DATE DUE

GRANGER'S®
INDEX TO POETRY

GRANGER'S®

INDEX TO POETRY

EIGHTH EDITION, COMPLETELY REVISED

AND ENLARGED, INDEXING ANTHOLOGIES

PUBLISHED THROUGH JUNE 30, 1985

EDITED BY WILLIAM F. BERNHARDT

COLUMBIA UNIVERSITY PRESS

NEW YORK   1986

GRANGER'S® INDEX TO POETRY

EIGHTH EDITION, COMPLETELY REVISED AND ENLARGED

PRINTED IN THE UNITED STATES OF AMERICA

Library of Congress Cataloging-in-Publication Data

Granger, Edith.
Granger's Index to poetry.
1. Poetry—Indexes. 2. English poetry—Indexes.
I. Bernhardt, William F. II. Title. III. Title:
Index to poetry.
PN1022.G7 1986 016.80881 85-32571
ISBN 0-231-06276-1

PREFACE

GRANGER'S® INDEX TO POETRY has been a standard reference work since its first appearance under the editorship of Edith Granger in 1904. In 1945 Columbia University Press took over the editing and publication of the work from A. C. McClurg & Co. in Chicago. The format was changed somewhat—prose works were omitted, titles and first lines were combined into a single alphabetical listing, and the Subject Index was greatly expanded—but the purpose remained unchanged: to assist the reader in identifying and locating poems or selections from poems appearing in the most generally accessible anthologies. Each entry in the Title and First Line Index is followed by alphabetical symbols for the anthologies in which the work appears. A Key to Symbols will be found in the front matter. No new symbol duplicates any used previously.

The Eighth Edition of GRANGER'S® returns to the cumulative format pursued in editions two through six, giving access to poems found in older anthologies, as well as to poems in collections published through June 1985. From the Sixth Edition, 212 volumes have been indexed; 111 volumes have been retained from the Seventh Edition; and 82 new volumes appearing since the Seventh Edition have been added—making a total of 405 volumes indexed here. Notable among the new volumes are several anthologies featuring contemporary American poets; collections of Asian American, Chicano, and American Indian poetry; an anthology of poetry written in American prisons; five new anthologies of women's verse, including one by black women; and six additions to the well-known series of anthologies from Oxford University Press.

In keeping with technological developments, the manuscript for this Eighth Edition of GRANGER'S® was prepared by word processor at the Press, and the information from individual disks was subsequently merged and sorted alphabetically to produce a computer file, which was printed for use in the editorial process. As a result, much of the tedious assembling of the basic material and of the elimination of repetitious entries was handled by the computer, thus expediting editorial work at the Press. Despite the new technology, however, the basic format of GRANGER'S® remains the same, so that librarians and other readers familiar with earlier editions should have no problem in using the new edition. With a minimum of fuss and a maximum of efficiency, Paul Lagassé guided the word processing operations at the Press, finding solutions to complications as they arose.

Once again, the Subject Index has been expanded to include many new topics. Our aim has been to be as specific as possible in assigning subject categories to poems, avoiding the pitfalls that imprecise or generalized headings can present to the indexer. Archie Hobson skillfully presided over the preparation of the Subject Index; see his headnote to that index for more detailed guidelines as to its use and information about its new features.

Continued from the Seventh Edition, and revised, is the designation of works recommended for priority acquisition by libraries. Since many libraries cannot acquire all or most of the anthologies indexed, they may be helped by the designation in the Key to Symbols of two asterisks for those works recommended for primary acquisition and by the designation of one asterisk for those works recommended for further acquisition. This feature is presented not as an infallible guide but as an aid to libraries with limited funds and no specialized requirements.

Assisting the Press in making the recommendations was a panel of experts consisting of Lillian Morrison, former Coordinator of Young Adult Services for the New York Public Library, poet, and anthologist; William Jay Smith, poet, critic, and anthologist; and William Katz, of the School of Information and Library Science at the State University of New York at Albany.

An accompanying page lists those individuals who assisted in the arduous and time-consuming tasks involved in the preparation of the new edition: marking and checking the anthologies, editing the voluminous printout for consistency and elimination of repetitions, and proofreading. For their assistance in a demanding job under pressure of deadlines, many thanks. Special thanks are due Judith Levey, head of the Reference Department at Columbia University Press, for handling so efficiently the many administrative details involved with such a project, and to Gerard Mayers, head of the Production Department at the Press, for his assistance in the myriad of production details.

January 1986 WILLIAM F. BERNHARDT

CONTENTS

PREFACE v

EXPLANATORY NOTES x

ABBREVIATIONS xi

KEY TO SYMBOLS xiii

TITLE AND FIRST LINE INDEX 1

AUTHOR INDEX 1393

SUBJECT INDEX 1733

EXPLANATORY NOTES

Each of the volumes of poetry indexed in GRANGER'S® is referred to by a short alphabetical abbreviation. These abbreviations, or symbols, are listed after the appropriate entries in the Title and First Line Index and mean that the relevant poem appears in that anthology. The complete title of the work and the essential publishing information can be found in the Key to Symbols.

The Author Index and the Subject Index are designed to be used in connection with the Title and First Line Index. A poem identified by title in the Author or Subject Index should be checked in the Title and First Line Index for the anthologies in which it appears.

Titles and first lines are arranged in one alphabetical listing in the Title and First Line Index. Titles are distinguished by initial capital letters on the important words. All first line entries are followed by the title of the poem, if there is a title. When the title and first line of a poem are identical, or nearly so, only the title is listed, although occasionally, for purposes of clarity, the first line has been added in quotation marks and in parentheses to the title entry.

Symbols are listed after both titles and first lines. However, more complete information as to translations, acts and scenes, abridgments, and variant titles is given in the title entry.

Indented listings below a title entry have the following significance: a single indentation indicates a *selection* from the above work; double indentation, within parentheses, signifies a *variant title* as used in the anthologies that follow.

Mother Goose rhymes are listed by first line only, rather than by the numerous arbitrary titles assigned to them by anthologists.

Generic title entries, such as Ode, Song, Sonnet, are followed by the first line in quotes for ease of identification. Such entries, of course, may also be located by first line listing.

Computerized printing has resulted in a change from earlier editions in the handling of titles and first lines beginning with "O" and "Oh." While in earlier editions such entries were filed as though all were spelled "O," in this edition such entries are filed separately, with cross-references where necessary. In a few instances words with variant spelling such as "honor" and "honour" are filed as though all followed standard American spelling. Names beginning "Mac," "Mc," and "M' " are filed as if all were spelled "Mac."

Chinese and old-style Japanese names in the Author Index are alphabeted, following standard practice, in uninverted form. Modern Japanese names, however, are inverted in the Western manner for filing purposes.

ABBREVIATIONS

abr.	abridged
ad.	adapted
add.	additional
arr.	arranged
at.	attributed
Bk.	book
br.	brief
ch.	chapter
comp.	compiled *or* compiler
comps.	compilers
cond.	condensed
diff.	different
fr.	from
frag.	fragment
incl.	included *or* including
introd.	introduction *or* introductory
ll.	lines
misc.	miscellaneous
mod.	modernized *or* modern
N.T.	New Testament
O.T.	Old Testament
orig.	original
par.	paraphrase *or* paraphrased
pr.	prose
Pt.	part
rev.	revised
sc.	scene
Sec.	section
sel.	selection
sels.	selections
sl.	slightly
st.	stanza
sts.	stanzas
tr.	translator, translation, *or* translated
trs.	translators *or* translations
var.	various
vers.	version *or* versions
wr.	wrong *or* wrongly

KEY TO SYMBOLS

Anthologies starred with two asterisks (**) are recommended for priority acquisition by small libraries, one star (*) for further acquisition. See PREFACE *for fuller explanation.*

AA American Anthology, An, 1787–1900. *Edmund Clarence Stedman, ed.* (1900) Houghton Mifflin Company

AAS Anchor Anthology of Sixteenth-Century Verse, The. *Richard S. Sylvester, ed.* (1974) Doubleday Anchor Books

ACP Anthology of Catholic Poets, An. *Shane Leslie, ed.* (Rev. ed., 1952) The Macmillan Company, *later pub. by* The Newman Press

AH American Hymns Old and New. *Albert Christ-Janer, Charles W. Hughes, and Carleton Sprague Smith, eds.* (1980) Columbia University Press (2 vols.; Vol. I, with music; Vol. II, notes on the hymns and biographies of the authors and composers)

AmFN America Forever New; a Book of Poems. *Sara Brewton and John E. Brewton, comps.* (1968) Thomas Y. Crowell Company

AmFP *American Folk Poetry; an Anthology. *Duncan Emrich, ed.* (1974) Little, Brown & Company

AmMo Amazing Monsters; Verses to Thrill and Chill. *Robert Fisher, ed.* (1982) Faber and Faber

AmNP American Negro Poetry. *Arna Bontemps, ed.* (Rev. ed., 1974) Hill and Wang

AmPA American Poetry Anthology, The. *Daniel Halpern, ed.* (1975) Avon Books

AmPP American Poetry and Prose. *Norman Foerster, Norman S. Grabo, Russel B. Nye, E. Fred Carlisle, and Robert Falk, eds.* (5th ed., 1970) Houghton Mifflin Company

AmSS American Sea Songs and Chanteys. *Frank Shay, ed.* (1948) W. W. Norton & Company. Edition of 1924, published by Doubleday, Doran & Company, had title Iron Men and Wooden Ships

AMV-80 Anthology of Magazine Verse and Yearbook of American Poetry; 1980 Edition. *Alan F. Pater, ed.* (1980) Monitor Book Company, Inc.

AMV-81 Anthology of Magazine Verse and Yearbook of American Poetry; 1981 Edition. *Alan F. Pater, ed.* (1981) Monitor Book Company, Inc.

AnAnS 1-2 Anchor Anthology of Seventeenth-Century Verse, The. Vol. I, *Louis L. Martz, ed.*; Vol. II, *Richard S. Sylvester, ed.* (1969) Doubleday Anchor Books

KEY TO SYMBOLS

AnIL	Anthology of Irish Literature, An. *David H. Greene, ed.* (1954) The Modern Library
AnIV	Anthology of Irish Verse, An. *Padraic Colum, ed.* (Rev. ed., 1948) Liveright Publishing Corporation
AnOE	Anthology of Old English Poetry, An. *Charles W. Kennedy, tr.* (1960) Oxford University Press
AP	American Poetry. *Gay Wilson Allen, Walter B. Rideout, and James K. Robinson, eds.* (1965) Harper & Row
APAS	Anthology of Poems on Affairs of State; Augustan Satirical Verse, 1660–1714. *George deF. Lord, ed.* (1975) Yale University Press
AS	American Songbag, The. *Carl Sandburg, comp.* (1927) Harcourt, Brace and Company
AWP	Anthology of World Poetry, An. *Mark Van Doren, ed.* (Rev. and enl. ed., 1936) Reynal & Hitchcock
BaBo	Ballad Book, The. *MacEdward Leach, ed.* (1955) Harper & Brothers
BALP	Black American Literature: Poetry. *Darwin T. Turner, ed.* (1969) Charles E. Merrill Publishing Company
BANP	Book of American Negro Poetry, The. *James Weldon Johnson, ed.* (Rev. ed., 1931) Harcourt, Brace and Company
BeLS	Best Loved Story Poems. *Walter E. Thwing, ed.* (1941) Garden City Publishing Company
BiP	Beginnings in Poetry. *William J. Martz, ed.* (2d ed., 1973) Scott, Foresman and Company
BIrV	*Book of Irish Verse, The; an Anthology of Irish Poetry from the Sixth Century to the Present. *John Montague, ed.* (1974) Macmillan Publishing Company (Also published as The Faber Book of Irish Verse)
BLPA	Best Loved Poems of the American People, The. *Hazel Felleman, ed.* (1936) Doubleday & Company
BLPL	*Best-Loved Poems in Large Print. *Virginia S. Reiser, ed.* (1983) G. K. Hall & Co.
BLRP	Best Loved Religious Poems, The. *James Gilchrist Lawson, comp.* (1933) Fleming H. Revell Company
BlSi	Black Sister; Poetry by Black American Women, 1746–1980. *Erlene Stetson, ed.* (1981) Indiana University Press
BLSo	**Best Loved Songs of the American People. (With music.) *Denes Agay, ed.* (1975) Doubleday & Company
BluL	Blues Line, The; a Collection of Blues Lyrics. *Eric Sackheim, comp.* (1969, paperback 1975) Schirmer Books
BoAN 1–2	Books of American Negro Spirituals, The; including The Book of American Negro Spirituals and The Second Book of Negro Spirituals. *James Weldon Johnson, ed.* (1925, 1926, 2 vols. in 1, 1940) The Viking Press

BoAnP — Book of Animal Poems, A. *William Cole, comp.* (1973) The Viking Press

BOLo — Black Out Loud; an Anthology of Modern Poems by Black Americans. *Arnold Adoff, ed.* (1970) The Macmillan Company

BoLoP — Book of Love Poetry, A. *Jon Stallworthy, ed.* (1974) Oxford University Press. Published in England under the title The Penguin Book of Love Poetry

BoNaP — Book of Nature Poems, A. *William Cole, comp.* (1969) The Viking Press

BoWoP — *Book of Women Poets from Antiquity to Now, A. *Aliki Barnstone and Willis Barnstone, eds.* (1980) Schocken Books

BPAW — Best Loved Poems of the American West. *John J. Gregg and Barbara T. Gregg, eds.* (1980) Doubleday & Company

BPo — Black Poets, The. *Dudley Randall, ed.* (1971) Bantam Books

BrPo — British Poetry 1880–1920; Edwardian Voices. *Paul L. Wiley and Harold Orel, eds.* (1969) Appleton-Century-Crofts

BrRo — Bread and Roses; an Anthology of Nineteenth- and Twentieth-Century Poetry by Women Writers. *Diana Scott, comp.* (1982) Virago Press

BrSi — *Breaking Silence; an Anthology of Contemporary Asian American Poets. *Joseph Bruchac, ed.* (1983) The Greenfield Review Press

BSV — Book of Scottish Verse, A. *Maurice Lindsay and R. L. Mackie, eds.* (3d ed., 1983) St. Martin's Press

BXAP — Brand-X Anthology of Poetry, The: Burnt Norton Edition. *William Zaranka, ed.* (1981) Apple-Wood Books, Inc.

CABA — College Anthology of British and American Poetry, The. *A. Kent Hieatt and William Park, eds.* (2d ed., 1972) Allyn and Bacon

CAD — City in All Directions; an Anthology of Modern Poems. *Arnold Adoff, ed.* (1969) The Macmillan Company

CaP — Canadian Poetry in English (Canadian Literature Series). *Bliss Carman, Lorne Pierce, and V. B. Rhodenizer, eds.* (Rev. and enl. ed., 1954) The Ryerson Press

CaPo — Cavalier Poets; Selected Poems. *Thomas Clayton, ed.* (1978) Oxford University Press

CAPP — Contemporary American Poetry. *A. Poulin, Jr., ed.* (1971) Houghton Mifflin Company

CavP — Cavalier Poets, The. *Robin Skelton, ed.* (1970) Oxford University Press

CBAP — Collins Book of Australian Poetry, The. *Rodney Hall, comp.* (1981, 1984) Fontana/Collins

CDC — Caroling Dusk; an Anthology of Verse by Negro Poets. *Countee Cullen, ed.* (1927) Harper & Brothers

CDW — *Carriers of the Dream Wheel; Contemporary Native American Poetry. *Duane Niatum, ed.* (1975) Harper & Row

CenHV	Century of Humorous Verse, A, 1850–1950 (Everyman's Library). *Roger Lancelyn Green, ed.* (1959) E. P. Dutton & Company
CH	Come Hither. *Walter de la Mare, comp.* (3d ed., 1957) Alfred A. Knopf
ChER	Choice of English Romantic Poetry, A. *Stephen Spender, ed.* (1947) The Dial Press
ChMP	Chatto Book of Modern Poetry, The, 1915–1955. *C. Day Lewis and John Lehmann, eds.* (New ed., 1959) Chatto & Windus
ChTr	Cherry-Tree, The. *Geoffrey Grigson, comp.* (1959) Phoenix House
CIP	Contemporary Irish Poetry; an Anthology. *Anthony Bradley, ed.* (1980) University of California Press
CMoP	Chief Modern Poets of Britain and America. *Gerald DeWitt Sanders, John Herbert Nelson, and M. L. Rosenthal, eds.* (5th ed., 1970) Macmillan Publishing Company
CNA	Celebrations; a New Anthology of Black American Poetry. *Arnold Adoff, ed.* (1977) Follett Publishing Company
CoAP	Contemporary American Poets, The; American Poetry since 1940. *Mark Strand, ed.* (1969) World Publishing Company
CoBMV	College Book of Modern Verse, A. *James K. Robinson and Walter B. Rideout, eds.* (1958) Row, Peterson and Company
CoMu	Common Muse, The; an Anthology of Popular British Ballad Poetry, XVth–XXth Century. *Vivian de Sola Pinto and Allan Edwin Rodway, eds.* (1957) Philosophical Library
ConAP	Contemporary American Poetry. *Donald Hall, ed.* (2d ed., 1972) Penguin Books
CoPo	Controversy of Poets, A; an Anthology of Contemporary American Poetry. *Paris Leary and Robert Kelly, eds.* (1965) Doubleday Anchor Books
CoSo	Cowboy Songs and Other Frontier Ballads. *John A. Lomax and Alan Lomax, eds.* (Rev. and enl. ed., 1938) The Macmillan Company
CrMA	Criterion Book of Modern American Verse, The. *W. H. Auden, ed.* (1956) Criterion Books
CTBA	Crazy to Be Alive in Such a Strange World; Poems about People. *Nancy Larrick, comp.* (1977) M. Evans and Company
CTC	Confucius to Cummings; an Anthology of Poetry. *Ezra Pound and Marcella Spann, eds.* (1964) New Directions
DBV	Devil's Book of Verse, The; Masters of the Poison Pen from Ancient Times to the Present Day. *Richard Conniff, ed.* (1983) Dodd, Mead & Company
DFF	Dont Forget to Fly; a Cycle of Modern Poems. *Paul B. Janeczko, comp.* (1981) Bradbury Press
DFT	Disenchantments; an Anthology of Modern Fairy Tale Poetry. *Wolfgang Mieder, ed.* (1985) Published for University of Vermont by University Press of New England

Symbol	Source
DiL	Divided Light: Father and Son Poems; a Twentieth-Century American Anthology. *Jason Shinder, ed.* (1983) The Sheep Meadow Press
DL	Death in Literature. *Robert F. Weir, ed.* (1980) Columbia University Press
DTC	Dylan Thomas's Choice; an Anthology of Verse Spoken by Dylan Thomas. *Ralph Maud and Aneirin Talfan Davies, eds.* (1963) New Directions
DTo	Dark Tower, The; Nineteenth Century Narrative Poems. *Dairine Coffey, comp.* (1967) Atheneum
DuDa	Dusk to Dawn; Poems of Night. *Helen Hill, Agnes Perkins, and Alethea Helbig, comps.* (1981) Thomas Y. Crowell Company
EaLo	Earth Is the Lord's, The; Poems of the Spirit. *Helen Plotz, comp.* (1965) Thomas Y. Crowell Company
EAS	English and American Surrealist Poetry. *Edward B. Germain, ed.* (1978) Penguin Books
EBCP	Eerdmans Book of Christian Poetry. *Pat Alexander, comp.* (1981) William B. Eerdmans Publishing Company
EBEV	Everyman's Book of English Verse. *John Wain, ed.* (1981) J. M. Dent & Sons Ltd.
EBVV	Everyman's Book of Victorian Verse. *J. R. Watson, ed.* (1982) J. M. Dent & Sons Ltd.
ElL	Elizabethan Lyrics. *Norman Ault, ed.* (3d ed., 1949) William Sloane Associates. Paperback edition of 1960 published by G. P. Putnam's Sons
ELP	English Lyric Poems, 1500–1900. *C. Day Lewis, ed.* (1961) Appleton-Century-Crofts
ELU	Eight Lines and Under; an Anthology of Short, Short Poems. *William Cole, ed.* (1967) The Macmillan Company
EnLoPo	English Love Poems. *John Betjeman and Geoffrey Taylor, comps.* (1957; paperback 1964) Faber and Faber
EnRePo	English Renaissance Poetry; a Collection of Shorter Poems from Skelton to Jonson. *John Williams, ed.* (1963) Doubleday Anchor Books
EnRP	English Romantic Poetry and Prose. *Russell Noyes, ed.* (1956) Oxford University Press
EnSB	English and Scottish Ballads (The Poetry Bookshelf). *Robert Graves, ed.* (1957) William Heinemann Ltd.
ErPo	Erotic Poetry; the Lyrics, Ballads, Idyls, and Epics of Love—Classical to Contemporary. *William Cole, ed.* (1963) Random House
ESPB	English and Scottish Popular Ballads. *Helen Child Sargent and George Lyman Kittredge, eds., from the collection of Francis James Child.* (1904, 1932, reissue, 1947) Houghton Mifflin Company
EtS	Eternal Sea, The; an Anthology of Sea Poetry. *W. M. Williamson, ed.* (1946) Coward-McCann

EvOK — Everybody Ought to Know. *Ogden Nash, ed.* (1961) J. B. Lippincott Company

EyDe — Eye's Delight; Poems of Art and Architecture. *Helen Plotz, comp.* (1983) Greenwillow Books

FaBoBa — *Faber Book of Ballads, The. *Matthew Hodgart, ed.* (1965; paperback 1971) Faber and Faber

FaBoBe — Family Book of Best Loved Poems, The. *David L. George, ed.* (1952) Doubleday & Company

FaBoCh — Faber Book of Children's Verse, The. *Janet Adam Smith, comp.* (1953; paperback 1963) Faber and Faber

FaBoCo — *Faber Book of Comic Verse, The. *Michael Roberts and Janet Adam Smith, eds.* (Rev. ed., 1974; paperback 1978) Faber and Faber

FaBoEE — Faber Book of Epigrams and Epitaphs, The. *Geoffrey Grigson, ed.* (1977) Faber and Faber

FaBoEn — Faber Book of English Verse, The. *John Hayward, ed.* (1958) Faber and Faber

Faber Book of Irish Verse, The. (1974) Faber and Faber (This book is the same as The Book of Irish Verse [BIrV]; see above)

Faber Book of Love Poems, The. (1975) Faber and Faber (This book is the same as The Gambit Book of Love Poems [GBL]; see below)

FaBoMo — *Faber Book of Modern Verse, The. *Michael Roberts, ed.* (4th ed., revised by Peter Porter, 1982) Faber and Faber

FaBoNo — *Faber Book of Nonsense Verse, The. *Geoffrey Grigson, ed.* (1979) Faber and Faber

Faber Book of Popular Verse, The. (1971) Faber and Faber (This book is the same as The Gambit Book of Popular Verse [GBP]; see below)

FaBoPa — Faber Book of Parodies, The. *Simon Brett, ed.* (1984) Faber and Faber

FaBoPP — Faber Book of Poems and Places, The. *Geoffrey Grigson, ed.* (1980) Faber and Faber

FaBoRV — Faber Book of Reflective Verse, The. *Geoffrey Grigson, ed.* (1984) Faber and Faber

FaBoTw — Faber Book of Twentieth-Century Verse, The. *John Heath-Stubbs and David Wright, eds.* (3d ed., 1975) Faber and Faber

FaBoUs — Faber Book of Useful Verse, The. *Simon Brett, ed.* (1981) Faber and Faber

FaBV — Family Book of Verse, The. *Lewis Gannett, ed.* (1961) Harper & Row

FaFP — Family Album of Favorite Poems, The. *P. Edward Ernest, ed.* (1959) Grosset & Dunlap

FaPo — Familiar Poems, Annotated. *Isaac Asimov.* (1977) Doubleday & Company

FaPON Favorite Poems Old and New. *Helen Ferris, ed.* (1957) Doubleday & Company

FaPoR Faber Popular Reciter, The. *Kingsley Amis, ed.* (1978) Faber and Faber

FAZ From A to Z; 200 Contemporary American Poets. *David Ray, ed.* (1981) Swallow Press/Ohio University Press

FB Forerunners, The; Black Poets in America. *Woodie King, Jr., ed.* (1975) Howard University Press

FF *Fine Frenzy; Enduring Themes in Poetry. *Robert Baylor and Brenda Stokes, eds.* (2d ed., 1978) McGraw-Hill Book Company

FIA Fiesta in Aztlan; Anthology of Chicano Poetry. *Toni Empringham, ed.* (1981) Capra Press

FiBHP Fireside Book of Humorous Poetry, The. *William Cole, ed.* (1959) Simon and Schuster

FiCP Fifty Contemporary Poets; the Creative Process. *Alberta T. Turner, ed.* (1977) David McKay Company

FiP Fifteen Poets; Chaucer to Arnold. (1941) Oxford University Press

FM Fellow Mortals; an Anthology of Animal Verse. *Roy Fuller, comp.* (1981) Macdonald and Evans Ltd.

FPL Favorite Poems in Large Print. *Virginia S. Reiser, ed.* (1981) G. K. Hall & Co.

FSN Favorite Songs of the Nineties; Complete Original Sheet Music for 89 Songs. *Robert A. Fremont, ed.* (1973) Dover Publications

FSW Folksinger's Wordbook. *Irwin Silber and Fred Silber, eds.* (1973) Oak Publications

FYAP *Fifty Years of American Poetry; Anniversary Volume for the Academy of American Poets. Introduction by Robert Penn Warren. (1984) Harry N. Abrams, Inc.

GBL Gambit Book of Love Poems, The. *Geoffrey Grigson, ed.* (1975) Gambit (Originally published in Great Britain by Faber and Faber as The Faber Book of Love Poems)

GBP Gambit Book of Popular Verse, The. *Geoffrey Grigson, ed.* (1971) Gambit (Also published as The Faber Book of Popular Verse)

GDP Good Dog Poems. *William Cole, comp.* (1981) Charles Scribner's Sons

GeTw Generation of 2000, The; Contemporary American Poets. *William Heyen, ed.* (1984) Ontario Review Press

GLGT Gladly Learn and Gladly Teach; Poems of the School Experience. *Helen Plotz, comp.* (1981) Greenwillow Books

GN Golden Numbers. *Kate Douglas Wiggin and Nora Archibald Smith, eds.* (1902) Doubleday, Doran & Company

GOA *Gift Outright, The; America to Her Poets. *Helen Plotz, ed.* (1977) Greenwillow Books

GoBC — Golden Book of Catholic Poetry, The. *Alfred Noyes, ed.* (1946) J. B. Lippincott Company

GoJo — Golden Journey, The; Poems for Young People. *Louise Bogan and William Jay Smith, comps.* (1965) Reilly & Lee Company

GoSl — Golden Slippers; an Anthology of Negro Poetry for Young Readers. *Arna Bontemps, comp.* (4th ed., 1941) Harper & Brothers

GoTL — Golden Treasury of Longer Poems, The (Everyman's Library). *Ernest Rhys, ed.* (Rev. ed., 1949) J. M. Dent & Sons Ltd.

GoTS — Golden Treasury of Scottish Poetry, The. *Hugh MacDiarmid, ed.* (1941) The Macmillan Company

GoYe — Golden Year, The; the Poetry Society of America Anthology, 1910–1960. *Melville Cane, John Farrar, and Louise Townsend Nicholl, eds.* (1960) The Fine Editions Press

GP — Geography of Poets, A; an Anthology of the New Poetry. *Edward Field, ed.* (1979) Bantam Books

GrPl — *Green Place, A; Modern Poems. *William Jay Smith, comp.* (1982) Delacorte Press/Seymour Lawrence

GTBS — Golden Treasury of the Best Songs and Lyrical Poems in the English Language. *Francis Palgrave, comp.* (1929) Oxford University Press

GTBS–P — Golden Treasury of the Best Songs & Lyrical Poems in the English Language, The. *Francis Turner Palgrave, comp. With a fifth book selected by John Press.* (5th ed., 1964) Oxford University Press

HAP — Harper Anthology of Poetry, The. *John Frederick Nims, ed.* (1981) Harper & Row

HBMV — Home Book of Modern Verse, The. *Burton Egbert Stevenson, ed.* (2d ed., 1953) Henry Holt and Company

HBV 1-2 — Home Book of Verse, The. *Burton Egbert Stevenson, ed.* (9th ed., 1953, 2 vols.) Henry Holt and Company

HBVY — Home Book of Verse for Young Folks, The. *Burton Egbert Stevenson, ed.* (Rev. and enl. ed., 1929) Henry Holt and Company

HeIP — Heath Introduction to Poetry, The. *Joseph de Roche, ed.* (2d ed., 1984) D. C. Heath and Company

HoAn — Hopwood Anthology, The; Five Decades of American Poetry. *Harry Thomas and Steven Lavine, eds.* (1981) The University of Michigan Press

HoPM — *How Does a Poem Mean? *John Ciardi and Miller Williams, eds.* (2d ed., 1975) Houghton Mifflin Company

IDB — I Am the Darker Brother; an Anthology of Modern Poems by Negro Americans. *Arnold Adoff, ed.* (1968) The Macmillan Company

IHMS — I Hear My Sisters Saying; Poems by Twentieth-Century Women. *Carol Konek and Dorothy Walters, eds.* (1976) Thomas Y. Crowell Company

ILwL In Love with Love; 100 of the Greatest Mystical Poems. *Anne Fremantle and Christopher Fremantle, eds.* (1978) Paulist Press

ImOP Imagination's Other Place; Poems of Science and Mathematics. *Helen Plotz, comp.* (1955) Thomas Y. Crowell Company

InMe Innocent Merriment; an Anthology of Light Verse. *Franklin P. Adams, comp.* (1942) McGraw-Hill Book Company

InPK Introduction to Poetry, An. *X. J. Kennedy, ed.* (3d ed., 1974) Little, Brown & Company

InPS Introduction to Poetry, An. *Louis Simpson, ed.* (2d ed., 1972) St. Martin's Press

InvP Invitation to Poetry; a Round of Poems from John Skelton to Dylan Thomas. *Lloyd Frankenberg, ed.* (1956) Doubleday & Company

InW Inventing a Word; an Anthology of Twentieth-Century Puerto Rican Poetry. *Julio Marzán, ed.* (1980) Columbia University Press (in association with The Center for Inter-American Relations)

IPY Irish Poetry after Yeats; Seven Poets. *Maurice Harmon, ed.* (1979) Little, Brown & Company

ISi I Sing of a Maiden; the Mary Book of Verse. *Sister M. Thérèse, ed.* (1947) The Macmillan Company

JB Jump Bad; a New Chicago Anthology. *Gwendolyn Brooks, ed.* (1971) Broadside Press

JCP Jacobean and Caroline Poetry; an Anthology. *T. G. S. Cain, ed.* (1981) Methuen

KiLC Kings, Lords, & Commons; an Anthology from the Irish. *Frank O'Connor, ed. and tr.* (1959) Alfred A. Knopf

LaA Late Augustans, The; Longer Poems of the Later Eighteenth Century (The Poetry Bookshelf). *Donald Davie, ed.* (1958) The Macmillan Company

LAuP Late Augustan Poetry. *Patricia Meyer Spacks, ed.* (1973) Prentice-Hall

LCAP *Longman Anthology of Contemporary American Poetry, The, 1950–1980. *Stuart Friebert and David Young, eds.* (1983) Longman

LFAC Light from Another Country, The; Poetry from American Prisons. *Joseph Bruchac, ed.* (1984) The Greenfield Review Press

LiSp Literature of Sports, A. *Tom Dodge, ed.* (1980) D. C. Heath and Company

LiTA Little Treasury of American Poetry, A. *Oscar Williams, ed.* (1948) Charles Scribner's Sons

LiTB Little Treasury of British Poetry, A. *Oscar Williams, ed.* (1951) Charles Scribner's Sons

LiTM Little Treasury of Modern Poetry, A, English and American. *Oscar Williams, ed.* (3d ed., 1970) Charles Scribner's Sons

LLLT Love Is Like the Lion's Tooth; an Anthology of Love Poems. *Frances McCullough, ed.* (1984) Harper & Row

LO Love. *Walter de la Mare, ed.* (1946) William Morrow & Company

LoBV London Book of English Verse, The. *Herbert Read and Bonamy Dobrée, comps.* (2d rev. ed., 1952) The Macmillan Company

LTB Leaving the Bough; 50 American Poets of the 80s. *Roger Gaess, ed.* (1982) International Publishers

MasP Master Poems of the English Language. *Oscar Williams, ed.* (1966) Trident Press

MAT Messages; a Thematic Anthology of Poetry. *X. J. Kennedy, ed.* (1973) Little, Brown & Company

MAYP *Morrow Anthology of Younger American Poets, The. *Dave Smith and David Bottoms, eds.* (1985) Quill (A Division of William Morrow & Company)

MeEL Medieval English Lyrics; a Critical Anthology. *R. T. Davies, ed.* (1964) Northwestern University Press

MeLP Metaphysical Lyrics & Poems of the Seventeenth Century; Donne to Butler. *Herbert J. C. Grierson, ed.* (1921) Oxford University Press

MePo Metaphysical Poets, The. *Helen Gardner, ed.* (1957) Penguin Books

MiAP Mid-Century American Poets. *John Ciardi, ed.* (1950) Twayne Publishers

MMA Men Who March Away; Poems of the First World War. *I. M. Parsons, ed.* (1965) The Viking Press

MoAB Modern American & Modern British Poetry. *Louis Untermeyer, ed., in consultation with Karl Shapiro and Richard Wilbur.* (Rev., shorter ed., 1955) Harcourt, Brace and Company

MoAmPo Modern American Poetry. *Louis Untermeyer, ed.* (8th rev. ed., 1962) Harcourt, Brace and Company

MoBrPo Modern British Poetry. *Louis Untermeyer, ed.* (7th rev. ed., 1962) Harcourt, Brace and Company

MoBS Modern Ballads and Story Poems. *Charles Causley, ed.* (1965) Franklin Watts, Inc. English edition, published in 1964 by Brockhampton Press Ltd., had title Rising Early

MoCV Modern Canadian Verse. *A. J. M. Smith, ed.* (1967) Oxford University Press

MOON Moonstruck; an Anthology of Lunar Poetry. *Robert Phillips, ed.* (1974) The Vanguard Press

MoPo Modern Poetry; American and British. *Kimon Friar and John Malcolm Brinnin, eds.* (1951) Appleton-Century-Crofts

MOS Moods of the Sea; Masterworks of Sea Poetry. *George C. Solley and Eric Steinbaugh, comps.* (1981) Naval Institute Press

MoShBr — Moon Is Shining Bright as Day, The; an Anthology of Good-humored Verse. *Ogden Nash, ed.* (1953) J. B. Lippincott Company

MoVE — Modern Verse in English, 1900–1950. *David Cecil and Allen Tate, eds.* (1958) The Macmillan Company

MP — Modern Poets, The; an American-British Anthology. *John Malcolm Brinnin and Bill Read, eds.* (1963) McGraw-Hill Book Company. Revised edition of 1970 has title Twentieth Century Poetry; American and British (1900–1970). *See* TwCP

NA — Nonsense Anthology, A. *Carolyn Wells, ed.* (1930) Charles Scribner's Sons. Paperback edition of 1958 published by Dover Publications

NaP — Naked Poetry; Recent American Poetry in Open Forms. *Stephen Berg and Robert Mezey, eds.* (1969) Bobbs-Merrill

NAs — Naked Astronaut, The; Poems on Birth and Birthdays. *René Graziani, ed.* (1983) Faber and Faber

NAWM 1–2 — Norton Anthology of World Masterpieces, The, Vols. I–II. *Maynard Mack, general ed.* (4th Continental ed., 1980) W. W. Norton & Company

NBM — 19th Century British Minor Poets. *W. H. Auden, ed.* (1966) Delacorte Press

NBP — New Black Poetry, The. *Clarence Major, ed.* (1969) International Publishers Company

NCEP — New Canon of English Poetry, A. *James Reeves and Martin Seymour-Smith, eds.* (1967) Barnes & Noble

NCSH — New Coasts & Strange Harbors; Discovering Poems. *Helen Hill and Agnes Perkins, comps.* (1974) Thomas Y. Crowell Company

NeAC — New American and Canadian Poetry. *John Gill, ed.* (1971) Beacon Press

NeAP — New American Poetry, The, 1945–1960. *Donald M. Allen, ed.* (1960) Grove Press

NeBP — New British Poets, The. *Kenneth Rexroth, ed.* (1949) New Directions

NeIP — New Irish Poets. *Devin A. Garrity, ed.* (1948) The Devin-Adair Company

NePA — New Pocket Anthology of American Verse from Colonial Days to the Present, The. *Oscar Williams, ed.* (1955) World Publishing Company

NePoAm — New Poems by American Poets. *Rolfe Humphries, ed.* (1953) Ballantine Books

NePoAm-2 — New Poems by American Poets #2. *Rolfe Humphries, ed.* (1957) Ballantine Books

NePoEA — New Poets of England and America. *Donald Hall, Robert Pack, and Louis Simpson, eds.* (1957) Meridian Books

KEY TO SYMBOLS

NePoEA-2 New Poets of England and America; Second Selection. *Donald Hall and Robert Pack, eds.* (1962) Meridian Books

NIP *Norton Introduction to Poetry, The. *J. Paul Hunter, ed.* (2d ed., 1981) W. W. Norton & Company. First edition had title The Norton Introduction to Literature: Poetry (NIL)

NMM No More Masks! An Anthology of Poems by Women. *Florence Howe and Ellen Bass, eds.* (1973) Doubleday Anchor Books

NMP New Modern Poetry, The; British and American Poetry since World War II. *M. L. Rosenthal, ed.* (1967) The Macmillan Company

NNaP New Naked Poetry, The; Recent American Poetry in Open Forms. *Stephen Berg and Robert Mezey, eds.* (1976) Bobbs-Merrill

NNP New Negro Poets U.S.A. *Langston Hughes, ed.* (1964) Indiana University Press

NoAM *Norton Anthology of Modern Poetry, The. *Richard Ellmann and Robert O'Clair, eds.* (1973) W. W. Norton & Company

NOBA *New Oxford Book of American Verse, The. *Richard Ellmann, ed.* (1976) Oxford University Press

NOBC New Oxford Book of Canadian Verse in English, The. *Margaret Atwood, comp.* (1982) Oxford University Press

NOBE *New Oxford Book of English Verse, The, 1250–1950. *Helen Gardner, ed.* (1972) Oxford University Press

NOBL *New Oxford Book of English Light Verse, The. *Kingsley Amis, ed.* (1978) Oxford University Press

NOCV New Oxford Book of Christian Verse, The. *Donald Davie, ed.* (1981) Oxford University Press

NOEC New Oxford Book of Eighteenth Century Verse, The. *Roger Lonsdale, ed.* (1984) Oxford University Press

NoP *Norton Anthology of Poetry, The. *Alexander W. Allison and others, eds.* (3d ed., 1983) W. W. Norton & Company

NPAW New Poetry of the American West. *Peter Wild and Frank Graziano, eds.* (1982) Logbridge-Rhodes, Inc.

NPGG 19 New American Poets of the Golden Gate. *Philip Dow, ed.* (1984) Harcourt Brace Jovanovich

NTCP *New Treasury of Children's Poetry, A; Old Favorites and New Discoveries. *Joanna Cole, comp.* (1984) Doubleday & Company

NU News of the Universe; Poems of Twofold Consciousness. *Robert Bly, comp.* (1980) Sierra Club Books

NYBP New Yorker Book of Poems, The. (1969) The Viking Press. Paperback edition of 1974 published by William Morrow & Company

NYP New York: Poems. *Howard Moss, ed.* (1980) Avon Books

OAEL 1–2 Oxford Anthology of English Literature, The, Vols. I–II. *Frank Kermode and John Hollander, general eds.* (1973) Oxford University Press (also published as six paperback vols.: Medieval English Literature, *J. B. Trapp, ed.;* The Literature of Renaissance England,

John Hollander and Frank Kermode, eds.; The Restoration and the Eighteenth Century, *Martin Price, ed.;* Romantic Poetry and Prose, *Harold Bloom and Lionel Trilling, eds.;* Victorian Prose and Poetry, *Lionel Trilling and Harold Bloom, eds.;* Modern British Literature, *Frank Kermode and John Hollander, eds.*)

OAEP — Oxford Anthology of English Poetry, An. *Howard Foster Lowry and Willard Thorp, eds.* (2d ed., 1956) Oxford University Press

OBAL — **Oxford Book of American Light Verse, The. *William Harmon, ed.* (1979) Oxford University Press

OBCA — *Oxford Book of Children's Verse in America, The. *Donald Hall, ed.* (1985) Oxford University Press

OBCP — Oxford Book of Christmas Poems, The. *Michael Harrison and Christopher Stuart-Clark, eds.* (1983) Oxford University Press

OBCV — Oxford Book of Canadian Verse in English and French, The. *A. J. M. Smith, ed.* (1960) Oxford University Press

OBEC — Oxford Book of Eighteenth Century Verse, The. *David Nichol Smith, ed.* (1926) Oxford University Press

OBET — Oxford Book of English Traditional Verse, The. *Frederick Woods, ed.* (1983) Oxford University Press

OBEV — Oxford Book of English Verse, The, 1250–1918. *Sir Arthur Quiller-Couch, ed.* (New ed., rev. and enl., 1939) Oxford University Press

OBMV — Oxford Book of Modern Verse, The, 1892–1935. *William Butler Yeats, ed.* (1936) Oxford University Press

OBNC — Oxford Book of Nineteenth-Century English Verse, The. *John Hayward, ed.* (1964) Oxford University Press

OBNV — Oxford Book of Narrative Verse, The. *Iona Opie and Peter Opie, eds.* (1983) Oxford University Press

OBRV — Oxford Book of Regency Verse, The, 1798–1837. *H. S. Milford, ed.* (1928) Oxford University Press. Edition of 1935 has title The Oxford Book of English Verse of the Romantic Period, 1798–1837

OBS — Oxford Book of Seventeenth Century Verse, The. *H. J. C. Grierson and G. Bullough, eds.* (1934) Oxford University Press

OBSC — Oxford Book of Sixteenth Century Verse, The. *E. K. Chambers, comp.* (1932) Oxford University Press

OBSV — Oxford Book of Satirical Verse, The. *Geoffrey Grigson, comp.* (1980) Oxford University Press

OBVE — Oxford Book of Verse in English Translation, The. *Charles Tomlinson, ed.* (1980) Oxford University Press

OBVV — Oxford Book of Victorian Verse, The. *Arthur Quiller-Couch, comp.* (1912) Oxford University Press

OBWP — *Oxford Book of War Poetry, The. *Jon Stallworthy, ed.* (1984) Oxford University Press

OCNZ Oxford Book of Contemporary New Zealand Poetry, The. *Fleur Adcock, comp.* (1982) Oxford University Press

OFD O Frabjous Day! Poetry for Holidays and Special Occasions. *Myra Cohn Livingston, ed.* (1977) Atheneum

OHFP One Hundred and One Famous Poems. *Roy J. Cook, comp.* (Rev. ed., 1958) Reilly & Lee Company; reprinted 1981 by Contemporary Books

OHIP Our Holidays in Poetry. *Mildred P. Harrington and Josephine H. Thomas, comps.* (1929) The H. W. Wilson Company

OLR One Little Room, an Everywhere; Poems of Love. *Myra Cohn Livingston, ed.* (1975) Atheneum

OnMSP 100 More Story Poems. *Elinor Parker, comp.* (1960) Thomas Y. Crowell Company

OnUR Once Upon a Rhyme; 101 Poems for Young Children. *Sara Corrin and Stephen Corrin, eds.* (1982) Faber and Faber

OnYI 1000 Years of Irish Poetry. *Kathleen Hoagland, ed.* (1947) The Devin-Adair Company

OuSiCo Our Singing Country; a Second Volume of American Ballads and Folk Songs. *John A. Lomax and Alan Lomax, comps.* (1941) The Macmillan Company

OxBA Oxford Book of American Verse, The. *F. O. Matthiessen, ed.* (1950) Oxford University Press

OxBB Oxford Book of Ballads, The. *James Kinsley, ed.* (1969) Oxford University Press

OxBC Oxford Book of Contemporary Verse, The, 1945–1980. *D. J. Enright, comp.* (1980) Oxford University Press

OxBChV Oxford Book of Children's Verse, The. *Iona Opie and Peter Opie, eds.* (1973) Oxford University Press

OxBI Oxford Book of Irish Verse, The; XVIIth Century–XXth Century. *Donagh MacDonagh and Lennox Robinson, comps.* (1958) Oxford University Press

OxBM Oxford Book of Medieval English Verse, The. *Celia Sisam and Kenneth Sisam, eds.* (1970) Oxford University Press

OxBoCh Oxford Book of Christian Verse, The. *Lord David Cecil, ed.* (1940) Oxford University Press

OxBoLi *Oxford Book of Light Verse, The. *W. H. Auden, ed.* (1938) Oxford University Press

OxBS Oxford Book of Scottish Verse, The. *John MacQueen and Tom Scott, comps.* (1966) Oxford University Press

OxBTC *Oxford Book of Twentieth-Century English Verse, The. *Philip Larkin, ed.* (1973) Oxford University Press

OxNR Oxford Nursery Rhyme Book, The. *Iona Opie and Peter Opie, comps.* (1955) Oxford University Press

PAH Poems of American History. *Burton Egbert Stevenson, ed.* (Rev. ed., 1922) Houghton Mifflin Company

PAI Poetry; an Introduction. *Ruth Miller and Robert A. Greenberg, eds.* (1981) St. Martin's Press

PAL Patriotic Poems America Loves. *Jean Anne Vincent, comp.* (1968) Doubleday & Company

PaPo Parlour Poetry; a Casquet of Gems. *Michael R. Turner, ed.* (1969) The Viking Press

Par Parodies; an Anthology from Chaucer to Beerbohm—and After. *Dwight Macdonald, ed.* (1960) The Modern Library

PB Poetry of Birds, The. *Samuel Carr, ed.* (1976) Taplinger Publishing Company

PBA Poems from Black Africa. *Langston Hughes, ed.* (1963) Indiana University Press

PBBP Penguin Book of Bird Poetry, The. *Peggy Munsterberg, ed.* First published by Allen Lane 1980; published in Penguin Books 1984

PBWP *Penguin Book of Women Poets, The. *Carol Cosman, Joan Keefe, and Kathleen Weaver, eds.* (1978) Penguin Books

PCat Poetry of Cats, The. *Samuel Carr, ed.* (1974) The Viking Press

PChr Poems of Christmas. *Myra Cohn Livingston, ed.* (1980) Atheneum

PCP Postcard Poems; a Collection of Poetry for Sharing. *Paul B. Janeczko, ed.* (1979) Bradbury Press

PDV Piping down the Valleys Wild; Poetry for the Young of All Ages. *Nancy Larrick, ed.* (1968) Delacorte Press

PeCV Penguin Book of Canadian Verse, The. *Ralph Gustafson, ed.* (Rev. ed., 1967) Penguin Books

PeD Pegasus Descending; a Book of the Best Bad Verse. *James Camp, X. J. Kennedy, and Keith Waldrop, eds.* (1971) The Macmillan Company

PeHV Penguin Book of Homosexual Verse, The. *Stephen Coote, ed.* (1983) Penguin Books

PeSA Penguin Book of South African Verse, The. *Jack Cope and Uys Krige, eds.* (1968) Penguin Books

PGD Poems for the Great Days. *Thomas Curtis Clark and Robert Earle Clark, comps.* (1948) Abingdon-Cokesbury Press

PH Poetry of Horses, The. *William Cole, comp.* (1979) Charles Scribner's Sons

PoA *Poetry Anthology, The, 1912–1977. *Daryl Hine and Joseph Parisi, eds.* (1978) Houghton Mifflin Company

PoAu 1–2 Poetry in Australia, Vols. I–II. Vol. I: From the Ballads to Brennan. *T. Inglis Moore, comp.* Vol. II: Modern Australian Verse. *Douglas Stewart, comp.* (1965) University of California Press

PoBA **Poetry of Black America, The; Anthology of the 20th Century. *Arnold Adoff, ed.* (1973) Harper & Row

PoCh — Poet's Choice. *Paul Engle and Joseph Langland, eds.* (1962) The Dial Press

PoDr — Poet Dreaming in the Artist's House, The; Contemporary Poems about the Visual Arts. *Emilie Buchwald and Ruth Roston, eds.* (1984) Milkweed Editions

PoEL 1–5 — **Poets of the English Language, Vols. I–V. *W. H. Auden and Norman Holmes Pearson, eds.* (1950) The Viking Press. Vol. I: Langland to Spenser; Vol. II: Marlowe to Marvell; Vol. III: Milton to Goldsmith; Vol. IV: Blake to Poe; Vol. V: Tennyson to Yeats

POL — Poems One Line and Longer. *William Cole, ed.* (1973) Grossman Publishers

PoLF — Poems That Live Forever. *Hazel Felleman, ed.* (1965) Doubleday & Company

PoM — Postmoderns, The; the New American Poetry Revised. *Donald Allen and George F. Butterick, eds.* (1982) Grove Press

PoNe — Poetry of the Negro, The, 1746–1970. *Langston Hughes and Arna Bontemps, eds.* (Rev. ed., 1970) Doubleday & Company

PoOW — Poems of the Old West; a Rocky Mountain Anthology. *Levette J. Davidson, ed.* (1951) The University of Denver Press

PoPl — Poetry for Pleasure; the Hallmark Book of Poetry. (1960) Doubleday & Company

PoPle — Poetry for Pleasure; a Choice of Poetry and Verse on a Variety of Themes. *Ian Parsons, ed.* (1977) W. W. Norton & Company

PoRA — Poems to Read Aloud. *Edward Hodnett, ed.* (Rev. ed., 1967) W. W. Norton & Company

PoSC — Poems for Seasons and Celebrations. *William Cole, ed.* (1961) World Publishing Company

PoSH — Poems of the Scottish Hills; an Anthology. *Hamish Brown, comp.* (1982) Aberdeen University Press

PP — Poems on Poetry; the Mirror's Garland. *Robert Wallace and James G. Taaffe, eds.* (1965) E. P. Dutton & Company

PPJ — Pocket Poems; Selected for a Journey. *Paul B. Janeczko, ed.* (1985) Bradbury Press

PPoe — Pleasures of Poetry, The. *Donald Hall, ed.* (1971) Harper & Row

PPON — Poems of Protest Old and New. *Arnold Kenseth, ed.* (1968) The Macmillan Company

PPP — Poetry: Past and Present. *Frank Brady and Martin Price, eds.* (1974) Harcourt Brace Jovanovich

Prf — Preferences; 51 American Poets Choose Poems from Their Own Work and from the Past. *Richard Howard, ed.* (1974) The Viking Press

PrIm — Practical Imagination, The; an Introduction to Poetry. *Northrop Frye, Sheridan Baker, and George Perkins.* (1983) Harper & Row

Psk Poetspeak; in Their Work, about Their Work. *Paul B. Janeczko, comp.* (1983) Bradbury Press

PSoN *Popular Songs of Nineteenth-Century America; Complete Original Sheet Music for 64 Songs. *Richard Jackson, ed.* (1976) Dover Publications (Published in Great Britain by Constable and Company)

PV Pith and Vinegar; an Anthology of Short Humorous Poetry. *William Cole, ed.* (1969) Simon and Schuster

QFR Quest for Reality; an Anthology of Short Poems in English. *Yvor Winters and Kenneth Fields, eds.* (1969) The Swallow Press

QQQ Of Quarks, Quasars, and Other Quirks; Quizzical Poems for the Supersonic Age. *Sara Brewton, John E. Brewton, and John Brewton Blackburn, eds.* (1977) Thomas Y. Crowell Company

RFM Room for Me and a Mountain Lion; Poetry of Open Space. *Nancy Larrick, comp.* (1974) M. Evans and Company

RHPC **Random House Book of Poetry for Children, The. *Jack Prelutsky, ed.* (1983) Random House

RoGo Roofs of Gold; Poems to Read Aloud. *Padraic Colum, ed.* (1964) The Macmillan Company

SaC Saturday's Children; Poems of Work. *Helen Plotz, comp.* (1982) Greenwillow Books

SBG Salt and Bitter and Good; Three Centuries of English and American Women Poets. *Cora Kaplan, ed.* (1975) Paddington Press Ltd.

SBVL Shivering Babe, Victorious Lord; the Nativity in Poetry and Art. *Linda Ching Sledge.* (1981) William B. Eerdmans Publishing Company

SCAP Seventeenth-Century American Poetry. *Harrison T. Meserole, ed.* (1968) Doubleday Anchor Books

SCV Six Centuries of Verse. *Anthony Thwaite, comp.* (1984) Thames Methuen

SD Sprints and Distances; Sports in Poetry and the Poetry in Sport. *Lillian Morrison, comp.* (1965) Thomas Y. Crowell Company

SeCePo Seven Centuries of Poetry; Chaucer to Dylan Thomas. *A. N. Jeffares, ed.* (1955) Longmans, Green & Company

SeCeV Seven Centuries of Verse, English and American. *A. J. M. Smith, ed.* (3d ed., rev. and enl., 1967) Charles Scribner's Sons

SeCP Seventeenth Century Poetry; the Schools of Donne and Jonson. *Hugh Kenner, ed.* (1964) Holt, Rinehart and Winston

SeCV 1–2 Seventeenth-Century Verse and Prose, Vols. I–II. Vol. I: 1600–1660; Vol. II: 1660–1700. *Helen C. White, Ruth C. Wallerstein, and Ricardo Quintana, eds.* (1951, 1952) The Macmillan Company.

ShM Shrieks at Midnight; Macabre Poems, Eerie and Humorous. *Sara Brewton and John E. Brewton, eds.* (1969) Thomas Y. Crowell Company

ShS Shantymen and Shantyboys; Songs of the Sailor and Lumberman. *William Main Doerflinger, comp.* (1951) The Macmillan Company

SiPS Silver Poets of the Sixteenth Century (Everyman's Library). *Gerald Bullett, ed.* (1947) J. M. Dent & Sons Ltd.

SiSoSe Sing a Song of Seasons; Poems about Holidays, Vacation Days, and Days to Go to School. *Sara Brewton and John E. Brewton, eds.* (1955) The Macmillan Company

SO Straight On Till Morning; Poems of the Imaginary World. *Helen Hill, Agnes Perkins, and Alethea Helbig, comps.* (1977) Thomas Y. Crowell Company

SoPo Sound of Poetry, The. *Mary C. Austin and Queenie B. Mills, eds.* (1963) Allyn and Bacon

SoSe *Sound and Sense; an Introduction to Poetry. *Laurence Perrine, ed., with the assistance of Thomas R. Arp.* (6th ed., 1982) Harcourt Brace Jovanovich

SOTS 70 on the 70's; a Decade's History in Verse. *Richard Snyder and Robert McGovern, eds.* (1981) The Ashland Poetry Press

SOTW *Sleeping on the Wing; an Anthology of Modern Poetry with Essays on Reading and Writing. *Kenneth Koch and Kate Farrell.* (1981) Random House

SpRo Speak Roughly to Your Little Boy; a Collection of Parodies and Burlesques, Together with the Original Poems, Chosen and Annotated for Young People. *Myra Cohn Livingston, ed.* (1971) Harcourt Brace Jovanovich

STE Songs from This Earth on Turtle's Back; Contemporary American Indian Poetry. *Joseph Bruchac, ed.* (1983) The Greenfield Review Press

STF Speaker's Treasury of 400 Quotable Poems, The. *Croft M. Pentz, comp.* (1963) Zondervan Publishing House

StPo Story Poems, New and Old. *William Cole, ed.* (1957) World Publishing Company

Str Strings; a Gathering of Family Poems. *Paul B. Janeczko, comp.* (1984) Bradbury Press

SUMH Scars Upon My Heart; Women's Poetry and Verse of the First World War. *Catherine W. Reilly, ed.* (1981) Virago Press

SUS Sung Under the Silver Umbrella. *Association for Childhood Education International.* (1935) The Macmillan Company

SUW Songs from Unsung Worlds; Science in Poetry. *Bonnie Bilyeu Gordon, ed.* (1985) Birkhäuser

SV Singular Voices; American Poetry Today. *Stephen Berg, ed.* (1985) Avon Books

SyP Symbolist Poem, The. *Edward Engelberg, ed.* (1967) E. P. Dutton & Company

TAP	*Treasury of American Poetry, The. *Nancy Sullivan, ed.* (1978) Doubleday & Company
TAT	Traveling America with Today's Poets. *David Kherdian, ed.* (1977) Macmillan Publishing Company
TDH	They've Discovered a Head in the Box for the Bread and Other Laughable Limericks. *John E. Brewton and Lorraine A. Blackburn, comps.* (1978) Thomas Y. Crowell Company
TEP	*Treasury of English Poetry, The. *Mark Caldwell and Walter Kendrick, eds.* (1984) Doubleday & Company
TiPo	Time for Poetry. *May Hill Arbuthnot, comp.* (Rev. ed., 1959) Scott, Foresman and Company
TrAS	Treasury of American Song, A. *Olin Downes and Elie Siegmeister, comps.* (2d ed., rev. and enl., 1943) Alfred A. Knopf
TrCP	Treasury of Christian Poetry, The. *Lorraine Eitel, comp., with Jeannine Bohlmeyer, Lynn M. Fauth, Gerald W. Healy, Daniel Taylor, and Christian Weintz.* (1982) Fleming H. Revell Company
TreF	Treasury of the Familiar, A. *Ralph L. Woods, ed.* (1942) The Macmillan Company
TreFS	Treasury of the Familiar, A Second. *Ralph L. Woods, ed.* (1950) The Macmillan Company
TreFT	Treasury of the Familiar, A Third. *Ralph L. Woods, ed.* (1970) The Macmillan Company
TrGrPo	Treasury of Great Poems, English and American, A. *Louis Untermeyer, ed.* (Rev. and enl. ed., 1955) Simon and Schuster
TrJP	Treasury of Jewish Poetry, A. *Nathan Ausubel and Marynn Ausubel, eds.* (1957) Crown Publishers
TrPWD	Treasury of Poems for Worship and Devotion, A. *Charles L. Wallis, ed.* (1959) Harper & Brothers
TRV	Treasury of Religious Verse, The. *Donald T. Kauffman, comp.* (1962) Fleming H. Revell Company
TTY	3000 Years of Black Poetry. *Alan Lomax and Raoul Abdul, eds.* (1970) Dodd, Mead & Company
TW	Tygers of Wrath; Poems of Hate, Anger, and Invective. *X. J. Kennedy, ed.* (1981) The University of Georgia Press
TwAmPo	Twentieth-Century American Poetry. *Conrad Aiken, ed.* (Rev. ed., 1963) The Modern Library
TwCP	Twentieth Century Poetry; American and British (1900–1970). *John Malcolm Brinnin and Bill Read, eds.* (1963, rev. ed., 1970) McGraw-Hill Book Company. Text edition entitled The Modern Poets; for the 1963 edition, *see* MP
TWSS	That's What She Said; Contemporary Poetry and Fiction by Native American Women. *Rayna Green, ed.* (1984) Indiana University Press

UnPo — *Understanding Poetry. *Cleanth Brooks and Robert Penn Warren, eds.* (4th ed., 1976) Holt, Rinehart and Winston

UnS — Untune the Sky; Poems of Music and the Dance. *Helen Plotz, comp.* (1957) Thomas Y. Crowell Company

UnTE — Uninhibited Treasury of Erotic Poetry, An. *Louis Untermeyer, ed.* (1963) The Dial Press

VGW — Voice That Is Great Within Us, The; American Poetry of the Twentieth Century. *Hayden Carruth, ed.* (1970) Bantam Books

ViBoFo — Viking Book of Folk Ballads of the English-speaking World, The. *Albert B. Friedman, ed.* (1956) The Viking Press

ViBoPo — Viking Book of Poetry of the English-speaking World, The. *Richard Aldington, ed.* (Rev., mid-century ed., 1958, in 2 vols.). The Viking Press

VLP — Victorian Literature: Poetry. *Donald J. Gray and G. B. Tennyson, eds.* (1976) Macmillan Publishing Company

VoR — Voices of the Rainbow; Contemporary Poetry by American Indians. *Kenneth Rosen, ed.* (1975) The Viking Press

VWA — Voices Within the Ark; the Modern Jewish Poets. *Howard Schwartz and Anthony Rudolf, eds.* (1980) Avon Books

WaaP — War and the Poet; an Anthology of Poetry Expressing Man's Attitudes to War from Ancient Times to the Present. *Richard Eberhart and Selden Rodman, eds.* (1945) The Devin-Adair Company

WaP — War Poets, The; an Anthology of the War Poetry of the 20th Century. *Oscar Williams, ed.* (1945) The John Day Company

WBLP — World's Best-loved Poems, The. *James Gilchrist Lawson, comp.* (1927) Harper & Brothers

WeW — Western Wind; an Introduction to Poetry. *John Frederick Nims, ed.* (2d ed., 1983) Random House

WGRP — World's Great Religious Poetry, The. *Caroline Miles Hill, ed.* (1934) The Macmillan Company

WHA — Winged Horse Anthology, The. *Joseph Auslander and Frank Ernest Hill, eds.* (1929) Doubleday & Company

WhC — What Cheer; an Anthology of American and British Humorous and Witty Verse. *David McCord, ed.* (1945) Coward-McCann

WHW — Wind Has Wings, The; Poems from Canada. *Mary Alice Downie and Barbara Robertson, eds.* (1968) Henry Z. Walck, Oxford University Press

WiR — Wind and the Rain, The; an Anthology of Poems for Young People. *John Hollander and Harold Bloom, eds.* (1961) Doubleday & Company

WOLT — Wetting Our Lines Together; an Anthology of Recent North American Fishing Poems. *Allen Hoey, ed., with Cynthia Hoey and Daniel J. Moriarty.* (1982) Tamarack Editions

WPE Women Poets in English, The; an Anthology. *Ann Stanford, ed.* (1972) McGraw-Hill Book Company

WPOW *Women Poets of the World. *Joanna Bankier and Deirdre Lashgari, eds.* (1983) Macmillan Publishing Company

WSC Why Am I Grown So Cold? Poems of the Unknowable. *Myra Cohn Livingston, ed.* (1982) Atheneum

WTO World Treasury of Oral Poetry, A. *Ruth Finnegan, ed.* (1978) Indiana University Press

YaD Yankee Doodles; a Book of American Verse. *Ted Malone, ed.* (1943) McGraw-Hill Book Company. Edition of 1948, published by the Garden City Publishing Company, has title The All-American Book of Verse

YeAr Year Around, The; Poems for Children. *Alice I. Hazeltine and Elva S. Smith, comps.* (1956) Abingdon Press

TITLE AND FIRST LINE INDEX

"A" (1–12), *sels.* Louis Zukofsky.
  "Giant sparkler,/ Lights of the river," 4. VGW
  "River that must turn full after I stop dying," 11. CoPo; VGW
A, a, a, a,/ Yet I love whereso I go. A Bachelor's Life. *Unknown.* OxBM
A, a, a, Domine Deus. David Jones. FaBoTw; NOCV
A, a noble failure, turns his critical wits on B. Names. D. J. Enright. FaBoCo
A. A violent order is disorder; and. Connoisseur of Chaos. Wallace Stevens. CABA
A and B. C. H. Sisson. OxBC
A B C, An. *Unknown. Fr.* The New England Primer. GBP
  ("In Adam's fall/ We sinned all.") OBCA
A B C Bunny, The. Wanda Gág. TiPo
A B C D. *Unknown.* OxNR
A, B, C, D, E, F, G. *Unknown.* OxNR
A, B, C, D, E, F, G. Alphabet. *Unknown.* FaBoUs
A B C D Goldfish. *Unknown.* NTCP
A B C for Grown Gentlemen, An. Chevalier de Boufflers, *tr. fr. French by* Leigh Hunt. GLGT
A.B.C. of Devotion, An. *Unknown.* MeEL
A B C's in Green. Leonora Speyer. HBMV; HBVY; OHIP
A Cappella. Michael Pettit. GrPl
A celuy que pluys eyme en mounde. To the One I Love Most [*or* Lines from Love Letters]. *Unknown.* MeEL; OBEV
A Clymene. Paul Verlaine, *tr. fr. French by* Arthur Symons. AWP
A' day aboot the hoose I work. Nocht o' Mortal Sicht. Bessie J. B. Macarthur. OxBS
A! Dere God, what may this be. On the Death of Edward III. *Unknown.* OxBM
A Deux. William Wood. ELU
A dis[h], a dis[h], a green grass. Green Grass. *Unknown.* CH; GBP; OxBoLi; OxNR; PoPle
A. E. Emily Brontë. *See* Two Children.
A. E. F. Carl Sandburg. CMoP; HBMV; MoAB; MoAmPo; WaaP
A. E. Housman and a Few Friends. Humbert Wolfe. FiBHP; WhC
  ("When lads have done with labor.") BXAP; Par; SpRo; WhC
"A 11." Louis Zukofsky. *Fr.* "A." VGW
$A = bh$ over 2. Homework for Annabelle. Phyllis McGinley. GLGT
A = pi r squared. Even Though. John Stone. AMV–81
A for Apple, big and red. The ABC Bunny. Wanda Gág. TiPo
"A 4." Louis Zukofsky. *Fr.* "A." VGW
A! [*or* Ah!] fredome [*or* freedom] is a noble thing! Freedom [*or* Fredome]. John Barbour. *Fr.* The Bruce. BSV; FaBoCh; GoTS; OBEV; OxBS; TrGrPo; ViBoPo
A ha ha ha! this world doth passe. Idle Fyno. *Unknown.* ChTr; PoEL–2
A ho! A ho!/ Love's horn doth blow. Song. Thomas Lovell Beddoes. *Fr.* The Bride's Tragedy. ChER
A. "I was a Have." B. "I was a 'Have-not.'" Equality of Sacrifice. Kipling. *Fr.* Epitaphs of the War. FaBoTw; NoP; OAEP; OBWP
A is an angel of blushing eighteen. The Alphabet. Charles Stuart Calverley. HBV–2
A Is an Apple. *Unknown.* WhC
A is for Acting, the shantyboy's life. The Shantyboy's Song. Kenneth Zwicker. ShS
A Is for Alpha: Alpha Is for A. Conrad Aiken. NePA
A is for ax [*or* axes], you very well know [*or* and that we all know]. The Lumberman's Alphabet. *Unknown.* AmFP; ShS
A is the aftermost part of the ship. The Sailors' Alphabet. *Unknown.* AmFP
A is the autograph bore. The Autograph Bore. Oliver Herford. TDH
A is to begin with, and A began with Adam. Genesis of Vowels. James Broughton. CrMA
A la Bourbon. Richard Lovelace. CaPo
A la Claire Fontaine (By Yonder Flowing Fountain). *Tr. fr. French by* Arthur Kevess. FSW
A la Promenade. Paul Verlaine, *tr. fr. French by* Arthur Symons. AWP; OBVE
À l'Ange Avantgardien. Francis Reginald. MoCV
A. M.—P.M. Theodore H. Hirschfield. AMV–81
À Madame, Madame B, Beauté Sexagenaire. Charles Sackville. APAS
A! Mercy, Fortune. *Unknown.* MeEL
A Mhic, ná Meabhraigh Éigse. *Unknown, tr. fr. Irish by* Máire MacEntee. OxBI
"A, my dere, a, my dere Son." Mary Weeps for Her Child. *Unknown.* OxBoLi
A peels an apple, while B kneels to God. A Primer of the Daily Round. Howard Nemerov. NYBP; WeW
A Perigord pres del muralh. Bertrans de Born, *tr. fr. Provençal by* Ezra Pound. CTC
A Quoi Bon Dire. Charlotte Mew. HBMV; OxBTC
A. R. U., *with music. Unknown.* AS
A Sè Stesso. Giacomo Leopardi, *tr. fr. Italian by* Lorna De' Lucchi. AWP
A Solis Ortus Cardine. Ford Madox Ford. ViBoPo
A soun tres chere et special. Lines from Love Letters, II. *Unknown.* OBEV
A.T. 30 lies in the siding. Ambulance Train 30. Carola Oman. SUMH
A Terre. Wilfred Owen. LiTM; MMA; OxBTC; PAI; WaP
A' things created have their uses. Strictures on the Economy of Nature. George Outram. FaBoCo
A to Amerous, to Adventurous, ne Angre the not to moche. The Alphabet of Aristotle. *At. to* Mayster Benet. FaBoUs
A tumbled down, and hurt his Arm, against a bit of wood. Alphabet. Edward Lear. FaBoNo
A.U.C. 334: about this date. Advice to Young Ladies. A. D. Hope. NoP
A, U, Hinny Burd. *Unknown.* GBP
A was an apple pie. The Alphabet. Kate Greenaway. HBVY
A was an apple pie, B bit it, C cut it. Mother Goose. FaBoUs; OxNR
A was an archer, who shot at a frog. Tom Thumb's [Picture] Alphabet. *Unknown.* FaBoUs; HBV–1; HBVY; OxBChV; OxNR
A was an Army, to settle disputes. A Single-Rhyme Alphabet. *Unknown.* FaBoUs
A was once an apple-pie. A Nonsense Alphabet [*or* An Alphabet]. Edward Lear. OxBChV; SoPo; SUS; TiPo
A ye wha are sae guid yoursel. *See* O ye wha are sae guid yoursel.
Aa the skippers of bonny Lothen. Young Allan. *Unknown.* ESPB
Aa went te Blaydon Races, 'twas on the ninth o' June. Blaydon Races. *Unknown.* ELP
Aardvark. Julia Fields. BOLo; CNA; OFD
Aaron. George Herbert. MeLP; MePo; OAEL–1; OAEP; OBS
Aaron Burr. Stephen Vincent Benét. InMe
Aaron Burr's Wooing. Edmund Clarence Stedman. PAH
Aaron Hatfield. Edgar Lee Masters. *Fr.* Spoon River Anthology. LiTA
Aaron Nicholas, Almost Ten. Janet Campbell Hale. VoR
Aaron Stark. E. A. Robinson. MoAB; MoAmPo
Aa's a broken-hairted keelman, and aa's ower heid in love. Cushie Butterfield. George Ridley. VLP
Abalone, *with music. Unknown.* AS
Abalone Song, The. George Sterling. BPAW
Abandonado, El, *with music. Unknown, tr. fr. Spanish by* Frank J. Dobie. AS
Abandoned, The. Arthur Symons. SyP
Abandoned Copper Refinery. Dan Gillespie. TAT
Abandoned Farmhouse. Ted Kooser. DFF; GP
Abandoned House, The. Patricia Hubbell. WSC
Abandoned House in Late Light. Chase Twichell. MAYP
Abandoned. My brother and I tiptoed. The Slaughterhouse Boys. William Meissner. AMV–81
Abandoned, Overgrown Cemetery in the Pasture near Our House, An. Gregory Orr. MAYP
Abandonment of Autos. Bruce Dawe. CBAP
Abasis. Christopher Middleton. *Fr.* Herman Moon's Hourbook. NePoEA–2
Abate, fair fugitive, abate thy speed. Daphne and Apollo. Ovid, *tr. by* Matthew Prior. *Fr.* Metamorphoses, I. NOEC
Abbess, The ("The abbess was of noble blood"). Sir Walter Scott. *Fr.* Marmion, II. GoBC
Abbey Asaroe. William Allingham. OnYI; OxBI
Abbey Church at Bath, The. Henry Harington. FaBoEE
Abbey Mason, The, *sel.* Thomas Hardy.
  "When longer yet dank death had wormed." PeD
Abbey Walk, The. Robert Henryson. BSV
Abbot is painting me so true. On His Portrait. William Cowper. EyDe

Abbot of Derry, The. John Bennett. HBMV
Abbot of Inisfalen, The. William Allingham. GN; HBV-2; OnMSP
Abbreviated Interviews with a Few Disgruntled Literary Celebrities. Reed Whittemore. FiBHP
Abbreviated Rumination. P. L. Jacobs. LFAC
Abdelazer, *sel.* Aphra Behn.
Song: "Love in fantastic triumph sate." HBV-1; NOBE; WPE
(Love Arm'd.) SBG
(Love in Fantastic Triumph Sat.) OAEP
(Song: Love Arm'd.) CavP
Abdelfatteh. E. A. Lacey. PeHV
Abdication of Fergus Mac Roy, The. Sir Samuel Ferguson. AnIL
Abdication Street Song. *Unknown.* PV
Abdolonymus the Sidonian. Jones Very. AP
Abduction, The. Stanley Kunitz. SV
Abdul A-Bul-Bul A-Mir. *Unknown.* TreF
(Abdul, the Bulbul Amir [*or* Ameer]). AS, *with music;* FSW
(Abdullah Bulbul Amir; or, Ivan Petrofsky Skovar.) BLPA; FPL
Abe Lincoln stood at the White House gate. Lord Lovel. *Unknown.* ViBoFo
A-Begging Buttermilk I Will Go. *Unknown.* OBET
Abel. Demetrios Capetanakis. GTBS-P; WaaP
Abel. Else Lasker-Schüler, *tr. fr. German by* Joachim Neugroschel. VWA
Abel was pure and woolly. Brothers. Dan Pagis, *tr. by* Shirley Kaufman. VWA
Abelard at Cluny. Grover Rees III. AMV-80
Abelard was: God is. Sic et Non. Sir Herbert Read. FaBoTw
Abel's Bride. Denise Levertov. VGW
Abenamar, Abenamar. *Unknown, tr. fr. Spanish by* Robert Southey. AWP
Aberdarcy: The Chaucer Road. Kingsley Amis. *Fr.* The Evans Country. NOBL
Aberdarcy: The Main Square. Kingsley Amis. *Fr.* The Evans Country. NOBL; OxBTC
Aberdeen, Mississippi Blues. *Unknown.* BluL
Aberdeen Train. Edwin Morgan. BSV
Abhorrent to all natural joys. Epigram: To Philaenis. Martial. PeHV
Abide, Good Men. *Unknown.* OxBM
Abide in Me, O Lord, and I in Thee, *with music.* Harriet Beecher Stowe. AH
Abide Not in the Realm of Dreams, *with music.* William Henry Burleigh. AH
Abide with Me. Henry Francis Lyte. BLRP; EBVV; FaBoBe; FaFP; FaPoR; HBV-2; ILwL; NOCV; TreF; VLP; WBLP; WGRP
(Hymn: "Abide with me; fast falls the eventide.") NBM
Abiding. A. B. Simpson. STF
Abiding Love, The. John White Chadwick. BLPA; FaBoBe
(Auld Lang Syne.) WGRP
Abiding snake. Prologue: Moments in a Glade. Alan Stephens. QFR
Abigail's Lamentation for the Loss of Mr. Harley. William Walsh. APAS
Abiku. Wole Soyinka. PBA
Abilene. *Unknown.* FSW
Abishag. Jacob Fichman, *tr. fr. Hebrew.* TrJP, *tr. by* Sholom J. Kahn; VWA, *tr. by* Robert Friend
Abishag. Rainer Maria Rilke, *tr. fr. German by* Jethro Bithell. AWP
Abishag. André Spire, *tr. fr. French by* Emanuel Eisenberg. TrJP
Abishag Writes a Letter Home. Itzik Manger, *tr. fr. Yiddish by* Ruth Whitman. VWA
Abla. Antara, *tr. fr. Arabic by* E. Powys Mathers. *Fr.* The Mu'allaqât. AWP
Abnegation. Martial, *tr. fr. Latin by* Thomas Moore. UnTE
(To Cloe.) AWP
Abnegation. Adrienne Rich. WPE
Abner Silver's "Pu-leeze! Mr. Hemingway!" Ring Lardner. OBAL
Abnormal Is Not Courage, The. Jack Gilbert. CoAP; NPGG
Aboard at a Ship's Helm. Walt Whitman. NePA; NOBA; OxBA
Abode of the nightingale is bare, The. Alone. Walter de la Mare. ChTr; EnLoPo
Abolitionist Hymn, *with music.* *Unknown.* TrAS
Abominable Baseball Bat, The. X. J. Kennedy. WSC
Aboriginal Sin. John Hay. NePoAm-2
Abortion. Ai. BoWoP
Abortion, An. Frank O'Hara. TAP
Abortion, The. Anne Sexton. CAPP; IHMS; MAT; NMM; VGW
Abortions will not let you forget. The Mother. Gwendolyn Brooks. BlSi; BPo; CAPP; GP; NMM
Abou Ben Adhem. Leigh Hunt. BeLS; BLPA; EnRP; FaBoBe; FaBV; FaFP; FaPoR; FPL; HBV-2; HBVY; NOBE; OBEV; OBVV; OHFP; TreF; TRV; WBLP; WGRP
(Abou Ben Adhem and the Angel.) FaBoRV; FaPON; GN
Abou Ben Adhem's name led all the rest. Holy Order. J. B. Boothroyd. FiBHP
About a fierce highwayman my story I will tell. Brennan on the Moor. *Unknown.* OuSiCo
About a fly. The Story. Charles Simic. NNaP
About a quarter to ten the door softly opened. Listening to Beethoven on the Oregon Coast. Henry Carlile. Psk
About a well-spring, in a little mead. Of Three Damsels in a Meadow. John Payne. OBVV
About a Year after He Got Married He Would Sit Alone in an Abandoned Shack in a Cotton Field Enjoying Himself. James Whitehead. GP
About an Excavation. Charles Reznikoff. NTCP; PCP; PrIm; VGW
About ane bank, where birdis on bewis. Alexander Montgomerie. *Fr.* The Cherry and the Slae. GoTS
About beef, for instance? Christmas. Leigh Hunt. OBCP
About Children. Phyllis McGinley. OBAL
About Feet. Margaret Hillert. RHPC
About fifty years since, in the days of our daddies. Paddy's Metamorphosis. Thomas Moore. OnYI
About four, a few flakes. Six Winter Privacy Poems. Robert Bly. LCAP
About Glenkindie and his man. Glenkindie. William Bell Scott. HBV-2
About her head or floating feet. My Father's Child. "Stuart Sterne." AA
About his brow the laurel and the bay. A Man! Clinton Scollard. OHIP
About in London. John Gay. *Fr.* Trivia; or, The Art of Walking the Streets of London. FaBoPP
About Marriage. Denise Levertov. NMM
About me the night, moonless, wimples the mountains. Vancouver Lights. Earle Birney. CaP
About mirrors in hotel rooms: one can say. Results of a Scientific Survey. Bruce Cutler. AMV-80; FAZ
About Motion Pictures. Ann Darr. GrPl
About mountains it is useless to argue. Alpine. R. S. Thomas. BoNaP; LiSp; POL; RFM
About My Poems. Donald Justice. PoA
About one month before my thirty-third. Thinking of You. Dick Lourie. NeAC
About Savannah. *Unknown.* PAH
About suffering, about adoration, the old masters. The Old and the New Masters. Randall Jarrell. InPK
About suffering they were never wrong. Musée des Beaux Arts. W. H. Auden. BiP; CABA; ChMP; CMoP; CoBMV; FaFP; FF; GTBS-P; HAP; HeIP; InPK; InPS; LiTB; LiTM; MoAB; MoPo; MP; NePA; NIP; NoAM; NOBE; NoP; OAEP; PAI; PoRA; PPP; PrIm; SCV; SeCePo; SeCeV; SoSe; TEP; TrCP; TreFT; TrGrPo; TwCP; WeW
About suffering you were wrong, Wystan. A Letter to Auden. Robert Phillips. AMV-81
About the august and ancient Square. Oxford Nights. Lionel Johnson. BrPo
About the Cool Water. Kenneth Rexroth. ErPo
About the cool water. Sappho, *tr. fr. Greek by* Kenneth Rexroth. OBVE
About the Cows. Roger Pfingston. FAZ
"About the dead, no murmur of dispraise." Elegy for a Bad Poet, Taken from Us Not Long Since. John Frederick Nims. TW
About the dog days folks complain. A Dog Day. Rachel Field. SiSoSe
About the fashions of the day. Hug Me Tight. John Kendall. WhC
About the Heavenly Life. Luis de Leon, *tr. fr. Spanish.* ILwL
About the hilltop how the clouds are cool. Summer Days. Roy Daniells. CaP
About the little chambers of my heart. Gone. Mary Elizabeth Coleridge. HBV-2; OBEV; OBNC; OBVV
"About the night on which a man said he would spend a 100 dollars." Epilogue: Anemone. Leslie Scalapino. *Fr.* Hmmmm. NPGG
About the Phoenix. James Merrill. NoAM
About the shark, phlegmatical one. The Maldive Shark. Herman Melville. AmPP; AP; MOS; NePA; NOBA; NoP; OxBA; PAI; PoEL-5; TAP; TW
About the Shelleys. *Unknown.* WhC
About the size of an old-style dollar bill. Poem. Elizabeth Bishop. FYAP
About the skull of the beloved, filled. Presentation Piece. Marilyn Hacker. AmPA
About the sweet bag of a bee. The Bag of the Bee. Robert Herrick. OAEP
About the Teeth of Sharks. John Ciardi. OBCA
About the time that taverns shut. The Ballad of Minepit Shaw. Kipling. PoPle
About the year of one B.C. Jonah and the Whale. *Unknown.* BLPA
About their prince each took his wonted seat. Pluto's Council. Tasso, *tr. by* Edward Fairfax. *Fr.* Godfrey of Bulloigne. OBSC
About this lady many fruitful trees. The Lady with the Unicorn. Vernon Watkins. LiTB; MP; TwCP
About this table/ Sat many hawk-eyed kings. Inscriptions at the City of Brass. *Unknown, tr. by* E. Powys Mathers. *Fr.* The Thousand and One Nights. AWP
About those wagon wheels. Wagon Wheels. S. E. LaMoure. AMV-81

About those who have recognized the range of choice. It Is Difficult Now to Speak of Poetry. George Oppen. NNaP
About to Die. *Gond Oral Tradition, tr. by* V. Elwin *and* S. Hivale. WTO
About twenty years ago. Wild Oats. Philip Larkin. InPS
About twilight we came to the whitewashed pub. East Coast Journey. James K. Baxter. NoP
About two thousand miles. Coming Home. John Stone. NIP
About us in white mist, ptarmigan. February Thaw. G. J. F. Dutton. PoSH
About Women. H. Phelps Putnam. TwAmPo
About Women's Liberation. María Saucedo, *tr. fr. Spanish by* Toni Empringham. FIA
About Yule, when [*or* quhen] the wind blew cule. Young Waters. *Unknown.* ESPB; OxBB
Above a stretch of still unravaged weald. The Garden Party. Donald Davie. NePoEA
Above a surface of stars. Metropolitan Night. Jorge Guillén, *tr. by* Barbara Howes. NYP
Above a world entrapped by fear. The Forgotten Star. Thomas Curtis Clark. PGD
Above, above. Behold. *Tr. fr. Hawaiian by* M. K. Pukui. WTO
Above all gifts we most should prize. Walter Savage Landor. FaBoEE
Above and below the ship, this blue. Becalmed. John Blight. PoAu-2
Above, below, in sky and sod. The Over-Heart. Whittier. NOCV; WGRP
Above Ben Loyal. Arthur Ball. PoSH
Above finespun, unruffled sheets. Lovebirds. William Jay Smith. ErPo
Above Inverkirkaig. Norman MacCaig. PoSH
Above It All. Philip Levine. NOBA
Above Machu Picchu, 129 Baker Street, San Francisco. Joseph Stroud. NPGG
Above me is the misty English sky. In the Lake Country. Kay Wissinger. AMV-80
Above me the abbey, grey arches on the cliff. Caedmon. Norman Nicholson. FaBoTw
Above my daughter in the tree. White Spider. Marita Garin. AMV-80
Above my desk/the Rabbi of Auschwitz. On a Drawing by Flavio. Philip Levine. VWA
Above my desk, whirring and [*or* but] self-important. Angel [*or* Another Angel]. James Merrill. ConAP; NoAM; PoA
Above my face is a map. The Cloud-Mobile. May Swenson. SO
Above my head the apples on my grandparents' tree. Skins. Elizabeth Spires. MAYP
Above my head the shields are stained with rust. The Lamp of Poor Souls. Marjorie Pickthall. HBV-2
Above Pate Valley. Gary Snyder. CoAP; ConAP; LCAP; NaP; NoP
Above Salerno. Ada Foster Murray. HBV-2
Above sleeping yard light, you wait. Raven at Lemon Creek Jail. Thomas Waltner. LFAC
Above Stromness, the Hills of Hoy rise proud. Lion Gate. Vera Rich. PoSH
Above the Arno. May Swenson. NYBP
Above the beach, the vineyard. The Flower. Robert Penn Warren. PoPl
Above the Bright Blue Sky, *sel.* Albert Midlane.
"There's a Friend for little children." OxBChV
Above the cloistral valley. The Sleeper. Clinton Scollard. HBV-2
Above the clouds the sun is warm. Flight 382. Doris Longman. AMV-81
Above the clumps where feather trees. At the Beginnings of the Andes. Barbara Ras. AMV-81
Above the Crags that fade and gloom. From a Window in Princes Street. W. E. Henley. EBVV
Above the Dock. T. E. Hulme. FaBoMo; GTBS-P
Above the Falls at Waimea. Don Johnson. MAYP
Above the fence-flowers, like a bloody thumb. Variations on Southern Themes. Donald Justice. SV
Above the fresh ruffles of the surf. The Sea. Hart Crane. Voyages, I. AmPP; AP; CABA; CMoP; CrMA; MOS; NoAM; NOBA; NoP; OxBA; TAP; VGW
Above the graves of countless millions slain. In the Name of Our Sons. Dorothy Gould. PGD
Above the hidden rocks all night. The Lighthouse. John Seller Anson. AMV
Above the High. Geoffrey Grigson. EnLoPo
Above the Hills of Time. Thomas Tiplady. TRV
Above the Medway. A. J. Munby. *Fr.* The Vales of the Medway. FaBoPP
Above the pines the moon was slowly drifting. Dickens in Camp. Bret Harte. BPAW; HBV-2
Above the plains. Of Only a Single Poem. G. J. F. Dutton. PoSH
Above the pools, above the valley of fears. Élévation. Baudelaire, *tr. by* Arthur Symons. AWP
Above the quiet dock in midnight. Above the Dock. T. E. Hulme. FaBoMo; GTBS-P
Above the quiet valley and unrippled lake. Spring Oak. Galway Kinnell. BoNaP; ELU; NePoAm
Above the rocking heads of the mothers. Nelly Sachs, *tr. fr. German by* Ruth *and* Matthew Mead. PBWP
Above the stream, grunting Staoineag stands. Staoineag. Leen Volwerk. PoSH
Above the violent park. A Star. George MacBeth. NYBP
Above the voiceful windings of a river. At the Grave of Henry Vaughan. Siegfried Sassoon. ChMP; CMoP; EaLo; GTBS-P; PoPle
Above the Wall. Susannah P. Malarkey. AMV-80
Above the weary waiting world. Christmas Song. Bliss Carman. PeCV; PoSC
Above them spread a stranger sky. The Indian's Welcome to the Pilgrim Fathers. Lydia Huntley Sigourney. AA
Above these bleak Wyoming plains. Winter Juniper. Joseph Langland. NePoEA
Above These Cares. Edna St. Vincent Millay. NoP
Above this bramble-overarched long lane. The Clearing. Robert Graves. NYBP
Above, through lunar woods a goddess flees. The Lovers. William Jay Smith. MoAmPo
Above yon sombre [*or* somber] swell of land. The Plough [*or* The Plow]. Richard Henry Horne. HBV-1; OBEV; OBVV
Above, you paint the sky. How to Paint a Perfect Christmas. Miroslav Holub, *tr. by* George Theiner *and* Ian Milner. OBCP
Abracadabra. Dorothy Livesay. WHW
Abraham. Stephen Mitchell. VWA
Abraham. Edwin Muir. EBCP
Abraham. Delmore Schwartz. VWA
Abraham. Eisig Silberschlag. VWA
Abraham and Hagar/ a marriage torn asunder. The Story of Abraham and Hagar. Edna Aphek, *tr. by* Yishai Tobin. VWA
Abraham and Isaac. Else Lasker-Schüler, *tr. fr. German.* BoWoP, *tr. by* Rosemarie Waldrop; VWA, *tr. by* Joachim Neugroschel
Abraham and Sarah. Itzik Manger, *tr. fr. Yiddish by* Stephen Garrin. VWA
Abraham built a town of sod. Abraham and Isaac. Else Lasker-Schüler, *tr. by* Rosemarie Waldrop. BoWoP
Abraham Davenport. Whittier. AmPP; NoP
Abraham in Egypt. Howard Schwartz. VWA
Abraham in the land of Eden. Abraham and Isaac. Else Lasker-Schüler, *tr. by* Joachim Neugroschel. VWA
Abraham Lincoln. A. S. Ames. OHIP
Abraham Lincoln. Joseph Auslander. YaD
Abraham Lincoln. Rosemary *and* Stephen Vincent Benét. PoSC; TiPo; YeAr
Abraham Lincoln. Henry Howard Brownell. GN
Abraham Lincoln. Bryant. *See* Death of Lincoln, The.
Abraham Lincoln. Samuel Valentine Cole. OHIP
Abraham Lincoln. Mildred Plew Meigs. PAL; TiPo
Abraham Lincoln. Edmund Clarence Stedman. PAH
Abraham Lincoln. Richard Henry Stoddard. AA; FaBoBe; GN; OHIP; PAH; PGD
Abraham Lincoln. Tom Taylor. HBV-2; PAH
Abraham Lincoln, the Dear President. The Dear President. John James Piatt. PAH
Abraham Lincoln, the Master. Thomas Curtis Clark. OHIP
Abraham Lincoln Walks at Midnight. Vachel Lindsay. AmFN; AmPP; CMoP; FaBV; FaFP; FaPON; GOA; HBV-2; LiTA; MoAmPo; MoVE; NoAM; NOBA; OFD; OHFP; OHIP; OxBA; PAH; PAI; PAL; PoPl; PPON; TAP; TreF; VGW
Abraham Lincoln was ten feet tall. Abraham Lincoln. Joseph Auslander. YaD
Abraham Sutskever. Seymour Mayne. VWA
Abraham's children played with shells. Hagar and Ishmael. Else Lasker-Schüler, *tr. by* Rosemarie Waldrop. BoWoP
Abraham's Daughter, *with music.* Septimus Winner. TrAS
Abraham's Knife. George Garrett. PoPl
Abraham's little sons played with seashells. Hagar and Ishmael. Else Lasker-Schüler, *tr. by* Joachim Neugroschel. VWA
Abram Bailey he'd three sons. Sir Lionel. *Unknown.* AmFP
Abroad. William Carlos Williams. TwAmPo
Abroad and at Home. Swift. DBV; WhC
(Epigram: "As Thomas was cudgeled one day by his wife.") FaBoEE
Abroad as I Was Walking. *Unknown.* OBET
Abroad as I was walking/All on a summer's day. Young Barnswell. *Unknown.* OBET
Abroad in the meadows to see the young lambs. Innocent Play. Isaac Watts. NOEC
Abroad on a winter's night there ran. A Christmas Legend. Frank Sidgwick. OHIP
Abroad Thoughts. Edward Blishen. NOBL
Abroad Thoughts from Home. Donald Hall. NePoEA

Abruptly All the Palm Trees. William Jay Smith. PoA
Absalom. Zerubavel Gilead, *tr. fr. Hebrew by* Dorothea Krook. VWA
Absalom and Achitophel, Pt. I. Dryden. NoP; OAEL-1; SeCV-2
Sels.
Achitophel: The Earl of Shaftesbury. NOBE
(Achitophel.) AWP, *br. sel.;* SeCePo; WHA, *br. sel.*
(Earl of Shaftesbury, The.) FaBoEn
(False Achitophel, The.) FiP
(Lord Shaftesbury.) LoBV
("Of these the false Achitophel was first.") HAP; InPS; PoEL-3; ViBoPo
(Shaftesbury.) OBS
Duke of Buckingham, The. FaBoEn
"In pious times, ere priestcraft did begin." HAP; NoP; OAEL-1; OAEP; SeCV-2
Malcontents, The. OBS
Popish Plot, The. ACP
"Some by their friends, more by themselves thought wise." OBSV
"Some of their chiefs were princes of the land." EBEV; SCV
"With all these loads of injuries oppressed." EBEV
Zimri: The Duke of Buckingham. NOBE; OBSV
("In the first rank of these did Zimri stand.") HAP; ViBoPo
(Zimri.) AWP; SeCePo
Absalom and Achitophel, Pt. II, *sels.* Nahum Tate *and* John Dryden.
"Next these, a troop of busy spirits press." Dryden. PPP; SeCV-2
Og and Doeg. AWP; FiP; TW
("Doeg, though without knowing how or why.") PoEL-3
Thomas Shadwell the Poet, 2 *ll.* ChTr
"To make quick way I'll leap o'er heavy blocks." Dryden. OBSV
Absence. Matthew Arnold. Switzerland, VI. OAEP
Absence. Jeannette Barnes. AMV-80
Absence. John Hoskins, *sometimes at. to* John Donne. MeLP
(Ode: "Absence, hear thou my protestation.") ElL
(Present in Absence.) GTBS; GTBS-P
Absence. Richard Jago. HBV-1; OBEV
Absence. Walter Savage Landor. *Fr.* Ianthe. EnRP; OBRV
Absence, The. Denise Levertov. NaP
Absence. Pierre Louÿs, *tr. fr. French by* Horace M. Brown. *Fr.* The Songs of Bilitis. UnTE
Absence. Claude McKay. CDC
Absence. Kathy Mangan. AMV-81
Absence. Peter Meinke. PPJ
Absence. Charlotte Mew. ChMP; MoAB; MoBrPo
Absence. Edwin Morgan. BSV
Absence. Shakespeare. *See* Sonnets, LVII.
Absence. Sir Philip Sidney. SiPS
Absence. *Unknown.* OBSC
Absence, The. Sylvia Townsend Warner. MoBrPo
Absence absenting causeth me to complain. Sir Thomas Wyatt. SiPS
Absence and Presence. Fulke Greville. Caelica, XLV. OBSC
("Absence, the noble truce.") EnRePo; NCEP; PoEL-1
Absence, hear thou my [*or* heare my] protestation. Absence [*or* Ode *or* Present in Absence]. John Hoskins, *sometimes at. to* John Donne. ElL; GTBS; GTBS-P; MeLP
Absence of Occupation. William Cowper. *Fr.* Retirement. OBEC
Absence, the noble truce. Absence and Presence. Fulke Greville. Caelica, XLV. EnRePo; NCEP; OBSC; PoEL-1
Absences. Philip Larkin. PoCh
Absent, The. Edwin Muir. NoAM
Absent Creation. D. S. Savage. NeBP
Absent Daughter. Barend Toerien, *tr. fr. Afrikaans by author.* PeSA
Absent from thee, I languish still. A Song [*or* Return]. Earl of Rochester. BoLoP; CavP; ELP; EnLoPo; FaBoEn; GBL; LoBV; MePo; NOBE; OBEV; OBS; SeCePo; SeCV-2; ViBoPo
Absent Lover, An. A. Godwin. *See* Song for My Lady.
Absent Lover. *Unknown, tr. fr. Xhosa by* A. C. Jordan. PBA
Absent-minded, in his shack. An Odd Old Man in Hackensack. *Unknown.* TDH
Absent-minded Professor. Howard Nemerov. ELU
Absent Ones, The. Maxine W. Kumin. PAI
Absent Star. Quinton Duval. FAZ
Absent, this morning. Aube Provençale. Marilyn Hacker. AmPA
Absent yet Present. Sir Edward Bulwer-Lytton. OBVV
Absinthe-Drinker, The. Arthur Symons. BrPo; FaBoTw
Absolute, An/ patience. The Breathing. Denise Levertov. NaP; RFM
Absolute and Abitofhell. Ronald Arbuthnott Knox. CenHV; FaBoCo
Absolute knowledge I have none. Source of News. *Unknown.* TreF
Absolute, pity the visionless. Address to an Absolute. Roy McFadden. NeIP
Absolute zero: the locust sings. Summer. Conrad Aiken. NoAM
Absolutely Ordinary Rainbow, An. Les A. Murray. CBAP
Absolution. Siegfried Sassoon. MMA
Absolution. Edward Willard Watson. AA
Absolvers, The. Robert Southey. *Fr.* A Vision of Judgement. EnRP
Abstemia. Gelett Burgess. NA
Abstinence. Kenneth Rosen. AmPA
Abstinence sows sand all over. Blake. *Fr.* Gnomic Verses. EBEV; FaBoEE; FF; GBL; TrGrPo; ViBoPo
Abstracted, sour, as he reaches across a dish. Scylla and Charybdis. Thomas Kinsella. OxBTC
Abstrosophy. Gelett Burgess. CenHV; NA
Abt Vogler. Robert Browning. GoTL; HBV-2; OAEL-2; OAEP; VLP; WGRP
Abu. Dudley Randall. BPo
Abu Nowas for the Barmacides. *Unknown, tr. fr. Arabic by* E. Powys Mathers. *Fr.* The Thousand and One Nights. AWP
Abysm past thinking on, chill. In Space-Time Aware. Abbie Huston Evans. GP
Abysmal corners will dis (be) located. Vitality. Maria Amalia Fonte Boa, *tr. by* Willis Barnstone *and* Nelson Cerqueira. BoWoP
Abyss, The. Baudelaire, *tr. fr. French by* Robert Lowell. SyP
Ac that most needen aren oure neighebores, and we nime good heede. *See* Most needy aren oure neighebores . . .
Academic. Theodore Roethke. CrMA; ELU; FaBoEE; MiAP; OBAL
Academic Affair. Brenda S. Stockwell. AMV-80
Academic Curse; an Epitaph. Wesli Court. TW
Academic Discourse at Havana. Wallace Stevens. MoPo
Academic Moon. Helen Bevington. GLGT
Academic Overture, The. Richmond Lattimore. GLGT
Acadia, *sel.* Joseph Howe.
"In ev'ry thought, in ev'ry wish I own." CaP
Acceleration near the Point of Impact. Joyce Carol Oates. GeTw
Accept each gift, though it be small. Lines for a Wedding Gift. Wesley Trimpi. NePoEA
Accept, my God, the praises which I bring. The Offering: Part One. Mary Lee, Lady Chudleigh. WPE
Accept this garland and this girl together. Double Gift. *Unknown, tr. by* Louis Untermeyer. UnTE
Accept, thou shrine of my dead saint. The Exequy [*or* Exequy on His Wife]. Henry King. AnAnS-2; BoLoP; CABA; FaBoEn; GBL; HAP; HBV-1; InvP; JCP; LoBV; MeLP; MePo; NOBE; NoP; OBEV; OBS; PoEL-2; PPoe; PrIm; QFR; SeCePo; SeCP; TEP; ViBoPo
Acceptance. Robert Frost. CMoP; OxBA
Acceptance. Langston Hughes. NePoAm-2
Acceptance Speech. Marvin Bell. AmPA
Acceptation. Margaret Junkin Preston. PAH
Accepting. Vassar Miller. FiCP
Accident, The. Len Gasparini. NeAC
Accident. Sydney Lea. NYP
Accident, The. Raymond Richard Patterson. CAD
Accident at Three Mile Island. Jim Barnes. AMV-81; FAZ
Accident Has Occurred, The. Margaret Atwood. NMM
Accident in Art. Richard Hovey. HBV-2
Accidentally. Maxine W. Kumin. RHPC
Accidents of Birth. William Meredith. NoP
Accidents will happen—still, in time. A Bedtime Story. [*or* If I Should Die before I Wake]. Robert Mezey. NePoEA; NYBP
Accidia. Henry Charles Beeching. OBVV
Acclamation, An. Sir John Davies. OxBoCh
Accommodating Lion, An. Tudor Jenks. OBCA
Accommodation. Anselm Parlatore. SUW
Accomplice, The. Ron Slate. AMV
Accomplices, The. Conrad Aiken. NOBA
Accomplished Facts. Carl Sandburg. WHA
Accomplishments. Cynthia MacDonald. DFF; GP
According to Brueghel. Landscape with the Fall of Icarus. William Carlos Williams. Pictures from Brueghel, II. LCAP; NIP; PPP
According to some learn'd opinions. Irish Antiquities. Thomas Moore. FaBoEE
"According to the Mighty Working." Thomas Hardy. CMoP
According to the silence, winter has arrived. Shepherd. William Stafford. PoA
According to the word of the Eternal Being. L'Imprévisibilité. Zinaida Hippius, *tr. by* Temira Pachmuss. PBWP
According to tradition. The Tryst. Christopher Morley. HBMV
Account of the Cruelty of the Papists, An. Benjamin Harris. SCAP
Accountability. Paul Laurence Dunbar. PoLF; YaD
Accountability. William Stafford. LCAP; NoP; NPAW
Accountant in His Bath, The ("The accountant dried his imperfect back"). Adrian Mitchell. NYBP
Accountants hover over the earth like helicopters. A Dream of Suffocation. Robert Bly. NaP
Accountings, The. Albert Goldbarth. GeTw
Accumulation of reefs, The. The Distances. Jim Carroll. PoA

Accursed power which stands on Privilege, The. On a General [*or* Great] Election. Hilaire Belloc. FaBoCo; FaBoEE; MoVE; NOBE; NOBL; OBSV; OxBoLi; OxBTC; WhC
Accursed [*or* Accurst] the man, whom fate ordains, in spite. The Pains of Education [*or* Against Education]. Charles Churchill. *Fr.* The Author. FaBoCo; TW
Accusation. Utahania, *tr. fr. Eskimo.* WTO
Accusation of the Inward Man, The. Edward Taylor. LiTA
Accused though I be without desert. Sir Thomas Wyatt. SiPS
Achaians have got Troy, upon this very day, The. Aeschylus, *tr. by* Richmond Lattimore. *Fr.* Agamemnon. WaaP
Ache of Marriage, The. Denise Levertov. FF; NoAM; NOBA; PoM; TAP
Ache of wide millions, The. Return of a Reaper. Alan Creighton. CaP
Achieving Perspective. Pattiann Rogers. MAYP
Achilles. Phillip Corwin. AMV-80
Achilles, *sel.* John Gay.
Song: "Think of dress in ev'ry light." OBEC
("Think of dress in every light.") InvP
Achilles. Ernest Myers. OBVV
Achilles Deatheridge. Edgar Lee Masters. AmFN
Achilles in Scyros, *sel.* Philip Bainbrigge.
Chorus of Scyrian Maidens. PeHV
Achilles Shows Himself in the Battle by the Ships. Homer, *tr. fr. Greek by* George Chapman. *Fr.* The Iliad, XVIII. OBS
Achilles spoke thus:/ "Atrides, and all." The Funeral Games for Patroclus: The Boastful Boxer. Homer, *tr. by* Ennis Rees. *Fr.* The Iliad, XXIII. LiSp
Achilles to Lycaon. Homer, *tr. fr. Greek by* Richmond Lattimore. *Fr.* The Iliad, XXI. WaaP
Achilles with wild fury in his heart. Homer, *tr. by* Robert Fitzgerald. *Fr.* The Iliad, XXIII. OBWP
Aching all over I believe I've got the pneumonia this time. Pneumonia Blues. *Unknown.* BluL
Achitophel: The Earl of Shaftesbury. Dryden. *Fr.* Absalom and Achitophel, Pt. I. NOBE
(Achitophel.) AWP, *br. sel.;* SeCePo; WHA, *br. sel.*
(Earl of Shaftesbury, The.) FaBoEn
(False Achitophel, The.) FiP
(Lord Shaftesbury.) LoBV
("Of these the false Achitophel was first.") HAP; InPS; PoEL-3; ViBoPo
(Shaftesbury.) OBS
Achtung. Sappho, *tr. fr. Greek by* Thomas Hardy. CTC
("Dead shalt thou lie; and nought," *tr. by* Thomas Hardy.) OBVE
("Deid sall ye ligg, and ne'er a memorie," *ad. by* Douglas Young.) OBVE
A'Chuilionn. A. G. Hutchison. PoSh
Acis and Galatea, *sels.* John Gay.
Love in Her Eyes. ELP
(Song: "Love in her eyes sits playing.") FaBoEn; OBEC
O Ruddier than the Cherry. ELP; ViBoPo
(Air: "O ruddier than the cherry.") NOEC
(Song: "O ruddier than the cherry.") HBV-1; NOBE; OBEC
Acme and Septimius. Catullus, *tr. fr. Latin by* Abraham Cowley. AWP; UnTE
(Ode: Acme and Septimius.) OBVE
Acon. Hilda Doolittle ("H. D."). VGW
Acoustics. Susan Griffin. *Fr.* Woman and Nature. NPGG
Acquainted with the Night. Robert Frost. AP; ChTr; CMoP; CoBMV; FPL; HAP; LiTM; MoAmPo; MP; NePA; NoAM; NOBA; PDV; PoLF; PPP; SoSe; TAP; TwCP; VGW; WeW
Acquiescence of Pure Love, The. William Cowper, *after the French of* Mme Guyon. ILwL
Acre of Grass, An. W. B. Yeats. CMoP; NoAM
Acres of Clams. *Unknown.* FSW
Acrobat. Rachel Field. *Fr.* A Circus Garland. SoPo
Acrobat. Edward Watkins. AMV-80
Acrobat from Xanadu disdained all nets, The. Dan Georgakas. FF
Acrobat on the border of the sea, An. The Woman That Had More Babies than That. Wallace Stevens. LiTA
Across a city from you, I'm with you. Adrienne Rich. Twenty-one Love Poems, XVI. PeHV
Across a pasture of yellow lillies. Blue Horses; West Winds. Anita Endrezze-Danielson. STE
Across a sage-grown upland. The Path of the Padres. Edith D. Osborne. AmFN
Across a sky suddenly mid-February blue. Cranes. J. R. S. Davies. POL
Across North Wales. Dafydd ap Gwilym Resents the Winter. Rolfe Humphries. NYBP
Across our road there used to lie. Malediction. Phyllis McGinley. DBV
Across Roblin Lake, two shores away. Wilderness Gothic. Alfred Purdy. MoCV; NOBC; NoP; PeCV
Across Space and Time. Charles Olson. PoM
Across the ages they come thundering. Say This of Horses. Minnie Hite Moody. PoLF
Across the alley from the alamo. Variation. Peter Wild. GP
Across the barrage, the cities of Europe remember. Homage of War. Bruce Williamson. NeIP
Across the bison-dotted plain. The Last Trail. Stanton A. Coblentz. BPAW
Across the blinded lowlands the beating rain blows chill. The Battle of the Swamps. Muriel Elsie Graham. SUMH
Across the bristled and sallow fields. The Hawk. Raymond Knister. OBCV
Across the correct perspective to the painted sky. Landscape. David Gascoyne. FaBoMo
Across the craggy indigo. Business as Usual 1946. A. J. M. Smith. NMP
Across the crests of the naked hills. Laramie Trail. Joseph Mills Hanson. BPAW; PoOW
Across the Delaware. Will Carleton. PAH
Across the dewy lawn she treads. Paean. Jonathan Henderson Brooks. CDC
Across the dim frozen fields of night. Night Train. Robert Francis. DuDa
Across the Door. Padraic Colum. HBV-1
Across the Eastern sky has glowed. The Crowing of the Red Cock. Emma Lazarus. AA; HBV-2
Across the empty garden-beds. The Sailing of the Sword. William Morris. OAEP; OBVV
Across the Field to Anne. Richard Burton. HBV-1
Across the fields of yesterday. Sometimes. Thomas S. Jones, Jr. HBV-1; TreFT; TRV
Across the flesh and feeling of soledad. Orisha. Jayne Cortez. BlSi
Across the floor flits the mechanical toy. Cirque d'Hiver. Elizabeth Bishop. LiTA; MiAP
Across the foaming river. The Bridge. Frederick Peterson. HBV-2
Across the grass I see her pass. The Milkmaid. Austin Dobson. HBV-1
Across the greening lawn. A Northern Spring. Gene Baro. NePoEA-2
Across the heavy sands running they came. Pan and Syrinx. W. R. Rodgers. NMP
Across the hills of Arcady. To Arcady. Charles Buxton Going. HBV-1
Across the hills to Grandma's house. You Take the Pilgrims, Just Give Me the Progress. Loyd Rosenfield. QQQ
Across the lonely beach we flit. *See* Across the narrow beach we flit.
Across the millstream below the bridge. The Blue Swallows. Howard Nemerov. BiP; NoP
Across the moorlands of the Not. Moorlands of the Not. *Unknown.* NA
Across the mud the line drags on and on. Ration Party. John Manifold. WaP
Across the narrow [*or* lonely] beach we flit. The Sandpiper. Celia Thaxter. AA; FaBoBe; FaPON; GN; HBV-1; HBVY; OBCA; OxBChV; WBLP
Across the night. From Creature to Ghost. Pauline Hanson. TAP
Across the open countryside. The Unsettled Motorcyclist's Vision of His Death. Thom Gunn. NePoEA-2; PoA
Across the Oregon plateau. Men against the Sky. John Haines. LCAP
Across the page of history. Lincoln Leads. Minna Irving. OHIP
Across the places deep and dim. The Road to Anywhere. Bert Leston Taylor. HBMV
Across the plain the wind whines through the sage. The Snowstorm. Pearl Riggs Crouch. BPAW; PoOW
Across the road. Flock. Lance Henson. VoR
Across the round field, under the dark male tower. The Lovers. Alex Comfort. NeBP; PoA
Across the sands of Syria. The Legend of the First Cam-u-el. Arthur Guiterman. CenHV
Across the sea will come Adze-head. Adze-Head. *Unknown, tr. by* James Carney. BIrV
Across the seas of Wonderland to Mogadore we plodded. Forty Singing Seamen. Alfred Noyes. OnMSP
Across the shimmering meadows. The Hawthorn Tree. Willa Cather. HBMV
Across the sky run streaks of white light, aching. Before Olympus. John Gould Fletcher. MoAmPo
Across the sky the daylight crept. Coventry Patmore. *Fr.* The Angel in the House, II, x. GBL
Across the snowy pastures of the estate. The Fox Who Watched for the Midnight Sun. Norman Dubie. LCAP; MAYP
Across the sombre prairie sea. Prairie. Herbert Bates. AA
Across the Stony Mountains, o'er the desert's drouth and sand. The Crisis. Whittier. PAH
Across the stony ridges. Ballad of the Drover. Henry Lawson. PoAu-1
Across the Straits. Rosemary Dobson. PoAu-2
Across the street, apples fill the gutter. When It Rains. H. A. Maxson. AMV-80
Across the street, my aunt has lost. Emergency at 8. Geof Hewitt. NeAC

Across the street—the freeway. Beneath the Shadow of the Freeway. Lorna Dee Cervantes. FIA
Across the swamps and marshlands of the hours. A Sea-Change: For Harold. Joseph Langland. LiTM
Across the swiffling waves they went. The Cruise of the *P. C.* *Unknown.* NA
Across the tracks in Cheyenne, behind the biggest billboard. A Long Way outside Yellowstone. Thomas McGrath. VGW
Across the trampled program-littered grass. After Commencement. Howard Nemerov. GLGT
Across the Western Ocean. *Unknown.* AmSS, *with music;* AS, *with music;* FSW
Across the wrack besprinkled bay. The Glaucous-Gull's Death. Daniel James O'Sullivan. NeIP
Across the years he could recall. The Secret Heart. Robert P. Tristram Coffin. PoSC
Across this dream of seas blue mountains fall. Between Seasons. Anne Welsh. PeSA
Across to the Peloponnese. James Welch. CDW
Across upon this undulated board of verdure chequered bright. The Five Unmistakable Marks. David Jones. In Parenthesis, VII. NoAM
Acrostic on Wharton, An. *Unknown.* OBSV
Acrostick on Mrs. Elizabeth Hull, An. John Saffin. SCAP
Acrostick on Mrs. Winifret Griffin, An. John Saffin. SCAP
A-Cruising We Will Go. *Unknown.* AmSS
Act, An. Kenneth Rosen. AmPA
Act, The. William Carlos Williams. ELU; SOTW; VGW
Act of Faith. Arturo Trías, *tr. fr. Spanish by* Julio Marzán. InW
Act of Love, The. Robert Creeley. GP; HAP
Act of Love. Nicholas Moore. NeBP
Act of Love. Vernon Scannell. ErPo
Act I/ Orlando hails. The Five-Minute Orlando Macbeth. George MacBeth. NOBL
Act II. Katherine Davis. PoPl
Actaeon. Arthur Hugh Clough. VLP
Actaeon. Rayner Heppenstall. FaBoTw
Actaeon. *Unknown. See* I Would I Were Actaeon.
Acteon. Ovid, *tr. fr. Latin by* Arthur Golding. *Fr.* Metamorphoses, III. CTC
Action. James Oppenheim. TrJP
Action of Electricity, The. Erasmus Darwin. *Fr.* The Economy of Vegetation. FaBoUs
Action of Invisible Ink, The. Erasmus Darwin. *Fr.* The Economy of Vegetation. FaBoUs
Action runs left to right, The. Movies, Left to Right. Robert Sward. NYBP
Action Would Kill It/A Gamble. Robert Adamson. CBAP
Actions. Marcel Schwob, *tr. fr. French by* William Brown Meloney. TrJP
Acton Beauchamp, Herefordshire. *Unknown.* FaBoPP; GBP
Actor, The. Thomas Snapp. NYBP
Actor's dead, and memory alone, The. J. B. H. C. Bunner. AA
Actress of emotional rôles, An. The Tattooed Man. Harry B. Smith. *Fr.* The Idol's Eye. InMe
Acts, *sel.* Bible, *N.T.*
Paul on the Road to Damascus, IX: 3-6. TreF
Acts of Youth, The. John Wieners. CoPo
Acts passed beyond the boundary of mere wishing. Stephen Spender. OxBTC
Actual evidence I have none. When the War Will End [*or* Rumors]. Reginald Arkell. InMe; TreFT
Actual Vision of Morning's Extrusion. Alan Dugan. PPP
Actuality. Sir John Suckling. *See* Sonnet: "Oh! for some honest lover's ghost."
Ad Chloen, M.A. Mortimer Collins. HBV-1
Ad Coelum. Harry Romaine. BLPA; FaBoBe
Ad Domnulam Suam. Ernest Dowson. HBV-1
Ad Finem. Heine, *tr. fr. German by* Elizabeth Barrett Browning. AWP
Ad Finem. Ella Wheeler Wilcox. BLPA; FPL
Ad Henricum Wottonem. Thomas Bastard. FaBoEE; FaBoPP
Ad Johannuelem Leporem, Lepidissimum, Carmen Heroicum. *Unknown.* FaBoNo
Ad Lesbiam. Catullus, *tr. fr. Latin by* Niall Sheridan. OxBI
Ad Leuconoen. Horace, *tr. fr. Latin by* Franklin P. Adams. Odes, I, 13. AWP
Ad Librum. Samuel Danforth, Jr. SCAP
Ad Limina. Joseph Campbell. BIrV
Ad Matrem. Julian Fane. HBV-1
Ad Matrem in Coelis. Linda Lyon Van Voorhis. GoBC
Ad Ministram. Horace. *See* Fie on Eastern Luxury!
Ad Patriam, *sel.* William Dudley Foulke.
Land of My Heart. PAL
("Land of my heart,/What future is before thee?") PGD
Ad Patriam. Clinton Scollard. PAH
Ad Persephonen. Franklin P. Adams. InMe
Ad Tusserum. *Unknown.* FaBoUs
Ad Xanthiam Phoceum. Horace, *tr. fr. Latin by* Franklin P. Adams. Odes, II, 4. AWP
Adage, An: "Gardener's rule applies to youth and age, The." H. J. Byron. FaBoUs
Adam. Anthony Hecht. CoPo; DiL
Adam. *Unknown. See* Adam Lay Ibounden.
Adam/ Had 'em. On [*or* Lines Written on] the Antiquity of Microbes. Strickland Gillilan. TreFT; WhC
Adam and Eve. Bible, *O.T.* Genesis, III: 7-II: 23. TreFT
Adam and Eve. Itzig Manger, *tr. fr. Yiddish by* Jacob Sonntag. TrJP
Adam and Eve. Milton. *Fr.* Paradise Lost, IV. SeCePo
Adam and Eve, *sels.* Karl Shapiro.
Recognition of Eve, The. MoAB
Sickness of Adam, The. AP; CoBMV; MoAB
Adam and Eve. C. H. Sisson. FaBoTw
Adam and Eve. *Unknown.* PoPle
(Epigram: "Whilst Adam slept, Eve from his side arose.") HBV-1
("While Adam slept, from him his Eve arose.") FaBoEE
Adam and Eve at the Garden Gate. Marsha Pomerantz. VWA
Adam and Eve, like us. A Circle. Theodore Spencer. NYBP
Adam and God. Anne Wilkinson. MoCV
Adam Bell, Clim of the Clough, and William of Cloudesly. *Unknown.* ESPB
(Adam Bel, Clym of the Cloughe, and Wyllyam of Cloudesle.) OxBB
Adam Birkett took his gun. Birkett's Eagle. Dorothy S. Howard. MoBS
Adam Driven from Eden. *Unknown.* OxBM
Adam, Eve and the Big Apple. Edward Watkins. AMV-81
Adam Fallen. Milton. *Fr.* Paradise Lost, XII. NOCV
(Banishment from Paradise.) TreFS
Adam in Love. Stephen Mitchell. VWA
Adam in the Garden Pinning [*or* Pinnin'] Leaves. *Unknown.* FSW; OuSiCo, *with music*
Adam, indignant, would not eat with Eve. Paradise Saved. A. D. Hope. OxBC
Adam is a pupil of mine. Athlete. Don Maynard. PoAu-2
Adam is clay, the dumb. Paradise. Chana Bloch. VWA
Adam Lay Ibounden [*or* Ibowndyn *or* Ybounden]. *Unknown.* ChTr; CTC; GoBC; HAP; InPS; NOBE; NOCV; NoP; OAEL-1; OAEP; OxBM; OxBoCh; OxBoLi; PoEL-1; PPoe; SeCeV; WeW
(Adam.) CH
(Adam Lay Bounden.) PAI
(Adam Lay in Bondage.) MeEL
("O Felix Culpa!") ACP
Adam, Lilith, and Eve. Robert Browning. HBV-1
"Adam, my child, my son." Adam. Anthony Hecht. CoPo; DiL
Adam on His Way Home. Robert Pack. ErPo
Adam scrivein, if ever it thee bifalle. To Adam, His Scribe. Chaucer. OAEL-1; OxBM
Adam Smith. E. C. Bentley. *Fr.* Clerihews. FaBoCo
Adam Speaks ("Oh, why did God,/Creator wise"). Milton. *Fr.* Paradise Lost, X. NU
Adam the goodliest man of men since born. A Scene in Paradise. Milton. *Fr.* Paradise Lost, IV. GN
Adam to Lilith. Christopher Brennan. *Fr.* Lilith. PoAu-1
Adam Unfallen. Milton. *Fr.* Paradise Lost, V. NOCV
Adam was de first man and Eve was de udder. *Unknown. Fr.* A Metrical Version of the Bible, Said to Have Been Composed by a Negro Christian in the State of Massachusetts, and Published in Louisville, Kentucky, in 1858. FaBoUs
Adam was my grandfather. For All Blasphemers. Stephen Vincent Benét. OxBA
Adam, who thought himself immortal still. The Discovery. Monk Gibbon. OnYI
Adams and Liberty. Robert Treat Paine. PAH
Adam's Apple. Coleman Barks. PPJ
Adam's Complaint. Denise Levertov. BoWoP; NNaP
Adam's Curse. W. B. Yeats. BIrV; CMoP; CoBMV; NoAM; NoP; OAEL-2; PP; SOTW; TEP; VLP
Adam's Death. Gabriel Levin. VWA
Adam's Dream. Howard Schwartz. VWA
Adam's Dying. Ridgely Torrence. FYAP
Adam's first wife had soft lips but no soul. Lilith. X. J. Kennedy. UnTE
Adam's Footprint. Vassar Miller. NePoEA; NIP
Adam's Hymn in Paradise. Joost van den Vondel, *tr. fr. Dutch by* Sir John Bowring. WGRP
Adam's Morning Hymn. Milton. *Fr.* Paradise Lost, V. WGRP
(Morning Hymn of Adam [and Eve].) OxBoCh; TrPWD, *shorter sel.*
Adam's Song of the Visible World. Ridgely Torrence. TrPWD
Adam's Song to Heaven. Edgar Bowers. ConAP; QFR
Adam's Task. John Hollander. NIP; NoP; PPP

Adapt Thyself. Shem-Tob ben Joseph Palquera, *tr. fr. Hebrew by* J. Chotzner. TrJP
Addendum to the Ten Commandments. *Unknown.* DBV
Adder's Epigrams. Colin Ellis. FaBoEE
Addict. Jack Montgomery. QQQ
Addict, The. Larry Rubin. GoYe
Addict, The. Anne Sexton. CTBA
Addio a la Mamma. Noe Jitrik, *tr. fr. Spanish by* Yishai Tobin. VWA
Addition to Kipling's "The Dead King (Edward VII), 1910." Max Beerbohm. FaBoEE
Additional Poem, An. John Ashbery. FaBoMo
Additional Verses to Hail Columbia. Oliver Wendell Holmes. PAH
Address. Alurista. PAI
Address. William Carlos Williams. DiL
Address Not Known. John Heath-Stubbs. ChMP
Address to a Child during a Boisterous Winter Evening. Dorothy Wordsworth. OxBChV
Address to a Haggis. Burns. ViBoPo
Address to a Mummy. Horace Smith. HBV-2; RoGo, *sl. abr.*
Address to an Absolute. Roy McFadden. NeIP
Address to Certain Gold Fishes. Hartley Coleridge. VLP
Address to Children. Theodore Hook. *See* Cautionary Verses to Youth of Both Sexes.
Address to His Elbow-Chair, New Cloath'd, An. William Somervile. OBEC
Address to Lady ———, Who Asked What the Passion of Love Was? Charles Morris. NOEC
Address to Miss Phillis Wheatley, An, *sel.* Jupiter Hammon.
"O come you pious youth! adore." AmPP
Address to Mr. Cross, of Exeter 'Change, on the Death of the Elephant. Thomas Hood. FM
Address to My Infant Daughter, *sel.* Wordsworth.
"Hast thou then survived." EvOK; Par
Address to My Soul. Elinor Wylie. AWP; LiTM; OxBA
Address to Plenty, *sel.* John Clare.
" 'Tis not great, what I solicit." OBRV
Address to the Crown. Charles L. O'Donnell. GoBC
Address to the Deil. Burns. EnRP; GoTS; LAuP; NOEC; OAEL-1; OAEP; OxBS; PoEL-4
Address to the New Tay Bridge, An. William McGonagall. PeD
Address to the Ocean. Byron. *See To the Ocean.*
Address to the Plebeians, An, *sel.* John Learmont.
"Poor crawlin' bodies, sair neglectit." NOEC
Address to the Refugees. John Malcolm Brinnin. GOA
Address to the Scholars of New England. John Crowe Ransom. GOA; LiTM; NePA
Address to the Soul Occasioned by a Rain, An. Edward Taylor. AP; OxBA; PoEL-3
(Let by Rain.) NOBA
Address to the Unco Guid, or the Rigidly Righteous. Burns. EnRP; HBV-1; LoBV; NOBE; NOCV; NoP; OAEP; OBEC; OxBS; SeCeV; TreFS; TrGrPo; ViBoPo
Address to the Vacationers at Cape Lookout, An. William Stafford. NYBP
Address to Venus. Lucretius, *tr. fr. Latin by* Spenser. *Fr.* De Rerum Natura *and fr.* The Faerie Queene, IV, 10. AWP
(Prayer to Venus.) EIL
Addressed to a Gentleman at Table, Who Kept Boasting of the Company He Kept. Burns. DBV; PV
(Toad-Eater, The, *sl. diff. vers.*) POL; TW
Addressed to a Young Lady. William Cowper. *See* To a Young Lady.
Addressed to Haydon. Keats. EnRP; OBNC
Addressing His Deaf Wife, Kansas, 1916. William Olsen. AMV-81
Ad-dressing of Cats, The. T. S. Eliot. FM
Adela Cathcart, *sel.* George Macdonald.
Sir Lark and King Sun, *fr. ch.* 16. GN; HBV-1; HBVY
Adelaide Crapsey. Carl Sandburg. HBMV
Adelaide Neilson. William Winter. AA
Adelita ("Adelita's the name of the lady"). *Unknown, tr. fr. Spanish by* F. S. Curtis, Jr. AS, *with music;* FSW
Adepts, The. Lawrence Durrell. *Fr.* Eight Aspects of Melissa. ErPo; NeBP
Adequacy. Elizabeth Barrett Browning. SBG
Adeste Fideles. *Unknown. See* O Come, All Ye Faithful.
Adew, my King, court, cuntrey, and my kin. To Henry Constable and Henry Keir. Alexander Montgomerie. OxBS
Adhesive Autopsy of Walt Whitman, The. Jonathan Williams. PoM
Adieu. Thomas Carlyle. HBV-1; OBRV
Adieu, adieu! my native shore. Childe Harold's Farewell to England. Byron. *Fr.* Childe Harold's Pilgrimage. OHFP; PoPl
Adieu, dear life! here am I left alone. On My Late Dear Wife. Jonathan Richardson. NOEC
Adieu, dear object of my love's excess. Orinda to Lucasia Parting, October, 1661, at London. Katherine Philips. OBS
Adieu, fair isle! I love thy bowers. Farewell to Cuba. Maria Gowen Brooks. AA
Adieu, Farewell Earth's Bliss. Thomas Nashe. *Fr.* Summer's Last Will and Testament. CH; EBEV; EIL; ELP; HAP; HeIP; InvP; LoBV; OAEP; PPoe; QFR; TEP; ViBoPo; WeW
(Death's Summons.) HBV-2
(Dust Hath Closed Helen's Eye.) SeCePo
(In a Time of Pestilence.) HoPM; TrGrPo
(In Plague Time.) FaBoCh; FaPoR; OBSC
(In Time of Pestilence.) DTC, NOBE; OBEV; PoPle
(In Time of Plague.) EnRePo
(Litany in Time of Plague, A.) CABA; DL; NIP; NoP; OAEL-1; PAI; PoRA; PPP; PrIm
(Lord, Have Mercy on Us.) ChTr
(Song.) FaBoEn; PoEL-2
(Song in Time of Plague.) SCV
Adieu, kind Life, though thou hast often been. Departure. May Riley Smith. AA
Adieu Love, Untrue Love. *Unknown. See* Unfaithful Shepherdess, The.
Adieu, my books! Adieu, bay-tree! An A B C for Grown Gentlemen. Chevalier de Boufflers, *tr. by* Leigh Hunt. GLGT
Adieu My Lovely Nancy. *Unknown.* OBET
Adieu, O daisy of delight. Adieu to His Mistress. Alexander Montgomerie. BSV
Adieu, Romauld! But thou canst not forget me. Ella Wheeler Wilcox. *Fr.* The Farewell of Clarimonde. PeD
Adieu, sweet Angus, Maeve and Fand. The Passing of the Shee. J. M. Synge. BIrV; FaBoEE; OnYI
Adieu the woods and waters' side. Lines on Leaving a Scene in Bavaria. Thomas Campbell. OBNC
Adieu to Belashanny [*or* Ballyshannon]! where I was bred and born. The Winding Banks of Erne [*or* Adieu to Belashanny]. William Allingham. AnIV; NBM; OxBI
Adieu to His Mistress. Alexander Montgomerie. BSV
Adieu to My Landlady, An. George Farewell. NOEC
Adieu to the pleasure of murder and whoring. Sir Thomas Armstrong's Last Farewell to the World. *Unknown.* APAS
Adieu to the Stone Walls, *with music. Unknown.* OuSiCo
"Adiew, madam my mother dear." Lord Maxwell's Last Goodnight. *Unknown.* ESPB
Adina. Harold Milton Telemaque. TTY
Adios. Donald C. Babcock. NePoAm-2
Adirondacs, The, *sel.* Emerson.
"We flee away from cities, but we bring." GLGT
Adjectives. Moishe Nadir, *tr. fr. Yiddish by* Joseph Leftwich. TrJP
Adjuration. Charles Enoch Wheeler. AmNP; PoNe
Adjustment. Whittier. WGRP
Adlatts parke is wyde and broad. Will Stewart and John. *Unknown.* ESPB
Adlestrop. Edward Thomas. BrPo; CH; FaBoPP; GoJo; HAP; LiTB; NOBE; OBEV; OxBTC
Admetus, from my marrow's core I do. Edna St. Vincent Millay. SBG
Administrator, An. Geoffrey Grigson. FaBoEE
Admiral. John Alexander Allen. NYBP
Admiral, admiral, sailing home. The Homing. John Jerome Rooney. AA
Admiral Benbow. *Unknown. See* Death of Admiral Benbow, The.
Admiral Byrd. Ogden Nash. InMe; YaD
Admiral Death. Sir Henry Newbolt. VLP
Admiral Hosier's Ghost. Richard Glover. HBV-2; NOEC; ViBoPo
Admiral, the prisoner of your giant's. Admiral. John Alexander Allen. NYBP
Admirals All. Sir Henry Newbolt. FaPoR; MOS
Admiral's Caravan, The, *sel.* Charles Edward Carryl.
Plaint of the Camel, The. EvOK; FaPON; HBV-2; HBVY; SoPo
(Camel's Complaint, The.) OBCA; OxBChV; RHPC
Admiral's Daughter, The. E. G. Burrows. HoAn
Admire Cranmer! Stevie Smith. NoAM
Admire the face of plastered stone. Quebec Farmhouse. John Glassco. NOBC; PeCV
Admire the old man, admire him, admire him. Admire Cranmer! Stevie Smith. NoAM
Admire thy wreath? And wherefore should I not. To a Plagiarist. Moses ibn Ezra, *tr. by* Solomon Solis-Cohen. TrJP
Admire, when you come here, the glimmering hair. Vuillard: "The Mother and Sister of the Artist." W. D. Snodgrass. CoAP
Admission. Henry Vaughan. AnAnS-1
Admonition. John Peale Bishop. TwAmPo
Admonition. Philip Stack. BLPA
Admonition for Spring. L. A. MacKay. CaP; OBCV; PeCV
Admonition to a Traveller. Wordsworth. GTBS; GTBS-P
Admonition to Montgomerie. James I, King of England. OxBS
Admonition to the Muse. Geoffrey Taylor. FaBoEE
Admonition to Young Lassies, An. Alexander Montgomerie. BSV

Admonitions. Lucille Clifton. BPo; InPS; NMM
Adobe House, An. Witter Bynner. BPAW
Adobe walls of the house, The. Woman. Ai. GP
Adolescence. Gregory Orr. Psk
Adolescence. P. K. Page. CaP; OBCV
Adolescence. Dennis Schmitz. FAZ
Adolescence—II. Rita Dove. AmPA
Adolescent night, breath of the town, The. Midsummer. Robert Fitzgerald. PoA
Adolph Hitler Meditates on the Jewish Problem. Oscar Hahn, *tr. fr. Spanish by* James Hoggard. AMV-81
Adon 'Olam. *Unknown, tr. fr. Hebrew by* F. De Sola Mendes. EaLo
Adonais. William Wallace Harney. AA; HBV-1
Adonais; an Elegy on the Death of John Keats. Shelley. CABA; ChER; EBEV; EnRP; FiP, *much abr.;* GoTL; HBV-2; HoPM; LoBV; MasP; NoP; OAEL-2; OAEP; OBRV; PoEL-4; TrGrPo; ViBoPo, *abr.;* WHA, *abr.*
Sels.
Go Thou to Rome. ChTr
(Grave of Keats, The.) FaBoPP
"He is made one with Nature." WGRP
"One remains, the many change and pass, The." SCV
(Lumen de Lumine.) GoBC
"Peace, peace! he is not dead, he doth not sleep." FaBoEn; LO
(Against Oblivion.) TreFS
(Elegy on the Death of John Keats, An.) OBNC
(Mourn Not for Adonais.) NoBE
Adonis. Hilda Doolittle ("H. D."). AP; AWP; LiTA; PoPl
Adonis, Dying. Praxilla, *tr. fr. Greek by* John Dillon. PBWP
("Most beautiful of things I leave is sunlight," *tr. by* Willis Barnstone.) BoWoP
Adorable paratroopess alights, The. Michael Silverton. POL
Adoration. Mme Guyon, *tr. fr. French.* STF; WGRP
(By Thy Life I Live.) TRV
Adoration. Christopher Smart. *Fr.* A Song to David. FaBoEn
Adoration of the Disk by King Akhnaten and Princess Nefer Neferiu Aten. *Unknown, tr. fr. Egyptian by* Robert Hillyer. *Fr.* The Book of the Dead. AWP; FaPON
Adoration of the Magi, The. Christopher Pilling. OBCP
Adoration of the Wise Men, The. Cecil Frances Alexander. HBVY
A-down the road and gun in hand. Whiskey Bill,—a Fragment. *Unknown.* BPAW
Adrian and Bardus. John Gower. *Fr.* Confessio Amantis, V. OxBM
Adrian Block's Song. Edward Everett Hale. PAH
Adriani Morientis ad Animam Suam. Emperor Hadrian. *See* Hadrian's Address to His Soul When Dying.
Adriatic. Robert Conquest. PP
Adrift. Elizabeth Dickinson Dowden. WGRP
Adsum. Richard Henry Stoddard. AA
Adult Lullaby, An. *Unknown.* MeEL
Adulterers and customers of whores. Womanisers. John Press. BoLoP; ErPo; NIP
Adulteries, murthers, robberies, thefts. Roger Williams. SCAP
Adultery. James Dickey. CAPP; TAP
Adultery. Alan Dugan. CAPP
Adultery at a Las Vegas Bookstore. Stephen Shu Ning Liu. BrSi
Adulthood. Nikki Giovanni. NMM
Adultness is thrust upon us. Bury Our Faces. Bob Millard. AMV-80
Adults Only. William Stafford. FF
Advance your choral motions now. Song: To the Masquers Representing Stars [*or* The Stars Dance]. Thomas Campion. *Fr.* The Lords' Mask. LoBV; OBSC
Advanced out toward the external from. Celestial Evening, October 1967. Charles Olson. *Fr.* The Maximus Poems. PoM
Advancement of Learning, An. Seamus Heaney. NCSH
Advantage of the Outside, The. Richard Eberhart. NePA
Advantages of Learning, The. Martial, *tr. fr. Latin by* Kenneth Rexroth. ErPo
Advantages of living with two cultures, The. Bonne Entente. F. R. Scott. FiBHP; OBCV; PeCV
Advantages of Washing, The. John Armstrong. *Fr.* The Art of Preserving Health. FaBoUs
Advent. W. H. Auden. *Fr.* For the Time Being; a Christmas Oratorio. OAEP; SBVL
Advent, *sel.* Brian Coffey.
"Awakening like return to Earth from Moon." CIP
Advent. William Everson. NeAP; TrCP
Advent. Christina Rossetti. TrCP; VLP
Advent; a Carol. Patric Dickinson. OBCP
Advent Lyrics, *sels. Unknown, tr. fr. Anglo-Saxon by* Charles W. Kennedy. *Fr.* Christ 1. AnOE
"Bless earth with Thine Advent, O Savior Christ!" VIII.
"Hail, O most worthy in all the world!" IX.
"O holy Jerusalem, Vision of peace," III.
". . .to the King./ Thou art the wall-stone the workers rejected," I.
Advent marriage doth thee deny. Close Season for Marriage. *Unknown.* FaBoUs
Advent 1955. John Betjeman. OBCP
Advent 1966. Denise Levertov. InPS; NNaP; Prf
Advent wind begins to stir, The. Advent 1955. John Betjeman. OBCP
Adventure. Harry Behn. TiPo
Adventure. Laura Benét. HBMV
Adventure. Guy Mason. CaP
Adventure. Grace Fallow Norton. HBMV
Adventurer, The. Odell Shepard. HBMV
Adventurers, The. May Byron. HBV-2
Adventurers, The. John Thompson. PoAu-2
Adventures of Huckleberry Finn, The, *sel.* "Mark Twain."
Emmeline Grangerford's "Ode to Stephen Dowling Bots, Dec'd." OBAL
(Ode to Stephen Dowling Bots, Dec'd.) FiBHP; NIP
Adventures of Isabel. Ogden Nash. CenHV; MoAmPo; MoShBr; OBAL; OBCA; OnMSP; OnUR; PDV; RHPC; TiPo
"Isabel met an enormous bear," *sel.* NTCP; ShM
Adventures of Master F. I., The, *sel.* George Gascoigne.
"And if I did, what then?" EBEV; ElL; FaBoEn; GBL; HAP; NCEP; NoP; PoEL-1
(Farewell, A.) LoBV; NOBE; OBSC
Adventures of Simon Swaugum, a Village Merchant, The. Philip Freneau. PoEL-4
Adventurous Muse, The. Isaac Watts. NOEC
Adversary, The. Phyllis McGinley. DBV; FaBoEE; OBCA
Advertisement. *Unknown.* FaBoUs
(Codfish, The.) RHPC
(It Pays to Advertise.) TreFT
Advertisement of a Lost Day. Lydia Huntley Sigourney. WBLP
Advertising Agency Song, The. *Unknown.* FaBoUs; PV
Advertising Epitaph: From Upton-on Severn, Gloucestershire. *Unknown. See* At Upton-on-Severn.
Advertising Epitaph: On a Quack. *Unknown.* FaBoUs
Advertising Epitaph: On One Lockyer, Inventor of a Patent Medicine. *Unknown.* FaBoUs
Advice. Yehuda Amichai, *tr. fr. Hebrew by* Ruth Nevo. VWA
Advice. Gwendolyn B. Bennett. BlSi; CDC
Advice. Ambrose Bierce. DBV
Advice. E. di Pasquale. AMV-81
Advice, The. Thomas Flatman. CavP
Advice. Walter Savage Landor. HBV-1
Advice, The. Sir Walter Ralegh. AAS; NCEP; SiPS
Advice, The. Charles Sackville. FaBoUs
Advice. Ruth Stone. NMM
Advice, The. *Unknown.* APAS
Advice against Travel. James Clarence Mangan. OBVV
Advice for good love: Don't love. Advice. Yehuda Amichai, *tr. by* Ruth Nevo. VWA
Advice from a Nightwatchman. Ian Healy. *Fr.* Poems from the Coalfields, II. PoAu-2
Advice from an Expert. John Kieran. InMe
Advice from Euterpe. Carter Revard. VoR
Advice from Poor Robin's Almanack. *Unknown.* OBCP
Advice of an Efficiency Expert, The. Augustus Young. CIP
Advice to a Blue-Bird. Maxwell Bodenheim. HBMV
Advice to a Fair Wanton. Ovid, *tr. fr. Latin by* Christopher Marlowe. Amores, III, 14. UnTE
("Seeing thou art faire, I barre not thy false playing.") OBVE
Advice to a Forest. Maxwell Bodenheim. TrJP
Advice to a Girl. Thomas Campion. *See* Never Love Unless You Can.
Advice to a Lady in Autumn. Earl of Chesterfield. FaBoUs; OBEC
(Advice to a Young Lady.) NoEC
Advice to a Lover. S. Charles Jellicoe. HBV-1
Advice to a Lover. *Unknown. See* Sea Hath Many Thousand Sands, The.
Advice to a Neighbour Girl. Yü Hsüan-chi, *tr. fr. Chinese by* Kenneth Rexroth *and* Ling Chung. PBWP
(For a Neighbor Girl, *tr. by* Geoffrey Waters.) BoWoP
Advice to a Painter. *Unknown.* APAS
Advice to a Prizefighter. Lucilius, *tr. fr. Greek by* Tom Dodge. LiSp
Advice to a Prophet. Richard Wilbur. AmPP; CAPP; CoPo; FYAP; MAT; MoAmPo; MP; NMP; NYBP; OBWP; OxBC; PPP; SUW; TwCP
Advice to a Raven in Russia. Joel Barlow. AmPP; NePA; NOBA; OBWP; OxBA
Advice to a Young Lady. Earl of Chesterfield. *See* Advice to a Lady in Autumn.
Advice to a Young Man (Of Letters) Who Doesn't Know How to Take Care of Himself. Irwin Edman. InMe
Advice to Bachelors. *Unknown, tr. fr. German by* Louis Untermeyer. UnTE

Advice to Bores. Abraham ibn Chasdai, *tr. fr. Hebrew by* J. Chotzner. TrJP
Advice to Colonel Valentine. Robert Graves. NYBP
Advice to Country Girls. *Unknown, tr. fr. German by* Louis Untermeyer. UnTE
Advice to Hotheads. Samuel ben Elhanan Isaac, Archevolti of Padua, *tr. fr. Hebrew by* A. B. Rhine. TrJP
Advice to Julia, *sels.* Henry Luttrell.
Dress. OBRV
Honeymoon, The. OBRV
Lovers and Friends. OBRV
Advice to Lovers. John Armstrong. *Fr.* The Oeconomy of Love; a Poetical Essay. NOEC
Advice to My Best Brother, Colonel Francis Lovelace. Richard Lovelace. CaPo
Advice to My Son. Peter Meinke. PAI; Psk
Advice to Small Children. Edward Anthony. RHPC
Advice to the Ladies. William Somervile. FaBoUs
Advice to the Ladies of London in the Choice of Their Husbands. *Unknown.* CoMu
Advice to the Old Beaux. Sir Charles Sedley. FaBoUs; SeCV-2
Advice to the Painter. Matthew Prior. APAS
Advice to the Same. Sir Philip Sidney. *See* Truth Doth Truth Deserve.
Advice to the Young. Miriam Waddington. NOBC
Advice to Travelers. Walker Gibson. NePoAm-2; PPJ
Advice to Young Children. Stevie Smith. ELU
Advice to Young Ladies. A. D. Hope. NoP
Adze-Head. *Unknown, tr. fr. Irish by* James Carney. BIrV
Ae boat anerlie nou. Largo. Sidney Goodsir Smith. NeBP
Ae Fond Kiss. Burns. BSV; CABA; ELP; EnRP; HBV-1; OAEL-1; OAEP; OBEC; OBEV; PoEL-4; PPP; SeCeV; TreFT; ViBoPo; WHA
(Farewell to Nancy.) FaFP; TreF
(Song: "Ae fond kiss, and then we sever.") BoLoP; NOEC
Ae weet forenicht i the yow-trummle. The Watergaw. "Hugh MacDiarmid." GoTS; NeBP; NoP
Aedh Hears the Cry of the Sedge. W. B. Yeats. *See* He Hears the Cry of the Sedge.
Aedh Tells of the Rose in His Heart. W. B. Yeats. *See* Lover Tells of the Rose in His Heart, The.
Aedh Thinks of Those Who Have Spoken Evil of His Beloved. W. B. Yeats. NoAM; VLP
(He Thinks of Those Who Have Spoken Evil of His Beloved.) CTC; ELU
Aedh Wishes for the Cloths of Heaven. W. B. Yeats. MoBrPo; NoAM; OBEV; OBVV
(He Wishes for the Cloths of Heaven.) CMoP; OLR; SOTW
Aegean. Louis Simpson. GrPl; NYBP
Aegean Islands 1940–41. Bernard Spencer. NeBP
Aeglamour's Lament. Ben Jonson. *Fr.* The Sad Shepherd. CH
Aelf-Scin, The. Michael McClure. PoM
(Aelf-scin, the Shining Scimmer the Gleam, the Shining, The.) CoPo
Aeliana's Ditty. Henry Chettle. *See* Of Cupid.
Aella; a Tragycal Enterlude, *sels.* Thomas Chatterton.
Minstrel's Song. HAP; HBV-1; LoBV; TrGrPo, *sl. abr.;* WHA
(My Love Is Dead.) WiR
(Mynstrelles Songe.) EnLoPo; EnRP; NOEC; OBEC
(O, Sing unto My Roundelay.) CH, *abr.;* LiTB
(Song: "O sing unto my roundelay.") LO, *abr.;* OBEV
("O! Synge untoe mie roundelaire.") NOBE
Mynstrelles Songe: "Angelles bee wrogte to bee of neidher kynd." EnLoPo
Song of the Three Minstrels. TrGrPo
("Budding floweret blushes at the light, The.") ViBoPo
(Mynstrelles Songe.) EnRP
Aeneas at Washington. Allen Tate. AP; FYAP; LiTA; MoPo; MoVE; NePA; NoAM; NOBA; OxBA
Aeneas built, in days of yore. Edward B. Goodwin. *Fr.* Roman History in Rhyme. FaBoUs
Aeneid. Claire McAllister. NePA
Aeneid, The, *abr.* Virgil, *tr. fr. Latin by* Allen Mandelbaum. NAWM-1
Sels.
"Affrayit, I glistnyt of sleip, and stert on feit," *fr.* II, *tr. into Middle English by* Gavin Douglas. OBVE
"Amyd the wod his modir met thame tway," *fr.* I, *tr. into Middle English by* Gavin Douglas. OBVE
"And now Aeneas charges straight at Turnus," *fr. XII, tr. by* Allen Mandelbaum. OBWP
"And oft the owle with rufull song complaind," *fr.* IV, *tr. by* the Earl of Surrey. OBVE
"And Turnus than, quhar he at erth dyd ly," *fr.* XII, *tr. into Middle English by* Gavin Douglas. OBVE
"Arms, and the man I sing, who forc'd by fate," *fr.* I, *tr. by* Dryden. OBVE
"As, sum tyme, dois the curser stert and ryn," *fr.* XI, *tr. into Middle English by* Gavin Douglas. OBVE
"As this convine and ordinance was mayd," *fr.* VIII, *tr. into Middle English by* Gavin Douglas. OBVE
"As when a fragment, from a mountain torn," *fr.* XII, *tr. by* Dryden. OBVE
"Attentively he heard us, while we spoke," *fr.* XI, *tr. by* Dryden. OBVE
"Batellis [*or* Batalis] and the man I will descrive [*or* wil discrive], The," *fr.* I, *tr. into Middle English by* Gavin Douglas. OBVE
(Batalis and the Man, The.) CTC
Battle of Actium, *fr.* VIII, *tr. by* Dryden. OBS
"Bot now the haisty, egir, and wild Dido," *fr.* IV, *tr. into Middle English by* Gavin Douglas. OBVE
"Dear Sister, my resentment had not been," *fr.* IV, *tr. by* Sir John Denham. OBVE
Destruction of Troy, The, *fr.* II, *tr. by* Sir John Denham. SeCV-1
Dido among the Shades, *fr.* VI, *tr. by* Dryden. OBS
Dido to Aeneas, *fr.* IV, *tr. by* Richard Stanyhurst. AnIV
Dido's Hunting, *fr.* IV, *tr. by* the Earl of Surrey. OBSC
"Eneas wonderit the greitnes of Cartaige," *fr.* I, *tr. into Middle English by* Gavin Douglas. OBVE
Entrance to Hell, The, *fr.* VI, *tr by* Gavin Douglas. GoTS
"Exulting in his strength, he seems to dare," *fr.* XI, *tr. by* Dryden. OBVE
Funeral Games for Anchises, The: Entellus, *fr.* V, *tr. by* Rolfe Humphries. LiSp
"Greeks' chieftains, all irked with the war, The," *fr.* II, *tr. by* the Earl of Surrey. OAEL-1
"Heaven, the earth, and all the liquid mayne, The," *fr.* VI, *tr. by* Sir Walter Ralegh. OBVE
"It was then night: the sound [*or* sounde] and quiet sleep [*or* slepe]," *fr.* IV, *tr. by* the Earl of Surrey. OAEL-1; PoEL-1
"Loe! formest of a rout that followed him," *fr.* II, *tr. by* the Earl of Surrey. OBVE
"Loud report through Lybian cities goes, The," *fr.* IV, *tr. by* Dryden. OBVE
Marcellus, *fr.* VI, *tr. by* Dryden. OBS
"Now manhood and garbroyls I chaunt," *fr.* I, *tr. by* Richard Stanyhurst. BIrV; OBVE
"Onto the hallowit steid bryng in, thai cry," *fr.* II, *tr. into Middle English by* Gavin Douglas. OBVE
"Prince, with wonder, sees the stately tow'rs, The," *fr.* I, *tr. by* Dryden. OBVE
Prologue to Book VII, the, *fr.* VII, *tr. by* Gavin Douglas. OxBS
"Quhen thou are careit to that cuntree," *fr.* III, *tr. into Middle English by* Gavin Douglas. OBVE
"Rang'd on the line opposed, Antonius brings," *fr.* VIII, *tr. by* Dryden. WaaP
Sixth Book of the Aeneis, The, *tr. by* Dryden. SeCV-2
"Then Mercury 'gan bend him to obey," *fr.* IV, *tr. by* the Earl of Surrey. ViBoPo
"There Charon stands, who rules the dreary coast," *fr.* VI, *tr. by* Dryden. OBVE
"They wished [*or* whisted] all, with fixed face attent," *fr.* II, *tr. by* the Earl of Surrey. LiTB; SiPS
"Thir riveris and thir watteris kepit war," *fr.* VI, *tr. into Middle English by* Gavin Douglas. OBVE
"Thus fell the King, who yet surviv'd the state," *fr.* II, *tr. by* Sir John Denham. OBVE
"To my prowd foe thus, sister, humblie saye," *fr.* II, *tr. by* the Earl of Surrey. OBVE
"Wee leave Creete Country; and our sayls unwrapped uphoysing," *fr.* III, *tr. by* Richard Stanyhurst. OBVE
Welcome to the Sun, *fr.* XII, *tr. by* Gavin Douglas. ACP
Aenigma on the Six Cases. *Unknown.* FaBoUs
Aeolian Harp. William Allingham. OnYI
Aeolian Harp, The. Samuel Taylor Coleridge. *See* Eolian Harp, The.
Aeolian Harp, The. Herman Melville. AmPP; AP
Aeons of history float. Prisoner. Marguerite George. GoYe
Aerial View of Louisiana. Cleopatra Mathis. *See* View of Louisiana.
Aeronaut to His Lady, The. Frank Sidgwick. WhC
Aerophorion, *sel.* Henry James Pye.
Air Balloon, The. NOEC
Aeroplane. Mary McBride Green. SoPo; TiPo
Aerosol. Harold Witt. SOTS
Aesop, *sel.* Sir John Vanbrugh.
In the Sprightly Month of May. UnTE
Aesop at Play. Phaedrus, *tr. fr. Latin by* Christopher Smart. AWP
Aesop [*or* Esope], mine author, makis mentio[u]n. The Tale [*or* Taill] of the Upland Mouse [*or* Uponlandis Mous] and the Burgess Mouse [*or* Burges Mous]. Robert Henryson. BSV; OBNV; OxBM
Aesop's Fable of the Frogs. La Fontaine, *tr. fr. French by* John Hookham Frere. OBVE

Aesthete, The. W. S. Gilbert. *See* Bunthorne's Song.
Aesthete to the Rose, The. *Unknown.* BXAP
Aesthete Weasel, The. Christian Morgenstern, *tr. fr. German by* Geoffrey Grigson. FaBoNo
Aesthetic. Norman Rosten. PoA
Aesthetic Point of View, The. W. H. Auden. OBAL
Aesthetics of the Moon. Jack Anderson. MOON
Aestivation [an Unpublished Poem by My Late Latin Tutor]. Oliver Wendell Holmes. *Fr.* The Autocrat of the Breakfast Table, *ch.* 11. InMe; NA; NOBL; OBAL; WhC
(Intramural Aestivation, or Summer in Town, by a Teacher of Latin.) ChTr; FaBoNo
Aetate XIX. Herman Charles Merivale. OBVV
Æthelstan King,/ Lord among Earls. The Battle of Brunanburh. *Unknown, tr. by* Tennyson. OBVE; OBWP; TrGrPo; WaaP
Æthelstan King, lord of eorls. The Battle of Brunanburh. *Unknown, tr. by* Charles W. Kennedy. AnOE
Aether. Allen Ginsberg. CoPo
Afar in the Desert. Thomas Pringle. HBV-1
Affable Irregular, An. The Road at My Door. W. B. Yeats. Meditations in Time of Civil War, V. BIrV; LiTB; NOBE
Affair of Honour. George Whalley. MoCV
Affaire d'Amour. Margaret Deland. HBV-1
Affection and Desire. Sir Walter Ralegh. *See* Conceit Begotten by the Eyes.
Affectionate Shepherd, The, *sels.* Richard Barnfield.
Daphnis to Ganymede. EIL
"If thou wilt love me, thou shalt be my boy." PBBP
Affection's charm no longer gilds. The Personified Sentimental. Bret Harte. NA
Affections, instincts, principles, and powers. Written in Butler's Sermons. Matthew Arnold. VLP
Affidavit in Platitudes. E. B. White. InMe
Affinity, The. Anna Wickham. HBMV
Affirmation. Helen Armstead Johnson. AmNP
Affirmations (I-III). Peter Viereck. MiAP
Affliction. Bible, *O.T.* Lamentations, III: 1-15. TrJP
Affliction. Sir John Davies. *Fr.* Nosce Teipsum. NOBE; OBSC
Affliction ("Broken in pieces all asunder"). George Herbert. AnAnS-1; JCP; LoBV
Affliction ("Kill me not every day"). George Herbert. TEP
Affliction ("When first thou didst entice to thee my heart"). George Herbert. AnAnS-1; CABA; JCP; LiTB; MeLP; MePO; NOBE; NoP; OBS; OxBoCh; SeCP
Affliction is a stormy deep. Submission in Affliction. *Unknown.* STF
Affliction of Margaret, The. Wordsworth. EnRP; GTBS; GTBS-P; OBRV; PoEL-4
Affliction of Richard, The. Robert Bridges. QFR
Afforestation. E. A. Wodehouse. FiBHP
Affrayit, I glistnyt of sleip, and stert on feit. Virgil, *tr. by* Gavin Douglas. *Fr.* The Aeneid, II. OBVE
Afoot. Sir Charles G. D. Roberts. CaP; HBV-1
Afoot and light-hearted I take to the open road. Song of the Open Road. Walt Whitman. FaFP; HBVY; NePA; NOBA; RFM; TiPo; TreFT; ViBoPo; WHA
Afore ye tak in hand this beuk. Lines Written in the Front of a Well-read Copy of Burns's *Songs:* To the Reader. *Unknown.* FaBoUs
Afraid. Walter de la Mare. WeW
Afraid of the sun, I hide behind my sleeve. For a Neighbor Girl. Yü Hsüan-chi, *tr. by* Geoffrey Waters. BoWoP
Afraid of the sunlight. Advice to a Neighbour Girl. Yü Hsüan-chi, *tr. by* Kenneth Rexroth *and* Ling Chung. PBWP
Afraid? Of whom am I afraid? Emily Dickinson. OHIP
Afreet ("*Afreet* I am afraid of"). David McCord. WSC
Afresh'd with paint the shop had glare. New Storefront. Russell Atkins. FB
Africa. Lewis Alexander. CDC
Africa. Maya Angelou. NIP
Africa. Lucille Clifton. CNA
Africa. David Diop, *tr. fr. French by* Ulli Beier. PBA; TTY
Africa. Claude McKay. BALP
Africa. Adèle Naudé. PeSA
Africa. Change Is Not Always Progress. Don L. Lee. TAP
Africa, my Africa. Africa. David Diop, *tr. by* Ulli Beier. PBA; TTY
Africa, you were once just a name to me. The Meaning of Africa. Abioseh Nicol. PBA
African Affair, The. Bruce McM. Wright. AmNP; NIP; PoBA; PoNe
African blues. Notes for a Speech. Amiri Baraka. CoPo
African Chief, The. Bryant. BLPA; PaPo; TreFS
African China. Melvin B. Tolson. PoBA
African Christmas. John Press. OBCP
African Dance. Langston Hughes. FaPON
African Day. Gloria de Sant'Ana, *tr. fr. Portuguese by* Allan Francovich *and* Kathleen Weaver. PBWP
African Dream. Bob Kaufman. AmNP; PoBA
African Easter. Abioseh Nicol. PBA
African Elegy, An. Robert Duncan. NoAM
African in Louisiana. Kojo Gyinaye Kyei. PBA
African Poems, *sel.* Don L. Lee.
"We're an Africanpeople." CNA
African Song, An. Thomas Chatterton. LoBV
African Things. Victor Hernández Cruz. InW
African Trader's Complaint, The. Dennis C. Osadebay. PBA
African Tramp, The. Geoffrey Haresnape. PeSA
Africa's Plea. Roland Tombekai Dempster. PBA; TTY
Africland. Oliver La Grone. FB
"Aften [*or* Aft] hae I playd at the cards and the dice." The Rantin Laddie. *Unknown.* BaBo (A *and* B *vers.*); ESPB
After. Robert Browning. TrGrPo
After. Caroline Grayson. BLRP
After. W. E. Henley. In Hospital, VI. BrPo
After. Ralph Hodgson. MoBrPo
After. Philip Levine. VWA
After. Philip Bourke Marston. HBV-1
After. Lizette Woodworth Reese. HBV-1
After. Michael Ryan. MAYP
After a banquet. The Cynneddf. Rolfe Humphries. CrMA
After a black day, I play Haydn. Allegro. Tomas Tranströmer, *tr. by* Robert Bly. EAS
After a Death. Gregory Orr. GeTw
After a dream in which your love's fullness. The Sapphire. W. S. Merwin. PoA
After a drifting day, visiting the bridge near Louisberg. Summer, 1960, Minnesota. Robert Bly. InPS
After a fearful maze where doubt. Chimera. Barbara Howes. MP; TwCP
After a Game of Squash. Samuel L. Albert. GoYe; NePoAm-2
After a heart disease, Aunt Li died. A Pair of Fireflies. Stephen Shu Ning Liu. BrSi
After a hundred years. Emily Dickinson. AWP; FaBoEn; MoPo; OxBA
After a Journey. Thomas Hardy. ChMP; CMoP; DTC; EBEV; ELP; EnLoPo; FaBoEn; FaBoPP; GBL; GTBS-P; MoVE; OBNC; OxBTC; PoEL-5
After a Lecture on Keats. Oliver Wendell Holmes. AA; ViBoPo
After a Line by John Peale Bishop. Donald Justice. *See* Grandfathers, The.
After a little I could not have told. The Song of the Tortured Girl. John Berryman. CoAP
After a long winter, giving/ each other nothing. Chiyo, *tr. fr. Japanese by* David Ray. BoWoP
After a month and a half without rain. August Rain. Robert Bly. LCAP; SV
After a Passage in Baudelaire. Robert Duncan. CMoP; PoA
After a soiree, with his dark head bent. Hazlitt Sups. Katharine Day Little. GoYe
After a Sultry Morning. Rodney Hall. *Fr.* The Owner of My Face. CBAP
After a supper of mountain rice. Hometown. Luis Cabalquinto. BrSi
After a thousand mazes overgone. A Sleeping Youth. Keats. *Fr.* Endymion. SeCePo
After a throbbing night, the house still dark, pull. Those of Pure Origin. Roy Fuller. FaBoMo
After a Time. Catherine Davis. NePoEA
After a while. The Widow Perez. Gary Soto. MAYP
After a while, in the larger cities, we. Normal as Two Ships in the Night. Walta Borawski. AMV-81
After a while it dawns on us. Historical Museum, Manitoulin Island. Lisel Mueller. PoA
After All. Donald Jeffrey Hayes. CDC
After all,/ One country, brethren! One Country. Frank Lebby Stanton. AA; PAL
After all and after all. After All. Donald Jeffrey Hayes. CDC
After all, Charlie, we shall see them go. Longshore Intellectual. Sean Lucy. CIP
After All These Years. May Sarton. AMV-81
After an age when thunderbolts and hail. Sonnet XVI. Louise Labé, *tr. by* Willis Barnstone. BoWoP
After an All-Night Cackle with Sloth and Co. I Enter Mansion and Greet the Dawn. Gary Gildner. GP
After an Eclipse of the Sun. Eugene Heimler, *tr. fr. Hungarian by* Peter Sherwood *and* Keith Bosley. VWA
After an evening of drinking. Ryókan. William Heyen. AMV-81
After an hundred and thirty years' nap. On the Erection of Shakespeare's Statue in Westminster Abbey. Pope. FaBoEE
After an Interval. Walt Whitman. AA
After Anacreon. Lew Welch. *Fr.* Taxi Suite. NeAP; PoM
After Annunciation. Anna Wickham. MoBrPo

After Apple-picking. Robert Frost. AmPP; AP; CMoP; CoBMV; FPL; LiTA; MoAB; MoAmPo; MoPo; MoVE; NoAM; NOBA; NU; OxBA; PAI; PPP; PrIm; RoGo; TAP; UnPo; ViBoPo
After Aughrim. Arthur Gerald Geoghegan. OnYI
After Aughrim. Emily Lawless. OBEV; OxBI
After Blenheim. Robert Southey. *See* Battle of Blenheim, The.
After Bombardment. John Pudney. WaP
After Bourlon Wood. Helen Dircks. SUMH
After breakfast and you'd left for school. Divorce. Bink Noll. MAT
After bringing forth eighteen. For a Shetland Pony Brood Mare Who Died in Her Barren Year. Maxine W. Kumin. PH
After casting the first act, checking sections. God and Man. Samuel Hazo. ELU
After centuries of dissecting. Lesbian Poem. Robin Morgan. IHMS
After Chagall. Renee Wenger. PoDr
After Christmas. W. H. Auden. *Fr.* For the Time Being. MoBrPo
After Christmas. Michael Richards. OBCP
After-Comers, The. Robert Traill Spence Lowell. AA
After Commencement. Howard Nemerov. GLGT
After Dark. Adrienne Rich. LCAP; LiTM; VGW
After dark/ Near the South Dakota border. Having Lost My Sons, I Confront the Wreckage of the Moon: Christmas, 1960. James Wright. CoAP
After Dark Vapours. Keats. EnRP; FaBoRV
("After dark vapours have oppress'd our plains.") TEP
(Sonnet.) OBNC
After days of putting down my poem. January. Ellen Bryant Voigt. NoP
After Death. Fanny Parnell. AnIV; OBVV; OnYI; OxBI
After Death. Charles Francis Richardson. AA
After Death. Christina Rossetti. GBL; TEP
After Death in Arabia. Sir Edwin Arnold. HBV-2; WGRP
After death nothing is, and nothing death. Seneca, *tr. by* the Earl of Rochester. *Fr.* Troades, II. EBEV; OBVE
After digging in the rubble of the ruined house. The Princess Casamassima. Daniel Hoffman. GLGT
After Dilettante Concetti. Henry Duff Traill. BXAP; CenHV; FaBoCo; HBV-1; Par
After dinner Erasmus. Bentley. *Fr.* Clerihews. CenHV
After dinner sit awhile. *Unknown.* FaBoUs
After dreaming some hours of the land of Cockaigne. Thomas Moore. *Fr.* The Fudge Family in Paris. BIrV
After Drinking All Night with a Friend, We Go Out in a Boat at Dawn to See Who Can Write the Best Poem. Robert Bly. NaP
After each quake. Crack in the Wall Holds Flowers. Adam David Miller. PoBA
After eight thousand years among the stars. Space-Wanderer's Homecoming. Peter Viereck. AMV-80
After Elegies. Jean Valentine. LCAP
After 11 years. The Most Beautiful Woman at My Highschool Reunion. Ellen Marie Bissert. PeHV
After Eli Whitney's gin. Southeast Arkanasia. Maya Angelou. SaC
After Emerson. *Unknown.* *See* Lives of Great Men.
After Ever Happily. Ian Serraillier. SO
After Experience Taught Me. W. D. Snodgrass. CoAP; OBWP
(After experience taught me that all the ordinary.) CAPP; PPP; TAP
After Five Years. Augustus Young. BIrV
After five years. The Ownership of the Night. Larry Levis. LCAP
After Floods on the Wharfe. Andrew Marvell. *Fr.* Upon Appleton House. FaBoPP
After Frost. Brian Patten. EBEV
After Galen. Oliver St. John Gogarty. FaBoEE; OBMV; PoRA
After Goliath. Kingsley Amis. NePoEA-2; NOBL; OxBTC; PoCh
After Grave Deliberation. Elizabeth Flynn. AMV-80
After great pain, a formal feeling comes. Emily Dickinson. AmPP; AP; BoWoP; CABA; HAP; InPS; LiTA; MoAB; MoAmPo; MoPo; MoVE; NePA; NIP; NOBA; NoP; PAI; PPoe; PrIm; SBG; TAP; UnPo
After great storms the calm returns. Sir Thomas Wyatt. SiPS
After Greece. James Merrill. ConAP; NOBA; NYBP
After Grey Vigils. George Santayana. Sonnets, XLIX. WHA
After Grief. Stanley Plumly. AmPA; DiL; LCAP
After having slain very many beasts. Sonnet XIX. Louise Labé, *tr. by* Willis Barnstone. BoWoP
After He Had Gone. Sylvia Townsend Warner. MoBrPo
After he sledged wife the man. Note in a Sanitorium. Ray Amorosi. FAZ
After he stripped off my clothes. Vallana, *tr. fr. Sanskrit by* Willis Barnstone. BoWoP
After Her Death. Anne Stevenson. HoAn
After her pills the girl slept and counted. Tally. Josephine Miles. NoAM
After her twelfth birthday. Woman's Liberation. Sister Maura. AMV-81
After his death we wade together. He Fishes with His Father's Ghost. Lewis Nordan. AMV-81
After his talking destroyed her. Antarctica. R. A. Simpson. CBAP
After Horace. Alfred Denis Godley. NOBL
After hot loveless nights, when cold winds stream. The Sisters. Roy Campbell. BoLoP; ChMP; ErPo; FaBoTw; MoVE; OBMV
After Hours. Robert Mezey. NaP
After I am dead/ Say this at my funeral. After My Death. Hayim Nachman Bialik, *tr. by* A. C. Jacobs. VWA
After I ate my dinner then I ate. Confession of a Glutton. Don Marquis. GDP
After I came down from the mountain, my Lord. Moses' Account. Milan Fuest, *tr. by* Andrè Ungar. VWA
After I got religion and steadied down. "Butch" Weldy. Edgar Lee Masters. *Fr.* Spoon River Anthology. NePA; SaC
After I Had Worked All Day. Charles Reznikoff. *Fr.* Five Groups of Verse. PrIm; VGW
After I Have Voted. Laura Jensen. AmPA
After I read you, I thought of every mortal. Poem to the Memory of H. L. Mencken. Baron Wormser. MAYP
After Illness. Vi Gale. GP
After it became obvious that the strange rain would never stop. Tentative Description of a Dinner to Promote the Impeachment of President Eisenhower. Lawrence Ferlinghetti. CoPo
After it happened. Poem for a Suicide. George Economou. DFF
After Jena. Thomas Hardy. *Fr.* The Dynasts. WaaP
After Jericho. R. S. Thomas. OxBC
After Johnson's Dance. Charles H. Souter. PoAu-1
After kicking on the swing. Li Ch'ing-chao, *tr. fr. Chinese by* Kenneth Rexroth *and* Ling Chung. BoWoP
After Laughter. Grace Buchanan Sherwood. GoYe
After Long Busyness. Robert Bly. PoA
After long journey in sun. Ear Is Not Deaf. Irene Dayton. GoYe
After Long Silence. W. B. Yeats. BoLoP; CMoP; ELU; EnLoPo; HeIP; HoPM; LiTM; OAEL-2; OBMV; PoPl; PPP; PrIm; UnPo
After long stormes and tempests sad assay. Amoretti, LXIII. Spenser. FaBoEn; OAEL-1; OAEP; OBSC
After Lorca. Robert Creeley. ConAP; InPS; LCAP; NaP; POL
After Lorca. Ted Hughes. PoA
After Love. Vincente Aleixandre, *tr. fr. Spanish by* Lewis Hyde. AMV
After Love. Maxine W. Kumin. NMM; TAP
After Making Love We Hear Footsteps. Galway Kinnell. DiL
After many scornes like these. What Hee Suffered. Ben Jonson. *Fr.* A Celebration of Charis. AnAnS-2; SeCP
After many strange thoughts. After Working. Robert Bly. NaP
After Mardi Gras. Sister Mary Honora. NePoAm-2
After Margrave died, nothing. History of a Literary Movement. Howard Nemerov. NePoEA; PP
After Mass. "Michael Field." WPE
After mass father rinsed the chalice with wine. 1955. Bruce Weigl. MAYP
After melon. *Unknown.* FaBoUs
After Midnight. Louis Simpson. NoAM
After Midnight. Charles Vildrac, *tr. fr. French by* Jethro Bithell. AWP
After midnight I heard a scream. By Night. Robert Francis. POL; VGW
After midnight the bright moon. Frost Warning. Ron McFarland. AMV-81
After midnight the charm. Party. Donald Justice. GP
After Midsummer. E. J. Scovell. OxBTC
After much dissension and strife. Peter's Tears. Thomas Hood. TreFT
After My Death. Hayim Nachman Bialik, *tr. fr.* Hebrew by A. C. Jacobs. VWA
After Night Flight. Robert Penn Warren. Mortmain, I. DiL
("In Time's concatenation and/Carnal conventicle.") NOBA; Prf
After night, the waking knowledge. Awaking. Stephen Spender. NYBP
After night there comes the day. Still He Sings. Allan Taylor. OBET
After night's thunder far away had rolled. Haymaking. Edward Thomas. BrPo; MoAB; MoBrPo; SeCePo
After noon, in the plaza, cries, shrill yells, running and breaking. Memorial Day. Josephine Miles. NoP
After one moment when I bowed my head. The Convert. G. K. Chesterton. GoBC
After our damp skins slid apart. Definition. Lauren Shakely. FYAP
After our fierce loving. The Profile on the Pillow. Dudley Randall. BPo; PoBA; TAP
After Our War. John Balaban. FAZ
After Paris, every city's just. The Next Time You Were There. Samuel Hazo. FAZ
After Passing the Examination. Meng Chiao, *tr. fr. Chinese by* Irving Y. Lo. GLGT
After Picking Rosehips. Harley Elliott. NeAC
After Plotinus. William Stafford. PoA
After Publication of Under the Volcano. Malcolm Lowry. FaBoTw
After Rabbi Akiba, Buxtorf, Herder. Commentaries on the Song of Songs. Judith Herzberg, *tr. by* Shirley Kaufman. VWA
After Rain. P. K. Page. NOBC

After Rain. Edward Thomas. NCSH
After rain. Mountain Study. Peter van Toorn. NOBC
After rain he ventures out. The Photographer. Roger Pfingston. PoDr
After rain, through afterglow, the unfolding fan. Train Ride. John Wheelwright. MoPo; TwAmPo; VGW
After Reading a Book on Abnormal Psychology. Ernest G. Moll. ELU
After Reading a Child's Guide to Modern Physics. W. H. Auden. NYBP
After Reading Certain Books. Mary Elizabeth Coleridge. EaLo
After Reading Homer. Digby Mackworth Dolben. GoBC
After Reading in a Letter Proposals for Building a Cottage. John Clare. OBRV
After Reading Nelly Sachs. Linda Pastan. VWA
After Reading St. John the Divine. Gene Derwood. LiTM; NePA; WPE
After Reading Sylvia Plath. Alta. IHMS
After reading the latest/ peace proposal. Ballet. Milton Kaplan. SOTS
After Reading the Life of Mrs. Catherine Stubbs in Isaac Ambrose's "War with the Devils." Isaac Hann. NOCV
After Reading the Reviews of "Finnegans Wake." Melville Cane. WhC
After Reading Twenty Years of Grantland Rice. Don Skene. InMe
After St. Augustine. Mary Elizabeth Coleridge. TrPWD; TRV
After scanning its face again and again. John Muir on Mt. Ritter. Gary Snyder. *Fr.* Myths and Texts: Burning. NOBA
After seven months in space, the astronauts. Down, Down, Down. Heather McHugh. SUW
After seventy-nine years in the same house. Departure. J. Charles Green. LFAC
After Sex. Greg Kuzma. GP
After Shakespeare. Alex Comfort. ErPo
After sharp words from the fine mind. The Flowering Bars. Charles Donnelly. CIP
After she/ had complained about. The Proposition. Paul Blackburn. ErPo
After she finished her first abortion. Margaret, Seen through a Picture Window. Judy Grahn. *Fr.* The Common Woman, VI. GP
After Shiki. Larry Eigner. FAZ
After Six Thousand Years. Victor Hugo, *tr. fr. French by* Selden Rodman. WaaP
After Snow. Walter Clark. NCSH
After so many concurring petitions. To the Five Members of the Honourable House of Commons. Sir John Denham. NCEP
After so many deaths to breathe again. Variations on a Theme by George Herbert. Marya Zaturenska. TrPWD
After so many decades of. . .of what? To Whom It May Concern. J. V. Cunningham. FYAP
After so many larger canvases. At the Louvre. E. L. Mayo. FAZ
After Some Day of Decision. Reed Whittemore. NePoEA
After some years Bohemian came to this. Epigram. J. V. Cunningham. VGW
After Speaking of One Dead a Long Time. Padraic Colum. GoYe
After Spending All Day at the National Museum of Art. Alan Britt. FAZ
After squid and cool white wine there is. Early Morning of Another World. Tom McKeown. AMV-80
After Storm. David Morton. HBMV
After such years of dissension and strife. Epigram [*or* Natural Tears *or* Dust to Dust]. Thomas Hood. FiBHP; HBV-1; ShM
After Summer. Philip Bourke Marston. HBV-1
After Sunday Dinner We Uncles Snooze. John Ciardi. HoAn
After Sunset. Grace Hazard Conkling. HBMV
After Sunset. Arthur Symons. *Fr.* At Dieppe. BrPo; SyP
After surmounting three-score and ten. My 71st Year. Walt Whitman. NAs
After Tempest. Percy MacKaye. FYAP
After Tennyson. Edward Lear. FaBoNo
After that war, when death had gone away. Joan Miró. Ruthven Todd. EAS
After the Agony in the Garden. Daryl Hine. PeCV
After the agony in the guest/ bedroom. Margaret Atwood. NeAC
After the Annunciation. Eileen Duggan. ISi
After the Anonymous Swedish. Jim Harrison. VGW
After the Armistice I was at Tours. First World War. Kenneth Slade Alling. NePoAm
After the Ball Is Over, *with music.* Charles Kassell Harris. BLSo, FSN, FSW
(After the Ball.) TreF
After the bars and the gates and the degradation. What Is Left? Assata Shakur. AMV
After the Battle. George Sylvester Viereck. GoYe
After the blast of lightning from the East. The End. Wilfred Owen. CH; FaBoRV; HBMV; MMA; MoVE
After the Blitz, 1941. J. R. Ackerley. PeHV
After the brief bivouac of Sunday. The Stenographers. P. K. Page. CaP; HeIP; LiTM; NoP; OBCV; PeCV
After the Broken Arm. Ron Padgett. ConAP; EAS
After the bronzed, heroic traveller. The Mapmaker on His Art. Howard Nemerov. NYBP
After the Burial. James Russell Lowell. AA; UnPo
After the burial-parties leave. The Hyaenas. Kipling. OBSV
After the celebrated carved misericords. Cromwell. Robert Francis. GP
After the Centennial. Christopher Pearse Cranch. PAH
After the centres' naked files, the basic line. The Lines. Randall Jarrell. CrMA
After the class I taught my father French. Ballet. Brenda Hillman. AMV-81
After the cloud embankments. Reconnaissance. Arna Bontemps. AmNP; BPo
After the Club-Dance. Thomas Hardy. At Casterbridge Fair, III. VLP
After the Comanches. *Unknown.* PAH
After the Cries of the Birds. Lawrence Ferlinghetti. CAPP
After the Dark. Enola Chamberlain. STF
After the darkness and storm. After. Caroline Grayson. BLRP
After the Dazzle of Day. Walt Whitman. NePA
After the Death of an Elder Klallam. Duane Niatum. CDW
After the Death of Her Daughter in Childbirth. Izumi Shikibu, *tr. fr. Japanese by* Edwin A. Cranston. PBWP
After the Deformed Woman Is Made Correct. Robert Lietz. AMV-80
After the Deluge. House of the Living. Claude Vigée, *tr. by* Henry Braun. VWA
After the Dentist. May Swenson. DFF; GP
After the doctor checked to see. First Practice. Gary Gildner. AmPA; InPK; LiSp; Psk; TW
After the door shuts and the footsteps die. A Hunt in the Black Forest. Randall Jarrell. CoAP; LCAP
After the dreadful Flood was past. The Tower of Babel. Nathaniel Crouch. OxBChV
After the event the rockslide. Clarity. A. R. Ammons. TAP
After the experience of waves. Ground Swell. G. Stanley Koehler. NePoAm-2
After the explosion or cataclysm, that big. The Eternal City. A. R. Ammons. EyDe
After the eyes that looked, the lips that spake. Lincoln at Gettysburg. Bayard Taylor. *Fr.* The Gettysburg Ode. OHIP; PAH
After the Fair. Thomas Hardy. At Casterbridge Fair, VII. CMoP; HAP; VLP
After the fall drive, the last. Montana Eclogue. William Stafford. NYBP
After the fall of the tree. After. Philip Levine. VWA
After the feast, my Shapcott, see. Oberon's Palace. Robert Herrick. CaPo
After the fiercest pangs of hot desire. Richard Duke. BoLoP
After the fifth day. Food Strike. Michael Hogan. GP
After the final no there comes a yes. The Well Dressed Man with a Beard. Wallace Stevens. BiP
After the Fire. Oliver Wendell Holmes. PAH
After the First Communion. Sunday Afternoon. Denise Levertov. ConAP; IHMS; PAI
After the First Frost. Lew Blockcolski. VoR
After the first powerful plain manifesto. The Express. Stephen Spender. CMoP; GoJo; LiTM; MoAB; MoBrPo; MoVE; MP; NIP; NoAM; PoPl; RoGo; SeCeV; TwCP
After the first shallows have dropped away. Daily the Ocean between Us. Patricia Goedicke. TAP
After the first sudden rain. Rains on the Island. Gabriel Preil, *tr. by* Robert Friend. VWA
After the five hour flight the confusion. Arrival: The Capital. Desmond O'Grady. NMP
After the Flood. Sir David Lindsay. *Fr.* The Monarche. OxBS
After the Flood. Arthur Rimbaud, *tr. fr. French by* Enid Rhodes Peschal. *Fr.* Illuminations. SOTW
After the Funeral. Dylan Thomas. CMoP; CoBMV; FaBoMo; InPK; MoVE; NoP; OAEL-2; OAEP
(In Memory of Ann Jones.) LiTB; MoAB; MoBrPo; MoPo; NeBP
After the Gale. Robert Bridges. *See* Who Has Not Walked upon the Shore.
After the Gentle Poet Kobayashi Issa. Robert Hass. GeTw
After the Golden Wedding, *sel.* James Kenneth Stephen.
"She's not a faultless woman; no!" EBVV
After the good fairy. The Birth of the Poet. Quandra Prettyman. BOLo
After the heaped piles and the cornsheaves waiting. Harvest and Consecration. Elizabeth Jennings. NePoEA-2
After the holiday we could finally understand. New Year's, 1978. Howard Nemerov. SOTS
After the honey drops of pearly showers. The Rose. William Hammond. OBS
After the horrors of Heathrow. 747 (London-Chicago). Robert Conquest. OxBC
After the Hunt. Detlev von Liliencron, *tr. fr. German by* Ludwig Lewisohn. AWP
After the Hurricane. Samuel Hazo. GrPl

After the Industrial Revolution, All Things Happen at Once. Robert Bly. CoAP; ConAP
After the "invitation" by the preacher she collapsed in the. Jim Harrison. *Fr.* Ghazals. NoAM
After the kill, there is the feast. Small Poem about the Hounds and the Hares. Lisel Mueller. GP
After the Killing. Dudley Randall. CNA; SoSe
After the Last Breath. Thomas Hardy. VLP
After the Last Bulletins. Richard Wilbur. CoAP; ConAP; MoAB; MoAmPo; NePoAm; NYBP; TrGrPo; ViBoPo
After the last class in the empty room. Room 000. William Stafford. GLGT
After the Last Dynasty. Stanley Kunitz. NMP; TAP
After the leaves have fallen, we return. The Plain Sense of Things. Wallace Stevens. InPS; PAI
After the light has set. The Return. George MacBeth. NYBP
After the Martyrdom. Scharmel Iris. HBV-2
After the May time and after the June time. Midsummer. Ella Wheeler Wilcox. HBV-1
After the men hunt. Dressing Game. Dennis Schmitz. NPGG
After the midnight unfolding of the White Rose. The Feast of Stephen. Kevin Nichols. OBCP
After the Movement. Peter Oresick. LTB
After the murder. The Last Quatrain of the Ballad of Emmett Till. Gwendolyn Brooks. CAPP; CNA; PoBA; WPE
After the murder, like parades of fools. Murder Mystery. David Wagoner. TwAmPo
After the Murder of Jimmy Walsh. Joan Murray. LTB
After the Navy and war. Wood Butcher. Norman Hindley. AMV-81
After the Night Hunt. James Dickey. PoA
After the palaces. May Sarton. *Fr.* A Nobleman's House. EyDe
After the Pangs of a Desperate Lover. Dryden. *Fr.* An Evening's Love, II, i. ELP; OAEP; UnTE; ViBoPo
(Love's Fancy.) ErPo
(Song: "After the pangs of a desperate lover.") FaBoEn
After the Party. Frances Cornford. ELU
After the Party. William Wise. FaPON
After the Persian. Louise Bogan. NePoAm; NYBP; PoA
After the planes unloaded, we fell down. The Dead in Europe. Robert Lowell. CMoP; DTC; LiTM; NePA; NePoEA; OxBA; OxBC
After the Pleasure Party. Herman Melville. AP; PoEL-5
After the poetry of outwaiting the line-up. Mexico City, 150 Pesos to the Dollar. Jim Mitsui. BrSi
After the Pow-Wow, *sel.* Harold Littlebird.
"I tell him how it used to be in Paguate." STE
After the Quarrel. Paul Laurence Dunbar. CDC
After the Quarrel. Barbara Gibson. FF
After the Quarrel. Adam Lindsay Gordon. OBVV
After the Rain. Edward A. Collier. BLRP
After the Rain. Stanley Crouch. CNA
After the Rain. Paul B. Janeczko. PCP
After the rain/ came the town ghost. Town Ghost. Lauris Edmond. OCNZ
After the rare arch-poet Jonson died [*or* dy'd]. Upon Mr. Ben Jonson: Epigram. Robert Herrick. CaPo; OAEP
After the red leaf and the gold have gone. A Spell before Winter. Howard Nemerov. LiTM
After the Release of Ezra Pound. Dannie Abse. NMP
After the Revolution. Marilyn Hacker. AmPA
After the rooster falls from the hen. Final Soliloquy on a Randy Rooster (in a Key of Yellow). Robert Peters. BXAP
After the satyr's twilight in the park. Homecoming—Massachusetts. John Ciardi. NYBP
After the Sea-Ship. Walt Whitman. MOS; NePA
After the sea, the harbor. Sequence. Edgar Daniel Kramer. BLRP
After the Seance. David Clewell. AMV-81
After the Second Operation. Patricia Goedicke. TAP
After the Seizer there were ten chiefs, and there was much warfare south and east. *Tr. fr. Delaware Indian by* Daniel G. Brinton. *Fr.* Walam Olum; or, Red Score. OBVE
After the shot the driven feathers rock. Rainbow. Robert Huff. NePoEA-2
After the Show. Sam Harrison. NeIP
After the Shower. Archibald Lampman. CaP
After the Spanish Chroniclers. William Bronk. GP
After the Speech to the Librarians. David Wagoner. NPAW
After the squealing brass. Saint's Parade. Robert Layzer. NePoEA
After the stars were all hung separately. The Book of How. Merrill Moore. MoAmPo
After the Storm. Elizabeth Bartlett. GoYe
After the storm, after the rain stopped pounding. Song of Napalm. Bruce Weigl. MAYP
After the Supper and Talk. Walt Whitman. MoAmPo
After the Surprising Conversions. Robert Lowell. AmPP; AP; CABA; CoBMV; ConAP; HAP; NePoEA; NoAM; NoP; PAI; PPP; SeCeV
After the Swimmer. Robert Wallace. LiSp
After the test they sent an expert. School Days. William Stafford. LCAP
After the third day, ash began to sift. Halflives. Daniel Hoffman. SOTS
After the thorns I came to the first page. The Sleeping Beauty; Variation of the Prince. Randall Jarrell. DFT; PoA
After the tiff there was stiff silence, till. The Lovers. W. R. Rodgers. BIrV
After the tumult and the blood. At Vshchizh. Fyodor Tyutchev, *tr. by* Charles Tomlinson. OBWP
After the Visit. Thomas Hardy. FaBoEn; NOBE; OBNC
After the War. Douglas Dunn. OxBC
After the War. Richard Le Gallienne. PAH
After the War. Hayim Naggid, *tr. fr. Hebrew by* Shlomo Vinner *and* Howard Schwartz. VWA
After the war—I hear men ask—what then? After the War. Richard Le Gallienne. PAH
After the whey-faced anonymity. South Country. Kenneth Slessor. CBAP
After the whipping, he crawled into bed. Portrait of a Boy. Stephen Vincent Benét. HBMV
After the wind. The Blizzard Ape. Kenneth Pitchford. CoPo
After the Winter. Claude McKay. BANP; IDB; PoBA; PoNe
After the winter thawed away, I rose. The Assignation. James Wright. NePoEA
After these words the Weather-Geat prince. Beowulf's Fight with Grendel's Mother. *Unknown, tr. by* Michael Alexander. *Fr.* Beowulf. WTO
After these years of lectures heard. To a Friend, on Her Examination for the Doctorate in English. J. V. Cunningham. TwAmPo; VGW
After they all leave. Surely You Remember. Dahlia Ravikovitch, *tr. by* Chana Bloch. VWA
After They Have Tired [of the Brilliance of Cities]. Stephen Spender. FaBoMo; LiTM
After they passed I climbed. A Story. William Stafford. NNaP; RFM
After They Put Down Their Overalls. Lenrie Peters. TTY
After this much time, it's still impossible. Spit. Charles Kenneth Williams. VWA
After those first days. Death of a Bird. Jon Silkin. BoAnP
After those reverend papers, whose soule is. To Sir H. W. [*or* Wotton] at His Going Ambassador to Venice. John Donne. MeLP; OBS
After three years—a 3-decker novel. Writing to Aaron. Denise Levertov. FAZ
After thy labour, take thine ease. The Mount of the Muses. Robert Herrick. CaPo
After Tonight. Gary Soto. GP
After Trinity. John Meade Falkner. OxBTC
After twenty-five years they drag you away. Mimosa. Cleopatra Mathis. MAYP
After Twenty Years. Fadwa Tuquan, *tr. fr. Arabic.* PBWP
After twenty years of expensive foods. Song for Mother's Day. T. S. Matthews. ELU
After two sittings, now our Lady State. The Last Instructions to a Painter. Andrew Marvell. APAS; OBSV
After Two Thousand Years. "Hugh MacDiarmid." DBV
After Two Years. Richard Aldington. HBV-1; MoBrPo; PoPl; WHA
After Vacation. Katherine Hanley. AMV-81
After Verlaine. Anselm Hollo. FAZ
After Visiting a Home for Disturbed Children. Lou Lipsitz. LTB
After Visiting the Tomb of Napoleon. Robert G. Ingersoll. TreF
After we fled away from the shuddering dock. On the Way to the Island. David Ferry. NePoAm-2
After we had burned on the water a while. Voice from Danang. Thomas Dillon Redshaw. MAT
After we had torn out. For a Marriage. Erica Jong. CTBA
After we knew that we were dead we sat down and cried a little. The Dead. Louis Dudek. NOBC
After we'd turned in they gathered round. Cow-Ponies. Maurice Lesemann. BPAW
After weeks of watching the roof leak. Gary Snyder. *Fr.* Hitch Haiku. InPK
After what had/ to be said. Drunk. Carroll Arnett. VoR
After Wings. Sarah Morgan Bryan Piatt. AA; HBV-1
After Winter. Sterling A. Brown. PoBA; PoNe
After Woman, The. Francis Thompson. ISi
After Work. John Oxenham. TRV
After Work. Gary Snyder. HoPM; NNaP
After Working. Robert Bly. NaP
After writing for an hour in the presbytery. James K. Baxter. Autumn Testament, 46. OCNZ
After X-Ray. Linda Pastan. POL
After years of relative clumsiness. Arachne. Judith Kazantzis. BrRo

After years of stock-car racing, running. Miami. Daniel Mark Epstein. MAYP
After you have enriched your soul. Jonathan Swift Somers. Edgar Lee Masters. *Fr.* Spoon River Anthology. OBAL
After you have gone. Renaming the Evening. Eric Pankey. AMV-81
After you left, I took the green. Absent Star. Quinton Duval. FAZ
After You, Madam. Alex Comfort. ErPo; UnTE
After Your Death. David James. AMV-80
After your death. Poem. William Knott. EAS
After you've been to bed together for the first time. Life Story. Tennessee Williams. PeHV
Afterbirth. Beryle Williams. PoDr
After-Glow, The. Mathilde Blind. OBNC
Afterglow. Jorge Luis Borges, *tr. fr. Spanish by* Norman Thomas di Giovanni. NYBP
Afterglow goldens the. The Mountain Afterglow. James Laughlin. VGW
Afterlives. Derek Mahon. CIP
Aftermath, An. Thomas Blackburn. NMP
Aftermath, The. Euripides, *tr. fr. Greek by* Richmond Lattimore. *Fr.* Iphigenia in Aulis. WaaP
Aftermath. Longfellow. AP; NOBA; TAP
Aftermath. Margaret McCulloch. PGD
Aftermath. Sylvia Plath. SBG
Aftermath. Siegfried Sassoon. BrPo; MoBrPo; TrJP; ViBoPo; WaP
Aftermath, The. William Carlos Williams. FAZ
Afternoon. Wendell Phillips Garrison. *Fr.* Post-Meridian. AA
Afternoon. Donald Hall. Str
Afternoon. Lucien Stryk. *Fr.* Zen Poems, after Shinkichi Takahashi. FAZ
Afternoon./ Teacher and nun, bleak refugee, a stone. Street Scene. Robert Mezey. LiTM
Afternoon,/ with just enough of a breeze for him to ride it. Robert Sund. BoAnP
Afternoon: Amagansett Beach. John Hall Wheelock. BoNaP; MoVE; NePA; PoRA
Afternoon at Cannes. Paul Davis. AMV-81
Afternoon cooking in the fall sun. Song. Robert Hass. AmPA
Afternoon dark increases with the clock, The. Late Tutorial. Vincent Buckley. PoAu-2
Afternoon deepening now, a dark animal growing. Hermit. David Baker. AMV-80
Afternoon foreclosing, see, The. The Swimmer. Irving Layton. PeCV
Afternoon in a Tree. Sister Maris Stella. GoBC
Afternoon in Anglo-Ireland. Bruce Williamson. NeIP
Afternoon in sultry summer, An. Amores (after Ovid). Jay Parini. MAYP
Afternoon in the Garden, An. Murray Edmond. OCNZ
Afternoon is dark and not with rain, The. The Breaking of the Day. Peter Davison. CoPo
Afternoon is invading my eyes. Drunken Poem. David Helwig. NOBC
Afternoon is the snack's own seasoning. Little Pudding. Mary M. Roberts. BXAP
Afternoon late summer, in a room, An. At My Grandmother's. David Malouf. PoAu-2
Afternoon of a Faun, The. Stéphane Mallarmé. *See* Après-Midi d'un faune, L'.
Afternoon on a Hill. Edna St. Vincent Millay. FaPON; GrPl; NTCP; OBCA; OxBA; PDV; SoPo
Afternoon Sleep. Robert Bly. NaP
Afternoon 3. Saburoh Kuroda. EAS
Afternoon turned dark early, The. During December's Death. Delmore Schwartz. NYBP
Afternoon wears on, The. Pastoral. David Wright. NYBP
Afternoon with Grandmother. Barbara A. Huff. FaPON
Afternoon with the heavy hours, The. The Traveller. Allen Tate. LiTM
Afternoons/ Brought coconut smell of gorse. John Betjeman. *Fr.* Summoned by Bells. FaBoPP
Afternoon's Angel. Seymour Mayne. VWA
Afternoons with Baedeker, *sels.* Osbert Lancaster.
Eireann. DBV; NOBL
English. FaBoCo; NOBL
French. FaBoCo; NOBL
Italian. FaBoCo
Manhattan. NOBL
After-Song. Richard Watson Gilder. AA; TrPWD
Afterthought. Elizabeth Jennings. OBCP
Afterthought. Justin Richardson. PV
After-Thought, The. Stevie Smith. OxBC
After-Thought. Wordsworth. The River Duddon, XXXIV. EnRP; FaBoEn; OBNC; OBRV; SeCePo
(After-Thought to "The River Duddon.") OAEP
("I thought of Thee, my partner and my guide.") FaBoRV
(To the River Duddon: After-Thought.) FaBoPP
(Valediction to the River Duddon.) NOBE
(Valedictory Sonnet to the River Duddon.) OBEV
Afterthoughts of Donna Elvira. Carolyn Kizer. NePoAm-2
Afterwake, The. Adrienne Rich. NOBA; Prf
Afterward. Mary Matheson. CaP
Afterward. Elizabeth Stuart Phelps Ward. HBV-2
Afterward he may take thought. The Airman. W. R. Rodgers. WaP
Afterwards. Margaret Postgate Cole. SUMH
Afterwards. "Violet Fane." HBV-2; OBVV
Afterwards. Thomas Hardy. BoNaP; CH; ChMP; ChTr; CMoP; EBEV; FaBoEn; FaBoRV; GTBS-P; InPS; LiTB; LiTM; MoAB; MoBrPo; MoVE; NOBE; NoP; OAEL-2; OAEP; OBNC; PoEL-5; PoPle; QFR; SeCeV; TreFT; TrGrPo; ViBoPo
Afterwards. Frances Ridley Havergal. BLRP
Afterwards, afterwards the wind between two mountains. Prelude. David Rosenmann-Taub, *tr. by* Charles Guenther. VWA
Afterwards, let us make riddles. Riddles. Patrick F. Kirby. GoBC
Afterwards, the compromise. After Love. Maxine W. Kumin. NMM; TAP
Afterwards there are dogends in. Sonnet. Maureen Duffy. PeHV
Afterwards, They Shall Dance. Bob Kaufman. PoNe; TwCP; VGW
Afterword, An: For Gwen Brooks. Don L. Lee. JB
Afterword: Song of Song. James Broughton. GP
Afton Water. Burns. BiP; BoNaP; FaBoPP; HeIP; LAuP; OAEP
(Flow Gently, Sweet Afton.) AWP; BLPL; FaBoBe; FaFP; FSW; HBV-1
(Sweet Afton.) CABA; EnRP; LiTB; TreF; TrGrPo
Aga Khan, The. Steve Orlen. Psk
Again. František Halas, *tr. fr. Czech by* Karl W. Deutsch. WaaP
Again. Charlotte Mew. MoAB; MoBrPo
Again. Jon Stallworthy. OxBC
Again, again, I sinful see. In Dream. J. M. Synge. SyP
Again and again I go away from you. J. Michael Yates. *Fr.* The Great Bear Lake Meditations. HoPM
Again and again I kiss thy gates at departing. Roma. Rutilius, *tr. by* Ezra Pound. CTC
Again and again I make the intolerable journey. The Repeated Journey. Thomas McGrath. NePoEA
Again and then again. . .the year is born. New Year's Day. Robert Lowell. AmPP; CABA; ConAP; LiTM; NePoEA; PPoe
Again as Evening's Shadow Falls, *with music.* Samuel Longfellow. AH
Again at Christmas did we weave. Tennyson. In Memoriam A. H. H., LXXVIII. PChr
Again, Christmas, bright colored lights. The Spirit. Doug Turner. AMV-81
Again Columbia's stripes, unfurl'd. *Enterprise* and *Boxer. Unknown.* PAH
Again for Hephaistos, the Last Time. Richard Howard. GP
Again heavy rain drives him home. Stepfather: A Girl's Song. Yusef Komunyakaa. Str
Again, his friend's death made the man sit still. John Berryman. NOBA
Again I hear that creaking step. My Familiar. John Godfrey Saxe. HBV-2; TreFS
Again I keep watch. Speak. Bea Opengart. AMV-80
Again I reply to the triple winds. January. William Carlos Williams. MoAB; MoAmPo
Again I see my bliss at hand. Meeting. Matthew Arnold. Switzerland, I. ELP; OAEP; VLP
Again I see you, ah my queen. Juana. Alfred de Musset, *tr. by* Andrew Lang. AWP
Again last night I dreamed the dream called laundry. The Mad Scene. James Merrill. CoAP; NoAM; NOBA; PoA; TAP
Again let me do a lot of extraordinary talking. The Song of the Militant Romance. Wyndham Lewis. FaBoTw; OxBTC
Again My Fond Circle of Doves. Baxter Hathaway. HoAn
Again? New tumults in my breast? Horace, *tr. by* Pope. Odes, IV, 1. PEHV
Again observing how my hands. Étude for Voice and Hand. Gabriel Levin. VWA
Again on the morrow morning doth Sigurd the Volsung ride. Sigurd Rideth to the Glittering Heath. William Morris. *Fr.* The Story of Sigurd the Volsung, II. PoEL-5
Again rejoicing Nature sees. Song. Burns. BoNaP; HBV-1
Again the ancient, meaningless. Gary Snyder. Myths and Texts: Logging, V. CAPP; NaP
Again the belt was off the flywheel. The Musician at His Work. Robert Currie. Str
Again the call of the winter birds. Poem for Carroll, Descendant of Chiefs. Lance Henson. VoR
Again the day. If the Stars Should Fall. Samuel Allen. IDB; NNP; PoBA
Again the light of. Epitaph: Snake River. Lance Henson. VoR
Again, the morning for a male is best. How to Conceive Boys. Claude Quillet, *tr. by* George Sewell. *Fr.* Callipaedia; or, The Art of Getting Beautiful Children. FaBoUs

Again the native hour lets down the locks. More Sonnets at Christmas, I. Allen Tate. LiTA; LiTM; NePA; WaP
Again the summer-fevered skies. Garfield's Ride at Chickamauga. Hezekiah Butterworth. PAH
Again the time and blood consuming sun crosses its corner. A Dawn Horse. William Harmon. FYAP
Again the wood, and long with-drawing vale. To Spring. Charlotte Smith. WPE
Again, the year's decline, midst storms and floods. Robert Bloomfield. *Fr.* The Farmer's Boy. OBRV
Again this morning trembles on the swift stream the image of the sun. Images. Kathleen Raine. NYBP
Again we smelled for days on end. Again. František Halas, *tr. by* Karl W. Deutsch. WaaP
Againe. Robert Herrick. SeCP
Against a falling snow. A Fear. Robert Francis. GP
Against a sharp spring sky. Sky Patterns. Jeannette Maino. AMV-80
Against a somber background, blue as midnight. The Offering of the Heart Tapestry from Arras, XV Century. Rolfe Humphries. FYAP
Against Absence. Sir John Suckling. CaPo
Against an elm a sheep was tied [*or* ty'd]. The Wild Boar and the Ram. John Gay. *Fr.* Fables. FM; NOEC; PAI; PPON
Against an Old Lecher. Sir John Harington. FaBoEE
Against Blame of Women. Gerald, Earl of Desmond, *tr. fr. Late Middle Irish by* the Earl of Longford. AnIL; BIrV
Against Borders. Yevgeny Yevtushenko, *tr. fr. Russian by* Anselm Hollo. CAD
Against Botticelli. Robert Hass. AmPA; NPGG
Against Broccoli. Roy Blount, Jr. OBAL
(Song against Broccoli.) PPJ
Against Constancy. Earl of Rochester. GBL
Against Consummation. Petronius Arbiter. *See* Doing a Filthy Pleasure Is.
Against Dark's Harm. Anne Halley. NMM
Against Death. Peter Redgrove. NMP
Against Education. Charles Churchill. *See* Pains of Education, The.
Against Friars. *Unknown.* OxBM
Against Fruition. Sir John Suckling. CaPo; ErPo
Against Fulfillment of Desire. *Unknown.* TrGrPo
Against Garnesche, *sel.* John Skelton.
"What, have ye kithéd you a knight, Sir Douglas the Doughty." ViBoPo
Against Gaudy-Bragging-Undoughty Daccus. John Davies of Hereford. FaBoEE
Against Gravity. Edith E. Cutting. AMV-80
Against Homosexuality. Thomas Gilbert. *Fr.* A View of the Town. In an Epistle to a Friend. NOEC
Against Hope. Abraham Cowley. *Fr.* The Mistress. LiTB; MeLP; OBS; SeCV-1
(On Hope.) MePo; NOBE
Against Idleness and Mischief. Isaac Watts. *See* How Doth the Little Busy Bee.
Against Indifference. Charles Webbe. HBV-1; OBEV
Against Irresolution. Richard Crashaw. *See* To the Noblest and Best of Ladies, the Countess of Denbigh.
Against Love. Katherine Philips. BoWoP; SBG; WPE
Against Marriage. *Unknown.* DBV
Against Marriage to His Mistress. William Walsh. FaBoUs
Against Minoan sunlight. Wishes for Her. Denis Devlin. CIP
Against Modesty in Love. Matthew Prior. ErPo
Against my love shall be, as I am now. Sonnets, LXIII. Shakespeare. OBSC
Against Oblivion. Shelley. *See* Elegy on the Death of John Keats, An.
Against Parting. Natan Zach, *tr. fr. Hebrew by* Jon Silkin. VWA
Against Platonick Love. *Unknown.* OBS
Against Proud Poor Phryna. John Davies of Hereford. FaBoEE
Against Quarrelling and Fighting. Isaac Watts. *See* Let Dogs Delight to Bark and Bite.
Against Romanticism. Kingsley Amis. NePoEA; NoAM
Against Seasons. Robert Mezey. NYBP
Against Slavery. William Cowper. *Fr.* The Task, II: The Timepiece. NOEC
("Oh for a lodge in some vast wilderness.") EnRP; OAEP
Against Still Life. Margaret Atwood. MoCV; NMM
Against summer, the leaf-lovely wide and lively trees. B-52's. Arnold Kenseth. PPON
Against Surrealism. James Wright. LCAP
Against Suspicion, *sel.* Mark Akenside.
Benevolence. OBEC
Against the Age. Louis Simpson. NePoEA-2
Against the Baron's Enemies. *Unknown.* *See* Song of Lewes, The.
Against the burly air I strode. Genesis. Geoffrey Hill. HAP; NePoEA; OAEL-2; OxBC
Against the clear intensity of dawn. Budding Spring. Jack Lindsay. PoAu-1
Against the day of sorrow. Trifle. Georgia Douglas Johnson. AmNP
Against the Evidence. David Ignatow. NNaP
Against the False Magicians. Thomas McGrath. NePoEA; PP
Against the Fear of Death. Lucretius, *tr. fr. Latin by* Rolfe Humphries. *Fr.* De Rerum Natura, III. DL, *abr.;* NAWM-1
Abr. versions, tr. by Dryden. AWP; FaBoRV; OAEL-1; OBVE
Fear of Death, The. LoBV
What Has This Bugbear Death. CTC
Against the flare and descant of the gas. Warning to a Guest. John Holloway. NePoEA
Against the Friars. *Unknown.* OxBM
Against the green flame of the hawthorn-tree. On Hampstead Heath. W. W. Gibson. HBV-1
Against the guide of Truth. Epigram V. *Unknown.* *Fr.* Duel with Verses over a Great Man. TrJP
Against the heavy yellow skies. Impression de Paris. Oscar Wilde. SyP
Against the Love of Great Ones. Sir John Denham. AnAnS-2
Against the Magpie. *Unknown.* GBP
("I crossed the pynot.") PBBP
Against the pure, reflective tiles. My Six Toothbrushes. Phyllis McGinley. GoYe
Against the rubber tongues of cows and the hoeing hands of men. Thistles. Ted Hughes. NoAM; OxBTC
Against the Silences to Come. Ron Loewinsohn. PoM
Against the stone breakwater. The Storm. Theodore Roethke. NCSH
Against the swart magnolias' sheen. Carolina Spring Song. Hervey Allen. HBMV
Against the Thieves of Liddesdale. Sir Richard Maitland. BSV
(Aganis the Thievis of Liddisdale.) GoTS
Against the window pane. Summer Rain. Sir Herbert Read. LiTM
Against Them Who Lay Unchastity to the Sex of Women. William Habington. *Fr.* Castara, II. AnAnS-2; JCP; MePo; OBS; SeCP
Against these turbid turquoise skies. Les Ballons. Oscar Wilde. SyP
Against what light. Black Dada Nihilismus. Amiri Baraka. PoM
Against Winter. Elaine Feinstein. VWA
Against Witches. *Unknown.* GBP
Against Women. Juvenal, *tr. fr. Latin by* Dryden. *Fr.* Satires, VI. UnTE
Against Women. *Unknown.* MeEL
Against Women either Good or Bad. Thomas Norton. EIL; ViBoPo
(Man May Live Thrice Nestor's Life, A.) InvP
Against Women Unconstant. Chaucer. NoP
(Ballade against Woman Inconstant, A.) CABA
Against Women's Fashions. John Lydgate. ACP
Agamemnon. Aeschylus, *tr. fr. Greek by* Louis MacNeice. NAWM-1
Sels.
Achaians Have Got Troy, upon This Very Day, The, *tr. by* Richmond Lattimore. WaaP
Chorus: "Great Fortune is an hungry thing," *tr. by* Gilbert Murray. AWP
God of War, Money Changer of Dead Bodies, The, *tr. by* Richmond Lattimore. PPON; WaaP
Hymn to Zeus, *tr. by* Gilbert Murray. WGRP
If I Were to Tell of Our Labours, Our Hard Lodging, *tr. by* Louis MacNeice. WaaP
Signal Fire, The, *tr. by* Dallam Simpson. CTC
Agamemnon's Tomb. Sacheverell Sitwell. LiTB; OBMV
"One by one, as harvesters, all heavy laden," *sel.* MoBrPo
Aganis the Thievis of Liddisdale. Sir Richard Maitland. *See* Against the Thieves of Liddesdale.
Agape the sooty collier stands. John Dalton. *Fr.* A Descriptive Poem, Addressed to Two Ladies at Their Return from Viewing the Mines, near Whitehaven. NOEC
Agatha. Alfred Austin. HBV-1
Agatha. Nadine Major. POL
Agatha Christie to. Said. George Starbuck. OBAL
Agatha Morley. Dust. Sydney King Russell. ShM
Agathon, *sel.* George Edward Woodberry.
Song of Eros. AA; HBV-1
Agbor Dancer. John Pepper Clark. PBA
Age. Abraham Cowley, *after the Greek of* Anacreon. AWP; CavP
Age? H. R. Hays. POL
Age, An. Laura Jensen. LCAP
Age. Rae Desmond Jones. CBAP
Age. Walter Savage Landor. ELU; FaBoEE; InPK; NBM; PoEL-4
Age. Philip Larkin. CMoP
Age. Marya Mannes. FAZ
Age. Sir Thomas More. EnRePo
Age. William Winter. HBV-1
Age, The/ requires this task. A Different Image. Dudley Randall. BPo; CNA; FF; NoAM; TAP

Age after age our bird through incense flies. Bird, Bird. Gene Derwood. LiTA
Age, and the deaths, and the ghosts. He Resigns. John Berryman. WeW
Age and Youth. Shakespeare. *See* Crabbed Age and Youth.
Age and Youth. *Unknown, tr. fr. German by* Louis Untermeyer. UnTE
Age being mathematical, these flowers, An. Tulips. Padraic Colum. ImOP
Age cannot reach me where the veils of God have shut me in. Immortality. Susan L. Mitchell. OnYI
Age cannot wither her whom not gray hairs. Evening. Wendell Phillips Garrison. *Fr.* Post-Meridian. AA
Age demanded an image, The. Hugh Selwyn Mauberley, II. Ezra Pound. HAP; MoAmPo; VGW
Age grips the body but the heart stays young. Love Is Bitter. *Unknown.* PeSA
Age in her embraces passed [*or* past], An. The Mistress; a Song. Earl of Rochester. CavP; EBEV; MePo; NOBE; OBS; ViBoPo
Age in Prospect. Robinson Jeffers. MoAB; MoAmPo
Age in Youth. Trumbull Stickney. NCEP
Age is a quality of mind. How Old Are You? H. S. Fritsch. PoLF
Age is dull and mean, The. Men creep. For Righteousness' Sake. Whittier. PoEL-4
Age Is Great and Strong, The. Victor Hugo, *tr. fr. French by* W. J. Robertson. WGRP
Age is when to a man. Samuel Beckett. *Fr.* Words and Music. BIrV
Age Not to Be Rejected. Robert Herrick. *See* To a Gentlewoman Objecting to Him His Grey Hairs.
Age of a Dream, The. Lionel Johnson. OBMV
Age of Animals, The. *Unknown.* FaBoUs
Age of Bronze, The, *sel.* Byron.
"Alas, the country! how shall tongue or pen." OBSV
Age of Bronze awoke now in brutality, The. John Heath-Stubbs. *Fr.* Artorius. EBEV
Age of Gold. Pietro Metastasio, *tr. fr. Italian by* Ezra Pound. CTC
Age of Innocence. Graham Hough. PoRA
"Age of Poetry is dead, The!" Tradition. Arthur Guiterman. DBV
Age of Reason, The. Jorie Graham. NPGG
Age of Reason, The. William Langland, *mod. by* Donald Attwater. *Fr.* The Vision of Piers Plowman. NOCV
Age of Sheen, The. Dorothy Hughes. NYBP
Age of the Butcher, The. Stuart Friebert. AMV-80
Age of Wisdom, The. Thackeray. *Fr.* Rebecca and Rowena. HBV-1; WhC
Ageanax. Edward Cracroft Lefroy. *Fr.* Echoes from Theocritus. OBVV
Aged Aged Man, The. "Lewis Carroll." *See* White Knight's Song, The.
Aged Carle, The. Sir Walter Scott. *See* Why Sit'st Thou by That Ruin'd Hall.
Aged catch their breath, The. Preface. W. H. Auden. LiTA
Aged Fisherman. Witter Bynner. GoYe
Aged Lover Discourses in the Flat Style, The. J. V. Cunningham. NoAM
Aged Lover Renounceth Love, The. Thomas, Lord Vaux. ElL; EnRePo; OAEL-1; OAEP; PoEL-1
(Image of Death, The.) GoTL; OBSC
Aged man, that mowes [*or* mows] these fields. A Dialogue betwixt Time and a Pilgrime [*or* Pilgrim]. Aurelian Townshend. AnAnS-2; MePo; NOBE; OAEL-1; OBS; PoEL-2; SeCP
Aged Pilot Man, The. "Mark Twain." OBAL
Aged Stranger, The. Bret Harte. AA; AmFN; TreFS
Aged twenty-six. Birthdays. C. J. Driver. PeSA
Aged Wino's Counsel to a Young Man on the Brink of Marriage, The. X. J. Kennedy. FF
Aged Woman to Her Sons, The. Babette Deutsch. AMV-81
Aged Writer, An. Roy McFadden. NeIP
Ageing Hunter, The. Avane, *tr. fr. Eskimo.* WTO
Ageless. *Unknown, tr. fr. Greek by* Louis Untermeyer. UnTE
Ageless, the Mantinean woman speaks. ". . .Discourse Heard One Day. . ." Donald C. Babcock. NePoAm-2
Agent of Love. A. K. Redwing. VoR
Agent Orange. Rita Brady Kiefer. SOTS
Agents, The. Robert Conquest. EAS
Ages and Ages Returning at Intervals. Walt Whitman. AP
Ages of Man, The. *At. to* Abraham ibn Ezra, *tr. fr. Hebrew by* Nina Davis Salaman. TrJP
Aghadoe. John Todhunter. AnIL; AnIV; OBVV; OxBI
Agincourt. Michael Drayton. BeLS; ElL; FaBoBe; FaBoCh; GoTL; HBV-2; OBEV; WHA
(Ballad of Agincourt, The.) EnRePo; FaPoR; OBNV; PoRA
(Battle of Agincourt, The.) GN
(To the Cambro-Britons and Their Harp, His Ballad of Agincourt.) OAEP; OBS; OBWP; PrIm
Agincourt Carol, The. *Unknown.* OAEL-1; OBET; OxBM
(Carol of Agincourt, A.) MeEL
("Deo gracias, Anglia.") EBEV
Aging. Randall Jarrell. PoA
Aging. Diane Wakoski. AMV-81
Aging Athlete, The. Neil Weiss. LiSp
Aging old queers are no treat. Limerick. *Unknown.* PeHV
Aging pilgrim on a, An. Kenneth Rexroth. *Fr.* On Flower Wreath Hill. GP
Aging Poet, on a Reading Trip to Dayton, Visits the Air Force Museum and Discovers There a Plane He Once Flew, The. Richard Snyder. Psk
Agitation of the air, An. End of Summer. Stanley Kunitz. CrMA; MoAmPo; Psk; VGW
Agitato ma Non Troppo. John Crowe Ransom. OxBA
Aglaia. Nicholas Breton. *Fr.* The Passionate Shepherd. OBSC
Aglaura, *sels.* Sir John Suckling.
Song: "No, no, fair heretic, it needs must be," *fr.* IV, i. AnAnS-2; CABA; CaPo; LoBV; OBS; PrIm
Why So Pale and Wan, Fond Lover? *fr.* IV, ii. AWP; BiP; HAP; HeIP; HoPM; NOBE; OBS; TrGrPo; UnPo; WHA
(Song: "Why so pale and wan, fond lover?") BoLoP; CABA; CaPo;HBV-1; InPS; PoPl; SeCV-1; ViBoPo
Agnes. Mah-do-ge Tohee. STE
Agnes lived with geraniums on the window-sills. Short Short Story. Josephine Jacobsen. NePoAm-2
Agnes looks through the window. The Home Place. Robert Currie. PPJ
Agnosco Veteris Vestigia Flammae. J. V. Cunningham. QFR; TwAmPo; VGW
Agnostic's Creed, The. Walter Malone. HBV-2
Agnosto Theo (To an Unknown God). Thomas Hardy. MoPo; WGRP
Agog, in rain house-deep. Apologia. Jean Garrigue. LiTA
Agonie [*or* Agony], The. George Herbert. AnAnS-1; JCP; MePo
(Philosophers Have Measured Mountains.) TRV
Agonies confirm His hour. Bahá'u'lláh in the Garden of Ridwan. Robert Hayden. PoBA
Agonizing Memory, The. Pierre Louys, *tr. fr. French. Fr.* Chansons de Bilitis. PeHV
Agony, The. George Herbert. *See* Agonie, The.
Agony, An. As Now. Amiri Baraka. AmPP; BALP; BPo; LiTM; PPP
Agony in the Garden, The. Felicia Dorothea Hemans. TrCP
Agreed that all these birds. All These Birds. Richard Wilbur. NOBA; Prf
Agricultural Irish Girl, The. *Unknown.* OnYI
Agricultural Show, Flemington, Victoria, The. "Furnley Maurice." CBAP
Agriculture, *sel.* Robert Dodsley.
Method of Preserving Hay from Being Mow-Burnt, or Taking Fire, A. FaBoUs
Aguinaldo. Bertrand Shadwell. PAH
Ah, all the sands of the earth lead unto heaven. Persian Miniature. William Jay Smith. CoAP; MoVE
Ah, Are You Digging on My Grave? Thomas Hardy. BoAnP; BrPo; DL; InPS; MoAB; MoBrPo; PAI; TEP
Ah, Be Not False. Richard Watson Gilder. AA; HBV-1; HBVY
Ah, be not vain! In yon flower-bell. Dewdrop, Wind and Sun. Joseph Skipsey. OBVV
Ah, bed! the field where joy's peace some do see. Astrophel and Stella, XCVIII. Sir Philip Sidney. EnLoPo; SiPS
Ah, Ben!/ Say how, or when. An Ode for Ben Jonson [*or* An Ode for Him]. Robert Herrick. AnAnS-2; AWP; CaPo; InvP; LoBV; NoP; OAEP; OBS; SeCP; SeCV-1; TrGrPo
Ah, blackbird, thou art satisfied. The Blackbird. *Unknown, tr. by* Kuno Meyer. AnIL; OnYI
Ah blessed plant! ah lucky creeper! Entwined. *Malay Oral Tradition, tr. by* R. J. Wilkinson *and* R. O. Winstedt. WTO
Ah, blessedness of work! the aimless mind. Work. Louis James Block. AA
Ah Bounce! ah gentle Beast! why wouldst thou dye. Lines on Bounce. Pope. FM
Ah, broken is the golden bowl! the spirit flown forever! Lenore. Poe. AA; AmPP; AP; LiTA; TreFS; WHA
Ah, but a good wife! Late Abed. Archibald MacLeish. NCSH
Ah! cease this kind persuasive strain. Ode to a Friend. William Mason. OBEC
Ah! cease to shroud the radiance of those cheeks. Dark Aspect and Prospect. *Unknown.* PeD
Ah child, no Persian-perfect art! Horace, *tr. by* Gerard Manley Hopkins. *Fr.* Odes. InPK; OBVE
Ah Chloris [*or* Cloris]! that [*or* could] I now could [*or* but] sit. Child and Maiden [*or* Song *or* To Chloris]. Sir Charles Sedley. *Fr.* The Mulberry Garden, III, ii. CavP; GTBS; GTBS-P; HBV-1; OAEP; OBEV; OBS; SeCV-2; ViBoPo
Ah, Christ, I love you rings to the wild sky. Sonnets at Christmas, II. Allen Tate. AP; HAP; LiTA; LiTM; NePA; PoNe; VGW
Ah, Classy Glossy, slick of paper as of prose. An Alexandrine Magazine. Howard Nemerov. SOTS

Ah, Clemence! when I saw thee last. La Grisette. Oliver Wendell Holmes. AA; HBV-1
Ah Cloris! that I now could sit. *See* Ah Chloris . . .
Ah, comic officer and gentleman. Elegy: E. W. L. E. Sissman. NYBP
Ah could we wake in mercy's name. Song for an Allegorical Play. John Ciardi. PoCh
Ah! County Guy, the hour is nigh. County Guy [*or* Serenade *or* Song]. Sir Walter Scott. *Fr.* Quentin Durward. CH; GTBS; GTBS-P; OAEP; OBRV
Ah, cruel maid, because I see. The Cruel Maid. Robert Herrick. CaPo
Ah dearest Love, for how long. Mechtild of Magdeburg, *tr. fr. German. Fr.* The Flowering Light of the Godhead. ILwL
Ah! dearest love, sweet home of all my fears. Keats. *Fr.* Ode to Fanny. ChER
Ah dextrous Chirurgeons, mitigate your plan. On Having Piles. Sir Walter Scott. FaBoEE
Ah, did he climb, that man, nigher to heaven than I. Dark Rapture. "Æ." SeCePo
Ah, did you once see Shelley plain. Memorabilia. Robert Browning. CABA; FaBoEn; FiP; HBV-2; LoBV; NoP; OAEL-2; OAEP; OBNC; PP; SeCePo; TreFT; WHA
Ah, dog. Here is my boot. Does it stink good? Timon Speaks to a Dog. Philip Hobsbaum. TW
Ah, drops of gold in whitening flame. To Daisies. Francis Thompson. HBV-1
Ah, dry those tears; they flow too fast. To Miss —— on the Death of Her Goldfish. Mr. Meredyth. FM
Ah, Fading Joy. Dryden. *Fr.* The Indian Emperor, IV, iii. ChTr; FiP; LoBV; OAEP; TreFT; ViBoPo
(Song: "Ah fading joy, how quickly art thou past!") PaBoEn; NoP
Ah! fair and lovely bloom the flowers of youth. Youth and Age. Mimnermus, *tr. by* John Addington Symonds. AWP
Ah! fair face gone from sight. Lionel Johnson. *Fr.* In Memory. FaBoEn; OBNC; PoEL-5
Ah, fair [*or* faire] Zenocrate, divine Zenocrate. Fair Is Too Foul an Epithet. Christopher Marlowe. *Fr.* Tamburlaine the Great, Pt. I, Act V, sc. ii. EBEV; LiTB; PoEL-2; ViBoPo
Ah false Amyntas, can that hour. Song. Aphra Behn. *Fr.* The Dutch Lover. WPE
Ah, Faustus,/ Now hast thou but one bare hour [*or* hower] to live. Christopher Marlowe. *Fr.* Doctor Faustus, V, ii. ChTr; HeIP; ILwL; PoEL-2; TrGrPo; ViBoPo; WHA
Ah, Flood of Life on which I am a wave. Watson Kirkconnell. *Fr.* The Tide of Life. CaP
Ah, flow on, flow on. Sail Peacefully Home. Simeon Frug. TrJP
Ah for the throes of a heart sorely wounded! The Damsel. Omar b. Abi Rabi'a, *tr. by* W. G. Palgrave. AWP
Ah! fredome [*or* freedom] is a noble thing! *See* A! fredome is a noble thing.
Ah, friend! 'tis true—this truth you lovers know. To Mr. Gay, Who Wrote Him a Congratulatory Letter on the Finishing His House. Pope. NOEC
Ah! gentle, fleeting, wav'ring sprite. Hadrian's Address to His Soul When Dying. Emperor Hadrian, *tr. by* Byron. OBVE
Ah gentle shepherd, thine the lot to tend. John Dyer. *Fr.* The Fleece. PoEL-3
Ah, gentle, tender lady mine! Thackeray. *Fr.* The Chronicle of the Drum. ViBoPo
Ah! Give Me, Lord, the Single Eye. Augustus Montague Toplady. OxBoCh
Ah, give us back our dear dead Land of Dreams! The Land of Dreams. Henry Martyn Hoyt. HBMV
Ah! Grandmother weaves! Grandmother Sleeps. Liz Sohappy Bahe. CDW
Ah, had you seen the Coolun. *See* O had you seen the Coolun.
Ah, happy blindness! Enion sees not the terrors of the uncertain. It Is Not So with Me. Blake. *Fr.* Vala; or, The Four Zoas. SeCePo
Ah, happy who have seen Him, whom the world. Francis W. Bourdillon. *Fr.* A Lost God. WGRP
Ah, happy youths, ah, happy maid. On a Picture by Poussin Representing Shepherds in Arcadia. John Addington Symonds. FaBoBe; HBV-1
Ah hate to see de evenin' sun go down. *See* I hate to see de ev'nin' sun go down.
Ah! he is fled! The Brittish Church. Henry Vaughan. AnAnS-1
Ah, here it is! the sliding rail. The Crooked Footpath. Oliver Wendell Holmes. *Fr.* The Professor at the Breakfast Table. HBV-2; TreF
Ah, how poets sing and die! Dunbar. Anne Spencer. BANP; CDC
Ah How Sweet It Is to Love. Dryden. *Fr.* Tyrannic Love, IV, i. HBV-1; HoPM; ViBoPo
(Song: "Ah how sweet it is to love.") CavP; FaBoEn
Ah! Hoyland, empress of my heart. Ode to Miss Hoyland. Thomas Chatterton. BXAP
Ah, I know what happiness is! Poem. Blanche Taylor Dickinson. CDC
Ah! I remember well (and how can I). Early Love. Samuel Daniel. *Fr.* Hymen's Triumph. ErPo
Ah, if I could, I'd dwell with you tonight. A Message. George Ives. PeHV
Ah! if we only dreamed how close they stand. Comfort. May Doney. HBMV
Ah in the thunder air. Trees in the Garden. D. H. Lawrence. CMoP; MoAB; MoBrPo; NoP
Ah—it's the skeleton of a lady's sunshade. The Sunshade. Thomas Hardy. OxBTC
Ah, Jack it was, and with him little Jill. Jack and Jill. Harriet S. Morgridge. *Fr.* Mother Goose Sonnets. AA
Ah, John, what changes since I saw thee last. Epitaph on John Murray, 1777. *Unknown.* BSV
Ah, June is here, but where is May. Unfulfillment. Frances Louisa Bushnell. AA
Ah! leave my harp and me alone. *Unknown.* SaC
Ah, Lenin, you were richt. But I'm a poet. Second Hymn to Lenin. "Hugh MacDiarmid." OAEL-2
Ah! liberal-handed lady, though. The Good Tradition. *Unknown, tr. by* Robin Flower. AnIL
Ah, life is good! and good thus to behold. Summons. Arthur Davison Ficke. Sonnets of a Portrait Painter, XIV. HBMV
Ah! light lovely lady with delicate lips aglow. At Mass. *Unknown, tr. by* Robin Flower. BIrV; OxBI
Ah! little flower, upspringing, azure-eyed. Fruitionless. Ina Coolbrith. AA
Ah! little fly, alighting fitfully. Calvus to a Fly. Charles Tennyson Turner. FM
Ah, little road, all whirry in the breeze. The Road. Helene Johnson. AmNP; BANP; BlS; CDC; PoNe
Ah, London! London! our delight. A Ballad of London. Richard Le Gallienne. FaBoPP; HBMV
Ah, look,/ How sucking their last sweetness from the air. The Divers. Peter Quennell. MoBrPo; MoVE
Ah! look an' zee how widely free. Air an' Light. William Barnes. VLP
Ah, look at all the lonely people! Eleanor Rigby. John Lennon *and* Paul McCartney. InPK; InPS; PPoe; PrIm; WTO
Ah Love! could you and I with Him conspire. Omar Khayyám, *tr. by* Edward Fitzgerald. *Fr.* The Rubáiyát of Omar Khayyám of Naishápúr. PoPl
Ah! Love, my Master, hear me swear. Of His Death. Meleager, *tr. by* Andrew Lang. AWP
Ah! Lovely Appearance of Death! *with music.* Charles Wesley. AH
Ah, Lucasta, why so bright. To Lucasta. Richard Lovelace. AnAnS-2; CaPo
Ah! Marvel not if when I come to die. For He Had Great Possessions. Richard Middleton. HBV-1
Ah! Matt.: old age has brought to me. Senex to Matt. Prior. James Kenneth Stephen. *Fr.* Two Epigrams. CenHV; FiBHP; WhC
Ah me,/ Was there a time. For Lucas Cranach's Eve. Adelaide Crapsey. QFR
Ah Me! Am I the Swaine. George Wither. OBS
Ah me! conceived in sin and born with sorrow. Childhood. Anne Bradstreet. *Fr.* The Four Ages of Man. SBG
Ah Me, Do You Remember Still. Agnes Mary Frances Robinson. WHA
Ah me, dread friends of mine—Love, Time, and Death. Love, Time and Death. Frederick Locker-Lampson. HBV-2
Ah me! full sorely is my heart forlorn. The School-Mistress. William Shenstone. GoTL; LaA; LAuP
Ah me! I cannot sleep at night. Foiled Sleep. "Marie Madelaine," *tr. by* Ferdinand E. Kappey. PeHV
Ah, me! I know how like a golden flower. The Grand Ronde Valley. Ella Higginson. AA
Ah me, if I grew sweet to man. The Tragic Mary Queen of Scots. "Michael Field." EnLoPo; OBMV
Ah me, my friend! it will not, will not last! Elegy: He Complains How Soon the Pleasing Novelty of Life Is Over [*or* Elegy XI]. William Shenstone. NOEC; OBEC
Ah me, the aspidistra grows dusty behind the window pane. In North Great George's Street. "Seumas O'Sullivan." BIrV
Ah me the hand upon the body. Legerdemain. Kenneth MacKenzie. PoAu-2
Ah Me! the Mighty Love. George Frederick Cameron. CaP
Ah me! those old familiar bounds! Ode on a Distant Prospect of Clapham Academy. Thomas Hood. BXAP
Ah! might I in some humble Kentish dale. Lines Written at Cambridge, to W. R., Esquire. Phineas Fletcher. *Fr.* To My Ever-honoured Cousin W. R., Esquire. EIL
Ah, moment not to be purchased. Bayard Taylor. *Fr.* The Sunshine of the Gods. AA
Ah, more than any priest, O soul, we too believe in God. Walt Whitman. *Fr.* Passage to India. WGRP
Ah Music, thou sweet sprite. To Music. William Kean Seymour. HBMV

Ah my Anthea! must my heart still break? To Anthea [*or* What Shame Forbids to Speak]. Robert Herrick. CaPo; UnTE
Ah my daughter, my grandchild! All You Others, Eat. Djurberaui, *tr. fr. Aborigine by* C. H. Berndt. WTO
Ah my dear angry [*or* deare angrie] Lord. Bitter-sweet. George Herbert. NOBE; NoP; OxBoCh; PAI; TrPWD
Ah! my heart, ah! what aileth thee. To His Heart. Sir Thomas Wyatt. OBSC; SiPS
Ah! my heart is weary waiting. Summer Longings. Denis Florence MacCarthy. HBV-1
Ah my Jill loves her nakedness. Marvelous. Allan Kaplan. POL
Ah my Perilla! do'st thou grieve to see. To Perilla. Robert Herrick. AnAnS-2; CaPo; OBS; SeCP; SeCV-1
Ah, necromancy sweet! Emily Dickinson. NOBA
Ah Night! blind germ of days to be. A Ballad of High Endeavor. *Unknown.* NA
Ah! no!/ You are not a soldierly upright row! Upon a Row of Old Books and Shoes in a Pawnbroker's Window. "Furnley Maurice." CBAP
Ah! no, no, it is nothing, surely nothing at all. The Wind. William Morris. NBM
Ah no; nor I myselfe: though my pure love. Sonnet. Richard Barnfield. Sonnets, XIX. PeHV
Ah! no, not these! Parentage. Alice Meynell. SBG
Ah, nobody knows. Frost. Stella Benson. OxBTC
Ah, not this marble, dead and cold. Washington's Monument, February 1885. Walt Whitman. OFD
Ah nuts! It's boring reading French newspapers. Les Luths. Frank O'Hara. NoAM; NOBA
Ah! on Thanksgiving Day, when from East and from West. The Pumpkin. Whittier. PoSC
Ah, Poor Bird. *Unknown.* FSW
Ah! poor intoxicated little knave. To a Fly, Taken out of a Bowl of Punch. "Peter Pindar." NOEC
Ah Posthumus! our years [*or* yeares] hence fly [*or* flye]. His Age, Dedicated to His Peculiar Friend, Master John Wickes, under the Name of Posthumus. Robert Herrick. CaPo; SeCP
Ah, ra, chickera. *Unknown.* OxNR
Ah, Raleigh, when thy breath thou didst resign. Britannia and Raleigh. John Ayloffe. APAS
Ah, Robin,/ Jolly Robin. Sir Thomas Wyatt. SiPS
Ah! sad wer we as we did peace. The Turnstile. William Barnes. CH; OBVV
Ah, see the fair chivalry come, the companions of Christ! Te Martyrum Candidatus. Lionel Johnson. ACP; HBV-2; OBMV; OxBoCh
Ah, Spain, already your tragic landscapes. The Spanish War. "Hugh MacDiarmid." CMop; NMP
Ah stay! ah turn! ah whither would you fly. Song. Congreve. *Fr.* The Fair Penitent (*by* Nicholas Rowe.) LoBV; OBEC
Ah, stay thy treacherous hand, forbear to trace. Verses on Sir Joshua Reynolds's Painted Window at New College, Oxford. Thomas Warton, the Younger. NOEC; OBEC; PoEL-3
Ah! Sun-Flower [Weary of Time]. Blake. *Fr.* Songs of Experience. AWP; CABA; EBEV; ELP; ELU; EnRP; FaBoRV; HAP; LAuP; NIP; NOEC; NoP; OAEL-2; OAEP; OBEC; OBNC; PoEL-4; PoPle; PPP; PrIm; SeCeV; TEP; UnPo; ViBoPo; WeW
(Sunflower, The.) ChTr; TrGrPo
Ah, sweet Content! where is thy mild [*or* mylde] abode? Content [*or* Sonnet]. Barnabe Barnes. Parthenophil and Parthenophe, LXVI. AAS; EIL; OBSC
Ah, Sweet Is Tipperary. Denis A. McCarthy. HBV-2
"Ah, sweet Kitty Neil, rise up from that wheel." Kitty Neil. John Francis Waller. HBV-1
Ah, sweet, thou little knowest how. Serenade. Thomas Hood. HBV-1
Ah, take these lips away; no more. Deadly Kisses. Pierre de Ronsard, *tr. by* Andrew Lang. AWP
Ah, Tam! gie me a Border burn. A Border Burn. J. B. Selkirk. *Fr.* Epistle to Tammus. PoSH
Ah, Teneriffe! Emily Dickinson. InPS
Ah, That I Were Far Away. Arthur Hugh Clough. *Fr.* Amours de Voyage. OBNC
(Upon Apennine Slope.) FaBoPP
Ah, that was but the wind. The Dead Bird. Andrew Young. FM
Ah, the blowfly is whining there, its maggots are eating the flesh. The Blowflies Buzz [*or* Djalbarmiwi's Song]. *Unknown, tr. by* Catherine Berndt. CBAP; WTO
Ah! then the grassy-meäded Maÿ. Zummer Stream. William Barnes. BoNaP
Ah, there is no abiding! Change. Mary Elizabeth Coleridge. MoVE
Ah! there's a house that I do know. Slow to Come, Quick a-Gone. William Barnes. VLP
Ah! there's the lily, marble pale. The Rose of May. Mary Howitt. HBV-1
Ah these are the poor. Street. George Oppen. GP
Ah, these with life so done with now, might deem. October. William Morris. *Fr.* The Earthly Paradise. VLP
Ah, those hours when by-gone sages. Half Hours with the Classics. H. J. DeBurgh. InMe
Ah, through the open door. Spring Morning. D. H. Lawrence. BrPo; CMoP; MoAB; MoBrPo
Ah! To be all alone in a little cell. The Desire for Hermitage. *Unknown, tr. by* Sean O'Faolain. AnIL
Ah to be alone and uninhibited! American against Solitude. Alan Dugan. CAPP
Ah, vale of woe, of gloom and darkness moulded. Song. Rachel Morpurgo, *tr. by* Nina Davis Salaman. TrJP
Ah, wake up mama: wake up and don't sleep so sound. Sweet Patuni. *Unknown.* BluL
Ah, wasteful woman, she that may. Unthrift [*or* Preludes, I]. Coventry Patmore. *Fr.* The Angel in the House. GoBC; HBV-1
Ah! weak and wide astray! Ah! shut in narrow doleful form. Blake. *Fr.* Jerusalem. OBRV
Ah, weary! I am called the laughing devil. Charles Heavysege. *Fr.* Saul. PeCV
Ah, well it is—since she is gone. Reply. Hartley Coleridge. OBRV
Ah well, the night. The Far North. Terry Savoie. AMV-80
Ah! were she pitiful as she is fair. Fawnia [*or* In Praise of His Loving and Best-beloved Fawnia]. Robert Greene. *Fr.* Pandosto. HBV-1; OBEV; OBSC; PoEL-2; TrGrPo; ViBoPo
Ah! what a weary race my feet have run. Sonnet: To the River Lodon [*or* Loddon]. Thomas Warton, the Younger. NOEC; OBEC; ViBoPo
Ah [*or* O], what avails the sceptred race! Rose Aylmer. Walter Savage Landor. AWP; BoLoP; CABA; CH; ELP; EnLoPo; EnRP; FaBoEn; FaFP; GBL; HAP; HBV-1; HeIP; HoPM; LiTB; LO; LoBV; NOBE; NoP; OAEL-2; OAEP; OBEV; OBNC; OBRV; OBVV; PoEL-4; RoGo; SeCeV; TEP; TreFS; TrGrPo; UnPo; ViBoPo; WeW; WHA
Ah, what can ail thee, wretched wight [*or* knight-at-arms]. *See* O what can ail thee, knight-at-arms.
Ah, what can be more stately. Walt Whitman. *Fr.* Crossing Brooklyn Ferry. AA
Ah! what is love? It is a pretty thing. The Shepherd's Wife's Song. Robert Greene. *Fr.* Greene's Mourning Garment. EIL; HAP; HBV-1; LoBV; OBSC; ViBoPo
Ah! what pleasant visions haunt me. The Secret of the Sea [*or* The Galley of Count Arnaldos]. Longfellow. EtS; OBEV; OBVV
Ah! what time wilt thou come? when shall that cry [*or* crie]. The Dawning. Henry Vaughan. MePo; NOCV; OxBoCh; TrPWD
Ah! What Woes Are Mine. Edmond O'Ryan, *tr. fr. Modern Irish by* Charlotte Brooke. OnYI
Ah, when I was a little boy, mama, 'bout 16 inches high. Stepfather Blues. *Unknown.* BluL
Ah, where, Kincora! is Brian the Great? Kincora. *Unknown, tr. by* James Clarence Mangan. AnIV
Ah! where must needy poet seek for aid. Swift. *Fr.* A Description of a City Shower. ViBoPo
Ah wherefore with infection should he live. Sonnets, LXVII. Shakespeare. PeHV
Ah! Why, because the Dazzling Sun. Emily Brontë. BrRo
Ah! why will my dear little girl be so cross. Washing and Dressing. Ann Taylor. FaBoUs
Ah, with the Grape my fading Life provide. Omar Khayyám, *tr. by* Edward Fitzgerald. *Fr.* The Rubáiyát of Omar Khayyám of Naishápúr. EBEV; GTBS-P
Ah! with what freedom [*or* freedome] could I once have pray'd. The Sigh. Nathaniel Wanley. OBS; OxBoCh
Ah Woe Is Me. Propertius, *tr. fr. Latin by* F. A. Wright. Elegies, I, 1. AWP
Ah Wretch! thou cry'st, ah! miserable me. Against the Fear of Death. Lucretius, *tr. by* Dryden. *Fr.* De Rerum Natura, III. FaBoRV
Ah yah, tair um bam, boo wah. Jungle Mammy Song. *Unknown.* AS
Ah, Yes, I Wrote the "Purple Cow." Gelett Burgess. DBV; FiBHP; PoPl
(Cing Ans Après.) HBV-2; OBAL; TreFS
(Confession.) FaBoNo
(Nonsense Quatrains.) CenHV
(Sequel to the Purple Cow.) FaBoCo
"Ah, yes, the works are busy on the Hook." A Hook for Leviathan. Norman Cameron. ChMP
Ah yes, when love allows. Hadewijch, *tr. fr. Dutch by* Frans van Rosevelt. PBWP
Ah! yesterday was dark and drear. Dare Quam Accipere. Mathilde Blind. OBVV
Ah, you are cruel. Neighbors. Anne Spencer. CDC
Ah, you beast of love. Hayden Carruth. VGW
Ah, you mistake me, comrades, to think that my heart is steel. Arnold at Stillwater. Thomas Dunn English. PAH
Ah (You Say), This Is Holy Wisdom. Hilda Doolittle ("H. D."). CrMA

Ahab Mohammed. James Matthew Legaré. AA
Ahab's gaily clad fisherfriends. Evil Is No Black Thing. Sarah Webster Fabio. PoBA
Ahasuerus. Joseph Roth, *tr. fr. German by* Erna Baber Rosenfeld. VWA
Ahead I bear; the Eagle of Gâl. The Lament for Urien. *Unknown, tr. by* Ernest Rhys. *Fr.* The Red Book of Hergest. OBMV
Ahkond of Swat, The. Edward Lear. *See* Akond of Swat, The.
Ahkoond of Swat, The. George Thomas Lanigan. *See* Threnody, A: "What, what, what . . ."
Ah'm Broke an' Hungry, *with music.* Lawrence Gellert. TrAS
Ah'm goin' whah nobody knows mah name, Lawd, Lawd! Levee Moan. *Unknown.* AS
Ah'm gonna build mahself a raft. De [*or* The] Blues Ain' Nothin'. *Unknown.* AS; TrAS
Ah'm sick, doctor-man, Ah'm sick! Calling the Doctor. John Wesley Holloway. BANP
Ahmed. James Berry Bensel. AA
Ahoy and ahoy, birds! Wings and Wheels. Nancy Byrd Turner. SoPo; SUS; TiPo
"Ahoy! and O-ho! and it's who's for the ferry?" Twickenham Ferry. Theophile Marzials. HBV-1
A-Hunting We Will Go. Henry Fielding. *Fr.* Don Quixote in England, II. HBV-1; ViBoPo
(Hunting Song.) OBEC; OxBoLi
Ai, ai, my small red man. Song of Welcome. Hermia Harris Fraser. CaP
Aid me Bellona, while the dreadful fight. The Battel of the Summer-Islands. Edmund Waller. AnAnS-2; SeCV-1
Aid me, kind Muse, so whimsical a theme. The Midshipman. William Falconer. MOS
Aideen. *Unknown, tr. fr. Irish by* Frank O'Connor. KiLC
Aidenn. Katrina Trask. AA
Aids for Latin. Gordon Perry. FaBoUs
Aids to Composition. Robert Conquest. PP
Aiken Drum. *Unknown.* FaBoCh; FaBoNo; OxNR
Aileen Aroon. Gerald Griffin. *See* Eileen Aroon.
Ailill the king is vanished. The Downfall of Heathendom. *Unknown, tr. by* Frank O'Connor. KiLC
Ailing fish moves in tired circles, An. Repose. Alfred Lichtenstein, *tr. by* Mary Zilzer. VWA
Ailing Parent, The. Lora Dunetz. NePoAm-2
Aim, The. Sir Charles G. D. Roberts. PeCV
Aim get your sights and its sound. Canto 7: First Thesis. Tom Weatherly. PoBA
Aim Was Song, The. Robert Frost. NoP; PP; SoSe
Aimee McPherson. *Unknown.* FSW
Aimirgin's Invocation. *At. to* Amergin. *See* Invocation to Ireland.
Aimless. Louis Palagyi, *tr. fr. Hungarian by* Watson Kirkconnell. TrJP
Ain' Go'n' to Study War No Mo', *with music. Unknown.* AS
(Study War No More.) FSW
Ain't been on Market Street for nothing. Ballad of the Hoppy-Toad. Margaret Walker. BlSi; FB; HoPM
Ain't Gonna Grieve My Lord No More. *Unknown.* FSW
Ain't Gonna Let Nobody Turn Me Round. *Unknown.* FSW
Ain't Gonna Rain, *with music. Unknown.* AS
Ain't gonna work on the railroad. Roll in My Sweet Baby's Arms. *Unknown.* FSW
Ain't got no money. Things About Comin' My Way. *Unknown.* FSW
Ain't I a Woman? Sojourner Truth. BlSi
Ain't It a Shame. *Unknown.* FSW
Ain't It Fine Today! Douglas Malloch. WBLP
(It's Fine Today.) BLPA
Ain't It Hard to Be a Right Black Nigger? *with music. Unknown.* OuSiCo
Ain't it hard to stumble. I'm a Stranger Here. *Unknown.* FSW
Ain't Nature Commonplace! Arthur Guiterman. FiBHP; InMe
Ain't No Grave Can Hold My Body Down. *Unknown.* AmFP
Ain't No More Cane on This Brazos. *Unknown.* FSW
Ain't No Tellin'. *Unknown.* BluL
Ain't no use to sit and cry. Sail Away Ladies. *Unknown.* FSW
Ain't Workin' Song, *with music. Unknown.* OuSiCo
Air. Amiri Baraka. SOTW
Air. Edwin Denby. CrMA
Air. Philip Dow. BXAP
Air. Kathleen Raine. MoAB; MoBrPo
Air. Tomaz Salamun, *tr. fr. Slovene by* Aleksandar Nejgebauer. VWA
Air: "Arise, arise, arise!" Henry Brooke. *Fr.* Jack the Giant Queller; an Antique History. NOEC
Air: "Cat bird singing." Robert Creeley. Prf
Air: "Flaxen-headed cow-boy, as simple as may be, A." John O'Keefe. NOEC
Air: "For often my mammy has told." Henry Brooke. *Fr.* Jack the Giant Queller; an Antique History. NOEC
Air: "Fox may steal your hens, sir, A." John Gay. *See* Soldier and a Sailor, A.
Air XXXV: "How happy could I be with either." John Gay. *Fr.* The Beggar's Opera. ViBoPo
Air: "I ne'er could any lustre [*or* luster] see." Sheridan. *Fr.* The Duenna. HBV-1; NOEC
Air: "Love of a woman, The." Robert Creeley. VGW
Air: "Naturally it is night." W. S. Merwin. CAPP; CoPo; NaP
Air: "O ruddier than the cherry." John Gay. *See* O Ruddier than the Cherry.
Air: Sentir avec Ardeur. Marie-Françoise-Catherine de Beauveau, Marquise de Boufflers, *tr. fr. French by* Ezra Pound. CTC; WPOW
Air: "Since laws were made for ev'ry degree." John Gay. *Fr.* The Beggar's Opera. NOEC
Air XXIII: "Sleep, O sleep." John Gay. *See* Song: "Sleep, O sleep."
Air: "Sportsmen keep hawks, and their quarry they gain, The." John Gay. *Fr.* Polly. NOEC
Air: "What a charming thing's a battle!" Isaac Bickerstaffe. *Fr.* The Recruiting Serjeant. NOEC
Air an' Light. William Barnes. VLP
Air [*or* Aire] and Angels. John Donne. AnAnS-1; EnRePo; JCP; MeLP; MePo; OAEL-1; OBS; Prf; SeCP; SeCV-1
Air as the fuel of owls. Snow. Iowa. Michael Dennis Browne. NYBP
Air Balloon, The. Henry James Pye. *Fr.* Aerophorion. NOEC
Air by Sammartini, An. Louis Dudek. OBCV
Air changes, blooms, The. Celebrating the Mass of Christian Burial. Cleopatra Mathis. LTB
Air, cold, The. Plowing at Full Moon. Leo Dangel. AMV-80
Air comes in tickly. Sneezing. Marie Louise Allen. SoPo
Air Field. Robert Siegel. GeTw
Air fresh, as it has been for days, The. The Color of Many Deer Running. Linda Gregg. NPGG
Air heaves at matter. Night Wind in Fall. W. R. Moses. NCSH
Air hides this morning, The. Agent Orange. Rita Brady Kiefer. SOTS
Air Is. John Michael Brennan. MAT
Air is, The/ Sucked clear of dross. January. H. R. Hays. EAS
Air is a mill of hooks, The. Mystic. Sylvia Plath. NYBP
Air is full of a farewell, The. On Leaving Ullswater. Kathleen Raine. NeBP
Air is full of diamond dust tonight, The. Frozen Fire. Floris Clarke McLaren. CaP
Air is like a butterfly, The. Easter. Joyce Kilmer. PDV; RHPC; SoPo; TiPo
Air is mild, not quite. A Sleep. Larry Eigner. CoPo
Air is one great dripping cloud, The. Tennis Pro. Lawrence Jay Dessner. AMV-81
Air is sweetest that a thistle guards, The. Variations: The Air Is Sweetest That a Thistle Guards. James Merrill. NePoEA
Air is thick with nerves and smoke, The. University Examinations in Egypt. D. J. Enright. MP; OxBTC; TwCP
Air is white and winds are crying, The. Snow Storm. Sister Mary Madeleva. GoBC
Air of June Sings, The. Edward Dorn. NeAP; PoM
Air of the museum, The. The Frozen Hero. Thomas H. Vance. NYBP
Air Plant, The. Hart Crane. MoAB; MoAmPo; NoP; PAI
Air Raid. Peter Wild. Psk
Air Sentry, The. Patrick Barrington. CenHV
Air Shaft. Ian Healy. *Fr.* Poems from the Coalfields. PoAu-2
Air Traveler. Lillian Morrison. RHPC
Air Vision, The. Jakov van Hoddis, *tr. fr. German by* Charles Guenther. VWA
Air was cleart with white and sable clouds, The. Robin at My Window. James Melville. *Fr.* The Black Bastill; or, A Lamentation of the Kirk of Scotland. BSV
Air was soft, the ground still cold, The. April 5, 1974. Richard Wilbur. GP
Air was vibrant around the hills, The. Leac A'Chlarsair. Lucy Taylor. PoSH
Air, which is not anything. Elements. Carolyn Wilson Link. GoYe
Airborne dragonfly, An. Hunter's Moon. Stephen Sandy. NYBP
Aircrews have had it and the war goes on. "For Whom the Bell Tolls." Gavin Ewart. WaP
Aire and Angells. John Donne. *See* Air and Angels.
Aire in Newfoundland-land is wholesome, good, The. The Pleasant Life in Newfoundland. Robert Hayman. NOBC
Airedale, erect beside the chauffeur of a Rolls-Royce, An. Fashions in Dogs. E. B. White. FiBHP; GDP
Airey-Force Valley. Wordsworth. VLP
Airline Breakfast, An. William Matthews. AMV-80; MAYP
Airliner. Francis Webb. CBAP
Airly Beacon. Charles Kingsley. EBVV; HBV-1; OBEV
Airman, The. W. R. Rodgers. WaP

Airman, R.F.C. Agnes Grozier Herbertson. SUMH
Airman Who Flew over Shakespeare's England, The. Hyam Plutzik. PoPl
Airplane, The ("An airplane has gigantic wings"). Rowena Bastin Bennett. FaPON
Airplane taxis down the field, The. Taking Off. Mary McB. Green. SoPo; TiPo
Airport. Martin Johnston. CBAP
Airport coffee tastes less of America, The. The Gulf. Derek Walcott. NoP
Air's advice is all, The. Prelude to Commencement. Marie de L. Welch. NYBP
Airs from the sea blown back. Ovid on the Dacian Coast. Dunstan Thompson. NYBP
Airs of Pei, *sel.* Confucius, *tr. fr. Chinese by* Ezra Pound.
 Efficient Wife's Complaint, The. CTC
Airs! that wander and murmur round. The Siesta. *Unknown, tr. by* Bryant. AWP
Airship. Hy Sobiloff. NePA
Airstrip in Essex, 1960, An. Donald Hall. InPS; LCAP; LiTM; PoCh
Airwaves. Warren Woessner. TAT
Airy Christ, The. Stevie Smith. NOCV
Airy, fairy Lilian. Lilian. Tennyson. HBV-1; PeD
Aishah Schechinah. Robert Stephen Hawker. GoBC; ISi; OBNC; OxBoCh
Aisling. Austin Clarke. AnIV
Aix-la-Chappelle, 1945. Edgar Bowers. NePoEA
Ajanta. Muriel Rukeyser. LiTA; LiTM; MiAP; MoAB; MoAmPo; NNaP; TwAmPo
Ajax, *sel.* Sophocles, *tr. fr. Greek.*
 Chorus: "Fair Salamis, the billow's roar," *tr. by* Winthrop Mackworth Praed. AWP
Ajax and Ulysses. James Shirley. *See* Contention of Ajax and Ulysses, The.
Ajax Samples, The. Laura Jensen. LCAP
Ajax the swift swerv'd never from the side. Homer, *tr. by* William Cowper. *Fr.* The Iliad, XIII. OBVE
Aka. Frederick Eckman. FAZ
Akathistos Hymn, The. *Unknown, tr. fr. Greek by* Vincent McNabb. ISi
Akawense. Phyllis Wolf. STE
Akedah, The. Matti Megged, *tr. fr. Hebrew by* Howard Schwartz. VWA
Akedah, The. Aliza Shenhar, *tr. fr. Hebrew by* Linda Zisquit. VWA
Akiba. Muriel Rukeyser. VWA
Akond of Swat, The. Edward Lear. CenHV; FaBoCh; FaBoCo; FaBoNo; FiBHP
 (Ahkond of Swat, The.) NA
Akriel's Consolation. William Pillin. AMV-80
Al Aaraaf. Poe. AP
 Sels.
 Song: "Young flowers were whispering in melody." NOBA
 Song from "Al Aaraaf" ("Neath blue-bell or streamer"). AmPP; NePA; OxBA
 Sonnet to Science. Prologue. InPK; NoP; TAP
Al Capone in Alaska. Ishmael Reed. TW
Al Fitnah Muhajir. Nazzam Al Sudan. NBP
Al the merier is that place. The Sun of Grace. *Unknown.* OxBM
Ala, mala, mink, monk. *Unknown.* OxNR
Alabado, *with music. Unknown, tr. fr. Spanish.* TrAS
Alabama, The. Maurice Bell. PAH
Alabama. Julia Fields. PoBA; PoNe
Alabama. Judy Dothard Simmons. CNA
Alabama, The. *Unknown.* ShS, 2 *vers., with music*
Alabama Bound. *Unknown.* BluL; FSW
Alabama Bus. *Unknown.* BluL
Alabama Centennial. Naomi Long Madgett. BALP; BPo
Alabama Earth. Langston Hughes. AmFN
Alabama, good-bye! I love thee well! A Missouri Maiden's Farewell to Alabama. "Mark Twain." InMe
Alabaster legs of the lonely woman, The. The Merry Window. Francis Scarfe. EAS
Alack! 'tis melancholy theme to think. The Irish Schoolmaster. Thomas Hood. BXAP
Aladdin. James Russell Lowell. HBV-1; RoGo; TreFT
Aladdin and the Jinn. Vachel Lindsay. Poems about the Moon, VI. TwAmPo
Alajire, we ask you to be patient. *Yoruba Oral Tradition, tr. by* Ulli Beier. WTO
Alamance. Seymour W. Whiting. PAH
Alarm, The. Hildebrand Jacob. NOEC
Alarm and time clock still intrude too early. And on This Shore. M. Carl Holman. AmNP; PoBA; PoNe
Alarm Clock, The. Mari Evans. BOLo
Alarm clocks tick in a thousand furnished rooms, The. North Infinity Street. Conrad Aiken. AP
Alarm sounds, The. The starting gates are empty. In the Silks. Diane Ackerman. MAYP
Alarmed Skipper, The. James Thomas Fields. EtS; HBV-2; YaD
 (Nantucket Skipper, The.) AmSS
Alarum. Urszula Koziol, *tr. fr. Polish by* Czeslaw Milosz. WPOW
Alarum, The. Sylvia Townsend Warner. MoBrPo
Alas! Sadi, *tr. fr. Persian by* L. Cranmer-Byng. *Fr.* The Gulistan. AWP
Alas, Alack. Walter de la Mare. EvOK; FaPON; OxBChV; TiPo
Alas! alas! the while. A Night with a Holy-Water Clerk. *Unknown.* MeEL
Alas! alas! thou turn'st in vain. Claim to Love. Giovanni Battista Guarini, *tr. by* Thomas Stanley. AWP
Alas, alas, well evil [*or* Allas, allas, wel ivel] I sped! Undo! *Unknown.* NOCV; OxBM
Alas! and am I born for this. On Liberty and Slavery. George Moses Horton. PoNe
Alas, and well-a-day! they are talking of me still. A Maori Girl's Song. Alfred Domett. OBVV
Alas! Carolina! J. Gordon Coogler. OBAL
Alas, dear Clio, every day. To Clio, from Rome. John Dyer. NOEC
Alas, dear heart! what hope had I. Love Me Again. *Unknown.* ElL
Alas! deceite that in truste is nowe. Trust Only Yourself. *Unknown.* MeEL
Alas, eheu, one question that sorely vexes. Ezra Pound. *Fr.* L'Homme Moyen Sensuel. OBSV
Alas! for all the pretty women who marry dull men. Meditation at Kew. Anna Wickham. FaBoTw; MoBrPo
Alas for him that for any of the vile rude world's estates. He Who Forsakes the Clerkly Life. *Unknown, tr. by* Standish Hayes O'Grady. *Fr.* The Life of St. Cellach of Killala. OnYI
Alas for me, who loved a falcon well! Sonnet: A Lady Laments for Her Lost Lover, by Similitude of a Falcon. *Unknown, tr. by* Dante Gabriel Rossetti. AWP
Alas! for Peter not a helping hand. Peter Grimes at Aldeburgh. George Crabbe. *Fr.* The Borough, Letter XXII. FaBoPP; OBRV
Alas! for the going of swiftness, for the feet of the running of thee. Johnny, I Hardly Knew Ye: In Swinburnese, *parody.* Robert Yelverton Tyrrell. OnYI
Alas! for the South. J. Gordon Coogler. HBV-1; OBAL
Alas for the voyage, O High King of Heaven. Farewell [*or* Colum-Cille's Farewell] to Ireland. *At. to* St. Colum-Cille, *tr. by* Douglas Hyde. AnIV; AWP
Alas! for them, their day is o'er. Indians. Charles Sprague. GN
Alas for Youth. Firdausi, *tr. fr. Persian by* R. A. Nicholson. AWP
Alas, have I not pain enough, my friend. Astrophel and Stella, XIV. Sir Philip Sidney. NoP; OAEL-1; SiPS
Alas! how dismal is my tale. The Curse of Doneraile. Patrick O'Kelly. DBV; OnYI
Alas, how easily things go wrong! Sweet Peril. George Macdonald. BLPA; FaBoBe; TreFS
Alas! how full of fear. The Fate of the Prophets. Longfellow. *Fr.* Christus; a Mystery. WGRP
Alas How Long ("Alas how long shall I and my maidenhead lie"). *Unknown.* ErPo
Alas, How Soon the Hours. Walter Savage Landor. *See* Plays.
Alas! I am seized by the shark, great shark! Love Is a Shark. *Tr. fr. Hawaiian by* N. B. Emerson. WTO
Alas, I am so faint I may not stand. The Desertion of Beauty and Strength. *Unknown. Fr.* Everyman. ACP
Alas, I draw breath heavily. An Old Woman's Song. Akjartoq, *tr. by* Knud Rasmussen; *tr. into English by* Tom Lowenstein. WPOW
Alas! if I think of her, my throat becomes. Love. Pierre Louys. *Fr.* Chansons de Bilitis. PeHV
Alas, Kind Element. Léonie Adams. MoVE
Alas! Madam, for Stealing of a Kiss. Sir Thomas Wyatt. BoLoP; OAEP
Alas! Mowler, the children's pride. Death of the Cat. Ian Serraillier. SO
Alas, my brothers. Hilda Doolittle ("H. D."). *Fr.* Helen in Egypt. NOBA
Alas! my child, where is the pen. The Hen. Oliver Herford. NA
Alas! my dear friend, what a state of affairs! Epistle of Condolence. Thomas Moore. OnYI
Alas, My God. Thomas Shepherd. *Fr.* For Communion with God. OxBoCh
 ("Alas, my God, that we should be," *shorter sel.*) TrPWD
Alas, my hart will brek in three. Fearful Death. *Unknown.* MeEL
Alas, my heart is black. The New Heart. *Unknown.* WGRP
Alas, my heart! mine eye hath wronged thee. Corydon to His Phyllis. Sir Edward Dyer. ElL
Alas! my Lord is going. Comfort in Extremity. Christopher Harvey. OxBoCh
Alas, my love, you [*or* ye] do me wrong. Greensleeves [*or* Lady Greensleeves]. *Unknown.* BLSo; FSW; GBL; PoEL-2; UnTE
Alas! noble Prince Leopold, he is dead! The Death of Prince Leopold. William McGonagall. EvOK
Alas, O King of Kings. The Song of the Heads. *Unknown, tr. by* Frank O'Connor. KiLC

Alas poor Death, where does thy great strength lye? Meditations for July 25, 1666. Philip Pain. SCAP
Alas! poor Fanny! wretched girl, alas! Fanny's Removal in 1714. John Winstanley. NOEC
Alas, poor heart, I pity thee. Medieval Norman Song. *Unknown, tr. by* John Addington Symonds. AWP
Alas, poor man, what hap have I. Sir Thomas Wyatt. SiPS
Alas! Poor Queen. Marion Angus. BSV; GoTS; OxBS
Alas, so all things now do hold [*or* thinges nowe doe holde] their peace. A Complaint by Night of the Lover Not Beloved [*or* Night]. Earl of Surrey, *after* Petrarch. AAS; AWP; EBEV; ElL; EnRePo; FaBoEn; LoBV; OAEL-1; OBSC; OBVE; SiPS; TEP
Alas, that ever that speche was spoken. *Unknown.* EnLoPo
Alas, that I should be. To My Infant Daughter. Yvor Winters. VGW
Alas, that I should die. Song of a Woman Abandoned by the Tribe. *Unknown, tr. by* Mary Austin. BPAW; WPE
Alas! that men must see. Love and Death. Margaret Deland. AA; HBV-2
Alas, that my heart is a lute. My Heart Is a Lute. Anne Barnard. HBV-1
Alas, the country! how shall tongue or pen. Byron. *Fr.* The Age of Bronze. OBSV
Alas the grief, and deadly woful smart! Sir Thomas Wyatt. SiPS
Alas, the moon should ever beam. The Water Lady. Thomas Hood. CH; HBV-1; ViBoPo
Alas! they had been friends in youth. The Scars Remaining [*or* Broken Friendship]. Samuel Taylor Coleridge. *Fr.* Christabel. OBNC; OBRV; TreFT
Alas 'tis true, I have gone here and there. Sonnets, CX. Shakespeare. EBEV; OAEP; OBSC; PeHV; ViBoPo
Alas! 'Tis Very Sad to Hear. Walter Savage Landor. GTBS-P; TW; WeW
Alas! too well we know our loss. Concerning Them That Are Asleep. R. W. Raymond. STF
Alas, unhappy land; ill-fated spot. Dirge of the Moolla of Kotal. George Thomas Lanigan. NA
Alas! what boots it that my noble steed. On a Distant Prospect of an Absconding Bookmaker. G. Rostrevor Hamilton. FaBoCo
Alas, what is the world? a sea of glass. Meditation 10. Philip Pain. NOBA
Alas [*or* Allas]! what shul we freres do. A Friar Complains [*or* The Friars' Retort]. *Unknown.* MeEL; OxBM
Alas, whence came this change of looks? Astrophel and Stella, LXXXVI. Sir Philip Sidney. SiPS
Alas! who knows or cares, my love. Laura's Song. Oliver Madox Brown. OBVV
Alas, with what tormenting fire. Of Death. Countess of Pembroke. *Fr.* Antonius. ElL
Alas! you son of her who is short-eared. Lion. *Unknown.* PeSA
Alaska. Joaquin Miller. PAH
Alaskan Mountain Poem #1. Leslie Silko. VoR
Alastor; or, The Spirit of Solitude. Shelley. EnRP; OAEL-2; OAEP
Sels.
"As an eagle grasped." ChER
"Earth, ocean, air, belovèd brotherhood!" FiP
(Invocation.) WHA
Alba. Samuel Beckett. BIrV
Alba ("Creeper grows over thorn"). Confucius, *tr. fr. Chinese by* Ezra Pound. *Fr.* Songs of T'ang. CTC
Alba ("As cool as the pale wet leaves"). Ezra Pound. GBL; HAP; SOTW; WeW
Alba ("When the nightingale to his mate"). Ezra Pound, *after the Provençal of* Arnaut Daniel. OBVE; VGW; WeW
Alba, *sel.* Robert Tofte. Love's Labour Lost. ElL
Alba. Derek Walcott. GoJo; PCP
Alba after Six Years. Christopher Middleton. NePoEA-2
Alba Innominata. *Unknown, tr. fr. French by* Ezra Pound. AWP
Alba: March. Marilyn Hacker. GP
Albany schmalbany. George Starbuck. PV
Albatross, The. Baudelaire, *tr. fr. French by* Richard Wilbur. SyP
Albatross. Charles Burgess. NePoAm-2
Albatross. Lele-io-Hoku, *tr. fr. Hawaiian by* S. H. Elbert *and* N. Mahoe. WTO
Albatross. Charles Warren Stoddard. AA; EtS
Albeit the Venice girls get praise. Ballad [*or* Ballade] of the Women of Paris. Villon, *tr. by* Swinburne. AWP; UnTE
"Albemarle" Cushing. James Jeffrey Roche. PAH
Albert Ayler: Eulogy for a Decomposed Saxophone Player. Stanley Crouch. PoBA
Albert Dürer. W. Leslie Nicholls. PV
Albert Sidney Johnston. Kate Brownlee Sherwood. PAH
Albert Sidney Johnston. Francis Orrery Ticknor. PAH
Alberta. *Unknown.* FSW
Albi, Ne Doreas. Horace, *tr. fr. Latin by* Austin Dobson. Odes I, 33. AWP
Albion & Albanius, *sel.* Dryden.
Song of the River Thames, A. FaBoEn
Albion Battleship Calamity, The. William McGonagall. BXAP; PeD
Albion's England, *sel.* William Warner.
Fate of Narcissus, The. OBSC
Albion's most lovely daughter sat on the banks of the. Mrs. Albion You've Got a Lovely Daughter. Adrian Henri. OxBTC
Albuera. Thomas Hardy. *Fr.* The Dynasts. WaaP
Album, The. C. Day Lewis. ChMP; EnLoPo; FaBoEn; OxBI; OxBTC
Album. Carol Papenhausen. AMV-81
Album Leaf. Stéphane Mallarmé, *tr. fr. French by* Keith Bosley. OBVE
Album of this season has poor pictures, The. Christmas at a Decade's End. Richard Snyder. SOTS
Alcaics; to H. F. B. Robert Louis Stevenson. NBM; OBEV; OBVV
Alceste in the Wilderness. Anthony Hecht. ConAP; PoA
Alcestis, *sel.* Euripides, *tr. fr. Greek by* A. E. Housman.
Strength of Fate, The. AWP
Alcestis. Isabel Williams Verry. GoYe
Alcestis in Ely. Nicholas Moore. NeBP
Alcestis on the Poetry Circuit. Erica Jong. AmPA
Alchemical Cupboard, The. Asa Benveniste. VWA
Alchemist, The. Louise Bogan. AWP; LLLT; MoAmPo
Alchemist, The. Richard Church. OxBTC
Alchemist, The, *sels.* Ben Jonson.
"Come on, sir. Now, you set your foot on shore," *fr.* II, i *and* ii. PoEL-2
"I will have all my beds blown up, not stuft," *fr.* II, i. EBEV
"No. I'll have no bawds," *fr.* II, ii. ViBoPo
Alchemist, The. Robert Kelly. CoPo
Alchemist, The. Ezra Pound. CMoP; LiTA; NePA; TwAmPo; WSC
Alchemist in the City, The. Gerard Manley Hopkins. NoP
Alchemy. Adelaide Love. PGD
Alchemy of Day, The. Anne Hébert, *tr. fr. French by* A. Poulin, Jr. BoWoP
Alcibiades to a Jealous Girl. Arthur Davison Ficke. HBMV
Alcide Pavageau. Miller Williams. TAT
Alcilia, *sel.* "J. C."
Frailty of Beauty, The. ElL
Alciphron and Leucippe. Walter Savage Landor. OBEV; VLP
Alcohol. Louis MacNeice. LiTM
Alcoholic. John Berryman. NOCV
Alcoholic. F. D. Reeve. NYBP
Alcyna met them at the outer gate. Ariosto, *tr. by* Sir John Harington. *Fr.* Orlando Furioso, VII. OBVE
Alcyone. Frances Laughton Mace. AA
Aldfrid's Itinerary through Ireland. *Unknown, tr. fr. Middle Irish by* James Clarence Mangan. OnYI
"I found in Munster, unfettered of any," *sel.*
(Prince Alfrid's Itinerary.) BIrV
Aldport (Mystery Tour). Kingsley Amis. *Fr.* The Evans Country. NOBL
(Terrible Beauty.) ErPo; NePoEA-2; PV
Alec Yeaton's Son. Thomas Bailey Aldrich. EtS; MOS
Aleph. Stuart Z. Perkoff. VWA
Aleph Bet, The. Fay Lipshitz. VWA
Aleph the cow with wide horns. The Letters of the Book. Rose Drachler. VWA
Alex, perhaps a colour of which neither of us had dreamt. Letter to Alex Comfort. Dannie Abse. FaBoTw; MP; TwCP
Alexander. Frederick Morgan. AMV-81
Alexander and Campaspe,*sels.* John Lyly.
Apelles' Song: "Cupid and my Campaspe played," *fr.* III, v. TrGrPo
(Cards and Kisses.) HoPM; NOBE; OBEV
(Cupid and Campaspe.) ElL; GTBS; GTBS-P; HBV-1; SeCeV; WHA
(Cupid and My Campaspe.) CABA; HeIP; NoP; PoRA
("Cupid and my Campaspe played.") GBL; OAEP; ViBoPo
(Song of Apelles.) OBSC
Serving Men's Song, A: "O! for a bowl of fat Canary," *fr.* I, iii. *Also in* A Mad World, My Masters (*by* Thomas Middleton). NOBE; OBSC
(Oh, for a Bowl of Fat Canary.) NoP; ViBoPo
Trico's Song: "What bird so sings," *fr.* V, i. OBSC; TrGrPo
(Song: "What bird so sings.") PBBP
(Spring, The.) CH
(Spring's Welcome.) OBEV
(Welcome to Spring.) NOBE
(What Bird So Sings.) ElL; ViBoPo
Alexander and the Gymnosophists. *Unknown.* OxBM
Alexander cut the knot. Alexander. Frederick Morgan. AMV-81
Alexander Graham Bell Did Not Invent the Telephone. Robert P. Tristram Coffin. TiPo
Alexander Jannai. Constantine Cavafy, *tr. fr. Greek by* Simon Chasen. TrJP
Alexander Selkirk. William Cowper. *See* Verses Supposed to Be Written by Alexander Selkirk . . .
Alexander the Great. *Unknown.* CH
Alexander to His Horse. Eleanor Farjeon. PH

Alexander's Feast; or, The Power of Music [*or* Musique]. Dryden. ACP; FaPo; FaPoR; FiP; GN; GoBC; GTBS; GTBS-P; HBV-2; LiTB; LoBV; NOBE; OAEL-1; OAEP; OBS; SeCeV; SeCV-2; TrGrPo; WHA; WiR

War, *br. sel.* TreFS

Alexandria. Lawrence Durrell. MoVE

Alexandrine Magazine, An. Howard Nemerov. SOTS

Alexandrite Ring, The. Margaret Ryan. AMV-81

Alexis, here she stayed; among these pines. Sonnet [*or* Spring Bereaved]. William Drummond of Hawthornden. ElL; HBV-1; OBEV; OBS

Alfa is nice. Her Roman eye. Safety at Forty; or, An Abecedarian Takes a Walk. L. E. Sissman. Prf

Alfonso Churchill. Edgar Lee Masters. *Fr.* Spoon River Anthology. GLGT

Alfonso was his name; his sad cantina. Skin Diving in the Virgins. John Malcolm Brinnin. NYBP; TAP

Alfred, a Masque, *sel.* James Thomson *and* David Mallet.

Rule, Britannia, *fr.* II, v. Thomson. FaPoR; GTBS; GTBS-P; HBV-2; NOEC; OAEP; OBEC; OBWP; TreF; WBLP

Alfred Corning Clark. Robert Lowell. NoAM

Alfred Lord Tennyson. Reed Whittemore. PP

Alfred the Harper. John Sterling. BeLS

Alfred was a ninny. Alfred Lord Tennyson. Reed Whittemore. PP

Alfred-Seeable Philadelphia Sky. Eli Siegel. CAD

Algernon Sidney's Farewell. *Unknown.* APAS

Algonkian Burial. Alfred Goldsworthy Bailey. OBCV

Algy Met a Bear. *Unknown.* FaPON; PoPle; RHPC

(Algy.) MoShBr; ShM

Ali. Lloyd M. Corbin, Jr. BOLo; CNA; PoBA

Ali Ben Shufti. Anthony Thwaite. OxBTC

Alibazan. Laura E. Richards. OBCA

Alibi. Arthur Guiterman. BXAP

Alibi. Hughes Mearns. *Fr.* Later Antigonishes. InMe

Alibi. Zoe A. Tilghman. BPAW

Alicante. Jacques Prévert, *tr. fr. French by* Lawrence Ferlinghetti. BoLoP

Alice. Herbert Bashford. HBV-1

Alice. Charles Cotton. *See* Resolution in Four Sonnets . . . Concerning Four Rural Sisters.

Alice B, *with music. Unknown.* AS

Alice Brand. Sir Walter Scott. *Fr.* The Lady of the Lake, IV. BeLS; HBV-2; HBVY; OnMSP

Alice Corbin Is Gone. Carl Sandburg. PoA

"Alice, dear, what ails you." A Frosty Night. Robert Graves. CH; MoAB; MoBrPo; MoBS; OxBTC

Alice Fell; or, Poverty. Wordsworth. BeLS; OBNV; SpRo

Alice, for whom my love is deep. Proof Positive. Deems Taylor. UnTE

Alice grown lazy, mammoth but not fat. Last Days of Alice. Allen Tate. NoAM; NOBA; OxBA; TwAmPo; UnPo

Alice in Wonderland. "Lewis Carroll." *See* Alice's Adventures in Wonderland.

Alice is tall and upright as a pine. Alice [*or* Two Rural Sisters]. Charles Cotton. *Fr.* Resolution in Four Sonnets . . . Concerning Four Rural Sisters. BoLoP; EnLoPo; PoEL-3; Prf; TrGrPo; UnTE

Alice Lee stood awaiting her lover one night. The Lips That Touch Liquor Shall Never Touch Mine. Harriet A. Glazebrook. PaPo

Alice on the croquet lawn. Matinal. Cilla McQueen. OCNZ

Alice on the croun o Bidean. On the Croun o Bidean. J. K. Annand. PoSH

Alice Ray. Sarah Josepha Hale. AA

Alice says we're marionettes. The Weight. William Aberg. LFAC

Alice, Where Art Thou? Wellington Guernsey. VLP

Alice's Adventures in Wonderland, *sels.* "Lewis Carroll."

Alice's Recitation, *fr. ch.* 10. FaBoNo; SpRo

" 'Tis the voice of the Lobster; I heard him declare." FaBoCo; NOBL; Par

(Lobster, The, *sl. diff.*) OxBChV

(Voice of the Lobster, The.) EvOK

Duchess's Lullaby, The, *fr. ch.* 6. FaBoNo; SpRo

(Lullaby, A.) RHPC

("Speak roughly to your little boy.") FaBoCh; FaBoCo; Par

Evidence Read at the Trial of the Knave of Hearts, *fr. ch.* 12. FaBoNo; FaFP; GTBS-P; NBM; OxBoLi

(Silence in Court.) FaBoCo

Father William, *fr. ch.* 5. BiP; BXAP; FaBoNo; FaBoPa; FaPON; FiBHP; FPL; GoJo; HBV-1; HoPM; InMe; LiTB; PDV; PoLF; PoRA; RHPC; SpRo; TreF; TrGrPo

(You Are Old, Father William.) OxBChV; UnPo; WhC

(" 'You are old, Father William,' the young man said.") FaBoCo; NOBL; Par; TiPo

How Doth the Little Crocodile, *fr. ch.* 2. FaBoCh; FaBoCo; FaBoEE; FaBoNo; FaFP; FaPON; MoShBr; NiP; NOBL; Par; ShM; SoPo; SpRo; TiPo; TreFS; WhC

(Crocodile, The.) HoPM; RHPC; TrGrPo

Lobster Quadrille, The, *from ch.* 10. MoShBr; OxBChV; Par; PoPle

(Mock Turtle's Song, The.) ChTr; FaBoNo; VLP, *2 versions*

(Whiting and the Snail, The.) HBV-1; HBVY

Mad Hatter's Song, The, *fr. ch.* 7. FaBoNo; SpRo

("Twinkle, twinkle, little bat!") NOBL; Par; WhC

Mouse's Tale, The, *fr. ch.* 3. FaBoNo

(Fury Said to a Mouse.) NoP

Turtle Soup, *fr. ch.* 10. FaBoNo; InMe; RHPC; SpRo

("Beautiful soup, so rich and green.") Par

Alice's Recitation. "Lewis Carroll." *Fr.* Alice's Adventures in Wonderland, *ch.* 10. FaBoNo; SpRo

" 'Tis the voice of the Lobster; I heard him declare," *sel.* FaBoCo; NOBL; Par

(Lobster, The, *sl. diff.*) OxBChV

(Voice of the Lobster, The.) EvOK

Alicia's Bonnet. Elisabeth Cavazza Pullen. AA

Alien. Helen Frazee-Bower. HBMV

Alien. Donald Jeffrey Hayes. AmNP

Alien. Archibald MacLeish. EtS

Alien. William Price Turner. OxBS

Alien wind that blew and blew, An. A Sleeping Beauty. James Whitcomb Riley. DFT

Alienation. Harry Kemp. HBMV

Alike from love and marriage hurry. Advice to Bachelors. *Unknown, tr. by* Louis Untermeyer. UnTE

Alimentary. Clifton Fadiman. PV

Alison. *Unknown. See* Alysoun ("Betwene Mersh and Averil").

Alison and Willie. *Unknown.* BaBo; ESPB

Alison Gross. *Unknown.* FaBoCh; OxBB; WSC

Alisoun. *Unknown. See* Alysoun ("Betwene Mersh and Averil").

Aliter. Confucius, *tr. fr. Chinese by* Ezra Pound. *Fr.* Songs of Ch'en. CTC

Alive or Not. Al Purdy. NOBC

Alive, this man was Manes, a common slave. Anyte, *tr. fr. Greek by* Willis Barnstone. BoWoP

Alive Together. Lisel Mueller. IHMS

Alive where I lie and hide. The Veteran. Louis O. Coxe. MoVE

Alkinoos, king and admiration of men. New Coasts and Poseidon's Son. Homer, *tr. by* Robert Fitzgerald. *Fr.* The Odyssey. WTO

All. Leona Gom. Str

All. Antoni Slonimski, *tr. fr. Polish by* Wanda Dynowska. TrJP

All/ fall it stuck. Horse. Randy Blasing. PH

All a green willow, willow, willow, *abr.* John Heywood. ElL

All after pleasures as I rid [*or* rode] one day. Christmas. George Herbert. OxBoCh; SBVL; SeCV-1; TrCP

All afternoon neither of us said. The Day the Air Was on Fire. Reg Saner. NPAW

All afternoon we lie, stretched out. Talking across Kansas. Paula Kwon. AMV-80

All, All a-Lonely. *Unknown.* ChTr; OxBoLi

All, All of a Piece [Throughout]. Dryden. *Fr.* The Secular Masque. ChTr; ELP; ELU; HAP; InPS

(Chorus: "All, all of a piece throughout.") ViBoPo

(Song.) WeW

All alone from his dark sanctum. Mahabalipuram. Louis MacNeice. NoAM

All alone on the hillside. The "Grey Horse Troop." Robert W. Chambers. HBV-2; PAH

All along the backwater. Duck's [*or* Ducks'] Ditty. Kenneth Grahame. *Fr.* The Wind in the Willows. FaPON; GoJo; MoShBr; NTCP; OxBChV; PDV; PoPle; RHPC; SoPo; SUS; TiPo

All along the rail. In Texas Grass. Quincy Troupe. PoBA

All along the valley, stream that flashest white. In the Valley of Cauteretz. Tennyson. BoLoP; NOBE; OBVV; VLP

All-American Guard, An. *Unknown.* TDH

All Animals Like Me. Raymond Souster. WHW

All are architects of Fate. The Builders. Longfellow. FaFP; OHFP; TreFS

All are but parts of one stupendous whole. Pope. *Fr.* An Essay on Man. WGRP

All are keen. Aideen. *Unknown, tr. by* Frank O'Connor. KiLC

All around him Patmos lies. Patmos. Edith M. Thomas. HBV-1

All Around Man. *Unknown.* BluL

All around me, the city was falling asleep. The Quick and the Dead. Ilarie Voronca, *tr. by* Edouard Roditi. VWA

All around the cobbler's bench. Pop! Goes the Weasel. *Unknown.* BLSo; FSW

All around the kitchen, cocky doodle doodle doo. Cocky Doodle Doodle Doo. *Unknown.* OuSiCo

All Around the Town, *sels.* Phyllis McGinley.

"B's the Bus." FaPON; SoPo; TiPo

"C is for the Circus." SoPo; TiPo

"E is the Escalator." TiPo
"F is the fighting Firetruck." FaPON
"J's the jumping Jay-walker." FaPON; RHPC
"P's the proud Policeman." TiPo
"R is for the Restaurant." TiPo
"U is for Umbrellas." TiPo
"W's for Windows." TiPo
All a-tremble she awoke. The Annunciation. Amrita Pritam, *tr. by* Khushwant Singh *and* Krishna Gorowara. WPOW
All beaded with dew. Gary Snyder. Myths and Texts: Hunting, VII. NaP
All beauty, resonance, integrity. Le Livre Est sur la Table. John Ashbery. EAS
All beginnings start right here. The Move Continuing. Al Young. PoBA
All Being Well. W. W. Gibson. OxBTC
All beneath the white-rose tree. The Three Captains. *Unknown, tr. by* Andrew Lang. AWP
All Bibles or sacred codes. The Voice of the Devil. Blake. *Fr.* The Marriage of Heaven and Hell. NU
All bones but yours will rattle when I say. The Sea-Serpent. James Robinson Planché. NA
All buildings are but monuments of death. Epigram: Fatum Supremum. *Unknown.* OBS
All busy punching tickets. Crickets. David McCord. NTCP; PDV
All but Blind. Walter de la Mare. FaPON; HBMV; MoAB; MoBrPo; PDV; WeW
All but unutterable Name! The Divine Presence. Aubrey Thomas De Vere. *Fr.* May Carols. GoBC
All children sound the same. The Core. John Holmes. MiAP
All Christian men in my behalf. On Sir John Calf. *Unknown.* FaBoEE
All Christians and Lay-Elders too. The Four-legg'd Elder; or, A Horrible Relation of a Dog and an Elder's Maid. Sir John Birkenhead. CoMu
All Christmas night upon the shelf. The Mouse. Hugh McCrae. PoAu-1
All Clowns Are Masked. Delmore Schwartz. The Repetitive Heart, III. LiTA; OxBA; ViBoPo
All craftsmen share a knowledge. They have held. Craftsmen. V. Sackville-West. OxBTC
All day a steady snow had drifted down. The Slide at the Empire Mine. Harriet L. Wason. PoOW
All day a strong wind blew. A Strong Wind. Austin Clarke. BoNaP
All day across the sagebrush flat. The Sheep-Herder. Charles Badger Clark, Jr. BPAW
All day and all day, as I sit at my measureless turning. The Mother's Song. Virginia Woodward Cloud. AA
All Day and All October. Laurence Lerner. PeSA
All day and many days I rode. A Wish. Hamlin Garland. AA
All day and night, save winter, every weather. Aspens. Edward Thomas. ChMP; InPS
All day at the lake we watched. The Collection. Bill Manhire. OCNZ
All day beneath the hurtling shells. The Dancers. W. W. Gibson. MMA
All day beside the shattered tank he'd lain. Reconciliation. C. Day Lewis. MP; NoAM; TwCP
All-day Bird, the artist, The. Claritas. Denise Levertov. VGW
All day, day after day, they're bringing them home. Homecoming. Bruce Dawe. CBAP
All day he slept, his mouth on pennyroyal. The Soldier in the Park. Elizabeth Riddell. CBAP
All day I bar you from my slightest thought. Compensation. Lizette Woodworth Reese. HBMV
All day I did the little things. The Blue Bowl. Blanche Bane Kuder. BLPA; FaBoBe
All day I follow. The Plowman. Raymond Knister. OBCV; PeCV
All day I have been completely alone, and now the night. Separation. D. S. Savage. NeBP
All Day I Hear [the Noise of Waters]. James Joyce. Chamber Music, XXXV. FaBoCh; MoBrPo; NoAM; OnYI; PoRA; SoSe; UnPo (Noise of Waters, The) FaPON; TiPo
All day I loved you in a fever, holding on to the tail of the horse. At Mid-Ocean. Robert Bly. LLLT
All day I tell my rosary. Love's Rosary. Alfred Noyes. HBV-1
All day I watch the stretch of burning sand. Le Repos en Egypte. Agnes Repplier. ISi
All day in exquisite air. Larks. Katharine Tynan. OnYI
All day it had been raining; now, the leaves. Hunt. Melvin Walker La Follette. NePoEA
All Day It Has Rained. Alun Lewis. GTBS-P; NOBE; OBWP; OxBTC
All day, knowing you dead. The Hours. John Peale Bishop. MoVE; OxBA
All day long/ The gray rain beating. Rain. "Seumas O'Sullivan." OnYI
All day long I glance against. The Old Lecher. Louis O. Coxe. TwAmPo
All day long I have been trying. Fall Letter. Dave Kelly. FAZ
All day long I have been working. Madonna of the Evening Flowers. Amy Lowell. PeHV; TreFT
All day long I played in an orchard. And of Laughter That Was a Changeling. Elizabeth Rendall. HBMV
All day long on the highway. The Highway. Louise Driscoll. HBV-1
All day long roved Hiawatha. The Death of Minnehaha. Longfellow. *Fr.* The Song of Hiawatha. AA
All day long the clouds formed in the peaks. First Winter Storm. William Everson. NU
All day long the clouds go by. Flight. George Johnston. WHW
All day long the guns at the forts. The Surrender of New Orleans. Marion Manville. PAH
All day long they have sat here. Composition in Black and White. Katha Pollitt. GrPl
All day long till the west was red. Making Port. J. T. McKay. EtS
All day my sheep have mingled with yours. Shepherdess. Norman Cameron. Three Love Poems, III. GBL; GTBS-P; OxBS
All day on the prairie in the saddle I ride. The Cowboy. *Unknown.* CoSo
All day pounding nails. The Horn Blow. Jeff Tagami. BrSi
All day rain fell. Ode on Contemplating Clapham Junction. Christopher Middleton. *Fr.* Herman Moon's Hourbook. NePoEA-2
All day she hurried to get through. Mis' Smith. Albert Bigelow Paine. PoLF
All day she sits behind a bright brass rail. The Travel Bureau. Ruth Comfort Mitchell. HBMV
All day subdued, polite. Negro Servant. Langston Hughes. VGW
All day swaying in the tower. Out from Lobster Cove. J. D. Reed. NeAC
All day the bees have come to the garden. Falling Asleep in a Garden. David Wagoner. AMV-81
All day the bird-song here has seemed. Random Reflections on a Summer Evening. John Hall Wheelock. NYBP
All day the coast of Africa was seen. To Naples. H. B. Mallalieu. WaP
All day the driftwood. Driftwood Dybbuk. Barbara F. Lefcowitz. VWA
All day the geese fly south. Starting Over. Shirley Kaufman. VWA
All day the gopher-killing boys. David. Eli Mandel. PeCV
All day the great guns barked and roared. Molly Pitcher. Laura E. Richards. PAH; YaD
All day the great planes gingerly descend. Air Field. Robert Siegel. GeTw
All day the guns had worked their hellish will. The Lark above the Trenches. Muriel Elsie Graham. SUMH
All day the irises have draped blue velvet. Elsdon. Freda Downie. FaBoPP
All day the light wind blew on the house. Day on Kind Continent. Robert David Cohen. NYBP
All day the mirrors kindle their brilliance. The Mirrors. Sophia de Mello Breyner Andresen, *tr. by* Allan Francovich. PBWP
All day the Nina sewed in this room. The Firstborn. Gary Soto. NPGG
All day the opposite house. The Opposite House. Robert Lowell. CMoP; NYP
All day the pigeons near the hangar door. The Pilot's Day of Rest. Lee Gerlach. HoAn
All day the red spit of the chain-shot tore. Evil. Arthur Rimbaud, *tr. by* Robert Lowell. *Fr.* Eighteen-seventy. OBWP
All day the stormy wind has blown. Take Heart. Edna Dean Proctor. HBV-2
All day the sun builds its temple. Dragon. Joseph Stroud. NPGG
All day the unnatural barking of dogs. The Dog. Valentin Iremonger. BIrV; NeIP
All day the waves assailed the rock. Nahant [*or* Waves]. Emerson. AA; AmPP
All day the wind has made love. On Lake Pend Oreille. Richard Shelton. NYBP
All day they loitered by the resting ships. The Wanderer. John Masefield. BrPo
All day to the loose tile behind the parapet. The Wasps' Nest. George MacBeth. OxBTC
All day today the sea gulls cried. Out in the Cold. George Starbuck. NYBP
All day under acrobat. Ruins under the Stars. Galway Kinnell. LCAP; NaP
All day we make our clockwise circle around the house. Washing Windows. Peter Wild. Str
All day we walked the streets. The Fifties. Ira Sadoff. AmPA
All Day We've Longed for Night. Sarah Webster Fabio. BlSi
All day you didn't cry or cry out and you felt like sleeping. Tall Windows. Robert Hass. NPGG
All do not seek the exalted fire. Earth and Fire. Vernon Watkins. NYBP
All dripping in tangles green. The Tuft of Kelp. Herman Melville. ChTr; FaBoEE; FaBoRV; MOS
All else for use, One only for desire. Deo Optimo Maximo. Louise Imogen Guiney. TrPWD
All-embracing, The. Frederick W. Faber. BLRP; TRV
All endeavor to be beautiful. Primer of Plato. Jean Garrigue. MoVE; NOBA

All evening, while the summer trees were crying. While the Summer Trees Were Crying [*or* Evening in Summer *or* Time, the Faithless]. Valentin Iremonger. AnIV; NeIP; OxBI
All evidence. In Winter. Paul Blackburn. NYP
All eyes were on Enceladus's face. Hyperion and Saturn. Keats. *Fr.* Hyperion. SeCePo
All fathers in Western civilization must have. The Father of My Country. Diane Wakoski. NoAM; TAP
All Fellows, *sel.* Laurence Housman.
"Dear love, when with a two-fold mind." WGRP
All fixed: early arrival at the flat. Nothing to Fear. Kingsley Amis. DBV; ErPo; OxBC
All Flesh. Francis Thompson. BrPo
All Flesh Is Grass. Bible, *O.T.* Isaiah, XL: 6-8. TrJP
All Flesh Is Grass, *sel.* Brenda G. Macrow.
When I Die. PoSH
All flesh is grass, and so are feathers too. Epitaphs on Two Piping-Bullfinches of Lady Ossory's [*or* Epitaph on Lady Ossory's Bullfinch]. Horace Walpole. ChTr; FaBoEE; NOEC
All flesh waxeth old as a garment. Bible, Apocrypha. *Fr.* Ecclesiasticus. OBVE
All folks, who pretend to religion and grace. The Place of the Damn'd. Swift. FaBoEE; OBSV
All Fools' Day. *Unknown.* SiSoSe; SoPo
All for Love. Byron. *See* Stanzas Written on the Road between Florence and Pisa.
All for Love, *sel.* Dryden.
Cleopatra and Antony. FiP
All for Love. *Unknown, tr. fr. German by* Louis Untermeyer. UnTE
All for the Cause. William Morris. VLP
All French folk, whereso'er ye be. If I Were King. Justin Huntly M'Carthy, *par. fr. the French of* Villon. *Fr.* If I Were King. HBV-1
All generous hearts lament. John Fitzgerald Kennedy. John Masefield. PAL
All gentlemen and yeomen good. Robin Hood and the Shepherd. *Unknown.* ESPB
All glorious as the rainbow's birth. Young Love. Gerald Massey. OBVV
All Goats. Elizabeth J. Coatsworth. BoAnP
All gods and goddesses, all looked up to. Meditation on the Nativity. Elizabeth Jennings. NAs
All God's Children Got Shoes. *Unknown.* FSW
All God's Chillun Got Wings. *Unknown.* BoAN-1, *with music;* TreFS
All God's spades wear dark shades. Its Curtains. Ted Joans. PoBA
All Gold. *Unknown, tr. fr. Irish by* Frank O'Connor. KiLC
All good things have not kept aloof. To ———. Tennyson. OBRV
All grave old men, and souldiers they had bene, but for age. Homer, *tr. by* George Chapman. *Fr.* The Iliad, III. OBVE
All Greece hates. Helen. Hilda Doolittle ("H. D."). BoWoP; LiTM; MoAmPo; MoVE; NOBA; NoP; PAI; SBG; TAP; TW
"All Green Things on the earth, bless ye the Lord!" Benedicite. Anna Callender Brackett. AA
All hail, once pleasing, once inspiring shade. Lines [*or* A Hymn] Written in Windsor Forest. Pope. EBEV; NOEC
All Hail the Power of Jesus' Name. Edward Perronet. *See* Coronation.
All Hail, Thou Noble Guest. Martin Luther, *tr. fr. German by* Arthur Tozer Russell *and* Catherine Winkworth. TrPWD
All hail! thou noble land. America to Great Britain. Washington Allston. AA; HBV-2
All hail to the town of Limerick. Hail to the Town of Limerick. Langford Reed. TDH
All hail! Unfurl the Stripes and Stars! God Save Our President. Francis DeHaes Janvier. PAH; PAL
All hallelujahs, Oh ye heav'nly quires. A Poem upon the Triumphant Translation of. . .Mrs. Anne Eliot. John Danforth. SCAP
All Hallows. Louise Glück. AmPA; NU
All Hands Unmoor! William Falconer. *Fr.* The Shipwreck. EtS
All has stilled, Magician Sleep having cast his spell. Those Last, Late Hours of Christmas Eve. Lou Ann Welte. PChr
All he owns is. Squirrel near Library. Genevieve Taggard. WPE
All he would have to say is. All. Leona Gom. Str
All heavy minds. Sir Thomas Wyatt. SiPS
All his friends had gotten a hole. First Holes Are Fresh. Vivian Shipley. AMV-81
All his hopes were hands, his ventures hands. The Hands. Tony Harrison. FaBoTw
All holy influences dwell within. The Children Band. Sir Aubrey De Vere. OBEV
All honor to that day which long ago. Washington's Birthday. Arthur J. Burdick. OHIP
All how silent and how still. Noon. John Clare. OBRV; SeCePo
All human race would fain be wits. On Poetry; a Rhapsody. Swift. HAP; OBSV; PoEL-3
All Human Things. Peter Schroeder. BXAP
All human [*or* humane] things are subject to decay. MacFlecknoe. Dryden. CABA; FiP; HAP; NOBE; NoP; OAEL-1; OAEP; OBS; OBSV; OxBoLi; PP; PPP; QFR; SCV; SeCV-2; TEP; TrGrPo; ViBoPo
All Hushed and Still within the House. Emily Brontë. FaBoCh; VLP
All I ask of a woman is that she. D. H. Lawrence. POL
All I can give you is broken-face gargoyles. Broken-Face Gargoyles. Carl Sandburg. AmPP; MoAmPo; OxBA
All I can offer now is a cracked china jug. Winter Offering. D. S. Savage. LiTB; NeBP
All I can say is—I saw it! Natural Magic. Robert Browning. VLP
All I could see from where I stood. Renascence. Edna St. Vincent Millay. FaFP; HBV-2; MoAB; MoAmPo; NePA; OHFP; PDV; TwAmPo
All I Do, de Church Keep a-Grumblin', *with music. Unknown.* BoAN-2
"All I do is dole out minutes." Gallop, Gallop to a Rhyme. Monica Shannon. SiSoSe
All I said was—Alexis is gorgeous. Epigram. Plato, *tr. by* Peter Jay. PeHV
All I want in this creation['s]. Black-eyed Susie. *Unknown.* AmFP; FSW
All I wanted/ was your/ love. To Mother and Steve. Mari Evans. BPo; PoBA
All I would say. On a Sea-Grape Leaf. Katherine Garrison Chapin. GrPl
All Ignorance Toboggans into Know. E. E. Cummings. NOBA; OxBA; WaP
All in a Garden Green. W. E. Henley. OBMV
All in a literary parleur. Bootie Black and the Seven Giants. Mike Cook. JB
All in All. Tennyson. *See* In Love, if Love Be Love.
All in Due Time. J. V. Cunningham. NIP
All in Green Went My Love Riding. E. E. Cummings. CMoP; FaBV; GoJo; HeIP; InPK; LiTA; LiTM; NePA; NoAM; NoP; OxBA; PAI; PoRA
(Song: "All in green went my love riding.") ViBoPo
All in our marriage garden. Our Wee White Rose. Gerald Massey. *Fr.* The Mother's Idol Broken. HBV-1
All in the April evening [morning, *wr.*]. Sheep and Lambs. Katharine Tynan. AnIV; HBV-2; OBEV; OBVV; OnYI; OxBI
All in the Downs. Tom Hood. CenHV
All in the Downs the fleet was moored [*or* moor'd]. Sweet William's Farewell to Black-eyed Susan [*or* Black-eyed Susan]. John Gay. AmFP; BeLS; BoLoP; EtS; GTBS; GTBS-P; HBV-1; MOS; NOEC; OBEC; RoGo; TreFS
All in the golden weather, forth let us ride to-day. The King's Highway. John S. McGroarty. BPAW; HBV-1
All in the leafy darkness, when sleep had passed me by. Care. Virginia Woodward Cloud. AA; HBV-2
All in the lilac-rain. In the Lilac-Rain. Edith M. Thomas. HBV-2
All in the merry month of May. Barbara Allen's Cruelty [*or* Barbry Ellen]. *Unknown.* FaBoBe; PrIM
All in the pleasant afternoon. The Lost Playmate. Abbie Farwell Brown. HBVY
All in this pleasant evening, together come are we. Old May Song. *Unknown.* CH
All intellectual eye, our solar round. James Thomson. *Fr.* To the Memory of Sir Isaac Newton. ImOP; NOEC
All Intents. Larry Eigner. VGW
All Ireland's now one vessel's company. Fearghal Og MacWard, *tr. by* the Earl of Longford. *Fr.* The Flight of the Earls, 1607. BIrV
All Is Best. Milton. *Fr.* Samson Agonistes. SeCePo
("All is best, though we oft doubt.") NOBE; OBEV; OBS; SeCeV
(Epilogue.) FaBoEn
All is divine/ which the Highest has made. The Queen of Seasons. Cardinal Newman. GoBC
All is dying; hearts are breaking. Unchanging Jesus. Karl Johann Philipp Spitta, *tr. by* R. Massie. BLRP
All Is God's. Jakov de Haan, *tr. fr. Dutch by* David Soetendorp. VWA
All is phantom that we mid fare. Phantasy. *Unknown.* ACP
All is quiet and the desert moon. Guard. Michael C. Martin. WaP
All is still/ Under the Pines. Under the Pines. Arthur S. Bourinot. OBCV
All is the same still. Earth and heaven locked in. Emily Brontë. C. Day Lewis. ChMP; GTBS-P
All Is Vanity. Bible, *O.T.* Ecclesiastes, I: 14-15; III: 19. TRV
All Is Vanity. *Unknown, at. to* Philip Rosseter. *See* Whether Men Do Laugh or Weep.
All Is Vanity, Saith the Preacher. Byron. TrCP
All Is Well. Arthur Hugh Clough. *See* Whate'er You Dream with Doubt Possest.
All it takes is girls. To Bring Spring. George Keithley. NPGG
All Jolly Fellows That Follow the Plough. *Unknown.* OBET
All joy to mortals, joy and mirth. Song. Aphra Behn. *Fr.* Emperor of the Moon. WPE
All June I bound the rose in sheaves. One Way of Love. Robert Browning. HBV-1

All kings, and all their favourites [*or* favorites]. The Anniversary [*or* The Anniversarie]. John Donne. AnAnS-1; BoLoP; HAP; HoPM; JCP; LiTB; MeLP, MePo; NOBE; NoP; OAEL-1; OAEP; OBS; PoPle; SeCeV; SeCP; SeCV-1; WeW
All kings are hollow. The Cool, Cool, Country. Shaw Neilson. PoAu-1
All-knowing God, 'Tis Thine to Know, *with music. Unknown.* AH
All-knowing Lamp. *Unknown, tr. fr. Greek by* Louis Untermeyer. UnTE
All Last Night. Lascelles Abercrombie. FaBoTw; HBV-1
All last winter, starved cattle. An Abandoned, Overgrown Cemetery in the Pasture near Our House. Gregory Orr. MAYP
All Legendary Obstacles. John Montague. BIrV; CIP; IPY
All lesser reasons for loving die away. Come to Birth. Abbie Huston Evans. NePoAm
All life, tumbled together in a storm. For Posterity. Kathleen Raine. NeBP
All look and likeness caught from earth. Phantom. Samuel Taylor Coleridge. OAEL-2; PoEL-4
All looks be pale, hearts cold as stone. A Lamentation. Thomas Campion. CH; OHIP
All loved and lovely women dear to rhyme. Immortals. David Morton. HBV-2
All Lovely Things. Conrad Aiken. PoRA
All matronly in her stoop, her wings canted. The Black Angel. Henri Coulette. NYBP
All meet here with us, finally. Ostriches and Grandmothers! Amiri Baraka. NeAP
All men are brothers and each people is my own. My Song to the Jewish People. Leib Olitski, *tr. by* Jacob Sonntag. TrJP
All men are locked in their cells. Fall Down. Calvin C. Hernton. CNA; PoBA
All men are wormes: but this no man. In silke. On Court-Worme. Ben Jonson. SeCP
All men from all lands. Inscription for a Wayside Spring. Frances Cornford. BrRo
All men know it, the young when the enemy in them. The Fear of Dying. John Holmes. MiAP
All month a smell of burning, of dry peat. July 1914. "Anna Akhmatova," *tr. by* Stanley Kunitz. WPOW
All Morning. Theodore Roethke. NaP
All Morning. Terry Stokes. AmPA
All morning he lay in the tight, dark room. Signature II. Joseph Stroud. NPGG
All morning I watched. David Martinson. *Fr.* Nineteen Sections from a Twenty Acre Poem. TAT
All morning long from inside the lobby. The Enormous Aquarium. Sherod Santos. MAYP
All morning the beast labors up from the valley. Sibyl. Joseph Stroud. NPGG
All morning the mist. Steady Rain. Lynn Merrill. AMV-80
All morning you squat in the weeds. Rescue. Ellen Bryant Voigt. NoP
All moveless stand the ancient cedar-trees. In the Dark. George Arnold. HBV-2
All moves within the visual frame. A Monument. Charles Madge. FaBoMo
All music, sauces, feasts, delights and pleasures. Thomas Traherne. *Fr.* Christian Ethics. UnS
All must be used. Barracks Apt. 14. Theodore Weiss. CoAP; NePoAm-2; TAP; TwAmPo
All my dark thoughts. Euclid Avenue. Charles Simic. LCAP
All my emprises have been fill'd with Thee. Walt Whitman. *Fr.* Prayer of Columbus. TRV
All my favourite characters have been. Mythology. Lawrence Durrell. DTC; OxBTC
All my future plans, dear. The Blue Room. Lorenz Hart. OBAL
All my life/ they have told me. To You. Frank Horne. *Fr.* Letters Found near a Suicide. BPo
"All my life I've wanted to be." Miss Crustacean. Robert Phillips. GeTw
All my life so far. Discoveries in Arizona. James Wright. NoP
All My Love [*or* Luve], Leave Me Not. *Unknown.* BSV; GoTS
All my neckties. Sooner or Later. John Digby. EAS
All my past life is mine no more. Love and Life. Earl of Rochester. BoLoP; CavP; ELP; EnLoPo; FaBoEn; FF; GBL; HAP; HBV-1; LoBV; MePo; NIP; NOBE; OBEV; OBS; PoEL-3; SeCV-2; TrGrPo; ViBoPo
All my pleasure is in catching of birds. The English Schoolboy. John Heywood. *Fr.* The Play of the Weather. ACP
All My Pretty Ones. Anne Sexton. CoPo; NoAM
All my research has shown. Wyvern. Charles Connell. AmMo
All my senses, like beacon's flame. Caelica, LVI. Fulke Greville. EnRePo; InvP; PoEL-1; QFR
All my sex life, I had been drifting. Royston Ellis. The Cherry Boy, I. PeHV
All my sheep/ Gather in a heap. Last Words before Winter. Louis Untermeyer. MoAmPo
All my shortcomings, in this year of grace. Dear Uncle Stranger. Conrad Aiken. NoAM; NOBA
All my stars forsake me. Song of the Night at Daybreak. Alice Meynell. CH
All my thoughts always speak to me of Love. Dante, *tr. by* Dante Gabriel Rossetti. La Vita Nuova, VI. AWP
All My Trials. *Unknown.* FSW
All names I will not mention, as you may understand. *Unknown.* OuSiCo
All Nature Has a Voice to Tell. James Gilchrist Lawson. BLRP
All Nature is a temple where the alive. Correspondences. Baudelaire, *tr. by* Allen Tate. AWP
All nature owns with one accord. Nature's Hymn to the Deity. John Clare. EBCP; VLP
All Nature seems at work. Slugs leave their lair. Work without Hope. Samuel Taylor Coleridge. BiP; BoNaP; EnRP; FiP; HBV-2; LoBV; NOBE; NoP; OBEV; OBRV; PAI; SaC; TEP
All Needs Met. J. H. Sammis. BLRP
All Night! Leon Baker. LFAC
All night/ you banged. To Poem. Lyn Lifshin. NeAC
All night a noise of leaping fish. The Fisher. Roderic Quinn. CBAP; PoAu-1
All night and all day the wind roared in the streets. Mid-Country Blow. Theodore Roethke. BoNaP
All night between my dreams the thought of you. Flight. Helen Frazee-Bower. Two Married, III. HBMV
All Night by the Rose. *Unknown.* GBL; HeIP
(Rose's Scent, The.) WiR
All night fell hammers, shock on shock. A London Fete. Coventry Patmore. EBVV; HAP; NBM
All night from the roof of the chieftain. Or Ever God Created Adam. *Malay Oral Tradition, tr. by* R. J. Wilkinson. WTO
All night had shout of men and cry. Easter Night. Alice Meynell. BrRo; OHIP
All night I am the doe, breathing. The Strange People. Louise Erdrich. TWSS
All night I clatter upon my creed. The Wife Who Would a Wanton Be. *Unknown.* FaBoCo
All night I could not sleep. *Tr. fr. Chinese by* Arthur Waley. *Fr.* Tzu Yeh Songs. BoWoP
All night I hear the hammers. The Students of Justice. W. S. Merwin. NaP
All Night I Heard. Gertrude MacGregor Moffatt. CaP
All night I lie awake and hear. Remembering. "Michael Lewis." *Fr.* Cherry Blossoms. UnTE
All night I raced the moon. Laurence Dakin. *Fr.* Tancred, II, i. CaP
All night I walked among your spirits, Richard. A Mourning Letter from Paris. Conrad Kent Rivers. BPo
All night I watched awake for morning. Dawn-Angels. Agnes Mary Frances Robinson. HBV-1
All night I wearied utterly of the pillow of darkness. In a Wood Clearing. Wilson MacDonald. CaP
All night I wore the phone, a dead scarf. Hello, Hello. William Matthews. PCP
All Night It Bullied You. C. K. Stead. *Fr.* A Small Registry of Births and Deaths. NAs
All Night Long. Nina Cassian, *tr. fr. Rumanian by* Herbert Kuhner. VWA
All Night Long ("All night long, all night long"). *Unknown.* FSW
All Night Long ("Paul and Silas bound in jail"). *Unknown.* AS, *with music*
(Keep Your Eyes on the Prize.) FSW
All Night Long Fooling Me. *Unknown.* AmFP
All night long into my sleeping bag's head pad the blood. The Far Side of Introspection. Al Lee. CoAP
All night long rocked in my bed. No One Is Asleep Even while Dreaming. Michelle Roberts. LFAC
All night long they race above my bed. Mares of Night. Virginia Long. AMV-81
All night long, through the starlit air and the stillness. The Cattle of His Hand. Wilbur Underwood. WGRP
All night rain fell. The Old Adam. William Rose Benét. YaD
All night the blind entrance of the children. Barren Poem. Michael Ryan. AmPA
All night the long rain encloses the house. Catechism Elegy. Margaret Gibson. MAYP
All night the men whipped the dead horse and then. Parable. Peggy Bennett. ELU
All night the pimp's cars slide past the burning mill. Homage to Elvis, Homage to the Fathers. Bruce Weigl. MAYP
All night the Shabbos candles. Labor. Lucille Day. VWA
All night the small feet of the rain. April. Dora Sigerson Shorter. HBMV; HBVY

All night the sound had. The Rain. Robert Creeley. CAPP; CoAP; ConAP; VGW
All night the surf bangs the coast. Green Frogs. David Rigsbee. AMV-81
All night the tall young man. Merlin and the Snake's Egg. Leslie Norris. WSC
All night the wind swept over the house. Winter Morning. William Jay Smith. BoNaP; NCSH
All night there had sought in vain. The Reminder. Léonie Adams. MoVE
All night they marched, the infantrymen under pack. 1935. Stephen Vincent Benét. MoAmPo
All night they whine upon their ropes and boom. Nocturne of the Wharves. Arna Bontemps. BANP; BPo; PoNe
All night, this headland. Sleepless at Crown Point. Richard Wilbur. WeW
All night upon the guarded hill. The Defence of Lawrence. Richard Realf. PAH
All night waiting, in an empty house. The Streets of Air. Malcolm Cowley. *Fr.* Blue Juniata. PoA
All-Night Waitress, The. Maura Stanton. AmPA
All-Nite Donuts. Albert Goldbarth. GeTw; MAYP
All of a row. *Unknown.* PBBP
All of a Sudden. Teresa de Jesús, *tr. fr. Spanish by* Maria A. Proser, Arlene Scully, *and* James Scully. WPOW
All of a sudden bicycles are toys. A Certain Age. Phyllis McGinley. NePoAm-2
All of a sudden the big nasturtiums. The Big Nasturtiums. Robert Beverly Hale. BoNaP; NYBP
All of Her. Samuel L. Albert. NePoAm-2
All of our fathers are old but lately. The Great Depression. Patricia Goedicke. GP
All of them asleep, the suspiring everywhere is audible weight. In the House of the Judge. Dave Smith. MAYP
All of them the wind took, all of them the light lured. Alone. Hayyim Nahman Bialik, *tr. by* Jessie Sampter. TrJP
All of us always turning away for solace. Delmore Schwartz. OxBA
All of us believe. The Question. W. H. Auden. SUW
All old women sometimes come to this. Old Women of Toronto. Miriam Waddington. NOBC
All on a Summer's Day. *Unknown.* PoPle
All on one summer's evening when the fever were a-dawning. The Grey Cock. *Unknown.* FaBoBa
All on the road to Alibazan. Alibazan. Laura E. Richards. OBCA
All One. Millen Brand. GP
All One in Christ. John Oxenham. *See* No East or West.
All One People. Carl Sandburg. AmFN
All or Nothing. Bayard Taylor. BXAP
All other joy of life he strove to warm. George Meredith. Modern Love, IV. OAEP
All Other Love Is like the Moon. *Unknown.* OxBM
All Our Joy Is Enough. Geoffrey Scott. OBMV
All our roads go nowhere. On Inhabiting an Orange. Josephine Miles. NoAM; PoA
All our stones like as much sun as possible. Forecast. Josephine Miles. CrMA; NoAM
All Out and Down. *Unknown.* BluL
All out for Illinois Central. Calling Trains. *Unknown.* AmFP
All out of doors looked darkly in at him. An Old Man's Winter Night. Robert Frost. AWP; HAP; HBMV; MoAB; MoAmPo; MoVE; NoAM; OxBA; VGW
All over America railroads ride through roses. Landscape as Metal and Flowers. Winfield Townley Scott. AmFN; GoJo; MiAP
All over the district, on leather couches. Walking through the Upper East Side. Erica Jong. NYP
All over the world, I wonder, in lands that I never have trod. Meditations of a Hindu Prince. Sir Alfred Comyns Lyall. WGRP
All over this unsettled country, bands. Wild Horse Jerry's Story. Sarah Elizabeth Howard. PoOW
All passes. Art alone. Austin Dobson, *after* Théophile Gautier. *Fr.* Ars Victrix. CTC
All Paths Lead to You. Blanche Shoemaker Wagstaff. BLPA; FaBoBe
All peacefully gliding. The Rapid. Charles Sangster. CaP; WHW
All people that on earth do dwell. Old Hundredth [*or* Scotch Te Deum *or* Psalm C]. William Kethe. BLSo; FaPoR; FSW; NOCV; WGRP
All perished—brides and infants. Song of a Jewish Boy. "M. J.," *tr. by* A. Glanz-Leyeless. TrJP
All phantoms of the day. Song. Robert Mezey. SUW
All Praise to Thee, *with music.* F. Bland Tucker. AH
All praise to Thee, my God, this night. An Evening Hymn. Thomas Ken. OBS, OxBChV
All praise your face, your verses none abuse. Horace Walpole. FaBoEE
All profits disappear: the gain. The Reckoning. Theodore Roethke. PoA
All Quiet. David Ignatow. ConAP
All Quiet along [*or* on] the Potomac. Ethel Lynn Beers, *sometimes at. to* Lamar Fontaine. AA; BeLS; FaBoBe; FaFP; PaPo; PSoN, *with music;* TrAS, *with music;* TreFS
(Picket-Guard, The.) HBV-2; PAH
All Revelation. Robert Frost. CABA; MoPo; NePA
All right, gentlemen who cry blue murder as always. Draft of a Reparations Agreement. Dan Pagis, *tr. by* Stephen Mitchell. VWA
All right, I may have lied to you, and about you. Love, 20 Cents the First Quarter Mile. Kenneth Fearing. HAP; WeW
All right, I'll die, my spirit is strong. Fear. Vittoria Aganoor Pompili, *tr. by* Brenda Webster. PBWP
All right now, listen to me right good. Unloading Rails. *Unknown.* AmFP
All right, open up in there!/ shout women's rights. For the ERA Crusaders. X. J. Kennedy. SOTS
All round about the door of your house. Regret and Refusal. *Tr. fr. Tewa Indian by* H. J. Spinden. WTO
All round the Browns stretched forty acres of potatoes. The Brown Family. Colleen Thibaudeau. NOBC
All round the horizon black clouds appear. On a Sea-Storm nigh the Coast. Richard Steere. SCAP
All round the room I waltzed with Ellen Taylor. Ellen Taylor. *Unknown.* OBET
All Ruin Is the Same. Emanuel Litvinoff. WaP
All Saints'. Edmund Yates. HBV-1
All Saints' Day, *sel.* Margherita Guidacci, *tr. fr. Italian by* Ruth Feldman *and* Brian Swann.
"All Saints' Day; November sky." PBWP
All Saints' Day, Nov. 1. Christopher Wordsworth. VLP
All saints revile her, and all sober men. The White Goddess. Robert Graves. MoBrPo; OAEL-2
All Scottish legends did his fancy fashion. Robert Burns. William Alexander. HBV-2
All Seasons in One. *Unknown.* TrGrPo
("April is in my mistress' face.") GBL; HeIP; OBSC
All seasons shall be sweet to thee. The Silent Icicles. Samuel Taylor Coleridge. *Fr.* Frost at Midnight. FaBoRV
All-seeing Intellect, The. Phineas Fletcher. *Fr.* The Purple Island, VI. JCP
All Service Ranks the Same with God. Robert Browning. Pippa Passes, Introd. TreFT
(Service.) TrGrPo
(Song: "All service ranks the same with God.") LoBV
All Shams. *Unknown.* APAS
All she took from her hand. The Return. Bruce Bennett Brown. TAT
All silence says music will follow. Onion Bucket. Lorenzo Thomas. PoBA
All Songs. B. Sanford Page. AMV-81
All Souls. D. H. Lawrence. FaBoRV
All Souls' Eve. Mary E. Mannix. GoBC
All Souls' Night. Frances Cornford. EnLoPo; OxBTC
All Souls' Night. W. B. Yeats. *Fr.* A Vision. MoVE
All souls that struggle and aspire. Whittier. *Fr.* The Shadow and the Light. TrPWD
All Splendor on Earth. Karin Kiwus, *tr. fr. German by* Almut McAuley. BoWoP
All such proclivities are tabulated. The Quiet Glades of Eden. Robert Graves. BoLoP; ErPo
All suddenly a stormy whirlwind blew. The Mask of Cupid. Spenser. *Fr.* The Faerie Queene, III, 12. OBSC
All-sufficient Christ, The. Bernice W. Lubke. BLRP
All summer I heard them. The Snakes of September. Stanley Kunitz. AMV-81
All summer long the people knelt. At the President's Grave. Richard Watson Gilder. PAH
All summer watch the children in the public garden. A Prospect of Children. Lawrence Durrell. *Fr.* Eight Aspects of Melissa. NeBP
All summer you have been. Poem for a Neighbor. Pat Therese Francis. AMV-81
All Sung. Richard Le Gallienne. OBVV
All that blazing day, swift-breasted swallows. Thunderstorm in South Dakota. Kay Boyle. WPE
All that blesses the step of the antelope. "Else a Great Prince in Prison Lies." Denise Levertov. NaP; PPP; VGW
All that doth flow we cannot liquid name. What Is Liquid. Margaret Cavendish, Duchess of Newcastle. FaBoUs
All That Glisters Is Not Gold. Shakespeare. *Fr.* The Merchant of Venice, II, vii. CTC
All That Glitters Is Not Gold. *Unknown.* TreFT
All that have two or but one ear. The Four-legg'd Quaker. *Unknown.* CoMu
All that he came to give. A Friend. Lionel Johnson. HBV-2
All That I Am, *with music.* Verna Arvey. AH
All that I am to Earth belongs. William Baylebridge. Life's Testament, XI. PoAu-1

All that I do is clumsy and ill timed. The Doppelganger [*or* Double-Goer]. Daryl Hine. MoCV; OBCV
All that I got from love. A Poem about Love. G. S. Fraser. NeBP
All that I had I brought. Exchanges. Ernest Dowson. OBMV
All that I know/ Of a certain star. My Star. Robert Browning. EvOK; FaPON; HBV-1; OAEP; SoSe; TrGrPo
All that I know of you is that you wore. The True Romance. Herbert Jones. HBMV
All that I may swynk or swet. Care Away. *Unknown.* OxBoLi
All that I ran from. The Mood. Quandra Prettyman. PoBA
All that I try to save him from. Sleep-Learning. Ruth Fainlight. NMM
All That Is, and Can Delight. Robert Farren. OxBI
All That Is Left. Basho, *tr. fr. Japanese by* Curtis Hidden Page. WaaP
("Old battle field, fresh with Spring flowers again.") AWP
All That Is Lovely in Men. Robert Creeley. NaP
All that is moulded of iron. Woodworker's Ballad. Herbert Edward Palmer. OBEV
All That Is Perfect in Woman. William Carlos Williams. BiP
All That Jazz. Yasmeen Jamal. LFAC
All That Matters. Walter Sorell. GoYe
All that matters is to be at one with the living God. Pax. D. H. Lawrence. TrCP
All that night I walked alone and wept. Gethsemane. Arna Bontemps. CDC
All that passes descends. The Gift of Gravity. Wendell Berry. GeTw
All that remains for me. Envoi. Arthur Symons. UnTE
All that remains now is her skeleton. From the Ice Age. Barbara Bloom. AMV-81
All that running water outside. The Marshes. Jane Mayhall. TAP
All That Summer. Lora Dunetz. NePoAm-2
All That Time. May Swenson. FF
All that was beautiful and just. In the Streets of Catania. Roger Casement. AnIV
All that we see, about, abroad. On the Universality and Other Attributes of the God of Nature. Philip Freneau. AP
All that which lies outside our sort of why. Objects. W. H. Auden. NePoAm-2
All That You Have Given Me, Africa. Anoma Kanié, *tr. fr. French by* Kathleen Weaver. PBWP
All That's Bright Must Fade. Thomas Moore. OxBI
All That's Past. Walter de la Mare. GoJo; MoAB; NOBE; OAEL-2; OAEP; OBMV; OxBTC; SeCeV; TreFT; TrGrPo; ViBoPo; WHA
All the/ outward and the inward. Body. Valerie Worth. FAZ
All the afternoon there has been a chirping of birds. Free Fantasia on Japanese Themes. Amy Lowell. MoAmPo
All the animals are looking over. An Evening Walk. William Stafford. NPAW
All the awnings at home had to be pulled down. Cleaning Day. Jose Kozer, *tr. by* David Unger. VWA
All the bells of heaven may ring. A Child's Laughter. Swinburne. BLPL; HBV-1; PoLF
All the bells were ringing. Christina Rossetti. *Fr.* Sing-Song. TiPo
All the birds have come again. Spring's Arrival. *Unknown.* FaPON
All the blues in the world. Australia. Michael Jackson. OCNZ
All the bones of the horses rise in moonlight. Song of Returnings. William Pitt Root. GeTw
All the boys of merry Lincoln. Hugh of Lincoln. *Unknown.* ACP
All the breath and the bloom of the year in the bag of one bee. Summum Bonum. Robert Browning. ELU; HBV-1; OHFP
All the cages are empty. The Two Selves. Margaret Avison. NoAM
All the cautionary tales of strange girls. Mythics. Helen Chasin. DFT; IHMS
All the clitorises are safely. Small Town. William Joyce. FAZ
All the convicts have their roaches lit. Starry Sky. Charles Simic. POL
All the day I worked and played. A Labourer's Wife. John Davidson. *Fr.* To the Street Piano. EBVV
All the days of my life. Lifelong. Rachel Boimwall, *tr. by* Howard Schwartz. VWA
All the Dead Dears. Sylvia Plath. CAPP; IHMS
All the Death-Room Needs. Michael Hartnett. CIP
All the different kinds of light. The Gods Must Not Know Us. Linda Gregg. NPGG
All the earth a hush of white. Nocturne. Amelia Josephine Burr. HBV-1
All the Farewells. Byron Vazakas. MoPo
All the field praises him. May 20: Very Early Morning. Luci Shaw. EBCP
All the flies are reading microscopic books. Serious Readers. Peter Redgrove. OxBC
All the Flowers of the Spring. John Webster. *Fr.* The Devil's Law Case. EIL; ELP; LiTB; OBS; PoEL-2; PoRA; ViBoPo
(Burial, The.) CH; LoBV
(Nets to Catch the Wind.) TrGrPo
(Song: "All the flowers of the spring.") HBV-2
(Vanitas Vanitatum.) NOBE; OBEV
All the forms are fugitive. Emerson. *Fr.* Woodnotes, II. WGRP
All the fruit is ripe, plunged in fire, cooked. Friedrich Hölderlin, *tr. fr. German by* Robert Bly. NU
All the full-moon night in the coomb. In the Night of the Full Moon. Carl Busse, *tr. by* Jethro Bithell. AWP
All the glorious Spring makes me color blind. Sorrow. Marie Tello Phillips. GoYe
All the golden air is full of balm and bloom. Hawthorn Dyke. Swinburne. VLP
All the here and all the there. Our Two Worthies. John Crowe Ransom. OBAL
All the Hills and Vales Along. Charles Hamilton Sorley. EBEV; FaBoCh; HBMV; MMA; MoBrPo; OBWP
All the Hosts of Heaven. Simeon ben Isaac ben Abun of Mainz, *tr. fr. Hebrew by* Nina Davis Salaman. TrJP
All the inventions that the world contains. Inventions. Samuel Butler. PV
All the long August afternoon. In August. William Dean Howells. GN
All the long forenoon, the loitering of insects. The Forenoon. Christopher Middleton. *Fr.* Herman Moon's Hourbook. NePoEA-2
All the Many is One. The Wild Geese. John Masefield. NoAM
All the materials of a poem. Lumber of Spring. Anne Ridler. NYBP
All the names I know from nurse. The Flowers. Robert Louis Stevenson. FaPON
All the new flowers flat. Cold Snap. Kathy Mangan. AMV-80
All the new thinking is about loss. Meditation at Lagunitas. Robert Hass. MAYP; NoP; NPGG
All the night sleep came not upon my eyelids. Sapphics. Swinburne. PoEL-5
All the Past We Leave Behind, *with music.* Walt Whitman. AH
All the perversions of the soul. A Small Farm. Michael Hartnett. CIP
All the Pretty Little Horses. *Unknown.* AmFP; FSW; OxBoLi
All the promises of the world are lies. The Promises of the World. Moses ibn Ezra, *tr. by* Solomon Solis-Cohen. *Fr.* The World's Illusion. TrJP
All the Roary Night. Kenneth Patchen. LiTM
All the Scenes of Nature Quicken. Christopher Smart. ELP
All the ships are sailing away without me. The Statue of Liberty. Edward Field. TAT
All the sisters of mercy. Canto Llano. Anita Endrezze Probst. CDW
All the skippers o Scarsburgh. Young Allan. *Unknown.* BaBo
All the Smoke. Eli Siegel. CAD; ELU; FiBHP
All the soft moon bends over. The Natural Mother. Jay MacPherson. CABA
All the soldiers marching along. Remembering Day. Mary Wight Saunders. YeAr
All the soul indrawn. Stéphane Mallarmé, *tr. fr. French by* Roger Fry. NAWM-2
All the Spirit Powers Went to Their Dancing Place. Gary Snyder. UnPo
All the things. The objects. Cold Term. Amiri Baraka. BPo; CNA; SOTW
All the Things You Are, *with music.* Oscar Hammerstein II. BLSo
All the time cold water fell. The Wheel. James Cole. FAZ
All the time they were praying. The Death Bed. Waring Cuney. CDC
All the trees they are so high. The Trees So High. *Unknown.* OxBoLi
All the trees were made. Mother. Barry Dempster. AMV-80
All the way/ on the road to Gary. The Helmet. Philip Levine. LCAP
All the way from Florence in the train. Walking in Nice. Patricia Traxler. AMV-81
All the Way from There to Here. Jack Gilbert. NPGG
All the Way My Saviour Leads Me. Fanny J. Crosby. FSW; STF
All the way to the hospital. The Almond Tree. Jon Stallworthy. NoP
All the way to Tir na n'Og are many roads that run. The King of Ireland's Son. Nora Hopper. AnIL
All the while, believe me, I prayed. Sappho, *tr. fr. Greek by* Willis Barnstone. BoWoP
All the while they were talking the new morality. The Encounter. Ezra Pound. PAI
All the whole world is living without war. Canzone: He Speaks of His Condition through Love. Folcachiero de' Folcachieri, *tr. by* Dante Gabriel Rossetti. AWP
All the wide air was trawled for cloud. L'Ile du Levant: The Nudist Colony. Barbara Howes. NePoAm-2; PoCh
All the woods are now in flower. The Wooing. *Unknown, tr. by* John Addington Symonds. UnTE
All the words that I utter. Where My Books Go. W. B. Yeats. OBEV; OBVV
All the World. *Unknown, tr. fr. Hebrew by* Israel Zangwill. TrJP
All the World Moved. June Jordan. NBP; PoBA
All the world shall come to serve Thee. All the World. *Unknown, tr. by* Israel Zangwill. TrJP
All the world's a school. Schoolmaster. George Rostrevor Hamilton. FaBoEE

All the World's a Stage. Sir Walter Ralegh. *See* What Is Our Life? A Play of Passion.
All the World's a Stage. Shakespeare. *Fr.* As You Like It, II, vii. FaPoR; FF; FiP; LiTB; MasP; NIP; PoLF; TrGrPo
(Seven Ages of Man, The.) FaFP; TreF
All their lives in a box! What generations. The Silkworms. Douglas Stewart. CBAP; PoAu-2
All these are your essence, you are their flesh and their force. Dick Diespecker. *Fr.* Between Two Furious Oceans. CaP
All These Birds. Richard Wilbur. NOBA; Prf
All these borders. Against Borders. Yevgeny Yevtushenko, *tr. by* Anselm Hollo. CAD
All these illegitimate babies. Valuable. Stevie Smith. OxBTC
All these maneuverings to avoid. Love's Stratagems. Donald Justice. NYBP
All these nights, all these traffic lights. Crossing with the Light. Dwight Okita. BrSi
All these on whom the sacred seal was set. An Unbeliever. Anna Hempstead Branch. WGRP
All these things are in my mind also, lady; but I fear still. Hektor to Andromache. Homer, *tr. by* Richmond Lattimore. *Fr.* The Iliad, VI. WaaP
All these years I have remembered a night. Grievance. Amy Lowell. ViBoPo
All Things Are a Flowing. R. P. Blackmur. TwAmPo
All Things Are Current Found. Henry David Thoreau. *Fr.* A Week on the Concord and Merrimack Rivers. ViBoPo
All things are doubly fair. Art. Théophile Gautier, *tr. by* George Santayana. AWP
All things are hushed, as Nature's self lay dead. Midnight. Dryden. ACP
All things are possible. Lake Walk at New Year's. Leigh Perez-Diotima. AMV-81
All Things Be Dear but Poor Mens Labour; or, The Sad Complaint of Poor People. *Unknown.* CoMu
"All things become thee, being thine," I think sometimes. Woman. Randall Jarrell. NoAM; NOBA
All Things Being Equal. J. Lee Humphrey. AMV-81
All Things Bright and Beautiful. Cecil Frances Alexander. FaPoR; OHIP; OxBChV; RHPC
(Creation, The.) FaPON
(Maker of Heaven and Earth.) VLP
All things burn with the fire of God. Revelation. Verne Bright. BLRP; WBLP
All Things Can Tempt Me. W. B. Yeats. CMoP
All things come alike to all. Bible, *O.T.* *Fr.* Ecclesiastes. NAWM-1
All things come to pass. My Name Is Afrika. Keorapetse Kgositsile. PoBA
All Things Confine. Hadewijch, *tr. fr. Dutch by* Frans van Rosevelt. PBWP
All things created, Moses writes. Josiah Chorley. *Fr.* A Metrical Index to the Bible. FaBoUs
All Things Decay and Die. Robert Herrick. CaPo
All Things Drink. Thomas Stanley, *after the Greek of* Anacreon. AWP
All Things Have Savour. *Unknown.* FaBoCo
All things return, Nietzsche said. The Recurrence. Edwin Muir. MoPo
All things shall perish from under the sky. Music Alone Shall Live. *Unknown.* FSW
All things that are on earth shall wholly pass away. The Love of God. Bernard Rascas, *tr. by* Bryant. WGRP
All things that go deep enough. The Ice Skin. James Dickey. NYBP
All things that pass. Passing and Glassing. Christina Rossetti. FaBoEn; OBNC
All things turned to Orpheus' hand. The Greater Music. Theodore Weiss. NePoAm-2
All things uncomely and broken, all things worn out and old. The Lover [*or* Aedh] Tells of the Rose in His Heart. W. B. Yeats. BrPo; CMoP; MoBrPo; ViBoPo; VLP
All Things Wait upon Thee. Christina Rossetti. GN
All things within this fading world hath end. Before the Birth of One of Her Children. Anne Bradstreet. BoWoP; MAT; NAs; NOBA; PAI; SBG; WPE; WPOW
All this day. Lunar Eclipse. Jessica Scarbrough. LFAC
All this indigo, nonviolent light will triumph. Sunday Evenings. John Hollander. NYBP; NYP
All this is one. My Faith. Ananda Acharya. WGRP
All this night shrill chanticleer. Chanticleer. William Austin. EBCP; OxBoCh
All this (said she) we know. Achilles Shows Himself in the Battle by the Ships. Homer, *tr. by* George Chapman. *Fr.* The Iliad, XVIII. OBS
All This Sunday Long. B. S. Johnson. ELU
All this time we have been drinking. Light Showers of Light. Kathryn Lindskoog. AMV-80
All this was, was. Verses on Accepting the World. Joseph Brodsky, *tr. by* Dimitry Pospielovsky *and* Keith Bosley. VWA
All those heads those ears those eyes. Song of the Old Woman. *Tr. fr. Eskimo by* Paul Emile Victor, *ad. by* Armand Schwerner. BoWoP
All those I love die young: Zoilus, I'll try. Balthasar Bonifacius. DBV
All those summers, waiting. Waiting for You to Come By. Simon J. Ortiz. CDW
All those treasures that lie in the little bolted box. Slow Movement. William Carlos Williams. PoA
All those who seek Thee tempt Thee. The Book of Pilgrimage. Rainer Maria Rilke, *tr. by* Jessie Lemont. ILwL
All those words that I've used for sixty-eight years. Symbols. Harry Roskolenko. FAZ
All those years that you ate and changed. Peasant. W. S. Merwin. NYBP
All thoughts, all passions, all delights. Love. Samuel Taylor Coleridge. BeLS; ChER; EnRP; GTBS; GTBS-P; HBV-1; LoBV; OAEP; OBEV; TreFT
All thro' the breathing night there seemed to flow. A Venetian Night. Hugo von Hofmannsthal, *tr. by* Ludwig Lewisohn. AWP
All thro' the Year. *Unknown.* BLRP
All through lunch Peter pinched at his crotch. Mission Tire Factory, 1969. Gary Soto. NPAW; NPGG
All through October. Indian Summer: Vermont. Anne Stevenson. NCSH
All through that summer at ease we lay. The Castle. Edwin Muir. LiTB
All through the garden I went and went. The Butterbean Tent. Elizabeth Madox Roberts. GoJo; SUS
All through the golden weather. A Song of Autumn. Rennell Rodd. HBV-1
All through the march, besides bag and blanket. Crazed Man in Concentration Camp. Agnes Gergely, *tr. by* Edwin Morgan. BoWoP
All through the Night. *Unknown, at. to* Harold Boulton; *also at. to* David Owen. FaPON, *shorter vers.;* FSW; TreFS, *sl. diff. vers.*
All through the night in silence they come and go. Charing Cross. Cecil Roberts. HBMV
All through the night my eyes have streamed with rain. Epigram. Strato, *tr. by* Sydney Oswald. PeHV
All through the night the happy sheep. The Happy Sheep. Wilfred Thorley. SoPo
All through the Rains. Gary Snyder. ConAP
All through the Stranger's Wood. Isaac Leibush Peretz, *tr. fr. Yiddish by* Joseph Leftwich. TrJP
All through the sultry hours of June. My Thrush. Mortimer Collins. HBV-1
All through the windless night the clipper rolled. John Masefield. Dauber, VI. CMoP
All Thumbs. David Giber. AMV-81
All to Myself. Wilbur Dick Nesbit. BLPA
All told the gray world. The Tall Toms. Edwin Honig. NePA
All Too Late. *Unknown.* OAEL-1; OxBM
("Whenne mine eyes misteth.") EBEV
All Too Little on Pictures. Charles Black. AMV-80
All travail of high thought. The Beginnings of Faith. Sir Lewis Morris. WGRP
All travellers at first incline. Stella's Birthday, 1720. Swift. OxBI; PoEL-3
All trembling in my arms Aminta lay. The Dream. Aphra Behn. *Fr.* A Voyage to the Isle of Love. PBWP
All Tropic Places Smell of Mold. Karl Shapiro. VGW
All Turns into Yesterday. *Unknown.* MeEL
All uncompelled, weightless as the notes. Caedmon. George Garrett. NePoAm-2
All under the leaves, the leaves of life. The Seven Virgins. *Unknown.* CH; ChTr; GBP; OBET; OBEV; OxBoCh
All up and down in shadow-town. The Shadows. Frank Dempster Sherman. AA
All Up and Down the Lines. Robert Cooperman. AMV-80
All upstarts, insolent in place. The Butterfly and the Snail. John Gay. *Fr.* Fables. FM
All veiled in black, with faces hid from sight. Mourning Women. Mathilde Blind. SBG
All Virgil's idylls end in sunsets; pale. The Voice. Edmund Wilson. NYBP
All wars are planned by old men. Two Sides of War. Grantland Rice. TreFT
All was as it is, before the beginning began, before. Jacob. Delmore Schwartz. VWA
All was as it was when I went in. Apopemptic Hymn. Dorothy Auchterlonie. PoAu-2
All was for you: and you are dead. Beyond. Lionel Johnson. BrPo
All was in flight. The Wind Was There. Bravig Imbs. EAS
All was play, all was sport. *Unknown, tr. by* Joseph Dunn. *Fr.* The Combat of Ferdiad and Cuchulain. OnYI
All Watched Over by Machines of Loving Grace. Richard Brautigan. MAT

All we make is enough. All Our Joy Is Enough. Geoffrey Scott. OBMV
All we were going strong last night this time. Sonnet. John Berryman. FaBoMo
All week, the maid tells me, bowing. A Walk in Kyoto. Earle Birney. GoYe
All were to little for the merchauntes hande. George Gascoigne. AAS
All wheels; a man breathed fire. The Celebration. James Dickey. VGW
All Which Isn't Singing Is Mere Talking. E. E. Cummings. VGW
All who have and have all can cry: "Peace!" Editorial Poem on an Incident of Effects Far-reaching. Russell Atkins. NBP
All who have loved, be sure of this from me. Richard Watson Dixon. *Fr.* Love's Consolation. OBNC
All who want to roam in Kansas. In Kansas. *Unknown.* FSW
All windows open, moths. Three Part Invention. Paul Blackburn. CoPo
All winter long you listened for the boom. The Stoic; for Laura von Courten. Edgar Bowers. CoAP; NePoEA; QFR
All winter through I bow my head. The Scarecrow. Walter de la Mare. MoBrPo; OxBTC
All winter your brute shoulders strained against collars, padding. Names of Horses. Donald Hall. HAP; LCAP; LLLT; PH
All wisdom and renown are worth. Summer Interlude. Lionel Stevenson. CaP
All women are beautiful as they rise. Poem for Easter. Robert Kelly. VGW
All women born are so perverse. Triolet. Robert Bridges. HBV-1; PV; SeCePo; TW
All women loved dance in a dying light. They Sing. Theodore Roethke. NYBP
All work and no play makes Jack a dull boy. *Unknown.* OxNR
All worldly shapes shall melt in gloom. The Last Man. Thomas Campbell. EnRP; OBRV
All ye poets of the age. Namby-Pamby. Henry Carey. FaBoNo; FaBoPa; NOEC; OBSV; Par
All Ye That Go Astray. Moses ibn Ezra, *tr. fr. Hebrew by* Solomon Solis-Cohen. *Fr.* The World's Illusion. TrJP
All ye that handle harp and viol. Chorus. Moses Hayyim Luzzatto, *tr. by* Nina Davis Salaman. *Fr.* Unto the Upright Praise. TrJP
All ye that lovely lovers be. Harvester's Song. George Peele. *Fr.* The Old Wives' Tale. TrGrPo
All ye that pass along Love's trodden way. Dante, *tr. by* Dante Gabriel Rossetti. La Vita Nuova, II. AWP
All ye that passe by this holy place. A Second Epitaph. *Unknown.* MeEL
All ye who, far from town, in rural hall. On a Wet Summer. John Codrington Bampfylde. NOEC
All ye who love the springtime. The Dawning o' the Year. Mary Elizabeth McGrath Blake. AA
All ye woods, and trees, and bowers. The God of Sheep [*or* To Pan]. John Fletcher. *Fr.* The Faithful Shepherdess. EIL; FaBoCh; TrGrPo
All ye young men, I pray draw near. The Gardener. *Unknown.* GBP
All year/ They have kept a careful record. The New Year for Trees. Howard Schwartz. VWA
All year the flax-dam festered in the heart. Death of a Naturalist. Seamus Heaney. HAP; NCSH; OxBC; WeW
All you ask is. Jonathan Williams. *Fr.* Strung Out with Elgar on a Hill. GP
All you can about animals as persons. What You Should Know to Be a Poet. Gary Snyder. NNaP; PoM
All you lords of Scottland ffaire. Tom Potts. *Unknown.* ESPB
All you on emigration bent. The Settler's Lament. *Unknown.* PoAu-1
All You Others, Eat. Djurberaui, *tr. fr. Aborigine by* C. H. Berndt. WTO
All you that are enamored of my name. Demos. E. A. Robinson. AP
All you that are low-spirited, I think it won't be wrong. A New Hunting Song. *Unknown.* OBET
All you that are single and wild in your ways. Old Maids. *Unknown.* AmFP
All you that are to mirth inclin'd, come tarry here a little while. The Country Girl's Policy; or, The Cockney Outwitted. *Unknown.* CoMu
All you that delight to spend some time. Little John a Begging. *Unknown.* ESPB
All you that desire to here of a jest. The Unfortunate Miller; or, The Country Lasses Witty Invention. *Unknown.* CoMu; OxBB
All you that in His house be here. Old Christmas. *Unknown.* OHIP
All you that to feasting and mirth are inclined. Old Christmas Returned. *Unknown.* GN; OHIP
All you violated ones with gentle hearts. For Malcolm X. Margaret Walker. BPo; CNA; PoBA
All you young men an' maidens come an' listen to my song. A New Song on the Taxes. *Unknown.* WTO
All Your Fortunes We Can Tell Ye. Ben Jonson. *Fr.* The Gypsies Metamorphosed. ChTr
All yow that crye O hone! O hone! A Lementable New Ballad upon the Earle of Essex Death. *Unknown.* CoMu
Allace depairting, grund of wo. Fairweill. *Unknown.* OxBS
Allace! So Sobir Is the Micht. Mersar. OxBS
Allah ("Allah gives light in darkness"). Siegfried August Mahlmann, *tr. fr. German by* Longfellow. AWP
Allah's Tent. Arthur Colton. HBV-2
Allalu Mo Wauleen. *Unknown.* AnIV
Allan Water. Matthew Gregory Lewis. HBV-1
Allas, allas, wel ivel I sped! *See* Alas, alas, well evil I sped!
Allas! my worthi maister honorable. Lament for Chaucer. Thomas Hoccleve. OBEV
Allas the Wo! Allas, the peynes stronge. Chaucer. *Fr.* The Canterbury Tales: The Knight's Tale. LO
Allas! what shul we freres do. *See* Alas! what shul we freres do.
Allatoona. *Unknown.* PAH
Alle bakbiteres hi wendeth to helle. Going to Hell. *Unknown.* OxBM
Alle that beth of herte trewe. The Death of King Edward I. *Unknown.* MeEL
Allegiance is assigned. Choice. J. V. Cunningham. VGW
Allegory, An. Barcroft Boake. CBAP
Allegory, An. David Ignatow. VGW
Allegory in Black. Carl Clark. JB
Allegory of the Adolescent and the Adult. George Barker. LiTB; MasP
Allegory of the Wolf Boy, The. Thom Gunn. OxBC
Allegro. "McM." InMe
Allegro. Tomas Tranströmer, *tr. fr. Swedish by* Robert Bly. EAS
Alleluia! Alleluia! Let the Holy Anthem Rise. *Unknown.* PoSC
Alleluia! Christ Is Risen Today, *with music.* John Henry Hopkins, Jr. AH
Alleluya. Rubén Darío, *tr. fr. Spanish by* Lysander Kemp. TTY
Allen Ginsberg Blesses a Bride and Groom; a Wedding Night Poem. Robert Peters. GP
(Blessing a Bride and Groom; a Wedding Night Poem.) BXAP
Allen said, I am searching for the true cadence. Helicon. John Hollander. NoAM
Allen-a-Dale. Sir Walter Scott. *Fr.* Rokeby, III. EnRP
Allergy. Walker Gibson. NePoAm
Alley, The; an Imitation of Spenser. Pope. NOEC
Alley Blues. *Unknown.* BluL
Alley Cat School. Frank Asch. RHPC
Alley of granite arkite pillars, The. Stones: Avesbury. Daisy Aldan. PoA
Alley-Walker. Joan Smith. AMV-80
Alleys. Sandra McPherson. MAYP
Allie ("Allie, call the birds in"). Robert Graves. FaPON; GoJo
Alligator, The. Mary Macdonald. RHPC
Alligator, The. Beatrice Ravenel. WPE
Alligator Bride, The. Donald Hall. ConAP; EAS
Alligator chased his tail, The. The Alligator. Mary Macdonald. RHPC
Alligator on the Escalator. Eve Merriam. SO
Alligator Pie. Dennis Lee. RHPC
Allison Gross. *Unknown.* CH; ESPB
Alliteration, or the Siege of Belgrade. *Unknown.* *See* Austrian Army, An.
Allow me just one short remark. The Boa. J. J. Bell. RHPC
All's ill and will be so. The Wind Is Ill. John Malcolm Brinnin. LiTA
All's over, then: does truth sound bitter. The Lost Mistress. Robert Browning. BoLoP; FaBoEn; FiP; HBV-1; NOBE; OBEV; OBNC; OBVV; PoPle
All's peace to-day at Beecher Isle. Beecher Island. Arthur Chapman. PoOW
All's Right with the World. Gerald Massey. EBVV
All's Vast. Francis Thompson. *Fr.* The Heart. MoAB; MoBrPo
(Correlated Greatness.) GTBS-P
("O nothing in this corporal earth of man.") OBMV
All's Well! William Allen Butler. HBV-2
All's Well. Harriet McEwen Kimball. AA
All's Well. Whittier. OBVV
All's Well That Ends Well, *sel.* Shakespeare.
"For I the ballad will repeat," *fr.* I, iii. BiP; ViBoPo
All's Well That Ends Well. *Unknown.* FaFP
Alluding to the One-armed Bandit. D. C. Berry. BXAP
Allusion to Horace, An; the Tenth Satire of the First Book. Earl of Rochester. APAS; OBS
Alma Mater. Mary Elizabeth Osborn. NePoAm
Alma Mater. Sir Arthur Quiller-Couch. OBVV
Alma Mater, Forget Me. William Cole. FiBHP
Alma Mater's Roll. Edward Everett Hale. AA
Alma; or, The Progress of the Mind, *sel.* Matthew Prior.
"In Britain's isles, as Heylyn notes." NOEC
Alma Redemptoris Mater. *At. to* Hermanus Contractus, *tr. fr. Latin by* Winfred Douglas. ISi
Alma to Her Sister. Linda Gregg. NPGG
Alma Venus, *sel.* Bernard O'Dowd.
"Door of existence, beacon of our haze." PoAu-1
Almae Matres. Andrew Lang. BSV; OBVV

Almanac. May Swenson. NYBP
Almanac Verse. Samuel Danforth. SCAP
Almanac Verse. *Unknown.* SCAP
Almanack for the Year of Our Lord, 1657, An. Samuel Bradstreet. SCAP
Almeria. Pablo Neruda, *tr. fr. Spanish by* Angel Flores. WaaP
Almightie Judge, how shall poore wretches brook. Judgement. George Herbert. AnAnS-1; SeCP
Almightly and all present Power. A Sergeant's Prayer. Hugh Brodie. PGD
Almighty and all merciable queen. La Prière de Nostre Dame. Chaucer, *mod. vers. by* Anselm M. Townsend. ISi
Almighty and everlasting God, we thank Thee. Prayer for Every Day. *Unknown, tr. by* Kweku Martin. PBA
Almighty crowd, thou shorten'st all dispute. Vox Populi. Dryden. *Fr.* The Medall. OBS
Almighty father! of high Heaven posses'd! The Lord's Prayer in Verse. Aaron Hill. FaBoUs
Almighty God, Fader of Hevene. A Prayer to the Trinity. *Unknown.* MeEL
Almighty God in Being Was, *with music.* Silas Ballou. AH
Almighty God, Thy Constant Care, *with music.* Henry S. Washburn. AH
Almighty God, Whose Justice Like a Sun. Hilaire Belloc. TrPWD
Almighty has dealt bitterly with me, The. The Great Sad One. Uri Zvi Greenberg, *tr. by* Robert Mezey *and* Ben Zion Gold. VWA
Almighty Lord, with One Accord, *with music.* Melancthon W. Stryker. AH
Almighty Maker God! Isaac Watts. *Fr.* Sincere Praise. TrPWD
Almighty Sovereign of the Skies! *with music.* Nathan Strong. AH
Almighty Spake, and Gabriel Sped, Th', *with music.* George Richards. AH
Almighty! What Is Man? Solomon ibn Gabirol, *tr. fr. Hebrew by* Emma Lazarus. TrJP
Almighty Wisdom made the land. The Sea Is His. Edward Sandford Martin. EtS
Almond Blossom. Sir Edwin Arnold. GN; HBV-1
Almond Blossom. D. H. Lawrence. FaBoPP
Almond Tree, The. Jon Stallworthy. NoP
Almost. Rachel Field. SUS
Almost afraid they led her in. Transfigured. Sarah Morgan Bryan Piatt. AA
Almost always ahead of us. Frog Hunting. Peter Cooley. MAYP
Almost as though the eggs run and leap back into their shells. Remembering Fire. Rodney Jones. MAYP
Almost at the equator. Once Only. Gary Snyder. SUW
Almost Everybody Is Dying Here: Only a Few Actually Make It. Daniel Berrigan. LFAC
Almost Grown. Ai. MAYP
Almost happy now, he looked at his estate. Voltaire at Ferney. W. H. Auden. LiTA; LiTM
Almost Human. C. Day Lewis. NoAM
Almost I, yes I hear. W. S. Graham. The Dark Dialogues, II. OxBS
Almost Ninety. Ruth Whitman. PCP
Almost Persuaded, *with music.* Philip Paul Bliss. AH
Almost reluctant, we approach the block. Thumbprint. Celeste Turner Wright. Psk
Almost sexless: the white skin. Girl in a Black Bikini. Allan Brown. AMV-80
Almost sheer fatigue. Early Pregnancy. Penelope Shuttle. BrRo
Almost singing, she stares past the crowd and flies. Old Woman Awaiting the Greyhound Bus. Duane Niatum. CDW
Almost twenty years. Drinking Cold Water. Peter Everwine. NNaP
Almost two years now I've been sleeping. After Elegies. Jean Valentine. LCAP
Almost yesterday, those gentle ladies stole. The Lost Ingredient. Anne Sexton. CoPo
Almswomen. Edmund Blunden. OBmV; OxBTC
Alnwick Castle. Fitz-Greene Halleck. AA
Aloe Plant, The. Henry Harbaugh. BLPA
Aloft he guards the starry folds. The Eagle of the Blue. Herman Melville. AA
Aloft in Heavenly Mansions, Doubleyou One. The Playboy of the Demi-World: 1938. William Plomer. OxBTC; PeHV; TW
Aloft, lightly on fingertips. Burial. Robert Francis. NCSH
Aloft upon an old basaltic crag. Kane. Fitz-James O'Brien. PAH
Aloft we all must go oh. John Damerlay. *Unknown.* ShS
Aloha. William Griffith. HBMV
Alone. "Anna Akhmatova," *tr. fr. Russian by* Stephen Berg. BoWoP
Alone. Hayyim Nahman Bialik, *tr. fr. Hebrew by* Jessie Sampter. TrJP
Alone. Chu Shu-chen, *tr. fr. Chinese by* Kenneth Rexroth. BoWoP
Alone. Walter de la Mare. ChTr; EnLoPo
Alone. John Farrar. YeAr
Alone. Robert Finch. CaP; PeCV
Alone. Jonathan Holden. Psk
Alone. James Joyce. InvP
Alone. Elsie Laurence. CaP
Alone. Itzik Manger, *tr. fr. Yiddish by* Ruth Whitman. VWA
Alone. Sappho, *tr. fr. Greek by* William Ellery Leonard. AWP
Alone. Siegfried Sassoon. *See* When I'm Alone.
Alone. E. J. Scovell. GBL
Alone. Richard Shelton. NYBP
Alone ("Alone! Alone!/I sit in the solitudes of the moonshades"). *Unknown.* NA
Alone, alone/ you are the eyes of midnight. The Mute City. Lazer Eichenrand, *tr. by* Gabriel Preil *and* Howard Schwartz. VWA
Alone, alone, about a dreadful wood. Advent. W. H. Auden. *Fr.* For the Time Being. OAEP
Alone am I, and alone I wish to be. Christine de Pisan, *tr. fr. French by* Julie Allen. BoWoP
Alone and Godless, stopped by the sudden edge. Patrick MacDonogh. *Fr.* Escape to Love. BIrV
Alone as I went up and doun. The Abbey Walk. Robert Henryson. BSV
Alone, at night, with all the world. Evil Nigger Waits for Lightnin'. Amiri Baraka. NoAM; NOBA
Alone at the end of green *allées,* alone. The Statues in the Public Gardens. Howard Nemerov. ConAP; EyDe
Alone by the Hearth. George Arnold. HBV-1
Alone by the Road's Edge. Diana O Hehir. NPGG
Alone far in the wilds and mountains I hunt. Walt Whitman. Song of Myself, X. SeCeV
Alone for the evening. Bringing Flowers. Roberta Spear. AmPA
Alone I tiptoe through the stars. Star Journey. Naomi Long Madgett. BPo
Alone I walked the ocean strand. A Name in the Sand. Hannah Flagg Gould. AA
Alone in a cold autumn I stood. Midstream. Mao Tse-tung, *tr. by* Earle Birney. MoCV
Alone in an Inn at Southampton, April the 25th, 1737. Aaron Hill. NOEC
Alone in April. James Branch Cabell. HBMV
Alone in greenwood must I roam. Hollin, Green Hollin. *Unknown.* GBP
Alone in the atoning belfry how I grieve. Giotto's Campanile. Guy Butler. PeSA
Alone in the dreary, pitiless street. Nobody's Child. Phila H. Case. TreF
Alone in the House. George Bogin. AMV-80
Alone in the night. Stars. Sara Teasdale. FaPON; HBMV; TiPo
Alone in this desert under the cold moon. If I Forget Thee. Emanuel Litvinoff. TrJP; VWA
Alone is delicious. Alone. Jonathan Holden. Psk
Alone Is the Hunter. Harold Littlebird. VoR
Alone no loneliness in the dream in the quiet. Alma to Her Sister. Linda Gregg. NPGG
Alone on Lykaion since man hath been. Mount Lykaion. Trumbull Stickney. *Fr.* Sonnets from Greece. MoVE; NePA; OxBA; TrGrPo
Alone on the jagged rock. November Day at McClure's. Robert Bly. NU
Alone on the lawn. The Dancing Cabman. J. B. Morton. MoShBr; NOBL
Alone on the shore in the pause of the nighttime. The Full Heart. Robert Nichols. BoNaP; HBMV
Alone on the tower. Diver. R. A. Simpson. CBAP
Alone one noon on a sheet of igneous rock. Myths. Guy Butler. PeSA
Alone she feeds the white swans. The Swans of Vadstena. Ralph Gustafson. MoCV
Alone the pallid cuckoo now. Pallid Cuckoo. David Campbell. CBAP; PoAu-2
Alone, upon the broad low bench, he sits. To Borglum's Seated Statue of Abraham Lincoln. Charlotte B. Jordan. OHIP
Alone walking/ And oft musing. The Bailey Beareth the Bell Away. *Unknown.* SeCePo
Alone walking,/ In thought pleining. Wishing My Death. *Unknown.* MeEL
Alone with God for one sweet, solemn hour. The Quiet Hour. Louise Hollingsworth Bowman. BLRP
Alone with the Dawn. Matthew Sweeney. AMV-80
Along a river-side, I know not where. The Washers of the Shroud. James Russell Lowell. AP; HBV-2
Along a road. Rain Clouds. Elizabeth-Ellen Long. RHPC
Along Ancona's hills the shimmering heat. Poppies in [*or* on] the Wheat. Helen Hunt Jackson. AA; BPAW
Along came the [*or* come that] F.F.V., the swiftest on the line. George Allen [*or* Engine 143]. *Unknown.* AmFP; FSW
Along East River and the Bronx. Ode to Walt Whitman. Federico García Lorca. PeHV
Along Highway 40, blare. The Shape of Autumn. Virginia Russ. GoYe
Along History. Muriel Rukeyser. NNaP
Along how many Main Streets have I walked. The Eternal Return. Robert Hillyer. NYBP
Along my ways of life you never came. Muna Lee. Sonnets, XII. HBMV
Along South Inlet. Greg Kuzma. WOLT

Along the avenue of cypresses. Giorno dei Morti. D. H. Lawrence. BrPo; FaBoRV, *abr.;* NOBE; SeCePo
Along the Banks, *with music.* Joel Barlow. AH
Along the blushing borders bright with dew. Spring Flowers. James Thomson. *Fr.* The Seasons: Spring. NOBE; OBEC
Along the cement walkway I pick up. Markings. Frank Steele. Psk
Along the country roadside, stone on stone. Stone Walls. Julie Mathilde Lippmann. AA
Along the dark, and silent night. The Bell-Man. Robert Herrick. OBS
Along the dark bank of the river. After the Night Hunt. James Dickey. PoA
Along the Field as We Came By. A. E. Housman. A Shropshire Lad, XXVI. HAP; HBV-1; MasP; MoAB; MoBrPo; OAEP; UnTE; WeW
Along the garden ways just now. A Love Symphony. Arthur O'Shaughnessy. HBV-1
Along the graceless grass of town. A Dead Harvest. Alice Meynell. MoVE
Along the highway street. A Mexican Scrapbook. Dave Oliphant. FAZ
Along the just-returning green. Wonder and a Thousand Springs. William Alexander Percy. HBMV
Along the lane beside the mead. A Pastoral. Norman Gale. HBV-1
Along the line of smoky hills. Indian Summer. Wilfred Campbell. CaP; NOBC; OBCV; PoPl; WHW
Along the pastoral ways I go. A Holiday. Lizette Woodworth Reese. AA
Along the path that skirts the wood. The Three Musicians. Aubrey Beardsley. VLP
Along the path where your light feet passed. Anath. Haim Guri, *tr. by* Naomi Nir *and* Howard Schwartz. VWA
Along the River. D. J. Enright. DFF
Along the river edge. Breathe on the Glass. Raymond Stineford. AMV-81
Along the Road. Robert Browning Hamilton. BLPA; BLPL; TreFS
Along the road all shapes must travel by. Prolonged Sonnet: In the Last Days of the Emperor Henry VII. Simone Dall' Antella, *tr. by* Dante Gabriel Rossetti. AWP
Along the roadside, like the flowers of gold. Prelude. Whittier. *Fr.* Among the Hills. AP; OxBA; PoEL-4
Along the sea-edge, like a gnome. The Sandpiper. Witter Bynner. HBMV; RHPC
Along the serried coast the Southerly raves. Sea-Grief. Dowell O'Reilly. PoAu-1
Along the shore the slimy brine-pits yawn. The Witch's Whelp. Richard Henry Stoddard. AA
Along the shore the tall, thin grass. In Memory of Colonel Charles Young. Countee Cullen. PoBA
Along the sprawled body of the derailed. Outside Fargo, North Dakota. James Wright. LCAP; NNaP
Along the Strand. Alfred Mombert, *tr. fr. German by* Jethro Bithell. TrJP
Along the thousand roads of France. The Good Joan. Lizette Woodworth Reese. FaPON; MoShBr
Along the turner turnpike at a rest stop between. Poem near Midway Truck Stop. Lance Henson. STE
Along the walks the sweet queens walk their dogs. Central Park West. Jack Spicer. PeHV
Along the woodland path we took. Where You Passed. Amelia Josephine Burr. HBMV
Along this path he walked, great Washington. At Mount Vernon. Thomas Curtis Clark. PAL; PGD
Alons au bois le may cueillir. Charles d'Orléans, *tr. fr. French by* W. E. Henley. AWP
Alonso to Ferdinand. W. H. Auden. *Fr.* The Sea and the Mirror. MoPo
Alonzo the Brave and Fair Imogine. Matthew Gregory Lewis. *Fr.* The Monk. OBEC
Aloof. Christina Rossetti. The Thread of Life, I. OBEV; OBVV; TrGrPo
("Irresponsive silence of the land, The.") NOBE
(Thread of Life, The.) FaBoEn; OBNC
Aloof, as if a thing of mood and whim. The Schreckhorn. Thomas Hardy. OAEL-2
Aloof upon the day's immeasured dome. The Black Vulture. George Sterling. BPAW; HBV-1; PB
Aloofe, aloofe, and come no neare. The Sea Marke. John Smith. SCAP
Alow and aloof. The Windy Night. Thomas Buchanan Read. GN
Alpaca pictures of the previous past. Confounded Nonsense. Tom Hood. FaBoNo
Alphabet, The. Charles Stuart Calverley. HBV-2
Alphabet, The. Kate Greenaway. HBVY
Alphabet ("A tumbled down, and hurt his Arm, against a bit of wood"). Edward Lear. FaBoNo
Alphabet, An ("A was once an Apple pie"). Edward Lear. *See* Nonsense Alphabet, A.
Alphabet, The. Karl Shapiro. NoAM; PoA; VWA
Alphabet ("A, B, C, D, E, F, G"). *Unknown.* FaBoUs
Alphabet ("Great A was alarmed at B's bad behaviour"). *Unkno* FaBoUs
("Great A was alarmed at B's bad behaviour.") OxNR
Alphabet Calendar of Amergin, The. *Unknown, tr. fr. Irish by* Ro Graves. BIrV
(Song of Amergin.) MOON
Alphabet Came to Me, The. Jerome Rothenberg. VWA
Alphabet of Aristotle, The. *At. to* Mayster Benet. FaBoUs
Alphabet of, The/ the trees. The Botticellian Trees. William Carl Williams. AmPP; LiTA
Alphabet rejoiced to hear, The. A Literary Squabble. James Robin Planché. CenHV
Alphabet Stew. Jack Prelutsky. RHPC
Alphabetical Song on the Corn Law Bill. *Unknown.* OxBoLi
Alphonso of Castile. Emerson. AP; NOBA
Alpine. R. S. Thomas. BoNaP; LiSp; POL; RFM
Alpine Descent. Wordsworth. *See* Simplon Pass, The.
Alpine Spirit's Song. Thomas Lovell Beddoes. OBNC
Alpine View. Melville Cane. PoPl
Alps. Rosanna Warren. MAYP
Alps on Alps. Pope. *Fr.* An Essay on Criticism, Pt. II. FaFP
Already autumn begins here in the mossy rocks. Thinking of "The Aut Fields." Robert Bly. NNaP
Already batter'd, by his lee they lay. The Sea Battle. Dryden. *Fr.* An Mirabilis. FiP
Already blushes on thy cheek. Nemesis. Emerson. NOBA
Already fallen plum-bloom stars the green. The Poor Man's Pig. Edmu Blunden. MoBrPo
Already I am no longer looked at with lechery or love. A Sunset of the C Gwendolyn Brooks. PBWP
Already I Feel the Emptiness. Edgar Jackson. Three Songs, III. LFAC
Already in the dew-wrapped vineyards dry. Among the Orchards. Archibald Lampman. PeCV
Already it's late summer. Sunbathers go. The Divine Insect. John Hall Wheelock. GoYe; NYBP
Already she seems bone thin. A Poem about Breasts. James Wright. TA
Already, through the splendour ere the morn. Virgil's Farewell to Dante. Dante, *tr. by* Laurence Binyon. *Fr.* Divina Commedia: Purgatorio. FaBoTw
Already we are both fans of the green and golden dragon. A Natural History of Dragons and Unicorns My Daughter and I Have Known. William Pitt Root. AMV-81
Als I me rode this endre day. The Singing Maid. *Unknown.* MeEL
Also Ulysses once—that other war. Kilroy. Peter Viereck. FF; MoAmPo; NIP; PoRA
Alta Quies. A. E. Housman. *See* Parta Quies.
Altar, The. George Herbert. AnAnS-1; HoPM; InPS; JCP; OAEL-1; SeCP; SeCV-1; TrCP; TrGrPo
Altar, The. Jean Starr Untermeyer. HBMV
Altar Prayers. *Tr. fr. Hawaiian by* N. B. Emerson. WTO
Altarpiece Finished, The. John Hollander. NoAM
Altars and Sacrifice. Jay Wright. FB
Altars in the Street, The. Denise Levertov. CAPP
Altarwise by Owl-Light. Dylan Thomas. CoBMV; LiTM; MasP
Sels.
"Altarwise by owl-light in the half-way house," I. CMoP; FaBoMo; MoAB; NoAM
"And from the windy West came two-gunned Gabriel," V. NoAM
"Death is all metaphors, shape in one history," II. CMoP; MoAB; NoAM
"First there was the lamb on knocking knees," III. CMoP
"From the oracular archives and the parchment," IX. CMoP; NoAM
"Let the tale's sailor from a Christian voyage," X. CMoP; FaBoMo; NoAM; OAEL-2
"Now stamp the Lord's Prayer on a grain of rice," VII. FaBoMo
"This was the crucifixion on the mountain," VIII. CMoP; NoAM
"What is the metre of the dictionary?" IV. CMoP; FaBoMo
Alter! When the hills do. Emily Dickinson. AA; AmPP; FaBoBe
Altered look about the hills, An. Emily Dickinson. OxBA; PPP
Alternative Endings to an Unwritten Ballad. Paul Dehn. FiBHP
Alternatives. Kingsley Amis. OxBC
Alternatives. Peter Cooley. AmPA
Although accustomed to picking them, it always. The Woman and the Aloe. Perseus Adams. PeSA
Although art is autonomous. On This Day I Complete My Fortieth Year. Peter Porter. NAs
Although as yet my cure be incomplete. James Branch Cabell. Retractions, I. HBMV
Although confused with details and a dunce. To a History Professor. *Unknown, tr. by* Louis Untermeyer. UnTE
Although crowds gathered once if she but showed her face. Fallen Majesty. W. B. Yeats. PoA
Although, great Queen, thou now in silence lie. In Honour of That High and

Mighty Princess Queen Elizabeth of Happy Memory. Anne Bradstreet. SBG
Although he has no form. Mukta Bai, *tr. fr. Marathi by* Willis Barnstone. BoWoP
Although his actions won him wide renown. Anonymous Gravestone. Erich Kästner, *tr. by* Patrick Bridgewater. ELU
Although I be the basest of mankind. St. Simeon Stylites. Tennyson. OAEL-2
Although I can see him still. The Fisherman. W. B. Yeats. BiP; CMoP; CoBMV; HAP; LiSp; NoAM
Although I cry and though my eyes still shed. Sonnet XIV. Louise Labé, *tr. by* Willis Barnstone. BoWoP
Although I do not hope to turn again. T. S. Eliot. Ash Wednesday, VI. FaBoEn
Although I do not know. Saigyo Hoshi, *tr. fr. Japanese by* Arthur Waley. AWP
Although I enter not. At the Church Gate. Thackeray. *Fr.* Pendennis. HBV-1
Although I feel its shape could knit my bones. The Shirt. Jon Silkin. NoAM
Although I had a check. Earl of Surrey. SiPS
Although I leave Braglu, I am close to it. I Djanggawul, am paddling. Djanggawul Song-Cycle. *Aborigine Oral Tradition, tr. by* R. M. Berndt. WTO
Although I mean it, and project the meaning. The Ice-Cream Wars. John Ashbery. PoA
Although I put away his life. Emily Dickinson. MoAmPo
Although I shelter from the rain. The Lamentation of the Old Pensioner. W. B. Yeats. HAP; InPK; PPON; TW; WeW
Although I was her pupil,/ even I reproach Myrtis. Korinna, *tr. fr. Greek by* Willis Barnstone. BoWoP. *See also* I blame Myrtis.
Although I'm oldest I can't. Daughter. Kimiko Hahn. BrSi
Although in a Crystal. Anselm Parlatore. SUW
Although it is a cold evening. At the Fishhouses. Elizabeth Bishop. CoAP; HAP; LCAP; LiTM; MoVE; NoP; NYBP; PoRA
Although it is night, I sit in the bathroom, waiting. Adolescence—II. Rita Dove. AmPA
Although it is not plainly visible to the eye. Fujiwara no Toshiyuki, *tr. by* Arthur Waley. *Fr.* Kokin Shu. AWP
Although it may appear archaic. Eppur Si Muove? Robert Hillyer. GoYe
Although it's cold no clothes I wear. *Unknown.* GBP
Although it's true. An Expanded Want Ad. Brad Leithauser. MAYP
Although lamps burn along the silent streets. James Thomson ("B. V."). The City of Dreadful Night, III. EBVV
Although Michaelmas Daisies bloom for a very long time. Gather Ye Rosebuds. Laurence Fowler. BXAP
Although my claws weaken. Sweetness. *Unknown, tr. by* John Montague. BIrV
Although my father's only child. Cecilia. *Unknown, tr. by* William McLennan. WHW
Although only a fool would mock. Queen Mother to New Queen. Robert Graves. OBSV
Although she feeds me bread of bitterness. America. Claude McKay. BALP; CDC; NIP; NoAM; PoBA; PoNe; TAP; TTY
Although some are afraid that to speak of a spade as a spade is a social mistake. Rigoletto. Newman Levy. OBAL
Although the aepyornis. He "Digesteth Harde Yron." Marianne Moore. CMoP; NoAM
Although the bed, by hollow shadowing. A Simpler Thing, a Chair. Robert Mezey. NePoEA
Although the house is gone, how well I know. Old House Place. Velma Sanders. AMV-80
Although the lattice had dropped loose. The Bride's Prelude. Dante Gabriel Rossetti. SeCePo
Although the night is damp. The Firefly Lights His Lamp. *Unknown.* SoPo
Although the ship's bell marks the time, it is. Concert at Sea. Hubert Creekmore. WaP
Although the snow still lingers. Last Snow. Andrew Young. OxBTC
Although thy blood be frozen, and thy scalp. To a Covetous Churl. Edward May. FaBoEE
Although thy hand and faith, and good works too. Change. John Donne. Elegies, III. EBEV; ViBoPo
Although Tormented. Kalonymos ben Judah, *tr. fr. Hebrew.* TrJP
Although what glitters. Two Paintings by Gustav Klimt. Jorie Graham. SV
Although you died in a distant land. Vigil. Marjorie Freeman Campbell. CaP
Although you mention Venice. For the Stranger. Carolyn Forché. MAYP
Although you move among them as a friend. The Coolin Ridge. William Bell. PoSH
Although your charms are many. To Natalie. Morrie Ryskind. HBMV
Altitudes. Richard Wilbur. CMoP
Alton Locke, *sel.* Charles Kingsley.
Sands of Dee, The, *fr. ch.* 26. BeLS; CH; EBVV; FaBoPP; FaPON; FaPoR; GN; HBV-1; PoPle; TreF; VLP; WBLP
Alulvan. Walter de la Mare. MoVE
Alumnus Football. Grantland Rice. FPL; PoLF
"You'll find the road is long and rough, with soft spots far apart," *sel.* TreFS
Always. Pablo Neruda, *tr. fr. Spanish by* Donald D. Walsh. OLR
Always/ Always. Poem to My Father. Joseph Stroud. NPGG
Always a third one's there. The Uninvited. Dorothy Livesay. NOBC
Always alone, star-told? Man. Samuel Greenberg. CrMA
Always at dusk, the same tearless experience. The Eyes of My Regret. Angelina Weld Grimké. CDC
Always Battling. Thomas O'Brien. NeIP
Always before, we sped in the same direction. The Queen. Kenneth Pitchford. NYBP; NYP
Always before Your Voice My Soul. E. E. Cummings. LiTA; MoAmPo; NePA; TwAmPo
Always Begin Where You Are. Thomas Hornsby Ferril. PrIm; VGW
Always driven, always in the bite of the blast. And Yet We Are Here! Karl Wolfskehl, *tr. by* Carol North Valhope *and* Ernst Morwitz. TrJP
Always expecting the winter. In Dream: The Privacy of Sequence. Ray A. Young Bear. CDW
Always Finish. *Unknown.* BLPA; FaBoBe; WBLP
(Perseverance.) TreFT
Always for thirty years now. Fish Peddler and Cobbler. Kenneth Rexroth. NNaP
Always, from My First Boyhood. John Peale Bishop. VGW
Always happy, always bright. The Commission Man. Robert V. Carr. BPAW
Always have these clear sounds been in your ear. Poem for You. Robert Pack. NePoEA
Always he sits in his accustomed place. Habitué. Helen Frith Stickney. GoYe
Always, here where I sleep, I hear the sound of the sea. The Sound of the Sea. John Hall Wheelock. EtS
Always hung on its plaque. Thermometer Wine. Robert Morgan. SUW
Always I have been a cottonwood. The Gathering. Dwayne Thorpe. AMV-81
Always I lay upon the brink of love. Judas. Vassar Miller. MoAmPo
Always—I tell you this they learned. House Fear. Robert Frost. *Fr.* The Hill Wife. VGW; WSC
Always in that valley in Wales I hear the noise. Waterfalls. Vernon Watkins. NoAM
Always in the Parting Year. Else Lasker-Schüler, *tr. fr. German by* Ralph Manheim. TrJP
Always in transit. Tenantry. George Scarbrough. TAT
Always I've loved the transient things that die. Unseen Flight. Markos Georgeou. AMV-80
Always lately on the rim of. Dream Girl. Karen Snow. HoAn
Always Modern Times. Bradford Stark. LTB
Always on Monday, God's [name is] in the morning papers. The Day after Sunday. Phyllis McGinley. MoAmPo; OBSV; UnPo
Always on the point of falling asleep. The Middle Ages. John Haines. LCAP
Always she goes like a captured wild bird. Sappho. Jack Cope. PeSA
Always she loved the sound of bells. Joan of Arc. Hugh McCrae. PoAu-1
Always She Moves from Me. Shirley Kaufman. WPE
Always the Following Wind. W. H. Auden. MoBrPo
Always the ghost of these will wake again. Oxford Bells. Sister Maris Stella. GoBC
Always the heavy air. The Lion-House. John Hall Wheelock. HBMV
Always the Melting Moon Comes. Margot Osborn. CaP
Always the same, when on a fated night. The Onset. Robert Frost. AP; CMoP; CoBMV; MoAB; MoAmPo; OxBA; PPP
Always the setting forth was the same. Odysseus. W. S. Merwin. NOBA; NoP
Always there is someone who has turned away. The Hermit. Howard Moss. NePoAm
Always there's some boy. Coda. Fred Johnson. CNA
Always to want to. The Tortoise. Cid Corman. InPK; VGW
Always too eager for the future, we. Next, Please. Philip Larkin. HeIP; MoBrPo; NePoEA
Always we have believed. Disguises. Elizabeth Jennings. NePoEA-2
Always We Watch Them. Paul Mariah. LFAC
Always within me lies. Homage to Ghosts. Jean Garrigue. TwAmPo
Always you begin the same. Nantucket's Widows. Richard Foerster. AMV-81
Always your body like a foreign country. Location. Knute Skinner. MAT
Alysoun ("Betwene Mersh [*or* March] and Averil"). GoBC; HAP; HeIP; OxBM

(Alison.) HAP; MeEL; NoP; OAEL-1; OBEV
(Alisoun.) CTC; PoEL-1
("Bytuene Mersh and Averil.") ViBoPo
Alysoun ("Lenten ys come with love to towne"). *Unknown.* *See* Lenten Is Come.
Am Driven Mad. Allen Polite. NNP
Am I. Message Clear. Edwin Morgan. NIP
Am I a king, that I should call my own. From My Arm-Chair. Longfellow. BLPA
Am I a stone and not a sheep. Good Friday. Christina Rossetti. OFD; PoEL-5; TRV
Am I alone—or is it you, my friend? Toussaint L'Ouverture. E. A. Robinson. PoNe
Am I despised because you say. To a Gentlewoman Objecting to Him His Grey Hairs [*or* Age Not to Be Rejected]. Robert Herrick. CaPo; JCP; OBS
Am I emptied, Lord, of self? Heartsearch. Evelyn K. Gibson. STF
Am I failing? For no longer can I cast. Modern Love, XXIX. George Meredith. CABA; GBL; OAEP
Am I mad, O noble Festus. The Distracted Puritan. Richard Corbet. OxBoLi
Am I sincere? I say I dote. To Anthea, Who May Command Him Anything New Style. Alfred Cochrane. HBV-1
Am I the slave they say. Soggarth Aroon. John Banim. GoBC
Am I thy gold? Or purse, Lord, for thy wealth. Edward Taylor. Preparatory Meditations, First Series, VI. AP; LiTA; NePA; OxBA; TAP; TrCP
Am I to become profligate as if I were a blonde? Meditations in an Emergency. Frank O'Hara. TAP
Am I too dangerous, that no man can let. D. B. Wyndham Lewis. *Fr.* If So the Man You Are. OBSV
Am I your only love—in the whole world—now? Tell Me Again. Nigâr Hanim, *tr. by* Tâlat S. Halman. PBWP
Am not I in blessed case. My Dear Lady. *Unknown.* EIL
Amagansett Beach Revisited. John Hall Wheelock. NYBP
Amalek. Friedrich Torberg, *tr. fr. German by* Erna Baber Rosenfeld. VWA
Amanda Barker. Edgar Lee Masters. *Fr.* Spoon River Anthology. NoAM
Amanda Dreams She Has Died and Gone to the Elysian Fields. Maxine W. Kumin. GP
Amanda is sending messages again. Amanda, Playing. C. W. Truesdale. PoDr
Amanda Is Shod. Maxine W. Kumin. PH
Amanda, Playing. C. W. Truesdale. PoDr
Amanda's Complaint. Philip Freneau. AP
Amantium Irae. Ernest Dowson. HBV-1
Amantium Irae [Amoris Redintegratio]. Richard Edwards. EIL; HBV-2; LoBV; OBEV; OBSC
Amarantha sweet and fair. To Amarantha, That She Would Dishevel Her Hair. Richard Lovelace. AnAnS-2; CaPo; HBV-1; HoPM; MePo; NIP; NoP; OBEV; SeCP; SeCV-1; TrGrPo; UnTE; ViBoPo
Amaryllis [*or* Amarillis]. Thomas Campion. *See* I Care Not for These Ladies.
Amasis. Laurence Binyon. OBVV
Amateur and muddled, as their sex goes. The Professionals. Geoffrey Grigson. PoA
Amateur Flute, The. *Unknown.* BXAP; Par; SpRo
Amateurs, we gathered mushrooms. Fall. Robert Hass. AmPA
Amaturus. William Johnson Cory. HBV-1
A-Maying, a-Playing. Thomas Nashe. *Fr.* Summer's Last Will and Testament. EIL
(Clownish Song, A.) OBSC
Amaze. Adelaide Crapsey. QFR
Amazement fills my heart to-night. Thanksgiving. Robert Nichols. MMA
Amazing Grace. Anselm Hollo. PoM
Amazing Grace. John Newton. BLSo, *with music*; FSW
Amazing monster! that, for aught I know. A Fish Replies [*or* Answers]. Leigh Hunt. *Fr.* The Fish, the Man, and the Spirit. FiBHP; MOS; MoShBr; NOBL; RoGo
Amazing Sight! The Saviour Stands. Henry Alline. *Fr.* Christ Inviting Sinners to His Grace. AH, *with music;* CaP
Amazing thing happened to me, An. A Sonnet. Daniil Kharms, *tr. by* George Gibian. FaBoNo
Ambarvalia, *sel.* Arthur Hugh Clough.
Pont-y-Wern. FaBoPP
Ambassador Puser the ambassador. Memorial Rain. Archibald MacLeish. AmPP; CMoP; LiTA; MoAB; MoAmPo; NoAM; OBWP; TwAmPo
Ambassadors, The. Paul Lawson. GP
Amber Bead, The. Robert Herrick. CaPo; ChTr
(Trapped Fly, A.) WiR
Amber Beads. Audrey Alexandra Brown. CaP
Amber the sky. Rokwaho. STE
Amber the wine. At the Party. Freda Laughton. NeIP
Ambiguous Dog, The. Arthur Guiterman. GDP
Ambiguous Time, I heard you sighing. Montgomery. J. C. Hall. ChMP
Ambition. Edith Agnew. TiPo
Ambition. Morris Bishop. AmFN
Ambition. W. H. Davies. MoBrPo; TrGrPo
Ambition. Robert Herrick. CaPo
Ambition. Aline Kilmer. HBMV
Ambition. Pope. DBV
Ambition. Shakespeare. King Henry VIII, *fr.* III, ii. TrGrPo
Ambition. Nathaniel Parker Willis. OBCA
Ambitious Ant, The. Amos R. Wells. OBCA
Ambitious Gorgons, wide-mouthed Lamians. John Marston. *Fr.* Satire V. ViBoPo
Amboyna; or, The Cruelties of the Dutch to the English Merchants, *sel.* Dryden.
"As needy gallants in the scriv'ners' hands," Prologue. OBSV
Ambrosia of Dionysus and Semele, The. Robert Graves. NYBP
Ambulance Call. Lorrie Goldensohn. AMV-81
Ambulance flies at a furious gait, The. Hell's Bells. Margaret Fishback. ShM
Ambulance men touched her cold, The. The Death of Marilyn Monroe. Sharon Olds. MAYP
Ambulance Train 30. Carola Oman. SUMH
Ambulances. Philip Larkin. FaBoTw; OxBC
Ambuscade. Hugh McCrae. PoAu-1
Ambushed by Angels. Gustav Davidson. GoYe
Ambushed myself discovered. Humility. Marie Luise Kaschnitz, *tr. by* Michael Hamburger. WPOW
Ameinias. John Simon. ELU
Amelia Mixed the Mustard. A. E. Housman. DBV; FaBoNo; RHPC; WhC
Amelia Street. Frank Ormsby. CIP
Amen. A. C. Benson. OBVV
Amen. F. G. Browning. BLRP
Amen. Alvaro Mutis, *tr. fr. Spanish by* James Normington. AMV-81
Amen. Jaime Sabines, *tr. fr. Spanish by* Steve Kowit. AMV-81
Amen. Richard W. Thomas. PoBA
Amend Me. *Unknown.* OxBM
Amendis to the Telyouris and Sowtaris for the Turnament Maid on Thame, The. William Dunbar. *See* Amends to the Tailors and Soutars.
Amendment. Thomas Traherne. SeCV-2
Amends for Ladies, *sel.* Nathaniel Field.
Rise, Lady Mistress, Rise! EIL
(Matin Song.) HBV-1
(Song: "Rise Lady Mistresse, rise.") OBS
Amends to Nature. Arthur Symons. HBMV
Amends to the Tailors and Soutars. William Dunbar. BSV
(Amendis to the Telyouris and Sowtaris for the Turnament Maid on Thame, The.) OBSV
America. Donald G. Babcock. NePoAm
America. Arlo Bates. *Fr.* The Torch-Bearers. AA; PAL
America. Bryant. *See* Oh Mother of a Mighty Race.
America. Arthur Cleveland Coxe. PAH
America. Robert Creeley. MAT
America. Sydney Dobell. OBVV
"Nor force nor fraud shall sunder us!" *sel.* HBV-2; PAL
America. Henry Dumas. BOLo; PoBA
America. Allen Ginsberg. CABA; CAPP; CoAP; NaP; NMP; NoAM; PoM; PPoe; PPP
America. Bobb Hamilton. BOLo
America. Claude McKay. BALP; CDC; NIP; NoAM; PoBA; PoNe; TAP; TTY
America. John Newlove. NOBC
America. Wendy Rose. CDW
America. Samuel Francis Smith. AA; BLSo, *with music*; FaBoBe; FaFP; FaPON; HBV-2; HBVY; PAL; PoLF; PSoN, *with music*; TreF; WBLP; YaD
America. Bayard Taylor. *Fr.* The National Ode, July 4, 1876. AA; PAL
America. Walt Whitman. GOA
America/ I/ carry/ you. The Pinta, the Nina and the Santa Maria. John Tagliabue. AmFN
America/ Is a fairyland fraud. America. Bobb Hamilton. BOLo
America; a Prophecy. Blake. OAEL-2
Empire Is No More, *sel.* EnRP
America, America! Delmore Schwartz. NYP
America at the end. The Children Grown. Haywood Jackson. SOTS
America Bleeds. Angelo Lewis. PoBA
America! dear brother land! Greeting from England. *Unknown.* PAH
America First! G. Ashton Oldham. PGD
America for Me. Henry van Dyke. BLPA; BLPL; FaFP; HBVY; OHFP; PAL; SoSe; TreFS; WBLP
America Greets an Alien. *Unknown.* PAL; PGD
"America, I Love You." Bert Kalmar *and* Harry Ruby. FiBHP; InMe
America Is Great Because. *At. to* Alexis de Tocqueville. TreFT

America is West and the wind blowing. Archibald MacLeish. *Fr.* American Letter. AmFN
America, it is to thee. From America. James M. Whitfield. BPo
America I've given you all and now I'm nothing. America. Allen Ginsberg. CABA; CAPP; CoAP; NaP; NMP; NoAM; PoM; PPoe; PPP
America, last hope of man and truth. Arlo Bates. *Fr.* The Torch-Bearers. PGD
America, my own! National Song. William Henry Venable. PAH
America, O Power benign, great hearts revere your name. Land of the Free. Arthur Nicholas Hosking. BLPA; PAL
America Prays. Arthur Gordon Field. PGD
America the Beautiful. Katharine Lee Bates. BLPA; EaLo; FaBoBe; FaBV; FaFP; FaPON; FSW; GOA; HBMV; HBVY; PAL; TAP; TreF; WBLP; WGRP; YaD
America the Beautiful. Stan Rice. NPGG
America, the land beloved. The Name of Washington. Arthur Gordon Field. PAL; PGD
America! thou fractious nation. A Proclamation. *Unknown.* PAH
America to England. George Edward Woodberry. AA
America to Great Britain. Washington Allston. AA; HBV-2
America was always promises. Archibald MacLeish. *Fr.* America Was Promises. AmFN
America was forests. America Was Schoolmasters. Robert P. Tristram Coffin. PAL
America Was Promises, *sels.* Archibald MacLeish.
"America was always promises." AmFN
"America was promises—to whom?" PAL
America Was Schoolmasters. Robert P. Tristram Coffin. PAL
America will never forgive you. H. Rap Brown. Henry Blakely. CNA
America, you ode for reality! America. Robert Creeley. MAT
American against Solitude. Alan Dugan. CAPP
American Ash. Stanley Plumly. GeTw
American Bandstand. Michael Waters. MAYP
American Boyhood, An. Jonathan Holden. Psk
American Child. Paul Engle. AmFN
American Commencement. Aram Boyajian. NeAC
American Dream, The, *sel.* Johnie Scott.
"'Speech, or dark cities screaming.'" NBP
American Dreams. Louis Simpson. GP
American Eagle, The. D. H. Lawrence. OAEL-2
American eagle is not aware he is, The. Eagle Plain. Robert Francis. AmFN
American Falls. Greg Keeler. WOLT
American Farm, 1934. Genevieve Taggard. VGW
American Flag, The. Joseph Rodman Drake. AA; FaBoBe; FaFP; GN; HBV-2; HBVY; PAH; PAL; PaPo; PGD; TreF; WBLP
American! frigate, a frigate of fame, An. Paul Jones's Victory. *Unknown.* AmFP; TrAS
American frigate from Baltimore came, An. Paul Jones. *Unknown.* PAH; PAL
American Girl, An. Brander Matthews. AA
American Gothic. Samuel Allen. *See* To Satch.
American Heartbreak. Langston Hughes. AmPP; BPo; CABA; LiTM
American Heritage. Robert Sward. OBAL
American Hero, The. Nathaniel Niles. *See* Bunker Hill.
American hero must triumph over, The. Eisenhower's Visit to Franco, 1959. James Wright. CAPP; NaP; NMP
American History. Michael S. Harper. BPo
American History. W. R. Moses. LiTA
American Independence. Francis Hopkinson. PAH
American Indian, The. *Unknown.* FaBoCo; FiBHP
American jump, American jump. *Unknown.* OxNR
American Landscape with Clouds & a Zoo. Jon Anderson. MAYP
American Laughter. Kenneth Allan Robinson. AmFN; TreFS
American Letter. Archibald MacLeish. AmPP; OxBA
"America is West and the wind blowing," *sel.* AmFN
American Lights Seen from Off Abroad. John Berryman. LCAP; OBAL
American muse, whose strong and diverse heart. Invocation. Stephen Vincent Benét. *Fr.* John Brown's Body. AmFN; CrMA; PAL
American Names. Stephen Vincent Benét. AmFN; GOA; OBAL; OxBA; TreFT; YaD
American Patriot's Prayer, The. *Unknown.* PAH
American Plan. John Malcolm Brinnin. GOA
American Poetry. Louis Simpson. ELU; NoAM; NOBA; PP; TAP
American Portrait: Old Style. Robert Penn Warren. FYAP
American Primitive. William Jay Smith. DiL; FF; InPK; MoAmPo; MP; NePoAm; NePoEA; PAI; PoPl; PPON; TwCP
American Rhapsody. Kenneth Fearing. MoAmPo
American Soldier, The. Philip Freneau. TAP
American Soldier's Hymn, The. *Unknown.* PAH
American Takes a Walk, An. Reed Whittemore. MoVE
American to France, An. Alice Duer Miller. HBMV
American Traveller, The. "Orpheus C. Kerr." FaBoCo; OBAL; WhC
American Twilights, 1957. James Wright. CoAP
American Vineyard. Mildred Cousens. GoYe
Americana XIII: "Captain Patterson, the folks back home." Carl Rakosi. InPS
Americana XVII: Reminder of William Carlos Williams, A. Carl Rakosi. InPS
Americana XV: Simplicity. Carl Rakosi. InPS
(Simplicity.) GP
Americana IX: "Your correspondent must be kidding when he says." Carl Rakosi. InPS
Americanized. Bruce Dawe. CBAP
Americans! Philip Freneau. *Fr.* Reflections. PPON
American's a hustler, for he says so, The. A Ballad of Abbreviations. G. K. Chesterton. NOBL
Americans Are Afraid of Lizards. Karl Shapiro. AmFN
Americans are always moving on. Stephen Vincent Benét. *Fr.* Western Star. AmFN
Americans in an Orange Grove. Arthur Vogelsang. MAYP
Americans pass by. Baja—Outside Mexicali. Michael McClure. GP
Americans, rejoice. Old Song Written during Washington's Life. *Unknown.* OHIP
America's Answer. R. W. Lilliard. BLPA; PAL
America's Gospel. James Russell Lowell. PGD
America's Prosperity. Henry van Dyke. PGD
America's Wounded Knee. Phillip William George. VoR
Americus, as he did wend. The Noble Tuck-Man. Jean Ingelow. NA
Ametas and Thestylis Making Hay-Ropes. Andrew Marvell. CavP; InvP; SeCP
Amid a wilderness of rock-piled towers. From Sappho's Death: Three Pictures by Gustave Moreau. T. Sturge Moore. SyP
Amid all Triads let it be confest. Epigram. Richard Garnett. OBVV
Amid conversation. I Go to Whiskey Bars. Raymond Thompson. LFAC
Amid curled leaves and green. Peach Tree with Fruit. Padraic Colum. BoNaP
Amid my bale I bathe in bliss. A Strange [*or* Straunge] Passion of a Lover. George Gascoigne. AAS; EnRePo
Amid the chapel's chequered gloom. Heliotrope. Harry Thurston Peck. AA; HBV-1
Amid the cloistered gloom of Aachen's aisle. The Opening of the Tomb of Charlemagne. Sir Aubrey De Vere. HBV-2
Amid the deafening traffic of the town. To a Passer-by. Baudelaire, *tr. by* C. F. MacIntyre. NAWM-2; SyP
Amid the Din of Earthly Strife. Henry Warburton Hawkes. TRV
Amid the fairest things that grow. Her Dwelling-Place. Ada Foster Murray. HBV-1
Amid the noncommitted compounds of the mind. Metagnomy. N. H. Pritchard. NBP
Amid the nut grove, still and brown. The Faerie's Child. Thomas Caulfield Irwin. OnYI
Amid the stony slapping of the waves. Barnacle Geese. Charles Higham. PoAu-2
Amid the thunders of the falling dark. The Coat of Fire. Edith Sitwell. OAEP
Amid this hot green glowing gloom. Interlude. Edith Sitwell. MoAB; MoBrPo
Amid Tibetan snows the ancient lama. What Hath Man Wrought Exclamation Point. Morris Bishop. NYBP
Amidst a wood of oaks with canvas leaves. Description of a Ninety Gun Ship. William Falconer. PeD
Amidst fruitless activity and fat idleness. Haifa Dovid Knut, *tr. by* Daniel Weissbort. VWA
Amidst the fairest mountain tops. Cynthia. Sir Edward Dyer. OBSC
Amiens's Song: "Blow, blow, thou winter wind." Shakespeare. *See* Blow, Blow, Thou Winter Wind.
Amiens's Song: "Under the greenwood tree." Shakespeare. *See* Under the Greenwood Tree.
Amiens's Song: "What shall he have that killed the deer?" Shakespeare. *See* Song: "What shall he have that kill'd the deer?"
Aminta, *sel.* Tasso, *tr. fr. Italian.*
Pastoral, A: "Oh happy golden age," *tr. by* Samuel Daniel. OAEL-1; OBSC; PoEL-2
(Golden Age, The, *tr. by* Leigh Hunt.) AWP
("O lovely age of gold!," *tr. by* Leigh Hunt.) OBVE
Amintas and Claudia; or, The Merry Shepherdess. *Unknown.* CoMu
Amish, The. William Doreski. SOTS
Amish, The. John Updike. OBAL
Amnesiac. Mark Osaki. BrSi
Amnesiac. Sylvia Plath. NYBP
Amo, Amas. John O'Keefe. ChTr; GBL
Amoeba Named Sam, An. *Unknown.* QQQ

Amoebaean Eclogues, *sel.* John Scott.
How to Fertilize Soil, *fr.* II. FaBoUs
Among/ of/ green. The Locust Tree in Flower. William Carlos Williams. SOTW
Among all lovely things my love had been. Wordsworth. GBL
Among Blackberries. Michael Waters. GeTw
Among branches. Gray Glove. Roo Borson. NOBC
Among Commuters. Jon Swan. NYP
Among Friends. Greg Kuzma. AMV-80
Among green shades and flowering ghosts, the remembrances of love. The Two Fires. Judith Wright. MoBrPo
Among Hawks. Lance Henson. VoR
Among High Hills. William Soutar. PoSH
Among his books he sits all day. A Tragedy. Edith Nesbit. HBV-1
Among His Effects We Found a Photograph. Ed Ochester. Str
Among Iron Fragments. Tuvia Ruebner, *tr. fr. Hebrew by* Robert Friend. VWA
Among left trucks, mailbags, churns. Homing Pigeons. Ted Walker. NYBP
Among other things, he smiles at lit lightbulbs. Seeing and Doing. John Dean. AMV-81
Among our country's outlaws. Jesse James. Rosemary *and* Stephen Vincent Benét. BPAW
Among our flocks of hard days. My Mother. Hayim Naggid, *tr. by* Rose Drachler. VWA
Among our young lass[i]es is [*or* there's] Muirland Meg. Muirland Meg [*or* She'll Do It]. Burns. ErPo; UnTE
Among Pelagian travellers. On the Circuit. W. H. Auden. NOBL; OxBTC
Among poppies in a field of maize. Death in the Corn. Detlev von Liliencron, *tr. by* C. F. MacIntyre. WaaP
Among rocks, I am the loose one. Night Song. Lisel Mueller. AMV-80
Among School Children. W. B. Yeats. AnIL; BLPL; CABA; ChMP; CMoP; CoBMV; FaBoEn; GTBS-P; HAP; LiTB; LiTM; MoAB; MoBrPo; MoVE; NIP; NoAM; NOBE; NoP; OAEL-2; OAEP; OxBTC; PPoe; PPP; PrIm; SeCeV; TrGrPo; WeW
Among Sharks. Al Lee. AmPA
Among snake-patterned swords Weland tasted sorrow. Deor. *Unknown, tr. by* John Wain. EBEV
Among Strangers. William Stafford. NNaP
Among stray quartz pebbles turned up. The Pheasant Hunter and the Arrowhead. Julian Gitzen. AMV-80
Among that band of Officers was one. Wordsworth. *Fr.* The Prelude, IX. ChER
Among the agents used by counterfeiters. There Is No Balm in Birmingham. Ann Deagon. NIP
Among the Anthropophagi. Ogden Nash. CenHV
(Funebrial Reflections.) ImOP
Among the Beautiful Pictures. Alice Cary. BLPA
Among the birds in the sky above. Nature in Couplets. Charlton Ogburn. GrPl
Among the bumble-bees in red-top hay. Adelaide Crapsey. Carl Sandburg. HBMV
Among the cigarettes and the peppermint creams. Far West. A. J. M. Smith. PeCV
Among the coffee cups and soup toureens walked Beauty. Jack Spicer. PeHV
Among the Daffadillies. Giles Farnaby. OAEP
Among the Ferns. Edward Carpenter. WGRP
Among the Finger Lakes. Robert Wallace. GrPl
Among the first to go are always a few. Only the Beards Are Different. Bruce Dawe. PoAu-2
Among the greatest plagues, one is the third day ague. Of Scolding Wives and the Third Day Ague. Henricus Selyns. SCAP
Among the guests who often stayed. Shelley. *Fr.* Peter Bell the Third. ChER
Among the high-branching, leafless boughs. The View from an Attic Window. Howard Nemerov. CoAP; ConAP
Among the hills of St. Jerome. At St. Jerome. Frances Harrison. WHW
Among the Hills, *sel.* Whittier.
Prelude: "Along the roadside, like the flowers of gold." AP; OxBA; PoEL-4
Among the iodoform, in twilight-sleep. The Leg. Karl Shapiro. DFF; HAP; MoAB; MoAmPo; TrGrPo; UnPo; WeW
Among the leaves the small birds sing. Lauds. W. H. Auden. TrCP
Among the Millet. Archibald Lampman. CaP; WHW
Among the Narcissi. Sylvia Plath. FaBoMo; SCV
Among the orchard weeds, from every search. Hen's Nest. John Clare. PBBP
Among the Orchards. Archibald Lampman. PeCV
Among the oxen (like an ox I'm slow). The Nativity. C. S. Lewis. EBCP; TrCP
Among the pickled foetuses and bottled bones. "Siena Mi Fe'; Disfecemi Maremma." Ezra Pound. *Fr.* Hugh Selwyn Mauberley. MoAmPo
Among the Pine Trees. Moshe Dor, *tr. fr. Hebrew by* Elaine Feinstein. VWA
Among the plastic flowers one honest one. The Woolworth Philodendron. Stephen Sandy. CoPo
Among the priceless gems and treasures rare. Pastel. Francis Saltus Saltus. AA
Among the rain. The Great Figure. William Carlos Williams. NoAM; QFR
Among the Roman love-poets, possession. Note on Propertius 1.5. Fleur Adcock. BoLoP
Among the rushes lived a mouse. The Needless Alarm. John Ruskin. FM
"Among the Savages. . ." Ralph Salisbury. STE
Among the Shades. Thomas Campion. *See* When Thou Must Home.
Among the signs of autumn I perceive. Tall Ambrosia. Henry David Thoreau. PoEL-4
Among the silver cornstalks. Eve. Robert L. Wolf. HBMV
Among the smoke and fog of a December afternoon. Portrait of a Lady. T. S. Eliot. HBMV; MP; TwAmPo; TwCP
Among the springs which flow from Ida's head. *Unknown, formerly at. to* Homer; *tr. by* Congreve. *Fr.* The Hymn to Venus. OBVE
Among the taller wood with ivy hung. The Vixen. John Clare. BoAnP
Among the thousand, thousand spheres that roll. Alcyone. Frances Laughton Mace. AA
Among the topless dancers. The Roses of Queens. Claire Nicholas White. NYP
Among the woods and tillage. Yattendon. Sir Henry Newbolt. HBMV
Among the Worst of Men That Ever Lived. Henry David Thoreau. PoEL-4
Among them marble where the man may lie. A Thurn. John Berryman. NOBA
Among these mountains, do you know. For Allan, Who Wanted to See How I Wrote a Poem. Robert Frost. PChr
Among these North Shore tennis tans I sit. Commencement, Pingree School. John Updike. Str
Among these tempests great and manifold. His Hope or Sheet-Anchor. Robert Herrick. CaPo
Among These Troopes of Christs Souldiers, Came. . .Mr. Roger Harlackenden. Edward Johnson. SCAP
Among These Turf-Stacks. Louis MacNeice. LiTB; SeCePo; WaP
(Turf-Stacks.) LiTM; OBMV
Among those joys, 'tis one at eve to sail. Sailing upon the River. George Crabbe. *Fr.* The Borough. OBNC
Among Those Killed in the Dawn Raid Was a Man Aged One Hundred. Dylan Thomas. MoPo
Among those things that make our love complete. Love's Immortality. Elsa Barker. *Fr.* The Spirit and the Bride. HBMV
Among those who promised us our honors. Palermo, Mother's Day, 1943. William Belvin. PoPl
Among thy fancies, tell me this. The Kisse. Robert Herrick. CavP
Among trees/ my father was a spruce. Family Photograph. Gerald Vizenor. VoR
Among twenty snowy mountains. Thirteen Ways of Looking at a Blackbird. Wallace Stevens. AP; BLPL; CABA; CMoP; CoBMV; HeIP; InPK; LiTM; NoAM; NOBA; NoP; PAI; SOTW; TAP; TwAmPo
Amongst the pure ones all. The Quaker's Song. *Unknown.* CoMu
Amor Loci. W. H. Auden. NOCV
Amor Mundi. Christina Rossetti. NBM; NoP; PoEL-5
Amor Mysticus. Sister Marcela de Carpio de San Felix, *tr. fr. Spanish by* John Hay. AWP
Amor Triumphans, *sel.* Arthur Symons.
Return, The. BrPo
Amores (after Ovid). Jay Parini. MAYP
Amores, *sels.* Ovid, *tr. fr. Latin.*
Apology for Loose Behavior, II, 4, *tr. by* Christopher Marlowe. UnTE
Corinnae Concubitus, I, 5, *tr. by* Christopher Marlowe. GBL
(Elegy: "In summer's heat and mid-time of the day.") BoLoP
("In summer's heat, and mid-time of the day.") EBEV; OBVE; UnTE
(Ovid's Fifth Elegy.) NCEP
Corinna, Having Tried, with Her Own Hand, *fr.* II, 13, *tr. by* Rolfe Humphries. NAs
"Cypassis, that a thousand ways trimm'st hair," II, 8, *tr. by* Christopher Marlowe. EBEV
"Does anyone these days respect the artist," III, 8, *tr. by* Guy Lee. NAWM-1
"Either she was foule, or her attire was bad," III, 6, *tr. by* Christopher Marlowe. OBVE
(Impotent Lover, The.) UnTE
(Shameful Impotence.) ErPo
"Graecinus (well I wot) thou told'st me once," II, 10, *tr. by* Christopher Marlowe. EBEV

("Graecinus, I blame you. Yours that memorable remark," *tr. by* Guy Lee.) NAWM-1
"I ask but right: let her that caught me late," I, 3, *tr. by* Christopher Marlowe. EBEV
"I Ovid poet of my wantonnesse," II, 1, *tr. by* Christopher Marlowe. OBVE
("Another collection of verse by the man from Sulmona," *tr. by* Guy Lee.) NAWM-1
"Now ore the sea from her old love comes she," I, 13, *tr. by* Christopher Marlowe. OBVE
"Offered a sexless heaven I'd say 'No thank you'," II, 9b, *tr. by* Guy Lee. NAWM-1
"Seeing thou art faire, I barre not thy false playing," III, 13, *tr. by* Christopher Marlowe. OBVE
(Advice to a Fair Wanton.) UnTE
"So that's my role—the professional defendant?" II, 7, *tr. by* Guy Lee. NAWM-1
"Yes, Atticus, take it from me," I, 9, *tr. by* Guy Lee. NAWM-1
"Your husband? Going to the same dinner as us?" I, 4, *tr. by* Guy Lee. NAWM-1
(Possessive Lover, The, *tr. by* Christopher Marlowe.) UnTE
(To His Mistress, *tr. by* Dryden.) BoLoP
"Your loveliness, I don't deny, needs lovers," III, 14, *tr. by* Guy Lee. NAWM-1
(Complaisant Swain, The, *tr. by* F.A. Wright.) AWP
Amoret. Mark Akenside. HBV-1; OBEV
Amoret. Congreve. *See* Hue and Cry after Fair Amoret, A.
Amoretti. Spenser. AAS
Sels.
I. "Happy ye leaves whenas those lily [*or* lilly] hands." EBEV; LoBV; NIP; OAEL-1
III. "The sovereign [*or* soverayne] beauty which I do[o] admire." EBEV; HBV-1; OAEL-1; OAEP; PoEL-1
V. "Rudely thou wrongst my dear heart's desire." ElL
VIII. "More than most fair [*or* fayre], full of the living fire [*or* fyre]." CABA; HBV-1; NoP; OAEP; TEP; TrGrPo
X. "Unrighteous Lord of love, what law is this." NoP
XV. "Ye tradeful merchants that, with weary toil." HeIP; LiTB; NIP; OAEL-1; TrGrPo
XVI. "One day as I unwarily did gaze." OAEL-1
XIX. "The merry cuckoo, messenger of spring." OBSC
XXIII. "Penelope, for her Ulysses' sake." NIP
XXIV. "When I behold that beauty's wonderment." HBV-1
XXV. "How long shall this like dying life endure." EnRePo
XXVI. "Sweet is the rose, but grows upon a brere." ElL
(Sweet and Sour.) HBV-2
XXVIII. "The laurel leaf which you this day do wear." CABA
XXX. "My Love is like to ice, and I to fire." ErPo; FF; FPL; LiTB; PAI; TrGrPo
XXXIV. "Like as a ship, that through the ocean wide." HBV-1; OBSC
(Sonnet: Lyke as a Ship.) EtS
XXXVII. "What guile is this, that those her golden tresses." NoP; OBSC; PAI; TrGrPo
XL. "Mark when she smiles with amiable cheer." OBSC
XLI. "Is it her nature or is it her will." OAEP
XLIV. "When those renoumed noble peers of Greece." CABA
XLVII. "Trust not the treason of those smiling looks." TrGrPo
LIII. "The panther, knowing that his spotted hide." EnRePo
LIV. "Of this world's threatre in which we stay." NIP; NoP; OAEL-1
LV. "So oft as I her beauty do behold." HBV-1; TrGrPo
LVIII. "Weak is the assurance that weak flesh reposeth."
(By Her That Is Most Assured to Herself.) EnRePo
LXII. "The weary year his race now having run." OBSC
LXIII. "After long storms and tempests sad assay." FaBoEn; OAEL-1; OAEP; OBSC
LXIV. "Com[m]ing to kisse her lyps, (such grace I found)." EBEV; LoBV; OAEL-1
LXVII. "Like [or Lyke] a huntsman after weary chase [*or* chace]." EnRePo; GBL; HeIP; NoP; OAEP; PoEL-1; SeCePo; TrGrPo
LXVIII. "Most glorious Lord of Life! that on this day." CABA; EBCP; ElL; EnRePo; HAP; HBV-1; LiTB; NOCV; NoP; OxBoCh; SeCeV; TrPWD
(Easter.) NoBE; OBEV
(Easter Morning.) OHIP; TRV
LXX. "Fresh Spring, the herald of love's mighty king." AWP; CABA; ChTr; ElL; FaBoEn; FF; HAP; HBV-1; NoP; OBEV; OBSC; SeCeV; ViBoPo
(Fresh Spring, the Herald.) LiTB
LXXII. "Oft when my spirit doth spread her bolder wings." OAEP; OBSC
LXXIII. "Being my selfe captyved here in care." LoBV
LXXV. "One day I wrote her name upon the strand." AWP; BLPL; BoLoP; CABA; EBEV; ElL; FiP; GBL; HAP; HBV-1; HeIP; NoP; OAEL-1; OAEP; PAI; SeCePo; SeCeV; ViBoPo; WeW
(One Day I Wrote Her Name.) LiTB
LXXVII. "Was it a dream, or did I see it plain?" NIP
LXXVIII. "Lacking my Love, I go from place to place." ElL; ViBoPo
LXXIX. "Men call you fair, and you do credit it." AWP; FaBoBe; HBV-1; NoP
(Sonnet). BLPL
LXXXI. "Fair is my Love, when her fair golden heares." ElL; NoP
LXXXII. "Joy of my life, full oft for loving you." HeIP
LXXXIII. "Let not one sparke of filthy lustfull fyre." TEP
LXXXVIII. "Since I have lacked the comfort of that light." EnRePo
LXXXIX. "Like as the culver on the bared bough." FF; GBL; PBBP
Amoris Exsul, *sels.* Arthur Symons.
Arques, XI. VLP
In the Bay, III. OBNC; PBBP
Amorist, The. *Unknown, tr. fr. Greek by* Louis Untermeyer. UnTE
Amorous Dialogue between John and His Mistress, An. *Unknown.* CoMu
(Amorous Dialogue between the Mistris and Her Aprentice, An.) UnTE
Amorous Leander, beautiful and young. Christopher Marlowe. *Fr.* Hero and Leander, First Sestiad. PeHV
Amorous Neptune. Christopher Marlowe. *Fr.* Hero and Leander, Second Sestiad. NOBE
Amorous Señor, The. Ogden Nash. TDH
Amorous shepherd lov'd a charming boy, An. Theocritus, *tr. by* T. Creech. Idylls, XXIII. PeHV
Amorous Silvy, The. *See* On a Time the Amorous Silvy.
Amorous Temper, An. John Trumbull. *Fr.* The Progress of Dulness. AmPP
Amos, *sel.* Bible, *O.T.*
O Ye That Would Swallow the Needy, VIII: 4-10. TrJP
Amour, *sels.* Paul Verlaine, *tr. fr. French by* John Gray.
Crucifix, A. SyP
Parsifal. PAI; SyP
Amours de Voyage, *sels.* Arthur Hugh Clough.
Ah, That I Were Far Away, Canto III, *introd.* OBNC
(Upon Apennine Slope.) FaBoPP
"Dear Eustatio, I write that you may write me an answer," *fr.* Canto I, i. EBVV
"*Dulce* it is, and *decorum,* no doubt, for the country to fall," *fr.* Canto II, ii. EBVV; OAEP
"Is it illusion? or does there a spirit from perfecter ages," Canto II, *introd.*-iv. EBEV
(Spirit from Perfecter Ages.) OBNC
Juxtaposition, Canto III, vi. OBNC
Letter from Rome, A, Canto I, v. LoBV
"Only think, dearest Louisa, what fearful scenes we have witnessed!" *fr.* Canto II, viii. EBVV
Rome, *fr.* Canto I. FaBoPP
"Rome disappoints me still; but I shrink and adapt myself to it," *fr.* Canto I, ii. EBVV
(Rome.) FaBoPP
"So, I have seen a man killed!" *fr.* Canto II, vii. EBVV
"There are two different kinds, I believe, of human attraction," Canto II, xi. GTBS-P
"Tibur is beautiful, too, and the orchard slopes, and the Anio," Canto III, xi. GTBS-P
(So Not Seeing I Sung.) OBNC
(Valley and Villa of Horace, The.) FaBoPP
"Victory, Victory! Yes, ah, yes, thou republican Zion," *fr.* Canto II, vi. EBVV
"What do the people say, and what does the government do?" Canto II, i. EBVV; OBSV, i-iv only
"When God makes a great Man he intends all others to crush him," *fr.* Canto II. OBSV
"Whither depart the souls of the brave that die in the battle," *fr.* Canto V, vi. OAEP
Ye Ancient Divine Ones, Canto I, x. OBNC
"Yes, we are fighting at last, it appears," *fr.* Canto II, v. EBVV
Amphibian. Amy Clampitt. SUW
Amphibious bedlam of mothers, The. What's Living? Linda Hogan. AMV-81
Amphibious Crocodile. John Crowe Ransom. OBAL
Amphimachos the Dandy. Vincent McHugh. NePoAm-2
Amphitryon, *sels.* Dryden.
Fair Iris and Her Swain. ViBoPo
Song, A: "Celia, that I once was blest." CavP
Song: "Fair Iris I love, and hourly I die." AWP
(Mercury's Song to Phaedra.) PoEL-3; SeCV-2
(Hourly I Die.) UnTE
Amphora, The. Fyodor Sologub, *tr. fr. Russian by* Babette Deutsch *and* Avrahm Yarmolinsky. AWP

Ample heaven of fabrik sure, The. A Summer's Day. Alexander Hume. CH
Ample make this bed. Emily Dickinson. AP; MoAB; MoAmPo; OxBA; PoEL-5
Amputation, The. Helen Sorrels. DFF
Amsterdam. Jean Garrigue. TAP
Amsterdam. Francis Jammes, *tr. fr. French by* Jethro Bithell. AWP
Robinson Crusoe Returns to Amsterdam, *sel.* FaPON
Amsterdam Letter. Jean Garrigue. NYBP
Amsterdam Street Scene, 1972. Raphael Rudnik. AMV-81
Amtrak. Elliot Fried. PPJ
Amurrika! Philip Appleman. BXAP
Amused contempt, is it, that scintillates. Juan de Pareja: Painted by Velazquez. Richard A. Long. AmNP
Amusing Our Daughters. Carolyn Kizer. VGW
Amy. James Matthew Legaré. AA
Amy Wentworth. Whittier. BeLS
Amyd the wod his modir met thame tway. Virgil, *tr. into Middle English by* Gavin Douglas. *Fr.* The Aeneid, I. OBVE
Amynta. Gilbert Elliot. HBV-1
Amyntas Led Me to a Grove. Aphra Behn. *See* Willing Mistress, The.
Amyntas, *sel.* Thomas Randolph, *tr. fr. Latin by* Leigh Hunt.
Song of Fairies Robbing an Orchard. OBRV
(Fairy Song.) HBV-1
An' Charlie he's my darling. Charlie He's My Darling. Burns. CH
An der Beach, an der Beach. An Unserer Beach. Kurt M. Stein. InMe
An die Musik. David Malouf. CBAP
An' I couldn't hear nobody pray, O, Lord. I Couldn't Hear Nobody Pray. *Unknown.* BoAN-1
An' O, for ane-and-twenty, Tam! O, for Ane-and-twenty. Burns. BSV
An Thou Were My Ain Thing, *sel.* Allan Ramsay.
"An thou were my ain thing." ViBoPo
An Unserer Beach. Kurt M. Stein. InMe
Anabasis. Rodney Nelson. AMV-81
Anabasis, *sel.* "St.-John Perse," *tr. fr. French by* T. S. Eliot.
"Such is the way of the world," IV. OBVE
Anabasis. Eithne Wilkins. NeBP
Anachronism. Oliver St. John Gogarty. FYAP
Anacreon to the Sophist. "B. H." InMe
Anacreon's Dove. Samuel Johnson, *after the Greek of* Anacreon. AWP
Anacreontic ("Born I was to be old"). Robert Herrick. CaPo; OAEP; OxBoLi
Anacreontic ("I must/ Not trust"). Robert Herrick. CaPo
Anacreontic on Drinking. Abraham Cowley. *See* Drinking.
Anacreontic, on Parting with a Little Child. Samuel Wesley. NOEC
Anacreontic to Flip. Royall Tyler. OBAL
Anacreontick, An. William Oldys. *See* On a Fly Drinking out of His Cup.
Anacreontics: Drinking. Abraham Cowley. *See* Drinking.
Anacreontics: The Epicure. Abraham Cowley. *See* Epicure, The ("Underneath this myrtle shade").
Anacreontics: The Swallow. Abraham Cowley. *See* Swallow, The.
Anacreontiques: The Grashopper. Abraham Cowley. *See* Grasshopper, The.
Anactoria, *sel.* Swinburne.
"Thee too the years shall cover; thou shalt be." ViBoPo
Anadarko John. Carroll Arnett. VoR
Anaesthesia. Jean Valentine. TAP
Anal erotic name Herman, An. Limerick. *Unknown.* PeHV
Analogous to floral pageantry. Land of the Free. Sister Mary Honora. NePoAm-2
Analogue of Unity in Multeity. Richard Eberhart. NoAM
Analogy. Brian Higgins. FaBoTw
Analysands. Dudley Randall. BPo; CABA
Analyst. David Fisher. NPGG
Ana(Mary-Army)gram. George Herbert. CABA; OAEL-1
Anansi son name Stan'-up-stick. Sweet Riley. *Unknown.* BaBo
Anarchist. Anthony Cronin. CIP
Anarchist. Norman Dugdale. BoAnP
Anarchist's Letter, An. Harald Wyndham. POL
Anasazi at Mesa Verde. Reg Saner. NPAW
Anastasis. Albert E. S. Smythe. CaP
Anath. Haim Guri, *tr. fr. Hebrew by* Naomi Nir *and* Howard Schwartz. VWA
Anathema of Cats. John Skelton. *Fr.* Phyllyp Sparowe. PCat
Anathemata, The, *sels.* David Jones.
Angle-Land, III. NoAM
"Did he meet Lud at the Fleet Gate? did count the top." EBEV
"Ship's master:/ before him, in the waist and before it." FaBoTw
Anatomie of the World, An. John Donne. *See* Anatomy of the World, An.
Anatomy. Gilbert Sorrentino. POL
Anatomy of Angels, The. Alden Nowlan. PeCV
Anatomy of Baseness, The, *sel.* John Andrews.
To the Detracted. EIL; LO, *longer sel.*
Anatomy of Happiness, The. Ogden Nash. LiTA; TAP
Anatomy of Humor, The. Morris Bishop. WhC
Anatomy of Melancholy, The, *sel.* Robert Burton.
Authors Abstract of Melancholy, The ("When I go musing all alone"). OBS
Anatomy of Monotony. Wallace Stevens. BiP
Anatomy [*or* Anatomie] of the World, An: The First Anniversary. John Donne. AnAnS-1; MasP
Sels.
Doth Not a Tenarif, or Higher Hill. ChTr
"She, she is dead; she's dead: when thou knowest this." JCP
Verse and Fame. FaBoRV
"When that rich Soule which to her heaven is gone." SeCV-1
Ancestor. Jimmy Santiago Baca. LFAC
Ancestor. Thomas Kinsella. BIrV
"Ancestor remote of Man, The." Man and the Ascidian. Andrew Lang. HBV-1
Ancestors, The. Anita Barrows. VWA
Ancestors, The. John Peale Bishop. PoA
Ancestors, The. Christopher Middleton. NMP
Ancestors. Dudley Randall. BPo; CNA
Ancestors. Harold Schimmel. VWA
Ancestors' Graves in Kurakawa. Joy Kogawa. BrSi
Ancestral Faces. Kwesi Brew. PBA
Ancestral Houses. W. B. Yeats. Meditations in Time of Civil War, I. ChMP; LiTB; MoVE; OAEL-2
Ancestral Weight. Alfonsina Storni, *tr. fr. Spanish by* Marti Moody. WPOW
Ancestry. Louis Daniel Brodsky. AMV-81
Anchises. Blanaid Salkeld. OxBI
Anchises, Paris, and Adonis too. Spoken by Venus on Seeing Her Statue Done by Praxiteles. *Unknown, tr. fr. Greek.* EyDe; FaBoEE
Anchor: "Oft I must strive with wind and wave." *Unknown, tr. fr. Anglo-Saxon by* Charles W. Kennedy. *Fr.* Riddles (Exeter Book). AnOE
Anchor is weighed, and the sails they are set, The. Away, Rio. *Unknown.* AmSS
Anchorage. Joy Harjo. STE; TWSS
Anchor's Aweigh, The, *with music. Unknown.* ShS
Anchorsmiths, The. Charles Dibdin. NOEC
Ancient. "Æ." SeCePo
Ancient Ballad of Chevy-Chase, The. *Unknown. See* Chevy Chase.
Ancient Barbarossa, the Kaiser Frederick old, The. Barbarossa. Friedrich Rückert, *tr. by* Elizabeth Craigmyle. AWP
Ancient bridge, and a more ancient tower, An. My House. W. B. Yeats. Meditations in Time of Civil War, II. LiTB
Ancient Castle, An. William Morris. *Fr.* Golden Wings. SeCePo
Ancient chestnut's blossoms threw, An. Alciphron and Leucippe. Walter Savage Landor. OBEV; VLP
Ancient Christmas Carol, An. *Unknown.* OHIP
Ancient Couple on Lu Mountain, The. Mark Van Doren. VGW
Ancient Custom, An. Anatoly Steiger, *tr. fr. Russian by* John Glad. VWA
Ancient Doctrine, The. Robert Browning. OBVV
Ancient Historian. Chris Wallace-Crabbe. PoAu-2
Ancient History. Arthur Guiterman. OBCA
Ancient Law, The. André Spire, *tr. fr. French by* Stanley Burnshaw. VWA
Ancient Lights. Austin Clarke. BIrV; CMoP; IPY; NMP; OxBI
Ancient long-horned bovine, An. The Last Longhorn. R. W. Hall. BPAW; CoSo
Ancient Mansion, The, *sels.* George Crabbe.
In Suffolk. FaBoPP
Spring to Winter. ChTr
Ancient Mariner, The: The Wedding Guest's Version of the Affair from His Point of View, The. *Unknown.* FaBoPa
Ancient Murderess Night. Anna Margolin, *tr. fr. Yiddish by* Ruth Whitman. VWA
Ancient Music. Ezra Pound. BXAP; DBV; FaBoCo; FaBoPa; FF; HeIP; LiTM; NePA; OBAL; OxBA; Par; PPON; SpRo; TW
Ancient nomadic snowman has rolled around. The Snowman. P. K. Page. NOBC
Ancient of Days. William Croswell Doane. AA; AH, *with music*
Ancient of Days. Anthony Rudolf. VWA
Ancient of Days bless the innocent. Clams. Stanley Moss. GP
Ancient of Days, old friend, no one believes you'll come back. Stone Canyon Nocturne. Charles Wright. LCAP
Ancient One, The. Charles Culhane. LFAC
Ancient pages of the Talmud. The Talmud. S. Frug, *tr. by* Alice Stone Blackwell. TrJP
Ancient Person, for whom I. A Song of a Young Lady to Her Ancient Lover. Earl of Rochester. BoLoP; CavP; EBEV; ErPo; GBL; MePo
Ancient Pistol, peacock Payne. Tennyson. FaBoEE

Ancient poets and their learned rhymes, The. An Answer to Some Verses Made in His Praise. Sir John Suckling. PP
Ancient Prayer, An. Thomas H. B. Webb, *after* A Prayer Found in Chester Cathedral. BLPA; FaBoBe
(Prayer, A: "Give us a good digestion, Lord.") STF
(Prayer Found in Chester Cathedral, A.) TreFS
Ancient Prophecy, An. Philip Freneau. PAH
Ancient readers of heaven's book, Th'. Of Cynthia. *Unknown.* OBSC
Ancient reservoir, The. The Reservoir. Edward Field. GP
Ancient saga tells us how, An. Dead Cow Farm. Robert Graves. BrPo
Ancient Sage, The. Tennyson. WGRP
Ancient songs, The/ Pass deathward mournfully. Choricos. Richard Aldington. HBMV
Ancient sowed an acorn from His mind, The. Oak. Philip Child. CaP
Ancient Speech, The. Kathleen Raine. *Fr.* Eileann Chanaidh. PoSH
Ancient story I'll tell you anon, An. King John and the Abbot [of Canterbury]. *Unknown.* EnSB; GN; HBV-2; TrGrPo
Ancient Thought, The. Watson Kerr. TRV; WGRP
Ancient to Ancients, An. Thomas Hardy. ChMP; CMoP; CoBMV; GTBS-P; LiTM; MoPo; MoVE; OxBTC
Ancient tutor, awaiting failure, The. The Clarity of Apples. Terry M. Perlin. AMV-80
Ancient Virgin, An. George Crabbe. *Fr.* The Parish Register. OBNC
Ancient Wisdom, Rather Cosmic. Ezra Pound. NOBA
Anciently in this village. Ivy and Holly. E. H. W. Meyerstein. ELU
Ancientness surrounds me. Death. Patty L. Harjo. VoR
And. Robert Creeley. LCAP
And. Ricardo Gonsalves. FIA
And a clam caught my little finger. The Little Girl That Lost a Finger. Gabriela Mistral, *tr. by* Muna Lee. FaPON
And after a while he'd say his head was a rose. Blossom. Stanley Plumly. GeTw
And after this quick bash in the dark. Portrait of a Young Girl Raped at a Suburban Party. Brian Patten. OxBTC
And afterwards, when honour has made good. Iris Tree. SUMH
And Again. Humphrey Evans. BXAP
And again, without snow, a new year. The Mudtower. Anne Stevenson. HoAn
"And all her silken flanks with garlands drest." Vlamertinghe; Passing the Château, July 1917. Edmund Blunden. MMA; OBWP
And all is well, though faith and form. Tennyson. In Memoriam, A. H. H., CXXVII. HBV-2
And all the sails hang limp. Comes Fog and Mist. William Hart-Smith. *Fr.* Christopher Columbus. PoAu-2
"And All the While the Sky Is Falling. . ." Lora Dunetz. NePoAm
And all the while they mocked him and reviled. The Martyr. Natalie Flohr. PGD
"And all the wickedness in this world that man might work or think." God's Mercy. William Langland, *mod. by* Donald Attwater. *Fr.* The Vision of Piers Plowman. NOCV
And all things are of God. God Was in Christ. Bible, *N.T.* *Fr.* Second Corinthians. TRV
And always through my window pane. Girl's Song. Marya Zaturenska. OLR
And an evening will come when I will leave. Plain Song. Benjamin Fondane, *tr. by* Matei Calinescu *and* Willis Barnstone. VWA
And answer made King Arthur, breathing hard. Tennyson. *Fr.* Idylls of the King: The Passing of Arthur. EBEV
And [*or* But] are ye sure the news is true? The Sailor's Wife [*or* The Mariner's Wife *or* There's Nae Luck about the House]. William Julius Mickle, *also at. to* Jean Adam. BeLS; BSV; GN; GTBS; GTBS-P; HBV-1; NOEC; OBEC; ViBoPo
And aren't those baby chicks. Chickens. Geof Hewitt. FAZ
"And Art Thou Come, Blest Babe?" *Unknown.* OxBoCh
And art thou come to this at last. Alexander McLachlan. *Fr.* To an Indian Skull. CaP
And art thou grieved, sweet and sacred Dove. Grieve Not the Holy Spirit. George Herbert. AnAnS-1
And as for me, though that my wit be lite [*or* thogh that I can but lyte]. Chaucer. *Fr.* The Legend of Good Women. CH; HeIP; ViBoPo
And as he journeyed, he came near Damascus. Paul on the Road to Damascus. Bible, *N.T.* *Fr.* Acts. TreF
And as I stood and cast aside mine eye. *Unknown.* *Fr.* The Flower and the Leaf. PBBP
And as I watch the fields. In the Distance. H. L. Van Brunt. FAZ
And as in winter time when Jove his cold-sharpe javelines throwes. Homer, *tr. by* George Chapman. *Fr.* The Iliad, XII. OBVE
And as, my friend, you ask me. Utah Carroll. *Unknown.* CoSo
And as our God the beasts had given in charge. Michael Drayton. *Fr.* Noah's Flood. PBBP
And as soon as it was morning the chief priests. Bible, *N.T.* *Fr.* St. Mark. DL
And as we came down the staircase. Valse Oubliée. John Heath-Stubbs. OxBTC
And as we spoke the Nicene Creed we were called out. Barnfire during Church. Robert Bly. NePoEA
And as we walked the grass was faintly stirred. Hawks. James Stephens. HBMV
And as when with the West-wind's flawes the sea thrusts up her waves. Homer, *tr. by* George Chapman. *Fr.* The Iliad, IV. OBVE
And at Lake Geneva, which is in Wisconsin. At Lake Geneva. Richard Eberhart. LiTA
And at the last I cast my mine eye aside. Lady of the Arbour. *Fr.* The Flower and the Leaf. WPE
And before hell mouth; dry plain/ and two mountains. Ezra Pound. *Fr.* Cantos, XVI. MoPo
And, behold, a certain lawyer stood up, and tempted him. The Good Samaritan. Bible, *N.T.* *Fr.* St. Luke. TreF
And, behold, two of them went that same day to a village called Emmaus. On the Road to Emmaus. Bible, *N.T.* *Fr.* St. Luke. TreFS
And believing she was a maid. The Faithless Wife. Federico García Lorca, *tr. by* A. L. Lloyd. BoLoP
And birds came crying. James Cunningham. *Fr.* The Narrator's Trance. JB
And boys, be in nothing so moderate as in love of man. Robinson Jeffers. *Fr.* Shine, Perishing Republic. TRV
And call ye this to utter what is just. Psalm LVIII: Si Vere Utique. Countess of Pembroke, *paraphrased fr.* Bible, *O.T.* BoWoP; NOCV; WPE
And can it be, that I should gain. Free Grace. Charles Wesley. NOCV
And Can the Physician. *Unknown.* *Fr.* Robin Goodfellow, Pt. II. ELP
(Song: "And can the physician make sick men well?") ElL; LoBV
And Canst Thou, Sinner, Slight, *with music.* Abby Bradley Hyde. AH
And change with hurried hand has swept these scenes. Sonnet [*or* Elegy in Six Sonnets]. Frederick Goddard Tuckerman. *Fr.* Sonnets. HAP; NOBA; QFR; TAP
And closeness, and the line between. Three inches. Distances. Albert Goldbarth. GeTw
And, constantly, I seek/ A poetry of facts. "Hugh MacDiarmid." *Fr.* The Kind of Poetry I Want. InPS
And cruell maid, because I see. The Cruell Maid. Robert Herrick. CavP
And David lamented with this lamentation over Saul and over Jonathan his son. David's Lament. Bible, *O.T.* *Fr.* Second Samuel. ChTr
And Death Shall Have No Dominion. Dylan Thomas. ChMP; CMoP; EaLo; LiTM; MoAB; MoBrPo; MoVE; NeBP; NoAM; OAEP; PPoe; SeCePo
And deep-eyed children cannot long be children. Ballad of the Outer Life. Hugo von Hofmannsthal, *tr. by* Jethro Bithell. AWP; TrJP
And Dick said, "Look what I have found!" Crescent Moon. Elizabeth Madox Roberts. SUS
And did ever a man go black with sun in a Belgian swamp. Nigger. Karl Shapiro. OxBA
And Did the Animals? Mark Van Doren. VGW
And Did Those Feet in Ancient Time. Blake. *Fr.* Milton. AWP; CABA; EnRP; FaBoCh; FaBv; HAP; HeIP; InPS; LoBV; MAT; NoP; OAEL-2; OAEP; OBRV; PAI; PoEL-4; PoRA; PrIm; SeCeV; ViBoPo; WGRP
(Jerusalem.) EaLo; EvOK; FaPoR; NOBE; NOCV; OBEV; WaaP
(New Jerusalem, A.) FaBoEn; FSW; LiTB; TrGrPo
(Preface.) PPoe
(Prelude.) OBNC
And did thy sapphire shallop slip. To a New-born Baby Girl. Grace Hazard Conkling. HBV-1
And did you know. Snowflakes. Clive Sansom. OBCP
And did you not hear of a jolly young waterman. The Jolly Young Waterman. Charles Dibdin. NOEC; PoPle
And did you not hear of a mirth that befell. Away to Twiver, Away, Away! *Unknown.* ElL
"And did you once see Shelley plain!" A Travelogue: Clovelly. Carolyn Wells. InMe
And did young Stephen sicken. Emmeline Grangerford's "Ode to Stephen Dowling Bots, Dec'd." "Mark Twain." *Fr.* The Adventures of Huckleberry Finn. FiBHP; NIP; OBAL
And do I see some cause a hope to feed. Astrophel and Stella, LXVI. Sir Philip Sidney. SiPS
And do our loves all perish with our frames. Immortality. Richard Henry Dana. AA
And do they so? have they a Sense. Rom. Cap. 8 Ver. 19. Henry Vaughan. AnAnS-1; MeLP; OBS
And don't bother telling me anything. César Vallejo, *tr. fr. Spanish by* Robert Bly. EAS
And dost thou faithlessly abandon me? The Unrealities. Schiller, *tr. by* James Clarence Mangan. AWP

And doun on knes anoon-ryght I me sette. This Fresshe Flour. Chaucer. *Fr.* The Legend of Good Women. SeCePo
And Dust to Dust. Charles David Webb. NePoAm-2
And each one to the advantage of her breasts. The Girl with 18 Nightgowns. Gregory Orr. POL
And early in the morning he came again into the temple. The Woman Taken in Adultery. Bible, *N.T.* *Fr.* St. John. TreFT
And ever must I fan this fire? Camoens. Herman Melville. ViBoPo
And every bird shew'd in his proper kind. Michael Drayton. *Fr.* The Owle. FM
And every prodigal greatness. The Flowering Urn. Laura Riding. LiTA
And every yeare a worlde my will did deeme. George Gascoigne. AAS
And ev'ry man 'neath his vine and fig tree. Vine and Fig Tree. Shalom Altman. FSW
And faces, forms and phantoms, numbered not. Elegy in Six Sonnets. Frederick Goddard Tuckerman. *Fr.* Sonnets. QFR
And Fall Shall Sit in Judgment. Audre Lorde. NNP
And first Morency, far famed water, you. Standish O'Grady. *Fr.* The Emigrant. CaP
And first, the lamp-posts whose burning match-heads. Jewish Main Street. Irving Layton. CaP; VWA
And for this freedom will be the freedom of all. A Free Nation. Edwin Markham. TRV
And for what, except for you, do I feel love? Wallace Stevens. *Fr.* Notes toward a Supreme Fiction. NOBA
And Forgive Us Our Trespasses. Aphra Behn. EBEV
And from the Citie Tegea there came the Paragone. Ovid, *tr. by* Arthur Golding. *Fr.* Metamorphoses, X. OBVE
And from the windy West came two-gunned Gabriel. Altarwise by Owl-Light, V. Dylan Thomas. NoAM
And from what distances, to this, are we come. Sungrazer. Alvin Greenberg. FAZ
And God created the great whales, and each. Milton. *Fr.* Paradise Lost, VII. EtS; MOS
And God looked down at God that day. My God, My God, Look upon Me. Chad Walsh. *Fr.* The Psalm of Christ. TrCP
And God said, Let the waters generate. Creation of the Animals. Milton. *Fr.* Paradise Lost, VII. FM
And God saw that the wickedness of man was great. Bible, *O.T.* *Fr.* Genesis. NAWM-1
And God spake all these words, saying. The Ten Commandments. Bible, *O.T.* *Fr.* Exodus. TreF
And God stepped out on space. The Creation. James Weldon Johnson. BALP; BANP; CDC; FaBV; MoAmPo; PoBA; PoPl; PoRA; TrCP; YaD
And Grow. John Hay. WaP
And Hannah prayed, and said. Hannah's Thanksgiving. Bible, *O.T.* *Fr.* First Samuel. BoWoP
And haply, bason'd in some unsunn'd cleft. Samuel Taylor Coleridge. *Fr.* To a Young Friend. ChER
And Happy Am I. Syd Scroggie. PoSH
And hast thou left old Jemmy in the lurch? A Satire upon the French King. Thomas Brown. APAS
And hasten Og and Doeg to rehearse. Og and Doeg. Dryden. *Fr.* Absalom and Achitophel, Pt. II. AWP
And Have the Bright Immensities, *with music.* Howard Chandler Robbins. AH
And have we done with war at last? Two Fusiliers. Robert Graves. MMA
And have we lost another friend? John Close. *Fr.* In Respectful Memory of Mr. Yarker. FaBoCo
And He Answered Them Nothing. Richard Crashaw. MePo
And he cast it down, down, on the green grass. The New Ghost. Fredegond Shove. ChMP; HBMV; MoVE; OxBoCh
And he continued more firmly, although with stronger emotion. Arthur Hugh Clough. *Fr.* The Bothie of Tober-na-Vuolich. VLP
And he is risen? Well, be it so. A Drizzling Easter Morning. Thomas Hardy. CMoP
And he looked up, and he saw the rich men casting their gifts. Bible, *N.T.* *Fr.* St. Luke. TreFT
And he [*or* Jesus] said, A certain man had two sons. The Prodigal Son. Bible, *N.T.* *Fr.* St. Luke. LO; TreF
And he said, So soule doth magnifie the Lord. Bible, *N.T.* *Fr.* St. Mark. OBVE
And he said to them all, If any man will come after me. On Taking Up One's Cross. Bible, *N.T.* *Fr.* St. Luke. TreFT
And he showed me a pure river of water of life. There Shall Be No Night. Bible, *N.T.* *Fr.* Revelation. TrGrPo
And he spake this parable unto certain which trusted. The Pharisee and the Publican. Bible, *N.T.* *Fr.* St. Luke. TreFT
And he went unto Ramah. There he met. The Dance of Saul with the Prophets. Saul Tchernichowsky, *tr. by* I. M. Lask. TrJP
And heaven did curse—they found him laid. Charlotte Brontë. *Fr.* Mementos. PeD
And heed not them that warn or chide thee. Hark! The Rosy Days Are Numbered. Moses ibn Ezra, *tr. by* Solomon Solis-Cohen. *Fr.* Wine-Songs. TrJP
And here face down beneath the sun. You, Andrew Marvell. Archibald MacLeish. AP; AWP; CMoP; CoBMV; FaBV; FYAP; HAP; HelP; HoPM; LiTA; LiTM; MoAB; MoAmPo; MoVE; MP; NoAM; NOBA; NoP; OxBA; PoRA; PPP; PrIm; SoSe; TreFT; TrGrPo; TwAmPo; TwCP; ViBoPo; WeW
And here I wish my soul died with my breath. Ovid, *tr. by* Henry Vaughan. *Fr.* Tristium, III, 3a. OBVE
And here is dear old Boston. The New Order. Phyllis McGinley. AmFN
And here the precious dust is laid [*or* layd]. Maria Wentworth [*or* The Inscription on the Tombe of the Lady Mary Wentworth]. Thomas Carew. AnAnS-2; CaPo; JCP; MeLP; MePo; OBS; SeCV-1
And here's good luck to the shanty boys. *Unknown.* OuSiCo
And here's the child's Dad. The Fount of Learning. *Unknown.* OxNR
And here's the happy, bounding flea. The Flea. Roland Young. PoPl; RHPC; WhC
And Him evermore I beheld. Follow Me. Longfellow. PGD
And Hiram of Tyre sent his servants unto Solomon. Bible, *O.T.* *Fr.* First Kings. EyDe
And his son Judas, who was called Maccabeus. Judas Maccabeus. Bible, Apocrypha. *Fr.* First Maccabees. TrJP
And how are the rats doing in the maze? Progress Report. Charles Simic. GeTw
And how beguile you? Death has no repose. James Elroy Flecker. *Fr.* The Golden Legend of Samarkand OxBTC
And how much of this. The Death of Nick Charles. Amiri Baraka. CoPo
And how will I forget. Eyes. Clarisse Nicoïdski, *tr. by* Stephen Levy. VWA
And I a beginner. Answer to Yo/Question. Sonia Sanchez. BPo
And I Am Old to Know. Pauline Hanson. TAP
And I bowed [*or* ich bowede.] my body and beheld all about [*or* bihelde al aboute]. A Vision of Nature. William Langland. *Fr.* The Vision of Piers Plowman. CTC; PoEL-1
"And I fare you well, Lady Ouncebell." Lord Lovel. *Unknown.* ESPB
And I had forgotten about the stars. Letter from Des Moines. Thomas Swiss. AMV-81
And I have come upon this place. L'An Trentiesme de Mon Eage [*or* Age]. Archibald MacLeish. LiTM; MoAmPo; MoVE; NePA; NoAM; NOBA; TwAmPo
And I have learned how diving's done. Fantasia. Dorothy Livesay. MoCV; OBCV
And I Have Loved Thee, Ocean! Byron. *See* Sea, The.
And I hear the pad of feet to the union hall. Thomas McGrath. Letter to an Imaginary Friend, Part One, II, 2. NNaP
And I, I was a good child on the whole. Elizabeth Barrett Browning. *Fr.* Aurora Leigh. BrRo
And "I Know Why the Caged Bird Sings"; a Villanelle. George Mosby, Jr. LFAC
And I made myself a surrogate wedding-day. The Sisters. Nicki Jackowska. BrRo
And I remember Spain. Louis MacNeice. *Fr.* Autumn Journal. OBWP
And I rode the Greyhound down to Brooklyn. Wild Strawberry. Maurice Kenny. STE
And I said to the man who stood at the gate of the year. M. Louise Haskins. *Fr.* The Gate of the Year. TreFS; TRV
And I saw a great white throne. The Last Judgment. Bible, *N.T.* *Fr.* Revelation. TreF
And I saw a new heaven and a new earth. The New Jerusalem. Bible, *N.T.* *Fr.* Revelation. TrGrPo
And I say nothing—no, not a word. My Sister Jane. Ted Hughes. OnUR; SO
And I say unto you, Ask, and it shall be given you. Effective Prayer. Bible, *N.T.* *Fr.* St. Luke. TreFT
And I standing in the shade. Petition. R. S. Thomas. FaBoMo
And I thought of how impossibly alone we were. After a Game of Squash. Samuel L. Albert. GoYe; NePoAm-2
And I took her down by the river. The Faithless Wife. Federico García Lorca, *tr. by* Robert O'Brien. ErPo
And I took myself for a walk in the woods that day. Family Outing—a Celebration. Nicki Jackowska. BrRo
And I was born with you, wasn't I, Blues? The Blues Don't Change. Al Young. NPGG
And I went down by that freight depot. Lost Lover Blues. *Unknown.* BluL
And I, woman, cloaked in blues. I, Woman. Irma McClaurin. BlSi
And ich bowede my body and bihelde al aboute. *See* And I bowed my body and beheld all about.
And if. Tangere. Theodore Enslin. CoPo

And if an eye may save or slay. Sir Thomas Wyatt. SiPS
And if any man should ask me. Deliverance. Frances Harper. WPOW
And if by such bright tokens. To Our Lady, the Ark of the Covenants. Raymond E. F. Larsson. ISi
And if death were only the eyelid. The Never Again. Charles Dobzynski, *tr. by* Anita Barrows. VWA
And if he ever should come back. The Last Words. Maurice Maeterlinck, *tr. by* Frederick York Powell. AWP; PoPl
And if he should come again. Ylen's Song. Richard Hovey. *Fr.* The Birth of Galahad. AA
"And if He's gone away," said she. Story. Dorothy Parker. InMe
And If I Did What Then? George Gascoigne. *Fr.* The Adventures of Master F. I. EBEV; ElL; FaBoEn; GBL; HAP; NCEP; NoP; PoEL-1 (Farewell, A.) LoBV; NOBE; OBSC
And, if I give thee honour due. Milton. *Fr.* L'Allegro. PoPle
And if I loved you Wednesday. Thursday. Edna St. Vincent Millay. InMe; PoA
And if Moishe Leib the poet should tell. Memento Mori. Moishe Leib Halpern, *tr. by* Ruth Whitman. VWA
And if my memory live when I am dead. Wedded Memories. Philip Bourke Marston. VLP
And if our lives spill. Elegy. Philip Dow. NPGG
And if the dead, and the dead. The Conspirators. Frederic Prokosch. LiTM; NePA; PrIm; WaP
"And if the name of 'Mage' offends these gentlemen." A Brief Introduction to the History of Culture. Weldon Kees. TwAmPo
And if tonight my soul may find her peace. Shadows. D. H. Lawrence. OAEP; OxBTC
And if ye stand in doubt. Colin Clout. John Skelton. OAEL-1
And, if you asked of him to say. Charles Stewart Calverley. *Fr.* Gemini and Virgo. FiBHP
And if you would ask me "Where do you find your songs." Hanukah. Jakov de Haan, *tr. by* David Soetendorp. VWA
And I'm going way down. The Gone Dead Train. *Unknown.* BluL
And I'm thinking how to get out. History. Myra Cohn Livingston. RHPC
And in conclusion I'll say. Goodbye. Bella Akhmadulina, *tr. by* Barbara Einzig. BoWoP
And in Her Morning. Jessica Agnes Powers. ISi
And in September, O what keen delight! Sonnets of the Months: September. Folgore da San Geminiano, *tr. by* Dante Gabriel Rossetti. AWP
And in That Drowning Instant. A. M. Klein. VWA
And in that land dwells a king. Sir Cawline. *Unknown.* ESPB
And in the frosty season, when the sun. On the Frozen Lake [*or* The Skaters *or* Skating]. Wordsworth. *Fr.* The Prelude. FaBoCh; GN; LiSp
And in the Hanging Gardens. Conrad Aiken. MoAB; MoAmPo
And in the midst of all, a fountaine stood. The Bower of Bliss. Spenser. *Fr.* The Faerie Queene, II, 12. CH
And in the morning the king loved you most. Arcanum One. Gwendolyn MacEwen. MoCV
And, in the night, the Spirit came. The Messenger. Alfred Noyes. GoBC
And in this swyving there nas noon hir pere. The Continuation of *The Cook's Tale.* William Zaranka. BXAP
And is he gone, whom these arms held but now. Quaerit Jesum Suum Maria. Richard Crashaw. ACP
And Is It Night? *Unknown.* ElL ("And is it night? Are they thine eyes that shine?") GBL
And is our life, a life wherein we borrow. Matthew X. 28. Roger Wolcott. SCAP
And is the great cause lost beyond recall? Faith. Ada Cambridge. PoAu-1
And is the water come? Sure't cannot be. Upon Sir John Lawrence's Bringing Water over the Hills. Sir John Suckling. CaPo
And is there care in heaven? and is there love? Guardian Angels [*or* The Bright Squadrons]. Spenser. *Fr.* The Faerie Queene, II, 8. GoBC; NOCV; OAEL-1; OBSC; OxBoCh
And is there then no earthly place. Thomas Moore. *Fr.* Rhymes on the Road. OBSV
And is this—Yarrow?—This the stream. Yarrow Visited. Wordsworth. EnRP; GTBS; GTBS-P; HBV-2
And Ishmael crouch'd beside a crackling briar. Ishmael. Herbert Edward Palmer. OBEV
And it all died down. From My Lai the Thunder Went West. Richard Ryan. CIP
And It Came to Pass at Midnight. Yannai, *tr. fr. Hebrew.* TrJP
And it came to pass in those days, that there went out a decree from Caesar Augustus. The First Christmas. Bible, *N.T.* *Fr.* St. Luke, II. NAWM-1; TreFS
And it came to pass, that, as Jesus sat at meat in his house. Jesus Eats With Sinners. Bible, *N.T.* Fr. St. Mark. TreFT
And it seemed, while we waited, he began to walk. Geoffrey Hill. Mercian Hymns, XXX. NoP
And it shall come to pass in the end of days. In the End of Days. Bible, *O.T.* *Fr.* Isaiah. TrJP
And it shall come to pass when the days shall grow long. When the Days Shall Grow Long. Hayyim Nahman Bialik, *tr. by* A. M. Klein. TrJP
And it's forty miles to Nicut Hill. Prince Robert. *Unknown.* AmFP
And it's hard to see the mountains. Can I Say. Dolly Bird. WPOW
And it's never mind, never mind, baby. Poor Man Blues. *Unknown.* BluL
And Jesus Don't Have Much Use for His Old Suitcase Anymore. Tom Kryss. NeAC
And Jesus said, A certain man had two sons. *See* And he said . . .
And Jesus said unto them, I am the bread of life: he that cometh to me shall never hunger; and he that believeth on me shall never thirst. I Am the Bread of Life. Bible, *N.T.* *Fr.* St. John. TreFS
And Joshua looks down on my face. Joshua's Face. Amir Gilboa, *tr. by* Shirley Kaufman. VWA
And just because he's human. United Front. Bertolt Brecht *and* Hans Eisler. FSW
And just by crossing the short sea. Channel Crossing. George Barker. ChMP; GTBS-P
And last night a man came in. Spring Street Bar. Mei-Mei Berssenbrugge. WPOW
And learn O voyager to walk. Seafarer. Archibald MacLeish. NoAM; NoP
And Lightly, like the Flowers. Pierre de Ronsard, *tr. fr. French by* W. E. Henley. AWP
And, like a dying lady, lean and pale. The Waning Moon [*or* The Moon]. Shelley. CH; ChER; FaBoCh; MOON; OBEV; PoPle; TrGrPo
And like thy father sing in tunefulness. A Barren Soul. Joseph Ezobi, *tr. by* D. I. Friedmann. *Fr.* The Silver Bowl. TrJP
And, lo! leading a blessed host comes one. Lincoln. Harriet Monroe. *Fr.* Commemoration Ode. AA
And lo! the sea that fleets about the land. The Sea Danceth. Sir John Davies. EtS
"And Lo, the Star!" Molly Anderson Haley. PGD
And long ere dinner-time I have. On a Day's Stint. Sir Walter Scott. NBM
And Los and Enitharmon builded Jerusalem weeping. Vala, Night the Ninth Being the Last Judgment. Blake. *Fr.* The Four Zoas. OAEL-2
And Los beheld the mild Emanation, Jerusalem, eastward bending. In Deadly Fear. Blake. *Fr.* Jerusalem. SeCePo
And Love Hung Still. Louis MacNeice. Trilogy for X, II. MoBrPo ("And love hung still as crystal over the bed.") CIP; GBL
And man is a spirit. Louis MacNeice. *Fr.* Holes in the Sky. TRV
"And Man is left alone with Man." 'Tis well! At the Worst. Israel Zangwill. WGRP
And Marie said, My soule doth magnifie the Lord. Bible, *N.T.* *Fr.* St. Luke. OBVE
And Mary said, "Before the void was filled." Ex Maria Vergine. Norbert Engels. ISi
And Mary stood beside the cross! Her soul. Mary at the Cross. Clyde McGee. PGD
And mathematics, fresh as May. Edmund Blunden. *Fr.* Reliques. ImOP
And may my humble dwelling stand. An Epistle. Matthew Green. *Fr.* The Spleen. LoBV
And Me happiest when I compose poems. The Birth of Tragedy. Irving Layton. MoCV; NoP; OBCV; PeCV
And me my winter's task is drawing over. Sonnet. Frederick Goddard Tuckerman. QFR
And mightier grew the joy to meet full-faced. Swimming. Swinburne. *Fr.* Tristram of Lyonesse. GN
And Monelle said: I will speak to you of actions. Actions. Marcel Schwob, *tr. by* William Brown Meloney. TrJP
And Monelle said: I will speak to you of moments. Moments. Marcel Schwob, *tr. by* William Brown Meloney. TrJP
And Monelle said: I will speak to you of things dead. Things Dead. Marcel Schwob, *tr. by* William Brown Meloney. TrJP
And mony ane sings o' grass, o' grass. *Unknown.* *Fr.* The Birth of Robin Hood. ViBoPo
And Mr. Ferritt. Judith Wright. MoBrPo
And Mrs. Stephanopoulos said oh yes I am happy. Armaments Race. Evangeline Paterson. AMV-81
And much fruit, the swan. See in the Midst of Fair Leaves. Marianne Moore. MoAB
And must we part, because some say. The Suspition upon His Over-much Familiarity with a Gentlewoman. Robert Herrick. CavP
And my dear one sat in the shadows. Ford Madox Ford. *Fr.* On Heaven. ViBoPo
And my love has come to me. Wendell Berry. *Fr.* 9 Verses of the Same Song. LLLT
And my poor fool is hang'd! No, no, no life! Death of Lear. Shakespeare. *Fr.* King Lear, V, iii. FiP

And my young sweetheart sat at board with me. Idyl. Alfred Mombert, *tr. by* Ludwig Lewisohn. AWP
And Naomi said/ Unto her two daughters-in-law. Naomi and Ruth. Bible, *O.T.* *Fr.* Ruth. TrJP
And nature, the old nurse, took. The Manuscripts of God. Longfellow. TRV
And next morning, at the medical center. One More Time. Patricia Goedicke. AMV-80
And night and distant travel; for the train. Last Evening. Rainer Maria Rilke, *tr. by* J. B. Leishman. OBWP
"And not to God the Father," he ends. In Church. Thomas Hardy. *Fr.* Satires of Circumstance. MoAB
And nothing can we call our own but death. Shakespeare. King Richard II, *fr.* III, ii. DL
"And Now." J. B. Boothroyd. FiBHP
And now,/ wherever I walk. The Beach. Robert Peters. GP
And now a fig for the lower house. Patrick Cary. JCP
And now Aeneas charges straight at Turnus. Virgil, *tr. by* Allen Mandelbaum. *Fr.* The Aeneid, XII. OBWP
And now all Nature seem'd in Love. On a Bank [*or* Banck] as I Sate a-Fishing; a Description of the Spring [*or* A May Day]. Sir Henry Wotton. AnAnS-2; CH; LoBV; OBS; SeCP
And now. An attempt. Behold the Lilies of the Field. Anthony Hecht. CoPo; NePoEA-2
And now at last. Robert E. Lee. Stephen Vincent Benét. *Fr.* John Brown's Body. AmFN
And now at length the joyful time drew on. Endymion's Convoy. Michael Drayton. *Fr.* Endimion and Phoebe. OBSC
And now, behold! as at the approach of the morning. The Celestial Pilot. Dante, *tr. by* Longfellow. *Fr.* Divina Commedia: Purgatorio. WGRP
And now Eurynome had bath'd the king. Homer, *tr. by* George Chapman. *Fr.* The Odyssey, XXIII. OBVE
"And Now Farley Is Going to Sing *While I Drink a Glass of Water!*" Albert Goldbarth. GeTw
And now four days the sun had seen our woes. The Great Fire. Dryden. *Fr.* Annus Mirabilis. FiP
And now gentlemen. The Base of All Metaphysics. Walt Whitman. NePA
And, now gives Time, her states description. George Chapman. *Fr.* Euthymiae Raptus; or, The Teares of Peace. PoEL-2
And now his well-known bow the master bore. Homer, *tr. by* Pope. *Fr.* The Odyssey, XXI. OBVE
And now I follow my father. Pursuit. Vern Rutsala. FAZ
And now I have another lad! The Danger of Writing Defiant Verse. Dorothy Parker. InMe
And now I, Meleager, am among them. Epigram. Meleager, *tr. by* Peter Whigham. PeHV
And now in Ellesmereland there sits. Ellesmereland II. Earle Birney. CABA
And now, kind friends, what I have wrote. Julia A. Moore. FaBoCo; FiBHP
And now, man-slaughtering Pallas tooke in hand. The End of the Suitors. Homer, *tr. by* George Chapman. *Fr.* The Odyssey, XXII. OBS; OBVE
And now my pampered beast. Epitaph for My Cat. Jean Garrigue. TAP
And now one prayer. *Unknown, tr. by* William Morris *and* Eirikr Magnusson. *Fr.* The Elder Edda: The Lay of Sigurd. OBVE
"And now," said the Governor, gazing First Thanksgiving Day. Margaret Junkin Preston. PAH
And now she cleans her teeth into the lake. Camping Out. William Empson. CMoP; FaBoMo; MoVE; OxBTC
And now take thought, my sonnet, who is he. Sonnets of the Months: Conclusion. Folgore da San Geminiano, *tr. by* Dante Gabriel Rossetti. AWP
And now th'art set wide ope, the speare's sad art. I Am the Door. Richard Crashaw. OAEP
And, now that every thing may in the proper place. Michael Drayton. *Fr.* Polyolbion, XIV. FM
And now the book is closed. Anne Waldman *and* Ted Berrigan. *Fr.* Memorial Day; a Collaboration. EAS
And now the dark comes on, all full of chitter noise. The Sound of Night. Maxine W. Kumin. BoNaP; DFF; WPE
And now the green household is dark. In the Tree House at Night. James Dickey. NoP
And now the heart/ overflows its beats. Beginning. Marcos Rodríguez Frese, *tr. by* Julio Marzán. InW
And now the purple dusk of twilight time. Star Dust. Mitchell Parish. BLSo
And now the Queene of women had intent. Homer, *tr. by* George Chapman. *Fr.* The Odyssey, XXI. OBVE
And now the riverbank. For the last time. Marina Tsvetayeva, *tr. by* Paul Schmidt. *Fr.* The Daughter of Jairus, VII. BoWoP
And now the riverbank. I cling. Marina Tsvetayeva, *tr. by* Paul Schmidt. *Fr.* The Daughter of Jairus, III. BoWoP
And now the sea-scoured temptress, having failed. The Re-Birth of Venus. Geoffrey Hill. NePoEA
And now the sun that through the horizon peeps. Christopher Marlowe. *Fr.* Hero and Leander, Second Sestiad. OAEL-1
And now the trembling light. Shoreham: Twilight Time [*or* Twilight Time]. Samuel Palmer. FaBoPP; NBM; OAEL-2
And now there is nothing left to celebrate. George Barker. Pacific Sonnets, XII. LiTM; NeBP
And now they are no longer. Enough! James Scully. LTB
And now they nigh approachèd to the stead. The Mermaids. Edmund Spenser. *Fr.* The Faerie Queene, II, 12. ChTr
And now 'tis time; for their officious haste. Heroique Stanzas, Consecrated to the Glorious Memory of His Most Serene and Renowned Highnesse, Oliver, Late Lord Protector of This Common-Wealth. Dryden. SeCV-2
"And now to God the Father," he ends. In Church. Thomas Hardy. *Fr.* Satires of Circumstance. DTC; MoBrPo; SCV
And now to the abyss I pass. Andrew Marvell. *Fr.* Upon Appleton House. OAEL-1
And now 'twas done. The Death of Crazy Horse. John G. Neihardt. BPAW
And now, unveiled, the toilet stands displayed. The Toilet. Pope. *Fr.* The Rape of the Lock. NOBE; OBEC
And now was Paris come/ From his high towres. Homer, *tr. by* George Chapman. *Fr.* The Iliad, VI. OBVE
And now we know/ why coaches rage. On the Death of the Evansville University Basketball Team in a Plane Crash December 31, 1977. Robert W. Hamblin. AMV-80
And now we walked along the solid mire. Dante, *tr. by* Robert Lowell. Divina Commedia: Inferno, XV. OBVE
And now we will write the praises of our Lady. Weddâsê Māryām. *Unknown, tr. by* Sir E. A. Wallis Budge. ISi
And now where're he strayes. Richard Crashaw. *Fr.* Saint Mary Magdalene. FaBoCo; Par
And now, with gleams of half-extinguished thought. Wordsworth. *Fr.* Tintern Abbey. ViBoPo
And now you live dispersed on ribbon roads. T. S. Eliot. *Fr.* The Rock. TiPo
And Now You're Ready Who While She Was Here. J. V. Cunningham, *after the Greek of* Skythinos. OBVE; TW
(Epigram: "And now you're ready who while she was here.") ErPo
And of Columbus. Horace Gregory. GOA; OFD
And of Laughter That Was a Changeling. Elizabeth Rendall. HBMV
And oft the owle with rufull song complaind. Virgil, *tr. by* the Earl of Surrey. *Fr.* The Aeneid, IV. OBVE
And oft, while wonder thrill'd my breast, mine eyes. Waterspout. Luis de Camoes, *tr. fr. Portuguese.* EtS
And oh! the jay our nest did yield. Day's Work a-Done. William Barnes. SaC
And oh, to think the sun can shine. Adelaide Neilson. William Winter. AA
And on My Eyes Dark Sleep by Night. "Michael Field." OBMV
And on My Return. Haim Guri, *tr. fr. Hebrew by* Mark Elliott Shapiro. VWA
And on that day, upon the heavenly scarp. Psalm VI [*or* Upon the Heavenly Scarp]. A. M. Klein. *Fr.* The Psalter of Avram Haktani. PeCV
And on the porch, across the upturned chair. The Poet at Seven. Donald Justice. TwAmPo
And on the wall was limned a mouldering corse. On the Wall. Immanuel di Roma, *tr. by* Solomon Solis-Cohen. TrJP
And on this day, which poets unto thee. Ovid, *tr. by* Henry Vaughan. *Fr.* Tristium, V, 3. OBVE
And on This Shore. M. Carl Holman. AmNP; PoBA; PoNe
And once again I was within that house. The Dream. John Peale Bishop. LiTA; LiTM
And $1.13 + tx. And. Ricardo Gonsalves. FIA
And one morning while in the woods. Between the World and Me. Richard Wright. AmNP; IDB; LiTM; NoAM; PAI; PoBA
And One Shall Live in Two. Jonathan Henderson Brooks. PoNe
And Only Our Shadow Walks with Us. Eithne Wilkins. NeBP
And/Or. Clarence Day. WhC
And other wonders. Geological Faults. Barbara Unger. AMV-81
"And other wond'rous works were done." The Ascension of Our Lord Jesus Christ. Christopher Smart. Hymns and Spiritual Songs, Hymn 14. NOCV
And Paradise does come. Joy. Gavin Bantock. OxBTC
And Paris be it or Helen dying. A Fragment on [*or* of] Death. Villon, *tr. by* Swinburne. AWP; CTC
And Pergamos,/ City of the Phrygians. Chorus. Euripides, *tr. by* Hilda Doolittle ("H. D"). *Fr.* Iphigenia in Aulis. AWP; OBVE
And Pilate wrote a title, and put it on the cross. Inscription on the Cross. Bible, *N.T.* *Fr.* St. John. TreFT

"And pray, who are you?" The Tax-Gatherer. John Banister Tabb. GN
"And ride in triumph through Persepolis!" Christopher Marlowe. *Fr.* Tamburlaine the Great, Pt. I, Act II, sc. v. TrGrPo; WHA
And Ronda with the old windows of the posadas. Yes. James Joyce. *Fr.* Ulysses. FF
And Ruth said, Intreat me not to leave thee. Intreat Me Not to Leave Thee. Bible, *O.T.* *Fr.* Ruth. FF; PoPl; TreF
And said I that my limbs were old. Love. Sir Walter Scott. *Fr.* The Lay of the Last Minstrel. BSV
And Sam he looked again, and Sam he saw. *Unknown.* *Fr.* The Coming of K——. VLP
And Samson grew old in days. Samson. Amir Gilboa, *tr. by* Stephen Mitchell. VWA
And "Science" said. The Dunce. Walter de la Mare. ImOP
And see th' expected hour is on the wing. Propsect of the Future Glory of America. John Trumbull. AmPP
And seeing the multitudes, he went up into a mountain. The Sermon on the Mount. Bible, *N.T.* *Fr.* St. Matthew. BiP; NAWM-1; PoPl; TreF
And semblably, though I go not upright. John Lydgate. *Fr.* The Fall of Princes: Epilogue. OxBM
And several strengths from drowsiness campaigned. The Sermon on the Warpland. Gwendolyn Brooks. BPo; LiTM; NOBA; PoBA
And shall I weep that Love's no more. Le Roi Est Mort. Agnes Mary Frances Robinson. OBVV
And shall it never be again, never? Not on nights filled. To See Him Again. Gabriela Mistral, *tr. by* Doris Dana. OLR
And Shall Trelawny Die? Robert Stephen Hawker. *See* Song of the Western Men, The.
And she aloof to laughter—till I don't know. Big, Fat Summer—and the Lean and Hard. Frederick Bock. NYBP
And she, being old, fed from a mashed plate. Old Woman. Iain Crichton Smith. BSV; FaBoTw; NePoEA-2; OxBTC
And she is beautiful, our daughter. To Our Daughter. Jennifer Armitage. BrRo
And she is with me—years roll, I shall change. Andromeda. Robert Browning. *Fr.* Pauline. OBRV
And she said. Ritratto. Ezra Pound. PP
And She Was Bad. Marvin Wyche, Jr. AmNP
And She Washed His Feet with Her Tears, and Wiped Them with the Hairs of Her Head. Sir Edward Sherburne, *after the Italian of* Giambattista Marino. ChTr; MeLP; OBS; OxBoCh
(Magdalen, The.) ACP; GoBC
And shores and strands and naked piers. Henry James at Newport. Weldon Kees. PoA
And should I thank you, my dear skin. Gratitude. Annette Lynch. FF
And silence/ And not another word. Monument to Pushkin. Joseph Brodsky, *tr. by* Dimitry Pospielovsky *and* Keith Bosley. VWA
And silence/ which proves. The End of Man Is His Beauty. Amiri Baraka. AmNP; BALP
And slowly answered Arthur from the barge. Tennyson. *Fr.* Morte d'Arthur (*also in* Idylls of the King: The Passing of Arthur). FaBoEn
And so an easier life our Cyclops drew. The Cyclops. Theocritus, *tr. by* Elizabeth Barrett Browning. Idylls, XI. AWP; OBVE
And so depart into dark. Homage to Ezra Pound. Gilbert Highet. BXAP; Par
And so for nights. The Night-blooming Cereus. Robert Hayden. FB; HoAn; NoP; NU
And so he called her Pigeon. Husband Betrayed. John Crowe Ransom. TwAmPo
And so I cross into another world. New Heaven and Earth. D. H. Lawrence. CMoP
And so I somehow-nohow played. Robert Browning. *Fr.* Fifine at the Fair. Par
And so I speak/ in place of that primordial cry. Monique Laederach, *tr. fr. French by* Charles Guenther. *Fr.* Penelope. BoWoP
And so it came to that last day. St. James' Grove. William Carlos Williams. TwAmPo
And so must I lose her whose mind. Prothalamium. Donagh MacDonagh. BIrV; NeIP
And so our royal relative is dead! A Dirge. William Augustus Croffut. InMe
And So Should You. Anna Temple Whitney. *See* Kneeling Camel, The.
And so that all these ages, these years. From the Domain of Arnheim. Edwin Morgan. BSV
And so the river moves. The Lost Children. Richard Eberhart. NePoAm-2
And so the things the country wants to see. Local Politics. Robert Pinsky. MAYP
And so they buried Lincoln? Strange and vain. Cenotaph of Lincoln. James T. McKay. OHIP
And so to a chambre full solacious. Dame Music. Stephen Hawes. *Fr.* The Pastime of Pleasure. PoEL-1
And so we two [*or* too] came where the rest have come. The Question. F. T. Prince. BoLoP; ChMP; GTBS-P; PeSA
And so you find them somewhat thin. The Old Songs. Sir Owen Seaman. InMe
And some are sulky, while some will plunge. Horses. Kipling. BoAnP; PH; POL
And some chose trade they fared the better. The Entertainment Industry. William Langland, *mod. by* Donald Attwater. *Fr.* The Vision of Piers Plowman. NOCV
"And something that . . . that is theirs—no longer ours." The Dispossessed. John Berryman. AP; PoCh; VGW
And sometimes in the cool night I see you are an animal. Ode for Soft Voice. Michael McClure. NeAP
And sometimes the speech. Invisible Trumpets Blowing. E. J. Pratt. *Fr.* Brébeuf and His Brethren. CaP
And spoke: coopers, craftsmen, shepherds. Great God Paused among Men. Daniel Berrigan. MAT
And, star and system rolling past. Tennyson. *Fr.* In Memoriam A. H. H., Epilogue. ImOP
And still I lie here. Song of the Invisible Corpse in the Field. Gregory Orr. LTB
And still the picnickers come on. Sunday in the Park. William Carlos Williams. *Fr.* Paterson. CrMA
And still they come and go: and this is all I know. Picture-Show. Siegfried Sassoon. CMoP
And still we stood and stared far down. Therefore Is the Name of It Called Babel. Sir Osbert Sitwell. MMA
And still you paint, and still I stand. The Painter's Mistress. James Elroy Flecker. BrPo
And Summer mornings the mute child, rebellious. Eleven. Archibald MacLeish. HAP; NCSH; WeW
And Summer turns her head with its dark tangle. Ralegh's Prizes. Robert Pinsky. MAYP
And that question which I have not asked. The Last. Ezra Zussman, *tr. by* D. Shnayorson. VWA
And That Will Be Heaven. Evangeline Paterson. EBCP
And That's All. *Unknown.* OxNR
And the Americans put Pound in a cage. The Cage. John Berryman. PoA
And the angel, taking some pains, told. Joseph's Suspicion. Rainer Maria Rilke. TrCP
And the betrayers of language. Ezra Pound. *Fr.* Cantos, XIV. MoPo
And the bitter storm augments; the wild winds wage. John Josselyn. SCAP
And the child, mine. Expectation. Aliza Shenhar, *tr. by* Linda Zisquit. VWA
And the Cock Begins to Crow, *with music.* Richard K. Avery. AH
And the Communists have nothing to offer but fat cheeks and eyeglasses and lying policemen. Kral Majales. Allen Ginsberg. GP; PoM
And the curtains, the lamp. True to a Dream. Donald Petersen. NePoEA-2
And the day arrives at last, my friends. Nightmare of a Cook. Chester Kallman. CrMA
And the days are not full enough. Ezra Pound. PCP
And the Dead. Sean Jennett. NeBP
And the Earth Rebelled. Yuri Suhl, *tr. fr. Yiddish by* Max Rosenfeld. TrJP
And "the earth under our feet." At Kenneth Burke's Place. William Carlos Williams. NOBA
And the first among them. Stony Brook Tavern. Ken Belford. NeAC
And the first grey of morning fill'd the east. Sohrab and Rustum. Matthew Arnold. DTo; OBNV; VLP
And the Gas Chamber Drones in the Distance. Greg Forker. LFAC
And the ground spoke when she was born. For Alva Benson, and for All Those Who Have Learned to Speak. Joy Harjo. TWSS
And the gud King held forth the way. Bruce Meets Three Men with a Wether. John Barbour. *Fr.* The Bruce. OxBM
And the Hotel Room Held Only Him. Mari Evans. PAI
And the hypocrites. Those Not Confused Are Prisoners of War. Noah Mitchell. LFAC
And the ladies dress in silk. On the High Cost of Dairy Products. James McIntyre. FiBHP
And the least of these. Handicapped. Daniel Berrigan. FAZ
And the lemon is tall. The sun is tall, and descends. Lemon. Mario Satz, *tr. by* Willis Barnstone. VWA
And the light, a wakened heyday of air. November Sunday Morning. Alvin Feinman. CoAP
And the Lord God formed man of the dust of the ground. Bible, *O.T.* *Fr.* Genesis. TreFT
And the Lord God planted a garden eastward in Eden. Bible, *O.T.* *Fr.* Genesis. OAEL-1
And the Lord said unto Samuel, How long wilt thou mourn for Saul. David and Goliath. Bible, *O.T. Fr.* First Samuel. TreFS
And the Lord Was Not in the Whirlwind. Louis MacNeice. *Fr.* Visitations: VII. EaLo

And the mist: and the rain in the west: and the wind steady. The Omelet of A. MacLeish. Edmund Wilson. NYBP; Par
And the mother, closing the exercise book. Poets Seven Years Old. Arthur Rimbaud, *tr. by* Kenneth Koch *and* Georges Guy. SOTW
And the new sun broke on fields of grain. My Life like Any Other. Philip Levine. AMV-81
And the next who came in was a sailor. When Johnson's Ale Was New. *Unknown.* ShS
And the Old Folks Said. Diane Mei Lin Mark. BrSi
And the Old Women Gathered. Mari Evans. BlSi; NNP; PoBA
And the order of the universe is reversed. Call to Order. Carol Burbank. SUW
And the place of their waiting a long burrow. David Jones. *Fr.* In Parenthesis. FaBoMo
And the raying sun from behind breaks out east. Heraclitus in the West. Charles G. Bell. NePoAm
And the robins. Variations on a Late October Day. George Mosby, Jr. LFAC
And the Russian women in blue towns. The Women Speaking. Linda Hogan. TWSS
And the Same Words. David Ignatow. NNaP
And the Seventh Dream Is the Dream of Isis. David Gascoyne. EAS
And the Silver Turns into Night. Nathan Yonathan, *tr. fr. Hebrew by* Richard Flantz. VWA
And the snake was/ talking to Eve. An Old Story. Rena Lee. VWA
And the stones in the Prague cemetery were so bored. The Drunken Stones of Prague. David Scheinert, *tr. by* Edouard Roditi. VWA
And the storm-fiends wild rave. Shelley. *Fr.* St. Irvyne. PeD
And the stranger at last stood before the monument of lava and anger. The Stone and the Blade of Grass in the Warsaw Ghetto. David Scheinert, *tr. by* Edouard Roditi. VWA
And the sun wields mercy. The Sun Wields Mercy. Charles Bukowski. MAT
And the traveller hopes: let me be far from any. Journey to Iceland. W. H. Auden. PoA
And the trunk: "So sweet those words to me that I." Pier delle Vigne. Dante, *tr. by* John Ciardi. *Fr.* Divina Commedia: Inferno, XIII. HoPM
And the two reservist guys went. Look, don't shoot. The Poem on Our Mother, Our Mother Rachel. Avot Yeshurun, *tr. by* Harold Schimmel. VWA
And the undecided question. The Lust for Murder. Gerda Penfold. GP
And the voice said: Walk. Little Falls. Robert Hogg. MoCV
And the way goes on in the worn earth. Prologue. Archibald MacLeish. *Fr.* Conquistador. NoAM
And the whole earth was of one language, and of one speech. Bible, *O.T.* *Fr.* Genesis. EyDe; NAWM-1
And the whole multitude of them arose. The Death of Jesus. Bible, *N.T.* *Fr.* St. Luke. TreF
And the Winner Is. Greg Forker. LFAC
And the woman sat on. About Women's Liberation. María Saucedo, *tr. by* Toni Empringham. FIA
And the World's Face. Julian Symons. WaP
And then fate strikes us. First our joys decay. Wilfrid Scawen Blunt. The Love Sonnets of Proteus, LXXV. VLP
And then he would lift this finest. Out-of-the-Body Travel. Stanley Plumly. AmPA; DiL; GeTw; LCAP
And then I pressed the shell. The Shell. James Stephens. BoNaP; CH; CMoP; MoAB; MoBrPo; MOS; MoShBr; MoVE
And then I sat me down, and gave the rein. Sonnet. Gustav Rosenhane, *tr. by* Sir Edmund Gosse. AWP
And then I wakened up in such a fright. Midnight. James Stephens. DTC
And then in mid-May the first morning of steady heat. Late Spring. Robert Hass. GeTw; MAYP
And Then It Rained. Mark Van Doren. BoNaP
And Then No More. Friedrich Rückert, *tr. fr. German by* James Clarence Mangan. AnIV; BIrV; BLPA
And then one day Hershey played by the door. You Are a Jew! Delmore Schwartz. *Fr.* Genesis. TrJP
And then she saw me creeping. Fossils. James Stephens. OnYI
And then the blue world daring onward. The Handball Players at Brighton Beach. Irving Feldman. NYP
And then the drug takes hold. Sleeping Pill. Diana O Hehir. AMV-81
And then the knife. Song of the Hanged. Eléni Vakaló, *tr. by* James Damaskos. PBWP
And then the old inhabitants, so kind. Fishing Village. Louis Dudek. *Fr.* Provincetown. MoCV
And then went down to the ship. Ezra Pound. Cantos, I. AmPP; CMoP; CoBMV; LiTA; MoAB; MoAmPo; MoVE; NoAM; NoP; OBVE; SeCeV; TrGrPo; VGW
And Then What. Dave Kelly. POL
And there are times truly. An Underdeveloped Country. D. J. Enright. NOBL
And there came two angels to Sodom at even. Bible, *O.T.* *Fr.* Genesis. HoPM
And there followed him a great company of people. Bible, *N.T.* *Fr.* St. Luke. LO
"And there goes the bell for the third month." The Fight of the Year. Robert McGough. OBCP
And there he was—/ the rhinoceros! Rhinoceros. William Hart-Smith. BoAnP
And there I found a gray and ancient ass. Pegasus Lost. Elinor Wylie. MoAmPo
And there I saw the seed upon the mountain. Preludes to Definition, I. Conrad Aiken. TwAmPo
And there I was. Not a dictionary. Northwest Airlines. Fred Chappell. HoPM
And there is nothing at all—neither fear. Natalya Gorbanyevskaya, *tr. fr. Russian by* Daniel Weissbort. BoWoP
And there it was once, on the banks. The Lake above Santos. Keith Wilson. GP
And there shall come forth a rod out of the stem of Jesse. The Rod of Jesse. Bible, *O.T.* *Fr.* Isaiah. AWP; OBVE; TrJP
And there she's leand her back to a thorn. The Cruel Mother. *Unknown.* ESPB
And there the knight stands, wringing his hands. St. Cuthbert Intervenes. "Thomas Ingoldsby." *Fr.* The Ingoldsby Legends. NBM
And there they were: with fire everywhere. A New Dance. S. E. Anderson. NBP
"And There Was a Great Calm." Thomas Hardy. ChTr; CMoP; FaBoRV; LiTM; OAEL-2
And there was complacency in heaven. Saints Lose Back. Nancy Willard. HoAn
And there was grass on the floor of the temple. Ezra Pound. *Fr.* Cantos, XXI. MoPo
And there was great mourning in Israel in every place. Great Mourning. Bible, Apocrypha. *Fr.* First Maccabees. TrJP
And there were in the same country shepherds abiding in the field. The First Christmas [*or* Christmas Eve *or* Tidings of Great Joy]. Bible, *N.T.* *Fr.* St. Luke. FaPON; PChr; SiSoSe; SoPo
And there were spring-faced cherubs that did sleep. The Sea of Death. *Unknown.* CH
And There Will I Be Buried. Thomas Davidson. BSV
And therefore praise I even the most high. James Branch Cabell. *Fr.* Retractions. HBMV
And therewith cast I doun mine eye again. Walking under the Tour. James I, King of Scotland. *Fr.* The Kingis Quair. SeCePo
And these few precepts in thy memory. Polonius to Laertes [*or* This above All]. Shakespeare. *Fr.* Hamlet, I, iii. GN; MasP; TrGrPo
And these mountains which my eyes have seen. The Seven Metal Mountains. Bible, Pseudepigrapha. *Fr.* Enoch. TrJP
And they both lived happily ever after. After Ever Happily. Ian Serraillier. SO
And they brought young children to him. Jesus and the Children. Bible, *N.T.* *Fr.* St. Mark. TreFT
And they had fixed the wedding day. Wordsworth. *Fr.* The Thorn. EvOK
And they have drown'd thee then at last! poor Phillis! On the Death of a Favourite Old Spaniel. Robert Southey. FM
And they have thrust our shattered dead away in foreign graves. The Martyrs of the *Maine.* Rupert Hughes. PAH
And They Shall Beat Their Swords into Plowshares. Bible, *O.T.* Micah, IV: 1-5. TreF
(Neither Shall They Learn War Any More.) TRV
And They Were Richt. Robert Garioch. BSV
And they were there in the City of Fire, enflamed. JuJu. Askia Muhammad Touré. PoBA
And this comely dame. John Skelton. *Fr.* Elinor Rumming. ViBoPo
And this I hate—not men, nor flag, nor race. The Hymn of Hate. Joseph Dana Miller. PGD
"And this is freedom!" cried the serf. Bondage. "Owen Innsley." AA
And this is [*or* Here's to] good old Boston. A Boston Toast [*or* On the Aristocracy of Harvard *or* To Boston]. John Collins Bossidy. AmFN; BLPA; CenHV; HBV-1; TreFS; WhC; YaD
And this is how you live: a woman, children. A Primary Ground. Adrienne Rich. NNaP
And this is it: the pause. Winding Down the War. Philip Appleman. SOTS
And This Is Love. Paula Reingold. IHMS
And This Is My Father. Marcus J. Grapes. AMV-80
And this is the organ which was made last. Skinning-the-Cat. Dennis Schmitz. NPGG
And this is the song that the white woman sings. Goosey Goosey Gander—

by Various Authors (Kipling's Version). William Percy French. CenHV
And this is the way the baby woke. The Way the Baby Woke. James Whitcomb Riley. AA
And this is the way they ring. Ringing the Bells. Anne Sexton. BiP; CAPP; FF; NMP; TAP; VGW
And this July—its nakedness burned out. Tansy for August. Theodore Enslin. CoPo
And this reft house is that the which he built. On a Ruined House in a Romantic Country. Samuel Taylor Coleridge. FaBoPa; Par
And thou, America,/ For the scheme's culmination. Song of the Universal. Walt Whitman. PGD
And Thou Art Dead. Byron. PoEL-4
(Elegy on Thyrza.) GTBS; GTBS-P
And thou art gone, most loved, most honored friend. On the Late S. T. Coleridge. Washington Allston. AA
And thou art now no longer near! To the Parted One. Goethe, *tr. by* Christopher Pearse Cranch. AWP
And thou, Dalhousie, the Great God of War. *Unknown.* FaBoCo
And thou hast walked about (how strange a story!) Address to a Mummy. Horace Smith. HBV-2; RoGo
And Thou, O Lord! by whom are seen. Whittier. *Fr.* The Eternal Goodness. TrPWD
And thou, O Virgin, Daughter, Mother, Bride. Appeal for Illumination. Luigi Pulci, *tr. by* Byron. Il Morgante Maggiore, Canto I, ii. ISi
And thou that art the flower of virgins all. Invocatio ad Mariam. Chaucer, *mod. vers. by* Frank Ernest Hill. *Fr.* The Canterbury Tales: The Prologue to the Second Nun's Tale. ISi
And thou wert sad—yet I was not with thee. Lines on Hearing That Lady Byron Was Ill. Byron. EBEV
And Thou! whom earth still holds, and will not yield. Wordsworth. William Wilberforce Lord. *Fr.* Ode to England. AA
And three baby barn swallows. After an All-Night Cackle with Sloth and Co. I Enter and Greet the Dawn. Gary Gildner. GP
And Three Hundred and Sixty-six in Leap Year. Ogden Nash. NePA
And through the Caribbean Sea. Margaret Danner. BPo
And thus as we were talking to and fro. Complaint [*or* Compleynt] of the Common Weill of Scotland. Sir David Lindsay. *Fr.* The Dreme. BSV; GoTS; OxBS
And thus continuing, she said. Wordsworth. *Fr.* The Sailor's Mother. Par
And thus declared that Arab lady. Solomon and the Witch. W. B. Yeats. NoAM
And Thus in Nineveh. Ezra Pound. PP; VGW
And thus went out this lamp of light. An Account of the Cruelty of the Papists. Benjamin Harris. SCAP
And timid, funny, brisk little bunny. Christina Rossetti. *Fr.* Sing-Song. TiPo
And to Her-Without-Bounds I send. Tribal Memories. Robert Duncan. Passages, I. NOBA
And to the Young Men. Merrill Moore. MoAmPo
And Tomorrow Wend Our Ways. *Malay Oral Tradition, tr. by* R. J. Wilkinson *and* R. O. Winstedt. WTO
And, truly, I would rather be struck dumb. Keats. *Fr.* Endymion. ViBoPo
And Truly It Is a Most Glorious Thing, *with music.* William Bradford. AH
And Turnus than, quhar he at erth dyd ly. Virgil, *tr. by* Gavin Douglas. *Fr.* The Aeneid, XII. OBVE
And two birdchildren. Poem for Thel—the Very Tops of Trees. Joseph Major. NBP
And walked across Potomac into Thebes. Effigy. Georgia Lee McElhaney. CoPo
And was it good for you this time? The Love-making: His and Hers. Eve Merriam. UnTE
And was it true,/ The stranger standing so. The Annunciation. John Duffy. ISi
And Was Not Improved. Lerone Bennett, Jr. CNA; PoBA
And wasna he a roguey. The Piper o' Dundee. *Unknown.* OxBS
And We Conquered. Rob Penny. PoBA
And we love Art for Art's sake. Art for Art's Sake. Marc Blitzstein. *Fr.* The Cradle Will Rock. TrJP
And we were speaking easily and all the light stayed low. In Judgment of the Leaf. Kenneth Patchen. VGW
And we will lace the. God Send Easter. Lucille Clifton. CNA
And welcom now (Great Monarch) to your own. Dryden. *Fr.* Astraea Redux. OBS
And What About the Children. Audre Lorde. PoBA
And what are we to do with the horses. Answer. Leah Goldberg, *tr. by* Robert Friend. VWA
And what are you that, wanting you. The Philosopher. Edna St. Vincent Millay. CMoP
And what I have learned. Duncan Spoke of a Process. Amiri Baraka. CAPP
And what if all Nature ratify this merciless outrage? Robert Bridges. *Fr.* Epistle II: To a Socialist in London. FM
And what is left for the others. What Is Left? István Vas, *tr. by* Emery George. VWA
And what is life? A Primer for Schoolchildren. Richard Weber. CIP
And what is love? It is a doll dress'd up. Modern Love. Keats. OBNC
And what is love? Misunderstanding, pain. Epigram. J. V. Cunningham. HAP; HoPM; NePoAm; PoA
And what is [*or* What is] so rare as a day in June? June [*or* A Day in June]. James Russell Lowell. *Fr.* The Vision of Sir Launfal. BLPL; FaBoBe; FaBV; FaFP; FaPON
And what Mantle dreams of. Even the Best. Gary Allan Kizer. LFAC
And what, my thoughtless sons, should fire you more. Britannia's Empire. James Thomson. *Fr.* Britannia. OBEC
And What of Me? Liz Sohappy Bahe. CDW
And what of you? You also shall not say. Insights. Catherine Davis. QFR
And what shall I bring back from such a voyage. Voyage. Stanislaw Wygodski, *tr. by* Isaac Komem. VWA
And What Shall You Say? Joseph Seamon Cotter, Jr. BANP; CDC; PoBA; PoNe
And What though Winter Will Pinch Severe. Sir Walter Scott. *Fr.* Old Mortality, *ch.* 19. EnRP
And what was the big room he walked in? Before a Fall. Geoffrey Grigson. EAS
And What with the Blunders. Kenneth Patchen. NaP
And when/ the cold white ness. Query. Ebon Dooley. PoBA
And when her broken thoughts went following after. Seven Sad Sonnets, V. Mary Aldis. HBMV
And When I Am Entombéd. Emerson. ViBoPo
And When I Lamented. Heine, *tr. fr. German by* Emma Lazarus. *Fr.* Homeward Bound. TrJP
And when I pay death's duty. Poem. Robin Blaser. NeAP
"And when it comis to the ficht." Bruce Addresses His Army. John Barbour. *Fr.* The Bruce, X. GoTS
And, when it was darkest, I came to a strong City. The Strong City. Alfred Noyes. *Fr.* The Last Voyage, Dedication. GoBC
And when my work is over, to Cheyenne then I'll head. Dodge City, the End of the Trial. *Unknown.* CoSo
And when that ballad lady went. A Road in Kentucky. Robert Hayden. LCAP; NCSH
And When the Green Man Comes. John Haines. ConAP; NCSH
And When the Prince Came. Robert Hillyer. DFT
And when the rain had gone away. The Bug. Marjorie Barrows. RHPC
And When the Revolution Came. Carolyn M. Rodgers. GP
And when the sun puts out his lamp. To the Mountains. Henry David Thoreau. PoEL-4
And when they asked her what she wanted to be. Vocation. Judith Herzberg, *tr. by* Manfred Wolf. WPOW
And when they came together in one place. Homer, *tr. by* Tennyson. *Fr.* The Iliad, IV. OBVE
And When They Fall. James J. Montague. HBMV
And when they see me coming. Beware of Larry Gorman. Larry Gorman. ShS
And when thou hast on foot the purblind hare. Poor Wat. Shakespeare. *Fr.* Venus and Adonis. OBSC
And when thy heart is resting. Emily Brontë. LO
And when we die at last. Heaven and Hell. *Unknown, tr. by* Edward Field. DL
And when you have forgotten the bright bedclothes. When You Have Forgotten Sunday: The Love Story. Gwendolyn Brooks. BPo; FF
And when you try to sleep. For Bill. Geof Hewitt. NeAC
And when you walk the world lifts up its head. To a Very Beautiful Lady. Ruthven Todd. BSV; NeBP
"And where have you been, my Mary?" The Fairies of the Caldon-Low. Mary Howitt. BeLS; HBV-1; HBVY
"And where now, Bayard, will thy footsteps tend?" Bayard Taylor. Whittier. HBV-2
And while my visitor prattled. Secret Thoughts. Christopher Morley. *Fr.* Translations from the Chinese. EvOK
And While We Are Waiting. Carolyn M. Rodgers. JB
And whilst the outer lake beneath the lash. Shelley. *Fr.* The Witch of Atlas. PBBP
And Who Has Seen a Fair Alluring Face. George Peele. ErPo
And who has seen the moon, who has not seen. Moonrise. D. H. Lawrence. LiTM; MOON; PoA
And who shall say. Magic. Thomas Wolfe. PoPl
And who shall separate the dust. Common Dust. Georgia Douglas Johnson. AmNP; PoBA; TTY
And why does Gratt teach English? Why, because. Professor Gratt. Donald Hall. OBAL
And why, in God's name, is that elegant bureau. Ballad of a Sweet Dream of Peace. Robert Penn Warren. TwAmPo

And why not I, as hee. To Himselfe and the Harpe. Michael Drayton. OBS
And why so coffined in this vile disguise. John Cleveland. *Fr.* The King's Disguise. JCP
And why to me this, thou lame Lord of fire. An Execration upon Vulcan. Ben Jonson. AnAnS-2; SeCP
And Will He [*or* A'] Not Come Again? Shakespeare. *Fr.* Hamlet, IV, v. PoEL-2; ViBoPo
(Ophelia's Songs, 2.) TrGrPo
And will she never hold her tongue. The Power of Silence. W. H. Davies. BrPo
And will they always be so tender, her. Swift Love, Sweet Motor. Hildegarde Flanner. WPE
And will they cast the altars down. In Portugal, 1912. Alice Meynell. NOCV; OxBoCh
"And will you cut a stone for him." The Stone. W. W. Gibson. MoBrPo
And wilt thou have me fashion into speech. Elizabeth Barrett Browning. Sonnets from the Portuguese, XIII. BrRo
And Wilt Thou Leave Me Thus? Sir Thomas Wyatt. ElL; EnLoPo; EnRePo; OAEP; SiPS
("And wylt thou leve me thus?") AAS
(Appeal, An [*or* The].) NOBE; OBEV; OBSC
(Earnest Suit, An.) GoBC
(Lover's Appeal, The.) GTBS; GTBS-P
(Say Nay.) LoBV
And with great fear I inhabit the middle of the night. The Acts of Youth. John Wieners. CoPo
And worth the blossoms that acacias. Poplar Tree. Padraic Colum. NePoAm
And would you gather turds. A History of Love. William Carlos Williams. VGW
And Would You See My Mistress' Face? *At. to* Thomas Campion. OAEP; OBSC
"And would you sign my copy sir?" "A Scotch?" The Poet at Fifty. Laurence Lerner. PeSA
And would'st thou reach, rash scholar mine. Zeal and Love. Cardinal Newman. TW
And wylt thow leve me thus? *See* And wilt thou leave me thus?
"And ye sall walk in silk attire." The Siller Croun. Susanna Blamire. HBV-1
And, yeah, brothers. I Sing of Shine. Etheridge Knight. BPo; GP
And Yet. Kadya Molodovsky, *tr. fr. Yiddish by* Seymour Levitan. VWA
And Yet. Arthur B. Rhinow. BLRP
And Yet. Errol B. Sloan. BLRP
And yet a kiss (like blubber)'d blur and slip. Love and Death. John Frederick Nims. HoPM; WeW
And yet, because thou overcomest so. Elizabeth Barrett Browning. Sonnets from the Portuguese, XVI. OAEP
And yet but lately have I seen, e'en here. A Winter-Piece. Ambrose Philips. SeCePo
And yet hath prayer, the heav'n-breathing foliage of faith. Ethick. Robert Bridges. *Fr.* The Testament of Beauty. OxBTC
And yet how lovely in thine age of woe. Greece. Byron. *Fr.* Childe Harold's Pilgrimage, II. OBRV
And yet I cannot reprehend the flight. To Delia, XXXII. Samuel Daniel. HBV-1; OAEP; OBEV
And yet the driving mirror shows me plain. To His Coy Mistress. W. J. Webster. BXAP
And yet the southern whale does some time come. The Whales. Marguerite Young. WPE
And yet this great wink of eternity. Voyages, II. Hart Crane. AmPP; CoBMV; DTC; FaBoEn; HAP; LiTM; MoAB; MoAmPo; MoPo; MOS; MoVE; NePA; NU; PPoe; PPP; TwAmPo; UnPo; VGW; ViBoPo
And Yet We Are Here! Karl Wolfskehl, *tr. fr. German by* Carol North Valhope *and* Ernst Morwitz. TrJP
And yet, where would we be without the American culture. Goodbye Nkrumah. Diane di Prima. PoM
And you are dead. The earth has not yet covered you. Isaac Leybush Peretz. Moishe Leib Halpern, *tr. by* Kathryn Hellerstein. VWA
And You Are There. Tom Clark. LiSp
And You as Well Must Die, Beloved Dust. Edna St. Vincent Millay. FPL; PoLF; PoRA; TAP
(Sonnet: "And you as well must die, beloved dust.") MasP
And you believed that I would do it so? Broken Monologue. "Michael Lewis." UnTE
And you, big rocket. November the Fifth. Leonard Clark. OnUR
And you came back. Samar Attar. *Fr.* The Return of the Dead. PBWP
And You, Helen. Edward Thomas. BoLoP
"And you, Sir Poet, shall you make, I pray." The Poet and the Child. Winifred Howells. AA
And you, whate'er your Fav'rite does, approve. Tibullus, *tr. by* John Dart. *Fr.* Odes, I, 4. PeHV
And you who love, you who attach yourselves. Conrad Aiken. *Fr.* Time in the Rock. ViBoPo
And you'll say a nation totters. G. D. H. Cole. *Fr.* Civil Riot. OxBTC
Andalusian merchant, that returns, The. *Unknown. Fr.* Wonders. FaBoCh
Andalusian Sereno, The. Francis Saltus Saltus. AA
Andante, ma Non Assai. Rufinus, *tr. fr. Greek by* Dudley Fitts. ErPo
Andante of Snakes, The. Arthur Symons. VLP
Andonis, My Daughter. Thomas Peacock. VoR
Andraitx—Pomegranate Flowers. D. H. Lawrence. NoAM; NoP
André. Charlotte Fiske Bates. PAH
Andre. Gwendolyn Brooks. TiPo
Andrea del Sarto. Robert Browning. CABA; CTC; HBV-1; NoP; OAEL-2; OAEP; PoEL-5; VLP; WHA
Andreas, *sel. Unknown, tr. fr. Anglo-Saxon by* Charles W. Kennedy.
St. Andrew's Voyage to Mermedonia. AnOE
Andrée Rexroth. Kenneth Rexroth. PrIm; VGW
André's Request to Washington. *Unknown.* PAH
André's Ride. Augustus Henry Beesly. HBV-2
Andrew. Thomas William Parsons. AA
Andrew and Maudlin, Rebecca and Will. A Ballad of Andrew and Maudlin. *Unknown.* CoMu
Andrew Gear of Sunderland. *Unknown.* FaBoCo
Andrew Jackson. Stephen Vincent Benét. InMe
Andrew Jackson. Martha Keller. AmFN
Andrew Jackson's Speech. Robert Bly. ConAP
Andrew Lammie. *See* Trumpeter of Fyvie, The.
Andrew Magrath's Reply to John O'Tuomy. Andrew Magrath, *tr. fr. Modern Irish by* John O'Daly, *vers. by* James Clarence Mangan. OnYI
Andrew M'Crie. Robert Fuller Murray. CenHV; FaBoCo
Andrew Rykman's Prayer, *sels.* Whittier.
"If there be some weaker one." TRV
"Make my mortal dreams come true." TrPWD
"Pardon, Lord, the lips that dare." TrPWD
Andrew's Bedtime Story. Ian Serraillier. DuDa
Androgynous child whose hair curls into flowers. The Total Influence or Outcome of the Matter: The Sun. Marge Piercy. WPOW
Andromache, *sel.* Euripides, *tr. fr. Greek by* George Allen.
Chorus: The Kings of Troy. WaaP
Andromache, I think of you! The stream. The Swan. Baudelaire, *tr. by* F. P. Sturm. SyP
Andromache's Lamentation. Homer, *tr. fr. Greek by* Congreve. *Fr.* The Iliad, XXIV. OBVE
Andromache's Wedding. Sappho, *tr. fr. Greek by* Willis Barnstone. BoWoP
Andromeda. Thomas Bailey Aldrich. AA
Andromeda. Robert Browning. *Fr.* Pauline. OBRV
Andromeda. Gerard Manley Hopkins. EBEV; FaBoMo; LiTB; VLP
Andromeda, *sel.* Charles Kingsley.
Nereids, The. NBM
Andromeda. James Jeffrey Roche. AA; HBV-2
Andromeda/ forgot. Sappho, *tr. fr. Greek by* Willis Barnstone. BoWoP
Andromeda, by Perseus saved and wed. Aspecta Medusa. Dante Gabriel Rossetti. VLP
Andy-Diana DNA Letter. Andrew Weiman. HAP
Andy's Gone with Cattle. Henry Lawson. PoAu-1
Ane Ballat of Our Lady. William Dunbar. *See* Ballad of Our Lady.
Ane doolie sessoun [*or* season] to ane cairfull [*or* careful] dyte. The Testament of Cresseid. Robert Henryson. BSV; GoTS; OxBS
Ane mornin when aw went te wark. The Row between the Cages. Thomas Armstrong. VLP
Ane Sang of the Birth of Christ, with the Tune of Baw Lula Low. Martin Luther, *tr. fr. German by* John Wedderburn. ChTr
Ane Satire [*or* Satyre] of the Three [*or* Thrie] Estaitis, *sels.* Sir David Lindsay.
"Have I nocht made ane honest shift." GoTS
"My patent pardouns ye may see." OBSV
(Pardoner's Sermon, The.) BSV
Ane Supplication in Contemptioun of Syde Taillis, *abr.* Sir David Lindsay. GoTS
Ane to Anither. Duncan Glen. PoSH
Anear the centre of that northern crest. The City's Queen. James Thomson ("B.V."). The City of Dreadful Night, XXI. FaBoEn; GTBS-P; NOBE; OAEP; VLP
Anecdote for Fathers. Wordsworth. EnRP
Anecdote from William IV Street. D. J. Enright. OxBC
Anecdote of the Jar. Wallace Stevens. AmPP; AP; CMoP; CoBMV; HeIP; HoPM; InPK; LiTA; MoAB; MoAmPo; MoVE; NePA; NIP; NoAM; NOBA; NoP; OxBA; PAI; PoA; PPP; PrIm; SOTW; TAP; UnPo
Anecdote of the Prince of Peacocks. Wallace Stevens. SOTW
Anecdote of the Sparrow. Robert Pack. NePA
Anecdote of 2 A.M. John Wain. NMP
Anemic pictures! Legend. Jules Laforgue, *tr. by* Louis Simpson. Prf

Anesthetist is singing, The. In the Operating Room. Alden Nowlan. NOBC
Angel, The ("I asked a thief. . ."). Blake. *See* I Asked a Thief.
Angel, The ("I dreamt a dream!"). Blake. *Fr.* Songs of Experience. CH; EnRP; LAuP
Angel, The. Alfred Hayes. TrJP
Angel. Brad Leithauser. FYAP; MAYP
Angel. James Merrill. ConAP; PoA
(Another Angel.) NoAM
Angel. Cardinal Newman. *Fr.* The Dream of Gerontius. GoBC; OxBoCh
"Angel." Robin Skelton. NMP
Angel. Gary Soto. AMV-80
Angel, The/ against a backdrop of gold. Renaissance/a Triptych. John Minczeski. PoDr
Angel and Stone. Howard Nemerov. NYBP
Angel and the Anchorite, The. Richard Shelton. NPAW
Angel and the girl are met, The. The Annunciation. Edwin Muir. CMoP; NOCV; PAI
Angel came by night, The. Adsum. Richard Henry Stoddard. AA
Angel came to me and said, An. A Memorable Fancy. Blake. *Fr.* The Marriage of Heaven and Hell. NU
Angel came to me and stood by my bedside, An. Nightmare, with Angels. Stephen Vincent Benét. MAT
Angel came to me, An. O Simplicitas. Madeleine L'Engle. *Fr.* Three Songs of Mary. EBCP; OBCP; PChr
Angel Describes Truth, An. Ben Jonson. *Fr.* Hymenaei. OBS
Angel Eye of Memory. John Malcolm Brinnin. PoA
Angel, hast thou betrayed me? Long ago. Vers la Vie. Arthur Upson. HBV-2
Angel in the House, The, *sels.* Coventry Patmore.
"Across the sky the daylight crept," *fr.* II, x. GBL
Attainment, The, *fr.* I iii. FaBoEE; GoBC; OBVV
Cathedral Close, The, *fr.* I, i. EBVV
(Salisbury; the Cathedral Close.) FaBoPP
Constancy Rewarded, *fr.* II, xi. VLP
(Constancy.) OBVV
County Ball, The, *fr.* II, iii. EBVV
Dean, The, *fr.* I, vi. VLP
Demonstration, A, *fr.* II, xi. VLP
Foreign Land, The, *fr.* II, ix. HBV-1
(Woman.) OBVV
Going to Church, *fr.* I x. LoBV
Honor and Desert, *fr.* II, iv. HBV-1
Impossibility, The, *fr.* I. i. VLP
In Love, at Stonehenge. FaBoPP
Joyful Wisdom, The, *fr.* I, x. HBV-2
Kiss, The, *fr.* II, viii. BoLoP; EnLoPo; FiBHP; OBVV; PoPle
Kites, The, *fr.* II, i. VLP
Love at Large, *fr.* I, ii. EBVV
Love Serviceable, *fr.* I, vi. EnLoPo
Love's Reality, *fr.* I, i. VLP
Married Lover, The, *fr.* II, xii. GoBC; HBV-1; OBEV; TreFT; TrGrPo; VLP
Nearest the Dearest, *fr.* II, i. HBV-1
Perspective, *fr.* II, i. FaBoEE; GBL
Platonic Love, *fr.* II, xi. VLP
Poet's Confidence, The, *fr.* I. i. VLP
Rainbow, The, *fr.* II, iii. GTBS-P
Revelation, The, *fr.* I, viii. EnLoPo; GBL; GTBS-P; HAP; NBM; OBNC
("Idle poet, here and there, An.") ViBoPO
Rose of the World, The, *fr.* I, iv. HBV-1
Sahara. EBVV
Spirit's Epochs, The, *fr.* I, viii. EBEV; GBL; GoBC
Tribute, The, *fr.* I, iv. EBEV; HBV-1; OBNC
" 'Twas when the spousal time of May," *fr.* II, vii. GBL
Unthrift, *fr.* I, vii. GoBC; HBV-1
Wedding, The, *fr.* II, xi. VLP
"Whirl'd off at last, for speech I sought," *fr.* II, xi. GBL
Angel, king of streaming morn. Sun. Henry Rowe. OBEV
Angel Michael, The. Anath Bental, *tr. fr. Hebrew by* Howard Schwartz. VWA
Angel of Death, The. *Unknown.* *See* There's a Man Goin' 'Round Takin' Names.
Angel of Patience, The. Whittier. WGRP
Angel of Peace, Thou Hast Wandered Too Long, *with music.* Oliver Wendell Holmes. AH
Angel of poets,/ Tell us how. Prayer for All Poets at This Time. Irwin Edman. TrPWD
Angel of the Agony. Cardinal Newman. *Fr.* The Dream of Gerontius. OxBoCh
Angel, robed in spotless white, An. Dawn. Paul Laurence Dunbar. AmNP; PoLF; PoNe
Angel Roll de Stone Away, De, *with music.* *Unknown.* BoAN-2
Angel said to me, The: "Why are you laughing?" Sarah. Delmore Schwartz. VWA
Angel slide your hand. A Poem in Yellow after Tristan Tzara. Jerome Rothenberg. PoM
Angel Spirits of Sleep. Robert Bridges. CH
(Spirits.) OBEV; OBVV
Angel stepping through her window said, An. L'Annunciazione. Ned O'Gorman. TwAmPo
Angel Surrounded by Paysans. Wallace Stevens. LCAP; PPP
Angel That Presided o'er My Birth, The. Blake. *Fr.* Gnomic Verses. InPK; NAs; OBRV; TrGrPo
Angel told Mary, An. A Christmas Carol. Harry Behn. PChr
Angel Unawares, An. *Unknown.* BLRP; TRV
Angela Davis. Alice S. Cobb. BlSi
Angela Honey (she wrote) I would it were not so. From Lois in London. Angela McCabe. AmPA
Angelic Guidance. Cardinal Newman. GoBC
Angelica and the Ork. Ariosto, *tr. fr. Italian by* Sir John Harington. *Fr.* Orlando Furioso, X. OBSC
Angelical whites of your eyes, The. Susan. Robin Magowan. EAS
Angelina. Paul Laurence Dunbar. HBV-2
Angelles bee wrogte to bee of neidher kynde. Mynstrelles Songe. Thomas Chatterton. *Fr.* Aella. EnLoPo
Angelo Orders His Dinner. Bayard Taylor. BXAP; Par
Angels. Dannie Abse. PoA
Angels. Richard Burns. VWA
Angels, The. William Drummond of Hawthornden. *Fr.* Flowers of Sion. GN; HBV-1
(Angels for the Nativity of Our Lord, The.) OxBoCh
(Nativitie, The.) OBS
Angels. Gertrude Hall. AA
Angels. Anne Szumigalski. NOBC
Angels, The. Marguerite Young. WPE
Angels/ might fall that way. Snowfall: Four Variations. George Amabile. NYBP
Angels and ministers of grace defend us! Shakespeare. *Fr.* Hamlet, I, iv. EBEV
Angels are bright still, though the brightest fell. Lucifer. D. H. Lawrence. OAEP
Angels are stooping, The. A Cradle Song. W. B. Yeats. PoPl
Angels, as well as birds, on silent wing. On Angels. W. W. Eustace Ross. MoCV
Angels Came a-Mustering, The. *Unknown, tr. fr. Hebrew by* Israel Zangwill. EaLo; TrJP
Angels' eyes, whom veils cannot deceive, The. Of the Blessed Sacrament of the Altar. Robert Southwell. OBEV
Angels for the Nativity of Our Lord, The. William Drummond of Hawthornden. *See* Angels, The.
Angels from the long ago. The Light Now Shineth. *Unknown.* STF
Angels, from the Realms of Glory. James Montgomery. OBRV
(Good Tidings of Great Joy to All People) HBV-2
(Nativity.) NOCV
Angels have no memory. God's Language. Ruth Fainlight. VWA
Angels have talked with him, and showed him thrones. The Mystic. Tennyson. OAEP; VLP
Angels in Heab'n Gwineter Write My Name, De, *with music.* *Unknown.* BoAN-2
Angels in Heav'n, as we may say. A Poem upon the Caelestial Embassy. Richard Steere. SCAP
Angels in high places, The. Azrael. Robert Gilbert Welsh. HBV-2
Angels in the House. Jerred Metz. VWA
Angels in Winter. Nancy Willard. FiCP; LCAP
Angels inhabit love songs. But they're sprites. The Anatomy of Angels. Alden Nowlan. PeCV
Angels of Buena Vista, The. Whittier. BeLS; PAH
Angel's Song. Charles Causley. OBCP
Angels' Song, The. Edmund Hamilton Sears. *See* It Came upon the Midnight Clear.
Angels Sung a Carol, The, *with music.* Edward Taylor. AH
Angels to the shepherds sang, The. A Carol. Fred E. Weatherly. YeAr
Angels walking under the palm trees. A Little Carol of the Virgin. Lope de Vega, *tr. by* Denise Levertov. PChr
Angels We Have Heard on High. *Unknown.* FSW; TreFS
Angels, where you soar. A Prayer. Alfred Noyes. PoPl
Angel's Whisper, The. Samuel Lover. OnYI
Angelus, The. Florence Earle Coates. HBV-2
Angelus inquit pastoribus. Now the Most High Is Born. James Ryman. MeEL
Angelus-Time near Dublin. William Bedell Stanford. NeIP
Anger. Robert Creeley. CoPo; NaP

Anger ("Anger in its time and place"). Charles *and* Mary Lamb. FaBoBe; HBV-1; HBVY
Anger now be your song, immortal one. The Iliad. Homer, *tr. by* Robert Fitzgerald. NAWM-1
Anger rises with metal filings, The. A Man All Grown Up Is Supposed To. Terry Stokes. AmPA
Anger that breaks a man down into boys, The. César Vallejo, *tr. fr. Spanish by* Robert Bly. EAS
Anger's Freeing Power. Stevie Smith. OxBC
Angina Pectoris. W. R. Moses. LiTA; NCSH
Anglais Mort a Florence. Wallace Stevens. AP
Angle-Land. David Jones. The Anathemata, III. NoAM
Angle of Geese. N. Scott Momaday. CDW; QFR
Angle of Vision. Martha Bosworth. AMV-80
Angle of Vision. Robert Rendall. OxBTC
Angler, The. John Chalkhill. HBV-1
Angler. Mark Vinz. WOLT
Angler named Ezekiel Hutt, An. Haulage. E. E. Nott-Bower. WhC
Angler's Ballad, The. Charles Cotton. CavP
Angler's Invitation, The. Thomas Tod Stoddart. GN; HBV-1
Angler's Reveille, The. Henry van Dyke. *Fr.* The Toiling of Felix. GN
Anglers Song, The (*in* Izaak Walton's The Compleat Angler). William Basse. LiSp; OBS
Angler's Song, The. John Dennys. *Fr.* The Secrets of Angling. ElL
Angler's Vade Mecum, An. John Engels. WOLT
Angler's Wish, An. Henry van Dyke. AA
Angler's Wish, The. Izaac Walton. *Fr.* The Compleat Angler. HBV-1
Anglican curate in want, An. Ronald Knox. FaBoNo
Anglicized Utopia. W. S. Gilbert. OBSV
Angling, a Day. Galway Kinnell. WOLT
Anglo-American Chainpoem. *Unknown.* EAS
Anglo-Eire Vignette. Patric Stevenson. NeIP
Anglo-Irishman's Complaint, An. *Unknown.* AnIL
Anglo-Saxon. E. L. Mayo. MiAP
Anglo-Saxon Race, The; a Rhyme for Englishmen. Martin Farquhar Tupper. PeD
Anglosaxon Street. Earle Birney. CABA; HeIP; NOBC
Angola Question Mark. Langston Hughes. BPo; TTY
Angora, The. Jim Gerard. AMV-80
Angrier than my now occasional. A Preface to the Memoirs. James Merrill. NOBA
Angry future like a winter builds, The. Poem on Hampstead Heath. Louis Adeane. NeBP
Angry nettle and the mild, The. The Plum Gatherer. Edna St. Vincent Millay. NoAM
Angry Poet, The. Frank O'Connor, *tr. fr. Irish.* CIP
Angry young husband called Bicket, An. Limerick. John Galsworthy. CenHV
Angst-ridden amorist, Fred, An. The Love Song of J. Alfred Prufrock. J. Walker. BXAP
Anguish. Stéphane Mallarmé, *tr. fr. French by* Arthur Symons. AWP; SyP
Anguish of a naked body is more terrible, The. A Prayer to the Lord Ramakrishna. James Wright. NNaP
Anguish of the earth absolves our eyes, The. Absolution. Siegfried Sassoon. MMA
Anguish'd Doubt Broods over Eden, The. Christopher Brennan. *Fr.* Lilith. PoAu-1
Anima. Diana O Hehir. NPGG
Animal. Max Eastman. FYAP
Animal Acts. Charles Simic. LCAP
Animal bones and some mossy tent rings. Lament for the Dorsets. Al Purdy. NoP
Animal Crackers. Christopher Morley. FaPON; SoPo; SUS; TiPo
Animal Fair. Philip Booth. NePoAm-2
Animal Fair. *Unknown.* AS, *with music;* BLPA; FaBoBe; FPL; MoShBr; NTCP; PoPle; RHPC; SoPo; YaD
Animal Howl, The. "M. J.," *tr. fr. Polish by* A. Glanz-Leyeless. TrJP
Animal I wanted, The. Kenneth Patchen. VGW
Animal Kingdom. Sydney Clouts. PeSA
Animal Magnetism; the Pseudo-Philosopher Baffled. Laurence Hynes Halloran. NOEC
Animal Pictures. Lawrence Locke. GrPl
Animal runs, it passes, it dies, The. And it is the great cold. Death Rites II. *Unknown, tr. by* C. M. Bowra. TTY
Animal sleeps and dreams, The. Sleep. Mei-mei Berssenbrugge. LTB
Animal Song. Heather McHugh. MAYP
Animal Store, The. Rachel Field. PDV; SoPo; TiPo
Animal That Drank Up Sound, The. William Stafford. VGW
Animal that I am, I come to call. The Man in the Dress Suit. Robert L. Wolf. HBMV
Animal, Vegetable and Mineral. Louise Bogan. FM; SBG
Animalcule, a Tale, The. Richard Savage. PeD
Animals, The. Stephen Berg. NaP
Animals, The. Josephine Jacobsen. GoYe
Animals. Robinson Jeffers. NU
Animals, The. Edwin Muir. CMoP; EBCP; EBEV; HeIP; MoBrPo; NoP
Animals, The. Charles Simic. GeTw
Animals. Walt Whitman. *See* I Think I Could Turn and Live with Animals.
Animals Are Passing from Our Lives. Philip Levine. CoAP; NoAM; NOBA; TAP; TW
Animals are silent in the hold, The. Noah's Song. Evan Jones. PoAu-2
Animals' Arrival, The. Elizabeth Jennings. PBWP
Animals' Carol, The. Charles Causley. NAs
Animals' Christmas, The. Philip Dacey. GP
Animals, hanging around in forms, The. On Visiting Central Park Zoo. Alan Dugan. NYP
Animals in That Country, The. Margaret Atwood. NoP
Animals in the Ark, The. *Unknown. Fr.* The Deluge. ChTr; GBP
Animals live in darkness, The. World of Darkness. Robert Chatain. PoA
Animals own a fur world. Adults Only. William Stafford. FF
Animals That Stand in Dreams, *sel.* Harley Elliott.
Panda, The. NeAC
Animals we have seen, all marvelous creatures, The. The Park in Milan. William Jay Smith. CAD; CoAP
Animals will never know, The. If They Spoke. Mark Van Doren. ImOP
Animation and Ego. Jody Swilky. AMV-80
Animula. T. S. Eliot. LiTB; MoVE; NAs; TwAmPo
Animula Vagula. A. Y. Campbell. HBMV
Animula Vagula, Blandula. Emperor Hadrian, *tr. fr. Latin by* Henry Vaughan. FaBoRV
Animula vagula blandula. Limerick. Conrad Aiken. FaBoNo; OBAL
Anishinabe children sing songs of sleep. For the Children. Thomas Peacock. VoR
Anishinabe Grandmothers. Gerald Vizenor. VoR
Ank'hor Vat. Denis Devlin. BIrV; CIP; IPY
Ankle, The. Anthony Euwer. *Fr.* The Limeratomy. HBMV
Anklet Song. *Tr. fr. Hawaiian by* N. B. Emerson. WTO
Ankotarinya. *Unknown, tr. fr. Aranda by* T. G. H. Strehlow. CBAP
Ann and the Fairy Song. Walter de la Mare. *Fr.* A Child's Day. FaBV
Ann, Ann!/ Come! quick as you can! Alas, Alack! Walter de la Mare. FaPON; EvOK; OxBchV; TiPo
Ann Eleanor, a child of ten. A Small Elegy. Richard Snyder. PCP
Ann Rutledge. Edgar Lee Masters. *See* Anne Rutledge.
Ann stood and watched the combers race to shore. Andrew Merkel. *Fr.* Tallahassee. CaP
Ann was astounded when. Claremont. Robert Peters. GP
Anna. Burns. TrGrPo; UnTE
Anna. Joe Johnson. CNA
Anna Elise. *Unknown.* OxNR
Anna-Marie, love, up is the sun. Sir Walter Scott. *Fr.* Ivanhoe. ViBoPo
Anna Playing in a Graveyard. Caroline Gilman. OBCA
Annabel Lee. Poe. AA; AmPP; AP; AWP; BeLS; BLPA; CH; DL; EtS; FaFP; FaPON; FPL; HBV-1; HBVY; HeIP; LiTA; NePA; NOBA; NoP; OBCA; OBVV; OnMSP; OxBA; PoPl; PrIm; RoGo; SeCeV; SpRo; TAP; TreF; TrGrPo; ViBoPo; WBLP
Annabel Lee, *parody.* Stanley Huntley. SpRo
Annales, *sel.* Ennius, *tr. fr. Latin by* John Wight.
"Like a Shower of Rain." WaaP
Annals of the trilled R, gently stroked L. The Harp of Renfrewshire. Douglas Dunn. BSV
Annan Water. *Unknown.* BaBo; CH; HBV-1
Anne. Lizette Woodworth Reese. AA
Anne,/ I think of you, the Massachusetts coast. Letters for the New England Dead. Mary Baron. HoAn
Anne and the Peacock. Noel Welch. FF
Anne Grenville, Countess Temple, Appointed Poet Laureate to the King of the Fairies. Horace Walpole. OBEC
Anne Hutchinson's Exile. Edward Everett Hale. PAH
Anne [*or* Ann] Rutledge. Edgar Lee Masters. *Fr.* Spoon River Anthology. AmFN; CMoP; FaFP; FaPo; HAP; LiTA; LiTM; MoAmPo; MOVE; NePA; NoAM; NOBA; OFD; OHFP; OxBA; PoPl; PoSC; TrGrPo
Anne says she dreams sometimes—and so do I. Silent Hill. Zilpha Keatley Snyder. WSC
Anne Sexton. Hans Juergensen. AMV-81
Annette Myers; or, A Murder in St. James's Park. *Unknown.* OxBoLi
Anniad, The. Gwendolyn Brooks. BlSi
Annie and Rhoda, sisters twain. The Sisters. Whittier. AWP
Annie and Willie's Prayer. Sophia P. Snow. BeLS; BLPA
Annie appears, arrayed. Hats. R. H. W. Dillard. GP
Annie Bolanny. *Unknown.* ChTr
Annie Breen, *with music. Unknown.* CoSo
Annie Died the Other Day. E. E. Cummings. ErPo

Annie Laurie. William Douglas, *revised by* Lady John Scott. FaBoBe; FaBV; FaFP; FSW; GN; HBV-1; PoPle; TreF; WBLP
Annie Shore and Johnnie Doon. Patrick Orr. HBV-1
Annihilation. Conrad Aiken. CrMA; GBL; MoAB; MoAmPo
Annihilation of Nothing, The. Thom Gunn. NePoEA-2; NoAM
Anniversarie, The. John Donne. *See* Anniversary, The.
Anniversary, The. Ai. GP
Anniversary [*or* Anniversarie], The. John Donne. AnAnS-1; BoLoP; HAP; HoPM; JCP; LiTB; MeLP; MePo; NOBE; NoP; OAEL-1; OAEP; OBS; PoPle; SeCeV; SeCP; SeCV-1; WeW
"Only our love hath no decay," *sel.* LO
Anniversary, An. Thomas Hardy. OxBTC
Anniversary. Richmond Lattimore. NYBP; PoCh
Anniversary, An. Richard Lovelace. *See* Anniversary on the Hymeneals of My Noble Kinsman . . .
Anniversary, The. Roberta Spear. MAYP
Anniversary. John Wain. MP; NePoEA-2; TwCP
Anniversary. Daniel Weissbort. VWA
Anniversary Approaches, An; of the Birth of God. David Wright. *Fr.* On the Margin. NAs
Anniversary of Death, An. John Wieners. PoM
Anniversary of the Great Retreat. Isabel C. Clarke. SUMH
Anniversary on the Hymeneals of My Noble Kinsman, Thomas Stanley, Esquire, An. Richard Lovelace. CaPo
(Anniversary, An.) LoBV
Anniversary Poem for the Cheyennes Who Fell at Sand Creek. Lance Henson. VoR
Anniverse, The; an Elegy. Henry King. JCP
Anno Domini, *sel.* Craig Raine.
Birth. NAs
Anno Domini. E. M. Walker. POL
Anno 1829. Heine, *tr. fr. German by* Charles Stuart Calverley. AWP
("I crave an ampler, worthier sphere.") OBVE
Annot and John, *orig. and mod. English prose. Unknown.* OxBM
Annot Lyle's Song: "Birds of omen." Sir Walter Scott. *Fr.* The Legend of Montrose, *ch.* 6. EnRP
Annotation for an Epitaph. Adrienne Rich. TwAmPo
Annotations of Auschwitz. Peter Porter. NMP
"London is full of chickens, on electric spits," *sel.* OxBTC
Annotators agree Composer X. A St. Cecilia's Day Epigram. Peter Porter. ELU
Announce it here with triple leading. Rarae Aves. Franklin P. Adams. WhC
Announced by all the trumpets of the sky. The Snow-Storm. Emerson. AA; AmPP; AP; BLPL; BoNaP; FaBoBe; GN; LiTA; NePA; NOBA; NoP; OHFP; OxBA; PoEL-4; PoLF; Prf; TAP; TiPo; TreFT; TrGrPo; UnPo; WiR
Announcement, The. George Ellenbogen. AMV-80
Annoying Miss Tillie McLush. Miss Tillie McLush. Joseph S. Newman. TDH
Ann's House. Dick Lourie. DFF
Annual Gaiety. Wallace Stevens. MoAB; MoAmP
Annual Legend. Winfield Townley Scott. CoAP; LiTA; LiTM; WaP
Annual Solution, The. Edwin Meade Robinson. InMe
Annuity, The. George Outram. HBV-2
Annul Wars. Rabbi Nahman of Bratzlav, *tr. fr. Hebrew by* Jacob Sloan. TrJP
Annunciation, The. Margaret Devereaux Conway. ISi
Annunciation, The. Abraham Cowley. *Fr.* Davideis. OxBoCh
Annunciation. John Donne. AnAnS-1; ISi; OBS; SBVL; TrCP
Annunciation, The. John Duffy. ISi
Annunciation. D. G. Jones. PeCV
Annunciation, The. Margot Kriel. PoDr
Annunciation. Sister Maura. TAT
Annunciation, The. W. S. Merwin. AP
Annunciation, The. Edwin Muir. CMoP; NOCV; PAI
Annunciation, The. Nerses, *tr. fr. Armenian by* W. H. Kent. ISi
Annunciation, The. Amrita Pritam, *tr. fr. Punjabi by* Khushwant Singh *and* Krishna Gorowara. WPOW
Annunciation. Rainer Maria Rilke, *tr. fr. German by* James Blair Leishman. OBVE
Annunciation, The. John Banister Tabb. ISi
Annunciation, The ("Gabriel, from Hevene-King"). *Unknown.* MeEL; OxBM
Annunciation, The ("Our lady went forth pondering"). *Unknown, tr. fr. German.* ISi
Annunciation Night. Abby Maria Hemenway. *Fr.* Mary of Nazareth. ISi
Annunciation over the Shepherds, *sel.* Rainer Maria Rilke, *tr. fr. German by* M. D. Herter Norton.
"Look up, you men. Men there at the fire." PChr
Annunciations. Geoffrey Hill. NePoEA-2
Annus Mirabilis, *sels.* Dryden.
"By viewing Nature, Natures hand-maid, Art." MOS
Fire of London. ChTr; FaBoEn, *shorter sel.*
Fourth Day's Battle, The. OBS
Great Fire, The. FiP
New London, The. FaBoCh; OBS
(London.) SeCePo
(London after the Great Fire, 1666.) NOBE
"Now van to van the foremost squadrons." OBWP
Sea Battle, The. FiP
"Swell'd with our late successes on the foe." EBEV
"Yet London, empress of the northern clime." ViBoPo
Annus Mirabilis. Philip Larkin. NIP; NOBL
Anodyne, An. Thomas Ken. OxBoCh
Anon out of the earth a fabric huge. Pandemonium and Its Architect. Milton. *Fr.* Paradise Lost, I. TreFS
Anon out of the north-est the noys bigynes. Jonah Is Cast into the Sea. *Unknown. Fr.* Patience. OxBM
Anon with gaping fearlessness they quaff. My Boots. Henry David Thoreau. PeD
Anonymous. John Banister Tabb. AA
Anonymous as cherubs. Two Voices in a Meadow. Richard Wilbur. NePoAm-2; PAI; UnPo
Anonymous Drawing. Donald Justice. CoAP; EyDe; HeIP; NePoEA-2
Anonymous Gravestone. Erich Kästner, *tr. fr. German by* Patrick Bridgewater. ELU
Anonymous—nor needs a name. Anonymous. John Banister Tabb. AA
Anonymous water can slide under the ground. Explanations. Lucille Clifton. GeTw
Another. Ellen Marie Bissert. PeHV
Another ("As loving hind that, hartless, wants her deer"). Anne Bradstreet. *See* Letter to Her Husband, Absent upon Public Employment.
Another. Abraham Cowley. *See* Epicure, The ("Underneath this myrtle shade").
Another. Robert Herrick. *See* To His Booke ("Who with thy leaves").
Another ("As I behold a winters evening air"). Richard Lovelace. SeCP
Another ("The Centaur, Syren, I foregoe"). Richard Lovelace. PoEL-3
Another ("Yes, every poet is a fool"). Matthew Prior. *See* Epigram: "Yes, every poet is a fool."
Another Academy. Charles Bukowski. TAT
Another and the Same. Samuel Rogers. *Fr.* Human Life. OBNC
Another Angel. James Merrill. *See* Angel.
Another armored animal—scale. The Pangolin. Marianne Moore. AP; CoBMV; CrMA; HAP; NoAM; NOBA; PBWP
Another [Epitaph on the Lady Mary Villiers] ("Purest soul that e'er was sent, The"). Thomas Carew. CaPo
(Other, An.) AnAn S-2; SeCV-1
Another [Epitaph on the Lady Mary Villiers] ("This little vault, this narrow room"). Thomas Carew. *See* Epitaph on the Lady Mary Villiers, An ("This little vault . . .").
Another [on the Snail.] Richard Lovelace. CaPo
Another Birthday. Ben Jonson. *See* Ode to Sir William Sydney, on His Birth-Day.
Another Canto. J. B. Morton. FaBoPa
Another Coast. David Wojahn. MAYP
Another collection of verse by the man from Sulmona. Ovid, *tr. by* Guy Lee. Amores, II, 1. NAWM-1
Another Color. Frank Stewart. AMV-81
Another cove of shale. On the Marginal Way. Richard Wilbur. CAPP; CoAP; NOBA
Another Cross. Stephen Gardner. AMV-80
Another Cynical Variation. "Helen." InMe
Another dawn, leaden. Words. Philip Levine. VWA
Another Day. Isabella Maria Brown. PoNe
Another day let slip! Its hours have run. The Wasted Day. Robert F. Murray. EBVV
Another day of standstill heat. Sheridan. Robert Lowell. DiL
Another Death. D. E. Borrell. FF
Another dreadful tale of woe as I will here unfold. Annette Myers; or, A Murder in St. James's Park. *Unknown.* OxBoLi
Another Dying Chieftain. Rayna Green. TWSS
Another Epitaph on an Army of Mercenaries. "Hugh MacDiarmid." DBV; NoAM; OBWP
Another Face. Ray A. Young Bear. CDW
Another Fan [Belonging to Mademoiselle Mallarmé]. Stéphane Mallarmé, *tr. fr. French by* Roger Fry. NAWM-2; SyP
Another four I've left yet to bring on. The Four Seasons of the Year. Anne Bradstreet. SCAP
Another Full Moon. Ruth Fainlight. BrRo
Another Generation. J. C. Squire. HBMV
Another Given: The Last Day of the Year. William Dickey. AMV-80

Another good cow-puncher has gone to meet his fate. Charlie Rutledge. *Unknown.* CoSo
Another Grace for a Child. Robert Herrick. *See* Grace for a Child.
Another guest that winter night. Prophetess. Whittier. *Fr.* Snow-bound. AA
Another hill town. Hotel Paradiso e Commerciale. John Malcolm Brinnin. MP; HoAn; NoAM; NYBP; PoCh; TwCP
Another. In Defence of Their Inconstancie. Ben Jonson. SeCP
Another Kind of Burning. Ruth Fox. NYBP
Another knight smote Saint Thomas in that self wound. Becket's Diadem. *Unknown.* ACP
Another Ladyes Exception Present at the Hearing. Ben Jonson. *Fr.* A Celebration of Charis. AnAnS-2; SeCP
Another Late Edition, *sel.* Olga Cabral.
This Morning the Sun. PPON
Another Letter to Her Husband, Absent upon Publick Employment. Anne Bradstreet. *See* Letter to Her Husband, A, Absent upon Public Employment.
Another Letter to Joseph Bruchac. Jack L. Anderson. LFAC
Another Little Drink. *Unknown.* TrAS, *with* Old Zip Coon
Another Man Done Gone. *Unknown.* *FSW*
Another Meeting. Lawrence A. Lucus. AMV-80
Another morning held up at the light. The World as Wave and Idea. Louis Coxe. SOTS
Another Mother and Child. Joe-Anne McLaughlin. FAZ
Another nickel in the slot. A Hero in the Land of Dough. Robert Clairmont. WhC
Another Night in the Ruins. Galway Kinnell. CoAP
Another Night on the Porch Swing. Cathleen Quirk. NMM
Another Night with Telescope. Leonard Cohen. PeCV
Another November. Stanley Plumly. LCAP
Another Ode to the North-East Wind. *Unknown.* Par
Another of the placid beauties! Natalya Nikolayevna Goncharov. Don Coles. NOBC
Another of the Same. Sir Walter Ralegh. SiPS
Another Old Song. Barney Bush. STE
Another on Her. Robert Herrick. SpRo
Another One for the Devil. David C. Childers. AMV-80
Another one of those puzzles. Rapunzel (Girl in a Tower). Eli Mandel. DFT
Another Poem about the Madness of Women. Tom Wayman. NOBC
Another Poem for Me. Etheridge Knight. NNaP
Another Poem on Absalom. Nathan Yonathan, *tr. fr. Hebrew by* Fichard Flantz. VWA
Another Prince Is Born. Adrian Mitchell. NAs
Another rejection. What ecstasy. The Necessity of Rejection. James Schevill. FAZ
Another Reply to "In Flanders Fields." J. A. Armstrong. BLPA; PAL
Another Return. Winfield Townley Scott. ELU
Another road. It seems sometimes. The Idiot. Keith Wilson. Psk
Another sate near him, whose harp of gold. Fenton Johnson. *Fr.* The Vision of Lazarus. BANP
Another season centers on this place. The Gourd Dancer. N. Scott Momaday. CDW; STE
Another September. Thomas Kinsella. BIrV; CIP; PoCh
Another shall hang from the gallows' height. *Unknown.* *Fr.* The Fortunes of Men. PBBP
Another shout from the wharves. Hilda Doolittle ("H. D."). *Fr.* Helen in Egypt. NOBA
Another side, umbrageous grots and caves. Paradise. Milton. *Fr.* Paradise Lost, IV. OBS
Another sin I had forgot. *Unknown.* PeD
Another Song ("For Jillian of Berry, she dwells on a hill"). Beaumont *and* Fletcher. *Fr.* The Knight of the Burning Pestle, IV, i. OBS
(Jillian of Berry.) ElL
Another Song ("Merry the green, the green hill shall be merry"). Donald Justice. ConAP; NePoEA-2; VGW
Another Song ("It is I that am under sorrow at this time"). William Ross, *tr. fr. Gaelic.* GoTS
Another Song of the Same Woman, to Some Partridges, Sent to Her Alive. Florencia del Pinar, *tr. fr. Spanish by* Julie Allen. BoWoP
Another Spirit Advances. Jules Romains, *tr. fr. French by* Joseph T. Shipley. AWP
Another Stone Poem. Philip Dacey. AMV-81
Another summer! Our Independence. Fourth of July in Maine. Robert Lowell. CAPP
Another Sunday Morning. Carter Revard. VoR
Another Sunset. John Minczeski. PoDr
Another Time. W. H. Auden. OxBA
Another time I'll let him pick his own. Eve's Version. James Harrison. AMV-81
Another to the Maids. Robert Herrick. OHIP
Another to the Same. Horace, *tr. fr. Latin by* William Browne. Odes, I, 5. WiR
("Tell me, Pyrrha, what fine youth.") OAEL-1
Another to Urania. Benjamin Colman. SCAP
Another Tribute to Wyatt. Earl of Surrey. *See* In the Rude Age.
Another True Maid. Matthew Prior. FaBoEE
Another uncle/ was a pathological liar. Family 8. Lyn Lifshin. NeAC
Another Villon-ous Variation. Don Marquis. HBMV
Another Way. Ambrose Bierce. AA
Another Weeping Woman. Wallace Stevens. MoVE
Another While. Morris Rosenfeld, *tr. fr. Yiddish.* TrJP
Another woman: a change of tears. Theodore Roethke. POL
Another Year. Frances Ridley Havergal. *See* Another Year Is Dawning.
Another Year. Oswald J. Smith. STF
Another year! another deadly blow! November, 1806. Wordsworth. OBRV; OBWP
Another Year Come. W. S. Merwin. NYBP; OFD; PAI; PCP
Another year has now been born. Another Year. Oswald J. Smith. STF
Another year has struck the vibrant chime. Washington. Mae Winkler Goodman. PGD
Another year I enter. A New Year's Promise. *Unknown.* BLRP
Another Year Is Dawning. Frances Ridley Havergal. WBLP
(Another Year.) BLRP; STF
Another year it may betide. *Unknown* HAP
Another youthful advocate of truth and right has gone. To the Memory of J. Horace Kimball. "Ada." BlSi
Anster Fair, *sel.* William Tennant.
On the Road to Anster Fair. OBRV
Answer. Leah Goldberg, *tr. fr. Hebrew by* Robert Friend. VWA
Answer, The. George Herbert. FaBoRV; TEP
Answer, The. Robinson Jeffers. CMoP; GoYe
Answer, The. Sara Teasdale. PoA
Answer. *Unknown.* *See* Reply, A.
Answer for Hope. Richard Crashaw. *See* For Hope.
Answer of Mr. Waller's Painter to His Many New Advisers, The. *Unknown.* APAS
Answer to a Child's Question. Samuel Taylor Coleridge. EnRP; FaBoBe; HBV-1; HBVY; OxBChV; PoPle
Answer that ye made to me, my dear, The. Sir Thomas Wyatt. SiPS
Answer to a Lady Advising Me to Retirement, An. Lady Mary Wortley Montagu. *See* In Answer to a Lady Who Advised Retirement.
Answer to Another Persuading a Lady to Marriage, An. Katherine Philips. CavP; HAP; WeW
(To One Persuading a Lady to Marriage.) OBEV
Answer to Cloe [*or* Chloe] Jealous. Matthew Prior. NOBE; OBEC; SeCePo
(Better Answer [to Cloe Jealous], A.) AWP; ELP; FaBoEn; NOEC; PoEL-3; SeCeV
(To Cloe [*or* Chloe] Jealous [a Better Answer].) HBV-1; ViBoPo
Answer to Marlowe. Sir Walter Ralegh.
See Nymph's Reply to the Shepherd, The.
Answer to Master Wither's Song, "Shall I, Wasting in Despair?" Ben Jonson. InMe
Answer to Some Verses Made in His Praise, An. Sir John Suckling. PP
Answer to the Parson, An. Blake. FaBoEE; OxBoLi
Answer to Voznesensky and Evtushenko. Frank O'Hara. HoAn; NNaP; PoM
Answer to Yo/ Question. Sonia Sanchez. BPo
Answer was, The. On the Way to Language. Michael Palmer. NPGG
Answered Prayer, The. Annie Johnson Flint. STF
Answering a Letter from a Younger Poet. Brewster Ghiselin. PoCh
Answering Dance. William Pitt Root. MAYP
Answering Li Ying Who Showed Me His Poems about Summer Fishing. Yü Hsüan-chi, *tr. fr. Chinese by* Geoffrey Waters. BoWoP
Answers, The. Robert Clairmont. SoPo; WhC
(When Did the World Begin.) GrPl
Answers. Elizabeth Jennings. NePoEA; OxBTC
Answers to the Snails. Arthur Solway. AMV-81
Ant, The. Richard Lovelace. CaPo
Ant, The. Ogden Nash. FaBV; OBAL
Ant and the Cricket, The. *Unknown.* HBV-1; HBVY
Ant has made himself illustrious, The. The Ant. Ogden Nash. FaBV; OBAL
Ant-Heap, The. A. C. Benson. EBVV
Ant on the tablecloth, An. Departmental. Robert Frost. GoYe; HeIP; HoPM; InPK; MoAB; MoAmPo; NIP; NOBA; NOBL; OBAL; SoSe
Ant-seething city, city full of dreams. The Seven Old Men. Baudelaire, *tr. by* Roy Campbell. OBVE
Ant Sun, The. Christopher Middleton. *Fr.* Herman Moon's Hourbook. NePoEA-2
Ant Trap, The. Joe Rosenblatt. NOBC
Ant Village, The. Marion Edey *and* Dorothy Grider. FaPON; TiPo
Antaeus; a Fragment. Wilfred Owen. PeHV

Antagonist, The. David Ferry. NePoAm-2
Antarctica. R. A. Simpson. CBAP
Ante Mortem. Robinson Jeffers. MoAmPo; MoVE
Ante Mortem. Syd Scroggie. PoSH
Ante-Bellum Sermon, An. Paul Laurence Dunbar. BALP; BPo
Antelope. William Jay Smith. TiPo
Ante-natal Dream. Patrick Kavanagh. NAs
Antenora. "Hugh MacDiarmid." SeCePo
Anteroom, The. Denise Levertov. NeBP
Anteroom: Geneva. Denis Devlin. CIP
Anteros. William Johnson Cory. OBVV
(Dirge, A: "Naiad; hid beneath the bank.") OBNC
Anterotics. W. E. Henley. In Hospital, XXVI. BrPo
Anthea bade me tie her shoe. The Shoe-tying. Robert Herrick. CaPo
Anthem: "Let us praise our Maker, with true passion extol Him." W. H. Auden. NOCV
Anthem for Doomed Youth. Wilfred Owen. BiP; BrPo; ChTr; CMoP; CoBMV; EBEV; EvOK; FaBoMo; FaBoRV; FaFP; GTBS-P; HAP; HBMV; HeIP; HoPM; LiTM; MoAB; MoBrPo; MoVE; NoAM; NOBE; NoP; OAEL-2; OAEP; OBEV; OBWP; OxBTC; PPP; SCV; SeCePo; SoSe; TreFT; TrGrPo; ViBoPo; WaP; WeW; WHA
Anthill, The ("The anthill lay unsheltered in the sun"). Donald G. Babcock. NePoAm
Ant-Hills. "Marian Douglas." OBCA
Anthologistics. Arthur Guiterman. InMe; WhC
Anthology of Nouns. Parker Tyler. PoA
Anthology Poem. Petra von Morstein, *tr. fr. German by* Rosemarie Waldrop. BoWoP
Anthony. Jane Shore. DFF
Anthony Wayne. Arthur Guiterman. TiPo
Anthropology in Fort Morgan, Colorado. Sam Hamod. TAT
Anthropophagites See a Sign on NC Highway 177 That Looks like Heaven, The. Jonathan Williams. OBAL
Anthropos apteros for days. The Labyrinth. W. H. Auden. LiTA; NePA
Anti-aircraft seen from a certain distance. Dam Neck, Virginia. Richard Eberhart. LiTA; MoAB; WaP
Antichrist. Edwin Muir. EaLo
Antichrist, or the Reunion of Christendom; an Ode. G. K. Chesterton. DBV; FaBoCo; NOBE; NOBL; OBSV; SeCePo
Antichrist, playing his lissome flute and merry. Armageddon. John Crowe Ransom. LiTA
Anticipation. Emily Brontë. OBNC
Anticipation. Lord De Tabley. ELP
Anticipation. Joseph Tusiani. GoYe
Anticipation of Sharks. Diane Wakoski. MAT
Antigone. Sophocles, *tr. fr. Greek by* T. H. Banks. NAWM-1
Thebes of the Seven Gates, *sel., tr. by* Dudley Fitts *and* Robert Fitzgerald. WaaP
Antigone and Helen—would they laugh. David P. Berenberg. *Fr.* Two Sonnets. HBMV
Antigone and Oedipus. Henrietta Cordelia Ray. BlSi
Antigone I. Herbert Martin. PoBA
Antigone VI. Herbert Martin. PoBA
Antigonish. Hughes Mearns. *See* Little Man Who Wasn't There, The.
Anti-Love Poems. Elizabeth Brewster. NOBC
Anti-Nostalgia. Henryk Grynberg, *tr. fr. Polish by* Isaac Komem. VWA
Antipastoral Memory of One Summer, An. Dave Smith. MAYP
Antipater of Thessalonica. Kenneth Rexroth. CrMA
Antipathy. Rowland Watkyns, *after the Latin of* Martial. FaBoEE
Antiphonal Hymn in Praise of Inanna. Enheduanna, *tr. fr. Sumerian*; *ad. by* Aliki *and* Willis Barnstone. BoWoP
Antiplatonick, The. John Cleveland. AnAnS-2; MePo; SeCP
Anti-Platonicke. George Daniel. CavP
Anti-Politician, The. Alexander Brome. CavP
Antiquary, The. Joseph Campbell. OxBTC
Antiquary. John Donne. EBEV; FF; InPK; NIP
Antiquary, The, *sels.* Sir Walter Scott.
Harlaw, *fr. ch.* 40. BSV
("Herring loves the merry moonlight, The," 1 *st.)* FaBoCh; PoPle
(Red Harlaw). OxBB
Why Sit'st Thou by That Ruin'd Hall, *fr. ch.* 10. EnRP
(Aged Carle, The.) OAEP
Antique Harvesters. John Crowe Ransom. AP; CoBMV; CrMA; FaBoEn; MoAB; MoAmPo; NoP; OxBA
Antique Indian should be Henry James, The. American Plan. John Malcolm Brinnin. GOA
Antique Shop. Carl Carmer. FaPON
Antiques. Walter de la Mare. PoA
Antiquitez de Rome. Joachim du Bellay. *See* Ruins of Rome.
Antiquity of Freedom, The. Bryant. AA; AP
Anti-Semanticist, The. Everett Hoagland. BPo
Antiseptic Baby and the Prophylactic Pup, The. Strictly Germ-proof. Arthur Guiterman. BLPA; HBV-2; TreF; TrJP; YaD
Antistrophe. William Hathaway. *Fr.* Rumplestiltskin Poems. DFT
Anti-Symbolist, The. Sidney Keyes. MoPo
Antlered forests, The. Ank'hor Vat. Denis Devlin. BIrV; CIP; IPY
Antoine and I Go Fishing. David Budbill. WOLT
Anton Leeuwenhoek was Dutch. The Microscope. Maxine W. Kumin. QQQ
Antonio. Laura E. Richards. MoShBr; OBCA; PDV; RHPC; SoPo; TDH; TiPo
Antonio and Mellida, *sel.* John Marston.
"My thoughts are fixed in contemplation." ViBoPo
Antonio, Antonio,/ Was tired of living alonio. Antonio. Laura E. Richards. MoShBr; OBCA; PDV; RHPC; SoPo; TDH; TiPo
Antonio's Revenge, *sel.* John Marston.
Prologue: "Rawish dank of clumsy winter ramps, The." LoBV; ViBoPo
Antonius, *sel.* Countess of Pembroke.
Of Death. ElL
Antony and Cleopatra. Henri Coulette. NePoEA
Antony and Cleopatra. William Haines Lytle. *See* Antony to Cleopatra.
Antony and Cleopatra, *sels.* Shakespeare.
"Barge she sat in, like a burnish'd throne, The," *fr.* II, ii. BiP; PPoe; SCV
(Cleopatra.) LiTB
(Cleopatra and Her Barge.) TreF
(Cleopatra's Barge.) TrGrPo
Cleopatra's Lament, *fr.* V, ii. UnPo
"Come, thou monarch of the vine," *fr.* II, vii. OAEP; ViBoPo
(Drinking Song.) OBSC
Death of Antony, *fr.* IV, xv. FiP
Death of Cleopatra, The, *fr.* V, ii. FiP; TreFS
(Cleopatra's Death.) TrGrPo
(Immortal Longings.) FaBoRV
"Eros, thou yet behold'st me?" *fr.* IV, xiv. EBEV
"Miserable change now at my end, The," *fr.* IV, xiii. EBEV; PoPle
Antony to Cleopatra. William Haines Lytle. AA; BeLS; FaPo; HBV-2
(Antony and Cleopatra.) BLPA; TreF
Antony's Oration. Shakespeare. *Fr.* Julius Caesar, III, iii. PoPl; TrGrPo
(Antony's Oration over Caesar's Body.) LiTB
(I Come to Bury Caesar.) WHA
(Mark Antony Addresses the Mob.) FaPoR
Antrim. Robinson Jeffers. BIrV; NOBA; VGW
Ants. Katharyn Machan Aal. AMV-80
Ants, The. John Clare. BoAnP
Ants. Lewis Hyde. AMV-80; FAZ
Ant's a centaur in his dragon world, The. Ezra Pound. *Fr.* The Pisan Cantos. FaBoEn
Ants, Although Admirable, Are Awfully Aggravating. Walter R. Brooks. RHPC
Ants and Others. Adrien Stoutenburg. BoAnP; FYAP; NYBP
Ants are walking under the ground, The. The People. Elizabeth Madox Roberts. GoJo; RHPC; SoPo; TiPo
Ants at the Olympics, The. Richard Digance. RHPC
Antwerp and Bruges. Dante Gabriel Rossetti. VLP
Antwerp: Musée des Beaux-Arts. Alan Ross. NYBP
Anvil of God's Word, The. John Clifford. BLRP; STF
(Anvil, The—God's Word.) BLPA
(God's Word.) TRV
(Hammers and Anvil.) WBLP
Anxiety about Dying. Alicia Ostriker. AMV-80
Anxiety Pastorale. Ted Schaefer. FAZ
Anxious bird in the lush, The. The Age of Reason. Jorie Graham. NPGG
Anxious Dead, The. John McCrae. OHIP
Anxious Farmer, The. Burges Johnson. BoNaP
Anxious Thought. Thomas Hoccleve. *Fr.* De Regimine Principum. OxBM
Any April. Cathy Beard. AMV-81
Any Complaints? Vernon Scannell. OxBTC
Any country is only a way of failing. Considerations. David Helwig. NOBC
Any Day Now. David McCord. QQQ; ShM
Any Father to Any Son. Francis Burdett Money-Coutts. OBVV
Any fool knows a Br'er in a rocker. Br'er Sterling and the Rocker. Michael Harper. LCAP
Any Lover, Any Lass. Richard Middleton. HBV-1; OBVV
Any Man to His Secretary. Hilary Corke. ErPo
Any Man's Advice to His Son. Kenneth Fearing. CMoP
Any Night. Philip Levine. AMV-80
Any of the several names. Eulogy for Populations. Ron Welburn. PoBA
Any Saint, *abr.* Francis Thompson. MoBrPo
Any Time. William Stafford. LCAP
Any Time, What May Hit You. T. R. Hummer. MAYP
Any way you hold them, they hurt. Pine Cones. Dave Smith. AMV-80
Any Wife or Husband. Carol Haynes. BLPA

Any Wife to Any Husband. Robert Browning. FaBoEn; OBNC; VLP
Anyhow, anyhow, anyhow my Lord! I'm Gwine Up to Heab'n Anyhow. *Unknown.* BoAN-2
Anyone Lived in a Pretty How Town. E. E. Cummings. AP; BiP; CABA; CMoP; CoBMV; EvOK; FPL; HAP; InPK; LiTA; LiTM; MoAB; MoAmPo; MoPo; MP; NiP; NOBA; NoP; PoA; PrIm; TAP; TwAmPo; TwCP; VGW; WeW
Anyone who has ever lived. Why I Can't Write My Autobiography. Rodger Kamenetz. VWA
Anything, God, but Hate. *Unknown.* TreFT
Anything Goes. Cole Porter. OBAL
Anything that promises good. First Hymn. John Gill. NeAC
Anything this/ recognizable. Downy Hair in the Shape of a Flame. Coleman Barks. PV
Anywhere I look/ the water has dominion. Dingman's Marsh. John Moore. NCSH
Anywhere Out of the World. Baudelaire, *tr. fr. French by* Arthur Symons. SyP
Anzac Cove. Leon Gellert. PoAu-1
Aodh Ruadh O'Domhnaill. Thomas McGreevy. AnIV; CIP; OBMV; OxBI
(Red Hugh.) OnYI
Aoibhinn, A Leabhrain, Do Thriall. *Unknown, tr. fr. Irish by* Flann O'Brien. AnIV; BIrV; OxBI
Apache Kid. Ned White. BPAW
Apart from my sisters, estranged. Cinderella. Olga Broumas. DFT
Apart from Oneself. Alejandra Pizarnik, *tr. fr. Spanish by* Yishai Tobin. VWA
Apartment Cats. Thom Gunn. GrPl
Apartment House. Gerald Raftery. AmFN
Apartment Hunter, The. Philip Schultz. NYP
Apartments on First Avenue. Cynthia Macdonald. NYP
Ape, The. Roland Young. PoPl; WhC
Ape, Lion, Fox and Ass, An. *Unknown.* OBET
Ape, the Monkey and Baboon Did Meet, The. *Unknown.* NCEP
Apelles' Song. John Lyly. *See* Cards and Kisses.
Apeneck Sweeney spreads his knees. Sweeney among the Nightingales. T. S. Eliot. AmPP; AP; CABA; ChMP; CMoP; CoBMV; FaBoMo; HAP; HeIP; InPK; InVP; LiTA; LiTM; MoVE; NePA; NoAM; NOBA; NOBE; NoP; OAEP; OBMV; OxBA; PPP; SeCeV; TwAmPo; WeW
Apes yawn and adore their fleas in the sun, The. The Jaguar. Ted Hughes. LiTM; PoPl
Apex. Nate Salsbury. InMe; WhC
Aphorisms. "Novalis," *tr. fr. German by* Charles E. Passage. NU
Aphrodite!/ Aphrodite of the blue sleep. Blue Sleep. Winifred Bryher. PoA
Aphrodite Metropolis. Kenneth Fearing. CAD
Aphrodite Pandemos. *Unknown, tr. fr. Greek by* Louis Untermeyer. UnTE
Apocalypse. D. J. Enright. NMP; OBSV
Apocalypse. Jean Lipkin. VWA
Apocalypse. John Frederick Nims. MiAP
Apocalypse. Francis Ernest Kobina Parkes. PBA
Apocalypse and Resurrection. John Bayliss. EAS
Apocrypha. Babette Deutsch. HBMV
Apocrypha. X. J. Kennedy. PV
Apocrypha. Stanley Moss. VWA
Apocryphal Apocalypse. John Wheelwright. MoVE
Apollo. James Wright. LCAP
Apollo and Daphne. W. R. Rodgers. ErPo; LiTB
Apollo and Daphne, *sel.* Paul Whitehead.
Hunting Song. OBEC; OxBoLi
Apollo 8. John Berryman. MOON
Apollo kept my father's sheep. A Daughter of Admetus. T. Sturge Moore. FaBoTw
Apollo now, Sol's carman, drives his stud. Evening; an Elegy. Horatio Smith. BXAP
Apollo 113. Diderik Finne. AMV-80
Apollo sings, his harpe resounds; give roome. Upon Master Fletcher's Incomparable Playes. Robert Herrick. OBS
Apollo then,/ With sudden scrutiny and gloomless eyes. Keats. *Fr.* Hyperion, III. OBRV
Apollo walks the deep roads back in the hills. Translation into the Original. Jack Gilbert. NPGG
Apollo's Song. Ben Jonson. *Fr.* The Masque of Augurs. LoBV
Apollo's Song. John Lyly. *Fr.* Midas. HBV-1
Apollyonists, The, *sel.* Phineas Fletcher.
Cambridge and the Cam. FaBoPP
Apologia. Herbert Farjeon. PV
Apologia. Jean Garrigue. LiTA
Apologia. David Gascoyne. ChMP
Apologia. Swinburne. VLP
Apologia Addressed to Ireland in the Coming Days. W. B. Yeats. *See* To Ireland in the Coming Times.
Apologia pro Poemate Meo. Wilfred Owen. ChMP; CoBMV; FaBoRV; LiTM; MoAB; MoBrPo
Apologia pro Vita Sua. A. R. Ammons. NOBA
Apologia pro Vita Sua. Samuel Taylor Coleridge. EnRP; PP
Apologia pro Vita Sua. Pope. *Fr.* Epistle to Dr. Arbuthnot. NOBE
Apologia pro Vita Sua. Sedulius Scottus, *tr. fr. Medieval Latin by* Helen Waddell. BIrV
Apologie for Having Loved Before, An. Edmund Waller. *See* Apology for Having Loved Before, An.
Apologie for the Precedent Hymnes on Teresa, An. Richard Crashaw. *See* Apology for the Foregoing Hymn, An.
Apologist's Evening Prayer, The. C. S. Lewis. TrCP
Apologue. Tony Connor. BoLoP
Apology. Anthony Cronin. CIP
Apology, The. Emerson. AmPP; AP
Apology. Vassar Miller. NePoEA
Apology, An. William Morris. *Fr.* The Earthly Paradise. AWP; OAEL-2; OAEP; OBNC
("Of Heaven or Hell I have no power to sing.") EBVV; LiTB; LoBV; ViBoPo
(Prologue: "Of Heaven or Hell I have no power to sing.") FaBoEn; NoP; VLP
(Singer's Prelude, The.) HBV-2
Apology, An. Diane Wakoski. TAP
Apology. Richard Wilbur. NePoAm; Psk
Apology. Wordsworth. *Fr.* Sonnets upon the Punishment of Death. VLP
Apology Addressed to the Critical Reviewers, The. Charles Churchill. LAuP
Apology for a Lost Classicism, An. John Ciardi. AMV-81
Apology for Actors, An, *sel.* Thomas Heywood.
Author to His Booke, The. OBS
Apology for Apostasy? Etheridge Knight. NeAC
Apology for Bad Dreams. Robinson Jeffers. AmPP; AP; CoBMV; LiTA; MoAB; MoAmPo; NOBA; OxBA; SeCeV; TwAmPo
Apology for Domitian. Robert Penn Warren. PAI
(Two Pieces after Suetonius.) NOBA
Apology for E. H. William Hathaway. FAZ
Apology [*or* Apologie] for Having Loved Before, An. Edmund Waller. MePo; OAEP
Apology for Loose Behavior. Ovid, *tr. fr. Latin by* Christopher Marlowe. Amores, II, 4. UnTE
Apology for the Foregoing Hymn, An. Richard Crashaw. JCP
(Apologie for the Precedent Hymnes on Teresa, An.) AnAnS-1
Apology for the Revival of Christian Architecture in England, An, *sel.* Geoffrey Hill.
Laurel Axe, The. NoP
Apology for Understatement. John Wain. NePoEA-2; OxBTC
Apology for Youth. Sister Mary Madeleva. PoPl
Apology of Genius. Mina Loy. QFR
Apology of the Young Scientists. Celia Dimmette. GoYe
Apology to My Lady. Edward Falco. AMV-80
Apology: Why Do I Write Today? William Carlos Williams. OxBA
Apon [*or* Upon] the midsummer evin [*or* even], mirriest of nichtis. The Tretis of the Tua Mariit Wemen and the Wedo. William Dunbar. BSV; GoTS; OxBS
Apopemptic Hymn. Dorothy Auchterlonie. PoAu-2
Apostasy. Aus of Kuraiza, *tr. fr. Arabic by* Hartwig Hirschfeld. TrJP
Apostasy. Mary Mills. NePoAm
Apostasy of One and But One Lady, The. Richard Lovelace. CaPo
Apostate, The. A. E. Coppard. OBMV
Apostle, citizen, and artisan! Love's Cosmopolitan. Annie Matheson. OBVV
Apostles of the hidden sun. The Last Supper. Oscar Williams. FaFP; LiTA; LiTM; NePA; TwAmPo
Apostrophe to a Pram Rider. E. B. White. InMe
Apostrophe to Death. Caelius Sedulius, *tr. fr. Latin by* George Sigerson. *Fr.* Carmen Paschale. OnYI
Apostrophe to Man. Edna St. Vincent Millay. DBV; SBG
Apostrophe to the Island of Cuba. James Gates Percival. PAH
Apostrophe to the Ocean ("Roll on, thou deep and dark blue ocean"). Byron. *See* To the Ocean.
Apostrophe to the Ocean ("There is a pleasure in the pathless woods"). Byron. *See* Sea, The.
Apostrophe to the Parret. E. H. Burrington. FaBoPP
Appalachian Convalescence. Robert Conquest. OxBC
Appalachian Front. Robert Lewis Weeks. AmFN; NYBP
Apparel of green woods and meadows gay. On Revisiting Cintra after the Death of Catarina. Luis de Camoes, *tr. by* Richard Garnett. AWP
Apparelled as a Paynim in pilgrim's wise. The Palmer. William Langland. *Fr.* The Vision of Piers Plowman. ACP
Apparent Failure. Robert Browning. NOBE

Apparently with no surprise. Emily Dickinson. AmPP; AP; CABA; NoP; PPP; SoSe; TrGrPo
Apparition. John Peale Bishop. MoVE
Apparition, The. John Donne. AnAnS-1; CABA; EnLoPo; EnRePo; GBL; HeIP; LoBV; MePo; NOBE; OAEL-1; OBEV; OBS; SCV; SeCP; SeCV-1; ViBoPo
Apparition. John Erskine. HBMV
Apparition. W. E. Henley. In Hospital, XXV. BrPo; TrGrPo
Apparition, The. Herman Melville. NoP
Apparition, The. Stephen Phillips. OBEV; OBVV
Apparition of His Mistress Calling Him to Elysium [*or* Elizium], The. Robert Herrick. AnAnS-2; CaPo; SeCP; SeCV-1
Apparition of Splendor. Marianne Moore. NePoAm
Apparition of these faces in the crowd, The. In a Station of the Metro. Ezra Pound. AmPP; CABA; CAD; HAP; HeIP; InPK; MoAB; MoAmPo; NIP; NoAM; NOBA; NoP; OxBA; PAI; TAP; UnPo; VGW; WeW
Apparitions. Thomas Curtis Clark. PGD; TRV
Apparitions, The. W. B. Yeats. CMoP; LiTM
Apparitions Are Not Singular Occurrences. Diane Wakoski. CoPo
Apparuit. Ezra Pound. TwAmPo
Appeal, The. Emily Brontë. LoBV
("If grief for grief can touch thee.") EnLoPo; OBNC
Appeal, The. Samuel Daniel. OLR
Appeal. Noémia da Sousa, *tr. fr. Portuguese. TTY, tr. by* Dorothy Guedes *and* Philippa Rumsey; WPOW, *tr. by* Alan Ryder
Appeal, An [*or* The]. Sir Thomas Wyatt. *See* And Wilt Thou Leave Me Thus?
Appeal by Unemployed Ex-Service Men, An. *Unknown.* OBET
Appeal for Illumination. Luigi Pulci, *tr. fr. Italian by* Byron. Il Morgante Maggiore, Canto I, ii. ISi
Appeal to Cats in the Business of Love, An. Thomas Flatman. EnLoPo; GBL; HAP; PCat
Appeal to Harold, The. H. C. Bunner. AA
Appeal to My Countrywomen, An. Frances E. W. Harper. BlSi
Appeal to the Moongod Nanna-Suen to Throw Out Lugalanne. Enheduanna, *tr. fr. Sumerian; ad. by* Aliki *and* Willis Barnstone. BoWoP
Appeal to the Phoenix. Louis Untermeyer. UnTE
Appear, O mother, was the perpetual cry. Invocation. Wilfred Watson. MoCV
Appear out of nowhere. Small Towns. Alejandro Murguía. FIA
Appearance, An. Sylvia Plath. CAPP
Appearance. Norman H. Russell. STE
Appearance and Reality. John Hollander. OBAL
Appeasement of Demeter, The. George Meredith. VLP
Appendix to the Anniad. Gwendolyn Brooks. BlSi
Appetite, The. Yom Kippur: Fasting. Ruth Whitman. OFD
Applauding youths laughed with young prostitutes. The Harlem Dancer. Claude McKay. BALP; BANP; BPo; FF; NoAM; TAP
Applause flutters onto the open air. A Snapshot for Miss Bricka. Robert Wallace. LiSp
Apple. Nan Fry. PPJ
Apple, The. Bruce Guernsey. PPJ
Apple, The. *At. to* Plato, *tr. fr. Greek.* WeW
Apple, The. Lady Margaret Sackville. OBVV
Apple, The. Ray Smith. TrCP
Apple a Day, An. Lee Blair. TDH
Apple a day, An. Health Food. *Unknown.* FaBoUs
Apple-Barrel of Johnny Appleseed, The. Vachel Lindsay. AmFN; OxBA
Apple Blight. Paul Zimmer. VGW
Apple Blossoms. Lucy Larcom. YeAr
Apple blossoms look like snow. A Comparison. John Farrar. FaPON
Apple Dumplings and a King, The. "Peter Pindar." OBEC; OBSV
Apple Gathering, An. Christina Rossetti. OBNC; OLR
Apple Hell. Mark Van Doren. PoA
Apple Offering. *Unknown, tr. fr. Greek by* Louis Untermeyer. UnTE
Apple Orchard in the Spring, An. William Martin. GN
Apple orchard smells like wine, An. Wise. Lizette Woodworth Reese. HBV-2
Apple Peeler. Robert Francis. CrMA; LCAP; NePoAm
Apple-pie, apple-pie. *Unknown.* OxNR
Apple Season. Frances Frost. SiSoSe
Apple-Seed John. Lydia Maria Child. OHIP
Apple Song. Frances Frost. FaPON; TiPo
Apple time, and the trees brittle with fruit. Picking Apples. Maurice Lindsay. BSV
Apple Tree, The. James K. Baxter. OxBC
Apple Tree, The. Beatrice Curtis Brown. SiSoSe
Apple-Tree, The. Nancy Campbell. AnIV
Apple-Tree, The. Brian Vrepont. PoAu-2
Apple trees are hung with gold, The. Endymion. Oscar Wilde. HBV-1
Apple Trees at Olema, The. Robert Hass. NPGG
Apple Wassail. *Unknown.* OBET
Apples. Donald Hall. LCAP
Apples. Shirley Kaufman. NMM
Apples. Lisel Mueller. NePoAm-2
Apples. Swift. *Fr.* Verses for Fruitwomen. AnIV; OnYI
(Verses Made for Women Who Cry Apples.) NCEP
Apples. Michael Waters. GeTw
Apples are seasoned, The. Apple Song. Frances Frost. FaPON; TiPo
Apples Be Ripe. *Unknown.* GBP
Apples, bright on the leafless bough. Apple Hell. Mark Van Doren. PoA
Apples in New Hampshire. Marie Gilchrist. BoNaP
Applicant, The. Sylvia Plath. MAT; NaP; NMM; NOBA; SBG; TwCP
Application for a Grant. Anthony Hecht, *ad. fr.* Horace. SaC
Apply for the position (I've forgotten now for what) I had. In Order To. Kenneth Patchen. NaP
Appoggiatura. Donald Jeffrey Hayes. AmNP; PoBA; PoNe
Appointed in the newe Moon. Jason and Medea. John Gower. *Fr.* Confessio Amantis. ACP
Appointed winners in a long-stretch'd game, The. To-Day and Thee. Walt Whitman. NePA
Appointment, The. Maxine W. Kumin. NMM
Appointment, The. L. A. G. Strong. OxBTC
Appointment, The. Sully-Prudhomme, *tr. fr. French by* Arthur O'Shaughnessy. OxBI
Appology, The. Countess of Winchilsea. SBG
Appraisal. Sara Teasdale. MoAmPo
Appreciation. Thomas Bailey Aldrich. AA
Appreciation. Harry Graham. PoPle
(Some Ruthless Rhymes, III.) CenHV
Appreciation. George Meredith. ViBoPo
Apprehension. *Unknown, tr. fr. Sanskrit by* Douglas Ainslie. OBVV
Apprehension this spring . . . the leaves, the leaves. Homage and Lament for Ezra Pound in Captivity. Robert Duncan. NOBA
Apprentice in the shop across from me, The. A Short Winter Tale. Natan Zach, *tr. by* Peter Everwine *and* Shula Starkman. VWA
Apprentice Painter, The. Jack Myers. AmPA
Apprenticed. Jean Ingelow. OBVV
Apprentices. Robin Munro. PoSH
Approach, The. Thomas Traherne. OxBoCh
("That childish thoughts such joys inspire.") AnAnS-1
"O Lord, I wonder at thy Lov," *sel.* TrPWD
Approach of Pharaoh, The. Caedmon, *tr. fr. Anglo-Saxon. Fr.* Genesis. ACP; WaaP
Approach of the Storm, The. *Tr. fr. Chippewa Indian by* Frances Densmore. OBVE
Approach of Winter. James Thomson. *Fr.* The Seasons: Winter. OBEC
("See, Winter comes, to rule the varied year.") NOEC; OAEP; TEP
Approach this court with deference. On Entering a Forest. Elinor Lennen. PGD
Approach to a City. William Carlos Williams. CAD; PoRA
Approach to Thebes, The. Stanley Kunitz. PoA
Approaches. George Macdonald. TRV
Approaches, The. W. S. Merwin. NOBA; Prf
Approaching America. J. C. Squire. HBMV
Approaching by the gate (Class of '79). Views of the Favorite Colleges. John Malcolm Brinnin. GLGT; LiTA; MoAB
Approaching death. William Carlos Williams. *Fr.* Asphodel, That Greeny Flower. FaBoMo
Approaching the laboratory gates. The Liberator. Lucien Stryk. GP
Approaching Washington Heights. James Reiss. NYP
Approve the traveler who never went. The Travelers. James Reeves. POL
Après le Bain. William Carlos Williams. OBAL
Après-midi d'un Faune, L'. Stephane Mallarmé, *tr. fr. French by* Aldous Huxley. AWP
Sels.
Eclogue, The, *tr. by* Roger Fry. NAWM-2; SyP
"Proud of my music, let me often make," *tr. by* Aldous Huxley. ErPo
Apricot Tree. Magda Isanos, *tr. fr. Rumanian by* Willis Barnstone *and* Matei Calinescu. BoWoP
April. Obadiah Cyrus Auringer. AA
April. Remy Belleau, *tr. fr. French by* Andrew Lang. AWP
April. Vidame de Chartres, *tr. fr. French by* Swinburne. AWP
April. Emerson. ViBoPo
April. Theodosia Garrison. HBMV
April. John Linthicum. AMV-80
April. Linda Pastan. Psk
April. Ezra Pound. CMoP
April. Dora Sigerson Shorter. HBMV; HBVY
April. Sara Teasdale. FaPON; PDV; PoSC; SoPo; TiPo; YeAr
April. Samuel Thompson. BIrV
April. Eunice Tietjens. SoPo; YeAr
April. Jean Valentine. TAP

April. Sir William Watson. *See* Song: "April, April,/ Laugh thy girlish laughter."
April. Yvor Winters. ELU; RFM
April Adoration, An. Sir Charles G. D. Roberts. HBV-1
April again and it is a year again. Elegy. Sidney Keyes. WaP
April again, and its message unvaried, the same old impromptu. The Burden of Junk. John Glassco. OBCV
April and Dying. Anne Reeve Aldrich. AA
April and May. Emerson. *Fr.* May-Day. GN; OHIP
April and May. Anne Robinson. SUS
April, and no one able to calculate. Patrick Kavanagh. The Great Hunger, IV. IPY
April, April,/ Laugh thy girlish laughter. Song [*or* April]. Sir William Watson. FaBV; GN; HBV-1; HBVY; OBEV; OBVV; PoSC; TreF; TrGrPo
April cold with dropping rain. April and May. Emerson. *Fr.* May-Day. GN; OHIP
April Day, An. Joseph S. Cotter, Jr. CDC
April, 1885. Robert Bridges. NBM; OxBTC
April Fantasie. Ellen Mackay Hutchinson Cortissoz. AA
April 5, 1974. Richard Wilbur. GP
April Fool. Elizabeth J. Coatsworth. YeAr
April Fool. Eleanor Hammond. SoPo
April Fool. Sam Hunt. OCNZ
April Fools' Day. Yusef Komunyakaa. MAYP
April Fools' Day. Marnie Pomeroy. PoSC
April Fool's Day, or, St. Mary of Egypt. John Berryman. Dream Songs, XLVII. NaP
April Fourth. Robert Mezey. NaP
April, Glengarry. Philip Coxon. PoSH
April, in another fortnight, metropolitan April. Piano Practice. Derek Walcott. NYP
April in England. Robert Browning. *See* Home-Thoughts from Abroad.
April Inventory. W. D. Snodgrass. AP; BiP; CABA; CAPP; CoAP; HAP; LiTM; MP; NePoEA; NoAM; NoP; PAI; PoPl; PPoe; PAI; TAP; TwCP
April is a laundress. April and May. Anne Robinson. SUS
April is a very unkind month, I am telling you. The Wasted Land. Edward Pygge. FaBoPa
April is in my mistress' face. All Seasons in One. *Unknown.* GBL; HeIP; OBSC; TrGrPo
April is no month for burials. Rite of Spring. Leo Kennedy. CaP
April is the cruellest [*or* cruelest] month, breeding. The Waste Land. T. S. Eliot. AmPP; AP; CABA; CMoP; CoBMV; FaBoMo; HAP; LiTA; LiTM; MasP; MoAB; MoAmPo; MoPo; MoVE; NePA; NOAM; NOBA; NOBE; NoP; OAEL-2; OAEP; OxBA; OxBTC; PPoe; TAP; UnPo
April Midnight. Arthur Symons. SyP
April Moment. Arthur Davison Ficke. Sonnets of a Portrait Painter, XI. HBMV
April Morning, An. Bliss Carman. HBMV; HBVY
April Mortality. Léonie Adams. MoAB; MoAmPo
"With all the drifting race of men," *sel.* TrGrPo
April 1940. Patrick Maybin. NeIP
April, 1942. Mark Van Doren. WaP
April 1962. Paul Goodman. NMP; VGW
April of the Ages, The. Digby Mackworth Dolben. GoBC
April, pride of woodland ways. April. Remy Belleau, *tr. by* Andrew Lang. AWP
April Puddle. Rowena Bennett. TiPo
April Rain. Mathilde Blind. HBV-1
April Rain. Robert Loveman. HBV-1; HBVY; SUS; TrJP
(Rain Song.) TreFT; WBLP
April Rain Song. Langston Hughes. FaPON; NTCP; OBCA; PDV; RHPC; SUS; TiPo
April Showers. James Stephens. TiPo
April 68. Sam Cornish. CNA
April Snow, The. Jones Very. AP
April this year, not otherwise. Song of a Second April. Edna St. Vincent Millay. CMoP; OxBA
April Weather. Lizette Woodworth Reese. HBMV
April what an ice-cold promise. Hudson Ferry. James Schuyler. NYP
April winds are magical, The. April. Emerson. ViBoPo
April world is misted with emerald and gold, The. Gypsy-Heart. Katharine Lee Bates. HBMV
Aprill. Spenser. *Fr.* The Shepheardes Calender. PoEL-1
Aprille is of al the months moste dyr. Burialle of the Dede. Martin Fagg. BXAP
Aprilly. Bert Leston Taylor. OBAL
April's blossoms launch. Two Weeks after an April Frost. Steven Helmling. AMV-80
April's sweet hand in the margins betrayed. Fifth Sunday after Easter. Thomas Kinsella. NMP
Apron, The. Stuart Friebert. FiCP
Apron of Flowers, The. Robert Herrick. CaPo; SeCV-1
Apron Strings. Marge Piercy. TAP
Aprons of Silence. Carl Sandburg. NoAM; NOBA
Aquarium. George T. Wright. NYBP
Aquarium, San Francisco, The. V. Sackville-West. SBG
Aquellos Vatos. Tino Villanueva. FIA
Aqui/ you can't loosen up. Real Deal Revelation. Raymond Ringo Fernandez. LFAC
Ar ne couthe ich sorwe none. A Prisoner's Prayer. *Unknown.* OxBM
Arab Love-Song, An. Francis Thompson. AWP; MoAB; MoBrPo
Arab Song. Richard Henry Stoddard. AA
Arab to His Favorite Steed, The. Caroline E. S. Norton. BeLS; TreFS
(Arab's Farewell to His Horse [*or* Steed], The.) BLPA; PaPo
Arabesque. Fred Johnson. PoBA
Arabia. Walter de la Mare. HBMV; WHA
Arabia. John Meade Falkner. OxBTC
Arabian Nights, The. *Unknown. See* Thousand and One Nights, The.
Arabian Proverb. *Unknown. See* He Who Knows.
Arabian Shawl, The. Katherine Mansfield. Two Nocturnes, I. HBMV
Arabs. Alfred Kreymborg. TwAmPo
Arabs complain—or so I have been told. For the Rain It Raineth Every Day. Robert Graves. NYBP
Arab's Farewell to His Horse [*or* Steed], The. Caroline E. S. Norton. *See* Arab to His Favorite Steed, The.
Arachne. Jody Aliesan. LTB
Arachne. Rose Terry Cooke. AA
Arachne. William Empson. InvP; MoVE; OBMV
Arachne. Judith Kazantzis. BrRo
Arac's Song. W. S. Gilbert. *Fr.* Princess Ida. FiBHP; WhC
Aran Islands. Irving Layton. NeAC
Aranda Song. *Unknown, tr. fr. Aranda by* T. G. H. Strehlow. CBAP
Arbasto, *sels.* Robert Greene.
Doralicia's Song. LoBV; OBSC
Whereat Erewhile I Wept, I Laugh. ElL
Arbeit Macht Frei. Dennis Schmitz. NPGG
Arbor Amoris. Villon, *tr. fr. French by* Andrew Lang. AWP
Arbor Day. Dorothy Brown Thompson. SiSoSe
Arbor Day Tree, An. *Unknown.* OHIP
Arbor Vitae. Coventry Patmore. *Fr.* The Unknown Eros, II, iii. GoBC; LoBV; NBM; OBNC; SeCePo; VLP
Arbor Vitae. Siegfried Sassoon. PoPle
Arbour, The. Anne Brontë. EBVV
Arc Inside and Out, The. A. R. Ammons. NoAM; NoP
Arcades, *sels.* Milton.
Song: "Nymphs and shepherds dance no more." FiP; ViBoPo
(Nymphs and Shepherds.) ELP
Song: "O'er [*or* O're] the smooth enamel[l]ed green." LoBV; OBEV; TrGrPo; ViBoPo
Arcades Ambo. Charles Stuart Calverley. BXAP
Arcadia, *sels.* Sir Philip Sidney.
Country Song, A. OBSC; SiPS
Cupid. SiPS
Echo. SiPS
Epithalamium: "Let mother earth now deck herself in flowers." SiPS
Geron and Histor. SiPS
Get Hence Foule Griefe. PoEL-1
(Contentment.) SiPS
Graven Thoughts. SiPS
In Vain, Mine Eyes. SiPS
Love and Jealousy. SiPS
Love and Reason. SiPS
"Loved I am, and yet complaine of Love." PoEL-1
(Complaint of Love.) SiPS
Madrigal: "Why dost thou haste away." OBSC; SiPS
My Sheep Are Thoughts. SiPS
"My true love hath my heart [*or* hart]." BoLoP; CH; FaBoBe; GBL; HBV-1; OAEP; PoEL-1; PoPle; ViBoPo; WHA
(Arcadian Duologue.) SiPS
(Bargain, The.) NOBE
(Ditty, A: "My true-love hath my heart, and I have his.") AWP; GTBS; GTBS-P
(Heart Exchange.) LiTB; LoBV
(Sonnet: "My true love hath my heart, and I have his.") ElL
(True Love.) ChTr
Night. SiPS
O Sweet Woods. FaBoRV; PoEL-1
(Delight of Solitariness.) LiTB
(Dorus's Song.) LoBv
(Solitariness.) OBSC; SiPS
Old Age. SiPS
Rural Poesy. Ell

Sapphics. SiPS
Shepherd Song: "As I my little flock on Ister bank." SiPS
Shepherd's Tale, A. SiPS
Since So Mine Eyes. SiPS
Sleep. OBSC; SiPS
(Sonnet: "Lock up, fair lids, the treasure of my heart.") EIL
Sweeter Saint I Serve, A. SiPS
Tale for Husbands, A. SiPS
Truth Doth Truth Deserve. HBV-1
(Advise to the Same.) SiPS
What Tongue Can Her Perfections Tell? EnRePo; SiPS
When Two Suns Do Appear. EnRePo; MOON; SiPS
Why Fear to Die? SiPS
(Since Nature's Works Be Good) OAEP
Wronged Lover, The. SiPS
"Ye goat-herd gods that love the grassy mountains." HAP; NOBE; NoP; OAEL-1
(Double Sestine.) LiTB; PoEL-1
Arcadia was of old (said he) a State. Rhotus on Arcadia. John Chalkhill. *Fr.* Thealma and Clearchus. OBS
Arcadian Duologue. Sir Philip Sidney. *See* My True Love Hath My Heart.
Arcady Revisited. Robert Funge. AMV-80
Arcana Sylvarum. Charles De Kay. AA
Arcanum One. Gwendolyn MacEwen. MoCV
Archaeological Picnic, The. John Betjeman. EnLoPo
Archaeologist of the Future, The. Leonard Bacon. WhC
Archaeologists. Real Faucher. AMV-80
Archaeology. Katha Pollitt. MAYP
Archaeology of a Marriage, The. Maxine W. Kumin. DFT
Archaeology of Love, The. Richard Murphy. EnLoPo
Archaic Apollo. William Plomer. ChMP
Archaic Torso of Apollo. Rainer Maria Rilke, *tr. fr. German by* Robert Bly. NU
Archangel, The. Byron. *Fr.* The Vision of Judgment. LoBV
("But bringing up the rear of this bright host.") OBRV
Archangel's silver panties glint as he flies, The. Michael. Sandra McPherson. LCAP
Archbishop Tait. *Unknown.* ChTr; FaBoNo
Archer, The. Clinton Scollard. FaPON
Archer, The. A. J. M. Smith. OBCV; PeCV
Archer, The. *Unknown, tr. fr. Sanskrit by* Douglas Ainslie. OBVV
Archer is wake, The! Peace on Earth. William Carlos Williams. LiTA; ViBoPo
Archers of the King. Sister Mary Genoveva. GoBC
Archery. Walter de la Mare. FaBoNo
Arches and Shadows. Annie Dillard. CTBA
Archetypes. Neal Bowers. AMV-81
Archibald MacLeish Suspends the Five Little Pigs. Louis Untermeyer. *Fr.* Mother Goose Up-to-Date. MoAmPo
Ar(chibald')s Poetica. Alan Ribback. BXAP
Archie o [*or* of] Cawfield [*or* Cafield] (*diff. vers.*). *Unknown.* AmFP; ESPB (A *and* B *vers.*); OxBS
Archilochos. John Tagliabue. FAZ
Archin' here and arrachin' there. Water Music. "Hugh MacDiarmid." GoTS
Architect. Louise Townsend Nicholl. EyDe
Architects of Dream. Lucia Trent. PGD
Architectural Masks. Thomas Hardy. EyDe
Archne. Richard Foerster. AMV-80
Archy a Low Brow. Don Marquis. *Fr.* Archys Life of Mehitabel. WhC
Archy and Mehitabel, *sels.* Don Marquis.
Archy at the Zoo. OBAL
Archy Confesses. EvOK, FiBHP
Cheerio My Deario. FaBoCo
Hen and the Oriole, The. EvOK; FiBHP
Old Trouper, The. FaBoCo
Trouble. TreFT
Wail of Archy, The.
"Gods i am pent in a cockroach." FiBHP
Warty Bliggins, the Toad. FiBHP
Archy at the Zoo. Don Marquis. *Fr.* Archy and Mehitabel. OBAL
Archy Confesses. Don Marquis. *Fr.* Archy and Mehitabel. EvOK; FiBHP
Archy Does His Part, *sel.* Don Marquis.
Fate Is Unfair. EvOK
Archy Experiences a Seizure. Don Marquis. *Fr.* Archys Life of Mehitabel. WhC
Archy, the Cockroach, Speaks. Don Marquis. *Fr.* Certain Maxims of Archy. FaPON
Archygrams. Don Marquis. *Fr.* Archys Life of Mehitabel. WhC
Archys Autobiography. Don Marquis. *Fr.* Archys Life of Mehitabel. CrMA
Archys Last Name. Don Marquis. *Fr.* Archys Life of Mehitabel. CrMA
Archys Life of Mehitabel, *sels.* Don Marquis.
Archy a Low Brow. WhC
Archy Experiences a Seizure. WhC
Archygrams. WhC
Archys Autobiography. CrMA
Archys Last Name. CrMA
Artists Shouldnt Have Offspring. CrMA
Ballade of the Under Side. InvP
Arctic Convoy. J. K. Annand. OxBS
Arctic honey blabbed over the report causing darkness, The. Leaving the Atocha Station. John Ashbery. CAPP
Arctic moon hangs overhead, The. The Wolf Cry. Lew Sarett. FaPON; RHPC
Arctic Ox, The. Marianne Moore. NYBP
Arctic raven tracks the caribou, The. Epigram. Raymond Wilson. PV
Arctic Tern in a Museum. Effie Lee Newsome. PoNe
Arctic Vision, An. Bret Harte. PAH
Arcturus is his other name. Emily Dickinson. FaBV; NOBA; SUW
Arcuconspicilla oves looks for perditas. She Lost Her Sheep. J. Moyr Smith. FaBoNo
Ardan Mór. Francis Ledwidge. *See* Herons, The.
Arden is not Eden, but Eden's rhyme. In Arden. Charles Tomlinson. OxBC
Ardent in love and cold in charity. A Man's Sliding Mood. "E." CBAP
Ardently down the backs of cousins. Hair. Maxine Silverman. VWA
Ardor. Gamaliel Bradford. HBMV
Ardour and Memory. Dante Gabriel Rossetti. The House of Life, LXIV. OAEL-2
Are all such off'rings, as are crusht, and bruis'd. Francis Quarles. FaBoEE
Are All the Children In? *Unknown.* STF
Are all these stones. Close-up. A. R. Ammons. PoA
Are at the end of our street. They. Donald Finkel. GP
Are generally over or around. Pockets. Howard Nemerov. NIP
Are God and Nature then at strife. Tennyson. *Fr.* In Memoriam A. H. H. TRV
Are not Abracadabra or anything slippery and remote. The Magic Words. Ronald Koertge. AMV-81
". . .Are not molesters of women" the book says. Pocket Guide for Service Men. Hubert Creekmore. WaP
Are the Children at Home? Margaret E. Sangster. HBV-1
Are the desolate, dark weeks. These. William Carlos Williams. AP; CoBMV; MoAmPo; NoAM; NOBA; NoP; OxBA
". . .Are the horns of the hall on fire?" The Battle of Finnsburg. *Unknown, tr. by* Charles W. Kennedy. AnOE
"Are the reindeer in the rain, dear?" Conversation between Mr. and Mrs. Santa Claus. Rowena Bennett. SiSoSe; TiPo
Are the Sick in Their Beds as They Should Be? Joan McIntosh. AMV-80
Are Then Regalities All Gilded Masks? Keats. *Fr.* Endymion, III. MOON
Are there birds twittering under the earth. Under the Earth. Abraham Sutskever, *tr. by* Ruth Whitman. VWA
Are there favoring ladies above thee? Valse Jeune. Louise Imogen Guiney. AA
Are there no roses in your garden. Jardin des Fleurs. Charles David Webb. NePoAm-2
Are there not twelve whole hours in every day. The Day of Denial. Jones Very. NOBA
Are these the astronauts who carried. A Farewell to the Moon. Ed Ochester. MOON
Are these the honors they reserve for me. Columbus in Chains. Philip Freneau. PAH
Are these the pope's grand tools? On the Murder of Sir Edmund Berry Godfrey. *Unknown.* APAS
Are these the strings that poets say. The Cat and the Lute. Thomas Master. PCat
Are these the tracks of some unearthly friend. Angelic Guidance. Cardinal Newman. GoBC
Are they clinging to their crosses. Antichrist, or the Reunion of Christendom; an Ode. G. K. Chesterton. DBV; FaBoCo; NOBE; NOBL; OBSV; SeCePo
Are They Dancing. Edward Dorn. NeAP; PoM
Are they exiles here from the rest of the world? What Do the Birds Think? Alfred Purdy. MoCV
Are They Not All Ministering Spirits? Robert Stephen Hawker. GoBC; HBV-1
Are They Shadows [That We See]? Samuel Daniel. *Fr.* Tethy's Festival. CH; EIL; InvP; LoBV; NoP; SeCeV
(Shadows.) NOBE; OBSC
(Song. "Are they shadowes that we see?" PoEL-2
Are we being fair, I wonder. Are We Thankful? *Unknown.* STF
Are we mere pieces in the hand. Fate. James Fenimore Cooper, Jr. HBMV

Are We Not the People, *sel.* Al-Samau'al ibn Adiya, *tr. fr. Arabic by* Hartwig Hirschfeld.
"Now listen to boasting which leaves the heart dazed." TrJP
Are we quite cut off from Thee? The Trial. Gershom Scholem, *tr. by* Jonathan Griffin. VWA
Are We Thankful? *Unknown.* STF
Are Women Fair? *At. to* Francis Davison. HBV-1
"Are Ye Right There, Michael?" (A Lay of the Wild West Clare.) Percy French. WTO
Are you a horror? With the Sun's Fire. David Ignatow. FAZ
Are you alive? The Pool. Hilda Doolittle. ("H. D."). CMoP
Are you almost disgusted with life, little man? How to Be Happy. *Unknown.* BLPA
Are you an active member. Do You Just Belong? *Unknown.* STF
Are you asking where I'm going with these sad faces. Poem with the Final Tune. Julia de Burgos, *tr. by* Julio Marzán. InW
"Are you asleep, Mother?" Mary's Vision. *Unknown, tr. by* Eleanor Hull. ISi
"Are you awake, Gemelli." Star-Talk. Robert Graves. BoNaP; GoJo; HBMV; MoBrPo; OxBTC
Are You Glad? *Mongol Oral Tradition, tr. by* C. R. Bawden. WTO
Are you going to Scarborough [*or* Wittingham] Fair? Scarborough [*or* Whittingham] Fair. *Unknown.* BLSo; FSW; GBP
Are you hot there too? Black Muslim Boy in a Hospital. James A. Emanuel. PoNe
Are You Just Back for a Visit or Are You Going to Stay? Francis Coleman Rosenberger. AMV-81
"Are you looking for someone, you who come pattering." Thoughts of Thomas Hardy. Edmund Blunden. PoCh
Are You looking for us? We are here. The 151st Psalm. Karl Shapiro. EaLo; VWA
"Are you ready, O Virginia." The Call to the Colors. Arthur Guiterman. PAH
Are you ready? soul said again. Two Trinities. Kenneth Mackenzie. CBAP
"Are you sad to think how often." Middle-aged Conversation. A. S. J. Tessimond. POL
Are you so weary? Come to the window. Wind in the Grass. Mark Van Doren. FaBV
Are you standing at "Wit's End Corner." Wit's End Corner. Antoinette Wilson. BLRP; STF
Are You the New Person Drawn toward Me? Walt Whitman. NePA; NoAM; PPP
Are You There, Mrs. Goose? John V. Hicks. AMV-80
Are you what your faire lookes expresse? Thomas Campion. AAS
Are you worsted in a fight? Laugh It Off. Henry Rutherford Elliot. WBLP
Are zebras black with broad white stripes. Zebra. William Jay Smith. TiPo
Areas. Leslie Scalapino. NPGG
Ares. Albert Ehrenstein, *tr. fr. German by* Babette Deutsch *and* Avram Yarmolinsky. TrJP
Ares at last has quit the field. Under Which Lyre, a Reactionary Tract for the Times. W. H. Auden. MoAB; MoBrPo; NOBL
Arethusa, The. Prince Hoare. FaPoR
Arethusa. Shelley. DTo; EnRP; GN; HBV-1; OBRV; WiR
Arf, Said Sandy. Charles Stetler. PPJ
Argalus and Parthenia, *sels.* Francis Quarles.
Authour's Dreame, The. OBS
Hos Ego Versiculos. OBS. *See also* Man's Mortality, *sl. diff. vers. at. to* Simon Wastell, *fr.* Microbiblion.
(Like as the Damask Rose.) LoBV
Argent Solipsism. Howard Blake. PoA
Argenteuil County. Peter Dale Scott. MoCV
Argentina in one swing of the bell skirt. The Beautiful Train. William Empson. MoVE
Argentine gaucho named Bruno, An. Limerick. *Unknown.* NOBL
Argument, An. Thomas Moore. BoLoP; EnLoPo
(Argument to Any Phillis or Cloë, An.) NIP
Argument, The. Jane P. Moreland. AMV-80
Argument. Mildred Weston. WhC
Argument against Metaphor. Gad Hollander. VWA
Argument begins the week we marry, The. The Argument. Jane P. Moreland. AMV-80
Argument of Democritus Platonissans, or the Infinitie of Worlds, The. Henry More. SeCV-2
Argument of His Book, The. Robert Herrick. AnAnS-2; AWP; CaPo; EBEV; HAP; HBV-2; HeIP; InVP; JCP; NoP; OAEL-1; OAEP; OBS; PoEL-3; PoPle; PoRA; SeCePo; SeCeV; SeCP; SeCV-1; TrGrPo; ViBoPo; WHA
("I sing of brooks, of blossoms, birds, and bowers.") TEP
Argument, An—of the Passion of Christ. Thomas Merton. CrMA
Argument of the refrigerator wakes me, The. The Refrigerator. Howard Moss. GP
Argument to Any Phillis or Cloë, An. Thomas Moore. *See* Argument, An.
Arguments against restraint, The. To His Dear Friend, Bones. Jay Parini. MAYP
Aria. Rolfe Humphries. NYBP
Aria. Delmore Schwartz. ErPo
Aria for Flute and Oboe. Joseph Langland. NePoEA
Aria Senza da Capo. Robert Finch. MoCV
Ariake, Japanese friend, I regard. To Ariake Kambara. Norman Rosten. NYBP
Ariana. Franklin Benjamin Sanborn. AA
Arid Husband, The. E. L. T. Mesens. EAS
Aridity. "Michael Field." OBMV; OxBoCh; TRV
Ariel. David Campbell. CBAP; PoAu-2
Ariel. Sylvia Plath. CABA; CMoP; HeIP; InPK; LCAP; NoAM; NOBA; NMP; NoP; PBWP
Ariel in the Cloven Pine. Bayard Taylor. AA
Ariel to Miranda:—Take. With a Guitar, to Jane [*or* To a Lady, with a Guitar]. Shelley. EnRP; GTBS; GTBS-P; HBV-2; OAEL-2
Ariel was glad he had written his poems. The Planet on the Table. Wallace Stevens. HAP
Ariel's Song: "Come unto these yellow sands." Shakespeare. *Fr.* The Tempest, I, ii. CTC; FaBoCh; GN; GoJo; LoBV; NOBE; TEP
("Come unto these yellow sands.") CH; ElL; HeIP; OBEV; OBSC; PoPle; SpRo; ViBoPo
(Fairy Songs.) HBV-1
(Song: "Come unto these yellow sands.") PoEL-2
Ariel's Song: "Full fathom five thy father lies." Shakespeare. *Fr.* The Tempest, I, ii. FaBoEn; GN; LoBV; NOBE; OBSC; SeCePo; TreFT
(Ariel's Dirge.) EvOK; GoJo
("Full fathom [*or* fadom] five thy father lies"). AWP; BiP; ChTr; EBEV; ElL; ELP; FaBoCh; HAP; HeIP; HoPM; InPK; InPS; LiTB; MOS; NoP; OAEP; OBEV; PAI; PoPle; PoRA; PPoe; SeCeV; TEP; ViBoPo; WHA
(Sea Dirge.) EtS; GTBS; GTBS-P; HBV-2; TrGrPo
(Song.) PoEL-2
Ariel's Song: "Where the bee sucks, there suck I." Shakespeare. *Fr.* The Tempest, V, i. GN; NOBE; OBSC; PDV
("Where the bee sucks, there suck I.") AWP; CABA; CH; CTC; ElL; EnRePo; FaBV; HeIP; NoP; OBEV; SeCeV; TiPo; TreFT; ViBoPo; WHA
(Fairy Songs.) HBV-1, HBVY
(Fairy's Life, A) PoPl
Ariosto. Osip Mandelstam, *tr. fr. Russian by* W. S. Merwin *and* Clarence Brown. OBVE
Arise and go now to the city of slaughter. The City of Slaughter. Hayyim Nahman Bialik, *tr. by* A. M. Klein. TrJP
Arise and Pick a Posy. *Unknown.* OBET
Arise and See the Glorious Sun, *with music.* Francis Hopkinson. AH
Arise, Arise. *Unknown.* OBET
Arise, arise, arise! Air. Henry Brooke. *Fr.* Jack the Giant Queller; an Antique History. NOEC
Arise faint Muse bring one heart-melting verse. An Elegie on the Deploreable Departure of the Honered and Truely Religious Chieftain John Hull. John Saffin. SCAP
Arise from your rope-strung bed, Clabe Mott. Clabe Mott. James Still. GrPl
Arise, My Soul! With Rapture Rise! *with music.* Samuel J. Smith. AH
Arise, O Glorious Zion, *with music.* William G. Mills. AH
Arise, O soul, and gird thee up anew. A Challenge. James Benjamin Kenyon. AA
Arise up on thy feet, O Quiet Heart! He Biddeth Osiris to Arise from the Dead. *Unknown, tr. by* Robert Hillyer. *Fr.* Book of the Dead. AWP
Arise ye daughters of a land. The Women's Marseillaise. F. E. M. Macaulay. BrRo
Arise, ye kings of Macha. *Unknown, tr. by* Joseph Dunn. *Fr.* The Combat of Ferdiad and Cuchulain. OnYI
Arise, Ye Saints of Latter Days, *with music. Unknown.* AH
Arise, ye sons of France, to glory! La Marseillaise. Claude Joseph Rouget de Lisle, *tr. fr. French.* FSW
Arise, you pris'ners of starvation. The Internationale. Eugene Potter *and* Pierre Degeyter. FSW
Arise! you who refuse to be bond-slaves. Chee Lai! (Arise!) *Unknown, tr. fr. Chinese.* FSW
Arisen from what childhood. The Phoenix of Mozart. Claude Vigée, *tr. by* Anthony Rudolf. VWA
Aristeides. Antipater, *tr. fr. Greek by* Charles Whibley. AWP
Aristocratic Trio, An. Judson France. PV
Aristocrats. Keith Douglas. FaBoMo; NePoEA; OBWP
Aristocrats of Labor. W. Stewart. PGD
Aristophanes' Symposium. Rita Mae Brown. IHMS

Aristotle to Phyllis. John Hollander. PoCh
Aristotle was a little man with/ eyes like a lizard. Humanities Lecture. William Stafford. GLGT; NNAP
Arithmetic ("Arithmetic is where numbers fly like pigeons in and out of your head"). Carl Sandburg. FaPON; ImOP; RHPC
Arithmetic. *Unknown.* TreFS
Arithmetic on the Frontier. Kipling. OBWP; VLP
Arithmetique nine digits, and no more. Upon the Losse of His Little Finger. Thomas Randolph. AnAnS-2
Arizona. Sharlot M. Hall. PAH
Arizona. *Unknown.* AmFP
Arizona Boys and Girls, The, *with music. Unknown.* CoSo
Arizona Highways. James Welch. CDW
Arizona Nature Myth. James Michie. NOBL
Arizona Poems, *sels.* John Gould Fletcher.
 Mexican Quarter, II. BPAW
 Rain in the Desert, VI. BPAW; NCSH
 Windmills, The, IV. CrMA
Arizona Village. Robert Stiles Davieau. AmFN
Arizona wind dries out my nostrils, The. The Hitchhiker. Ai. GeTw
Arjuna said:/ How shall I in battle against Bhisma. *Unknown. Fr.* The Bhagavad-Gita. DL
Ark, The, *sels.* Jay Macpherson.
 Ark Anatomical. NOBC
 Ark Apprehensive. NOBC
 Ark Artefact. NOBC
 Ark Articulate. NOBC
 Ark Astonished. NOBC
 Ark Overwhelmed. NOBC
 Ark Parting. NOBC
 Ark to Noah. NOBC
 ("I wait, with those that rest.") PoA
Ark, The. Milton. *Fr.* Paradise Lost, XI. EtS
Ark Anatomical. Jay Macpherson. *Fr.* The Ark. NOBC
Ark and the *Dove,* The. Daniel Sargent. EtS
Ark Apprehensive. Jay Macpherson. *Fr.* The Ark. NOBC
Ark Artefact. Jay Macpherson. *Fr.* The Ark. NOBC
Ark Articulate. Jay Macpherson. *Fr.* The Ark. NOBC
Ark Astonished. Jay Macpherson. *Fr.* The Ark. NOBC
Ark noisy with children, The. Noah. Chana Bloch. VWA
Ark of the Covenant. Louise Townsend Nicholl. ImOP
Ark Overwhelmed. Jay Macpherson. *Fr.* The Ark. NOBC
Ark Parting. Jay Macpherson. *Fr.* The Ark. NOBC
Arkansas. Jackman Young. TAT
Arkansas Traveler, The ("Oh, once upon a time in Arkansas"). *Unknown.* FSW
Arkansas Traveller, The ("How do you do?"), *with music.* Mose Case. PSoN
Arkansaw Traveler, The ("My name it is Bill Stafford"). *Unknown.* ViBoFo
Arlington Cemetery Looking toward the Capitol. Winthrop Palmer. GoYe
Arlo Will. Edgar Lee Masters. *Fr.* Spoon River Anthology. LiTA
Arm, Arm, Arm, Arm! John Fletcher. *Fr.* The Mad Lover. ElL
Armada, The [a Fragment]. Macaulay. BeLS; FaBoCh; FaPoR; GN; HBV-2; OBRV; WBLP
 "Night sank upon the dusky beach, and on the purple sea," *sel.* OBNC
Armada, 1588, The. John Wilson. OxBChV
Armada of Thirty Whales, An. Daniel G. Hoffman. NePa
Armadillo, The [—Brazil]. Elizabeth Bishop. NoAM; NOBA; NoP; NYBP; TAP; VGW
Armageddon. John Crowe Ransom. LiTA
Armageddon, Armageddon, *sel.* Paul Muldoon.
 "When Oisin came back to Ireland." CIP
Armagh. W. R. Rodgers. NoAM
Armaments Race. Evangeline Paterson. AMV-81
Armand Dussault. Wilson MacDonald. WhC
Arme, Arme, Arme, Arme, great Neptune rowze, awake. John Smith of His Friend Master John Taylor. John Smith. SCAP
Armed Vision. N. P. Van Wyk Louw, *tr. fr. Afrikaans by* Jack Cope *and* Uys Krige. PeSA
Armed we go. we are the dancers. A Tryptych for Jan Bockelson. John Oliver Simon. NeAC
Armful, The. Robert Frost. CMoP
Armies in the Fire. Robert Louis Stevenson. EBVV
Arming of Pigwiggen, The. Michael Drayton. *See* Pigwiggin Arms Himself.
Armistice. Elizabeth Daryush. AMV-81
Armistice. Paul Dehn. OxBTC
Armistice. Charles Buxton Going. HBMV
Armistice. Sophie Jewett. AA
Armistice. Eunice Mitchell Lehmer. PGD
Armistice. Thomas Lodge. *See* For Pity, Pretty Eyes, Surcease.
Armistice Day. Charles Causley. OBWP
Armistice Day. John Freeman. MMA
Armistice Day. Lucia Trent. PGD
Armistice Day Vow. Dorothy Gould. PGD
Armless, The. Don Welch. AMV-81
Armor. James Dickey. CoAP
Armorer's Daughter, The. Debora Greger. MAYP
Armorer's Song, The. Harry Bache Smith. AA; OHIP
Armorial. Ralph Gustafson. MoCV; PeCV
Armour's Undermining Modesty. Marianne Moore. AP; CoBMV
Armoury, An. Alcaeus, *tr. fr. Greek by* Gilbert Highet. WaaP
Arms and the Boy. Wilfred Owen. BrPo; CABA; CMoP; FaFP; HAP; LiTB; LiTM; MoAB; MoBrPo; OAEL-2; OAEP; WaP; WeW
Arms and the man I sing, and sing for joy. Epigram. J. V. Cunningham. NePoAm
Arms, and the man I sing, who forc'd by fate. Virgil, *tr. by* Dryden. *Fr.* The Aeneid, I. OBVE
Arms at my side like some inadequate sign. Mountain Town—Mexico. Eldon Grier. NOBC
Arms in cool dresses shine, boys' throats are bare. In a London Schoolroom. James Kirkup. GLGT
Arms reversed and banners craped. A Dirge for McPherson. Herman Melville. AP; PAH; PoEL-5
Arms seem clumsy at first, The. The Fever Toy. Charles Wright. AmPA
Armstrong at Fayal, The. Wallace Rice. PAH
Armstrong Spring Creek. Lloyd Davis. AMV-81
Army Corps on the March, An. Walt Whitman. InPS; PAL; PoLF; PPoe
Army Correspondent's Last Ride. George Alfred Townsend. AA
Army in the dust, An. Drummer Boy. William Stafford. FAZ
Army, Navy. *Unknown.* OxNR
Army of the Lord. I'm a Soldier in the Army of the Lord. *Unknown.* AmFP
Army returned home wet with sunlight, The. One Night Away from Day. John Digby. EAS
Army was ours that spring, The. Landing in England. North Pickenham. Coman Leavenworth. *Fr.* Norfolk Memorials, I. LiTA
Arnold at Stillwater. Thomas Dunn English. PAH
Arnold, Master of the *Scud.* Bliss Carman. EtS
Arnold, the Vile Traitor ("Arnold the name, as heretofore"). *Unknown.* PAH
Arnold von Winkelried. James Montgomery. *See* Make Way for Liberty.
Arnold, warm with God. The Last Warmth of Arnold. Gregory Corso. CoPo; NoAM
Around, above my bed, the pitch-dark fly. Truth. Howard Nemerov. HoPM; LiTM; MoVE
Around, around the sun we go. Mother Goose's Garland. Archibald MacLeish. OBAL
Around bend after bend. Not of School Age. Robert Frost. GLGT
Around Cape Horn, *with music. Unknown.* AmSS
Around his open grave from near and far. Harry Edward Mills. *Fr.* Convicted. PeD
Around islands of jade and malachite. The Wave Symphony. Arthur Davison Ficke. *Fr.* Four Japanese Paintings. PoA
Around me roar and crash the pagan isms. The Pagan Isms. Claude McKay. BPo
Around me the images of thirty years. The Municipal Gallery Revisited. W. B. Yeats. GTBS-P; LiTB; OxBTC
Around my garden the little wall is low. Losing a Slave-Girl. Po Chü-i, *tr. by* Arthur Waley. AWP
Around Thanksgiving. Rolfe Humphries. OFD
Around the battlements go by. War on the Periphery. George Johnston. NOBC; PeCV
Around the bend we streaked it with the leaders swingin' wide. The Oro Stage. Henry Herbert Knibbs. BPAW
Around the Block. Keith Waldrop. AMV-80
Around the Child. Walter Savage Landor. HBV-1
Around the Corner ("Around the corner I have a friend"). Charles Hanson Towne. PoLF
Around the Corner. *Unknown.* FSW
Around the fire one wintry night. The Beggar Man. Lucy Aikin. OxBChV
Around the fireplace, pointing at the fire. On Falling Asleep by Firelight. William Meredith. NoAM; NYBP
Around the Fish: After Paul Klee. Howard Moss. MoPo
Around the headland, at the end. The Lives of Gulls and Children. Howard Nemerov. NePoEA
Around the house the flakes fly faster. Birds at Winter Nightfall. Thomas Hardy. ELU; MoBrPo
Around the Kitchen Table. Gary Gildner. Str
Around the little park. Back to Life. Thom Gunn. NoP
Around the quays, kicked off in twos. Fishing Boats in Martigues. Roy Campbell. FaBoEE; FaBoPP
Around the rick, around the rick. *Unknown.* OxNR
Around the rocky headlands, far and near. The Sea's Voice. William Prescott Foster. EtS

Around the vase of Life at your slow pace. The Vase of Life. Dante Gabriel Rossetti. The House of Life, XCV. SyP
Around their legs girl athletes twist. Girl Athletes. Haniel Long. HBMV
Around this lovely valley rise. Midsummer. John Townsend Trowbridge. AA; HBV-1; HBVY
Around us speeches of birds. I tremble. Lines to a Tree. Judah Leib Teller, *tr. by* Gabriel Preil *and* Howard Schwartz. VWA
Around us summer wrote its last farewell. September Afternoon. Margaret Haley Carpenter. GoYe
Around were all the roses red. Spleen. Paul Verlaine, *tr. by* Ernest Dowson. AWP; SyP
Around You, Your House. William Stafford. NPAW
Arous'd and angry, I'd thought to beat the alarum, and urge relentless war. Epigraph to "Drum-Taps." Walt Whitman. PAI
Arouse, arouse, ye friends of right. The World Hymn. J. Gilchrist Lawson. WBLP
A-Roving ("In Amsterdam there lived a maid"). *Unknown. See* Fair Maid of Amsterdam, The.
A-Roving ("In Plymouth Town there lived a maid"). *Unknown.* UnTE
A-Roving ("Now, a-roving, a-roving"), *vers. II, with music. Unknown.* ShS
Arraigned before his worldly gods. The Execution of Cornelius Vane. Sir Herbert Read. BrPo; NoAM
Arraignment. Helen Gray Cone. AA
Arraignment of a Lover, The. George Gascoigne. AAS
Arraignment of Paris, The, *sels.* George Peele.
Dirge: "Welladay, welladay, poor Colin, thou art going to the ground." ElL
(Shepherd's Dirge, The.) OBSC
Fair and Fair. ElL; OBEV
(Oenone and Paris.) NOBE
(Song of Oenone and Paris.) OBSC
Not Iris in Her Pride. ViBoPo
O Gentle Love. ElL
(Colin's Passion of Love.) OBSC
Oenone's Complaint. ElL
Arran. *Unknown, tr. fr. Old Irish by* Kenneth Jackson. ChTr; FaBoPP; FaBoCh, *tr. by* Kuno Meyer
Arrange the scene with only a shade of difference. An Incident. Douglas Le Pan. MoCV; PeCV
Arranged by two's as peaches are. Nine Nectarines and Other Porcelain. Marianne Moore. OxBA
Arrangements with Earth for Three Dead Friends. James Wright. NIP
Arras. P. K. Page. MoCV; OBCV
Arrest of Oscar Wilde at the Cadogan Hotel, The. John Betjeman. CMoP; DTC; EBEV; InvP; MoBrPo; NoAM; NoP; OxBTC
Arrested like marble horses. A Frieze. John Peale Bishop. MoPo
Arrival, The. Alexander McLachlan. *Fr.* The Emigrant. NOBC
Arrival. John Wain. EBEV
Arrival and Departure. Charles Eglington. PeSA
Arrival at Santos. Elizabeth Bishop. OxBC
Arrival at the Waldorf. Wallace Stevens. NYP; PP
Arrival in Hell. Ricarda Huch, *tr. fr. German by* Susan C. Strong. PBWP
Arrival, New York Harbor. Robert Peters. GOA
Arrival of My Mother, The. Keith Wilson. DFF; GP
Arrival of the Bee Box, The. Sylvia Plath. FaBoMo; NaP
Arrival: The Capital. Desmond O'Grady. NMP
Arrivals and Departures. Melvin Walker La Follette. CoPo
Arrivals at a Watering-Place. Winthrop Mackworth Praed. NOBL
Arrivals, Departures. Philip Larkin. MoBrPo
Arriv'd now at our ship, we launch'd, and set. Ulysses Hears the Prophecies of Tiresias. Homer, *tr. by* George Chapman. *Fr.* The Odyssey, XI. LoBV
Arrive. The Ladies from the Ladies' Betterment League. The Lovers of the Poor. Gwendolyn Brooks. BiP; CAPP; NoAM; NOBA
Arrived from scattered cities, several lands. Shipment to Maidanek. Ephim G. Fogel. OBWP; TrJp
Arrived in heaven, when his sands were run. The Crusader. Dorothy Parker. ShM
Arrived upon the downs of asphodel. Classic Encounter. "Christopher Caudwell." OxBTC
Arriving. Daniel Halpern. HoPM
Arriving. Gabriel Preil, *tr. fr. Hebrew by* Robert Friend. VWA
Arrogance Repressed. John Betjeman. FiBHP
Arrow, The. Clarence Urmy. HBMV
Arrow and the Song, The. Longfellow. AA; FaFP; HBV-2; HBVY; PoPl; TreF
Arrow of Desire, The. *Gond Oral Tradition, tr. by* V. Elwin *and* S. Hivale. WTO
Arrow rides upon the sky, An. Love Song. Samuel Allen. NNP
Arrowhead Christian Center and No-Smoking Luncheonette. Janet Sylvester. MAYP
Arrowheads. Leona Gom. AMV-81
Arrows of the narrow moon flock down direct, The. Communion of Saints: The Poor Bastard under the Bridge. Marie Ponsot. VGW
Arrowy Dreams. Witter Bynner. GOA
Arroyo. Tom Weatherly. PoBA
Ars. Marina Tsvetayeva, *tr. fr. Russian by* Willis Barnstone *and* Edward Brown. BoWoP
Ars Amoris. J. V. Cunningham. QFR
Ars Longa. Which is crueller. The Peacock Room. Robert Hayden. FB
Ars Poetica. Horace. *See* Art of Poetry, The.
Ars Poetica. X. J. Kennedy. ErPo; NIP; PP; PV
Ars Poetica. Archibald MacLeish. AmPP; AP; AWP; BiP; CoBMV; CMoP; FPL; HAP; HeIP; HoPM; InPK; LiTA; LiTM; MoAB; MoAmPo; NIP; NOBA; NoP; OxBA; PAl; PoA; PoPl; PoRA; PP; SeCeV; SoSe; TAP; TwAmPo; WeW
Ars Poetica. Arturo Trías, *tr. fr. Spanish by* Julio Marzán. InW
Ars Poetica. Victor van Vriesland, *tr. fr. Dutch by* Adriaan J. Barnouw. TrJP
Ars Poetica. Adam Wazyk, *tr. fr. Polish by* Isaac Komem. VWA
Ars Poetica about Ultimates. Tram Combs. MP; TwCP
Ars Victrix. Austin Dobson, *after the French of* Théophile Gautier. HBV-2; HBVY; SyP; VLP
"All passes. Art alone," *sel.* CTC
Arsenal at Springfield, The. Longfellow. AmPP; AP; HBV-2; WaaP
"Were half the power, that fills the world with terror," *sel.* PGD
Arsenic. Howard Moss. CoAP; NYBP
Arson and Cold Lace. Worth Long. NBP
Art. Ambrose Bierce. InPK
Art. Hjalmar Flax, *tr. fr. Spanish by* Julio Marzán. InW
Art. Théophile Gautier, *tr. fr. French by* George Santayana. AWP
Art. Denise Levertov. CAPP
Art. Herman Melville. AmPP; AP; NOBA; ViBoPo
Art. Alfred Noyes. OBEV
Art. Lilla Cabot Perry. AA
Art. James Thompson. OBVV
Art. *Unknown.* BLPA
Art above Nature, to Julia. Robert Herrick. AnAnS-2
Art and Civilization. Robert Conquest. NoAM
Art and Life. Lola Ridge. HBMV
Art and Reality. James Simmons. CIP
Art as meagre as a quilt, An. The Spare Quilt. John Peale Bishop. GOA
Art for Art's Sake. Marc Blitzstein. *Fr.* The Cradle Will Rock. TrJP
Art Gallery. John Dickson. AMV-81
Art has nothing to do with perfect circles. C. K. Stead. *Fr.* Walking Westward. OCNZ
Art has taught this man to writhe in marble. Carrara. Philip Murray. NePoAm
Art in America. Theodore Weiss. AMV-80
Art is unmade/ To nature and the wild again. An Open Air Performance of "As You Like It." E. J. Scovell. ChMP
Art Master, An. John Boyle O'Reilly. AA
Art of Angling, The, *sels.* Thomas Barker. FaBoUs
Baits for Various Fish.
How to Catch Trout.
Methods of Cooking Trout.
Art of Biography, The. E. C. Bentley. *Fr.* Clerihews. CenHV; FiBHP; NOBL; PV
Art of Cookery, The, *sel.* William King.
"Far from the parlour have your kitchen plac'd." FaBoUs
Art of Dancing, The, *sels.* Soame Jenyns. FaBoUs
"Dare I in such momentous points advise."
"Now haste, my Muse, pursue thy destin'd way."
Art of Enforced Deprivation, The. Alta. GP
Art of Happiness, The. Edward Young. *Fr.* Night Thoughts, VIII. POL
(Happiness an Art.) OBEC
Art of Holding On, The. Dwight Okita. BrSi
Art of losing isn't hard to master, The. One Art. Elizabeth Bishop. HAP; SoSe
Art of Love, The. Samuel Butler. *Fr.* Hudibras. FaBoEn
Art of Love, The. Richard Grossman. AMV-81
Art of Love, The, *sels.* Kenneth Koch.
"Life is full of horrors and hormones." GP
"To win the love of women one should first discover." NNaP
Art of Love, The, *sels.* Ovid, *tr. fr. Latin.*
"Attend, ye nymphs, by wedlock unconfin'd," *tr. by* Congreve. FaBoUs
"In Cupid's school whoe'er would take a degree," *tr. by* Dryden. UnTE
"Kiss, if you can: Resistance if she make," *tr. by* Dryden. ErPo
"You, who in Cupid's rolls inscribe your name," *tr. by* Dryden. FaBoUs
Art of Making Puddings, The, *sel.* William King.
"Sometimes the frugal matron seems in haste." FaBoUs
"Art of Our Necessities Is Strange, The." Forrest Izard. WhC
Art of Picasso, The. Salvador Dali, *tr. fr. Spanish by* David Gascoyne. EAS

Art of Poetry, The, *sel.* Dryden.
"Rash author, 'tis a vain presumptuous crime." PP
Art of Poetry, The, *sels.* Horace, *tr. fr. Latin.*
"As woods whose change appeares," *tr. by* Ben Jonson. OBVE
"Should some ill painter, in a wild design," *tr. by* John Oldham. OBVE
Art of Poetry, An. James McAuley. NOCV
Art of Poetry, The [*or* Art Poëtique]. Paul Verlaine, *tr. fr. French by* Arthur Symons. AWP; SyP
Art of Politics [*or* Politicks], The, *sel.* James Bramston.
Time's Changes. NOEC; OBEC
Art of Preserving Health, The, *sels.* John Armstrong.
Advantages of Washing, The. FaBoUs
Blest Winter Nights. OBEC
Dangers of Sexual Excess, The. FaBoUs
Home of the Naiads, The. OBEC
Madness. NOEC
Transience. NOEC
Urban Pollution. NOEC
Art of the Sonnet, *sels.* Gil Orlovitz.
"If I could rise and see my father young." DiL
"Night comes. Day runs for its life into my eyes." PoA
Art of War, The, *sel.* Joseph Fawcett.
Feast of Blood, The. NOEC
Art of Wenching, The, *sel.* *Unknown.*
"Be punctual then to know." NOEC
Art photographer alone, The. Quantum. Martin Johnston. CBAP
Art Poëtique. Paul Verlaine. *See* Art of Poetry, The.
Art thou a Statist in the van. A Poet's Epitaph. Wordsworth. EnRP; OBRV
Art thou afraid the adorer's prayer. Walter Savage Landor. GBL
Art Thou Gone in Haste? *Unknown.* *Fr.* The Thracian Wonder. ElL; ELP; OxBoLi
(Chase, The, *at. to* William Rowley.) CH
(Love Pursued.) GBL
(Pursuit of Love.) ChTr
Art thou gone so far. Ode: The Spirit Wooed. Richard Watson Dixon. OBNC
Art Thou Heywood. John Heywood. NCEP
Art thou not hungry for thy children, Zion. To Zion. Judah Halevi, *tr. by* Maurice Samuel. AWP
Art thou pale for weariness. To the Moon. Shelley. BoNaP; ChER; EnRP; GTBS; GTBS-P; LoBV; MOON; PPP; TrGrPo; ViBoPo
Art thou poor, yet has thou golden slumbers? Sweet Content [*or* The Happy Heart *or* The Basket-Maker's Song]. Thomas Dekker. *Fr.* The Pleasant Comedy of Patient Grissell, I, i. CH; ElL; GTBS; GTBS-P; HAP; HBV-2; InPS; LoBV; OAEP; OBEV; OBSC; TreFT; TrGrPo; UnPo; ViBoPo; WHA
Art thou some wingëd Sprite, that, fluttering round. To a Maple Seed. Lloyd Mifflin. AA
Art Thou That She. *Unknown.* ViBoPo
Art Thou the Same. Frances Dorr Tatnall. AA
Art Work. Ronald Wallace. PPJ
Artegall and Radigund. Spenser. *Fr.* The Faerie Queene, V, 5. OBSC
"Artemidora! Gods invisible." The Death of Artemidora. Walter Savage Landor. *Fr.* Pericles and Aspasia. EnRP; OBNC; SeCeV; ViBoPo
Artemis. Peter Davison. ErPo
Artemis. Dulcie Deamer. PoAu-1
Artemis, Artemis: there is fading. The Night-Walker. Horace Gregory. MOON
Artemis Prologizes. Robert Browning. LoBV
Arteries Juicy with Blood. Osip Mandelstam, *tr. fr. Russian by* James Greene. *Fr.* Lines Concerning the Unknown Soldier. NAs
Arthritic farmer and a calf watch Dr. Graves, The. These Obituaries of Rattlesnakes Being Eaten by the Hogs. Roger Weingarten. AmPA
Arthur. Ogden Nash. FiBHP; NoP
Arthur. William Winter. AA
Arthur McBride. *Unknown.* GBP; OBET
Arthur Mitchell. Marianne Moore. PoNe
Arthur O'Bower has broken his bands [*or* band]. The Wind [*or* The High Wind]. *Unknown.* ChTr; FaBoCh; GBP; OxNR
Arthur Ridgewood, M.D. Frank Marshall Davis. BPo
Arthur with a lighted taper. Wallace Irwin. *Fr.* Science for the Young. ShM
Arthur's Disillusionment. Tennyson. *Fr.* Idylls of the King. TreFS
Arthur's Seat, *sel.* Thomas Mercer.
"Where is the gallant race that rose." OxBS
Artichoke. Henry Taylor. MAYP
Artichoke for Montesquieu, An. Jorie Graham. NPGG
Articles of War. Dunstan Thompson. WaP
Artificer. X. J. Kennedy. TwCP
Artificial Beauty. Lucianus, *tr. fr. Greek by* William Cowper. AWP
Artificial Death, II. Elizabeth Ann James. SOTS
Artificial Intelligence. Adrienne Rich. SUW
Artificial Teeth. Solyman Brown. *Fr.* Dentologia; a Poem on the Diseases of the Teeth and Their Proper Remedies. FaBoUs
Artillerie [*or* Artillery]. George Herbert. InPS; NoP; PoEL-2; SeCV-1
Artillery Shoot. James Forsyth. WaP
Artisan, The. Alice Brown. TrPWD
Artisan didn't collect his gear and say, The. The Makers. Richard Kell. CIP
Artist, The. Stewart Brisby. LFAC
Artist, An. Robinson Jeffers. VGW
Artist, The. Peter Meinke. PoDr
Artist. Ernestine Mercer. InMe
Artist, The. Sir Walter Alexander Raleigh. DBV; WHC
Artist, The. William Carlos Williams. InPS; LCAP; NYBP; PAI
Artist and Ape. Gordden Link. GoYe
Artist and his luckless wife, The. The Artist. Sir Walter Alexander Raleigh. DBV; WhC
Artist as Cuckold, The. *Unknown, tr. by* Louis Untermeyer. UnTE
Artist Draws a Peach, An. Patricia Hampl. PoDr
Artist has slipped her spiral shell, The. "That First Gulp of Air We All Took When First Born." Nancy Paddock. PoDr
Artist must leave these woods now, The. The Departure. Reed Whittemore. TAP
Artist on Penmaenmawr, The. Charles Tennyson Turner. FaBoPP; OBNC
Artist, that underneath my table. The Spider. Edward Littleton. NOEC
Artists East and West. Diana Chang. BrSi
Artists Shouldnt Have Offspring. Don Marquis. *Fr.* Archys Life of Mehitabel. CrMA
Artorius, *sels.* John Heath-Stubbs.
"Age of Bronze awoke now in brutality, The." EBEV
"It was the virgin Zennora, who dwelt." EBEV
Art's Variety. David McFadden. NeAC
Arundel Tomb, An. Philip Larkin. HeIP; NePoEA-2; PPP
As a bathtub lined with white porcelain. The Bathtub. Ezra Pound. NIP; WeW
As a Beauty I Am Not a Star. Anthony Euwer. *Fr.* The Limeratomy. InvP
(Face, The.) HBMV; NePA; OBAL; TreF
(Limerick: "As a beauty I'm not a great star.") HBV-2; HBVY
(My Face.) FaFP; NePA; PoLF; WhC
As a Bell in a Chime. Robert Underwood Johnson. AA
As a Black Child I was a dreamer. Four Sheets to the Wind and a One-Way Ticket to France, 1933. Conrad Kent Rivers. AmNP; CABA. *See also* As a child/ I bought a red scarf.
As a boy. Now I Am a Man. Russell Marano. AMV-80
As a boy with a richness of needs I wandered. Clifford Dyment. OxBTC
As a boy you outdrove the masters. To an Aging Charioteer. Leontius Scholasticus, *tr. by* Tom Dodge. LiSp
As a Buddhist tried for months. Genitori. David Ray. TW
As a child/ I bought a red scarf. Four Sheets to the Wind and a One-Way Ticket to France. Conrad Kent Rivers. BPo; IDB; NNP; PoBA; PoNe
As a child holds a pet. Port Bou. Stephen Spender. MoPo; MP; TwCP
As a child I was. Woman. Elouise Loftin. PoBA
As a child of cedar, hemlock, and the sea. No One Remembers Abandoning the Village of White Fir. Duane Niatum. CDW
As a child running loose. Learning to Speak. Peter Everwine. NNaP
As a Child Seeing a Cardinal. John Gill. NeAC
As a child, they could not keep me from wells. Personal Helicon. Seamus Heaney. IPY
As a critic the poet Buchanan. On Robert Buchanan, Who Attacked Him under the Pseudonym of "Thomas Maitland." Dante Gabriel Rossetti. FaBoEE
As a dancer dancing in a shower of roses before her King. The Joys of Art. Rachel Annand Taylor. OBVV
As a dare-gale skylark scanted in a dull cage. The Caged Skylark. Gerard Manley Hopkins. CMoP; FM; LiTM; MoAB; MoBrPo; MoPo; OBMV; PBBP; SoSe
As a fond mother, when the day is o'er. Nature. Longfellow. AA; AP; BoNaP; FaBoBe; FPL; HBV-1; PoLF; TAP; TreFT; TrGrPo; TRV; WHA
As a friend to the children commend me the yak. The Yak. Hilaire Belloc. FaBV; FaPON; HBVY; InMe; MoBrPo; NA; NOBL; OxBChV; TreFS
As a gray hawk's eyes. Hawk's Eyes. Yvor Winters. PoA
As a Great Prince. Edwin Honig. NoAM
As a guest who may not stay. In Memory of James T. Fields. Whittier. OBVV
As a hungry fledgling, who sees and hears. Vittoria Colonna, *tr. fr. Italian by* Brenda Webster. WPOW
As a lamp of fine crystal, wonderfully wrought. Radclyffe Hall. *Fr.* Forgotten Island. PeHV
As a little fat man of Bombay. *Unknown.* OxBChV

As a man who soon must be without. Hunger. Gaspara Stampa, *tr. by* Brenda Webster. WPOW
As a mote in at a minster door, so mighty were its jaws. Jonah. *Unknown. Fr.* Patience. ACP
As a naked man I go. In [*or* The] Waste Places. James Stephens. HBV-2; MoAB; MoBrPo; MoVE
As a pale phantom with a lamp. Moonlight. Longfellow. MOON
As a Plane Tree by the Water. Robert Lowell. AP; CMoP; CoAP; CoBMV; CrMA; DTC; LiTM; MoAB; MoAmPo; NePa; NePoEA; NoAM; NOBA; OxBA; TrGrPo
As a Possible Lover. Amiri Baraka. AmNP
As a queen sits down, knowing that a chair will be there. Walking to Sleep. Richard Wilbur. LCAP; NYBP
As a rule, man is a fool [*or* man's a fool]. Man Is a Fool [*or* Generalization]. Joseph Capp. FaFP; TreFT, *diff. vers.*
As a Seal upon Thy Heart. Bible, *O.T.* The Song of Solomon, VIII: 6-7. TrJP
As a signet of carbuncle in a setting of gold. Music. Bible, Apocrypha. *Fr.* Ecclesiasticus. TrJP
As a sloop with a sweep of immaculate wing on her delicate spine. Buick. Karl Shapiro. BiP; CMoP; DFF; HoPM; MiAP; MoAB; TrGrPo; ViBoPo
As a torn paper might seal up its side. The Pruned Tree. Howard Moss. NYBP
As a twig trembles, which a bird. She Came and Went. James Russell Lowell. AA; HBV-1; ViBoPo
As a white candle. The Old Woman. Joseph Campbell. AWP; GoBC; HBMV; MoBrPo; OnYI; OxBI; OxBTC; TreFT; ViBoPo
As a white stone draws down the fish. Behaviour of Fish in an Egyptian Tea Garden. Keith Douglas. FaBoMo
As a young Child, whose Mother, for a jest. The Child's Purchase. Coventry Patmore. ISi
As Adam Early in the Morning. Walt Whitman. AP; OxBA; PAI
As Aesop was with boys at play. Aesop at Play. Phaedrus, *tr. by* Christopher Smart. AWP
As after noon, one summer's day. Cupid's [*or* Cupid] Mistaken. Matthew Prior. InMe; ViBoPo
As Ah walked oot, yah Sunday morn. Bleeberrying. Jonathan Denwood. MoBS
As All Things Pass. Diana Bickston. LFAC
As an eagle grasped/ In folds of the green serpent. Shelley. *Fr.* Alastor. ChER
As an egg, when broken, never. Thomas Holley Chivers. *Fr.* To Allegra Florence in Heaven. BXAP; PeD
As an intruder I trudged with careful innocence. Old Mansion. John Crowe Ransom. HeIP; NOBA; OxBA
As an Old Mercer. Mahlon Leonard Fisher. HBV-1
As an old traveller, I am indebted to paper-bound thrillers. Calling Spring VII-MMMC. Ogden Nash. FaBoCo
As an unperfect actor on the stage. Sonnets, XXIII. Shakespeare. BiP; HBV-1; InvP; OAEP
As And to Aus, and Aus to Bis. The Passionate Encyclopedia Britannica Reader to His Love. "Maggie." InMe
As Ann came in one summer's day. The Sleeper. Walter de la Mare. MoAB; MoBrPo; SeCeV
As, at a railway junction, men. Sic Itur. Arthur Hugh Clough. EBVV; NCEP
As at noon[e] Dulcina rested. On Dulcina [*or* Come to Me Soon]. *At. to* Sir Walter Ralegh. CoMu; UnTE
As aw was gannin to Durham. Durham Old Women. *Unknown.* GBP
As Bad as a Mile. Philip Larkin. ELU; InPK; OxBC
As beautiful Kitty one morning was tripping. Kitty of Coleraine. *Unknown, at. to* Charles Dawson Shanly. HBV-1; OnYI
As bees, that when the skies are calm and fair. Bees and Monks. John Hookham Frere. *Fr.* King Arthur and His Round Table. OBRV
As beneath the moon I walked. The Whisperers. W. W. Gibson. HBV-2
As billows upon billows roll. The Surrender at Appomattox. Herman Melville. PAH
As bird to nest, when, moodily. Sarasvati. James Stephens. NoAM
As Birds Are Fitted to the Boughs. Louis Simpson. BoLoP; NePoEA; OLR
As black as ink and isn't ink. *Unknown.* OxNR
As boring as the fact of a marvelous friend. The Rainy Season. William Meredith. NePoEA
As Brothers Live Together. Longfellow. *Fr.* The Song of Hiawatha, I. TreFT
As bryght Phebus, scheyn soverane hevynnys e. The Prologue to Book VII. Virgil, *tr. by* Gawin Douglas. *Fr.* The Aeneid, VII. OxBS
As by the dead we love to sit. Emily Dickinson. NePA
As by the instrument she took her place. Virtuosa. Mary Ashley Townsend. AA
As by the streams of Babylon. Bible, *O.T.* Psalm CXXXVII, *paraphrased by* Thomas Campion. OAEL-1
As cages, think of department stores and certain zoos. Cages. Marvin Solomon. NYBP
As Camels Who Have Become Thirsty. Ilmi Bowndheri, *tr. fr. Somali by* M. F. Abdillahi *and* B. W. Andrzejewski. WTO
As careful mothers do to sleeping lay. On the Deputy of Ireland's Child. Sir John Davies. FaBoEE
As Catholics make of the Redeemer. Brand Speaks. Ibsen, *tr. by* C. H. Herford. *Fr.* Brand. WGRP
As cedars beaten with continual storms. George Chapman. *Fr.* Bussy d'Ambois. ViBoPo
As Celia rested in the shade. A Pastorall Dialogue. Thomas Carew. AnAnS-2; CavP
As children bring their broken toys. Reproof. *Unknown.* STF
As Chloris [*or* Cloris] full of harmless thoughts. A Song. Earl of Rochester. ErPo; TEP; UnTE
As clever Tom Clinch, while the rabble was bawling. Clever Tom Clinch Going to Be Hanged. Swift. CoMu; FaBoBa; SeCeV
As Cloe came into the room t'other day. A [*or* The] Lover's Anger. Matthew Prior. ErPo; UnTE
As commanded, I looked for my origin. The Search. Michael Hamburger. VWA
As Concerning Man. Alexander Radcliffe. OBSV
As convicts go, when it is time, to cells. The Convict. Anthony Frisch. CaP
As cool as the pale wet leaves. Alba. Ezra Pound. GBL; HAP; SOTW; WeW
"As cruel as a Turk: Whence came." On Mammon. Herman Melville. *Fr.* Clarel. OxBA
As Cupid in a garden strayed. The Bee. *Unknown.* TrAS
As custome was, the pepill far and neir. The Assembly of the Gods. Robert Henryson. *Fr.* The Testament of Cresseid. PoEL-1
As dainty a sight as ever I did see? Ballade of Boys Bathing. Frederick Rolfe. PeHV
As darkness/ is my shelter. The Voice of the Power of This World. Gregory Hall. NU
As Day Begins to Wane. Helena Coleman. CaP
As day did darken on the dewless grass. The Wind at the Door. William Barnes. ELP; GBL; GTBS-P; LO; PoEL-4
As Dick and I. Lines Left at Mr. Theodore Hook's House in June, 1834. Richard H. Barham. FaBoUs
As difference blends into identity. Josephine Miles. NoAM
As doctors give physic by way of prevention. For My Own Monument [*or* For His Own Epitaph]. Matthew Prior. FaBoEE; HBV-1; LoBV; OBEC; OBEV
As Dolly and her favorite swain. The Unfortunate Reminder. William Pattison. UnTE
As doth his heart who travels far from home. To a Young Child. Eliza Scudder. AA
As Down a Lone Valley, *with music.* Timothy Dwight. AH
As down the torrent of an angry flood. The Story of the Pot and the Kettle. Charles Montagu. APAS
As down through Cupid's garden for pleasure I did walk. The 'Prentice Boy. *Unknown.* AmFP
As down through Moore's field one evening I went. The Silk Weaver's Daughter. *Unknown.* AmFP
As down thru Sally's garden one evening as I chanced to stray. Sally's Garden. *Unknown.* AmFP
As due by many titles I resigne. John Donne. Holy Sonnets, II. AnAnS-1; JCP; MasP; MePo; OBS
As dusk comes on, I almost hope to meet. Robert Hillyer. *Fr.* A Letter to Charles Townsend Copeland: Le Baron Russell Briggs. GLGT
As dyed in blood the streaming vines appear. Woodbines in October. Charlotte Fiske Bates. AA
As, even today, the airman, feeling the plane sweat. Icarus. Valentin Iremonger. BIrV; CIP; NeIP; OnYI; OxBI
As fair as morn, as fresh as May. *Unknown.* GBL
As far as statues go, so far there's not. From Trollope's Journal. Elizabeth Bishop. GOA
As fine a piece of furniture. Central. Ted Kooser. Psk
As fire, unfound ere pole approaches pole. William Baylebridge. Love Redeemed, LXXXVIII. PoAu-1
As Firmly Cemented Clam-Shells. Basho, *tr. fr. Japanese by* Nobuyuki Yuasa. PAI
As flame streams upward, so my longing thought. He Made Us Free. Maurice Francis Egan. AA
As Flows the Rapid River, *with music.* Samuel Francis Smith. AH
As fly the shadows o'er the grass. The Irish Wolf-Hound. Denis Florence MacCarthy. GDP
As for Me, I Delight in the Everyday Way. Joseph Stroud. NPGG
As for me, my Nanna ignores me. Condemning the Moongod Nanna. Enheduanna, *tr. fr. Sumerian.* BoWoP

As for my life, I've led it. A Placid Man's Epitaph. Thomas Hardy. MoBrPo
As for the birds and the beasts, the men in bygone times. William Langland. *Fr.* The Vision of Piers Plowman, Passus XII. PBBP
As Fowlers Lie in Wait. Bible, *O.T.* Jeremiah, V: 26–31. TrJP
As Freedom Is a Breakfastfood. E. E. Cummings. CMoP; LiTA; LiTM; MAT; NOBA; OxBA; TAP; TwAmPo; VGW
As from an ancestral oak. Similes for Two Political Characters of 1819. Shelley. InPS; TW
As from the Dorset shore I travell'd home. The White Horse of Westbury. Charles Tennyson Turner. EBEV; VLP
As from the moist and gelid sleep. George Darley. *Fr.* Nepenthe. OnYI
As gay for you to take your father's ax. To a Young Wretch. Robert Frost. OFD
As Gentle Dews Distill, *with music.* George Rogers. AH
As good to write, as for to lie and groan. Astrophel and Stella, XL. Sir Philip Sidney. SiPS
As grit swirls in the wind the word spreads. The Center of Attention. Daniel Hoffman. FYAP; UnPo
As growth of form or momentary glance. Transfigured Life. Dante Gabriel Rossetti. The House of Life, LX. VLP
As hang two mighty thunderclouds. The Guns in the Grass. Thomas Frost. PAH
As Happy Dwellers by the Seaside Hear. Celia Thaxter. EtS
As hath been, lo, these many generations. First Travels of Max. John Crowe Ransom. MoAmPo
As He Came near Death. Roy Fisher. FaBoMo
As he climbs down our hill, my kestrel rises. Esyllt. Glyn Jones. DTC
As he comes from one of those small houses. The Fisherman. George Bruce. BSV
As He Is. W. H. Auden. MoPo
As He Lay Dying. Randolph Stow. BoAnP
As he learned the land. The Farmer. Terry Stokes. POL
As he left the ship he saw this, only this. The Descent of the Vulture. Marya Zaturenska. WPE
As he moves the mine-detector. Hunting Civil War Relics at Nimblewill Creek. James Dickey. ConAP; GOA
As he said vanity, so vain say I. The Vanity of All Worldly Things. Anne Bradstreet. NoP; SCAP
As he that loves oft looks on the dear form. On the "Vita Nuova" of Dante. Dante Gabriel Rossetti. VLP
As he trudged along to school. The Story of Johnny Head-in-Air. Heinrich Hoffmann. OxBChV; TiPo
As hearts have broken, let young hearts break. Little Dirge. Jean Starr Untermeyer. HBMV
As Helen Once. Muna Lee. HBMV
As Hermes once took to his feathers light. On a Dream. Keats. EnRP
As his great wings the albatross. Albatross. Charles Burgess. NePoAm-2
As Holy Kirke makes mind. The Nativity. *Unknown.* MeEL
As honest Jacob on a night. The Patriarch. Burns. CoMu
As honey to wine/ wine, honey. Epigram. Meleager, *tr. by* Peter Whigham. PeHV
As I am,/ I should be able to. Missing Beat. Carolyn M. Rodgers. JB
As I am a Rhymer. On My Joyful Departure from the City of Cologne. Samuel Taylor Coleridge. FaBoCo; InvP; TW; WhC
As I Am My Father's. Rose Drachler. VWA
As I am not. Posterity. Cyril Dabydeen. BrSi
As I am now so you will [*or* must] be. A Curt Addendum. *Unknown.* ShM; WhC
As I am unhappy. Yosano Akiko, *tr. fr. Japanese by* Glenn Hughes *and* Yozan T. Iwasaki. WPOW
As I approach the Big Rock Hole. Last Day of the Trip. Lloyd Davis. WOLT
As I beheld a winters evening air. Another. Richard Lovelace. SeCP
As I cam in by Dunidier. The Battle of Harlaw. *Unknown.* ESPB
"As I cam in by Glasgow [*or* boney Glassgow] town." Glasgow Peggie. *Unknown.* BaBo; ESPB
As I cam thro the Garrioch land. The Battle of Harlaw (B *vers.*). *Unknown.* ESPB
As I Came Down from Lebanon. Clinton Scollard. AA; HBV-2
As I came down Mount Tamalpais. Clarence Urmy. AA; HBMV
As I came down Talbingo Hill. Bullocky Bill. *Unknown.* PoAu-1
As I came down the Cano'gate. Merry May the Keel Row. *Unknown.* GBP
As I came down the hillside. Despair. Edward Bliss Reed. HBMV
As I came down to the long street by the water. South Street. Francis E. Falkenbury. EtS
As I came home through Drury's woods. Cold Fear. Elizabeth Madox Roberts. WPE
As I came in by Fiddich-side. Willie Macintosh. *Unknown.* ESPB
As I came in by Turra market. Barnyards of Delgaty. *Unknown.* FSW
As I Came O'er Cairney Mount. Burns. CoMu
(My Bonnie Highland Laddie.) UnTE
As I came o'er the Devil's Stair. Southward Bound. J. F. A. Burt. PoSH
As I came out of the New York Public Library. Nuns in the Wind. Muriel Rukeyser. NNaP
As I came over London Bridge. Geordie. *Unknown.* OBET
As I Came Over the Grey, Grey Hills. Joseph Campbell. AnIL
As I came over Windy Gap. Running to Paradise. W. B. Yeats. OxBoLi
As I came past the Brimham Rocks. The Song of Nidderdale. Dorothy Una Ratcliffe. HBMV
As I came round the harbor buoy. The Long White Seam. Jean Ingelow. GN; HBV-1
As I came through Sandgate. The Keel Row. *Unknown.* PoPle
As I Came Through the Desert. James Thomson. ("B.V."). *Fr.* The City of Dreadful Night. LiTB; NBM
("As I came through the desert thus it was.") BSV
As I came to the edge of the woods. Come In. Robert Frost. AmPP; BoNaP; FaBV; LiTA; LiTM; MoAB; MoAmPo; NOBA; NoP; TrGrPo
As I came to the sea wall that August day. On the Sea Wall. C. Day Lewis. SeCePo
As I came up the sandy road that lifts above the sea. The Spell. Henry Martyn Hoyt. HBMV
As I descended black, impassive rivers. The Drunken Boat. Arthur Rimbaud, *tr. by* Stephen Stepanchev. NAWM-2; SyP
As I did walk abroad one time. The Mourning Conquest; or, The Woman's Sad Complaint, and Doleful Cry to See Her Love in Fainting Fits to Lye. *Unknown.* CoMu
As I did walke my selfe alone. King James and Brown. *Unknown.* ESPB
As I drive to the junction of lane and highway. At Castle Boterel. Thomas Hardy. DTC; EBEV; FaBoEn; GTBS-P; MoVE; NOBE; OBNC; SCV
As I Ebb'd with the Ocean of Life. Walt Whitman. AmPP; LoBV; NOBA; PrIm; TAP
As I gaed down to Collistown. The Cunning Clerk. *Unknown.* OxBB
As I gaed in by the Duke o' Athole's gates. The Duke o' Athole's Nurse. *Unknown.* OxBB
As I gaed in yon greenwood-side. The Duke of Athole's Nurse. *Unknown.* BaBo
As I Gird on for Fighting. A. E. Housman. CMoP
As I Grew Older. Langston Hughes. AmPP; BANP
As I Grow Older and Fatten on Myself. Joseph Carson. AMV-80
As I have seene when on the breast of Thames. Praise of Poets. William Browne. *Fr.* Brittania's Pastorals, II, Song 2. OBS
As I hear it, now when there is company. Grandmother and Grandson. W. S. Merwin. NePoEA-2
As I in hoary [*or* hoarie] winter's night stood shivering in the snow. The Burning Babe. Robert Southwell. ACP; AnAnS-1; CABA; CH; EIL; FaBoCh; FABoEn; GoBC; HAP; HBV-1; HeIP; InPS; LiTB; LoBV; MePo; NAs; NOBE; NOCV; NoP; OAEL-1; OBCP; OBEV; OBSC; OxBoCh; PAI; PoEL-2; PPoe; PrF; SBVL; SeCePo; TrCP; TrGrPo; ViBoPo
As I lay asleep in Italy. The Mask of Anarchy. Shelley. EnRP; OBSV; SCV
As I lay awake in the white moonlight. Sleepyhead. Walter de la Mare. TiPo
As I Lay Musing ("As I lay musing all alone"). *Unknown.* CoMu
(Friar and the Fair Maid, The, *shorter vers.*) UnTE
(Friar in the Well, The, A *and* B *vers.*) ESPB
As I lay musing all alone/ upon my resting bed. The Poore [*or* Poor] Man Payes [*or* Pays] for All. *Unknown.* CoMu; OBET
As I Lay Quiet. Margaret Widdemer. GoYe
As I Lay Sleeping. *Unknown.* TrGrPo
As I Lay upon a Night. *Unknown.* SBVL
(Jesus Reassures His Mother.) MeEL
As I lay upon a night. My Thought Was on a Maid So Bright. *Unknown.* ISi
As I Lay with My Head in Your Lap Camerado. Walt Whitman. OxBA
As I Laye a-Thynkynge. "Thomas Ingoldsby." HBV-2
(Last Lines.) OBVV
As I leaned at my window. The Song of Samuel Sweet. Charles Causley. OBNV
As I leaned to retrieve. The Savage Beast. William Carlos Williams. TW
As I lie in bed. A Prayer. Joseph Seamon Cotter, Jr. BANP
As I lie roofed in, screened in. On the Porch. Harriet Monroe. SUMH
As I listened from a beach-chair in the shade. Their Lonely Betters. W. H. Auden. GoJo
As I look back upon your first embrace. Surrender. Amelia Josephine Burr. HBV-1
As I look in the mirror. An Israeli Soldier's Nightmare. Alison B. Carb. AMV-80
As I look out from the desk window. Laura St. Martin. FF
As I looked out of my window. Run Little Dogies [*or* Run Along, You Little Dogies]. *Unknown.* BPAW; OuSiCo

As I looked, the poplar rose in the shining air. The Deceptive Present, the Phoenix Year. Delmore Schwartz. BoNaP
As I mark a set of essays. Assignment: Descriptive Essay. Gary Willis. AMV-81
As I my little flock on Ister Bank. Shepherd Song. Sir Philip Sidney. *Fr.* Arcadia. SiPS
As I once came from Tottingham. Tottingham Frolic. *Unknown.* UnTE
As I one evening [*or* ev'ning] sat before my cell. Artillerie [*or* Artillery]. George Herbert. InPS; NoP; PoEL-2; SeCV-1
As I one morning shaving sat. The Cat and the Boot; or, An Improvement upon Mirrors. *Unknown.* FaBoUs
As I Out Rode. *Unknown.* SBVL
As I pass through my incarnations in every age and race. The Gods of the Copybook Headings. Kipling. FaPoR; OBSV; OHPF; OxBTV; TW
As I pass'd [*or* passed] by a river side [*or* riverside]. The Carnal and the Crane. *Unknown.* ESPB; OBET
As I passed by a willow tree. The Willow Tree. *Unknown.* OBET
As I passed by [*or* rode out by] Tom Sherman's bar-room. The Cowboy's Lament [*or* the Dying Cowboy]. *Unknown.* FaBoBa; ViBoFo
As I Pondered in Silence. Walt Whitman. WHA
As I reach to close each book. Against the Evidence. David Ignatow. NNaP
As I ride, as I ride. Through the Metidja to Abd-el-Kadr. Robert Browning. PeD
As I rode out by Tom Sherman's bar-room. *See* As I passed by Tom Sherman's Bar-room.
As I rode out one evening down by a river side. Two Lovers Discoursing. *Unknown.* ShS
As I roll back from you. Blank Verse for a Fat Demanding Wife. Jim Lindsey. TW
As I Roved Out ("As I roved out on a May morning"). *Unknown.* DTC
(Johnny's the Lad I Love.) AnIV; OxBoLi
As I roved out impatiently. In the Ringwood. Thomas Kinsella. CMoP; NMP; OxBI
As I roved out on a summer's morning. Castle Hyde [*or* Castlehyde]. *Unknown.* FaBoPP; OnYI
As I roved out one summer's morning, speculating most curiously. Colleen Rue. *Unknown.* BIrV; OnYI
As I rowed out to the light-house. The Light-House Keeper's White-Mouse. John Ciardi. PDV
As I rummaged thro' the attic. My Trundle Bed. J. G. Baker. BLPA; FaBoBe
As I sail home to Galveston. A Sailor's Song. Hazel Harper Harris. EtS
As I sail o'er life's wide ocean. The Pilot. *Unknown.* STF
As I Sat at My Spinning-Wheel. *Unknown.* CoMu
As I Sat at the Café. Arthur Hugh Clough. *Fr.* Spectator ab Extra (*also in* Dipsychus). ELP
("As I sat at the café I said to myself.") FaBoCo; FiBHP; GTBS-P; NBM; OAEL-2; OxBoLi
(How Pleasant It Is to Have Money.) NOBE
(So Pleasant It Is to Have Money.) SeCePo
As I sat by my window last evening. Miss Foggerty's Cake. *Unknown.* BLPA
As I sat down one ev'nin' in a timber-town café [*or* small café]. The Frozen Logger. *At. to* James Stevens. BPAW; FSW; OBAL
As I sat down t' play a game o' coon can. Po' Boy. *Unknown.* TrAS
As I sat down to breakfast in state. The Country Clergyman's Trip to Cambridge. Macaulay. OBSV; OxBoLi
As I sat in a lonesome grove. The Little Dove. *Unknown.* AmFP
As I sat in the gloaming. The Voice. Walter de la Mare. WSC
As I Sat on a Sunny Bank. *Unknown.* ChTr; OxBoLi, *abr.*
(Carol.) OxNR, *abr.*
(Sunny Bank.) GBP
As I Sat under a Sycamore Tree. *Unknown.* LiTB; ViBoPo
(I Saw Three Ships.) ACP
As I sd to my/ friend. I Know a Man. Robert Creeley. CAPP; ConAP; CoPo; InPK; InPS; MAT; NOBA; PoM; PPP
As I see them now and then. Mardi Gras / Grandmothers—Portrait in Red and Black Crayon. James Nolan. Str
As I seize the ladder by its shoulder. Remembering My Father. Jonathan Holden. Str
As I sent over the water. *Unknown.* PBBP
As I Set Down to Play Tin-Can, *with music.* *Unknown.* OuSiCo
As I sit here reflecting on my life. The Nuclear Family. Melvin Douglass Brown. LFAC
As I sit looking out of a window of the building. The Instruction Manual. John Ashbery. HAP; NeAP; NoAM; NOBA; PoM; SOTW; WeW
As I sit on a log here in the woods among the clean-faced beeches. Choir Practice. Ernest Crosby. AA
As I Step over a Puddle at the End of Winter, I Think of an Ancient Chinese Governor. James Wright. CAPP; NaP
As I stood/ Ling'ring upon the threshold, half-concealed. Xantippe. Amy Levy. BrRo
As I stood at the door. The College of Surgeons. James Stephens. AnIL
As I stray'd o'er the common on Cork's rugged border. Mary Le More. George Nugent Reynolds. OnYI
As I strayed in the shade of the Buachaille. The Last of the Grand Old Masters. Tom Patey. PoSH
As I strole the city, oft I. Swift. *Fr.* The Legion Club. BIrV
As I strolled out one evening just as the sun went down. The Farmer and the Shanty Boy. *Unknown.* AmFP
As I strolled out one evening, out for [*or* upon] a night's career. The Fire Ship [*or* The Fireship]. *Unknown.* AmSS; FSW
As I sunbathe in the prison yard. Reaching. William Carson Fagg. LFAC
As I sunk the lobster-pots. Fisherman's Luck. W. W. Gibson. EtS
As I talk to these children hovering on the verge. Fledglings. William Meredith. GLGT
As I talk with learned people. A Spade Is Just a Spade. Walter Everette Hawkins. PoBA
As I view the leaf, my theme is not the shades of meaning. My Own House. David Ignatow. AMV-80
As I walk out of the *La Belle.* Simply. Laura Chester. NPGG
As I walk through the streets. Prayer. F. S. Flint. TrPWD
As I Walk'd by Myself. *Unknown.* *See* As I Walked by Myself.
As I walk'd thinking through a little grove. Catch: On a Wet Day [*or* On a Wet Day]. Franco Sacchetti, *tr. by* Dante Gabriel Rossetti. AWP; BoNaP
As I walked between Bolton and Bury. The New Bury Loom. *Unknown.* OBET
As I walked by a forest side. Stag-Hunt. *Unknown.* OxBM
As I Walked [*or* Walk'd] by Myself. *Unknown.* ChTr; FaBoEE; OxNR
(Song on King William III, A.) NA
As I walked down by the river. A Ballad for Katharine of Aragon. Charles Causley. FaBoTw; NePoEA
As I walked down on Broadway. Can't You Dance the Polka? *Unknown.* FSW
As I walked down yon meadow, I carelessly did stray. A British Man-of-War. *Unknown.* OBET
As I walked fforth one morninge. Christopher White. *Unknown.* ESPB
As I walked forth one morning fair. The Wanton Seed. *Unknown.* OBET
As I walked forth one summer's morn, all in the month of June. Brave Collier Lads. *Unknown.* OBET
As I Walked in the Woods. *Unknown.* UnTE
As I walked me this endurs day. Here I Sit Alone. *Unknown.* OxBoCh
As I walked my pardner to the gate today. The Gate. Yasmeen Jamal. LFAC
As I walked one May morning. Down by the Riverside. *Unknown.* OBET
As I Walked Out. *Unknown.* *See* Git Along Little Dogies.
As I Walked Out in the Streets of Laredo. *Unknown.* *See* Cowboy's Lament, The.
As I walked out in yonder dell. The Elfin Knight. *Unknown.* ViBoFo
As I walked out of a London Bridge. Geordie. *Unknown.* FSW
As I walked out of St. James's Hospital. The Bad Girl's Lament. *Unknown.* ViBoFo
As I walked out one cold winter night. The Lass of Roch Royal. *Unknown.* ViBoFo
As I Walked Out One Evening. W. H. Auden. ChMP; FF; HeIP; InPK; LiTM; MP; NOBE; NoP; OAEP; PrIm; SeCeV; TwCP; UnPo
(Song: "As I walked out one evening.") OAEL-2; MoAB; MoBrPo
As I walked out one evening, all in the month of May. The Banks of Claudy. *Unknown.* AmFP
As I walked out one evening down by the Strawberry Lane. Captain Wedderburn's Courtship. *Unknown.* AmFP
As I walked out one evening late, a-drinking of sweet wine. My Old True Love. *Unknown.* OuSiCo
As I walked out one May morning,/ One May morning betimes. Searching for Lambs. *Unknown.* OBET
As I walked out one May morning,/ One May morning early. Seventeen [*or* I'm Seventeen] Come Sunday. *Unknown.* OBET; UnTE
As I walked out one May morning,/ When May was all in bloom. The Bold Fisherman [*or* The Royal Fisherman]. *Unknown.* BaBo; GBP
As I walked out one May morning/ When May was white in bloom. Cupid the Ploughboy. *Unknown.* OBET
As I walked out one May morning,/ When the small birds sang so sweet. The Lover Proved False. *Unknown.* AmFP
As I walked out one midsummer's morning. The Banks of Sweet Primroses. *Unknown.* ELP
As I Walked Out One Morning. *Unknown.* AmFP
As I walked out one morning/All in the month of May. The Banks of Claudy. *Unknown.* OBET
As I walked out one morning down by the Sligo dock. Yellow Meal. *Unknown.* ShS

As I walked out one morning for pleasure. *See* As I was a-walking one morning for pleasure.
As I walked out one morning in May. Archie o Cawfield. *Unknown.* AmFP
As I walked out one morning, just as day was dawning. As I Walked Out One Morning. *Unknown.* AmFP
As I walked out one morning on the fourteenth of July. The Mower. *Unknown.* OBET
As I walked out one night, it being dark all over. The Sailor's Return. *Unknown.* OxBoLi
As I walked out one summer's day to view the fields and the lizards springing. The Husband with No Courage in Him. *Unknown.* FSW
As I walked out one summer's evening. John Riley. *Unknown.* OuSiCo
As I walked out that sultry night. Full Moon. Robert Graves. FaBoEn; NOBE
As I walked out upon the road one day. Poor Old Man. *Unknown.* ShS
As I walked the heights of Meelin on a tranquil autumn day. The Fairy Harpers. James B. Dollard. CaP
As I walked through my garden. Butterfly. Hilda Conkling. TiPo
As I Walked through the Meadows. *Unknown.* OBET
As I walked through the rumorous streets. Vistas. Odell Shepard. HBMV
As I wandered on the beach. The Great Blue Heron. Carolyn Kizer. CoAP; NePoEA-2; WPE
As I wandered round the homestead. My Mother's Prayer. T. C. O'Kane. BLPA; FaBoBe
As I wandered through the eight hundred and eight streets of the city. Streets. Amy Lowell. SBG
As I was a-goin' over Gilgary Mountain. Whiskey in the Jar. *Unknown.* FSW
As I was a-going to Strawberry Fair. Strawberry Fair. *Unknown.* OBET
As I was a-gwine down the road. *See* As I was goin' . . .
As I was a-hoeing, a-hoeing my lands. The Six Badgers. Robert Graves. GoJo; GrPl; WSC
As I was a-roaming for pleasure one day. The Little Mohee. *Unknown.* BaBo
As I was a-roving one morning in spring. The Mantle So Green. *Unknown.* AmFP
As I was a-walkin'/ All by the seashore. Little Mohee. *Unknown.* AmSS
As I was a-walkin' [*or* walking] down Paradise Street. Blow the Man Down. *Unknown.* AmSS (*vers.* II); AS
As I was a-walking/ One morning in spring. The Pretty Ploughboy [*or* The Lark in the Morning]. *Unknown.* ChTr; GBP
As I was a-walking by Saint James Hospital. Young Man Cut Down in His Prime (St. James Hospital). *Unknown.* FSW
As I was a walking, I cannot tell where. Narcissus, Come Kiss Us! *Unknown.* ErPo
As I was a-walking on Westminster Bridge. *Unknown.* OxNR
As I was a-walking on yon far distant shore. The Indian Lass. *Unknown.* OBET
As I was a-walking one midsummer's morning. The Plains of Waterloo. *Unknown.* OBET
As I was a-walking one morning down by the Clarence dock. Heave Away, *vers.* I. *Unknown.* ShS
As I was a-walking one morning in the spring. The Sign of the Bonny Blue Bell. *Unknown.* OBET
As I was a-walking [*or* walked out] one morning for pleasure. Git Along Little Dogies [*or* Whoopee-Ti-Yi-Yo]. *Unknown.* AS; BPAW; CoSo; FaPON; FSW; MoShBr; TiPo; TreF
As I was a-walking the other day. The Shoemaker. *Unknown.* FaPON; SoPo
As I was a-walking to Nottingham Fair. Nottingham Fair. *Unknown.* AmFP
As I was carving images from clouds. Opifex. Thomas Edward Brown. OBVV
As I was cast in my ffirst sleepe. Young Andrew. *Unknown.* ESPB; OxBB
As I was climbing Ardán Mór. The Herons [*or* Ardan Mór]. Francis Ledwidge. ACP; AnIV; AWP; OnYI; OxBI
As I was coming down the stair. *Unknown.* CenHV
As I was driving my waggon one day. Gee Ho, Dobin. *Unknown.* CoMu
As I was falling down the stair. Alibi. Hughes Mearns. *Fr.* Later Antigonishes. InMe
As I was fishing off Pondy Point. Jim Desterland. Hyam Plutzik. VGW
As I was goin' [*or* a-gwine] down the road. Turkey in the Straw. *Unknown.* AS; BLSo; FaFP; GBP; TrAS; TreFS; YaD
As I was going along, long, long. Mother Goose. OxNR
As I was going by Charing Cross. King Charles the First. *Unknown.* CH; FaBoCh; GBP; OxNR
As I was going down the lane. Ballad of No Proper Man. Daniel Hoffman. MAT
As I was going o'er London Bridge. Mother Goose. OxNR
As I was going o'er Tipple Tine. *Unknown.* OxNR
As I was going over Mulberry Mountain. Mulberry Mountain. *Unknown.* AmFP
As I was going to Banbury. *Unknown.* OxNR
As I was going to Bethlehem town. Bethlehem Town. Eugene Field. WBLP
As I was going to Derby. The Derby Ram. *Unknown.* FaBoNo; GBP; OxNR; ViBoFo
As I Was Going to Saint Ives. Daniel G. Hoffman. NYBP
As I was going to St. Ives. Mother Goose. HBV-1; HBVY; NTCP; OxNR; SoPo
As I was going to sell my eggs. Mother Goose. OxNR
As I was going to town. Me Alone. Lula Lowe Weeden. CDC
As I was going up Pippen Hill. Mother Goose. OxNR
As I was going up the hill. Jack the Piper. *Unknown.* ChTr; GBP; OxNR
As I was going [*or* walking] up the stair. The Little Man Who Wasn't There [*or* Antigonish *or* I Met a Man]. Hughes Mearns. BLPL; FaBoCo; FaFP; FaPON; InMe; OnUR; PoLF; RHPC; SoPo; WhC
As I was hiking past the woods, the cool and sleepy summer woods. Out There Somewhere. Henry Herbert Knibbs. BLPA
As I Was Laying on the Green. *Unknown.* FiBHP; InPK; WhC
As I was letting down my hair. The Lady with Technique. Hughes Mearns. *Fr.* Later Antigonishes. FiBHP; InMe; WhC
As I was lumb'ring down de street. Lubly Fan. Cool White. TrAS
As I was musing by myself alone. Mirth and Melancholy. Margaret Cavendish, Duchess of Newcastle. WPE
As I was old sometime and sometime young. Time's Mutability. Bertolt Brecht, *tr. by* Martin Esslin. ELU
As I was on the high-road. Wet or Fine. Amory Hare. HBMV
As I was out up on the road one day. Sacramento, *vers.* II. *Unknown.* ShS
As I was playing on the green. *Unknown.* WhC
As I was robbing Chelsea Bank. Crime Notes. Hughes Mearns. *Fr.* Later Antigonishes. InMe
As I was rumbling through the mountain rift. Reward of Virtue. Arthur Guiterman. InMe
As I was sailing down the coast. The High Barbaree. Laura E. Richards. SoPo; SUS
As I was sitting by the fire, talking to old Reilly's daughter. Reilly's Daughter. *Unknown.* FSW
As I was sitting in my chair. The Perfect Reactionary. Hughes Mearns. NTCP; WhC
As I was sitting with a jug and spoon. The Jug of Punch. Francis McPeake. FSW
As I was, so be ye. Epitaph. *Unknown.* TreFS
As I was spittin' into the Ditch aboard o' the *Crocodile.* "Soldier an' Sailor Too." Kipling. MOS
As I Was Standing in the Street. *Unknown.* NTCP
As I was traveling one morning in May. The Bachelor's Lay. *Unknown.* OuSiCo
As I was travelling toward the city of satisfactions. The City of Satisfactions. Daniel Hoffman. CoPo; Prf
As I was waiting for the bus. Sight Unseen. Kingsley Amis. ErPo; NePoEA-2
As I was wa'king all alone. *See* As I was walking all alone.
As I was walkin' an' a-ramblin' one day. The Wild Rippling Water. *Unknown.* FaBoBa
As I Was Walkin' down Wexford Street, *with music. Unknown.* AS
As I was walkin' the jungle round, a-killin' of tigers an' time. A Ballad. Guy Wetmore Carryl. BXAP; InMe; Par
As I was walking/ I came upon. Kore. Robert Creeley. ConAP; CoPo; InPK; InPS; NMP
As I was walking all alane [*or* alone]. The Twa Corbies. *Unknown.* AWP; BSV; CABA; CH; ELP; EnSB; ESPB; FaBoBa; FaBoCh; GoTS; GTBS; GTBS-P; HAP; HBV-2; InPk; NoP; OBEV; OxBS; PAI; PBBP; PoPle; PPP; SeCePo; SeCeV; UnPo; ViBoFo (8 *vers.*)
As I was walking [*or* wa'king] all alone [*or* alane]. The Wee Wee Man. *Unknown.* CH; EBEV; ELP; ESPB; FaBoCh; GBP; OAEL-1; OxBB
As I was walking among the fires of hell. A Memorable Fancy. Blake. *Fr.* The Marriage of Heaven and Hell. NU
As I was walking down by the seashore. The Lover's Lament for Her Sailor. *Unknown.* AmFP
As I was walking down Covent Garden. The Buck's Elegy. *Unknown.* OBET
As I was walking down Paradise Street. *See* As I was a-walkin' down Paradise Street.
As I was walking down the street. Buffalo Gals. *Unknown.* BLSo; FSW
As I was walking I met a woman. An Old Air. F. R. Higgins. AnIL
As I was walking in a field of wheat. *Unknown.* OxNR
As I was walking mine alane. Archie o [*or* of] Cawfield. *Unknown.* ESPB; OxBS
As I was walking mine alane. The Wee Wee Man. *Unknown.* *See* As I was walking all alone.
As I was walking one midsummer morning. O Dear O. *Unknown.* ErPo

As I was walking one morn at my ease. What's the Life of a Man? *Unknown.* OBET
As I was walking one morning in spring. I Shall Be Married on Monday Morning. *Unknown.* ErPo
As I was walking out one morning, I met a buxom lass. Buxom Lass. *Unknown.* ErPo
As I was walking out upon the road one day. Sacramento, *vers.* III. *Unknown.* ShS
As I was walking up the stair. *See* As I was going up the stair.
As I was walking up the street. O Mally's Meek, Mally's Sweet. Burns. GN; HBV-1
As I watch the moon. Native African Revolutionaries. Paul Jones. AMV-80
As I Went a-Walkin' down Ratcliffe Highway, *2 vers., with music. Unknown.* ShS
As I Went a-Walking One Fine Summer's Evening, *with music. Unknown.* OuSiCo
As I went a-walking one fine summer's morning. The Shoofly. Felix O'Hare. AmFP
As I went by a dyer's door. The Dyer. *Unknown.* ChTr; OxNR
As I went by St. James's, I heard a bird sing. An Excellent New Ballad Called the Prince of Darkness. *Unknown.* APAS
As I went down by Hastings Mill I lingered in my going. Hastings Mill. Cecily Fox-Smith. HBV-1
As I went down the hill along the wall. Meeting and Passing. Robert Frost. OxBA
As I went down the hill I heard. The Voice. Norman Gale. HBV-1; OHIP
As I went down through Dublin City. Dublin: The Old Squares. Padraic Colum. NePoAm
As I went down to Darby-town. The Ram of Darby. *Unknown.* OuSiCo
As I Went Down to David's Town, *with music.* George Craig Stewart. AH
As I went down to Dymchurch Wall. In Romney Marsh. John Davidson. BSV; EBVV; FaBoPP; GoTS; OBVV; OxBTC; PoPle; ViBoPo
As I went down to Rotten Lake I remembered. Rotten Lake Elegy. Muriel Rukeyser. MoPo; NePA
As I went down to the huckleberry picnic. The Kicking Mule. *Unknown.* AmFP
As I went down to the mowin' field. Fod. *Unknown.* AmFP
As I went down to the old depot. The Maid Freed from the Gallows. *Unknown.* ViBoFo
As I went eastward, while the zun did zet. Lowshot Light. William Barnes. VLP
As I went on Yol Day. Jankin, the Clerical Seducer. *Unknown.* MeEL
As I went out a crow. The Last Word of a Bluebird. Robert Frost. FaPON; GoJo; GrPl; SO; TiPo
As I went out a-walking to breathe the pleasant air. Rolly Trudum. *Unknown.* AmFP
As I Went Out for a Ramble, *with music. Unknown.* OuSiCo
As I went out in Dublin City. Wheel of Fortune. *Unknown.* FSW
As I went out one evening. The Mermaid. *Unknown.* OuSiCo
As I went out one May morning. Bird in a Cage. *Unknown.* GBP
As I went out one morning early, to breathe the sweet and pleasant air. John Riley. *Unknown.* FSW
As I went out one morning to breathe [*or* take] the morning [*or* pleasant] air. Lolly Too-Dum. *Unknown.* FSW; OuSiCo
As I went out, so I came in. *Unknown.* GBP
As I went out walking for pleasure one day. The Little Mohea. *Unknown.* AmFP
As I went out walking upon a fine day. Little Mohee. *Unknown.* FSW
As I went over London Bridge. Riddle. *Unknown.* ChTr
As I went over the Far Hill. Beyond Rathkelly. Francis Carlin. HBMV
As I went over the water. *Unknown.* OxNR
As I went over Tipple Tyne. Riddle. *Unknown.* ChTr
As I went owre the Hill o' Hoos. *Unknown.* GBP
As I went through a garden gap. Mother Goose. HBV-1; HBVY
As I went through the marshes. A Doe at Evening. D. H. Lawrence. BrPo
As I Went to Bonner. *Unknown.* OxBoLi; OxNR
As I went to Totnam. The Maid of Tottenham. *Unknown.* CoMu
As I went up by Heartbreak Road. Heartbreak Road. Helen Gray Cone. HBMV
As I went up by Ovillers. Ballad of the Three Spectres. Ivor Gurney. OBWP
As I went up the Brandy hill. *Unknown.* OxNR
As I went up the humber jumber. *Unknown.* FaBoNo
As I went up to Craigbilly Fair. Craigbilly Fair. *Unknown.* ChTr; GBP
"As I went up to London." Going Up to London. Nancy Byrd Turner. HBMV
As I went walking/ The road from town. Song in Spring. Louis Ginsberg. YeAr
As I wer readen ov a stwone [*or* stuone]. Readen ov a Head-Stwone [*or* The Head-Stone]. William Barnes. CH; HBV-2; OBVV
As I work at the pump, the wind heavy. Mother. Seamus Heaney. NAs
As I'd Nothing Else to Do. Herbert Fry. TreFS
As if a cast of grain leapt back to the hand. An Event. Richard Wilbur. TwAmPo
As If a Phantom Caress'd Me. Walt Whitman. GBL
As if he had been poured. The Grauballe Man. Seamus Heaney. CIP
As if he had crawled from the sea. Warrior with Shield. Michael Dennis Browne. PoDr
As if I carried a charm. Her Going. Shirley Kaufman. PCP
As if I didn't have enough. Small Aircraft. Bella Akhmadulina, *tr. by* Daniel Halpern. BoWoP
As if inside. Seal Pups. Nora Dauenhauer. TWSS
As if it were/ forever that they move, that we. Merritt Parkway. Denise Levertov. AmPP; NeAP; PoM
As if it were a scene made-up by the mind. Often I Am Permitted to Return to a Meadow. Robert Duncan. CMoP; HeIP; NMP; NOBA; NU
As if it's been waiting until he can't have it. Eating. Reginald Gibbons. MAYP
As if passages of stone. Coyote Brother Song. Annette Arkeketa West. TWSS
As if some irremediable poison. London. J. R. Rowland. CBAP
As if somebody ordered it. Tashkent Breaks into Bloom. "Anna Akhmatova," *tr. by* Richard McKane. BoWoP
As if the trees were not indifferent. Gathered at the River. Denise Levertov. SV
As If You Had Never Been. Richard Eberhart. EyDe
As I'm sitting all alone in the gloaming. Bantry Bay. James Lyman Molloy. OnYI
As imperceptibly as grief. Emily Dickinson. AP; CMoP; FaBoEn; HBVY; LiTA; NOBA; NoP; PBWP; PoEL-5; QFR
As in a dream of flood from which we rose intact but alone. The Break. E. N. Sargent. NYBP
As in a duskie and tempestuous night. Sonnet. William Drummond of Hawthornden. FaBoEn; OBS
As in a pot the milk turns sour. The Shattering of Love. *Gond Oral Tradition, tr. by* V. Elwin *and* S. Hivale. WTO
As in a Rose-Jar. Thomas S. Jones, Jr. PoLF
As in a thunderstorm at night. Waiting. Robert Pack. PPJ
As in a Watteau fete of rose and silver blue. The Tempest. Marya Zaturenska. MoAmPo
As in smooth oil the razor best is whet. Epigram. *Unknown.* HBV-1
As in the age of shepherd king and queen. Dans l'Allée [*or* The Avenue]. Paul Verlaine, *tr. by* Arthur Symons. AWP; SyP
As in the cool-air'd road I come by. My Love's Guardian Angel. William Barnes. GBL; NBM; PoEL-4
As in the gardens, all through May, the rose. His Lady's Tomb. Pierre de Ronsard, *tr. by* Andrew Lang. AWP
As in the house I sate [*or* sat]. Poverty. Thomas Traherne. OxBoCh; Prf; TEP; TrCP
As in the Land of Darkness. Robert Miklitsch. AMV-80
As in the lonely night. The Setting of the Moon. Giacomo Leopardi, *tr. by* John Heath-Stubbs. MOON
As in the Midst of Battle There Is Room. George Santayana. AWP; NePA
As in the night I restless lie. An Anodyne. Thomas Ken. OxBoCh
As in the Old Days, Passages 8. Robert Duncan. PoM
As in Their Time. Louis MacNeice. POL
As in your innocent eyes last night. Birthday Poem, November 4th. John Thompson, Jr. WaP
As inward love breeds outward talk. The Anglers Song (*in* Izaak Walton's The Compleat Angler). William Basse. LiSp; OBS
As Is the Sea Marvelous. E. E. Cummings. MOS
As it befell in midsummertime. Sir Andrew Barton. *Unknown.* EnSB
As it befell on a bright holiday. The Bitter Withy. *Unknown.* ChTr; GBP
As it befell upon one time. Hughie Grame. *Unknown.* ESPB
As it fell on a holy-day. John Dory. *Unknown.* ESPB
As it fell one holy-day [*or* on a light holyday *or* high holyday]. Little Musgrave and Lady Barnard. *Unknown.* ErPo; ESPB; FaBoBa; InvP; OBET; OxBB; ViBoFo
As it fell out in [*or* on] a long summer's day. Fair Margaret and Sweet William. *Unknown.* ESPB; OxBB
As it fell out on a holiday. The Holy Well. *Unknown.* OBET
As it fell out on a holy day [*or* high holiday *or* upon a bright holiday]. The Bitter Withy. *Unknown.* BaBo; FaBoBa; NOCV; NoP; OAEP; OBET; SBVL; ViBoFo
As it fell out one May morning. The Holy Well. *Unknown.* FaBoCh; GBP; NOCV; OxBoCh
As it fell out upon a day [*or* one day]. Dives and Lazarus. *Unknown.* ELP; ESPB; FaBoBa; OBET; OxBB
As It Fell upon a Day. Richard Barnfield. *Fr.* The Passionate Pilgrim. GBL; PBBP; ViBoPo
(Nightingale, The.) AWP; GTBS; GTBS-P
(Ode, An.) ElL; LoBV; OBSC

(Philomel.) CH; HBV-1; NOBE; OBEV
As it fell upon a day. A Vision of Truth. J. C. Squire. NOBL
As it is true that I, like all, must die. Scene-Shifter Death. Mary Devenport O'Neill. NeIP
As It Looked Then. E. A. Robinson. CMoP; NePA; NoAM
As It Was. Lilla Cabot Perry. Meeting after Long Absence, II. AA
As itt beffell in midsumer-time. Sir Andrew Barton. *Unknown.* ESPB; OxBB; ViBoFo
As Jack, the jolly plowboy, was plowing of his land. The Jolly Plowboy. *Unknown.* AmFP
As Jack walked out of London city. Jack the Jolly Tar. *Unknown.* AmFP
As Jock the Leg and the merry merchant. Jock the Leg and the Merry Merchant. *Unknown.* ESPB
As Joe Gould says in. E. E. Cummings. FiBHP
As Joseph knocked upon his door. No Room. Dorothy Conant Stroud. STF
As Joseph Was a-Walking [*or* a-Waukin']. *Unknown.* OHIP; ViBoPo
(Cherry Tree Carol, The.) PChr
(Christmas Carol.) GN; HBV-1; HBVY
As Julia once a-slumbering lay. The Captived Bee; or, The Little Filcher. Robert Herrick. CaPo
As junco is with winter. Different Winter. Louise Townsend Nicholl. NePoAm-2
As Kaethe Kollwitz knew. Death Swoops. Kenneth Pitchford. CoPo
As Kingfishers Catch Fire [Dragonflies Draw Flame]. Gerard Manley Hopkins. CMoP; EaLo; EBEV; EBVV; FaBoMo; LiTM; NOCV; NoP; PrIm; VLP
(What I Do Is Me.) MoAB; MoBrPo
As Lambs into the Pen. Dorothy Wellesley. FaBoTw
As landscapes richen after rain, the eye. Foliage of Vision. James Merrill. MoPo; VGW
As late I journey'd o'er the extensive plain. Life. Samuel Taylor Coleridge. EnRP
As late I lay within an arbour sweet. A Poem of a Maid Forsaken. *Unknown.* PBBP
As laurel leaves that cease not to be green. The Promise of a Constant Lover. *Unknown.* ElL
As life improved, their poems. Postscript. R. S. Thomas. FaBoMo; OxBC
As life runs on, the road grows strange. Sixty-eighth Birthday. James Russell Lowell. PCP; PoEL-5
As Like the Woman as You Can. W. E. Henley. HBV-1
As little Jenny Wren/ Was sitting by the shed. Mother Goose. OxNR
As lonely I strayed by the banks of the river. Lost Jimmie Whalen. *Unknown.* BaBo
As long as I continue weeping. Sonnet. Louise Labé, *tr. by* Joan Keefe *and* Richard Terdiman. PBWP
As long as I go forth on ships that sail. A Seaman's Confession of Faith. Harry Kemp. TrPWD
As long as I live. Me. Walter de la Mare. FaPON; RHPC; TiPo
As long as people. On Wearing Ears. William J. Harris. BOLo
As long as the blade has never. Shame. Arthur Rimbaud, *tr. by* Louise Varèse. SyP
As Long as the Heart Beats. Christine Zawadiwsky. AMV-81
As long as they were standing, they were all that passion dares. The Cubistic Lovers. Charles Edward Eaton. AMV-81
As long as we look forward, all seems free. The Western Approach. Howard Nemerov. TAP
As long as you allowed her complete liberty. The Incentive. Martial, *tr. by* Louis Untermeyer. UnTE
As love and I, late harbour'd in one inn. Michael Drayton. GBL
As love is cause of joy. Love. Anthony Munday. *Fr.* Zelanto, the Fountain of Fame. OBSC
As loving hind that (hartless) wants her deer. A Letter [*or* Another Letter] to Her Husband, Absent upon Public [*or* Publick] Employment. Anne Bradstreet. OxBA; SBG; SCAP; WPE
As mad sexton's bell, tolling. Song on the Water. Thomas Lovell Beddoes. *Fr.* Death's Jest Book. FaBoCh
As man and his motor have brought it about. Streamlined Stream-Knowledge. Arthur W. Bell. WhC
As many, Mother, are your moods and forms. Bernard O'Dowd. *Fr.* The Bush. PoAu-1
As Mars and Minerva were viewing of some implements. Under the Rose. *Unknown.* OBET
As May was opening the rosebuds. Birth of the Foal. Ferenc Juhász, *tr. by* David Wevill. BoAnP; PH
As me and me marrer was gannin' te work. The Collier's Rant. *Unknown.* OBET
"As men from men." Despondency Corrected. Wordsworth. *Fr.* The Excursion, IV. EnRP
As men who fought for home and child and wife. The Battle of Oriskany. Charles D. Helmer. PAH
As men who see a city fitly planned. Proofs of Buddha's Existence. *Unknown.* WGRP
As much for the seatide ages of my sons. The Alchemical Cupboard. Asa Benveniste. VWA
As my eyes search the prairie. Spring Song. *Tr. fr. Chippewa Indian by* Frances Densmore. OBVE
As my new life begins, I start smiling at the people around me. Farewell to Kurdistan. Rosemary Tonks. OxBTC
As "Name of individual, partnership, or corporation to whom paid." Royalties. D. J. Enright. NOBL
As Nature H——'s clay was blending. On a Certain Effeminate Peer. John Winstanley. FaBoEE
As near beauteous Boston lying. A New Song. *Unknown.* PAH
As near Portobello lying. Admiral Hosier's Ghost. Richard Glover. HBV-2; NOEC; ViBoPo
As needy gallants in the scriv'ners' hands. Dryden. *Fr.* Amboyna; or, The Cruelties of the Dutch to the English Merchants. OBSV
As Night Comes On. Cecil Cobb Wesley. GoYe
As night drew on, and, from the crest. Winter Night. Whittier. *Fr.* Snow-bound. TrGrPo
As oceans are to porpoises. The Snowfish. Edward Field. GrPl
As Ocean's Stream. Fyodor Tyutchev, *tr. fr. Russian by* Babette Deutsch *and* Avrahm Yarmolinsky. AWP
As o'er my latest book I pored. Printer's Error. P. G. Wodehouse. FiBHP
As o'er the hill we roam'd at will. Wanderers. Charles Stuart Calverley. CenHV
As oft as I behold and see. Earl of Surrey. SiPS
As often as some where before my feet. Francis Daniel Pastorius. SCAP
As on a window late I cast mine eye. Love-Joy. George Herbert. OAEL-1
As on Euphrates shady banks we lay. Paraphrase on the Psalms of David: Psalme CXXXVII. George Sandys. OBS
As on my bed at dawn I mused and pray'd. The Lattice at Sunrise. Charles Tennyson Turner. OBVV
As on Serena's Panting Breast. *Unknown.* UnTE
As on the bank the poor fish lies. The Restless Heart. *Unknown.* WGRP
As on the cross, the Saviour hung. Deep Spring. *Unknown.* AmFP
As on the gauzy wings of fancy flying. Oliver Wendell Holmes. *Fr.* The Iron Gate. AA
As on the Heather. Reinmar von Hagenau, *tr. fr. German by* Jethro Bithell. AWP
As on the highway's quiet edge. The Coast: Norfolk. Frances Cornford. OxBTC
As once, if not with light regard. Ode on the Poetical Character. William Collins. EnRP; LAuP; NOEC; OAEL-1; OAEP; PoEL-3; TEP
As once in black[e] I disrespected walked. On a Maid [*or* Maide] of Honour Seen by a Scholar in Somerset Garden. Thomas Randolph. JCP; MePo
As once in heaven Dante looked back down. The Backward Look. Howard Nemerov. OxBC
As one abandoned on a barren shore. To Rotenham. August, Graf von Platen, *tr. by* Reginald Bancroft Cooke. PeHV
As one advances up the slow ascent. Solitude. Philip Henry Savage. AA
As one, at midnight, wakened by the call. Prelude. W. W. Gibson. MoBrPo
As one by one the singers of our land. The Succession. Frances Laughton Mace. AA
As one grows older and Caesar, Hitler. The Walk Home. Reed Whittemore. ConAP
As One Non-Combatant to Another. George Orwell. OxBTC
As One Put into the Packet-Boat. John Ashbery. HAP
As one that for a weary space has lain. The Odyssey. Andrew Lang. HBV-2; LoBV; OBEV; OBNC; OBVV; PoLF; PoRA; ViBoPo; WHA
As one that strives, being sick, and sick to death. To Celia, upon Love's Ubiquity. Thomas Carew. AnAnS-2
As One Who Bears beneath His Neighbor's Roof. Robert Hillyer. MoAmPo
As one who came with ointments sweet. Spikenard. Laurence Housman. TrPWD
As one who cleaves the circumambient air. Timon of Archimedes. Charles Battell Loomis. NA
As one who cons at evening o'er an album all alone. James Whitcomb Riley. *Fr.* An Old Sweetheart of Mine. TreFS
As one who follows a departing friend. Last Days. Elizabeth Stoddard. AA
As one who hangs down-bending from the side. A Dedicated Spirit. Wordsworth. *Fr.* The Prelude. SeCePo
As one who has sailed across an unknown sea. The Solitary. Rainer Maria Rilke, *tr. by* C. F. MacIntyre. TrJP
As one who held herself a part. Sister. Whittier. *Fr.* Snow-bound. AA
As one who, long by wasting sickness worn. Hope. William Lisle Bowles. EnRP

As one who walks in sleep, up a familiar lane. The Road. John Gould Fletcher. HBMV
As One Who Wanders into Old Workings. C. Day Lewis. FaBoMo; LiTM
As one whose country is distraught with war. Conflict. Caroline Clive. OBVV
As other men, so I myself do muse. Michael Drayton. Idea, IX. JCP
As our king lay musing on his bed. King Henry Fifth's [*or* Henry V's] Conquest of France. *Unknown.* ESPB; OBET
As over muddy shores a dragon flock. The Fear. Lascelles Abercrombie. OBMV
As Oyster Nan Stood by Her Tub. *Unknown.* CoMu
As patience paints the flower red, so grass. And Grow. John Hay. WaP
As pilot well expert in perilous wave. The Cave of Mammon. Spenser. *Fr.* The Faerie Queene, II, 7. OAEL-1; PoEL-1
As pioneering children, when no rain. Wagon Train. E. L. Mayo. MiAP
As pools beneath stone arches take. Invocation. John Drinkwater. HBMV; PoA
As power and wit will me assist. Sir Thomas Wyatt. SiPS
As praiseworthy/ the power of breathing. Lorine Niedecker. VGW
As Ralph and Nick i'th'field were plowing. The Plowman. *Unknown.* APAS
As red as a starling's his peepers. The Opium-Den. *Malay Oral Tradition, tr. by* R. J. Wilkinson *and* R. O. Winstedt. WTO
As regions may be known by their moths. Protective Colors. William Logan. AMV-81
As Rimbaud said, I thought today sitting in the library. Leslie Scalapino. *Fr.* Hmmmm. NPGG
As rising from the vegetable World. James Thomson. *Fr.* The Seasons: Spring. PoEL-3
As Rivers of Water in a Dry Place. Anna Bunston de Bary. HBMV
As Rochefoucauld his maxims drew. Verses on the Death of Dr. Swift, D.S.P.D., Occasioned by Reading a Maxim in Rochefoucauld. Swift. LoBV; MasP; NOEC; PoEL-3; TEP
As rock to sun or storm. Poem. Niall Sheridan. OnYI
As Rocks Rooted. Howard G. Hanson. AMV-80
As round as an apple, as deep as a cup. Mother Goose. OxNR; TiPo
As round as an apple, as deep as a pail. *Unknown.* OxNR
As round their dying father's bed. The Father and His Children. *Unknown.* OxBChV
As Sand. Natan Zach, *tr. fr. Hebrew by* Jon Silkin. VWA
As sea-foam blown of the winds, as blossom of brine that is drifted. H. C. Bunner. *Fr.* Home, Sweet Home, with Variations. CenHV; InMe; OBAL
As seventh sign, the antique heavens show. Feast of the Ram's Horn. Harvey Shapiro. VGW
As Severn lately in her ebbs that sank. The Severn. Michael Drayton. *Fr.* The Baron's War, Canto I. ChTr
As Shadows Cast by Cloud and Sun, *with music.* Bryant. AH
As Shakespeare couldn't write his plays. By Deputy. Arthur St. John Adcock. CenHV
As She Feared It Would Be. Lilla Cabot Perry. Meeting after Long Absence, I. AA
As she shook her little fist. The Death of the Novel. David Young. AmPA
As shepherd and shepherdess, how many summers had we. Out of That Sea. David Ferry. NePoAm-2
As shining sand-drift. An Epitaph. Margaret Sackville. HBMV
As ships, becalmed at eve, that lay. Qua Cursum Ventus. Arthur Hugh Clough. EtS; HBV-2; MoS; OAEP; OBEV; OBVV; TreFT; VLP
As shows the air when with a rainbow graced. Upon Julia's Ribband. Robert Herrick. CaPo
As silent as a mirror is believed. Legend. Hart Crane. CABA; MoVE; NoAM; OxBA; SyP; TwAmPo
As simple an act. Way Out West. Amiri Baraka. NeAP; NMP; PoBA
As sinewy as biltong, as narrow. My Grandmother. Perseus Adams. PeSA
As Sir Launfal made morn through the darksome gate. Sir Launfal and the Leper. James Russell Lowell. *Fr.* The Vision of Sir Launfal. GN
As Sisyphus against the infernal steep. Byron. *Fr.* English Bards and Scotch Reviewers. OBSV
As slow our ship her foamy track. The Journey Onwards. Thomas Moore. GTBS; GTBS-P; HBV-2; SeCePo
As slowly and sadly I strayed by the river. Lost Jimmie Whalen. *Unknown.* AmFP
As slowly, as carefully as a wading bird. The Water Lily. David Wagoner. PoDr
As snow in summer, and as rain in harvest. Bible, *O.T.* Proverbs, XXVI. BiP
As soft as silk, as white as milk. Mother Goose. GBP; HBV-1; HBVY; OxNR; PoPle
As some brave admiral, in former war. The Disabled [*or* Maimed] Debauchee. Earl of Rochester. BoLoP; CABA; HAP; NCEP; NOBL; OBSV; PoEL-3; PPP; WeW
As some day it may happen that a victim must be found. Ko-Ko's Song [*or* They'll None of 'Em Be Missed]. W. S. Gilbert. *Fr.* The Mikado. LiTB; VLP
As some fond virgin, whom her mother's care. Epistle to Miss Blount [*or* To a Young Lady], on Her Leaving the Town after the Coronation. Pope. BoLoP; EBEV; NOBE; NOEC; NoP; OBEC; PoEL-3; PPP; SeCeV
As some heroes bold, I will unfold, together were conversing. Grand Conversation on Brave Nelson. *Unknown.* OBET
As some lone miser visiting his store. Real Happiness. Goldsmith. *Fr.* The Traveller. OBEC
As Some Mysterious Wanderer of the Skies. Henry Jerome Stockard. AA
As some women love jewels. Ode to a Lebanese Crock of Olives. Diane Wakoski. GP
As Sometimes in a Dead Man's Face. Tennyson. In Memoriam A. H. H., LXXIV. LiTB
As sometimes with a sable cloud. The First Meeting. Lord Herbert of Cherbury. AnAnS-2
As soon/ as a squirrel. Song for Thrift Week. Mildred Weston. WhC
As soon/ Seek roses in December, ice in June. Byron. *Fr.* English Bards and Scotch Reviewers. DBV
As Soon as Ever Twilight Comes. Walter de la Mare. SiSoSe
As soon as he came home, straightway Pygmalion did repair. Pygmalion's Statue Comes to Life. Ovid, *tr. by* Arthur Golding. *Fr.* Metamorphoses. OAEL-1
As soon as I could I have called you together. The Queen's Speech. Arthur Mainwaring. APAS
As soon as I lie down in my soft bed. Sonnet IX. Louise Labé, *tr. by* Willis Barnstone. BoWoP
As soon as I'm in bed at night. Mrs. Brown. Rose Fyleman. OxBChV; TiPo
As soon as the fire burns red and low. The Sleepy Dog. Josephine Daskam Bacon. SUS
As soon as the idea of the Flood had subsided. After the Flood. Rimbaud, *tr. by* Enid Rhodes Peschal. *Fr.* Illuminations. SOTW
As soon as Wolf began to feel. Little Red Riding Hood and the Wolf. Roald Dahl. DFT
As Spring the Winter. Anne Bradstreet. EBCP
(As Spring the Winter Doth Succeed, *with music.*) AH
As, sum tyme, dois the curser stert and ryn. Virgil, *tr. by* Gavin Douglas. *Fr.* The Aeneid, XI. OBVE
As summer ends and leaves fall like dust. A Cantor's Dream before the High Holy Days. Martin Robbins. VWA
As Sun, as Sea. James Sullivan. AMV-81
As sunbeams stream through liberal space. Woodnotes, II. Emerson. NOBA; OHIP
As supple as a tiger's skin. The Prayer Rug. Sara Beaumont Kennedy. HBMV
As sure as shooting. From the Brothers Grimm to Sister Sexton to Mother Goose; One Transmogrification. David Cummings. BXAP
As sure as we have a fatherland. Fellow-Citizens. Verner von Heidenstam, *tr. by* Charles Wharton Stork. PoPl
"As surely as I hold your hand in mine." Brown Boy to Brown Girl. Countee Cullen. PoBA
As Tate grows old some child will fondle him. From Gestures to the Dead. John Wheelwright. MoVE
As that Arabian bird (whom all admire). William Browne. *Fr.* Britannia's Pastorals, I, Song 4. OAEL-1
As the Allied tanks trod Germany to shard. May, 1945. Peter Porter. OxBC
As the black storm upon the mountain-top. Residence in London. Wordsworth. *Fr.* The Prelude, VII. HAP; PoEL-4
As [*or* When] the blackbird in the spring. Aura Lea [*or* Lee]. W. W. Fosdick. BLSo; PSoN
As the body denies the means to look. Epigram. Pernette du Guillet, *tr. by* Joan Keefe *and* Richard Terdiman. PBWP
As the bow unto the cord is. Longfellow. *Fr.* The Song of Hiawatha. TRV
As the brown mowers strode across the field. The Swathe Uncut. John Hewitt. NeIP
As the cat/ climbed over. Poem. William Carlos Williams. CABA; FaPON; InPK; InPS; InvP; NoP; PAI; PDV
As the chameleon, who is known. The Chameleon. Matthew Prior. OBSV
As the clouds that are so light. The Clouds That Are So Light. Edward Thomas. FaBoTw
As the coin of her ear-ring. June Song of a Man Who Looks Two Ways. Leslie Daiken. NeIP
As the crest of some slow-arching wave. Lincolnshire Shores. Tennyson. *Fr.* The Last Tournament. FaBoPP
As the Crow Flies, *sel.* Samuel Hoffenstein.
"How much we pay to say, *Je suis.*" WhC
As the Day Breaks. Ernest McGaffey. AA
As the Dead Prey upon Us. Charles Olson. NeAP

As the deep blue of heaven brightens into stars. God's Promises. *Unknown.* BLRP
As the dust from the wet dream of a nation. Written in Unbridled Repugnance near Sioux Falls, Alabama—April 30, 1974. A. K. Redwing. VoR
As the fireman said. Riding the Elevator into the Sky. Anne Sexton. NYP
As the flight of a river. Absent yet Present. Sir Edward Bulwer-Lytton. OBVV
As the fog lifts over. Snacks. Ronald P. Tanaka. BrSi
As the gods began one world, and man another. Snakecharmer. Sylvia Plath. NePoEA-2; PP
As the golden grass burns out. September Evening, 1938. William Plomer. SeCePo
As the gook woman howls. In the Mourning Time. Robert Hayden. BPo
As the guests arrive at my son's party. Rite of Passage. Sharon Olds. MAYP
As the hand moves over the harp, and the strings speak. Inspiration. *Unknown, tr. by* J. Rendel Harris. *Fr.* Solomon, VI. WGRP
As the Hart Panteth. Bible, *O.T.* Psalms, XLII. TrJP
("As the hart panteth after the water brooks.") AWP; TRV
(My Soul Thirsteth for God.) TrGrPo
(Search, The, *Moulton, Modern Reader's Bible.)* WGRP
As the Holly Groweth Green. Henry VIII, King of England. ViBoPo
(Green Groweth the Holly.) EBEV; PChr, *diff. vers.;* SBVL; TrGrPol
(Holly, The.) CTC; OBSC
(Love Ever Green.) MeEL
As the image of the sun. Estuary. Ted Walker. NYBP
As the insect from the rock. The Making of Man. John White Chadwick. AA
As the leaves say. Free Will. Walter Clark. NCSH
As the Mist Leaves No Scar. Leonard Cohen. NoP
As the mute nightingale in closest groves. To the Blessed Virgin Mary. Gerald Griffin. OnYI
As the night ended. My Son, My Son. Seymour Cain. AMV-81
As the poem drifts under the cry of the sea. Adriatic. Robert Conquest. PP
As the poets have mournfully sung. The Aesthetic Point of View. W. H. Auden. OBAL
As the poor end of each dead day drew near. He Liked the Dead. Malcolm Lowry. OxBTC
As the proud horse with costly trappings gay. Shortening Sail. William Falconer. *Fr.* The Shipwreck, II. EtS; MOS
As the Queen and Prince Albert, so buxom and all pert. Old England Forever and Do It No More. *Unknown.* GBP
As the rain falls. Rain. William Carlos Williams. AP; CoBMV
As the rains of spring. Izumi Shikibu, *tr. fr. Japanese by* Edwin A. Cranston. PBWP
As the sin that was sweet in the sinning. The Poets at Tea, III. Barry Pain. Par
As the slanting sun drowsed lazily. Cape Coloured Batman. Guy Butler. PeSA
As the snow falls I brush it away. A Snowfall. Richard Eberhart. FiCP
As the stars hide in the light before daybreak. Avoiding News by the River. W. S. Merwin. NaP
As the stores close, a winter light. February Evening in New York. Denise Levertov. InPS; NoAM
As the story goes,/ the Jews bought for themselves. The Jews in Hell. Isaac Goldemberg, *tr. by* David Unger. VWA
As the sun declined the snow at our feet. Prose Poem. Humphrey Jennings. EAS
As the sun, its globe compressed in. Rannoch Moor. Malcolm MacGregor. PoSH
As the sunbeams stream through liberal space. *See* As sunbeams stream through liberal space.
As the sunlight in the sky. For the Cultural Campaign. Chimedin Jigmed, *tr. by* C. R. Bawden. WTO
As the swamp cooler breathes. A Sale of Smoke. Roberta Spear. AmPA
As the sweet sweat of roses in a still. The Comparison. John Donne. ErPo; TEP
As the Team's Head-Brass. Edward Thomas. GTBS-P; MMA; OBWP; OxBTC; PoPle
As the through-train of words with white-hot whistle. Express. W. R. Rodgers. MoVE
As the Transatlantic tourists. The Doves of Venice. Laurence Hutton. AA
As the tree does not end. Appearance. Norman H. Russell. STE
As the Twig Is Bent. Pope. *Fr.* Moral Essays, Epistle I. TreF
As the used anger drips from his hands like blood. The Murderer. Paul Petrie. NYBP
As the war-trumpet drowns the rustic flute. Pindar. Antipater, *tr. by* John Addington Symonds. AWP
As the wind at play with a spark. Louisa May Alcott. Louise Chandler Moulton. AA
As the Window Darkens. Laura Jensen. LCAP
As the wise men of old brought gifts. The Gift. William Carlos Williams. NePoAm-2; PoPl
As the Word came to prophets of old. Prophets for a New Day. Margaret Walker. BPo
As the World Turns. Larry Mollin. NeAC
As the young phoenix, duteous to his sire. Renewal. "Michael Field." OBVV
As there, along the elmy hedge, I go. Troubles of the Day. William Barnes. GTBS-P
As they came from the East. Kings and Stars. John Erskine. TrCP
As they came in by the Eden side. The Slaughter of the Laird of Mellerstain. *Unknown.* ESPB
As things be/come. Word Poem (Perhaps Worth Considering). Nikki Giovanni. BOLo; PoBA
As this convine and ordinance was mayd. Virgil, *tr. by* Gavin Douglas. *Fr.* The Aeneid, VIII. OBVE
As Thomas was cudgel'd one day by his wife. Abroad and at Home [*or* Epigram]. Swift. DBV; FaBoEE; WhC
As those of old drank mummia. Mummia. Rupert Brooke. BrPo
As those we love decay, we die in part. Finis [*or* On the Death of a Particular Friend]. James Thomson. *Fr.* On the Death of Mr. William Aikman the Painter. BSV; OBEC; OBEV
As those who are not athletic at breakfast day by day. Nature Morte. Louis MacNeice. NoAM
As though an aged person were to wear. Elegy for the Monastery Barn. Thomas Merton. CoPo; VGW
As threads spilling dew-drops. The Dolphins. Hamish Maclaren. EtS
As thro' the Land at Eve We Went. Tennyson. *Fr.* The Princess. LiTB; OBVV; TreFS
(Reconciliation, The.) HBV-1
(Song: "As thro' the land at eve we went.") OAEP
As through the Void we went I heard his plumes. The Doors. Lloyd Mifflin. AA
As thus the snows arise, and, foul and fierce. Winter. James Thompson. *Fr.* The Seasons. SeCePo
As Thy Days. Grant Colfax Tullar. BLRP
As Thy Days So Shall Thy Strength Be. "George Klingle." BLRP; TRV
As Time One Day by Me Did Pass. Henry Vaughan. AnAnS-1; MeLP; SeCV-1
As to a bird's song she were listening. Deaf. H. C. Bunner. AA
As to a sacrament/ Quiet I go. Love's Language. Donagh MacDonagh. NeIP
As to Being Alone. James Oppenheim. TrJP
As to His Choice of Her. Wilfrid Scawen Blunt. *See* To Manon, as to His Choice of Her.
As to kidnap the Congress has long been my aim. General Howe's Letter. *Unknown.* PAH
As to Marshals, and Statesmen, and all their whole lineage. French Cookery. Thomas Moore. *Fr.* The Fudge Family in Paris. OBRV
As to naps. Perambulator Poems, VI. David McCord. WhC
As to that poet (if so great a one as he). A Letter from the Country to a Friend in Town. John Oldham. PP
As to the blooming prime. To Favonius. Edmund Bolton. OBSC
As Toilsome I Wander'd Virginia's Woods. Walt Whitman. HBV-2; SeCeV; ViBoPo
As Tom and his wife were discoursing one day. Too Candid by Half. John Godfrey Saxe. HBV-1
As Tom the porter went up Ludgate Hill. Tom the Porter. John Byrom. NOEC
As Tommy Snooks and Bessy Brooks. Mother Goose. HBV-1; HBVY; OxNR
As tongueless Echo in the pastoral vale. To the Greek Anthologists. George Rostrevor Hamilton, *after* Satyros. FaBoEE
As t'other night in bed I thinking lay. The Dream of the Cabal; a Prophetical Satire. *Unknown.* APAS
As Tranquil Streams, *with music.* Marion Franklin Ham. AH
As travellours when the twilight's come. The Pilgrimage. Henry Vaughan. AnAnS-1; NCEP
As true as I was born into. Halfway. Maxine W. Kumin. GoYe
As Turpin was riding across the moor. Dick Turpin and the Lawyer. *Unknown.* ViBoFo
As twilight fell. I Saw a Ghost. Joan Boilleau. TiPo
As two men were a-walking, down by the sea-side. The Duke of Grafton. *Unknown.* ChTr; GBP
As unto Francis poverty. Brother Juniper. Blanche Mary Kelly. GoBC
"As unto the bow the cord is." Hiawatha's Wooing. Longfellow. *Fr.* The Song of Hiawatha, X. BeLS; TreFS
As Vesta Was from Latmos Hill Descending. *Unknown.* OAEP
As virtuous men pass mildly away. A Valediction: Forbidding Mourning. John Donne. AnAnS-1; BLPL; CABA; EnRePo; FaBoEn; FF; HAP; HeIP; HoPM; InPK; InPS; JCP; LiTB; MasP; MeLP; MePo; NIP;

NOBE; NoP; OAEL-1; OAEP; OBS; PAI; PoEL-2; PoPle; PPoe; PPP; PrIm; SeCeV; SeCP; SeCV-1; SoSe; TEP; TreFT; UnPo; WeW
As vonce I valked by a dismal svamp. The Old Cove. Henry Howard Brownell. PAH
As We Are So Wonderfully Done with Each Other. Kenneth Patchen. ErPo
As we came through the gate to look at the few new lambs. Ravens. Ted Hughes. NAs
As we climb to the church of Galilee. The Church of Galilee. Muriel Rukeyser. *Fr.* The Gates. GP
As We Dance Round. *Unknown.* CH
As we entered by that door. Dirge of the Lone Woman. Mary M. Colum. AnIV
As we get older we do not get any younger. Chard Whitlow. Henry Reed. BXAP; DTC; FaBoCo; FaBoNo; FaBoPa; FiBHP; LiTM; MoBrPo; NOBL; NoP; OxBTC; Par; UnPo
As we lay musing in our beds. The Mermaid. *Unknown.* BaBo; ESPB
As we live, we are transmitters of life. We Are Transmitters. D. H. Lawrence. OxBTC
As we marched down to Fernario. Peggy-O. *Unknown.* FSW
As we paced along/ Upon the giddy footing of the hatches. Shakespeare. King Richard III, *fr.* I, iv. MOS
As we rowed from our ships and set foot on the shore. The Savages. Josephine Miles. LiTM
As we rush, as we rush in the train. In the Train. James Thomson ("B. V."). *Fr.* Sunday at Hampstead. ViBoPo
As we sailed down the Chyannel of old Engeland. Let Go the Reef Tackle. *Unknown.* ShS
As we sailed on the water blue. Whisky Johnny. *Unknown.* AS
As we stood on the crushed stone. A Conversation. Barbara Howes. IHMS
As we wax older on this earth. The Things That Are More Excellent. Sir William Watson. OHFP
As we went/ I felt a scruple, which I durst not vent. The Poet Questions Peace. George Chapman. *Fr.* Euthymiae Raptus; or, The Tears of Peace. JCP
As we were marching to Quebec. Marching to Quebec. *Unknown.* AmFP
As we withered ferns. Ballade of Dead Friends. E. A. Robinson. AA
As wearied pilgrims, once possessed. His Own Epitaph. Robert Herrick. CaPo
As Weary Pilgrim, Now at Rest. Anne Bradstreet. PoEL-3; SCAP
(Longing for Heaven.) LiTA
As Well as They Can ("As well as it can, the hooked fish while it dies"). A. D. Hope. GrPl
As wet as a fish—as dry as a bone. Similes. *Unknown.* HBVY
As, when a beauteous nymph decays. Stella's Birthday, 1725. Swift. NOEC; PP
As when a fragment, from a mountain torn. Virgil, *tr. by* Dryden. *Fr.* The Aeneid, XII. OBVE
As When a Man. Tennyson. *Fr.* A Dream of Fair Women. ChER
("As when a man that sails in a balloon.") OBRV
(Balloon, The.) RoGo
As when a Scout. New Worlds. Milton. *Fr.* Paradise Lost, III. OBS
As when a stone is dropped in water, the harmonies of the universe. Buddha. Daniel Hoffman. CoPo
As, when a tree's cut down, the secret root. Prologue to "The Tempest." Dryden. NoP
As when a wretch, (who conscious of his crime). Priam and Achilles. Homer, *tr. by* Pope. *Fr.* The Iliad, XXIV. OBEC
As when an architect some palace wall. Homer, *tr. by* William Cowper. *Fr.* The Iliad, XVI. OBVE
As when desire, long darkling, dawns, and first. Bridal Birth. Dante Gabriel Rossetti. *Fr.* The House of Life. OAEP
As when devouring flames some forest seize. Homer, *tr. by* William Cowper. *Fr.* The Iliad, II. OBVE
"As When Emotion Too Far Exceeds Its Cause." Gloria C. Oden. AmNP
As when far off the warbled strains are heard. LaFayette. Samuel Taylor Coleridge. EnRP
As when his first beams tremble in the sky. Dante, *tr. by* Laurence Binyon. Divina Commedia: Purgatorio, XXVII. NAWM-1
As when it happ'neth that some lovely town. Sonnet: Content and Resolute. William Drummond of Hawthornden. JCP
As when, of amorous night uncertain birth. A Summer Storm. Charles Whitehead. OBRV
As when of frequent bees. Homer, *tr. by* George Chapman. *Fr.* The Iliad, II. OBVE
As when rooting in a bin. Dick, a Maggot. Swift. TW
As when some dire usurper Heav'n provides. The Fire of London. Dryden. *Fr.* Annus Mirabilis. ChTr
As When Some Hungry Fledgling Hears and Sees. Vittoria da Colonna, *tr. fr. Italian by* Barbara Howes. BoWoP
("Like a hungry fledgeling that watches and hears," *tr. by* Lynne Lawner.) PBWP
As when some wayfaring man passing a wood. A Devonshire Walk. William Browne. *Fr.* Britannia's Pastorals, I, Song 5. FaBoPP
As When the Blowfish Perishing. Linda Gregg. NPGG
As when the moon hath comforted the night. George Chapman. *Fr.* The Conspiracy of Charles, Duke of Byron. MOON; ViBoPo
As when the winds, ascending by degrees. Homer, *tr. by* Pope. *Fr.* The Iliad, IV. OBVE
As when, to one who long hath watched, the morn. Sonnet. John Codrington Bampfylde. NOEC
As when two men have loved a woman well. Lost on Both Sides. Dante Gabriel Rossetti. The House of Life, XCI. NOP; SeCePo; VLP
As when two monarchs of the brindled breed. Paul Whitehead. *Fr.* The Gymnasiad, or Boxing Match. NOEC
As when, upon a trancèd summer-night. Keats. *Fr.* Hyperion. ViBoPo
As white's the blossom on the rise. The Love-sick Lass. "Hugh MacDiarmid." BSV
As William and Mary stood by the seaside. William and Mary. *Unknown.* AmFP
As William walking with his wife was seen. A Fair Exchange. La Fontaine. UnTE
As Winter, fleeing. The Fearless. Mortimer J. Adler. PoA
As wishing all about us sweet. On St. Winefred. Gerard Manley Hopkins. SaC
As, with enforced yet unreluctant pace. The Social Future. John Kells Ingram. OnYI
As with Gladness Men of Old. William Chatterton Dix. FaPoR
As with the picture puzzle of an angler. The Big One. Edward Morin. WOLT
As with varnish red and glistening. Casualty. W. E. Henley. In Hospital, XIII. BrPo; VLP
As withereth the primrose by the river. A Palinode. Edmund Bolton. ElL; InvP; OBSC; PoEL-2; PrIm
As woods whose change appeares. Horace, *tr. by* Ben Jonson. *Fr.* The Art of Poetry. OBVE
As Wulfstan said on another occasion. Speech for the Repeal of the McCarran Act. Richard Wilbur. CMoP; GOA; NePoAm
As Ye Came from the Holy Land. *Unknown, sometimes at. to* Sir Walter Ralegh. *See* As You Came from the Holy Land.
As ye go through these palm-trees. A Song of the Virgin Mother. Lope de Vega, *tr. by* Ezra Pound. AWP
As ye see, a mountaine lion fare. Sarpedon's Speech. Homer, *tr. by* George Chapman. *Fr.* The Iliad, II. OBS
As years do grow, so cares increase. To Mistress Anne Cecil, upon Making Her a New Year's Gift, January 1, 1567-8. William Cecil, Lord Burghley. ElL; OBSC
As Yet. Vincente Rodríguez Nietzche, *tr. fr. Spanish by* Julio Marzán. InW
As yonder lamp in my vacated room. The Lamp. Charles Whitehead. OBEV; OBVV
As you all know, tonight is the night of the full moon. 12 o'Clock News. Elizabeth Bishop. GP; OxBC
As you are walking. Hey Fella Would You Mind Holding This Piano a Moment. William J. Harris. GP
As You [*or* Ye] Came from the Holy Land [of Walsingham]. *Unknown, sometimes at. to* Sir Walter Ralegh. AAS; ChTr; ElL; EnLoPo; GBL; HAP; InPS; LoBV; NoP; OBEV; PoEL-2; PoPle; PrIm; TrGrPo; ViBoPo
(Holy Land of Walsinghame, The.) EnSB
(Lover's Complaint, A.) FaBoEn
(Walsingham[e].) BoLoP; FaBoCh; LiTB; NOBE; OBSC; PPP; SeCeV
As You Come In. Anne Marriott. NOBC
As you drank deep as Thor, did you think of milk or wine? Fish Food. John Wheelwright. LiTA; MOS; TwAmPo
As you know, I have not lost you. Orpheus to Eurydice. Frederick Morgan. AMV-80
As you lay in sleep. Cartography. Louise Bogan. PoPl
As You Leave Me. Etheridge Knight. ConAP; FF; NNaP
As You Leave the Room. Wallace Stevens. AP
As you lie there in the shadows of the room. After Love. Vicente Aleixandre, *tr. by* Lewis Hyde. AMV-80
As You Like It, *sels.* Shakespeare.
All the World's a Stage, *fr.* II, vii. FaPoR; FF; FiP; LiTB; MasP; NIP; PoLF; TrGrPo
(Seven Ages of Man, The.) FaFP; TreF
Blow, Blow, Thou Winter Wind, *fr.* II, vii. AWP; CH; ChTr; ElL; ELP; EnRePo; FaFP; GBL; GTBS; GTBS-P; HBV-2; HelP; InPS; LiTB; NOBE; NoP; OAEL-1; OAEP; OBEV; PPoe; PrIm; SeCeV; TreF; ViBoPo; WHA; WiR
(Amiens's Song.) OBSC
(Song: "Blow, blow, thou winter wind.") CTC; FiP; PoEL-2
(Songs of the Greenwood.) TrGrPo
"Come apace, good Audrey. I will fetch up your goats, Audrey," *fr.* III, iii. PP

"Fool, a fool, A! I met a fool i' the forest," *fr.* II, vii. TreFT
(Motley's the Only Wear.) TrGrPo
"If it do come to pass," *fr.* II, v. ViBoPo
It Was a Lover and His Lass, *fr.* V, iii. AWP; BiP; CH; EIL; ELP; FSW; GBL; GTBS; GTBS-P; HBV-1; HeIP; InPK; InPS; LiTB; LoBV; NOBE; NoP; OBEV; OLR; PPoe; UnTE; ViBoPo
(Country Song.) TrGrPo
(Pages' Song, The.) OBSC; SeCePo
(Song: "It was a lover and his lass.") CTC; FiP
Orlando's Rhymes, *fr.* III, ii. OBSC
Song: "If the scorn of your bright eyne," *fr.* IV, iii. CTC
Under the Greenwood Tree, *fr.* II, v. AWP; BoNaP; CH; EIL; ELP; EnRePo; FaBoBe; FaFP; FaPON; GN; GTBS; GTBS-P; HBV-1; HeIP; HoPM; InPS; LiTB; NoP; OAEL-1; OAEP; OBEV; OHIP; SeCeV; TiPo; TreFS; UnPo; ViBoPo; WHA; WiR
(Amiens's Song.) OBSC
(Song: "Under the greenwood tree.") CTC; FiP
(Songs of the Greenwood.) TrGrPo
Uses of Adversity, The, *fr.* II, i. LiTB; TreFS; TrGrPo
"Wedding is great Juno's crown," *fr.* V, iv. ViBoPo
"What shall he have that killed the deer?" *fr.* IV, ii. ViBoPo
(Amiens's Song.) OBSC
(Song: "What shall he have that kill'd the dear?") CTC
"Why should this a desert be?" *fr.* III, ii. CTC
As You Like It. Theodore Weiss. TAP
As you read, a white bear leisurely. To the Reader. Denise Levertov. AmPP; CoPo; PoM; VGW
As you say (not without sadness), poets don't see, they feel. Karl Shapiro. *Fr.* The Bourgeois Poet. PP
Asante Sana, Te Te. Thadious M. Davis. BlSi
Ascend my shoulders, firmly keep thy seat. *Unknown, formerly at. to* Homer; *tr. by* Thomas Parnell. *Fr.* The Battle of the Frogs and Mice. OBVE
Ascendancy. Herbert A. Simmons. NBP
Ascending Red Cedar Moon. Duane Niatum. CDW
Ascension, The. Joseph Beaumont. OxBoCh
Ascension. Denis Devlin. BlrV
Ascension-Day. Henry Vaughan. AnAnS-1; OxBoCh
Ascension-Hymn ("Dust and clay"). Henry Vaughan. AnAnS-1; SeCV-1; TrCP
Ascension Hymn ("They are all gone"). Henry Vaughan. *See* They Are All Gone into the World of Light.
Ascension, The: 1925. John Malcolm Brinnin. Str
Ascension of Our Lord Jesus Christ, The. Christopher Smart. Hymns and Spiritual Songs, Hymn 14. NOCV
Ascent. Wendell Berry. AP
Ascent. Donald G. Saunders. PoSH
Ascent to the Sierras. Robinson Jeffers. OxBA
Ascention. John Donne. AnAnS-1; OBS
Ascetic, The. Victor J. Daley. PoAu-1
Ascot Waistcoat. David McCord. FiBHP
(Sportif.) NYBP
Ase I me rod this ender day. The Five Joys of Mary. *Unknown.* MeEL
Ash. George MacBeth. NMP
Ash and the Oak, The. Louis Simpson. ConAP; NePoAm
Ash-Glory. Paul Celan, *tr. fr. German by* Joachim Neugroschel. VWA
Ash Grove, The. *Unknown.* FSW
Ash-heap of four cultures. Conon in Alexandria. Lawrence Durrell. MoPo
Ash in the air. Ash in everyone's mouth. Wake. Elizabeth Spires. AMV-80
Ash on an old man's sleeve. T. S. Eliot. *Fr.* Four Quartets: Little Gidding. FaBoTw
Ash Wednesday. Daniel Burke. AMV-80
Ash Wednesday. T. S. Eliot. AP; CoBMV; LiTA; MoAB; MoAmPo; MoPo; OxBA; SeCeV; TwAmPo; VGW
Sels.
"Although I do not hope to turn again." FaBoEn
"At the first turning of the second stair." NoAM; NOBA
"Because I do not hope to turn again." OxBoCh
"If the lost word is lost, if the spent word is spent." OxBoCh
"Lady, three white leopards sat under a juniper-tree." LO, LoBV
Ash Wednesday. Christina Rossetti. TrCP; VLP
Ashboughs. Gerard Manley Hopkins. VLP
Ashby. John Reuben Thompson. AA
Ashcake. Thomas Nelson Page. AA
Ashen feelers of the frigid morrow, The. The Specter. Ernst Hardt, *tr. by* Jethro Bithell. AWP
Ashen man on ashen cliff above the salt halloo. Statue against a Clear Sky. Wallace Stevens. *Fr.* New England Verses. EyDe
Ashes. Philip Levine. AMV-80
Ashes, ashes, all fall down. Children's Lenten Wisdom. James A. Houck. AMV-80
Ashes have waited for me in the ash tray, The. Homecoming Blues. Vassar Miller. GP
Ashes of Life. Edna St. Vincent Millay. BLPL; FaBoBe; HBV-1
Ashes of Roses. Elaine Goodale Eastman. AA; HBV-1
Ashes of roses, forsythia bones. Changes of Life. Constance Urdang. VWA
Ashkelon. Anthony Rudolf. VWA
Ashland Tragedy, The, 2 *versions.* Elijah Adams. AmFP
Ashokan. Dachine Rainer. NePoAm
Ashore. "Laurence Hope." HBV-1
Ashtabula Disaster, The. Julia Moore. EvOK; OBAL
Ashville Junction, Swannanoa tunnel. Swannonoa Tunnel. *Unknown.* FSW
Asia on the one side. This Narrow Stage. Theodore Weiss. NoAM
Asian Desert. Dorothy Wellesley. OBMV
Asian Peace Offers Rejected without Publication. Robert Bly. CAPP; NaP; NoAM
Asians Dying, The. W. S. Merwin. CAPP; CoAP; NaP; NOBA; NYBP
Aside. Alan Dugan. PoA
Aside. R. S. Thomas. OxBC
Aside from ashcans & halljohns & pigeoncoops. Eastside Incidents. Gregory Corso. GP; NYP
Asides from the Clowns, *sel.* Jules Laforgue, *tr. fr. French by* William Jay Smith.
"My clear-cut heart, my tender soul." PoPl
Asides on the Oboe. Wallace Stevens. AP; FaBoMo; MoAB; MoAmPo
A-Sitting on a Gate. "Lewis Carroll." *See* White Knight's Song, The.
Ask and Have. Samuel Lover. HBV-1; TreFS
Ask, and Ye Shall Receive. Mrs. Havens. BLRP
Ask any question in this town. "Round Cape Horn." *Unknown.* EtS
Ask if I love thee? Oh, smiles cannot tell. Margaret to Dolcino. Charles Kingsley. HBV-1
Ask, is it well, O thou consumed of fire. The Burning of the Law. Meïr of Rothenburg, *tr. by* Nina Davis Salaman. TrJP
Ask Me. William Stafford. FiCP; NPAW
Ask Me No More. Tennyson. *Fr.* The Princess, Pt. VI. HBV-1; LiTB; UnTE
("Ask me no more: the moon may draw the sea.") GBL; OBNC; PoEL-5; TreFT; TrGrPo
(Song.) OAEP
Ask me no more, my truth to prove. Winter Song. Elizabeth Tollet. NOEC
Ask Me No More Where Jove Bestows. Thomas Carew. AWP; ELP; HAP; OAEP; PoRA; SeCePo; TEP; WHA
(Song: "Ask [*or* Aske] me no more where Jove bestows.") AnAnS-2; CABA; CaPo; CavP; CH; EnLoPo; FaBoEn; FaFP; GBL; HBV-1; HeIP; HoPM; InPS; LiTB; LoBV; MasP; MeLP; MePo; NOBE; NoP; OBEV; OBS; PAI; PoEL-3; PoPle; PPP; SeCP; SeCV-1; TreFT; TrGrPo; ViBoPo
Ask me no more, why there appears. Pyms Anarchy. *At. to* Thomas Jordan. OBS
Ask me not for the semblance of my loue. She Dwelt among the Untrodden Ways. J. C. Squire. BXAP
Ask me why I send you here. The Primrose. Robert Herrick, *wr. at. to* Thomas Carew. FaBoUs; HBV-1; OBEV; ViBoPo
Ask night how it feels to be dark. To Be Black, to Be Lost. Hannah Kahn. GoYe
Ask No Return. Horace Gregory. Chorus for Survival, XIV. MoAmPo
("Ask no return for love that's given."). TwAmPo; VGW
Ask not for whom the bells toll. Donne Redone. Joseph Paul Tierney. ShM
Ask not my name, O friend! A Nameless Epitaph. Matthew Arnold. VLP
Ask not overmuch for fair. He That Loves a Rosy Cheek. Heinrich von Rugge, *tr. by* Jethro Bithell. AWP
Ask not the cause why sullen Spring. Song to a Fair Young Lady, Going Out of the Town in the Spring. Dryden. CABA; HBV-1; OBEV; OBS
Ask Not to Know This Man. Ben Jonson. CABA
(Little Shrub Growing By, A.) EnRePo; TW
Ask Not Ungainly. Horace, *tr. fr. Latin by* Ezra Pound. Odes, I, 11. CTC
Ask not why hearts turn magazines of passions. A Funeral Elogy, upon. . .Mrs. Anne Bradstreet. John Norton. SCAP
Ask nothing more of me, sweet. The Oblation. Swinburne. HBV-1; VLP
Ask of the sun. Louis Zukofsky. NoAM
Ask the Empresse of the night. The Magnet. Thomas Stanley. MePo; NOBE
Ask what kind of war it is. What Kind of War? Larry Rottman. POL
Ask you what provocation I have had? Satire [*or* The Defence of Satire *or* The Power of Ridicule]. Pope. *Fr.* Epilogue to the Satires. NOBE; NOEC; OBEC; OBSV
Askest, "How long thou shalt stay?" The Visit. Emerson. NOBA
Askest thou of these graves? They'll tell thee. Gheluvelt. Robert Bridges. BrPo

Asking for Ruthie. Judy Grahn. GP; NMM
Asking what, asking what?—all a boy's afternoon. Debate: Question, Quarry, Dream. Robert Penn Warren. VGW
Asleep. Wilfred Owen. MMA
Asleep. William Winter. AA
Asleep at the Switch. George Hoey. BeLS; PaPo
Asleep he wheezes at his ease. Roger the Dog. Ted Hughes. RHPC
Asleep in the Deep. Arthur J. Lamb. FSN, *with music;* TreFT
Asleep, my love? Shakespeare. *Fr.* A Midsummer Night's Dream, V, i. CTC
Asleep or waking is it? for her neck. Laus Veneris. Swinburne. VLP
Asleep while the children howl and the house burns. Goddess. Judith Johnson Sherwin. BoWoP
Asleep within the deadest hour of night. To ———. Robert Nichols. HBMV
A-sleepin' at length on the sand. The Sea Serpant. Wallace Irwin. FiBHP
Asmodai [*or* Asmodeus]. Geoffrey Hill. FaBoTw; NePoEA
Asolando, *sels.* Robert Browning.
  Epilogue: "At the midnight in the silence of the sleep-time." FaBoEn; FaBV; FiP; HBV-2; HBVY; NOBE; OAEP; OBNC; OBVV; OHFP; TEP; TreFT; TrGrPo; ViBoPo; VLP
  Prologue: "Poet's age is sad, The: for why?" OAEL-2; VLP
Aspatia's Song. Beaumont *and* Fletcher. *Fr.* The Maid's Tragedy, II, i. AWP; HAP; HBV-1; NOBE; OBEV; OBS; PoPle; TrGrPo
  (I Died True.) CH
  (Lay a Garland on My Hearse.) GBL; OAEP; WHA
Aspect of Love, Alive in the Ice and Fire, An. Gwendolyn Brooks. BPo; CAPP; PAI; TAP
Aspecta Medusa. Dante Gabriel Rossetti. VLP
Aspects. Norman MacCaig. BSV; OxBS
Aspects of Robinson. Weldon Kees. CoAP; NaP; NYBP; NYP; TwAmPo
Aspects of Some Forsythia Branches. Ralph Gustafson. PeCV
Aspects of Spring in Greater Boston. George Starbuck. Poems from a First Year in Boston, II. NYBP
Aspects of the Pines. Paul Hamilton Hayne. AA; HBV-1
Aspects of the World like Coral Reefs. William Bronk. VGW
Aspen and the Stream, The. Richard Wilbur. NYBP
Aspens. Edward Thomas. ChMP; InPS
Aspens and the maples now, The. Valentine's Day. Aileen Fisher. YeAr
Aspens glisten, The. Spring Again. Ronald Wallace. PPJ
Aspen's Song, The. Yvor Winters. POL
Aspens yesterday, The. Did You Not See. Alex Kuo. BrSí
Asphalt morning found him, The; he was dead. Raccoon on the Road. Joseph Payne Brennan. GoYe
Asphodel. David Malouf. CBAP
Asphodel, That Greeny Flower, *sels.* William Carlos Williams.
  "Approaching death." FaBoMo
  "Of asphodel, that greeny flower." CMoP; PP
Aspiration. Mário de Andrade, *tr. fr. Portuguese by* John Nist. TTY
Aspiration, The. John Norris. LoBV; OxBoCh
Aspiration. John Banister Tabb. LO
Aspiration. Edward William Thomson. OBVV
Aspiring Man, by learned pens. Brief Essay on Man. Arthur Guiterman. OBAL
Asra, The. Heine. *See* Azra, The.
Ass, The ("The ass/ is decidedly middlecrass"). Edwin Allan. PoPl; WhC
Ass, The. Moses Mendes. *Fr.* The Chaplet. TrJP
Ass-Face. Edith Sitwell. OBMV
Ass in the Lion's Skin, The ("An ass put on a lion's skin and went"). Aesop, *tr. fr. Greek by* William Ellery Leonard. AWP
Ass will with his long ears fray, An. Samuel Butler. FaBoEE
Assailant. John Raven. BPo
Assassination, The. Robert Hillyer. MoAmPo; OFD
Assassination. Don L. Lee. AmNP; BOLo; FF; NeAC; OFD; PoBA
Assassination of President McKinley, The. Paul Blackburn. NYP
Assassination Poems. John Ridland. MAT; OFD
Assassination Raga. Lawrence Ferlinghetti. CAPP
Assassin's Fatal Error, The. Lawrence Raab. AmPA
Assault on the Fortress, The. Timothy Dwight. PAH
Assay a Friend. *Unknown.* OxBM
Assemble, all ye maidens, at the door. Elegy on a Lady, Whom Grief for the Death of Her Betrothed Killed. Robert Bridges. CoBMV; OBEV; OBVV; VLP
Assembling of the Fays, The. Joseph Rodman Drake. *Fr.* The Culprit Fay. GN
Assembly. W. S. Merwin. GP
Assembly: Harlem School. Eugene T. Maleska. GoYe
Assembly of Ladies, The, *sel.* Lady of the Assembly.
  Palace of Pleasant Regard, The. WPE
Assembly of the Gods, The. Robert Henryson. *Fr.* The Testament of Cresseid. PoEL-1
Assert ten barren love day made. A Play on Words. Eugene Field. WhC
Asses' milk, half a pint, take at seven, or before. Advice to a Lady [*or* Young Lady] in Autumn. Earl of Chesterfield. FaBoUs; NOEC; OBEC
"Asshole" and "shit" were always on her lips. A Lady. W. D. Snodgrass. TW
Assignation, The, *sel.* Dryden.
  Long betwixt Love and Fear. ViBoPo
Assignation, The. Juana de Ibarbourou, *tr. fr. Spanish by* Brian Swann. PBWP
Assignation, The, *sel.* Poe.
  To One in Paradise. AA; AmPP; AP; BLPL; BoLoP; HBV-1; LiTA; LO; NePA; OBEV; OBRV; OBVV; OxBA; PoLF; TAP; TrGrPo; ViBoPo; WHA
Assignation, The. James Wright. NePoEA
Assignation with a Somnambulist. John Manifold. CBAP
Assignment: Descriptive Essay. Gary Willis. AMV-81
Assisi. Alfred Noyes. GoBC
Assistance, The. Paul Blackburn. NeAP; PoM
Assistant editor of *Crewel World,* The. The New York Woman. L. E. Sissman. MAT
Assorted Relishes. Richard Armour. WhC
Ass's hoof alone can hold, An. On Burning a Dull Poem. Swift. TW
Assuming the Name of Any Next Child. John Tagliabue. AMV-80
Assumpta Est Maria. Liam Brophy. ISi
Assumpta Maria. Francis Thompson. ISi
Assumption, The. Sir John Beaumont. ACP; GoBC
Assumption, The. John Gilland Brunini. ISi
Assumption. Padraic Fallon. BIrV
Assumption, The. John Banister Tabb. ISi
Assumption, The. *Unknown.* OxBM
Assunpink and Princeton. Thomas Dunn English. PAH
Assurance, An. Nicholas Breton. OBSC
  (Say That I Should Say I Love Thee.) EIL
Assurance. George Herbert. OxBoCh
Assurance. Ida Norton Munson. PGD
Assynt. Alan Gilchrist. PoSH
Assyrian came down like the wolf on the fold, The. The Destruction of Sennacherib. Byron. BeLS; BLPA; BLPL; EnRP; EvOK; FaBoBe; FaBoCh; FaFP; FaPo; FaPON; FaPoR; FF; GN; HAP; HBV-2; NIP; NoP; OAEP; OBWP; OnMSP; PAI; PaPo; PoLF; TrCP; TreF; WBLP; WeW; WGRP
Assyrian King in peace, with foul desire, The. The Portrait of Henry VIII [*or* Sardanapalus]. Earl of Surrey. AAS; ACP; SiPS
Aster ("My star, star-gazing?—if only I could be"). Plato, *tr. fr. Greek by* Peter Jay. PeHV
Aster ("You were the morning star among the living"). Plato, *tr. fr. Greek by* Peter Jay. PeHV
Asteroid Light, The. *Unknown.* FSW
Astonished poplars hide. Paysage Moralisé. John Hollander. ErPo; NePoEA
Astræa. Whittier. AA
Astraea at the Capitol. Whittier. PAH
Astraea Redux, *sels.* Dryden.
  "And welcom now (Great Monarch) to your own." OBS
  "Now with a general peace the world was blest." OBS
Astride on steel. Motorcycle. Benjamin Sturgis Pray. GoYe
Astrologer Argues Your Death, The. Charles deGravelles. AMV-81
Astrologer's Song, An. Kipling. MoBrPo
Astrology. Tom Marshall. PeCV
Astronaut's Choice. M. M. Darcy. QQQ
Astronomer's Journal, An. Jane Shore. PoA
Astronomers of Mont Blanc, The. Edgar Bowers. PoA; QFR
Astronomy. A. E. Housman. OBWP
Astrophel, *sel.* Spenser.
  "Such skill, matcht with such courage as he had." OBWP
Astrophel and Stella. Sir Philip Sidney. AAS; SiPS (*Sonnets,* I-CVIII, *and 9 Songs*)
  Sonnets.
  I. "Loving in truth, and fain in verse my love to show." AWP; BLPL; CABA; EBEV; FaBoEn; GBL; HAP; HBV-1; LiTB; MasP; NoP; OAEL-1; OAEP; OBSC; PP; SeCePo; SeCeV; TEP; TreFT; TrGrPo; ViBoPo
  II. "Not at the first sight, nor with a dribbed shot." OAEL-1
  III. "Let dainty wits cry on the Sisters nine." OAEL-1; OBSC
  V. "It is most true that eyes are formed to serve." OAEL-1; OBSC
  VII. "When Nature made her chief work, Stella's eyes." CABA; NIP
  XI. "In truth, O Love, with what a boyish kind." EIL; InvP
  XIV. "Alas, have I not pain enough, my friend." NoP; OAEL-1
  XV. "You that do search for every purling spring." OAEL-1; OBSC
  XX. "Fly, fly, my friends, I have my death wound; fly." OAEL-1; TEP
  XXI. "Your words, my friend, right helpful caustics, blame." CABA; TEP
  XXII. "In highest way of heaven the Sun did ride." OBSC

XXIV. "Rich fools there be, whose base and filthy heart." OAEP
XXV. "The wisest scholar of the wight most wise." NoP; OAEL-1
XXVI. "Though dusty wits dare scorn astrology." OAEL-1
XXVIII. "You that with allegory's curious frame." InPK; OAEL-1
XXXI. "With how sad steps, O Moon, thou climb'st the skies!" AWP; BoLoP; CH; ChTr; ElL; EnLoPo; EnRePo; FaBoEn; GBL; HAP; HBV-1; HeIP; InPK; InPS; InvP; MAT; MOON; NoP; OAEP; OBSC; PoEL-1; PoRA; PPoe; PPP; SeCeV; TEP; TrGrPo; ViBoPo; WeW; WHA
(His Lady's Cruelty.) OBEV
(Languishing Moon, The.) BoNaP
(Moon, The.) LoBV
(To the Sad Moon.) NOBE
XXXIII. "I might—unhappy word—oh me, I might." OAEL-1; OBSC
XXXV. "What may words say, or what may words not say." CABA
XXXIX. "Come sleep! O sleep, the certain knot of peace." CABA; ElL; EnRePo; HBV-1; NIP; NoP; OAEP; OBSC; PoRA; PPP; SCV; TEP; TreFS; TrGrPo; ViBoPo; WHA
(Sleep.) LoBV; OBEV
(To Sleep.) NOBE
XLI. "Having this day my horse, my hand, my lance." EnRePo; HAP; OAEP; OBSC
XLVII. "What, have I thus betrayed my liberty?" GBL; NIP; NoP; PoEL-1
(Yoke of Tyranny, The.) TrGrPo
XLVIII. "Soul's joy, bend not those morning stars from me." NoP
XLIX. "I on my horse, and Love on me, doth try." NoP; OAEL-1
LII. "Strife is grown between Virtue and Love, A." NoP
LIV. "Because I breathe not love to every one." OAEP; OBSC; TrGrPo
LIX. "Dear, why make you more of a dog than me?" GBL; OAEP; PrIm
LXII. "Late tired with woe, even ready for to pine." HBV-1
LXIII. "O grammar-rules, O now your virtues show."
(Grammar-Rules.) FaBoUs
LXIV. "No more, my dear, no more these counsels try." HBV-1; OBSC
LXVIII. "Stella, the only planet of my light." OBSC
LXIX. "O joy too high for my low style to show!" TrGrPo
LXXI. "Who will in fairest book of Nature know." CABA; NoP; OAEL-1
LXXIII. "Love still a boy and oft a wanton is." HBV-1; OAEP
LXXIV. "I never drank of Aganippe well." CABA; EnRePo; HeIP; OBSC
LXXXII. "Nymph of the garden where all beauties be." InvP
LXXXIII. "Good brother Philip, I have borne you long." PBBP
LXXXIV. "Highway, since you my chief Parnassus be." ElL; EnRePo; OAEP; OBSC
(Highway, The.) LiTB; OBEV
XC. "Stella, think not that I by verse seek fame." OBSC
XCVIII. "Ah bed! the field where joy's peace some do see." EnLoPo
XCIX. "When far-spent night persuades each mortal eye." CABA; OBSC
CIII. "O happy Thames that didst my Stella bear!" HBV-1
CVII. "Stella! since thou so right a princess art." HBV-1; NoP
CIX. "Thou blind man's mark, thou fool's self-chosen snare." *Sometimes considered part of* Astrophel and Stella. CABA; ErPo; HeIP; PPP
(Desire.) LiTB; MasP; NOBE
CX. "Leave me, O Love, which reachest but to dust." *Sometimes considered part of* Astrophel and Stella. CABA; FaBoRV; GBL; HeIP; LiTB; OxBoCh; PPP; SeCePo; TreFT; WHA
(Splendidis Longum Valedico Nugis.) LO; NOBE
Songs.
First Song: "Doubt you to whom my Muse these notes intendeth." HBV-1; OBSC
(To Stella.) ElL; WHA
Third Song: "If Orpheus voyce had force to breathe such musickes love." PoEL-1
Fourth Song: "Only joy, now here you are." ElL; EnRePo; GBL; HAP; InvP; NoP; OBSC; UnTE
Sixth Song: "O you that hear this voice." OBSC
Eighth Song: "In a grove most rich of shade." OAEP; OBSC; SiPS
Eleventh Song: "Who is it that this dark night." ElL; EnRePo; OBSC; PoEL-1; TEP; ViBoPo
(Underneath My Window.) SeCePo
(Voices at the Window.) NOBE; OBEV; PoPle
Asunder shall the clouds be rolled. The Day of Judgment. Dugald Buchanan. GoTS
Aswelay. Norman Henry Pritchard II. PoBA
A-swell within her billowed skirts. The Mad Woman of Punnet's Town. L. A. G. Strong. MoBrPo
Asylum. David R. Clark. PPON
Asylum. John Freeman. OBMV
At a Bach Concert. Adrienne Rich. NePoEA; NIP
At a bend in the Bally-Dale road. The Last Families in the Cabins. Millen Brand. GP
At a Child's Baptism. Vassar Miller. GoJo
At a Chinaman's Grave. Wing Tek Lum. BrSi
At a Concert of Music. Conrad Aiken. MoAB; MoAmPo; UnS
At a Country Dance in Provence. Harold Monro. OBVV
At a Country Fair. John Holmes. MoShBr
At a Country Hotel. Howard Nemerov. PoRA
At a Cowboy Dance. James Barton Adams. BPAW; HBV-2; PoOW
At a Friends' Meeting. Mary Elizabeth Coleridge. WPE
At a gay reception given in a mansion grand and old. The Moth and the Flame. George Taggart. FSN; TreF
At a Georgia Camp Meeting, *with music.* Kerry Mills. BLSo
At a Hasty Wedding. Thomas Hardy. VLP
At a Jewish wedding. The Homeless. Joan Joffe Hall. AMV-81
At a Loss. James L. Weil. GoYe
At a Low Mass for Two Hot-Rodders. X. J. Kennedy. Psk
At a March against the Vietnam War. Robert Bly. EAS
At a Modernist School. Morris Bishop. TDH
At a Month's End. Swinburne. VLP
At a Parade. F. T. Prince. NeBP; WaP
At a party of university people. Double Exposure. Ian Young. NeAC; PeHV
At a pleasant evening party I had taken down to supper. Ferdinando and Elvira. W. S. Gilbert. FaBoCo; FaBoNo; FiBHP
At a Potato Digging. Seamus Heaney. IPY
At a Private Showing in 1982. Maxine Kumin. SV
At a Reading. Thomas Bailey Aldrich. OBAL
At a roundup on the Gily. The Legend of Boastful Bill. Charles Badger Clark, Jr. BPAW
At a Ruined Croft. John Manson. PoSH
At a Solemn Music [*or* Musick]. Milton. GTBS; GTBS-P; HBV-2; HeIP; LoBV; NOBE; OAEP; OBEV; OBS; PoEL-3; SeCeV
(Blest Pair of Sirens.) OxBoCh
"Blest pair of Sirens, pledges of Heaven's joy," *sel.* UnS
At a Solemn Musick. Delmore Schwartz. TwAmPo
At a spring well [*or* springe wel] under a thorn. The Spring under a Thorn [*or* The Virgin]. *Unknown.* GBP; MeEL
At a Summer Hotel. Isabella Gardner. GrPl
At a Time. Ray Mathew. PoAu-2
At a university women's sort of charity fair. The Fortune Teller. John Holmes. NePoAm-2
At a Vacation Exercise, *sel.* Milton.
"Hail native language, that by sinews weak." JCP; OBS; PP
At a Watering Place. Thomas Hardy. CMoP
At a Welsh Waterfall. Gerard Manley Hopkins. FaBoPP
At a Window. Carl Sandburg. FaBoBe; HBMV; TrPWD
At Aberdeen. *Unknown. See* Epitaph: "Here lie I, Martin Elginbrodde."
At alarming bell daybreak, before. Eilean Ni Chuilleanain. *Fr.* Site of Ambush. CIP
At an Exhibition of Historical Paintings, Hobart. Vivian Smith. CBAP
At anchor in Hampton Roads we lay. The *Cumberland.* Longfellow. AA; EtS; PAH
At Annika's Place. Siv Widerberg, *tr. fr. Swedish by* Verne Moberg. NTCP
At April. Angelina Weld Grimké. BlSi
At Arley. Andrew Young. FaBoPP
At Arm's Length. Shirley Bossert. FAZ
At Baia. Hilda Doolittle ("H. D."). LiTA; NOBA; TwAmPo
At Ballyshannon, Co. Donegal. William Allingham. FaBoPP
At Barstow. Charles Tomlinson. NoAM; TwCP
At Beautyes barre as I dyd stande. The Arraignment of a Lover. George Gascoigne. AAS
At Bedtime. Mariana Griswold Van Rensselaer. HBMV
At Beltane, when ilk body bownis. Peblis to the Play. *Unknown.* GoTS
At Best. John Boyle O'Reilly. AA
At Bethlehem. John Banister Tabb. *Fr.* The Child. AA
At Bickford's. Gerald Stern. NYP
At Birth. Anthony Thwaite. NePoEA-2
At blackest night to come alone in rain. The Wind of the Cliff Ka Hea. Phyllis Thompson. FAZ
At Boot Hill in Tombstone, Arizona. *Unknown.* ShM
At break of day I chanced to stray. The Oul' Gray Mare. *Unknown.* AnIV
At breakfast a husband is cheery or blue. Sentimental Journey. "Elspeth." WhC
At breakfast I had french toast. On First Knowing God. Reed Whittemore. *Fr.* The Seven Days. GP
At Brill on the hill. *Unknown.* GBP; OxNR
At Bungendore. James McAuley. PoAu-2
At Cambridge. Audrey McGaffin. NePoAm
At Camino. Timothy Sheehan. SUW
At Candlemas. Charles Causley. OBCP
At Carbis Bay. Arthur Symons. FaBoPP
At Carmel. Mary Austin. AmFN

At Carmel Highlands. Janet Lewis. PoA
At Casterbridge Fair, *sels.* Thomas Hardy.
After the Club-Dance, III. VLP
After the Fair, VII. CMoP; HAP; VLP
Ballad-Singer, The, I. BoLoP; OLR; VLP
Former Beauties, II. FaBoEn; NoAM; OBMV; OBNC
At Castle Boterel. Thomas Hardy. DTC; EBEV; FaBoEn; GTBS-P; MoVE; NOBE; OBNC; SCV
At Castle Wood. Emily Brontë. ViBoPo
At Cato's Head in Russell Street. On the Fly-Leaf of a Book of Old Plays. Walter Learned. HBV-1
At Chadwicks Bar and Grill. Lance Henson. STE
At Chappaqua. Joel Benton. AA
At Cheyenne. Eugene Field. BPAW
At Christmas. Robert Duncan. NoAM
At Christmas, when old friends are meeting. Good Will to Men—Christmas Greetings in Six Languages. Dorothy Brown Thompson. OBCP
At Christmastide. Laura Simmons. PGD
At Church Next Sunday. *Unknown.* BLRP
At Cockcrow. Lizette Woodworth Reese. TrPWD
At Common Dawn. Vivian Locke Ellis. CH
At Communion. Madeleine L'Engle. TrCP
At cool of day, with God I walk. Eventide. Caroline Atherton Briggs Mason. TreFS
At Cooloolah. Judith Wright. MoBrPo
At Cosmo/ the sky is swarming with color. The Parents-without-Partners Picnic. Ted Schaefer. FAZ
At counters where I eat my lunch. Marble-Top. E. B. White. FiBHP; OBAL; WhC
At court I met it, in clothes brave enough. On Something, That Walks [*or* Walkes] Somewhere. Ben Jonson. PAI; SeCP; SeCV-1
At Cove on the Crooked River. William Stafford. ConAP; LiTM; NaP
At Creçy by Somme in Ponthieu. Creçy. Francis Turner Palgrave. BeLS; HBV-2
At Dante's Grave. Ezra Zussman, *tr. fr. Hebrew by* D. Shnayorson. VWA
At Darien Bridge. James Dickey. NoP
At Dawn. Arthur Symons. OBNC
At Dawn. J. M. Synge. SyP
At dawn a knot of sea-lions lies off shore. Animals. Robinson Jeffers. NU
At dawn crowed the cock. Cock. Aharon Amir, *tr. by* Bernhard Frank. AMV-81
"At dawn," he said, "I bid them all farewell." The Volunteer. Elbridge Jefferson Cutler. AA
At dawn I squat on the garage. Sound. Jim Harrison. VGW
At dawn of day I saw a man. *See* At dawn today I saw a man come out of a saloon.
At dawn of the day the Creator. Gaspara Stampa, *tr. fr. Italian by* J. Vitiello. BoWoP
At Dawn of the Year. "George Klingle". PGD
At dawn she lay with her profile at that angle. Daybreak. Stephen Spender. BoLoP; DFF
At dawn, the joyful choir of bells. Ave-Maria Bells. Charles Warren Stoddard. ISi
At Dawn the Light Will Come. N. P. Van Wyk Louw, *tr. fr. Afrikaans by* Uys Krige *and* Jack Cope. PeSA
At dawn the ridge emerges massed and dun. Attack. Siegfried Sassoon. MoBrPo; NOBE; OxBTC
At dawn the sea monster slept. Explorations/ Bronchitis: The Rosario Beach House. Aleida Rodríguez, *tr. by* Toni Empringham. FIA
At Dawn the Virgin Is Born. Lope de Vega, *tr. fr. Spanish by* W. S. Merwin. PChr
At dawn three shearsmen. Bernie's Quick-Shave (1968). Sydney Lea. MAYP
At dawn today [*or* of day] I saw a man come out of a saloon. The Drunkard's Doom. *Unknown.* AS; FSW
At dawn, when England's childish tongue. Dandelion. Annie Rankin Annan. HBV-1
At Dawning, *with music.* Nelle Richmond Eberhart. BLSo
At Daybreak. Siegfried Sassoon. PeHV
At daybreak, when the falcon claps his wings. Ballad Written for a Bridegroom. Villon, *tr. by* Swinburne. AWP
At Day's End. *Unknown.* TreFT
At day's light. In Autumn. Jon Anderson. AmPA
At dead of night, after an evening ball. The Duchess of York's Ghost. *Unknown.* APAS
At dead of night, the sailors sprawled on deck. Nearing La Guaira. Derek Walcott. TTY
At Delft. Charles Tomlinson. NYBP
At Delos. Duncan Campbell Scott. PeCV
At Delphos shrine one did a doubt propound. Upon Master Edmund Spenser. Francis Beaumont. FaBoEE
At Devlin's Siding. Barcroft Boake. CBAP
At Dieppe, *sels.* Arthur Symons.
After Sunset. BrPo; SyP
Grey and Green. FaBoPP; SyP
On the Beach. VLP
Rain on the Dawn. BrPo; OBNC; OBVV; SyP
At Dingle Bank. Edward Lear. WhC
(Dingle Bank.) FaBaNo
At dinner, she is hostess, I am host. George Meredith. Modern Love, XVII. HeIP; NoP; OAEP
At Dirty Dick's and Sloppy Joe's. Song of the Master and Boatswain. W. H. Auden. *Fr.* The Sea and the Mirror. BoLoP; DTC; FaBoTw; MOS
At Dover Cliffs [July 20, 1787]. William Lisle Bowles. EnRP; ViBoPo
(Dover Cliffs.) HBV-2
(Sonnet: At Dover Cliffs.) OBEC
At Drugger's Head, without a puff. From a Tobacco Wrapper. *Unknown.* FaBoUs
At Dunwich. Anthony Thwaite. MoBS
At dusk/ from the island in the river. If the Owl Calls Again. John Haines. BoAnP; BoNaP; CoAP; ConAP; HeIP; LCAP; NCSH; NU
At dusk and long-distance they are the mouths. Tide Pools. Dave Smith. AMV-81
At dusk heavy clouds grieve the long day. Poem to the Tune of "Tsui hua yin." Li Ch'ing-chao, *tr. by* Marsha Wagner. WPOW
At each level. Lamb and Bear; Jet Landing. Laurence Lieberman. DiL
At Eagle Farm I stand at the passenger gate. Flights. Roger McDonald. CBAP
At early dawn I once had been. The Dawning of the Day. *Unknown, tr. by* Edward Walsh. OnYI
At Early Morn. Binga Dismond, *fr. the French of* Catulle Mendes. PoNe
At early morning, clear and cold. The Troopship. Lionel Johnson. EBVV
At Ease. Walter de la Mare. ChMP; GTBS-P
At Easter Time. Laura E. Richards. OHIP
At eight I was brilliant with my body. Black Hair. Gary Soto. NPGG
At 8:00 he rises, bathes, and dresses. Mr. Eliot's Day. Robert Francis. NYBP
At eighteen, the U.S. Navy eye chart. The Pornography Box. Dave Smith. DiL
At Eighty. Rosamund Stanhope. AMV-80
At eighty/ reading lines. Heavy, Heavy—What Hangs Over? Kenneth Burke. POL
At 85. Richard Ardinger. AMV-81
At Eighty-seven. Dachine Rainer. NePoAm
At eighty-six she takes to pressing flowers. Foxfire. Nancy Willard. IHMS
At eighty they took the scales. At Eighty. Rosamund Stanhope. AMV-80
At Elsdon. George Chatt. FaBoPP
At Epidaurus. Lawrence Durrell. LiTB; MoPo
At Euston. A. M. Harbord. PoSH
At Eutaw Springs the valiant died. To the Memory of the Brave Americans [*or* Eutaw Springs]. Philip Freneau. AA; AmPP; AP; BeLS; PAH; PAL; PoLF
"At eve should be the time," they said. Datur Hora Quieti. Robert Stephen Hawker. GoBC
At eve the horse is freed of plough or wain. An Evening Falls. James Stephens. SUS
At even, when the hour drew nigh at which we say farewell. Epigram. Strato, *tr. by* Sydney Oswald. PeHV
At evening I pause, neglected pen. "Who Then Is Crazy?" Barry Spacks. GP
At evening, sitting on this terrace. Bat. D. H. Lawrence. BrPo; GTBS-P; HAP; OAEL-1
At evening when the lamp is lit. The Land of Story-Books. Robert Louis Stevenson. FaBoBe; FaPON; HBV-1; HBVY; TiPo; TreFS
At every hour I wake. Night. Aldo Camerino, *tr. by* Anita Barrows. VWA
At every stroke his brazen fins do take. The Whale. John Donne. *Fr.* The Progress of the Soul. ChTr
At Farringford. Tennyson. *Fr.* To the Rev. F. D. Maurice. FaBoPP
At Ferns Castle. Padraic Colum. NePoAm
At fifty, I approach myself. In a Dream. David Ignatow. GP
At First. C. H. Sisson. OxBC
At first blush, discomfiting. Diehard. Judith Moffett. PoA
At first cock-crow. The Neighbors. Theodosia Garrison. HBMV
At first, he wondered why he should be spared. The Madman. Constance Urdang. PoPl
At first I could remove the bandages. Under the Catalpa Trees. Gary Young. AMV-81
At first I prayed for Light. The Larger Prayer [*or* Prayer—Answer]. Ednah D. Cheney. BLRP; STF; WGRP
At first I thought a pest. Armour's Undermining Modesty. Marianne Moore. AP; CoBMV
At first I thought some animal, wounded. Near Barbizon. Galway Kinnell. NePoAm-2

At first I was given centuries. Margaret Atwood. HAP; NMM; WPOW
At first I was worried about you. When I Held You to My Chest, You Fit. Jack Myers. AmPA
At first I went apart. And now I see. Tammuz. Rayner Heppenstall. WaP
At first I would not reply, and my shame showed upon my cheeks. Remorse. Pierre Louÿs, *tr. by* Horace M. Brown. *Fr.* The Songs of Bilitis. UnTE
At first it will seem tame. Money. Victor Contoski. GP
At first light. The Print-out. Howard Nemerov. AMV-80
At first nothing is. Nothing Is. Sun-Ra. PoBA
At first she thought it a fantastic dream. Ballade of Charon and the River Girl. J. B. Morton. WhC
At First Sight. Robert Graves. FaBoEE
At first there all sea-water on the top land. On the Creation and Ontogony. *Unknown, tr. by* C. S. Rafinesque. *Fr.* The Wallum Olum. LiTA
At first was neither Being nor Nonbeing. The Song of Creation. *Tr. fr. Sanskrit by* Raimundo Panikkar. *Fr.* Vedic Hymns. ILwL
At first we sat imprisoned in this place. Conversation in Black and White. May Sarton. GoYe
At first when I heard the old song. I Heard the Old Song. B. W. Vilakazi. PeSA
At first when we saw a girl. Sunday Afternoon. Philip Levine. NaP
At five in the afternoon. Lament for Ignacio Sanchez Mejías. Federico García Lorca, *tr. by* A. L. Lloyd. OBVE
At five in the morning, as jolly as any. The Miner's Doom. *Unknown.* AmFP
At five o'clock he milks the cow. The Breakfast Song. Emilie Poulsson. HBVY
At five of this winter morn the hound and I. Ceremony. Howard Nemerov. AMV-80
At five precisely in the afternoon. Crossing. Archibald MacLeish. POL
At 5:10 a.m. Uncle Henry. Dream 1971. Victor Contoski. GP
At five this morn, when Phoebus raised his head. Tunbridge Wells. Earl of Rochester. FaBoPP; OBSV
At Florence. Wordsworth. VLP
At Flores in the Azores, Sir Richard Grenville lay. The *Revenge* [*or* A Ballad of the Fleet]. Tennyson. BeLS; DTo; EBVV; FaBoCh; FaPo; FaPoR; HBV-2; OAEP; OBWP; OnMSP; PoRA
At focus in the national. The Monument and the Shrine. John Logan. LCAP
At Fotheringay. Robert Southwell. PoEL-2
(Decease, Release: Dum Morior Orior.) NCEP
At 4:00 A.M., I drove to American Falls. American Falls. Greg Keeler. WOLT
At four in the morning the smoke of the forded river. While We Slept. David Wolff. TrJP
At four o'clock. Roosters. Elizabeth Bishop. CrMA; LiTM; NePA
At four o'clock in the afternoon. Surfaces. Jane Mayhall. NYP
At four o'clock in the morning. Waking Time. Ivy O. Eastwick. SiSoSe; TiPo
At four o'clock it's dark. In Winter. Michael Ryan. MAYP
At four p.m. small fingers moved the dial to one-six-"O." Riders. Linda Peavy. PH
At 4:30 AM/ she rose. Ntozake Shange. *Fr.* For Colored Girls Who Have Considered Suicide When the Rainbow Is Enuf. BoWoP
At 14th Street and First Avenue. Strawberries in Mexico. Ron Padgett. EAS
At Francis Allen's on the Christmas-eve. The Epic. Tennyson. VLP
At Fredericksburg. John Boyle O'Reilly. PAH
At Fyvie's yetts there grows a flower. The Trumpeter of Fyvie [*or* Andrew Lammie]. *Unknown.* ESPB; OxBB
At Galway Races. W. B. Yeats. LiSp
At Gettysburg full anonymity. Yugoslav Cemetery. Celeste Turner Wright. DFF; WPE
At Gibraltar (*Sonnets* I *and* II). George Edward Woodberry. AA; GN
"England, I stand on thy imperial ground," *sel.* HBV-2
At Glan-y-Wern. Arthur Symons. Intermezzo: Pastoral, IV. VLP
At Glastonbury. Henry Kingsley. *See* Magdalen.
At Glendalough lived a young saint. St. Kevin. *Unknown, at. to* Samuel Lover. WTO
At God's Command. Joseph Rolnik, *tr. fr. Yiddish by* Keith Bosley. VWA
At Golgotha I stood alone. Edwin John Ellis. *Fr.* Himself. OBMV
At Grand Canyon's Edge. David Ray. TAT
At Grandfather's. Clara Doty Bates. OBCA
At Grass. Philip Larkin. HAP; NePoEA; OxBTC; WeW
At Great Torrington, Devon. *Unknown.* FaBoCo; ShM
("Here lies a man who was killed by lightning.") FaBoEE
At Guaymas I born in this various world. The Pinto. Owen Wister. BPAW
At Gull Lake: August, 1810. Duncan Campbell Scott. NOBC; OBCV
At Hadleigh, Suffolk. *Unknown.* FaBoCo
At half-past five—the earth cooling. Bachelor Farmer. Roger McDonald. CBAP
At half-past three a single bird. Emily Dickinson. AP; MoAmPo; OxBA
At Hallowmas, whan nights grow lang. Hallow-Fair. Robert Fergusson. OxBS
At Hans Christian Andersen's Birthplace, Odense, Denmark. Maurice Lindsay. BSV
At Haroun's court it chanced, upon a time. The World's Way. Thomas Bailey Aldrich. HBV-1
At hawthorn-time in Wiltshire travelling. Lob. Edward Thomas. MoVE
At Henry's bier let some thing fall out well. John Berryman. *Fr.* Dream Songs. CAPP; NoP
At her departure his disdain return'd. Homer, *tr. by* Dryden. *Fr.* The Iliad, I. OBVE
At Her Fair Hands. Walter Davison. ElL; WHA
(How Can the Heart Forget Her.) HBV-1; OBEC
(Ode: "At her fair hands how have I grace entreated.") BoLoP; OBSC
At her step the water-hen. Fragment. Dante Gabriel Rossetti. FM
At Her Window. Frederick Locker-Lampson. HBV-1; OBVV
At His Father's Grave. John Ormond. FaBoTw
At his right hand. Poet. Linda Pastan. DFF
At home alone, O Nomades. Home, Sweet Home, with Variations, III. H. C. Bunner. CenHV; InMe; OBAL
At home, as in no other city, here. Oxford. Keith Douglas. NePoEA
At home at Annika's place. At Annika's Place. Siv Widerberg, *tr. by* Verne Moberg. NTCP
At Home in Dakar. Margaret Danner. BlSi; FB
At Home in Heaven. James Montgomery. HBV-2; VLP
At Home in Heaven. Robert Southwell. AnAnS-1
At home, in my flannel gown, like a bear to its floe. 90 North. Randall Jarrell. AP; CoAP; CoBMV; FYAP; MoAB; MoPo; MoVE; NoAM; NOBA; TAP
At home the hearth lies in sorrow such as this. The God of War. Aeschylus. *Fr.* Agamemnon. PPON
At home the sea is in the town. The Sea Eats the Land at Home. Kofi Awoonor. CAD
At It. R. S. Thomas. OxBC
At Ithaca. Hilda Doolittle ("H. D."). VGW
At its margin. Ode to Arnold Schoenberg. Charles Tomlinson. NePoEA-2
At its own distance. Siciliana: The Landings at Gela. G. Stanley Koehler. NePoAm-2
At Jacob's well a stranger sought. Jacob's Well. *Unknown.* OBET
At Kenneth Burke's Place. William Carlos Williams. NOBA
At Kirk Yetholm. Dave Calder. PoSH
At Knaresborough. Donald Davie. NePoEA
At Lake Geneva. Richard Eberhart. LiTA
At Last. Syd Scroggie. PoSH
At Last. Richard Henry Stoddard. HBV-1
At Last. Katrina Trask. AA
At Last. Whittier. AP; TreFS; TrPWD; WGRP
(To Paths Unknown.) TRV
At last a juggler is led out under the stars. The Initiate. W. S. Merwin. NNaP
At last her face was turned to him who knew. Seven Sad Sonnets, II. Mary Aldis. HBMV
At last I am alone. At One o'Clock in the Morning. Baudelaire, *tr. by* Arthur Symons. SyP
At last I bless the hours. Rosemarie Newcombe. POL
At last I can figure out the nature of that whisking sound. Fate in Incognito. Michael Benedikt. OBAL
At last I found the monastery. A young. Abstinence. Kenneth Rosen. AmPA
At last I have a Sabine farm. My Sabine Farm. Eugene Field. InMe
At last I have ceased repining, at last I accept my fate. The Agnostic's Creed. Walter Malone. HBV-2
At last I put off love. He Abjures Love. Thomas Hardy. OBNC
At last love has come. I would be more ashamed. Sulpicia, *tr. fr. Latin by* Aliki *and* Willis Barnstone. BoWoP
At last, my old, inveterate foe. To Melancholy. Countess of Winchilsea. WPE
At last, O thou serene retreat. To Retirement. Luís de León, *tr. by* Thomas Walsh. TrJP
At last our dull Earth listens. Earth Listens. Katharine Lee Bates. PGD
At last she calls to mind where hangs a piece. Troy Depicted. Shakespeare. *Fr.* The Rape of Lucrece. OBSC
At last the beef appears in sight. Edward Chicken. *Fr.* The Collier's Wedding. NOEC
At last the dawn throws the forest in relief. After the Agony in the Garden. Daryl Hine. PeCV
At Last the Secret Is Out. W. H. Auden. SeCePo
At last to be identified! Resurgam. Emily Dickinson. WGRP
At last Wayman gets the girl into bed. Wayman in Love. Tom Wayman. NIP; NOBC

At last we are met—but I hope with no other. The Pacific Engagement. *Unknown. Fr.* Bungiana. WhC
At Last We Killed the Roaches. Lucille Clifton. GP; NIP
At last we parley: we so strangely dumb. George Meredith. Modern Love, XLVI. OAEP
At last withdraw your cruelty. Sir Thomas Wyatt. SiPS
At last year's Jungle Olympics. The Ants at the Olympics. Richard Digance. RHPC
At last you yielded up the album, which. Lines on a Young Lady's Photograph Album. Philip Larkin. EnLoPo; HAP; HeIP; OAEL-1; WeW
At least a hundred times. For Edward Hicks. David Helwig. NOBC
At least at night, a streetlight. So Long. William Stafford. PPJ
At least, it was a life of swords. Comrades. Lionel Johnson. HBV-2
At least 100 seabirds attended my grandmother's funeral. My Grandmother's Funeral. Thomas Lux. WeW
At least—to pray—is left—is left. Emily Dickinson. AP
At Leeds. *Unknown.* FaBoCo; PV; WhC
At length a reverend sire among them came. The Ark. Milton. *Fr.* Paradise Lost, XI. EtS
At length arrived, your book I take. On Receiving a Copy of Mr. Austin Dobson's "Old World Idylls." James Russell Lowell. AP
At length, by so much importunity pressed [*or* press'd]. The Lover; a Ballad. Lady Mary Wortley Montagu. NoP; OBEC
At length, my Lord, I have the bliss. Thomas Moore. *Fr.* The Fudge Family in Paris. OBSV
At length nigh to the sea they drew. Spenser. *Fr.* The Faerie Queene, V, 2. NoP
At length old age came on her. Old Poulter's Mare. *Unknown.* PeD
At Length the Busy Day Is Done, *with music.* Francis Hopkinson. AH
At length the finished garden to the view. James Thomson. *Fr.* The Seasons: Spring. ViBoPo
At length the soft nocturnal minutes fly. The Bricklayer's Labours. Robert Tatersal. NOEC
At length the term's ending. A Letter. Sir Arthur Quiller-Couch. CenHV
At length their long kiss severed, with sweet smart. Nuptial Sleep. Dante Gabriel Rossetti. *Fr.* The House of Life. EBVV; LoBV; VLP
At Length There Dawns the Glorious Day, *with music.* Ozora S. Davis. AH
At length they came into a larger space. The Cave of Mammon. Spenser. *Fr.* The Faerie Queene, II, 7. FiP
At length 'tis done, the glorious conflict's done. On the Late Successful Expedition against Louisbourg. Francis Hopkinson. PAH
At length we have settled a pastor. Wanted, a Minister's Wife. *Unknown.* BLPA; TreFS
At length with jostling, elbowing, and the aid. Byron. *Fr.* The Vision of Judgment. OBRV; OBSV
At Liberty. Anne S. Perlman. SUW
At liberty I sit and see. The Lover in Liberty Smileth at Them in Thraldom, That Sometime Scorned His Bondage. *Unknown.* EIL
At Lincoln. Oscar Fay Adams. AA
At Lindos. May Sarton. WPE
At Little Virgil's Window. Edwin Markham. TRV
At Long Last. Lindsay Patterson. CNA
At Lord's. Francis Thompson. EBVV; LiSp
At Loschwitz above the city. The Birch-Tree at Loschwitz. Amy Levy. TrJP
At low tide like this how sheer the water is. The Bight. Elizabeth Bishop. NYBP
At lucky moments we seem on the brink. W. H. Auden. PV
At Lulworth Cove a Century Back. Thomas Hardy. ChMP
At Magnolia Cemetery. Henry Timrod. *See* Ode: "Sleep sweetly in your humble graves."
At Majority. Adrienne Rich. NePoEA-2
At Manhood End the older dead lie thick. Manhood End. Anthony Thwaite. NMP
At Marshfield. William Cleaver Wilkinson. *Fr.* Webster; an Ode. AA
At Masada. Ernest Neufeld. AMV-81
At Mass. Vachel Lindsay. VGW
At Mass. *Unknown, tr. fr. Irish by* Robin Flower. OxBI
("Ah! light lovely lady with delicate lips aglow.") BIrV
At Matyne houre in midis of the nicht. Honour with Age. Walter Kennedy. OxBS
At Max Gate. Siegfried Sassoon. NoAM
At meat, or hearing you deplore. Consumer's Report. X. J. Kennedy. FiCP
At Melville's Tomb. Hart Crane. AP; CoBMV; HAP; MoAmPo; MOS; NePA; NoAM; NoP; PoA; SeCeV; TAP; UnPo; VGW
At Mexican Springs. Laura Tohe. STE
At Mid-Ocean. Robert Bly. LLLT
At midday/ sparrows gossip on. For Years. Ralph J. Mills, Jr. AMV-80
At midday the birds doze. The Hermit Picks Berries. Maxine W. Kumin. RFM
At midday they looked up and saw their death. George Barker. Pacific Sonnets, VII. LiTM; MasP; MOS; WaP
At Midnight. Frank Dempster Sherman. AA
At midnight by the stream I roved. Lewti. Samuel Taylor Coleridge. EnRP
At midnight Death dismissed the chancellor. Lines on the Death of Bismarck. John Jay Chapman. PoEL-5
At midnight, flaking down like chromium. Closing Time. David Wagoner. NYBP
At midnight I awoke. Clams. Ishigaki Rin, *tr. by* Hiroaki Sato. PBWP
At midnight, in his guarded tent. Marco Bozzaris. Fitz-Greene Halleck. AA; BeLS; GN; HBV-2; HoPM; TreF; WBLP
At midnight in the alley. The Tom-Cat. Don Marquis. BoAnP; PoRA
At midnight, in the garden never planted. They Also Stand. . . Merrill Moore. CrMA
At midnight, in the month of June. The Sleeper. Poe. AA; AmPP; AP; LiTA; NePA; NOBA; OBVV; OxBA; PoEL-4; TAP; TrGrPo
At midnight, sudden, dim-lit isolation. The Crow-Marble Whores of Paris. James Schevill. NMP
At midnight the heart's. A. M.—P. M. Theodore H. Hirschfield. AMV-81
At midnight when cattle are sleeping. The Cowboy's Meditation. *Unknown.* CoSo
At Midnight's Hour I Raised My Head. Henry David Thoreau. PoEL-4
At Midsummer. Norman Dubie. MAYP
At mile marker 5 on Highway 89. Armstrong Spring Creek. Lloyd Davis. AMV-81
At minus tide the music. Poke-Pole Fishing. Dennis Schmitz. AmPA
At Mrs. Appleby's. Elizabeth Upham McWebb. SiSoSe; TiPo
At Monday dawn, I climbed into my skin. Diary. David Wagoner. CoAP
At moost mischief. *See* At most mischief.
At morn, at noon, at twilight dim. Hymn. Poe. ISi
At Morning an Iris. Patrick Evans. NeBP
At morning from the coldness of Mount Brandon. Aisling. Austin Clarke. AnIV
At morning we all look out. Hedge Life. James Dickey. LCAP
At most [*or* moost] mischief. My Lute and I. Sir Thomas Wyatt. MeEL; SiPS
At Mount Rushmore I looked up into one. X. J. Kennedy. *Fr.* Edgar's Story. OFD
At Mount Vernon. Thomas Curtis Clark. PAL; PGD
At My Father's Grave. "Hugh MacDiarmid." ELU; GTBS-P
At my father's wake. Desmet, Idaho, March 1969. Janet Campbell Hale. STE; VoR
At My Grandmother's. David Malouf. PoAu-2
At My Mother's Bedside. Marcia Lee Masters. WPE
At My Mother's Knee. *Unknown.* STF
At My Nativity. Shakespeare. King Henry IV, Pt. I, *fr.* III, i. NAs
At My Whisper. Lyle Donaghy. AnIV
At my windowpane a bird. That Is All I Heard. "Yehoash," *tr. by* Isidore Goldstick. TrJP
At Nebra, by the Unstrut. The Inn of Care. Samuel Waddington. OBVV
At new age fifty. A Phoenix at Fifty. Lawrence Ferlinghetti. NAs
At Newmarket. Samuel Bishop. PV
At Night. Bella Akhmadulina, *tr. fr. Russian by* Daniel Halpern *and* Albert Todd. BoWoP
At Night. Rachel Boimwall, *tr. fr. Yiddish by* Gabriel Preil *and* Howard Schwartz. VWA
At Night. Frances Cornford. MoBrPo
At Night. Richard Eberhart. Str
At Night. Margherita Guidacci, *tr. fr. Italian by* Marina La Palma. WPOW
At Night. Alice Meynell. CH; HBV-1; OBVV
(To W. M.) GoBC
At Night. George Edgar Montgomery. AA
At Night. Alan Proctor. FAZ
At night, alone, the animals came and shone. The Animals. Josephine Jacobsen. GoYe
At night and in the wind and the rain. Refugees. Chaim Grade, *tr. by* Marc Kaminsky. VWA
At night, as drough the mead I took my way. To Me. William Barnes. NBM; PoEL-4
At night Babylon is remembered. Apocalypse. Jean Lipkin. VWA
At night, by the fire. Domination of Black. Wallace Stevens. AmPP; AP; CoBMV; MoAB; MoAmPo; OxBA; TwAmPo
At night Chinamen jump. Poem. Frank O'Hara. NoAM; NOBA
At night in each other's arms. Love's Vision. Edward Carpenter. WGRP
At night in Piazza Navona, I used to lie supine. Going Back. Salvatore Quasimodo, *tr. by* Rina Ferrarelli. AMV-81
At night my shoes look at me. My Mother's Shoes. Rayzel Zychlinska, *tr. by* Marc Kaminsky. VWA
At night, sometimes, when I cannot sleep. A Chosen Light. John Montague. IPY

At night, the coffeepot stands upended in the rack. Parachute. Dwight Okita. BrSi
At night the day is constantly woken up. Work. Andrei Codrescu. EAS
At night the factories. Varick Street. Elizabeth Bishop. NYP
At night the gold and black slashed bees come. Gold and Black. Michael Ondaatje. NoP
At night the mountains look like huge. Moving Again. William Matthews. NPAW
At night the sand wears a corsage of flesh. Casino Beach. Thomas Rabbitt. MAYP
At night the ticking of the clock. The Clock. Jean Jaszi. SoPo
At night the wallpaper shakes. At Night. Margherita Guidacci, *tr. by* Marina La Palma. WPOW
At night through the city in a song. For Them All. John Hall Wheelock. HBMV
At night what things will stalk abroad. Lux in Tenebris. Katharine Tynan. OxBI; TrPWD
At night when ale is in. Of Drunkenness. George Turberville. NoP
At night when dying proceeds to sever all seams. Landscape of Screams. Nelly Sachs, *tr. by* Michael Roloff. NYBP
At night when sick folk wakeful lie. The Dead Coach. Katharine Tynan. HBV-2
At night, when the black water-hen. The Heron. John Lyle Donaghy. NeIP
At night while. Black Warrior. Norman Jordan. PoBA
At Nightfall. Charles Hanson Towne. BLPA; FaBoBe
At 9:42 on this May morning. A House of Readers. Jim Wayne Miller. GP; PPJ
At nine from behind the door. Serenade for Strings. Dorothy Livesay. NAs
At nine in the morning there passed a church. Faintheart in a Railway Train. Thomas Hardy. CTC; EnLoPo
At Nine o'Clock in the Spring. Elissa Bishop. AMV-80
At noon in the desert a panting lizard. At the Bomb Testing Site. William Stafford. CoAP; LiTM; NoP; OBWP
At noon the sun puffed up, outsize. Idyll. Francis Webb. PoAu-2
At noon they talk of evening and at evening. Cypresses. Robert Francis. LCAP
At noon, Tithonus, withered by his singing. The Wedding. Conrad Aiken. CMoP; TAP
At once, from hence, my lines and I depart. To Mr. T. W. John Donne. PP
At once with him they rose. Hell. Milton. *Fr.* Paradise Lost, II. OBS
At once with resolution held. John Trumbull. *Fr.* M'Fingal. AmPP
At one glance/ I loved you. Mihri Hatun, *tr. fr. Turkish by* Tâlat S. Halman. PBWP
At 100 Mile House the cowboys ride in rolling. The Cariboo Horses. Alfred Purdy. HeIP; NOBC
At One o'Clock in the Morning. Baudelaire, *tr. fr. French by* Arthur Symons. SyP
At one point of the journey, a memorable one. A Valentine. Hal Summers. ChMP
At one the wind rose. Night-Music. Philip Larkin. InPS
At one time. A Sometimes Love Poem. George Leong. BrSi
At Only That Moment. Alan Ross. ErPo
At Paris it was, at the Opera there. Aux Italiens. "Owen Meredith." BeLS; BLPA; BLPL; FaBoBe; HBV-1; TreFS
At parties I want to get even. The Odd Woman. Madeline DeFrees. GP
At Parting. Heine, *tr. fr. German by* Dwight Durling. NAWM-2
At Parting. Swinburne. HBV-1; ViBoPo
At Pavia, a visitation of some sorrow. Boethius' dungeon. Geoffrey Hill. Mercian Hymns, XVIII. FaBoMo
At Penshurst ("Had Sacharissa lived when mortals made"). Edmund Waller. AnAnS-2; OAEL-1
(At Penshurst Another.) SeCV-1
At Penshurt ("While in the park I sing, the listning deer"). Edmund Waller. AnAnS-2; OAEP
At Perigord near to the wall. A Perigord pres del muralh. Bertrans de Born, *tr. by* Ezra Pound. CTC
At Piccadilly Circus. Vivian de Sola Pinto. OBMV
At Polwart on the Green. Polwart on the Green. Allan Ramsay. NOEC
At Pompeii. Shelley. *Fr.* Ode to Naples. FaBoPP
At Pont-Aven, Gauguin's Last Home in France. Andrew Grossbardt. AMV-81
At Port Royal. Whittier. PAH
Song of the Negro Boatman, *sel.* GN
At Potterne, Wiltshire. *Unknown.* DBV; FaBoCo
At pre-dawn, colored like the nose of a bullet. Off Molokai. Norman Hindley. WOLT
At present I still have. Exit Lines. George Jonas. NeAC
At Prime Jesus was y-led. William of Shoreham. *Fr.* Hours of the Passion. ACP
At Quebec. Jean Blewett. CaP
At Queensferry. W. E. Henley. VLP
At Quincey's moat the squandering village ends. Almswomen. Edmund Blunden. OBMV; OxBTC
At Rest in the Blast. Marianne Moore. MoAB; MoAmPo
At Richmond the people walked along by the river. Mr. Symons at Richmond, Mr. Pope at Twickenham. Julian Symons. WaP
At Robert Fergusson's Grave, October 1962. Robert Garioch. OxBS
At Roblin Lake. Alfred Purdy. PeCV
At Rochdale. Ian Young. NeAC
At Rochecoart/ Where the hills part. Provincia Deserta. Ezra Pound. CrMA; OxBA
At Sagamore the Chief lies low. Sagamore. Corinne Roosevelt Robinson. HBMV
At St. Jerome. Frances Harrison. WHW
At Saint Patrick's Purgatory. Donnchadh Mor O'Dala, *tr. fr. Middle Irish by* Sean O'Faolain. AnIL; OnYI
At Sainte-Marguerite. Trumbull Stickney. LiTA; MoVE; NCEP; OxBA; TwAmPo
At school, during class. Graffiti in a University Restroom: "Killing People Is Easier than Writing Poetry." Jim Mitsui. BrSi
At school I sometimes read a book. My Education. James Kenneth Stephen. WhC
At Sea. James Whitcomb Riley. MOS
At Sea. Jean Toomer. BALP
At Sea. John T. Trowbridge. EtS
At sea in the dome of St. Paul's. Homage to Wren. Louis MacNeice. EyDe
At Sestos Hero dwelt, Hero the fair[e]. Hero the Fair[e]. Christopher Marlowe. *Fr.* Hero and Leander. FaBoEn; WHA
At Set of Sun. "George Eliot." *See* Count That Day Lost.
At Set of Sun. Mary Ashley Townsend. AA
At setting day and rising morn. Song. Allan Ramsay. HBV-1
At seven in the summer evenings. Plaza Reál with Palmtrees. Paul Blackburn. NoAM
At seventeen I spent cold cash. Hearthside Story. X. J. Kennedy. CoPo
At seventeen your. Maryuma. Frank Lamont Phillips. AmNP
At 79th and Park. Barbara Howes. NYP
At several times the speed of light. Gemini Jones. Willard R. Espy. FaBoUs
At Shakespeare's Grave. Irving Browne. AA
At Shelley's birth. To Shelley. John Banister Tabb. AA
At six I lived for spells. What For. Garrett Kaoru Hongo. MAYP
At six o'clock. The Sound of Morning in New Mexico. Reeve Spencer Kelley. AmFN
At six o'clock we were waiting for coffee. A Miracle for Breakfast. Elizabeth Bishop. LiTA; MiAP
At six, when April chills our hands and feet. Elektra on Third Avenue. Marilyn Hacker. MAYP; NYP
At sixteen I came West, riding. A Living Pearl. Kenneth Rexroth. LiTM
At sixteen she was a potential celebrity. Clara. Ezra Pound. DTC
At sixteen years she knew no care. Butterflies. John Davidson. HBV-1
At sixty, it might be well to start. The Collector. Desirée Flynn. BrRo
At Slim's River. John Haines. NPAW
At stated .ic times. Composed in the Composing Room. Franklin P. Adams. NIP; OBAL
At Staufen. Michael Hamburger. VWA
At steeplecock height. Quebec. Eldon Grier. PeCV
At Su K'wa K'e there used to bloom a flower. Lost Love. *Tr. fr. Tewa Indian by* H. J. Spinden. WTO
At such a time, in such a spot. Emily Brontë. VLP
At summer eve, when Heaven's ethereal bow. Thomas Campbell. *Fr.* The Pleasures of Hope. EnRP
At Summer's End. Saul Hillel Benjamin. AMV-81
At Sunset. Louis V. Ledoux. HBV-1
At sunset I have a vision of 10,000 carabaos. The New Manong. Luis Syquia. BrSi
At sunset my brown nightingales. Nightingales. Grace Hazard Conkling. HBMV
At sunset my foot outreached the mounting Pacific's. Swimming in the Pacific. Robert Penn Warren. AMV-80
At sunset only swamp. The Slough of Despond. Robert Lowell. SyP
At Swindon. Reginald Brett. PeHV
At table yonder sits the man we seek. At the Mermaid Inn. Charles Lotin Hildreth. AA
At Tara [*or* Tarah] today, in this awful hour. St. Patrick's Hymn before Tara [*or* Tarah]. James Clarence Mangan. EnRP; GoBC
At Tauba's death I swore. Lamenting Tauba. Laila Akhyaliyya, *tr. fr. Arabic by* Willis Barnstone. BoWoP
At tea in cocktail weather. Publisher's Party. Phyllis McGinley. OBAL
At ten a clock, when I the fire rake. Epigram. Francis Daniel Pastorius. SCAP

At ten A.M. the young housewife. The Young Housewife. William Carlos Williams. HeIP; NoAM; NoP; TAP
At ten I saw a black horse running. Black Horse Running. Noel Maureen Valis. AMV-80
At Thames faire port. Praise of Poets. William Browne. *Fr.* Britannia's Pastorals, II, Song 1. OBS
At That Moment. Raymond R. Patterson. CABA; PoBA
At that soft pale hour. Encounter in Jerusalem. Fay Lipshitz. VWA
At the age of nineteen I was digging the land. The Kerry Recruit. *Unknown.* FSW
At the Airport. John Malcolm Brinnin. MoAB
At the Airport in Dallas. Stephen Mooney. TAT
At the airport, ready to leave on my little trip. The Fear of Flying. Mona Van Duyn. NMM
At the Algonquin. Howard Moss. Psk
At the Altar. Robert Lowell. Between the Porch and the Altar, IV. InPK; InPS
At the Altar-Rail. Thomas Hardy. *Fr.* Satires of Circumstance. MoAB; MoBrPo
At the Appointed Hour They Came. Michael Smith. CIP
At the Aquarium. Max Eastman. FaPON; HBMV; WGRP
At the back of the houses there is the wood. The House in the Wood. Randall Jarrell. LCAP
At the Back of the North Wind, *sel.* George Macdonald.
Baby, The, *fr. ch.* 23. FaPON; HBV-1; HBVY; TreF; TRV
(Song: "Where did you come from, baby dear?") PaPo
At the bad time, nothing betrays outwardly the harsh findings. December Blues. Robert Pinsky. MAYP
At the Badr Trench. Safiya bint Musafir, *tr. fr. Arabic by* Bridget Connelly *and* Deirdre Lashgari. WPOW
At the Ball! Charles H. Webb. OBAL
At the Ball Game. Roswell Martin Field. InMe
At the Ball Game. William Carlos Williams. CMoP; LiSp; NoAM; NOBA ("Crowd at the ball game, The.") OxBA
At the Band Concert. John Malcolm Brinnin. PoA
At the barren heart of midnight. Nocturn. W. E. Henley. In Hospital, XXVII. BrPo
At the Battery Sea-Wall. Clifford James Laube. GoYe
At the beginning I noticed. A Stone Diary. Pat Lowther. NOBC
At the beginning of winter a cold spirit comes. *Tr. fr. Chinese by* Arthur Waley. BoWoP
At the Beginnings of the Andes. Barbara Ras. AMV-81
At the big trumpet, we must all put on. Rise and Shine. Richmond Lattimore. NYBP
At the black wood's corner, not one green bud. Pluviose. Julian Bell. ChMP
At the blackboard I had missed. Zimmer's Head Thudding against the Blackboard. Paul Zimmer. PCP
At the boarding house where I live. Folk Song. *Unknown.* ShM
At the Bomb Testing Site. William Stafford. CoAP; LiTM; NoP; OBWP
At the bottom of the twisted. Poem for Lorry. Gerald Hausman. CTBA
At the Bottom of the Well. Louis Untermeyer. GoJo
At the British Museum. Richard Aldington. MoBrPo
At the British War Cemetery, Bayeux. Charles Causley. OBWP; OxBC
At the Cannon's Mouth. Herman Melville. PAH
At the Cantina. Gary Soto. MAYP
At the Carnival. Anne Spencer. BANP; BlSi; CDC; NoAM; PoNe
At the Cedars. Duncan Campbell Scott. CaP; NOBC
At the center, a dark star. Apple. Nan Fry. PPJ
At the Center of Everything Which Is Dying. Patricia Goedicke. FAZ
At the ceremony of *Emobo*. Ceremony. Kattie M. Cumbo. BlSi
At the Church Gate. Thackeray. *Fr.* Pendennis. HBV-1
At the close of a winter day. The Rhyme of the Three Captains. Kipling. BeLS
At the Closed Gate of Justice. James David Corrothers. BANP
At the Comedy. Arthur Stringer. HBV-1
At the corner of Wood Street, when daylight appears. The Reverie of Poor Susan. Wordsworth. CH; EnRP; GTBS; GTBS-P; HBV-1; OxBoLi; WiR
At the court of the miracle-working Rabbi of Sadagora. Father. Rose Ausländer, *tr. by* Ewald Osers. VWA
At the Cross. *Unknown.* STF
At the cross her station keeping. Stabat Mater. *At. to* Jacopone da Todi, *tr. fr. Latin.* TreFS; WGRP
At the Crossroads. Richard Hovey. HBV-2
At the crossroads/ of my gaping dreams. Trembling. Aliza Shenhar, *tr. by* Linda Zisquit. VWA
At the cross-roads I came upon the delinquent moon. Templeogue. Blanaid Salkeld. NeIP
At the Crucifixion. *Unknown.* OxBM
At the cry of the first bird/ They began to crucify Thee, O cheek like a swan. The Crucifixion. *Unknown, tr. by* Kuno Meyer. OxBI
At the cry of the first bird/ They began to crucify Thee, O Swan! The Crucifixion. *Unknown, tr. by* Howard Mumford Jones. OnYI
At the Dark Hour. Paul Dehn. BoLoP; WaP
At the dawn I seek Thee. Morning Song. Solomon ibn Gabirol, *tr. by* Nina Davis Salaman. TrJP
At the dead centre of the boundless plain. Edwin Muir. *Fr.* Variations on a Time Theme. MoVE
At the dead end of a road twisting snakelike. Party at Bannon Brook. Alden Nowlan. NeAC
At the Dog Show. Christopher Morley. MoShBr
At the door of his hut sat Massasoit. The Peace Message. Burton Egbert Stevenson. PAH
At the door of Mercy Sighing, *with music.* Thomas Mackellar. AH
At the Doors. Der Nistor, *tr. fr. Yiddish by* Joseph Leftwich. TrJP
At the Draper's. Thomas Hardy. *Fr.* Satires of Circumstance. MoAB; MoBrPo
At the earliest ending of winter. Not Ideas about the Thing but the Thing Itself. Wallace Stevens. HAP; LCAP; TAP; ViBoPo
At the edge of all the ages. The Song of Finis. Walter de la Mare. MoBrPo
At the edge of her sofa. Rapist. José Y. Terán Jr. LFAC
At the Edge of the Bay. Thomas Caldecot Chubb. EtS
At the Edge of the Day. Clarence Urmy. HBMV
At the Edge of the Jungle. Patrick Lane. NOBC
At the edge of the macadam parking lot. Getting By on Honesty. Stephen E. Smith. AMV-80
At the edge of this pale. Waiting Carefully. Nancy P. Kamm. AMV-80
At the edge of tide. The Sandpiper. Frances Frost. RHPC
At the Edge of Town. William Stafford. NNaP
At the end of a freight train rolling away. Late Lights in Minnesota. Ted Kooser. TAT
At the end of a full day of walking we found. Passion. Galway Kinnell. NePoAm
At the end of a long-walled garden. The Cottage Hospital. John Betjeman. GTBS-P; MoBrPo; MoVE; NOBE; UnPo
At the end of everything, I walk Milwaukee. Walking Milwaukee. Harold Witt. HoAn; TAT
At the end of life paralysis or those creeping teeth. Bog and Candle. Robert D. Fitzgerald. CBAP
At the end of my yard there is a vat. Riddle. *Unknown.* ChTr
At the end of October. The Snake. Wendell Berry. GeTw
At the end of our streets is sunrise. The City by the Sea. George Sterling. BPAW
At the End of Spring. Yü Hsüan-chi, *tr. fr. Chinese by* Geoffrey Waters. BoWoP
At the end of summer. Forty Pounds of Blackberries Equals Thirteen Gallons of Wine. Robert D. Hoeft. AMV-80
At the end of Tarriers' Lane, which was the street. Wm. Brazier. Robert Graves. NOBL
At the End of the Affair. Maxine W. Kumin. TAP
At the end of the bough! Sweet Apple. James Stephens. CMoP
At the End of the Day. Richard Hovey. HBVY
At the end of the day. Nothing Strange. Tom Kryss. NeAC
At the end of the garden. Pumpkins. John Cotton. BoNaP
At the end of the garden walk. The Cold Green Element. Irving Layton. NOBC; NoP; OBCV
At the end of the third act, poetry gutters down. After Shakespeare. Alex Comfort. ErPo
At the end of the war I arose. The Driver. James Dickey. VGW
At the End of Things. Arthur Edward Waite. WGRP
"Cast away fear," *sel.* TRV
At the Entrance. Douglas Stewart. CBAP
At the equinox when the earth was veiled in a late rain. Continent's End. Robinson Jeffers. AWP; FaBV; ImOP; TwAmPo
At the far end of a trip north. Nooksack Valley. Gary Snyder. NaP
At the feast of Belshazzar and a thousand of his lords. The Handwriting on the Wall. Knowles Shaw. BLPA
At the feeder, suddenly strange birds. Everything. James Paul. HoAn
At the field's edge. The White Hare. Lilian Bowes-Lyon. OxBTC; PoPle
At the Fillmore. Philip Levine. NNaP
At the first hour from dawn. Journey through the Night. John Holloway. NePoEA
At the first peep of dawn she roused me! The Wanderer: Paterson—the Strike. TwAmPo
At the first sound the Golden sun arises from the deep. Enitharmon Revives with Los. Blake. *Fr.* Vala; or, The Four Zoas. OBNC
At the first stepping-stone, the past of water. The Stepping Stones. Conrad Aiken. CrMA
At the first strokes of the fiddle bow. The Wheel. Wendell Berry. GeTw
At the first turning of the second stair. Ash Wednesday, III. T. S. Eliot. NoAM; NOBA
At the Firth of Lorne. Iain Crichton Smith. BSV

At the Fishhouses. Elizabeth Bishop. CoAP; HAP; LCAP; LiTM; MoVE; NoP; NYBP; PoRA
At the focus of thought there is no face. The Crystal Skull. Kathleen Raine. NeBP
At the foot of a great pine, in the wild country. Reconciliation. John Hall Wheelock. CrMA
At the foot of Meetinghouse Hill. Bricking the Church. Robert Morgan. MAYP
At the foot of the Cathedral of Burgos. Autobiography. Gloria Fuertes, *tr. by* Philip Levine. PBWP
At the foot of the stairs. Hope. William Dickey. GDP; POL
At the foot of yon mountain, where the fountain doth flow. Red River Shore. *Unknown.* CoSo
At the foot of yonder mountain where the fountains do flow. The Green Briar Shore. *Unknown.* AmFP
At the ford, while grass-green frogs. Charming the Moon. James DenBoer. MAT
At the Fountain. Marcabrun, *tr. fr. French by* Harriet Waters Preston. AWP
At the Front. John Erskine. HBMV
At the frontier the long train slows to a stop. The Frontier. John Hewitt. BIrV
At the Funeral of Great-Aunt Mary. Robert Bly. Str
At the Garden Gate. David McCord. FaPON
At the Gate. Chaucer. *Fr.* Troilus and Criseyde. SeCePo
At the Gate of Heaven. Byron. *See* Vision of Judgment, The.
At the gate of old Granada, when all its bolts are barred. The Lamentation for Celin. *Unknown, tr. by* John Gibson Lockhart. AWP
At the gate of the West I stand. Scum o' the Earth. Robert Haven Schauffler. HBV-2
At the gathered ends of rooty paths. The Island in the Evening. Fairfield Porter. PoA
At the Golden Ball and Lillie's Head. To Saffold's Customers. *At. to* John Case. FaBoUs
At the Grave of a Land-Shark. Ernest G. Moll. DBV; WhC
At the Grave of Burns. Wordsworth. EnRP
At the Grave of Champernowne. John Albee. HBV-2
At the Grave of Henry James. W. H. Auden. LiTA; MoPo; NoP
At the Grave of Henry Vaughan. Siegfried Sassoon. ChMP; CMoP; EaLo; GTBS-P; PoPle
At the Grave of My Brother. William Stafford. Str
At the Grave of Walker. Joaquin Miller. AA
At the Great Wall of China. Edmund Blunden. GTBS-P
At the grey dawn, amongst the falling leaves. A Bird from the West. Dora Sigerson Shorter. OBVV
At the Hacienda. Bret Harte. AA
At the heart of the cyclone tearing the sky. The Place of Peace. Edwin Markham. TreFT; TRV
At the Heich Kirk-Yaird, *sel.* Alastair MacKie.
Passin Ben Dorain. PoSH
At the Holi festival of color. Mira Bai, *tr. fr. Hindi by* Willis Barnstone *and* Usha Nilsson. BoWoP
At the Indian Killer's Grave. Robert Lowell. NOBA; VGW
At the inn there was no room. The Loan of a Stall. James L. Duff. ISi
At the instant. Any April. Cathy Beard. AMV-81
At the instant of drowning he invoked the three sisters. The Three Fates. Rosemary Dobson. BoWoP
At the Jewish Cemetery in Prague. Oscar Levertin, *tr. fr. Swedish by* Richard Burns *and* Göran Printz-Pahlson. VWA
At the Jewish Museum. Olga Cabral. PoDr
At the Jewish Museum. Linda Pastan. VWA
At the jungle's edge, torn open. Lan Nguyen; the Uniform of Death, 1971. David Mura. BrSi
At the Keyhole. Walter de la Mare. DTC; MoAB; MoBrPo
At the king's gate the subtle noon. Coronation. Helen Hunt Jackson. AA; BeLS; GN; HBV-2
At the kiss of my heel. The Gentled Beast. Dilys Laing. PH
At the large foot of a fair hollow tree. The Country-Mouse. Abraham Cowley, *after* Horace. OBVE; SeCP
At the Last. Philip Bourke Marston. HBV-1
At the last, tenderly. The Last Invocation [*or* The Imprisoned Soul]. Walt Whitman. HBV-2; MoAmPo; OBEV; OxBA; PoEL-5; TreFT; TrGrPo; TrPWD; TRV; WGRP
At the Lavender Lantern. Charles Divine. HBMV
At the Lincoln Tomb. John H. Bryant. PGD
At the Long Island Jewish Geriatric Home. Jorie Graham. NPGG
At the long tables of time. The Jugs. Paul Celan, *tr. by* Christopher Middleton. OBVE
At the Loom. Robert Duncan. *Fr.* Passages. VGW
At the Lord's Table waiting, robed and stoled. An Incident. Frederick Tennyson. GoBC
At the Louvre. E. L. Mayo. FAZ
At the Manger Mary Sings. W. H. Auden. *Fr.* For the Time Being; a Christmas Oratorio. EBCP; ILwL; SBVL
At the Mermaid Inn. Charles Lotin Hildreth. AA
At the Mid Hour of Night. Thomas Moore. AnIV; FaBoEn; GoBC; HBV-1; NBM; NOBE; OAEP; OBEV; OBNC; OBRV; OxBI; PoEL-4; TreFS; ViBoPo
("At the mid hour of night, when stars are weeping, I fly.") GTBS; GTBS-P
At the midnight in the silence of the [*or* at] sleep-time. Epilogue. Robert Browning. *Fr.* Asolando. FaBoEn; FaBV; FiP; HBV-2; HBVY; NOBE; OAEP; OBNC; OBVV; OHFP; TEP; TreFT, TrGrPo; ViBoPo; VLP
At the Midsummer, when the hay was down. Four Years. Dinah Maria Mulock Craik. HBV-1
At the Millinery Shop. Daniel Mark Epstein. MAYP
At the Moated Grange. Shakespeare. *See* Take, O Take Those Lips Away.
At the Montejo Palace in Merida. A Lesson in Hammocks. James Schevill. FAZ
At the Movies. Florence Ripley Mastin. SUMH
At the muezzin's call for prayer. Ad Coelum. Harry Romaine. BLPA; FaBoBe
At the Museum. John Malcolm Brinnin. EyDe
At the Museum of Modern Art. May Swenson. NYP
At the Nadir. Gerta Kennedy. PoPl
At the National Black Assembly. Amiri Baraka. GP
At the Natural History Museum. William Meredith. NYP
At the Nature-Strip. Judith Rodriguez. CBAP
At the New Year. Kenneth Patchen. LiTM
At the next vacancy for God, if I am elected. In Place of a Curse. John Ciardi. HoAn
At the Ninth Hour. John Lancaster Spalding. *Fr.* God and the Soul. AA
At the Nursing Home. John Cain. FAZ
At the Ocean's Verge. Ralph Gustafson. OBCV
At the officers' table, for half an hour afterwards, port. Class Incident from Graves. Alan Brownjohn. OxBTC
At the old concert hall on the Bowery [*or* Bow'ry]. She Is More to Be Pitied than Censured. William B. Gray. BeLS; BLPA; FSN; FSW; TreF
At the Party. Patricia Goedicke. FAZ
At the Party. Freda Laughton. NeIP
At the periphery and fringe. Wedding. Dorothy Livesay. PeCV
At the Piano. Swinburne. *See* John Jones.
At the Place of the Roman Baths. "Richard Scrace." CaP
At the Place of the Sea. Annie Johnson Flint. BLPA; STF
(Red Sea Place in Your Life, The.) BLRP
At the Playground. William Stafford. LCAP
At the Poem Society a black-haired man stands up to say. Fresh Air. Kenneth Koch. CAPP; NeAP; NNaP; NoAM; PP
At the point of shining feathers. The Night a Sailor Came to Me in a Dream. Diane Wakoski. TAP; VGW
At the Portal. Frances Ridley Havergal. BLRP
At the post office he sees Joe McInnes. Quiet Desperation. Louis Simpson. SV
At the President's Grave. Richard Watson Gilder. PAH
At the river's edge I study my form and face. Reflections. Merle Molofsky. AMV-81
At the road's end glimmer the station lights. Fetching the Wounded. Laurence Binyon. MMA
At the Roadside. John Knoepfle. FAZ
At the Roman Baths, Bath. Edward Lucie-Smith. NePoEA-2
At the round earth's imagined [*or* imagin'd] corners, blow. Holy Sonnets, VII. John Donne. AnAnS-1; BLPL; CABA; ChTr; EaLo; EBCP; EBEV; EnRePo; FaBoEn; FaBoRV; HAP; HeIP; InPS; JCP; LiTB; LoBV; MasP; MeLP; MePo; NOBE; NoP; OAEL-1; OAEP; OBS; OxBoCh; PAI; PoEL-2; PoPle; PPoe; PPP; QFR; SeCeV; SeCP; SeCV-1; TEP; TreFT; ViBoPo
At the Salon. Florence Wilkinson Evans. HBV-2
At the Salvation Army. Simon J. Ortiz. *Fr.* From Sand Creek. STE
At the San Francisco Airport. Yvor Winters. HeIP; InPK; NIP; NOBA; QFR
At the Scenic Drive-in. David McAleavey. SUW
At the screen door. Mrs. Green. David Huddle. PPJ
At the Sea's Edge. Gwen Harwood. CBAP
At the Seaside. Robert Louis Stevenson. FaPON; NTCP; OxBChV; SUS; TiPo
At the segregated party. Evening in the Suburbs. Stella Barnett. PV
At the Shelter-Stone. Brenda G. Macrow. PoSH
At the Ship. R. P. Lister. FiBHP
At the Shrine. Richard Kendall Munkittrick. AA
At the side of the little black crosses. Funeral Notices. Alfonsina Storni, *tr. by* Dorothy Scott Loos. AMV-81
At the siege of Belle Isle. Mother Goose. OxNR
At the Sign-Painter's. Jared Carter. FYAP

At the Slackening of the Tide. James Wright. CABA; MOS; UnPo; VGW
At the Smithsonian. Vanessa Haley. AMV-81
At the song's beginning. Violet. John Hollander. FYAP
At the Spa. James H. Bowden. AMV-81
At the summit of perception. Prince Henry the Navigator. Sydney Clouts. PeSA
At the Symphony. Robert Nathan. HBMV
At the Tavern. *Unknown.* OxBM
At the Telephone Club. Henri Coulette. CoAP
At the Theater. Rachel Field. FaPON
At the Theater. A. P. Herbert. FiBHP
At the third hour always. Rain. Paul Murray. BIrV
At the time it seemed unimportant: he was lying. The Day. Roy Fuller. OxBTC
At the time of Matines, Lord, thu were itake. The Hours of the Passion. *Unknown.* MeEL
At the time of puberty I had obsessions. Ralph Chubb. *Fr.* The Sun Spirit. PeHV
At the time of the white dawn. Song of the Fallen Deer. *Tr. fr. Pima Indian by* Frank Russell. OBVE
At the time there were those who said with a wink. The Father. Desmond O'Grady. NoAM
At the time when blossoms. *Tr. fr. Chinese by* Arthur Waley. *Fr.* Tzu Yeh Songs. BoWoP
At the time when the earth became hot. Birth of Sea and Land Life. Keaulumoku, *tr. by* M. W. Beckwith. *Fr.* The Kumulipo; a Creation Chant. WTO
At the Tomb of Rachel. "Yehoash," *tr. fr. Yiddish by* Isidore Goldstick. TrJP
At the Tomb of Washington. Clinton Scollard. OHIP
At the Tombs of the House of Savoy. William Jay Smith. NePoAm-2
At the top of a low hill. Hampstead; the Horse Chestnut Trees. Thom Gunn. NoP
At the top of my street the attorneys abound. Conversation in Craven Street, Strand. James Smith *and* Sir George Rose. FaBoCo
At the top of the house the apples are laid in rows. Moonlit Apples. John Drinkwater. BoNaP; OBMV; OxBTC; PoRA
At the Top of the Road. Charles Buxton Going. HBV-2
At the top of the stairs. Beatrix Is Three. Adrian Mitchell. NAs
At the top of the world, where fields of snow. Mrs. Santa Claus' Christmas Present. Alice S. Morris. PoSC
At the Tourist Center in Boston. Margaret Atwood. NoP
At the track the horses run. The Track. Nicholas Christopher. MAYP
At the Trough. Arthur Gregor. FAZ
At the Un-National Monument along the Canadian Border. William Stafford. HAP; HeIP
At the Vent Haven Museum in Fort Mitchell. "And Now Farley Is Going to Sing *While I Drink a Glass of Water!*" Albert Goldbarth. GeTw
At the village emporium in Woodstock. Limerick. Frederick Winsor. WhC
At the Washing of My Son. David Ray. DiL
At the Water Zoo. E.V. Knox. BoAnP
At the Well. Malka Heifetz Tussman, *tr. fr. Yiddish by* Marcia Falk. VWA
At the Western Shore. Sarah Youngblood. IHMS
At the Western Wall. Barbara F. Lefcowitz. VWA
At the White Mass. Lilies. Padraic Colum. NePoAm
At the window holding. Saint. Stéphane Mallarmé, *tr. by* Roger Fry. NAWM-2; SyP
At the windows, you look out. Synthesizing Several Abstruse Concepts with an Experience. Carol Poster. BXAP
At the Woodpile. Raymond Henri. SaC
At the Worst. Israel Zangwill. WGRP
"Evil is here? That's work for us to do," *sel.* TRV
At the worst place in the hills above the city. The Birthday Dream. James Dickey. NAs
At the "Ye That Do Truly." Charles Williams. NOCV; OxBoCh
At the Zoo. Walter de la Mare. BoAnP
At the Zoo. A. A. Milne. FaPON; TiPo
At the Zoo. Thackeray. NTCP; OxBChV
At the Zoo. Israel Zangwill. TrJP
At thee the Mocker sneers in cold derision. The Maid of Orleans. Schiller, *tr. by* James Clarence Mangan. AWP
At Their Place. Paul Mariah. LFAC
At Thermopylae. Simonides. *See* On the Spartan Dead at Thermopylae.
At these high words great heaven began to shake. A Prayer Brings Rain. Tasso, *tr. by* Edward Fairfax. *Fr.* Godfrey of Bulloigne. OBSC
At thieves I bark; at lovers wag my tail. *Unknown, after the Latin of* Joachim du Bellay. FaBoEE
At thirty, when the faiths give out. On When McCarthy Was a Wolf among a Nation of Queer-Queers. Alan Dugan. GP
At Thirty Years. Byron. *Fr.* Don Juan. FiP
At thirty-five, I get by. Catching-Up. David Walker. FAZ
At this Adonis smiles as in disdain. Shakespeare. *Fr.* Venus and Adonis. EBEV
At this hour the soul floats weightlessly. Poor Angels. Edward Hirsch. MAYP
At this moment hundreds of women. The Watch. Marge Piercy. GeTw
At this moment in time. They Flee from Me That Sometime Did Me Seek. Gavin Ewart. OxBC
At This Moment of Time. Delmore Schwartz. TwAmPo
At this range, it's really monumental. Grass. Alfred Corn. MAYP
At this th' impatient hero sowrly smil'd. Homer, *tr. fr. Greek by* Dryden. *Fr.* The Iliad, I. OBVE
At this the last yet second meeting. The Encounter. Lawrence Durrell. *Fr.* Eight Aspects of Melissa. NeBP
At this time I find the bed very arid. The Reason for Poetry. Nancy Morejón, *tr. by* Anita Whitney. WPOW
At Thomas Hardy's Birthplace, 1953. James Wright. ConAP
At 3 a.m. I run my tongue. Death's Head. Phyllis Gotlieb. NOBC
At three in the morning. Pointed Boots. Christopher Middleton. *Fr.* Herman Moon's Hourbook. NePoEA-2
"At thy door I'm knocking." Au Clair de la Lune. *Unknown.* FSW
At thy nativity a glorious quire. Milton. *Fr.* Paradise Regained, I. PChr
At Tide Water. Sir Charles G. D. Roberts. PeCV
At Timber Line. Frank H. Mayer. PoOW
At Times I Feel like a Quince Tree. John Robert Quinn. AMV-81
At times I resort, beyond man's discerning. Wind. *Unknown, tr. by* Charles W. Kennedy. *Fr.* Riddles (Exeter Book). AnOE
At times I thought the country itself was a cloud. England. Mary Jo Salter. AMV-80
At Timon's Villa. Pope. *Fr.* Moral Essays, Epistle IV.
("At Timon's villa let us pass a day.") OBSV
(Epistle to Richard Boyle, Earl of Burlington, An.) NOEC
(Timon's Villa.) OBEC
At Toledo. Arthur Symons. BrPo
At Torrey Pines State Park. Jerome Mazzaro. FiCP
At Tripolis. Constance Carrier. WPE
At Trumpingtoun, not [*or* nat] fer fro[m] Cantebrigge. The Mill at Trumpington. Chaucer. *Fr.* The Canterbury Tales: The Reeve's Tale. OxBM; ViBoPo
At Twelfth Night twilight now. Twelfth Night. Philip Booth. NePoEA
At twelve bell answers bell. Angelus-Time near Dublin. William Bedell Stanford. NeIP
At 12 o'clock in the afternoon. Epigram. Meleager, *tr. by* Sydney Oswald. PeHV
At twelve, the disintegration of afternoon. What We See Is What We Think. Wallace Stevens. SyP
At 12:30 sharp. Almost Everybody Is Dying Here: Only a Few Actually Make It. Daniel Berrigan. LFAC
At 21. Eugene L. Belisle. AMV-81
At twenty-one Jupe ran away. Slave Story. Hodding Carter. PoNe
At twenty she was brilliant and adored. Pathedy of Manners. Ellen Kay. SoSe
At Twilight. Peyton Van Rensselaer. AA
At twilight I went into the street. Descending Figure. Louise Glück. GeTw
At twilight time, when the lamps are lit. Father Coyote. George Sterling. BPAW
At two a.m. Truck Drivers. Terri Haag. CTBA
At two a.m. a thing, jumping out of a manhole. News Report. David Ignatow. ErPo; TwCP
At 2 a.m. the world is populated. Night Shift. Naomi Shihab Nye. GP
At two-thirty on this bright afternoon. The Longing. William Goodreau. AMV-80
At Upton-on-Severn. *Unknown.* FaBoCo
(Advertising Epitaph: From Upton-on-Severn, Gloucestershire.) FaBoUs
("Beneath this stone, in hope of Zion.") FaBoEE
At Vallauris and Vence, Picasso and Matisse. Picasso and Matisse. Robert Francis. NePoAm
At Veronica's. Robert Peterson. NeAC
At Viscount Nelson's lavish funeral. 1805. Robert Graves. ChMP; EvOK; FaBoCh; OBSV
At Vshchizh. Fyodor Tyutchev, *tr. fr. Russian by* Charles Tomlinson. OBWP
At War. Russell Atkins. AmNP
At War. Charles Madge. FaBoMo
At Wednesbury there was a cocking. The Wednesbury Cocking. *Unknown.* EnSB; FaBoBa
At whiles (yea oftentimes) I muse over. Dante, *tr. by* Dante Gabriel Rossetti. La Vita Nuova, IX. AWP
At White River. John Haines. FiCP
At Winchester was a wedding. The Winchester Wedding. Thomas D'Urfey. CavP

At Wonder Donut. Laureen Mar. BrSi
At Woodlawn I heard the dead cry. The Lost Son. Theodore Roethke. AP; CoBMV; DiL; HAP; LiTM; MiAP; MoPo; NePA; TrGrPo; TwAmPo; VGW
At Woodward's Gardens. Robert Frost. ImOP; PoA
At words poetic, I'm so pathetic. You're the Top. Cole Porter. OBAL; UnPo
At work his arms wave like a windmill. The Secretary. Peter Redgrove. OxBTC
At Year's-End. Richard Wilbur. *See* Year's End.
At your burial. In Its Place. Carol Stager. AMV-80
At your entreaty, I at last have writ. Maidenhead. "Ephelia." WPE
At your light side trees shy. Poem. William Knott. EAS
Atalanta. Ovid, *tr. fr. Latin by* Rolfe Humphries. *Fr.* Metamorphoses, X. LiSp
Atalanta in Calydon, *sels.* Swinburne.
  Before the Beginning of Years. FaFP; HBV-1; HeIP; LiTB; MasP; NoP; OAEP; WHA
    (Chorus: "Before the beginning of years.") EBVV; LoBV; OBEV; OBVV; TRV; ViBoPo
    (Man.) TrGrPo
  Chorus: "Who hath given man speech? or who hath set therein." OAEL-2; ViBoPo
  Death of Meleager, The. OBVV
  "Maiden, and mistress of the months and stars." PoEL-5
  When the Hounds of Spring [Are on Winter's Traces]. FaBoBe; HBV-1; HeIP; LiTB; MasP; NoP; PrIm; TEP; TreF; TrGrPo; WHA
    (Chorus: "When the hounds of spring are on winter's traces.") AWP; CTC; EBVV; EvOK; FaBoEn; GTBS-P; HAP; NOBE; OAEL-2; OBEV; PoPle; SeCeV; ViBoPo; WeW
    (Hounds of Spring, The.) FaBV
Atalanta in Camden-Town. "Lewis Carroll." CenHV
Atalanta's Race. William Morris. DTo
Atameros. John Beevers. EAS
Ataraxia. Bert Leston Taylor. HBMV; InMe
Atavism. Richard Lake. NCSH
Atavism. Elinor Wylie. HBMV; PoA; SBG
Athalie, *sel.* Racine, *tr. fr. French by* Charles Randolph.
  "God whose goodness filleth every clime, The." WGRP
Athanasia. Oscar Wilde. BrPo
Atheist. E. Y. Harburg. PV
Atheist's Prayer, The. Miguel de Unamuno, *tr. fr. Spanish.* ILwL
Atheist's Tragedy, The, *sels.* Cyril Tourneur.
  Epitaph on a Soldier. ElL
  "Walking next day upon the fatal shore." ViBoPo; WaaP
    Soldier's Death, A, *shorter sel.* SeCePo
Atheling Grange; or, The Apotheosis of Lotte Nussbaum. William Plomer. OBNV
Athelstan King,/ Lord among Earls. *See* Æthelstan King.
Athene's Song. Eavan Boland. CIP
Athenian Garden, An. Trumbull Stickney. NCEP
Athens. Milton. *Fr.* Paradise Regained, IV. OBS
Athens, a fragile kingdom by the foam. Triumph. John Crowe Ransom. HBMV
Athirst in spirit, through the gloom. The Prophet. Pushkin, *tr. by* Babette Deutsch *and* Avrahm Yarmolinsky. AWP; EaLo
Athlete. Don Maynard. PoAu-2
Athlete, one vacation, An. An Accommodating Lion. Tudor Jenks. OBCA
Athletes. Walker Gibson. LiSp
Athol Brose. Thomas Hood. FaBoCo
Athwart the island here, from sea to sea. Inscriptions for the Caledonian Canal. Robert Southey. NBM
Athwart the sky a lowly sigh. London. John Davidson. NOBE; OBNC
Atlantic Charter, A.D. 1620-1942. Francis Brett Young. *Fr.* The Island. AmFN; PAL
Atlantic is a stormy moat, and the Mediterranean, The. The Eye. Robinson Jeffers. AP; CoBMV; CrMA; FaBoEn; LiTA; LiTM; NOBA; OxBA; WaP
Atlantid islands, phantom-fair. Frederic William Henry Myers. *Fr.* Teneriffe. OBVV
Atlantides, The. Henry David Thoreau. *Fr.* A Week on the Concord and Merrimack Rivers. ViBoPo
Atlantis. W. H. Auden. PoPl
Atlantis. Hart Crane. *Fr.* The Bridge. LiTM; MoPo; NePA; NYP; TwAmPo
Atlantis, *sel.* Louis Dudek.
  Marine Aquarium, The. MoCV
Atlas, The, *sels.* Kenneth Slessor. PoAu-2
  Dutch Seacoast.
  King of Cuckooz, The.
  Mermaids.
  Post-Roads.
Atoll in the Mind, The. Alex Comfort. LiTB; LiTM; SeCePo
Atom from Atom. Emerson. *Fr.* Fragments on Nature and Life. ImOP
Atomic Courtesy. Ethel Jacobson. FaFP; QQQ; ShM
Atomic holocaust! Fall out! Consequences of conflagration. Of How Scientists Are Often Ahead of Others in Thinking, While the Average Man Lags Behind; and How the Economist (Who Can Only Follow in the Footsteps of the Average Man Looking for Clues to the Future), Remains Thoroughly out of It. Michael Benedikt. SUW
Atonement, The. Milton. *Fr.* Paradise Lost, III. OBS
Atop a tower I pitched a silken thing. Parachuting Thoor Ballylee. William Zaranka. BXAP
Atop its mound frosted white. "Among the Savages. . ." Ralph Salisbury. STE
Atrocious Pun, An. *Unknown.* RHPC; TDH
Atrocity, The/ Of the great elephant. The Elephant. Sandra Hochman. BoAnP
Attack, The. Thomas Buchanan Read. PAH
Attack. Siegfried Sassoon. MoBrPo; NOBE; OxBTC
Attack me, Father, now. Prayer for Peace. Johnstone G. Patrick. TrPWD
Attack of the Crab Monsters. Lawrence Raab. AmPA; NoP
Attainment. Madison Cawein. WGRP
Attainment, The. Coventry Patmore. *Fr.* The Angel in the House, I, iii. FaBoEE; GoBC; OBVV
Attainment. Ella Wheeler Wilcox. WGRP
Attempt at Jealousy, An. Marina Tsvetaeva, *tr. fr. Russian by* Robert Perelman *and* Aleksandar Petrov. WPOW
Attend, all ye who list to hear our noble England's praise. The Armada. Macaulay. BeLS; FaBoCh; FaPoR; GN; HBV-2; OBRV; WBLP
Attend church? Of course we do. Attending Church. *Unknown.* STF
Attend my fable if your ears be clean. Roy Campbell. *Fr.* The Wayzgoose. OBSV
Attend my lays, ye ever honour'd nine. An Hymn to the Morning. Phillis Wheatley. TAP
Attend my words, my gentle knave. Stans Puer ad Mensam. Sir Walter Alexander Raleigh. WhC
Attend, ye mournful Parents, while. Another to Urania. Benjamin Colman. SCAP
Attend, ye nymphs, by wedlock unconfin'd. Ovid, *tr. by* Congreve. *Fr.* The Art of Love. FaBoUs
Attend, Young Friends, While I Relate. *Unknown.* AmFP
Attending Church. *Unknown.* STF
Attending to some inexpressible wish. Nude with Green Chair. Antony Oldknow. AMV-81
Attention. Adrienne Rich. TAP
Attention, architect! Message from a Mouse, Ascending in a Rocket. Patricia Hubbell. RHPC
Attentive eyes, fantastic heed. A Poet. Thomas Hardy. NoAM
Attentively he heard us, while we spoke. Virgil, *tr. by* Dryden. *Fr.* The Aeneid, XI. OBVE
Attic, The. Charles Bruce. *Fr.* The Flowing Summer. CaP
Attic, The. Henri Coulette. NePoEA-2; PoPl; PoRA
Attic, The ("The attic and the cedar closet—nostalgia!"). Richard Eberhart. *Fr.* Burr Oaks. MoAB
Attic Landscape, The. Herman Melville. NOBA; OBAL
Attic maid! with honey fed. To the Swallow. William Cowper, *after* Euenus. OBVE
Attica Is. Stewart Brisby. LFAC; SOTS
Atticus. Pope. *Fr.* Epistle to Dr. Arbuthnot. AWP; InPK; NOBE; OBEC; SeCePo; TW; WHA
  ("Peace to all such! but were there one whose fires.") ViBoPo
Attila's spirit rides again the red roads of the East. Ave, Vita Nostra! Clifford James Laube. ISi
Attired in black, spangled with flames of fire. The Spirit of Night. Thomas Rogers. ElL
Attis. Catullus, *tr. fr. Latin by* Peter Whigham. OBVE
Attorney General, An. Ambrose Bierce. DBV
Attorney was taking a turn, An. The Briefless Barrister. John Godfrey Saxe. ShM
Attraction. *Unknown.* STF
Attraction. Ella Wheeler Wilcox. PeD
Attractions of a Fashionable Irish Watering-Place, The. Francis Sylvester Mahony. FaBoPP; NBM
Atween the world o' licht. Scotland. William Soutar. OxBS
Au Clair de la Lune, *with music.* *Unknown, tr. fr. French by* "C. F. M." FSW
Au Jardin des Plantes. John Wain. NePoEA-2; OxBTC
Au Tombeau de Mon Père. Ronald McCuaig. PoAu-2
Aubade: Donna Anna to Juan, Still Asleep. Richard Howard. PoA
Aubade: "Hark! Hark! the lark at heaven's gate sings." Shakespeare. *See* Hark! Hark! the Lark.

Aubade: "Having bitten on life like a sharp apple." Louis MacNeice. NIP; ViBoPo
Aubade: "Hours before dawn we were woken by the quake." William Empson. FaBoMo; FaBoTw; LiTB; OxBTC
Aubade: "I work all day, and get half drunk at night." Philip Larkin. SoSe
Aubade: "Jane, Jane,/ Tall as a crane." Edith Sitwell. CMoP; MoAB; MoBrPo; NoAM; PoRA
Aubade: Lake Erie. Thomas Merton. NYBP
Aubade: "Lark now leaves his watery [*or* wat'ry] nest, The." Sir William Davenant. *See* Lark Now Leaves His Wat'ry Nest, The.
Aubade: "Long ago when I shouted in red letters." Ruth Lechlitner. AMV-80
Aubade: "My bed rocks me gently." Dilys Laing. NMP
Aubade: N.Y.C. Robert Wallace. HoPM
Aubade: "She wakes long before he does. A fierce shock." Mekeel McBride. MAYP
Aubade: "Stay, O sweet, and do not rise." *Unknown, at. to* John Donne. *See* Break of Day.
Aubade: The Desert. Frederick Bock. PoA
Aubade: "What dawn is it?" Karl Shapiro. GP; VGW
Aubade after the Party. Tom O'Grady. FAZ
Aubade for Hope. Robert Penn Warren. MoAmPo
Aube Provençale. Marilyn Hacker. AmPA
Aubrey Bodine's crosswater shot of Menchville. The Perspective and Limits of Snapshots. Dave Smith. MAYP
Auburn. Goldsmith. *Fr.* The Deserted Village. OBEC; SeCePo
(Sweet Auburn.) LiTB; NOBE
("Sweet Auburn! loveliest village of the plain.") TreFS; ViBoPo
(Village, The.) TrGrPo
Auburn. Paul Verlaine, *tr. fr. French by* Lawrence M. Bensky. ErPo
Aucassin and Nicolete. Francis William Bourdillon. HBV-1
Aucassin and Nicolette. *Unknown, tr. fr. French by* Edward Francis Moyer *and* Carey DeWitt Eldridge. NAWM-1
Who Would List, *sel. tr. by* Andrew Lang. CTC
"Auchanachie Gordon is bonny and braw." Lord Saltoun and Auchanachie. *Unknown.* BaBo; ESPB
Auction. William Heyen. MAYP
Auction Sale, The. Henry Reed. MoBrPo
Auctioneer. Carl Sandburg. PDV
Auctioneer of parting, The. Emily Dickinson. AP; PoEL-5
Auctioneer's Handbill, An. William Hall. FaBoUs
Auden ("Auden is dead, and leaves"). Raymond Roseliep. SOTS
Auden, MacNeice, Day Lewis, I have read them all. British Leftish Poetry, 1930-40. "Hugh MacDiarmid." CMoP; FaBoTw; NMP; NoAM
Audiences. Robert Hollander. GLGT
Auditors In. Patrick Kavanagh. OxBI
Auditory Hallucinations. Joyce Mansour, *tr. fr. French by* Carol Cosman. PBWP
Audubon, Drafted. Amiri Baraka. PPP; TTY
Auf dem Wasser zu Singen. Stephen Spender. EnLoPo
Auf meiner Herzliebsten Äugelein. Heine, *tr. fr. German by* Richard Garnett. AWP
Auf Wiedersehen. Donald Jeffrey Hayes. CDC
Auf Wiedersehen. James Russell Lowell. AA; HBV-1
Augsburg Adoration, The. Randall Jarrell. NYBP
Auguries for Three Women. Jacquelyne Crews. AMV-81
Auguries of Innocence. Blake. BiP; BLPL; CABA; EBEV; EnRP; FaBoCh; FaBoEn; FaBV; FaFP; FaPoR; FM; LAuP; LiTB; LoBV; MasP; OAEL-1; OAEP; OBNC; OBRV; OxBoLi; PoEL-4; RHPC; SeCeV; TrGrPo; WHA
Sels.
"God appears, and God is Light." TRV
Robin Redbreast in a Cage, A. SiSoSe; TreFT
(Three Things to Remember.) MoShBr
To See a World in a Grain of Sand. ImOP; InPK; PPoe; TreFS; TRV; ViBoPo; WGRP
August. Laurence Binyon. SyP
August. Folgore da San Gemignano, *tr. fr. Italian by* Dante Gabriel Rossetti. *Fr.* Sonnets of the Months. CTC
August. Robert Frost. BXAP
August. Francis Ledwidge. OxBI
August. Louis MacNeice. FaBoEn; LiTM; PoPle
August. Katherine Pyle. OBCA
August. Adrienne Rich. NNaP; PBWP
August. Roy Scheele. PPJ
August ("The sixth was August"). Spenser. *Fr.* The Faerie Queene, VII, 7. GN
August ("Tell me, Perigot"). Spenser. *Fr.* The Shepheardes Calender. OAEP
August. Swinburne. WiR
August. Celia Thaxter. FaPON; YeAr
August. John Updike. *Fr.* A Child's Calendar. OBCA; RHPC
August. Helen Maria Winslow. YeAr
August. Elinor Wylie. MoAB; MoAmPo
August/ Fresno 1973. Roberta Spear. AmPA
August Afternoon. Marion Edey. YeAr
August Afternoon. Nancy Remaly. CTBA
August and on the vine eight melons sleeping. Eight Melons. Malcolm Cowley. TwAmPo
August and the drive-in picture is packed. Dear John Wayne. Louise Erdrich. TWSS
August, another year and the same. To an Estranged Wife. Gary Young. AMV-81
August, at an Upstairs Window. Harold McCurdy. AMV-80
August at the Lake. David Young. AmPA
August 18. Joanne Kyger. PoM
August Evenings in Hatteras. Gabriele Glang. WOLT
August for the People. W. H. Auden. WaP
(Birthday Poem) NAs
August for the people and their favourite islands. Birthday Poem. W. H. Auden. NAs
August from My Desk. Roland Flint. AmFN
August. Hear/ the cicadas. Speaking for Them. Hayden Carruth. GP
August heat. Haiku. Gerald Vizenor. VoR
August is a lazy girl. August Smiles. Elizabeth J. Coatsworth. SiSoSe
August is nearly over, the people. Louis MacNeice. *Fr.* Autumn Journal. CMoP
August Midnight, An. Thomas Hardy. BrPo
August Night. Elizabeth Madox Roberts. YeAr
August Night. Sara Teasdale. MoAmPo
August Night, 1953. Elizabeth B. Harrod. NePoEA
August night thick and black on us, The. Pelvic Meditation. Bruce Smith. AMV-80
August, 1914. John Masefield. HBV-2
August 1914. Isaac Rosenberg. EBEV; NOBE; OBWP; OxBTC
August on Sourdough, a Visit from Dick Brewer. Gary Snyder. SOTW
August Rain. Robert Bly. LCAP; SV
August, revered,/ Our nation's sire. His Task—and Ours. Dorothy Gould. PGD
August 2. Norman Jordan. PoBA
August Second Syndrome Poem, The. J. A. Hines. LFAC
August 6, 1945. City of Hiroshima. The Day after Trinity. Richard Oyama. BrSi
August Smiles. Elizabeth J. Coatsworth. SiSoSe
August 13, 1966. Daryl Hine. GP
August 'twas, the twenty-fifth. Bar's Fight, August 28, 1746. Lucy Terry. BlSi; BPo; PoNe
August 12, 1952. Charles Fishman. AMV-81
August Was Foggy. Gary Snyder. NNaP
August wind rides Spain tonight in a fierce saddle, The. Casa de Pollos. Kathleen Fraser. AmPA
Augustus was a chubby lad. The Story of Augustus Who Would Not Have Any Soup. Heinrich Hoffmann, *tr. fr. German.* FaBoUs; GoJo; HBV-1; HBVY; MoShBr; OxBChV; RHPC; ShM; SpRo; TiPo
Auld Daddy Darkness. James Ferguson. HBV-1; HBVY; OxBChV
Auld Deil cam to the man at the pleugh, The. The Farmer's Curst Wife. *Unknown.* ESPB
Auld Hammus knapped his whunstane chips. A Border Forecast. William Landles. PoSH
Auld House, The. Lady Nairne. HBV-2
Auld House, The. William Soutar. OxBS
Auld Lang Syne. Burns. AWP; BiP; BLPL; BLSo, *with music;* BSV; EnRP; FaFP; FSW; GoTS; HBV-1; LAuP; LiTB; NOBE; OAEP; OBEC; OBEV; OxBS; PoLF; TEP; TreF
Auld Lang Syne. John White Chadwick. *See* Abiding Love, The.
Auld Man's Mear's Dead, The. Patrick Birnie. GoTS
Auld Matrons. *Unknown.* BaBo; ESPB
Auld mune on her back, The. Leander Stormbound. Sydney Goodsir Smith. OxBS
Auld Noah was at hame wi' them a'. Parley of Beasts. "Hugh MacDiarmid." BoAnP; MoBrPo; NoAM; NoP; OBMV
Auld Robin Gray. Lady Anne Lindsay. BeLS; BSV; CH; GoTS; GTBS; GTBS-P; HBV-1; NOEC; OBEC; OBEV; ViBoPo; WPE
Auld Sanct-Aundrians—Brand the Builder. Tom Scott. BSV
Auld Sang. William Soutar. OxBS
Auld Seceder Cat, The. *Unknown. See* There Was a Presbyterian Cat.
Auld wife sat at her ivied door, The. Ballad. Charles Stuart Calverley. BXAP; CenHV; FaBoCo; FaBoNo; FiBHP; HBV-1; InMe; NA; Par; SpRo; VLP; WhC; WiR
Auld wumman cam' in, a mere rickle o' banes, An. Old Wife in High Spirits. "Hugh MacDiarmid." CMoP; NMP; OxBTC
Auncient Acquaintance, Madam, The. John Skelton. PoEL-1
("Auncient acquaintance, madam, betwen us twayn, The.") AAS
Aunt, The. Daniel Berrigan. TwAmPo

Aunt Alice in April. William H. Matchett. CTBA
Aunt Beulah's Wisdom. Earl Gene Box. LFAC
Aunt Cora. Kenneth Pitchford. CoPo
Aunt Eliza. Harry Graham. ChTr; DBV; FaFP; NA; WhC
Aunt Eliza. *Unknown.* ShM
Aunt Elsie's Night Music ("Aunt Elsie hears"). Mary Oliver. Str
Aunt Gladys's Home Movie No. 31, Albert's Funeral. Jim Wayne Miller. Str
Aunt Helen. T. S. Eliot. OBAL; PoA
Aunt Jane. Alden Nowlan. SoSe
Aunt Jane Allen. Fenton Johnson. IDB; PoBA; PoNe
Aunt Jane, of whom I dreamed the nights it thundered. Aunt Jane. Alden Nowlan. SoSe
Aunt Jemima of the Ocean Waves. Robert Hayden. LCAP; PoBA
Aunt Jennifer's Tigers. Adrienne Rich. HeIP; NIP; NoP
Aunt Laura Moves toward the Open Grave of Her Father. Joseph de Roche. HeIP
Aunt Liza/ Yes? Me, Colored. Peter Abrahams. *Fr.* Tell Freedom. PBA
Aunt Mary. Robert Stephen Hawker. OHIP
Aunt Maud. Harry Graham. *See* Waste.
Aunt Melissa. R. T. Smith. Str
Aunt Nerissa's Muffin. Wallace Irwin. FiBHP
Aunt Rhody. *Unknown. See* Old Gray Goose, The.
Aunt Rose—now—might I see you. To Aunt Rose. Allen Ginsberg. CABA; LiTM; NoP; PAI; VGW
Aunt Selina. Carol Haynes. HBMV; HBVY
Aunt Sponge and Aunt Spiker. Roald Dahl. RHPC
Aunt Sue's Stories. Langston Hughes. DuDa
Aunt Tabitha. Oliver Wendell Holmes. CenHV
Aunt was on the garden seat. The Fox Rhyme. Ian Serraillier. ELU
Aunt Zillah Speaks. Herbert Palmer. FaBoTw
Auntie Bridge and Uncle Pat. Geoffrey Lehmann. *Fr.* Ross's Poems. CBAP
Auntie, did you feel no pain. Appreciation [*or* Some Ruthless Rhymes, III]. Harry Graham. CenHV; PoPle
Aura amara, L'. Arnaut Daniel, *tr. fr. Provençal by* Ezra Pound. CTC
Aura Lea [*or* Lee], *with music.* W. W. Fosdick. BLSo; PSoN
Auras of Delight. Coventry Patmore. The Unknown Eros, II, xi. ACP; LoBV; OBVV
Auras on the Interstates. Gerald Vizenor. STE
Aurelia. Robert Nichols. OBMV
Aureng-Zebe, *sels.* Dryden.
  Prologue: "Our Author by experience finds it true." FiP; OBS; OxBoLi; PP; SeCeV; SeCV-2
  When I Consider Life, *fr.* IV, i. FiP
Aurora. Emily Dickinson. *See* Of bronze and blaze.
Aurora, *sels.* Earl of Stirling.
  Madrigal: "When in her face mine eyes I fix." ElL
  "O happy Tithon! if thou know'st thy harp." OBEV
  Sonnet: "Cleare moving cristall, pure as the Sunne beames," XXV. OxBS
  Sonnet: "I envy not Endymion now no more." ElL
  Sonnet: "Ile give thee leave my love, in beauties field," XXVI. OxBS
  Sonnet: "Let others of the world's decaying tell." ElL
  Sonnet: "Oh, if thou knew'st how thou thyself dost harm." ElL
  (To Aurora.) FaFP; GTBS; GTBS-P
  Sonnet: "Then whilst that Latmos did contain her bliss." ViBoPo
Aurora Borealis. Edouard Roditi. EAS
Aurora, lady grey. A Simple Pastoral. George Alexander Stevens. NOEC
Aurora Leigh, *sels.* Elizabeth Barrett Browning.
  "And I, I was a good child on the whole." BrRo
  "Books, books, books!" WPOW
  "Critics say that epics have died out, The." PBWP
  "Earth crammed with heaven." TRV
  Florence. FaBoPP
  "I had a little chamber in the house." FaBoPP
  "I learnt the collects and the catechism." TEP
  Olives and Mountains. FaBoPP
  Reading. GN
  "So it was./ I broke the copious curls upon my head." GLGT
  "Then, land!—then England! oh, the frosty cliffs." FaBoPP
  " 'There it is!/ You play beside a death-bed like a child.' " BrRo
  "Truth, so far, in book; the truth which draws." WGRP
  Tuscan Life. FaBoPP
Auroras of Autumn, The, *sels.* Wallace Stevens. CMoP
  "Farewell to an idea . . . A cabin stands."
  "This is where the serpent lives, the bodiless."
  "Unhappy people in a happy world, An."
Auschwitz from Colombo. Anne Ranasinghe. VWA
Auspex. James Russell Lowell. AP; HBV-1; NePA; OBVV; PoEL-5; TAP
Auspice of Jewels. Laura Riding. LiTA; NoAM
Auspicious night. Courtesan with Fan. Elizabeth Spires. MAYP
Austere the Music of My Songs. Fyodor Sologub, *tr. fr. Russian by* Babette Deutsch *and* Avrahm Yarmolinsky. AWP
Austerity of Poetry. Matthew Arnold. OAEP; OBVV
  (Jacopone da Todi.) GoBC
Australasia, *sel.* William Charles Wentworth.
  "Land of my birth! though now, alas! no more." PoAu-1
Australia. A. D. Hope. NoP
Australia. Michael Jackson. OCNZ
Australia. Bernard O'Dowd. PoAu-1
Australia 1970. Judith Wright. CBAP
Australian, The. Arthur H. Adams. PoAu-1
Australian Dream, The. David Campbell. CBAP
Australian Transcripts, *sels.* "Fiona Macleod." FM
  Bell-Bird, The.
  Mid-Noon in January.
  Wood-Swallows, The.
Australia's on the Wallaby. *Unknown.* PoAu-1
Austrian Army, An. *Unknown, at. to* Alaric A. Watts. FaBoCo; FiBHP; NOBL
  (Alliteration, or the Siege of Belgrade.) ChTr
  (Siege of Belgrade, The.) BLPA; HBV-2; TreF
Aut Neutrum . . . Vel Duos. Rufinus Domesticus, *tr. fr. Latin by* Dudley Fitts. OLR
Autant en Emporte le Vent. Marguerite de Navarre, *tr. fr. French by* Aline Allard. PBWP
Autet e bas. Arnaut Daniel, *tr. fr. Provençal by* Ezra Pound. CTC
Authentic, The! Shadows of it. Matins. Denise Levertov. AmPP; CoPo; IHMS; NoAM; NOBA
Author, The, *sels.* Charles Churchill.
  "Gods! with what pride I see the titled slave." OBSV
  Pains of Education, The. FaBoCo
  (Against Education.) TW
  "When with much pains this boasted learning's got." OBSV
Author Apologizes to a Lady for His Being a Little Man, The. Christopher Smart. BoLoP
Author Consults a Critic and Sells His Manuscript, The. Francis Hawling. *Fr.* The Signal; or, A Satire against Modesty. NOEC
Author Loving These Homely Meats, Specially, viz.: Cream, Pancakes, Buttered Pippin-Pies, The. *Fr.* The Scourge of Folly. John Davies of Hereford. ElL; FaBoNo
  (Buttered Pippin-Pies.) ChTr
  (Homely Meats.) FaBoCh
Author of *Christine,* The. Richard Howard. CoAP
Author, of His Own Fortune, The. Sir John Harington. FaBoEE
Author of light, revive my dying spright. Thomas Campion. AAS
Author to Her Book, The. Anne Bradstreet. AmPP; AP; InPK; NePA; NOBA; NoP; OxBA; SCAP; TAP
Author to His Body on Their Fifteenth Birthday, 29.ii.80, The. Howard Nemerov. NAs
Author to His Book, The. George Alsop. SCAP
Author to His Booke, The. Thomas Heywood. *Fr.* An Apology for Actors. OBS
Author to His Wife, of a Woman's Eloquence, The. Sir John Harington. BoLoP; ErPo
Author to the Reader, The. Randall Jarrell. OxBC
Author Unknown. William Montgomerie. OxBS
Authority. William Reed Huntington. AA
Authority is a disease, and cure. Samuel Butler. FaBoEE
Author's Abstract of Melancholy, The. Robert Burton. *Fr.* The Anatomy of Melancholy. OBS
Authors and actors and artists and such. Bohemia. Dorothy Parker. CrMA
Author's Apology, The. T. Carmi, *tr. fr. Hebrew by* Marcia Falk. VWA
Author's Early Life, The. Julia A. Moore. PeD
Author's Entreaty for His Lay. Eysteinn Asgrímsson, *tr. fr. Icelandic by* Eirik Magnusson. *Fr.* Lilya. ISi
Author's Epitaph, The. *Unknown.* FiBHP
Author's Epitaph, Made by Himselfe, The. Sir Walter Ralegh. *See* Even Such Is Time.
Author's Epitaph, An. Written by Himself. Abel Evans. FaBoEE
Authors—essayist, atheist, novelist, realist, rimester. Tennyson. *Fr.* Locksley Hall Sixty Years After. PeD
Author's favourite pipe am I, An. The Pipe. Sir John Squire. PoPl
Author's Mock-Song to Mark Anthony, The. John Cleveland. AnAnS-2
Authors of the Town, The, *sel.* Richard Savage.
  "First, let me view what noxious nonsense reigns." OBSV
Author's Reply, The. Sir Carr Scroope. APAS
Author's Resolution, The. George Wither. *See* Shall I, Wasting in Despair.
Authour's Dreame, The. Francis Quarles. *Fr.* Argalus and Parthenia. OBS
Auto Mobile. A. R. Ammons. FF; InPK; OBAL
Auto Wreck. Karl Shapiro. BiP; CMoP; FF; LiTM; MiAP; MoVE; NePA; NIP; PoPl; VGW

Autobiographia Literaria. Frank O'Hara. NNaP; NOBA
Autobiographical. A. M. Klein. MoCV
Autobiographical Fragment. Kingsley Amis. NePoEA-2
Autobiography. Sonja Akesson, *tr. fr. Swedish by* Ingrid Claréus. BoWoP
Autobiography. Charles Causley. LiTM
Autobiography. Mbella Sonne Dipoko. TTY
Autobiography. Janet Dubé. BrRo
Autobiography. Gloria Fuertes, *tr. fr. Spanish by* Philip Levine. PBWP
Autobiography. Dan Pagis, *tr. fr. Hebrew by* Robert Friend. VWA
Autobiography. Dorothy Parker. WhC
Autobiography, An. Ernest Rhys. OBEV; OBVV
Autobiography, Chapter XVII: Floating the Big Piney. Jim Barnes. STE
Autobiography, Chapter XII: Hearing Montana. Jim Barnes. AMV-81
Autobiography: Hollywood. Charles Reznikoff. *Fr.* Going To and Fro and Walking Up and Down. VWA
Autobiography: Last Chapter. Jim Barnes. CDW
Autobiography of a Lungworm. Roy Fuller. NoAM; NoP; OxBC
Autochthon. Sir Charles G. D. Roberts. CaP
Autocrat of the Breakfast-Table, The, *sels.* Oliver Wendell Holmes.
Aestivation [an Unpublished Poem, by My Late Latin Tutor], *fr. ch.* 11. InMe; NA; NOBL; OBAL; WhC
(Intramural Aestivation, or Summer in Town, by a Teacher of Latin.) ChTr; FaBoNo
Chambered Nautilus, The, *fr. ch.* 4. AA; AmPP; AP; EtS; FaBoBe; FaFP; FPL; GN; HBV-2; HoPM; LiTA; MOS; NePA; NOBA; NoP; OBVV; OHFP; PoEL-5; PoLF; PrIm; Tref; WGRP
Contentment, *fr. ch.*11. AmPP; AP; HBV-1; InMe; OxBA; Tref
Deacon's Masterpiece, The; or, The Wonderful "One-Hoss Shay," *fr. ch.* 11. AmPP; AP; BeLS; FaBoBe; FaFP; FaPo; FPL; HBV-1; HBVY; InMe; LiTA; MoShBr; NePA; NOBA; OBAL; OBCA; OHFP; OxBA; PaPo; PoLF; PoRA; TAP; WBLP; YaD
(One-Hoss Shay, The.) TreF
Living Temple, The, *fr. ch.* 7. AA; AP
Voiceless, The, *fr. ch.* 12. AA; ViBoPo
Autograph, An. James Russell Lowell. AA
Autograph, An. Whittier. AA
Autograph Book/ Prophecy. Anne Halley. NMM
Autograph Bore, The. Oliver Herford. TDH
Autolycus as Peddler. Shakespeare. *See* Lawn as White as Driven Snow.
Autolycus' Song (in Basic English). Richard L. Greene. SpRo; WhC
Autolycus's Song ("Jog on, jog on . . ."). Shakespeare. *See* Jog On, Jog On.
Autolycus's Song ("Lawn as white as driven snow"). Shakespeare. *See* Lawn as White as Driven Snow.
Autolycus's Song ("When daffodils begin to peer"). Shakespeare. *See* When Daffodils Begin to Peer.
Automatic fingers write, The. Séance. Francis King. PoA
Automobile, The. Russell Edson. LCAP
Automobile Mechanics. Dorothy W. Baruch. FaPON; SoPo; TiPo
Automobiles/ In/ a/ row. Stop-Go. Dorothy W. Baruch. FaPON; SUS; TiPo
Autonomous. Mark Van Doren. LiTA
Autosonic Door. Dorothy Brown Thompson. GoYe
Autres Bêtes, Autres Moeurs. Ogden Nash. *See* Turtle, The.
Autumn. Bella Akhmadulina, *tr. fr. Russian by* Barbara Einzig. BoWoP
Autumn. D. R. Beeton. PeSA
Autumn. Roy Campbell. GTBS-P; MoBrPo; OBMV; OxBTC
Autumn. William Carpenter. Psk
Autumn ("Summer is gone and all the merry noise.") John Clare. SaC
Autumn ("The thistledown's flying. . ."). John Clare. BoNaP; HAP; NBM; NU; PoEL-4; WeW
Autumn. Edwin Curran. HBMV
Autumn. Walter de la Mare. OxBTC
Autumn. Emily Dickinson. *See* Morns are meeker than they were, The.
Autumn. Thomas Hood. BLPL; LiTB; OBEV; OBRV; ViBoPo
(Ode: Autumn.) OAEL-2; OBNC; PoEL-4; UnPo; VLP
(Ode to Autumn.) HBV-1
Autumn. Patricia Hubbell. PDV
Autumn. T. E. Hulme. FaBoMo; LoBV; MOON; SeCePo; ViBoPo
Autumn. Philip Levine. NNaP
Autumn. Detlev von Liliencron, *tr. fr. German by* Ludwig Lewisohn. AWP
Autumn. Longfellow. OBVV
Autumn. Itzig [*or* Itzik] Manger, *tr. fr. Yiddish.* TrJP, *tr. by* Joseph Leftwich; VWA, *tr. by* Ruth Whitman
Autumn. Thomas Nashe. *Fr.* Summer's Last Will and Testament. ElL; EnRePo; LoBV; OAEL-1; OBSC; QFR; TrGrPo
Autumn. Pushkin, *tr. fr. Russian by* Max Eastman. AWP
Autumn. Rainer Maria Rilke, *tr. fr. German by* C. F. MacIntyre. TrJP
Autumn. Elizabeth Madox Roberts. YaD
Autumn. W. R. Rodgers. NeBP
Autumn. Christina Rossetti. BrRo
Autumn. Vernon Scannell. OxBTC
Autumn. Thomas W. Shapcott. CBAP
Autumn. Shelley. CH
Autumn. Princess Shikishi, *tr. fr. Japanese by* Hiroaki Sato. PBWP
Autumn. Stevie Smith. ELU
Autumn. William Jay Smith. NePoAm
Autumn. Spenser. *Fr.* The Faerie Queene. GN
Autumn. Rabindranath Tagore. WGRP
Autumn. Allen Tate. *Fr.* Seasons of the Soul. MoVE
Autumn. James Thomson. *Fr.* The Seasons. FM; LoBV; OAEP
Sels.
"But see the fading many-colour'd woods." EnRP
"Here the rude clamour of the sportsman's joy." PBBP
Lavinia. OBEC
Love of Nature. OBEC
Moonlight in Autumn. OBEC
Autumn! Nancy Byrd Turner. YeAr
Autumn ("Autumn's good, a cosy season"). *Unknown, tr. fr. Irish by* Frank O'Connor. KiLC; PoSC
Autumn ("I at my window sit, and see"). *Unknown.* NOEC
Autumn ("Woman full of wile"). *Unknown. See* Growing Old.
Autumn. Jean Starr Untermeyer. HBMV; MoAmPo
Autumn. Sir William Watson. OBVV
Autumn. Frances Winwar. GoYe
Autumn. Humbert Wolfe. PoLF
Autumn; a Dirge. Shelley. HBV-1
Autumn; an Ode. Charles Gullans. NePoEA
Autumn Begins in Martins Ferry, Ohio. James Wright. CAPP; InPS; NaP; POL
Autumn Birds. John Clare. PBBP
Autumn Breeze, An. William Hamilton Hayne. AA
Autumn Burial; a Meditation. Charles Gullans. QFR
Autumn Change. John Clare. VLP
Autumn Chapter in a Novel. Thom Gunn. FaBoMo; OxBTC
Autumn, cloud blades on the horizon. Clear after Rain. Tu Fu, *tr. by* Kenneth Rexroth. PoPl
Autumn Color. Tom Robinson. YeAr
Autumn comes on slippered feet. Autumn's Fete. Alice Sutton McGeorge. YeAr
Autumn comes to its senses. October. Fredric Koeppel. AMV-80
Autumn Complaint. Stéphane Mallarmé, *tr. fr. French by* George Moore. SyP
Autumn constellations, The. Moon Festival. Tu Fu, *tr. by* Kenneth Rexroth. NaP
Autumn, Crystal Eye. Margot Ruddock. OBMV
Autumn, Dark Wanderer. Elizabeth Daryush. QFR
Autumn Dawn. Antonio Machado, *tr. fr. Spanish by* Jean Rogers Longland. PoPl
Autumn Day, An. Sorley MacLean. AMV-81
Autumn Day. Rainer Maria Rilke, *tr. fr. German by* C. F. MacIntyre. TrJP
Autumn Eve. Amelia Andriello. SiSoSe
Autumn Evening. George Anthony. EAS
Autumn Fancies. *Unknown.* FaPON
Autumn Fashions. Edith M. Thomas. YeAr
Autumn Fires. Robert Louis Stevenson. SUS; TiPo; YeAr
Autumn Garden, An. Bliss Carman. HBV-1
Autumn has a mother. Usually an Old Female Is the Leader. Tom Hennen. FAZ
Autumn has turned the dark trees toward the hill. Quail in Autumn. William Jay Smith. Psk
Autumn hath all the summer's fruitful treasure. Autumn. Thomas Nashe. *Fr.* Summer's Last Will and Testament. ElL; EnRePo; LoBV; OAEL-1; OBSC; QFR; TrGrPo
Autumn House, The. George M. Brady. OnYI
Autumn Idleness. Dante Gabriel Rossetti. The House of Life, LXIX. GBL; OAEL-2
Autumn Imagined. Donald Davie. PoA
Autumn in the West. William Davis Gallagher. AA
Autumn is for older men. Adios. Donald C. Babcock. NePoAm-2
Autumn is in the air. London Interior. Harold Monro. BrPo
Autumn is over the long leaves that love us. The Falling of the Leaves. W. B. Yeats. VLP
Autumn is the blue of the wall: being sheltered by little deaths. Apart from Oneself. Alejandra Pizarnik, *tr. by* Yishai Tobin. VWA
Autumn is weary, halt, and old. The October Redbreast. Alice Meynell. MoBrPo
Autumn Journal, *sels.* Louis MacNeice.
"And I remember Spain." OBWP
"August is nearly over, the people." CMoP
"Conferences, adjournments, ultimatums." OxBTC; WaP
"Nightmare leaves fatigue." AnIL; BIrV
"Shelley and jazz and lieder and love and hymn-tunes." NOBL
Autumn Journey. Denise Levertov. NeBP
Autumn Leaves. Janie Screven Heyward. HBMV

Autumn Leaves, The. *Unknown.* NA
Autumn Leaves. Charles H. Webb. OBAL
Autumn leaves are falling, The. The Autumn Leaves. *Unknown.* NA
Autumn light, light of afternoon, the crows. For My Grandfather. Richard Robbins. AMV-81
Autumn made colors burn, The. Venus Khoury-Gata, *tr. fr. French by* Willis Barnstone. BoWoP
Autumn met me today as I walked over Castle Hill. The Stand-to. C. Day Lewis. OBWP
Autumn Morning at Cambridge. Frances Cornford. HBMV; MoVE; OBVV; PoRA
Autumn Morning in Shokoku-ji, An. Gary Snyder. *Fr.* Four Poems for Robin. HAP; NNaP; NoAM; NOBA; NoP; SOTW; VGW
Autumn Mushrooms. Kenneth Mackenzie. CBAP
Autumn Music. Gabriel Preil, *tr. fr. Hebrew by* Howard Schwartz. VWA
Autumn 1940. W. H. Auden. LiTA
Autumn, 1914. Mary Webb. SUMH
Autumn on the Upper Thames. William Morris. *See* Fair Is the World.
Autumn Orchard. Catherine Haydon Jacobs. AMV-80
Autumn-pallid sun looks down, The. The End Is Now. "Marie Madelaine," *tr. by* Ferdinand E. Kappey. PeHV
Autumn Park, An. David Gascoyne. MoPo
Autumn Poem. Anthony Cronin. CIP
Autumn Rain. D. H. Lawrence. BrPo
Autumn Rain. Kenneth Rexroth. NU
Autumn Refrain. Wallace Stevens. LiTA
Autumn resumes the land, ruffles the woods. The Laurel Axe. Geoffrey Hill. *Fr.* An Apology for the Revival of Christian Architecture in England. NoP
Autumn Road, An. Glenn Ward Dresbach. HBMV
Autumn Scene. Basil Dowling. BoNaP
Autumn seems to cry for thee, The. Helen. "Susan Coolidge." AA
Autumn Sequence. Adrienne Rich. VGW
Autumn Song. Edward Dowden. OnYI
Autumn Song. Elizabeth-Ellen Long. SiSoSe
Autumn Song. Dante Gabriel Rossetti. ViBoPo
Autumn Song. Stephen Stepanchev. FAZ
Autumn Song. Johann Ludwig Tieck, *tr. fr. German by* James Clarence Mangan. AWP
Autumn Song on Perry Street. Lloyd Frankenberg. GrPl
Autumn Squall—Lake Erie. Lola Ingres Russo. AmFN
Autumn Testament, *sels.* James K. Baxter. OCNZ
"After writing for an hour in the presbytery," 46.
"Bodies of the young are not the flower, The," 19.
"Creek has to run muddy before it can run clear, The!" 15.
"I think the Lord on his axe-chopped cross," 29.
"Life can be a hassle. Are you free of it, Monsignor," 32.
"Rata blooms explode, the bow-legged tomcat, The," 42.
"To pray for an easy heart is no prayer at all," 22.
Autumn: the ninth year of Yüan Ho. The Temple. Po Chü-i, *tr. by* Arthur Waley. OBMV
Autumn-time has come, The. My Triumph. Whittier. NOBA
Autumn time is with us, The. Autumn in the West. William Davis Gallagher. AA
Autumn upon us was rushing, The. Ravings. Tom Hood. BXAP; Par
Autumn Walk, An. Witter Bynner. GoYe
Autumn was cold in Plymouth town. Her Picture. Ellen Mackay Hutchinson Cortissoz. AA
Autumn Wind, The. John Clare. BoNaP
Autumn Wind, The ("Autumn wind rises; white clouds fly"). Emperor Wu Ti, *tr. fr. Chinese by* Arthur Waley. FaBoCh
Autumn wind's a pirate, The. Pirate Wind. Mary Jane Carr. SiSoSe
Autumn Woods. James S. Tippett. SUS; TiPo
Autumnal. Horatio Colony. TwAmPo
Autumnal. Louis O. Coxe. TwAmPo
Autumnal, The. John Donne. Elegies, IX. InPS; JCP; OAEP; PoEL-2; SeCV-1; TEP; ViBoPo
Autumnal. Ernest Dowson. EBVV; OBNC
Autumnal Consummation. Patric Stevenson. NeIP
Autumnal Evening, An. "Fiona Macleod." PoSC; SyP
Autumnal Moon, The. James Thomson. *Fr.* The Seasons: Autumn. NOBE
Autumnal Ode. Aubrey Thomas De Vere. OBNC
Autumnal Song. Walter Savage Landor. *See* Very True, the Linnets Sing.
Autumnal Spring Song. Vassar Miller. NePoEA
Autumnall. Joseph Bennett. NePA
Autumn's bright moon. Haiku. Kaga no Chiyo, *tr. by* R. H. Blyth. PBWP
Autumn's Fete. Alice Sutton McGeorge. YeAr
Autumn's good, a cosy season. Autumn. *Unknown, tr. by* Frank O'Connor. KiLC; PoSC
Autumn's Mirth. Samuel Minturn Peck. GN
Autumn's Processional. Dinah Maria Mulock Craik. GN
Autumn's wind on suthering wings, The. The Autumn Wind. John Clare. BoNaP
Autumnus. Joshua Sylvester. ElL; OBS; SoSe
Aux Carmélites. Katharine Tynan. OnYI
Aux Italiens. "Owen Meredith." BeLS; BLPA; BLPL; FaBoBe; HBV-1; TreFS
Avalanche. Adrien Stoutenburg. NYBP
Avalon. Audrey McGaffin. NePoAm
Avant Garde. Louis Dudek. *Fr.* Provincetown. MoCV
Avarice. George Herbert. FaBoRV; LiTB
Avast, honest Jack! now, before you get mellow. The Battle of Erie. *Unknown.* PAH
Ave. Dante Gabriel Rossetti. GoBC; ISi; OxBoCh
Ave atque Vale. Dryden. *Fr.* Sigismonda and Guiscardo. OBS
Ave atque Vale. Thomas S. Jones, Jr. HBV-2
Ave atque Vale. *Malay Oral Tradition, tr. by* R. J. Wilkinson *and* R. O. Winstedt. WTO
Ave atque Vale. Swinburne. NOBE; OAEL-2; OAEP; OBEV; OBNC; SyP; ViBoPo; VLP
Ave atque Vale. Rosamund Marriott Watson. HBV-1
Ave, Caesar! W. E. Henley. In Hospital, XIV. BrPo
Ave Caesar. Robinson Jeffers. MoVE; NoAM; NOBA; OxBA
Ave Eva. John Wheelwright. MoPo
Ave Imperatrix! Oscar Wilde. HBV-2
Ave Maria. Byron. *Fr.* Don Juan, III. ISi
Ave Maria. Henriette Charasson, *tr. fr. French by* Frederic Thompson. ISi
Ave Maria. Hart Crane. *Fr.* The Bridge. MoPo; NePA; NoAM; NOBA
Ave Maria. Frank O'Hara. NNAP; NoP; PoM
Ave Maria. Sir Walter Scott. *See* Hymn to the Virgin.
Ave-Maria Bells. Charles Warren Stoddard. ISi
Ave Maria! blessed be the hour! Ave Maria. Byron. *Fr.* Don Juan, III. ISi
Ave Maria, Gratia Plena. Oscar Wilde. ISi
Ave Maria! Maiden mild! Hymn to the Virgin [*or* Ave Maria]. Sir Walter Scott. *Fr.* The Lady of the Lake, III. EnRP; GoBC; ISi
Ave Maris Stella ("Ave maris stella, the star of the sea"). *Unknown.* CTC
Ave Maris Stella ("Star of ocean fairest"). *Unknown, tr. fr. Latin.* ISi
Ave! Nero Imperator. Duffield Osborne. AA
Ave Regina Coelorum. *Unknown, tr. fr. Latin by* Winfred Douglas. ISi
Ave, Vita Nostra! Clifford James Laube. ISi
'Ave you 'eard o' the Widow at Windsor. The Widow at Windsor. Kipling. BrPo; NoP; OAEP
Avenge, O Lord, thy slaughtered [or slaughter'd] saints, whose bones. On the Late Massacre [*or* Massacher] in Piedmont [*or* Piemont]. Milton. AWP; BiP; CABA; FaPo; GTBS; GTBS-P; HAP; HBV-2; HeIP; InPK; JCP; LiTB; LoBV; NIP; NOBE; NOCV; NoP; OAEL-1; OAEP; OBS; OBWP; PAI; PoEL-3; SeCeV; TW; OAEP; OBS; OBWP; PAI; POEL-3; PPoe; PPP; SeCeV; TW; UnPo; ViBoPo; WaaP; WeW; WHA
Avenger, The. James Wright. TwAmPo
Avengers, The. Robert Graves. HBMV
Avengers, The. Edwin Markham. MoAmPo
Avenue, The. Paul Verlaine. *See* Dans l'Allée.
Avenue Bearing the Initial of Christ into the New World, The. Galway Kinnell. CoPo
Sels.
"Behind the Power Station on 14th, the held breath," 14. NaP
"Children set fires in ashbarrels," 9. NaP
"First Sun Day of the year. Tonight," 4. NaP
"Fishmarket closed, the fishes gone into flesh, The," 11. ConAP; NaP; NMP
"From the Station House," 3. NMP
"In sunlight on the Avenue," 2. LiTM; NMP
"In the pushcart market, on Sunday," 6. NaP; NMP
"Pcheek pcheek pcheek pcheek pcheek," 1. CAD; LiTM; NePoEA-2
"Promise was broken too freely, The," 8. NaP
Avenue Y. Anita Barrows. VWA
Avenues, The. David St. John. AMV-80; MAYP
Average Man, The. Margaret Elizabeth Sangster. WBLP
Avert, High Wisdom, never vainly wooed. On the Danger of War. George Meredith. PPON
Aviemore. Janet Waller. PoSH
Avis. Ted Morison. AMV-81
Avocado Pit, The. Carl Rakosi. FAZ
Avoid and pass us by, O curse. An Imprecation against Foes and Sorcerers. *Unknown, tr. by* A. A. MacDonnell. WSC
Avoid the reeking herd. The Eagle and the Mole. Elinor Wylie. AWP; BoWoP; HBMV; LiTA; LiTM; MoAB; MoAmPo; TreFT; UnPo; ViBoPo; WHA
Avoidances. Ron Welburn. PoBA
Avoiding News by the River. W. S. Merwin. NaP
Avondale Mine Disaster, The. *Unknown.* AmFP; BaBo; ViBoFo

Avremele, when will we have our own child? Abraham and Sarah. Itzik Manger, *tr. by* Stephen Garrin. VWA
Aw/ You so ugly. Ugly Chile. Clarence Williams. TW
Aw, quit yer cryin', kid—I know it's tough. Cell-Mates. Louis Untermeyer. HBMV
Aw, Sally Brown, I been a long while a-courtin' ya. Sally Brown, *vers.* II. *Unknown.* ShS
Aw was young and lusty. Sair Fyel'd, Hinny. *Unknown.* GBP
Awa te the hulls, awa. Feels. J. C. Milne. PoSH
Awaits no solar quadriga. The Welcome. Freda Laughton. NeIP
Awake! Jack Black. BXAP
Awake. Mary Elizabeth Coleridge. OBNC
Awake! W. R. Rodgers. LiTM; WaP
Awake! Walther von der Vogelweide, *tr. fr. German by* Jethro Bithell. AWP
Awake./ Your youth is passing like smoke. A Lamentation. Carl Rakosi. VWA
Awake, Aeolian lyre, awake. The Progress of Poesy. Thomas Gray. AWP; EnRP; GTBS; GTBS-P; HBV-2; LAuP; NOEC; OAEP; OBEC; OBEV; PP; ViBoPo
Awake, alone, aware. Insomniac Poem. Ron Loewinsohn. NeAP
Awake, arise,/ Pull out your eyes. Mother Goose. OxNR
Awake! arise! shake off thy dreams! To My Native Land. James Clarence Mangan. AnIL
Awake, arise, the hour is come. A Radical War Song. Macaulay. OBSV
Awake! arise, ye men of might! To Arms. Park Benjamin. PAH
Awake, Arise, You Drowsy Sleeper. *Unknown.* AmFP
Awake, Awake! Thomas Campion. ELP
Awake! Awake! John Ruskin. *Fr.* Song of the Dawn. HBV-2
Awake! Awake! The Bells. William Young. *Fr.* Wishmakers' Town. AA
Awake, awake! for my track is red. The Song of the Flume. Anna M. Fitch. BPAW
Awake, awake, good people all. May Carol. *Unknown.* OBET
Awake! awake! my gallant friends. The Battle of Tippecanoe. *Unknown.* PAH
Awake, awake, my little boy! The Land of Dreams. Blake. BeLS; CH; OBRV
Awake, awake, my Lyre! A Supplication. Abraham Cowley. *Fr.* Davideis. GTBS; GTBS-P
Awake, awake, O Church of God! The Clarion-Call. *Unknown.* BLRP
Awake! awake! the stars are pale, the east is russet gray. Awake! Awake! John Ruskin. *Fr.* Song of the Dawn. HBV-2
Awake, awake! thou heavy sprite. Awake, Awake! Thomas Campion. ELP
Awake, awake to love and work! G. A. Studdert-Kennedy. TRV
Awake, awake, ye drowsy souls. New Year's Carol. *Unknown.* OBET
Awake, faire Muse; for I intend. An Ode. William Browne. OBS
Awake! for morning in the bowl of night. The Rubáiyát of Omar Khayyám of Naishápúr. Omar Khayyám, *tr. by* Edward Fitzgerald. EBVV; FaPoR; HAP; HeIP; LoBV; OxBI; PrIm; WEW.*See also* Wake! for the Sun who scattered into flight.
Awake! For Sweeney in pyjamas bright. Awake! Jack Black. BXAP
Awake, glad heart! get up, and sing. Christ's Nativity. Henry Vaughan. AnAnS-1; SBVL
Awake (great Sir) the Sun shines heer. On New-Years Day 1640, to the King. Sir John Suckling. SeCV-1
Awake, like a hippopotamus with eyes bulged. Monday. William Stafford. NYBP
Awake, Mine Eyes! *Unknown.* ElL
("Awake, mine eyes, see Phoebus bright arising.") PBBP
Awake, My Fair. Judah Halevi, *tr. fr. Hebrew by* Alice Lucas. TrJP
Awake, My Heart, to Be Loved. Robert Bridges. GTBS-P; HBV-1; MoAB; MoBrPo; NOBE; OBEV; OBVV
Awake, My Lute! C. S. Lewis. CenHV; FaBoNo
Awake, my St. John! leave all meaner things. Pope. An Essay on Man, Epistle I. NoP; OAEP; PoEL-3; PrIm
Awake, My Soul! Philip Doddridge. WGRP
Awake, My Soul. Moses ibn Ezra, *tr. fr. Hebrew by* Solomon Solis-Cohen. *Fr.* Wine-Songs. TrJP
Awake, My Soul. Thomas Ken. *See* Morning Hymn.
Awake My Soul, Betimes Awake, *with music.* Isaac Chanler. AH
Awake, My Soul! In Grateful Songs, *with music.* Andrew Fowler. AH
Awake, my soul, let's to the tavern go. Awake, My Soul. Moses ibn Ezra, *tr. by* Solomon Solis-Cohen. *Fr.* Wine-Songs. TrJP
Awake, my soul; stretch every nerve. Awake, My Soul! Philip Doddridge. WGRP
Awake now,/ Fully sensible of my own chains. View from the Window. Jane McCoy. AMV-80
Awake, O [*or* Oh,] north wind. Bible, *O.T.* *Fr.* The Song of Solomon. FaPON; SUS
Awake, O rain, O sun, O night. Ending. *Tr. fr. Hawaiian by* K. Luomala. WTO
Awake, oh Heaven, for (lo) the heavens conspire. Cyril Tourneur. MOON
Awake or sleeping (for I know not which). An Old-World Thicket. Christina Rossetti. SBG
Awake sad heart, whom sorrow ever drowns. The Dawning. George Herbert. AnAnS-1
Awake sound sleeper! hark, what dismal knells. Upon the Death of His Much Esteemed Friend Mr. Jno Saffin Junr. Grindall Rawson. SCAP
Awake! the dawn is on the hills! Morning Serenade. Madison Cawein. HBV-1
Awake! The day is coming now. Awake! Walther von der Vogelweide, *tr. by* Jethro Bithell. AWP
Awake thee, my Bessy, the morning is fair. Song. James Joseph Callanan. OnYI
Awake thee, my lady-love. Serenade. George Darley. *Fr.* Sylvia. HBV-1
Awake to the cold light. March. Hart Crane. BoNaP
Awake, ye forms of verse divine! The National Paintings. Fitz-Greene Halleck *and* Joseph Rodman Drake. *Fr.* The Croaker Papers. AA
Awake, ye nations, slumbering supine. Sonnets Written in the Fall of 1914. George Edward Woodberry. HBV-2; PAH
Awake yee westerne nymphs, arise and sing. Samuel Danforth. SCAP
Awakened War God, The. Margaret Widdemer. WGRP
Awakening, The. Conrad Aiken. *Fr.* The Kid. MoVE
Awakening. Robert Bly. ConAP; NaP
Awakening, The. Robert Creeley. NeAP
Awakening. John Haines. EAS
Awakening, The. Don Marquis. HBMV
Awakening, The. Angela Morgan. OHIP
Awakening. David Robinson. AMV-81
Awakening. Margaret E. Sangster. AA
Awakening. Lucien Stryk. SV
Awakening, The. *Unknown.* *See* On a Time the Amorous Silvy.
Awakening—/ Voices of birds. Nelly Sachs, *tr. from German by* Ruth *and* Matthew Mead. PBWP
Awakening like return to Earth from Moon. Brian Coffey. *Fr.* Advent. CIP
Awakening of Dermuid, The. Austin Clarke. *Fr.* The Vengeance of Finn. AnIV
Awakening of Man, The. Robert Browning. *Fr.* Paracelsus, V. WGRP
Awakening swan grows tired at last, The. The Swan. Sir Edmund Gosse. SyP
Awaking. Stephen Spender. NYBP
Awaking muscle of a race asleep. Maceo. Luis Lloréns Torres, *tr. by* Julio Marzán. InW
A-walking and a-talking. The Cuckoo (B *vers.*). *Unknown.* OBET
Award. Ray Durem. BPo; CABA; IDB; PoBA; SoSe; TTY
"Well, old spy," *sel.* NNP
Aware. D. H. Lawrence. BoNaP; MoBrPo
Aware Aware. Tram Combs. MP; TwCP
Aware that summer baked the water clear. Skykomish River Running. Richard Hugo. PoA
Aware to the dry throat of the wide hell in the world. King David Dances. John Berryman. OxBC
Awareness. Don L. Lee. BOLo; PoBA
Away. Walter de la Mare. NoP
Away! Robert Frost. NOBA
Away. Josephine Miles. GP
Away. James Whitcomb Riley. BLRP; TreFT; TRV; WGRP
(He Is Not Dead.) BLPA; FPL
Away. Lucien Stark. GP
Away above a Harborful. Lawrence Ferlinghetti. *Fr.* Pictures of a Gone World. BoLoP; ErPo; NMP; PoM
Away! away!/ Tempt me no more, insidious Love. The Complaint. Mark Akenside. OBEV
Away, away from city and street. Away Out West. Sharlot M. Hall. BPAW
Away, away in the Northland. A Legend of the Northland. Phoebe Cary. HBV-1; HBVY; OBCA; OnMSP
Away beyond the Jarboe house. Strange Tree. Elizabeth Madox Roberts. BoNaP; FaPON; GrPl; WSC
Away by the haunts of the Yang-tse-boo. The Rhyme of the Kipperling. Sir Owen Seaman. CenHV
A-way by the river so clear. Little Moses. *Unknown.* FSW
Away, Delights. Beaumont *and* Fletcher. *Fr.* The Captain, III, iv. ElL; NOBE; OBEV; ViBoPo
(Sad Song, The.) FaBoEn; GBL
Away despair; my gracious Lord doth heare. The Bag. George Herbert. AnAnS-1; SeCP
Away down deep and away up high. At the Playground. William Stafford. LCAP
Away down South in old Tennessee. A Long Time Ago, *vers.* I. *Unknown.* ShS
Away down South where I was born. A Long Time Ago, *vers.* II. *Unknown.* ShS

Away down yonder in the Wahee Mountains. The Oregon Trail. *Unknown.* BPAW
Away, fond thing! tempt me not more! To Plautia. Sir Aston Cokayne. CavP
Away, for we are ready to a man! Epilogue. James Elroy Flecker. *Fr.* The Golden Journey to Samarkand. NOBE
Away from friends, away from home. The Wanderer's Grave. Rufus B. Sage. BPAW; PoOW
Away from You. Cecilia Meireles, *tr. fr. Portuguese by* Harriet Zinnes. AMV-81
Away, haul away, Oh, haul away together. Haul Away, Joe *Unknown.* AmSS
Away, haul away, rock and roll me over. Haul Away, Joe, *vers.* I. *Unknown.* ShS
Away in a Manger. *Unknown, at. to* Martin Luther. AH, *with music;* FSW; TreFS
(Cradle Hymn.) FaPON; OHIP; SUS
Away; let nought to Love displeasing. Winifreda. *Unknown.* HBV-1; OBEC; OBEV
Away loose-reined careers of Poetry! Urian Oakes. *Fr.* An Elegie upon That Reverend . . . Mr. Thomas Shepard. NOCV
Away, Melancholy. Stevie Smith. OxBTC; PBWP
Away my verse! and never fear. To His Verse. Walter Savage Landor. OBVV
Away out in old Texas, that great Lone Star State. Only a Cowboy. *Unknown.* CoSo
Away Out West. Sharlot M. Hall. BPAW
Away, Rio, *with music. Unknown.* AmSS
Away! the moor is dark beneath the moon. Stanzas—April, 1814 [*or* Remorse]. Shelley. ChER; EnRP; FiP; LoBV; OAEP; OBEV; OBNC
Away thou fondling motley humorist. John Donne. Satires, I. OAEP
Away to the brook. The Angler's Ballad. Charles Cotton. CavP
Away to Twiver, Away, Away! *Unknown.* ElL
Away, useless trifles! Of the Sad Lot of the Humanists in Paris. George Buchanan. GoTS
Away Vane World. Alexander Montgomerie. NOCV
Away, way down on the old Swaunee. Yale Boola! A. M. Hirsh. FSN
Away We Go. Aileen Fisher. TiPo
Away with all whimsical bubbles of air. Botany Bay. John Freeth. NOEC
Away with Bloodshed. A. E. Housman. ShM; WhC
Away with Funeral Music. Robert Louis Stevenson. TreFT
Away with Rum. *Unknown.* FSW
Away with silks, away with lawn. Clothes Do but Cheat and Cozen Us. Robert Herrick. CaPo; ErPo
Away with these self-loving lads. [Song to *or* Of His] Cynthia. Fulke Greville. Caelica, LII. ElL; ELP; EnRePo; NoP; OBSC; ViBoPo
"Away with you, away with you, James de Grant!" James Grant. *Unknown.* ESPB
Away with your fictions of flimsy romance. The First Kiss of Love. Byron. HBV-1
Away, ye gay landscapes, ye gardens of roses! Lachin y Gair. Byron. OxBS
Away yee barb'rous woods; how ever yee be plac't. Michael Drayton. *Fr.* Polyolbion, Third Song. OBS
Aweary Am I. Abu-l-Ala al-Maarri, *tr. fr. Arabic by* R. A. Nicholson. AWP
Awéé'. Nia Francisco. STE
Awesome are the works of God. The Works of God. Moses ibn Ezra, *tr. by* Solomon Solis-Cohen. TrJP
Awful Fix. *Unknown.* BluL
Awful line between north and south, The. Poem Written before Mother's Day for Mrs. Lopez from the South. R. Wayne Hardy. LFAC
Awful Mother, The. Susan Griffin. NPGG
Awful Responsibility, An. Keith Preston. PoPl; WhC
Awful shadow of some unseen power, The. Hymn to Intellectual Beauty. Shelley. BiP; BLPL; EnRP; HAP; HeIP; NoP; OAEL-2; OAEP; OBNC; OBRV
Awhile she lay all passive to the touch. An Indian Mother About to Destroy Her Child. James Montgomery. PaPo
Awkward Goodbyes. Vassar Miller. FAZ
Awkward was she yesterday. The Maiden. Peter Hille, *tr. by* Jethro Bithell. AWP
Ax. Charles Simic. GP
Ax was sharpe, the stokke was harde, The. Epigram on the Year 1390-1. *Unknown.* NIP
Axe angles, An/ From my neighbor's ashcan. Junk. Richard Wilbur. HAP; InPK; NoP; SaC; WeW
Axe has cut the forest down, The. Conquest [*or* The Wilderness Is Tamed]. Elizabeth J. Coatsworth. AmFN; FaPON
Axe-Helve, The. Robert Frost. OxBA
Axe of the Pioneer, The. Isabella Valancy Crawford. CaP
Axe rings in the wood, The. Remembered Morning. Janet Lewis. WPE
Axes/ After whose stroke the wood rings. Words. Sylvia Plath. ConAP; LCAP
Axioms. Gad Hollander. VWA
Axle quits, An. Metal Fatigue. Adam Le Fevre. AMV-81
Axle Song. Mark Van Doren. MoPo
Axolotl, The. David McCord. FiBHP; OBAL; WhC
Ay. Tennyson. *Fr.* The Window; or, The Song of the Wrens. PBBP
Ay ant lak pie-plant pie so wery vell. Sonnet on Stewed Prunes. William F. Kirk. WhC
Ay, ay, and away she goes. Highland Laddie. *Unknown.* ShS
Ay, ay; good man, kind father, best of friends. *See* Aye, the good man, kind father, best of friends.
Ay, ay, O ay—the winds that bend the brier! Tristram's Song. Tennyson. *Fr.* Idylls of the King: The Last Tournament. FaBoRV
Ay, Ay, This Is the Day. *Unknown.* OxBM
Ay, besherewe yow [*or* beshrew you!] be [*or* by] my fay. Mannerly Margery Mylk and Ale. John Skelton. AAS; FaBoNo; NoP
Ay, but to die, and go we know not where. The Fear of Death. Shakespeare. *Fr.* Measure for Measure, III, i. TreFT
Ay! drop the treacherous mask! throw by. Butler's Proclamation. Paul Hamilton Hayne. PAH
Ay, Dwainie!—My Dwainie! Dwainie. James Whitcomb Riley. *Fr.* The Flying Islands of the Night. AA
Ay, it is fitting on this holiday. Ode in Memory of the American Volunteers Fallen for France. Alan Seeger. PAH
Ay, let it rest! And give us peace. The Gospel of Peace. James Jeffrey Roche. PAH
Ay Me, Alas. *Unknown.* FaBoCh
(Ay Me, Alas, Heigh Ho!)
(Madrigal.) OxBoLi
Ay me, alas! the beautiful bright hair. Canzone: His Lament for Selvaggia. Cino da Pistoia, *tr. by* Dante Gabriel Rossetti. AWP
Ay me, ay me, I sigh to see the scythe afield. A Proper Sonnet, How Time Consumeth All [Earthly] Things [*or* Sic Transit]. *Unknown, at. to* Thomas Proctor. ChTr; ElL; FaBoRV; OBSC; TrGrPo
Ay me! for aught that I could ever [*or* ever I could] read. The Course of True Love. Shakespeare. *Fr.* A Midsummer Night's Dream, I, i. TreFS; WHA
Ay me, how many perils doe enfold. Spenser. *Fr.* The Faerie Queene, I, 8. OAEL-1
Ay me! whilst thee the shores and sounding seas. Milton. *Fr.* Lycidas. Prf
"Ay, not at home, then, didst thou say?" A Call on Sir Walter Raleigh. Sarah Morgan Bryan Piatt. AA
Ay, Oliver! I was but seven, and he was eleven. Echo and the Ferry. Jean Ingelow. EBVV
Ay or Nay? Ralph Schomberg. *Fr.* The Judgment of Paris. TrJP
Ay, screen thy favourite dove, fair child. A Child Screening a Dove from a Hawk. Letitia Elizabeth Landon. VLP
Ay, shout and rave, thou cruel sea. Herndon. S. Weir Mitchell. PAH
Ay, since beyond these walls no heavens there be. Herbert Trench. *Fr.* To Arolilia. LO
Ay, so it is in every brain. To a Young Brother. Maria Jane Jewsbury. OxBChV
Ay, tear her tattered ensign down! Old Ironsides. Oliver Wendell Holmes. AA; AP; BLPA; EtS; FaBoBe; FaFP; FaPo; FaPON; FPL; GN; GOA; HBV-2; HBVY; MOS; PAH; PAL; PoPl; TAP; TreF; YaD
Ay—There It Is! Emily Brontë. ChER
("Aye, there it is! It wakes to-night.") VLP
Ay, this is freedom!—these pure skies. The Hunter of the Prairies. Bryant. AA; LiSp
Ay! thou look'st cold on me, pomp-loving Moon. To the Moon. George Darley. MOON
Ay, 'Tis Thus. *Unknown, tr. fr. Hebrew by* Israel Zangwill. TrJP
Ay, 'twas here, on this spot. Atalanta in Camden-Town. "Lewis Carroll." CenHV
Ay! Unto thee belong. Theocritus. Annie Fields. AA
Ay Waukin O. Burns. NOEC
(Simmer's a Pleasant Time.) PoEL-4
Ayaiyaja/ This why, I wonder. It Is Hard to Catch Trout. Piuvkaq, *tr. fr. Eskimo.* WTO
Aye, aye, lads, we fought 'em. "Off Manilly." Edmund Vance Cooke. PAH
Aye, back at Leady-Day, you know. Leady-Day, an' Ridden House. William Barnes. VLP
"Aye! I am a poet and upon my tomb." And Thus in Nineveh. Ezra Pound. PP; VGW
"Aye, squire," said Stevens, "they back him at evens." How We Beat the Favourite. Adam Lindsay Gordon. CBAP
Aye, the good man, kind father, best of friends. "Bona de Mortuis." Thomas Lovell Beddoes. ELU; TW
Aye, There's Hills. Hamish Brown. PoSH

Aye up at the feast, by Melhill's brow. Melhill Feast. William Barnes. OBNC
Aye Waukin' O! *Unknown.* BSV; GoTS
Ayee! Ai! This [is] heavy earth on our shoulders. Burying Ground by the Ties. Archibald MacLeish. *Fr.* Frescoes for Mr. Rockefeller's City. GOA; MoAmPo
Ayii, Ayii,/ I walked on the ice of the sea. *Unknown, tr. fr. Eskimo.* RFM
Ayii, Ayii/ The great sea has set me in motion. *Unknown, tr. fr. Eskimo.* RFM
Aylmer's Field. Tennyson. VLP
Leolin and Edith, *sel.* GN
Ayohu Kanogisdi. Carroll Arnett. STE
Azalea, The. Coventry Patmore. The Unknown Eros, I, vii. ELP; GBL; GoBC
Azaleas. Harriet McEwen Kimball. AA
Azaleas are funny plants. Spring Morning: Waking. Emily Seelbinder. AMV-81
Azaleas—whitest of white! White Azaleas. Harriet McEwen Kimball. AA; HBV-1
Aziola, The. Shelley. EBEV; PBBP
A-zlay, A-zlay, you who have clambered the mountains, A-zlay. Navajo Song. Maynard Dixon. BPAW
Azouou. Mririda n'Ait Attik, *tr. fr. Berber into French by* René Euloge; *English vers. by* Daniel Halpern *and* Paula Paley. WPOW
Azra, The. Heine, *tr. fr. German by* John Hay. AWP
(Asra, The, *tr. by* Ernst Feise.) NAWM-2
Azrael. Robert Gilbert Welsh. HBV-2
Aztec City, The. Eugene Fitch Ware. AA; HBV-2
Aztec Figurine. John Beecher. GP
Aztec sacrifice, An. Le Musée Imaginaire. Charles Tomlinson. NePoEA-2
Azure, I come! from the caves of death withdrawn. Helen, the Sad Queen. Paul Valéry, *tr. by* Joseph T. Shipley. AWP
Azure striation swirls beyond the stones. La Fontaine de Vaucluse. Marilyn Hacker. FYAP
Azured [*or* Azur'd] vault, the crystal circles bright, The. Heaven and Earth [*or* Sonnet]. James I, King of England. ChTr; EIL; MOON; SeCePo
Azzoomm, azzoomm loud and strong. Riding in an Airplane. Dorothy W. Baruch. FaPON

B

B. Larry Eigner. NeAP
BC:AD. U. A. Fanthorpe. OBCP
B-52's. Arnold Kenseth. PPON
B is for beautiful Bella. Beautiful Bella. *Unknown.* TDH
B Negative. X. J. Kennedy. ConAP; NePoEA-2
B Stands for Bear. Hilaire Belloc. *Fr.* A Moral Alphabet. ShM
B, taught by Pope to do his good by stealth. A Misconception. James Russell Lowell. OBAL
B was a beggarly bear. A Beggarly Bear Carolyn Wells. TDH
Baa, baa, black sheep, have you any wool? Mother Goose. FaBoBe; FaFP; HBV-1; HBVY; OxNR; SoPo; TiPo
Baa, baa, black sheep, where'd you leave your lamb? *Unknown.* AmFP
Baal Shem Tov. A. M. Klein. CaP; TrJP
Bab-Lock-Hythe. Laurence Binyon. MoVE
Babe, The. Monk Gibbon. OxBI
Babe is born all of a May, A. Three Christmas Carols, I. *Unknown.* ACP
Babe Jesu lying/ On my little pallet lonely. Saint Ita's Fosterling. *At. to* Saint Ita, *tr. by* Robin Flower. OnYI
Babe was laid in the Manger, The. A Nativity. Kipling. NAs
Babe, with a cry brief and dismal, The. Edward Gorey. OBAL
Babel. Gary Pacernik. AMV-81
Babes in the Wood ("My dear, do you know"). *Unknown.* OxBChV
Babes in the Wood, The ("Now ponder well, you parents dear"). *Unknown.* HBV-1; HBVY; OBNV
(Children in the Wood, The.) EnSB
Babi Yar. Lev Ozerov, *tr. fr. Russian by* Daniel Weissbort. VWA
Babiaantje, The. F. T. Prince. ChMP; MoBrPo
Babie, The. Jeremiah Eames Rankin, *wr. at. to* Hugh Miller. AA; HBV-1
Babies, The. Mark Strand. GeTw; NYBP
Babies of the Pioneers. Eunice W. Luckey. BPAW
Baboon. *Unknown, tr. fr. Hottentot.* PeSA
Baboon. *Zulu Oral Tradition, tr. by* C. *and* W. Leslav. WTO
Baboon 2. *Unknown, tr. fr. Hottentot.* PeSA
Babushka. Edith M. Thomas. OnMSP
Baby. Elaine Goodale Eastman. AA
Baby. Florence Kiper Frank. HBMV
Baby, The. Sir William Jones. *See* Epigram: "On parent knees, a naked new-born child."
Baby, The. George Macdonald. *Fr.* At the Back of the North Wind, *ch.* 23. FaPON; HBV-1; HBVY; TreF; TRV
(Song: "Where did you come from, baby dear.") PaPo
(Where Did You Come From [Baby Dear].) BLPA; FaFP; OxBChV
Baby. Joyce Carol Oates. GeTw
Baby, The. James Reaney. *Fr.* A Sequence in Four Keys. NAs
Baby, The. Ann Taylor. OHIP
Baby,/ You shall be free. Kadia the Young Mother Speaks. Jessie Sampter. TrJP
Baby and I. *Unknown.* OxNR
Baby and Mary. *Unknown.* NA
Baby at my breast, The. Against Dark's Harm. Anne Halley. NMM
Baby at Play. *Unknown.* HBV-1; HBVY
Baby, baby, naughty baby. Mother Goose. NOBL; OxNR
Baby Bell. Thomas Bailey Aldrich. HBV-1
Baby brought us luck, The. Lucky. Cathy Song. BrSi
Baby cat is soft and sweet, A. Cats. Marchette Chute. SoPo
Baby Cobina. Gladys May Casely Hayford. CDC
Baby, depend upon it. Shade. Charles Lynch. CNA
Baby did you hear about the bad luck. Bad Luck Blues. *Unknown.* BluL
Baby Goes to Boston, The. Laura E. Richards. TiPo
Baby got here once who before, A. The Rampage. C. K. Williams. GeTw
Baby I am, A. Awéé'. Nia Francisco. STE
Baby I can see just what's on your mind. Mind Reader Blues. *Unknown.* BluL
Baby I'm going/ down town. Sic 'Em Dogs On. *Unknown.* BluL
Baby, I'm going up town. Hunkie Tunkie. *Unknown.* BluL
Baby I'm sick. I need. Night Thoughts: Baby & Demon. Gwen Harwood. CBAP
Baby is born [*or* borne], us bliss [*or* blis] to bring, A. Dear Son, Leave Thy Weeping [*or* Jesus Comforts His Mother]. *Unknown.* CTC; MeEL
Baby is sleeping so cozy and fair. Rock-a-bye Baby. Effie I. Canning. FSN
Baby-Land. George Cooper. HBV-1; HBVY
Baby Lon; or, The Bonnie Banks o' Fordie. *Unknown. See* Babylon; or, The Bonnie Banks o' Fordie.
Baby lying on his mother's breast, A. Man's Pillow. Irving Browne. AA
Baby May. William Cox Bennett. HBV-1
Baby Mine. *Unknown.* FSW
Baby Mine, *with music.* Charles Mackey. BLSo
Baby moon, a canoe, a silver papoose, The. Early Moon. Carl Sandburg. BPAW
Baby picked from an ash barrel by the night police, The. Chicago Boy Baby. Carl Sandburg. NAs
Baby Pictures of Famous Dictators. Charles Simic. GeTw; WeW
Baby, Please Don't Go. *Unknown.* FSW
Baby Running Barefoot. D. H. Lawrence. NoP
Baby Sardine, A. Spike Milligan. OnUR
Baby sat on the window-seat. Baby and Mary. *Unknown.* NA
Baby Seed Song. Edith Nesbit. FaPON; HBV-1; HBVY
Baby-Sermon, A. George Macdonald. OxBChV
Baby Show, De. Wilson MacDonald. WhC
Baby Sleeps. Samuel Hinds. HBV-1
Baby Song. Thom Gunn. NAs
Baby Talk. Anna Bird Stewart. RHPC
Baby Ten Months Old Looks at the Public Domain, A. William Stafford. NYBP
Baby Toes. Carl Sandburg. FaPON; SUS
Baby Tortoise. D. H. Lawrence. BoAnP; CMoP
Baby Villon. Philip Levine. CoAP; NaP
Baby wades alone across the lawn, The. Errantry. Robert Fitzgerald. NYBP
Baby wants his breakfast. Baby's Breakfast. Emilie Poulsson. HBV-1; HBVY
Baby was sleeping, A. The Angel's Whisper. Samuel Lover. OnYI
Baby watched a ford, whereto, A. Wagtail and Baby. Thomas Hardy. HBMV
Baby wept, The. Baby Sleeps. Samuel Hinds. HBV-1
Baby you know I get high. Not Quite Spring. Lyn Lifshin. NeAC
Babyhood. Josiah Gilbert Holland. *Fr.* Bitter-sweet. AA
Babylon. "Æ." HBMV
Babylon. Robert Graves. HBMV
Babylon. Ralph Hodgson. BrPo; HBMV
Babylon. Robert Eyres Landor. *Fr.* The Impious Feast. OBRV
Babylon. Viola Taylor. HBV-1
Babylon ("King and Queen of Cantelon"). *Unknown.* ChTr
Babylon ("There were three ladies lived in a bower"). *Unknown. See* Babylon; or, The Bonnie Banks o' Fordie.
Babylon and Sion (Goa and Lisbon). Luis de Camoes, *tr. fr. Portuguese by* Richard Garnett. AWP
Babylon; or, The Bonnie Banks o' Fordie. *Unknown.* AmFP BaBo (A *and* B *vers.*); ESPB

(Baby Lon; or, The Bonnie Banks o' Fordie.) SeCePo
(Babylon, *with music.*) OxBB
Babylon Revisited. Amiri Baraka. BPo; NoAM; TW
Babylonian Sorrows. Heine, *tr. fr. German by* Aaron Kramer. NAWM-2
Baby's Breakfast. Emilie Poulsson. HBV-1; HBVY
Baby's Dance, The. *At. to* Mother Goose *and also to* Ann Taylor. OxBChV
("Dance, little baby, dance up high.") OxNR
Baby's Debut, The. Horace Smith *and* James Smith. OBRV; Par
Baby's Drinking Song. James Kirkup. NTCP
Baby's feet, like sea-shells pink, A. Swinburne. Étude Réaliste, I. FaPON; GN; HBV-1; WeW
"Baby's in jail; the animal day plays alone." Charles Henri Ford. MoVE
Babysitters, The. Sylvia Plath. NoP
Baccalaureate. David McCord. BXAP; OBAL; SpRo; WhC
Bacchae, *sel.* Euripides, *tr. fr. Greek. by* Gilbert Murray.
Home of Aphrodite, The. AWP
Bacchanal. Peter De Vries. BXAP; NIP; NOBL; OBAL
Bacchanal. Irving Layton. OBCV
Bacchanalia; or, The New Age, *sels.* Matthew Arnold.
"Epoch ends, the world is still, The," II. OAEL-2
First-born Star, The. FaBoRV
Bacchante to Her Babe, The. Eunice Tietjens. HBMV
Bacchus. Emerson. AmPP; AP; AWP; HBV-2; LiTA; NOBA; OBEV; OxBA; PoEL-4; ViBoPo
Bacchus. William Empson. NoAM; PoCH
Sels.
"God who fled down with a standard yard, The." PoA
"Herm whose length measured degrees of heat, The." PoA
Bacchus. Thomas Love Peacock. *Fr.* Rhododaphne. OBRV
Bacchus in Tuscany, *sel.* Francesco Redi, *tr. fr. Italian by* Leigh Hunt.
Bacchus's Opinion of Wine, and Other Beverages. AWP; OBVE
Bacchus, let me drink no more. A Hymn to Bacchus. Robert Herrick. JCP
Bacchus must now his power resign. A Drinking-Song. Henry Carey. OBEV
Bacchus, the father of drunken Nowls. The Man in the Moon Drinks Clarret. *Unknown.* CoMu
Bacchus's Opinion of Wine, and Other Beverages. Francesco Redi, *tr. fr. Italian by* Leigh Hunt. *Fr.* Bacchus in Tuscany. AWP; OBVE
Bacchylides. George Meason Whicher. AA
Bachelor. William Meredith. NoAM
Bachelor Bold and Young. *Unknown.* AmFP
Bachelor Farmer. Roger McDonald. CBAP
Bachelor growls when his peace is, The. A Token of Attachment. J. Adair Strawson. TDH
Bachelor Hall. Eugene Field. BLPA; FPL
Bachelor's Ballade, The. David Fisher Parry. InMe
Bachelor's Complaint, The. *Unknown.* AmFP
Bachelor's Hall. John Finley. HBV-2
Bachelor's Lament, The. *Unknown.* OxNR
Bachelor's Lay, The, *with music. Unknown.* OuSiCo
Bachelor's Life, A. *Unknown.* OxBM
Bachelor's Song, The. Thomas Flatman. *See* On Marriage.
Back. W. W. Gibson. TreFT
Back. Weldon Kees. NaP; PrIm; TwAmPo
Back. Angela McCabe. AmPA
Back. Robert Mezey. AmPA
Back Again for the Holidays. John Betjeman. *Fr.* Summoned by Bells. FaBoPP
Back Again from Yucca Flats. Reeve Spencer Kelley. AmFN
Back Again, Home. Don L. Lee. BALP; BPo
Back and Forth. Lucy Sprague Mitchell. FaPON
Back and forth, back and forth. Fall 1961. Robert Lowell. OBWP; VGW
Back and forth on the criss-crossing walks. A Little Something for William Whipple. Dave Oliphant. FAZ
Back and Side Go Bare, Go Bare. *At. to* William Stevenson. *Fr.* Gammer Gurton's Needle. HeIP; InvP; LiTB; OAEP; ViBoPo
(Drinking Song.) WiR, *at. to* John Still
(In Praise of Ale.) TrGrPo
(Jolly Good Ale and Old.) HBV-2; NoP; OBEV; SeCeV
(Of Jolly Good Ale and Old.) ElL
(Song of Ale, A.) OBSC
Back Country. Joyce Carol Oates. Psk
Back from the line one night in June. Corporal Stare. Robert Graves. BrPo
Back from the Paved Way. Robert D. Fitzgerald. PoAu-2
Back from the trebly crimsoned field. Wanted—a Man. Edmund Clarence Stedman. PAH
Back Gnawing Blues. *Unknown.* BluL
Back home. Manong Federico Delos Reyes and His Golden Banjo. Al Robles. BrSi
Back home the black women are all beautiful. W. W. Amiri Baraka. HeIP; NBP; NOBA; PAI; PoBA
Back in a melon-pink. Great-Grandma. Carol Shields. Str
Back in a yard where play has grooved a ditch. Old Men Pitching Horseshoes. X. J. Kennedy. AMV-81
Back in back of the back country. Alabama. Judy Dothard Simmons. CNA
Back in Black Mountain a child will smack your face. Black Mountain Blues. *Unknown.* BluL
Back in *tachanka* days, when Red and Green. Makhno's Philosophers. John Manifold. CBAP
Back in the dear old thirties' days. The Poet of Bray. John Heath-Stubbs. NOBL
Back in the States. Louis Simpson. AMV-81
Back in the years when Phlagstaff, the Dane, was monarch. The Rejected "National Hymns." "Orpheus C. Kerr." InMe; OBAL
Back into the Garden. Sarah Webster Fabio. BlSi
Back Lane. R. D. Murphy. PoAu-2
Back of the beating hammer. The Thinker. Berton Braley. BLPA; WBLP
Back of the dam, under. The Town of Hill. Donald Hall. FiCP; TAP
Back of the door the child is playing that. Resolution. W. S. Merwin. NYBP
Back of the loaf is the snowy flour. "Give Us This Day Our Daily Bread." Maltbie D. Babcock. TRV
Back of the mind is a small hotel, The. The Small Hotel. Michael Longley. CIP
Back out of all this now too much for us. Directive. Robert Frost. AmPP; AP; BLPL; CABA; CMoP; CoBMV; CrMA; HAP; LiTA; LiTM; MasP; MAT; MoAB; MoAmPo; NePA; NoAM; NOBA; NoP; PPP; PrIm; SeCeV
Back Road. Bruce Guernsey. AMV-81
Back Road Farm. Charles Bruce. CaP
Back Room Joys. Justin Richardson. FiBHP
Back she came through the trembling dusk. Folk-Song. Louis Untermeyer. HBV-1
Back through clouds. Train Tune. Louise Bogan. NePoAm
Back to Arizona. Earl Alonzo Brininstool. BPAW
Back to back, stud poker & an open/ pot. Twin Aces. Keith Wilson. Psk
Back to Base. Jenny Joseph. BrRo
Back to Dublin. R. A. D. Ford. CaP; MoCV
Back to Griggsby's Station. James Whitcomb Riley. BLPA; BLPL
Back to Life. Thom Gunn. NoP
Back to silent big soap flakes. Don't Hope to Gain by What Has Preceded. Joanne Kyger. PoM
Back to the Angels. William Walter De Bolt. AMV-81
Back to the bewildering vision. Kinship. Sir Charles G. D. Roberts. CaP
Back to the flower-town, side by side. In Memory of Walter Savage Landor. Swinburne. HBV-2; PoEL-5
Back to the Ghetto. Jacob Glatstein, *tr. fr. Yiddish by* Joseph Leftwich. TrJP
Back to the green deeps of the outer bay. The Herring Weir. Sir Charles G. D. Roberts. *Fr.* Songs of the Common Day. NOBC; PeCV
Back water at Blytheville. High Water Everywhere: 2. *Unknown.* BluL
Back Water Blues. *Unknown.* BluL; FSW
Back water done rose around Sumner, now, The. High Water Everywhere: 1. *Unknown.* BluL
Back water rising: southern people can't make no time. Rising High Water Blues. *Unknown.* BluL
Back when I was still trying. The Fisherman. Will Wells. AMV-80
Back will go the head with the dark curls. Castanets. Bernard Spencer. WeW
Back wings, The/ of the. Between Walls. William Carlos Williams. HoPM; SOTW; TAP; VGW
Back Yard, July Night. William Cole. BoNaP
Backed correctly into a corner. A Cappella. Michael Pettit. GrPl
Backgammon, *sel.* Olga Broumas.
"Long history." SUW
Backgrounds to Italian Paintings: Fifteenth Century. Anne Ridler. WPE
Backlash Blues, The. Langston Hughes. BPo
Backroad leafmold stonewall chipmunk. Silent Poem. Robert Francis. FiCP; LCAP
Backstage, eating bananas. Carmen Miranda. Frank Polite. GP
Backtracking/ Fifty miles past Bakersfield. Visiting Father. Genny Lim. BrSi
Backward & down into inbetween as Vicki says. Mean Drunk Poem. Sharon Thesen. NOBC
Backward among the dusky years. Compassion. Thomas Hardy. FM
Backward—Forward. *Unknown.* BLRP
Backward Look, The. Howard Nemerov. OxBC
Backward Spring, A. Thomas Hardy. PPP
Backward, turn backward, O time, in your flight. Rock Me to Sleep

[,Mother]. Elizabeth Akers Allen. AA; BLPA; BLPL; FaBoBe; FaFP; HBV-1; OBCA; PaPo; TreF; WBLP
Backward, turn backward, O Time with your wheels. Two Parodies. *Unknown.* CoSo
Backward we look regretful, forward we glance with dread. Resurgam. W. Nelson Bitton. BLRP
Backwater Pond: The Canoeists. W. S. Merwin. PoPl
Backwoods Hero, A, *sel.* Alexander McLachlan.
"Where yonder ancient willow weeps." CaP
Backyard Swing. Janet Campbell Hale. STE
Bacon and Eggs. A. P. Herbert. WhC
Bacon's Epitaph, Made by His Man. *At. to* John Cotton. PAH; SCAP
Bacteria legs, bacteria mouths. World of Bacteria. Sakutaro Hagiwaro, *tr.* by Graeme McD. Wilson. AMV-80
Bad and Good. Alexander Resnikoff. NTCP
Bad Apple, The. Bruce Bennett. LTB
Bad Bishop Jegon. *Unknown.* GBP
Bad Boy, The, *with music. Unknown.* CoSo
Bad breed of the natives with their hates, The. D. C. Karl Shapiro. NYBP
Bad company is a disease. Rowland Watkyns. FaBoEE
Bad Day on the Boulder. Lloyd Davis. WOLT
Bad Dream. Louis MacNeice. NoAM
Bad Dreams, *sels.* Robert Browning.
"Last night I saw you in my Sleep," I. OAEP
"This was my dream! I saw a forest," III. OAEL-2; VLP
Bad Example. Isabella Fey. BoAnP
Bad Girl Blues. *Unknown.* BluL
Bad Girl's Lament, The. *Unknown.* ViBoFo
Bad Habit, The. Charles Henri Ford. EAS
Bad Joke, A. Martial, *tr. fr. Latin by* Louis Untermeyer. UnTE
Bad Kittens, The. Elizabeth J. Coatsworth. FaPON; OBCA
Bad Luck Blues ("Baby did you hear about the bad luck"). *Unknown.* BluL
Bad Luck Blues ("I want to go home and I ain't got sufficient"). *Unknown.* BluL
Bad Luck to This Marching. Charles James Lever. OnYI
Bad Man Ballad. *Unknown.* AmFP
Bad Man from the Brazos, The. *Unknown.* CoSo
Bad Morning. Langston Hughes. OBAL
Bad Mother, The. Susan Griffin. NPGG
Bad news has come to town, bad news is carried. Montcalm and Wolfe. *Unknown.* AmFP
Bad Old Days, The. Kenneth Rexroth. NNaP; NoAM; PAI
Bad Season Makes the Poet Sad, The. Robert Herrick. AnAnS-2; CABA; CaPo; LiTB; OAEP; PrIm; SeCeV
Bad Sleeper, A. Paul Verlaine, *tr. fr. French by* François Pirou. PeHV
Badger ("When midnight comes a host of dogs and men"). John Clare. EnRP; HAP; LiSp; LiTB; NBM; NCEP; NoP; NU; OAEL-2; PAI; PoEL-4; PrIM; VLP; WeW; WiR
Badger ("Badger grunting on his woodland track, The"), *longer version.* FM; InPS
Badgers, The. Seamus Heaney. CIP
Badman of the Guest Professor. Ishmael Reed. BPo
Badminton. Sir Alfred Comyn Lyall. *Fr.* Studies at Delhi. OBVV
Baedeker for Metaphysicians. Brian Higgins. FaBoTw
Baffled for just a day or two. Emily Dickinson. PAI
Baffled Knight, The. *Unknown.* ESPB; ViBoFo
(Courteous Knight, The, *with music.*) OxBB
(There Was a Knight [and He Was Young].) CoMu; UnTE
Bag, The. George Herbert. AnAnS-1; SeCP
Bag of the Bee, The. Robert Herrick. OAEP
Bag of Tools, A. R. L. Sharpe. BLPA; TreFT; YaD
Bagatelle, A. James Reeves. POL
Bagel, The. David Ignatow. ConAP; FF; TwCP
Baggot Street Deserta. Thomas Kinsella. CIP; CMoP; IPY; NMP
Bagley Wood. Lionel Johnson. VLP
Bagman O'Reilly's Curse. Les A. Murray. TW
Bagpipe Man, The. Nancy Byrd Turner. TiPo
Bagpipe Music. "Hugh MacDiarmid." OAEL-2
Bagpipe Music. Louis MacNeice. CMoP; GTBS-P; LiTB; LiTM; NoAM; NOBE; NOBL; NoP; OnYI; OAEL-2; OAEP; OBSV; OxBTC; SeCePo; SeCeV; ViBoPo
Bagpipes. *Unknown.* OxNR
Bags of Meat. Thomas Hardy. BoAnP; FM
Bags Packed and We Expected This. Ramona Wilson. VoR
Baguio Poems, *sel.* Harry Roskolenko.
Waiting for God. FAZ
Bah! Walter de la Mare. BoAnP
Bah! I have sung women in three cities. Cino. Ezra Pound. VGW
Bah! spite of Fate, that says us nay. The Indolent. Paul Verlaine, *tr. by* Arthur Symons. SyP
Bahamas. George Oppen. NYBP
Baha'u'llah in the Garden of Ridwan. Robert Hayden. PoBA
Bahnhofstrasse. James Joyce. NoAM
Bailey Beareth the Bell Away, The. *Unknown. See* Maidens Came, The.
Bailiff, The. Ebenezer Elliott. *Fr.* The Splendid Village. NBM
Bailiff's Daughter of Islington, The. *Unknown.* AmFP; ESPB; FaBoBa; FSW; GN; HBV-2; OAEP; OBET; OxBB, *with music;* OxBoLi; ViBoFo, *with music*
Bairnies cuddle doon at nicht, The. Cuddle Doon. Alexander Anderson. GN; HBV-1; OHFP
Bait Shop. Thomas Reiter. WOLT
Bait [*or* Baite], The. John Donne. CABA; ErPo; HoPM; InPK; InPS; NIP; OAEL-1; OAEP; PoRA; TEP; WhC
Baith Gud[e] and Fair and Womanlie [*or* Womanly]. *Unknown.* GoTS; OxBS
Baits for Various Fish. Thomas Barker. *Fr.* The Art of Angling. FaBoUs
Baja. Gerald Stern. SV
Baja—Outside Mexicali. Michael McClure. GP
Baked potato's, The. Diner. A. R. Ammons. POL
Baker's Boy, The. Mary Effie Lee Newsome. CDC
Baker's Dozen of Wild Beasts, A, *sels.* Carolyn Wells. OBCA
Bath-Bunny, The.
Corn-Pone-y, The.
Cream-Puffin, The.
Mince-Python, The.
Baker's Duzzen uv Wize Sawz, A. Edward Rowland Sill. FaBoBe; FaFP; HBV-1; HBVY; InMe; TreFS
Baker's Tale, The. "Lewis Carroll." *Fr.* The Hunting of the Snark. EBEV
Baking Day. Rosemary Joseph. Str
Balaam. John Keble. OBNC; OBVV
Balaam's Blessing. Bible, *O.T.* Numbers, XXIV: 5-9. TrGrPo
("How goodly are the tentes of Jacob.") OBVE, *tr. by* William Tyndale
Balaclava. *Unknown.* OBET
Balade: "Hide [*or* Hyd], Absalon, thy gilte tresses clear." Chaucer. *Fr.* The Legend of Good Women: Prologue. AWP; ChTr; FiP; GBL; LoBV; NOBE; OBEV; SeCeV
("Hide [*or* Hyd], Absolon, thy gilte tresses clere.") EBEV; HAP; OAEL-1; OxBM
(Lady without Paragon, A.) MeEL
Balade de [*or* of] Bon Conseyl [*or* Conseil *or* Conseill]. Chaucer. TrGrPo; ViBoPo
(Ballad of Good Counsel) ACP; GoBC, *sl. mod. vers. by* Wordsworth
(Ballade of Good Counsel, *mod. by* Henry van Dyke.) TrGrPo
(Truth.) AWP; NoP; OAEP; OxBM
(Truth Shall Set You Free.) MeEL
Balade Simple. John Lydgate. GBL
Balalaika. Norman Dubie. AmPA
Balance. Philip Schultz. MAYP
Balance, The. Judith Johnson Sherwin. GP
Balance of Europe, The. Pope. SeCeV
Balanced a row of peas on it. My Grandaddy Mostly with His Knife. David Huddle. GrPl
Balanced Bait in Handy Pellet Form, A. Allen Curnow. OCNZ
Balancing of gaudy broad pavilions, The. Irradiations, IV. John Gould Fletcher. TwAmPo
Balancing spaces are not disturbed, The. The Known Soldier. Kenneth Patchen. WaaP
Balancing 'twixt earth and sky. The Pole-Vaulter. *Unknown.* LiSp
Balankin was as gude a mason. Lamkin. *Unknown.* ESPB
Balboa. Nora Perry. PAH
Balboa, the Entertainer. Amiri Baraka. NoAM
Balcon, Le. Baudelaire, *tr. fr. French by* Lord Alfred Douglas. AWP
Balcony Poems, The. Douglas Smith. AMV-81
Balcony with Birds, A. Howard Moss. NePoEA
Bald-bare, bone-bare, and ivory yellow: skull. The U.S. Sailor with the Japanese Skull. Winfield Townley Scott. LiTM; MiAP; NMP; WaP
Bald Cavalier, The. *Unknown.* OxBChV
Bald heads forgetful of their sins. The Scholars. W. B. Yeats. CMoP; NoP; OAEL-2; PoA
Bald Spot, The. Wesley McNair. AMV-81
Balder, *sels.* Sydney Dobell.
Chanted Calendar, A. HBV-1; HBVY; OBEV
(Procession of the Flowers, The.) GN
"Was this world built for happiness, that man." PeD
Balder Dead, *sel.* Matthew Arnold.
Second Asgard, The. FiP
Balder's Wife. Alice Cary. AA
Baldpate Pond. E. F. Weisslitz. NYBP
Baldy Bane. W. S. Graham. NePoEA
Baldy Green. *Unknown.* PoOW
Balearic Idyll. Frederick Packard. FiBHP
Bale-fire kindled in the night, A. Carlyle and Emerson. Montgomery Schuyler. AA

Balgu Song. *Unknown, tr. fr. Balgu by* Clancy McKenna. CBAP
Balinda's Dance. Louise Erdrich. TWSS
Balkis. Lascelles Abercrombie. *Fr.* Emblems of Love: Judith. HBV-2
(Song: "Balkis was in her marble town.") MoBrPo
Ballgame, The. Amiri Baraka. DiL
Ball Game. Richard Eberhart. LiSp
Ball of fire shoots through the tamarack, A. The Scarlet Tanager. Joel Benton. AA
Ball Poem, The. John Berryman. CoAP; FF; LiSp; MoAmPo; NoAM; NOBA; NoP
Ball will bounce, but less and less, A. Juggler. Richard Wilbur. CMoP; LiTM; MoAB; NCSH; NePA; NePoEA; NYBP; TAP
Ballad, A: "As I was walkin' the jungle round, a-killin' of tigers an' time." Guy Wetmore Carryl. BXAP; InMe; Par
Ballad: "Auld wife sat at her ivied door, The." Charles Stuart Calverley. BXAP; CenHV; FaBoCo; FaBoNo; FiBHP; HBV-1; InMe; Par; SpRo; VLP; WhC; WiR
(Auld Wife, The.) NA
Ballad: "Blackbird has built in the pasture agen, The." John Clare. *Fr.* Child Harold. VLP
Ballad: "Father, through the dark that parts us." Roy Fuller. ELU
Ballad: "Follow, follow me into the South." Marjorie Allen Seiffert. HBMV
Ballad: "He passed by with another." Gabriela Mistral, *tr. fr. Spanish by* Doris Dana. OLR
Ballad: "He said: 'The shadows darken down.'" May Kendall. HBV-1
Ballad: "I put my hat upon my head." Samuel Johnson. NOBL
Ballad: "I want to know the unity in all things." A. R. Ammons. GP
Ballad: "In the summer even." Harriet Prescott Spofford. HBV-1
Ballad: "It was Earl Haldan's daughter." Charles Kingsley. GN
Ballad: "Mother mine, Mother mine, what do you see?" Annemarie Ewing. NePoAm
Ballad: "My lady was found mutilated." Leonard Cohen. OBCV
Ballad: "Noble Ritter Hugo, Der." Charles Godfrey Leland. *See* Ballad by Hans Breitmann.
Ballad: "Oh, come my joy, my soldier boy." Henry Treece. WaP
Ballad: "O! shairly ye hae seen my love." William Soutar. NeBP
Ballad: "O What Is That Sound." W. H. Auden. *See* O What Is That Sound.
Ballad: "Of all the girls that e'er were seen." John Gay. CoMu; ErPo
Ballad: "Roses in my garden, The." Maurice Baring. HBV-1
Ballad: "'Twas when the seas were roaring." John Gay. *Fr.* The What D'Ye-Call-It. HBV-1; ViBoPo
('Twas When the Seas Were Roaring.) HAP
Ballad: "What's that approaching like dust like poverty." Charles Simic. LCAP
Ballad against the Enemies of France. Villon, *tr. fr. French by* Swinburne. AWP
Ballad by Hans Breitmann. Charles Godfrey Leland. BXAP; CenHV; NOBL
(Ballad: "Noble Ritter Hugo, Der.") PaPo
(Ballad of the Mermaid.) FiBHP
Ballad Called Perkin's Figary, A. *Unknown.* APAS
Ballad Called the Haymarket Hectors, A. *Unknown.* APAS
Ballad for a Boy, A. William Johnson Cory. OxBChV
(Two Captains, The.) FaPoR
Ballad for Gloom. Ezra Pound. LiTM; MoAmPo; NePA; OBVV
Ballad for Katharine of Aragon, A. Charles Causley. FaBoTw; NePoEA
Ballad for Sue Ellen Westerfield, The. Robert Hayden. NoAM
Ballad for the Unknown Soldier. Allan Taylor. OBET
Ballad from the Seven Dials Press, A. *Unknown.* CoMu; VLP
Ballad in Blank Verse of the Making of a Poet, A, *sel.* John Davidson.
Greenock. BSV
Ballad in Blonde Hair Foretold. Robert Bagg. NePoAm-2
Ballad in "G," A. Eugene Fitch Ware. PoLF
Ballad, November 1680, Made upon Casting the Bill against the Duke of York, A. *Unknown.* APAS
Ballad of a Barber, The. Aubrey Beardsley. PAI; SyP
Ballad of a Bun, A. Sir Owen Seaman. CenHV
Ballad of a Mine, A. Robin Skelton. MoBS
Ballad of a Nun, A. John Davidson. BeLS; HBMV; MoBrPo; OnMSP
Ballad of a Strange Thing. H. Phelps Putnam. MoVE; OxBA
Ballad of a Sweet Dream of Peace. Robert Penn Warren. TwAmPo
Ballad of Abbreviations, A. G. K. Chesterton. NOBL
Ballad of Adam's First, The. Leland Davis. HBMV
Ballad of Agincourt, The. Michael Drayton. *See* Agincourt.
Ballad of All [the] Trades, A. *Unknown.* CoMu; ErPo; UnTE
Ballad of an Empty Table. Tom Kryss. NeAC
Ballad of Andrew and Maudlin, A. *Unknown.* CoMu
Ballad of Another Ophelia. D. H. Lawrence. ChTr; CoBMV; MoVE
Ballad of Badmen. Owen Dodson. FB
Ballad of Ballymote, The. Tess Gallagher. GP
Ballad of Banners (1944), The. John Lehmann. MoBS
Ballad of Barnaby, The. W. H. Auden. OBNV
Ballad of Bedlam. *Unknown.* NA
Ballad of Billie Potts, The. Robert Penn Warren. NOBA; OxBA
Ballad of Billy Rose, The. Leslie Norris. MoBS
Ballad of Billy the Kid, The. Henry Herbert Knibbs. BPAW
Ballad of Birmingham. Dudley Randall. BPo; HeIP; InPK; NIP; NoAM
Ballad of Bouillabaisse, The. Thackeray. HBV-1; InMe; OBEV; OBVV; ViBoPo
"This Bouillabaisse a noble dish is," *sel.* FaBoUs
Ballad of Bunker Hill, The. Edward Everett Hale. PAH
Ballad of Camden Town, The. James Elroy Flecker. HBV-1
Ballad of Captain Kidd, The. *Unknown.* *See* Captain Kidd.
Ballad of Cassandra Brown, The. Helen Gray Cone. InMe
Ballad of Charity, The. Charles Godfrey Leland. InMe
Ballad of Chickamauga, The. Maurice Thompson. PAH
Ballad of Chicken Bill, The. F. E. Vaughn. PoOW
Ballad of Chocolate Mabbie, The. Gwendolyn Brooks. CAPP
Ballad of Christmas, A. Walter de la Mare. OBCP
Ballad of Culinary Frustration. Phyllis McGinley. FiBHP
Ballad of Dead Ladies, A. Justin Huntly M'Carthy, *par. fr. the French of* Villon. *Fr.* If I Were King, *ch.* 9. HBV-1
Ballad of Dead Ladies, The. Villon, *tr. fr. French by* Dante Gabriel Rossetti. AWP; CTC; FaFP; GoBC; HBV-1; PoRA; PrIM; ViBoPo
(Ballade of Dead Ladies, *tr. by* Andrew Lang.) HBV-1
(Ballat o the Leddies o Langsyne, *tr. by* Tom Scott.) OBVE
(Snows of Yester-Year, The.) WiR
Ballad of Dead Men's Bay, The. Swinburne. MOS
Ballad of Dead Yankees, The. Donald Petersen. HeIP; LiSp
Ballad of Don Juan Tenorio and the Statue of the Comendador. Roy Campbell. PeSA
Ballad of Douglas Bridge. Francis Carlin. AnIV; HBMV; OxBI
Ballad of Downal Baun, The. Padraic Colum. SUS
Ballad of Dowsabell, The. Michael Drayton. *See* Cassamen and Dowsabell.
Ballad of Dreamland, A. Swinburne. HBV-1
Ballad of East and West, The. Kipling. BeLS; BLPL; BrPo; FaBoBe; FaBV; FaPoR; HBV-2; OBNV
"Oh, East is East, and West is West," *sel.* TRV
Ballad of Faith. William Carlos Williams. OBAL
Ballad of Father Gilligan, The. W. B. Yeats. AnIV; EaLo; EBVV; HBV-2; MoBrPo; OnYI; PoRA
Ballad of Father O'Hart, The. W. B. Yeats. *See* Priest of Coloony, The.
Ballad of Fisher's Boardinghouse, The. Kipling. PoRA
Ballad of François Villon, A. Swinburne. PoEL-5; PoRA
Ballad of Good Counsel. Chaucer. *See* Balade de Bon Conseyl.
Ballad of Hampstead Heath, The. James Elroy Flecker. MoBrPo
Ballad of Heaven, A. John Davidson. BeLS
Ballad of Hector in Hades. Edwin Muir. NoAM; NOBE
Ballad of Hell, A. John Davidson. HBMV; HoPM; MoBrPo; WHA
(Christmas Eve.) EBVV; OHIP
Ballad of Heroes, A. Austin Dobson. HBV-2; HBVY; OHIP
Ballad of High Endeavor, A. *Unknown.* NA
Ballad of Hiram Hover, The. Bayard Taylor. BXAP; FaBoCo; OBAL
Ballad of Ho Chi Minh. Ewan MacColl. FSW
Ballad of Human Life. Thomas Lovell Beddoes. BeLS
Ballad of Imitation, The. Austin Dobson. HBV-1
Ballad of Ira Hayes. Peter La Farge. MAT
Ballad of Ishmael Day, The. *Unknown.* PAH
Ballad of John Cable and Three Gentlemen. W. S. Merwin. CoAP; NePoEA; NOBA
Ballad of John Silver, A. John Masefield. EvOK
Ballad of Johnny Appleseed, A. Helmer O. Oleson. SiSoSe; TiPo
Ballad of Judas Iscariot, The. Robert Buchanan. HBV-2
Ballad of Keith of Ravelston, The. Sydney Dobell. *Fr.* A Nuptial Eve. HBV-2; OBEV; OBVV
Ballad of Kynd Kittok, The. William Dunbar. BSV; GoTS; OxBoLi
Ballad of Ladies' Love, Number Two. Villon, *tr. fr. French by* John Payne. ErPo
Ballad of Lager Bier, The. Edmund Clarence Stedman. OBAL
Ballad of Life, A. Swinburne. HBV-1
Ballad of London, A. Richard Le Gallienne. FaBoPP; HBMV
Ballad of Longwood Glen, The. Vladimir Nabokov. NYBP
Ballad of Low-lie-down. Madison Cawein. HBV-1
Ballad of Luna, Luna. Federico García Lorca, *tr. fr. Spanish by* William B. Logan. SOTW
Ballad of Manila Bay, A. Sir Charles G. D. Roberts. PAH
Ballad of Mary Baldwin, The. Stephen Sandy. MAT
Ballad of Master McGrath, A. *Unknown.* FaBoBa
(Master McGrath.) OBET
Ballad of Minepit Shaw, The. Kipling. PoPle
Ballad of Mistress Death. Denis Devlin. NMP
Ballad of Mrs. Noah, The. Robert Duncan. NoAM; NOBA
Ballad of Nat Turner, The. Robert E. Hayden. BALP; BPo; VGW

Ballad of New Orleans, The. George Henry Boker. PAH
Ballad of No Proper Man. Daniel Hoffman. MAT
Ballad of O'Bruadir, The. F. R. Higgins. EtS; OBMV
Ballad of Oriskany, The. Obadiah Cyrus Auringer. AA
Ballad of Orleans, A. Agnes Mary Frances Robinson. HBV-2
Ballad of Our Lady. William Dunbar. ACP; ISi, *mod. vers. by* E. M. Clerke.
(Ane Ballat of Our Lady.) OxBS
(Hymn to Mary, A.) MeEL
"Empryce of prys, imperatrice," *sel.* EBEV
Ballad of Paco Town, The. Clinton Scollard. PAH
Ballad of Past Meridian, A. George Meredith. OAEL-2; VLP
Ballad of Persse O'Reilly, The. James Joyce. *Fr.* Finnegans Wake. FaBoBa; LiTB
Ballad of Private Chadd, The. A. A. Milne. CenHV
Ballad of Pug-nosed Lil, The. Robert H. Fletcher. BPAW
Ballad of Queensland (Sam Holt), A. G. H. Gibson. PoAu-1
Ballad of Reading Gaol, The. Oscar Wilde. BeLS; BrPo; DTo; HBV-2; OBNV; OnYI; TreF
Sels.
"He did not wear his scarlet coat." MoBrPo; NOBE; OBMV; OBNC
"In Debtor's Yard the stones are hard." ViBoPo
"In Reading gaol by Reading town." FaFP; LiTB; PoPl
"There is no chapel on the day." EBVV; OxBI
"Yet each man kills the thing he loves." TEP; TrGrPo; WHA
Ballad of Red Fox, The. Melvin Walker La Follette. BoAnP; NePoEA
Ballad of Redhead's Day, A. Richard Butler Glaenzer. PAH
Ballad of Remembrance, A. Robert Hayden. AmNP; BPo; IDB; PoBA; PoNe
Ballad of Sally in Our Alley, The. Henry Carey. *See* Sally in Our Alley.
Ballad of Sam Hall. *Unknown. See* Sam Hall.
Ballad of Sarsfield, A. Aubrey Thomas De Vere. GoBC; HBV-2
Ballad of Sir Brian and the Three Wishes, The. Newman Levy. FiBHP
Ballad of Sir John Franklin, A. George Henry Boker. AA; HBV-2; OnMSP
Ballad of Sir Patrick Spens, The. *Unknown.* EtS; RoGo
Ballad of Springhill (The Springhill Mine Disaster). Ewan MacColl *and* Peggy Seeger. FSW
Ballad of Sue Ellen Westerfield, The. Robert Hayden. AmPP
Ballad of Sweet P, The. Virginia Woodward Cloud. PAH
Ballad of the Angel, The. Theodosia Garrison. HBV-1
Ballad of the Boat, The. Richard Garnett. HBV-2
Ballad of the Boll Weevil, The. *Unknown. See* Ballit of de Boll Weevil, De.
Ballad of the Boston Tea-Party, A. Oliver Wendell Holmes. PAH; PAL
Ballad of the Captains, A. E. J. Brady. EtS
Ballad of the Children of the Czar, The. Delmore Schwartz. MiAP
Ballad of the Common Man. Alfred Kreymborg. PAL
Ballad of the Conemaugh Flood, A. Hardwick Drummond Rawnsley. PAH
Ballad of the Cool Fountain. *Unknown, tr. fr. Spanish by* Edwin Honig. BoWoP
Ballad of the Courtier and the Country Clown, A. *Unknown.* CoMu
Ballad of the Cross, The. Theodosia Garrison. HBMV; HBVY
Ballad of the Dark Ladie, The. Samuel Taylor Coleridge. EnRP
Ballad of the Days of the Messiah. A. M. Klein. TrJP
Ballad of the D-Day Dodgers. *Unknown.* WTO
(D-Day Dodgers, The.) FSW
Ballad of the Despairing Husband. Robert Creeley. NeAP; NoP; OBAL
Ballad of the Double Bed. Eve Merriam. UnTE
Ballad of the Drinker in His Pub. N. F. van Wyk Louw, *tr. fr. Afrikaans by* Uys Krige, Jack Cope, *and* Ruth Miller. PeSA
Ballad of the Drover. Henry Lawson. PoAu-1
Ballad of the Epiphany. Charles Dalmon. HBMV; OnMSP
Ballad of the Faded Field. Robert Burns Wilson. AA
Ballad of the Faithful Clerk. Albert Stillman. DBV; InMe
Ballad of the Fleet, A. Tennyson. *See Revenge,* The.
Ballad of the Flood. Edwin Muir. MoBS
Ballad of the French Fleet, A. Longfellow. AA; HBV-2; PAH
Ballad of the Gibbet. Villon, *tr. by* Andrew Lang. AWP
Ballad of the Gold Country, A. Helen Hunt Jackson. BPAW
Ballad of the Golden Bowl. Sara Henderson Hay. OnMSP
Ballad of the Good Lord Nelson, A. Lawrence Durrell. ErPo; LiTM
Ballad of the Goodly Fere. Ezra Pound. CMoP; HBV-2; LiTA; LiTM; MoAB; MoAmPo; MoBS; NePA; NoAM; OFD; PoRA; TrCP; TrGrPo
Ballad of the Harp-Weaver, The. Edna St. Vincent Millay. WSC
Ballad of the Hidden Dragon, *abr. Unknown, tr. fr. Chinese.* WTO
Ballad of the Hoppy-Toad. Margaret Walker. BlSi; FB; HoPM
Ballad of the Hyde Street Grip. Gelett Burgess. BPAW
Ballad of the Icondic. John Ciardi. OBAL
Ballad of the Landlord. Langston Hughes. NOBA
Ballad of the Lincoln Penny. Alfred Kreymborg. YaD
Ballad of the Little Black Hound. Dora Sigerson Shorter. OnYI
Ballad of the Londoner. James Elroy Flecker. EnLoPo
Ballad of the Long-legged Bait. Dylan Thomas. CoBMV; SeCeV
Ballad of the Lords of Old Time. Villon, *tr. fr. French by* Swinburne. AWP
Ballad of the Mermaid. Charles Godfrey Leland. *See* Ballad by Hans Breitmann.
Ballad of the Morning Streets. Amiri Baraka. CNA; SOTW
Ballad of the Mouse. Robert Wallace. NYBP
Ballad of the Oedipus Complex. Lawrence Durrell. FaBoCo
Ballad of the Outer Life. Hugo von Hofmannsthal, *tr. fr. German by* Jethro Bithell. AWP; TrJP
Ballad of the Oysterman, The. Oliver Wendell Holmes. AP; EtS; FaFP; HBV-2; HBVY; MOS; MoShBr; TreFS
Ballad of the Rising in the North, A. *Unknown.* ACP
Ballad of the Strange and Wonderful Storm of Hail, A. *Unknown.* CoMu
Ballad of the Tempest. James Thomas Fields. BeLS; BLPL; EtS; FaBoBe; HBV-1; HBVY; PoLF; YaD
(Captain's Daughter, The.) FaFP
(Tempest, The.) TreF
Ballad of the Ten Casino Dancers. Cecilia Meireles, *tr. fr. Portuguese by* James Merrill. BoWoP
Ballad of the Three Coins. Vernon Watkins. NoAM
Ballad of the Three Spectres. Ivor Gurney. OBWP
Ballad of the Two Tapsters. Vernon Watkins. MoBS
Ballad of the White Horse, The, *sels.* G. K. Chesterton.
"Before the gods that made the gods." ACP
Harp of Alfred, The. MoVE
King Alfred Answers the Danes. OxBoCh
Songs of Guthrum and Alfred, The. HBV-2
Ballad of the Women of Paris. Villon, *tr. fr. French by* Swinburne. AWP
(Ballade of the Women of Paris.) UnTE
Ballad of Tonopah Bill, The. *Unknown.* BPAW
Ballad of Trees and the Master, A. Sidney Lanier. AA; AP; EBCP; FPL; GoBC; HBV-2; LiTA; NOBA; OxBA; PoEL-5; PoLF; TreFT; TRV; WGRP
(Into the Woods My Master went, *with music.*) AH
Ballad of Villon and Fat Madge, The. Villon, *tr. fr. French by* Swinburne. OBVE
Ballad of William Bloat, The. *Unknown.* DBV; NOBL
(Belfast Linen.) WTO
Ballad of William Sycamore, The. Stephen Vincent Benét. HBMV; MoAmPo; PoRA; TreFT
Ballad of Yukon Jake, The. Edward E. Paramore, Jr. BeLS; BLPA
Ballad on the Taxes, A. Edward Ward. OxBoLi; PPON
Ballad on the Times, A. Henry Hall. APAS
Ballad-Singer, The. Thomas Hardy. At Casterbridge Fair, I. BoLoP; OLR; VLP
Ballad to a Traditional Refrain. Maurice James Craig. BIrV; SeCePo
Ballad to Queen Elizabeth, A. Austin Dobson. OBVV
(Ballade of the Armada, A.) FaPoR
Ballad to the Tune of Bateman, A. Sir Charles Sedley. CoMu
Ballad to the Tune of "The Cut-Purse," A. Swift. PP
Ballad [*or* Ballade] upon a Wedding, A. Sir John Suckling. AnAnS-2; CABA; CaPo; CavP; CoMu; EBEV; FaBoBa; HBV-1; InvP; JCP; LoBV; NoP; OBS; Par; SeCeV; SeCP; SeCV-1; UnTE; ViBoPo
Bride, The, *sel.* TrGrPo
Ballad upon the Popish Plot, A. John Gadbury. CoMu
Ballad Which Anne Askew Made and Sang When She Was in Newgate, The. Anne Askew. WPE
Ballad with an Ancient Refrain. *Unknown.* NA
Ballad Written for a Bridegroom. Villon, *tr. fr. French by* Swinburne. AWP
Ballade: "Brother humans who live on after us." Villon, *tr. fr. French by* Galway Kinnell. NAWM-1
(Ballat o the Hingit, *tr. by* Tom Scott.) OBVE
Ballade: "Outcast bones from a thousand biers." Don Marquis. WhC
Ballade: "Pretty maid she died, she died, in love-bed as she lay, The." Paul Fort, *tr. fr. French by* Frederick York Powell. AWP
(Pretty Maid, The.) OBMV
Ballade against Woman Inconstant, A. Chaucer. *See* Against Women Unconstant.
Ballade-Catalogue of Lovely Things, A. Richard Le Gallienne. HBMV
Ballade de Marguerite. *Unknown, tr. fr. French by* Oscar Wilde. AWP
Ballade des Belles Milatraisses. Rosalie Jonas. BlSi
Ballade d'une Grande Dame. G. K. Chesterton. OxBoLi
Ballade Made in the Hot Weather. W. E. Henley. MoBrPo
(Made in the Hot Weather.) GN
Ballade of a Friar. Clément Marot, *tr. fr. French by* Andrew Lang. HBV-1
Ballade of a Summer Hotel. "Junia." WhC
Ballade of a Talked-off Ear. Dorothy Parker. DBV
Ballade of Andrew Lang. Dugald Sutherland MacColl. CenHV
Ballade of Any Father to Any Son, A. J. C. Squire. WhC
Ballade of Beauties. Alexander Scott. BSV
Ballade of Big Plans. Dorothy Parker. InMe

Ballade of Boys Bathing. Frederick Rolfe. PeHV
Ballade of Charon and the River Girl. J. B. Morton. WhC
Ballade of Dead Actors. W. E. Henley. EBVV; OBMV
Ballade of Dead Friends. E. A. Robinson. AA
Ballade of Dead Ladies, The. Villon. *See* Ballad of Dead Ladies, The.
Ballade of Diminishing Control, A. J. C. Squire. WhC
Ballade of England. Louis MacNeice. NYBP
Ballade of Evolution, A. Grant Allen. EBVV
Ballade of Expansion. Hilda Johnson. PAH
Ballade of Faith. Tom MacInnes. CaP
Ballade of Good Counsel. Chaucer. *See* Balade de Bon Conseyl.
Ballade of Hell and of Mrs. Roebeck. Hilaire Belloc. MoVE
Ballade of Illegal Ornaments. Hilaire Belloc. ACP
Ballade of Islands, A. Lucy Catlin Robinson. AA
Ballade of Ladies' Love. Villon, *tr. fr. French by* John Payne. UnTE
Ballade of Ladies' Names. W. E. Henley. HBV-1
Ballade of Liquid Refreshment. E. C. Bentley. FaBoCo
Ballade of Lost Objects. Phyllis McGinley. PoCh; PoRA
Ballade of Middle Age. Andrew Lang. HBV-1
Ballade of My Lady's Beauty. Joyce Kilmer. HBV-1
Ballade of Sayings. W. S. Merwin. NNaP
Ballade of Schopenhauer's Philosophy. Franklin P. Adams. HBMV
Ballade of Soporific Absorption. J. C. Squire. InMe
Ballade of Suicide, A. G. K. Chesterton. FiBHP; HBV-1; InMe
Ballade of the Ancient Wheeze. Nate Salsbury *and* Newman Levy. InMe
Ballade of the Armada, A. Austin Dobson. *See* Ballad to Queen Elizabeth, A.
Ballade of the Dreamland Rose. Brian Hooker. HBMV
Ballade of the Fair Helm-Maker. Villon, *tr. fr. French by* John Payne. UnTE
Ballade of the Goth. Sir Walter Alexander Raleigh. WhC
Ballade of the Heresiarchs. Hilaire Belloc. MoVE
Ballade of the Incompetent Ballade-Monger, The. James Kenneth Stephen. VLP
Ballade of the Nurserie, A. John Twig. NA
Ballade of the Old-Time Engine. Eda H. Vines. QQQ
Ballade of the Poetic Life. J. C. Squire. OBMV; WhC
Ballade of the Primitive Jest. Andrew Lang. HBV-1
Ballade of the Scottyshe Kynge, A. John Skelton. CoMu; FaBoBa
Ballade of the Session after Camarillo. David Galler. NMP
Ballade of the Under Side. Don Marquis. InvP
Ballade of the Women of Paris. Villon. *See* Ballad of the Women of Paris.
Ballade of Unfortunate Mammals. Dorothy Parker. InMe
Ballade of Villon and Fat Margot. Villon, *tr. fr. French by* John Payne. UnTE
Ballade of Youth and Age. W. E. Henley. VLP
Ballade on Eschatology. Sister Mary Madeleva. GoYe
Ballade to His Mistress. Villon, *tr. fr. French by* Norman Cameron. WeW
Ballade to My Psychoanalyst. Kenneth Lillington. FiBHP
Ballade to Our Lady. Alexander Barclay. *Fr.* The Ship of Fools. ISi
Ballade to Our Lady of Czestochowa. Hilaire Belloc. ACP; ISi
Ballade to Rosamund. Chaucer. *See* To Rosamond.
Ballade Tragique à Double Refrain. Max Beerbohm. OBSV
Ballade un Peu Banale. A. J. M. Smith. MoCV
Ballade upon a Wedding, A. Sir John Suckling. *See* Ballad upon a Wedding, A.
Ballant o' the Laird's Bath, The. Douglas Young. BSV
Ballat o the Hingit. Villon. *See* Ballade: "Brother humans who live on after us."
Ballat o the Leddies o Langsyne. Villon. *See* Ballad of Dead Ladies, The.
Ballata: Concerning a Shepherd-Maid. Guido Cavalcanti, *tr. fr. Italian by* Dante Gabriel Rossetti. AWP
Ballata: He Reveals, in a Dialogue, His Increasing Love for Mandetta. Guido Cavalcanti, *tr. fr. Italian by* Dante Gabriel Rossetti. AWP
Ballata: He Will Gaze upon Beatrice. Dante, *tr. fr. Italian by* Dante Gabriel Rossetti. AWP
(Sonnet: "Because mine eyes can never have their fill.") GoBC
Ballata: His Talk with Certain Peasant-Girls. Franco Sacchetti, *tr. fr. Italian by* Dante Gabriel Rossetti. AWP
Ballata: In Exile at Sarzana. Guido Cavalcanti, *tr. fr. Italian by* Dante Gabriel Rossetti. AWP
Ballata V: "Light do I see within my Lady's eyes." Guido Cavalcanti, *tr. fr. Italian by* Ezra Pound. CTC
Ballata: Of a Continual Death in Love. Guido Cavalcanti, *tr. fr. Italian by* Dante Gabriel Rossetti. AWP
Ballata: Of His Lady among Other Ladies. Guido Cavalcanti, *tr. fr. Italian by* Dante Gabriel Rossetti. AWP
Ballata: Of True and False Singing. *Unknown, tr. fr. Italian by* Dante Gabriel Rossetti. AWP
Ballata: One Speaks of the Beginning of His Love. *Unknown, tr. fr. Italian by* Dante Gabriel Rossetti. AWP
Ballatetta. Ezra Pound. VGW
Ballet. Brenda Hillman. AMV-81
Ballet. Milton Kaplan. SOTS
Ballet. *Unknown.* TDH
Ballet of de [*or* the] Boll Weevil, De. *Unknown.* *See* Ballit of De Boll Weevil, De.
Ballet of the Fifth Year, The. Delmore Schwartz. MoAB; MP; OxBA; TwCP
Ballet under the Stars. Robert Stewart. FAZ
Ballinderry. *Unknown.* WTO
Balliol Rhymes, *sels. Var. authors.*
"First come I. My name is Jowett." Henry Charles Beeching. CenHV; FaBoCo; FaBoEE; GLGT; NOBL; PoPle
"I am a most superior person. Henry Charles Beeching. CenHV
"I am Andrew Cecil Bradley." Cecil Arthur Spring-Rice. CenHV
"I am Branson; Nature's laws." Henry Charles Beeching *and* John Bowyer Nichols. FaBoEE
"I am featly-tripping Lee." Henry Charles Beeching. CenHV; FaBoEE; GLGT
"I am Huxley, blond and merry." John Bowyer Buchanan Nichols. CenHV
"I am rather tall and stately." *Unknown.* FaBoEE; NOBL
"I am the Dean, and this is Mrs. Liddell." *Unknown.* FaBoEE
"I am the Dean of Christ Church, Sir." Cecil Arthur Spring-Rice. CenHV; FaBoCo; FaBoEE; NOBL
"I'm the great Sir William Anson." *Unknown.* FaBoEE
"My name is George Nathaniel Curzon." John William Mackail *and* Cecil Arthur Spring-Rice. FaBoCo; FaBoEE; NOBL
"Old tips come out as good as new." John William Mackail. CenHV
"Positivists ever talk in s-/Uch an epic style as Dawkins." John William Mackail. FaBoEE
"Roughly, so to say, you know." John William Mackail. CenHV
"Upright and shrewd, more woo'd of fame." Henry Charles Beeching. CenHV
Ballit of de Boll Weevil, De. *Unknown.* NOBA
(Ballad of the Boll Weevil, The.) FSW; TrAS, *with music*
(Ballet of de Boll Weevil, De, *with music.*) AS
(Ballet of the Boll Weevil, The.) ViBoFo (*A vers.; B vers., with music*)
(Boll Weevil Song, The, *with music.*) AS; BLSo
Balloon, The. Karla Kuskin. PDV
Balloon, The. Tennyson. *See* As When a Man.
Balloon Faces. Carl Sandburg. CMoP
Balloon Man, The. Dorothy Aldis. TiPo
Balloon Man, The. Rose Fyleman. SoPo; SUS
Balloon Man. Jessica N. North. SoPo
Balloon of the Mind, The. W. B. Yeats. POL
Balloons. Sylvia Plath. NCSH
Balloons hang on wires in the Marigold Gardens, The. Balloon Faces. Carl Sandburg. CMoP
Ballot, The. John Pierpont. AA
Ballroom Dancing Class. Phyllis McGinley. MoShBr
Ballroom was filled with fashion's throng, The. A Bird in a Gilded Cage. Arthur J. Lamb. BLSo; FSN; FSW; TreFT
Ball's Bluff. Herman Melville. OBWP
Balls in an over, six you know. Aids for Latin. Gordon Perry. FaBoUs
Ball's lost, lost, gone. The Lost Ball. Lucy Sprague Mitchell. TiPo
Ballydavid Pier. Thomas Kinsella. BIrV
Ballykinlar: May 1940. Patrick Maybin. NeIP
Ballymurphy. *Unknown.* FSW
Ballynahinch. George Canning. FaBoCo
Ballyshannon foundered off the coast of Cariboo, The. Etiquette. W. S. Gilbert. CenHV; FaBoCh; FaBoCo; FiBHP; VLP
Balm in Gilead. *Unknown.* FSW
Balme. Spenser. *Fr.* The Faerie Queene, I, 11. CH
Balmy spring wind, A. Four Haiku [*or* Haiku]. Richard Wright. FAZ; NoAM
Baloo, loo, lammy, now baloo, my dear. Lullaby. Lady Nairne. HBV-1
Balow. *Unknown.* OBEV
(By-low, My Babe, *abr.*) TrGoPo
(Lady Anne Bothwell's Lament.) HBV-1
Balow, my Babe, weep not for me. The New Balow. *Unknown.* CoMu
Balsham Bells. Kenrick Prescot. NOEC
Balthasar's Song. Shakespeare. *See* Sigh No More, Ladies.
Balulalow. James, John, *and* Robert Wedderburn. LoBV; OxBoCh
(Cradle Song: "O my deir hert, young Jesus sweit.") EaLo; OBEV
Bam, Bam, Bam. Eve Merriam. PDV
Bambi-eyed rich girls. Poem for Edie Sedgwick Who Slept in a Swimming Pool. Stewart Brisby. LFAC
Bambini picking daisies in the new spring grass. Daisies of Florence. Kathleen Raine. NYBP
Bamboo. William Plomer. PeSA
Ban of Time there is no disobeying, The. Lament. Gelett Burgess. InMe

Bañalbufar, a Brazier, Relativity, Cloud Formations & the Kindness & Relentlessness of Time. Paul Blackburn. CoPo
Banana. Charles G. Bell. ErPo; NePoAm-2
Banana. Adrian Mitchell. PV
Banana leaves are burning. "Containing Communism." Charlie Cobb. PoBA
Banana-stuffed, the ape behind the brain. After Sunday Dinner We Uncles Snooze. John Ciardi. HoAn
Bananananananana. William Cole. RHPC
Bananas ripe and green, and ginger-root. The Tropics in New York. Claude McKay. AmNP; NoAM; PoBA; PoNe; TTY
Band, The. Carl Dennis. AMV-80
Band in the Pines, The. John Esten Cooke. AA
Band makes a tunnel of the open street. The Bands and the Beautiful Children. P. K. Page. PeCV
Band Music. John Fuller. NePoEA-2
Band of Gideon, The. Joseph S. Cotter, Jr. BANP; CDC
Band o' Gideon, De, *with music. Unknown.* BoAN-1
Band of the bold were gathered together, The. The Parting of the Red Sea. *Unknown, tr. by* Charles W. Kennedy. *Fr.* Exodus. AnOE
Band Played On, The. John F. Palmer. BLSo, *with music;* FSN, *with music;* FSW; OBAL; TreF
Band Played Waltzing Matilda, The. Eric Bogle. OBET
Banded Cobra, The. C. Louis Leipoldt, *tr. fr. Afrikaans by* Uys Krige, Jack Cope, *and* Ruth Miller. PeSA
Bandersnatch is a strange affair, The. Wash-Day Wonder. Dorothy Faubion. QQQ
Bandinello slouches on a chair. Geo-Politics. Alvaro Cardona-Hine. PoDr
Bandit. A. M. Klein. WHW
Bandog, The. Walter de la Mare. BrPo; EvOK; TiPo
Bands and the Beautiful Children, The. P. K. Page. PeCV
Bang, bang, bang. The History of the Flood. John Heath-Stubbs. MoBS; OxBTC
Bangkok. F. R. Scott. MoCV; OBCV
Banish the scent of sherry and cigars. After the Party. Frances Cornford. ELU
Banished, dispossessed dead, The. Litany of the Rooms of the Dead. Franz Werfel, *tr. by* Edith Abercrombie Snow. TrJP
Banished Duke of Grantham, The. *Unknown.* EnSB
Banished Gods, The. Derek Mahon. OxBC
Banished thrush, the homeless rook, The. Nature in War-Time. S. Gertrude Ford. SUMH
Banishment, The ("So spoke our Mother Eve, and Adam heard"). Milton. *Fr.* Paradise Lost, XII. NOBE; OBS
(Exit from Eden, The.) FaBoRV
Banishment from Paradise ("Descended Adam to the bower where Eve"). Milton. *See* Adam Fallen.
Banishment from Ur. Enheduanna, *tr. fr. Sumerian; ad. by* Aliki *and* Willis Barnstone. BoWoP
Banjo, The. Robert Winner. FF
Banjo Player, The. Fenton Johnson. BANP; PoNe
Bank of the Arkansaw, The, *with music. Unknown.* OuSiCo
Bank swallows veer and dip, The. The Siskins. Theodore Roethke. PB
Bank Thief, The. J. R. Farrell. BeLS; BLPA
Bankers Are Just like Anybody Else, except Richer. Ogden Nash. LiTA
Banking Coal. Jean Toomer. PoNe
Bankis of Helicon, The, *sel. Unknown.* "Declair, ye bankis of Helicon." OxBS
Bankrupt. Cortlandt W. Sayres. PoLF
Banks fou, braes fou. *Unknown.* GBP
Banks o' Doon, The. Burns. BoLoP; BSV; HBV-1; LoBV; NOBE; NOEC; OBEC; OBEV; PrIm; TreFS; TrGrPo; ViBoPo; WBLP; WHA
(Bonie Doon.) NoP; PAI
(Bonnie Doon.) HBV-1
(Ye Banks and Braes [o' Bonnie Doon].) CH; ELP; GTBS; GTBS-P
(Ye Flowery Banks [o' Bonnie Doon].) AWP; EnRP; OAEP; OBEC; PoEL-4; UnPo
Banks of a River, The. Abraham Sutskever, *tr. fr. Yiddish by* Ruth Whitman. VWA
Banks of Champlain, The. *Unknown.* AmFP
Banks of Claudy, The. *Unknown.* AmFP; OBET
Banks of Dee, The. *Unknown.* AmFP
Banks of Dundee, The. *Unknown.* BaBo
Banks of Gaspereaux, The. *Unknown.* BaBo
(Banks of the Gaspereaux, The.) AmFP; ShS
Banks of Marble. Les Rice. FSW
Banks of Newfoundland, The. *Unknown.* GBP; ShS, *with music*
Banks of [the] Sacramento, The, *with music. Unknown.* AmSS; AS
Banks of Sweet Dundee, The. *Unknown.* AmFP
Banks of Sweet Primroses, The. *Unknown.* ELP
Banks of the Condamine, The. *Unknown.* FaBoBa; GBP; PoAu-1
Banks of the Gaspereaux, The. *Unknown.* *See* Banks of Gaspereaux, The.
Banks of the Nile, The. *Unknown.* OBET
Banks of the Ohio. *Unknown.* FSW
Banks of the Roses, The. *Unknown.* FSW; ShS, *with music*
Banks of the Sacramento, The. *Unknown.* *See* Banks of Sacramento, The.
Banks of Wye, The, *sels.* Robert Bloomfield.
Coracle Fishers, The. OBNC
Meandering Wye. OBNC
Banner of England, not for a season, O banner of Britain, hast thou. The Defence of Lucknow. Tennyson. BeLS
Banner of Freedom high floated unfurled, The. The *United States* and *Macedonian. Unknown.* PAH
Banner of the Jew, The. Emma Lazarus. AA; TrJP
Bannockburn. Burns. *See* Scots Wha Hae.
Bannockburn. Sir Walter Scott. *Fr.* The Lord of the Isles. BSV
Banquet, The. George Herbert. AnAnS-1
Banquet, The. Keats. *Fr.* Lamia. SeCePo
Banquet, A. Sotades, *tr. fr. Greek by* Charles Duke Yonge. FaBoUs
Banquet-cups, of many a hue and shape, The. The Respite. Maria Gowen Brooks. *Fr.* Zophiël. AA
"Banquet of the Century, The" in Persepolis. Alamgir Hashmi. SOTS
Bansha Peeler wint won night, A. The Peeler and the Goat. *Unknown.* AnIL
Banshee, The. John Todhunter. OnYI
Bantam Husband, The, *with music. Unknown.* OuSiCo
Bantams in Pine-Woods. Wallace Stevens. CMoP; InPS; MoVE; NOBA; OxBA; SeCeV; UnPo
Bantry Bay. James Lyman Molloy. OnYI
Baptism. Charles G. Bell. AmFN
Baptism. Claude McKay. PoNe
Baptism. Alden Nowlan. POL
Baptism. Dale Zieroth. NOBC
Baptist, The. William Drummond of Hawthornden. *See* For the Baptist.
Bar, The. *Unknown.* STF
Bar close as you can, and bolt fast too your door. No Lock against Lechery. Robert Herrick. CaPo
Bar Harbor. Marita Garin. AMV-81
Bar is closed and I come, The. Night on Clinton. Robert Mezey. AmPA; NaP
Bar is crossed, The; but Death—the pilot—stands. Becalmed. John Banister Tabb. AA
Bar Kochba. Emma Lazarus. TrJP
Bar Mitzvah. Isaac Goldemberg, *tr. fr. Spanish by* David Unger. VWA
Bar Mitzvah. Steve Orlen. GP
Bar my girlfriend works in is a dive, The. The Lights Go On. Mark McCloskey. AMV-80
Bar Not the Door. Thomas Campion. UnTE
Bar to heaven, a door to hell, A. The Bar. *Unknown.* STF
Barabbas, Judas Iscariot. The Morning After. Dorothy Wellesley. OBMV
Barbara. Alexander Smith. BSV; GoTS; HBV-1; OBVV
Barbara Allen [*or* Allan]. *Unknown.* BeLS; BSV; CABA; EnSB; FaBoBa; FaFP; FSW; OBET; TrAS, *with music;* TreF; ViBoFo (A *and* C *vers.;* B *vers., with music*)
(Barbara Allen's Cruelty.) FaBoBe; HBV-2; OBEV; ViBoPo
(Barbra Allen, *with music.*) AS; BLSo
(Barbry Ellen.) PrIm
(Bonny Barbara Allan [*or* Allen].) AmFP; AWP; BiP; BoLoP; CH; ESPB (A *and* B *vers.*); HeIP; InPk; LiTB; NoP (A *vers.*); OxBB, *with music;* PAI; TrGrPo
(Sir John Graeme and Barbara Allan.) OxBoLi
Barbara Frietchie. Whittier. AP; BeLS; CTC; FaBoBe; FaBV; FaFP; FaPo; FaPON; FaPoR; FPL; GN; HBV-2; HBVY; NOBA; OBAL; OBCA; PAH; PAL; PaPo; PoLF; PoSC; TreF; TrGrPo; WBLP; YaD
Barbara's Land Revisited—August 1978. Geary Hobson. STE
Barbarians. John Fowles. POL
Barbarians must we always be? Observing a Vulgar Name on the Plinth of an Ancient Statue. Walter Savage Landor. EyDe
Barbarossa. Friedrich Rückert, *tr. from German.* AWP, *tr. by* Elizabeth Craigmyle; WSC, *tr. by* John W. Thomas
Barbecue Blues. *Unknown.* BluL
Barbed Wire. Eithne Wilkins. NeBP
Barbed Wire Fence Meditates upon the Goldfinch, A. Don McKay. NOBC
Barber, The. Roy Fuller. NoAM
Barber, The. John Gray. SyP
Barber, barber, shave a pig. Mother Goose. EvOK; HBV-1; HBVY; OxNR
Barber shaved the mason, The. *Unknown.* OxNR
Barber snips and snips, The. Barber's Clippers. Dorothy Baruch. SoPo
Barber, Spare Those Hairs. John Love, Jr. YaD
Barberries. Mary Aldis. HBMV
Barberries ripe. Chant for Skippers. Katharine Gallagher. SiSoSe
Barberry-Bush, The. Jones Very. AP
Barber's, The. Walter de la Mare. GoJo; SoPo; SUS
Barber's Clippers. Dorothy Baruch. SoPo

Barber's Cry, *with music.* *Unknown.* TrAS
Barbershop. Martin Gardner. RHPC
Barber shop is blank, The. Through the Barber Shop Window. Violet Anderson. CaP
Barbie Doll. Marge Piercy. DFF; NIP
Barbra Allen. *Unknown.* *See* Barbara Allen.
Barbry Ellen. *Unknown.* *See* Barbara Allen.
Barcarole of James Smith, The. Herbert S. Gorman. HBMV
Barcarolle. Arthur O'Shaughnessy. NBM
Bard. Gavin Bantock. FaBoTw
(Love, Reason, Hate.) NCEP
Bard. Theodore Black. AMV-81
Bard, The. Blake. *See* Hear the Voice of the Bard.
Bard, The. Thomas Gray. EnRP; GTBS; GTBS-P; LAuP; NOBE; NOEC; OAEL-1; OAEP; OBEC
"On a rock, whose haughty brow," *sel.* SeCePo
Bard, The. James Shirley. ErPo
Bard is buried here, not strong, but sweet, A. The Epitaph of Eusthenes. Edward Cracroft Lefroy. *Fr.* Echoes from Theocritus. AWP; OBVV
Bard of Armagh, The. *Unknown.* *See* Bold Phelim Brady, the Bard of Armagh.
Bard who is singing of Wollombi Jim, The. Jim the Splitter. Henry Kendall. PoAu-1
Bard whom pilf'red pastorals reknown, The. Pope. *Fr.* An Epistle to Dr. Arbuthnot. OBSV
Bards, The. Walter de la Mare. DTC; FaBoNo; NOBL; PV
Bards, The. Robert Graves. DTC; FaBoMo; LiTM; SeCePo; ViBoPo
(Lust in Song.) OxBI
Bard's Chant. James Shirley. *Fr.* Saint Patrick for Ireland. ACP
Bards falter in shame, their running verse. The Bards. Robert Graves. LiTM; ViBoPo. *See also* Their cheeks are blotched for shame, their running verse.
Bards of Passion and of Mirth. Keats. OBEV
(Ode: "Bards of passion and of mirth.") ChER; EnRP; OAEP; OBRV
(Ode on the Poets.) GTBS; GTBS-P
(To the Poets.) HBV-2; ViBoPo
Bard's Song, The. Sir Robert Stapylton. SeCePo
Bards We Quote, The. Bert Leston Taylor. HBMV; WhC
Bare Almond-Trees. D. H. Lawrence. FaBoPP
Bare Arms of Trees, The. John Tagliabue. Psk
Bare branches tremble, The. Tzu Yeh, *tr. fr. Chinese by* Kenneth Rexroth *and* Ling Chung. WPOW
Bare-handed, I hand the combs. Stings. Sylvia Plath. NaP
Bare room, The. Lost. David Fisher. NPGG
Bare skin is my wrinkled sack. The Shrouded Stranger. Allen Ginsberg. NeAP
Bare soul will tramp, The. Footprints. Hamish Brown. PoSH
Bare that breathes the northern blast, The. *See* Bear that breathes the northern blast, The.
Bare trees, The/ alternate. Larry Eigner. PoM
Barefoot and ragged, with neglected hair. On a Fair Beggar. Philip Ayres. EnLoPo; OBS
Barefoot Boy, A. James Whitcomb Riley. FaFP
Barefoot Boy, The. Whittier. AA; FaBoBe; FPL; GN; HBV-1; HBVY; LiTA; OBAL; OBCA; OBVV; OHFP; PoLF; TreF; WBLP, *abr.*
"Blessings on thee, little man," *sel.* FaPON; PoPL
Barefoot boy, A! I mark him at his play. A Barefoot Boy. James Whitcomb Riley. FaFP
Barefoot Days. Rachel Field. FaPON; YeAr
Barefoot I went and made no sound. The Viper. Ruth Pitter. FaBoTw
Barefoot, in unaccustomed clouts or skirts of raw muslin. The New Saddhus. Robert Pinsky. MAYP
Barefoot through the bazaar. Sindhi Woman. Jon Stallworthy. OxBC
Barefoot tramp on a stone, A. On My Wandering Flute. Abraham Sutskever, *tr. by* Ruth Whitman. VWA
Barefoot without a stitch she walks. Dance with Banderillas. Richard Duerden. NeAP
Barely a twelvemonth after. The Horses. Edwin Muir. CMoP; HAP; MoBrPo; NMP; NoAM; NoBE; NoP; OAEL-2; OxBTC; PPoe; TEP; WeW
Barely acceptable in grammar. Man and Wife Is One Flesh. Ann Deagon. NIP
Barely tolerated, living on the margin. Soonest Mended. John Ashbery. Prf
Barely twelve years old. In Memory of My Arab Grandmother. Evelyn Arcad Zerbe. WPOW
Bargain. Louise Driscoll. HBMV
Bargain, The. Sir Philip Sidney. *See* My True Love Hath My Heart.
Bargain. Ruth Stone. GP
Barge glided, The. Vision. Israel Zangwill. TrJP
Barge Horse, The. Seán Jennett. PH
Barge she sat in, like a burnished throne, The. Cleopatra. Shakespeare. *Fr.* Antony and Cleopatra, II, ii. BiP; LiTB; PPoe; SCV; TreF; TrGrPo
Barges on the Hudson. Babette Deutsch. WPE
Barine, the Incorrigible. Horace, *tr. fr. Latin by* Louis Untermeyer. Odes, II, 8. UnTE
Bark. Don Welch. GP
Bark leaps love-fraught from the land, The. The Thousand Islands. Charles Sangster. *Fr.* The St. Lawrence and the Saguenay. NOBC; OBCV
Bark smells like pineapple. Foxtail Pine. Gary Snyder. CoPo; NaP; NU
Bark that bare me through foam and squall. Boatman's Hymn. *At. to* Andrew Magrath, *tr. by* Sir Samuel Ferguson. OnYI
Bark that held the prince went down, The. He Never Smiled Again. Felicia Dorothea Hemans. HBV-2
Barking sound the shepherd hears, A. Fidelity. Wordsworth. FM
Barks the melancholy dog. Wakeful in the Township. Elizabeth Riddell. PoAu-2
Barley straw's good fodder. *Unknown.* FaBoUs
Barley-Break, A. Sir John Suckling. CaPo; SeCV-1
(Love, Reason, Hate.) NCEP
Barley-Break; or, Last in Hell. Robert Herrick. CaPo
Barmenissa's Song. Robert Greene. FaBoRV
Barn, The. Wendell Berry. EyDe
Barn, The. Edmund Blunden. MoBrPo; SeCePo
Barn, The. Elizabeth J. Coatsworth. OBCP; SoPo
Barn, The. Seamus Heaney. HAP
Barn, The. Stephen Spender. CMoP
Barn, The. Edward Thomas. EyDe
Barn Fire. Thomas Lux. LCAP
Barn in Winter, The. Claire Harris MacIntosh. CaP
Barnabooth Enters Russia. Paul Hoover. AMV-81
Barnacle Geese. Charles Higham. PoAu-2
Barney Bodkin broke his nose. *Unknown.* OxNR
Barney Google. Billy Rose. OBAL
Barney McGee. Richard Hovey. HBV-2; InMe; OBAL; TreFS
Barney O'Hea. Samuel Lover. OnYI
Barney's Invitation. Philip Freneau. PAH
Barnfire during Church. Robert Bly. NePoEA
Barnfloor and Winepress. Gerard Manley Hopkins. ACP
Barns grow slowly out of the dark. Lenox Christmas Eve 68. Sam Cornish. CNA
Barnsley and District. Donald Davie. OxBC
Barnyard, The. Maude Burnham. TiPo
Barnyard, The. *Unknown.* *See* Barnyard Song.
Barnyard Melodies. Fred Emerson Brooks. OBAL
Barnyard Song, *with music.* *Unknown.* TrAS
(Barnyard, The.) AmFP
(Farmyard Song, A, *arr. by* Maria Hastings.) SoPo
("I had a cat and the cat pleased me.") OxNR
Barnyards of Delgaty. *Unknown.* FSW
Baron has decided to mate the monster, The. The Bride of Frankenstein. Edward Field. CoAP; HeIP
Baron of Brackley, The. *Unknown.* ESPB (A *and* B *vers.*)
(Baron of Braikley, The, *with music.*) OxBB
Baron of Buchlyvie. Buchlyvie. *Unknown.* GBP; TW
Baron of [*or* o] Leys, The. *Unknown.* ESPB; OxBB, *with music*
Baron of Smaylho'me rose with day, The. The Eve of Saint John. Sir Walter Scott. EnRP; PoEL-4
Baron Renfrew's Ball. Charles Graham Halpine. PAH
Baroness Mu Impeded in Her Wish to Help Famine Victims in Wei. Confucius, *tr. fr. Chinese by* Ezra Pound. *Fr.* Yung Wind. CTC
Baron's Last Banquet, The. Albert Gorton Greene. AA; BeLS
Baron's War, The, *sel.* Michael Drayton. Seven, The, *fr.* I. ChTr
Baroque Comment. Louise Bogan. CrMA
Baroque Gravure, A. Thomas Merton. CoPo
Baroque-handled and sharp. The Compasses. George MacBeth. NePoEA-2
Baroque Wall-Fountain in the Villa Sciarra, A. Richard Wilbur. AmPP; BiP; CAPP; MP; NePoEA; NoP; NYBP; PoCh; TwCP
Barracks Apt. 14. Theodore Weiss. CoAP; NePoAm-2; TAP; TwAmPo
Barracks-square, washed clean with rain, The. In Barracks. Siegfried Sassoon. FaBoTw
Barrage. Richard Aldington. BrPo
Barred Islands. Philip Booth. NePoEA
Barrel-Organ, The. Alfred Noyes. BLPL; FaBV; HBV-2; MoBrPo; PoRA; TreF, *sl. abr.*
Barrels of blue potato-spray, The. Spraying the Potatoes. Patrick Kavanagh. BIrV; IPY; NoP; OxBI
Barren. Rachel, *tr. fr. Hebrew by* L. V. Snowman. TrJP
Barren cross-ties of penny-whistle twigs. Affirmation. Helen Armstead Johnson. AmNP
Barren Moors, The. William Ellery Channing. AA
Barren Poem. Michael Ryan. AmPA

Barren Shore, The. Coventry Patmore. GBL
Barren Soul, A. Joseph Ezobi, *tr. fr. Spanish by* D. I. Friedmann. *Fr.* The Silver Bowl. TrJP
Barren Spring. Dante Gabriel Rossetti. The House of Life, LXXXIII. FaBoEn; NoP; OAEL-2; OBNC; PoEL-5; VLP
(Sonnet: Barren Spring.) EBVV
Barricade—a wall—a stronghold, A. The Breech. Michael McClure. NeAP
Barricades. Michael S. Harper. PoBA
Barricades, The. Denise Levertov. NeBP
Barrier, The. Claude McKay. BANP
Barrier stone has rolled away, The. Easter. Edwin L. Sabin. OHIP; PoSC
Barriers Burned. Charles K. Field. BPAW
Bar-Room Matins. Louis MacNeice. EaLo; NYBP
Bars Fight, August 28, 1746. Lucy Terry. BlSi; BPo; PoNe
Bars on Eighth Avenue in Harlem, The. Harlem Gallery: From the Inside. Larry Neal. BPo
Bars on my cell have rusted, The. Rust. Michael Hogan. LFAC
Barter. Marie Blake. PoPl
Barter. Sara Teasdale. FaBV; FaPON; SoSe; TreFS
Barter. Margaret Widdemer. HBMV; WGRP
Bartholdi Statue, The. Whittier. PAH
Bartholomew. Norman Gale. HBV-1; HBVY
Bartholomew Benjamin Bunting. The Singular Sangfroid of Baby Bunting. Guy Wetmore Carryl. NA
Bartholomew is very sweet. Bartholomew. Norman Gale. HBV-1; HBVY
Barthram's Dirge. *Unknown.* FaBoRV
Bartleme Fair. George Alexander Stevens. ELP; NOEC
Bartley Costello, eighty years old. Gaeltacht. Pearse Hutchinson. BIrV
Bartol. Amos Bronson Alcott. AA
Baruch, *sel.* Bible, Apocrypha.
Path of Wisdom, The, III: 9-IV: 4. TrJP
Bas Bleu, *sel.* Hannah More.
Conversation. OBEC
Bas-Relief. Carl Sandburg. CrMA
Base Chapel, Lejeune 4/79. Archie Hobson. AMV-81
Base Details. Siegfried Sassoon. DBV; FF; HeIP; MMA; MoBrPo; NIP; SoSe
Base metal hanger by your master's thigh! One Writing against His Prick. *Unknown.* TW
Base of All Metaphysics, The. Walt Whitman. NePA
Base Stealer, The. Robert Francis. GoJo; LiSp; NCSH; NTCP; RHPC
Base words are uttered only by the base. W. H. Auden. PV
Baseball. Tom Clark. LiSp
Baseball. Frank Dempster Sherman. OBCA
Baseball and Classicism. Tom Clark. LiSp
Baseball and Writing. Marianne Moore. BoWoP; LiSp
Baseball in spring. Play Ball! Robert Francis. AMV-80
Baseball Pitcher. Mabel M. Kuykendall. LiSp
Baseball's Sad Lexicon. Franklin P. Adams. FaFP; InMe; TreFS
Basement Watch, The. Thomas Tolnay. AMV-80
Bashful Earthquake, The, *sel.* Oliver Herford.
If This Little World To-night. ShM
(Proem.) AA
Basho, coming. The Snow Party. Derek Mahon. CIP; OxBC
Basia, *sels.* Johannes Secundus, *tr. fr. Latin.*
Neaera's Kisses, *tr. by* John Nott. UnTE
Insatiate, The, *tr. by* John Nott. UnTE
"Not alwayes give a melting kiss," *tr. by* Thomas Stanley. OBVE
Basic. Ray Durem. PoNe
Basic Communication. Thomas Hornsby Ferril. NePoAm-2
Basic themes of lyric poetry are seven, The. Seven. Nicanor Parra, *tr. by* Miller Williams. POL
Basic Writing 702. John Paul Minarik. LFAC
Basilisk, The. Philip Child. CaP
Basket Maker's Song. Thomas Dekker. *See* Sweet Content.
Basket of dirty clothes, A. Repetition of Words and Weather. Ruth Stone. BoWoP
Basketball. Nikki Giovanni. RHPC
Basketball. James Lewisohn. LFAC
Basketball. Stephen Vincent. LiSp; NeAC
Basketball Star. Karama Fufuka. RHPC
Baskets of ripe fruit in air. Gardener Janus Catches a Naiad. Edith Sitwell. MoAB; MoBrPo
Basking Shark. Norman MacCaig. BoAnP
Bast. William Rose Benét. HBMV
Bastard King of England, The. *Unknown.* FSW
Bastard, The, *sel.* Richard Savage.
"In gayer hours, when high my fancy ran." NOEC; OBSV
(Bastard's Lot, The.) OBEC
Bat. D. H. Lawrence. BrPo; GTBS-P; HAP; OAEL-2
Bat, The. Frank Jacobs. RHPC
Bat, The. Ogden Nash. PV
Bat, The. Ruth Pitter. FM
Bat, The. Theodore Roethke. GoJo; OBCA; PAI; PDV; RHPC; WSC
Bat, The. Edith Sitwell. FaBoMo
Bat, The. Roberta Spear. AmPA; MAYP
Bat, The. Ellen Bryant Voigt. MAYP
Bat and the Scientist, The. J. S. Bigelow. QQQ
Bat Angels. Larry Levis. AmPA
Bat, bat, come under my hat. Mother Goose. OxNR
Bat is born, A. Bats. Randall Jarrell. BiP; GrPl; NTCP; NU; OBCA; PAI; RFM
Bat is dun, with wrinkled wings, The. Emily Dickinson. FM
Bat of rather uncertain age, A. The Bat and the Scientist. J. S. Bigelow. QQQ
Batalis and the Man, The. Virgil, *tr. fr. Latin by* Gavin Douglas. *Fr.* The Aeneid, I. CTC
("Batellis and the man I will descrive, The.") OBVE
Batata and rice. Tiempo Muerto. Ricardo Alonso. SaC
Batchelor leads an easy life, A. Good and Bad Wives. *Unknown.* CoMu
Batches of New Leaves. Jonathan London. AMV
Batellis and the man I will descrive, The. Virgil, *tr. by* Gavin Douglas. *Fr.* The Aeneid, I. OBVE
Bath, The. Harry Graham. CenHV; ShM
Bath. Lincoln Kirstein. NoAM
Bath, The. R. C. Lehmann. GDP
Bath, The. Joel Oppenheimer. NeAP
Bath, The. Gary Snyder. DiL; GP; NNaP; TAP
Bath, The; or, The Western Lass, *sel.* Thomas Durfey.
Dialogue, between Crab and Gillian. NOEC
Bath-Bunny, The. Carolyn Wells. *Fr.* A Baker's Dozen of Wild Beasts. OBCA
Bathe me O God in thee, mounting to thee. Walt Whitman. *Fr.* Passage to India. TrPWD
Bathed Is My Blood. Oliver La Grone. NNP
Bather in a Painting, A. Ashton Greene. NePoAm
Bathers, The. Hart Crane. SyP
Bathers. Terence Tiller. ChMP; NeBP
Bathing Girl, A. Johannes V. Jensen, *tr. fr. Danish by* Charles Wharton Stork. PoPl
Bathing herself, a girl with silver feet. The Young Bather. *Unknown, tr. by* Louis Untermeyer. UnTE
Bathing in inversion. Winter Developing. Nora Dauenhauer. TWSS
Bathing of Oisin's Head, The. *Unknown, tr. fr. Early Modern Irish by* Eoin MacNeill. AnIL
Bathing Song. Anne Ridler. NYBP
Bathing the Aged. Paul Monette. AmPA
Bathing with Father. Doug Fetherling. NeAC
Bathos, The. Richard Porson. FaBoEE
Baths of Rome and Babylon. A City Song. John Hanlon Mitchell. CaP
Bathsheba came out to the sun. Telling the Bees. Lizette Woodworth Reese. AA
Bathsheba! to whom none ever said scat. For a Little Girl Mourning Her Favorite Cat. Whittier. PCat; POL
Bathtub [*or* Bath Tub], The. Ezra Pound. NIP; WeW
Bathtub Gin. Philip H. Rhinelander. WhC
Bathtubs. Richmond Lattimore. NYBP
Bats, The. Robert Hillyer. GoYe
Bats. Randall Jarrell. BiP; GrPl; NTCP; NU; OBCA; PAI; RFM
Bats. George MacBeth. NoAM
Bats are creepy; bats are scary. The Bat. Frank Jacobs. RHPC
Batson, *with music. Unknown.* OuSiCo
Batt he gets children, not for love to reare 'em. Upon Batt. Robert Herrick. AnAnS-2; FaBoEE
Battel of the Summer-Islands, The. Edmund Waller. AnAnS-2
"Aid me Bellona, while the dreadful fight," *sel.* SeCV-1
Batter my heart, three person'd God; for, you. John Donne. Holy Sonnets, XIV. AnAnS-1; BiP; BLPL; CABA; EaLo; EBEV; EnRePo; FaFP; FF; GoBC; HAP; HEIP; HoPM; IlwL; InPK; InPS; JCB; LiTB; MaSP; MeLP; MePo; NIP; NOBE; NoP; OAEL-1; OAEP; OBS; OxBoCh; PAI; PoEL-2; PPoe; PPP; PrIm; SeCePo; SeCeV; SeCP; SeCV-1; SoSe; TEP; TrCP; TreFT; TrGrPo; TrPWD
Batter'd, wreck'd old man, A. Prayer of Columbus. Walt Whitman. AmPP; WGRP
Battered roof where stars went tripping, A. The Sleepers. F. W. Harvey. MMA
Batteries Out of Ammunition. Kipling. *Fr.* Epitaphs of the War. MMA
Battery grides and jingles, The. The Day's March. Robert Nichols. MMA
Battery Moving Up to a New Position from Rest Camp: Dawn. Robert Nichols. MMA
Battery Park, High Noon. Ben Belitt. NYP
Batte's Song. Michael Drayton. *Fr.* The Shepherd's Garland, Eclogue VII. LoBV

Battle, A. Isabella Valancy Crawford. NOBC
Battle, The. W. H. Davies. BrPo
Battle. Robinson Jeffers. *See* May-June, 1940.
Battle, The ("But as they left the dark'ning heath"). Sir Walter Scott. *Fr.* Marmion, VI. ELP
Battle, The ("By this, though deep the evening fell"). Sir Walter Scott. *See* Flodden.
Battle, The ("Not far advanced was morning day"). Sir Walter Scott. *Fr.* Marmion, VI. EnRP
(Marmion and Douglas.) WHA
Battle, The. Louis Simpson. OBWP
Battle, The. *Unknown, at. to* Chu Yuan. *See* Hymn to the Fallen.
Battle Autumn of 1862, The. Whittier. PAH
Battle Ballad, A. Francis Orrery Ticknor. PAH
Battle Cry. John G. Neihardt. HBMV
Battle Cry. William Henry Venable. PAH
Battle Cry of Freedom, The. George Frederick Root. FaBoBe; FSW; PAH; PSoN, *with music*; TreFS; YaD
Battle Eve of the [Irish] Brigade, The. Thomas Osborne Davis. AnIV; OnYI
Battle-Flag, The. Mary Evelyn Moore Davis. BPAW
Battle-Flag of Sigurd, The. Dora Greenwell. OBVV
Battle Hymn. Michael Altenburg, *tr. fr. German by* Catherine Winkworth. WGRP
Battle Hymn of the Republic, The. Julia Ward Howe. AA; BLPA; BLSO, *with music;* CH; EaLo; FaBoBe; FaFP; FaPo; FaPON; FaPoR; FSW; GN; HBV-2; HBVY; NePA; NOBA; NOCV; OBWP; OHIP; PAH; PAL; PSoN, *with music;* SCV; TAP; TrAS, *with music;* TreF; WBLP; WGRP; WPE; YaD
(Battle Hymn of the American Republic.) OBVV
(Mine Eyes Have Seen the Glory.) AH, *with music;* TRV
Battle Hymn of the Spanish Rebellion. L. A. Mackay. OBCV
Battle in the Clouds, The. William Dean Howells. PAH
Battle of Actium. Virgil, *tr. fr. Latin by* Dryden. *Fr.* The Aeneid, VIII. OBS
Battle of Agincourt, The. Michael Drayton. *See* Agincourt.
Battle of Antietam Creek, The. *Unknown.* AmFP
Battle of Aughrim, The, *sels.* Richard Murphy.
"Deep red bogs divided." CIP
Planter. BIrV
Rapparees. BIrV
"Who owns the land where musket-balls are buried." IPY
Battle of Baltimore, The. *Unknown.* PAH
Battle of Bannockburn, The. John Barbour. *Fr.* The Bruce. BSV
Battle of Bennington, The. Thomas P. Rodman. PAH
Battle of Blenheim, The. Robert Southey. BeLS; EnRP; FaBV; FaPoR; FPL; GN; HBV-2; HBVY; InMe; OBNC; OBRV; OBWP; PaPo; PoLF; TreF; TrGrPo; WBLP
(After Blenheim.) GTBS; GTBS-P; TRV
Battle of Bothwell Bridge, The. *Unknown.* OxBB, *with music*
(Bothwell Bridge.) ESPB
Battle of Bridgewater, The. *Unknown.* PAH
Battle of Brunanburh. *Unknown, tr. fr. Anglo-Saxon by* Tennyson. OBVE; OBWP; TrGrPo; WaaP;
——*Tr. by* Charles W. Kennedy. AnOE
"Then the Northmen fled in their nailed ships," *sel.* PBPP
Battle of Bull Run, The. *Unknown.* AmFP
Battle of Bunker Hill, The. *Unknown.* PAH
Battle of Charleston Harbor, The. Paul Hamilton Hayne. PAH
Battle of Charlestown, The. Henry Howard Brownell. PAH
Battle of Dunbar, The (1296). *Unknown.* OxBM
Battle of Erie, The. *Unknown.* PAH
Battle of Eutaw, The. William Gilmore Simms. PAH
Battle of Finnsburg, The. *Unknown, tr. fr. Anglo-Saxon by* Charles W. Kennedy. AnOE
Battle of Gettysburg, The. Stephen Vincent Benét. *Fr.* John Brown's Body. BeLS
Battle of Glentilt (1847), The. Sir Douglas Maclagan. PoSH
Battle of Harlaw, The. *Unknown.* ESPB (A *and* B *vers.*)
Battle of Hohenlinden, The. Thomas Campbell. *See* Hohenlinden.
Battle of Ivry, The. Macaulay. *See* Ivry.
Battle of King's Mountain, The. *Unknown.* PAH
Battle of La Prairie, The. William Douw Schuyler-Lighthall. PAH
Battle of Lake Champlain, The. Philip Freneau. PAH
Battle of Lookout Mountain, The. George Henry Boker. PAH
Battle of Lovell's Pond, The. Longfellow. PAH
Battle of Maldon, The. *Unknown, tr. fr. Anglo-Saxon by* Charles W. Kennedy. AnOE; OAEL-1; OBWP, *tr. by* Kevin Crossley-Holland
Battle of Manila, The. Richard Hovey. PAH
Battle of Monmouth, The. Thomas Dunn English. PAH
Battle of Monmouth, The. "R. H." PAH
Battle of Morris' Island, The. *Unknown.* PAH
Battle of Murfreesboro, The. Kinahan Cornwallis. PAH
Battle of Muskingum, The; or, The Defeat of the Burrites. William Harrison Safford. PAH
Battle of Naseby, The. Macaulay. HBV-2; OBRV
Battle of Navarino, The. *Unknown.* CoMu
Battle of New Orleans, The. Thomas Dunn English. PAH
Battle of New Orleans, The. *Unknown.* AmFP
Battle of Oriskany, The. Charles D. Helmer. PAH
Battle of Otterburn, The. *Unknown.* ESPB (A, B, *and* C *vers.*); HBV-2; OnMSP
(Battle of Otterbourne, The.) BSV; FaBoCh; GoTS; OxBB, *with music*
"Yt fell abowght the Lamasse tyde," *sel.* OxBS
Battle of Philiphaugh, The. *Unknown.* ESPB
Battle of Plattsburg, The. *Unknown.* PAH
Battle of Plattsburg Bay, The. Clinton Scollard. PAH
Battle of Queenstown, The. William Banker, Jr. PAH
Battle of Shiloh, The. *Unknown.* AmFP
Battle of Similes, A. *Malay Oral Tradition, tr. by* R. J. Wilkinson *and* R. O. Winstedt. WTO
Battle of Sole Bay, The. *Unknown.* GBP
Battle of Somerset. Cornelius C. Cullen. PAH
Battle of Stonington on the Seaboard of Connecticut, The. Philip Freneau. PAH
Battle of the Baltic, The. Thomas Campbell. EnRP; FaPoR; GN; GTBS; GTBS-P; HBV-2; NBM; OBEV; RoGo
Battle of the *Bonhomme Richard* and the *Serapis.* Walt Whitman. Song of Myself, XXXV-XXXVI. MOS; UnPo
(John Paul Jones.) PAL
(Old-Time Sea-Fight, An.) OnMSP
("Would you hear of an old-time sea-fight?") SeCeV; TrGrPo
Battle of the Cowpens, The. Thomas Dunn English. PAH
Battle of the Frogs and Mice, The, *sel.* *Unknown, formerly at. to* Homer; *tr. fr. Greek by* Thomas Parnell.
"Ascend my shoulders, firmly keep thy seat." OBVE
Battle of the Jarama, The. Pablo Neruda, *tr. fr. Spanish by* Angel Flores. WaaP
Battle of the Kegs, The. Francis Hopkinson. OBAL
(British Valor Displayed.) PAH
Battle of the King's Mill. Thomas Dunn English. PAH
Battle of the Swamps, The. Muriel Elsie Graham. SUMH
Battle of Tippecanoe, The. *Unknown.* PAH
Battle of Trenton, The. *Unknown.* PAH
Battle of Valparaiso, The. *Unknown.* PAH
Battle of Waterloo, The. Byron. *See* Waterloo.
Battle Pledge. *Somali Oral Tradition, tr. by* M. Laurence. WTO
Battle Problem. William Meredith. NoAM; NYBP
Battle rent a cobweb diamond-strung, The. Range-finding. Robert Frost. CABA; NIP; NoAM; NoP; OBWP
Battle Report. Bob Kaufman. AmNP; CAD; TTY
Battle Royal between Dr. Sherlock, Dr. South, and Dr. Burnet, The. William Pittis. APAS
Battle Song. Ebenezer Elliott. OBRV
Battle Song. Macuilxochitl, *tr. fr. Nahuatl by* Miguel León-Portilla; *English vers. by* Catherine Rodriquez-Nieto. WPOW
Battle Song. Robert Burns Wilson. PAH
Battle-Song of Failure. Amelia Josephine Burr. HBMV
Battle-Song of the *Oregon.* Wallace Rice. PAH
Battle Songs of the King Tshaka. *Unknown, tr. fr. Zulu.* PeSA
Battle Within, The. Christina Rossetti. TRV
(Who Shall Deliver Me?) OxBoCh
Battle Won Is Lost. Phil George. GrPl
Battlefield. Richard Aldington. MMA; OBWP
Battle-Field, The. Bryant. AA; FPL; PAL; PoLF
"Truth, crushed to earth, shall rise again," *sel.* TRV
(Truth, the Invincible.) TreF
Battlefield, The. Emily Dickinson. *See* They dropped like flakes, they dropped like stars.
Battle-Field, The. Lloyd Mifflin. PAH
Battles nor songs can from oblivion save. Immortality. Lizette Woodworth Reese. AA; HBMV; HBVY
Battleship of Maine. *Unknown.* FSW
Batyushkov. Osip Mandelstam, *tr. fr. Russian by* W. S. Merwin *and* Clarence Brown. OBVE
Baucis. Erinna, *tr. fr. Greek by* Richard Garnett. AWP
Baucis and Philemon. Katherine Hoskins. PoA
Baucis and Philemon. Ovid, *tr. fr. Latin by* Dryden. *Fr.* Metamorphoses, VIII. AWP; OAEL-1
Baucis and Philemon. Swift, *after* Ovid.. GoTL; GN; NOEC; OAEL-1; OBEC
("Then Lelex rose, an old experienc'd man.") OBVE
Baudelaire. Delmore Schwartz. MP; TwCP; VGW
Baudelaire in Brussels. Anthony Cronin. BIrV

Bavarian Gentians. D. H. Lawrence. CMoP; FaBoCh; FaBoMo; GoJo; GTBS-P; HAP; InPK; InPS; LiTB; NoAM; NoP; NOBE; OAEL-2, 2 *versions;* OAEP; PAI; PPoe; SeCeV; SOTW; ViBoPo
Baviad, The, *sel.* William Gifford.
Della Cruscans, The. OBEC
Bawl of a steer, The. The Cowboy's Life. *At. to* James Barton Adams. AmFN; BPAW; CoSo; SoPo; TiPo
Baxter Bickerbone of Burlington. On Learning to Adjust to Things. John Ciardi. OBCA
Bay Bank. A. R. Ammons. DFF
Bay Fight, The. Henry Howard Brownell. PAH
Bay is not blue but somber yellow, The. Self-Criticism in February. Robinson Jeffers. AmPP
Bay of Biscay, The. *Unknown.* AmFP
Bay Poem. Lance Henson. VoR
Bay Psalm Book, The, *sels.* *Unknown.*
Psalm 1. SCAP
Psalm 19. SCAP
Psalm 23. OBCA
Psalm 103. SCAP
Psalm 107. SCAP
Psalm 121. OBCA
Bay Violets. Sister Maris Stella. GoBC
Bayadere, The. Francis Saltus Saltus. AA
Bayard Taylor. Whittier. HBV-2
Baying Hounds, The. Mary Gilmore. PoAu-1
Bayonet and the Needle, The. Eliezer Steinbarg, *tr. fr. Yiddish by* Curt Leviant. VWA
Bayonne Turnpike to Tuscarora. Allen Ginsberg. NNaP
Be a god, your spirit cried. To William Blake. Olive Tilford Dargan. HBMV
Be a Monster. Roy Fuller. AmMo
Be Absolute for Death. Shakespeare. *Fr.* Measure for Measure, III, i. FaBoRV
Be aisy an' list to a chune. Tim the Dragoon. Sir Arthur Quiller-Couch. WhC
"Be alive," they say, when I. On Rape Unattempted. Alan Dugan. NoAM
Be always drunken. Nothing else matters. Be Drunken. Baudelaire, *tr. by* Arthur Symons. SyP
Be always in time. *Unknown.* OxNR
Be assured, the Dragon is not dead. Vanity. Robert Graves. GTBS-P
Be Beautiful, Noble, like the Antique Ant. José Garcia Villa. CrMA; TwAmPo
Be Careful What You Say. Joseph Kronthal. STF
Be composed—be at ease with me—I am Walt Whitman. To a Common Prostitute. Walt Whitman. MoAmPo; ViBoPo
Be Cool, Baby. Rob Penny. PoBA
Be Daedalus. Nanina Alba. PoBA; PoNe
Be dark, be deep, wait there for me between. The Upper Lake. Francis Stuart. NeIP
Be Different to Trees. Mary Carolyn Davies. FaPON; HBMV; HBVY (Be Deferent to Trees.) OHIP
Be Drunken. Baudelaire, *tr. fr. French by* Arthur Symons. SyP
Be dumb ye infant chimes, thump not the metal. Great Tom. Richard Corbet. OxBoLi
Be dumb you beggars of the rhythming trade. The Hecatomb to his Mistress. John Cleveland. AnAnS-2
Be ever meek and humble, nor essay. The Meek and the Proud. Abraham ibn Chasdai, *tr. by* J. Chotzner. TrJP
Be extra careful by this door. The Whisperer. Mark Van Doren. MoAmPo; UnTE
Be Friendly. Walter E. Isenhour. STF
Be Frugal. Richard Church. OxBTC
Be gay, be merry, and don't be wary of milking the modest minute. Samuel Hoffenstein. *Fr.* Song, on Reading That the Cyclotron Has Produced Cosmic Rays. ShM
Be glad in heart, grow great before the Lord. A Brave-hearted Maid. *Unknown, tr. by* Mother Margaret Williams. ISi
Be glaid, al ye that luvaris bene. Four May Poems, IV. *Unknown.* OxBS
Be Glorified Eternally, *with music.* Balthasar Hoffman, *tr. fr. German by* Sheema Z. Buehne. AH
Be gone ye blockheads, Heraclitus cries. Diogenes Laertius, *tr. fr. Greek by* Samuel Johnson. GLGT
Be governour baith guid and gratious. To the Queen. Lord Darnley. OxBS
Be happy for me, girls,/ my mother-in-law is dead! *Tr. fr. Arabic by* Willis Barnstone. BoWoP
Be his memory forever green and rich. Baal Shem Tov. A. M. Klein. CaP; TrJP
Be in me as the eternal moods. Doria. Erza Pound. MoAB; MoAmPo; MoVE; ViBoPo
Be it not mine to steal the cultured flower. Simple Nature. George John Romanes. HBV-1
Be it right or wrong, these men among. The Nut-brown Maid. *Unknown.* OBEV; OBSC
Be just, and fear not. For a Patriot. Shakespeare. King Henry VIII, *fr.* III, ii. PGD
Be just (domestick monarchs) unto them. George Alsop. SCAP
Be kind and tender to the Frog. The Frog. Hilaire Belloc. FaBoBe; FaBV; FaPON; FiBHP; GoJo; HBV-2; NTCP; InMe; MoShBr; NA; OxBChV; RHPC
Be kind, good sir, and I'll lift my sark. Confucius, *tr. by* Ezra Pound. *Fr.* Songs of Cheng. CTC
Be kind to all dumb animals. Humane Thought. Rebecca McCann. YaD
Be kind to her. To End Her Fear. John Freeman. OBMV
Be kind to me. Sappho, *tr. fr. Greek by* Mary Barnard. PeHV
Be kind to the panther! for when thou wert young. The Panther. *Unknown.* NA
Be kind to yourself, it is only one. Who Be Kind To. Allen Ginsberg. NNaP
Be life what it has been, and let us hold. To His Wife. Ausonius, *tr. by* Terrot Reaveley Glover. AWP
Be like the Bird. Victor Hugo, *tr. fr. French.* FaPON; SoPo; SUS; TiPo
Be merry, all birds, today. Ay. Tennyson. *Fr.* The Window; or, The Song of the Wrens. PBBP
Be mute, this autumn; gather in the world. In March. Philip Martin. PoAu-2
Be natural. The Name. Robert Creeley. CoPo
Be near me when my light is low. Tennyson. In Memoriam A. H. H., L. EBVV; ELP; HAP; LiTB; NOCV; NoP; PoEL-5; SCV
Be near to me, O white shadowless Light of my soul's swift venture. Psalm to the Holy Spirit. A. M. Sullivan. TrPWD
Be neither song, nor game, nor feast. Ring Out, Wild Bells. Tennyson. *Fr.* In Memoriam A. H. H., CV-CVI. WiR
Be not afeard [*or* afeared]: the isle is full of noises. Caliban [*or* To Dream Again]. Shakespeare. *Fr.* The Tempest, III, ii. FiP; TrGrPo
Be not afraid, O Dead, be not afraid. Struthers Burt. The Land, III. HBMV
Be not afraid of every stranger. A Spell. George Peele. *Fr.* The Old Wives' Tale. ChTr
Be not afraid to pray—to pray is right. Prayer. Hartley Coleridge. TreFT
Be not dismayed, whate'er betide. God's Goodness. C. D. Martin. WBLP
Be not frighted with our fashion. All Your Fortunes We Can Tell Ye. Ben Jonson. *Fr.* The Gypsies Metamorphosed. ChTr
Be not proud, but now incline. The Changes to Corinna. Robert Herrick. JCP
Be not proud of your sweet body. *Gond Oral Tradition, tr. by* V. Elwin *and* S. Hivale. WTO
Be Not Silent. David ben Meshullam, *tr. fr. Hebrew.* TrJP
Be not sparing. Herrings. Swift. *Fr.* Verses for Fruitwomen. AnIV; OnYI
Be not thou so foolish nice. Invitation to Dalliance. *Unknown.* FaBoEE
Be not too certain, life! The Hill. Horace Holley. WGRP
Be not too forward, painter; 'tis. To the Painter Preparing to Draw M. M. H. James Shirley. CavP
Be not too proud, imperious dame. The Defiance. Thomas Flatman. OBS
Be of Good Cheer; I Have Overcome the World. Bible, *N.T.* St. John, XVI: 19-33. TreFS
Be of good cheer, spirit of Myrrha! To a Courtesan a Thousand Years Dead. Paul Eldridge. PoA
Be Off! Stevie Smith. OxBC
Be pitiful, my God! Mea Culpa. "Ethna Carbery." TrPWD
Be plain in dress, and sober in your diet. Good Advice. Lady Mary Wortley Montagu. FaBoEE; POL
Be Present at Our Table, Lord. *Unknown, at. to.* John Cennick. BLRP; TreFT
(John Wesley's Grace before Meals, *at to* John Wesley.) TreFT
Be proud as Spaniards! Leap for pride ye fleas! On Donne's Poem "To a Flea." Samuel Taylor Coleridge. FM
Be punctual then to know. *Unknown.* *Fr.* The Art of Wenching. NOEC
Be quick, be quick, my eyes, my ears. Harvesting. Selma Robinson. InMe
Be Quiet, Sir! *Unknown.* ErPo
(Cautious Struggle, The.) UnTE
Be real, show organs, show blood, Oh let me. Oh Ease Oh Body-Strain Oh Love Oh Ease Me Not! Wound-Bore. Michael McClure. CoPo
Be reasonable, my pain, and think with more detachment. Inward Conversation. Baudelaire, *tr. by* Robert Bly. InPK
Be Sad, My Heart. Francis Quarles. NIP
Be seated first thing upon awakening. Direction from Zulu. Daniel Halpern. FAZ
Be silent, secret, and conceal. Silentium. Fyodor Tyutchev, *tr. by* Avrahm Yarmolinsky. PoPl
Be slow. Fold the daily news. A Nickle Bet. Etheridge Knight. CAD

Be staid; be careful; and be not too free. Week-end. Harold Monro. SeCePo
Be Still. William Ward Ayer. BLRP
Be Still. Betsy W. Kline. STF
"Be still and know that I am God!" Be Still. William Ward Ayer. BLRP
Be Still as You Are Beautiful. Patrick MacDonogh. AnIV; NeIP; OxBI
Be still: be still: nor dare. A Holy Hill. "Æ." AWP
Be Still, My Heart. *Unknown.* STF
Be still, my heart, and listen. Khristna and His Flute. "Laurence Hope." HBV-1
Be still, my little, dancing feet. A Song of Diligence. Helen Frazee-Bower. HBMV
Be Still, My Soul. Katharina von Schlegel, *tr. fr. German by* Jane L. Borthwick. TRV
Be still, my soul, be still; the arms you bear are brittle. A. E. Housman. A Shropshire Lad, XLVIII. MoAB; MoBrPO; OAEL-2; OAEP; OBNC; TrGrPo
Be still, my soul: the Lord is on thy side. Be Still, My Soul. Katharina von Schlegel, *tr. by* Jane L. Borthwick. TRV
Be Still. The Hanging Gardens Were a Dream. Trumbull Stickney. LiTA; NCEP; NePA; TwAmPo
Be still, while the music rises about us: the deep enchantment. At a Concert of Music. Conrad Aiken. MoAmPo; MoAB; UnS
Be Strong. Maltbie Davenport Babcock. AH, *with music;* BLPA; FaBoBe; FaFP; OHFP; WBLP
Be sure you paint. Alluding to the One-armed Bandit. D. C. Berry. BXAP
Be swift, dear heart, in saying. Kindness. *Unknown.* STF
Be Thankful. Mark Bullock. STF
Be Thankful unto Him. Bible, *O.T.* Psalms, C. *See* Psalm of Praise, A.
Be the Best of Whatever You Are. Douglas Malloch. BLPA; YaD
Be the mistress of my choice. What Kind of Mistress He Would Have. Robert Herrick. CaPo; TrGrPo; UnTe
Be the New Year sweet and short. Prosit Neujahr. George Santayana. InMe
Be then your counsels, as your subject, great. To the Federal Convention. Timothy Dwight. PAH
Be this the fate/ Of the man who would shut his gate. A Curse on a Closed Gate. James H. Cousins, *fr. the Irish.* AnIV
Be thou at peace this night. Nocturne. Edward L. Davison. CH
Be Thou My Guide. Florence Earle Coates. TrPWD
Be Thou my vision, O Lord of my heart. A Prayer. *Unknown, tr. by* Eleanor Hull. OnYI
Be thou our country's Chief. A National Hymn. John William DeForest. *Fr.* Miss Ravenel's Conversion. PAL
Be thou praised, my Lord, with all Thy creatures. Praise of Created Things. St. Francis of Assisi. FaPON
Be thou then my beauty named. Thomas Campion. AAS
Be True. Horatius Bonar. FaBoBe; GN; HBV-2; TRV
(Honesty.) HBVY
Be True to Your Condition in Life. John Audelay. MeEL
Be Useful. George Herbert. GN
Be vengeance wholly left to powers divine. Conversion [*or* Worldly Vanity]. Dryden. *Fr.* The Hind and the Panther. ACP; FiP
Be ware, squier, yeman, and page. Service Is No Heritage. *Unknown.* OxBM
Be wary, lad; the road up which you go. To a Negro Boy Graduating. Eugene T. Maleska. PoNe
Be wary of the loathsome troll. The Troll. Jack Prelutsky. RHPC
Be who you are and will be. For Each of You. Audre Lorde. CNA
Be Wise and Fly Not. Thomas Campion. UnTE
Be wise to day, 'tis madness to defer. Procrastination. Edward Young. *Fr.* Night Thoughts. OBEC
Be with me, Beauty, for the fire is dying. On Growing Old. John Masefield. CMoP; FaFP; FPL; HBMV; LiTB; LiTM; MoAB; MoBrPo; PoLF; PoRA; TreFS; ViBoPo; WHA
Be with Me, Lord. George Macdonald. *Fr.* Diary of an Old Soul. TrCP
Be with me, Luis de San Angel, now. Ave Maria. Hart Crane. *Fr.* The Bridge. MoPo; NePA; NoAM; NOBA
Be with us, Lord, at eventide. Grace at Evening. Edwin McNeill Poteat. TrPWD; TRV
Be Ye in Love with April-Tide. Clinton Scollard. AA; HBV-1
Be you to others kind and true. Our Saviour's Golden Rule. Isaac Watts. OxBChV
Be your words made, good Sir, of Indian ware. Astrophel and Stella, XCII. Sir Philip Sidney. SiPS
Beach, The. Robert Peters. GP
Beach at Veracruz, The. George Bowering. NeAC
Beach Burial. Kenneth Slessor. CBAP; PoAu-2
Beach Fire. Frances M. Frost. TiPo
Beach Homos, The. Forrest Anderson. PeHV
Beach House. Mary Rita Hurley. PoPl
Beach in August, The. Weldon Kees. VGW
Beach Talk. Norman MacCaig. PoA
Beachcomber. George Mackay Brown. OxBC
Beached on the meadow, close by the sea's/ Accustomed lap. The Old Boat. Lenore Pratt. CaP
Beached Whales off Margate. Stephen Dunn. LTB
Beachhead Preachment. Ahmos Zu-Bolton. AMV-81
Beachy Head, *sels.* Charlotte Smith.
"I once was happy, when, while yet a child." WPE
"On thy stupendous summit, rock sublime!" SBG
Beacon, The. Arthur Gregor. GP
Beacon Light. Leslie Savage Clark. PGD
Beacons, The. Henry Hart Milman. *Fr.* Samor. OBRV
Because of body's hunger are we born. Sehnsucht. Anna Wickham. MoBrPo
Beadle's Testimony, The. Jerome Rothenberg. NNaP
Beads, The. Jaime Jacinto. BrSi
Beads from Blackpool. Anne Ridler. NMP
Beagles. W. R. Rodgers. FaBoTw; GDP; OnYI
Beagle's Cry, The. *Unknown, tr. fr. Late Middle Irish by* Eoin MacNeill. OnYI
Beak, The. Elizabeth Smither. OCNZ
Beaks of Eagles, The. Robinson Jeffers. NOBA
Beale Street. Langston Hughes. PPP
Beale Street, Memphis. Thurmond Snyder. NNP
Beam of Light, A. John Jerome Rooney. AA
Bean Eaters, The. Gwendolyn Brooks. BlSi; CAPP; GrPl; HAP; HeIP; MAT; NoP; PoBA; PrIm; TAP; TTY; WeW
Bean Spasms. Ted Berrigan. EAS
Bean Vield, The. William Barnes. VLP
Beans, Bacon and Gravy. *Unknown.* FSW
Beans in Blossom. John Clare. VLP
Bean-Stalk, The. Edna St. Vincent Millay. WSC
Bear, The. Robert Frost. MoAmPo; MoAB; NoAM
Bear, The. Ted Hughes. FaBoMo
Bear, The. Galway Kinnell. CoAP; NNaP; RFM; TAP; VGW
Bear, The. N. Scott Momaday. CDW
Bear, The. Ann Stanford. WSC
Bear a Horn and Blow It Not. *Unknown.* OxBM
Bear and the Squirrels, The. Christopher Pearse Cranch. OBCA
Bear cub, chained and tethered to a stake, A. Squaring the Circle. Louis O. Coxe. NYBP
Bear Dance. Ron Rogers. STE
Bear down lightly. To Destiny. *Unknown, tr. by* Frances Herskovits. EaLo
Bear down under the cliff, A. This Poem Is for Bear. Gary Snyder. Myths and Texts: Hunting, VI. NaP; NOBA; NU
Bear him, comrades, to his grave. Burial of Barber. Whittier. PAH
Bear, however hard he tries, A. Teddy Bear. A. A. Milne. OnUR
Bear Hunt, The. Margaret Widdemer. FaPON
Bear Hunting. Aua, *tr. fr. Eskimo.* WTO
Bear in Mind, O Ye Recording Angels. Norman Cameron. ELU
Bear in mind. Drum. Langston Hughes. MoAmPo
Bear me to Dictaeus. Acon. Hilda Doolittle ("H. D."). VGW
Bear on the Delhi Road, The. Earle Birney. BoAnP; HeIP; MoCV; NOBC; NoP; NYBP; PoCh; PrIm
Bear part with me most straight and pleasant tree. Morea's Sonnet. Mary Sidney Wroth, Countess of Montgomery. *Fr.* Urania. WPE
Bear puts both arms around the tree above her, The. The Bear. Robert Frost. MoAB; MoAmPo; NoAM
Bear sleeps in a cellar hole, A. New Hampshire. Donald Hall. LCAP; NePoEA-2
Bear Song. John R. Swanton. BPAW
Bear [*or* Bare] that breathes [*or* breaks] the northern blast, The. Upon a Wasp Chilled [*or* Child] with Cold. Edward Taylor. FaBoEn; NOBA; NOCV; PoEL-3
Bear That Came to the Wedding, The. Howard McCord. GP
Bear Who Came to Dinner, The. Adrien Stoutenburg. SO
Bear who eats with a silver spoon, A. Animal Acts. Charles Simic. LCAP
Bear with me, Master, when I turn from Thee. Prayer. Edith Lovejoy Pierce. TrPWD
Bearded goldfish move about the bowl, The. Goldfish. Howard Nemerov. BoAnP
Bearded grass waves in the summer breeze, The. Death and Night. James Benjamin Kenyon. AA
Bearded man seated on a camp-stool, A. The Photographer. Louis Simpson. LCAP
Bearded Oaks. Robert Penn Warren. LiTM; MoAmPo; MoVE; MP; NoAM; NOBA; PAI; PoA; TAP; TwCP
Bearer of Evil Tidings, The. Robert Frost. NoAM
Bearer of finches and clouds, pale atmosphere. Oxygen. Joan Swift. NYBP
Bearhug. Michael Ondaatje. PPJ

Bearing their birds and gardens on their hats. L'Après Midi d'une Fille aux Cheveux de Lin. Ronald McCuaig. PoAu-2
Bears. Adrienne Rich. NCSH; NePoEA; NYBP; PAI
Bears. Arthur Guiterman. PoRA
Bears and Waterfalls. May Sarton. GP
Bears are kept by hundreds within fences, are fed cracked, The. Elizabeth's War with the Christmas Bear; 1601. Norman Dubie. LCAP; MAYP
Bear's Blood. Ileana Malancioiu, *tr. fr. Rumanian by* Stavros Deligiorgis. BoWoP
Bear's Song, The. *Unknown, tr. fr. Haida Indian by* Constance Lindsay Skinner. AWP
(Three Songs from the Haida: The Bear's Song.) BPAW
Beast, The. Brian Patten. AmMo
Beast, The. Theodore Roethke. SO
Beast and bird must bow aside. Epilogue for a Masque of Purcell. Adrienne Rich. NePoEA; NYBP
Beast Enough. Robert Billings. AMV-81
Beast in the Space, The. W. S. Graham. FaBoTw; PoA
Beast, I've known you. Ode to the Alien. Diane Ackerman. SUW
Beast Section, The. Welton Smith. PoBA
Beast stands at my eye, A. The Naked Land. Kenneth Patchen. EAS
Beast That Rode the Unicorn, The. Conny Hannes Meyer, *tr. fr. German by* Herbert Kuhner. VWA
Beast with Chrome Teeth, The. Thurmond Snyder. NNP
Beasts. Paul Engle. PoCh
Beasts, The. Walt Whitman. *See* I Think I Could Turn and Live with Animals.
Beasts. Richard Wilbur. AmPP; CrMA; LCAP; MP; NePoAm; NU; PPoe; PPP; TwAmPo; TwCP
Beasts and Birds. Adelaide O'Keeffe. OxBChV
Beasts Are Very Wise, The. Kipling. BoAnP
Beasts in their major freedom. Beasts. Richard Wilbur. AmPP; CrMA; LCAP; MP; NePoAm; NU; PPoe; PPP; TwAmPo; TwCP
Beasts of Boston, The. Betty Lowry. AMV
Beasts onely capable of sense, enjoy. John Ford. *Fr.* The Broken Heart, IV, ii. PoEL-2
Beat! Beat! Drums! Walt Whitman. AP; BiP; FaBV; FPL; InPK; InPS; NoP; OBWP; PoLF
Beat hell out of it. Paterson: Episode 17. William Carlos Williams. OxBA
Beat on proud billowes, Boreas blow. Loyalty Confin'd. Sir Roger L'Estrange. OBS
Beat on the tom-toms, and scatter the flowers. The Bride. "Laurence Hope." HBV-1
Beat Poem by an Academic Poet. Vassar Miller. WPE
Beat the drums of skins. War Comes. Zalman Schneour, *tr. by* Joseph Leftwich. TrJP
Beat the drums of tragedy for me. Fantasy in Purple. Langston Hughes. BANP; CDC
Beat the knife on the plate and the fork on the can. Going In to Dinner. Edward Shanks. OxBTC; OBMV
Beata l'Alma. Sir Herbert Read. FaBoMo
Beaten and baffled man, A. The Black Knight. John Todhunter. OBVV
Beaten, beaten, beaten, beaten. The Copper Song. Hermia Harris Fraser. CaP
Beaten like an old hound. Mad Day in March. Philip Levine. NYBP
Beaten Path, The. Anne Goodwin Winslow. HBMV
Beatific Sea, The. Thomas Campbell. EtS
Beating, The. T. R. Hummer. MAYP
Beating, The. Ann Stanford. WPE
Beating Heart, The. Heine, *tr. fr. German by* Louis Untermeyer. UnTE
Beating heart! we come again. At Her Window. Frederick Locker-Lampson. HBV-1; OBVV
Beatitudes, The. Bible, *N.T.* *Fr.* St. Matthew TrGrPo
("Blessed are the poore in spirit: for theirs is the kingdome of heaven.") OBVE
Beatnik Limernik. Norman R. Jaffray. TDH
Beatrice is gone up into high Heaven. Sonnet. Dante, *tr. by* Dante Gabriel Rossetti. *Fr.* La Vita Nuova. GoBC
Beatrice's Last Words. Shelley. *Fr.* The Cenci. FiP
Beatrix Is Three. Adrian Mitchell. NAs
Beatus Vir. Richard Le Gallienne. HBMV; OHIP
Beaucourt Revisited. A. P. Herbert. MMA
Beauing, belle-ing, dancing, drinking. The Rakes of Mallow. *Unknown.* OnYI
Beauregard. Mrs. C. A. Warfield. PAH
Beau's Receipt for a Lady's Dress, The. *Unknown.* CoMu
Beau's Reply. William Cowper. FaBoCh
Beauté, La. Baudelaire, *tr. fr. French by* Lord Alfred Douglas. AWP
Beauteous Ethel's father has a, The. A Piazza Tragedy. Eugene Field. FiBHP
Beauteous, Yea Beauteous More than These. Christopher Smart. *Fr.* A Song to David. EaLo
Beautie and the life, The. *See* Beauty and the life, The.
Beautie, I know, is good, and bloud is more. Ben Jonson. *Fr.* An Epistle to Lady Rutland. FaBoEn
Beautie, sweet love, is like the morning dewe. *See* Beauty, sweet love, is like the morning dew.
Beauties, Have Ye Seen This Toy. Ben Jonson. *Fr.* The Hue and Cry after Cupid. OAEP
(Cupid.) InMe
(Venus' Runaway.) HBV-1
Beauties of Santa Cruz, The, *sel.* Philip Freneau.
"Sick of thy northern glooms, come, shepherd, seek." AmPP
Beautiful. W. A. Bixler. WBLP
Beautiful, The. W. H. Davies. ELU
Beautiful, The. John Aylmer Dorgan. AA
Beautiful, The. F. S. Woodley. PeHV
Beautiful always the littoral line. The Innocent. Gene Derwood. NePA; WaP
Beautiful American Word, Sure, The. Delmore Schwartz. CrMA; LiTA; VGW
Beautiful and blond they come, the Californians. The Californians. Theodore Spencer. NYBP; TW
Beautiful and happy girl, A. Memories. Whittier. AP; OBVV
Beautiful are the fingers of the loved one. When She Plays upon the Harp or Lute. Moses ibn Ezra, *tr. by* Solomon Solis-Cohen. TrJP
Beautiful as the flying legend of some leopard. Judith of Bethulia. John Crowe Ransom. CrMA; DTC; FaBoMo; FYAP; LiTA; LiTM; MoPo; NePA; NoAM; NOBA
Beautiful as the pomegranate is the white face of Ophrah. The Hot Flame of My Grief. Moses ibn Ezra, *tr. by* Solomon Solis-Cohen. TrJP
Beautiful, beautiful brown eyes. Beautiful Brown Eyes. *Unknown.* FSW
Beautiful, Beautiful Mother, give. Immaculate Palm. Joseph Joel Keith. ISi
Beautiful Bella. *Unknown.* TDH
Beautiful black man, A. Sleeping Beauty. Charles Johnson. DFT
Beautiful Black Men. Nikki Giovanni. BPo; NMM
Beautiful Black Women. Amiri Baraka. BPo; PoM
Beautiful Brown Eyes. *Unknown.* FSW
Beautiful cashier's white face has risen once more, The. Before the [*or* a] Cashier's Window in a Department Store. James Wright. CoAP; MAT; NYBP; NYP
Beautiful Changes, The. Richard Wilbur. CMoP; CoAP; InPS; NIP; SeCeV
Beautiful Creatures Brief as These. Douglas G. Jones. MoCV
Beautiful, delicate bright gazelle, The. A Love-Song. Walter James Turner. OBMV
Beautiful Dreamer. Stephen Collins Foster. BiP; BLSo, *with music;* FSW
Beautiful Evelyn Hope is dead! Evelyn Hope. Robert Browning. HBV-1; TrGrPo; VLP
Beautiful evening, early summer, A. It's Time. Ian Wedde. Earthly: Sonnets for Carlos, 2. OCNZ
Beautiful eyes of the dead, The. Carried Away. Anne Elder. CBAP
Beautiful faces are those that wear. Beautiful Things. Ellen P. Allerton. BLPA; WBLP
Beautiful girl said something in your praise, A. To a Friend on His Marriage. F. T. Prince. LiTM
Beautiful habitations, auras of delight! Auras of Delight. Coventry Patmore. *Fr.* The Unknown Eros. ACP; LoBV; OBVV
Beautiful Hands. *Unknown, at. to* Ellen M. H. Gates. TreF
(My Mother's Hands.) TreFS
Beautiful Horses, The. Donald Hall. NePoAm-2
Beautiful is fair, the just is fair, The. Fair and Unfair. Robert Francis. VGW
Beautiful is she, this woman. Love Song. *Unknown, tr. by* Constance Lindsay Skinner. AWP
Beautiful Is the Loved One. Moses ibn Ezra, *tr. fr. Hebrew by* Solomon Solis-Cohen. TrJP
Beautiful Isle of Somewhere. Jessie B. Pounds. FSN, *with music;* TreFT
Beautiful ladies through the orchard pass. Les Demoiselles de Sauve. John Gray. VLP
Beautiful lady named Psyche, A. Limerick [*or* A Lady Named Psyche]. *Unknown.* TDH; WhC
Beautiful Lawn Sprinkler, The. Howard Nemerov. PCP
Beautiful, lo, the summer clouds. Song of the Blue-Corn Dance. *Tr. by* Natalie Curtis. WTO
Beautiful mother is bending, The. Nativity Song. Jacopone da Todi. OHIP
Beautiful must be the mountains whence ye come. Nightingales. Robert Bridges. BrPo; CMoP; CoBMV; FaBoEn; HBMV; LiTB; LiTM; MoAB; MoBrPo; MoPo; NOBE; OAEL-2; OBEV; OBMV; OBNC; OBVV; PoPl; PBBP; SeCeV; TrGrPo; UnPo; VLP
Beautiful, my delight. To Be Sung on the Water. Louise Bogan. MoVE; PrIm; VGW

Beautiful natural blossoms. To a Beautiful Pear Tree. James Wright. HAP
Beautiful Necessity, The, *sel.* Claude Bragdon.
Point, the Line, the Surface and Sphere, The, 2 *ll.* ImOP
Beautiful Negress, The. Ruth Pitter. MoVE
Beautiful new railway bridge of the silvery Tay. An Address to the New Tay Bridge. William McGonagall. PeD
Beautiful Night, A. Thomas Lovell Beddoes. *Fr.* Fragments Intended for the Dramas. ChER; LoBV
(Lines: "How lovely is the heaven of this night.") NBM
Beautiful, O beautiful/ In all the mountain passes. The April of the Ages. Digby Mackworth Dolben. GoBC
Beautiful place is the town of Lo-yang, A. Lo-yang. Emperor Ch'ien Wen-ti, *tr. by* Arthur Waley. AWP
Beautiful Poultry. Ian Wedde. OCNZ
Beautiful railway bridge of the silvery Tay!/ With your numerous arches. The Railway Bridge of the Silvery Tay. William McGonagall. PeD
Beautiful railway bridge of the silv'ry Tay!/ Alas! I am very sorry to say. The Tay Bridge Disaster. William McGonagall. EvOK; PeD
Beautiful rain falls, the unheeded angel, The. In Time. Kathleen Raine. NeBP; WPE
Beautiful River, *with music.* Robert Lowry. PSoN
(Shall We Gather at the River?) AH
Beautiful Ruined Orchard, The. Daniel Berrigan. FYAP
Beautiful! Sir, you may say so. Chiquita. Bret Harte. AA; BPAW
Beautiful Snow. John Whittaker Watson. BLPA; TreF; WBLP
Beautiful soup, so rich and green. Turtle Soup. "Lewis Carroll." *Fr.* Alice's Adventures in Wonderland. FaBoNo; InMe; Par; RHPC; SpRo
Beautiful star in heav'n so bright. Star of the Evening. James M. Sayles. Par; SpRo
Beautiful sun that giveth us light. Beautiful. W. A. Bixler. WBLP
Beautiful Sunday. "Jake Falstaff." BoNaP
Beautiful Swimmer, The. Walt Whitman. PeHV
Beautiful, tender, wasting away for sorrow. Luscious and Sorrowful. Christina Rossetti. PoEL-5; SeCePo
Beautiful thing/ I saw you. William Carlos Williams. *Fr.* Paterson. CMoP
Beautiful Things. Ellen P. Allerton. BLPA; WBLP
Beautiful, through clear skies newly blue. Spring Landscape. Melvin Walker La Follette. NePoEA-2
Beautiful Toilet, The. Ezra Pound, *after the Chinese.* OBVE
Beautiful Train, The. William Empson. MoVE
Beautiful was the appearance of Cormac in that assembly. Cormac Mac Airt Presiding at Tara. *Unknown, tr. by* Douglas Hyde. BIrV
Beautiful, which mocked his fond pursuing, The. The Beautiful. John Aylmer Dorgan. AA
Beautiful Woman. Dale Zieroth. NOBC
Beautiful woman, a cup of wine, and a garden, A. Joy of Life. Moses ibn Ezra, *tr. by* Solomon Solis-Cohen. *Fr.* The Book of Tarshish. TrJP
Beautiful Woman Who Sings, The ("The beautiful woman at Laguna"). Paula Gunn Allen. TWSS
Beautiful woman, you crown the hours. Beautiful Woman. Dale Zieroth. NOBC
Beautiful World, The. W. L. Childress. OHIP
Beautiful you rise upon the horizon of heaven. The Hymn to the Sun. Akhenaton, *tr. by* J. E. Manchip White. TTY
Beautiful Young Nymph Going to Bed, A. Swift. DBV; NIP; NOEC; UnTE
Corinna, Pride of Drury-Lane, *sel.* PPON
Beautiful Youth. Gottfried Benn, *tr. fr. German by* Joachim Neugroschel. POL
Beautifull Mistress, A. Thomas Carew. OBS
Beautifully Janet slept. Janet Waking. John Crowe Ransom. CABA; CMoP; InPK; MoAB; MoAmPo; NoAM; NoP; NCSH; TAP
Beauty. Kenneth Slade Alling. HBMV
Beauty. Paul David Ashley. LFAC
Beauty. Basho, *tr. fr. Japanese by* Harold G. Henderson. SoPo
Beauty. Baudelaire, *tr. fr. French by* Elaine Marks. NAWM-2
Beauty. Laurence Binyon. MoBrPo
Beauty. Abraham Cowley. LiTB; PoEL-2; TrGrPo
Beauty. E-Yeh-Shure'. FaPON; TiPo
Beauty. Giovanni Battista Guarini. *See* Of Beauty.
Beauty, The, *sel.* Thomas Hardy.
"O do not praise my beauty more." PeD
Beauty. Peter Hille, *tr. fr. German by* Jethro Bithell. AWP
Beauty. Isaac Rosenberg. TrJP
Beauty. Sappho. *See* One Girl.
Beauty. Spenser. *Fr.* An Hymne in Honour of Beautie. OBSC
(Soul Is Form, *abr.*) GOBC
Beauty. Joel Elias Spingarn. HBMV
Beauty. Thomas Stanley, *after the Greek of* Anacreon. AWP; OBVE
Beauty. *Unknown. Fr.* The Passionate Pilgrim, XIII. OBSC
Beauty. Walt Whitman. WeW
Beauty. Elinor Wylie. OxBA
Beauty, a silver dew that falls in May. Epigram. *Unknown.* OBSC
Beauty, Alas, Where Wast Thou Born. *At. to* Thomas Lodge *and to* Robert Greene. EIL
Beauty all stainless, a pearl of a maiden, A. The Geraldine's Daughter. Egan O'Rahilly, *tr. by* James Clarence Mangan. AnIL; OnYI
Beauty and Duty. Ellen S. Hooper. *See* Duty.
Beauty and Love. Andrew Young. GBL
Beauty and Sadness. Cathy Song. MAYP
Beauty and Terror. Lesbia Harford. CBAP; PoAu-1
Beauty and the Bird. Dante Gabriel Rossetti. FM
Beauty [*or* Beautie] and the life, The. Madrigal [*or* Her Passing]. William Drummond of Hawthornden. EIL; OBEV; PoEL-2
Beauty and youth, with manners sweet, and friends. On the Grave of a Young Cavalry Officer Killed in the Valley of Virginia. Herman Melville. AP
Beauty, arise, show forth thy glorious shining! A Bridal Song. Thomas Dekker, *and others. Fr.* The Pleasant Comedy of Patient Grissill. EIL; OBSC; TrGrPo
Beauty as a Shield. Elsie Robinson. BLPA
Beauty Bathing. Anthony Munday. *See* Beauty Sat Bathing.
Beauty blue and beauty white. Shopping Day. Orrick Johns. InMe
Beauty calls and gives no warning. Evensong. Ridgely Torrence. HBV-1
Beauty Clear and Fair. John Fletcher. *Fr.* The Elder Brother, III, v. OAEP; OBEV; OBS; ViBoPo
Beauty depends on simplicity. The Inner Man. Plato. PoPl
Beauty does not walk through lovely days. Beauty and Terror. Lesbia Harford. CBAP; PoAu-1
Beauty Extolled [*or* Extoll'd]. *Unknown, at. to* Henry Noel *and to* William Strode. ChTr; OBS
(Gaze Not on Swans.) ELP
(On His Mistress.) PoEL-2
Beauty goes out to meet a greater beauty. Dying. Jessie Holt. PGD
Beauty had first my pride. The Star. Willoughby Weaving. HBMV; HBVY
Beauty I Would Suffer For. Marge Piercy. NIP
Beauty Imposes. Shaw Neilson. PoAu-1
Beauty in Trouble. Robert Graves. NYBP
Beauty in woman; the high will's decree. Sonnet: He Compares All Things with His Lady, and Finds Them Wanting. Guido Cavalcanti, *tr. by* Dante Gabriel Rossetti. AWP
Beauty in Worship. *Unknown. Fr.* A Poem, in Defence of the Decent Ornaments of Christ-Church. . . OBS
Beauty Is a Witch. Shakespeare. *Fr.* Much Ado about Nothing, II, i. TrGrPo
Beauty Is but a Painted Hell. Thomas Campion. BiP
Beauty is but a vain and doubtful good. Beauty. *Unknown. Fr.* The Passionate Pilgrim, XIII. OBSC
Beauty Is Ever to the Lonely Mind. Robert Nathan. HBMV
Beauty Is Most at Twilight's Close. Pär Lagerkvist, *tr. fr. Swedish by* G. Kenneth Laycock. PoPl
Beauty is never satisfied. Mythmaking. Kathleen Spivack. NMM
Beauty Is Not Bound. Thomas Campion. *See* Give Beauty All Her Right
Beauty is not caused—it is. Emily Dickinson. LiTA
Beauty is seen. Beauty. E-Yeh-Shure'. FaPON; TiPo
Beauty is still immortal in our eyes. The Immortal. Majorie Pickthall. CaP
Beauty like hers is genius. Not the call. Genius in Beauty. Dante Gabriel Rossetti. *Fr.* The House of Life. OAEP
Beauty may be the path for highest good. The Straight Road. Ellen Hooper. HBV-2
Beauty no other thing is than a beam. The Definition of Beauty. Robert Herrick. CaPo
Beauty of Israel is slain upon thy high places, The. David's Lament [*or* How Are the Mighty Fallen]. Bible, *O.T. Fr.* Second Samuel. AWP; FF; OBVE; OBWP; TrGrPo; WaaP
Beauty of Job's Daughters, The. Jay Macpherson. MoCV; NOBC; PoCh
Beauty of manhole covers, The—what of that? Manhole Covers. Karl Shapiro. AmFN; GoJo; GP; NCSH
Beauty of, The/ the terrible faces. Apology: Why Do I Write Today? William Carlos Williams. OxBA
Beauty of the Friend it was that taught me, The. Makhfi, *tr. fr. Farsi by* Paul Whalley. WPOW
Beauty of the northern dawns, The. Christine. John Hay. AA
Beauty of the Ship, The. Walt Whitman. MOS
Beauty of the Stars, The. Moses ibn Ezra, *tr. fr. Hebrew by* Solomon Solis-Cohen. TrJP
Beauty of the unused, The. Unspeakable. Margaret Avison. NOBC
Beauty of the world hath made me sad, The. The Wayfarer. Padraic Pearse. OxBI
Beauty of Things, The. Robinson Jeffers. PoA
Beauty Rohtraut. Eduard Möricke, *tr. fr. German by* George Meredith. AWP; OBVE

Beauty Sat Bathing [by a Spring]. Anthony Munday. *Fr.* Primaleon of Greece. ElL; UnTE
(Beauty Bathing.) NOBE; OBEV
(Colin.) GTBS; GTBS-P
(To Colin Clout.) OAEP; OBSC; ViBoPo
Beauty, Since You So Much Desire. Thomas Campion. ErPo; OAEL-1
(Place of Cupid's Fire, The.) UnTE
Beauty, Sleeping. Arthur Freeman. DFT
Beauty [*or* Beautie], sweet love, is like the morning dew. Sonnet. Samuel Daniel. To Delia, XLII [XLVII]. ElL; EnRePo; FaBoEn; HBV-1; NOBE; OBEV; OBSC; ViBoPo
Beauty That All Night Long, A. Jalal ed-Din Rumi, *tr. fr. Persian by* Edward Fitzgerald. AWP
Beauty! thou art a wanderer on the earth. Behold, O Aspasia! I Send You Verses. Walter Savage Landor. *Fr.* Pericles and Aspasia. LoBV; OBNC; ViBoPo
Beauty, thou wild fantastic ape. Beauty. Abraham Cowley. LiTB; PoEL-2; TrGrPo
Beauty, Time and Love. Samuel Daniel. *See* Fair Is My Love.
Beauty—a beam, nay, flame. Fading Beauty. Giambattista Marini, *tr. by* Samuel Daniel. AWP
Beauty—be not caused—it is. Emily Dickinson. TAP
Beauty's Hands Are Cool. Karle Wilson Baker. GoYe
Beauty's Self. *Unknown. See* My Love in Her Attire.
Beauty—what is it? A perfume without name. Arthur Davison Ficke. *Fr.* Epitaph for the Poet V., III. HBMV
Beaver Island Boys, The, *with music. Unknown.* OuSiCo
Beaver Pond. Anne Marriott. NOBC
Beaver roars hoarse with meltin' snows. Mr. Hosea Biglow to the Editor of the Atlantic Monthly. James Russell Lowell. *Fr.* The Biglow Papers, 2d series, No. X. PoEL-5
Beaver Sign. Kenneth Porter. NePoAm
Beaver's Story, The. Vernon Watkins. NYBP
Be-Bop Boys. Langston Hughes. OBAL
Becalmed. John Blight. PoAu-2
Becalmed. John Banister Tabb. AA
Because. Edward Fitzgerald. HBV-1
Because. Paul Johnson. AMV-81
Because. James McAuley. CBAP
Because. Edward Teschemacher. FSN, *with music;* TreFT
Because. B. W. Vilakazi, *tr. fr. Zulu.* PeSA
Because a woman's lips were red. History. Paul Tanaquil. HBMV
Because all this food is grown in the store. Picketing Supermarkets. Tom Wayman. NIP
Because beer tingles. Beer Drops. Melba Joyce Boyd. BlSi
Because dusk comes. Saskatchewan Dusk. C. M. Buckaway. AMV-80
Because everything I build is built on the miracle. The Miracle. Chaim Grade, *tr. by* Ruth Whitman. VWA
Because, forsooth, you're young and fair. To His Young Mistress. Anacreon, *tr. by* Abraham Cowley. UnTE
Because God put His adamantine fate. Failure. Rupert Brooke. ILwL
Because Going Nowhere Takes a Long Time. Kenneth Patchen. NaP
Because he had spoken harshly to his mother. Revelation. Robert Penn Warren. LiTA; MoPo; NePA; NoAM; TwAmPo
Because he is young. Okura, *tr. fr. Japanese by* Arthur Waley. *Fr.* Manyo Shu. AWP
Because He Liked to Be at Home. Kenneth Patchen. NaP
Because He Lives. Adele Lathrop. BLRP
Because he puts the compromising chart. Zola. E. A. Robinson. MoVE; NePA; OxBA
Because he sent a head of cattle on. The Island and the Cattle. Nicholas Moore. EAS
Because he studied texts. The Poor Shammes of Berditchev. Rochelle Ratner. VWA
Because he was a butcher and thereby. Reuben Bright. E. A. Robinson. MoAmPo; MoAB; NePA; NOBA; NoP; TAP; TrGrPo
Because he was armored. In Days of New. Elizabeth Bartlett. AMV-81
Because He Was Tempted. *Unknown.* STF
Because his madness had outgrown the world. The Kabbalist. Deborah Eibel. VWA
Because his soup was cold, he needs must sulk. House-Mates. Leon Gellert. CBAP
Because I am a woman. Muse Poem. Kathryn Van Spanckeren. FF
Because I am idolatrous and have besought. Epigram. Ernest Dowson. ACP
"Because I am mad about women." The Wild Old Wicked Man. W. B. Yeats. AnIL; CMoP
Because I believe in the community of little children. The Massacre of the Innocents. William Jay Smith. EaLo
Because I breathe not love to every one. Astrophel and Stella, LIV. Sir Philip Sidney. OAEP; OBSC; SiPS; TrGrPo
Because I Could Not Dump. Andrea Paterson. BXAP
Because I could not stop for death. Emily Dickinson. AmPP; AP; AWP; BoWoP; CABA; CMoP; DL; EBCP; FF; FPL; HAP; HeIP; LiTA; LiTM; MasP; MoAB; MoAmPo; MoPo; MoVE; NIP; NePA; NoAM; NoP; OxBA; PAI; PBWP; PoEL-5; SBG; SCV; SeCeV; SoSe; SOTW; TAP; TreFS; TRV; TwAmPo; UnPo; WeW; WGRP; WPE
Because I do not always know. A Prayer for Charity. Edwin O. Kennedy. TrPWD
Because I do not hope to turn again. Ash-Wednesday, I. T. S. Eliot. AP; CoBMV; LiTA; MoAB; MoAmPo; MoPo; OxBA; OxBoCh; SeCeV; TwAmPo; VGW
Because I feel that, in the Heavens above. To My Mother. Poe. AP; NePA; OxBA
Because I had loved so deeply. Compensation. Paul Laurence Dunbar. AmNP; BPo; HBV-2; PoNe
Because I have been given much. Because of Thy Great Bounty. Grace Noll Crowell. TrPWD
Because I have loved life, I shall have no sorrow to die. A Song of Living. Amelia Josephine Burr. HBV-2
Because I know deep in my own heart. Song. Pauli Murray. BlSi
Because I Liked You Better. A. E. Housman. GBL; OxBTC; PeHV
Because I Live. Evelyn Ames. GoYe
Because I love and serve a whore *sans glose.* Ballade of Villon and Fat Margot. Villon, *tr. by* John Payne. UnTE
Because I oft in dark abstracted guise. Astrophel and Stella, XXVII. Sir Philip Sidney. SiPS
Because I once beat you up. For a Far-out Friend. Gary Snyder. NeAP; PoM
Because I Paced My Thought. John Hewitt. CIP
Because I think not ever to return. Ballata: In Exile at Sarzana. Guido Cavalcanti, *tr. by* Dante Gabriel Rossetti. AWP
Because I used to shun. The Spark. Joseph Plunkett. AnIV; AWP
Because I waddle when I walk. The Dachshund. Edward Anthony. GDP
Because I was content with these poor fields. Musketaquid. Emerson. AP
Because I work not, as logicians work. Magic. Lionel Johnson. VLP
Because in Argentina. For Refugio Talamante. Ed Ochester. LTB
Because in This Sorrowing Statue of Flesh. Kenneth Patchen. NaP
Because in Vietnam the vision of a Burning Babe. Advent 1966. Denise Levertov. InPS; NNaP; Prf
Because it is lunchtime. Planting Trout in the Chicago River. Dennis Schmitz. NPGG
Because it is the day of Palms. Palm Sunday: Naples. Arthur Symons. BrPo
Because language dreams in metaphors. Charming. William Matthews. MAYP
Because mine eyes are fashioned so. Vagabonds. "Marie Madelaine," *tr. by* Ferdinand E. Kappey. PeHV
Because mine eyes can never have their fill. Ballata: He Will Gaze upon Beatrice [*or* Sonnet]. Dante, *tr. by* Dante Gabriel Rossetti. AWP; GoBC
Because My Faltering Feet. Hilaire Belloc. Sonnets, XVII. OxBoCh
(Her Faith.) GoBC
Because my grief seems quiet and apart. Sonnet. Robert Nathan. TrJP
Because my joy is less than joy. Courage. Helen Frazee-Bower. HBMV
Because my shelter must not be known. Cricket. No Ch'ŏn-myŭng, *tr. by* Ko Won. PBWP
Because my will is simple as a window. The Blessed Virgin Mary Compared to a Window. Thomas Merton. ISi
Because no one has ever asked. Mythology. Michael Waters. MAYP
Because of Clothes. Laura Riding. LiTA; NoAM
Because of Her Who Flowered So Fair. Leonard Feeney. *Fr.* Song for a Listener. ISi
Because of long depression and a sudden urge. Midnight and Ten Minutes. Shlomo Vinner, *tr. by* Laya Firestone *and* Howard Schwartz. VWA
Because of the memory of one we held dear. In a Province. F. T. Prince. MoVE
Because of the steepness. Mountain Brook. Elizabeth J. Coatsworth. RHPC
Because of Thy Great Bounty. Grace Noll Crowell. TrPWD
Because of You. Sophia Almon Hensley. HBV-1
Because of you we will be glad and gay. Julian Grenfell. Maurice Baring. HBMV
Because of your long neck. Deer. No Ch'ŏn-myŭng, *tr. by* Ko Won. PBWP
Because on the branch that is tapping my pane. In the Hospital. Arthur Guiterman. WGRP
Because One Is Always Forgotten. Carolyn Forché. MAYP
Because our lives are cowardly and sly. The Road. James Stephens. HBMV
Because Our Past Lives Every Day. Ed Lipman. LFAC
Because river-fog. River-Fog. Kiyowara Fukuyabu, *tr. by* Arthur Waley. *Fr.* Shui Shu. AWP; FaPON
Because San Quentin Killed Two More Today. Ed Lipman. LFAC

Because she breathed too wildly in the sun. The Sixth Hell. Jerome Rothenberg. *Fr.* The Seven Hells of Jigoku Zoshi. NNaP
Because she was a white girl. The Death of Janis Joplin. Robert Phillips. SOTS
Because She Would Ask Me Why I Loved Her. Christopher Brennan. CBAP
Because Sometimes You Can't Always Be So. Kenneth Patchen. NaP
Because the Chiricahuas formed a haven. Warriors. Michael Hogan. LFAC
Because the cithole hath a thousand tones. Soul-Severance. St. John Hankin. FaBoPa
Because the ground-creature looked so sad. The Little Green Blackbird. Kenneth Patchen. PoCh
Because the light this morning is recondite. Cold Glow: Icehouses. David Wojahn. AMV-81; MAYP
Because the moon became my mother. Lament. Joseph Stroud. NPGG
Because the paint is not the shadow of branches. Camouflage. John Manifold. WaP
Because the pleasure-bird whistles after the hot wires. January 1939. Dylan Thomas. EAS
Because the rose must fade. Song. Richard Watson Gilder. HBV-2
Because the shadows are sepia. 1930. Kathleen Fraser. NPGG
Because the shadows deepened verily. At the Last. Philip Bourke Marston. HBV-1
Because the Three Moirai Have Become the Three Maries. Constance Urdang. MOON
Because the warden is a cousin, my. Deer Hunt. Judson Jerome. RFM
Because the warm honey. Sanctuary. Bruce Boyd. NeAP
Because their fathers had been drilled. The Last Republicans. Austin Clarke. CIP
Because there are avenues. After Tonight. Gary Soto. GP
Because there is safety in derision. The Apparitions. W. B. Yeats. CMoP; LiTM
Because there was a man somewhere in a candystripe silk shirt. Homage to the Empress of the Blues. Robert Hayden. CABA; CNA; LCAP; PoBA; PoNe
Because there was no other place. Flee on Your Donkey. Anne Sexton. NYBP
Because they are not. The Deceptrices. William Carlos Williams. NYBP
Because They Were Very Poor That Winter. Kenneth Patchen. NaP
Because this is the way our world goes under. On Why I Would Betray You. Jorie Graham. AMV-81
Because, this month, when napkins, pretty spoons. Roman Presents. Martial, *tr. by* James Michie. OBCP
Because thou canst not see. The Philosopher to His Mistress. Robert Bridges. LiTM; OAEP; PoEL-5
Because thou wast the daughter of a king. To Saint Catherine. Henry Constable. GoBC
Because time is a fiction in the mind. Miklos Radnoti. Willis Barnstone. VWA
Because time kept. Pre Domina. Jean Lipkin. PeSA
Because time subdues sharp angles and closes wounds. Burial. Paulin Joachim, *tr. by* Oliver Bernard. TTY
Because we are all. Judas, Peter. Luci Shaw. AMV
Because we breathe the same birds of sand. Brotherhood. José Luis Vega, *tr. by* Julio Marzán. InW
Because we do. Together. Paul Engle. RHPC
Because We Do Not See. *Unknown.* BLRP
Because we live in the browning season. Kopis'taya. Paula Gunn Allen. STE; TWSS
Because we love bare hills and stunted trees. Hound Voice. W. B. Yeats. SyP
Because we suspected/ the pillow would say "I know." Lady Ise, *tr. fr. Japanese by* Etsuko Terasaki *and* Irma Brandeis. BoWoP
Because we were baffled. The White Bird. Wilfred Watson. MoCV
Because women are expected to keep silent about. On Stripping Bark from Myself. Alice Walker. LTB
Because ye have broken your own chain. The Curse. Elizabeth Barrett Browning. *Fr.* A Curse for a Nation. WPOW
Because you are going. Emily Dickinson. MoAmPo
Because you are simple people, kindly and romantic. Fourth Act. Robinson Jeffers. LiTA; WaP
Because you are to me a song. Passing Love. Langston Hughes. BiP
Because You Asked about the Line between Prose and Poetry. Howard Nemerov. WeW
Because you come to me with naught save love. Because. Edward Teschemacher. FSN; TreFT
Because you have increased my hurt. The Storm. Robert David Cohen. NYBP
Because you have no fear to mingle. To a Sparrow. Francis Ledwidge. HBMV
Because you have thrown off your prelate lord. On the New Forcers of Conscience under the Long Parliament. Milton. CABA
Because you left her name unnamed. Joseph Mary Plunkett. Wilfrid Meynell. ISi
Because you love me I have much achieved. Encouraged. Paul Laurence Dunbar. TRV
Because you made me glad, I was the net. Affirmations. Peter Viereck. MiAP
Because you once beat me up. Melon-Slaughterer; or, A Sick Man's Praise for a Well Woman. Robert Peters. BXAP
Because you passed, and now are not. A Ballad of Heroes. Austin Dobson. HBV-2; HBVY; OHIP
Because You Prayed. "C. B. B." STF
Because you threw rocks at me on Backbone Mountain. Night Song from Backbone Mountain. Daniel Mark Epstein. TAT
Because your voice was at my side. James Joyce. Chamber Music, XVII. OLR
Because You're You, *with music.* Henry Blossom. BLSo
Becket, *sels.* Tennyson.
 Duet: "Is it the wind of the dawn that I hear." GBL
 Prologue: "Over! the sweet summer closes." GBL
Becket's Diadem. *Unknown.* ACP
Beckett Kit, The. Linda Gregg. AmPA
Beckie, my luve!—What is't, ye twa-faced tod? Sonnet. George Campbell Hay. OxBS
Beckon Me, Ye Cuillins. K. G. P. Hendrie. PoSH
Becky Deem. *Unknown.* BluL
Beclouded. Emily Dickinson. *See* Sky is low, the clouds are mean, The.
Becoming a Dad. Edgar A. Guest. BLPL; PoLF
Becoming a Frog. Paul R. Jones. DFT
Becoming a Nun. Erica Jong. MAYP
Becoming an Eskimo isn't hard once you must. Bum's Rush. Michael Dransfield. CBAP
Becoming Is Perfection. Tom Johnson. AMV-81
Becoming Real. Barry Goldensohn. AMV-81
Bed, The. A. D. Hope. NoAM; OxBC
Bed, The. James Merrill. NePoEA
Bed, The. Dennis Saleh. NeAC
Bed, The. Karl Shapiro. NYBP
Bed at Ostend at 5 A.M. Charles Stuart Calverley. *Fr.* Dover to Munich. NOBL
Bed Book, The, *sel.* Sylvia Plath.
 "These are the beds." RHPC
Bed Charm. *Unknown.* *See* Before Sleeping.
Bed in Summer. Robert Louis Stevenson. GoJo; OxBChV; PoPl; TreFT
Bed is the boon for me! Old Lizette on Sleep. Agnes Lee. HBMV
Bed of Campanula, A. "John Crichton." CaP
Bed without a Woman, A. Raymond Souster. ELU; ErPo
Bedbug, The. Tony Harrison. PV
Bedded in tranquility. Voice of the Crocus. Mildred N. Hoyer. AMV-80
Bedelia, *with music.* William Jerome. FSN
Bedford Level. John Dyer. *Fr.* The Fleece, II. FaBoPP
Bedlam; a Poem on His Majesty's Happy Escape from His German Dominions, *sel.* *Unknown.*
 "What mean these loud aerial cracks I hear?" NOEC
Bedlam Hills. Vivian Smith. PoAu-2
Bedlamite, The. Thomas Mozeen. NOEC
Bedouin Song. Bayard Taylor. AA; FaBoBe; HBV-1; PaPo; TreFT
Bedouin springs from his horse, A. Into the Book. Martin Grossman. VWA
Bedouins of the Skies, The. James Benjamin Kenyon. AA
Bedpost, The. Robert Graves. SO
Bed-ridden, laid by an age's malady. Final Poem. Robert Bhain Campbell. MoPo; NePA
Beds are made close to a wall flat. Saturday Morning. Richard Howard. ErPo
Beds of Fleur-de-Lys, The. Charlotte Perkins Gilman. AA
Bed Time. Peter Davison. UnPo
Bedtime. Francis Erskine, Earl of Rosslyn. HBV-1; HBVY (Bed-time.) OBVV
Bedtime. Eleanor Farjeon. SoPo; TiPo
Bedtime. Ian Hamilton Finlay. BSV
Bed-Time. Ralph M. Jones. HBMV
Bedtime. Denise Levertov. IHMS; NaP; TwCP
Bedtime. Hillel Schwartz. AMV-81
Bed-Time Song. Emilie Poulsson. HBV-1; HBVY
Bedtime Stories. Lilian Moore. NTCP
Bedtime Story. Lou Lipsitz. VGW
Bedtime Story. George MacBeth. NePoEA-2; NoAM; SoSe
Bedtime Story, A. Robert Mezey. NePoEA (If I Should Die before I Wake). NYBP
Bedtime Story for My Son. Peter Redgrove. NePoEA-2

Bee, The. James Dickey. LiSp; SoSe
Bee, The. Emily Dickinson. *See* Like trains of cars.
Bee, The. John Fandel. GoYe
Bee, The. Charles Fitzgeffry. *Fr.* Sir Francis Drake. ElL
Bee, The. Henry Hawkins. ACP
Bee. X. J. Kennedy. OBCA
Bee, The, *with music. Unknown.* TrAS
Bee and the Petunia, The. Katherine Hoskins. ErPo
Bee his burnished carriage, A. Emily Dickinson. NOBA
Bee! I'm expecting you! Emily Dickinson. BoAnP; SO; SOTW
Bee-logic: each small life. Kindergarten. Dennis Schmitz. NPGG
Bee Meeting, The. Sylvia Plath. InPS; PPP; WPE
Bee-Orchis, The. Andrew Young. ChTr
Bee Song. Carl Sandburg. PDV
Bee, the Ant, and the Sparrow, The. Nathaniel Cotton. OxBChV
Bee to the heather, The. Song. Sir Henry Taylor. OBVV
Bee upon a briar-rose hung, A. The Flesh-Fly and the Bee. Coventry Patmore. FaBoEE
Bee Wassail. *Unknown.* OBET
Bee-Wisp, The. Charles Tennyson Turner. FM
Beech, The. Andrew Young. BoNaP
Beech Leaves. James Reeves. OnUR
Beech Tree's Petition, The. Thomas Campbell. HBV-1
Beecher Island. Arthur Chapman. PoOW
Beef. Leon Stokesbury. GP
Beef Sandwich in Randy's on Michigan Ave. Chicago Allegory. Stewart Parker. CIP
Beehive. Jean Toomer. IDB; PoBA; TTY
Beehould a cluster to itt selfe a vine. William Alabaster. AnAnS-1
Bee-keeper kissed me, The. *Unknown, tr. fr. Spanish by* W. S. Merwin. BoWoP
Beekeeper's Daughter, The. Sylvia Plath. IHMS
Beekeeper's Dream, The. Katharine Auchincloss Lorr. SUW
Beela by the Sea. Leroy F. Jackson. RHPC
Been in dat jailhouse, expectin' a fine. Sun Gonna Shine in My Door Some Day. *Unknown.* OuSiCo
Been in the Pen So Long. *Unknown.* AS, *with music;* FSW
Been on the hummer since ninety-four. A.R.U. *Unknown.* AS
Been out in the lifeboat often? The Lifeboat. George R. Sims. PaPo
Been to Pike's Peak, lost all my dimes. Soliloquy of the Returned Gold Adventurer. "Syntax." PoOW
Beeny Cliff. Thomas Hardy. OBNC
Beer. Charles Stuart Calverley. BXAP; CenHV; FaBoCo
"But Hark! a sound is stealing on my ear," *sel.* FiBHP
Beer. George Arnold. AA; OBAL; TreFT
Beer Drops. Melba Joyce Boyd. BlSi
Bees, The. Monk Gibbon. OnYI
Bees, The. Lola Ridge. FaPON
Bees and a honeycomb in the dried head of a horse. In Tall Grass. Carl Sandburg. PoA
Bees and Monks. John Hookham Frere. *Fr.* King Arthur and His Round Table. OBRV
Bees Awater. Robert Morgan. WeW
Bees, bees of paradise. Bee Wassail. *Unknown.* OBET
Bees build around red liver. A Poor Christian Looks at the Ghetto. Czeslaw Milosz, *tr. by author.* NIP
Bees build in the crevices, The. The Stare's Nest by My Window. W. B. Yeats. Meditations in Time of Civil War, VI. BIrV; GTBS-P; LiTB; NOBE
Bees hummed and rooks called hoarsely outside the quiet room. Gervais. Margaret Adelaide Wilson. SUMH
Bees in the clover are making honey, and I am making my hay, The. The Mower in Ohio. John James Piatt. AA
Bees in the late summer sun. Bee Song. Carl Sandburg. PDV
Bees in the weatherboards. The Young Wife. C. K. Stead. OCNZ
Bees inside Me. Laura Chester. NPGG
Bees of Middleton Manor, The. May Probyn. GoBC
Bees over the gooseberry bushes. The Bees. Lola Ridge. FaPON
Bees' Song, The. Walter de la Mare. WhC
Beethoven. John Hall Wheelock. PoA
Beethoven's Death Mask. Stephen Spender. OxBTC
Beetle, The, *sel.* James Whitcomb Riley.
"Shrilling locust slowly sheathes, The." FaPON
Beetle Bemused. R. P. Lister. PV
Beetle loves his unpretending track, The. Wordsworth. *Fr.* Liberty. FaBoCo; FiBHP; Par
Beetle on the Shasta Daylight. Shirley Kaufman. NYBP; WPE
Beetles,/ noisy bumble bees. Come Visit My Garden. Tom Dent. NNP
Beets. Alden Nowlan. PeCV
Before. Albert Goldbarth. MAYP
Before. W. E. Henley. In Hospital, IV. BrPo; MoBrPo; VLP
Before. Ann Stanford. GP
Before/ and After. Jewel C. Latimore. JB
Before/ I opened my mouth. On Reading Poems to a Senior Class at South High. D. C. Berry. SoSe
Before a Cashier's Window in a Department Store. James Wright. *See* Before the Cashier's Window in a Department Store.
Before a Fall. Geoffrey Grigson. EAS
Before a Saint's Picture. Walter Savage Landor. OxBChV
Before a Statue of Achilles. George Santayana. HBV-2
Before Action. Leon Gellert. CBAP
Before Action. William Noel Hodgson. WGRP
Before Agincourt ("Now entertain conjecture of a time"). Shakespeare. *Fr.* King Henry V, *prologue to* IV. FaBoRV
(Before Agincourt ["From camp to camp, through the foul womb of night"].) ChTr
("Now entertain conjecture of a time.") EBEV; WaaP
Before an audible sound, an almost recognizable. Prelude to Memorial Song: 100 Years Later. Phillip William George. VoR
Before an Old Painting of the Crucifixion. N. Scott Momaday. QFR
Before Bannockburn. John Barbour. *Fr.* The Bruce. OxBS
Before Bannockburn. Burns. FaBoCh
Before Bed. Keith Waldrop. InPK
Before Breakup on the Chena outside Fairbanks. David McElroy. Psk
Before Dawn. Elinor Chipp. HBMV
Before Dawn. Horace Hamilton. NYBP
Before dawn i rose thirsty. Other. Lance Henson. VoR
Before Dawn in the Woods. Marguerite Wilkinson. HBMV
Before Day. Siegfried Sassoon. WGRP
Before daybreak, before dew breaks. Youth. Barend Toerien. PeSA
Before Disaster. Yvor Winters. HoPM; QFR
Before father shot the moon out. Hunting at Dusk. Doug Cockrell. Str
Before God's footstool to confess. Judgement. *Unknown.* TreFT
Before Good-bye. P. Wolny. PPJ
Before Harvest. Robert Fitzgerald. PoPl
Before He formed a star. His Plan. *Unknown.* STF
Before he pass'd from mortal view. Solemn Rondeau. Charles Dent Bell. OBVV
Before her supper where she sits. The Daughter at Evening. Robert Nathan. HBMV
Before Him weltered like a shoreless sea. Judgment Day. William Dean Howells. AA
Before history. Brightness. Heather McHugh. GeTw
Before I began to burn. Interval with Fire. Dorothy Livesay. CaP
Before I came across the sea. The Native Irishman. *Unknown.* OnYI
Before I crossed the sound. The Paps of Jura. Andrew Young. PoSH
Before I got my eye put out. Emily Dickinson. LiTA; LiTM
Before I had a face. The Man Who Buys Hides. Dennis Schmitz. LCAP
Before I joined the Army. Death and the Fairies. Patrick MacGill. HBMV
Before I Knocked and Flesh Let Enter. Dylan Thomas. FaBoTw
Before I laughed with him. What She Said. Maturai Eruttalan Centamputan, *tr. by* A. K. Ramanujan. BoLoP
Before I left my spot. Sunset. David Allan Evans. PPJ
Before I melt. The Snowflake. Walter de la Mare. NCSH; RHPC
Before I saw the Spring. Spring in Hiding. Frances Frost. YeAr
Before I set sail, I will not fail. Skin the Goat's Curse on Carey. *Unknown.* BIrV; TW
Before I sigh my last gasp, let me breathe. The Will. John Donne. EBEV; LiTB; MePo; OAEP
Before I Stumbled. Francis Carlin. HBMV
Before I trust my fate to thee. A Woman's Question. Adelaide Anne Procter. HBV-1
Before I was a travelled bird. Regarding (1) the U. S. and (2) New York. Franklin P. Adams. HBMV
Before I woke I knew her gone. Robert Nichols. *Fr.* The Flower of Flame. OBMV
Before I woke, the customed thews. Male Torso. Christopher Middleton. NePoEA-2
Before Invasion, 1940. John Betjeman. MoVE
Before Life and After. Thomas Hardy. FaBoRV
Before man came to blow it right. The Aim Was Song. Robert Frost. NoP; PP; SoSe
Before Meat/ O Thou, who kindly doth provide. A Poet's Grace. Burns. TrPWD
Before mine eye to feede my greedy will. George Gascoigne. AAS
Before morning you shall be here. Alba. Samuel Beckett. BIrV
Before my bright window. Winter. Mani Leib, *tr. by* Keith Bosley. VWA
Before my drift-wood fire I sit. Burning Drift-Wood. Whittier. MOS
Before My Face the Picture Hangs. Robert Southwell. *See* Upon the Image of Death.
Before my feet the ploughshare rolls the earth. Winter Ploughing. William Everson. NU

Before my lady's window gay. Medieval Norman Song. *Unknown, tr. by* John Addington Symonds. AWP
Before my light goes out for ever if God should give me a choice of graces. Impenitentia Ultima. Ernest Dowson. BrPo; HBV-1
Before Olympus. John Gould Fletcher. MoAmPo
Before one drop of angry blood was shed. Non-Combatant. Cicely Hamilton. SUMH
Before our eyes a pageant rolled. After the Centennial. Christopher Pearse Cranch. PAH
Before our lives divide for ever. The Triumph of Time. Swinburne. VLP
Before Passover. Seymour Mayne. NOBC
Before remembrance we moved here, withheld. The Font in the Forest. Léonie Adams. CrMA
Before Rereading Shakespeare's Sonnets. T. Sturge Moore. BrPo
Before Salamis. William Bedell Stanford. NeIP
Before Sedan. Austin Dobson. TreFS
Before Sentence Is Passed. R. P. Blackmur. LiTA
Before she has her floor swept. Portrait by a Neighbor. Edna St. Vincent Millay. FaPON; MoShBr; OBCA; PDV; TiPo
Before she saw him in the wood. The Quickening. Stella Weston Tuttle. GoYe
Before Sleep. Anne Ridler. NeBP
Before Sleeping. *Unknown.* CH; TreF
(Bed Charm.) HBVY
("Matthew, Mark, Luke, and John/ Bless the bed that I lie on.") FaBoCh; OxNR
(Prayer: "Matthew, Mark . . .") OxBoLi
(White Paternoster.) GBP
Before St. Anno. A Good Bishop. *Unknown, tr. by* William Taylor. WGRP
Before Sunrise in Winter. Edward Rowland Sill. AA
Before sunrise. Song for My Name. Linda Hogan. STE; TWSS
Before Sunset. Swinburne. VLP
Before that my loved one. Apprehension. *Unknown, tr. by* Douglas Ainslie. OBVV
Before the Actual Cold. Ray A. Young Bear. VoR
Before the altar of the world in flower. Sacrament. Margaret Sackville. SUMH
Before the Anaesthetic; or, A Real Fright. John Betjeman. EBCP; SeCePo
Before the Barn-Door Crowing. John Gay. *Fr.* The Beggar's Opera. ELU; PBBP
(Song.) ErPo; PoEL-3
Before the Beginning. Christina Georgina Rossetti. OxBoCh
(Last Prayer.) OBVV
Before the Beginning of Years. Swinburne. *Fr.* Atalanta in Calydon. FaFP; HBV-1; LiTB; MasP; NoP; OAEP; WHA
(Chorus.) EBVV; HeIP; LoBV; OBEV; OBVV; TRV; ViBoPo
(Man.) TrGrPo
Before the beginning Thou hast foreknown the end. Before the Beginning [*or* Last Prayer]. Christina Rossetti. OxBoCh
Before the Big Storm. William Stafford. NaP
Before the Birth of One of Her Children. Anne Bradstreet. BoWoP; MAT; NAs; NOBA; PAI; SBG; WPE; WPOW
Before the blond horsemen rode into our village. An Event. Edward Field. CoAP
Before the Breaking. Lee Pennington. AMV-81
Before the bright sun rises over the hill. The Gleaner. Jane Taylor. OxBChV
Before the Carnival. Thom Gunn. NePoEA
Before the [*or* a] Cashier's Window in a Department Store. James Wright. CoAP; MAT; NYBP; NYP
Before the cathedral in grandeur rose. How the Great Guest Came. Edwin Markham. BeLS; BLPA; BLPL
Before the children say goodnight. The Happy Family. John Ciardi. DuDa
Before the dawn-wind swept the troubled sky. A Vision. Geoffrey Dearmer. HBMV
Before the days of duty. The Silver Racer. Joseph Colin Murphey. AMV-80
Before the Dive. Elizabeth Kempf. AMV-81
Before the Fall. Milton. *Fr.* Paradise Lost, IV. NIP
("She, as a veil down to the slender waist.") ErPo
Before the falling summer sun. Musings. William Barnes. HAP; NOBE; OBNC
Before the Feast of Shushan. Anne Spencer. BANP; BlSi
Before the Flowers of Friendship Faded Faded, *sel.* Gertrude Stein.
"I love my love with a v." PeHV
Before the glare o' dawn I rise. The Shearer's Wife. Louis Esson. PoAu-1
Before the gods that made the gods. G. K. Chesterton. *Fr.* The Ballad of the White Horse. ACP
Before the grass could be planted. Building in Nova Scotia. Stephen Dunn. GP
Before the Great Void, we burn the fragrant incense. To Purity and Truth. *Unknown, tr. by* William C. White. TrJP
Before the Ikon of the Mother of God. Constantine of Rhodes, *tr. fr. Greek by* G. R. Woodward. ISi
Before the living bronze Saint-Gaudens made. *See* Before the solemn bronze . . .
Before the Mirror. Swinburne. OBVV
"Glad, but not flush'd with gladness,"*sel.* OBEV
Before the moon should circlewise close both her horns in one. Medea Casts a Spell to Make Aeson Young Again. Ovid, *tr. by* Arthur Golding. *Fr.* Metamorphoses. MOON
Before the Mountain. Elizabeth Libbey. AmPA
Before the Pacific. Blanca Varela, *tr. fr. Spanish by* Willis Barnstone. BoWoP
Before the Paling of the Stars. Christina Rossetti. HBVY; TrCP
Before the Poetry Reading. Louis Simpson. OxBC
Before the prim old mirror. Hair-dressing. Louis Untermeyer. UnTE
Before the Rain. Thomas Bailey Aldrich. GN
Before the Rain. Amélie Rives. AA
Before the Roman came to Rye or out to Severn strode. The Rolling English Road. G. K. Chesterton. EvOK; FaBoCh; HBMV; NOBE; NOBL; OBEV; OBMV; OxBTC; SeCeV
Before the sixth day of the next new year. On the [*or* A Prognostication upon] Cards and Dice. Sir Walter Ralegh. EnRePo; SiPS
Before the solemn [*or* living] bronze Saint Gaudens made. An Ode in Time of Hesitation. William Vaughn Moody. AP; HBV-2; OxBA; PAH
Before the starry threshold of Jove's court. Comus. Milton. OAEL-1; OAEP
Before the Statue of a Laughing Man. William C. Bowie. AMV-81
Before the Statue of Apollo. Saul Tchernichowsky, *tr. fr. Hebrew by* L. V. Snowman. TrJP
Before the stirring of the notes at the lecture. Madonna of the Dons. Arthur MacGillivray. ISi
Before the Storm. Richard Dehmel, *tr. fr. German by* Ludwig Lewisohn. AWP
Before the Storm. Kenneth O. Hanson. CoAP
Before the Stuff Comes Down. Gary Snyder. HeIP
Before the sun goes down. Astrid Hjertenaes Andersen, *tr. fr. Norwegian by* Nadia Christensen. BoWoP
Before the sun rose at yester-dawn. Kitty Bhan. Edward Walsh. ACP
Before the Thaw. John Gill. NeAC
Before the thing begins we have. Poetry Reading. Vernon Scannell. NOBL
Before the urchin well could go. The Fair Thief. Charles Wyndham. HBV-1
Before the War. Marilyn Hacker. AmPA
Before the War. James Pendergast. AMV-81
Before the war. From Our Album. Lawson Fusao Inada. AmPA
Before the World Was Made. W. B. Yeats. GTBS-P
Before their quaintly carven doors were smashed. Short History of Twentieth-Century Scholarship. John Wain. GLGT
Before, there is water. Water. Edmond Jabès, *tr. by* Anthony Rudolf. VWA
Before, there was one. Birth. Constance Urdang. VWA
Before they ripen into diffused spririts. Katerina Anghelaki-Rooke, *tr. fr. modern Greek by* Kimon Friar. NU
Before this fever of the almost cold. Mirror. Peter De Vries. PoA
Before this longing. Her Longing. Theodore Roethke. NU
Before thy door too long of late. Extremum Tanain. Horace, *tr. by* Austin Dobson. Odes, III, 10. AWP
Before Thy Throne. William Boyd Carpenter. TRV
Before time they were sound. Grandfathers. Dennis Shady. LFAC
Before Trinity Church. The Assassination of President McKinley. Paul Blackburn. NYP
Before Vespasian's regal throne. Death of Gaudentis. "Harriet Annie." WBLP
Before Vicksburg. George Henry Boker. PAH
Before Waterloo. Thomas Hardy. *Fr.* The Dynasts. MoAB; WaaP
(Eve of Waterloo, The.) OBWP
("Eyelids of eve fall together at last, The.") OAEL-2
Before we shall again behold. Endimion Porter and Olivia. Sir William Davenant. MeLP; MePo; NOBE; OBS
Before you kissed me only winds of heaven. The Kiss. Sara Teasdale. HBV-1
Before you step out. I Hope I Don't Have You Next Semester, But. Edwin S. Godsey. HoPM
Before your mouth was fringed with hair. Epigram: On a Slanderer. Martial. PeHV
Before Your Waking. Anna Gréki, *tr. fr. French by* Anita Barrows. WPOW
Beforehand. Witter Bynner. HBMV
Beg Parding. *Unknown.* ChTr
Bega. Majorie Pickthall. CaP

Begetting. Dorothea Spears. PeSA
Begetting of Cain, The. Hyam Plutzik. VWA
Beggar, The. H. L. Doak. HBMV
Beggar, The. Adrian Mitchell. FaBoTw
Beggar, The. Thomas Moss. NOEC
Beggar. Nicanor Parra, *tr. fr. Spanish by* Miller Williams. CAD
Beggar, The. *Unknown.* OBET
Beggar Boy, The. Cecil Frances Alexander. OxBChV
"Beggar," he sayes. Little John a Begging. *Unknown.* ESPB
Beggar in dirt. Dervish. Georgia Lee McElhaney. CoPo
Beggar-Laddie, The. *Unknown.* ESPB
Beggar Maid, The. Tennyson. BeLS; HBV-1; OnMSP
Beggar Man, The. Lucy Aikin. OxBChV
Beggar on the Beach, The. Horace Gregory. NMP
Beggar shouts his martial wares, The. The Beggar. Adrian Mitchell. FaBoTw
Beggar to Beggar Cried. W. B. Yeats. CMoP; NoAM
Beggar to Mab, the Fairy [*or* Fairie] Queen, The. Robert Herrick. CaPo; WSC
Beggar to the graveyard hied, A. Poverty. *Unknown, tr. by* Arthur W. Ryder. *Fr.* The Panchatantra. AWP
Beggar Wind, The. Mary Austin. BoNaP
Beggar Woman, The. William King. NOEC
Beggarly Bear, A. Carolyn Wells. TDH
Beggarman's Song, A, *sel.* *Tr. fr. Gaelic by* Frank O'Connor.
"Would God that I and my darling." WTO
Beggars. Rhys Carpenter. HBMV
Beggars. Francis Davidson. CH
Beggars. Ella Higginson. AA
Beggars' Bush, *sel.* John Fletcher.
Cast Our Caps and Cares Away. ViBoPo
Beggars in the stories of old. Fairy Tales. Itzik Manger, *tr. by* Miriam Waddington. VWA
Beggar's Opera, The John Gay. OAEL-1
Sels.
Air: "Fox may steal your hens, sir, A," *fr.* I, i. NOEC
(Soldier and a Sailor, A.) TEP
Air XXXV: "How happy I could be with either," *fr.* II, ii. ViBoPo
Air: "Since laws were made for ev'ry degree," *fr.* III, xiii. NOEC
Before the Barn-Door Crowing, *fr.* II, i. ELU; PBBP
(Song: "Before the barn-door crowing.") ErPo; PoEL-3
Highwaymen, The, *fr.* II, i. WiR
"If the heart of a man is deprest with cares," *fr.* II, ii. EnLoPo
(If the Heart of a Man.) ELP; HeIP
Modes of the Court, The, *fr.* III, iv. HeIP
"O Polly, you might have toy'd and kist," *fr.* I, i. EnLoPo
Song: "Can love be controll'd by advice?" *fr.* I, viii. LoBV
Song: "If any Wench Venus's Girdle wear," *fr.* I, i. PoEL-3
Song: "Thus when the Swallow, seeking Prey," *fr.* II, ii. PoEL-3
Song: "Youth's the season made for joys," *fr.* II, i. OBEC
(Youth and Love.) NOBE
(Youth's the Season.) WiR
"Were I laid on Greenland's coast," *fr.* I, i. EnLoPo
(Macheath and Polly.) LoBV; NOEC
(Over the Hills and Far Away.) BLSo, *with music;* NOBE; PrIm
(Song:"Were I laid on Greenland's coast.") OBEC; OxBoLi; PoEL-3; SeCeV
What Shall I Do to Show How Much I Love Her? *fr.* I, vii. TEP
Would You Have a Young Virgin? *fr.* II, i. TEP
Beggar's Serenade. John Heath-Stubbs. BoLoP; ErPo; NeBP
Beggar's Song. Gregory Orr. LTB
Begging. Henry Vaughan. AnAnS-1
Begging Another, on Colour of Mending the Former. Ben Jonson. *Fr.* A Celebration of Charis. AnAnS-2; OAEP; PoEL-2; SeCP
(For Love's Sake.) UnTE
Begging on North Main. Dabney Stuart. AMV-81
Begin again. There is no law which says. Five Epigrams. Donald Hall. NePoAm-2
Begin before birth with swept-back fins. The Matin Pandemoniums. Richard Eberhart. NYBP
Begin by parting your hair. Parting; a Game. Lynn Sukenick. NMM
Begin, ephebe, by perceiving the idea. Wallace Stevens. *Fr.* Notes toward a Supreme Fiction. NOBA
Begin Summer. Ingrid Jonker, *tr. fr. Afrikaans by* Jack Cope *and* Uys Krige. PeSA
Begin the Day with God ("Every morning lean thine arms awhile"). *Unknown.* TRV
Begin the day with God. Rules for Daily Life. *Unknown.* STF
Begin to charm, and as thou strok'st mine ears. To Music. Robert Herrick. CaPo
Begin unto my God with timbrels. With Timbrels. Bible, Apocrypha. *Fr.* Judith. TrJP
Beginner, The. Kipling. *Fr.* Epitaphs of the War. FaBoTw
Beginner/ Perpetual beginner. What Can I Tell My Bones? Theodore Roethke. AmPP; NOBA
Beginners. Walt Whitman. AA
Beginning. Alden Nowlan. NeAC; NOBC
Beginning. Marcos Rodríguez Frese, *tr. fr. Spanish by* Julio Marzán. InW
Beginning. David Rokeah, *tr. fr. Hebrew by* Robert Mezey. VWA
Beginning, The. Wallace Stevens. VGW
Beginning and an End, A. Edouard Roditi. VWA
Beginning by Example, *sel.* Christopher Gilbert.
Blue. FYAP
Beginning I will praise a fine beginning. The Goods She Can Carry: Canticle of Her Basket Made of Reeds. Gibbons Ruark. MAYP
Beginning in half darkness. The Morning Track. Edward Parone. NYBP
Beginning my fortieth year. Beyond the Presidency. Morgan Gibson. FF
Beginning My Studies. Walt Whitman. OxBA
Beginning of a Long Poem on Why I Burned the City, The. Lawrence Benford. NBP; TTY
Beginning of an Undergraduate Poem. *Unknown.* FaBoCo
Beginning of eternity, the end of time and space, The. Rhyming Riddle. *Unknown.* TreFT
Beginning of the End, The. Gerard Manley Hopkins. VLP
Beginning of the End, The. Jon Stallworthy. OxBC
Beginning, The: Some landscape & words about nature. Kirk Lonegren's Home Movie Taking Place Just North of Prince George, with Sound. Sharon Thesen. NOBC
Beginning storm sets my blood racing, A. Lives. Cyril Dabydeen. BrSi
Beginning the Year at Rosebud, S.D. Roberta Hill. CDW; TWSS
Beginning to dangle beneath. In the Marble Quarry. James Dickey. AmFN; NoP
Beginning to Live. Ruth Stone. GP
Beginning to Squall. May Swenson. RFM
Beginning with C in the dank school basement. Mr. Brunt. Robert Siegel. GeTw
Beginnings. Erez Biton, *tr. fr. Hebrew by* Judith Katz. VWA
Beginnings, *sel.* Robert Hayden.
"Plowdens, Finns." CNA
Beginnings of Faith, The. Sir Lewis Morris. WGRP
Beg-Innish. J. M. Synge. MoBrPo; OnYI; OxBI
Begins the crying. Guitar. Federico García Lorca, *tr. by* Keith Waldrop. InPK
Begins with the *ooo ooo* of a mourning dove. Holy Thursday. Charles Wright. GeTw
Begot by butchers, but by bishops bred. On Cardinal Wolsey [*or* Cacophonous Couplet on Cardinal Wolsey]. *Unknown.* DBV; FaBoCo
Begotten by the meeting of rock with rock. Sea Holly. Conrad Aiken. AP; LiTM; NePA
Begotten of the Spleen. Charles Simic. LCAP
Begun before Easter. . ./ Sign of the Fish. Thomas McGrath. Letter to an Imaginary Friend, Part Two, VI, 4. NNaP
Behave Yoursel' before Folk. Alexander Rodger. HBV-1
Behaviour of Fish in an Egyptian Tea Garden. Keith Douglas. FaBoMo
Behaviour of Money. Bernard Spencer. LiTB
Behind a web of bottles, bales. The Gombeen. Joseph Campbell. BIrV
Behind an unfrequented glade. Matthew Prior. *Fr.* The Turtle and the Sparrow. PBBP
Behind glass in Mexico. Five Poems for Dolls, I. Margaret Atwood. NIP
Behind glass, my room is neat. Out of Chaos Out of Order Out. Michele Roberts. BrRo
Behind her, mesquite and caliche dirt. Yaqui Women: Three Generations. Rick Casillas. GP
Behind her not the quivering of a leaf. Circe. A. D. Hope. PPP
Behind him lay the gray Azores. Columbus. Joaquin Miller. AA; BeLS; EtS; FaBoBe; FaFP; FaPON; GN; HBV-2; HBVY; MOS; OHFP; PAL; PaPo; PGD; PPP; TreF; YaD; YeAr
Behind him spreads the horizoned shore. On a Landscape of Sestos. Carlos Baker. *Fr.* A Visit to the Art Gallery. EyDe
Behind him the hotdogs split and drizzled. Suicide off Egg Rock. Sylvia Plath. NMP; PPP
Behind his dinner jacket. He's Doing Natural Life. Conyus. PoBA
Behind King's Chapel what the earth has kept. At the Indian Killer's Grave. Robert Lowell. NOBA; VGW
Behind me the house was asleep. Happening. Edwin Honig. NePA
Behind me—dips eternity. Emily Dickinson. AP; PBWP
Behind our house there is a mere. The White Drake. *Unknown, tr. by* John Glassco. WHW
Behind shut doors, in shadowy quarantine. The First Time. Karl Shapiro. ErPo; VGW
Behind, sun, before, shadow! Silhouette. Annette M'Baye, *tr. by* Kathleen Weaver. PBWP
Behind That Wall My Roommate Fucks His Girl. Geof Hewitt. NeAC; POL

Behind that white brow. To a Dead Journalist. William Carlos Williams. QFR
Behind the calm famous faces knowledge of what crimes? Collapsible. Tom Raworth. EAS
Behind the Falls. William Stafford. RFM
Behind the Glass Wall. Harold Norse. PeHV
Behind the granite church. Fugue. Constance Carrier. GoYe
Behind the hilltop drops the sun. John Vance Cheney. Evening Songs, IV. AA
Behind the house the upland falls. After the Pleasure Party. Herman Melville. AP
Behind the Kokusai Theatre in Nihonmachi. Dreams in Progress. Richard Oyama. BrSi
Behind the leaves of redbud and sycamore, dangling. This Town. James Paul. HoAn
Behind the Line. Edmund Blunden. ChMP
Behind the Log, *sel.* E. J. Pratt.
"There is a language in a naval log." MoCV
Behind the New Jersey shore. Obon by the Hudson. Richard Oyama. BrSi
Behind the Plough. James H. Cousins. OxBI
Behind the Power Station on 14th, the held breath. Galway Kinnell. *Fr.* The Avenue Bearing the Initial of Christ into the New World. NaP
Behind the Stove. James Hearst. TAT
Behind the tree, behind the house, behind the stars. Seen in a Glass. Kathleen Raine. ChMP
Behind the wall of St. John's in the city. The Garden at St. John's. May Swenson. NePoEA; PoPl
Behind the Waterfall. Winifred Welles. TiPo
Behind the wild-bird's throat. Wood-Thrush. John Hall Wheelock. NePoAm
Behind thy pasteboard, on thy battered hack. Don Quixote. Austin Dobson. HBV-2; HBVY
Behind you/ a riot of pallid orphans. Small Country. Claribel Alegria, *tr. by* Aliki *and* Willis Barnstone. BoWoP
Behold. *Tr. fr. Hawaiian by* M. K. Pukui. WTO
Behold a [*or* the] critic, pitched like the castrati. Pipling. Theodore Roethke. NePA; TW
Behold! a giant am I! The Windmill. Longfellow. MoShBr
Behold a hag whom Life denies a kiss. Opportunity. Madison Cawein. AA
Behold! a new white world! A New Year. Dora Sigerson Shorter. YeAr
Behold, a silly [*or* little] tender babe. New Prince, New Pomp. Robert Southwell. AnAnS-1; ELP; GN; NOBE; NOCV; OBSC; OHIP; SBVL; TrCP
Behold, a virgin shall conceive. The Messiah. Bible, *O.T.* *Fr.* Isaiah. AWP
Behold a woman! The Justified Mother of Men. Walt Whitman. OHIP
Behold a Wonder Here! *Unknown.* OBSC; TrGrPo
"Behold another singer!" Criton said. "Song to the Gods, Is Sweetest Sacrifice." Annie Fields. AA
Behold, bless ye the Lord. Bible, *O.T.* Psalms, CXXXIV. TRV
Behold, four Kings in majesty rever'd. The Playing Cards. Pope. *Fr.* The Rape of the Lock, III. ChTr
Behold from sluggish winter's arm. Primo Vere. Giosuè Carducci, *tr. by* John Bailey. AWP
Behold, God is great, and we know him not. Bible, *O.T.* *Fr.* Job. ImOP
Behold he comes to make thy people groan. Pasquin to the Queen's Statue at St. Paul's. William Shippen. APAS
Behold her seven hills loom white. Resurge San Francisco. Joaquin Miller. PAH
Behold her, single in the field. The Solitary Reaper. Wordsworth. AWP; BLPL; CABA; CH; ChER; EnRP; FaBoCh; FaBoEn; FaPoR; FiP; GN; GTBS; GTBS-P; HAP; HBV-1; InPS; LiTB; LoBV; NOBE; NoP; OAEL-2; OAEP; OBEV; OBNC; OBRV; PAI; PoEL-4; PoPle; PoRA; PPP; RoGo; SCV; SeCeV; SoSe; TEP; TreF; TrGrPo; UnPo; WeW; WHA
Behold him now his genuine colours wear. Sonnet: To the Departing Spirit of an Alienated Friend. Anna Seward. PeHV
Behold, how eager this our little boy. Of the Boy and Butterfly. Bunyan. NIP; OxBChV
Behold, how good and how pleasant it is. To Dwell Together in Unity. Bible, *O.T.* Psalms, CXXXIII. AWP; TreFT; TrJP; TRV
Behold, I have a weapon. Shakespeare. *Fr.* Othello, V, ii. BiP
Behold! in various throngs the scribbling crew. Byron. *Fr.* English Bards and Scotch Reviewers. EnRP; OAEL-2
Behold, love, thy power how she despiseth! Sir Thomas Wyatt. GBL
Behold me waiting—waiting for the knife. Before. W. E. Henley. In Hospital, IV. BrPo; MoBrPo; VLP
Behold, my dearest, how the fragrant rose. To Her Love. Edward May. FaBoEE
Behold, my Samsons are returning, and the gates of Gaza are on their shoulders. My Samsons. Haim Guri, *tr. by* Mark Elliott Shapiro. VWA
Behold, my servant shall deal prudently. Bible, *O.T.* *Fr.* Isaiah. NAWM-1
Behold, O Aspasia! I Send You Verses. Walter Savage Landor. *Fr.* Pericles and Aspasia. LoBV; OBNC
("Beauty! thou art a wanderer on the earth.") ViBoPO
Behold, O Man. Spenser. *Fr.* The Faerie Queene, II, 6. EIL
Behold, O world, the toiling man. Edwin Markham. *Fr.* The Toiler. PGD
Behold once more with serious labor here. To the Reader. Samuel Daniel. OBSC; PP
Behold, One of Several Little Christs. Kenneth Patchen. NaP
Behold Pelides with his yellow hair. Before a Statue of Achilles. George Santayana. HBV-2
Behold, slow-settling o'er the lurid grove. The Storm. James Thomson. *Fr.* The Seasons: Summer. LoBV
Behold that which I have seen. Enjoy the Good. Bible, *O.T.* *Fr.* Ecclesiastes. TreFT
Behold the barren reef, which an earthquake hath just left dry. Martin Farquhar Tupper. *Fr.* Of Invention. VLP
Behold the birds of the heaven. God Provides. Bible, *N.T.* *Fr.* St. Matthew. BLRP
Behold the brand of beauty tossed! The Dancer. Edmund Waller. TrGrPo
Behold the child, by Nature's kindly law. Pope. *Fr.* An Essay on Man, IV. FaBoRV; POL
Behold the Cot! where thrives th' industrious swain. George Crabbe. *Fr.* The Parish Register, I. OBRV
Behold the critic, pitched like the castrati. *See* Behold a critic . . .
Behold the Deeds! H. C. Bunner. HBV-2; InMe
Behold the dental artist's bright array. Artificial Teeth. Solyman Brown. *Fr.* Dentologia; a Poem on the Diseases of the Teeth and Their Proper Remedies. FaBoUs
Behold the duck. The Duck. Ogden Nash. MoShBr; WhC
Behold the ever-tim'rous hare. April. Samuel Thompson. BIrV
Behold the fatal day arrive! Swift. *Fr.* Verses on the Death of Dr. Swift. SCV; ViBoPo
Behold the father is his daughter's son. The Nativity of Christ. Robert Southwell. EBCP
Behold the flag! Is it not a flag? The Rejected "National Hymns." "Orpheus C. Kerr." OBAL
Behold, the Grave of a Wicked Man. Stephen Crane. The Black Riders, XXV. TAP
(Why?) AA
Behold the hippopotamus! The Hippopotamus. Ogden Nash. FaBV; OnUR
Behold the house of Sir William Forbes. The Pentland Hills. *Unknown.* GBP
Behold the Lilies of the Field. Anthony Hecht. CoPo; NePoEA-2
Behold the Man! *Unknown.* STF
Behold the man alive in me. Ecce Homo. Witter Bynner. WGRP
Behold the mansion reared by Daedal Jack! The Domicile of John. Pope. InMe
Behold, the Meads. Guillaume de Poitiers, *tr. fr. French by* Harriet Waters Preston. AWP
Behold the mighty dinosaur. The Dinosaur. Bert Leston Taylor. ImOP
Behold! the mother bird. The Assumption. John Banister Tabb. ISi
Behold the Mount of Olives and the Greek cloister. Jerusalem. Antoni Slonimski, *tr. by* Isaac Komem. VWA
Behold the portal: open wide it stands. The Garden Where There Is No Winter. Louis James Block. AA
Behold the ravens on the trees. Contentment. Benjamin Schlipf. BLRP
Behold the rocky wall. The Two Streams. Oliver Wendell Holmes. *Fr.* The Professor at the Breakfast Table. AP
Behold the Sea, *sel.* Aaron Kurtz.
They Got You Last Night. PPON
Behold, the Shade of Night Is Now Receding, *with music.* St. Gregory the Great, *tr. fr. Latin by* Ray Palmer. AH
Behold the tormented and the fallen angel. Beethoven. John Hall Wheelock. PoA
Behold the wicked little barb. The Question Mark. Persis Greely Anderson. WhC
Behold the wonders of the mighty deep. The Sea. *Unknown.* NA; RHPC
Behold the works of William Morris. Rondel. *Unknown.* BXAP; Par
Behold these woods, and mark, my sweet. A Pastoral Courtship. Earl of Rochester. UnTe
Behold this brief hexagonal. Text. Audrey Wurdemann. FYAP
Behold This Dreamer. Elizabeth Bartlett. NePoAm-2
Behold this fleeting world, how all things fade. An Epitaph of the Death of Nicholas Grimald. Barnabe Googe. EnRePo
Behold this needle when the arctic stone. On the Needle of a Sundial. Francis Quarles. OBS; TrGrPo
Behold this ruin! 'Twas a skull. To a Skeleton. Anna Jane Vardhill. BLPA

Behold those wingèd images. A Legend of the Hive. Robert Stephen Hawker. EBVV
Behold, Thou Art Fair. Bible, *O.T.* The Song of Solomon, IV. BiP; TrJP (1-7)
Behold through the veil of distance a pleasing image. Jonathan. Rachel, *tr. by* L. V. Snowman. TrJP
Behold thy darling, which thy lustfull care. Francis Quarles. Emblems, V, 8. AnAnS-1
Behold upon the swelling seas. A-Cruising We Will Go. *Unknown.* AmSS
Behold, we have gathered together our battleships, near and afar. "Mene, Mene, Tekel, Upharsin." Madison Cawein. PAH
Behold what furies still. Chorus. Samuel Daniel. *Fr.* Cleopatra. LoBV
Behold with Joy, *with music.* Elhanan Winchester. AH
Behold within our Hayden Planetarium. Ode to the Hayden Planetarium. Arthur Guiterman. ImOP
Behold, within the leafy shade. The Sparrow's Nest. Wordsworth. EnRP
Behold yon hill, how it is swell'd with pride. Describes the Place Where Cynthia Is Sporting Herself. Philip Ayres. EnLoPo
Behold yon mountain's hoary height. To Thaliarchus. Horace, *tr. by* Dryden. Odes, I, 9. AWP; CavP; OBVE
Behold yon new-born infant, griev'd. The Ignorance of Man. James Merrick. OxBoCh
Behold you not this globe, this golden bowl. Thomas Dekker. *Fr.* Old Fortunatus. ViBoPo
Beholde, how good and joyfull a thinge it is. Bible, *O.T.* Psalms, CXXXIII. OBVE
Beholde me, I pray thee, with all thine whole reson. Wofully Araide. *Unknown.* MeEL
Beholders, The. James Dickey. AP
Beholding element, in whose pure eye. The Aspen and the Stream. Richard Wilbur. NYBP
Bei Hennef. D. H. Lawrence. BrPo
Being, The. James Dickey. NMP
Being a Christian. *Unknown.* STF
Being a Giant. Robert Mezey. GrPl
Being a modest man, you wanted. For My Father. Philip Whalen. DiL
Being Adult. Bill Zavatsky. POL
Being at last on our way. Departure. William Hart-Smith. *Fr.* Christopher Columbus. PoAu-2
Being awake still and not unhappy. Selichos. Francis Landy. VWA
Being Born Is Important. Carl Sandburg. NAs
Being Called For. Rosemary Dobson. CBAP
Being Forsaken of His Friend He Complaineth. "E. S." ElL
Being Gypsy. Barbara Young. SoPo
Being Herded Past the Prison's Honor Farm. David Wagoner. SoSe
Being his resting place. A Dog Sleeping on My Feet. James Dickey. PP
Being homeward bound on the mighty deep. Lady Franklin's Lament, *vers.* I. *Unknown.* ShS
Being in thought of love, I chanced to see. Ballata: He Reveals, in a Dialogue, His Increasing Love for Mandetta. Guido Cavalcanti, *tr. by* Dante Gabriel Rossetti. AWP
Being my selfe captyved here in care. Amoretti, LXXIII. Spenser. LoBV
Being Natural. Carl Rakosi. GP
Being now three or four years more than sixty. The World's Wonders. Robinson Jeffers. NePA
Being on the road wasn't so bad. Has Been. Alice F. Worsley. AMV-80
Being one day at my window all alone. The Visions. Petrarch, *tr. by* Spenser. *Fr.* Sonnets to Laura: Songs. AWP
Being Refused Local Credit. Paula Rankin. MAYP
Being Sad. Orban Veli Kanik, *tr. fr. Turkish by* Talat Sait Halman. LLLT
Being set, let's sport a while, my fair. Thomas Randolph. *Fr.* A Pastoral Courtship. ViBoPo
Being set on the idea. Atlantis. W. H. Auden. PoPl
Being Somebody. Edwin Honig. TAP
Being to Timelessness as It's to Time. E. E. Cummings. HAP; NePA
Being with Men. Linda Gregg. NPGG
Being with you. Margaret Atwood. *Fr.* The Circle Game. MoCV
Being without quality. Vox Humana. Thom Gunn. NePoEA-2
Being witless it said no prayer. The Death of an Angel. Russell Edson. LCAP
Being you, you cut your poetry from wood. The Egg Boiler. Gwendolyn Brooks. PoBA
Being your slave, what should I do but tend. Sonnets, LVII. Shakespeare. GTBS; GTBS-P; HAP; OBEV; PeHV; PoEL-2; ViBoPo
Beinn A' Ghlo. Bill Tulloch. PoSH
Beinn Naomh, *sel.* Kathleen Raine.
Summit, The, IV. OxBS
Beirut-Hell Express, The, *sel.* Etel Adnan.
"Human race is going to the cemetery, The." WPOW
Bel m'es quan lo vens m'alena. Arnaut Daniel, *tr. fr. French by* Harriet Waters Preston. AWP
Belated Violet, A. Oliver Herford. AA
Belden Hollow. Leslie Nelson Jennings. GoYe
Belfast: High Street. Padraic Colum. NePoAm
Belfast Linen. *Unknown. See* Ballad of William Bloat, The.
Belfast Lough. *Unknown, tr. fr. Irish by* John Montague. BIrV
Belfry, The. Laurence Binyon. CH
Belfry of Bruges, The. Longfellow. HBV-2
Belief. A. R. Ammons. GOA
Belief. Ruth Fitch Bartlett. InMe
Belief. Josephine Miles. NoAM; TAP
Belief and Unbelief. Robert Browning. *Fr.* Bishop's Blougram's Apology. FaBV
Belief in Plan of Thee. Walt Whitman. TRV
Believe and Take Heart. John Lancaster Spalding. AA
"Believe in me," the Prophet cried. Infallibility. Thomas Stephens Collier. AA
Believe It. John Logan. LCAP
Believe me, every hour e'en yet I dream. To Schmidlein. August, Graf von Platen, *tr. by* Reginald Bancroft Cooke. PeHV
Believe me, I say to the gentleman with the pince-nez. In the Library. Elizabeth Brewster. OBCV
Believe me, I understand your refusal. Letter to Pasternak. Ralph Pomeroy. CoPo
Believe Me, If All Those Endearing Young Charms. Thomas Moore. BLPA; ELP; EnRP; FaBoBe; FaBV; FaFP; FPL; FSW; HBV-1; LiTB; OBNC; OBRV; OnYI; PoEL-4; PoPl; TEP; TreF; WBLP
Believe me, knot of gristle, I bleed like a tree. Give Way, Ye Gates. Theodore Roethke. CMoP; NMP
Believe me, Love, this vagrant life. To Cordelia. Joseph Stansbury. CaP; NOBC
Believe me, sir, I'd like to spend whole days. Martial, *tr. fr. Latin by* J. V. Cunningham. OBVE
Believe me. Elmer Ruiz. Peter Oresick. LTB
Believe Not. Isaac Leibush Peretz, *tr. fr. Yiddish by* Solomon Liptzin. TrJP
Believe not, Fair, that I can prove untrue. William Diaper. *Fr.* Nereides; or, Sea-Eclogues, I. PeD
Believe not that the world is for naught, made. Believe Not. Isaac Leibush Peretz, *tr. by* Solomon Liptzin. TrJP
Believe the Bible. A. B. Simpson. STF
Belinda lived in a little white house. The Tale of Custard the Dragon. Ogden Nash. FaPON; OBCA; OnUR; PoPl; PoRA; TiPo
Belisarius. Longfellow. PoEL-5; WiR
Belita. Alberto Ríos. LTB
Bell, A. Clinton Scollard. AA
Bell-Bird, The. "Fiona Macleod." *Fr.* Australian Transcripts. FM
Bell-Birds. Henry Kendall. PoAu-1
Bell-Bottom [*or* bottomed] Trousers. *Unknown.* AmSS; FSW; UnTE
Bell diphthonging in an atmosphere, A. A Dubious Night. Richard Wilbur. CAPP
Bell horses, bell horses, what time of day? Mother Goose. OxNR; SiSoSe; TiPo
Bell in the Orthodox Steeple, A. Thomas Waltner. LFAC
Bell, my silver tonguèd bell. Theme. Carl Spitteler, *tr. by* Margarete Münsterberg. PoPl
Bell-rope that gathers God at dawn, The. The Broken Tower. Hart Crane. AmPP; AP; CMoP; CoBMV; LiTM; MoAB; MoAmPo; MoPo; MoVE; NoAM; NOBA; NoP; OxBA; SyP; TrGrPo
Bell sings, "Children! Children!", A. A Bell in the Orthodox Steeple. Thomas Waltner. LFAC
Bell Speech. Richard Wilbur. AP; CABA; MoAB; MoAmPo; MoVE
Bell that tolls my syllables can tell, The. S. S. *City of Benares.* G. S. Fraser. NeBP
Bell Too Heavy to Ring. Tom Kryss. NeAC
Bell Tower. Léonie Adams. MoAB; MoAmPo; PoPl
Bell Weather. Lewis Turco. AMV-80
Bella and the Golem. Rossana Ombres, *tr. fr. Italian by* Edgar Pauk. VWA
Bella Ciao. *Unknown, tr. fr. Italian.* FSW
Bella was young and Bella was fair. Unhappy Bella. *Unknown.* ErPo
Belle, *with music. Unknown.* OuSiCo
Belle de Jour. George Melly. FaBoPa
Belle of the Balkans, The. Newman Levy. FiBHP
Belle of the Ball-Room, The. Winthrop Mackworth Praed. *Fr.* Every-Day Characters. EnRP; FaBoCo; HBV-1; InMe
"Our love was like most other loves," *sel.* ViBoPo
Belle Saison, La. Jacques Prévert, *tr. fr. French by* Lawrence Ferlinghetti. CAD
Belle Starr. *Unknown.* BPAW
Bellerophon, *sel.* Euripides, *tr. fr. Greek by* John Addington. Symonds.
There Are No Gods. EaLo
Bellies bitter with drinking the/ Weak tears. Final Chorus. Archibald MacLeish. *Fr.* Panic. MoAmPo
Belling the Cat. William Langland. *Fr.* The Vision of Piers Plowman. OxBM

Bellman, The. Robert Herrick. CaPo; CH; OBS; PoPle
Bell-man of night, if I about shall go. Cock-Crow. Robert Herrick. PBBP
Bellman's Song, The. *Unknown.* EBEV; EIL; SeCePo
Bellow of good Master Bull, The. Ballade un Peu Banale. A. J. M. Smith. MoCV
Bellows Maker of Oxford, The. John Hoskyns. FaBoEE
Bellringing was another. To My Father. Tony Curtis. AMV-81
Bells, The. Poe. AA; FaFP; FPL; GN; HBV-2; LiTA; NePA; OBAL; OBCA; OHFP; PoLF; TAP; TreF; WBLP
Sels.
"Hear the mellow wedding bells." PoPl
"Hear the sledges with the bells." FaPON; SpRo
Bells. Duncan Campbell Scott. CaP
Bells, The. *Unknown.* FiBHP
Bells, The. William Young. *Fr.* Wishmakers' Town. AA
Bells are booming down the bohreens. Ireland with Emily. John Betjeman. GTBS-P; OxBTC
Bells assault the maiden air, The. Ou Phrontis. Charles Causley. NePoEA
Bells at Midnight, The. Thomas Bailey Aldrich. PAH
Bells for John Whiteside's Daughter. John Crowe Ransom. AP; CMoP; CoBMV; CrMA; DTC; FF; HAP; HeIP; HoPM; InPK; InPS; LiTA; LiTM; MoAB; MoAmPo; MoVE; NePA; NIP; NoAM; NOBA; NoP; OxBA; PAI; PPON; PPP; PrIm; SoSe; TAP; TreFT; TwAmPo; UnPo; VGW; WeW
Bells have wide mouths and tongues, but are too weak. Upon a Ring of Bells. Bunyan. CH
Bells in the Country. Robert Nathan. HBMV
Bells of Heaven, The. Ralph Hodgson. BrPo; EaLo; GoJo; LiTM; MoAB; MoBrPo; NOBE; OBEV; PPON; SiSoSe; TreFT
Bells of London, The. *Unknown.* EvOK; HBV-1; HBVY; PoPle; PoRA
("Gay go up and gay go down.) OxNR
(London Bells.) ChTr; LiTB; OxBoLi
Bells of Lynn, The. Longfellow. AA
Bells of Oseney, The. Chanson of the Bells of Oseney. Cale Young Rice. HBV-2
Bells of Ostend, The. William Lisle Bowles. *See* Sonnet: At Ostend.
Bells of Peace, The. Aileen Fisher. SiSoSe
Bells of Ste. Anne des Monts, The. Leo Cox. CaP
Bells of San Blas, The. Longfellow. OxBA
Bells of Shandon, The. Francis Sylvester Mahony. ACP; AnIV; CH; ChTr; GoBC; HBV-2; OBEV; OBRV; OBVV; RoGo; TreFS
(Shandon Bell, The.) OnYI
Bells of Sunday rang us down, The. Song. John Ciardi. WaP
Bells of the New Year. Arthur Gordon Field. PGD
Bells of waiting Advent ring, The. Christmas. John Betjeman. EBCP; OBCP; OxBTC
Bells ov Alderburnham, The. William Barnes. EBVV
Bells their Christmas message send o'er earth, The. Perpetual Christmas. Arthur Gordon Field. PGD
Belly Dancer. Diane Wakoski. NIP
Belly of the Land, The. Luci Tapahonso. STE
Belongings, The. Theodore Enslin. CoPo
Beloved, The. May Probyn. GoBC
Beloved, The. Katharine Tynan. HBV-2
Beloved,/ my parents mock me. Freely, from a Song Sung by Jewish Women of Yemen. Stephen Levy. VWA
Beloved, and he sweetly thus goes on. A Pulpit to Be Let. *Unknown.* PAAS
Beloved, do you pity not my doleful case. Lament of the Mangaire Sugach. Andrew Magrath, *tr. by* Edward Walsh. OnYI
Beloved dog, in from the wet. Birthday. James Merrill. NAs
Beloved friends! More glorious times than ours. To My Friends. Schiller, *tr. by* James Clarence Mangan. AWP
Belovèd, from the Hour That You Were Born. Corinne Roosevelt Robinson. HBMV
Beloved, gaze in thine own heart. The Two Trees. W. B. Yeats. BrPo; OAEL-2; VLP
Beloved, it is good. Dream Song. *Tr. by* Francis Densmore. OBVE
Belovèd, It Is Morn. Emily Henrietta Hickey. GoBC; OnYI
(Song: "Belovèd, it is morn!") OBVV
Beloved land is yon land in the east, A. Deirdre's Farewell to Scotland. *Unknown, tr. by* Whitley Stokes *and* Kuno Meyer. OnYI
Beloved, let us love: love is of God. Love Is of God. Horatius Bonar. TRV
Beloved, Let Us Once More Praise the Rain. Conrad Aiken. Preludes for Memnon, VII. LiTA; TwAmPo; UnPo
Beloved, may your sleep be sound. Lullaby. W. B. Yeats. BoLoP; FaBoTw; OBMV
Beloved, my beloved, when I think. Sonnets from the Portuguese, XX. Elizabeth Barrett Browning. OAEP; WPE
Beloved person must I think, The. Ki no Akimine, *tr. by* Arthur Waley. *Fr.* Kokin Shu. AWP
Beloved, thou hast brought me many flowers. Sonnets from the Portuguese, XLIV. Elizabeth Barrett Browning. EBVV; OAEP; OBNC; WPE
Beloved to the Spouse, The. William Baldwin. *See* Christ to His Spouse.
Beloved's Image, The. *Tr. fr. Hawaiian by* M. W. Beckwith. WTO
Below Bald Mountain. Janice Townley Moore. AMV-80
Below fair Peebles, on the river's side. Alexander Pennecuik. *Fr.* A Marriage betwixt Scrape, Monarch of the Maunders, and Blobberlips, Queen of the Gypsies. NOEC
Below lies one whose name was traced in sand. My Epitaph. David Gray. EBVV; OBVV
Below me the city was in flames. The Improved Binoculars. Irving Layton. NOBC
Below me trees unnumber'd rise. John Dyer. *Fr.* Grongar Hill. FaBoEn
Below Mount T'ui K'oy, Home of the Gods, Todos Santos Cuchumatán, Guatemalan Highlands. Joseph Stroud. NPGG
Below my father's house lies a river valley. Seeing in the Dark. Matthew Brennan. AMV-81
Below the dancing larches freckled. "Adam Drinan." *Fr.* Men of the Rocks. OxBS
Below the down the stranded town. A Cinque Port. John Davidson. BrPo; PoPle; VLP
Below the gardens and the darkening pines. At Carmel Highlands. Janet Lewis. PoA
Below, the river scrambled like a goat. God's Little Mountain. Geoffrey Hill. NePoEA
Below the thunders of the upper deep. The Kraken. Tennyson. AmMo; CABA; NoP; OAEL-2; OBNC; OBRV; PoEL-5; SyP; VLP; WiR; WSC
Below thir stanes lie Jamie's banes. On a Noisy Polemic. Burns. FaBoEE
Belshazzar's Feast. Bible, *O.T.* Daniel, V: 1-31. TreF
Be'mi'ster. William Barnes. EBVV
Ben. Thomas Wolfe. NCSH
Ben Alder 1963-1977. Des Hannigan. PoSH
Ben Allah Achmet; or, The Fatal Tum. W. S. Gilbert. VLP
Ben-Arabie was the Camel. Exile. Virna Sheard. PeCV
Ben Backstay. *Unknown.* AmSS
Ben Battle was a soldier bold. Faithless Nelly Gray. Thomas Hood. BXAP; EnRP; FaBoCo; HBV-2; InME; NA; NOBL; ShM; TreF; VLP
Ben Bolt. Thomas Dunn English. AA; FaBoBe; FaFP; HBV-1; TreF
(Ben Bolt; or, Ah! Don't You Remember.) FSW; PSoN, *with music*
Ben Franklin munched a loaf of bread while walking down the street. Benjamin Franklin 1706-1790. Rosemary Benét *and* Stephen Vincent Benét. FaPON; TiPo
Ben Hall was out on the Lachlan side. The Death of Ben Hall. Will H. Ogilvie. PoAu-1
Ben Hur, *sel.* Lew Wallace.
Song: " 'Wake not, but hear me, love!' " AA
Ben Jonson Entertains a Man from Stratford. E. A. Robinson. AmPP; MoAB; MoAmPo; MoPo; TwAmPo
Ben. Johnsons Sociable Rules for the Apollo. Ben Jonson, *tr. fr. Latin by* Alexander Brome. SeCV-1
Ben Karshook's Wisdom. Robert Browning. OAEP
Ben Milam. William H. Wharton. PAH
Ben Nevis is a mountain. The Harlot. Hamish Brown. PoSH
Ben Plays Hide and Seek in the Deep Woods. Geof Hewitt. FAZ
Bench of Boors, The. Herman Melville. OBAL
Bench, the sewermouth, the hydrant placed, The. Northern Boulevard. Edwin Denby. CrMA
Benches are broken, the grassplots brown and bare, The. South End. Conrad Aiken. CMoP; HoPM; MoVE; OxBA
Bend as the bow bends, and let fly the shaft. Conrad Aiken. CMoP
Bend back thy bow, O Archer, till the string. The Archer. A. J. M. Smith. OBCV; PeCV
Bend low again, night of summer stars. Summer Stars. Carl Sandburg. RFM; YeAr
Bend low, O dusky night. To-Night. Louise Chandler Moulton. AA
Bend now thy body to the common weight. The Breaking. Margaret Steele Anderson. HBV-1
Bend the neck back quickly. Killing Rabbits. Ed Ochester. LTB
Bend willow, willow bend down deep. Willow Bend and Weep. Herbert Clark Johnson. PoNe
Bendemeer. Thomas Moore. *See* By Bendemeer's Stream.
Bending, I bow my head. Combing. Gladys Cardiff. CDW; STE
Bending sails shall whiten on the sea, The. The Ships. Theodore Maynard. EtS
Bendix. John Updike. NYBP
Beneath a churchyard yew. O Sweet Anne Page. William Shenstone. SeCePo
Beneath a Cool Shade. Aphra Behn. UnTE
Beneath a holm repaired two jolly swains. Corydon and Thyrsis. Virgil, *tr. by* Dryden. Eclogues, VII. AWP
Beneath a Myrtle Shade. Dryden. *Fr.* The Conquest of Granada. UnTE
(Song of the Zambra Dance.) ErPo; OAEP; PoEL-3

(Zambra Dance, The.) SeCV-2
Beneath a thundery glaze. Walter James Turner. *Fr.* The Seven Days of the Sun. OBMV
Beneath all the statistics. New York. Federico García Lorca, *tr. by* Robert Bly. NU; NYP
Beneath an Indian palm a girl. The Palm-Tree and the Pine. Richard Monckton Milnes. HBV-1
Beneath him with new wonder now he views. Milton. *Fr.* Paradise Lost, IV. PPP
Beneath its morning caul, this ravaged land. Dakota Badlands. Elizabeth Landeweer. AmFN
Beneath my palm-trees, by the river side. The Song of the Indian Maid. Keats. *Fr.* Endymion, IV. NOBE; ViBoPo
Beneath our consecrated elm. The New-come Chief. *Unknown. Fr.* Under the Old Elm. PAH
Beneath our feet and o'er our head. The Holy Field. Henry Hart Milman. OxBoCh
Beneath our feet, the shuddering bogs. On Yes Tor. Sir Edmund Gosse. CH
Beneath salt beaked birds. Corn-Woman Remembered. Judith Mountain Leaf Volborth. TWSS
Beneath the barren artifice of red. City Girl. Maxwell Bodenheim. HBMV
Beneath the blistering tropical sun. Wheeler's Brigade at Santiago. Wallace Rice. PAH
Beneath the branch of the green may. Medieval Norman Song. *Unknown, tr. by* John Addington Symonds. AWP
Beneath the branches of the olive yard. Etruscan Tombs. Agnes Mary Frances Robinson. WHA
Beneath the burning brazen sky. The Ute Lover. Hamlin Garland. AA
Beneath the cement foundations. Washyuma Motor Hotel. Simon J. Ortiz. GP
Beneath the curious gaze of all the dead. The Gown. Mary Carolyn Davies. HBMV
Beneath the Cypress Shade. Thomas Love Peacock. *See* Grave of Love, The.
Beneath the deep my broken timbers lie. The Spirit of the *Bluenose.* Claire Harris MacIntosh. CaP
Beneath the fabric of leaves. The Spring. Ellen Bryant Voigt. MAYP
Beneath the flat and paper sky. Clowns' Houses. Edith Sitwell. SyP
Beneath the golden cope of dawn. The Shepherd of Meriador. Wilfred Rowland Childe. HBMV
Beneath the low-hung night cloud. The *Three Bells.* Whittier. EtS
Beneath the Malebolge lies Hastings Street. Christ Walks in This Infernal District Too. Malcolm Lowry. MoCV; NOBC
Beneath the marmalade, muffins, and tea. Sunday Review Section. Baron Wormser. MAYP
Beneath the Memnonian shadows of Memphis, it rose from the slime. The Reed. Henry Bernard Carpenter. AA
Beneath the midnight moon of May. The Night Watch. William Winter. AA
Beneath the Mound. R. T. Smith. STE
Beneath the ocean's sapphire lid. The Gardens of the Sea. George Sterling. EtS
Beneath the sagging roof. Ezra Pound. Hugh Selwyn Mauberley, X. MoAmPo
Beneath the same bush rests his brother. Epitaphs on Two Piping-Bullfinches of Lady Ossory's. Horace Walpole. FaBoEE
Beneath the shadow of dawn's aerial cope. Hope and Fear. Swinburne. FaBoBe; HBV-2
Beneath the Shadow of the Freeway. Lorna Dee Cervantes. FIA
Beneath the silent chambers of the earth. Hell. Abraham Cowley. *Fr.* Davideis, I. OxBoCh
Beneath the snow the broad sad wastelands. Winter Day. Susannah Fried, *tr. by* Anthony Rudolf. VWA
Beneath the softly falling snow. The Changing Road. Katharine Lee Bates. HBV-2
Beneath the umbrageous shadow of a shade. A Pastoral; in the Modern Style. "Worcester." NOEC
Beneath the warrior's helm, behold. On an Intaglio Head of Minerva. Thomas Bailey Aldrich. HBV-1; InMe
Beneath the waters of the sea. The Mock Turtle's Song, *early version.* "Lewis Carroll." *Fr.* Alice's Adventures in Wonderland. VLP
Beneath the willow wound round with ivy. Hops. Boris Pasternak, *tr. by* Jon Stallworthy *and* Peter France. BoLoP
Beneath their flames, cities of candelabra. The Chestnut Avenue at Alton House. Charles Tomlinson. FaBoTw
Beneath these alien stars. Pioneer Woman. Vesta Pierce Crawford. BPAW; PoOW
Beneath these fruit-tree boughs that shed. The Green Linnet. Wordsworth. EnRP; GTBS; GTBS-P; HBV-1; PBBP
Beneath these plains. West of Chicago. John Dimoff. RFM
Beneath these poppies buried deep. Epitaph on Robert Southey [*or* a Well-known Poet]. Thomas Moore. DBV; FaBoCo; FaBoEE; InMe; PP
Beneath these shades, beside yon winding steam. On Visiting the Graves of Hawthorne and Thoreau. Jones Very. AP; TAP
Beneath these stones repose the bones. On an Old Toper Buried in Durham Churchyard, England. *Unknown.* ShM
Beneath these sun-warm'd pines among the. A South Coast Idyll. Rosamund Marriott Watson. OBVV
Beneath this mound Charles Crocker now reposes. Ambrose Bierce. DBV
Beneath this plain pine board is lying. Joshua Hight. *Unknown.* ShM
Beneath this silent stone is laid. Epitaph on a Talkative Old Maid. Benjamin Franklin. WhC
Beneath this smooth stone. Erected to the Memory of Mr. Jonathan Gill, Esq. *Unknown.* DBV; FaBoEE
Beneath this sod lie the remains. Epitaph on a Young Poet Who Died before Having Achieved Success. Amy Lowell. OBAL
Beneath this stone a Poet Laureate lies. Epitaph on William Whitehead. *Unknown.* FaBoEE
Beneath this stone does William Hazlitt lie. W. H. *Eheu!* Samuel Taylor Coleridge. FaBoEE
Beneath this stone in hopes of Zion. At Upton-on-Severn [*or* Advertising Epitaph]. *Unknown.* FaBoCo; FaBoEE; FaBoUs
Beneath this stone lies Cath'rine Gray. On an Old Woman Who Sold Pots. *Unknown.* PAI
Beneath this stone lies one good man; and when. An Epitaph. W. H. Davies. ChMP
Beneath this stone lies the body of Hengist. Hengest Cyning. Jorge Luis Borges, *tr. by* Norman Thomas di Giovanni. NYBP
Beneath this stone our baby lies. *Unknown.* WhC
Beneath this stony roof reclined. Inscription in a Hermitage. Thomas Warton, the Younger. HBV-1
Beneath this tent, clutching this glass of beer. Blues for an Old Blue. Walker Gibson. NYBP
Beneath those parts, where stretching to its bound. The Process of Conception. Claude Quillet, *tr. by* George Sewell. *Fr.* Callipaedia; or, The Art of Getting Beautiful Children. FaBoUs
Beneath thy spell, O radiant summer sea. The Sea's Spell. Susan Marr Spalding. AA; EtS
Beneath Thy Wing. Hayyim Nahman Bialik, *tr. fr. Hebrew by* Helena Frank. TrJP
Beneath Time's roaring cannon. When the Mississippi Flowed in Indiana. Vachel Lindsay. CMoP
Beneath yon birch with silver bark. The Ballad of the Dark Ladie. Samuel Taylor Coleridge. EnRP
Beneath yon larkspur's azure bells. The Blue-Bird. Herman Melville. BLPL; NOBA
Beneath yon ruin'd abbey's moss-grown piles. The Solemn Noon of Night. Thomas Warton, the Younger. *Fr.* The Pleasures of Melancholy. NOEC; OBEC; SeCePo
Benedicite. Anna Callender Brackett. AA
Benedicite, What Dreamed [*or* Dremid] I This Night? *Unknown.* HAP; NCEP; PoEL-1
(Dream, A.) OBSC
Benedictine Garden, A. Alice Brown. HBV-1
Benediction. Bible, *O.T.* Numbers, VI: 24-26. TrGrPo
(Blessing of the Priests.) TrJP
("Lorde blesse the and kepe the, The," *tr. by* William Tyndale.) OBVE
Benediction. William Freedman. VWA
Benediction. Donald Jeffrey Hayes. AmNP; PoNe
Benediction. Bob Kaufman. PoNe
Benediction. Stanley Kunitz. VGW
Benediction. Myra Sklarew. VWA
Benediction. Mark Turbyfill. PoA
Benediction for the Felt. *Mongol Oral Tradition, tr. by* C. R. Bawden. WTO
Benediction for the Tent. *Mongol Oral Tradition, tr. by* C. R. Bawden. WTO
Benefactors, The. Sara Henderson Hay. DFT
Benefits and Abuse of Alcohol, The. Eubulus, *tr. fr. Greek by* Richard Cumberland. FaBoUs
Benevolence. Mark Akenside. *Fr.* Against Suspicion. OBEC
Bengal. *Unknown. See* Limerick: "There once was a man of Bengal."
Benicasim. Sylvia Townsend Warner. OBWP
Benighted to the Foothills of the Cairngorms. Olive Fraser. PoSH
Benign Neglect/ Mississippi, 1970. Primus St. John. PoBA
Benjamin. Ogden Nash. NePA
Benjamin Franklin Hazard. Edgar Lee Masters. *Fr.* The New Spoon River. GOA
Benjamin Franklin 1706-1790. Rosemary Benét *and* Stephen Vincent Benét. FaPON; TiPo
Bennachie. Charles Murray. PoSH
Bennie's kisses left me cold. Georgie Porgie. Franklin P. Adams. HBMV
Bennington. W. H. Babcock. PAH

Bens camp by the road-side, The. Passin Ben Dorain. Alastair MacKie. *Fr.* At the Heich Kirk-Yaird. PoSH
Bent and heavy with rain. Roadside near Moscow. R. A. D. Ford. PeCV
Bent benches, no lockers, nor nowhere near nozzles enough. Bath. Lincoln Kirstein. NoAM
Bent double, like old beggars under sacks. Dulce et Decorum Est. Wilfred Owen. CABA; CMoP; CoBMV; DL; FaBoTw; FaBV; FF; HeIP; HoPM; InPK; InvP; LiTB; LiTM; MMA; MoAB; MoBrPo; NIP; NoAM; NoP; OAEL-2; OAEP; OBWP; PPON; PPP; PrIm; TW; UnPo; WaP
Bent old men and women and dirty children scavenging. Environment. Lionel Kearns. NOBC
Bent over, staggering in panic or despair. Tableau. Judith Wright. CBAP
Bent Sae Brown, The. *Unknown.* ESPB
Bent Tree. Peter Serchuk. AMV-80
Bents and Broom, The. *Unknown.* OxBB
Beowulf. Kingsley Amis. FaBoCo; OxBC
Beowulf. Richard Wilbur. CrMA
Beowulf. *Unknown, tr. fr. Anglo-Saxon by* Charles W. Kennedy. OAEL-1
Sels.
Beowulf and Wiglaf Slay the Dragon, *tr. by* Charles W. Kennedy. AnOE
Beowulf's Death, *tr. by* Charles W. Kennedy. AnOE
Beowulf's Fight with Grendel's Mother, *tr. by* Michael Alexander. WTO
Fire-Dragon and the Treasure, The, *tr. by* Charles W. Kennedy. AnOE
Funeral Pyre, The, *tr. by* Charles W. Kennedy. AnOE
Grendel, *tr. by* Burton Raffel. NU
Lay of Finn, The, *tr. by* Charles W. Kennedy. AnOE
"Oft in the hall I have heard my people," *tr. by* Charles W. Kennedy. HeIP
Tale of Sigemund, The, *tr. by* Charles W. Kennedy. AnOE
"What! We of Spear-Danes in spent days," *tr. by* C. K. Scott-Moncrieff. ViBoPo
Beppo; a Venetian Story. Byron. OBNV, *abr;* OBSV
Sels.
"England! with all thy faults I love thee still." UnPo
Italy. OBRV; SeCePo
(Italy versus England.) NOBE
" 'Tis known, at least it should be, that throughout." NOBL
Bequest. S. Gale Gilburt. AMV-81
Bequest of His Heart, A. Alexander Scott. *See* Hence, Hairt, with Her That Must Depairt.
Berceuse. Amy Clampitt. SUW
Bereaved. James Whitcomb Riley. AA
Bereaved Maid, The. *Unknown. See* Corpus Christi Carol ("Lully, lullay . . .").
Bereaved of all, I went abroad. Emily Dickinson. TwAmPo
Bereaved Swan, The. Stevie Smith. FaBoNo; FaBoTw
Bereaved years, they've settled to this, The. Evening Harbour. Tom Paulin. AMV-81
Bereavement. Elizabeth Barrett Browning. WPE
Bereavement of the Fields. Wilfred Campbell. CaP
Bereft. Robert Frost. LiTM; MoAB; MoAmPo; OxBA; SoSe; TwAmPo
Bereft. Thomas Hardy. BoLoP; NoAM
Bereft Child's First Night. Frances Bellerby. POL
Berg, The. Herman Melville. AmPP; AP; InPK; LiTA; NOBA; NoP; PoEL-5; TAP
Berkeley, Madison, Ann Arbor, Kent. William Stafford. SOTS
Berkeley Pier, The. John Addiego. AMV-81
Berlin Interior with Jews, 1939. Lynn Emanuel. MAYP
Bermondsey Tragedy, The. *Unknown.* VLP
Bermuda Suite. Winfield Townley Scott. MiAP
Bermudas. Andrew Marvell. AnAnS-1; AWP; CABA; CH; ChTr; FaBoCh; FaBoEn; GN; HBV-2; JCP; LoBV; MePo; MOS; NOBE; NOCV; NoP; OAEP; OBEV; OBS; PAH; PAI; SeCeV; SeCP; SeCV-1; ViBoPo
(Song of the Emigrants [in Bermuda].) GTBS; GTBS-P; OxBoCh
Bernard. Raymond Souster. POL
Bernard reads late, alone; and twilight falls. The Vision of St. Bernard. M. Whitcomb Hess. ISi
Bernie's Quick-Shave (1968). Sydney Lea. MAYP
Berries. Walter de la Mare. MoBrPo; TiPo
Berries, The. William Heyen. GeTw; MAYP
Berry Picking. Irving Layton. MoCV; NoP
Bert Schultz. Colin Thiele. PoAu-2
Beryl. Lyn Lifshin. NeAC
Beset Wife, The. Robert Farren. OxBI
Beshrew that heart that makes my heart to groan. Sonnets, CXXXIII. Shakespeare. InvP
Beside a chapel I'd a room looked down. Dread. J. M. Synge. BoLoP; MoBrPo
Beside a fall there is a round wood pipe. Jean Garrigue. POL
Beside a narrow trail in the blue. Dream of the Lynx. John Haines. NU
Beside a runnel build my shed. After Reading in a Letter Proposals for Building a Cottage. John Clare. OBRV
Beside dim wharves, the battered ships are dreaming. Old Ships. Louis Ginsberg. HBMV
Beside he was a shrewd Philosopher. Hudibras the Sectarian. Samuel Butler. *Fr.* Hudibras. SeCePo
Beside her ashen hearth she sate her down. The Fortunate One. Harriet Monroe. AA
Beside his heavy-shouldered team. Bullocky. Judith Wright. CBAP; PoAu-2; SeCePo
Beside his wife at Passover in spring. Passover Eve. Fania Kruger. GoYe
Beside me,—in the car,—she sat. Natura Naturans. Arthur Hugh Clough. HAP; VLP
Beside me she sat, hand hooked and hovering. An Egyptian Passage. Theodore Weiss. CoPo; TAP
Beside that tent and under guard. Geronimo. Ernest McGaffey. AA; BPAW; PAH
Beside the Bed. Charlotte Mew. MoAB; MoBrPo; TrGrPo; WPE
Beside the bed where parting life was laid. The Village Preacher. Goldsmith. *Fr.* The Deserted Village. TrGrPo
Beside the Blackwater. Norreys Jephson O'Conor. HBMV
Beside the broad, gray Thames one lies. Laleham: Matthew Arnold's Grave. Lionel Johnson. FaBoPP
Beside the Brokenstraw or Licking Creek. John Chapman. Richard Wilbur. OxBC
Beside the crater and the tattered palm. The Dead in Melanesia. Randall Jarrell. MiAP
Beside the dead I knelt for prayer. Christus Consolator. Rossiter W. Raymond. HBV-2
Beside the haunted lake where nereids seem. Mademoiselle Richarde. Edith Sitwell. MoVE
Beside the horse troughs, General Grant. Hens. Alden Nowlan. POL
Beside the idle summer sea. Rondel: Beside the Idle Summer Sea. W. E. Henley. OBNC
Beside the landsman knelt a dame. The Manor Lord. George Houghton. AA
Beside the Line of Elephants. Edna Becker. RHPC
Beside the lone river. Little Big Horn. Ernest McGaffey. PAH
Beside the Mead of Memories. The Dead Quire. Thomas Hardy. OAEP
Beside the mountain roads, the men. Blue Smoke. Frances Frost. SiSoSe
Beside the pleasant Mills of Trompington. Wordsworth. *Fr.* The Prelude, III. OBRV
Beside the pool where shadows flit. The Fool of Love. *Unknown, tr. by* Louis Untermeyer. UnTE
Beside the pounding cataracts. The City of the End of Things. Archibald Lampman. NOBC; OBCV
Beside the rail, despite the gale. The Missing Link. Oliver Herford. CenHV
Beside the rivers of the midnight town. Madrigal. John Frederick Nims. MiAP
Beside the Road. Ken Belford. NeAC
Beside the road to Texas. The Road to Texas. Berta Hart Nance. BPAW
Beside the Seaside, *sel.* John Betjeman.
"Green shutters, shut your shutters! Windyridge." OxBTC
Beside the slew the poplars play. A Prairie Water Colour. Duncan Campbell Scott. OBCV
Beside the stolid opaque flow. The Gravel-Pit Field. David Gascoyne. NeBP
Beside the ungathered rice he lay. The Slave's Dream. Longfellow. FaPoR; OBVV; PoNe
Beside the very view of Notre Dame's. Notre Dame Perfected by Reflection. Harold Witt. HoAn
Beside yon straggling fence that skirts the way. The Village Schoolmaster. Goldsmith. *Fr.* The Deserted Village. GLGT; OBEC; TrGrPo
Besides drinking and telling lies. Man and Machine. Robert Morgan. Str
Besides the autumn poets sing. Emily Dickinson. OxBA
Besieged. Zalman Schneour, *tr. fr. Yiddish by* Joseph Leftwich. TrJP
Besieged Heart, The. Sir John Suckling. *See* 'Tis Now, Since I Sat Down Before.
Besom-Man, The. Joseph Campbell. OnYI
Bespoke for weeks, he turned up some morning. Thatcher. Seamus Heaney. IPY
Bess. William Stafford. GP; NNaP; NoP;
Bess and Her Spinning-Wheel. Burns. BSV
Besse Bunting. *Unknown.* MeEL
Bessie Bell and Mary Gray. *Unknown. See* Bessy Bell and Mary Gray.
Bessie Carmichael School health day fair. Pan-Asian Holiday Tour. Luis Syquia. BrSi
Bessy [*or* Bessie] Bell and Mary Gray (*ballad*). *Unknown.* BSV; ESPB; OxBB, *with music;* ViBoFo
("O Bessie Bell and Mary Gray.") LO
Bessy Bell and Mary Gray. Mother Goose. OxNR

Best, The. Elizabeth Barrett Browning. *See* Best Thing in the World, The.
Best? Siv Widerberg, *tr. fr. Swedish by* Verne Moberg. NTCP
Best and brightest, come away. The Invitation. Shelley. CH; GTBS; GTBS-P; HBV-1; OBEV; OBRV; SeCeV
Best and the Worst, The. *Unknown.* TreFT
Best Choice, The. *Unknown.* STF
Best comedy of the season, The. Christmas Myth, 1973. Robert McGovern. SOTS
Best Dance Hall in Iuka, Mississippi, The. Thomas Johnson. FAZ
Best dance is the dance of the eastern clans, The. *Somali Oral Tradition, tr. by* B. W. Andrzejewski *and* I. M. Lewis. WTO
Best Firm, The. Walter G. Doty. HBVY; HBV-1
Best for Me, The. *Unknown.* STF
Best for Us, The. Olive H. Burnett. STF
Best Friend, The. W. H. Davies. OBMV
Best Friends. Judith Hemschemeyer. AMV-81
Best Game the Fairies Play, The. Rose Fyleman. SoPo
Best Line Yet, The. Edward Allen. InPK; POL
Best Loved of Africa. Margaret Danner. PoBA; PoNe
Best Memory Course, The. *Unknown.* STF
Best of All, The. Fanny Crosby. BLRP
Best of All. *Unknown.* WBLP
Best of both worlds being got, The. Poets' Corner. Robert Graves. FaBoEE
Best of Show. Barbara Howes. GDP
Best of thy sex! if sacred friendship can. To Phylocles, Inviting Him to Friendship. "Ephelia." WPE
Best of Two Worlds. Basil Boothroyd. BoAnP
Best Old Fellow in the World, The. *Unknown.* AmFP
Best Religion, The. Heine, *tr. fr. German by* Emma Lazarus. *Fr.* Tannhäuser. TrJP
Best Road of All, The. Charles Hanson Towne. HBMV
Best slave, The. Alcestis on the Poetry Circuit. Erica Jong. AmPA
Best Thing in the World, The. Elizabeth Barrett Browning. EBVV
(Best, The.) OBVV
Best thing in the world but I better be quick about it, The. Biotherm. Frank O'Hara. CoPo
Best Time for Conception, The. Claude Quillet, *tr. fr. Latin by* George Sewell. *Fr.* Callipaedia; or, The Art of Getting Beautiful Children. FaBoUs
Best Treasure, The. John J. Moment. TRV
"Best way to go, The," said my muffled-up friend. March Hares. Walter de la Mare. FaBoNo
Best work is made, The. Art. Denise Levertov. CAPP
Bestiary. A. M. Klein. OBCV
Bestiary, A. Kenneth Rexroth. OBAL
Sels.
Deer. HoPM PBBP
Fox. NNaP
Herring. HoPM
Horse. NNaP
Lion. HoPM
Raccoon. NNaP
(Racoon.) FiBHP
Vulture. NNaP
Wolf. NNaP
You. HoPM
Bestiary, The, *sels. Unknown, tr. fr. Middle English.* PBBP
Nature of the Eagle, The.
Nature of the Turtle Dove, The.
Bestiary for the Fingers of My Right Hand. Charles Simic. AmPA; LCAP
Bête Humaine. Francis Brett Young. CH; HBMV
Beth Appleyard's Verses. Peter De Vries. OBAL
Beth Gêlert. William Robert Spencer. BeLS; GDP; TreFS
(Beth Gêlert; or, The Grave of the Greyhound.) BLPA; OBNV
Bethel. A. J. H. Duganne. PAH
Bethlehem. William Canton. *See* Carol: "When the herds were watching."
Bethlehem Town. Eugene Field. WBLP
"Unto a Child in Bethlehem-town," *sel.* PGD
Bethou Me, Said Sparrow. Wallace Stevens. Notes toward a Supreme Fiction, XVI. CrMA; NePA
("Bethou me, said sparrow, to the crackled blade.") LiTM; MoPo
Bethsabe's Song. George Peele. *Fr.* David and Bethsabe. EnRePo; NOBE; OBSC; OxBoLi; SeCeV
(Bethsabe Bathing.) ElL; LoBV; TrGrPo
(Hot Sun, Cool Fire.) NoP
("Hot sun[ne], cool[e] fire, tempered with sweet air[e].") GBL; PoEL-2; TEP
Betjeman at the Post Office. Stanley J. Sharpless. FaBoPa
Betjeman, 1984. Charles Causley. FaBoCo; NOBL; OxBTC
Betrayal. Hester H. Cholmondeley. TRV
(Still as of Old.) PGD
Betrayal, The. Alice Furlong. AnIV
Betrayal. Sidney Lanier. *Fr.* The Jaquerie. AA
Betrayal. John Banister Tabb. ACP
Betrayal. Sir Thomas Wyatt. *See* How Should I Be So Pleasant.
Betrayal of the Rose, The. Edith M. Thomas. AA
Betrayed Maiden, The. *Unknown.* OBET
Betrothal, A. E. J. Scovell. GBL
Betrothed. Louise Bogan. LLLT
Betrothed, The. Kipling. HBV-1
Betrothed, The, *sel.* Sir Walter Scott.
"Woman's faith, and woman's trust." ViBoPo
Betsey and I Are Out. Will Carleton. PaPo
Betsy from Pike. *Unknown.* *See* Sweet Betsy from Pike.
Betsy, if pencil erasers could sing. 110 Year Old House. Ed Ochester. Psk
Betsy Jane's Sixth Birthday. Alfred Noyes. SiSoSe
Betsy's Battle Flag. Minna Irving. PAH
Better a bug in the dust underfoot. The Child in the Rug. John Haines. DFF; GP
Better a day in Oxbridge. Stanley J. Sharpless. BXAP
Better Answer (to Cloe Jealous), A. Matthew Prior. *See* Answer to Cloe Jealous.
Better Bargain, The. Congreve. UnTE
Better born than married, misled. The Grandmother. Wendell Berry. DFF; GP; SaC
Better disguised than the leaf-insect. The Lake. Ted Hughes. FaBoTw; NYBP
Better it were had you borne black earth, o mother, rather than me. Mother of Man. Vesna Param, *tr. by* Mary Coote. PBWP
Better it were, my brother. Man to Man. John McClure. HBMV
Better never trouble Trouble. Trouble. David Keppel. FaFP; FPL; PoLF; TreF; WBLP
Better not go to these deep woods. The Great Fountains. Anne Hébert, *tr. by* Willis Barnstone. BoWoP
Better not to go back to the village. The Malefic Return. Ramón López Velarde, *tr. by* Samuel Beckett. OBVE
Better one bird in hand than ten in the wood. Of Birds and Birders. John Heywood. PBBP
Better one thin frail line of friendship in a letter. The Letter. John Blight. CBAP
Better Path, The. Bible, *O.T.* Ecclesiastes, VII: 1-5. TreFS
("It Is Better . . .", 1-9.) TrJP
Better Resurrection, A. Christina Rossetti. EBCP; HBV-2; OxBoCh; TrPWD; VLP
Better than a closet martinet. What Happened? John Wieners. PoM
Better than Gold ("Better than grandeur, better than gold"). Abram Joseph Ryan. FaFP
Better than granite, Spoon River. Aaron Hatfield. Edgar Lee Masters. *Fr.* Spoon River Anthology. LiTA
Better the book against the rock. Three Poems about Children. Austin Clarke. CIP
Better the empty sorrow in the dark. Night of Rain. Bernice Lesbia Kenyon. HBMV
Better they never learned to read! The Misogynist. Jean Morgan. FF
Better to be the rock above the river. La Crosse at Ninety Miles an Hour. Richard Eberhart. AmFN
Better to live as a rogue and a bum. Mahsati, *tr. fr. Farsi by* Deirdre Lashgari. WPOW
Better to see your cheek grown hollow. Madman's Song. Elinor Wylie. MoAB; MoAmPo; MOON; PoRA
Better to Spit on the Whip than Stutter Your Love like a Worm. Colette Inez. TW
Better trust all and be deceived. Faith. Frances Anne Kemble. FaBoBe; HBV-2; OBVV
Better Way, The. Walter Leaf. FaBoCo
Better, Wiser and Happier. Ella Wheeler Wilcox. WBLP
Betty and Dupree. *Unknown.* *See* Dupree.
Betty at the Party. *Unknown.* OnUR
Betty Botter bought some butter. *Unknown.* OxNR
Betty Fuller cried and said, Hit me. A Local Man Remembers Betty Fuller. James Whitehead. GP
Betty told Dupree, "Daddy, I want a diamond ring." Dupree [*or* Betty and Dupree]. *Unknown.* FSW; OuSiCo
Betty Zane. Thomas Dunn English. PAH; PAL
Betuix twell houris and ellevin. *See* Betwix twell houris and eleven.
Between a Contractor and His Wife. *Unknown.* NOEC
Between a Good Hat and Good Boots. Kell Robertson. TAT
Between a sunny bank and the sun. Two Houses. Edward Thomas. ChMP; FaBoCh
Between an Unemployed Artist and His Wife. *Unknown.* NOEC
Between Birthdays. Ogden Nash. OnUR
Between Botallack and the light. A Ballad of a Mine. Robin Skelton. MoBS

Between Brielle and Manasquan. Oliver St. John Gogarty. OnYI
Between Cellini's Perseus and the Sabine Rape. More Nudes for Florence. Harold Witt. ErPo
Between dawn and the Opera. Clandestine Work. Yvan Goll, *tr. by* Anthony Rudolf. VWA
Between decision and ensuing act. Birdwatcher. Henry Treece. WaP
Between dinner and death, the crowds shadow the loom of steel. Park Avenue. Robert Fitzgerald. NYP
Between extremities. Vacillation. W. B. Yeats. MoVE; NoAM
Between fields of popcorn. "America, I Love You." Bert Kalmar *and* Harry Ruby. FiBHP; InMe
Between five and fifty. Praise. Jane Cooper. TAP
Between God's Eyelashes. José Garcia Villa. CrMA
Between great coloured vanes the butterflies. Wings. Judith Wright. CBAP
Between Here and Illinois. Ralph Pomeroy. Psk
Between Leaps. Brad Leithauser. MAYP
Between Life and Death. Frantisek Gottlieb, *tr. fr. Czech by* Ewald Osers. VWA
Between Me and Anyone Who Can Understand. Sharon Scott. JB
Between me and the sunset, like a dome. The Man against the Sky. E. A. Robinson. AmPP; AP; CMoP; CoBMV; LiTA; MoVE; OxBA; TwAmPo
Between me and the wood. Ark Artefact. Jay Macpherson. *Fr.* The Ark. NOBC
Between my eyes and hers so thin the screen. George Edward Woodberry. Ideal Passion, XXXVII. HBMV
Between my finger and my thumb. Digging. Seamus Heaney. BIrV; CIP; IPY; TwCP
Between my lips the taste of night-time blends. The Realm of Touching. Alan Bold. BSV
Between my love and me there runs a thread. Irene Rutherford McLeod. *Fr.* Sonnets. HBMV
Between Our Folding Lips. Thomas Edward Brown. PeD
Between Ourselves. Audre Lorde. WPOW
Between painting a roof yesterday and the hay. Independence Day. Wendell Berry. OFD
Between rebellion as a private study and the public. Last Poem [*or* Poem]. Charles Donnelly. BIrV; CIP
Between Rivers and Seas. Lance Henson. VoR
Between Seasons. Anne Welsh. PeSA
Between such animal and human heat. The Partner. Theodore Roethke. NePA; NePoAm
Between the Acts. Stanley Kunitz. ELU
Between the cloud and the ground. Clouds and Clay. Valerie Gillies. PoSH
Between the dark and the daylight. If. Franklin P. Adams. OBAL
Between the dark and the daylight. The Children's Hour. Longfellow. AA; FaBoBe; FaBV; FaFP; FaPON; FPL; HBV-1; HBVY; OBAL; OBCA; OHFP; PoEL-5; PoLF; PoPl; TreF; WBLP
Between the dark silent trees. Dionysius. Sophia de Mello Breyner Andresen, *tr. by* Allan Francovich. PBWP
Between the earth and the drowned platinum. The Battle of the Jarama. Pablo Neruda, *tr. by* Angel Flores. WaaP
Between the erect and solemn trees. The Temple of the Trees. J. D. C. Pellow. PGD
Between the exhiliration of Beginning. The Middle-Time. Lona M. Fowler. TRV
Between the falling leaf and rose-bud's breath. The Term of Death. Sarah Morgan Bryan Piatt. AA
Between the first pangs and the last of love. This Little Vigil. Charles G. Bell. NePoAm
Between the fosse and inner wall. The Defender. Arthur M. Sampley. GoYe
Between the gardening and the cookery. A Bookshop Idyll. Kingsley Amis. NePoEA; OxBTC
Between the green bud and the red. Prelude to "Songs before Sunrise." Swinburne. VLP
Between the Karim Shahir. Rochelle Owens. CoPo
Between the midnight and the morn. The Secret Muse. Roy Campbell. PeSA
Between the moondrawn and the sundown here. On the Cliffs. Swinburne. VLP
Between the mountains and the sea. Santa Barbara. Francis Fisher Browne. AA
Between the perfect. Somewhere the Equation Breaks Down. Daniel Berrigan. NYBP
Between the Porch and the Altar. Robert Lowell. MiAP; NePoEA
Sels.
At the Altar, IV. InPK; InPS
Katherine's Dream, III. ConAP
Between the railway and the mine. The Blackberry. Norman Nicholson. MoBrPo
Between the rough hills of gabbro and the cold sea. In Our Time. Michael Roberts. WaP
Between the Sunken Sun and the New Moon. Paul Hamilton Hayne. AA
Between the sunset and the sea. Mary Beaton's Song. Swinburne. *Fr.* Chastelard. HBV-1
Between the Tides. Emily Sargent Councilman. AMV-80
Between the Traveller and the Setting Sun. Henry David Thoreau. PoEL-4
Between the turnpike and the avenue. The Road the Crows Own. Susan Astor. AMV-81
Between the two follies I return and return to. Vincent O'Sullivan. Brother Jonathan, Brother Kafka, 44. OCNZ
Between the under and the upper blue. Seagulls. Robert Francis. RFM
Between the Walls of the Valley. Elisabeth Peck. AmFN
Between the walls, the brim. Terce. James McMichael. PoA
Between the wheeze of her torpor and the wind of her falling. Faintly and from Far Away. Vassar Miller. CoPo
Between the World and Me. Richard Wright. AmNP; IDB; LiTM; NoAM; PAI; PoBA
Between their sandspit ends. Barred Islands. Philip Booth. NePoEA
Between them is the land of broken colors. The Black Horse Rider. Pierre Loving. EAS
Between thirty and forty, one is distracted by the Five Lusts. On Being Sixty. Po Chü-i, *tr. by* Arthur Waley. AWP
Between town and the. The Quarry Pool. Denise Levertov. VGW
Between trains, on this day of snow. At the Roman Baths, Bath. Edward Lucie-Smith. NePoEA-2
Between Two Furious Oceans, *sel.* Dick Diespecker.
"All these are your essence, you are their flesh and their force." CaP
Between two golden tufts of summer grass. Lying in the Grass. Sir Edmund Gosse. EBVV; OBVV
Between two mighty hills a sheer. The Eagle. "Fiona Macleod." *Fr.* Transcripts from Nature. FM
Between Two Prisoners. James Dickey. AP
Between Two Worlds. Rosemary Thomas. NYBP
Between Us. Stephen Berg. NaP
Between Walls. William Carlos Williams. HoPM; SOTW; TAP; VGW
Betweens. Norman MacCaig. EAS
Betwene March [*or* Mersh] and Averil. *See* Bytuene Mersh and Averil.
Betwix [*or* Betuix] twell houris and eleven. Amends to the Tailors and Soutars. William Dunbar. BSV; OBSV
Betwixt mine eye and heart a league is took. Shakespeare. Sonnets, XLVII. EyDe
Betwixt the quarters, flows a golden sea. Battle of Actium. Virgil, *tr. by* Dryden. *Fr.* The Aeneid, VIII. OBS
Betwixt two billows of the downs. The Winnowers. Robert Bridges. OAEP
Betwixt two ridges of plowed-land sat Wat. The Hunting of the Hare. Margaret Lucas, Duchess of Newcastle. FM
Beulah Land. Edgar P. Stites. *See* I've Reached the Land of Corn and Wine.
Beulah Louise. William Jay Smith. TDH
Beverley Maid and the Tinker, The. *Unknown.* CoMu
Beverly Hills, Chicago. Gwendolyn Brooks. VGW
Bewail with me, all ye that have professed. On the Death of Phillips. *Unknown.* OBSC
Bewailing in my chamber thus allone. He Sees His Beloved [*or* The Coming of Love]. James I, King of Scotland. *Fr.* The Kingis Quair. BSV; GoTS; PoEL-1
Bewar, squier, yeman, and page. A Warning to Those Who Serve Lords. *Unknown.* MeEL
Beware, beware the snare of "victory." Victory. Roger Axford. PGD
Beware: Do Not Read This Poem. Ishmael Reed. BPo; CNA; NCSH; NIP; NoP; PAI; PoBA; WSC
Beware Fair Maide. *At. to* Joshua Sylvester. OBS
Beware, My Child. Shel Silverstein. PDV
Beware of Dogmas. Ebenezer Elliott. FaBoEE
Beware of Figs. Nicophon, *tr. fr. Greek by* Charles Duke Yonge. FaBoUs
Beware of Larry Gorman, *with music.* Larry Gorman. ShS
Beware of the man who denounces ambition. Seventeen Warnings in Search of a Feminist Poem. Erica Jong. AmPA
Beware of those. Diane DiPrima. *Fr.* Revolutionary Letters. GP
Beware, Oh, Take Care. *Unknown.* FSW
Beware, take heede, take heede, beware, beware. How Collingbourne Was Cruelly Executed for Making a Foolish Rhyme. William Baldwin. NCEP
Beware the deadly Sitting habit. Cave Sedem! Theodore F. MacManus. HBV-2
Beware the Months of Fire. Patrick Lane. NeAC
Bewick and Graham. *Unknown.* BaBo; ESPB
(Bewick and the Graeme, The, *with music.*) OxBB

(Graeme and Bewick.) EnSB
Bewick Finzer. E. A. Robinson. AP; CMoP; CoBMV; MoAB; MoAmPo; PPP
Bewildered in our buying throng. Patrum Propositum. Robert Fitzgerald. GOA
Bewildered with the broken tongue. Words in Time. Archibald MacLeish. CrMA; NePA; PoCh; PoRA
Bewilderingly, from wildly shaken cloud. Internal Firesides. Mathilde Blind. FM
Bewilderment at the Entrance of the Fat Boy into Eden, A. Daryl Hine. NOBC; OBCV
Bewteis of Fute-Ball, The. *Unknown.* FaBoCo; GoTS; OxBS
(Bewtis of the Fute-Ball, The.) BSV
Bewty of hir amorus ene, The. Off Womanheid Ane Flour Delice. *Unknown.* OxBS
Beyond. Lionel Johnson. BrPo
Beyond. Hannah Parker Kimball. AA
Beyond a low wall. Tortoise. Joanne de Longchamps. BoAnP
Beyond all this, the wish to be alone. Wants. Philip Larkin. GTBS-P; NoP
Beyond Belief. Tom Luhrmann. AMV-81
Beyond, beneath, within, wherever blood. A Quintina of Crosses. Chad Walsh. TrCP
Beyond, beyond the mountain line. Dreams. Cecil Frances Alexander. OnYI
Beyond Biology. Robert Francis. NePoAm
Beyond earshot of others, furtively. The Conspirators. Kenneth Burke. TwAmPo
Beyond Feith Buidhe. Hamish Brown. PoSH
Beyond her window in October sun. Farm Wife. Matt Field. AMV-81
Beyond Kerguelen. Henry Kendall. PoAu-1
Beyond Magdalen and by the Bridge, on a place called there the Plain. By Magdalen Bridge, Oxford. Gerard Manley Hopkins. FaBoPP
Beyond Memory. Monny de Boully, *tr. fr. Serbo-Croat by* Aleksander Nejgebauer. VWA
Beyond Nagel's Funeral Parlor. "The Elizabethans Called It Dying." James Schuyler. NeAP; PoM
Beyond Possession. Elizabeth Jennings. NePoEA
Beyond Rathkelly. Francis Carlin. HBMV
Beyond Recall. Mary Emily Bradley. AA
Beyond Religion. Lucretius, *tr. fr. Latin by* William Ellery Leonard. AWP
Beyond the Alps. Robert Lowell. NOBA
Beyond the Atlas roams a glutton. The Glutton. Robert Graves. CMoP; TW
Beyond the blue, the purple seas. The Hunter. W. J. Turner. HBMV
Beyond the bourn of mortal death and birth. At Last. Katrina Trask. AA
Beyond the Chagres. James Stanley Gilbert. PoLF
Beyond the Chiltern coast, this church. Edlesborough. Anne Ridler. NeBP
Beyond the doorway of the tiny room. Blue Homespun. Frank Oliver Call. CaP
Beyond the East the sunrise, beyond the West the sea. Wander-Thirst. Gerald Gould. HBV-1; TiPo
Beyond the edge of the sepia. Lament for a Cricket Eleven. Kenneth Allott. OxBTC
Beyond the End. Denise Levertov. NeAP; VGW
Beyond the ferry water. Ferry Hinksey. Laurence Binyon. HBV-1
Beyond the field where crows cawed at a hawk. Two Lives and Others. Winfield Townley Scott. PoPl
Beyond the Firehouse. Patrick Worth Gray. AMV-80
Beyond the great valley an odd instinctive rising. Ascent to the Sierras. Robinson Jeffers. OxBA
Beyond the hour we counted rain that fell. Old Countryside. Louise Bogan. HAP; LiTA; NePA; TwAmPo; WPE
Beyond the Hunting Woods. Donald Justice. ConAP; NCSH; NePoEA; NYBP; PoPl
Beyond the image of the willow. The Importance of Poetry, or the Coming Forth from Eternity into Time. Hyam Plutzick. PP
Beyond the inmost barriers of the brain. The Owl. Edward Davison. PoA
Beyond the iron-barred fence. A City Graveyard. Joyce Carol Oates. DFF
Beyond the last gate, where I made my first halt. On Scafell Pike. Ted Walker. NYBP
Beyond the last horizon's rim. The Hills of Rest. Albert Bigelow Paine. HBV-2; WGRP
Beyond the last house, where home was. American Portrait: Old Style. Robert Penn Warren. FYAP
Beyond the Last Lamp. Thomas Hardy. MoVE; NOBE; OBNC
Beyond the low marsh-meadows and the beach. The Pines and the Sea. Christopher Pearse Cranch. AA; HBV-1
Beyond the murk that swallows me. Irene Rutherford McLeod. *Fr.* The Rebel. WGRP
Beyond the narrow window. The Tree-Top Road. May Riley Smith. HBV-2
Beyond the Nigger ("Beyond the outstretched hands"). Sterling Plumpp. PoBA
Beyond the porcelain fence of the pleasure garden. A Year Passes. Amy Lowell. MOON
Beyond the Potomac. Paul Hamilton Hayne. PAH
Beyond the Presidency. Morgan Gibson. FF
Beyond the primitive powers of pain, of love at last. In Praise of Robert Penn Warren. David Lehman. AMV-81
Beyond the sea, I know not where. Vivérols. David Starr Jordan. AA
Beyond the Smiling and the Weeping. Horatius Bonar. HBV-2
(Little While, A.) VLP
Beyond the sphere which spreads to widest space. Dante, *tr. by* Dante Gabriel Rossetti. La Vita Nuova, XXIX. AWP; CTC
Beyond the stone wall. Jug Brook. Ellen Bryant Voigt. MAYP
Beyond the Tapestries. Norma Farber. GoYe
Beyond the turning sea's far foam. At War. Russell Atkins. AmNP
Beyond the vague Atlantic deep. Our Mother Tongue. Richard Monckton Milnes. GN
Beyond the Wall. J. J. Maloney. LFAC
Beyond the white dust flushed by the carriers. Patrol; Buonamary. Bernard Gutteridge. WaP
Beyond the yard the barn is hulking. My Father Dragged by Horses. T. Alan Broughton. AMV-80
Beyond Wars. David Morton. PAH
Beyond Winter. Emerson. RHPC
Beyond Words. Robert Frost. TW; WeW
Bhagavad-Gita, The, *sels.* *Unknown, tr. fr. Sanskrit.*
"Arjuna said:/ How shall I in battle against Bhisma," *tr. by* Franklin Edgerton. DL
Never the Spirit Was Born, *tr. by* Sir Edwin Arnold. TreFT
One, The, *tr. by* Raimundo Panikkar. ILwL
Bi a forrest as I gan fare. By a Forest. *Unknown.* NCEP
Biafra. L. V. Mack. PoBA
Biafran, *sertanejo*, Pakistani. Retreat. Amy Bushnell. AMV-80
Bianca, *sel.* Arthur Symons.
"Her cheeks are hot, her checks are white," I. UnTE; VLP
Bianca among the Nightingales. Elizabeth Barrett Browning. BrRo; GTBS-P
Bible, The, *sel.* David Levi, *tr. fr. Italian by* Mary A. Craig.
"Thou, Zion, old and suffering." TrJP
Bible, The. Sir Walter Scott. *See* Book of Books, The.
Bible, The. Dorothy Conant Stroud. STF
Bible, The. Whittier. *Fr.* Miriam. TreFT
(Book Our Mothers Read, The.) BLRP; TRV
Bible is an antique volume, The. Emily Dickinson. NoP
Bible says Sennacherib's campaign was spoiled, The. Sonnet. C. S. Lewis. TrCP
Bible soothes the harried soul, The. Travelling Companions. Richard Armour. GrPl
Bibliolaters, *sel.* James Russell Lowell.
God Is Not Dumb. WGRP
Bibliomaniac's Prayer, The. Eugene Field. AA
Bibliotheca Bodleiana. Geoffrey Grigson. GBL
Bibulous eagle behind me at the ball game, The. One to Nothing. Carolyn Kizer. OBAL
"Biby's" Epitaph. *Unknown.* FiBHP
Bicause I have the still kept fro lyes and blame. Petrarch, *tr. fr. Italian by* Sir Thomas Wyatt. OBVE
Bicycle, The. Stan Rice. NPGG
Bicycle Built for Two, A (Daisy Bell). Harry Dacre. *See* Daisy Bell.
Bicycle Rider, The. Thomas W. Shapcott. CBAP
Bicycles go by in twos and threes, The. Inniskeen Road; July Evening. Patrick Kavanagh. IPY; NoAM; NoP
Bicycles! Tricycles! John Banister Tabb. OBAL
Bicycling Song. Henry Charles Beeching. GN
Bid a strong ghost stand at the head. A Prayer for My Son. W. B. Yeats. EBEV; NAs
Bid Adieu to Maidenhood. James Joyce. Chamber Music, XI. OBEV
(Bid Adieu, Adieu, Adieu.) OnYI
(Bid Adieu to Girlish Days.) HBV-1
Bid me not go where neither suns nor show'rs. A Valediction. William Cartwright. OBS
Bid me remember, O my gracious Lord. Mary Elizabeth Coleridge. *Fr.* Death. TrPWD
Bid me to live, and I will live. To Anthea, Who May Command Him Anything. Robert Herrick. AnAnS-2; CaPo; CavP; GTBS; GTBS-P; HBV-1; JCP; LoBV; NOBE; OAEL-1; OAEP; OBEV; OBS; SeCP; SeCV-1; TrGrPo; ViBoPo
Bid the din of battle cease! The Message of Peace. Julia Ward Howe. PGD

Bid your Papa Goodnight. Sweet exhibition! Mrs. Hopley, on Seeing Her Children Say Goodnight to Their Father. Gerard Manley Hopkins. FaBoEE
Bidding Prayer, A ("Bidde we with milde stevene"). *Unknown.* OxBM
Biddy, Biddy, *with music.* *Unknown.* OuSiCo
Bide a Wee! John Oxenham. TRV
Bide thou thy time! The Patient Church. Cardinal Newman. GoBC
Bidean Nam Bian. A. M. Dobson. PoSH
Biftek aux Champignons. Henry Augustin Beers. AA; HBV-1
Big Apple Blues. *Unknown.* BluL
Big Baboon, The. Hilaire Belloc. MoBrPo; MoShBr
Big Bell in Zion, The. Theodore Henry Shackleford. BANP
Big Ben is cracked, we needs must own. To Disraeli. Shirley Brooks. NOBL
Big Bessie Throws Her Son into the Street. Gwendolyn Brooks. VGW
Big Billie Potts was big and stout. The Ballad of Billie Potts. Robert Penn Warren. NOBA; OxBA
Big black Angus bull. Seventh Georgic. George Economou. POL
Big blue-jean, the summer-bored boy next door, The. Carry Me Back. John Holmes. AmFN; NePoAm-2
Big box,/ Little box. *Unknown.* OxNR
Big Boy came. Catch. Langston Hughes. NoAM
Big breakers roll over the sea. Breakers over the Sea. *Malay Oral Tradition, tr. by* R. O. Winstedt. WTO
Big Brother. Elizabeth Madox Roberts. FaPON
Big bull-dyke, surly and sallow, A. Limerick. *Unknown.* PeHV
Big Chief Blues. *Unknown.* BluL
Big Chief Wotapotami. David McCord. WhC
Big City Glissando. Nicholas Christopher. NYP
Big Clock, The. *Unknown.* SoPo; TiPo
Big Crash Out West. Peter Viereck. PoPl
Big Daddy Lipscomb, who used to help them up. Say Goodbye to Big Daddy. Randall Jarrell. LiSp; PoNe
Big Dam. W. R. Moses. AmFN
Big Dog. Philip Booth. BoAnP; GDP
Big Dream, Little Dream. Louis Simpson. POL
Big Engines, The. Chorus. Jack Kerouac. *Fr.* Mexico City Blues. NeAP
Big, Fat Summer—and the Lean and Hard. Frederick Bock. NYBP
Big Fat Woman, *with music.* *Unknown.* OuSiCo
Big Five-Gallon Jar, The, *with music.* *Unknown.* ShS
Big Friend of the Stones. Steve Orlen. Psk
Big Fun. Diane Burns. STE; TWSS
Big Grave Creek. Cid Corman. HoAn
Big guns again. Imperator Victus. Hart Crane. OxBA
Big house,/ Little house. *Unknown.* OxNR
Big iron horse with lifted head. The Little Boy to the Locomotive. Benjamin R. C. Low. HBMV
Big-jawed bluefish, ravenous, sleek muscle slamming, The. Night Fishing for Blues. Dave Smith. LiSp
Big Man. Mason Jordan Mason. PoNe
Big Momma. Don L. Lee. BPo; CNA
Big mountains sit still in the afternoon light, The. Sinners. D. H. Lawrence. ViBoPo
Big Nasturtiums, The. Robert Beverly Hale. BoNaP; NYBP
Big Night Blues. *Unknown.* BluL
Big old houses have passed away. Sometimes I Think of Maryland. Jodi Braxton. CNA
Big One, The. Luis Cubalquinto. BrSi
Big One, The. Edward Morin. WOLT
Big Ralph from Rolfe had a black Corvette. The True Ballad of the Great Race to Gilmore City. Phil Hey. Psk
Big Road Blues. *Unknown.* BluL
Big Rock Candy Mountains, The, *diff. versions.* *Unknown.* AmFP; ChTr; FSW; GBP; NOBA; OBAL; TreFT
Big Rock Jail. *Unknown.* BluL
Big rocks into pebbles. Rocks. Florence Parry Heide. NTCP
Big Sheep Knocks You About. Sharon Bryan. MAYP
Big Ship Sailing, A. *Unknown.* FSW
Big star, and that other, The. Leaflets. Adrienne Rich. NoAM
Big Steamers. Kipling. Par
Big steel tourist shield says maybe, The. On a Field at Fredericksburg. Dave Smith. GeTw
Big stones of the cistern behind the barn, The. Twilights. James Wright. LCAP; NaP
Big strong work horses working every day. Work Horses. Edith Newlin Chase. SoPo
Big Sunflower, The, *with music.* Bobby Newcomb. BLSo
Big Swing-Tree Is Green Again, The. Mary Jane Carr. SiSoSe
Big Thompson Can[y]on. Jean Milne Gower. PoOW
Big Trimmer, The. Ronald P. Tanaka. BrSi
Big trucks for steel beams. Trucks. James S. Tippett. FaPON
Big trucks with apples. Country Trucks. Monica Shannon. FaPON; TiPo
Big Turtle, A. *Unknown.* SoPo
Big water main, The. In War. Mason Jordan Mason. PoNe
Big Wind. Theodore Roethke. AmPP; CMoP; GoJo; InvP; NCSH; NoP; PPoe; ViBoPo; VGW
Big with great purposes and proud, they sat. Homer, *tr. by* William Cowper. *Fr.* The Iliad, VIII. OBVE
Big Woman. *Unknown.* BluL
Big yellow trolley limbers along. There Are So Many Ways of Going Places. Leslie Thompson. FaPON; SoPo
Big young bareheaded woman, A. Proletarian Portrait. William Carlos Williams. OBAL; TAP
Bigamist born in Zambezi, A. Lessons in Limericks, I. David McCord. InMe
Bigerlow, *with music.* *Unknown.* AS
Bigger Day, The. G. E. Bishop. WBLP
Biggest Killing, The. Edward Dorn. CoPo; VGW
Bight, The. Elizabeth Bishop. NYBP
Bigler, The, *with music.* *Unknown.* AmSS; OuSiCo
Biglow Papers, The, *sels.* James Russell Lowell.
  1st Series, No. I.
    Letter, A ("Thrash away, you'll hev to rattle"). OxBA
    (Mr. Hosea Biglow Speaks.) PAH
    ("Thrash away, you'll hev to rattle.") AmPP
      Ez fer War, 4 *sts.* PPON
  1st Series, No. II.
    Letter, A ("This kind o' sogerin' ain't a mite like our October trainin' "). OxBA
  1st Series, No. III.
    What Mr. Robinson Thinks. AA; AmPP; HBV-1; InMe; PAH; YaD
  1st Series, No. V.
    Debate in the Sennit, The. HBV-1; PAH
  1st Series, No. VI.
    Candidate's Creed, The, *abr.* YaD
  1st Series, No. VII.
    Candidate's Letter, The. AA
  2d Series, Introduction.
    Courtin', The. AA; AmPP; BeLS; HBV-1; InMe; NOBA; OBAL; OBVV; TreFS
  2d Series, No. II.
    Jonathan to John. PAH
  2d Series, No. IV.
    Rev. Homer Wilbur's "Festina Lente." OBAL
  2d Series, No. VI.
    Sunthin' in the Pastoral Line. AP
      Spring, *sel.* FaBV
  2d Series, No. X.
    Mr. Hosea Biglow to the Editor of the Atlantic Monthly. AA, *abr.;* PoEL-5
Bigness of cannon, The. La Guerre. E. E. Cummings. MoAB; MoAmPo
Bijou. Vern Rutsala. DFF
Biking at night with no lights. To Maynard on the Long Road Home. W. D. Ehrhart. LTB
Bile Them Cabbage Down. *Unknown.* AmFP; FSW
Bilitis. Pierre Louÿs, *tr. fr. French by* Horace M. Brown. *Fr.* The Songs of Bilitis. UnTE
Bill. Peter Kocan. CBAP
Bill/ exists. A Personality Sketch: Bill. Ronda Davis. JB
Bill/ Was ill. Careless Talk. Mark Hollis. FiBHP
Bill and Joe. Oliver Wendell Holmes. AA; HBV-2
Bill and Parson Sim. *Unknown.* BPAW
Bill Bailey Won't You Pleases Come Home. Hughie Cannon. BLSo, *with music;* FSN, *with music;* FSW; OBAL
Bill dug a well. A Narrative. Theodore Spencer. WhC
Bill Groggin's Goat. *Unknown.* *See* Goat, The.
Bill Haller's Dance. Robert V. Carr. PoOW
Bill Jones had been the shining star upon his college team. Alumnus Football. Grantland Rice. FPL; PoLF
Bill Jupp lies 'ere, aged sixty year. From the Greek Anthology. L. A. G. Strong. DBV; WhC
Bill learned to play tunes on a comb. A Nuisance at Home. *Unknown.* TDH
Bill Munson's wife was sick, you see. The Cowboy and the Stork. Robert V. Carr. BPAW
Bill Peters, the Stage Driver. *Unknown.* CoSo
Bill Riley was a cowboy and a quicker shot than him. Bill and Parson Sim. *Unknown.* BPAW
Bill the Whaler. Will Lawson. PoAu-1
Bill Venero, *with music.* *Unknown.* CoSo
Billiards. Laurie Blauner. AMV-81
Billiards. Walker Gibson. LiSp; NePoAm
Billings and Cooings from "The Berkeley Barb." Mona Van Duyn. GP

Billowy headlands swiftly fly, The. Battle-Song of the *Oregon.* Wallace Rice. PAH
Billy. Harry Graham. *See* Tender-heartedness.
Billy Barlow. *Unknown.* FSW; OuSiCo, *with music*
Billy Boy. *Unknown.* AmFP; BLPA; HoPM; OBET
("Where have ye [*or* you] been all the day,/ Billy Boy?") LO; OxNR; OxNR
Billy Budd, Foretopman, *sel.* Herman Melville.
Billy in the Darbies. HAP; LoBV; NCEP; NOBA; OxBoLi; PoEL-5
Billy Could Ride. James Whitcomb Riley. PH
Billy goat's a handsome gent, The. The Goat. Roland Young. BoAnP; WhC
Billy Grimes. *Unknown.* AmFP
Billy, He's in Trouble. James Barton Adams. YaD
Billy, in one of his nice new sashes. Tender-heartedness. Harry Graham. Some Ruthless Rhymes, II. CenHV; FaBoCo; FaFP; RHPC; TreFT; WhC. *See also* Little Willie, in the best of sashes.
Billy in the Darbies. Herman Melville. *Fr.* Billy Budd, Foretopman. HAP; LoBV; NCEP; NOBA; OxBoL; PoEL-5
Billy Lyons and Stack O'Lee. *Unknown.* BluL
Billy Magee Magaw. *Unknown.* *See* Three Ravens, The.
Billy the Kid. Jack Spicer. CoPo
Billy the Kid ("Billy was a bad man"). *Unknown.* BPAW; CoSo
Billy the Kid ("I'll sing you a true song of Billy the Kid"). *Unknown.* BPAW; CoSo, *with music;* FaBoBe; FSW
Billy the Kid or William H. Bonney. N. Howard Thorp. BPAW
Billy Venero heard them say. Bill Venero. *Unknown.* CoSo
Billy was a bad man. Billy the Kid. *Unknown.* BPAW; CoSo
Billy was born for a horse's back! Billy Could Ride. James Whitcomb Riley. PH
Billy's Rose ("Billy's dead, and gone to glory"). George R. Sims. PaPo
Bim Bam. Dorothy Rosenberg. PoNe
Bind us the Morning, mother of the stars. Thefts of the Morning. Edith M. Thomas. AA
Bind your straight hair. Thessalian. Winifred Bryher. PoA
Binding Arbitration. Robert Wrigley. SOTS
Bindlestiff. Edwin Ford Piper. HBMV
Bind-Weed. "Susan Coolidge." GN
Bindweed, The. Walter de la Mare. BrPo
Bingen on the Rhine. Caroline Elizabeth Sarah Norton. BeLS; BLPA; HBV-2; TreF; WBLP
Bingo. *Unknown.* CH; FSW
Bingo Has an Enemy ("Bingo is kind and friendly"). Rose Fyleman. TiPo
Binker ("Binker—What I call him—is a secret of my own"). A. A. Milne. PoPl
Binni the Meshuggener. Danny Siegel. VWA
Binnorie. *Unknown.* *See* Two Sisters, The.
Binocular owl, The. The Woods at Night. May Swenson. DuDa
Binoculars I'd meant for birds. Between Leaps. Brad Leithauser. MAYP
Binsey Poplars (Felled 1879). Gerard Manley Hopkins. BoNaP; BrPo; CoBMV; EBVV; ELP; FaBoPP; InPS; MoVE; NoAM; NoP; PAI; VLP
Biographical Note. Gabriel Preil, *tr. fr. Hebrew by* Howard Schwartz. VWA
Biography. Amiri Baraka. TAP
Biography. Charles Bruce. CaP
Biography. A. M. Klein. TrJP
Biography, *sel.* John Masefield.
"Other bright days of action have seemed great." OxBTC
Biography. Maura Stanton. MAYP
Biography. Jan Struther. InMe
Biography for Beginners. E. C. Bentley. *See* Clerihews.
Biography for Traman, *sel.* Winfield Townley Scott.
"Let us record/ The evenings when we were innocents of twenty." ErPo
Biography of an Agnostic. Louis Ginsberg. TrJP
Biography of Southern Rain. Kenneth Patchen. VGW
Biological, The/ and dynastic phenomenon. The Art of Picasso. Salvador Dali, *tr. by* David Gascoyne. EAS
Biology Lesson. John D. Engle, Jr. AMV-80
Bio-poetic Statement. Carroll Arnett. STE
Biothanatos. Joseph Beaumont. OBS
Biotherm. Frank O'Hara. CoPo
Birch. Louis Simpson. ELU
Birch begins to crack its outer sheath, The. A Young Birch. Robert Frost. BoNaP; LiTA
Birch-Tree at Loschwitz, The. Amy Levy. TrJP
Birch-tree trunks are white as plaster casts, The. Lyre. Patrick White. AMV-80
Birch tree, you remind me. Birch. Louis Simpson. ELU
Birch Trees. John Richard Moreland. HBMV; HBVY; OHIP; RHPC
Birches. Robert Frost. AmPP; BiP; CMoP; FaBV; FPL; HBMV; HeIP; LiTA; LiTM; MoAB; MoAmPo; MoVE; NIP; NoAM; NoP; OxBA; PAI; PoLF; PoPl; PoRA; TAP; TreF; TrGrPo; TwAmPo
Birches stand in their beggar's row, The. February; the Boy Breughel. Norman Dubie. LCAP
Birches that dance on the top of the hill, The. Parenthood. John Farrar. OHIP
Bird, A. Emily Dickinson. *See* Bird came down the walk, A.
Bird, The. Robert Greacen. NeIP
Bird, The. Moishe Leib Halpern, *tr. fr. Yiddish by* John Hollander. PPP
Bird, The. Samuel Hoffenstein. FiBHP; PV
Bird, The. Max Michelson. TrJP
Bird. Agnes Nemes Nagy, *tr. fr. Hungarian by* Bruce Berlind. BoWoP
Bird, The. Charles Simic. AmPA
Bird, The. Louis Simpson. NePoEA-2
Bird, The. Rabindranath Tagore. PoPl
Bird, The. Henry Vaughan. AnAnS-1; FM; LoBV; OBEV; PoEL-2; SeCV-1
(To a Bird after a Storm.) TRV
Bird, a man, a loaded gun, A. *Unknown.* WhC
Bird and the Muse. Marya Zaturenska. PoA
Bird and the Tree, The. Ridgely Torrence. HBMV; PoNe
Bird at Dawn, The. Harold Monro. MoBrPo
Bird at Night. Marion Ethel Hamilton. GoYe
Bird, Bird. Gene Derwood. LiTA
Bird, bird don't edge me in. The Reply. Theodore Roethke. NoP; NYBP
Bird calls me, A. The Bird. Charles Simic. AmPA
Bird came down the walk, A. Emily Dickinson. AmPP; AP; BiP; BLPL; CABA; CMoP; FaPON; FF; FM; GoJo; InvP; LiTA; LiTM; MoAmPo; NOBA; NoP; NTCP; OBAL; OBCA; OxBA; PB; PDV; PoLF; PoRA; SeCeV; SoPo; TiPo; TreFT; TwAmPo
Bird Catcher, The. *Unknown, tr. fr. Egyptian by* Ulli Beier. TTY
Bird comes, A/ delicately as a little girl. Yosano Akiko, *tr. fr. Japanese by* Kenneth Rexroth *and* Ikuko Atsumi. WPOW
Bird flew tangent-wise to the open window, A. The Bird. Robert Greacen. NeIP
Bird flies and I gum it to a concept, A. Letter to Anne Ridler. G. S. Fraser. OxBS
Bird flying past my head said previous previous, The. Conrad Aiken. *Fr.* Time in the Rock; or, Preludes to Definition, LXII. VGW
Bird from the West, A. Dora Sigerson Shorter. OBVV
Bird in a Cage. *Unknown.* AS, *with music;* GBP
Bird in a Gilded Cage, A. Arthur J. Lamb. BLSo, *with music*; FSN, *with music*; FSW; TreFT
Bird in my bower, A. Song. Francis Howard Williams. AA
Bird in my heart is calling through a far-fled, tear-grey sea, The. Blanid's Song. Gordon Bottomley. *Fr.* The Crier by Night. BrPo
Bird in Search of a Cage, A. Robert Pack. NePoEA
Bird in the Bush, A. Lord Kennet. PV
Bird in the Room, The. Rudolph Chambers Lehmann. HBMV; HBVY
Bird inside a Box, A. William Stafford. NPAW
Bird is lost, The. Yardbird's Skull. Owen Dodson. AmNP; CNA; IDB; PoBA; VGW
Bird is my neighbor, a whimsical fellow and dim, The. The Crane Is My Neighbor. Shaw Neilson. CBAP; PoAu-1
Bird kept saying that birds had once been men, The. On an Old Horn. Wallace Stevens. LiTA
Bird, Let Loose in Eastern Skies, The. Thomas Moore. HBV-2
"Bird Lives": Charles Parker in St. Louis. Michael S. Harper. AmPA
Bird, most likely a sparrow, A. Two Birds. Kathleen Linnell. AMV-81
Bird Nest Bound. *Unknown.* BluL
Bird of Dawning, The. Shakespeare. *See* Christmas.
Bird of Juno glories in his plumes, The. Verses under a Peacock Portrayed in Her Left Hand. Robert Greene. PBBP
Bird of Night, The. Randall Jarrell. DuDa; NCSH; RFM
Bird of Paradise, The. W. H. Davies. BrPo; MoVE
Bird of Power. Jim Tollerud. VoR
Bird of the bitter bright grey golden morn. A Ballad of François Villon. Swinburne. PoEL-5; PoRA
Bird of the moths! that radiant wing. The Butterfly. Robert Stephen Hawker. EBVV
Bird of the wilderness. The Skylark. James Hogg. GN; HBV-1; HBVY; PBBP
Bird on Briar. *Unknown.* OxBM
Bird on Nellie's Hat, The, *with music.* Arthur J. Lamb. FSN
Bird on the wire was an accident, The. Falling in Love. Jon Anderson. MAYP
Bird-Scene at a Rural Dwelling, A. Thomas Hardy. FM
Bird-shaped island, with secretive bird-voices. New Guinea. James McAuley. NOCV; PoAu-2
Bird sings the selfsame song, A. The Selfsame Song. Thomas Hardy. CMoP; PBBP
Bird Sings to Establish Frontiers, A. Jack Gilbert. NPGG
Bird Song. *See* Birdsong.
Bird that flies to climates crisper, The. Spring. Oscar Williams. LiTA

Bird that I don't know, A. A Country Life. Randall Jarrell. MiAP; MoAmPo
Bird walks by the shore, The. Northern Water Thrush. D. G. Jones. PeCV
Bird Was Singing, A. Dietmar von Aist, *tr. fr. German by* Jethro Bithell. AWP
Birdwatcher. Henry Treece. WaP
Bird Watcher. Ronald Wallace. PPJ
Birdwatchers of America. Anthony Hecht. CoPo; HoPM; NoAM; NOBA; PPP
Bird watchers top my honors list. Up from the Egg; the Confessions of a Nuthatch Avoider. Ogden Nash. BoAnP; FiBHP; PoRA
Bird with a Broken Wing, The. Hezekiah Butterworth. WBLP
Bird with bone on the outside, The. The Eggs. Peter Redgrove. NAs
Bird-witted. Marianne Moore. CMoP; FM
Bird-Woman of the ultra-world. Lilith. Yvan Goll. VWA
Bird you caught me, with blue feathers, The. Letter: The Japanese, to Her Husband at War. William Walsh. PoPl
Birdcatcher, The. Ralph Hodgson. MoBrPo
Birdie McReynolds. Samuel Hoffenstein. BXAP
Birdie with a yellow bill, A. Time to Rise. Robert Louis Stevenson. OxBChV; SiSoSe
Birdies, can there be any doubt. November. James Reaney. *Fr.* A Suit of Nettles. OBCV
Birdless heaven, seadusk, one lone star, A. Tutto è Sciolto. James Joyce. OBMV; OxBI
Bird-like, my heart was glad to soar and vault. Voyage to Cythera. Baudelaire, *tr. by* John Gray. SyP
Birds, The. *Aborigine Oral Tradition, tr. by* R.M. Berndt. *Fr.* The Moon-Bone Cycle. WTO
Birds, The, *sel.* Aristophanes. , *tr. fr. Greek by* Swinbume.
Chorus of Birds. AWP
(Grand Chorus of Birds.) PoEL-5
Birds, The ("Thou hearest the nightingale begin the song of spring"). Blake. *See* Vision of Beulah, The.
Birds, The ("Where thou dwellest, in what grave"). Blake. CH; OBRV
Birds. Robinson Jeffers. AP; CoBMV; TwAmPo; VGW
Birds. D.H. Lawrence. BoAnP
Birds. "Lywelyn. "PoAu-2
Birds. Ruth Miller. PeSA
Birds. "Moira O'Neill." HBV-1
Birds. "Seumas O'Sullivan." Ox; OxBI
Birds, The. David Posner. NYBP
Birds, The. J. C. Squire. HBMV
"O let your imagination turn," *sel.* PBBP
Birds. Richard Henry Stoddard. AA; HBV-1
Birds, The ("From out of a wood did a cuckoo fly"). *Unknown, tr. fr. Czechoslovakian.* PChr
Birds ("Wild pigeon of the leaves"). *Unknown, tr. fr. Arabic by* E. Powys Mathers. *Fr.* The Thousand and One Nights. AWP
Birds, The/ confused by the angle. December Eclipse. Margo Lockwood. Psk
Birds against the April wind, The. What the Birds Said. Whittier. NOBA
Birds All Singing. Norman MacCaig. ChMP
Birds all the sunny day. Nest Eggs. Robert Louis Stevenson. FM
Birds and Bees. *Unknown, tr. fr. German by* Louis Untermeyer. UnTE
Birds and Fishes. Robinson Jeffers. NoP
Birds and leaves disconnect in Fall. Zimmer in Fall. Paul Zimmer. PPJ
Birds and periodic blood. 5:30 A.M. Adrienne Rich. NMM; NOBA
Birds and Roses Are Birds and Roses. William Heyen. GeTw
Birds and sunlight. Yellow. De Leon Harrison. PoBA
Birds Are Drowsing on the Branches. Leah Rudnitsky, *tr. fr. Yiddish by* David G. Roskies. VWA
Birds are flowers flying. Mirrorment. A. R. Ammons. PCP
Birds are of passage now. Words for the Raker of Leaves. Léonie Adams. PoCh
Birds are our angels—out of heaven. Birds. "Llywelyn." PoAu-2
Birds are singing round my window. Birds. Richard Henry Stoddard. AA; HBV-1
Birds are the life of the skies. Birds. D. H. Lawrence. BoAnP
Birds, The—are they worth remembering? Wingtip. Carl Sandburg. PCP
Birds at Winter Nightfall. Thomas Hardy. ELU; MoBrPo
Birds' Ball, The. C. W. Bardeen. BLPA
Birds, birds, birds. Beat Poem by an Academic Poet. Vassar Miller. WPE
Birds, birds—birds, birds, birds. Siege at Stony Point. Horace Gregory. FAZ
Birds come like fishes out of the air, The. Prey to Prey. David Rowbotham. CBAP
Birds' Courting Song, The, *with music. Unknown.* TrAS
Birds drip from the trees. Daybreak. Bert Meyers. EAS
Bird's egg, a green branch, A. That's June. Mary F. Butts. YeAr
Birds far-off and open in the evening. The Gentle Hill. Salvatore Quasimodo, *tr. by* Allen Mandelbaum. PoPl
Birds feed on birds, beasts on each other prey. Wretched Man. Earl of Rochester. *Fr.* A Satire against Mankind. SeCePo
Birds find their way. Migration. Joseph Bruchac. AMV-81
Birds go fluttering in the air, The. The Silent Snake. *Unknown.* FaPON; TiPo
Birds have been singing today, The. In February. John Addington Symonds. YeAr
Birds have come back again early in the morning, in the spring. Homecoming. Wislawa Szymborska, *tr. by* Benjamin Sher. AMV-81
Birds have hid, the winds are low, The. John Vance Cheney. Evening Songs, I. AA
Birds I beheld building nests in the bushes. William Langland. *Fr.* The Vision of Piers Plowman, Passus XI. PBBP
Birds in a whirl, drift to the rooftops. Gary Snyder. Myths and Texts: Hunting, III. NaP
Birds in Snow. Hilda Doolittle ("H. D."). PoA
Birds in Spring. James Thomson. *Fr.* The Seasons: Spring. OBEC
Birds in the Fens. Michael Drayton. *Fr.* Polyolbion. ChTr
("Duck, and mallard first, the falconers onely sport, The.") FM
Birds in the first light twitter and whistle, The. A Little Morning Music. Delmore Schwartz. BoNaP; NYBP
Birds in the Night. Luis Cernuda, *tr. fr. Spanish by* Erskine Lane. PeHV
Birds in the Wood. *Unknown.* HAP
Birds in their little nests agree. Hilaire Belloc. POL
Birds' Lament. John Clare. PoEL-4
Bird's Nest, A. Erez Biton, *tr. fr. Hebrew by* Judith Katz. VWA
Bird's Nest, The. John Drinkwater. EvOK; PDV; SoPo
Bird's Nest, The. Elizabeth Turner. OHIP
Birds' Nests. John Clare. OAEL-2; VLP
Birds' Nests. Edward Thomas. HeIP
Birds of America, The. James Broughton. AmFN; BoAnP
Birds of Arles, The. David Fisher. NPGG
Birds of Bethlehem, The. Richard Watson Gilder. AA
Birds of Killingworth, The. Longfellow. *Fr.* Tales of a Wayside Inn: The Poet's Tale. OnMSP; OxBA
"Do you ne'er think what wondrous beings these?" *sel.* WBLP
Birds of omen dark and foul. Annot Lyle's Song. Sir Walter Scott. *Fr.* The Legend of Montrose, *ch.* 6. EnRP
Birds of Paradise, The. John Peale Bishop. GoJo
Birds of Scotland, The, *sel.* James Grahame.
"With earliest spring, while yet in mountain cleughs." PBBP
Birds of the Air, The. Hollis Freeman. STF
Birds of the forest are calling for thee, The. Gypsy Love Song. Harry B. Smith. FSN
Birds of Tin, The. Charles Madge. EAS; NeBP
Birds' Rondel, The. Chaucer. *See* Now Welcome, Somer.
Birds sang sweet as ony bell, The. Sir Aldingar. *Unknown.* ESPB
Birds saw the people walking along, The. The Birds. *Aborigine Oral Tradition, tr. by* R. M. Berndt. *Fr.* The Moon-Bone Cycle. WTO
Birds sleeping gently, The. Alice, Where Art Thou? Wellington Guernsey. VLP
Birds stayed not their singing. Armistice Day. John Freeman. MMA
Birds their love-notes warble, The. Alice Ray. Sarah Josepha Hale. AA
Birds their quire apply, The; airs, vernal airs. The Eternal Spring. Milton. *Fr.* Paradise Lost, IV. GN
Birds, trees and flow'rs they bring to me. J. C. Squire. *Fr.* The Swallow. BXAP
Birds turned, The. Wrapped Hair Bundles. Tauhindauli. STE
Birds Waking. W. S. Merwin. NOBA
Birdsong. Blake. *See* Vision of Beulah, The.
Bird Song. John Hay. NePoAm-2
Bird Song. Laura E. Richards. HBV-1
Bird Song. Betsy Rosenberg. VWA
Birdsong. Shakespeare. *Fr.* The Merchant of Venice. PB
Birdsong. James Burns Singer. FaBoTw
Birdsville Track, The, *sel.* Douglas Stewart.
"Oh the corrugated-iron town." CBAP
Birdwatcher. *See* Bird Watcher.
Birkett's Eagle. Dorothy S. Howard. MoBS
Birks of Aberfeldy, The. Burns. CTC; ViBoPo
Birks of Endermay, The. David Mallet. OBEC
Birlinn Chlann-Raghnaill. Alexander MacDonald, *tr. fr. Gaelic by* "Hugh MacDiarmid." GoTS
Birmingham. Julia Fields. PoNe
Birmingham. Louis MacNeice. CMoP; MoAB; MoBrPo
Birmingham. Margaret Walker. PoBA
Birmingham and Wolverhampton. James Woodhouse. *Fr.* The Life and Lucubrations of Crispinus Scriblerus. NOEC
Birmingham Jail. *Unknown.* *See* Down in the Valley.
Birmingham 1963. Raymond R. Patterson. CNA; GP; PoBA

Birmingham Sunday. Langston Hughes. PoNe
Birmingham. The city bell tower chimes one. Letters from Birmingham. Harold Bond. TAT
Birth. Edith Bruck, *tr. fr. Italian by* Ruth Feldman *and* Brian Swann. BoWoP
Birth, A. James Dickey. NOBA
Birth, The. Rosemary Dobson. PoAu2
Birth. Amir Gilboa, *tr. fr. Hebrew.* OFD, *tr. by* Robert Mezey *and* Shula; VWA, *tr. by* Stephen Mitchell
Birth. Langston Hughes. NAs
Birth. George Ella Lyon. Str
Birth. Gabriela Melinescu, *tr. fr. Rumanian by* Willis Barnstone *and* Matei Calinescu. BoWoP
Birth. Harold Monro. *Fr.* Strange Meetings. PoA
Birth. Craig Raine. *Fr.* Anno Domini. NAs
Birth. Grace Raymond. AA
Birth. Constance Urdang. VWA
Birth-Bond, The. Dante Gabriel Rossetti. The House of Life, XV. OAEP
Birth by Anesthesia. George Scarbrough. GoYe
Birth-Dues. Robinson Jeffers. MoAB; MoAmPo
Birth in a Narrow Room, The. Gwendolyn Brooks. BlSi; NAs; PoNe
Birth of a Country. Agnes Gergely, *tr. fr. Hungarian by* Emery George. VWA
Birth of a Great Man. Robert Graves. NYBP
Birth of a Shark, The. David Wevill. TwCP
Birth of Galahad, The, *sel.* Richard Hovey.
Ylen's Song. AA
Birth of John Henry, The. Melvin B. Tolson. *Fr.* Harlem Gallery. BPo
("Night John Henry is born an ax, The.") TTY
Birth of Love. Robert Penn Warren. UnPo
Birth of Moshesh, The. David Granmer T. Bereng, *tr. fr. Sotho by* Dan Kunene *and* Jack Cope PeS; TTY
Birth of Rainbow. Ted Hughes. NAs
Birth of Robin Hood, The. *Unknown.* OAEL-1; OxBB
(Willie and Earl Richard's Daughter, A, B, *and* C *vers.*) ESPB
"And mony ane sings o' grass, o' grass," *sel.* ViBoPo
Birth of Saint Patrick, The. Samuel Lover. HBV-2; PoSC
Birth of Sea and Land Life. Keaulumoku, *tr. fr. Hawaiian by* M. W. Beckwith. *Fr.* The Kumulipo; a Creation Chant. WTO
Birth of the Foal. Ferenc Juhász, *tr. fr. Hungarian by* David Wevill. BoAnP; PH
Birth of the Poet, The. Quandra Prettyman. BOLo
Birth of the Squire, The; an Eclogue. John Gay. NOEC; PoEL-3
Birth of Tragedy, The. Irving Layton. MoCV; NoP; OBCV; PeCV
Birth of Venus. Constance Urdang. PoA
Birth of Venus, The. *Unknown.* EtS
Birth Report. X. J. Kennedy. *Fr.* Snapshots. NAs
Birth seems like chance, and life appears uncertain. Lincoln. Rembrandt William B. Ditmars. HBMV
Birthday. Earle Birney. NAs
Birthday. John Ciardi. NAs
Birthday, The Philip Dacey. AmPA
Birthday, A. Rachel Field. SiSoSe; TiPo
Birthday. P. J. Kavanagh. NAs
Birthday. D. H. Lawrence. NAs
Birthday. James Merrill. NAs
Birthday, A. Edwin Muir. BSV; NAs
Birthday, A. Christina Rossetti. AWP; BLPL; CH; FaFP; InvP; LiTB; LoBV; NAs; NOBE; OAEL-2; OAEP; OBEV; OBVV; OLR; TreFS; TrGrPo; ViBoPo; VLP; WHA; WiR; WPE
Birthday. William Stafford. NAs
Birthday. Yevgeny Yevtushenko, *tr. fr. Russian by* Peter Levi *and* Robin Milner-Gulland. NAs
Birthday Cake. Aileen Fisher. PDV
Birthday Candle, A. Donald Justice. NYBP
Birthday Card for a Psychiatrist. Mona Van Duyn. IHMS
Birthday Child, The. Rose Fyleman. FaPON; SiSoSe
Birthday Crown, The. William Alexander. OBVV
Birthday Dream, The. James Dickey. NAs
Birthday Gifts. Herbert Asquith. OFD; SiSoSe
Birthday in Hospital, A. Elizabeth Jennings. NAs
Birthday Memorial to Seventh Street, A. Audre Lorde. CNA
Birthday Ode to Mr. Alfred Austin, A. Sir Owen Seaman. NOBL
Birthday of but a single pang. Emily Dickinson. NAs; OFD
Birthday of Catharine Tufton, The, *sel.* Countess of Winchilsea.
Portrait, The. OBEC
Birthday on Deathrow. Harold LaMont Otey. LFAC
Birthday Party. Patti Patton. AMV-80
Birthday Poem. W. H. Auden. *See* August for the People.
Birthday Poem. Al Young. NPGG
Birthday Poem for Thomas Hardy. C. Day Lewis. CoBMV
Birthday Poem from Venice. Patricia Beer. OxBC
Birthday Poem, November 4th. John Thompson, Jr. WaP
Birthday Prayer, A. John Finley. TrPWD
Birthday Sonnet. Elinor Wylie. MoAB; MoAmPo
Birthday: Tara Regina. George Mosby, Jr. AMV-81
Birthday Verses Written in a Child's Album. James Russell Lowell. OxBChV
Birthdays. Marchette Chute. SiSoSe
Birthdays. Hilde Domin, *tr. fr. German by* Tudor Morris. BoWoP
Birthdays. C. J. Driver. PeSA
Birthdays from the ocean one desert april noon. That "Craning of the Neck." Isabella Gardner. NePA; WPE
Birthdays? yes, in a general way. Sincere Flattery of R. B. James Kenneth Stephen. FaBoPa; InMe; NOBL; Par
Birthing: 2000. Pancho Aguila. LFAC
Birthnight, The; to F. Walter de la Mare. NAs
Birthplace. Duane Big Eagle. STE
Birthplace, The. Robert Frost. EyDe; OFD
Birthplace. Tahereh Saffarzadeh, *tr. fr. Farsi by* Deirdre Lashgari. WPOW
Birthplace; New Rochelle. George Oppen. DiL
Birthplace Revisited. Gregory Corso. CAD; NeAP; PoM; VGW
Birthright. John Drinkwater. CH; HBV-2; OxBTC; WHA
Birthright. Geraldine Kudaka. BrSi
Birthsong. Jessica Scarbrough. LFAC
Bishop and a bold dragoon, A. A Recent Dialogue. Thomas Moore. NBM
Bishop and His Portmanteau, The. *Unknown.* DBV
Bishop Blomfield's First Charge to His Clergy. *At. to* Sydney Smith. FaBoEE
Bishop Blougram's Apology. Robert Browning. OBNC; PoEL-5; VLP
Sels.
Belief and Unbelief. FaBV
"When the fight begins with himself." TRV
Bishop Butler of Kilcash. *Unknown.* OnYI
Bishop Doane on His Dog. George Washington Doane. BLPA; FaBoBe
Bishop Hatto [and the Rats]. Robert Southey. *See* God's Judgment on a Wicked Bishop.
Bishop of Atlanta, The: Ray Charles. Julian Bond. AmNP; CNA; NIP
Bishop of Canterbury, The. *Unknown.* AmFP
Bishop of Chester, The. On Dr. Keene, Bishop of Chester. Thomas Gray. FaBoEE
Bishop of El Salvador is dead, murdered by no one knows who, The. Rusia en 1931. Robert Hass. MAYP
Bishop of Rum-ti-Foo, The. W. S. Gilbert. CenHV
Bishop Orders His Tomb at Saint Praxed's Church, The. Robert Browning. AWP; CABA; EBVV; FiP; HAP; HBV-1; HeIP; NoP; OAEL-2; OAEP; OBAL; PPoe; PPP; PrIm; SeCeV; TEP; ViPoPo
Bishop sat in lordly state and purple cap sublime, The. Tangmalangaloo. P. J. Hartigan. PoAu-1
Bishop seduces the world with his voice, The. The Bishop of Atlanta: Ray Charles. Julian Bond. AmNP; CNA; NIP
Bishop tells us, The: "When the boys come back." "They." Siegfried Sassoon. CMoP; HBMV; OBSV; OBWP
Bishop Winterbourne. Walter de la Mare. FaBoNo
Bishop's hand on a widow's breast, A. Russell Lucas. BXAP
Bishop's Harp, The. Robert Manning. ACP
Bishop's Last Directions, The. *Unknown.* DBV
("Tell my priests, when I am gone.") WhC
Bishop's See, The. *Unknown.* CoMu
Bison, The. Hilaire Belloc. FaBoNo; NA
Bit an apple on its red. Green Red Brown and White. May Swenson. VGW
Bit of color against the blue, A. A Song for Our Flag. Margaret E. Sangster. FaFP
Bit of East within a Chinese wall. Chinatown. Anna Blake Mezquida. BPAW
Bit of talcum, A. Reflection on Babies. Ogden Nash. FaBoUs
Bit of the Book, A. Margaret E. Sangster. TRV
Bit of yarrow and then of rue, A. Bouquet in Dog Time. Hayden Carruth. GrPl
Bitch-Kitty, The. Jonathan Williams. PoM
Bite, and the taste of tongues. The Empty Pain-Killer Bottles. Tom Raworth. EAS
"Bite deep and wide, O Axe, the tree." Isabella Valancy Crawford. *Fr.* Malcolm's Katie. OBCV
Biter Bit, The. William Edmonstoune Aytoun. InMe
Biting air. Winter Days. Gareth Owen. OBCP
Biting Through. Traise Yamamoto. BrSi
Bits of Straw. John Clare. WiR
(Song: "I peeled bits of straw and I got switches too.") VLP
Bitten to dust are the savage feathers of fire. To a Seaman Dead on Land. Kay Boyle. PoA
Bitter air, The. L'aura amara. Arnaut Daniel, *tr. by* Ezra Pound. CTC

Bitter batter boop! The Last Cry of the Damp Fly. Dennis Lee. NTCP
Bitter bitter. A Judezmo Writer in Turkey Angry. Stephen Levy. VWA
Bitter black bitterness. Poem (No Name No. 2). Nikki Giovanni. BOLo
Bitter Bread. Osip Mandelstam, *tr. fr. Russian by* James Greene. VWA
Bitter for Sweet. Christina Rossetti. GBL
Bitter Herbs. Alta. NMM
"Bitter in sooth is the wind to-night." The Viking. Whitley Stokes. OnYI
Bitter king in anger to be gone, A. Like an Old Proud King in a Parable. A. J. M. Smith. OBCV
Bitter morning, A. Haiku. J. W. Hackett. BoAnP
Bitter Question. Arthur R. Macdougall, Jr. PGD
Bitter rain in my courtyard. Wu Tsao, *tr. fr. Chinese by* Kenneth Rexroth *and* Ling Chung. BoWoP
Bitter Sanctuary. Harold Monro. FaBoMo; LiTB; OBMV
Bitter the storm to-night. The Vikings. *Unknown.* ChTr
Bitter the wind tonight. The Vikings. *Unknown, tr. by* John Montague. BIrV
Bitter was it, Oh to view. *Unknown. Fr.* A Lament for the Priory of Walsingham. ChTr
Bitter Withy, The. *Unknown.* BaBo; ChTr; FaBoBa; GBP; NOCV; NoP; OAEP; OBET; SBVL; ViBoFo, *with music*
Bitter year it was, A. What woman ever. The Wreath. Robert Graves. BoLoP
Bitterness of days like these we know, The. Salutamus. Sterling A. Brown. CDC
Bitter-sweet. George Herbert. NOBE; NoP; OxBoCh; PAI; TrPWD
Bitter-sweet, *sels.* Josiah Gilbert Holland.
Cradle Song: "What is the little one thinking about?" HBV-1 (Babyhood.) AA
Hymn: "For Summer's bloom and Autumn's blight." TrPWD
Bitwene Mersh and Averil. *See* Bytuene Mersh and Averil.
Bivouac. Alun Lewis. ChMP
Bivouac of the Dead, The. Theodore O'Hara. AA; BLPA; HBV-2; PAH; PAL; TreF
Bivouac on a Mountain Side. Walt Whitman. AA; AP; ChTr; OxBA; PAL; PoLF
Bix to Buxtehude to Boulez. The Victor Dog. James Merrill. NoP
Bizarre Apollo, half what Henry dreamed. Apollo 8. John Berryman. MOON
Black. Nicholas Rinaldi. AMV-80
Black/ wings sun glanced. Leaving Smoke's. Gordon Henry. STE
Black A, white E, red I, green U, blue O—vowels. Vowels. Arthur Rimbaud, *tr. by* Kenneth Koch. SOTW
Black absence hides upon the past. Stanzas. John Clare. EnLoPo
Black All Day. Raymond Patterson. BOLo; PoBA.
Black an' White. William Barnes. VLP
Black and glossy as a bee and curled was my hair. Ambapali, *tr. fr. Pali by* A. L. Basham. WPOW
Black and Gold. Nancy Byrd Turner. SoPo; TiPo; YeAr
Black and tan—yeah, black and tan. Dancing Gal. Frank Marshall Davis. FB
Black and White. Leonard Adame. SoSe
Black and White. Esther Lilian Duff. HBMV
Black and White. Tom Schmidt. NeAC
Black and White Shuffle. Harry Elmore Hurd. WhC
Black and yellow. Bumble Bee. Margaret Wise Brown. PDV
Black Angel, The. Henri Coulette. CoAP; NYBP
Black Army, The. S. E. K. Mqhayi, *tr. fr. Xhosa by* C. M. Mcanyangwa *and* Jack Cope. PeSA
Black Art. Amiri Baraka. BPo; CAPP; NIP
Black Art, The. Anne Sexton. PoA
Black as a battering-ram the massive head. Buffalo. Roy Daniells. CaP
Black as the centre of an eye, the centre, a blackness. Marina Tsvetayeva, *tr. by* Elaine Feinstein *and* Angela Livingstone. *Fr.* Insomnia. PBWP
Black ash. Pine Point, You Are. Gordon Henry. STE
Black Bagatelles, *sels.* Rodney Hall. CBAP
My Coffin Is a Deckchair.
October.
They're Dying Just the Same in Station Homesteads.
World Is a Musician's Cliff House, The.
Black Ball Line, The, *with music. Unknown.* AmSS
(Blow, Boys, Blow, *vers.* IV, *diff. vers.*) ShS
Black Bart. *Unknown.* BPAW
"Black Bart, P08." Ambrose Bierce. BPAW
Black Bastill, The; or, A Lamentation of the Kirk of Scotland, *sel.* James Melville.
Robin at My Window. BSV
Black Bear sang, drumming on a log. Moon of Huckleberries. Phillip William George. VoR
Black bear sits alone, A. Galway Kinnell. *Fr.* Lastness. DiL; GP
Black beauty, which above that common light. Sonnet of Black Beauty. Lord Herbert of Cherbury. AnAnS-2; MePo
Black biplane crashes into [or through] the window, The [*or* A]. Love Poem. Gregory Orr. GeTw; MAT
Black, black, black is the color of my true love's hair. Black Is the Color [of My True Love's Hair]. *Unknown.* TreFT
Black, black, the sheen of his back and shoulders. Toro. W. S. Merwin. NePA
Black Blues. Bloke Modisane. PBA
Black Book, The, *sel.* John Berryman.
"Grandfather, sleepless in a room upstairs." VGW
Black Book of Carmarthen, The, *sel. Unknown, tr. fr. Welsh by* Ernest Rhys.
Song of the Graves, The. OBMV
Black Bottom Bootlegger, The. Esther M. Leiper. TAT
Black Bourgeoisie. Amiri Baraka. BPo
Black Boy. Norman Rosten. TrJP
Black boy/ let me get up from the white man's table of fifty sounds. PSI. Melvin B. Tolson. PoBA
Black boy, the night hides you. Black Boy. Norman Rosten. TrJP
Black brother, think you life so sweet. Time to Die. Ray Garfield Dandridge. BANP; PoBA
Black Bull of Aldgate. Tennyson. TW
Black Cat. Lora Dunetz. NePoAm-2
Black cat, sweet brother. For James Baldwin. Kay Boyle. NMM
Black cat yawns, The. Cat. Mary Britton Miller. PCat; RHPC; SoPo; SUS; TiPo
Black centipedal bugs. Letter with a Black Border. Sandra McPherson. GeTw
Black Church on Sunday. Joseph M. Mosley, Jr. NBP
Black cock crowed, The. Two o'Clock. Katharine Pyle. *Fr.* The Wonder Clock. OBCA
Black con getting out with me stood there, The. Getting Out. J. J. Maloney. LFAC
Black Cottage, The. Robert Frost. VGW
Black Crispus Attucks taught. Dark Symphony. Melvin B. Tolson. AmNP; BALP; PoNe
Black crosses on the skyline, like a squad heedless of levies. Erris Coast, 1943. Hugh Connell. NeIP
Black, crumbling rock. Dead scree. The dolorous wind. Climb in Torridon. Brenda G. Macrow. PoSH
Black Dada Nihilismus. Amiri Baraka. PoM
Black Death, The. Philip Dacey. GP
Black Dog. Ray A. Young Bear. CDW
Black Draftee from Dixie, The. Carrie Williams Clifford. BlSi
Black Earth. Marianne Moore. *See* Melancthon.
Black-eyed Susan. John Gay. *See* Sweet William's Farewell to Black-eyed Susan.
Black-eyed Susie. *Unknown.* AmFP; FSW
Black eyes if you seem dark. To Her Eyes. Lord Herbert of Cherbury. JCP; OBS
Black Faced Sheep, The. Donald Hall. LCAP; SV
Black Fear. Elizabeth Woody. STE
Black Finger, The. Angelina Weld Grimké. AmNP; PoBA
Black Flags Are Fluttering. David Vogel, *tr. fr. Hebrew by* A. C. Jacobs. VWA
"Black folks have got to be superhuman." A Poem about Beauty, Blackness, Poetry. Linda Brown Bragg. CNA
Black fool, why winter here? These frozen skies. Advice to a Raven in Russia [December, 1812]. Joel Barlow. AmPP; NePA; NOBA; OBWP; OxBA
Black gal,/ she took a knife. My Black Gal Blues. *Unknown.* BluL
Black Girl, De. *Unknown.* GBP
Black girl black girl. Blackberry Sweet [*or* Black Magic]. Dudley Randall. BOLO; CNA; HAP; InPS; NBP; NCSH; OLR; PoBA; WeW
Black Girl Goes By, A. Emile Roumer, *tr. fr. French by* Edna Worthley Underwood. TTY
Black greyed into white a nightmare of bicycling. That Which We Call a Rose. Michael Dransfield. CBAP
Black grows the southern sky, betokening rain. Sudden Shower. John Clare. OBRV; PoSC
Black guard motions me into an airway full, A. City Jail. J. J. Maloney. LFAC
Black Hair. Gary Soto. NPGG
Black-haired girl, The. The Yawn. Paul Blackburn. CTBA; ELU
Black Hat, The. Clayton Eshleman. VGW
Black Hawk in Hiding. George Keithley. NPGG
Black hen of the night, The. The Four Cardinal Times of Day. Rene Daumal, *tr. by* Jan Pallister. AMV-81
Black Hills are threatening to run dry, The. Western Movies. Jeffry Jensen. AMV-80
Black Hills Survival Gathering, 1980. Linda Hogan. STE; TWSS
Black history. The Living Truth. Sterling Plumpp. PoBA
Black Holes. James A. Perkins. SOTS
Black Horse Blues. *Unknown.* BluL

Black Horse Rider, The. Pierre Loving. EAS
Black Horse Running. Noel Maureen Valis. AMV-80
Black Humor. Archibald MacLeish. NCSH
Black I am and much admired. *Unknown.* OxNR
Black in blazonry means. The Buffalo. Marianne Moore. PoA
Black iron fence closes the graves in, A. Visiting Emily Dickinson's Grave with Robert Francis. Robert Bly. LCAP
Black Is a Soul. Joseph Blanco White. IDB; PoBA
Black Is Best. Larry Thompson. BOLo; PoBA
Black is; slavery was; I am. This Child Is the Mother. Gloria C. Oden. BlSi
Black is the beauty of the brightest day. Divine Zenocrate [*or* To Entertain Divine Zenocrate]. Christopher Marlowe. *Fr.* Tamburlaine the Great, Pt. II. ChTr; ViBoPo; WHA
Black Is the Color [of My True Love's Hair]. *Unknown.* FF; FSW; GBP; TreFT
Black is the first nail I ever stepped on. Negritude. James A. Emanuel. BPo; CNA
Black is the night. What Is Black? Mary O'Neill. NTCP
Black is what the prisons are. The African Affair. Bruce McM. Wright. AmNP; NIP; PoBA; PoNe
Black Jack Davey [*or* Davy]. *Unknown. See* Wraggle Taggle Gipsies, The.
Black Jackets. Thom Gunn. HeIP; MP; TwCP
Black Jam for Dr. Negro. Mari Evans. BPo; PoBA
Black Jess. Peter Kane Dufault. NYBP
Black Job, A, *sel.* Thomas Hood.
"History of human-kind to trace, The." VLP
Black key. White key. Unrelenting Flood. William Matthews. GeTw
Black Knight, The. John Todhunter. OBVV
Black Lightning. Arthur Sze. BrSi
Black, long-tailed, The. The Yellow Season. William Carlos Williams. MoAB; MoAmPo
Black Lotus. Alicia Ley Johnson. NBP
Black luggie, lammer bead. Against Witches. *Unknown.* GBP
Black Madonna, The. Albert Rice. CDC
Black Magdalens. Countee Cullen. BANP
Black Magic. Dudley Randall. *See* Blackberry Sweet.
Black Magic. Sonia Sanchez. BPo
Black Mail. Alice Walker. AmPA
Black Majesty. Countee Cullen. PoBA; VGW
Black Mammies. John Wesley Holloway. BANP
Black Man, A. Sam Cornish. CNA; PoBA
Black man in a white dress shirt. Man's World Dissolving. Derek Butler. LFAC
Black man is hugging me around the throat from behind, A. Father and Son. David Ignatow. DiL
Black Man Speaks, The. Langston Hughes. TreFT
Black Man Talks of Reaping, A. Arna Bontemps. AmNP; BANP; BPo; CDC; FB; IDB; PoBA; PoNe
Black Man's Feast. Sarah Webster Fabio. PoBA; PoNe
Black Man's Son, The. Oswald Durand, *tr. fr. French by* Edna Worthley Underwood. TTY
Black Maps. Mark Strand. PoA
Black Marble. Arthur O'Shaughnessy. SyP
Black Marigolds. Bilhana, *formerly at. to* Chauras, *tr. fr. Sanskrit by* E. Powys Mathers. AWP; ErPo, *abr.*
Black men bleeding to death inside themselves. Eulogy for Alvin Frost. Audre Lorde. CNA
Black Mesa, The. James Merrill. PoA
Black Mesa. Ron Rogers. STE
Black milk of dawn we drink it at dusk. Death Fugue. Paul Celan, *tr. by* Joachim Neugroschel. VWA
Black milk of daybreak we drink it at nightfall. Fugue of Death. Paul Celan, *tr. by* Christopher Middleton. OBVE
Black milk of the dawn we drink it evenings. Death Fugue. Paul Celan, *tr. by* Clement Greenberg. TrJP
Black Money. Tess Gallagher. GeTw; LTB
Black Mountain Blues. *Unknown.* BluL
Black mountains pricked with pointed pine. The Watershed. Alice Meynell. SBG
Black Muslim Boy in a Hospital. James A. Emanuel. PoNe
Black Narcissus. Gerald W. Barrax. PoBA
Black night./ White snow. Alexander Blok, *tr. fr. Russian by* Babette Deutsch *and* Avrahm Yarmolinsky. *Fr.* The Twelve. AWP
Black November Turkey, A. Richard Wilbur. BoAnP; LCAP; MoAB; NCSH
Black on flat water past the jonquil lawns. The Black Swan. James Merrill. MoPo
Black one, last as usual, swings her head, The. Fetching Cows. Norman MacCaig. BoAnP; OxBC
Black Panther, The. John Hall Wheelock. FF; HBMV; LiTM
Black Patch on Lucasta's Face, A. Richard Lovelace. AnAnS-2; CaPo; SeCP
Black Pebble, The. James Reeves. PDV
Black People! Amiri Baraka. BPo
Black people think. Awareness. Don L. Lee. BOLo; PoBA
Black People: This Is Our Destiny. Amiri Baraka. CAPP; CNA
Black people, we rainclouds. We Rainclouds. Marvin Wyche, Jr. AmNP
Black Pierrot, A. Langston Hughes. OLR
Black pitchy night, companion of my woe. Sonnet. Michael Drayton. Idea's Mirrour, LXX [XLV]. LoBV; OBSC
Black Plateau, The. W. S. Merwin. NNaP
Black Poet, White Critic. Dudley Randall. BPo; CABA; ConAP
Black Poetry Day, A. Alicia Loy Johnson. BOLo
Black poets should live—not leap. For Black Poets Who Think of Suicide. Etheridge Knight. CNA; HeIP; PoBA
Black Pony Eating Grass. Robert Bly. FAZ
Black Poplar-Boughs. John Freeman. HBMV
Black Power. Alvin Saxon. PoBA
Black Power Poem. Ishmael Reed. BPo
Black Pride. Margaret Goss Burroughs. BlSi
Black reapers with the sound of steel on stones. Reapers. Jean Toomer. BPo; CDC; HAP; InPK; NoAM; PoBA; PPP; WeW
Black Regiment, The. George Henry Boker. GN; HBV-2; PAH
Black Riders, The, *sels.* Stephen Crane.
Ancestry, XXII. AA
"Behold, from the land of the farther suns," XXIX. AP
Behold, the Grave of a Wicked Man, XXV. TAP
"Black riders came from the sea," I. AP; TAP
(Black Riders, The.) AA
Blades of Grass, The, XVIII. AP; MoAmPo; PoPl; TreFT
Book of Wisdom, The, XXXVI. HoPM; MoAmPo
"God fashioned the ship of the world carefully," VI. AP; MOS
God in Wrath, A, XIX. AP; TAP
"God lay dead in heaven," LXVII. AmPP; AP
"I looked here," VIII. AP
"I saw a man pursuing the horizon," XXIV. AmPP; AP; FF; HoPM; LiTA; LiTM; MAT; MoAmPo; NePA; NOBA
"I stood musing in a black world," XLIX. AP
I Stood upon a High Place, IX. AP; LiTA; NePA
"I stood upon a highway," XXXIV. AP
"If I should cast off this tattered coat," LXVI. AP
In the Desert, III. AP; FaBoEE; LiTM; NOBA; PAI; TAP
(Four Poems, I.) CrMA
(Heart, The.) InPK; HoPM; MoAmPo; TW
It Was Wrong to Do This, Said the Angel, LIV. AP; LiTA; NePA; PAI
Learned Man, A, XX. LiTA; MoAmPo; NePA
"Livid lightnings flashed in the clouds," XXXIX. AP
"Love walked alone," XLI. AP
Man Saw a Ball of Gold in the Sky, A, XXXV. EvOK; LiTA; NePA; PoPl
"Man went before a strange God, A," LI. AP
"Many red devils ran from my heart," XLVI. AP; TAP
Many Workmen, XXXI. LiTA; NePA; TAP
"Ocean said to me once, The," XXXVIII. MOS
"Places among the stars," XXIII. AP
"Sage lectured brilliantly, The," III. YaD
'Scaped, LXV. AA
"Should the wide world roll away," X. AmPP; AP; BiP
"There was, before me," XXI. AP
"There was crimson clash of war," XIV. AP
"Think as I Think," XLVII. WeW
"'Truth,' said a traveller," XXVIII. AP
"Upon the road of my life," LX. AP
"Well then, I hate Thee, unrighteous picture," XII. AP
Why? XXV. AA
Youth in Apparel That Glittered, A, XXVII. LiTA; NePA
(Content.) AA
(Youth, A.) MoAmPo
Black robes, hoods gold scarlet purple, bright heads. The Academic Overture. Richmond Lattimore. GLGT
Black Rock of Kiltearn, The. Andrew Young. FaBoTw
Black Rocks. Laureen Mar. BrSi
Black Rook in Rainy Weather. Sylvia Plath. LiTM; MP; NePoEA-2; NIP; PP
Black Sailor's Chanty. Charles Keeler. EtS
Black Sheep. Richard Burton. AA; HBV-2
Black Silk. Tess Gallagher. MAYP
Black Sister. Kattie M. Cumbo. BlSi
Black Sketches. Don L. Lee. NeAC
Black skin against bright green. Black Sister. Kattie M. Cumbo. BlSi
Black skull-caps. Dying under a Fall of Stars. Mark Elliott Shapiro. VWA

Black-smocked smiths, smattered with smoke. Blacksmiths. *Unknown.* WiR
Black Snake, The. Patricia Hubbell. PDV
Black Snake. *Unknown.* BluL
Black Soldier Remembers, A. Horace Coleman. FAZ
Black Soldier's Civil War Chant. *Unknown. See* Negro Soldier's Civil War Chant.
Black Soul of the Land. Lance Jeffers. FB
Black spirits and white, red spirits and gray. Thomas Middleton. *Fr.* The Witch, V, i. WSC
Black Spring. Robert Lowell, *ad. fr. Russian of* Innokenti Annensky. NaP
Black spruce and Norway pine. Pare Lorentz. *Fr.* The River. AmFN
Black Star Line. Henry Dumas. CNA; PoBA
Black steel carcass in a field of sheep, A. Scrap Iron. Raymond Durgnat. PCP
Black Students. Julia Fields. NBP
Black swallows swooping or gliding. The Skaters. John Gould Fletcher. MoAmPo
Black Swan, The. Randall Jarrell. CMoP; NMP
Black Swan, The. James Merrill. MoPo
Black Taffy. Peggy Susberry Kenner. JB
Black Tail Range, The, *with music.* *Unknown.* CoSo
Black Tambourine. Hart Crane. AP; CoBMV; InPK; NoAM; OxBA; PPP; TAP
Black Tarn. V. Sackville-West. SBG
Black Thing. *Unknown.* CoMu
Black Tower, The. W. B. Yeats. CMoP
Black Tragedy lets slip her grim disguise. Masks. Thomas Bailey Aldrich. AA
Black trees. The banks fill with shadow. For My Father. Stephen Berg. DiL
Black Trumpeter. Henry Dumas. PoBA
Black Venus of the Dead, what Sun of Night. Elegy for Dylan Thomas. Edith Sitwell. PoA
Black Virgin, The. G. K. Chesterton. ISi
Black Vulture, The. George Sterling. BPAW; HBV-1; PB
Black walnuts litter the grass. Poem for Dorothy Holt. Susan Irene Rea. AMV-81
Black Warrior. Norman Jordan. PoBA
Black was the color of the peddler's wagon. Needles and Pins. Mark Van Doren. SO
Black wave the trees in the forest. Adventure. Laura Benét. HBMV
Black Wedding Song. A. Gwendolyn Brooks. CNA
Black wings and white in the hollow. Behind the Plough. James H. Cousins. OxBI
Black within, and red without. Mother Goose. GBP; OxNR
Black Woman. Georgia Douglas Johnson. BALP
Black Woman. Naomi Long Madgett. BlSi; FB; OLR; PoBA
Black Woman. Léopold Sédar Senghor, *tr. fr. French by* Anne Atik. TTY
Blackberries sweet and dusty. Someplace Else. Marge Piercy. NeAC
Blackberry, The. Norman Nicholson. MoBrPo
Blackberry Fold. *Unknown. See* Squire and Milkmaid; or, Blackberry Fold.
Blackberry-picking. Seamus Heaney. BoNaP
Blackberry Sweet. Dudley Randall. BOLo; HAP; InPS; NBP; NCSH; WeW
(Black Magic.) CNA; OLR; PoBA
Blackberry Winter. Peter Huggins. AMV-81
Blackberry Winter. John Crowe Ransom. OxBA; PoRA
Blackberrying. Sylvia Plath. HAP; NoAM; NOBA; NYBP
Blackbird, The. William Barnes. HBV-1
Blackbird, The. Henry Charles Beeching. OBVV
Blackbird, The. W. E. Henley. Echoes, XVIII. HBV-1; MoBrPo; TrGrPo
(To A. D.) HoPM; ViBoPo.
Blackbird, The. A. E. Housman. A Shropshire Lad, VII. HBV-1
(When Smoke Stood Up from Ludlow.) MoBrPo
Blackbird. Christopher Leach. BoAnP
Blackbird, The. Tennyson. FM; PB; PBBP
Blackbird, The. Frederick Tennyson. HBV-1
Blackbird, The ("Ah, blackbird, thou art satisfied"). *Unknown, tr. fr. Middle Irish by* Kuno Meyer. AnIL; OnYI
Blackbird, The ("In midst of woods or pleasant grove"). *Unknown.* ElL
Blackbird, The ("On a fair summer's morning of soft recreation"). *Unknown.* OnYI
Blackbird, The. Humbert Wolfe. FaPON; GoJo; GrPl; HBMV; HBVY; RHPC; SUS; TiPo
Blackbird, blackbird in the cage. The Bird and the Tree. Ridgely Torrence. HBMV; PoNe
Blackbird by Belfast Lough, The. *Unknown, tr. fr. Irish by* Frank O'Connor. KiLC
Blackbird has built in the pasture agen, The. Ballad. John Clare. *Fr.* Child Harold. VLP
Blackbird of Derrycairn, The. *Unknown, tr. fr. Irish by* Austin Clarke. BIrV; NeLP
Blackbird of Litir Lone, The. On Not Hearing the Birds Sing in Ireland. Padraic Colum. NePoAm
Blackbird sang, the skies were clear and clean, The. At Queensferry. W. E. Henley. VLP
Blackbird Singing, A. R. S. Thomas. BoAnP
Blackbird singing in the tree, The. Best of Two Worlds. Basil Boothroyd. BoAnP
Blackbird startles from the homestead hedge, The. John Clare. *Fr.* Child Harold. VLP
Blackbird Suddenly, A. Joseph Auslander. TiPo
Black-bird whistles from the thorny brake, The. Birds in Spring. James Thomson. *Fr.* The Seasons: Spring. OBEC
Blackbird Winter. Annette Arkeketa West. TWSS
Blackbirds and Thrushes. *Unknown.* GBP
Blackbirds fat with winter. Blackbird Winter. Annette Arkeketa West. TWSS
Blackbirds feeding in a field of grass. White Whales Specked Black. Randolph Outlaw. LFAC
Blackbird's Song. *Unknown.* GBP
Blackcaps pipe among the reeds, The. Before the Rain. Amélie Rives. AA
Blackcock, The. Joanna Baillie. PBBP
Blacken thy heavens, Jove. Prometheus. Goethe, *tr. by* John S. Dwight. AWP
Blackened and bleeding, helpless, panting, prone. Chicago. Bret Harte. PAH
Blackfish Poem. Milton Acorn. NeAC
Blackfoot Sin-ka-ha. William S. Lewis. BPAW
Blackfriars. Eleanor Farjeon. OxBChV
Blackheads. Knute Skinner. GP
Blackie Thinks of His Brothers. Stanley Crouch. PoBA
Blackleg Miner[s], The. *Unknown.* GBP; OBET; VLP
Blacklisted. Carl Sandburg. SaC
Blackman/ midway in the night. Midway in the Night: Blackman. Eugene B. Redmond. GP
Blackmen: Who Make Morning. Angela Jackson. CNA
Blackmwore Maidens. William Barnes. HBV-1
Black'on frowns east on Maidon. After the Club-Dance. Thomas Hardy. At Casterbridge Fair, III. VLP
Black-out. Robinson Jeffers. LiTA; LiTM; NePA; WaP
Blackpool Breezes. *Unknown.* CoMu
Blackshawled women of New Mexico, The. Old Women beside a Church. Keith Wilson. Psk
Blacksmith, The ("A blacksmith, courted me, nine months and better"). *Unknown.* OBET
Blacksmith Pain. Otto Julius Bierbaum, *tr. fr. German by* Jethro Bithell. AWP
Blacksmiths, The. *Unknown.* CABA; OxBM; TW, *mod. vers. by* Wesli Court; WiR
(Smoke-blackened Smiths.) MeEL
(Swarte-smeked Smithes.) HAP
Blacksmith's boy went out with a rifle, The. Legend. Judith Wright. SO
Blacksmith's Song, The. *Unknown.* GBP
Blackstone Rangers, The. Gwendolyn Brooks. BALP; NoAM; PoBA
"There they are," *sel.* CAD
Blackwater Mountain. Charles Wright. GeTw
Blade of a knife, The. Nocturne. Richard Murphy. IPY
Blade of Grass Sings to the River, The. Leah Goldberg, *tr. fr. Hebrew by* Robert Friend. TrJP
Blades. C. K. Williams. GeTw
Blades of Grass, The. Stephen Crane. The Black Riders, XVIII. MoAmPo; PoPl; TreFT
Blades of Harden, The. Will H. Ogilvie. *Fr.* Whaup o' the Rede. GoTS
Bladyn's Song of Cloten. Charles M. Doughty. *Fr.* The Dawn in Britain. PoEL-5
Blah, Blah, Blah. Ira Gershwin. OBAL
Blake Leads a Walk on the Milky Way. Nancy Willard. OBCA
Blake saw a treeful of angels at Peckham Rye. Mad Blake. William Rose Benét. HBMV
Blakeney people, The. The People of Blakeney. *Unknown.* GBP
Blame me not, Sweet, if here and there. Alibi. Arthur Guiterman. BXAP
Blame not my cheeks, though pale with love they be. Thomas Campion. AAS; UnPo
Blame Not My Lute for He Must Sound [*or* Sownde]. Sir Thomas Wyatt. AAS; EBEV; ElL; EnRePo; OAEL-1; SiPS
(Lute Obeys, The.) OBSC; QFR
Blanaid's Song ("Blanaid loves roses"). Joseph Campbell. OxBI
Blancheflour and Jellyflorice. *Unknown.* ESPB
Blanid's Song. Gordon Bottomley. *Fr.* The Crier by Night. BrPo
Blank Book Letter, The. Samuel Greenberg. LiTA
Blank Verse for a Fat Demanding Wife. Jim Lindsey. TW

Blanket around Her, The. Joy Harjo. TWSS
Blanket Injun, The. Arthur Chapman. BPAW
Blanket loosens, The. Now, before Shaving. Aaron Kramer. AMV-81
Blantyre Explosion, The. *Unknown.* OBET
Blare of trumpet and roll of drum! The Victor. William Young. HBMV
Blast of War. Shakespeare. *See* Once More unto the Breach.
Blast of wind, a momentary breath, A. The Life of Man. Barnabe Barnes. *Fr.* A Divine Century of Spiritual Sonnets. EBEV; OBSC
Blasted Herb, The. Meshech Weare. PAH
Blasted with sighs, and surrounded with tears. Twicknam [*or* Twickenham] Garden. John Donne. AnAnS-1; EBEV; EnLoPo; FaBoPP; LoBV; MeLP; MePo; OBS; PoEL-2; SeCP; TEP
Blasting from Heaven. Philip Levine. CoAP
Blasts rip newspaper grey Mannahatta's mid day air spires. Friday the Thirteenth. Allen Ginsberg. NNaP
Blatant as factory buildings. Marina Tsvetayeva, *tr. by* Elaine Feinstein *and* Angela Livingstone. *Fr.* Poem of the End. PBWP
Blauen Veilchen der Äugelein, Die. Heine, *tr. fr. German by* James Thomson. AWP
Blaydon Races. *Unknown.* ELP
Blazing Heart, The. Alice Williams Brotherton. AA
Blazing white shirts of the white men, The. Race Riot, Tulsa, 1921. Sharon Olds. MAYP
Blazon Columbia's emblem. Columbia's Emblem. Edna Dean Proctor. GN
Bleached wood massed in bone piles. Kalaloch. Carolyn Forché. AmPA
Bleak and barren mountains keep, The. Loch Coruisk (Skye). "Fiona Macleod." SyP
Bleak season was it, turbulent and bleak. The Sunbeam Said, Be Happy. Wordsworth. *Fr.* The Recluse, I. FaBoRV
Bleak the February light. Kingdom of Heaven. Léonie Adams. MoAB; MoAmPo
Bleat of Protest. Mildred Weston. FiBHP
Bled/ holding on/ to details. Monogram 23. Martina Werner, *tr. by* Rosemarie Waldrop. BoWoP
Bleeberrying. Jonathan Denwood. MoBS
Bleecker Street. Jean Garrigue. NYP; TAP
Blemishes. James Hart. AMV-81
Blend of mirth and sadness, A. The Masterpiece. Walter Malone. PGD
Blenheim. Joseph Addison. *Fr.* The Campaign. OBEC
(Poem to His Grace the Duke of Marlborough, A.) OBWP
Blenheim, *sel.* John Philips.
War Poetry. NOEC
Blennerhassett's Island. Thomas Buchanan Read. *Fr.* The New Pastoral. PAH
Bless earth with Thine Advent, O Saviour Christ! Advent Lyrics, VIII. *Unknown, tr. by* Charles W. Kennedy. *Fr.* Christ 1. AnOE
Bless Him ("Bless Him, O constant companions"). *Unknown, tr. fr. Hebrew by* Israel Abrahams. TrJP
Bless the four corners of this house. House Blessing. Arthur Guiterman. TiPo; TrPWD
Bless the Lord, O my soul/ O Lord my God. Bible, *O.T.* Psalms, CIV. NAWM-1; OHIP; TrJP; WGRP
Bless the Lord, O my soul; and all that is within me. Bible, *O.T.* Psalms, CIII. AWP
Bless This House ("Bless this house, O Lord, we pray"). Helen Taylor. TreFT; TRV, 1 *st.*
Bless Thou this year, O Lord! Prayer [*or* A Prayer for a Happy New Year]. A. S. C. Clarke. BLRP; PGD
Bless you, bless you, burnie-bee. Mother Goose. OxNR
Bless you God our God. The Fringes. Harris Lenowitz. VWA
Bless you, Mother. On the Appeal from the Race of Sheba: II. Léopold Sédar Senghor, *tr. by* John Reed *and* Clive Wake. TTY
Bless'd art Thou, O Lord of all. Prayer before Sleep. Alice Lucas. TrJP
Blessed. Soné, *tr. fr. Hebrew by* David Kuselewitz. TrJP
Blessed/ are the injured animals. Blessing[s]. Linda Hogan. STE; TWSS
Blessed above women/ shall Jael the wife of Heber the Kenite be. Song of Deborah. Bible, *O.T. Fr.* Judges. WPOW
Blessed and Resting Uncle. Harley Elliott. NeAC
Blessed angell not a word replies, The. Ariosto, *tr. by* Sir John Harington. *Fr.* Orlando Furioso, XIV. OBVE
Blessed are the eyes that see. My Peace I Give unto You. G. A. Studdert-Kennedy. EBCP
Blessed are the poor[e] in spirit: for theirs is the kingdom[e] of heaven. The Beatitudes. Bible, *N.T. Fr.* St. Matthew. OBVE; TrGrPo
Blessed are they of the Easter faith. Easter Beatitudes. Clarence M. Burkholder. BLRP
Blessed are they that have eyes to see. Some Blesseds. John Oxenham. WGRP
Blessed are they who sow but do not reap. Blessed. Soné, *tr. by* David Kuselewitz. TrJP
Blessed Are Those Who Sow and Do Not Reap. Avraham Ben-Yitzhak, *tr. fr. Hebrew by* A. C. Jacobs. VWA
Blessed Art Thou, O Lord. *Unknown, tr. by* Theodor H. Gaster. *Fr.* The Dead Sea Scrolls. TrJP
Blessed art thou that beholdest the depths, and sittest upon the cherubims. The Song of the Three Holy Children. Bible, Apocrypha. ILwL
Blessed Assurance, *with music.* Fanny Crosby. AH
Blessed be that lady bright. A Cause for Wonder. *Unknown.* MeEL
Blessed Be the Holy Will of God. *Unknown, tr. fr. Modern Irish by* Douglas Hyde. OnYI
Blessed Be the Paps Which Thou Hast Sucked. Richard Crashaw. *See* Luke XI: Blessed Be the Paps Which Thou Hast Sucked.
Blessed Bible, sacred treasure. The Best of All. Fanny Crosby. BLRP
Blessed Comforter Divine, *with music.* Lydia Huntley Sigourney. AH
Blessed Damozel, The. Dante Gabriel Rossetti. AWP; BLPL; EBVV; GoTL; HBV-2; LiTB; LoBV; MasP; NOBE; NoP; OAEL-2; OAEP; OBEV; OBNC; OBVV; OHFP; PoEL-5; SeCeV; TEP; TrGrPo; VLP; WHA
"Blessed damozel leaned out, The," *sel.* SpRo
Blessed is every one that feareth the Lord. Bible, *O.T.* Psalms, CXXVIII. TRV
Blessed Is Everyone, *with music. Unknown.* AH
Blessed Is God. Bible, Apocrypha, *tr. fr. Greek by* D. C. Simpson. Tobit, XIII. TrJP
Blessed is he who has found the break-weed. Handful of Ashes. Ilya Rubin, *tr. by* Linda Zisquit. VWA
Blessed is the man, O Virgin Mary. Psalter of the Blessed Virgin Mary. St. Bonaventure, *tr. by* Sister Mary Emmanuel. ISi
Blessed is the man that walketh not in the counsel of the ungodly [*or* wicked]. The Godly and the Ungodly [*or* The Tree and the Chaff]. Bible, *O.T.* Psalms, I. AWP; BiP; TreF; WGRP
Blessed land of Judea! thrice hallowed of song. Palestine. Whittier. WBLP
Blessed Lord, What It Is to Be Young. David McCord. NTCP
Blessed Mary, moder virginal. A Short Prayer to Mary. *Unknown.* MeEL
Blessed Match, The. Hannah Senesh, *tr. fr. Yiddish.* TrJP
Blessed Name, The. George W. Bethune. *See* There Is No Name So Sweet on Earth.
Blessed Nearness. Mary Bullock. STF
Blessed Offendor [*or* Offendour]: who thyself hast tried [*or* haist try'd]. To Saint Mary Magdalen. Henry Constable. LoBV; PoEL-2
Blessed poster girl leaned out, The. The Poster Girl. Carolyn Wells. BXAP; HBV-1; InMe
Blessed the match that was burned. The Blessed Match. Hannah Senesh. TrJP
Blessed Trinity have pity! Childless. Giolla Brighde MacNamee, *tr. by* Frank O'Connor. BIrV; KiLC
Blessed Virgin Compared to the Air We Breathe, The. Gerard Manley Hopkins. BrPo; ISi; MoPo; OxBoCh; VLP
Blessed Virgin Mary Compared to a Window, The. Thomas Merton. ISi
Blessed Virgin's Expostulation, The. Nahum Tate. ISi
Blessed with a joy that only she. The Gift of God. E. A. Robinson. AP; CoBMV; MoAB; MoAmPo; OxBA; TwAmPo
Blessing, The. Ruth Berman. AMV-81
Blessing. Linda Hogan. STE
(Blessings.) TWSS
Blessing, A. Mekeel McBride. MAYP
Blessing. Melvin Wilk. VWA
Blessing, A. James Wright. ConAP; GrPl; HeIP; InPK; LLLT; NaP; NoAM; NOBA; NoP; PPP; TwCP
Blessing a Bride and Groom; a Wedding Night Poem. Robert Peters. *See* Allen Ginsberg Blesses a Bride and Groom; a Wedding Night Poem.
Blessing, and Honor. Horatius Bonar. TRV
Blessing at Kellenberger Road. Maxine Kent Valian. AMV-80
Blessing his handiwork, his drawbridge closed. Artificer. X. J. Kennedy. TwCP
Blessing in Disguise, A. John Ashbery. PoM
Blessing Mrs. Larkin. Margery Mansfield. GoYe
Blessing of St. Francis, The. Sister Maura. CaP
Blessing of the Firstborn. Howard Schwartz. VWA
Blessing of the Priests. Bible, *O.T. See* Benediction.
Blessing on Little Boys. Arthur Guiterman. TrPWD
Blessing on the Cows, A. "Seumas O'Sullivan." BoAnP
Blessing on the hand of women! *See* Blessings on the hand . . .
Blessing on you, Mrs. Larkin, for planting my trees! A. Blessing Mrs. Larkin. Margery Mansfield. GoYe
Blessing over Food. Hayyim Nahman Bialik. YeAr
Blessing the Hounds. Mary Winter. GoYe
Blessing without Company. *Unknown.* BPo; POL
Blessings. Linda Hogan. *See* Blessing.
Blessings Are. Cid Corman. GP

Blessings in abundance come. The Good-Night, or Blessing. Robert Herrick. CaPo
Blessings of Surrender, The. Mary J. Helphingtine. STF
Blessings on all the kids who improve the signs in the subways. Graffiti. Edward Field. CABA; CoPo
Blessings on Doneraile. Patrick O'Kelly. OnYI
Blessings [*or* Blessing] on the hand of women! The Hand That Rocks the Cradle Is the Hand That Rules the World. William Ross Wallace. BLPL; FaFP; PoLF; TreF; WBLP
Blessings on thee, little man. The Barefoot Boy. Whittier. AA; FaBoBe; FaPON; FPL; GN; HBV-1; HBVY; LiTA; OBAL; OBCA; OBVV; OHFP; PoLF; PoPl; TreF; WBLP
Blessings That Remain, The. Annie Johnson Flint. BLRP
Blest are the pure in heart. Purity of Heart. John Keble. BLRP
Blest are your North parts, for all this long time. To Mr. I. L. John Donne. SeCP
Blest as th' immortal gods is he. Fragment of Sappho. *Unknown, tr. by* Ambrose Philips. OBEC
Blest be God/ who did create. Blessing over Food. Hayyim Nahman Bialik. YeAr
Blest be Mother bind your hand on my head on the eve. The Poem on the Guilt. Avot Yeshurun, *tr. by* Harold Schimmel. VWA
Blest be the bric-a-brac that still survives. In the Shadowy Whatnot Corner. Robert Silliman Hillyer. NePoAm
Blest be the day, and blest the month and year. Petrarch, *tr. by* Joseph Auslander. Sonnets to Laura: To Laura in Life, XLVII. NAWM-1
Blest be the God of love. Even-Song. George Herbert. AnAnS-1; FaBoEn
Blest Be the Tie That Binds. John Fawcett. HBV-2
Blest Be the Wondrous Grace, *with music.* George Barrell Cheever. AH
Blest, Blest and Happy He. *Unknown.* BSV; GBL; GoTS
Blest infant bud, whose blossome-life. The Burial of an Infant. Henry Vaughan. OAEP
Blest is t' bride at t' sun shines on. Wedding and Funeral. *Unknown.* GBP
Blest is the boy who has a room. Window to the East. Virginia Moran Evans. AMV-80
Blest is the man who loves and after early play. Boys and Sport. Solon, *tr. by* John Addington Symonds. PeHV
Blest Is the Man Whose Tender Breast, *with music.* Abijah Davis. AH
Blest leaf! whose aromatic gales dispense. In Imitation of Pope. Isaac Hawkins Browne. *Fr.* A Pipe of Tobacco. BXAP; OBEC; Par
Blest Order, which in power dost so excell. The Priesthood. George Herbert. AnAnS-1
Blest pair of Sirens, pledges of heaven's joy. At a Solemn Music[k]. Milton. GTBS; GTBS-P; HBV-2; HeIP; LoBV; NOBE; OAEP; OBEV; OBS; OxBoCh; PoEL-3; SeCeV
Blest Retirement. Goldsmith. *Fr.* The Deserted Village. OBEC
("Sweet Auburn! parent of the blissful hour.") EBEV
Blest Spirit of Calm that dwellest in these woods! Charles Sangster. *Fr.* Sonnets Written in the Orillia Woods, August 1859. PeCV
Blest statesman he, whose mind's unselfish will. Wordsworth. VLP
Blest Winter Nights. John Armstrong. *Fr.* The Art of Preserving Health, III. OBEC
Bleue Maison. Edmund Blunden. BrPo
B'lieve I'll take me a walk 'round the corner. Take a Walk around the Corner. *Unknown.* BluL
Blight. Arna Bontemps. BANP; CDC
Blight. Emerson. AP; NOBA; NoP
Blight rests in your face, The. To a Publisher. . .Cut-out. Amiri Baraka. NeAP
Blighted apples will not shine. Apple Blight. Paul Zimmer. VGW
"Blighters." Siegfried Sassoon. CMoP; FaBoTw; MMA; MoVE; NoAM
Blin' Man Stood on de Road an' Cried, De, *with music.* *Unknown.* BoAN-1
(Blind Man, *with music.*) TrAS
Blind, The. Baudelaire, *tr. fr. French by* T. Sturge Moore. SyP
Blind. Harry Kemp. HBMV
Blind Adolphus. Angela McCabe. AmPA
Blind as the song of birds. Lines to a Blind Girl. Thomas Buchanan Read. AA
Blind Bartimaeus at the gates. Jericho's Blind Beggar. Longfellow. WBLP
Blind Beggar of Bednall (Bethnal) Green, The. *Unknown.* BaBo
(Blind Beggar, The, *diff. vers.*) AmFP
Blind Boy, The. Colley Cibber. GTBS; GTBS-P; HBV-1; NOEC; OBEC; OxBChV; RoGo; TreFS
Blind Boy's Pranks, The. William Thom. OBEV
Blind but Happy. Fanny Crosby. TRV
Blind Date. Conrad Aiken. DL; MoVE; ViBoPo
Blind Fiddler, The. *Unknown.* FSW
Blind folding their dollar, The. Braille. Gerald Costanzo. AMV-81
Blind for the lamp she's smashed and the riving tears. Nuit Blanche. Katherine Hoskins. NMP
Blind Girl. W. S. Merwin. NePoEA-2
Blind girl, A. Black Lightning. Arthur Sze. BrSi
Blind girl singing on the radio, A. Singing in the Dark. Irma Wassall. PoNe
Blind, I Speak to the Cigarette. Joanne de Longchamps. GoYe
Blind Leading the Blind, The. Lisel Mueller. IHMS
Blind Linnet, The. Robert Buchanan. FM
Blind Louise. George Washington Dewey. AA
Blind Love. Shakespeare. *See* Sonnets, CXLVIII.
Blind Man. Michael Hamburger. NePoEA-2
Blind Man, The. James Lewisohn. LFAC
Blind Man. *Unknown.* *See* Blin' Man Stood on de Road an' Cried, De.
Blind Man, The, *sel.* Judith Wright.
Country Dance. CBAP
Blind Man at the Fair, The. Joseph Campbell. AnIV; AWP
Blind man, blind man. *Unknown.* OxNR
Blind man draws his curtains for the night, The. Rooming House. Ted Kooser. POL
Blind man, A. I can stare at him. A Solitude. Denise Levertov. NePoEA-2
Blind Man Lay beside the Way, *with music.* *Unknown.* AS
Blind man, standing on the bridge, as grey, The. Bridge of the Carousel. Rainer Maria Rilke, *tr. by* John Drury. AMV-80
Blind-Man's Buff. Blake. WiR
Blindman's Buff. Peter Viereck. LiTM; MiAP; MoAmPo
Blind men add the figures, draw the maps, The. Great Powers Conference. Edith Lovejoy Pierce. PGD
Blind Men and the Elephant, The. John Godfrey Saxe. BLPA; FaBoBe; FPL; HBV-1; HBVY; OBCA; OnMSP; OnUR; TreF; WBLP
Blind Mr. Klugel loves the baritone of Mr. Cantini. The Follies. Daniel Mark Epstein. MAYP
Blind Old Woman. Clarence Major. PoBA
Blind, palsied, halting, speechless, mad. An Old Folks Home. Paul Lake. AMV-81
Blind Panorama of New York. Federico García Lorca, *tr. fr. Spanish by* Ben Belitt. NYP
Blind Psalmist, The. Elizabeth Clementine Kinney. AA
Blind Samson. William Plomer. PeSA
Blind Sheep, The. Randall Jarrell. NYBP; OBAL
Blind Steersmen. Francis Ernest Kobina Parkes. PBA
Blind Thamyris, and blind Maeonides. Ode to the Human Heart. Laman Blanchard. InMe; NA; NOBL
Blind with love, my daughter. Pain for a Daughter. Anne Sexton. SoSe; WeW
Blinded and deafened by the seas. Meditation. Blanaid Salkeld. OnYI
Blinded Bird, The. Thomas Hardy. BiP; CMoP; EaLo; LiTM; NoAM
Blinded parson gingering down the neo-Gothic steps, A. The Four. Geoffrey Grigson. WaP
Blinded Soldier to His Love, The. Alfred Noyes. PoPl
Blindest buzzard that I know, The. A Sketch. Christina Rossetti. GTBS-P
Blinding spot burned on the snow, A. Mistress of the Matchless Mine. Clyde Robertson. PoOW
Blinding sun at ten o'clock, The. The Church. Edwin Ford Piper. WGRP
Blindman. *See* Blind Man.
Blindness. Delmira Agustini, *tr. fr. Spanish by* D. M. Pettinella. PBWP
Blindness of Samson, The. Milton. *Fr.* Samson Agonistes. LiTB
Blisful lyf, a paisible and a swete, A. The Former Age. Chaucer. OxBM
Bliss. Eleanor Farjeon. RHPC
Bliss. George Johnston. NOBC
Bliss for which our spirits pine, The. The True Heaven. Paul Hamilton Hayne. WGRP
Bliss of man, The (could pride that blessing find). Pope. *Fr.* An Essay on Man, Epistle I. NOEC; NU
"Blissful," quoth [*or* said] I, "can [*or* may] this be true?" The Queen of Courtesy. *Unknown.* *Fr.* The Pearl. ACP; ISi, *mod. vers. by* Stanley Perkins Chase
Blistered and dry was the desert I trod. The Palm. Roy Campbell. MoBrPo
Blistering proof lies in the enclosed rose and the black-eyed susan, The. Summer Mansions. Ruth Herschberger. HoAn
Blisters with pride swelled. Dryden. *Fr.* Upon the Death of the Lord Hastings. PeD
Blithe and bonny country lass, A. Coridon's Song. Thomas Lodge. *Fr.* Rosalynde. UnTE
"Blithe-fronted, lofty, young too, wilt thou, day." The Swan. Stéphane Mallarmé, *tr. by* T. Sturge Moore. SyP
Blithe Mask, The. Dollett Fuguet. TRV
Blithe the bright dawn found me. John O'Dwyer of the Glen. *Unknown, tr. by* Thomas Furlong. AnIV
Blizzard Ape, The. Kenneth Pitchford. CoPo
Bloated/ on rotten eggs. The Skunk. Philip Dow. BXAP
Bloated Biggaboon, The. Henry Cholmondeley-Pennell. NA

Block City. Robert Louis Stevenson. EyDe; FaPON; NTCP; SoPo; TiPo
Block the cannon; let no trumpets sound! Sunset Horn. Myron O'Higgins. AmNP; PoNe
Blockhouse. Olga Kirsch, *tr. fr. Afrikaans by* Jack Cope. PeSA
Blocking the Pass. Charles Madge. FaBoMo
Blocks. Frank O'Hara. EAS
Blocks, The/ which are the buildings and walls. Comforted by Limestone. Edward Dorn. *Fr.* Oxford. NOBA
Blok: Let Me Learn the Poem. Aram Boyajian. NeAC
Blond. Joseph de Roche. HeIP
Blond cowl terse as a blunt threat to injure, The. Love among the Manichees. William Dickey. PoCh
Blond Hair at the Edge of the Pavement. Michael Smith. CIP
Blond witch, The. The Roots of Revolution in the Vegetable Kingdom. Constance Urdang. GP
Blondel. Clarence Urmy. AA; HBMV
Blood. Ray Bremser. NeAP
Blood. Barney Bush. STE
Blood, The. Nina Cassian, *tr. fr. Rumanian.* VWA, *tr. by* Herbert Kuhner; WPOW, *tr. by* Laura Schiff
Blood falling in drops to the earth. Where Are the Men Seized in This Wind of Madness? Alda do Espirito Santo, *tr. by* Alan Ryder. TTY; WPOW
Blood flows in me, but what does it have to do. Living by the Red River. James Wright. NNaP
Blood has soaked the bone which hides the stone, The. Clive James. *Fr.* Peregrine Prykke's Pilgrimage. FaBoPa
Blood Horse, The. "Barry Cornwall." GN; HBV-1; PH
Blood Hound Blues. *Unknown.* BluL
Blood Is Thicker than Water. Wallace Rice. PAH
Blood locked as I am, sun bound, and hot as a pistol. Life Must Burn. John Hay. NePoAm
Blood Marksman and Kureldei the Marksman. *Tatar (Turkic) Oral Tradition, tr. fr. German and Russian versions by* Norman Cohn. WTO
Blood on the Saddle. *Unknown.* FSW
(Trail End.) CoSo
Blood on the Sails. Phil *and* June Colclough. OBET
Blood Red Roses. *Unknown.* FSW
Blood-red the aloes flank. Farm Gate. Uys Krige, *tr. by* Uys Krige *and* Jack Cope. PeSA
Blood-Sister. Adrienne Rich. NoP
Blood-strained Banders, The. *Unknown.* AmFP; OuSiCo, *with music*
Blood Supply in New York City Is Low, The. Terry Stokes. NYP
Blood thudded in my ears. I scuffed. First Confession. X. J. Kennedy. ConAP; NCSH; NePoEA-2; NIP; PPP
Blood to Blood. Alvin Aubert. GP
Blood will not serve. A Poem for Heroes. Julia Fields. CNA
Blood, wine, and glee. The Dance of the Sword. *Unknown, tr. by* Tom Taylor. WaaP
Bloodhound, The. Edward Anthony. GDP
Bloodhounds look like sad old judges, The. Nice Day for a Lynching. Kenneth Patchen. PoNe
Blood-letting, The. Joy Harjo.. TWSS
Bloods and bucks of this lewd town, The. Horace, *tr. fr. Latin.* Odes, I, 25. OBVE
Bloody, A/ egg yolk. A burnt hole. Out of the Sea, Early. May Swenson. RFM
Bloody and a sudden end, A. John Kinsella's Lament for Mrs. Mary Moore. W. B. Yeats. CMoP; DTC; LiTM; MoAB; NoP; OAEL-2; OAEP
Bloody, and stained, and with mothers' cries. The Innocents. Jay Macpherson. OBCV
Bloody Brother, The, *sels.* John Fletcher, *and others.*
Drink To-Day, and Drown All Sorrow, *fr.* II, ii. OAEP
(Drink To-day.) HBV-2; ViBoPo
(Drinking Song.) ElL
Take, Oh, Take Those Lips Away, *fr.* V, ii, *st.* 1 *also in* Shakespeare's Measure for Measure. NoP
(Hide, Oh, Hide Those Hills of Snow, *st.* 2.) ViBoPo
(Love Song.) FaBoEn
(Song: "Take, oh take those Lips away.") PoEL-2
Bloody Conquests of Mighty Tamburlaine, The. Christopher Marlowe. *Fr.* Tamburlaine the Great, Pt. II, Act IV, sc. iii. ChTr
(Emperor of the Threefold World.) TrGrPo.
("Forward, then, ye jades!") ViBoPo
Bloody Cranesbill on the Dunes. E. J. Scovell. ChMP
Bloody day subsided, A: the volcano's lips. Postlude: For Goya. Ramon Guthrie. NMP
Bloody Injians, The. *Unknown.* CoSo
Bloody Pause. Astra. BrRo
Bloody Sire, The. Robinson Jeffers. CMoP; LiTM; NePA; PoA
Bloody trunk [*or* Bloudy trunck] of him who did possess[e], The. The Fall [*or* A Great Favorit Beheaded]. Sir Richard Fanshawe, *after the Spanish of* Luis de Góngoro. *Fr.* Il Pastor Fido. MePo; OBS; OBVE
Bloom. Alfred Kreymborg. HBMV
Bloom is result. To Meet a flower. Emily Dickinson. PoEL-5
Bloom Street. Angela McCabe. AmPA
Blooming Nelly. Burns. UnTE
Blooming Sally. *Unknown.* OBET
Blooms such as wither at finger-touch. Brian Coffey. *Fr.* Muse, June, Related. BIrV
Blossom, The. Blake. *Fr.* Songs of Innocence. GoJo; PB; PBBP
Blossom [*or* Blossome], The. John Donne. AnAnS-1; AWP; LiTB; MeLP; OBS; SeCP; UnPo
Blossom. Stanley Plumly. GeTw
Blossom, The. Shakespeare. *See* On a Day—Alack the Day.
Blossom is in her hair. Flowers. *Gond Oral Tradition, tr. by* V. Elwin *and* S. Hivale. WTO
Blossom of the almond trees. Almond Blossom. Sir Edwin Arnold. GN; HBV-1
Blossom of the Soul, The. Robert Underwood Johnson. AA
Blossom on the plum. March. Nora Hopper. HBV-1
Blossom Time. Wilbur Larremore. AA
Blossome, The. John Donne. *See* Blossom, The.
Blossoms. Frank Dempster Sherman. OBCA
Blossoms closed into buds, The. Adam's Dream. Howard Schwartz. VWA
Blossoms crowd the branches: too beautiful to endure. Spring-gazing Song. Hsüeh T'ao, *tr. by* Carolyn Kizer. BoWoP
Blossoms dropped before we really saw them, The. The Quick. Sean Jennett. NeBP
Blossoms have fallen, The. Princess Shikishi, *tr. fr. Japanese by* Donald Keene. BoWoP
Blossoms of babies. Handfuls. Carl Sandburg. AP
Blot in the 'Scutcheon, A, *sel.* Robert Browning.
Earl Mertoun's Song. HBV-1; OBEV; PoPle
("There's a woman like a dew-drop, she's so purer than the purest.") UnTE
Bloudy trunck of him who did possesse, The. *See* Bloody trunk of him who did possess, The.
Blouzelinda's Funeral. John Gay. *Fr.* The Shepherd's Week. OBEC
Blow Away the Morning Dew. *Unknown.* OBET
Blow, blow over me, sweet-scented breath. Wind of the Prairie. Grace Clementine Howes. GoYe
Blow! blow! The winds are so hoarse they cannot blow! Storm at Sea. Sir William Davenant. RoGo
Blow, Blow, Thou Winter Wind. Shakespeare. *Fr.* As You Like It, II, vii. AWP; CH; ChTr; ElL; ELP; EnRePo; GBL; GTBS; GTBS-P; HBV-2; HEIP; InPs; LiTB; NOBE; NoP; OAEL-1; OAEP; OBEV; PPoe; PrIm; SeCeV; TrGrPo; ViBoPo; WHA; WiR
(Amiens's Song.) OBSC
(Blow, Thou Winter Wind.) FaFP; TreF
(Song: "Blow, blow, thou winter wind.") CTC; FiP; PoEL-2
Blow, blow, ye spicy breezes. Ambrose Bierce. *Fr.* The Devil's Dictionary. OBAL
Blow, Boys, Blow ("I served my time in the Black Ball Line"). *Unknown.* *See* Black Ball Line, The.
Blow, Boys, Blow ("Now, it's blow, you winds"), *with music.* *Unknown.* ShS (*vers.* III)
Blow, Boys, Blow ("Oh, a Yankee ship came down the river"). *Unknown.* ShS (*vers.* II); TrAS, *with music*
Blow, Boys, Blow ("Oh, blow away, I long to hear you"), *with music.* *Unknown.* ShS (*vers.* I)
(Blow, Bullies Blow, *diff. vers.*) AmSS, *with music*
Blow, Bugle! Thomas Curtis Clark. PGD
Blow, Bugle, Blow. Tennyson. *See* Splendor Falls, The.
Blow, bugle, blow! Bugle Song of Peace. Thomas Curtis Clark. WBLP; WGRP
Blow, Bugles, Blow. John S. McGroarty. HBV-2
Blow, Bullies, Blow. *Unknown.* *See* Blow, Boys, Blow ("Oh, blow away . . .")
Blow Gabriel. *Unknown.* BluL
Blow gently over my garden. The Beloved. Katharine Tynan. HBV-2
Blow High! Blow Low! Charles Dibdin. HBV-1
Blow Me Eyes! Wallace Irwin. HBMV; InMe
Blow, Northern Wind. *Unknown.* GBL; OBEV; OxBM
(Love for a Beautiful Lady.) MeEL
Blow out the candles of your cake. For K. R. on Her Sixtieth Birthday. Richard Wilbur. NoP
"Blow out the light," they said, they said. Temper. Rose Fyleman. OxBChV
Blow out, you bugles, over the rich dead! The Dead. Rupert Brooke. 1914, III. HBV-2; OBWP; TreF; WGRP
Blow softly down the valley. The King of Ireland's Cairn. "Ethna Carbery." WPE
Blow Softly, Thrush. Joseph Russell Taylor. HBV-1
(Veery-Thrush, The.) AA

Blow the Candle Out ("It was late last Saturday evening"). *Unknown.* FaBoBa
Blow the Candle Out (The Jolly Boatsman). *Unknown.* AmFP
Blow the Candles Out ("When I was apprenticed in London"). *Unknown.* FSW
Blow the fife and clarinet. Jonathan Bing Dances for Spring. Beatrice Curtis Brown. SiSoSe
Blow the fire, blacksmith. *Unknown.* OxNR
Blow the Man Down. *Unknown.* AmFP; AmSS, 2 *vers., with music;* AS; BLSo, *with music;* FSW; ShS, 5 *vers. with music;* TrAS, *with music*
Blow the Stars Home. Eleanor Farjeon. PDV
Blow the Winds, I-Ho. *Unknown.* GBP; OxBoL
Blow, Thou Winter Wind. Shakespeare. *See* Blow, Blow, Thou Winter Wind.
Blow, West Wind. Robert Penn Warren. *Fr.* Notes on a Life to Be Lived. NoAM
Blow, wind, blow! and go, mill, go! Mother Goose. HBV-1; OxNR; SoPo; TiPo
Blow, Winds ("Blow, winds, and crack your cheeks!"). Shakespeare. *Fr.* King Lear, III, ii. TrGrPo; WHA
(King Lear to the Storm.) TreFT
(Lear's Speech to the Storm.) TW
Blow, Ye Winds [in the Morning]. *Unknown.* AmFP; AmSS, *with music;* FSW
Blow Ye Winds Westerly. *Unknown.* FSW
(Boston, Come-All-Ye, The, *with music.*) TrAS
(Fishes, The.) GBP
(Song of the Fishes, *with music.*) AmSS
Blow Your Trumpets, Angels. John Donne. *See* Holy Sonnets, VII.
Blowflies Buzz, The. *Unknown, tr. fr. Djambarbingu dialect by* Catherine Berndt. WTO
(Djalbarmiwi's Song.) CBAP
Blowflies explode from nowhere as I walk. The Swarm. Richard Moore. SUW
Blowing Bubbles. William Allingham. GN
(Bubble, The.) OnYI
Blown [*or* Blowne] in the morning, thou shalt fade ere noon. A Rose [*or* The Rose of Life]. Sir Richard Fanshawe. *Fr.* Il Pastor Fido. AWP; CavP; HBV-1; OBEV; OBS; PoEL-2; SeCePo
Blown out of the prairie in twilight and dew. Coyote. Bret Harte. BPAW
Blows the Wind Today. Robert Louis Stevenson. BSV; CH; LoBV; PoSH
(To S. R. Crockett.) EBVV; FaBoEn; FaBoPP; NOBE; OBNC
Bludy Serk, The. Robert Henryson. OxBoCh
Blue. Christopher Gilbert. *Fr.* Beginning by Example. FYAP
Blue/ on/ blue. Pinay. Virginia Cerenio. BrSi
Blue Alert. Eve Merriam. PCP
Blue and the Gray, The. Francis Miles Finch. AA; BLPA; BLPL; FaBoBe; HBV-2; PAH; PAL; PaPo; TreF; WBLP
Blue and White. Mary Elizabeth Coleridge. OBEV; OBVV
Blue Animals, The. Jon Anderson. AmPA
Blue are the beautiful skies! Sweeping the Skies. Elizabeth Anna Hart. CenHV
Blue as the blowpipe's petal of flame. Blue Flag. Dorothy Donnelly. NYBP
Blue Bell. *See* Bluebell.
Blue Black. Bloke Modisane. PBA
Blue-black flare at the bottom, The. Blue Bottle. Patricia Hampl. AMV-81
Blue-black mountains are etched, The. The Chance. Arthur Sze. BrSi
Blue Blood. James Stephens, *after the Irish of* David O'Bruaidar. MoAB; MoBrPo; OBMV; OxBI
Blue-blooded Mauser's first cousin, The. Guns. Ronald Crowe. AMV-81
Blue, blue is the grass about the river. The Beautiful Toilet. Ezra Pound, *after the Chinese.* OBVE
Blue Bog Children. Roger Weingarten. AmPA
Blue Bonnets over the Border. Sir Walter Scott. *See* Border Ballad.
Blue Booby, The. James Tate. AmPA; EAS; NoAM; NoP
Blue Bottle. Patricia Hampl. AMV-81
Blue Bottle, *with music. Unknown.* OuSiCo
Blue boughs, green fruit. The Furnished Room. James Merrill. NOBA
Blue Bowl, The. Blanche Bane Kuder. BLPA; FaBoBe
Blue-Butterfly Day. Robert Frost. RFM
Blue calf tethered. *Gond Oral Tradition, tr. by* V. Elwin *and* S. Hivale. WTO
Blue Church, The. Peter Balakian. AMV-80
Blue Closet, The. William Morris. NBM; VLP
Blue Coat, A. Gertrude Stein. *Fr.* Tender Buttons. PBWP
Blue Cockerel. W. S. Merwin. TwAmPo
Blue crane fishing in Cooloolah's twilight, The. At Cooloolah. Judith Wright. MoBrPo
Blue day, A/ a blue jay. March. Elizabeth J. Coatsworth. PDV; RHPC
Blue diamonds. Captured Bird. George Rachow. LFAC
Blue dusk ran between the streets: my love was winged within my mind, The. Babylon. "Æ." HBMV
Blue eagle and the demon of the steppes, The. The Staircase with a Hundred Steps. Benjamin Péret. EAS
Blue expanse of hyacinthine bloom, The. Memories of a Dorset Childhood in the 1730's. Thomas Cole. *Fr.* The Life of Hubert. NOEC
Blue Ey'd Mary. *Unknown.* CoMu
Blue-eyed and bright of face but waning fast. Staff-Nurse: New Style. W. E. Henley. In Hospital, X. BrPo; NBM
Blue-eyed Girl. *Unknown.* AmFP
Blue-eyed Mary. Mary E. Wilkins Freeman. OBCA
Blue-eyed Precinct Worker, The. Henri Coulette. MAT
Blue-eyed was Elf the minstrel. The Harp of Alfred. G. K. Chesterton. *Fr.* The Ballad of the White Horse. MoVE
Blue, faded purple, horizon mount, The. Peace. Samuel Greenberg. CrMA
Blue Flag. Dorothy Donnelly. NYBP
Blue Flag, The. Chris Miller. FaBoPa
Blue-Fly, The. Robert Graves. CMoP; MoVe; NoAM; NYBP
Blue Fly. Joaquim Maria Machado de Assis, *tr. fr. Portuguese by* Frances Ellen Bruckland. TTY
Blue Funk. Joel Oppenheimer. NeAP
Blue-geese, white-geese, you may say. Hilda Doolittle ("H. D."). *Fr.* The Flowering of the Rod. NOBA
Blue Ghosts. Stanley Snaith. ChMP
Blue Gift, The. David Perkins. NCSH
Blue Girls. John Crowe Ransom. ChTr; CMoP; GBL; LiTA; MoAB; MoAmPo; MoVE; NoAM; PrIm; TAP; TreFT; TwAmPo; VGW; WeW
Blue go up and blue go down. American Lights, Seen from Off Abroad. John Berryman. LCAP; OBAL
Blue gulf all around us. The Burial of the Dane. Henry Howard Brownell. AA; HBV-1
Blue Heron, The. Theodore Goodridge Roberts. CaP; NOBC; OBCV; PeCV
Blue Heron. Don Welch. GP
Blue hill is my desire, The. Hwang Chin-i, *tr. fr. Korean by* Ko Won. PBWP
Blue Hills beneath the Haze. Charles Goodrich Whiting. AA
Blue-Hole, The. Charles G. Bell. GrPl
Blue Homespun. Frank Oliver Call. CaP
Blue Horse, The. Melvin Walker La Follette. NePoEA
Blue Horses. Ed Roberson. PoBA
Blue Horses; West Winds. Anita Endrezze-Danielson. STE
Blue in the west the mountain stands. Vickery's Mountain. E. A. Robinson. MoAmPo
Blue iris, A. Shining. Kathleen Spivack. AMV-81
Blue is Our Lady's colour. Blue and White. Mary Elizabeth Coleridge. OBEV; OBVV
Blue is this night of stars. Inquietude. Pauli Murray. BlSi
Blue Island Intersection. Carl Sandburg. MoAmPo
Blue Jay [*or* Bluejay]. Robert Francis. ELU; LCAP; PCP
Blue Jay, The. D. H. Lawrence. FM
Blue jay [*or* Bluejay], fly to my windowsill! Invitation. Harry Behn. FaPON; SoPo
Blue jay scuffling in the bushes follows, The. On the Move. Thom Gunn. CMoP; HAP; LiTM; MP; NePoEA-2; NIP; NMP; NoP; OAEL-2; OxBTC; PPP; TwCP
Blue jay with a crest on his head, The. The Blue Jay. D. H. Lawrence. FM
Blue Jeaned Rock Queen in Search of Happiness on a Blind Thursday at 1/3 Speed and Crying, A. A. K. Redwing. VoR
Blue jumped a rabbit, run him one solid mile. Rabbit Foot Blues. *Unknown.* BluL
Blue Juniata, *sel.* Malcolm Cowley.
Streets of Air, The. PoA
Blue laguna rocks and quivers, The. Port of Holy Peter. John Masefield. OBMV
Blue landing lights make. Our Ground Time Here Will Be Brief. Maxine W. Kumin. AMV-81
Blue Lantern. Cathy Song. MAYP
Blue light, morning. This Decoration. Hayden Carruth. NNaP
Blue like Death. James Welch. CDW
Blue Max. Harvey Shapiro. GP
Blue Meridian, The. Jean Toomer. PoNe
Sels.
Brown River, Smile. AmNP; PoBA
"Each new American." BALP
Blue Moles. Sylvia Plath. BiP; NePoEA-2
Blue Monday. *Unknown.* AmFP
Blue Moonshine. Francis G. Stokes. NA
Blue Mountain. Roberta Hill. VoR

Blue mountains to the north of the walls. Taking Leave of a Friend. Li Po, *tr. by* Ezra Pound. SOTW; TwAmPo
Blue Owl Song. Alfred Kittner, *tr. fr. German by* Herbert Kuhner. VWA
Blue Peter. Stanislaus Lynch. OnYI
Blue pickup, A. Landscape, New Mexico. Kell Robertson. TAT
Blue, pink and yellow houses, and, afar. Tropical Town. Salomón de la Selva. HBV-2
Blue Ribbon at Amesbury, A. Robert Frost. NePA
Blue Ridge. Elizabeth Hodges. AMV-81
Blue Ridge, The. Harriet Monroe. HBMV
Blue Ridge. Ellen Bryant Voigt. MAYP
Blue robe on their shoulder[s], A. The Seven Fiddlers. Sebastian Evans. EBVV; OnMSP
Blue Room, The. Lorenz Hart. OBAL
Blue Ruth: America. Michael S. Harper. PoBA
Blue shadow of dawn settles, The. A Blessing. Mekeel McBride. MAYP
Blue sky and bluer sea with its white teeth showing. Sand Dunes and Sea. John Richard Moreland. HBMV
Blue sky, blue noon, and the secret line is flung. The Sounding. Conrad Aiken. CrMA
Blue sky, green fields, and lazy yellow sun! Spring Passion. Joel Elias Springarn. HBV-1
Blue Sleep. Winifred Bryher. PoA
Blue Sleigh. Winfield Townley Scott. MP; NePoAm
Blue Smoke. Frances Frost. SiSoSe
Blue smoke eclipsed, The. Eclipse. Amir Rashidd. NBP
Blue Sparks in Dark Closets. Richard Snyder. Psk
Blue Squills. Sara Teasdale. HBMV
Blue Stones. Larry Levis. DiL
Blue Swallows, The. Howard Nemerov. BiP; NoP
Blue Symphony. John Gould Fletcher. TwAmPo
Blue-Tail Fly, The. *Unknown.* BLSo, *with music;* FaFP; FSW; GBP; TreFT; ViBoFo
(Jim Crack Corn; or, The Blue Tail Fly.) PSoN, *with music*
Blue Tanganyika. Lebert Bethune. PoBA
Blue toads are dying all over Minnesota. Walking through a Cornfield in the Middle of Winter I Stumble over a Cow Pie and Think of the Sixties Press. Barbara Harr. BXAP
Blue Train for the South—but the Green Train for us, The. The Green Train. E. V. Rieu. SO
Blue Tropic. Luis Cabalquinto. BrSi
Blue unsolid tongue, if you could talk. The Overturned Lake. Charles Henri Ford. EAS
Blue Valentine, A. Joyce Kilmer. ISi
Blue water; upon it two possible movements. The Landfall. James Dickey. PoA
Blue Waves. David St. John. MAYP
Blue waves are sleeping, The. Serenade. James Joseph Callanan. OnYI
Blue wave's slumber and the rocky brow, The. Olive Grove. James Merrill. NePoAm
Blue West, The. Dahlia Ravikovich, *tr. fr. Hebrew by* Chana Bloch. PBWP
Blue Whale, The. Robert Watson. MAT
Blue Wing, The. Donald Hall. ConAP
Blue Winter. Robert Francis. LCAP
Bluebeard's Closet. Rose Terry Cooke. AA
Bluebeard's Wife. Daryl Hine. NoAM
Bluebell. Geoffrey Taylor. NeIP
Bluebells. Lucia Clark Markham. HBMV
Bluebells for Love. Patrick Kavanagh. IPY
Blue Bells of Scotland, The. *Unknown.* FWS, *ad. by* Annie McVicar *and* Dorothy Jordan; HBV-2; TreFS
Blue-Bird, The. Herman Melville. BLPL; NOBA
Blue-Bird, The. Alexander Wilson. AA
Bluebird, Bluebird, Fly through My Window. *Unknown.* FSW
Bluebird lives in yonder tree, A. To Miguel de Cervantes Saavadra. Richard Kendall Munkittrick. AA
Bluejay. *See* Blue jay.
Blueline. Ken Belford. NeAC
Bluely, bluely, styles from stone chimneys crippling smoke. In Memory of My Father. James Agee. DiL
Blueprint. D. B. Steinman. GoYe
Blues. John Fuller. NOBL
Blues. Horace Mungin. BOLo
Blues. Quandra Prettyman. BOLo
Blues/ Never climb a hill. Get Up, Blues. James A. Emanuel. AmNP; BOLo; PoBA
Blues Ain' Nothin', The [*or* De], *with music. Unknown.* AS; TrAS
Blues and Bitterness. Lerone Bennett, Jr. FF; NNP; PoBA
Blues Ballad. Kenneth Pitchford. *Fr.* Good for Nothing Man. CoPo
Blues Don't Change, The. Al Young. NPGG
Blues for an Old Blue. Walker Gibson. NYBP
Blues for Benny Kid Paret. Dave Smith. LiSp
Blues for Bessie. Myron O'Higgins. PoNe
Blues for Sister Sally. Lenore Kandel. NMM
Blues is a fine/ sister. Blues. Horace Mungin. BOLo
Blues is the black o' the face, The. Black Blues. Bloke Modisane. PBA
Blues lady/ with the beaded face. Grinding Vibrato. Jayne Cortez. BlSi
Blues meant Swiss-Up, The. Riding across John Lee's Finger. Stanley Crouch. PoBA
Blues Note. Bob Kaufman. CNA; NIP; PoBA
Blues Today, The. Mae Jackson. BOLo; PoBA
Bluff Henry the Eighth to six spouses was wedded. Henry VIII. *Unknown.* FaBoUs
Bluffalo, The. Jane Yolen. RHPC
Bluish, pale, The. Moontan. Mark Strand. NYBP
Blum. Dorothy Aldis. MoShBr
Blurry Cow. Chase Twichell. MAYP
Blurt, Master Constable, *sels.* Thomas Middleton.
"Love for such a cherry lip." ViBoPo
(Lips and Eyes.) HBV-1
(Song: "Love for such a cherry lip.") ElL
Midnight. ElL; SeCePo
True Love Ditty, A. ElL
Blush as of roses, A. Le Marais du Cygne. Whittier. PAH
Blush is on the flower, and the bloom is on the tree, The. My Own Cáilin Donn. George Sigerson. FaBoBe; HBV-1
Blushing rose and purple flower, The. Song [*or* A Song of Pleasure]. Philip Massinger. *Fr.* The Picture. UnTE; ViBoPo
Blyth Aberdeane, throw beriall of all tounis. To Aberdein. William Dunbar. FaBoPP
Blythsome Bridal, The. *Unknown, at. to* Francis Sempill. GBP
Bo peeper. *Unknown.* OxNR
Boa, The. J. J. Bell. RHPC
Boadicea [an Ode]. William Cowper. BeLS; FaPo; FaPoR; HBV-2
Boar, The. Robert Kelly. CoPo
Boar and the Dromedar, The. Henry Beissel. WHW
Boar of Badenoch and the Sow of Atholl, The. Naomi Mitchison. PoSH
Board Meets, The. John Gloag. FiBHP
Board of War has quelled the mutiny, The. To the Minister Liu. Yu Hsuan-chi, *tr. by* Geoffrey Waters. BoWoP
Boarder, The. Frederick Feirstein. NYP
Boarder, The. Louis Simpson. PoPl
Boarding, The. Denis Johnson. AMV-80; MAYP
Boarding nettings are triced for fight, The. Jack Creamer. James Jeffrey Roche. PAH
Boar's Head, The. *Unknown.* OxBM
(Boar's Head Carol, The.) MeEL
Boast no more fond Love, thy power. A Song. Thomas D'Urfey. CavP
Boast not proud English, of thy birth and blood. Roger Williams. GOA; SCAP
Boast of Masopha. Z. D. Mangoaela, *tr. fr. Sotho.* PeSA
Boastful Husbandman. *Unknown, tr. fr. German by* Louis Untermeyer. UnTE
Boasting Drunk in Dodge, The. *Unknown.* CoSo
Boasting of Sir Peter Parker, The. Clinton Scollard. PAH
Boat, The. Caroline Gilman. OBCA
Boat, The. Robert Kelly. CoPo
Boat, The. Robert Pack. CoAP; DiL; NePoEA-2
Boat-Haven, Co. Mayo. Geoffrey Taylor. NeIP
Boat is chafing at our long delay, The. Song. John Davidson. OBEV; OBVV; PoPle
Boat-load of emigrant Huns, A. The Wreck of the Deutschland. David Annett. BXAP
Boat Poem. Bernard Spencer. FaBoTw; OxBTC
Boat Sails Away, The. Kate Greenaway. MoShBr
Boat Song. Sir Walter Scott. *See* Hail to the Chief Who in Triumph Advances!
Boatman, The. Jay Macpherson. MoCV; OBCV
Boatman dance, boatman sing. Boatman's Dance. Daniel Decatur Emmett. FSW
Boatman, have they crossed? "Not all." Doom Ferry. Sir Arthur Quiller-Couch. EBVV
Boatman's Dance. Daniel Decatur Emmett. FSW
Boatman's Hymn. *At. to* Andrew Magrath, *tr. fr. Modern Irish by* Sir Samuel Ferguson. OnYI
Boatman's Song, The. Thomas Hardy. *Fr.* The Dynasts. WaaP
Boats. Rowena Bastin Bennett. SoPo; TiPo
Boats Are Afloat, The. Chu Hsi, *tr. fr. Chinese by* Kenneth Rexroth. NaP
Boats at Night. Edward Shanks. CH
Boats go out and the boats come in, The. The Fisher's Widow. Arthur Symons. HBV-1
Boats in a Fog. Robinson Jeffers. MOS; NoP; OxBA
Boats in the backyards, The. In the Fishing Village. Sheila Nickerson. WOLT

Boats sail on the rivers. The Rainbow. Christina Rossetti. *Fr.* Sing-Song. OxBChV; SoPo; TiPo
Boats that carry sugar. Freight Boats. James S. Tippett. FaPON
Boatswain! The Tempest. Shakespeare. OAEL-1
Bob Anderson, My Beau. *Unknown.* PAH
Bob McKinney. *Unknown.* BluL
Bob, nothing in me wants to tell you again. Homosexual Sonnets. Kenneth Pitchford. GP
Bob Southey! You're a poet—poet-laureate. Dedication [*or* Dedication to the Poet Laureate *or* Invocation *or* Southey and Wordsworth]. Byron. *Fr.* Don Juan. CTC; EnRP; FiP; LoBV; OAEL-2; OAEP; OBSV; PPoe; TrGrPo
Bob Stanford. *Unknown.* CoSo
Bob-tailed Flush, A. John R. Painter. BPAW
Bob was bathing in the Bay. Some Ruthless Rhymes, V. Harry Graham. CenHV
Bob White. George Cooper. HBVY
Bobber. Raymond Carver. GeTw
Bobbie's Cat. Gerald Locklin. GP
Bobbing in the waters of the womb. The Buddha in the Womb. Erica Jong. MAYP
Bobbing with the crowds. The Urban Experience: Part One. Lew Blockcolski. VoR
Bobby Blue. John Drinkwater. FaPON; SoPo
Bobby Campbell. *Unknown.* FSW
Bobby Shaftoe's gone to sea. Mother Goose. FSW; GBP; HBV-1; OxNR
Bobby's First Poem. Norman Gale. FiBHP; MoShBr; PV
Bob-ing split-able heads. Solitary Visions of a Kaufmanoid. James Cunningham. JB
Bobolink, The. Thomas Hill. HBV-1
Bobolink! Max Schling, Max Schling, Lend Me Your Green Thumb. Ogden Nash. PV
Bobolink! that in the meadow. The Bobolink. Thomas Hill. HBV-1
Bobolinks, The. Christopher Pearse Cranch. AA; GN
Boddynge flourettes bloshes atte the lyghte, The. *See* Budding floweret blushes at the light, The.
Bodhisattva Undoes Hell, A. Jerome Rothenberg. CoPo
Bodies of rusted cars hold. Nymphing through Car Windows (East Gallatin). Greg Keeler. WOLT
Bodies of the young are not the flower, The. James K. Baxter. Autumn Testament, 19. OCNZ
Bodies on fire. Black Hills Survival Gathering, 1980. Linda Hogan. STE; TWSS
Bodies that gleam like rare bronze in the fire. The War Dance. Robert V. Carr. PoOW
Bodiless, nameless God. Prayer of the Young Stoic. Stephen P. Dunn. TrPWD
Bodily Beauty. George Rostrevor Hamilton. HBMV
Body, The. William Bronk. VGW
Body, The. Robert Herrick. CaPo
Body. Valerie Worth. FAZ
Body, The/ of/ Benjamin Franklin. Epitaph. Benjamin Franklin. TRV
Body black in the rock spine of Quinag. Marry the Lass? Andrew Greig. PoSH
Body fat as my forearm, blunt-arrowed head. Snake Handling Religious Service. Charles Wright. *Fr.* Tattoos. GP
Body Fished from the Seine. Gregory Corso. GP
Body full of bees. "I Don't Hear Any Melody Breathing I Hear." John Gill. NeAC
Body is like a November birch facing the full moon, The. Solitude Late at Night in the Woods. Robert Bly. BiP; VGW
Body Is like Roots Stretching, The. Charles Reznikoff. VWA
Body is the soul's poor house, or home, The. The Body. Robert Herrick. CaPo
Body Is the Victory and the Defeat of Dreams, The. Katerina Anghelaki-Rooke, *tr. fr. Greek by* Philip Ram. WPOW
Body keeps spilling its sweet, heavy freight, The. Snow Train. Louise Erdrich. TWSS
Body lies under the ground. Dirge. Gavin Bantock. OxBTC
Body, long oppressed, The. This Corruptible. Elinor Wylie. MoAB; MoAmPo
Body my house. Question. May Swenson. HeIP; LiTM; NePoEA; PrIm; VGW
Body of a Rook. David Wevill. MoCV
Body perishes, the heart stays young, The. Old Age. *Zulu Oral Tradition, tr. by* H. Tracey. WTO
Body Politic, The. Donald Hall. MP; NePoEA
Body slumbers, humble as the dead, The. Lines in Order to Be Slandered. Paul Verlaine, *tr. by* T. Sturge Moore. SyP
Body will not reject plastic, The. The Therapeutist. Beth Bentley. AMV-80
Body's Beauty. Dante Gabriel Rossetti. The House of Life, LXXVIII. HBV-1; OAEL-2; TrGrPo; VLP
(Lilith.) PoEl-5
Body's Freedom. Helen Nelville. NePA
Body's products become, The. Dido. John Ashbery. *Fr.* Two Sonnets. CAPP; VGW
Body's Speech, The. Donal MacCarthy, 1st Earl Clancarty, *tr. fr. Irish by* Frank O'Connor. KiLC
Bofors A.A. Gun, The. Gavin Ewart. WaP
Bog. Leen Volwerk. PoSH
Bog and Candle. Robert D. Fitzgerald. CBAP
Bog Lands, The. William A. Byrne. AnIV
Bog Queen. Seamus Heaney. PAI
Bogac Bân. Darrell Figgis. AnIV
Bogey. Lee L. Berkson. AMV-81
Bogeyman, The. Jack Prelutsky. RHPC
Boggy Creek. *Unknown. See* Buffalo Skinners, The.
Boggy wood as full of springs as trees, A. The Idea of Entropy at Maenporth Beach. Peter Redgrove. FaBoMo
Bogland. Seamus Heaney. IPY; NoP
Bogs, purgatory, wolves and ease, by fame. Barten Holyday. FaBoEE
Bogus-Boo, The. James Reeves. AmMo; RHPC
Bohemia. Dorothy Parker. CrMA
Bohemian Girl, The, *sels.* Alfred Bunn.
When Other Lips and Other Hearts. TreF
I Dreamt I Dwelt in Marble Halls. TreFS
Bohemian Hymn, The. Emerson. WGRP
Bohemians, The. Ivor Gurney. MMA
Bohernabreena. Leslie Daiken. OnYI
Bohunkus. *Unknown.* YaD
Boisterous Poem about Poetry, A, *sel.* John Wain.
"I have a notion that the world is round." PP
Boke of Two Ladies, *sel.* David Morton.
Petition for a Miracle. ISi
Bolakins was a very fine mason. Lamkin. *Unknown.* AmFP
Bold, amiable, ebon outlaw, grave and wise. To a Crow. Robert Burns Wilson. AA
Bold Captain of the Body-Guard. Zagonyi. George Henry Boker. PAH
Bold Dragoon, A ("In the dragon's ride from out the north"). *Unknown.* OBET
Bold Dragoon, The ("My father is a knight and a man of high renown"). *Unknown.* OBET
Bold Fenian Men, The. *Unknown.* FSW
Bold Fisherman, The. *Unknown.* BaBo
Bold General Wolfe. *Unknown.* OBET
Bold Jack Donahue. *Unknown.* AmFP; FSW
Bold Lanty was in love, you see, with lively Rosie Carey. Lanty Leary. *Unknown.* ChTr
Bold Manning, *with music.* *Unknown.* ShS
Bold McCarthy. *Unknown. See City of Baltimore,* The.
Bold Pedlar and Robin Hood, The. *Unknown.* AmFP; ESPB
Bold Phelim Brady, the Bard of Armagh. *Unknown.* OnYI
(Bard of Armagh, The.) FSW
Bold *Princess Royal*, The, *with music.* *Unknown.* ShS (2 *vers.*)
Bold Reynard the Fox. *Unknown.* OBET
Bold Robert Emmet. Tom Maguire. OnYI
Bold Soldier, The. *Unknown.* FSW
Bold Troubleshooters. Peter Veale. NOBL
Bolding Vedas! Shanks New Nisa! Place-Names of China. Alan Bennett. FaBoPa; NOBL
Boldness[e] in Love. Thomas Carew. AnAnS-2;CaPo; ErPo; MePo; SeCV-1; UnTE
Boll Weevil Song, The. *Unknown. See* Ballit of de Boll Weevil, De.
Boll-weevil's coming, and the winter's cold. November Cotton Flower. Jean Toomer. CDC; NoAM; UnPo
Bologna, and Byron. Samuel Rogers. *Fr.* Italy. OBRV
Bolshevik who never gave heed to queen or to king, A. Sorley Maclean. Dain do Eimhir, XXX. NeBP
Bolsum Brown, *with music.* *Unknown.* AS
Bolt and bar the shutter. Mad as the Mist and Snow. W. B. Yeats. ChTr
Bomb Disposal, The. Ciaran Carson. CIP
Bombardment. Richard Aldington. MMA
Bombardment. D. H. Lawrence. MMA
Bombardment of Bristol, The. *Unknown.* PAH
Bomber, The ("Bomber climb out on the roof"). Robert Lowell. WaaP
Bombers. C. Day Lewis. CMoP; MoAB
Bombers spread out, temperature steady, The. War and Silence. Robert Bly. CAPP
Bombing Casualties: Spain. Sir Herbert Read. PPON
Bon jour, bon jour a vous! A Call for a Song. *Unknown.* OxBM
Bon Mot, A. *Unknown.* ErPo; POL

"Bon soir, ma chérie." Comrades in Arms: Conversation Piece. *Unknown.* ErPo
"Bona de Mortuis." Thomas Lovell Beddoes. ELU; TW
Bonac. John Hall Wheelock. MoVE
Bondage. "Owen Innsley." AA
Bondmen of Mizraim/ Were our fathers. Flowering without End. Stefan Zweig, *tr. by* Eden *and* Cedar Paul. *Fr.* Jeremiah. TrJP
Bond-slave to Christ, and in my bonds rejoicing. Paul. John Oxenham. TRV
Bone-aged is my white horse. Song [*or* Song—Talysarn]. Brenda Chamberlain. NeBP; NeIP
Bone and Skin, two millers thin. On Two Monopolists. John Byrom. FaBoCo; FaBoEE
Bone China. R. P. Lister. NYBP
Bone Poem. Nancy Willard. HoAn
Bone that has no marrow, The. Emily Dickinson. TAP
Bone Thoughts on a Dry Day. George Starbuck. GoYe; MP; NYBP; TwCP
Bone Yard. Jim Barnes. CDW
"Boneless tongue, so small and weak, The." The Tongue. Phillips Burrows Strong. TreFT; WBLP
Bones. Walter de la Mare. FiBHP; ShM
Bones, The. W. S. Merwin. ConAP; LiTM; NePoEA-2
Bones. Frederick Morgan. FAZ
Bones. Carl Sandburg. MOS
Bones are all there waiting their hour, The. After X-Ray. Linda Pastan. POL
Bones go under the soil, under the soil, The. Bones. Frederick Morgan. FAZ
Bones in the Desert. Ned White. BPAW
Bones of a French Lady in a Museum. Richard Gillman. NePoAm
Bones of Chuang Tzu, The. Chang Heng, *tr. fr. Chinese by* Arthur Waley. AWP
Bones of Incontention, The. Robert David Cohen. NYBP
Bones of My Father, The. Etheridge Knight. DiL
Bones of our fathers, The. Talking to the Townsfolk in Ideal, Georgia. Isaac J. Black. CNA
Boney, *with music.* *Unknown.* AmSS; ShS (2 *vers.*)
(Boney Was a Warrior.) FSW
Bonfire, The. Robert Frost. InvP
Bongaloo, The. Spike Milligan. AmMo
Bonhoeffer in his skylit cell. Christmas Trees. Geoffrey Hill. NOCV
Bonhomme Richard and *Serapis,* The. Philip Freneau. PAH
Bonie Doon. Burns. *See* Banks o' Doon, The.
Bonnard; a Novel. Richard Howard. CoAP; NYBP
Bonne Entente. F. R. Scott. FiBHP; OBCV; PeCV
Bonner's Ferry Beggar. Duane Clark. AMV-81
Bonnets So Blue. *Unknown.* OBET
Bonnie Annie. *Unknown.* ESPB (A *and* B *vers.*)
Bonnie Annie Livieston. *Unknown.* OxBB
Bonnie Black Bess. *Unknown.* *See* Dick Turpin and Black Bess.
Bonnie Blue Flag, The. Annie Chambers Ketchum. PAH
Bonnie Blue Flag, The, *with music.* Harry Macarthy. BLSo; PSoN
Bonnie, bonnie bairn who sits poking in the ase, The. Castles in the Air. James Ballantine. HBV-1
Bonnie Bower, The. *Unknown.* *See* Lament of the Border Widow, The.
Bonnie Broukit Bairn, The. "Hugh MacDiarmid." FaBoCh; HAP; InPS
Bonnie Charlie's now awa. Will Ye No Come Back Again? Lady Nairne. BSV
Bonnie Doon. Burns *See* Banks o' Doon, The.
Bonnie Dundee. Sir Walter Scott *See* Bonny Dundee.
Bonnie Earl of Moray [*or* Murray], The. *Unknown.* *See* Bonny Earl of Murray, The.
Bonnie George Campbell. *Unknown.* AmFP; AWP; CH; ELP; EnRP; FaBoBa; GBP; HBV-2; NoP (C *vers.*); OxBB, *with music*
(Bonny George Campbell.) BSV; GoTS; OxBoLi; PoPle; ViBoPo
(Bonnie James Campbell.) BaBo (A *and* B *vers.*); ESPB (A, B, C, *and* D *vers.*)
Bonnie House o' Airlie, The. *Unknown.* ESPB; OBEV; OxBB, *with music;* OxBS
Bonnie James Campbell. *Unknown.* *See* Bonnie George Campbell.
Bonnie Kilmeny gaed up the glen. *See* Bonny Kilmeny . . .
Bonnie Laddie's Lang a-Grouwin', The. *Unknown.* OxBS
Bonnie lassie, will ye go. The Birks of Aberfeldy. Burns. CTC; ViBoPo
Bonnie Lesley. Burns. CTC; GTBS; GTBS-P; NOBE; OBEC; OBEV
(O Saw Ye Bonny Lesley.) HVB-1
(Saw Ye Bonie Lesley.) OxBS
Bonnie "No" with smiling looks again, A. An Admonition to Young Lassies. Alexander Montgomerie. BSV
Bonnie Ship *The Diamond,* The. *Unknown.* FSW
Bonnie Wee Thing. Burns. HBV-1
Bonniest Bairn in a' the Warl', The. Robert Ford. GN
Bonniest lass that ye meet neist, The. For A' That an' A' That. *At. to* Burns. CoMu; UnTE
Bonny at Morn. *Unknown.* GBP
Bonny Baby Livingston. *Unknown.* BaBo; ESPB (A *and* C *vers.*)
Bonny Barbara Allan. *Unknown.* *See* Barbara Allen.
Bonny Bee Hom. *Unknown.* ESPB
Bonny Birdy, The. *Unknown.* ESPB
Bonny Brown Girl, The. *Unknown.* *See* Brown Girl, The.
Bonny Bunch of Roses [O], The. *Unknown.* FaBoBa; OxBoLi
Bonny burgh is Edinbro', the city brave and bright, A. Edinburgh. Arthur Guiterman. WhC
Bonny Dundee. Sir Walter Scott. *Fr.* The Doom of Devorgoil, II, ii. EnRP; FaBoCh; OBRV; OxBoLi; OxBS; SeCeV
(Bonnie Dundee.) HBV-2; Par, *abr.*
Bonny Earl of Livingston, The. *Unknown.* *See* Fair Mary of Wallington.
Bonny Earl of Murray [*or* o' Murray], The. *Unknown.* ESPB (A *and* B *vers.*); FaBoBa; HBV-2; OBEV; OxBB, *with music;* OxBS; PoPle; PrIm; ViBoFo
(Bonnie Earl of Moray [*or* Murray], The.) FaBoCh; FSW; OBS
(Bonny Earl o' Moray, The.) BSV; ELP; GoTS
Bonny Eloise. C. W. Elliot *and* J. R. Thomas. FSW
Bonny fine maid of a noble degree, A. Robin Hood and Maid Marian. *Unknown.* ESPB
Bonny George Campbell. *Unknown.* *See* Bonnie George Campbell.
Bonny Grey, The. *Unknown.* GBP
"Bonny heir, and the well-faird heir, The." The Heir of Linne. *Unknown.* BaBo; ESPB
Bonny Hind, The. *Unknown.* ESPB; ViBoFo
(Bonny Heyn, The.) OxBB
Bonny John Seton. *Unknown.* ESPB
Bonny Keel Laddie, The. *Unknown.* GBP
Bonny [*or* Bonnie] Kilmeny gaed up the glen. Kilmeny. James Hogg. *Fr.* The Queen's Wake. BSV; GoTS; HBV-2; OBEV; OBRV
Bonny Lass of Anglesey, The. *Unknown.* ESPB (A *and* B *vers.*)
Bonny Lassie O! John Clare. CH
Bonny Lizie Baillie. *Unknown.* BaBo; ESPB
Bonny Moorhen, The. *Unknown.* GBP
Bonsai [*or* Bonzai] tree, The. A Work of Artifice. Marge Piercy. IHMS; Psk
Bonum Est Mihi Quod Humiliasti Me, *abr.* Earl of Surrey. SiPS
Bony. Simon J. Ortiz. CDW
Bony black face, The. Esperanza. James Scully. LTB; NYP
Bonzai tree, The. *See* Bonsai tree, The.
Bood is beabig brighdly, love, The. To Bary Jade. Charles Follen Adams. OBAL
"Boogie with O. O. Gabugah." Al Young. NPGG
Boogie-woogie Ballads. St. Clair McKelway. PoNe
Book, A ("He ate and drank the precious words"). Emily Dickinson. *See* He ate and drank the precious words.
Book, A. ("There is no frigate like a book"). Emily Dickinson. *See* There is no frigate like a book.
Book, The. William Drummond of Hawthornden. *See* Book of the World, The.
Book, The. William Carson Fagg. LFAC
Book, The. Winfred Ernest Garrison. TRV
Book, A. Hannah More. PoSC
(Riddle, A: "I'm a strange contradiction.") GN
Book, A. Lizette Woodworth Reese. YeAr
Book, The. Henry Vaughan. JCP; SeCV-1
Book, a friend, a song, a glass, A. William Thompson. *Fr.* The Happy Life. ViBoPo
Book and Bookplate. John Masefield. WhC
Book-burning Pit, The. Lo Yin, *tr. fr. Chinese by* Edward H. Schafer. GLGT
Book I Held Grew Cold, The. Ernst Toller, *tr. fr. German by* Ashley Dukes. TrJP
Book lay unread in my lap, The. Going Home. Maurice Kenny. STE
Book-Lender's Lament. *Unknown.* FaBoUs
Book may be a flower, A. A Book. Lizette Woodworth Reese. YeAr
Book mites are eating the bindings. The Insect Shuffle Method. Gary Tapp. AMV-80
Book Moth: "A moth ate a word. To me it seemed." *Unknown, tr. fr. Anglo-Saxon by* Charles W. Kennedy. *Fr.* Riddles (Exeter Book). AnOE
Book of Books, The. Sir Walter Scott. *Fr.* The Monastery, *ch.* 12. TreFT
(Bible, The.) BLRP; TRV
(Sir Walter Scott's Tribute.) WBLP
Book of Gawain, The. Jack Spicer. *Fr.* The Holy Grail. PoM
Book of God's Madness, The, *sel.* Ralph Chubb.
"Liveliest effigy of the human race." PeHV
Book of How, The. Merrill Moore. MoAmPo
Book of Hunting, *sels.* Julians Barnes. WPE
"Time of grease beginneth at Midsummer day."

"When ye hunt at the roe, then shall ye see there."
"Wheresoever ye fare by frith or by fell."
Book of Job and a Draft of a Poem to Praise the Paths of the Living, The. George Oppen. NNaP
Book of Kells, The. Padraic Colum. BIrV
Book of Kells, The. Howard Nemerov. EaLo
Book of Leinster, *sel.* Comac, *tr. fr. Old Irish by* George Sigerson.
Heavenly Pilot, The. On YI
Book of Los, The, *sel.* Blake.
Immortal, The, *fr. ch.* II. LiTB; LoBV
Book of Merlin, The. Jack Spicer. CoPo
Book of Music, A. Jack Spicer. PoM
Book of Mysteries, The. Anthony Barnett. VWA
Book of Percival, The. Jack Spicer. CoPo
Book of Persephone, The, *sels.* Robert Kelly. PoM
Dance, The, 17.
"Earth is a woman who imagines us. She sings," 10.
Fourth Ode to Persephone, 16.
Glade, The, 18.
"Persephone is the woman buried," 11.
Second Ode to Persephone, 9.
Third Ode to Persephone, 14.
Versions, 12.
Book of Pilgrimage, The. Rainer Maria Rilke, *tr. fr. German by* Jessie Lemont. ILwL
Book of Rights, *sel. Unknown, tr. fr. Middle Irish by* James Clarence Mangan.
Testament of Cathaeir Mor, The. OnYI
Book of Songs. *Tr. fr. Chinese. See* Shih Ching.
Book of Tarshish, The, *sel.* Moses ibn Ezra, *tr. fr. Hebrew by* Solomon Solis-Cohen.
Joy of Life. TrJP
Book of the Dead, *sels. Unknown, tr. fr. Egyptian by* Robert Hillyer.
Adoration of the Disk by King Akhnaten and Princess Nefer Neferiu Aten. AWP
"Cattle roam again across the field, The." FaPON
Dead Man Ariseth and Singeth a Hymn to the Sun, The. AWP
He Approacheth the Hall of Judgment. AWP
He Asketh Absolution of God. AWP
He Biddeth Osiris to Arise from the Dead. AWP
He Cometh Forth into the Day. AWP
He Commandeth a Fair Wind. AWP
He Defendeth His Heart against the Destroyer. AWP
He Embarketh in the Boat of Ra. AWP
He Entereth the House of the Goddess Hathor. AWP
He Establisheth His Triumph. AWP
He Holdeth Fast to the Memory of His Identity. AWP
He Is Declared True of Word. AWP
He Is like the Lotus. AWP; EaLo
(Death as a Lotus Flower, *tr. by* Ulli Beier.) TTY
He Is like the Serpent Saka. AWP
He Kindleth a Fire. AWP
He Knoweth the Souls of the East. AWP
He Knoweth the Souls of the West. AWP
He Maketh Himself One with Osiris. AWP
He Maketh Himself One with the God Ra. AWP
He Maketh Himself One with the Only God, Whose Limbs Are the Many Gods. AWP
He Overcometh the Serpent of Evil in the Name of Ra. AWP
He Prayeth for Ink and Palette That He May Write. AWP
He Singeth a Hymn to Osiris, the Lord of Eternity. AWP
He Singeth in the Underworld. AWP
He Walketh by Day. AWP
Other World, The. AWP
Book of the Dead, Prayer 14. Mei Berssenbrugge. GP
Book of the Duchess[e], The, *sels.* Chaucer.
Dream, The. FiP
"Me thoughte thus: that it was May." PBBP
(May Morning.) WHA, *longer sel., mod. vers.*
Book of the Native, The, *sel* Sir Charles G. D. Roberts.
When the Sleepy Man Comes. HBV-1; HBVY
Book of the Two Married Women and the Widow, The, *sel.* William Dunbar.
Widow Speaks, The. PoEL-1
Book of the World, The. William Drummond of Hawthornden. HBV-1
(Book, The.) CH
(Lessons of Nature, The.) GTBS; GTBS-P
(World, The.) OBS
Book of Thel, The. Blake. ChER; EnRP; LAuP; NoP; OAEL-2; OBNC; PoEL-4; TEP
Sels.
Thel's Motto, 4 *ll.* ChTr
"Why cannot the ear be closed to its own destruction?" FaBoEn
Book of True Love, The, *sel.* Jean Ruiz, Archpriest of Hita, *tr. fr. Spanish by* Hubert Creekmore.
"When you're together with her, and you have a good excuse." ErPo
Book of Verses, A. Mordecai Marcus. AMV-80
Book of verses underneath the bough, A. Omar Khayyám, *tr. by* Edward Fitzgerald. *Fr.* The Rubáiyát of Omar Khayyám. HoPM; NOBE; OBEV; OBVV; SeCePo; SeCeV
Book of Wisdom, The. Stephen Crane. The Black Riders, XXXVI. HoPM; MoAmPo
Book Our Mothers Read, The. Whittier *See* Bible, The.
Book Reviews. Russell Davies. FaBoEE
Book Rises Out of the Fire, The. Edmond Jabès, *tr. fr. French by* Rosemarie Waldrop. VWA
Book slides from the shelf, pops open, The. A Book of Verses. Mordecai Marcus. AMV-80
Book was dull, its pictures, The. The Bride. Ralph Hodgson. HBMV
Book was writ of late called *Tetrachordon,* A. On the Detraction Which Followed upon My Writing Certain Treatises. Milton. SeCeV
Book you made, The. Love. Patrick Lane. NeAC
Booker T. and W. E. B. Dudley Randall. NoAM
Booker Washington Trilogy, The, *sels.* Vachel Lindsay.
John Brown, II. MoAmPo
Simon Legree—a Negro Sermon, I. HBMV; InMe; LiTA; MoVE; NePA; TAP
(Negro Sermon, a—Simon Legree.) MoAmPo
Bookmark. St. Theresa of Avila. *See* Lines Written in Her Breviary.
Bookra. Charles Dudley Warner. AA; HBV-2
Books. William Baer. AMV-81
Books. George Crabbe. *Fr.* The Library. OBEC
Books. Eleanor Farjeon. YeAr
Books. Wordsworth. *Fr.* The Prelude, V. PoEL-4
Books Are bridges. Golden Spurs. Virginia Scott Miner. SiSoSe
Books Are Keys. Emilie Poulsson. SiSoSe
Books, books, books! Elizabeth Barrett Browning. *Fr.* Aurora Leigh, I. WPOW
Books Fall Open. David McCord. OBCA
Books I have are made of lead, The. David McCord. Convalescence, VIII. WhC
Books, lips, hands. Hypodermic Release. Del Corey. AMV-81
Bookshop Idyll, A. Kingsley Amis. NePoEA; OxBTC
Bookworm, The. Walter de la Mare. TiPo
Bookworms, The. Burns. ChTr; ELU; FaBoEE; FiBHP
Boom! Howard Nemerov. LiTM; MP; NIP
Boom. Julian Lee Rayford. AMV-80
Boom/ The shrill whistle of the wolf. Bird of Power. Jim Tollerud. VoR
Boom above my knees lifts, and the boat, The. Sailing to an Island. Richard Murphy. IPY; NMP
Boomer Johnson. Henry Herbert Knibbs. BPAW
Boomerang. John Perreault. EAS
Boon, A. William Meredith. NePoEA
Boon Nature to the woman bows. The Tribute. Coventry Patmore. *Fr.* The Angel in the House. EBEV; HBV-1; OBNC
Boosting the Booster ("Boost your city, boost your friend"). *Unknown.* WBLP
Boot and a shoe and a slipper, A. High and Low. John Banister Tabb. TDH
Boot and Saddle ("Boot, saddle, to horse, and away!"). Robert Browning. Cavalier Tunes, III. HBV-2; OAEP; SoSe
Boot-soles and overalled haunches to the street. Janitor Working on Threshold. Margaret Avison. PeCV
Booth Killed Lincoln. *Unknown.* AmFP; OFD
Booth led boldly with his big bass drum. General William Booth Enters into Heaven. Vachel Lindsay. AmPP; CMoP; HBV-2; LiTA; LiTM; MoAB; MoAmPo; MoPo; NoAM; NOBA; OxBA; PoA; SeCeV; TAP; TreFS; TrGrPo; WGRP
Boothbay Whale, The. *Unknown.* FSW
Bootie Black and the Seven Giants. Mike Cook. JB
Boots. Kipling. BLPA; FaPoR; FPL; MoBrPo; WHA
Boots,/ Shoes. *Unknown.* OxNR
Boots and Saddles. Nicolas Saboly, *tr. fr. Provençal.* OHIP
Bop Lyrics. Allen Ginsberg. OBAL
Bo-peep/ Little Bo-peep. *Unknown.* OxNR
Bordello, Revisited. Eve Triem. GP
Border Ballad, A. Thomas Love Peacock. BXAP
Border Ballad. Sir Walter Scott. *Fr.* The Monastery, *ch.* 25. GN; HBV-2
(Blue Bonnets over the Border.) OxBS
(Border March.) EnRP
(March, March, Ettrick and Teviotdale.) BSV; ViBoPo
Border Burn, A. J. B. Selkirk. *Fr.* Epistle to Tammus. PoSH
Border Forecast, A. William Landles. PoSH
Border March. Sir Walter Scott *See* Border Ballad.
Border River. Alfred Goldsworthy Bailey. CaP

Border Widow's Lament, The. *Unknown. See* Lament of the Border Widow, The.
Bordering Manuscript. James Applewhite. PoA
Border Line. Langston Hughes. PoCh
Borderline Ballad. Richard Weber. PPON
Boreas blows on his high wood whistle. In Winter. C. H. Bretherton. InMe
Bored. Horatio Brown. PeHV
Bored lifeguard shrugs, The. Chippewa Lake Park. Warren Woessner. TAT
Bored Ostrich, The. *Unknown.* TDH
Bored with his wife that fatal day. The Brockton Murder; a Page out of William James. Knute Skinner. TW
Bores hed in hands [*or* hondes] I bring, The. The Boar's Head [*or* The Boar's Head Carol]. *Unknown.* MeEL; OxBM
Borges. Willis Barnstone. AMV-80
Borgia, thou once wert [*or* were] almost too august. On Seeing a Hair of Lucretia Borgia [*or* On Lucretia Borgia's Hair]. Walter Savage Landor. CABA; EnRP; HAP; InPK; OAEP; WeW
Boring executors approach their locks, The. Poem against Catholics. James Fenton *and* John Fuller. OBSV
Boris is dead. The fatalist parrot. Obituary. Weldon Kees. BoAnP
Born Again. Forugh Farrokhzad, *tr. fr. Persian by* Jascha Kessler *and* Amin Banani. PBWP
Born are we of fire. Mothers and Children. Orrick Johns. HBMV
Born by a whim. Signature. Dorothy Livesay. OBCV
Born from a world of tyrants beneath the western sky. Free America. Joseph Warren. FSW
Born I was to be old. Anacreontic. Robert Herrick. CaPo; OAEP; OxBoLi
Born[e] I was to meet with age. On Himself[e]. Robert Herrick. ChTr; FaBoEE; SeCV-1
Born in a fence-corner. Tumbling Mustard. Malcolm Cowley. AmFN
Born in a hovel, trained in hardship's school. Abraham Lincoln. A. S. Ames. OHIP
Born in a trance, we wake, observe, inquire. Another and the Same. Samuel Rogers. *Fr.* Human Life. OBNC
Born in my mouth, the naked beast leaned out. A Warning to My Love. David Wagoner. NePoEA-2
Born in the garret, in the kitchen bred. A Sketch [from Private Life]. Byron. OBNC; OBRV
Born in the purple the red grouse cry. The Kingship of the Hills. Will H. Ogilvie. PoSH
Born in the quarter-night, brash. Delta Traveller. Charles Wright. AmPA; LCAP
Born in wealth and wealthily nursed. Thomas Hood. *Fr.* Miss Kilmansegg and Her Precious Leg. EBVV
Born, nurtured, wedded, prized, within the pale. La Fayette. Dolly Madison. PAH; PAL
Born of the sorrowful of heart. For Paul Laurence Dunbar. Countee Cullen. Four Epitaphs, 3. BALP; CDC
Born on the Colorado. *Unknown.* CoSo
Born over there, in mist, not even God. Grandfather. Willis Barnstone. VWA
Born to these gentle stones and grass. Urn Burial. Ted Hughes. EBEV
Born was the island. *Tr. fr. Hawaiian.* WTO
Born with all arms, he sought a separate peace. The Deserter. John Manifold. CBAP; WaP
Born with the Vices. Thomas D'Urfey. *See* To Cynthia; a Song.
Born without a Chance. Edmund Vance Cooke. BLPA
Born Yesterday. Philip Larkin. NAs
Borne on a whispered sigh. Fallen Leaves. Kathryn Munro Tupper. CaP
Borough, The, *sels.* George Crabbe.
  "Can scenes like these withdraw thee from thy wood," *fr.* Letter I. OBRV
  Caroline, The, *fr.* Letter XI. SeCePo
  "Now is it pleasant in the summer-eve," *fr.* Letter IX. FM; OBRV
  Peter Grimes, Letter XXII. EnRP; OBNV; POEL-4; TEP
    (Poor of the Borough, The; Peter Grimes.) NoP
    "Alas, for Peter not a helping hand," *sel.* OBRV
    (Peter Grimes at Aldeburgh.) FaBoPP
    "He built a mud-wall'd hovel, where he kept," *sel.* SaC
  "Thus by himself compell'd to live each day," *sel.* FaBoEn; NOBE; OBNC; SeCePo
  Sailing upon the River, *fr.* Letter IX. OBNC
  Schools, Letter XXIV. CTC
  Slum Dwelling, *fr.* Letter XVIII. OBNC
  Suffolk Shore, The, *fr.* Letter XXIII. FaBoPP
  Vicar, The, *fr.* Letter III. OBNC; OBSV
  Winter Storm at Sea, The, *fr.* Letter I. EtS
  Winter Views Serene, *fr.* Letter IX. OBNC
"Borrowed." *Unknown.* BLRP
  (Cross Was His Own, The, 4 *sts.*) BLPA
Borrowed light went through the dark, The. Jack Rabbit. Adrien Stoutenburg. BoAnP
Borrowed wings on his ankles. Perseus. Louis MacNeice. CoBMV; LiTM
Borrower of Salt, The. Oscar Williams. *Fr.* Variations on a Theme. LiTA; NePA
Borrowing. Emerson. WhC
Borrowing Days, The. *Unknown.* GBP
Bosky Steer, The. Henry Herbert Knibbs. BPAW
Bos'n Hill. John Albee. AA
Bosnia. November. And the mountain roads. Sarajevo. Lawrence Durrell. GTBS-P
Bosom/ that was meant to bloom, A. I'll Tell You What a Flapper Is. Anne Hobson Freeman. GrPl
Bosom of, A/ green buds. Mare Nostrum. Joel Oppenheimer. NeAP
Boss, The. James Russell Lowell. OBAL; SaC
Boss comes up to me with a five dollar bill, The. Get Thee behind Me, Satan. Lee Hays, Millard Lampell, *and* Pete Seeger. FSW
Boss he had a yaller gal. Git Along Down to Town. *Unknown.* AmFP
Boss I just discovered what. Archys Last Name. Don Marquis. *Fr.* Archys Life of Mehitabel. CrMA
Boss I saw a picture. Archy a Low Brow. Don Marquis. *Fr.* Archys Life of Mehitabel. WhC
Boss knows what shape I'm in, The. He tells me. Drunk Last Night with Friends, I Go to Work Anyway. Philip Dow. NPGG
Boss Machine-Tender after Losing a Son, The. Paul Corrigan. AMV-81
Boss's Wife, The. *Unknown.* CBAP
Boston ("And this is good old Boston"). John Collins Bossidy. *See* Boston Toast, A.
Boston ("I come from the city of Boston"). *At. to* Samuel C. Bushnell. OBAL; OxBoLi. *See also* Boston Toast, A.
Boston. John Boyle O'Reilly. PAH
Boston Ballad, A. Walt Whitman. OBAL
Boston Boy Went out to Yuma, A. "D. D." ShM
Boston Burglar, The. *Unknown.* AmFP; CoSo, *with music;* FSW; ViBoFo
Boston Charlie. Walt Kelly. FiBHP; GoJo
Boston Come-All-Ye, The. *Unknown. See* Blow Ye Winds Westerly.
Boston Evening Transcript, The. T. S. Eliot. InPK; NePA
Boston has a festival. In the Public Garden. Marianne Moore. NOBA
Boston Hymn. Emerson. PAH; PAL; TRV; WGRP
Boston in Distress. *Unknown.* NOEC
Boston, Lincolnshire. *Unknown.* FaBoPP; GBP
Boston. Lord God, the ocean never to windward. George Starbuck. Poems from a First Year in Boston. NePoEA-2; TwAmPo
Boston Nursery Rhymes. Joseph Cook. InMe; QQQ; SpRo
Boston Toast, A. John Collins Bossidy. BLPA; YaD
  ("And this is good old Boston.") CenHV
  (Boston.) AmFN
  (Boston, *sl. diff. version:* "I come from the city of Boston.") FaBoCo; FaBoEE; OBAL (*At. to* Samuel C. Bushnell); OxBoLi (*At. to* Samuel C. Bushnell)
  (On the Aristocracy of Harvard.) HBV-1; WhC
  (To Boston.) TreFS
Boswell by my bed. Reading in War Time. Edwin Muir. WaP
Bosworth Field, *sel.* Sir John Beaumont.
  Richard III's Speech. JCP
Bot now the haisty, egir, and wild Dido. Virgil, *tr. by* Gavin Douglas. *Fr.* The Aeneid, IV. OBVE
Bot of ane bowrd in to bed I sall yow breif yit. William Dunbar. *Fr.* The Tretis of the Tua Mariit Wemen and the Wedo. EBEV
Bo-talee rode easily among his enemies. The Fear of Bo-talee. N. Scott Momaday. STE
Botanic Garden, The, *sels.* Erasmus Darwin.
  Pt. I. The Economy of Vegetation.
    Immortal Nature. OBEC
    Steam Power. NOEC; OBEC
  Pt. II. The Loves of the Plants.
    Nightmare. NOEC
    Vegetable Loves. OBEC
Botanist's Vision, The. Sydney Dobell. VLP
Botany Bay. John Freeth. NOEC
Botany Bay ("Come all you men of learning"). *Unknown.* ViBoFo
Botany Bay ("Farewell to old England"). *Unknown.* FSW; PoAu-1
Botany Lesson. F. D. Reeve. AMV-80
Both Cherokee and Samek saw you, and tell. Bear Dance. Ron Rogers. STE
Both gentlemen, or yoemen bould. A True Tale of Robin Hood. *Unknown.* ESPB
Both Less and More. Richard Watson Dixon. LoBV
Both my child. Teitoku, *tr. fr. Japanese by* Nobuyuki Yuasa. OFD
Both My Grandmothers ("Both my grandmas came from far away"). Edward Field. Str
Both old and young, I pray lend an ear. The Nightingale. *Unknown.* ShS

Both Plutarch and Pausanius tell a story. Kleomedes. David Wright. NoAM
Both skyed. Japanese Print. Austin Clarke. IPY
Both were so shy. Two. Robert Canzoneri. HoPM
Both you two have. To the Yew and Cypress to Grace His Funeral. Robert Herrick. QFR
Bothie of Tober-na-Vuolich, The, *sels.* Arthur Hugh Clough.
"And he continued more firmly, although with stronger emotion," *fr.* Bk. VII. VLP
"Philip returned to his books, but returned to his Highlands after," *fr.* Bk. IX. VLP
"There is a stream, I name not its name," *fr.* Bk. III. BoNaP; VLP
(Highland Glen near Loch Ericht, A.) FaBoPP
Bothwell Bridge. *Unknown. See* Battle of Bothwell Bridge, The.
Botticellian Trees, The. William Carlos Williams. AmPP; LiTA
Bottle, The. Walter de la Mare. MoPo
Bottle, The. Al Levine. GrPl
Bottle, coarse tumbler, loaf of bread. Still Life. Walter de la Mare. EyDe
Bottle of Chianti, The. Raymond Souster. ELU
Bottle of perfume that Willie sent, The. Limerick. *Unknown.* WhC
"Bottle Should Be Plainly Labeled 'Poison.'" Sara Henderson Hay. GoYe
Bottle Up and Go. *Unknown.* FSW
Bottled [*or* Bottled: New York]. Helene Johnson. BlSi; CDC; PoBA
Bottles are empty, the breakfast was good, The. The Morning After. Heine, *tr. by* Louis Untermeyer. ErPo; UnTE
Bottomed by tugging combs of water. The Swan. W. R. Rodgers. NeBP; NMP; NoAM
Bottom's Dream. Philip Dow. NPGG
Bottom's Song. Shakespeare. *Fr.* A Midsummer Night's Dream, III, i. CTC
("Ousel cock so black of hue, The.") PB; ViBoPo
("Woosel cock so black of hue, The.") PBBP
Boudoir Lament. Yü Hsüan-chi, *tr. fr. Chinese by* Geoffrey Waters. BoWoP
Bough will bend, the leaf will sometime fall, The. Fable. Mary Mills. NePoAm
Boughs do shake and the bells do ring, The. *Unknown.* OxNR
Boughs, the boughs are bare enough, The. Winter with the Gulf Stream. Gerard Manley Hopkins. CMoP; NoAM; SyP; VLP
Bought. Francis Douglas Davison. NeBP
Bought/ from the flower-peddler's tray. Tune: Magnolia Blossom. Li Ching-chao, *tr. by* C. H. Kwôck *and* Vincent McHugh. PBWP
Bought at the drug store, very cheap; and later pawned. Green Light. Kenneth Fearing. VGW
Bought Embrace, A. G. S. Fraser. WaP
Bought Locks. Martial, *tr. fr. Latin by* Sir John Harington. AWP
Boulder Dam. May Sarton. SaC
Bounce, buckram, velvet's dear. *Unknown.* OxNR
Bounce to Fop; an Heroick Epistle from a Dog at Twickenham to a Dog at Court. Pope. FM
Bouncing Ball. Sara Ruth Watson. SoPo
Bouncing! bouncing! on the beds. In the Motel. X. J. Kennedy. RHPC; Str
Bound. Theodore Roethke. PoA
Bound and free. Eudaimon. Kathleen Raine. PBWP
Bound by unnatural sleep. Fairy Tales. Jane Flanders. DFT
Bound Down to Newfoundland, *with music. Unknown.* ShS
Bound in a moonlight circle. The 49 Stomp. Lew Blockcolski. VoR
Bound lion, almost blind from meeting their gaze and popcorn. Riverdale Lion. John Robert Colombo. PeCV
Bound No'th Blues. Langston Hughes. AmNP; BiP
Bound to his torment on the wheel that turns. The Dream. "Michael Field." SyP
Bound to my heart as Ixion to the wheel. Dirge for the New Sunrise. Edith Sitwell. *Fr.* Three Poems of the Atomic Bomb. CMoP; EaLo; MoAB; MoBrPo; SeCePo
Boundaries. Carrol B. Fleming. SUW
Boundaries. Roberta Spear. MAYP
Bounded unbrokenly by summer weather. The Made Lake. Louise Townsend Nicholl. NePoAm-2
Bountiful in charity. Praise of Mary. *Unknown, tr. by* Henry Sorg. ISi
Bounty. Josephine Miles. NoAM
Bounty of Jehovah Praise, The, *with music.* George Sandys. AH
Bounty of Our Age, The. Henry Farley. FaBoCh; SeCePo
("To see a strange [*or* quaint] outlandish fowl.") FaBoEE; ViBoPo
Bouquet for Jerry Ford, A. Mordecai Marcus. SOTS
Bouquet in Dog Time. Hayden Carruth. GrPl
Bouquet of Belle Scavoir. Wallace Stevens. MoAB; MoAmPo
Bouquets. Robert Francis. DFF; GP
Bourbons. Walter Savage Landor. OBSV
Bourgeois Poet, The, *sels.* Karl Shapiro.
"As you say (not without sadness), poets don't see, they feel." PP
"Bourgeois poet closes the door of his study and lights his pipe, The." PP
Bourne, The. Christina Rossetti. ELP; FaBoEn; HBV-2; LoBV; OBNC
Bourtree, bourtree, crookit rung. The Elder, or Bourtree [*or* The Elder Tree]. *Unknown.* ChTr; GBP
'Bout th'husband oke, the vine. To Castara, upon an Embrace. William Habington. AnAnS-2
Bout with Burning. Vassar Miller. LiTM; MoAmPo; NePoEA
Bouzouki. Kenneth O. Hanson. GP
Bow all desires—even unknown ones—I had. After Reading a Book on Abnormal Psychology. Ernest G. Moll. ELU
Bow Down, Mountain, *with music.* Norma Farber. AH
Bow down, my song, before her presence high. Thysia, III. Morton Luce. HBV-1
Bow down my soul in worship very low. Russian Cathedral [*or* St. Isaac's Church, Petrograd]. Claude McKay. AmNP; CDC; PoBA
Bow Down Your Head and Cry. *Unknown.* CoSo; WTO
Bow-wow, says the dog. *Unknown.* OxNR
Bow, wow, wow,/ Whose dog art thou? Mother Goose. OxNR; TiPo
Bowed by the weight of centuries he leans. The Man with the Hoe. Edwin Markham. AA; BLPA; BLPL; EaLo; FaFP; HBV-2; LiTA; MoAmPo; OHFP; PPON; PrIm; SaC; TreF; TrGrPo; TRV; WBLP; WGRP
Bower of Bliss, The. Spenser. *Fr.* The Faerie Queene, II, 12. CH; FaBoEn; FiP; LoBV; OBSC; PoEL-1
("Eftsoones they heard a most melodious sound.") NOBE
(Gather the Rose.) WHA
Bower of Peace, The. Robert Southey. *Fr.* Ode Written during the War with America, 1814. PAH
Bowery, The. Charles Hale Hoyt. FSN, *with music;* TreF; YaD
Bowery. David Ignatow. CTBA
Bowge of Courte, The. John Skelton. AAS
Bowl. Wallace Stevens. PAI
Bowl of Roses, A. W. E. Henley. MoBrPo
Bowline, The. A. P. Herbert. WhC
Bowling-Green, The, *sel.* William Somervile.
"Where fair Sabrina's wand'ring currents flow." NOEC
Bowling Green. *Unknown.* FSW
Bows glided down, and the coast, The. Ballad of the Long-legged Bait. Dylan Thomas. CoBMV; SeCeV
Box for Tom, A. James Tate. FiCP
Boxcar Poem, The ("The boxcars drift by"). David Young. AmPA
Box cars run by a mile long. Work Gangs. Carl Sandburg. SaC
Boxer bitch is pregnant, The. Geisha. Gary Gildner. GP; POL
Boxer Loses Face and Fortune. Lucilius, *tr. fr. Greek by* Tom Dodge. LiSp
Boxer Shorts Named Champion. Melvin Douglass Brown. LFAC
Boxer Turned Bartender, The. Gary Allan Kizer. LFAC
Boxes break, The/ At the corners. Christmas Ornaments. Valerie Worth. PChr
Boy, A. John Ashbery. DiL; NeAP
Boy, The. Eugene Field. NA
Boy, The; or, Son of Rip-off. Malcolm Glass. BXAP
Boy Actor, The. Noel Coward. OxBTC
Boy and the Flute, The. Björnstjerne Björnson, *tr. fr. Norwegian by* Sir Edmund Gosse. AWP; PoPl
Boy and the Geese, The. Padraic Fiacc. NeIP
Boy and the Lantern, The, *abr.* Evaristo Ribera Chevremont, *tr. fr. Spanish by* Julio Marzán. InW
Boy and the Mantle, The. *Unknown.* ESPB; OxBB; UnTE
Boy and the Parrot, The. John Hookham Frere. OxBChV
Boy and the Snake, The. Charles *and* Mary Lamb. OxBChV
Boy and the Wolf, The. John Hookham Frere. HBV-1; HBVY
Boy at a Certain Age. Robert Francis. DFF
Boy at Target Practice; a Contemplation. W. R. Moses. NYBP
Boy at the Window. Richard Wilbur. NoP
Boy Breaking Glass. Gwendolyn Brooks. NoAM; NoP
Boy! Bring an Ounce. Isaac Hawkins Browne. *Fr.* A Pipe of Tobacco. BXAP
("Boy! bring an ounce of Freeman's best.") Par
Boy, bring me candles on a silver salver. Candles. Hélène Swarth, *tr. by* Jonathan Crewe. WPOW
Boy Brittan. Forceythe Willson. PAH
Boy brought in the logs to start the fire, The. Mesón Brujo. E. A. Lacey. PeHV
Boy called to his team, The. Late Autumn. Andrew Young. MoVE
Boy claims he saw you on a bicycle last week, A. The Use of Fiction. Naomi Shihab Nye. MAYP
Boy drove into the city, his wagon loaded down, A. The Little Black-eyed Rebel. Will Carleton. FaPON; PAH
Boy from his bedroom-window, The. At Ballyshannon, Co. Donegal. William Allingham. FaBoPP
Boy from Rome, Da. T. A. Daly. FaPON
Boy had run all the way home, The. Mending Crab Pots. Dave Smith. GeTw
Boy He Had an Auger, A, *with music. Unknown.* AS

Boy, I detest the Persian pomp. The Preference Declared. Horace, *tr. by* Eugene Field. Odes, I, 38. InPK
Boy, I hate their empty shows. Persian Fopperies [*or* Simplicity]. Horace, *tr. by* William Cowper. Odes, I, 38. AWP; InPK; OBVE
Boy in Ice. Laurie Lee. NYBP
Boy in the Lamont Poetry Room, Harvard. D. G. Jones. PeCV
Boy in the Roman Zoo. Archibald MacLeish. NCSH
Boy is as old as the stars, A. To My God in His Sickness. Philip Levine. NNaP
Boy looked out of eyes like Euclid's eyes, The. Form Was the World. Maurice English. NYBP
Boy-mad no longer. Epigram. Rufinus, *tr. by* Alan Marshfield. PeHV
Boy-Man. Karl Shapiro. NYBP; SoSe
Boy named Simon sojourned in a dale, A. Simple Simon. Harriet S. Morgridge. AA
Boy of eighteen years mid myrtle-boughs, A. Le Jeune Homme Caressant Sa Chimère. John Addington Symonds. OBVV
Boy of fifteen, A. Honi Soit Qui Mal Y Pense. Ian Young. PeHV
Boy of Quebec, The. *At. to* Kipling. FaBoNo
(Limerick: "There was a small boy of Quebec.") HBV-2; HBVY
("There was a young man of Quebec.") FaBoCo
Boy Playing an Organ. Francis Sweeney. GoBC
Boy, presuming on his intellect, A. At Woodward's Gardens. Robert Frost. ImOP; PoA
Boy Reciter, The. David Everett. *See* Tall Oaks from Little Acorns Grow.
Boy rehearsing the Continental Stroll, The. American Bandstand. Michael Waters. MAYP
Boy Remembers in the Field. Raymond Knister. CaP; NOBC
Boy Riding Forward Backward. Robert Francis. LCAP; NePoAm-2
Boy Serving at Table, The. John Lydgate. OxBChV
Boy should have an open fireplace, A. A Boy's Need. Herbert Clark Johnson. PoNe
Boy sits in the classroom, The. Learning Experience. Marge Piercy. FF
Boy stood in the supper-room, The. *Unknown.* CenHV
Boy stood on the burning deck, The. Casabianca. Felicia Dorothea Hemans. BeLS; BLPA; EtS; FaBoBe; FaBoPa; FaFP; FaPON; FPL; HBV-2; HBVY; PaPo; TreF; WBLP
Boy stood on the burning deck, The/ Eating peanuts by the peck. Peanuts. *Unknown.* FaFP
Boy stood on the burning deck, The/ His feet were covered with blisters. A Fragment. *Unknown.* FaBoPa
Boy stood on the burning deck, The/ His fleece was white as snow. Familiar Lines. *Unknown.* FiBHP
Boy stoops, picking greens with his mother, A. Greens. David Ray. VGW
Boy that is good, The [*or* A]. The Description of a Good Boy. Henry Dixon. OxBChV; OxNR, *st.* 1
Boy that is truthful and honest, A. The Boy We Want. *Unknown.* WBLP
Boy Thirteen, A. Jeff Irish. DL
Boy Trash Picker. Jim Howard. FAZ
Boy Wandering in Simms' Valley. Robert Penn Warren. DFF; SoSe
Boy was lying upside-down from me, The. Too Dark. Mark McCloskey. PoA
Boy Washington, The. Dorothy Brown Thompson. SiSoSe
Boy watched the sun, The. Driving Home after a Funeral. Gregory Orr. GeTw
Boy We Want, The. *Unknown.* WBLP
Boy who fell into the Morning Glory Pool, The. Morning Glory Pool. Sandra McPherson. LCAP
Boy who has crawled, The. Green Pastures. Dick Allen. AMV-80
Boy Who Laughed at Santa Claus, The. Ogden Nash. CenHV
Boy Who Smells like Cocoa, A. Robert Hershon. NeAC
Boy who throws the ball, The. The Beadle's Testimony. Jerome Rothenberg. NNaP
Boy, whose little, confiding hand. The Locomotive to the Little Boy. Benjamin R. C. Low. HBMV
Boy with a Cart, The, *sel.* Christopher Fry.
"In our fields, fallow and burdened, in grass and furrow." LiTB
Boy with a Hammer. Russell Hoban. PCP
Boy with His Hair Cut Short. Muriel Rukeyser. InPK; LiTM; MoAB; MP; PoPl; RoGo; TwAmPo; TwCP; VGW; WPE
Boyang the Wandering Recluse. Al Robles. BrSi
Boyhood. Wordsworth. *Fr.* The Prelude. WHA
Boyne Walk, The. F. R. Higgins. OxBI
Boyne Water, The. *Unknown.* AnIV; FaPoR; OnYI
Boys, The. Oliver Wendell Holmes. HBV-1; WBLP
Boys. Winifred M. Letts. HBMV
Boys/ I don't promise you nothing. Admonitions. Lucille Clifton. BPo; InPS; NMM
Boys and girls come out to play. Mother Goose. OxNR
Boys and girls, we pledge allegiance. Dianae Sumus in Fide. Catullus, *tr. by* Horace Gregory. MOON
Boys and Sport. Solon, *tr. fr. Greek by* John Addington Symonds. PeHV
Boys are comin' to town, The!—Whoop la! Comin' to Town. Robert V. Carr. BPAW
Boys, are ye calling a toast to-night? Admiral Death. Sir Henry Newbolt. VLP
Boys. Black. Gwendolyn Brooks. CNA
Boys Brushed By, The. Catherine Gonick. AMV-80
Boys, by Girls Held in Their Thighs. John Peale Bishop. ErPo
Boys' cocks, Diodore. Epigram. Strato, *tr. fr. Greek by* Thomas Meyer. PeHV
Boys flying kites haul in their white-winged birds. Words. *Unknown.* PoLF
Boys in October. Irving Layton. OBCV
Boys in sporadic but tenacious droves. The Horse Chesnut Tree. Richard Eberhart. CMoP; CrMA; LiTM; MoAB; MoAmPo; NePA; NePoAm; PoPl
Boy's Mother, A. James Whitcomb Riley. HBVY; OHIP
Boys' Names. Eleanor Farjeon. SUS; TiPo
Boy's Need, A. Herbert Clark Johnson. PoNe
Boys of Mullabaun [*or* Mullaghbawn], The. *Unknown.* BIrV; GBP
Boys of Sanpete County, The. *Unknown.* AmFP
Boys of the Island, The, *with music.* Larry Gorman. ShS
Boys of These Men Full Speed. Muriel Rukeyser. NNaP
Boys of Tyre are beautiful, The. Epigram. Meleager, *tr. by* Peter Whigham. PeHV
Boys of Wexford, The. *Unknown.* ELP
Boy's Place, A. Rose Burgunder. PDV
Boy's Prayer, A. Henry Charles Beeching. *See* Prayers.
Boy's Song, A. James Hogg. CH; FaPON; FaPoR; HBV-1; HBVY; MoShBr; OBEV; OnUR; OxBChV; PoPle; WiR
Boy's Summer Song, A. Paul Laurence Dunbar. SiSoSe
Boys, these aches and pains will make us men. Rainer Maria Rilke Returns from the Dead to Address the Junior Military School at Sankt Pölten. John Engman. LTB
Boy's Will, Joyful Labor without Pay, and Harvest Home, *sel.* Robert Penn Warren.
Work. SaC
Boysick (by gadzooks thunderstruck), The. The Honey Lamb. Jonathan Williams. PoM
Bozzy and Piozzi, *sel.* "Peter Pindar."
Introduction and Anecdotes. PoEL-3
Braced against the rise and fall of ocean. Korea Bound, 1952. William Childress. AmFN
Braced in the sinewy vigour of thy breed. The Horse and His Rider. Joanna Baillie. NOEC
Bracelet, The. Thomas Stanley. AnAnS-2
Bracelet of Grass, The. William Vaughn Moody. AP
Bracelet, The: To Julia. Robert Herrick. HBV-1; OBEV; TrGrPo
Bracelets of cold spume wreath my city ankles. Finisterra. Bayla Winters. AMV-81
Bracken Hills in Autumn. "Hugh MacDiarmid." NoP
Bracken on the hillside. November. Aileen Fisher. SiSoSe; TiPo
Brackish reach of shoal off Madaket, A. The Quaker Graveyard in Nantucket. Robert Lowell. AP; CMoP; CoBMV; HAP; LiTM; MiAP; MoAB; MoPo; MoVE; MOS; NePA; NMP; NoAM; NOBA; NoP; OxBA; SeCeV; TAP; TwAmPo; UnPo; ViBoPo
Braddan Vicarage. Thomas Edward Brown. FaBoPP
Braddock's Fate, with an Incitement to Revenge. Stephen Tilden. PAH
Brady (A *and* B *vers.*), *with music.* *Unknown.* AS
Braemar. Galway Kinnell. PoA
Braes o' Gleniffer, The. Robert Tannahill. OBRV
Braes o' Yarrow, The. *Unknown.* *See* Dowie Houms o' Yarrow, The.
Braes of Yarrow, The. William Hamilton. OBEC
Braes of Yarrow, The. John Logan. BSV; GTBS; GTBS-P; HBV-1; OBEC
Braggart! Denis Wrafter. OnYI
Braggart March stood in the season's door, The. The Passing of March. Robert Burns Wilson. HBV-1
Braggin' Bill's Fortytude. *At. to* C. Wiles Hallock. BPAW
Brahma. Emerson. AA; AmPP; AP; AWP; BiP; EaLo; HAP; HBV-2; ILwL; LiTA; NePA; NOBA; NoP; OBEV; OBVV; OxBA; PAI; PoRA; SeCeV; TAP; TreF; TrGrPo; UnPo; ViBoPo; WGRP; WHA
Brahma. Andrew Lang. BXAP; CenHV; FaBoCo; NOBL
Brahma, the World Idea. *Unknown, tr. fr. Vedic by* Romesh Dutt. *Fr.* The Rig-Veda. WGRP
(Song of Creation, *tr. by* Raimundo Panikkar.) ILwL
Brahms, The. Herbert Morris. NePoAm-2
Brahms/ stabbed me in the ear. St. Julien's Eve. James Cunningham. JB
Braid Claith. Robert Fergusson. BSV; GoTS; NOEC; OBEC; OxBS
Braille. Gerald Costanzo. AMV-81
Brain. Coleman Barks. PPJ
Brain Cells, The. Donald Hall. TAP
Brain Coral. Lois Bassen. SUW

Brain forgets, but the blood will remember, The. The Dark Chamber. Louis Untermeyer. MoAmPo; WHA
Brain is wider than the sky, The. Emily Dickinson. MoAB; MoAmPo; NIP; NoAM; OxBA
Brain itself in its skull, The. Harsh Climate. Charles Simic. LCAP
Brain, the blood, the busy thews, The. William Baylebridge. Life's Testament, II. PoAu-1
Brain, within its groove, The. Emily Dickinson. AP; NoAM; NOBA
Brainstorm. Howard Nemerov. HAP; NCSH; NoAM
Brainwashing Dramatized. Don Johnson. PoNe
Brakes, like young stag's horns, come up in Spring, The. London versus Epping Forest. John Clare. *Fr.* Child Harold. FaBoPP
Branch, The. Stanley Moss. DiL
Branch of may, it does look gay, A. May Song. *Unknown.* OBET
Branch of the apple-tree from Emain, A. *Unknown, tr. by* Kuno Meyer. *Fr.* The Voyage of Bran. AnIL
Branches Back Into. Ken Belford. NeAC
Branches ripped by a storm tide. Walking the Beach. Sarah Youngblood. IHMS
Brand, *sel.* Ibsen, *tr. fr. Norwegian by* C. H. Herford.
Brand Speaks, *br. sel.* WGRP
Brand Fire New Whaling Song Right from the Pacific Ocean. *Unknown.* EtS
Branding Iron Herd, The. Ralph Rigby. PoOW
Brandish't sword of God before them blaz'd, The. Expulsion from Paradise. Milton. *Fr.* Paradise Lost, XII. ChTr
Brandy Leave Me Alone. *Unknown.* FSW
Branwell's Sestina. James Reaney. *Fr.* A Suit of Nettles. MoCV
Brasch wrote, "these islands" and I. An Excellent Memory. Allen Curnow. OCNZ
Brash and bare and whistling cold. Song of January. Gerta Kennedy. PoPl
Brass and parrot feathers. Oshun, the River Goddess. *Yoruba Oral Tradition, tr. by* Ulli Beier. WTO
Brass band blares, The. Circus. Eleanor Farjeon. SUS
Brass Horse, The. Drummond Allison. FaBoTw
Brass Spittoons. Langston Hughes. AmNP; BANP; MoAmPo; NoAM
Brasses jangle and the hausers tighten, The. The Barge Horse. Seán Jennett. PH
Brassica (oleracea) is a cabbage. Cabbage. Rosemary Norman. BrRo
Bratzlav Rabbi to His Scribe, The. Jacob Glatstein, *tr. fr. Yiddish by* Jacob Sloan. TrJP
Brave and high-souled Pilgrims, you who knew no fears. Thanksgiving Day. Annette Wynne. OHIP
Brave as a falcon and as merciless. To Manon, Comparing Her to a Falcon [*or* The Falcon]. Wilfrid Scawen Blunt. The Love Sonnets of Proteus, II. ACP; OBVV
Brave as the firstborn flame upsprings the statue. At the Salon. Florence Wilkinson Evans. HBV-2
Brave at Home, The. Thomas Buchanan Read. *Fr.* The Wagoner of the Alleghanies. HBV-2
Brave College is hanged, the chief of our hopes. The Whig's Lamentation for the Death of Their Dear Brother College. *Unknown.* APAS
Brave Collier Lads. *Unknown.* OBET
Brave Donahue. *At. to* Jack Donahue. PoAu-1
Brave flowers, that I could gallant it like you. A Contemplation upon Flowers. Henry King. BoNaP; ELP; HBV-1; LoBV; MeLP; MePo; NoP; OBEV; OBS; SeCP; TrGrPo
Brave infant of Saguntum, clear[e]. To the Immortal Memory and Friendship of That Noble Pair, Sir Lucius Cary and Sir Henry Morison. Ben Jonson. AnAnS-2; NOBE; NoP; OAEL-1; OBS; PoEL-2; SeCP; SeCV-1
Brave Kelso, he's considered great. Julia E. Moore. *Fr.* Grand Rapids Cricket Club. PeD
Brave Knight, A. Mary Mapes Dodge. TDH
Brave lads in olden musical centuries. Alcaics; to H. F. B. Robert Louis Stevenson. NBM; OBEV; OBVV
Brave little bird that fears not God, A. The Meadow Lark. Hamlin Garland. AA
Brave Lord Willoughby. *Unknown. See* Lord Willoughby.
Brave Man, The. Wallace Stevens. SOTW
Brave men have followed. The Flag Speaks. Emily Greene Balch. PGD
Brave New World. Archibald MacLeish. NOBA; OFD; OxBA
Brave New World. Shakespeare. *Fr.* The Tempest, V, i. TrGrPo
Brave news is come to town. *Unknown.* OxNR
Brave Old Duke of York, The. *Unknown. See* Noble Duke of York, The.
Brave Old Oak, The. Henry Fothergill Chorley. FaBoBe; HBV-1
Brave Old Ship, the *Orient,* The. Robert Traill Spence Lowell. AA; FaBoBe
Brave Old World. Elisabeth Lambert. FaFP
Brave Paulding and the Spy. *Unknown.* PAH
Brave Rover. Max Beerbohm. GDP
Brave Teuton, though thy awful name. Schemmelfennig. Bret Harte. OBAL
Brave weathercock, I see thou'lt set thy nose. Upon the Weathercock. Bunyan. OxBChV
Brave Wolfe. *Unknown.* BaBo (A *and* B *vers.*); PAH; TrAS, *with music;* ViBoFo
Brave young city by the Balboa seas, The. Twilight at the Heights. Joaquin Miller. AA
Brave youth, to whom Fate in one hour. For a Picture Where a Queen Laments over the Tomb of a Slain Knight. Thomas Carew. CaPo
Brave-hearted Maid, A. *Unknown, tr. fr. Anglo-Saxon by* Mother Margaret Williams. ISi
Bravely from Fairyland he rode, on furlough. The Broken Girth. Robert Graves. BIrV
Bravery runs in my family. Coward. A. R. Ammons. OBAL
Bravest Battle, The. Joaquin Miller. WBLP
(Mothers of Men, The.) PGD
Bravest names for fire and flames, The. General John. W. S. Gilbert. NA
Braving the Wilds All Unexplored, *with music.* Robert Freeman. AH
Brawling of a sparrow in the eaves, The. The Sorrow of Love. W. B. Yeats. OAEL-2; TEP
Brazen Tongue. William Rose Benét. MoAmPo
Brazil, January 1, 1502. Elizabeth Bishop. NoAM
Brazos River, The. *Unknown.* PrIm
Bread. Stanley Burnshaw. TrJP
Bread. James Dickey. LCAP
Bread. Nancy Keesing. PoAu-2
Bread. A. M. Klein. PeCV
Bread. W. S. Merwin. EAS
Bread. Gabriela Mistral, *tr. fr. Spanish by* Allan Francovich *and* Kathleen Weaver. WPOW
Bread. Constance Urdang. GP
Bread and Music. Conrad Aiken. *See* Music I Heard.
Bread and Wine, *sel.* Friedrich Hölderlin, *tr. fr. German by* Robert Bly.
"Oh friend, we arrived too late." NU
Bread Hot from the Oven, The. John Thompson. NOBC
Bread Is Born. Anne Hébert, *tr. fr. French by* Maxine W. Kumin. BoWoP
Bread Loaf to Omaha, Twenty-eight Hours. Patrick Worth Gray. TAT
Bread of Brotherhood. Lucia Trent. PGD
Bread of Heaven, on Thee We Feed. Josiah Conder. TrCP; VLP
Bread of Life, The. Mary A. Lathbury. *See* Break Thou the Bread of Life.
Bread of Our Affliction, The. Martin Grossman. VWA
Bread that bringeth strength I want to give, The. I Shall Not Pass Again This Way. *Unknown.* BLRP; TreF; WBLP
Breadth. Circle. Desert. Monarch. Month. Wisdom. John Hollander. PoA
Break, The. E. N. Sargent. NYBP
Break and trail home. The Girl I Left behind Me. *Unknown.* AmFP
"Break, Break, Break." J. C. Squire. BXAP
Break, Break, Break. Tennyson. AWP; BiP; BLPL; CABA; CH; DL; EtS; FaBoBe; FaBoEn; FaBV; FaPoR; FF; FiP; GoJo; GTBS-P; HAP; HBV-1; HeIP; LiTB; MOS; NIP; NOBE; NoP; OAEP; OBNC; PoEL-5; PoPl; PoRA; PPoe; PrIm; TEP; TreF; TrGrPo; WBLP; WeW; WHA
Break forth, break forth, O Sudbury town. Lydia. Lizette Woodworth Reese. AA
Break forth in song, ye trees. Centennial Hymn. John Pierpont. PAL
Break not his sweet repose. A Soldier's Grave. John Albee. AA
Break not my loneliness, O Wanderer! The Dove's Loneliness. George Darley. OBNC
Break not the slumbers of the bride. An Hymeneal Song on the Nuptials of the Lady Anne Wentworth and the Lord Lovelace. Thomas Carew. CaPo
Break [*or* Breake] of Day (" 'Tis true, 'tis day; what through it be"). John Donne. CABA; EnRePo; ErPo; LiTB
Break of Day ("Stay, O sweet, and do not rise"). John Donne. EIL; TrGrPo
(Aubade.) BoLoP; NOBE
(Daybreak.) OBEV
Break of Day. Shaw Neilson. PoAu-1
Break of Day in the Trenches. Isaac Rosenberg. BrPo; FaBoMo; GTBS-P; MMA; MoBrPo; NIP; NOBE; NoP; OAEL-2; OBWP; PoA; SeCePo; ViBoPo; VWA; WaP; WaaP
"Break off your argument." The Shape of a Bird. Laurence Whistler. MoVE
Break the News to Mother. Charles Kassel Harris. FSN, *with music;* TreFS
Break thou my heart, ah, break it. Arab Song. Richard Henry Stoddard. AA
Break Thou the Bread of Life. Mary A. Lathbury. AH, *with music;* TRV
(Bread of Life, The.) STF
Break—break it open; let the knocker rust. Dedication to the Generation Knocking at the Door. John Davidson. BrPo
Breakdown, The. Sherod Santos. MAYP

Breake now my heart and dye! Oh no, she may relent. Thomas Campion. AAS
Breakers of Broncos. Lew Sarett. BPAW
Breakers over the Sea. *Malay Oral Tradition, tr. by* R. O. Winstedt. WTO
Breakfast. W. W. Gibson. OBMV; OxBTC
Breakfast. Thom Gunn. OxBC
Breakfast. Robin Shectman. AMV-80
Breakfast for Barbarians, A. Gwendolyn MacEwen. NOBC
Breakfast in a Bowling Alley in Utica, New York. Adrienne Rich. CoPo
Breakfast Song, The. Emilie Poulsson. HBVY
Breakfast Song in Time of Diet. Stoddard King. OBAL
Breakfast Time. James Stephens. SUS
Breakfast with Gerard Manley Hopkins. Anthony Brode. BXAP; FaBoPa; FiBHP; NOBL; Par
Breaking. J. Alexander Allan. PoAu-2
Breaking, The. Margaret Steele Anderson. HBV-1
Breaking Green. Michael Ondaatje. NOBC
Breaking Ground in Me. Tom Kryss. NeAC
Breaking of the Day, The. Peter Davison. CoPo
Breaking Off from Waiting. Clarisse Nicoïdski, *tr. fr. Judezmo by* Stephen Levy. VWA
Breaking Point. Sylvia Auxier. GoYe
Breaking Silence. Janice Mirikitani. BrSi
Breaking the morning ice on the well's bucket was no great hardship. On the Pilgrim's Way in Kent, as It Leads to the Coldrum Stones. Asphodel. BrRo
Breaking through the first door, he found. Seven Dreams. John Bayliss. EAS
Breaking Tradition. Janice Mirikitani. BrSi
Breaking waves dashed high, The. The Landing of the Pilgrim Fathers in New England. Felicia Dorothea Hemans. BeLS; BLPA; FaBoBe; FaBV; FaFP; FaPo; FaPON; GN; HBV-2; HBVY; OHIP; PAH; PAL; PaPo; PGD; SBG; TreF; WBLP; WPE
Breakings. Henry Taylor. GrPl
Breaks up in obelisks on the river. Ice. Ai. FYAP
Breakthrough. Carolyn M. Rodgers. BPo
Breakthrough. John Sinclair. NBP
Break-up, The. A. M. Klein. NOBC
Breakwaters. Ted Walker. NYBP
Breast, The. Anne Sexton. CABA
Breast/ below ground. The Dance. Robert Kelly. The Book of Persephone, 17. PoM
Breast/ Is best. Note on Feeding. *Unknown.* FaBoUs
Breastdown fluttering in the breeze. Sparrow in Winter. Shinkichi Takahashi, *tr. by* Lucien Stryk *and* Takashi Ikemoto. NU
Breastplate of St. Patrick, The. *At. to* St. Patrick. *See* Deer's Cry, The.
Breasts. Tess Gallagher. AmPA
Breasts. Donald Hall. OBAL
Breasts. Charles Simic. NNaP
Breasts. Barbara Unger. DFT
Breasts of a barmaid of Crale, The. Limerick. *Unknown.* NOBL
Breasts of Mnasidice, The. Pierre Louys, *tr. fr. French. Fr.* Chansons de Bilitis. PeHV
Breath, A. "Madeline Bridges." AA
Breath. Reginald Gibbons. MAYP
Breath. Heather McHugh. GeTw
Breath can fan love's flame to burning. A Breath. "Madeline Bridges." AA
Breath in My Nostrils. Lance Jeffers. CNA
Breath of Air, A. James Wright. NOBA; PoPl
Breath of Hampstead Heath. Edith M. Thomas. AA
Breath of life imbued those few dim days, The. Fragment. Jessie Fauset. CDC
Breath of my life, The—no less. Epigram. Meleager, *tr. by* Peter Whigham. PeHV
Breath of Night, The. Randall Jarrell. CrMA
Breath on the Oat. Joseph Russell Taylor. HBV-2; PAH
Breathe Dust. Fred Wah. NOBC
Breathe in experience, breathe out poetry. Poem Out of Childhood. Muriel Rukeyser. NMM
Breathe not, hid Heart: cease silently. To an Unborn Pauper Child. Thomas Hardy. CoBMV; FaBoRV; GTBS-P; LiTB; NAs; ViBoPo
Breathe on the Glass. Raymond Stineford. AMV-81
Breathe, trumpets, breathe. Requiem. George Lunt. AA
Breathers, The. James Reiss. AmPA
Breathes There a Man. Samuel Hoffenstein. PoPl; WhC
("Breathes there a man with hide so tough.") FiBHP
Breathes There the [*or* a] Man [with Soul So Dead]. Sir Walter Scott. *Fr.* The Lay of the Last Minstrel, VI. BLPA; EnRP; FaFP; FPL; OAEP; OBRV; OxBS; PGD; TreF
(Innominatus.) OBEV; PAL
(Love of Country.) OHFP; PaPo; WBLP
(My Native Land.) GN
(My Own, My Native Land!) BSV
(Native Land.) TrGrPo
(Patriot, The.) FaPoR; OBNC
(Patriotism.) NOBE; TRV
Breathing, The. Denise Levertov. NaP; RFM
Breathing do I draw that air to me. Song of Breath. Peire Vidal, *tr. by* Ezra Pound. AWP
Breathing his last music, Mozart is supposed. Lost Letter to James Wright, with Thanks for a Map of Fano. Gibbons Ruark. MAYP
Breathing something German at the end. The Gift to Be Simple. Howard Moss. ImOP; MP; Psk; TwCP
Breathing the Strong Smell. Harold Norse. PeHV
Breathless, we flung us on the windy hill. The Hill. Rupert Brooke. HBV-1; MoBrPo; OxBTC; ViBoPo
Breathless when the breeze deserts them. Cuban Refugees on Key Biscayne. Barbara Winder. TAT
Breaths. Birago Diop, *tr. fr. French by* Anne Atik. TTY
Brébeuf and His Brethren, *sels.* E. J. Pratt.
"Fury of taunt was followed by fury of blow, The." PeCV
Invisible Trumpets Blowing. CaP
Martyrdom of Brébeuf and Lalemant, 16 March 1649, The. NOBC; OBCV
Brébeuf and His Brethren. F.R. Scott. NOBC
Brecon Beacons and the Black Mountains, The. Henry Vaughan. FaBoPP
Bred in a low place, lord of little deeds. A Man of Men. Leonard Charles Van Noppen. PGD
Bredon Hill. A. E. Housman. A Shropshire Lad, XXI. BrPo; EBVV; FaBoPP; MoAB; MoBrPo; SoSe; TreF; VLP; WHA
Breech, The. Michael McClure. NeAP
Breech Birth. Nora Dauenhauer. TWSS
Breed's described, The: Now, Satire, if you can. Daniel Defoe. *Fr.* The True-born Englishman, Pt. II. OBSV
Breeze and Billow. Albert Durrant Watson. CaP
Breeze blows o'er the lake, A. Herons. *Unknown.* SUS
Breeze has swelled the whitening sail, The. Song of the Pilgrims. Thomas Cogswell Upham. PAH
Breeze is blowing, The. *Tr. fr. Maori by* A. Armstrong *and* R. Ngata. WTO
Breeze is sharp, the sky is hard and blue, The. Frederick Goddard Tuckerman. Sonnets, II, xiv. AP
Breeze stops, the afternoon heat rises, The. The Field. David Huddle. Str
Breeze was crisp and the sea lay blue, The. The Pirates' Fight. Joseph Schull. *Fr.* The Legend of Ghost Lagoon. CaP
Breeze wipes creases off my forehead, A. Poem in June. Milton Acorn. WHW
Breezes went steadily thro' the tall pines, The. Nathan Hale. *Unknown.* PAH
Breezeways in the tropics winnow the air. A Letter from the Caribbean. Barbara Howes. CoAP; UnPo
Breitmann in Politics, *sel.* Charles Godfrey Leland.
"Dere's a liddle fact in hishdory vitch few hafe oonershtand." OBAL
Brendan Gone. Padraic Fiacc. CIP
Brendan, holy Brendan of the blessed beard. Saint Brendan's Prophecy. *Unknown, tr. by* Thomas Crofton Croker. OnYI
Brennan on the Moor. *Unknown.* AmFP; BaBo; FaBoBa; FSW; GBP; OnYI; OuSiCo, *with music;* ViBoFo, *with music*
Brennbaum. Ezra Pound. *Fr.* Hugh Selwyn Mauberley. MoAmPo
Brent; a Poem to Thomas Palmer Esq. William Diaper. *Sels.* FaBoPP
"Had mournful Ovid been to Brent condemned." OBSV
"Happy are you, whom Quantock overlooks." NOEC; OBSV
Br'er Sterling and the Rocker. Michael Harper. LCAP
Brereton Omen, The, *sel.* Felicia Dorothea Hemans.
"Yes! I have seen the ancient oak." CTC
Brest Left Behind. John Chipman Farrar. PAH
Bretagne had not her peer. In the province far or near. Lady of Castlenoire. Thomas Bailey Aldrich. BeLS
Breton Afternoon. Ernest Dowson. OBNC
Breughel's Winter. Walter de la Mare. SeCePo
Brevard Fault. Robert Morgan. SUW
Brevities. Siegfried Sassoon. PoLF
Brew your potion, mix your spell. Comrade in Arms. T. Inglis Moore. PoAu-2
Brewer, A. *Unknown.* FaBoCo; WhC
Brewer's Man, The. L. A. G. Strong. DBV; DTC; ELU; FaBoCo; FiBHP; WhC
Brewing of Soma, The. Whittier. PoEL-4
"Dear Lord and Father of mankind," *sel.* AH, *with music;* NOCV; TrPWD; TRV
(Prayer: "Dear Lord and Father of mankind.") TreFT
Brian O'Linn. *Unknown.* FaBoBa; FaBoNo; OnYI
(Bryan O'Lynn.) GBP
Brick, The. Paul Roche. NYBP

Brick distinguishes this country. Amsterdam Letter. Jean Garrigue. NYBP
Brick not used in building, A. Naomi Replansky. POL
Brick plant like a school, The. The winter set. L. E. Sissman. *Fr.* Parents in Winter. DiL
Bricking the Church. Robert Morgan. MAYP
Bricklayer tells the busdriver, The. The Continuity. Paul Blackburn. CAD; NeAP
Bricklayer's Labours, The. Robert Tatersal. NOEC
Bricklay'r throws his trowel by, The. Religion and the Lower Classes. Evan Lloyd. *Fr.* The Methodist. NOEC
Brickster, The. *Unknown.* OBET
Brid one brere, brid, brid one brere. Bird on Briar. *Unknown.* OxBM
Bridal bed, The. Above it. Jenny Mastoráki, *tr. fr. Modern Greek by* Nick Germanacos. PBWP
Bridal Birth. Dante Gabriel Rossetti. The House of Life, II. OAEP
Bridal Couch. Donald J. Lloyd. NIP
Bridal Morn [*or* Morning], The. *Unknown. See* Maidens Came, The.
Bridal Pair, The. William Young. *Fr.* Wishmakers' Town. AA
Bridal Song ("Cynthia, to thy power"). Beaumont *and* Fletcher. *Fr.* The Maid's Tragedy, I, ii. OBEV
Bridal Song ("Hold back thy hours"). Beaumont *and* Fletcher. *Fr.* The Maid's Tragedy, I, ii. ElL; ErPo; TrGrPo
(Hold Back Thy Hours.) UnTE; ViBoPo
Bridal Song ("Now, Sleep, bind fast the flood of air"). George Chapman. *Fr.* The Masque of the Middle Temple and Lincoln's Inn. ElL
Bridal Song ("O! Come, soft rest of cares, come Night"). George Chapman. *Fr.* Hero and Leander, Fifth Sestiad. NOBE; OBEV
(Song.) ViBoPo
Bridal Song, A. Thomas Dekker, *and others. Fr.* The Pleasant Comedy of Patient Grissill. OBSC; TrGrPo
(Beauty, Arise.) ElL
Bridal Song, A. Fletcher *and* Shakespeare. *Fr.* Two Noble Kinsmen, I, i. ElL; NOBE; OBEV; OBSC
(Roses Their Sharp Spines.) ViBoPo
Bridal Song, A. Shelley. OBRV
Bridal Song to Amala. Thomas Lovell Beddoes. *Fr.* Death's Jest Book, IV, iii. GBL; OBVV
(Epithalamia.) PoEL-4
(Song: "We have bathed, where none have seen us.") ChER; FaBoEn; OBNC
(Songs at Amala's Wedding.) LoBV
Bride, The. Bella Akhmadulina, *tr, fr. Russian by* Stephan Stepanchev. BoWoP; PBWP
Bride, The. Ambrose Bierce. AA
Bride, A. Harry Fainlight. BoLoP
Bride, The. Ralph Hodgson. HBMV
Bride, The. "Laurence Hope." HBV-1
Bride, The. D. H. Lawrence. NoAM; OxBTC
Bride, The. Ruth Comfort Mitchell. HBMV
Bride, The. Sir John Suckling. *Fr.* A Ballad upon a Wedding. TrGrPo
Bride cam' out o' the byre, The. Wooed and Married and A'. Alexander Ross. HBV-1
Bride loved old words, and found her pleasure marred. Five Epigrams. J. V. Cunningham. OBAL; UnTE
Bride of Abydos, The. Byron. OAEP
"Winds are high on Helle's wave, The," *sel.* OBRV
Bride of Frankenstein, The. Edward Field. CoAP; HeIP
Bride of Lammermoor, The, *sel.* Sir Walter Scott.
Lucy Ashton's Song, *fr. ch.* 3. BSV; EnRP; GoTS; NOBE; OBEV; OxBS
(Look Not Thou.) OBRV
Bride Song. Christina Rossetti. *Fr.* The Prince's Progress. OBEV; OBVV; WPE
("Too late for love, too late for joy.") ViBoPo
Bridegroom, The. Kipling. *Fr.* Epitaphs of the War. FaBoEE
Bridegroom Dick, *sel.* Herman Melville.
"Where's Commander All-a-Tanto?" PoEL-5
Bridegroom of Cana, The. Marjorie Pickthall. CaP; TrCP
Brides, The. A. D. Hope. HAP; InPK; PAI
Bride's Farewell, The: Two Songs. *Gond Oral Tradition, tr. by* V. Elwin *and* S. Hivale. WTO
Bride's Prelude, The. Dante Gabriel Rossetti. SeCePo
Bride's Toilette, The. Ellen Mackay Hutchinson Cortissoz. AA
Bride's Tragedy, The, *sels.* Thomas Lovell Beddoes.
"Dear, I could weep, but that my brain is dry." LO
Poor Old Pilgrim Misery. EnRP
Song: "A ho! A ho!/ Love's horn doth blow." ChER
Bridesmaid. Robley Wilson, Jr. AMV-80
Bridge. A. R. Ammons. CoAP
Bridge, The. Hart Crane. LiTA
Sels.
Atlantis. LiTM; MoPo; NePA; NYP; TwAmPo
Ave Maria. MoPo; NePa; NoAm; NOBA
Cape Hatteras.
"Nasal whine of power whips a new universe." MoAB
Power: Cape Hatteras. MoAmPo
Cutty Sark. FaBoMo
Powhatan's Daughter.
Dance, The. LiTM; MoAB; MoAmPo; OxBA; TwAmPo; SeCeV
Harbor Dawn, The. MoPo; NePA; NYP; OxBA
Indiana. TwAmPo
River, The. AmPP; AP; CMoP; CoBMV; GOA; MoAB; MoAmPo; NoAM; NOBA; OxBA; PrIm; TwAmPo; ViBoPo
"Down, down—born pioneers in time's despite." TrGrPo
Van Winkle. AmPP; CrMA; FaBV; MoAB; MoAmPo
Quaker Hill. LiTM
Three Songs.
National Winter Garden. ErPo; InPS; LiTM; OxBA
To Brooklyn Bridge. AP; BLPL; CABA; CoBMV; CrMA; EyDe; FaBoEn; InPS; LiTM; MoAB; MoAmPo; MoPo; NePA; NOBA; NYP; OxBA; PoPl; PrIm; SeCeV
(Proem: To Brooklyn Bridge.) AmPP; CMoP; HAP; HeIP; NoAm; NoP; TAP; WeW
Tunnel, The. AP; CMoP; MAT; MoAB; MoAmPo; NePA; NYP; OxBA
Bridge, The. Longfellow. HBV-2; TreF
Bridge, The. Frederick Peterson. HBV-2
Bridge, The. James Thomson. Sunday up the River, II. OBVV
Bridge, The. Derek Walcott. NYP
Bridge, and a hot concrete road, A. The Desert of Love. Janos Pilinszky, *tr. by* Ted Hughes *and* János Csokits. OBVE
Bridge Builder, The. Will Allen Dromgoole. BLPA; TreFS; TRV
(Building the Bridge.) WeW
(Building the Bridge for Him.) STF
Bridge from Brooklyn, The, *sel.* Raymond Henri.
"Roebling, his life and mind reprieved enough." EyDe
Bridge-Guard in the Karroo. Kipling. OBWP
Bridge of Death, The. *Unknown, tr. fr. French by* Andrew Lang. AWP
Bridge of Heraclitus, The. George Reavey. BIrV
Bridge of Sighs, The. Thomas Hood. BeLS; EBEV; EnRP; FaPoR; FPL; GTBS; GTBS-P; HBV-2; OBEV; OBVV; PeD; TreF; WBLP; WHA
Bridge of the Carousel. Rainer Maria Rilke, *tr. fr. German by* John Drury. AMV-80
Bridge says, The: Come across, try me; see how good I am. Potomac Town in February. Carl Sandburg. EvOK
Bridges. Rhoda W. Bacmeister. SoPo
Bridges and Tunnels. Beth Bentley. EyDe
Bridges are essential in a place. Covered Bridge. Robert P. Tristram Coffin. AmFN
Bridges are for going over water. Over and Under. William Jay Smith. TiPo
Bridgework. Annette Lynch. FF
Brief Autumnal. *Unknown, tr. fr. Greek by* Dudley Fitts. PAI; WeW
Brief Elegie on My Dear Son John, A. John Saffin. SCAP
Brief Essay on Man. Arthur Guiterman. OBAL
Brief Farewell. Anthony Delius. PeSA
Brief History. Olga Hampel Briggs. GoYe
Brief Introduction to the History of Culture, A. Weldon Kees. TwAmPo
Brief Journey West, The. Howard Nemerov. NoAM
Brief, on a flying night. Chimes. Alice Meynell. CH; MoBrPo; SBG; WHA; WPE
Brief Reflection on the Insect. Miroslav Holub, *tr. fr. Czech by* Stuart Friebert *and* Dana Hóbová. SUW
Brief Sermon, A. *Unknown.* TreFS
Briefless Barrister, The. John Godfrey Saxe. ShM
"Brigade Must Not Know, Sir, The!" *Unknown.* PAH
Brigadier. A. J. M. Smith. MoCV; NMP
Brigg, The. Robin Skelton. NMP
Briggflatts, *sels.* Basil Bunting.
Coda. OAEL-2
"Grass caught in willow tells the flood's height," IV. FaBoMo; NoAM
"Light lifts from the water," *fr.* V. OAEL-2
Brigham Young. *Unknown.* CoSo (A *and* B *vers.*); FSW
Bright Abandon. Tessa Sweazy Webb. GoYe
Bright are the days which the Fates hold in store for us. To William (Whom We Have Missed). P. G. Wodehouse. NOBL
Bright are the heavens, the narrow bay serene. The Indian's Grave. George J. Mountain. CaP
Bright as the day, and like the morning fair. Cloe. George Granville. FaBoCo; FaBoEE; NIP
Bright as Venus' golden star. The Insatiate. Johannes Secundus, *tr. by* John Nott. *Fr.* Basia. UnTE
Bright axe breaks the silence in the wood, The. Tree Felling. George Woodcock. NeBP
Bright Babe! whose awfull beautyes [*or* beauties] make. In the Glorious

Epiphanie of Our Lord God [*or* A Hymne for the Epiphanie]. Richard Crashaw. AnAnS-1; PoEL-2
Bright Be the Place of Thy Soul! Byron. HoPM
Bright be the skies that cover thee. To Laura W——, Two Years Old. Nathaniel Parker Willis. HBV-1
Bright berries on the roadside. On the March. Richard Aldington. BrPo
Bright books! the perspectives to our weak sights. To His Books. Henry Vaughan. QFR
Bright breaks the warrior o'er the ocean wave. The Ocean Wanderer. *Unknown.* NA
Bright captures, wing-shimmers, facts. Spider. Richmond Lattimore. PP
Bright cards above the fire bring no friends near. Christmas 1944. Denise Levertov. NeBP
Bright clasp of her whole hand around my finger. To My Daughter. Stephen Spender. DFF
Bright Clouds. Edward Thomas. BrPo
Bright college years with pleasure rife. Yale Boola! H. S. Durand. FSN
Bright-coloured, mirror-plated, strung with lights. Merry-go-round. James McAuley. CBAP
Bright drips the morning from its trophied nets. Sonnet of Fishes. George Barker. FaBoMo
Bright eyes and laughing lips. Rain. Patrick F. Kirby. GoBC
Bright Flower! whose home is everywhere. To the Daisy. Wordsworth. EnRP
Bright-haired Spirit! Golden Brow! Onward to Far Ida. George Darley. *Fr.* Nepenthe. OBNC
Bright Hillside, The. Rhoda Coghill. NeIp; OxBI
Bright, hot day, A. Late June. The bus from Rome. La Banditaccia, 1979. Rika Lesser. MAYP
Bright Is the Ring of Words. Robert Louis Stevenson. BrPo; OBNC; TrGrPo
Bright little maid in [*or* of] St. Thomas, A. St. Thomas [*or* Limerick]. *Unknown, at. to* Ferdinand G. Christgau. HBV-2; TDH
Bright mirror I braved, The: the devil in it. Cleopatra to the Asp. Ted Hughes. EBEV
Bright moon illumines the night-prospect, A. *Tr. fr. Chinese by* Arthur Waley. BoWoP
Bright moon lifts from the Mountain of Heaven, The. The Moon at the Fortified Pass. Li Po, *tr. by* Witter Bynner *and* Kiang Kang-hu. WaaP
Bright on the banners of lily and rose. Welcome to the Nations. Oliver Wendell Holmes. PAH
Bright portalles of the skie. An Hymne of the Ascension. William Drummond of Hawthornden. OBS
Bright Queen of Heaven, God's Virgin Spouse. The Knot. Henry Vaughan. ISi
Bright ran thy line, O Galloway. Lord Galloway. Burns. DBV; OxBoLi
Bright scene, A; a summer morning. A Minor Victorian Painter. John Hewitt. CIP
Bright sea washed beneath her feet, The. The Return. Annie Fields. AA
Bright shadows of true Rest! some shoots of blisse. Son-Dayes. Henry Vaughan. SeCP
Bright shine the golden summits in the light. A Calm Sea. Robert Southey. EtS
Bright shines the sun on Clinch's Hill. The Vance Song. *Unknown.* OuSiCo
Bright shines the sun; play, beggars, play! In Praise of a Beggar's Life [*or* A Song in Praise of a Beggar's Life *or* Play, Beggars, Play!]. "A. W." ElL; OBSC; TrGrPo; WHA
Bright spark, shot from a brighter place. The Starre. George Herbert. AnAnS-1
Bright Sparkles in de Churchyard. *Unknown.* AA
Bright Squadrons, The. Spenser. *See* Guardian Angels.
Bright Star. Keats. *See* Bright Star! Would I Steadfast as Thou Art!
Bright star of beauty! on whose eyelids sit. Idea, IV. Michael Drayton. HBV-1
Bright Star, Would I Were Steadfast [*or* Stedfast] as Thou Art! Keats. BLPL; CABA; EnLoPo; GBL; GTBS; GTBS-P; HAP; InPK; InPS; LiTB; NIP; OAEL-2; PPoe; PPP; PrIm; SCV; SeCeV; TreFS; TrGrPo; ViBoPo
(Bright Star.) EnRP; NoP; WHA
(His Last Sonnet.) LoBV
(Last Sonnet.) ChER; HBV-2; NOBE; OBEV
(Sonnet: "Bright Star.") FABV; FiP; OAEP; OBNC; PoEL-4
(Written on a Blank Page in Shakespeare's Poems [Facing "A Lover's Complaint"].) FaBoEn; OBRV
Bright tulips, we do know. To a Bed of Tulips. Robert Herrick. CaPo
Bright vocabularies are transient as rainbows. Precious Moments. Carl Sandburg. MoAmPo
Bright Was the Morning. Thomas D'Urfey. OBS
Bright waves scour the wound of Carthage, The. Rome Remember. Sidney Keyes. MoAB
Bright white street lights, The. Allegory in Black. Carl Clark. JB
Bright Winter Morning. Chris Klein. AMV-81
Brightest and Best of the Sons of the Morning. Reginald Heber. GN; HBV-1; WGRP
(Hymn.) NBM
Brightest morning of summer, The. The Graveyard Road. Tom McKeown. HoAn
Brightest of the Bright, The. Egan O'Rahilly, *tr. fr. Irish by* James Clarence Mangan. BIrV
Brightly colored for a new season. Merry-go-round. Oliver Jenkins. GoYe
Brightly shone the sun in my hut. Those Who Lost Everything. David Diop, *tr. by* Langston Hughes. PBA
Brightly the sun of summer shone. Memory. Anne Brontë. EBVV
Brightness. Heather McHugh. GeTw
Brightness as a Poignant Light. David Ignatow. DiL
Brightness of Brightness. Egan O'Rahilly, *tr. fr. Irish by* Frank O'Connor. KiLC
"Brigid is a caution, sure!"—What's that ye say? Her Sister. Moira O'Neill. OxBTC
Brignall Banks. Sir Walter Scott. *Fr.* Rokeby, III. EnRP; OBEV
(Edmund's Song.) PoRA
(Outlaw, The.) GTBS; GTBS-P
(Song: "O Brignall banks are wild and fair.") HBV-2; OAEP; OBRV
Brilliant-bellied newt flashes, The. Summer Matures. Helene Johnson. PoNe
Brilliant kernel of the night, The. Robert Louis Stevenson. *Fr.* The Light-Keeper. EBVV
Brilliant seaside glitters its farewell, The. A Summer Gone. Howard Moss. NePoEA
Brindabella. Douglas Stewart. PoAu-2
Bring a leaf to me. Invitation Standing. Paul Blackburn. VGW
Bring a Torch, Jeanette, Isabella. Nicholas Saboly, *tr. fr. Provençal.* OHIP
Bring cypress, rosemary and rue. Grover Cleveland. Joel Benton. PAH
Bring Daddy home. *Unknown.* OxNR
Bring down the moon for genteel Janet. Goodbye Now, or, Pardon My Gauntlet. Ogden Nash. FiBHP
Bring 'Em Home. Barbara Dane *and others.* FSW
Bring every child. Christmas Songs. Gerta Kennedy. PoPl
Bring flowers, to strew again. Ode for Decoration Day. Henry Peterson. OHIP
Bring from the craggy haunts of birch and pine. Song [*or* O Mighty, Melanchonly Wind]. John Todhunter. OBVV; OnYI
Bring Good Ale. *Unknown. See* Bring Us In Good Ale.
Bring hemlock, black as Cretan cheese. Epigram. Robert Hillyer. WhC
Bring Home the Poet. Patrick MacDonough. OnYI
Bring Kateen-beug [*or* Kateen-beag] and Maurya Jude. Beg-Innish. J. M. Synge. MoBrPo; OnYI; OxBI
Bring me a cup of good red wine. Rinaldo. Henry Peterson. AA
Bring Me a Little Water, Sylvie. Leadbelly (Huddie Ledbetter). FSW
"Bring me a long sharp knife for we are in danger." The Sunflowers. Douglas Stewart. POL
Bring me men to match my mountains. Sam Walter Foss. *Fr.* The Coming American. AmFN; BLPA; FaBoBe
Bring me my dead! Tennyson. Thomas Henry Huxley. HBV-2
Bring me my rose-buds, drawer, come. A Frolic. Robert Herrick. FaBoEE
"Bring me soft song," said Aladdin. Aladdin and the Jinn. Vachel Lindsay. Poems about the Moon, VI. TwAmPo
Bring Me the Cup. Moses ibn Ezra, *tr. fr. Hebrew by* Solomon Solis-Cohen. *Fr.* Wine-Songs. TrJP
Bring me the sunset in a cup. Emily Dickinson. AP; MoAmPo; NOCV
Bring me to the blasted oak. Crazy Jane and the Bishop. W. B. Yeats. CMoP; LiTM
Bring me wine, but wine which never grew. Bacchus. Emerson. AmPP; AP; AWP; HBV-2; LiTA; NOBA; OBEV; OxBA; PoEL-4; ViBoPo
Bring now the last flower in to warm this room. At My Mother's Bedside. Marcia Lee Masters. WPE
Bring, O Morn, thy music! Bring, O night, thy hushes! "Who Wert and Art and Evermore Shalt Be." William Channing Gannett. TrPWD
Bring out all the set ideas. Borderline Ballad. Richard Weber. PPON
Bring out the hemlock! bring the funeral yew! Dirge of the Munster Forest. Emily Lawless. OBVV; OnYI
Bring out the tall tales now that we told. Ghost Story. Dylan Thomas. OBCP
Bring that red mouth of yours. Madrigal de Verano. Federico García Lorca, *tr. by* Paul Blackburn. ErPo
Bring the camera closer in. Focus. Documentary. Joseph Stroud. NPGG
Bring the comb and play upon it. Marching Song. Robert Louis Stevenson. FaPON; TiPo
Bring the good old bugle, boys, we'll sing another song. Marching through Georgia. Henry Clay Work. FaPoR; FSW; PAH; PSoN
Bring the holy crust of bread. Charmes. Robert Herrick. WSC
Bring the North. William Stafford. LCAP
Bring the Soul Blocks. Victor Hernandez Cruz. CAD

Bring the War Home. William Matthews. GeTw
Bring Them Not Back. James Benjamin Kenyon. AA
Bring to me then all passionate, crimson flowers. She Plans Her Funeral. Louise Morey Bowman. CaP
Bring to me white roses, roses, pinks and lavender. The Patchwork Quilt. Dora Sigerson Shorter. HBMV
Bring Torches. A. M. Stephen. CaP
Bring Us In Good Ale. *Unknown.* CH; EBEV; FaBoCo; MeEL; OAEL-1; OxBM; ViBoPo
(Bring Good Ale.) SeCePo
Bring Your Own Victim. Allen Curnow. OCNZ
Bring your shears and clip him well. Vinegaroon. Witter Bynner. BPAW
Bringer of sun, arrower of evening, star-begetter and moon-riser. Hymnal. Harold Vinal. TrPWD
Bringing Flowers. Roberta Spear. AmPA
Bringing Him Up. Lord Dunsany. PV
Bringing in the Sheaves. Knowles Shaw. FSW
Bringing Our Sheaves. Elizabeth Akers Allen. HBV-2
Bringing Up Babies. Roy Fuller. RHPC
Brisk Chaunticleer his matins had begun. A Morning-Piece; or, An Hymn for the Hay-Makers. Christopher Smart. NOEC
Brisk Girl, The. *Unknown. See* There Was a Brisk Girle.
Brisk Young Widow, A. *Unknown.* OBET
Brissit brawnis and broken banis. The Bewteis [*or* Bewtis] of the Fute-Ball. *Unknown.* BSV; FaBoCo; GoTS; OxBS
Bristling beard was his peculiarity, A. His Hirsute Suit. Frank Sidgwick. WhC
Bristol. Richard Savage. FaBoPP
Bristol and Clifton. John Betjeman. CMoP
Bristowe Tragedie; or, The Dethe [*or* Death] of Syr Charles Bawdin. Thomas Chatterton. EnRP; OBEC; OxBB
Britain. Goldsmith. *Fr.* The Traveller; or, A Prospect of Society. NOEC
Britannia, *sel.* James Thomson.
Britannia's Empire ("And what, my thoughtless sons, should fire you more."). OBEC
Britannia ("Heavens! What a goodly prospect spreads around."). James Thomson. *See* Happy Britannia.
Britannia and Raleigh. John Ayloffe. APAS
Britannia now lament for our hero that is dead. Lamentation on the Death of the Duke of Wellington. *Unknown.* OBET
Britannia Rules of Orthography. "Firth." InMe; WhC
Britannia rules the waves. On a Parisian Boulevard [*or* England and America, II]. James Kenneth Stephen. DBV; InMe; NOBL
Britannia to Columbia. Alfred Austin. *See* To America.
Britannia's Baby. D. H. Lawrence. NAs
Britannia's daughters, much more fair than nice. Edward Young. *Fr.* Love of Fame, the Universal Passion. OBSV
Britannia's Empire. James Thomson. *Fr.* Britannia. OBEC
Britannia's gallant streamers. Yankee Thunders. *Unknown.* PAH
Britannia's isles proclaim. To the First of August. Ann Plato. BlSi
Britannia's Pastorals, *sels.* William Browne.
"As that Arabian bird (whom all admire)," *fr.* I, Song 4. OAEL-1
Course of the Tavy, The, *fr.* I, Song 2. FaBoPP
Devonshire Walk, A, *fr.* I, Song 5. FaBoPP
Frolic Mariners of Devon, The, *fr.* II, Song 3. ChTr
Gentle Nymphs, Be Not Refusing, *fr.* I, Song 3. ElL; ViBoPo
Glide Soft, Ye Silver Floods, *fr.* II, Song 1. ElL
Memory ("Marina's gone, and now sit I"), 7 *sts. fr.* III, Song 1. HBV-1
(Celadyne's Song.) OBS
(So Shuts the Marigold Her Leaves, *shorter sel.*) ChTr
Memory ("So shuts the marigold her leaves"), 3 *sts. fr.* III, Song 1. OBEV
("So shuts the marigold her leaves.") ViBoPo
"Mounting lark, day's herald, got on wing, The," *fr.* I, Song 3. PBBP
"Muses' friend, The (grey-eyed Aurora), yet," *fr.* II, Song 2. JCP
Praise of Poets, *fr.* II, Songs 1 *and* 2. OBS
Shall I Tell You Whom I Love? *fr.* II, Song 2. ElL
(Song: "Shall I tell you whom I love?") HBV-1
Brither-men wha eftir us live on. Ballat o the Hingit. Villon, *tr. by* Tom Scott. OBVE
British, The. A. S. J. Tessimond. ChMP
British Army now carries two rifles, The. Identification in Belfast (I.R.A. Bombing). Robert Lowell. OxBC
British Church, The. George Herbert. AnAnS-1
British Commerce. James Thomson. *Fr.* Liberty, IV. OBEC
British Commerce. John Dyer. *Fr.* The Fleece, IV. OBEC
British Grenadier, The ("Come, come fill up your glasses"). *Unknown.* PAH
British Grenadiers, The ("Some talk of Alexander, and some of Hercules"). *Unknown.* FSW; HBV-2; OxBoLi; OBEC
British in branding their betters, The. Lessons in Limericks, II. David McCord. InMe
British Journalist, The. Humbert Wolfe. DBV; FiBHP; PV
("You cannot hope.") FaBoEE; OxBTC
British Leftish Poetry, 1930-40. "Hugh MacDiarmid." CMoP; FaBoTw; NMP; NoAM
British Lyon Roused, The. Stephen Tilden. PAH
British Man-of-War, A. *Unknown.* OBET
British Museum Reading Room, The. Louis MacNeice. LiTM; MoAB; MoBrPo; NOBE; SeCePo; WaP
British Prison Ship, The, *sel.* Philip Freneau.
Hospital Prison Ship, The, III. AmPP
British puss demurely mews, The. Philological. John Updike. ELU
British, the Ethiopians, and the Italians are squabbling, The. Our Country Is Divided. Faarah Nuur, *tr. fr. Somali by* B. W. Andrzejewski *and* I. M. Lewis. WTO
British Valor Displayed. Francis Hopkinson. *See* Battle of the Kegs, The.
Britomart in the House of Busirane. Spenser. *Fr.* The Faerie Queene, III, 11-12. FiP
Briton Who Shot at His King, A. David Ross. ShM
Britons grown big with pride. A Poem Containing Some Remarks on the Present War. *Unknown.* PAH
Brittain's Ida, *sel.* Phineas Fletcher.
Song: "Fond men! whose wretched care the life soon ending." ElL
Brittan's Remembrancer, *sel.* George Wither.
"I know that if thou please thou canst provide." SeCV-1
Brittish Church, The. Henry Vaughan. AnAnS-1
Brittle Beauty. Earl of Surrey. TrGrPo
("Brittle beauty [*or* beautie], that nature made so frail[e].") AAS; EnLoPo; SiPS
(Frailty and Hurtfulness of Beauty, The.) AAS; HoPM
Brittle hollow stalks of sunflower, The. Nature Green Shit. Gary Snyder. LCAP
Brittle streets, with midnight walking flung, The. Sonnet on a Still Night. J. V. Cunningham. PoA
"Broad acres, sir." You hear them in my talk. At Knaresborough. Donald Davie. NePoEA
Broad-Ax, The. Walt Whitman. *Fr.* Song of the Broad-Ax. MoAmPo
Broad-backed hippopotamus, The. The Hippopotamus. T. S. Eliot. AWP; HoPM; LiTB; OBMV; PAI; PoPl; VGW
Broad bars of sunset-slanted gold. Ballad of the Faded Field. Robert Burns Wilson. AA
Broad beach, The/ Sea wind and the sea's irregular rhythm. Afternoon: Amagansett Beach. John Hall Wheelock. BoNaP; MoVE; NePA; PoRA
Broad field darkens, but, still moving round, The. Central Park. Howard Nemerov. NYP
Broad is the gate and wide the path. The Bath. Harry Graham. CenHV; ShM
Broad Is the Road. Isaac Watts. AH, *with music*
("Broad is the road that leads to death.") AmFP
Broad shadows fall. On all the mountain side. A Sunset at Les Éboulements. Archibald Lampman. OBCV
Broads. David R. Slavitt. BXAP
Broadway. Walt Whitman. NYP
Broadway Pageant, A. Walt Whitman. NYP
Brobdingnag. Adrien Stoutenburg. NYBP
Brobinyak has dragon eyes, The. What You Will Learn about the Brobinyak. John Ciardi. EvOK
Brocadós and Damasks, and Tabbies, and Gawzes. An Excellent New Song on a Seditious Pamphlet. Swift. CoMu
Broccoli. Tom Schmidt. GP
Brockton Murder, The; a Page out of William James. Knute Skinner. TW
Broke and Hungry. *Unknown.* BluL
Broken, a/ tremble like. Suicid/ing(ed) Indian Women. Paula Gunn Allen. TWSS
Broken, The. W. S. Merwin. LCAP
Broken altar, Lord, Thy servant rears, A. The Altar. George Herbert. AnAnS-1; HoPM; InPS; JCP; OAEL-1; SeCP; SeCV-1; TrCP; TrGrPo
Broken Appointment, A. Thomas Hardy. BiP; DTC; GBL; NoAM; NoP; OAEP
Broken Bodies. Louis Golding. HBMV
Broken Bowl, The. James Merrill. PoA
Broken Bowl, The. Jones Very. AP
Broken-down Digger, The. *Unknown.* PoAu-1
Broken-down Squatter, The. *Unknown.* PoAu-1
Broken-Face Gargoyles. Carl Sandburg. AmPP; MoAmPo; OxBA
Broken Friendship. Samuel Taylor Coleridge. *See* Scars Remaining, The.
Broken from the bursting bough. The Apple. Ray Smith. TrCP
Broken Girth, The. Robert Graves. BIrV
Broken Gull, A. John Moore. NCSH
Broken Heart, The. Thomas Beedome. OBS
Broken Heart, The. John Donne. EBEV
Broken Heart, The, *sels.* John Ford.
"Beasts onely capable of sense, enjoy," *fr.* IV, ii. PoEL-2
Can You Paint a Thought? *fr.* III, ii. InvP; OAEP; PoEL-2; ViBoPo

"Glories, pleasures, pomps, delights, and ease," *fr.* V, iii. ViBoPo
(Dirge.) LoBV
(Song, A.) OBS
"Oh, no more, no more, too late," *fr.* IV, iii. ELP; GBL; LO; PoEL-2; ViBoPo
(Love's Martyrs.) NOBE
(Song.) LoBV; OBS; SeCePo
Broken Heart, Broken Machine. Richard E. Grant. PoBA
Broken-hearted Gardener, The. *Unknown.* ChTr; GBP
Broken Home, The. James Merrill. HAP; NoAM; NOBA; NYBP; PPP; WeW
Broken Home. William Stafford. NNaP
Broken in pieces all asunder. Affliction. George Herbert. AnAnS-1; JCP; LoBV
Broken lamps! After Visiting a Home for Disturbed Children. Lou Lipsitz. LTB
Broken Monologue. "Michael Lewis," *tr. fr. German.* UnTE
Broken One, The. John Holmes. MiAP
Broken pillar of the wing jags from the clotted shoulder, The. Hurt Hawks. Robinson Jeffers. AmPP; AP; CMoP; CoBMV; FYAP; LiTA; LiTM; MoAB; MoAmPo; MoVE; NoAM; NOBA; NoP; OxBA; PAI; PrIm; TAP; UnPo
Broken Pitcher, The. William Edmondstoune Aytoun. InMe
Broken Sky. Carl Sandburg. PCP
Broken snow should leave the traces, The. The Snow. Robert Creeley. AP
Broken Soldier, The. Katharine Tynan. SUMH
Broken Song, A. "Moira O'Neill." OBVV
Broken String, The. *Unknown, tr. fr. Bushman by* W. H. I. Bleek. PeSA
Broken the pot, there's still the jar. The Loves of the Birds. *Malay Oral Tradition, tr. by* R. J. Wilkinson *and* R. O. Winstedt. WTO
Broken Token, The. *Unknown. See* Pretty Fair Maid, A.
Broken Tower, The. Hart Crane. AmPP; AP; CMoP; CoBMV; LiTM; MoAB; MoAmPo; MoPo; MoVE; NoAM; NOBA; NoP; OxBA; SyP; TrGrPo
Broken Treaties, *sel.* Victor Contoski.
"Kiss the one you love." GP
Broken wagon wheel that rots away beside the river, A. Pioneers. Badger Clark. FaBoBe
Brome, brome on hill. The Broomfield Hill. *Unknown.* CH
Bronc Peeler's Song. *Unknown.* CoSo
Broncho Dan halts midway of the stream. A Health at the Ford. Robert Cameron Rogers. AA; FaBoBe
Broncho That Would Not Be Broken, The. Vachel Lindsay. BPAW; NePA; PH; RoGo
Broncho versus Bicycle. John Wallace Crawford. BPAW
Bronco Busting, Event #1. May Swenson. LiSp; PH
Brontosaurus. Gail Kredenser. RHPC
Bronze Head, A. W. B. Yeats. LiTB
Bronze Statuette of Kwan-yin, A. Charles Wharton Stork. GoYe
Bronzes. Carl Sandburg. EyDe
Bronzeville Man with a Belt in the Back. Gwendolyn Brooks. IDB; PoBA
Brooding Grief. D. H. Lawrence. CMoP; LoBV
Brooding Likeness. Louise Glück. MAYP
Brooding of Sigurd, The. William Morris. *Fr.* The Story of Sigurd the Volsung. SeCePo
Brooding on the eightieth letter of Fors Clavigera. Geoffrey Hill. Mercian Hymns, XXV. HAP
Brooding upon its unexerted power. Gas and Hot Air. Morris Bishop. OBAL
Brook, The. William Wilberforce Lord. AA
Brook, The; an Idyl, *sel.* Tennyson.
Brook, The. BoNaP; FaBV; FaPON; GN; GoJo; PoPle
(Brook's Song. The.) FaBoBe; FaFP; HBV-1; HBVY; TreF
Brook, The. Edward Thomas. MoVE; OAEL-2; SeCeV
Brook, The, *sel.* William Bull Wright.
"Through his million veins are poured." AA
Brook and road, The/ Were fellow-travellers. The Simplon Pass. Wordsworth. *Fr.* The Prelude, VI. OBRV; SyP
Brook in February, The. Sir Charles G. D. Roberts. BoNaP; OBCV; WHW
Brook in the City, A. Robert Frost. OxBA
Brook in Winter, The. James Russell Lowell. *Fr.* The Vision of Sir Launfal. GN
("Down swept the chill wind from the mountain peak.") TreF
Brook Song. James Herbert Morse. AA
Brook, would thou couldst flow. Brook Song. James Herbert Morse. AA
Brookfield, *sel.* William E. Marshall.
"But see this happy village festival." CaP
Brooklyn at Santiago, The. Wallace Rice. PAH
Brooklyn Bridge. Vladimir Mayakovsky, *tr. fr. Russian by* Vladimir Markov *and* Merrill Sparks. NYP
Brooklyn Bridge, The. Edna Dean Proctor. PAH
Brooklyn Bridge. Sir Charles G. D. Roberts. PAH
Brooklyn Bridge at Dawn. Richard Le Gallienne. HBMV
Brooklyn Heights. John Wain. LiTM; NYP; OxBTC
Brooklyn Summer. Lou Lipsitz. LTB
Brooklyn Theater Fire, The. *Unknown.* AmFP
Brooklynese Champion. Margaret Fishback. WhC
Brook's Song, The. Tennyson. *Fr.* The Brook. FaBoBe; FaFP; HBV-1; HBVY; TreF
Brookside, The. Richard Monckton Milnes. HBV-1; TreFS
Broom Balancing. Kathleen Fraser. RHPC
Broom Flower, The. Mary Howitt. HBV-1
Broom, Green Broom. *Unknown.* LiTB; OxBoLi; PoRA
(Green Broom, *sl. diff. vers.*) CH
Broom of Cowdenknows, The. *Unknown.* ESPB (A *and* B *vers.*)
Broom out the floor now, lay the fender by. June. Francis Ledwidge. BIrV; HBMV; OnYI
Broom pods crackling in the heat. A Picture. D. C. Cuthbertson. PoSH
Broomfield Hill, The. *Unknown.* AmFP; CH; ESPB (A *and* B *vers.*); OxBB; *with music;* ViBoFo
Broomfield Wager, The. *Unknown.* OBET
Brooms. Dorothy Aldis. SoPo
Brooms. Charles Simic. AmPA; LCAP; NNaP, *early version*
Broomstick bat, The. Stickball. Virginia Schonborg. RHPC
Broomstick Train, The, *sel.* Oliver Wendell Holmes.
"Look out! Look out, boys! Clear the track!" FaPON
Brother, The. Peter Everwine. FYAP; NNaP
Brother. Jewel C. Latimore. JB
Brother, The. Semion Yakovlevich Nadson, *tr. fr. Russian by* H. Badanes. TrJP
Brother. Richard Shelton. Str
Brother Alberto, one hot summer day. Pietro Aretino, *tr. fr. Italian.* PeHV
Brother and Sister. "Lewis Carroll." ChTr; FaBoNo; ShM
Brother and Sister, *abr.* "George Eliot." GN
Brother Ass, Brother Ass, you are full of fancies. James K. Baxter. Jerusalem Sonnets, 36. OCNZ
Brother Astolfo sated appetite. Pietro Aretino, *tr. fr. Italian.* PeHV
Brother Baptis' on Woman Suffrage. Rosalie Jonas. BlSi
Brother Bulleys, let us sing. The Bullfinches. Thomas Hardy. PB
Brother, Can You Spare a Dime? E. Y. Harburg. SaC
Brother, come! And What Shall You Say? Joseph Seamon Cotter, Jr. BANP; CDC; PoBA; PoNe
Brother Fire. Louis MacNeice. MoAB; NoAM; NOBE; OAEP; WaaP
Brother Green. *Unknown.* AmFP
Brother, Hast Thou Wandered Far, *with music.* James Freeman Clarke. AH
Brother humans who live on after us. Ballade. Villon, *tr. by* Galway Kinnell. NAWM-1
Brother-in-Law, The. Larry Rubin. GP; TW
Brother Jonathan, Brother Kafka, *sels.* Vincent O'Sullivan. OCNZ
"Between the two follies I return and return to," 44.
"Day bloated with statistics, A. A quarter of the States," 35.
"Everyman true to himself as Whitman—and that goes," 31.
"I begin to get like a guy in the movies—I eat," 15.
"My landlady has been to Hawaii. I look at her diamante," 33.
"On the day my father died a flame-tree," 8.
"This talking of death in itself is getting over," 9.
"To be in a place for spring and not have lived its winter," 13.
"Young bee falls between my window, A," 32.
Brother Jonathan's Lament for Sister Caroline. Oliver Wendell Holmes. HBV-2; PAH
Brother Juniper. Blanche Mary Kelly. GoBC
Brother, Lift Your Flag with Mine. Josephine Daskam Bacon. PoSC
Brother Noah, *with music.* *Unknown.* AmSS
Brother of mine, good monk with cowled head. Thomas à Kempis. Lizette Woodworth Reese. AA
Brother of My Heart. Galway Kinnell. FAZ
Brother shout your country's anthem. Hymn for Nations. *Unknown.* FSW
Brother, sing your country's anthem. Brother, Lift Your Flag with Mine. Josephine Daskam Bacon. PoSC
Brother Solon's Hunting Song. Thomas D'Urfey. *Fr.* The Marriage-Hater Match'd, II, i. CavP
Brother, Though from Yonder Sky, *with music.* James Henry Bancroft. AH
Brother to the firefly. Morning Light (The Dew-Drier). Mary Effie Lee Newsome. AmNP; CDC; PoBA; PoNe
Brotherhood. Edwin Markham. PGD
Brotherhood, *sel.* Sir Lewis Morris.
"There shall come from out this noise of strife and groaning." PGD
Brotherhood. José Luis Vega, *tr. fr. Spanish by* Julio Marzán. InW
Brotherhood. "J. J. W." PeHV
Brotherhood is not by the blood certainly, The. Speech to Those Who Say Comrade. Archibald MacLeish. OxBA
Brotherhood. Bible, *N.T.* First John, II: 9-11; IV: 20-21. TreFT
Brothers. Robert Currie. Psk
Brothers. Solomon Edwards. NNP

Brothers, The. John Holloway. NMP
Brothers. Gerard Manley Hopkins. OAEP
Brothers. James Weldon Johnson. BANP
Brothers, The. Edwin Muir. GTBS-P; HeIP; NoP; PrIm
Brothers. Dan Pagis, *tr. fr. Hebrew by* Shirley Kaufman. VWA
Brothers (I). James Reiss. AMV-81
Brothers, The. Charles Sprague. AA
Brothers/ brothers/ everywhere. Utopia. Jewel C. Latimore. BPo
Brothers/ i/ under/overstand. The Revolutionary Screw. Don L. Lee. GP
Brothers and men that shall after us be. Ballad of the Gibbet. Villon, *tr. by* Andrew Lang. AWP
Brothers, celebrate with me this morning. Ash Wednesday. Daniel Burke. AMV-80
Brothers in blood! They who this wrong began. To the United States of America. Robert Bridges. HBV-2; PAH
Brothers, let us discover our hearts again. Open Letter. Owen Dodson. BALP
Brothers, my teeth hurt. Strictly for Posterity. Charles Simic. NNaP
Brothers Together in Winter. Harley Elliott. NeAC
Brought back from the tedium of dying. Return of a Popular Statesman. Vincent Buckley. CBAP
Brought here in slave ships and pitched overboard. Love Your Enemy. Yusef Iman. BPo; TTY
Brought up as I was to ask of the weather. Point Grey. Daryl Hine. NOBC
Broughty Wa's. *Unknown.* ESPB
Brow bender, Eye peeper. Baby at Play. *Unknown.* HBV-1; HBVY
Brow, brow, brenty. *Unknown.* OxNR
Brow of Nephin, The. *Unknown, tr. fr. Modern Irish by* Douglas Hyde. AnIL
Brown Adam. *Unknown.* ESPB (A *and* B *vers.*); OxBB, *with music*
Brown and furry. The Caterpillar. Christina Rossetti. *Fr.* Sing-Song. FaPON; GoJo; OxBChV; RHPC; SoPo; SUS
Brown arms of the mothering plateau, The. The Lowveld. Charles Eglington. PeSA
Brown Baby Cobina, with his large black velvet eyes. Baby Cobina. Gladys May Casely Hayford. CDC
Brown Bear, The. Mary Austin. FaPON; PoSC
Brown Beauty, The. Lord Herbert of Cherbury. AnAnS-2
Brown bed of earth, still fresh and warm with love. John Gould Fletcher. Irradiations, VIII. TwAmPo
Brown Bird, The. Walt Whitman. *See* Out of the Cradle Endlessly Rocking.
Brown Boy to Brown Girl. Countee Cullen. PoBA
Brown bunny sits inside his burrow. The Rabbit. Edith King. HBMV; SoPo
Brown-dappled fawn, The. The Fawn in the Snow. William Rose Benét. MoAmPo
Brown earth-line meets gray heaven. In November. Anne Reeve Aldrich. AA
Brown enormous odor he lived by, The. The Prodigal. Elizabeth Bishop. CoAP; InvP; LCAP; LiTM; MoAB; MP; NYBP; PPP; TwCP
Brown-eyed Lee, *with music. Unknown.* CoSo
Brown-faced nurse has murmured something unintelligible, The. Microscosmos. Susan Miles. OxBTC
Brown Family, The. Colleen Thibaudeau. NOBC
Brown field jabbed a finger into the grove of cottonwoods, A. Firefly. George Uba. BrSi
Brown from the sun's mid-afternoon caress. Spectrum. William Dickey. ELU
Brown Girl, The ("I am as brown as brown can be"). *Unknown.* BaBo (A *and* C *vers.*); ELP; ESPB (A *and* B *vers.*); OBET
(Bonny Brown Girl, The.) OxBB
Brown girl chanting Te Deums on Sunday. Ruth. Pauli Murray. NMM
Brown Girl Dead, A. Countee Cullen. TAP
Brown Girl or Fair Eleanor, The. *Unknown. See* Lord Thomas and Fair Annet.
Brown in the snow, a car with a heater. Strangers. William Stafford. NNaP
Brown Is My Love. *Unknown.* EIL
("Brown is my love, but graceful.") GBL; OBSC
(Song Set by Nicholas Yonge.) CTC
Brown Jug, The. Francis Fawkes. ViBoPo
Brown like Us. Gary Soto. NPGG
Brown lived at such a lofty farm. Brown's Descent; or, The Willy-Nilly Slide. Robert Frost. EvOK; MoAmPo; PoRA; WhC
Brown o' San Juan. H. C. Bunner. *Fr.* Home, Sweet Home with Variations. InMe; OBAL
Brown of Ossawatomie. Whittier. HBV-2; PAH
Brown old man with a green thumb, A. He Was. Richard Wilbur. NCSH; SaC
Brown owl sits in the ivy bush, The. The Great Brown Owl. Jane Euphemia Browne. OxBChV
Brown paper worn next to the skin. B. L. Howarth. BXAP
Brown Penny. W. B. Yeats. BoLoP; CMoP; ELP; FaBoCh; LLLT; OLR
Brown River, Smile. Jean Toomer. *Fr.* The Blue Meridian. AmNP; PoBA
Brown Robin ("The king but an' his nobles a' "). *Unknown.* ESPB (A *and* B *vers.*); OxBB, *with music*
Brown Robyn's Confession ("It fell upon a Wodensday [*or* Wednesday]"). *Unknown.* ESPB; GBP
(Brown Robin's Confession.) ACP
(Brown Robyn.) CH
Brown, sad-coloured hillside, where the soil, A. The Sower. Sir Charles G. D. Roberts. CaP; OBCV
Brown sails of fishing boats. The Fishing Fleet. Lincoln Colcord. HBMV
Brown semicolons move doggedly. The Ant Trap. Joe Rosenblatt. NOBC
Brown Skin Girl. *Unknown.* BluL
Brown Thrush, The. Lucy Larcom. FaPON; HBV-1; HBVY; OBCA
Brownies' Celebration, The. Palmer Cox. OBCA
Browning at Asolo. Robert Underwood Johnson. AA
Browning, old fellow, your leaves grow yellow. In a Copy of Browning. Bliss Carman. HBMV
Brown's Descent; or, The Willy-Nilly Slide. Robert Frost. EvOK; MoAmPo; PoRA; WhC
Brown's Ferry Blues. *Unknown.* FSW
Brown's for Lalage, Jones for Lelia. Ballade of Ladies' Names. W. E. Henley. HBV-1
Brown's wife, herself a normal type. Family Life. Allan M. Laing. FiBHP
Brownsville Blues. *Unknown.* BluL
Br-r-r-am-m-m, rackety-am-m, OM, *Am.* What the Motorcycle Said. Mona Van Duyn. NIP
Bruadar and Smith and Glinn. *Unknown, tr. fr. Irish by* Douglas Hyde. AnIV
(Curse, A.) BIrV
Bruce, The, *sels.* John Barbour.
Battle of Bannockburn, The. BSV
Before Bannockburn. OxBS
Bruce Addresses His Army. GoTS
Bruce Consults His Men. GoTS
Bruce Meets Three Men with a Wether. OxBM
Freedom [*or* Fredome]. BSV; FaBoCh; GoTS; OBEV; OxBS; TrGrPo
("A! fredome is a noble thing!") ViBoPo
"Storys to rede ar delitabill." OxBS
Bruce and the Spider. Bernard Barton. BeLS
Bruce Consults His Men. John Barbour. *Fr.* The Bruce. GoTS
Bruce Meets Three Men with a Wether. John Barbour. *Fr.* The Bruce. OxBM
Bruce to His Men at Bannockburn. Burns. *See* Scots Wha Hae.
Bruce's March to Bannockburn. Burns. *See* Scots Wha Hae.
Bruckner. James Camp. MAT
Bruised by a heel he strove to die. The Death of a Snake. William Plomer. ELU
Bruised by the masseur's final whack. Health and Fitness. J. B. Morton. FaBoCo
Bruised Titans, The. Keats. *Fr.* Hyperion; a Fragment. OBNC
("Just at the self-same beat of Time's wide wings.") OBRV
Bruises. Coleman Barks. PPJ
Brumana. James Elroy Flecker. BrPo
Brummell at Calais. John Glassco. MoCV; PeCV
Bruno. *Unknown.* TDH
Brush Up Your Shakespeare. Cole Porter. OBAL
Brushes and paints are all I have. Quatrains. Gwendolyn B. Bennett. CDC
Brushing back the curls from your famous brow. The Copulating Gods. Carolyn Kizer. Prf
Brusque shoulders and bluff beard. Tudor Portrait. Richmond Lattimore. EyDe
Brussels and Oxford. William Hurrell Mallock. EBVV
Brussels in Winter. W. H. Auden. OxBTC
Brussels, 1919. Carola Oman. SUMH
Brut, The, *sel.* Layamon.
Death of Arthur, The, *orig. and mod. English prose.* OxBM
Bruton Town. *Unknown. See* In Brunton Town.
Brutus Explains Why He Murdered Caesar. Shakespeare. *Fr.* Julius Caesar, III, ii. TreFT
Bryan, Bryan, Bryan, Bryan. Vachel Lindsay. CMoP; CrMA; LiTA; OxBA; OxBoLi
Bryan O'Lynn. *Unknown. See* Brian O'Linn.
Bryan's Last Battle. *Unknown.* AmFP
Bryant. James Russell Lowell. *Fr.* A Fable for Critics. AP; NOBA; TAP
Brying us in good ale, and brying us in good ale. *See* Bring Us In Good Ale.
Brynbwrla. Kingsley Amis. *Fr.* The Evans Country. NOBL

B's the Bus. Phyllis McGinley. *Fr.* All Around the Town. FaPON; SoPo; TiPo
Buachaille Etive Mor and Buachaille Etive Beag. Naomi Mitchison. PoSH
Bubba Esther, 1888. Ruth Whitman. AMV-81
Bubble, The. William Allingham. *See* Blowing Bubbles.
Bubble, The. John Banister Tabb. AA
Bubble, The; a Song. Robert Herrick. CaPo
Bubble-breasted swells the dome. Frascati's. Aldous Huxley. ViBoPo
Bubble, Bubble, light and airy. Bubbles. George H. Shorey. PoPl
Bubble Gum. Nina Payne. RHPC
Bubble of the silver-springing waves, The. The Poetic Land. William Caldwell Roscoe. OBVV
Bubbles. George H. Shorey. PoPl
Bubbles soar and die in the sterile bottle, The. Notes for the Chart in 306. Ogden Nash. NYBP
Bubbling brook doth leap when I come by, The. Nature. Jones Very. AP; HBV-1
Bubbling Wine. Abu Zakariya, *tr. fr. Arabic by* A. J. Arberry. TTY
Buccaneer, The. Nancy Byrd Turner. TiPo
Bucephalus is neighing me a love song. Hossolalia. Mildred Luton. PH
Buchlyvie. *Unknown.* GBP; TW
Buck has a headache. Tony ate. The Garden of Earthly Delights. Charles Simic. NoP
Buck in the Snow, The. Edna St. Vincent Millay. BoAnP; CrMA
Buckaroo Sandman. *Unknown.* BPAW
Buckdancer's Choice. James Dickey. NoAM; NOBA; NoP; NYBP; PoNe
Buckee Bene. *Unknown.* CH
Bucket, The. Samuel Woodworth. *See* Old Oaken Bucket, The.
Bucket in the Well. Connie Wanek. AMV-80
Bucket of Sea-Serpents. Howard Ant. GoYe
Buckeye Jim. *Unknown.* FSW
Bucking Bronco. *Unknown.* AmFP; BPAW (*At. to* Belle Starr); CoSo; FSW
Buckingham Palace. A. A. Milne. OxBChV; PDV
Buckinghamshire. *Unknown.* GBP
Buckle the spur and belt again. Lofty Lane. Edwin Gerard. PoAu-1
Buckles glitter, billies lean, The. American Twilights, 1957. James Wright. CoAP
Bucko-Mate. Samuel Schierloh. GoYe
Buck's Elegy, The. *Unknown.* OBET
Buckskin Joe. *Unknown.* CoSo
Bucolic. W. S. Merwin. NMP
Bucolic Eclogues, *sel.* Ethel Anderson.
Waking, Child, While You Slept. PoAu-2; WPE
Bucyrus. John Holmes. CrMA; NePoAm
Bud, The/ stands for all things. Saint Francis and the Sow. Galway Kinnell. FYAP
Bud fantasies, dreams of an ear of corn. Paean to Eve's Apple. James Liddy. CIP
Buddha. Daniel Hoffman. CoPo
Buddha. Arno Holz, *tr. fr. German by* William Ellery Leonard. AWP
Buddha. Herman Melville. HeIP
Buddha at Kamakura, The. Kipling. LoBV
Buddha in the Womb, The. Erica Jong. MAYP
Buddha is not more strange. In a Warm Bath. Carl Rakosi. TAP
Buddha took some Autumn leaves. Kenneth Rexroth. *Fr.* The City of the Moon. GP
Buddha's Birthday: April 8, 1819. Issa, *tr. fr. Japanese by* Nobuyuki Yuasa. *Fr.* Oraga Haru. OFD
Buddha's Death Day: February 15, 1815. Issa, *tr. fr. Japanese by* Nobuyuki Yuasa. *Fr.* Oraga Haru. OFD
Buddhist Priest, A. Ho Xuan Huong, *tr. fr. Vietnamese by* Nguyen Ngoc Bich *and* Burton Raffel. PBWP
Budding [*or* Boddynge] floweret blushes at the light, The. Song of the Three Minstrels [*or* Mynstrelles Songe]. Thomas Chatterton. *Fr.* Aella. EnRP; TrGrPo; ViBoPo
Budding Spring. Jack Lindsay. PoAu-1
Budding-Time Too Brief. Evaleen Stein. AA
Budgie Finds His Voice. Wendy Cope. FaBoPa
Budmouth Dears. Thomas Hardy. *Fr.* The Dynasts, Pt. III. CH; MoVE; PoPle
("When we lay where Budmouth Beach is.") LO
Buen Matina. Sir John Salusbury. EIL
Buena Vista. Albert Pike. PAH
Buffalo. Louis Daniel Brodsky. AMV-80
Buffalo. Florence Earle Coates. PAH
Buffalo. Roy Daniells. CaP
Buffalo. Henry Dumas. PoBA
Buffalo. Charles Eglington. PeSA
Buffalo, The. Marianne Moore. PoA
Buffalo Bill's. E. E. Cummings. AmPP; CABA; CMoP; HeIP; InPK; LiTA; NePA; NOBA; PAI; TAP; VGW
(Buffalo Bill's Defunct.) AmFN
(Portrait.) InPS; MoAB; MoAmPo; NIP
Buffalo Boy. *Unknown.* AmFP; FSW
Buffalo breathed quietly inside, The. The Crow-Children Walk My Circles in the Snow. Ray A. Young Bear. CDW
Buffalo, buffalo, buffalo, buffalo. Death Chant. Peter Blue Cloud. VoR
Buffalo Creek. J. Le Gay Brereton. PoAu-1
Buffalo Dance. Alice Corbin, *after Chippewa Indian.* BPAW
Buffalo Dusk. Carl Sandburg. BPAW; GOA; OBCA; PDV; RFM; RHPC; TiPo
Buffalo Girls. *Unknown.* AmFP
(Buffalo Gals.) BLSo, *with music;* FSW
Buffalo Hunters, The. *Unknown.* CoSo
Buffalo—Isle of Wight Power Cable. Anselm Hollo. PoM
Buffalo loomed at the far loop of the field, The. The Difference. Winfield Townley Scott. NePoAm
Buffalo Marrow on Black. Lance Henson. STE
Buffalo Moon and Sun-Go-Under. Reservation. David McCord. WhC
Buffalo Skinners, The. *Unknown.* AmFP; AS, *with music;* BPAW; CoSo, *with music,* FSW; GBP; ViBoFo
(Boggy Creek, *cowboy vers.*) CoSo
Buffalo Trace. Robert Morgan. GeTw
Buffaloes are gone, The. Buffalo Dusk. Carl Sandburg. BPAW; GOA; OBCA; PDV; RFM; RHPC; TiPo
Buffel's Kop. Roy Campbell. ChMP; PeSA
Bufo. Pope. *Fr.* Epistle to Dr. Arbuthnot. OBEC
("Proud as Apollo on his forked hill.") OBSV
Bug, The. Marjorie Barrows. RHPC
Bug in a Jug. *Unknown.* RHPC
Bug Sat in a Silver Flower, A. Karla Kuskin. RHPC
Bugger Burns, *with music. Unknown.* OuSiCo
Bugle, The. Tennyson. *See* Splendor Falls, The.
Bugle and battle-cry are still. Happy Death. John Freeman. HBMV
Bugle calls coiling through the rocky valley. A Northern Legion. Sir Herbert Read. SeCePo
Bugle Song. Tennyson. *See* Splendor Falls, The.
Bugle Song of Peace. Thomas Curtis Clark. WBLP; WGRP
Bugle sounds the measured call to prayers, The. Sunday: New Guinea. Karl Shapiro. AmFN; PoPl
Bugler boy from barracks, A (it is over the hill). The Bugler's First Communion. Gerard Manley Hopkins. NoAM; OAEP; PeHV
Bugler named Dougal MacDougal, A. Edouard. Ogden Nash. NePA
Bugler sent a call of high romance, The. The Last Post. Robert Graves. MMA
Bugler's First Communion, The. Gerard Manley Hopkins. NoAM; OAEP; PeHV
Bugles!/ And the Great Nation thrills and leaps to arms! The Call of the Bugles. Richard Hovey. AA
Bugs. Will Stokes. MoShBr
Bugs, *sels.* Mary Ann Hoberman. OBCA
Cockroach.
Combinations.
Bugville team was surely up against a rocky game, The. Casey—Twenty Years Later. S. P. McDonald. BLPA
Buick. Karl Shapiro. BiP; CMoP; DFF; HoPM; MiAP; MoAB; TrGrPo; ViBoPo
Buik of Alexander, The, *sel.* John Barbour.
Prologue to the Avowis of Alexander. OxBS
Build a little fence of trust. Today. Mary Frances Butts. TreFT; TRV
"Build at Kallundborg by the sea." Kallundborg Church. Whittier. BeLS
Build for yourself a strong box. Then Laugh. Bertha Adams Backus. BLPA; TreFT; WBLP; YaD
"Build me straight, O worthy Master!" The Building of the Ship. Longfellow. EtS
Build thee more stately mansions, O my soul. Oliver Wendell Holmes. *Fr.* The Chambered Nautilus. TRV
Builder builded a temple, A. Two Temples. Hattie Vose Hall. BLPA
Builder, in building the little house. The Kitchen Chimney. Robert Frost. EyDe
Builder Kachina; Home-going. Wendy Rose. TWSS
Builder of continents, The. "Ping Hsin," *tr. by* Kai-yu Hsu. *Fr.* The Stars. WPOW
Builder, The. Caroline Giltinan. HBMV
Builder, The. Francis Sherman. CaP
Builder, The. Willard Wattles. HBMV
Builders. Purd E. Deitz. TRV
Builders. Hortense Flexner. HBMV
Builders, The. Longfellow. FaFP; OHFP; TreFS
Builders, The, *sel.* Henry van Dyke.
"Grant us the knowledge that we need." TrPWD
Builders, The. Judith Wright. SeCePo
Builder's Lesson, A. John Boyle O'Reilly. PoLF
Building, The. As You Come In. Anne Marriott. NOBC

Building a Person. Stephen Dunn. FAZ
Building a Skyscraper. James S. Tippett. OnUR
Building for Eternity. N. B. Sargent. BLPA
Building in Nova Scotia. Stephen Dunn. GP
Building in Stone. Sylvia Townsend Warner. MoBrPo
Building of a New Church, The. *Unknown.* EyDe
(On the Building of a New Church.) FaBoEE
Building of the *Long Serpent,* The. Longfellow. *Fr.* Tales of a Wayside Inn: The Musician's Tale, Pt. I. EtS
Building of the Nest, The. Margaret E. Sangster. HBV-1; HBVY
Building of the Ship, The. Longfellow. EtS
Sels.
Ship of State, The. FaBoBe; HBVY; OHIP; PAL
(O Ship of State.) FaFP
(Republic, The.) AA; PAH; WGRP
(Sail On, O Ship of State.) FaPON; TreF
("Thou, too, sail on, O Ship of State!") MOS; PGD; YaD
"Then the Master with a gesture." OHFP
Building of the Skyscraper, The. George Oppen. GOA
Building Society Blues. Roger Roughton. EAS
Building the Bridge for Him. Will Allen Dromgoole. *See* Bridge Builder, The.
Buildings, The. Wendell Berry. EyDe
Buildings. Daniela Gioseffi. FAZ
Buildings are all womanly, The. Their roofs. The Buildings. Wendell Berry. EyDe
Buke of the Howlat, The, *sel.* Sir Richard Holland.
"Roye Robert the Bruss the rayke he avowit, The." OxBS
Bulb, A. Richard Kendall Munkittrick. AA; POL
Bulbs strung along. Christmas Lights. Valerie Worth. PChr
Bulbul, The ("The bulbul hummeth like a book"). Sir Owen Seaman. NA
Bulge, The. George Johnston. MoCV; PV
Bulging in petticoats in May she comes. The Dandelion Gatherer. Robert Francis. PPJ
Bulkeley, Hunt, Willard, Hosmer, Meriam, Flint. Hamatreya. Emerson. AmPP; AP; HeIP; MAT; NOBA; NoP; OxBA; PoEL-4; PrIm; SeCeV; TAP. *See also* Minott, Lee, Willard . . .
Bull, A. Babette Deutsch. BoAnP; LiSp
Bull, The. Ralph Hodgson. BrPo; LiTM; MoAB; MoBrPo; MoVE; OBMV; OxBTC; WHA
Bull, The. Freda Laughton. NeIP
Bull, The. V. Sackville-West. WPE
Bull, The. William Carlos Williams. LiTM; MoVE; MP; NoP; TwCP
Bull, The. Judith Wright. GrPl; PoAu-2
Bull, A./ A fence. Kandinsky: "Improvisation No. 27." Edward Tick. PoDr
Bull be took bad, Th', says old Sam—wunnot fancy 'is fodder. From My Rural Pen. T. S. Watt. FiBHP
Bull Calf, The. Irving Layton. InPK; OBCV; PeCV
Bull Fight, The. Byron. *Fr.* Childe Harold's Pilgrimage, I. LiSp
Bull Moose, The. Alden Nowlan. CABA; NOBC
Bull Moses, The. Ted Hughes. NoP
Bull-voiced young fellow of Pawling, A. Hog-calling Competition. Morris Bishop. RHPC; TDH
Bull with the fierce eyes that none dares look at. Praises of King George VI. A. Z. Ngani, *tr. by* Jack Cope. PeSA
Bullard's Song, The. *Unknown.* OBET
Bulldog on the Bank, The. *Unknown.* FSW
Bulldozer, The. Robert Francis. PPJ
Bulldozer, The. Donald A. Stauffer. WaP
Bulldozers. Frederick Dec. PCP
Bulletin of the boarding school, The. Under All This Slate. James Hayford. NePoAm-2
Bullets splat downrange. On Teaching David to Shoot. Walter McDonald. AMV-80
Bullfinches, The. Thomas Hardy. PB
Bullfrog. Ted Hughes. NYBP; RFM
Bullfrog Blues. *Unknown.* BluL
Bullfrogs. David Allan Evans. Psk
Bullocky. Judith Wright. CBAP; PoAu-2; SeCePo
Bullocky Bill. *Unknown.* PoAu-1
Bulls and cows roam white. Counting. Michael Collier. SUW
Bulls by day. The Bulldozer. Robert Francis. PPJ
Bull's excited by another bull, The. Superbull. Harold Witt. FAZ
Bull's Eye: the water cries out. Stone and the Obliging Pond. Felix Pollak. POL
Bull's eyes and targets. *Unknown.* OxNR
Bullwhacker, The. *Unknown.* CoSo
Bully, A. *Malay Oral Tradition, tr. by* R. J. Wilkinson. WTO
Bully, The. *At. to* the Earl of Rochester *and to* Thomas D'Urfey. InvP
(Song: Noble Name of Spark, The.) SeCePo
Bully ship and a bully crew, A. Sacramento. *Unknown.* FSW
Bully ship and bully crew, A. Lowlands, *vers.* III. *Unknown.* ShS
Bully Song, The, *with music.* Charles E. Trevathan. BLSo
Bum. W. Dayton Wedgefarth. BLPA
Bumble Bee. Margaret Wise Brown. PDV
Bumblebeaver, The. Kenyon Cox. TiPo
Bumi. Amiri Baraka. PoBA
Bumper of good liquor, A. Sheridan. *Fr.* The Duenna, II, iii. WhC
Bumper Sticker, The, on His Pickup Said, "I'm a Lover, I'm a Fighter, I'm a Wild Bull Rider." Eldon Ray Fox. LiSp
Bumpity doun in the corrie gaed whuddran the pitiless whun stane. Sisyphus. Robert Garioch. BSV; PoSH
Bums are the spirit of us parked in ratty old hotels. Bowery. David Ignatow. CTBA
Bums, on Waking. James Dickey. NYBP
Bum's Rush. Michael Dransfield. CBAP
Bunch Grass #37. Robert Sund. NU
Bunch of Grapes, The. George Herbert. AnAnS-1
Bunch of grass, a wild rose, A. That's July. Mary F. Butts. YeAr
Bunch of Larks, The. Robert Leighton. EBVV
Bunch of Roses, A. John Banister Tabb. HBVY
Bunch of the boys were whooping it up in the Dixie-Belle, on Lex, A. The Tale of the Dixie-Belle. Frank Chase. InMe
Bunch of the boys were whooping it up in the Malamute saloon, A. The Shooting of Dan McGrew. Robert W. Service. BeLS; FaBoBe; FaFP; FPL; PoLF; PoRA; TreF; WHW
Bunches of Grapes. Walter de la Mare. GoJo; GrPl; HBV-1; HBVY; MoShBr; OxBChV; SUS; TiPo
Bundle is a funny thing, A. Bundles. John Farrar. TiPo
Bundle of orange flames, A. Old Miniatures. Leo Vroman. VWA
Bundles. John Farrar. TiPo
Bundles. Carl Sandburg. MoAmPo
Bungaloid Growth. Colin Ellis. FaBoEE
Bungalows, The. John Ashbery. CoAP
Bungiana, *sel.* *Unknown.*
Pacific Engagement, The. WhC
Bunhill's Fields. Anne Ridler. NeBP
Bunker Hill. George Henry Calvert. BeLS; FaBoBe; PAH
Bunker Hill, *with music.* Nathaniel Niles. BLSo; TrAS
(American Hero, The.) WaaP
(Why Should Vain Mortals Tremble, *with music.*) AH
Bunker's Hill, or the Soldier's Lamentation. John Freeth. NOEC
Bunky Boy Bunky Boy Who's My Little Bunky Boy. Larry Mollin. NeAC
Bunnies are a feeble folk, The. A Bunny Romance. Oliver Herford. OBCA
Bunny. Christopher Fahy. TAT
Bunny Romance, A. Oliver Herford. OBCA
Buns harden like pomanders. The Great Aunts of My Childhood. Alice Fulton. Str
Bunthorne's Song. W. S. Gilbert. *Fr.* Patience. FiBHP; LiTB; NBM; OAEL-2
(Aesthete, The.) EBVV; VLP
Bunyip, The. Douglas Stewart. AmMo
Bunyip and the Whistling Kettle, The. John Manifold. LiTB; PoAu-2; WaP
Buoy-Bell, The. Charles Tennyson Turner. EtS
Buoy like a man in a red sou'wester, A. Beginning to Squall. May Swenson. RFM
Buoys begin clanging like churches. The River That Is East. Galway Kinnell. NYP
Burbank with a Baedeker; Bleistein with a Cigar. T. S. Eliot. HBMV
Burd Ellen and Young Tamlane. *Unknown.* ESPB
Burd Helen was her mother's dear. Broughty Wa's. *Unknown.* ESPB
Burd Isabel and Earl Patrick. *Unknown.* BaBo; ESPB
Burden, The. Francesca Yetunde Pereira. PBA
Burden of Decision, The. Peter Everwine. NNaP
Burden of Junk, The. John Glassco. OBCV
Burden of Love, The. "Owen Innsley." AA
Burden of Nineveh, The. Dante Gabriel Rossetti. OAEP
Bureaucratic Limerick ("The Bureau of Labor Statistics"). William Harmon. OBAL
Burgeis, thou haste so blowen atte the cole. Too Much Sex. *Unknown.* MeEL
Burgess was drunk when he was admitted. The Hospital—Retrospections. Kenneth Mackenzie. CBAP
Burgesses of Calais, The. Laurence Minot. ACP
Burglar Bill. "F. Anstey." CenHV; FiBHP
Burglar of Babylon, The. Elizabeth Bishop. NYBP
Burial. Robert Francis. NCSH
Burial. Paulin Joachim, *tr. fr. French by* Oliver Bernard. TTY
Burial. May Sarton. GP
Burial, The. Mark Thalman. AMV-80
Burial. Mark Van Doren. MoBS

Burial. Alice Walker. AmPA; PrIm
Burial, The. John Webster. *See* All the Flowers of the Spring.
Burial at Sea. E. J. Pratt. *Fr.* The *Roosevelt* and the *Antinoe.* CaP
Burial, Green, A. Marcia Southwick. MAYP
Burial in Flanders, The. Robert Nichols. PeHV
Burial in the Sand. Nancy Sullivan. NIP
Burial of a Fisherman in Hydra. Grace Schulman. BoWoP
Burial of an Infant, The. Henry Vaughan. OAEP
Burial of an Irish President. Austin Clarke. BIrV; IPY
Burial of Barber. Whittier. PAH
Burial of King Cormac, The. Sir Samuel Ferguson. AnIL; OnYI
Burial of Latané, The. John R. Thompson. PAH
Burial of Moses, The. Cecil Frances Alexander. BeLS; BLPA; BLRP; GN; HBV-2; WBLP
Burial of Saint Brendan, The. Padraic Colum. OxBI
Burial of Sir John Moore after [*or* at] Corunna, The. Charles Wolfe. AnIV; ChTr; EnRP; FaBoRV; FaFP; FaPoR; GN; GTBS; GTBS-P; HBV-2; HBVY; NOBE; OBEV; OBRV; OBWP; OnYI; OxBI; PaPo; PoRA; RoGo; TreF; WaaP; WBLP; WHA
Burial of the Bachelor, The. *Unknown.* FaBoPa
Burial of the Dane, The. Henry Howard Brownell. AA; HBV-1
Burial of the Linnet, The. Juliana Horatia Ewing. OxBChV
Burial of the Spirit of a Young Poet. Richard Hughes. MoBrPo
Burial of the Young Love. Waring Cuney. BANP
Buriall. Henry Vaughan. SeCV-1
Burialle of the Dede. Martin Fagg. BXAP
Burials. George Crabbe. *Fr.* The Parish Register, Pt. III. OAEL-1, abr.
Sels.
Ancient Virgin, An. OBNC
Lady of the Manor. NOBE; OBNC
"My record ends." OBRV
Burials. Geoffrey Grigson. PoA
Buried at Springs. James Schuyler. CoAP; PoM
Buried beneath his poems, here lies. The Wandering Jew. Benjamin Fondane, *tr. by* Edouard Roditi. VWA
Buried Child, The. Dorothy Wellesley. *Fr.* Deserted House. DTC
(Epilogue: "He is not dead nor liveth.") OBMV
Buried in noontime traffic. The Glade. Robert Kelly. The Book of Persephone, 18. PoM
Buried in the shades of horrid night. On His Late Espoused Saint. Sir Kenelm Digby. ACP
Buried Lake, The. Allen Tate. CrMA
Buried Life, The. Matthew Arnold. OAEL-2; OAEP; SeCeV; VLP
Buried Stream, The. James K. Baxter. OxBC
Buried under a flat stone, but beside. Patty, 1949-1961. Sharon Mayer Libera. IHMS
Burke and Wills. Ken Barratt. PoAu-2
Burlesque Ode, on the Author's Clearing a New House of Some Workmen, A, *sel.* George Keate.
"Midst the fair range of buildings which, new-reared." NOEC
Burlesque of Lope De Vega. Samuel Johnson. *See* If the Man Who Turnips Cries.
Burly, dozing humble-bee. The Humble-Bee. Emerson. AA; FaPON; FM; GN; HBV-1; HBVY; NOBA; OxBA
Burma Hills. Bernard Gutteridge. WaP
Burman Lover, The. Calder Campbell. *See* Ossian's Serenade.
Burn Down the Icons. Grace Schulman. GP
Burn drowns steadily in its own downpour, The. Waterfall. Seamus Heaney. NoAM
Burn Out Burn Quick. Abraham Reisen, *tr. fr. Yiddish by* Joseph Leftwich. TrJP
Burn Ovid with the rest. Lovers will find. Penal Law. Austin Clarke. BoLoP; ELU; GTBS-P; IPY; NoAM; PAI
Burn stilly, thou; and come with me. To a Candle. Walter de la Mare. ChMP; ELP
Burncombe Hollow. William Barnes. OBNC
Burned and dusty garden said, The. An Athenian Garden. Trumbull Stickney. NCEP
Burned Bridge, The. Ruth Stone. WPE
Burned in this element. Letter II. W. S. Graham. NePoEA
Burnet's Character. *Unknown.* APAS
Burning. Galway Kinnell. CoAP
Burning, *abr.* Gary Snyder. *Fr.* Myths and Texts. NeAP; PoM
Sels.
"He's out stuck in a bird's craw," IV. NaP
" 'If, after attaining Buddhahood, anyone in my land,' " X. NaP
"John Muir on Mt. Ritter," VIII. NOBA
"Night here, a covert," IX. NaP
Second Shaman Song, I. NOBA
"Sourdough mountain called a fire in," XVII. NaP; NoP
"Spikes of new smell driven up nostrils," XIII. NaP
"Stone-flake and salmon," XV. NaP
Burning/ burning/ burning. Crow's Last Stand. Ted Hughes. InPS
Burning against the Wind. Judith Minty. GeTw
Burning and Fathering; Accounts of My Country. Jack Gilbert. NPGG
Burning, The—at first—would be probably worst. Heaven and Hell. James Kenneth Stephen. CenHV
Burning Babe, The. Robert Southwell. ACP; AnAnS-1; CABA; CH; ElL; FaBoCh; FaBoEn; GoBC; HAP; HBV-1; HelP; InPS; LiTB; LoBV; MePo; NAs; NOBE; NOCV; NoP; OAEL-1; OBCP; OBEV; OBSC; OxBoCh; PAI; PoEL-2; PPoe; Prf; SBVL; SeCePo; TrCP; TrGrPo; ViBoPo
Burning Bush. Karle Wilson Baker. HBMV
Burning Bush. Martin Feinstein. TrJP
Burning Bush, The. Norman Nicholson. EaLo; EBCP; NeBP; SeCePo
Burning Bush, The. Henry van Dyke. TRV
Burning Drift-Wood. Whittier. MOS
Burning Hills. Michael Ondaatje. NOBC; NoP
Burning in the Night. Thomas Wolfe, *arr. in verse by* John S. Barnes. AmFN
Burning Love Letters. Howard Moss. DFF; HoPM
Burning Mountain. W. S. Merwin. NYBP
Burning of Auchindown. *Unknown.* *See* Willie Macintosh.
Burning of Books, The. Bertolt Brecht, *tr. fr. German by* H. R. Hays. PoPl
Burning of Jamestown, The. Thomas Dunn English. PAH
Burning of Paper instead of Children, The. Adrienne Rich. LCAP
Burning of the Birds, The. Shirley Kaufman. GP
Burning of the Law, The. Meïr of Rothenburg, *tr. fr. Hebrew by* Nina Davis Salaman. TrJP
Burning of the Leaves, The. Laurence Binyon. ChMP; DTC; GTBS-P; MoVE; NOBE; OxBTC
Burning of the Temple, The. Isaac Rosenberg. FaBoMo; TrJP
Burning Oneself In. Adrienne Rich. NYP
Burning Sand of Sinai. Nelly Sachs, *tr. fr. German by* Keith Bosley. VWA
Burning Shit at An Khe. Bruce Weigl. MAYP
Burning the Cat. W. S. Merwin. NIP
Burning the Christmas Greens. William Carlos Williams. AP; CoBMV; LiTM; MoPo; NePA; NoAM; NOBA; TwAmPo
Burning the Letters. Gwendolyn Grew. HoPM
Burning the Letters. Randall Jarrell. MiAP; MoAB; MoAmPo
Burning the Root. Margaret Gibson. MAYP
Burning the Small Dead. Gary Snyder. CAPP; NNaP
Burning the Tomato Worms. Carolyn Forché. AmPA
Burnished, burned-out, still burning as the year. The Public Garden. Robert Lowell. AP; NoP; PoRA; TAP
Burnished silver mask hangs in white air, The. On a Celtic Mask by Henry Moore. Horace Gregory. PoA
Burns. Fitz-Greene Halleck. AA
Burns and His Highland Mary, *with music.* *Unknown.* ShS
Burn's Log Camp, *with music.* *Unknown.* ShS
Burnt. Boris Slutsky, *tr. fr. Russian by* Daniel Weissbort. VWA
Burnt Bush, The. Jack R. Clemo. FaBoTw
Burnt Debris. Thomas Sessler, *tr. fr. German by* Herbert Kuhner. VWA
Burnt Norton. T. S. Eliot. *Fr.* Four Quartets. CMoP; LiTM; MoAB; MoAmPo; MoPo; TwAmPo
"Words move, music moves," *sel.* UnS; ViBoPo
Burnt Offering to Your Greenstone Eyes, Tangaroa, A. Hone Tuwhare. OCNZ
Burnt Ship, A. John Donne. EBEV; InPK; OBWP; WaaP
Burr Oaks, *sel.* Richard Eberhart.
Attic, The. MoAB
Burro, The. J. J. Gibbons. PoOW
Burro once, sent by express, A. Advice to Travelers. Walker Gibson. NePoAm-2; PPJ
Burro with the Long Ears. *Unknown, tr. fr. Navajo Indian by* Hilda Faunce Wetherill. FaPON
Burrowing deep into the earth until the grave is complete. Wolf. Peter Blue Cloud. VoR
Burst of iris so that, A. Iris. William Carlos Williams. InPS; LCAP; WeW
Burst of steam from the pipes in the morning startles me, A. The Two of Cups. Emmett Jarrett. NeAC
Bury Her at Even. "Michael Field." OBMV
Bury Him Deep. Thomas Lovell Beddoes. TW
(Fragment: "Bury him deep. So damned a work should lie.") ELU
Bury Me beneath the Willow. *Unknown.* FSW
Bury me deep when I am dead. Requiescat. Rosamund Marriott Watson. HBV-1
Bury Me in a Free Land. Frances E. W. Harper. BPo
Bury Me in America. Arno Karlen. FAZ
Bury Me Not on the Lone Prairie. *Unknown.* BPAW; FaBV; FaFP; FSW; TrAS, *with music;* TreF
(Dying Cowboy, The.) CoSo, *with music;* FaBoBe
(Lone Prairie, The.) ViBoFo

(Oh, Bury Me Not on the Lone Prairie, *with music.*) AS
Bury Me Out on the Prairie. *Unknown.* BPAW; CoSo, *with music*
"Bury me," the bishop said. St. Swithin. Daniel Henderson. HBMV; ShM
Bury Our Faces. Bob Millard. AMV-80
Bury the corngod. Throw yr shovel. The Eternal Return. Alan Loney. OCNZ
Bury the dragon's teeth! Bury Them. Henry Howard Brownell. PAH
Bury the Great Duke. Ode on the Death of the Duke of Wellington. Tennyson. HBV-2; OBVV; VLP
Bury Them. Henry Howard Brownell. PAH
Bury your heart in some deep green hollow. Saturday Market. Charlotte Mew. HBMV; WPE
Burying Blues for Janis. Marge Piercy. GeTw; NeAC
Burying Ground by the Ties. Archibald MacLeish. Frescoes for Mr. Rockefeller's City, III. GOA; MoAmPo
Bus, The. Leonard Cohen. CAD; HeIP
Bus Ride. Lenore Kandel. NMM
Bus Ride. Selma Robinson. *Fr.* Ferry Ride. FaPON
Bus Stop. Donald Justice. FYAP; LCAP
Bus Stop. Vincent O'Sullivan. OCNZ
Bus Trip, The. Joel Oppenheimer. NeAP
Busby, Whose Verse No Piercing Beams, No Rays. Richard Moore. TW
Bush, The, *sels.* Bernard O'Dowd.
"As many, Mother, are your moods and forms." PoAu-1
"To other eyes and ears you are a great." CBAP
Bush Aboon Traquair, The. John Campbell Shairp. OBVV
Bush Christening, A. A. B. Paterson. PoAu-1
Bush-Fiddle, The. Judith Green. PoAu-2
Bush Justice. Charles Harpur. CBAP
Bush land scrub land. The Country North of Belleville. Al Purdy. NOBC
Bush on Mount Venus, The. Donald Finkel. CoPo
Bush that has most briers and bitter fruit, The. The Barberry-Bush. Jones Very. AP
Bush was on that dump, A. The Burnt Bush. Jack R. Clemo. FaBoTw
Bush, The. Yes. It burned like they say it did. Deuteronomy. Robert Bringhurst. NOBC
Bushed. Earle Birney. MoCV; NOBC; NoP; OBCV; PeCV
Bushed. Charles Lillard. NOBC
Bushed. Barry McKinnon. NOBC
Bushes and Briars. *Unknown.* OBET
Bushes lean in the wind, The. Need of an Angel. Raymond Souster. CaP
Bushman's Song, A. A. B. Paterson. PoAu-1
Bushman's stature is not great, The. The Fat-buttocked Bushmen. Earnest A. Hooton. WhC
Bushranger, A. Kenneth Slessor. CBAP
Bushrangers, The. Edward Harrington. PoAu-1
Busie old foole, unruly Sunne. *See* Busy old fool, unruly Sun.
Business, The. Robert Creeley. CAPP
Business as Usual. Mark Vinz. Str
Business as Usual 1946. A. J. M. Smith. NMP
Business Is Business. Berton Braley. WBLP
Business Life, The. David Ignatow. NNaP; TW
Business Man's Prayer, A. William Ludlum. BLRP
Business men with awkward hips. The City. John Betjeman. TEP
Business of the lambing ewes would make me, The. Eagles over the Lambing Paddock. Ernest G. Moll. PoAu-2
Business Trips. Laurie Taylor. AMV-80
Businessman of Alicante, The. Philip Levine. NaP
Busk ye, busk ye, my bony bony bride. The Braes of Yarrow. William Hamilton. OBEC
Buson, Goshun, Kinkoku. Artists East and West. Diana Chang. BrSi
Busses are bright yellow and have brought, The. The Dream about Junior High School in America. Dick Lourie. NeAC
Bussy D'Ambois, *sels.* George Chapman.
"As cedars beaten with continual storms," *fr.* I, i. ViBoPo
"Ile sooth his plots: and strow my hate with smiles," *fr.* IV, ii. PoEL-2
"I long to know/ How my dear mistress fares," *fr.* V, iii. ViBoPo
"Now all the peacefull regents of the night," *fr.* II, ii. PoEL-2
"Now shall we see, that nature hath no end," *fr.* V, ii. PoEL-2
Pilot, The ("Man is a torch borne in the wind, a dream"), *fr.* I, i. EtS
Bustan, The, *sels.* Sadi, *tr. fr. Persian by* Sir Edwin Arnold. AWP
Dancer, The.
Great Physician, The.
Buster Keaton. Michael McFee. AMV-81
Buster Keaton & the Cops. George Keithley. NPGG
Bustin' down the canyon. Billy the Kid or William H. Bonney. N. Howard Thorp. BPAW
Bustle in a house, The. Emily Dickinson. AP; ELU; FaBV; FPL; HAP; HeIP; NePA; NoP; OxBA; PoEL-5; PoLF; WGRP
Busts and bosoms have I known. *Unknown.* ErPo; PV
Busy ant works hard all day, The. Ants, Although Admirable Are Awfully Aggravating. Walter R. Brooks. RHPC
Busy Body, The. Rachel Field. InMe
Busy Carpenters. James S. Tippett. SoPo
Busy, curious, thirsty fly! On a Fly Drinking out of [*or* from] His Cup [*or* An Anacreontick]. William Oldys. FaFP; OBEC; OBEV; TrGrPo; ViBoPo
Busy Heart, The. Rupert Brooke. HBV-1; MoBrPo
Busy in study be thou, child. Demeanour. *Unknown.* OxBChV
Busy is the life of the weaving woman! Song of the Weaving Woman. Yüan Chen, *tr. by* Wu-chi Liu. SaC
Busy Man Speaks, A. Robert Bly. ConAP
Busy Old Fool. Ian Kelso. BXAP
Busy [*or* Busie] old fool, unruly sun. The Sun [*or* Sunne] Rising. John Donne. AnAnS-1; BiP; BoLoP; CABA; EnRePo; FF; GBL; HAP; HeIP; InPS; InvP; JCP; LiTB; LoBV; MeLP; MePo; NIP; NOBE; NoP; OAEL-1; OAEP; PAI; PoEl-2; PoPle; PPP; SCV; SeCePo; SeCeV; SeCP; SeCV-1; SoSe; TEP; TrGrPo; UnTE; WeW
Busy with love, the bumble bee. Meleager, *tr. fr. Greek by* Peter Whigham. BoLoP
But/ he" i/ staring. E. E. Cummings. NoAM
But a large quantity of brandy. A Small Faculty Stag for the Visiting Poet. Earle Birney. OxBC
But ae braithless note. Sydney Goodsir Smith, *after the French of* Tristan Corbière. *Fr.* The Gangrel Rymour and the Pairdon of Sanct Anne. OBVE
But afar on the headland exalted. Swinburne. By the North Sea, VII. VLP
But ah! let me under some Kentish hill. Phineas Fletcher. *Fr.* The Purple Island. ViBoPo
But are these landscapes to be imagined. Letters to Walt Whitman, IX. Ronald Johnson. VGW
But are ye sure the news is true? *See* And are ye sure the news is true?
But Art Thou Come, Dear Saviour? *Unknown.* OxBoCh
But as I lay this other night waking. Sir Thomas Clanvowe. *Fr.* The Cuckoo and the Nightingale. PBBP
But as she sat allone and thoughte thus. Criseyde Sees Troilus Return from Battle. Chaucer. *Fr.* Troilus and Criseyde, II. OxBM
But as they left the dark'ning heath. Sir Walter Scott. *Fr.* Marmion. ELP
But Bacchus was not so content: he quyght forsooke their land. King Midas. Ovid, *tr. by* Arthur Golding. *Fr.* Metamorphoses, XI. CTC
But be contented: when that fell arrest. Sonnets, LXXIV. Shakespeare. OBSC
But black is the colour of my true love's hair. Black Is the Colour. *Unknown.* GBP
But bringing up the rear of this bright host. The Archangel. Byron. *Fr.* The Vision of Judgment. LoBV; OBRV
But can see better there, and laughing there. "Pygmies Are Pygmies Still, Though Percht on Alps." Gwendolyn Brooks. PoNe
But chief by numbers of industrious hands. A Nation's Wealth. John Dyer. *Fr.* The Fleece, III. OBEC
But Choose. John Holmes. MiAP
But did not paradise itself contain. Age of Innocence. Graham Hough. PoRA
But do not let us quarrel any more. Andrea del Sarto. Robert Browning. CABA; CTC; HBV-1; NoP; OAEL-2; OAEP; PoEL-5; VLP; WHA
But do the threat'ning clouds precipitate. A Method of Preserving Hay from Being Mow-Burnt, or Taking Fire. Robert Dodsley. *Fr.* Agriculture. FaBoUs
But does every man feel like this at forty. The Second Life. Edwin Morgan. OxBS
But don't you know it, my dear. Looking at a Picture on an Anniversary. Thomas Hardy. EyDe
But ere sterne conflict mixt both strengths, faire Paris stept before. Homer, *tr. by* George Chapman. *Fr.* The Iliad, III. OBVE
But Fear Thou Not, O Jacob. Bible, *O.T.* Jeremiah, XLVI: 27-28. TrJP
But for a breathing-space the witch. The Witch. W. W. Gibson. *Fr.* Skye. PoSH
But for a brief/ Moment, a poised minute. A Grasshopper. Richard Wilbur. HAP; HoPM; WeW
But for an hour's sleep in a filthy bed. Recall. Reed Whittemore. NYBP
But for Lust. Ruth Pitter. FaBoTw; OxBTC
But for the broken firing pin. Spider Reeves. Henry Carlile. Psk
But for the steady wash of rain. No Country You Remember. Robert Mezey. FF
But for your Terror. To Death. Oliver St. John Gogarty. FaBoEE; OBMV
But Gebir when he heard of her approach. Walter Savage Landor. *Fr.* Gebir, I. OBRV
But give me for my soul, those beauteous maids. Those Beauteous Maids. Moses ibn Ezra, *tr. by* Solomon Solis-Cohen. TrJP
But give me holly, bold and jolly. Christina Rossetti. *Fr.* Sing-Song. TiPo
But give them me, the mouth, the eyes, the brow! Orpheus and Eurydice. Robert Browning. CTC

But God has no machine. Eclogue: Queen Elizabeth's Day. John Davidson. BrPo
But God's Own Descent. Robert Frost. *Fr.* Kitty Hawk. EaLo
But, gracious [*or* gratious] God! how well dost Thou provide. The Church's Testimony. Dryden. *Fr.* The Hind and the Panther. ACP; TrPWD
But grant, in public, men sometimes are shown. Woman's Ruling Passions. Pope. *Fr.* Moral Essays, Epistle II. OBEC
But grant, the virtues of a temp'rate prime. Life's Last Scene. Samuel Johnson. *Fr.* The Vanity of Human Wishes. OBEC; SeCePo
But, grant thy poetry should find success. John Oldham. *Fr.* A Satire. ViBoPo
But, gratious God, how well dost thou provide. *See* But, gracious God. . .
But half of me is woman grown. To a Vagabond. Constance Davies Woodrow. CaP
But hark! a sound is stealing on my ear. Charles Stuart Calverley. *Fr.* Beer. FiBHP
But hark! the cry is Astur. Horatius. Macaulay. *Fr.* Lays of Ancient Rome. OBWP
But, hark, 'tis late; the Whistlers knock from Plough. Evening Prayer. Edward Benlowes. *Fr.* Theophila. FaBoEn
But hark! What hubbub now is this that comes. Charles Harpur. *Fr.* The Temple of Infamy. PoAu-1
But harken, my America, my own. The Errand Imperious. Edwin Markham. PAL; PGD
But he comes! the Messiah of royalty comes! George the Fourth in Ireland. Byron. OBRV
But he followed the pair to Pawtucket. Limerick. *Unknown.* TreF
But he his wonted pride. Satan and His Host. Milton. *Fr.* Paradise Lost, I. OBS
But He Was Cool; or, He Even Stopped for Green Lights. Don L. Lee. AmNP; BPo; NoAM; PoBA
"But hear. If you stay, and the child be born." In the Restaurant. Thomas Hardy. *Fr.* Satires of Circumstance. MoAB; MoBrPo
But here, at starting, I must just premise. John Moultrie. *Fr.* Sir Launfal. OBRV
"But hold y . . . hold y . . ." says Robin. The Jolly Pinder of Wakefield. *Unknown.* ESPB
But how can I describe the doleful sight. Vision of Sorrow. Thomas Sackville. *Fr.* Induction to "The Mirror for Magistrates." LoBV
But How It Came from Earth. Conrad Aiken. MoAB; MoAmPo
But how many merry monthes be in the yeere? Robin Hood and the Curtal Friar. *Unknown.* ESPB
But how shall I, unblamed, express. Dress. Henry Luttrell. *Fr.* Advice to Julia. OBRV
But how shall we this union well expresse? In What Manner the Soule Is United to the Body [*or* The Soul and the Body]. Sir John Davies. *Fr.* Nosce Teipsum. CTC; LiTB; NOBE; OBSC; PoEL-2
But I Am Growing Old and Indolent. Robinson Jeffers. AP; NoAM; NOBA; TAP
But I Do Not Need Kindness. Gregory Corso. CoPo; NeAP
But I knew it: a verse is a magic helmet. The Seven-League Boots. Ilarie Voronca, *tr. by* Willis Barnstone *and* Matei Calinescu. VWA
But I Shall Weep. Beatrice Redpath. CaP
But I think the king of that country comes out from his tireless host. The Gospel of Labor. Henry van Dyke. WGRP
But I was dead, an hour or more. Escape. Robert Graves. BrPo; MoBrPo
But if a man should eat green figs at noon. Beware of Figs. Nicophon, *tr. by* Charles Duke Yonge. FaBoUs
But if I look the ice is gone from the lake. Spring of the Thief. John Logan. BiP; CAPP; NNaP
But if I were a dandelion weed. It's True I'm No Miss America. Stephanie Slowinsky. AMV-80
But if that I may have truly. A Song of Ale. *At. to* William Stevenson. *Fr.* Gammer Gurton's Needle. OBSC
But if the darkness and corruption leave. Christina Rossetti. *Fr.* Remember. LO
But if there be a power too just and strong. Dryden. *Fr.* Religio Laici. NOCV
But in the crowding darkness not a word did they say. The Old-Marrieds. Gwendolyn Brooks. AmNP; PoBA
But in the dome of mighty Mars the red. The Knight's Tale. Chaucer, *tr. by* Dryden. *Fr.* The Canterbury Tales. OBWP
But in the end one tires of the high-flown. About the Phoenix. James Merrill. NoAM
But in the last days it shall come to pass. And They Shall Beat Their Swords into Plowshares [*or* Neither Shall They Learn War Any More]. Bible, *O.T.* *Fr.* Micah. TreF; TRV
But it was right that she. His Wife. Shirley Kaufman. LCAP
But, John, have you seen the world, said he. Angle of Vision. Robert Rendall. OxBTC
But, knowing now that they would have her speak. The Defence of Guenevere. William Morris. OAEP; TEP; VLP
But let applause be dealt in all we may. The Vicar. George Crabbe. *Fr.* The Borough. OBNC
But lo! at length the day is lingered out. Francis Thompson. *Fr.* Sister Songs. OBMV
But, lo! from forth a copse that neighbours by. The Courser and the Jennet. Shakespeare. *Fr.* Venus and Adonis. FM; LoBV; NOBE; OBSC; PH; PoPle
But lo we see, we touch, sayeth John. Of the Holy Eucharist. *Unknown.* ACP
"But, Lord," she said, "my shoulders still are strong." At the Top of the Road. Charles Buxton Going. HBV-2
But love, first learnèd in a lady's eyes. Shakespeare. *Fr.* Love's Labour's Lost, IV, iii. PP
But love whilst that thou mayst be loved again. To Delia, XXXVII. Samuel Daniel. EIL; NoP; OBSC
But Man, Proud Man. Shakespeare. *See* Isabella Condemns Tyranny.
But mind, but thought/ If these have been the master part of us. Life and Thought. Matthew Arnold. *Fr.* Empedocles on Etna. FiP
But most by numbers judge a poet's song. Poetical Numbers [*or* Sound and Sense]. Pope. *Fr.* An Essay on Criticism. FaBoUs; HAP; NIP; OBEC; PP; SeCePo
But most of all subdued, or fearful least. James Hurdis. *Fr.* The Favourite Village. PBBP
But my good little man, you have made a mistake. To a Boy-Poet of the Decadence. Sir Owen Seaman. CenHV; FiBHP
But nearer night than you, my younger. Solomon and Morolph, Their Last Encounter. Oscar Levertin, *tr. by* Richard Burns *and* Göran Printz-Pahlson. VWA
But no, the familiar symbol, as that the/ curtain. Time in the Rock, XCII. Conrad Aiken. VGW
But not so odd. Cecil Browne. DBV
But now at thirty years my hair is grey. Growing Old. Byron. *Fr.* Don Juan, I. NOBE; SCV
But now Athenian mountains they descry. The Shipwreck. William Falconer. GoTL
"But now farewell. I am going a long way." Tennyson. *Fr.* Morte d'Arthur. FaBoRV
But now more serious let me grow. Matthew Green. *Fr.* The Spleen. PoEL-3
But now Mr. Ferritt. And Mr. Ferritt. Judith Wright. MoBrPo
But now my Muse toyled with continuall care. Sonnet. Richard Barnfield. Sonnets, XX. PeHV
But now, no longer deaf to honour's call. Homer, *tr. by* Pope. *Fr.* The Iliad, VI. OBVE
But now the dentist cannot die. Andrew Lang. CenHV
But now the gentle dew-fall sends abroad. Looking down on Nether Stowey. Samuel Taylor Coleridge. *Fr.* Fears in Solitude. FaBoPP
But now the salmon-fishers moist. Carrying Their Coracles. Andrew Marvell. *Fr.* Upon Appleton House. ChTr
But now the wholesome music of the wood. Vivien's Song. Tennyson. *Fr.* Idylls of the King. OAEL-2
But, O immortals! What had I to plead. Christopher Smart. *Fr.* Hymn to the Supreme Being on Recovery from a Dangerous Fit of Illness. NOEC
But O, my Muse, what numbers wilt thou find. Blenheim [*or* A Poem to His Grace the Duke of Marlborough]. Joseph Addison. *Fr.* The Campaign. OBEC; OBWP
But O! the freedom, pleasure and the ease. On Giving Up Smoking. Lawrence Spooner. *Fr.* A Looking-Glass for Smokers. NOEC
But of all the plagues, the greatest is untold. Juvenal, *tr. fr. Latin by* Dryden. *Fr.* Satires, VI. OBSV
But oh! o'er all, forget not Kilda's race. St. Kilda. William Collins. *Fr.* Ode on the Popular Superstitions of the Highlands. FaBoEn
But Once. Theodore Winthrop. AA
But once upon a time. Cranach. Sir Herbert Read. BrPo; FaBoMo
But one apocalyptic lion's whelp (in flesh). There Is No Opera like "Lohengrin." John Wheelwright. NYBP; WhC
But one of the whole mammoth-brood still kept. Keats. *Fr.* Hyperion, I. OBRV
But only to be memories of spiritual gate. Immortality. Samuel Greenberg. LiTA
But peaceful was the night. Milton. *Fr.* On the Morning of Christ's Nativity. FaBoCh
But Perhaps. Nelly Sachs, *tr. fr. German by* Ruth *and* Matthew Mead. BoWoP
But piteous things we are—when I am gone. Robert Nichols. *Fr.* Sonnets to Aurelia. OBMV
"But plett a wand o bonnie birk." Sweet William's Ghost. *Unknown.* ESPB
But poets are name-proud craftsmen; Greeks and Jews. Karl Shapiro. *Fr.* Essay on Rime. PP

But pretty though as/ roses is. Three Sayings from Highlands, North Carolina. Jonathan Williams. OBAL
But Robin he walkes in the greene fforest. Robin Hood and the Butcher. *Unknown.* ESPB
But say thou very woman, why to me. To His Unconstant Friend. Henry King. AnAnS-2
But see here comes thy reverend Sire. Milton. *Fr.* Samson Agonistes. EBEV
But see the fading many-colour'd woods. James Thomson. *Fr.* The Seasons: Autumn. EnRP; LoBV
But see this happy village festival. William E. Marshall. *Fr.* Brookfield. CaP
But Sgurr nan Gillean the best Sgurr of them. Sgurr Nan Gillean. Sorley MacLean. *Fr.* The Cuillin. PoSH
But, sires, o word forgat I in my tale. Chaucer. *Fr.* The Canterbury Tales: The Pardoner's Tale. EBEV
But, soft! What light through yonder window breaks. Shakespeare. *Fr.* Romeo and Juliet, II, ii. MOON
But some one will ask, "How are the dead raised?" Bible, *N.T.* *Fr.* First Corinthians. DL
But, Still, He. Henry N. Lucas. AMV-81
"But Still in Israel's Paths They Shine." Carter Revard. VoR
But still the thunder of Los peals loud and thus the thunder's cry. Blake. *Fr.* Jerusalem. OAEL-2
But sweet sister Death has gone debauched today and stalks. David Jones. *Fr.* In Parenthesis. OBWP
But teeming women, when desire grows strong. Cravings during Pregnancy. M. Saint-Marthe. *Fr.* Paedotrophiae; or, The Art of Bringing Up Children. FaBoUs
But That Is Another Story. Donald Justice. CoAP; NePoEA-2
But that Thou art my wisdom, Lord. Submission. George Herbert. JCP
"But that was nothing to what things came out." Welsh Incident. Robert Graves. CMoP; NOBE; OxBTC; WSC
But That Was Yesterday. Aileen Fisher. SoPo
But that which most I wonder at, which most. Innocence. Thomas Traherne. AnAnS-1
But the broad light glares and beats. Tennyson. *Fr.* Maud. SyP
But the chief/ Are poets. Poets. Mark Akenside. *Fr.* The Pleasures of Imagination, IV. OBEC
But the Copperbelt night is a snake. The Leader. Dorothy Livesay. MoCV; PeCV
But the kitten, how she starts. Wordsworth. *Fr.* The Kitten and Falling Leaves. PCat
But the light returns. Dreams. André Breton, *tr. by* Robert Duncan. InPS
But the men who are now dying. Breakthrough. John Sinclair. NBP
But the morn to the noon hath fallen, and the afternoon to the eve. The Brooding of Sigurd. William Morris. *Fr.* The Story of Sigurd the Volsung. SeCePo
But the vast pile th' amazed vulgar views. The Destruction of Troy. Virgil, *tr. by* Sir John Denham. *Fr.* The Aeneid, II. SeCV-1
But Thee, but Thee, O sovereign Seer of time. Sidney Lanier. *Fr.* The Crystal. TrPWD
But Then and There the Sun Bore Down. N. Scott Momaday. CDW
But then there comes that moment rare. Voices of the Air. Katherine Mansfield. HBMV
But there are richer entanglements. Love and Friendship. Keats. *Fr.* Endymion, I. OBRV
But there is no black jaw which cannot be broken by our word. Kenneth Patchen. *Fr.* The Journal of Albion Moonlight. NaP
But there is one, they say. He Walks in Peace. *Unknown, at. to* Lao-tzu. *Fr.* Tao Teh King. TRV
But there was/ once/ a time. Eleni Vakalo, *tr. fr. Greek by* John Stathatos. WPOW
But they're crazy, I'm telling you. Those Zionists. Crescenzo del Monte, *tr. by* Barbara Garvin. VWA
But this by sure experiment we know. Of the Pythagorean Philosophy. Ovid, *tr. by* Dryden. *Fr.* Metamorphoses, XV. FM
But this fruit-dish (I suppose it is for fruit). A Good Thing. Ray Mathew. CBAP
But, this I found. Robert Norwood. *Fr.* The Man of Kerioth. CaP
But this is learning; to have skill to throw. Learning. George Chapman. *Fr.* Euthymiae Raptus; or, The Tears of Peace. SeCePo
But this, so feminine? Donald Davie. *Fr.* The Forests of Lithuania. OxBTC
But thou, Israel, My servant. Israel, My Servant. Bible, *O.T.* *Fr.* Isaiah. TrJP
But thou my deere sweet-sounding lute be still. Diella, XVI. Richard Lynche. AAS
But to His Mother Mary. Milton. *Fr.* Paradise Regained, II. ISi
But to reach the archimedean point. "Mysticism Has Not the Patience to Wait for God's Revelation." Richard Eberhart. MoPo; NoAM
But to see now how strangely things sometimes turn out. "Thomas Ingoldsby." *Fr.* The Ingoldsby Legends: A Lay of St. Gengulphus. VLP
But Troy, alas, methought above them all. Troy. Thomas Sackville. *Fr.* Induction to "The Mirror for Magistrates." SeCePo
But twelve short years you lived, my son. His Son. Callimachus, *tr. by* G. B. Grundy. AWP
But Two There Are. C. Day Lewis. OxBI
But unto him came swift calamity. Frederick Goddard Tuckerman. Sonnets, II, ix. AP
But, venture on the darkness; and within. A Fauxbourg. George Croly. OBRV
But Venus first. Sister Juana Ines de la Cruz, *tr. by* Samuel Beckett. *Fr.* First Dream. BoWoP
But was the language alive? The Test. Robert Friend. GP
But we are set to strive to make our mark. Sonnet. Frederick Goddard Tuckerman. Sonnets, III, xv. TrCP
But We Shall Bloom. Haim Guri, *tr. fr. Hebrew by* David Kuselewitz. TrJP
But well away, so is mine heart woe. To Chaucer. Thomas Hoccleve. *Fr.* De Regimine Principum. ACP
But what, by the fur on your satin sleeves. The Retort Discourteous. Stephen Vincent Benét. HBMV
But what dark flag. Shark's Fin. Eithne Wilkins. NeBP
But what is happening I see. The Birds of Arles. David Fisher. NPGG
But when Grandpa, the miner, came back from the States. Une Vie. Pentti Saarikoski, *tr. by* Anselm Hollo. ELU
But when I looked further. Maps to Nowhere. David Rosenberg. VWA
But when I waked, I saw that I saw not. A Storm at Sea. John Donne. *Fr.* The Storm. NOBE; PoPle
But when it was my turn to wrestle with the angel. Under the Ladder to Heaven. Elizabeth Fenton. NMM
But when that comely he covered his wits. The Temptation of Sir Gawain. *Unknown.* *Fr.* Sir Gawain and the Green Knight. ACP
But when the golden-thron'd Aurora made. *Unknown, formerly at. to* Homer; *tr. by* Congreve. *Fr.* The Hymn to Venus. OBVE
But when the next day brake from under ground. Percivale's Quest. Tennyson. *Fr.* Idylls of the King. OAEL-2
But when the Pharisees had heard that he had put the Sadducees. The Great Commandment. Bible, *N.T.* *Fr.* St. Matthew. TreFT
But when the water roars around us. The Ocean. Louis Dudek. *Fr.* Provincetown. MoCV
But when with her white horses day shone fair. Salamis. Aeschylus, *tr. by* G. M. Cookson. *Fr.* The Persians. WaaP
But where began the change; and what's my crime? George Meredith. Modern Love, X. NBM; PoEL-5
But where shall wisdom be found? Bible, *O.T.* *Fr.* Job. TreFT
But where to find the happiest spot below. The First, Best Country. Goldsmith. *Fr.* The Traveller. GN
But wherefore do not you a mightier waie. Sonnets, XVI. Shakespeare. FaBoEn
"But who art thou, with curious beauty graced." Opportunity. Machiavelli, *tr. by* James Elroy Flecker. AWP
But who considers well will find indeed. Andrew Marvell. *Fr.* The Loyal Scot. ViBoPo
But who is this, what thing of sea or land? Delilah. Milton. *Fr.* Samson Agonistes. SeCePo
But who the melodies of morn can tell? Nature and the Poets. James Beattie. *Fr.* The Minstrel. OBEC; SeCePo; ViBoPo
But who tipped the sand out of your shoes. Burning Sand of Sinai. Nelly Sachs, *tr. by* Keith Bosley. VWA
But whoso may, thrice happy man him hold. Spenser. *Fr.* An Hymn of Heavenly Beauty. WGRP
But why are you sleeping, your wispy black hair. Anima. Diana O Hehir. NPGG
"But why do you go?" said the lady, while both sate under the yew. Lord Walter's Wife. Elizabeth Barrett Browning. BeLS; HAP
But will you woo this wild-cat? Petruchio Is Undaunted by Katharina. Shakespeare. *Fr.* The Taming of the Shrew, I, ii. TreFT
But word is come to Warrington. Sir John Butler. *Unknown.* ESPB
But yesterday she played with childish things. The Dead Child. George Barlow. OBVV
But yesterday the earth drank like a child. A Letter to His Friend Isaac. Judah Halevi, *tr. by* Emma Lazarus. TrJP
But yesterday, when from the bath he stept. Epigram. Strato, *tr. by* Sydney Oswald. PeHV
But you can Life upon the Poor bestow. To a Good Physician. William Wycherley. ACP
But You, My Darling, Should Have Married the Prince. Kathleen Spivack. AmPA; NMM
But you, Thomas Jefferson. Brave New World. Archibald MacLeish. NOBA; OFD; OxBA
"But, you're so/ different," they said of. The Photograph the Cat Licks. Beatrice Walter. NMM

Butch, a black cocker spaniel, collected. A History of the Pets. David Huddle. PPJ
Butch Is Back. Earl Gene Box. LFAC
"Butch" Weldy. Edgar Lee Masters. *Fr.* Spoon River Anthology. NePA; SaC
Butcher, The. Hugo Williams. OxBTC
Butcher, a bald guy, The. Kicking from Centre Field. David McFadden. NeAC
Butcher Boy, The. *Unknown.* AmFP; BaBo; ViBoPo
(Butcher's Boy, The.) FSW
Butcherboy. Tom Schmidt. NeAC
Butcher carves veal for two, The. The Butcher. Hugo Williams. OxBTC
Butcher Shop. Charles Simic. AmPA; LCAP; NNaP
Butcher's Boy, The. *Unknown. See* Butcher Boy, The.
Butcher's Wife. Herbert Scott. GP
Butchery. Sandra McPherson. LCAP
Butler's Proclamation. Paul Hamilton Hayne. PAH
Butter. Tom Schmidt. NeAC
Butter and ink. Note on Modern Journalism during the Last Campaign. E. L. Mayo. FAZ
Butterbean Tent, The. Elizabeth Madox Roberts. GoJo; SUS
Buttercup Cow. Elizabeth Rendall. TiPo
Buttercup nodded and said good-by. August. Celia Thaxter. FaPON; YeAr
Buttercup, the cow, had a new baby calf. The New Baby Calf. Edith Newlin Chase. SoPo; TiPo
Buttercups. Louis Ginsberg. HBVY
Buttercups. Wilfrid Thorley. FaPON; HBV-1; HBVY; OBVV
Buttercups about the rocks and the sky. The Pass. John Logan. LCAP
Buttercups and Daisies. Mary Howitt. HBV-1; HBVY; OHIP; OxBChV
Buttercups, buttercups/ What do you hold? Buttercups. Louis Ginsberg. HBVY
Buttered Pippin-Pies. John Davies of Hereford. *See* Author Loving These Homely Meats, The.
Butterflies. John Davidson. HBV-1
Butterflies. Haniel Long. HBMV
Butterflies. Clive Sansom. BoAnP
Butterflies, butterflies. Corn-grinding Song. *Unknown, tr. by* Natalie Curtis. AWP; SUS
Butterflies flutter and flit o'er the bay. Unique among Girls. *Malay Oral Tradition, tr. by* R. J. Wilkinson *and* R. O. Winstedt. WTO
Butterfly. Peter Armstrong. PCP
Butterfly, The. Margaret Avison. OBCV
Butterfly, The. Gray Burr. CoPo
Butterfly. Hilda Conkling. TiPo
Butterfly, The. Pavel Friedmann, *tr. fr. Czech by* Dennis Silk. VWA
Butterfly, The. Robert Stephen Hawker. EBVV
Butterfly, The. Alice Archer James. AA
Butterfly, The. Kikaku, *tr. fr. Japanese by* Harold G. Henderson. SoPo
Butterfly. D. H. Lawrence. SOTW
Butterfly, The. Adelaide O'Keefe. HBV-1; HBVY
Butterfly, The. Alice Freeman Palmer. HBV-1
Butterfly. William Jay Smith. GoJo; TiPo
Butterfly, a [*or* the] cabbage-white, The. Flying Crooked. Robert Graves. FaBoMo; LiTM; MP; PCP; TwCP
Butterfly, an idle thing, The. The Butterfly. Adelaide O'Keefe. HBV-1; HBVY
Butterfly and the Bee, The. William Lisle Bowles. HBV-1; HBVY
Butterfly and the Caterpillar, The. Joseph Lauren. OnMSP
Butterfly and the Snail, The. John Gay. *Fr.* Fables. FM
Butterfly Bones; or, Sonnet against Sonnets. Margaret Avison. LiTM
Butterfly, butterfly, butterfly, butterfly. Butterfly Song. *Tr. by* Frances Densmore. OBVE
Butterfly in Church, A. George Marion McClellan. BANP
Butterfly in the Fields. Joseph Campbell. BoAnP
Butterfly it's, The/ a crazy toy. Butterfly. Peter Armstrong. PCP
Butterfly maidens. Lahpu, *tr. fr. Hopi Indian by* Natalie Curtis. WTO
Butterfly on Rock. Irving Layton. NOBC
Butterfly, one summer morn, A. The Butterfly and the Caterpillar. Joseph Lauren. OnMSP
Butterfly Song. *Tr. fr. Acoman Indian by* Frances Densmore. OBVE
Butterfly, the cabbage-white, The. *See* Butterfly, a cabbage-white, The.
Butterfly, the wind blows sea-ward, strong beyond the garden wall! Butterfly. D. H. Lawrence. SOTW
Butterfly's Ball, The. William Roscoe. OnUR; OxBChV; RHPC
Butterfly's Ball and the Grasshopper's Feasts, The. The Peacock "At Home." Catherine Ann Dorset. OxBChV
Buttermilk Hill. *Unknown.* FSW
Butternut and walnut. Hillside Pause. Catharine Morris Wright. GoYe
Butter's Etymological Spelling Book ("Butter's books I ne'er have read"). Hartley Coleridge. GLGT
Buttery, sugary, syrupy waffle, A. The Groaning Board. "Pink." InMe
Button to chin. *Unknown.* FaBoUs; OxNR
Buttons. Walter de la Mare. DTC; FaBoNo
Buttons, a farthing a pair. Mother Goose. OxNR
Buxom Joan. Congreve. *See* Soldier and a Sailor, A.
Buxom Lass. *Unknown.* ErPo
Buxom Young Dairy Maid, The. *Unknown.* OBET
Buxom young fellow from London came down, A. Nine Times a Night. *Unknown.* OBET
Buy a fresh chicken. Sweet 'n Sour. Genny Lim. BrSi
Buy Me an Ounce and I'll Sell You a Pound. E. E. Cummings. NCSH; OxBA
Buy my English posies! The Flowers. Kipling. OBVV
Buy One Now. D. J. Enright. NOBL
Buy the paper, take it home. Coming and Going. Mitchell Goodman. VGW
Buy tobacco, buy tobacco. *Unknown.* PBBP
Buy Us a Little Grain. Christine Lavant, *tr. fr. German by* Michael Hamburger. WPOW
Buying a Record. Robert Peters. BXAP
Buying a Shop on Dizengoff. Erez Biton, *tr. fr. Hebrew by* Judith Katz. VWA
Buying the book at last. Stopping the Heart. Murray Edmond. OCNZ
Buying the Dog. Michael Ondaatje. Str
Buying wood from Mrs. Lalo Roybal. Manly Diversion. Karl Kopp. GP
Buz, Quoth the Blue Fly. Ben Jonson. *Fr.* Oberon, the Fairy Prince. NA; TEP
("Buzz, quoth the blue fly," *sl. diff.*) OxNR
(Catch, A.) ElL
(Satyrs' [*or* Satyres] Catch, The.) FaBoNo; FM
(Song of the Satyrs.) PoPle
Buzz. Jim Tollerud. VoR
Buzz Plane, The. Robert Francis. TW
Buzz saw snarled and rattled in the yard, The. "Out, Out." Robert Frost. CABA; DL; FF; HAP; HeIP; OxBA; PAI; PPoe; SoSe; UnPo; VGW; WeW
Buzzard. Michael Daugherty. PoSH
Buzzard finds no fault with itself, A. In Praise of a Guilty Conscience. Wislawa Szymborska, *tr. by* Grazyna Drabik *and* Austin Flint. AMV-81
Buzzards, The. Martin Armstrong. HBMV
Buzzards over Pondy Woods, The. Pondy Woods. Robert Penn Warren. MoAmPo
Buzzing, buzzing, buzzing, my golden-belted bees. The Bees of Middleton Manor. May Probyn. GoBC
Buzzing Doubt, The. Donald L. Hill. NCSH
Bwagamoyo. Lebert Bethune. PoBA
Bwoat, The. William Barnes. VLP
By/ birds/ bird flocks. Divination. Jerred Metz. VWA
By a bank as I lay. Dawn. *Unknown.* OBSC; PBBP
By a Bank of Pinks and Lilies. *Unknown.* ErPo
By a Chapel as I Came. *Unknown.* ChTr; GBP; OxBM
By a clear well, within a little field. Of Three Girls and of Their Talk. Boccaccio, *tr. fr. Italian by* Dante Gabriel Rossetti. *Fr.* Sonnets. AWP
By a dim road, o'ergrown with dry thin grass. Cut It Down. Mary Elizabeth Coleridge. MoVE
By a dismal cypress lying. A Song from the Italian. Dryden. *Fr.* The Kind Keeper. SeCV-2
By a flat rock on the shore of the sea. The Rock. *Unknown, tr. by* Geoffrey Grigson. ChTr; GBL
By a Forest. *Unknown.* NCEP
(Hare, The.) OxBM
By a gentle river laid. Love's Arithmetic. Sir Edward Sherburne. CavP
By a grey stone pile. The Old. George Mosby, Jr. LFAC
By a Lake in Minnesota. James Wright. AmFN
By a peninsula the painter sat. Conduct. Samuel Greenberg. CrMA; LiTA
By a peninsula the wanderer sat and sketched. Emblems of Conduct. Hart Crane, *after* Samuel Greenberg. LiTA; LiTM; NePA
By a Rich Fast Moving Stream. John Tagliabue. ELU
By a route obscure and lonely. Dream-Land. Poe. AmPP; AP; LiTA; NePA; NOBA; OxBA; TAP
By a window overlooking tv antennas and bakery. Reflections on the Death of a Parrot. Jaime Jacinto. BrSi
By Achmelvich Bridge. Norman MacCaig. OxBS
By all means sing of love, but if you do. The Truest Poetry Is the Most Feigning; or, Ars Poetica for Hard Times. W. H. Auden. NYBP
By all-star orchestra, they dine in space. Space Shuttle. Diane Ackerman. MAYP; SUW
By all the glories of the day. Before Action. William Noel Hodgson. WGRP
By all the laws. The Tree Is Father to the Man. Lou Lipsitz. NCSH
By all the published facts in the case. About Children. Phyllis McGinley. OBAL

By an alley lined with tumble-down shacks. Mexican Quarter. John Gould Fletcher. Arizona Poems, II. BPAW
By and By ("By and by, I'm gwinter lay down my heavy load"), *with music.* *Unknown.* BoAN-1
By and By ("By and by, star shines down on number one"). *Unknown.* FSW
By and by. Epitaph on a Waiter [*or* On a Waiter]. David McCord. NIP; OBAL; PPJ; WhC
By April mist. Spring Song. Katharine O'Brien. GoYe
By archy/ the roach that scurries. Ballade of the Under Side. Don Marquis. *Fr.* Archys Life of Mehitabel. InvP
By Arthur's Dale as late I went. Bonny Bee Hom. *Unknown.* ESPB
By Babel's Streams, *with music.* Philip Freneau. AH
By banks where burned awhile the rose. Renascence. Muredach J. Dooher. OnYI
By Bendemeer's Stream. Thomas Moore. (Bendemeer.) FSW; OBRV
By Blue Ontario's Shore, *sels.* Walt Whitman.
"I swear I begin to see the meaning of these things!" *fr.* XV. (Marches Now the War Is Over.) InPS
"I will confront these shows of the day and the night!" *fr.* XVIII. (Marches Now the War Is Over.) InPS
Poet, The, IX-XVII. MoAmPo
"Rhymes and rhymers pass away," *fr.* XIII. (Marches Now the War Is Over.) InPS
By bluster, graft, and doing people down. A Tribute to the Founder. Kingsley Amis. DBV; NePoEA-2
By Candlelight. Sylvia Plath. SBG
By Canoe through the Fir Forest. James Dickey. NYBP
By Cavité on the bay. The Battle of Manila. Richard Hovey. PAH
By channels of coolness the echoes are calling. Bell-Birds. Henry Kendall. PoAu-1
By Chickamauga's crooked stream the martial trumpets blew. The Ballad of Chickamauga. Maurice Thompson. PAH
By Clyde's bonny banks where I sadly did wander. The Blantyre Explosion. *Unknown.* OBET
By Cobequid Bay. Alexander Louis Fraser. CaP
By Coelia's Arbor. Sheridan. OnYI
By Cool Siloam's Shady Rill. Reginald Heber. ELP; NOCV; OxBoCh
By copse and hedgerow, waste and wall. Knapweed. A. C. Benson. HBV-1
By dark severance the apparition head. Painted Head [*or* Painting; a Head]. John Crowe Ransom. AP; CoBMV; CrMA; LiTA; LiTM; MoAB; MoAmPo; MoPo; MoVE; NoAM; NOBA; OxBA
By day & also by night & you are. Ian Wedde. Earthly: Sonnets for Carlos, 10. OCNZ
By day Golgotha sleeps, but when night comes. Night at Gettysburg. Don C. Seitz. OHIP
By day my timid passions stand. Serenade. Richard Middleton. HBV-1
By day she woos me, soft, exceeding fair. The World. Christina Rossetti. BoWoP; VLP
By day the bat is cousin to the mouse. The Bat. Theodore Roethke. GoJo; OBCA; PAI; PDV; RHPC; WSC
By day the fields and meadows cry. The Poet's Call. Thomas Curtis Clarke. WGRP
By day the skyscraper looms in the smoke and sun and has a soul. Skyscraper. Carl Sandburg. PoPl
By day your high gates are closed. Seal of Fire. Mordecai Temkin, *tr. by* Jeremy Garber. VWA
By death's favor. Epitaph on an Engraver. Henry David Thoreau. EyDe
By Deputy. Arthur St. John Adcock. CenHV
By dim light, there not being much. Obligatory Love Poem. P. L. Jacobs. LFAC
By dint of color. A Dab of Color. Theodore Weiss. VGW
By divination came the Dorians. In Arcadia. Lawrence Durrell. MoBrPo
By ear, he sd. Maximus of Gloucester, To You. Charles Olson. *Fr.* The Maximus Poems. NeAP
By easy slope to west as if it had. Cheyenne Mountain. Helen Hunt Jackson. BPAW; PoOW
By-Election Idyll. Peter Dickinson. FiBHP
By every ebb of the river-side. Pisgah. Willard Wattles. WGRP
By every light, in every pose. In God's Eternal Studios. Paul Shivell. *Fr.* The Studios Photographic. HBV-2
By fall the vines have crawled out. Pumpkin. Robert Morgan. GeTw
By fate, not option, frugal Nature gave. Xenophanes. Emerson. NOBA
By favorable breezes fanned. Cythère. Paul Verlaine, *tr. by* Arthur Symons. AWP; SyP
By feathers green, across Casbeen. The Phoenix. A. C. Benson. OBEV; OBVV
By Fiat of Adoration. Oscar Williams. LiTM; NePA
By Frazier Creek Falls. Gary Snyder. GOA
By Gentle Love. *Unknown.* TRV
By Godde and Seynt Johne I sweare ye. The Eternale Footeman's Tale. George Moor. BXAP
By granting charters of peace. An Anglo-Irishman's Complaint. *Unknown.* AnIL
By Hallucination Visited. Robert Horan. EAS
By hard journeys in a dead land. Omphalos: The Well. Seán Jennett. NeIP
By Heaven 'tis false, I am not vain. The Defiance. Aphra Behn. EnLoPo
By Heaven's! 'twas bravely done! Spoken Extempore. Earl of Rochester. SeCePo
By Her Aunt's Grave. Thomas Hardy. *Fr.* Satires of Circumstance. MoAB; MoBrPo
By Her That Is Most Assured to Her Self. Spenser. *See* Amoretti, LVIII.
By Heraclides. *Unknown, tr. fr. Greek by* William Cowper. OBVE
By Herndyke Mill there haunts, folks tell. The Silver Bird of Herndyke Mill. Edmund Blunden. GoTL
By Him. Ben Jonson. TRV
By him lay heavy sleep, the cousin of death. Sleep. Thomas Sackville. *Fr.* The Induction to "The Mirror for Magistrates." WHA
By his commandement hee maketh the snow to fall apace. Bible, Apocrypha. *Fr.* Ecclesiasticus. OBVE
By hook, by crook, by hair of head. Primary Education. Phyllis McGinley. GLGT
By illness pent in lime-tree bower. Lines Written near Linton, on Exmoor. Daniel Hoffman. BXAP
By itself and from a distance. The Brick. Paul Roche. NYBP
"By Jesus Christ" he said. Of Flowers. Alan Loney. OCNZ
By June our brook's run out of song and speed. Hyla Brook. Robert Frost. BoNaP; TwAmPo
By Killarney's lakes and fells, em'rald isles and winding bays. Killarney. Edward Falconer. TreFS
By landscape reminded once of his mother's figure. Prologue. W. H. Auden. NoAM
By Langley bush I roam, but the bush hath left its hill. Enclosure. John Clare. *Fr.* Remembrance. NBM
By late in spring the cottonmouths and rattlers. Coon Hunt, Sixth Month (1955). Sydney Lea. MAYP
By leave of my eyes that watched the bereaving. Pledge. Avraham Shlonsky, *tr. by* Francis Landy. VWA
By Loe Pool. Arthur Symons. VLP
By Logan's streams that rin sae deep. Logan Braes. John Mayne. OxBS
By loss in play men oft forget. The Gambler's Repentance. Gerald, Baron of Offaly. AnIV
By lost Clonard the river meads still hold. Clonard. Thomas S. Jones, Jr. HBMV
By love was my eye opened. How Beautiful You Are: 3. Elaine Edelman. IHMS
By-low, My Babe. *Unknown.* *See* Balow.
By Magdalen Bridge, Oxford. Gerard Manley Hopkins. FaBoPP
By Master Saville who, conceivably, from the accuracy of his drawing. *The River Map* and We're Done. Charles Olson. *Fr.* The Maximus Poems. CoPo
By Memory Inspired. *Unknown.* AnIV
By mid-afternoon, the hot sun. Stockton Lake; Stockton, Missouri. Mark Sanders. WOLT
By mid-day it was warm enough; she climbed. Aunt Alice in April. William H. Matchett. CTBA
By miracles exceeding power of man. Crucifying. John Donne. AnAnS-1; OBS
By Moonlight. *Unknown, tr. fr. French by* Louis Untermeyer. UnTE
By moonlight. Conversation Piece. Robert Graves. GrPl
By myself walking. Hypochondriacus. Charles Lamb. BXAP
By nature shy, by nature. Whispering Clouds. Mariquita Platov. AMV-80
By Nebo's lonely mountain. The Burial of Moses. Cecil Frances Alexander. BeLS; BLPA; BLRP; GN; HBV-2; WBLP
By Night. Philip Jerome Cleveland. TRV
By Night. Robert Francis. POL; VGW
By night around my temple grove. Buddha. Arno Holz, *tr. by* William Ellery Leonard. AWP
By night on my bed I sought him whom my soul loveth. On My Bed I Sought Him. Bible, *O.T.* *Fr.* The Song of Solomon. TrJP
By night they haunted a thicket of April mist. Spectral Lovers. John Crowe Ransom. GBL; HeIP
By night we lingered on the lawn. Tennyson. In Memoriam A. H. H., XCV. HAP; LoBV; NoP; OBNC; PoEL-5
By none but me can the tale be told. The White Ship. Dante Gabriel Rossetti. OBNV; VLP
By Now. Ralph Salisbury. STE
By now I should be entering on the supreme stage. Pilgrim's Problem. C. S. Lewis. TrCP
By now you will have met. Voice. W. S. Merwin. NNaP

By numbers here from shame or censure free. Poverty in London. Samuel Johnson. *Fr.* London. ChTr; NOEC; OBEC; OBSV; ViBoPo
By orange grove and palm-tree, we walked the southern shore. Hemlock Mountain. Sarah N. Cleghorn. HBV-1
By our first strange and fatal interview. On His Mistress [*or* Elegy on His Mistress]. John Donne. Elegies, XVI. AnAnS-1; BoLoP; EBEV; GBL; LiTB; LoBV; MeLP; MePo; NOBE; PoEL-2; SeCeV; SeCP; SeCV-1; ViBoPo
By pain of stone and wearing down of bronze. Upon This Rock. Ruthven Todd. PoA
By plain analogy we're told. Ambrose Bierce. DBV
By-Products. Baron Wormser. MAYP
By proud New York and its man-piled Matterhorns. Proud New York. John Reed. HBMV; PoA
By Rail through Istria. Robert Conquest. NoAM
By Rail through the Earthly Paradise, Perhaps Bedfordshire. Denise Levertov. NNaP
By rays sharper than the sharpest angle. Noon Glare. Matthew Brennan. AMV-80
By reason of despair we set forth behind you. The Murder of Moses. Karl Shapiro. EaLo
By Return Mail. Richard Aldridge. NePoAm-2
By runnels and sea-dipped clover, easing. Green Island. William Logan. MAYP
By Saint [*or* Saynt] Mary, my lady. To [*or* In Praise of] Mistress [*or* Maystres] Isabel Pennell. John Skelton. *Fr.* The Garlande of Laurell. AAS; CH; NaS; NOBE; OAEP; OBEV; OBSC; OxBoLi; PoEL-1; SeCeV; TrGrPo; ViBoPo
By Sandy Waters. Jesse Stuart. AmFN
By Saturday I said you would be better on Sunday. The Operation. Robert Creeley. NaP
By scattered rocks and turbid waters shifting. The Mountain Heart's-Ease. Bret Harte. HBV-1
By seven vineyards on one hill. The Mystic. Witter Bynner. HBV-1
By sloth on sorrow fathered. Lollocks. Robert Graves. ChTr; DTC; EvOK
By some derision of wild circumstance. Reunion. E. A. Robinson. NoAM; NOBA
By some peculiar force centrifugal. To a Book. Elinor Wylie. LiTA
By some sad means, when reason holds no sway. Philip Freneau. *Fr.* The House of Night. PoEL-4
By special lens, photo-electric cells. A Different Speech. Louise Townsend Nicholl. ImOP
By Stubborn Stars, *sels.* Kenneth Leslie.
"Silver herring throbbed thick in my seine, The." ErPo; OBCV; PeCV
(Sonnet.) NOBC
"Warm rain whispers, but the earth knows best, A." PeCV
By such an all-embalming summer day. Near Helikon. Trumbull Stickney. LiTA; NCEP; TwAmPo
By Talland Church as I did go. The Planted Heel. Sir Arthur Quiller-Couch. EBVV
By that evening window where. Verses for the 60th Birthday of T. S. Eliot. George Barker. ChMP
By that withering oak. Daybreak. Frank Lamont Phillips. CNA
By the Arno. Oscar Wilde. EBVV
By the Babe Unborn. G. K. Chesterton. NAs
"By the Babylonish waters." By the Waters of Babylon. Heine, *tr. by* Charles Godfrey Leland. *Fr.* Hebrew Melodies. TrJP
By the banks of the roses my love and I sat down. Banks of the Roses. *Unknown.* FSW
By the beard of the Prophet the Bashaw swore. How We Burned the *Philadelphia.* Barrett Eastman. PAH
By the Beautiful Sea. Thomas Cole. NePoAm-2
By the Bivouac's Fitful Flame. Walt Whitman. AP; NoAM; NoP; OxBA
By the blue taper's trembling light. A Night-Piece on Death. Thomas Parnell. NOEC; OBEC
By the blue wooden sea. Switchback. Edith Sitwell. PBWP
By the Bridge. Ted Walker. NYBP
By the city dead-house by the gate. The City Dead-House. Walt Whitman. InPK
By the Conemaugh. Florence Earle Coates. PAH
By the cross of expiation. Stabat Mater. *At. to* Jacapone da Todi, *tr. by* Aubrey Thomas De Vere. ISi
By the Deep Nine. *At. to* W. Pearce *and to* Charles Dibdin. *See* Heaving the Lead.
By the Deep Sea. Byron. *See* Ocean, The ("Oh! that the desert were my dwelling place").
By the dry road the fathers cough and spit. The Brief Journey West. Howard Nemerov. NoAM
By the Exeter River. Donald Hall. MoBS
By the fierce flames of love I'm in a sad taking. A Love Song. Royall Tyler. TAP
By the Fire-Side. Robert Browning. EBVV; OAEL-2; VLP
By the Flat Cup. Horace, *tr. fr. Latin by* Ezra Pound. Odes, I, 31. CTC
By the flow of the inland river. The Blue and the Gray. Francis Miles Finch. AA; BLPA; BLPL; FaBoBe; HBV-2; PAH; PAL; PaPo; TreF; WBLP
By the gas-fire, kneeling. Olga Poems. Denise Levertov. LCAP; NNaP
By the gate with star and moon. Medallion. Sylvia Plath. HeIP; NoP
By the glim of a midwinterish early morning. Son and Father. C. Day Lewis. EaLo
By the great stones we chose our ground. In Love, at Stonehenge. Coventry Patmore. *Fr.* The Angel in the House. FaBoPP
By the grim grace of the Puritans she had been brought. Sarah Threeneedles. Katharine Lee Bates. HBMV
By the high steel hospital bed. Miss Alderman. Robert Winner. GP
By the highway the stream downslope. Runoff. A. R. Ammons. PPP
By the Hoof of the Wild Goat. Kipling. *Fr.* Plain Tales from the Hills. OBNC
(Predestination.) LoBV
By the impulse of my will. Magnetism. Emma Lazarus. SBG
By the Isar, in the twilight. River Roses. D. H. Lawrence. BrPo; CMoP; GBL; OAEL-2; ViBoPo
By the Klondike River. Alan Coren. OnUR
By the Lake. Lawrence Durrell. *Fr.* Eight Aspects of Melissa. NeBP
By the lake the orchards lie. Intermezzo. Robert Silliman Hillyer. NePoAm
By the lamplit stall I loitered, feasting my eyes. Sight. W. W. Gibson. MoBrPo
By the little river. The Willows. Walter Prichard Eaton. FaPON; HBMV; OHIP
By the Margin of the Great Deep. "Æ." HBMV; OBEV; OBVV
By the margin of the ocean, one morning [*or* one pleasant evening] in the month of June. The Bonny Bunch of Roses O. *Unknown.* FaBoBa; OxBoLi
By the merest chance, in the twilight gloom. What My Lover Said. Homer Greene. AA; HBV-1; TreFS
By the Moon. *Unknown, at. to* John Lyly *and to* Thomas Ravenscroft. *Fr.* The Mayde's Metamorphosis. CH
(Fairy Dances, 1.) ElL
By the morning hours. The Morning Hours. *Unknown, tr. by* Mohammed Marmaduke Pickthall. PoPl
By the new Boot's, a tool-chest with flagpoles. Aberdarcy: The Main Square. Kingsley Amis. NOBL; OxBTC
By the newly bulldozed logging road, for a hundred yards. Working against Time. David Wagoner. MAT
By the North Gate, the wind blows full of sand. Lament of the Frontier Guard. Li Po, *tr. by* Ezra Pound. AP; CoBMV; OBVE; OBWP; TwAmPo; VGW; WaaP
By the North Sea, *sels.* Swinburne.
"But afar on the headland exalted," VII. VLP
"Land that is lonelier than ruin, A," I. PoEL-5; VLP
Suffolk, *fr.* III. FaBoPP
Where Dunwich Used to Be, *fr.* VI. FaBoPP
By the old Moulmein Pagoda, lookin' eastward to [*or* lazy at] the sea. Mandalay. Kipling. BrPo; FaBV; FPL; HBV-2; LiTB; MoBrPo; NOBE; TreF; TrGrPo
By the Pacific Ocean. Joaquin Miller. AA
By the pale marge of Acheron. Villanelle of Acheron. Ernest Dowson. VLP
By the Pool. Allen Grossman. AMV-80
By the Pool at the Third Rosses. Arthur Symons. In Ireland, II. FaBoPP; OBNC; VLP
By the Potomac. Thomas Bailey Aldrich. PAH
By the public hook for the private eye. River Song. Weldon Kees. NoAM; PPP; TwAmPo
By the purple haze that lies. Indian Summer. Susanna Moodie. CaP
By the Rio Grande. The Rio Grande. Sacheverell Sitwell. SeCePo
By the River Eden. Kathleen Raine. NYBP
By the rivers [*or* waters] of Babylon [*or* Babel], there we sat down. Bible, *O.T* Psalms, CXXXVII. AWP; NAWM-1; OAEL-1, 2 *versions*; OBVE; TrGrPo; TrJP
By the Road. Geoffrey Grigson. OxBTC
By the Road to the Air-Base. Ivor Winters. CrMA
By the road to the contagious hospital. Spring and All [*or* Poem]. William Carlos Williams. AP; CABA; CMoP; CoBMV; HAP; LiTM; MoAB; MoAmPo; MoVE; NoAM; NOBA; OxBA; PPoe; QFR; TAP; UnPo
By the rosy cliffs of Devon, on a green hill's crest. Where Love Is. Amelia Josephine Burr. HBV-1
By the rude bridge that arched the flood. Concord Hymn [*or* Hymn]. Emerson. AA; AmFN; AmPP; AP; AWP; BLPA; BLPL; FaBoBe; FaBoEn; FaFP; FaPo; FaPON; FaPoR; GN; GOA; HAP; HBV-2; HBVY; HeIP; LiTA; NePA; NOBA; NoP; OBWP; OHFP; OxBA;

PAH; PAI; PAL; PoPl; SeCeV; TAP; TreF; TrGrPo; ViBoPo; WaaP; YaD
By the sad waters of separation. Exile. Ernest Dowson. BoLoP; BrPo
By the Salt Margin. Abbie Huston Evans. NePoAm
By the Saltings. Ted Walker. NYBP
By the sands of Rio Bravo. The Smugglers. Owen Wister. BPAW
By the Sea. Emily Dickinson. *See* I started early, took my dog.
By the Sea. Richard Watson Dixon. OBNC
By the Sea. Christina Rossetti. BoNaP; MOS
By the Sea. Wordsworth. *See* It Is a Beauteous Evening.
By the seven stars of her halo. Lady of O. James J. Galvin. ISi
By the shores of Gitche [*or* Gitchee] Gumee. Hiawatha's Childhood. Longfellow. *Fr.* The Song of Hiawatha. FaPON; OHFP; SpRo; TiPo; TreF; WBLP
By the side of a green stagnate pool. A Pastoral. G. A. Stevens. CoMu; ErPo
By the side of a murmuring stream an elderly gentleman sat. The Elderly Gentleman. George Canning. NA
By the Statue of King Charles at Charing Cross. Lionel Johnson. BrPo; FaBoRV; HBV-2; MoBrPo; NBM; NOBE; OBEV; OBMV; OBNC; OBVV; PoEL-5; RoGo; VLP
By the time he's suited. Cold Fact. Dick Emmons. PoPl
By the time you read this. Letter. W. S. Merwin. HAP
By the time you swear you're his. Unfortunate Coincidence. Dorothy Parker. BXAP; FaBoUs; NoP; PoPl; SBG; TreF; WhC
By the Turnstile. John Francis O'Donnell. NBM
By the wall o' the gearden, a-stannen chalk white. Black an' White. William Barnes. VLP
By the Waterfall. Friedrich Adler, *tr. fr. German by* Jethro Bithell. TrJP
By the Waters of Babylon. Benjamin Fondane, *tr. fr. French by* Edouard Roditi. VWA
By the Waters of Babylon. Heine, *tr. fr. German by* Charles Godfrey Leland. *Fr.* Hebrew Melodies. TrJP
By the Waters of Babylon, *sels.* Emma Lazarus. WPE
Currents.
Exodus, The (August 3, 1492).
By the waters of Babylon we sat down and wept. Super Flumina Babylonis. Swinburne. OBVV; PoEL-5; VLP
By the waters of Babylon we sat downe and weapte. *See* By the rivers of Babylon, there we sat down.
By the waters of Life we sat together. An Old Man's Idyl. Richard Realf. AA; HBV-1
By the Waters of Minnetonka, *with music.* J. M. Cavanass. BLSo
By the wave rising, by the wave breaking. The Crow. P. K. Page. WHW
By the wayside, on a mossy stone. Old. Ralph Hoyt. AA
By the wayside, three crows sat on a cross. Adam on His Way Home. Robert Pack. ErPo
By the Weir. W. W. Gibson. MoVE
By the wells. Zippora Returns to Moses at Rephidim. Rose Drachler. VWA
By the Wood. Robert Nichols. ChMP; HBMV; MMA
By these presents be it known. Anne Grenville, Countess Temple, Appointed Poet Laureate to the King of the Fairies. Horace Walpole. OBEC
By these slow shadows and the frosted air. Calvinist Autumnal. Elizabeth B. Harrod. NePoEA
By thine own tears thy song must tears beget. The Song-Throe. Dante Gabriel Rossetti. The House of Life, LXI. VLP
By this bright bank the easy noon. The River Glideth in a Secret Tongue. Anthony Ostroff. NePoAm-2
By this cold shuddering fit of fear. The Glen of Silence. "Hugh MacDiarmid." CMoP; NeBP
By this he knew she wept with waking eyes. Modern Love, I. George Meredith. EnLoPo; HBV-1; HeIP; HoPM; NBM; NoP; OAEL-2; OAEP; PoEL-5; VLP
By this, Leander, being near the land. Christopher Marlowe. *Fr.* Hero and Leander, Second Sestiad. EBEV; ErPo
By this low fire I often sit to woo. Frederick Goddard Tuckerman. Sonnets, I, xxv. AP
By this, the dreadfull beast drew nigh to hand. The Death of the Dragon. Spenser. *Fr.* The Faerie Queene, I, 11. WHA
By this, though deep the evening fell. Flodden [*or* The Battle]. Sir Walter Scott. *Fr.* Marmion. BSV; PoEL-4
By this time long-gowned Lumen walked abroad. William Rankins. *Fr.* Satyrus Peregrinans. OBSV
By those soft tods of wool[l]. A Conjuration, to Electra. Robert Herrick. GBL; PoEL-3
By thy cold breast and serpent smile. Byron. *Fr.* Manfred. DBV
By Thy Life I Live. Mme Guyon. *See* Adoration.
By thys fyre I warme my handys. The Months. *Unknown.* ChTr
By Tre, Pol and Pen. Cornishmen. *Unknown.* FaBoUs
By two black eyes my heart was won. Rondeau. *Unknown.* FaBoCo
By viewing Nature, Natures hand-maid, Art. Dryden. *Fr.* Annus Mirabilis. MOS
By Vows of Love Together Bound, *with music.* Eleazar Thompson Fitch. AH
By Wauchopeside. "Hugh MacDiarmid." EBEV
By Way of Preface. Edward Lear. *See* How Pleasant to Know Mr. Lear.
By way of pretext. Yakamochi, *tr. fr. Japanese. Fr.* Manyo Shu. AWP
By ways remote and distant waters sped. On the Burial of His Brother. Catullus, *tr. by* Aubrey Beardsley. AWP
By Wellesbourne and Charlcote ford. Women Singing. Sir Henry Taylor. OBVV
By what appalling dim upheaval. Simon Gerty. Elinor Wylie. OBAL
By what astrology of fear or hope. Longfellow. *Fr.* To a Child. FaBoEn
By what bold passion am I rudely led. Sir William Davenant. *Fr.* Gondibert, I. FaBoEn; OBS
By what glass of resemblance may we see. Sonnet. William Alabaster. SBVL
By what sends. Children's Rhymes. Langston Hughes. BOLo; BPo
By what word's power, the key of paths untrod. Heart's Hope. Dante Gabriel Rossetti. The House of Life, V. HBV-1
By Winter Seas. George Brandon Saul. AMV-80
By World Laid Low. *Unknown, tr. fr. Irish.* ChTr
By yellow Chame, where all the Muses reign. Cambridge and the Cam. Phineas Fletcher. *Fr.* The Apollyonists. FaBoPP
By yon bonnie banks and by yon bonnie braes. Loch Lomond. Lady John Scott. FSW; TreFS
By Yon Burn Side. Robert Tannahill. HBV-1
By yonder flowing fountain. A La Claire Fontaine (By Yonder Flowing Fountain). *Tr. fr. French by* Arthur Kevess. FSW
By your breasts. Conversation between the Chevalier de Chamilly and Mariana Alcoforado in the Manner of a Song of Regret. The Three Marias, *tr. by* Helen R. Lane. BoWoP
By your unnumbered charities. Hospital for Defectives. Thomas Blackburn. GTBS-P; OxBTC
Bye Baby Brother. Stevie Smith. TW
Bye, baby bunting. Mother Goose. HBV-1; HBVY; OxNR; SoPo; SpRo, TiPo; TrAS, *with music*
Bye baby bunting. Rhyme for Astronomical Baby. Joseph Cook. *Fr.* Boston Nursery Rhymes. InMe; QQQ; SpRo
Bye Bye Baby Blues. *Unknown.* BluL
Bye, bye, baby bunting/ Your daddy's gone a-hunting. *Unknown.* OxNR
Bye-o, baby, bye. Mama's Gone to the Mail Boat. *Unknown.* OuSiCo
Byfield Rabbit, The. Katherine Hoskins. SaC
Bygones. Bert Leston Taylor. HBMV
By'm By, *with music. Unknown.* AS
B'york! but it's lovely under the leaf. Spring Song. Donald Finkel. NYBP
Byre. Norman MacCaig. BoAnP; BSV
Byrnies, The. Thom Gunn. NePoEA-2; NoAM; OxBTC
Byron. J. Gordon Coogler. OBAL
Byron, *sel.* Joaquin Miller.
In Men Whom Men Condemn as Ill. HBV-2; PoLF; TreFT
Byron in Greece. Norman Rosten. HoAn
Byron Recollected at Bologna. Samuel Rogers. *Fr.* Italy. OBNC
Byron vs. DiMaggio. Peter Meinke. LiSp
Byron's Conspiracy. *See* Conspiracy of Charles, Duke of Byron, The. George Chapman.
Byrontown, *with music.* Larry Gorman. ShS
By's beard the Goat, by his bush-tail the Fox. Of Kate's Baldness. John Davies of Hereford. FaBoEE
Bystander, The. Rosemary Dobson. CBAP
Bystanders. William Matthews. NPAW
Bytuene Mersh[e] [*or* Betwene March] and [*or* ant] Averil. Alysoun [*or* Alison *or* Alisoun]. *Unknown.* CTC; GoBC; HAP; HeIP; MeEL; NoP; OAEL-1; OBEV; OxBM; PoEL-1; ViBoPo
By-ways, The/ of my oaten straw? Hayseed. Theodore Weiss. TwAmPo
Byzantium. W. B. Yeats. CABA; CMoP; CoBMV; EBEV; FaBoEn; FaBoMo; HAP; InPS; LiTM; LoBV; MoAB; MoBrPo; MoPo; NIP; NoAM; NOBE; NoP; OAEL-2; OAEP; OnYI; OxBTC; PPP; SeCePo; SeCeV; TEP
Byzantium Burning. Jack Gilbert. NPGG

C

CCC, The ("CCC campers near West Cummington"). Thomas Whitbread. NYBP
C. C. Rider, *with music. Unknown.* AS (A *and* B *vers.*)
C. G. Jung's "First Years." Thomas Kinsella. IPY
C Is for Charms. Eleanor Farjeon. WSC
C is for Curious Charlie. Curious Charlie. Isabel Frances Bellows. TDH

C Is for the Circus. Phyllis McGinley. *Fr.* All Around the Town. SoPo; TiPo
C. L. M. John Masefield. HBV-1; LiTM; MoBrPo; OxBTC
(To His Mother: C. L. M.) OBVV
C.S.A. Commissioners, The. *Unknown.* PAH
C Stands for Civilization. Kenneth Fearing. TrJP
C was papa's gray cat. Edward Lear. PCat
Ca' the Yowes. Burns. EnRP
(Hark! the Mavis.) OBEV
Ca' the Yowes to the Knowes. Isobel Pagan. OBEV
Ca' the Yowes to the Knowes. *Unknown.* OxBS
Cabbage. Rosemary Norman. BrRo
Cabbage tree heads, they nod. An Ordinary Day beyond Kaitaia. Kendrick Smithyman. OCNZ
Cabbages catch at the moon. Nocturn Cabbage. Carl Sandburg. DuDa
Cabdriver's Smile, The. Denise Levertov. NYP
Cabin Creek Flood, The. *Unknown.* AmFP
Cabin in Minnesota, A. Marvin Bell. HoPM
Cabin North of It All, The. James McMichael. AmPA
Cable cars swing up the hill, The. San Francisco. Mary Austin. BPAW
Cable Hymn, The. Whittier. PAH
Cables entangling her. She Is Far from the Land. Thomas Hood. DTC; FaBoNo; WiR
Caboose Thoughts. Carl Sandburg. CMoP
Cachalot, The, *sels.* E. J. Pratt.
"Thousand years now had his breed, A." MoCV; OBCV
"Where Cape Delgado strikes the sea." CaP; MoCV
Cackle, cackle, Mother Goose. *Unknown.* OxNR; PBBP
Cackling, smelling of camphor, crumbs of pink icing. Muse. David Wagoner. PoA
Cacoëthes Scribendi. Oliver Wendell Holmes. AA
Cacophonous Couplet on Cardinal Wolsey. *Unknown.* *See* On Cardinal Wolsey.
Cactus towers, straight and tall, The. In Mexico. Evaleen Stein. AA
Cadenus and Vanessa, *sels.* Swift.
"Cupid tho' all his darts were lost." OxBI
Flattery. TreFT
(" 'Tis an old maxim of the schools.") PV
Cadenza. Ted Hughes. CMoP; NYBP
Cadenza. Miriam Waddington. CaP
Cader Idris at Sunset. Charles Tennyson Turner. FaBoPP
Cadgwith. Lionel Johnson. OBVV
"Mary star of the sea!" III. ISi
Cadmus and Harmonia. Matthew Arnold. *Fr.* Empedocles on Etna, II, ii. OBVV
("Far, far from here.") GTBS-P
(Song of Callicles, The.) FiP
Caedmon. George Garrett. NePoAm-2
Caedmon. Norman Nicholson. FaBoTw
Caedmon's Hymn. Caedmon, *tr. fr. Anglo-Saxon.* EBCP; EBEV, *tr. by* Sally Purcell; OAEL-1; TEP, *tr. by* Walter Kendrick
(Hymn: "Now we must praise heaven—kingdom's Guardian.") TrCP
(Hymn: "Now we should praise Heaven—kingdom's guard," *tr. by* D. K. Fry.) PAI
Caelia, *sel.* Sir David Murray.
Sonnet: "Ponder thy cares, and sum them all in one." ElL
Caelica, *sels.* Fulke Greville.
"Absence, the noble truce," XLV [XLIV]. EnRePo; NCEP; PoEL-1
(Absence and Presence.) OBSC
"All my senses, like beacon's flame," LVI. EnRePo; InvP; PoEL-1; QFR
"Away with these self-loving lads," LII. EnRePo
(Cynthia.) OBSC
(Of His Cynthia.) ElL; ELP; NoP
(Song to His Cynthia.) ViBoPo
"Caelica, I overnight was finely used," XXXVIII. AAS; EnRePo
(Sonnet: "Caelica, I overnight was finely used.") JCP
"Caelica, when I did see you every day," LXIII. AAS
"Caelica, while you doe sweare you love me best," LXI. NCEP
"Cupid, thou naughty [*or* naughtie] boy, when thou wert loathed," XII. EnRePo; NCEP
"Cynthia, because your horns look diverse ways," LIV. MOON
"Down[e] in the depth of mine iniquity," XCIX [C]. EnRePo; PPoe; QFR
(Sonnet: "Downe in the depth of mine iniquity.") OBS
"Earth with thunder torn[e], with fire blasted, The," LXXXVI [LXXXVII]. AAS; EnRePo; QFR
(Sonnet: "Earth with thunder torn, with fire blasted, The.") JCP
"Eternal[l] Truth, almighty, infinite," XCVII [XCVIII]. EnRePo; OxBoCh
(Sonnet: "Eternall Truth, almighty, infinite.") OBS
"Faction, that ever dwells," XXIX. EnRePo
(Love and Fortune.) OBSC
"Farewell, sweet boy; complain not of my truth," LXXXIV [LXXXV]. EnRePo; FaBoRV; GBL; NCEP; QFR
(Farewell to Cupid.) OBSC
"Fie [*or* Fye], foolish Earth, think[e] you the heaven wants glory," XVI. EnRePo; PoEL-1
(Love's Glory.) OBSC
Golden age was when the world was young, The, XLIV. OAEL-1
"I offer wrong to my beloved Saint," XVIII. NCEP
"I, with whose colors [*or* colours] Myra dressed [*or* dress'd] her head," XXII. EnRePo; GBL; HAP; InvP; QFR
(Myra.) ElL; LoBV; NOBE; OBEV; OBSC; PoPle
(To Myra.) LiTB; ViBoPo
"In night, when colors [*or* colours] all to black[e] are cast," C. AAS; EnRePo; OAEL-1; QFR
"In the time when herbs and flowers," LXXVI.
(Caelica and Philocell.) OBSC
"In the window of a grange," LXXIV.
(Love and Honour.) OBSC
"In those years when our sense, desire and wit," XCVI. NOCV
"Juno, that on her head Loves liverie carried," XI. NCEP
"Love is the peace, whereto all thoughts do[e] strive," LXXXV. AAS
(Sonnet: "Love is the peace, whereto all thoughts do strive.") JCP
"Love, the delight of all well-thinking minds," I. OBSC
"Man, dream[e] no more of curious mysteries," LXXXVIII [LXXXIX]. EnRePo; MePo; QFR
(Sonnet: "Man, dream[e] no more of curious mysteries.") JCP; OBS
"Manicheans did no idols make, The," LXXXIX. NOCV
"Men, that delight to multiply desire," XCIV.
(Sonnet: "Men, that delight to multiply desire.") OBS
"Merlin, they say, an English prophet borne," XXIII. NCEP
"More than most fair, full of that heavenly fire," III. ElL
(To His Lady.) OBSC
"Nurse-life wheat, within his green[e] husk[e] growing, The," XL. AAS; EnRePo; NCEP
(Sonnet: "Nurse-life wheat within his green husk growing, The.") JCP
(Youth and Maturity.) OBSC
"O false and treacherous Probability," CIII [CIV]. AAS; OxBoCh
(Sonnet: "O false and treacherous Probability.") OBS
"Sathan, no woman, yet a wandring spirit," XXI. NCEP
"Sion lies [*or* Syon lyes] waste, and thy Jerusalem," CIX [CX]. EnRePo; NoP; OxBoCh; PoEL-1
"Three things there be in man's opinion dear[e]," CV [CVI]. LiTB; NOCV; PoEL-1
(Sonnet: "Three things there be in mans opinion deare.") OBS
"When all this All doth pass from age to age," LXIX. EBEV; EnRePo
"Whenas [*or* When as] man's life, the light of human[e] lust," LXXXVII [LXXXVIII]. LiTB; MePo; OxBoCh; PoEL-1
(Sonnet: "When as man's life, the light of human lust.") OBS
"Who ever sailes neere to Bermuda coast," LIX. NCEP
"Who grace, for zenith had, from which no shadowes grow," LXXXIII. PoEL-1
(Despair.) OBSC
"World, that all contains, is ever moving, The," VII. EnRePo; NIP
(Change.) OBSC
"Wrapped [*or* Wrapp'd] up, O Lord, in man's degeneration," XCVIII [XCIX]. EnRePo; OxBoCh; QFR
"You little stars [*or* starres] that live in skies," IV. ElL; NCEP; NoP
(His Lady's Eyes.) OBSC
"You that seek what life is in death," LXXXII [LXXXIII]. EnRePo
(Time and Eternity.) OBSC
Caelica and Philocell. Fulke Greville. Caelica, LXXVI. OBSC
Caelica, I overnight was finely used. Sonnet. Fulke Greville. Caelica, XXXVIII. AAS; EnRePo; JCP
Caelica, when I did see you every day. Caelica, LXIII. Fulke Greville. AAS
Caelica, while you doe sweare you love me best. Caelica, LXI. Fulke Greville. NCEP
Caelius, my Lesbia, that one, that only Lesbia. Catullus, *tr. fr. Latin by* Horace Gregory. NAWM-1
Caenlochan. Helen B. Cruickshank. PoSH
Caesar. W. S. Merwin. LCAP; NaP
Caesar. Paul Valéry, *tr. fr. French by* C. F. MacIntyre. WaaP
Caesar, afloat with his fortunes! The Turtle. *Unknown.* PAH
Caesar and Pompey, *sel.* George Chapman.
"Poor slaves, how terrible this death is to them!" ViBoPo
Caesar Remembers. William Kean Seymour. HBMV
Caesar, serene Caesar, your foot on all. Caesar. Paul Valéry, *tr. by* C. F. MacIntyre. WaaP
Caesar, that proud man. Caesar Remembers. William Kean Seymour. HBMV
Caesura. Kenneth Mackenzie. CBAP
Cafe in Warsaw. Allen Ginsberg. HAP
Café Tableau. May Swenson. ErPo
Cafes. Robert B. Smith. LFAC

Cage, The. Elizabeth Bartlett. NePoAm-2
Cage, The. John Berryman. PoA
Cage, The. David Gascoyne. EAS
Cage, The. John Montague. CIP
Cage, The. James Stephens. OxBTC
Cage, The. Avner Treinin, *tr. fr. Hebrew by* A. C. Jacobs. VWA
Caged back of iron grilles. Maiden Lane. Al Lee. NYP
Caged Bird, The. Arthur Symons. BrPo
Caged in old woods, whose reverend echoes wake. Captivity. Samuel Rogers. FaBoEn; OBNC
Caged Rats. Ebenezer Elliott. EBEV; VLP
Caged Skylark, The. Gerard Manley Hopkins. CMoP; FM; LiTM; MoAB; MoBrPo; MoPo; OBMV; PBBP; SoSe
Cages. Marvin Solomon. NYBP
Cain. Irving Layton. MoCV; PeCV
Cain Shall Not Slay Abel Today on Our Good Ground. Malcolm Lowry. OBCV; PeCV
Cain's eyes are not gracious to God. Abel. Else Lasker-Schüler, *tr. by* Joachim Neugroschel. VWA
Cain's Song. Donald Finkel. VWA
Caint call your name. The Hermit Cackleberry Brown, on Human Vanity. Jonathan Williams. OBAL; PoM
Cairngorm, November 1971. Martyn Berry. PoSH
Cairo Jag. Keith Douglas. NePoEA
Caisson Song, The. Edmund L. Gruber. PAL; TreF
(Caissons Go Rolling Along, The.) BLSo, *with music*
Cakes and Ale. *Unknown. See* I Gave Her Cakes; I Gave Her Ale.
Calabash wherein she served my food, The. The Serving Girl. Gladys May Casely Hayford. CDC
Calais, August 15, 1802. Wordsworth. NAs
Calais Sands. Matthew Arnold. OAEP
Calamiterror, *sel.* George Barker.
"Meandering abroad in the Lincolnshire meadows day," VI. EAS
Calamity. F. R. Scott. PeCV
Calamity Jane Greets Her Dreams. Kathleen Lignell. AMV-80
Calamity of seals begins with jaws, The. Seals at High Island. Richard Murphy. CIP; IPY
Calculating Female. Jill Hellyer. POL
Calculation, The. David Wagoner. NYBP
Calder, A. Karl Shapiro. EyDe
Caldwell of Springfield. Bret Harte. PAH
Caledonia. Colleen J. McElroy. BlSi
Caledonia. Anthony Powell. NOBL
Caledonian Market, The. William Plomer. ChMP
Calendar. Cecil Bodker, *tr. fr. Danish by* Nadia Christensen *and* Alexander Taylor. BoWoP
Calendar is ironic, The. The stripper dances. The Dancing Sunshine Lounge. Thomas Rabbitt. MAYP
Calenture. Alastair Reid. NYBP; PrIm
Calf came two days ago, The. The New Calf. Frances Downing Vaughan. AMV-80
Calf-deep in spruce dust. Dulcimer Maker. Carolyn Forché. SaC
Calf-Path, The. Sam Walter Foss. HBV-1; HBVY; PoLF
Calf, the Goat, the Little Lamb, The. Samuel Hoffenstein. DBV
Caliban. Shakespeare. *Fr.* The Tempest, III, ii. FiP
(To Dream Again.) TrGrPo
Caliban in the Coal Mines. Louis Untermeyer. HBV-2; MoAmPo; PDV; PoPl; TreFS; TrJP; TRV
Caliban upon Setebos; or, Natural Theology in the Island. Robert Browning. AWP; EBEV; NoP; OAEL-2; OAEP; VLP; WGRP
Calico-pale paddocks through the window, The. Song for Past Midnight. Geoffrey Lehmann. CBAP
Calico Pie. Edward Lear. FaBoCh; FaPON; SoPo; TrGrPo; WhC
Califas/ baby blue skies. Heading for Eugene. Lorenza Schmidt. FIA
California. Thomas Lake Morris. AA
California. Joseph Philip Robson. VLP
California. Lydia Huntley Sigourney. PAH
California, *with music. Unknown.* AS
California Dead. G. E. Murray. MAYP
California Idyl, A. Ernest McGaffey. BPAW
California Joe. Jack Crawford. CoSo
California #2. Victor Hernández Cruz. TAT
California Oaks, The. Yvor Winters. GOA
California Phrasebook, The. Dennis Schmitz. AmPA; NPGG
California Quail in January. Will C. Jumper. GrPl
California song, A. Song of the Redwood-Tree. Walt Whitman. AmPP
California Stage Company, The. *Unknown.* CoSo
California, This Is Minnesota Speaking. Stephen Dunn. GP
California Winter, *sel.* Karl Shapiro.
"This land grows the oldest living things." AmFN
Californian, The. *Unknown. See* Sacremento.
Californians, The. Theodore Spencer. NYBP; TW
Californy Stage. *Unknown.* BPAW
Caligula. Robert Lowell. CoPo
Caliph shot a gazelle, The. Humorous Verse. Abu Dolama, *tr. by* Raoul Abdul. TTY
Call, The. Thomas Curtis Clark. PGD
Call, The. Daniel Corkery. OnYI
Call, The. James Dickey. NePoEA-2
Call, The. John Hall. FaBoEn; MeLP; MePo; OBS; ViBoPo
Call, The. Reginald Wright Kauffman. HBV-1
Call, The. Charlotte Mew. ChMP
Call, The. Thomas Osbert Mordaunt. *See* Sound, Sound the Clarion.
Call, The. Jessie Pope. SUMH
Call, The. Jules Supervielle, *tr. fr. French by* Geoffrey Gardner. NU
Call, The. *Unknown.* OBEV
Call across the Valley of Not Knowing, The, *sel.* Galway Kinnell.
"Of that time in a Southern jail." GP
"Call All." *Unknown.* PAH
Call all hands to man the capstan. Rolling Home, *vers.* I. *Unknown.* ShS
Call down the hawk from the air. The Hawk. W. B. Yeats. PoA
Call for a Song, A. *Unknown.* OxBM
Call for the Robin Redbreast and the Wren. John Webster. *Fr.* The White Devil, V, iv. ChTr; EBEV; FaBoCh; HAP; HeIP; NoP; OAEP; PAI; PoEL-2; PoRA; PrIm; SeCePo; SeCeV; ViBoPo
(Cornelia's Song.) InPS; OBS; TrGrPo
(Dirge, A: "Call for the robin-redbreast and the wren.") ElL; FaBoEn; HBV-2; LiTB; NOBE; OBEV; WHA
(Land Dirge, A.) CH; GTBS; GTBS-P; LoBV
Call from the Afterworld. Jozef Habib Gerez, *tr. fr. Turkish by* Musa Moris Farhi *and* Anthony Rudolf. VWA
Call him drunken Ira Hayes, he won't answer any more. Ballad of Ira Hayes. Peter La Farge. MAT
Call Him the Lover and call me the Bride. The Song the Body Dreamed in the Spirit's Mad Behest. William Everson. ErPo
Call is for belief, The. The Fundament Is Shifted. Abbie Huston Evans. NYBP
Call It a Good Marriage Robert Graves. BoLoP
Call it a louse—I'm. Cid Corman. VGW
Call it neither love nor spring madness. Without Name. Pauli Murray. AmNP; PoBA; PoNe
Call it not vain—they do not err. The Minstrel Responds to Flattery. Sir Walter Scott. *Fr.* The Lay of the Last Minstrel, V. OBNC; OBRV
Call it survival. Canteen Pimpin'. Yasmeen Jamal. LFAC
Call John the Boatman, *with music. Unknown.* ShS
"Call Junius!" From the crowd a shadow stalk'd. Byron. *Fr.* The Vision of Judgment. OBRV
Call Martha Corey. The Trial. Longfellow. *Fr.* Giles Corey of the Salem Farms. PAH
Call me friend or foe. The Comrade. Lee Wilson Dodd. HBMV
Call me Ishmael and listen. Ishmael. Gabriel Levin. VWA
Call me no more. His Lachrimae or Mirth, Turn'd to Mourning. Robert Herrick. SeCV-1
Call me no more, O gentle stream. To a River in the South. Sir Henry Newbolt. CH
Call Me Not Back from the Echoless Shore. *Unknown.* BLPA
Call Me Not Dead. Richard Watson Gilder. HBV-2; WGRP
Call me not false, beloved. The Bridegroom. Kipling. *Fr.* Epitaphs of the War. FaBoEE
Call me the Valiant heading west on Fourteen into the frozen. Ford Pickup. David Allan Evans. PPJ
Call me Zamboni. Nights my job is hockey. Rink Keeper's Sestina. George Draper. PrIm
Call no faith false which e'er has brought. Tolerance. Sir Lewis Morris. OBVV
Call not thy wanderer home as yet. Germinal. "Æ." BIrV; MoBrPo; OBEV; OBMV
Call of the Bugles, The. Richard Hovey. AA
Call of the Christian, The. Whittier. NOCV
Call of the Morning, The. George Darley. OnYI
Call of the River Nun, The. Gabriel Okara. PBA
Call of the Spring, The. Alfred Noyes. SUS
Call of the Wild, The. Robert W. Service. CaP
Call on Sir Walter Raleigh, A. Sarah Morgan Bryan Piatt. AA
Call Out My Number. Julia de Burgos, *tr. fr. Spanish by* Julio Marzán. InW
"Call Rose Costara!" The Night Court. Ruth Comfort Mitchell. HBV-2
Call the cows home! Thunder. Walter de la Mare. BoNaP
Call the Horse, Marry. *Unknown.* OBET
Call the roller of big cigars. The Emperor of Ice-Cream. Wallace Stevens. AmPP; AP; BiP; CABA; CMoP; CoBMV; FaBoMo; FF; HAP; InPK; LiTA; MoPo; MoVE; NePA; NIP; NoAM; NOBA; NoP; OxBA; PAI; TAP; ViBoPo; WeW
Call the seller of used cars. Sunday Service. Michael Heffernan. BXAP

Call to a Scot, The. Ruth Guthrie Harding. HBV-2
Call to Action, A. Callinus, *tr. fr. Greek by* T. F. Higham. WaaP
Call to Action, A. Ch'iu Chin, *tr. fr. Chinese by* Kenneth Rexroth *and* Ling Chung. PBWP
Call to Arms, A. Mary Raymond Shipman Andrews. PAH
Call to Conflict. *Unknown.* STF
Call to Order. Carol Burbank. SUW
Call to Pentecost, A. Inez M. Tyler. BLRP
Call to the Colors, The. Arthur Guiterman. PAH
Call to the Strong, The. William Pierson Merrill. BLRP
Call to the Wild, A. Lord Dunsany. OnYI
Callahan, *with music. Unknown.* OuSiCo
Call—call—and bruise the air. Expression. Isaac Rosenberg. MoBrPo
Called Away. Richard Le Gallienne. SoPo; SUS
("I meant to do my work today.") TiPo
Called Back. Emily Dickinson. *See* Just lost, when I was saved.
Called from my room to a death. The Stringer. James Brasfield. AMV-81
Called Proud. Walter Savage Landor. GBL
Caller Herrin'. Lady Nairne. HBV-1; OxBS
Caller of the Buffalo. Mary Austin. BPAW
Caller rain frae abune. Douglas Young, *after the Greek of* Sappho. OBVE
Callicles' Song. Matthew Arnold. *See* Song of Callicles, The.
Calligram, 15 May 1915. Guillaume Apollinaire, *tr. fr. French by* O. Bernard. OBWP
Calling all butterflies of every race. Pod of the Milkweed. Robert Frost. LiTM
Calling black people. SOS. Amiri Baraka. BPo; CNA; PoBA
Calling Home the Scientists. Wendy Rose. AMV-81
Calling in the Cat. Elizabeth J. Coatsworth. BoAnP; PCat
Calling Lucasta from Her Retirement. Richard Lovelace. CaPo
Calling Myself Home. Linda Hogan. TWSS
Calling Spring VII-MMMC. Ogden Nash. FaBoCo
Calling the Doctor. John Wesley Holloway. BANP
Calling, the heron flies athwart the blue. The Creek-Road. Madison Cawein. AA
Calling the Roll. Nathaniel Graham Shepherd. *See* Roll-Call.
Calling to mind[e], mine eie long went about [*or* my eyes went long about]. The Excuse. Sir Walter Ralegh. AAS; SiPS
Calling to mind[e] since first my love begun. Michael Drayton. Idea, LI. EnRePo; NOBE; OBSC; PoEL-2
Calling Trains. *Unknown.* AmFP
Calliope, *with music. Unknown.* AS
Calliope in the Labour Ward. Elaine Feinstein. BrRo
Callipaedia; or, The Art of Getting Beautiful Children, *sels.* Claude Quillet, *tr. fr. Latin by* George Sewell.
How to Conceive Boys. FaBoUs
Process of Conception, The. FaBoUs
Calloused grass lies hard, The. By the Road to the Air-Base. Ivor Winters. CrMA
Callow young were huddling in the nests, The. Scorned. Alexander Smith. OBVV
Callypso Speaks. Hilda Doolittle ("H. D."). SBG
Calm. Aldo Camerino, *tr. fr. Italian by* Anita Barrows. VWA
Calm. Stanton A. Coblentz. EtS
Calm [*or* Calme], The. John Donne. LoBV; MePo; MOS
Calm, The/ Cool face. Suicide's Note. Langston Hughes. CDC; DFF
Calm after Storm. Frank Yerby. AmNP
Calm and Full the Ocean. Robinson Jeffers. WaP
Calm as that second summer which precedes. Charleston. Henry Timrod. AA; AmPP; AP; NOBA; OxBA; PAH; TAP
Calm as the Cloudless Heaven. "Christopher North". EtS
Calm Death, God of crossed hands and passionless eyes. Death. George Pellew. AA
Calm down, my sorrow, we must move with care. Meditation. Baudelaire, *tr. by* Robert Lowell. InPK; NAWM-2
Calm is all nature as a resting wheel. Written in Very Early Youth. Wordsworth. EnRP
Calm is the landscape when the storm has passed. Peace in the Welsh Hills. Vernon Watkins. ChMP; GTBS-P; OxBTC
Calm is the morn without a sound. In Memoriam A. H. H., XI. Tennyson. ChTr; EBEV; EBVV; ELP; FaBoEn; FaBoPP; FaBoRV; FiP; LiTB; NOBE; OBNC; PoEL-5; SeCeV; TrGrPo
Calm martyr of a noble cause. Jefferson Davis. Walker Meriwether Bell. PAH
Calm Morning at Sea. Sara Teasdale. EtS; MOS
Calm of heaven rests upon my heart, The. Blessed Nearness. Mary Bullock. STF
Calm on the bosom of thy God. Dirge [*or* A Death-Hymn]. Felicia Dorothea Hemans. *Fr.* The Siege of Valencia. HBV-2; OBEV; OBRV
Calm, on the Listening Ear of Night, *with music.* Edmund Hamilton Sears. AH
Calm Sea, A. Robert Southey. EtS
Calm Soul of All Things. Matthew Arnold. *Fr.* Lines Written in Kensington Gardens. TrPWD; TRV; WGRP
Calm the boy sleeps, though death is in the clouds. Infant Noah. Vernon Watkins. NeBP
Calm [*or* Calme] was the day, and through the trembling air [*or* ayre]. Prothalamion. Spenser. AAS; AWP; ChTr; EBEV; ElL; EnRePo; FaBoEn; FaBoPP; GoTL; GTBS; GTBS-P; HAP; HBV-1; LiTB; LoBV; NIP; NoP; OBEV; OBSC; PPoe; PPP; SeCePo; ViBoPo; WHA
Calm was the even, and clear [*or* cleer] was the sky [*or* skie]. A Song. Dryden. *Fr.* An Evening's Love, IV, i. CavP; FF; OAEP; SeCV-2
Calm was the evening and clear was the sky (*longer vers.*). Amintas and Claudia; or, The Merry Shepherdess. *Unknown.* CoMu
Calm Winter Sleep. Hilary Corke. MP; NYBP
Calme, The. John Donne. *See* Calm, The.
Calmly beside her tropic strand. Charleston. Paul Hamilton Hayne. PAH
Calmly We Walk through This April's Day. Delmore Schwartz. *See* For Rhoda.
Calton Weaver, The. *Unknown.* FSW
Calumet Early Evening. Annette Arkeketa West. TWSS
Calumny. Frances Sargent Osgood. AA; HBV-2
Calvary. Mary Hallet. PGD
Calvary. E. A. Robinson. MoAmPo; OFD; TreFS; WGRP
Calvary. Libby Stopple. GoYe
Calvary, *with music. Unknown.* AH; BoAN-1, *diff. sts.*
Calvary and Easter. " Susan Coolidge." PGD; WBLP
(Easter Song, An.) BLRP; TRV
Calverly's. E. A. Robinson. NoAM
Calvin in the Attic Cleans. Craig Weeden. AMV-81
Calvin in the Casino. Turner Cassity. NIP
Calvinist Autumnal. Elizabeth B. Harrod. NePoEA
Calvinist in Love, A. Jack R. Clemo. ChMP
Calvinist Sand. Alexander Scott. OxBS
Calvus to a Fly. Charles Tennyson Turner. FM
Calypso. Richard Kell. CIP
Calypso. William Carlos Williams. NePoAm-2
Calypso/ Is a bit of a dipso. Forever Ambrosia. Christopher Morley. OBAL
Calypsomania. Anthony Brode. FiBHP
Calypso's Island. Archibald MacLeish. MoAB; NoP
Calypso's Song to Ulysses. Adrian Mitchell. GBL
Calyx of the Oboe Breaks, The. Conrad Aiken. NYBP
(Music.) AP
Cam' Ye By [the Salmon Fishers]. *Unknown.* CH; GBP
Cambrian, *sels.* Eeva-Liisa Manner, *tr. fr. Finnish by* Jaakko A. Ahokas. PBWP
"If they wanted freedom."
"To move over shifting borders."
"Turn the page of stone and there."
Cambric Shirt, The. *Unknown.* *See* Elfin Knight, The.
Cambridge, an outdoor library stack of bricks. Vale. John Ciardi. MiAP
Cambridge and the Alps. Wordsworth. *Fr.* The Prelude, VI. PoEL-4
Cambridge and the Cam. Phineas Fletcher. *Fr.* The Apollyonists. FaBoPP
Cambridge Ladies Who Live in Furnished Souls, The. E. E. Cummings. *Fr.* Sonnets—Realities. AmPP; HeIP; InPK; MoVE; NoAM; NOBA; NoP; OBAL; OxBA; PAI; PPON; TAP; ViBoPo
Cambridge people rarely smile. Rupert Brooke. *Fr.* The Old Vicarage, Grantchester. DBV
Cambridge Songs, *sel.* *Tr. fr. Latin by* Willis Barnstone.
"Wind is thin." BoWoP
Camden Magpie. Hugh McCrae. PoAu-1
Camden, most reverend head, to whom I owe. To William Camden. Ben Jonson. AnAnS-2; AWP; JCP; OBS; SeCV-1
Came first, five hundred miles from port. Approaching America. J. C. Squire. HBMV
Came in my full youth to the midnight cave. Ajanta. Muriel Rukeyser. LiTA; LiTM; MiAP; MoAmPo; MoAB; NNaP; TwAmPo
Came, on a Sabbath morn [*or* noon], my sweet. Meet We No Angels, Pansie? Thomas Ashe. HBV-1; OBVV
Came such a long way. Postcards from Rotterdam. Carolyn Kizer. GP
Came the morning of that day. Sumter. Edmund Clarence Stedman. PAH
Came the relief. "What, sentry, ho!" Relieving Guard. Bret Harte. RoGo
Came to lakes; came to dead water. A Field of Light. Theodore Roethke. LiTM; MP; TwCP
Came to me. Rudaki, *tr. fr. Persian by* Basil Bunting. BoLoP; OBVE
Came You Not from Newcastle. *Unknown.* GBP
Camel. Alan Brownjohn. RHPC
Camel. Gene Derwood. NePA
Camel. Laila Akhyaliyya, *tr. fr. Arabic by* Willis Barnstone. BoWoP
Camel. W. S. Merwin. NePA
Camel. Mary Britton Miller. TiPo
Camel, The. Ogden Nash. CenHV; SoPo
Camel. Jon Stallworthy. BoAnP

Camel at the close of day, The. The Kneeling Camel [*or* And So Should You *or* Submission and Rest]. Anna Temple Whitney. BLPA; BLRP; STF
Camel has a single hump, The. The Camel. Ogden Nash. CenHV; SoPo
Camel-Rider, The. *Unknown, tr. fr. Arabic by* Wilfrid Scawen Blunt. AWP
Camel, with practical views, A. Sole-hungering Camel. Oliver Herford. TDH
Camelopard, The. Hilaire Belloc. FaBoNo
"Camels are coming, The." huzza, huzza! The Camels Have Come. *Unknown.* PoOW
Camel's Complaint, The. Charles Edward Carryl. *See* The Plaint of the Camel.
Camels Have Come, The. *Unknown.* PoOW
Camel's Hump, The. Kipling. *Fr.* Just-So Stories. EvOK
(Hump, The.) OxBChV
Camels of the Kings. Leslie Norris. OBCP
(Camels, the Kings' Camels, The.) PChr
Cameo, The. Edna St. Vincent Millay. FYAP; LiTA; MoAmPo; UnPo; WPE
Cameo No. II. June Jordan. BPo
Camera. Ted Kooser. Psk
Camera at the crossing sees the city. Gauley Bridge. Muriel Rukeyser. NNaP
Camerados. Bayard Taylor. Par; UnPo
Camoens. Herman Melville. ViBoPo
Camoens in the Hospital. Herman Melville. ViBoPo
Camões, alone, of all the lyric race. Luis de Camões. Roy Campbell. FaBoTw; PeSA
Camoes and the Debt. Sophia de Mello Breyner Andresen, *tr. fr. Portuguese by* Willis Barnstone *and* Nelson Cerqueira. BoWoP
Camouflage. Amy Clampitt. SUW
Camouflage. John Manifold. WaP
Camp. Patrick Anderson. OBCV
Camp Hymn, The. Mary S. Edgar. TRV
(Prayer-Poem, A.) BLRP
Camp in the Prussian Forest, A. Randall Jarrell. AP; CMoP; MiAP; MoAmPo; NMP; OBWP; OxBC
Camp meeting took place, in a wide open space, A. At a Georgia Camp Meeting. Kerry Mills. BLSo
Camp Notes, *sels.* Mitsuye Yamada. WPOW
In the Outhouse.
On the Bus.
Camp of Souls, The. Isabella Valancy Crawford. NOBC
Camp within the West, The. Roderic Quinn. PoAu-1
Campaign, The, *sel.* Joseph Addison.
Blenheim. OBEC
(Poem to His Grace the Duke of Marlborough, A.) OBWP
Campaign, The. Josephine Miles. WPE
Campaign Promise. Henry Taylor. TW
Campañero, The, *with music. Unknown.* ShS
Campaspe. John Lyly. *See* Alexander and Campaspe.
Campbells Are Comin', The. *Unknown.* FSW
Campers from Fayetteville & Toledo. Reno, 2 A.M. Sam Hamill. TAT
Campi Flegrei. Barend Toerien, *tr. fr. Afrikaans by author.* PeSA
Campidoglio. Robert Garioch, *after the Italian of* Giuseppe Belli. OBVE
Camping at Thunder Bay. David Fedo. AMV-81
Camping Out. William Empson. CMoP; FaBoMo; MoVE; OxBTC
Camping Out on Rainy Mountain. Jim Barnes. CDW
Camp's asleep and thro' the gloom, The. Silhouette in Sepia. Robert V. Carr. PoOW
Camptown. John Ciardi. WaP
Camptown Races, The [*or* De]. Stephen Collins Foster. FSW; PSoN, *with music;* TrAS, *with music*
(Gwine to Run All Night; or, De Camptown Races.) OBAL
Campus, The. David Posner. NYBP
Campus in Summer, A. Reed Whittemore. GLGT
Campus on the Hill, The. W. D. Snodgrass. AP; LiTM; MP; NIP; NoAM; TAP; TwCP
Can a bell ring in the heart. When Death Came April Twelve 1945. Carl Sandburg. AP
Can a mere human brain stand the stress and the strain. Capsule Philosophy. Felicia Lamport. QQQ
Can anyone lend me two twelve-pound rats? Wanted. Shel Silverstein. PV
Can death be faithful or the grave be just. The Resurrection. Nathaniel Wanley. LoBV
Can death be sleep, when life is but a dream. On Death. Keats. SyP
Can flame beget white steel. She Contrasts with Herself Hippolyta. Hilda Doolittle ("H. D."). SBG
Can freckled August, drowsing warm and blonde. The Rain-Crow. Madison Cawein. AA
Can. Hist. Earle Birney. OxBC
Can I easily say. Sisters. Adrienne Rich. IHMS
Can I Forget? ("Can I forget the sickle mune.") Sidney Goodsir Smith. NeBP; SeCePo
Can I forget the sweet days that have been. Days That Have Been. W. H. Davies. FaBoPP
Can I not come to Thee, my God, for these. To His Ever-loving God. Robert Herrick. AnAnS-2; TrPWD
Can I not sin, but thou wilt be. To His Conscience. Robert Herrick. AnAnS-2; NoP; OxBoCh; PoEL-3
Can I Not Sing. *Unknown.* ViBoPo
(Jolly Shepherd Wat, The.) NOBE: OxBM; SBVL
(Shepherd upon a Hill, The.) GoBC
(Shepherd upon the Hill, The.) OxBoCh
Can—I—poet. For Some Poets. Mae Jackson. BOLo; PoBA
Can I Say. Dolly Bird. WPOW
Can I see another's woe. On Another's Sorrow. Blake. *Fr.* Songs of Innocence. AWP; EBCP; EnRP; FaBV; PoEL-4; ViBoPo
"Can I Tempt You to a Pond Walk?" James Schuyler. PoA
Can I, who have for others oft compiled. Of My Dear Son [*or* Deare Sonne], Gervase Beaumont. Sir John Beaumont. JCP; NOBE; OBS; ViBoPo
Can it be possible no words shall welcome. Comforting Lines. *Unknown.* STF
Can it be right to give what I can give? Sonnets from the Portuguese, IX. Elizabeth Barrett Browning. CTC; HBV-1
Can Life Be a Blessing. Dryden. *Fr.* Troilus and Cressida. SeCePo; ViBoPo
(Song: "Can life be a blessing.") NoP; SeCV-2
Can. Lit. Earle Birney. CABA; NOBC
Can love be controll'd by advice? Song. John Gay. *Fr.* The Beggar's Opera. LoBV
Can one love a boulder. Highland Loves. Rennie McOwan. PoSH
Can-Opener. David McAleavey. AMV-81
Can scenes like these withdraw thee from thy wood. George Crabbe. *Fr.* The Borough, Letter I. OBRV
Can the Circle Be Unbroken? *Unknown.* FSW
Can the lover share his soul. Epithalamium. W. J. Turner. OBMV
Can the Mole Take. C. Day Lewis. OBMV
Can there be a moon in heaven to-night. Isabelle. James Hogg. BXAP; Par
Can these movements which move themselves. Belly Dancer. Diane Wakoski. NIP
Can u walk away from ugly. Positives for Sterling Plumpp. Don L. Lee. JB; PoBA
Can we believe—by an effort. Cities. Hilda Doolittle ("H. D."). ViBoPo
Can we fail to be touched by the thought. Sanctuary. J. B. Boothroyd. FiBHP
Can we not force from widowed [*or* widdowed] poetry. An Elegy [*or* Elegie] upon the Death of the Dean[e] of [St.] Paul's, Dr. John Donne. Thomas Carew. AnAnS-2; CABA; CaPo; JCP; MeLP; MePo; NoP; OAEL-1; OBS; PP; SeCP; SeCV-1
Can white birds sing? An ornithologist. No White Bird Sings. John Ciardi. AMV-80
Can ye [*or* you] play me Duncan Gray. Duncan Gray [*or* The Thrusting of It]. Burns. CoMu; ErPo; UnTE
Can Ye Sew Cushions? *Unknown.* FaBoCh
Can You Change a Shilling? Toni Del Renzio. EAS
Can you dance? Music. Eleanor Farjeon. TiPo
Can you hear the music of the letters of the alphabet? Life of the Letters. Emily Borenstein. VWA
Can you keep it so. Starlings. Norman MacCaig. BoAnP
Can you make me a cambric shirt. *Unknown.* OxNR
Can You Paint a Thought? John Ford. *Fr.* The Broken Heart, III, ii. InvP; OAEP; PoEL-2; ViBoPo
Can you play me, Duncan Gray? Burns. *See* Can ye play me . . .
Can you recall an ode to June. A Drawing-Room Ballad. Henry Duff Traill. CenHV
Can your foreigner's nose smell mullets. Who Among You Knows the Essence of Garlic? Garrett Hongo. HoAn
Can Zone; or, The Good Food Guide. Rika Lesser. MAYP
Cana. Thomas Merton. TrCP
Cana Revisited. Seamus Heaney. FaBoMo
Canaan. Muriel Spark. NYBP
Canada. Sir Charles G. D. Roberts. PeCV
Canada-I-O [*or* Canaday I. O.] ("Come all ye jolly lumbermen and listen to my song"). *Unknown, at. to* Ephraim Braley. AmFP; BaBo; FSW, *short version*; ViBoFo, *with music*
Canada-I-O ("There was a gallant lady all in her tender youth"). *Unknown.* AmFP
Canadian Authors Meet, The. F. R. Scott. NOBC; OBCV; WHC
Canadian Boat Song, A. Thomas Moore. GoBC; HBV-1; OBRV
Canadian Boat Song. *Unknown, at. to* John Galt *and also to* "Christopher North." BLPA; BSV; CaP; FaBoCh; FaPoR; GoTS; OBEV; OBNC; OBRV; OxBS

Canadian Exile, The. Antoine Gerin-Lajoie, *tr. fr. French-Canadian by* John Boyd. CaP
Canadian Farmer. Genevieve Bartole. CaP
Canadian Herd-Boy, The. Susanna Moodie. OBCV
Canadian Prairies View of Literature, The. David Donnell. NOBC
Canadian Rossignol, The. Edward William Thomson. CaP
Canadians. Ivor Gurney. FaBoTw
Canadice Lake. Bob Mondy. WOLT
Canal, The. Aldous Huxley. HBMV
Canal Bank, The. James Stephens. GrPl
Canal Bank Walk. Patrick Kavanagh. CIP; CMoP; FaBoTw; IPY; MoBrPo; NoAM
Canal Street. John Wheelwright. PoA
Canal Street, Chicago. Clyde Fixmer. TAT
Canaries in the morning, orchestras/ In the afternoon. Academic Discourse at Havana. Wallace Stevens. MoPo
Canaries were his hobby. The Glass Blower. James Scully. MP; NYBP; TwCP
Canary, The. Ogden Nash. DFF; FiBHP; RHPC
Canary, The. Elizabeth Turner. OxBChV
Canary-birds feed on sugar and seed. The Plaint of the Camel [*or* The Camel's Complaint]. Charles Edward Carryl. *Fr.* The Admiral's Caravan. EvOK; FaPON; HBV-2; HBVY; OBCA; OxBChV; RHPC; SoPo
Canary, its woe to assuage, A. The Conservative Owl. Oliver Herford. TDH
Canberra in April. J. R. Rowland. PoAu-2
Cancel My Subscription. J. A. Hines. LFAC
Cancelled Stanza of the Ode on Melancholy. Keats. SyP
Cancer Cells, The. Richard Eberhart. HAP; LiTM; MiAP
Cancer Match, The. James Dickey. GP
Cancer Patient. Jessica Powers. AMV-81
Cancer Research. Anselm Parlatore. SUW
Cancer's a Funny Thing. J. B. S. Haldane. OxBTC
Cancion: "O love, I never, never thought." John II of Castile, *tr. fr. Spanish by* George Tichnor. AWP
Cancion: "When I am the sky." Denise Levertov. PoM
Candaules, King of Lydia. The Queen of Lydia. C. H. Sisson. OxBC
Candid Friend, The. George Canning. TreFT
("Give me the avowed, the erect, the manly foe.") TreFS
Candid Man, The. Stephen Crane. MoAmPo
Candid Physician, The. John C. Lettsom. *See* On Dr. Isaac Letsome.
Candida ("Candida is one today."). Patrick Kavanagh. NAs
Candidate, The. Allamae Ezell. AMV-80
Candidate, The. Thomas Gray. PPP
Candidate: Now, Mr. Echo, will you vote for me? By-Election Idyll. Peter Dickinson. FiBHP
Candidate's Creed, The. James Russell Lowell. *Fr.* The Biglow Papers, 1st Series, No. VI. YaD
Candidate's Letter, The. James Russell Lowell. *Fr.* The Biglow Papers, 1st Series, No. VII. AA
Candle. Jacob Isaac Segal, *tr. fr. Yiddish by* Seymour Mayne. VWA
Candle, A. Sir John Suckling. ErPo
Candle, a Saint, The. Wallace Stevens. PoRA
Candle and Book. Nina Willis Walter. TRV
Candle-blossoms of horse-chestnut left, The. What Trinkets? Thomas Hornsby Ferril. NePoAm-2
Candle, candle,/ Burning bright. Christmas Chant. Isabel Shaw. SiSoSe
Candle fit the glass, The. Yahrzeit Candle. Jean Nordhaus. AMV-81
Candle Flame, The. Janet Lewis. CrMA
Candle Indoors, The. Gerard Manley Hopkins. LiTB; LiTM; OxBoCh; PoEL-5
Candle-lighting Song. Arthur Ketchum. HBMV
Candle lit in darkness of black waters, A. On the Lake. V. Sackville-West. ChMP; MoVE; OBMV; SBG
Candle Song. Anna Elizabeth Bennett. GoYe
Candle takes the first desperate, The. Homage to Chagall. Duane Niatum. CDW
Candlemas. Alice Brown. AA
Candles. Sylvia Plath. NMM
Candles. Hélène Swarth, *tr. fr. Dutch by* Jonathan Crewe. WPOW
Candles. *Unknown.* GoBC
Candles Draw Well after All, The. Laura Jensen. LCAP
Candles. Red tulips, ninety [*or* sixty] cents the bunch. Recipe for an Evening Musicale [*or* Evening Musicale]. Phyllis McGinley. OBAL; WhC
Candles splutter, The; and the kettle hums. The Still Small Voice. A. M. Klein. OBCV; PeCV
Candor. H. C. Bunner. HBV-1
Candy/ Is dandy. Reflections on Ice-breaking. Ogden Nash. BLPL; FaBoCo; FaFP; LiTM; NePA; NoP; OBAL
Candy Man Blues. *Unknown.* BluL; FSW
Cane-bottomed Chair, The. Thackeray. HBV-2; PaPo
Canedolia. Edwin Morgan. FaBoCo; PoSH
Canine Amenities. *Unknown.* GDP
Canis Major. Robert Frost. *Fr.* A Sky Pair. MoAB; MoAmPo
Canned Heat Blues. *Unknown.* BluL
Canner, exceedingly canny, A. Limerick [*or* Two Limericks, I]. Carolyn Wells. FaPON; HBV-2; HBVY; YaD
Cannibal Flea, The. Tom Hood. SpRo
Cannibal Hymn, The. *Unknown, tr. fr. Egyptian by* Samuel A. B. Mercer. TTY
Cannibalee; a Po'em of Passion. Charles Fletcher Lummis. *See* Poe-'em of Passion, A.
Cannibalism. Diana Chang. WPOW
Cannibals' Grace before Meat, The. Charles Dickens. FaBoNo
Cannily/ the mists smoor. Kythans. Stewart McGavin. PoSH
Cannily, Cannily. *Unknown.* FSW
Canning Time. Robert Morgan. Str
Cannon Arrested. Michael S. Harper. CNA; FAZ
Cannon Park. Mark St. Germain. PCP
Cannon's brazen lips are cold, The. To Pius IX. Whittier. TW
Canny bord ower there. Rape. Tom Pickard. FaBoTw
Canny moment, lucky fit. The Nativity Chant. Sir Walter Scott. *Fr.* Guy Mannering. ChTr; FaBoCh; NAs
Canoe, The. Isabella Valancy Crawford. OBCV; OnYI
(Said the Canoe.) NOBC
Canoe. Keith Douglas. NeBP
Canoe-hauling Chant. *Tr. fr. Maori by* Apirana Ngata. WTO
Canoe Song at Twilight. Laura E. McCully. CaP
Canoe-Trip. Douglas Le Pan. CaP; OBCV; PeCV
Canogait kirkyaird in the failing year. At Robert Fergusson's Grave, October 1962. Robert Garioch. OxBS
Canonical black-coats, like birds of a feather. Vox Clero.APAS
Canonical Hours. William Dickey. CoAP
Canonicus and Roger Williams. *Unknown.* PAH
Canonization, The. John Donne. AnAnS-1; BiP; BLPL; CABA; EIL; EnLoPo; EnRePo; HAP; JCP; LiTB; MasP; MePo; NIP; NOBE; NoP; OAEL-1; OBS; PoEL-2; PPoe; PPP; SeCeV; SeCP; SeCV-1; TrGrPo; UnPo; UnTE; ViBoPo
(Canonisation, The.) LoBV; SeCePo; TEP
Canopic Jar. Rika Lesser. MAYP
Canopus. Bert Leston Taylor. FiBHP; HBMV; InMe; NOBL; WhC
Canopy of nerve ends. Epiderm. Michael Dransfield. CBAP
Canso Strait, *with music. Unknown.* ShS
Canst thinke the cargoe wherewith ship is fraught. Upon the Decease of Mrs. Anne Griffin. John Fiske. SCAP
Canst thou by searching find out God? Job's Comforters. Bible, *O.T.* (*Moulton, Modern Readers' Bible*). *Fr.* Job. WGRP
Canst Thou Draw Out Leviathan with an Hook. Allen Curnow. OCNZ
Canst thou draw out leviathan with an hook[e]? Leviathan. Bible, *O.T. Fr.* Job. MOS; OBVE; TrGrPo
Canst thou imagine where those spirits live. Shelley. *Fr.* Prometheus Unbound. WSC
Canst thou indeed be he that still would sing. Dante, *tr. by* Dante Gabriel Rossetti. La Vita Nuova, XIII. AWP
Canst thou love and lie alone? The Courtier's Good-Morrow to His Mistress. *Unknown.* EIL
Canst thou love me, lady? Love. Charles Stuart Calverley. FiBHP
Canst thou not minister to a mind diseas'd. Shakespeare. *Fr.* Macbeth, V, iii. TRV
Canst work i' th' ground so fast? Anarchist. Norman Dugdale. BoAnP
Can't. Harriet Prescott Spofford. PAH
Can't make excuses for you, Cinque. Cinque. Janet Campbell Hale. VoR
"Can't see out of my left eye." Spinning. Al Purdy. NOBC
Can't tell my future/ I can't tell my past. Future Blues. *Unknown.* BluL
Can't They Dance the Polka! *with music. Unknown.* ShS
Can't we find some way/ to meet again. To Ibn Zaidun. Wallada, *tr. by* James Monroe *and* Deirdre Lashgari. WPOW
Can't You Dance the Polka? *Unknown.* FSW
Can't You Live Humble? *with music. Unknown.* BoAN-2
Cantata for Two Lovers. Helga Sandburg. UnTE
Cante Hondo. Ellen de Young Kay. NePoEA
Canteen Pimpin'. Yasmeen Jamal. LFAC
Canter has two stride patterns, one on the right lead and one on the left, The. The Flying Change. Henry Taylor. MAYP
Canterbury Tales, The, *sels.* Chaucer.
Prologue. NoP; OAEL-1; OAEP; PPP, *abr.*; SeCeV; TRV, *mod. version by* H.C. Leonard
Clerk of Oxford, The. OxBM
("Clerk ther was of Oxenford also, The.") GLGT; InPS; TrGrPo; ViBoPo
("Student came from Oxford town also, A," *mod. vers. by* Louis Untermeyer.) TrGrPo
"Frankeleyn was in his compaignye, A." ViBoPo

"Frere ther was, a wantowne and a merye, A." BiP
("There was a Friar, a wanton one and merry," *mod. version by* Nevill Coghill.) BiP
"Good man was ther of religioun, A." NOCV; PAI
(Good Parson, The, *mod. version by* H. C. Leonard.) WGRP
(Poor Parson, The.) ACP
(Poure Persoun, The.) GoBC
"Knyght [*or* Knight] ther was, and that a worthy man, A." BiP; InPS; TrGrPo
("Knight there was, and that a worthy man, A," *mod. vers. by* Louis Untermeyer.) TrGrPo
("There was a Knight, a most distinguished man," *mod. version by* Nevill Coghill.) BiP
"Marchant was ther with a forked berd, A." CTC, *abr.;* ViBoPo
"Miller[e] was a stout carl, for the nones, The." TrGrPo; ViBoPo
("Miller, stout and sturdy as the stones, The," *mod. vers. by* Louis Untermeyer.) TrGrPo
"Monk ther was, a fair for the maistrye [*or* maistrie], A." CTC, *abr.;* TrGrPo
("Monk there was, a monk of mastery, A," *mod. vers. by* Louis Untermeyer.) TrGrPo
Prioress, The. OxBM
(Madame Eglantine.) NOBE
("Ther[e] was also a Nonne, a Prioresse.") CTC, *abr.;* TrGrPo; ViBoPo
("There also was a nun, a Prioress," *mod. vers. by* Louis Untermeyer.) TrGrPo
Reeve, The. OxBM
"Sergeant of the Lawe, war and wys, A." CTC
Shipman, The. ACP; EtS
("Shipman was ther, woning fer by weste, A.") MOS
"Whan that Aprill[e] with his shoures soote," *br. sels.* ChTr; CTC; FiP; GoBC; InPS; NIP; SCV; TrGrPo; ViBoPo
(When April with Its Sweet Showers.) PrIm
("When in April the sweet showers fall," *mod. vers. by* Nevill Coghill.) TEP
("When the sweet showers of April follow March," *mod. vers. by* Louis Untermeyer.) TrGrPo
Wife of Bath, The. OxBM
("Good Wif was ther of biside Bathe, A.") BiP; EBEV; InPS; PPoe; ViBoPo
("Good Wyf was ther of bisyde Bathe, A.") TrGrPo
("There was a Wife from Bath, a well-appearing," *mod. vers. by* Louis Untermeyer.) TrGrPo
("Worthy woman from beside Bath city, A," *mod. version by* Nevill Coghill.) BiP
"With him ther was his sone, a young Squyer." TrGrPo
("With him there was his son, a youthful Squire," *mod. vers. by* Louis Untermeyer.) TrGrPo
"With hym ther rood a gentil Pardoner." BiP
("He and a gentle Pardoner rode together," *mod. version by* Nevill Coghill.) BiP
("This Pardoner had hair as yellow as wax," *mod. version by* Nevill Coghill.) SCV
Clerk's Tale, The.
Patient Griselda, *mod. by* Edward Hodnett. PoRA
Cook's Tale, The. BXAP
Franklin's Prologue, The. OAEL-1
Franklin's Tale, The. OAEL-1; OAEP
Introduction to the Man of Law's Prologue. FiP
Knight's [*or* Knightes] Tale, The. GoTL; OBWP, *mod. version by* Dryden
"Allas the wo! Allas, the peynes stronge." LO
Manciple's Tale, The.
Controlling the Tongue. OxBChV
Lat Take a Cat. ChTr
(Mice before Milk.) PCat
Merchant's Tale, The, *mod. version by* Frank Ernest Hill. UnTE, *abr.*
Miller's Prologue, The. OAEL-1
Miller's [*or* Milleres] Tale, The. OAEL-1; OxBoLi; TEP, *mod. vers. by* Nevill Coghill
"Fair was this yonge wyf, and therwithal." EBEV
Nun's Priest's Prologue, The. OAEL-1
Nun's Priest's [*or* Nonne Preestes] Tale, The. FiP; NoP; OAEL-1; OAEP; PoEL-1; SeCeV; TrGrPo, *orig. and mod. version by* Frank Ernest Hill
(Cock and the Hen, The.) OBNV
Chauntecleer. PB
"His comb was redder than the fine coral." PBBP
"There liv'd, as authors tell, in days of yore," *mod. version by* Dryden. OBVE
"This Chauntecleer stood hye up-on his toos." FiP
"Oure hoste gan to swere as he were wood." NoP; OAEL-1
Pardoner's Prologue, The. NoP; OAEL-1; OAEP
Pardoner's Tale, The. BiP, *mod. version by* Nevill Coghill; FiP; HAP, *abr.*; NoP; OAEL-1; OAEP; PoEL-1; SCV, *mod. version by* Nevill Coghill
"But, sires o word forgat I in my tale." EBEV
Death and the Three Revellers. OBNV
("These rioters, of whom I make my rime," *mod. version.*) WHA
(Three Revellers Search for Death.) OxBM
Prioress's Tale, The. ACP; GoBC, *mod. version by* Wordsworth; ISi, *mod. version by* Frank Ernest Hill; LoBV; OAEP; OxBoCh
Prologue of the Prioress's Tale, The. GoBC, *mod. by* Wordsworth *and incl. in* The Prioress' Tale; OxBoCh, incl. in The Prioress's Tale
"Invocation: O mother-maid! O maiden-mother free!" *mod. version by* Frank Ernest Hill. ISi
Two Invocations of the Virgin, II. ACP
Prologue to Sir Thopas. Par
Prologue to the Man of Law's Tale. FiP
Prologue to the Second Nun's Tale, The.
Invocatio Ad Mariam, *mod. vers. by* Frank Ernest Hill. ISi
"Thou maid and mother, daughter of thy Son." GoBC
Two Invocations of the Virgin, I. ACP
Reeve's Tale, The. UnTE, *mod. vers. by* Frank Ernest Hill
"At Trumpyngtoun nat fer from Cantebrigge." ViBoPo
Mill at Trumpington, The. OxBM
Sir Thopas. Par
(Tale of Sir Thopas, The.) BXAP
Wife of Bath's Prologue, The. OAEL-1; OxBoLi, *abr.*
(Prologue to the Wife of Bath's Tale, The.) PoEL-1
"If poor (you say) she drains her husband's purse," *mod. version by* Pope. OBSV
"My fifthe housbonde, god his soule blesse!" FiP
Wife's Fifth Husband, The. OxBM
Wife of Bath's Tale, The. OAEL-1
"In th'olde dayes of the Kyng Arthour." ViBoPo
Cantica: Our Lord Christ: Of Order. St. Francis of Assisi, *tr. fr. Italian by* Dante Gabriel Rossetti. AWP; OBVE
(Of Order in Our Lord Christ.) GoBC
Canticle. Wendell Berry. AP
Canticle. William Griffith. HBMV; HBVY
Canticle. James McAuley. PoAu-2
Canticle. Michael McClure. NeAP; PoM
Canticle. Francis Quarles. *See* My Beloved Is Mine, and I Am His.
Canticle of Darkness. Wilfred Watson. MoCV
Canticle of the Rose, The. Edith Sitwell. NoAM
Canticle of the Sun. St. Francis of Assisi, *tr. fr.* Italian. PAI, *tr. by* P. Robinson; TreFS, *tr. by* Matthew Arnold; WGRP, *tr. by* Maurice Francis Egan
(Cantico del Sole, *tr. by* Ezra Pound.) CTC; OBAL
(Song of the Creatures, *tr. by* Matthew Arnold.) GoBC
Canticle to Apollo, A. Robert Herrick. CaPo
Canticle to the Waterbirds, A. William Everson. NeAP; PoM
Canticles to Men. Marya Mannes. AMV-80
(First, The.) FAZ
Cantico del Sole. St. Francis of Assisi. *See* Canticle of the Sun.
Cantiga. Gil Vicente, *tr. fr. Portuguese and Spanish by* Thomas Walsh. ISi
Canto Amor. John Berryman. CoAP; MoAmPo; MoPo; MoVE; NePA; VGW
Canto Cantare Cantavi Cantatum. Rita Mae Brown. PeHV
Canto Llano. Anita Endrezze Probst. CDW
Cantor sings, The. Yom Kippur. Lucille Day. VWA
Cantor was reading Psalms, The. Requiem after Seventeen Years. Dahlia Ravikovitch, *tr. by* Chana Bloch. VWA
Cantor's Dream before the High Holy Days, A. Martin Robbins. VWA
Cantos, *sels.* Ezra Pound.
"And before hell mouth; dry plain/ and two mountains," *fr.* XVI. MoPo
"And the betrayers of language," *fr.* XIV. MoPo
"And then went down to the ship," I. AmPP; CMoP; CoBMV; LiTA; MoAB; MoAmPo; MoVE; NoAM; NoP; OBVE; SeCeV; TrGrPo; VGW
"And there was grass on the floor of the temple," *fr.* XXI. MoPo
"Ant's a centaur in his dragon world, The," *fr.* LXXXI. FaBoEn
"Eleanor (she spoiled in a British climate)," VII. NoAM; NOBA
" 'From the colour the nature,' " XC. VGW
"Hang it all, Robert Browning," II. AmPP; CoBMV; HAP; MoAB; MoAmPo; NePA; NoAM; NOBA; OxBA; PoA; TwAmPo
"Has he tempered the viol's wood," *fr.* LXXXII. HAP
"I sat on the Dogana's steps," III. TAP
"Jungle:/ Glaze green and red feathers, jungle," *fr.* XX. MoPo
"Kung walked/ by the dynastic temple," XIII. CMoP; FaBoMo
"Oh to be in England now that Winston's out," *fr.* LXXX. PoA
Said Jim X . . ., *fr.* XII. NAs
"Scientists are in terror, The," *fr.* CXV. FaBoMo
"She is submarine, she is an octopus," *fr.* XXIX. MoPo
"Skin-flakes, repetitions, erosions," *fr.* XV. MoPo
"So that the vines burst from my fingers," XVII. LoBV; OBMV

"Then a partridge-shaped cloud over dust storm," *fr.* CXIII. NYBP
"Tudor indeed is gone and every rose," *fr.* LXXX. FaBoTw
"What thou lovest well remains," *fr.* LXXXI. CMoP; FaBoTw; InPS; MoAB; NePA; NOBE; OxBA; SeCeV; ViBoPo
"Who even dead, yet hath his mind entire!" XLVII. CMoP; CrMA; MoPo; VGW
"With Usura," XLV. CMoP; LiTM; MoPo; NePA; NOBA; TW
"Yet/ Ere the season died a-cold," *fr.* LXXXI. MoVE
"Zeus lies in Ceres' bosom," LXXXI. FaBoMo; NoAm; NOBA; VGW
Cantos, *sels.* Tom Weatherly. PoBA
Coon Fire, 5.
First Thesis, 7.
Gullfish, 4.
Cantus: "When Alexander our kynge was dede." *Unknown. See* Death of Alexander, The.
Canvas leaves, the painted trees, The. Midsummer Night's Dream. Byron Vazakas. NePA
Canyon is deep shade beneath, The. Shasta. Witter Bynner. BPAW
Canzone: Donna Mi Priegha. Guido Cavalcanti, *tr. fr. Italian by* Ezra Pound. CTC
(Donna Me Prega.) OBVE
Canzone: He Beseeches Death for the Life of Beatrice. Dante, *tr. fr. Italian by* Dante Gabriel Rossetti. AWP
Canzone: He Perceives His Rashness in Love, but Has No Choice. Guido Guinicelli, *tr. fr. Italian by* Dante Gabriel Rossetti. AWP
Canzone: He Speaks of His Condition through Love. Folcachiero de' Folcachieri, *tr. fr. Italian by* Dante Gabriel Rossetti. AWP
Canzone: His Lament for Selvaggia. Cino da Pistoia, *tr. fr. Italian by* Dante Gabriel Rossetti. AWP
Canzone: His Portrait of His Lady, Angiola of Verona. Fazio degli Uberti, *tr. fr. Italian by* Dante Gabriel Rossetti. AWP
Canzone: Of His Dead Lady. Giacomino Pugliesi, *tr. fr. Italian by* Dante Gabriel Rossetti. AWP
Canzone: Of His Love, with the Figure of a Sudden Storm. Prinzivalle Doria, *tr. fr. Italian by* Dante Gabriel Rossetti. AWP
Canzone: Of the Gentle Heart. Guido Guinicelli, *tr. fr. Italian by* Dante Gabriel Rossetti. AWP; CTC; OBVE
Canzone: To Love and to His Lady. Guido delle Colonne, *tr. fr. Italian by* Dante Gabriel Rossetti. AWP
Canzone: "When shall we learn, what should be clear as day." W. H. Auden. LiTA; MoVE
Canzonet. *Unknown.* ElL
("See, see, mine own sweet jewel.") LO
Canzonetta: A Bitter Song to His Lady. Pier Moronelli da Fiorenza, *tr. fr. Italian by* Dante Gabriel Rossetti. AWP; OBVE
Canzonetta: He Will Neither Boast nor Lament to His Lady. Jacopo da Lentino, *tr. fr. Italian by* Dante Gabriel Rossetti. AWP
Canzonetta: Of His Lady, and of His Making Her Likeness. Jacopo da Lentino, *tr. fr. Italian by* Dante Gabriel Rossetti. AWP
Canzonetta: Of His Lady in Absence. Giacomino Pugliesi, *tr. fr. Italian by* Dante Gabriel Rossetti. AWP
Caoilte. *Unknown, tr. fr. Irish by* Frank O'Connor. KiLC
Caow-hand with a gun or two, A. Western Formula. *Unknown.* PoOW
Cap and Bells, The. W. B. Yeats. BrPo; ChTr; MoAB; MoBrPo; NoAM; NoP; OnMSP; OBVV; WSC
Capability Brown. William Cowper. SaC
Cape Ann. T. S. Eliot. Landscapes, V. BiP; EvOK; GoJo
Cape Ann. *Unknown.* FSW; BLSo, *with music*
Cape Ann; a View. John Malcolm Brinnin. NYBP
Cape Coast Castle Revisted. Jo Ann Hall-Evans. BlSi
Cape Cod Girls ("Cape Cod girls they've got no combs"). *Unknown.* AmSS; FSW; TrAS, *with music*
(Codfish Shanty, The.) GBP
Cape Coloured Batman. Guy Butler. PeSA
Cape Hatteras, *sel.* Hart Crane. *Fr.* The Bridge.
"Nasal whine of power whips a new universe." MoAB
Capilano ("Capilano, in the canyon"). A. M. Stephen. CaP
Capital. Heather McHugh. MAYP
Capital ship for an ocean trip, A. The *Walloping Window-Blind* [*or* A Nautical Ballad *or* A Capital Ship]. Charles Edward Carryl. *Fr.* Davy and the Goblin. FaPON; FSW; HBV-2; InMe; NA; OBAL; OBCA; TreFS; WhC. *See also* Oh a capital ship for an ocean trip.
Capital Square. Patrick Anderson. OBCV
Capitals Are Rocked, The. Nikolai Nekrasov, *tr. fr. Russian by* Babette Deutsch *and* Avrahm Yarmolinsky. AWP
"Cap'n." Arthur Wallace Peach. EtS
Cap'n & Me. Leon Baker. LFAC
Cap'n, I Believe, *with music. Unknown.* AS
Capped arbiter of beauty in this street. For the Marriage of Faustus and Helen (III). Hart Crane. FaBoMo; LiTM
Capriccio. Babette Deutsch. HBMV
Capriccio Dramatico, Il, *sel.* Lorenzo da Ponte, *tr. fr. Italian by* John Mazzinghi.
To an Artful Theatre Manager. TrJP
Capricious wind stirs Shannon's. An Irish Wind. Zelma S. Dennis. AMV-80
Capstan Chantey, A. Edwin James Brady. HBMV
Capsule Philosophy. Felicia Lamport. QQQ
Captain, The, *sels.* Beaumont *and* Fletcher.
Away, Delights, *fr.* III, iv. ElL; NOBE; OBEV; ViBoPo
("Away delights, go see some other dwelling.") LO
(Sad Song, The.) FaBoEn; GBL
Tell Me Dearest, What is Love? ElL; ViBoPo
(What Is Love?) HBV-1
Captain, The, *abr.* John G. C. Brainard. EtS
Captain, The. Tennyson. MOS
Captain, The. Blanca Varela, *tr. fr. Spanish by* Lynne Alvarez. WPOW
Captain, The. Jon Manchip White. NePoEA
Captain,/ what are you doing. George Simic. Charles Simic. DiL
Captain Arthur Phillip and the Birds. Lex Banning. PoAu-2
Captain bold in [*or* from] Halifax, that [*or* who] dwelt in country quarters, A. Unfortunate Miss Bailey [*or* Miss Bailey's Ghost]. George Colman, the Younger. DTC; FaBoBa; FiBHP; FSW; GBP; OxBoLi; ViBoFo
Captain Bover. *Unknown.* GBP
Captain Bunker. *Unknown.* AmFP
Captain Captain. *Unknown.* BluL
Captain Car. *Unknown. See* Edom o' Gordon.
Captain Carpenter. John Crowe Ransom. AP; CoBMV; FaBoMo; HoPM; LiTA; LiTM; LoBV; MasP; MoAB; MoAmPo; MoVE; MP; NePA; NoAM; NOBA; OxBA; PPoe; SeCeV; TwAmPo; TwCP
Captain Craig, *sel.* E. A. Robinson.
"I doubt if ten men in all Tilbury Town." PoEL-5
Captain Death. *Unknown.* CoMu
Captain Hall. *Unknown.* GBP
Captain Jinks. William Horace Lingard. BLPA; BLSo, *with music*; FaFP; FSW; TreF
Captain Jones' Invitation. Philip Freneau. MOS
Captain Kelly Lets His Daughter Go to Be a Nun. Thomas Butler Feeney. PoPl
Captain Kidd. *Unknown.* AmFP, *longer vers.*; FSW, *diff. vers.*; MoShBr, *shorter vers.*; TrAS, *with music*; ViBoFo
(Ballad of Captain Kidd, The.) AmSS, *with music*
Captain Molly. William Collins. PAL
Captain of St. Kitts, The. Beulah May. EtS
Captain of the *Shannon* came sailing up the bay, The. The *Shannon* and the *Chesapeake.* Thomas Tracy Bouvé. PAH
Captain of the Western wood. Madroño. Bret Harte. AA
Captain of the Years. Arthur R. Macdougall, Jr. TRV
"Captain, oh, captain, what will you give me." The Low-Down, Lonesome Low. *Unknown.* OuSiCo
Captain or colonel, or knight in arms. When the Assault Was Intended to the City [*or* Sonnet]. Milton. GTBS; GTBS-P; NoP; OAEL-1; RoGo
Captain Patterson, the folks back home. Americana XIII. Carl Rakosi. InPS
Captain Reece. W. S. Gilbert. CenHV; EvOK; FiBHP; GN; HBV-2
Captain Spud and His First Mate, Spade. John Ciardi. OBCA
Captain Stood on the Carronade, The. Frederick Marryat. *Fr.* Snarleyyow; or, The Dog Fiend. EtS; HBV-2; MOS
(The Old Navy.) PaPo
Captain Stratton's Fancy. John Masefield. MoBrPo; OBEV
Captain Sword. Leigh Hunt. GN
Captain: the weathervane's rusted. Widow's Walk. Elizabeth Spires. MAYP
Captain Ward and the *Rainbow. Unknown.* BaBo; ESPB; OBET; ViBoFo
Captain Wattle and Miss Roe. Charles Dibdin. OxBoLi
Captain! we often heretofore. To Our House-Dog Captain. Walter Savage Landor. NBM; PoEL-4
Captain Wedderburn's Courtship. *Unknown.* AmFP; ESPB (A *and* B *vers.*); ViBoFo (A *and* B *vers.*)
Captain Went Below, The. *Unknown.* AmSS
Captain's Daughter, The. James Thomas Fields. *See* Ballad of the Tempest.
Captain's Feather, The. Samuel Minturn Peck. AA
Captivated by the strange, buzzing. Open Range. Thomas Mitchell. AMV-81
Captive, The. William Franklin. LFAC
Captive. Peretz Hirshbein, *tr. fr. Yiddish by* Joseph Leftwich. TrJP
Captive. Marion Strobel. ErPo
Captive Dove, The. Anne Brontë. EBVV
Captive of Love, A. Ovid, *tr. fr. Latin by* Christopher Marlowe. Elegies, I, 2. AWP
Captive Ships at Manila, The. Dorothy Paul. PAH
Captive Stone, The. Jim Barnes. CDW
Captived Bee, The; or, The Little Filcher. Robert Herrick. CaPo

Captive's Hymn, The. Edna Dean Proctor. PAH
Captivity, The; an Oratorio, *sels.* Goldsmith.
Hope, *fr.* II. OBEC; TreFT
Memory, *fr.* I. OBEC; OBEV
(Song: "O memory, thou fond deceiver.") ViBoPo
Captivity. Samuel Rogers. FaBoEn; OBNC
Captivity Narrative, September 1981. Adrian C. Louis. STE
Capture of Edwin Alonzo Boyd, The. Peter Miller. MoCV
Capture of Little York. *Unknown.* PAH
Captured. Archibald MacLeish. HBMV
Captured Bird. George Rachow. LFAC
Caput apri refero. The Boar's Head [*or* The Boar's Head Carol]. *Unknown.* MeEL; OxBM
Car/ I give you over to. Car Wash. Myra Cohn Livingston. NTCP
Car Cemetery, The. Ciaran Carson. CIP
Car conveys us where we've been, The. Moving between Beloit and Monroe. Bink Noll. GrPl
Car is also, A/ a high-speed hermitage. Portrait of the Autist as a New World Driver. Les A. Murray. CBAP
Car is heavy with children, The. The Road Back. Anne Sexton. NYBP
Car loaded. Leaving Home. Shirley Cochrane. AMV-80
Car-tape machine, The. Road Hazard. Rayna Green. TWSS
Car Wash. Myra Cohn Livingston. NTCP
Carat of the first radiance. Lightning Bug. Robert Morgan. GeTw
Caravaggio Dying, Porto Ercole, July 1610, Aged 36, *sel.* Edward Lucie-Smith.
"My own head. Seen in mirrors. Cleanly axed," II. PeHV
Caravan, The. Gwendolyn MacEwen. MoCV
Caravati's Junkyard. Elizabeth Morgan. GrPl
Carcassonne. Gustave Nadaud, *tr. fr. French by* John R. Thompson. BLPA; FaBoBe; HBV-1
Card comes to tell you, A. Non Piàngere, Liù. Peter Porter. OxBC
Card Dealer, The. Dante Gabriel Rossetti. NBM; VLP
Card Game, A; Kinjiro Sawada. Patricia Y. Ikeda. BrSi
Card of Invitation to Mr. Gibbon, at Brighthelmstone, 1781, A. William Hayley. OBEC
Card-Players, The. Philip Larkin. OxBC
Card-Players, The. David Ray. VGW
Card table in the library stands ready, A. Lost in Translation. James Merrill. FYAP
Cardinal. Barbara Howes. DFF
Cardinal, A. W. D. Snodgrass. PP
Cardinal, The. Robert Penn Warren. *Fr.* Kentucky Mountain Farm. MoVE
Cardinal and the Dog, The. Robert Browning. VLP
Cardinal Bembo's Epitaph on Raphael. Thomas Hardy, *after the Latin of* Pietro Bembo. EyDe; FaBoEE
Cardinal Bird, The. William Davis Gallagher. AA
Cardinal Fisher. John Heywood. ACP
Cardinal Ideograms. May Swenson. OBCA
Cardinal, lover of shade. The Cardinal. Robert Penn Warren. *Fr.* Kentucky Mountain Farm. MoVE
Cardinal Wolsey's Farewell. Shakespeare *and probably* John Fletcher. *Fr.* King Henry VIII. LiTB; TreF
(Farewell to Greatness.) TrGrPo
(Wolsey's Farewell to His Greatness.) OHFP
Cardinal's Dog, The. John Glassco. MoCV
Cardrona Valley. Ian Wedde. OCNZ
Cards and Kisses. John Lyly. *Fr.* Alexander and Campaspe, III, v. HoPM; NOBE; OBEV
(Apelles' Song.) TrGrPo
(Cupid and Campaspe.) ElL; GTBS; GTBS-P; HBV-1; SeCeV; WHA
(Cupid and My Campaspe.) CABA; HeIP; NoP; PoRA
("Cupid and my Campaspe played.") GBL; OAEP; ViBoPo
(Song of Apelles.) OBSC
Care. Virginia Woodward Cloud. AA; HBV-2
Care. Josephine Miles. NYBP
Care. Richard Murphy. IPY
Care and heavy thought weigh me down. Estat ai en greu cossirier. Beatriz de Dia, *tr. by* Paul Blackburn. ErPo
Care Away ("Care away, away, away,/ Care away for evermore!"). *Unknown.* OxBM; OxBoLi
Care away, away, away,/ Murninge away! I Am Forsaken. *Unknown.* OxBM
Care-Charmer Sleep. Samuel Daniel. *Fr.* To Delia. LiTB; LoBV; OAEL-1
("Care-charmer sleep[e], son[ne] of the sable night.") AAS; EnRePo; GTBS; GTBS-P; HBV-1; InPS; NIP; NOBE; NoP; OAEP; OBSC; TreFS; TrGrPo
(Sonnet: "Care-charmer sleep[e], son[ne] of the sable night.") ElL; FaBoEn; PoEL-2; ViBoPo
Care-charmer sleep[e], sweet ease in restless misery [*or* restles miserie]. Sleep. Bartholomew Griffin. Fidessa, More Chaste than Kind, XV. AAS; NIP; OBSC
Care-charming Sleep, [Thou Easer of All Woes]. John Fletcher. *Fr.* The Tragedy of Valentinian, V, ii. ELP; FaBoRV; OAEP; TrGrPo; ViBoPo
(Into Slumbers.) SeCePo
(Invocation to Sleep.) WHA
(Song: "Care-charming sleep, thou easer of all woes.") LoBV; OBS; PoEL-2
(Song for the Sick Emperor.) FaBoEn
(Song to Sleep.) OxBoLi
(Thou Easer of All Woes.) TreFT
(To Sleep.) PoRA
Care of Bees, The. Virgil, *tr. fr. Latin by* Dryden. *Fr.* Georgics, IV. FaBoUs
Careful Angler, The. Robert Louis Stevenson. LiSp; SoSe
Careful Husband, The. *Unknown, tr. fr. Late Middle Irish by* the Earl of Longford. OnYI; OxBI
Careful man I ought to be, A. Service Supreme. *Unknown.* STF
Careful[l] observers may foretell the hour. A Description of a City Shower. Swift. HeIP; LoBV; MAT; NOEC; NoP; OAEL-1; OBSV; OnYI; PCat; PPP; SeCePo; SeCeV; TEP; UnPo
Carefully she opened her tunic. The Breasts of Mnasidice. Pierre Louys. *Fr.* Chansons de Bilitis. PeHV
Careless/ but not fearless. Walter Lew. *Fr.* Urn I: Silent for Twenty-five Years, the Father of My Mother Advises Me. BrSi
Careless and still. The Rabbit Hunter. Robert Frost. GDP; LiSp
Careless Content. John Byrom. HBV-2; NOEC; OBEC
Careless for an instant I closed my child's fingers in the jamb. Fingers in the Door. David Holbrook. NePoEA-2
Careless Gallant, The. Thomas Jordan. *See* Let Us Drink and Be Merry.
Careless Good Fellow, The. John Oldham. APAS; SeCV-2
Careless I lived, accepting day by day. Epitaph on a Vagabond. Alexander Gray. HBMV
Careless Love. Stanley Kunitz. WaP
Careless Love. *Unknown.* AS, *with music*; BluL; BLSo, *with music*; FSW; TrAS, *with music*; UnPo; UnTE
Careless Lover, The. Sir John Suckling. CavP
Careless Niece, The. Carolyn Wells. ShM
Careless seems the great Avenger. James Russell Lowell. *Fr.* The Present Crisis. TreFT; TRV
Careless Talk. Mark Hollis. FiBHP
Careless Willie. *Unknown.* FaPON
Careless young driver, McKissen, A. Stop! Lee Blair. TDH
Careless young lad down in Natchez, A. Ouch! *Unknown.* TDH
Careless Zookeeper, The. *Unknown.* TDH
Carelesse Nurse Mayd, The. Thomas Hood. FaBoNo; VLP
Carentan O Carentan. Louis Simpson. CoAP; MoBS; NMP; NOBA; OBWP; PrIm
Cares of Majesty, The. Shakespeare. King Henry IV, Pt. II, *fr.* III, i. LiTB; TreF
(O Gentle Sleep.) FaBoRV
(Soliloquy on Sleep.) FiP
Caresses. Elsa Barker. *Fr.* The Spirit and the Bride. HBMV
Cargoes. John Masefield. BLPL; CMoP; FaBV; FaPo; FaPON; FaPoR; LiTM; MoAB; MoBrPo; MOS; NOBE; OBEV; OBMV; OBVV; PAI; PoRA: RoGo; SeCeV; TEP; TreF
Cargoes of the Radanites. Harry Alan Potamkin. TrJP
Carhop floated up, The. Chicken. Dave Etter. MAT
Caria and Philistia considered. Cry Faugh! Robert Graves. CoBMV; MoBrPo
Cariboo Horses, The. Alfred Purdy. HeIP; NOBC
Caries. Solyman Brown. *Fr.* Dentologia; a Poem on the Diseases of the Teeth and Their Proper Remedies. FaBoUs
Caring ("Caring is loving, motionless"). F. R. Scott. PeCV
Carious Exposure. Gladys Cardiff. CDW
Carl Hamblin. Edgar Lee Masters. *Fr.* Spoon River Anthology. CMoP; LiTA; LiTM; OBSV; PAI
Carle He Came o'er the Croft, The. Allan Ramsay. OxBS
Carlino! what art thou about, my boy? To My Child Carlino. Walter Savage Landor. NoP; OBRV
Carlon the King, our Emperor Charlemayn. The Song of Roland. *Unknown, tr. by* Dorothy L. Sayers. NAWM-1
Carlyle and Emerson. Montgomery Schuyler. AA
Carlyle combined the lit'ry life. Thomas Carlyle. *Unknown.* FiBHP
Carlyle on Burns. William Jeffrey. *Fr.* On Glaister's Hill. OxBS
Carmarthen Bar. John Malcolm Brinnin. HoAn
Carmel Point. Robinson Jeffers. NoP
Carmen. Victor Hernandez Cruz. CAD; PoBA
Carmen. Newman Levy. FiBHP
Carmen Bellicosum. Guy Humphreys McMaster. AA; GN; HBV-2; PAH; PAL
Carmen Elegiacum. Thomas Morton. SCAP

Carmen Miranda. Frank Polite. GP
Carmen Miranda died on my seventh birthday. The Death of Carmen Miranda. Stephen E. Smith. AMV-81
Carmen Paschale [*or* Easter Song], *sels.* Caelius Sedulius, *tr. fr. Latin.*
Apostrophe to Death, *tr. by* George Sigerson. OnYI
Christ Quiets the Tempest, *tr. by* George Sigerson. OnYI
Hail, Maiden Root, *tr. by* Raymond F. Roseliep. ISi
Invocation: "Eternal God omnipotent! The One," *tr. by* George Sigerson. OnYI
Slaughter of the Innocents by Order of King Herod, The, *tr. by* George Sigerson. OnYI
Carmen Possum. *Unknown.* BLPA
Carmen Saeculare. Charles H. Sisson. , *after the Latin of* Horace. OBVE
Carmina Amico, *sels.* Edward James.
"He had a many-coloured glance like flowers." PeHV
"You have returned. You have returned, my joy." PeHV
Carmina Burana, *sels. Unknown, tr. fr. Latin.*
Gaudeamus Igitur, *tr. by* John Addington Symonds. GLGT; HBV-2
"I loved/ secretly," *tr. by* Willis Barnstone. BoWoP
In the Balance. *tr. by* George F. Whicher. OLR
"Let's away with study," *tr. by* Helen Waddell. NAWM-1
"O happy hour," *tr. by* Helen Waddell. NAWM-1
Carnal and the Crane, The. *Unknown.* ESPB; OBET
Carnal Knowledge. Thom Gunn. BoLoP
Carnal Knowledge. Gwen Harwood. CBAP
Carnation, The. Paul Hannigan. POL
Carnation Milk is the best in the land. The Virtues of Carnation Milk. David Ogilvy. OBAL
Carnations and Butterflies. Pope. *Fr.* The Dunciad. NOEC
Carnegie Hall: Rescued. Marianne Moore. *See* Glory.
Carnival is over, The. The high tents. Sunday Night in Santa Rosa. Dana Gioia. GrPl
Carnival Songs, *sel.* Lorenzo de' Medici, *tr. fr. Italian by* Richard Aldington.
Triumph of Bacchus and Ariadne. CTC
Carnival was a sick, The. The Indian Graveyard. Ramona Weeks. TAT
Carol, A: "Angels to the shepherds sang, The." Fred E. Weatherly. YeAr
Carol: "Deep in the fading leaves of night." W. R. Rodgers. ChMP; DTC; OBCP
Carol: "Fire is what's precious now." Alison Boodson. NeBP
Carol: Five Joys of the Virgin, The. *Unknown.* ACP; ISi
Carol, A: "He came all so still." *Unknown.* HBV-1; HBVY
(Ancient Christmas Carol, An.) OHIP
("He came all so still.") PChr
Carol: "I sing of a maiden." *Unknown. See* I Sing of a Maiden.
Carol: "I was a lover of turkey and holly." Anne Wilkinson. OBCV
Carol: "Mary laid her Child among." Norman Nicholson. NeBP; OBCP
Carol, A: "Mary the Mother/ Sang to her Son." Lizette Woodworth Reese. HBMV
Carol: "Mary, the mother, sits on the hill." Langdon E. Mitchell. OHIP
Carol: "Month can never forget the year, The." John McClure. HBMV
Carol: "My lady went to Canterbury." *Unknown.* FaBoCo; FaBoNo
Carol: "Now is the world withdrawn all." Howard Nemerov. TrCP
Carol, A: "Sweet music, sweeter far." Edmund Bolton. OxBoCh
Carol: "There was a boy bedded in bracken." John Short. DTC; FaBoCh; FaBoTw
Carol: "Villagers all, this frosty tide." Kenneth Grahame. *See* Christmas Carol: "Villagers all . . ."
Carol: "Vines branching stilly." Louise Imogen Guiney. Five Carols for Christmastide, II. OBVV
("Vines branching stilly.") ISi
Carol: "We saw him sleeping in his manger bed." Gerald Bullett. HBVY
Carol: "When the herds were watching." William Canton. HBVY; OHIP
(Bethlehem.) YeAr
Carol, every violet has. Epilogue. Alfred Noyes. *Fr.* The Flower of Old Japan. MoBrPo
Carol for Advent. John Heath-Stubbs. OxBC
Carol for Children, A. Ogden Nash. EaLo
Carol for Christmas Day, A. William Byrd. SBVL
Carol for Christmas Day, A. Francis Kinwelmersh. SBVL
Carol for His Darling on Christmas Day. Derek Stanford. NeBP
Carol for Saint Stephen's Day, A. *Unknown. See* St. Stephen and Herod.
Carol for the Last Christmas Eve. Norman Nicholson. OBCP
Carol for Twelfth Day, A. *Unknown.* OHIP
Carol in Praise of the Holly and Ivy. *Unknown. See* Holly and Ivy ("Holly and Ivy made a great party").
Carol, in the Park, Chewing on Straws. Judy Grahn. The Common Woman, IV. PeHV; WPOW
Carol Naïve. John McClure. HBMV
Carol of Agincourt, A. *Unknown. See* Agincourt Carol.
Carol of Death, The. Walt Whitman. *See* Death Carol.
Carol of Patience. Robert Graves. OBCP
Carol of St. George, A. *Unknown.* MeEL
Carol of the Birds. *Unknown, tr. fr. French.* OHIP
Carol of the Brown King. Langston Hughes. PChr; SBVL
Carol of the Numbers. *Unknown.* AmFP
(Dilly Song, The.) GBP; OBET
(Green Grow the Rushes.) FSW
(Green Grow the Rushes O.) OxBoLi
Carol of the Poor Children, The. Richard Middleton. OBCP
Carol of the Russian Children. *Unknown, tr. fr. Russian.* OHIP
Carol of the Three Kings. W. S. Merwin. PChr
Carol to Our Lady, A. *Unknown. See* I Sing of a Maiden.
Carol Took Her Clothes Off. Bill Messenger. CTBA
Carolers. Nancy G. Westerfield. AMV-81
Carolina. Henry Timrod. PAH
Carolina Spring Song. Hervey Allen. HBMV
Carolinas, The. David Ray. TAT
Caroline, The. George Crabbe. *Fr.* The Borough. SeCePo
Caroline and Her Young Sailor Bold. *Unknown.* AmFP
Caroline, II: To The Evening Star. Thomas Campbell. *See* To the Evening Star ("Gem of the crimson-colour'd even").
Caroline of Edinboro' Town. *Unknown.* AmFP
Caroline Pink. *Unknown.* PoPle
Carousel, The. Gloria C. Oden. AmNP; PoBA
Carp are secrets, The. Lifting Illegal Nets by Flashlight. William Stafford. NNaP
Carpe Diem. Thomas Lodge. *See* Pluck the Fruit and Taste the Pleasure.
Carpe Diem. Shakespeare. *Fr.* Twelfth Night, II, iii. GTBS; GTBS-P
Carpenter. George Mackay Brown. OxBC
Carpenter, The. George Macdonald. TrPWD; TRV
Carpenter, The. Michael Perkins. POL
Carpenter, The. Mary Brent Whiteside. TrCP
Carpenter Christ. Mildred Fowler Field. PGD
Carpenter, he worked with wood, A. Carpenter of Eternity. E. Merrill Root. PGD
Carpenter is intent on the pressure of his hand, The. El Greco: Espolio. Earle Birney. MoCV; PeCV
Carpenter of Eternity. E. Merrill Root. PGD
Carpenter of Galilee, The. Hilda W. Smith. TRV
Carpenter's made a hole, The. A Hole in the Floor. Richard Wilbur. NoAM; NOBA; SoSe
Carpenter's Real Anguish, The. Stephen Gardner. AMV-81
Carpenter's Son, The. A. E. Housman. A Shropshire Lad, XLVII. CoBMV; MoAB; MoBrPo; SpRo
Carpenter's son, carpenter's son. Craftsman. Luci Shaw. TrCP
Carpenter's Wife, The. *Unknown. See* Demon Lover, The.
Carpet-Weavers' Lament, The. *Unknown.* OBET
Carpets cover many floors where I come from. To Vietnam. Charlie Cobb. PoBA
Carrara. Philip Murray. NePoAm
Carrefour. Amy Lowell. BoWoP
Carriage brushes through the bright, The. Solo for Ear-Trumpet. Edith Sitwell. MoAB; MoBrPo
Carriage from Sweden, A. Marianne Moore. HAP; LiTA; LiTM; MoAB; MP; NePA; TwCP; WeW
Carrickfergus. Louis MacNeice. AnIL; FaBoPP; NoAM; OnYI
Carried Away. Anne Elder. CBAP
Carried her unprotesting out the door. The Rites for Cousin Vit. Gwendolyn Brooks. *Fr.* The Womanhood. BPo; HAP; WeW; WPE
Carrier Indians. Ken Belford. NOBC
Carrier Letter. Hart Crane. BoLoP
Carrier's Address. *Unknown.* PoOW
Carriers of the Dream Wheel. N. Scott Momaday. CDW
Carrion, A. Baudelaire, *tr. fr. French by* Allen Tate. AWP
Carrion. Harold Monro. *Fr.* Youth in Arms. MMA
Carrion Comfort. Gerard Manley Hopkins. CABA; HeIP; InPK; LiTB; MoVE; NoAM; NoP; OAEL-2; OAEP; OxBoCh; PoEL-5; PPP; TEP
("Not, I'll not, carrion comfort, Despair, not feast on thee.") CMoP
(Sonnet.) FaBoEn; OBNC
(Terrible Sonnets, I, The.) MoPo
Carrion crow sat upon an oak, The. Mother Goose. OxNR; PBBP, *sl. diff. version, with 2 add. sts.*
Carrion Crow, The. Thomas Lovell Beddoes. *See* Song: "Old Adam, the carrion crow."
Carrion-eater's nobility calls back from God, The. A Dreamed Realization. Gregory Corso. NeAP; PoM; VGW
Carroll's Sword. *At. to* Dallan MacMore. *See* Song of Carroll's Sword The.
Carrot has a green fringed top, A. Vegetables. Rachel Field. SoPo
Carrot headed boys. Malcom, Iowa. Charles Itzin. FAZ
Carrouse to the Emperor, the Royal Pole, and the Much-wronged Duke of Lorrain, A. *Unknown.* CoMu
Carrousel Tune. Tennessee Williams. OBAL

Carrowmore. "Æ." HBMV
(Gates of Dreamland, The.) HBV-2
Carry Her over the Water. W. H. Auden. FaBoTw
Carry Me Back. John Holmes. AmFN; NePoAm-2
Carry Me Back to Old Virginny. James A. Bland. BLSO, *with music*; FaBoBe; FaFP; PSoN, *with music*; TreF
(Old Virginny.) FaBV
Carry me back to Ole Virginny. First Families Move Over! Ogden Nash. FaBoCo
Carry me out. Discharged. W. E. Henley. In Hospital, XXVIII. BrPo
Carry On! Robert W. Service. HBV-2
Carry your garden. The Serpent Muses. Peggy Henderson. NMM
Carry your grief alone. Alone. Robert Finch. CaP; PeCV
Carrying a hammer on a quiet street. The Planting. Harley Elliott. NeAC
Carrying generations of lust on his tiny feet. Agent of Love. A. K. Redwing. VoR
Carrying my world. Father. Myra Cohn Livingston. NTCP
Carrying Their Coracles. Andrew Marvell. *Fr.* Upon Appleton House. ChTr
Carrying their packages of groceries in particular. Old Men and Old Women Going Home on the Street Car. Merrill Moore. MoAmPo
Cars/ In the Park. Central Park Tourney. Mildred Weston. AmFN
Cars are wicked, poets think. Man on Wheels. Karl Shapiro. PCP
Cars collide and erupt luggage and babies. In Laughter. Ted Hughes. InPS
Cars disappearing from the driveway, carrying. After the Seance. David Clewell. AMV-81
Car's in the Hall, The. Morris Bishop. TDH
Cars in the mirror come swiftly forward, The. Rear Vision. William Jay Smith. NYBP
Cars once steel and green, now old. Louis Zukofsky. VGW
Carta Canadensis. Ralph Gustafson. PeCV
Cartagena de Indias. Earle Birney. MoCV
Carter, The. *Unknown.* OBET
Carthon; a Poem. James Macpherson. EnRP
Carthusians. Ernest Dowson. VLP
Cartload of Shoes, A. Abraham Sutskever, *tr. fr. Yiddish by* David G. Roskies. VWA
Cartography. Louise Bogan. PoPl
Cartography. Joel Oppenheimer. CoPo
Cartoon. Jim Simmerman. AMV-81
Caruso: a voice. Sleeping with Women. Kenneth Koch. NoAM; PoM
Carved by a mighty race whose vanished hands. The Sphinx Speaks. Francis Saltus Saltus. AA
Carved by Obadiah Verity. Don Welch. PoDr
Carved in cheap marble, milky & veined. The Lamb. Keith Wilson. Psk
Carved on an Areca Nut. Ho Xuan Huong, *tr. fr. Vietnamese by* Nguyen Ngoc Bich *and* Burton Raffel. PBWP
Carver, The. Conrad Aiken. *Fr.* Priapus and the Pool. HBMV
Carving on the jamb of an embrasure, A. The Priory of St. Saviour, Glendalough. Donald Davie. OxBC
Caryatid. Léonie Adams. LiTM; MoVE
Caryophyllaceae, The. Spring Coming. A. R. Ammons. HeIP; InPK
Caryo's sweet smile Dianthus proud admires. Erasmus Darwin. *Fr.* The Loves of the Plants. PeD
Casa d'Amunt. Alastair Reid. NePoEA
Casa de Pollos. Kathleen Fraser. AmPA
Casabianca. Felicia Dorothea Hemans. BeLS; BLPA; EtS; FaBoBe; FaFP; FaPON; FPL; HBV-2; HBVY; PaPo; TreF; WBLP
Casanova. Richard Usborne. POL
Cascade, The. Edgell Rickword. ChMP; FaBoTw
Cascadilla Falls. A. R. Ammons. NIP; NOBA
Cascading streamers down of palest green. Weeping Willow. Richard Aldridge. NePoAm-2
Case, The. H. R. Hays. EAS
Case. Phyllis Janowitz. AMV-81
Case, A. Hughes Mearns. *See* Little Man Who Wasn't There, The.
Case at Sessions, A. Walter Savage Landor. OBSV
Case for the Miners, The. Siegfried Sassoon. SaC
Case History. Arthur W. Bell. WhC
"Case of Assault," A. Lydia Stephanou, *tr. fr. Modern Greek by* Kimon Friar. BoWoP
Case of Thomas More, The. Sister Mary St. Virginia. GoBC
Case to the Civilians, A. *Unknown.* FaBoEE
Cased in your bone and plaster. The Succubus. Harriet Rose. BrRo
Casey at the Bat. Ernest Lawrence Thayer. BeLS; BLPA; FaBoBe; FaFP; FaPON; FPL; HBV-2; InMe; LiSp; OBAL; OBCA; PaPo; PoPl; PoRA; TreF; YaD
Casey Jones. Edward Vincent Swart. PeSA
Casey Jones ("Come all you muckers and gather here"). *Unknown.* AmFP
Casey Jones ("Come all you rounders, if you want [*or* for I want you] to hear"). *Unknown.* AS, *with music*; BeLS; FaBV, *arr. by* T. Lawrence Siebert; OxBoLi; TreF; TrGrPo; ViBoFo (A, B, C, D, E, F, *and* G *vers.*)
Casey Jones has left today. Casey Jones. Edward Vincent Swart. PeSA
Casey Jones (Union). Joe Hill. FSW
Casey Jones was a brave engineer. Casey Jones (D *vers.*). *Unknown.* ViBoFo
Casey Jones was engineer. Casey Jones (F *vers.*). *Unknown.* ViBoFo
Casey Jones was long and tall. Casey Jones (E *vers.*). *Unknown.* ViBoFo
Casey—Twenty Years Later. *Unknown, at. to* S. P. McDonald. BLPA
Casey's Daughter at the Bat. Al Graham. InMe
Casey's Revenge. James Wilson. BLPA; OnMSP; TreFS
Casey's Table d'Hote. Eugene Field. PoOW
Cash In. Sharlot M. Hall. BPAW
Cash Only, No Refund, No Return. Daniel Mark Epstein. MAYP
Cashed in his chips. Epitaph for a Man from Virginia City. Kenneth Porter. NePoAm-2
Cashel of Munster. *Unknown, at. to* William English, *tr. fr. Modern Irish by* Sir Samuel Ferguson. AnIV: BIrV; GBL; OBEV; OBVV; OnYI; OxBI
Casida of the Rose. Federico García Lorca, *tr. fr. Spanish by* Robert Bly. NU
Casino. W. H. Auden. MoPo
Casino Beach. Thomas Rabbitt. MAYP
Casket Song, A. Shakespeare. *See* Tell Me Where Is Fancy Bred.
Cassamen and Dowsabell. Michael Drayton. *Fr.* The Shepherd's Garland, Eclogue VIII. OBSC
(Ballad of Dowsabell, The.) LoBV
(Dowsabel.) UnTE
Cassandra. Louise Bogan. HAP; MoAmPo; MoVE; PBWP; SBG; VGW
Cassandra. Robinson Jeffers. HeIP; LiTA; LiTM; NePA; WaP
Cassandra. E. A. Robinson. CMoP; LiTA; LiTM; NePA; NoAM; OxBA; PPON; SeCeV
Cassandra Southwick. Whittier. PAH
Cassie O'Lang. *Unknown.* ShM
Cassinus and Peter. Swift. OAEL-1; PPP
Cassius Hueffer. Edgar Lee Masters. *Fr.* Spoon River Anthology. NoAM; OxBA
Cassius Poisons Brutus's Mind. Shakespeare. *Fr.* Julius Caesar, I, ii. TreFS
Cast a cold eye. W. B. Yeats. *Fr.* Under Ben Bulben. FaBoEE
Cast all your cares on God; that anchor holds. Tennyson. *Fr.* Enoch Arden. TRV
Cast aside dull books and thought. Invitation to the Dance. *Unknown, tr. by* John Addington Symonds. UnTE
Cast away fear. Arthur Edward Waite. *Fr.* At the End of Things. TRV
Cast Down, but Not Destroyed. *Unknown.* PAH
Cast on the field from their full height. Second Shadow. Theodore Roethke. PoA
Cast on the water by a careless hand. The Cocoa-Tree. Charles Warren Stoddard. AA
Cast on 120 stitches,/ Rep. to the end of the row. On a Grey-haired Old Lady Knitting at an Orchestral Concert. " Furnley Maurice." CBAP
Cast Our Caps and Cares Away. John Fletcher. *Fr.* Beggars' Bush. ViBoPo
Cast out, amid so many companions. The Comet. Emil Makai, *tr. by* André Ungar. VWA
Cast Thy Bread upon the Waters. Bible, *O.T.* Ecclesiastes, XI. AWP (1-6); NAWM-1 (*complete*); OBEV (1-8)
(Life's Uncertainty, 1-8.) TreFS
Cast Thy Bread upon the Waters, *with music.* Phoebe A. Hanaford. AH
Cast wide the folding doorways of the East. From the Night of Forebeing. Francis Thompson. OBVV
Castanets. Bernard Spencer. WeW
Castara. William Habington. *Poems indexed separately by titles and first lines.*
Castara, see that dust, the sportive wind. To Castara, upon Beautie. William Habington. *Fr.* Castara, II. AnAnS-2; SeCP
Castaway, The. William Cowper. CABA; ELP; EnRP; FaBoEn; FiP; HeIP; LAuP; MOS; NOBE; NOEC; NoP; OAEL-1; OAEP; OBEC; PoEL-3; PPoe; PPP
Castaway. John Nerber. PoA
Castaway, A, *sel.* Augusta Webster.
"Well, well, I know the wise ones talk and talk." BrRo
Castellated, tall. The Bat. Edith Sitwell. FaBoMo
Castiglione has many a frontier. The Road to Bologna. Roy Macnab. PeSA
Castile. Miguel de Unamuno, *tr. fr. Spanish by* Eleanor L. Turnbull. PoPl
Castilian. Elinor Wylie. HBMV
Casting All Your Care upon God, for He Careth for You. Thomas Washbourne. OxBoCh
Casting All Your Care upon Him. *Unknown.* STF
Casting at Night. Allen Hoey. AMV-80; WOLT

Casting from the Miami causeway. The Osprey Suicides. Laurence Lieberman. HoAn
Casting, up a salt creek in the sea-rank air. San Pedro Road. Robert Hass. GeTw; WOLT
Castle, The. Sidney Alexander. PoNe
Castle, The. Edwin Muir. LiTB
Castle by the Sea, The. Ludwig Uhland, *tr. fr. German by* Longfellow. AWP
Castle Hyde [*or* Castlehyde]. *Unknown.* FaBoPP; OnYI
Castle of Chillon, The, *sel.* Byron.
"Eternal Spirit of the chainless Mind!" PoPl
Castle of Indolence, The, *sels.* James Thomson.
"Doors that knew no shrill alarming bell, The," *fr.* I. ViBoPo
"In lowly dale, fast by a river's side," *fr* I. EnRP; NOEC; ViBoPo
(Enchanted Ground.) BSV
(Land of Indolence, The.) OBEC; SeCePo
Indifference to Fortune, *fr.* II. OBEC
"O mortal man, who livest here by toil," *fr.* I. LAuP
Praise of Industry, The, *fr.* II. OBEC
"Sometimes the pencil, in cool airy halls," *fr.* I. PoEL-3
Sons of Indolence, *fr.* I. OBEC
Witching Song, A, *fr.* I. OBEC
Wondrous Show, A, *fr.* I. OBEC
Castle of Thorns, The. Yvor Winters. NoAM
Castle Rock. Frederick Morgan. AMV-81
Castled crag of Drachenfels, The. Byron. *Fr.* Childe Harold's Pilgrimage, III. ViBoPo
Castlehyde. *Unknown. See* Castle Hyde.
Castles. A. Glanz-Leyeles, *tr. fr. Yiddish.* TrJP, *tr. by* Joseph Leftwich; VWA, *tr. by* Keith Bosley
Castles in the Air. James Ballantine. HBV-1
Castles in the Air. Thomas Love Peacock. HBV-1
Castles with lofty. Soldier's Song. Goethe, *tr. by* Bayard Taylor. *Fr.* Faust. AWP
Castoff Skin. Ruth Whitman. InPK
Casual glance on me, The. Old Essex Door. Agnes MacCarthy Hickey. GoYe
Casual Gold. Maud E. Uschold. SoPo; YeAr
Casual Meeting. Sam Bradley. AMV-81
Casual Song, A. Roden Noel. HBV-1
Casualty. Seamus Heaney. IPY
Casualty. W. E. Henley. In Hospital, XIII. BrPo; VLP
Casualty. Winifred M. Letts. SUMH
Casualty. Robert Nichols. MMA
Casualty. Diana Witherby. ChMP
Cat. Dorothy W. Baruch. SoPo; SUS; TiPo
Cat, The. Baudelaire, *tr. fr. French by* Roy Campbell. PoPl
Cat, The! Joseph Payne Brennan. ShM
Cat, The. Charles Stuart Calverley. *Fr.* Sad Memories. ChTr
Cat, The. Richard Church. BoAnP; PCat
Cat, The. W. H. Davies. NOBE; PCat
Cat. Eleanor Farjeon. OnUR
Cat, The. Oliver Herford. FaBV
Cat, The. William Matthews. AmPA
Cat. Mary Britton Miller. PCat; RHPC; SoPo; SUS; TiPo
Cat. Joe Rosenblatt. NOBC
Cat. Lytton Strachey. PCat
Cat, A. Edward Thomas. BoAnP; BrPo
Cat, A/ I keep, that plays about my. Robert Herrick. PCat
Cat!/ Scat! Cat. Eleanor Farjeon. OnUR
Cat and Mouse. Ted Hughes. EaLo
Cat and the Bird, The. George Canning. ChTr
Cat and the Bird, The. Marvin Solomon. NePoAm-2
Cat and the Boot, The; or, An Improvement upon Mirrors. *Unknown.* FaBoUs
Cat and the Fish, The. Thomas Gray. *See* Ode on the Death of a Favourite Cat Drowned in a Tub of Gold Fishes.
Cat and the Lute, The. Thomas Master. PCat
Cat and the Moon, The. W. B. Yeats. CMoP; FaBoCh; GoJo; PCat; RoGo
Cat and the Rain, The. Swift. *Fr.* A Description of a City Shower. PCat
Cat and the Weather. May Swenson. HAP; WeW
Cat as Cat, The. Denise Levertov. NOBA
Cat at the Cream. *Unknown.* GBP; POL
Cat Ballerina Assoluta. Emilie Glen. GoYe
Cat bird singing. Air. Robert Creeley. Prf
Cat by the fireside, purring, A. Herbs in the Attic. Marilyn Waniek. AMV-81; MAYP
Cat, Caged and Shrunken, The. Arthur Freeman. BoAnP
Cat Came Back, The. Harry S. Miller. FSN, *with music*; FSW
Cat Goddesses. Robert Graves. MoVE; NYBP
Cat Heard the Cat-Bird, The. John Ciardi. SO
Cat, if you go outdoors you must walk in the snow. On a Night of Snow. Elizabeth J. Coatsworth. MoAmPo; MoShBr; OBCA
Cat in Despondency, A. *Unknown.* RHPC
Cat in the Box, The. Anne Rae Jonas. SUW
Cat in the cold, so eager to come in. Will You, Won't You. Mark Van Doren. NCSH
Cat in the Snow. Aileen Fisher. NTCP
Cat into Lady. La Fontaine, *tr. fr. French by* Edmund Marsh. PCat
Cat is placed in a box, A. The Cat in the Box. Anne Rae Jonas. SUW
Cat May Look at a King, A. *Unknown.* OxBoLi
Cat Morgan Introduces Himself. T. S. Eliot. NOBL
Cat of Cats, The. William Brighty Rands. OxBChV; RHPC
(Kitty: What She Thinks of Herself.) MoShBr
Cat of Many Years. Gertrude May Lutz. AMV-80
Cat of the House, The. Ford Madox Ford. PCat
Cat on Couch. Barbara Howes. DFF; NCSH
Cat on my bosom, The. The Cat as Cat. Denise Levertov. NOBA
Cat on the Porch at Dusk. Dorothy Harriman. GoYe
Cat or Stomp. Laura Tohe. STE
Cat runs races with her tail, The. Signs of Winter. John Clare. BoNaP; OAEL-2; PoSC; WiR
Cat said, A/ on the corner. Vietnam #4. Clarence Major. BOLo; FF; PoBA
Cat sat asleep by the side of the fire, The. *Unknown.* OxNR
Cat sat quaintly by the fire, A. Hearth. Peggy Bacon. FaPON
Cat sits on the pavement by the house, A. The Lonely Man. Randall Jarrell. OxBC
"Cat spreads herself, The." Six Haiku for Graham V. Phillips Who First Said the First One. Robert Phillips. GrPl
Cat takes a look at the weather. Cat and the Weather. May Swenson. HAP; WeW
Cat that comes to my window sill, The. That Cat. Ben King. FiBHP
Cat That Followed His Nose, The. John Kaye Kendall. CenHV
Cat walks on the barracks roof, A. Bus Stop. Vincent O'Sullivan. OCNZ
Cat was once a weaver, The. What the Gray Cat Sings. Arthur Guiterman. MoShBr
Cat went here and there, The. The Cat and the Moon. W. B. Yeats. CMoP; FaBoCh; GoJo; PCat; RoGo
Cat! who hast pass'd [*or* past] thy grand climacteric. To a Cat [*or* On Mrs. Reynolds's Cat]. Keats. FaBoCh; FM; PCat
Cat with yellow eyes doesn't yet realize, The. Getting Up. Stephen Dobyns. MAYP
Cataclysmic if it were so. "What You See Is Me." Barbara Gibbs. NYBP
Catacombs. István Vas, *tr. fr. Hungarian by* Jascha Kessler. VWA
Cataldo Mission. Richard Hugo. FAZ
Catalogue. Hilde Domin, *tr. fr. German by* Tudor Morris. VWA
Catalogue, *sel.* Rosalie Moore.
"Cats sleep fat and walk thin." NTCP
Catalogue. Louis Untermeyer. HBMV
Catalogue Army. Naomi Shihab Nye. MAYP
Catalpa, in you a song, a cache. Catalpa Tree. Miriam Waddington. MoCV; OBCV
Catalpa Tree. Padraic Colum. NePoAm
Catalpa Tree. Miriam Waddington. MoCV; OBCV
Catalpa tree with a trunk like monolith. Catalpa Tree. Padraic Colum. NePoAM
"Catamount Tavern" is lively to-night, The. Parson Allen's Ride. Wallace Bruce. PAH
Cataract. Margoret Smith. NYBP
Cataract at Lodore, The. Helen Bevington. SpRo
Cataract of Lodore, The. Robert Southey. GN; HBV-1; OxBChV; SpRo; TEP; TreFS; WBLP
Cataract, whirling to the precipice, The. Fragment. John Clare. BoNaP
Catastrophe. Edwin Brock. NMP
Catch, A. Henry Aldrich. *See* Reasons for Drinking.
Catch. Robert Francis. HeIP; InPK; LiSp; NCSH; PP
Catch, The. Brewster Ghiselin. HAP
Catch, A. Tom Hood. CenHV
Catch. Langston Hughes. NoAM
Catch, A. Ben Jonson. *See* Boz, Quoth the Blue Fly.
Catch, A. Thomas Love Peacock. *See* Three Men of Gotham.
Catch, A. Richard Henry Stoddard. AA
Catch, The/ fishing for lunkers. Fishing the Big Hole. John Holbrook. WOLT
Catch a floater, catch an eel. Beela by the Sea. Leroy F. Jackson. RHPC
Catch a Little Rhyme. Eve Merriam. OBCA; PDV
Catch by the Hearth, A. *Unknown.* OHIP
Catch her and hold her if you can. Defiance. Walter Savage Landor. HBV-1; VLP
Catch him coming off the thing after a state of the union. Strategies. Welton Smith. NBP; PoBA
Catch him, crow! Carry him, kite! *Unknown.* OxNR

Catch of Shy Fish, A. Gwendolyn Brooks. CAPP
Catch: On a Wet Day. Franco Sacchetti, *tr. fr. Italian by* Dante Gabriel Rossetti. AWP
(On a Wet Day.) BoNaP
Catch the blues song. Transformation. Quincy Troupe. CNA
Catch-22 Test, A. John L. Sellers. LFAC
Catch What You Can. Jean Garrigue. VGW
Catching a Horse. Barbara Winder. PH
Catching One Clear Thought Alive. Paula Gunn Allen. WPOW
Catching Soft Craws. William J. Vernon. WOLT
Catching-up. David Walker. FAZ
Catching yourself, hands lathery. In the Round. Theodore Weiss. NMP
Catechism Elegy. Margaret Gibson. MAYP
Catechism, 1958. W. M. Ransom. CDW
Catechisms: Talking with a Four-year-old. George Ella Lyon. Str
Caterpillar, The. Anselm Hollo. FAZ
Caterpillar. R. E. Rashley. CaP
Caterpillar, [The]. Christina Rossetti. *Fr.* Sing-Song. FaPON; GoJo; OxBChV; RHPC; SoPo
("Brown and furry.") SUS
Caterpillar and the Ant, The. Allan Ramsay. SeCePo
Caterpillars. John Freeman. ChMP
Catfish, The. Michael Waters. WOLT
Cathedral, A. Stanislav Vinaver, *tr. fr. Serbo-Croat by* Vasa D. Mihailovich. VWA
Cathedral Close, The. Coventry Patmore. *Fr.* The Angel in the House. EBVV
(Salisbury; the Cathedral Close.) FaBoPP
Cathedral window was a cliché, The. Lumière. H. L. Van Brunt. AMV–81; LTB
Cathedrals. W. S. Doxey. AMV–80
Cathemerinon, *sel.* Prudentius, *tr. fr. Latin by* Raymond F. Roseliep.
O Noble Virgin, *Hymn* XI, *verses* 53–60. ISi
Catherine. Karla Kuskin. NTCP; PDV
Catherine, describing a perfect circle. Virgin Martyrs. John Heath-Stubbs. OxBC
Catherine Kinrade. Thomas Edward Brown. OBVV
Catherine Ogg. Edgar Lee Masters. *Fr.* The New Spoon River. GLGT
Catherine said "I think I'll bake." Catherine. Karla Kuskin. NTCP; PDV
Cathexis. F. J. Bryant, Jr. PoBA
Cathleen. *Unknown, tr. fr. Irish by* Thomas MacIntyre. BIrV
Cathleen Sweeping. George Johnston. NOBC
Catholic Amen, The. Christopher Smart. *Fr.* A Song to David. GoBC
("He sang of God—the mighty source.") TRV
Catholic Bells, The. William Carlos Williams. CMoP; NOBA; OxBA
Catholic Church, The. Dryden. *Fr.* The Hind and the Panther, II. OBS
Catkin. *Unknown.* TiPo
(Little Gray Pussy.) SoPo
Catkins, like caterpillars slung arow. Lost Lane. Dorothy Wellesley. WPE
Cato, *sel.* Joseph Addison.
Cato's Soliloquy, *fr.* V, i. TreFS; WBLP
Cato. C. H. Sisson. NOCV
Cato's Address to His Troops in Lybia. Lucan, *tr. fr. Latin by* Nicholas Rowe. *Fr.* Pharsalia, IX. OBEC
Cato's Soliloquy. Joseph Addison. *Fr.* Cato, V, i. TreFS; WBLP
Cats. Marchette Chute. SoPo
Cats. Eleanor Farjeon. PCat; PDV; RHPC
Cats. Robert Francis. DFF
Cats, The. Weldon Kees. NaP
Cats. Francis Scarfe. BoAnP; NeBP
"Those who love cats which do not even purr," *sel.* PCat
Cats. A. S. J. Tessimond. BoAnP; PCat
Cats and Dogs. Howard Moss. OBAL
Cats and Egypt. Andrew Hudgins. AMV–81
Cats and kittens, kittens and cats. Country Barnyard. Elizabeth J. Coatsworth. RHPC
Cats are home tonight, The. Unblinking eyes. On Sitting Up Late, Watching Kittens. Eric W. Paff. AMV–81
Cats caught a yellow-vented bulbul, The. Parliament of Cats. D. J. Enright. NMP
Cat's Conscience, A. *Unknown.* PoLF
Cat's electric fur, The. The Cat, Caged and Shrunken. Arthur Freeman. BoAnP
Cat's Eyes. Francis Scarfe. PCat
Cats I scorn, who sleek and fat. A True Cat. Anna Seward. PCat
Cat's Meat. Harold Monro. OBMV
Cat's Menu. Richard Shaw. RHPC
Cats, no less liquid than their shadows. Cats. A. S. J. Tessimond. BoAnP; PCat
Cats of Kilkenny, The. *Unknown.* RHPC
Cat's purr, A. At the Loom. Robert Duncan. *Fr.* Passages. VGW
Cats purr. I Speak, I Say, I Talk. Arnold L. Shapiro. GrPl
Cats sleep/ Anywhere. Cats. Eleanor Farjeon. PCat; PDV; RHPC
Cats sleep fat and walk thin. Rosalie Moore. *Fr.* Catalogue. NTCP
Cat's Song, The. *Unknown.* GBP
Cats' Tea-Party, The. Frederick E. Weatherly. TiPo
Cats walk neatly. Cats. Robert Francis. DFF
Cattail fluff. Porous. William Carlos Williams. NYBP
Cattle. Berta Hart Nance. BPAW
Cattle. Peter Skrzynecki. CBAP
Cattle. *Unknown.* SoPo
Cattle in the common field, The. On the Heights. Walter Savage Landor. FaBoEE
Cattle of His Hand, The. Wilbur Underwood. WGRP
Cattle roam again across the fields, The. Adoration of the Disk. *Unknown, at. to* King Akhnaten *and* Princess Nefer Neferiu Aten, *tr. by* Robert Hillyer. *Fr.* Book of the Dead. FaPON
Cattle Show. " Hugh MacDiarmid." BSV; FaBoMo; GoTS; HAP; MoBrPo; OBMV; OxBTC
Cattle Thief, The. Pauline Johnson. WPOW
Cattle-trains edge along the river, bringing morning on a white vibration. Ceiling Unlimited. Muriel Rukeyser. MoAmPo
Catullus Talks to Himself. Catullus, *tr. fr. Latin by* Louis Untermeyer. UnTE
Catullus to Lesbia. James Reeves. ErPo
Catullus, you're a fool, I said. Catullus Talks to Himself. Catullus, *tr. by* Louis Untermeyer. UnTE
Catwalk. Daniel L. Klauck. LFAC
Catwise. Philip Booth. NePoAm-2
Caucasus, The ["The Caucasus lay vast in light"). Boris Pasternak, *tr. fr. Russian by* Eugene M. Kayden. PoPl
Caughnawaga Beadwork Seller, The. William Douw Lighthall. CaP
Caught and composed, motionless blue, behind. The Desire of Water. Mark Jarman. PoA
Caught at hanger's ends the limp. Goodwill, Inc. Dennis Schmitz. AmPA
Caught between two streams of traffic, in the gloom. T. S. Eliot. Robert Lowell. NoAM; NOBA
Caught in the centre of a soundless field. Myxomatosis. Philip Larkin. CMoP; ELU; NMP; NoAM; NoP
Caught in the glib catcher's net. Sockeye Salmon. Ronald Hambleton. CaP; OBCV
Caught in the Pocket. William D. Barney. LiSp
Caught Jupiter, that old benefic. The Incubation. Al Zolynas. LTB
Caught off first, he leaped to run to second, but. Ball Game. Richard Eberhart. LiSp
Caught on the shoulders of Bunn Mhor on a slope. Soaring. Cal Clother. PoSh
Caught Stealing a Dahlia. *Unknown.* TDH
Caught still as Absalom. Chagrin. Isaac Rosenberg. ChMP; MoBrPo; VWA
Caught upon a thousand thorns, I sing. 1934. Richard Eberhart. TwAmPo
Caught without wife and mother, child. Getting Drunk with Daughter. Robert Huff. NePoEA-2
Cauld are the ghaisties in yon kirk yaird. Ghaisties. Robert Garioch. NeBP
Cauld blaws the wind frae east to west. Up in the Morning Early. Burns. PoSC
Cauld blows the wind frae north to south. Cold Blows the Wind. John Hamilton. CH
Cauld, cauld is Alnack. Benighted to the Foothills of the Cairngorms. Olive Fraser. PoSH
Cauld Cornwood. *Unknown.* GBP
Cauld Lad of Hilton, The. *Unknown.* OxBoLi
(Cauld Lad's Song, The.) ChTr
(Ghost's Song, The.) FaBoCh
(Song of the Cauld Lad of Hylton.) GBP
(Wandering Spectre, The.) CH
Cauld Lad's Song, The. *Unknown. See* Cauld Lad of Hilton, The.
Cauliflower, The. John Haines. GP; InPK
Cauliflower-eared Spartan. Reading and Talking. Louis Zukofsky. *See* For want of a nail.
Cause for Wonder, A. *Unknown.* MeEL
Cause nobody deals with Aretha—a mother with four children. Poem for Aretha. Nikki Giovanni. BPo; PoBA
"Cause of loving God is God alone, The." The One Thing Needful. Vassar Miller. PoCh
Cause of Our Joy. Sister Maris Stella. ISi
Cause of This I Know Not. Haniel Long. HBMV
Causes are in Time, The; only their issue. The Allegory of the Wolf Boy. Thom Gunn. OxBC
Causes of Color, The. Ann Rae Jonas. SUW
Causeway. Allan Block. TAT

Caution ("Listen, lass, if you would be"). *Unknown, tr. fr. German by* Louis Untermeyer. UnTE
Caution to Everybody, A. Ogden Nash. *See* Consider the Auk.
Caution to Poets, A. Matthew Arnold. FaBoUs; PV
Cautionary Limerick. *Unknown.* FaBoUs
Cautionary Tale, A. Anne Wilkinson. OBCV; PeCV
Cautionary Verses to Youth of Both Sexes. Theodore Hook. HBV-2; OxBChV
(Address to Children.) FaBoUs
Cautious Gunslinger, The. An Idle Visitation. Edward Dorn. *Fr.* Gunslinger. NOBA
Cautious Lovers, The, *sel.* Countess of Winchilsea.
To Silvia. HBV-1
Cautious Struggle, The. *Unknown. See* Be Quiet, Sir!
Cautious yet unafraid, twirling lightly. Shadow Dirge. R. P. Dexter. LiSp
Cautiously, hoping that nobody sees. In Columbus, Ohio. John Matthias. AMV-80
Cavalier. Richard Bruce. CDC
Cavalier Lyric. James Simmons. InPK; POL
Cavalier Tunes, *sels.* Robert Browning.
Boot and Saddle, III. HBV-2; OAEP; SoSe
Give a Rouse, II. HBV-2; OAEP
Marching Along, I. HBV-2; OAEP
Cavalier's Escape, The. Walter Thornbury. FaBoBe; GN; HBV-2
Cavalier's Song. Robert Graham. *See* If Doughty Deeds.
Cavalier's Song, The. William Motherwell. GN; HBV-2
Cavalry Crossing a Ford. Walt Whitman. AA; AmPP; AP; CABA; ChTr; HeIP; InPK; InPS; NoAM; NoP; OxBA; PAI; PoPl; PPP; TAP; UnPo
Cave, The. Glenn W. Dresbach. RFM
Cave-Boy, The. Laura E. Richards. FaPON
Cave-Drawing, The. Vernon Watkins. LiTB
Cave of Despair, The. Spenser. *Fr.* The Faerie Queene, I, 9. LoBV; NOBE; OBNV
("Ere long they come, where that same wicked wight.") OAEL-1
(To Be or Not to Be.) FaBoEn
Cave of Mammon, The. Spenser. The Faerie Queene, II, 7. FiP, *sts.* 21-32; PoEL-1
("As pilot well expert in perilous wave.") OAEL-1
Cave of Night, The, *sel.* John Montague.
"Rifled honeycomb, The." CIP
Cave of Staffa, I ("We saw, but surely, in the motley crowd"). Wordsworth. VLP
Cave of Staffa, II ("Ye shadowy beings, that have rights and claims"). Wordsworth. VLP
Cave Sedem! Theodore F. MacManus. HBV-2
Cave we found, but vacant all within, The. Homer, *tr. by* Pope. *Fr.* The Odyssey, IX. OBVE
Caved-in cardboard box, The. Words, like Spiders. P. Wolny. PCP
Cavern, The. Charles Tomlinson. CMoP; NMP
Caverns of the Grave I've Seen, The. Blake. NCEP
Caverns there were within my mind, which sun. Wordsworth. *Fr.* The Prelude, III. FaBoPP
Caves. David Baker. MAYP
Caves, The. Michael Roberts. ChMP
Caviar comes from the virgin sturgeon. The Virgin Sturgeon. *Unknown.* FSW
Caw, caw, caw. Poem/Ditty-Bop. Carolyn M. Rodgers. JB
Caw Caw Caw. The Sea and Ourselves at Cape Ann. Lawrence Ferlinghetti. PoM
Cawsand Bay. *Unknown.* PoPle
Caxtons are mechanical birds with many wings. A Martian Sends a Postcard Home. Craig Raine. NoP
Cean[n] Dubh Deelish. *Unknown. See* Dear Dark Head.
Cean-Salla. James Clarence Mangan. OnYI
Cease rude Boreas blust'ring railers. The Tempest. *Unknown.* AmFP
Cease, Then, My Tongue! Spenser. ILwL
Cease then, nor order *imperfection* name. Whatever Is, Is Right. Pope. *Fr.* An Essay on Man, Epistle I. OBEC
Cease your labors, lovers of boys. Epigram. *Unknown.* PeHV
Ceaselessly he watched TV. The Addict. Jack Montgomery. QQQ
Ceaselessly the weaver, Time. The Weaver. William H. Burleigh. BLPA
Cecil County. Ron Welburn. PoBA
Cecilia. *Unknown, tr. fr. French by* William McLennan. WHW
Cedar. Robert Morgan. GeTw
Cedar and jagged fir. The Lonely Land. A. J. M. Smith. CaP; NOBC
Cedar at first, then a splay of staghorn put to the torch. Burning the Root. Margaret Gibson. MAYP
Cedar Mountain. Annie Fields. PAH
Cedar Needles. Chase Twichell. MAYP
Cedar River, The. Reginald Gibbons. MAYP
Cedar took over an hour of digging, The. In the Dream of the Body. David Keller. AMV-80
Cedar Waxwing. William H. Matchett. ELU
Cedars of Lebanon, The. Alphonse Marie Louis de Lamartine, *tr. fr. French by* Toru Dutt. AWP
Ceiling, The. Theodore Roethke. EyDe
Ceiling of his bedroom, The. Cartography. Joel Oppenheimer. CoPo
Ceiling Unlimited. Muriel Rukeyser. MoAmPo
Celadyne's Song. William Browne. Britannia's Pastorals, III, Song 1. OBS
(Memory.) HBV-1
(So Shuts the Marigold Her Leaves.) ChTr
Celan. Asya, *tr. fr. Yiddish by* Gabriel Preil *and* Howard Schwartz. VWA
Celan. Anthony Barnett. VWA
Celandine. Edward Thomas. OxBTC
Celanta at the Well of Life. George Peele. *See* Song at the Well, The.
Celebrant. David Mitchell. OCNZ
Celebrants, The, came chanting, "God is dead!" The Death of God. Howard Nemerov. OxBC
Celebrated Return. Clarence Major. AmNP
Celebrating the Freak. Cynthia Macdonald. Psk
Celebrating the Mass of Christian Burial. Cleopatra Mathis. LTB
Celebration. Elizabeth Newton Sachs. AMV-81
Celebration. Leonard Cohen. ErPo
Celebration, The. James Dickey. VGW
Celebration, The. Robert Mezey. FAZ
Celebration, A. May Sarton. NePoAm-2
Celebration. Ray A. Young Bear. CDW
Celebration for My Mother. Wendy Rose. CDW
Celebration in the Plaza, The. Adrienne Rich. NePoEA; TwAmPo
Celebration 1982. Terri Meyette Wilkins. LFAC
Celebration of Charis [in Ten Lyric Pieces (*or* Lyrick Peeces)], A. Ben Jonson. AnAnS-2; SeCP
Sels.
Begging Another, on Colour of Mending the Former. OAEP; PoEL-2
(For Love's Sake.) UnTE
His Excuse for Loving. EnRePo; JCP; PoEL-2; QFR; SeCV-1
How He Saw Her. EnRePo; OAEP; QRF; SeCV-1
Triumph of Charis, The. CABA; ELP; GoBC; InPS; LiTB; LoBV; NOBE; NoP; PoPle; SeCeV; WHA
(Her Triumph.) CTC; EBEV; ElL; FaBoEn; HBV-1; JCP; OAEP; PoEL-2; PrIm; SeCV-1; ViBoPo
("See the chariot at hand here of Love.") InvP
(Triumph, The.) OBEV
So White, So Soft, So Sweet, *sel.* TrGrPo; UnTE
("Have you seen but a bright lily grow.") FaBoCh
(So Sweet Is She.) GN
Celebrations. Austin Clarke. IPY; OxBI
Celery. Ogden Nash. FaBoUs; FaPON; RHPC
Celestial Body. Louise Townsend Nicholl. NePoAm
Celestial choir, enthron'd in realms of light. To His Excellency, General Washington [*or* His Excellency General Washington]. Phillis Wheatley. OFD; PoNe; SBG; WPE
Celestial City, The. Giles Fletcher the Younger. Christ's Victory and Triumph, IV. NOBE; OBS
Celestial Country, The. Bernard of Cluny. *See* Jerusalem.
Celestial Evening, October 1967. Charles Olson. *Fr.* The Maximus Poems. PoM
Celestial Love, *sel.* Emerson.
Love's Nobility. TreF
Celestial Love. Michelangelo, *tr. fr. Italian by* John Addington Symonds. AWP
Celestial Passion, The. Richard Watson Gilder. AA
Celestial Pilot, The. Dante, *tr. fr. Italian by* Longfellow. *Fr.* Divina Commedia: Purgatorio. WGRP
Celestial Queen. Jacopo Sannazaro, *tr. fr. Latin by* John C. Eustace. *Fr.* De Partu Virginis, Book III. ISi
Celestial Surgeon, The. Robert Louis Stevenson. BrPo; EBCP; EBVV; HBV-2; HBVY; MoBrPo; TreFS; TrGrPo; TrPWD; TRV; ViBoPo; WGRP
Celestial Wisdom. Juvenal, *tr. fr. Latin by* Samuel Johnson. The Satires, X. AWP
Celestine. Robert Fitzgerald. MoVE
Celestine Silvousplait Justine de Mouton Rosalie. Propinquity Needed. Charles Battell Loomis. InMe
Celia. Ellen Bass. NMM
Celia Bleeding, to the Surgeon. Thomas Carew. AnAnS-2; PeD; SeCP
Celia Celia. Adrian Mitchell. FaBoEE
Celia, Celia, your name is like cilia. Celia. Ellen Bass. NMM
Celia Singing. Thomas Carew. OAEP
Celia Singing. Thomas Stanley. AnAnS-2
Celia, that I once was blest. A Song. Dryden. *Fr.* Amphitryon. CavP
Celia's Home-coming. Agnes Mary Frances Robinson. OBEV; OBVV
Celimena, of my heart. A Song [*or* Damon and Celimena]. Dryden. *Fr.* An Evening's Love. CavP; InvP

Celinda, by what potent art. Song. Thomas Stanley. CavP
Cell, The. George Rostrevor. TrPWD
Cell. Dennis Shady. LFAC
Cell by cell the baby made herself, the cells. Sara in Her Father's Arms. George Oppen. GP; NNaP
Cell Lay inside Her Body, The. Murray Edmond. A Patching Together, 3. NAs
Cell-Mates. Louis Untermeyer. HBMV
Cell of Himself, The. Arthur Freeman. TwCP
Cell-Rap #27. Raymond Ringo Fernandez. LFAC
Cell so small, A. Cell. Dennis Shady. LFAC
Cell Song. Etheridge Knight. NNaP; PoBA
Cello, The. Richard Watson Gilder. AA
Cello Entry. Paul Celan, *tr. fr. German by* Joachim Neugroschel. VWA
Cello sobs, the symphony begins, The. The Festival. Frederic Prokosch. LiTA; WaP
'Cellos, setting forth apart, The. At the Symphony. Robert Nathan. HBMV
Cells Breathe in the Emptiness. Galway Kinnell. NaP; VGW
Cells hold mock convention in the brain, The. Lobotomy. Kenneth Pitchford. PoA
Celluloid of a photograph holds them well, The. Six Young Men. Ted Hughes. OBWP
Celt in Me, The. Keith Wilson. GP
Celtic Cross. Norman MacCaig. OxBS
Celtic Cross, The. Thomas D'Arcy McGee. OnYI
Celtic Fringe, The. Stevie Smith. FaBoNo
Celtic Lyric, The. J. C. Squire. BXAP
Celts, The. Thomas D'Arcy McGee. OnYI; OxBI
Celts, The. Stevie Smith. NoP
Cemeteries are places for departed souls. Lines Written at the Grave of Alexander [*or* Alexandre] Dumas. Gwendolyn B. Bennett. CDC; PoNe
Cemetery, A. Emily Dickinson. *See* This quiet Dust was Gentlemen and Ladies.
Cemetery at Academy, California, The. Philip Levine. NaP; NYBP
Cemetery in New Mexico, A. A. Alvarez. VWA
Cemetery Is, The. Audrey McGaffin. NePoAm-2
Cemetery Nights. Stephen Dobyns. SV
"Cemetery stone New England autumn, The." Voices of Heroes. Horace Gregory. OFD
Cenci, The. Shelley. EnRP
Sels.
Beatrice's Last Words. FiP
Cenci's Curse upon His Daughter, The. TW
Cenotaph, The. Charlotte Mew. MMA; SUMH; WPE
Cenotaph, The. Ursula Roberts. SUMH
Cenotaph of Lincoln. James T. McKay. OHIP
Censorship. Philip Brasfield. LFAC
Censorship. John Ciardi. TW
Censorship. Arthur Waley. OxBTC; WaP
Censorship would have this pen. Censorship. Philip Brasfield. LFAC
Centaur, The. Theodore Roethke. NePoAm-2
Centaur, The. May Swenson. GrPl; MP; NePoAm-2; NMM; PH; SO; TwAmPo; TwCP
Centaur does not need a horse, The. The Centaur. Theodore Roethke. NePoAm-2
Centaur Overheard, The. Edgar Bowers. ConAP
Centaur, siren [*or* syren], I forgo [*or* foregoe], The. Another. Richard Lovelace. CaPo; PoEL-3
Centaur Song. Hilda Doolittle ("H. D."). VGW
Centaur Song. Stanley Moss. DiL
Centaur, syren, I foregoe, The. *See* Centaur, siren, I forgo, The.
Centaurs, The. James Stephens. AmMo
Centenarian's Story, The. Walt Whitman. CTC
Centennial Hymn. Bryant. PAH
Centennial Hymn. John Pierpont. PAL
Centennial Hymn. Whittier. AA; PAH; PAL
Centennial Meditation of Columbia, The. Sidney Lanier. PAH
Dear Land of All My Love, *sel.* GN; HBVY
("Long as thine art shall love true love.") PGD
Center of America, The. Robert Siegal. AMV-81
Center of Attention, The. Daniel Hoffman. FYAP; UnPo
Center of the Garden, The. Ann Stanford. AMV-80
Centerfold Reflected in a Jet Window. Sandra McPherson. GeTw; MAYP
Centipede, The. Samuel Hopkins Adams. InMe
Centipede, A. Mrs. Edward Craster. *See* Centipede Was Happy Quite, A.
Centipede, The. A. P. Herbert. CenHV
Centipede, The. Ogden Nash. FaPON
Centipede adown the street, The. Archy at the Zoo. Don Marquis. *Fr.* Archy and Mehitabel. OBAL
Centipede along the threshold crept, The. The Haunted House. Thomas Hood. WiR
Centipede is not complete, The. About Feet. Margaret Hillert. RHPC
Centipede is not quite nice, The. The Centipede. A. P. Herbert. CenHV
Centipede Was Happy Quite, A. Mrs. Edward Craster. SoPo
(Centipede, A.) OnUR; TiPo
(Puzzled Centipede, The.) FaPON
(Quandary.) TreFS
Central. Ted Kooser. Psk
Central Heating System. Stephen Spender. GrPl
Central Park. Robert Lowell. LiTM; NYP
Central Park. Howard Nemerov. NYP
Central Park, 1916. Pamela Stewart. NYP
Central Park *Some People (3 P.M.).* Nancy Morejón, *tr. fr. Spanish by* Sylvia Carranza. PBWP
Central Park South. Donald Revell. NYP
Central Park Tourney. Mildred Weston. AmFN
Central Park West. Stanley Moss. PCP
Central Park West. Jack Spicer. PeHV
Centre of equal daughters, equal sons. America. Walt Whitman. GOA
Centuries Are His, The. Georgia Moore Eberling. TRV
Century ago deep dripping galleries were gutted, A. The Old Bing. Stanley Roger Green. BSV
Century Farms. Once upon a Nag. Michael Beirne McMahon. PH
Century of Couplets, A, *sel.* Richard Chenevix Trench.
"Who praises God the most, what says he more than he." OBRV
Century of evening prayers, A. Over to God. Stephen Harrigan. FAZ
Century Piece for Poor Heine, A. John Logan. NNaP
Century since, out in the West, A. Betty Zane. Thomas Dunn English. PAL
Century was fading fast, A. That Little Hatchet. C. Butler-Andrews. PeD
Cerberus. H. L. Van Brunt. FAZ
Ceremonial Band, The. James Reeves. OnUR
Ceremonial Ode Intended for a University. Lascelles Abercrombie. OBVV
Ceremonies for Candlemas Day, The. Robert Herrick. OAEP
Ceremonies for Candlemas[se] Eve. Robert Herrick. CaPo; JCP; OAEP; OBS
Ceremonies for Christmas[se]. Robert Herrick. AnAnS-2; GN; HBV-1; OHIP; TEP
(Yule Log.) OBCP
"Wassail the trees, that they may bear," *sel.* PChr
Ceremony. Kattie M. Cumbo. BlSi
Ceremony. Johari M. Kunjufu. BlSi
Ceremony. Vassar Miller. NePoEA
Ceremony. Howard Nemerov. AMV-80
Ceremony. William Stafford. LCAP
Ceremony. Richard Wilbur. CoAP; MiAP; NoAM; PP
Ceremony after a Fire Raid. Dylan Thomas. CMoP; CoBMV; MoPo; WaP
Ceremony must be found, The. Speaking of Poetry. John Peale Bishop. LiTA; OxBA; PP; TwAmPo
Ceremony upon Candlemas Eve. Robert Herrick. OBCP
Cernunnos. Hugh Maxton. CIP
Certain Age, A. Phyllis McGinley. NePoAm-2
Certain Choices. Richard Shelton. Psk
Certain dark underground eyes. Picture of Loot. Alan Sillitoe. OxBTC
Certain days wash ashore from the sea. Good Memory. Sotero Rivera-Avilés, *tr. by* Julio Marzán. InW
Certain Dead. John Haines. LCAP
Certain great statesman, whom all of us know, A. Ballynahinch. George Canning. FaBoCo
Certain Lady, A. Dorothy Parker. NIP
Certain Maxims of Archy. Don Marquis. InMe; OBAL
Archy, the Cockroach, Speaks, *sel.* FaPON
Certain Maxims of Hafiz. Kipling. HBV-1
Certain Mercies. Robert Graves. CoBMV; GTBS-P
Certain old party of Moultrie, A. A Strong Feeling for Poultry. Roy Blount, Jr. TDH
Certain pasha, dead five thousand years, A. A Turkish Legend. Thomas Bailey Aldrich. GN; HBV-2; HBVY
Certain Peace, A. Nikki Giovanni. CNA
Certain people would not clean their buttons. The Bohemians. Ivor Gurney. MMA
Certain poets/ have written good poems. On the Poet's Leer. David Ray. NePoEA-2
Certain portions of the heart. Anatomy. Gilbert Sorrentino. POL
Certain Presbyterian Pair, A. The Presbyterian Wedding. *Unknown.* CoMu; ErPo
Certain presuppositions are altered. Upland. A. R. Ammons. NOBA
Certain Slant of Light, A. Emily Dickinson. *See* There's a certain slant of light.
Certain True Woords Spoken Concerning One Benet Corbett [after Her Death]. Richard Corbett. AnAnS-2; SeCP
Certain violinist had a beautiful violin, A. Falling Upwards. David Shapiro. AMV-81

Certain women, I think, are born. International Motherhood Assoc. M. L. Hester. AMV-81
Certain Young Gourmet, A. Charles Cuthbert Inge. TDH
(Limerick: "Certain young gourmet of Crediton, A.") CenHV; WhC
Certain Young Lady, A. Washington Irving. FaBoBe; HBV-1
Certain Young Man of Great Gumption, A. *Unknown.* ShM
Certain youthful lady in Thoulouse, A. Sonnet: Of the Eyes of a Certain Mandetta. Guido Cavalcanti, *tr. by* Dante Gabriel Rossetti. AWP
Certainly there was something to their stories. Childe Roland, etc. Elder Olson. OBAL
Certainties. Helen Frazee-Bower. Two Married, IV. HBMV
Certainties. Margaret Widdemer. HBMV
Certainty. Evelyn Hardy. HBMV
Certainty before Lunch. John Berryman. LCAP; OxBC
Certainty Enough. Amelia Josephine Burr. HBMV
Certified Copy. Ann Deagon. NIP
Cervantes. E. C. Bentley. EvOK
("People of Spain think Cervantes, The.") CenHV; FiBHP
Cervantes, Dostoievsky, Poe. A Poem Intended to Incite the Utmost Depression. Samuel Hoffenstein. DBV; FaBoCo
Cervera. Bertrand Shadwell. PAH
Cerveteri road. Elena Clementelli, *tr. by* Ruth Feldman *and* Brian Swann. *Fr.* Etruscan Notebook. PBWP
Cerylas, jesting, called his pretty jade. Hors d'Oeuvre. Deems Taylor. UnTE
César Franck. Joseph Auslander. HBMV
'Cession's stahted on de gospel way, De. A Spiritual. Paul Laurence Dunbar. BPo
C'est un grand Monsieur Pussy-Cat. Monsieur Pussy-Cat, Blackmailer. Stevie Smith. PCat
Cetewayo, chief of the Zulus. Footnote. Anthony Delius. PeSA
Cethegrande is a fis. The Whale. *Unknown.* OxBM
Ceylon. A. Hugh Fisher. HBV-2
Cézanne. Gertrude Stein. TAP
Chace, The. William Somervile. *See* Chase, The.
Chaeronean Plutarch, to thy deathless praise. Plutarch. Agathias, *tr. by* Dryden. AWP
Chaff, The. W. S. Merwin. PPP
Chagrin. Isaac Rosenberg. ChMP; MoBrPo; VWA
Chahcoal Man, *with music. Unknown.* AS
Chain. Audre Lorde. BlSi
Chain Gang Blues. *Unknown.* WTO
Chain Gang Trouble. *Unknown.* BluL
Chain I gave was fair to view, The. From the Turkish. Byron. HBV-1
Chain Letters. Alice Fulton. LTB
Chain of Pearl, A, *sel.* Lady Diana Primrose.
Fourth Pearl, The: Temperance. WPE
Chained by stern duty to the rock of state. Lincoln. S. Weir Mitchell. PAH
Chained in the market-place he stood. The African Chief. Bryant. BLPA; PaPo; TreFS
Chains, my good lord: in your raised brows I read. Tennyson. *Fr.* Columbus. OFD
Chains that bind my thinking, The. The Searching. Alice S. Cobb. BlSi
Chair, Dog, and Clock. Hilary Corke. NYBP
Chair she sat in, like a burnished throne, The. A Game of Chess. T. S. Eliot. *Fr.* The Waste Land. SCV
Chairman of many committees. Clubwoman. Mary Carter Smith. PoNe
Chairs. Henry Petroski. PoDr
Chairs. Valerie Worth. NTCP
Chaitivel, *sel.* Arthur O'Shaughnessy.
Sarrazine's Song to Her Dead Lover. HBV-1
Chalk Angel, The. Dennis Schmitz. NPGG
Chalk from Eden. Howard Moss. NePA
Chalk mark sex of the nation, on walls we drummers. Three Modes of History and Culture. Amiri Baraka. NoAM
Chalk-Pit, The. Edward Thomas. BrPo
Challenge. Sterling A. Brown. CDC
Challenge. Thomas Curtis Clark. PGD
Challenge, A. James Benjamin Kenyon. AA
Challenge, The. Grenville Kleiser. BLRP
Challenge, The. Longfellow. AP
Challenge. Kenton Foster Murray. HBV-1
Challenge, The. Calvin Murry. LFAC
Challenge, The. Pope. PoEL-3
Challenge, The. *Unknown, tr. fr. Spanish by* Louis Untermeyer. UnTE
Challenge comes, The. The Challenge. Grenville Kleiser. BLRP
Challengers. Alfred Dorn. GoYe
Chamber Music. John Ditsky. AMV-81
Chamber Music. James Joyce. *Poems indexed separately by titles and first lines.*
Chamber over the Gate, The. Longfellow. AP
Chamber-Pot Rhyme. *Unknown.* GBP
Chamber Scene. Nathaniel Parker Willis. HBV-1
Chambered Nautilus, The. Oliver Wendell Holmes. *Fr.* The Autocrat of the Breakfast-Table, *ch.* 4. AA; AmPP; AP; EtS; FaBoBe; FaFP; FPL; GN; HBV-2; HBVY; HoPM; LiTA; MOS; NePA; NOBA; NoP; OBVV; OHFP; PoEL-5; PoLF; PrIm; TreF; WGRP
"Build thee more stately mansions, O my soul," *sel.* TRV
Chambermaid's Second Song, The. W. B. Yeats. ErPo
Chambers of Jerusalem. Yehuda Karni, *tr. fr. Hebrew by* Jeremy Garber. VWA
Chameleon. Paul Engle. CrMA
Chameleon, The. A. P. Herbert. FaPON
Chameleon. Gordon LeClaire. EtS
Chameleon, The. James Merrick, *after* De la Motte. HBV-1
Chameleon, The. Matthew Prior. OBSV
Chameleon changes his color, The. The Chameleon. A. P. Herbert. FaPON
Chameleon, knowing I am near. Chameleon. Paul Engle. CrMA
Chameleons saw an arc of color, The. The Lord's Chameleons. Peter Klappert. AmPA
Chamois, The. Hilaire Belloc. FaBoNo
Chamonix. George Hookham. OBVV
Champ de Manœuvres. Sir Herbert Read. BrPo
Champagne. Rita Dove. MAYP
Champagne Charlie, *with music. At. to* George Leybourne. BLSo; PSoN
Champagne Rosée. John Kenyon. OBEV; OBRV; OBVV
Champion of those who groan beneath. To William Lloyd Garrison. Whittier. PAH
Champs d'Honneur. Ernest Hemingway. PoA
Chance, The. John Holmes. NePoAm-2
Chance, The. Arthur Sze. BrSi
Chance adjustment of my car mirror, A. In a Mirror. Marcia Stubbs. MAT
Chance Meeting. Susan Griffin. NPGG
Chancellor's Nightmare, The. W. S. Gilbert. *See* Nightmare.
Chancery Suit, A. Sir George Rose. FaBoCo
Chances, The, *sel.* John Fletcher.
"Merciless love, whom nature hath denied," *fr.* III, ii. GBL
Chances, The. Wilfred Owen. MMA; OxBTC
Chances. Brenda S. Stockwell. AMV-81
Chances of Rhyme, The. Charles Tomlinson. FaBoMo; PoA
Chandelier as Protagonist, The. William Virgil Davis. AMV-80
Chandeliers hemorrhage, Tritons, The. Figures in a Ruined Ballroom. George Hitchcock. VGW
Chandler's Wife, The. *Unknown.* FSW
Chang-an in utter confusion. War in Chang-an City. Wang Tsan, *tr. by* Rewi Alley. PPON
Chang'd, yet Constant. Thomas Stanley. AnAnS-2
Change. Mary Elizabeth Coleridge. MoVE
Change, The. Abraham Cowley. *Fr.* The Mistress. AnAnS-2; FaBoEn; MeLP; MePo; OBS; SeCP; SeCV-1
Change. John Donne. Elegies, III. EBEV; ViBoPo
Change. Earl of Essex. *See* Change Thy Mind. . .
Change. Robert Graves. OxBTC
Change. Fulke Greville. *Fr.* Caelica, VII. OBSC
("World, that all contains, is ever moving, The.") EnRePo; NIP
Change. William Dean Howells. AA
Change. Raymond Knister. CaP; OBCV; PeCV
Change, The. David O'Bruadair, *tr. fr. Irish by* Austin Clarke. BIrV
Change./ like if u were a match I wd light u. A Poem to Complement Other Poems. Don L. Lee. BPo; NoAM
Change and Immutability. Syd Scroggie. PoSH
Change Is Not Always Progress. Don L. Lee. TAP
Change is the circumstance of our delight. The Prism. H. A. Pinkerton. NePoAm
Change, move, dead clock, that this fresh day. Small Prayer. Weldon Kees. PoA; VGW
Change of Address. Kathleen Fraser. NYBP
Change of Heart, A. Valine Hobbs. SiSoSe
Change of Life. Constance Urdang. VWA
Change of School. Elizabeth Smither. OCNZ
Change of Venue. Jill Clockadale. AMV-80
Change Should Breed Change. William Drummond of Hawthornden. OBEV; OxBoCh
Change Thy Mind since She Doth Change. Earl of Essex. ElL
(Change.) OBSC
Change-up. Don L. Lee. CNA; PoBA
Changed. Charles Stuart Calverley. FiBHP
Changed to Corinna, The. Robert Herrick. JCP
Changed Woman, The. Louise Bogan. HBMV
Changeful Beauty. *Unknown, tr. fr. Greek by* Andrew Lang. EnLoPo
Changeless Shore. Sarah Leeds Ash. GoYe

Changeling, The. Charlotte Mew. CH
Changeling, The, *sels.* Thomas Middleton.
"Here we are, if you have any more," *fr.* V, iii. PoEL-2
"What makes your lip so strange?" *fr.* III, iv. PoEL-2
Changeling VIII. Kristjana Gunnars. NOBC
Changelings. Mary Thacher Higginson. AA
Changes. "Owen Meredith." PoLF
Changes, The. Robert Pinsky. NPGG
Changes around the Bay. Michael Palmer. NPGG
Changing. Mary Ann Hoberman. RHPC
Changing guests, each in a different mood, The. Inclusiveness. Dante Gabriel Rossetti. The House of Life, LXIII. NBM; NCEP; SyP; VLP
Changing Road, The. Katharine Lee Bates. HBV-2
Changing Wind, The. Julian Orde. NeBP
Changsha Shoe Factory. Willis Barnstone. SaC
Channel Crossing. George Barker. ChMP; GTBS-P
Channel Firing. Thomas Hardy. BiP; BrPo; CABA; CMoP; CoBMV; EBEV; HAP; HeIP; InPK; LiTB; MoPo; NIP; NoAM; NoP; OAEL-2; OAEP; OxBTC; PAI; PoEL-5; PoRA; PPON; PrIm; SeCeV; SoSe; UnPo; WaaP
Channel moon went down, as ignorance, The. The Outlanders. Andrew Glaze. NYBP
Channel Passage, A. Rupert Brooke. MOS
Channel Passage, A. Swinburne. VLP
Channel U.S.A.—Live. Adrien Stoutenburg. AmFN
Channel Water. Virginia Scott Miner. AMV-80
Channing. Amos Bronson Alcott. AA
Chanson de Rosemonde. Richard Hovey. HBV-1
Chanson d'Or. Ann Hamilton. HBMV
Chanson Innocent[e]. E. E. Cummings. *See* Chansons Innocentes.
Chanson Naïve. John McClure. HBMV
Chanson of the Bells of Oseney. Cale Young Rice. HBV-2
Chanson un Peu Naïve. Louise Bogan. HBMV
Chansons d'Automne. Paul Verlaine, *tr. fr. French by* Arthur Symons. AWP
Chansons de Bilitis, *sels.* Pierre Louys, *tr. fr. French.*
Agonizing Memory, The. PeHV
Breasts of Mnasidice, The. PeHV
Complaisant Friend, The. PeHV
Love. PeHV
Meeting, The. PeHV
Penumbra. PeHV
Chansons Innocentes, *sels.* E. E. Cummings.
"In Just-/ Spring when the world is mud," I. AmPP; CAD; FaBV; FaPON; HeIP; InPK; MoAB; MoAmPo; MoShBr; NCSH; NIP; NoP; PrIm; SoSe; WeW
"Little tree," II. NTCP; OBCP; PChr; PDV; PoSC; RoGo
Chant for Dark Hours. Dorothy Parker. SBG
Chant for Reapers. Wilfrid Thorley. OBEV; OBVV
Chant for Skippers. Katharine Gallagher. SiSoSe
Chant for Young/Brothas and Sistuhs, A. Sonia Sanchez. BPo
Chant-Pagan. Kipling. OAEP; VLP
Chant of Departure; [a Missionary's Prayer]. Alfred Barrett. GoBC; ISi
Chant of Hate against England, A. Ernst Lissauer, *tr. fr. German by* Barbara Henderson. HBV-2
Chant Out of Doors, A. Marguerite Wilkinson. TrPWD
Chant Royal from a Copydesk. Rufus Terral. InMe
Chant Royal of High Virtue. Sir Arthur Quiller-Couch. HBV-2
Chant Royal of the Dejected Dipsomanic. Don Marquis. HBMV
Chant to Io. Tiwai Paraone, *tr. fr. Maori by* A. Alpers. WTO
Chanted Calendar, A. Sydney Dobell. *Fr.* Balder. HBV-1; HBVY; OBEV
(Procession of the Flowers, The.) GN
Chantey of Notorious Bibbers. Henry Morton Robinson. InMe
Chanticleer. William Austin. EBCP; OxBoCh
Chanticleer. John Farrar. SoPo; TiPo
Chanticleer. Margaret Irvin. PoAu-2
Chanticleer. Katharine Tynan. HBV-1; HBVY; TiPo
Chanticleer makes canticles. Chanticleer. Margaret Irvin. PoAu-2
Chanting Cherubs, The—a Group by Greenough. Richard Henry Dana. AA
Chanting in Tibet has not ceased, The. Moirè. Michael McClure. EAS
Chanting sun, as ever, rivals, The. Prologue in Heaven. Goethe, *tr. by* Louis MacNeice. *Fr.* Faust. NAWM-2
Chants Communal, *sel.* Horace Traubel.
What Can I Do? TrJP
Chants, incense, and the glory pass and die. December 26. George Edward Hoffman. PGD
Chanuke, O Chanuke ("Chanukah, O Chanukah, O holiday so fair"). *Tr. fr. Yiddish.* FSW
Chaos. Pope. *See* Triumph of Dullness, The.
Chap has a shark up in Sparkill, A. The Sick Shark. Morris Bishop. TDH
Chapel, as the pivot of this valley, The. For the Altarpiece of the Roseau Valley Church, Saint Lucia. Derek Walcott. NoP
Chapel's cowbell, The. Crusoe's Island. Derek Walcott. NoAM
Chaperon, The. H. C. Bunner. AA; HBV-1
Chaplet, The, *sels.* Moses Mendes.
Ass, The. TrJP
Philanderer, The. TrJP
Chaplet of Southernwood, A, *sel.* John Gambril Nicholson.
"I love him wisely if I love him well." PeHV
Chaplinesque. Hart Crane. AP; CMoP; CrMA; LiTM; NoAM; NOBA; OxBA; VGW
Chapter Heading. Ernest Hemingway. PoA
Chapter of Kings, The. John Collins. FaBoUs
Character, A. Charlotte Fiske Bates. AA
Character, A. Blake. *See* Her Whole Life Is an Epigram.
Character. Emerson. AA; LiTA
Character of a Certain Whig, The. William Shippen. APAS
Character of a Critic. Charles Churchill. *See* Critical Fribble, A.
Character of a Good Parson, The. Dryden. NOCV
Character of a Happy Life, The. Sir Henry Wotton. AnAnS-2; EIL; FaPoR; GTBS; GTBS-P; HBV-2; HBVY; LiTB; NOBE; OBEV; OBS; TreF; TrGrPo; ViBoPo
(Happy Life, The.) WGRP
Character of a landscape stands always in a mysterious relation, The. Poem. Charles Madge. EAS
Character of a Trimmer, The. *Unknown.* APAS
Character of Holland, The, *abr.* Andrew Marvell. NOBL
"Holland, that scarce deserves the name of land," *sel.* ChTr; OBSV
Character of Love Seen as a Search for the Lost, The. Kenneth Patchen. NaP; VGW
Character of the Happy Warrior. Wordsworth. EnRP; FaBoBe; FaFP; HBV-2; HBVY; LiTB; LoBV; OBRV; TreF
Characteristics of a Child Three Years Old. Wordsworth. OBRV
Characters of great and small, The. The Skeleton in the Cupboard. Frederick Locker-Lampson. HBV-1
Characters of Women. Edward Young. *Fr.* Love of Fame. OBEC
Characters of Women: Flavia, Atossa, and Cloe. Pope. *Fr.* Moral Essays, Epistle II. OBEC
Charade. Winthrop Mackworth Praed. GN
Charcoal-Burner, The. Sir Edmund Gosse. OBVV
Charcoal Man, *with music. Unknown.* TrAS
Chard Whitlow. Henry Reed. BXAP; DTC; FaBoCo; FaBoNo; FaBoPa; FiBHP; LiTM; MoBrPo; NOBL; NoP; OxBTC; Par; UnPo
Charge. Christopher Gilbert. MAYP
Charge, The. Denise Levertov. NePoEA-2
Charge, A. Herbert Trench. HBV-2; OBEV; OBVV
Charge, The. Jay Wright. DiL; FB
Charge at Santiago, The. William Hamilton Hayne. PAH
Charge by the Ford, The. Thomas Dunn English. PAH
Charge of the Light Brigade, The. Tennyson. BeLS; BLPA; FaBoBe; FaBV; FaFP; FaPo; FaPoR; FaPON; FPL; GN; HBV-2; HBVY; HoPM; NIP; OBWP; OHFP; PaPo; PoPl; PrIm; TEP; TreF; WBLP
Charge the Can Cheerily. *Unknown.* AmSS
Charge to Keep I Have, A. Charles Wesley. HBV-2
Charge to the Poets, A, *sel.* William Whitehead.
"If nature prompts you, or if friends persuade." OBSV
Charges I seek, dependent things. Nursing the Hide. Carol Dunne. AMV-81
Charing Cross. Cecil Roberts. HBMV
Chariot, The. Emily Dickinson. *See* Because I could not stop for death.
Chariot rode on the mountain top, The. Great Day. *Unknown.* FSW
Chariots. Witter Bynner. HBMV
Charis guesse, and doe not misse. Clayming a Second Kisse by Desert. Ben Jonson. *Fr.* A Celebration of Charis. AnAnS-2; SeCP
Charis one day in discourse. Urging Her of a Promise. Ben Jonson. *Fr.* A Celebration of Charis. AnAnS-2; SeCP
Charitas Nimia; or, The Dear[e] Bargain. Richard Crashaw. AnAnS-1; JCP; MePo; NOCV; OxBoCh
Charité Espérance et Foi. Earle Birney. OxBC
Charity. Pope. *Fr.* An Essay on Man, Epistle III. OBEC
("For forms of government let fools contest.") POL; ViBoPo
Charity. *At. to* Edward Wallis Hoch. BLPA
(Good and Bad.) TreFS
Charity in Thought. Samuel Taylor Coleridge. WhC
Charity lotteries for dream houses, The. Judith Wright. Habitat, VI. CBAP
Charity Overcoming Envy. Marianne Moore. NYBP
Charlemagne. Longfellow. FaFP
Charles at the Siege. George Hetherington. AnIV
Charles Atlas, I heard you were dead. Dynamic Tension. Steve Sanfield. SOTS
Charles Carville's Eyes. E. A. Robinson. CMoP; NePA; OxBA
Charles Donnelly, *sel.* Donagh MacDonagh.
"Of what a quality is courage made." CIP

Charles gave Elizabeth a dodo. Of a Certain Green-eyed Monster. Esther Lilian Duff. HBMV
Charles Guiteau. *Unknown.* AmFP, 2 *versions*; FSW; ViBoFo
Charles Gustavus Anderson, *vers.* I, *with music.* *Unknown.* ShS
Charles Gustavus Anderson, *vers.* II. *At. to* Joseph Keating. ShS
Charles Harpur in his journals long ago. Extinct Birds. Judith Wright. PBWP
Charles! my slow heart was only sad, when first. Sonnet to a Friend Who Asked, How I Felt When the Nurse First Presented My Infant to Me. Samuel Taylor Coleridge. EnRP
Charles river reaps here like a sickle, The. Professor Kelleher and the Charles River. Desmond O'Grady. CIP; NoAM
Charles the Fifth and the Peasant. Robert Lowell, *after the French of* Paul Valéry. MiAP
Charles the First, *sels.* Shelley.
"Heigho! the lark and the owl," *fr.* sc. v. PBBP
Song, A: "Widow bird sate mourning for her love," *fr.* sc. v. FaBoEn; LoBV; NOBE; OBNC; PoEL-4; PoPle
(Widow Bird, A.) CH; FaPON
("Widow bird sate mourning for her love, A.") ELP; GTBS; GTBS-P; LO; OBRV: SeCeV
Charles II. Andrew Marvell. *Fr.* Last Instructions to a Painter. OBS
("Paint last the King, and a dead shade of night.") OBSV
Charles II. *Unknown.* FaBoEE
(Historical Poem, An.) APAS
Charles XII [of Sweden]. Samuel Johnson. *Fr.* The Vanity of Human Wishes. NOBE; OBEC
("On what foundation stands the warrior's pride.") OBWP; ViBoPo
Charles used to watch Naomi, taking heart. Laboratory Poem. James Merrill. InPK; MAT; MP; NePoEA-2; TwCP
Charleston. Richard Watson Gilder. PAH
Charleston. Paul Hamilton Hayne. PAH
Charleston. Henry Timrod. AA; AmPP; AP; NOBA; OxBA; PAH; TAP
Charleston Blues. *Unknown.* BluL
Charleston Garden, A. Henry Bellamann. PoLF
Charleston in the 1860s. Adrienne Rich. CoAP
Charleston, South Carolina, baby is where I was was born. Charleston Blues. *Unknown.* BluL
Charleville. Arthur Rimbaud, *tr. fr. French by* John Gray. SyP
Charley Barley, butter and eggs. *Unknown.* OxNR
Charley, Charley. *Unknown.* OxNR
Charley Warlie had a cow. *Unknown.* OxNR
Charlie Chaplin Went to France. *Unknown, at. to* Carl Withers. FaFP; MoShBr
Charlie Cherry. *Unknown.* BluL
Charlie died today. Eulogy for a Tough Guy. Daniel L. Klauck. LFAC
Charlie, He's My Darling. Burns. CH; ViBoPo
(Charlie Is My Darling.) FSW; HBV-2
Charlie Johnson in Kettletown. Claude Clayton Smith. WOLT
Charlie MacPherson. *Unknown.* ESPB
Charlie Piecan. F. Murray *and* F. Leigh. OxBoLi
Charlie Rutledge. *Unknown.* CoSo
Charlie Wolf used to whittle skinning knives. Halcyon Days. Jim Barnes. CDW
Charlotte Brontë." Susan Coolidge." OBCA
Charlotte Brontë said, "Wow, sister! *What* a man!" Limerick. Victor Gray. NOBL
Charlotte Corday. Charles Tomlinson. OxBC
Charlotte Nicholls. Jack Clemo. NAs
Charlottie liv'd on a mountain top in a bleak and lonely spot. The Frozen Girl. *Unknown.* AS
Charlton Heston. Elliot Fried. AMV-80
Charm, A. Dryden. ChTr
Charm, A. Robert Herrick. ChTr
Charm. Miklos Radnoti, *tr. fr. Hungarian by* Steven Polgar, Stephen Berg, *and* S. J. Marks. LLLT
Charm, The. Shakespeare. *See* Thrice the Brinded Cat Hath Mewed.
Charm a single charm is doubtful, A. Nothing Elegant. Gertrude Stein. *Fr.* Tender Buttons. PBWP
Charm against a Magpie, A. *Unknown.* ChTr
(Dove, The.) GBP
Charm against the Toothache, A. John Heath-Stubbs. InPK; MP; NePoEA; TwCP
Charm against Wens, *orig. and mod. English prose.* *Unknown.* OxBM
Charm: Bleeding. *Unknown.* FaBoUs
Charm: Burns. *Unknown.* FaBoUs
Charm: Corns. *Unknown.* FaBoUs
Charm for Our Time, A. Eve Merriam. QQQ
Charm for Spring Flowers, A. Rachel Field. TiPo
Charm: Hiccups. *Unknown.* FaBoUs
Charm is the measure of attraction's power. What Is Charm? Louisa Carroll Thomas. BLPA
Charm me asleep, and melt me so. To Music [*or* Musique], to Becalm[e] His Fever. Robert Herrick. CaPo; GoJo; HBV-2; OBEV; OBS; QFR; SeCV-1; UnS
Charm of my life, my dearest care. Epigram. Martial, *tr. by* Brian Hill. PeHV
Charm of rouge on fragile cheeks, The. Maquillage. Arthur Symons. VLP
Charm[e], or an Allay for Love, A. Robert Herrick. FaBoCh; FaBoUs
Charm'd with a drink which Highlanders compose. Athol Brose. Thomas Hood. FaBoCo
Charme. Ben Jonson. *See* Witches' Charms, The.
Charme, or an Allay for Love, A. Robert Herrick. *See* Charm, or an Allay for Love, A.
Charmed as a brown wicker nest. Reflections on a Womb Which Is Called "Vacant." Jeanine Hathaway. IHMS
Charmed by a girl's soft ears. Downy Hair. Lucien Stryk. *Fr.* Zen Poems, after Shinkichi Takahashi. FAZ
Charmes. Robert Herrick. WSC
Charmides, *sel.* Edmund St. Gascoigne Mackie.
"Up leaps the lark. Delightful Spring once more." PeHV
Charming. William Matthews. MAYP
Charming Beauty Bright. *Unknown.* AmFP
Charming oysters I cry. Oysters. Swift. ErPo
Charming the Moon. James DenBoer. MAT
Charming, the movement of girls about a May-pole in May. Men Working. Edna St. Vincent Millay. SaC
Charming Woman, The. Helen Selina Sheridan. OBRV; WPE
Charming young woman named Pat, A. Limerick. *Unknown.* NIP
Charms for a Sudden Stitch. *Unknown, tr. fr. Anglo-Saxon by* Charles W. Kennedy. AnOE
Charms for Unfruitful Land. *Unknown, tr. fr. Anglo-Saxon by* Charles W. Kennedy. AnOE
Charms of Nature, The. Joseph Warton. *Fr.* The Enthusiast. OBEC; SeCePo
Charms, that call down the moon from out her sphere. To Music, to Becalm a Sweet-sick Youth. Robert Herrick. CaPo
Charnwood Forest. Michael Drayton. *Fr.* Polyolbion, the Sixth and Twentieth Song. FaBoPP
Charon. Louis MacNeice. FaBoTw
Charon! Thou slave! Thou fool! Thou Cavalier! A Mock Charon. Richard Lovelace. CaPo
Charon's Cosmology. Charles Simic. GeTw; NoP
Chart, The. Walter de la Mare. CoBMV
Charter Boat. Norman Hindley. WOLT
Chartivel, *sel.* Marie de France, *tr. fr. French.*
"Hath any loved you well, down there," *tr. by* Arthur O'Shaughnessy. EnLoPo; WPOW
(Sarrazine's Song to Her Dead Lover.) HBV-1
(Song from "Chartivel.") AWP
Chartless. Emily Dickinson. *See* I never saw a moor.
Chartres. Raymond Henri. View of the Cathedral, I. EyDe
Charwoman. Ben Belitt. SaC
Chase, The. J. V. Cunningham. LiSp; NoAM
Chase, The. W. H. Davies. BrPo
Chase, The. *Unknown, at. to* William Rowley. *See* Art Thou Gone in Haste?
Chase, The. Sir Walter Scott. *Fr.* The Lady of the Lake, I. EnRP
("Harp of the North! that mouldering long hast hung.") OAEP; ViBoPo
Chase, The, *sel.* William Somervile.
Hare-hunting. NOEC; OBEC
Chased from my calling to this hackneyed trade. James Kennedy. *Fr.* The Exile's Reveries. NOEC
Chasing the Paper-Shamans. Wendy Rose. TWSS
Chasm. A. R. Ammons. OBAL
Chasm, A. Michael Silverton. PV
Chaste Arabian Bird, The. Earl of Rochester. ErPo
Chaste Cloris doth disclose the shames. Cloris and Mertilla. Michael Drayton. *Fr.* The Muses Elizium. LoBV
Chaste Florimel. Matthew Prior. BoLoP; ErPo
Chaste Maid in Cheapside, A, *sel.* Thomas Middleton.
Parting. ElL
Chaste maids which haunt fair Aganippe's well. Lament. William Drummond of Hawthronden. *Fr.* Tears on the Death of Moeliades. LoBV
Chaste, pious, prudent Charles the Second. The History of Insipids. John Freke. APAS
Chastelard, *sel.* Swinburne.
Mary Beaton's Song. HBV-1
Chastity. Milton. *Fr.* Comus. OBS
Chateau Papineau. S. Frances Harrison. CaP
Chatterers in Church. *Unknown.* *See* Tutivillus, the Devil.
Chattering finch and water-fly. The Skeleton. G. K. Chesterton. FaBoTw
Chattering swallow! what shall we. The Swallow. Thomas Stanley. AWP

Chaucer. Benjamin Brawley. BANP
Chaucer. Longfellow. AA; AP; AWP; HeIP; InvP; NePA; NOBA; NoP; OBEV; OBVV; OxBA; PoRA; PP; PrIm; TrGrPo; TAP
Chaucer, Langland, Douglas, Dunbar with all your. Ode to the Medieval Poets. W. H. Auden. PoA
Chaucer's Complaint to His Empty Purse. Chaucer. *See* Complaint of Chaucer to His Purse, The.
Chauffeur of Lilacs, The. George Hitchcock. GP
Chaunt of the Brazen Head, The, *sel.* Winthrop Mackworth Praed.
"I think the thing you call Renown." OBSV
Chauntecleer. Chaucer. *Fr.* The Canterbury Tales: The Nun's Priest's Tale. PB
Chavez. Mildred McNeal Sweeney. HBV-2
Che Sara Sara. Victor Plarr. HBV-1
Cheat of Cupid, The; [or, The Ungentle Guest]. Robert Herrick, *after the Greek of* Anacreon. AWP; OBVE; SeCeV
Check. James Stephens. AnIL; HBMV; OnUR; RHPC; SiSoSe; SUS; TiPo
Check to Song. "Owen Meredith." *See* Going Back Again.
Checking the Firing. R. T. Smith. AMV-80
Checking the traps. The Ice-fishing House: Long Lake, Minnesota. Michael S. Harper. TAT
Cheddar Pinks. Robert Bridges. ChMP; MoVE; SeCePo
Chee Lai! (Arise!) *Unknown, tr. fr. Chinese.* FSW
Cheeks as red as the blooming rose. Shady Grove. *Unknown.* FSW
Cheeks as soft as July peaches. Baby May. William Cox Bennett. HBV-1
Cheer and salute for the Admiral, and here's to the Captain bold, A. The Men behind the Guns. John Jerome Rooney. AA; BLPA; EtS; FaBoBe; HBV-2; PAH; YaD
Cheer for the Consumer. Nixon Waterman. OBAL
Cheer of the *Trenton,* The. Walter Mitchell. EtS
Cheer up, all you young men. Brave Wolfe. *Unknown.* BaBo
Cheer up, cheer up! my own Jeannette, tho' far away I go. Jeannot's Answer. Charles Jeffries. BLPA
Cheer up, cheer up, you sons of toil, and listen to my song. Striking Times. *Unknown.* OBET
Cheer up, my [*or* ye] young men all [*or* your hearts, young men]; let nothing fright you. Brave Wolfe. *Unknown.* BaBo; PAH; TrAS; ViBoFo
Cheered with this hope, to Paris I returned. Residence in France. Wordsworth. *Fr.* The Prelude, X. PoEL-4
Cheerfu' supper done, wi' serious face, The. The Cotter's Saturday Night. Burns. WGRP
Cheerful and industrious beast, A. The Bumblebeaver. Kenyon Cox. TiPo
Cheerful arn he blaws in the marn, The. The Cheerful Horn. *Unknown.* CH
Cheerful Chilterns, The. Frank Sidgwick. BXAP
Cheerful Horn, The. *Unknown.* CH
Cheerful Welcome, A. *Unknown. See* What Cheer?
Cheerfulness. *Unknown. See* I'm Glad.
Cheerio My Deario. Don Marquis. *Fr.* Archy and Mehitabel. FaBoCo
Cheerios. Peter Meinke. GP
Cheer'ly, Man, *with music. Unknown.* AmSS
Cheers. Eve Merriam. LiSp
Cheese it is a peevish elf. *Unknown.* FaBoUs
Cheese-Mites Asked, The. *Unknown.* WhC
Cheetie-Poussie-Cattie, O. *Unknown. See* There Was a Were Bit Mousikie.
Chef whose hat is celluloid and green, A. Owed to Dickens, 1956. Jan Burroway. NePoAm-2
Chekhov Comes to Mind at Harvard. William T. Freeman. AMV-81
Chelmsfords Fate. Benjamin Tompson. SCAP
Chelsea Churchyard. Ralph J. Mills, Jr. FAZ
Chelsea, The. Derek Walcott. NYP
Chemist to His Love, The. *Unknown.* InMe; QQQ
Chemistry of Character, The. Elizabeth Dorney. BLPA
Chenille. James Dickey. NoAM
Chequer-board of mingled light and shade, A? Life's Chequer-Board. John Oxenham. TRV
Cher Maître:/ Neither my explication. A Letter to Wilbur Frohock. Daniel Hoffman. CoPo
Chercheuses de Poux, Les. Arthur Rimbaud, *tr. fr. French by* T. Sturge Moore. AWP
(Lice-Finders, The, *tr. by* T. Sturge Moore.) SyP
(Lice-Hunters, The, *tr. by* Robert Lowell.) NAWM-2; SyP
(Lice-Hunters, *tr. by* Ezra Pound.) NAWM-2
(Lice Seekers, The, *tr. by* Kenneth Koch *and* Georges Guy.) SOTW
(Seekers of Lice, The, *tr. by* Wallace Fowlie.) NAWM-2
Cherokee Dean, The. Norman H. Russell. STE
Cherrie-Ripe. Robert Herrick. *See* Cherry Ripe.
Cherries, *sel.* Edward Brathwaite.
So When the Hammers of the Witnesses of Heaven Are Raised All Together. NAs
Cherries. Zalman Schneour, *tr. fr. Yiddish by* Joseph Leftwich. TrJP
Cherries, The; a Parable. Thomas Moore. OBSV
Cherry. Gene Baro. ErPo
Cherry and pear are white. The Crowns. John Freeman. CH
Cherry and the Slae, The, *sel.* Alexander Montgomerie.
"About ane bank, where birdis on bewis." GoTS
Cherry blossom spring festival. Sushi-Okashi and Green Tea with Mitsu Yashima. Al Robles. BrSi
Cherry-Blossom Wand, The. Anna Wickham. MoBrPo
Cherry Blossoms, *sels.* "Michael Lewis," *after the Chinese.* UnTE
Cursing and Blessing.
Leaving.
Living and Dying.
Longing.
Remembering.
Cherry blossoms, The. Spring. Princess Shikishi, *tr. by* Hiroaki Sato. PBWP
Cherry Boy, The, *sels.* Royston Ellis.
"All my sex life, I had been drifting," 1. PeHV
"It was an international rage," 6. PeHV
Cherry Fair, The. *Unknown. See* Farewell, This World.
Cherry-lipt Adonis in his snowie shape. Sonnet. Richard Barnfield. Sonnets, XVII. PeHV
Cherry-Pit. Robert Herrick. OAEP
Cherry-ripe. Thomas Campion. *See* There Is a Garden in Her Face.
Cherry-ripe. Robert Herrick. CaPo; CH; ELP; OBEV; PAI; TEP
(Cherrie-ripe.) CavP, SeCP; SeCV-1
Cherry Robbers. D. H. Lawrence. MoAB; MoBrPo
Cherry Tree, The. Thom Gunn. Psk
Cherry Tree. Christina Rossetti. *See* Oh, Fair to See.
Cherry-Tree Carol, The (*diff. versions*). *Unknown.* AmFP (4 *versions*); ChTr; EBEV; ELP; EnSB; ESPB (A *and* B *versions*); FaBoBa; FSW; GBP; HeIP; LoBV; OAEL-1, *with music;* OAEP; OBET; OFD; OnMsP; OxBB, *with music;* OxBoCh; OxBoLi; SBVL; SeCeV; TrGrPo; ViBoFo, *with music*
(Joseph Was an Old Man.) OBCP; ViBoPo
Cherry Tree Carol, The ("As Joseph Was a-walking"). *Unknown. See* As Joseph Was a-Walking.
Cherry tree is down, and dead, that was so high, The. Small Dark Song. Philip Dacey. PPJ
Cherry Trees, The. Edward Thomas. OBWP
("Cherry trees bend over and are shedding, The.") PoPle
Cherry trees, mindless of the field, The. The Orchard. Michael Spence. AMV-80
Cherry year, A. *Unknown.* OxNR
Cherrylog Road. James Dickey. CoAP; CABA; HAP; InPK; InPS; NIP; NYBP; PrIm; TwCP; WeW
Cherubic Pilgrim, The. "Angelus Silesius," *tr. fr. German.* WGRP
Cherwell Waterlily, The. Frederick W. Faber. GoBC
Chesapeake. Gerta Kennedy. NYBP
Chesapeake and the *Shannon,* The ("The *Chesapeake* so bold"). *Unknown.* PAH; ViBoFo, *with music*
Cheshire Cat. Kenneth Allott. NeBP
Cheshire for men. English Counties. *Unknown.* POL
Chess-Board, The. "Owen Meredith." HBV-1; OBVV
"Chessie," the Chesapeake and Ohio's. Our Flag Was Still There. Richard Tillinghast. MAYP
Chesspieces. Joseph Campbell. OxBI
Chester. William Billings. *See* Let Tyrants Shake Their Iron Rod.
Chestnut Avenue at Alton House, The. Charles Tomlinson. FaBoTw
Chestnut Casts His Flambeaux, [and the Flowers,] The. A. E. Housman. BrPo; CMoP; LiTB; MoAB; MoBrPo; NoAM; OAEP; OBMV; PPP; PrIm
Chestnut Stands. Rachel Field. SiSoSe
Chestnut tree stands in the line of sight, A. St. Asaph's. Kingsley Amis. OxBTC
Chestnut vendor, The. Karl Szelki. PCP
Chevalier Malheur, Le. Paul Verlaine, *tr. fr. French by* John Gray. *Fr.* Sagesse. SyP
Chevaliers de la Table Ronde. *Unknown, tr. fr. French.* FSW
Chevy Chase ("God prosper long our noble king"). *Unknown.* FaBoBa; HBV-2; OBET; ViBoFo, *with music*
(Chevy-Chace.) GN
(Hunting of the Cheviot, The.) BaBo (B *and* C *vers.*); ESPB; OAEP
Chevy Chase ("The Percy out of Northumberland"). *Unknown.* EnSB, *sl. diff. vers.;* OxBB; ViBoPo; WHA
(Ancient Ballad of Chevy-Chase, The.) EnRP
(Hunting of the Cheviot, The.) BaBo (A *vers.*); ESPB
"Chew Mail Pouch." D. L. Klauck. AMV-81
Chewing Chawing Gum. *Unknown.* AmFP
(Chewing Gum.) FSW
Cheyenne, *with music. Unknown.* CoSo
Cheyenne Mountain. Helen Hunt Jackson. BPAW; PoOW
Chez Brébant. Francis Alexander Durivage. AA

Chez Jane. Frank O'Hara. CoAP; NeAP; NoAM; NOBA; PoA
Chez Madame. Sam Harrison. NeIP
Chez-Nous. A. G. Austin. PoAu-2
Chi ama, crede: mother. Study No. X. Pierre Coupey. PeCV
Chiaroscuro. Carole Bergé. ErPo
Chic desolation of the/ factory. The Emergency Room. David Fisher. NPGG
Chic Freedom's Reflection. Alice Walker. NMM
Chicago. Bret Harte. PAH
Chicago. Galway Kinnell. NePoAm
Chicago. John Boyle O'Reilly. PAH
Chicago. Lola Ridge. PoA
Chicago. Carl Sandburg. AmPP; AP; BiP; BLPL; CMoP; FaBV; HBMV; LiTM; MoAB; MoAmPo; MoVE; NePA; NoAM; NOBA; NoP; OxBA; PoA; PoPl; TAP; TreF; UnPo; ViBoPo; VGW; YaD
Chicago. Whittier. PAH
Chicago Allegory. Stewart Parker. CIP
Chicago Boy Baby. Carl Sandburg. NAs
Chicago *Defender* Sends a Man to Little Rock, The. Gwendolyn Brooks. AmNP; PoBA
Chicago: Near West-Side Renewal. Dennis Schmitz. AmPA
Chicago Picasso, The. Gwendolyn Brooks. *Fr.* Two Dedications. BPo; EyDe; LiTM
Chicago Poem. Lew Welch. NeAP; PoM
Chicago ran a fever of a hundred and one that groggy Sunday. The Shooting of John Dillinger outside the Biograph Theater, July 22, 1934. David Wagoner. CoAP; FYAP
Chicago, Summer Past. Richard Snyder. Psk
Chicago we could have imagined for ourselves, The. Trading Chicago. Charles O. Hartman. AMV-80
Chick! my naggie. *Unknown.* OxNR
Chickadee. Hilda Conkling. TiPo
Chickadee, The. Emerson. FaPON
Chickadee in the apple tree, The. Chickadee. Hilda Conkling. TiPo
Chickadees, The. John Hay. NePoAm-2
Chickadees/ round suet balls. Winter, New Hampshire. David Kherdian. TAT
Chicken. Walter de la Mare. TiPo
Chicken. Dave Etter. MAT
Chicken. Dennis Kelly. PeHV
Chicken blessed and caressed. *Unknown.* *Fr.* A Collection of Hymns . . . of the Moravian Brethren. NOEC
Chicken. How shall I tell you what it is. A Presentation of Two Birds to My Son. James Wright. DiL; PPP
Chicken-Licken. Maya Angelou. FF
Chicken Soup Therapy: Its Mode of Action. Caroline Breese Hall. SUW
Chickens. Geof Hewitt. FAZ
Chickens, The. *Unknown.* *See* Five Little Chickens.
Chickens a-crowin' on Sourwood Mountain. Sourwood Mountain. *Unknown.* AS; FSW; GBP; TrAS
Chickens Are a-Crowing, The, *with music.* *Unknown.* TrAS
Chickens crowing for midnight. It's Almost Day. Leadbelly (Huddie Ledbetter). FSW
Chickens the Weasel Killed. William Stafford. NaP
Chickens they are crowing, a-crowing, a-crowing, The. The Chickens Are a-Crowing. *Unknown.* TrAS
Chicken-skin, delicate, white. On a Fan That Belonged to the Marquise de Pompadour. Austin Dobson. HBV-1; OBVV; ViBoPo
Chickitten Gitten! Ted Joans. GP
Chickory. Zerubavel Gal'ed, *tr. fr. Hebrew.* TrJP
Chide, chide no more away. Expectation [*or* Destiny]. Thomas Stanley. AnAnS-2; LoBV; OBS
"Chief, The." W. E. Henley. In Hospital, XV. BrPo
Chief, chief, that I am. Bear Song. John R. Swanton. BPAW
Chief defect of Henry King, The. Henry King, [Who Chewed Bits of String, and Was Early Cut Off in Dreadful Agonies]. Hilaire Belloc. CenHV; DTC; FaBoNo; FaBoUs; HBMV; ShM
Chief Leschi of the Nisqually. Duane Niatum. CDW; STE
Chief of organic numbers! On Seeing a Lock of Milton's Hair [*or* Lines on Seeing a Lock of Milton's Hair]. Keats. PeD; PP
Chief of the West, Darkling, The. David Knight. MoCV
Chief Petty Officer. Charles Causley. OxBTC
Chiefe use then in man of that he knowes, The. Fulke Greville. *Fr.* Of Human Learning. OBS
Chiefly to Mind Appears. C. Day Lewis. MoAB; MoBrPo
Chiefs of State marched up the hill, The. Alpine View. Melville Cane. PoPl
Chieftain Iffucan of Azcan in caftan. Bantams in Pine-Woods. Wallace Stevens. CMoP; InPS; MoVE; NOBA; OxBA; SeCeV; UnPo
Chieftain to the Highlands bound, A. Lord Ullin's Daughter. Thomas Campbell. BeLS; EnRP; FaPON; FaPoR; GN; GTBS; GTBS-P; HBV-2; HBVY; OBRV; RoGo; TreF; WBLP
Chiffons! *with music.* William Samuel Johnson. HBV-1
Child, A. Richard Watson Gilder. AA
Child, The. Donald Hall. NePoEA-2; NCSH
Child, The. George Keithley. NPGG
Child, A. Mary Lamb. OBEV
Child. Tom MacIntyre. CIP
Child, The. W. S. Merwin. NoAM
Child, The. Frank Ormsby. AMV-81
Child. Sylvia Plath. PBWP
Child, The. Ivor Popham. EaLo
Child. Carl Sandburg. TRV
Child. E. N. Sargent. NYBP
Child, The, *sels.* John Banister Tabb.
 At Bethlehem. AA
 To his Mother. AA
 "Where were ye, Birds, that bless His name." AA
Child, The. George Edward Woodberry. Wild Eden, XXX. AA
Child, A/ Curious and innocent. To Robert Louis Stevenson. W. E. Henley. MoBrPo
Child,/ You are my brother. The Mists Are Rising Now. Hasye Cooperman. GoYe
Child (a boy) bouncing, A. To. William Carlos Williams. OBAL
Child Accepts, A. Michael Hamburger. NMP
Child alone a poet is, The. Babylon. Robert Graves. HBMV
Child an' the Mowers, The. William Barnes. VLP
Child, and all children. To a Christmas Two-Year-Old. Luci Shaw. TrCP
Child and Boatman. Jean Ingelow. *Fr.* Songs on the Voices of Birds. FM
Child and Maiden. Sir Charles Sedley. *Fr.* The Mulberry Garden, III, ii. GTBS; GTBS-P
 ("Ah Cloris! that I now could sit.") CavP; OAEP; OBS
 (Song: "Ah Chloris [*or* Cloris]! that I now could sit.") SeCV-2; ViBoPo
 (To Chloris.) HBV-1; OBEV
Child and the Mariner, The. W. H. Davies. CH
Child and the Shadow, The. Elizabeth Jennings. NePoEA-2
Child at Winter Sunset, The. Mark Van Doren. NCSH
Child awaits the angel, The. The Angel. Alfred Hayes. TrJP
Child Bearers, The. Anne Sexton. BoWoP
Child Bearing. Charles Ghigna. AMV-81
Child Beater. Ai. BoWoP
Child-Bride, The. Joyce Carol Oates. GeTw
Child, Child. Sara Teasdale. HBV-1
Child Compassion, The. Margot Ruddock. OBMV
Child Crying. Anthony Thwaite. NePoEA-2
Child crying in the night, A. Unintelligible Terms. Charles Simic. NoP
Child devoted to sacred study, pale, A. For Arthur Gregor. Edward Field. FAZ
Child! do not throw this book about! Dedication on the Gift of a Book to a Child. Hilaire Belloc. EBEV; HBVY
Child draws the outline of a body, A. Portrait. Louise Glück. Str
Child Dying, The. Edwin Muir. ChMP; FaBoTw; GTBS-P
Child, feverish, frowning, only saw red, The. The Lice-Hunters. Arthur Rimbaud, *tr. by* Robert Lowell. NAWM-2; SyP
Child grabbed my hand and made me run with him, The. Into the Wind. Winfield Townley Scott. NMP
Child had been struck by two bullets in the head, The. Memory of the Night of the Fourth. Victor Hugo, *tr. by* Mary Ann Caws. NAWM-2
Child Harold, *sels.* John Clare.
 Ballad: "Blackbird has built in the pasture agen, The." VLP
 "Blackbird startles from the homestead hedge, The." VLP
 London versus Epping Forest. FaBoPP
 Northamptonshire Fens. FaBoPP
 Stanzas from "Child Harold." OBNC
 (In Epping Forest.) FaBoPP
Child I left your class to have, The. For Elizabeth Bishop. Sandra McPherson. GeTw; MAYP
Child, I warn thee in all wise. Symon's Lesson of Wisdom for All Manner of Children. *Unknown.* OxBChV
Child, I will give you rings to wear. Declaration. Arthur Symons. *Fr.* Violet. BrPo; ViBoPo
Child Ill, A. John Betjeman. DTC
Child in Adam's field I dreamed away, A. Edwin Muir. *Fr.* Variations on a Time Theme. NoAM
Child in the Garden, The. Henry van Dyke. HBV-1
Child in the Rug, The. John Haines. DFF; GP
Child in the Street, The. John James Piatt. AA
Child Is Born, A. *Unknown.* STF
Child is born amonges man, A. Hand by Hand We Shall Us Take. *Unknown.* SBVL
"Child Is Father to the Man, The." Gerard Manley Hopkins. FaBoCo
 (Triolet.) NOBL
Child is holy and most wise, The. The Child. Ivor Popham. EaLo

Child is like a rare bird, A. Praise of a Child. *Yoruba Oral Tradition, tr. by* Ulli Beier *and* B. Gbadamosi. WTO
Child Is like a Sailor Cast Up by the Sea, The. Lucretius, *tr. fr. Latin by* C. H. Sisson. *Fr.* De Rerum Natura. NAs
Child is not dead, The. The Child Who Was Shot Dead by Soldiers at Nyanga. Ingrid Jonker, *tr. by* Jack Cope *and* Uys Krige. PeSA
Child is on my shoulders, The. Laughing Child. Carl Sandburg. CTBA; PCP
Child, is thy father dead? Song. Ebenezer Elliott. SaC
Child Jesus to Mary the Rose, The. John Lydgate. GoBC; ISi
Child-King, The. Morris Wintchevsky, *tr. fr. Yiddish by* Alter Brody. TrJP
Child like mustard seed, The. War-Baby. D. H. Lawrence. NAs
Child Maurice. *Unknown.* ESPB (A, B, *and* D *vers.*)
(Childe Maurice.) TrGrPo; ViBoFo
Child most infantine, A. A Child of Twelve. Shelley. *Fr.* The Revolt of Islam. GN
Child-Musician, The. Austin Dobson. GN
Child My Choice, A. Robert Southwell. EBCP; GoBC; HBV-2; OxBoCh
Child Naming Flowers. Robert Hass. MAYP; NPGG
Child need not be very clever, A. Grandpa Is Ashamed. Ogden Nash. PV
Child Next Door, The ("The child next door has a wreath on her hat"). Rose Fyleman. FaPON
Child Noryce is a clever young man. Child Maurice (B *vers.*). *Unknown.* ESPB
Child of a day, thou knowest not. On a Child. Walter Savage Landor. OBVV
Child of Blue. Michael Hogan. LFAC
Child of death. Praises of the King of Oyo. *Yoruba Oral Tradition, tr. by* Ulli Beier. WTO
Child of God. *Unknown.* FSW
Child of Hers, A. T. Walking Eagle Marietta. LFAC
Child of Loneliness. Norman Gale. WGRP
Child of Misfortune! Offspring of the Muse! On the Death of Dermody, the Poet. Henry Kirke White. PeD
Child of my winter, born. Heart's Needle. W. D. Snodgrass. CAPP; ConAP; CoPo; MoAmPo
Child of Our Time. Eavan Boland. CIP
Child of patient industry. Invitation to the Bee. Charlotte Smith. OxBChV
Child of Peace, The. Selma Lagerlof, *tr. fr. Swedish by* Charles Wharton Stork. PoPl
Child of silence and shadow. Yvonne Caroutch, *tr. fr. French by* David Cloutier. BoWoP
Child of sin and sorrow. Exhortation. Thomas Hastings. AA
Child of the frightened face. Frightened Face. Marion Strobel. HBMV
Child of the gorgeous East, whose ardent suns. To an Egyptian Boy. H. W. Berry. WhC
Child of the season of adventure, child of the heart. Child. E. N. Sargent. NYBP
Child of the World. Edna L. S. Barker. GoYe
Child of To-Day, A. James Buckham. AA
Child of Twelve, A. Shelley. *Fr.* The Revolt of Islam. GN
Child on the Judgment Seat, The. Elizabeth Rundle Charles. BLPA
Child on Top of a Greenhouse. Theodore Roethke. ELU; LCAP; MiAP; NCSH; PoPl; VGW
Child Owlet. *Unknown.* ESPB
Child Poem. Annette Arkeketa West. TWSS
Child Reads an Almanac, The ("The child reads on; her basket of eggs stands by"). Francis Jammes, *tr. fr. French by* Ludwig Lewisohn. AWP; FaPON
Child said, A, *What is the grass?* Grass. Walt Whitman. Song of Myself, VI. AA; BLPL; NePA; NoP; TrGrPo
Child saw the bombers skate, The. Come to the Stone. Randall Jarrell. VGW
Child Screening a Dove from a Hawk, A. Letitia Elizabeth Landon. VLP
Child should always say what's true, A. Whole Duty of Children. Robert Louis Stevenson. EvOK; FaBoUs; HBV-1; HBVY; OxBChV; TreFS
Child skipping jump on the quay at the mill, A. Poor Old Horse. David Holbrook. NePoEA-2
Child That Has a Cold [We May Suppose], A. Thomas Dibdin. ChTr; FaBoNo; PV
Child, the current of your breath is six days long. Unknown Girl in the Maternity Ward. Anne Sexton. CoPo; NoAM; NAs
Child to His Sick Grandfather, A. Joanna Baillie. NOEC
Child was gone, The: the mother stood alone. Madonna of the Empty Arms. Maurice Francis Egan. ISi
Child Waters. *Unknown.* ESPB (A *and* B *vers.*); FaBoBa; OAEP; OBET; OxBB; ViBoFo
Child, weary of thy baubles of to-day. The Human Plan. Charles Henry Crandall. AA
Child Who Was Shot Dead by Soldiers at Nyanga, The. Ingrid Jonker, *tr. fr. Afrikaans by* Jack Cope *and* Uys Krige. PeSA
Child, who went gathering the flowers of death. Haroun Al-Rachid for Heart's-Life. *Unknown, tr. by* E. Powys Mathers. *Fr.* The Thousand and One Nights. AWP
Child with a Cockatoo. Rosemary Dobson. CBAP
Child with a wrench is, A/ moving. A Junkie with a Flute in the Rain. David Fisher. NPGG
Child with Shell. R. G. Everson. PeCV
Child with Six Fingers. Carol Muske. AmPA
Child with the hungry eyes. Beggars. Ella Higginson. AA
Child, you were and/ you learned to be. With the Bait of Bread. Helene Pilbosian. AMV-81
Child, you were conceived in my upstairs room. To a Child Born in Time of Small War. Helen Sorrells. WPE
Childbirth. Ted Hughes. NAs
Childcity, Aprilcity. Paris. Gregory Corso. VGW
Childe Harold ("Where rose the mountains, there to him were friends"). Byron. *Fr.* Childe Harold's Pilgrimage, III. OBRV
Childe Harold to the dark tower, L-two. The Letter. John Holmes. NePoAm
Childe Harold's Farewell to England. Byron. *Fr.* Childe Harold's Pilgrimage. OHFP; PoPl
Childe Harold's Pilgrimage, *sels.* Byron.
Bull Fight, The, *fr.* I. LiSp
"Castled crag of Drachenfels, The," *fr.* III. ViBoPo
Childe Harold ("Where rose the mountains, there to him were friends"), *fr.* III. OBRV
Childe Harold's Farewell to England, *fr.* I. OHFP; PoPl
Dying Gladiator, The, *fr.* IV. NOBE
"Egeria, sweet creation of some heart," *fr.* IV. ViBoPo
Fame, *fr.* IV. FiP
Greece, *fr.* II. OBRV
"He that has sail'd upon the dark blue sea," *fr.* II. MOS
"I have not loved the world, not the world me," *fr.* III. OBRV
(Poet and the World, The.) SeCePo
"I stood in Venice, on the Bridge of Sighs," IV. EnRP, *abr.;* OAEP, *abr.;* OBRV, *9 sts.;* ViBoPo, 3 *sts.*
(On the Bridge of Sighs, 4 *sts.*) FaBoPP
(Venice, 4 *sts.*) HBV-2
"Is thy face like thy mother's, my fair child!" III. ChER, 15 *sts.;* EnRP; OAEL-2, *abr.;* OAEP
It Is the Hush of Night, *fr.* III. LiTB
(Lake Leman ["Clear, placid Leman! thy contrasted lake"], *sl. diff. sel.*) OBNC
(Night.) LoBV
"Lake Leman woos me with its crystal face," *fr.* III. InPS
(Lake Leman.) PoEL-4
Napoleon, *fr.* III. OBRV
"Oh love! no habitant of earth thou art," *fr.* IV. OAEL-2; ViBoPo
(Fatal Spell, The.) OBNC
Rome, by Metella's Tomb, *fr.* IV. FaBoPP
Sky, Mountains, River! *fr.* III. WHA
"Stop!—for thy tread is on an empire's dust!" *fr.* III. InPS
Ocean, The, *sl. diff. sels. fr.* IV. FaBV; PoEL-4; TrGrPo
(Address to the Ocean.) TreFS
(And I Have Loved Thee, Ocean!) WHA
(Apostrophe to the Ocean.) EtS; OHFP; WBLP
(By the Deep Sea.) OBNC
(Deep and Dark Blue Ocean.) ChTr
(Roll On, Thou Dark Blue Ocean.) FaPON
(Roll On, Thou Deep and Dark Blue Ocean.) FiP
(Sea, The.) BLPL; FaBoBe; HBV-1; LiTB
(There Is a Pleasure in the Pathless Woods.) MOS; OBRV; TreF; ViBoPo
(To the Ocean.) GN; WGRP
To Eddleston, *fr.* II. PeHV
To England, *fr.* IV. WHA
To Ianthe, *dedication.* FaBoEn
(Dedication: To Ianthe.) OBNC
Voltaire and Gibbon, *fr.* III. OBRV
Wandering Outlaw, The, *fr.* III. FiP
Waterloo, *sl. diff. sels. fr.* III. FiP; OBRV; TrGrPo; WaaP; WHA
(Battle of Waterloo, The.) FaFP; TreF
(Eve of Waterloo, The.) BeLS; FaBoBe; FaBoCh; FaBoEn; FaBV; HBV-2; NOBE; OBNC
(Night before the Battle of Waterloo, The.) WBLP
(Night before Waterloo, The.) GN
("There was a sound of revelry by night.") EBEV; OBWP; ViBoPo
Childe Maurice. *Unknown. See* Child Maurice.
Childe Roland, etc. Elder Olson. OBAL
"Childe Roland to the Dark Tower Came." Robert Browning. DTo; NoP; OAEL-2; OAEP; OBNV; PPP; SeCeV; VLP
Childe Rolandine. Stevie Smith. BrRo

Childe Watters in his stable stoode. Child Waters. *Unknown.* ESPB; FaBoBa; OAEP; OxBB; ViBoFo
Childheart, time alone is not enough. A Late Spring. James Scully. NYBP
Childhood. Jens Baggesen, *tr. fr. Danish by* Longfellow. AWP
Childhood. Anne Bradstreet. *Fr.* The Four Ages of Man. SBG
Childhood. Edith Bruck, *tr. fr. Italian by* Anita Barrows. VWA
Childhood. Frances Cornford. OxBTC
Childhood. Donald Justice. LCAP
Childhood. Jewel C. Latimore. JB
Childhood. Donagh MacDonagh. NeIP
Childhood. Sir Thomas More. *See* I Am Called Childhood.
Childhood. Edwin Muir. CMoP; HeIP; NoP; SeCePo
Childhood. Ned O'Gorman. PoPl
Childhood. Sir Herbert Read. BrPo
Childhood. Rainer Maria Rilke, *tr. fr. German by* M. D. Herter Norton. SOTW
Childhood, *sel.* Arthur Rimbaud, *tr. fr. French by* T. Sturge Moore. *Fr.* Illuminations.
"This idol with black eyes and yellow hair." SyP
Childhood. Sherod Santos. AMV-81
Childhood, A. Stephen Spender. NeBP
Childhood. Maura Stanton. MAYP
Childhood. John Banister Tabb.. HBV-1
Childhood. Thomas Traherne. TrGrPo
Childhood. Henry Vaughan. OxBoCh
Childhood. Margaret Walker. BOLo; IHMS; PBWP; PoBA; WPOW
Childhood and School-Time. Wordsworth. The Prelude, I. FaBoEn; NOBE; NOP; OBNC; OBRV
Sels.
"Dust as we are, the immortal spirit grows." SCV
"Fair seed-time had my soul, and I grew up." HAP
(Introduction—Childhood and School-Time.) PoEL-4
(On the Solitary Fells . . .) FaBoPP
In Patterdale. FaBoRv
"Moon was up, the lake was shining clear, The." FaBoEn
On Ullswater. FaBoPP
On Windemere; Bowness Bay and Belle Isle. FaBoPP
Oh There Is a Blessing in This Gentle Breeze. TreFT
"One summer evening (led by her) I found. FiP; NU; OBRV; ViBoPo
(One Summer Evening,) FiP
"Poet, gentle creature as he is, The." PP
Skating. CH; GN
(On the Frozen Lake.) FaBoCh
(Skaters, The.) LiSP
"Wisdom and Spirit of the universe." NOBE
(Boyhood.) WHA
(Influence of Natural Objects.) AWP; LoBV; OBRV
Wordsworth Skates on Esthwaite Water. FaBoPP
Childhood Fled. Charles Lamb. EnRP
Childhood in Jacksonville, Florida. Jane Cooper. TAP
Childhood is when the mouth tastes earth. Childhood. Ned O'Gorman. PoPl
Childhood of an Equestrian, The. Russell Edson. AmPA
Childhood remembrances are always a drag. Nikki-Rosa [*or* Nikki-Roasa]. Nikki Giovanni. AmNP; BlSi; CAD; HeIP; IHMS; NBP; NoAM; NYP; PAI; PoBA; TAP
Childish Game, A. Reinmar von Hagenau, *tr. fr. German by* Jethro Bithell. AWP
Childish Prank, A. Ted Hughes. OAEL-2; OxBC
Childless. Giolla Brighde MacNamee, *tr. fr. Irish by* Frank O'Connor. BIrV; KiLC
Childless Father, The. Wordsworth. CH
Childless Witch, A. Raquel Chalfi, *tr. fr. Hebrew by* Alexandra Meiri *and* Myra Glazer Schotz. VWA
Childlessness. James Merrill. ConAP
Childlike Heart. Ellen Weston Catlin. PGD
Children, The. Charles Monroe Dickinson. AA; HBV-1
Children, The. Clifford Dyment. ChMP
Children. Russell Edson. AmPA
Children, The. William Heyen. GeTw; GP
Children, The. Susan MacDonald. IHMS
Children, The. William Soutar. BSV
Children, The. Constance Urdang. CoAP; IHMS
Children, The. Mark Vinz. DFF; GP
Children, The. William Carlos Williams. NePoAm-2
Children/ They teach to walk. Training on the Shore. Shlomo Vinner, *tr. by* Laya Firestone *and* Howard Schwartz. VWA
Children among the Hills. Linda Gregg. NPGG
Children and pets, please note. In a Closed Universe. James Hayford. NePoAm-2
Children and Sir Nameless, The. Thomas Hardy. NoP
Children are dumb to say how hot the day is. The Cool Web. Robert Graves. AWP; ChMP; GTBS-P; NIP; NoAM; NoP; OxBTC; PoA; PrIm; SCV
Children ask questions, The. Probity. David Swanger. FAZ
Children Band, The. Sir Aubrey De Vere. OBEV
Children begin at green dawn nimbly to build. The Altars in the Street. Denise Levertov. CAPP
Children, behold the chimpanzee. The Chimpanzee. Oliver Herford. CenHV; FaBV; FiBHP; NA
Children believe in clover, magic numbers. The Sacred Children. H. R. Hays. EAS
Children born of fairy stock. I'd Love to Be a Fairy's Child. Robert Graves. FaPON; HBVY; PDV; SoPo
Children, Children Everywhere. Jack Prelutsky. RHPC
Children conceived when two nightgowns. The Submarine Bed. John Peale Bishop. LiTA
Children do not ask the proper questions. Leaping into the Gulf. Patricia Beer. OxBC
Children, do you ever. My Other Me. Grace Denio Litchfield. AA; HBV-1
Children enter, The. Sundown at Darlington 1878. Lance Henson. VoR
Children go forward with their little satchels, The. The School Children. Louise Glück. AmPA; WeW
Children, Go Where I Send Thee. *Unknown.* FSW
Children Grown, The. Haywood Jackson. SOTS
Children, if you dare to think. Warning to Children. Robert Graves. FaBoCh; FaFP; NoP; OAEL-2; SO
Children in the Market-Place. Henry van Dyke. TRV
Children in the Wood, The. *Unknown. See* Babes in the Wood, The.
Children know how to do it, The. Feeding the Fire. Donald Finkel. VWA
Children Look at the Parents, The. A. S. J. Tessimond. ChMP
Children March, The. Elizabeth Riddell. CBAP
Children model the dust. In a City Square. Eleanor Glenn Wallis. NePoAm-2
Children Not Kept at Home. Joyce Carol Oates. DFF
Children now awake to birds. Lines for the Margin of an Old Gospel. Sheila Wingfield. ChMP
Children of Auschwitz. Naum Korzhavin, *tr. fr. Russian by* Daniel Weissbort. VWA
Children of Darkness. Robert Graves. NoAM
Children of dreams are in terror, The. A Text for These Distracted Times. Rodney Hall. CBAP
Children of Greenock, The. W. S. Graham. FaBoTw
Children of Israel prayed for [*or* wanted] bread, The. Old Sam's Wife [*or* On the Wife of a Parish Clerk]. *Unknown.* ChTr; ShM
Children of Light. Robert Lowell. AP; CMoP; MoAB; OxBA; PoPl
Children of Love. Harold Monro. MoBrPo
Children of my happier prime. Immolated. Herman Melville. ViBoPo
Children of Night. Richard Shelton. FiCP
Children of Stare, The. Walter de la Mare. BrPo
Children of the cold sun and the broken horizon. The City. Ben Maddow. WaP
Children of the Czar, The. The Ballad of the Children of the Czar. Delmore Schwartz. MiAP
Children of the Heavenly King. John Cennick. WGRP
Children of the Night, The. E. A. Robinson. NePA; OxBA
Children of the Owl and the Pussy-Cat, The. Edward Lear. FaBoNo
Children of the Poor, The. Gwendolyn Brooks. *Fr.* The Womanhood.
Sels.
"People who have no children can be hard," 1 *and* 2. PoA; WPE
"What shall I give my children? who are poor," 2. BALP; PoCh
(What Shall I Give My Children?) BPo
Children of the State, The. James Lewisohn. LFAC
Children of the Sun. Fenton Johnson. BANP
Children of the world are on the march, The. The Children March. Elizabeth Riddell. CBAP
Children of yesterday. Song of Hope. Mary Artemisia Lathbury. BLPA
Children on the corner, The. City. Raymond Biasotti. AMV-80
Children picking up our bones. A Postcard from the Volcano. Wallace Stevens. AP; CABA; HAP; LiTA; WeW
Children play with doll Katchinas, The. Hopi Woman. Lillian White Spencer. BPAW
Children: Private Ward. W. E. Henley. In Hospital, XVIII. BrPo
Children set fires in ashbarrels. Galway Kinnell. *Fr.* The Avenue Bearing the Initial of Christ into the New World. NaP
Children take longer to die. A Snapshot of Uig in Montana. Richard Hugo. NPAW
Children, the Sandbar, That Summer. Muriel Rukeyser. LCAP
Children they move stand, The. Clear. Angelo Lewis. PoBA
Children Waking: Indian Hill Station. Ralph Nixon Currey. PeSA
Children walk. City. Jane Stembridge. NMM
Children wandered up and down, The. The Cruise of the *Mystery.* Celia Thaxter. OBCA

Children we have not borne. To My Daughter the Junkie on a Train. Audre Lorde. CNA
Children were frightened by crescendoes, The. A Fete. Larry Eigner. NeAP
Children were shouting together, The. Frolic. "Æ." FaPON; MoBrPo
"Children who paddle where the ocean bed shelves steeply." Advice to Young Children. Stevie Smith. ELU
Children, why do you fear, why turn away? For Miriam. Marjorie Oludhe Macgoye. WPOW
Children, you are very little. Good and Bad Children. Robert Louis Stevenson. EBVV; FaBoCh; FaFP; HBV-1; HBVY; NBM; OxBChV; TreF
Children's Bells, The. Eleanor Farjeon. CH
Children's Carol, The. Eleanor Farjeon. PChr; RHPC
Children's Crusade, The. Philip Levine. NaP
Children's Crusade 1939. Bertolt Brecht, *tr. fr. German by* Michael Hamburger. MoBS
Children's Elegy. Muriel Rukeyser. *Fr.* Eighth Elegy. LCAP
Children's Ghosts, The. Winifred M. Letts. HBMV
Children's Hour, The. Longfellow. AA; FaBoBe; FaBV; FaFP; FaPON; FPL; HBV-1; HBVY; OBAL; OBCA; OHFP; PoEL-5; PoLF; PoPl; TreF; WBLP
Children's Lenten Wisdom. James A. Houck. AMV-80
Children's Letters, The. Dorothy Livesay. NOBC
Children's Rhymes. Langston Hughes. BOLo; BPo; InPS
Children's Runes and Omens. *Unknown.* MAT
("Hinx, minx, the old witch winks.") OxNR
Children's Song. Arye Sivan, *tr. fr. Hebrew by* David Shevin. VWA
Children's Song. Ford Madox Ford. HBV-1
Children's Song, The. *Unknown.* FaPON
Children's voices in the orchard. New Hampshire. T. S. Eliot. Landscapes, I. BiP; FaBoCh; GTBS-P; LoBV; WeW
Child's a plaything for an hour, A. A Child. Mary Lamb. OBEV
Child's Calendar, A, *sels.* John Updike.
August. OBCA; RHPC
May. OBCA
Child's Christmas Day, A. *Unknown.* OBCP
Child's Christmas without Jean Cocteau, A. David Fisher. NPGG
Child's cough scratches at my heart, The—my head. New York—December, 1931. Babette Deutsch. ImOP
Child's Day, A, *sels.* Walter de la Mare.
Ann and the Fairy Song. FaBV
"Softly, drowsily." SoPo; SUS
Child's Dream, The. Susan Ludvigson. AMV-80; MAYP
Child's Evening Hymn. Sabine Baring-Gould. *See* Now the Day Is Over.
Child's Evening Prayer, A. Samuel Taylor Coleridge. *See* Pains of Sleep, The.
Child's First Grief, The. Felicia Dorothea Hemans. BLPA
(First Grief, The.) CH
Child's Game. Judson Jerome. DuDa
Child's Grace, A. Burns. FaPON; MoShBr
(Two Graces: "Some hae meat that canna eat.") FaBoCh
Child's Grace, A. Robert Herrick. *See* Grace for a Child.
Child's Heritage, The. John G. Neihardt. HBV-1
Child's Laughter, A. Swinburne. BLPL; HBV-1; PoLF
Child's Memory. Terri Meyette Wilkins. LFAC
Child's Nativity, A. John N. Morris. GP
Child's Natural History, *sels.* Oliver Herford.
Some Geese. FiBHP; NA
(Geese.) HBV-2
Mon-Goos, The. AA; HBV-2
Seal, A. HBV-2; HBVY
Yak, The. HBV-2; HBVY
Child's Pet, A. W. H. Davies. CH
Child's plaything for an hour, A. Parental Recollections. Charles Lamb. OBRV
Child's Prayer, A. John Banister Tabb. FaPON; TreF; YaD
Child's Prayer, A. Francis Thompson. *See* Ex Ore Infantium.
Child's Prayer, A. *Unknown.* BLRP
Child's Present to His Child-Saviour, A. Robert Herrick. *See* To His Saviour, a Child, a Present by a Child.
Child's Purchase, The. Coventry Patmore. ISi
Child's Question, The. Emily Dickinson. *See* Will there really be a morning?
Child's Question, A. Emma Huntington Nason. AA
Child's Sight, The. Hy Sobiloff. VGW
Child's Song. Robert Lowell. NMP
Child's Song. Thomas Moore. GoBC; OxBI; SUS; ViBoPo
(Garden Song, A.) BoNaP
Child's Song. Swinburne. OBVV
Child's Song in Spring. Edith Nesbit. HBV-1; OHIP; OxBChV
Child's Song of Christmas, A. Marjorie Pickthall. HBV-1; HBVY; YeAr
Child's Song to Her Mother, A. Winifred Welles. HBMV
Child's Talk in April. Christina Rossetti. GN
Child's Thought, A. Bertha Moore. PaPo
Child's Thought of God, A. Elizabeth Barrett Browning. FaPON; TRV
Child's Thought of Harvest, A." Susan Coolidge." OHIP; PoSC
Child's Visit to the Biology Lab, A. Kathleen Spivack. AmPA
Child's Winter Evening, A. Gwen John. CH
Child's wisdom is in saying, The. The Child's Sight. Hy Sobiloff. VGW
Child's Wish, A. Abram Joseph Ryan. AA
Child's Wish Granted, The. George Parsons Lathrop. AA; HBV-1
Child's World, The. William Brighty Rands. *See* Wonderful World, The.
Chile. Susan Griffin. NPGG
Chilean Elegies, The: 5. The Interior. Tom Wayman. NOBC
Chiliasm. Richard Eberhart. EaLo
Chill, chill! Winter. *Unknown, tr. by* Frank O'Connor. KiLC
Chill New England sunshine, The. The Death of Goody Nurse. Rose Terry Cooke. PAH
Chill of the Eve. James Stephens. OnYI
Chilled by Different Winds. Alice Mackenzie Swaim. AMV-80
Chilled by the Blasts of Adverse Fate, *with music.* Jacob Duché. AH
Chilled by the Present, its gloom and its noise. Sonnets from China, XVIII. W. H. Auden. PPP
Chilled in this Irish pub I wish my loves. John Berryman. *Fr.* Dream Songs. FaBoMo; LCAP
Chilled into a serenity. To an Icicle. Blanche Taylor Dickinson. CDC
Chilled with salt dew, tossed on dark waters deep. A Mermaiden. Thomas Hennell. FaBoTw
Chilly Water, *with music. Unknown.* BoAN-2
Chilly Winds, *with music. Unknown.* OuSiCo; TrAS
Chilterns, The. Rupert Brooke. MoBrPo
Chimera. Barbara Howes. MP; TwCP
Chimera, The. Alfred Mombert, *tr. fr. German by* Erna Baber Rosenfeld. VWA
Chimes. Alice Meynell. CH; MoBrPo; SBG; WHA; WPE
Chimes. Dante Gabriel Rossetti. OBNC
Chimney, breathing a little smoke, A. February. James Schuyler. NeAP
Chimney of my neighbour's house. Soliloquy to Absent Friends. Douglas G. Jones. MoCV
Chimney Swallows. Horatio Nelson Powers. HBV-1
Chimney Sweeper, The ("A little black thing among the snow"). Blake. *Fr.* Songs of Experience. CABA; LAuP; NOEC; OAEL-2; PPoe; PPP; SaC; TEP
Chimney Sweeper, The ("When my mother died I was very young"). Blake. *Fr.* Songs of Innocence. CH; EnRP; FF; HeIP; InPK; LAuP; NOEC; OAEL-2; OxBChV; PAI; PPoe; PPP; SaC; SoSe; TEP
Chimney Sweeper, The. *Unknown.* AmFP
Chimney-Sweeper's Complaint, The. Mary Alcock. NOEC
Chimneys: colder. Reindeer Report. U. A. Fanthorpe. OBCP
Chimneys, rank on rank, The. Evening. Richard Aldington. MoBrPo; MOON; SeCePo
Chimpanzee, The. Oliver Herford. FaBV; FiBHP; NA
("Children behold the chimpanzee.") CenHV
Chimpanzee, The/ Is a most embarrassing animal to see. Muriel Sly. FiBHP
Ch'in Chia's Wife's Reply. *Tr. fr. Chinese by* Arthur Waley. BoWoP
Chin in, I doubt the praying mantis prays. The Chance. John Holmes. NePoAm-2
China Policy, The. Carl Rakosi. FAZ
Chinaman's Chance, A. Marilyn Chin. BrSi
Chinashop at seaborde. Civility a Bogey. Margaret Avison. NOBC
Chinatown. Anna Blake Mezquida. BPAW
Chinatown Chant. Tom MacInnes. CaP
Chinatown Games. Wing Tek Lum. BrSi
Chinatown Talking Story. Kitty Tsui. BrSi
Chinese Baby Asleep. Dorothy Donnelly. NCSH
Chinese Banyan, The. William Meredith. NePoEA
Chinese Camp, Kamloops (circa 1883). Andrew Suknaski. NOBC
Chinese Graves in Beechworth Cemetery, The. Philip Mead. AMV-81
Chinese Mural, A. Carlos Baker. *Fr.* A Visit to the Art Gallery. EyDe
Chinese Nightingale, The. Vachel Lindsay. HBMV; MoAmPo; NePA
Chinese Poems: Arthur Waley." C. A. Fair." PeSA
Chinese Serenade for the Ut-Kam and Tong-Koo, *sel.* Thomas Holley Chivers.
"Tu Du,/ Skies blue." PeD
Chinese, to whom the eighteenth-century English, The. The Fashionable Heart. Jack Gilbert. NPGG
Chinese Vase, A. Edward Hirsch. AMV-80
Chinese Winter. F. R. Higgins. BIrV
Chinese written character, The. Signature. Carol Orlock. AMV-81
Ching a Ring. James Planché. NOBL
Chinless and slouched, gray-faced, and slack of jaw. For an Early Retirement. Donald Hall. TW

Chinoiserie. Charles Wright. AmPA
Chinoiseries. Amy Lowell. PoRA
Chip. George Starbuck. OBAL
("Clippety cloppity.") PV
Chip on His Shoulder, A. *Unknown.* BLPA; WBLP
Chipeta. Eugene Field. PoOW
Chipeta's Ride. John W. Taylor. PoOW
Chipmunk chewing the Chippendale. Exit, Pursued by a Bear. Ogden Nash. NYBP
Chipmunk's Day, The. Randall Jarrell. OBCA; NCSH; RHPC
(Chipmunk's Song, The.) PDV
("In and out the bushes, up the ivy.") BoAnP
Chipmunks jump, and/Greensnakes slither. Valentine. Donald Hall. GrPl; LLLT; NTCP; PCP
Chipmunk's Song, The. Randall Jarrell. *See* Chipmunk's Day, The.
Chippewa Lake Park. Warren Woessner. TAT
Chippewa Love Song. *Tr. fr. Chippewa Indian by* Frances Densmore, *ad. by* Willis Barnstone. BoWoP
Chiquita. Bret Harte. AA; BPAW
Chisel in hand stood a sculptor boy. Life Sculpture. George Washington Doane. BLPA; OHFP; WBLP
Chisholm Trail, The. *Unknown. See* Old Chisholm Trail, The.
Chivalrous Shark, The. Wallace Irwin. *See* Rhyme of the Chivalrous Shark.
Chivalry. "Æ." ViBoPo
Chivalry at a Discount. Edward Fitzgerald. HBV-1
"Chkk! chkk!" hopper-grass. Confucius, *tr. by* Ezra Pound. *Fr.* Shao and the South. CTC
Chloe. Burns. GN; HBV-1
Chloe. Charles Mordaunt, Earl of Peterborough. *See* I Said to My Heart.
Chloe. Pope. *Fr.* Moral Essays. AWP; NOBE
("'Yet Cloe sure was formed without a spot.'") ErPo; OBSV
Chloe Divine. Thomas D'Urfey. HBV-1; OBEV
(Chloe.) UnTE
(Chloe's a Nymph.) PoPle
Chloe found Amyntas lying. Rondelay [*or* Kiss Me, Dear]. Dryden. CavP; UnTE; ViBoPo
Chloe, the contours of your bust. To Chloe. Earnest Albert Hooten. UnTE
Chloe, why wish you that your years. To Chloe, Who Wished Herself Young Enough for Me [*or* Who for His Sake Wished Herself Younger]. William Cartwright. HBV-1; JCP; LiTB; MePo; OBS; ViBoPo
Chloe's a Nymph in flowery groves. Chloe Divine. Thomas D'Urfey. HBV-1; OBEV; PoPle; UnTE
Chloride of Lime and Charcoal. Louis Zukofsky. CoPo
Chloris, *sels.* William Smith.
"Some in their harts their mistris colours bears," XXIX. AAS
Sonnet: "My Love, I cannot thy rare beauties place." ElL
To the Most Excellent and Learned Shepheard Collin Cloute, *dedication.* AAS
Chloris and Hilas. Made to a Saraban. Edmund Waller. SeCV-1
Chloris Farewell. Edmund Waller. *See* Song: "Chloris! farewell. Now I must go."
Chloris, forbear a while. Song. Henry Bold. GBL
Chloris in the Snow. William Strode. *See* On Chloris Walking in the Snow.
Chloris made my heart to stop. A Winter Madrigal. Morris Bishop. InMe
Chloris, 'Tis Not in Your Power. Sir George Etherege. OBS
Chloris, when I to thee present. A Song. *Unknown.* OBS
Chloris, whilst thou and I were free. Sonnet. Charles Cotton. ViBoPo
Chock House Blues. *Unknown.* BluL
Chocolate Cake. Nina Payne. RHPC
Chocolate Chocolate. Arnold Adoff. RHPC
Chocolate Easter bunny. Patience. Bobbi Katz. RHPC
Chocolate Soldiers, The. Calvin Forbes. MAT; MAYP
Chocolates. Louis Simpson. LCAP; OxBC
Choctaw Chief Helps Plan a Festival, A. Jim Barnes. TAT
Choeses me boue er plach yoang. Foreign Literature. Thackeray. FaBoNo
Choice. A. R. Ammons. PAI
Choice, The. Hilary Corke. MP; NYBP
Choice. J. V. Cunningham. VGW
Choice. Emily Dickinson. *See* Of all the souls that stand create.
Choice. John Farrar. SiSoSe
Choice, The. John Masefield. MoAB; MoBrPo
Choice. Angela Morgan. PoLF
Choice, The. Frederick Morgan. AMV-81
Choice, The. John Norris. CavP
Choice, The. John Pomfret. NOEC; OBEC
Choice, The. Dante Gabriel Rossetti. The House of Life, LXXI-LXXIII. HBV-2; OBVV; ViBoPo
"Eat thou and drink," LXXI. WHA
"Think thou and act," LXXIII. GTBS-P; OBEV; WHA
Choice, A. Edward de Vere, Earl of Oxford. OBSC
(Doubtful Choice, A.) ElL
(Epigram: "Were I a king, I could command content.") FaBoEE
Choice, The. George Wither. OBEV
Choice, The. W. B. Yeats. CMoP; NoAM; OxBTC
Choice of the Cross, The. Dorothy L. Sayers. *Fr.* The Devil to Pay. TrCP
Choice of Weapons, A. Stanley Kunitz. LiTM; VGW
Choice soul, in whom, as in a glass, we see. The Doom of Beauty. Michelangelo, *tr. by* John Addington Symonds. AWP
Choir Invisible, The." George Eliot." OBVV; OHFP; WBLP
("O [*or* Oh], may I join the choir invisible.") EBVV; HBV-2; OBNC; TreFS; TRV; WGRP
Choir of bright beauties in spring did appear, A. The Lady's Song. Dryden. SeCeV
Choir of Day, The. Blake. *See* Vision of Beulah, The.
Choir of spirits on a cloud, A. William Baylebridge. Life's Testament, XVII. PoAu-1
Choir Practice. Ernest Crosby. AA
Choirmaster's Burial, The. Thomas Hardy. DTC
Choirs of Heaven are tokened in a harp-string, The. The Counsels of O'Riordan, the Rann Maker. T. D. O'Bolger. AnIV
Chomei at Toyama. Basil Bunting. OxBTC
Choo a choo a choo tooth. The Cannibals' Grace before Meat. Charles Dickens. FaBoNo
Chook, chook, chook, chook, chook. *Unknown.* OxNR
Choose. Verna Bishop. STF
Choose Life. Bible, *O.T.* Deuteronomy, XXX: 15-19. TreFT
Choose me your valentine. To His Mistress[e]. Robert Herrick. OFD; ViBoPo
Choose now among this fairest number. Song. William Browne. GBL
Choose Something like a Star. Robert Frost. MoAB; MoAmPo; PoCh
Choose the darkest part o' the grove. Incantation to Oedipus [*or* A Spell]. Dryden. *Fr.* Oedipus, III, i. OFD; WiR; WSC
Choose You a Seat 'n' Set Down, *with music. Unknown.* OuSiCo
Choose you this day whom you will serve. Choose. Verna Bishop. STF
Choosing. Eleanor Farjeon. TiPo
Choosing a Death. Alberta Turner. LCAP
Choosing a Mast. Roy Campbell. FaBoTw; PeSA
Choosing a Name. Charles *and* Mary Lamb. HBV-1; OxBChV
Choosing a Name. Anne Ridler. NOBE
Choosing a Wet-Nurse. M. Saint-Marthe, *tr. fr. French. Fr.* Paedotrophiae; or, The Art of Bringing Up Children. FaBoUs
Choosing Coffins. Raymond Souster. MoCV
Choosing Shoes. ffrida Wolfe. SoPo; SUS; TiPo
Choosing the Devil. Linda Gregg. NPGG
Choosing Their Names. Thomas Hood. PCat
Chop-Cherry. Robert Herrick. EnLoPo; UnTE
Chopin Prelude. Eleanor Norton. HBMV
Chopping Fire-Wood. Robert Pack. NePoEA-2
Chops. Alan Dixon. BoAnP
Chops Are Flyin. Stanley Crouch. NBP
Choral Symphony Conductor. Carol Coates. CaP
Chorale: "Often had I found her fair." A. D. Hope. ErPo; UnTE
Chords knotted together like insane nouns, The. You (IV). Tom Clark. EAS
Choric Song: "There is sweet music here that softer falls." Tennyson. *Fr.* The Lotos-Eaters. HeIP; OBNC
(Choric Song of the Lotus-Eaters.) FaFP; ViBoPo
(Song of the Lotus-Eaters.) NOBE; OBEV; WHA
(There Is Sweet Music Here.) FaBV
Choricos. Richard Aldington. HBMV
Choristers Training, *orig. and mod. English prose. Unknown.* OxBM
Chorus: "All, all of a piece throughout." Dryden. *See* All, All of a Piece.
Chorus: "All ye that handle harp and viol." Moses Hayyim Luzzatto, *tr. fr. Hebrew by* Nina Davis Salaman. *Fr.* Unto the Upright Praise. TrJP
Chorus: "And Pergamos,/ City of the Phrygians." Euripides, *tr. fr. Greek by* Hilda Doolittle ("H. D."). *Fr.* Iphigenia in Aulis. AWP
("And Pergamos,/city of the Phrygians.") OBVE
Chorus: "Before the beginning of years." Swinburne. *See* Before the Beginning of Years.
Chorus: "Behold what furies still." Samuel Daniel. *Fr.* Cleopatra. LoBV
Chorus: "Big Engines, The." Jack Kerouac. *Fr.* Mexico City Blues. NeAP
Chorus: "Doom is dark and deeper than any sea-dingle." W. H. Auden. *See* Wanderer, The. GTBS-P
Chorus: "Essence of Existence, The." Jack Kerouac. *Fr.* Mexico City Blues. NeAP
Chorus: "Fair Salamis, the billow's roar." Sophocles, *tr. fr. Greek by* Winthrop Mackworth Praed. *Fr.* Ajax. AWP
Chorus: "Glenn Miller and I were heroes." Jack Kerouac. *Fr.* Mexico City Blues. NeAP
Chorus: "Got up and dressed up." Jack Kerouac. *Fr.* Mexico City Blues. NeAP
Chorus: "Great Fortune is an hungry thing." Aeschylus, *tr. fr. Greek by* Gilbert Murray. *Fr.* Agamemnon. AWP

Chorus: "Hail to the Headlong! the Headlong Ap-Headlong!" Thomas Love Peacock. *Fr.* Headlong Hall. OBRV
Chorus: "How dost thou wear and weary out thy days." Samuel Daniel. *Fr.* The Tragedie of Philotas. OBSC
Chorus: "If I drink water while this doth last." Thomas Love Peacock. *Fr.* Crotchet Castle. ViBoPo
Chorus: Kings of Troy, The. Euripides, *tr. fr. Greek by* George Allen. *Fr.* Andromache. WaaP
Chorus: "Life of Life! thy lips enkindle." Shelley. *See* Life of Life.
Chorus: "Love's multitudinous boneyard." Jack Kerouac. *Fr.* Mexico City Blues. NeAP
Chorus: "Nobody knows the other side." Jack Kerouac. *Fr.* Mexico City Blues. NeAP
Chorus: "Oh, may my constant feet not fail." Sophocles, *tr. fr. Greek by* Robert Whitelaw. *Fr.* Oedipus Rex. WGRP
Chorus: "O wearisome condition of humanity." Fulke Greville. *See* Chorus Sacerdotum.
Chorus: "Old Man Mose." Jack Kerouac. *Fr.* Mexico City Blues. NeAP
Chorus: "Only awake to Universal Mind." Jack Kerouac. *Fr.* Mexico City Blues. NeAP
Chorus: "Praise be man, he is existing in milk." Jack Kerouac. *Fr.* Mexico City Blues. NeAP
Chorus: "Saints, I give myself up to thee." Jack Kerouac. *Fr.* Mexico City Blues. NeAP
Chorus: "Since you have come thus far." C. Day Lewis. *Fr.* Noah and the Waters. OAEP
Chorus: "Spring all the Graces of the age." Ben Jonson. *Fr.* Neptune's Triumph. OBS
Chorus: "Summer holds, The: upon its glittering lake." W. H. Auden. *Fr.* The Dog beneath the Skin. OxBTC
Chorus: "Sweet are the ways of death to weary feet." Lord De Tabley. *Fr.* Medea. NBM; OBEV; OBVV
Chorus: "Then thus we have beheld." Samuel Daniel. *Fr.* Cleopatra. OBSC
Chorus: "Throned are the gods, and in." Lord De Tabley. *Fr.* Philoctetes. NBM
Chorus: "To throw away the key and walk away." W. H. Auden. *Fr.* Paid on Both Sides. MoBrPo
(Walking Tour, The.) CMoP
Chorus: "Vain man, born to no happiness." Sidney Godolphin. LoBV
Chorus: "Void that's highly embraceable, The." Jack Kerouac. *Fr.* Mexico City Blues. NeAP
Chorus: "We do not wish anything to happen." T. S. Eliot. *Fr.* Murder in the Cathedral. OxBTC
Chorus: "We have not been happy, my Lord, we have not been too happy." T. S. Eliot. *Fr.* Murder in the Cathedral. OxBTC
Chorus: "What man is he that yearneth." Sophocles, *tr. fr. Greek by* A. E. Housman. *Fr.* Oedipus at Colonus. AWP
Chorus: "Wheel of quivering meat, The." Jack Kerouac. *Fr.* Mexico City Blues. NeAP
("Wheel of quivering meat, The.") PoM
Chorus: "When the hounds of spring are on winter's traces." Swinburne. *See* When the Hounds of Spring.
Chorus: "Who hath given man speech? or who hath set therein." Swinburne. *Fr.* Atalanta in Calydon. OAEL-2; ViBoPo
Chorus: "World's great age begins anew, The." Shelley. *Fr.* Hellas. FaBoEn; HBV-2; LoBV; OAEP; OBRV; PoEL-4; SeCeV
(Chorus from "Hellas.") AWP
(Choruses from "Hellas," 4.) EnRP
(Final Chorus, The.) SeCePo
(Hellas.) ChTr; OBEV
(New World, A.) TrGrPo
(World's Great Age [Begins Anew], The.) FiP; HeIP; NoP; TEP; TreFS
("World's great age begins anew, The.") EBEV; HAP; NOBE; OAEL-2
Chorus: "Worlds on worlds are rolling ever." Shelley. *See* Worlds on Worlds.
Chorus: "Yea, the coneys are scared by the thud of hoofs." Thomas Hardy. *See* Field of Waterloo, The.
Chorus: "You are the town and we are the clock." W. H. Auden. *Fr.* The Dog beneath the Skin. OxBTC
Chorus for Survival, *sel.* Horace Gregory.
"Ask no return for love that's given," XIV. TwAmPo; VGW
(Ask No Return.) MoAmPo
Chorus from a Play. W. H. Auden. *See* Wanderer, The.
Chorus from a Tragedy. Leonard Bacon. ViBoPo
Chorus from "Hellas." Shelley. *See* Chorus: "World's great age begins anew, The."
Chorus from "The Rock"—III. T. S. Eliot. *Fr.* The Rock. LiTB
("Word of the Lord came unto me, saying.") TRV
Chorus of Angels. Cardinal Newman. *Fr.* The Dream of Gerontius. NBM
(Fifth Choir of Angelicals.) GoBC
("Praise to the holiest in the height.") NOCV; PoEL-5
Chorus of Birds. Aristophanes, *tr. fr. Greek by* Swinburne. *Fr.* The Birds. AWP
(Grand Chorus of Birds.) PoEL-5
Chorus of Satyrs, Driving Their Goats. Euripides, *tr. fr. Greek by* Shelley. *Fr.* Cyclops. AWP
Chorus of Scyrian Maidens. Philip Bainbrigge. *Fr.* Achilles in Scyros. PeHV
Chorus of Sirens. George Darley. *See* Mermaidens' Vesper-Hymn, The.
Chorus of Spirits. George Darley. *Fr.* Sylvia; or, The May Queen. OnYI
Chorus of Spirits. Shelley. *Fr.* Prometheus Unbound, I. LoBV
Chorus of the Archangels, The. Goethe. *See* Prologue in Heaven.
Chorus of the Elements. Cardinal Newman. *See* Elements, The.
Chorus of the Rescued. Nelly Sachs, *tr. fr. German.* VWA, *tr. by* Harry Zohn; WPOW, *tr. by* Ruth Mead *and* Matthew Mead
Chorus of the Unborn. Nelly Sachs, *tr. fr. German by* Ruth Mead *and* Matthew Mead. NYBP
Chorus of the Years. Thomas Hardy. *See* Field of Waterloo, The.
Chorus Primus: Wise Counsellors. Fulke Greville. *Fr.* Mustapha. OBS
Chorus Quintus: Tartarorum. Fulke Greville. *Fr.* Mustapha. OBS
Chorus Sacerdotum. Fulke Greville. *Fr.* Mustapha. FaBoEn; InvP; JCP; MePo; NOBE; OAEL-1; OBS; PoEL-1; PPP; SeCePo
(Chorus: "O wearisome condition of humanity.") ViBoPo
(O Wearisome Condition of Humanity.) HAP; LiTB; SeCeV
Chorus Speaks Her Words as She Dances, The. Linda Gregg. NPGG
Chorus Tertius: Of Time; Eternitie. Fulke Greville. *Fr.* Mustapha. OBS
Choruses from "Hellas". Shelley. *Fr.* Hellas. EnRP
Chosen, The. Carl Dennis. AMV-81
Chosen. W. B. Yeats. BoLoP; CMoP
Chosen, The—Kalgoorlie, 1894. Fay Zwicky. VWA
Chosen Light, A. John Montague. IPY
Chosen of God. Stefan Zweig, *tr. fr. German by* Eden *and* Cedar Paul. *Fr.* Jeremiah. TrJP
Chosen People, The. W. N. Ewer. DBV
("How odd/ Of God.") FaBoEE
Chosen Three, on Mountain Height, The, *with music.* David H. Ela. AH
Chou and the South. Confucius, *tr. fr. Chinese by* Ezra Pound. *Fr.* The Classic Anthology. CTC
Chough, The. James Reaney. CABA; OBCV; PeCV
Chough. Rex Warner. PoRA
Chough and crow to roost are gone, The. The Outlaw's Song [*or* Song of the Outlaws]. Joanna Baillie. OBEV; OBRV
Chough, said a dictionary, The. The Chough. James Reaney. CABA; OBCV; PeCV
Choyce, The. Thomas Beedome. CavP
Christ 2, *sels.* Cynewulf, *tr. fr. Anglo-Saxon.*
Maiden Ring-Adorned, A, *tr. by* Mother Margaret WilliamsISi
Voyage of Life, The, *tr. by* Charles W. Kennedy. AnOE; MOS
Christ. Greg Forker. LFAC
Christ. Daniel Hoffman. CoPo
Christ, The. John Oxenham. TRV
Christ 1, *sel.* *Unknown, tr. fr. Anglo-Saxon by* Charles W. Kennedy. AnOE
Advent Lyrics.
"Bless earth with Thine Advent, O Saviour Christ! VIII.
"Hail, O most worthy in all the world!' IX.
"O holy Jerusalem, Vision of peace," III.
". . . to the King./ Thou art the wall-stone rejected," I.
Christ 3, *sel.* *Unknown, tr. fr. Anglo-Saxon by* Charles W. Kennedy.
Last Judgment, The. AnOE
Christ Alone. Shel Helsley. STF
Christ Alone. Theodore Monod. *See* None of Self and All of Thee.
Christ and his Mother, heavenly maid. Founder's Day. Robert Bridges. OBVV
Christ and Satan, *sel.* *Unknown, tr. fr. Anglo-Saxon by* Charles W. Kennedy.
Lamentations of the Fallen Angels. AnOE
Christ and the Little Ones. Julia Gill. BLPA
Christ and the Pagan. John Banister Tabb. TrCP
Christ bears a thousand crosses now. Quatrain. Charles G. Blanden. PGD
Christ, by dark clouds of worldliness concealed. Prayer before Meat. Una W. Harsen. TrPWD
Christ Calls Man Home. *Unknown.* MeEL
Christ child lay on Mary's lap, The. A Christmas Carol. G. K. Chesterton. FaFP; GoBC; HBV-1; HBVY; OBCP; OHIP; SUS
Christ Church Meadows, Oxford. Donald Hall. NYBP
Christ claims our help in many a strange disguise. The Man of Sorrows. *Unknown.* PGD
Christ Climbed Down. Lawrence Ferlinghetti. SBVL; VGW
Christ comes to mind and comes across the mind. Burns Singer. Sonnets for a Dying Man, XXXIX. NePoEA-2
Christ Complains to Sinners. *Unknown.* *See* Seven Sins, The.
Christ-Cross Rhyme, A. Robert Stephen Hawker. GoBC
Christ Crucified. Richard Crashaw. GoBC; OBEV

Christ for Everything. R. A. Belsham. STF
Christ for the World! We Sing, *with music.* Samuel Wolcott. AH
Christ gave a yoke, a sword, a cross. Gifts. Chauncey R. Piety. PGD
Christ God who savest man, save most. Count Gismond. Robert Browning. VLP
Christ has no hands but our hands. The World's Bible. Annie Johnson Flint. STF; TRV
Christ hath a garden walled around. Isaac Watts. FaBoCh
Christ His Cross shall be my speed! A Christ-Cross Rhyme. Robert Stephen Hawker. GoBC
Christ! I am Christ's! and let the name suffice you. Frederick W. H. Myers. *Fr.* Saint Paul. TRV
Christ I Wudint Know Normal if I Saw It When. Bill Bissett. NOBC
Christ in Alabama. Langston Hughes. PoBA
Christ in Flanders. Lucy Whitmell. SUMH
Christ in the Clay-Pit. Jack Clemo. EBCP; GTBS-P
Christ in the Universe. Alice Meynell. ACP; GoBC; HBMV; MoBrPo; NOBE
Christ in You. *Unknown.* STF
Christ Inviting Sinners to His Grace, *sel.* Henry Alline.
"Amazing sight, the Savior stands." AH, *with music;* CaP
Christ is a nigger. Christ in Alabama. Langston Hughes. PoBA
Christ Is Arisen. Goethe, *tr. fr. German. Fr.* Faust. TrCP
(Easter Chorus, *diff. sel., tr. by* Bayard Taylor.) WGRP
Christ Is Coming. W. Macomber. STF
Christ Is Crucified Anew. John Richard Moreland. PGD
Christ Is Risen! D. H. Dugan. BLRP
Christ is the Fact of facts, the Bible's Theme. The Greatest Person in the Universe. Daniel L. Marsh. BLRP
Christ keep the Hollow Land. Song. William Morris. *Fr.* The Hollow Land. ChTr; NBM; PoEL-5
Christ made a trance on Friday view. Good Friday. *Unknown.* ChTr
Christ [*or* Crist] made [*or* maketh] to man a fair present. Divine Love [*or* Christ's Gift to Man *or* Love Unlike Love]. *Unknown.* ACP; MeEL; OAEL-1; OxBM
Christ, My Beloved. William Baldwin. EIL; ELP; NOCV; OxBoCh
(Spouse to the Beloved, The.) OBSC
Christ, my Life, my Only Treasure. During His Courtship. Charles Wesley. NOCV
Christ, My Salvation. Eva Gray. STF
Christ of His gentleness. In the Wilderness. Robert Graves. CH; MoAB; MoBrPo; SeCePo
Christ of Judea, look thou in my heart! Richard Watson Gilder. *Fr.* Credo. TrPWD
Christ of the Andes, The, *sel.* Edwin Markham.
"O Christ of Olivet, you hushed the wars." TrPWD
Christ Our Example in Suffering. James Montgomery. HBV-2
Christ Quiets the Tempest. Caelius Sedulius, *tr. fr. Latin by* George Sigerson. *Fr.* Carmen Paschale. OnYI
Christ risen was rarely recognized by sight. For They Shall See God. Luci Shaw. TrCP
Christ the Lord is risen to-day. Easter Hymn. Charles Wesley. OHIP; TRV
Christ, the Man. W. H. Davies. WGRP
Christ, the Refuge of the Soul. Charles Wesley. *See* Jesus, Lover of My Soul.
Christ! These are her angels! The Unicorn and the Lady. Jean Garrigue. NYBP
Christ to His Spouse. William Baldwin. EIL; NOCV; OxBoCh
(Beloved to the Spouse, The.) OBSC
Christ Unconquered, *sel.* Arthur J. Little
Invocation: "Mother of God, mother of man reborn," Bk. IX. ISi
Christ Walking on the Water. W. R. Rodgers. AnIL; MoAB; NoAM; OxBI
Christ Walks in This Infernal District Too. Malcolm Lowry. MoCV; NOBC
Christ was born on Christmas day. Christmas Carol. Thomas Helmore. OHIP
Christ was your lord and captain all your life. To His Father. Robinson Jeffers. DiL
Christ washed the feet of Judas! The Feet of Judas. George Marion McClellan. BANP; PoNe
Christ, wha'd ha'e been Chief Rabbi gin he lik't. Up to Date. "Hugh MacDiarmid." FaBoCo
Christ, when a child, a garden made. A Legend. *Unknown, at. to* Peter Ilich Tchaikovsky, *tr. by* Nathan Haskell Dole. OHIP
Christ, Whose Glory Fills the Skies. Charles Wesley. *See* Morning Hymn, A.
Christ will prove the true attraction. Attraction. *Unknown.* STF
Christ with me, Christ before me, Christ behind me. Phyllis Garlick. *Fr.* St. Patrick. TRV
Christ wow/ now I get. Insight. Lionel Kearns. PeCV
Christabel. Samuel Taylor Coleridge. EnRP; GoTL; OAEL-2; OAEP
Sels.
"Alas! they had been friends in youth," *fr.* Pt. II. OBRV
(Broken Friendship.) TreFT
(Scars Remaining, The.) OBNC
Christabel and Geraldine, *fr.* Pt. I. PeHV
"Little child, a limber elf, A," *fr.* Pt. II. LoBV; ViBoPo
" 'Tis the middle of night by the castle clock," Pt. I. CH, ll. 1-65; FiP; OBRV; SeCePo, ll. 1-70; WHA
Christchurch Bells. *Unknown.* OBET
Christchurch, N. Z. Earle Birney. OxBC
Christendom. Thomas Traherne. PoEL-2
"Things Native sweetly grew," *sel.* FaBoEn
Christening, A. Donald Davie. OxBC
Christening-Day Wishes for My God-Child. Robert P. Tristram Coffin. OFD
Christenings. Peter Porter. NAs
Christian, Be Up, *with music.* Robert Nathan. AH
Christian Ethics, *sels.* Thomas Traherne.
"All music, sauces, feasts, delights and pleasures." UnS
Contentment. NOCV
(Contentment Is a Sleepy Thing.) OxBoCh
For Man to Act. OxBoCh
("For man to act as if his soul did see.") NOCV
Mankind Is Sick. OxBoCh
Christian Freedom. George Matheson. *See* Christ's Bondservant.
Christian Is a Man Who Feels, A. Thomas R. Ybarra. WhC
Christian Life, The. Samuel Longfellow. WGRP
Christian Pilgrim's Hymn, The. William Williams. WGRP
(Divine Hand, The.) BLRP
Christian Scientist, high-buttoned mind. Miss Ada. Christopher Fahy. TAT
Christian, seek not yet repose. Watch and Pray. Charlotte Elliott. STF
Christian Soldier, The, *sel.* G. A. Studdert-Kennedy.
"Peace does not mean the end of all our striving." TRV
Christian Year, The, *sels.* John Keble.
Eleventh Sunday after Trinity. VLP
Third Sunday in Lent. VLP
Christiana. Peter Redgrove. OxBC
Christians at War. John F. Kendrick. TW
Christians awake, salute the happy morn. A Hymn for Christmas Day. John Byrom. NOCV; OBEC; PoEL-3; SBVL
Christian's "Good-Night," The. Sarah Doudney. BLPA
Christians have always been pilgriming. "Faith and Practice." John Balaban. GOA
Christians have had two thousand years, The. After Two Thousand Years." Hugh MacDiarmid." DBV
Christian's New-Year Prayer, The, *sel.* Ella Wheeler Wilcox.
"If my vain soul needs blows and bitter losses." TrPWD
Christians Reply to the Phylosopher, The. Sir William Davenant. MeLP
Life and Death, *sel.* OBS
Christians were on the earth ere Christ was born. An Early Christian. Robert Barnabas Brough. OBVV
Christina. Louis MacNeice. BoLoP; OxBI, *abr.*
Christine. John Hay. AA
Christine to Her Son. Christine de Pisan, *tr. fr. French by* Barbara Howes. BoWoP
Christmas. John Betjeman. EBCP; OBCP; OxBTC
Christmas. Marchette Chute. SiSoSe
Christmas. George Herbert. OxBoCh; SBVL; SeCV-1; TrCP
Christmas. Leigh Hunt. OBCP
Christmas. Gertrude von Le Fort, *tr. fr. German by* Margaret Chanler. ISi
Christmas. Shakespeare. *Fr.* Hamlet, I, i. ChTr
(Bird of Dawning, The.) FaBoRV
(Gracious Time, The.) GN
("Some say that ever 'gainst that season comes.") OFD; PChr
Christmas. Nahum Tate. *See* While Shepherds Watched Their Flocks by Night.
Christmas Amnesty. Edith Lovejoy Pierce. PGD
Christmas and Common Birth. Anne Ridler. FaBoTw
Christmas Antiphones, *sel.* Swinburne.
"Thou whose birth on earth." PGD; TrPWD; TRV
Christmas at a Decade's End. Richard Snyder. SOTS
Christmas at Babbitt's. Henry Hallam Tweedy. TRV
Christmas at Melrose. Leslie Pinckney Hill. BANP
Christmas at Sea. Robert Louis Stevenson. BLPL; BrPo; CH; EBVV; EtS; FaBoBe; FaBV; HBV-1; MOS; OBVV
Christmas at Vail: On Staying Indoors. Pat Monaghan. AMV-80
Christmas Bells. Longfellow. BLRP; EBCP; FaFP; FaPON; HBV-1; HBVY; OBCP; PChr, *st.* 1; PGD, *abr.*; TreFT; TRV; WBLP
(I Heard the Bells on Christmas Day.) AH, *with music;* NTCP; PoSC
Christmas bells, awake and ring. Christmas Morning. Harry Behn. PChr

Christmas Bills. Joseph Hatton. OBCP
Christmas Birthday. Grace Ellen Glaubitz. SiSoSe
Christmas Candle, The. Kate Louise Brown. SoPo
Christmas candles confuse the dusk. Central Park, 1916. Pamela Stewart. NYP
Christmas Card. Ted Hughes. OBCP
Christmas Carol, A: "Angel told Mary, An." Harry Behn. PChr
Christmas Carol: "As Joseph was a-walking [*or* a-waukin']." *Unknown. See* As Joseph Was a-Walking.
Christmas Carol, A: "Christ child lay on Mary's lap, The." G. K. Chesterton. FaFP; GoBC; HBV-1; HBVY; OBCP; OHIP; SUS
Christmas Carol: "Christ was born on Christmas day." Thomas Helmore. OHIP
Christmas Carol, A: "Everywhere, everywhere, Christmas tonight." Phillips Brooks. OHIP; SoPo
(Christmas Everywhere.) BLPP; FaFP; OHFP; WBLP
Christmas Carol: "From the starry heav'ns descending." J. R. Newell. BLRP
Christmas Carol: "God bless the master of this house." *Unknown.* OHIP; SiSoSe; TiPo
("God bless the master of this house.") OxNR
(Grace, A.) MoShBr
(Souling Song.) OBET
Christmas Carol, A: "In the bleak mid-winter." Christina Rossetti. ChTr; OHIP; SBVL
(In the Bleak Mid-Winter.) OxBoCh; SUS; TRV
"What can I give Him," *st.* 5. PChr
(My Gift.) FaPON; SiSoSe
Christmas Carol: "Lacking samite and sable." May Probyn. ACP; GoBC; HBMV; ISi; OBVV
Christmas Carol, A: "Shepherds went their hasty way." Samuel Taylor Coleridge. ISi; OxBoCh
Christmas Carol, A: "So now is come our joyful'st feast." George Wither. OBS; ViBoPo
(Our Joyful Feast.) OHIP; SiSoSe
Christmas Carol: "Thank God, thank God, we do believe." Christina Rossetti. PChr
Christmas Carol, A: "There's a song in the air!" Josiah Gilbert Holland. AA; GN; HBVY; OHIP
(There's a Song in the Air.) TRV
Christmas Carol, A: "Three damsels in the queen's chamber." Swinburne. SBVL
Christmas Carol: "Three outas from the bleak Karoo." D. J. Opperman, *tr. fr. Afrikaans by* Anthony Delius. PeSA
Christmas Carol, A: "Thys ender nyght." *Unknown.* TrGrPo, *abr.*
(Thys Endris Nygth.) OAEP.
Christmas Carol: "Villagers all, this frosty tide." Kenneth Grahame. *Fr.* The Wind in the Willows. FaPON; PChr
(Carol.) OHIP
Christmas Carol, A: " 'What means this glory round our feet.' " James Russell Lowell. PGD
Christmas Carol, A: "What sweeter music can we bring." Robert Herrick. *See* Christmas Caroll, Sung to the King, A . . .
Christmas Carol, A: "When Christ was born in Bethlehem." *Unknown, tr. fr. Italian by* Longfellow. OHIP
Christmas Caroll Sung to the King in the Presence at White-Hall, A. Robert Herrick. GoJo
(Christmas Carol, A: "What sweeter music can we bring.") SBVL
Sels.
"Darling of the world is come, The." PChr
"What sweeter music can we bring." PChr
Christmas Carols. Patricia Beer. OxBC
Christmas Carols. Edmund Hamilton Sears. *See* It Came upon the Midnight Clear.
Christmas Chant. Isabel Shaw. SiSoSe
Christmas Childhood, A. Patrick Kavanagh. AnIL; IPY; OxBI
"My father played the melodion," *sel.* DTC; PChr
Christmas comes but once a year. Mother Goose. OxNR; SoPo
Christmas Comes to Moccasin Flat. James Welch. CDW; GP; MAT
Christmas Cradlesong, A. Lope de Vega, *tr. fr. Spanish by* George Ticknor. PoPl
Christmas Creek. Henry Kendall. CBAP
Christmas Dawn at Sea, A. Evan Morgan. EtS
Christmas Day. Roy Fuller. OBCP
Christmas Day. Christopher Smart. *Fr.* Hymns and Spiritual Songs, Hymn XXXII. ChTr; OBCP
Christmas Day. Andrew Young. OBCP
Christmas Day in the Workhouse. George R. Sims. BeLS; BLPA; TreF
(In the Workhouse.) OBCP
(In the Workhouse: Christmas Day.) PaPo
Christmas Day Is Come. Luke Wadding. OxBI
Christmas Day; the Family Sitting. John Meade Falkner. NOCV; OxBTC
Christmas declares the glory of the flesh. Christmas and Common Birth. Anne Ridler. FaBoTw
Christmas Dinner. Michael Rosen. OBCP
Christmas dinner was at two, The. A Summer Christmas in Australia. Douglas Sladen. OBCP
Christmas 1898, *sel.* Lewis Morris.
" 'Tis nigh two thousand years." TrPWD
Christmas Eve. A. R. Ammons. NAs
Christmas Eve. Patricia Beer. OBCP
Christmas Eve. Bible, *N.T.* St. Luke. *See* First Christmas, The.
Christmas Eve. Liam P. Clancy. ISi
Christmas Eve. John Davidson. *See* Ballad of Hell, A.
Christmas Eve. C. Day Lewis. EaLo
Christmas Eve. John Drinkwater. HBMV
Christmas Eve. Marion Edey. YeAr
Christmas Eve. Eugene Field. OHIP
Christmas Eve. Ted Kooser. GP
Christmas Eve. Catherine Parmenter. PGD
Christmas Eve. Karl Shapiro. NYBP
Christmas Eve. Robert Siegel. GeTw
Christmas Eve. *Unknown.* TRV
Christmas-Eve and Easter-Day, *sel.* Robert Browning.
Earth Breaks Up. TrCP
Christmas Eve, and it's silent tonight. December 24, 1979. Roger Weaver. SOTS
Christmas Eve, and twelve of the clock. The Oxen. Thomas Hardy. BiP; CMoP; CoBMV; EBEV; HAP; HBMV; InPK; LiTM; MoAB; MoBrPo; NoAM; NOBE; OAEL-2; OAEP; OBCP; OxBTC; PChr; PPoe; PPP; SoSe; WeW
Christmas Eve—Another Ceremony. Robert Herrick. OHIP
Christmas Eve Choral, A. Bliss Carman. ISi
Christmas Eve in France. Jessie Redmond Fauset. BANP
Christmas Eve in Nineteen-fourteen. Christmas 1914. Mike Harding. OBET
Christmas Eve in Whitneyville [1955]. Donald Hall. DiL; UnPo
Christmas Eve Service at Midnight at St. Michael's. Robert Bly. NNaP
Christmas Eve under Hooker's Statue. Robert Lowell. AP; CAPP; ConAP; FF; NePA; OxBA
Christmas Everywhere. Phillips Brooks. *See* Christmas Carol, A: "Everywhere, everywhere, Christmas tonight."
Christmas Family Reunion. Peter De Vries. NOBL
Christmas Folk-Song, A. Lizette Woodworth Reese. FaPON; HBMV; HBVY; OBCA; OHIP; OnMSP; SUS; TrCP
Christmas Ghost-Story, A. Thomas Hardy. OBWP
Christmas Greeting. *Unknown. See* Old Christmas Greeting, An.
Christmas Hymn, A. Cecil Frances Alexander. *See* Once in Royal David's City.
Christmas Hymn, A. Alfred Domett. GN; HBV-1; WGRP
(Christmas Hymn, 1837, A.) OBVV
"It is the calm and solemn night!" *sel.* PGD
Christmas Hymn, *sel.* St. Ephrem, *tr. fr. Syriac by* W. H. Kent.
"Virgin truly full of wonder." ISi
Christmas Hymn, A. Richard Wilbur. CoPo; OBCP; OFD; PChr; TrCP
Christmas Hymn, 1837, A. Alfred Domett. *See* Christmas Hymn, A.
Christmas in England. Sir Walter Scott. *See* Christmas in the Olden Time.
Christmas in Freelands. James Stephens. TrCP
Christmas in the Heart. *Unknown.* OHIP; SiSoSe
Christmas in the Olden Time. Sir Walter Scott. *Fr.* Marmion, *introd. to* VI. GoBC
(Christmas in England, *abr.*) GN
(Heap on More Wood!) OBCP
("Heap on more wood!—the wind is chill.") TiPo
(Old Christmastide.) SiSoSe
Christmas in the Wood. Frances Frost. TrCP
Christmas is coming [*or* a-coming],/ The geese are getting fat. *Unknown.* NTCP; OxNR; PChr; SoPo
Christmas is here. The Mahogany Tree. Thackeray. HBV-2
Christmas is in the air. Five Days Old. Francis Webb. PoAu-2
Christmas Is Really for the Children. Steve Turner. EBCP; OBCP
Christmas Is Remembering. Elsie Binns. SiSoSe
Christmas Island. Katharine Lee Bates. HBMV; HBVY
Christmas Landscape. Laurie Lee. OBCP
Christmas Legend, A. Frank Sidgwick. OHIP
Christmas Letter Home. G. S. Fraser. OxBTC
Christmas Lights. Valerie Worth. PChr
Christmas Lullaby. Ulrich Troubetzkoy. YeAr
Christmas Lullaby for a New-born Child. Yvonne Gregory. AmNP
Christmas Mass for a Little Atheist Jesus. Claude Maillard, *tr. fr. French by* Maxine W. Kumin *and* Judith Kumin. BoWoP
Christmas Message, A. Gavin Ewart. FaBoMo
Christmas Morn. *Unknown, tr. by* Ruth Sawyer. *See* Words from an Old Spanish Carol.

Christmas Morning. Harry Behn. PChr
Christmas Morning. Steven Lautermilch. AMV-80
Christmas Morning. Elizabeth Madox Roberts. MoAmPo; PChr; PoSC; SUS
Christmas Morning I. Carol Freeman. PChr; PoBA; TTY
(Gift.) PoNe
Christmas Mourning. Vassar Miller. CoPo; MoAmPo
Christmas Myth, 1973. Robert McGovern. SOTS
Christmas Night. Hugh MacCawell, *tr. fr. Irish by* Frank O'Connor. KiLC
Christmas Night. Lawrence Sail. OBCP
Christmas Night in the Quarters, *sel.* Irwin Russell.
Fust Banjo, De. AA; BLPA; HBV-2
Christmas Night of '62. William Gordon McCabe. AA
Christmas night: the solstice storm. The Narrows of Birth. William Everson. PoM
Christmas 1959 et Cetera. Gerald W. Barrax. OFD; PChr
Christmas 1944. Denise Levertov. NeBP
Christmas 1942. Eric Irvin. PoAu-2
Christmas 1914. Mike Harding. OBET
Christmas 1970. Spike Milligan. OBCP
Christmas, 1916. M. Winifred Wedgwood. SUMH
Christmas: 1924. Thomas Hardy. FaBoEE; OBCP; PV
Christmas Now Is Drawing Near. *Unknown.* OBET
Christmas Ornaments. Valerie Worth. PChr
Christmas Package, A, *sels.* David McCord.
"My stocking's where." PChr; RHPC
"That broken star." PChr
Christmas Pageant. Margaret Fishback. PoSC
Christmas Prayer, A. Molly Anderson Haley. PGD
Christmas Prayer, A. Herbert H. Hines. PGD
Christmas Prayer, A. George Macdonald. PChr; SUS
Christmas Prayer. Madeline Morse. PGD
Christmas Prayer, A. Robert Louis Stevenson. TrCP
Christmas Present, The. Patricia Hubbell. PDV
Christmas Rede. Jane Barlow. OBVV
Christmas, season of streamers, coloured lights. Christmas Story (1980). Pat Arrowsmith. BrRo
Christmas Sermon, A, *sel.* Robert Louis Stevenson.
To Be Honest, to Be Kind. PoLF
Christmas Shopping. Louis MacNeice. OBCP
Christmas Silence, The. Margaret Deland. OHIP
Christmas Singing. Elsie Williams Chandler. SiSoSe
Christmas Song. Bliss Carman. PeCV; PoSC
Christmas Song. Eugene Field, *wr. at. to* Lydia Avery Coonley Ward. OHIP; YeAr
(Why Do the Bells of Christmas Ring.) SoPo
Christmas Song. Elizabeth-Ellen Long. SiSoSe
Christmas Songs. Gerta Kennedy. PoPl
Christmas Sonnet, A. E. A. Robinson. EaLo
Christmas star burns overhead, The. Childlike Heart. Ellen Weston Catlin. PGD
Christmas Story (1980). Pat Arrowsmith. BrRo
Christmas Thank You's. Mick Gower. OBCP
Christmas, the Year One, A.D. Sara Henderson Hay. PoRA
Christmas Tree, The. Patricia Beer. OBCP
Christmas Tree, A. William Burford. NePA; SoSe
Christmas Tree. Stanley Cook. OBCP
Christmas Tree, The. Peter Cornelius. PChr
Christmas Tree. Aileen Fisher. PDV
Christmas Tree. Laurence Smith. OBCP
Christmas Tree in the Nursery, The. Richard Watson Gilder. HBVY; OHIP
Christmas Trees, The. Mary F. Butts. OHIP
Christmas Trees. Geoffrey Hill. NOCV
Christmas Trees (A Christmas Circular Letter). Robert Frost. BiP
Christmas twigs crispen and needles rattle, The. New Year's Poem. Margaret Avison. LiTM; NOBC; OBCV
Christmas was in the air and all was well. Karma. E. A. Robinson. AmPP; AP; CMoP; CoBMV; HeIP; MoAB; MoAmPo; NoAM; OFD; TrCP
"Christo et Ecclesiae" 1700. Oliver Wendell Holmes. *Fr.* Two Sonnets: Harvard. AP
Christofero had a mind. The Great Discovery. Eleanor Farjeon. PoSC
Christofo Columbo, *with music. Unknown.* AmSS
Christofo Colombo was a hungry man. Mysterious Biography. Carl Sandburg. OFD; SiSoSe
Christographia 35. Eugene Warren. AMV-80
Christophe. Russell Atkins. PoNe
Christopher at Birth. Michael Longley. CIP
Christopher Columbus. Franklin P. Adams. InMe
Christopher Columbus, *sels.* William Hart-Smith.
Cipangu. PoAu-2
Comes Fog and Mist. PoAu-2
Departure. PoAu-2
Space. PoAu-2
Waterspout, The. PoAu-2
Christopher Marlowe. Michael Drayton. *Fr.* To Henry Reynolds, of Poets and Poesy. ChTr
Christopher Marlowe. Swinburne. TrGrPo
Christopher of the Shenandoah, A. Edith M. Thomas. PAH
Christopher Robin goes/ Hoppity, hoppity. Hoppity. A. A. Milne. FaBV; NTCP; TiPo
Christopher Street Liberation Day, June 28, 1970. Fran Winant. PeHV
Christopher White. *Unknown.* ESPB
Christ's Bondservant. George Matheson. STF; TRV
(Christian Freedom). TrPWD
Christ's Coming. *Unknown. See* Coming of Christ, The.
Christ's Descent into Hell. Rainer Maria Rilke, *tr. fr. German by* James Wright *and* Sarah Youngblood. Prf
Christ's Gift to Man. *Unknown. See* Divine Love.
Christ's Kirk on the Green. *At. to* James V, King of Scotland. OxBS
Christ's Life Our Code, *with music.* Benjamin Copeland. AH
Christ's Love-Song. *Unknown.* OxBM
Christ's Nativity. Henry Vaughan. AnAnS-1; SBVL
Christ's Plea to Mankind. *Unknown.* OxBM
Christ's Prayer in Gethsemane. *Unknown.* SeCePo
Christ's Reply. Edward Taylor. *Fr.* God's Determinations. PoEL-3
Christ's Resurrection and Ascension. Philip Doddridge. NOCV
Christ's Sleeping Friends. Robert Southwell. AnAnS-1
Christ's Tear Breaks My Heart. *Unknown. See* Lovely Tear of Lovely Eye.
Christ's Victory and Triumph, *sels.* Giles Fletcher.
Christ's Triumph after Death, IV.
Celestial City, The. NOBE; OBS
Easter Morn. EIL; NOCV
"Had I a voice of steel to tune my song." LoBV
Halcyon's Nest, The FaBoPP
Heavenly Jerusalem, The. OxBoCh
Christ's Triumph over Death, III.
On the Crucifixion. EBCP; OxBoCh
"So down the silver streams of Eridan." LoBV
Christ's Victory in Heaven, I.
Excellency of Christ. WGRP
(He Is a Path.) TRV
Mercy Pleads for Mankind. JCP
"She was a virgin of austere regard." ViBoPo
Christ's Victory on Earth, II.
"His haire was blacke and in small curls did twine." SeCV-1
"Love is the blossom where there blows." LO; ViBoPo
(Wooing Song.) EIL; HBV-1; OBEV
Christus; a Mystery, *sels.* Longfellow.
Fate of the Prophets, The, *fr.* I, Introitus. WGRP
Flight into Egypt, The, *fr.* II, 3. OBVV
Christus Consolator. Rossiter Worthington Raymond. HBV-2
Christus Mattaeum et Discipulos Alloquitur. Sir Edward Sherburne. ACP
Christus natus est! the cock. The Animals' Carol. Charles Causley. NAs
Chrome Babies Eating Chocolate Snowmen in the Moonlight. A. K. Redwing. VoR
Chromis. Phineas Fletcher. *Fr.* Piscatorie Eclogues. LoBV
Chromo. Sarah Webster Fabio. CNA
Chronicle, The. Abraham Cowley. *See* Chronicle, The; a Ballad.
Chronicle. Edward Dorn. TAT
Chronicle, *sel.* Robert of Gloucester.
Town against Gown at Oxford. OxBM
Chronicle, A. *Unknown.* BLPL; NA
Chronicle, The; a Ballad. Abraham Cowley. SeCV-1
(Chronicle, The.) GoTL; ViBoPo
Chronicle "Green Sheet" dries out, The. News. Dennis Schmitz. NPGG
Chronicle of the Drum, The, *sel.* Thackeray.
"Ah, gentle, tender lady mine!" ViBoPo
Chronicler, The. Alexander Bergman. TrJP
Chronicles: Number Three. Mei Berssenbrugge. GP
Chronology. Turner Cassity. PoA
Chronos, Chronos, mend thy pace. The Secular Masque. Dryden. PoEL-3; PrIm; SeCeV; SeCV-2
Chrysalides. Thomas Kinsella. BIrV; NoAM
Chrysalis, A. Mary Emily Bradley. AA; HBV-1
Chrysanthemum Show, The. C. Day Lewis. MoVE
Chrysanthemums/ come in spring too, now. For Murasaki. Josephine Jacobsen. FAZ
Chrysothemis. Henry Reed. MoVE
Chuck Will's Widow Song. *Unknown.* BPo
"Chuff! chuff! chuff!" An' a mountain-bluff. A Song of Panama. Damon Runyon. PAH
Chug! Puff! Chug! Tugs. James S. Tippett. FaPON

Chugachimute I Love the Name. Rochelle Owens. CoPo
Chums, The. Theodore Roethke. NoAM
Church, The. Edwin Ford Piper. WGRP
Church, The. Jules Romains, *tr. fr. French by* Jethro Bithell. WGRP
Church,/ Chapel. *Unknown.* OxNR
Church and Church-Yard at Night. Robert Blair. *Fr.* The Grave. OBEC
("See yonder hallowed fane, the pious work.") ViBoPo
Church and clergy here, no doubt, The. Swift. DBV
Church and State. W. B. Yeats. CMoP
Church and the World walked far apart, The. The Church Walking with the World. Matilda C. Edwards. BLPA
Church at little Winwick, The. Winwick, Lancashire. GBP
Church Bell in the Night, The. *Unknown, tr. fr. Old Irish by* Kuno Meyer. AnIL
(Church Bell at Night, The, *tr. by* Howard Mumford Jones.) OnYI
Church Bells. Berton Braley. TDH
Church bells are ringing, The. Sunday up the River, IV. James Thomson ('B. V.'). OAEP
Church bells in gray air. Sundays. Marieve Rugo. AMV-81
Church Burning: Mississippi. James A. Emanuel. PoBA; PoNe
Church do zeem a touchèn zight, The. Vo'k a-Comen into Church. William Barnes. OxBoCh
Church Floor[e], The. George Herbert. AnAnS-1; EBEV; MeLP; OAEL-1; OBS; SeCePo; SeCeV
Church Going. Philip Larkin. CMoP; GTBS-P; InPK; LiTM; MoBrPo; MP; NePoEA; NIP; NoAM; NoP; OAEL-2; PAI; PPP; PrIm; SCV; TwCP; UnPo
Church in the Heart, The. Morris Abel Beer. TRV
Church is a business, and the rich, The. After Lorca. Robert Creeley. ConAP; InPS; LCAP; NaP; POL
"Church is dead, The," said brother Brown. The Pastor's Friend. *Unknown.* STF
Church Lock and Key. George Herbert. AnAnS-1
Church Militant, *sel.* George Herbert.
L'Envoy: "King of glory, King of heaven." AnAnS-1
Church Monuments. George Herbert. AnAnS-1; CABA; HAP; JCP; NOCV; NoP; OAEL-1; QFR
Church Mouse, The. Gerald Bullett. BoAnP
Church Mouse commends: tapeworms and slugs grow wings. Critics and Poets. Geoffrey Grigson. FaBoEE
Church Musick. George Herbert. AnAnS-1; SeCV-1; UnS
Church of a Dream, The. Lionel Johnson. OAEL-2; OBMV
Church of England, The. Dryden. *Fr.* The Hind and the Panther, I. OBS
Church of England's Glory, The. *Unknown.* APAS
Church of Galilee, The. Muriel Rukeyser. *Fr.* The Gates. GP
Church of San Antonio de la Florida, The. Paul Petrie. NYBP
Church of the Revolution, The. Hezekiah Butterworth. PAH
Church of the Sacred Heart, The. Ashton Greene. NePoAm
Church of Vice-Morcate, The. View by Color Photography on a Commercial Calendar. William Carlos Williams. LCAP
Church on Comiaken Hill, The. Richard Hugo. LCAP; Prf
Church Poem. Joyce Carol Thomas. CNA
Church Porch, The. George Herbert. AnAnS-1
"Let vain or busy thoughts have there no part," *sel.* TRV
Church Romance, A. Thomas Hardy. FaBoTw; NOBE; OxBTC; VLP
Church Scene, The. Longfellow. *Fr.* Evangeline. TreF
Church Street wears ever a smile, from having watched bright belles. Streets. Douglas Goldring. HBMV
Church the Garden of Christ, The. Isaac Watts. NOCV
Church Today, The. Sir William Watson. WGRP
Church tower crowned the town, A. The Glass Town. Alastair Reid. NYBP
Church Triumphant, The. John Addington Symonds. *See* These Things Shall Be.
Church Universal, The. Samuel Longfellow. WGRP
Church Walking with the World, The. Matilda C. Edwards. BLPA
Church Windows, The. George Herbert. *See* Windows, The.
Church-Windows, The. *Unknown. Fr.* A Poem, in Defence of the Decent Ornaments of Christ-Church, Oxon, Occasioned by a Banbury Brother, Who Called Them Idolatries. OBS
Churches are best for prayer, that have least light. Dark Churches. John Donne. *Fr.* A Hymn to Christ, at the Author's Last Going into Germany. FaBoRV
Churches, lord, all the dark churches, The. Crag Jack's Apostasy. Ted Hughes. EaLo
Churches of Rome and of England, The. Dryden. *Fr.* The Hind and the Panther, I. ACP
("Milk white Hind, immortal and unchang'd, A.") SeCV-2
Church's One Foundation, The. Samuel J. Stone. TreFT; VLP; WGRP
Church's one foundation, The. Battle Hymn of the Spanish Rebellion. L. A. Mackay. OBCV
Church's Restoration, The. Hymn. John Betjeman. FaBoPa
Church's Testimony, The. Dryden. *Fr.* The Hind and the Panther, I. ACP
("But, gratious God, how well dost thou provide.") TrPWD
Churchyard, The. Robert Buchanan. HBV-2
Churchyard. Robert Hass. NPGG
Churchyard leans to the sea with its dead, The. The Old Churchyard of [*or* at] Bonchurch. Philip Bourke Marston. EBVV; HBV-2; NBM; OBNC; OBVV
Churchyard of St. Mary Magdalene, Old Milton. John Heath-Stubbs. NePoEA
Churchyard on the Sands, The. Lord De Tabley. CH, *abr.*; FaBoPP; GBL; HBV-1; LoBV; OBNC
Churl that wants another's fare, The. The Dog in the River. Phaedrus, *tr. by* Christopher Smart. AWP
Churning the compost, dazed. To Earth. James Applewhite. PoA
Cibber! write all thy verses upon glasses. Pope. FaBoEE
Cicada, The. H. M. Green. PoAu-1
Cicada. John Haines. NPAW
Cicada, The. Ou-yang Hsiu, *tr. fr. Chinese by* Arthur Waley. AWP
Cicada. Adrien Stoutenburg. NYBP; RFM
Cicada-Shell. Basho, *tr. fr. Japanese.* SoPo
Cicadas are dying, The. Homecoming Celebration. Rosemary Catacalos. AMV-80
Cicadas in brambled foliage, The. The House-Builders. Kamala Das. PBWP
Cider and Vesalius. John Peck. AmPA
Cider Song. Mildred Weston. BoNaP
Cid's Rising, The. Felicia Dorothea Hemans. OBRV
Cigales. Richard Wilbur. NePoEA; NoAM; NOBA
Cigar Smoke, Sunday, after Dinner. Louise Townsend Nicholl. FYAP; NePoAm
Cigarette, A. *Mongol Oral Tradition, tr. by* C. R. Bawden. WTO
Cigarette for the Bambino. Gavin Ewart. WaP
Cigarette my girl is smoking, A. Jealousy. *Malay Oral Tradition, tr. by* R. J. Wilkinson *and* R. O. Winstedt. WTO
Cigarette Poem, The. Faye Kicknosway. IHMS
Cigarette smoke floated. Milne's Bar. Norman MacCaig. FaBoTw
Cigarettes Will Spoil Yer Life, *with music. Unknown.* AS
Cimabuella. Bayard Taylor. BXAP
Cincinnati. Cid Corman. GP
Cincirinella Had a Mule. *Unknown, tr. fr. Italian by* Maria Cimino. FaPON
Cinco de Mayo, 1862. A. A. Rios. GP
Cincophrenicpoet. Bob Kaufman. PoNe
Cinderella. Feroz Ahmed-ud-Din. DFT
Cinderella. Olga Broumas. DFT
Cinderella. Randall Jarrell. DFT; LCAP
Cinderella. Roger Mitchell. DFT
Cinderella. Cynthia Pickard. DFT; PoPl
Cinderella. Sylvia Plath. DFT
Cinderella. Ruby C. Saunders. BlSi
Cinderella Grass. Aileen Fisher. DFT
Cinderella Liberated. Anne Hussey. DFT
Cinderella's Song. Elizabeth Madox Roberts. DFT
Cindy. *Unknown.* BLSo, *shorter version, with music*; FSW; TrAS, *with music*; TreFS
Cinema at the Lighthouse. Henri Coulette. *Fr.* The War of the Secret Agents. NePoEA-2
Cinéma Vérité. Dorothy Walters. IHMS
Cinnamon and sugar man, Andrew Young, A. Status Symbols. Anne Sostrom. SOTS
Cinnamon Peeler, The. Michael Ondaatje. NOBC
Cino. Ezra Pound. VGW
Cinq Ans Après. Gelett Burgess. *See* Ah, Yes, I Wrote "The Purple Cow."
Cinquain: A Warning. Adelaide Crapsey. *See* Warning, The.
Cinque. Janet Campbell Hale. VoR
Cinque Port, A. John Davidson. BrPo; PoPle; VLP
Cinque Ports, The. *Unknown.* FaBoUs
Cipangu. William Hart-Smith. *Fr.* Christopher Columbus. PoAu-2
Circa 1814. David Staudt. AMV-80
Circe. Lord De Tabley. VLP
Circe. Hilda Doolittle ("H. D."). PoRA
Circe. William Gibson. PoA
Circe. A. D. Hope. PPP
Circe. Louis MacNeice. OBMV
Circle, The. Carol Coates. CaP
Circle, The. Jean Garrigue. LiTA; MoPo
Circle, A. Theodore Spencer. NYBP
Circle, A/ and, in this circle, another. A Circular Cry. Edmond Jabes, *tr. by* Anthony Rudolf. VWA
Circle, a Square, a Triangle and a Ripple of Water, A. Jane Cooper. TAP
Circle Begins, A. Harold Littlebird. STE
Circle Game, The, *sels.* Margaret Atwood.
"Being with you." MoCV

"Returning to the room." MoCV
"Summer again." MoCV
Circle of Struggle. William Pitt Root. NYBP
Circle to the left, Old Brass Wagon. Old Brass Wagon. *Unknown.* AS
Circles. Elizabeth Knies. AMV-80
Circles. Carl Sandburg. AmFN
Circles never fully round, but change, The. Perspective of Co-ordination. Arthur Davison Ficke. PoA
Circlet, The. The Numbers. Joel Oppenheimer. CoPo
Circling shadow on the measured dial, The. Chronology. Turner Cassity. PoA
Circling upon his star. The Sleepwalker. Nelly Sachs, *tr. by* Michael Hamburger. NYBP
Circuit Breaker. Sid Gary. QQQ
Circuit closes, The. House and heart. Winter Night. Louis O. Coxe. NYBP
Circuit Judge, The. Edgar Lee Masters. *Fr.* Spoon River Anthology. FaBoEE
Circular Cry, A. Edmond Jabes, *tr. fr. French by* Anthony Rudolf. VWA
Circulation, The. Thomas Washbourne. NOCV
Circulation of the Blood, The. Sir Richard Blackmore. *Fr.* Creation. FaBoUs
Circumambulation of Mt. Tamalpais. Andrew Hoyem. PoA
Circumcision, The. Linda Zisquit. VWA
Circumstance. Thomas Bailey Aldrich. AA
Circumstance. Laurie Stroblas. AMV-80
Circumstance without Pomp. John Kendall. WhC
Circus. Eleanor Farjeon. SUS
Circus, The. Milton Kaplan. GoYe
Circus, The. Elizabeth Madox Roberts. FaPON; SoPo
Circus, The. E. B. White. InMe
Circus Animals' Desertion, The. W. B. Yeats. BiP; CMoP; FaBoMo; FaBoTw; LiTB; MAT; NiP; NoAM; NOBE; NoP; OAEL-2; OAEP; OxBTC; PAI; PP; PrIm; TEP
Circus Dancer, A. Celia Dropkin, *tr. fr. Yiddish by* Howard Schwartz. VWA
Circus Garland, A, *sels.* Rachel Field.
Acrobat. SoPo
Equestrienne. OBCA
(Girl on the Milk-White Horse, The.) SoPo
Gunga. OBCA
(Elephant, The.) SoPo
Next Day. SoPo
(Epilogue: "Nothing now to mark the spot.") OBCA
Parade. OBCA; SoPo
Performing Seal, The. OBCA; RHPC; SoPo; TiPo
Circus Lion. C. Day Lewis. BoAnP; PoPle
Circus Maximus. George Bowering. PeCV
Circus of battleships carrying heavy laughter, A. Celebrated Return. Clarence Major. AmNP
Circus Parade, The. Olive Beaupré Miller. SoPo; TiPo
Circus Parade, The. Katherine Pyle. OBCA
Circus-Postered Barn, The. Elizabeth J. Coatsworth. MoAmPo
Circus Ringmaster's Apology to God, The. Norman Dubie. MAYP
Circus Ship *Euzkera,* The. Walker Gibson. FiBHP
Circus was never meant for children, The. The Circus. Milton Kaplan. GoYe
Cirque d'Hiver. Elizabeth Bishop. LiTA; MiAP
Cirrus bow of surf is blown, The. A Fantasy of Little Waters. James Scully. NYBP
Cit, a Common-Council-Man by place, The. What Is't to Us? Charles Churchill. *Fr.* Night; an Epistle to Robert Lloyd. SeCePo
Citation and Examination of William Shakespeare, The, *sel.* Walter Savage Landor.
Maid's Lament, The. HBV-1; OBEV; OBNC; OBRV; OBVV
Cities, The. "Æ." OBMV
Cities. Hilda Doolittle ("H. D."). ViBoPo
Cities and Science. David McCord. AmFN
Cities and Seas. Norman Jordan. PoNe
Cities and Thrones and Powers. Kipling. *Fr.* Puck of Pook's Hill. FaBoEn; GoJo; MoVE; NOBE; OBNC; OxBTC; PoEL-5; SeCeV; VLP
Cities and towns, ye haunts of wretchedness! Industrial Evils. Joseph Cottle. *Fr.* Malvern Hills. NOEC
Cities are walled. It is a cruel land. Memory. Babette Deutsch. PoA
Cities are washed into time, The. John Oliver Simon. NeAC
Cities behind Glass. Linda Hogan. STE
Cities Drowned. Sir Henry Newbolt. CH
Cities #8, *sel.* Victor Hernandez Cruz.
"Little cousins/ play on your." BOLo
Cities of dream wander under the bark of a December forest, The. A December Forest. Vesna Krmpotic, *tr. by* Vasa D. Mihailovich. WPOW
Cities send to one another saying, The: "My sons are mad." Blake. *Fr.* Vala; or, The Four Zoas. ViBoPo
Citizen. Louis Grudin. NePA
Citizen, The. Vilma Howard. NNP
Citizen. Chris Wallace-Crabbe. CBAP
Citizen and the Red Lion of Brentford, The. Christopher Smart. NCEP
Citizen, myself, or personal friend. More Sonnets at Christmas, IV. Allen Tate. WaP
Citizenship; Form 8889512, Sub-Section Q. G. K. Chesterton. OxBoLi
Cit's Country Box, The. Robert Lloyd. NOEC
City, The. "Æ." WGRP
City, The. John Betjeman. TEP
City. Raymond Biasotti. AMV-80
City. Joseph Bruchac. CDW
City, The. Robert Creeley. LCAP
City. Langston Hughes. FaPON; PDV; RHPC
(City: San Francisco.) AmFN
City, The. David Ignatow. PCP
City, The. Ben Maddow. WaP
City. Timothy P. Mocarski. AMV-81
City, The. Frank Mason North. *See* Where Cross the Crowded Ways of Life.
City, The. Linda Pastan. NYP
City. Jane Stembridge. NMM
City. Joseph Stroud. NPGG
City, The. James Thomson ("B. V."). *See* Proem: "Lo, thus, as prostrate, 'In the dust I write.' "
City Afternoon. John Ashbery. HeIP
City Afternoon. Barbara Howes. AmFN
City asleep. The City Dump. Felice Holman. RHPC
City bred. Moon. Frances Horovitz. BrRo
City Butterfly. Charles Siebert. NYP
City by the Sea, The. George Sterling. BPAW
City Child, The. Tennyson. OxBChV
City Church, The. "E. H. K." WGRP
City, City. Marci Ridlon. RHPC
City Clerk, The. Thomas Ashe. EBVV; OBVV
City clocks point out the hours, The. Belfast: High Street. Padraic Colum. NePoAm
City Dead-House, The. Walt Whitman. InPK
City Dump, The. Felice Holman. RHPC
City Eclogue, A. "W. J." NOEC
City Flower, A. Austin Dobson. TEP
City Girl. Maxwell Bodenheim. HBMV
City Graveyard, A. Joyce Carol Oates. DFF
City had withdrawn into itself, The. Christmas Trees (A Christmas Circular Letter). Robert Frost. BiP
City has streets, The. City Streets and Country Roads. Eleanor Farjeon. SoPo; TiPo
City! I am true son of thine. Glasgow. Alexander Smith. BSV
City in the Sea, The. Poe. AA; AmPP; AP; FaBoEn; HBV-2; LiTA; MAT; MOS; NePA; NOBA; NoP; OxBA; PoEL-4; SCV; TAP; TrGrPo; ViBoPo; WHA
(Doomed City, The.) OBRV
City is of Night, The; perchance of Death. James Thomson ("B. V."). The City of Dreadful Night, I. EBVV; LiTB; OAEP; PoEL-5; ViBoPo; VLP
City Jail. J. J. Maloney. LFAC
City Life. D. H. Lawrence. CAD; OAEP
City Lights. Rachel Field. FaPON; PDV; RHPC
City Limits, The. A. R. Ammons. NoAM; NOBA; NoP; NYP
City, Lord, Where Thy Dear Life, The, *with music.* William E. Dudley. AH
City, The: Midnight. Bruce Dawe. PoAu-2
City Mouse and the Garden Mouse, The. Christina Rossetti. *Fr.* Sing-Song. FaBoBe; FaPON; HBV-1; HBVY; NTCP
("City mouse lived in a house, The.") SUS; TiPo
City Nights: In Bohemia. Arthur Symons. SyP
(In Bohemia.) BrPo
City Nights: In the Train. Arthur Symons. SyP
(In the Train.) VLP
City of ascensions, A. A Jerusalem Notebook. Harvey Shapiro. AMV-81
City of Baltimore, The, *with music. Unknown.* ShS
City of Beggars, The. Alfred Hayes. WaP
City of Dreadful Night, The, *abr.* James Thomson ("B. V."). OBNC
Sels.
"Although lamps burn along the silent streets," III. EBVV
"Anear the centre of that northern crest," XXI. FaBoEn; GTBS-P; OAEP; VLP
(City's Queen, The.) NOBE
"As I came through the desert thus it was," *fr.* IV. BSV; LiTB; NBM
"City is of Night, The; perchance of Death," I. EBVV; LiTB; OAEP; PoEL-5; ViBoPo; VLP
"He stood alone within the spacious square," IV. WiR

"I sat me weary on a pillar's base," XX. BSV; NBM; OAEP; VLP
"Large glooms were gathered in the mighty fane," XIV. EBEV; OAEL-2; OAEP
"Mansion stood apart in its own ground, The," X. BSV
"Mighty river flowing dark and deep, The," XIX. EBVV
"Of all things human which are strange and wild," XIII. LoBV; ViBoPo
Proem: "Lo, thus, as prostrate, 'In the dust I write.'" GoTS; OAEP; OxBS; ViBoPo; VLP
(City, The.) NOBE
"What men are they who haunt these fatal glooms," XI. EBVV
City of Esteli, The. June 10. Magdalena de Rodriguez, *tr. by* Nina Serrano. WPOW
City of Falling Leaves, The. Amy Lowell. SUS; TiPo; TwAmPo
City of God. Samuel Johnson. AA; FaPoR; TRV; WGRP
City of God, The. Francis Turner Palgrave. WGRP
City of Light. Nahum Bomze, *tr. fr. Yiddish by* Gabriel Preil *and* Howard Schwartz. VWA
City of mist and rain and blown gray spaces. Edinburgh. Alfred Noyes. HBV-2
City of Orgies. Walt Whitman. NYP
City of Prague, The. William Jeffery Prowse. CenHV
City of Satisfactions, The. Daniel Hoffman. CoPo; Prf
City of Slaughter, The. Hayyim Nahman Bialik, *tr. fr. Hebrew by* A. M. Klein. TrJP
City of tense and stricken faces. Jackson, Mississippi. Margaret Walker. FB
City of the Dead, The. Richard Burton. HBV-2
City of the End of Things, The. Archibald Lampman. NOBC; OBCV
City of the Moon, The, *sel.* Kenneth Rexroth.
"Buddha took some Autumn leaves." GP
City of the Soul, The. Lord Alfred Douglas. HBMV
Each New Hour's Passage Is the Acolyte, *sel.* WHA
City, Oh, City! Jack Prelutsky. RHPC
City Pigeons. Helen Chasin. WeW
City planners. To the New Annex to the Detroit County Jail. Richard W. Thomas. PoBA
City Rain. Rachel Field. SoPo; TiPo
City Rat and the Country Rat, The. La Fontaine. *See* Town Rat and the Country Rat, The.
City Rises, The. James Cunningham. JB
City rises, The. A Poem for Democrats. Amiri Baraka. CAPP
City Roofs. Charles Hanson Towne. BLPA
City: San Francisco. Langston Hughes. *See* City.
City Shower in Imitation of Virgil's Georgics, A. Swift. *See* Description of a City Shower, A.
City shuffles through the snow, the whirling snow, and I, indifferent, The. Dead of Winter. Anthony Towne. NYBP
City Song, A. John Hanlon Mitchell. CaP
City Songs. Mark Van Doren. NYBP
City Sparrow. Jane Mayhall. TAP
City squats on my back, The. Route Six. Stanley Kunitz. AMV-80
City-Storm. Harold Monro. MoBrPo
City Streets and Country Roads. Eleanor Farjeon. SoPo; TiPo
City Traffic. Eve Merriam. PDV
City Tree, The. Isabella Valancy Crawford. CaP
City Trees. Vere Dargan. PGD
City Trees. Edna St. Vincent Millay. FaPON
City Walk-up, Winter 1969. Carolyn Forché. MAYP
City which thou seest no other deem, The. Rome. Milton. *Fr.* Paradise Regained, IV. OBS
City, whose streets are wavering reflections. Canal Street. John Wheelwright. PoA
City without Smoke. Edwin Denby. NYP
City without Walls. W. H. Auden. NYBP; NYP
City yawns, The. Sunrise. Frank Asch. RHPC
City's Crown, The. William Dudley Foulke. HBMV; WGRP
City's Queen, The. James Thomson ("B. V."). The City of Dreadful Night, XXI. NOBE
("Anear the centre of that northern crest.") FaBoEn; GTBS-P; OAEP; VLP
City's taken off her winter things, The. Spring. Vladimir Mayakovsky, *tr. by* Babette Deutsch. CAD
Civil Defense. Kenneth Burke. OBAL
Civil Elegies, *sel.* Dennis Lee.
"Often I sit in the sun and brooding over the city, always." NOBC
Civil Irish and Wild Irish. Laoiseach Mac an Bhaird, *tr. fr. Late Middle Irish by* Kenneth Jackson. AnIL
Civil Riot, *sel.* G. D. H. Cole.
"And you'll say a nation totters." OxBTC
Civil Servant, A. Robert Graves. InPK
Civil Service, The. William Langland, *mod. by* Donald Attwater. *Fr.* The Vision of Piers Plowman. NOCV
Civil War. Charles Dawson Shanly. HBV-2; PAH
Civil War. Mark Van Doren. MoVE
Civil Wars, The, *sel.* Samuel Daniel.
"It was upon the twilight of that day," *fr.* VIII. OBWP
Civile, res ago [*or* si ergo]. See, Will, 'Ere's a Go. *Unknown.* ChTr; FaBoNo; WhC
Civilian. Josephine Miles. WPE
Civilian for a pause of hours. Goodmorning with Light. John Ciardi. WaP
Civilities of Lamplight. Charles Tomlinson. OxBC
Civility a Bogey. Margaret Avison. NOBC
Civilization. Tom Schmidt. NeAC
Civilization and Its Discontents. John Ashbery. CAPP; LCAP; TwCP
Civilization is hooped together, brought. Meru. W. B. Yeats. InPS; NoAM; OAEL-2; PoA
Civilized, crying how to be human again: this will tell you how. Signpost. Robinson Jeffers. GoYe; ViBoPo
Civilizing the Child. Lisel Mueller. CTBA
Clabe Mott. James Still. GrPl
Clack your beaks you cormorants and kittiwakes. A Canticle to the Waterbirds. William Everson. NeAP; PoM
Clad All in White. Abraham Cowley. *Fr.* The Mistress. SeCV-1
Clad in the wealthy robes his genius wrought. On Shakespeare and Voltaire. Thomas Holcroft. NOEC
Claim That Has the Canker on the Rose, The. Joseph Plunkett. OxBI
Claim to Love. Giovanni Battista Guarini, *tr. fr. Italian by* Thomas Stanley. AWP
Clair de Lune. Anthony Hecht. NYBP
Clair de Lune. Arthur Symons. SyP
Clair de Lune. Paul Verlaine, *tr. fr. French by* Arthur Symons. AWP; MOON
Clamb ape mountain backwards. To Be Quicker. Don L. Lee. JB
Clamdigger, The. Dionis Coffin Riggs. TAT
Clamming. Reed Whittemore. NYBP; TAP
Clamour of the wind making music. St. Columcille, *tr. fr. Irish by* John Montague. BIrV
Clams. Stanley Moss. GP
Clams. Ishigaki Rin, *tr. fr. Japanese by* Hiroaki Sato. PBWP
Clancy. David Wagoner. PH
Clancy of the Overflow. A. B. Paterson. PoAu-1
Clandestine Work. Yvan Goll, *tr. fr. French by* Anthony Rudolf. VWA
"Clang!" goes the high-framed, feather-tufted gong. "Tan Ta Ra, Cries Mars . . ." David Wagoner. NePoAm-2
Clap, clap the double nightcap on! William Gifford. Walter Savage Landor. FaBoEE; GTBS-P
Clap hands, clap hands/ Hie, Tommy Randy. *Unknown.* OxNR
Clap hands, clap hands/ Till father comes home. *Unknown.* OxNR
Clap hands, Daddy comes/ With his pocket full of plums. *Unknown.* OxNR
Clap hands, Daddy's coming/ Up the waggon way. *Unknown.* OxNR
Clap hands with festal joy, O holy people. Hymn for Laudes Feast of Our Lady of Good Counsel. *Unknown, tr. by* Sister Maura. ISi
Clap Your Hands for Herod. Josef Hanzlik, *tr. fr. Czech by* Ian Milner. OBCP
Clapping her platter stood plump Bess. Chicken. Walter de la Mare. TiPo
Clapping the door to, in the little light. Charwoman. Ben Belitt. SaC
Clara. Ezra Pound. DTC
Clare Coast. Emily Lawless. OxBI
Clare de Kitchen. *Unknown.* BLPA
Clarel, *sels.* Herman Melville.
Epilogue: "If Luther's day expand to Darwin's year." AP; ImOP
Of Rome. OxBA
On Mammon. OxBA
Prelusive. AmPP
Sodom. AmPP
Ungar and Rolfe. OxBA
Claremont. Robert Peters. GP
Clarence ("Clarence Lee from Tennessee"). Shel Silverstein. OBCA
Clarence Mangan. Thomas Kinsella. CIP
Clarence Short Bull died. Sitting Bull's Will versus the Sioux Treaty of 1868 and Monty Hall. A. K. Redwing. VoR
Clarendon had law and sense. On the Young Statesmen. Charles Sackville. APAS
Clare's Dragoons. Thomas Osborne Davis. OnYI
Clari, the Maid of Milan, *sel.* John Howard Payne.
Home, Sweet Home! AA; BLPA; BLSo; FaBoBe; FaFP; FSW; HBV-2; PaPo; PSoN; TreF; WBLP
Claribel. Tennyson. PeD
Clarified into present. The Exchanges II. Robert Kelly. CoPo
Clarimonde. Théophile Gautier, *tr. fr. French by* Lafcadio Hearn. AWP
Clarinda's Indifference at Parting with Her Beauty. Countess of Winchilsea. SBG

Clarion-Call, The. *Unknown.* BLRP
Claritas. Denise Levertov. VGW
Claritas. Gerrye Payne. NWP
Clarity. A. R. Ammons. TAP
Clarity of Apples, The. Terry M. Perlin. AMV-80
Clark Colven and his gay ladie. Clerk Colvill. *Unknown.* ESPB
Clark Sanders. *Unknown.* *See* Clerk Saunders.
Clash of arms which shook the Persian state, The. Abdolonymus the Sidonian. Jones Very. AP
Clash of salutation. As keels thrust into shingle. Geoffrey Hill. Mercian Hymns, XVI. NoP
Clash with Cliches, A. Vassar Miller. AMV-80; FAZ
Clasp her and hold her and love her. At Sunset. Louis V. Ledoux. HBV-1
Clasp you the God within yourself. The Last Round. Anna Wickham. MoBrPo
Clasping of Hands. George Herbert. ILwL; PoEL-2
Class, The. Josephine Jacobsen. GP
Class Dismissed. *Unknown, tr. fr. Greek by* Louis Untermeyer. UnTE
Class Incident from Graves. Alan Brownjohn. OxBTC
Class of 19—. Frederick Dec. PCP
Class was history, that's, The. Before. Albert Goldbarth. MAYP
Classic. A. R. Ammons. NOBA
Classic Anthology, The, *sel.* Confucius, *tr. fr. Chinese by* Ezra Pound.
Chou and the South. CTC
Classic Ballroom Dances. Charles Simic. GeTw; LCAP
Classic Case, A. Gilbert Sorrentino. NeAP
Classic Encounter." Christopher Caudwell." OxBTC
Classic Idyll, A. Avraham Huss, *tr. fr. Hebrew by* Mark Elliott Shapiro. VWA
Classic landscapes of dreams are not, The. The Snowfall. Donald Justice. NePoEA-2; VGW
Classic Ode, A. Charles Battell Loomis. NA
Classic Scene. William Carlos Williams. OxBA
Classic Waits for Me, A. E. B. White. BXAP; NYBP; Par; SpRo; WhC
Classical Autumn. Robert Clayton Casto. AMV-81
Classical engine of death moves my day, The. Hurrying me. Burning and Fathering; Accounts of My Country. Jack Gilbert. NPGG
Classical key, A. Cubist Blues in Poltergeist Major. Allan F. Kipp. AMV-81
Classical Quatrain, A. Paul Goodman. VGW
Classical Style, The. Michael Palmer. NPGG
Classroom in October. Elias Lieberman. GoYe
Claud Halcro's Invocation. Sir Walter Scott. *Fr.* The Pirate. NBM
Claude Allen. *Unknown.* AmFP
Claudio's Lament. Shakespeare. *See* Epitaph: "Done to death by slanderous tongues" *and* Song: "Pardon, goddess of the night."
Claudius Gilbert. John Wilson. SCAP
Claus von Stauffenberg. Thom Gunn. OBWP
Clausa Germanis Gallia. Millen Brand. GP
Clavering. E. A. Robinson. CrMA; HBMV; OxBA
Claws on cement. Cerberus. H. L. Van Brunt. FAZ
Clay. E. V. Lucas. HBV-1
Clay and Water. Sandra Hochman. Str
Clay Hills. Jean Starr Untermeyer. HBMV
Clay is the word and clay is the flesh. Patrick Kavanagh. *Fr.* The Great Hunger. IPY; NoAM; OxBTC
Clay Jug, The. Kabir, *ad. fr. Hindi by* Robert Bly. NU
Clay, sand, and rock, seem of a diff'rent birth. Barten Holyday. FaBoEE
Clayming a Second Kisse by Desert. Ben Jonson. *Fr.* A Celebration of Charis. AnAnS-2; SeCP
Clean as a lady. Tulip. Humbert Wolfe. MoBrPo
Clean birds by sevens. A Charm against a Magpie [*or* The Dove]. *Unknown.* ChTr; GBP
Clean Clara. William Brighty Rands. HBV-2; HBVY
Clean de ba'n an' sweep de flo'. Uncle Eph's Banjo Song. James Edwin Campbell. BANP
Clean Hands. Austin Dobson. TrPWD
Clean in the light, with nothing to remember. Aspects. Norman MacCaig. BSV; OxBS
Clean the spittoons, boy. Brass Spittoons. Langston Hughes. AmNP; BANP; MoAmPo; NoAM
Clean thin hollow of breast. Reflections. Anita Barrows. NMM
Cleaning Day. José Kozer, *tr. fr. Spanish by* David Unger. VWA
Cleaning Fish. Richard Behm. WOLT
Cleaning Ship. Charles Keeler. EtS
Cleaning the Well. Paul Ruffin. Str
Cleaning Up. Edward Dyson. PoAu-1
Cleaning Up, Clearing Out. Daniel Ross Bronson. AMV-80
Cleaning woman opened the rusty door, A. The Church of San Antonio de la Florida. Paul Petrie. NYBP
Cleanliness. Charles *and* Mary Lamb. OxBChV
Cleanliness is godliness. The Blessing. Ruth Berman. AMV-81
Cleanly rush of the mountain air, The. The Dead Knight. John Masefield. CH; GTBS-P
Cleanly, sir, you went to the core of the matter. A Correct Compassion. James Kirkup. ChMP; FaBoTw; ImOP; OxBTC; SeCePo
Cleanness, *sel.* *Unknown, tr. fr. Middle English by* Brian Stone.
"He who would acclaim Cleanness in becoming style." NOCV
Cleansing Fires. Adelaide Anne Proctor. WGRP
Cleanthes of Andros, The. To a Greek Ship in the Port of Dublin. William Bedell Stanford. NeIP
Clear. Angelo Lewis. PoBA
Clear after Rain. Tu Fu, *tr. fr. Chinese by* Kenneth Rexroth. PoPl
Clear air and grassy lea. Early Morning at Bargis. Hermann Hagedorn. HBV-1
Clear Air of October, The. Robert Bly. NaP; NoAM
Clear and cool, clear and cool. The Tide River. Charles Kingsley. *Fr.* The Water Babies. BoNaP; GN; HBV-1; OxBChV
Clear and gentle stream! Elegy. Robert Bridges. BrPo; OAEP
Clear as air, the western waters. The Grave of Rury. Thomas W. Rolleston. AnIL; AnIV; OnYI
Clear Bright. Li Ch'ing-chao, *tr. fr. Chinese by* Kenneth Rexroth. BoWoP
Clear bright morning, with its scented air, The. The Fair Morning. Jones Very. NOBA
Clear brown eyes, kindly and alert, with 12-20 vision, The. Portrait. Kenneth Fearing. MoAmPo
Clear cool note of the cuckoo which has ousted the legitimate nest-holder, The. Sincere Flattery of W. W. (Americanus) [*or* Imitation of Walt Whitman]. James Kenneth Stephen. FaBoPa; FiBHP; HBV-1; InMe; NOBL; Par; SpRo; WhC
Clear Eyes. Walter de la Mare. MoVE; ViBoPo
Clear frost succeeds, and thro' the blew serene. James Thomson. *Fr.* The Seasons: Winter. FaBoEn
Clear [*or* Cleere] had the day been [*or* bin] from the dawn[e]. A Fine Day [*or* Lines *or* The Sixt Nimphall]. Michael Drayton. *Fr.* The Muses' Elysium. GN; LoBV; OBS
Clear Midnight, A. Walt Whitman. HAP
Clear moon arcs, The. Red Rock Ceremonies. Anita Endrezze Probst. VoR
Clear Night. Charles Wright. GeTw
Clear Night, Small Fire, No Wind. Reg Saner. NPAW
Clear night, thumb-top of a moon, a back-lit sky. Clear Night. Charles Wright. GeTw
Clear nights, the massive. War Bride. Douglas Worth. FF
Clear, noon sky at midsummer is God's eye, A. Cosmic Eye. A. K. Redwing. VoR
Clear obsession that holds up the walls, The. Addressing His Deaf Wife, Kansas, 1916. William Olsen. AMV-81
Clear ocean seems, The. The Double Vision of Manannan. *Unknown, tr. by* John Montague. BIrV
Clear or Cloudy, Sweet as April Showering. *Unknown.* EIL; OBSC
Clear, placid Leman! thy contrasted lake. Lake Leman. Byron. *Fr.* Childe Harold's Pilgrimage. OBNC
Clear ringing of a bell. New Years and Old. Maud Frazer Jackson. PGD
Clear Rock's Chisholm Trail, *with music.* *Unknown.* CoSo
Clear sky may tell it wrong, A. The Choice. Frederick Morgan. AMV-81
Clear the field for the grand tournament of the nations! The Tournament of Man. Ernest Crosby. PGD
Clear—the senses bright—sitting in the black chair—Rocker. Peyote Poem, I. Michael McClure. NeAP; PoM
Clear, the shaken water. After the Swimmer. Robert Wallace. LiSp
Clear the way and build the road! The Road. Zalman Schneour, *tr. by* Joseph Leftwich. TrJP
Clear water in a brilliant bowl. The Poems of Our Climate. Wallace Stevens. MoPo; MP; NoP; OxBA; PP; TrGrPo; TwCP
Clear water of the imperial pond, The. Ise Tayu, *tr. fr. Japanese by* Kenneth Rexroth *and* Ikuko Atsumi. BoWoP
Cleare moving cristall, pure as the Sunne beames. Sonnet. Earl of Stirling. Aurora, XXV. OxBS
Cleared Land, A, *sel.* Robin Fulton.
More than People. PoSH
Clearing, The. Amiri Baraka. CoPo
Clearing, The. Peter Everwine, *after the Nahuatl.* NNaP
Clearing, The. Robert Graves. NYBP
Clearing at Dawn. Li Po, *tr. fr. Chinese by* Arthur Waley. AWP
Clearing brush away. Taking to the Woods. Henry Taylor. MAYP
Clearing in the forest. The Lincoln-Child. James Oppenheim. HBMV
Cleator Moor. Norman Nicholson. FaBoTw; NeBP
Cleavage. A. R. Ammons. OBAL
Cleavage. Louise Townsend Nicholl. NePoAm
Cleere had the day bin from the dawne. *See* Clear had the day been from the dawn.

Cleitagoras. Leonidas of Tarentum, *tr. fr. Greek by* William M. Hardinge. AWP
Clement Attlee. Michael Benedikt. InPS
Clementine. *Unknown. See* Oh, My Darling Clementine.
Cleo on the Section Gang. The Park. Robin Blaser. CoPo
Cleobulus' Epitaph. Simonides, *tr. fr. Greek by* Richmond Lattimore. PoPl
Cleombrotus retired from the ring. The Retired Boxer. Lucilius, *tr. by* Tom Dodge. LiSP
Cleomenes, *sel.* Dryden.
No, No, Poor Suffering Heart, *fr.* II, ii. LiTB; LoBV; QFR; ViBoPo
(One Happy Moment.) OBEV
(Song: "No, no, poor suff'ring Heart no Change endeavour.") SeCV-2
Cleon. Robert Browning. OAEL-2; OAEP; VLP
Cleonicos. Edward Cracroft Lefroy, *after the Greek of* Theocritus. *Fr.* Echoes from Theocritus. AWP
Cleopatra, *sels.* Samuel Daniel.
Chorus: "Behold what furies still." LoBV
Chorus: "Then thus we have beheld." OBSC
O Fearfull, Frowning Nemesis. PoEL-2
Cleopatra. Shakespeare. *Fr.* Anthony and Cleopatra, II, ii. LiTB
("Barge she sat in, like a burnish'd throne, The.") BiP; PPoe; SCV
(Cleopatra and Her Barge.) TreF
(Cleopatra's Barge.) TrGrPo
Cleopatra. William Wetmore Story. AA
Cleopatra. Swinburne. BeLS
Cleopatra and Antony. Dryden. *Fr.* All for Love. FiP
Cleopatra and Her Barge. Shakespeare. *See* Cleopatra.
Cleopatra Dying. Thomas Stephens Collier. BLPA; BLPL; FaBoBe; TreFT
Cleopatra to the Asp. Ted Hughes. EBEV
Cleopatra, who thought they maligned her. Limerick. Newton Mackintosh. NA
Cleopatra's Barge. Shakespeare. *See* Cleopatra.
Cleopatra's Death. Shakespeare. *See* Death of Cleopatra.
Cleopatra's Lament. Shakespeare. *Fr.* Antony and Cleopatra, V, ii. UnPo
Clepsydra. Charles Cotton. CavP
Clergyman [*or* Evangelical vicar], in want, A. Limerick. Ronald Arbuthnott Knox. CenHV; OxBoLi; WhC
Clergyman out in Dumont, A. Limerick. Morris Bishop. WhC
Clergyman told from his text, A. Who's Next? *Unknown.* TDH
Cleric Courts His Lady, A. *Unknown.* MeEL
Clerical Cabal, The. *Unknown.* APAS
Clerical Oppressors. Whittier. PAH; PPON
Clerihew: "Spinoza/ Collected curiosa." *Unknown.* NOBL
Clerihews, *sels.* E. C. Bentley.
"Adam Smith." FaBoCo
"After dinner Erasmus." CenHV
"Art of Biography, The." CenHV; FiBHP; NOBL; PV
" 'Dear me!' exclaimed Homer." FiBHP
"Digestion of Milton, The." PV
"Dr. Clifford." CenHV
"Geoffrey Chaucer." PV
George Hirst. PoPle
"George the Third." DBV; FaBoCo; FiBHP; NOBL; OxBoLi; PV
"Great Duke of Wellington, The." CenHV
"Great Emperor Otto, The." PV
"I am not Mahomet." NOBL
" 'I quite realized,' said Columbus." FiBHP
"If only Mr. Roosevelt." CenHV
"Intrepid Ricardo, The." CenHV
"John Stuart Mill." FaBoCo; FiBHP
(J. S. Mill.) OxBoLi; WhC
Liszt. UnS
"Mr. Bernard Shaw." CenHV
"Mr. Hilaire Belloc." CenHV
" 'No,' said Charles Peace." NOBL
" 'No, sir,' said General Sherman." NOBL
"People of Spain think Cervantes, The." CenHV; FiBHP
(Cervantes.) EvOK
Professor James Dewar, F.R.S. PoPle
"Sir Christopher Wren." CenHV; FaBoCo; FiBHP; InMe; InPK; MoShBr; PV; WhC
"Sir Humphry Davy." CenHV; FaBoCo; ImOP
"Sir Walter Raleigh." CenHV
" 'Susaddah!' exclaimed Ibsen." PV
"There exists no proof as." NOBL
"What I like about Clive." CenHV; NOBL
(Lord Clive.) MoShBr; PoPle; WhC
Clerimont's Song. Ben Jonson. *See* Still to Be Neat.
Clerk Colvill. *Unknown.* EnSB; ESPB (A *and* B *vers.*); FaBoBa; GBP; OxBB; ViBoFo
Clerk of Oxford, The. Chaucer. *Fr.* The Canterbury Tales: Prologue. OxBM
("Clerk ther was of Oxenford, A.") GLGT; InPS; TrGrPo; ViBoPo
("Student came from Oxford town also, A," *mod. vers. by* Louis Untermeyer.) TrGrPo
Clerk Saunders (*diff. versions*). *Unknown.* ESPB (A, B, *and* F *vers.*); FaBoBa; OAEP; OBEV; OxBS; SeCeV; ViBoFo
(Clark Sanders.) OxBB
Clerk Ther Was of Cauntebrigge Also, A. Walter William Skeat. BXAP; Par
Clerk ther was of Oxenford also, A. The Clerk of Oxford. Chaucer. *Fr.* The Canterbury Tales: Prologue. GLGT; InPS; OxBM; TrGrPo; ViBoPo
Clerke ther was, a puissant wight was hee, A. Ye Clerke of Ye Wethere. *Unknown.* BXAP
Clerks, The. E. A. Robinson. AA; CABA; MoAB; MoAmPo; MoVE; PoEL-5
Clerk's Twa Sons o Owsenford, The. *Unknown.* ESPB
Clevedon Church. Andrew Lang. BSV; GoTS, *abr.*
Cleveland Lyke Wake Dirge, The. *Unknown. See* Lyke Wake Dirge, A.
Clever Chinese say they read, The. Cat's Eyes. Francis Scarfe. PCat
Clever man builds a city, A. Woman. *Unknown, tr. by* H. A. Giles. *Fr.* Shi King. AWP
Clever Peter and the Ogress. Katherine Pyle. OBCA
Clever Skipper, The. *Unknown.* AmFP
Clever Tom Clinch Going to Be Hanged. Swift. CoMu; FaBoBa; SeCeV
Clever Woman, A. Mary Elizabeth Coleridge. BrRo
Cliches with worn wit combined. On a Lover of Books. Geoffrey Grigson. FaBoEE
Click Go the Shears, Boys. *Unknown.* PoAu-1
Click o' the Latch. Nancy Byrd Turner. HBMV
Clickbeetle. Mary Ann Hoberman. RHPC
Clickety-Clack. Paul Blackburn. NoAM
Clickety-clack. Song of the Train. David McCord. FaPON; NTCP; SoPo
Clickstone. Rokwaho. STE
Client meeting at twelve, that lot of layabouts. Nine o'Clock Thoughts on the 73 Bus. Peter Porter. POL
Cliff Dwelling, The. Arthur W. Monroe. PoOW
Cliff gave way and the slope shifted ground, The. The Trees in the Road. James Still. GrPl
Cliff Klingenhagen. E. A. Robinson. AmPP; AP; CoBMV; HBMV; MoAB; MoAmPo; TreFS
Cliff-locked port and a bluff sea wall, A. Reid at Fayal. John Williamson Palmer. PAH
Cliff Rose, The. Ernest Fewster. CaP
Cliff-Top, The. Robert Bridges. BoNaP
Cliffs/ Cliffs. Thorn Piece. Amy Lowell. PeHV
Cliffs that rise a thousand feet. Sailing Homeward. Chan Fang-sheng, *tr. by* Arthur Waley. AWP; FaBoCh
Cliffside Path, The. Swinburne. A Midsummer Holiday, VI. VLP
Clifton Chapel. Sir Henry Newbolt. OBEV; OBVV
Clifton Grove, *sel.* Henry Kirke White.
"Lo! in the West, fast fades the ling'ring light." OBNC
Climate of Paradise, The. Louis Simpson. NOBA
Climate of Thought, The. Robert Graves. MoAB; ViBoPo
Climax of passion, the dancers are trembling, The. Rumba. José Zacarías Tallet, *tr. by* Sangodare Akanji. TTY
Climb/ through my hair, climb in. Rapunzel. Olga Broumas. DFT
Climb at Court for me that will. Senec. Traged. ex Thyeste Chor. 2. Seneca, *tr. by* Andrew Marvell. *Fr.* Thyestes, II. OBVE; SeCV-1
Climb in Torridon. Brenda G. Macrow. PoSH
Climb then by spiral stairways of cold thought. The Ghost in the Cellarage. John Heath-Stubbs. NeBP
Climb to Snowdon, The. Wordsworth. *Fr.* The Prelude, XIV. FaBoRV
("In one of these excursions, travelling then.") EBEV
(Snowdon Sunrise, The.) FaBoPP
Climber Surveys His Mountain, The. Hugh Ouston. PoSH
Climbers, The. Elizabeth Jennings. NePoEA
Climbers are fools, forget. Magma. G. J. F. Dutton. PoSH
Climbing. Daniel Mark Epstein. AMV-80
Climbing. Gloria Fuertes, *tr. fr. Spanish by* Philip Levine. PBWP
Climbing. Jennifer Maiden. CBAP
Climbing from the Lethal dead. Orpheus. Yvor Winters. MoVE; NOBA; VGW
Climbing in Glencoe. Andrew Young. LiSp
Climbing mountains. Human Dilemma. Jim Rosemergy. AMV-80
Climbing northward. The Herds. W. S. Merwin. NaP; NYBP
Climbing Rope, The. Alice V. Stuart. PoSH
Climbing sun had drunk the shade, The. Blue Ghosts. Stanley Snaith. ChMP
Climbing the rutted path, the lights of the town. The Phases of Darkness. Paul Petrie. TAP
Climbing the staircase. Simplicity. Louis Simpson. InPS; Prf

Climbing the stairway gray with urban midnight. Effort at Speech. William Meredith. NYP; Prf; WeW
Climbing through the January snow, into the Lobo Canyon. Mountain Lion. D. H. Lawrence. BoAnP; OxBTC; RFM
Climbing up the hillside beneath the summer stars. Man in Nature. William Roscoe Thayer. AA
Climbing You. Erica Jong. PoA
Climbing Zero Gully. David J. Morley. PoSH
Climbs hobbling. A Very Old Woman. Clayton Eshleman. MAT
Clime of the brave! the high heart's home. New England. George Denison Prentice. AA
Cling to Me. John Le Gay Brereton. PeHV
Cling together in your dust: the frost. Earthly Love. Joseph Bennett. NePA
Clinging to my breast, no stronger. Spinster's Lullaby. Vassar Miller. BoWoP; NMM
Clinic Day. Jo Barnes. BrRo
Clinic: Examination. Audrey Conard. AMV-80
Clinical. W. E. Henley. In Hospital, XI. BrPo
Clink! Clink! Clink!/ The song of the hammer and drill. The Miner. Alfred Castner King. PoOW
Clink of the Ice, The. Eugene Field. InMe
Clinton South of Polk. Carl Sandburg. AmFN
Clio's Protest. Sheridan. FaBoEE
Clip-clop go water-drops and bridles ring. Nude in a Fountain. Norman MacCaig. OxBS
Clipper, The. Thomas Fleming Day. EtS
Clipper Loitered South, The. John Masefield. *Fr.* Dauber. EtS
Clipper Ships. John Anderson. EtS
Clippety cloppety,/ Cesare Borgia. Chip. George Starbuck. OBAL; PV
Clippity clop, clippity clop. The Milkman. Jane W. Krows. SoPo
Clitta, clatta, clatta, clatter. Thomas Holley Chivers. *Fr.* Railroad Song. PeD
Cloak, The. Violet Anderson. CaP
Clock, The. Felice Holman. GrPl
Clock, The. Jean Jaszi. SoPo
Clock. Harold Monro. BrPo
Clock, The. Francis Scarfe. NeBP
Clock-a-Clay. John Clare. EBEV; FaPON; LiTB; LoBV; NBM; OAEL-2; OBNC; PoEL-4; SeCeV; VLP; WHA
(Clock-o'-Clay.) TrGrPo
Clock in the Square, A. Adrienne Rich. HeIP; NIP
Clock is striking autumn at the apple vendor's fair, The. Autumn. Patricia Hubbell. PDV
Clock-o'-Clay. John Clare. *See* Clock-a-Clay.
Clock of my days winds down, The. The Alligator Bride. Donald Hall. ConAP; EAS
Clock says, The, "When will it be morning?" After Lorca. Ted Hughes. PoA
Clock shows nearly five, The. To a Salesgirl, Weary of Artificial Holiday Trees. James Wright. NYBP
Clock stopped, A. Emily Dickinson. AmPP; AP; NCEP; NoP; PoEL-5; TwAmPo
Clock stops ticking, The. Stroke. Mike Lowery. Psk
Clock Symphony. John Frederick Nims. MiAP
Clock Time by the Geyser. John White. ShM
Clock Tower, The. Colleen Thibaudeau. WHW
Clock within us, speaking time, The. Making Love, Killing Time. Anne Ridler. NMP
Clock without Hands. John Frederick Nims. PoA
Clocked with the sun and by his journey paced. Homestead—Winter Morning. Mary Ballard Duryee. GoYe
Clocking Hen, The. *Unknown.* HBVY
Clocks. Louis Ginsberg. TrJP
Clocks. Malka Locker, *tr. fr. Yiddish by* Jeremy Garber. VWA
Clocks. Carl Sandburg. CrMA
Clocks are chiming in my heart, The. Past. John Galsworthy. HBV-1
Clocks begin, civicly simultaneous, The. At Delft. Charles Tomlinson. NYBP
Clock's Song, The. Rose Hawthorne Lathrop. AA
Clock's untiring fingers wind the wool of darkness, The. Cradle Song [for Miriam]. Louis MacNeice. MoAB; MoBrPo; NAs
Clockwork beings, winding out their lives. Insects. Isidor Schneider. TrJP
Clockwork skating Wordsworth on the ice, A. Xmas for the Boys. Gavin Ewart. OBSV
Clod, The. Edwin Curran. HBMV
Clod and the Pebble, The. Blake. *Fr.* Songs of Experience. CABA; EBCP; EnLoPo; EnRP; FaBoEn; FaBV; InPS; LAuP; LoBV; NOBE; NoP; OAEP; OBEC; OBNC; PAI; PrIm; SCV; TEP; TrGrPo; ViBoPo
Cloe ("Bright as the day, and like the morning fair"). George Granville. FaBoCo; FaBoEE; NIP
Cloe, blooming sweet as May. To Cloe. Hildebrand Jacob. NOEC
Cloe, by your command, in verse I write. A Letter from Artemisa in the Town, to Cloe, in the Country. Earl of Rochester. SeCV-2
Cloe's the wonder of her sex. To Cloe. George Granville. FaBoEE (*At. to* Charles Sackville); POL; PV
Clogged ashtray a dead lung, A. Grass, Grass. George Bowering. NeAC
Cloister. Conrad Aiken. Preludes for Memnon, XX. MoAB; MoAmPo ("So, in the evening, to the simple cloister.") LiTA; TwAmPo
Cloistered. Alice Brown. AA
Cloisters. Anthony Barnett. VWA
Cloisters, The. Samuel Yellen. NePoAm
Clonakilty. *Unknown.* FaBoEE
Clonard. Thomas S. Jones, Jr. HBMV
Clonfeacle. Paul Muldoon. CIP
Clonmacnoise. Angus O'Gillan. *See* Dead at Clonmacnois, The.
Clonmel Jail. *Unknown, tr. fr. Irish by* Valentin Iremonger. BIrV
Clora come view my soul, and tell. The Gallery. Andrew Marvell. AnAnS-1; MeLP; NoP; OBS
Clorinda and Damon. Andrew Marvell. AnAnS-1; SeCP
Cloris and Mertilla. Michael Drayton. *Fr.* The Muses' Elysium. LoBV
Cloris, I cannot say your eyes. To Cloris. Sir Charles Sedley. BoLoP
Cloris, it is not thy disdaine. To the Tune of, In Fayth I Cannot Keepe My Father's Sheepe [*or* Song]. Sidney Godolphin. MeLP; OBS
Clorox Kid, The. Kirk Robertson. GP
Close by the basement door-step. A Toad. Elizabeth Akers Allen. OBCA
Close by the careless worker's side. Work. G. A. Studdert-Kennedy. EBCP
Close by those meads, for ever crowned with flowers. Ombre at Hampton Court. Pope. *Fr.* The Rape of the Lock. FaBoPP; FiP; OBEC; OBSV; OxBoLi
Close Clan, The. Mark Van Doren. GoYe
Close gray sky, A. The Lark. Lizette Woodworth Reese. HBMV
Close his eyes; his work is done! Dirge for a Soldier. George Henry Boker. AA; HBV-2; OBVV; PAH; PeD; WaaP
Close in the hollow bank she lies. The Stockdove. Ruth Pitter. SeCePo
Close keep your lips, if that you meane. To Women, to Hide Their Teeth, if They Be Rotten or Rusty. Robert Herrick. FaBoUs
Close now the door; shut down the light. The Supremer Sacrifice." Furnley Maurice." CBAP
Close now thine eyes, and rest secure. A Good-Night. Francis Quarles. OBS; TrGrPo
Close of Day, The. Wesley Curtwright. CDC
Close on the edge of a midsummer dawn. A Shadow of the Night. Thomas Bailey Aldrich. AA
Close Quarters. John Banister Tabb. OBAL
Close Season for Marriage. *Unknown.* FaBoUs
Close softly thine arms about me like a girdle. Endearments. Pierre Louÿs, *tr. by* Horace M. Brown. *Fr.* The Songs of Bilitis. UnTE
Close thine eyes, and sleep secure. On a Quiet Conscience. Charles I, King of England. CH; PoPle
Close to Me. Gabriela Mistral, *tr. fr. Spanish by* Langston Hughes. PoPl
Close to nature my brother, your thoughts ring softly. To an Indian Poet. Patty L. Harjo. VoR
Close to the frontier of Eternity is my patrimony. The Migrant. Donald G. Babcock. NePoAm
Close to the gates a spacious garden lies. The Gardens of Alcinous. Homer, *tr. by* Pope. *Fr.* The Odyssey, VIII. OAEL-1; OBVE
Close to the sod. The Snowdrop. Anna Bunston de Bary. HBMV
Close-up. A. R. Ammons. PoA
Close up the casement, draw the blind. Shut Out That Moon. Thomas Hardy. BrPo; CMoP; MoVE; NoAM; NOBE; ViBoPo
Close-ups of Summer. Norman MacCaig. OxBC
Close Your Eyes! Arna Bontemps. AmNP; CDC; FB; PoBA; PoNe
Close your sleepy eyes. My Little Buckaroo. *Unknown.* BPAW
Closed Door, The. Theodosia Garrison. BLPA
Closed eyes can't see the white roses. Give Them the Flowers Now. *Unknown.* WBLP
Closed is that curious ear by Death's cold hand. Thomas Gray's View of Nature. William Mason. *Fr.* The English Garden, III. NOEC
Closed like confessionals, they thread. Ambulances. Philip Larkin. FaBoTw; OxBC
Closed System, The. Larry Eigner. VWA
Closed window looks down, A. Ka 'Ba. Amiri Baraka. BPo; CAPP; CNA; TAP
Closed World, The. Denise Levertov. NoP
Closer First to Earth. Anne Hazlewood-Brady. IHMS
Closer I come to their huge black-and-white sides, the less, The. Being Herded Past the Prison's Honor Farm. David Wagoner. SoSe
Closes and courts and lanes. Song. John Davidson. BrPo; HBV-2
Closest to men, thou pitying Son of Man. To Jesus of Nazareth. Frederic Lawrence Knowles. TrPWD
Closing of the Rodeo, The. William Jay Smith. GOA; MP; NePoEA; SaC; TwCP

Closing Piece. Rainer Maria Rilke, *tr. fr. German by* M. D. Herter Norton. PCP
Closing Prayer. Johnstone G. Patrick. TrPWD
Closing Scene, The. Thomas Buchanan Read. AA; HBV-2
Closing Time. James Michie. NePoEA-2
Closing Time. David Wagoner. NYBP
Clote, The (Water-Lily). William Barnes. ELP; PoEL-4
Cloth of Gold, The, *sel.* M. Krishnamurti.
"Now the last step! Behold." PeD
Cloth of Gold. Francis Reginald. MoCV
Cloth-plant grew till it covered the thorn bush, The. Widow's Lament, *tr. fr. Chinese by* Arthur Waley. *Fr.* Shih Ching. BoWoP
Cloth was laid in the Vorkhouse hall, The. The Workhouse Boy. *Unknown.* GBP; VLP
Clothed in yellow, red and green. *Unknown.* OxNR
Clother of the lily, feeder of the sparrow. A Prayer [*or* They Toil Not neither Do They Spin]. Christina Rossetti. OBVV; TrPWD
Clothes, The. Rayzel Zychlinska, *tr. fr. Yiddish by* Marc Kaminsky. VWA
Clothes Do but Cheat and Cozen Us. Robert Herrick. CaPo; ErPo
Clothes in which you saw me, The. The Clothes. Rayzel Zychlinska, *tr. by* Marc Kaminsky. VWA
Clothes make no sound when I tread ground. A Riddle. *Unknown, tr. fr. Anglo-Saxon.* ChTr
Clothes Maketh the Man. Theodore Weiss. NoAM
Clothes Pit, The. Douglas Dunn. OxBTC
Clothing's New Emperor, The. Donald Finkel. NePoEA
Cloud, The. Shelley. BLPL; ChER; EnRP; FaPON; GN; HBV-1; ImOP, *abr.*; LiTB; NoP; OAEP; OBRV; OHFP; PoEL-4; SeCeV; TreF; TrGrPo; ViBoPo
Orbed Maiden, *sel.* MOON
Cloud and Flame. John Berryman. AP
Cloud-backed heron will not move, The. The Heron. Vernon Watkins. ChMP; GTBS-P; MP; TwCP; UnPo
Cloud-bank lies in a red-gold ring, The. Judith Remembers. Maxwell Anderson. *Fr.* Judith of Minnewaulken. WHA
Cloud-capp'd towers, the gorgeous palaces, The. Shakespeare. *Fr.* The Tempest, IV, i. PoPl
Cloud capped peaks fill the eyes. On a Visit to Ch'ung Chen Taoist Temple. Yu Hsüan-chi, *tr. by* Kenneth Rexroth *and* Ling Chung. PBWP
Cloud Chamber, The. Arthur Sze. BrSi
Cloud—cloud—cloud—hurls. It. Gary Snyder. LCAP
Cloud Country. James Merrill. NePoEA
Cloud doth gather, the green wood roar, The. Thekla's Song. Schiller, *tr. by* Samuel Taylor Coleridge. *Fr.* The Piccolomini. AWP
Cloud Factory, The. John Haines. EAS
Cloud-Flower Lullaby, The. *Tr. fr. Tewa Indian by* H. J. Spinden. WTO
Cloud in Trousers, A, *abr.* Vladimir Mayakovsky, *tr. fr. Russian by* Peter Bogdanoff. SOTW
Cloud is the post office between continents, The. To Modigliani to Prove to Him That I Am a Poet. Max Jacob, *tr. by* Wallace Fowlie. TrJP
Cloud lay cradled near the setting sun, A. The Evening Cloud. John Wilson. HBV-1
Cloud-maidens that float on forever. Song of the Clouds. Aristophanes, *tr. by* Oscar Wilde. *Fr.* The Clouds. AWP
Cloud-Mobile, The. May Swenson. SO
Cloud moved close, A. The bulk of the wind shifted. The Visitant. Theodore Roethke. CMoP; NMP; PPoe; UnPo
Cloud of Carmel, The. Jessica Agnes Powers. ISi
Cloud of dust on the long white road, A. The Teams. Henry Lawson. CBAP; PoAu-1
Cloud of grasshoppers, A. Credo. Leonard Cohen. PeCV
Cloud of Unknowing, The. Philip Murray. NePoAm-2
Cloud of witnesses, A. To whom? To what? A Fanfare for the Makers. Louis MacNeice. NOBE
Cloud Parade, The. Laura Jensen. LCAP
Cloud-piles o'er Kona's sea whet my joy, The. Fathomless Is My Love. Kalola, *tr. fr. Hawaiian by* N. B. Emerson. WTO
Cloud possessed the hollow field, A. The High Tide at Gettysburg. Will Henry Thompson. AA; BeLS; BLPA; FaBoBe; HBV-2; PAH; PAL; PaPo; TreFS
Cloud-puffball, torn tufts, tossed pillows. That Nature Is a Heraclitean Fire and of the Comfort of the Resurrection. Gerard Manley Hopkins. BiP; BrPo; CABA; CoBMV; FaBoMo; GTBS-P; LiTB; MoAB; MoPo; MoVE; NoP; OAEL-2; OAEP; PoEL-5; TEP; VLP
Cloud-riders leap for Normandy. On the Cliff. Hal Summers. ChMP
Cloud River. Charles Wright. GeTw
Cloudburst and Soaring Moon." Hugh MacDiarmid." NoAM
Cloudburst and steady downpour now. Gifts of Rain. Seamus Heaney. IPY
Clouded Morning, The. Jones Very. AP; NOBA
Clouded sun on coolin' morn. The Trail Herd. *Unknown.* BPAW
Clouded with snow. Winter. Walter de la Mare. OAEL-2; OBMV
Clouds. Dorothy Aldis. SoPo
Clouds, The, *sel.* Aristophanes, *tr. fr. Greek.*
Song of the Clouds, *tr. by* Oscar Wilde. AWP
Clouds. Norman Ault. HBVY
Clouds. Rupert Brooke. BrPo; MoVE; OBEV; OBMV; OxBTC
Clouds. John Jay Chapman. EtS
Clouds, The. William Croswell. AA
Clouds. Philip Levine. LCAP
Clouds, The. Mirabai, *tr. fr. Medieval Hindi; English version by* Robert Bly. NU
Clouds. James Reaney. WHW
Clouds. *Unknown.* SoPo
Clouds, The. Arthur Vogelsang. MAYP
Clouds, The. William Carlos Williams. MoPo; VGW
Clouds and Clay. Valerie Gillies. PoSH
Clouds are giving way: bushes. April. John Linthicum. AMV-80
Clouds are scudding across the moon, The. Storm Song. Bayard Taylor. EtS; HBV-1
Clouds are swirling, clouds are straying. Phantoms of the Steppe. Pushkin, *tr. by* Edna Worthley Underwood. WSC
Clouds darken the plain. Hand. Edouard Roditi. EAS
Clouds dissolve into blueness. Hearing of the End of the War. Richard Tillinghast. MAYP
Clouds fell. Song in White. Anne Le Dressay. AMV-80
Clouds fill the sky. The Morning after . . . Love. Kattie M. Cumbo. BlSi
Clouds grow clear, the pine-wood glooms and stills, The. A Summer Evening. Archibald Lampman. PeCV
Clouds Have Left the Sky, The. Robert Bridges. CH
Clouds in the sky at twilight. The Violin Calls. Florence Randal Livesay. CaP
Clouds, lingering yet, extend in solid bars. Composed by the Side of Grasmere Lake. Wordsworth. ChER
Clouds of Evening. Robinson Jeffers. MoAmPo
Clouds scattered across the sky all so far away. The Words. Lee Harwood. EAS
Clouds spout upon her. Rain on a Grave. Thomas Hardy. CoBMV; HBV-1; OAEP
Clouds stretch into their. Daybreak on a Pennsylvania Highway. John Daunt. AMV-80
Clouds That Are So Light, The. Edward Thomas. FaBoTw
Clouds, the source of rain, one stormy night, The. Lost in Heaven. Robert Frost. MoAmPo
Clouds, torsos, shells, peppers, trees, rocks, smokestacks. Edward Weston in Mexico City. Philip Dacey. LTB; PoDr
Clouds were fishbone, The. Walden in July. Donald Junkins. NYBP
Clouds, which rise with thunder, slake, The. All's Well. Whittier. OBVV
Clove, salmon knocking. For Lerida. David St. John. AmPA
Clover, The. Margaret Deland. AA
Clover. John Banister Tabb. AA
Clover-burr was two feet high, and the billabongs were full, The. Irish Lords. Charles H. Souter. PoAu-1
Clovers, The. Jean Garrigue. MoPo
Clown, The. Dorothy Aldis. PDV
Clown, The. Donald Hall. NYBP
Clown, The. Mary Catherine Rose. SoPo
Clown, The: He Dances in the Clearing by Night. Ramon Guthrie. NMP
Clownish Song, A. Thomas Nashe. *See* A-Maying, a-Playing.
Clownlike, happiest on your hands. You're. Sylvia Plath. FaBoTw; NAs; NCSH
Clown's Baby, The." Margaret Vandegrift." PaPo
Clowns' Houses. Edith Sitwell. SyP
Clowns in a garish air. On panicky pedals. The Necromancers. John Frederick Nims. PoCh
Clown's Song, The ("Come away, come away, death"). Shakespeare. *See* Come Away, Come Away, Death.
Clown's Song ("O mistris mine where are you roming?"). Shakespeare. *See* O Mistress Mine, Where Are You Roaming?
Cloying sea envelopes man at birth, A. Adventure. Guy Mason. CaP
Club 82: Lisa. Cynthia Kramer Genser. NYP
Clubby! thou surely art, I ween. Verses on a Cat. Charles Daubeny. HBV-1
Clubwoman. Mary Carter Smith. PoNe
Clue, The. Charlotte Fiske Bates. AA
Clumsy. J. B. Lee. TDH
Clumsy in his drunken joints. Animal Pictures. Lawrence Locke. GrPl
Clustered in the forest around. Kenneth Rexroth. *Fr.* On Flower Wreath Hill. GP
Clustering rainbow-grapes. Balloon Man. Jessica N. North. SoPo
Clustering up on my Christmas steps. Carolers. Nancy G. Westerfield. AMV-81
Clusters in Thy vineyard turn to gold, O God, The. Grape-gathering. Abraham Shlonsky, *tr. by* I. M. Lask. TrJP

Clusters of ruins on vine-shoots of steel. Grave at Cassino. Noah Stern, *tr. by* Harold Schimmel. VWA
Clyde's Water[s], *diff. versions. Unknown.* BSV; OxBB, *with music*
(Mother's Malison, The; or, Clyde's Water.) BaBo; ESPB (A *and* B *vers.*)
"C'mon, get out." Sunflower Rock. Paul Blackburn. NoAM
C'mon godamya c'mon gimme that pussy! Chickitten Gitten! Ted Joans. GP
Coach. Eleanor Farjeon. DFT
Coach,/ Carriage. *Unknown.* OxNR
Coach into Pumpkin. Dorothy E. Reid. DFT
Coach is at the door at last, The. Farewell to the Farm. Robert Louis Stevenson. FaPON; TiPo
Coachman's Yarn, The. E. J. Brady. PoAu-1
Coal. Audre Lorde. BlSi; CNA; NoP; PoBA
Coal black woman fry no meat for me. Seven Sister Blues. *Unknown.* BluL
Coal Diggin' Blues. *Unknown.* AmFP
Coal Fire in Winter, A. Thomas McGrath. NU
Coal for Mike. Bertolt Brecht, *tr. fr. German by* H. R. Hays. PoPl
Coal Loadin' Blues. *Unknown.* AmFP
Coal Mine Disaster's Last Trapped Man Contemplates Salvation, The. William Meissner. AMV-80
Coal Miner's Child, The, *with music. Unknown.* OuSiCo
Coal Miner's Goodbye, A. *Unknown.* AmFP
Coal Miner's Grace. Jay Divine. AMV-80
Coal-Owner and the Pitman's Wife, The. *Unknown.* CoMu
Coal-white bird appeares this spring, A. Almanac Verse. Samuel Danforth. SCAP
Coame, Malkyn, Hurle Thine Oyz at Hodge Trillindle. *Unknown.* NCEP
Coarse/ jocosity/ catches the crowd. Archy Confesses. Don Marquis. *Fr.* Archy and Mehitabel. EvOK; FiBHP
Coast, The: Norfolk. Frances Cornford. OxBTC
Coast of Peru, The. *Unknown.* EtS; FSW; ShS
Coast to Coast. Adrienne Rich. NIP
Coast View, A, *sel.* Charles Harpur.
"Dead city walls may pen us in, but still." CBAP
Coastguard House, The. Robert Lowell, *ad. fr. the Italian of* Eugenio Montale. NaP
Coasting toward Midnight at the Southeastern Fair. David Bottoms. AMV-81
Coastline. Elaine Feinstein. BrRo
Coastwise Lights, The. Kipling. EtS
Coat, A. W. B. Yeats. CABA; CMoP; LiTM; NoAM; PoEL-5
Coat of Arms. Alan Dugan. DiL
Coat of Fire, The. Edith Sitwell. OAEP
Coax Me, *with music.* Andrew Sterling. FSN
Cob, thou nor soldier, thief, nor fencer art. To Pertinax Cob. Ben Jonson. JCP
"Cobalt and umber and ultramarine." The Paint Box. E. V. Rieu. RHPC; SO
Cobb Would Have Caught It. Robert Fitzgerald. GrPl; HAP; InvP; MP; TwCP; WeW
Cobbe's Prophecies. *Unknown.* NA
Cobbler, The. Eleanor Alletta Chaffee. SoPo; TiPo
Cobbler bent at his wooden foot, The. John Masefield. *Fr.* Reynard the Fox. ViBoPo
Cobbler, cobbler, mend my shoe. Mother Goose. OxNR
Cobbler in Willow Street, The. George O'Neil. HBMV
Cobbler's Song, The. *At. to* Charles Tilney. *Fr.* Locrine. OBSC
Coble o Cargill, The. *Unknown.* ESPB
Coblerone I'm told, A. Mutton and Leather. *Unknown.* CoMu
Cobra is the night image of a chinese water-print. North Express. Joyce Mansour, *tr. by author.* WPOW
Cocaine Bill and Morphine Sue. *Unknown. See* Cocaine Lil.
Cocaine Blues. *Unknown.* FSW
Cocaine Lil. *Unknown.* AS, *with music*; MAT; TrAS, *with music*
(Cocaine Bill and Morphine Sue.) FSW
(Cocaine Lil and Morphine Sue.) GBP; OxBoLi
Cock. Aharon Amir, *tr. fr. Hebrew by* Bernhard Frank. AMV-81
Cock, The. Ewa Lipska, *tr. fr. Polish by* Peter Jay *and* Geri Lipschultz. VWA
Cock-a-doodle-do! 'tis the bravest game. Cock-throwing. Martin Lluellyn. PBBP
Cock a doodle doo! / My dame has lost her shoe. Mother Goose. HBVY; OxNR
Cock-a-doodle-doo the brass-lined rooster goes [*or* says]. Dog. John Crowe Ransom. InPS; LiTA; OBAL
Cock-a-Hoop. Isabella Gardner. WPE
Cock Again, The. Kikaku, *tr. fr. Japanese by* Harold G. Henderson. SoPo
Cock and his hen perching in the night, A. The Cock and the Hen. John Heywood. PBBP
Cock and the Bull, The. Charles Stuart Calverley. BXAP; FaBoCo; FaBoNo; FaBoPa; InMe; NA; Par; VLP, *abr.*
Cock and the Fox, The. La Fontaine, *tr. fr. French by* Elizur Wright. AWP
Cock and the Hen, The. Chaucer. *See* The Nun's Priest's Tale.
Cock and the Hen, The. John Heywood. PBBP
Cock before Dawn. Norman MacCaig. OxBC
Cock, cock, cock, cock. *Unknown.* OxNR; PBBP
Cock-Crow. Ralph Nixon Currey. PeSA
Cock-Crow. Robert Herrick. PBBP
Cock-Crow. Edward Thomas. GTBS-P; MoAB; MoBrPo
Cockcrow. Eithne Wilkins. NeBP
Cock-crow clouds wave like nebulous fingers, The. Morning from My Office Window. John A. Wood. AMV-81
Cock-crowing. Henry Vaughan. AnAnS-1; MePo; OAEL-1; PBBP; SeCV-1
Cock Crowing in a Poulterer's Shop, A. John Ferguson. BoAnP
Cock crows, The. Depression before Spring. Wallace Stevens. OBAL; SOTW
Cock crows [*or* Cocks crow] in the morning [*or* morn] to tell us to rise. Mother Goose. HBVY; PBBP; TiPo
Cock doth crow, The/ To let you know. Mother Goose. OxNR; TiPo
Cock doth crow, the wind doth blow, The. Mother Goose. GBP
Cock gaid to Rome, seeking shoon, seeking shoon, The. *Unknown.* PBBP
Cock is crowing, The. Written in March [*or* The Merry Month of March]. Wordsworth. BoNaP; EnRP; EvOK; FaPON; GoJo; HBV-1; HBVY; MoShBr; NTCP; SoPo; SUS; TiPo; UnPo; YeAr
Cock of Glory is the *coq français,* The. The French, 1870–1871. *Unknown.* FaBoEE
Cock of the Game, The. *Unknown.* OBET
Cock Robin got up early. *Unknown.* OxNR; PBBP
Cock shall crow, The. Ditty. Robert Louis Stevenson. TrGrPo
Cock sparrow with a sweet, The. Rocking. A. R. Ammons. GP
Cock-throwing. Martin Lluellyn. PBBP
Cockayne Country. Agnes Mary Frances Robinson. OBVV
Cockcrow. *See* Cock Crow.
Cocker of Snooks, A. Phyllis Gotlieb. NOBC
Cockerel. *Unknown. See* I Have a Gentle Cock.
Cockies of Bungaree. *Unknown.* PoAu-1
Cockles and Mussels (Molly Malone). *Unknown, ad. by* James Morehead. ELP; OnYI
(Molly Malone.) FSW
Cockle-Shell and Sandal-Shoon. Herbert T. J. Coleman. CaP
Cockley Moor, Dockray, Penrith. Norman Nicholson. NeBP
Cockney of the North, The. Harry Graham. CenHV
Cockney rounds the corner, laundry pins, A. The Don. Barbara Howes. GLGT
Cockpit in the Clouds. Dick Dorrance. FaPON; RHPC; TiPo
Cockroach. Mary Ann Hoberman. *Fr.* Bugs. OBCA
Cockroach stood by the mickle, The. Archy Experiences a Seizure. Don Marquis. *Fr.* Archys Life of Mehitabel. WhC
Cockroaches. Kaye Starbird. RHPC
Cocks crow in the morn. *See* Cock crows in the morning.
Cock's on the wood pile, The. *Unknown.* OxNR
Cocktail is a pleasant drink, The. R-E-M-O-R-S-E. George Ade. FiBHP; OBAL; TreFT
Cocky Doodle Doodle Doo, *with music. Unknown.* OuSiCo
Cocoa Morning. Bob Kaufman. AmNP
Cocoa-Tree, The. Charles Warren Stoddard. AA
Coconut, The. "Ande." FiBHP
Coconut. Mario Satz, *tr. fr. Spanish by* Willis Barnstone. VWA
Coconut for Katerina, A. Sandra McPherson. FiCP; LCAP
Cocoon. David McCord. OBCA
Cocoon. Ishigaki Rin, *tr. fr. Japanese by* Ayusawa Takako. WPOW
Cocooning, The. Frédéric Mistral, *tr. fr. Provençal by* Harriet Waters Preston. *Fr.* Mirèio. AWP; PoPl
Cocteau's Opium: 1 ("Still, no one has paid much tribute to the man"). Donald Finkel. CoPo
Cocteau's Opium: 2 ("Picasso, who knows everything, will tell you"). Donald Finkel. CoPo
Cod-Fisher, The. Joseph C. Lincoln. EtS
Cod Liver Oil [*or* Ile]. *Unknown.* FSW; OuSiCo, *with music*
Coda. Basil Bunting. *Fr.* Briggflatts. OAEL-2
Coda. Fred Johnson. CNA
Coda. Dorothy Parker. DBV; InMe; SBG; TreFS
Coda. Ezra Pound. NOBA
Coda. James Tate. AmPA; NYBP
Coda. William Carlos Williams. NOBA
Coda: Revising History. Paul Mariani. MAYP
Code, The. Robert Frost. InPS; OBNV; PoA; UnPo
Code of Morals, A. Kipling. FaBoCo
Code of the Cow Country. S. Omar Barker. PoOW
Codes. Diana Chang. BrSi

Codes. Lois Seyster Montross. HBMV
Codfish lays ten thousand [*or* a million] eggs, The. Advertisement [*or* It Pays to Advertise *or* The Codfish]. *Unknown.* FaBoUs; RHPC; TreFT
Codfish Shanty, The. *Unknown. See* Cape Cod Girls.
Codicil. Mabel MacDonald Carver. GoYe
Codicil. Ruth Stone. BoWoP
Codicil. Derek Walcott. NoAM
Cod-piece that will house, The. Shakespeare. *Fr.* King Lear, III, ii. ViBoPo
Coelia, *sels.* William Percy.
"It shall be sayd I dy'de for Coelia," XIX. AAS
(Sonnet: "It shall be said I died for Coelia!") EIL
"Relent, my deere, yet unkind Coelia," XVII. AAS
Coesper erat: tunc lubriciles ultravia circum. Mors Iabrochii. *Unknown.* NA
Coeur de Lion to Berengaria. Theodore Tilton. AA
Coffee. J. V. Cunningham. MoAmPo; PrIm; VGW
Coffee and jasmine on a tray. Convalescence. James McAuley. CBAP
Coffee cups cool on the Vicar's harmonium. A Game of Consequences. Paul Dehn. ErPo; FiBHP; NOBL
Coffee that they give us, The. Gee, but I Want to Go Home. *Unknown.* FSW
Coffin, The. Heine, *tr. fr. German by* Louis Untermeyer. AWP
Coffin-Worm, The. Ruth Pitter. MoBrPo
Coilyear, gudlie in feir, tuke him be the hand, The. *Unknown. Fr.* Rauf Coilyear. OxBS
Coin, The. Sara Teasdale. HBMV; TiPo
Coin in the Fist. Florence Kerr Brownell. GoYe
Coins and Coffins under My Bed. Diane Wakoski. CoPo
Coins handsome as Nero's; of good substance and weight. Geoffrey Hill. Mercian Hymns, XI. FaBoMo; HAP
Cois na Teineadh. T. W. Rolleston. AnIV
Cokaygne. *Unknown. See* Land of Cockayne, The.
Cokby, Part Two. Jerome Rothenberg. NNaP
Cokkils. Sydney Goodsir Smith. OxBS; PoA
Cold. Robert Francis. LCAP; NePoAm-2; PoA
Cold, The. Lance Henson. CDW
Cold. Dorothy Roberts. NOBC
Cold and brilliant streams the sunlight on the wintry banks of Seine. Funeral of Napoleon I. Sir John H. Hagarty. CaP
Cold and clear-cut face, why come you so cruelly meek. Tennyson. *Fr.* Maud. SyP
Cold and Heat. *Tr. fr. Hawaiian by* M. W. Beckwith. WTO
Cold and holy oak. Rumba of the Three Lost Souls. Charles Madge. NeBP
Cold and starry darkness moans, A. Ghosts. Harry Behn. RHPC
Cold and the colors of cold: mineral, shell. Cold. Robert Francis. LCAP; NePoAm-2; PoA
Cold April, A. *Unknown.* FaBoUs
Cold Are the Crabs. Edward Lear. FaBoNo; GoJo; VLP
(Sonnet, A: "Cold are the crabs that crawl on yonder hills.") CenHV
Cold as no love, and wild with all negation. Stevie Smith. FaBoEE
Cold as no plea. The Death Sentence. Stevie Smith. NoP
Cold as the breath of winds that blow. Lucasta's World. Richard Lovelace. CaPo; SeCP
Cold as the thin Marquis who bit when kissing. The Lucifer. Guy Glover. CaP
Cold blast at the casement beats, The. The Heart's Summer. Epes Sargent. AA
Cold blood or warm, crawling or fluttering. Pet Shop. Louis MacNeice. BoAnP
Cold-blooded Creatures. Elinor Wylie. ImOP; SBG
Cold-blooded in warm waters, my Nurse. Among Sharks. Al Lee. AmPA
Cold blows the blast—the night's obscure. George Colman the Younger. *Fr.* The Maid of the Moor; or, The Water-Fiends. NOEC
Cold Blows the Wind. John Hamilton. CH
Cold blows the wind to my true-love [*or* tonight, sweetheart]. The Unquiet Grave. *Unknown.* FaBoBa; FSW; OBET; ViBoFo
Cold blows the winter wind: 'tis Love. Love at the Door. Meleager, *tr. by* John Addington Symonds. AWP
Cold, clear, and blue, the morning heaven. The Morning Star. Emily Brontë. ChTr
Cold, coiled line of mottled lead, A. Massasauga. Hamlin Garland. AA; BPAW
Cold, cold!/ Cold tonight is broad Moylurg. A Song of Winter. *Unknown, tr. by* Kuno Meyer. AnIL; CH; OnYI
Cold. Cold. Cold winds and colder heart. A Knight of Ghosts and Shadows. Dunstan Thompson. NePA
Cold, cold is the north wind and rude is the blast. The Battle of Lovell's Pond. Longfellow. PAH
Cold, cold the year draws to its end. Old Poem. *Unknown, tr. by* Arthur Waley. AWP; BoWoP
Cold Colloquy. Patrick Anderson. Poem on Canada, V. CaP; NOBC; PeCV
"Cold coming we had of it, A." Journey of the Magi. T. S. Eliot. CABA; DTC; EaLo; EBCP; FaBoCh; FaBoMo; FaFP; HAP; HeIP; LiTM; MoAB; MoAmPo; MP; NePA; NIP; NOCV; NoP; OAEP; OBCP; OBMV; OxBTC; PAI; PChr; PPoe; SBVL; SoSe; TAP; TrGrPo; TwCP
Cold, deserted and silent. *Unknown. Fr.* Winter on Black Mingo. FiBHP
Cold drool on his chin, warm drool in his lap, a sigh. A Dimpled Cloud. Frederick Seidel. FYAP
Cold earth slept below, The. Lines. Shelley. ChER; EnRP; LoBV; NCEP; SyP
Cold eyelids that hide like a jewel. Dolores. Swinburne. VLP
Cold Fact. Dick Emmons. PoPl
Cold Fear. Elizabeth Madox Roberts. WPE
Cold Feet in Columbus. William Heath. TAT
Cold felt cold until our blood, The. Phantasia for Elvira Shatayev. Adrienne Rich. LiSp
Cold Fire. George Starbuck. NYBP
Cold Front. Peter Sharpe. AMV-80
Cold Front, A. William Carlos Williams. NAs
Cold Glow: Icehouses. David Wojahn. AMV-81; MAYP
Cold, gray light of the dawning, The. Ticonderoga. V. B. Wilson. PAL
Cold Green Element, The. Irving Layton. NOBC; NoP; OBCV
Cold grey hills they bind me around, The. The King on the Tower. Ludwig Uhland, *tr. by* Thackeray. OBVV
Cold grey walls. San Francisco County Jail Cell B-6. Conyus. PoBA
Cold had a corpulent pig, A. A Corpulent Pig. Marnie *and* Harnie Wood. TDH
Cold has put blue horses where lambs were, The. Blue Horses. Ed Roberson. PoBA
Cold Heaven, The. W. B. Yeats. AWP; CTC; GTBS-P; HAP; MoVE; NoAM; OAEL-2; OAEP; TEP; WeW
Cold in the earth—and the deep snow piled above thee. Remembrance [*or* R. Alcona to J. Brenzaida]. Emily Brontë. BLPL; BoLoP; BoWoP; BrRo; CH; EBEV; EBVV; EnLoPo; FaBoEn; FaFP; HAP; HBV-1; LiTB; LO; MasP; NOBE; NoP; OAEP; OBNC; OxBI; PBWP; PoEL-5; TEP; TreFT; TrGrPo; VLP; WeW; WPE
Cold Irish Earth, The. Knute Skinner. InPK
Cold Iron. Kipling. OnMSP
Cold limbs of the air, The. A Mountain Wind. "Æ." AWP
Cold moon hangs to the sky by its horn, The. The Night of the Dance. Thomas Hardy. BrPo
Cold moon led us coldly, The. Shooting Ducks in South Louisiana. Richard Tillinghast. MAYP
Cold morning early. Two Mornings. Lawrence McGaugh. PoBA
Cold Night, A. Bernard Spencer. WaP
Cold night held the clandestine, A. Dreambooks. Alfred Corn. DFT
Cold night, the sidewalk we walk on icy, A. Christmas Eve Service at Midnight at St. Michael's. Robert Bly. NNaP
Cold nights on the farm, a sock-shod. On the Disadvantage of Central Heating. Amy Clampitt. AMV-80
Cold nights outside the taverns in Wyoming. Accountability. William Stafford. LCAP; NoP; NPAW
Cold Oxford unfamiliar now, around. Above the High. Geoffrey Grigson. EnLoPo
Cold rain, a steady wind. The Day the Beatles Lost One to the Flesh-eating Horse. Dave Kelly. FAZ
Cold remote islands, The. Night. Louise Bogan. UnPo
Cold Rendering, A. *Unknown.* BXAP
Cold, Sharp Lamentation. Douglas Hyde, *tr. fr. Irish by* Lady Gregory. OBMV
Cold shuttered loveless star, skulker in clouds. News of the World I. George Barker. LiTB
Cold slope is standing in darkness, The. December Night. W. S. Merwin. CAPP
Cold, smoldering, The. A Love Dirge to the Whitehouse. Bob Fletcher. NBP
Cold Snap. Kathy Mangan. AMV-80
Cold Spring, A. Elizabeth Bishop. MP; TwCP
Cold stings your bare cheeks and arms, The. To a Cactus Seller. Anwar Shaul, *tr. by* Yoffee Berkovitz. VWA
Cold Term. Amiri Baraka. BPo; CNA; SOTW
Cold, the dull cold! What ails the sun. A Seamark. Bliss Carman. PeCV
Cold transparent ham is on my fork, The. Sonnet to Vauxhall. Thomas Hood. PoEL-4
Cold was the night wind, drifting fast the snows fell. The Widow. Robert Southey. NOEC; OBEC
Cold Water. Donald Hall. NCSH
Cold Water Flat. Philip Booth. NePoAm
Cold Wave Blues. *Unknown.* BluL
Cold-Weather Love. Ronald Everson. MoCV

Cold winds swept the mountain's height, The. The Mother in the Snow-Storm. Seba Smith. PaPo
Cold winter now is in the wood. Elizabeth J. Coatsworth. TiPo
Colder Fire. Robert Penn Warren. *Fr.* To a Little Girl, One Year Old, in a Ruined Fortress. LiTM; MOVE
Colder the Air, The. Elizabeth Bishop. MiAP
Coldly, sadly descends. Rugby Chapel. Matthew Arnold. OAEP; OxBoCh; PoEL-5; VLP; WGRP
Coldness, The. Jon Silkin. CABA; VWA
Cold's the Wind. Thomas Dekker. *Fr.* The Shoemaker's Holiday, V, iv. ViBoPo
(Drinking Song.) TrGrPo
(Hey Derry Derry.) SeCePo
(Saint Hugh.) OBSC
(Troll the Bowl!) EIL
Cole, that unwearied prince of Colchester. Variations of [*or* on] an Air: After [Alfred] Lord Tennyson. G. K. Chesterton. FaBoPa; NOBL; Par
Cole Younger. *Unknown.* AmFP; BeLS; FSW
Colebrook Dale, *sel.* Anna Seward.
"While neighbouring cities waste the fleeting hours." NOEC
Colenso Rhymes for Orthodox Children. Bret Harte. OBAL
Coleridge. Aubrey Thomas De Vere. GoBC
Coleridge. Theodore Watts-Dunton. HBV-2; OBVV
Coleridge caused his wife unrest. Theme and Variation. Peter De Vries. NYBP
Coleridge Crossing the Plain of Jars; 1833. Norman Dubie. LCAP
Coleridge received the person from Porlock. Thoughts about the Person from Porlock. Stevie Smith. FaBoCo; NoP
Cole's Island. Charles Olson. *Fr.* The Maximus Poems. PoM
Colin. Anthony Munday. *See* Beauty Sat Bathing.
Colin and Lucy. Thomas Tickell. OBEC
Colin Clout, *sels.* John Skelton.
"And if ye stand in doubt." OAEL-1
"Doctors that learned be." OBSV
Prelates, The. TrGrPo
Colin Clout's Come Home Again, *sels.* Spenser.
Colin Clout at Court. OBSC
Her Heards Be Thousand Fishes. ChTr
"Of loves perfection perfectly to speake." OAEL-1
Colin, my deare, when shall it please thee sing. November. Spenser. *Fr.* The Shepheardes Calender. PoEL-1
Colin, you can tell my words are crippled now. James K. Baxter. Jerusalem Sonnets, 37. OCNZ
Colin's Complaint. Nicholas Rowe. OBEC
Colin's Passion of Love. George Peele. *See* O Gentle Love.
Coliseum, The. Poe. AmPP; AP; NOBA
Colkelbie Sow, *sel.* *Unknown.*
"Penny lost in the lak, The." OxBS
Collage for Richard Davis, A—Two Short Forms. De Leon Harrison. PoBA
Collages and Compositions. Richmond Lattimore. PP
Collapsars. Sandra McPherson. LCAP
Collapsible. Tom Raworth. EAS
Collapsible lover, the spider in iniquitousness, The. Anthology of Nouns. Parker Tyler. PoA
Collar, The. George Herbert. AnAnS-1; AWP; BiP; BLPL; CABA; EaLo; EBEV; FaBoEn; HAP; HBV-2; HeIP; InPS; JCP; LiTB; LoBV; MasP; MeLP; MePo; NIP; NOBE; NOCV; NoP; OAEL-1; OAEP; OBS; OxBoCh; PAI; PoEL-2; PoPle; PoRA; PPoe; PPP; SCV; SeCePo; SeCeV; SeCP; SeCV-1; TEP; TrGrPo; ViBoPo; WeW; WHA
Collar-Bone of a Hare, The. W. B. Yeats. OxBTC
Collect Calls. Diana Bickston. LFAC
Collect the silver on a Sunday. The Lucky Coin. Austin Clarke. NeIP
Collection, The. Bill Manhire. OCNZ
Collection of Emblemes, Ancient and Moderne, A, *sel.* George Wither.
"Why, silly Man! so much admirest thou." SeCV-1
Collection of Hymns . . . of the Moravian Brethren, A, *sels.* *Unknown.*
"Chicken blessed and caressed." NOEC
"What does a bird in Cross's air." NOEC
Collective Portrait, The. Robert Finch. MoCV
Collector, The. Richard Behm. AMV-81
Collector, The. Desirée Flynn. BrRo
Collector, The. Raymond Souster. ErPo; OBCV
Collector, The. Robert F. Whisler. AMV-81
Collector of lost beads, buttons, bird bones. The Pack Rat. Robert Pack. PPP
Collectors are abroad, the nets are spread. At the Museum. John Malcolm Brinnin. EyDe
Colleen Oge Asthore. *Unknown.* OnYI
Colleen Rue. *Unknown.* BIrV; OnYI
College Cat, The. Alfred Denis Godley. CenHV
College Colonel, The. Herman Melville. AA; OBWP
College Formal: Renaissance Casino. Langston Hughes. BALP
College of flunkeys, and a few gentlemen. John Berryman. GLGT
College of Surgeons, The. James Stephens. AnIL
College Song. Ed Anthony. InMe
Colley fell ill, and is no more! On an Insignificant Fellow. Lord Curzon. PV
Colley's Run-I-O. *Unknown.* AmFP
(Jolly Lumbermen, The, *with music.*) TrAS
Collie puppies in a dooryard. Wonder. Bernard Raymund. GDP
Collier, The. Vernon Watkins. DTC; FaBoTw; MoVE
Collier Lad's Lament, The. *Unknown.* OBET
Collier Lass, The. Frankie Armstrong. BrRo
Colliers' March, The. John Freeth. OBET
Collier's Rant, The. *Unknown.* OBET
Collier's Wedding, The, *sel.* Edward Chicken.
"At last the beef appears in sight." NOEC
Collier's Wife, The. D. H. Lawrence. OxBTC
Collies, The. Edward Anthony. GDP
Collige Rosas. W. E. Henley. *See* O Gather Me the Rose.
Collin my deere and most entire beloved. To the Most Excellent and Learned Shepheard Collin Cloute. William Smith. Chloris: Dedication. AAS
Collision: two seconds before, I saw the dark. Night Mare. Anita Endrezze-Danielson. STE
Colloque Sentimental. Paul Verlaine, *tr. fr. French by* Ernest Dowson. BrPo
(Sentimental Colloquy, *tr. by* Alan Conder.) LO
(Sentimental Conversation.) SyP, *tr. by* Ernest Dowson; WSC, *tr. by* Lloyd Alexander
Colloquial. Rupert Brooke. BrPo
Colloquy. Weldon Kees. NaP; NYBP
Colloquy at Peniel. W. S. Merwin. NePoEA
Colloquy in Black Rock. Robert Lowell. AP; CAPP; CoBMV; MiAP; MoAB; MoAmPo; NoAM
Colloquy of the Ancients, The, *sel.* *Unknown, tr. fr. Late Middle Irish by* Standish Hayes O'Grady *and* Kuno Meyer, *arr. by* Kathleen Hoagland.
"MacLugach! says Finn." OnYI
Colloquy with a King-Crab. John Peale Bishop. LiTA; MoPo
Colloquy with God, A. Sir Thomas Browne. *Fr.* Religio Medici. OBS
(Evening Hymn.) OxBoCh
Colloquy with Gregory on the Balcony, A. Howard Moss. FAZ
Collusion between a Alegaiter and a Water-Snaik. J. W. Morris. NA
Colly, My Cow. *Unknown.* EvOK
Colm had a cat. The Pets. Robert Farren. OxBI
Cologne. John Bate. NeBP
Cologne. Samuel Taylor Coleridge. DBV; FaBoEE; HBV-1; InMe; PV; TW; WhC
Cologne. Hilde Domin, *tr. fr. German by* Tudor Morris. VWA
Colombine. Hugh McCrae. PoAu-1
Colombo. March. The city white fire. Auschwitz from Colombo. Anne Ranasinghe. VWA
Colonel, The. Carolyn Forché. OBWP
Colonel B. Constance Carrier. NePoAm-2
Colonel B. Afforestation. E. A. Wodehouse. FiBHP
Colonel Chartres. John Arbuthnot. *See* Epitaph on Colonel Francis Chartres.
Colonel Cold strode up the line. Winter Warfare. Edgell Rickword. OBWP; OxBTC
Colonel Ellsworth. Richard Henry Stoddard. PAH
Colonel Fantock. Edith Sitwell. MoAB; MoBrPo; MoVE; OBMV
Colonel Fazackerley. Charles Causley. OnUR; RHPC
Colonel from Cheltenham stopped everyone, A. W. H. Auden. *Fr.* A Happy New Year. OBSV
Colonel in a casual voice, The. Gallantry. Keith Douglas. OBWP
Colonel rode by his picket-line, The. The Two Wives. William Dean Howells. AA
Colonel Sharp. *Unknown.* BaBo
Colonels here in solemn manner meet, The. Thomas Brown. FaBoEE
Colonel's Soliloquy, The. Thomas Hardy. OBWP
Colonial Set. Alfred Goldsworthy Bailey. OBCV
Colonialism ("The colonialist governments"). Cabdullaahi Qarshe, *tr. fr. Somali by* J. W. Johnson. WTO
Colonus' Praise. Sophocles, *tr. fr. Greek by* W. B. Yeats. *Fr.* Oedipus at Colonus. OBVE
Colophon. Oliver St. John Gogarty. OBMV
Colophon for Lan-t'ing Hsiu-hsi. John Peck. AmPA
Color, The. John Haines. GP
Color. Langston Hughes. BOLo
Color. Christina Rossetti. *Fr.* Sing-Song. SoPo
Color Alone Can Speak. Louise Townsend Nicholl. NePoAm
Color Blind. Carol Paine. PV
Color—caste—denomination. Emily Dickinson. EaLo; TAP
Color gladdens all your heart, The. Sympathy. Althea Gyles. HBV-1

Color in the Wheat. Hamlin Garland. BPAW
(Dakota Wheat-Field, A.) OBCA
Color it/ blue funk. Chromo. Sarah Webster Fabio. CNA
Color of leaves. The Underside of Trees. Charlotte DeClue. TWSS
Color of Many Deer Running, The. Linda Gregg. NPGG
Color of silence is the oyster's color, The. Earliness at the Cape. Babette Deutsch. FYAP; NePoAm-2; NYBP
Color of stone when leaves are yellow, The. Autumn. William Jay Smith. NePoAm
Color of the flowers, The/ has faded. Ono no Komachi, *tr. fr. Japanese by* Kenneth Rexroth. BoWoP
Color of the ground was in him, the red earth, The. Edwin Markham. *Fr.* Lincoln, the Man of the People. PGD
Color of the year spills down the street, The. November Walk. Susanne Doyle. AMV-81
Color of walls of scratches of cracks of brightness. The Aelf-scin, the Shining Scimmer the Gleam, the Shining. Michael McClure. CoPo
Colorado. John D. Dillenback. PoOW
Colorado. Robert Fitzgerald. MoPo
Colorado Sand Storm, A. Eugene Field. PoOW
Colorado Trail, The. *Unknown.* AS, *with music*; CoSo, *with music*; FSW
Coloratura. Geoff Page. AMV-81
Coloratura Named Luna, A. J. F. Wilson. TDH
Colored folks work on the Mississippi. Ol' Man River. Oscar Hammerstein II. BLSo
Colored pictures/ of all things to eat: dirty. The Songs of Maximus. Charles Olson. *Fr.* The Maximus Poems. NeAP; NoAM
Coloring Margarine. William Hathaway. AMV-81
Colors. Yevgeny Yevtushenko, *tr. fr. Russian by* Robin Milner-Gulland *and* Peter Levi. LLLT
Colors for Mama. Barbara Mahone. CNA; PoBA
Colors in the sun, colors at night, the Army, Navy and Marines. The Lagoon. Ashton Greene. NePoAm
Colors of Night, The. N. Scott Momaday. STE
Colors of the Dark One have penetrated Mira's body, The. Why Mira Can't Go Back to Her Old House. Mirabai, *English version by* Robert Bly. NU
"Colors," she said, "are never so fine." The Green and the Black. Anthony Bailey. NYBP
Colors shifting. Time of Fish Dying. Gabriela Melinescu, *tr. by* Stavros Deligiorgis. BoWoP
Colors we depend on are, The. The Love Bit. Joel Oppenheimer. CoPo; PoM
Colosseum. Harold Norse. TrJP
Colossus, The. Sylvia Plath. CAPP; LiTM; MP; NePoEA-2; NoAM; NOBA; NoP; TAP
Colour it cherry-red and call it Death-Wish Valley—that's the message. Loveliest of Counties, Shropshire Now. Ian Sainsbury. BXAP
Colour of God's Face, The, *sels.* Dorothy Livesay.
Land, The. PeCV
People, The: Village. PeCV
Coloured lanterns lit the trees, the grass, The. Episode of a Night of May. Arthur Symons. *Fr.* Scènes de la Vie de Bohème. BrPo
Coloured long-shore fishermen unfurl, The. The Gamblers. Anthony Delius. PeSA
Colours of Love, The. Denis Devlin. IPY; OxBI
Colours of the setting sun, The. The Sliprails and the Spur. Henry Lawson. PoAu-1
Coltish horseplay of the locker room, The. The Feast of Stephen. Anthony Hecht. HAP; NoP
Coltrane must understand how. Soul. D. L. Graham. PoBA
Colts ("Colts behind their mothers"). *Unknown, tr. fr. Japanese.* SUS
Columbia. Timothy Dwight. HBV-2; PAH
(Star of Columbia, *with music.*) TrAS
Columbia ("Thus down a lone valley with cedars o'erspread"). *Unknown.* AmFP
Columbia, appear! To thy mountains ascend. Perry's Victory—A Song. *Unknown.* PAH
Columbia College, 1796. Joseph Shippey. PeD
Columbia, Columbia, to glory arise. Columbia [*or* Star of Columbia]. Timothy Dwight. HBV-2; PAH; TrAS
Columbia, the Gem of the Ocean. David T. Shaw. FaBoBe; FSW; PAL
(Red, White and Blue, The.) WBLP
Columbia, Trust the Lord, *with music.* *Unknown.* AH
Columbiad, The, *sel.* Joel Barlow.
"Eager he look'd. Another train of years," *fr.* X. AmPP
(One Centred System.) AP
Columbian poet, whom we've all respected. Letter to an American Visitor. Alex Comfort. OxBTC
Columbia's Agony." Orpheus C. Kerr." OBAL
Columbia's Emblem. Edna Dean Proctor. GN
Columbine, The. Jones Very. AP; NOBA
Columbus. Arthur Hugh Clough. AmFN; PoSC
Columbus. Edward Everett Hale. PAH
Columbus. Percy Hutchison. EtS
Columbus. Leroy F. Jackson. SiSoSe
Columbus, *sel.* James Russell Lowell.
"One day more/ These muttering shoalbrains leave the helm to me." PGD
Columbus. Joaquin Miller. AA; BeLS; EtS; FaBoBe; FaFP; FaPON; GN; HBV-2; HBVY; MOS; OHFP; PAH; PAL; PaPo; PGD; TreF; YaD; YeAr
Columbus. Ogden Nash. NoP; OFD
Columbus. Muriel Rukeyser. GOA
Columbus. Schiller, *tr. fr. German by* Erika Gathmann Koessler. OFD
Columbus. Lydia Huntley Sigourney. AA; HBV-2; PAH
Columbus, *sel.* Tennyson.
"Chains, my good lord: in your raised brows I read." OFD
Columbus and the Mayflower. Richard Monckton Milnes. PAH
Columbus and the Mermaids. Elizabeth J. Coatsworth. GOA
Columbus at the Convent. John T. Trowbridge. PAH
Columbus discovered America. A Concise History of the World. Ira Sadoff. AmPA
Columbus Dying. Edna Dean Proctor. PAH
Columbus in Chains. Philip Freneau. PAH
Columbus is remembered by young men. And of Columbus. Horace Gregory. GOA; OFD
Columbus looked; and still around them spread. The First American Congress. Joel Barlow. PAH
Columbus looks towards the New World. Space. William Hart-Smith. *Fr.* Christopher Columbus. PoAu-2
Columbus Never Knew. Gail Brook Burket. PGD
Columbus Reaches Juana, 1492. Ralph Gustafson. NOBC
Columbus sailed over the ocean blue. Columbus. Leroy F. Jackson. SiSoSe
Columbus sailed the ocean blue. *Unknown.* FaBoUs
Columbus Stockade Blues. Woody Guthrie. FSW
Columbus the World-Giver. Maurice Francis Egan. PGD
Columbus to Ferdinand. Philip Freneau. OBCA; PAH
Columcille the Scribe. *At. to* St. Columcille. *See* St. Columcille the Scribe.
Colum-Cille's Farewell to Ireland. *At. to* St. Columcille. *See* Farewell to Ireland.
Columcille's Greeting to Ireland, *abr.* *At. to* St. Columcille, *tr. fr. Middle Irish by* William Reeves *and* Kuno Meyer. OnYI
Column A. Michael Silverton. PV
Columns and Caryatids. Carolyn Kizer. WPE
Com home againe! Christ Calls Man Home. *Unknown.* MeEL
Com my swete, com my flowr. The Assumption. *Unknown.* OxBM
Com out, Lazer, what-so befalle! Come Out, Lazurus! *Unknown.* OxBM
Coma. Dennis Schmitz. NPGG
Comanche. Gary Gildner. PH
Comanche Ghost Dance: An Impression. Lance Henson. VoR
Comarnad it is a very bonny place. Richie Story. *Unknown.* ESPB
Comb, The. Walter de la Mare. FaBoRV
Comb or womb of what we lay down nightly, A. The People's Choice: The Dream Poems II. Amiri Baraka. BiP
Combat, The. Edwin Muir. ChMP; CMoP; LiTB; MoBrPo; NOBE
Combat, The. Thomas Stanley, *after the Greek of* Anacreon. AWP
Combat of Ferdiad and Cuchulain, The, *sels.* *Unknown, tr. fr. Middle Irish by* Joseph Dunn.
"All was play, all was sport." OnYI
"Arise, ye kings of Macha." OnYI
"Ravens shall pick." OnYI
"Roll of a chariot, The." OnYI
Combat raged not long, but ours the day, The. The Burial of Latané. John R. Thompson. PAH
Combe, The. Edward Thomas. FM; GTBS-P
Combed by the cold seas, Bering and Pacific. Love Letter from an Impossible Land. William Meredith. WaP
Combination of Wagner and burlesque. Job. Eli Mandel. PeCV
Combinations. Mary Ann Hoberman. *Fr.* Bugs. OBCA
Combing. Gladys Cardiff. CDW; STE
Comcomly's Skull. Jim Barnes. STE
Come! William Barnes. CH
Come a landsman, a pinsman, a tinker or a tailor. Old Maid's Song. *Unknown.* FSW
"Come a little nearer, Doctor, thank you, let me take the cup." The Old Sergeant. Forceythe Willson. AA; BeLS
Come again to the place. After the Visit. Thomas Hardy. FaBoEn; NOBE; OBNC
Come, all brother sailors, I hope you'll draw nigh. The Beaver Island Boys. *Unknown.* OuSiCo
Come all fair maids both far and near and listen unto me. Tragic Verses. *Unknown.* CoMu
Come all gallant [*or* you gallant] seamen that unite a meeting. The Death of

Nelson [*or* A New Song Composed on the Death of Lord Nelson]. *Unknown.* CoMu; OxBoLi
Come all good people, I'd have you draw near. Naomi Wise. *Unknown.* ViBoFo
Come, all my boys and listen, a song I'll sing to you. The *Bigler.* *Unknown.* OuSiCo
Come all my fair ones. Jack Tar. *Unknown.* ShS
Come, all my good people, and listen to my song. Tittery-Irie-Aye. *Unknown.* AmFP
Come all my jolly seamen, likewise the landsmen, too. The *Cumberland* and the *Merrimac.* *Unknown.* AmFP
Come all of you blooming country lads and listen unto me. Country Hirings. *Unknown.* OBET
Come all of you bold shanty boys, and list while I relate. The Jam on Gerry's Rock. *Unknown.* BaBo
Come all of you good workers. Which Side Are You On? Florence Reese. FSW
Come all of you, my brother scouts. The Old Scout's Lament. William F. Drannan. CoSo; PoOW
Come all of you people, I pray you draw near. The Arizona Boys and Girls. *Unknown.* CoSo
Come all old maids that are squeamish. Eurynome. Jay MacPherson. NMP; OBCV; PV
Come all that loves good company. The Merry Hoastess. *Unknown.* CoMu
Come all who desire to hear of a jest. The Foolish Miller. *Unknown.* UnTE
Come, all ye bold Americans, to you the truth I tell. The Surrender of Cornwallis. *Unknown.* PAH
Come all ye bold sailors [*or* young sailormen *or* you young sailors]/ Who sail [*or* cruise] round Cape Horn [*or* who've rounded the Horn]. The Coast of Peru. *Unknown.* EtS; FSW; ShS
Come all ye [*or* you] bold sailors that follow the lakes. Red Iron Ore. *Unknown.* AS; FSW
Come all ye [*or* you] bold undaunted ones who brave the winter's frost [*or* cold]. Fifteen Ships on Georges Banks. *Unknown.* AmFP; BaBo
Come all ye boys of Liverpool I'd have you to beware. Van Dieman's Land. *Unknown.* BaBo
Come All Ye Fair and Tender Ladies. *Unknown.* AmFP
Come All Ye Fair and Tender Maidens. *Unknown.* *See* Little Sparrow.
Come all ye foreign strolling gentry. Four Epigrams on the Naturalization Bill. John Byrom. NOBL
Come all ye gentle [*or* you tender] Christians [*or* you Christian people], wherever you may be. Charles Guiteau. *Unknown.* AmFP; FSW; ViBoFo
Come all ye gents vot cleans the plate. Jeames of Buckley Square. Thackeray. VLP
Come, all ye good people, my story to hear. Poor Ellen Smith. *Unknown.* AmFP
Come all ye Irish gentlemen, a story I would tell. How We Built a Church at Ashcroft. Jack Leahy. PoOW
Come all ye jolly boatsman boys. Blow the Candle Out. *Unknown.* AmFP
"Come all ye jolly fellows, who delight in a gun." Polly Vaughn. *Unknown.* AmFP
Come all ye jolly lumbermen and listen to my song. Canada-I-O [*or* Canaday I. O.]. *Unknown, at. to* Ephraim Braley. AmFP; BaBo; FSW; ViBoFo
Come all ye jolly lumbermen who lumbered on Gaspereaux. *See* Come all you jolly lumbermen, I'd have you for to know.
Come all ye jolly sailors bold. Captain Ward and the Rainbow. *Unknown.* ViBoFo
Come, all ye jolly sailors bold. The *Arethusa.* Prince Hoare. FaPoR
Come all ye jolly shepherds. When the Kye Comes Hame. James Hogg. HBV-1; OxBS
Come all ye knights, ye knights of Molites. The Sons of Levi. *Unknown.* AmFP
Come all ye lads and lassies and listen to me a while. The Maid of the Sweet Brown Knowe. *Unknown.* AnIV; OnYI
Come all ye lads who know no fear. Barney's Invitation. Philip Freneau. PAH
Come all ye Lewiston fac'try girls. The Factory Girl's Come-All-Ye. *Unknown.* AmFP; OBAL
Come all ye maids of Simcoe, give ear to what I write. The Maids of Simcoe. *Unknown.* ShS
Come All Ye Mourning Pilgrims, *with music.* John A. Granade. AH
Come, All Ye People, *with music.* George R. Seltzer. AH
Come all ye railroad section men. Jerry, Go an' Ile That Car. *Unknown.* AS
Come, all ye seamen [*or* you sailors] bold. The Death of Admiral Benbow [*or* Admiral Benbow]. *Unknown.* CoMu; EnSB; GBP
Come all ye sons of Brittany. Braddock's Fate, with an Incitement to Revenge. Stephen Tilden. PAH
Come all ye [*or* you] true born shanty-boys, wherever you may be [*or* whoever that ye be]. The Jam on Gerry's Rock [*or* Young Monroe at Gerry's Rock]. *Unknown.* AmFP; AmSS; AS; FaBoBa; FSW; ViBoFo
Come all ye true-bred Irishmen. The *City of Baltimore.* *Unknown.* ShS
Come all ye Yankee sailors, with swords and pikes advance. The *Constellation* and the *Insurgente.* *Unknown.* PAH
Come all ye young fellows of Prince Edward Island. The Boys of the Island. Larry Gorman. ShS
Come all ye [*or* you] young fellows that [*or* who] follow the sea. Blow the Man Down. *Unknown.* BLSo; ShS, *vers.* II
Come all ye young fellows that follow the sea. The Black Ball Line. *Unknown.* AmSS
Come all ye young females, I pray you'll attend. Sally Monroe. *Unknown.* ShS
Come all ye young people and all my relations. Mr. Davis's Experience. *Unknown.* AmFP
Come all ye young people [*or* all young men and ladies], come fathers and mothers, too. The Rowan County Crew. *At. to* James William Day. AmFP; OuSiCo
Come all ye young sailor men [*or* you bold fishermen], listen to me. Blow Ye Winds Westerly [*or* Song of the Fishes *or* The Boston Come-All-Ye]. *Unknown.* AmSS; FSW; TrAS
Come all ye young sailormen who've rounded the Horn. *See* Come all ye bold sailors/ Who sail round Cape Horn.
Come, All Ye Youths. Thomas Otway. *Fr.* The Orphan. OAEP
Come all you blessed Christians dear. A Ballad from the Seven Dials Press. *Unknown.* CoMu; VLP
Come All You Bold Canadians, *with music.* *Unknown.* ShS
Come all you bold fisherman, listen to me. *See* Come all ye young sailor men . . .
Come all you bold ox teamsters. Teamster's Song. *Unknown.* TrAS
Come all you bold robbers and open your ears. Quantrell. *Unknown.* CoSo
Come all you bold sailors that follow the lakes. *See* Come all ye bold sailors . . .
Come, all you bold undaunted men. Jack Donahoe. *Unknown.* CoSo
Come all you bold, undaunted ones. *See* Come all ye bold undaunted ones . . .
Come all you bonny boys. The Bullard's Song. *Unknown.* OBET
Come all you booze buyers, if you want to hear. Kentucky Bootlegger. *Unknown.* FSW
Come all you brave Americans. Brave Paulding and the Spy. *Unknown.* PAH
Come all you brave Annapolis boys. Corbitt's Barkentine. *At. to* Tom Reynolds. ShS
Come, all you brave gallants, and listen a while. Robin Hood and the Butcher. *Unknown.* ESPB
Come all you brave sailors, that sails on the Main. The Famous Fight at Malago; or, The Englishmen's Victory over the Spaniards. *Unknown.* CoMu
Come all you brave soldiers, both valiant and free. On Independence. Jonathan Mitchell Sewall. PAH
Come all you brave young shanty-boys. James Whaland. *Unknown.* AS
Come all you British hearts of oak, and listen unto me. The Glorious Victory of Navarino! *Unknown.* CoMu
Come all you Christian people, wherever you may be. *See* Come all ye gentle Christians, wherever you may be.
Come all you cockers, far and near. The Bonny Grey. *Unknown.* GBP
Come All You Fair and Tender Ladies. *Unknown.* *See* Little Sparrow.
Come all you fair and tender maids. Rue. *Unknown.* FSW
Come all you fair gallants, fair gallants attend. Pretty Polly of Topsham. *Unknown.* AmFP
Come all you fine young fellows with hearts so warm and true. Flat River Girl. *Unknown.* AS
Come all you gallant heroes, I'd have you lend an ear. Major André. *Unknown.* AmFP
Come all you gallant poachers that ramble void of care. Van Dieman's Land. *Unknown.* CoMu; FaBoBa; FSW; OBET (B *vers.*)
Come all you gallant seamen that unite a meeting. *See* Come all gallant seamen . . .
Come all you girls and all you boys [*or* Come all you joky boys]. Kitty Morey [*or* Katy Dorey]. *Unknown.* AmFP; OuSiCo
Come all you good fellows wherever you be. The Rackets around the Blue Mountain Lake. *Unknown.* FSW
Come all you good old boys and listen to my rhymes. Lackey Bill. *Unknown.* CoSo
Come all you good people/ From all over the World. Lula Vires. *Unknown.* AmFP
Come all you good people of every degree. The Bermondsey Tragedy. *Unknown.* VLP
Come all you hardy sons of toil, pray lend an ear to me. The History of Prince Edward Island. Larry Gorman. ShS

Come all you hearty roving blades, and listen to my song. The Frolicsome Parson Outwitted. *Unknown.* CoMu
Come all you heroes, where'er you be. The Dying Sergeant. *Unknown.* AmFP
Come all you humane countrymen, with pity lend an ear. Charles Gustavus Anderson, *vers.* II. *At. to* Joseph Keating. ShS
Come all you joky boys. *See* Come all you girls and all you boys.
Come all you jolly [*or* old time] cowboys [*or* skinners] and listen to my song. The Buffalo Skinners [*or* Boggy Creek]. *Unknown.* BPAW; CoSo; FSW; GBP; ViBoFo
Come all you jolly cowboys that follow the bronco steer. The Crooked Trail to Holbrook. *Unknown.* CoSo
Come all you jolly dogs, in the Grapes, and King's Head, and/ Green Man, and Bell taps. Tom Tatter's Birthday Ode. Thomas Hood. LoBV
Come all you jolly fellows, come listen to my song. The Shanty Boys and the Pine. *Unknown.* AmFP
Come all you jolly freighters that ever hit the road [*or* that has freighted on the road]. Freighting from Wilcox to Globe. *Unknown.* AmFP; CoSo
Come all you jolly-hearted sailors. False Nancy. *Unknown.* AmFP
Come all you jolly highwaymen and outlaws of the land. Bold Jack Donahue. *Unknown.* AmFP
Come all you jolly jokers, if you want to have some fun. The Great American Bum. *Unknown.* FSW
Come all you jolly lumbermen, and listen to my song. Colley's Run-I-O [*or* The Jolly Lumbermen]. *Unknown.* AmFP; TrAS
Come all you [*or* ye] jolly lumbermen, I'd have you for to know [*or* who lumbered on Gaspereaux]. The Banks of the Gaspereaux. *Unknown.* AmFP; BaBo; ShS, *diff. vers.*
Come all you jolly ploughmen. The Painful Plough. *Unknown.* OBET
Come all you jolly railroad men, and I'll sing you if I can. Way Out in Idaho. *Unknown.* AmFP; BPAW; OuSiCo
Come all you jolly river boys, I'll have you all draw near. The Jam on Gerry's Rock, *vers.* I. *Unknown.* ShS
Come all you jolly sailormen that follow the salt sea. The Schooner *Blizzard.* *At. to* Henry Burke. ShS
Come all you jolly seamen who plough that restless deep. Jimmy Judge. *Unknown.* AmFP
Come all you jolly shanty boys that work the shanty and go. Turner's Camp on the Chippewa. *Unknown.* AmFP
Come all you jolly skinners and listen to my song. *See* Come all you jolly cowboys and listen to my song.
Come all you jolly travellers that's out of work, just mind. Cockies of Bungaree. *Unknown.* PoAu-1
Come all you Lachlan men, and a sorrowful tale I'll tell. The Streets of Forbes. *Unknown.* CBAP
Come all you lads of high renown and listen my story. Country Statutes. *Unknown.* OBET
Come all you Louisiana girls and/ listen to my noise. The Texian Boys. *Unknown.* CoSo
Come all you loyal Unionists, wherever you may be. Virginia's Bloody Soil. *Unknown.* AmFP
Come all you maids that live at a distance. I Live Not Where I Love. *Unknown.* OBET
Come all you married couples gay. The Dunmow Flitch of Bacon. *Unknown.* OBET
Come all you melancholy folks and listen unto me. The Melancholy Cowboy. *Unknown.* CoSo
Come all you men and maidens. Rufus Mitchell's Confession. *Unknown.* AmFP
Come all you men and maidens dear, to you I will relate. The Lexington Miller. *Unknown.* BaBo
Come all you men of Arkansas, a tale to you I'll sing. Annie Breen. *Unknown.* CoSo
Come all you men of learning. Botany Bay. *Unknown.* ViBoFo
Come all you Mill-town rowdies that drink and have no fear. Tomah Stream. Larry Gorman. ShS
Come all you muckers and gather here. Casey Jones. *Unknown.* AmFP
Come all you old cow-punchers, a story I will tell. A Man Named Hods. *Unknown.* CoSo
Come all you old time cowboys and listen to my song. *See* Come all you jolly cowboys and listen to my song.
Come all you old-timers and listen to my song. John Garner's Trail Herd. *Unknown.* CoSo
Come all you people from every land. Ellen Flannery. *Unknown.* AmFP
Come all you pretty fair maids. Green Willow, Green Willow. *Unknown.* AmFP
Come all you pretty fair maids, I pray you attend. My New Garden Field. *Unknown.* AmFP
Come all you pretty girls, to you these lines I'll write. The Buffalo Hunters. *Unknown.* CoSo
Come all you rambling sailor lads and listen unto me. The *Flying Cloud,* *vers.* I. *Unknown.* ShS
Come all you range riders and listen to me. The Range Riders. *Unknown.* CoSo
Come all you rounders if you want [*or* for I want you] to hear. Casey Jones. *Unknown.* AS; BeLS; FaBV; OxBoLi; TreF; TrGrPo; ViBoFo (A *and* B *vers.*)
Come all you sailors bold. *See* Come, all ye seamen bold.
Come, all you sailors of the southern waters. Phantoms All. Harriet Prescott Spofford. AA
Come all you saucy landladies, what makes you look so gay? The Royal Light Dragoon. *Unknown.* OBET
Come all you sons of Erin, attention now I crave. Morrissey and the Russian Sailor. *Unknown.* AS
Come all you sons of freedom and listen to my theme. Once More a-Lumbering Go. *Unknown.* AmFP
Come, all you sons of Liberty, that to the seas belong. The *General Armstrong.* *Unknown.* PAH
Come all you swaggering farmers, whoever you may be. The Times Have Altered. *Unknown.* CoMu
Come all you tender Christians, wherever you may be. *See* Come all ye gentle Christians . . .
Come all you Texas Rangers wherever you may be. The Texas Rangers. *Unknown.* BPAW; CoSo; FSW; OuSiCo
Come all you thoughtless young men, a warning take by me. The Murder of Maria Marten. *Unknown.* CoMu; OBET
Come, all you true boys from the river. Johnny Stiles; or, The Wild Mustard River. *Unknown.* OuSiCo
Come all you true lovers and the truth I'll unfold. The Jolly Young Sailor and the Beautiful Queen. *Unknown.* ShS
Come all you true-born shanty boys, wherever ye [*or* you] may be. *See* Come all ye true born shanty-boys . . .
Come all you wild and wicked youths. Van Dieman's Land. *Unknown.* OBET (A *vers.*)
Come all you wild young people and listen to my song. Young Edwin in the Lowlands Low. *Unknown.* BaBo; OBET
Come all you woolly waddies. The Harrington Barn Dance. *Unknown.* CoSo
Come all you worthy gentlemen that may be standing by. Comfort and Tidings of Joy. *Unknown.* FSW
Come all you young and handsome ladies. Little Sparrow. *Unknown.* AmFP
Come all you young Canadian boys, wherever that you be. The Jam on Jerry's Rock, *vers.* II. *Unknown.* ShS
Come, all you young companions. Young Companions. *Unknown.* CoSo
Come all you young fellows [*or* gallants] that follow the gun. Young Molly Ban [*or* Bawn]. *Unknown.* FaBoBa; OnYI
Come all you young fellows who follow the sea. *See* Come all ye young fellows that follow the sea.
Come, all you young gallants that follow the gun. *See* Come all you young fellows that follow the gun.
Come All You Young Ladies and Gentlemen. *Unknown.* OBET
Come all you young ladies and make no delay. *Unknown.* OxNR
Come all you young men from the Nashwaak. Young Forbest. *Unknown.* ShS
Come all you young men [*or* people] who handle a [*or* the] gun. Molly Bawn [*or* Shooting of His Dear]. *Unknown.* BaBo; OxBoLi
Come all you young people/ That live far and near. The Murder of Goins. *Unknown.* AmFP
Come all you young people, a story I will tell [*or* I pray you draw near]. Naomi (Omie) Wise. *Unknown.* AmFP; BaBo
Come all you young people who handle the gun. *See* Come all you young men who handle a gun.
Come all you young rebels and list while I sing. The Patriot Game. Dominic Behan. FSW
Come all you young sailors who cruise round Cape Horn. *See* Come all ye bold sailors/ Who sail round Cape Horn.
Come, all young girls [*or* along girls], pay attention [*or* and listen] to my noise. Kansas Boys. *Unknown.* AS; FSW
Come all young men and ladies, fathers and mothers, too. *See* Come all ye young people, come fathers and mothers, too.
Come all young men and maidens, come listen to my rhyme. Caroline of Edinboro' Town. *Unknown.* AmFP
Come, all young men, taking warning by me. Married and Single Life. *Unknown.* AmFP
Come along, boys, and listen to my tale. The Old Chisholm Trail. *Unknown.* BeLS; BPAW; CoSo; FaBoBe; TreFT
Come along, fatty-calf. Prodigal's Return. Ralph D. Eberly. AMV-80
Come along get you ready. A Hot Time in the Old Town [*or* There'll Be a Hot Time]. Joe Hayden. BLSo; FSN; YaD
Come along girls and listen to my noise. *See* Come, all young girls, pay attention to my noise.
Come along in then, little girl! From a Very Little Sphinx. Edna St. Vincent Millay. OBAL

Come along, 'tis the time, ten or more minutes past. Spectator ab Extra: Le Diner. Arthur Hugh Clough. OBSV; OxBoLi
Come an' Meet Me wi' the Children on the Road. William Barnes. VLP
Come and buy/ Have a try! Dorothy Brown Thompson. SiSoSe
Come and get your quinine, and come and get your pills. Words for Army Bugle Calls: Sick Call. *Unknown.* TreF
Come and Go with Me to That Land. *Unknown.* FSW
Come and let me make thee glad. The Builder. Francis Sherman. CaP
Come and let us live my deare. Out of Catullus. Catullus, *tr. by* Richard Crashaw. CavP; OBVE
Come and see her as she stands. Fanny. Anne Reeve Aldrich. HBV-1
Come and see the chimney-pots, etched against the light! Paris; the Seine at Night. Charles Divine. HBMV
"Come and you shall see." Shadow. Ann Mars. GoYe
Come apace, good Audrey. I will fetch up your goats, Audrey. Shakespeare. *Fr.* As You Like It, III, iii. PP
Come, arm ye! Come, arm ye! The Garibaldi Hymn. Luigi Mercantini. WBLP
Come at dawn, good friend. *Unknown, tr. fr. Spanish by* Willis Barnstone. BoWoP
Come away,/ Make no delay. Dooms-Day. George Herbert. JCP; SeCP; SeCV-1
Come Away, Come Away, Death. Shakespeare. *Fr.* Twelfth Night, II, iv. ElL; ELP; GBL; NOBE; NoP; OAEP; PoPle; ViBoPo; WHA
(Clown's Song, The.) CTC
(Come Away, Death.) PoRA; SeCeV
(Dirge.) OBEV
(Dirge of Love.) GTBS; GTBS-P
(Feste's Song.) OBSC
(Love's Despair.) TrGrPo
(Song.) FiP; PoEL-2
Come Away, Come, Sweet Love. *At. to* John Dowland. EnRePo; OAEP; OBSC; PoEL-2
(Come Away, Sweet Love.) LoBV
(To His Love.) ElL; ELP; GBL
Come Away, Death. Shakespeare. *See* Come Away, Come Away, Death.
Come Away, Sweet Love. *At. to* John Dowland. *See* Come, Away, Come, Sweet Love.
Come away to the skies. For His Wife, on Her Birthday. Charles Wesley. NOCV
Come Back. Arthur Hugh Clough. NCEP
Come Back. Henry William Herbert. AA
Come Back. W. S. Merwin. NaP
Come back again, my olden heart! Come Back. Arthur Hugh Clough. NCEP
Come back and bring my life again. Come Back. Henry William Herbert. AA
"Come back at dead of night and speak to me." The Two Societies. John Hall Wheelock. PoCH
Come back before the birds are flown. The Recall. James Russell Lowell. AP
Come Back Blues. Michael S. Harper. PoBA
Come Back, Lincoln. Chauncey R. Piety. PGD
Come Back to Erin. Charlotte Alington Barnard. TreFS
Come back to me. Another Night with Telescope. Leonard Cohen. PeCV
Come back to me, who wait and watch for you. Monna Innominata. Christina Rossetti. VLP
Come back, ye wandering Muses, come back home. On [*or* Proem to] the Hellenics. Walter Savage Landor. *Fr.* The Hellenics. EnRP; ViBoPo
Come balmy sleep! tired nature's soft resort. To Sleep. Charlotte Smith. WPE
Come, Blessed Bird. *Unknown.* NCEP
Come boyes, fill us a bumper, we'l make the Nation roare. The Courtier's Health; or, Merry Boys of the Times. *Unknown.* CoMu
Come, Break with Time. Louise Bogan. MoAmPo
Come, break your heart, then, with the world's beauty. Sic Transit Gloria Mundi. James Wreford Watson. CaP
Come, brethren of the water. The Powte's Complaint. *Unknown.* GBP
Come, bring with a noise. Ceremonies for Christmas[se] [*or* Yule Log]. Robert Herrick. AnAnS-2; GN; HBV-1; OBCP; OHIP; TEP
Come, brother, come. Let's lift it. Cotton Song. Jean Toomer. BPo; CDC
Come, brothers! rally for the right! The Bonnie Blue Flag. Annie Chambers Ketchum. PAH
Come, butter, come. Mother Goose. OxNR
Come Buy! Come Buy! Shakespeare. *See* Lawn as White as Driven Snow.
Come buy my fine wares. Apples [*or* Verses Made for Women Who Cry Apples]. Swift. *Fr.* Verses for Fruitwomen. AnIV; NCEP; OnYI
Come, Captain Age. Sarah N. Cleghorn. HBMV
Come, Celia, let's agree at last. Song. John Sheffield. HBV-1
Come, chearfull day, part of my life, to mee. Thomas Campion. *See* Come, Cheerful Day!
Come, cheer up, my lads, like a true British band. A Song. *Unknown.* PAH
Come, cheer up, my lads! 'tis to glory we steer. Heart of Oak. David Garrick. HBV-2; NOEC; OBEC; OxBoLi
Come, Cheerful Day! Thomas Campion. ElL
("Come, chearfull day, part of my life, to mee.") AAS
Come child, and with your sunbeam gaze assign. The Green Eye. James Merrill. PoA
Come, children, hear the joyful sound. The Big Bell in Zion. Theodore Henry Shackleford. BANP
Come, children, listen to me now. The Cow. *Unknown.* FaBoUs
Come, Chloe, and Give Me Sweet Kisses. Sir Charles Hanbury Williams, *after the Latin of* Martial. HBV-1; UnTE
(Epigram of Martial Imitated, An.) OBEC
Come, choose your road and away, my lad. The Call of the Spring. Alfred Noyes. SUS
Come Christmas. David McCord. PChr
Come close to me, dear Annie, while I bind a lover's knot. Pot and Kettle. Robert Graves. HBMV
Come, come away. Upon a Delaying Lady. Robert Herrick. PoPle
Come, come away, to the Tavern I say. *Unknown.* OBS
Come, come dear Night! Love's mart of kisses. Epithalamion Teratos. George Chapman. *Fr.* Hero and Leander. ElL; LoBV
Come, come fill up your glasses. The British Grenadier. *Unknown.* PAH
Come, come Flipote; it's time I left this place. Tartuffe; or, The Impostor. Molière, *tr. by* Richard Wilbur. NAWM-2
Come, come, my love, the bush is growing. With Garments Flowing. John Clare. GBL
Come, come, no time for lamentation now. Death of Samson [*or* No Time for Lamentation Now]. Milton. *Fr.* Samson Agonistes. ChTr; FaBoRV; FiP
"Come, Come," Said Tom's Father. Thomas Moore. *See* Epigram: " 'Come, come,' said Tom's father, 'at your time of life.' "
Come, come, what doe I here? Henry Vaughan. AnAnS-1; MePo; SeCV-1
"Come!" cried Helen, eager Helen. Sisters. Eleanor Farjeon. FaPON
"Come!" cried my mind and by her might. The Wanderer: Clarity. William Carlos Williams. TwAmPo
"Come," cried the Voice, "it is already Spring." Mary, Mary. Anthony C. Deane. FaBoPa
Come, cropper lads of great renown. The Cropper Lads. *Unknown.* OBET
Come cuddle close in daddy's coat. The Fairy Folk. Robert Bird. HBV-1; HBVY
Come, cut thy throte, and have thy throte-ball out! Lovers' Debouchment. William Zaranka. BXAP
Come dally me, darling, dally me with kisses. Psyche to Cupid: Her Ditty. James Broughton. ErPo
Come dance a jig. Mother Goose. OxNR
Come Dance with Kitty Stobling. Patrick Kavanagh. NoAM
Come dance with me. South of the Border. Virginia Real Nicholas. AMV-80
Come, dark-eyed Sleep, thou child of Night. And on My Eyes Dark Sleep by Night. "Michael Field." OBMV
Come, day, glad day, day running out of the night. Glad Day. Louis Untermeyer. TrJP
Come day, go day. Traveller's Ditty. Miriam Allen deFord. HBMV
Come, dear Amanda, quit the town. To Amanda. James Thomson. BSV
Come, dear children, let us away. The Forsaken Merman. Matthew Arnold. BeLS; EBEV; EtS; FaBoCh; FaPoR; FiP; GN; HBV-1; MOS; OAEP; OBNV; OBVV; PoPle; ViBoPo; VLP; WHA
Come, dear old comrade, you and I. Bill and Joe. Oliver Wendell Holmes. AA; HBV-2
Come, Death, I'd have a word with thee. Motley. Walter de la Mare. HoPM; MMA
Come, Death—My Lady Is Dead. *At. to* Charles d'Orléans MeEL
Come, doleful owl, the messenger of woe. *Unknown.* PBBP
Come Down. George Macdonald. TrPWD
Come down at dawn from windless hills. Sunrise on Rydal Water. John Drinkwater. HBV-1; LiTM
Come down, come down, my Lord, come down. My Lord's a-Writin' All de Time. *Unknown.* BoAN-1
"Come down, come down," said the farmer to his son. The Yorkshire Bite. *Unknown.* BaBo
Come down, come down to the Square. The Cat That Followed His Nose. John Kaye Kendall. CenHV
Come down, dear love, be quick. A Lover's Words. Vernon Watkins. DTC
Come down from heaven to meet me when my breath. Invocation. Siegfried Sassoon. MoBrPo
Come down from the Cross, my soul, and save thyself. Descent from the Cross. "Michael Field." WPE
Come down, O Christ, and help me! reach thy hand. E Tenebris. Oscar Wilde. BrPo; CABA; MoBrPo; TreFT; TrPWD

Come Down, O Maid, [from Yonder Mountain Height]. Tennyson. *Fr.* The Princess, Pt. VII. CABA; EBVV; FF; GTBS-P; OAEL-2; OBEV; OBNC; OBVV; TreFT; ViBoPo; WHA
(Idyl, An.) TrGrPo
(Shepherd's Song.) LoBV
(Song.) FaBoEn; OAEP; SeCeV
Come down, ye graybeard mariners. A Cry from the Shore. Ellen Mackay Hutchinson Cortissoz. AA
Come Down, You Bunch of Roses, Come Down, *with music.* *Unknown.* ShS
Come, drunks and drug-takers; come, perverts unnerved! Several Voices out of a Cloud. Louise Bogan. MoVE
Come, each death-doing dog who dares venture his neck. Hot Stuff. Edward Botwood. PAH
Come, Every Soul, *with music.* John H. Stockton. AH
Come, Ev'ning, once again, season of peace. Evening. William Cowper. *Fr.* The Task, IV. OBEC
Come! fill a fresh bumper, for why should we go. Ode for a Social Meeting. Oliver Wendell Holmes. OBAL
Come, fill the beaker, while we chaunt a pean of old days. Fort Duquesne. Florus B. Plimpton. PAH
Come, fill the cup, and in the fire of spring. Omar Khâyyâm, *tr. by* Edward Fitzgerald. *Fr.* The Rubâiyât of Omar Khâyyâm of Naishâpûr. FaBoRV; FaBV; TEP; TreF; WGRP; WHA
Come fleetly, come fleetly, my hookabadar. Cossimbazar. Henry S. Leigh. NA
Come follow, follow me. The Fairy Queen [*or* The Queen of Fairies]. *Unknown.* PoPle; ViBoPo
Come follow, heart upon your sleeve. A Maine Trail. Gertrude Huntington McGiffert. HBV-1
Come, Follow Me. Thomas Campion. EnRePo
Come, follow me by the smell. Onions [*or* Onyons]. Swift. *Fr.* Verses for Fruitwomen. AnIV; BIrV; FaBoUs; OnYI
Come forth, and let us through our hearts receive. Foliage. Felicia Dorothea Hemans. OBRV
Come Forth, Come Forth! "Christopher North." OBRV
Come forth! for Spring is singing in the boughs. April Moment. Arthur Davison Ficke. Sonnets of a Portrait Painter, XI. HBMV
Come forth from thy oozy couch. Imitation of Julia A. Moore. "Mark Twain." OBAL
Come forth, old lion, from thy den. On Himself. Walter Savage Landor. FaBoEE
Come forth, you workers! Rèveille. Lola Ridge. HBMV; WPE
Come forthe, sire sergeaunt, with your stately mace. The Dance. John Lydgate. *Fr.* The Dance of Death. PoEL-1
Come, freemen of the land. Put It Through. Edward Everett Hale. PAH
Come, freighted heart, within this port. Lovemusic. Carolyn Kizer. ErPo
Come, friendly bombs, and fall on Slough. Slough. John Betjeman. DBV; MoBrPo
Come friends and listen to my song. The Three Tall Men. *Unknown.* OBET
Come, Friends and Neighbors, Come, *with music.* Lewis Hartsough. AH
Come, friends, if you will listen, a story I will tell. The Sherman Cyclone. *Unknown.* AmFP
Come from a distant country. At Birth. Anthony Thwaite. NePoEA-2
Come from my first, ay, come! Charade. Winthrop Mackworth Praed. GN
Come from thy palace, beauteous Queen of Greece. Invocation. Thomas Randolph. MOON
Come, Gaze with Me upon This Dome. E. E. Cummings. NoAM; OxBA
Come, Gentle Death! Thomas Watson. *Fr.* Hecatompathia. EIL
Come, gentle sleep, death's image though thou art. Thomas Warton, the Younger, *tr. fr. Latin by* Wordsworth. OBVE
Come, gentle Spring, ethereal mildness, come. Spring. James Thomson. *Fr.* The Seasons. LAuP
Come, gentle tripe, the hungry carter's joy. Tripe. J. B. Morton. InMe
Come, gentle Zephyr, tricked with those perfumes. George Peele. *Fr.* David and Bethsabe. ViBoPo
Come, gentlemen all, and listen a while. Robin Hood and the Bishop. *Unknown.* ESPB
Come, gentlemen Tories, firm, loyal, and true. Sir Henry Clinton's Invitation to the Refugees. Philip Freneau. PAH
Come, Georgia boy, come listen to my song. Georgia Boy. *Unknown.* OuSiCo
Come gie's a sang, Montogomery cry'd. Tullochgorum. John Skinner. BSV; GoTS; OBEC; OxBS
Come, Gorgo, put the rug in place. "Michael Field." *Fr.* Variations on Sappho. PeHV
Come Green Again. Winfield Townley Scott. PoPl
Come, guard this night the Christmas-pie. Christmas Eve—Another Ceremony. Robert Herrick. OHIP
Come, Happy Children, *with music.* *Unknown.* AH
Come Harken unto Me, *with music.* *Unknown.* AH
Come . . . have do with dillying. Shrine to What Should Be. Mari Evans. NNP
Come, heavy souls, oppressed that are. Casting All Your Care upon God, for He Careth for You. Thomas Washbourne. OxBoCh
"Come here, come here, you freely feed." Kemp Owyne [*or* Kempion]. *Unknown.* ESPB (B *vers.*); OxBB
Come here, Denise. Denise. Robert Beverly Hale. GDP; GrPl
Come Here, Lord! *with music.* *Unknown.* BoAN-2
"Come here, my boy; hould up your head." The Irish Schoolmaster. James A. Sidney. FiBHP
Come here, said my hostess, her face making room. A Literary Dinner. Vladimir Nabokov. FiBHP; OBAL
Come here, thou proud pretender unto arts. There's Life in a Mussel; a Meditation. George Farewell. NOEC
Come here, you nigoramus. Dolly's Lesson. *Unknown.* FaBoUs
Come Hither. John Clare. NoP
Come hither all sweet maidens soberly. Sonnet: On a Picture of Leander. Keats. EnRP
Come hither and behold this lady's face. Laura Sleeping. Louise Chandler Moulton. AA
Come hither Apollo's bouncing girl. Square-Cap. John Cleveland. AnAnS-2
Come hither, Child! and rest. Villanelle of Sunset. Ernest Dowson. BrPo
Come hither, Evan Cameron! The Execution of Montrose. William Edmondstoune Aytoun. HBV-2; OnMSP
Come hither lads, and hearken, for a tale there is to tell. The Day Is Coming, *parody.* Sir Walter Besant. CenHV
Come hither lads, and hearken, for a tale there is to tell. The Day Is Coming. William Morris. OAEP; WGRP
Come Hither, My Dear One. John Clare. ELP
Come hither, Sir John, my picture is here. On a Lady Who Beat Her Husband. *Unknown.* FiBHP
Come hither, Topham, come, with a hey, with a hey. A Raree Show. Stephen College. APAS
Come hither, womankind and all their worth. Kissing. Lord Herbert of Cherbury. EnLoPo; ViBoPo
Come hither ye dreamers of dreams. The Vision. Daniel Defoe. APAS
Come hither, ye who thirst. Come Hither. John Clare. NoP
Come Hither, You That Love. John Fletcher. ELP
Come, Holy Babe! Mary Dickerson Bangham. PGD
Come, Holy Dove/ Descend on silent pinion. Hymn to the Holy Spirit. Richard Wilton. OxBoCh
Come, Holy Ghost! thou fire divine! Veni, Sancte Spiritus. *Unknown, at. to* Robert II, King of France, *tr. by* Catharine Winkworth. HBV-2
Come Holy Spirit, Dove Divine, *with music.* Adoniram Judson. AH
Come, holy tortoise shell. Sappho, *tr. fr. Greek by* Willis Barnstone. BoWoP
Come Home. *Unknown, tr. fr. Zulu by* Jack Cope. PeSA
Come Home, Come Home! Arthur Hugh Clough. HAP
Come Home, Father. Henry Clay Work. *See* Father, Dear Father, Come Home with Me Now.
Come home with me a little space. Christmas at Melrose. Leslie Pinckney Hill. BANP
Come home with white gulls waving across gray. Winter Landscape. Stephen Spender. MoAB; MoBrPo
Come, Hooker, come forth of thy native soile. Yee Shall Not Misse of a Few Lines in Remembrance of Thomas Hooker. Edward Johnson. SCAP
Come, human dogs, interfertilitate. The Eugenist. Robert Graves. FaBoEE
Come, I will make the continent indissoluble. For You, O Democracy. Walt Whitman. TrGrPo
Come In. Robert Frost. AmPP; BoNaP; FaBV; LiTA; LiTM; MoAB; MoAmPo; NOBA; NoP; TrGrPo
Come In. Isaiah Shembe, *tr. fr. Zulu by* H. Tracey. WTO
Come in at the low-silled window. Being Called For. Rosemary Dobson. CBAP
Come in, come in, you old true love. False True Love. *Unknown.* FSW
Come in, she said, but. Invitation. Victor Contoski. PV
Come in sweet grief. Tricked Again. Ridhiana. NBP
Come in the evening, or come in the morning. The Welcome. Thomas Osborne Davis. HBV-1; TreFT
Come in, the ford is roaring on the plain. Enid's Song. Tennyson. *Fr.* Idylls of the King: The Marriage of Geraint. FaBoRV
Come in this hour to set my spirit free. Before Day. Siegfried Sassoon. WGRP
Come in, Tom longtail, come short hose and round. Tom Long. *Unknown.* EBEV
Come inside the weather. By Hallucination Visited. Robert Horan. EAS
Come into Animal Presence. Denise Levertov. AP; HeIP; InPK; NaP; NU
Come into dinner squalls the dame. Snaps for Dinner, Snaps for Breakfast, and Snaps for Supper. George Moses Horton. OBAL
Come into the garden, Kate. The Tryst. Edward Valpy Knox. CenHV

Come into the Garden, Maud. Tennyson. Maud, Pt. I, xxii. EBVV; FaBV; FiP; HBV-1; NOBE; OAEL-2; OBVV; PaPo; TreF
(Maud.) OBEV
(Song from "Maud.") AWP
Come into the orchard, Anne. Swinburne. FaBoNo
Come, John, sit thee down I have somewhat to say. An Amorous Dialogue between John and His Mistress [*or* the Mistris and Her Aprentice]. *Unknown.* CoMu; UnTE
Come join hand in hand, brave Americans all. The Liberty Song. John Dickinson. BLSo; TrAS
Come, keen iambic[k]s, with your badger's feet. John Cleveland. *Fr.* The Rebel Scot. OBS; ViBoPo
Come knock your heads against this stone. An Epitaph. Blake. TEP
Come ladies and gentlemen, listen to my song. Robert's Farm. *Unknown.* FSW
Come lads and listen to my song, a song of honest toil. The English Labourer. *Unknown.* OBET
Come, Landlord, Fill the Flowing Bowl. *Unknown.* OxBoLi
Come lasses and lads, take leave of your dads. The Rural Dance about the Maypole. *Unknown.* GBP; OxBoLi
Come Laugh with Me. *Gond Oral Tradition, tr. by* V. Elwin *and* S. Hivale. WTO
Come learn with me the fatal song. The Mighty Heart. Emerson. *Fr.* Woodnotes, II. AA
Come leave the loathed stage. Ode to Himself[e]. Ben Jonson. AnAnS-2; OAEL-1; OBS; SeCP
Come! leave this sullen state, and let not wine. Henry Vaughan. *Fr.* To His Retired Friend. ViBoPo
Come leave thy care, and love thy friend. The Anti-Politician. Alexander Brome. CavP
Come, Lesbia, let us live and love. Catullus, *tr. fr. Latin by* Horace Gregory. NAWM-1
Come, let me write. And to what end? To ease. Astrophel and Stella, XXXIV. Sir Philip Sidney. SiPS
Come let us be going my brothers. Come Home. *Unknown, tr. by* Jack Cope. PeSA
Come! let us draw the curtains. Autumn. Humbert Wolfe. PoLF
Come, let us drink away the time. A Song of Sack [*or* Ode]. *At. to* Charles Cotton. CavP; OBS
Come, Let Us Find. W. H. Davies. HBMV
Come, let us join our friends above. The Ever-living Church. Charles Wesley. STF
Come, Let Us Kiss and Part. Michael Drayton. *See* Idea: "Since there's no help, come let us kiss and part."
Come, Let Us Make Love Deathless. Herbert Trench. HBMV; OBVV
Come, let us mount the breezy down. Harvest Home. Frederick Tennyson. OBVV
Come, let us now resolve at last. The Reconcilement. John Sheffield. OBEV
Come, let us pity those who are better off than we are. The Garret. Ezra Pound. PoPl; SOTW
Come, let us plant the apple-tree. The Planting of the Apple-Tree. Bryant. AA; GN; HBV-1; HBVY; OHIP; PoSC
Come let us rejoice. About Savannah. *Unknown.* PAH
Come, let us sigh a requiem over love. Robert Nichols. *Fr.* Sonnets to Aurelia. OBMV
Come, let us sing! it is time for summer. For an Eskimo. Annie Charlotte Dalton. CaP
Come, Let Us Tune Our Loftiest Song, *with music.* Robert A. West. AH
Come, let us walk. Spring in Virginia. Ramona Wilson. VoR
Come, let's go climb on that jasmine-mantled rock. What Her Girlfriend[s] Said to Her. Okkur Macatti, *tr. by* A. K. Ramanujan. BoWoP; PBWP
Come, let's to bed. Mother Goose. GBP; OxBoLi; OxNR
Come light and listen, you gentlemen all. Robin Hood and the Beggar, I. *Unknown.* ESPB
Come, list and hark, the bell doth toll. The Passing Bell. Thomas Heywood. *Fr.* The Rape of Lucrece. FaBoRV
Come listen a while and give ear to my song. Hard Times. *Unknown.* AmFP
Come listen a while, you gentlemen all. Robin Hood Newly Revived. *Unknown.* ESPB
Come, listen all unto my song. How Cyrus Laid the Cable. John Godfrey Saxe. PAH
Come, listen, all you gals and boys. Jump Jim Crow. Thomas D. Rice. BLSo
Come listen, and hear me tell/ the end of a tale so true. The Lass of Lynn's New Joy, for Finding a Father for Her Child. *Unknown.* CoMu
Come listen and I'll tell you. The Yankee Privateer. Arthur Hale. PAH
Come listen awhile, and I'll sing you a song. The Silly Old Man. *Unknown.* CoMu; TW
Come listen, good neighbors of every degree. The Liberty Pole. *Unknown.* PAH
Come listen, good people, to what I shall say. A Ballad Called Perkins's Figary. *Unknown.* APAS
Come listen, O Love, to the voice of the dove. The Voice of the Dove. Joaquin Miller. AA
Come listen to a ranger, you kind-hearted stranger. The Disheartened Ranger. *Unknown.* CoSo
Come listen to another song. The Old Scottish Cavalier. William Edmondstoune Aytoun. GN; HBV-2
Come listen to me, you gallants so free. Robin Hood and Allen [*or* Allin]-a-Dale. *Unknown.* ESPB; FaBoBe; GBP; HBV-2; MoShBr
Come listen to my ditty/ 'Twill not detail you long. Baldy Green. *Unknown.* PoOW
Come listen to my story, Molly Bawn. Molly Bawn and Brian Oge. *Unknown.* OnYI
Come, listen to my story, ye landsmen, one and all. Raging Canawl. *Unknown.* AS
Come, listen to my tragedy, good people, young and old. Henry Green [*or* Mary Wyatt and Henry Green]. *Unknown.* AmFP; BaBo
Come listen to the story of brave Lathrop and his men. The Lamentable Ballad of the Bloody Brook. Edward Everett Hale. HBV-2; PAH
Come listen, ye Whigs, to my pitiful moan. The Salamanca Doctor's Farewell. *Unknown.* APAS
Come, Little Babe. Nicholas Breton. *See* Cradle Song: "Come, little babe. . ."
"Come, little cottage girl, you seem." The Poets at Tea, VI. Barry Pain. Par
Come, little Drummer Boy, lay down your knapsack here. The Soldier's Friend. George Canning *and* John Hookham Frere. OBEC; Par
Come, little John, tell me the lovely tale. Whom Jesus Loved. John Barford. PeHV
Come, Little Leaves. George Cooper. FaPON
Come live and be merry. Laughing Song. Blake. *Fr.* Songs of Innocence. SoPo
Come Live with Me. Naomi Marks. BXAP
Come, Live with Me and Be My Love. C. Day Lewis. Two Songs, II. BoLoP; CoBMV; HAP; NoAM; OBMV
(Song: "Come live with me and be my love.") NIP; NoP
"Come live with me and be my love." Bacchanal. Peter De Vries. BXAP; NIP; NOBL; OBAL
Come live with me and be my love. That Strain Again. Ronald Hambleton. CaP
Come live with me[e] and be[e] my love. The Bait[e]. John Donne. CABA; ErPo; HoPM; InPK; InPS; NIP; OAEL-1; OAEP; PoRA; TEP; WhC
Come live with me[e] and be my Love. The Passionate Shepherd [*or* Sheepheard] to His Love [*or* The Shepherd to His Love *or* The Shepherd's Plea]. Christopher Marlowe. AAS; AWP; BiP; BoLoP; CABA; CTC; ElL; ELP; FaBoBe; FaBoEn; FaFP; FF; FPL; GN; GTBS; GTBS-P; HAP; HBV-1; HeIP; HoPM; InPK; InPS; LiTB; LoBV; NIP; NOBE; NoP; OAEL-1; OAEP; OBEV; OBSC; OLR; PAI; PoLF; PoRA; PPoe; PPP; SCV; SeCePo; SeCeV; SiPS; TreF; TrGrPo; UnTE; ViBoPo; WeW; WHA
Come live with me and be my whore. The Wooing Rogue. *Unknown.* CoMu
Come live with me and be my wife. A Modern Romance. Paul Engle. PoPl
Come live with me and be my wife. The Passionate Shepherd to His Love. Delmore Schwartz. NIP
Come, love, for now the night and day. Song for Autumn. Andrew Young. GBL
Come, Love, Let's Walk. *Unknown.* ElL
Come lovely and soothing death. Death Carol [*or* The Carol of Death]. Walt Whitman. *Fr.* When Lilacs Last in the Dooryard Bloom'd. DL; SCV; WHA
Come, lovely Muse, desert for me. Invocation. Samuel Hoffenstein. BXAP
Come, madam, come, all rest my powers defy. Going to Bed [*or* Elegie *or* To His Mistress Going to Bed]. John Donne. Elegies, XIX. AnAnS-1; BoLoP; EBEV; EnRePo; ErPo; GBL; JCP; LiTB; MePo; NoP; OAEL-1; PPP; SeCP; TEP; UnTE
Come! Marget, come!—the team is at the gate! The Country Lovers; or, Isaac and Marget Going to Town, on a Summer's Morning. George Smith. NOEC
Come marvel at my ox. Song of Praise for an Ox. Abraham Sutskever, *tr. by* Ruth Whitman. VWA
Come, me canny Tynesiders, an' lissen. The Strike. *Unknown.* OBET
Come Michaelmas. A. Newberry Choyce. HBMV
Come, Micky and Molly and dainty Dolly. The Flitch of Dunmow. James Carnegie. HBV-2
Come, Muse, migrate from Greece and Ionia. The Muse in the New World. Walt Whitman. *Fr.* Song of the Exposition. MoAmPo; PP

Come muster, my lads, your mechanical tools. The New Roof. Francis Hopkinson. PAH
Come, my brothers. The Only Tourist in Havana Turns His Thoughts Homeward. Leonard Cohen. CABA; MoCV; NoAM
Come, My Celia [Let Us Prove]. Ben Jonson. *Fr.* Volpone, III, vii. CABA; EIL; FaBV; FF; HeIP; NIP; NoP; OBVE; TEP; TrGrPo; WHA
(Song: To Celia.) AnAnS-2; BiP; EnRePo; ErPo; JCP; OAEL-1, *with music*; OBS; SeCeV; SeCP; SeCV-1
(To Celia.) FaBoEn; LoBV; OAEP; UnTE
Come (my dear) whilst youth conspires. Time Recover'd. Thomas Stanley, *after* Girolamo Casone. OBVE
Come, my fine cat, against my loving heart. The Cat. Baudelaire, *tr. by* Roy Campbell. PoPl
Come, my friends. Tennyson. *Fr.* Ulysses. TRV
Come my friends and listen unto me. The Parson Grocer. *Unknown.* CoMu
Come my friends come. Call from the Afterworld. Jozef Habib Gerez, *tr. by* Musa Moris Farhi *and* Anthony Rudolf. VWA
Come, my lad, and sit beside me: we have often talked before. The Story of a Stowaway. Clement Scott. PaPo
Come, my little Robert, near. Cleanliness. Charles *and* Mary Lamb. OxBChV
Come, my Lucasia, since we see. Friendship's Mystery; to My Dearest Lucasia. Katherine Philips. PeHV; ViBoPo
"Come my own one, come my fond one." The Saucy Sailor. *Unknown.* OBET
Come, my pretty little Muse. On My Pretty Marten. Charles Cotton. FM
Come, my songs, let us express our baser passions. Further Instructions. Ezra Pound. MP; PoA; TwCP
Come, my tan-faced children. Pioneers! O Pioneers! Walt Whitman. FaBoBe; WHA
Come, mysterious night. A Hymn to Night. Max Michelson. TrJP
Come near me, for the night. Microcosmos, XL. Nigel Heseltine. NeBP
"Come, neighbours, no longer be patient and quiet." The Riot; or, Half a Loaf Is Better than No Bread. Hannah More. NOEC
Come night. News from Mount Amiata. Robert Lowell. NaP
Come not again! I dwell with you. The Flown Soul. George Parsons Lathrop. AA
Come Not Near. Mary Elizabeth Osborn. NePoAm-2
Come Not Near My Songs. *Unknown, tr. fr. Shoshone Indian by* Mary Austin. AWP; OLR; WPE
(Song of a Passionate Lover.) BPAW
Come not the earliest petal here, but only. Quiet. Marjorie Pickthall. NOBC; OBCV
Come Not the Seasons Here. E. J. Pratt. NoP; PeCV
Come Not to Me for Scarfs. Aurelian Townshend. AnAnS-2
Come Not When I Am Dead. Tennyson. FaBoRV; GBL
(Go By.) OBNC
Come now, and let us wake them: time. Serenade. *Unknown, tr. by* Jethro Bithell. AWP
Come now behold. The Glory of and Grace in the Church Set Out. Edward Taylor. *Fr.* God's Determinations. AmPP; AP
Come now each gen'rous feeling heart. The Framework-knitters Lamentation. *Unknown.* CoMu
Come now! You supercilious detractors of America. Meredith Phyfe. Edgar Lee Masters. *Fr.* The New Spoon River. GOA
Come, O come, my life's delight. My Life's Delight. Thomas Campion. EIL; InvP; OBSC; TrGrPo
Come, O Friend, to Greet the Bride. Heine, *after the Hebrew of* Solomon Halevi Alkabez, *tr. fr. German by* Louis Untermeyer. *Fr.* Hebrew Melodies. TrJP
Come, O Lord, Like Morning Sunlight. Milton S. Littlefield. TrPWD
Come, O Sabbath Day, *with music.* Gustav Gottheil. AH
Come, O Thou Traveller Unknown. Charles Wesley. *See* Wrestling Jacob.
Come o'er the hills, and pass unto the wold. A Winter Hymn—to the Snow. Ebenezer Jones. OBNC
Come o'er the stream, Charlie. McLean's Welcome. James Hogg. OxBS
Come off to the stable, all you who are able. Words for Army Bugle Calls: Stable Call. *Unknown.* TreF
Come, oh come in pious laies. Hymne I: A Generall Invitation to Praise God. George Wither. *Fr.* Hallelujah; or, Britain's Second Remembrancer. SeCV-1
Come, Oh, come, my life's delight. *See* Come, O come, my life's delight.
Come on! Come on! This hillock hides the spire. Sunday Afternoon Service in St. Enodoc Church, Cornwall. John Betjeman. MoVE; NOCV
Come On Home. Sharon Scott. JB
Come On in My Kitchen. *Unknown.* BluL
Come on in now and get in this hip shaking contest. Hip Shakin' Strut. *Unknown.* BluL
Come on, mama/ Out to the edge of town. Bird Nest Bound. *Unknown.* BluL
Come on, my fellow pilgrims, come. *At. to* Sarah Lancaster. AmFP
Come on out of there with your hands up, Charlie. Patriotic Ode on the Fourteenth Anniversary of the Persecution of Charlie Chaplin. Bob Kaufman. PoBA
Come on, sir; here's the place. Stand still. How fearful. Dover, the Samphire Cliff. Shakespeare. *Fr.* King Lear, IV, vi. FaBoPP
Come on, sir. Now, you set your foot on shore. Ben Jonson. *Fr.* The Alchemist, II, i *and* ii. PoEL-2
Come on then, ye dwellers by nature in darkness. Chorus of Birds [*or* Grand Chorus of Birds]. Aristophanes, *tr. by* Swinburne. *Fr.* The Birds. AWP; PoEL-5
Come, on thy swaying feet. The Spirit of the Fall. Danske Bedinger Dandridge. AA
Come on, ye critics! Find one fault who dare. On Mr. Edward Howard, upon His British Princes. Charles Sackville. OBSV
Come, Ophrah, fill my cup—but not with wine. The Splendor of Thine Eyes. Moses ibn Ezra, *tr. by* Solomon Solis-Cohen. TrJP
Come out and climb the garden path. Luriana, Lurilee. Charles Elton. PoPle
Come out and hear the waters shoot, the owlet hoot. Apprenticed. Jean Ingelow. OBVV
Come out and walk. The last few drops of light. A Night Piece. Edward Shanks. HBMV
"Come out and watch the nighthawks fly." Waiting for Nighthawks in Illinois. Roger Pfingston. FAZ
Come out come out come out. Moon Eclipse Exorcism. *Unknown, tr. by* Armand Schwerner. MOON
Come Out, Come Out, Ye Souls That Serve. Christopher Brennan. *Fr.* The Wanderer. PoAu-1
Come out for a while and look from the outside in. Christmas Eve. C. Day Lewis. EaLo
Come Out into the Sun. Robert Francis. NYBP
Come Out, Lazarus! *Unknown.* OxBM
Come out o' door, 'tis Spring! 'tis May. May. William Barnes. PoSC
Come out of Crete/ and find me here. Sappho, *tr. fr. Greek by* Guy Davenport. OBVE
Come out of the Golden Gate. Old Counsel. Herman Melville. FaBoRV
Come out of the shrubs now. Hagar to Ishmael. Deborah Eibel. VWA
Come out, 'tis now September. The Ripe and Bearded Barley. *Unknown.* BoNaP; ChTr; GBP
"Come out with me!" cried the little red sled. The Little Red Sled. Jocelyn Bush. SoPo; TiPo
Come over the born bessy. A Songe betwene the Quenes Majestie and Englande. William Birche. CoMu
Come Painter, you and I, you know, dare do. Old England. Nahum Tate. APAS
Come, pass about the bowl to me. The Royalist. Alexander Brome. CavP
"Come, Philomele, that sing'st of ravishment." Shakespeare. *Fr.* The Rape of Lucrece. PBBP
Come, Phyllis, I've a cask of wine. To Phyllis. Eugene Field. InMe
Come play with me. To a Squirrel at Kyle-na-no. W. B. Yeats. FaPON; FM; PDV; RHPC
Come play with me said the sun. Play. Frank Asch. NTCP
Come praise Colonus' horses, and come praise. Colonus' Praise. Sophocles, *tr. by* W. B. Yeats. *Fr.* Oedipus at Colonus. OBVE
Come, Precious Soul, *with music.* *Unknown.* AH
Come, put off your gown of smooth lilac. Winter and Red Berries. Nicholas Moore. NeBP
Come rede me, dame, come tell me, dame. Nine Inch Will Please a Lady. Burns. ErPo
Come, rejoice, 'tis Easter Day! Christ Is Risen! D. H. Dugan. BLRP
Come, Rest in This Bosom. Thomas Moore. EnRP
(Stricken Deer, The.) GoBC
Come ride and ride to the garden. Lady Gregory. SUS
Come, Ride with Me to Toyland. Rowena Bennett. SiSoSe
Come right in this house, Will Johnson! Mrs. Johnson Objects. Clara Ann Thompson. BlSi
Come, rouse up, ye bold-hearted Whigs of Kentucky. Old Tippecanoe. *Unknown.* PAH
Come rude Boreas, blustering railer, list ye landsmen all to me. Rude Boreas. *Unknown.* OBET
Come, Sable Night. *Unknown.* EnRePo
"Come saddle me my fastest steed." Geordie. *Unknown.* AmFP
Come, Said My Soul. Walt Whitman. NOBA
"Come!" said Old Shellover. Old Shellover. Walter de la Mare. OxBChV; PoPle
Come sail with me o'er the golden sea. The Lord of the World. G. A. Studdert-Kennedy. PGD
Come sapless blossom, creep not stil on earth. The Sap. Henry Vaughan. AnAnS-1
Come Saturday morning, we bring ourselves. Women Hoping for Rain. David Tillinghast. AMV-81

Come, see the Dolphin's anchor forged! 'tis at a white heat now. The Forging of the Anchor. Sir Samuel Ferguson. HBV-1
Come, see thy friend, retir'd without regret. Nil Admirari. Congreve. OBEC
Come, Shepherds, Come! John Fletcher. *Fr.* The Faithful Shepherdess. ElL; ErPo
Come, Silence, thou sweet reasoner. Silence. James Herbert Morse. AA
Come, Sirrah Jack, Ho! *Unknown.* NCEP; OAEP
Come, sit thee down by these cool streams. Then Lose in Time Thy Maidenhead. *Unknown.* ErPo
Come, Sleep. Beaumont *and* Fletcher. *Fr.* The Woman-Hater III, i. ElL; ELP
(Lullaby: "Come sleep, and with the sweet deceiving.") FaBoEn
(Sleep.) HBV-2
Come, sleep, O sleep, the certain knot of peace. Astrophel and Stella, XXXIX. Sir Philip Sidney. CABA; ElL; EnRePo; HBV-1; LoBV; NIP; NOBE; NoP; OAEP; OBEV; OBSC; PoRA; PPP; SCV; SiPS; TEP; TreFS; TrGrPo; ViBoPo; WHA
Come slowly, Eden. Emily Dickinson. CMoP; UnTE
Come Slowly, Paradise. James Benjamin Kenyon. AA
Come small creatures of low estate, friskily moving. To the Field Mice. Richard Eberhart. BoAnP
Come, sons of Mars, who thirst for blood. A Drinking-Song, against All Sorts of Disputes in Drinking. William Wycherley. SeCV-2
Come, sons of summer, by whose toil[e]. The Hock-Cart, or Harvest Home. Robert Herrick. AnAnS-2; CaPo; EBEV; JCP; OAEP; OBS; SeCP; SeCV-1; ViBoPo
Come, sound up your trumpets and beat up your drums. The Young Earl of Essex's Victory over the Emperor of Germany. *Unknown.* ESPB; OBET
Come, Spirit of Thy Holy Love. My Heart's Desire. *Unknown.* STF
Come, spread foam rubber on the floor. I Can't Have a Martini, Dear, but You Take One. Ogden Nash. PoRA
Come, sprite, and dance! The sun is up. The Bacchante to Her Babe. Eunice Tietjens. HBMV
Come spur [*or* spurre] away. An Ode to Mr. [*or* Master] Anthony Stafford to Hasten Him into the Country [*or* Ode on Leaving the Great Town]. Thomas Randolph. AnAnS-2; FaBoEn; GoTL; HBV-1; NOBE; OBEV; OBS; ViBoPo
Come, stack arms, men! Pile on the rails. Stonewall Jackson's Way. John Williamson Palmer. AA; HBV-2; PAH
Come, stir the fire. Safe. James Walker. OBCP
Come, Stumpy, old man, we must shift while we can. The Broken-down Squatter. *Unknown.* PoAu-1
Come! supper is ready. The Good Moolly Cow. Eliza Lee Follen. OBCA
"Come, surly fellow, come! A song!" The Haunted House. Robert Graves. OxBI
Come swallow your bumpers, ye Tories, and roar. Massachusetts Song of Liberty. *At. to* Mrs. Mercy Warren. PAH
Come, sweetheart, come. *Unknown, tr. fr. Latin by* Helen Waddell. NAWM-1
Come take up your hats, and away let us haste. The Butterfly's Ball. William Roscoe. OnUR; OxBChV; RHPC
Come the little clouds out of the Ice-Caves. Rain Chant. Louis Mertins. BPAW
Come, the wind may never again. D.G.C. to J.A. Emily Brontë. BrRo; EnLoPo, 1 *st.*
Come then, and like two doves with silv'rie [*or* silvery] wings. The Apparition of His Mistress[e] Calling Him to Elizium [*or* Elysium]. Robert Herrick. AnAnS-2; CaPo; SeCP; SeCV-1
Come then! and while the slow icicle hangs. Winter's Frosty Pangs. Henry Vaughan. *Fr.* To His Retired Friend, an Invitation to Brecknock. FaBoRV
Come then, as ever, like the wind at morning! Invocation to Youth. Laurence Binyon. OBEV; OBVV
Come then, my friend! my genius come along. Henry St. John, Viscount Bolingbroke. Pope. *Fr.* An Essay on Man, Epistle IV. OBEC
Come, Thou Almighty King. Charles Wesley. WGRP
Come, thou monarch of the vine. A Drinking Song. Shakespeare. *Fr.* Antony and Cleopatra, II, vii. OAEP; OBSC; ViBoPo
Come thou, who art the wine and wit. His Winding-Sheet. Robert Herrick. CaPo; HBV-2; OBEV
Come through the quiet fields; April again. April 1940. Patrick Maybin. NeIP
Come to Birth. Abbie Huston Evans. NePoAm
Come to Britain; a Humble Contribution to the Movement. A. P. Herbert. WhC
Come to conquer. Cold Water Flat. Philip Booth. NePoAm
Come to Jesus. Frederick William Faber. VLP
(God Our Father.) WGRP
Come to Me. *Gond Oral Tradition, tr. by* V. Elwin *and* S. Hivale. WTO
Come to me, angel of the weary hearted! To Sleep. Frances Sargent Osgood. AA
Come to Me, Beloved. Digby Mackworth Dolben. OxBoCh
(Homo Factus Est.) TrPWD
Come to me broken dreams and all. The Still Voice of Harlem. Conrad Kent Rivers. CNA; IDB; NNP; PoBA
Come to Me, Dearest. Joseph Brenan. HBV-1
Come to me, Eros, if you needs must come. To the God of Love. E. V. Knox. HBMV; NOBL
Come to me from Crete to this holy temple. Sappho, *tr. fr. Greek by* Richmond Lattimore. WPOW
Come to me God; but do not come. To God. Robert Herrick. AnAnS-2
Come to me, grief, for ever. A Funerall Song. *Unknown.* CH
Come to me in my dreams, and then. Longing. Matthew Arnold. FPL; HBV-1; OAEP; PoLF
Come to me in the night—we shall sleep closely together. A Love Song. Else Lasker-Schüler, *tr. by* Michael Gillespie. BoWoP
Come to me in the silence of the night. Echo. Christina Rossetti. BoLoP; CH; EBVV; ELP; GBL; LoBV; NIP; NOBE; NoP; OAEL-2; OBNC; PoEL-5; SeCeV; ViBoPo
Come to Me Soon. *At. to* Sir Walter Ralegh. *See* On Dulcina.
Come to me when the swelling wind assails the wood with a sealike roar. Late Light. Edmund Blunden. EnLoPo
Come to my window in the evening twilight. Sunset. Hayyim Nahman Bialik, *tr. by* Helena Frank. TrJP
Come to our well-run desert. W. H. Auden. *Fr.* For the Time Being. TRV
Come to Sunny Prestatyn. Sunny Prestatyn. Philip Larkin. CABA; NoAM
Come to term the started child shocks. Mustipara: Gravida 5. Marie Ponsot. VGW
Come to the festal board tonight. The Festal Board. *Unknown.* BLPA; TreFS
Come to the judgment, golden threads. The Judgment of the May. Richard Watson Dixon. OBNC
Come to the Stone. Randall Jarrell. VGW
Come to the window & see sweet dawn shine on this wonder; a man. Bottom's Dream. Philip Dow. NPGG
Come to your heaven, you heavenly choirs [*or* quires]. New Heaven, New War[re]. Robert Southwell. AnAnS-1; LoBV; MePo; NOBE; NoP; OBSC; OxBoCh; SBVL
Come townsmen all and women too. Funny Rigs of Good and Tender-hearted Masters. *Unknown.* OBET
Come trotting up. Foal. Mary Britton Miller. PDV; PH
"Come, try your skill, kind gentlemen." The Gipsy Girl. Ralph Hodgson. MoBrPo
Come Turn to Mee, Thou Pretty Little One. *Unknown.* CoMu
Come unto Me ("Come unto Me, said Jesus"). Flora Osgood. STF
Come unto Me (" 'Come unto Me,' said One below"). John Stuart. STF
Come unto me, all ye that labour and are heavy laden. My Yoke Is Easy. Bible, *N.T.* *Fr.* St. Matthew. TreFS
Come unto Me, When Shadows Darkly Gather, *with music.* Catharine H. Watterman. AH
Come unto me, ye heroes. Saratoga Song. *Unknown.* PAH
Come unto these yellow sands. Paul Dehn. SpRo
Come unto these yellow sands. Ariel's Song [*or* Fairy Songs *or* Song]. Shakespeare. *Fr.* The Tempest, I, ii. CH; CTC; ElL; FaBoCh; GN; GoJo; HBV-1; HeIP; LoBV; NOBE; OBEV; OBSC; PoEL-2; PoPle; SpRo; TEP; ViBoPo
Come unto Us Who Are . . . Laden. Harry Roskolenko. FAZ
Come up England by a different line. I Remember, I Remember. Philip Larkin. FaBoPP
Come Up from the Fields, Father. Walt Whitman. MoAmPo; OBWP; OxBA; PPP; UnPo
Come up in the orchard with grass to your knees. Apple Season. Frances Frost. SiSoSe
Come Up, Methuselah. C. Day Lewis. OBMV
Come up, my horse, to Budleigh Fair. *Unknown.* OxNR
Come up to me at early dawn. Invitation. Solomon ibn Gabirol, *tr. by* Israel Zangwill. TrJP
Come, virgin tapers of pure wax. Epithalamium. Richard Crashaw. NOCV; ViBoPo
Come Visit My Garden. Tom Dent. NNP
Come visit my pancake collection. The Pancake Collector. Jack Prelutsky. OBCA
Come walk with me. Walk on a Winter Day. Sara Van Alstyne Allen. YeAr
Come walk with me along this willowed lane. May. Henry Sylvester Cornwell. HBV-1
Come, Walter Savage Landor, come this way. Landor. John Albee. AA
Come, warm your hands. Driftwood. Witter Bynner. FYAP
Come Wary One. Ruth Manning-Sanders. CH
Come, we shepherds [*or* shepheards], whose blest sight. In the Holy Nativity

of Our Lord God [*or* Hymn of the Nativity *or* The Nativity]. Richard Crashaw. AnAnS-1; CABA; HAP; MeLP; MePo; OBS; OxBoCh; PoEL-2; SBVL; SeCeV; SeCV-1; WGRP
Come wench, are we almost at the well. Fair Maiden. George Peele. *Fr.* The Old Wives' Tale. PoEL-2
Come, when no graver cares employ. To the Rev. F. D. Maurice. Tennyson. GTBS-P; VLP
Come when the leaf comes, angle with me. The Angler's Invitation. Thomas Tod Stoddart. GN; HBV-1
Come when you're called. Mother Goose. HBV-1; HBVY; OxNR
Come Where My Love Lies Dreaming. Stephen Collins Foster. TreFS
"Come, wife," said good old Farmer Gray. The Little Dog under the Wagon. *Unknown.* PoLF
Come with Me. Robert Bly. CAPP; NoAM; NOBA
Come with Me into Winter's Disheveled Grass. Karen Swenson. GrPl
Come with rain, O loud Southwester! To the Thawing Wind. Robert Frost. OxBA
Come with the Spring-time, forth fair maid, and be. The Meddow Verse; or, Aniversary to Mistris Bridget Lowman. Robert Herrick. SeCV-1
Come, Woeful Orpheus. *Unknown.* EnRePo
Come, workers! Poets, artists, dreamers, more and more. Angela Morgan. *Fr.* Let Us Declare! PGD
Come, worthy Greek, Ulysses, come. Ulysses and the Siren. Samuel Daniel. CABA; ElL; EnRePo; HAP; LoBV; NOBE; NoP; OBEV; OBSC; PoEL-2; TEP; ViBoPo
Come, Ye Disconsolate. Thomas Moore. WGRP
Come, ye heavy states of night. *Unknown.* OBSC
Come ye hither all, whose taste. The Invitation. George Herbert. AnAnS-1
Come, Ye Lads, Who Wish to Shine. *Unknown.* PAH
Come ye old English huntsmen that love noble sport. The Old Pack. *Unknown.* APAS
Come, ye thankful people, come. Harvest Home. Henry Alford. WGRP
Come you fatall sisters three. Whipping Cheare. *Unknown.* FaBoBa
Come you gallants all, to you I do call. Robin Hood's Chase. *Unknown.* ESPB
Come you ladies and you gentlemen and listen to my song. Hard Times in the Country. *Unknown.* OuSiCo
Come, You Pretty False-eyed Wanton. Thomas Campion. ELP; OBSC
Come, You Whose Loves Are Dead. Beaumont *and* Fletcher. *Fr.* The Knight of the Burning Pestle, IV, iv. ElL
Comedian, The. Irving Layton. AMV-81
Comedian as the Letter C, The. Wallace Stevens. NePA; OxBA; TwAmPo
Comedian Said It, The. Duff Bigger. FAZ
Comedy. Mark Van Doren. NePoAm-2
Comely and capable one of our race. On the Portrait of a Woman about to Be Hanged. Thomas Hardy. CMoP
Comes a brown. Corkby, Part Two. Jerome Rothenberg. NNaP
Comes a cry from Cuban water. Cuba Libre. Joaquin Miller. PAH
Comes a dun in the morning and raps at my door. The Poet and the Dun. William Shenstone. PP
Comes a time. The Poet in Old Age Fishing at Evening. Desmond O'Grady. CIP
Comes Fall. Robert Nathan. HBMV
Comes Fog and Mist. William Hart-Smith. *Fr.* Christopher Columbus. PoAu-2
Comes home dull with coal-dust deliberately. Her Husband. Ted Hughes. OxBC
Comes not the springtime here. Come Not the Seasons Here. E. J. Pratt. NoP; PeCV
Comes the deer to my singing. Hunting-Song. *Unknown, tr. by* Natalie Curtis. AWP; PAI
Comes the lure of green things growing. Afoot. Sir Charles G. D. Roberts. CaP; HBV-1
Comes the New Year; wailing the north winds blow. Thysia, XVI. Morton Luce. HBV-1
Comes the time. Algonkian Burial. Alfred Goldsworthy Bailey. OBCV
Comes the time when it's later. A Wicker Basket. Robert Creeley. CAPP; HAP; NoAM; NoP
Comes to knock and knock again. Galileo Galilei. William Jay Smith. PoCh
Comes walking barefoot. Sojourner Truth. Robert Hayden. *Fr.* Stars. CNA
Comes Winter, the Sea Hunting. Norman Dubie. MAYP
Comet, The. Emil Makai, *tr. fr. Hungarian by* André Ungar. VWA
Comet, The. Michael Palmer. NPGG
Comet at Yell'ham, The. Thomas Hardy. CMoP; GBL
(Comet at Yalbury or Yell'ham, The.) VLP
Comets and Princes. Samuel Johnson. FaBoEE
Comfort. Elizabeth Barrett Browning. HBV-2; TRV
Comfort. May Doney. HBMV
Comfort. Margaret Widdemer. GoYe
Comfort and Tidings of Joy. *Unknown.* FSW
Comfort but a queer companion, A. Woman. *Unknown, tr. by* Louis Untermeyer. UnTE
Comfort in Affliction. William Edmonstoune Aytoun. InMe
Comfort in Extremity. Christopher Harvey. OxBoCh
Comfort in Puirtith. Helen B. Cruickshank. OxBS
Comfort me with stars, not apples. Star Drill. T. Inglis Moore. PoAu-2
Comfort of the Fields. Archibald Lampman. CaP
Comfort of the Trees, The. Richard Watson Gilder. PAH
Comfort Stop, A. Tony Beyer. OCNZ
Comfort thee, O thou mourner, yet awhile! To the Sister of Elia. Walter Savage Landor. HBV-2
Comfort thyself, my woful heart. Sir Thomas Wyatt. SiPS
Comfort to a Youth That Had Lost His Love. Robert Herrick. NOBE; OBEV
Comfort Ye, Comfort Ye My People. Bible, *O.T.* Isaiah, XL. EaLo; OBVE; TreFS; TrJP
Comforted. Amy Carmichael. TRV
Comforted by Limestone. Edward Dorn. *Fr.* Oxford. NOBA
Comforters, The. Dora Sigerson Shorter. CH; HBMV
Comforting Lines. *Unknown.* STF
Comic Adventures of Old Mother Hubbard and Her Dog, The. Sarah Catherine Martin. *See* Old Mother Hubbard.
Comical Revenge, The, *sels.* Sir George Etherege.
Song: "If she be not as kind as fair." CavP
Song: "Ladies, though to your conqu'ring eyes," *fr.* V, iii. HBV-1; OBS
Comin' o' the Spring, The. Lady John Scott. BSV
Comin' thro' [*or* through] the Rye (*diff. versions*). Burns. FaFP; FSW; HBV-1; LiTB; OxBS; SpRo; TreF; UnTE; WBLP
Comin' through the craigs o' Kyle. Owre the Muir amang the Heather. Jean Glover. HBV-1
Comin' to Town. Robert V. Carr. BPAW
Coming. Philip Larkin. MoBrPo; OxBTC
Coming Across. Mehri, *tr. fr. Farsi by* Deirdre Lashgari. WPOW
Coming American, The, *sel.* Sam Walter Foss.
"Bring me men to match my mountains." AmFN; BLPA; FaBoBe
Coming and Going. Mitchell Goodman. VGW
Coming and Going. Louis Johnson. OCNZ
Coming and the Appearing, The. *Unknown.* STF
Coming around the corner of a dark trail . . . what was wrong with the valley? The Inquisitors. Robinson Jeffers. MoAmPo
Coming around the Horn. John A. Stone. AmFP
Coming at an end, the lovers. A Book of Music. Jack Spicer. PoM
Coming Awake. D. H. Lawrence. BrPo
Coming Back. Joseph Bruchac. CDW
Coming Back. Linda Gregg. NPGG
Coming Back Home. Ray A. Young Bear. CDW
Coming back one evening through deserted fields. Through All Your Abstract Reasoning. Brian Patten. FaBoTw
Coming back over the col between. Strength through Joy. Kenneth Rexroth. FYAP; VGW
Coming Back to America. James Dickey. NYBP; NYP
Coming back to school again. Getting Back. Dorothy Brown Thompson. SiSoSe
Coming back to this generous island. Returning to Store Bay. Barbara Howes. Psk
Coming by evening through the wintry city. At a Bach Concert. Adrienne Rich. NePoEA; NIP
Coming Child, The. Richard Crashaw. TRV
Coming down the mountain in the twilight. Where the Hayfields Were. Archibald MacLeish. DuDa
Coming Down to It. Malcolm Glass. BXAP
Coming from the south. Six Ten Sixty-nine. Conyus. PoBA
Coming from the woods. Haiku. Richard Wright. FAZ
Coming Home. John Stone. NIP
Coming Home, Detroit, 1968. Philip Levine. TAT
Coming Home from Camp. Lonny Kaneko. BrSi
Coming home, I find you still in bed. Abortion. Ai. BoWoP
Coming Home in March. Harold Littlebird. STE; VoR
Coming home on a summer night. Small Moon. Howard Nemerov. PCP
Coming home to the white. Alba: March. Marilyn Hacker. GP
Coming home with the last load I ride standing. Emergency Haying. Hayden Carruth. NNaP
Coming Homeward out of Spain. Barnabe Googe. ElL; EnRePo
Coming in again, you know the town by boards it makes eyes touch. Autobiography: Last Chapter. Jim Barnes. CDW
Coming in splendor through the golden gate. This Is the Last. Gilbert Waterhouse. PGD
Coming into the store at first angry. The Man Who Finds That His Son Has Become a Thief. Raymond Souster. NOBC; OBCV
Coming late, as always. The Poem. W. S. Merwin. PP
Coming of Age. John Logan. DiL

Coming of Age in the County Jail. Carter Revard. VoR
Coming of Christ, The. *Unknown.* ACP
(Christ's Coming.) OxBM
Coming of Dusk upon a Village in Haiti, The. Henry Rago. HoPM
Coming of Good Luck, The. Robert Herrick. ELU; FaBoEE; JCP
Coming of His Feet, The. Lyman W. Allen. BLPA
Coming of Light, The. Mark Strand. PPJ
Coming of Love, The. James I, King of Scotland. *See* He Sees His Beloved.
Coming of Spring, The. Nora Perry. HBVY; SoPo
(Coming of the Spring, The.) YeAr
Coming of that limpid star is twice, The. Sonnet VI. Louise Labé, *tr. by* Willis Barnstone. BoWoP
Coming of the Cold, The. Theodore Roethke. OBCP
Coming of the King, The. *Unknown. See* Guest, The.
Coming of the Plague, The. Weldon Kees. NaP; VGW
Coming of the Spring, The. Nora Perry. *See* Coming of Spring, The.
Coming of the White Man, The. Patrick Anderson. Poem on Canada, II. CaP; MoCV
Coming of War, The: Actaeon. Ezra Pound. CMoP; PoA
Coming of Wisdom with Time, The. W. B. Yeats. FaBoEE; PAI; POL; SoSe
Coming Out. Jacqueline Lapidus. IHMS
Coming out from a movie. Catwise. Philip Booth. NePoAm-2
Coming Out Of. Robert Duncan. EAS
Coming out of the house on a fresh March morning. March 1st. Kathleen Spivack. NYBP
Coming out of the mountains of a summer evening. St. Gervais. Michael Roberts. FaBoCh
Coming out of you. Out of You. Rodney Phillips. POL
Coming over the rise, passing. On the Farm. Barbara Winder. PH
Coming Suddenly to the Sea. Louis Dudek. NOBC
Coming to cottonwoods, an. Prospecting. A. R. Ammons. ConAP
Coming [*or* Comming] to kiss[e] her lips [*or* lyps], (such grace I found). Amoretti, LXIV. Spenser. EBEV; LoBV; OAEL-1
Coming to see the cherries. After Shiki. Larry Eigner. FAZ
Coming together. Recreation. Audre Lorde. NIP; NoP
Coming Up and Falling Down. Stephen Vincent. NeAC
Coming up England by a different line. I Remember, I Remember. Philip Larkin. NOBL
Coming upon it unawares. Pittsburgh. Witter Bynner. AmFN
Cominius, you reprobate old goat. Catullus, *tr. fr. Latin by* James Michie. DBV
Command the stones in a loud voice. How to Amuse a Stone. Richard Shelton. AMV-80
Commander Lowell. Robert Lowell. DiL; VGW
Commanding a Telephone to Ring. Jack Anderson. AMV-81
Commanding Elephants. Philip Levine. NaP
Commemoration. Claude McKay. BANP
Commemoration. Sir Henry Newbolt. FaBoTw; OBVV
Commemoration Ode, The. James Russell Lowell. *See* Ode Recited at the Harvard Commemoration.
Commemoration Ode, *sels.* Harriet Monroe.
Democracy. AA
Lincoln. AA
Two Heroes. OHIP
Washington. AA; FaBoBe
Commemorative of a Naval Victory. Herman Melville. AP; HAP; MOS; UnPo
Commencement. Constance Carrier. WPE
Commencement, Pingree School. John Updike. Str
Commendations of Mistress Jane Scrope, The. John Skelton. *Fr.* Phyllyp Sparrowe. OBSC
("How shall I report.") ViBoPo
Comment. Dorothy Parker. *Fr.* Some Beautiful Letters. InMe; NIP; OBAL
Commentaries on the Song of Songs. Judith Herzberg, *tr. fr. Dutch by* Shirley Kaufman. VWA
Commentary, *sel.* W. H. Auden.
"Some of our dead are famous, but they would not care." MoPo
Comments. Peggy Susberry Kenner. JB
Commercial Candour. G. K. Chesterton. WhC
Commercial Traveller. Lauris Edmond. OCNZ
Comming of K——, The, *sel. Unknown (Staff of Beeton's Annual).*
"And Sam he looked again, and Sam he saw." VLP
Comming to kisse her lyps, (such grace I found.) *See* Coming to kiss her lips . . .
Commingling sky, A. Freely Espousing. James Schuyler. NeAP; NoP
Commissary Report. Stoddard King. ShM
Commission. Ezra Pound. BoLoP; MP; NIP; TwCP
Commission Man, The. Robert V. Carr. BPAW
Commissioner bet me a pony, The—I won. Songs of the Squatters. Robert Lowe. PoAu-1
Commitment. James Russell Lowell. *See* Slaves.
Commitment in a City. Margaret Tsuda. CTBA
Committee, The. C. Day Lewis. BiP; CMoP
Committee, The—now a permanent body. Dream. Marianne Moore. NYBP
Committee's fat, The. Un-American Investigators. Langston Hughes. BPo
Common Bill. *Unknown.* AmFP; AS, *with music;* FSW
Common Blessings. Thomas Curtis Clark. TrPWD
Common Cormorant, The. Christopher Isherwood. FaBoCh; FaBoCo; FaBoNo; FiBHP; RHPC; WhC
(Common Cormorant or Shag, The.) ChTr
(Cormorant, The.) PoPle
Common Dawn. Guy Butler. PeSA
Common Dust. Georgia Douglas Johnson. AmNP; PoBA; TTY
Common Form. Kipling. *Fr.* Epitaphs of the War. FaBoEE; FaBoTw; PV
Common Grave, The. James Dickey. CoAP
Common Ground, A. Denise Levertov. PoM
"Not 'common speech,'" *sel.* PP
Common Inference, A. Charlotte Perkins Gilman. AA; WGRP
Common Light, A. Steve Orlen. Str
Common Living Dirt, The. Marge Piercy. GeTw
Common Lot, The. Adelbert Sumpter Coats. TrPWD
Common Man, The. Goldsmith. *Fr.* The Deserted Village. TreFT
("Ill fares the land, to hastening ills a prey.") OBSV; TRV
Common Man, The. A. J. M. Smith. NOBC
Common Poem, A. Carolyn M. Rodgers. CNA
Common Road, The. Silas H. Perkins. BLPA; FaBoBe
Common Sense. Thomas Field. AA
Common Sense. Harry Graham. *See* Mr. Jones.
Common Sense and Genius. Thomas Moore. NBM
Common speech is, spend and God will send, The. Gascoigne's Memories, III. George Gascoigne. EnRePo
Common Street, The. Helen Gray Cone. HBV-2
Common Woman, The, *sels.* Judy Grahn.
Carol, in the Park, Chewing on Straws, IV. PeHV; WPOW
Ella, in a Square Apron, along Highway 80, II. NMM
Margaret, Seen through a Picture Window, VI. GP
Vera, from My Childhood, VII. GP
Commonplace. "Susan Coolidge." TreFT
Commonplace, The. Walt Whitman. MoAmPo; TrGrPo
Commonplace Day, A. Thomas Hardy. PoPle
Commonplace I sing, The. The Commonplace. Walt Whitman. MoAmPo; TrGrPo
"Commonplace life, A," we say, and we sigh. Commonplace. "Susan Coolidge." TreFT
Commonplaces. Kipling. HBV-1
Commons' Petition to Charles II, The. Earl of Rochester. FaBoCo
Commonwealth. Ambrose Bierce. DBV
Commonwealth of Birds, The. James Shirley. GoBC
Commonwealth of the Bees, The. Shakespeare. King Henry V, *fr.* I, ii. GN
Commonwealth of Toil, The. Ralph Chaplin. FSW
Commotion of these waves, however strong, cannot disturb, The. Louis Dudek. Europe, XCV. OBCV
Communal. Mary Fullerton. PoAu-1
Communication. Elizabeth Jennings. NePoEA
Communication in Whi-te. Don L. Lee. BPo
Communication of His Thirtieth Birthday. Marvin Bell. CoAP
Communication to Nancy Cunard, A. Kay Boyle. PoNe
Communication to the City Fathers of Boston. George Starbuck. NYBP
Communion. Edward Dowden. TrPWD
Communion. J. L. Spicer. BLRP
Communion. John Banister Tabb. WGRP
Communion Hymn, A. Alice Freeman Palmer. TrPWD
Communion of Saints: The Poor Bastard under the Bridge. Marie Ponsot. VGW
Communism. Ella Wheeler Wilcox. PeD
Commuter. E. B. White. PV; TreFT; WhC
(Commuters.) FaBoCo
Commuter's Entry in a Connecticut Diary. Robert Penn Warren. AMV-81
Companion, The. E. A. Robinson. NoAM
Companion Fear is at my side. The News. "Sec." TRV
Companions. Charles Stuart Calverley. FaBoCo; HBV-1; NA; NOBL
Companions, The. Howard Nemerov. NYBP
Companions were we in the grove and glen! Frederick Goddard Tuckerman. Sonnets, II, viii. AP
Companionship. Maltbie D. Babcock. STF
Companionship. Mary Elizabeth Coleridge. NBM
Company of mountains, an upthrust of mountains, A. Kinloch Ainort. Sorley MacLean. PoSH
Company of Scholars, The. Helen Bevington. GLGT

Company of vessels on the sea, A. Battle Problem. William Meredith. NoAM; NYBP
Company One Keeps, The. *At. to* Aimor R. Dickson. *See* Judged by the Company One Keeps.
Compare a stick with the wood. Family Screams. Hy Sibiloff. TwAmPo
Comparison, The. Thomas Carew. AnAnS-2; CavP
Comparison, The. John Donne. ErPo; TEP
Comparison, A. John Farrar. FaPON
Comparison, The, *sel. Unknown.*
"Let dirty streets be paved with flow'ry green." NOEC
Comparison, A ("We fear to judge a watermelon"). *Unknown.* STF
Comparison and Complaint, The. Isaac Watts. TrPWD
Comparison of Love to a Streame Falling from the Alpes. Sir Thomas Wyatt. FaBoEn
Comparison of the Life of Man, A. Richard Barnfield. OBSC
Comparisons. Christina Rossetti. OxBChV
Compasses, The. George MacBeth. NePoEA-2
Compassion. Thomas Hardy. FM
Compassionate eyes had our brave John Brown. John Brown; a Paradox. Louise Imogen Guiney. PAH
Compassionate Fool, The. Norman Cameron. GTBS-P; OxBTC
Compatience perses, reuth and marcy stoundes. The Passion of Jesus. *Unknown.* MeEL
Compel Them to Come In. Leonard Dodd. BLRP
Compelled by calamity's magnet. Aftermath. Sylvia Plath. SBG
Compelled to Love. Walter Stone. ErPo
Compensation. James Edwin Campbell. BANP
Compensation. Thomas Stephens Collier. AA
Compensation. Paul Laurence Dunbar. AmNP; BPo; HBV-2; PoNe
Compensation. Emerson. AmPP; AP; FPL; LiTA; NOBA; TAP
Compensation. Gerald Gould. HBMV
Compensation. Robinson Jeffers. MoAB; MoAmPo
Compensation. Virginia Maughan Kammeyer. AMV-80
Compensation. Lizette Woodworth Reese. HBMV
Compensation. Celia Thaxter. HBV-1
Competing not so much with one another. Watching Gymnasts. Robert Francis. LiSp
Complacencies of the peignoir, and late. Sunday Morning. Wallace Stevens. AmPP; AP; BiP; BLPL; CABA; CMoP; CoBMV; CrMA; FaBoEn; HAP; HeIP; LiTA; LiTM; MasP; MoAB; MoAmPo; MoVE; NePA; NIP; NOBA; NoP; OxBA; PoA; PPoe; QFR; SeCeV; TAP; TwAmPo; WeW
Complacent Cliff-Dweller, The. Margaret Fishback. PoLF
"Complaine my lute, complaine on him." A Pleasant New Ballad of Two Lovers. *Unknown.* CoMu
Complaint, The. Mark Akenside. OBEV
Complaint. Ian Hamilton. NoAM
Complaint. Joseph Bennett. LiTA
Complaint. Samuel Taylor Coleridge. *See* Good Great Man, The.
Complaint. Rufinus Domesticus, *tr. fr. Greek by* Dudley Fitts. OLR
Complaint. William Carlos Williams. QFR
Complaint, A. Wordsworth. NOBE; OBRV; PoEL-4
Complaint. James Wright. NOBA; TAP; VGW
Complaint, The; or, Night Thoughts. Edward Young. *See* Night Thoughts.
Complaint about Exile, A. Mairi MacLeod, *tr. fr. Gaelic by* Joan Keefe. PBWP
Complaint by Night of the Lover Not Beloved, A. Earl of Surrey, *after the Italian of* Petrarch. AWP; EIL; FaBoEn; TEP
("Alas, so all things [*or* thinges] now[e] do[e] hold[e] their peace.") AAS; EBEV; EnRePo; OAEL-1; OBVE; SiPS
(Complaint by Night). LoBV
(Night.) OBSC
Complaint of a Lover Forsaken of His Love, The. *Unknown.* *See* Green Willow, The.
Complaint of a Lover Rebuked. Petrarch. *See* Love That Doth Reign and Live within My Thought.
Complaint of a Young Girl. Wang Chung-ju, *tr. fr. Chinese by* Kenneth Rexroth. PCP
Complaint of Chaucer to His Purse, The. Chaucer. InPK; OAEL-1; OxBM; ViBoPo
(Chaucer's Complaint to His Empty Purse, *mod. vers. by* Louis Untermeyer.) TrGrPo
(Complaint [*or* Compleinte] of Chaucer to His Empty Purse [*or* Purs], The.) GoBC, *mod. vers. by* Belle Cooper; TrGrPo; WHA, *mod. vers.*
(Complaint to His Purse.) CABA; NoP
(Song to His Purse for the King, A.) MeEL
Complaint of Henrie Duke of Buckinghame, The. Thomas Sackville. *See* Induction to "A Mirror for Magistrates."
Complaint of Love. Sir Philip Sidney. *Fr.* Arcadia. SiPS
("Loved I am, and yet complaine of Love.") PoEL-1
Complaint of New Amsterdam, The. Jacob Steendam. PAH
Complaint of Rosamond, The, *abr.* Samuel Daniel. OAEP
Sels.
Henry's Lament. OBSC
Lonely Beauty. CTC; OBSC
Rosamond's Appeal. OBSC
Complaint of the Absence of Her Lover Being upon the Sea. Earl of Surrey. EIL; ELP; GBL; OBEV
(Lady Complains of Her Lover's Absence, A.) SiPS
("O happie dames, that may embrace.") AAS; EBEV
(Seafarer, The.) NOBE; OBSC
Complaint of the Common Weill of Scotland. Sir David Lindsay. *Fr.* The Dreme. BSV; GoTS
(Compleynt of the Comoun Weill of Scotland, The.) OxBS
Complaint of the Fair Armouress [*or* Armoress], The. Villon, *tr. fr. French by* Swinburne. AWP; CTC; OBVE; UnTE; VLP
(Old Lady's Lament for Her Youth, The, *tr. by* Robert Lowell.) BoLoP
Complaint of the Fisherman's Wife. Sheila Nickerson. WOLT
Complaint of the Morpethshire Farmer, The. Basil Bunting. CTC
Complaint of Troilus, The. Chaucer. *Fr.* Troilus and Criseyde. NOBE; OBEV
Complaint That His Ladie after She Knew of His Love Kept Her Face Alway Hidden from Him. Earl of Surrey. *See* Cornet, The.
Complaint to His Purse. Chaucer. *See* Complaint of Chaucer to His Purse, The.
Complaints of Poverty, The, *sel.* Nicholas James.
"May poverty, without offence, approach." NOEC
Complaisant Friend, The. Pierre Louys, *tr. fr. French. Fr.* Chansons de Bilitis. PeHV
Complaisant Swain, The. Ovid, *tr. fr. Latin by* F. A. Wright. Amores, III, 14. AWP
Compleat Angler, The, *sel.* Izaac Walton.
Angler's Wish, The. HBV-1
Compleint of Chaucer to His Empty Purse, The. Chaucer. *See* Complaint of Chaucer to His Purse, The.
Complement, The. Thomas Carew. CavP
Complete earth, A. The Avocado Pit. Carl Rakosi. FAZ
Complete in Thee, No Work of Mine, *with music.* Aaron R. Wolfe. AH
Complete Lover, The. William Browne. HBV-1
(Song: "For her gait, if she be walking.") OBEV
Complete Misanthropist, The. Morris Bishop. FiBHP; FPL; TW
Completion. Eunice Tietjens. HBMV
Compleynt of the Comoun Weill of Scotland, The. Sir David Lindsay. *See* Complaint of the Common Weill . . .
Compliance. Ambrose Bierce. DBV
Complicity. Tess Gallagher. GeTw
Complicity killed you. I know. I know. Closer First to Earth. Anne Hazlewood-Brady. IHMS
Compliment, The. William Habington. ACP
Compliment to the Ladies, A. Blake. BXAP
Compliment upon a crutch, A. To a Lady, with a Present of a Walking-Stick. John Hookham Frere. FaBoUs
Compline. Debora Greger. AMV-81
Compline. Patrick F. Kirby. GoBC
Compline. Duncan Campbell Scott. GoBC
Components. Roger McDonald. CBAP
Compose compose beds. Sacred Emily Gertrude Stein. OBAL
Composed at Neidpath Castle, the Property of Lord Queensberry, 1803. Wordsworth. GTBS; GTBS-P
Composed at thirty, my funeral oration: Here lies. A Funeral Oration. David Wright. MP
Composed by the Sea-Side, near Calais, August 1802. Wordsworth. EnRP; OAEP
Composed, generally defined. The Map. Mark Strand. NYBP
Composed in the Composing Room. Franklin P. Adams. NIP; OBAL
Composed in the Tower before his execution. "More Light! More Light!" Anthony Hecht. CoAP; ConAP; HAP; NePoEA-2; NoAM; NOBA; NoP; OBWP; SoSe; TwCP; UnPo; VGW; VWA
Composed on the Theme "Willows by the Riverside." Yü Hsüan-chi, *tr. fr. Chinese by* Jan W. Walls. WPOW
(Poem to the Tune "Riverbank Willows," *tr. by* Geoffrey Waters.) BoWoP
Composed upon an Evening of Extraordinary Splendour and Beauty. Wordsworth. EnRP; OAEL-2
Composed upon Westminster Bridge, September 3, 1802. Wordsworth. AWP; BiP; BLPL; CABA; ChTr; EnRP; EyDe; FaBoCh; FaBoPP; FaBoRV; FaBV; FaFP; FF; HAP; HeIP; InPK; InPS; InvP; NoP; OAEL-2; OAEP; OBNC; OBRV; PAI; PoEL-4; PoLF; PoPl; PPP; PrIm; TEP; TrGrPo; UnPo; WeW
(Earth Has Not Anything to Show More Fair.) WHA
(Sonnet Composed upon Westminster Bridge, September 3, 1802.) FiP; HBV-2

(Upon Westminster Bridge.) FaPoR; GTBS; GTBS-P; LiTB; NOBE; OBEV; SCV; SeCeV; TreF
(Westminster Bridge.) LoBV; PoRA; ViBoPo
Composed While under Arrest. Mikhail Yuryevich Lermontov, *tr. fr. Russian by* Max Eastman. AWP
Composer's Winter Dream, The. Norman Dubie. LCAP
Composing scales beside the rails. The Harmonious Heedlessness of Little Boy Blue. Guy Wetmore Carryl. BoAnP
Composition. Peter Blue Cloud. VoR
Composition for a Nativity. John Ciardi. MiAP
Composition in Black and White. Katha Pollitt. GrPl
Composition in Late Spring. Irving Layton. PeCV
Composition of Pat Young, The. Pat Young. Kenneth MacKenzie. PoAu-2
Compost. James Grainger. *Fr.* The Sugar Cane. NOEC
(How to Fertilize Soil.) FaBoUs
Compost Heap, The. Vernon Watkins. NYBP
Compounded in confusion. The New Litany. Rita Mae Brown. PeHV
Compozishun—to James Herndon and Others. Ronald J. Goba. NCSH
Compromise. Laurence McKinney. InMe
Compromised by sorrow. Elegy for Chief Sealth. Duane Niatum. CDW
Compulsive Qualifications, *sels.* Richard Howard.
"Richard, may I ask a question? What is an episteme?" PoA
"Richard, what will it be like when you ask the questions?" PoA
Computation, The. John Donne. OAEP
Computer. Otto Orban, *tr. fr. Hungarian by* Emery George. VWA
Computer's First Christmas Card, The. Edwin Morgan. FaBoCo; NIP; PChr
Comrade, The. Lee Wilson Dodd.
Comrade in Arms. T. Inglis Moore. PoAu-2
Comrade Jesus. Ralph Cheyney. PGD
Comrade Jesus. Sarah N. Cleghorn. HBMV; WGRP
Comrade, Remember. Raymond Kresensky. PGD
Comrade Rides Ahead, A. Douglas Malloch. HBMV
Comrade, with your finger on the playback switch. The Bedbug. Tony Harrison. PV
Comrade, within your tent of clay. Comrade, Remember. Raymond Kresensky. PGD
Comradery. Madison Cawein. AA
Comrades. Henry Ames Blood. AA
Comrades. Henry R. Dorr. PAH
Comrades. Laurence Housman. HBV-2
Comrades. Lionel Johnson. HBV-2
Comrades, *with music.* Felix McGlennon. FSN
Comrades. George Edward Woodberry. HBV-2
Comrades as We Rest Within. Ronald Hambleton. CaP
Comrades in Arms: Conversation Piece. *Unknown.* ErPo
Comrades, leave me here a little, while as yet 'tis early morn. Locksley Hall. Tennyson. BLPL; EBEV; FaBoBe; FaFP; HBV-2; OAEL-2; OAEP; VLP; WHA
Comrades of risk and rigour long ago. Prisoners. F. W. Harvey. MMA
Comrades of the Cross. Willard Wattles. HBMV
Comrades, the morning breaks, the sun is up. Hafiz, *tr. by* Richard Le Gallienne. Odes, II. AWP
Comrades, when the air is sweet. At a Country Dance in Provence. Harold Monro. OBVV
Comrades, you may pass the rosy. The Lay of the Lovelorn [*or* Cry]. William Edmonstoune Aytoun *and* Sir Theodore Martin. CenHV; FaBoCo; VLP
Comus; a Masque Presented at Ludlow Castle. Milton. OAEL-1, *with music;* OAEP
Sels.
Chastity. OBS
"O foolishnes of men! that lend their ears." ViBoPo
(Comus's Praise of Nature.) PoEL-3, *longer sel.*
Sabrina Fair. EBEV; ELP; FaBoCh, *much abr.*; GN; PoEL-3
(Sabrina.) CH, *abr.*; NOBE; OBEV; OBS
(Song: "Sabrina fair.") Ecs; LoBV; SeCeV; ViBoPo
"Star that bids the shepherd fold, The." FaBoCh; OBEV; PPoe; ViBoPo, *longer sel.;* WHA
(Comus' Invocation to His Readers.) TrGrPo
(Comus Speaks.) NOBE
(Invocation of Comus, The.) OBS, *longer sel.*
(Mask, A.) FiP
(Song: "Star that bids the shepherd fold, The.") SeCeV, *longer sel.*
Song: "Sweet Echo, sweetest Nymph, that livest unseen." LoBV; SeCeV; ViBoPo
(Echo.) OBEV; OBS
(Lady Sings, The.) NOBE
(Lady's Song.) TrGrPo
(Sweet Echo, Sweetest Nymph.) ELP
Temperance and Virginity. OBS
"To the ocean now I fly." OBEV; OBS; ViBoPo
(Farewell of the Attendant Spirit.) TrGrPo
(Song: "To the ocean now I fly.") SeCeV
(Spirit Epiloguizes, The.) NOBE
Concealed within the shady wood. To Cara, after an Interval of Absence. Thomas Moore. PeD
Concealment, The: Ishi, the Last Wild Indian. William Stafford. NaP
Conceit Begotten by the Eyes. Sir Walter Ralegh. EnRePo; SiPS
(Affection and Desire.) OBSC
Conceit upon the Feet. William Zaranka. BXAP
Conceited Man, A. *Gond Oral Tradition, tr. by* V. Elwin *and* S. Hivale. WTO
Conceits, *sels.* Arlo Bates.
Kitty's Laugh. AA
Kitty's "No." AA
Concentred here th' united wisdom shines. The Federal Convention. *Unknown.* PAH
Concentric. Richard Kostelanetz. TAP
Concept of Force, The. Robert Sargent. SUW
Conception. Waring Cuney. BANP
Conception. Josephine Miles. GP
Conception is interesting, The: to see, as though reflected. Wet Casements. John Ashbery. PoM
Concepts and Their Bodies (The Boy in the Field Alone). Pattiann Rogers. MAYP
Concerning brave captains. Great-Heart. Kipling. HBV-2
Concerning Love. Josephine Preston Peabody. WhC
Concerning Mme. Robert. Deems Taylor, *tr. fr. French.* UnTE
Concerning One Responsible Negro with Too Much Power. Nikki Giovanni. BPo
Concerning the Awakening of My Soul. Henriette Roland-Holst, *tr. fr. Dutch by* Jonathan Crewe. WPOW
Concerning the Dead. Mark Halperin. FAZ
Concerning the Dead Women: The Munitions Plant Explosion: June, 1918. Elizabeth Libbey. AmPA
Concerning the Nature of Love. Lucretius, *tr. fr. Latin by* Dryden. *Fr.* De Rerum Natura. ErPo
Concerning Them That Are Asleep. R. W. Raymond. STF
Concerning Unnatural Nature: An Inverted Form. Hollis Summers. ErPo
Concerning your letter in which you ask. With Mercy for the Greedy. Anne Sexton. CAPP
Concert. Michael Arvey. AMV-81
Concert, The. Phyllis McGinley. YeAr
Concert. Helen Quigless. NBP
Concert. Robert Sward. VGW
Concert at Sea. Hubert Creekmore. WaP
Concert at the Station. Osip Mandelstam, *tr. fr. Russian by* Andrew Glaze. AMV-81; VWA
Concert-hall creaked like a full-dress shirt, The. Unfamiliar Quartet. Stephen Vincent Benét. WhC
Concert Party. Siegfried Sassoon. MMA
Concert Scene. John Logan. NePoEA-2
Concertmaster. Richard Burgin. AMV-81
Concise History of the World, A. Ira Sadoff. AmPA
Conclusion, The: "Even such is time, that takes in trust." Sir Walter Ralegh. *See* Even Such Is Time.
Conclusion, The: "How slow time moves when torment stops the clock!" Delmore Schwartz. TwAmPo
Conclusion: "If what began (look far and wide) will end." John Frederick Nims. PoA
Conclusion: "Image dance of change, An." Siegfried Sassoon. MoBrPo
Conclusion: "It was a Summer's night, a close warm night." Wordsworth. *Fr.* The Prelude. FaBoEn; OBNC
(Conclusion: "It was a close, warm, breezeless summer night.") PoEL-4
Conclusion: "Now have I brought a woork too end which neither Joves fierce wrath." Ovid, *tr. fr. Latin by* Arthur Golding. *Fr.* Metamorphoses, XV. CTC; OBVE
Conclusion of the Whole Matter, The. Ridgely Torrence. *Fr.* The House of a Hundred Lights. HBV-2
Conclusive Voyage, The. Juan Ramón Jiménez, *tr. fr. Spanish by* H. R. Hays. PoPl
Concord Hymn. Emerson. AA; AmFN; AmPP; AP; AWP; BLPA; BLPL; FaBoBe; FaBoEn; FaFP; FaPo; FaPON; FaPoR; GN; GOA; HAP; HBV-2; HBVY; HeIP; LiTA; NePA; NOBA; NoP; OBWP; OHFP; OxBA; PAH; PAI; PAL; SeCeV; TAP; TreF; TrGrPo; WaaP; YaD
(Hymn Sung at the Completion of the Battle Monument.) PoPl
"By the rude bridge that arched the flood," *sel.* ViBoPo
Concordance. Paul Violi. AMV-81
Concrete Cat. Dorthi Charles. InPK
Concrete Mixers. Patricia Hubbell. PDV; RHPC
Concrete Poem, A. Anthony Mundy. PV

Concubine, The, *sels.* William Julius Mickle.
Sunset. OBEC
Wild Romantic Dell, A. OBEC
Condemnation. Thich Nhat Hanh. PPON
Condemned, The. Edward Howland. AA
Condemned, The. Edmond Jabès, *tr. fr. French by* Jack Hirschman. VWA
Condemned [*or* Condemn'd] to hope's delusive mine. On the Death [*or* Lines on the Death] of Mr. [*or* Dr.] Robert Levet, a Practiser in Physic. Samuel Johnson. EBEV; FaBoEn; HBV-2; HeIP; InPS; LAuP; NOBE; NOEC; NoP; OAEL-1; OBEC; OBEV; PoEL-3; PPP; SCV; TEP
Condemned Women. Baudelaire. *See* Women Damned.
Condemning the Moongod Nanna. Enheduanna, *tr. fr. Sumerian; ad. by* Aliki *and* Willis Barnstone. BoWoP
Condition, The. T. Carmi, *tr. fr. Hebrew by* Peter Everwine *and* Shula Starkman. VWA
Conditions. José Luis Vega, *tr. fr. Spanish by* Julio Marzán. InW
Condoms keep catching at the river's/ skirt. In Mysterious Ways. Faye Kicknosway. GeTw
Condone. Ambrose Bierce. DBV
Condor, The. Michael Hogan. LFAC
Condors. Padraic Colum. GoJo
Conduct. Samuel Greenberg. CrMA; LiTA
Conductor Bradley. Whittier. PaPo
Conductor when he receives a fare, The. The Passenjare. Isaac H. Bromley. FiBHP
Conductor's cocked twig turns out, The. Orchestra. Reg Saner. AMV-80
Conductor's hands were black with money, The. Charon. Louis MacNeice. FaBoTw
Conemaugh. Elizabeth Stuart Phelps Ward. PAH
Conestoga. George E. Murphy, Jr. AMV-81
Coney Island Life, A. James L. Weil. AmFN
Coney Island of the Mind, A, *sels.* Lawrence Ferlinghetti.
Away above a Harborful. ErPo
"Constantly risking absurdity." CAPP; LiTM; NeAP; PoM; TAP
Fortune. CAD
"Frightened/ by the sound of my own voice." NoAM; TAP
Funny Fantasies Are Never So Real as Oldstyle. ErPo
In a Surrealist Year. PAI; PPON
In Golden Gate Park That Day. NoAM; PAI
In Goya's Greatest Scenes. FF; HeIP; LiTM; NeAP; NMP; NoAM; PoM; TAP
"Pennycandystore beyond the El, The." BiP; CAD; CAPP; CTBA; HeIP; PoM; TAP
"Poet's yes obscenely seeing, The." LiTM
"Sometime during eternity." CAPP; NoAM
"This life is not a circus where." PPP
"What could she say to the fantastic foolybear." CAPP
"Wounded wilderness of Morris Graves, The." NeAP
Confab. Kenneth Rosen. AmPA
Confederate veterans came to town. John Beecher. *Fr.* To Live and Die in Dixie. GP
Conference, The, *sel.* Charles Churchill.
Conscience. OBEC
Conference among ourselves we called, A. George Gascoigne. *Fr.* The Fruits of War. OBWP
Conference-meeting through at last, The. The Doorstep. Edmund Clarence Stedman. HBV-1
Conferences, adjournments, ultimatums. Louis MacNeice. *Fr.* Autumn Journal. OxBTC; WaP
Confess Jehovah, *with music. Unknown.* TrAS
Confess, Marpessa. Robert Graves. TEP
Confess We All, before the Lord, *with music.* John Wilson. AH
Confess'd from yonder slow-extinguish'd clouds. Summer Evening and Night. James Thomson. *Fr.* The Seasons: Summer. OBEC
Confessio Amantis, *sels.* John Gower.
Adrian and Bardus, *fr.* V. OxBM
Ceix and Alceone, *fr.* IV. OxBM
Jason and Medea, *fr.* V. ACP
Medea's Magic, *fr.* V. OxBM
Parting of Venus and Old Age, The, *fr.* VIII. PoEL-1
Confessio Fidei. Dryden. *See* Private Judgment Condemned.
Confession. Elsa Barker. *Fr.* The Spirit and the Bride. HBMV
Confession. Gelett Burgess. *See* Ah, Yes I Wrote the "Purple Cow."
Confession. Lucille Clifton. GeTw
Confession, The. Peter Cooley. AmPA
Confession. Donald Jeffrey Hayes. CDC
Confession. George Herbert. AnAnS-1; JCP
Confession, The. "Thomas Ingoldsby." FiBHP
Confession, A. Robert Mezey. AmPA; NaP
Confession. Charles d'Orléans. *See* My Ghostly Father, I Me Confess.
Confession. Ralph Pomeroy. CoPo
Confession. D. S. Savage. NeBP
Confession, A. Paul Verlaine, *tr. fr. French by* Arthur Symons. WGRP
Confession, The. Wen Yi-tuo, *tr. fr. Chinese.* ChTr
Confession in Holy Week. Christopher Morley. HBMV
Confession of a Glutton. Don Marquis. GDP
Confession of a Stolen Kiss. Charles d'Orléans. *See* My Ghostly Father, I Me Confess.
Confession of Faith. Elinor Wylie. MoAmPo; SBG
Confession Overheard in a Subway. Kenneth Fearing. LiTA; LiTM; WaP
Confession Stone, The. Owen Dodson. TTY
Confession to J. Edgar Hoover. James Wright. CAPP; ConAP
Confession to Settle a Curse. Rosemarie Waldrop. TW
Confessional, The. Robert Browning. ViBoPo
Confessional, The. *Unknown, tr. fr. Latin by* Louis Untermeyer. UnTE
Confessions. Elizabeth Barrett Browning. OBVV
Confessions. Robert Browning. ELP; GTBS-P; NOBE; PoPle; ViBoPo
Confessions of a Born Spectator. Ogden Nash. LiSP
Confessions of the Life Artist. Thom Gunn. CMoP
Confessor, The. G. G. Belli, *tr. fr. Italian by* Harold Norse. ErPo
Confide ye aye in Providence. Its Ain Drap o' Dew. James Ballantine. HBV-2
Confidence. *Unknown.* BLRP
Confidential. Winfield Townley Scott. ELU
Confines of a city block, The. Construction. Karl Shapiro. PCP
Confirmation, The. Edwin Muir. OxBS
Confirmation, The. Karl Shapiro. ErPo
Confirmers, The. A. R. Ammons. TAP
Conflict. Caroline Clive. OBVV
Conflict, The. C. Day Lewis. LiTB; LiTM; MoAB; MoBrPo; NoP
Conflict. F. R. Scott. CaP; PeCV
Conflict of Convictions, The. Herman Melville. AP; NOBA
Conformers, The. Thomas Hardy. ViBoPo
Confounded Nonsense. Tom Hood. FaBoNo
Confrontation. John Hart. POL
Confrontations of March. H. C. Dillow. AMV-80
Confronting a longing. Poem to My Death. Julia de Burgos, *tr. by* Grace Schulman. BoWoP
Confusion. Christopher Hervey. BXAP; Par
Conger Eel, The. Patrick MacGill. OnYI
Congo, The. Vachel Lindsay. CMoP; FaFP; LiTA; MoAB; MoAmPo; NoAM; NOBA; OxBA; PoNe; PoRA; TAP; TreF (I *and* III); WHA (I *and* III)
Congratulations. Ordinance on Winning. Naomi Lazard. GP
Conjecture, A. Charles Francis Richardson. AA
Conjergal Rights. Thomas Edward Brown. *Fr.* In the Coach. VLP
Conjugation of the Verb, "To Hope." Lou Lipsitz. FiCP
Conjuration. Agnes Gergely, *tr. fr. Hungarian by* Emery George. VWA
Conjuration, to Electra, A. Robert Herrick. GBL; PoEL-3
Conjuring Roethke. James Tate. OBAL
Connacht Caoine, A. *Unknown, tr. fr. the Irish.* AnIV
Connais-Tu le Pays? Richard Shelton. NYBP
Connaught Rangers, The. Winifred M. Letts. HBMV
Connecticut Elm, The. Emma Swan. PoPl
Connecticut River, The. Reuel Denney. TwAmPo
Connecticut summers recede and flow. Vanished. Steve Eng. AMV-81
Connection, The. Daniil Kharms, *tr. fr. Russian by* George Gibian. FaBoNo
Connoisseur of Chaos. Wallace Stevens. CABA; LiTM; MoPo; SUW
Connoisseur of pearl, A. African China. Melvin B. Tolson. PoBA
Connolly. Liam MacGowan. OnYI
Conon in Alexandria. Lawrence Durrell. MoPo
Conor the king. The King of Ulster. *Unknown, tr. by* Frank O'Connor. KiLC
"Conquer the gloomy night of thy sorrow." Defiance. Solomon ibn Gabirol, *tr. by* Emma Lazarus. TrJP
Conquered. Zoë Akins. HBMV
Conquered Banner, The. Abram J. Ryan. AA; HBV-2; PAH; TreF
Conquered the flower-maidens, and the wide embrace. Parsifal. Paul Verlaine, *tr. by* John Gray. *Fr.* Amour. PAI; SyP
Conqueror Worm, The. Poe. *Fr.* Ligeia, *prose tale.* AA; AP; AWP; BLPL; HBV-2; LiTA; NOBA
(Emperor Worm, The.) DL
Conquerors, The. Harry Kemp. HBV-2
Conquerors, The. Phyllis McGinley. DBV
Conqueror's Grave, The. Bryant. AA
Conquest. Elizabeth J. Coatsworth. AmFN
(Wilderness Is Tamed.) FaPON
Conquest. Philippe Desportes, *tr. fr. French.* AWP
(His Lady's Might.) OBSC
Conquest, The. Oliver St. John Gogarty. OBMV
Conquest. Georgia Douglas Johnson. AmNP
Conquest, A. Walter Herries Pollock. OBVV

Conquest of Granada, The, *sels.* Dryden.
Epilogue: "They who have best succeeded on the stage," *fr.* Pt. II. FiP; SeCV-2
Love, *fr.* Pt. II, Act III, sc. iii. FiP
Song of the Zambra Dance, *fr.* Pt. I, Act III, sc. i. ErPo; OAEP; PoEL-3
(Beneath a Myrtle Shade.) UnTE
(Zambra Dance, The.) SeCV-2
Conquistador. Georgia Lee McElhaney. CoPo
Conquistador, *sel.* Archibald MacLeish.
Prologue: "And the way goes on in the worn earth." NoAM
Conrad. Antoni Slonimski, *tr. fr. Polish by* Isaac Komem. VWA
Conrad in Twilight. John Crowe Ransom. OxBA
Conscience. Charles Churchill. *Fr.* The Conference. OBEC
Conscience, The. Anthony Euwer. *Fr.* The Limeratomy. HBMV
Conscience. George Herbert. AnAnS-1
Conscience. Melech Ravitch, *tr. fr. Yiddish by* Keith Bosley. VWA
Conscience. Sir Edward Sherburne. ACP
Conscience. Charles William Stubbs. BLPA
Conscience. Henry David Thoreau. *Fr.* A Week on the Concord and Merrimack Rivers. HBV-2
Conscience, The. Anna Wickham. POL
Conscience-Curst, The! "F. Anstey." CenHV
Conscience is instinct bred in the house. Conscience. Henry David Thoreau. *Fr.* A Week on the Concord and Merrimack Rivers. HBV-2
Conscience-Keeper, The. William Young. *Fr.* Wishmakers' Town. AA
Conscience's Song. Robert Wilson. *See* New Brooms.
Conscientious Objector. Edna St. Vincent Millay. WPOW
Conscientious Objector, The. Karl Shapiro. OxBA
Conscious. Wilfred Owen. MMA
Conscripts of the Dream, *sel.* Edwin Markham.
"Give thanks, O heart, for the high souls." PGD
Consecration. Patrick F. Kirby. GoBC
Consecration, A. John Masefield. HBMV; MoAB; MoBrPo; NoAM; WHA
Consecration. Benjamin Schmolck. BLRP
Consecration. *Unknown.* TRV
Consecration of the House. W. S. Fairbridge. PoAu-2
Consejos y Documentos al Rey Dom Pedro, *sel.* Santob de Carrion, *tr. fr. Spanish.*
Jewish Poet Counsels a King, A. TrJP
Consequences. William Meredith. NoAM
Conservancies. Josephine Miles. GP
Conservative, A. Charlotte Perkins Gilman. AA; HBV-1
Conservative. Harold Witt. AMV-80
Conservative, out on his motor, A. On the Wrong Side. A. W. Webster. TDH
Conservative Owl, The. Oliver Herford. TDH
Conservative Shepherd to His Love, The. Jack D'Arcy. InMe
Conserves. David Mus. *Fr.* The Joy of Cooking. PoA
Conserving the Magnitude of Uselessness. A. R. Ammons. NoAM
Consider. Christina Rossetti. GN; TRV
Consider a Move. Michael Ryan. MAYP
Consider a new habit—classical. Arras. P. K. Page. MoCV; OBCV
Consider fish: magnesium flows, slowly on the whole. Ecological Lecture. Burton Raffel. AMV-81
Consider, if you can/ the heads. On Viewing a Florist's Whimsy at Fifty-ninth and Madison. Margaret Fishback. WhC
Consider me a memory, a dream that passed away. Recessional. Georgia Douglas Johnson. CDC; PoNe
Consider, O my soul, what morn is this! A Meditation for Christmas. Selwyn Image. OBEV
Consider our Disneyland tour by the Yangtze. Tours. Stephen Shu Ning Liu. AMV-80
Consider the Auk. Ogden Nash. QQQ
(Caution to Everybody, A.) NePA
Consider the Lilies. Dorothy Donnelly. HoAn
Consider the Lilies. William Channing Gannett. *See* He Hides within the Lily.
Consider the lowering Lynx. Limerick. Langford Reed. CenHV
Consider the mysterious salt. In Time like Air. May Sarton. NYBP
Consider the sages who pulverize boulders. P Is for Paleontology. Milton Bracker. FiBHP; InMe; WhC
Consider the sea's listless chime. The Sea-Limits. Dante Gabriel Rossetti. EtS; MOS; NBM; OAEL-2; VLP
Consider them both in paradise. W. H. Auden & Mantan Moreland. Al Young. NPGG
Consider them, my soul, how horrible! The Blind. Baudelaire, *tr. by* T. Sturge Moore. SyP
Consider These, for We Have Condemned Them. C. Day Lewis. LiTB; LiTM; SeCePo
Consider This and in Our Time. W. H. Auden. FaBoMo; LiTB
Consider this my love: we are. While Waiting for Kohoutek. Christopher Erb. SOTS
Consider this small dust, here in the glass. The Hour Glass. Ben Jonson. BLPL; LiTB
Consider Well. Sir Thomas More. ACP; GoBC
Considerable Speck, A. Robert Frost. MoAB; MoAmPo; OBAL; PPP; WhC
Considerate Crocodile, The. Amos R. Wells. OBCA
Consideration for Others. Christopher Smart. *See* Mutual Subjection.
Considerations. David Helwig. NOBC
Consideratus Considerandus. John Saffin. SCAP
Considered Reply to a Child, A. Jonathan Price. BoLoP
Considering the Bleakness. Moishe Leib Halpern, *tr. fr. Yiddish by* Richard J. Fein. VWA
Considering the Death of John Wayne. Louis Phillips. SOTS
Considering the Snail. Thom Gunn. GrPl; LiTM; MP; NePoEA-2; TwCP
Consignee of silent storms and unseen lightning. Lynx. R. A. D. Ford. CaP
Consolation. Anthony Cronin. IBM
Consolation. Arthur Guiterman. BXAP
Consolation, A. Shakespeare. *See* Sonnets, XXIX.
Consolation. Earl of Surrey. NOBE; OBSC
(When Raging Love.) EnRePo
("When raging [*or* ragying] love with extreme pain [*or* payne].") AAS; EBEV; EnLoPo; SiPS; TEP
Consolation. *At. to* Lilla M. Alexander. *See* There Is Never a Day So Dreary.
Consolation, The. Edward Young. *Fr.* Night Thoughts, IX. NOEC
Consolation in July. Rayner Heppenstall. NeBP
Consolation in War. Lewis Mumford. NYBP
Consolation of Philosophy, The, *sels.* Boethius, *tr. fr. Latin.*
"Happy he whose eyes have view'd," *fr.* III, 12, *tr. by* Samuel Johnson. OBVE
"Happy That First White Age When We[e]," II, 5, *tr. by* Henry Vaughan. OBVE; PAI
(Metrium V.) PPON
Happy Too Much, *fr.* II, *tr. by* Elizabeth I, Queen of England. CTC
"He that hath set his headlong heart," *tr. by* Helen Waddell. NAWM-1
"He who has made his reckoning with life," *tr. by* Helen Waddell. NAWM-1
"O Father, give the spirit power to climb," *tr. by* Helen Waddell. NAWM-1
"O Maker of the starry world," *tr. by* Helen Waddell. NAWM-1
"O thou whose pow'r o'er moving worlds presides," III, 9, *tr. by* Samuel Johnson. OBVE; TrPWD
"Though countless as the grains of sand," II, 2, *tr. by* Samuel Johnson. OBVE
Consolations of Art. Roy Fuller. OxBC
Consolations of Philosophy. Derek Mahon. BIrV; CIP
Consolatory! St. John Emile Clavering Hankin. CenHV
Consolatory Poem Dedicated unto Mr. Cotton Mather, A. Nicholas Noyes. SCAP
Consorting with Angels. Anne Sexton. NMM
Conspiracy, The. Robert Creeley. PPJ
Conspiracy of Charles, Duke of Byron, The, *sels.* George Chapman.
"As when the moon hath comforted the night," *fr.* III, i. MOON; ViBoPo
"Give me a spirit that on life's rough sea," *fr.* III, i. ViBoPo
(Master Spirit, The.) EtS
Conspirators, The. Kenneth Burke. TwAmPo
Conspirators, The. Frederic Prokosch. LiTM; NePA; PrIm; WaP
Constable Calls, A. Seamus Heaney. IPY
Constance Kent. *Unknown.* OBET
Constancies. *Unknown, tr. fr. German by* Louis Untermeyer. UnTE
Constancy. Samuel Daniel. *Fr.* Hymen's Triumph. OBSC
Constancy. Sidney Godolphin. *See* Constancye.
Constancy. John Boyle O'Reilly. OnYI
Constancy. Coventry Patmore. *See* Constancy Rewarded.
Constancy. Earl of Rochester. CavP; HBV-1; OBEV; OBS
Constancy. Sir John Suckling. *See* Constant Lover, The.
Constancy. Minor Watson. HBV-2
Constancy. Sir Thomas Wyatt. OBSC
("Perdie, I said it not.") EnRePo; SiPS
("Perdye I said yt not.") PoEl-1
Constancy of a Lover, The. George Gascoigne. EnRePo; QFR
Constancy Rewarded. Coventry Patmore. The Angel in the House, II, xi, 4. VLP
(Constancy.) OBVV
Constancye. Sidney Godolphin. MePo
Constant, The. A. R. Ammons. HAP; WeW
Constant. Emily Dickinson. *See* Alter! When the hills do.
Constant Bridegrooms, The. Kenneth Patchen. CrMA; LiTM; NaP
Constant Cannibal Maiden, The. Wallace Irwin. OBAL
Constant Defender. James Tate. MAYP
Constant Farmer's Son, The. *Unknown.* OBET

Constant Labor, A. James W. Thompson. BPo
Constant Lover, The. Louis Simpson. NYBP
Constant Lover, The. Sir John Suckling. AWP; CaPo; FaBV; FaFP; FPL; HBV-1; HeIP; JCP; LiTB; NOBE; OBEV; OLR; SeCePo; TreFS; TrGrPo
(Constancy.) LoBV
(Out upon It!) NoP; OBS; PAI; PoEL-3; PoRA; SCV
(Out upon It! I Have Loved.) BoLoP; CABA; ErPo; FF; NIP; SeCeV; TEP
(Poem, A: "Out upon it! I have loved.") ViBoPo
(Poem with the Answer, A.) CaVP
(Sir J. S.) AnAnS-2; SeCV-1
(Song: "Out upon it, I have lov'd.") MeLP; MePo; SeCP; WHA
Constant Lover, The. Aurelian Townsend. *See* Though Regions Far Divided.
Constant North, The. J. F. Hendry. NeBP; OxBS
Constant Penelope sends to thee, careless Ulysses. Ovid, *tr. fr. Latin.* EnLoPo; GBL; OAEL-1
Constant Swain and Virtuous Maid, The. *Unknown.* HBV-1
Constant to none, but ever false to me. An Elegye. Thomas Campion. AAS
Constantine's Vision of the Cross. Cynewulf, *tr. fr. Anglo-Saxon by* Charles W. Kennedy. *Fr.* Elene. AnOE
Constantly near you, I never in my entire. The Horse Show. William Carlos Williams. CMoP; NOBA; TAP; VGW
Constantly risking absurdity. Lawrence Ferlinghetti. *Fr.* A Coney Island of the Mind. CAPP; LiTM; NeAP; PoM; TAP
Constellation, The. Henry Vaughan. SeCV-1
Constellation and the *Insurgente,* The. *Unknown.* PAH
Constitution and the *Guerrière,* The. *Unknown.* AmFP; AmSS, *with music;* FSW; PAH; ViBoFo
Constitution for a League of Nations. Arthur Guiterman. InMe
Constitution's Last Fight, The. James Jeffrey Roche. PAH
Constricted by my tortured thought. Prayer before Study. Theodore Roethke. TrPWD
Constructed Space, The. W. S. Graham. PoA
Construction. Virginia Schonborg. QQQ
Construction. Karl Shapiro. PCP
Construction #13. Judith Johnson Sherwin. NoAM
Consumed. James Tate. MAT
Consumer's Report. X. J. Kennedy. FiCP
Consumer's Report, A. Peter Porter. FaBoCo; NOBL
Consummate Happiness. Wordsworth. *Fr.* The Prelude, IV. OBNC
Consummation. Elsa Barker. *Fr.* The Spirit and the Bride. HBMV
Consummation. Thomas Traherne. SeCV-2
Consummation. *Unknown, tr. fr. Greek by* Louis Untermeyer. UnTE
Consummation of their lawless pleasure, The. Their Beginning. C. P. Cavafy, *tr. by* John Mavrogordato. PeHV
Contact. Dorothy Livesay. CaP
Contagiousness of Dreams, The. Diane Middlebrook. AMV-81
Container, The. Cid Corman. VGW
"Containing Communism." Charlie Cobb. PoBA
Contemplate all this work of Time. In Memoriam A. H. H., CXVIII. Tennyson. EBVV; FF; SeCeV
Contemplation. Francis Thompson. BrPo; LoBV
Sels.
"Nature one hour appears a thing unsexed." OBNC
"River has not any care, The." FaBoEn
Contemplation of Our State in Our Deathbed. John Donne. *Fr.* Of the Progresse of the Soule; the Second Anniversarie. OBS
("Think then, my soul, that death is but a groom.") OxBoCh
Contemplation upon Flowers, A. Henry King. BoNaP; ELP; HBV-1; LoBV; MeLP; MePo; NoP; OBEV; OBS; SeCP; TrGrPo
Contemplation would make a good life, keep it strict, only. The Cruel Falcon. Robinson Jeffers. BiP
Contemplations. Anne Bradstreet. AmPP; AP; SCAP; WPE, *abr.*
Sels.
"I wist not what to wish, yet sure thought I." PBWP
"Mariner that on smooth waves doth glide, The." WPOW
"O Time the fatal wrack of mortal things." PBWP; WPOW
"Shall I then praise the heavens, the trees, the earth." PBWP
"Silent alone, where none or saw, or heard." PBWP
"So he that saileth in this world of pleasure." WPOW
"Some time now past in the Autumnal Tide." PoEL-3, *abr.*
"When I behold the heavens as in their prime." PBWP
Contemplative Quarry, The. Anna Wickham. HBMV
Contemplative Sentry, The. W. S. Gilbert. *Fr.* Iolanthe. FiBHP
Contemporania, *sel.* Ezra Pound.
Tenzone. PoA
Contemporary. Hortense Flexner. PoA
Contemporary Muse, The. Edgell Rickword. OBSV
Contemporary Nursery Rhyme. *Unknown.* PV; SpRo
Contemporary Poets. Byron. *Fr.* Don Juan, XI. OBRV
Contemporary Song. Theodore Spencer. LiTA
Contempt for Dylan Thomas, A. Wilfred Watson. PeCV
Contempt for the World. Bernard of Cluny. *See* De Contemptu Mundi.
Contempt of Poetry, The. Spenser. *See* October.
Contempt of the World. *Unknown.* *See* Ubi Sunt Qui ante Nos Fuerunt?
Contend in a sea which the land partly encloses. The Yachts. William Carlos Williams. AmPP; AP; BiP; CMoP; CoBMV; HeIP; LiSp; LiTA; LiTM; MasP; MoAmPo; MoPo; MOS; NePA; NoAM; NOBA; NoP; OxBA; PPP; SeCeV; TwAmPo; ViBoPo
Contending with her streams, renascent stars. Aria for Flute and Oboe. Joseph Langland. NePoEA
Content. Barnabe Barnes. Parthenophil and Parthenophe, LXVI. OBSC
("Ah, sweet content, where is thy mylde abode?") AAS
(Sonnet: "Ah, sweet Content! where is thy mild abode?") EIL
Content. Thomas Campion. OBSC
Content. Earl of Essex. *See* See Happy Were He.
Content. Norman Gale. HBV-1
Content. Thomas, Lord Vaux. *See* Of a Contented Mind.
Content. Geffrey Whitney. EIL
(Song: "In crystal towns and turrets richly set.") ACP
Content and Rich. Robert Southwell. OBSC
Content Thyself with Thy Estate. *Unknown.* EIL
Content within his wigwam warm. Canonicus and Roger Williams. *Unknown.* PAH
Contented at Forty. Sarah N. Cleghorn. HBMV
Contented Bachelor, The. John Kendall. InMe
Contented John. Jane Taylor. HBV-1; HBVY
Contented Man, The. Pope. *See* Ode on Solitude.
Contented Mind, A. Joshua Sylvester. HBV-2
Contented wi' Little. Burns. BSV
Contention between Four Maids Concerning That Which Addeth Most Perfection to That Sex. Sir John Davies. SiPS
Contention betwixt a Wife, a Widow, and a Maid, A. Sir John Davies. OBSC; SiPS
Contention of Ajax and Ulysses, The, *sel.* James Shirley.
Glories of Our Blood and State, The, *fr.* sc. iii. CavP; ChTr; FaBoRV; HAP; InvP; JCP; NoP; OBS; PoPle; PoRA; PPP; TrGrPo; ViBoPo; WaaP
(Death the Leveller.) BLPL; FaPoR; FF; GTBS; GTBS-P; LiTB; LoBV; NOBE; OBEV; PPON; SeCeV; UnPo
(Death's Final Conquest.) HBV-2
(Dirge: "Glories of our blood and state, The.") ACP; AWP; OAEL-1; PoEL-2; TreFT
(Of Death.) WHA
(Our Blood and State.) GoBC
(Song: "Glories of our blood and state, The.") FaBoEn
Contentions. *Unknown.* *See* It Was a Lording's Daughter.
Contentment. Nathaniel Cotton. OxBChV
Contentment. Lawrence E. Estes. AMV-80
Contentment. Owen Felltham. CavP
Contentment. Oliver Wendell Holmes. *Fr.* The Autocrat of the Breakfast Table, *ch.* 11. AmPP; AP; HBV-1; InMe; OxBA; TreF
Contentment. Burges Johnson. GDP
Contentment. Mark Osaki. BrSi
Contentment. Benjamin Schlipf. BLRP
Contentment. Sir Philip Sidney. *See* Get Hence Foule Griefe.
Contentment. Thomas Traherne. *Fr.* Christian Ethics. NOCV
("Contentment is a sleepy thing.") OxBoCh
Contentment of Willoughby, The. Frances Alexander. GoYe
Contentment; or, The Happy Workman's Song. John Byrom. OBEC
Contentment, parent of delight. A Cure for the Spleen. Matthew Green. *Fr.* The Spleen. OBEC
Continental Crossing. Dorothy Brown Thompson. AmFN
Continent's End. Robinson Jeffers. AWP; FaBV; ImOP; TwAmPo
Continual Conversation with a Silent Man. Wallace Stevens. LiTM; NePA; NoP
Continual deprivation, now. Deprivation. H. A. Pinkerton. NePoAm
Continuance, The. William Bronk. GP
Continuation of *The Cook's Tale,* The. William Zaranka. BXAP
Continuaunce/ of remembraunce. A Lover Left Alone. *Unknown.* MeEL
Continuing City, The. Laurence Housman. WGRP
Continuity. "Æ." MoBrPo; NBM
Continuity, The. Paul Blackburn. CAD; NeAP
Continuous, a medley of old pop numbers. The Songs. Martin Bell. FF
Continuum. Denise Levertov. LCAP
Contours of Fixation, The. Weldon Kees. NaP
Contra Mortem, *sel.* Hayden Carruth.
"Wherever shadow falls wherever the drowning." PoA
Contrapuntalist, A/ composer of chorales. Melchior Vulpius. Marianne Moore. AP
Contrary, The. Alexander Brome. CavP

Contrary Mary. Nancy Byrd Turner. HBMV; HBVY
Contrary Theses (I). Wallace Stevens. OxBA
Contrary to popular belief, the potato. The Potato Eaters. Frank Graziano. PoDr
Contrary Waiter, The. Edgar Parker. RHPC
Contrast, The. Helen Gray Cone. AA
Contrast, The; the Parrot and the Wren. Wordsworth. FM
Contretemps, The. Thomas Hardy. CMoP; LiTM
Contrite Heart, The. William Cowper. PoEL-3; TrPWD
(Lord Will Happiness Divine, The.) NOCV; OxBoCh
Contrition twines me like a snake. Fulani Cattle. John Pepper Clark. PBA
Contrivances, The, *sel.* Henry Carey.
Maiden's Ideal of a Husband, A. HBV-1
Controlling the Tongue. Chaucer. *Fr.* The Canterbury Tales: The Manciple's Tale. OxBChV
Conundrum. Carl Clark. JB
Conundrum of the Workshops, The. Kipling. HBV-1; MoBrPo
Convalescence. Amy Lowell. SUMH
Convalescence. James McAuley. CBAP
Convalescence, I-VIII. David McCord.
Convalescent, The. Cicily Fox Smith. SUMH
Convenant. Paul Auster. VWA
Convenanter's Lament for Bothwell Brigg, The. Winthrop Mackworth Praed. OBRV
Convent, The. "Seumas O'Sullivan." POL
Convent Cemetery, Mount Carmel. Sister Mary St. Virginia. GoBC
Convent of Pleasure, The, *sel.* Margaret Cavendish, Duchess of Newcastle.
Song: "My cabinets are oyster-shells." WPE
Convent Threshold, The. Christina Rossetti. MasP; NoP; PoEL-5
Conventicle. Gerrit Lansing. CoPo
Convention. Agnes Lee. HBMV
Convention Song. *Unknown.* PAH
Convergence of the Twain, The; Lines on the Loss of the *Titanic.* Thomas Hardy. BiP; BrPo; CoBMV; FaBoTw; HeIP; InPK; LiTB; LiTM; MoAB; MoBrPo; MoPo; MOS; MoVE; NoAM; NoP; OAEL-1; OAEP; OxBTC; PAI; PrIm; SeCeV; TEP
Conversation. Ai. LTB
Conversation. John Berryman. LiTA; LiTM; NePA; WaP
Conversation. Buson, *tr. fr. Japanese.* NTCP
Conversation. Berenice C. Dewey. InMe
Conversation. Nikki Giovanni. CTBA
Conversation, A. Barbara Howes. IHMS
Conversation. David McCord. GrPl; SO
Conversation. Louis MacNeice. TEP
Conversation. K. Malley. AMV-80
Conversation. Hannah More. *Fr.* Bas Bleu. OBEC
Conversation. Gyorgy Raba, *tr. fr. Hungarian by* Jascha Kessler. VWA
Conversation. Anne Robinson. SUS
Conversation, A. Dylan Thomas. RFM
Conversation between Mr. and Mrs. Santa Claus. Rowena Bennett. SiSoSe; TiPo
Conversation between the Chevalier de Chamilly and Mariana Alcoforado in the Manner of a Song of Regret. The Three Marias, *tr. fr. Portuguese by* Helen R. Lane. BoWoP
Conversation brings us so close! Opening. Looking into a Face. Robert Bly. NOBA
Conversation Galante. T. S. Eliot. HBMV
Conversation in Avila. Phyllis McGinley. EaLo
Conversation in Black and White. May Sarton. GoYe
Conversation in Craven Street, Strand. James Smith *and* Sir George Rose. FaBoCo
Conversation in the Drawing Room, The. Weldon Kees. EAS; TwAmPo
Conversation of Prayer, The. Dylan Thomas. EBEV; GTBS-P; NoP
Conversation Piece. Arthur Freeman. ErPo
Conversation Piece. Robert Graves. GrPl
Conversation with a Countryman. Antoni Slonimski, *tr. fr. Polish by* Isaac Komem. VWA
Conversation with an April Fool. Rowena Bennett. SiSoSe
Conversation with God. Jeanine Hathaway. AMV-80
Conversation with Rain. Louise D. Gunn. GoYe
Conversation with Three Women of New England. Wallace Stevens. NePA
Conversation with Washington. Myra Cohn Livingston. OFD
Conversational. *Unknown.* FiBHP
Conversational Reformer, The. Harry Graham. InMe; YaD
Conversations are simple, The: about food. Under the Window: Ouro Preto. Elizabeth Bishop. NYBP
Conversations between Here and Home. Joy Harjo. TWSS
Conversations from the Nightmare. Carol Lee Sanchez. TWSS
Conversations in Courtship, *sel.* *Unknown, tr. fr. Egyptian into Italian by* Boris de Rachewitz, *tr. into English by* Ezra Pound.
"Darling, you only, there is no duplicate." CTC
Conversing with Paradise. Howard Nemerov. PoDr
Conversion. Frances Angermayer. PoLF; TreFS
(Last Thoughts of a Fighting Man.) PGD
Conversion. Dryden. *Fr.* The Hind and the Panther. ACP
(Worldly Vanity.) FiP
Conversion. Geof Hewitt. NeAC
Conversion. T. E. Hulme. FaBoMo; LoBV; ViBoPo
Convert, The. G. K. Chesterton. GoBC
Convert, The. Margaret Danner. BPo
Converts, The. Chana Bloch. AMV-81
Convert's but a fly, that turns about, A. Samuel Butler. FaBoEE
Convex face of the black countries, The. The First Psalm. Bertolt Brecht, *tr. by* Robert Bly. NU
Convict, The. Anthony Frisch. CaP
Convict, The. *Unknown.* CoSo
Convict of Clonmel [*or* Clonmala], The. *Unknown, tr. fr. Modern Irish by* Jeremiah Joseph Callanan. AnIL; AnIV; NBM; OnYI; OxBI
Convicted, *sel.* Harry Edward Mills..
"Around his open grave from near and far." PeD
Conviction, The. J. M. Synge. SyP
Convicts' Ball, The. Ambrose Bierce. BPAW
Convict's Lament on the Death of Captain Logan, A. *Unknown.* PoAu-1
Convicts working on the frontier forts, The. On the Danube. Robert Conquest. NMP
Convinced by Sorrow. Elizabeth Barrett Browning. *Fr.* The Cry of the Human. BLRP; WBLP
Convoy, The. Juan Antonio Corretjer, *tr. fr. Spanish by* Julio Marzán. InW
Convoy. William Jay Smith. WaP
Convulsions came; and, where the field. The Apparition. Herman Melville. NoP
Coo-Coo, *with music.* *Unknown.* AS
Coogan's Wood. Francis Stuart. NeIP
Cook, The. Ray A. Young Bear. CDW
Cook County. Archibald MacLeish. CrMA
(Weather.) MoAmPo
Cook's Tale, The. Chaucer. *Fr.* The Canterbury Tales. BXAP
Cooks who'd roast a sucking-pig. Roasted Sucking Pig. *Unknown.* BXAP
Cooky-Nut Trees, The. Albert Bigelow Paine. OBCA
Cool black nights thru redwoods. First Party at Ken Keseys with Hell's Angels. Allen Ginsberg. ConAP
Cool, Cool, Country, The. Shaw Neilson. PoAu-1
Cool Gold Wines of Paradise, The. Robert Farren. AnIV; SeCePo
Cool, Grey City of Love, The. George Sterling. BPAW
Cool in summer's heat. The Well: Two Songs. *Gond Oral Tradition, tr. by* V. Elwin *and* S. Hivale. WTO
Cool it Mag. Margaret Are You Drug. George Starbuck. MAT
Cool shadows blanked dead cities, falling. Falling. Bob Kaufman. PoBA
Cool sky opens like a hand, The. William Blake Sees God. Roy McFadden. NeIP
Cool small evening shrunk to a dog bark and the clank of a bucket, A. Full Moon and Little Frieda. Ted Hughes. OxBC
Cool to the wrist. Six Divine Circles. Gail Ghai. AMV-81
Cool Tombs. Carl Sandburg. AmPP; AP; BLPL; CMoP; HAP; HBMV; HeIP; MoAB; MoAmPo; NoAM; NOBA; PAL; PoLF; TAP; TrGrPo; TwAmPo; ViBoPo; WHA
Cool Tombs. Edward Thomas. MoVE
Cool Web, The. Robert Graves. AWP; ChMP; GTBS-P; NIP; NoAM; NoP; OxBTC; PoA; PrIm; SCV
Cool with the touch of autumn, waters break. Lament for My Brother on a Hayrake. James Wright. TwAmPo
Coole Park and Ballylee, 1931. W. B. Yeats. CMoP; GTBS-P; NoAM; OBMV; PPP
Coole Park, 1929. W. B. Yeats. OAEL-2; OBMV; OxBI
Cooleen, The. Douglas Hyde. OBVV
Coolie Chinee, The. Septimus Winner. OBAL
Coolin Ridge, The. William Bell. PoSH
Coolness will come to their children, A. John Haines. *Fr.* Forest without Leaves. NPAW
Coolun, The. Maurice O'Dugan, *tr. fr. Late Middle Irish by* Sir Samuel Ferguson. AnIV; OnYI; OxBI
Coon Can (Poor Boy), *with music.* *Unknown.* AS
Coon explains it. Evolution. Rochelle Owens. CoPo
Coon Hunt, Sixth Month (1955). Sydney Lea. MAYP
Coon Song. A. R. Ammons. NoAM; NOBA
Cooney Potter. Edgar Lee Masters. *Fr.* Spoon River Anthology. CTBA; SaC
Coo-pe-coo. *Unknown.* PBBP
Cooper. James Russell Lowell. *Fr.* A Fable for Critics. AP; NOBA; OxBA; TAP
Cooper & Bailey Great London Circus, The. Robert Hershon. MAT
Cooper o' Dundee, The. *Unknown.* CoMu

Cooper, whose name is with his country's woven. Red Jacket. Fitz-Greene Halleck. AA
Co-operation. J. Mason Knox. BLPA; YaD
Cooper's Hill. Sir John Denham. AnAnS-2; SeCP; SeCV-1
Sels.
"My eye descending from the Hill, surveys." OAEL-1; ViBoPo
(Thames from Cooper's Hill, The.) OBS; SeCePo
Thames, The. FaBoEn
"There Faunus and Sylvanus keep their courts." JCP
Coosaponakeesa (Mary Mathews Musgrove Bosomsworth), Leader of the Creeks, 1700-1783. Rayna Green. TWSS
Cootchie. Elizabeth Bishop. NIP
Coots. Joseph Bruchac. FAZ
Coots are awash, The. Lake Harriet: Wind. Laurie Taylor. AMV-81
Cop, The/ with a cold. High-cool/2. James Cunningham. JB
Cop holds me up like a fish, The. Fish. Larry Levis. AmPA
Cop slumps alertly on his motorcycle, The. Corner. Ralph Pomeroy. CAD; CoPo; NYP
Copacetic Mingus. Yusef Komunyakaa. MAYP
Copernican System, The. Thomas Chatterton. FaBoUs
Cophetua. "Hugh MacDiarmid." OxBS; POL
Cophetua was a merry King. King Cophetua and the Beggar Maid. Don Marquis. HBMV; InMe
Coplas. *Unknown, tr. fr. Spanish.* FSW
Coplas about the Soul Which Suffers with Impatience to See God, *sel.* St. John of the Cross,. *tr. fr. Spanish by* Roy Campbell.
"I live without inhabiting/ Myself." OBVE
Copper-Beech and Butter-Fingers. Pearse Hutchinson. CIP
Copper cobra comes out of his slit, The. The Banded Cobra. C. Louis Leipoldt, *tr. by* Uys Krige, Jack Cope, *and* Ruth Miller. PeSA
Copper-green Phillip. Captain Arthur Phillip and the Birds. Lex Banning. PoAu-2
Copper Song, The. Hermia Harris Fraser. CaP
Copperhead, The. David Bottoms. AMV-81; MAYP
Coppersmith. Richard Murphy. IPY
Cops and Robbers. Bill Middleton. AMV-80
Coptic Poem. Lawrence Durrell. FaBoCo
Copulate. The Indomitable. Carl Rakosi. GP
Copulating Gods, The. Carolyn Kizer. Prf
Copy of an Intercepted Despatch from His Excellency Don Strepitoso Diabolo. Thomas Moore. NBM; OBSV
Copy of Non Sequitors, A. *Unknown.* FaBoNo
Copy of the Last Verses Made by Dr. Wild, Author of "Iter Boreale," A, *sel.* Robert Wild.
"Devils can change their shapes, but not their natures." DBV
Copy of Verses, A. John Wilson. SCAP
Copy of Verses Sent by Cleone to Aspasia, A. Walter Savage Landor. *Fr.* Pericles and Aspasia. LoBV
Coquette, The. Aphra Behn. TrGrPo
(Coquet, The.) ViBoPo
Coquettes with doctors; hoards her breath. The Old Beauty. Phyllis McGinley. FaBoEE
Cor Cordium. Swinburne. VLP
Cora Punctuated with Strawberries. George Starbuck. NCSH; NMP
Coracle, The. Lucan, *tr. fr. Latin by* Sir Walter Ralegh. ChTr
Coracle Fishers, The. Robert Bloomfield. *Fr.* The Banks of Wye. OBNC
Coral Grove, The. James Gates Percival. AA; EtS; GN
Coral Reef, The. Laurence Lieberman. CoAP
Coralville, in Iowa. Marvin Bell. FAZ
Corbie and the Crow, The. *Unknown.* PoPle
Corbitt's Barkentine, *with music. At. to* Tom Reynolds. ShS
Corda Concordia, *sel.* Edmund Clarence Stedman.
Quest. AA
Cordate head meanders through himself, The. Pit Viper. N. Scott Momaday. CDW
Cordoba. Asher Mendelssohn. VWA
Cordova. Ibn Zaydun, *tr. fr. Arabic by* H. A. R. Gibb. AWP
Core, The. John Holmes. MiAP
Coridon and Phillis. Robert Greene. *Fr.* Perimedes. OBSC
(Phillis and Coridon.) HBV-1
Coridon's Song. John Chalkhill. HBV-1; ViBoPo
Coridon's Song. Thomas Lodge. *Fr.* Rosalynde. UnTE
Corinna. Thomas Campion. *See* When to Her Lute Corinna Sings.
Corinna. *Unknown.* FSW
Corinna Bathes. George Chapman. *Fr.* Ovid's Banquet of Sense. OBSC
(Natures Naked Jem.) FaBoEn
Corinna, from Athens, to Tanagra. Walter Savage Landor. *Fr.* Pericles and Aspasia. OBEV; OBVV
(Corinna to Tanagra.) OBNC; OBRV; ViBoPo, *abr.*
(Corinna, to Tanagra, from Athens.) NOBE
Corinna Goes a-Singing. Frank Sidgwick. WhC
Corinna, Having Tried, with Her Own Hand. Ovid, *tr. fr. Latin by* Rolfe Humphries. *Fr.* Amores, II, 13. NAs
Corinna in Vendome. Pierre de Ronsard, *tr. fr. French by* Robert Mezey. BoLoP; ErPo
Corinna, pride of Drury-Lane. A Beautiful Young Nymph Going to Bed. Swift. DBV; NIP; NOEC; PPON; UnTE
Corinna, to Tanagra, from Athens. Walter Savage Landor. *See* Corinna, from Athens, to Tanagra.
Corinnae Concubitus. Ovid. *See* In Summer's Heat.
Corinna's Going a-Maying. Robert Herrick. AnAnS-2; BiP; BoNaP; CABA; CaPo; HAP; HBV-1; JCP; NIP; NOBE; NoP; OAEL-1; OAEP; OBEV; OBS; PoEL-3; PoPle; PPP; PrIm; SeCeV; SeCP; SeCV-1; TEP; TreFT, *abr.*; TrGrPo; WHA
Corinne at the Capitol. Felicia Dorothea Hemans. BrRo
Coriolan, *sel.* T. S. Eliot.
Triumphal March. OBWP; WaaP
Cormac Mac Airt Presiding at Tara. *Unknown, tr. fr. Irish by* Douglas Hyde. BIrV
Cormorant, The. Christopher Isherwood. *See* Common Cormorant, The.
Cormorant in Its Element, The. Amy Clampitt. SUW
Cormorant still screams, The. Late. Louise Bogan. PBWP; VGW
Cormorants. John Blight. CBAP
Corn. Sidney Lanier. AP
Corn-blossom maidens. Masahongva, *tr. fr. Hopi Indian by* Natalie Curtis. WTO
Corn Cañon. Patric Stevenson. NeIP
Corn Crake, The. James H. Cousins. OnYI
(Corncrake, The.) BoAnP
Corn does not hurry, and the black grape swells. Second Wisdom. Henry Morton Robinson. GoYe
Corn-grinding Song ("Butterflies, butterflies"). *Unknown, tr. fr. Laguna Indian by* Natalie Curtis. AWP; SUS
Corn-grinding Song ("This way from the North"). *Unknown, tr. fr. Tewa Indian by* N. Barnes. WTO
Corn-grinding Song ("Yonder, yonder see the fair rainbow"). *Unknown, tr. fr. Hopi Indian. See* Rainbow, The.
Corn Harvest, The. William Carlos Williams. Pictures from Brueghel, VII. PPP
Corn Husker, The. Pauline Johnson. CaP
Corn-Planter. Maurice Kenny. STE
Corn-Pone-y, The. Carolyn Wells. *Fr.* A Baker's Dozen of Wild Beasts. OBCA
Corn Rig[g]s Are Bon[n]ie. Burns. *See* Rigs o' Barley, The.
Corn Song, The. John Wesley Holloway. BANP
Corn-Song, The. Whittier. GN; OHIP
Corn-Woman Remembered. Judith Mountain Leaf Volborth. TWSS
Corncrake, The. James H. Cousins. *See* Corn Crake, The.
Cornelia, *sel.* Thomas Kyd.
Of Fortune, *abr.* EIL
Cornelian, The. Byron. PeHV
Cornelia's Song. John Webster. *See* Call for the Robin Redbreast and the Wren.
Cornelia's Window. Julie Kane. AMV-81
Corner, The. Rita Johnson. AMV-80
Corner. Ralph Pomeroy. CAD; CoPo; NYP
Corner bank has lost a great window, The. High Wind at the Battery. Ralph Pomeroy. NYBP
Corner Boys. Bryan MacMahon. OnYI
Corner Knot, The. Robert Graves. NYBP
Corner Lot. Sharon Bryan. MAYP
Corner Meeting. Langston Hughes. CAD
Corner of the Field, The. Frances Cornford. ELU
Corner Seat. Louis MacNeice. MoVE
Corner Stone, The. Walter de la Mare. BrPo
Cornered and trapped, The. For Mack C. Parker. Pauli Murray. PoBA
Cornet, The. Earl of Surrey. OBSC
(Complaint That His Ladie after She Knew of His Love Kept Her Face Alway Hidden from Him, *sl. diff.*) PoEL-1
("I never saw you, madam, lay apart.") AAS; SiPS
Cornfield. Leo Cox. CaP
Cornfield, The. Elizabeth Madox Roberts. GoJo; SUS
Cornfield Myth. Mary Goose. STE
Cornfields in Accra. Ama Ata Aidoo. WPOW
Cornhusk bag. Talking Designs. Liz Sohappy Bahe. CDW
Cornish Emigrant's Song, The. Robert Stephen Hawker. EBVV
Cornish Litany, A. *Unknown. See* Litany for Halloween.
Cornish Magic. Ann Durell. FaPON
Cornishmen. *Unknown.* FaBoUs
Cornwallis. Tony Beyer. OCNZ
Cornwallis led a country dance. The Dance [*or* Cornwallis's Country Dance]. *Unknown.* PAH; TrAS, *with* Yankee Doodle
Cornwallis's Surrender. *Unknown.* PAH

Coromandel Fishers. Sarojini Naidu. EtS
Corona. Paul Celan, *tr. fr. German by* Joachim Neugroschel. VWA
Coronach. Alexander Scott. OxBS
Coronach ("He is gone on the mountain"). Sir Walter Scott. *Fr.* The Lady of the Lake, III. BSV; CH; EnRP; GTBS; GTBS-P; HBV-2; OAEP; OBRV; OHIP; TreFS; TrGrPo; ViBoPo; WHA; WiR
Coronary Thrombosis. William Price Turner. OxBS
Coronation. Helen Hunt Jackson. AA; BeLS; GN; HBV-2
Coronation. Edward Perronet. BLSo, *with music;* HBV-2; TreFS; WGRP
(All Hail the Power of Jesus' Name.) NOCV
Coronation Day at Melrose. Peter Bladen. PoAu-2
Coronemus Nos Rosis Antequam Marcescant. Thomas Jordan. *See* Let Us Drink and Be Merry.
Coroner's Jury. L. A. G. Strong. OxBTC
Coronet, The. Andrew Marvell. AnAnS-1; LoBV; MeLP; MePo; NCEP; NOCV; NoP; OBS; OxBoCh; PoPle; PP; SeCV-1
Coronet for His Mistress Philosophy, A, *sel.* George Chapman.
"Muses that sing Love's sensual empery," I. ElL; LoBV
(Love and Philosophy.) OBSC; SeCePo
Corporal. Ambrose Bierce. *Fr.* The Devil's Dictionary. DBV
("Fiercely the battle raged, and, sad to tell.") OBAL
"Corporal Green!" the orderly cried. Roll-Call [*or* Calling the Roll]. Nathaniel Graham Shepherd. AA; HBV-2; OBCA; OHIP
Corporal Pym. Walter de la Mare. FaBoEE
Corporal Stare. Robert Graves. BrPo
Corporate Entity. Archibald MacLeish. OBAL
Corposant. Peter Redgrove. NePoEA-2; OxBTC
Corps d'Esprit. Heather McHugh. AmPA
Corpse-bearing. Thomas Ashe. EBVV
Corpse, clad with carefulness. Of Misery. Thomas Howell. EIL; FF
Corpse-Keeper, The. *Unknown, tr. fr. Catalan by* W. S. Merwin. BoWoP
Corpse-Plant, The. Adrienne Rich. CoPo
Corpses in the Wood. Ernst Toller, *tr. fr. German by* E. Ellis Roberts. TrJP
Corpulent Pig, A. Marnie *and* Harnie Wood. TDH
Corpus Christi Carol, The ("Heron flew east, the heron flew west, The"). *Unknown. See* Heron, The.
Corpus Christi Carol ("Lully, lullay [*or* lulley], lully, lullay [*or* lulley]"). *Unknown.* ChTr; EBEV; FaBoBa; GBP; HAP; MeEL; NOBE; NoP; NU; OAEL-1; OxBM; SCV
(Bereaved Maid, The.) TrGrPo
(Corpus Christi.) FaBoBa
(Falcon, The.) ACP; LiTB; NU; OxBoCh; SeCeV; ViBoPo
(Knight of the Grail, The.) OBEV
(Lully, Lulley, Lully, Lulley.) CH; EBEV; HAP; LoBV; OAEP; WeW
(Over Yonder's a Park [Corpus Christi].) BaBo (A *vers.*)
Corpus Christi Carol, The ("Over yonder's a park, which is newly begun"). *Unknown.* GBP
(Over Yonder's a Park [Corpus Christi].) BaBo (B *vers.*)
Corral, The. Earle Thompson. STE
Correct Compassion, A. James Kirkup. ChMP; FaBoTw; ImOP; OxBTC; SeCePo
Correction, A. Robert Frost. WhC
Correlated Greatness. Francis Thompson. *See* All's Vast.
Correspondence:/ when I have sad thoughts. Lady Ise, *tr. fr. Japanese by* Etsuko Terasaki *and* Irma Brandeis. BoWoP
Correspondence between Mr. Harrison in Newcastle and Mr. Sholto Peach Harrison in Hull. Stevie Smith. FaBoNo; OxBC
Correspondence School Instructor Says Goodbye to His Poetry Students, The. Galway Kinnell. NOBA; NoP; TAP
Correspondences. Baudelaire, *tr. fr. French.* AWP, *tr. by* Allen Tate; NAWM-2, *tr. by* Anthony Hartley; SyP, *tr. by* Arthur Symons
Correspondences. Robert Duncan. PoM
Corrib: An Emblem. Donald Davie. PoCh
Corridor, The. Thom Gunn. NePoEA; PPP
Corridor was empty, The. March 23, 1982; Tuesday Night. Thomas Waltner. LFAC
Corridors of the soul! Rebirth. Antonio Machado, *tr. by* Robert Bly. NU
Corries. Janet M. Smith. PoSH
Corroded flat as hills allow. Bedlam Hills. Vivian Smith. PoAu-2
Corrs, The. Tom MacIntyre, *tr. fr. Irish.* CIP
Corrupt Man in the French Pub, The. Brian Higgins. OxBTC
Corruption. Henry Vaughan. AnAnS-1; FaBoEn; JCP; NOCV; OAEL-1; OBS; OxBoCh; Prf; SeCP; SeCV-1
Corrymeela. "Moira O'Neill." AnIV; AWP; HBV-2
Corsage Bouquet, A. Charles Henry Lüders. HBV-1
Corsair, The, *sel.* Byron.
Summer, *fr.* III. OBRV
(Sunset over the Aegean.) OBNC
Corsons Inlet. A. R. Ammons. CoAP; NoAM; NOBA; NoP; PPP
Cortège. Paul Verlaine, *tr. fr. French by* Arthur Symons. AWP; OBVE
Cortege for Colette. Jean Garrigue. NYBP
Cortège for Rosenbloom. Wallace Stevens. TwAmPo
Cortes. A. A. Rios. GP
Coruisk. W. C. Smith. PoSH
Corydon and Thyrsis. Virgil, *tr. fr. Latin by* Dryden. Eclogues, VII. AWP
Corydon, Arise, My Corydon! *Unknown. See* Phyllida's Love-Call.
Corydon to His Phyllis. Sir Edward Dyer. ElL
Corydon's Complaint. Samuel Pordage. CavP
Corydon's Farewell, on Sailing in the Late Expedition Fleet. *Unknown.* NOEC
Corythos, *sel.* Walter Savage Landor.
Helen and Corythos. LoBV
Cosher Bailey's Engine. *Unknown.* FSW
Cosmetic. Gretchen Herbkersman. AMV-80
Cosmic Eye. A. K. Redwing. VoR
Cosmic Fabric, The. Yakov Polonsky, *tr. fr. Russian by* Avrahm Yarmolinsky *and* Cecil Cowdery. EaLo
Cosmic Leviathan, that monstrous fish. Cosmogony. Edgell Rickword. FaBoTw
Cosmogony. D. C. Berry. BXAP
Cosmogony. Edgell Rickword. FaBoTw
Cosmologists are wrong, The. Creation Myths. Burton Raffel. AMV-80
Cossimbazar. Henry S. Leigh. NA
Cost, The. Anthony Hecht. OxBC
Cost, The. Flora L. Osgood. STF
Cost-of-Living Mother Goose, The. Dow Richardson. QQQ
Cost of Pretending, The. Peter Davison. TW
Cosy fire is bright and gay, The. The Poets at Tea, IV. Barry Pain. Par
Cot, The. Grover Amen. NYBP; NYP
Côte d'Azur. Katherine Hoskins. NYBP
Cottage, The. Jones Very. OxBA
Cottage Hospital, The. John Betjeman. GTBS-P; MoBrPo; MoVE; NOBE; UnPo
Cottage in the Wood, A. Russell Edson. LCAP
Cottage Street, 1953. Richard Wilbur. FaBoMo
Cottage was a thatch'd one, The. Little Jim. Edward Farmer. PaPo
Cottager, The, *sel.* John Clare.
"True as the church clock hand the hour pursues." OBRV
Cottager to Her Infant, The. Dorothy Wordsworth. CH; HBV-1; OxBChV
Cottager's Complaint, [on the Intended Bill for Enclosing Sutton-Coldfield], The. John Freeth. NOEC; OBET
Cotter's Saturday Night, The. Burns. BeLS; EnRP; FaBoBe; HBV-2; LAuP; OAEP; OBEC, *abr.*; PoLF; WGRP
Cotton blouse you wear, your mother said, The. McDonogh Day in New Orleans. Marcus B. Christian. AmNP; PoNe
Cotton Boll, The. Henry Timrod. AA; AmPP
Cotton Eye Joe, *with music. Unknown.* OuSiCo
(Cotton-eyed Joe).FSW
Cotton-Mill Colic, *with music. Unknown.* OuSiCo
Cotton Song. Jean Toomer. BPo; CDC
Cottonmouth Country. Louise Glück. CoAP; GeTw
Cottonmouth white faces survey the marshes. Okeechobee. John Allison. GrPl
Cottonwood Leaves. Badger Clark. TiPo
Cottonwood, willow, and briar. Leaves like Fish. Gladys Cardiff. CDW; TWSS
Couch, The. Fred W. Wright, Jr. AMV-80
Coughing in a shady grove. Ipecacuanha. George Canning. ChTr; FaBoNo
Coughing up blood. Differences. Ray A. Young Bear. NU
Could all this be forgotten? Yes, a schism. Keats. *Fr.* Sleep and Poetry. ChER
Could but this be brought into your ken. Technique. Langdon Elwyn Mitchell. *Fr.* To a Writer of the Day. AA
Could every time-worn heart but see Thee once again. To the Child Jesus. Henry van Dyke. TrPWD
Could he have made Priscilla share. Llewellyn and the Tree. E. A. Robinson. BeLS; HBMV
Could Homer come himself, distressed and poor. Epigram on the Refusal of the University of Oxford to Subscribe to His Translation of Homer. William Cowper. TW
Could I Believe. Ewart Milne. OxBI
Could I bring back lost youth again. Florine. Thomas Campbell. BSV
Could I but retrace. Tanka (I-VIII). Lewis Alexander. CDC
Could I find out/ The woman's part in me! Shakespeare. *Fr.* Cymbeline. DBV
Could I pluck down Aldebaran. The Unloved to His Beloved. William Alexander Percy. HBMV
Could I remove the stones from the river? Song of Longing. *Gond Oral Tradition, tr. by* V. Elwin *and* S. Hivale. WTO
Could I Say I Touched You. Harold Littlebird. VoR
Could I take me to some cavern for mine hiding. O for the Wings of a Dove. Euripides, *tr. by* Gilbert Murray. *Fr.* Hippolytus. AWP

Could It Have Been a Shadow? Monica Shannon. FaPON; RHPC; SoPo; TiPo
Could love for ever. Stanzas. Byron. HBV-1; ViBoPo
Could Man Be Drunk for Ever. A. E. Housman. *Fr.* A Shropshire Lad. LiTM; OBMV; PPP
Could not once blinding me, cruel, suffice? Samson to His Delilah. Richard Crashaw. TrGrPo
Could she come back who has been dead so long. Separation. Alice Learned Bunner. *Fr.* Vingtaine. AA
Could then the babes from yon unshelter'd cot. Sonnet. Thomas Russell. OBEC
Could Time, his flight reversed, restore the hours. William Cowper. *Fr.* On the Receipt of His Mother's Picture. WHA
Could We. *Unknown.* STF
Could we but draw back the curtains. If Only We Understood. *Unknown.* STF
Could we only see the goodness. Could We. *Unknown.* STF
Could ye come back to me, Douglas, Douglas. Douglas, Douglas, Tender and True [*or* Too Late]. Dinah Maria Mulock Craik. BLPA; HBV-1; OBVV; TreF
Could you bid an acorn. Lover's Reply to Good Advice. Richard Hughes. MoBrPo
Could you catch a little fish, son. Father and Son. Richard Eberhart. DiL
Could You Do That? Burns. UnTE
Could you indeed come lightly. Song for a Departure. Elizabeth Jennings. NMP
Could you not drink her gaze like wine? The Card-Dealer. Dante Gabriel Rossetti. NBM; VLP
Could you, so arrantly of earth, so cool. Animal. Max Eastman. FYAP
Could You Spare Some Time for Jesus? Lester Knickman. STF
Could you tell me the way to Somewhere. Somewhere. Walter de la Mare. FaPON
Couldst thou, Great Fairy, give to me. The Pines. Harriet Prescott Spofford. AA
Could'st thou (O Earth) live thus obscure, and now. George Alsop. SCAP
Councell Given to Master Bartholmew Withipoll. George Gascoigne. AAS
Council of Horses, The. John Gay. GN
Council of Satan, The. Milton. *Fr.* Paradise Lost, I. PoEL-3
Councils. Marge Piercy. NeAC
Counsel, The. Alexander Brome. CavP
Counsel. Mary Evelyn Moore Davis. HBV-2
Counsel. Roselle Mercier Montgomery. HBMV
Counsel of Moderation, A. Francis Thompson. MoBrPo
Counsel to Girls. Robert Herrick. *See* To the Virgins, to Make Much of Time.
Counsel to Girls. Archibald Stodart-Walker. *Fr.* The Moxford Book of English Verse. CenHV
Counsel to Unreason. Léonie Adams. PoA
Counselor, The. Dorothy Parker. InMe
Counsels of O'Riordan, the Rann Maker, The. T. D. O'Bolger. AnIV
Counsels of Sigrdrifa. *Unknown.* *See* Part of the Lay of Sigrdrifa.
Count bell rings, The. State Prison 5:00 P.M. Thomas G. Nickens. LFAC
Count each affliction, whether light or grave. Sorrow. Aubrey Thomas De Vere. BLPA; GoBC; HBV-2; WGRP
Count Filippo, *sels.* Charles Heavysege.
"Now let the drums roll muffled; let the bells'." PeCV
"Who is lord of lordly fate." PeCV
Count Gismond. Robert Browning. VLP
Count me o'er earth's chosen heroes—they were souls that stood alone. James Russell Lowell. *Fr.* The Present Crisis. WGRP
Count not his broken pledges as a crime. Lloyd George. *Unknown.* FaBoCo
Count on dead fingers of time the years that pass. Poem for Garcia Lorca. George Woodcock. NOBC
Count Orlo in England. Jon Manchip White. NePoEA
Count That Day Lost. "George Eliot." TreFT
(At Set of Sun.) PoPl; TRV
Count the sighs, and count the teares. The Broken Heart. Thomas Beedome. OBS
Count the white horses you meet on the way. White Horses. Eleanor Farjeon. PDV; PH
Count this among my heartfelt wishes. Fish Story. Richard Armour. LiSp
Count up those books whose pages you have read. Indolence. Vernon Watkins. FaBoTw
Count William's Escapade. Guillaume de Poitiers, *tr. fr. Provençal by* Hubert Creekmore. ErPo
Countdown takeoff. To the Moon and Back. William Plomer. MOON
Countee Cullen. Eugene T. Maleska. PoNe
Countenance like lightning, why do you stand. Colloquy at Peniel. W. S. Merwin. NePoEA
Counter-Attack. Siegfried Sassoon. BrPo; MoBrPo; WaP
Counter-Serenade: She Invokes the Autumn Instant. Peter Viereck. CrMA
Counterpart, The. Elizabeth Jennings. LiTM
Counterparts. Stephen Dobyns. PoA
Counterpoint, A. Robert Creeley. NeAP
Counterpoint. Owen Dodson. PoNe
Counters. Elizabeth J. Coatsworth. SoPo; SUS
Countershadow, The. Philip Booth. NYBP
Countersign. Arthur Ketchum. HBMV
Countess Laura. George Henry Boker. BeLS
Countesse of Douglas out of her boure she came, The. The Knight of Liddesdale. *Unknown.* ESPB
Counting. Michael Collier. SUW
Counting. Fenton Johnson. AmNP
Counting on Flowers. John Ciardi. PP
Counting-out Rhyme. Edna St. Vincent Millay. GoJo; MoShBr
Counting Out Rhyme ("Round about, round about"). *Unknown.* SpRo
("Round about, round about/ Maggotty pie.") OxNR; PBBP
Counting-out Rhyme ("Zeenty, peenty, heathery, mithery"). *Unknown.* ChTr
("Zeenty, peenty, heathery, mithery.") GBP
Counting-out Rhyme for March. Frances Frost. YeAr
Counting-out Rhymes. *Unknown.* FaPON
Counting Sheep. Russell Edson. FiCP; LCAP
Counting Sheep. Aileen Fisher. SoPo
Counting Small-Boned Bodies. Robert Bly. CAPP; EAS; NaP
Counting the Beats. Robert Graves. DTC; ELP; GBL; GTBS-P; HAP; OxBTC; ViBoPo; WeW
Counting the Mad. Donald Justice. ConAP; FF; NePoEA; NIP; PAI; PPON; UnPo
Countless gold of a merry heart, The. Riches. Blake. TrGrPo
Countless stars, which to our human eye, The. The Starry Host. John Lancaster Spalding. *Fr.* God and the Soul. AA; HBV-2
Countless things escape easily out of me. Afternoon 3. Saburoh Kuroda. EAS
Countrie men of England, who live at home with ease. Saylors for my Money. Martin Parker. CoMu
Countries tears, be ye my spring, The; my hill. To the Memory of the Learned and Reverend, Mr. Jonathan Mitchell. Francis Drake. SCAP
Country, The/ was back in the hands of the patriots. Poem. Fred Levinson. AmPA
Country and Town. Charles Morris. NOEC
Country Barnyard. Elizabeth J. Coatsworth. RHPC
Country Bedroom, The. Frances Cornford. MoBrPo
Country Boy in Winter, A. Sarah Orne Jewett. OBCA
Country Burying (1919). Robert Penn Warren. LiTM
Country Cemetery. Freda Newton Bunner. AMV-80
Country Clergy, The. R. S. Thomas. GTBS-P; OxBTC
Country Clergyman's Trip to Cambridge, The. Macaulay. OBSV; OxBoLi
Country Club Romance, A. Derek Walcott. OxBC
Country Club Sunday. Phyllis McGinley. CrMA
Country Curate, The. Henry Taylor. NOEC
Country Dance. Edith Sitwell. NoAM
Country Dance, A. Charles Tennyson Turner. VLP
Country Dance. Judith Wright. *Fr.* The Blind Man. CBAP
Country Doctor, The. Will M. Carleton. BLPA
Country Faith, The. Norman Gale. HBV-1; OBEV; OBVV; WGRP
Country folk who pass have said to me, The. The Grave. John Lyle Donaghy. NeIP
Country Girl's Policy, The; or, The Cockney Outwitted. *Unknown.* CoMu
Country Glee. Thomas Dekker. *See* Haymakers, Rakers.
Country God, A. Edmund Blunden. MoBrPo
Country Gods. Cometas, *tr. fr. Greek by* T. F. Higham. FaBoCh
Country Greeting. Frank Steele. Psk
Country Gulliver, A. The Reports Come In. J. D. Reed. NYBP
Country Hirings. *Unknown.* OBET
Country House, The. Louis Simpson. NOBA
Country Inn, The, *sel.* Joanna Baillie.
Song: "Though richer swains thy love pursue." OBRV
Country is like a tobacco lung, The. E.P.A. Pancho Aguila. LFAC
Country is no country I have seen, The. Civil War. Mark Van Doren. MoVE
Country Justice, The. John Langhorne. LaA
Sels.
Apology for Vagrants. OBEC
Gypsies. NOEC
Poor, The. NOEC
Country lad and bonny lass, A. Have-at a Venture. *Unknown.* CoMu; ErPo
Country Landscape. Sherod Santos. AMV-80
Country Letter. John Clare. NCEP
Country Life. Horace, *tr. fr. Latin by* Dryden. *Fr.* Epodes. AWP
Country Life, A. Randall Jarrell. MiAP; MoAmPo
Country life is sweet, A! The Useful Plow. *Unknown.* HBV-1

Country Life, A: To His Brother, Master Thomas Herrick. Robert Herrick. CaPo; SeCP; SeCV-1
Country Lovers, The. *Unknown. See* Lavender Blue.
Country Lovers, The; or, Isaac and Marget Going to Town, on a Summer's Morning. George Smith. NOEC
Country Man, The, *sel.* George Farewell.
"Crunking crane heard high amongst the clouds, The." NOEC
Country Mouse, The. Abraham Cowley, *after the Latin of* Horace. OBVE; SeCP
Country Mouse and the City Mouse, The. Richard Scrafton Sharpe. OxBChV
Country North of Belleville, The. Al Purdy. NOBC
Country Nun. Geoff Page. CBAP
Country of a Thousand Years of Peace, The. James Merrill. PoCh
Country of desolation between junctions. Junk. William Zaranka. AMV-80
Country of hunchbacks!—where the strong, straight spine. Sonnet to Gath. Edna St. Vincent Millay. BoWoP; CMoP; MoAB; MoAmPo
Country of No Lack. Jean Starr Untermeyer. MoAmPo
Country of Water. Bernice Ames. WPE
Country Pleasures. Martial, *tr. fr. Latin by* F. A. Wright. AWP
Country Reverie. Carol Coates. CaP
Country rings around with loud alarms, The. The Militia. Dryden. *Fr.* Cymon and Iphigenia. OBSV
Country Roads. Rolf Jacobsen, *tr. by* Robert Bly. NU
Country roads are yellow and brown. Street Lanterns. Mary Elizabeth Coleridge. PoRA
Country Song. Nicholas Breton. *See* Report Song, A.
Country Song. Shakespeare. *See* It Was a Lover and His Lass.
Country Song, A. Sir Philip Sidney. *Fr.* Arcadia. OBSC; SiPS
Country Stars. William Meredith. GrPl
Country Statutes. *Unknown.* OBET
Country Store, The. *Unknown.* BLPA
Country Summer. Léonie Adams. GoJo; LiTM; MoAB; MoAmPo; MoPo; MoVE; TrGrPo; TwAmPo; ViBoPo
Country Thought. Sylvia Townsend Warner. MoBrPo
Country Towns. Kenneth Slessor. CBAP; PoAu-2
Country Trucks. Monica Shannon. FaPON; TiPo
Country vegetables scorn, The. Vegetables. Eleanor Farjeon. FaPON; TiPo
Country Villa. Jean Garrigue. TAP
Country Walk, A. Thomas Kinsella. CIP; CMoP; NMP
Country Walk. Geoffrey Taylor. OxBI
Country Ways. Marcia Masters. Impressions of My Father, I. GoYe
Country Wedding, The. *Unknown.* HBV-1
Country Wedding, The (A Fiddler's Story). Thomas Hardy. UnPo
Country-Western Music. Ted Kooser. TAT
Country without a Mythology, A. Douglas Le Pan. MoCV; NOBC
Country Wooing, *sel.* J. C. Squire.
"So lay the youth with Mary in his arms." BXAP
Countryman's Return, The. Dylan Thomas. OxBTC
Countryman's Wooing, A. Theocritus, *tr. fr. Latin by* Charles Stuart Calverley. ErPo
Country's Crisis, The. Brian Merriman, *tr. fr. Modern Irish by* David Marcus. *Fr.* The Midnight Court. BIrV
Countrywoman of Mine, A. Elaine Goodale Eastman. AA
County Ball, The. Coventry Patmore. *Fr.* The Angel in the House, II, iii. EBVV
County Ball, The, *sel.* Winthrop Mackworth Praed.
County Member, The. OBNC
County Guy. Sir Walter Scott. *Fr.* Quentin Durward. OAEP; OBRV
(Serenade, A.) GTBS; GTBS-P
(Song: "Ah County Guy, the hour is nigh.") CH
County Jail, The. Jimmy Santiago Baca. LFAC
County Mayo. Anthony Raftery, *tr. fr. Irish.* AnIL, *tr. by* James Stephens; KiLC; *tr. by* Frank O'Connor
County Member, The. Winthrop Mackworth Praed. *Fr.* The County Ball. OBNC
County of Mayo, The. *At. to* Thomas Flavell [*or* Lavelle], *tr. fr. Modern Irish by* George Fox. AnIV; BIrV; OBEV; OnYI; OxBI
County Roads. Thomas Rabbitt. MAYP
County Sligo. Louis MacNeice. OnYI
(Sligo and Mayo.) FaBoPP
Coup d'Etat. Ruth Herschberger. LiTA
Coup de Grâce. A. D. Hope. DFT; PPP
Coup de Grace, The. Edward Rowland Sill. AA
Couple, The. Ana Blandiana, *tr. fr. Rumanian by author and* William M. Murray. WPOW
Couple, The. Sandra Hochman. CTBA; NYBP
Couple, The. Joel Oppenheimer. CoPo
Couple. Walter Stone. NYBP
Couple. Mary Swope. AMV-81
Couple Overhead, The. William Meredith. HoPM; NoAM; TW
Couple Upstairs, The. Hugo Williams. POL
Couples sought (enclose photographs please). Billings and Cooings from "The Berkeley Barb." Mona Van Duyn. GP
Couplets for WCW. Martha Christina. AMV-80
Couplets 20 [*or* XX]. Robert Mezey. FYAP; NU
Courage. Matthew Arnold. OAEL-2
Courage. Stopford Brooke. WGRP
Courage. Helen Frazee-Bower. HBMV
Courage. Paul Gerhardt. *See* Give to the Winds Thy Fears.
Courage. Sadi, *tr. fr. Persian by* Sir Edwin Arnold. *Fr.* The Gulistan. AWP
Courage, All. Edwin Markham. HBMV
Courage, brother! do not stumble. Trust in God and Do the Right. Norman Macleod. BLRP; PaPo; TreFT
Courage, dear Moll! and drive away despair. À Madame, Madame B, Beauté Sexagenaire. Charles Sackville. APAS
Courage for the Pusillanimous. Paul Roche. GoYe
"Courage!" he said, and pointed toward the land. The Lotos-Eaters. Tennyson. CABA; ChTr; FiP; GoTL; HBV-2; LiTB; NoP; OAEL-2; OAEP; OBRV; OnMSP; PoEL-5; SeCeV; TEP; TreFT; VLP
Courage Means Running. William Empson. LiTB
Courage, my soul, now learn to wield. A Dialogue between the Resolved Soul and Created Pleasure. Andrew Marvell. AnAnS-1; MeLP; MePo; OAEL-1; OBS; SeCP; SeCV-1
Courage, my Soul! now to the silent wood. Peace. Bhartrihari, *tr. by* Paul Elmer More. AWP
Courage: your tongue has left. Stutterer. Alan Dugan. CAPP; NYBP
Coureurs de Bois. Douglas Le Pan. CaP; MoCV; NOBC
Couriers, The. Sylvia Plath. LCAP
Course, The. Robert Huff. CoAP
Course bread and water's most their fare. Roger Williams. SCAP
Course of a Particular, The. Wallace Stevens. PPoe; QFR
Course of each life must vary, The. Bread of Brotherhood. Lucia Trent. PGD
Course of the Tavy, The. William Browne. *Fr.* Britannia's Pastorals, I. FaBoPP
Course of True Love, The. Shakespeare. *Fr.* A Midsummer Night's Dream, I, i. TreFS; WHA
Courser and the Jennet, The. Shakespeare. *Fr.* Venus and Adonis. LoBV; NOBE
("But lo, from forth a copse that neighbours by.") FM; PH; PoPle
(Courser, The.) OBSC
Court, The. *Unknown.* APAS
Court and Country Love. *Unknown.* UnTE
Court considered the country's crisis, The. The Country's Crisis. Brian Merriman, *tr. by* David Marcus. *Fr.* The Midnight Court. BIrV
Court Historian, The. Walter Thornbury. HBV-1; OBVV
Court is kept att leeue London, The. Hugh Spencer's Feats in France. *Unknown.* ESPB
Court Lady, A. Elizabeth Barrett Browning. BeLS; HBV-2
Court of Charles II, The. Pope. *Fr.* To Augustus. OBEC
Court of Neptune, The. John Hughes. EtS
Court of Sapience, *sel.* John Lydgate.
Lament. PoEL-1
Court We Live On, The. Bill Tremblay. TAT
Courteous kind gallants all. Sir Walter Rauleigh His Lamentation. *Unknown.* CoMu
Courteous Knight, The. *Unknown. See* Baffled Knight, The.
Courteous pagan shall condemne, The. Roger Williams. SCAP
Courteously self-assured, although alone. Charlotte Corday. Charles Tomlinson. OxBC
Courtesan with Fan. Elizabeth Spires. MAYP
Courtesies of good-morning and good-evening. On Dwelling. Robert Graves. CMoP; FaBoMo; MoVE
Courtesy. Hilaire Belloc. ACP; HBMV
Courtesy. Coventry Patmore. OBVV
Courthouse in the center of town, A. A Return from the Wars. Frederick Bock. SOTS
Courthouse Square. Herbert Merrill. AmFN
Courtier's a Riddle, A. Ralph Schomberg. *Fr.* The Judgment of Paris. TrJP
Courtier's Good-Morrow to His Mistress, The. *Unknown.* ElL
Courtier's Health, The; or, Merry Boys of the Times. *Unknown.* CoMu
Courtier's Life, The. Sir Thomas Wyatt. FaBoEE
Courtin', The. James Russell Lowell. *Fr.* The Biglow Papers, 2d series, *introd.* AA; AmPP; BeLS; HBV-1; InMe; NOBA; OBAL; OBVV; TreFS
Courts wait, wide open, The. Mismatch. Carl Lindner. AMV-80
Courtship. Alexander Brome, *after the Latin of* Catullus. CavP
Courtship. Alice Corbin. BPAW
Courtship. Diana O Hehir. NPGG

Courtship. Mark Strand. GP
Courtship, Merry Marriage, and Picnic Dinner of Cock Robin and Jenny Wren, The. *Unknown.* HBV-1
Courtship of Miles Standish, The. Longfellow. BeLS; TreFS
Sels.
Expedition to Wessagusset, The. PAH
War-Token, The. PAH
Courtship of the Yonghy-Bonghy-Bo, The. Edward Lear. EnLoPo; EvOK; FaBoNo; HBV-2; OAEL-2; OnMSP; WiR
(Yonghy-Bonghy-Bo, The.) NA
Courtyard in Winter. John Montague. IPY
Cousin Ella Goes to Town. George Ella Lyon. Str
Cousin Jack Song. *At. to* Charley Tregonning. AmFP
Cousin Jeannette hands. Midwife. Earl Gene Box. LFAC
Cousin Nancy. T. S. Eliot. OBAL
Cousins. Paula B. Cullen. AMV-81
Covenant, The. James Cunningham. JB
Coventry Carol. *Unknown.* EBCP; ELP; MeEL; OFD; PChr
Cover. Frances Frost. SUS
Cover Her Face. Thomas Kinsella. CIP; IPY
Cover my eyes with your palm. Ruth Miller. *Fr.* Cycle. PeSA
Covered Bridge. Robert P. Tristram Coffin. AmFN
Covered Wagon, The. Lena Whittaker Blakeney. BPAW
Covered with snow, the herd, with none to guide. Without the Herdsman. Diotimus, *tr. by* John William Burgon. AWP
Covered with yellow leaves. Memory Gardens. Allen Ginsberg. NNaP
Covertly under the line tree aspen. Epithalamium for Cavorting Ghosts. Dachine Rainer. NePoAm-2
Covet. Ambrose Bierce. DBV
Covetousness. Peter Idley. OxBChV
Covey of cotton-dressed, apple-breasted girls, A. Wax. Winfield Townley Scott. ErPo
Covey struts across the chrome-green roof, The. California Quail in January. Will C. Jumper. GrPl
Cow, The. Oliver Herford. *Fr.* More Animals. NA
Cow. Janet Reed McFatter. GrPl
Cow, The. Ogden Nash. CenHV; NoP; RHPC
Cow, The. Bernard O'Dowd. PoAu-1
Cow, The. Jack Prelutsky. RHPC
Cow, The. Theodore Roethke. FiBHP; OBAL; OBCA
Cow, The. Robert Louis Stevenson. BrPo; FaPON; FM; NTCP; OxBChV; SoPo; SUS; TiPo
Cow, The. Ann Taylor *or* Jane Taylor. HBV-1; HBVY; OxBChV
Cow, The. *Unknown.* FaBoUs
Cow and a calf, A. *Unknown.* OxNR
Cow Ate the Piper, The. *Unknown.* GBP
Cow-bosses are good-hearted chunks, The. Dogie Song. *Unknown.* CoSo
Cow Camp on the Range, A. *Unknown.* CoSo
Cow-Chace, The. John André. PAH
Cow Dance. Bruce Beaver. PoAu-2
Cow eats green grass, The. Response to Rimbaud's Later Manner. T. Sturge Moore. OBMV; SyP
Cow has a cud, The. David McCord. TiPo
Cow in Apple Time, The. Robert Frost. CABA; MoAB; MoAmPo; PoLF
Cow is of the bovine ilk, The. The Cow. Ogden Nash. CenHV; NoP; RHPC
Cow is too well known, I fear, The. The Cow. Oliver Herford. *Fr.* More Animals. NA
Cow-lady, or sweet lady-bird. Lines to a Lady-Bird. Lord De Tabley. FM
Cow mainly moos as she chooses to moo, The. The Cow. Jack Prelutsky. RHPC
Cow Pissing. Robert Morgan. GeTw
Cow-Ponies. Maurice Lesemann. BPAW
Cow Time. Monica Shannon. SiSoSe
Cow walks away from him, The. Thomas in the Fields. Lois Moyles. NYBP
Cow wandering in the bare field, The. Randall Jarrell. MoVE
Coward. A. R. Ammons. OBAL
Coward, The. Kipling. *Fr.* Epitaphs of the War. FaBoEE; FaBoTw; OAEP
Coward, The. Eve Merriam. TrJP
Coward, The. Stephen Spender. NoAM
Coward—of heroic size. Grizzly. Bret Harte. AA; BPAW
Cowards die many times before their deaths. The Death of Cowards [*or* That Men Should Fear]. Shakespeare. *Fr.* Julius Caesar, II, ii. FF; TreFS; TrGrPo
Cowards fear to die, but courage stout. On the Snuff of a Candle. Sir Walter Ralegh. FaBoEE; SiPS
Cowboy, The. John Antrobus. AA; FaBoBe; FaPON
Cowboy, The ("All day on the prairie in the saddle I ride"), *with music.* *Unknown.* CoSo (2 *vers.*)
Cowboy ("I'm wild and woolly"). *Unknown.* ChTr
Cowboy, The ("It was only a few short years ago"). *Unknown.* CoSo
Cowboy, The ("Oh, a man there lives on the Western plains"). *Unknown.* BPAW; CoSo
Cowboy and His Love, The, *with music.* John Milton Hagen. CoSo
Cowboy and the Stork, The. Robert V. Carr. BPAW
Cowboy at Church, The, *with music.* *Unknown.* CoSo
Cowboy at Work, The. *Unknown.* CoSo
Cowboy Dance Song, A. *Unknown.* CoSo
Cow-Boy Fun. Wallace D. Coburn. PoOW
Cowboy Graces. *Unknown.* CoSo
Cowboy has his bunkie, The. The Sheep-Herder's Lament. Arthur Chapman. BPAW
Cowboy hat, and underneath, A. Belle Starr. *Unknown.* BPAW
Cowboy he lay on the prairie, A. The Dry-landers. *Unknown.* CoSo
Cowboy Jack, *with music.* *Unknown.* CoSo
Cowboy Song. Charles Causley. NePoEA; PoRA
Cowboy stands beneath, The. Vaquero. Edward Dorn. NeAP; PoM
Cowboy Talks to a Pitching Horse. *Unknown.* CoSo
Cowboy Up to Date, The. Charles F. Thomas, Jr. CoSo
Cowboy's Ball, The. Henry Herbert Knibbs. PoOW
Cowboys' Christmas Ball, The. William Lawrence Chittenden. BPAW; CoSo, *with music*
Cowboys, come and hear a story of Roy Bean in all his glory. Roy Bean.. BeLS; BPAW; CoSo; OBAL
Cowboy's Dance Song, The, *with music.* *Unknown.* CoSo
Cowboy's Dream, The ("Last night as I lay on the prairie"). *Unknown, at. to* Charles J. Finger. BPAW; CoSo, *with music;* FSW, *shorter version*
Cowboy's Fate, The. Wallace D. Coburn. PoOW
Cowboy's Gettin'-up Holler, *with music.* *Unknown.* CoSo; TrAS
Cowboy's Lament, The (*diff. versions*). *Unknown.* BLSo, *with music;* BPAW; ChTr; CoSo (A, B *and* C *vers., all with music*); FaFP; GBP; TreFS; ViBoFo (A *and* B *vers.*)
(As I Walked Out in the Streets of Laredo, *with music.*) AS
(Dying Cowboy, The.) FaBoBa
(Streets of Laredo, The.) AmFP; FSW
Cowboy's Life, The. *At. to* James Barton Adams, *ad. by* John A. *and* Alan Lomax. AmFN; BPAW; CoSo; SoPo; TiPo
Cowboy's Life Is a Very Dreary Life, The. *Unknown.* AmFP
(Kansas Line, The ["A cowboy's life is a dreary, dreary life"], *longer version, with music.*) CoSo
Cowboy's Meditation, The. *Unknown.* CoSo
Cowboy's Salvation Song. Robert V. Carr. PoOW
Cow-Boy's Song, The. Anna Maria Wells. OBCA
Coweta County Courthouse, The. James Miller Robinson. AMV-80
Cowhorn-crowned, shockheaded, cornshuck-bearded. The Knight, Death, and the Devil. Randall Jarrell. CrMA; WeW
Cowled with a news-sheet in his asphalt cage. At the Zoo. Walter de la Mare. BoAnP
Cowman's Prayer, The, *with music.* *Unknown.* CoSo
Cowper's Grave. Elizabeth Barrett Browning. HBV-2; OBVV
Cowper's Three Hares. Charles Tennyson Turner. FM
Cows. James Reeves. NTCP; PoSC
Cows Are Coming Home in Maine. Robert P. Tristram Coffin. DuDa
Cows at Night, The. Hayden Carruth. SV
Cows bring in the last light, The. The Black Plateau. W. S. Merwin. NNaP
Cows! Cows! With ears like mouths of telephones! Band Music. John Fuller. NePoEA-2
Cows graze. Horses Graze. Gwendolyn Brooks. CNA; GP
Cows Grazing at Sunrise. William Matthews. AMV-81; NPAW
Cows in Vatra Dornii lumber on the grass-wet, The. Hertza. Benjamin Fondane, *tr. by* Matei Calinescu *and* Willis Barnstone. VWA
Cows low in the pasture on the hill, The. The Song of the Robin. Beatrice Bergquist. SUS
Cows near the Graveyard, The. Howard Nelson. NU
Cows they had, many, like heavy clouds drifting in the meadow. The Wheelbarrow. Russell Edson. LCAP
Coxcomb Bird, The. Pope. *Fr.* Moral Essays. LiTB
Coy Clelia, veil those charming eyes. To Clelia. Matthew Coppinger. CavP
Coy in a covert of the glossy bracken. Illusion. Sir Edmund Gosse. SyP
Coy Lass Dress'd Up in Her Best, The. *Unknown.* ErPo
Coy nature (which remain'd, tho [*or* though] aged grown). Ode upon Doctor Harvey. Abraham Cowley. Par; PoEL-2
Coy Shepherdess, The; or, Phillis and Amintas. *Unknown.* CoMu
Coyote. Bret Harte. BPAW
Coyote, The. Carter Revard. VoR
Coyote/ pineneedles. Vihio Images. Judith Mountain Leaf Volborth. TWSS
Coyote/ running. Sweat Song. Peter Blue Cloud. STE; VoR
Coyote and the Locust, The. *Unknown.* *See* Locust, The.
Coyote and the Star. Arthur Guiterman. BPAW

Coyote Brother Song. Annette Arkeketa West. TWSS
Coyote, Coyote, Please Tell Me. Peter Blue Cloud. STE
Coyote kicks back. Agnes. Mah-do-ge Tohee. STE
Coyote's Daylight Trip. Paula Gunn Allen. TWSS
Cozzo Grillo. H. B. Mallalieu. WaP
Crab, The. Conrad Aiken. BoAnP
Crab-Apple. Ethel Talbot. TiPo
Crab Orchard Sanctuary; Late October. Thomas Kinsella. IPY
Crab Tree, The. Oliver St. John Gogarty. AnIL; OxBI
Crabbed Age and Youth. Shakespeare. The Passionate Pilgrim, XII. HBV-1; InPS; LiTB; NIP; OBEV; TreFS; UnTE; ViBoPo
(Age and Youth.) ElL; FaBoEn
("Crabbed age and youth cannot live together.") GBL
(Madrigal, A: "Crabbed age and youth.") GTBS; GTBS-P
(Youth and Age.) OBSC
Crabbing. Marky Daniel. AMV-81
Crabbing. Norman Levine. CaP; OBCV
Crack, The. Michael Goldman. NYBP
Crack in our hearth of land, The. Brevard Fault. Robert Morgan. SUW
Crack in the Wall Holds Flowers. Adam David Miller. PoBA
Crack ran through our hearthstone long ago, A. The Refugees. Edwin Muir. NoAM
Cracked cedar, The. Elephants. Patrick Lane. NeAC
Cracked is the very foundation. Epigram: To Charinus, a Catamite. Martial. PeHV
Crackling embers on the hearth are dead, The. Night. Hartley Coleridge. NCEP
Crackling Twig, The. James Stephens. *See* Satyr, The.
Cracks, The. Robert Creeley. ConAP
Cracks on the walls, The. Star Blanket. Ray A. Young Bear. CDW
Cradle and the Cross, The. A. S. Reitz. STF
Cradle and Throne. *Unknown.* STF
Cradle Hymn. *At. to* Martin Luther. *See* Away in a Manger.
Cradle Hymn, A. Isaac Watts. HBV-1, *sl. abr.*; LoBV; OBEC; OBEV, *sl. abr.*; OxBChV, *abr.*; PoEL-3; SBVL; SoPo, *abr.*; SUS, *abr.*; TreFS, *sl. abr.*
(Cradle Song, A.) EBCP, *abr.*; OxBoCh, *abr.*
Cradle Song, A: "Angels are stooping, The." W. B. Yeats. PoPl
Cradle Song: "Clock's untiring fingers wind the wool of darkness, The." Louis MacNeice. MoAB; MoBrPo
(Cradle Song for Miriam.) NAs
Cradle Song, A: "Come, little babe, come, silly soul." Nicholas Breton. HBV-1; NOBE; OBEV
(Come, Little Babe.) PPoe
(Sweet Lullaby, A.) ElL; OBSC; ViBoPo
Cradle Song: "Curled like a hoop in sleep." Lawrence Durrell. NAs
Cradle Song: "Fear not the atom in fission." Samuel Hoffenstein. DBV
Cradle Song: "From groves of spice." Sarojini Naidu. FaPON
Cradle Song, A: "Golden slumbers kiss your eyes." Thomas Dekker. *See* Golden Slumbers.
Cradle Song, A: "Hush! my dear, lie still and slumber." Isaac Watts. *See* Cradle Hymn, A.
Cradle Song: "Imagine lamenting our longing, no." Yona Wallach, *tr. fr. Hebrew by* Leonore Gordon. VWA
Cradle Song: "Lord Gabriel, wilt thou not rejoice." Josephine Preston Peabody. HBV-1
Cradle Song: "Lullaby, my little one." Carl Michael Bellman. FaPON
Cradle-Song: "Madonna, Madonna [*or* Madonnina]." Adelaide Crapsey. HBMV; ISi
Cradle Song, A: "O men from the fields." Padraic Colum. GoBC; ISi; OnYI; OxBi
(Lullaby.) WTO
Cradle Song: "O my deir hert, young Jesus sweit." James, John, *and* Robert Wedderburn. *See* Balulalow.
Cradle Song: "Sleep enfold thee,/ Jesukin." James L. Duff. ISi
Cradle Song: "Sleep, my child, my little daughter." *Unknown, tr. fr. Yiddish by* Joseph Leftwich. TrJP
Cradle Song: "Sleep, my darling, sleep." Louis MacNeice. OxBI; PoPl
Cradle Song: "Sleep, sleep, beauty bright." Blake. EnRP; FPL; HBV-1; HBVY; OBEC; OBEV; PoLF; PoPl
Cradle Song, A: "Sweet dreams, form a shade." Blake. *Fr.* Songs of Innocence. EnRP; LAuP; OAEP; OBCP; SBVL; ViBoPo
Cradle Song: "What does little birdie say." Tennyson. *See* What Does Little Birdie Say.
Cradle Song: "What is the little one thinking about?" Josiah Gilbert Holland. *Fr.* Bitter-sweet. HBV-1
(Babyhood.) AA
Cradle Song for Miriam. Louis MacNeice. *See* Cradle Song: "Clock's untiring fingers wind the wool of darkness, The."
Cradle Song of the Elephants. Adriano del Valle, *tr. fr. Spanish by* Alida Malkus. FaPON
Cradle Song of the Virgin. *Unknown.* *See* Virgin's Song, The.
Cradle Will Rock, The, *sel.* Marc Blitzstein.
Art for Art's Sake. TrJP
Cradled and warm, fur-warm, in the she-wolf's lair. Wolf-Boy. David Malouf. CBAP
Craftsman, The. Marcus B. Christian. PoNe
Craftsman. Luci Shaw. TrCP
Craftsmen. V. Sackville-West. OxBTC
Crafty Farmer, The. *Unknown.* AmFP; BaBo; ESPB
Crafty Miss of London, The; or, The Fryar Well Fitted. *Unknown.* CoMu; OxBB
Crag Jack's Apostasy. Ted Hughes. EaLo
Craigbilly Fair. *Unknown.* ChTr; GBP
Cramped like sardines on the Queens, and sedated. Tourists. Howard Moss. FiBHP; NYBP
Cranach. Sir Herbert Read. BrPo; FaBoMo
Cranberry Song, The. Barney Reynolds. AmFP
Crane. Joseph Langland. NYBP
Crane, The. Charles Tomlinson. MoBrPo
Crane Is My Neighbour, The. Shaw Neilson. CBAP; PoAu-1
Cranes. J. R. S. Davies. POL
Cranes, The. Po Chü-i, *tr. fr. Chinese by* Arthur Waley. OBVE
Crane's Ascent, The. Nick Bozanic. AMV-81
Cranes of Ibycus, The. Emma Lazarus. AA
Cranial Nerves, The. *Unknown.* FaBoUs
Crankadox leaned o'er the edge of the moon, The. Craqueodoom [*or* Spirk Troll-Derisive]. James Whitcomb Riley. NA; OBAL
Cranmer. C. H. Sisson. FaBoTw
Cranmer's Prophecy of Queen Elizabeth. Shakespeare. King Henry VIII, *fr.* V, v. WGRP
Crapshooters. Carl Sandburg. VGW
Craqueodoom. James Whitcomb Riley. OBAL
(Spirk Troll-Derisive.) NA
Crashed through the woods that lumbering Coach. The dust. The Last Coachload. Walter de la Mare. SeCePo
Crashing sky has swept old paths aside, The. Make Way! Florence Crocker Comfort. PGD
Crass Times Redeemed by Dignity of Souls. Peter Viereck. MiAP
"Tenderness of dignity of souls, The," *sel.* HoPM
Craven. Sir Henry Newbolt. HBV-2; HBVY; PAH
Craving of Samuel Rouse for clearance to create, The. The Slave and the Iron Lace. Margaret Danner. AmNP; BPo
Cravings during Pregnancy. M. Saint-Marthe, *tr. fr. French. Fr.* Paedotrophiae; or, The Art of Bringing Up Children. FaBoUs
Crawdad. *Unknown.* FSW
Crawl Blues. Vincent McHugh. ErPo
Crawl, crawl, clock on the wall. Pendulum Rhyme. Selma Robinson. InMe
Crawl into Bed. Quandra Prettyman. BOLo
Crawl, laugh. Issa, *tr. fr. Japanese by* Nobuyuki Yuasa. OFD
Crawlers, The. Keaulumoku, *tr. fr. Hawaiian by* M. W. Beckwith. *Fr.* The Kumulipo; a Creation Chant. WTO
Crawlin' aboot like a snail in the mud. The Image o' God. Joe Corrie. OxBS
Craw's Killed the Poussie, O, The! *Unknown.* BoAnP
Crayon House. Muriel Rukeyser. EyDe
Crazed by the suck and roar. Calypso. Richard Kell. CIP
Crazed Girl, The. W. B. Yeats. InPS
Crazed Man in Concentration Camp. Agnes Gergely, *tr. fr. Hungarian by* Edwin Morgan. BoWoP
Crazed Moon, The ("Crazed through much child-bearing"). W. B. Yeats. MOON
Crazy/ to be alive in such a strange. Lawrence Ferlinghetti. CTBA; FF
Crazy Arithmetic. D'Arcy Thompson. FaBoCo
Crazy as hell and typical of us. Making Contact. John Manifold. CBAP
Crazy Bill to the Bishop. Robert Peters. BXAP
Crazy bookcase, placed before, A. Epilogue to the Breakfast-Table Series. Oliver Wendell Holmes. *Fr.* The Poet at the Breakfast Table. AA
Crazy Dogholkoda. Mary TallMountain. TWSS
Crazy Horse Returns to South Dakota. Harley Elliott. NeAC
Crazy Horse: The Last Morning. Lance Henson. VoR
Crazy Jane and Jack the Journeyman. W. B. Yeats. CMoP
Crazy Jane and the Bishop. W. B. Yeats. CMoP; LiTM
Crazy Jane Grown Old Looks at the Dancers. W. B. Yeats. CMoP; EBEV
Crazy Jane on God. W. B. Yeats. CMoP; EBEV; MoAB; OxBTC
Crazy Jane on the Day of Judgment. W. B. Yeats. CMoP; SOTW
Crazy Jane on the Mountain. W. B. Yeats. CMoP
Crazy Jane Reproved. W. B. Yeats. CMoP
Crazy Jane Talks with the Bishop. W. B. Yeats. BoLoP; CABA; CMoP; CoBMV; EBEV; ErPo; InPK; NoAM; NoP; OAEL-2; OAEP; PAI; PPP
Crazy Movie. Gregorio Barrios, *tr. fr. Spanish by* Toni Empringham. FIA
Crazy pier, a roof of splinters, The. The Union Barge on Staten Island. Louis Simpson. NYP

Crazy Song to the Air of "Dixie," *with music.* "Andy Lee." AS
Crazy tugs, The. East River. Rosemary Thomas. AmFN
Crazy World, The. William Gay. PoAu-1
Creaking by pancake plateaus. Conestoga. George E. Murphy, Jr. AMV-81
Cream of phosphorescent light, A. Jonah. Aldous Huxley. ChTr
Cream-Puffin, The. Carolyn Wells. *Fr.* A Baker's Dozen of Wild Beasts. OBCA
Cream sours in this weather. Are You There, Mrs. Goose? John V. Hicks. AMV-80
Creamcheese babies square and downy as bolsters. The Peaceable Kingdom. Marge Piercy. TwCP
Cream-cups, butter-cups. A Little Song of Spring. Mary Austin. YeAr
Created, The. Jones Very. NOCV; QFR
Created by the poet to sing my song. The Reaper. Robert Duncan. CrMA
Created for whose sake? The praying. Don't Sit under the Apple Tree with Anyone Else but Me. Robert Pack. CoPo; FF
Created purely from glass the saint stands. In Piam Memoriam. Geoffrey Hill. NePoEA-2; OxBC
Created Universe, The. Mark Akenside. *See* Nature's Influence on Man.
Creation, The. Cecil Frances Alexander. *See* All Things Bright and Beautiful.
Creation, The. Bible, *O.T.* *Fr.* Genesis. TreF (I:1-II:3)
("In the beginning God created the heaven and the earth.") ImOP (I:1-31); NAWM-1 (I-IV)
Creation. Ambrose Bierce. AA
Creation, *sel.* Sir Richard Blackmore.
Circulation of the Blood, The. FaBoUs
Creation, The. Abraham Cowley. *Fr.* Davideis, I. OBS
Creation, The. James Weldon Johnson. BALP; BANP; CDC; FaBV; MoAmPo; PoBA; PoPl; PoRA; TrCP; YaD
Up from the Bed of the River, *sel.* EaLo
Creation, The. *Maori Oral Tradition, tr. by* Richard Taylor. WTO
Creation. Louise Townsend Nicholl. GoYe
Creation. Alfred Noyes. GoBC; OBVV
Creation, The: According to Coyote. Simon J. Ortiz. CDW
Creation Myths. Burton Raffel. AMV-80
Creation of Birds, The. Milton. *Fr.* Paradise Lost, VII. PB
("Meanwhile the tepid caves and fens and shores.") PBBP
Creation of Man, The. *Maori Oral Tradition, tr. by* John White. WTO
Creation of My Lady, The. Francesco Redi, *tr. fr. Italian by* Sir Edmund Gosse. AWP
Creation of the Animals. Milton. *Fr.* Paradise Lost, VII. FM
Creation of the Child. Susan Litwack. VWA
Creation of the Moon, The. *Unknown, tr. fr. Amazonian Indian by* W. S. Merwin. MOON
Creation's and Creator's crowning good. To the Body. Coventry Patmore. The Unknown Eros, XL. GoBC; OAEL-2; OxBoCh; PoEL-5; VLP
Creation's crust and crumb, breaking of bread. Bread. A. M. Klein. PeCV
Creation's Lord, We Give Thee Thanks, *with music.* William deWitt Hyde. AH
Creation's mildest charms are there combined. Britain. Goldsmith. *Fr.* The Traveller; or, A Prospect of Society. NOEC
Creative Force. Maude Miner Hadden. GoYe
Creative Process, The. Mark Akenside. *Fr.* The Pleasures of Imagination. NOEC
Creator of Infinities, *with music.* Chadwick Hansen. AH
Creator Spirit, by whose aid. Veni Creator Spiritus. *Unknown, at. to* Charlemagne, *to* Hrabanus Maurus, *and to* St. Gregory the Great, *paraphrased by* Dryden. AWP; FaPoR; GoBC; HBV-2; ILwL; SeCV-2; WGRP
Creator Spirit come. Pagan Rites. Paul Goodman. *Fr.* North Percy. DiL
Creatrix. Anna Wickham. MoBrPo
Creature half horse, half human, A. Centaur Song. Stanley Moss. DiL
Creature in the Classroom, The. Jack Prelutsky. RHPC
Creature to pet and spoil, A. Kob Antelope. *Yoruba Oral Tradition, tr. by* Ulli Beier. WTO
Creatures. Maxine W. Kumin. BoAnP
Creatures that we met this morning, The. Discovery of the New World. Carter Revard. VoR
Creçy. Francis Turner Palgrave. BeLS; HBV-2
Credences of Summer. Wallace Stevens. AP; CoBMV
Credibility. John Ciardi. InPK
Credit. *Unknown.* STF
Creditor, The. Louis MacNeice. EaLo
Credo. Leonard Cohen. PeCV
Credo. Zona Gale. TrPWD
Credo. Brewster Ghiselin. PoA
Credo, *sel.* Richard Watson Gilder.
"Christ of Judea, look thou in my heart!" TrPWD
Credo. Robinson Jeffers. MoAB; MoAmPo; PoPl
Credo. Georgia Douglas Johnson. BALP; PoBA
Credo. "Seumas O'Sullivan." OnYI
Credo. John Oxenham. BLRP
Credo. E. A. Robinson. AmPP; AP; CMoP; LiTM; MoAmPo; NePA; OxBA; TAP; TrCP; TreFT; WGRP
Credo. Arthur Symons. OBVV
Credo, A. Thackeray. HBV-2
Creed. Walter Lowenfels. PoNe
Creed, A. Norman McLeod. WGRP
Creed, A. Edwin Markham. BLPA; BLPL; FaBoBe; FaFP; PoPl; TreFS
Creed, A. John Masefield. HBMV; WGRP
Creed. Anne Spencer. CDC
Creed. Mary Ashley Townsend. BLPA; FaBoBe
Creed, A. *Unknown.* *See* My Daily Creed.
Creed of Mr. Nicholas Culpeper. Patricia Beer. OxBC
Creede. Cy Warman. BPAW; PoOW
Creeds. Karle Wilson Baker. HBMV; WGRP
Creeds. Willard Wattles. HBMV
Creek, The. W. W. E. Ross. MoCV; OBCV
Creek has to run muddy before it can run clear, The! James K. Baxter. Autumn Testament, 15. OCNZ
Creek of the Four Graves, The, *sels.* Charles Harpur.
"I verse a settler's tale of olden times." CBAP
"Settler in the olden times went forth, A." PoAu-1
Creek-Road, The. Madison Cawein. AA
Creek, shining, The. The Creek. W. W. E. Ross. MoCV; OBCV
Creep afore Ye Gang. James Ballantine. HBV-1
Creep into thy narrow bed. The Last Word. Matthew Arnold. CABA; FaBoEn; FiP; HBV-2; NOBE; OAEL-2; OBNC; OBVV; PoEL-5; TreFT; TrGrPo; VLP; WHA
Creeper, The. Tom Schmidt. NeAC
Creeper grows over thorn. Alba. Confucius, *tr. by* Ezra Pound. *Fr.* Songs of T'ang. CTC
Creeps in half wanton, half asleep. Wagner. Rupert Brooke. FaBoTw; NOBL
Cremation. Robinson Jeffers. ELU
Cremation of Sam McGee, The. Robert W. Service. BLPL; FaFP; NOBC; OBNV; PoLF; ShM; TreF
Crematorium. John Betjeman. PoA
Cremona. Sir Arthur Conan Doyle. HBV-2
Creole Girl. Leslie Morgan Collins. PoNe
Creole Slave-Song, A. Maurice Thompson. AA
Crepe de Chine. Tennessee Williams. NYBP
Crepe paper christmas. Star Child Suite. Paula Gunn Allen. TWSS
Crêpes Flambeau. Tess Gallagher. AMV-81; MAYP
Crept side by side beyond the thresh. Epithalamium. Vassar Miller. NePoEA
Crepuscular. Richard Howard. TwCP
Crescent Moon. Elizabeth Madox Roberts. SUS
Crescent Moon, The. *Unknown.* MOON
("In Mornigan's park there is a deer.") GBP
(Riddle: "In Mornigan's park there is a deer.") ChTr
Crescenzio, the Pope's Legate at the High Council, Trent. The Cardinal and the Dog. Robert Browning. VLP
Cresseid's Complaint against Fortune. Robert Henryson. *Fr.* The Testament of Cresseid. MeEL
Cressid. Nora Perry. AA
Cressida's Leprosy. Robert Henryson. *Fr.* The Testament of Cresseid. SeCePo
Crest and crowning of all good, The. Brotherhood. Edwin Markham. PGD
Crest Jewel, The. James Stephens. AnIL; MoAB; MoBrPo
Crested and ruffed and stiff with whistling frills. Ganymede. William Plomer. PeHV
Crethis. Callimachus, *tr. fr. Greek by* Richard Garnett. AWP
Creüsa cried for, through the tomb of Troy. Aeneid. Claire McAllister. NePA
Crew-Cuts. Donald Hall. MAT
Crew is changed, the stone's face notched in darkness, The. Weldon Kees. *Fr.* The Hourglass. NYP
Crew Practice on Lake Bled, in Jugoslavia. James Scully. NYBP
Crib, The. Robert Finch. OBCP
Cricket, The. Vincent Bourne, *tr. fr. Latin by* William Cowper. HBV-1; HBVY; PoLF
Cricket. No Ch'ŏn-myŭng, *tr. fr. Korean by* Ko Won. PBWP
Cricket. Clinton Scollard. HBV-2
Cricket, The. Frederick Goddard Tuckerman. FM; NOBA; QFR
Cricket; an Heroic Poem, *sel.* James Dance.
"When the returning sun begins to smile." NOEC
Cricket and the greshope wenten hem to fight, The. Nonsense. *Unknown.* EBEV; OxBM
Cricket Bowler, A. Edward Cracroft Lefroy. OBVV

Cricket, chirring in the autumn twilight. Cricket. Clinton Scollard. HBV-2
Cricket Kept the House, The. Edith M. Thomas. OBCA
Cricket on a rubbish-tip, A. Winter Cricket. John Heath-Stubbs. OBCP
Cricket[s] sang, The. Emily Dickinson. SOTW; TwAmPo
Crickets. David McCord. NTCP; PDV
Crickets. Aram Saroyan. MAT
Crickets. Valerie Worth. RHPC
Crickets and locusts, cicadas. Rosalía de Castro, *tr. fr. Galician by* Benjamin de Castro. PBWP
Crickets are making/ The merriest din. September [Is Here]. Edward Bliss Reed. HBMV; HBVY; YeAr
Cricket's Story, The. Emma Huntington Nason. HBV-1; HBVY
Cried the navy-blue ghost. Four in the Morning. Edith Sitwell. NoAM
Crier, The. Michael Drayton. EIL; InvP; OAEP; WhC
(Cryer, The.) PoEL-2
Crier by Night, The, *sel.* Gordon Bottomley.
Blanid's Song. BrPo
Crime Club. Weldon Kees. NaP
Crime Note. Hughes Mearns. *Fr.* Later Antigonishes. InMe
Crimes of Lizzie Borden, The. *Unknown. See* Lizzie Borden.
Crimes of Lugalanne. Enheduanna, *tr. fr. Sumerian*; *ad. by* Aliki *and* Willis Barnstone. BoWoP
Crimes of Passion: The Phone Caller. Terry Stokes. AmPA
Crimes of Passion: The Slasher. Terry Stokes. AmPA
Criminality of War, The. Edward Young. PGD
("One to destroy, is murder by the law.") FF
Crimp and whorl of conch, The. A Mantelpiece of Shells. Ruthven Todd. NYBP
Crimson Cherry Tree, The. Henry Treece. WaP
Crimson nor yellow roses, nor. Eros D'Aute. Theodore Wratislaw. GBL
Crimson roses burn and glow, The. Vigil. Richard Dehmel, *tr. by* Ludwig Lewisohn. AWP
Crimson Tent. John Dos Passos. PoA
Crinog, melodious is your song. To Crinog. *Unknown, tr. by* Kuno Meyer. AnIL; OnYI
Cripple Creek. *Unknown.* AmFP; FSW
Cripple Dick upon a stick. *Unknown.* OxNR
Cripple for Life, The; or, The Poor Volunteer. *Unknown.* AmFP
Crippled Child at the Window. Melissa Cannon. AMV-80
Crippled for life at seventeen. Pluck. Eva Dobell. SUMH
Crippler, The. Danny Siegel. VWA
Cripples. Nina Cassian, *tr. fr. Romanian by* Herbert Kuhner. VWA
Cripples. J. D. Reed. NeAC
Criseyde Sees Troilus Return from Battle. Chaucer. *Fr.* Troilus and Criseyde, II. OxBM
Crisis, The. Robert Creeley. FF; PPP
Crisis. G. S. Fraser. NeBP
Crisis, The. Whittier. PAH
Crisp, The/ pale green. Salad La Raza. Janet Campbell Hale. VoR
Crispus Attucks. Robert Hayden. CNA
Crispus Attucks. John Boyle O'Reilly. PAH
Crispus Attucks McCoy. Sterling A. Brown. BPo
Crist. Cynewulf. *See* Christ 2.
Crist made to man a fair present. *See* Christ made to man a fair present.
Cristina. Robert Browning. OAEP
Critic, The. John Farrar. SoPo
Critic, A. Walter Savage Landor. ChTr; DBV; FaBoEE
Critic advises, A. Black Poet, White Critic. Dudley Randall. BPo; CABA; ConAP
Critic and Poet. Robert F. Murray. DBV
("Every critic in the town.") POL
Critic of the days of yore, The. Narcissus and Some Tadpoles. Victor J. Daley. PoAu-1
Critic on the Hearth, The. L. E. Sissman. TW
Critical Fribble, A. Charles Churchill. *Fr.* The Rosciad. OBEC
(Character of a Critic.) NOEC
(Criticaster, A.) FaBoEn
Critical Observations. Archibald MacLeish. OBAL
Criticaster, A. Charles Churchill. *See* Critical Fribble, A.
Critics. George Crabbe. PP
Critics. Martial, *tr. fr. Latin by* Sir John Harington. AWP
Critics, The. Theodore Spencer. NYBP
Critics. Swift. *Fr.* On Poetry; a Rhapsody. OBEC; SeCePo
("Hobbes clearly proves that every creature.") HAP; PP; SCV
Critics and Connoisseurs. Marianne Moore. AmPP; CMoP; NePA; NoAM; NOBA; OxBA
Critics and Poets. Geoffrey Grigson. FaBoEE
Critics!—appalled, I venture on the name. Second Epistle to Robert Graham. Burns. DBV
Critics avaunt! Tobacco is my theme. In Imitation of Young. Isaac Hawkins Browne. *Fr.* A Pipe of Tobacco. OBEC
Critics cry unfair, The. In Defense of Black Poets. Conrad Kent Rivers. BOLo; BPo
Critics: in your sight. Sister Juana Inés de la Cruz, *tr. by* Judith Thurman. *Fr.* A Satirical Romance. PBWP
Critic's Rules, The. Robert Lloyd. *Fr.* Shakespeare; an Epistle to David Garrick, Esq. OBEC
Critics say that epics have died out, The. Elizabeth Barrett Browning. *Fr.* Aurora Leigh, V. PBWP
Critics sipping cups of tea. Obituary. Anthony Brode. FiBHP
Critter. W. M. Ransom. CDW
Croak of a raven hoar, The! Mammon Marriage. George Macdonald. BoLoP; EBVV; NBM; OBVV
Croaker Papers, The, *sels.* Fitz-Greene Halleck *and* Joseph Rodman Drake.
Man Who Frets at Worldly Strife, The. AA
National Paintings, The. AA
Ode to Fortune. AA
Crockery. Julia Budenz. AMV-80
Crockett. William Jay Smith. TDH
Crocodile, The. "Lewis Carroll." *See* How Doth the Little Crocodile.
Crocodile, The. Oliver Herford. OBCA; TDH
Crocodile. William Jay Smith. OBCA
Crocodile once dropped a line, A. The Crocodile. Oliver Herford. OBCA
Crocodile wept bitter tears, The. Crocodile. William Jay Smith. OBCA
Crocus, The. Walter Crane. RHPC; SoPo
Crocus. Alfred Kreymborg. HBMV
Crocus. Joan Murray. AMV-80
Crocus armies from the dead, The. Veni Coronaberis. Geoffrey Hill. NoP
Crocus Night. James Schuyler. PoM
Crocus, while the days are dark, The. The Year. Coventry Patmore. EBVV
Crocuses, The. Frances E. W. Harper. BlSi
Crocuses. Jōsa, *tr. fr. Japanese.* TiPo
Crocuses in the Square. Extras. Richard Burton. AA
Crofters few but crafty. Shore Tullye. Robert Rendall. OxBS
Crois was made al of reed, A. Prologue to a Translation. John Trevisa. OxBM
"Crom Cruach and his sub-gods twelve." The Burial of King Cormac. Sir Samuel Ferguson. AnIL; OnYI
Cromek. Blake. FiBHP; PV
(On Cromek.) FaBoCo; PoPle
Cromwell. Robert Francis. GP
Cromwell Dead. Andrew Marvell. *Fr.* A Poem upon the Death of Oliver Cromwell. ChTr
("I saw him dead, a leaden slumber lies.") JCP; OBS; ViBoPo
Cromwell, I charge thee, fling away ambition. Ambition. Shakespeare. King Henry VIII, *fr.* III, ii. TrGrPo
Cromwell, I did not think to shed a tear. Wolsey [*or* Wolsey's Regrets]. Shakespeare. King Henry VIII, *fr.* III, ii. FaBoRV; TreFS
Cromwell, our chief of men, who through a cloud. To the Lord General[1] Cromwell, May 1652 [*or* To Oliver Cromwell]. Milton. CABA; NoP; OBS; SeCeV; TrGrPo; ViBoPo
Crooked/ beneath a denim. Dreams. Charles Cooper. PoBA
Crooked bank still winds to something new, The. Sneyd Davies. *Fr.* A Voyage to Tintern Abbey. NOEC
Crooked Carol. Norma Farber. POL
Crooked Footpath, The. Oliver Wendell Holmes. *Fr.* The Professor at the Breakfast Table. HBV-2; TreF
Crooked gables. In Chagall's Village. Rose Ausländer, *tr. by* Ewald Osers. VWA
Crooked Gun, The, *with music. Unknown.* OuSiCo
Crooked heels. The Cobbler. Eleanor Alletta Chaffee. SoPo; TiPo
Crooked Old Woman. Self-Portrait. Judith Mountain Leaf Volborth. TWSS
Crooked paths go every way, The. The Goat Paths. James Stephens. AnIV; AWP; CH; GoJo; LiTB; OxBI; UnPo; WHA
Crooked Trail to Holbrook, The. *Unknown.* CoSo
Crop plane stalls its engines, The. The Hours. Susan Tichy. MAYP
Cropdusting, The. William Zaranka. BXAP
Cropped, grey, too-small, bullet, Prussian head, A. Pigeon. Roy Fuller. PB
Cropper Lads, The. *Unknown.* OBET
Croppy Boy, The. William B. McBurney. OnYI
Croppy Boy, The. *Unknown.* AmFP; AnIL; AnIV; FaBoBa; FSW; OxBoLi
Crops are all in and the peaches are rotting, The. Plane Wreck at Los Gatos (Deportee). Woody Guthrie. InPK; PrIm; WTO
Croquet. David Huddle. Str
Cross. Langston Hughes. AmNP; BANP; IDB; LiTM; PoBA; PoLF; SoSe; TAP
Cross, The. Charles N. Pace. BLRP
Cross, The. Allen Tate. AP; AWP; MoAmPo; MoVE; OxBA
Cross and the Tomb, The. Annie Johnson Flint. STF
Cross and the Tree, The. William L. Stidger. PGD

Cross at the morning. Once and Upon. Madeline Gleason. NeAP
Cross-eyed Lover, The. Donald Finkel. Prf
Cross is such a simple thing, The. The Cross. Charles N. Pace. BLRP
Cross leaves marks the tree we fancy, A. An Owl Is an Only Bird of Poetry. Robert Duncan. NeAP; PoM
Cross-legged in my pinafore. That Mulberry Wine. Janet Sylvester. MAYP
Cross-legged on his bed. Son. James A. Emanuel. PoNe
Cross of boy with man within is an, The. On a Prize Crucifix by a Student Sculptor. Robert Logan. CAPP
Cross of Gold, The. David Gray. AA
Cross of Snow, The. Longfellow. AP; HeIP; NOBA; OxBA; TAP
Cross Patch/ Draw the latch. Mother Goose. ChTr; EvOK; GBP; OxNR
Cross Spider, The. May Swenson. SUW
Cross, the Cross, The. Tortoise-Shell. D. H. Lawrence. CMoP; FM; OAEL-2
Cross, the Cross is tainted, The! O most Just. The Temptation of Saint Anthony. Arthur Symons. BrPo
Cross, the icon, The. The Paradox. Francesca Yetunde Pereira. PBA
Cross Ties. X. J. Kennedy. CoPo; HoPM
Cross Was His Own, The. *Unknown.* *See* "Borrowed."
Cross-bars and posts, the echo of distant bells. Football Field: Evening. J. A. R. McKellar. LiSp
Crossbow wanted a child. The Children's Crusade. Philip Levine. NaP
Crosse, The. George Herbert. AnAnS-1
Crosse of Jesu Christ be ever oure spede. An A.B.C. of Devotion. *Unknown.* MeEL
Crossed Apple, The. Louise Bogan. BiP; HeIP
Crossed Swords, The. Nathaniel Langdon Frothingham. AA
Crossedroads. Martin Staples Shockley. FF
Crosses. Robert Herrick. CaPo
Crossing. Anthony Barnett. VWA
Crossing, The. Paul Blackburn. NYBP
Crossing. Philip Booth. AmFN; GOA
Crossing. Archibald MacLeish. POL
Crossing. J. Robert Oppenheimer. SUW
Crossing a Creek. Herbert Clark Johnson. PoNe
Crossing Alone the Nighted Ferry. A. E. Housman. ChMP; FaBoRV; GTBS-P; NOBE; NoP
Crossing at Fredericksburg, The. George Henry Boker. PAH
Crossing Boston Common. Louise Dyer Harris. WhC
Crossing Brooklyn Ferry. Walt Whitman. AmPP; AP; CABA; LiTA; NoAM; NOBA; NoP; NYP; TAP
Sels.
"Ah, what can be more stately." AA
"Crowds of men and women attired in the usual costumes." CTBA
Crossing Kansas by Train. Donald Justice. NYBP
Crossing Portsmouth Bridge. Alan Chong Lau. BrSi
Crossing Raquette Lake at Night. Greg Kuzma. WOLT
Crossing the Atlantic. Anne Sexton. MOS; NoAM
Crossing the Bar. Tennyson. BiP; BLRP; CABA; DL; EBVV; EtS; FaBoEn; FaBoRV; FaBV; FaFP; FaPoR; FF; FiP; FPL; HBV-2; HBVY; HeIP; InPK; LiTB; MOS; NOBE; NoP; OAEL-2; OAEP; OBEV; OBNC; OBVV; OHFP; PAI; PoLF; PoRA; SoSe; TEP; TrCP; TreF; TrGrPo; TRV; ViBoPo; VLP; WBLP; WGRP; WHA
Crossing the Border into Canada. Joy Harjo. STE
Crossing the Colorado River into Yuma. Simon J. Ortiz. TAT
Crossing the County Line. Elizabeth Randall-Mills. GoYe
Crossing the Park. Howard Moss. NYBP
Crossing the Plains. Joaquin Miller. AA; BPAW; GN
Crossing the shallow holdings high above sea. The Hungry Grass. Donagh MacDonagh. BIrV; NeIP; OxBI
Crossing the street. The Broken Home. James Merrill. HAP; NoAM; NOBA; NYBP; PPP; WeW
Crossing the Tropics. Herman Melville. AA
Crossing the Western Ocean to the edge of the world. After the Spanish Chroniclers. William Bronk. GP
Crossing there under the trees with leaden pace. False Enchantment. Jean Starr Untermeyer. MoAmPo
Crossing West Texas (1966). Kell Robertson. TAT
Crossing with the Light. Dwight Okita. BrSi
Crotalus. Bret Harte. AA
Crotalus Rex. Brewster Ghiselin. MoVE
Crotchet Castle, *sels.* Thomas Love Peacock.
Chorus: "If I drink water while this doth last." ViBoPo
"He took castle and towns; he cut short limbs and lives." DBV
In the Days of Old. HBV-1
Priest and the Mulberry-Tree, The. GN; OnMSP
Crouched beneath a snowbound sky. The Grey Ones. Louis MacNeice. CMoP
Crouched by the casino like a white rabbit. Sugar Daddy. Elizabeth Smither. OCNZ
Crouched in the yard. Pastoral. Ellen Bryant Voigt. MAYP
Crouched [*or* Crouch'd] on the pavement close by Belgrave Square. West London. Matthew Arnold. FF; OAEP
Crouched up beneath a crowd of Grampian hills. Highland Shooting Lodge. Maurice Lindsay. PoSH
Crow, The. Rita Boumí-Pappás, *tr. fr. Modern Greek by* Kimon Friar. PBWP
Crow, The. William Canton. HBV-1
Crow, The. Robert Creeley. TW
Crow, The. P. K. Page. WHW
Crow and Pie. *Unknown.* ESPB
Crow and the Fox, The. La Fontaine, *tr. fr. French by* Edward Marsh. AWP
Crow and the Nighthawk, The. Watson Kirkconnell. CaP
Crow Blacker than Ever. Ted Hughes. TEP
Crow-Children Walk My Circles in the Snow, The. Ray A. Young Bear. CDW
Crow, crow, get out of my sight. *Unknown.* PBBP
Crow doth sing as sweetly as the lark, The. Birdsong. Shakespeare. *Fr.* The Merchant of Venice. PB
Crow flew so fast, The. Haiku. Richard Wright. FAZ
Crow, in pulpit lone and tall. In the Pauper's Turnip-Field. Herman Melville. PoEL-5
Crow in the cage in the dining-room, The. The Crow. Robert Creeley. TW
Crow Jane. Amiri Baraka. PoM
Crow lies over the cornfield, The. Ballad in Blonde Hair Foretold. Robert Bagg. NePoAm-2
Crow-Marble Whores of Paris, The. James Schevill. NMP
Crow on the fence. *Unknown.* PBBP
Crow Resting. Edward Pygge. BXAP; FaBoPa
Crow Sat on the Willow, The. John Clare. VLP
Crow sat perched upon an oak, A. The Crow and the Fox. La Fontaine, *tr. by* Edward Marsh. AWP
Crow, Straight Flier, but Dark. Laya Firestone. VWA
Crow Voices. Gail Tremblay. AMV-81
Crow will tumble up and down, The. Crows in Spring. John Clare. EnRP
Crowd, The. John Masefield. OxBTC
Crowd at the ball game, The. At the Ball Game. William Carlos Williams. CMoP; LiSp; NoAM; NOBA; OxBA
Crowd back the hills and give me room. Soul Lifted. Albert Durrant Watson. CaP
Crowd fear: blown paper and uprooted ferns. The Spring Festival on the River. John Peck. AmPA
Crowded balcony and she, A. Big City Glissando. Nicholas Christopher. NYP
Crowded gravestones. Chelsea Churchyard. Ralph J. Mills, Jr. FAZ
Crowded Out. Florence White Willett. STF
Crowded steps, a sea of white faces. Sacrifice. Thomas Kinsella. IPY
Crowded Ways of Life. Walter S. Gresham. BLPA
Crowdieknowe. "Hugh MacDiarmid." InPS; NoAM; NoP; OxBS
Crowdpleasers/ coming down the aisles. Goosepimples. Coleman Barks. PV
Crowds. Baudelaire, *tr. fr. French by* Arthur Symons. SyP
Crowds. Virginia Schonborg. RHPC
Crowds of men and women attired in the usual costumes. Walt Whitman. *Fr.* Crossing Brooklyn Ferry. CTBA
Crowds pushing. Crowds Virginia Schonborg. RHPC
Crowing of the Red Cock, The. Emma Lazarus. AA; HBV
Crown me with roses whilest I live. Abraham Cowley. , *after the Greek of* Anacreon. *Fr.* The Epicure ("Underneath this myrtle shade"). OBVE
Crown of Days. *Unknown, tr. fr. Hebrew by* Herbert Loewe. TrJP
Crown of Happiness. Anne Hébert, *tr. fr. French by* Willis Barnstone. BoWoP
Crown of Windflowers, A. Christina Rossetti. OxBChV
Crown Prince of Dullness, The. Dryden. *Fr.* MacFlecknoe. NOBE
Crowned. Amy Lowell. HBV-1
Crowned, girdled, garbed, and shod with light and fire. Christopher Marlowe. Swinburne. TrGrPo
Crowned Heart, The. Sir Robert Ayton. *See* Upon a Diamond Cut in Form of a Heart . . .
Crowned Poet, A. Anne Reeve Aldrich. AA
Crowned with flowers, I saw fair Amarillis. *Unknown.* EnLoPo
Crowning a bluff where gleams the lake below. Pontoosuce. Herman Melville. NOBA
Crowning Gift, The. Gladys Cromwell. HBMV
Crowning of Dreaming John, The. John Drinkwater. HBMV
Crowns, The. John Freeman. CH
Crows, The. Louise Bogan. SBG
Crows. Philip Booth. DFF
Crows. Tom Clark. DFF
Crows, The. John Engels. AMV-81

Crows, The. Zulfikar Ghose. BoAnP
Crows. David McCord. MoAmPo; PDV; RFM; TiPo
Crows. Charles Simic. GeTw
Crows, The. Maria Valli. CBAP
Crows. William Witherup. PCP; POL
Crows are come again to pick my eyes, The. Soliloquy on Death. F. K. Fiawoo. PBA
Crow's Ditty. *Unknown.* GBP
Crow's First Lesson. Ted Hughes. InPS; NoAM
Crow's harsh dissyllables. A Valediction. Melvin Walker La Follette. CoPo
Crows in Spring. John Clare. EnRP
Crow's Last Stand. Ted Hughes. InPS
Crows mark, The. African Day. Gloria de Sant'Ana, *tr. by* Allan Francovich *and* Kathleen Weaver. PBWP
Crow's Nest. Richard F. Armknecht. GoYe
Crow's Way. Duane Niatum. CDW
Crows will stick their beaks into anything. The Crows. Zulfikar Ghose. BoAnP
Crucial Stew. Colette Inez. FAZ
Crucified Lord, you swim upon your cross. Lachrimae Verae. Geoffrey Hill. *Fr.* Lachrimae. NoP
Crucified to the World. *Unknown.* MeEL
Crucifix, The. Sir Herbert Read. BrPo
Crucifix, A. Paul Verlaine, *tr. fr. French by* John Gray. *Fr.* Amour. SyP
Crucifixion. Eva Gore Booth. WGRP
Crucifixion. Waring Cuney. BANP
Crucifixion. Hugh O. Isbell. PGD
Crucifixion. "Marie Madelaine," *tr. fr. German by* Ferdinand E. Kappey. PeHV
Crucifixion, The. Alice Meynell. OxBoCh
Crucifixion. Mrs. Roy L. Peifer. STF
Crucifixion, The ("At the cry of the first bird"). *Unknown, tr. fr. Middle Irish.* OnYI, *tr. by* Howard Mumford Jones; OxBI, *tr. by* Kuno Meyer
Crucifixion, The ("I sike [al] when I singe"). *Unknown. See* I Sigh When I Sing.
Crucifixion ("They [*or* Dey] crucified my Lord"). *Unknown.* BoAn-1, *with music;* BPo; TAP; TrGrPo
(They Crucified My Lord.) STF
Crucifixion to the World by the Cross of Christ. Isaac Watts. *See* When I Survey the Wondrous Cross.
Cruciform. Winifred Welles. LO; NYBP
Crucifying. John Donne. AnAnS-1; OBS
Crude Foyer. Wallace Stevens. LiTM; NePA
Cruel, and fair! when this soft down. To Ligurinus. Horace, *tr. by* Sir Edward Sherburne. Odes, IV, 10. CavP
Cruel arrows gone, The. Fleche. Larry Eigner. VGW
Cruel Boys. Gary Soto. NPGG
Cruel Brother, The. *Unknown.* AmFP; ESPB (A *and* B *vers.*); OxBB, *with music;* ViBoFo
Cruel, but composed and bland. Matthew Arnold. *Fr.* Matthias. POL
Cruel, Clever Cat. Geoffrey Taylor. ChTr; FaBoEE
Cruel Falcon, The. Robinson Jeffers. BiP
Cruel Frederick. Heinrich Hoffmann, *tr. fr. German.* SpRo
Cruel girls we loved, The. Mothers and Daughters. David Campbell. POL
Cruel Maid, The. Robert Herrick. CaPo
(Cruell Maid, The.) CavP
Cruel Mother, The. *Unknown.* AmFP; ESPB (A, B, C, *and* P *vers.*); FaBoBa; FSW; InPK; OBET; OxBB; *with music;* ViBoFo
Cruel Sister, The. *Unknown. See* Two Sisters, The.
Cruel War Is Raging, The. *Unknown.* FSW
Cruel You Be. George Puttenham. ElL
Cruell Maid, The. Robert Herrick. *See* Cruel Maid, The.
Cruell Mistris, A. Thomas Carew. AnAnS-2
Cruelty. T. R. Hummer. MAYP
Cruelty has a human heart. A Divine Image. Blake. *Fr.* Songs of Experience. ChTr; NoP; OBNC; TEP
Cruise of the *Fair American,* The. *Unknown.* PAH
Cruise of the *Monitor,* The. George Henry Boker. PAH
Cruise of the *Mystery*, The. Celia Thaxter. OBCA
Cruise of the *P. C.,* The. *Unknown.* NA
Cruisers, destroyers, carriers align. Victory Parade. George Edward Hoffman. PGD
Cruiskeen Lawn, The. *Unknown.* HBV-2; OnYI
Crumbled rock of London is dripping under, The. Sonnet. Roy Fuller. PoA
Crumbling a dark leaf between darker fingers. Midewiwan. Phyllis Wolf. STE
Crumbling centuries are thrust, The. The Jewels. Austin Clarke. MoAB
Crumbling into this world. Venice. James Wright. AMV-81
Crumbling is not an instant's act. Emily Dickinson. AmPP; AP; NOBA; PPP
Crumbs. Walter de la Mare. SoPo
Crumbs for the robin; well he knew. The Robin. William Bell Scott. FM
Crumbs or the Loaf. Robinson Jeffers. CMoP
Crunking crane heard high amongst the clouds, The. George Farewell. *Fr.* The Country Man. NOEC
Crusade. Hilaire Belloc. GoBC
Crusader, The. Dorothy Parker. ShM
Crusaders knew the Holy Places, The. Jenny Mastoraki, *tr. fr. Modern Greek by* Nikes Germanakos. BoWoP; PBWP
Cruse, The. Louise Townsend Nicholl. NYBP
Crush the manroot, swallow what you desire. Learning the Spells; a Diptych. Anita Endrezze Probst. CDW
Crushed by that just contempt his follies bring. On Poet Ninny. Earl of Rochester. APAS
Crushed by the waves upon the crag was I. Sea Dirge. Archias of Byzantium, *tr. by* Andrew Lang. AWP
"Crusher" never scared me, The. Tho that giant. Elegy. Alan Loney. OCNZ
Crushing of a thousand petals, Lord, The. The Poet Prays. Grace Noll Crowell. TrPWD
Crusoe's Island. Derek Walcott. NoAM
Crust of Bread, The. *Unknown.* HBV-1; HBVY
Crust of bread and a corner to sleep in, A. Life. Paul Laurence Dunbar. AmNP; CDC
Crustaceans. Roy Fuller. NeBP; NoAM
Crusty Critics. George Crabbe. *Fr.* The Library. OBEC
Crutches. Robert Herrick. CaPo
Cry-Bird Journey, The. Stan Rice. NPGG
Cry, Crow. Sonnet. Hayden Carruth. NNaP
Cry Faugh! Robert Graves. CoBMV; MoBrPo
Cry for a Disused Synagogue in Booysens. Mannie Hirsch. VWA
Cry for Light, A. *Unknown.* BLRP
Cry from the Battlefield. Robert Menth. ISi
Cry from the Canadian Hills, A. Lillian Leveridge. BLPA
Cry from the Ghetto, A. Morris Rosenfeld, *tr. fr. Yiddish by* Charles Weber Linn. TrJP
Cry from the green-grained sticks of the fire, A. Surview [Cogitavi Vias Meas]. Thomas Hardy. ChMP; LO
Cry from the Shore, A. Ellen Mackay Hutchinson Cortissoz. AA
Cry in Distress, A ("My God, my God, why hast Thou forsaken me?"). Bible, *O.T.* Psalms, XXII: 1-15. TrGrPo
Cry in my mouth wakes me, The (thirty years later). It Comes during Sleep. Philip Dow. NPGG
Cry, The, is: "Back to God!" Without respite. The Homeward Journey. L. Aaronson. TrJP
Cry Kismet! and take heart. Erôs is gone. James Branch Cabell. Retractions, XII. HBMV
Cry left your mouth, A. Mouth. Clarisse Nicoïdski, *tr. by* Stephen Levy. VWA
Cry of a Dreamer, The. John Boyle O'Reilly. BLPA; TreFS
(Cry of the Dreamer, The.) OnYI
Cry of an Aged One, The. Ray Fraser. NeAC
Cry of Generations, The. Mordechai Husid, *tr. fr. Yiddish by* Seymour Mayne *and* Rivka Augenfeld. VWA
Cry of the Age, The. Hamlin Garland. WGRP
Cry of the Child, The. William Zaranka. BXAP
Cry of the Children, The. Elizabeth Barrett Browning. EBVV; HBV-1; OAEP; ViBoPo; VLP
"They look up with their pale and sunken faces," *sel.* NBM
Cry of the Daughter of My People, The. Bible, *O.T.* Jeremiah, VIII: 18-23. TrJP
Cry of the Dreamer, The. John Boyle O'Reilly. *See* Cry of a Dreamer, The.
Cry of the Human, The, *sel.* Elizabeth Barrett Browning.
Convinced by Sorrow. BLRP; WBLP
Cry of the Lovelorn, The. William Edmonstoune Aytoun *and* Sir Theodore Martin. *See* Lay of the Lovelorn, The.
Cry of the Peoples, The. Alter Brody. TrJP
Cry of the raven rang over the moor, The. Bobby Campbell. *Unknown.* FSW
Cry of those being eaten by America, The. Those Being Eaten by America. Robert Bly. CoAP; NaP
Cry out for Sakhr when a dove with necklaces. Elegy for Her Brother Sakhr. Al-Khansa, *tr. fr. Arabic by* Willis Barnstone. BoWoP
Cry, A!—someone is knocked. At 79th and Park. Barbara Howes. NYP
Cry to Arms, A. Henry Timrod. PAH
Cry to Mary, A. St. Godric. MeEL
Cry went through me like a stab of a knife, A. W. H. Auden. *Fr.* A Happy New Year. OBSV
Cryer, The. Michael Drayton. *See* Crier, The.
Cryin' ain't goin' down this big road by myself. Big Road Blues. *Unknown.* BluL
Cryin' canned heat. Canned Heat Blues. *Unknown.* BluL

Cryin' I ain't goin' down the dark road by myself. Dark Road Blues. *Unknown.* BluL
Cryin', who's that yonder. Maggie Campbell Blues. *Unknown.* BluL
Crying. Galway Kinnell. NTCP
Crying Asia! that famous place. The Marriage of Hector and Andromache. Sappho, *tr. by* Guy Davenport. OBVE
Crying in Early Infancy, *sels.* John Tranter.
"It's bad luck with a coughing baby." CBAP
"Spy bears his bald intent like a maniac, The." CBAP
Crying only a little bit. Crying. Galway Kinnell. NTCP
Crystal, The. George Barker. LiTM; OBMV
Crystal, The. Titus Munson Coan. AA
Crystal. Faye Kicknosway. IHMS
Crystal, The, *sels.* Sidney Lanier.
"But Thee, but Thee, O sovereign Seer of time." TrPWD
"Oh, what amiss may I forgive in Thee." TRV
Crystal and silver. The Islands of the Ever Living. *Unknown, tr. by* Padraic Colum. AnIV
Crystal Cabinet, The. Blake. CH; FaBoCh; NCEP; OAEL-2; OBNC; OBRV; PAI; PoEL-4
Crystal Gazer, The. Sara Teasdale. MoAmPo
Crystal Lithium, The. James Schuyler. PoM
Crystal Night. Denise Levertov. *Fr.* During the Eichmann Trial. NMP
Crystal Palace, The. Thackeray. InMe
Crystal parting the meads. The River in the Meadows. Léonie Adams. MoAB; MoAmPo;
Crystal Skull, The. Kathleen Raine. NeBP
Crystallization of color spreads, A. Aurora Borealis. Edouard Roditi. EAS
Crystals like Blood. "Hugh MacDiarmid." HAP; InPS; NoP
Cu Chuimne in youth. *Unknown, tr. fr. Irish by* John V. Kelleher. BIrV
Cuatro Generales, Los (The Four Insurgent Generals). *Unknown, tr. fr. Spanish.* FSW
Cuba. Lawrence Kearney. AMV-81
Cuba. Harvey Rice. PAH
Cuba. Edmund Clarence Stedman. PAH
Cuba, disheveled, naked to the waist. On a Monument to Martí. Walter Adolphe Roberts. TTY
Cuba Libre. Joaquin Miller. PAH
Cuba, 1962. Ai. AmPA
Cuba to Columbia. Will Carleton. PAH
Cuban Refugees on Key Biscayne. Barbara Winder. TAT
Cubes. Mary Fullerton. PoAu-1
Cubic Triolet, A. *Unknown.* PV
Cubical Domes, The. David Gascoyne. EAS
Cubist Blues in Poltergeist Major. Allan F. Kipp. AMV-81
Cubist Portrait. Marjorie Allen Seiffert. PoA
Cubistic Lovers, The. Charles Edward Eaton. AMV-81
Cubs of bears a living lump appear, The. The Phoenix Self-born. Ovid, *tr. by* Dryden. *Fr.* Metamorphoses, XV. ChTr
Cucaracha, La (The Cockroach), *with music.* *Unknown, tr. fr. Spanish.* AS; TrAS
Cuccu Song. *Unknown.* *See* Cuckoo Song.
Cuchillo. Joy Harjo. TWSS
Cuchulain Comforted. W. B. Yeats. CMoP; LiTM; OAEL-2
Cuchulain's Fight with the Sea. W. B. Yeats. *See* Death of Cuchulain, The.
Cuchullain's Lament over Fardiad. *Unknown, tr. fr. Middle Irish by* George Sigerson. AnIV
(Cuchulain's Lament for Ferdiad.) AnIL
Cuckoo! Hilaire Belloc. MoVE
Cuckoo, The. Patrick Reginald Chalmers. BoAnP; CenHV
Cuckoo, The. Gerard Manley Hopkins. MoAB; MoBrPo
(Fragment: "Repeat that, repeat.") ELU; FM
("Repeat that, repeat.") PBBP
Cuckoo. R. P. Lister. BoAnP
Cuckoo, The. Frederick Locker-Lampson. HBV-1
Cuckoo, The. Edward Thomas. BrPo
Cuckoo, The ("A-walking and a-talking"). *Unknown.* OBET (B *vers.*)
Cuckoo, The ("The cuckoo is a bonny [*or* fine *or* funny *or* merry *or* pretty] bird"), *sl. diff. versions.* *Unknown.* AmFP; ChTr; FSW; GBP; OBET (2 *vers.*); PoPle
("Cuckoo is a merry bird, The.") OxNR; PBBP
Cuckoo ("In former days my father and mother"). *Unknown, tr. fr. Anglo-Saxon by* Charles W. Kennedy. *Fr.* Riddles (Exeter Book). AnOE
Cuckoo. Andrew Young. ChTr
Cuckoo and the Nightingale, The, *sel.* Sir Thomas Clanvowe.
"But as I lay this other night waking." PBBP
Cuckoo, cherry tree. *Unknown.* PBBP
Cuckoo clock on the nursery wall, The. Ticking Clocks. Rachel Field. TiPo
Cuckoo comes in April, The. *Unknown.* OxNR
"Cuckoo! The," cried my child, the while I slept. The Oocuck. Justin Richardson. BoAnP; FiBHP
Cuckoo, cuckoo!/ In April skies were blue. Cuckoo Song. Katharine Tynan. OnYI
Cuckoo, cuckoo!/ Is it thy double note I hear. Cuckoo. Andrew Young. ChTr
Cuckoo, cuckoo/ What do you do? *Unknown.* OxNR; PBBP
Cuckoo, cuckoo, cherry tree. *Unknown.* OxNR
Cuckoo is a bonny [*or* fine *or* funny *or* merry *or* pretty] bird, The. The Cuckoo. *Unknown.* AmFP; ChTr; FSW; OBET (2 *vers.*); OxNR; PBBP; PoPle
Cuckoo, noisy among the Shenbaka flowers. Andal, *tr. fr. Tamil by* Willis Barnstone. BoWoP
Cuckoo, scabbèd gowk. *Unknown.* PBBP
Cuckoo she's a pretty bird, The. *See* Cuckoo is a bonny bird, The.
Cuckoo Sings, The. Shakespeare. *See* When Daisies Pied and Violets Blue.
Cuckoo Song. Katharine Tynan. OnYI
Cuckoo [*or* Cuccu] Song. *Unknown.* ChTr; NOBE; NoP; OBEV; SpRo; TrGrPo
(Now the Summer's Come, *mod. English version.*) HAP
(Sing Cuccu.) ViBoPo
(Sumer Is Icumen In.) AWP; BiP; EBEV; FF; GBP; HAP; HeIP; InPS; InvP; MeEL; NIP; OAEL-1; OxBM; SeCePo; SeCeV; TreFT
(Summer Is a-Coming In.) FSW
("Summer is icummen in.") TEP
("Summer is y-comen in.") PBBP
Cuckoo-throb, the heartbeat of the Spring, The. Ardour and Memory. Dante Gabriel Rossetti. The House of Life, LXIV. OAEL-2
Cuckoo Waltz, *with music.* *Unknown.* AS
Cuckoo, when the lambkins bleat, The. The Cuckoo. Patrick Reginald Chalmers. BoAnP; CenHV
Cuckoos. Andrew Young. ChTr
Cuckoo's a bonny bird, The. *See* Cuckoo is a bonny bird, The.
Cuckoo's double note, The. Wiltshire Downs. Andrew Young. ChMP; GTBS-P; OxBTC
Cuddie [*or* Cuddy], for shame hold up thy heavy[e] head. October [*or* The Contempt of Poetry]. Spenser. *Fr.* The Shepheardes Calender. OAEL-1; OBSC; PP
Cuddle Doon. Alexander Anderson. GN; HBV-1
Cudgelled but Contented Cuckold, The. La Fontaine. UnTE
Cudworth's Undergraduate Ode to a Bare Behind. John Ower. AMV-81
Cuento. Carlos Cumpian. FIA
Cui Bono? Thomas Carlyle. HBV-2; OBRV; WGRP
Cuillin, The, *sel.* Sorley MacLean.
Sgurr Nan Gillean. PoSH
Cuisine Bourgeoise. Wallace Stevens. LiTA
Culbin Sands. Andrew Young. GTBS-P; OxBS; OxBTC
Cullen ("Cullen renounced his cradle at fifteen"). P. K. Page. CaP
Culloden and After. Iain Crichton Smith. OxBS
Culprit Fay, The, *sels.* Joseph Rodman Drake.
Assembling of the Fays, The. GN
Elfin Song. AA
Fairy Dawn. GN
Fairy in Armor, A. FaPON
Fay's Crime, The. GN
Fay's Sentence, The. AA; GN
First Quest, The. AA
(Fay's Departure, The, *shorter sel.*) GN
"If the spray-bead gem be won." GN
Second Quest, The. AA
Throne of the Lily-King, The. GN
Cult of the Celtic, The. Anthony C. Deane. BXAP; NOBL
Cultivated Signals types. Footnote to Enright's "Apocalypse." Martin Bell. FaBoMo
Cultivation of Christmas Trees, The. T. S. Eliot. OFD
Cultural Exchange. Langston Hughes. BPo; PoBA; PoNe
Cultural Notes. Kenneth Fearing. CMoP
Cultural Presupposition, The. W. H. Auden. CABA; PAI
Culture in the Slums. W. E. Henley. CenHV; HBV-1; InMe
Cultured gentleman, mature, congenial, refined. Personal. Samuel Yellen. NYBP
Cultured Girl Again, The. Ben King. FiBHP; OBAL
Cum, listen w'ile yore Unkel sings. 'Ittle Touzle Head. Ray Garfield Dandridge. BANP
Cumberbunce, The. Paul West. NA
Cumberland, The. Longfellow. AA; EtS; PAH
Cumberland, The. Herman Melville. PAH
Cumberland and the *Merrimac,* The, 2 *versions.* *Unknown.* AmFP
Cumberland Gap ("Cumberland Gap is a noted place"). *Unknown.* AmFN
Cumberland Gap ("Lay down boys, take a little nap"). *Unknown.* FSW
Cumberland Station. Dave Smith. MAYP
Cumberland's Crew, The. *Unknown.* AmFP; ShS, *with music*

Cummerbund, The. Edward Lear. CenHV
Cumnor Hall. William Julius Mickle. BeLS; OBEC; OxBB
"Dews of summer night did fall, The," *sel.* ViBoPo
Cunjah Man, De. James Edwin Campbell. BANP
Cun-ne-wa-bum—"one who looks on stars." Portrait of a Cree. "Katherine Hale." CaP
Cunning as a woman beautiful as a snake shy as an idol. Another Poem on Absalom. Nathan Yonathan, *tr. by* Richard Flantz. VWA
Cunning Clerk, The, *with music. Unknown.* OxBB
Cunning Cobbler Done Over, The. *Unknown.* CoMu
Cunning, wise, cautious, folly is, by which. Upon the Most Useful Knowledge, Craft or Cunning, Which Is More Wisdom, as 'Tis Less Wit. William Wycherly. SeCV-2
Cup, The. John Oldham, *after the Greek of* Anacreon. AWP
Cup, The. John Townsend Trowbridge. HBV-1
Cup capsizes along the formica, A. In the Snack-Bar. Edwin Morgan. FF
"Cup for hope, A!" she said. Three Seasons. Christina Rossetti. HBV-1
Cup I sing is a cup of gold, The. The Cup. John Townsend Trowbridge. HBV-1
Cup is bound to spill, a saucer to break, A. Yankee Poet. Robley Wilson, Jr. AMV-81
Cup of Happiness, The. Gilbert Thomas. TrPWD
Cup of O'Hara, The. Turlough Carolan, *tr. fr. Modern Irish by* Sir Samuel Ferguson. OnYI
(When Kian O'Hara's Cup Was Passed to Turlough O'Carolan.) AnIV
Cupbearer, O victorious Falcon, come! Qorratu'l-Ayn, *tr. by* Deirdre Lashgari. *Fr.* He the Beloved. WPOW
Cupbearer Speaks, The. Goethe, *tr. fr. German by* John Weiss. *Fr.* West-Easterly Divan, Bk. 9. PeHV
Cupboard, The. Walter de la Mare. FaPON; NTCP; SoPo; TiPo
Cupid. Ben Jonson. *See* Beauties, Have Ye Seen This Toy.
Cupid. Sir Philip Sidney. *Fr.* Arcadia. SiPS
Cupid. *Unknown.* ElL
Cupid a Plowman. Moschus. *See* Cupid Turned Plowman.
Cupid and Campaspe. John Lyly. *See* Cards and Kisses.
Cupid and Death, *sels.* James Shirley.
Victorious Men of Earth. OBS; TrGrPo
(Death, the Conqueror.) GoBC
(Death's Emissaries.) LoBV
(Death's Subtle Ways.) HBV-2
(Last Conqueror, The.) GTBS; GTBS-P
(Song.) FaBoEn
Love's Victories. GoBC
Cupid and My Campaspe. John Lyly. *See* Cards and Kisses.
Cupid and Venus. Mark Alexander Boyd. *See* Fra Bank to Bank, Fra Wood to Wood I Rin.
Cupid as he lay among. The Wounded Cupid. Robert Herrick. AWP; OBVE; OFD
Cupid, because thou shin'st in Stella's eyes. Astrophel and Stella, XII. Sir Philip Sidney. SiPS
Cupid, beware, there'll come a day. Warning to Cupid. *Unknown, tr. by* Louis Untermeyer. UnTE
Cupid did cry, his mother chid him so. The Compliment. William Habington. ACP
Cupid Drowned. Leigh Hunt. HBV-1
Cupid, dumb idol, peevish saint of love. Idea, XXVI. Michael Drayton. EnRePo
Cupid-faced hooligan standing on tiptoe, The. Amsterdam Street Scene, 1972. Raphael Rudnik. AMV-81
Cupid Far Gone. Richard Lovelace. CaPo
Cupid in a Bed of Roses. *Unknown.* ElL
Cupid Mistaken. Matthew Prior. *See* Cupid's Mistaken.
Cupid Stung ("Cupid once upon a bed"). Thomas Moore. HBV-1
Cupid the Ploughboy. *Unknown.* OBET
Cupid tho' all his darts were lost. Swift. *Fr.* Cadenus and Vanessa. OxBI
Cupid, thou naughty [*or* naughtie] boy, when thou wert loathed. Caelica, XII. Fulke Greville. EnRePo; NCEP
Cupid Turned Plowman. Moschus, *tr. fr. Greek by* Matthew Prior. AWP
(Cupid a Plowman.) OBVE
Cupid Ungodded. James Shirley. GoBC
Cupidon. William Jay Smith. NePoEA
Cupids Call. James Shirley. ErPo
Cupid's Darts. A. P. Herbert. CenHV
Cupid's Indictment. John Lyly. *Fr.* Galathea. ElL
(Song of Diana's Nymphs, A.) OBSC
Cupid's Mistaken. Matthew Prior. ViBoPo
(Cupid Mistaken.) InMe
Cupid's Pastime. Francis Davison. UnTE
Cupid's Revenge, *sel.* Beaumont *and* Fletcher.
Lovers Rejoice [*or* Rejoyce]! ElL; FaBoEn
Cupping her chin and lying there, the Bren. Defensive Position. John Manifold. MoBrPo
Cups of Illusion. Henry Bellamann. HBMV
Cur foretells the knell of parting day, The. Ambrose Bierce. *Fr.* The Devil's Dictionary. OBAL
Curate Thinks You Have No Soul, The. St. John Lucas. BLPA
Curate's Kindness, The. Thomas Hardy. CoBMV
Curb for stubborn steed. Earliest Christian Hymn. Clement of Alexandria, *tr. by* Edward H. Plumptre. WGRP
Curbstones are to balance on. What They Are For. Dorothy Aldis. SoPo
Cure All, The. Don L. Lee. CAD
Cure for Fault-finding, A. Strickland W. Gillilan. *See* Watch Yourself Go By.
Cure for Poetry, A. *Unknown. See* Seven Wealthy Towns.
Cure for the Spleen, A. Matthew Green. *Fr.* The Spleen. OBEC
Curé in his windy gown, The. Saint Francis. John Peale Bishop. EaLo
Cure me with quietness. For Sleep, or Death. Ruth Pitter. TrPWD
Curé's Progress, The. Austin Dobson. HBV-1
Curfew. Paul Eluard, *tr. fr. French by* Quentin Stevenson. BoLoP
Curfew. Longfellow. AA; OxBA
Curfew, A: December 13, 1981. Amy Clampitt. SUW
Curfew Must Not Ring Tonight. Rose Hartwick Thorpe. BeLS; BLPA; BLPL; FaBoBe; FaPON; HBV-2; PaPo; TreF; WBLP
Curfew tolls the knell of parting day, The. Elegy Written in a Country Churchyard. Thomas Gray. AWP; BiP, CABA; DL; EBEV; EnRP; FaBoBe; FaBoEn; FaBoPP; FaBoRV; FaFP; FaPoR; FPL; GN; GoTL; GTBS; GTBS-P; HAP; HBV-2; HBVY; HeIP; InPK; InPS; LaA; LAuP; LiTB; LoBV; MasP; NOBE; NOEC; NoP; OAEL-1; OAEP; OBEC; OBEV; OHFP; PAI; POEL-3; PoLF; PPoe; PPP; PrIm; SCV; SeCeV; TEP; TreF; TrGrPo; UnPo; ViBoPo; WBLP; WeW; WHA
Curfew tolls the knell of parting day, The. If Gray Had Had to Write His Elegy in the Cemetery of Spoon River Instead of in That of Stoke Poges, *parody.* J. C. Squire. BXAP; FaBoPa; WhC
Curfew tolls the knell of parting day, The. Diversions of the Re-Echo Club. Carolyn Wells. OBAL
Curio's rich sideboard seldom sees the light. On a Stingy Beau. John Winstanley. FaBoEE
Curiosity. Harry Behn. SoPo
Curiosity. Alastair Reid. SoSe
Curiosity, *sels.* Charles Sprague.
Fiction. AA
News, The. AA
Curiosity-Shop, The. Peter Redgrove. OxBC
Curiosity's not in me head. On Reading: Four Limericks. Myra Cohn Livingston. TDH
Curious Charlie. Isabel Frances Bellows. TDH
Curious child, who dwelt upon a tract, A. Wordsworth. *Fr.* The Excursion. WGRP
Curious, curious Tiggady Rue. Tiggady Rue. David McCord. TiPo; WSC
Curious Discourse That Passed between the Twenty-five Letters at Dinner-Time, A. *Unknown.* FaBoUs
Curious fly. Bug in a Jug. *Unknown.* RHPC
Curious is this stonework! The Fates destroyed it. The Ruin. *Unknown, tr. by* Gavin Bone. EBEV
Curious knot God made in paradise, A. Upon Wedlock and Death of Children. Edward Taylor. AmPP; AP; NoP
Curious Something. Winifred Welles. TiPo
Curious twists, The. Energy for a New Thang. Ernie Mkalimoto. NBP
Curious wits, seeing dull pensiveness, The. Astrophel and Stella, XXIII. Sir Philip Sidney. SiPS
Curled in his black-ringed tail. The Dance of Gray Raccoon. Arthur Guiterman. BPAW
Curled like a hoop in sleep. Cradle Song. Lawrence Durrell. NAs
Curled up and sitting on her feet. L'Eau Dormante. Thomas Bailey Aldrich. HBV-1
Curls powdered with chalk like a black roman bust. Native Working on the Aerodrome. Roy Fuller. NeBP
Curly Joe. *Unknown.* BPAW
Curly Locks! Curly Locks! wilt thou be mine? Mother Goose. HBV-1; HBVY; OxNR; SoPo
Curr dhoo, curr dhoo. Mother Goose. OxNR
Current, The. James Merrill. NYBP
Current freed for a while. Listening to Confucius. Henryk Grynberg, *tr. by* Isaac Komem. VWA
Currente Calamo. Arthur Hugh Clough. *Fr.* Mari Magno. LoBV
Currents. Emma Lazarus. *Fr.* By the Waters of Babylon. WPE
Curricle and hansom, The. The Great Garret, or 100 Wheels. James McMichael. AmPA
Curriculum Vitae. Ingeborg Bachmann, *tr. fr. German by* Jerome Rothenberg. BoWoP
Curse, The. Elizabeth Barrett Browning. *Fr.* A Curse for a Nation. WPOW
Curse, The. John Donne. OAEP; TW
Curse, A. Irving Feldman. TW

Curse, The. Robert Francis. TW
Curse. Robert Greacen. TW
Curse, The. John Hollander. UnPo
Curse, The. J. M. Synge. ChTr; DBV; FaBoCo; FaBoEE; PV; TreFT; TW
Curse, A. *Unknown. See* Bruadar and Smith and Glinn.
Curse, The; a Song. Robert Herrick. CaPo
Curse against the Owner, A. Barton Sutter. TW
Curse for a Nation, A. Elizabeth Barrett Browning. SBG; WPE
Sels.
Curse, The. WPOW
Prologue. WPOW
Curse God and Die, You Said to Me. Archibald MacLeish. *Fr.* J. B. EaLo
Curse him who digs in yellow leaves. Academic Curse; an Epitaph. Wesli Court. TW
Curse of a Fisherman's Wife. Lila Chalpin. AMV-80
Curse of Cromwell, The. W. B. Yeats. BIrV; SeCePo
Curse of Doneraile, The. Patrick O'Kelly. DBV, *abr.*; OnYI
Curse of Faint Praise, The. Irwin Edman. InMe
Curse of Kehama, The, *sels.* Robert Southey.
Kehama's Curse. OBNC
("I charm thy life.") LoBV; OBRV
Love Indestructible. OBNC
("They sin who tell us Love can die.") OBRV
"Stream descends on Meru mountain, A." OBRV
"Two forms inseparable in unity." OBRV
Curse of the Cat Woman. Edward Field. CABA; WeW
Curse on a Closed Gate, A. James H. Cousins, *fr. the Irish.* AnIV
Curse on Mine-Owners, A. *Unknown.* TW
Curse on the Cat, A. John Skelton. *Fr.* Phyllyp Sparowe. EvOK
(O Cat of Carlish Kind.) ChTr
Curse on the star, dear Harry, that betrayed. An Epistle from a Half-Pay Officer in the Country to His Friend in London. Richardson Pack. NOEC
Curse on Uruk, A. Enheduanna, *tr. fr. Sumerian; ad. by* Aliki *and* Willis Barnstone. BoWoP
Curse upon Edward, The. Thomas Gray. OBEV
Curse upon that faithless maid, A. Song. Aphra Behn. *Fr.* Emperor of the Moon. WPE
Cursed Be the Day. Bible, *O.T.* Jeremiah, XX: 14-18. TrJP
Curses. Joseph Duemer. AMV-80
Cursing and Blessing. "Michael Lewis," *after the Chinese. Fr.* Cherry Blossoms. UnTE
Cursive crawl, the squared-off characters, The. Writing. Howard Nemerov. NYBP
Cursor Mundi, *sel. Unknown.*
Pound of Flesh, The. OxBM
Curt Addendum, A. *Unknown.* ShM
("As I am now, so you must be.") WhC
Curtain! Paul Laurence Dunbar. CenHV
Curtain, The (Old Tabor Grand Opera House). Jean Milne Gower. PoOW
Curtain. Lance Henson. VoR
Curtain Poem, The. Edwin Brock. NMP
Curtain rises on Act II, The. Act II. Katherine Davis. PoPl
Curtain Speech. Michael Braude. AMV-81
Curtains are of lace, softening darkness, The. Curtains for a Spinster. Walter H. Kerr. NePoAm-2
Curtains drawn back, the door ajar. Robinson at Home. Weldon Kees. CoAP; NYBP; TwAmPo
Curtains for a Spinster. Walter H. Kerr. NePoAm-2
Curtains in the House of the Metaphysician, The. Wallace Stevens. PoA
Curtains Now Are Drawn, The. Thomas Hardy. CMoP
Curtains of rock. Orpheus in the Underworld. David Gascoyne. FaBoTw
Curtains were half drawn, the floor was swept, The. After Death. Christina Rossetti. GBL; TEP
Curvd lines toe-drawn, round cornered squares, The. Hop, Skip, and Jump. Gary Snyder. LCAP
Curving, leaping line of light, A. Prairie Fires. Hamlin Garland. OBCA
Cushendall. *Unknown.* WTO
Cushie Butterfield. George Ridley. VLP
Cushla Ma Chree. John Philpot Curran. HBV-2
Cushy cow, bonny, let down thy milk. Mother Goose. GBP; OxNR
Custard the Dragon. Ogden Nash. *See* Tale of Custard the Dragon, The.
Custer 1 ("You, Custer, you hated"). Alison Baker. FAZ
Custer 2 ("In this picture/ Custer is wearing"). Alison Baker. FAZ
Custer. Edmund Clarence Stedman. BPAW; PAH
Custer Lives in Humbolt County. Janet Campbell Hale. STE; VoR
Custer Must Have Learned to Dance. Elizabeth Woody. STE
Custer's Last Charge. Frederick Whittaker. BPAW; HBV-2; OnMSP; PAH; PoLF
Custom of the World, The. Louis Simpson. BoLoP
Customer's blowing, A. All-Nite Donuts. Albert Goldbarth. GeTw; MAYP
Customs. Juan Gelman, *tr. fr. Spanish by* Yishai Tobin. VWA
Customs Change. *Unknown.* OxBChV
Customs seal on my travel bag, The. Debussy and Proust. John Tagliabue. FAZ
Cut. David J. Feela. AMV-81
Cut. Sylvia Plath. CABA; CAPP; InPK; TAP
Cut down that timber! Bells, too many and strong. The Planster's Vision. John Betjeman. PoPl
Cut Flower, A. Karl Shapiro. BoNaP; HAP; WeW
Cut from the joints of this immense. The Night. Lawrence Durrell. *Fr.* Eight Aspects of Melissa. NeBP
Cut Grass. Philip Larkin. OxBC; PrIm
Cut is the branch that might have grown full straight. Christopher Marlowe. *Fr.* Doctor Faustus, Epilogue. ViBoPo
Cut It Down. Mary Elizabeth Coleridge. MoVE
Cut Lilac. Tony Beyer. OCNZ
Cut out/ the insides. Hegel. Amiri Baraka. CoPo
Cut the Cables. Robert Burns Wilson. PAH
Cut the Grass. A. R. Ammons. HAP; PPP; TAP; WeW
Cut thistles in May. *Unknown.* FaBoUs; OxNR
Cut your nails [*or* them] on Monday, [you] cut them for news [*or* health]. *Unknown.* HBV-1; OxNR
Cutter risen from the mollusks, it is a god, A. The Memoirs. Carl Rakosi. PoA
Cutting Edge, The. Philip Levine. NYBP
Cutting that jungle road from Lugardville. Surveyor. Guy Butler. PeSA
Cutting Wood on Shell Creek. Gretel Ehrlich. MAYP
Cuttings ("Sticks-in-a-drowse droop over sugary loam"). Theodore Roethke. LCAP; NoAM; NOBA; TAP; UnPo
Cuttings ("This urge, wrestle, resurrection of dry sticks"). Theodore Roethke. LCAP; NoAM; NOBA; PPoe; TAP; UnPo
(Cuttings, Later.) AP
Cutty Sark. Hart Crane. *Fr.* The Bridge. FaBoMo
Cutty Wren, The. *Unknown.* FSW; GBP; NCEP; OxBoLi; WiR
Cwa een like milk-wort and bog-cotton hair! Milk-Wort and Bog Cotton. "Hugh MacDiarmid." BSV; NeBP
Cwmrhydyceirw Elegiacs. Vernon Watkins. PoA
Cyanide jar seals life, as sonnets move, The. Butterfly Bones; or, Sonnet against Sonnets. Margaret Avison. LiTM
Cyclamen, The. Arlo Bates. AA; HBV-1
Cycle. Langston Hughes. FaPON
Cycle. Frank Lonergan. AMV-81
Cycle, *sels.* Ruth Miller.
"Cover my eyes with your palm." PeSA
"Dropped leaf, The." PeSA
"To eat pain like bread is a condition." PeSA
Cycle: Seven War Poems. Sean Jennett. WaP
I Was a Labourer, *sel.* OnYI
Cycle sings, A. Nature. Walter Stone. NYBP
Cycle was closed and rounded, A. Bennington. W. H. Babcock. PAH
Cycles, Cycles. Suzanne Berger Rioff. NMM
Cycling to Dublin. Robert Greacen. OnYI
Cyclist, The. Lawrence Kearney. AMV-80
Cyclists, The. Amy Lowell. WPE
Cyclone, The. Stewart Brisby. LFAC
Cyclone at Sea, A. William Hamilton Hayne. AA
Cyclone Blues. *Unknown.* CoSo
Cyclops, *sels.* Euripides, *tr. fr. Greek by* Shelley.
Chorus: Love Song. AWP
Chorus of Satyrs, Driving Their Goats. AWP
Cyclops. Ovid, *tr. fr. Latin by* Arthur Golding. *Fr.* Metamorphoses, XIII. CTC
Cyclops, The. Theocritus, *tr. fr. Greek by* Elizabeth Barrett Browning. Idylls, XI. AWP
("And so an easier life our Cyclops drew.") OBVE
Cyder, *sels.* John Philips.
How to Catch Wasps. FaBoUs
Pruning. FaBoUs
Cygnet crested on the purple water, The. Similes. Edward Moxon. OBRV
Cymbals clash. Harlem Sounds: Hallelujah Corner. William Browne. AmNP
Cymbals crash, The. A Victory Dance. Alfred Noyes. PoLF
Cymbeline, *sels.* Shakespeare.
"Could I find out/ The woman's part in me!" *fr.* II, v. DBV
Fear No More the Heat o' the Sun, *fr.* IV, ii. AWP; CH; ChTr; EBEV; EIL; ELP; EnRePo; FaFP; FF; GBL; HAP; HeIP; InPK; InPS; LiTB; LoBV; NoP; OAEP; PAI; PoPle; PoRA; PPoe; PrIm; QFR; RoGo; SCV; SeCeV; SoSe; TrGrPo; ViBoPo; WHA
(Dirge: "Fear no more the heat o' the sun.") HBV-2; OAEL-1
(Dirge for Fidele.) NOBE

(Fidele.) GTBS; GTBS-P; OBEV
(Fidele's Dirge.) FaBoCh; OBSC
(Lament for Imogen.) TreF
(Lament of Guiderius and Arviragus.) FaBoEn
(Song: "Fear[e] no more the heat[e] o' the sun.") CTC; FiP; PoEL-2
Hark! Hark! the Lark, *fr.* II, iii. AWP; CH; ChTr; EnRePo; FaBoCh; FaBV; FaFP; FaPON; HBV-1; HeIP; LiTB; LoBV; NIP; NoP; PrIm; SeCeV; TreF; TrGrPo; ViBoPo; WHA
(Aubade: "Hark! hark! the lark at heaven's gate sings.") OBEV
(Morning Song, A.) GN
(Song: "Hark! hark! the lark at heaven's gate sings.") EIL; FiP
(Song to Imogen.) OBSC
"With fairest flowers,/ Whilst summer lasts," *fr.* IV, ii. EBEV
Cymbeline, Tempest, Much Ado, Verona. Memoria Technica for the Plays of Shakespeare. *Unknown.* FaBoUs
Cymochles and Phaedria. Spenser. *Fr.* The Faerie Queene, II, 6. OBSC
Cymon and Iphigenia. Dryden. OBNV
Sels.
Militia, The. OBSV
Power of Love, The. OBS
Cynara. Ernest Dowson. *See* Non Sum Qualis Eram Bonae sub Regno Cynarae.
Cynic, The. Theodosia Garrison. HBMV
Cynic, The. St. George Tucker. OBAL
Cynical Ode to an Ultra-cynical Public. Charles MacKay. DBV
Cynical Portraits. Louis Paul. InMe
Cynics say that every rose, The. The Wisdom of Folly. Ellen Thorneycroft Fowler. HBV-2
Cynicus to W. Shakspere. James Kenneth Stephen. *Fr.* Two Epigrams. CenHV; WhC
Cynisca. *Unknown, tr. fr. Greek by* Tom Dodge. LiSp
Cynneddf, The. Rolfe Humphries. CrMA
Cynotaph, The. "Thomas Ingoldsby." *Fr.* The Ingoldsby Legends. FM
Cynthia. Edward Benlowes. *Fr.* Theophila; or, Love's Sacrifice. MOON
Cynthia. Sir Edward Dyer. OBSC
Cynthia ("Away with these self-loving lads"). Fulke Greville. *See* Of His Cynthia.
Cynthia, because your horns look diverse ways. Caelica, LIV. Fulke Greville. MOON
Cynthia in the Snow. Gwendolyn Brooks. TiPo
Cynthia Matz, with my finger in your cunt. Each Day. David Ignatow. NNaP
Cynthia on Horseback. Philip Ayres. EnLoPo
Cynthia, Queen of seas and lands. The Mariner's Song. Sir John Davies. OBSC
Cynthia, to thy power and thee. Bridal Song. Beaumont *and* Fletcher. *Fr.* The Maid's Tragedy. OBEV
Cynthia's Revels, *sels.* Ben Jonson.
Glove, The, *fr.* IV. EIL
("Thou more than most sweet glove.") GBL
Hymn to Diana, *fr.* V, vi. AWP; CH; ChTr; EIL; EnRePo; GTBS; GTBS-P; HAP; MOON; NOBE; OBEV; OBS; PoPle; PoRA; QFR; SeCP; TrGrPo; WHA; WiR
(Hesperus' Hymn[e] to Cynthia.) JCP; LoBV; SeCV-1
(Hesperus' Song.) GN
(Hymn[e], The: "Queene and Huntress, chaste, and faire.") AnAnS-2; PoEL-2; ViBoPo
(Hymn to Cynthia.) PrIm; SeCePo
("Queen[e] and huntress[e], chaste and fair[e].") CABA; HeIP; NoP; OAEL-1; OAEP
(Song: To Cynthia.) HBV-1
Slow, Slow, Fresh Fount, *fr.* I, ii. ChTr; EIL; ELP; InPK; NoP; OAEL-1; OAEP; OBS; PrIm; SeCeV; WHA
(Echo's Lament for Narcissus.) CH
(Echo's [*or* Eccho's] Song.) JCP; LoBV; SeCV-1; TrGrPo
(Song: "Slow, slow, fresh fount, keepe time with my salt teares.") AnAnS-2; EnRePo; FaBoEn; PoEL-2; SeCP; ViBoPo
(Song of Echo.) GoBC
Song: "O, that joy so soon should waste!" *fr.* IV, iii. ViBoPo
(Kiss, The.) HBV-1; UnTE
Cypassis, that a thousand ways trimm'st hair. Ovid, *tr. by* Christopher Marlowe. Amores, II, 8. EBEV
Cypress Curtain of the Night, The. Thomas Campion. LoBV
Cypress Grove. Austin Clarke. IPY
Cypress Grove Blues. *Unknown.* BluL
Cypress stood up like a church, The. Bianca among the Nightingales. Elizabeth Barrett Browning. BrRo; GTBS-P
Cypress swamp around me wraps its spell, The. Down the Bayou. Mary Ashley Townsend. AA
Cypresses. Robert Francis. LCAP
Cypresses. D. H. Lawrence. FaBoPP
Cyprian Woman, A. Margaret Widdemer. HBV-2
Cyrano de Bergerac, *sels.* Edmond Rostand, *tr. fr. French by* Brian Hooker.
Cyrano de Bergerac Discusses His Nose, *fr.* I. TreFS
"Love, I love beyond," *fr.* III. OLR
Cyriack, this three years' day these eyes, though clear. To Mr. Cyriack Skinner upon His Blindness. Milton. OBS; TrGrPo
Cyriack, whose grandsire, on the royal bench. To Cyriack Skinner [*or* Sonnet]. Milton. GTBS; GTBS-P; LoBV; NoP; OBEV; OBS
Cythère. Paul Verlaine, *tr. fr. French by* Arthur Symons. AWP
(Cythera.) SyP
Cywdd to Morvydd, The. David ap Gwilim, *tr. fr. Welsh.* NOEC

D

D Blues. Calvin C. Hernton. PoBA
D. C. Karl Shapiro. NYBP
D-Dawn. Margaret McGarvey. GoYe
D-Day Dodgers, The. *Unknown. See* Ballad of the D-Day Dodgers.
D. G. C. to J. A. Emily Brontë. BrRo
"Come, the wind may never again," 1 *st.* EnLoPo
D. H. Lawrence and James Joyce. Humbert Wolfe. FaBoEE
D. L. & W.'s Phoebe Snow, The. *Unknown.* TreF
D Minor, The. E. L. Mayo. MiAP
DNA Lab. Michael Spence. SOTS
DOA in Dulse. Diane Burns. STE
"D. O. M." Sir Henry Wotton. *See* Eternal Mover.
D-Y Bar. James Welch. CDW; STE
Da Capo. H. C. Bunner. HBV-1
Da Silva Gives the Cue. Walter Hart Blumenthal. TrJP
Dab of Color, A. Theodore Weiss. VGW
Dabbling in the Dew. *Unknown.* CH; UnTE
Daccus is all bedaub'd with golden lace. Against Gaudy-Bragging-Undoughty Daccus. John Davies of Hereford. FaBoEE
Dachau. John Malcolm Brinnin. GP
Dachshund, The. Edward Anthony. GDP
Dachshunds ("The dachshund leads a quiet life"). William Jay Smith. OBAL
Dad. Elaine Feinstein. VWA
Dad, a Home Guard, when in liquor. *Unknown.* WhC
Dad and the Cat and the Tree. Kit Wright. OnUR
Dad he said the White Sox. Two Hopper. Ron Ikan. Str
Dada would have liked a day like this. Lawrence Ferlinghetti. *Fr.* Pictures of the Gone World. NeAP
Daddy. Lucille Clifton. NIP
Daddy. Rose Fyleman. SiSoSe
Daddy. Sylvia Plath. BiP; BoWoP; CAPP; CMoP; CoAP; InPK; InPS; LiTM; NaP; NIP; NMM; NMP; NoAM; NOBA; NoP; PAI; PrIm; TW; TwCP; UnPo
Daddy and Mummy. Life Story. Tomioka Taeko, *tr. by* Harry *and* Lynn Guest *and* Kajima Shozo. WPOW
Daddy drinks/ lots of/ beer. Idle Chatter. Charles Cooper. BOLo
Daddy Fell into the Pond. Alfred Noyes. FaPON; PDV; RHPC
Daddy fixed breakfast [*or* the breakfast]. Mummy Slept Late and Daddy Fixed Breakfast. John Ciardi. PDV; RHPC
Daddy had a little boy. Does Daddy Go? *Unknown.* STF
Daddy rides the rodeo, while pride rides on a tiny brown face. Childs Memory. Terri Meyette Wilkins. LFAC
Daddy Shot a Bear, *with music. Unknown.* OuSiCo
Daddy sits/ in his brown. Sunflowers and Saturdays. Melba Joyce Boyd. BlSi
Daddyboy/ trickster hero. Daring. Carol Konek. IHMS
Dad's Greatest Job. *Unknown.* STF
Dae what ye wull ye canna parry. "Hugh MacDiarmid." *Fr.* A Drunk Man Looks at the Thistle. EBEV
Daedalus. Ovid, *tr. fr. Latin by* Arthur Golding. *Fr.* Metamorphoses, VIII. CTC
("Now in this while gan Daedalus a weariness to take.") OBVE
Daedalus. Alastair Reid. NCSH; NYBP
Daemon, The. Louise Bogan. NYBP
Daemon, The, *sel.* Mikhail Yuryevich Lermontov, *tr. fr. Russian.*
"On the sightless seas of ether," *tr. by* Babette Deutsch *and* Avrahm Yarmolinsky. AWP
Daemon Lover, The. *Unknown. See* Demon Lover, The.
Daemon of the World, The, *sel.* Shelley.
Trackless Deeps, The, *fr.* Pt. II. EtS
Daffadowndilly has come up to town. *See* Daffy-down-dilly is new come to town.
Daffodils. Ruth Guthrie Harding. HBMV
Daffodils. Michael Heffernan. AMV-80
Daffodils. Kikurio, *tr. fr. Japanese.* SoPo; SUS; TiPo

Daffodils. Lizette Woodworth Reese. AA
Daffodils. Wordsworth. *See* I Wandered Lonely as a Cloud.
Daffodils,/ That come before the swallow dares. Shakespeare. *Fr.* The Winter's Tale, IV, iii. TiPo
Daffodil's Return. Bliss Carman. CaP
Daffy-down-dilly is new come to town [*or* Daffadowndilly has come up to town]. Mother Goose. NTCP; OxNR; SoPo; TiPo
Daft Days, The. Robert Fergusson. BSV; NOEC
Daft Jean. Sydney Dobell. VLP
Dafydd ap Gwilym Resents the Winter. Rolfe Humphries. NYBP
Dagger, The ("A dagger rests in a drawer"). Jorge Luis Borges, *tr. fr. Spanish by* Norman Thomas di Giovanni. NYBP
Dagger. Mikhail Yuryevich Lermontov, *tr. fr. Russian by* Max Eastman. AWP
Dago, the Injun, the Chink, the Jew, The. Uncultivated Accent. *Unknown.* DBV
Dagonet's Canzonet. Ernest Rhys. HBV-1
Daguerreotype of a Grandmother. Celeste Turner Wright. Str
Daguerreotype Taken in Old Age. Margaret Atwood. BoWoP
Dahlias. Padraic Colum. GoJo; NePoAm
Dai horse neighs against the bleak wind of Etsu, The. South-Folk in Cold Country. Ezra Pound, *after the Chinese.* CrMA; OBVE
Daily Courage Doesn't Count. Alta. GP
Daily Grind, The. Fenton Johnson. AmNP
Daily Growing. *Unknown.* FSW
Daily I Fall in Love with Waitresses. Elliot Fried. GP
Daily I listen to wonder and woe. Ballade of a Talked-off Ear. Dorothy Parker. DBV
Daily Manna, The. Sara Henderson Hay. GoYe
Daily News. Tom Clark. EAS
Daily Paradox. Sara Henderson Hay. InMe
Daily the Drum. Anne Wilkinson. NOBC
Daily the Ocean between Us. Patricia Goedicke. TAP
Daily the wind-flowers age, and so do I. Weaving Love-Knots. Hsüeh T'ao, *tr. by* Carolyn Kizer. BoWoP
Daily Trials. Oliver Wendell Holmes. PoEL-5
Daily Wages. Amrita Pritam, *tr. fr. Punjabi by author and* Charles Brasch. PBWP
Daily walked the fair and lovely. The Azra. Heine, *tr. by* John Hay. AWP
Daily went the Sultan's beauteous. The Asra. Heine, *tr. by* Ernst Feise. NAWM-2
Daily with You. Annie Johnson Flint. BLRP
Dain do Eimhir, *sels.* Sorley Maclean. NeBP
"Bolshevik who never gave heed to queen or to king, A," XXX.
"I do not see the sense of my toil putting thoughts in a dying tongue," LV.
"I gave you immortality and what did you give me?" XIX.
"I walked with my reason out beside the sea: we were together," XXII.
"Multitude of the skies, gold riddle of millions of stars," XVII.
"You were dawn on the Cuillin and benign day on the Clarach," LIV.
Dain Eile, *sel.* Sorley Maclean.
"My eye is not on Calvary, nor on Bethlehem the Blessed." NeBP
Dainty fine bird, that art encaged there. *See* Dainty Sweet Bird.
Dainty little maiden, whither would you wander? The City Child. Tennyson. OxBChV
Dainty Miss Apathy. Pooh! Walter de la Mare. HAP
Dainty Sang, A. Allan Ramsay. *Fr.* The Gentle Shepherd. OBEC
(Jocky Said to Jeany.) BSV
Dainty Sweet Bird. *Unknown.* EnRePo; NCEP
(Prisoners.) ElL
Dainty young heiress of Lincoln's Inn Fields, The. Charles Sackville. POL
Dairymaid and Her Milk-Pot, The. La Fontaine, *tr. fr. French by* Marianne Moore. NAWM-2
Daisies, The. Bliss Carman. BoNaP; HBV-1
Daisies. Alden Nowlan. NeAC
Daisies, The. James Stephens. AnIV; AWP
Daisies. Valerie Worth. PCP
Daisies. Andrew Young. GoJo
Daisies of Florence. Kathleen Raine. NYBP
Daisy, The. Burns. *See* To a Mountain Daisy.
Daisy, The. Tennyson. EnLoPo; OBNC; OBVV; PoEL-5
Daisy. Francis Thompson. AWP; BeLS; BrPo; FaBV; GoBC; HBV-1; MoAB; MoBrPo; OBEV; OBNC; OBVV; WHA
Daisy. William Carlos Williams. MoAB; MoAmPo;
Daisy, The. Marya Zaturenska. GrPl; MoAmPo
"Daisy and Lily." Waltz. Edith Sitwell. *Fr.* Façade. OAEP
Daisy Bell; or, A Bicycle Built for Two, *with music.* Harry Dacre. BLSo; FSN
(Bicycle Built for Two, A.) FSW
(Daisy Bell.) TreF
Daisy Fraser. Edgar Lee Masters. *Fr.* Spoon River Anthology. CMoP; HAP; MoVE
Daisy's Song. Keats. BoNaP
Dakota Badlands. Elizabeth Landeweer. AmFN
Dakota: Five Times Six. Joseph Hansen. NYBP
Dakota Land. *Unknown.* AS, *with music;* BPAW; CoSo, *with music;* FSW
Dakota: October, 1822, Hunkpapa Warrior. Rod Taylor. WeW
Dakota Wheat-Field, A. Hamlin Garland. *See* Color in the Wheat.
Dalesman's Litany, The. *Unknown.* OBET
Daley's Dorg Wattle. W. T. Goodge. GDP; PoAu-1
Dallán Dé! Dallán Dé! Butterfly in the Fields. Joseph Campbell. BoAnP
Dalliance of the Eagles, The. Walt Whitman. AA; AmPP; BiP; BoAnP; CABA; FaBoEn; FM; HAP; HeIP; InPK; NoP; POL; PPoe; PPP; PrIm; TAP
Dalyaunce. *Unknown.* CH
Dam Bellona, The. Der Blinde Junge. Mina Loy. QFR
Dam, Glen Garry, The. Robert Symmons. PoSH
Dam Neck, Virginia. Richard Eberhart. LiTA; MoAB; WaP
Damage You Have Done, The. Ellis Ayitey Komey. PBA
Damages, Two Hundred Pounds. Thackeray. OBSV
Dame. Susan Astor. AMV-80
Dame, dame! the watch is set. The Witches' Charms [*or* Sabbath]. Ben Jonson. *Fr.* The Masque of Queens. ElL; WSC
Dame, get up and bake your pies. *Unknown.* OxNR
"Dame, how the moments go." The Bride's Toilette. Ellen Mackay Hutchinson Cortissoz. AA
Dame Jane a sprightly nun and gay. The Penitent Nun. John Lockman. ErPo; UnTE
Dame Liberty Reports from Travel. Dorothy Cowles Pinkney. GoYe
Dame Music. Stephen Hawes. *Fr.* The Pastime of Pleasure. PoEL-1
Dame Nature. Spenser. *Fr.* The Faerie Queene, VII, 7. PoEL-1
Dame, said the Panther, times are mended well. Dryden. *Fr.* The Hind and the Panther, II. PoEL-3
Dame Trot and her cat. Mother Goose. OxNR
Dame Wiggins of Lee. *Unknown, at. to* Richard Scrafton Sharpe *and to* Mrs. Pearson. FaBoNo; OxBChV
(Dame Wiggins of Lee and Her Seven Wonderful Cats.) FaBoBe
Damelus' [*or* Damelias'] Song to [*or* of] His Diaphenia. *At. to* Henry Constable, *and to* Henry Chettle. *See* Diaphenia.
Dames of France are fond and free, The. The Girl I Left behind Me. Thomas Osborne Davis. AmSS; FaBoBe; FaFP; HBV-1; OnYI; TreF
Damis, an author cold and weak. Epigram. *Unknown.* HBV-1
Damisel, rest thee wel. A Student Courting. *Unknown.* OxBM
Damit blackman. Domestics. Kattie M. Cumbo. BlSi
Damn blue eyes. Damn the street. Curses. Joseph Duemer. AMV-80
Damn fool feeling her up. Wreck. Noel Polk. AMV-81
Damn it all! all this our South stinks peace. Sestina: Altaforte. Ezra Pound. CMoP; CoBMV; FaBoTw; LiTA; MoAB; MoAmPo; NOBA; SoSe; SOTW
Damn that celibate farm, that cracker-box house. Censorship. John Ciardi. TW
Damnation follows death in other men. On Poets. Pope. FaBoEE
Damnation of Vancouver, *sel.* Earle Birney.
Speech of the Salish Chief. OBCV
Damned Minoan crevices, that I clog them up! Paranoia in Crete. Gregory Corso. NeAP
Damned ship lurched and slithered, The. Quiet and quick. A Channel Passage. Rupert Brooke. MOS
Damned Women. Baudelaire, *tr. fr. French by* Roy Campbell. BoLoP
Damocles. Robert Graves. NYBP
Damon and Celimena. Dryden. *See* Song, A: "Celimena, of my heart."
Damon and Cupid. John Gay. EnLoPo; SeCeV
Damon and Pythias. Robert Creeley. LCAP
Damon come drive thy flocks this way. Clorinda and Damon. Andrew Marvell. AnAnS-1; SeCP
Damon died young; no bell was tolled for him. Toll the Bell for Damon. Maxwell Anderson. InMe
Damon forbear, and don't disturb your Muse. The Court. *Unknown.* APAS
Damon the Mower. Andrew Marvell. AnAnS-1; JCP; OAEL-1
Damp fallen leaves smell of ripe bananas, The. Walking Home at Night. Daniel Weissbort. VWA
Damp swell of dunes that turn into flour, The. A New Genesis. Avraham Shlonsky, *tr. by* Francis Landy. VWA
Dampe, The. John Donne. SeCP
Damsel, The. Omar b. Abi Rabi'a, *tr. fr. Arabic by* W. G. Palgrave. AWP
Dan Bartholmew's Dolorous Discourses. George Gascoigne. EnRePo
Dan Ellis's Boys. *Unknown.* AmFP
Dan Taylor, *with music. Unknown.* CoSo
Dan, the Dust of Masada Is Still in My Nostrils. Ruth Whitman. VWA
Dana Point. Brewster Ghiselin. AMV-81
Danaë. Barbara Howes. WPE
Dance, The. Amiri Baraka. CoPo
Dance, The. *At. to* Thomas Campion. ElL; FaBoCh; LoBV

Dance, The. Hart Crane. *Fr.* The Bridge: Powhatan's Daughter. LiTM; MoAB; MoAmPo; OxBA; SeCeV; TwAmPo
Dance, The. Robert Duncan. NeAP
Dance, The. Daniel Halpern. MAYP
Dance, The. Robert Kelly. The Book of Persephone, 17. PoM
Dance, The. Rudolph Chambers Lehmann. HBMV
Dance, The. John Lydgate. *Fr.* The Dance of Death. PoEL-1
Dance, The. Theodore Roethke. *Fr.* Four for Sir John Davies. CrMA; NePoAm
Dance, The. Spenser. *See* Dance of the Graces, The.
Dance, The. Mark Strand. GeTw
Dance, The. *Unknown.* PAH
(Cornwallis's Country Dance, *abr., with* Yankee Doodle.) TrAS
Dance, The. William Carlos Williams. AmPP; CMoP; GoJo; GrPl; HAP; HeIP; InPK; LiTM; NCSH; NIP; NoAM; NOBA; NoP; OxBA; PAI; POL; PrIm; SoSe; TAP; WeW
Dance a baby diddy. Mother Goose. OxNR
Dance and Eye Me (Wicked)ly My Breath a Fixed Sphere. Rochelle Owens. NMM
Dance begins with the sun descending, The. Marrakech. Richard Eberhart. LiTM
Dance Called David, The. Theodore Weiss. CoPo
Dance Chant, A ("Hail! Hail! Hail!"). *Unknown, tr. fr. Iroquois Indian by* E. S. Parker. WGRP
Dance Chant, A ("O Wahkonda [Master of Life] pity me!"). *Unknown, tr. fr. Osage Indian by* D. G. Brinton. WGRP
Dance, dance in this museum case. Love Song to Eohippus. Peter Viereck. MoAmPo
Dance Figure. Ezra Pound. HeIP; MoAB; MoAmPo; TwAmPo
Dance for Ma Rainey, A. Al Young. NBP
Dance for Militant Dilettantes, A. Al Young. PoBA
Dance for Rain, A. Witter Bynner. BPAW
Dance grows, The. The Dead. Jay Wright. FB
Dance Hymn. Isaiah Shembe, *tr. fr. Zulu by* B. G. M. Sundkler. WTO
Dance in the township hall is nearly over, The. Country Dance. Judith Wright. *Fr.* The Blind Man. CBAP
Dance Instructions for a Young Girl. Kimiko Hahn. BrSi
Dance is on the Bridge of Death, The. The Bridge of Death. *Unknown, tr. by* Andrew Lang. AWP
Dance like a jackrabbit. The Inside Chance. Marge Piercy. LTB
Dance, little baby, dance up high. The Baby's Dance. *At. To* Mother Goose, *and also to* Ann Taylor. OxBChV; OxNR
Dance of Death, The. Austin Dobson. HBV-2
Dance of Death, The, *sel.* John Lydgate.
Dance, The. PoEL-1
Dance of Despair, The. Hayyim Nahman Bialik, *tr. fr. Hebrew by* A. M. Klein. TrJP
Dance of Dust, The. Louis Untermeyer. BXAP
Dance of Gray Raccoon, The. Arthur Guiterman. BPAW
Dance of Love, The. Sir John Davies. *Fr.* Orchestra; or, A Poem of Dancing. ElL; SeCePo
Dance of Saul with the Prophets, The. Saul Tchernichowsky, *tr. fr. Hebrew by* I. M. Lask. TrJP
Dance of the Abakweta. Margaret Danner. PoNe
Dance of the Daughters of Herodias, The. Arthur Symons. BrPo
Dance of the Elephants, The. Michael Harper. LCAP
Dance of the Graces, The. Spenser. *Fr.* The Faerie Queene, VI, 10. OBSC
(Dance, The, *shorter sel.*) TrGrPo
Dance of the Infidels. Al Young. PoBA
Dance of the Macabre Mice. Wallace Stevens. CMoP; NePA; NOBA; OxBA; SeCeV
Dance of the Rain, The. Eugène Marais, *tr. fr. Afrikaans by* Jack Cope *and* Uys Krige. PeSA
Dance of the Sevin Deidly Synnis [*or* Seven Deadly Sins], The. William Dunbar. BSV; GoTS; OxBS
Dance of the Sword, The. *Unknown, tr. fr. Breton by* Tom Taylor. WaaP
Dance on Pushback. James Still. GrPl
Dance-Song. Jaroslav Seifert, *tr. fr. Czech by* Paul Jagasich *and* Tom O'Grady. AMV-81
Dance Song. *Unknown, tr. fr. Chinese by* Arthur Waley. FaBoCh
Dance-Song of the Lightning. *Unknown, tr. fr. Hottentot.* PeSA
Dance, Thumbkin, dance. Mother Goose. OxNR
Dance to your [*or* thee] daddy [*or* daddie], *diff. versions.* Mother Goose. FSW; OBET; OxNR (2 *vers.*); PoPle; TiPo, 1 *st.*
Dance with Banderillas. Richard Duerden. NeAP
Dancer, The. Joseph Campbell. OBMV; OxBI
Dancer, The. Sadi, *tr. fr. Persian by* Sir Edwin Arnold. *Fr.* The Bustan. AWP
Dancer, The. W. J. Turner. OBMV
Dancer, The. Edmund Waller. TrGrPo
Dancer, The. Al Young. PoBA
Dancer dips and holds, A. The sun. The Berkeley Pier. John Addiego. AMV-81
Dancer: Four Poems. Paul Engle. AMV-80
Dancer from the Dance, The. Suzanne Juhasz. IHMS
Dancer quarrels with solid air, The. Dancer: Four Poems. Paul Engle. AMV-80
Dancers, The. Babette Deutsch. HBMV
Dancers, The. W. W. Gibson. MMA
Dancers, The. Edith Sitwell. SUMH
Dancers at the Moy. Paul Muldoon. BIrV
Dancers Inherit the Party, The. Ian Hamilton Finlay. FF
Dancer's Life, A. Donald Justice. LCAP
Dancers of Colbek, The. Robert Mannyng. *Fr.* Handlyng Synne. OxBM
Dances of Death, *sel.* Alexander Blok, *tr. fr. Russian by* Jon Stallworthy *and* Peter France.
"Night, street, a lamp, a chemist's window." OBVE
Dancing, The. Gerald Stern. DiL
Dancing. Yang Kuei-fei, *tr. fr. Chinese by* Florence Ayscough *and* Amy Lowell. FaPON
Dancing at Whitsun. Austin John Marshall. OBET
Dancing Bear, The. Rachel Field. NTCP
Dancing Bear, The. Albert Bigelow Paine. OBCA
Dancing Bear, The. Robert Southey. FM
Dancing [*or* Dauncing], bright lady, then began to be. The Praise of Dancing. Sir John Davies. *Fr.* Orchestra; or, A Poem of Dancing. FaBoEn; NOBE; PoEL-2
Dancing Cabman, The. J. B. Morton. MoShBr; NOBL
Dancing, drinking, gambling, fighting. Off Guard. *Unknown.* CoSo
Dancing Faun, The. Robert Cameron Rogers. AA
Dancing Gal. Frank Marshall Davis. FB
Dancing Girl, A. Frances Sargent Osgood. AA
Dancing-Girl's Song. Kshetrayya, *tr. fr. Teluga by* Tambimuttu *and* R. Appalaswamy. BoWoP
Dancing on the edge of a razor blade. Ming the Merciless. Jessica Hagedorn. BrSi
Dancing Partners. Philip Child. CaP
Dancing School. Jonathan Holden. Psk
Dancing Sea, The. Sir John Davies. *Fr.* Orchestra. ChTr
(Sea Danceth, The.) EtS
Dancing Seal, The. W. W. Gibson. HBMV; OnMSP
Dancing Sunshine Lounge, The. Thomas Rabbitt. MAYP
Dancing the Shout to the True Gospel; or, The Song Movement Sisters Don't Want Me to Sing. Rita Mae Brown. NMM; PeHV
Dancing with such salacious gestures. Familiarity Breeds Indifference. Martial, *tr. by* Louis Untermeyer. UnTE
Dandelion. Annie Rankin Annan. HBV-1
Dandelion. Hilda Conkling. FaPON; PDV; TiPo
Dandelion Gatherer, The. Robert Francis. PPJ
Dandelion stares, The. The Little Dandelion. Lula Lowe Weeden. CDC
Dandelions. John Albee. AA
Dandelions, The. Helen Gray Cone. HBV-1
Dandelions. Frances M. Frost. TiPo
Dandelions. Gerda Mayer. POL
Dandelions. Howard Nemerov. DFF; NePA; TwAmPo
Dandelions for Chains ("Dandelions meet me wherever I am"). Sarah Kirsch, *tr. fr. German by* Michael Hamburger. WPOW
Dandelions purr in their sleep. Of Dandelions & Tourists. Joe Rosenblatt. NOBC
Dandelions, wrecked on their stems, The. Late Dandelions. Ben Belitt. NYBP
Dandoo, *with music. Unknown.* TrAS
Dandy Horse, The. *Unknown.* OBET
Dandy O, The. *Unknown.* CoMu
Dane-Geld. Kipling. OxBTC
Danebury. *Unknown.* PeHV
Danger. Theodora L. Paine. PGD
Danger is silent in the bloodless square. Capital Square. Patrick Anderson. OBCV
Danger of Writing Defiant Verse, The. Dorothy Parker. InMe
Danger stalks on such nights, the moon is dangerous. The Lunar Tides. Marya Zaturenska. MOON
"Dangerous Condition": Sign on Inner-City House. Russell Atkins. CNA
Dangerous Music, A. Michael Knoll. LFAC
Dangers of drifting while driving in a daze, The. In a Motion. Laura Chester. NPGG
Dangers of Sexual Excess, The. John Armstrong. *Fr.* The Art of Preserving Health. FaBoUs
Daniel, *sel.* Bible, *O.T.*
Belshazzar's Feast, V: 1-31. TreF
Daniel. Vachel Lindsay. ChTr
(Daniel Jazz, The.) TrGrPo
Daniel and Abigail. Epitaph. Miguel de Barrios. TrJP

Daniel at Breakfast. Phyllis McGinley. OBSV
Daniel Boone. Stephen Vincent Benét. AmFN; GOA; PoPI
Daniel Boone. Arthur Guiterman. FaPON; MoShBr
Daniel Defoe. Walter Savage Landor. NCEP
Daniel Gray. Josiah Gilbert Holland. AA; HBV-2
Daniel Jazz, The. Vachel Lindsay. *See* Daniel.
Daniel Saw de Stone, *with music. Unknown.* BoAN-2
Daniel Webster. Oliver Wendell Holmes. PAH
Daniel Webster's Horses. Elizabeth J. Coatsworth. AmFN; MoAmPo; OBCA; PH
Danish Wit. John Hollander. PV
Dank, limber verses, stuft with lakeside sedges. Some of Wordsworth. Walter Savage Landor. ChTr
Dankwerts, scholarship boy from the slums. Living? Our Supervisors Will Do That for Us! David Holbrook. NePoEA-2
Danny. Malcolm Cowley. PoA
Danny Boy. *Unknown.* FSW
Danny Deever. Kipling. BrPo; EBVV; FaBoBa; FaPoR; FPL; GTBS-P; HBV-2; InPS; LiTB; MoBrPo; NOBE; OAEP; OxBoLi; OxBTC; PoLF; SCV; SeCePo; TEP; TreFS; TrGrPo; UnPo; VLP; WaaP
Danny Murphy. James Stephens. OnUR; RoGo
Danny was a rascal. The Buccaneer. Nancy Byrd Turner. TiPo
Danny's Wooing. David McKee Wright. PoAu-1
Dans l'Allée. Paul Verlaine, *tr. fr. French by* Arthur Symons. AWP (Avenue, The.) SyP
Danse Russe. William Carlos Williams. CMoP; InPK; InPS; NOBA; NoP; PPP; TAP
Dante. Bryant. ViBoPo
Dante, *sel.* Robert Duncan.
"I know a little language of my cat, tho Dante says." PoM
Dante ("Oft have I seen at some cathedral door"). Longfellow. *See* Oft Have I Seen at Some Cathedral Door.
Dante ("Tuscan, that wanderest through the realms of gloom"). Longfellow. AA
Dante. Michelangelo, *tr. fr. Italian by* Longfellow. AWP
Dante, a sigh that rose from the heart's core. To Dante Alighieri: He Reports, in a Feigned Vision, the Successful Issue of Lapo Gianni's Love. Guido Cavalcanti, *tr. by* Dante Gabriel Rossetti. AWP
Dante Alighieri, a dark oracle. Inscription for a Portrait of Dante. Boccaccio, *tr. by* Dante Gabriel Rossetti *Fr.* Sonnets. AWP; GoBC
Dante Alighieri, Cecco, your good friend. Sonnet: To Dante Alighieri on the Last Sonnet of the Vita Nuova. Cecco Angiolieri da Siena, *tr. by* Dante Gabriel Rossetti. AWP
Dante Alighieri, if I jest and lie. Sonnet: To Dante Alighieri (He Writes to Dante, Then in Exile at Verona, Defying Him as No Better than Himself). Cecco Angiolieri da Siena, *tr. by* Dante Gabriel Rossetti. AWP
Dante Alighieri in Becchina's praise. Sonnet: He Rails against Dante, Who Had Censured His Homage to Becchina. Cecco Angiolieri da Siena, *tr. by* Dante Gabriel Rossetti. AWP
Dante had the right idea. If Justice Moved. Bettie M. Sellers. TW
Dante, if thou within the sphere of Love. To Dante in Paradise, after Fiammetta's Death. Boccaccio, *tr. by* Dante Gabriel Rossetti. *Fr.* Sonnets. AWP; GoBC (*in* Fiammetta)
Dante, whenever this thing happeneth. To Dante Alighieri: He Conceives of Some Compensation in Death. Cino da Pistoia, *tr. by* Dante Gabriel Rossetti. AWP
Danube orchards, The. The Peachtree. Denise Levertov. *Fr.* During the Eichmann Trial. CAPP
Danube to the Severn gave, The. The Hushing of the Wye. Tennyson. *Fr.* In Memoriam A. H. H. EBVV; FaBoPP; FF; GTBS-P; LoBV
Danville Girl. *Unknown.* FSW
Daphnaida, *sel.* Spenser.
"She fell away in her first ages spring." PoPle
(Elegy: "She fell away in her first ages spring.") OBEV
Daphne. Bliss Carman. OBCV
Daphne. Hildegarde Flanner. HBMV
Daphne. Thomas S. Jones, Jr. OHIP
Daphne. John Lyly. *Fr.* Midas. ElL
Daphne. Claire McAllister. TwAmPo
Daphne. Selden Rodman. PoNe
Daphne. Edith Sitwell. HBMV
Daphne. Swift. NOBL
Daphne and Apollo. George Macy. InMe
Daphne and Apollo. Ovid, *tr. fr. Latin by* Matthew Prior. *Fr.* Metamorphoses, I. NOEC
Daphne knows, with equal ease. Daphne. Swift. NOBL
Daphne Stillorgan. Denis Devlin. CIP
Daphnis Came on a Summer's Day. *Unknown.* ViBoPo
Daphnis to Ganymede. Richard Barnfield. *Fr.* The Affectionate Shepherd. ElL
Dappled horse stood at the edge of the meadow, A. The Grey Horse. James Reeves. PH
Dappled sky, a world of meadows, A. Jean Ingelow. *Fr.* Divided. OBNC
Dappling shadows on the summer grass. Kensington Gardens. Viviane Verne. SUMH
Dar was ole Mister Johnson, he had trouble of his own. The Cat Came Back. Harry S. Miller. FSN
Darby and Joan. St. John Honeywood. AA
Darby and Joan are [*or* were] dressed in black. *Unknown.* OxNR; PoPle
Darby Ram, The. *Unknown. See* Derby Ram, The.
Dare I in such momentous points advise. Soame Jenyns. *Fr.* The Art of Dancing. FaBoUs
Dare not to farre Castara, for the shade. To Castara, Ventring to Walke Too Farre in the Neighbouring Wood. William Habington. AnAnS-2
Dare Quam Accipere. Mathilde Blind. OBVV
Dare we despair? Through all the nights and days. He Leads Us Still. Arthur Guiterman. OHIP
Daredevil. Kirby Congdon. PeHV
Darest Thou Now O Soul. Walt Whitman. AA; HBV-2; NePA; TrGrPo; TRV; ViBoPo; WGRP
Darien. Sir Edwin Arnold. PAH
Daring. Carol Konek. IHMS
Darius Green and His Flying-Machine. John Townsend Trowbridge. BeLS; BLPL; FaBoBe; HBV-2; HBVY; InMe; MoShBr; OBAL; OBCA; OxBChV; PoLF; YaD
Darius the Mede was a king and a wonder. Daniel [*or* The Daniel Jazz]. Vachel Lindsay. ChTr; TrGrPo
Dark, The. Roy Fuller. DuDa
Dark. Eloise Klein Healy. AMV-80
Dark, The. William Heyen. EyDe
Dark abdomen upraised. Answering Dance. William Pitt Root. MAYP
Dark accurate plunger down the successive knell. The Subway. Allen Tate. AP; NoAM; NOBA; NYP
Dark an' stormy may come de wedder. Slave Marriage Ceremony Supplement. *Unknown.* BPo; POL; TAP
Dark and Falling Summer, The. Delmore Schwartz. NYBP
Dark and lugubrious, his eyes. The Condor. Michael Hogan. LFAC
Dark and more dark the shades of evening fell. Sonnet: Composed after a Journey across the Hamilton Hills, Yorkshire. Wordsworth. ChER
Dark and the Fair, The. Stanley Kunitz. PoCh
Dark Angel. Elizabeth Bartlett. NePoAm-2
Dark Angel, The. Lionel Johnson. ACP; GTBS-P; LiTB; MoBrPo; NOBE; OAEL-2; OBMV; VLP; WHA
Dark angel of the night, you come on folded wings. Dark Angel. Elizabeth Bartlett. NePoAm-2
Dark Angel, with thine aching lust. The Dark Angel. Lionel Johnson. ACP; GTBS-P; LiTB; MoBrPo; NOBE; OAEL-2; OBMV; VLP; WHA
Dark Area. Russell Atkins. FB
Dark as the clouds of even. The Black Regiment. George Henry Boker. GN; HBV-2; PAH
Dark as wells, his eyes. Long Person. Gladys Cardiff. CDW; STE; TWSS
Dark Aspect and Prospect. *Unknown.* PeD
Dark Birds, The. Bert Meyers. VWA
Dark, black robe. Invitation (To the Night and All Other Things Dark). Ronda Davis. JB
Dark brain. Poem to the Man on My Fire Escape. Diane Wakoski. CoPo
Dark branches. Alaskan Mountain Poem # 1. Leslie Marmon Silko. VoR
Dark Brother, The. Lewis Alexander. CDC
Dark brother touches me, The. Will Inman. *Fr.* 108 Tales of a Po'Buckra. GP
Dark brown is the river. Where Go the Boats? Robert Louis Stevenson. FaBoBe; FaBoCh; GoJo; NTCP; OxBChV; SoPo; SUS; TiPo; TreFT
Dark bull quartered in my eye. Jerome Rothenberg. *Fr.* Three Landscapes. CoPo
Dark Cat, The. Audrey Alexandra Brown. CaP
Dark Cavalier, The. Margaret Widdemer. HBMV
Dark Chamber, The. Louis Untermeyer. MoAmPo; WHA
Dark Château, The. Walter de la Mare. BrPo
Dark Churches. John Donne. *Fr.* A Hymn to Christ, at the Author's Last Going into Germany. FaBoRV
Dark Conclusions. Ruth Stone. BoWoP
Dark Corner. Graham Hough. NMP
Dark Country, A. Derek Mahon. BIrV
Dark Danny. Ivy O. Eastwick. FaPON; TiPo
Dark, deep, and cold the current flows. Plaint [*or* The Land Which No One Knows]. Ebenezer Elliott. HBV-2; OBEV; OBVV
Dark, deeply. A red. Inside the River. James Dickey. PoA
Dark Dialogues, The, *sels.* W. S. Graham. OxBS
"Almost I, yes, I hear," II.
"Now in the third voice," III.
Dark Earth and Summer. Edgar Bowers. QFR

Dark Eleanor and Henry sat at meat. The Rose of the World. John Masefield. PoRA
Dark eyed/ O woman of my dreams. Dance Figure. Ezra Pound. HeIP; MoAB; MoAmPo; TwAmPo
Dark-eyed Canaller. *Unknown. See* Dark-eyed Sailor, The.
Dark-eyed Gentleman, The. Thomas Hardy. MoAB; MoBrPo; UnPo; VLP
Dark-eyed Lad Columbus. Nancy Byrd Turner. SiSoSe
Dark-eyed Sailor, The. *Unknown.* FSW; ShS, *with music*
(Dark-eyed Canaller, *with music.*) OuSiCo
Dark eyes, wonderful, strange and dear they shone. The Half Door. "Seumas O'Sullivan." AnIV
Dark fell the night, the watch was set. Alfred the Harper. John Sterling. BeLS
Dark figures, lunged ahead, The. The Moral. Theodore Weiss. Prf
Dark Flows the River. Arthur S. Bourinot. CaP
Dark Forest, The. Edward Thomas. NoP
Dark-fringed eyelids slowly close, The. Tucking the Baby In. Curtis May. HBV-1
Dark Girl Dressed in Blue, The. *Unknown.* BeLS
Dark Girl's Rhyme, The. Dorothy Parker. InMe
Dark Glass, The. Dante Gabriel Rossetti. The House of Life, XXXIV. HBV-1
Dark gray clouds, The. Natalia M. Belting. PDV
Dark green truck on the cement platform, The. Train Window. Robert Finch. OBCV; PeCV
Dark-haired girl, who holds my thoughts entirely, The. Peggy Browne. Turlough O'Carolan, *tr. by* Austin Clarke. BIrV
Dark Hand, A. Itzik Manger, *tr. fr. Yiddish by* David G. Roskies *and* Hillel Schwartz. VWA
Dark Hills, The. E. A. Robinson. AP; CoBMV; FaFP; GoJo; HAP; LiTA; LiTM; MoAB; MoAmPo; NePA; NoAM; WeW; WHA
Dark hills. Night Fishing. Greg Kuzma. WOLT
Dark House, The. *Unknown.* NTCP
Dark house, by which once more I stand. In Memoriam A. H. H., VII. Tennyson. EBVV; FaBoEn; GTBS-P; HAP; InPK; LiTB; NOBE; NoP; OBNC; PeHV; PoEL-5; PPoe; SCV; SeCeV; UnPo
Dark in the Reich of the Blond. William Heyen. MAYP
Dark is kind and cozy, The. God's Dark. John Martin. PoLF
Dark is no more than a blanket, The. Wind. Hamish Brown. PoSH
Dark is shattered, The. New Things and Old. Sister Mary Madeleva. GoBC
Dark is soft, like fur. Rhyme for Night. Joan Aiken. DuDa
Dark is the face of Harriet. Harriet Tubman. Margaret Walker. PoNe
Dark is the forest and deep, and overhead. The Dark Forest. Edward Thomas. NoP
Dark is the house, the hall, the mirror silent. Garden Party. Mary Mills. NePoAm
Dark is the sapphire night. Half-Light. Jean Percival Waddell. CaP
Dark is the stair, and humid the old walls. The Belfry. Laurence Binyon. CH
Dark Lady, The. *Unknown.* OxBM
Dark Lord of Savaiki, The, *abr.* Alistair Campbell. OCNZ
Dark Man, The. Nora Hopper. HBV-1
Dark Morning, The. Thomas Merton. PoA
Dark Mountains. Milton Lockyer, *tr. fr. Yindjibarndi by* Frank Wordick. CBAP
Dark narrow stairway, A. Sleeping Beauty. Laurie Sheck. DFT
Dark Night, The. St. John of the Cross, *tr. fr. Spanish by* John Frederick Nims. WeW
(Obscure Night of the Soul, The, *tr. by* Arthur Symons.) AWP; OBMV
(Songs of the Soul in Rapture at Having Arrived at the Height of Perfection, Which Is Union with God by the Road of Spiritual Negation, *tr. by* Roy Campbell.) PAI
("Upon a darksome night," *tr. by* E. Allison Peers.) ErPo
(Upon a Gloomy Night, *tr. by* Roy Campbell.) BoLoP; OBVE; PeSA
("Upon an obscure night," *tr. by* Arthur Symons.) ILwL
Dark Palace, The. Alice Milligan. AnIV
Dark People. Kattie M. Cumbo. BOLo
Dark Phrases. Ntozake Shange. BlSi
Dark Pines under Water. Gwendolyn MacEwen. NOBC
Dark Planet, The. John Heath-Stubbs. OAEL-2
Dark plume fetch me from yon blasted yew, A. Return. Wordsworth. *Fr.* The River Duddon. HAP
Dark Prophesy: I Sing of Shine. Etheridge Knight. *See* I Sing of Shine.
Dark, puckered hole: a purple carnation. Sonnet: To the Asshole. Arthur Rimbaud *and* Paul Verlaine, *tr. by* J. Murat *and* W. Gunn. PeHV
Dark Rapture. "Æ." SeCePo
Dark red roses in a honeyed wind swinging. June. Nora Hopper. YeAr
Dark Road, The. Ethel Clifford. HBV-2
Dark Road Blues. *Unknown.* BluL
Dark Romance. Lucha Corpi, *tr. fr. Spanish by* Catherine Rodriguez-Nieto. WPOW
Dark Room. Fredrick Zydek. AMV-80
Dark Rosaleen. *Unknown, at. to* Hugh O'Donnell, *tr. fr. Irish by* James Clarence Mangan. ACP; AnIL; AnIV; AWP; BIrV; CH; EnRP; HBV-2; OBEV; OBVV; OnYI; OxBI; ViBoPo
Dark Rosaleen, *sels.* David McKee Wright. PoAu-1
"My love is the voice of a song," IX.
"On a shining silver morning long ago," I.
Dark Scent of Prayer, The. Rose Drachler. VWA
Dark Shadows. John Hall. NBP
Dark sky blowing over, A. The Elm's Home. William Heyen. MAYP
Dark Song. A. R. Ammons. MAT
Dark Song. Edith Sitwell. CMoP; FaBoTw; PBWP
Dark Stag, The. Isabella Valancy Crawford. NOBC; PeCV
Dark streets are deserted, The. After Midnight. Louis Simpson. NoAM
Dark suffocates the world; but such. An Autumn Park. David Gascoyne. MoPo
Dark swimmers, The. Larry Eigner. PoM
Dark Symphony. Melvin B. Tolson. AmNP; BALP; PoNe
Dark Testament. Pauli Murray. AmNP; BlSi
Dark theme keeps me here, A. In Evening Air. Theodore Roethke. NYBP; TAP
Dark, thinned, beside the wall of stone. In Time of Grief. Lizette Woodworth Reese. AA
Dark Thoughts Are My Companions. J. V. Cunningham. *See* Epigram: "Dark thoughts are my companions. I have wined."
Dark-time. The little ones like bees. Little Lullaby. Irving Feldman. NYBP
Dark to me is the earth. Dark to me are the heavens. The Desolate City. *Unknown, tr. by* Wilfrid Scawen Blunt. AWP; OBEV; OBVV
Dark was the day for Childe Rolandine the artist. Childe Rolandine. Stevie Smith. BrRo
Dark was the forest, dark was the mind. The Awakening. Conrad Aiken. The Kid, VII. MoVE
Dark Was the Night. *Unknown.* AmFP
Dark was the sky, and not one friendly star. Death. Philip Freneau. *Fr.* The House of Night. AP
Dark waters churn amongst us. C. G. Jung's "First Years." Thomas Kinsella. IPY
Dark Way Home, The: Survivors. Michael S. Harper. CNA
Dark wind batters the door, A. Rose Red to Snow White. Joan Colby. DFT
Dark Wings. James Stephens. PoA
Dark Wood. Ian Wedde. OCNZ
Dark World, A. E. J. Scovell. MoVE
Darkened bedroom, the double bed, The. Driving Wheel. Sherley Anne Williams. BlSi
Darkened farmhouse is asleep, The. Saving the Harvest. Geoffrey Lehmann. CBAP
Darkened hut outlined againt the sky, A. The Sunrise of the Poor. Robert Burns Wilson. AA
Darkened in the Soul. Napa, *tr. fr. Eskimo.* WTO
Darkened Windows. Ronald Bottrall. PoA
Darkening Hotel Room. Alfred Corn. MAYP
Darkening the azure roof of Nero's world. Domine Quo Vadis? Sir William Watson. WGRP
Darkling Chicken, The. Robert Peters. BXAP
Darkling Elves, The. Jack Prelutsky. RHPC
Darkling Thrush, The. Thomas Hardy. BrPo; CMoP; CoBMV; EBVV; EvOK; FaFP; FPL; HAP; HBMV; InPS; LiTB; LiTM; MasP; MoAB; MoBrPo; MoPo; NIP; NoAM; NOBE; NoP; OAEL-2; OAEP; OBEV; OBNC; OBVV; PAI; PBBP; PPP; RoGo; SeCeV; SoSe; TEP; TreFT; TrGrPo; UnPo; VLP; WaP
Darkly their glibs o'erhang. The Fate of King Dathi. Thomas Osborne Davis. OnYI
Darkmotherscream. Andrei Voznesensky, *tr. fr. Russian by* Robert Bly *and* Vera Dunham. NU
Darkness. Byron. EnRP; LiTB; OAEL-2; OAEP; PoEL-4; TEP
Darkness. Joseph Campbell. BIrV
Darkness, The. Lionel Johnson. BrPo
Darkness. Greg Kuzma. WOLT
Darkness and snow descend. Advent. W. H. Auden. *Fr.* For the Time Being; a Christmas Oratorio. SBVL
Darkness and death? Nay, Pioneer, for thee. Walt Whitman. Francis Howard Williams. AA
Darkness begins a/ retreat. After Christmas. Michael Richards. OBCP
Darkness came o'er like chaos; and the sun. The Hailstorm in June 1831. John Clare. VLP
Darkness comes out of the earth. Twilight. D. H. Lawrence. OBMV
Darkness comes to the shore. Darkness. Greg Kuzma. WOLT
Darkness crumbles away, The. Break of Day in the Trenches. Isaac Rosenberg. BrPo; FaBoMo; GTBS-P; MMA; MoBrPo; NIP; NOBE; NoP; OAEL-2; OBWP; PoA; SeCePo; ViBoPo; VWA; WaaP; WaP

Darkness dwells around Dunlathmon. Oithona; a Poem. James Macpherson. LAuP
Darkness encloses the concert hall. Choral Symphony Conductor. Carol Coates. CaP
Darkness falls like a wet sponge. The Picture of Little J. A. in a Prospect of Flowers. John Ashbery. ConAP; PPP
Darkness has called to darkness, and disgrace. As a Plane Tree by the Water. Robert Lowell. AP; CMoP; CoAP; CoBMV; CrMA; DTC; LiTM; MoAB; MoAmPo; NePA; NePoEA; NoAM; NOBA; OxBA; TrGrPo
Darkness has dawned in the east. Choruses from "Hellas," 3. Shelley. *Fr.* Hellas. EnRP
Darkness is closing around us, The. In Orbit. Henry Taylor. BXAP
Darkness is not dark, nor sunlight the light of the sun. Foal. Vernon Watkins. OxBTC
Darkness like a guillotine, The. Nightfall on Sedgemoor. Andrew Young. FaBoPP
Darkness Music. Muriel Rukeyser. BoWoP
Darkness presses all around, The. Government! Tuta Nihoniho, *tr. by* A. Armstrong. WTO
Darkness refuses the amnesia. Night Crackles. Elizabeth Woody. STE
Darkness reigned. Sacrifice. Nana Issaia, *tr. by* Helle Tzalopoulou Barnstone. BoWoP
Darkness rolls upward, The. Blue Symphony. John Gould Fletcher. TwAmPo
Darkness: the rain sluiced down; the mire was deep. The Redeemer. Siegfried Sassoon. MMA; WGRP
Darkness was a richness in the room, The. From a Childhood. Rainer Maria Rilke, *tr. by* C. F. MacIntyre. TrJP
Darkness wears off, and, dawning into light. The Figures on the Frieze. Alastair Reid. ErPo; NYBP
Darky Sunday School. *Unknown.* OxBoLi
Darlin'. *Unknown.* FSW
Darlin' Corey. *Unknown. See* Darling Cory.
Darling,/ why couldn't you have told me. End of the Affair. Curtis W. Casewit. AMV-80
Darling/ you are not at all. Surfaces. Peter Meinke. Str
Darling, at last my tiny lute. Ad Persephonen. Franklin P. Adams. InMe
Darling, at the beautician's you buy. A Valentine for a Lady. Lucillius, *tr. by* Dudley Fitts. OFD
Darling! Because My Blood Can Sing. E. E. Cummings. InvP; OxBA
Darling [*or* Darlin'] Cor[e]y. *Unknown.* AmFP; FSW; OuSiCo, *with music* (Darling Cora, *with music.*) TrAS
Darling, each morning a blooded rose. Corinna in Vendome. Pierre de Ronsard, *tr. by* Robert Mezey. BoLoP; ErPo
Darling here's my head. The Balance. Judith Johnson Sherwin. GP
Darling, I am growing old. Silver Threads among the Gold. Eben Eugene Rexford. BLSo; FaFP; FSW; PSoN; TreF
Darling I steal, and with hushed footsteps slow. Midnight at Baiae; a Dream Fragment of Imperial Rome. John Addington Symonds. PeHV
Darling, I won't be your hot love. Sulpicia, *tr. fr. Latin by* Aliki *and* Willis Barnstone. BoWoP
Darling, If You Only Knew. Edward Newman Horn. ErPo
Darling, my darling!—It was mother singing low. At Bedtime. Mariana Griswold Van Rensselaer. HBMV
Darling Nelly Gray. Benjamin Russel Hanby. BLSo, *with music;* FSW; PSoN, *with music;* TrAS, *with music;* TreFS
Darling of God[s] and Men, beneath the gliding stars. Lucretius, *tr. by* Basil Bunting. *Fr.* De Rerum Natura. NoAM; PoPl
Darling of the world is come, The. Robert Herrick. *Fr.* A Christmas Carol, Sung to the King in the Presence at White-Hall. PChr
Darling one was naked and, knowing my wish, The. Jewels. Baudelaire, *tr. by* David Paul. NAWM-2
Darling, Tell Me Yes. John Godfrey Saxe. HBV-1
Darling, you only, there is no duplicate. *Unknown, tr. by* Ezra Pound. *Fr.* Conversations in Courtship. CTC
Darned Mounseer, The. W. S. Gilbert. *Fr.* Ruddigore. NOBL
Dar's a lazy, sorta hazy. Sprin' Fevah. Ray Garfield Dandridge. BANP
Dart, The. *Unknown.* GBP
Dart, here's a man. The River Dart. *Unknown.* GBP
Dart of Izdabel prevails, The! 'twas dipped. The Dying Indian. Joseph Warton. NOEC
Dartmoor. Coventry Patmore. NBM
Dartmouth Winter-Song. Richard Hovey. AA
Darwin and Mendel laid on man the chains. Progress. David McCord. ImOP
Darwin on Species. *Unknown.* FaBoUs
Darwinism in the Kitchen. *Unknown.* FiBHP
Darwinity. Herman C. Merivale. InMe; NA
Das Kapital. Amiri Baraka. PoM
Das Liebesleben. Thom Gunn. ErPo
Das Schloss. Lincoln Kirstein. NoAM
Dash back that ocean with a pier. Tennyson. *Fr.* Mechanophilus. FaBoCo
Dash for the Colors, The. Frederick G. Webb. BeLS
Dashing thro' [*or* through] the snow in a one-horse open sleigh. Jingle Bells [*or* The One Horse Open Sleigh]. James S. Pierpont. BLSo; FaFP; FSW; PSoN; TreF; YaD
Dasius, chucker-out/ at the Turkish Baths. Martial, *tr. fr. Latin by* Peter Porter. OBVE
Dat Sunshine Special comin' around de bend. C. C. Rider. *Unknown.* AS
Data, data, data. Transfigured Night. Ralph Gustafson. MoCV
Dated Valmont 10-16/ october 1849. Eugene Delacroix Says. Edward Dorn. NoAM
Dates. *Unknown, tr. fr. Arabic by* E. Powys Mathers. *Fr.* The Thousand and One Nights. AWP; FaPON
Dates on bridges, The. History and Abstraction. Thomas Lux. AmPA
Datur Hora Quieti. Robert Stephen Hawker. GoBC
Datur Hora Quieti. Sir Walter Scott. GTBS; GTBS-P
Dauber, *sels.* John Masefield.
"All through the windless night the clipper rolled," VI. CMoP
Clipper Loitered South, The, *fr.* IV. EtS
Rounding the Horn, *fr.* VI. EtS; MoAB; MoBrPo; WHA
Daufuskie. Mari Evans. BlSi
Daughter. Kimiko Hahn. BrSi
Daughter. Ellen Bryant Voigt. AMV-80
Daughter at Evening, The. Robert Nathan. HBMV
"Daughter, how the door is creaking." Evening Prayer. Arthur Fitger, *tr. by* Jethro Bithell. AWP
Daughter of Admetus, A. T. Sturge Moore. FaBoTw
Daughter of Debate, The. Elizabeth I, Queen of England. *See* Doubt of Future Foes, The.
Daughter of Egypt, veil thine eyes! Song. Bayard Taylor. AA
Daughter of her whose face, and lofty name. Sonnets to Miranda, I. Sir William Watson. HBV-1
Daughter of Jairus, The, *sels.* Marina Tsvetayeva, *tr. fr. Russian by* Paul Schmidt. BoWoP
"And now the riverbank. For the last time," VII.
"I catch the movement of his lips," V.
"Our last bridge," VIII.
"Past factory workshops, empty," IX.
"Rain. A heavy mane," XII.
"To lose it all at once," XI.
Daughter of Jove, relentless power. Hymn to Adversity. Thomas Gray. EnRP; GTBS; GTBS-P; OBEC
Daughter of Mendoza, The. Mirabeau B. Lamar. AA; BPAW; HBV-1
Daughter of Night, chaotic Queen! Ode to the German Drama. *Unknown.* NOEC
Daughter of the ancient Eve. The After Woman. Francis Thompson. ISi
Daughter of the Regiment, The. Clinton Scollard. PAH
Daughter of th'Italian heaven! Corinne at the Capitol. Felicia Dorothea Hemans. BrRo
Daughter, take this amulet. Mwana Kupona Msham, *tr. fr. Swahili by* J. W. Allen, *ad. by* Deirdre Lashgari. *Fr.* Poem to Her Daughter. WPOW
Daughter, this small stiletto which I found. The Gift. Ann Darr. PAI
"Daughter, thou art come to die." A Very Old Song. "William Laird." HBV-1
Daughter to that good Earl, once President. To the Lady Margaret Ley [*or* Sonnet]. Milton. GTBS; GTBS-P; OBEV; OBS
Daughters. Astra. BrRo
Daughters, daughters, do ye grieve? Thammuz. William Vaughn Moody. AP
Daughters, in the wind's boisterous roughing. Vernal Equinox. Ruth Stone. MoAmPo
Daughters of Blum, The. Charles Wright. CoAP
Daughters of Jove, whose voice is melody. Hymn to Selene. *Unknown, tr. by* Shelley. *Fr.* Homeric Hymns. AWP
Daughters of the Horseleech, The. Stanley Kunitz. CrMA; TW
Daughters of the Seraphim led round their sunny flocks, The. The Book of Thel. Blake. EnRP; LAuP; NoP; OAEL-2; OBNC; PoEL-4; TEP
Daughters of Time, the hypocritic Days. Days. Emerson. AA; AmPP; AP; HAP; HeIP; LiTA; NOBA; NoP; OBVV; OxBA; PoEL-4; SeCeV; TAP; TreFT; TrGrPo; ViBoPo; WHA
Daughters of War. Isaac Rosenberg. BrPo
Daughter's Rebellion, The. Francis Hopkinson. PAH
Daughters Will You Marry? *Unknown.* FSW
Dauncing (bright lady) then began to be. *See* Dancing, bright lady . . .
D'Avalos' Prayer. John Masefield. MOS; TrPWD
Davening. Rochelle Ratner. VWA
Daventry Wonder, The. "Agricola." NOEC
David. Earle Birney. CaP; NOBC
David. Mary Carolyn Davies. HBMV
David. Walker Gibson. CrMA; NePoAm
David. Eli Mandel. PeCV

David and Bethsabe, *sels.* George Peele.
Bethsabe's Song, *fr.* sc. i. EnRePo; NOBE; OBSC; OxBoLi; SeCeV
(Bethsabe Bathing.) EIL; LoBV; TrGrPo
(Hot Sun, Cool Fire.) NoP
("Hot Sun[ne], cool[e] fire, tempered with sweet air[e].") GBL; PoEL-2; TEP
"Come, gentle Zephyr, tricked with those perfumes," *fr.* sc. i. ViBoPo
"Now comes my lover tripping like the roe," *fr.* sc. i. ViBoPo
"Now for the crown and throne of Israel," *fr.* sc. xii. ViBoPo
David and Goliath. Bible, *O.T.* First Samuel, XVI, XVII: 1-51. TreFS
David and Goliath. Nathaniel Crouch. OxBChV
David and I that summer cut trails on the Survey. David. Earle Birney. CaP; NOBC
David and Jonathan. Abraham Cowley. *Fr.* Davideis, II. PeHV
David and Solomon. James Ball Naylor. *See* King David and King Solomon.
David Drummond's destinie. The Coble o Cargill. *Unknown.* ESPB
David Garrick. Goldsmith. *Fr.* Retaliation. NOEC; OBEC; SeCeV
("Here lies David Garrick, describe him who can.") DBV
David Garrick, the Actor, to Sir John Hill. David Garrick. *See* On Sir John Hill, M.D., Playwright.
David Homindae. Marjorie Stamm Rosenfeld. AMV-80
David Hume ate a swinging great dinner. On the Author of the *Treatise of Human Nature.* James Hay Beattie. FaBoCo
David in April. Betty Booker. PPJ
David Jazz, The. Edwin Meade Robinson. HBMV
David sang to his hooknosed harp. King David. Stephen Vincent Benét. HBMV
David the king was grieved and moved. David's Lamentation. William Billings. AmFP; TrAS
David was a shepherd lad, beautiful as you. David. Mary Carolyn Davies. HBMV
David was a Young Blood, David was a striplin'. The David Jazz. Edwin Meade Robinson. HBMV
Davideis, *sels.* Abraham Cowley.
Annunciation, The, *fr.* II. OxBoCh
Creation, The, *fr.* I. OBS
David and Jonathan, *fr.* II. PeHV
Hell, *fr.* I. OxBoCh
Power of Numbers, The, *fr.* I. OBS
Supplication, A, *fr.* III. GTBS; GTBS-P
"With sober pace an heav'enly Maid walks in," *fr.* III. SeCV-1
David's Lament. Bible, *O.T.* Second Samuel, I: 19-27. ChTr; FF; TrGrPo; TrJP
("Beauty of Israel is slaine upon thy high places, The.") OBVE; OBWP
(David's Lament for Saul and Jonathan.) AWP
(How Are the Mighty Fallen.) WaaP
David's Lament for Jonathan. Peter Abelard, *tr. fr. Latin by* Helen Waddell. NAWM-1; PeHV
David's Lament for Saul and Jonathan. Bible, *O.T.* *See* David's Lament.
David's Lamentation. William Billings. AmFP; TrAS, *with music*
Davis Matlock. Edgar Lee Masters. *Fr.* Spoon River Anthology. LiTA: LiTM
Davy and the Goblin, *sels.* Charles Edward Carryl.
My Recollectest Thoughts, *fr. ch.* 7. HBV-2; HBVY; NA
Robinson Crusoe, *fr. ch.* 11. AA; HBV-2; HBVY; TreFT
(Robinson Crusoe's Story.) BeLS; FiBHP; InMe; PoRA
Walloping Window-Blind, The, *fr. ch.* 8. InMe: MoShBr; NA; OBCA; TreFS; WhC
(Capital Ship, A.) FSW
(Nautical Ballad, A.) FaPON; HBV-2; OBAL
Davy Crockett in his woodman dress. Lament for the Alamo. Arthur Guiterman. AmFN
Davy Davy Dumpling. *Unknown.* OxNR
Dawlish Fair. Keats. PoPle
Dawn. Gordon Bottomley. MoBrPo
Dawn. Louis Dudek. PeCV
Dawn. Paul Laurence Dunbar. AmNP; PoLF; PoNe
Dawn. John Ford. *See* Fly Hence, Shadows.
Dawn. Federico García Lorca, *tr. fr. Spanish by* William B. Logan. SOTW
Dawn. George B. Logan, Jr. HBV-1
Dawn. *Malay Oral Tradition, tr. by* R. J. Wilkinson. WTO
Dawn. John Masefield. BrPo
Dawn. Constance Ortmayer. SaC
Dawn. Alejandra Pizarnik, *tr. fr. Spanish by* Alina Rivero. VWA
Dawn. Rachel, *tr. fr. Hebrew by* A. M. Klein. TrJP
Dawn. Arthur Rimbaud, *tr. fr. French by* Enid Rhodes Peschal. SOTW
Dawn. Frederick George Scott. CaP; PoPl
Dawn. Frank Dempster Sherman. TRV
Dawn. David Shevin. VWA
Dawn ("By a bank as I lay"). *Unknown.* OBSC
("By a bank as I lay.") PBBP
Dawn ("Thou enemy of love"). *Unknown, tr. fr. Greek by* Louis Untermeyer. UnTE
Dawn. William Carlos Williams. MoAB; MoAmPo; PoPl
Dawn, The. W. B. Yeats. MoVE
Dawn/ rose like a hand at the edge of dark. Crazy Horse: The Last Morning. Lance Henson. VoR
Dawn: a good wind blows from the sea. Semantic. Robert Conquest. TEP
Dawn amid Scotch Firs. "Fiona Macleod." SyP
Dawn—and a magical stillness: on earth, quiescence profound. Dawn on the Headland. Sir William Watson. HBV-1
Dawn and Dark. Norman Gale. HBV-1
Dawn: and foot on the cold stair treading. Aubade for Hope. Robert Penn Warren. MoAmPo
Dawn; and the jew's-harp's sawing seesaw song. Pilots, Man Your Planes. Randall Jarrell. MoAB; MoAmPo
Dawn—and the mist across the silent lane. A Hillside Farmer. John Farrar. HBMV
Dawn-Angels. Agnes Mary Frances Robinson. HBV-1
Dawn Boy's Song. *Unknown, tr. fr. Navaho Indian by* Washington Matthews. FaBV
Dawn breaking as I woke. Alba. Derek Walcott. GoJo; PCP
Dawn breeze, The. Sand Paintings. Alice Corbin. BPAW
Dawn came wild with rain, and all day long, The. Moonlight on Lake Sydenham. Wilson MacDonald. CaP
Dawn comes cold, The: the haystack smokes. Dawn. John Masefield. BrPo
Dawn cried out: the brutal voice of a bird. In All These Acts. William Everson. NoP
Dawn drives the dreams away, yet some abide. Omnia Somnia. Rosamund Marriott Watson. HBV-1
Dawn drizzle ended dampness steams from. Anglosaxon Street. Earle Birney. NOBC
Dawn. First light tearing. Clouds. Philip Levine. LCAP
Dawn from the foretop! Dawn from the barrel! The Ice-Floes. E. J. Pratt. CaP
Dawn has flashed up the startled skies. Forgotten Dead, I Salute You. Muriel Stuart. SUMH
Dawn Has Yet to Ripple In. Melville Cane. MoAmPo
Dawn Hippo. Sydney Clouts. PeSA
Dawn Horse, A. William Harmon. FYAP
Dawn in Britain, The, *sels.* C. M. Doughty.
Bladyn's Song of Cloten. PoEL-5
Gauls Sacrifice, The. FaBoTw
Hymn to the Sun. FaBoTw
Roman Officer Writes, A. FaBoTw
Dawn in Inishtrahull. D. J. O'Sullivan. OnYI
Dawn in January. Lance Henson. CDW
Dawn in New York comes. Dawn. Federico García Lorca, *tr. by* William B. Logan. SOTW
Dawn in the Heart of Africa. Patrice Emery Lumumba. PBA; TTY
Dawn is dense with twitter. Wings at Dawn. Joseph Auslander. HBMV
Dawn is here. Now I must go. Leaving. "Michael Lewis." *Fr.* Cherry Blossoms. UnTE
Dawn is, in essence, sinister as fire. Dew. Jennifer Maiden. CBAP
Dawn is lonely for the sun, The. Chanson de Rosemonde. Richard Hovey. HBV-1
Dawn is not distant, The. Longfellow. *Fr.* Tales of a Wayside Inn: The Saga of King Olaf. TRV
Dawn is smiling on the dew that covers, The. The Genesis of Butterflies. Victor Hugo, *tr. by* Andrew Lang. AWP
Dawn of a bright June morning. Mass of Love. *Unknown, tr. by* Anna Pursche. PoPl
Dawn of a pleasant morning in May. Lee to the Rear. John Randolph Thompson. PAH
Dawn of Day. William Browne. *Fr.* The Shepherd's Pipe. EIL
Dawn of Day, The. Keaulumoku, *tr. fr. Hawaiian by* M. W. Beckwith. *Fr.* The Kumulipo; a Creation Chant. WTO
Dawn of Jaffa Pigeons, A. Eli Bachar, *tr. fr. Hebrew by* Jeremy Garber. VWA
Dawn of Love, The. Henrietta Cordelia Ray. BlSi
Dawn of the Space Age. John Ciardi. OBAL
Dawn of Womanhood. Harold Monro. HBV-1
Dawn on Mid-Ocean. John Hall Wheelock. EtS
Dawn on the East Coast. Alun Lewis. OBWP
Dawn on the Headland. Sir William Watson. HBV-1
Dawn on the Lievre, The. Archibald Lampman. CaP
Dawn on the Night-Journey. Dante Gabriel Rossetti. NCEP
Dawn peered through the pines as we dashed at the ford. Riding with Kilpatrick. Clinton Scollard. PAH
Dawn shakes the candle, shoots a flame. May It Be. Boris Pasternak, *tr. by* C. M. Bowra. TrJP
Dawn Song—St. Patrick's Day. Violet Alleyn Storey. YeAr

Dawn songs in the dews of young orange trees. In England's Green & (a Garland and a Clyster). Jonathan Williams. CoPo
Dawn that cares for nobody. February. W. S. Merwin. NNaP
Dawn the sun steadily rose. The One Who Is Within. Nia Francisco. STE
Dawn turned on her purple pillow. A December Day. Sara Teasdale. YeAr
Dawn Wail for the Dead. Kath Walker. CBAP
Dawn Walk. Edward Hirsch. MAYP
Dawn was apple-green, The. Green. D. H. Lawrence. ELU; GBL; MoBrPo; PoA
Dawndrizzle ended dampness steams from. Anglosaxon Street. Earle Birney. CABA; HeIP
Dawne to darke. Lines for a Sundial. Thomas Herbert Warren. OBVV
Dawning, The. George Herbert. AnAnS-1
Dawning, The. Henry Vaughan. MePo; NOCV; OxBoCh; TrPWP, *abr.*
Dawning Fair, Morning Wonderful, *with music. Unknown.* AH
Dawning o' the Year, The. Mary Elizabeth McGrath Blake. AA
Dawning of morn, the daylight's sinking, The. Thee, Thee, Only Thee. Thomas Moore. GBL; OBNC
Dawning of the Day, The. James Clarence Mangan. GoBC
Dawning of the Day, The. *Unknown, tr. fr. Modern Irish by* Edward Walsh. OnYI
Dawning sun; The/ Shines down on the dunes. Siilenboor. *Mongol Oral Tradition, tr. by* C. R. Bawden. WTO
Dawn's Awake, The! Otto Leland Bohanan. BANP
Dawns I Have Seen. Ivor Gurney. FaBoPP
Dawn's precise pronouncement waits, The. The Edge of Day. Laurie Lee. NYBP
Day, The. George M. Brady. NeIP
Day, The. Witter Bynner. PGD
Day, The. Roy Fuller. OxBTC
Day, The. John Glassco. MoCV
Day, The/ is ready to close. Saturday Night in the Village. Giacomo Leopardi, *tr. by* Robert Lowell. OBVE
Day, a night, an hour of sweet content, A. Content. Thomas Campion. OBSC
Day; a Pastoral. John Cunningham. OBEC
(Morning.) NOEC
Day after Day. Rabindranath Tagore. *Fr.* Gitanjali. OBMV
Day after day/ The muffled shuttling of Her blood. Our Lady's Labor. John Duffy. ISi
Day after day after day. The Prison Guard [*or* Poems from Prison, 1]. J. J. Maloney. FAZ; LFAC
Day after day, alone on a hill. The Fool on the Hill. John Lennon *and* Paul McCartney. PPoe
Day after day it goes on. How Much Longer? Robert Mezey. OBWP
Day after day, O lord of my life, shall I stand before thee face to face? Day after Day. Rabindranath Tagore. *Fr.* Gitanjali. OBMV
Day after day they caught rain in the smoke-hole. Two Animals, One Flood. Diane Glancy. STE
Day after decapitation, The. The Head. Padraic Fallon. CIP
Day after Sunday, The. Phyllis McGinley. MoAmPo; OBSV; UnPo
Day after Trinity, The. Richard Oyama. BrSi
Day after you left, The. Disintegration. Richard Shelton. DFF
Day agone, as I rode sullenly, A. Dante, *tr. by* Dante Gabriel Rossetti. La Vita Nuova, IV. AWP
Day and Night. Lewis Alexander. CDC
Day and night are never weary. Greek Epigram. Ezra Pound. MoAB; MoAmPo
Day and Night Handball. Stephen Dunn. AmPA; LiSp
Day and night I wander widely through the wilderness of thought. God. Gamaliel Bradford. TRV; WGRP
Day and Night My Thoughts Incline. Richard Henry Stoddard. *See* Jar, The.
Day and night she dances. Shulamit in Her Dreams. Marcia Falk. VWA
Day and then a week passed by, A. The Cardinal Bird. William Davis Gallagher. AA
Day arrives of the autumn fair, The. A Sheep Fair. Thomas Hardy. Prf
Day at the beach. Littoral. Hjalmar Flax, *tr. by* Julio Marzán. InW
Day at the Races, A. Louis Phillips. PH
Day Aviva Came to Paris, The. Irving Layton. MoCV
Day before April, The. Mary Carolyn Davies. FaPON; SUS
Day before Christmas. Marchette Chute. NTCP
Day before Christmas, The. Raymond Souster. PeCV
Day before the houses sank beneath the waves, The. The Day the Houses Sank. Constance Urdang. MAT
Day Begins, A. Denise Levertov. DFF; NaP
Day Begins at Governor's Square Mall. Leon Stokesbury. MAYP
Day begins to droop, The. Winter Nightfall. Robert Bridges. MoAB; MoBrPo; OBEV
Day bloated with statistics, A. A quarter of the States. Vincent O'Sullivan. Brother Jonathan, Brother Kafka, 35. OCNZ
Day breaks, clear and still, The. Early. Bruce Bennett. WOLT
Day breaks on England down the Kentish hills. The Dying Patriot. James Elroy Flecker. HBMV; ViBoPo
Day breaks, your mind aches, The. For No One. John Lennon *and* Paul McCartney. WTO
Day by Day. A. G. Fisher. STF
Day by Day. Julia Harris May. BLRP
Day by Day. Stephen F. Winward. TRV
Day by day I float my paper boats/ one by one down the running stream. Paper Boats. Rabindranath Tagore. FaPON
Day by day, oh Master, make me. Day by Day. A. G. Fisher. STF
Day by Day the Manna Fell. Josiah Conder. TrCP; VLP
Day by day the Organ-Builder in his lonely chamber wrought. The Legend of the Organ-Builder. Julia C. R. Dorr. BeLS; BLPA; FaBoBe
"Day by day," the promise reads. Day by Day. Stephen F. Winward. TRV
Day Concludes Burning, The. Desmond O'Grady. CIP
Day creeps down. The moon is creeping up. The Man on the Dump. Wallace Stevens. HAP
Day Dawn of the Heart. *Unknown.* PGD
Day dawns with scent of must and rain, The. Mirror in February. Thomas Kinsella. CIP; GTBS-P; NoAM
Day Death Comes, The. Faiz Ahmed Faiz, *tr. fr. Pakistani by* Naomi Lazard. AMV-81
Day dies beautiful, The. Made to See. John Nist. AMV-80
Day does not come with violence. Deer in Aspens. Kay DeBard Hall. GoYe
Day draws to an end, The. The Author's Apology. T. Carmi, *tr. by* Marcia Falk. VWA
Day Dream. *See* Daydream.
Day Duke Raised, The. Quincy Troupe. LTB
Day Flight. Jack Davis. CBAP
Day for Anne Frank, A. C. K. Williams. GeTw
Day goes down red darkling, The. Desolate. Gerald Massey. EBVV
Day grows hot, and darts his rays, The. Noon Quatrains. Charles Cotton. LoBV
Day had awakened all things that be. Daybreak. Shelley. GN
Day had fled, the moon arose, The. George Gordon McCrae. *Fr.* Mamba the Bright-eyed. PoAu-1
Day had lapsed to twilight, The. Peter Titheradge. Teatime Variations: After A. E. Housman. FaBoPa
Day has barred her windows close, and gangs wi' quiet feet. East Coast Lullaby. Lady Anne Lindsay. EtS
Day has her star, as well as Night. The Two Stars. W. H. Davies. MoBrPo
Day he first spoke to me of love, The. When He Spoke to Me of Love. M. A. Mokhomo, *tr. by* Dan Kunene *and* Jack Cope. PeSA
Day in a Long Hot Summer, A. Yuri Kageyama. BrSi
Day in Autumn, A. R. S. Thomas. BoNaP
Day in, day out. Corner Boys. Bryan MacMahon. OnYI
Day in Ireland, A. *Unknown, tr. fr. Irish by* Michael Cavanagh. AnIV
Day in June, A. James Russell Lowell. *See* June ("What is so rare as a day in June").
Day in melting purple dying. Song of Egla. Maria Gowen Brooks. AA
Day in My Union Suit, A. Michael Pettit. MAYP
Day in the City, A. L. E. Sissman. NYBP
Day in the Life, A. John Lennon *and* Paul McCartney. PPoe
Day in the Life, A. Stef Pixner. BrRo
Day is a Negro, The. Day and Night. Lewis Alexander. CDC
Day is again begun. Unrest. Richard Watson Dixon. OBNC
Day is broke, The! Melpomene, begone. Iter Boreale. Robert Wild. APAS
Day is cold, and dark, and dreary, The. The Rainy Day. Longfellow. AWP; FPL; HBV-2; PoLF; PoPl; TreFT
Day is colorless like Swiss characters in a novel, The. For Guillaume Apollinaire. William Meredith. CoAP
Day Is Coming, The, *parody.* Sir Walter Besant. CenHV
Day Is Coming, The. William Morris. OAEP; WGRP
Day is curled about again [*or* agen], The. An Anniversary on the Hymeneals of My Noble Kinsman, Thomas Stanley, Esquire. Richard Lovelace. CaPo; LoBV
Day is dark, The. Sehnsucht; or, What You Will. "Corinna." FiBHP; InMe
Day is dark and dreary, The. If. Franklin P. Adams. OBAL
Day Is Done, The, *parody.* Phoebe Cary. BXAP; OBAL
Day Is Done, The. Longfellow. BLPA; FaBoBe; FaFP; FPL; HBV-2; NOBA; OHFP; OxBA; PoPl; PoRA; TreF; TrGrPo
Day is done, The. Evening Hymn. Elizabeth Madox Roberts. TiPo
Day is done, gone the sun. God Is Nigh. *Unknown.* TRV
Day is done, the winter sun, The. At Castle Wood. Emily Brontë. ViBoPo
Day is drawing to its fall, A. First Sight of Her and After. Thomas Hardy. PoEL-5

Day Is Dying in the West. Mary A. Lathbury, *also at. to* William F. Sherwin. AH, *with music;* TreFT; TRV; WGRP
Day is ended, The. Ere I sink to sleep. All's Well. Harriet McEwen Kimball. AA
Day Is Gone, The. Keats. EnRP
Day is late enough you could stand, The. American Ash. Stanley Plumly. GeTw
Day is ours together, The. Full Moon. Galway Kinnell. NePoAm-2
Day is over, The. Evening Twilight. Baudelaire, *tr. by* Arthur Symons. SyP
Day is over, Mother, see, The. Compline. Patrick F. Kirby. GoBC
Day is past and gone, The. Evening Shade. John Leland. AH; AmFP
Day is past, the sun is set, The. Evening. Thomas Miller. OxBChV
Day is quenched, and the sun is fled, The. A Song of Doubt. Josiah Gilbert Holland. WGRP
Day is the children's friend. The Prejudice against the Past. Wallace Stevens. LiTM
Day is tired with idleness and awe, The. Solstice. Charles Weekes. OnYI
Day is turning ghost, The. A Commonplace Day. Thomas Hardy. PoPle
Day is warm, The. June. Aileen Fisher. PDV
Day Lady Died, The. Frank O'Hara. CAPP; HoAn; NeAP; NoAM; NOBA; NoP; NYP; PAI; PoM; SOTW
Day later than he said in the letter, A. The Light Passages. Debora Greger. MAYP
Day like blank paper, The. The Six Hundred Thousand Letters. Harvey Shapiro. VWA
Day, like our souls, is fiercely dark. Battle Song. Ebenezer Elliott. OBRV
Day of anger after the holy night, The. News from a Pacified Area. James K. Baxter. OxBC
Day of Atonement. Jack Myers. VWA
Day of Battle, The. A. E. Housman. A Shropshire Lad, LVI. OHIP; WaaP
Day of Days, The. William Morris. VLP
Day of Denial, The. Jones Very. NOBA
Day of Doom, The. Michael Wigglesworth. SCAP
"Then to the bar, all they drew near," *sel.* OBCA
Day of glory! Welcome day! The Fourth of July. John Pierpont. PAH; PAL; YeAr
Day of God! Thou Blessed Day, *with music.* Hannah Flagg Gould. AH
Day of hunting done. Twilight in California. Philip Dow. AmPA
Day of Inverlochy, The. Iain Lom, *tr. fr. Gaelic.* GoTS
Day of Judgement [*or* Judgment], The. Swift. BIrV; FaBoEn; FaBoRV; InPK; NOBE; NOEC; OAEL-1; OBSV; PPP; TW
(On the World.) AnIV
Day of Judgement [*or* Judgment], The. Isaac Watts. HAP; LoBV; NOBE; NOEC; NoP; OBEC; OBEV; SeCePo
Day of Judgement, The. Edward Young. OxBoCh
Day of Judgment, The. Dugald Buchanan, *tr. fr. Gaelic.* GoTS
Day of Judgment, The. Thomas of Celano. *See* Dies Irae.
Day of Love, A. Dante Gabriel Rossetti. The House of Life, XVI. VLP
Day of my double birth, if such the year. John Thelwall. *Fr.* Lines Written at Bridgewater, 27 July 1797. NOEC
Day of my life! Where can she get! Good-Night, Babette! Austin Dobson. HBV-1; OBVV
Day of Notes, A. J. Charles Green. LFAC
Day of Renewal. Louis MacNeice. NAs
Day of Resurrection, The. St. John of Damascus, *tr. fr. Greek by* John Mason Neale. TrCP
(Resurrection, The.) PGD
Day of sunny face and temper, A. Big Bessie Throws Her Son into the Street. Gwendolyn Brooks. VGW
Day of tender memory, A. Memorial Day. Emma A. Lent. WBLP
Day of the Crucifixion, The. "Hugh MacDiarmid." PV
Day of the fête, The—and what a day for it. School Cadets. Anne Elder. CBAP
Day of the king most righteous. The Day of Wrath. St. Columcille, *tr. by* Helen Waddell. OxBI
Day of the Night, The. James Scully. LTB
Day of the Pancreas, The. David McFadden. NeAC
Day of the Parade. Alan Chong Lau. BrSi
Day of These Days. Laurie Lee. BoNaP; MoVE
Day of Wrath, The. St. Columcille, *tr. fr. Latin by* Helen Waddell. OxBI
Day of wrath, that day of burning. Dies Irae. Thomas of Celano, *tr. by* Abraham Coles. AA; HBV-2
Day on Kind Continent. Robert David Cohen. NYBP
Day Returns, The. Burns. HBV-1
Day Returns, The. Robert Louis Stevenson. TRV
Day she visited the dissecting room, The. Two Views of a Cadaver Room. Sylvia Plath. CMoP; GoYe; NMP
Day spread her lap and bade me choose. The Little Searcher. Donna Bowen. AMV-80
Day that ends the world will be the one, The. Like a Whisper. Ethan Ayer. GoYe
Day That I Have Loved. Rupert Brooke. FPL; PoLF
Day that I was christened, The. Godmother. Dorothy Parker. PoRA
Day that my dear came to us, The. Early Mornings. *Unknown, tr. by* Louis Untermeyer. AS
Day the Air Was on Fire, The. Reg Saner. NPAW
Day the Beatles Lost One to the Flesh-eating Horse, The. Dave Kelly. FAZ
Day the fat woman, The. The Beach in August. Weldon Kees. VGW
Day the Houses Sank, The. Constance Urdang. MAT
Day the Tide, The. Philip Booth. CoAP
Day the T.V. Broke, The. Gerald Jonas. QQQ
Day, The—the Way. John Oxenham. TRV
Day the wind is white shall I be free, The. Apostasy. Mary Mills. NePoAm
Day the wind was hardly, A. Letter VI. W. S. Graham. ChMP; FaBoMo
Day They Busted the Grateful Dead, The. Richard Brautigan. MAT
Day Thou Gavest, Lord, Is Ended, The. John Ellerton. EBVV; FaPoR
Day time failed began as usual, The. Burial of a Fisherman in Hydra. Grace Schulman. BoWoP
Day transports fallen snows, muddied, mildewed, ruined, The. Spring over the City. Anne Hébert, *tr. by* Kathleen Weaver. PBWP
Day turns heavily on its axis, The. Encirclement. Mieczyslaw Jastrun, *tr. by* Benjamin Sher. AMV-81
Day Twenty-three. Victor Coleman. NOBC
Day was here when it was his to know, The. The New Tenants. E. A. Robinson. NoAM
Day was so bright, The. Miroslav Holub, *tr. by* George Theines *and* Ian Milner. *Fr.* A Dog in the Quarry. BoAnP; GDP
Day was when I did not keep myself in readiness, The. Rabindranath Tagore. *Fr.* Gitanjali. ILwL
Day when Charmus ran with five, The. A Mighty Runner. E. A. Robinson. LiSp; OBAL
Day when I can not, A. Poem. James Lewisohn. LFAC
Day when it will not matter, The. The Day. John Glassco. MoCV
Day will come when I will, The. A Farewell to a Southern Melody. Huang O, *tr. by* Kenneth Rexroth *and* Ling Chung. BoWoP
Day will return with a fresher boon. A Song of Faith. Josiah Gilbert Holland. WGRP
Day will rise and the sun from eastward. Song. George Campbell Hay. OxBS
Day will soon be gone, The. Fujiwara no Michinobu, *tr. by* Curtis Hidden Page. *Fr.* Hyaku-Nin-Isshu. AWP
Day with sky so wide, A. The Motion of the Earth. Norman Nicholson. ImOP
Day with the Foreign Legion, A. Reed Whittemore. CoAP; ConAP; LiTM; NePoEA
Day you appeared I began to speak, The. To Your Question. Duane Niatum. CDW
Day You Are Born, The. Cathy Song. BrSi
Day You Are Reading This, The. William Stafford. PoA
Day you came, The. Breasts. Tess Gallagher. AmPA
Day you came naked to Paris, The. The Day Aviva Came to Paris. Irving Layton. MoCV
Day, you have bruised and beaten me. The New Moon. Sara Teasdale. MOON
Day you shot yourself, The. On a Friend's Suicide. Michael Yots. AMV-81
Dayak Man Making Fishtrap. Carol Rubenstein. WOLT
Daybreak. Frances Cornford. FM
Daybreak. John Donne. *See* Break of Day. ("Stay, O sweet")
Daybreak. Galway Kinnell. LCAP
Daybreak. Longfellow. FPL; HBV-2; PoLF; TreFT
Daybreak. Bert Meyers. EAS
Daybreak. Phillip Yellowhawk Minthorn. STE
Daybreak. Frank Lamont Phillips. CNA
Daybreak. Carl Sandburg. PDV
Daybreak. Shelley. GN
Daybreak. Samuel F. Smith. *See* Morning Light Is Breaking, The.
Daybreak. Stephen Spender. BoLoP; DFF
Daybreak comes first. Daybreak. Carl Sandburg. PDV
Daybreak in Alabama. Langston Hughes. AmFN; CNA
Daybreak on a Pennsylvania Highway. John Daunt. AMV-80
Daybreak: the household slept. Father and Child. Gwen Harwood. CBAP; WPE
Daybreak upon the hills! Peace. Adeline D. T. Whitney. PAH
Day-Breakers, The. Arna Bontemps. AmNP; CDC; IDB; PoBA; PoNe
Day Dream, A. Emily Brontë. VLP
Day-Dream, The. Dante Gabriel Rossetti. SyP
Daydream. A. S. J. Tessimond. SeCePo
Day-Dreamer. *Unknown, ad. fr. German by* Louis Untermeyer. TiPo
Daydreamers. Norma L. Davis. PoAu-2

Day Dreams, or Ten Years Old. Margaret Johnson. BLPA
Dayley Island. Frederick Seidel. CoPo
Daylight Saving Time. Phyllis McGinley. RHPC
Daylights. Rosanna Warren. MAYP
Day-long cold hard rain drove, The. Surviving. James Welch. CDW; STE
Daylong this tomcat lies stretched flat. Esther's Tomcat. Ted Hughes. OxBC; PCat
Days. Karle Wilson Baker. TiPo
Days, The. Paul Blocklyn. AMV-80
Days. Emerson. AA; AmPP; AP; HAP; HeIP; LiTA; NOBA; NoP; OBVV; OxBA; PoEL-4; SeCeV; TAP; TreFT; TrGrPo; ViBoPo; WHA
Days, The. Theodosia Garrison. HBMV
Days. Philip Larkin. EBEV; FaBoMo; OxBC
Days after daffodils were up. Easter Snowfall. Harry Behn. TiPo
Days Ago. Dianne Hai-Jew. BrSi
Days and Nights. T. Sturge Moore. HBMV
Days are clear, The. Stay, June, Stay! Christina Rossetti. *Fr.* Sing-Song. TiPo; YeAr
Days are cold, the nights are long, The. The Cottager to Her Infant. Dorothy Wordsworth. CH; HBV-1; OxBChV
Days are sad, it is the holy tide, The. The Holy Tide. Frederick Tennyson. OBEV; OBVV
Days are short, The. January. John Updike. PDV; RHPC
Day's at end and there's nowhere to go, The. More Sonnets at Christmas, II. Allen Tate. LiTA; LiTM; NePA; SBVL; WaP
Days dawn on us that make amends for many. The Interpreters. Swinburne. PoEL-5
Days drift by, The—as ships drift out to sea. In Summer. Charles Hanson Towne. HBMV
Day's End. Laurence Binyon. OBVV
Day's End. Lesbia Harford. PoAu-1
Day's end. A Midas sack of cloud has spilled. Nothing Gold Can Stay. Norma Farber. AMV-81
Days get shorter and. God Is Here Again. Charles Angoff. AMV-80
Days Gone By, The. James Whitcomb Riley. OBCA; TreF
Days grow and the stars cross over, The. Darkness Music. Muriel Rukeyser. BoWoP
Days grow shorter, the nights grow longer, The. Interlude [*or* Growing Old]. Ella Wheeler Wilcox. BLPA; FPL; HBV-2
Day's grown old, the fainting sun, The. Evening [*or* Evening Quatrains *or* Summer Evening]. Charles Cotton. ChTr; LoBV; PoEL-3; TrGrPo; WiR
Days have kept on coming, The. Daddy. Lucille Clifton. NIP
Days in White. Ingeborg Bachmann, *tr. fr. German by* Daniel Huws. BoWoP
Days like this, off Jake's, the August fog. Jake's Wharf. Philip Booth. NYBP
Day's March, The. Robert Nichols. MMA
Days, my grandfather said to me, The. Angle of Vision. Martha Bosworth. AMV-80
Days of Bute and Grafton's fame, The. The Eight-Day Clock. Alfred Cochrane. HBV-1
Days of 1896. C. P. Cavafy, *tr. fr. Greek by* Edmund Keeley *and* Philip Sherrard. PeHV
Days of Forty-nine, The. *Unknown.* BPAW; CoSo, *with music;* FSW; PAH
Days of My Youth. St. George Tucker. AA; HBV-1
Days of 1956. Robin Magowan. EAS
Days of 1978. Gerald Stern. AMV-81
Days of 1964. James Merrill. CoAP
Days of Our Youth, The. *Unknown, tr. fr. Arabic by* Wilfrid Scawen Blunt. AWP
Days of spring are here, The! The eglantine. Hafiz, *tr. by* Gertrude Lowthian Bell. Odes, X. AWP
Days of the Unicorns, The. Phyllis Webb. NOBC
Days of the Week. *Unknown. See* Propitious Days for Wedding.
Days of yore, The—both good and ill. Braggin' Bill's Fortytude. *At. to* C. Wiles Hallock. BPAW
Days pass easy over these ancient hills. We Are a People. Lance Henson. VoR
Day's swim done, we found some grass and flung, The. A Serendipity of Love. Richard Aldridge. NePoAm-2
Days That Have Been. W. H. Davies. FaBoPP
Days Too Short. W. H. Davies. MoBrPo
Days went by, The. I took up the old days. Tuscan Life. Elizabeth Barrett Browning. *Fr.* Aurora Leigh, VII. FaBoPP
Days Were Great as Lakes. David Vogel, *tr. fr. Hebrew by* A. C. Jacobs. VWA
Day's Work a-Done. William Barnes. SaC
Dayseye hugging the earth, The. Daisy. William Carlos Williams. MoAB; MoAmPo
Daysleep. Virginia E. Smith. AMV-81
Dazel'd thus, with height of place. *See* Dazzled thus. . .
Dazzle. Dorothy Roberts. NOBC
Dazzle on the sea, my darling, The. Leaving Barra. Louis MacNeice. EBEV
Dazzled. Arthur Sze. BrSi
Dazzled blood, The. Faustus Triumphant. Thom Gunn. FaBoMo
Dazzled [*or* Dazel'd] thus with height of place. Upon the Sudden Restraint of the Earl[e] of Somerset, Then Falling from Favor [*or* Favour]. Sir Henry Wotton. AnAnS-2; ELP; JCP; MePo; NOBE; NoP; OBS; SeCP
De Aegypto. Ezra Pound. VGW
De Amore. Ernest Dowson. OBNC
"Lord over life and all the ways of breath," *sel.* TrPWD
De Civitate Hominum. Thomas MacGreevy. CIP
De Clerico et Puella. *Unknown.* OxBM
De Coenatione Micae. Martial, *tr. fr. Latin by* Robert Louis Stevenson. FaBoCh
De Consolatione Philosophiae. Boethius. *See* Consolation of Philosophy.
De Contemptu Mundi, *sels.* Bernard of Cluny, *tr. fr. Latin.*
Jerusalem, *tr. by* John Mason Neale. HBV-2; OBVV
(Celestial Country, The.) GoBC, *longer sel.*
(Jerusalem the Golden.) VLP; WGRP, *shorter sel.*
"Scarcely believe things shameful to utter which yet I shall speak of." PeHV
De Guiana, Carmen Epicum. George Chapman. OBSC
"De Gustibus." Robert Browning. HBV-2; InPS; OAEP
Italy of the South, *sel.* FaBoPP
De Gustibus. St. John Emile Clavering Hankin. CenHV; LiSp
De Imagine Mundi. John Ashbery. FaBoMo
De Mexico ha venido, *with music. Unknown, tr. fr. Spanish.* TrAS
De Morte. Sir Henry Wotton. OBS
"De Mortuis Nil Nisi Bonum." Richard Realf. HBV-2
De Naevo in Facie Faustinae. Thomas Bastard. FaBoEE
De Partu Virginis, *sel.* Jacopo Sannazaro, *tr. fr. Latin by* John C. Eustace
Celestial Queen, *fr.* Book III. ISi
De Ponto, *sels.* Ovid, *tr. fr. Latin by* Henry Vaughan. OBVE
"Shall I complain or not? Or shall I mask," *fr.* IV, 3a.
"You have consum'd my language, and my pen," III, 7.
De Profundis. Bible, *O.T.* Psalms, CXXX. BLRP; TreF; WGRP
("Out of the deep have I called unto thee, O Lord.") ILwl
(Out of the Depths.) TrJP
(Song of Supplication, A.) TrGrPo
De Profundis, *sel.* Elizabeth Barrett Browning.
"Whatever's lost, it first was won." TrPWD
De Profundis. David Gascoyne. *Fr.* Miserere. NeBP
De Profundis. "Hugh MacDiarmid." SeCePo
De Profundis. Dorothy Parker. ErPo
De Profundis. Amos N. Wilder. TrPWD
De Profundis Clamavi. Baudelaire, *tr. fr. French by* Arthur Symons. SyP
De Regimine Principum, *sels.* Thomas Hoccleve.
Lament for Chaucer and Gower. OxBM
(Hoccleve's Lament for Chaucer and Gower, *abr.*) OAEP
("O maister deere and fader reverent!") EBEV
Prologue: "Musing upon the restless bisinesse." PoEL-1
(Anxious Thought.) OxBM
To Chaucer. ACP
De Rerum Natura (On the Nature of Things), *sels.* Lucretius, *tr. fr. Latin.*
Address to Venus, *fr.* I, *tr. by* Spenser, *fr.* The Faerie Queene, IV, 10. AWP
("Darling of God[s] and Men, beneath the gliding stars," *tr. by* Basil Bunting.) NoAM; PoPl
(Prayer to Venus, *tr. by* Spenser.) EIL
Against the Fear of Death, *fr.* III, *tr. by* Rolfe Humphries. DL, *abr.*; NAWM-1
Abr. versions, tr. by Dryden. AWP; FaBoRV; OAEL-1; OBVE
(Fear of Death, The.) LoBV
(What Has This Bugbear Death.) CTC
"Child is like a sailor cast up by the sea, The," *tr. by* C. H. Sisson. NAs
Concerning the Nature of Love, *fr.* IV, *tr. by* Dryden. ErPo
(Nature of Love, The.) UnTE
"Delight of humane kind, and gods above," *fr.* I, *tr. by* Dryden. OBVE
"Now since the members of the world we view," *fr.* I, *tr. by* Thomas Creech. OBVE
No Single Thing Abides, *tr. by* W. H. Mallock. AWP; ImOP, *abr.*
Suave Mari Magno, *tr. by* W. H. Mallock. AWP
De Roberval, *sels.* John Hunter-Duvar.
"Here, then, we stand, on the Canadian shore." CaP
La Belle Sauvage. OBCV
Twilight Song. WHW
De Se. John Weever. FaBoEE
De Senectute. Franklin P. Adams. HBMV
De Tea Fabula. Sir Arthur Quiller-Couch. CenHV
Deacon Morgan. Naomi Long Madgett. BlSi
Deacon's Masterpiece, The; or, The Wonderful "One-Hoss Shay." Oliver

Wendell Holmes. *Fr.* The Autocrat of the Breakfast Table, *ch.* 11. AmPP; AP; FaFP; FaPo; FPL; HBV-1; HBVY; InMe; LiTA; MoShBr; NePA; NOBA; OBAL; OBCA; OHFP; OxBA: PaPo; PoLF; PoRA; TAP; WBLP
(One-Hoss Shay, The.) TreF
(Wonderful "One-Hoss Shay," The.) BeLS; FaBoBe; YaD
Deacon's wife was a bit desirish, The. Pride of Ancestry. Robert Frost. OBAL
Dead, The. Mathilde Blind. OBVV; SBG; WGRP
Dead, The ("Blow out, you bugles, over the rich dead!"). Rupert Brooke. 1914, III. HBV-2; OBWP; TreF; WGRP
Dead, The ("These hearts were woven of human joys and cares"). Rupert Brooke. 1914, IV. BrPo; CH; HBV-2; LiTB; MMA; PoA; SeCeV
Dead. Rhoda Coghill. OnYI
Dead, The. C. Day Lewis. MP; TwCP
Dead, The. Louis Dudek. NOBC
Dead, The. Charles Heavysege. *See* How Great unto the Living Seem the Dead.
Dead. Lionel Johnson. BrPo; FaBoEn; OBNC; PoEL-5
Dead, The. David Morton. PAH
Dead, The. A. J. M. Smith. NOBC
Dead, The. Mark Strand. HeIP
Dead, The. Jones Very. AA; AP; HAP; NOBA; OxBA; TAP
Dead, The. John Williams. NePoAm-2
Dead, The. Jay Wright. FB
Dead abide with us, The! Though stark and cold. The Dead. Mathilde Blind. OBVV; SBG; WGRP
Dead and the Living One, The. Thomas Hardy. MMA
Dead at Clonmacnois, The. Angus O'Gillan, *tr. fr. Irish by* Thomas William Rolleston. AnIL; FaBoPP; HBV-2; OBEV; OBVV; OnYI; OxBI
(Clonmacnoise.) AnIV; OBMV
Dead beast, turned up, The. The Well-travelled Roadway. John Newlove. NeAC
Dead Bird. David R. Slavitt. BXAP
Dead Bird, The. Andrew Young. FM
Dead birds fell, but no one had seen them fly, The. Some Dreams They Forgot. Elizabeth Bishop. NoAM
Dead Boy. John Crowe Ransom. CMoP; FaBoMo; LiTA; MP; NoAM; NoP; OxBA; TwCP
Dead boy living among men as a man, A. A Head. James Schuyler. NoAM; PoM
Dead Bride, The. Geoffrey Hill. TW
Dead Brother, The. *Unknown.* EnSB
Dead Butterfly, The. Denise Levertov. NoP
Dead by the Side of the Road, The. Gary Snyder. HAP
Dead Calm and Mist, A. "Fiona Macleod." SyP
Dead Center. Chester Kallman. PoA
Dead Center. Ruth Whitman. NYBP
Dead Child, The. George Barlow. OBVV
Dead Child, The. Ernest Dowson. BrPo
Dead Cities Speak to the Living Cities, The. Edmond Fleg, *tr. fr. French by* Anthony Rudolf. VWA
Dead city walls may pen us in, but still. Charles Harpur. *Fr.* A Coast View. CBAP
Dead Cleopatra lies in a crystal casket. Conrad Aiken. Discordants, IV. PoA
Dead Coach, The. Katharine Tynan. HBV-2
Dead Color. Charles Wright. LCAP
Dead Cow Farm. Robert Graves. BrPo
Dead Crab, The. Andrew Young. BSV; FaBoTw; FM; LoBV
Dead dancer, how is this?—the laurel here. Vernon Castle. Harriet Monroe. HBMV
Dead! dead! the Child I lov'd so well! On the Death of His Son. Charles Wesley. NOCV
Dead do not specially depress me, The. At Morning an Iris. Patrick Evans. NeBP
Dead Dog. Vernon Scannell. OxBC
Dead Drunk Blues. *Unknown.* BluL
Dead Eagle, The. Thomas Campbell. EnRP
Dead Embryos. Judit Tóth, *tr. fr. Hungarian by* Laura Schiff. WPOW
Dead Faith, The. Fanny Heaslip Lea. HBV-2; WGRP
Dead Feast of the Kol-Folk, The. Whittier. PoEL-4
Dead Fiddle, The. Humbert Wolfe. TrJP
Dead Fires. Jessie Redmond Fauset. BANP; PoNe
Dead Fly. Eilean Ni Chuilleanain. CIP
Dead Girl. Anna Hajnal, *tr. fr. Hungarian by* Jascha Kessler. VWA
Dead Hand. W. S. Merwin. CAPP; InPK
Dead hangs the fruit on that tall tree. Burial of the Spirit of a Young Poet. Richard Hughes. MoBrPo
Dead Harvest, A. Alice Meynell. MoVE
Dead heat rises for weeks, The. In the Middle of August. Edward Hirsch. MAYP
Dead here look upon the light from caves, The. Girod Street Cemetery: New Orleans. Harry Morris. GoYe
Dead Heroes. Karoniaktatie. STE
Dead Heroes, The. Isaac Rosenberg. MoBrPo
Dead Horse, The. Cecília Meireles, *tr. fr. Portuguese by* James Merrill. PBWP
Dead Horse, The, *with music. Unknown.* AmSS; AS
Dead Host's Welcome, The. John Fletcher. *Fr.* The Lover's Progress. TrGrPo
('Tis Late and Cold.) ViBoPo
Dead in Bloody Snow. Meridel Le Sueur. GP
Dead in Europe, The. Robert Lowell. CMoP; DTC; LiTM; NePA; NePoEA; OxBA; OxBC
Dead in Melanesia, The. Randall Jarrell. MiAP
Dead in Queens lean westward from their stones, The. A Day in the City. L. E. Sissman. NYBP
Dead in the cold, a song-singing thrush. Last Rites. Christina Rossetti. OxBChV; RHPC
Dead in the Sierras. Joaquin Miller. AA; BPAW
Dead in via, The. La Préface. Charles Olson. PoM
Dead in Wars and in Revolutions. Mary Devenport O'Neill. NeIP
Dead! Is it possible? He, the bold rider. Custer's Last Charge. Frederick Whittaker. BPAW; HBV-2; OnMSP; PAH; PoLF
Dead is the roll of the drums. Abraham Lincoln. Henry Howard Brownell. GN
Dead Jews, dead Jews, just points now an underground. Dime Call. Albert Goldbarth. VWA
Dead King, A. Swinburne. VLP
Dead Knight, The. John Masefield. CH; GTBS-P
Dead Lady Canonized, The. Amiri Baraka. CAPP
Dead Leaf, A. Howard Moss. NYBP; NYP
Dead leaves, one-time fair, The. A Word to the West End. Thomas Ashe. EBVV
Dead lemon like a cowled old woman crouching in the cold, A. For *Under the Volcano.* Malcolm Lowry. NOBC
Dead Letter, A. Austin Dobson. HBV-1
Dead Liebknecht, The. "Hugh MacDiarmid," *after the German of* Rudolf Leonhard. OBVE
Dead, long dead. Tennyson. *Fr.* Maud. OAEL-2; SyP
Dead Love. Mary Mathews Adams. AA
Dead Make Rules, The. Mary Carolyn Davies. HBMV
Dead man, A/ who never caused others to die. W. H. Auden. *Fr.* Marginalia. OAEL-2
Dead Man Ariseth and Singeth a Hymn to the Sun, The. *Unknown, tr. fr. Egyptian by* Robert Hillyer. *Fr.* Book of the Dead. AWP
Dead Man Dragged from the Sea, The. Carl Gardner. PoBA
Deadman's Dirge. George Darley. *See* Sea Ritual, The.
Dead Man's Dump. Isaac Rosenberg. BrPo; FaBoMo; GTBS-P; LiTM; MMA; MoPo; NoP; OBWP; TrJP; VWA; WaP
Dead Man's Song, Dreamed by One Who Is Alive. Paulinaoq, *tr. fr. Eskimo.* WTO
Dead March, A. Cosmo Monkhouse. HBV-2
"Play me a march," *sel.* OBVV
Dead Marine. Louis O. Coxe. WaP
Dead Marten, The. Walter Savage Landor. FM
"Dead means somebody has to kiss you." Reading the Brother's Grimm to Jenny. Lisel Mueller. DFT
Dead Men, The. Sophia de Mello Breyner Andresen, *tr. fr. Portuguese by* Allan Francovich. PBWP
Dead men are wisest, for they know. The Wise. Countee Cullen. PoNe
Dead men of 'ninety-two, also of 'ninety-three. Sonnet. Arthur Rimbaud, *tr. by* Norman Cameron. WaaP
Dead Men Tell No Tales. Haniel Long. HBMV
Dead Mole, A. Andrew Young. FM; GTBS-P
Dead Moon, The. Danske Bedinger Dandridge. AA
Dead Musicians. Siegfried Sassoon. BrPo
Dead Neck. Sue Standing. AMV-81
Dead of the Wilderness, The. Hayyim Nahman Bialik, *tr. fr. Hebrew by* Maurice Samuel. AWP
Dead of the World, The. Jeanne Finlay. AMV-81
Dead of Winter. Anthony Towne. NYBP
Dead on the Desert. Harrison Conrard. BPAW
Dead on the War Path. *Tr. fr. Tewa Indian by* H. J. Spinden. WTO
Dead! One of them shot by the sea in the east. Mother and Poet. Elizabeth Barrett Browning. HBV-2; SBG
Dead Pan, The. Elizabeth Barrett Browning. VLP
Dead Past, A. *At. to* C. C. Munson. BLRP; WBLP
Dead Pig, The. *Unknown.* FaBoNo
Dead Player, The. Robert Burns Wilson. AA
Dead Poet, The. Lord Alfred Douglas. HBMV; PeHV; ViBoPo
Dead Poet, The. Al Purdy. NOBC

Dead poets, philosophs, priests. Walt Whitman. *Fr.* Starting from Paumanok. InPS
Dead poets stalk the air. Rainy Night at the Writers' Colony. Josephine Jacobsen. TAP
Dead Ponies. Brenda Chamberlain. NeBP; WPE
Dead President, The. Edward Rowland Sill. PAH
Dead Prospector, The. Arthur Chapman. BPAW
Dead Quire, The. Thomas Hardy. OAEP
Dead Ride Fast, The. R. P. Blackmur. MoPo
Dead scents I couldn't bear bore. Year of the Bird. Brian Swann. AmPA
Dead Sea, The. Henryk Grynberg, *tr. fr. Polish by* Isaac Komem. VWA
Dead Sea Scrolls, The, *sels. Unknown, tr. fr. Hebrew.* TrJP
Blessed Art Thou, O Lord, *tr. by* Theodore H. Gaster.
Lo, I Am Stricken Dumb, *tr. by* Theodore H. Gaster.
My Soul in the Bundle of Life, *tr. fr. the French vers. by* E. Margaret Rowley.
Though Mine Eye Sleep Not, *tr. by* Theodore H. Gaster.
Dead Seal. Alfred Purdy. MoCV; NoAM
Dead Seal near McClure's Beach, The. Robert Bly. NNaP; NU
Dead Shall Be Raised Incorruptible, The. Galway Kinnell. NOBA
"In the Twentieth Century of my trespass on earth," 4. GP; TW
Dead shall rise again, The. The Raising of Lazarus. Lucille Clifton. CNA
Dead shalt thou lie; and nought. Achtung. Sappho, *tr. by* Thomas Hardy. CTC; OBVE
Dead Sheep, The. Andrew Young. FM
Dead sheep/ beside the highway. Preparations. Leslie Silko. VoR
Dead Ship of Harpswell, The. Whittier. EtS
Dead Singer, The. Mary Ashley Townsend. AA
Dead Sister, The. Caroline Gilman. OBCA
Dead smell the rain gives, The. Cut Lilac. Tony Beyer. OCNZ
Dead Snake. William Jay Smith. NePoAm-2
Dead Soldier. Nicolás Guillén, *tr. fr. Spanish by* Langston Hughes. TTY
Dead Soldier, A. George Edgar Montgomery. AA
Dead Soldiers. James Fenton. OBWP
Dead Solomon, The. John Aylmer Dorgan. AA
Dead Sparrow, The. William Cartwright. BoAnP; CH
(Lesbia on Her Sparrow.) CavP
Dead Statesman, A. Kipling. *Fr.* Epitaphs of the War, 1914–18. FaBoEE; OAEP
Dead Still. Andrei Voznesensky, *tr. fr. Russian by* Richard Wilbur. BoLoP
Dead, they'll burn you up with electricity. Marcus Argentarius. Kenneth Rexroth. CrMA
Dead Tribune, The. Denis Florence MacCarthy. ACP
Dead Warrior, A. Laurence Housman. HBMV
Dead Wasp. Kenneth Slade Alling. NePoAm
Dead Weasel, A. David Helwig. NOBC
Dead "Wessex" the Dog to the Household. Thomas Hardy. FM
Dead Wingman, The. Randall Jarrell. MiAP
Dead woman lay in her first night's grave, The. The Dead and the Living One. Thomas Hardy. MMA
Dead wood with its load of stones. The Water-Wheel. Jack R. Clemo. ChMP
Dead Words, The. Vernon Watkins. LiTM
Dead young man stood up in his grave, The. Articles of War. Dunstan Thompson. WaP
Deader they die here, or at least. Fall Comes in Back-Country Vermont. Robert Penn Warren. NYBP; VGW
Deadfall. Martha Keller. GoYe
Deadly destructive to my man and me. The Conscience. Anna Wickham. POL
Deadly Kisses. Pierre de Ronsard, *tr. fr. French by* Andrew Lang. AWP
Dead's right grain, The. The Future and the Ancestor. Andrée Chedid, *tr. by* Samuel Hazo *and* Mirène Ghossein. WPOW
Deadsong. Don Domanski. NOBC
Deaf. H. C. Bunner. AA
Deaf. Barry O. Higgs. PeSA
Deaf-and-Dumb School. Anthony Delius. PeSA
Deaf children were monkey-nimble, fish-tremulous and sudden, The. Deaf School. Ted Hughes. NoP
Deaf, giddy, helpless, left alone. On His Own Deafness. Swift. BIrV; FaBoEE
Deaf is like. Deaf. Barry O. Higgs. PeSA
Deaf School. Ted Hughes. NoP
Deaf to God, who calls and walks. Doomsday Morning. Genevieve Taggard. MoAmPo
Deaf to the bustle of the street, soporifically. The Jewish Cemetery. Cesar Tiempo, *tr. by* Angela McEvan-Alvarado. VWA
Deafness. Richard Ryan. BIrV
Dealer, bewitched by gain-promising dreams, A. Bush Justice. Charles Harpur. CBAP
Dean, The. Coventry Patmore. *Fr.* The Angel in the House, I, vi. VLP
Dean, adult education may seem silly. Lucretius versus the Lake Poets. Robert Frost. GLGT
Dean and prebendary, A. The Battle Royal between Dr. Sherlock, Dr. South, and Dr. Burnet. William Pittis. APAS
Dean, if we believe report, The. Swift. *Fr.* Verses on the Death of Dr. Swift. FaBoEn
Dean Inge. Humbert Wolfe. FaBoEE
(On Dean Inge.) ChTr
Dean of Paul's did search for his wife, The. Fragment of a Song on the Beautiful Wife of Dr. John Overall. *Unknown.* BoLoP
Dean-bourn, a Rude River in Devon, by Which Sometimes He Lived ("Dean-bourn, farewell; I never look to see"). Robert Herrick. *See* To Dean-bourn, a Rude River in Devon.
Dean's Lady, The. George Crabbe. LoBV
Dear/ Diana. Andy-Diana DNA Letter. Andrew Weiman. HAP
Dear ———, I'll gie ye some advice. To an Artist. Burns. EyDe
Dear Alice! you'll laugh when you know it. The Talented Man. Winthrop Mackworth Praed. EnRP; FiBHP; HBV-1; NOBL
Dear America. Robert Peterson. PPON
Dear and great Angel, wouldst thou only leave. The Guardian-Angel. Robert Browning. GoBC; HBV-2
Dear Ann, I think I am losing my husband. Help Is on the Way. Herbert Scott. GP
Dear Ann, wherever you are. For Ann Scott-Moncrieff. Edwin Muir. GTBS-P
"Dear as remembered kisses after death." Constancy. Minor Watson. HBV-2
Dear as the Moon. *Gond Oral Tradition, tr. by* V. Elwin *and* S. Hivale. WTO
Dear Auntie/ Oh, what a nice jumper. Christmas Thank You's. Mick Gower. OBCP
Dear, back my wounded heart restore. The Divorce. Thomas Stanley. AnAnS-2; MeLP
Dear, beauteous Death! the jewel of the just. Henry Vaughan. LO
Dear Bill,/ When I search the past for you. A Letter to William Carlos Williams. Kenneth Rexroth. NNaP; PP
Dear Black Head. *Unknown. See* Dear Dark Head.
Dear boy, you will not hear me speak. Pangloss's Song [A Comic-Opera Lyric]. Richard Wilbur. AP; NePoAm-2; NoAM; OxBC
Dear Brethren, Are Your Harps in Tune? *with music.* Eunice Smith. AH
Dear Brook, farewell! To-morrow's noon again. Wordsworth. *Fr.* An Evening Walk. EnRP
Dear brother Robin, this comes from us all. Country Letter. John Clare. NCEP
Dear brother, would you know the life. A Letter. Emerson. OxBA
Dear charming nymph, neglected and decried. Farewell to Poetry. Goldsmith. *Fr.* The Deserted Village. OBEC
Dear child of nature, let them rail! To a Young Lady. Wordsworth. EnRP
Dear child, these words which briefly I declare. The Maiden's Best Adorning. *Unknown.* OxBChV
Dear Child Whom I Begot. J. V. Cunningham. NAs
"Dear children," they asked in every town. The Wise Men Ask the Children the Way [*or* The Kings from the East]. Heine, *tr. by* Geoffrey Grigson. OBCP
Dear Chloe, how blubber'd is that pretty face! *See* Dear Cloe, how blubbered is that pretty face!
Dear chorister, who from those shadows sends. *See* Dear quirister, who from those shadows sends.
Dear Citizens,/ I heard the newsboys shouting "Europe! Europe!" The True, the Good and the Beautiful. Delmore Schwartz. MiAP
Dear Claudia, this is a love note written to you. To Ellen. Charles Stetler. PPJ
Dear Cleo, I can't complain about your absence. To the Muse. Philip Whalen. PoM
Dear Clive, I've meant to scribble you a letter. Letter to Myself. Christopher Reid. FaBoPa
Dear Cloe [*or* Chloe], how blubbered is that pretty face! Answer to Cloe [*or* Chloe] Jealous [*or* A Better Answer *or* To Chloe Jealous]. Matthew Prior. AWP; ELP; FaBoEn; HBV-1; NOBE; NOEC; OBEC; PoEL-3; SeCePo; SeCeV; ViBoPo
Dear common flower, that grow'st beside the way. To the Dandelion. James Russell Lowell. AP; FaPON; HBV-1; HBVY; GN
Dear Companion. *Unknown.* FSW
Dear Country Cousin. E. G. Burrows. HoAn
Dear creature by the fire a-purr. Cat. Lytton Strachey. PCat
Dear critic, who my lightness so deplores. To a Captious Critic. Paul Laurence Dunbar. BPo
Dear Cynthia, though thou bear'st the name. To Cynthia. On Her Changing. Sir Francis Kynaston. MePo
Dear Dark Head. *Unknown, tr. fr. Irish by* Sir Samuel Ferguson. AnIV; OnYi; OxBI; UnTE

(Cean[n] Dubh Deelish.) GBL; OBVV; SeCePo
(Dear Black Head.) BIrV
Dear Dave: Rain five days and I love it. Letter to Wagoner from Port Townsend. Richard Hugo. NNaP
Dear, dear, dear. The Thrush's Song. *Unknown, tr. by* William MacGillivray. CH
Dear Denise: Long way from, long time since Boulder. Letter to Levertov from Butte. Richard Hugo. NNaP
Dear Dennice: I'm this close but the pass is tough this year. Letter to Scanlon from Whitehall. Richard Hugo. NNaP
Dear, Do Not Your Fair Beauty Wrong. Thomas May. ViBoPo
Dear Doll, while the tails of our horses are plaiting. Miss Biddy Fudge to Miss Dorothy. Thomas Moore. *Fr.* The Fudge Family in Paris. NBM
Dear Dolly, stay thy scampering joints one minute. Ode to a Country Hoyden. "Peter Pindar." NOEC
Dear dreamer, that I may plunge. Another Fan [Belonging to Mademoiselle Mallarmé]. Stéphane Mallarmé, *tr. by* Roger Fry. NAWM-2; SyP
Dear Erin, how sweetly thy green bosom rises! Cushla Ma Chree. John Philpot Curran. HBV-2
Dear Eustatio, I write that you may write me an answer. Arthur Hugh Clough. *Fr.* Amours de Voyage, Canto I, i. EBVV
Dear Fanny. Thomas Moore. HBV-1; InMe
Dear, farewell, a little while. Anacreontic, on Parting with a Little Child. Samuel Wesley. NOEC
Dear Father/ hear and bless. Margaret Wise Brown. PDV
Dear father and dear mother: Let me crave. Erotion. Martial, *tr. by* Kirby Flower Smith. AWP
Dear Father Christmas. Russell Davies. FaBoPa
Dear Father, Look Up. "Orpheus C. Kerr." OBAL
Dear father, mother, sister, come listen while I tell. The Ashland Tragedy. Elijah Adams. AmFP
"Dear Father, tell me, Why are Worms?" Why? Walter de la Mare. FiBHP
Dear fellow-artist, why so free. To a Young Beauty. W. B. Yeats. CMoP
Dear fellow castaway, the cruise ships. Weathering the Depths. Al Lee. AmPA
Dear Female Heart. Stevie Smith. FaBoEE
Dear Fergusson—They've Ramsay's statue clean. Letter to Robert Fergusson. Alexander Scott. OxBS
Dear Folks. Patrick Kavanagh. FaBoTw
Dear Fred: I hope this finds you, Marge and children O.K. Letter to Garber from Skye. Richard Hugo. AMV-81.
Dear Friend,/ I hear this town does so abound. An Epistolary Essay from M. G. to O. B. upon Their Mutual Poems. Earl of Rochester. APAS
Dear friend! Believe me, Love's not always blind. Love Has Eyes. William Forster. CBAP
Dear friend, I fear my heart will break. Out of French. Sir Charles Sedley. FaBoEE
Dear [*or* Deare] friend, sit down: the tale is long and sad. Love Unknown. George Herbert. JCP; Prf
Dear friend! whose holy, ever-living lines. The Match. Henry Vaughan. AnAnS-1
Dear Friend, Whose Presence in the House, *with music.* James Freeman Clarke. AH
Dear Friends and Patrons of the *Denver News!* Carrier's Address. *Unknown.* PoOW
Dear friends, let your disease be what God will. Saffold's Cures. *At. to* Thomas Saffold. FaBoUs
Dear Fronto, famed alike in peace and war. Country Pleasures. Martial, *tr. by* F. A. Wright. AWP
Dear galway/ it is flooding here, in missouri. A Poem to Galway Kinnell. Etheridge Knight. NNaP
Dear gentle soul, who went so soon away. Luís de Camoes, *tr. fr. Portuguese by* Roy Campbell. BoLoP
Dear George,/ At last the blowfly's buzz retreats. Letter to a Friend. John Thompson. PoAu-2
Dear Gill I ne'er thought till last night. The New Married Couple; or, A Friendly Debate between the Country Farmer and His Buxome Wife. *Unknown.* CoMu
Dear Girl. Gregory Corso. NoAM
Dear God,/ give us a flood of water. The Prayer of the Little Ducks. Carmen Bernos de Gasztold. PDV
Dear God, another day is done. An Evening Prayer. *Unknown.* STF
Dear God, I humbly pray. Prayer of a Beginning Teacher. Ouida Smith Dunnam. TrPWD
Dear God, my little boy of three. A Father's Prayer. *Unknown.* STF
Dear God our Father, at Thy knee confessing. For Deeper Life. Katharine Lee Bates. TrPWD
Dear Grandmamma, with what we give. Grandmamma's Birthday. Hilaire Belloc. DBV; ELU; FiBHP; PoPl
Dear, had the world in its caprice. Respectability. Robert Browning. EnLoPo; ViBoPo
Dear Happy Souls, *with music.* Eunice Smith. AH
Dear Harp of My Country. Thomas Moore. AnIL; EnRP; OAEP
Dear, heavn-designing soul! To a Young Gentle-Woman, Councel Concerning Her Choice. Richard Crashaw. OBS
Dear hope! Earth's dowry and heaven's debt! For Hope [*or* Answer for Hope *or* M. Crashaw's Answer for Hope *or* On Hope]. Richard Crashaw. LiTB; MeLP; MePo; NOBE; OBS; SeCV-1; ViBoPo
Dear, I could weep, but that my brain is dry. Thomas Lovell Beddoes. *Fr.* The Bride's Tragedy. LO
Dear, I do not count it flighty. To a Lady across the Way. E. B. White. InMe
Dear, I must be gone. Parting. W. B. Yeats. FaBoTw
Dear If I with Guile. Thomas Campion. NCEP
Dear, if unsocial privacies obsess me. Epigram. J. V. Cunningham. VGW
Dear, If You Change. *Unknown.* EIL; EnRePo
("Dear, if you change, I'll never choose again.") EnLoPo; InvP; OBSC
(Deare, If You Change.) PoEL-2
Dear, if you love me, hold me most your friend. A Sonnet. Alice Duer Miller. AA
Dear Italy! The sound of thy soft name. Italian Rhapsody. Robert Underwood Johnson. HBV-2
Dear J. D.: One should think of Chief Joseph here. Letter to Reed from Lolo. Richard Hugo. NNaP
Dear Jesus! ever at my side. The Nearest Friend. Frederick W. Faber. TreFS
Dear Jim: This is as far as I ever chased a girl. Letter to Welch from Browning. Richard Hugo. NNaP
Dear John, Dear Coltrane. Michael S. Harper. AmPA; GeTw; NIP
Dear John: This is a Dear John Letter from booze. Letter to Logan from Milltown. Richard Hugo. NNaP
Dear John Wayne. Louise Erdrich. TWSS
Dear John, whoever now takes pen to write. James McAuley. *Fr.* A Letter to John Dryden. CBAP
Dear Jonno. A Trip on the Staten Island Ferry. Audre Lorde. CNA
Dear kindly Sergeant Krupke. Gee, Officer Krupke. Stephen Sondheim. OBAL
Dear Knight, how great a drudge is he. Hudibras and Milton Reconciled. William Somervile. NOEC
Dear Kong. Fay Wray to the King. Judith Rechter. NMM
Dear Ladies of Cincinnati, The. Anne Stevenson. HoAn
Dear Lady,/ you have been selected. Chain Letters. Alice Fulton. LTB
Dear Land of All My Love. Sidney Lanier. *Fr.* The Centennial Meditation of Columbia. GN; HBVY
("Long as thine art shall love true love.") PGD
Dear Land of Hope, thy hope is crowned. Land of Hope and Glory. A. C. Benson. FaPoR
Dear Lillian! (The "dear" one risks). To Lillian Russell. Bert Leston Taylor. WhC
Dear little child, this little book. With a First Reader. Rupert Hughes. HBMV
Dear little Dorothy, she is no more. Dorothy. Rose Hawthorne Lathrop. AA
Dear little house, dear shabby street. To the Little House. Christopher Morley. HBMV
Dear little tree that we plant to-day. An Arbor Day Tree. *Unknown.* OHIP
Dear Lizbie Browne. To Lizbie Browne. Thomas Hardy. DTC; ELP
Dear Lord! accept a sinful heart. Self-Acquaintance. William Cowper. NOCV
Dear Lord and Father of Mankind. Whittier. *Fr.* The Brewing of Soma. AH, *with music;* NOCV; TrPWD; TRV
(Prayer: "Dear Lord and Father of mankind.") TreFT
Dear Lord—before I take my place. A Driver's Prayer. *Unknown.* STF
Dear Lord, Behold Thy Servants, *with music.* Hosea Ballou I. AH
Dear Lord, for all in pain. For All in Pain. Amy Carmichael. TRV
Dear Lord, I do not hesitate. A Business Man's Prayer. William Ludlum. BLRP
Dear Lord! Kind Lord! James Whitcomb Riley. *See* Love's Prayer.
Dear Lord, receive my son, whose winning love. Of His Dear Son, Gervase. Sir John Beaumont. *Fr.* Of My Dear Son, Gervase Beaumont. GoBC; OBEV
Dear Lord, thy table is outspread. The Master's Invitation. Anson Davies Fitz Randolph. AA
Dear Lord, Whose serving-maiden. Hymn. Josephine Preston Peabody. TrPWD
Dear Lord's best interpreters, The. In Earthen Vessels. Whittier. BLRP; TRV
Dear loss! since thy untimely fate. Henry King. *Fr.* The Exequy. LO; WHA
"Dear love, dost thou sleep fairly?" Parting at Morning. Dietmar von Aist, *tr. by* Frank C. Nicholson. AWP
Dear [*or* Deare] love, for nothing less[e] than thee. The Dream[e]. John

Donne. AnAnS-1; EIL; InvP; LiTB; LoBV; MeLP; MePo; OAEL-1; OAEP; OBEV; OBS; SeCP
Dear love, when with a two-fold mind. Laurence Housman. *Fr.* All Fellows. WGRP
"Dear love, why should you weep." A Lost World. Robert Graves. NYBP
Dear Lucy, you know what my wish is. Persicos Odi [*or* Ad Ministram]. Horace, *tr. by* Thackeray. Odes, I, 38. HBV-2; OBEV; OBVE
Dear Madam, did you never gaze. On Mites; to a Lady. Stephen Duck. FM
Dear Madam, you have seen this play. At the Theater. A. P. Herbert. FiBHP
Dear Maiden. Heine, *tr. fr. German by* John Todhunter. AWP
Dear Mamma, if you just could be. A Lesson for Mamma. Sydney Dayre. OBCA; OxBChV
Dear March, come in! Emily Dickinson. YeAr
Dear marshes, by no hand of man/ Laboriously sown. Flood-Time on the Marshes. Evaleen Stein. AA
Dear Martin Folkes, dear scholar, brother, friend. John Byrom. *Fr.* A Full and True Account of a Horrid and Barbarous Robbery. NOBL
Dear Marvin: Months since I left broke down and sobbing. Letter to Bell from Missoula. Richard Hugo. NNaP
Dear Master, in Whose Life I See. John Hunter. TRV
"Dear me!" exclaimed Homer. E. C. Bentley. *Fr.* Clerihews. FiBHP
Dear me! what signifies a pin. The Pin. Ann Taylor. HBV-1; HBVY; OxBChV
Dear Men and Women. John Hall Wheelock. NYBP; Prf
Dear Messrs. Tippins, what is feared by you. Reply to a Creditor. George Harding. FaBoUs
Dear Miss Dix, I am a young man of half-past thirty-seven. Two and One Are a Problem. Ogden Nash. FiBHP
Dear Miss Miller. Letter to a Substitute Teacher. Gary Gildner. Psk
Dear Mister Congressman. Bob Dylan. MAT
Dear Mr. Editor: I wish to say. A Grievance. James Kenneth Stephen. BXAP; FaBoPa; HBV-1; Par
Dear Mr. Noman, does it ever strike you. On Noman, a Guest. Hilaire Belloc. DBV; FaBoEE; PV
Dear Mistress, do not grieve for me. Leo to His Mistress. Henry Dwight Sedgwick. BLPA
Dear Mrs. McKinney of the Sixth Grade. David Kherdian. GLGT
Dear Molly, why so oft in tears? Horace, *tr. by* George Stepney. Odes, III, 7. OBVE
Dear Mother. Emmett Jarrett. NeAC
Dear mother, dear mother, the Church is cold. The Little Vagabond. Blake. *Fr.* Songs of Experience. OBSV; SeCeV
Dear Mother, I attempt to write you a letter. A Letter from School. Thomas Love Peacock. FaBoUs
Dear Mother of the Savior, yet remaining. Last Antiphon: To Mary. James J. Donohue. ISi
"Dear Mother," said a little fish. The Little Fish That Would Not Do as It Was Bid. Jane *and* Ann Taylor. OHIP
Dear murdered comrades, not in vain. Tulips from Their Blood. Edwin Brooks. NBP
Dear, my familiar hand in love's own gesture. Epigram. J. V. Cunningham. PV
Dear my friend and fellow-student, I would lean my spirit o'er you! Lady Geraldine's Courtship. Elizabeth Barrett Browning. DTo
Dear native brook! wild streamlet of the west! Sonnet: To the River Otter. Samuel Taylor Coleridge. ChER; OAEL-2
Dear Night! this world's defeat. Henry Vaughan. *Fr.* The Night. TrGrPo
Dear object of my love, whose manly charms. Pretty Maids Beware! *Unknown.* CoMu
Dear object of my love, whose pow'rful charms. Sarah Hazard's Love Letter. John Ellis. NOEC
Dear! of all happy in the hour, most blest. Safety. Rupert Brooke. 1914, II. BrPo; EnLoPo; HBV-2
Dear Old Dad. Eva Gilbert Shaver. STF
Dear old equivocal and closest friend. The Author to His Body on Their Fifteenth Birthday, 29.ii.80. Howard Nemerov. NAs
Dear Old Girl, *with music.* Richard Henry Buck. FSN
Dear old ladies whose cheeks are pink, The. Autumn Leaves. Janie Screven Heyward. HBMV
Dear Old Mothers. Charles S. Ross. PGD
Dear Old Stockholm. Al Young. NPGG
Dear, on a day of dumb rain. Rain. Howard Moss. ErPo
Dear Patty, Dear Tania. Richard Mathews. GP
Dear Paulus it's a busy trade of late. Lines Descriptive of Thomson's Island. Benjamin Lynde. SCAP
Dear Phoebus, hear my only vow. The Poetess's Bouts-Rimés. *Unknown.* NOEC
Dear Possible. Laura Riding. LiTA
Dear President, The. John James Piatt. PAH
Dear Queenie, though it breaks my heart. The Handmaid of Religion. Edgell Rickword. OBSV
Dear quirister [*or* chorister], who from those shadows sends. Sonnet [*or* To the Nightingale]. William Drummond of Hawthornden. HBV-1; ViBoPo
Dear Rat,/ Never in all my life have I seen. Letters from an Irishman to a Rat. Christopher Logue. BoAnP
Dear Reader. Peter Meinke. Psk
Dear Reader. James Tate. EAS
Dear reliques of a dislodg'd soul, whose lack. Death's Lecture at the Funeral of a Young Gentleman. Richard Crashaw. SeCP
Dear Reynolds! as last night I lay in bed. Epistle to John Hamilton Reynolds. Keats. OBNC
Dear Samson,/ I put your hair. Love Letter. Carole C. Gregory. BlSi
Dear Saviour, If These Lambs Should Stray, *with music.* Abby Bradley Hyde. AH
Dear singer of our fathers' day. To John Greenleaf Whittier. William Hayes Ward. AA
Dear Sir,—You wish to know my notions. The Candidate's Letter. James Russell Lowell. *Fr.* The Biglow Papers, 1st Series, VII. AA
Dear Sir, your astonishment's odd. A Reply. *Unknown.* FaBoCo; NOBL; PoPle
Dear Sirs:/ Of course I'll come. I've packed my galoshes. In Response to Executive Order 9066: All Americans of Japanese Descent Must Report to Relocation Centers. Dwight Okita. BrSi
Dear Sirs: Is it not time we formed a Boston. Communication to the City Fathers of Boston. George Starbuck. NYBP
Dear sister! Dear Ismene! How many evils. Antigone. Sophocles, *tr. by* T. H. Banks. NAWM-1
Dear Sister, my resentment had not been. Virgil, *tr. fr. Latin by* Sir John Denham. *Fr.* The Aeneid, IV. OBVE
Dear Smith, the sleest, paukie thief. Epistle to James Smith [*or* To James Smith]. Burns. BSV; HoPM; OBEC
Dear son/ have you received the papers back. A Letter from Home. John Paul Minarik. LFAC
Dear son:/ when you left us you left. The Father in Tennessee. J. Edgar Simmons. TAT
Dear Son, Leave Thy Weeping. *Unknown.* CTC
(Jesus Comforts His Mother.) MeEL
Dear Son, when the warm multitudes cry. Alonso to Ferdinand. W. H. Auden. *Fr.* The Sea and the Mirror. MoPo
Dear soul be strong! Richard Crashaw. *Fr.* On a Prayer Book Sent to Mrs. M.R. ErPo
Dear steps may die away. Room. Robert Finch. MoCV
Dear stranger, reading this small, true book. Strength to War. Stephen Stepanchev. WaP
Dear sugar, dear tea, and dear corn. The Four Dears. Ebenezer Elliott. SaC
Dear, they are praising your beauty. Praise. "Seumas O'Sullivan." HBV-1
Dear, They Have Poached the Eyes You Loved So Well. Rupert Brooke. WhC
Dear Thomas, didst thou never pop. A Simile. Matthew Prior. FaBoEn; NOEC
Dear, Though the Night Is Gone. W. H. Auden. BoLoP; InvP
Dear, though to part it be hell. To Dianeme. Robert Herrick. CaPo
Dear, though your mind stand so averse. Hear Me Yet. *Unknown.* ElL
Dear tiger lily, fanged and striped! you are the bravest. The Return. Conrad Aiken. NePA
Dear to me were the three sides. The Wife of Aed mac Ainmirech, King of Ireland, Laments Her Husband. *Unknown, tr. by* Myles Dillon. AnIL
Dear [*or* Deere] to my soul[e]! then leave me not forsaken! Sonnet. Henry Constable. *Fr.* Diana. AAS; EIL; OBSC
Dear Tom, this brown jug that now foams with mild ale. The Brown Jug. Francis Fawkes. ViBoPo
Dear Uncle Stranger. Conrad Aiken. NoAM; NOBA
Dear urge no more that killing cause. To One That Pleaded Her Own Want of Merit [*or* To Celia Pleading Want of Merit]. Thomas Stanley. MeLP; OBS
Dear voyager, a lucky star be thine. Ageanax. Edward Cracroft Lefroy. *Fr.* Echoes from Theocritus. OBVV
Dear wanton, when the moon made light our bed. Mother of Men. Stephen Southwold. HBMV
Dear Was He. *Unknown, tr. fr. Late Middle Irish by* Standish Hayes O'Grady. *Fr.* The Life of St. Cellach of Killala. OnYI
Dear, when I did from you remove. Madrigal. Lord Herbert of Cherbury. EIL
Dear, when I went with you. A Song of Two Wanderers. Marguerite Wilkinson. HBMV
Dear, when the sun is set. Give Me Not Tears: Joy. Rose Hawthorne Lathrop. AA
Dear, when we sit in that high, placid room. Touché. Jessie Redmond Fauset. BlSi; CDC

Dear, when you see my grave. Give Me Not Tears: Despair. Rose Hawthorne Lathrop. AA
Dear Whizz, I remember you at St. Mark's in '39. To Auden on His Fiftieth. Richard Eberhart. GLGT; NAs
Dear Whoever-You-Are-That-You-Are. A Letter from the Pygmies. Theodore Weiss. VGW
Dear, why make you more of a dog than me? Astrophel and Stella, LIX. Sir Philip Sidney. GBL; OAEP; PrIm; SiPS
Dear [*or* Deare *or* Deere], why should you command [*or* commaund] me to my rest. Idea, XXXVII. Michael Drayton. AAS; ElL; FaBoEn; HBV-1; LiTB; NOBE; OAEP; OBSC; PoEL-2; ViBoPo
"Dear wife, I don't suppose you understand." The First Goodbye Letter. James Simmons. AMV-81
Dear wife, last midnight, whilst I read. Dibdin's Ghost. Eugene Field. AA
Dear wife, let me have a fire made. Sir T. J.'s Speech to His Wife and Children. *Unknown.* CoMu
Dear youth, too early lost, who now art laid. On the Death of a Young and Favorite Slave. Martial, *tr. by* Goldwin Smith. AWP
Deare friend sit down, and bear awhile this shade. The Palm-Tree. Henry Vaughan. AnAnS-1
Deare friend, sit down, the tale is long and sad. *See* Dear friend, sit down. . .
Deare if I with guile would guild a true intent. Dear If I with Guile. Thomas Campion. NCEP
Deare, If You Change. *Unknown. See* Dear, If You Change.
Deare Lelipa, where hast thou bin so long. The Seventh Nimphall. Michael Drayton. *Fr.* The Muses Elizium. AnAnS-2
Deare love, for nothing lesse than thee. *See* Dear love, for nothing less than thee.
Deare, why should you command me to my rest. *See* Dear, why should. . .
Dearest and nearest brother. Stephen Spender. Elegy for Margaret, VI. FaBoEn
Dearest, Do Not You Delay Me. John Fletcher. *Fr.* The Spanish Curate. ViBoPo
Dearest Friend, Thou Art in Love. Heine, *tr. fr. German by* Emma Lazarus. *Fr.* Homeward Bound. TrJP
Dearest in friendship, if you'll know. My Happy Life. Mildmay Fane, Earl of Westmorland. CavP
Dearest, it was a night. The Birthnight; to F. Walter de la Mare. NAs
Dearest love, do you remember. Weeping, Sad and Lonely [*or* When This Cruel War Is Over]. Charles C. Sawyer. AmFP; FSW; TrAS
Dearest Man-in-the-Moon. Erica Jong. MOON
Dearest of all the heroes! Peerless knight. Don Quixote. Arthur Davison Ficke. HBMV
Dearest of thousands, now the time drawes neere. His Charge to Julia at His Death. Robert Herrick. SeCV-1
"Dearest Papa," says my boy to me. The Legend of the Easter Eggs. Fitz-James O'Brien. BeLS
Dearest Poets, The. Leigh Hunt. HBV-2
Dearest Reader. Michael Palmer. NPGG
Dearest Spot on Earth, The. W. T. Wrighton. FaBoBe
Dearest, these household cares remit. The Blackbird. Henry Charles Beeching. OBVV
Dearest thy tresses are not threads of gold. The Comparison. Thomas Carew. AnAnS-2; CavP
Dearest, when your lovely head. But I Shall Weep. Beatrice Redpath. CaP
Death. Maltbie D. Babcock. *See* Emancipation.
Death. Maxwell Bodenheim. TrJP
Death. Emily Brontë. OBNC; VLP
("Death, that struck when I was most confiding.") EBVV
Death. Howard Byatt. FF
Death. Madison Cawein. AA
Death. John Clare. GTBS-P
Death. Florence Earle Coates. HBV-2
Death, *sel.* Mary Elizabeth Coleridge.
"Bid me remember, O my gracious Lord." TrPWD
Death. Emily Dickinson. *See* Bustle in a house, The, *and also* Death is a dialogue between.
Death. John Donne. *See* Death Be Not Proud.
Death. Philip Freneau. *Fr.* The House of Night. AP
Death. Roy Fuller. NoAM
Death. *Gond Oral Tradition, tr. by* V. Elwin *and* S. Hivale. WTO
Death. Patty L. Harjo. VoR
Death. George Herbert. AnAnS-1; JCP; MePo; NoP; OBS; SeCP; SeCV-1
Death. Thomas Hood. *See* Sonnet: "It is not death, that sometime in a sigh."
Death. Mildred Jeffrey. AMV-80
Death, A. Elizabeth Jennings. NMP
Death. L. E. Jones. POL
Death. William Knott. EAS
Death. Walter Savage Landor. *See* Death Stands above Me.
Death. Sir Thomas More. EnRePo
Death. James Oppenheim. WGRP
Death. George Pellew. AA
Death. Darwin T. Turner. BALP
Death ("I am a stranger in the land"). *Unknown.* BLPA; FPL
Death ("O death, rock me asleep"). *Unknown. See* O Death, Rock Me Asleep.
Death ("Once he will miss, twice he will miss"). *Unknown, tr. fr. Arabic by* E. Powys Mathers. *Fr.* The Thousand and One Nights. AWP
Death. Henry Vaughan. NCEP
Death. William Carlos Williams. OxBA; VGW
Death. Charles Wright. FiCP
Death. W. B. Yeats. ChMP
Death/ Is nothing to us, has no relevance. Against the Fear of Death. Lucretius, *tr. by* Rolfe Humphries. *Fr.* De Rerum Natura, III. DL; NAWM-1
Death!/ Plop. A Tragedy. Théophile Marzials. PeD
Death./ The death of a million. Pastoral. Ron Loewinsohn. NeAP
Death Again. T. Hope. BXAP
Death, always cruel, Pity's foe in chief. Dante, *tr. by* Dante Gabriel Rossetti. La Vita Nuova, III. AWP
Death, and change, and darkness everlasting. Where Dunwich Used to Be. Swinburne. *Fr.* By the North Sea, VI. FaBoPP
Death and Co. Sylvia Plath. CMoP; ConAP; FF; LCAP; PrIm
Death and darkness, get you packing. Easter Hymn. Henry Vaughan. AnAnS-1; EBCP; PoPle
Death and Doctor Hornbook. Burns. OxBS
Death and Empedocles 444 B.C. Horace Gregory. PoA
Death, and it is broken. The Instrument. Kathleen Raine. PoA
Death and Love. Ben Jonson. *See* Karolin's Song.
Death and Night. James Benjamin Kenyon. AA
Death and Resurrection. George Croly. WGRP
Death and the Arkansas River. Frank Stanford. FiCP
Death and the Cobbler. *Unknown.* APAS
Death and the Fairies. Patrick MacGill. HBMV
Death and the Lady. Léonie Adams. MoAB; MoAmPo
Death and the Maiden. *Unknown, tr. fr. Irish by* Frank O'Connor. KiLC
Death and the Plowman. Sidney Keyes. OxBTC
Death and the Three Revellers. Chaucer. *Fr.* The Canterbury Tales: The Pardoner's Tale. OBNV
("These rioters, of whom I make my rime," *mod. version.*) WHA
(Three Revellers Search for Death.) OxBM
Death-angel smote Alexander McGlue, The. Mr. Slimmer's Funeral Verses for the *Morning Argus* [*or* Out of the Hurly-Burly]. "Max Adeler." CenHV; OBAL
Death as a Lotus Flower. *Unknown. See* He Is like the Lotus.
Death as History. Jay Wright. PoBA
Death at Daybreak. Anne Reeve Aldrich. AA
Death at the headlands, Hesiod, long ago. Hesiod, 1908. Alexander Mair. GoTS
Death Balloon, The. Patricia Goedicke. FAZ
Death, Be Not Proud. John Donne. Holy Sonnets, X. BiP; ChTr; DL; FaBV; FaFP; FF; FPL; GoBC; HAP; HBV-2; InvP; LiTB; NIP; PoRA; PrIm; TreFS; TrGrPo; TRV; WeW; WHA
(Death.) OBEV; PPON
("Death be not proud, though some have called thee.") CABA; EnRePo; FaBoRV; HeIP; JCP; LoBV; MasP; MeLP; MePo; NOBE; NoP; OAEL-1; OAEP; OBS; PAI; PoEL-2; PPoe; PPP; SCV; SeCeV; SeCP; SeCV-1; TEP; TrCP; ViBoPo
(On Death.) EBCP
(Sonnet: "Death be not proud, though some have called thee.") AnAnS-1; ElL; FaBoEn
Death be not proud, thy hand gave not this blow. Elegy. Lucy Harington, Countess of Bedford. WPE
Death, become a shewolf. Crown of Happiness. Anne Hébert, *tr. by* Willis Barnstone. BoWoP
Death Bed. *See* Deathbed.
Death before forty's no bar. Lo! Obit on Parnassus. F. Scott Fitzgerald. InMe; NYBP; PrIm; WhC
Death Bells. *Unknown.* BluL
Death by Drowning. Elizabeth Brewster. NOBC
Death by Rarity. Marguerite Young. LiTA
Death by Water. T. S. Eliot. The Waste Land, IV. OBVE
Death calls me—Sweet, it might be good. Babylonian Sorrows. Heine, *tr. by* Aaron Kramer. NAWM-2
Death Carol. Walt Whitman. *Fr.* When Lilacs Last in the Door-Yard Bloom'd. WHA
(Carol of Death, The.) DL
("Come, lovely and soothing death.") SCV
Death-cell, A? The shack of the coastguards. The Coastguard House. Robert Lowell. NaP

Death Chant. Peter Blue Cloud. VoR
Death Circus, The. John Tranter. CBAP
Death Come to My House He Didn't Stay Long, *with music. Unknown.* BoAN-2
Death Comes for the Old Cowboy. Kevin Clark. AMV-81
Death comes in quantity from solved. The Tolerance of Crows. Charles Donnelly. CIP
Death Comes to the Salesman. Louis Daniel Brodsky. AMV-81
Death, death; O amiable lovely death! Shakespeare. *Fr.* King John, III, iv. TreFT
Death Deposed. William Allingham. OnYI
Death designs swirl high above faces that are of disbelief. War Walking Near. Ray A. Young Bear. CDW
Death devours all lovely things. Passer Mortuus Est. Edna St. Vincent Millay. CMoP; MoAmPo; OxBA
Death did not come to my mother. Conception. Josephine Miles. GP
Death, Don't Be Boring. Roy Kelly. BXAP
Death-doomed. Will Carleton. PaPo
Death for the Dark Stranger. Thomas McGrath. VGW
Death from Cancer. Robert Lowell. *Fr.* In Memory of Arthur Winslow. MP; TwCP
Death Fugue. Paul Celan. *See* Fugue of Death.
Death himself. LMFBR. Gary Snyder. PoM
Death-Hymn, A. Felicia Dorothea Hemans. *See* Dirge: "Calm on the bosom of thy God."
Death I recant, and say, unsaid by me. Elegy on Mistress Boulstred. John Donne. JCP
Death, I repent. Two Invocations of Death, I [*or* Invocation of Death]. Kathleen Raine. MoAB; OxBTC
Death, if thou wilt, fain would I plead with thee. A Dialogue. Swinburne. PoEL-5
Death in Hospital, A. John Lehmann. ChMP
Death in Leamington. John Betjeman. NoP; PoPl
Death in Life. Thomas, Lord Vaux. *See* No Pleasure without Some Pain.
Death-in-Love. Dante Gabriel Rossetti. The House of Life, XLVIII. SyP; VLP
Death in the Corn. Detlev von Liliencron, *tr. fr. German by* C. F. MacIntyre. WaaP
Death in the Desert, A. Robert Browning. GoTL; OxBoCh
"For life, with all it yields of joy and woe," *sel.* TRV
Death in the Desert, A. Charles Tomlinson. FF
Death in the Home. T. Sturge Moore. BrPo
Death in the Streets, A. Mario Petaccia. LFAC
Death in this tomb his weary bones hath laid. Death's Epitaph. Philip Freneau. *Fr.* The House of Night. AA
Death in Yorkville. Langston Hughes. PoBA
Death Invited. May Swenson. BoAnP; LiSp; WPE
Death Invoked. Philip Massinger. *Fr.* The Emperor of the East. ACP
(Sad Song, A.) OBS
(Song: "Why art thou slow, thou rest of trouble, Death.") ViBoPo
Death is a dialogue between. Emily Dickinson. WGRP
Death Is a Door. Nancy Byrd Turner. BLPA
Death Is a Second Cousin Dining with Us Tonight. Geraldine Kudaka. BrSi
"Death is a voyage," I heard it lightly told. O Mariners! Archibald Rutledge. EtS
Death is all metaphors, shape in one history. Dylan Thomas. Altarwise by Owl-Light, II. CMoP; MoAB; NoAM
Death is another milestone on their way. The Funeral. Stephen Spender. CMoP; MoAB; MoBrPo; NoAM
Death is asleep. Riddles and Lies. Christine Zawadiwsky. AMV-80
Death Is Awful. *Unknown.* BluL
Death is before me today. Dying. A. Alvarez. VWA
Death is great. Closing Piece. Rainer Maria Rilke, *tr. by* M. D. Herter Norton. PCP
Death is more than. One X. E. E. Cummings. FaBoMo
Death is not a dream; death lives. Death. Darwin T. Turner. BALP
Death is not a period. Thesis. William Walter De Bolt. AMV-80
Death is only an old door. Death Is a Door. Nancy Byrd Turner. BLPA
Death is stronger than all the governments. Death Snips Proud Men. Carl Sandburg. CMoP
Death is the cook of nature, and we find. Margaret Cavendish, Duchess of Newcastle. *Fr.* Nature's Cook. PBWP
Death is the strongest of all living things. Warning to One. Merrill Moore. MoAmPo; TrGrPo; YaD
Death killed the rich. *Yoruba Oral Tradition, tr. by* W. Abimbola WTO
Death-Lace. David Ray. MAT
Death lay in ambush. Christopher Okigbo. *Fr.* Distances. TTY
Death lies on her like an untimely frost. Frost on the Flower. Shakespeare. *Fr.* Romeo and Juliet. FaBoRV
Death Looks Down. Linda Gregg. NPGG
Death May Be Very Gentle. Oliver St. John Gogarty. PoRA
Death may leap on a sunny day. Raymond Thompson. LFAC
Death, my lifes Mistress, and the soveraign Queen. To His Mistress for Her True Picture. Lord Herbert of Cherbury. AnAnS-2; SeCP
Death never troubled Damocles. Damocles. Robert Graves. NYBP
Death News. Allen Ginsberg. NoAM
Death of a Bird. Jon Silkin. BoAnP; NePoEA
Death of a Cat, The, *sels.* Louis MacNeice. PCat
"For he was our puck, our miniature lar."
"To begin with he was a beautiful object."
Death of a Cat. James Schevill. NMP
Death of a Fair Girl. Alpheus Butler. PeD
Death of a Friend. Pauli Murray. PoBA
Death of a Hind. Alasdair Maclean. PoSH
Death of a Jazz Musician. William Jay Smith. NePoAm-2
Death of a Naturalist. Seamus Heaney. HAP; NCSH; OxBC; WeW
Death of a Negro Poet, The. Conrad Kent Rivers. BPo
Death of a Poet. Charles Causley. OxBTC
Death of a Snake, The. William Plomer. ELU
Death of a Soldier, The. Wallace Stevens. OBWP; OFD; QFR
Death of a Son. Jon Silkin. FF; GTBS-P; NePoEA; NoAM; OxBTC; VWA
Death of a Toad, The. Richard Wilbur. AP; BiP; CABA; CMoP; LiTM; MiAP; MoVE; NMP; NoAM; NoP; PoA; TwAmPo
Death of a Vermont Farm Woman. Barbara Howes. MoAmPo
Death of a Warrior, The. Jenny Mastoraki, *tr. fr. Modern Greek by* Kimon Friar. BoWoP
Death of a Whale. John Blight. CBAP; PoAu-2
Death of a Young Son by Drowning. Margaret Atwood. BoWoP; NOBC
Death of Admiral Benbow, The. *Unknown.* CoMu; GBP
(Admiral Benbow.) EnSB
Death of Adonis, The. Philip Ayres, *after the Greek of* Theocritus. OBVE
Death of Adonis, The. Shakespeare. *See* Lo! Here the Gentle Lark.
Death of Ailill, The. Francis Ledwidge. OnYI
Death of Alexander, The. *Unknown.* OxBS
(Cantus: "When Alexander our kynge was dede.") BSV
(When Alexander Our King Was Dead.) GoTS
(When Alysandyr Our King Was Dede.) FaBoCh
Death of an Aircraft. Charles Causley. MoBS
Death of an Angel, The. Russell Edson. LCAP
Death of an Elephant, The. Gianfranco Pagnucci. NU
Death of an Irishwoman. Michael Hartnett. CIP
Death of an Old Man, The. Michael Hamburger. NePoEA
Death of Antony. Shakespeare. *Fr.* Antony and Cleopatra, IV, xv. FiP
Death of Artemidora, The. Walter Savage Landor. *Fr.* Pericles and Aspasia. EnRP; OBNC; SeCeV
("Artemidora! Gods invisible.") ViBoPo
Death of Arthur, The. Layamon. *Fr.* The Brut. OxBM
Death of Azron, The. Alice Wellington Rollins. AA
Death of Ben Hall, The. Will H. Ogilvie. PoAu-1
Death of Buckingham, The. Pope. *See* Duke of Buckingham, The.
Death of Carmen Miranda, The. Stephen E. Smith. AMV-81
Death of Cleopatra. Shakespeare. *Fr.* Antony and Cleopatra, V, ii. FiP; TreFS
(Cleopatra's Death.) TrGrPo
(Immortal Longings.) FaBoRV
Death of Colman, The. Thomas Frost. PAH
Death of Cowards, The. Shakespeare. *Fr.* Julius Caesar, II, ii. TreFS
("Cowards die many times before their deaths.") FF
(That Men Should Fear.) TrGrPo
Death of Crazy Horse, The. John G. Neihardt. BPAW
Death of Cuchulain, The. W. B. Yeats. ChTr; GoTL
(Cuchulain's Fight with the Sea, *diff. vers.*) AnIL
Death of Custer, The. "Captain Jack" Crawford. PoOW
Death of Daphnis, The. Theocritus, *tr. fr. Greek by* Charles Stuart Calverley. Idylls, I. AWP
Death of David, The. Hayyim Nahman Bialik, *tr. fr. Hebrew by* Herbert Danby, *ad. by* Sholom J. Kahn. TrJP
Death of Death, The. Shakespeare. *See* Sonnets, CXLVI.
Death of Digenes Akritas, The. John Heath-Stubbs. NePoEA
Death of Dr. King. Sam Cornish. CNA; OFD; PoBA
Death of Don Pedro, The. *Unknown, tr. fr. Spanish by* John Gibson Lockhart. AWP
Death of Europe, The. Charles Olson. NeAP
Death of Eurydice and Orpheus' Journey to Hell, The. Ovid, *tr. fr. Latin by* George Sandys. *Fr.* Metamorphoses. JCP
Death of faithful Dobbin I deplore, The. An Elegy on the Death of Dobbin, the Butterwoman's Horse. Francis Fawkes. NOEC
Death of Fathers, The. Theodore Weiss. DiL; SV
Death of Friends, The. Adele Levi. GoYe
Death of Gaudentis. "Harriet Annie." WBLP
Death of General Pike, The. Laughton Osborn. PAH

Death of General Uncebunke, The; a Biography in Little, *sel.* Lawrence Durrell.
"My uncle sleeps in the image of death." FaBoMo
Death of God, The. Howard Nemerov. OxBC
Death of Goody Nurse, The. Rose Terry Cooke. PAH
Death of Grant, The. Ambrose Bierce. AA
Death of Haidée, The. Byron. *Fr.* Don Juan, IV. FiP; WHA, *longer sel.*
Death of Hamlet. Shakespeare. *See* I Am Dead, Horatio.
Death of Harrison, The. Nathaniel Parker Willis. PAH
Death of Hector, The. Homer, *tr. fr. Greek by* George Chapman. *Fr.* The Iliad, XXII. OBS
Death of Hoel, The. Thomas Gray. NOEC
Death of Janis Joplin, The. Robert Phillips. SOTS
Death of Jefferson, The. Hezekiah Butterworth. PAH
Death of Jesus, The. Bible, *N.T.* Luke, XXIII: 1-46. TreF
Death of Justice, The. Walter Everette Hawkins. PoBA
Death of King Edward I, The. *Unknown.* MeEL
Death of King Edward VII, The. *Unknown.* OxBoLi
Death of King George V. John Betjeman. *See* "New King Arrives in His Capital by Air. . ."—*Daily Newspaper.*
Death of Kings, The. Shakespeare. King Richard II, *fr.* III, ii. TrGrPo
(Let's Talk of Graves.) FaBoRV
("Let's talk of graves, of worms, and epitaphs") PPoe
(Richard II's Dejection.) TreFS
Death of Leander, The. Thomas Hood. *Fr.* Hero and Leander. EnRP
Death of Lear. Shakespeare. *Fr.* King Lear, V, iii. FiP
Death of Leonidas, The. George Croly. BeLS
Death of Lesbia's Bird, The. Catullus, *tr. fr. Latin by* Samuel Taylor Coleridge. AWP
(Death of the Starling, The.) PBBP
Death of Lincoln, The. Bryant. AP; TAP
(Abraham Lincoln.) PAH
(To the Memory of Abraham Lincoln.) OHIP
Death of Little Boys. Allen Tate. LiTA; MoAB; MP
Death of Lord Warriston, The. *Unknown.* OxBB
Death of Lyon, The. Henry Peterson. PAH
Death of Marilyn Monroe, The. Sharon Olds. MAYP
Death of Meleager, The. Swinburne. *Fr.* Atalanta in Calydon. OBVV
Death of Minnehaha, The. Longfellow. *Fr.* The Song of Hiawatha. AA
Death of Morgan, The. *Unknown.* FaBoBa
Death of Moses, The. *Unknown, tr. fr. Hebrew by* Alice Lucas. TrJP
Death of My Aunt. *Unknown.* OxBoLi
Death of Myth-making, The. Sylvia Plath. PoA
Death of Nelson, The. *Unknown.* OxBoLi
(New Song Composed on the Death of Lord Nelson, A.) CoMu
Death of Nick Charles, The. Amiri Baraka. CoPo
Death of Old Joe Yazzie, The. Ron Rogers. STE
Death of Othello. Shakespeare. *Fr.* Othello, V, ii. FiP
(Othello's Farewell.) TreFS
Death of Parcy Reed, The. *Unknown.* ESPB
Death of Peter Esson, The. George Mackay Brown. NePoEA-2
Death of Polybius Jubb, The. Roy Campbell. WhC
Death of Prince Leopold, The. William McGonagall. EvOK
Death of Professor Backwards, The. X. J. Kennedy. SOTS
Death of Puck, The. Eugene Lee-Hamilton. HBMV; OBVV
Death of Queen Jane, The. *Unknown.* AmFP (2 *versions*); ESPB (A *and* B *vers.*); OBET; ViBoFo
(Queen Jane.) FSW
Death of Richard Wagner, The. Swinburne. LoBV
Death of Rimbaud. David Fisher. NPGG
Death of Robert, Earl of Huntingdon, *sel.* Anthony Munday.
Robin Hood's Funeral. WiR
(Dirge: "Weep, weep, ye woodmen, wail.") CTC; OBSC
(Song: "Weep, weep, ye woodmen, wail.") ElL
(Weep, Weep, Ye Woodmen.) CH
Death of Robin Hood, The ("Robin dwelt in greene wood"). *Unknown.* EnSB
Death of Robin Hood, The ("When Robin Hood and Little John"). *Unknown. See* Robin Hood's Death.
Death of Saint Guthlac. Cynewulf, *tr. fr. Anglo-Saxon. Fr.* Guthlac. ACP
Death of Samson. Milton. *Fr.* Samson Agonistes. ChTr
("Come, come, no time for lamentation now.") FiP
(No Time for Lamentation Now.) FaBoRV
Death of Samuel Adams, The. *Unknown.* AmFP
Death of Sir Nihil, book the *n*th. Tywater. Richard Wilbur. CMoP; ConAP; LiTA; LiTM; MiAP; MoAB; NePA
Death of Slavery, The. Bryant. AA
Death of Sohrab, The. Matthew Arnold. *Fr.* Sohrab and Rustum. FiP
Death of Tammuz, The. Saul Tchernichowsky, *tr. fr. Hebrew.* TrJP, *tr. by* L. V. Snowman; VWA, *tr. by* Mark Elliott Shapiro
Death of the Ball Turret Gunner, The. Randall Jarrell. AP; BiP; CMoP; CoBMV; ELU; FF; HAP; HoPM; InPK; LCAP; LiTM; MiAP; MoAmPo; NAs; NIP; NMP; NoAM; NOBA; NoP; OBWP; OxBA; PAI; PoPl; PPP; PrIm; SeCeV; SoSe; TAP; UnPo; VGW; WaaP; WaP
Death of the Bird, The. A. D. Hope. PoAu-2
Death of the Bronx, The. Chana Bloch. MAYP
Death of the Cat. Ian Serraillier. SO
Death of the Craneman, The. Alfred Hayes. LiTA; NCSH; WaP
Death of the Day. Walter Savage Landor. NoP
Death of the Dragon, The. Spenser. *Fr.* The Faerie Queene, I, 11. WHA
Death of the Epileptic Poet Yesenin, The. Aram Boyajian. NeAC
Death of the First Man, The. Nancy Sullivan. NIP
Death of the Flowers, The. Bryant. AA; BLPL; BoNaP; GN; HBV-1; OBCA; PoLF; TreF; WBLP
Death of the Gods, The; an Ode Written in Imitation of Pindar. L. Ker. NOEC
Death of the Hired Man, The. Robert Frost. AmPP; CMoP; HoPM; MoAB; MoAmPo; NoP; OxBA; SeCeV; SoSe; TrGrPo
Home, *br. sel.* TRV
(Home Defined.) TreF
Death of the innocent by the innocent. On Reading Gene Derwood's "The Innocent." Willard Maas. NePA
Death of the Lincoln Despotism. *Unknown.* PAH
Death of the Moon. David Wagoner. PoA
Death of the Novel, The. David Young. AmPA
Death of the Old Year, The. Tennyson. HBV-1
"Full knee-deep lies the winter snow," *sel.* PoSC
Death of the Sailor's Wife, The. Fred Barton. AMV-80
Death of the Sheriff, The. Robert Lowell. MoAB; MoAmPo
(Noli Me Tangere.) LCAP
Death of the Starling, The. Catullus. *See* Death of Lesbia's Bird, The.
Death, of thee do I make my moan. To Death, of His Lady. Villon, *tr. by* Dante Gabriel Rossetti. AWP
Death of Urgan, The. Swinburne. *Fr.* Tristram of Lyonesse. WHA
Death of Venus, The. Robert Creeley. NOBA
Death of Vitellozzo Vitelli, The. Irving Feldman. MP; TwCP
Death of Warren, The. Epes Sargent. PAH
Death of Will, The. Charles Tomlinson. OxBC
Death of Wolfe, The. *Unknown.* PAH
Death of Wyatt, The. Earl of Surrey. *See* Divers Thy Death.
Death of Yeats, The. George Barker. LiTB
Death on a Crossing. Evangeline Paterson. EBCP
Death on a Live Wire. Michael Baldwin. MoBS
Death on the Farm. Cary Waterman. GP
Death, reaping the mad world, his crimson blade. The Foiled Reaper. William Kean Seymour. HBMV
Death Rites II. *Unknown, tr. by* C. M. Bowra. TTY
Death Rode a Pinto Pony. Whitney Montgomery. BPAW
Death Room, The. Robert Graves. NYBP
Death Row. Charles Culhane. LFAC
Death Seed. Ricarda Huch, *tr. fr. German by* Susan C. Strong. PBWP
Death Sentence, The. Stevie Smith. NoP
Death shall be death forever unto thee. Forever Dead. Sappho, *tr. by* William Ellery Leonard. AWP
Death; She Was Always Here. Yona Wallach, *tr. fr. Hebrew by* Leonore Gordon. VWA
Death, since I find not one with whom to grieve. Canzone: He Beseeches Death for the Life of Beatrice. Dante, *tr. by* Dante Gabriel Rossetti. AWP
Death Snips Proud Men. Carl Sandburg. CMoP
Death Song, A. Paul Laurence Dunbar. BANP; CDC; PoLF; PoNe
Death Song. Robert Stephen Hawker. OBNC; OBRV; OBVV
Death Song. Alonzo Lewis. PAH
Death Songs. L. V. Mack. PoBA
Death Sonnet I. Gabriela Mistral, *tr. fr. Spanish by* David Garrison. BoWoP
Death speaks:/ When men my scythe and darts supply. Thomas Parnell. *Fr.* Night Piece on Death. OnYI
Death Stands above Me. Walter Savage Landor. EnRP; LiTB; NOBE; OAEP; PoEL-4; SoSe
(Death.) FaBV; HBV-2
("Death stands above me, whispering low.") NoP; OBNC
(On Death.) OAEL-2; TrGrPo
(On His Own Death.) OBVV
Death stately came to a young man. Death Deposed. William Allingham. OnYI
Death Sting Me Blues. *Unknown.* BluL
Death stretched down two hands. Casualty. Diana Witherby. ChMP
Death Swoops. Kenneth Pitchford. CoPo
Death, that is small respecter of distinction. Trainwrecked Soldiers. John Frederick Nims. MiAP
Death, that struck when I was most confiding. Death. Emily Brontë. EBVV; OBNC; VLP

Death, the black wizard of the center. The Turnaround for Higherground. Pancho Aguila. LFAC
Death, the Conqueror. James Shirley. *See* Victorious Men of Earth.
Death the Consequence of the Fall. Dryden. *Fr.* The State of Innocence. NOCV
Death, the friend behind phenomenon. A Game of Chance. Howard Moss. PoA
Death the Leveller. James Shirley. *See* Glories of Our Blood and State, The.
Death, tho I see him not, is near. *See* Death, though I see him not, is near.
Death, Thou Hast Seized Me. Isaac Luzzatto, *tr. fr. Hebrew by* Nina Davis Salaman. TrJP
Death, thou wast once an uncouth hideous thing. Death. George Herbert. AnAnS-1; JCP; MePo; NOP; OBS; SeCP; SeCV-1
Death, though [*or* tho] I see him not, is near. Age. Walter Savage Landor. ELU; FaBoEE; InPK; NBM; PoEL-4
Death, thou'rt a cordial old and rare. The Stirrup-Cup. Sidney Lanier. AA; AmPP; WHA
Death thresholded old man hold. Double Ritual. Dachine Rainer. CrMA
Death to the Lady said. Death and the Lady. Léonie Adams. MoAB; MoAmPo
Death to Us, A. Jon Silkin. NePoEA
Death to Van Gogh's Ear! Allen Ginsberg. CABA; NaP; VGW
Death took my father. Manos Karastefanís. James Merrill. TAP
Death Valley. Jack H. Lee. BPAW
Death Valley Blues. *Unknown.* BluL
Death-Wake or Lunacy, The, *sel.* Thomas Stoddart.
Mirthful Lunacy. OBNC
Death walks through the mind's dark woods. Poem. Henry Treece. NeBP
Death Was a Woman. Sydney King Russell. GoYe
Death was there, sitting by the roadside. Climbing. Gloria Fuertes, *tr. by* Philip Levine. PBWP
Death Watchers, The. Alice Ryerson. AMV-80
Death, when I am ready, I. Pause en Route. Thomas Kinsella. OxBI
Death, when you come to me, tread with a footstep. So Might It Be. John Galsworthy. BLPL; PoLF
Death, why hast thou made life so hard to bear. Canzone: Of His Dead Lady. Giacomino Pugliesi, *tr. by* Dante Gabriel Rossetti. AWP
Death, why so cruel [*or* soe crewill]? What! no other way. Bacon's Epitaph, Made by His Man. *At. to* John Cotton. PAH; SCAP
Death will make his entry into your body which is so beautiful. Death. *Gond Oral Tradition, tr. by* V. Elwin *and* S. Hivale. WTO
Death with a Coda. Giuseppe Gioachino Belli, *tr. fr. Italian by* Miller Williams. AMV-81
Death with his sad hands. Death of Rimbaud. David Fisher. NPGG
Death you are a dreadful fellow. Death, Don't Be Boring. Roy Kelly. BXAP
Death, you are so much more powerful. Stone Words for Robert Lowell. Richard Eberhart. AMV-80
Death-Bed, A. James Aldrich. AA; HBV-2
Death Bed, The. Waring Cuney. CDC
Deathbed, A. John Hawthorn. *Fr.* The Journey and Observations of a Countryman. NOEC
Death-Bed, The. Thomas Hood. EnRP; GTBS; GTBS-P; HBV-2; NOBE; OBEV; OBNC; OBRV; OBVV; TreFS
Death Bed. Thomas Kinsella. CIP
Death-Bed, The. Siegfried Sassoon. LiTM; MMA; MoVE; PoPle
Death-Bed Reflections of Michel-Angelo. Hartley Coleridge. EyDe
Death-Bed Song. *Unknown.* AmFP
Deathless Aphrodite, throned in flowers. Ode to Aphrodite. Sappho, *tr. by* William Ellery Leonard. AWP
Deathless Ones, The. Eleanor Glenn Wallis. NePoAm
"Deathless Principle, Arise." Augustus Montague Toplady. OxBoCh
Death's Blue-eyed Girl. Linda Pastan. PPJ
Death's but one more to-morrow. Thou art gray. Of One Who Seemed to Have Failed. S. Weir Mitchell. AA
Death's Emissaries. James Shirley. *See* Victorious Men of Earth.
Death's Epitaph. Philip Freneau. *Fr.* The House of Night. AA
Death's Final Conquest. James Shirley. *See* Glories of Our Blood and State, The.
Death's Gwinter Lay His Cold Icy Hands on Me, *2 vers., with music. Unknown.* BoAN-2
Death's Head. Phyllis Gotlieb. NOBC
Death's-Head Moth. Stanley Roger Green. BSV
Death's head on your hand you neede not weare, A. Thomas Dudley, Ah! Old Must Dye. *Unknown.* SCAP
Death's Jest Book; or, The Fool's Tragedy, *sels.* Thomas Lovell Beddoes.
Bridal Song to Amala ("We have bathed"), *fr.* IV, iii. GBL; OBVV
(Epithalamia.) PoEL-4
(Song.) ChER; FaBoEn; OBNC
(Songs at Amala's Wedding.) LoBV
Dirge: "If thou wilt ease thine heart," *fr.* II, ii. LiTB; LO; OBNC; OBRV; PoEL-4
(If Thou Wilt Ease Thine Heart.) EnRP
(Wolfram's Dirge.) NOBE; OBEV
Dirge: "Swallow leaves her nest, The," *fr.* I, iv. LoBV; OBVV; PoEL-4
(Song from the Waters.) NOBE
(Voice from the Waters, A.) OBNC; OBRV
Dirge: "We do lie beneath the grass," *fr.* V, iv. OBNC; WiR
(Sibilla's Dirge.) NBM; NOBE
(We Do Lie beneath the Grass.) ELP
"Durst thou again say life and soul has lifted," *fr.* III, iii. LO
"Fair and bright assembly, A: never strode," *fr.* II, iii. CTC
"I never knew before/ The meaning of this love," *fr.* II, iii. LO
L'Envoi: "Who findeth comfort in the stars and flowers." LO; OBNC
Mandrake's Song ("Folly hath now turned out the door"), *fr.* I, i. NBM
"My will lies there, my hope, and all my life," *fr.* II, ii. LO
Song: "Old Adam, the carrion crow," *fr.* V, iv. ChER; EBEV; LiTB; OAEL-2; OBRV; PBBP; PoEL-4
(Carrion Crow, The.) TrGrPo; WiR
(Old Adam.) ELP
(Old Adam, the Carrion Crow.) EnRP
(Wolfram's Song.) OBVV
Song by Isbrand, *fr.* III, iii. OBNC; PrIm
(Squats on a Toad-Stool under a Tree.) InvP
Song on the Water. FaBoCh
"Then all the minutes of my life to come," *fr.* II, iv. LO
To Sea, to Sea! *fr.* I, i. EtS
(Mariner's Song.) OBVV
(Sailor's Song.) HBV-1
(Song from the Ship.) OBRV
(To Sea.) CH
Death's Lecture at the Funeral of a Young Gentleman. Richard Crashaw. SeCP
Deaths of Paragon, Indiana, The. John Woods. CoPo
Death's Subtle Ways. James Shirley. *See* Victorious Men of Earth.
Death's Summons. Thomas Nashe. *See* Adieu, Farewell Earth's Bliss.
Death's the Classic Look. John Ciardi. PoA
Death's Transfiguration. Israel Zangwill. TrJP
Death's Vision, *sel.* John Reynolds.
Mysteries Revealed after Death. NOEC
Death's Warning to Beauty. *Unknown, tr. fr. Early Modern Irish by* Robin Flower. AnIL
Deathward. John Lyle Donaghy. BIrV
Deathwatch. Michael S. Harper. AmPA; PoBA
Debate between Arjuna and Sri Krishna. *Unknown, tr. fr. Sanskrit by* Swami Prabhavananda *and* Christopher Isherwood. WaaP
Debate in the Sennit, The. James Russell Lowell. The Biglow Papers, 1st Series, No. V. HBV-1; PAH
Debate: Question, Quarry, Dream. Robert Penn Warren. VGW
Debate with the Rabbi. Howard Nemerov. PoPl
Debora Sleeping. William Logan. MAYP
Deborah danced, when she was two. Experience. Aline Kilmer. HBMV
Deborah Lee. Yvonne. CNA
Debout, *sel.* Tchicaya U Tam'si, *tr. fr. French by* E. S. Yntema.
"Here is the stream again under the rainbow." PBA
Debridement: Operation Harvest Moon: *On Repose.* Michael S. Harper. GeTw
Debt, The. Paul Laurence Dunbar. AmNP; BANP; CABA; CDC; SoSe; TRV
Debt. *Gond Oral Tradition, tr. by* V. Elwin *and* S. Hivale. WTO
Debt is paid, The. The Past. Emerson. FaBoCh; FPL; LiTA; PoEL-4; TAP
Debts. Jessie B. Rittenhouse. HBMV
Debussy and Proust. John Tagliabue. FAZ
Debutante was sitting in the parlor of her flat, A. Song: "Don't Tell Me What You Dreamt Last Night." Franklin P. Adams. FiBHP
Debutantrum. William Rose Benét. InMe
Decade, A. Amy Lowell. MoAmPo; PoPl
Decades behind me. A Right-of-Way: 1865. William Plomer. DTC
Decanter of Madeira, Aged 86, to George Bancroft, Aged 86, A. S. Weir Mitchell. AA; ViBoPo
Decay. George Herbert. AnAnS-1; SeCP; SeCV-1
Decay of a People, The. William Gilmore Simms. AA
Decay of Piety. Wordsworth. TrCP
Decayed Monastery, A. Thomas Dermody. OnYI
Decayed Time. Jean Wahl, *tr. fr. French by* Charles Guenther. VWA
Decease, Release: Dum Morior Orior. Robert Southwell. *See* At Fotheringay.
Deceased. Cid Corman. PCP; VGW
Deceased, The. Keith Douglas. FaBoTw
Deceav'd and undeceav'd to be. The Self-Deceaver. Thomas Stanley, *after the Spanish of* Juan Perez de Montalvan. OBVE

Deceitful Brownskin Blues. *Unknown.* BluL
Deceitful snow, made of the gray sea. December Storm. John Hay. NePoAm
Deceiving world, that with alluring toys. A Palinode. Robert Greene. *Fr.* Greene's Groatsworth of Wit. OBSC
December. John Clare. OBCP
December. Aileen Fisher. SiSoSe
December. Robert Francis. LCAP
December. William Caulfield Irwin. NBM
December. Keats. *See* In a Drear-nighted December.
December. Maurice Kenny. STE
December. Ron Padgett. EAS
December. Christina Rossetti. YeAr
December. James Schuyler. NoAM
December. Gary Snyder. InPS
December among the Vanished. W. S. Merwin. NaP
December, and the closing of the year. Christmas Eve in Whitneyville, 1955. Donald Hall. DiL; UnPo
December Blues. Robert Pinsky. MAYP
December Day, A. Sara Teasdale. YeAr
December Day, Hoy Sound. George Mackay Brown. OxBS
December Eclipse. Margo Lockwood. Psk
December 18, 1975. Michael Hogan. FAZ
December 18th. Anne Sexton. *Fr.* Eighteen Days without You. CAPP
December 15, 1811. Poem for My Family: Hazel Griffin and Victor Hernandez Cruz. June Jordan. BPo
December Forest, A. Vesna Krmpotic, *tr. fr. Croatian by* Vasa D. Mihailovich. WPOW
December Fragments. Richmond Lattimore. PChr
December, my dear, on the road to Nijmegen. The Road to Nijmegen. Earle Birney. OBCV
December narrows our day to a thread of light. Song in the Cold Season. Samuel French Morse. PoA
December Night. W. S. Merwin. CAPP
December, nightfall at three-thirty. Swan. Donald Hall. LCAP
December 1970. John Tagliabue. GP
December: Of Aphrodite. W. S. Merwin. NePoEA
December: Prayer to St. Nicholas. John Heath-Stubbs. OBCP
December Stillness. Siegfried Sassoon. CMoP
December Storm. John Hay. NePoAm
December sun sits low over hedgerows, glitter. What Shines in Winter Burns. T. R. Hummer. MAYP
December Sunset. Jonathan Holden. FAZ
December: the trees chafing. Mile Hill. Dennis Schmitz. LCAP
December 21st. Jean Valentine. LCAP
December 24 and George McBride Is Dead. Richard Hugo. HoPM
December 24, 1979. Roger Weaver. SOTS
December 26. George Edward Hoffman. PGD
Decent Burial. Lois Seyster Montross. HBMV
Decent docent doesn't doze, The. History of Education. David McCord. NIP; OBAL; WhC
Deception. Alfred Corn. PoA
Deceptions. Philip Larkin. CABA; CMoP; ErPo; GTBS-P; NePoEA; NMP
Deceptive Grin of the Gravel Porters, The. Gavin Ewart. FaBoMo
Deceptive Present, the Phoenix Year, The. Delmore Schwartz. BoNaP
Deceptrices, The. William Carlos Williams. NYBP
Deciduous Branch. Stanley Kunitz. TwAmPo
Decision, The. Owen Dodson. PoNe
Decision. Theodore Roethke. VGW
Decision, A. Edith Södergran, *tr. fr. Swedish by* Jaakko O. Ahokas. PBWP
Deck out. You. John Tagliabue. GP
Deck the Halls. *Unknown.* FSW
Deck thyself, maiden. Esthonian Bridal Song. Johann Gottfried von Herder, *tr. by* W. Taylor. AWP
Deck us all with Boston Charlie. Boston Charlie. Walt Kelly. FiBHP; GoJo
Decks. Robert Phillips. GeTw; NYP
Decks awash,/ Mast-top dipping. Archilochus, *tr. fr. Latin by* Guy Davenport. OBVE
Declaimer, The. Henry Baker. NOEC
Declair, ye bankis of Helicon. *Unknown.* *Fr.* The Bankis of Helicon. OxBS
Declaration. Arthur Symons. *Fr.* Violet. BrPo; ViBoPo
Declaration, The. Nathaniel Parker Willis. OBAL
Declaration at Forty. Judson Crews. UnTE
Declare, my pretty maid. The Philanderer. Moses Mendes. *Fr.* The Chaplet. TrJP
Declension. Stephen Sandy. PoA
Declining of a Gallant, The. *Unknown.* FaBoUs
Decorating the Soldiers' Graves. Minot J. Savage. OHIP
Decoration. Louise Bogan. MoAB; MoAmPo
Decoration. Thomas Wentworth Higginson. AA; OHIP
Decoration Day. George Hurlbut Barbour. OHIP
Decoration Day. Julia Ward Howe. OHIP
Decoration Day. Longfellow. OHIP; PoSC
Decoration Day. Bennie Lee Sinclair. TAT
Decorations climbing up the loft on a wobbly ladder. My Christmas; Mum's Christmas. Sarah Forsyth. OBCP
Decoy. John Ashbery. PoM
Decoys, The. W. H. Auden. CMoP; SyP
Decrees of God, The. Chao Ying-tou, *tr. fr. Chinese by* William C. White. TrJP
Decrepit Old Gasman, A. *Unknown.* FaFP
(Limerick: "Decrepit old gas man named Peter, A.") SoSe
Dedicated, The. Philip Larkin. OxBC
Dedicated Dancing Bull and the Water Maid, The, *sel.* Stevie Smith.
"Hop hop, thump thump." WPE
Dedicated Spirit, A. Wordsworth. *Fr.* The Prelude. SeCePo
Dedication, A, *sel.* Karin Boye, *tr. fr. Swedish by* Nadia Christensen.
"I feel your steps in the hall." PBWP
Dedication: "Bob Southey! You're a poet—poet-laureate." Byron. *Fr.* Don Juan. CTC; EnRP; OAEL-2; OAEP; OBSV
("Bob Southey! You're a poet—poet-laureate.") PPoe
(Dedication to the Poet Laureate, *abr.*) FiP
(Invocation.) LoBV
(Southey and Wordsworth.) TrGrPo
Dedication: "Eugenius, thy son, who guards the Rock." Pope Eugenius III, *tr. fr. Latin by* Raymond F. Roseliep. ISi
Dedication: "Had there been peace there never had been riven." Drummond Allison. FaBoTw
Dedication, A: "He was, through boyhood's storm and shower." G. K. Chesterton. FiBHP
Dedication, The: "Health to great Gloucester—from a man unknown." Charles Churchill. OBSV
(Dedication to the Sermons, The.) QFR
Dedication: "Holy Jesus, Thou art born." Victoria Saffelle Johnson. GoBC; TrPWD
Dedication: "I speak with a proud tongue of the people who were." Patrick MacGill. *See* Slainthe!
Dedication: "I would the gift I offer here." Whittier. *Fr.* Songs of Labor. OxBA
Dedication: "In my dreams we are always together." Richard Stull. AMV-81
Dedication, A: "Life of my learning, fire of all my Art." Mary Elizabeth Coleridge. TrPWD
Dedication, The: "Lord, my first fruits present themselves to thee." George Herbert. AnAnS-1; OAEP
Dedication, A: "Lucilla, saved from shipwreck on the seas." Claire McAllister. TwAmPo
Dedication, The: "My God, thou that didst dye for me." Henry Vaughan. AnAnS-1
Dedication, A: "My new-cut ashlar takes the light." Kipling. HBV-2; OBVV
Dedication: "Sea gives her shells to the shingle, The." Swinburne. VLP
Dedication: "Some nine years gone, as we dwelt together." Swinburne. VLP
Dedication II: "Strongest and the noblest argument, The." Sir John Davies. *Fr.* Nosce Teipsum. SiPS
Dedication: "Tall unpopular men." Oliver St. John Gogarty. OBMV
Dedication: "These to His Memory—since he held them dear." Tennyson. *Fr.* Idylls of the King. CABA; VLP
Dedication, A: "They are rhymes rudely strung with intent less." Adam Lindsay Gordon. CBAP; PoAu-1
Dedication: " 'They shall not die in vain,' we said." Ralph Gustafson. CaP
Dedication: "This little book, my God and King." Sir James Chamberlayne. CavP
Dedication: "Thou, whose unmeasured temple stands." Bryant. BLRP
(How Amiable Are Thy Tabernacles!) TrPWD
("Thou, whose unmeasured temple stands.") TRV
Dedication: To Ianthe. Byron. *See* To Ianthe.
Dedication: To Leigh Hunt, Esq. Keats. *See* To Leigh Hunt, Esq.
Dedication I: "To that clear majesty which in the north." Sir John Davies. *Fr.* Nosce Teipsum. SiPS
(To Queen Elizabeth.) OBSC
Dedication: "When I have ended, then I see." Laurence Housman. TrPWD
Dedication for a Book of Criticism. Yvor Winters. GLGT
Dedication for a Building. Alan Dugan. CAD; NYP
Dedication of the Chronicles of England and France. Robert Fabyan. ISi
Dedication of the Cook. Anna Wickham. MoBrPo
Dedication of the Illustrations to Blair's "Grave," *sel.* Blake.
Door of Death, The. ChTr
(To the Queen.) EnRP
Dedication on the Gift of a Book to a Child. Hilaire Belloc. EBEV; HBVY

Dedication to G**** H******* Esq., A, *sel.* Burns.
"Morality, thou deadly bane." OBSV
Dedication to Hunger. Louise Glück. GeTw
Dedication to Leigh Hunt. Keats. *See* To Leigh Hunt, Esq.
Dedication to My Wife, A. T. S. Eliot. BoLoP; FF
Dedication to "Songs of the Springtides." Swinburne. VLP
Dedication to the Final Confrontation. Lloyd M. Corbin, Jr. PoBA
Dedication to the Generation Knocking at the Door. John Davidson. BrPo
Dedication to the Poet Laureate. Byron. *See* Dedication: "Bob Southey! You're a poet—Poet-laureate."
Dedication to the Sermons, The. Charles Churchill. *See* Dedication, The: "Health to great Gloucester—from a man unknown."
Dedications [*of* Orchestra]. Sir John Davies. SiPS
To His Very Friend, Master Richard Martin, I.
To the Prince, II.
Dedicatory: "Somewhere, sometime, in an April twilight." Willa Cather. WPE
Dedicatory Ode, *sel.* Hilaire Belloc.
They Say That in the Unchanging Place. PoLF
Dedicatory Sonnet to S. T. Coleridge. Hartley Coleridge. OAEL-2
Dee dee dee dee dee wee weee eeeeee wee we. Communication in Whi-te. Don L. Lee. BPo
Deean Tractorman, Clear, The. Edith Anne Robertson. OxBS
Deean Tractorman, Deleerit, The. Edith Anne Robertson. OxBS
Deed of Lieutenant Miles, The. Clinton Scollard. PAH
Deeds of Kindness. Epes Sargent, *sometimes at. to* Fanny Crosby. HBV-1; HBVY
Deeds of Valor at Santiago. Clinton Scollard. HBV-2; PAH
Deeds That Might Have Been, The. Wilfrid Scawen Blunt. *Fr.* In Vinculis. TrGrPo
Deem as ye list, upon good cause. Sir Thomas Wyatt. SiPS
Deem not, because you see me in the press. Sonnets, XI. George Santayana. TrGrPo
Deem not, devoid of elegance, the sage. Sonnet: Written in a Blank Leaf of Dugdale's "Monasticon" [*or* Sonnet]. Thomas Warton, the Younger. Sonnets, III. OBEC; SeCePo
Deep, The. John G. C. Brainard. AA; EtS
Deep affections of the breast, The. The Parrot. Thomas Campbell. FM
Deep and Dark Blue Ocean. Byron. *See* Sea, The.
Deep and soft and far off over country. Before Harvest. Robert Fitzgerald. PoPl
Deep asleep, perfect immobility, no apparent evidence of consciousness or of dream. Waking Jed. C. K. Williams. DiL
Deep black against the dying glow. An Autumnal Evening. "Fiona Macleod." PoSC; SyP
Deep Blue Sea. *Unknown.* FSW
Deep Calling, The. John Rothfork. WOLT
Deep cradled in the fringed mow to lie. Theophany. Evelyn Underhill. WGRP
Deep Dark Night, The. Tennyson. *Fr.* The Devil and the Lady. SeCePo
Deep Dark River. Lloyd Roberts. CaP
Deep in a distant bay, and deeply hidden. The Lonely Isle. Claudian, *tr. by* Howard Mumford Jones. AWP
Deep in a Rose's glowing heart. Sent with a Rose to a Young Lady. Margaret Deland. AA
Deep in a vale, a stranger now to arms. The American Soldier. Philip Freneau. TAP
Deep in a vale where rocks on every side. Sonnet. Gustav Rosenhane, *tr. by* Sir Edmund Gosse. AWP
Deep in Alabama earth. Alabama Earth. Langston Hughes. AmFN
Deep in love. Bhavabhūti, *tr. fr. Sanskrit by* W. S. Merwin *and* J. Moussaieff Masson. LLLT
Deep in my heart I hear them, the gaunt hounds pacing. The Hounds of the Soul. Louis Ginsberg. TrJP
Deep in my soul there roared the crashing thunder. Calm after Storm. Frank Yerby. AmNP
Deep in the air the past appears. The Greeks. Tom Clark. PoA
Deep in the back ways of my mind I see them. My Great-Grandfather's Slaves. Wendell Berry. GeTw
Deep in the brown bosom. Bangkok. F. R. Scott. MoCV; OBCV
Deep in the fading leaves of night. Carol. W. R. Rodgers. ChMP; DTC; OBCP
Deep in the forest there is a pond. After the Anonymous Swedish. Jim Harrison. VGW
Deep in the Georgia night when all. Georgia Towns. Daniel Whitehead Hicky. AmFN
Deep in the grass there lies a dead gazelle. Maytime. *Unknown, tr. by* L. Cranmer-Byng. *Fr.* Shi King. AWP
Deep in the heart of the forest the lily of Yorrow is growing. The Lily of Yorrow. Henry van Dyke. AA
Deep in the heart of the lake. Water Music. Alun Lewis. ChMP
Deep in the hill the gold sand burned. A Ballad of the Gold Country. Helen Hunt Jackson. BPAW
Deep in the oven, where the two had shoved her. Juvenile Court. Sara Henderson Hay. DFT
Deep in the shady sadness of a vale. Hyperion. Keats. ChER; EnRP; FaBoEn; FiP; LoBV; OAEL-2; OAEP; OBNC; OBRV; PoEL-4; TrGrPo
Deep in the Siberian mine. Message to Siberia. Pushkin, *tr. by* Max Eastman. AWP; TTY
Deep in the study. The Phoenix. Ogden Nash. CenHV; NePA
Deep in the wave is a coral grove. The Coral Grove. James Gates Percival. AA; EtS; GN
Deep in the windless/ wood. Buson, *tr. fr. Japanese by* Harry Behn. WSC
Deep in the winter plain, two armies. Two Armies. Stephen Spender. ChMP; CoBMV; OBWP; OxBTC; SeCeV; WaP
Deep in the wood I made a house. August. Katherine Pyle. OBCA
Deep in [*or* into] the woods we'll go. Heart of the Woods. Wesley Curtright. GoSl; PoNe
Deep in their roots, all flowers keep the light. Theodore Roethke. POL
Deep in these Ozark hills, dark-limbed. Caves. David Baker. MAYP
Deep in this grave her bones remain. Reflections, Written on Visiting the Grave of a Venerated Friend. Ann Plato. BlSi
Deep in your cheeks. Origins. Keorapetse Kgositsile. PoBA
Deep inside me, someone sits at the harp. Someone Sits at the Harp. Jon Lang. AMV-81
Deep into the woods we'll go. *See* Deep in the woods we'll go.
Deep lane, poor families; I have few friends. At the End of Spring. Yü Hsüan-chi, *tr. by* Geoffrey Waters. BoWoP
Deep lines of honour all can hit. The Portrait. Countess of Winchilsea. *Fr.* The Birthday of Catharine Tufton. OBEC
Deep music of the ancient forest! Sancta Silvarum. Lionel Johnson. BrPo
Deep Night. Juan Ramón Jiménez, *tr. fr. Spanish by* Robert Bly. NYP
Deep on the convent-roof the snows. St. Agnes' Eve. Tennyson. GoBC; HBV-2; LiTB; OAEP; OBEV; OBVV; OxBoCh
Deep red bogs divided. Richard Murphy. *Fr.* The Battle of Aughrim. CIP
Deep River ("Deep river, my home is over Jordan"). *Unknown.* BoAN-1, *with music;* BPo; FSW; TAP; TrAS, *with music*
Deep-Sea Cables, The. Kipling. VLP
Deep-Sea Fishing. "Hugh MacDiarmid." SeCePo
Deep Sea Soundings. Sarah Williams. EtS; WGRP
Deep seclusion of this forest path, The. Enchantment. Madison Cawein. HBV-1
Deep Spring. *Unknown.* AmFP
Deep Stuff. Keith Preston. WhC
Deep-sworn Vow, A. W. B. Yeats. CMoP; ELU; OAEL-2; PCP; UnPo
Deep Water. *Unknown.* FSW
Deep Well, *sel.* Roland Robinson.
"I am at Deep Well where the spirit-trees." CBAP
Deep well knows it certainly, The. World-Secret. Hugo von Hofmannsthal, *tr. by* Charles Wharton Stork. TrJP
Deep wooden note, A. Overheard. Denise Levertov. PoM
Deeper in the Tank—the Last Middle East Crisis, 1972. Eugene Ruggles. SOTS
Deeper into the Forest, *sel.* Roy Daniells.
"I never swung a staff and deep, oh deep." PeCV
Deeper Seas, The. Henry Bellamann. EtS
Deeper than sleep but not so deep as death. Night Feeding. Muriel Rukeyser. MiAP; NMM; WPE
Deeper than the narwhal sinketh. The Sea-Deeps. Thomas Miller. EtS
Deepest Bow, The. Marie Takvan, *tr. fr. Norwegian by* Harold P. Hansen. AMV-81
Deepest Sensuality, The. D. H. Lawrence. NoAM
Deeply repentant of my sinful ways. Gaspara Stampa, *tr. fr. Italian by* Lorna de'Lucchi. WPOW
Deer, The. Asya, *tr. fr. Yiddish by* Gabriel Preil *and* Howard Schwartz. VWA
Deer, The. Mary Austin. FaPON
Deer. John Drinkwater. CH
Deer. No Ch'ŏn-myŭng, *tr. fr. Korean by* Ko Won. PBWP
Deer. Kenneth Rexroth. *Fr.* A Bestiary. HoPM
Deer, The. Laurie Sheck. AMV-80
Deer and the Snake, The. Kenneth Patchen. MoAmPo
Deer are gentle and graceful. Deer. Kenneth Rexroth. *Fr.* A Bestiary. HoPM
Deer at the Roadside. Iain Crichton Smith. *Fr.* Deer on the High Hills—a Meditation. PoSH
Deer carcass hangs from a rafter, The. Gathering the Bones Together. Gregory Orr. AmPA; GeTw; Psk
Deer feed on. Upon Leaving the Parole Board Hearing. Conyus. PoBA
Deer Hunt. Judson Jerome. RFM
Deer Hunt, Salt Lake Valley. Helen Handley. GrPl
Deer in Aspens. Kay DeBard Hall. GoYe

Deer in the Bush. Chana Bloch. MAYP
Deer is humble, lovely as God made her, The. The Deer and the Snake. Kenneth Patchen. MoAmPo
Deer is patience, The. The Deer. Laurie Sheck. AMV-80
Deer Isle. Philip Booth. BiP; VGW
Deer, lightning, bluebird, toad. Beneath the Mound. R. T. Smith. STE
Deer-of-the-Waters: he laboured hard on his grammar. Red Indian Corpse. Peter Redgrove. OxBC
Deer on Pine Mountain, The. Onakatomi no Yoshinobu, *tr. fr. Japanese by* Kenneth Rexroth. *Fr.* Shui Shu. PAI
("Deer which lives, The," *tr. by* Arthur Waley.) AWP
Deer on the High Hills—a Meditation, *sel.* Iain Crichton Smith.
Deer at the Roadside. PoSH
Deer on the Mountain. Grace Fallow Norton. HBMV
Deer Sing, *sel.* Confucius, *tr. fr. Chinese by* Ezra Pound.
Fraternitas. CTC; OBVE
Deer Song. Leslie Silko. VoR
Deer were bounding like blown leaves, The. Fire on the Hills. Robinson Jeffers. CMoP
Deer which lives, The. Onakatomi no Yoshinobu. *See* Deer on Pine Mountain, The.
Deere to my soule, then leave me not forsaken. *See* Dear to my soul . . .
Deere, why should you commaund me to my rest. *See* Dear, why should. . .
Deer's Cry, The. *At. to* St. Patrick, *tr. fr. Old Irish by* Whitley Stokes, John Strachan, *and* Kuno Meyer. AnIL; OnYI; WGRP
(Breastplate of St. Patrick, The.) OxBI, *tr. by* Cecil Frances Alexander
(St. Patrick's Breatsplate.) AnIV, *tr. by* Kuno Meyer; FaBoCh, *abr., tr. by* Cecil Frances Alexander
"I bind unto myself to-day," *sel.* TRV
Deevil's Waltz, The. Sydney Goodsir Smith. FaBoTw
Defeat. Witter Bynner. PoNe
Defeat, A. Denise Levertov. PBWP
Defeat and Victory. Wallace Rice. PAH
Defeat may serve as well as victory. Victory in Defeat. Edwin Markham. BLPL; PoLF; PoPl; TreFT
Defeat of the Rebels. Robert Graves. WaP
Defence of Guenevere, The. William Morris. OAEP; TEP; VLP
Defence of Lawrence, The. Richard Realf. PAH
Defence of Lucknow, The. Tennyson. BeLS
Defence of Satire, The. Pope. *See* Satire: "Ask you what provocation I have had?"
Defence of the Alamo, The. Joaquin Miller. BPAW; HBV-2; OnMSP; PAH
(Defense of the Alamo, The.) BeLS; FaBoBe
Defend Us, Lord, from Every Ill, *with music.* John Hay. AH
Defender, The. Arthur M. Sampley. GoYe
Defender of his country, The—the founder of liberty. Epitaph on Washington. *Unknown.* OHIP
Defense of the Alamo, The. Joaquin Miller. *See* Defence . . .
Defense Rests. Vassar Miller. MoAmPo
Defensive Position. John Manifold. MoBrPo
Defiance, The. Aphra Behn. EnLoPo
Defiance, The. Thomas Flatman. OBS
Defiance. Solomon ibn Gabirol, *tr. fr. Hebrew by* Emma Lazarus. TrJP
Defiance. Walter Savage Landor. HBV-1; VLP
Defiant One, The. Alice Morrey Bailey. AMV-80
Defiled Is My Name Full Sore. *At. to* Anne Boleyn. WPE
Definition. Lauren Shakely. FYAP
Definition for Blk/ Children. Sonia Sanchez. PoBA
Definition of Beauty, The. Robert Herrick. CaPo
Definition of Love, The. Andrew Marvell. AnAnS-1; BLPL; BoLoP; EBEV; FaBoEn; GBL; HoPM; InPK; InPS; JCP; LiTB; LoBV; MeLP; MePo; NOBE; NoP; OAEL-1; OAEP; OBEV; OBS; PoEL-2; SeCePo; SeCeV; SeCP; SeCV-1; TEP; TreFT; TrGrPo; UnPo; WHA
Definition of My Brother. W. S. Graham. NeBP
Definition of Nature. Eugene Redmond. PoBA
Definition of the Soul. Boris Pasternak, *tr. fr. Russian by* Babette Deutsch. TrJP
Definitions of the Word *Gout.* Tina Koyama. BrSi
Deflective rhythm under seas. Einstein among the Coffee-Cups. Louis Untermeyer. WhC
Deflowered forever. Here the Stem Rises. Daniel Berrigan. TwAmPo
Deformed Mistress, The. Sir John Suckling. BXAP; ErPo
Deftly, admiral, cast your fly. Song. W. H. Auden. GTBS-P
Degas. Paul Monette. AmPA
Degenerate Age, A. Solomon ibn Gabirol, *tr. fr. Hebrew by* Emma Lazarus. TrJP
Degenerate Douglas! O the unworthy lord! Composed at Neidpath Castle, the Property of Lord Queensberry, 1803. Wordsworth. GTBS; GTBS-P
Degli Sposi. Rika Lesser. FYAP
Degrees of Gray in Philipsburg. Richard Hugo. CoAP; NoP; NPAW
Degrees of Shade. H. A. Pinkerton. NePoAm
Deh was a princess propose to be married. The Maid Freed from the Gallows. *Unknown.* ViBoFo
Deid is now that divour and dollin in erd. The Widow Speaks. William Dunbar. *Fr.* The Book of the Two Married Women and the Widow. PoEL-1
Deid sall ye ligg, and ne'er a memorie. Douglas Young, *after the Greek of* Sappho. OBVE
Deidre's Lament for the Sons of Usnach. *Unknown.* *See* Deirdre's Lament for the Sons of Usnagh.
Deigne at my hands this crown of prayer and praise. La Corona. John Donne. AnAnS-1; OBS
De'il cam fiddling thro' [*or* through] the town, The. The De'il's Awa' wi' the Exciseman [*or* The Exciseman]. Burns. GoTS; OAEP; ViBoPo
Deil o' Bogie, The. Sir Alexander Gray. BSV
De'il's Awa' wi' the Exciseman, The. Burns. OAEP; ViBoPo
(Exciseman, The.) GoTS
Deirdre. James Stephens. AWP; CMoP; HBMV; NoAM; OBMV; PoRA; ViBoPo
Deirdre, *sel.* W. B. Yeats.
" 'Why is it,' Queen Edain said." ViBoPo
Deirdre and the Poets. Ewart Milne. NeIP
Deirdre's Farewell to Alba. *Unknown, tr. fr. Middle Irish by* Sir Samuel Ferguson. OnYI
(Deirdre's Farewell to Scotland, *tr. by* Whitley Stokes *and* Kuno Meyer). OnYI
Deirdre's Lament for the Sons of Usnagh. *Unknown, tr. fr. Middle Irish by* Sir Samuel Ferguson. OnYI
(Deidre's Lament for the Sons of Usnach, *tr. by* Sir Samuel Ferguson.) SeCePo
(Deirdre's Lament, *tr.* by Whitley Stokes *and* Kuno Meyer). OnYI
Deirdre's Song at Sunrise. Sister Maura. CaP
Deities and Beasts. John Updike. ELU
Deity of Love Incorporate, A. Edward Taylor. *Fr.* Preparatory Meditations, First Series. TAP
Déjà Vu. Shirley Kaufman. LCAP
Deja Vu. J. B. Mulligan. AMV-80
Dejected Lover, The. George Crabbe. *Fr.* Tales of the Hall. FaBoEn
(Sad Lover, The.) OBNC
Dejection. Robert Bridges. QFR
Dejection; an Ode. Samuel Taylor Coleridge. CABA; EnRP; FaBoEn; FiP; HBV-2; LiTB; LoBV; MasP; NOBE; NoP; OAEL-2; OAEP; OBNC; OBRV; PoEL-4; PPP
(Letter to Sara Hutchinson, A, *longer vers.*) NCEP
"Well! If the Bard was weather-wise, who made," *sel.* SeCePo
Dekunle, handsome man, hail! Omobayode Arowa, *tr. fr. Yoruba.* *Fr.* Dirge for Fajuyi. WTO
Del Cascar. William Stanley Braithwaite. BANP; CDC
Delacroix pentit Chopin's heid. Ye Mongers Aye Need Masks for Cheatrie. Sydney Goodsir Smith. OxBS
Delay. Charlotte Fiske Bates. AA
Delay. Elizabeth Jennings. InPK; NePoEA; OxBTC
Delay Has Danger. George Crabbe. *See* Tales of the Hall.
Delayed till she had ceased to know. Emily Dickinson. AA
Delaying Tactics. Christopher Wiseman. AMV-81
Delfica. Gérard de Nerval, *tr. fr. French by* Andrew Hoyem. NU
Delia. Samuel Daniel. *See* To Delia.
Delia Holmes ("Delia, Delia, why didn't you run?"). *At. to* "Whistling Bill" Ruff. AmFP
Delia Very Angry. *Unknown.* NOEC
Delia's Gone. Blind Blake (Blake Alphonso Higgs). FSW
Deliberately, long ago/ the carcasses. From an Old House in America. Adrienne Rich. NNaP
Delicate Balance, A. Laura Schreiber. AMV-80
Delicate eyes that blinked blue Rockies all ash. On Neal's Ashes. Allen Ginsberg. PoM
Delicate fabric of bird song, A. May Day. Sara Teasdale. BoNaP; PoSC
Delicate girl was eager to air, The. Princess Elizabeth of Bohemia, as Perdita. Frank O'Hara. PoA
Delicate Impasse, A. Kenneth John Atchity. AMV-80
Delicate Mother Kangaroo. D. H. Lawrence. GrPl
Delicate, Plummeting Bodies, The. Stephen Dobyns. FYAP
Delicate the Toad. Robert Francis. DuDa
Delicate young Negro stands, A. Anonymous Drawing. Donald Justice. CoAP; EyDe; HeIP; NePoEA-2
Deliciae Sapientiae de Amore. Coventry Patmore. The Unknown Eros, II, ix. OxBoCh
Delicious Beauty. John Marston. UnTE
(Song: "Delicious beauty that doth lie.") ElL
Delight in books from evening. Francis Daniel Pastorius. SCAP
Delight in Disorder. Robert Herrick. AnAnS-2; BiP; CABA; CaPo; CavP; EnLoPo; ErPo; FaBoEn; FaBV; FF; HAP; HBV-1; HeIP; InMe; InPK;

InPS; JCP; LiTB; LoBV; NIP; NOBE; NoP; OAEL-1; OAEP; OBEV; OBS; PAI; PoPle; PoRA; PPoe; PP; PPP; PrIm; SeCePo; SeCeV; SeCP; SeCV-1; TreFS; TrGrPo; ViBoPo; WeW; WHA
(Sweet Disorder.) AWP; BLPL
("Sweet disorder in the dress, A.") EBEV; GTBS; GTBS-P; TEP
Delight of humane kind, and gods above. Lucretius, *tr. by* Dryden. *Fr.* De Rerum Natura, I. OBVE
Delight of Solitariness, The. Sir Philip Sidney. *See* Solitariness.
Delight Song of Tsoai-Talee, The. N. Scott Momaday. CDW; GrPl; STE
Delightful, book, your trip. Aoibhinn, A Leabhráin, Do Thriall. *Unknown, tr. by* Flann O'Brien. AnIV; BIrV; OxBI
Delightful change from the town's abode. Barnyard Melodies. Fred Emerson Brooks. OBAL
Delightful I think it to be in the bosom of an isle. St. Columcille's Island Hermitage. *Unknown, tr. by* Kenneth Jackson. AnIL
Delightful to be on the Hill of Howth. Columcille's Greeting to Ireland. *At. to* St. Columcille, *tr. by* William Reeves *and* Kuno Meyer. OnYI
Delights of the bottle and charms of old wine, The. Love and Wine. Thomas Shadwell. UnTE
Delights of the Door, The. Francis Ponge, *tr. fr. French by* Robert Bly. NU
Delilah. Kipling. BrPo
Delilah. Milton. *Fr.* Samson Agonistes. SeCePo
Delilah Aberyswith was a lady—not too young. Delilah. Kipling. BrPo
Delilie was a woman, fine an' fair. Samson. *Unknown.* OuSiCo
Delineaments of the Giants, The. William Carlos Williams. *Fr.* Paterson. NoAM
("Paterson lies in the valley under the Passaic Falls.") TAP
Delirium in Vera Cruz. Malcolm Lowry. FaBoTw; OxBTC
Deliver Me. Amy Carmichael. STF
(Flame of God, *sl. diff. vers.*) STF
Deliver Me, O Lord, from My Daily Bread. Jeanne Murray Walker. AMV-80
Deliver us from apple pies. Grandmother's Apple Pies. Bruce Weston Munro. PeD
Deliverance. William James Dawson. OBVV
Deliverance. Frances Harper. WPOW
Deliverance from a Fit of Fainting. Anne Bradstreet. TAP
Deliverance of Jehovah, The. Bible, *O.T.* (*Moulton, Modern Readers' Bible*). Psalms, XXVII. WGRP
"Lord is my light and my salvation, The," 1, 4, 14. TreFT
Deliverer, The. Milton. *Fr.* Samson Agonistes. OBS
("Oh [*or* O] how comely it is and how reviving.") NOBE; NOCV; OBEV; SeCeV
Delivering Children. David Holbrook. NePoEA-2
Dell, The. Gavin Ewart. OxBC
Della Cruscans, The. William Gifford. *Fr.* The Baviad. OBEC
Delos. Lawrence Durrell. NeBP
Delphic and Theban and Corinthian. Four Legs, Two Legs, Three Legs. William Empson. MoPo
Delphic Hymn to Apollo. Swinburne. VLP
Delphine. Teresa Anderson. LTB
Delta, The. Michael Dennis Browne. NYBP
Delta Farmer in a Wet Summer. James Whitehead. TAT
Delta lies unchanged, flat, The. View [*or* Aerial View] of Louisiana. Cleopatra Mathis. MAYP; TAT
Delta Traveller. Charles Wright. AmPA; LCAP
Deluded mortals, whom the great. A Libel on Doctor Delaney and a Certain Great Lord. Swift. NCEP
Delug'd with tears, by what you heard before. To My Honoured Patron Humphery Davie. Benjamin Tompson. SCAP
Deluge. John Clare. BoNaP
Deluge, The, *sel.* *Unknown.*
Animals in the Ark, The. ChTr; GBP
Deluge, The. *Unknown, tr. fr. Lenape Indian by* C. S. Rafinesque. *Fr.* The Wallum Olum. LiTA
Delusions of the days that once have been. Prologue. Longfellow. *Fr.* Giles Corey of the Salem Farms. PAH
Delusions VI. Charles Madge. NeBP
Delve deep amongst the musty muniments. Nicolas Gatineau. Arthur S. Bourinot. CaP
Dem Bones, *with music.* *Unknown.* OuSiCo
Demagogue, The. Phyllis McGinley. FaBoEE
Demands of the Muse. Vernon Watkins. PoA
Deme as Ye List Uppon Goode Cause. Sir Thomas Wyatt. PoEL-1
Demeanour. *Unknown.* OxBChV
Dementia Praecox. Morris Bishop. PoA
Demeter and Persephone. Tennyson. VLP
Demeter devastated our good land. The Appeasement of Demeter. George Meredith. VLP
Demiurge's Laugh, The. Robert Frost. OxBA
Democracy. Harriet Monroe. *Fr.* Commemoration Ode. AA
Democratic Barber, The; or, Country Gentleman's Surprise. John Parrish. NOEC
Demogorgon's Speech. Shelley. *Fr.* Prometheus Unbound. LoBV
("This is the day, which down the void abysm.") SeCeV
Demolition. Philip Raisor. AMV-81
Demon, Demon, you have dumped me. Her Love Poem. Lucille Clifton. GP
Demon-Lover, The. James Abraham Hillhouse. *Fr.* Hadad. AA
Demon Lover, The. Adrienne Rich. IHMS
Demon Lover, The. *Unknown.* CABA; EnSB; HAP; LiTB; MAT; UnPo; WeW
(Carpenter's Wife, The.) OAEL-1, *with music;* OBET, *diff. vers.*; OxBB, *with music*
(Daemon Lover, The.) MOS, *diff. vers.*; NU
(House Carpenter, The.) AmFP; AS, *with music*
(House Carpenter's Wife, The.) FSW
(James Harris, *diff. vers.*) BaBo (A, B, C, *and* D *vers.*); ESPB (A, D, *and* F *vers.*); FaBoBa; ViBoFo (A *vers.*; B *vers., with music*)
Demon of the Mirror, The. Bayard Taylor. BeLS
Demonstration. Margaret Finefrock. AMV-80
Demonstration, A. Coventry Patmore. *Fr.* The Angel in the House, II, xi. VLP
Demos. E. A. Robinson. AP
Den of the Titans, The. Keats. *Fr.* Hyperion. WHA
Denial, A. Elizabeth Barrett Browning. GBL; OBNC
Denial. George Herbert. JCP; NOBE; NoP; OAEL-1
(Deniall.) AnAnS-1; FaBoEn; MePo; PoEL-2
Denials 1. Jane Somerville. AMV-80
Denied, she screamed in rage, and ran away. You Can't Be Wise. Paul Engle. PoPl
Denied the shelter of air and the power. A Broken Gull. John Moore. NCSH
Denise. Robert Beverly Hale. GDP; GrPl
Denise: A Letter Never Sent. Henri Coulette. *Fr.* The War of the Secret Agents, VIII. NePoEA-2
Dennis was hearty when Dennis was young. The Grand Match. Moira O'Neill. HBMV
Denouement. Ruth Stone. BoWoP
Dense on the stream the vapours lay. The Mowers: An Anticipation of the Cholera, 1848. Charles Mackay. EBVV
Dentist, The. Rose Fyleman. SoPo; TiPo
Dentist, A. *Unknown.* FaBoCo; FaBoEE; TreFT; WhC
(Epitaph on a Dentist.) OxBoLi; TreFS
Dentists continue to water their lawns even in the rain. The Great Society. Robert Bly. CAD; NoAM; NYP; PAI
Dentist's Window, A. James K. Baxter. OxBC
Dentologia; a Poem on the Diseases of the Teeth and Their Proper Remedies, *sels.* Solyman Brown. FaBoUs
Artificial Teeth.
Caries.
Tartar.
Value of Dentistry, The.
Denunciation, A. Mahammed Abdille Hassan, *tr. fr. Somali by* B. W. Andrzejewski. WTO
Denunciation; or, Unfrock'd Again. Philip Whalen. NeAP
Deny Yourself. Christopher Morley. YaD
Deo Gracias. *Unknown.* OxBM
Deo gracias, Anglia. The Agincourt Carol [*or* A Carol of Agincourt]. *Unknown.* EBEV; MeEL; OxBM
Deo Opt. Max. George Sandys. *Fr.* Paraphrase on the Psalms of David. OBS
Deo Optimo Maximo. Louise Imogen Guiney. TrPWD
Deor. *Unknown, tr. fr. Anglo-Saxon.* EBEV, *tr. by* John Wain; TEP, *tr. by* Walter Kendrick
(Deor's Lament, *tr. by* Charles W. Kennedy.) AnOE; OAEL-1
Depairt, depairt, depairt [*or* Departe, departe, departe]. Lament of the Master of Erskine [*or* A Lament; 1547]. Alexander Scott. BSV; CH; GBL
Depart from Me. Mary Elizabeth Coleridge. TrPWD
Departe, departe, departe. *See* Depairt . . .
Departed, The. John Banister Tabb. AA
Departed Friend, A. Julia A. Moore. FiBHP
Departed friend, I do not come. Exequy: To Peter Allt. Kildare Dobbs. OBCV
Departed Friends. Henry Vaughan. *See* They Are All Gone into the World of Light.
Departed out of parlement echone. The Despair of Troilus. Chaucer. *Fr.* Troilus and Criseyde, IV. LoBV
Departed—to the judgment. Emily Dickinson. CABA
Departmental. Robert Frost. GoYe; HeIP; HoPM; InPK; MoAB; MoAmPo; NIP; NOBA; NOBL; OBAL; SoSe
Departure. Kingsley Amis. NePoEA

Departure. Carolyn Forché. AMV-80
Departure. J. Charles Green. LFAC
Departure. William Hart-Smith. *Fr.* Christopher Columbus. PoAu-2
Departure. George Hitchcock. GP
Departure. Genny Lim. BrSi
Departure, A. Derek Mahon. CIP
Departure. Edna St. Vincent Millay. MoAmPo
Departure, The. Robert Pack. NePoEA
Departure. Coventry Patmore. The Unknown Eros, I, viii. ACP; HBV-1; LO; NOBE; OBEV; OBNC; OBVV; SeCePo; TreFT; VLP
Departure, The. Jeremy Robson. VWA
Departure. May Riley Smith. AA
Departure, The. Frank Steele. PPJ
Departure, The. Reed Whittemore. TAP
Departure, The; an Elegy. Henry King. SeCP
Departure in the Dark. C. Day Lewis. ChMP; CoBMV; MoPo; MP; TwCP
Departure of the Good Daemon, The. Robert Herrick. FaBoRV
Departure Platform. Kenneth Allott. NeBP
Departure's Girl-Friend. W. S. Merwin. ConAP; LCAP
Depending on his mood & the hour of the day. Aka. Frederick Eckman. FAZ
Deportation. "M. B.," *tr. fr. Polish by* A. Glanz-Leyeless. TrJP
Deposition by John Wilmot, A. Vincent McHugh. ErPo
Deposition from Beauty, A. Thomas Stanley. HBV-1
Deposition from Love, A. Thomas Carew. AnAnS-2; CaPo; CavP; MeLP; OAEP; OBS
Depot, The. Lewis Turco. GrPl
Depot Blues ("Standing at the station"). *Unknown.* BluL
Depot Blues ("Well look a-here, honey"). *Unknown.* AmFP
Depot in Rapid City. Roberta Hill. BoWoP
Deprecating Parrots. Beulah May. EtS
Depreciating Her Beauty. Wilfrid Scawen Blunt. The Love Sonnets of Proteus, VI. OBMV
Depressed by a Book of Bad Poetry, I Walk toward an Unused Pasture and Invite the Insects to Join Me. James Wright. ConAP
Depressed by the Death of the Horse That He Bought from Robert Bly. Henry Taylor. BXAP
Depression. Robert Bly. NaP
Depression. Rex Burwell. AMV-80
Depression. "Michael Field." SyP
Depression, *sel.* Charles Reznikoff.
"Simple soul, who so early in the morning." CTBA
Depression before Spring. Wallace Stevens. OBAL; SOTW
Deprivation. H. A. Pinkerton. NePoAm
Depriv'd of root, and branch and rind. A Maypole. Swift. NCEP
Deprived of his enemy, shrugged to a standstill. John Berryman. *Fr.* Dream Songs. CAPP; LCAP
Deprived of the green of that exclusive golf course, the scotch. Epistle to the Gentiles. Alfred Hayes. TrJP
Depths, The. Denise Levertov. NaP; NU
Depths of Sorrow, The. *Gond Oral Tradition, tr. by* V. Elwin *and* S. Hivale. WTO
Der Blinde Junge. Mina Loy. QFR
Der Deitcher's Dog, *with music.* Septimus Winner. PSoN
Der Heilige Mantel von Aachen. Benjamin Francis Musser. ISi
Der lived a king inta da aste. King Orfeo. *Unknown.* ESPB; OxBB; OxBoLi
Deranged. Padraic Fiacc. NeIP
Derby Ram, The. *Unknown.* AmFP; FaBoNo; GBP; ViBoFo, *with music*
("As I was going to Derby.") OxNR
(Darby Ram, The.) FSW
(Ram of Darby, The.) OuSiCo, *with music*
Derbyshire Bluebells. Sacheverell Sitwell. ChMP
Derelict. Young E. Allison. BLPA; EtS; FaBoBe; FaFP; HBMV; OnMSP; TreFS
Derelict, The. Lucius Harwood Foote. AA
Derelict. Henry Johnson. LFAC
Derelict, The. Kipling. BrPo
Derelict. Elisabeth Cavazza Pullen. AA
Dere's a beeg jam up de reever, w'ere rapide is runnin' fas'. The Log Jam. William Henry Drummond. NOBC
Dere's a Han' Writin' on de Wall, *with music.* *Unknown.* BoAN-2
Dere's a liddle fact in hishdory vitch few hafe onnershtand. Charles Godfrey Leland. *Fr.* Breitmann in Politics. OBAL
Dere's a star in de Eas' on Christmas morn. *See* There's a star in the East on Christmas morn.
Dere's No Hidin' Place Down Dere. *Unknown.* BoAN-1, *with music;* BPo
(No Hiding Place.) FSW
Derry. Seamus Deane. CIP
Dervish. Georgia Lee McElhaney. CoPo
Dervorgilla's supremely lovely daughter. Portrait with Background. Oliver St. John Gogarty. OBMV
Derwent; an Ode, *sel.* John Carr.
Memories of Childhood. NOEC
Des a little cabin. A Little Cabin. Charles Bertram Johnson. BANP
Des plu sages de la tere. Four Wise Men on Edward II's Reign. *Unknown.* OxBM
Descartes and the Stove. Charles Tomlinson. FaBoMo
Descend, Fair Sun! George Chapman. *Fr.* The Masque of the Middle Temple and Lincoln's Inn. EIL
Descend from heav'n Urania, by that name. Invocation to Urania. Milton. *Fr.* Paradise Lost, VII. EBEV; FiP; OBS
Descend from that pneumatic pedestal. To a Loudmouth Pontificator. Ray Mizer. TW
Descend, silent spirit. Prayer to the Snowy Owl. John Haines. BoAnP
Descend, Ye Nine. Pope. *Fr.* Ode on St. Cecilia's Day. GN
Descended, Adam to the bower where Eve. Adam Fallen [*or* Banishment from Paradise]. Milton. *Fr.* Paradise Lost, XII. NOCV; TreFS
Descended of an ancient line. To Maecenas [*or* Horat. Ode 29. Book 3]. Horace, *paraphrased by* Dryden. *Fr.* Odes. AWP; OBVE; SeCV-2
Descending. Valentin Iremonger. *See* Going down the Mountain.
Descending. Robert Pack. NePoEA-2
Descending Figure. Louise Glück. GeTw
Descent. Helen Frazee-Bower. Two Married, II. HBMV
Descent, The. William Carlos Williams. HAP; MoAB; PoCh; WeW
Descent for the Lost. Philip Child. CaP
Descent from the Cross. "Michael Field." WPE
Descent into Hell, The. William Langland. *Fr.* The Vision of Piers Plowman. PoEL-1
Descent of Odin, The; an Ode from the Norse Tongue. Thomas Gray. LAuP
Descent of the Vulture, The. Marya Zaturenska. WPE
Descent of Winter, The (Section 10/30). William Carlos Williams. InPK
Descent on Middlesex, The. Peter St. John. PAH
Descent to Bohannon Lake. Jim Barnes. FAZ
Describes the Place Where Cynthia Is Sporting Herself. Philip Ayres. EnLoPo
Description, A. Lord Herbert of Cherbury. AnAnS-2; SeCP
Description and Praise of His Love Geraldine. Earl of Surrey. OAEP
("From Tuscan[e] came my lady's worthy race.") AAS; SiPS
Description of a City Shower, A. Swift. HeIP; LoBV; MAT; NOEC; NoP; OAEL-1; OBSV; OnYI; PPP; SeCePo; SeCeV; TEP
(City Shower in Imitation of Virgil's Georgics, A.) UnPo
Sels.
"Ah! where must needy poet seek for aid." ViBoPo
Cat and the Rain, The, 4 *ll.* PCat
Description of a Good Boy, The. Henry Dixon. OxBChV
("Boy that is good, A," *st.* 1.) OxNR
Description of a New England Spring. John Josselyn. SCAP
Description of a Ninety Gun Ship. William Falconer. PeD
Description of a Strange (and Miraculous) Fish, A. Martin Parker. CoMu
Description of a Summer's Eve. Henry Kirke White. OBRV
Description of an Author's Bedchamber, A. Goldsmith. BIrV
Description of an Irish Feast, The. Hugh MacGowran. *See* O'Rourke's Feast.
Description of Beauty, A. Samuel Daniel, *after the Italian of* Giambattista Marini. OBSC
Enjoy Thy April Now, *sel.* EIL; ELP
Description of Castara, The. William Habington. *Fr.* Castara. AnAnS-2; CavP
("Like the violet, which alone.") HBV-1
Description of Elizium, The. Michael Drayton. *Fr.* The Muses Elizium. AnAnS-2; OAEL-1
Description of Elysium. James Agee. CrMA
Description of His Ugly Lady, A. Thomas Hoccleve. *See* Hoccleve's Humorous Praise of His Lady.
Description of London, A. John Bancks. NOEC
Description of Love, A. Sir Walter Ralegh. EIL; ELP; OAEL-1; OBSC; UnTE
(Now What Is Love.) FPL; HBV-1; PoLF
Description of Maidenhead, A. Earl of Rochester. NOBL; UnTE
Description of Sir Geoffrey Chaucer, The. Robert Greene. *Fr.* Greene's Vision. CTC; OBSC
(Sir Geoffrey Chaucer.) FaBoCh
Description of Spring [Wherein Each Thing Renews Save Only the Lover]. Earl of Surrey. *See* Soote Season, The.
Description of Spring in London, A. *Unknown.* NOEC
Description of the Contrarious Passions in a Lover. Petrarch, *tr. fr. Italian by* Sir Thomas Wyatt. Sonnets to Laura: To Laura in Life, CIV. FF; OAEP; TrGrPo
(I Find No Peace.) LiTB
("I find [*or* fynde] no peace, and all my war is done.") AAS; OAEL-1; OBVE; PPoe
(Love's Inconsistency.) AWP

(Sonnet: "I find no peace, and all my war is done.") SiPS
Description of the Morning, A. Swift. CABA; EBEV; FaBoEn; FF; HAP; HeIP; NIP; NOBE; NOEC; NoP; OAEL-1; PAI; PPP; Prf; SeCeV; SoSe; TEP; ViBoPo; WeW
Description of Tyme, A. Alexander Montgomerie. OxBS
Description of Wallace, A. Henry the Minstrel. *Fr.* Schir William Wallace, IX. GoTS
Descriptive Poem, Addressed to Two Ladies at Their Return from Viewing the Mines, near Whitehaven, A, *sel.* John Dalton.
Agape the sooty collier stands. NOEC
Desdemona's Song. Shakespeare. *Fr.* Othello, IV, iii. LoBV
Dese Bones Gwine to Rise Again. *Unknown.* AS, *with music;* OxBoLi
Desert. Agnes Gergely, *tr. fr. Hungarian by* Emery George. VWA
Desert, The. Henry Herbert Knibbs. BPAW
Desert around. Desert. Treason of Sand. Hemda Roth, *tr. by* Mariana Potasman. VWA
Desert Bloom. Gertrude Thomas Arnold. BPAW
Desert Claypan. Frederick T. Macartney. PoAu-1
Desert Flowers. Keith Douglas. FaBoTw
Desert Gulls. Dan Gillespie. TAT
Desert Holy Man. John Beecher. TAT
Desert in the Sea. Brian Swann. AmPA
Desert Lark, The. Eugène Marias, *tr. fr. Afrikaans by* Uys Krige *and* Jack Cope. PeSA
Desert March. Gerda Norvig. VWA
Desert moves out on half the horizon, The. The Supper after the Last. Galway Kinnell. NOBA; PoCh; TwAmPo
Desert of Love, The. János Pilinszky, *tr. fr. Hungarian by* Ted Hughes *and* János Csokits. OBVE
Desert Places. Robert Frost. AmPP; AP; BiP; CABA; CMoP; CoBMV; MoAB; MoAmPo; MoVE; NCSH; NoAM; NOBA; OxBA; PPP; TAP; TwAmPo; UnPo
Desert River. Patricia Benton. GoYe
Desert Shipwreck. Barbara Leslie Jordan. GoYe
Desert Song ("There's no hiding here in the glare of the desert"). Glenn Ward Dresbach. BPAW
Desert Song ("When I came on from Santa Fe"). John Galsworthy. BPAW
Desert Stone. Miriam Waddington. VWA
Desert Tortoise. Byrd Baylor. RHPC
Desert Warfare. Michael Longley. CIP
Deserted and scorned, the proud Marlborough sate. The False Favorite's Downfall. *Unknown.* APAS
Deserted Buildings under Shefford Mountain. John Glassco. OBCV
Deserted Garden, The. Elizabeth Barrett Browning. HBV-1
Deserted Garden. The. Ann Stanford. AMV-81
Deserted Home, A. Sidney Royse Lysaght. CH
Deserted Home, The. *Unknown, tr. fr. Irish by* Kuno Meyer. OxBI
(Ruined Nest, The.) OnYI
Deserted Homestead, The. Loren C. Eiseley. PoA
Deserted House, The. Mary Elizabeth Coleridge. CH; MoVE
Deserted House, *sel.* Dorothy Wellesley.
Epilogue: "He is not dead nor liveth." OBMV
(Buried Child, The.) DTC
Deserted Kingdom, The. Lord Dunsany. AnIV
Deserted Mountain, The. *Unknown, tr. fr. Irish by* John Montague. BIrV
Deserted Pasture, The. Bliss Carman. HBV-1
Deserted Shrine. Avner Treinin, *tr. fr. Hebrew by* E. A. Levenston. VWA
Deserted Village, The. Goldsmith. BeLS; EnRP; FaFP; GoTL; HBV-2;LaA; LAuP; LoBV, *abr.*; MasP; NOEC; NoP; OAEL-1; OAEP; OnYI; OxBI; PoEL-3; TEP
Sels.
"Even now the devastation is begun." EBEV
Farewell to Poetry. OBEC
"Ill fares the land, to hastening ills a prey." OBSV; TRV, 2 *ll.*
(Ill Fares the Land, 6 *ll.*) TreFT
"O luxury! Thou curst by Heaven's decree." BIrV
"Sweet Auburn! loveliest village of the plain." TreFS; ViBoPo
(Auburn.) OBEC; SeCePo
(Sweet Auburn.) LiTB; NOBE
(Village, The.) TrGrPo
"Sweet Auburn! parent of the blissful hour." EBEV
(Blest Retirement.) OBEC
Sweet, Smiling Village. PPON
"Sweet was the sound when oft at evening's close." FaBoEn
Village Parson, The. OBEC; WGRP
("Near yonder copse, where once the garden smiled.") TRV
(Village Preacher, The.) TrGrPo
Village Schoolmaster, The. OBEC; TrGrPo
Still the Wonder Grew, 4 *ll.* TreF
"Yes! let the rich deride, the proud disdain." OBSV
Deserted Village, The. Robin Hyde. WPE
Deserter, The. Joseph S. Cotter, Jr. CDC
Deserter, The. John Philpot Curran. *See* Deserter's Lamentation, The.
Deserter, The. A. E. Housman. OBMV; SeCeV
Deserter, The. Winifred M. Letts. SUMH
Deserter, The. John Manifold. CBAP; WaP
Deserter, The. Bayard Taylor. PaPo
" 'Deserter!' Well, Captain, the word's about right." The Deserter. Bayard Taylor. PaPo
Deserter's Lamentation, The. John Philpot Curran. FaBoRV; SeCePo
(Deserter, The.) ViBoPo
(Let Us Be Merry before We Go.) AnIV
Desertion of Beauty and Strength, The. *Unknown. Fr.* Everyman. ACP
Desertion of the Women and Seals, The. George Mackay Brown. OxBC
Deserts. Leigh Hanes. GoYe
Deservings. *Unknown.* HBV-2
Desideravi. Theodore Maynard. HBMV
Desideria. Wordsworth. *See* Surprised by Joy.
Desiderium. Phineas Fletcher. *Fr.* The Purple Island, I. OBS
Design. Robert Frost. AP; BLPL; CABA; CMoP; CoBMV; CrMA; HeIP; InPK; InPS; NIP; NoAM; NOBA; NoP; PAI; PPP; PrIm; SeCeV; SoSe; TAP
Design, The. Clarence Major. PoBA
Design. Peter Redgrove. OxBC
Design for a Bowl. Anacreon, *tr. fr. Greek by* Thomas Moore. UnTE
Design for a Stream-lined Sunrise. Sister Mary Madeleva. GoBC
Design for Mediæval Tapestry. A. M. Klein. CaP
Design for Peace. Janet Norris Bangs. PGD
Designer sits, head in hand, The. Design. Peter Redgrove. OxBC
Desire. "Æ." ILwL; OBMV; TrPWD
Desire. Matthew Arnold. WGRP
Desire. Isaac de Botton, *tr. fr. Judezmo by* Stephen Levy. VWA
Desire. William Cornish. OBSC; SeCeV
(Knight and the Lady, The.) NOBE
(Latet Anguis.) OBEV
Desire. Pierre Louÿs, *tr. fr. French by* Horace M. Brown. *Fr.* The Songs of Bilitis. UnTE
Desire. Kathleen Raine. MoPo
Desire. Sir Philip Sidney. *See* Thou Blind Man's Mark.
Desire. Thomas Traherne. OxBoCh
("For giving me desire.") LO
Desire, The. Katharine Tynan. HBV-1
Desire flickers like candles in the wind. Age. Marya Mannes. FAZ
Desire for a woman took hold of me in the night. Song. *Unknown.* LLLT
Desire for Hermitage, The. *Unknown, tr. fr. Old Irish by* Sean O'Faolain. AnIL
Desire is a witch. C. Day Lewis. CMoP
Desire Is Dead. D. H. Lawrence. FaBoEE
Desire of Water, The. Mark Jarman. PoA
Desire that all men have is all my love. Love and Marriage. Ray Mathew. PoAu-2
Desire, though thou my old companion art. Astrophel and Stella, LXXII. Sir Philip Sidney. SiPS
Desired Swan-Song, The. Samuel Taylor Coleridge. *See* On a Bad Singer.
Desiree,/ I find it most bitter that you. Denise: A Letter Never Sent. Henri Coulette. *Fr.* The War of the Secret Agents, VIII. NePoEA-2
Desire's Government. "A. W." EIL
Desires of Men and Women. John Berryman. LiTM
Desk, The. David Bottoms. MAYP
Desk, The. Cid Corman. VGW
Desmet, Idaho, March 1969. Janet Campbell Hale. STE; VoR
Desnos Reading the Palms of Men on Their Way to the Gas Chambers. Stephen Berg. VWA
Desolate. Sydney Dobell. NBM; OBNC
Desolate. Gerald Massey. EBVV
Desolate. Claude McKay. CDC
Desolate and lone. Lost. Carl Sandburg. AmPP; CMoP; PDV; PoPl; WHA
Desolate City, The. *Unknown, tr. fr. Arabic by* Wilfrid Scawen Blunt. AWP; OBEV; OBVV
Desolate Lover, The. Eileen Shanahan. NeIP
Desolate Rhythm of Dying Recurs, The. Michael Smith. CIP
Desolate Shore, A. W. E. Henley. SyP
Desolate that cry as though world were unworthy. Chough. Rex Warner. PoRA
Desolate windmill, eyelid of the distance. The Windmill. Lord De Tabley. NBM
Desolation. Amy Lowell. PoA
Desolation in Zion. Bible, *O.T.* Lamentations, I: 12-17. TrJP
Desolation Is a Delicate Thing. Elinor Wylie. MoAmPo
Desolation Row. Bob Dylan. InPS
Despair. Fulke Greville. *Fr.* Caelica. OBSC
("Who grace, for zenith had, from which no shadowes grow.") PoEL-1
Despair. Denise Levertov. NNaP

Despair. Olive E. Lindsay. SUMH
Despair. Edward Bliss Reed. HBMV
Despair. Spenser. *Fr.* The Faerie Queene, I, 9. SeCePo
Despair. Tennyson. VLP
Despair and Hope. Israel Zangwill. TrJP
Despair in Seascape. Richmond Lattimore. TwAmPo
Despair is big with friends I love. Consequences. William Meredith. NoAM
Despair is given me. Where Fled. John Wieners. CoPo
Despair of all, and hope for none! Despair and Hope. Israel Zangwill. TrJP
Despair of Troilus, The. Chaucer. *Fr.* Troilus and Criseyde, IV. LoBV
Despairing beside a clear stream. Colin's Complaint. Nicholas Rowe. OBEC
Despairing Embrace, The. Pierre Louÿs, *tr. fr. French by* Horace M. Brown. *Fr.* The Songs of Bilitis. UnTE
Despairing Lover, The. William Walsh. ELP; FaBoCh; NOBL; OBEC; OxBoLi
Desperado, The ("I'm a howler from the prairies of the West"). *Unknown.* CoSo; TreFS
Desperado, The ("There was a desperado from the wild and woolly West"). *Unknown.* FSW
Despisals. Muriel Rukeyser. NMM; Prf
Despise the World. *Unknown.* MeEL
Despised and Rejected. Katharine Lee Bates. TrCP
Despite someone starving somewhere. Euphoria, Euphoria. Mark DeFoe. AMV-80
Despite strangulated cries. Slick. Daniel Hoffman. SOTS
Despite the drums we were ready to go. The Mountaineers. Dannie Abse. PP
Despondency Corrected. Wordsworth. *Fr.* The Excursion, IV. EnRP
Desponding Phyllis [*or* Phillis] was endu'd. Phyllis; or, The Progress of Love. Swift. OAEL-1; OBSV; PoEL-3
Desponding Soul's Wish, The. John Byrom. OBEC; TrPWD
Despot treads thy sacred sands, The. Carolina. Henry Timrod. PAH
Despot's heel is on thy shore, The. My Maryland [*or* Maryland, My Maryland]. James Ryder Randall. AA; FaBoBe; FaFP; FaPo; HBV-2; PAH; PSoN; TreF
Destinations. Josephine Jacobsen. WPE
Destined to war from very infancy. Epitaphs, VI. Gabriello Chiabrera, *tr. by* Wordsworth. AWP
Destinie. Abraham Cowley. MeLP
Destiny. Sir Edwin Arnold. PoLF
Destiny. Harrison Smith Morris. AA
Destiny. Thomas Stanley. *See* Expectation.
Destiny of Nations, The, *sels.* Samuel Taylor Coleridge.
"'Even so' (the exulting Maiden said)." ChER
"For what is Freedom, but the unfettered use." EnRP
Destiny of the Poet. Claude Vigée, *tr. fr. French by* Anthony Rudolf. VWA
Destroyer of Destroyers, The. Wallace Rice. PAH
Destroying Angel. Hilary Corke. NYBP
Destruction of Bulfinch's House, The. Stephen Sandy. CoPo
Destruction of Jerusalem by the Babylonian Hordes, The. Isaac Rosenberg. VWA
Destruction of Letters. Babette Deutsch. WPE
Destruction of Sennacherib, The. Byron. BeLS; BLPA; BLPL; EnRP; EvOK; FaBoBe; FaBoCh; FaFP; FaPo; FaPON; FaPoR; FF; GN; HAP; HBV-2; NIP; NoP; OAEP; OBWP; OnMSP; PAI; PoLF; TrCP; TreF; WBLP; WeW; WGRP
(Sennacherib.) PaPo
Destruction of Troy, The. Virgil, *tr. fr. Latin by* Sir John Denham. *Fr.* The Aeneid, II. SeCV-1
Destructive caries comes with secret stealth. Caries. Solyman Brown. *Fr.* Dentologia; a Poem on the Diseases of the Teeth and Their Proper Remedies. FaBoUs
Detachment is a virtue, teachers say. Ballade on Eschatology. Sister Mary Madeleva. GoYe
Detail, The. Cid Corman. PCP
Detail from an Annunciation by Crivelli. Rosemary Dobson. PoAu-2
Detective Work. Wendy Rose. TWSS
Determination. John Henrik Clarke. CNA; PoBA
Determination. *Unknown.* *Fr.* Sir Andrew Barton. TreFT
Determinism. Maurice Evan Hare. *See* Limerick: "There once was a man who said, 'Damn!'"
Detestable race, continue to expunge yourself, die out. Apostrophe to Man. Edna St. Vincent Millay. DBV; SBG
Detroit. Donald Hall. AmFN
Detroit City. Jill Witherspoon Boyer. CNA
Detroit Conference of Unity and Art. Nikki Giovanni. HoPM
Deus ex Machina. Richard Armour. QQQ
Deus Noster Ignis Consumens. Laurence Housman. HBMV
Deuteronomy, *sels.* Bible, *O.T.*
Choose Life, XXX: 15-19. TreFT
"For the Lordes parte is his folke," XXXII: 9-15, *tr. by* William Tyndale. OBVE
Give Ear, Ye Heavens, XXXII: 1-43. TrJP
Deuteronomy. Robert Bringhurst. NOBC
Developers at Crystal River. James Merrill. AMV-81
Developing a Wife. Andrew Taylor. CBAP
Development. Robert Browning. VLP
"My father was a scholar and knew Greek," *sel.* GLGT
Development of Idiotcy, A. Ebenezer Jones. OBNC
Deviator, The. Bertram Warr. OBCV
Devil, The. *Unknown.* STF
Devil and the Angel, The, *sel.* Rosemary Dobson.
Methuselah. PoAu-2
Devil and The Farmer's Wife, The. *Unknown.* FSW; TrAS, *with music*
Devil and the Governor, The, *sel.* William Forster.
"In New South Wales, as I plainly see." CBAP; PoAu-1
Devil and the Lady, The, *sel.* Tennyson.
Deep Dark Night, The. SeCePo
Devil-Dancers, The. William Plomer. PeSA
Devil Got My Woman. *Unknown.* BluL
Devil, having nothing else to do, The. On Lady Poltagrue, a Public Peril. Hilaire Belloc. FaBoCo; MoBrPo; POL; PV; TreFT; WhC
Devil! I tell thee without nubbs or jubbs. After Reading the Life of Mrs. Catherine Stubbs in Isaac Ambrose's "War with the Devils." Isaac Hann. NOCV
Devil now knew his proper cue, The. Shelley. *Fr.* Peter Bell the Third. OBSV
Devil sprang from box. Jack-in-the-Box. Elder Olson. NePA
Devil to Pay, The, *sel.* Dorothy L. Sayers.
Choice of the Cross, The. TrCP
Devil was given permission one day, The. The History of Arizona: How It Was Made and Who Made It. Charles O. Brown. BPAW
Devil was more generous than Adam, The. Samuel Butler. FaBoEE
Devil, we're told, in hell was chained, The. Hell in Texas. *Unknown.* BLPA; BPAW
Devilish Mary. *Unknown.* AmFP; FSW; OuSiCo, *with music*
Devils. Norman Mailer. OBAL
Devil's Advice to Story-Tellers, The. Robert Graves. LiTM; NoAM
Devil's Bag, The. James Stephens. WSC
Devils can change their shapes, but not their natures. Robert Wild. *Fr.* A Copy of the Last Verses Made by Dr. Wild, Author of "Iter Boreale." DBV
Devil's Dictionary, The, *sels.* Ambrose Bierce. OBAL
"Blow, blow, ye spicy breezes."
"Cur foretells the knell of parting day, The."
"Fiercely the battle raged and, sad to tell."
(Corporal.) DBV
"Hail, holy Lead!—of human feuds the great."
"Megaceph, chosen to serve the State."
"Once I seen a human ruin."
"'One night,' a doctor said, 'last fall.'"
"Spelling reformer indicted, A."
"There's a man with nose."
Devil's Law Case, The, *sels.* John Webster.
All the Flowers of the Spring. EIL; ELP; LiTB; OBS; PoEL-2; PoRA; ViBoPo
(Burial, The.) CH; LoBV
(Nets to Catch the Wind.) TrGrPo
(Song: "All the flowers of the spring.") HBV-2
(Vanitas Vanitatum.) NOBE; OBEV
"O, I shall run mad!" LO
Devil's Nine Questions, The. *Unknown.* AmFP; WSC
Devil's Thoughts, The. Robert Southey *and* Samuel Taylor Coleridge. FaBoCo, *abr.*; OBSV; OxBoLi, *abr.*
(Devil's Walk, The, *shorter vers.*) PV
"He saw a lawyer killing a viper," *sel., at. to* Richard Porson. DBV
Devil's Tribute to Moling, The, *sel.* *Unknown, tr. fr. Old Irish by* Whitley Stokes *and* John Strachan.
Holy Man, The. OnYI
Devoide of reason, thrale to foolish ire. Thomas Lodge, *after* Pierre de Ronsard. Phyllis, XXXI. AAS
Devon to Me. John Galsworthy. HBMV
Devonshire Rhyme, A. *Unknown.* SiSoSe
Devonshire Scenes. Coventry Patmore. *Fr.* Tamerton Church-Tower; or, First Love. FaBoPP
Devonshire Song, A. *Unknown, at. to* William Strode. OBS; PoEL-2, *sl. diff. vers.*
Devonshire Walk, A. William Browne. *Fr.* Britannia's Pastorals, I, Song 5. FaBoPP

Devotion ("Follow thy fair sun"). Thomas Campion. *See* Follow Thy Fair Sun.
Devotion ("Follow your saint"). Thomas Campion. *See* Follow Your Saint.
Devotion. *Unknown.* *See* Fain Would I Change That Note.
Devotional Incitements. Wordsworth. OxBoCh
Devotions of the Fowls, *sel.* John Lydgate.
"Then I heard a voice celestial." PBBP
Devouring Time, blunt thou the lion's paws [*or* lyons pawes]. Sonnets, XIX. Shakespeare. AWP; ChTr; EBEV; MAT; OAEL-1; OBSC; PoEL-2; TrGrPo; WHA
Devout Fits. John Donne. *See* Sonnet: "Oh, to vex me. . ."
Devout Lover, A. Thomas Randolph. HBV-1; HoPM; OBEV
Devout Man Prays to His Relations, The. William Herebert. MeEL
Devout Prayer of the Passion, A. *Unknown.* MeEL
Devoutly worshipping the oak. Canticle. William Griffith. HBMV; HBVY
Dew. Jennifer Maiden. CBAP
Dew. Charles Reznikoff. *See* Let Other People Come as Streams.
Dew is gleaming in the grass, The. Among the Millet. Archibald Lampman. CaP; WHW
Dew is on the grasses, dear, The. Youth. Georgia Douglas Johnson. BANP; PoNe
Dew is on the heather, The. The Captain's Feather. Samuel Minturn Peck. AA
Dew it trembles on the thorn, The. Silent Love. John Clare. EnRP
Dew of the rouge-flower, The. Haiku. Kaga no Chiyo, *tr. by* R. H. Blyth. PBWP
Dew on a Dusty Heart. Jean Starr Untermeyer. MoAmPo
Dew on the bamboos. Song. *Unknown, tr. by* E. Powys Mathers. LLLT
Dew Sat on Julia's Hair. Robert Herrick. ELP
Dew, the rain and moonlight, The. A Net to Snare the Moonlight. Vachel Lindsay. PoLF
Dew was falling fast, the stars began to blink, The. The Pet Lamb. Wordsworth. OxBChV
Dewdrop of the darkness born, A. The Immaculate Conception. John Banister Tabb. ISi
Dewdrop, Wind and Sun. Joseph Skipsey. OBVV
Dewdrops. John Clare. VLP
Dewdrops hang from leaf and stem. May Thirtieth. *Unknown.* PoSC
Dewey and His Men. Wallace Rice. PAH
Dewey at Manila. Robert Underwood Johnson. HBV-2; PAH
Dewey in Manila Bay. R. V. Risley. PAH
Dews drop slowly and dreams gather, The: unknown spears. The Valley of the Black Pig. W. B. Yeats. ChTr
Dews of summer night[e] did fall[e], The. Cumnor Hall. William Julius Mickle. BeLS; OBEC; OxBB; ViBoPo
Dewy Dawn from old Tithonus' bed, The. Jabberwocky; as the Author of "The Faerie Queene" Might Have Written It. Junius Cooper. InMe
Dexter. Joan Byers Grayston. PH
Dey Got Each and de Udder's Man. *Unknown.* WTO
Dey had a gread big pahty down to Tom's de othah night. The Party. Paul Laurence Dunbar. AmNP
Dey is times in life when Nature. When de Co'n Pone's Hot. Paul Laurence Dunbar. BANP
Dey lynched him, shore dey lynched him. Paternal. Ernest J. Wilson, Jr. PoNe
Dey tell me Joe Turner he done come [*or* Joe Turner's come and gone]. Joe Turner [Blues]. *Unknown.* AS; TrAS
Dey was hard times jes fo' Christmas round our neighborhood one year. An Indignation Dinner. James David Corrothers. BANP; PoNe
Dey was talkin' in de cabin, dey was talkin' in de hall. When Dey 'Listed Colored Soldiers. Paul Laurence Dunbar. BPo
Dey's a so't o' threatenin' feelin' in de blowin' of de breeze. Soliloquy of a Turkey. Paul Laurence Dunbar. BPo
Deze eatin' folks may tell me ub de gloriz ub spring lam'. Hog Meat. Daniel Webster Davis. BANP
Dhows, The. Francis Brett Young. EtS
Diagnosis of our hist'ry proves, A. The Rejected "National Hymns." "Orpheus C. Kerr." InMe; OBAL
Dial Tone, The. Howard Nemerov. NYBP
Dial Tone. Felix Pollak. PPJ
Dialect Quatrain. Marcus B. Christian. AmNP
Dialectics of Flight. John Hall Wheelock. NePoAm-2
Dialectique. Hugh Maxton. CIP
Dialogue. Agathias Scholasticus, *tr. fr. Greek by* Dudley Fitts. OLR
Dialogue. John Erskine. HBMV
Dialogue. George Herbert. MePo; OBEV; OBS; SeCV-1
Dialogue, A. David Ignatow. NNaP
Dialogue. Howard Nemerov. NYBP; PoPl
Dialogue, A. Pope. POL
Dialogue. Adrienne Rich. TAP
Dialogue, A. Swinburne. PoEL-5
Dialogue after Enjoyment. Abraham Cowley. BoLoP
Dialogue between a Squeamish Cotting Mechanic and His Sluttish Wife, in the Kitchen. Edward Ward. *Fr.* Nuptial Dialogues. NOEC
Dialogue, between Crab and Gillian. Thomas D'Urfey. *Fr.* The Bath; or, The Western Lass. NOEC
Dialogue between Horace and Lydia, A. Horace, *tr. fr. Latin by* Robert Herrick. Odes, III, 9. OBVE
Dialogue between King William and the Late King James on the Banks of the Boyne, A. Charles Blount. APAS
Dialogue between Mary and Gabriel. W. H. Auden. *Fr.* For the Time Being; a Christmas Oratorio. ISi
Dialogue between Strephon and Daphne, A. Earl of Rochester. CavP; SeCV-2
Dialogue between the Lovelorn Sir Hugh and Certain Ladies of Venice, A. Thomas Deloney. UnTE
Dialogue between the Resolved Soul, and Created Pleasure, A. Andrew Marvell. AnAnS-1; MeLP; MePo; OAEL-1; OBS; SeCP; SeCV-1
Dialogue between the Soul and Body, A. Andrew Marvell. AnAnS-1; HAP; JCP; MeLP; MePo; NoP; OAEL-1; OBS; OxBoCh; PoEL-2; PPP; SeCP; SeCV-1; TEP; WeW
Dialogue between Thyrsis and Dorinda, A. Andrew Marvell. SeCP
Dialogue betweene Araphill and Castara, A. William Habington. AnAnS-2
Dialogue betwixt God and the Soul, A. *At. to* Sir Henry Wotton, *after* Horace. MeLP; OBS; OxBoCh
Dialogue betwixt Time and a Pilgrime [*or* Pilgrim], A. Aurelian Townshend. AnAnS-2; MePo; NOBE; OAEL-1; OBS; PoEL-2; SeCP
Dialogue 4 1 Voice Only. Doug Fetherling. NeAC
Dialogue from Plato, A. Austin Dobson. HBV-1
Dialogue I'll tell you as true as my life, A. The Coal-Owner and the Pitman's Wife. *Unknown.* CoMu
Dialogue: Lover and Lady. Ciullo d'Alcamo, *tr. fr. Italian by* Dante Gabriel Rossetti. AWP
Dialogue of Self and Soul, A. W. B. Yeats. CABA; CMoP; FaBoMo; LiTB; LiTM; MasP; MoBrPo; NoAM; OAEP
"Living man is blind and drinks his drop, A," *sel.* DTC
Dialogue—2 Dollmakers. Gregory Corso. NeAP
Dialogue with a Door. Catullus, *tr. fr. Latin by* John Nott. UnTE
Diameter of the bomb was thirty centimeters, The. Lament. Yehuda Amichai, *tr. by* Ruth Nevo. VWA
Diamond Cut Diamond. Ewart Milne. FaBoCh; NeIP; PCat
Diamond, The, is a ship my lads. The Bonnie Ship *The Diamond.* *Unknown.* FSW
Diamond Joe, *with music.* *Unknown.* CoSo; OuSiCo
Diamond of a morning, A. Morning Song. Sara Teasdale. MOON
Diamonds are forever so I gave you quartz. The Hardness Scale. Joyce Peseroff. LLLT
Dian, Isis, Artemis, whate'er thy name. W. J. Turner. *Fr.* The Seven Days of the Sun. OBMV
Dian, that fain would cheer her friend the Night. Astrophel and Stella, XCVII. Sir Philip Sidney. SiPS
Diana, *sels.* Henry Constable.
"Dear [*or* Deere] to my soul! then leave me not forsaken!" AAS; EIL; OBSC
"Fair sun, if you would have me praise your light." OBSC
"Grace full of grace, though in these verses here." OBSC
"Hope, like the hyena [*or* hyaena], coming to be old." EnLoPo; OBSC
"If ever sorrow spoke from soul that loves." EIL
"Miracle of the world, I never will deny." NIP; OBSC
"My lady's presence makes the roses red." EIL; HBV-1; NIP; OBSC
"My tears are true, though others be divine." OBSC
"Needs must I leave and yet needs must I love." InvP; OBSC
"Not that thy hand is soft, is sweet, is white." OBSC
"Ready to seek out death in my disgrace." OBSC
"Sun, his journey ending in the west, The." OBSC
"To live in hell, and heaven to behold." AAS; HBV-1; OBSC
"Whilst Echo cries [*or* eccho cryes], 'What shall become of me [*or* mee]?' " AAS; OBSC
"You secret vales, you solitary fields." OBSC
Diana, *sel.* Jorge de Montemayor, *tr. fr. Spanish by* Bartholomew Young.
Song: "Shepherd, who can pass such wrong." EIL
Diana. Sir Walter Ralegh. OBSC
(Homage to Diana.) WiR
(Shepherd's Praise of Diana, The.) SiPS
Diana. Ernest Rhys. OBVV
Diana Cecyll, that rare beauty thou dost show. To Mrs. Diana Cecyll. Lord Herbert of Cherbury. AnAnS-2
Diana Fitzpatrick Mauleverer James. Miss James. A. A. Milne. MoShBr; TiPo
Diana guardeth our estate. Hymn to Diana. Catullus, *tr. by* Richard Claverhouse Jebb. AWP
Dianae Sumus in Fide. Catullus, *tr. fr. Latin by* Horace Gregory. MOON
Diana's Hunting-Song. Dryden. *Fr.* The Secular Masque. SeCePo

Diane de Poitiers, Josephine and Pompadour. Mother Goose Rhyme. Kenneth Rexroth. ErPo
Diapered in hospital linen. The Recovery Room: Lying-in. Helen Chasin. IHMS
Diaphenia. *At. to* Henry Constable *and also to* Henry Chettle. CH; ElL; GoBC; GTBS; GTBS-P; NOBE
(Damelus' [*or* Damelias'] Song to [*or* of] His Diaphenia.) ElP; FaBoEn; HBV-1; OBSC; PoEL-2; ViBoPo
Diary. Charlotte DeClue. TWSS
Diary, *sel.* Ethel Romig Fuller.
"Old Year is a diary where is set, The." PGD
Diary. David Wagoner. CoAP
Diary of a Church Mouse. John Betjeman. OxBTC
Diary of a Raccoon. Gertrude Ryder Bennett. GoYe
Diary of Amanda McFadden, The. Linda Hogan. TWSS
Diary of an Old Soul, *sels.* George Macdonald. TrCP
Be with Me, Lord.
That Thou Art Nowhere to Be Found.
This Day Be with Me.
Diary of the Sailors of the North, A. David Shulman, *tr. fr. Hebrew by author.* VWA
Diary of the Waning Moon, The, *sel.* Abutsu the Nun, *tr. fr. Japanese by* Edwin O. Reischauer.
"Shore wind is cold on my travel clothes, The." PBWP
Diaspora, The. W. H. Auden. *See* Jew Wrecked in the German Cell, The.
Diaspora Jews. Rachel Boimwall, *tr. fr. Yiddish by* Gabriel Preil *and* Howard Schwartz. VWA
Dibdin's Ghost. Eugene Field. AA
Dicamus Bona Verba. Tibullus, *tr. fr. Latin by* Constance Carrier. NAs
Dichterliebe. Robert Klein Engler. AMV-81
Dichtung und Wahrheit. Allen Curnow. OCNZ
Dick, a Maggot. Swift. TW
Dick and Jane. Judith Kroll. AmPA
Dick and Will and Charles and I. Autumn. Elizabeth Madox Roberts. YaD
Dick Hairbrain Learns the Social Graces. John Trumbull. *Fr.* The Progress of Dulness. AmPP
"Dick, I marvel much why in every plat." The "Gloria Patri." John Heywood. ACP
Dick is the one with the weenie. Dick and Jane. Judith Kroll. AmPA
Dick Johnson Reel, The. "Jake Falstaff." EvOK; WhC
Dick o' the Cow. *Unknown.* ESPB; OxBB, *with music*
Dick Turpin and Black Bess ("When fortune's blind goddess"). *Unknown.* AmFP
(Bonnie Black Bess.) BPAW; CoSo, *with music*
Dick Turpin and the Lawyer ("As Turpin was riding across the moor"). *Unknown.* ViBoFo
Dick Turpin's Ride ("Dick Turpin bold! Dick, hie away"). *Unknown.* OBET
(My Bonny Black Bess.) CoMu
Dickens in Camp. Bret Harte. BPAW; HBV-2
Dickery, dickery, dare. Mother Goose. OxNR
"Dictates of nature prove school-knowledge weak, The." Repentance. George Alexander Stevens. NOEC
Dictionaries cannot. Luck. Elaine Epstein. AMV-81
Dictionary Is an *His*torian, The: A Found Political Poem. Judith McCombs. IHMS
Dictum: For a Masque of Deluge. W. S. Merwin. AP; NoAM
Did all the lets and bars appear. The March into Virginia. Herman Melville. AP; BLPL; HAP; LiTA; NoP; TAP; TrGrPo; ViBoPo; WaaP
Did any one plan this? At Roblin Lake. Alfred Purdy. PeCV
Did any seer of ancient time forbode. The Steam Threshing Machine. Charles Tennyson Turner. VLP
Did Bethlehem's stable loathe. Come, Holy Babe! Mary Dickerson Bangham. PGD
Did but the law appoint us one. A Popular Functionary. Charles Dibdin. NOEC
Did Chaos form,—and water, air, and fire. Genesis. John Hall Ingham. AA
Did he meet Lud at the Fleet Gate? did he count the top. David Jones. *Fr.* The Anathemata. EBEV
Did he strike soundings off Vecta Insula? Angle-Land. David Jones. The Anathemata, III. NoAM
Did I ever tell you that Mrs. McCave. Too Many Daves. "Dr. Seuss." OBCA; RHPC
Did I ever think. Ono no Takamura, *tr. by* Arthur Waley. *Fr.* Kokin Shu. AWP
Did I follow Truth wherever she led. Herman Altman. Edgar Lee Masters. *Fr.* Spoon River Anthology. OxBA
Did I hear the news from Custer? The Death of Custer. "Captain Jack" Crawford. PoOW
Did I love thee? I only did desire. Rondo. George Moore. UnTE
Did I, my lines intend for publick view. The Introduction. Countess of Winchilsea. SBG; WPOW
Did I reach the pinnacle of success. Willis Beggs. Edgar Lee Masters. *Fr.* The New Spoon River. SaC
Did I stand on the bald top of Nefin. The Brow of Nephin. *Unknown, tr. by* Douglas Hyde. AnIL
Did I this morn devoutly pray. Self-Examination. *Unknown.* FaBoUs
Did it yell. Cicada-Shell. Basho. SoPo
Did ivver ye see the like o' that? Pride. Violet Jacob. OxBS
Did love sojourn with you long. Black and White. Esther Lilian Duff. HBMV
Did Not. Thomas Moore. BoLoP; ErPo; NBM
(Quantum Est Quod Desit.) EnLoPo
Did not each poet amorous of old. Troubadours. Arthur Davison Ficke. Sonnets of a Portrait Painter, X. HBMV
Did Not the Heavenly Rhetoric of Thine Eye. Shakespeare. *Fr.* Love's Labour's Lost, IV, iii. LiTB
(Sonnet: "Did not the heavenly rhetoric of thine eye.") ViBoPo
Did our best moment last. Emily Dickinson. NOBA
Did she in summer write it, or in spring. Words on the Windowpane. Dante Gabriel Rossetti. SyP
Did she mean that much to him that he was. Achilles. Phillip Corwin. AMV-80
Did Shriner die or make it to New York? A Disappearance in West Cedar Street. L. E. Sissman. TwCP
Did the harebell loose her girdle. Emily Dickinson. FaBV
Did the people of Viet Nam. What Were They Like? Denise Levertov. HeIP; NIP; OBWP; PAI; PPON; VGW; WPE
Did they catch as it were in a Vision at shut of the day. Jezreel. Thomas Hardy. NoP
"Did they dare, did they dare, to slay Eoghan Ruadh O'Neill?" Lament for the Death of Eoghan Ruadh [*or* Owen Roe] O'Neill. Thomas Osborne Davis. AnIV; OnYI; OxBI
Did They Help Me at the State Hospital for the Criminally Insane? Mbembe Milton Smith. FAZ
Did they send me away from my cat and my wife. Gunner. Randall Jarrell. OFD; PAI
Did Ya Hear? Yasmeen Jamal. LFAC
Did ye ever hear o guid Earl o Bran. Earl Brand. *Unknown.* ESPB
Did ye ever sleep at the foot o' the bed. Sleepin' at the Foot o' the Bed. Luther Patrick. BLPA
Did ye hear of the Widow Malone. The Widow Malone. Charles James Lever. HBV-2
Did You? William Cole. RHPC
Did you deserve a quiet death? did you. Dream of a Decent Death. G. A. Borgese. NePoAm
Did you eever iver ever. Hand-clapping Rhyme. *Unknown.* NTCP
Did you ever. Backyard Swing. Janet Campbell Hale. STE
Did you ever come to the place. Mother's Love. Ross B. Clapp. WBLP
Did You Ever, Ever, Ever. *Unknown.* AS, *with music*; FaBoNo; GBP
Did You Ever Go Fishing? *Unknown.* RHPC
Did you ever go to meetin', Uncle Joe, Uncle Joe? Uncle Joe [*or* Hop Up, My Ladies]. *Unknown.* FSW; OuSiCo
Did you ever hear about Cocaine Lil? Cocaine Lil [and Morphine Sue]. *Unknown.* AS; GBP; MAT; OxBoLi; TrAS
Did You Ever Hear an English Sparrow Sing? Bertha Johnston. BLPA
Did you ever hear of Captain Wattle? Captain Wattle and Miss Roe. Charles Dibdin. OxBoLi
Did you ever hear of Editor Whedon. Daisy Fraser. Edgar Lee Masters. *Fr.* Spoon River Anthology. CMoP; HAP; MoVE
Did you ever hear tell of sweet Betsy from Pike. Sweet Betsy from Pike. *Unknown.* CoSo; FaBoBa
Did you ever hear the story 'bout Willy the Weeper? Willy the Weeper. *Unknown.* AS; FSW
Did you ever hear the story of how one stormy night. The Stampede. Wallace D. Coburn. PoOW
Did you ever look. Raccoons. Aileen Fisher. PDV
Did you ever note the beauty of the soft New England grasses. A Painter in New England. Charles Wharton Stork. HBMV
Did you ever see a muskrat, Sally Ann? Sally Ann. *Unknown.* FSW
Did you ever see an alligator. Arlo Will. Edgar Lee Masters. *Fr.* Spoon River Anthology. LiTA
Did you ever see two Yankees. Give My Regards to Broadway. George M. Cohan. BLSo; FSN
Did you ever sit and ponder, sit and wonder, sit and think. Life's a Funny Proposition after All. George M. Cohan. PoLF
Did you ever think as a [*or* the] hearse rolls by. The Hearse Song. *Unknown.* AS; FSW
Did you ever think how queer. A Birthday. Rachel Field. SiSoSe; TiPo
Did you ever think you'd like to. Honest, Wouldn't You? *Unknown.* WBLP

Did you ever wait for daylight when the stars along the river. The Shallows of the Ford. Henry Herbert Knibbs. BPAW
Did you go at all to Chicago? The Stockyard. J. C. Squire. OxBTC
Did you hear of the curate who mounted his mare. The Priest and the Mulberry-Tree. Thomas Love Peacock. *Fr.* Crotchet Castle. GN; OnMSP
Did you hear of the fight at Corinth. The Eagle of Corinth. Henry Howard Brownell. PAH
Did you hear of the Widow Malone. The Widow Malone. Charles Lever. TreFS
Did you make the bluebells ring. The Road to School. Joy M. Lane. AMV-81
Did You Not See. Alex Kuo. BrSi
Did you see my wife, did you see, did you see. *Unknown.* OxNR
Did you see Paidin. The Besom-Man. Joseph Campbell. OnYI
Did you tackle that trouble that came your way. How Did You Die? Edmund Vance Cooke. BLPA; OHFP; PeD
Did you think of us this morning. Who Prayed? *Unknown.* STF
Did young Stephen sicken. Ode to Stephen Dawling Bots, Dec'd. "Mark Twain." *Fr.* The Adventures of Huckleberry Finn. NIP
Didactic Sonnet. Melvin Walker La Follette. NePoEA; PoA
Diddie Wa Diddie. *Unknown.* BluL
Diddle, diddle, dumpling, my son John. Mother Goose. OxNR
Diddlety, diddlety, dumpty. Mother Goose. OxNR
Didn' My Lord Deliver Daniel? *Unknown.* *See* Didn't My Lord. . .
Didn' Ol' John Cross the Water on His Knees? *with music.* *Unknown.* OuSiCo
Didn't acknowledge receipt. The Suicide. Joyce Carol Oates. Psk
Didn't He Ramble. Will Handy. FSW
Didn't My Lord Deliver Daniel? *Unknown.* AH, *with music*; BoAN-1, *with music*; FSW
(Didn' My Lord Deliver Daniel? *with music.*) TrAS
Didn't Old Pharaoh Get Los'? *with music.* *Unknown.* BoAN-1
Dido. John Ashbery. *Fr.* Two Sonnets. CAPP; VGW
Dido among the Shades. Virgil, *tr. fr. Latin by* Dryden. *Fr.* The Aeneid, VI. OBS
Dido My Dear, Alas, Is Dead. Spenser. *Fr.* The Shepheardes Calender: November. ChTr
Dido: Swarming. Kathleen Spivack. PoA
Dido to Aeneas. Virgil, *tr. fr. Latin by* Richard Stanyhurst. *Fr.* The Aeneid, IV. AnIV
Dido with the driven hair. The Beaten Path. Anne Goodwin Winslow. HBMV
Dido's Hunting. Virgil, *tr. fr. Latin by* the Earl of Surrey. *Fr.* The Aeneid, IV. OBSC
Didst thou not find the place inspired. Upon My Lady Carlisle's [*or* Carliles] Walking in Hampton Court Garden. Sir John Suckling. AnAnS-2; CaPo; NoP
Didyma. *Unknown, tr. fr. Greek by* Louis Untermeyer. UnTE
Didymus. Louis MacNeice. EaLo
Die, die my shriek, you will not be heard. Die My Shriek. Aaron Kushniroff, *tr. by* Joseph Leftwich. TrJP
Die in de Fiel', *with music.* *Unknown.* BoAN-1
Die My Shriek. Aaron Kushniroff, *tr. fr. Yiddish by* Joseph Leftwich. TrJP
Die Neuen Heiligen, *sel.* John Updike.
"Kierkegaard, a/ cripple and a Dane." DBV
Die Not, Fond Man. *Unknown.* ElL
Die, pussy, die. *Unknown.* OxNR
Die wild country, like the eaglehawk. Australia 1970. Judith Wright. CBAP
Died from fatigue, three laundresses together all. *Unknown.* FaBoEE
Died of Love. *Unknown.* OBET
Died, Sir Charles Wetherell's laundress, honest Sue. *Unknown.* FaBoEE
Diehard. Judith Moffett. PoA
Diella, *sels.* Richard Lynche.
"But thou my deere sweet-sounding lute be still," XVI. AAS
Love's Despair ("I *know,* within my mouth, for bashful fear"), XIII. ElL
"What sugred termes, what all-perswading arte," IV. AAS
Dies Irae. Thomas of Celano, *tr. fr. Latin.* AA, *tr. by* Abraham Coles; AWP, *tr. by* Richard Crashaw; GoBC, *par. by* Sir Walter Scott; HBV-2, *tr. by* Abraham Coles; WGRP, *tr. by* Wentworth Dillon
(Day of Judgment, The, *tr. by* Richard Crashaw.) OBVE
(That Day of Wrath, That Direful Day, *tr. unknown.*) AH, *with music*
Diet, The. Maureen Burge. BrRo
Dietary Advice. *Unknown.* FaBoUs
Dieu Qu'Il la Fait. Charles d'Orléans, *tr. fr. French by* Ezra Pound. AWP
Difference, A. Tom Clark. HoAn
Difference, The. Benjamin Franklin. WhC
Difference, The. Stoddard King. OBAL
Difference, The. Tadhg Dall O'Huiginn, *tr. fr. Irish by* Robin Flower. BIrV
Difference, The. Laura E. Richards. HBV-1; HBVY
Difference, The. Winfield Townley Scott. NePoAm
Difference, The. *Unknown.* STF
Difference between a Lie and the Truth, The. Ronald James Dessus. LFAC
Difference between despair, The. Emily Dickinson. NoAM; NoP; QFR
Difference between reacting to a storm, The. Storm and Quiet. Richard Eberhart. AMV-81
Difference of Zoos, A. Gregory Corso. VGW
Differences. Ray A. Young Bear. NU
Differences. Paul Laurence Dunbar. TreFS
Differences between rich and poor, king and queen. Rank. Lincoln Kirstein. OBWP
Different. Clere Parsons. FaBoTw
Different Bicycles. Dorothy W. Baruch. FaPON; SUS; TiPo
Different Image, A. Dudley Randall. BPo; CNA; FF; NoAM; TAP
Different Persuasions. Marge Piercy. *See* Nothing More Will Happen.
Different Speech, A. Louise Townsend Nicholl. ImOP
Different task remains, A; the secret paths. Poetic Genius. Mark Akenside. *Fr.* The Pleasures of Imagination. NOEC
Different wind, taller skies, A. Footsteps of Spring. Hayyim Nahman Bialik, *tr. by* Ruth Nevo. VWA
Different Winter. Louise Townsend Nicholl. NePoAm-2
Difficult Adjustment, A. Lauris Edmond. OCNZ
Difficult Guest, A. Carroll Watson Rankin. TDH
Difficult Times. Bertolt Brecht, *tr. fr. German by* Martin Esslin. ELU
Difficult to recall an emotion that is dead. The Patient Is Rallying. Weldon Kees. NaP
Difficulties of Translation, The, *abr.* Gavin Douglas. *Fr.* Prologues to the Aeneid. GoTS
Difficulty to think at the end of day, The. A Rabbit as King of the Ghosts. Wallace Stevens. SOTW
Difficulty was, it was, The. In the Beginning Was a Word. Robert Graves. PoA
Difficulty with all, The. Knight, with Umbrella. Elder Olson. FiBHP
Diffugere Nives. Horace, *tr. fr. Latin by* A. E. Housman. Odes, IV, 7. OBVE
Diffugere Nives, 1917. Maurice Baring. HBMV
Dig My Grave. *Unknown.* AmFP; FSW; OuSiCo, *with music*
Digestion of Milton, The. E. C. Bentley. *Fr.* Clerihews. PV
Diggers, The. W. S. Merwin. EAS
Digging. Edward Thomas. BrPo; MoAB; MoBrPo; OxBTC
Digging. Seamus Heaney. BIrV; CIP; IPY; TwCP
Digging earth for puddles, she would wake stranded. Steps. Roberta Hill. VoR
Digging for China. Richard Wilbur. GoJo; GrPl; MP; NCSH; TwCP
Digging for Indians. Gary Gildner. AmPA
Digging Out the Roots. Duane Niatum. STE
Dignified things, may I your leaves implore. To the Respective Judges. *Unknown.* APAS
Dignity of Labor, The. Robert Bersohn. PoPl; WhC
Dignity of Man, The—Lesson #1. Walter H. Kerr. NePoAm-2
Dilemma. Patricia Beer. OxBC
Dilemma. David Ignatow. VGW
Dilemma. Dorothy Parker. InMe
Dilemma of the Elm. Genevieve Taggard. MoAmPo
Diligent in the burnt fields above the sea. Find. Josephine Miles. NoP; WPE
Dillar, a dollar, A,/ A ten o'clock scholar. Mother Goose. FaBoBe; FaFP; GLGT; HBV-1; HBVY; OxNR; TiPo
Dilly Dilly Piccalilli. Clyde Watson. NTCP
Dilly Song, The. *Unknown.* *See* Carol of the Numbers.
Dim afternoon December afternoon. December. Robert Francis. LCAP
Dim, as the borrow'd beams of moon and stars. Religio Laici. John Dryden. AnAnS-2; FiP; LoBV; OAEL-1; OBS; OxBoCh; SeCV-2; ViBoPo
Dim boy claps because the others clap, The. The Freaks at Spurgin Road Field. Richard Hugo. LCAP
Dim, gradual thinning of the shapeless gloom. The Troops [*or* Prelude: The Troops]. Siegfried Sassoon. ChMP; CMoP
Dim light of daybreak now. Dawn Wail for the Dead. Kath Walker. CBAP
Dim sea glints chill, The. The Sign-Post. Edward Thomas. ViBoPo
Dim stars wheeled above the frontier post, The. The Gold Seekers. Marion Muir Richardson. PoOW
Dim the light in your faces: be passionless in the room. The Image. Richard Hughes. OBMV
Dim wind pillared the hills: stiller than mist it seemed. Sunrise Trumpets. Joseph Auslander. TrJP
Dime Call. Albert Goldbarth. VWA
Dime store. The goldfish swam in the murky. Kite. Laura Jensen. LCAP
Dimidium Animae Meae. Charles A. Brady. GoYe
Diminutivus Ululans. Francis MacNamara. OxBI
Dimme eyes, deaf ears, cold stomach shew. Verses Found in Thomas Dudley's Pocket after His Death. Thomas Dudley. SCAP

Dimmest and brightest month am I. December. Christina Rossetti. YeAr
Dimpled and flushed and dewy pink he lies. Baby. Elaine Goodale Eastman. AA
Dimpled Cloud, A. Frederick Seidel. FYAP
Din of work is subdued, The. Lullaby. W. H. Auden. FaBoMo
Dinah. A. R. Ammons. PV
Dinch me, dark God, having smoked me out. John Berryman. *Fr.* Dream Songs. CAPP
Diner. A. R. Ammons. POL
Diners in the Kitchen, The. James Whitcomb Riley. GDP; OBAL
Ding dang, bell rang. *Unknown.* OxNR
Ding Dong. A. C. Hilton. BXAP; Par
Ding Dong. *Unknown. Fr.* Swetnam, the Woman-Hater. ElL
Ding, dong, bell,/ Pussy's in the well. Mother Goose. OxNR; SoPo; TiPo
Ding dong didero,/ Blow big bellows. Smith's Song. George Sigerson. OnYI
Ding-dong! ding-dong!/ Merry, merry, go the bells. Song from Fragment of an Eccentric Drama. Henry Kirke White. OBRV
Ding-dong, ding-dong, ding-dong./ Here lies a kitten. Dirge for a Righteous Kitten. Vachel Lindsay. SUS
Ding Dong Dollar. Hamish Henderson. FSW
Dingle Bank. Edward Lear. *See* At Dingle Bank.
Dingle dingle doosey. *Unknown.* OxNR
Dingman's Marsh. John Moore. NCSH
Dingty diddlety. Mother Goose. OxNR
Dingy donkey, formal and unchanged, A. A Fable. John Hookham Frere. FaBoCo
Dining Out with Doug and Frank. James Schuyler. NYP
Dining-Room Tea. Rupert Brooke. BrPo; MoBrPo
Dining with his older daughter. Waiters. Mary Ann Hoberman. RHPC
Disintegration. Richard Shelton. DFF
Dinkey-Bird, The. Eugene Field. AA; AmMo; HBVY; NA; TreFS
Dink's Song. *Unknown.* ErPo; FSW; OxBoLi
Dinky. Theodore Roethke. OBAL; OBCA; RHPC
Dinna Ask Me. John Dunlop. HBV-1
Dinner, The. Gregory Orr. POL
Dinner at Lüchow's. The invisible man. Lüchow's and After. L. E. Sissman. NYP
Dinner Guest. Oscar Williams. TwAmPo
Dinner Guest: Me. Langston Hughes. BPo
Dinner's over. Now he mumbles at. Commerical Traveller. Lauris Edmond. OCNZ
Dinnshenchas, *sels. Unknown, tr. fr. Middle Irish by* Edward Gwynn.
 Enchanted Fawn, The. OnYI
 Story of Macha, The, *tr. by* Sir Samuel Ferguson. OnYI
 Tara. OnYI
Dino Campana and the Bear. Edward Hirsch. MAYP
Dinosaur. Bonnie Hearn. AMV-80
Dinosaur, The. Carl S. Junge. SoPo
Dinosaur, The. Bert Leston Taylor. ImOP
Dinosaur, an ancient beast, The. So Big! Max Fatchen. AmMo
Dinosaur died, was consumed by the soil, The. Pre-History Repeats. Robert J. McKent, Jr. QQQ
Dinosaur Spring. Marilyn Waniek. MAYP
Dinosaur Tracks in Beit Zayit. Shirley Kaufman. FiCP
Dinosaurs. Carolyn Stoloff. NYBP
Dinosaurs. Valerie Worth. NTCP
Dinosaurs are not all dead, The. Steam Shovel. Charles Malam. NTCP; RHPC
Dinosaurus courteously, The. Leaving the Dance. Alexander Whitaker. NIP
Diodorus is nice, isn't he, Philocles? Epigram. Meleager, *tr. by* Peter Whigham. PeHV
Diodorus Siculus. *Unknown.* ErPo; PV
Diogenes. Max Eastman. HBV-2
Dion of Tarsus. *Unknown, tr. fr. Greek by* Alma Strettell. AWP
Dionysius. Sophia de Mello Breyner Andresen, *tr. fr. Portuguese by* Allan Francovich. PBWP
Dionysus. Irving Layton. ErPo
Dioramacist does not know, The. The Museum of the Second Creation. Sandra McPherson. LCAP
Dip, dip, allebadar. *Unknown.* GBP
Dip, dip, dip. *Unknown.* GBP
Dip down upon the northern shore. Spring. Tennyson. In Memoriam A. H. H., LXXXIII. EBVV; HBV-1; ViBoPo
Dipper, The. Phoebe Hesketh. PoSH
Dipsychus, *sels.* Arthur Hugh Clough.
 "As I sat at the café, I said to myself," *fr.* Pt. II, sc. ii, *also in* Spectator ab Extra. ELP; FaBoCo; FiBHP; NBM; OAEL-2; OxBoLi
 (How Pleasant It Is to Have Money.) NOBE
 (So Pleasant It Is To Have Money.) SeCePo
 (Spectator ab Extra, 3 *sts.*) GTBS-P
 "I dreamt a dream; till morning light," *fr.* Pt. I, sc. v. OAEP, *abr.*
 Isolation, *fr.* Pt. II, sc. ii. OBVV
 "O let me love my love unto myself alone," *fr.* Pt. II, sc. ii. OAEP
 "There Is No God," the Wicked Saith, *fr.* Pt. I, sc. v. NBM; TreFS
 (Spirit's Song, The.) LoBV
 (There Is No God.) BLPL; NOBE
 "Yes, it is beautiful ever, let foolish men rail at it never," *fr.* Pt. II, sc. ii. VLP
 "Yet I could think, indeed, the perfect call," *fr.* Pt. II, sc. v. OBNC
Diptych. Velma West Sykes. IHMS
Dirce. Walter Savage Landor. *Fr.* Pericles and Aspasia, CCXXX. AWP; CTC; EBEV; EnRP; FaBoEE; FaBoEn; GBL; HAP; LiTB; LoBV; NOBE; NoP; OAEL-2; OAEP; OBEV; OBNC; OBRV; PoEL-4; PoPle; PoRA; SeCeV; TreFT; TrGrPo; ViBoPo; VLP; WeW; WHA; WhC
 (Stand Close Around.) ChTr
Dirdum drum. The Cat's Song. *Unknown.* GBP
Dire Dilemma, A. Pope. *Fr.* Epistle to Dr. Arbuthnot. WHA
Dire is the violence of ocean waves. The Worst Horror. Euripides, *tr. by* John Addington Symonds. DBV
Direct Song. Eve Merriam. UnTE
Direct This Day. Thomas Ken. TRV
Direction. Barbara Guest. WPE
Direction. Roberta Hill. CDW
Direction from Zulu. Daniel Halpern. FAZ
Directions. William Matthews. AmPA
Directions. Onitsura, *tr. fr. Japanese by* Harold G. Henderson. SoPo
Directions for Dreamfishing. Martin Johnston. CBAP
Directions for Making a Birth-Day Song, *sel.* Swift.
 To Form a Just and Finish'd Piece. NAs
Directions that you took. Old Haven. Jean Garrigue. WPE
Directions to a Rebel. W. R. Rodgers. LiTM
Directions to the Nomad. James Welch. CDW
Directive. Robert Frost. AmPP; AP; BLPL; CABA; CMoP; CoBMV; CrMA; HAP; LiTA; LiTM; MasP; MAT; MoAB; MoAmPo; NePA; NoAM; NOBA; NoP; PrIm; PPP; SeCeV
Diretro al Sol. Charles G. Bell. NePoAm
Dirge, A: "And so our royal relative is dead!" William Augustus Croffut. InMe
Dirge: "Body lies under the ground." Gavin Bantock. OxBTC
Dirge, A: "Call for the robin-redbreast and the wren." John Webster. *See* Call for the Robin Redbreast and the Wren.
Dirge: "Calm on the bosom of thy God." Felicia Dorothea Hemans. *Fr.* The Siege of Valencia. HBV-2; OBEV
 (Death-Hymn, A.) OBRV
Dirge: "Come away, come away, death." Shakespeare. *See* Come Away, Come Away, Death.
Dirge: "Fear no more the heat o' the sun." Shakespeare. *See* Fear No More the Heat o' the Sun.
Dirge, A: "Glories of our blood and state, The." James Shirley. *See* Glories of Our Blood and State, The.
Dirge: "Glories, pleasures, pomps, delights, and ease." John Ford. *See* Glories, Pleasures.
Dirge: "He lies in state." Austin Clarke. CIP
Dirge: "Her house is become like a man dishonoured." Bible, Apocrypha. First Maccabees, II: 8-14. TrJP
Dirge: "I make this dirge for you Miss Mary Binning I miss you." *Unknown, tr. fr. Hawaiian by* Armand Schwerner. BoWoP
Dirge: "If thou wilt ease thine heart." Thomas Lovell Beddoes. *Fr.* Death's Jest-Book, II. LiTB; LO; OBNC; OBRV; PoEL-4
 (If Thou Wilt Ease Thine Heart.) EnRP
 (Wolfram's Dirge.) NOBE; OBEV
Dirge: "It is the endless dance of the dead." Quincy Troupe. PoBA
Dirge: "Just at the blackest bit of my depression." Hazel Townson. PV
Dirge, A: "Naiad, hid beneath the bank." William Johnson Cory. *See* Anteros.
Dirge: "Never the nightingale." Adelaide Crapsey. HBV-1
Dirge: "1-2-3 was the number he played but today the number came 3-2-1." Kenneth Fearing. FF; HeIP; HoPM; InPK; NIP; PoRA; TrJP
Dirge: "Room for a soldier! lay him in the clover." Thomas William Parsons. *See* Dirge for One Who Fell in Battle.
Dirge, A: "Rough wind, that moanest loud." Shelley. CABA; ChTr; EnRP; InPK; NOBE; OAEP; PoRA; SoSe; TEP; TrGrPo; WiR; WHA
Dirge: "Softly!/ She is lying/ With her lips apart." Charles Gamage Eastman. AA
Dirge: "Swallow leaves her nest, The." Thomas Lovell Beddoes. *Fr.* Death's Jest-Book, I. LoBV; OBVV; POEL-4
 (Song from the Waters.) NOBE
 (Voice from the Waters, A.) OBNC; OBRV
Dirge: "Tuck the earth, fold the sod." William Alexander Percy. HBMV
Dirge: "Wail! wail ye o'er the dead!" George Darley. *Fr.* Sylvia; or, The May Queen. OBRV

Dirge: "We do lie beneath the grass." Thomas Lovell Beddoes. *Fr.* Death's Jest Book. OBNC; WiR
(Sibilla's Dirge.) NOBE
(Sybilla's Dirge.) NBM
(We Do Lie beneath the Grass.) ELP
Dirge: "Weep, weep, ye woodmen, wail." Anthony Munday. *See* Robin Hood's Funeral.
Dirge: "Welladay, welladay, poor Colin, thou art going to the ground." George Peele. *Fr.* The Arraignment of Paris. EIL
(Shepherd's Dirge, The.) OBSC
Dirge: "What shall her silence keep?" Madison Cawein. AA
Dirge, A: "Why were you born when the snow was falling?" Christina Rossetti. ChTr; EBVV; LoBV; SBG; VLP
Dirge for a Righteous Kitten. Vachel Lindsay. SUS
Dirge for a Soldier. George Henry Boker. AA; HBV-2; OBVV; PAH; PeD; WaaP
Dirge for Ashby. Margaret Junkin Preston. PAH
Dirge for Fajuyi, *sel.* Omobayode Arowa, *tr. fr. Yoruba.*
"Dekunle, handsome man, hail!" WTO
Dirge for Fidele. Shakespeare. *See* Fear No More the Heat o' the Sun.
Dirge for McPherson, A. Herman Melville. AP; PAH; PoEL-5
Dirge for One Who Fell in Battle. Thomas William Parsons. AA; GN; HBV-2
(Dirge: "Room for a Soldier! lay him in the clover.") PAH
Dirge for Small Wilddeath. Judith Moffett. LTB
Dirge; for the Barrel-Organ of the New Barbarism. Louis Aragon, *tr. fr. French by* Selden Rodman. WaaP
Dirge for the New Sunrise. Edith Sitwell. *Fr.* Three Poems of the Atomic Bomb. CMOP; EaLo; MoAB; MoBrPo; SeCePo
Dirge for the Ninth of Ab. *Unknown, tr. fr. Hebrew by* Nina Davis Salaman. TrJP
Dirge for the Year. Shelley. GN; HBV-1; HBVY
Dirge for Three Trumpets. *Unknown (Chainpoem).* EAS
Dirge for Two Veterans. Walt Whitman. MoAmPo; PoEL-5
(Two Veterans.) GN
Dirge in "Cymbeline." William Collins.
See Song from Shakespeare's "Cymbeline," A.
Dirge in Woods. George Meredith. FF; OAEP; OBEV; OBNC; OBVV; VLP; WHA; WiR
(Dirge in the Woods.) LoBV; SeCeV
Dirge is sung, the ritual said, The. I. H. B. William Winter. AA
Dirge of Alaric the Visigoth. Edward Everett. BeLS
Dirge of Love. Shakespeare. *See* Come Away, Come Away, Death.
Dirge of O'Sullivan Bear. *Unknown. See* Lament for O'Sullivan Beare, The.
Dirge of the Lone Woman. Mary M. Colum. AnIV
Dirge of the Moolla of Kotal. George Thomas Lanigan. NA
Dirge of the Munster Forest. Emily Lawless. OBVV; OnYI
Dirge of the Three Queens. Fletcher *and* Shakespeare.. *See* Funeral Song.
Dirge on the Death of Art O'Leary. *Unknown. See* Lament for Art O'Leary.
Dirge Sung at Death. *Tr. fr. Maori by* John White. WTO
Dirge upon the Death of the Right Valiant Lord, Bernard Stuart, A. Robert Herrick. SeCV-1
Dirge without Music. Edna St. Vincent Millay. CMoP; DL; LiTA; LO; NePA; NoAM; PPON; SBG; TrGrPo
Dirge Written for a Drama. Thomas Lovell Beddoes. EnRP
Dirigible, The. Ralph W. Bergengren. FaPON; SoPo
Dirigible, The. Chris Wallace-Crabbe. CBAP
Dirt Doctor, The. Melvin Douglass Brown. LFAC
Dirt Dumping. "Mark Twain." TDH
(Limerick: "Man hired by John Smith and Co., A.") FaBoNo
Dirt road rose abruptly through a wood, The. Snake Hill. Jay Parini. AMV-81; MAYP
Dirt sticks under fingernails. Pulling Weeds. Eric Chock. BrSi
Dirt under the fingernails of the window-ledge. Spring Street in '58. Derek Walcott. NYP
Dirtiest Man in the World, The. Shel Silverstein. OBCA
Dirty-billed Freeze Footy, The. Judith Hemschemeyer. Str
Dirty Dozens, The. *Unknown.* BluL
Dirty Floor, The. Edward Field. CoAP
(Floor Is Dirty, The.) NeAP
Dirty Jim. Jane Taylor. HBV-1; HBVY
Dirty Joke. D. L. Klauck. LTB
Dirty Little Accuser, The. Norman Cameron. OxBS
Dirty money and the sleazy hearts, The. The Matadors. Josephine Jacobsen. TAP
Dirty picture, a photograph, possibly a tintype, from the turn of the century, even before, A. Floor. C. K. Williams. GeTw
Dirty river by religious explorers, The. Mystic River. John Ciardi. NYBP
Dirty socks in dirty sneakers. Sorting, Wrapping, Packing, Stuffing. James Schuyler. NoAM
Dirty water reflects too. Momma's Not Gods Image. Noah Mitchell. LFAC
Dirty Word, The. Karl Shapiro. CoAP; InPK; MiAP; PoA; PoCh
Dis Aliter Visum; or, Le Byron de Nos Jours. Robert Browning. VLP
Dis Mornin', Dis Evenin', So Soon. *Unknown. See* Tell Old Bill.
Dis sun are hot. This Sun Is Hot. *Unknown.* BPo
Disabled. Wilfred Owen. BiP; BrPo; CMoP; FF; InPS; LiTM; MMA; NIP; NoAM; OxBTC; WaP
Disabled Debauchee, The. Earl of Rochester. BoLoP; HAP; NOBL; OBSV; PPP; WeW
(Maimed [*or* Maim'd] Debauchee, The.) CABA; NCEP; PoEL-3
Disagreeable Feature, A. Edwin Meade Robinson. HBMV
Disagreeable Man, The. W. S. Gilbert. FiBHP
Disappearance in West Cedar Street, A. L. E. Sissman. TwCP
Disappointment, A. Joanna Baillie. NOEC
Disappointment, The. *At. to* Aphra Behn *and to* Earl of Rochester. SBG; UnTE
Disappointment. Thomas Stephens Collier. AA
Disappointment. John Boyle O'Reilly. ACP; OnYI
Disappointment, The. Jane Taylor. FaBoUs
Disappointment. Edith Lillian Young. TRV; WBLP
(Disappointment—His Appointment.) BLRP
Disarm the Hearts. Ethel Blair Jordan. PGD
Disarmament, *sel.* Whittier.
" 'Put up the sword!' The voice of Christ once more." PGD
Disarmed. Laura Redden Searing. AA
Disarticulated/ arm torn out. Last Affair: Bessie's Blues Song. Michael S. Harper. GeTw; LCAP
Disaster. Charles Stuart Calverley. CenHV; FM; HBV-1; SpRo
Disasters numb within us, The. Life at War. Denise Levertov. NMM; VGW
Discerning the Lord's Body. Carrie Judd Montgomery. STF
Discharged. W. E. Henley. In Hospital, XXVIII. BrPo
Disciple, The. Oscar Wilde. OAEL-2
Discipleship. C. O. Bales. STF
Discipline. George Herbert. FPL; HBV-2; LiTB; LoBV; MeLP; MePo; NOBE; NOCV; NoP; OBEV; OBS; OxBoCh; PAI; PoLF; SeCePo; SeCeV; TrGrPo; ViBoPo
Disciplined in the school of hard campaigning. Horace, *tr. by* James Michie. Odes, II, 7. OBWP
Disclaimer of Prejudice. Eli Siegel. PV
Disco Chinatown. Yuri Kageyama. BrSi
Discomfort in High Places. Sydney Tremayne. PoSH
Disconnection, The. Rita Mae Brown. IHMS
Disconnections, The. John Engels. WOLT
Disconsolate and sad. Platonick Love. Lord Herbert of Cherbury. AnAnS-2; OBS
Disconsolate I/ from the thinning line. Witness to Death. Richmond Lattimore. VGW
Discontented Student, The. St. George Tucker. OBAL
Discontents in Devon. Robert Herrick. AnAnS-2; CaPo; OAEP; POL; SeCV-1
Discord and darkness—but the Song and the Star. Pilgrimage. Elinor Lennen. PGD
Discord in Childhood. D. H. Lawrence. ELU
Discordants, *sels.* Conrad Aiken.
"Dead Cleopatra lies in a crystal casket," IV. PoA
"Music I heard with you was more than music, " I. AWP; CMoP; LiTM; NOBA
(Bread and Music.) MoAB; MoAmPo
(Music I Heard.) BLPL; FaFP; HBV-1; LiTA; TreFT
(Music I Heard with You.) OxBA; PoRA
Discouraged. Lucille Stanaback. STF
". . .Discourse Heard One Day. . ." Donald C. Babcock. NePoAm-2
Discourse of the Wanderer, and an Evening Visit to the Lake. Wordsworth. *Fr.* The Excursion, IX. EnRP
Discourse on the Real. Samuel Yellen. NePoAm
Discovered in Mid-Ocean. Stephen Spender. MoBrPo
(Icarus.) NoAM; PrIm
Discoverer, The. Arthur Gordon Field. PGD
Discoverer, The. Edmund Clarence Stedman. AA; HBV-1
Discoveries. Vernon Watkins. LiTM; WaP
Discoveries in Arizona. James Wright. NoP
Discovering. Sharon Scott. JB
Discovering God Is Waking One Morning. John L'Heureux. BoNaP
Discovery. Hilaire Belloc. DBV; ViBoPo
Discovery. Hildegarde Flanner. HBMV
Discovery, The. Monk Gibbon. OnYI
Discovery, The. Gwendolyn MacEwen. NOBC
Discovery, The. Cardinal Newman. OBRV

Discovery, The. J. C. Squire. OFD; PoSC
(Sonnet: "There was an Indian, who had known no change.") CH; FaPON
(There Was an Indian.) AmFN
Discovery of LSD a True Story, The. Anselm Hollo. PoM
Discovery of San Francisco Bay. Richard Edward White. PAH
Discovery of the New World. Carter Revard. VoR
Discovery of the Pacific, The. Thom Gunn. HeIP
Discovery of This Time. Archibald MacLeish. LiTA; WaP
Discovery of Tradition, The. Lawson Fusao Inada. LTB
Discretions of Alcibiades. Robert Pinsky. NPGG
Discriminations, The; Virtuous Amusements and Wicked Demons. Jim Bogan. PoDr
Discriminator, The. Vernon Scannell. OxBC
Discussion of the Vicissitudes of History under a Pine Tree, A. Katha Pollitt. MAYP
Disdain. Sir Thomas Wyatt. *See* If in the World There Be More Woe.
Disdain Me Not. Sir Thomas Wyatt. EnRePo
("Disdain me not without desert.") SiPS
Disdain Me Still. William Herbert, Earl of Pembroke. ElL
Disdain [*or* Disdaine] Returned. Thomas Carew. AWP; CaPo; CavP; HBV-1; OBS; SeCV-1; TEP; TrGrPo; ViBoPo, 2 *sts.*
(He That Loves a Rosy Cheek.) FaBV; 2 *sts.*; LiTB; PoPle
(True Beauty, The.) GTBS; GTBS-P
(Unfading Beauty, The.) OBEV
Disdainful Mistress, The. *Malay Oral Tradition, tr. by* R. J. Wilkinson *and* R. O. Winstedt. WTO
Disdainful Shepherdess, The. *Unknown. See* Phillida Flouts Me.
Disdaining butterflies. The Woman Who Loved Worms. Colette Inez. NMM
Disdains Zenocrate to live with me? Christopher Marlowe. *Fr.* Tamburlaine the Great. ViBoPo
Diseases of Bath, The; a Satire, *sel. Unknown.*
"If to the Pump Room in the morn we go." NOEC
Diseases of the Moon. Doug Fetherling. NeAC; POL
Disenchantment. Charles Leonard Moore. AA
Disgrace he'd brought on an ancient name. "Rake" Windermere. Leonard Pounds. PaPo
Disguise upon disguise, and then disguise. Soul unto Soul Glooms Darling. Charles Leonard Moore. AA
Disguised in my mouth as a swampland. In the Morning. Jayne Cortez. BlSi
Disguises. Thomas Edward Brown. VLP; WGRP
Disguises. Elizabeth Jennings. NePoEA-2
Dish for a Poet, A. *Unknown.* OBCP
Dish for the bishop, a crushed and bitter dish, A. Almeria. Pablo Neruda, *tr. by* Angel Flores. WaaP
Disheartened Ranger, The. *Unknown.* CoSo
Dishonest men are always the rage. Antistrophe. William Hathaway. *Fr.* Rumplestiltskin Poems. DFT
Dishonest Miller, The. *Unknown.* AmFP
Dishonor. Edwin Denby. ErPo
Disillusion. Maureen Burge. BrRo
Disillusioned. "Lewis Carroll." CenHV
(My Fancy.) FaBoCo
Disillusionment. Claribel Alegria, *tr. fr. Spanish by* Darwin Flakoll. AMV-80
Disillusionment of Ten o'Clock. Wallace Stevens. CMoP; CrMA; FF; InPK; InPS; NIP; OxBA; PAI; PPoe; SOTW
Disillusion. *Tr. fr. Tewa Indian by* H. J. Spinden. WTO
Disingenuous, The/ Charm of living. Limb and Mind. John Waller. NeBP
Disinherited, The, *sel.* Mary Gilmore.
"Sudden autumn winds, like hounds, The." PoAu-1
Dislike of Tasks. Richmond Lattimore. SaC
Dismal and purposeless and gray. Pain. St. John Lucas. HBV-2
Dismantled Ship, The. Walt Whitman. AmPP; CABA; MOS; NoAM; NoP; OxBA
Dismiss the instruments that for your pleasure. Music in Venice. Louis Simpson. NYBP
Dismiss your apprehension, pseudo bard. At Shakespeare's Grave. Irving Browne. AA
Dismissal. Thomas Campion. *See* Hours of Sleepy Night, The.
Dismissal. Peter Redgrove. NMP
Dismissing Progress and Its Progenitors. George Reavey. EAS
Dismissing reports and men, he put pressure on the wax. Geoffrey Hill. Mercian Hymns, XIV. HAP
Disobedience. A. A. Milne. NTCP
Disobliging Bear, The. Carolyn Wells. TDH
Disordering, The. Lynda Yates. AMV-81
Dispatch Number Nine. Doug Fetherling. NeAC
Dispatch Number Sixteen. Doug Fetherling. NeAC
Dispatch Number Sixty. Doug Fetherling. NeAC
Dispensary, The, *sels.* Sir Samuel Garth.
"How impotent a deity am I!" OBSV
"Oft has this planet rolled around the sun." OBSV
"One doctor, singly like the sculler plies," 4 *ll.* DBV
"This wight all mercenary projects tries." OBSV
Displacement. Horace Hamilton. AMV-80
Display thy breasts, my Julia: there let me. Upon Julia's Breasts. Robert Herrick. CaPo; NoP
Disposed to wed, e'en while you hasten, stay. Marriages. George Crabbe. *Fr.* The Parish Register. FaBoUs
Dispossessed, The. John Berryman. AP; PoCh; VGW
Dispossessed, The. Thomas Kinsella. NOCV
Dispossessed Poet. Monk Gibbon. OnYI
Dispraise of a Courtly Life. Sir Philip Sidney. LoBV; OAEP
Dispraise of Absalom, The. *Unknown, tr. fr. Irish by* Robin Flower. BIrV; OxBI
Dispraise of Love, and Lover's Follies. "A. W." ElL; HBV-1; OBSC
(Dispraise of Love.) TrGrPo
("If love be life, I long to die.") LO
Dispute of the Heart and Body of François Villon, The. Villon, *tr. fr. French by* Swinburne. AWP; OBVE
Dispute over Suicide, A. *Unknown, tr. fr. Egyptian by* T. Eric Peet. TTY
Disquieting Muses, The. Sylvia Plath. NMM; SBG
Dissatisfaction with Metaphysics. William Empson. CMoP
Dissembler, The. Abraham Cowley. AnAnS-2
Dissembler. Charles Shaw. GoYe
Dissenters' Thanksgiving for the Late Declaration, The. *Unknown.* APAS
Dissolution, The. John Donne. OAEP; SeCV-1
Dissolving, the coals shift. Rain swaddles us. The Ruin. Charles Tomlinson. NePoEA-2
Dissonance. Cedric Whitman. AMV-80
Distaff, The. Erinna, *tr. fr. Greek by* Marylin Arthur. WPOW
Distance. Robert Creeley. CoPo
Distance. Anthony Delius. PeSA
Distance. Peter Everwine. NNaP
Distance brings proportion. From here. Tao in the Yankee Stadium Bleachers. John Updike. LiSp
Distance doesn't matter, Francisco. Extracts: From the Journal of Elisa Lynch. Maura Stanton. AmPA
Distance drums your words into my ears, The; it's good. Autobiography, Chapter XII: Hearing Montana. Jim Barnes. AMV-81
Distance from the Sea, A. Weldon Kees. NoAM
Distance is swept by the smooth. Radar. Alan Ross. DFF; FF
Distance sheltered upon tubes of foam. The Ghost of the Cargo Boat. Pablo Neruda, *tr. by* Donald D. Walsh. WSC
Distance Spills Itself. Yocheved Bat-Miriam, *tr. fr. Hebrew by* Robert Friend. VWA
Distances, The. Jim Carroll. PoA
Distances. Albert Goldbarth. GeTw
Distances. Jeremy Kingston. NYBP
Distances, The. W. S. Merwin. NOBA
Distances, *sel.* Christopher Okigbo.
"Death lay in ambush." TTY
Distances, The. Charles Olson. NeAP; NoP
Distances don't matter. On the Road to Paradise. Garrett Hongo. HoAn
Distances They Keep, The. Howard Nemerov. BoAnP
Distances to the Friend, The. Jonathan Williams. NeAP
Distant and long have I waited without going. To Mackinnon of Strath. Iain Lom. GoTS
Distant as the Duchess of Savoy. *Unknown.* MeEL
Distant Drum, The. Calvin C. Hernton. BOLo; CTBA; FF; NNP; TTY
Distant Fury of Battle, The. Geoffrey Hill. NoP
Distant Orgasm, The. James Tate. AmPA
Distant Runners, The. Mark Van Doren. GOA; LiTA; LiTM; MoAmPo; NePA
Distant Seychelles are not so remote, The. Eireann. Osbert Lancaster. *Fr.* Afternoons with Baedeker. DBV; NOBL
Distant View. Uys Krige, *tr. fr. Afrikaans by* Uys Krige *and* Jack Cope. PeSA
Distant View of England from the Sea. William Lisle Bowles. EnRP
Distant Winter, The. Philip Levine. VGW
Distant Wisconsin. Tree Poem on My Wife's Birthday. Tom Hanna. FAZ
Distich. Shuraikh, *tr. fr. Arabic.* TrJP
Distinction. Mark A. De Wolfe Howe. AA
Distinction. Charles Tomlinson. CMoP
Distinguish carefully between these two. The Justice of the Peace. Hilaire Belloc. OBSV
Distinguished old one-legged colonel, A. The One-legged Colonel. *Unknown.* TDH
Distortions. Pearse Hutchinson. CIP
Distracted Puritan, The. Richard Corbet. OxBoLi

Distracted with care. The Despairing Lover. William Walsh. ELP; FaBoCh; NOBL; OBEC; OxBoLi
Distraction. Henry Vaughan. NCEP; SeCP
Distractions and the Human Crowd. Stevie Smith. OxBC
Distress. Susan Griffin. NPGG
Distribution of Honours for Literature. Walter Savage Landor. FaBoEE
District school, not far away, A. The Smack in School. William Pitt Palmer. HBV-2
Distrust. Robert Herrick. CaPo
Disturb me not, oh bouyant youths! *Tr. fr. Maori by* John White. WTO
Disturb the sanctuary. Paperweight Escape. Stephen Todd Booker. LFAC
Disturbed by consciousness. Satori. Gayl Jones. BlSi
Disturbing it is/ To take your stick sedately talking. The River Walk. Padraic Fallon. OxBI
Disused Shed in Co. Wexford, A. Derek Mahon. CIP; OxBC
Disused Temple, The. Norman Cameron. ChMP; OxBS; OxBTC
Dithering towards the horizon. Horizon without Landscape. Tom Lowenstein. VWA
Dithyramb in Retrospect. Peter Hopegood. PoAu-2
Ditty: "Cock shall crow, The." Robert Louis Stevenson. TrGrPo
Ditty, A: "I went into my garden to gather some herbs." Berth Jacobs, *tr. fr. Dutch by* Jonathan Crewe. WPOW
Ditty, A: In Praise of Eliza, Queen of the Shepherds. Spenser. *Fr.* The Shepheardes Calender: April. OBEV
(Ditty, A: "See where she sits upon the grassy green.") FaBoCh
("See where she sits upon the grassy green.") ViBoPo
Ditty, A: "My true-love hath my heart, and I have his." Sir Philip Sidney. *See* My True Love Hath My Heart.
Ditty: "O holy Love, religious saint!" Sir Robert Chester. *Fr.* Love's Martyr. ElL
Ditty, A: "Peace, peace, peace, make no noise." John Day. *Fr.* Humour Out of Breath. ElL
Ditty, A: "See where she sits upon the grassy green." Spenser. *See* Ditty, A: In Praise of Eliza, Queen of the Shepherds.
Ditty, The: "Young Colin Clout." John Gay. *See* Tuesday; or, The Ditty.
Ditty in Imitation of the Spanish, A. Lord Herbert of Cherbury. AnAnS-2; ElL
(Ditty in Imitation of the Spanish "Entre Tanto Que L'Avril.") OBS
Ditty of the Six Virgins, The. Thomas Watson. *See* With Fragrant Flowers We Strew the Way.
Divan, The. Richard Henry Stoddard. AA
Dive. Langston Hughes. CAD; NYP
Dive could come who was its fledgling first, The. Nijinsky. Parker Tyler. PoA
Dive for dreams. E. E. Cummings. OLR
Diver. Robert Francis. LiSp
Diver, The. Robert Hayden. AmPP; BPo; LiSp; MOS
Diver, The. John Frederic Herbin. CaP
Diver, The. E. L. Mayo. CoAP
Diver, The. Leonard E. Nathan. ErPo
Diver, The. Nikos Phocas, *tr. fr. Greek by* Kimon Friar. AMV-81
Diver, The. W. W. E. Ross. NOBC; OBCV; PeCV; WHW
Diver. R. A. Simpson. CBAP
Diver go down. Diver. Robert Francis. LiSp
Diverging now (as if his quest had been). Wordsworth. *Fr.* The Excursion, II. OBRV
Divers, The. Peter Quennell. MoBrPo; MoVE
Divers Doth Use, as I Have Heard and Know. Sir Thomas Wyatt. OAEP
("Dyvers dothe use as I have heard and kno.") AAS
(Sonnet: "Divers doth use (as I have heard and know).") SiPS
Divers Thy Death. Earl of Surrey. NCEP
(Death of Wyatt, The.) SiPS
("Dyvers thy death doo dyverslye bemone.") AAS
Diversely passioned is the lover's heart. The Eleventh Property. Sir Thomas More. *Fr.* The Twelve Properties or Conditions of a Lover. EnRePo
Diversions for an Unhappy Princess. *Unknown. Fr.* The Squyer of Lowe Degre. OxBM
Diversions of the Re-Echo Club. Carolyn Wells. OBAL
Diverting History of John Gilpin, The. William Cowper. BeLS; FaBoBe; FiP; GN; HBV-2; HBVY; InMe; LAuP; OBEC; OBNV; PoPle; RoGo; TreFS
(John Gilpin.) InvP; ViBoPo
Dives and Lazarus. *Unknown.* AmFP; ELP; ESPB; FaBoBa; OBET; OxBB
(Dives and Laz'us.) TTY
Dives, when you and I go down to Hell. To Dives. Hilaire Belloc. HBMV; OBSV
Divide your bread in two. Heavenly Jerusalem, of the Earth. Leah Goldberg, *tr. by* Robert Friend VWA
Divided. David Gray. AA
Divided. Jean Ingelow. HBV-1; SpRo; VLP
"Dappled sky, a world of meadows, A," *sel.* OBNC
Divided Heart, The. George Wither. *Fr.* Fair Virtue, the Mistress of Philarete. TrGrPo
Dividends. Hubert Creekmore. WaP
Dividing the Field. William Aberg. LFAC
Dividing the House. James Richardson. AMV-81
Divina Commedia, *sels.* Dante, *tr. fr. Italian.*
Inferno, *tr. by* Mark Musa. NAWM-1
"And now we walked along the solid mire," XV, *tr. by* Robert Lowell. OBVE.
("Now the hard margin bears us on, while steam," *tr. by* Dorothy L. Sayers.) PeHV
Canto I, *ll.* 1-21, *tr. fr. Italian by 5 diff. trs.* HoPM
Francesca and Paolo, *fr.* V, *tr. by* Byron. TreFT
"Like fire-flies that the peasant on the hill," *fr.* XXVI, *tr. by* Laurence Binyon. Prf
Pier delle Vigne, XII, *tr. by* John Ciardi. HoPM
Paradiso, *much abr., tr. by* Laurence Binyon. NAWM-1
"I raised my eyes aloft, and I beheld," 4 *ll.* TRV
Saint Bernard's Prayer to Our Lady, *fr.* XXXIII, *tr. by* Louis How. ISi
Saints in Glory, The, *fr.* XXXI, *tr. by* Henry F. Cary. WGRP
"Within the deep and luminous subsistence of the High Light," *fr.* XXXIII. ILwL
Purgatorio
"As when his first beams tremble in the sky," XXVII, *tr. by* Laurence Binyon. NAWM-1
Celestial Pilot, The, *fr.* II, *tr. by* Longfellow. WGRP
"Earnest to explore within and all around," *fr.* XXVIII, *tr. by* Shelley. OBVE
"In that hour when the heat of day no more," XIX, *tr. by* Laurence Binyon. NAWM-1
"Now hoisteth sail the pinnace of my wit," I-II, *tr. by* Laurence Binyon. NAWM-1
"Now when those Seven of the First Heaven stood still," XXX-XXXI, *tr. by* Laurence Binyon. NAWM-1
Virgil's Farewell to Dante, *fr.* XXVII, *tr. by* Laurence Binyon. FaBoTw
Divina Commedia (*poems introductory to* Longfellow's *tr. of the* Divine Comedy, I-VI). Longfellow. AmPP; AP; NePA; OxBA; TAP
Sels.
"How strange the sculptures that adorn these towers," II. GoBC
(Three Sonnets on the Divina Commedia.) SeCeV
"I enter, and I see thee in the gloom," III. GoBC
"I lift mine eyes, and all the windows blaze," IV[V]. GoBC
(Three Sonnets on the Divina Commedia.) SeCeV
"O star of morning and of liberty," V[VI]. GoBC
"Oft have I seen at some cathedral door," I. GoBC; HAP; HBV-2; TreF; ViBoPo
(Dante.) OBEV
(Three Sonnets on the Divina Commedia.) SeCeV
"With snow-white veil and garments as of flame," IV. TreFT
Divination. Jerred Metz. VWA
Divination by a Daffadill [*or* Daffodil]. Robert Herrick. CaPo; CavP; OBS; SeCV-1
Divine Abundance. *Unknown.* BLRP
Divine Awe. George Edward Woodberry. Wild Eden, XVI. AA
Divine Blacksmith, The. Matthew Prior. FaBoNo
Divine Century of Spiritual Sonnets, A, *sels.* Barnabe Barnes.
Life of Man, The. OBSC
("Blast of wind, a momentary breath, A.") EBEV
World's Bright Comforter, The. OxBoCh
(God's Virtue.) NOCV; OBSC
(Sonnet: "World's bright comforter, whose beamsome light, The.") ElL
Divine destroyer, pity me no more. A la Bourbon. Richard Lovelace. CaPo
Divine Hand, The. William Williams. *See* Christian Pilgrim's Hymn, The.
Divine Harmony, The. Shakespeare. *Fr.* The Merchant of Venice, V, i. GoBC
Divine Image, A ("Cruelty has a Human heart"). Blake. *Fr.* Songs of Experience. ChTr; NoP; OBNC; TEP
Divine Image, The ("To mercy pity peace and love"). Blake. *Fr.* Songs of Innocence. EBCP; EnRP; FaBoEn; LAuP; NOBE; NOEC; NoP; OAEL-2; OAEP; OBEC; OBNC; OxBoCh; PoEL-4; PPP; TEP; TRV; ViBoPo; WGRP
("To mercy pity peace and love.") LO
Divine Insect, The. John Hall Wheelock. GoYe; NYBP
Divine Love. Michael Benedikt. AmPA; CoAP; ConAP
Divine Love. *Unknown.* OAEL-1; OxBM
(Christ's Gift to Man, *abr.*) ACP
(Love unlike Love.) MeEL
Divine Love. Charles Wesley. *See* Love Divine, All Loves Excelling.
Divine Lover, The. Charles Wesley. *See* Jesus, Lover of My Soul.
Divine Mistris, A. Thomas Carew. AnAnS-2

Divine Office of the Kitchen, The. Cecily Hallack. BLRP; PoLF; TreFT. *See also* Lord of All Pots and Pans and Things.
Divine Presence, The. Aubrey Thomas De Vere. May Carols, Pt. I, iii. GoBC
Divine Rapture, A. Francis Quarles. *See* My Beloved Is Mine, and I Am His.
Divine winds upon the waters, The. Hai. Stuart Z. Perkoff. VWA
Divine Wooer, The, *sel.* Phineas Fletcher.
"Me Lord? can'st Thou mispend." TrPWD
Divine Zenocrate. Christopher Marlowe. *Fr.* Tamburlaine the Great, Pt. II, Act II, sc. iii. WHA
("Black is the beauty of the brightest day.") ViBoPo
(To Entertain Divine Zenocrate.) ChTr
Divinely shapen cup, thy lip. On a Greek Vase. Frank Dempster Sherman. AA
Divinely Superfluous Beauty. Robinson Jeffers. HeIP; MoAmPo; PoPl
Diviners, The. Mary Oliver. WPE
Diving for Pearls. Traise Yamamoto. BrSi
Diving into the Wreck. Adrienne Rich. HeIP; MOS; NIP; NoAM; NOBA; NoP
Divinities. W. S. Merwin. PoA
Division. John Ratti. NYBP
Division of Parts, The. Anne Sexton. NePoEA-2
Divorce. Kate Jennings. AMV-80
Divorce. Erica Jong. GP
Divorce. Bink Noll. MAT
Divorce, The. Thomas Stanley.
Divorce. Anna Wickham. MoBrPo
Divorce. Siv Widerberg, *tr. fr. Swedish by* Verne Moberg. CTBA
Divorce Dress, The. Jeanne Finley. AMV-80
Divorce of a Lover, The ("Divorce me nowe good death"). George Gascoigne. AAS
Divorced, but friends again at last. The Onion, Memory. Craig Raine. NoP
Dixie ("I wish I was in the land of cotton"). Daniel Decatur Emmett. BLSo, *with music*; FaFP; FaPON; FSW, *with music*; HBV-2; TrAS, *with music*; TreF; TrGrPo; YaD
(Dixie's Land.) PSoN
Dixie ("Southrons, hear your country call you"). Albert Pike. AA; HBV-2; PAH
Dixon, a Choctaw, twenty years of age. A Savage. John Boyle O'Reilly. AA
Dizzy Giraffe, The. *Unknown.* TDH
Djalbarmiwi's Song. *Unknown.* *See* Blowflies Buzz, The.
Djanggawul Song-Cycle, *much abr.* *Aborigine Oral Tradition, tr. by* R. M. Berndt. WTO
Do. Melvin B. Tolson. *See* On the Founding of Liberia.
Do all the good you can. John Wesley's Rule [*or* A Rule]. John Wesley. FaFP; HBVY; TreFT
Do alley cats go. Alley Cat School. Frank Asch. RHPC
Do any thing anything you will. Pigeon. Elouise Loftin. CNA
Do as they do in the Isle of Man. The Isle of Man. *Unknown.* GBP
Do' a-stan'in' on a jar, fiah a-shinnin' thoo. Howdy, Honey, Howdy! Paul Laurence Dunbar. PoLF
Do [*or* Doe] but consider this small dust. The Hourglass [*or* The Houre-Glasse]. Ben Jonson. EnLoPo; EnRePo; NIP; OAEL-1; SeCP
Do Come Back Again, *with music.* *Unknown.* OuSiCo
Do diddle di do. Jim Jay. Walter de la Mare. BrPo; CenHV; HBMV; SD; SiSoSe
Do Don't Touch-a My Garment, Good Lord, I'm Gwine Home, *with music.* *Unknown.* BoAN-2
Do explain to us. Return to Dachau. B. Z. Niditch. AMV-81
Do gorillas have birthdays? Questions My Son Asked Me, Answers I Never Gave Him. Nancy Willard. LCAP
Do I give off in the wee. The Sickness of Friends. Henri Coulette. NYBP
Do I Love Thee? John Godfrey Saxe. HBV-1
Do I love you? A Love Song. Raymond Richard Patterson. BOLo
Do I prefer to forget it? This middle stretch. Day of Renewal. Louis MacNeice. NAs
Do I Really Pray? John Burton. STF
"Do I see a hat in the road?" I said. The Old Sussex Road. Ian Serraillier. NTCP
Do I sleep? Do I dream? De Tea Fabula. Sir Arthur Quiller-Couch. CenHV
Do I sleep? do I dream? Further Language from Truthful James [*or* Truthful James]. Bret Harte. CenHV; FaBoCo; NOBL
Do I venture away too far. Song. Keith Douglas. NePoEA
Do It Now. Berton Braley. BLPA; FaFP; WBLP
Do It Now ("He was going to be all that a mortal should be"). *Unknown.* STF
Do It Now ("If you've got a job to do"). *Unknown.* BLPA; FaFP; WBLP
Do It Right. Samuel O. Buckner. WBLP
Do it, then. If you do. It. Richmond Lattimore. PP
Do It Yrself. Larry Eigner. NeAP; PoM
Do Li A. *Unknown.* GBP
"Do look at those pigs as they lie in the straw." The Pigs. Jane Taylor. FM
Do, Lord, Remember Me. *Unknown.* AmFP
Do my Johnny Boker. Johnny Boker. *Unknown.* FSW; ShS
Do Not Accompany Me. Shimon Halkin, *tr. fr. Hebrew by* Ruth Nevo. VWA
Do not account that for thine own. Isabella Whitney. *Fr.* A Sweet Nosegay, or Pleasant Posy. WPE
Do Not Ask. Christine Lavant, *tr. fr. German by* Michael Hamburger. WPOW
Do not ask: where? We Go. Karl Wolfskehl. TrJP, *tr. by* Carol North Valhope *and* Ernst Morwitz; VWA, *tr. by* Harry Zohn
Do not ask me, charming Phillis. By a Bank of Pinks and Lilies. *Unknown.* ErPo
Do not awake the academic scholars. Morning. Patrick Kavanagh. GLGT
Do not bathe her in blood. An Abortion. Frank O'Hara. TAP
Do not be a lost dog. Dogs of Santiago. Eugene McCarthy. BoAnP; GDP
Do not chafe at social rules. The Lonely Cloud of Care. Coventry Patmore. *Fr.* The Victories of Love, II, vii. FaBoRV
Do not come when I am dead. My Hereafter. Juanita De Long. WGRP
Do not conceal[e] thy [*or* those] radiant eyes. To Cynthia, on Concealment of Her Beauty. Sir Francis Kynaston. CavP; HBV-1; MeLP; MePo; NOBE; OBS; ViBoPo
Do not conceive that I shall here recount. A Virgin Declares Her Beauties. Francesco da Barberino, *tr. by* Dante Gabriel Rossetti. AWP; ErPO
Do not crouch to-day and worship. The Present. Adelaide Anne Proctor. WGRP
Do not delude yourself that they are kind. The Benefactors. Sara Henderson Hay. DFT
Do not despair, my sister, of a brother's process. Under Our Own Wings. Nellie Wong. BrSi
Do not despair. For Johnny. John Pudney. OBWP
Do not disdain, O straight up-raised pine. Graven Thoughts. Sir Philip Sidney. *Fr.* Arcadia. SiPS
Do Not Embrace Your Mind's New Negro Friend. William Meredith. WaP
Do not enforce the tired wolf. Prelude to an Evening. John Crowe Ransom. AP; CoBMV; EAS; MoAB; MoAmPo; MoPo; MoVE; NePA; OxBA; PoCh
Do Not Expect Again a Phoenix Hour. C. Day Lewis. CMoP; FaBoMo; LiTB; LiTM; MoAB; MoBrPo; OxBI; OxBTC; PoRA
(Do Not Expect Again.) NoAM
("Do not expect again a phoenix hour.") CMoP; OxBTC
Do not fear, my love; no danger. Precaution. Heine, *tr. by* Louis Untermeyer. UnTE
Do not fear to put thy feet. The River-God's Song [*or* Song]. John Fletcher. *Fr.* The Faithful Shepherdess, III, i. ElL; FaPON; MoShBr; OBS
Do Not Go Gentle ("Do not go gentle into Death's esteemed vale"). Tim Hopkins. BXAP
Do Not Go Gentle into That Good Night. Dylan Thomas. BiP; CABA; ChMP; CoBMV; DL; FaFP; FF; HAP; HeIP; HoPM; InPK; InPS; LiTM; MoAB; MoBrPo; MoVE; MP; NIP; NoAM; NOBE; NoP; OAEL-2; OxBTC; PAI; PPON; PrIm; SCV; SeCeV; SoSe; TEP; TreFT; TW; TwCP; UnPo; ViBoPo; WeW
Do not hold my few years. So We've Come at Last to Freud. Alice Walker. IHMS
Do not hurry; have faith. Have Faith. Edward Carpenter. WGRP
Do not imagine that the exploration. The Discovery. Gwendolyn MacEwen. NOBC
Do not jump on ancient uncles. Rules. Karla Kuskin. RHPC
Do not leave me, Lord, do not let the field lie fallow. Prayer for the Useless Days. Edith Lovejoy Pierce. TrPWD
Do not let any woman read this verse! Deirdre. James Stephens. AWP; CMoP; HBMV; NoAM; OBMV; PoRA; ViBoPo
Do not look for him. Elegy. Leonard Cohen. HeIP
Do not lose sight. You Who Occupy Our Land. Manuela Margarido, *tr. by* Allan Francovich. WPOW
Do not love me, my friend. Love Song. Flavien Ranaivo, *tr. by* Miriam Koshland. PBA
Do Not, Oh, Do Not Prize. *Unknown.* ElL
("Do not, O do not prize thy beauty at too high a rate.") OBSC
(Pride Is the Canker.) TrGrPo
Do not pay too much attention to the stupid old body. The Stupid Old Body. Edward Carpenter. WGRP
Do not pay too much attention to the wandering lunatic mind. The Wandering Lunatic Mind. Edward Carpenter. WGRP
Do not place frill or border or bouquet. At the Jewish Cemetery in Prague. Oscar Levertin, *tr. by* Richard Burns *and* Göran Printz-Pahlson. VWA

Do not rumple my top-knot. The Coy Lass Dress'd Up in Her Best. *Unknown.* ErPo
Do not spend your time in fretting. When Things Go Wrong. *Unknown.* STF
Do not stifle me with the strange scent. Alien. Donald Jeffrey Hayes. AmNP
Do not suddenly break the branch, or. Usk. T. S. Eliot. Landscapes, III. BiP; FaBoCh; NOCV
"Do not take a bath in Jordan." Scotch Rhapsody. Edith Sitwell. MP; TwCP
Do not take your piece. Bio-poetic Statement. Carroll Arnett. STE
Do Not Think. Carol Freeman. CNA
Do not think I am not grateful for your small. Gratitude. Louise Glück. HeIP
Do Not Torment Me, Woman ("Do not torment me, woman, for your honour's sake do not pursue me"). *Unknown, tr. fr. Late Middle Irish by* Kenneth Jackson. AnIL
Do not torment me, woman, let us set our minds at one. Reconciliation. *Unknown, tr. by* Kenneth Jackson. AnIL
Do not tremble, wife. The Mistress Addresses the Wife. Naomi Replansky. GP
Do not trust him gentle lady. The Gipsy's Warning. *Unknown.* BeLS
Do not waste your pity, friend. A Wasted Sympathy. Winifred Howells. AA
Do not waste your time. To a Boy. *Unknown, tr. by* Frank O'Connor. KiLC
Do not weep, maiden, for war is kind. War Is Kind, I. Stephen Crane. AmPP; BiP; FPL; HBV-2; LiTA; LiTM; NOBA; OBWP; PAL; PoLF; TAP; ViBoPo; WaaP
Do not worry if I scurry from the grill-room in a hurry. Cupid's Darts. A. P. Herbert. CenHV
Do Nothing till You Hear from Me. David Henderson. CNA; PoBA
Do skyscrapers ever grow tired. Skyscrapers. Rachel Field. FaPON
Do Something. *Unknown.* STF
Do the Baby Cake-Walk. Clyde Watson. NTCP
Do the Dead Know What Time It Is? Kenneth Patchen. HoPM; MoAmPo
Do the wife and baby travelling to see. The Sick Nought. Randall Jarrell. OxBA
Do They Miss Me at Home? Caroline Atherton Briggs Mason. TreFS
Do They Think of Me at Home. Joseph Edward Carpenter. FaBoBe; TreFS
Do They Whisper behind My Back? Delmore Schwartz. LiTA
Do We Not Hear Thy Footfall? Amy Carmichael. TRV
Do What Thy Manhood Bids Thee Do. Sir Richard Francis Burton. TreFS
Do What You Will. Dorothy Hobson. GoBC
Do ye hear the children weeping, O my brothers. The Cry of the Children. Elizabeth Barrett Browning. EBVV; HBV-1; OAEP; ViBoPo; VLP
Do ye ken hoo to fush for the salmon? Master and Man. Sir Henry Newbolt. OxBTC; WhC
Do ye ken John Peel with his coat so gray? *See* D'ye ken John Peel with his coat so gay?
Do you/ dig ray/ charles. Ray Charles. Sam Cornish. CNA
Do you ask me how I prove. The Heart's Proof. James Buckham. BLRP; WBLP
Do you ask me what I think of. What I Think of Hiawatha. J. W. Morris. Par; SpRo
Do you ask what the birds say? The sparrow, the dove. Answer to a Child's Question. Samuel Taylor Coleridge. EnRP; FaBoBe; HBV-1; HBVY; OxBChV; PoPle
Do you blame me that I loved him? A Double Standard. Frances E. W. Harper. BlSi
Do you come to me to bend me to your will. A Woman to Her Lover. Christina Walsh. BrRo
Do you ever hear it? Afterword: Song of Song. James Broughton. GP
Do you ever think of me, Kitty Kline? Kitty Kline. *Unknown.* AmFP
Do You Fear the Wind? Hamlin Garland. AA; HBV-1; HBVY; PoPl; TreFT; YaD
Do you feel your heart discouraged as you pass along the way? When Thou Passest through the Waters. Henry Crowell. BLRP
Do you forget the shifting hole. To a Defeated Saviour. James Wright. NePoEA
Do you have a sweet thought, Cerinthus. Sulpicia, *tr. fr. Latin by* Aliki *and* Willis Barnstone. BoWoP
Do you hear the blue owl shriek? Blue Owl Song. Alfred Kittner, *tr. by* Herbert Kuhner. VWA
Do you hear the cry as the pack goes by. Wind-Wolves. William D. Sargent. RHPC; TiPo
"Do you herd sheep?" old gramma sighed. How Low Is the Lowing Herd. Walt Kelly. FiBHP
Do You Just Belong? *Unknown.* STF
Do you know how the people of all the land. From Potomac to Merrimac. Edward Everett Hale. PAH
Do you know, I would quietly. Rainer Maria Rilke, *tr. fr. German by* M. D. Herter Norton. OLR
Do you know me now? From the Ballad of Evil. N. P. Van Wyk Louw, *tr. by* Anthony Delius. PeSA
Do you know my/ slap-a-hand. Main Man Blues. Eugene B. Redmond. GP
Do you know my children. A Message from Reverend Fat Back Made Possible by the International Society of Social Suckers. Melvin Douglass Brown. LFAC
Do you know of the dreary land. The River Fight. Henry Howard Brownell. PAH
Do you know that once. Overnight Guest. Ramona Wilson. VoR
Do you know that your soul is of my soul such part. To My Son [*or* Like Mother, like Son]. Margaret Johnston Grafflin. BLPA; SoSe
Do you know the old man who. The Wild Flower Man. Lu Yu, *tr. by* Kenneth Rexroth. NaP
Do you know there's lots of people. Get into the Boosting Business. *Unknown.* WBLP
Do you know what. Fancy. Robert Creeley. NOBA
Do you know what is bad? Bad and Good. Alexander Resnikoff. NTCP
Do you know where I got my song? My Song. Hayyim Nahman Bialik, *tr. by* Ruth Nevo. VWA
Do you know you have asked for the costliest thing. A Woman's Question. Lena Lathrop, *wr. at. to* Elizabeth Barrett Browning. BLPA; WBLP
Do you look for a rainbow, Love, in this wet weather. Wet Weather. Patricia Low. VGW
Do You Love Me? Robert Watson. POL
Do you love me. Question. *Unknown.* PoSC; RHPC
"Do you love me?" I asked. The Toad. Gerald Locklin. GP
Do you 'member way last summer? You Kicked and Stomped and Beat Me. *Unknown.* OuSiCo
Do you ne'er think what wondrous beings these? Longfellow. *Fr.* The Birds of Killingsworth. WBLP
"Do you not find something very strange about him?" The Assassination. Robert Hillyer. MoAmPo; OFD
Do you not hear her song. Daphne. Thomas S. Jones, Jr. OHIP
Do you not hear me calling, white deer with no horns! Mongan Laments the Change That Has Come upon Him and His Beloved. W. B. Yeats. VLP
"Do you not hear the Aziola cry?" The Aziola. Shelley. EBEV; PBBP
Do you not see the Christmas star. Song of the Wise Men. Edith Lovejoy Pierce. PGD
"Do you not wish to renounce the Devil?" Epigram. Armand Lanusse, *tr. by* Langston Hughes. PoNe; TTY
Do you, now, as the news becomes known. Pay-off. Kenneth Fearing. CMoP
Do You Plan to Speak Bantu? Ogden Nash. FiBHP
Do You Remember. Thomas Haynes Bayly. HBV-1
Do you remember/ How you won. To James. Frank Horne. *Fr.* Letters Found near a Suicide. BPo
Do you remember/ That afternoon. Envoy. W. E. Henley. BrPo
Do you remember a long time ago. Cotton-eyed Joe. *Unknown.* FSW
Do you remember an inn. Tarantella. Hilaire Belloc. CH; FaBoCh; GoBC; MoBrPo; MoShBr; OBMV; SpRo
Do you remember how I beat on the door. A Door. W. S. Merwin. LCAP
Do you remember how the twilight stood. To Butterfly. William Alexander Percy. HBMV
Do you remember how we came that day. The Heights. Helen Frazee-Bower. Two Married, I. HBMV
Do you remember, long ago. After Aughrim. Arthur Gerald Geoghegan. OnYI
Do You Remember Me? Walter Savage Landor. *Fr.* Ianthe. EnRP; ViBoPo
("Do you remember me? or are you proud?") OBNC
(Ianthe's Question.) OBEV
Do you remember Mr. Goodbeare, the carpenter. Elegy for Mr. Goodbeare. Sir Osbert Sitwell. MoBrPo
Do you remember, my sweet, absent son. The Child's Wish Granted. George Parsons Lathrop. AA; HBV-1
Do you remember one immortal. To F. C. in Memoriam Palestine. G. K. Chesterton. HBMV
Do you remember that day of the roaring storm. Mountaineering Bus. Rennis McOwan. PoSH
Do You Remember That Night? *Unknown, tr. fr. Irish by* Eugene O'Curry. AnIV; BlrV; OnYI; OxBI
Do you remember the lizard? The Lizard. Rona Murray. NOBC
Do you remember the meadow-field. The Meadow-Field. Charles Sangster. *Fr.* Pleasant Memories. OBCV
Do you remember when you heard. Do You Remember. Thomas Haynes Bayly. HBV-1

Do you remember, when you were first a child. Message from Home. Kathleen Raine. ImOP; WPE
Do you say/ its progesterone. What Do You Say When a Man Tells You, You Have the Softest Skin. Mary Mackey. FF
Do you see them? I mean the Dead. Haunted Odysseus: The Last Testament. Horace Gregory. MoVE
Do you seek to bind me, ye gods. The Sword of Tethra. William Larminie. *Fr.* Moytura. OnYI
Do you think/ you must work signs. Instructions for the Messiah. Myra Sklarew. VWA
Do you think of me at all. Dead "Wessex" the Dog to the Household. Thomas Hardy. FM
Do you think that odes and sermons. Sexsmith the Dentist. Edgar Lee Masters. *Fr.* Spoon River Anthology. NePA
Do you think we skip. The Zobo Bird. Frank A. Collymore. AmMo; GoJo
Do you want to know his name? The Porch. R. S. Thomas. NOCV
Do you wish the world were better? Better, Wiser and Happier. Ella Wheeler Wilcox. WBLP
Do your days seem long, your pleasures few. He Cares. Owen C. Salway. STF
Doan't You Be What You Ain't. Edwin Milton Royle. BLPA
Dobbin. George Bowering. NOBC
Dobbin Dead. William Barnes. VLP
Dobe Bill, he came a-riding. The Killer. *Unknown.* CoSo
Dock-Leaves. William Barnes. VLP
Docker. Seamus Heaney. NoAM; TW
Dockery and Son ("'Dockery was junior to you'"). Philip Larkin. NoAM
Doctor asked him if he dreamed at night, The. The Patient. Nicholas Moore. EAS
Doctor Bill Williams. Ernest Walsh. InvP
Dr. Birch and His Young Friends, *sel.* Thackeray.
  End of the Play, The. FaFP; GN; TreF
Doctor Blenn. Ambrose Bierce. DBV
Doctor Bottom was preparing to leave. Medical Aid. Walter Hard. BXAP; WhC
Dr. Clifford. E. C. Bentley. *Fr.* Clerihews. CenHV
Dr. Coppelius. Wrey Gardiner. NeBP
Dr. Dimity Is Forced to Complain. Cynthia Macdonald. SUW
Dr. Dimity Lectures on Unusual Cases. Cynthia Macdonald. SUW
Dr. Dimity's head hurts. He refuses to use a stronger word. Dr. Dimity Is Forced to Complain. Cynthia Macdonald. SUW
Doctor, doctor, it fits real fine. Vet's Rehabilitation. Ray Durem. PoBA
Dr. Donne. Kenneth Slade Alling. NePoAm
Doctor Emmanuel ("Doctor Emmanuel Harrison-Hyde"). James Reeves. PV; RHPC
Doctor Faustus. Geoffrey Hill. NePoEA-2; NMP
Doctor Faustus. Christopher Marlowe. OAEL-1
  Sels.
  "Ah, Faustus,/ Now hast thou but one bare hour to live," fr. V, ii. ChTr; HeIP; ILwL; ViBoPo
    (End of Doctor Faustus, The). PoEL-2
    (End of Faustus, The.) TrGrPo
    (Faustus Faces His Doom.) TreFT
    (Finale.) WHA
  "Cut is the branch that might have grown full straight," *fr.* Epilogue. ViBoPo
  "Was this the face that launched a thousand ships?" *fr.* V, i. EBEV; GBL; HeIP; NIP; TreF, 3 *ll.*; TrGrPo; ViBoPo
    (Face of Helen, The.) FaBV
    (Helen). BLPL; FaFP; LiTB; WHA
    (Helen of Troy.) FF
Doctor Faustus was a good man. Mother Goose. GLGT
Doctor Fell. Thomas Brown, *after the Latin of* Martial. ChTr; DBV; FaBoCo; FaBoEE; FaFP; TreFT
  ("I do not like thee, Doctor Fell.") OxNR
  ("I do not love thee, Dr. Fell.") MoShBr; NIP; OBVE; WhC
  (Non Amo Te.) AWP; ImOP
Doctor Fell in a Deep Well, A. *Unknown.* ShM
Doctor Foster is a good man. *Unknown.* OxNR
Doctor Foster went to Gloucester [*or* Glo'ster]. Mother Goose. OxBoLi; OxNR
Doctor Freud. David Lazar. FSW
"Dr. Halley never eat any thing." Edmond Halley. Roy Fuller. OxBC
Dr. Hu/ speaks. Norman Mailer. ELU
Doctor Johnson. Soame Jenyns. FaBoEE; OBSV
  (Epitaph on Dr. Johnson.) ELU
Dr. Joseph Goebbels. W. D. Snodgrass. *Fr.* The Führer Bunker. TW
Doctor loves the patient, The. The Bed. A. D. Hope. NoAM; OxBC
Doctor Major. Lionel Johnson. BrPo
Dr. Newman with the crooked pince-nez. Grotesque. Robert Graves. DTC
Dr. Potatohead Talks to Mothers. Judith Johnson Sherwin. NoAM
Doctor punched my vein, The. Scyros. Karl Shapiro. HoPM; LiTA; LiTM; MoVE; NePA; SeCeV; WaP
Doctor Rebuilds a Hand, The. Gary Young. AMV-80; SUW
Doctor said, count to ten, The. Flight. Ruth Whitman. SO
Dr. Sigmund Freud Discovers the Sea Shell. Archibald Macleish. BiP; PPON; SoSe
Dr. Syntax in Search of the Picturesque, *sels.* William Combe.
  "First, the middle, and the last, The." OBRV
  "Hail, favour'd casement!—where the sight." OBRV
  In Search of the Picturesque. OBRV
Dr. Unlikely, we love you so. Horror Movie. Howard Moss. NePoEA-2
Doctor Who Sits at the Bedside of a Rat, The. Josephine Miles. VGW
Dr. Wild's Ghost. *Unknown.* APAS
Doctor, you say there are no haloes. Monet Refuses the Operation. Lisel Mueller. FYAP
Doctor's aseptic popsicle stick, The. Tonsilectomy. James W. Rivers. AMV-81
Doctors attended behind each chair. W. H. Auden. *Fr.* A Happy New Year. OBSV
Doctors' Row. Conrad Aiken. AP; HAP; NYP; PoPl
Doctor's Story, The. Will M. Carleton. BLPA
Doctors tender of their fame, The. Swift. *Fr.* Verses on the Death of Doctor Swift. NOBL
Doctors that learned be. John Skelton. *Fr.* Colin Clout. OBSV
Doctors, white as candles, say, The. Bone Poem. Nancy Willard. HoAn
Doctrine has wound of lovers' limbs. Chalk from Eden. Howard Moss. NePA
Document. Tuvia Ruebner, *tr. fr. Hebrew by* Harold Schimmel. VWA
Documentary. Joseph Stroud. NPGG
Documentary on Airplane Glue, A. David Henderson. MAT
Documentary on Brazil, The. Alfred Corn. MAYP
Documentation. Michael Palmer. NPGG
Doddledy, doodledy, doodledy, dan. *Unknown.* OxNR
Dodger, The. *Unknown.* AmFP; GBP; OuSiCo, *with music*
  (Dodger Song, The.) FSW
Dodo, The ("Dodo used to walk around"). Hilarie Belloc. ChTr
Dodo. Henry Carlile. GP; Psk
Dodo, The. Edward Lucie-Smith. POL
Dodona's Oaks Were Still. Patrick MacDonogh. NeIP
Doe. Philip Dow. NPGG
Doe at Evening, A. D. H. Lawrence. BrPo
Doe but consider this small dust. *See* Do but consider. . .
Doe, doe! Lay of the Deserted Influenzaed. Henry Cholmondeley-Pennell. InMe
Doe not their prophane orgies heare. To Castara. William Habington. AnAnS-2
Doe of the mountains east. Mother/Deer/Lady. Harold Littlebird. VoR
Doeg, though without knowing how or why. John Dryden *and* Nahum Tate. *Fr.* Absalom and Achtophel, Part II. PoEL-3
Does a tear fall from the eye. Tragedy. Howard Moss. NePoEA
Does Almighty God know about His sneaky competition? Peek-a-Boo. Robert Lowenstein. AMV-81
Does anyone these days respect the artist. Ovid, *tr. by* Guy Lee. Amores, III, 8. NAWM-1
Does Daddy Go? *Unknown.* STF
Does It Matter? Siegfried Sassoon. MoBrPo; PAI; PPON; WaP
Does it wear a yarmulka? What Is a Jewish Poem? Myra Sklarew. VWA
Does man love Art? Man visits Art, but squirms. The Chicago Picasso. Gwendolyn Brooks. *Fr.* Two Dedications. BPo; EyDe; LiTM
Does morning always *have* to come? The Second Hymn to the Night. "Novalis," *tr. by* Robert Bly. *Fr.* Hymns to the Night. NU
Does nature bear a tyrant's breast? John Langhorne. *Fr.* Owen of Carron. FaBoCo
Does the Eagle know what is in the pit? The Book of Thel. Blake. ChER; ChTr (4 *ll.*)
Does the lily flower open? Star Song of the Bushman Women. *Unknown, tr. by* W. H. I. Bleek. PeSA
Does the road wind up-hill all the way? Up-Hill. Christina Rossetti. BLPA; CH; EBVV; FaBoBe; FaBoRV; FPL; HAP; HBV-2; LoBV; NOBE; NoP; OAEL-2; OAEP; OBEV; OBNC; OBVV; PoRA; PPP; TrCP; TreFS; TrGrPo; ViBoPo; VLP; WeW; WGRP; WHA; WiR; WPE
Does the Spearmint Lose Its Flavor on the Bedpost Overnight? Billy Rose. OBAL
Does the typewriter type. Truth. Susan Fromberg Schaeffer. IHMS
Does your heart go back to Galway, to the Blazers and stone walls. Blue Peter. Stanislaus Lynch. OnYI
Doesn't he realize/ that I am not/ like the swaying kelp. Ono no Komachi, *tr. fr. Japanese by* Kenneth Rexroth *and* Ikuko Atsumi. BoWoP; WPOW
Doesn't It Seem to You. Gevorg Emin, *tr. fr. Armenian by* Martin Robbins. AMV-81

Dog. D. C. Berry. BXAP
Dog, The. W. H. Davies. GDP; MoBrPo
Dog, The. Frederick William Faber. FM
Dog. Lawrence Ferlinghetti. HoPM
Dog, The. Oliver Herford. FaBV
Dog, The. Valentin Iremonger. BIrV; NeIP
Dog. Ingrid Jonker, *tr. fr. Afrikaans by* Jack Cope *and* William Plomer. PBWP
Dog. Harold Monro. MoBrPo
Dog, The. Ogden Nash. GDP
Dog. John Crowe Ransom. InPS; LiTA; OBAL
Dog. William Jay Smith. GoJo
Dog, The. *Unknown.* WBLP
Dog, A. Charlotte Zolotow. GDP
Dog Alive. Harold Witt. BoAnP
Dog and the Water-Lily, The. William Cowper. OAEP
Dog and Tiger. Eliezer Greenberg, *tr. fr. Yiddish by* Stanley Kunitz. BoAnP
Dog around the Block. E. B. White. GDP
Dog barked; then the woman stood in the doorway, The. Roan Stallion. Robinson Jeffers. BeLS
Dog barks from a cloud, The. Adolescence. Gregory Orr. Psk
Dog beneath the cherry-tree, The. The Ambiguous Dog. Arthur Guiterman. GDP
Dog beneath the Skin, The, *sels.* W. H. Auden. OxBTC
Chorus: "The summer holds: upon its glittering lake."
Chorus: "You are the town and we are the clock."
Dog body and cat mind, The. Jenny Joseph. BrRo
Dog called Sesamë slewed out. Stray Dog, near Ecully. Margaret Avison. OBCV; PoA
Dog Child, The. Keaulumoku, *tr. fr. Hawaiian by* M. W. Beckwith. *Fr.* The Kumulipo; a Creation Chant. WTO
Dog comes home with a mouth full, The. Pain. Robert Wrigley. AMV-81
Dog Creek Mainline ("Dog Creek: cat track and bind splay"). Charles Wright. AmPA; LCAP
Dog Day, A. Rachel Field. SiSoSe
Dog Day Vespers. Charles Wright. LCAP
Dog, Dog in My Manger. George Barker. LiTM
Dog emerges from the flies, A. Nino, the Wonder Dog. Roy Fuller. FF
Dog from Malta, The. Tymnes. *See* Maltese Dog, A.
Dog gazes back at me, The. The pair of rats. Another Color. Frank Stewart. AMV-81
Dog Hospital. Peter Wild. AmPA; GP
Dog howled and howled, The. Alison Prince. POL
Dog in the Fountain. Raymond Souster. GDP
Dog in the Quarry, A, *sel.* Miroslav Holub, *tr. fr. Czech by* George Theiner *and* Ian Milner.
"Day was so bright, The." BoAnP; GDP
Dog in the River, The. Phaedrus, *tr. fr. Latin by* Christopher Smart. AWP
Dog in Us, The. John Barnie. AMV-81
Dog is a faithful, intelligent friend, The. The Song Called "His Hide Is Covered with Hair." Hilaire Belloc. FaBoNo; FM
Dog is cousin to the wolf, but more acceptable, The. Dog and Tiger. Eliezer Greenberg, *tr. by* Stanley Kunitz. BoAnP
Dog is man's best friend, The. An Introduction to Dogs. Ogden Nash. MoShBr
Dog Lake with Paula. Richard Hugo. WOLT
Dog loved its churlish life, The. Lupercalia. Ted Hughes. CMoP; NMP
Dog means dog. Blum. Dorothy Aldis. MoShBr
Dog, Midwinter. Raymond Souster. GDP
Dog must see your corpse, The. The last thing that you feel. Dog Prospectus. Peter Redgrove. OxBC
Dog Named Ego, the Snowflakes as Kisses, A. Delmore Schwartz. LiTM; MiAP
(Dog Named Ego, A.) LiTA
Dog of Art, The. Denise Levertov. NoAM
Dog Parade, The. Arthur Guiterman. BoAnP; GDP
Dog Prospectus. Peter Redgrove. OxBC
Dog Sacrifice at Lake Ronkonkoma. William Heyen. AmPA
Dog Sleeping on My Feet, A. James Dickey. PP
Dog stops barking after Robinson has gone, The. Robinson. Weldon Kees. NaP; NoAM; NYBP; TwAmPo
Dog, that has ten years of breath, A. The Last Years. W. H. Davies. FM
Dog that is beat has a right to complain, The. On Sir Henry Clinton's Recall. *Unknown.* PAH
Dog, The. The book. The glass. Poem Following Discussion of Brain. Stan Rice. NPGG
Dog, the lightning frightened us, dark house and both of us. Jim Harrison. *Fr.* Ghazals. InPS
Dog-tired, suisired, will now my body down. The Poet's Final Instructions. John Berryman. VGW
Dog trots freely in the street, The. Dog. Lawrence Ferlinghetti. HoPM
Dog Wanted. Margaret Mackprang Mackay. GDP
Dog was there, outside her door, The. The Dog. W. H. Davies. GDP; MoBrPo
Dog who knew the winter felt no spleen, The. The Watcher. Ruth Stone. NYBP
Dog will come when he is called, The. Beasts and Birds. Adelaide O'Keeffe. OxBChV
Dog will often steal a bone, A. A Cat's Conscience. *Unknown.* PoLF
Dog Yoga. Charles Wright. LCAP
Dogchain Gang, The. Stan Rice. NPGG
Doggerel by a Senior Citizen. W. H. Auden. NOBL
Dogget Gap. *Unknown.* AmFP
Doggies went to the mill, The. *Unknown.* OxNR
Doggin' Me Around Blues. *Unknown.* BluL
Dogie Song, *with music. Unknown.* CoSo
Dogrose. Patric Stevenson. NeIP
Dogs. Susan Griffin. NPGG
Dogs and Cats and Bears and Bats. Jack Prelutsky. RHPC
Dogs and Weather. Winifred Welles. FaPON; TiPo
Dogs are quite a bit like people. Dog. William Jay Smith. GoJo
Dogs Are Shakespearean, Children Are Strangers. Delmore Schwartz. NoAM
Dogs barking, dust awhirling. Hail and Farewell. Anne Higginson Spicer. HBMV
Dog's Best Friend Is His Illiteracy, A. Ogden Nash. BoAnP
Dog's Cold Nose, The. Arthur Guiterman. GDP; TiPo
Dog's Death, A. J. C. Squire. FM
Dog's Death. John Updike. PsK
Dogs greet me, I descend, The. I Come Home Wanting to Touch Everyone. Stephen Dunn. AMV-81
Dogs of Santiago. Eugene McCarthy. BoAnP; GDP
Dog's violent sneeze, The. Haiku. Richard Wright. FAZ
Dogskin Rug. Adrien Stoutenburg. GP
Dogwood Blossoms. Peter Blue Cloud. STE
Dogwood Blossoms. George Marion McClellan. BANP
Dogwood flakes. Variations Done for Gerald Van de Wiele. Charles Olson. NeAP; NoAM; NOBA; NoP
Doing, a Filthy Pleasure Is, and Short. Petronius Arbiter, *tr. fr. Latin by* Ben Jonson. BoLoP; CABA; ErPo; LLLT; OBVE
(Against Consummation.) UnTE
(Epigram from Petronius.) OAEL-1
(Fragmentum Petronius Arbiter, Translated.) HeIP
Doing my wash. Wash Day. Larry Mollin. NeAC
Doing Railroads for *The Rocky Mountain News.* Cy Warman. PoOW
Doing the Dubhs. *Unknown.* PoSH
Doing what the moon says, he shifts his chair. Orkney Interior. Ian Hamilton Finlay. NMP
Doing 70 on Interstate 94. Bread Loaf to Omaha, Twenty-eight Hours. Patrick Worth Gray. TAT
Dolcino to Margaret. Charles Kingsley. HBV-1
(Hey, Nonny!) OBVV
Dole of the King's Daughter, The. *Unknown, tr. fr. French by* Oscar Wilde. AWP
Dolgelley Hotel, The. Thomas Hughes. FaBoCo
("If ever you go to Dolgelly.") CenHV
Doll, The. Robert Friend. GP
Doll, The. Gregory Orr. AmPA
Doll, don't be too proud of those eyes. To Vanity. Darwin T. Turner. PoNe
Doll House, The. Darlene Button Kitzman. AMV-81
Doll in the doll-maker's house, A. The Dolls. W. B. Yeats. BrPo; CMoP; NoAM
Doll Song. "Lewis Carroll." SoPo
Doll Thy Ale. *Unknown.* OxBM
Dollar and a Half a Day, A, *with music. Unknown.* TrAS
Dollar Bill. John Frederick Nims. MiAP
Dollar Dog, The. John Ciardi. GDP
Dollar I Gave, A. *Unknown.* STF
Dollmaker, snug in your house. The Doll. Robert Friend. GP
Dolls. David St. John. LCAP
Dolls, The. W. B. Yeats. BrPo; CMoP; NoAM
Doll's boy's asleep. E. E. Cummings. DuDa
Doll's faces are rosier but these were children. Bombing Casualties: Spain. Sir Herbert Read. PPON
Doll's hair concealing, A. Partial Resemblance. Denise Levertov. CoAP; NaP
Dolls Play at Hansel and Gretel, The. William Dickey. DFT
Dolls' Wash, The. Juliana Horatia Ewing. OxBChV
Dolly's Lesson. *Unknown.* FaBoUs
Dolomites. J. C. Milne. PoSH
Dolor. Theodore Roethke. AmPP; AP; BiP; CABA; CMoP; CoBMV; HeIP; HoPM; InPK; InPS; LiTM; MoVE; NMP; NoAM; PoA
(Dolour.) PPON

Dolores. Swinburne. VLP
"We shift and bedeck and bedrape us," *sel.* UnTE
Dolphin. Robert Lowell. NOBA
Dolphin plunge, fountain play. Invocation. Louis MacNeice. SO
Dolphin Seen Alone. Richmond Lattimore. BoAnP
Dolphins, The. Hamish Maclaren. EtS
Dom Pedro, The. *Unknown.* AmFP
"Domaine Public." Geoffrey Hill. OxBC
Dome of Sunday, The. Karl Shapiro. AP; CMoP; CoAP; CoBMV; LiTM; MoAB; MoAmPo; MoPo; NePA; NoAM; OxBA; WaP
Dome Poem. Dave Smith. PoA
Domed with the azure of heaven. Vapour and Blue. Wilfred Campbell. CaP
Domenic Darragh walked the land. The Mountainy Childer. Elizabeth Shane. HBMV
Domestic Asides; or, Truth in Parentheses. Thomas Hood. EnRP
Domestic: Climax. Merrill Moore. ErPo
Domestic Didactics by an Old Servant. Thomas Hood. OBRV; VLP
Domestic Duties. Richard Emil Braun. NoAM
Domestic Quarrel. Sally McInerney. GrPl
Domestic Scene. Michael Hartnett. BIrV
Domestic Science. *Unknown.* WBLP
Domestic Stones, The (fragment). Hans Arp, *tr. fr. French by* David Gascoyne. EAS
Domestics. Kattie M. Cumbo. BlSi
Domicile of John, The. Pope. InMe
Domicilium. Thomas Hardy. FaBoPP
Domination of Black. Wallace Stevens. AmPP; AP; CoBMV; MoAB; MoAmPo; OxBA; TwAmPo
Domine, Quo Vadis? *Unknown.* ACP
Domine Quo Vadis? Sir William Watson. WGRP
Domineering Eagle and the Inventive Bratling, The. Guy Wetmore Carryl. OBAL
Dominic came riding down, sworded, straight and splendid. The Lovers of Marchaid. Marjorie Pickthall. HBV-1
Dominic Francis Xavier Brotherton-Chancery. Pastoral. Gavin Ewart. OxBC
Dominic Has a Doll. E. E. Cummings. PoPl
Dominion of Australia, The. Brunton Stephens. PoAu-1
Dominus Illuminatio Mea. Richard Doddridge Blackmore. OBEV; OBVV; TreFS
Domus Caedet Arborem. Charlotte Mew. PBWP
Don, The. Barbara Howes. GLGT
Don Baty, the Draft Resister. Muriel Rukeyser. NNaP
Don Giovanni, *sel.* Lorenzo da Ponte, *tr. fr. Italian by* Natalie MacFarren.
"Giovinette, Che Fate All'Amore." TrJP
Don Giovanni on His Way to Hell ("The oxen have voices"). Jack Gilbert. NPGG
Don Giovanni on His Way to Hell II ("How could they think women a recreation"). Jack Gilbert. NMP; NPGG
Don Juan, *sels.* Byron.
At Thirty Years, *fr.* I. FiP
Ave Maria, Canto III. ISi
("But now at thirty years my hair is grey," *sl. diff. sel.*) SCV
(Growing Old.) NOBE
Contemporary Poets, *fr.* XI. OBRV
Death of Haidée, The, *fr.* IV. FiP; WHA
Dedication: "Bob Southey! You're a poet—poet-laureate." CTC; EnRP; OAEL-2; OAEP; OBSV
("Bob Southey! You're a poet—Poet laureate.") PPoe
(Dedication to the Poet Laureate.) FiP
(Invocation: "Bob Southey! You're a poet—Poet laureate.") LoBV
(Southey and Wordsworth.) TrGrPo
"Don Juan had got out on Shooter's Hill," *fr.* XI. OAEP
(Juan in England.) FiP
Don Juan's Education, *fr.* I. WHA
Donna Julia, *fr.* I. PoEL-4
Duke of Wellington, The ("You are 'the best of cut-throats'—do not start"). DBV
Evening, *after* Sappho, *fr.* III. TrGrPo
(Hesperus the Bringer.) AWP
"For me, I know nought; nothing I deny," *fr.* XIV. OBRV
"Fourth day came, but not a breath of air, The," *fr.* II. ChER
Fragment: "I would to heaven that I were so much clay," *on the back of the poet's MS of* I. CTC; FiP; NOBL; NoP; OAEL-2; OAEP; PrIm
Gulbeyaz, *fr.* V. PoEL-4
Haidee ("One of the two, according to your choice"), *fr.* IV. SeCePo
"Hail, Muse! et caetera.—We left Juan sleeping," *fr.* III. OAEL-2
"He who has seen the wild tornado sweep," *fr.* XVII. PeD
"I know that what our neighbours call *longueurs*," *fr.* II. OBSV
"I want a hero: an uncommon want," I. EnRP; NoP; OAEL-2, *abr.*; OAEP, *abr.*
"I wonder if his appetite was good?" *fr.* V. OAEL-2
"In her first passion woman loves her lover," *fr.* I. ErPo; UnTE
"In the great world—which, being interpreted," *fr.* XI. OxBoLi
Isles of Greece, The, *fr.* III. AWP; ChTr; FaBoEn; FaPoR; FiP; HBV-2; LiTB; NOBE; OBEV; OBRV: RoGo; SeCeV; TreFS; ViBoPo; WHA
"It was the cooling hour, just when the rounded," *fr.* II. ViBoPo
(Haidée.) OBRV
(Haidée and Don Juan.) OBNC
"Juan embark'd—the ship got under way," *fr.* II. MOS
"Juan knew several languages—as well," *fr.* XI. OAEL-2
Lady Adeline Amundeville, *fr.* XIII. PoEL-4
Lambro's Return, *fr.* III. OBRV
" 'Let there be light!' said God, and there was light!" *fr.* VII. OBWP
"Man's love is of man's life a thing apart," *fr.* I. TreF
"Milton's the prince of poets—so we say," *fr.* III. NOBL; OAEL-2
My Days of Love Are Over, *fr.* I. FaBoEn; OBNC
Norman Abbey, *fr.* XIII. OBRV
"Nothing so difficult as a beginning," *fr.* IV. EnRP; OAEL-2
(Romantic to Burlesque, *shorter sel.*) FiP
"O love! O glory! what are you who fly," *fr.* VII. OAEL-2
"Oh Wellington! (Or 'Villainton,' for Fame)," *fr.* IX. OBSV; OxBoLi
(On Wellington.) FiP
(Wellington) OBRV
"Oh ye! who teach the ingenuous youth of nations," *fr.* II. EnRP
"Old Lambro pass'd unseen a private gate," *fr.* III. EnRP
"Over the stones still rattling, up Pall Mall," *fr.* XI. NOBL
Poetical Commandments, *fr.* I. FiP; OBRV
("If ever I should condescend to prose.") OxBoLi
(Poet's Credo.) SeCePo
"Sagest of women, even of widows, she," *fr.* I. NOBL
Shipwreck, The, *fr.* II. OBRV; WHA
"Shore looked wild, without a trace of man, The," *fr.* II. HAP
Sun Set, and Up Rose the Yellow Moon, The, *fr.* I. MOON
"Their poet, a sad trimmer, but no less," *fr.* III. OAEP
"They tell me 'tis decided; you depart," *fr* I. ViBoPo
"They were alone once more; for them to be," *fr.* IV. EBEV
"Though somewhat large, exuberant, and truculent," *fr.* IX. OAEL-2
" 'Tis pleasing to be schooled in a strange tongue," *fr.* II. ViBoPo
". . .'Tis sweet to hear," *fr.* I. ViBoPo
(First Love) OBRV
"To our theme.—The man who has stood on the Acropolis," *fr.* XI. InPS; OBSV
" 'Twas midnight—Donna Julia was in bed," *fr.* I. BiP; UnTE
" 'Twas on a summer's day—the sixth of June," *fr.* I. PPP
"Why call the miser miserable?" *fr.* XII. UnPo
" 'Whom the gods love die young' was said of yore," *fr.* IV. OAEP
"You know, or you don't know, that great Bacon saith," *fr.* XIV. NOBL
"Young unmarried man, with a good name, A," *fr.* XII. NOBL
Don Juan. Lucius Harwood Foote. AA
Don Juan. D. H. Lawrence. PoA
Don Juan had got out on Shooter's Hill. Juan in England. Byron. *Fr.* Don Juan, XI. FiP; OAEP
Don Juan has ever the grand old air. Don Juan. Lucius Harwood Foote. AA
Don Juan in Hell. Baudelaire, *tr. fr. French by* James Elroy Flecker. AWP; SyP
Don Juan's Address to the Sunset. Robert Nichols. OBMV
Don Juan's Education. Byron. *Fr.* Don Juan, I. WHA
Don Larsen's Perfect Game. Paul Goodman. LiSp
Don Leon, *sel.* *Unknown.*
"Then, say, was I or nature in the wrong." PeHV
Don' Let Yo' Watch Run Down, *with music.* *Unknown.* AS
Don Quixote. Craven Langstroth Betts. AA
Don Quixote. Austin Dobson. HBV-2; HBVY
Don Quixote. Arthur Davison Ficke. HBMV
Don Quixote in England, *sels.* Henry Fielding.
A-Hunting We Will Go, *fr.* II. HBV-1; ViBoPo
(Hunting Song.) OBEC; OxBoLi
Roast Beef of Old England, The. OBEC
Don Surly, to aspire the glorious name. On Don Surly. Ben Jonson. FaBoEE
Donal o' Dreams has no bed for his sleeping. The Fiddler. Edna Valentine Trapnell. HBMV
Donal[l] Oge: Grief of a Girl's Heart. *Unknown, tr. fr. Modern Irish by* Lady Gregory. GBL; OnYI; OxBI
(Donal Ogue, *tr. by* Frank O'Connor.) KiLC
(Grief of a Girl's Heart, The, *tr. by* Lady Gregory.) ChTr; OLR; PBWP
Donald. Henry Abbey. AA
Donald Caird. Sir Walter Scott. BSV
Donald, he's come to this town. Dugall Quin. *Unknown.* ESPB
Donald of the Isles. *Unknown.* *See* Lizie Lindsay.
Done For. Rose Terry Cooke. AA

Done Foun' My Los' Sheep, *with music.* *Unknown.* BoAN-1
Done Is a Battle. William Dunbar. NoP
(Done Is a Battell on the Dragon Blak.) HAP
(Done Is a Battle on the Dragon Black.) BSV
(Hymn of the Resurrection, A.) MeEL
(Lord Is Risen, The.) NOBE
(Of the Resurrection of Christ.) OxBoCh
(On the Resurrection of Christ.) NOCV; OxBS; PoEL-1
Done to death by slanderous tongues. Epitaph [*or* Claudio's Lament]. Shakespeare. *Fr.* Much Ado about Nothing, V, iii. CTC; OBSC
Done with myself, I asked. Coma. Dennis Schmitz. NPGG
Doney-Gal ("Traveling up the lonesome trail"). *Unknown.* BPAW
Doney Gal ("We're alone Doney Gal, in the rain and the hail"). *Unknown.* CoSo, *with music*; FSW; OuSiCo, *with music*
Dong with a Luminous Nose, The. Edward Lear. AmMo; CenHV; ChTr; EBVV; FaBoCo; FaBoNo; FaBV; NBM; PoEL-5; VLP; WiR
Donibristle Moss Moran Disaster, The. *Unknown.* WTO
Donkey, The. G. K. Chesterton. ACP; EBCP; FaBV; FaPoR; FPL; GoBC; HBVY; MoBrPo; OBEV; PoLF; TreFT; WGRP
Donkey, The. Theodore Roethke. GrPl; OBCA
Donkey, The. *Unknown.* RHPC
Donkey. Mark Van Doren. EaLo
Donkey and the Lapdog, The. La Fontaine, *tr. fr. French by* Marianne Moore. OBVE
Donkey doctor came covered with rain, The. Big Friend of the Stones. Steve Orlen. Psk
Donkey, donkey, do not bray. *Unknown.* OxNR
Donkey Riding. *Unknown.* WHW
Donkey sat down on the roadside, The. Time Out. John Montague. BoAnP
Donkey Will Carry You, A. Jakov Steinberg, *tr. fr. Hebrew by* Mark Elliott Shapiro. VWA
Donkeys. Edward Field. BoAnP
Donna. Paula Gunn Allen. TWSS
Donna Julia. Byron. *Fr.* Don Juan, I. PoEL-4
Donna Me Prega. Guido Cavalcanti. *See* Canzone: Donna Mi Priegha.
Donne Redone. Joseph Paul Tierney. ShM
Donne, the delight of Phoebus, and each Muse. To John Donne. Ben Jonson. AnAnS-2; OAEP; OBS; SeCV-1
Donner Party, The, *sel.* George Keithley.
"Old Graves fell asleep." NPGG
Don's Holiday. G. Rostrevor Hamilton. FaBoCo
Don't. James Jeffrey Roche. HBV-1
Don't. *Unknown.* STF
Don't Answer the Phone for Me the Same. Gerald Locklin. GP
Don't ape what must be born in one. The Donkey and the Lapdog. La Fontaine, *tr. by* Marianne Moore. OBVE
Don't ask a geologist about rocks. No More Soft Talk. Diane Wakoski. FF; IHMS
Don't ask me how he managed. The Worm. Raymond Souster. WHW
Don't ask me what to wear. Sappho, *tr. fr. Greek by* Mary Barnard. PBWP
Don't Ask Me Who I Am. James A. Randall, Jr. BPo
Don't ask where is wisdom to be sought as ecstatic music. The Undertaking. Gerrit Lansing. CoPo
Don't be afraid of dying. The glass of water. Couplets, XX. Robert Mezey. FYAP; NU
Don't be afraid, she tells us. Dogs. Susan Griffin. NPGG
Don't Be Foolish Pray. *Unknown.* CoMu
Don't Be Sorrowful, Darling. Rembrandt Peale. HBV-1
Don't blame me, ladies, if I've loved. No sneers. Sonnet XXIV. Louise Labé, *tr. by* Willis Barnstone. BoWoP
Don't bother a bit, you are only a dream you are having. A Real Question Calling for a Solution. Robert Penn Warren. PPP
Don't bother telling me about the programs. TV. John Forbes. CBAP
Don't call to me father. To My Dead Father. Frank O'Hara. DiL
"Don't Care" and "Never Mind" ("'Don't care' is no friend of mine"). John Kendrick Bangs. FaFP
Don't care didn't care. *Unknown.* GBP
Don't care when you go. Someday Baby. *Unknown.* BluL
Don't Copy Cat. "Mark Twain." TreFT
Don't dress for it. Chiyo, *tr. fr. Japanese by* David Ray. BoWoP
Don't drive me out of my mind. Second Honeymoon. *Unknown, tr. by* Augustus Young. BIrV
Don't Ever Cross a Crocodile. Kaye Starbird. PDV
Don't ever grab/ old crusty crab. The Crab. Conrad Aiken. BoAnP
Don't Ever Seize a Weasel by the Tail. Jack Prelutsky. RHPC
Don't Fish in My Sea. *Unknown.* BluL
Don't Forget. Stephen Berg. PoA
Don't forget the crablike/ hands. The Hands. Denise Levertov. NeAP; PoM
Don't get discouraged when you hear. Don't. *Unknown.* STF
Don't get the wrong idea. Eyewitness. Rodney Hall. PoAu-2
Don't Give Up. *Unknown.* FaFP
Don't give up hoping when the ship goes down. Hang to Your Grit! Louis E. Thayer. WBLP
Don't go. Larry Eigner. PoM
Don't Grow Old. Allen Ginsberg. DiL
Don't Grow Weary, Boys. *Unknown.* CoSo
Don't hand me over with a word, Toihau. Reply to a Marriage Proposal. Irihapeti Rangi te Apakura, *tr. by* Roger Oppenheim *and* Allen Curnow. PBWP
Don't hide too far Geof. Ben Plays Hide and Seek in the Deep Woods. Geof Hewitt. FAZ
Don't Hope to Gain by What Has Preceded. Joanne Kyger. PoM
Don't hurry spring. Spring Song. Rod McKuen. CAD
Don't knock at my door, little child. Black Woman. Georgia Douglas Johnson. BALP
Don't know why I. Angola Question Mark. Langston Hughes. BPo; TTY
Don't let me lose you. How Tuesday Began. Kathleen Fraser. CTBA; NYBP
Don't let them die out. Now Poem. For Us. Sonia Sanchez. CNA; PoBA
Don't Let Your Deal Go Down. *Unknown.* FSW
Don't, like the cat, try to get more out. Don't Copy Cat. "Mark Twain." TreFT
Don't lock me in wedlock, I want. About Marriage. Denise Levertov. NMM
Don't look at his hands now. Stonecarver. Carole Oles. Str
Don't Look Now but Mary Is Everybody. Peter Viereck. LiTA
Don't look, the woman says. Tarantula. Diana O Hehir. NPGG
Don't love me, my sweet. Song of a Common Lover. Flavien Ranaivo, *tr. by* Alan Ryder. TTY
Don't mind the train or the rollin' sea. The Grey Funnel Line. Cyril Tawney. OBET
Don't neglect the quiet hour. Communion. J. L. Spicer. BLRP
Don't offend. Song of the Breed. Carroll Arnett. STE
Don't pull off my boots and pull off my hat. The Dying Desperado. *Unknown.* CoSo
Don't pull that bud, it yet may grow. To George Pulling Buds. Adelaide O'Keeffe. FaBoUs
Don't Quit. *Unknown.* BLPA; FPL; STF
Don't Say. Moshe Yungman, *tr. fr. Yiddish by* Marcia Falk. VWA
Don't Say You Like Tchaikowsky. Paul Rosner. FiBHP
Don't scold me, ladies, if I have loved. Sonnet XXIV. Louise Labé, *tr. by* Carol Cosman. PBWP
Don't seek me where the myrtles bloom! My Camping Ground. Morris Rosenfeld, *tr. by* Aaron Kramer. TrJP
"Don't send my boy to Harvard, the dying mother said." Old College Song with Variant Lines to Suit. *Unknown.* TreFT
Don't Show Me. Ruth Beker. VWA
Don't sing: a song. Drops of Gall. Gabriela Mistral, *tr. by* David Garrison. BoWoP
Don't Sing Love Songs. *Unknown.* FSW
Don't Sit under the Apple Tree with Anyone Else but Me! Robert Pack. CoPo; FF
Don't Sleep. Ingrid Jonker, *tr. fr. Afrikaans by* Elizabeth Jones. WPOW
Don't Steal. Ambrose Bierce. POL
Don't step/ so lightly. Break. The Cracks. Robert Creeley. ConAP
Don't suppose that the weightless phantom. The Titans. Betti Alver, *tr. by* Willis Barnstone *and* Felix Oinas. BoWoP
Don't Talk about It, *with music.* *Unknown.* OuSiCo
Don't Tell Bad Dreams Says Tita's Mother. John Oliver Simon. NeAC
Don't Tell Me That I Talk Too Much! Arnold Spilka. RHPC
Don't tell your friends about your indigestion. How Are You? [*or* Of Tact] Arthur Guiterman. MoShBr; WhC
"Don't touch me!" I scream at passers-by. Natalya Gorbanyevskaya, *tr. fr. Russian by* Daniel Weissbort. LLLT
Don't touch me. The Hermaphrodite's Song. Lorna Mitchell. BrRo
Don't touch that fruit, Eve. Paradise Lost. Stanley J. Sharpless. BXAP
Don't Trouble Trouble. Mark Guy Pearse. WBLP
Don't wait for the wind to blow you through the door. Moving In. Paul Engle. PoA
Don't Wanna Be. Sonia Sanchez. CNA
Don't Want No Hungry Woman. *Unknown.* BluL
Don't waste your time in longing. Shine Just Where You Are. *Unknown.* STF
Don't waste your time in looking for. Long Gone. Jack Prelutsky. RHPC
"Don't wear that snake." The Rattlesnake Band. Robert J. Conley. STE
Don't worry/ One night we'll find that deserted kinema. If Life's a Lousy Picture, Why Not Leave before the End. Roger McGough. OxBTC
Don't worry about growing old. Prayerwheel: 2. David Meltzer. NeAP
Don't worry baby. Broken Heart, Broken Machine. Richard E. Grant. PoBA
Don't Worry if Your Job Is Small. *Unknown.* RHPC
Dont Worry Yr Hair. Bill Bissett. NOBC

Don't You Be like the Foolish Virgin, *with music. Unknown.* AH
Don't you care for my love? she said bitterly. Intimates. D. H. Lawrence. BoLoP
Don't You Hurry Worry with Me, *with music. Unknown.* OuSiCo
Don't you let my good girl catch you here. Ain't No Tellin'. *Unknown.* BluL
Don't You Like It? *with music. Unknown.* OuSiCo
Don't you love farce? All those bedroom doors. Adam, Eve and the Big Apple. Edward Watkins. AMV-81
Don't you love my baby, mam. Infant Song. Charles Causley. NAs; OxBC
Don't you remember sweet Alice, Ben Bolt. Ben Bolt. Thomas Dunn English. AA; FaBoBe; FaFP; HBV-1; TreF
"Don't you take no sail off 'er," the Ol' Man said. What the Old Man Said. C. Fox Smith. EtS
Don't you think it's probable. Little Talk. Aileen Fisher. FaPON
Don't you trouble trouble till trouble troubles you. Don't Trouble Trouble. Mark Guy Pearse. WBLP
Don't You Weep after Me. *Unknown.* FSW
Don'ts. D. H. Lawrence. LiTB; LiTM; NoAM; OxBoLi
Donzella and the *Ceylon*, The, *with music. At. to* Daniel Smith. ShS
Dooley Is a Traitor. James Michie. NePoEA-2; OxBTC
Doom. Arthur O'Shaughnessy. OBVV
Doom-devoted. Louis Golding. HBMV
Doom Ferry. Sir Arthur Quiller-Couch. EBVV
Doom Is Dark. W. H. Auden. *See* Wanderer, The.
Doom of Beauty, The. Michelangelo, *tr. fr. Italian by* John Addington Symonds. AWP
Doom of Devorgoil, The, *sel.* Sir Walter Scott.
Bonny Dundee, *fr.* II, ii. EnRP; FaBoCh; OBRV; OxBoLi; OxBS; SeCeV
(Bonnie Dundee.) HBV-2; Par, *abr.*
Doom-Well of St. Madron, The. Robert Stephen Hawker. VLP
Doomed City, The. E. L. Mayo. FAZ
Doomed City, The. Poe. *See* City in the Sea, The.
Doomed in the depths to dwell. Thanksgiving. David Abenatar Melo, *tr. by* Henry Hart Milman. TrJP
Doomed Man, The. Joseph Addison Alexander. TRV
(Hidden Line, The.) BLPA
Dooms-Day. George Herbert. JCP; SeCP; SeCV-1
Doomsday. Elinor Wylie. CrMA
Doomsday Morning. Genevieve Taggard. MoAmPo
Doon Deeside cam Inverey. The Baron of Braikley. *Unknown.* OxBB
Door, The. Robert Creeley. NaP; NeAP; NoAM; PoM; VGW
Door, The. Mary Carolyn Davies. HBMV
Door, The. Robert Graves. LiTB
Door, A. W. S. Merwin. EAS; LCAP
Door, The. Mark Strand. NoAM
Door, The. L. A. G. Strong. MoBrPo
Door, The. Charles Tomlinson. PoA
Door and the Window, The. Henry Reed. NeBP
Door and Window Bolted Fast. Mani Leib, *tr. fr. Yiddish by* Joseph Leftwich. TrJP
Door behind me was you, The. You, I. Tom Clark. EAS
Door closed against the splinters. Old Seawoman. Gordon LeClaire. CaP
Door closed, The. The Sweat. Nila NorthSun. STE
Door creaks in the house, A. Outside the window. Scenario. D. S. Savage. NeBP
Door is before you again and the shrieking, The. The Door. Mark Strand. NoAM
Door is on the latch tonight, The. Christmas Eve. *Unknown.* TRV
"Door is shut fast, The." Who's In. Elizabeth Fleming. RHPC
Door it opened slowly, The. Story of Isaac. Leonard Cohen. VWA
Door of Death, The. Blake. *Fr.* Dedication of the Illustrations to Blair's "Grave." ChTr
(To the Queen.) EnRP
Door of existence, beacon of our haze. Bernard O'Dowd. *Fr.* Alma Venus. PoAu-1
Door slam, The. After the First Frost. Lew Blockcolski. VoR
Door still swinging to, and girls revive, The. A Dream of Fair Women. Kingsley Amis. FF; MP; NMP; NoAM; OAEL-2
Door sunk in a hillside, with a bolt, A. The Icehouse in Summer. Howard Nemerov. NoAM
Door that someone opened wide, The. The Message. Jacques Prévert, *tr. by* John Frederick Nims. WeW
Door was bolted and the windows of my porch, The. The Milkman. Isabella Gardner. NePA
Door was shut, as doors should be, The. Jack Frost. "Gabriel Setoun." HBV-1; HBVY
Door was shut, The. I looked between. Shut Out. Christina Rossetti. VLP
Doorbell buzzed, The. It was past three o'clock. The Australian Dream. David Campbell. CBAP
Doorbell rang, The. It was Death. Alone in the House. George Bogin. AMV-80
Doorbells. Rachel Field. FaPON; TiPo
Doorman. Martin Galvin. SUW
Door-Mats. Mary Carolyn Davies. HBMV; YaD
Doors. Therese Plantier, *tr. fr. French by* Willis Barnstone *and* Elene Kolb. BoWoP
Doors. Tom Clark. ConAP
Doors, The. Lloyd Mifflin. AA
Doors are locked, The. House. For Sale. Leonard Clark. RHPC
Doors close fly. Dry July. Arnold Adoff. CAD
Doors flapped open in Ulysses' house, The. The Return. Edwin Muir. CMoP
Doors of that city are ninety feet high, The. The Retarded Children Find a World Built Just for Them. Diana O Hehir. NPGG
Doors of the Temple. Aldous Huxley. HBMV
Doors open, The/ and the heat undoes itself. In the Beach House. Anne Sexton. PPP
Doors opened with a silent scream. The Spirit of 34th Street. Peggy Shriver. AMV-80
Doors that knew no shrill alarming bell, The. James Thomson. *Fr.* The Castle of Indolence. ViBoPo
Doors, where my heart was used to beat. Tennyson. In Memoriam A. H. H., CXIX. NoP; OBNC; PoEL-5; SCV
Doorstep, The. Edmund Clarence Stedman. HBV-1
Doorway to Time in Three Voices. Luis Palés Matos, *tr. fr. Spanish by* Rachel Benson. InW
Dopefiends Trip. Hector Angulo. FIA
Dopey sez to Doc. Snow White. Ed Ochester. GP
Doppelganger, The. Daryl Hine. OBCV
(Double-Goer, The.) MoCV
Dora versus Rose. Austin Dobson. NOBL
Dora Williams. Edgar Lee Masters. *Fr.* Spoon River Anthology. HAP
Doralicia's Song. Robert Greene. *Fr.* Arbasto. LoBV; OBSC
Doran's Ass. *Unknown.* OnYI
Dorcas. George Macdonald. OBVV
Dorchester Giant, The. Oliver Wendell Holmes. FaPON; OnMSP
Doré knew this overhang. View from the Gorge. Ben Belitt. NYBP
Doretha wore the short blue lace last night. The Reception. June Jordan. NMM
Doria. Ezra Pound. MoAB; MoAmPo; MoVE; ViBoPo
Doric. Anghelos Sikelianos, *tr. fr. Modern Greek by* Edmund Keeley *and* Philip Sherrard. ErPo
Doricha. Poseidippus, *tr. fr. Greek by* E. A. Robinson. AWP; FaBoEE; OBVE
Dorinda's sparkling wit, and eyes. Song [*or* Dorinda *or* On the Countess of Dorchester]. Charles Sackville. APAS; CavP; OBEV; OBS; SeCePo; SeCV-2
Doris. Congreve. NOEC
Doris; a Pastoral. Arthur Joseph Munby. HBV-1
Doris and Philemon, *sel.* J. C. Squire.
"Now the declining fulgent orb of day." BXAP
Doris, I that could repell. The Snow-Ball. Thomas Stanley. CavP
Dormouse and the Doctor, The. A. A. Milne. WhC
Dornröschen (The Sleeping Beauty). Hayden Carruth. DFT
Doron's Description of Samela. Robert Greene. *Fr.* Menaphon. LoBV; PoEL-2
(Samela.) ElL; GBL; HBV-1; NOBE; OBEV; OBSC; ViBoPo
Doron's Jigge. Robert Greene. *Fr.* Menaphon. PoEL-2
(Jig, A.) ElL
Dorothea. Sarah N. Cleghorn. HBMV
Dorothy. Rose Hawthorne Lathrop. AA
Dorothy Q. Oliver Wendell Holmes. AA; AP; HBV-1; InMe; NOBA; TreFS
Dorus's Song. Sir Philip Sidney. *See* Solitariness.
Dory Miller. Sam Cornish. CNA
Dose of a mere, The. The Discovery of LSD a True Story. Anselm Hollo. PoM
Dosn't thou 'ear my 'erse's legs, as they canters awaäy? Northern Farmer: New Style. Tennyson. BiP; VLP
Dosser in Springtime, The. Douglas Stewart. ErPo
Dost deem him weak that owns his strength is tried? The Strong. John Vance Cheney. AA
Dost not thou Castara read. A Dialogue betweene Araphill and Castara. William Habington. AnAnS-2
Dost see how unregarded now. Sonnet. Sir John Suckling. AnAnS-2; CaPo; ELP
"Dost tha hear my horse's feet, as he canters away?" Lord Tennyson and Lord Melchett. D. H. Lawrence. FaBoEE
Dost think he whom thy liberal table drew. Martial. Thomas Heyrick. CavP
Dost thou deem that thyself. "Te Judice." Frederick George Scott. PeCV

Dost thou know who made thee? The Lamb. Blake. *Fr.* Songs of Innocence. InPS; PAI. *See also* Little lamb, who made thee?
Dost thou remember ever, for my sake. Mathilde Blind. *Fr.* Love in Exile. OBNC
Dost Thou Remember Me? Emily Dickinson. *See* Savior! I've no one else to tell.
Dostoievsky's Daughters. Michael Hamburger. NAs
Doth it not thrill thee, poet. The Passionate Reader to His Poet. Richard Le Gallienne. HBV-2
Doth most humbly show it. The Humble Petition of Poor Ben to the Best of Monarchs, Masters, Men, King Charles. Ben Jonson. PP
Doth Not a Tenarif, or Higher Hill. John Donne. *Fr.* Anatomy of the World: The First Anniversary. ChTr
Doth some one say that there be gods above? There Are No Gods. Euripides, *tr. by* John Addington Symonds. *Fr.* Bellerophon. EaLo
Doth then the world go thus, doth all thus move? William Drummond of Hawthornden. BSV; GTBS; GTBS-P
Double, The. Irving Feldman. NYBP
Double Axe, The. Anne Hazlewood-Brady. IHMS
Double Ballad of Good Counsel, A. Villon, *tr. fr. French by* Swinburne. AWP
Double Ballade of Primitive Man. Andrew Lang *and* Edward Burnett Tylor. CenHV
Double-barreled Ding-Dong-Bat. Dennis Lee. RHPC
Double boiler fixed on fiery wheels, A. On Shakespeare Critics. A. D. Hope. *Fr.* Dunciad Minor, V. OxBC
Double, double toil and trouble. Song of the Witches. Shakespeare. *Fr.* Macbeth, IV, i. RHPC
Double Duty. W. E. Farbstein. PoPl; WhC
Double Entendre. J. F. Wilson. TDH
Double Exposure. Ian Young. NeAC; PeHV
Double Feature. Theodore Roethke. DFF
"Double flesh/ Double way." Freud: Dying London, He Recalls the Smoke of His Cigar Beginning to Sing. James Schevill. TAP
Double Fortress, The. Alfred Noyes. GoBC
Double Gift. *Unknown, tr. fr. Greek by* Louis Untermeyer. UnTE
Double-Goer, The. Daryl Hine. *See* Doppelganger, The.
Double-headed Snake, The. John Newlove. MoCV
Double-Header. John Stone. TAT
Double L and single T. The Spelling of Elliot. *Unknown.* FaBoUs
Double Looking Glass, The. A. D. Hope. CBAP
Double Monologue. Adrienne Rich. NePoEA-2
Double Ode. Muriel Rukeyser. LCAP
Double Play, The. Robert Wallace. LiSp; PP
Double Ritual. Dachine Rainer. CrMA
Double Sestine. Sir Philip Sidney. *See* Ye Goatherd Gods.
Double Shame, The. Stephen Spender. LiTB; LiTM
Double Standard, The. Franklin P. Adams. OBAL
Double Standard, A. Frances E. W. Harper. BlSi
Double Take at Relais de L'Espadon. Thadious M. Davis. BlSi
Double Transformation, The. Goldsmith. OBNV
Double Tree, The. Winfield Townley Scott. PoPl
Double Vision, The. C. Day Lewis. NoAM
Double Vision of Manannan, The. *Unknown, tr. fr. the Irish by* John Montague. BIrV
Doubt. Elinor Chipp. HBMV
Doubt. Margaret Deland. TrPWD
Doubt. Fernand Gregh, *tr. fr. French by* Ludwig Lewisohn. WGRP
Doubt. Helen Hunt Jackson. WGRP
Doubt. Robert Cameron Rogers. AA
Doubt. Tennyson. *See* In Memoriam A.H.H.: "You say, but with no touch of scorn."
Doubt me, my dim companion! Emily Dickinson. ViBoPo
Doubt no longer miracles. Miracles. Arna Bontemps. PoNe
Doubt of Future Foes, The. Elizabeth I, Queen of England. CTC; PBWP; WPE
(Daughter of Debate, The.) OBSC
Doubt of Martyrdom, A. Sir John Suckling. *See* Sonnet: "Oh! for some honest lover's ghost."
Doubt you to whom my Muse these notes intendeth. To Stella. Sir Philip Sidney. Astrophel and Stella, First Song. ElL; HBV-1; OBSC; SiPS; WHA
Doubter, The. Richard Watson Gilder. TrPWD
Doubter's Prayer, The. Anne Brontë. TrPWD; WGRP
Doubtful Choice, A. Edward de Vere, Earl of Oxford. *See* Choice, A.
Doubting. Louis Simpson. NNaP
Doubting Heart, A. Adelaide Anne Procter. HBV-2
Doubts. Rupert Brooke. CH
Dough Roller Blues. *Unknown.* BluL
Douglas, Douglas, Tender and True. Dinah Maria Mulock Craik. BLPA; TreF
(Douglas.) OBVV
(Too Late.) HBV-1
Douglas Tragedy, The, *diff. versions. Unknown.* HBV-2; NoP (B *vers.*); OxBB, *with music*; TrGrPo
(Earl Brand.) AmFP; BaBo (A *and* B *vers.*); ESPB; (A, B, *and* F *vers.*) FSW; OxBB; ViBoFo (A *and* B *vers.*)
(Earl Brand [The Douglas Tragedy].) FaBoBa
Douglass was someone who. Frederick Douglass: 1817-1895. Langston Hughes. BPo
Doun throu the sea. Cokkils. Sydney Goodsir Smith. OxBS; PoA
Dove. Norma Farber. PChr
Dove, The. Judah Halevi, *tr. fr. Hebrew by* Amy Levy. TrJP
Dove, A. Ted Hughes. OxBC
Dove, The. Keats. *See* I Had a Dove.
Dove, The. Ewan MacColl. OBET
Dove, The. *Unknown. See* Charm against a Magpie, A.
Dove alone expresses, The. Thomas Campion. *Fr.* What Harvest Half So Sweet Is. PBBP
Dove Apologizes to His God for Being Caught by a Cat, The. Anthony Eaton. PeSA
Dove-Breeder, The. Ted Hughes. PAI
Dove it is a pretty bird, she sings as she flies, The. The Dove. Ewan MacColl. OBET
Dove of Dacca, The. Kipling. GN
Dove of liberty sat on an egg, The. The American Eagle. D. H. Lawrence. OAEL-2
Dove of New Snow, The. Vachel Lindsay. MoAmPo
Dove of rarest worth, A. The Dove. Judah Halevi, *tr. by* Amy Levy. TrJP
Dove returns, The; it found no resting place. Where We Must Look for Help. Robert Bly. ConAP; NePoEA
Dove says, Coo, coo, The. Mother Goose. OxNR; PBBP
Dove walks with stick feet, The. Pastoral. Kenneth Patchen. NaP
Dover Beach. Matthew Arnold. AWP; BiP; BLPA; CABA; DTC; EaLo; EBVV; EtS; FaBoBe; FaBoEn; FaBoPP; FaBoRV; FaBV; FaFP; FF; FiP; FPL; GTBS-P; HAP; HBV-2; HeIP; HoPM; InPK; InPS; InvP; LiTB; LoBV; MasP; MAT; MOS; NIP; NOBE; NoP; NU; OAEL-2; OAEP; OBNC; OBVV; PAI; PoEL-5; PoPl; PoPle; PoRA; PPoe; PPON; PPP; Prf; PrIm; SCV; SeCePo; SeCeV; SoSe; TEP; TreFS; TrGrPo; TRV; UnPo; ViBoPo; VLP; WeW; WHA
"Dover Beach"—a Note to That Poem. Archibald MacLeish. FF
Dover Bitch, The. Anthony Hecht. BXAP; CABA; MAT; NePoEA-2; NIP; NOBA; NOBL; OBAL; PP; PPP; UnPo; VGW
Dover Cliffs. William Lisle Bowles. *See* At Dover Cliffs.
Dover, Sandwich, and Winchelsea. The Cinque Ports. *Unknown.* FaBoUs
Dover, the Samphire Cliff. Shakespeare. *Fr.* King Lear, IV, vi. FaBoPP
Dover to Munich, *sels.* Charles Stuart Calverley.
"Bed at Ostend at 5 A.M." NOBL
"Farewell, farewell! Before our prow." NOBL
"On, on the vessel steals." NOBL
Doves. Joachim Neugroschel. VWA
Doves, The. Katharine Tynan. AnIV; AWP
Doves flit by in their flocks of thousands. Sick unto Death of Love. *Malay Oral Tradition, tr. by* R. J. Wilkinson *and* R. O. Winstedt. WTO
Dove's Loneliness, The. George Darley. OBNC
Dove's Nest. Joseph Russell Taylor. HBV-1
Doves of Venice, The. Laurence Hutton. AA
Dove's Song in Winter. *Zulu Oral Tradition, tr. by* B. W. Vilakazi. WTO
Dovid,/ my twenty-/ three year old son. In the Year of Two Thousand. Menke Katz. AMV-81
Dowager. John Montague. IPY
Dowager Semibreve sat by the fire, The. First Lessons in Musical Time. *Unknown.* FaBoUs
Dowie Houms o' [*or* of] Yarrow, The. *Unknown.* BSV; GoTS; OBEV; OBS; OxBS
(Braes o' [*or* of] Yarrow, The.) BaBo; ESPB (A *and* E *vers.*); OxBB, *with music*; ViBoFo
(Dowie Dens of Yarrow, The.) FSW
Down/ a/ deep/ well. The Grasshopper. David McCord. GrPl
Down/ Down into the fathomless depths. Black Is a Soul. Joseph White. IDB; PoBA
Down a blackened alley. La Llorona. Greg Pape. AmPA
Down a broad river of the western wilds. Indian Woman's Death-Song. Felicia Dorothea Hemans. SBG
"Down a down!" Phoebe's Sonnet. Thomas Lodge. ViBoPo
Down a hill, then up a hill. An Autumn Road. Glenn Ward Dresbach. HBMV
Down a street in the town where I went. Shapes, Vanishings. Henry Taylor. AMV-81; MAYP
Down a Sunny Easter Meadow. Nancy Byrd Turner. SiSoSe; SoPo
Down among the Wharves. Eleanore Myers Jewett. EtS
Down and Out. Clarence Leonard Hay. BeLS; BLPA
Down around the quay they lie, the ships that sail to sea. The Port o' Heart's Desire. John S. McGroarty. HBV-1

Down at the Docks. Kenneth Koch. PrIm; VGW
Down at the hall at midnight sometimes. Dance. Lula Lowe Weeden. CDC
Down Below. Joan Aiken. WSC
Down by the bridge/ They sit and wait. Water-Front. Cecil French Salkeld. OnYI
Down by the brook which glides through yonder vale. Robin; a Pastoral Elegy. John Dobson. NOEC
Down by the church-way walk, and where the brook. An Ancient Virgin. George Crabbe. *Fr.* The Parish Register. OBNC
Down by the gate of the orchard. Spring Whistles. Lucy Larcom. OBCA
Down by the Glenside. Peadar Kearney. AnIV
Down by the ocean side where ships were sailing. The Nightingales of Spring. *Unknown.* AmFP
Down by the Old Mill Stream. John Read. TreFS
Down by the railroad in a green valley. Eye-Witness. Ridgely Torrence. HBMV
Down by the river. *Unknown.* OxNR
Down by the Riverside. *Unknown.* OBET
Down by the Salley Gardens. W. B. Yeats. CMoP; CTC; EBVV; EnLoPo; FSW; HBV-1; NoAM; OBEV; OBVV; OnYI; OxBI; PoEL-5; PrIm; SoSe
(Old Song Resung, An.) MoAB; MoBrPo
Down by the waterside stand a house and a plat. *Unknown.* GBP
Down by the weeping willow. *See* Down by yon weeping willow.
Down by the Wild Mustard River. The Wild Mustard River. *Unknown.* AmFP
Down by yon garden green. The Laird of Wariston. *Unknown.* ESPB
Down by yon [*or* the] weeping willow. Florella [*or* Fair Florella], or, The Jealous Lover. *Unknown.* AmFP; BaBo, A *vers.*; ViBoFo
"Down cellar," said the cricket. The Potatoes' Dance. Vachel Lindsay. FaPON; SUS
Down Dip the Branches. Mark Van Doren. DuDa
Down! Down! Eleanor Farjeon. NTCP; SoPo; SUS; TiPo
Down down across the open sea to Shikoku. Ancestors' Graves in Kurakawa. Joy Kogawa. BrSi
Down, down—born pioneers in time's despite. Hart Crane. *Fr.* The Bridge: The River. TrGrPo
Down, Down Derry Down, *with music.* *Unknown.* AS
Down, Down, Down. Heather McHugh. SUW
Down, Down, Down, *with music.* William Keating. OuSiCo
Down drop of the blackbird, The. Three Spring Notations on Bipeds. Carl Sandburg. AWP
Down every passage of the cloister hung. Upon the Death of George Santayana. Anthony Hecht. CoPo; NePA
Down flew the shaft of the god. A Love Affair. Arnold Bennett. OxBTC
Down from his post in the tower. Across the Straits. Rosemary Dobson. PoAu-2
Down from the Country. John Blight. CBAP
Down from the purple mist of trees on the mountain. The Bull Moose. Alden Nowlan. CABA; NOBC
Down here now/ summer's burnt skeins. In Blanco County. Russell T. Fowler. AMV-80
Down hill I came, hungry, and yet not starved. The Owl. Edward Thomas. LiTB
Down Home. Randolph Outlaw. LFAC
Down in a Coal Mine. J. B. Geoghegan. AmFP; TreFS
Down in a deep dark ditch sat an old cow munching a beanstalk. Hexameter and Pentameter. *Unknown.* ChTr; FaBoNo
Down in a garden olden. The Rose's Cup. Frank Dempster Sherman. AA
Down in a garden sits my dearest Love. The Riddle. *Unknown.* UnTE
Down in a green and shady bed. The Violet. Jane Taylor. HBV-1; HBVY; TreF
Down in a lonesome valley. Fair Florella; or, The Jealous Lover (B *vers.*). *Unknown* BaBo
Down in a meadow fresh and gay. Picking Lilies. *Unknown.* OBET
Down in a Wine Vault. Don Marquis. WhC
Down in Alabam'; or, Aint I Glad I Got Out de Wilderness. *At. to* J. Warner. PSoN
Down in Alabama I was born. Roll the Cotton Down, *vers.* II. *Unknown.* ShS
Down in Carlisle there lived a lady. The Lady of Carlisle. *Unknown.* AmFP; FSW; OuSiCo
Down in Dallas. X. J. Kennedy. CoPo; FF; OFD
Down in Dumbarton there wonnd a rich merchant. Bonnie Annie (B *vers.*). *Unknown.* ESPB
Down in front of Casey's old brown wooden stoop. The Sidewalks of New York. James W. Blake. BLPA; BLSo; FaBoBe; FSN; FSW; TreFS; YaD
Down in green valleys a town in Yorkshire. Bonnets So Blue. *Unknown.* OBET
Down in Lehigh Valley. *Unknown.* TreF
Down in London where I was raised. Barbara Allen.FaBoBa
Down in New Mexico, where the plains are brown and sere. Old Buck's Ghost. Frank Benton. PoOW
Down in old Kentucky. Ballad of the Lincoln Penny. Alfred Kreymborg. YaD
Down in our cellar on a Monday and a Tuesday. Old Ellen Sullivan. Winifred Welles. FaPON; TiPo
Down in some lone valley, in some lonesome place. Pretty Saro. *Unknown.* FSW
Down in some lonesome piney grove. Lonesome Dove. *Unknown.* AmFP
Down in St. Louis at 12th and Carr. Brady. *Unknown.* AS
Down in the bleak December bay. The Mayflower. Erastus Wolcott Ellsworth. AA; FaBoBe; HBV-2; PAH
Down in the deep, dumb worlds are waiting, silent. Letter to My Wife. Miklós Radnóti, *tr. by* Emery George. VWA
Down in the dell. Idyl: Sunrise. Henrietta Cordelia Ray. BlSi
Down [*or* Downe] in the depth of mine iniquity. The Saving God [*or* Sonnet]. Fulke Greville. *Fr.* Caelica. EnRePo; LoBV; OBS; PPoe; QFR
Down in the Forest. *Unknown.* OBET
Down in the hole we go, boys. Lament while Descending a Shaft. *Unknown.* AmFP
Down in the Hollow. Aileen Fisher. SoPo; SUS
Down in the jungle/ Living in a tent. *Unknown.* WTO
Down in the jungle [*or* jungles] lived a maid. Under the Bamboo Tree. Bob Cole. BLSo; FSN
Down in the land of the center-fire saddle. Up the Trail. *Unknown.* CoSo
Down in the Lonesome Garden. *Unknown.* BPo
Down in the meadow, sprent with dew. Revelation. Alice Brown. *Fr.* The Road to Castaly. WGRP
Down in the mine, in the dark, dismal drift. Only a Miner. *Unknown.* AmFP
Down in the rushes beside the pool. The Frogs' Singing-School. E. T. Carbell. SoPo
Down in the silent hallway. Unsatisfied Yearning. Richard Kendall Munkittrick. GDP; InMe
Down in the south, by the waste without sail on it. Beyond Kerguelen. Henry Kendall. PoAu-1
Down in the Valley. *Unknown.* AS, *with music*; BLSo, *with music*; FaFP; FSW; TreFT; WTO
(Birmingham Jail.) GBP
Down in the water meadows Riley. Riley. Charles Causley. SO
Down in the west the shadows rest. Canoe Song at Twilight. Laura E. McCully. CaP
Down in the Willow Garden. *Unknown.* FSW
Down in Yon Forest. *Unknown.* FSW
Down in yon garden sweet and gay. Willy Drowned in Yarrow. *Unknown.* GTBS; GTBS-P
Down in Yonder Meadow. *Unknown.* CH; PoPle
Down [*or* Downe] lay the shepherd swain. Hye Nonny Nonny Noe. *Unknown.* FaBoCo; NOBL
Down Loudon Lanes, with swinging reins. Mosby at Hamilton. Madison Cawein. PAH
Down mountain roads like scars across a fist. At Tripolis. Constance Carrier. WPE
Down near the end of a wandering lane. A Rhyme of the Dream-Maker Man. William Allen White. PoLF
Down Newport Street, last Sunday night. Newport Street, E. Douglas Goldring. HBMV
Down on the beach we separate. The Hinge. Sheila Cowing. AMV-81
Down on the beach when the tide is out. Treasures. Mary Dixon Thayer. SoPo
Down on the flat of the lake. Lake Harvest. Raymond Knister. PeCV
Down on the riverbank. Landscape Workers. Harley Elliott. LTB
Down on your knees, boys, holystone the decks. Cleaning Ship. Charles Keeler. EtS
Down-Pullers, The. Walter E. Isenhour. STF
Down Route 2, the farmers. Spring. Linda McCarriston. AMV-81
Down South on the Rio Grande. *Unknown.* CoSo
Down streams of centuries grown old. Women of My Land. Frankie Armstrong. BrRo
Down stucco sidestreets. Dublinesque. Philip Larkin. OxBC
Down swept the chill wind from the mountain peak. The Brook in Winter. James Russell Lowell. *Fr.* The Vision of Sir Launfal: Prelude to Pt. II. GN; TreF
Down the assembly line they roll and pass. The Brides. A. D. Hope. HAP; InPK; PAI
Down the Bayou. Mary Ashley Townsend. AA
Down the blue night the unending columns press. Clouds. Rupert Brooke. BrPo; MoVE; OBEV; OBMV; OxBTC
Down the bright stream the fairies float. The Last Voyage of the Fairies. William H. Davenport Adams. HBVY

Down the centuries, eternal. From a Venetian Sequence. Adèle Naudé. PeSA
Down the close, darkening lanes they sang their way. The Send-off. Wilfred Owen. BrPo; InPS; LiTB; MoAB; MoBrPo; MoVE; OBWP; OxBTC
Down the coast south of here. Earth. Jim Tollerud. VoR
Down the court thudding hard through the center. Basketball. James Lewisohn. LFAC
Down the dawn-brown. The Current. James Merrill. NYBP
Down the dead streets of sun-stoned Frederiksted. The Virgins. Derek Walcott. OxBC; SoSe
Down the dimpled green-sward dancing. Song. George Darley. OnYI
Down the dripping pathway dancing through the rain. Rainy Song. Max Eastman. FaBoBe; HBMV
Down the flightline. Beyond the Firehouse. Patrick Worth Gray. AMV-80
Down the Glimmering Staircase. Siegfried Sassoon. *Fr.* Vigils. PoLF
Down the goldenest of streams. Mater Amabilis. Emma Lazarus. OHIP
Down the green hill-side fro' the castle window. Lady Jane. Sir Arthur Quiller-Couch. FiBHP; InMe; WhC
Down the lane by the Butts in the headlights. Delivering Children. David Holbrook. NePoEA-2
Down the Little Big Horn. Francis Brooks. PAH
Down the long hall she glistens like a star. Venus of the Louvre. Emma Lazarus. AA; SBG
Down the long path beneath the garden wall. A Dream. V. Sackville-West. MoVE
Down the M4. Dannie Abse. OxBC
Down the Mississippi. John Gould Fletcher. AmFN; LiTA
Down the Mississippi steamed the *Whippoorwill.* Steamboat Bill. *Unknown.* FSW
Down the Ohio the flatboats go. Anthony Wayne. Arthur Guiterman. TiPo
Down the quiet eve. Music. W. E. Henley. In Hospital, XXIII. BrPo
Down the Rain Falls. Elizabeth J. Coatsworth. SoPo
Down the rivers, o'er the prairies. As Brothers Live Together. Longfellow. *Fr.* The Song of Hiawatha, I. TreFT
Down the road rides a German lad. The Three Lads. Elizabeth Chandler Forman. SUMH
Down the road someone is practicing scales. Sunday Morning. Louis MacNeice. CoBMV; FaBoMo; HeIP; LiTB; MoAB; MoBrPo; MoVE; NIP
Down the rock chute into the tombs of the kings. This Is the Life. Louis MacNeice. NoAM
Down the slide. Sliding. Marchette Chute. TiPo
Down the sultry arc of day. Description of a Summer's Eve. Henry Kirke White. OBRV
Down the wintry mountain. Dinah Maria Mulock Craik. *Fr.* Highland Cattle. GN
Down the Wolf river. Feasts of Death, Feasts of Love. Stuart Z. Perkoff. NeAP
Down the world with Marna! The Wander-Lovers. Richard Hovey. AA; HBV-1
Down the Yellowstone, the Milk, the White and Cheyenne. Pare Lorentz. *Fr.* The River. AmFN
Down there a poor woman. The Potter. *Unknown, tr. by* Halim El-Dabh. TTY
Down there where I was. The Story of My Life. Carroll Arnett. VoR
Down through the ancient Strand. Scherzando. W. E. Henley. London Voluntaries, III. BrPo
Down through the snow-drifts in the street. The Boy. Eugene Field. NA
Down through the spheres there came the Name of One. The Path of the Stars. Thomas S. Jones, Jr. WGRP
Down thy valleys, Ireland, Ireland. Ireland, Ireland. Sir Henry Newbolt. FaPoR
Down to Sleep. Helen Hunt Jackson. GN
Down to the Puritan marrow of my bones. Puritan Sonnet. Elinor Wylie. Wild Peaches, IV. BoWoP; FPL; MoAB; MoAmPo; TrGrPo
Down to the Sacred Wave, *with music.* Samuel Francis Smith. AH
Down toward the deep-blue water, marching to throb of drum. Your Lad, and My Lad. Randall Parrish. PAH
Down underground. The Indictment. Frederick Fanning Ayer. PeD
Down valley a smoke haze. Mid-August at Sourdough Mountain Lookout. Gary Snyder. HAP; MAT; NaP; NCSH; NoP; TAP
Down Wall Street. The Workers Rose on May Day or Postcript to Karl Marx. Audre Lorde. GP
Down, Wanton, Down! Robert Graves. BoLoP; CMoP; ErPo; FaBoTw; HeIP; LiTM; NoAM; NoP; OAEL-2; TEP
Down Went McGinty. Joseph Flynn. FSN, *with music*; TreF; YaD
Down went the gunner, a bullet was his fate. Praise the Lord and Pass the Ammunition! Frank Loesser. YaD
Down Wind against the Highest Peaks. Clarence Major. NBP
Down with him! chain him! bind him fast! On the Capture and Imprisonment of Crazy Snake, January, 1900. Alexander L. Posey. BPAW
Down with the lambs. *Unknown.* OxNR
Down with the rosemary and bay[e]s. Ceremonies for Candlemas[se] Eve. Robert Herrick. CaPo; JCP; OAEP; OBS
Down with the rosemary, and so. Ceremony upon Candlemas Eve. Robert Herrick. OBCP
Down, you mongrel, Death! The Poet and His Book. Edna St. Vincent Millay. MoAmPo; NePA
Downe in the depth of mine iniquity. Fulke Greville. *See* Down in the depth of mine iniquity.
Downe lay the shepherd swaine. *See* Down lay the shepherd swain.
Downe to the King's most bright-kept Baths they went. Homer, *tr. by* George Chapman. *Fr.* The Odyssey, IV. CTC
Downfall of Charing Cross, The. *Unknown.* FaBoCo
Downfall of Heathendom, The. *Unknown, tr. fr. Irish by* Frank O'Connor. KiLC
Downfall of Piracy, The. *At. to* Benjamin Franklin. PAH
Downfall of the Chancellor, The. *Unknown.* APAS
Downfall of the Gael, The. Fearflatha O'Gnive, *tr. fr. Late Middle Irish by* Sir Samuel Ferguson. AnIV; AWP; OnYI
Downfall of the Tyrant. Bible, *O.T.* Isaiah, XIV: 4-19. TrGrPo
Downhill I came, hungry, and yet not starved. The Owl. Edward Thomas. ChTr; DTC; EBEV; FaBoRV; FaBoTw; FF; GTBS-P; NoAM; NOBE; NoP; OAEL-2; PoPle; PPoe; SoSe; UnPo
Downing his drink to toasts of cut-rate jokes. 3 for 25. William Jay Smith. WaP
Downright Country-Man, The; or, The Faithful Dairy Maid. *Unknown.* CoMu
Downs and tender-tinted cliffs are lost, The. The Needles' Lighthouse from Keyhaven, Hampshire. Charles Tennyson Turner. FaBoPP
Downs will lose the sun, white alyssum, The. Head and Bottle. Edward Thomas. BrPo
Downstairs, a door. Summer Storm. John Montague. IPY
Downstream they have killed the river and built a dam. The Fish Counter at Bonneville. William Stafford. AmFN
Downtown-Boy Uptown. David Henderson. NNP; PoNe
Downtown in the city where I was born. The Last Job I Held in Bridgeport. D. W. Donzella. TAT
Downward through the evening twilight. Hiawatha's Childhood. Longfellow. *Fr.* The Song of Hiawatha. FaBV
Downwards. C. K. Williams. GeTw
Downwards we hurried fast. Alpine Descent. Wordsworth. *Fr.* The Prelude, VI. WHA
Downwind the lion catches scent. The Sleeping Gypsy. Nick Johnson. PoDr
Downy Hair. Lucien Stryk. *Fr.* Zen Poems, after Shinkichi Takahashi. FAZ
Downy Hair in the Shape of a Flame. Coleman Barks. PV
Dow's Flat. Bret Harte. FaBoBe; HBV-2
Dowsabel. Michael Drayton. *See* Cassamen and Dowsabell.
Doxology. Bert Leston Taylor. OBAL
Doxy, oh! thy glaziers shine. The Maunder's Praise of His Strowling Mort. *Unknown.* OxBoLi
Doze, The. James Reeves. AmMo
Dozen machines, A. A Time for Building. Myra Cohn Livingston. PDV
Dozen sandaled saints I see, A. So Runs Our Song. Mary Eva Kitchel. PGD
Dozens of girls would storm up. Embraceable You. Ira Gershwin. BLSo
Drab drugget paths protect these polished floors. Fantasia on a Wittelsbach Atmosphere. Siegfried Sassoon. MoVE
Draft Horse, The. Robert Frost. CMoP; HeIP; HoPM; PAI
Draft of a Reparations Agreement. Dan Pagis, *tr. fr. Hebrew by* Stephen Mitchell. VWA
Draft Riot, The. Charles De Kay. PAH
Drafts. Nora Bomford. SUMH
Drafts for a Quatrain. Edmund Wilson. OBAL
Dragging in Winter. David McElroy. AmPA
Dragging the Main. David Ray. TAT
Dragon, The. Spenser. *Fr.* The Faerie Queene, I, 11. SeCePo
Dragon. Joseph Stroud. NPGG
Dragon, The. Carolyn Wells. TDH
Dragon Country: To Jacob Boehme. Robert Penn Warren. PPP
Dragon Lesson. James Hearst. AMV-80
Dragon of the Seas, The. Thomas Nelson Page. PAH
Dragon Skate. Gladys Cardiff. CDW
Dragon that our seas did raise his crest, The. Of the Great and Famous . . . Sir Francis Drake, and of My Little-Little Selfe. Robert Hayman. CH; FaBoCh; NoP
Dragon, who was a great wag, A. The Dragon. Carolyn Wells. TDH
Dragonfly, The. Louise Bogan. HeIP; NIP

Dragonfly, The. Chisoku, *tr. by* Harold G. Henderson. SoPo
Dragonfly, A. Eleanor Farjeon. FaPON; OnUR; PDV; RHPC
Dragon-Fly, The. Walter Savage Landor. OBEV; OBVV
(Lines to a Dragon-Fly.) FM; OBNC; OBRV
Dragonfly, The. Howard Nemerov. PoA
Dragonfly, The. Theodore Harding Rand. CaP
Dragon-fly and I together, The. Two of a Trade. Samuel Willoughby Duffield. AA
Dragon's Hoard, The. J. R. R. Tolkien. AmMo
Draherin O Machree. *Unknown.* AnIV
Drake's Drum ("Drake he's in his hammock an' a thousand mile[s] away"). Sir Henry Newbolt. EtS; FaBoCh; FaPoR; HBV-2; HBVY; OBMV; OBVV; PaPo; PoRA; TreF; VLP
Drama's vitallest expression is the common day. Emily Dickinson. NOBA
Dramatic Fragment. Trumbull Stickney. ELU; OxBA
("Sir, say no more.") InPK
Dramatis Personae, *sel.* Robert Browning.
Epilogue: "On the first of the Feast of Feasts." VLP
Drank lonesome water. Lonesome Water. Roy Helton. AmFN; MoAmPo
Draped in khaki, Jurgis. Jurgis Petrakas, the Workers' Angel, Organizes the First Miner's Strike in Exeter, Pennsylvania. Anthony Petrosky. FYAP
Drat my hateful birthday. Sulpicia, *tr. fr. Latin by* John Dillon. PBWP
Draw a historical parallel. Entrance Exams. "Cuthbert Bede." FaBoNo
Draw a Pail of Water. *Unknown.* MoShbr; OxNR
Draw back the cradle curtains, Kate. The King of the Cradle. Joseph Ashby-Sterry. HBV-1
Draw closer to me, God, than were I one. Prayer of an Unbeliever. Lizette Woodworth Reese. TrPWD
Draw me nere [*or* near], draw me nere [*or* near]. The Juggler [*or* Magician] and the Baron's Daughter [*or* The Jolly Juggler]. *Unknown.* EBEV; MeEL; NoP; OxBM
Draw near [*or* neer]/ You lovers that complain. The Exequies. Thomas Stanley. AnAnS-2; MeLP; OBS
Draw near to the tables, ye that wear the cloaks. A Connacht Caoine. *Unknown.* AnIV
Draw near, young men, and learn of me. McAfee's Confession. *Unknown.* AmFP
Draw neer/ You lovers that complain. *See* Draw near . . .
Draw up the papers, lawyer. Betsey and I Are Out. Will Carleton. PaPo
Drawer, The. George MacBeth. NePoEA-2
Drawing-Room Ballad, A. Henry Duff Traill. CenHV
Drawing Wildflowers. Jorie Graham. NPGG
Drawings by Children. Lisel Mueller. PoDr
Drawn blinds and flaring gas within. City Nights: In Bohemia [*or* In Bohemia]. Arthur Symons. BrPo; SyP
Drawn from his refuge in some lonely elm. Squirrel in Sunshine. William Cowper. BoAnP
Dray, The. Laurence Binyon. SyP
Drayman, The. Walt Whitman. *Fr.* Song of Myself. PoNe
Dread. J. M. Synge. BoLoP; MoBrPo
Dread are the death-pale Kings. Still-Heart. Frank Pearce Sturm. OBMV
Dread of Death. John Audelay. *See* In His Utter Wretchedness.
Dreadful case of murder, A. Execution of Alice Holt. *Unknown.* OxBoLi
Dreadful Dinotherium he, The. Hilaire Belloc. *Fr.* A Moral Alphabet. NOBL
Dreadful Fate of Naughty Nate, The. John Kendrick Bangs. OBCA
"Dreadful Has Already Happened, The." Mark Strand. NoAM
Dreadnought, The. *Unknown.* AmFP; AmSS, *with music;* ShS (2 *vers.*), *with music*
Dream, A [*or* The]. William Allingham. BlrV, *abr.*; OxBI
Dream, A. Bella Akhmadulina, *tr. fr. Russian by* Jean Valentine *and* Olga Carlisle. BoWoP
Dream, A. Matthew Arnold. GBL; GTBS-P; SeCePo
Dream, The. Aphra Behn. *Fr.* A Voyage to the Isle of Love. PBWP
Dream, The. "Brian Bendo." NOEC
Dream, The. John Peale Bishop. LiTA; LiTM
Dream, A. Blake. *Fr.* Songs of Innocence. CH; EnRP; LAuP; PoPle
Dream, The. Louise Bogan. LiTA; LiTM; MAT; MoAB; MoAmPo; SBG
Dream, A. Emily Brontë. NBM
Dream, A, *sel.* Burns.
Guid-Mornin to Your Majesty! NAs
Dream, The. Byron. BeLS; ChER; TEP
Dream, The. Chaucer. *Fr.* The Book of the Duchesse. FiP
("Me thoughte thus: that it was May.") PBBP
Dream, A. Hugh Connell. NeIP
Dream. Richard Watson Dixon. EBEV; LoBV; VLP
Dream. Stephen Dobyns. MAYP
Dream [*or* Dreame], The ("Dear[e] love, for nothing less[e] than thee"). John Donne. AnAnS-1; ElL; InvP; LiTB; LoBV; MeLP; MePo; OAEL-1; OAEP; OBEV; OBS; SECP
Dream. Solomon Edwards. NNP; PoNe
Dream. Joseph Eliyia, *tr. fr. Greek by* Rae Dalven. VWA
Dream, The. "Michael Field." SyP
Dream, The. David Ignatow. CoAP; MAT; NNaP; PAI; VWA
Dream. Nana Issaia, *tr. fr. Modern Greek by* Helle Tzalopoulou Barnstone. BoWoP
Dream [*or* Dreame], The. Ben Jonson. NOBE; PoEL-2
Dream, A. Keats. *Fr.* The Fall of Hyperion, I. OBNC; OBRV
Dream, A. Elizabeth Clementine Kinney. AA
Dream. Josephine Miles. PoA
Dream, The. Francis Burdett Money-Coutts. OBVV
Dream. Marianne Moore. NYBP
Dream, The. Paul Petri. TAP
Dream, The. Theodore Roethke. LLLT; MoVE; NIP; NoP; NYBP; UnPo
Dream, A. V. Sackville-West. MoVE
Dream. William Jay Smith. MoVE
Dream, The. Helen Spalding. ChMP
Dream, A, *sels.* Rachel Speght. WPE
"I sought, I found, she asked me what I would."
"My grief, quoth I, is called Ignorance."
"Quoth she, I wish I could prescribe your help."
"Upon a sudden, as I gazing stood."
Dream, The. Arthur Symons. SyP
Dream, A. Charles Tomlinson. OxBC
Dream, A ("*Benedicte,* what dreamed I this night?"). *Unknown. See* Benedicte, What Dreamed I This Night.
Dream, The ("I dreamed that, buried in my fellow clay"). *Unknown.* NOEC
Dream, The ("Last night I had a dream bad 'cess to my dreaming"). *Unknown.* WTO
Dream, The ("Last night I supped on lobster; it nearly drove me mad"). *Unknown.* OxBoLi
Dream, A ("Me thought I was in wildernesse walking al one"). *Unknown. Fr.* Mum and the Sothsegger. OxBM
Dream, A. Charles Williams. OBEV
Dream about an Aged Humorist, A. Aaron Zeitlin, *tr. fr. Yiddish by* Ruth Whitman. VWA
Dream about Junior High School in America, The. Dick Lourie. NeAC
Dream about Sunsets. Anabelle Hébert. GrPl
Dream after Touring the Tokyo Tokei. Joy Kogawa. BrSi
Dream and the Blood, The. Louis Untermeyer. UnTE
Dream and the Song. James David Corrothers. BANP
Dream as Reported, A. Virginia Earle. GoYe
Dream Barker. Jean Valentine. PrIm; VGW
Dream Boogie. Langston Hughes. AmPP
Dream Called Life, The. Pedro Calderon de la Barca, *tr. fr. Spanish by* Edward Fitzgerald. AWP
Dream Data. Robert Duncan. NeAP
Dream Deferred. Langston Hughes. *See* Harlem ("What happens to a dream deferred").
Dream, Dump-Heap, and Civilization. Robert Penn Warren. NoP
Dream-fair, beside dream waters, it stands alone. The Shadow House of Lugh. "Ethna Carbery." AnIV
Dream Fantasy. "Fiona Macleod." WGRP
Dream Farmer. Jill Witherspoon Boyer. CNA
Dream Feast, The (Three Poems). Anita Endrezze Probst. VoR
Dream Fishing. Jim Thomas. WOLT
Dream fluently, still brothers, who when young. To the Etruscan Poets. Richard Wilbur. OxBC
Dream-Follower, The. Thomas Hardy. VLP
Dream Girl. Karen Snow. HoAn
Dream House, The. Marjorie Allen Seiffert. HBMV
Dream in a dream the heavy soul somewhere. Canto Amor. John Berryman. CoAP; MoAmPo; MoPo; MoVE; NePA; VGW
Dream in Early Spring, A. Fredegond Shove. MoVE
Dream is a cocktail at Sloppy Joe's, The. Havana Dreams. Langston Hughes. PoNe
"Dream is the thought in the ghost, The." George Meredith. *Fr.* A Faith on Trial. WGRP
Dream is vague, The. Beale Street. Langston Hughes. PPP
Dream it was in which I found myself, A. The Dream Called Life. Pedro Calderon de la Barca, *tr. by* Edward Fitzgerald. AWP
Dream Land. Frances Anne Kemble. OBVV
Dreamland, *sel.* Charles Mair.
"We are not wholly blest who use the earth." CaP
Dream-Land. Poe. AmPP; AP; LiTA; NePA; NOBA; OxBA
(Dreamland.) TAP
Dream Land. Christina Rossetti. BrRo; VLP
Dream-Love. Christina Rossetti. CH; HAP; NBM; PoEL-5
Dream Motorcycle, The. Pete Winslow. PV
Dream 1971. Victor Contoski. GP
Dream not of noble service elsewhere wrought. Life's Common Duties. Minot J. Savage. WBLP
Dream Observed, A. Anne Ridler. NeBP
Dream of a Baseball Star. Gregory Corso. NoAM; VGW

Dream of a Boy Who Lived at Nine Elms, The. William Brighty Rands. OxBChV
Dream of a Decent Death. G. A. Borgese. NePoAm
Dream of a Girl Who Lived at Sevenoaks, The. William Brighty Rands. OxBChV
Dream of Aengus Og, The. Eleanor Rogers Cox. HBMV
Dream of Artemis, A, *sel.* Francis Ledwidge.
"God, whose kindly hand doth sow." TrPWD
Dream of Burial, A. James Wright. NaP
Dream of Dakiki, The. Firdausi, *tr. fr. Persian by* A. V. Williams Jackson. WGRP
Dream of Death, A. "Owen Innsley." AA
Dream of Death, A. W. B. Yeats. GBL
Dream of Eugene Aram, The. Thomas Hood. BeLS; HBV-2
(Dream of Eugene Aram, the Murderer, The.) EnRP
Dream of Fair Women, A. Kingsley Amis. FF; MP; NoAM; NMP; OAEL-2
Dream of Fair Women, A, *sel.* Tennyson.
As When a Man. ChER
("As when a man that sails in a balloon.") OBRV
(Balloon, The.) RoGo
Dream of Flowers, A. Titus Munson Coan. AA
Dream of Flying Comes of Age, The. Howard Nemerov. BiP
Dream of Gerontius, The, *sels.* Cardinal Newman.
Angel ("My work is done"). GoBC
Angel ("Softly and gently, dearly-ransom'd soul"). OxBoCh
Angel of the Agony ("Jesu! by that shuddering dread which fell on Thee"). OxBoCh
"Jesu, Maria—I am near to death." ACP
"Now let the golden prison ope its gates," *conclusion.* VLP
"O Lord, how wonderful in depth and height." VLP
"Praise to the Holiest in the height." NOCV; PoEL-5
(Chorus of Angels.) NBM
(Fifth Choir of Angelicals.) GoBC
Soul before God, The. OxBoCh
Dream of Governors, A. Louis Simpson. NYBP
Dream of Horses, A. Ted Hughes. NePoEA-2
Dream of Jealousy, A. Seamus Heaney. CIP
Dream of Judgement, A. Douglas Dunn. OxBC
Dream of mine flew over the mead, A. The Dream-Follower. Thomas Hardy. VLP
Dream of November, A. Sir Edmund Gosse. SyP
Dream of Rebirth. Roberta Hill. CDW; TWSS
Dream of Suffocation, A. Robert Bly. NaP
Dream of the Cabal, The; a Prophetical Satire. *Unknown.* APAS
Dream of the Cross, The. *Unknown. See* Dream of the Rood, The.
Dream of the Forgotten Lover. Lucia Fox, *tr. fr. Spanish by* R. Maghan. BoWoP
Dream of the Lynx. John Haines. NU
Dream of the Romaunt of the Rose, The. Guillaume de Lorris, *tr. fr. French by* Chaucer. *Fr.* The Romance of the Rose. LoBV
Dream of the Rood, The. *Unknown, at. to* Cynewulf, *tr. fr. Anglo-Saxon.* ACP; AnOE, *tr. by* Charles W. Kennedy; NOCV, *tr. by* Michael Alexander; OAEL-1, *tr. by* Charles W. Kennedy
(Dream of the Cross, The, *tr. by* Sally Purcell.) EBEV
Dream of the Unknown, A. Shelley. GTBS; GTBS-P
Dream of the walls of a cave. The Fossil. John Lyle Donaghy. NeIP
Dream of Venus, A. Bion, *tr. fr. Greek by* Leigh Hunt. AWP
Dream of waking in some sleeper's eye, A. Hiroshima. Margaret Rockwell. PPON
Dream of Winter. George Mackay Brown. FaBoTw
Dream of Women, A. Carolyn Maisel. IHMS
Dream of Wrecks, A. Shakespeare. King Richard III, *fr.* I, iv. ChTr
(Methought I Saw a Thousand Fearful Wrecks, *shorter sel.*) Ets
Dream on stone. Afternoon's Angel. Seymour Mayne. VWA
Dream, or the Type of the Rising Sun, A. Jean Adams. NOEC
Dream-Pedlary. Thomas Lovell Beddoes. CH; EnRP; FaBoBe; HAP; LiTB; LoBV; NOBE; OBEV; OBNC; OBRV; OBVV; PoEL-4; TreFS; TrGrPo; ViBoPo; WiR
Dream Record: June 8, 1955. Allen Ginsberg. ConAP; NOBA
Dream Sequence, Part 9. Naomi Long Madgett. BPo
Dream Song. Lewis Alexander. PoBA; PoNe
Dream-Song. Walter de la Mare. PoPle
Dream Song. Richard Middleton. HBV-1
Dream Song. *Tr. fr. Pawnee Indian by* Frances Densmore. OBVE
Dream Songs. John Berryman. *Poems indexed separately by titles and first lines.*
Dream the Great Dream. Florence Earle Coates. HBMV
Dream-Teller, The. Padraic Gregory. HBMV; OnYI
Dream Tryst. Richard Le Gallienne. HBMV
Dream 2: Brian the Still-Hunter. Margaret Atwood. BoWoP
Dream Variation [*or* Variations]. Langston Hughes. AmNP; BALP; CDC; HAP; IDB; NOBA; PoBA; PoNe; PoPl; WeW
Dream within a Dream, A. Poe. AmPP; AP; BLPL; ChTr; GBL; NOBA; OxBA; SyP; TAP; TrGrPo
Dreambooks. Alfred Corn. DFT
Dreame, The. John Donne. *See* Dream, The ("Dear love, for nothing less than thee").
Dreame, The. Ben Jonson. *See* Dream, The.
Dreamed Realization, A. Gregory Corso. NeAP; PoM; VGW
Dreamer, The. Dorothy Gould. PGD
Dreamer, The. Thomas Nunan. WBLP
Dreamer of Dreams. William Herbert Carruth. PoLF
Dreamer, waiting for darkness with sorrowful, drooping eyes. Forward. Edna Dean Proctor. HBV-2
Dreamers, The. Theodosia Garrison. HBMV
Dreamers. Siegfried Sassoon. BrPo; HBMV; MoBrPo; NoAM
Dreamers and the Sea, The. Eithne Wilkins. *Fr.* Parzival. NeBP
Dreamers Cry Their Dream, The. Lucia Trent. PGD
Dreamers turn, The. The Dreamers and the Sea. Eithne Wilkins. *Fr.* Parzival. NeBP
Dreamers upon the hilltops, The. The Dreamers Cry Their Dream. Lucia Trent. PGD
Dreaming about Freedom. Jimmy Santiago Baca. AMV-80
Dreaming America. Joyce Carol Oates. GeTw
Dreaming in marble all the castle lay. Of Nicolette. E. E. Cummings. HBMV
Dreaming in the Trenches. William Gordon McCabe. AA
Dreaming of honeycombs to share. Waiting. Harry Behn. SiSoSe; TiPo
Dreaming Trout, The. Charles Bruce. *Fr.* The Flowing Summer. CaP
Dreaming with a Friend. Stephen Berg. NaP
Dreaming you say thank you. Voices That Have Filled My Day. Fay Chiang. BrSi
Dreamland. *See* Dream Land.
Dreamlike leap, A. For the Record. Roy Blount, Jr. OBAL
Dreams. Cecil Frances Alexander. OnYI
Dreams. André Breton, *tr. fr. French by* Robert Duncan. InPS
Dreams. Charles Cooper. PoBA
Dreams. Victor J. Daley. PoAu-1
Dreams. Nikki Giovanni. CNA; PoBA
Dreams. Robert Herrick. CaPo; HAP
Dreams. Langston Hughes. RHPC
Dreams. Poe. AmPP; OxBA; TAP
Dreams. Arthur Symons. PoA
Dreams. Israel Zangwill. TrJP
Dreams are old before you, The. It Is Finished. Barney Bush. STE
"Dreams Are the Royal Road to the Unconscious." Paul Goodman. PoA
Dreams fled away, this country bedroom, raw. Another September. Thomas Kinsella. BIrV; CIP; PoCh
Dreams go fast and far. To Dark Eyes Dreaming. Zilpha Keatley Snyder. RHPC
Dreams in Progress. Richard Oyama. BrSi
Dreams in War Time, *sel.* Amy Lowell.
"I dug a grave under an oak-tree." BoWoP
Dreams of Auschwitz. Boris Slutsky, *tr. fr. Russian by* Daniel Weissbort. VWA
Dreams of the Dreamer, The. Georgia Douglas Johnson. CDC
Dreams of the Sea. W. H. Davies. EtS
Dreams of Water. Donald Justice. LCAP; NYBP
Dreams Old and Nascent. D. H. Lawrence. WGRP
Dreams that delude with flying shade men's minds. We Are Such Stuff as Dreams. Petronius Arbiter, *tr. by* Howard Mumford Jones. AWP
Dreamscape. Philip Booth. FiCP
Dreamscape in Kümmel. Harold Witt. NYBP
Dreamwater. Hilde Domin, *tr. fr. German by* Tudor Morris. VWA
Dreamy crags with raucous voices croon, The. Hymn to the Sunrise. *Unknown.* NA
Dreamy in a darkling bar. Ode to a Nightingale. Roy Kelly. BXAP
Dreary and brown the night comes down. Columbus at the Convent. John T. Trowbridge. PAH
Dreary Black Hills, The (*diff. versions*). *Unknown.* AmFP; AS, *with music*; BPAW; CoSo, *with music*; FSW
Dreary Change, The. Sir Walter Scott. FaBoPP; OAEL-2; OBNC
("Sun upon the Weirdlaw Hill, The.") BSV
Dred of deth, sorow of sin. In His Utter Wretchedness [*or* Dread of Death]. John Audelay. MeEL; OxBM
Dredged in a net the slender god. Archaic Apollo. William Plomer. ChMP
Dree Night, The. *Unknown.* ChTr
Dregs. Ernest Dowson. HBV-1; NCEP; OBMV; SeCePo
Dreme, The, *sels.* Sir David Lindsay.
Complaint [*or* Compleynt] of the Common Weill of Scotland, The. BSV; GoTS; OxBS

Of the Realme of Scotland. OxBS
Drenched earth has a warm, sweet radiance all her own, The. The Robin's Egg. Annie Charlotte Dalton. CaP
Dress. Henry Luttrell. *Fr.* Advice to Julia. OBRV
Dress, The. Christopher Middleton. NMP
Dress, The. Mark Strand. GeTw
Dress Me, Dear Mother. Avraham Shlonsky, *tr. fr. Hebrew by* Robert Mezey. VWA
Dress me in green. *Unknown, tr. fr. Spanish by* Willis Barnstone. BoWoP
Dress of Fire, A. Dahlia Ravikovitch, *tr. fr. Hebrew by* Chana Bloch. VWA
Dress of Spring, The. May Justus. YeAr
Dress that my brother has put on is thin, The. "The Lady of Sakanoye." *Fr.* Manyo Shu. AWP
Dresscessional, A. Carolyn Wells. WBLP
Dressed in his clumsy, stiff, aquatic clothes. The Diver. E. L. Mayo. CoAP
Dressed man and a naked man, A. George Orwell. EBEV
Dressed up in my melancholy. Song. M. Carl Holman. AmNP; PoNe
Dresses. Kathleen Fraser. NMM
Dressing. Henry Vaughan. AnAnS-1
Dressing Game. Dennis Schmitz. NPGG
Dressing Stations, The. Norman Dubie. AmPA
Dressmaker's Dummy as Scarecrow, The. Barbara Howes. DFF
Dried Apple Pies. *Unknown.* BLPA
Dried blowfish crumbling now, a pocket, A. Only One. Ralph Burns. PoDr
Dried Fruit. Philip Dow. BXAP
Dried sinks and hot. Caravati's Junkyard. Elizabeth Morgan. GrPl
Dried to a pit of meanness. Ten Week Wife. Rhoda Donovan. Str
Dried up old cactus. June. Elaine Feinstein. BrRo
Driest place in the yard's, The. Self-Projection. A. R. Ammons. FAZ
Drift descends like rattling dust, The. Avalanche. Adrien Stoutenburg. NYBP
Drifter off Tarentum, A. Kipling. *Fr.* Epitaphs of the War. FaBoEE; MMA; PoPle
Drifter, The. *Unknown.* CoSo
Drifters. Bruce Dawe. CBAP
Drifting. D. Maitland Bushby. BPAW
Drifting. Thomas Buchanan Read. AA; GN; HBV-1
Drifting. Kathleen Spivack. IHMS
Drifting and innocent and like snow. Christmas Letter Home. G. S. Fraser. OxBTC
Drifting Away. Charles Kingsley. OxBoCh
Drifting night in the Georgia pines. O Daedalus, Fly Away Home. Robert Hayden. BiP; HAP; IDB; NCSH; PoBA; PoNe; WeW
Drifting outside in a pall of smoke. Forever. Raymond Carver. GeTw
Drifting Sands and a Caravan. Yolande Langworthy. BLPA
Drifting we wake. Snow. Nan Fry. PPJ
Driftwood. Witter Bynner. FYAP
Driftwood. Daniel Smythe. RFM
Driftwood, *abr.* Trumbull Stickney. HBV-2
Driftwood Dybbuk. Barbara F. Lefcowitz. VWA
Drill Man Blues. George Sizemore. AmFP; WTO
Drill, The. Harry Brown. WaaP
Drill, Ye Tarriers, Drill! *At. to* Thomas F. Casey. FSW
Drilling in Russell Square. Edward Shanks. OBMV
Drilling Missed Holes. Don Cameron. PoOW
Drink. William Carlos Williams. OxBA
Drink and dance and laugh and lie. The Flaw in Paganism. Dorothy Parker. DBV
Drink! drink! to whom shall we drink? The Old Man's Carousal. James Kirke Paulding. AA
Drink, Friends. Moses ibn Ezra, *tr. fr. Hebrew by* Solomon Solis-Cohen. *Fr.* Wine-Songs. TrJP
Drink, gossips mine! we drink no wine. Medieval Norman Song. *Unknown, tr. by* John Addington Symonds. AWP
Drink (ingurgitate, engulph, engorge, gulp). A Thesaurus Nightmare. J. Willard Ridings. WhC
Drink me. Thirst. Musa Moris Farhi. VWA
Drink of Water, A. Seamus Heaney. OxBC
Drink that rotgut, drink that rotgut. Drinking Song. *Unknown.* CoSo
Drink to Me Only with Thine Eyes. Ben Jonson. *See* To Celia ("Drink to me only. . .").
Drink To-Day. John Fletcher, *and others.* *Fr.* The Bloody Brother. HBV-2; ViBoPo
(Drink To-Day, and Drown All Sorrow.) OAEP
(Drinking Song). ElL
Drink, unhappy lover, drink. Epigrams. Meleger, *tr. fr. Greek by* Peter Whigham. PeHV
Drink with Something in It, A. Ogden Nash. PoPl
Drinke and be merry, merry, merry boyes. The Songe. Thomas Morton. SCAP
Drinker. Patrick Anderson. PeCV
Drinking. Abraham Cowley, *after the Greek of* Anacreon. BLPL; CABA; FF; HBV-2; LoBV; MePo; NOBE; OBEV; OBVE; PAI; PoPle; SeCePo; SeCP; SeCV-1; TrGrPo; WhC
(Anacreontic on Drinking.) SeCePo
(Anacreontics: Drinking.) HeIP
(Thirsty Earth, The.) WiR
Drinking. Virginia R. Terris. FAZ
Drinking Alone in the Moonlight. Li Po, *tr. fr. Chinese by* Amy Lowell *and* Florence Ayscough. AWP
Drinking Cold Water. Peter Everwine. NNaP
Drinking Fountain. Marchette Chute. TiPo
Drinking hot saké. Gary Synder. *Fr.* Hitch Haiku. InPK
Drinking Song. Alexander Brome. PoPle
Drinking Song. Burns. *Fr.* The Jolly Beggars. TrGrPo
Drinking-Song, A. Henry Carey. OBEV
Drinking Song. Thomas Dekker. *See* Cold's the Wind.
Drinking Song. John Fletcher, *and others.* *See* Drink To-Day.
Drinking Song. Jim Harrison. WOLT
Drinking Song. Anthony Hecht. NMP
Drinking Song, A. Shakespeare. *Fr.* Antony and Cleopatra, II, vii. OBSC
("Come, thou monarch of the vine.") OAEP; ViBoPo
Drinking Song. James Kenneth Stephen. NOBL
Drinking Song. *At. to* William Stevenson. *See* Back and Side Go Bare, Go Bare.
Drinking Song ("Drink that rotgut, drink the rotgut"). *Unknown.* CoSo
Drinking Song, A ("If ever your spirits are damp, low"). *Unknown.* FaBoUs
Drinking Song ("She tells me with claret she cannot agree"). *Unknown.* NOBL
Drinking Song ("Tappster, fill another ale"). *Unknown.* OxBM
Drinking Song, A. W. B. Yeats. BoLoP; OAEL-2; POL
Drinking-Song, against All Sorts of Disputes in Drinking, A. William Wycherley. SeCV-2
Drinking the Wind. Tan Ying, *tr. fr. Chinese by* Kenneth Rexroth *and* Ling Chung. WPOW
Drinking Time. D. J. O'Sullivan. OnYI
Dripping June, A. *Unknown.* FaBoUs
Drips surprise, The. They talk too. Fag-End. Philip O'Connor. EAS
Drive, The. Janet Reed McFatter. GrPl
Drive Away Blues. *Unknown.* BluL
Drive Imagining. Arthur Vogelsang. MAYP
Drive It On, *with music.* *Unknown.* OuSiCo
Drive on, sharp wings, and cry above. The Redshanks. Julian Bell. OBMV
Drive the pilings deep! Beach House. Mary Rita Hurley. PoPl
Drive-ins are out, to start with. Movie-Going. John Hollander. CoAP; NYP; PPP
Driven from the soil of France, a female came. Sonnet: September 1, 1802. Wordsworth. ChER
Driven in by autumn's sharpening air. Wordsworth. *Fr.* The Redbreast. PBBP
Driver, The. James Dickey. VGW
Driver in Italy, The. Nicholas Christopher. MAYP
Driver rubbed at his nettly chin, The. To the Four Courts, Please. James Stephens. BIrV; HBMV; MoAB; MoBrPo; UnPo
"Driver, what stream is it?" I asked, well knowing. The Lordly Hudson. Paul Goodman. CoAP; NMP; NYP; VGW
Drivers are washing the concrete mixers, The. Concrete Mixers. Patricia Hubbell. PDV; RHPC
Drivers of Boston, The. June Gross. AMV-80
Driver's Prayer, A. *Unknown.* STF
Drivin' steel, drivin' steel. Hammer Man. *Unknown.* AS
Drivin' Steel, *with music.* *Unknown.* AS
Driving at Dawn. William Heyen. SaC
Driving By. Robert Wallace. LiSp
Driving Cattle to Casas Buenas. Roy Campbell. PeSA
Driving Cross-Country. X. J. Kennedy. TwCP
Driving down from the turf bog in the rain. Merchandise. Seán Jennett. NeIP
Driving down the concrete vein. The White Man Pressed the Locks. James C. Kilgore. InPK
Driving; Driven. David McAleavey. AMV-80
Driving, driven. The Driver in Italy. Nicholas Christopher. MAYP
Driving Home. Jonathan London. AMV-81
Driving Home after a Funeral. Gregory Orr. GeTw
Driving Home the Cows. Kate Putnam Osgood. AA; BeLS; HBV-2; PAH; TreFS
Driving, I come for a while. Late at Night. William Stafford. NNaP
Driving in Oklahoma. Carter Revard. VoR
Driving in the Park. *Unknown.* OxBoLi
Driving into Enid. Michael Van Walleghen. FYAP

Driving late at night I pass. Sleep. Dana Naone. CDW
Driving North from Kingsville, Texas. Naomi Shihab. TAT
Driving North from Savannah on My Birthday. Paul Zimmer. AMV-81
Driving Saw-Logs on the Plover, *with music. Unknown.* AS
Driving the Mule. *Unknown. See* My Sweetie's a Mule in the Mine.
Driving the new road to Buck's Lake. Coming of Age. John Logan. DiL
Driving through Minnesota during the Hanoi Bombings. Robert Bly. NoP
Driving through New England. Lucille Clifton. GOA
Driving through the Pima Indian Reservation. Paul H. Cook. AMV-80
Driving to Santa Barbara. Light Rain. Christopher Buckley. AMV-81
Driving to Sauk City. Warren Woessner. TAT
Driving to the Beach. Joanna Cole. RHPC
Driving to Town Late to Mail a Letter. Robert Bly. BoNaP; ELU; HeIP; InPK; NaP; VGW
Driving toward the Lac Qui Parle River. Robert Bly. ConAP; LCAP; NaP; NCSH; NoP
Driving Wheel. Sherley Anne Williams. BlSi
Drizzling Easter Morning, A. Thomas Hardy. CMoP
Dromedary, The. Hilaire Belloc. WhC
Dromedary, The. A. Y. Campbell. HBMV
Dromedary. François Dodat, *tr. fr. French by* Bert *and* Odette Meyers. BoAnP
Dromedary is a cheerful bird, The. The Dromedary. Hilaire Belloc. WhC
Drone of airplane neared, and dimmed away, The. Immanent. Walter de la Mare. PoA
Drone v. Worker. Ebenezer Elliott. NBM; OBSV
Droning a drowsy syncopated tune. The Weary Blues. Langston Hughes. BALP; FaBV; InPK; NoAM; NOBA; NoP; PoNe
Droop under doves' wings silent, breathing shapes. The Night Nurse Goes Her Round. John Gray. LoBV; OBNC
Drooping, the labourer-ox. Winter. James Thomson. *Fr.* The Seasons. FM
Drop a kernel of corn on a rock. Epilog. Wendy Rose. *Fr.* Lost Copper. TWSS
Drop a Pebble in the Water. James W. Foley. BLPA
Drop an unkind word or careless. The Difference. *Unknown.* STF
Drop, Drop, Slow Tears. Phineas Fletcher. *See* Hymn: "Drop, drop, slow tears."
Drop fell on the apple tree, A. Emily Dickinson. BoNaP
Drop of Dew, A. Shmuel Halkin, *tr. fr. Yiddish by* Jacob Sonntag. TrJP
Drop of Ink, A. Joseph Ernest Whitney. AA
Drop of sepia in the fragrant vase, The. Dusk. Abraham Z. Lopez-Penha, *tr. by* Thomas Walsh. TrJP
Drop, one drop, how sweetly one fair drop, A. On Dives. Richard Crashaw. ACP
Drop the Wires. Hugh Seidman. AmPA
Drop Thy Still Dews. Whittier. ILwL
Drop your offering in the box. Candles. *Unknown.* GoBC
Dropped leaf, The. Ruth Miller. *Fr.* Cycle. PeSA
Dropped petals of a broken lotus-moon. No Less than Prisoners. Frederick T. Macartney. CBAP
Dropping back with the ball ripe in my palm. The Passer. George Abbe. LiSp
Dropping Your Aitches. Joseph Warren Beach. NYBP
Drops of Gall. Gabriela Mistral, *tr. fr. Spanish by* David Garrison. BoWoP
Drosophila wing of the morning moon, The. Mushroom Hunting in Late August, Peterborough, N.H. Michael Blumenthal. MAYP
Drought. Oumar Bar, *tr. fr. French by* Kathleen Weaver. PBWP
Drought. David Holbrook. OxBTC
Drought. Frederick E. Laight. OBCV
(Soliloquy.) CaP
Drove-Road, The. W. W. Gibson. OxBTC
Drover, A. Padraic Colum. AnIL; AnIV; AWP; HBV-1; MoBrPo; OBMV; OxBI; ViBoPo
Droving Man. Thea Astley. PoAu-2
Drowned, The. Norman MacCaig. OxBC
Drowned, The. Stephen Spender. MOS
Drowned Lady, The. *Unknown.* ChTr
Drowned Mariner, The. Longfellow. AA
Drowned Sailor. Neufville Shaw. CaP
Drowned Seaman, The. Maude Goldring. HBMV
Drowning in Spanish. Tom Schmidt. NeAC
Drowning is not so pitiful. Emily Dickinson. CMoP
Drowning of Conaing, The. *Unknown, tr. fr. Old Irish by* Frank O'Connor. AnIL
Drowning Poet, The. James Merrill. PP
Drowning with Others. James Dickey. CoPo
Drowsily come the sheep. Slumber Song. Louis V. Ledoux. FaPON; HBMV
Drowsy Herodotus holds him there, The. Ancient Historian. Chris Wallace-Crabbe. PoAu-2
Drowsy Sleeper, The. *Unknown. See* Who's That at My Bedroom Window?
Drowsy sun went slowly to his rest, The. Evening. James Stephens. MoBrPo
Drug Clerk, The. Eunice Tietjens. HBMV
Drug of the incomprehensible. The Bad Habit. Charles Henri Ford. EAS
Drug Store. Karl Shapiro. CMoP; MoVE; MP; OxBA; TwCP
Drug Store. John V. A. Weaver. HBMV; YaD
Drugged. Walter de la Mare. BrPo
Drugs are a tuition. Going to School in France or America. Tom Clark. ConAP
Druid, The. John Banister Tabb. AA
Drum. Langston Hughes. MoAmPo
Drum, The. John Scott of Amwell. *See* I Hate That Drum's Discordant Sound.
Drum for Ben Boyd, A, *sel.* Francis Webb.
Papuan Shepherd, A. PoAu-2
Drum Majah, De. Ray Garfield Dandridge. BANP
Drum on your drums, batter on your banjos. Jazz Fantasia. Carl Sandburg. MoAB; MoAmPo; PoNe; TwAmPo
Drum, The: The Narrative of the Demon of Tedworth. Edith Sitwell. FaBoTw
Drumdelgie. *Unknown.* GBP
Drumdrumdrum, A. The Wall. Gwendolyn Brooks. *Fr.* Two Dedications. PoBA
Drumlin Woodchuck, A. Robert Frost. GoYe; NoAM; NOBA
Drummer, The. Anna Robinson. SUS
Drummer Boy. William Stafford. FAZ
Drummer-Boy and the Shepherdess, The ("Drummer-boy, drummer-boy, where is your drum?"). William Brightly Rands. MoShBr
Drummer Boy of Shiloh, The. *Unknown.* AmFP
Drummer Hodge. Thomas Hardy. AWP; BrPo; CoBMV; EBEV; GTBS-P; HAP; InPS; NoAM; NoP; OBWP; PAI; SeCeV; VLP; WeW
Drumochter. Anne B. Murray. PoSH
Drums gather and humble us beyond escape. Belief. A. R. Ammons. GOA
Drums in Scotland. Richard Hugo. LCAP
Drunk. Carroll Arnett. VoR
Drunk,/ you move. Last Born. Judith Kirkwood. Str
Drunk and senseless in his place. Ramon. Bret Harte. BeLS
Drunk as drunk on turpentine. Pablo Neruda, *tr. fr. Spanish by* Christopher Logue. BoLoP
Drunk I have been. And drunk I was that night. To Laura Phelan: 1880-1906. Leon Stokesbury. MAYP
Drunk in the Furnace, The. W. S. Merwin. CAPP; LiTM; MAT; MP; NePoEA-2; NoAM; NoP; TwCP
Drunk Last Night. *Unknown.* FSW
Drunk Last Night with Friends, I Go to Work Anyway. Philip Dow. NPGG
Drunk Man Looks at the Thistle, A, *sel.* "Hugh MacDiarmid."
"Dae what ye wull ye canna parry." EBEV
Drunk on sour cherries, the harlequin of birds. Cedar Waxwing. William H. Matchett. ELU
Drunkard, The. Bible, *O.T.* Proverbs, XXIII: 29-35. TrJP
Drunkard, The. Philip Levine. NePoEA-2
Drunkard, A. *Unknown.* OxBM
Drunkard and the Pig, The. *Unknown.* OBAL
Drunkard cannot meet a cork, A. Emily Dickinson. InPS
Drunkard to His Bottle, A. Joseph Sheridan Le Fanu. OnYI
Drunkards, The. Malcolm Lowry. NYBP
Drunkards, The ("The drunkards are rolling in slowly"). Jalal ed-Din Rumi, *ad. fr. Persian by* Robert Bly. NU
Drunkard's Doom, The. *Unknown.* AS, *with music*; FSW
Drunken Boat, The. Arthur Rimbaud, *tr. fr. French by* Stephan Stepanchev. NAWM-2; SyP
Drunken Dee, The. Syd Scroggie. PoSH
Drunken Fisherman, The. Robert Lowell. AmPP; AP; CMoP; CrMA; LiTA; LiTM; MoPo; MoVE; NOBA; OxBA; TwAmPo; VGW
Drunken Lover. Owen Dodson. AmNP
Drunken Man, The. Stephen Orlen. MAYP
Drunken night in my house with a, A. Dream Record: June 8, 1955. Allen Ginsberg. ConAP; NOBA
Drunken Poem. David Helwig. NOBC
Drunken Preacher's Sermon, The. James Reaney. *Fr.* A Suit of Nettles. PeCV
Drunken Rose, The. Amarou, *tr. fr. Sanskrit by* E. Powys Mathers. AWP
Drunken Sailor, The; or, Early in the Morning. *Unknown. See* What Shall We Do with a Drunken Sailor?
Drunken Stones of Prague, The. David Scheinert, *tr. fr. French by* Edouard Roditi. VWA
Drunken Streets. Malka Locker, *tr. fr. Yiddish by* Jeremy Garber. VWA
Drunken sun, The/ totters among the clouds. Orgy (That Is, Vegetable Market, at Sarno). Gina Labriola, *tr. by* Edgar Pauk. WPOW

Drunkenness of Pain, The. Aliza Shenhar, *tr. fr. Hebrew by* Linda Zisquit. VWA
Drunkenness of youth has passed like a fever, The. Inscriptions at the City of Brass. *Unknown, tr. by* E. Powys Mathers. *Fr.* The Thousand and One Nights. AWP
Dry. Samuel Hoffenstein. BXAP
Dry afternoon scraping the rooftops, The. Summer Street. Ana Ilce, *tr. by* Steven White. AMV-81
Dry August and warm. *Unknown.* FaBoUs
Dry Be That Tear. Sheridan. OnYI
Dry brown coughing beneath their feet, The. Beverly Hills, Chicago. Gwendolyn Brooks. VGW
Dry Gapa dingy general store. Western Town. David Wadsworth Cannon, Jr. PoNe
Dry July. Arnold Adoff. CAD
Dry Land Blues. *Unknown.* BluL
Dry-Landers, The, *with music. Unknown.* CoSo
Dry leaves, soldier, dry leaves, dead leaves. The Wars. Conrad Aiken. *Fr.* The Soldier. WaaP
Dry Loaf. Wallace Stevens. CrMA; NOBA; OxBA; PoRA
Dry-Point. Philip Larkin. CMoP; NMP
Dry Salvages, The. T. S. Eliot. *Fr.* Four Quartets. CABA; LiTB; NoP; OxBA; SeCePo
"Lady, whose shrine stands on the promontory," IV. ISi
Dry vine leaves burn in an angle of the wall. The Thousand Things. Christopher Middleton. NePoEA-2
Dry Your Tears, Africa! Bernard Dadié, *tr. fr. French by* Donatus Ibe Nwoga. TTY
Dryad Song. Margaret Fuller. WGRP
Dryad's home was once the tree, A. On Sivori's Violin. Frances Sargent Osgood. AA
Drying-Green, The. Douglas Dunn. BSV
Drynaun, Dhun, The. *Unknown.* GBP
Du Bartas: His Divine Weeks and Works, *sels.* Joshua Sylvester.
Fifth Day of the First Week, The.
"Pretty lark, climbing the welkin clear." PBBP
Seventh Day of the First Week, The.
"There on his knee, behind a box tree shrinking." PBBP
Du bist wie eine Blume. Heine, *tr. fr. German by* Kate Freiligrath Kroeker. *Fr.* Homeward Bound. AWP
Dual Site, The. Michael Hamburger. MP; NePoEA-2; TwCP
Duality. Dannie Abse. NoAM
Duality. Arthur Sherburne Hardy. AA
Duality. Katherine Thayer Hobson. GoYe
Dubious Night, A. Richard Wilbur. CAPP
Dublin. Louis MacNeice. CIP; FaBoPP; OxBI; OxBTC
Dublin Ballad, A: 1916. "Dermot O'Byrne." AnIV; OxBI
Dublin Bay. Ewart Milne. NeIP
Dublin Doggerel. Richard Conniff. DBV
Dublin Made Me. Donagh MacDonagh. AnIV; NeIP; OxBI; OxBTC
Dublin: The Old Squares. Padraic Colum. NePoAm
Dublinesque. Philip Larkin. OxBC
Dubrovnik Poem (Emilio Tolentino). Anthony Rudolf. VWA
"Ducats take, The! I'll sign the bond today." Two Argosies. Wallace Bruce. AA
Duchess of Malfi, The, *sels.* John Webster.
"Farewell Cariola!" *fr.* IV, ii. LO
Hark, Now Everything Is Still, *fr.* IV, ii. ElL; HAP; InPS; LoBV; NoP; QFR; SeCePo; ViBoPo
(Hark.) CH
(Hearke, Now Every Thing Is Still.) OBS
(Shrouding of the Duchess of Malfi, The.) NOBE; OBEV
(Summons to Execution.) FaBoEn
"I am come to make thy tomb," *fr.* IV, ii. ChTr
Madman's Song, The, *fr.* IV, ii. ElL
(Song: "Oh, let us howl some heavy note.") InvP
"What hideous noyse was that?" *fr.* IV, ii. PoEL-2
"Yond's the Cardinall's window: This fortification," *fr.* V, iii. PoEL-2
Duchess of York's Ghost, The. *Unknown.* APAS
Duchess's Lullaby, The. "Lewis Carroll." *See* Speak Roughly to Your Little Boy.
Duck, The. Richard Digance. RHPC
Duck. John Lyle Donaghy. BIrV; OxBI
Duck, The. Edith King. HBVY
Duck, The. Ogden Nash. MoShBr; WhC
Duck. Valerie Worth. NTCP
Duck and a drake, A. Mother Goose. OxNR
Duck, and mallard first, the falconers' only sport, The. Birds in the Fens. Michael Drayton. *Fr.* Polyolbion. ChTr; FM
Duck and the Kangaroo, The. Edward Lear. OxBChV
Duck-chasing. Galway Kinnell. MP; NMP; TwCP; VGW
Duck in Central Park. Frances Higginson Savage. GoYe
Duck is whiter than whey is, The. Quack! Walter de la Mare. TiPo
Duck Pond at Mini's Pasture, a Dozen Years Later, The. Philip Dow. AmPA; NPGG
Duck who had got such a habit of stuffing, A. The Notorious Glutton. Ann Taylor. OxBChV
Ducks. Robert Bly. PV
Ducks. Frederick William Harvey. OnUR
"When God had finished the stars and whirl of coloured suns," *sel.* EBCP
Ducks. Phoebe Hesketh. BoAnP
Ducks, The. Alice Wilkins. TiPo
Duck's-assed and leather-jacketed. The Execrators. David Galler. NMP
Ducks at Dawn. James S. Tippett. SiSoSe; SoPo; TiPo
Duck's [*or* Ducks'] Ditty. Kenneth Grahame. *Fr.* The Wind in the Willows. FaPON; GoJo; MoShBr; NTCP; OxBChV; PDV; PoPle; RHPC; SoPo; SUS; TiPo
Ducks down in the Meadow. William Stafford. NPAW
Ducks in the Millpond, *with music. Unknown.* OuSiCo
Ducks in the mill-pond eating up moss. Don't Grow Weary, Boys. *Unknown.* CoSo
Due Date. Seymour Cain. AMV-80
Due North. Benjamin R. C. Low. EtS; HBMV
Due of the Dead, The. Thackeray. OBWP
Duel, The. Abraham Cowley. AnAnS-2
Duel, The. Eugene Field. BeLS; CenHV; FaBoBe; FaFP; FaPON; FPL; HBV-1; HBVY; MoShBr; OBAL; OBCA; OHFP; OnMSP; PoLF; PoPl; PoRA; RHPC; SoPo; TiPo; TreF
Duel, The. Richard Lovelace. CaPo
Duel, The. Harold Trowbridge Pulsifer. HBMV
Duel, The. *Unknown.* ShM
Duel in the Park. Lisa Grenelle. GoYe
Duel with Verses over a Great Man, *sels. Unknown, tr. fr. Hebrew.* TrJP
"Against the guide of Truth," Epigram V.
"Forgive us, son of Amram, be not wroth," Epigram III.
"Here lies a man, and still no man," Epitaph I.
"Thou fool profane, be silent!" Epigram II.
"Thou Guide to doubt, be silent evermore," Epigram I.
"What thought ye to burn, when ye kindled the pyre," Epigram IV.
Duellist, The, *sel.* Charles Churchill.
"First, The (entitled to the place)." OBSV
Duenna, The, *sels.* Sheridan.
Air: "I ne'er could any lustre [*or* luster] see," *fr.* I, ii. HBV-1; NOEC
"Bumper of good liquor, A," *fr.* II, iii. WhC
"If a daughter you have, she's the plague of your life," *fr.* I, iii. DBV
Song: "Had I a heart for falsehood fram'd," *fr.* I, v. HBV-1; OBEC
Duérmete, Niño Lindo. *Tr. fr. Spanish.* FSW
Duet, A. T. Sturge Moore. OBEV; OBVV
Duet. Leonora Speyer. HBMV
Duet. Tennyson. *Fr.* Becket. GBL
Dufferin, Simcoe, Grey. Margaret Atwood. AMV-81
Duffy's Hotel, *with music. Unknown.* ShS
Dugall Quin. *Unknown.* ESPB (A *and* B *vers.*)
Dug-out, The. Siegfried Sassoon. CH; MoBrPo; MoVE; OHIP; Waap; WaP
Duino Elegies, *sel.* Rainer Maria Rilke, *tr. fr. German by* David Young.
"It's one thing/ to sing the beloved," III. NAWM-2
"Duke" and the "Count," The. Richard Fewell. AMV-81
Duke Is the Lad, The. Thomas Moore. OnYI
(Duke Is the Lad to Frighten a Lass, The.) TW
Duke of [*or* o'] Athole's Nurse, The. *Unknown.* BaBo; ESPB (A *and* B *vers.*); OxBB, *with music*
Duke of Benevento, The. Sir John Henry Moore. OBEC
Duke of Buckingham, The. Dryden. *See* Zimri: The Duke of Buckingham.
Duke of Buckingham, The. Pope. *Fr.* Moral Essays, Epistle III. NOBE; OBEC
(Death of Buckingham, The.) FiP
Duke of Gordon's Daughter, The ("The Duke of Gordon has three daughters"). *Unknown.* ESPB
Duke of Grafton, The. *Unknown.* ChTr; GBP
Duke of Marlborough, The. *Unknown.* OBET
Duke of Parma's Ear. Eli Siegel. ELU
Duke of Plaza-Toro, The. W. S. Gilbert. *Fr.* The Gondoliers. FaPON; FiBHP
Duke of Wellington, The. Byron. *Fr.* Don Juan. DBV
Duke of York's Statue, The. Walter Savage Landor. FaBoEE
Duke William was a wench's son. Song of Duke William. Hilaire Belloc. FaBoNo
Duke's Song, The. Mary Sidney Wroth, Countess of Montgomery. *Fr.* Urania. WPE
Dulce et Decorum? Elinor Jenkins. SUMH
Dulce et Decorum. T. P. Cameron Wilson. HBMV
Dulce et Decorum Est. Wilfred Owen. CABA; CMoP; CoBMV; DL; FaBoTw; FaBV; FF; HeIP; HoPM; InPK; InvP; LiTB; LiTM; MMA;

MoAB; MoBrPo; NIP; NoAM; NoP; OAEL-2; OAEP; OBWP; PPON; PPP; PrIm; TW; UnPo; WaP
Dulce it is, and *decorum,* no doubt, for the country to fall. Arthur Hugh Clough. *Fr.* Amours de Voyage, Canto II, ii. EBVV; OAEP
Dulcimer Maker. Carolyn Forché. SaC
Dule's i' This Bonnet o' Mine, The. Edwin Waugh. HBV-1
Dull and hard the low wind creaks. Suburb. Harold Monro. HBV-1
Dull as I was, to think that a court fly. A Black Patch on Lucasta's Face. Richard Lovelace. AnAnS-2; CaPo; SeCP
"Dull day, A." Wait till Then. Mark Van Doren. SO
Dull day darkens to its close, The. The sheen. Sonnet VII. "Fiona Macleod." SyP
Dull heap, that thus thy head above the rest dost rear. Stonehenge. Michael Drayton. *Fr.* Polyolbion. FaBoPP
Dull Is My Verse. Walter Savage Landor. PoEL-4
Dull masses of dense green. Down the Mississippi. John Gould Fletcher. AmFN; LiTA
Dull people, A. From Colony to Nation. Irving Layton. CABA; NOBC
Dull soul aspire. To the Soul. John Collop. TrGrPo
"Dull sublunary lovers . . . " Nocturne: Lake Huron. Conor Kelly. AMV-80
Dull, Sullen Prisoners. Pope. *See* Most Souls, 'Tis True, but Peep Out Once an Age.
Dull to myself, and almost dead to these. The Bad Season Makes the Poet Sad. Robert Herrick. AnAnS-2; CABA; CaPo; LiTB; OAEP; PrIm; SeCeV
Dull unwashed windows of eyes. A Poem Some People Will Have to Understand. Amiri Baraka. BPo; NOBA
Dulled by the slow glare of the yellow bulb. A Wartime Dawn. David Gascoyne. LiTM; MoVE
Dulnesse. George Herbert. AnAnS-1
Dum Vivimus Vigilamus. Charles Henry Webb. AA
Dum Vivimus, Vivamus. Philip Doddridge. *See* Live While You Live.
Dumain's Rhymes. Shakespeare. *See* On a Day—Alack the Day.
Dumb,/ Bloodied, the severed. A Grafted Tongue. John Montague. BIrV; CIP
Dumb are the trumpets, cymbals. Solomon. Heine, *tr. by* Emma Lazarus. TrJP
Dumb Dick. Leslie A. Fiedler. ErPo
Dumb, Dumb, Dumb. *Unknown.* OnYI
Dumb genius blows. From Another Room. Gregory Corso. NeAP
Dumb Soldier, The. Robert Louis Stevenson. OxBChV
Dumb World, The. W. H. Davies. BoAnP; OxBTC
Dumbarton's Drums. *Unknown.* FSW
Dumbfounding, The. Margaret Avison. NOBC
Dumbo rescue report: the weather was dirty. Time Zones for Forty-four. Donald A. Stauffer. WaP
Dummer the shepherd sacrific'd. Epitaph. Cotton Mather. SCAP
Dump, The. Greg Kuzma. PoA
Dumpy Duck. Lucy Larcom. OBCA
Dun-Colour. Ruth Pitter. FM; MoVE
(Dun-Color.) PoRA
Duna. Marjorie Pickthall. HBV-2
Dunbar. Anne Spencer. BANP; CDC
Duncan and Brady, *with music. Unknown.* OuSiCo
Duncan and his brother was playing pool. Brady. *Unknown.* AS
Duncan, Duncan was a-tendin' the bar. Duncan and Brady. *Unknown.* OuSiCo
Duncan Gray. Burns. BSV; CoMu; ErPo; GoTS; GTBS; GTBS-P; OBEC
(Thrusting of It, The.) UnTE
Duncan Spoke of a Process. Amiri Baraka. CAPP
Dunce, The. Walter de la Mare. ImOP
Dunce Song 6. Mark Van Doren. DuDa
Dunciad, The, *sels.* Pope
Carnations and Butterflies. NOEC
"In vain, in vain—the all-composing hour," *fr.* IV. EBEV; SCV; ViBoPo
(Chaos.) LoBV
(Reign of Chaos, The.) FiP
(Triumph of Dullness [*or* Dulness], The.) NOBE; NOEC; NoP; OBEC
"Mighty Mother and her son who brings, The," *fr.* I. OBSV
"Next bidding all draw near on bended knees," *fr.* IV. OBSV
"Yet, yet a moment, one dim ray of light," IV. OAEL-1; PoEL-3
Young Traveller Is Presented to the Goddess Dulness, A, *fr.* IV. NOEC
Dunciad Minor, *sels.* A. D. Hope.
"Now Muse assist me, aptly to describe," *fr.* Bk. V. BXAP
On Shakespeare Critics, *fr.* Bk. V. OxBC
Duncton Hill. Hilaire Belloc. GoBC
Dunderbeck. *Unknown.* FSW
Dundonnel Mountains. Andrew Young. PoSH
Dunes are graying that were blackest. Aubade: The Desert. Frederick Bock. PoA
Dunlavin Green. *Unknown.* FaBoBa
Dunmow Flitch of Bacon, The. *Unknown.* OBET
Dunna thee tell me it's his'n, mother. Whether or Not. D. H. Lawrence. MoBrPo
Duns Scotus. Thomas Merton. CoPo
Duns Scotus's Oxford. Gerard Manley Hopkins. EBEV; EyDe; FaBoPP; GTBS-P; NoAM; OBMV; PoEL-5; VLP
Duo. Olive Tilford Dargan. HBMV
Duomo, Milan. Raymond Henri. View of the Cathedral, II. EyDe
Duplicity of Women, The. John Lydgate. MeEL
Dupree. *Unknown.* OuSiCo, *with music;* ViBoFo (A *and* B *vers.*)
(Betty and Dupree, *ad. by* Brownie McGhee.) FSW
Durable Bon Mot, The. Keith Preston. HBMV
Duraluminum dove dives, The. Summary of the Distance between the Bomber and the Objective. Walter Benton. WaP
Durand of Blonden. Ludwig Uhland, *tr. fr. German by* James Clarence Mangan. AWP
Durant Jail, The, *with music* ("The Durant jail beats no jail at all"). *Unknown.* CoSo
Durban, Birmingham. Question and Answer. Langston Hughes. BPo
Dürer; Innsbruck, 1495. "Ern Malley." CBAP
Dürer would have seen a reason for living. The Steeple-Jack. Marianne Moore. *Fr.* Part of a Novel, Part of a Poem, Part of a Play. AP; BoWoP; CMoP; CoBMV; CrMA; FaBoMo; HAP; MoPo; NoAM; NOBA; NoP; OxBA; PBWP; SBG; TwAmPo; WeW; WPE
Dürer's Piece of Turf. Norbert Krapf. PoDr
Durham Field. *Unknown.* ESPB
Durham Lock-out, The. *Unknown.* CoMu
Durham Old Women. *Unknown.* GBP
Duriesdyke. Swinburne. OxBB
During a Chorale by César Franck. Witter Bynner. HBMV
During December's Death. Delmore Schwartz. NYBP
During His Courtship. Charles Wesley. NOCV
During one period I remember. Eveningsong 2. Ramona Wilson. VoR
During the Depression my grandmother. One Foot in the Door. Anne Elder. CBAP
During the dream. Fidelity. Jerry Kass. AMV-80
During the Eichmann Trial, *sels.* Denise Levertov.
Crystal Night. NMP
Peachtree, The. CAPP
During the Great Debates, he tried a joke. Campaign Promise. Henry Taylor. TW
During the holidays. Holidays. Eva Mylonas, *tr. by* Kimon Friar. BoWoP
During the night. Viewing Russian Peasants from a Leningrad-bound Train. Roger Gaess. LTB
During the Pageant at Medicine Lodge. Charles G. Ballard. VoR
During the plague I came into my own. Tarantula or the Dance of Death. Anthony Hecht. CoAP
During the season of cut organs we. Initiation. Jayne Cortez. PoBA
During the strike, the ponies were brought up. The Ponies. W. W. Gibson. PH
During the War. William Kloefkorn. *Fr.* Loony. GP
During the winter she began. Division. John Ratti. NYBP
During Wind and Rain. Thomas Hardy. CMoP; ELP; GTBS-P; HAP; InPK; NIP; OAEL-2; OxBTC; PoPle; PPP; QFR; SeCeV; TEP
Durst thou again say life and soul has lifted. Thomas Lovell Beddoes. *Fr.* Death's Jest Book; or, The Fool's Tragedy. LO
Dusk. Ken Belford. NeAC
Dusk. Angelina Weld Grimké. CDC
Dusk. DuBose Heyward. HBMV
Dusk. Abraham Z. Lopez-Penha, *tr. fr. Spanish by* Thomas Walsh. TrJP
Dusk. Archibald MacLeish. HBMV
Dusk. Gabriela Mistral, *tr. fr. Spanish by* David Garrison. BoWoP
Dusk. Marcia Southwick. MAYP
Dusk/ Above the/ water. Swan and Shadow. John Hollander. NoP; PoA
Dusk/ no dawns, and silver linings. No Dawns. Julianne Perry. PoBA
Dusk Chant. Judith Mountain Leaf Volborth. TWSS
Dusk grew on the window. Taking the Train Home. William Matthews. GeTw
Dusk in the Domain. Dorothea MacKellar. PoAu-1
Dusk in Winter. W. S. Merwin. NaP
Dusk made a thrust at my heart. The Star. Grace Hazard Conkling. HBMV
Dusk of Horses, The. James Dickey. AP; LiTM; NYBP
Dusk of the Revolutionaries. John Haines. NPAW
Dusk Song. William H. A. Moore. BANP
Dusk-haired and gold-robed o'er the golden wine. For "The Wine of Circe" by Edward Burne-Jones. Dante Gabriel Rossetti. VLP
Duskier than the clouds that lie. Willy to Jinny. Joseph Skipsey. VLP
Dusky night rides down the sky, The. A-Hunting We Will Go [*or* Hunting Song]. Henry Fielding. *Fr.* Don Quixote in England, II. HBV-1; ViBoPo

Dusky owl in velvet moth-like flight, A. Night on the Shore. Marie Carmichael Stopes. SUMH
Dust. "Æ." HBMV; WGRP
Dust. Rupert Brooke. HBV-1; MoBrPo; OBVV; OxBTC
Dust. Waring Cuney. CDC
Dust, The. Gertrude Hall. AA
Dust, The. Lizette Woodworth Reese. HBMV
Dust. Sydney King Russell. ShM
Dust. André Spire, *tr. fr. French by* Jethro Bithell. TrJP
Dust. Kathleen Spivack. BoWoP
Dust. Randolph Stow. CBAP; PoAu-2
Dust always blowing about the town. A Peck of Gold. Robert Frost. BPAW; PDV; SO
Dust and clay. Ascension-Hymn. Henry Vaughan. AnAnS-1; SeCV-1; TrCP
Dust are our frames; and, gilded dust, our pride. Aylmer's Field. Tennyson. VLP
Dust as we are, the immortal spirit grows. Wordsworth. *Fr.* The Prelude, I. SCV
Dust blows up and down, The. The Dust. Lizette Woodworth Reese. HBMV
Dust Bowl. Robert A. Davis. IDB
Dust Bowl. Langston Hughes. PoA
Dust Dethroned, The. George Sterling. *Fr.* Three Sonnets on Oblivion. HBV-2
Dust hangs thick upon the trail, The. The Cowboy and His Love. John Milton Hagen. CoSo
Dust Hath Closed Helen's Eye. Thomas Nashe. *See* Adieu, Farewell Earth's Bliss.
Dust of Snow. Robert Frost. CMoP; MoShBr; OxBA; PAI; PDV; PrIm; RHPC; SoSe; TAP; TiPo; UnPo; WeW
Dust of the Overland Trail, The. James Barton Adams. PoOW
Dust of Timas, The. Sappho, *tr. fr. Greek by* E. A. Robinson. AWP
Dust on my hair and face. Irrigation. Susan Tichy. MAYP
Dust on Spring Street. Louis Grudin. NoP
Dust thou art, but dust carefully. Ralph Hodgson. *Fr.* Flying Scrolls. FaBoTw
Dust to Dust. Thomas Hood. *See* Epigram: "After such years of dissension and strife."
Dust to Dust. Walter de la Mare. TrPWD
Dust Will Settle, The. Luci Tapahonso. STE
Duster, dust away, my friend. Dust. André Spire, *tr. by* Jethro Bithell. TrJP
Dusting. Rita Dove. MAYP
Dusting of the Books, The. Dorothy Hughes. GoYe
Dustman, The. Frederic Edward Weatherly. HBV-1
Dusty Answer, A. George Meredith. *See* Modern Love: "Thus piteously Love closed what he begot."
Dusty black beetle, A. Robert Sund. BoAnP
Dusty light falls through windows. Cities behind Glass. Linda Hogan. STE
Dutch, The. George Canning. DBV
Dutch April. Daniel Halpern. GrPl
Dutch in the Medway, The. Andrew Marvell. *Fr.* Last Instructions to a Painter. OBS
Dutch Lover, The, *sels.* Aphra Behn.
  Song: "Ah false Amyntas, can that hour." WPE
  Willing Mistress, The. SBG; UnTE; ViBoPo
  (Amyntas Led Me to a Grove.) ErPo
Dutch Lullaby, A. Eugene Field. *See* Wynken, Blynken, and Nod.
Dutch Picture, A. Longfellow. EtS; HBVY; MoShBr
  (Simon Danz.) OBVV
Dutch Proverb, A. Matthew Prior. FaBoEE; NOEC; POL
Dutch Seacoast. Kenneth Slessor. *Fr.* The Atlas. PoAu-2
Dutchess of Monmouth's Lamentation for the Loss of Her Duke, The. *Unknown.* CoMu; FaBoBa
Dutchesse of Malfy, The. John Webster. *See* Duchess of Malfi, The.
Dutchman, The. Don Welch. WOLT
Duties of Man, The. Bible, *N.T.* Romans, XII: 3-21 TreF
Duty. Arthur Hugh Clough. EBVV
Duty. Emerson. *Fr.* Voluntaries, III. FaFP; GN; HBV-1; TreF; YaD
  (So Nigh Is Grandeur.) HBVY; TreFS
  ("So nigh is grandeur to our dust.") TRV
Duty. Ellen S. Hooper. BLPA; TreFS
  (Beauty and Duty.) HBV-2
Duty. Edwin Markham. HBMV; HBVY
Duty is a path of pain and peril. Motherhood. William L. Stidger. PGD
Duty lies in your desk. Hating Your Life. John N. Morris. CABA
Duty—that's to say, complying. Duty. Arthur Hugh Clough. EBVV
Duty to Death, LD. Dick Roberts. WaP
Dvonya. Louis Simpson. NNaP; NOBA
Dwainie. James Whitcomb Riley. *Fr.* The Flying Islands of the Night. AA
Dwarf, The. Gerald Locklin. DFT; GP
Dwarf barefooted, chanting, The. The Peasants. Alun Lewis. LiTM; PPP
Dwarf of Disintegration. Oscar Williams. LiTM; MoPo; NePA; PoCH
Dwarf pines; the wild plum on the wind-grassed shore. Colloquy with a King-Crab. John Peale Bishop. LiTA; MoPo
Dwarfed limb, A. The Copperhead. David Bottoms. AMV-81; MAYP
Dwell, awful Silence, on the shady hills. Pan Piping. Plato, *tr. by* Thomas Stanley. FaBoEE
Dwell with Me, Lovely Images. Theodore Maynard. GoBC
Dwelling, The. Moshe Dor, *tr. fr. Hebrew by* Dennis Johnson. VWA
Dwelling-Place, The. Henry Vaughan. MeLP; OBS; OxBoCh; TrPWD; WGRP
Dwindling Forest of Arden, The. Michael Drayton. *Fr.* Polyolbion, Thirteenth Song. FaBoPP
D'ye [*or* Do ye] ken John Peel with his coat so gay [*or* gray]? John Peel. John Woodcock Greaves. CH; FSW; OxBoLi
D'ye ken the big village of Balmaquhapple. The Village of Balmaquhapple. James Hogg. BSV; FaBoCo; FaBoPP
Dyer, The. *Unknown.* ChTr
  ("As I went by a dyer's door.") OxNR
Dying. A. Alvarez. VWA
Dying. Emily Dickinson. *See* I heard a fly buzz—when I died.
Dying. Jessie Holt. PGD
Dying. Robert Pinsky. AMV-81; MAYP
Dying Airman, The. *Unknown.* FaBoNo; FaFP; OxBoLi
  (Handsome Young Airman, The.) AS, *with music*
Dying: An Introduction. L. E. Sissman. NYBP
Dying Californian, The. *Unknown.* AmFP; BPAW; TrAS, *with music*
Dying Child, The. John Clare. EnRP; NCEP; TrGrPo
Dying Child's Request, The. Hannah F. Gould. OBCA
Dying Christian to His Soul, The. Pope, *par. fr. the Latin of* Emperor Hadrian. AWP; GoBC; HBV-2; OBEV; TreF
  (Vital Spark of Heavenly Flame.) BLPL; LiTB
Dying Cowboy, The ("As I rode out by Tom Sherman's bar-room"). *Unknown.* *See* Cowboy's Lament, The.
Dying Cowboy, The ("O [*or* Oh] bury me not on the lone prairie"). *Unknown.* *See* Bury Me Not on the Lone Prairie.
Dying Cowboy of Rim Rock Ranch, The, *with music.* *Unknown.* CoSo
Dying day pinches the tot. Daily News. Tom Clark. EAS
Dying Desperado, The. *Unknown.* CoSo
Dying Father's Farewell, The. *Unknown.* *See* Time Is Swiftly Rolling On, The.
Dying figure against the sky, A. Calvary. Mary Hallet. PGD
Dying firelight slides along the quirt, A. The End of the Weekend. Anthony Hecht. ConAP; FaBoMo; HAP; LiTM; NePoEA-2; WeW
Dying Fisherman's Song, The. *Unknown.* TreFT
Dying for love is out of fashion. Return to Astolat. Gail White. AMV-81
Dying Garden, The. Howard Nemerov. Psk
Dying Gaul, The. Desmond O'Grady. BIrV
Dying Girl, The. Richard D'Alton Williams. OnYI
Dying Gladiator, The. Byron. *Fr.* Childe Harold's Pilgrimage, IV. NOBE
Dying Hobo, The. *Unknown.* AmFP
Dying Hogger, The, *with music.* *Unknown.* AS
Dying Hymn. Alice Cary. HBV-2
Dying Indian, The. Joseph Warton. NOEC
Dying Lover, The. Richard Henry Stoddard. HBV-1
Dying Man in His Garden, The. George Sewell. GTBS; GTBS-P
Dying Mine Brakeman, The. Orville Jenks. AmFP
Dying Patriot, The. James Elroy Flecker. HBMV; ViBoPo
Dying Prostitute, The; an Elegy. Thomas Holcroft. NOEC
Dying Ranger, The, *with music.* *Unknown.* CoSo
  (Dying Soldier, The, *diff. vers., with music.*) ShS
Dying Reservist, The. Maurice Baring. HBV-2
Dying Sergeant, The. *Unknown.* AmFP
Dying Soldier, The. *Unknown.* *See* Dying Ranger, The.
Dying Speech of an Old Philosopher. Walter Savage Landor. *See* On His Seventy-fifth Birthday.
Dying Stockman, The. *Unknown.* PoAu-1; ViBoFo
Dying sun, shine warm a little longer! Lament for Pasiphae. Robert Graves. FaBoTw
Dying sun, The. Prison Graveyard. Etheridge Knight. LFAC
Dying Swan, The. T. Sturge Moore. OBMV; SeCePo; SyP
Dying Swan, The. Tennyson. PBBP; WiR
Dying Swan, The. *Unknown.* ChTr
Dying Thief. Itzik Manger, *tr. fr. Yiddish by* Stephen Garrin. VWA
Dying tiger, A—moaned for drink. Emily Dickinson. PeD
Dying! To be afraid of thee. Emily Dickinson. MoPo
Dying under a Fall of Stars. Mark Elliott Shapiro. VWA
Dying Viper, A. "Michael Field." FM
Dying Wife to Her Husband, A. Moses ibn Ezra, *tr. fr. Hebrew.* TrJP
Dying Words of Stonewall Jackson, The. Sidney Lanier. PAH
Dyke-Builder, The. Henry Treece. LiTB; WaP

Dykes, The. Kipling. OBWP; VLP
Dykes in the Garden. Sharon Barba. PeHV
Dylan Thomas. T. O. Maglow. InPK
Dylan, Who Is Dead. Samuel Allen. PoBA
Dynamic Tension. Steve Sanfield. SOTS
Dynamite Song. *Unknown.* AmFP
Dynasts, The, *sels.* Thomas Hardy.
After Jena, *fr.* Pt. II, Act I, sc. vii. WaaP
Albuera, *fr.* Pt. II, Act VI, sc. iv. WaaP
Chorus: "Yea, the coneys are scared the thud of hoofs," *fr.* Pt. III, Act VI, sc. viii. LoBV
(Before Waterloo.) MoAB; WaaP
(Chorus of the Years.) CMoP
(Field of Waterloo, The, *shorter sel.*) FaBoCh
"Eyelids of eve fall together at last, The," *fr.* Pt. III, Act VI, sc. viii. OAEL-2
Field of Talavera, The, *fr.* Pt. II, Act IV, sc. iv. CMoP
Men Who March Away, *fr.* Pt. I, Act I, sc. i. CH
Night of Trafalgar, The, *fr.* Pt. I, Act V, sc. vii. ChTr; FaBoCh; MoBrPo; MOS; OBMV
(Boatman's Song, The.) WaaP
(Trafalgar.) CH
"When we lay where Budmouth Beach is," *fr.* Pt. III, Act II, sc. i. LO
(Budmouth Dears.) CH; MoVE; PoPle
Dysynni Valley, The. Daniel Hoffman. CoPo
Dyvers dothe use as I have hard and kno. *See* Divers doth use as I have heard and know.
Dyvers thy death doo dyverslye bemone. *See* Divers Thy Death.

E

E. B. B. James Thomson. HBV-2
(One-Hoss Shay, The.) TreF
E is the Escalator. Phyllis McGinley. *Fr.* All Around the Town. TiPo
E. Jarvis-Thribb (17) and Keith's Mum. On the Tercentenary of Milton's Death. Gavin Ewart. OxBC
E.P.A. Pancho Aguila. LFAC
E. P. Ode pour l'Election de Son Sepulchre. Ezra Pound. Hugh Selwyn Mauberley, I. AmPP; AP; CABA; CMoP; CoBMV; CrMA; FaBoEn; HAP; InPS; LiTA; LiTM; MasP; MoAmPo; MoPo; MoVE; NePA; NoAM; NOBA; NoP; PP; SeCeV; TAP; VGW
("For three years, out of key with his time.") OxBA; UnPo
(Pour l'Election de Son Sepulchre, I-V.) FaBoMo
E Questo il Nido in Che la Mia Fenice? A. D. Hope. OxBC
E Tenebris. Oscar Wilde. BrPo; CABA; MoBrPo; TrPWD
"Come down, O Christ, and help me! reach thy hand, *sel.*" TreFT
È, the Feasting Florentines. Daniel Hoffman. VGW
E to the X dy! dx! Engineer's Yell (University of California). *Unknown.* WhC
E Uni Que A The Hi A Tho, Father. Roberta Hill. VoR
'E was sittin' on a door-step. The Road to Vagabondia. Dana Burnet. PoLF
'E was warned agin 'er. The Sergeant's Weddin'. Kipling. OxBTC
Each a Part of All. Augustus Wright Bamberger. WBLP
Each and All. Emerson. AA; AmPP; AP; AWP; BLPL; HBV-2; NePA; NOBA; OHFP; OxBA; TAP; WGRP
Each atom is an idea. Atoms are the floating part of all material. The Life of Particles. Michael Benedikt. SUW
Each beast can choose his fere according to his mind. Of a Lady That Refused to Dance with Him. Earl of Surrey. SiPS
Each beat of the drum's a round drop of rain. Santo Domingo Corn Dance. R. P. Dickey. TAT
Each Bird Walking. Tess Gallagher. MAYP; SV
Each body has its art, its precious prescribed. "Still Do I Keep My Look, My Identity. . ." Gwendolyn Brooks. PoA
Each care-worn face is but a book. The Strangers. Jones Very. OxBA
Each creation. Afterbirth. Beryle Williams. PoDr
Each dawn is clear. Gary Snyder. Myths and Texts: Logging, VIII. NaP; NMP
Each Day. David Ignatow. NNaP
Each day/ ungently leads. Separation. P. Wolny. DFF
Each day, a certain hour. In Disguise. Joseph Rolnik, *tr. by* Keith Bosley. VWA
Each day brings its toad, each night its dragon. Jerome. Randall Jarrell. PPP
Each day, dear love, my road leads far. The Homing Heart. Daniel Henderson. HBMV
Each day I live, each day the sea of light. Poem against the Rich. Robert Bly. CAPP; NMP; NoAM; NOBA
Each day I lure the hummingbirds. The Ritual. Joy Gwillim. AMV-80
Each day I open the cupboard. The Routine. Paul Blackburn. ELU
Each day I walk with wonder. A Prayer. Clinton Scollard. TrPWD
Each day into the upper air. Election Reflection. M. Keel Jones. PV
Each day is an iceberg. Nightdream. Charles Wright. LCAP
Each Day Is Anxious. "Anna Akhmatova," *tr. fr. Russian by* Judith Hemschemeyer *and* Anne Wilkinson. AMV-81
Each day the earth turns, each day. As for Me, I Delight in the Everyday Way. Joseph Stroud. NPGG
Each day the string that joined their natural selves. The Cat and the Bird. Marvin Solomon. NePoAm-2
Each day the terror wagon. War. Richard Shelton. PPJ
Each day the tide withdraws; chills us; pastes. Wreaths. Geoffrey Hill. PoA
Each day to her a miracle. Mother. *Unknown.* PGD
Each day was like another. Ballad of the Hidden Dragon. *Unknown, tr. fr. Chinese.* WTO
Each day we settle for a little less. Less Is More. Vern Rutsala. AMV-80
Each day, when the glow of sunset. Are the Children at Home? Margaret E. Sangster. HBV-1
Each dusk I saw, while those I loved the most. The Owl. V. Sackville-West. SBG
Each eve earth falleth down the dark. The Day of Days. William Morris. VLP
Each face in the street is a slice of bread. Bread. W. S. Merwin. EAS
Each face its own phantom. Cartagena de Indias. Earle Birney. MoCV
Each Found Himself at the End Of. . . Ebbe Borregaard. NeAP
Each gesture. A Reason. Robert Creeley. NaP
Each golden note of music greets. Moonlight Song of the Mocking-Bird. William Hamilton Hayne. AA
Each hath his drug for sorrow. To Each His Own. Margaret Root Garvin. HBV-2
Each house had its ghost. Sigmund Freud. Howard Nemerov. PoA
Each, in himself, his hour to be and cease. Credo. Arthur Symons. OBVV
Each in His Own Tongue. William Herbert Carruth. BLPA; HBV-2; OHFP; TRV; WBLP; WGRP
Each inmost peece in me is thine. Bible, *O.T., paraphrased by* Countess of Pembroke. *Fr.* Psalms, CXXXIX. OBVE
Each instant of his life a task, he never rests. The Poet. James Kirkup. PP
Each is beautiful. Tell Our Daughters. Besmilr Brigham. IHMS
Each known mile comes late. The Train Runs Late to Harlem. Conrad Kent Rivers. IDB; PoBA
Each lover's longing leads him naturally. To Dante Alighieri: He Interprets Dante's Dream. Cino da Pistoia, *tr. by* Dante Gabriel Rossetti. AWP
Each man has/ his own way. The End Bit. Jim Burns. FF
Each man me telleth I change most my devise. Sonnet. Sir Thomas Wyatt. SiPS
Each man to his forced march; this is mine. Hitchhiker. Jack Marshall. NYBP
Each moment. Wind and Impulse. Duane Big Eagle. STE
Each moment of the long-liv'd day. Catullus, *tr. fr. Latin by* Tom Brown. OBVE
Each Morning. Amiri Baraka. *Fr.* Hymn for Lanie Poo. IDB; NNP; PoBA
Each morning I lift my blind to stare. Urban Roses. Ted Isaac. PoPl
Each morning the birds awake me. Morning Vigil. Phillip William George. VoR
Each morning they bring me the condemned man's brekker. Analogy. Brian Higgins. FaBoTw
Each new American. Jean Toomer. *Fr.* The Blue Meridian. BALP
Each New Hour's Passage Is the Acolyte. Lord Alfred Douglas. *Fr.* The City of the Soul. WHA
Each night we hear the sound. Sounds. Paul David Ashley. LFAC
Each object by a few short years how changed! A Visit to the Author's Paternal Seat. Richard Polwhele. *Fr.* The Influence of Local Attachment. NOEC
Each of them must have terrified. In Memory of the Utah Stars. William Matthews. GeTw; MAYP; NPAW; Psk
Each of us is like Balboa: once in all our lives do we. Rare Moments. Charles Henry Phelps. AA
Each of us like you. Adonis. Hilda Doolittle ("H. D."). AP; AWP; LiTA; PoPl
Each of us pursues his trade. The Scholar and the Cat. *Unknown, tr. by* Frank O'Connor. KiLC
Each of us waking to the window's light. Exile. Donald Hall. NePA
Each one shall sit at table with his own cup and spoon. A Practical Program for Monks. Thomas Merton. CoPo
Each other we meet but live grief rises early. Definition of My Brother. W. S. Graham. NeBP
Each pale Christ stirring underground. Words for a Resurrection. Leo Kennedy. OBCV; PeCV

Each person lies in their bed, restless. Tonight Everyone in the World Is Dreaming the Same Dream. Susan Litwack. VWA
Each poet with a different talent writes. Earl of Roscommon. *Fr.* An Essay on Translated Verse. FaBoUs
Each prisoner is so sad in the glare. The Line-up. Joan Swift. FiCP
Each return is a blessing. Gnostology. Sam Hamill. AMV-81
Each Saturday, our father downtown to work. Arrowhead Christian Center and No-Smoking Luncheonette. Janet Sylvester. MAYP
Each soldier as he passes looks at their breasts. Namkwin Pul. Bernard Gutteridge. WaP
Each soul should go to its own college. The Learning Soul. Reed Whittemore. GLGT
Each spring there was the well to be cleaned. Cleaning the Well. Paul Ruffin. Str
Each storm-soaked flower has a beautiful eye. Rain. Vachel Lindsay. CMoP
Each subtlety hard for the pedant to solve. Coming Across. Mehri, *tr. by* Deirdre Lashgari. WPOW
Each summer, the alien evangelist comes. The Evangelist. Bennie Lee Sinclair. TAT
Each, the issue of a passioned kiss. On a Row of Nuns in a Cemetery. R. G. Howarth. ELU
Each time, greenbones, you pressed the neat trigger. Boy at Target Practice; a Contemplation. W. R. Moses. NYBP
Each time his will abdicated. Possession. Lynne Lawner. ErPo
Each time I return to this place. The Marsh. Marcia Southwick. MAYP
Each time we lose grief, friend, we are free from joy & cross into eternity. Goodbye "Hello." Philip Dow. NPGG
Each to Each. Melville Cane. GoYe
Each way the turn. The Turn. Robert Creeley. LCAP
Each with each has borne in patience. To Edom. Heine. TrJP
Each year for a short season. Folk Wisdom. Thomas Kinsella. TwCP
Each year, the court expands. The Old Pro's Lament. Paul Petrie. LiSp; TAP
Eachie, peachie, pearie, plum. *Unknown.* GBP
Eadie, *with music. Unknown.* OuSiCo
Eadwacer. *Unknown, tr. fr. Anglo-Saxon.* PBWP, *tr. by* Kemp Malone; WPE
(Wulf and Eadwacer.) BoWoP, *tr. by* Willis Barnstone *and* Elene Kolb; CIP, *ad. by* Richard Ryan; TrGrPo
Eager he look'd. Another train of years. One Centred System. Joel Barlow. *Fr.* The Columbiad, X. AmPP; AP
Eager note on my door said, "Call me," The. Poem. Frank O'Hara. EAS; NoAM; NOBA
Eager Spring. Gordon Bottomley. MoBrPo
Eager to breathe out. Mocking Song against Qaqortingneq. Piuvkaq, *tr. fr. Eskimo.* WTO
Eagerly/ Like a woman hurrying to her lover. Four Glimpses of Night. Frank Marshall Davis. AmNP; NoP; PoBA; PoNe
Eagle, The. Richard Blessing. AMV-80
Eagle. Tom Bowker. PoSH
Eagle, The. "Fiona Macleod." *Fr.* Transcripts from Nature. FM
Eagle. Robin Skelton. NOBC
Eagle, The. Tennyson. CABA; CH; FaBoCh; FaPON; FF; FiP; FM; GN; GoJo; GTBS-P; HBV-1; HeIP; InPK; NoP; NTCP; OAEL-2; OAEP; PAI; PB; PBBP; PDV; PoPle; PPoe; PrIM; RHPC; SeCePo; SeCeV; SUS; SyP; TreFT; TrGrPo; UnPo; WiR
Eagle, The. Andrew Young. ELU; PoSH
Eagle and the Beetle, The. La Fontaine, *tr. fr. French by* Elizur Wright. OBVE
Eagle and the Mole, The. Elinor Wylie. AWP; BoWoP; HBMV; LiTA; LiTM; MoAB; MoAmPo; TreFT; UnPo; ViBoPo; WHA
Eagle and Vulture, The. Thomas Buchanan Read. PAH
Eagle Converses with Chaucer, The. Chaucer. *Fr.* The House of Fame. OxBM
Eagle, did ye see him fall, The? The Eagle's Fall. Charles Goodrich Whiting. AA
Eagle-Feather Fan, The. N. Scott Momaday. CDW; STE
Eagle for an Emperor. Falconry. Anne Wilkinson. MoCV; OBCV
Eagle into swayback Ganymede. L'Aigle a Deux Jambes. Turner Cassity. GP
Eagle is my power, The. The Eagle-Feather Fan. N. Scott Momaday. CDW; STE
Eagle of Corinth, The. Henry Howard Brownell. PAH
Eagle of Pengwern. *Unknown, tr. fr. Welsh by* Gwyn Williams. PBWP
Eagle of the armies of the West, The. The Flight of the War-Eagle. Obadiah Cyrus Auringer. AA
Eagle of the Blue, The. Herman Melville. AA
Eagle Plain. Robert Francis. AmFN
Eagle so caught in some bursting cloud, An. Shelley. *Fr.* Prometheus Unbound. PBBP
Eagle soars in the summit of heaven, The. T. S. Eliot. *Fr.* The Rock. OBMV
Eagle Song. Gordon Bottomley. *Fr.* Suilven and the Eagle. MoBrPo
Eagle Sonnets, *sels.* Clement Wood. HBMV
"Flower of the dust am I: for dust will flower," VII.
"I am a tongue for beauty, Not a day," XIX.
"I have been sure of three things all my life," III.
"O bitter moon, O cold and bitter moon," IX.
"We are the singing shadows beauty casts," XX.
"When down the windy vistas of the years," XI.
Eagle Squadron. Vern Rutsala. AMV-80
Eagle, stooping from yon snow-blown peaks, The. Inscription. Whittier. GOA
Eagle That Is Forgotten, The. Vachel Lindsay. AWP; CMoP; HBV-2; LiTA; MoAB; MoAmPo; NePA; NOBA; OxBA; TwAmPo; ViBoPo; WHA
Eagle Valor, Chicken Mind. Robinson Jeffers. ELU; LiTA; OxBA; WaP
Eagle! why soarest thou above that tomb? Spirit of Plato [*or* Plato's Tomb]. *Unknown, tr. by* Shelley. AWP; FaBoCh; OBVE
Eagles, The. Jones Very. TAP
Eagles. Elizabeth Woody. STE
Eagles and Isles. W. W. Gibson. PoSH
Eagle's Fall, The. Charles Goodrich Whiting. AA
Eagles gather on the place of death, The. The Eagles. Jones Very. TAP
Eagles have practically left America, The. Inability to Depict an Eagle. Richard Eberhart. GOA
Eagle's nest on the head of an old redwood, An. The Beaks of Eagles. Robinson Jeffers. NOBA
Eagles on a Half. *Unknown.* BluL
Eagles over the Lambing Paddock. Ernest G. Moll. PoAu-2
Eagle's shadow runs across the plain, The. Zebra. "Isak Dinesen." GoJo; RFM
Eagle's Song, The. Mary Austin. GOA
Eagle's Song, The. Richard Mansfield. HBV-2; HBVY; PAH
Eagles, that wheel above our crests. The Cedars of Lebanon. Alphonse Marie Louis de Lamartine, *tr. by* Toru Dutt. AWP
Eaper Weaper. *Unknown.* DBV; FaBoNo; OxBoLi
Ear Is Not Deaf. Irene Dayton. GoYe
Ear-Maker and the Mould-Mender, The. La Fontaine. UnTE
Ear the answer, The. The Hill of Intrusion. W. S. Graham. NePoEA
Ear to the earth. Figure and Ground. Elton Glaser. AMV-80
Earl Bothwell. *Unknown.* ESPB
Earl Brand. *Unknown. See* Douglas Tragedy, The.
Earl Crawford. *Unknown.* BaBo; ESPB
Earl March look'd on his dying child. The Maid of Neidpath [*or* Song]. Thomas Campbell. GoTS; GTBS; GTBS-P; HBV-1
Earl Mar's Daughter. *Unknown.* GN; HBV-2
(Earl of Mar's Daughter, The.) BaBo; CH; ESPB
Earl Mertoun's Song. Robert Browning. *Fr.* The Blot in the 'Scutcheon. HBV-1; OBEV; PoPle
("There's a woman like a dew-drop, she's so purer than the purest.") UnTE
Earl o' Quarterdeck, The. George Macdonald. BeLS; EtS
Earl of Aboyne, The. *Unknown.* BaBo; ESPB
Earl of Errol, The. *Unknown.* ESPB
Earl of Mar's Daughter, The. *Unknown. See* Earl Mar's Daughter.
Earl of Shaftesbury, The. Dryden. *See* Achitophel: The Earl of Shaftesbury.
Earl of Surrey to Geraldine, The. Michael Drayton. OBSC
Earl of Westmoreland, The. *Unknown.* ESPB
Earl of Wigton had three daughters, The. Richie Story. *Unknown.* BaBo; ESPB
Earl Percie of Northumberland. Chevy Chase. *Unknown.* EnSB
Earl Richard had but ae daughter. The Kitchie-Boy. *Unknown.* BaBo
Earl Rothes. *Unknown.* BaBo; ESPB
Earl stood on two legs when he had one to spare. Cash Only, No Refund, No Return. Daniel Mark Epstein. MAYP
Earle Douglasse for this day doth with the Percies stand, The. Michael Drayton. *Fr.* Polyolbion. OBS
Earlier in the evening the moon. The Moon. Robert Creeley. VGW
Earliest Christian Hymn. Clement of Alexandria, *tr. fr. Greek by* Edward H. Plumptre. WGRP
Earliest morning, switching all the tracks. Love Lies Sleeping. Elizabeth Bishop. NYP
Earliest Spring. William Dean Howells. OBEV; OBVV
(In Earliest Spring.) AA; FaBoBe
Earliest Spring. Denise Levertov. LCAP
Earliness at the Cape. Babette Deutsch. FYAP; NePoAm-2; NYBP
Early. Bruce Bennett. WOLT
Early and late the backdrop is for joy. This World. Abbie Huston Evans. NePoAm
Early April. Robert Frost. YeAr

Early Bacon. Archibald Stodart-Walker. *Fr.* The Moxford Book of English Verse. CenHV
Early before the day doth spring. Of Astraea. Sir John Davies. *Fr.* Hymns to Astraea. TrGrPo
Early bird got up and whet his beak, The. A Birthday Ode to Mr. Alfred Austin. Sir Owen Seaman. NOBL
Early blossoms—could a single. Permanence in Change. Goethe, *tr. by* John Frederick Nims. HoPM
Early Bluebird, An. Maurice Thompson. AA
Early Christian, An. Robert Barnabas Brough. OBVV
Early Chronology. Siegfried Sassoon. GLGT
Early Copper. Carl Sandburg. HeIP
Early Death. Hartley Coleridge. HBV-2; OBEV; TreFS
Early dew woos the half-opened flowers, An. Haroun's Favorite Song. *Unknown, tr. by* E. Powys Mathers. *Fr.* The Thousand and One Nights. AWP
Early Discoveries. David Malouf. CBAP
Early Dutch. Jennie M. Palen. GoYe
Early, each morning, Martha Blake. Martha Blake at Fifty-one. Austin Clarke. CIP; IPY
Early, Early Easter Day. Aileen Fisher. SiSoSe
Early, Early in the Spring, *diff. versions. Unknown.* OBET
(Earlye, Earlye, in the Spring.) AmFP
(Early in the Spring.) AmFP
Early Electric! With what radiant hope. The Metropolitan Railway. John Betjeman. EBEV; OxBTC
Early Evening Quarrel. Langston Hughes. UnPo
Early Fall: The Adirondacks. Carolyne Wright. AMV-81
Early Frogs, The. Harry Edward Mills. PeD
Early have a miser's insinuating rub, The. Timers. Flora J. Arnstein. GoYe
Early I rose. Love Song. *Unknown, tr. by* Mary Austin. AWP; LiTA
Early Illinois Winter, An. Alex Kuo. BrSi
Early in spring the little General came. The Little General. Edwin Muir. BSV
Early in the Morning. Louis Simpson. ConAP; LCAP
Early in the morning at seven o'clock. Drill Ye Tarriers, Drill. *At. to* Thomas F. Casey. FSW
Early in the Morning, *with music. Unknown.* AmSS
Early in the Spring. *Unknown. See* Early, Early in the Spring.
Early in the spring when the snow is all gone. A Trip to The Grand Banks. Amos Hanson. AmFP; ShS
Early in the Springtime. *Unknown.* OBET
Early Influences. Mark Akenside. *Fr.* The Pleasures of Imagination. OBEC
Early January. W. S. Merwin. VGW
Early June. R. P. Dickey. TAT
Early Losses; a Requiem. Alice Walker. BlSi
Early Love. Samuel Daniel. *Fr.* Hymen's Triumph. ErPo
Early Lynching. Carl Sandburg. MoAmPo
Early Meadow-Rue. Stanley Plumly. LCAP
Early Moon. Carl Sandburg. BPAW
Early Morn. W. H. Davies. CH
Early Morning, The. Hilaire Belloc. BoNaP; HBMV; HBVY
Early Morning. Morris Bishop. PV
Early Morning. Philip Dow. DFF
Early morning. Ojisan after the Stroke; Three Notes to Himself. Tina Koyama. BrSi
Early Morning at Bargis. Hermann Hagedorn. HBV-1
Early Morning Meadow Song. Charles Dalmon. CH; HBMV
Early Morning of Another World. Tom McKeown. AMV-80
Early morning over Rouen, hopeful. Rouen. May Wedderburn Cannan. OBWP; OxBTC; SUMH
Early morning quick coffee and bran. "Quick Now, Here, Now, Always." William J. Rewak. AMV-81
Early Morning Woman. Joy Harjo. TWSS
Early Mornings, *with music. Unknown, tr. fr. Spanish by* Louis Untermeyer. AS
Early, my God, without delay. Isaac Watts. AmFP
Early News. Anna Maria Pratt. AA
Early Nightingale. John Clare. PBBP
Early on a Monday [*or* Sunday] morning. Kevin Barry. *Unknown.* AS; FSW
Early One Morning. Edward Thomas. MoVE
Early One Morning. *Unknown.* ChTr; FSW, *longer version*
Early one morning. Voodoo on the Un-Assing of Janis Joplin. Carolyn M. Rodgers. JB
Early one morning just about 4 o'clock. Titanic Blues. *Unknown.* BluL
Early one morning, just as the sun was rising. Early One Morning. *Unknown.* ChTr; FSW
Early one morning the bay will be full of pelicans. The Pelicans My Father Sees. Sister Maris Stella. GoBC
Early Pregnancy. Penelope Shuttle. BrRo
Early Purges, The. Seamus Heaney. NCSH
Early Rising. John Godfrey Saxe. BLPL; HBV-2; InMe; PoLF; WhC
Early Saturdays. Rowing. Ed Ochester. Str
Early Spring. Sidney Keyes. MoBrPo
Early Spring. Tennyson. HBV-1; HBVY
Early Summer Sea-Tryst. Frederick T. Macartney. CBAP
Early sun on Beaulieu water. Youth and Age on Beaulieu River, Hants. John Betjeman. ChMP; FaBoTw; MP; TwCP
Early Supper. Barbara Howes. DuDa; GoJo; GrPl; NCSH; PoPl
Early that afternoon, as we keep. The "Portland" Going Out. W. S. Merwin. NYBP
Early this morning. The Strangers. Audrey Alexandra Brown. WHW
Early this morning when you knocked upon my door. Me and the Devil Blues. *Unknown.* BluL
Early thou goest forth, to put to rout. To a "Tenting" Boy. Charles Tennyson Turner. OBNC
Early Thoughts. William Edward Hartpole Lecky. OnYI
Early Thoughts of Marriage. Nathaniel Cotton. OxBChV
(Marriage.) FaBoUs
Early to bed and early to rise. New Proverb. Shirley Brooks. FaBoNo
Early to bed and early to rise. *Unknown.* FaBoBe; FaBoUs
Early to meet you, watching a man. The Last Fish. Barry Spacks. AMV-80
Early Unfinished Sketch. Austin Clarke. ErPo
Early, up without breakfast. Moving. Janet Reed McFatter. GrPl
Early wagons left no sign, The. The Trail into Kansas. W. S. Merwin. GOA
Early Waking. Léonie Adams. LiTM; MoVE
Early Warning. Shirley Marks. QQQ
Early Winter. Weldon Kees. NaP
Earlye, Earlye, in the Spring. *Unknown. See* Early, Early in the Spring.
Earnest, earthless, equal, attuneable. Spelt from Sibyl's Leaves. Gerard Manley Hopkins. BrPo; CMoP; CoBMV; FaBoMo; LiTM; MoPo; OAEL-2; PrIm
Earnest Liberal's Lament, The. Ernest Hemingway. OBSV
(Ernest Liberal's Lament, The.) OBAL
Earnest Suit, An. Sir Thomas Wyatt. *See* And Wilt Thou Leave Me Thus?
Earnest to explore within and all around. Dante, *tr. by* Shelley. *Fr.* Divina Commedia: Purgatorio, XXVIII. OBVE
Earning high wages? Yus. Munition Wages. Madeline Ida Bedford. SUMH
Ears. Sonja Åkesson, *tr. fr. Swedish by* Joanna Bankier. WPOW
Ears, The. Anthony Euwer. *Fr.* The Limeratomy. HBMV
Ears cocked wide. Two at Showtime. Suzanne Brabant. PH
Ears in the Turrets Hear. Dylan Thomas. FaBoTw
Earth. Bryant. AP
Earth, The. Emerson. AA
Earth. Jim Tollerud. VoR
Earth, The. Jones Very. OxBA
Earth ("Grasshopper, your fairy [*or* tiny] song"). John Hall Wheelock. HBMV; LiTA; MoAmPo
Earth ("A planet doesn't explode"). John Hall Wheelock. LiTM; PV; SoSe
Earth, The/ is a wonderful. Poem for Friends. Quincy Troupe. PoBA
Earth a flower. For Nothing. Gary Snyder. NNaP
Earth Abideth Forever, The. Bible, *O.T.* Ecclesiastes, I: 4-7. FaPON
Earth and Fire. Wendell Berry. FF; GP
Earth and Fire. Vernon Watkins. NYBP
Earth and I Gave You Turquoise. N. Scott Momaday. CDW; PoPl; UnPo
Earth and Man, The. Stopford Augustus Brooke. HBV-2; OnYI
Earth and Sky. Euripides, *tr. fr. Greek by* C. M. Bowra. EaLo
Earth and Sky. Eleanor Farjeon. PoSC; SUS
Earth and water, air and stars. Immortality. Nicolai Maksimovich Minsky, *tr. by* Babette Deutsch. TrJP
Earth around him, The: he within his life. Adam in Love. Stephen Mitchell. VWA
Earth Asks and Receives Rain, The. Phyllis Haring. PeSA
Earth Breaks Up. Robert Browning. *Fr.* Christmas-Eve and Easter-Day. TrCP
Earth Buried. Kenneth Mackenzie. CBAP
Earth Changes. Kent Shire. AMV-80
Earth Cycle Dream, The. Phillip Yellowhawk Minthorn. STE
Earth darkens and is beaded. Quod Tegit Omnia. Yvor Winters. MoVE; QFR
Earth does not ever grow fat, The. Ngoni Burial Song. *Unknown.* PeSA
Earth does not lack. W. H. Davies Simplifies the Simplicities He Loves. Louis Untermeyer. WhC
Earth does not understand her child. The Return. Edna St. Vincent Millay. LiTA; MoAB; MoAmPo; MoPo; NoAM; OxBA; PoPl
Earth draws her breath so gently, heaven bends. The Marriage of Earth and Heaven. Jay Macpherson. OBCV
Earth Dweller. William Stafford. LCAP

Earth Felicities, Heavens Allowances. Richard Steere. SCAP
Earth from her winter slumber breaks. Decoration Day. Julia Ward Howe. OHIP
Earth gave Thee a cradle, O Christ, and a cross. Cradle and Throne. *Unknown.* STF
Earth gets its price for what Earth gives us. James Russell Lowell. *Fr.* The Vision of Sir Launfal. TreF
Earth goes on the earth glittering in gold, The. Inscribed in Melrose Abbey. *Unknown.* FaBoEE; FaBoRV
Earth grown old, yet still so green. Advent. Christina Rossetti. TrCP; VLP
Earth grows white with harvest, The; all day long. The Harvest of the Sea. John McCrae. EtS
Earth Has Not Anything to Show More Fair. Wordsworth. *See* Composed upon Westminster Bridge, September 3, 1802.
Earth has not anything to show more fair. On Mrs. W——. Nicolas Bentley. DBV; FiBHP
Earth Has Shrunk in the Wash. William Empson. CMoP
Earth holds the sunlit. For Spring. D. G. Jones. NOBC
Earth in Spring, The. Judah Halevi, *tr. fr. Hebrew by* Edward G. King. TrJP
Earth is a beautiful place, The. The Third Sermon on the Warpland. Gwendolyn Brooks. BPo
Earth is a place on which England is found, The. Geography. G. K. Chesterton. *Fr.* Songs of Education. HBMV; OBSV
Earth is a woman who imagines us. She sings. Robert Kelly. The Book of Persephone, 10. PoM
Earth is dark where you rest. Dark Earth and Summer. Edgar Bowers. QFR
Earth Is Enough. Edwin Markham. TreFS; TRV
Earth Is the Lord's, The. Bible, *O.T.* Psalms, XXIV. AWP; EaLo; FaPON; TreFT; TrJP
(Lift Up Your Heads.) TrGrPo
Earth keeps some vibration going, The. Fiddler Jones. Edgar Lee Masters. *Fr.* Spoon River Anthology. CMoP; LiTA; NoAM; OxBA; TAP; TrGrPo
Earth labored, and lo! Man lay in her lap. Afterthought. Justin Richardson. PV
Earth, Late Choked with Showers, The. Thomas Lodge. *Fr.* Scilla's Metamorphosis. ElL; ViBoPo
(Melancholy.) OBSC
Earth lay like one revealed. Thunder over Earth. Horatio Colony. TwAmPo
Earth lies here in giant folds and creases, The. High Wheat Country. Elijah L. Jacobs. AmFN
Earth Listens. Katharine Lee Bates. PGD
Earth, My Likeness. Walt Whitman. NePA; OxBA
Earth now is green, and heaven is blue. To the Spring. Sir John Davies. *Fr.* Hymns Astraea. ElL
Earth, ocean, air, belovèd brotherhood! Alastor; or, The Spirit of Solitude. Shelley. EnRP; FiP; OAEL-2, *abr.*; OAEP; WHA
Earth out of Earth. *Unknown.* *See* Earth upon Earth.
Earth Psalm. Denise Levertov. PPP
Earth rais'd up her head. Earth's Answer. Blake. *Fr.* Songs of Experience. EnRP; InPS; LAuP; NOEC; OAEL-2
Earth rebelled, The./ The good and patient earth. Yuri Suhl, *tr. by* Max Rosenfeld. TrJP
Earth, receive an honoured guest. W. H. Auden. *Fr.* In Memory of W. B. Yeats. ChMP; ChTr; FaBoRV; FaBoTw
Earth rolls on through empty space, its journey's never done, The. The Ramble-eer. *Unknown.* PoAu-1
Earth runs furrows under my skin, The. New Graveyard: Jerusalem. Shirley Kaufman. VWA
Earth seems a desolate mother, The. March. Charles Henry Webb. AA
Earth, Sky. Sydney Clouts. PeSA
Earth Song. Thomas Peacock. VoR
Earth, that let us in, was soft as fern, The. En Route. E. L. Mayo. MiAP
Earth to earth, and dust to dust. Death and Resurrection. George Croly. WGRP
Earth Took of Earth. *Unknown.* HAP
Earth Trembles Waiting. Blanche Shoemaker Wagstaff. PoLF
Earth tremor. I felt an earth tremor. On the Wallowy. Laura Chester. NPGG
Earth Tremor in Lugano. James Kirkup. NYBP
Earth turns, The/ like a rainbow. When You Read This Poem. Pinkie Gordon Lane. BlSi
Earth upon Earth. *Unknown.* ChTr
(Earth out of Earth.) MeEL
(Memento Homo Quod Cinis Es et in Cinerem Reverteris.) FaBoRV
Earth Walk. William Meredith. MAT
Earth was form'd, but in the womb as yet, The. Milton. *Fr.* Paradise Lost, VII. MOS
Earth was my home, but even there I was a stranger. The Flight of Apollo. Stanley Kunitz. MOON
Earth was not Earth before her sons appeared. Appreciation. George Meredith. ViBoPo
Earth will be going on a long time, The. Lute Music. Kenneth Rexroth. TAP
Earth, with all its fullness, is the Lord's, The. Poor for Our Sakes. Mary Brainerd Smith. BLRP
Earth, with its dark and dreadful ills. Dying Hymn. Alice Cary. HBV-2
Earth with thunder torn[e], with fire blasted, The. Sonnet. Fulke Greville. *Fr.* Caelica. AAS; EnRePo; JCP; QFR
Earth Worm, The. Denise Levertov. NOBA
Earth, you have had great lovers in your hour. Poets. Hortense Flexner. HBMV
Earthborn. Peter McArthur. CaP
Earthly Illusion. Louise Leighton. GoYe
Earthly Love. Joseph Bennett. NePA
Earthly nouris [*or* hourrice *or* nurrice] sits and sings, An. *See* Eartly nourris sits and sings, An.
Earthly Paradise, The, *sels.* William Morris.
  Apology, An. AWP; OAEL-2; OAEP; OBNC
    ("Of Heaven or Hell I have no power to sing.") EBVV; LiTB; LoBV; NoP; ViBoPo
    (Prologue: "Of Heaven or Hell I have no power to sing.") FaBoEn; VLP
    (Singer's Prelude, The.) HBV-2
  March ("He ended; and midst those who heard were some"). VLP
  May. VLP
  "O June, O June, that we desired so." ViBoPo
  October. OBNC; VLP
    "O love, turn from the unchanging sea, and gaze." FaBoEn
  Outlanders, The. EBVV
    (Minstrels and Maids.) GN
    ("Outlanders, whence ye lust?") OxBoCh
  Prologue: The Wanderers. EBVV
  Road of Life, The. OBNC
  Song: "Fair is the night, and fair the day." HBV-1
  Song from "Ogier the Dane." OAEP
    ("In the white-flowered hawthorn brake.") ViBoPo
  "Under a bent when the night was deep." PChr
  Written in a Copy of "The Earthly Paradise," Dec. 25, 1870. VLP
Earthly props are useless. Props. John Oxenham. TRV
Earthly roses at God's call have made, The. On the Death of a Pious Lady. Olof Wexionius, *tr. by* Sir Edmund Gosse. AWP
Earthly: Sonnets for Carlos, *sels.* Ian Wedde. OCNZ
  "By day & also by night & you are," 10.
  " 'Hello' his first word," 53.
  " 'If thy wife is small bend down to her &,' " 9.
  It's Time, 2.
Earthly tree a heavenly fruit it bare, An. A Carol for Christmas Day. William Byrd. SBVL
Earthquake. R. A. D. Ford. NOBC
Earthquake, The. *Tr. fr. Zuni Indian by* K. Kennedy. WTO
Earth's Answer. Blake. *Fr.* Songs of Experience. EnRP; InPS; LAuP; NOEC; OAEL-2
Earth's Bondman. Betty Page Dabney. GoYe
Earth's crammed with heaven. Elizabeth Barrett Browning. *Fr.* Aurora Leigh. TRV
Earth's first Adam, he lay in the grass. Adam and Eve. Itzig Manger, *tr. by* Jacob Sonntag. TrJP
Earth's Night. William Allingham. TRV
Earth's shadow crosses the full-/moon. Lunar Eclipse. Diane Glancy. STE
Earthworms. Parody. Martha Paley Francescato, *tr. by* Willis Barnstone. BoWoP
Earthy Anecdote. Wallace Stevens. CMoP; GoJo; RFM
Eartly [*or* Earthly] nourris [*or* nouris *or* nourrice *or* nurrice] sits and sings, An. The Great Silkie of Sule Skerry [*or* The Silkie o' Sule Skerrie]. *Unknown.* ChTr; ESPB; EtS; FaBoBa; FaBoCh; FSW; GBP; MAT; MOS; ViBoFo
Ease. William Cowper. *Fr.* The Task, I. TEP
Ease is the pray'r of him who, in a whaleboat. Sapphics: At the Mohawk-Castle, Canada. Thomas Morris. NOEC
Ease It to Me Blues. *Unknown.* BluL
Easier. James Harrison. AMV-80
Easiest Way, The. *Unknown, tr. by* Louis Untermeyer. UnTE
Easily to the old. Exit. Wilson MacDonald. CaP; ViBoPo
Easing the ring down her finger, he hears noon. The Ring. Robert Pack. FAZ
East and the South have ruled us long, The. Andrew Jackson. Stephen Vincent Benét. InMe
East Anglian Bathe. John Betjeman. NoP

East Anglian Fen. George Crabbe. *Fr.* Tales of the Hall: Delay Has Danger. FaBoPP
East Bronx. David Ignatow. ConAP
East Coast—Canada. Elizabeth Brewster. CaP
East Coast Journey. James K. Baxter. NoP
East Coast Lullaby. Lady Anne Lindsay. EtS
East Coker. T. S. Eliot. *Fr.* Four Quartets. ChMP; HAP; MoVE; NePA; PPP; VGW
East Hampton: The Structure of Sound. Philip Appleman. NYP
East is a clear violet mass, The. A Street Scene. Lizette Woodworth Reese. OBCA
East London. Matthew Arnold. OAEP; WGRP
East-northeaster pounds the coast tonight, The. Euroclydon. Abbie Huston Evans. NePoAm
East River. Rosemary Thomas. AmFN
East St. Louis Blues. *Unknown.* AmFP
East unrolled a sheet of gold, The. As Helen Once. Muna Lee. HBMV
East Virginia. *Unknown.* FSW; OuSiCo, *with music*
East wind./ A straight line of spruce roaring. Unusual Things. Tom Hennen. FAZ
East Wind asperges Boston with Lynn's sulphurous brine, An. Father. John Wheelwright. DiL; UnPo
Easter. Elizabeth J. Coatsworth. YeAr
Easter. Mary Carolyn Davies. OHIP
Easter ("I got me flowers to straw thy way"). George Herbert. CH; FaBoCh; FaBoEn; NOBE; OBEV; OBS; OHIP; TrGrPo; TRV
Easter ("Rise, heart! thy Lord is risen"). George Herbert. AnAnS-1; SeCV-1; TrCP
Easter. Joyce Kilmer. PDV; RHPC; SoPo; TiPo
Easter. John G. Neihardt. *See* Easter, 1923.
Easter. Howard Nemerov. NoP
Easter. Frank O'Hara. EAS
Easter. Edwin L. Sabin. OHIP; PoSC
Easter. Spenser. *See* Amoretti, LXVIII.
Easter. Robert Whitaker. PGD
Easter Beatitudes. Clarence M. Burkholder. BLRP
Easter Bunny Blues, The, or All I Want for Xmas Is the Loop. Ebon Dooley. PoBA
Easter Canticle, An. Charles Hanson Towne. OHIP; TrPWD
Easter Carol: "O Earth! throughout thy borders." George Newell Lovejoy. OHIP; PGD
Easter Carol, An: "Spring bursts to-day." Christina Rossetti. OHIP
Easter Chorus. Goethe. *See* Christ Is Arisen.
Easter Communion. Gerard Manley Hopkins. BrPo; OFD
Easter dawn! Morning, Noon, And. Hawley Truax. NYBP
Easter Day, Naples, 1849. Arthur Hugh Clough. OAEP; VLP
Easter Day II. Arthur Hugh Clough. OAEP; VLP
"Weep not beside his tomb," *sel.* PGD
Easter-Day. Henry Vaughan. AnAnS-1
Easter, Day of Christ Eternal. Maurice Moore. STF
Easter Day was a holiday. Sir Hugh. *Unknown.* ViBoFo
Easter Day we got up early. Early, Early Easter Day. Aileen Fisher. SiSoSe
Easter duck and Easter chick. Some Things That Easter Brings. Elsie Parrish. SoPo
Easter Egg. Alan Kieffaber. AMV-80
Easter Eve. James Branch Cabell. HBMV
Easter Eve. Muriel Rukeyser. NePA; VGW
(Easter Eve, 1945.) MiAP
Easter Flood. Brenda S. Stockwell. AMV-81
Easter has come around. W. D. Snodgrass. *Fr.* Heart's Needle. ConAP; NePoEA; NMP
Easter Hymn. A. E. Housman. CABA; ChMP; EaLo; EBEV; MoAB; OAEP; OFD
Easter Hymn, An. Richard Le Gallienne. OHIP
Easter Hymn. Henry Vaughan. AnAnS-1; EBCP; PoPle
Easter Hymn. Charles Wesley. OHIP; TRV
Easter in the Woods. Frances Frost. SiSoSe
Easter Island. Frederick George Scott. OBCV
Easter Joy. Nancy Byrd Turner. YeAr
Easter lilies! Can you hear. On Easter Day. Celia Thaxter. FaPON; YeAr
Easter Monday. Eleanor Farjeon. SUMH
Easter Monday. Michael McFee. AMV-80
Easter Monday. Christina Rossetti. NOCV
Easter Morn. Giles Fletcher. *Fr.* Christ's Victory and Triumph. ElL; NOCV
Easter Morning. A. R. Ammons. NoP
Easter Morning. Bible, *N.T.* St. Matthew, XXVIII:1-10. TreF
Easter Morning. Spenser. *See* Amoretti, LXVIII.
Easter Night. Alice Meynell. BrRo; OHIP
Easter, 1916. W. B. Yeats. BrPo; CABA; ChMP; CMoP; CoBMV; FaBoMo; FaPoR; HAP; InPS; LiTM; MoAB; NIP; NoAM; NOBE; NoP; OAEL-2; OBWP; OxBI; OxBTC; PPoe; PPP; SeCeV
Easter, 1923. John G. Neihardt. HBMV; OHIP
Easter Parade. Marchette Chute. SiSoSe
Easter Poem. Kathleen Raine. LiTB
Easter Snowfall. Harry Behn. TiPo
Easter Song, An. "Susan Coolidge." *See* Calvary and Easter.
Easter Song. Mary A. Lathbury. OHIP
Easter Song, An. *Unknown.* OxBM
Easter Sunday. Sedulius Scottus, *tr. fr. Latin by* Helen Waddell. OFD
Easter Sunday, 1945. G. A. Borgese. NePoAm
Easter Thought. Leo Cox. CaP
Easter Week. Charles Kingsley. OHIP
Easter Week. *Unknown.* OnYI
Easter Wings. George Herbert. AnAnS-1; CABA; HAP; HeIP; InPK; InPS; LiTB; MeLP; MePo; NIP; NoP; OAEL-1; OAEP; OBS; PAI; PoEL-2; PP; PPP; SeCP; TEP; TrCP; WeW
Easter Zunday. William Barnes. VLP
Eastern guard tower. Haiku. Etheridge Knight. BPo; NeAC; NoAM; TAP
Eastern Serenade. William E. Aytoun *and* Sir Theodore Martin. InMe
Eastern Tempest. Edmund Blunden. MoBrPo
Eastmuir king, and Wastmuir king. Fause Foodrage (C *vers.*). *Unknown.* ESPB
Eastmure king, and the Westmure King, The. Fause Foodrage (B *vers.*). *Unknown.* ESPB
Eastside Chick with Drive. Albert Spector. CTBA
Eastside Incidents. Gregory Corso. GP; NYP
Eastward, etched in purple by a sun. Appalachian Convalescence. Robert Conquest. OxBC
Eastward far anon. The Beacons. Henry Hart Milman. *Fr.* Samor. OBRV
Eastward I Stand, Mercies I Beg. *Unknown, tr. fr. Anglo-Saxon by* Sarah Plotz. EaLo
Eastward to Eden. Edgar Bogardus. POL
Easy as a Bat. *Gond Oral Tradition, tr. by* V. Elwin *and* S. Hivale. WTO
Easy as cove-water rustles its pebbles and shells. Part of a Letter. Richard Wilbur. CMoP
Easy Decision, An. Kenneth Patchen. CTBA
Easy Does It. Henry Chapin. FAZ
Easy Poem, An. Terry Kennedy. AMV-80
Easy Rider. *Unknown.* FSW
Easy Rider Blues. *Unknown.* BluL
Easy thing, O Power Divine, An. The Things I Miss. Thomas Wentworth Higginson. TrPWD
Eat/ 300 feet. The Anthropophagites See a Sign on NC Highway 177 That Looks like Heaven. Jonathan Williams. OBAL
Eat and Walk. James Norman Hall. BLPA
Eat but simple food; go for early rising. Advice from an Expert. John Kieran. InMe
Eat 'Em Up Smith Tells All in South Africa. Judith Johnson Sherwin. NoAM
Eat-It-All Elaine. Kaye Starbird. PDV; RHPC
"Eat my cake, eat," cried the young. To the Last Wedding Guest. Horace Gregory. NYBP
Eat no green apples or you'll droop. Advice to Small Children. Edward Anthony. RHPC
Eat thou and drink; to-morrow thou shalt die. The Choice, 1. Dante Gabriel Rossetti. The House of Life, LXXI. HBV-2; OBVV; ViBoPo; WHA
Eat with Care. *Unknown.* FaBoUs
Eat your meat and save the skin. Cowboy Graces. *Unknown.* CoSo
Eaten Heart, The. *Unknown, tr. fr. Middle English by* Pearl London. *Fr.* The Knight of Curtesy. TrGrPo
'Eathen, The. Kipling. OxBTC
Eating. Reginald Gibbons. MAYP
Eating Bamboo-Shoots. Po Chü-i, *tr. fr. Chinese by* Arthur Waley. OBVE
Eating Fish. George Johnston. WHW
Eating Lechon, with My Brothers and Sisters. Luis Cabalquinto. BrSi
Eating out alone, one makes solitude. Tokyo West. Alfred Corn. NYP
Eating Poetry. Mark Strand. GrPl; MAT; NoAM; PPP; TAP
Eating Song. Sir Walter Alexander Raleigh. WhC
Eating the eggs for a buck eighty. At Grand Canyon's Edge. David Ray. TAT
Eating the living germs of grasses. Song of the Taste. Gary Snyder. LCAP
Eau-Forte. F. S. Flint. OxBTC
Ebb. John Lyle Donaghy. NeIP
Ebb/ with the flow. Daufuskie. Mari Evans. BlSi
Ebb and Flow. George William Curtis. AA; HBV-2
Ebb and Flow, The. Edward Taylor. AmPP; AP; SCAP

Ebb slips from the rock, the sunken, The. Night. Robinson Jeffers. AP; AWP; CoBMV; LiTA; MoAmPo; MoPo; NOBA; OxBA; WHA
Ebb Tide. Majorie Pickthall. CaP
Ebb Tide, The. Robert Southey. OBNC
Ebb tide has come for me. The Hag of Beare. *Unknown, tr. by* John Montague. BIrV; CIP; PBWP
Ebb tide to me as of the sea! The Old Woman of Beare, *abr. Unknown, tr. by* Kuno Meyer. OnYI
Ebb-tide to me as to the sea; old age brings me reproach. The Hag of Beare. *Unknown, tr. by* Lady Gregory. OBVE
Ebbed and flowed the muddy Pei-ho by the gulf of Pechili. Blood Is Thicker than Water. Wallace Rice. PAH
Ebbing, the wave of the sea. The Woman of Beare. *Unknown, tr. by* Stephen Gwynn. AnIV
Ebbs from soiled fields the last drab vestige of snow. February. D. S. Savage. NeBP
Ebenezer, The, *with music. Unknown.* ShS
Ecce Homo. Witter Bynner. WGRP
Ecce Homo. David Gascoyne. *Fr.* Miserere. ChMP; LiTM; NeBP; OBWP
Ecce in Deserto. Henry Augustin Beers. AA
Ecce Puer. James Joyce. BIrV; EBEV; NAs; NoAM; PoPl; TrCP
Eccentric old person of Slough, An. Limerick. George Robey. CenHV
Eccho, The. Richard Leigh. MePo
Ecchoing Green, The. Blake. *See* Echoing Green, The.
Eccho's Song. Ben Jonson. *See* Slow, Slow, Fresh Fount.
Ecclesiastes, *sels.* Bible, *O.T*
 "All things come alike to all," IX: 2-12. NAWM-1
  "I returned, and saw under the sun," 11-12. Prf
  Live Joyfully, 7-11. TreFS
 "Cast thy bread upon the waters," XI. AWP (1-6); NAWM-1; OBVE (1-8)
  (Life's Uncertainty, 1-10.) TreFS
  Light Is Sweet, The, 7. FaPON
 Enjoy the Good, V: 18-20. TreFT
 "It is better . . .," VII: 1-9. TrJP
  (Better Path, The, 1-5.) TreFS
 Remember Now Thy Creator, XII: 1-8. AWP; ChTr; OBVE
  (Remember Then Thy Creator.) TrJP
  (Youth and Age.) TrGrPo
 To Everything There Is a Season, III: 1-8. FF; NAWM-1; OBVE; PoPl
  ("For everything there is a season.") DL
  (Time for Everything, A.) TrGrPo
 "Vanity of vanities, saith the Preacher, vanity of vanities; all is vanity," I: 2-II: 24. NAWM-1; TrJP (I: 2-9)
  All Is Vanity, I: 14-15; III: 19. TRV
  Earth Abideth Forever, The, I: 4-7. FaPON
  Words of the Preacher, The, I: 2-11. TreFS
Ecclesiastes. Morris Bishop. HBMV
Ecclesiastes. G. K. Chesterton. MoBrPo
Ecclesiastes. Joseph Langland. NePoEA; PoPl
Ecclesiastes. Derek Mahon. BIrV; CIP
Ecclesiastical Chronicle, An, *sel.* John Heath-Stubbs.
 "Year of Our Lord two thousand one hundred and seven, The." NOBL
Ecclesiastical Sonnets, *sels.* Wordsworth.
 Inside of King's College Chapel, Cambridge, Pt. III, XLIII. EnRP; GoBC; OAEP; OBNC; OBRV; OxBoCh
  (Within King's College Chapel, Cambridge.) GTBS; GTBS-P
 Mutability, Pt. III, XXXIV. CABA; EBEV; EnRP; HeIP; InPK; LiTB; NOBE; NoP; OAEL-2; OBEV; OBRV; PoEL-4; PrIm; SeCeV
Ecclesiasticus, *sels.* Bible, Apochrypha.
 "All flesh waxeth old as a garment," XIV: 17-18. OBVE
 "By his commandment hee maketh the snow to fall apace," XLIII: 13-26. OBVE
 "I am the mother of fair love," XXIV: 24-28, *Douay vers.* ISi
 "Let us now praise famous men," XLIV: 1-15. ChTr; OBVE
  (Our Fathers.) TrJP
 Music, XXXII: 5-6. TrJP
 O Death, XLI: 1-4. TrJP
 Test of Men, The, XXVI: 5-8. TrJP
Ech, Sic a Pairish. *Unknown.* FaBoCo; FiBHP
Eche man me telleth I chaunge moost my devise. Sir Thomas Wyatt. AAS
Echo. *See also* Eccho.
Echo. Walter de la Mare. MoVE; OBMV; SeCeV
Echo. Viscountess Grey of Fallodon. CH
Echo. Elizabeth Stanton Hardy. GoYe
Echo. Milton. *See* Song: "Sweet Echo, sweetest nymph, that livest unseen."
Echo. Thomas Moore. ELP; GoBC; OxBI
 (Echoes.) GTBS; GTBS-P
Echo. Christina Rossetti. BoLoP; CH; EBVV; ELP; GBL; LoBV; NIP; NOBE; NoP; OAEL-2; OBNC; PoEL-5; SeCeV; ViBoPo
Echo. Sir Philip Sidney. *Fr.* Arcadia. SiPS
Echo. Mildred Weston. BoNaP
Echo always mocks the sound, The. Rabindranath Tagore. *Fr.* Epigrams. PoA
Echo and the Ferry. Jean Ingelow. EBVV
Echo Canyon. *Unknown.* AmFP
Echo, I ween, will in the wood reply. A Gentle Echo on Woman. Swift. FaBoCo; NU; OLR; OnYI
Echo in a Church. Lord Herbert of Cherbury. AnAnS-2
Echo Poem. M. Allan. FiBHP
Echo, the beating of the tide. Prophecy on Lethe. Stanley Kunitz. PoA
Echo to a Rock. Lord Herbert of Cherbury. PoEL-2
Echoes. W. E. Henley. *Poems indexed separately by titles and first lines.*
Echoes. Emma Lazarus. SBG
Echoes. Thomas Moore. *See* Echo.
Echoes from Theocritus, *sels.* Edward Cracroft Lefroy, *after the Greek of* Theocritus.
 Ageanax, VI. OBVV
 Cleonicos, XXVII. AWP
 Epitaph of Eusthenes, The, XXVIII. AWP; OBVV
 Flute of Daphnis, XXIII. AWP; OBVV
 Grave of Hipponax, XXX. AWP
 Monument of Cleita, The, XXIX. AWP
 Sacred Grove, A, XXIV. AWP
 Summer Day in Old Sicily, A, V. OBVV
 Sylvan Revel, A, XXV. AWP
 Thyrsis, XXVI. AWP
Echoes of Childhood. Alice Corbin. PoNe
Echoing Cliff, The. Andrew Young. PoSH
Echoing [*or* Ecchoing] Green, The. Blake. *Fr.* Songs of Innocence. CABA; CH; LAuP; OBEC; PoSC; UnPo; WiR
Echo's Lament for Narcissus. Ben Jonson. *See* Slow, Slow, Fresh Fount.
Echo's Song. Ben Jonson. *See* Slow, Slow, Fresh Fount.
Eclipse. William Carson Fagg. LFAC
Eclipse. Anita Endrezze Probst. CDW
Eclipse. Amir Rashidd. NBP
Eclipse. Ed Roberson. PoNe
Eclipse. Tomaz Salamun, *tr. fr. Slovene by* Michael Scammel *and* Veno Taufer. VWA
Eclipse. Timothy Sheehan. SUW
Eclipse, The. Henry Vaughan. HBV-2
Eclipse of Faith, The. Theodore Dwight Woolsey. AA
Eclipses. Nancy Sullivan. TAP
Ecliptic, The: Cancer; or, The Crab, *sel.* Joseph Gordon Macleod.
 "Moonpoison, mullock of sacrifice." NeBP
Eclogue: Common a-Took In, The. William Barnes. VLP
Eclogue: "Late 'twas in June, the fleece when fully grown." Michael Drayton. *Fr.* The Shepherd's Garland, Eclogue IX (1606 ed.). OBSC
Eclogue: "Lycon begin—begin the mournful tale." William Diaper. *Fr.* Nereides; or, Sea-Eclogues. SeCePo
Eclogue: "No one dies cleanly now." Frederic Prokosch. ViBoPo
Eclogue IV: Poet, The, *sel.* Charles Jenner.
 Soliloquy in the Suburbs, A. NOEC
Eclogue: Queen Elizabeth's Day. John Davidson. BrPo
Eclogue: Two Farms in Woone. William Barnes. NBM
Eclogue: "What makes you look so black, so glum, so cross?" Edward Lear. FaBoNo
Eclogue: "Whores are afraid to cross the street, The." David Bergman. AMV-80
Eclogue for Christmas, An. Louis MacNeice. FaBoMo; MoPo; MoVE; NoAM; OBMV
Eclogue to Mr. Johnson, An, *sel.* Thomas Randolph.
 Poetry and Philosophy. OBS
Eclogues. Dennis Schmitz. NPGG
Eclogues, *sels.* Virgil, *tr. fr. Latin.*
 Corydon and Thyrsis, VII, *tr. by* Dryden. AWP
 Lycidas and Moeris, IX, *tr. by* Dryden. AWP
 Messiah, The, IV, *tr. by* Dryden. AWP
  (Sicilian Muse, I Would Try Now a Somewhat Grander Theme, *tr. by* C. Day Lewis.) NAs
  ("Sicilian Muses, sing we greater things," *tr. by* Sir John Beaumont.) OBVE
  "For thee little boy, will the earth pour forth gifts," *tr. by* James Laughlin. PoPl
  Sibylline Prophecy, The, *tr. by* Thomas Walsh. ISi
 Shepherd's Gratitude, The, I, *tr. by* Charles Stuart Calverly. AWP
Eco Right. Walt Gavenda. QQQ
Ecole St. Luc. Ray Fraser. NeAC
Ecological Lecture. Burton Raffel. AMV-81
Ecology. X. J. Kennedy. *See* Vulture.
Economy of Vegetation, The, *sels.* Erasmus Darwin. FaBoUs
 Action of Electricity, The.
 Action of Invisible Ink, The.
 Protection of Plants, The.

Ecstacy, The. John Donne. *See* Ecstasy, The.
Ecstasie, rash production of the thoughts. George Darley. *Fr.* Errors of Ecstasie. OnYI
Ecstasies of Dialectic, The. Howard Nemerov. TwAmPo
Ecstasy, The. Al-Hallaj, *tr. fr. Persian.* ILwL
Ecstasy, The. John Donne. BoLoP; CABA; EnRePo; FPL; HAP; InPS; JCP; LiTB; LoBV; NOBE; NoP; OAEL-1; OBEV; PPoe; PrIm; TEP; TrGrPo; UnTE; ViBoPo
(Ecstacy, The.) SeCePo; SeCeV
(Extasie, The.) AnAnS-1; EnLoPo; FaBoEn; MasP; MeLP; MePo; OBS; PoEL-2; SeCP; SeCV-1
Ecstasy. Duncan Campbell Scott. CaP
Ecstasy. Hélène Swarth, *tr. fr. Dutch by* Jonathan Crewe.
Ecstasy. Arthur Symons. UnTE
Ecstasy. Rachel Annand Taylor. GoTS
Ecstasy. W. J. Turner. CH
Ecstasy. *Unknown. See* Oh, When Shall I See Jesus?
Ecstatic bird songs pound. Dawn. William Carlos Williams. MoAB; MoAmPo; PoPl
Eczema. David Slavitt. TW
Ed and Sid and Bernard. Edward MacDuff. QQQ
Ed Shreckongost. Ed Ochester. TAT
Eddi, priest of St. Wilfrid. Eddi's Service. Kipling. OBCP; PoPle
Eddie and Eve. Charles Bukowski. GP
Eddington's universe goes phut. Richard Tolman's Universe. Leonard Bacon. ImOP
Eddi's Service. Kipling. OBCP; PoPle
Eddystone Light, The. *Unknown.* FSW
Eden. Lev Mak, *tr. fr. Russian by* Daniel Weissbort. VWA
Eden. Milton. *Fr.* Paradise Lost, IV. FaBoEn
Eden. D. M. Thomas. NCSH
Eden. Thomas Traherne. AnAnS-1; PoEL-2; SeCV-2; TrGrPo
Eden-Gate. Sydney Dobell. OBVV
Eden Is a Zoo. Margaret Atwood. WPE
Eden: Or One View of It. Theodore Spencer. NePA
Eden Revisited. Vassar Miller. FAZ; GP
Edenhall. "Susan Coolidge." OBCA
Edenlike as your name. Edge. John Montague. IPY
Eden's Courtesy. C. S. Lewis. EBCP
Edgar A. Guest Considers "The Good Old Woman Who Lived in a Shoe" and the Good Old Truths Simultaneously. Louis Untermeyer. *Fr.* Mother Goose Up-to-Date. NIP; PoPl
(Edgar A. Guest Considers "The Old Woman Who Lived in a Shoe" and the Good Old Verities at the Same Time.) FiBHP; OBAL; WhC
(Edgar A. Guest Syndicates the Old Woman Who Lived in a Shoe.) MoAmPo
Edgar Guest. Oscar Williams. PP
Edgar's Story, *sel.* X. J. Kennedy.
"At Mount Rushmore I looked up into one." OFD
Edge, The. James K. Bowen. AMV-80
Edge, The. Ann Chandonnet. AMV-81
Edge. Robert D. Fitzgerald. CBAP
Edge. John Montague. IPY
Edge. Sylvia Plath. TAP
Edge, The. Lola Ridge. OnYI
Edge of Day, The. Laurie Lee. NYBP
Edge of Town, The. William Clamurro. AMV-81
Edge-Hill; or, The Rural Prospect Delineated and Moralised, *sel.* Richard Jago.
Iron Industry in Birmingham, The. NOEC
Edgehill Fight. Kipling. PoPle
Edges of the stones are sharp, The. The Builder. Caroline Giltinan. HBMV
Edi be thu, Hevene Quene. *See* Edy be thou, Hevene-Quene.
Edinburgh. Arthur Guiterman. WhC
Edinburgh. Alfred Noyes. HBV-2
Edinburgh after Flodden, *sel.* William Edmonstoune Aytoun.
"Then the Provost he uprose." OBWP
Edinburgh from the Pentland Hills. Sir Walter Scott. *Fr.* Marmion, IV. FaBoPP
Edinburgh Spring. Norman MacCaig. NMP
Edith. William Ellery Channing. AA; HBV-2
Edith and Harold. Arthur Gray Butler. OBVV
Edith Cavell. George Edward Woodberry. HBMV
Edith Sitwell Assumes the Role of Luna. Robert Francis. MOON
Edith, the silent stars are coldly gleaming. Edith. William Ellery Channing. AA; HBV-2
Editor sat in his easy chair, The. The Editor's Tragedy. St. John Emile Clavering Hankin. CenHV
Editor Whedon. Edgar Lee Masters. *Fr.* Spoon River Anthology. CMoP; CrMA; FaBoEE; NoAM; NOBA; OBSV; OxBA
Editorial Poem on an Incident of Effects Far-reaching. Russell Atkins. NBP
Editor's Tragedy, The. St. John Emile Clavering Hankin. CenHV
Editor's Wooing, The. "Orpheus C. Kerr." OBAL
Edlesborough. Anne Ridler. NeBP
Edmond Halley. Roy Fuller. OxBC
Edmonton, thy cemetery. Stevie Smith. OxBTC
Edmund Burke. Goldsmith. *Fr.* Retaliation. DBV; InvP; NOEC; OBEC; SeCeV
("Here lies our good Edmund, whose genius was such.") FaBoEE
Edmund Clerihew Bentley. William Jay Smith. PV
Edmund Davie 1682; Annagram. Benjamin Tompson. SCAP
Edmund Pollard. Edgar Lee Masters. *Fr.* Spoon River Anthology. ErPo
Edmund's Song. Sir Walter Scott. *See* Brignall Banks.
Edna St. Vincent Millay Exhorts Little Boy Blue. Louis Untermeyer. *Fr.* Mother Goose Up-to-Date. MoAmPo
Edom o' Gordon. *Unknown.* BSV; HBV-2; OxBB, *with music*
(Captain Car.) ESPB (A, B, F, *and* H *vers.*); FaBoBa; OAEP; ViBoFo (A *and* B *vers.*)
Edouard. Ogden Nash. NePA
Edser. Spike Milligan. TDH
Educated Love Bird, The. Peter Newell. FiBHP
Education. Pauline Barrington. SUMH
Education. Don L. Lee. AmNP; BALP
Education of Nature, The. Wordsworth. GTBS; GTBS-P
Educational Administration Professor's Prayer, The. Gerald Bobango. AMV-80
Educational Music or Erosion. William H. Schubert. AMV-81
Edward. *Unknown.* AmFP; BiP; BSV; CABA; CH; EBEV; ELP; ESPB (A *and* B *vers.*); FaBoBa; FSW, *modern vers.*; GoTS; HoPM; InPK; NoP (B *vers.*); OAEP; OxBS; PAI; PoEL-1; PPoe; PrIm; SoSe; TrGrPo; TW; ViBoPo (A *and* B *vers.*)
(Edward, Edward.) EnRP; FaPoR; HAP; HBV-2; InPS; LiTB; NOBE; OBEV; OxBB; PoRA; SeCeV; TreFS; WeW; WHA
"Edward back from the Indian Sea." Neglectful Edward. Robert Graves. BrPo; MoBrPo
Edward Gray. Tennyson. OBVV
Edward Hopper Retrospective, The. Tony Quagliano. PoDr
Edward Lear. W. H. Auden. InvP
Edward Lear in February. Christopher Middleton. TwCP
Edward the Dyke and Other Poems, *sel.* Judy Grahn.
"In the place where." PeHV
Edward the Second, *sel.* Christopher Marlowe.
"I must have wanton poets, pleasant wits." ViBoPo
Edward the Third had seven sons. The Ballad of Banners (1944). John Lehmann. MoBS
Edward Weston in Mexico City. Philip Dacey. LTB; PoDr
Edwardian Hat. Betty Parvin. POL
Edwardus Comes Clarendoniae. Bibliotheca Bodleiana. Geoffrey Grigson. GBL
Edwin A. Nelms. Sheryl L. Nelms. Str
Edwin Booth. Alice Brown. HBV-2
Edwin in the Lowlands Low. *Unknown. See* Young Edwin in the Lowlands Low.
Edy be thou [*or* Edi be thu], Hevene-Quene. In Praise of Mary [Queen of Heaven]. *Unknown.* MeEL; OxBM
Eee wah-wah-wah-wah-wah. Talking to Myself. *Unknown.* BluL
"Eek/ a nigger." At the National Black Assembly. Amiri Baraka. GP
Eek!/ Her legs are caught in something. The Orlando Commercial. George MacBeth. NOBL
Eel, The. Walter de la Mare. ShM
Eel, The. Eugenio Montale, *tr. fr. Italian.* NaP, *tr. by* Robert Lowell; WeW, *shorter vers., tr. by* John Frederick Nims
Eel, The. Ogden Nash. FaBV; FaPON; NTCP
Eels and Tortoises. William Diaper, *after the Greek of* Oppian. *Fr.* Halieutica. NOEC
("Strange the formation of the eely race.") OBVE
Eemis-Stane, The. "Hugh MacDiarmid." BSV; NeBP
E'en as a lovely flower. Du bist wie eine Blume. Heine, *tr. by* Kate Freiligrath Kroeker. *Fr.* Homeward Bound. AWP
E'en as the flowers do wither. *Unknown.* OBSC
E'en like two little bank-dividing brooks. *See* Ev'n like two . . .
E'en this, Lord, didst thou bless. Insomnia. John Banister Tabb. TrPWD
Eena, meena, mina, mo. *See* Eenie, meenie, minie, mo.
Eenie, meenie, mackeracka. *Unknown.* OxNR
Eenie, meenie, minie, mo. Counting-out Rhymes. *Unknown.* FaPON
(Eena, meena, mina, mo.) OxNR
Eenity, feenity, fickety, feg. *Unknown.* OxNR
Eeny, weeny, winey, wo. *Unknown.* OxNR
Ees, last Whit-Monday, I an' Meary. Whitsuntide an' Club Walken. William Barnes. VLP

Ees, twer at Liady-Day, ya know. Liady-Day an' Ridden House. William Barnes. OBRV
Ef I had 'bout—fo'ty-five dollahs. John Henry. *Unknown.* ViBoFo
Ef [*or* If] I had wings like Noah's dove. Dink's Song. *Unknown.* ErPo; FSW; OxBoLi
Effect of Example, The. John Keble. HBV-2; HBVY
Effective Prayer. Bible, *N.T.* St. Luke, XI: 9-13. TreFT
Effendi. Michael S. Harper. CNA; PoBA
Effervescence and Evanescence. Keith Preston. OBAL
Efficiency Apartment. Gerald W. Barrax. PoBA
Efficient Wife's Complaint, The. Confucius, *tr. fr. Chinese by* Ezra Pound. *Fr.* Airs of Pei. CTC
Effie. Sterling A. Brown. BANP
Effigy. Georgia Lee McElhaney. CoPo
Effingham, Grenville, Raleigh, Drake. Admirals All. Sir Henry Newbolt. FaPoR; MOS
Effort at Speech. William Meredith. NYP; Prf; WeW
Effort at Speech between Two People. Muriel Rukeyser. FYAP; MoAB; MoAmPo; MP; PAI; TrGrPo; TrJP; TwCP; WeW
Effortlessly Democratic Santa Fe Trail. Martha Baird. PoPl
Eftsoones they heard a most melodious sound. The Bower of Bliss [*or* Gather the Rose]. Spenser. *Fr.* The Faerie Queene, II, 12. FaBoEn; LoBV; NOBE; OBSC; SCV; ViBoPo; WHA
Eftsoons they saw an hideous host array'd. Sea Monsters. Spenser. *Fr.* The Faerie Queene, II, 12. ChTr
Egan O Rahilly. *Unknown, at. to* Egan O'Rahilly, *tr. fr. Irish by* James Stephens. EBEV; NoAM; OBMV; SeCePo
Egeria, sweet creation of some heart. Byron. *Fr.* Childe Harold's Pilgrimage, IV. ViBoPo
Egg, The. George Bowering. NeAC
Egg-and-Dart. Robert Finch. OBCV
Egg and the Machine, The. Robert Frost. CABA; MoAmPo
Egg Boiler, The. Gwendolyn Brooks. PoBA
Egg is a grand thing for a journey, An. How the Hen Sold Her Eggs to the Stingy Priest. Nancy Willard. LCAP
Egg is smooth and very pale, The. The Inefficacious Egg. Roy Bishop. HBMV
Egg of Nothing, The. John Taylor. AMV-81
Egg sat on the workbench, The. The Egg. George Bowering. NeAC
Egg Thoughts. Russell Hoban. *See* Soft-boiled Egg.
Egg won't roll well, An. An Airline Breakfast. William Matthews. AMV-80; MAYP
Eggleston was a taxi-driver. Cynical Portraits. Louis Paul. InMe
Eggplants Have Pins and Needles, The. Novella Matveyeva, *tr. fr. Russian by* Daniel Weissbort. WPOW
Eggs, The. Peter Redgrove. NAs
Eggs and Marrowbone. *Unknown.* FSW
Eggs boiling in a pot. Divorce. Erica Jong. GP
Eggs from a chain store grocery. One No. 7. John Frederick Frank. GoYe
Eggstravagance, An. Oliver Wendell Holmes. *See* Limerick: "Reverend Henry Ward Beecher, The."
Egnatius, because his teeth are white. Catullus, *tr. fr. Latin by* James Michie. DBV
Egnatius has fine teeth, and those. Catullus, *tr. fr. Latin by* Walter Savage Landor. OBVE
Ego. Philip Booth. MP; TwCP
Ego. Norman MacCaig. GTBS-P
Ego. Robert Siegel. GeTw; PoA
Ego Dominus Tuus. W. B. Yeats. CMoP
Ego Sum. Gelett Burgess. InMe
Ego Tripping. Nikki Giovanni. NoAM; Psk
Egocentric. Stevie Smith. FaBoNo
Egoism. W. Craddle. FiBHP; WhC
Egoist Dead, The. Elizabeth Brewster. CaP
Egotism. Edward Sanford Martin. AA
Egotist, The. H. A. C. Evans. POL
Egrets. Judith Wright. GoJo; NCSH
Egypt. Hilda Doolittle ("H. D."). HBMV
Egyptian banks, an avenue of clay. Flighting for Duck. William Empson. MoPo
Egyptian Lotus, The. Arthur Wentworth Hamilton Eaton. AA
Egyptian Passage, An. Theodore Weiss. CoPo; TAP
Egyptian Pulled Glass Bottle in the Shape of a Fish, An. Marianne Moore. PBWP
Egyptian Serenade. George William Curtis. HBV-1
Egyptians say, the sun has twice, The. Samuel Butler. *Fr.* Hudibras, II, 3. ImOP
Egypt's Might Is Tumbled Down. Mary Elizabeth Coleridge. CH
Eheu Fugaces. "Thomas Ingoldsby." FaBoEE; NBM; OxBoLi
Eichmann. Douglas Blazek. LTB
Eichmann before his death. Construction #13. Judith Johnson Sherwin. NoAM
8:00 A.M. Monday Morning. William Welsh. SOTS
Eight and already bored. Indian Mounds. Angela Peace. AMV-80
Eight Aspects of Melissa, *sels.* Lawrence Durrell.
  Adepts, The. ErPo; NeBP
  By the Lake. NeBP
  Encounter, The. NeBP
  Night, The. NeBP
  Petron, the Desert Father. NeBP
  Prospect of Children, A. NeBP
  Rising Sun, The. NeBP
  Visitations. MoBrPo; NeBP
8-Ball at the Twilight. David Baker. MAYP
Eight bells! Eight bells! their clear tone tells. All's Well! William Allen Butler. HBV-2
Eight-Day Clock, The. Alfred Cochrane. HBV-1
Eight days went by, eight days. Soothsay. William Carlos Williams. TwAmPo
Eight fingers. The Difference. Laura E. Richards. HBV-1; HBVY
Eight hands across, form a ring. Mississippi Sawyer. *Unknown.* AmFP
Eight-legged aerialists, The. Spiders. Diane Ackerman. MAYP
Eight Lines for a Script Girl. George Jonas. NeAC
Eight lines of clergymen converged. Colonel B. Constance Carrier. NePoAm-2
Eight Melons. Malcolm Cowley. TwAmPo
Eight Miles South of Grand Haven. Dave Kelly. AMV-80
Eight o'Clock. A. E. Housman. BrPo; CABA; CMoP; InPK; LoBV; MoAB; MoBrPo; NoAM; NoP; PAI; SoSe; TrGrPo
Eight o'clock. Christina Rossetti. *Fr.* Sing-Song. TiPo
Eight o'Clock Bells. *Unknown.* PoPle
Eight Sandbars on the Takano River. Gary Snyder. CoPo
Eight-toes, teetering. Magpie. Peter Davison. GrPl
Eight Volunteers. Lansing C. Bailey. PAH
Eight Witches. B. J. Lee. RHPC
Eight years ago this May. A Spring Night in Shokoku-ji. Gary Snyder. *Fr.* Four Poems for Robin. NNaP; NoAM; NOBA; NoP; SOTW; VGW
Eight years gone & the welfare building is a parking ramp. Balance. Philip Schultz. MAYP
Eight years old, crouched in a corner, eyeing the other askance. Party. Constance Carrier. NePoAm-2
Eight young pigs in a row look at me from the trough. The Laughing Faces of Pigs. Fred Lape. BoAnP
Eighteen. Maria Banus, *tr. fr. Rumanian by* Willis Barnstone *and* Matei Calinescu. BoWoP; VWA
Eighteen. Sister Mary Honora. NePoAm-2
Eighteen Days without You, *sel.* Anne Sexton.
  December 18th. CAPP
1887. A. E. Housman. CoBMV; FaPoR; NIP; PrIm; UnPo; VLP
1805. Robert Graves. ChMP; EvOK; FaBoch
Eighteen-forty-three. *Unknown.* FaBoCo
Eighteen hundred and ninety-one,/ 'Fore I workses, I'd ruther be hung. Ain't Workin' Song. *Unknown.* OuSiCo
Eighteen-ninety. E. Richard Shipp. PoOW
1892-1941. Louis Zukofsky. PoA
Eighteen-seventy, *sels.* Arthur Rimbaud, *tr. fr. French.*
  Evil, *tr. by* Robert Lowell. OBWP
  Napoleon after Sedan, *tr. by* Robert Lowell. OBWP
  Poster of Our Dazzling Victory at Saarbrucken, A, *tr. by* Robert Lowell. OBWP
  Sleeper in the Valley, The. OBWP, *tr. by* Robert Lowell; WaaP, *tr. by* Selden Rodman
  (Sleeper of the Valley, The, *tr. by* Ludwig Lewisohn.) AWP
  To the French of the Second Empire, *tr. by* Robert Lowell. OBWP
1864. Richard Howard. CABA
Eighteen sixty nine being the date of the year [*or* and the year]. A Ballad of Master McGrath [*or* Master McGrath]. *Unknown.* FaBoBa; OBET
1867: Last Sounds. Gerry O'Egan. POL
1863, my great grandmother. Generations. Judy Dothard Simmons. CNA
18,000 Feet. Ed Roberson. PoNe
Eighteen Verses Sung to a Tatar Reed Whistle, *sels.* Ts'ai Yen, *tr. fr. Chinese by* Kenneth Rexroth *and* Ling Chung.
  "I have no desire to live, but I am afraid of death," XI. WPOW
  "I never believed that in my broken life," XIII. BoWoP; WPOW
  "I was born in a time of peace," I. BoWoP; PBWP; WPOW
  "Seventeenth stanza, The. My heart aches, my tears fall," XVII. WPOW
  "Sun sets, The. The wind moans," VII. BoWoP; WPOW
  "Tatar chief forced me to become his wife, A," II. WPOW
18 West 11th. James Merrill. NYP
Eighteen years you beat me over the head. Brothers (I). James Reiss. AMV-81
Eighteenth of October, The. The Fire of Frendraught. *Unknown.* ESPB; OxBB; ViBoPo

Eighth Air Force. Randall Jarrell. FF; MiAP; MoVE; NoAM; NoP; NOBA; OBWP; PoCh
Eighth child of an eighth child, your wilful advent. Birth of a Great Man. Robert Graves. NYBP
Eighth day was the wedding, The. The First Wedding in the World. Joel Rosenberg. VWA
Eighth Elegy, *sel.* Muriel Rukeyser.
Children's Elegy. LCAP
Eighth Song: "In a grove most rich of shade." Sir Philip Sidney. *See* Astrophel and Stella: Eighth Song.
Eighth Street West. Rachel Field. SiSoSe
Eighty and nine with their captain. The Charge by the Ford. Thomas Dunn English. PAH
Eighty-four years ago. Birthday Party. Patti Patton. AMV-80
'Eighty-nine was bad. Graves at Elkhorn. Richard Hugo. UnPo
80-Proof A.R. Ammons. SUW
Eighty years ago a woman passed. Tomorrow Is a Birthday. Gwendolen Haste. GoYe
Eileann Chanaidh, *sel.* Kathleen Raine.
Ancient Speech, The. PoSH
Eileen Aroon ("Fain would I ride with thee"). Carrol O'Daly, *tr. fr. Middle Irish or fr. Late Middle Irish by* George Sigerson. OnYI
Eileen Aroon ("When like the early rose"). Gerald Griffin. AnIV; GoBC; HBV-1; OBVV
(Aileen Aroon.) OnYI
"When like the rising day," *sel.* OBEV
Eileen of four. The Clock's Song. Rose Hawthorne Lathrop. AA
Einstein. Archibald MacLeish. MoPo; TwAmPo
"He lies upon his bed," *sel.* ImOP
Einstein among the Coffee-Cups. Louis Untermeyer. WhC
Einstein's Father. D. L. Klauck. LTB
Eire. William Drennan. OnYI
Eire. David O'Bruadair, *tr. fr. Irish by* Austin Clarke. BIrV
Eireann. Osbert Lancaster. *Fr.* Afternoons with Baedeker. DBV; NOBL
Eisenhower's Visit to Franco, 1959. James Wright. CAPP; NaP; NMP
Either get out of my house or conform to my tastes, woman. Martial, *tr. fr. Latin by* James Michie. FaBoEE
Either he is an excellent critic. Little Roach Poem. C. W. Truesdale. PoDr
Either she was foul, or her attire was bad. Shameful Impotence [*or* The Impotent Lover]. Ovid, *tr. by* Christopher Marlowe. Amores, III, vii. ErPo; OBVE; UnTE
Either to keep the thinking in. Country Ways. Marcia Masters. Impressions of My Father, I. GoYe
Either we're liberals or we truly do. Death with a Coda. Giuseppe Gioachino Belli, *tr. by* Miller Williams. AMV-81
Either you will. Prospective Immigrants Please Note. Adrienne Rich. GOA; VGW
"Ej Blot til Lyst." William Morton Payne. AA
Ejected Wife, The. *Tr. fr. Chinese by* Arthur Waley. OBVE
El Aghir. Norman Cameron. *See* Green, Green Is El Aghir.
El Alamein Revisited. Roy Macnab. PeSA
El Camino Verde. Paul Blackburn. CoPo
El Capitan-General. Charles Godfrey Leland. AA; HBV-2; YaD
El Dorado. Richard Ryan. BIrV
El Emplazado. William Henry Venable. PAH
El Greco. E. L. Mayo. HoPM; MiAP
El Greco: Espolio. Earle Birney. MoCV; PeCV
El Gusano. Irving Layton. PeCV
El Hombre. William Carlos Williams. CABA; CMoP; LiTA
El Ropero. Antonio di Montorio. TrJP
El Vaquero. Lucius Harwood Foote. AA
Elaboration, The. Bill Manhire. OCNZ
Elaine's Song. Tennyson. *See* Song of Love and Death, The.
El-a-noy, *with music.* *Unknown.* AS; TrAS
(Elanoy.) FSW
Elbows in wine-slops, news of the ocean isles. Cipangu. William Hart-Smith. *Fr.* Christopher Columbus. PoAu-2
Elbucks on the herbour waa. Mongol Quine. Alastair Mackie. BSV
Elder Brother, The, *sel.* John Fletcher.
"Beauty clear and fair," *fr.* III, v. OAEP; OBEV; OBS; ViBoPo
Elder Edda, The, *sels.* *Unknown, tr. fr. Old Norse* by William Morris *and* Eirikr Magnusson.
First Lay of Gudrun, The. AWP
First Lay of Gudrun, The: "Gudrun Laments over Sigurd." OBVE
Lay of Sigurd, The. AWP
And now one prayer." OBVE
Part of the Lay of Sigrdrifa. OBVE
(Counsels of Sigrdrifa.) AWP
Voluspo, *tr. by* Henry Adams Bellows. AWP
"Elder Father, though thine eyes." The Holy of Holies. G. K. Chesterton. TRV; WGRP
Elder, or Bourtree, The. *Unknown.* GBP
(Elder Tree, The.) ChTr
Elder Tree. Conrad Aiken. AP
Elderberry Flute Song. Peter Blue Cloud. STE
Elderly Gentleman, The. George Canning. NA
Elders at their services begin, The. Epigram. J. V. Cunningham. NePoAm
Elder's Reproof to his Wife, An. 'Abdillaahi Muuse, *tr. fr. Somali by* B. W. Andrzjewski *and* I. M. Lewis. TTY; WTO
Eldest is calling, The. Tip-of-the-Single-Feather. Velema, *tr. by* B. H. Quain. WTO
Eldest son bestrides him, The. The Undertaker's Horse. Kipling. FaBoNo; FM
Eldorado. Poe. AmPP; AP; AWP; FaBoBe; FaBoCh; FPL; HBV-2; NePA; NOBA; NoP; OxBA; PAI; TAP; WiR
Eleanor Rigby. John Lennon *and* Paul McCartney. InPK; InPS; PPoe; PrIm; WTO
Eleanor (she spoiled in a British climate). Ezra Pound. Cantos, VII. NoAM; NOBA
Eleazar Wheelock. Richard Hovey. OBAL; WhC
Elected Kaiser, burgher and a knight. Charles the Fifth and the Peasant. Robert Lowell, *after the French of* Paul Valéry. MiAP
Elected Knight, The. *Unknown, tr. fr. Danish by* Longfellow. AWP
Elected Silence. Siegfried Sassoon. MoBrPo
Elected Silence, sing to me. The Habit of Perfection. Gerard Manley Hopkins. ACP; BrPo; CoBMV; LiTB; MoAB; MoBrPo; NoAM; NoP; OAEP; OBEV; OBMV; PoPle; PoRA; TrGrPo; UnS; ViBoPo; VLP
Election, An. Mordecai Marcus. SOTS
Election, The. Robert Pack. CoPo
Election Address, An. James Kenneth Stephen. NBM
Election Reflection. M. Keel Jones. PV
Election Songs. *Yoruba Oral Tradition, tr. by* Ulli Beier. WTO
Election Time. *Unknown.* FaBoPa
Electra. Francis Howard Williams. AA
Electric Cop, The. Victor Hernandez Cruz. PoBA
Electric Sign Goes Dark, An. Carl Sandburg. HBMV
Electric Storm. Michael C. Martin. WaP
Electric Telegraph, The. Thomas Baker. *Fr.* The Steam Engine; or, The Power of Flame. FaBoUs
Electrically, cleanly. January. Richard A. Hawley. AMV-80
Electricity Is Funny! John Currier. GrPl
Electrocution. Lola Ridge. WPE
Electrocution Script. P. L. Jacobs. LFAC
Electronic baby born to be. Dream after Touring the Tokyo Tokei. Joy Kogawa. BrSi
Elegance. Christopher Smart. Hymns for the Amusement of Children, Hymn 13. NOCV
Elegant use of foliage and grace, An. More. Gertrude Stein. *Fr.* Tender Buttons. PBWP
Elegiac. James Gates Percival. AA
(It Is Great for Our Country to Die.) HBV-2
Elegiac Sonnet. Charlotte Smith. *See* Sonnet Written at the Close of Spring.
Elegiac Stanzas, Suggested by a Picture of Peele Castle, in a Storm. Wordsworth. ChER; FaBoPP; HBV-2; NoP; OAEL-2; OAEP; OBRV
(Elegiac Stanzas.) EnRP; OBNC
(Nature and the Poet.) GTBS; GTBS-P
Elegiack Verse on. . .Mr. Elijah Corlet. Nehemiah Walter. SCAP
Elegie: Autumnal, The. John Donne. *See* Autumnal, The.
Elegie: "Goe stop the swift-wing'd moments in their flight." William Habington. AnAnS-2
Elegie: Going to Bed. John Donne. *See* Going to Bed.
Elegie: His Parting from Her. John Donne. *See* His Parting from Her.
Elegie: His Picture. John Donne. *See* His Picture.
Elegie, An: "Let me be what I am, as Virgil cold." Ben Jonson. PoEL-2; SeCP
Elegie, An: "Love, give me leave to serve thee, and be wise." Thomas Randolph. MePo
Elegie VII: "Natures lay ideot, I taught thee to love." John Donne. *See* Elegy: "Nature's lay idiot, I taught thee to love."
Elegie: On His Mistris. John Donne. *See* On His Mistress.
Elegie, An: "Though beautie be the marke of praise." Ben Jonson. *See* Elegy, An: "Though beauty be the mark of praise."
Elegie, An: " 'Tis true, I'm broke! Vowes, oathes, and all I had." Ben Jonson. AnAnS-2
Elegie XIX: To His Mistris Going to Bed. John Donne. *See* Going to Bed.
Elegie Made by Mr. Aurelian Townshend in Remembrance of the Ladie Venetia Digby, An. Aurelian Townshend. AnAnS-2; SeCP
Elegie on the Deploreable Departure of the Honered and Truely Religious Chieftain John Hull, An. John Saffin. SCAP
Elegie on the Lady Jane Pawlet, Marchion. of Winton, An. Ben Jonson. SeCP

Elegie upon That Reverend . . . Mr. Thomas Shepard, An. Urian Oakes. SCAP
"Away loose-reined careers of poetry!" *sel.* NOCV
Elegie upon the Death of His Owne Father, An. Richard Corbett. AnAnS-2
Elegie upon the Death of the Deane of Pauls, Dr. John Donne, An. Thomas Carew. *See* Elegy upon the Death of the Dean of Paul's, Dr. John Donne, An.
Elegie upon the Death of the Lord Hastings, An. Sir John Denham. SeCV-1
Elegie upon the Death of the Reverend Mr. Thomas Shepard, An. Urian Oakes. *See* Elegie upon That Reverend . . .
Elegies. André Chénier, *tr. fr. French by* Arthur Symons. AWP
"Every Man has his sorrows; yet each still," I.
"Well, I would have it so. I should have known," III.
"White nymph wandering in the woods by night, A," II.
Elegies, *sels.* John Donne.
Autumnal[l], The, IX. InPS; JCP; OAEP; PoEL-2; SeCV-1; TEP; ViBoPo
Change, III. EBEV; ViBoPo
Elegy: "Nature's lay idiot, I taught thee to love," VII. NoP
(Elegie: "Nature's lay ideot, I taught thee to love.") SECP
Going to Bed, XIX. AnAnS-1; EBEV; BGL; LiTB; PPP
(Elegy [*or* Elegie]: Going to Bed.) EnRePo; MePo
(Elegie XIX: To His Mistris Going to Bed.) SeCP
(To His Mistress [*or* Mistris] Going to Bed.) BoLoP; ErPo; JCP; NoP; OAEL-1; TEP; UnTE
His Parting from Her, XII. EBEV
(Elegie: His Parting from Her.) OBS
His Picture, V. FaBoEn; MePo; OBS
(Elegy [*or* Elegie] V: His Picture.) EnRePo; MeLP
Jealousy, I. FF
(Jealosie.) AnAnS-1
Love's Progress, XVIII. LiTB; OAEL-1; ViBoPo
On His Mistress [*or* Mistris], XVI. AnAnS-1; BoLoP; EBEV; LiTB; PoEL-2; SeCeV; ViBoPo
(Elegy [*or* Elegy] on His Mistress.) GBL; LoBV; MeLP; MePo; SeCV-1
(Elegie XVI: On His Mistress.) SeCP
(To His Mistress Desiring to Travel with Him as His Page.) NOBE
Perfume, The, IV. AnAnS-1; SeCP
Elegies, *sels.* Ovid, *tr. fr. Latin.*
Captive of Love, I, 2, *tr. by* Christopher Marlowe. AWP
Lente, Lente, I, 14, *tr. by* Kirby Flower Smith. AWP
To Verse Let Kings Give Place, *fr.* XV, *tr. by* Christopher Marlowe. ChTr
Elegies, *sels.* Propertius, *tr. fr. Latin.* AWP
Ah Woe Is Me, I, 1, *tr. by* F. A. Wright.
Hylas, I, 20, *tr. by* F. A. Wright.
Revenge to Come, III, 25, *tr. by* Kirby Flower Smith.
Elegies for the Hot Season. Sandra McPherson. AmPA
Elegy XI: "Ah me, my friend! it will not, will not last!" William Shenstone. *See* Elegy: He Complains How Soon . . .
Elegy: "And if our lives spill." Philip Dow. NPGG
Elegy: "April again and it is a year again." Sidney Keyes. WaP
Elegy: "Clear and gentle stream!" Robert Bridges. BrPo; OAEP
Elegy: " 'Crusher' never scared me, The. Tho that giant." Alan Loney. OCNZ
Elegy: "Death be not proud, thy hand gave not this blow." Lucy Harington, Countess of Bedford. WPE
Elegy: "Do not look for him." Leonard Cohen. HeIP
Elegy: E. W. L. E. Sissman. NYBP
Elegy: "Fled is the swiftness of all the white-footed ones." Joseph Auslander. TrJP
Elegy: "Floods of tears well from my deepest heart, The." Immanuel di Roma, *tr. fr. Italian by* J. Chotzner. TrJP
Elegy, An: "Friend, whose unnatural early death." David Gascoyne. FaBoTw; MP; TwCP
Elegy: "Gnu up at the zoo, The." John Hall Wheelock. NYBP
Elegy XIX: Going to Bed. John Donne. *See* Going to Bed.
Elegy, An: "Good people all, with one accord." Goldsmith. *See* Elegy on That Glory of Her Sex, Mrs. Mary Blaize, An.
Elegy: He Complains How Soon the Pleasing Novelty of Life Is Over. William Shenstone. OBEC
(Elegy XI: "Ah me, my friend! it will not, will not last!") NOEC
Elegy: "Her face like a rain-beaten stone on the day she rolled off." Theodore Roethke. CTBA; DFF; NCSH
Elegy V: His Picture. John Donne. *See* His Picture.
Elegy XXIII: "How does it help me if, with flawless art." Louise Labé, *tr. fr. French by* Raymond Oliver. WPOW
Elegy: "I die for Your holy word without regret." Antonio Enriquez Gomez, *tr. fr. Spanish.* TrJP
Elegy XIII: "I got her in the Black Bull." Sydney Goodsir Smith. *Fr.* Under the Eildon Tree. BSV
Elegy: "I know but will not tell." Alan Dugan. AP; CAPP; DiL
Elegy: "I must wait for a stranger to knock on my door." David Ignatow. NNaP
Elegy: "I remember the feel of a hammer." Robert Winner. DiL
Elegy: "I stood between two mirrors when you died." William Jay Smith. NePoEA
Elegy, An: "I will not weep, for 'twere as great a sin." Henry King. AnAnS-2
Elegy, An: "In early winter before the first snow." E. J. Scovell. ChMP
Elegy: "In my collection, the words are, we use." Alan Loney. OCNZ
Elegy: "In pain she bore the son who her embrace." Moses ibn Ezra, *tr. fr. Hebrew by* Solomon Solis-Cohen. TrJP
Elegy: In Spring, *sel.* Michael Bruce.
"Now spring returns: but not to me returns." BSV
Elegy: "In summer's heat and mid-time of the day." Ovid. *See* In Summer's Heat.
Elegy: Ise Lamenting the Death of Empress Onshi. Lady Ise, *tr. fr. Japanese by* Etsuko Terasaki *and* Irma Brandeis. BoWoP
Elegy: "Jackals prowl, the serpents hiss, The." Arthur Guiterman. InMe
Elegy: "Let them bury your big eyes." Edna St. Vincent Millay. Memorial to D.C., V. CMoP; HBMV; MoAB; MoAmPo; NePA; PoRA
("O, loveliest throat of all sweet throats.") OxBA
Elegy, The: "Madam, no more! The time has come to eat." A. D. Hope. ErPo; NoP
Elegy IX: "My dear, observe the rose! though she desire it." William Bell. NePoEA
Elegy: "My father was born with a spade in his hand and traded it." John Ciardi. DiL
Elegy: "My prime of youth is but a frost of cares." Chidiock Tichborne. ChTr; EBEV; LoBV; NOBE; OBSC; WeW
(Elegy, Written with His Own Hand in the Tower before His Execution.) DL; InPK; PAI
(His Elegy.) PPoe
(Lament the Night before His Execution, A.) HBV-1
(On the Eve of His Execution.) TrGrPo
(Retrospect.) ACP; GoBC
(Tichborne's Elegy.) ElL; FaBoRV; FF; HAP; HeIP; InPS; NoP; OAEL-1
(Written on the Eve of Execution.) LiTB; TreFT
(Written the Night before His Execution.) SCV; ViBoPo
Elegy: "My Thompson, least attractive character." Howard Nemerov. PPJ
Elegy: "My thoughts impelled me to the resting-place." Moses ibn Ezra, *tr. fr. Hebrew by* Emma Lazarus. TrJP
Elegy: "Narrowing of knowledge to one window to a door, A." William Montgomerie. *See* Elegy for William Soutar.
Elegy: "Nature's lay idiot, I taught thee to love." John Donne. Elegies, VII. NoP
(Elegie VII: "Natures lay ideot, I taught thee to love.") SeCP
Elegy: "No more, no more Jewish townships in Poland." Antoni Slonimski, *tr. fr. Polish by* Isaac Komem. VWA
Elegy, An: "Noon is beautiful, The: the perfect wheel." Yvor Winters. VGW
Elegy: "Nor Hammond's love nor Shenstone's was sincere." John Maclaurin. NOEC
Elegy X: "Now Christendom bids her cathedrals call." William Bell. NePoEA
Elegy: "O snatch'd away in beauty's bloom!" Byron. GTBS; GTBS-P
(Oh! Snatched [*or* Snatch'd] Away in Beauty's Bloom.) EnRP; FiP; HBV-1; LoBV; OBRV
Elegy: "O spare a tear for poor Tom Hood." Martin Fagg. *See* Elegy on Thomas Hood.
Elegy: "Out on the roads of sky the moon stands poised." Roy McFadden. NeIP
Elegy: "Pages of history open, The." Sandra M. Gilbert. PoA
Elegy V: Separation of Man from God. George Barker. LiTB
(Elegy: "These errors loved no less than the saint loves arrows.") FaBoTw
(Sacred Elegy V.) MoPo
Elegy, An: "She fell away in her first ages spring." Spenser. *Fr.* Daphnaïda. OBEV
("She fell away in her first ages spring.") PoPle
Elegy, An: "Since you must go, and I must bid farewell." Ben Jonson. EnRePo; LoBV
Elegy: "Somebody left the world last night, I felt it." Olga Broumas. LTB
Elegy: Summer-House on the Mound, The. Robert Bridges. GoTL
Elegy: "These errors loved no less than the saint loves arrows." George Barker. *See* Elegy V: Separation of Man from God.
Elegy: "They are lang deid, folk that I used to ken." Robert Garioch. OxBS
Elegy: "Those reckless hosts rush to the wells." Baruch of Worms, *tr. fr. Hebrew.* TrJP

Elegy, An: "Though beauty be the mark of praise." Ben Jonson. EnRePo; NoP; OBEV; QFR
(Elegie, An: "Though beautie be the marke of praise.") SeCV-1
Elegy: Three. Seamus Deane. CIP
Elegy: To Spring, *sel.* Michael Bruce.
"Farewell, ye blooming fields! ye cheerful plains!" NOEC
Elegy: "Tonight the moon is high, to summon all." William Bell. FaBoTw
Elegy: "Waxen and the false grace of tulips, The." G. S. Fraser. NeBP
Elegy: "Way the hell-bent years consume my pleasure, The." Pushkin, *tr. fr. Russian by* Robley Wilson, Jr. AMV-81
Elegy: "When in the mirror of a permanent tear." Gene Derwood. *See* Elegy on Gordon Barber.
Elegy: "When the old ones die." Karoniaktatie. STE
Elegy: "Whenever we touched, I thought of the Lying-in Hospital." Robert Layzer. NePoEA; PoPl
Elegy: "While walking at dusk in a strange city." Pinhas Sadeh, *tr. fr. Hebrew by* Gabriel Preil *and* Howard Schwartz. VWA
Elegy: "Who keeps the owl's breath? Whose eyes desire?" David St. John. LCAP
Elegy: "Whole tribe dies, A." Duane Big Eagle. STE
Elegy: "Wood is bare, The: a river-mist is steeping." Robert Bridges. EBVV; OAEP; PoPle
Elegy: "Youd make capital of." Alan Loney. OCNZ
Elegy and Flame. Horace Gregory. FYAP
Elegy and Kaddish. David Rosenmann-Taub, *tr. fr. Spanish by* Charles Guenther. VWA
Elegy before Death. Edna St. Vincent Millay. CMoP; LiTA; LiTM
Elegy for a Bad Poet, Taken from Us Not Long Since. John Frederick Nims. TW
Elegy for a Countryman. Padraic Fallon. NeIP
Elegy for a Cricket. J. V. Cunningham. NoAM
Elegy for a Dead Confederate. Robert McGovern. SOTS
Elegy for a Dead Soldier. Karl Shapiro. AP; CoBMV; HAP; LiTM; MiAP; OBWP; OxBA; WaaP; WaP
Epitaph: "Underneath this wooden cross there lies," *sel.* OFD
Elegy for a Diver. Philip Booth. LiSp
Elegy for a Diver. Peter Meinke. Psk
Elegy for a Nature Poet. Howard Nemerov. BoNaP; HoPM; PP
Elegy for a Puritan Conscience. Alan Dugan. CAPP; NoAM
Elegy for a School-Friend. Augustus Young. BIrV
Elegy for a Woman Who Remembered Everything. David Wagoner. DFF
Elegy for Alfred Hubbard. Tony Connor. SoSe
Elegy for an Estrangement. John Holloway. NePoEA
Elegy for Bella, Sarah, Rosie, and All the Others. Sonya Dorman. GOA
Elegy for Bob Marley, An. William Matthews. MAYP
Elegy for Chief Sealth. Duane Niatum. CDW
Elegy for D. H. Lawrence, An. William Carlos Williams. NoAM
Elegy for Doctor Dunn. Lord Herbert of Cherbury. AnAnS-2
Elegy for Dylan Thomas. Edith Sitwell. PoA
Elegy for Ezra. Raymond Roseliep. SOTS
Elegy for Former Students. Virginia Scott Miner. AMV-81
Elegy for 41 Whales Beached in Florence, Ore., June, 1979. Linda Bierds. AMV-81
Elegy for Helen Trent. Paris Leary. CoPo
Elegy for Her Brother Sakhr. Al-Khansa, *tr. fr. Arabic.* BoWoP, *tr. by* Willis Barnstone; WPOW, *tr. by* Bridget Connelly
Elegy (for Himself). Moses Rimos of Majorca, *tr. fr. Hebrew by* Israel Abrahams. TrJP
Elegy for Jack Bowman. Joseph Bruchac. CDW
Elegy for Jane. Theodore Roethke. AmPP; AP; BiP; CoAP; FF; GLGT; HAP; InPK; InPS; LiTM; MoAB; MoAmPo; MP; NePA; NoP; PAI; PPoe; TAP; TwAmPo; TwCP; WeW
Elegy for Margaret, *sel.* Stephen Spender.
"Dearest and nearest brother," VI. FaBoEn
Elegy for Minor Poets. Louis MacNeice. PP
Elegy for Mr. Goodbeare. Sir Osbert Sitwell. MoBrPo
Elegy for My Father. Robert Louthan. AMV-80
Elegy for My Father. Howard Moss. CoAP; DiL; LiTM; NePoEA; VWA
Elegy for My Father. Mark Strand. DiL; GeTw; LCAP
Sels.
Empty Body, The. UnPo
New Year, The. UnPo
Your Shadow. Prf
Elegy for My Father, *sel.* Irving Wexler.
"When Friday nights are lucky, you." DiL
Elegy for N. N. Czeslaw Milosz. SV
Elegy for Our Dead. Edwin Rolfe. WaP
Elegy for the Duke of Marmalade. Luis Palés Matos, *tr. fr. Spanish by* Julio Marzán. InW
Elegy for the Forgotten Oldsmobile. Adrian C. Louis. STE
Elegy for the Giant Tortoises. Margaret Atwood. BoWoP
Elegy for the Monastery Barn. Thomas Merton. CoPo; VGW
Elegy for the Silent Voices and the Joiners of Everything. Kenneth Patchen. NaP
Elegy for the Wife of a Friend. Yü Hsüan-chi, *tr. fr. Chinese by* Geoffrey Waters. BoWoP
Elegy for Two Banjos. Karl Shapiro. LiTA; TrJP; WaP
Elegy for W. C. W., the Lovely Man, An. John Berryman. *Fr.* Dream Songs. NoP
Elegy for William Soutar. William Montgomerie. NeBP
(Elegy: "Narrowing of Knowledge to one window to a door, A.") OxBS
Elegy for Yards, Pounds, and Gallons. David Wagoner. PoA
Elegy in a Country Churchyard. G. K. Chesterton. DBV; EvOK; FaPoR; HBMV; MMA; MoBrPo; OBWP; TreFT; TrGrPo; ViBoPo; WhC
Elegy in a Firelit Room. James Wright. TwAmPo
Elegy in a Presbyterian Burying-Ground. R. N. D. Wilson. BIrV
Elegy in a Theatrical Warehouse. Kenneth Fearing. NYBP
Elegy in Memory of the Worshipful Major Thomas Leonard Esq, An. Samuel Danforth, Jr. SCAP
Elegy in Six Sonnets. Frederick Goddard Tuckerman. *Fr.* Sonnets. QFR
Elegy in the Cemetery of Spoon River instead of in That of Stoke Poges. J. C. Squire. *See* If Gray Had Had to Write His Elegy . . .
Elegy Is Preparing Itself, An. Donald Justice. HoPM
Elegy Just in Case. John Ciardi. MiAP; MP; TwAmPo; TwCP
Elegy, Montreal Morgue. Goodridge MacDonald. CaP
Elegy of Fortinbras. Zbigniew Herbert, *tr. fr. Polish by* Czeslaw Milosz. OBVE
Elegy on a Dead Mermaid Washed Ashore at Plymouth Rock. Robert Hillyer. EtS
Elegy on a Lady, Whom Grief for the Death of Her Betrothed Killed. Robert Bridges. CoBMV; OBEV; OBVV; VLP
Elegy on a Lap-Dog, An. John Gay. HBV-1
Elegy on a Nordic White Protestant. John Gould Fletcher. PoNe
Elegy on Albert Edward the Peacemaker. *Unknown.* CoMu
Elegy on an Australian Schoolboy, *sel.* Zora Cross.
"O brother in the restless rest of God!" PoAu-1
Elegy on Any Lady by George Moore. Max Beerbohm. FaBoEE
Elegy on Ben Jonson [*or* Johnson], An. John Cleveland. MeLP; OBS
Elegy on Captain Matthew Henderson, *sel.* Burns.
"Mourn, ye wee songsters o' the wood." PBBP
Elegy on Gordon Barber. Gene Derwood. FaFP; NePA; TwAmPo
(Elegy: "When in the mirror of a permanent tear.") LiTA; LiTM
Elegy on Herakleitos. Callimachus, *tr. fr. Greek by* Dudley Fitts. InPK
Elegy on His Mistress. John Donne. *See* On His Mistress.
Elegy on Mistress Boulstred. John Donne. JCP
Elegy on Mrs. Mary Blaize. Goldsmith. *See* Elegy on That Glory of Her Sex, Mrs. Mary Blaize, An.
Elegy on Shakespeare. William Basse. FaBoRV; OBS
(On Mr. Wm. Shakespeare.) ElL; ViBoPo
Elegy on That [*or* the] Glory of Her Sex, Mrs. Mary Blaize, An. Goldsmith. FaBoNo; HBV-2; LAuP;OAEP; OBEC; OnYI; TreFT
(Elegy, An: "Good people all, with one accord.") InMe; NA
(Elegy on Mrs. Mary Blaize.) WhC
(Mrs. Mary Blaize.) FaBoCo
Elegy on the Death of a Mad Dog, An. Goldsmith. *Fr.* The Vicar of Wakefield, *ch.* 17. BeLS; BLPA; FaBoBe; FaBoCh; FaBoCo; FaFP; FPL; GDP; GN; HBV-2; HBVY; LAuP; NA; NOBE; NOEC; OAEP; OBEC; OBNV; PoPle; RoGo; ShM; TEP; TreF
Elegy on the Death of Dobbin, the Butterwoman's Horse, An. Francis Fawkes. NOEC
Elegy on the Death of Furuhi, An. Yamamoue Okura, *tr. fr. Japanese.* DL
Elegy on the Death of Her Husband. Anne Howard, Duchess of Arundel. WPE
Elegy on the Death of John Keats, An. Shelley. *Fr.* Adonais. OBNC
(Against Oblivion.) TreFS
(Mourn Not for Adonais.) NOBE
("Peace, peace! he is not dead, he doth not sleep.") FaBoEn; Lo
Elegy on the Death of Sidney. *At. to* Fulke Greville *and to* Sir Edward Dyer. *See* Epitaph on Sir Philip Sidney.
Elegy on the Dust. Thom Gunn. NoAM
Elegy on the Eve. George Barker. WaaP
Elegy on the Glory of Her Sex, Mrs. Mary Blaize, An. Goldsmith. *See* Elegy on That Glory of Her Sex, Mrs. Mary Blaize, An.
Elegy on the Lady Venetia Digby, Wife of Sir Kenelm Digby, *sel.* Ben Jonson.
Picture of Her Mind, The. GoBC
Elegy on the Late King of Patagonia, An. St. John Emile Clavering Hankin. CenHV
Elegy on the Loss of U.S. Submarine S4. H. C. Canfield. *See* On the Loss of U.S. Submarine S4.
Elegy on Thomas Hood. Martin Fagg. FaBoPa; NOBL
(Elegy: "O spare a tear for poor Tom Hood.") BXAP
Elegy on Thyrza. Byron. *See* And Thou Art Dead.

Elegy, or Friend's Passion for His Astrophil, An, *sels.* Matthew Royden.
On Sir Philip Sidney. EIL
"Upon the branches of those trees." PBBP
Elegy over a Tomb. Lord Herbert of Cherbury. AnAnS-2; EIL; FaBoEn; MeLP; MePo; NOBE; OBEV; OBS; PoEL-2; QFR; ViBoPo
Elegy, to an Old Beauty, An. Thomas Parnell. NOEC
Elegy to His Mistress. Ovid. *See* In Summer's Heat.
Elegy to the Memory of an Unfortunate Lady. Pope. ACP; FiP; HBV-2; LO; NOBE; NOEC; OAEL-1; OBEC; OBEV; SeCeV; TEP
"Most souls, 'tis true, but peep out once an age," *sel.* CH; ELU; PAI
(Dull, Sullen Prisoners.) FaBoRV
Elegy to the Sioux. Norman Dubie. MAYP
Elegy upon My Best Friend, An. Henry King. AnAnS-2
Elegy upon the Death of Doctor Donne, Dean of Paul's, An. Thomas Carew. *See* Elegy upon the Death of the Dean of Paul's, Dr. John Donne.
Elegy upon the Death of That Holy Man of God Mr. John Allen, An. Edward Taylor. PoEL-3
Elegy upon the Death of the Dean of Paul's, Dr. John Donne, An. Thomas Carew. JCP; NoP
(Elegie upon the Death of the Deane of Pauls, Dr. John Donne, An.) AnAnS-2; MeLP; MePo; OBS; SeCP; SeCV-1
(Elegy upon the Death of the Dean of St. Paul's, Dr. John Donne.) CABA; CaPo
(Elegy upon the Death of Doctor Donne, Dean of Paul's, An.) OAEL-1; PP
On the Death of Donne, *sel.* NOBE
Elegy upon the Most Incomparable King Charles the First, An, *sel.* Henry King.
"Thou from th' enthroned martyrs blood-stain'd line." OBS
Elegy while Pruning Roses. David Wagoner. AMV-80
Elegy Written at the Sea-Side, and Addressed to Miss Honoria Sneyd. Anna Seward. PeHV
Elegy Written in a Country Churchyard. Thomas Gray. AWP; BiP; CABA; DL; EBEV; EnRP; FaBoBe; FaBoEn; FaBoPP; FaBoRV; FaFP; FaPoR; FPL; GN; GoTL; GTBS; GTBS-P; HAP; HBV-2; HBVY; HeIP; InPK; InPS; LaA; LAuP; LiTB; LoBV; MasP; NOBE; NOEC; NoP; OAEL-1; OAEP; OBEC; OBEV; OHFP; PAI; PoEL-3; PoLF; PPoe; PPP; PrIm; SCV; SeCeV; TEP; TreF; TrGrPo; UnPo; ViBoPo; WBLP; WeW; WHA
Elegy Written in a Country Coal-Bin. Christopher Morley. OBAL
Elegy Written on a Frontporch. Karl Shapiro. MoPo
Elegy, Written with His Own Hand in the Tower before His Execution. Chidiock Tichborne. *See* Elegy: "My prime of youth is but a frost of cares."
Elegy Wrote in the Tower, 1554, *shorter vers.* John Harington. EIL
Elegye, An: "Constant to none, but ever false to me." Thomas Campion. AAS
Elektra on Third Avenue. Marilyn Hacker. MAYP; NYP
Element. P. K. Page. MoCV; PeCV
Element of air was out of hand, The. Interlude. Theodore Roethke. MiAP
Element that utters doves, angels and cleft flames. Air. Kathleen Raine. MoAB; MoBrPo
Elemental. D. H. Lawrence. NoP
Elementary. Jim Tollerud. VoR
Elementary Cosmogony. Charles Simic. NNaP
Elementary Scene, The. Randall Jarrell. CMoP; LCAP
Elementary School Classroom [*or* Class Room] in a Slum, An. Stephen Spender. CoBMV; FF; GLGT; LiTB; MoAB; MoBrPo; MoPo; MP; NIP; OAEP; PPON; TrGrPo; TWCP; UnPo
(Elementary School Classroom, An.) FaBoMo
Elements, The. W. H. Davies. MoBrPo; OBVV
Elements, The. Tom Lehrer. FaBoUs
Elements. Carolyn Wilson Link. GoYe
Elements, The. Cardinal Newman. GoBC; OBRV
(Chorus of Elements.) OBVV
Elements have merged into solicitude, The. The Racer's Widow. Louise Glück. AmPA; GeTw; LiSp; NYBP
Elements of Grammar. Calvin C. Hernton. NBP
Elements of San Joaquin, The. Gary Soto. NPGG
Elena's Song. Sir Henry Taylor. *Fr.* Philip van Artevelde, II. OBEV; OBRV; OBVV
Elene, *sels.* Cynewulf, *tr. fr. Anglo-Saxon by* Charles W. Kennedy. AnOE
Constantine's Vision of the Cross.
Helena Embarks for Palestine.
Eleonora Duse as Magda. Laurence Binyon. SyP
Elephant, The. Herbert Asquith. SoPo; SUS; TiPo
Elephant, The. Hilaire Belloc. SoPo; TiPo
Elephant. Alan Brownjohn. OnUR
Elephant, The. Rachel Field. *See* Gunga.
Elephant, The. Sandra Hochman. BoAnP
Elephant, The. A. E. Housman. *See* Elephant, or the Force of Habit, The.
Elephant. David McFadden. WHW
Elephant, The ("Elephant carries a great big trunk"). *Unknown.* OnUR
Elephant [I], The ("Elephant who brings death"). *Unknown. See* Erin.
Elephant [II], The ("Elephant hunter, take your bow!"). *Unknown, tr. by* C. M. Bowra. TTY
Elephant ("Tall-topped acacia, you, full of branches"). *Unknown, tr. fr. Hottentot.* PeSA
Elephant always carries his trunk, The. The Elephant's Trunk. Alice Wilkins. SoPo; TiPo
Elephant and the Bookseller, The. John Gay. LoBV
Elephant and the Flea, The. *See* Way Down South. *Unknown.*
Elephant and the Giraffe, The. Charlotte Osgood Carter. TDH
Elephant carries a great big trunk, The. The Elephant. *Unknown.* OnUR
Elephant is in love with the millimeter, The. What the Violins Sing in Their Baconfat Bed. Jean Arp, *tr. by* John Frederick Nims. WeW
Elephant Is Slow to Mate, The. D. H. Lawrence. InPK; LiTB; LiTM; NoAM; PoPl; PPP; TEP
Elephant of long service to a circus, An. The Retirement of the Elephant. Russell Edson. AmPA
Elephant of Moissel, hear my pious prayer. Léopold Sédar Senghor, *tr. by* Ellen Conroy Kennedy. *Fr.* Return of the Prodigal Son. GrPl
Elephant, or the Force of Habit, The. A. E. Housman. NOBL; PV; WhC
(Elephant, The.) FaBV
Elephant Rock. Primus St. John. PoBA
Elephant Sat on Some Kegs, An. J. G. Francis. TDH
Elephant, the huge old beast, The. The Elephant Is Slow to Mate. D. H. Lawrence. InPK; LiTB; LiTM; NoAM; PoPl; PPP; TEP
Elephant to the Girl in Bertram Mills' Circus, The. Anthony Cronin. CIP
Elephant who brings death. Erin [*or* The Elephant]. *Unknown, tr. by* Gbadamosi *and* Ulli Beier. PBA; TTY
Elephants. Patrick Lane. NeAC
Elephants are born with so much clothing. Ivory Paper Weight. Adrien Stoutenburg. GP
Elephants Are Different to Different People. Carl Sandburg. MoAmPo
Elephants from the Sea. Ian Young. NeAC
Elephants in the Circus. D. H. Lawrence. BoAnP
Elephants May Parade before Your House. *Gond Oral Tradition, tr. by* V. Elwin *and* S. Hivale. WTO
Elephant's Trunk, The. Alice Wilkins. SoPo; TiPo
Elephants walking. Holding Hands. Lenore M. Link. FaPON; MoShBr; NTCP; RHPC; SoPo
Eletelephony. Laura E. Richards. FaPON; GoJo; NTCP; OBCA; OnUR; OxBChV; PDV; RHPC; SoPo; TiPo; YaD
Elevated Train, The. James S. Tippett. SUS
Élévation. Baudelaire, *tr. fr. French by* Arthur Symons. AWP
Elevator Landscapes, *sels.* Stephen Vincent. NeAC
Floor: Five.
Floor: O.
Elevator Man Adheres to Form, The. Margaret Danner. PoBA; PoNe
Elevator operator. Mr. 'Gator. N. M. Bodecker. NTCP; OnUR
Elevator rises, Negro men, The. Poem to Negro and Whites. Maxwell Bodenheim. PoNe
Elevator stops at every floor, The. Neuteronomy. Eve Merriam. QQQ
Eleven. Archibald MacLeish. HAP; NCSH; WeW
Eleven Addresses to the Lord, *abr.* John Berryman. OxBC
Sels.
"Master of beauty, craftsman of the snowflake," I. PAI; UnPo
Prayer for the Self, A, VIII. PPP
"Sole watchman of the flying stars, guard me," III. UnPo
"1100 Exposition." Newsletter from My Mother. Michael S. Harper. PoBA
Eleven o'clock, and the curtain falls. End of the Comedy. Louis Untermeyer. PoA
Eleven Tanka, *sel.* Lady Ise, *tr. fr. Japanese by* Burton Watson.
Sleeping with Someone Whom Came in Secret. LLLT
11th and Last Book of the Ocean to Cynthia, The. Sir Walter Ralegh. NCEP
(Ocean to Cynthia, The, *sl. abr.*) OBSC
(Ocean's Love to Cynthia, The, *sl. abr.*) SiPS
Eleventh Property, The. Sir Thomas More. *Fr.* The Twelve Properties or Conditions of a Lover. EnRePo
Eleventh Song: "Who is it that this dark[e] night." Sir Philip Sidney. *See* Astrophel and Stella: Eleventh Song.
Eleventh Sunday after Trinity. John Keble. *Fr.* The Christian Year. VLP
Elf and the Dormouse, The. Oliver Herford. AA; FaBoBe; FaPON; HBV-1; HBVY; OnMSP; RHPC; SoPo; TiPo
Elf-light, owl-light. Dusk in the Domain. Dorothea MacKellar. PoAu-1
Elf Night. Ron Rogers. STE
Elf Owl. Mary Austin. BPAW
Elfer Hill. *Unknown, tr. fr. Danish by* Robert Jamieson. AWP
Elfin Knight, The ("As I walked out in yonder dell"). *Unknown.* ViBoFo
Elfin Knight, The ("Elphin Knight sits on yon hill, The"). ESPB

Elfin Knight, The ("Go tell him to clear me one acre of ground"). *Unknown.* AmFP; WSC
(Cambric Shirt, *diff. vers.*) BaBo; FSW
("Can you make me a cambric shirt.") OxNR
Elfin Knight, The ("My plaid awa, my plaid awa"). BaBo; CH; FaBoBa; GBP; ViBoFo
Elfin Skates. Eugene Lee-Hamilton. OBVV
Elfin Song. Joseph Rodman Drake. *Fr.* The Culprit Fay. AA
Elfin Town. Rachel Field. WSC
Elgin Cathedral Epitaph. *Unknown. See* Epitaph: "Here lie I, Martin Elginbrodde."
Elgonyi say, there are big dreams and little dreams, The. Big Dream, Little Dream. Louis Simpson. POL
El-Hajj Malik El-Shabazz. Robert Hayden. CNA; PoBA
Eli, Eli. Judith Wright. CBAP
Eli, Eli, lama sabacthani? At the Ninth Hour. John Lancaster Spalding. *Fr.* God and the Soul. AA
Eli the Thatcher. Max Beerbohm *and* William Rothenstein. FaBoNo
Elihu. Alice Cary. PaPo
Elijah Speaking. Doug Fetherling. NOBC
Elijah's mantle fell upon. A Little Song of Work. Sarah Elizabeth Sprouse. BLRP
Elinda's Glove. Richard Lovelace. OBS
(Ellinda's Glove.) CaPo
Elinor Rumming. John Skelton. *See* Tunnyng of Elynour Rummyng, The.
Elinor Wylie fell in love with Shelley. A Thought in Time. Robert Hillyer. NYBP
Elinoure and Juga. Thomas Chatterton. LAuP
Eliot Cass was from Boston, Mass. The Old School Tie-up. Laurence McKinney. WhC
Elisa. Spenser. *Fr.* The Shepheardes Calender: April. OBSC
(Lay to Eliza, The.) NOBE
Elisa, or an Elegy upon the Unripe Decease of Sir Antony Irby, *sel.* Phineas Fletcher.
"My dearest Betty, my more lovéd heart." ViBoPo
Elixir, The. George Herbert. AnAnS-1; FaBoCh; GN; NoP; OHIP; TrGrPo; WGRP
(Elixer, The.) SeCV-1
Eliza. Erasmus Darwin. PaPo
Eliza and Anne were extremely distress'd. The Bird's Nest. Elizabeth Turner. OHIP
Eliza Telefair. Jocelyn Macy Sloan. GoYe
Elizabeth. Valentin Iremonger. *See* This Houre Her Vigill.
Elizabeth. George Brandon Saul. HBMV
Elizabeth. Sylvia Townsend Warner. MoAB; MoBrPo
Elizabeth, Elspeth, Betsy and Bess. Mother Goose. *See* Elizabeth, Lizzy, Betsy, and Bess.
Elizabeth, frigidly stretched. This Houre Her Vigill [*or* Elizabeth *or* Recollection in Autumn]. Valentin Iremonger. CIP; NeIP; OnYI; OxBI; OxBTC
Elizabeth her frock has torn. Think before You Act. Mary Elliott. HBVY
Elizabeth in Italy. Richard Weber. BoLoP
(In Memoriam II, Elizabeth in Italy.) ErPo
Elizabeth L. H. Ben Jonson. *See* Epitah on Elizabeth, L.H.
Elizabeth, Lizzy [*or* Elspeth], Betsy, and Bess. Mother Goose. HBV-1; HBVY; OxNR
Elizabeth of Bohemia. Sir Henry Wotton. *See* On His Mistress, the Queen of Bohemia.
"Elizabeth the Beloved." Elizabeth. Sylvia Townsend Warner. MoAB; MoBrPo
Elizabethan Tragedy; a Footnote. Howard Moss. NePoEA
"Elizabethans Called It Dying, The." James Schuyler. NeAP; PoM
Elizabeth's War with the Christmas Bear [1601]. Norman Dubie. LCAP; MAYP
Elk Ghosts; a Birth Memory. Dave Smith. GeTw
Ella, fell a/ Maple tree. Picnic. Hugh Lofting. GoJo; SUS
Ella, in a Square Apron, along Highway 80. Judy Grahn. *Fr.* The Common Woman. NMM
Ella of the Cinders. Mary Blake French Crouch. DFT
Ella Speed. *Unknown.* AmFP
Ellas and the Statues. Gülten Akin, *tr. fr. Turkish by* Nermin Menemencioglu. PBWP
Ellen Flannery. *Unknown.* AmFP
Ellen Irwin; or, The Braes of Kirtle. Wordsworth. PeD
Ellen M'Jones Aberdeen. W. S. Gilbert. HBV-2; InMe
Ellen Taylor. *Unknown.* OBET
Ellesmereland I ("Explorers say that harebells rise"). Earle Birney. CABA
Ellesmereland II ("And now in Ellesmereland there sits"). Earle Birney. CABA
Ellinda's Glove. Richard Lovelace. *See* Elinda's Glove.
Elliott Hawkins. Edgar Lee Masters. *Fr.* Spoon River Anthology. OxBA
Ellis Park. Helen Hoyt. HBMV
Ellora. Leonard Nathan. GP
Ellsworth. *Unknown.* PAH
Elm. Sylvia Plath. NoAM; NOBA; NoP
(Elm Speaks, The.) NYBP
Elm, The. Odell Shepard. HBMV
Elm Beetle, The. Andrew Young. LoBV
Elm is turned to crystal, The. Weather. William Meredith. NYBP
Elm lets fall its leaves before the frost, The. The Pine. Augusta Webster. HBV-1; OHIP
Elm Speaks, The. Sylvia Plath. *See* Elm.
Elmer Ruiz. Peter Oresick. LTB
Elms are bad, sinister trees. Breakwaters. Ted Walker. NYBP
Elms have to fight, The. Home Movies. Carter Revard. VoR
Elm's Home, The. William Heyen. MAYP
Eloïsa to Abelard. Pope. LoBV; OAEP; PoEL-3; TEP
Sels.
Eloïsa ("How happy is the blameless vestal's lot?"). OBEC
(Vestal, The.) ACP
Eloïsa ("What scenes appear where-e'er I turn my view"). SeCePo
Eloïsa's Prayer for Abelard. GoBC
"How oft, when pressed to marriage, have I said." ViBoPo
Eloquent are the hills: their power speaks. The Green Lake. Michael Roberts. ChMP
Eloquent as stuck drawers, we come out. Dividing the House. James Richardson. AMV-80
Eloquent between the formal hedges. Affair of Honour. George Whalley. MoCV
Elphin knight sits on yon hill, The. The Elfin Knight. *Unknown.* ESPB
Elsa Wertman. Edgar Lee Masters. *Fr.* Spoon River Anthology. NoAM; OxBA; PAI
Elsdon. Freda Downie. FaBoPP
"Else a Great Prince in Prison Lies." Denise Levertov. NaP; PPP; VGW
Elsewhere. Linda Pastan. VWA
Elsewheres. Donald Justice. LCAP
Elsie Marley is grown so fine. *Unknown.* OxNR
Elusive Maid, The. Abraham ibn Chasdai, *tr. fr. Hebrew by* J. Chotzner. TrJP
Elustrious Dame whose vertues rare doe shine. An Acrostick on Mrs. Elizabeth Hull. John Saffin. SCAP
Elver Fishers. Ivor Gurney. FaBoPP
Elves' Dance, The. *Unknown, at. to* John Lyly *and to* Thomas Ravenscroft. *Fr.* The Mayde's Metamorphosis. CH; FaPON
Elvin's Blues. Michael S. Harper. BPo
Elwha River, The. Gary Snyder. NoAM
Elysee. Larry Eigner. VGW
Elysian glade. Developers at Crystal River. James Merrill. AMV-81
Elysium is as far as to. Emily Dickinson. CABA; FaBoEn; GrPl; MoAB; MoAmPo; OLR; OxBA; WPE
(Suspense.) AWP
Emancipation. Maltbie D. Babcock. BLRP; WBLP
(Death.) WGRP
Emancipation. *Unknown.* BLPA; FPL
Emancipation from British Dependence. Philip Freneau. PAH
Emancipation Group, The, *sel.* Whittier.
"Let man be free! The mighty word." PGD
Emancipation of George-Hector (a Colored Turtle), The. Mari Evans. AmNP
Emancipators, The. Randall Jarrell. PoA; WaP
Emaricdulfe. "E. C." ElL
Embalming is so intricate these days. And Dust to Dust. Charles David Webb. NePoAm-2
Embankment, The. T. E. Hulme. EBEV; ELU; FaBoMo; GTBS-P; OxBTC
(Fantasia of a Fallen Gentleman on a Cold Bitter Night on the Embankment.) SeCePo
Embarcation. Thomas Hardy. BrPo; OBWP
Embarkation, The. Longfellow. *Fr.* Evangeline. PAH
Embarrassed Judge. *Unknown, tr. fr. Greek by* Louis Untermeyer. UnTE
Embarrassing Episode of Little Miss Muffet, The. Guy Wetmore Carryl. FaPON; OBCA; OnMSP
Embassy of doves, An. Late. Helen Salz. GoYe
Embers of the day are red, The. Evensong. Robert Louis Stevenson. TreFT; TrPWD; TRV
Emblazoned bleak in austral skies. Southern Cross. Herman Melville. LiTA
Emblem of England's ancient faith. To an Oak Tree. Sir Walter Scott. *Fr.* Waverley. OBNC
Emblem of Two Foxes, An. Barry Spacks. HoPM
Emblems. Douglas Dunn. FaBoMo
Emblems, *sels.* Francis Quarles.
"Behold thy darling, which thy lustful care," V, 8. AnAnS-1
Emblem ("'Tis but a foil at best, and that's the most"), II, 14. LoBV

Epigram: "My soul, thy love is dear: 'twas thought a good," *fr.* V, 4. OAEL-1
Epigram: "Paul's midnight voice prevailed; his music's thunder," *fr.* V, 10. LoBV
"Great All in all, that art my rest, my home," IV, 3. TrPWD
"How shall my tongue expresse that hallow'd fire," V, 11. AnAnS-1
Like to the Arctic Needle, V, 4. NOCV; OxBoCh
(I Am My Beloved's, and His Desire Is towards Me.) OBS
("Like to the arctic needle that doth guide.") EBEV; OAEL-1
My Beloved Is Mine, and I Am His; He Feedeth among the Lillies, V, 3. MePo; NOBE; OBS; TrGrPo, *abr.*
(Canticle.) FaBoEn
(Divine Rapture, A.) HBV-2; OBEV
("E'en [*or* Ev'n] like two little bank-dividing brook[e]s.") LO; MeLP
"My soule is like a bird; my flesh, the cage," V, 10. AnAnS-1
Wherefore Hidest Thou Thy Face, and Holdest Me for Thine Enemie? III, 7. MePo; OBS
("Why dost Thou shade thy lovely face? Oh why.") TrPWD
Wilt Thou Set Thine Eyes upon That Which Is Not? II, 5. OBS
(False World, Thou Liest.) SeCePo
(Vanity of the World, *abr.*) PPON
"World's a floore, whose swelling heapes retaine, The," II, 7. AnAnS-1
Emblems. Allen Tate. AWP; VGW
Emblems of Conduct. Hart Crane, *after* Samuel Greenberg. LiTA; LiTM; NePA
Emblems of Evening. Robert Horan. CrMA
Emblems of Love, *sels.* Lascelles Abercrombie.
Balkis. HBV-2
Epilogue: "What shall we do for Love these days?" HBV-1; MoBrPo; OBVV
Small Fountains. CH
Hymn to Love. OBEV; OBVV
Woman's Beauty, *fr.* Vashti. MoBrPo
Embodied close, the lab'ring Grecian train. Homer, *tr. by* Pope. *Fr.* The Iliad, V. OBVE
Embodiment of what, The. Lyric. Arthur Gregor. TAP
Embrace the Blade. Joyce Mansour, *tr. fr. French by* Carol Cosman. PBWP
Embraceable You, *with music.* Ira Gershwin. BLSo
Embracing low-falutin. The Countryman's Return. Dylan Thomas. OxBTC
Embro to the Ploy. Robert Garioch. OxBS
Embroidery. Maria Jacobs. AMV-80
Embroidery, An. Denise Levertov. DFT; NMM; NU
Embryo. Mary Ashley Townsend. AA; HBV-2
Emer, he is your man, now. Fand Yields Cuchulain to Emer. *Unknown, tr. by* Sean O'Faolain. AnIL
Emerald April, September's gold. Song of the Seasons. Blanche De Good Lofton. YeAr
Emerald cages a jungle, The. Prologue for a Bestiary. Ronald Perry. NePoEA-2
Emerald is as green as grass, An. Flint. Christina Rossetti. *Fr.* Sing-Song. OxBChV; RHPC; TiPo
Emeralds are singing on the grasses, The. How Many Heavens. Edith Sitwell. TrCP
Emergency. Isabel Fiske Conant. HBMV
Emergency at 8. Geof Hewitt. NeAC
Emergency Haying. Hayden Carruth. NNaP
Emergency Maker, The. David Wagoner. NePoEA-2
Emergency Room, The. David Fisher. NPGG
Emerges daintily, the skunk. The Wood Weasel. Marianne Moore. CMoP
Emerging from the inmost hideout. Splendor. Shin Shalom, *tr. by* Abraham BirmanVWA
Emerging from the naked labyrinth. August 13, 1966. Daryl Hine. GP
Emeritus, n. Henri Coulette. FF
Emerson. Amos Bronson Alcott. AA
Emerson. Mary Mapes Dodge. AA
Emerson. James Russell Lowell. *Fr.* A Fable for Critics. AmPP; AP; NOBA; OxBA; TAP
("There comes Emerson first, whose rich words, every one.") PP
Emerson, strolling through the Louvre. Art in America. Theodore Weiss. AMV-80
Emigrant, The, *sels.* Alexander McLachlan.
Arrival, The. NOBC
Song: "Old England is eaten by Knaves." NOBC; OBCV
Emigrant, The, *sels.* Standish O'Grady.
"And first Morency, far famed water, you." CaP
Old Nick in Sorel. OBCV
Winter in Lower Canada. NOBC; OBCV
Emigrant Song. "S. Ansky," *tr. fr. Yiddish by* Joseph Leftwich. TrJP
Emigrant's Child, The. Lyman H. Sproull. PoOW
Emigrant's Dying Child, The. G. W. Patton. BPAW
Emigration. Anita Barrows. NMM
Emigration of the Fairies, The, *sel.* John Hunter-Duvar.
"First halt. They heard within a sugar patch." CaP
Emigravit. Helen Hunt Jackson. AA
Emilia. Sarah N. Cleghorn. HBV-1
Emily Brontë. C. Day Lewis. ChMP; GTBS-P
Emily Carr. Wilfred Watson. MoCV; NOBC; OBCV
Emily Dickinson. Inger Hagerup, *tr. fr. Norwegian by* Harold P. Hansen. AMV-81
Emily Dickinson. Michael Longley. CIP
Emily Dickinson Postage Stamp. Lynn Strongin. NMM
Emily Geiger. *Unknown.* BLPL; PoLF; PAL
Emily Hardcastle, Spinster. John Crowe Ranson. CMoP
Emily, John, James, and I ("Emily Jane was a nursery maid"). W. S. Gilbert. InMe; WhC
Emily Sparks. Edgar Lee Masters. *Fr.* Spoon River Anthology. GLGT
Emily wandered through town and folks said that she saw. Old Emily. Hyacinthe Hill. GoYe
Emily's Haunted Housman. David Cummings. BXAP
Eminence becomes you. Now when the rock is struck. To T. S. Eliot. Emanuel Litvinoff. VWA
Eminent Critic. John Frederick Nims. TW
Emma. Goldsmith. OnYI
Emma. Yvonne. CNA
Emma Lee's husband beat her up. Conversations between Here and Home. Joy Harjo. TWSS
Emmeline Grangerford's "Ode to Stephen Dowling Bots, Dec'd." "Mark Twain." *Fr.* The Adventures of Huckleberry Finn. OBAL
(Ode to Stephen Dowling Bots, Dec'd.) FiBHP; NIP
Emmett Till. James A. Emanuel. CNA; NIP; PoBA
Emmonsail's Heath in Winter. John Clare. FaBoEn; PoEL-4
Emmy ("Emmy's exquisite youth and her virginal air"). Arthur Symons. HBV-1; OBNC; OBVV; TreF
Empedocles. George Meredith. VLP
Empedocles came coughing through the smoke. To the Thoughtful Reader. William Meredith. NoAM
Empedocles on Etna. Matthew Arnold. VLP
"Far far from here," fr. I, 2. GTBS-P
(Cadmus and Harmonia.) OBVV
(Song of Callicles, The.) FiP
"Fulness of life and power of feeling," *fr.* II. OAEP
"It is so small a thing," fr. I, 2. OBEV; OBVV
Life and Thought, *fr.* II. FiP
Song of Callicles ("Through the black, rushing smoke-bursts"), fr. II. NOBE: OAEL-2; OBEV; OBVV.
(Callicles' Song.) ChTr; LoBV
(Not Here, O Apollo.) FaBoRV
(Song for Apollo.) FiP
(Song of the Muses, The.) WiR
Empedocles on Etna. H.B. Mallalieu. PoA
Emperor, The. Tu Fu, *tr. fr. Chinese by* E. Powys Mathers. AWP
Emperor Hadrian to His Soul, The. Emperor Hadrian. *See* Hadrian's Address to His Soul When Dying.
Emperor Nap he would set off, The. The March to Moscow. Robert Southey. FaBoCo
Emperor of Ice-cream, The. Wallace Stevens. AmPP; AP; BiP; CABA; CMoP; CoBMV; FaBoMo; FF; HAP; InPK; LiTA; MoPo; MoVE; NePA; NIP; NoAM; NOBA; NOP; OxBA; PAI; TAP; ViBoPo; WeW
Emperor of the East, The, *sel.* Philip Massinger.
Song: "Why art thou slow, thou rest of trouble, Death," *fr.* V, iii. ViBoPo
(Death Invoked.) ACP
(Sad Song, A.) OBS
Emperor of the Moon, *sels.* Aphra Behn.
Song: "All joy to mortals, joy and mirth." WPE
Song: "Curse upon that faithless maid, A." WPE
Song: "When maidens are young, and in their spring." FF
Emperor of the Threefold World. Christopher Marlowe. *See* Bloody Conquests of Mighty Tamburlaine, The.
Emperor Worm, The. Poe. *See* Conqueror Worm, The.
Empire Builders. Archibald MacLeish. OxBA
Empire Is No More. Blake. *Fr.* America; a Prophecy. EnRP
Empire of Dreams. Charles Simic. LCAP
"Empire to be lost or won, An!" Whitman's Ride for Oregon. Hezekiah Butterworth. PAH
Empires. Francis Burdett Money-Coutts. OBVV
Employee, The. Rudi Holzapfel. DBV
Employment ("He that is weary, let him sit"). George Herbert. JCP; OBS; OxBoCh; SeCP; TEP
Employment ("If as a flowre doth spread and die"). George Herbert. SeCV-1
Employments of Life, The. John Gay. PV
Empress, The. Diane Wakoski. CoPo
Empress Brand Trim, The: Ruby Reminisces. Sherley Anne Williams. BlSi

Empress Poppaea, The. *Unknown.* PV
Empryce of prys, imperatrice. William Dunbar. *Fr.* Ane Ballat of Our Lady. EBEV
Emptied and pearly skulls. The Statue and the Perturbed Burghers. Denis Devlin. OnYI
Emptied with weeping. At the Badr Trench. Safiya bint Musafir, *tr. by* Bridget Connelly *and* Deirdre Lashgari. WPOW
Empties Coming Back. Angelo De Ponciano. BLPA
Empty Apartment, The. Aaron Zeitlin, *tr. fr. Yiddish by* Ruth Whitman. VWA
Empty Bed Blues. Bessie Smith. OBAL; UnPo
Empty Body, The. Mark Strand. *Fr.* Elegy for My Father. UnPo
Empty carousel in a deserted place, An. The Carousel. Gloria C. Oden. AmNP; PoBA
Empty Dwelling Places. Kenneth Patchen. PoA
Empty Glen, The. R. Crombie Saunders. OxBS
Empty green wine bottles wink. Night Out, Tom Cat. Charles deGravelles. AMV-81
Empty House, The. Walter de la Mare. BrPo
Empty House, The. Russell Hoban. WSC
Empty House, The. Harold Monro. BrPo
Empty House, The. Stephen Spender. NYBP; PCP
Empty House, The. Max Williams. CBAP
Empty, illusory life. The Enchanted Region; or, Mistaken Pleasures. Walter Harte. EBEV
Empty Kettle. Louis (LittleCoon) Oliver. STE
Empty lap, an hour to tea, An. Anno Domini. E. M. Walker. POL
Empty my heart, Lord, of daily vices. Invocation. Theodore Spencer. TrPWD
Empty Pain-Killer Bottles, The. Tom Raworth. EAS
Empty Saddles. *Unknown.* BPAW
Empty sickbed, An. Haiku. Richard Wright. FAZ
Empty sky, a world of heather, An. Divided. Jean Ingelow. HBV-1; SpRo; VLP
Empty Threat, An. Robert Frost. RFM
Empty Vessel. "Hugh MacDiarmid." FaBoTw; NoP; OxBS
Empty Woman, The. Gwendolyn Brooks. IHMS
Emulation, The. Sarah Fyge Egerton. NOEC
Emus. Mary Fullerton. BoAnP; PoAu-1
En Bateau. Paul Verlaine, *tr. fr. French by* Arthur Symons. AWP
En Garde, Messieurs. William Lindsey. AA
En las Internas Entrañas. St. Theresa of Ávila, *tr. fr. Spanish by* Father Benedict Zimmerman. WPOW
En Route. E. L. Mayo. MiAP
En Route. Duncan Campbell Scott. NOBC; OBCV
En route to the picnic they drive through their history. Picnic; the Liberated. M. Carl Holman. PoBA; PoNe
En Voyage. Caroline Atwater Mason. *See* Whichever Way the Wind Doth Blow.
Enacting someone's notion of themselves. Aunt Jemima of the Ocean Waves. Robert Hayden. LCAP; PoBA
Enamel Girl, The. Genevieve Taggard. HBMV; MoAmPo
Enamored [*or* Enamoured] Architect of Airy Rhyme. Thomas Bailey Aldrich. AA; HBV-2
Enamored so of form, of calculation. Of the Mathematician. Alice Clear Matthews. GoYe
Enamoured of the Miniscule. Michael Hartnett. BIrV
Enchainment. Arthur O'Shaughnessy. HBV-1
(Song: "I went to her who loveth me no more.") OBNC
Enchanted Fawn, The. *Unknown, tr. fr. Middle Irish by* Edward Gwynn. *Fr.* Dinnshenchas. OnYI
Enchanted Ground. James Thomson. *See* Land of Indolence, The.
Enchanted Halibut, The. Sheila Nickerson. WOLT
Enchanted Heart, The. Edward Davison. HBMV
Enchanted Island, The. Luke Aylmer Conolly. OBRV
Enchanted Knight, The. Edwin Muir. MoVE
Enchanted Lyre, The. George Darley. *See* Solitary Lyre, The.
Enchanted Region, The; or, Mistaken Pleasures. Walter Harte. EBEV
Enchanted Shirt, The. John Hay. BLPA; GN; PaPo
Enchanted Spring, The. George Darley. BoNaP; NBM
Enchantment. Lewis Alexander. PoBA
Enchantment. Madison Cawein. HBV-1
Enchantment, The. Thomas Otway. HBV-1; OBEV; ViBoPo
Enchantment, The. Theocritus, *tr. fr. Greek by* Thomas Creech. Idylls, II. CTC; OBVE
Enchantress Circe, with a potent wine, The. To a Lady. J. B. Morton. POL
Enchantress, touch no more that strain. Music and Memory. John Albee. AA
Encinctured with a twine of leaves. The Fruit Plucker [*or* In a Moonlight Wilderness *or* A Fragment]. Samuel Taylor Coleridge. CH; FaBoCh; OBNC; SeCeV
Encircled by the traffic's roar. In a Restaurant, 1917. Eleanour Norton. SUMH
Encirclement. Mieczyslaw Jastrun, *tr. fr. Polish by* Benjamin Sher. AMV-81
Enclosed in a circle. The Pact. Larry Rubin. AMV-81
Enclosed the lacquered, coiling snake. The Zoo in the City. Sara Van Alstyne Allen. GoYe
Enclosure. John Clare. *Fr.* Remembrance. NBM
Encomium upon a Parliament, An. Daniel Defoe. APAS
Encompass me, my lover. The Constant North. J. F. Hendry. NeBP; OxBS
Encompassed by a thousand nameless fears. As Day Begins to Wane. Helena Coleman. CaP
Encounter, The. Paul Blackburn. NeAP
Encounter. Denis Devlin. BIrV; OnYI
Encounter, The. Lawrence Durrell. *Fr.* Eight Aspects of Melissa. NeBP
Encounter. Geraldine Hammond. IHMS
Encounter. Uys Krige, *tr. fr. Afrikaans by author.* PeSA
Encounter. Dorothy Livesay. AMV-81
Encounter. Vassar Miller. GP
Encounter, The. Ezra Pound. PAI
Encounter, The. Edgell Rickword. OxBTC
Encounter in Jerusalem. Fay Lipshitz. VWA
Encounter in Safed. Moshe Yungman, *tr. fr. Yiddish by* Gabriel Preil *and* Howard Schwartz. VWA
Encounter in the Cage Country. James Dickey. BiP; CAPP
Encounter with Hunger. Brian Vanderlip. AMV-81
Encountering God. Walt Whitman. *Fr.* Song of Myself, XLVIII. TreFT
Encouraged. Paul Laurence Dunbar. TRV
Encouragement[s] to a Lover. Sir John Suckling. *See* Why So Pale and Wan?
Encouragement to Exile. Petronius Arbiter, *tr. fr. Latin by* Howard Mumford Jones. AWP
End, The. Walter de la Mare. OAEP
End, The. Allen Ginsberg. ConAP
End, The. Walter Savage Landor. *See* On His Seventy-fifth Birthday.
End, The. A. A. Milne. SiSoSe
End, The. Wilfred Owen. CH; FaBoRV; HBMV; MMA; MoVE
End, The. Wallace Rice. AA
End, An. Christina Rossetti. FaBoRV; GBL
End, The. Mark Van Doren. ViBoPo
End, The. Marguerite Wilkinson. HBMV
End Bit, The. Jim Burns. FF
End came as I drove it down the road, The. Last of the Poet's Car. Tony Connor. OxBTC
End came easy for most of us, The. The Man from Washington James Welch. CDW; GP
End Is near the Beginning, The. David Gascoyne. EAS
End Is Now, The. "Marie Madelaine," *tr. fr. German by* Ferdinand E. Kappey. PeHV
End of a Day in the Provinces, The. Jules Laforgue, *tr. fr. French by* Margaret Crosland. SyP
End of a Leave, The. Roy Fuller. NeBP
End of a long stillness. Dawn in January. Lance Henson. CDW
End of a Meaningful Relationship, The. Kurt J. Fickert. AMV-81
End of a War, The. Sir Herbert Read. OBMV; WaP
End of Another Home Holiday. D. H. Lawrence. DTC; EBEV; FaBoMo; MoVE
End of April, The. Robert Fuller Murray. CenHV
End of August. Gregory Orr. MAYP
End of Being, The. Seneca, *tr. fr. Latin by* H. C. Leonard. WGRP
End of Clonmacnois, The. *Unknown, tr. fr. Irish by* Frank O'Connor. CIP; KiLC
End of Doctor Faustus, The. Christopher Marlowe. *Fr.* Doctor Faustus. PoEL-2
("Ah, Faustus,/Now hast thou but one bare hour to live.") ChTr; HeIP; ILwL; ViBoPo
(End of Faustus, The.) TrGrPo
(Finale.) WHA
End of everything approaches, The. Doomsday. Elinor Wylie. CrMA
End of Exploring, The. David Campbell. SeCePo
End of Fall, The. Francis Ponge, *tr. fr. French by* Robert Bly. NU
End of Faustus, The. Christopher Marlowe. *See* End of Doctor Faustus, The.
End of February. Bañalbufar, a Brazier, Relativity, Cloud Formations & the Kindness & Relentlessness of Time, All Seen through a Window while Keeping the Feet Warm at the Same Time As. Paul Blackburn. CoPo
End of His Work, The. Robert Herrick. CaPo
End of Love, The. George Meredith. *See* Male in Love: "By this he know she wept with waking eyes."
End of Man Is Death, The. Moses ibn Ezra, *tr. fr. Hebrew by* Solomon Solis-Cohen. TrJP
End of Man Is His Beauty, The. Amiri Baraka. AmNP; BALP

End of My Sister's Guggenheim, The. John Malcolm Brinnin. GLGT
End of October after a rain, The. Sonship. John C. Rezmerski. FAZ
End of Play. Robert Graves. EBEV
End of Season. Robert Penn Warren. TwAmPo
End of September. The Sign. Paul Blackburn. TAT
End of Sorrow, The. Edmond Fleg, *tr. fr. French by* Humbert Wolfe. *Fr.* The Wall of Weeping. TrJP
End of Steel. Thomas Saunders. CaP
End of Summer. Stanley Kunitz. CrMA; MoAmPo; Psk; VGW
End of Summer, The. Edna St. Vincent Millay. BoNaP
End of Summer, The. Judith Minty. FiCP; GeTw
End of Summer. Berl Pomerantz, *tr. fr. Hebrew by* Harold Schimmel. VWA
(End) of Summer (1966). William Knott. EAS
End-of-Summer-Poem. Rowena Bastin Bennett. FaPON; SiSoSe
End of Term. *Unknown.* PoPle
End of the Affair. Curtis W. Casewit. AMV-80
End of the Affair. Geoffrey Grigson. GBL
End of the Comedy. Louis Untermeyer. PoA
End of the Flower World (A.D. 2300). Stanley Burnshaw. TrJP
End of the Indian Poems, The. Stanley Plumly. GOA
End of the Line. John Taylor. FAZ
End of the Parade, The. William Carlos Williams. NYBP
End of the Play, The. Thackeray. Dr. Birch and His Young Friends, *epilogue.* FaFP; GN; TreF
End of the Season on a Stormy Day—Oban. Iain Crichton Smith. NePoEA-2
End of the Seers' Convention. Kenneth Fearing. LiTA
End of the Story, The. Terence Tiller. ChMP; NeBP
End of the Street, The. John Haines. LCAP
End of the Suitors, The. Homer, *tr. fr. Greek by* George Chapman. *Fr.* The Odyssey, XXII. OBS
("And now man-slaughtering Pallas tooke in hand.") OBVE
End of the War in Merida. Anthony Ostroff. FAZ
End of the Way, The. Harriet Cole. BLRP
End of the Weekend, The. Anthony Hecht. ConAP; FaBoMo; HAP; LiTM; NePoEA-2; WeW
End of the World, The. Bible, *O.T.* Jeremiah, IV: 19-26. PPON
End of the World, The. Gordon Bottomley. BrPo; CH; MoBrPo; MoVE
End of the World. Else Lasker-Schüler, *tr. fr. German by* Willis Barnstone *and* Michael Gillespie. BoWoP
End of the World, The. Archibald MacLeish. AP; BLPL; CMoP; CoBMV; HoPM; InPK; LiTM; MAT; MoAB; MoAmPo; NCSH; NePA; NoAM; NOBA; OBAL; OxBA; PAI; TAP; TrGrPo; VGW
End of the World. Jakov van Hoddis, *tr. fr. German by* Edouard Roditi. VWA
End of the Year, The. Su Tung-p'o, *tr. fr. Chinese by* Kenneth Rexroth. PoPl
End of the year fell chilly, The. New Year's Eve. A. E. Housman. VLP
End of World War One, The. Sharon Olds. AMV-81
End over end, a leaping. Amphibian. Amy Clampitt. SUW
End Song. Ruth Krauss. LLLT
End to all I've ever had to say, An. Endpiece. *Unknown, tr. by* Frank O'Connor. KiLC
End was more of a melting, The. The Death of Will. Charles Tomlinson. OxBC
End was quick and bitter, The. Quick and Bitter. Yehuda Amichai, *tr. by* Assia Gutmann. BoLoP
End Which Comes, The. Sir Edwin Arnold. *Fr.* The Light of Asia. LoBV
End will come swiftly in an early autumn. Final Autumn. Josephine W. Johnson. NePA
Endearments. Pierre Louÿs, *tr. fr. French by* Horace M. Brown. *Fr.* The Songs of Bilitis. UnTE
Endimion. John Lyly. *See* Endymion.
Endimion and Phoebe, *sels.* Michael Drayton. OBSC
Endymion's Convoy.
Phoebe on Latmus.
Endimion Porter and Olivia. Sir William Davenant. MePo; NOBE
(Song: "Before we shall again behold.") MeLP
(Song: Endimion Porter and Olivia.) OBS
Ending, The. Paul Engle. NYBP
Ending. Norman Jordan. PoNe
Ending. *Tr. fr. Hawaiian by* K. Luomala. WTO
Endless. Muriel Rukeyser. NYBP
Endless Chain, An. Abraham Reisen, *tr. fr. Yiddish by* Keith Bosley. VWA
Endless cycle of idea and action, The. T. S. Eliot. *Fr.* The Rock. TRV
Endless mime goes on, The; new faces come. The Play. James B. Kenyon. HBV-2
Endless part of disintegration, The. The Wisdom of Insecurity. Richard Eberhart. NePA
Endless Song, The. Ruth McEnery Stuart. OBAL
Endlessly over the water. The Sweetness of Nature. *Unknown, tr. by* Frank O'Connor. KiLC
Endlessly, time-honoured irritant. Dry-Point. Philip Larkin. CMoP; NMP
Endpiece. *Unknown, tr. fr. Irish by* Frank O'Connor. KiLC
Ends of dreams are acts of completion, The. The Armless. Don Welch. AMV-81
Ends of the Hibiscus burgeon, The. Song of a Sick Child. *Malay Oral Tradition, tr. by* R. J. Wilkinson *and* R. O. Winstedt. WTO
Endurance. Elizabeth Akers Allen. HBV-2
Endurance. Carolyn Forché. SV
Endurance Test. Dacre Balsdon. DBV; FiBHP
Endure what life God gives and ask no longer span. Sophocles, *tr. by* W. B. Yeats. *Fr.* Oedipus at Colonus. DTC; OBMV
Enduring is the bust of bronze. The Duke of York's Statue. Walter Savage Landor. FaBoEE
Enduring Music, The. Harold Vinal. EtS
Endymion [a Poetic Romance], *sels.* Keats.
"And truly, I would rather be struck dumb," *fr.* I. ViBoPo
Are Then Regalities All Gilded Masks? *fr.* III. MOON
"Beneath my palm-trees, by the river side," *fr.* IV. ViBoPo
"He saw far in the concave green of the sea," *fr.* III. EtS
Here Is Wine, *fr.* II. OBRV
Hymn to Pan, *fr.* I. ChER; OBRV; PoEL-4
Life Again. SeCePo
Love and Friendship, *fr.* I. OBRV
"Muse of native land! loftiest Muse!" *fr.* IV. EnRP
"O Moon! the oldest shades 'mong oldest trees," *fr.* III. EnRP
"O sovereign power of love! O grief! O balm!" *fr.* II. EnRP; OBNC; ViBoPo
Sleeping Youth, A, *fr.* II. SeCePo
Song of the Indian Maid, *fr.* IV. NOBE; OAEP; OBEV
(O Sorrow! *abr.*) CH
(Song: "O Sorrow," *shorter sel.*) LoBV
("To Sorrow/ I bade good-morrow," *shorter sel.*) OBRV
"Thing of beauty is a joy for ever, A," *fr.* I. BLPL; CTC; EnRP; FaBV; FaFP; FiP; LiTB; NIP; OAEP; OBNC; OBRV; PoPl; PrIm; TreF; TrGrPo; TRV; ViBoPo
Endymion. Longfellow. AA; HBV-1
Endymion, *sel.* John Lyly.
Song by Fairies. OAEP
(Fairy Song, A.) OBSC
Endymion. Oscar Wilde. HBV-1
Endymion's Convoy. Michael Drayton. *Fr.* Endimion and Phoebe. OBSC
Eneas wonderit the greitnes of Cartaige. Virgil, *tr. by* Gavin Douglas. *Fr.* The Aeneid, I. OBVE
Enemy, The. John Waller. NeBP
Enemy, Enemy. Cecil J. Mullins. AMV-80
Enemy forces are in wild flight, The. Defeat of the Rebels. Robert Graves. WaP
Enemy of life, decayer of all kind, The. Epigram. Sir Thomas Wyatt. SiPS
Enemy who wears, The. Fourteenth Birthday. Phyllis McGinley. NePoAm-2
Enemy's Portrait, The. Thomas Hardy. EyDe; TW
Energetic Women. D. H. Lawrence. InPS
Energy. Victor Hernández Cruz. PoBA
Energy for a New Thang. Ernie Mkalimoto. NBP
Energy of Light, The. John Hay. NePoAm-2
Enfant perdu. Heine, *tr. fr. German by* Lord Houghton. AWP
Enfors we us with all our might. A Carol of St. George. *Unknown.* MeEL
Enfranchising cable, silvered by the sea. Granite and Steel. Marianne Moore. NYBP
Engagement, The. Arthur Hugh Clough. NBM
Engine. James S. Tippett. SoPo; SUS
Engine, The; a Manual. Michael Dobberstein. AMV-81
Engine Driver's Story, The. William Wilkins. BeLS
Engine Failure. Timothy Corsellis. WaP
Engine 143. *Unknown. See* George Allen.
Engineers. Jimmy Garthwaite. SoPo
Engineer's dream, holding water, an. The Water Tower. James Paul. AMV-81
Engineer's Story, The. Eugene J. Hall. PaPo
Engineer's Story, The. *Unknown.* BeLS
Engineer's Yell (University of California). *Unknown.* WhC
Engines thrum in their agile wilderness, The. Old World, New World. Harry Roskolenko. AMV-81
England. William Cowper. *Fr.* The Task, II. FiP; OBEC
(Love of England.) LoBV
England. Richard Edwin Day. AA
England. Gerald Massey. HBV-2
England. George Edgar Montgomery. AA
England. Marianne Moore. CrMA; LiTA; MoAB; MoAmPo; TwAmPo
England. Cardinal Newman. ACP; GoBC
England. Mary Jo Salter. AMV-80
England. *Unknown.* ELU

England and America. James Kenneth Stephen. InMe
Sels.
On a Parisian Boulevard. DBV; NOBL
On a Rhine Steamer. NBM; NOBL; TW
England and America, 1863. Richard Monckton Milnes. EBVV
England and America in 1782. Tennyson. PAH; PAL
England and Switzerland 1802. Wordsworth. *See* Thought of a Briton on the Subjugation of Switzerland.
England! Awake! Awake! Awake! Blake. *Fr.* Jerusalem, IV, Prologue. EnRP; NoP; OBRV
(Prelude.) OBNC
England, 1802 ("Great Men have been among us . . ."). Wordsworth. *See* Great Men Have Been among Us.
England, 1802 ("It is not to be thought that the flood"). Wordsworth. *See* It Is Not to Be Thought Of.
England, 1802 ("Milton! thou should'st be living at this hour"). Wordsworth. *See* London 1802.
England, 1802 ("O Friend! I know not which way I must look"). Wordsworth. *See* Written in London, September 1802.
England, 1802 ("When I have borne in memory what has tamed"). Wordsworth. *See* When I Have Borne in Memory.
England Expects. Ogden Nash. DBV
England Expects? Sir Owen Seaman. NOBL
England, I stand on thy imperial ground. At Gibraltar. George Edward Woodberry. AA; GN; HBV-2
England in 1819. Shelley. CABA; EnRP; FF; MAT; NIP; NOBE; NoP; OAEL-2; OBRV; TrGrPo; TW; UnPo
(Sonnet: England in 1819.) FiP; OAEP; PPP; SeCePo; SeCeV
England, look up! Thy soil is stained with blood. Martyrdom of Father Campion. Henry Walpole. ACP; GoBC
England, My England. W. E. Henley. BLPL; HBV-2; MoBrPo; OBEV; OBVV; PoLF; TreF
England, my England—you have been my tutrix. W. H. Auden. *Fr.* Letter to Lord Byron. OBSV
England Reclaimed, *sel.* Sir Osbert Sitwell.
"Sound out, proud trumpets." ViBoPo
England! the time is come when thou shouldst wean. Sonnet. Wordsworth. ViBoPo
England, unlike junior nations. Remember Suez? Adrian Mitchell. OxBTC
England, Unprepared for War. Mark Akenside. *Fr.* An Ode to the Countty Gentlemen of England. OBEC
England, we love thee better than we know. Gibraltar. Richard Chenevix Trench. OBRV; OBVV
"England! with all thy faults I love thee still." Byron. *Fr.* Beppo; a Venetian Story. UnPo
England, with all thy faults, I love thee still. England [*or* Love of England]. William Cowper. *Fr.* The Task, II. FiP; LoBV; OBEC
England with its baby rivers and little towns, each with its abbey or its cathedral. England. Marianne Moore. CrMA; LiTA; MoAB; MoAmPo; TwAmPo
England's Darling; or, Great Britain's Joy and Hope on That Noble Prince James, Duke of Monmouth. *Unknown.* CoMu
England's Dead. Felicia Dorothea Hemans. HBV-2
England's Difficulty. Seamus Heaney. CIP
England's Heart. Martin Farquhar Tupper. PaPo
England's Heroical Epistles, *sels.* Michael Drayton.
Epistle of Rosamond to King Henry the Second, The. AnAnS-2
King Henry to Rosamond. OBSC
(Henry to Rosamond.) AnAnS-2
England's ingratitude still blots. What Jenner Said on Hearing in Elysium That Complaints Had Been Made of His Having a Statue [in Trafalgar Square]. Shirley Brooks. EyDe; FaBoEE
England's lads are miniature men. Boy-Man. Karl Shapiro. NYBP; SoSe
England's Prayer. William Blundell. GoBC
England's Sovereigns in Verse. *Unknown.* BLPA
England's sun was slowly setting. Curfew Must Not Ring Tonight. Rose Hartwick Thorpe. TreF; WBLP
England's Triumph. *Unknown.* CoMu
English. Osbert Lancaster. *Fr.* Afternoons with Baedeker. FaBoCo; NOBL
English, The. *Unknown.* GBP
English Are Frosty, The. Alice Duer Miller. *Fr.* The White Cliffs. PoLF
English Are So Nice, The! D. H. Lawrence. NoP
English Ballad, on the Taking of Namur by the King of Great Britain, 1695, An. Matthew Prior. PoEL-3
English Bards, and Scotch Reviewers, *sels.* Byron.
"As Sisyphus against the infernal steep." OBSV
"As soon/ Seek roses in December, ice in June." DBV
"Behold! in various throngs the scribbling crew." EnRP; OAEL-2
"Illustrious Holland! hard would be his lot." OBRV; OBSV
"Next comes the dull disciple of thy school." OBRV; PP
(That Idiot, Wordsworth.) DBV
William Lisle Bowles. OBNC
English Beach Memory: Mr. Thuddock. Sir Osbert Sitwell. NYBP
English Counties. *Unknown.* POL
English Elegy, An. Daryl Hine. NoAM
English Fog, The. John Dyer. *See* English Weather.
English Garden, The, *sels.* William Mason.
How to Build a Ha-ha. FaBoUs
Landscape, *fr.* I. OBEC
Thomas Gray's View of Nature, *fr.* III. NOEC
English Girl. *Unknown, tr. fr. Chinese by* E. Powys Mathers. OBMV
English History in Rhyme, or a Rhyming Epitome of the History of England, from B.C. 55 to A.D. 1872, *sel.* Edward B. Goodwin.
"Growth of Heptarchy we trace, The." FaBoUs
English Horn. Laurence McKinney. WhC
English Labourer, The. *Unknown.* OBET
English lad, who, reading in a book, An. Keats. Lizette Woodworth Reese. AA
English Language, The, *abr.* William Wetmore Story. GN
English Liberal. Geoffrey Taylor. FaBoEE
English Mother, An. Robert Underwood Johnson. HBV-2
English Padlock, An. Matthew Prior. FaBoEn; OBEC
English Poetry. Samuel Daniel. *Fr.* Musophilus; or, Defence of All Learning. OBSC
(Heavenly Eloquence.) NOBE
English Race, The. Daniel Defoe. *Fr.* The True-born Englishman. OBEC
English Retort, The. *Unknown.* OxBM
English Schoolboy, The. John Heywood. *Fr.* The Play of the Weather. ACP
English sparrow, pert and free, An. A Card of Invitation to Mr. Gibbon, at Brighthelmstone, 1781. William Hayley. OBEC
English Succession, The. *Unknown.* OxBChV
English Thornton. Edgar Lee Masters. *Fr.* Spoon River Anthology. OxBA
English Train, Summer. Ralph Pomeroy. GP
English Weather. John Dyer. *Fr.* The Fleece, I. OBEC
(English Fog.) TrGrPo
English Wood, An. Robert Graves. BrPo
Englishman, The. G. K. Chesterton. WhC
Englishman, The. Eliza Cook. PaPo
Englishman, The. W. S. Gilbert. *Fr.* H. M. S. Pinafore. NOBL
Englishman in Italy, The. Robert Browning. PoEL-5
Piano di Sorrento, *sel.* FaBoPP
(Englishman in Italy, The ["Time for rain! for your long hot dry autumn"].) SeCePo
Englishman in the old days, An. Carl Sandburg. *Fr.* The People, Yes. FYAP
Englishman with an Atlas, An; or, America the Unpronounceable. Morris Bishop. GOA
Engraved on the Collar of a Dog Which I Gave to His Royal Highness. Pope. *See* Epigram Engraved on the Collar of a Dog Given to His Royal Highness.
Enid's Song. Tennyson. *Fr.* Idylls of the King: The Marriage of Geraint. FaBoRV
Enigma. Kenneth Burke. TwAmPo
Enigma, The. Richard Eberhart. NYBP
Enigma. Jessie Redmond Fauset. PoNe
Enigma. Hugh McCrae. PoAu-1
Enigma. Richard Murphy. CIP
Enigma. R. S. Thomas. ChMP
Enigma for Christmas Shoppers. Phyllis McGinley. PoPl
(Enigma in Altman's.) WhC
Enigma Variations, The. Paul Petrie. NYBP
Enigmas. Pablo Neruda, *tr. fr. Spanish by* Robert Bly. NU
Enigmatic moon has at long last died, The. Stevedore. Leslie M. Collins. AmNP
Enigmatic Traveler, The. Byron Vazakas. AMV-80
Enion Replies from the Caverns of the Grave. Blake. *Fr.* Vala; or, The Four Zoas. OBNC
Enitharmon Revives with Los. Blake. *Fr.* Vala; or, The Four Zoas. OBNC
(Enitharmon's Song.) ChTr
Enjoy the Good. Bible, *O.T.* Ecclesiastes, V: 18-20. TreFT
Enjoy Thy April Now. Samuel Daniel. *Fr.* A Description of Beauty. ElL; ELP
Enjoyment. Theognis, *tr. fr. Greek by* John Hookham Frere. AWP
Enjoyment, The. *Unknown.* ErPo
Enkindled Spring, The. D. H. Lawrence. NoAM
Enlightenment. Robert V. Carr. BPAW
Enlightenment, The. Patricia Sheppard. AMV-81
Enmeshed in steel stands a stone. The Captive Stone. Jim Barnes. CDW
Ennui. Langston Hughes. OBAL; OBCA

Ennui. Peter Viereck. NYBP
Enoch, *sels.* Bible, Pseudepigrapha. TrJP
Seven Metal Mountains, The, LII: 6–9.
Wisdom's Plight, XLII: 1–3.
Enoch. Jones Very. HAP
Enoch Arden. Tennyson. BeLS
Sels.
"Cast all your cares on God; that anchor holds." TRV
November in the Isle of Wight. FaBoPP
Enormous Aquarium, The. Sherod Santos. MAYP
Enormous cloud-mountains that form over Point Lobos and into the sunset. Clouds of Evening. Robinson Jeffers. MoAmPo
Enough! Bunyan. *See* Shepherd Boy Sings, The.
Enough. Digby Mackworth Dolben. EBVV
Enough. Arthur Gregor. TAP
Enough. Tom Masson. OBAL
Enough. Marianne Moore. NOBA
Enough! James Scully. LTB
Enough; and leave the rest to fame. An Epitaph [*or* An Epitaph upon ———]. Andrew Marvell. CavP; LO; LoBV; OBEV; PoPle
Enough! Let this season end. Enough. Arthur Gregor. TAP
Enough Not One. Benjamin Franklin. TRV
Enough of a day has come to pass. Inner-City Lullaby Russell Atkins. CNA
Enough of those who study the oblique. A Good Resolution. Roy Campbell. OBSV
Enough of Thought, Philosopher. Emily Brontë. NCEP
"Enough," she said. But the dust still rained around [*or* about] her. Dust. Randolph Stow. CBAP; PoAu-2
Enough! we're tired, my heart and I. My Heart and I. Elizabeth Barrett Browning. HBV-1
Enough! Why should a man bemoan. Per Iter Tenebricosum. Oliver St. John Gogarty. AnIL; OBMV; OxBI
Enough: you have the dream, the flame. Due North. Benjamin R. C. Low. EtS; HBMV
Enquiring fields, courtesies, The. Pastoral. Allen Tate. AP
Enquiry, The. John Dyer. OBEC
Enraging Griefs, though you most divers be. October 14, 1644. Lord Herbert of Cherbury. AnAnS-2
Enraptured I Gaze, *with music.* Francis Hopkinson. BLSo
Enrica, 1865. Christina Rossetti. TEP
Enrich My Resignation. Hart Crane. PoA
Ensamples of Our Savior. Robert Southwell. PoEL-2
Enslav'd, the daughters of Albion weep: a trembling lamentation. Visions of the Daughters of Albion. Blake. OAEL-2
Enslaved. Claude McKay. BALP; BPo
Entailed Farm, The. John Glassco. MoCV; NOBC
Entanglement. Francis Sparshott. MoCV
Enter and learn the story of the rulers. Inscriptions at the City of Brass. *Unknown, tr. by* E. Powys Mathers. *Fr.* The Thousand and One Nights. AWP; WaaP
Enter Harlem. Walk with de Mayor of Harlem. David Henderson. PoBA
Enter into His gates with thanksgiving. Giving Thanks. Bible, *O.T.* Pslams, C. BLRP
Enter No (Silence Is the Blood Whose Flesh). E. E. Cummings. AP
Enter Patient. W. E. Henley. In Hospital, I. BrPo
Enter the chilly no-man's land of about. The Ghost's Leavetaking. Sylvia Plath. NePoEA-2
Enter the dream-house, brothers and sisters, leaving. Newsreel. C. Day Lewis. MoAB; MoBrPo
Entered in the Minutes. Louis MacNeice. LiTB
Entering casually the precincts of the Cathedral. Alcestis in Ely. Nicholas Moore. NeBP
Entering here, I hope the confetti. Unitarian Easter. Sandra McPherson. MAYP
Entering the Body, *sel.* Stephen Berg.
"Rising without names today." NaP
Entering the darkened room. Fugue. Kathleen Spivack. AMV-80
Entering the Desert; Big Circles Running. Wendy Rose. TWSS
Entering the hall, she meets the new wife. The Ejected Wife. *Tr. fr. Chinese by* Arthur Waley. OBVE
Entering the publisher's warehouse, a foreign young lady. Anecdote from William IV Street. D. J. Enright. OxBC
Entering the Room. Roger Pfingston. PoDr
Enterprise and *Boxer. Unknown.* PAH
Entertainment Industry, The. William Langland, *mod. by* Donald Attwater. *Fr.* The Vision of Piers Plowman. NOCV
Entertainment of War, The. Roy Fisher. FaBoMo
Entertainment, or Porch-Verse, at the Marriage of Master Henry Northleigh and the Most Witty Mistress Lettice Yard, The. Robert Herrick. CaPo
Entertainment to James, *sel.* Thomas Dekker.
Troynovant. OBSC
Enthroned above the world although he sit. Immanence. Richard Hovey. TRV; WGRP
Enthused by flickers and coots. Bird Watcher. Ronald Wallace. PPJ
Enthusiast, The; an Ode. William Whitehead. OBEC
Enthusiast, The; or, The Lover of Nature. Joseph Warton. EnRP; LAuP; PoEL-3
Sels.
Charms of Nature, The. OBEC; SeCePo
"Ye green-robed Dryads, oft at dusky eve." FaBoEn; NOEC
Entire country is overrun with private property, The. Gypsy. Josephine Miles. NoAM
Entirely. Louis MacNeice. CMoP; LiTB
Entombed in my heart no blood flows to you. Poem. Margery Dodson. AMV-80
Entoptic Colours (1817). Goethe, *tr. fr. German by* Christopher Middleton. SUW
Entrain airport: New York, Chicago, west. Valediction to My Contemporaries. Horace Gregory. MoAmPo
Entrance and exit wounds are silvered clean. Recalling War. Robert Graves. CMoP; CoBMV; LiTM; MMA; NoAM; OAEL-2; OBWP; WaP
Entrance Exams. "Cuthbert Bede." FaBoNo
Entrance to Hell, The. Virgil, *tr. fr. Latin into Scottish by* Gavin Douglas. *Fr.* The Aeneid, VI. GoTS
Entrapped inside a submarine. H. C. Canfield. *Fr.* On the Loss of U.S. Submarine S4. FaBoCo; FiBHP
Entreat Me Not to Leave Thee. Bible, *O.T. Fr.* Ruth. *See* Intreat Me Not to Leave Thee.
Entrepreneur chicken shed his tail feathers, surplus, The. Josephine Miles. NoAM
Entropy. Theodore Spencer. ImOP
Entwined. *Malay Oral Tradition, tr. by* R. J. Wilkinson *and* R. O. Winstedt. WTO
Entwined on the bed in the dark. Two Shapes. Arthur Gregor. TAP
Enueg I ("Exeo in a spasm"). Samuel Beckett. CIP
Enueg II ("World world world world/ And the face grave"). Samuel Beckett. NoAM
Enviable Isles, The. Herman Melville. AA; FaBoBe
Envied by us all. Maple Leaves. Shiko, *tr. by* Harold G. Henderson. SoPo
Envies, The. George Bowering. NOBC
Envious Critick, The. William Wycherley. PV
Envious wits, what hath been mine offence. Astrophel and Stella, CIV. Sir Philip Sidney. SiPS
Environment. Lionel Kearns. NOBC
Environs. Larry Eigner. NeAP
Envoi: "All that remains for me." Arthur Symons. UnTE
Envoi: "Fly, white butterflies, out to sea." Swinburne. *See* White Butterflies.
Envoi: "Go, dumb-born book." Ezra Pound. *See* Envoi (1919).
Envoi: "God, thou great symmetry." Anna Wickham. MoBrPo
Envoi: "Hear me, whom I betrayed." J. V. Cunningham. VGW
Envoi: "I am the Prince." Charles Causley. FF
Envoi: "I strove with none, for none was worth my strife." Walter Savage Landor. *See* On His Seventy-fifth Birthday
Envoi: "I warmed both hands before the fire of Life." D. B. Wyndham Lewis. FiBHP
Envoi: "My country is not a country." Eli Mandel. NOBC
Envoi: "Oh, seek me not within a tomb." John G. Neihardt. HBV-2; WGRP
Envoi: "Running out of town on a rail is too good for." E. L. Mayo. FAZ
Envoi: "Take of me what is not my own." Kathleen Raine. NeBP; NOBE
Envoi: "What has want to give." Kathleen Raine. WPE
Envoi (1919). Ezra Pound. *Fr.* Hugh Selwyn Mauberly. AmPP; AP; CABA; CMoP; CoBMV; CTC; HAP; InPS; LiTA; LiTM; MasP; MoPo; NoAM; NOBA; NoP; SeCeV; TAP; UnPo; VGW
(Envoi: "Go, dumb-born book.") MoAB; MoAmPo; NePA; OxBA
Envoy: "Do you remember." W. E. Henley. BrPo
Envoy, The: "Go, litel book, go litel myn tregedie." Chaucer. *Fr.* Troilus and Criseyde, V. FiP
("Go, litel book [*or* bok], go litel myn tragedie [*or* tragedye].") OAEL-1; ViBoPo
(Go, Little Book.) OxBM
Envoy: "Go, little book, and wish to all." Robert Louis Stevenson. HBV-2; TreFT
(Go Little Book.) MoBrPo
(Wishes.) OBEV; OBVV
Envoy: "Go, songs, for ended is our brief, sweet play." Francis Thompson. HBV-2; MoBrPo
(Go Songs.) FaBV
Envoy: "Good Night, at last." Robert Duncan. *Fr.* Passages. VGW
Envoy: "Have little care that life is brief." Bliss Carman. HBV-2

Envoy: "If homely virtues draw from me a tune." James Weldon Johnson. TrPWD
Envoy: "Legend of Felix is ended, the toiling of Felix is done, The." Henry van Dyke. *Fr.* The Toiling of Felix. BLPA
Envoy: "On Meall nan Con, the Peak of the Dogs." Alasdair MacLean. PoSH
Envoy: "Sweet World, if you will hear me now." David Gray. AA
Envoy: "They are not long, the weeping and the laughter." Ernest Dowson. *See* Vitae Summa Brevis Spem Nos Vetat Incohare Longam.
Envoy: "Whose furthest footstep never strayed." Richard Hovey. *Fr.* More Songs from Vagabondia. AA; HBV-2
Envy. Charles *and* Mary Lamb. OxBChV
Envy. Spenser. *Fr.* The Faerie Queene, I, 4. TW
Envy of Poor Lovers, The. Austin Clarke. CIP; CMoP; IPY; NMP
Envy the Old. Mark Van Doren. Prf
Envying the Pelican. Richard Weber. CIP
Eolian Harp, The. Samuel Taylor Coleridge. EnRP; OAEL-2
(Aeolian Harp, The.) NoP
Eons ago, when the earth was still yeasty. Leopard. Gretchen Kreps. RHPC
Eph Kate was a cow-punchin' boy. Salty Dogs. *Unknown.* CoSo
Ephelia to Bajazet. Sir George Etherege. APAS
Ephemera. W. B. Yeats. BrPo
Ephraim the Grizzly. Arthur Guiterman. BPAW
Epic. Patrick Kavanagh. BIrV; CIP; IPY; OxBI
Epic, The. Tennyson. VLP
Epic of Gilgamesh, The, *sels.* *Unknown, tr. fr. Babylonian.*
"Gilgamesh washed his grimy hair, polished his weapons," *tr. by* E. A. Speiser. Prf
"Hear me, great ones of Uruk," *tr. by* N. K. Sandars. DL
Seduction of Engadu, The, *tr. by* Willia Ellery Leonard. ErPo
Epicedium. J. Corson Miller. HBMV; PAH
Epicedium. Horace L. Traubel. AA
Epicoene; or, The Silent Woman, *sel.* Ben Jonson.
Still to Be Neat [Still to Be Dressed (*or* Drest)], *fr* I, i, *tr. fr. the Latin of* Jean Bonnefons. CABA; ElL; FF; GBL; HAP; HeIP; JCP; NIP; NoP; OAEP; PAI; PoPle; PrIm; SeCePo; TEP; TreFT; WeW; WHA
(Clerimont's Song). InPS; LoBV; OAEL-1; PPP; SeCP; SeCV-1; TrGrPo
(Simplex Munditiis.) AWP; GoBC; HBV-1; HoPM; NOBE; OBEV
(Song: "Still to be neat, still to be dressed [*or* drest].") AnAnS-2; EnRePo; OBS; ViBoPo
Epicure, The ("Fill the bowl with rosy, wine"). Abraham Cowley, *after the Greek of* Anacreon. HBV-2; OBS; SeCP
(Epicure after Anacreon, The.) CavP
(Today Is Ours.) TrGrPo
Epicure, The ("Underneath this myrtle shade"). Abraham Cowley, *after the Greek of* Anacreon. AWP; OBEV
(Another.) SeCP
"Crown me with roses whilest I live," *sel.* OBVE
Epicure, Dining at Crewe, An. *Unknown.* NTCP
(Limerick: "Epicure, dining at Crewe, An.") CenHV; WhC
Epicure, The, Sung by One in the Habit of a Town Gallant. Thomas Jordan. *See* Let Us Drink and Be Merry.
Epicurean, The. Sir Francis Hastings Doyle. OBVV
Epicurean. William James Linton. EBVV
Epicurean Ode, An. John Hall. MeLP; MePo
Epiderm. Michael Dransfield. CBAP
Epidermal Macabre. Theodore Roethke. NoAM; TW
Epigram: "After some years Bohemian came to this." J. V. Cunningham. VGW
Epigram: "After such years of dissension and strife." Thomas Hood. HBV-1
(Dust to Dust.) ShM
(Natural Tears.) FiBHP
Epigram V: "Against the guide of Truth." *Unknown, tr. fr. Hebrew. Fr.* Duel with Verses over a Great Man. TrJP
Epigram: "All I said was—Alexis is gorgeous." Plato, *tr. fr. Greek by* Peter Jay. PeHV
Epigram: "All through the night my eyes have streamed with rain." Strato, *tr. fr. Greek by* Sydney Oswald. PeHV
Epigram: "Amid all Triads let it be confest." Richard Garnett. OBVV
Epigram: "And now I, Meleager, am among them." Meleager, *tr. fr. Greek by* Peter Whigham. PeHV
Epigram: "And now you're ready who while she was here." J. V. Cunningham. *See* And Now You're Ready Who While She Was Here.
Epigram: "And what is love? Misunderstanding, pain." J. V. Cunningham. HoPM; HAP; NePoAm; PoA
Epigram: "Arms and the man I sing, and sing for joy." J. V. Cunningham. NePoAm
Epigram: "Artic raven tracks the caribou, The." Raymond Wilson. PV
Epigram: "As honey in wine/wine, honey." Meleager, *tr. fr. Greek by* Peter Whigham. PeHV
Epigram: "As in smooth oil the razor best is whet." *Unknown.* HBV-1
Epigram: "As the body denies the means to look." Pernette du Guillet, *tr. fr. French by* Joan Keefe *and* Richard Terdiman. PBWP
Epigram: "As Thomas was cudgeled one day by his wife." Swift. *See* Abroad and at Home.
Epigram: "At even, when the hour drew nigh at which we say farewell." Strato, *tr. fr. Greek by* Sydney Oswald. PeHV
Epigram: "At 12 o'clock in the afternoon." Meleager, *tr. fr. Greek by* Sydney Oswald. PeHV
Epigram: "Beauty, a silver dew that falls in May." *Unknown.* OBSC
Epigram: "Because I am idolatrous and have besought." Ernest Dowson. ACP
Epigram: "Boy-mad no longer." Rufinus, *tr. fr. Greek by* Alan Marshfield. PeHV
Epigram: "Boys' cocks, Diodore." Strato, *tr. fr. Greek by* Thomas Meyer. PeHV
Epigram: "Boys of Tyre are beautiful, The." Meleager, *tr. fr. Greek by* Peter Whigham. PeHV
Epigram: "Breath of my life, The—no less." Meleager, *tr. fr. Greek by* Peter Whigham. PeHV
Epigram: "Bring hemlock, black as Cretan cheese." Robert Hillyer. WhC
Epigram: "But yesterday, when from the bath he stept." Strato, *tr. fr. Greek by* Sydney Oswald. PeHV
Epigram: "Cease your labors, lovers of boys." *Unknown, tr. fr. Greek.* PeHV
Epigram: "Charm of my life, my dearest care." Martial, *tr. fr. Latin by* Brian Hill. PeHV
Epigram: " 'Come, come,' said Tom's father, 'at your time of life.' " Thomas Moore. DBV; HBV-1
("Come, Come," Said Tom's Father.) WhC
(Joke Versified, A.) FaBoCo
(On Taking a Wife.) TreF
Epigram: "Damis, an author cold and weak." *Unknown.* HBV-1
Epigram: "Dark thoughts are my companions. I have wined." J. V. Cunningham. VGW
(Dark Thoughts Are My Companions.) TW
("Dark thoughts are my companions, I have wined.") QFR
Epigram: "Dear, if unsocial privacies obsess me." J. V. Cunningham. VGW
Epigram: "Dear, my familiar hand in love's own gesture." J. V. Cunningham. PV
Epigram: "Diodorus is nice, isn't he, Philocles?" Meleager, *tr. fr. Greek by* Peter Whigham. PeHV
Epigram: " 'Do you not wish to renounce the Devil?' " Armand Lanusse, *tr. fr. French by* Langston Hughes. PoNe; TTY
Epigram: "Drink, unhappy lover, drink." Meleager, *tr. fr. Greek by* Peter Whigham. PeHV
Epigram: Dutch, The. George Canning. OxBoLi
Epigram: "Elders at their services begin, The." J. V. Cunningham. NePoAm
Epigram: "Enemy of life, decayer of all kind, The." Sir Thomas Wyatt. SiPS
Epigram, An: "Epigram should be, An—if right." William Walsh. NIP
Epigram: "Even if I try not to ogle a boy in the street." Strato, *tr. fr. Greek.* PeHV
Epigram: "Face that should content me wonders well, A." Sir Thomas Wyatt. CTC; EnLoPo; OBSC
Epigram: Fatum Supremum. *Unknown.* OBS
Epigram: "For Hekabé and the women of Ilion." Plato, *tr. fr. Greek by* Peter Jay. PeHV
Epigram III: "Forgive us, son of Amram, be not wroth." *Unknown, tr. fr. Hebrew. Fr.* Duel with Verses over a Great Man. TrJP
Epigram: "Friend, on this scaffold Thomas More lies dead." J. V. Cunningham.
("Friend, on this scaffold Thomas More lies died.") InPK
Epigram: "Fruit of all the service that I serve, The." Sir Thomas Wyatt. SiPS
Epigram: "Gathering the bloom of all the fairest boys that be." Strato, *tr. fr. Greek by* Sydney Oswald. PeHV
Epigram: "Give me a boy whose tender skin." Martial, *tr. fr. Latin by* Brian Hill. PeHV
Epigram: "Glad youth had come thy sixteenth year to crown." Ausonius, *tr. fr. Latin.* PeHV
Epigram: Go, Happy Rose. Martial, *tr. fr. Latin by* Brian Hill. PeHV
Epigram: "God bless the King—I mean the faith's defender!" John Byrom. *See* Jacobite Toast, A.
Epigram: "Golden casket I designed, A." John Swanick Drennan. BIrV
Epigram: "Golden one is gone from the banquets, The." Hilda Doolittle ("H. D."). PoA
Epigram: "Good Fortune, when I hailed her recently." J. V. Cunningham. PV

Epigram: "Great woe, fire & war come on me." Skythinos, *tr. fr. Greek by* Thomas Meyer. PeHV
Epigram: "He who in his pocket hath no money." *Unknown.* HBV-1
Epigram: "Here lie I, Martin Elginbrodde." *Unknown, at. to* George Macdonald. *See* Epitaph: "Here lie I, Martin Elginbrodde."
Epigram: "Here lies a great and mighty king." Earl of Rochester. *See* King's Epitaph, The.
Epigram: "Here lies my wife. Eternal peace." J. V. Cunningham. NePoAm
("Here lies my wife. Eternal peace.") NIP; OBAL
Epigram: "Here lies my wife: here let her lie!" Dryden. *See* Epitaph Intended for His Wife.
Epigram: "Hetero-sex is best for the man of a serious turn of mind." Marcus Argentarus, *tr. fr. Greek by* Fleur Adcock. PeHV
Epigram: "Homer was poor. His scholars live at ease." J. V. Cunningham. VGW
Epigram: "How shall I know if my love lose his youth." Strato, *tr. fr. Greek by* Sydney Oswald. PeHV
Epigram: "How we desire desire! Joy of surcease." J. V. Cunningham. VGW
Epigram: "I am his Highness' dog at Kew." Pope. *See* Epigram Engraved on the Collar of a Dog Given to His Royal Highness.
Epigram: "I am provoked." Strato, *tr. fr. Greek by* W. G. Shepherd. PeHV
Epigram: "I celebrate Rhegion, Italy's tip, licked by." *Unknown, tr. fr. Greek by* Peter Jay. PeHV
Epigram: "I change, and so do women too." *Unknown. See* Written on a Looking-Glass.
Epigram: "I delight in the prime of a boy of twelve." Strato, *tr. fr. Greek by* Thomas Meyer. PeHV
Epigram: "I dined with Demetrius last night." Automedon, *tr. fr. Greek.* PeHV
Epigram: "I don't care for women." *Unknown, tr. fr. Greek.* PeHV
Epigram: "I had gone broke, and got set to come back." J. V. Cunningham. NePoAm; PV
("I had gone broke, and got set to come back.") QFR
(Three Epigrams.) MoAmPo
Epigram: " 'I hardly ever ope my lips,' one cries." Richard Garnett. HBV-1
Epigram: "I like them pale, fair or honey-skinned." Strato, *tr. fr. Greek.* PeHV
Epigram: "I loved thee beautiful and kind." Robert, Earl Nugent. NOEC
(I Loved Thee.) FiBHP
Epigram: "I married in my youth a wife." J. V. Cunningham. *See* I Married in My Youth a Wife.
Epigram: "I was thirsty." Meleager, *tr. fr. Greek by* Sydney Oswald. PeHV
Epigram: "I who by day am function of the light." J. V. Cunningham. *See* Motto for a Sun Dial.
Epigram: " 'I would,' says Fox, 'a tax devise.' " Sheridan. HBV-1
Epigram: "If a man who turnips cries." Samuel Johnson. *See* If the Man Who Turnips Cries.
Epigram: "If men be judged wise." Joseph Solomon del Medigo, *tr. fr. Hebrew.* TrJP
Epigram: "If wisdom, as it seems it is." J. V. Cunningham. QFR
Epigram: "If you see someone beautiful." Adaios, *tr. fr. Greek by* Alistair Elliot. PeHV
Epigram: "In whose will is our peace? Thou happiness." J. V. Cunningham. VGW
("In whose will is our peace? Thou happiness.") QFR
Epigram: "Insomuch, Bassa, as I never saw." Martial, *tr. fr. Latin.* PeHV
Epigram: "It is true that I held Thero fair." Meleager, *tr. fr. Greek by* Peter Whigham. PeHV
Epigram: "Joy is the blossom, sorrow is the fruit." Walter Savage Landor. *See* Joy Is the Blossom.
Epigram: "Just as he is growing a beard." Flaccus, *tr. fr. Greek.* PeHV
Epigram: "King George, observing with judicious eyes." Joseph Trapp. FaBoCo
("King, observing with judicious eyes, The.") FaBoEE
Epigram: "King to Oxford sent a troop of horse, The." Sir William Browne. FaBoCo; FaBoEE
(Oxford and Cambridge.) WhC
Epigram: "Kissing Hippomenes, I crave." Paulos, *tr. fr. Greek by* Andrew Miller. PeHV
Epigram: "Lasses, like nuts at bottom brown." Allan Ramsay. FaBoEE
Epigram: "Life flows to death as rivers to the sea." J. V. Cunningham. VGW
("Life flows to death as rivers to the sea.") POL
Epigram: "Life is a jest, and all things show it." John Gay. *See* My Own Epitaph.
Epigram: "Like when the burning sun doth rise." Strato, *tr. fr. Greek by* Sydney Oswald. PeHV
Epigram: Likeness, The. Martial, *tr. fr. Latin by* Brian Hill. PeHV
Epigram: "Listen, you know the pains of love." Meleager, *tr. fr. Greek by* Peter Whigham. PeHV
Epigram: "Lo! Beauty flashed forth sweetly; from his eyes." Meleager, *tr. fr. Greek by* Sydney Oswald. PeHV
Epigram: "Long hair, endless curls trained by the devoted." Strato, *tr. fr. Greek by* Teddy Hogge. PeHV
Epigram: "Lord Pam in the church (cou'd you think it) kneel'd down." Swift. NCEP
Epigram: "Love brought me quietly in the dreaming night." Meleager, *tr. fr. Greek by* Sydney Oswald. PeHV
Epigram: "Love signed the contract blithe and leal." John Swanwick Drennan. BIrV
Epigram: "Lux my fair falcon, and your fellows all." Sir Thomas Wyatt. *See* Lux, My Fair Falcon.
Epigram: "Man who goes for Christian resignation, The." J. V. Cunningham. NePoAm; PV
Epigram: "Me Polytimus vexes and provokes." Martial, *tr. fr. Latin.* PeHV
Epigram: "Member of the modern great, A." John Cunningham. FaBoEE
Epigram: "Midas, they say, possessed the art of old." "Peter Pindar." DBV; ELU; NIP
Epigram: "Milo's from home; and, Milo being gone." Martial, *tr. fr. Latin by* Elijah Fenton. OBVE
Epigram: Mistake, The. Theodore Roethke. *See* Mistake, The.
Epigram: "Most inexplicable the wiles of boys I deem." Rhianus, *tr. fr. Greek by* Sydney Oswald. PeHV
Epigram: "My better half, why turn a peevish scold." Martial, *tr. fr. Latin.* PeHV
Epigram: "My heart still hovering round about you." Robert, Earl Nugent. NOEC
Epigram: "My soul, sit thou a patient looker-on." Francis Quarles. NOBE; PoPle
(Epigram: Respice Finem.) OBEV
(My Soul, Sit Thou a Patient Looker-on.) NIP
(Respice Finem.) TreFT
Epigram: "Naked I came, naked I leave the scene." J. V. Cunningham. *See* Epitaph for Someone or Other.
Epigram: "Need from excess—excess from folly growing." Samuel Bishop. NOEC
Epigram: "Nicander, ooh, your leg's got hairs!" Alkaios, *tr. fr. Greek by* Tony Harrison. PeHV
Epigram: "No truer word, save God's, was ever spoken." Walter Savage Landor. HBV-1
(No Truer Word.) TreF
Epigram: "Nobles and heralds, by your leave." Matthew Prior. *See* Epitaph on Himself.
Epigram: "Now art thou fair, Diodorus." Strato, *tr. fr. Greek by* Sydney Oswald. PeHV
Epigram: "O Diodorus, in a storm of spring." *Unknown, tr. fr. Greek by* Sydney Oswald. PeHV
Epigram: Of Treason. Sir John Harington. *See* Of Treason.
Epigram: "Oh! trouble not Menèdemos by guile." Strato, *tr. fr. Greek by* Sydney Oswald. PeHV
Epigram: On a Slanderer. Martial, *tr. fr. Latin.* PeHV
Epigram: On Hedylus. Martial, *tr. fr. Latin.* PeHV
Epigram: On Inclosures. *Unknown. See* On Inclosures.
Epigram: "On parent knees, a naked new-born child." Sir William Jones, *after the Sanskrit of* Kalidasa. FaBoEE; OBEV; PoPl; PoPle
(Baby, The.) TreFS
(Moral Tetrastich, A.) OBEC
(On Parent Knees.) HBV-1
Epigram: On Sir Francis Drake. *Unknown.* OBS
Epigram: On Sir Roger Phillimore. *Unknown.* FaBoCo
Epigram: "One boy alone in all the world for me." Meleager, *tr. fr. Greek by* Sydney Oswald. PeHV
Epigram: "Passing the flower-stalls there did I perceive." Strato, *tr. fr. Greek by* Sydney Oswald. PeHV
Epigram: "Paul's midnight voice prevail'd; his music's thunder." Francis Quarles. *Fr.* Emblems, V, 10. LoBV
Epigram: "Perchance some coming after." Strato, *tr. fr. Greek by* Sydney Oswald. PeHV
Epigram: "Philosopher, whom dost thou most affect." Richard Garnett. HBV-1
Epigram: Political Reflexion. Howard Nemerov. *See* Sparrow in the Zoo, The.
Epigram: "Poverty? wealth? seek neither." Kassia, *tr. fr. Greek by* Patrick Diehl. WPOW
Epigram: "Quoth Satan to Arnold: 'My worthy good fellow.' " *Unknown.* PAH
Epigram: "Reincarnating Pythagoras, say." Ausonius, *tr. fr. Latin.* PeHV
Epigram: Respice Finem. Francis Quarles. *See* Epigram: "My soul, sit thou a patient looker-on."
Epigram: Riddle, A. Martial, *tr. fr. Latin by* Brian Hill. PeHV
Epigram: "Rudely forced to drink tea, Massachusetts, in anger." *Unknown.* PAH

Epigram: "Sighs are my food, drink are my tears." Sir Thomas Wyatt. SiPS
Epigram: "Since first you knew my am'rous smart." Robert, Earl Nugent. NOEC
Epigram: "Since I'm completely drunk." *Unknown, tr. fr. Greek by* Peter Jay. PeHV
Epigram: "Sir, I admit your general rule." Pope, *also at. to* Samuel Taylor Coleridge *and to* Matthew Prior. FaBoEE; FiBHP; HBV-1; LiTB; TreF
Epigram: "Some say, compared to Bononcini." John Byrom. *See* Epigram on Handel and Bononcini.
Epigram: "Stolen kisses, wary eyes." Strato, *tr. fr. Greek.* PeHV
Epigram: "Swans sing before they die." Samuel Taylor Coleridge. *See* On a Bad Singer.
Epigram: "There was this gym-teacher." Strato, *tr. fr. Greek by* Teddy Hogge. PeHV
Epigram: "This house, where once a lawyer dwelt." William Erskine. *See* This House Where Once a Lawyer Dwelt.
Epigram: "This Humanist whom no beliefs constrained." J. V. Cunningham. VGW
("This Humanist whom no beliefs constrained.") ELU
Epigram: "This is my curse, Pompous, I pray." J. V. Cunningham. PV
("This is my curse, Pompous, I pray.") HAP
Epigram: "Those snooty boys in all their purple drag!" Strato, *tr. fr. Greek by* Tony Harrison. PeHV
Epigram I: "Thou Guide to doubt, be silent evermore." *Unknown, tr. fr. Hebrew. Fr.* Duel with Verses over a Great Man. TrJP
Epigram II: "Thou fool profane, be silent!" *Unknown, tr. fr. Hebrew. Fr.* Duel with Verses over a Great Man. TrJP
Epigram: "Three things must epigrams, like bees, have all." *Unknown.* NIP
Epigram: "Thy eyes are sparks, Lycines, god-like made." Strato, *tr. fr. Greek by* Sydney Oswald. PeHV
Epigram: "Thy nags (the leanest things alive)." Matthew Prior. FaBoEE
Epigram: "Time heals not: it extends a sorrow's scope." J. V. Cunningham. VGW
Epigram: "Time was when once upon a time, such toys." Glaukos, *tr. fr. Greek by* Peter Jay. PeHV
Epigram: " 'Tis highly rational, we can't dispute." Richard Garnett. HBV-1
Epigram: " 'Tis human fortune's happiest height, to be." Sir William Watson. TreFT
Epigram: To Charinus, a Catamite. Martial, *tr. fr. Latin.* PeHV
Epigram: To Dindymus. Martial, *tr. fr. Latin by* Brian Hill. PeHV
Epigram: "To John I ow'd great obligation." Matthew Prior. FaBoCo; FaBoEE; FaFP; OBVE
(Quits.) AWP
Epigram: To Labienus. Martial, *tr. fr. Latin.* PeHV
Epigram: To Lygdus. Martial, *tr. fr. Latin,* PeHV
Epigram: To Papilus. Martial, *tr. fr. Latin.* PeHV
Epigram: To Philaenis. Martial, *tr. fr Latin.* PeHV
Epigram: To Phoebus. Martial, *tr. fr. Latin.* PeHV
Epigram: To Polycharmus. Martial, *tr. fr. Latin.* PeHV
Epigram: "Tom's sickness did his morals mend." Matthew Prior. FaBoEE
Epigram: "Treason doth never prosper; what's the reason?" Sir John Harington. *See* Of Treason.
Epigram: " 'Twas not so in my time,' surly Grumio exclaims." Samuel Bishop. NOEC
Epigram: "Wealth covers sin—the poor." Kassia, *tr. fr. Greek by* Patrick Diehl. WPOW
Epigram: "Were I a king, I could command content." Edward de Vere, Earl of Oxford. *See* Choice, A.
Epigram: "What is an epigram? a dwarfish whole." Samuel Taylor Coleridge. HBV-1
(What Is an Epigram?) NIP; PV
("What is an epigram? a dwarfish whole.") FaBoEE
Epigram: " 'What? rise again with all one's bones.' " Samuel Taylor Coleridge. HBV-1
Epigram IV: "What thought ye to burn, when ye kindled the pyre." *Unknown, tr. fr. Hebrew. Fr.* Duel with Verses over a Great Man. TrJP
Epigram: "When Bibo thought fit from the world to retreat." Matthew Prior. FaBoEE
Epigram: "When doctrines meet with general approbation." David Garrick. HBV-1
Epigram: "When Eve upon the first of men." Thomas Hood. , *wr. at. to* Thomas Moore *See* Reflection, A.
Epigram: "When Graphicus sat by the baths." Strato, *tr. fr. Greek.* PeHV
Epigram: "When 'mongst the youths you lately came." *Unknown, tr. fr. Greek by* Sydney Oswald. PeHV
Epigram; "When other ladies to the shades go down." Pope. *See* On Certain Ladies.
Epigram: "When Pontius wished an edict might be passed." Matthew Prior. DBV
Epigram: "When whelmed the altar, priest and creed." Sir William Watson. WGRP
Epigram: "Whilst Adam slept, Eve from his side arose." *Unknown. See* Adam and Eve.
Epigram: "Who hath heard of such cruelty before?" Sir Thomas Wyatt. AAS; SiPS
Epigram: "Who killed Kildare? Who dared Kildare to kill?" Swift. *See* Who killed Kildare? Who Dared Kildare to Kill?
Epigram: "Why all the racket, you chattering birds?" *Unknown, tr. fr. Greek by* Thomas Meyer. PeHV
Epigram: "With death doomed to grapple." Byron. *See* Epitaph for William Pitt.
Epigram: "Within this mindless vault." J. V. Cunningham. VGW
Epigram: "Woman working hard and wisely, A." Kassia, *tr. fr. Greek by* Patrick Diehl. WPOW
Epigram: "World is full of care, much like unto a bubble, The." Nathaniel Ward. POL
Epigram: "Yes, every poet is a fool." Matthew Prior. FaBoEE
(Another.) FaBoCo
Epigram: "You ask me how Contempt who claims to sleep." J. V. Cunningham. ErPo; ELU; NePoAm
Epigram: "You beat your pate, and fancy wit will come." Pope. HBV-1; TreFT
("You beat your pate, and fancy wit will come.") FaBoEE; PoPle
Epigram: "You were a pretty boy once, Archestratus, and." Philip of Thessalonica, *tr. fr. Greek by* Edith Morgan. PeHV
Epigram: "You wonder why Drab sells her love for gold?" J. V. Cunningham. NePoAm
Epigram Engraved on the Collar of a Dog Given [*or* Which I Gave] to His Royal Highness. Pope. FaBoCo; FaBoEE; FM; InPK; NOEC; NTCP; PAI; PoPle
(Engraved on the Collar of a Dog Which I Gave to His Royal Highness.) CABA; ChTr; LiTB; OxBoLi; SeCeV; SoSe
(Engraved on the Collar of His Highness' Dog.) WhC
(Epigram: "I am His Highness' dog at Kew.") HBV-1; TreFS
(His Highness's Dog.) RHPC
Epigram for the Dead at Tegea. *Unknown, tr. fr. Greek by* Richmond Lattimore. WaaP
Epigram from Petronius. Petronius Arbiter. *See* Doing, a Filthy Pleasure Is, and Short.
Epigram in a Maid of Honour's Prayer-Book. Pope. FaBoEE
Epigram of Martial, Imitated, An. Sir Charles Hanbury Williams. *See* Come, Chloe, and Give Me Sweet Kisses.
Epigram on a Lawyer's Desiring One of the Tribe to Look with Respect to a Gibbet. Robert Fergusson. OxBS
Epigram on an Academic Visit to the Continent. Richard Porson. OxBoLi; WhC
(On an Imaginary Journey to the Continent.) PV
(Porson's Visit to the Continent.) FaBoCo; FaBoEE
Epigram on an Academic Visit to the Continent. *Unknown.* OxBoLi
(On a German Tour, *sl. diff.*) FiBHP
Epigram on Elphinstone's Translation of Martial's Epigrams. Burns. *See* On Elphinston's Translation . . .
Epigram on Fasting. Swift. OBVE
Epigram on Florio. John Winstanley. FaBoEE
Epigram on Handel and Bononcini. John Byrom. FaBoEE; OBEC
(Epigram: "Some say, compared to Bononcini.") NOBL
(Epigram on the Feuds between Handel and Bononcini.) NOEC
Epigram on John Bull. Byron. *See* World Is a Bundle of Hay, The.
Epigram on Milton. Dryden. *See* Lines Printed under the Engraved Portrait of Milton.
Epigram on Miltonicks. Samuel Wesley. OBEC; POL
Epigram on One Who Made Long Epitaphs. Pope. FaBoEE
Epigram on Scolding. Swift. FaBoEE
Epigram on the Feuds between Handel and Bononcini. John Byrom. *See* Epigram on Handel and Bononcini.
Epigram on the First of April. John Winstanley. NOEC
Epigram on the Poor of Boston Being Employed in Paving the Streets, 1774. *Unknown.* PAH
Epigram on the Refusal of the University of Oxford to Subscribe to His Translation of Homer. William Cowper. TW
Epigram on the Unknown Inventor of Scissors. L. E. Jones. POL
Epigram on the Year 1390-1. *Unknown.* NIP
Epigram on Two Ladies. Sophia Burrell. ErPo; POL
Epigram on Voltaire. Edward Young. FaBoCo
(Extempore to Voltaire Criticising Milton.) ViBoPo
Epigram on Woman, An. Philip Ayres. FaBoEE
Epigram should be, An—if right. An Epigram. William Walsh. NIP
Epigram to King Charles for an Hundred Pounds He Sent Me in My Sickness, An. Ben Jonson. OAEP
Epigram to the Queen Then Lying In, An. Ben Jonson. SBVL
Epigrams, *sels.* Martial, *tr. fr. Latin by* Rolfe Humphries. GLGT.
"Schoolmaster, give your simple mob a break," X, lxii.
"To whom should you entrust your son," V, lvi.

Epigrams [I-IX]. Howard Nemerov. OBAL
Epigrams. Francis Daniel Pastorius. SCAP
Epigrams, *sel.* Rabindranath Tagore.
"Echo always mocks the sound, The." PoA
Epigrams and Epitaphs, *sel.* C. S. Lewis.
"Save yourself. Run and leave me. I must go back," *fr.* 6. EBEV
Epigrams must be curt, nor seem. Walter Savage Landor. FaBoEE
Epigrams on Priapus. *Unknown.* ErPo
Epigraph: "I give you the end of a golden string." Blake. *See* To the Christians.
Epigraph from *The Judge Is Fury.* J. V. Cunningham. QFR
Epigraph to "Drum-Taps." Walt Whitman. PAI
Epilog: "Drop a kernel of corn on a rock." Wendy Rose. *Fr.* Lost Copper. TWSS
Epilog: "Like the ears of wheat in a wheat-field growing." Heine. *See* Epilogue: "Like the stalks of wheat in the fields."
Epilogue: "All is best, though we oft doubt." Milton. *See* All Is Best.
Epilogue: Anemone. Leslie Scalapino. *Fr.* Hmmmm. NPGG
Epilogue: "At the midnight in the silence of the [*or* at] sleep-time." Robert Browning. *Fr.* Asolando. FaBoEn; FaBV; FiP; HBV-2; HBVY; NOBE; OAEP; OBNC; OBVV; TEP; TreFT; ViBoPo; VLP
(Epilogue to Asolando.) OHFP; TrGrPo
Epilogue: Author to Reader. Henri Coulette. *Fr.* The War of the Secret Agents, XII. NePoEA-2
Epilogue: "Away, for we are ready to a man!" James Elroy Flecker. *Fr.* The Golden Journey to Samarkand. NOBE
Epilogue: "Carol, every violet has." Alfred Noyes. *Fr.* The Flower of Old Japan. MoBrPo
Epilogue: "Giver of bliss and pain, of song and prayer." William Alexander Percy. TrPWD
Epilogue: "Have I spoken too much or not enough of love?" Richard Aldington. BrPo
Epilogue: "He is not dead nor liveth." Dorothy Wellesley. *See* Buried Child, The.
Epilogue: "Heaven, which man's generations draws." Francis Thompson. *Fr.* A Judgment in Heaven. MoAB; MoBrPo
Epilogue: "Hold! are you mad? you damned, confounded dog!" Dryden. *See* Epilogue to "Tyrannick Love."
Epilogue: "I am sure this Jesus will not do." Blake. *Fr.* The Everlasting Gospel. OBRV
Epilogue, An: "I have seen flowers come in stony places." John Masefield. FaBoEE; OxBTC
Epilogue: "I thought I had found a swan." Denise Levertov. LLLT
Epilogue: "I, too, sing America." Langston Hughes. *See* I, Too.
Epilogue: "I too was a little child once." Joseph Eliyia, *tr. fr. Greek by* Rae Dalven. VWA
Epilogue: "If Luther's day expand to Darwin's year." Herman Melville. *Fr.* Clarel. AP; ImOP
Epilogue: "If we shadows have offended." Shakespeare. *Fr.* A Midsummer Night's Dream, V, ii. OBSC
Epilogue: "Like the stalks of wheat in the fields." Heine, *tr. fr. German by* Emma Lazarus. *Fr.* The North Sea. TrJP
(Epilog: "Like the ears of wheat in a wheat-field growing, *tr. by* Louis Untermeyer.) AWP
Epilogue: "My bibliography has grown." Dallas Wiebe. TW
Epilogue: "Nothing now to mark the spot." Rachel Field. *See* Next Day.
Epilogue: "Now my charms are all o'erthrown." Shakespeare. *Fr.* The Tempest, V, i. CTC
Epilogue: "Now the hungry lion roars." Shakespeare. *See* Now the Hungry Lion Roars.
Epilogue: "O chansons foregoing." Ezra Pound. OxBA
Epilogue: " 'O where are you going?' said reader to rider." W. H. Auden. *See* O Where Are You Going?
Epilogue: "On the first of the Feast of Feasts." Robert Browning. *Fr.* Dramatis Personae. VLP
Epilogue: "Painted autumn overwhelms, The." John Meade Falkner. FaBoPP
Epilogue: "Phoenix on the hot sirocco's breath." H. B. Mallalieu. PoA
Epilogue: " 'Poets pour us wine, The.' " Robert Browning. VLP
Epilogue: " 'Terence, this is stupid stuff.' " A. E. Housman. *See* Terence, This Is Stupid Stuff.
Epilogue: "That death might not be casual." James Burns Singer. FaBoTw
Epilogue: "There's something in a stupid ass." Byron. Par
Epilogue: "They who have best succeeded on the stage." Dryden. *Fr.* The Conquest of Granada, Pt. II. FiP; SeCV-2
Epilogue: "Those blessèd structures, plot and rhyme." Robert Lowell. NoP
Epilogue: "Thus far, with rough and all-unable pen." Shakespeare. *Fr.* King Henry V. CTC
Epilogue: "Time is a thing." Stephen Spender. MoBrPo
Epilogue: To the Accuser Who Is the God of This World. Blake. *See* Epilogue: "Truly, my Satan, thou art but a dunce."
Epilogue: "Truly, my Satan, thou art but a dunce." Blake. *Fr.* The Gates of Paradise. CABA; HAP; OAEL-2; OBNC; WeW
(Epilogue: To the Accuser Who Is God of This World.) FaBoEn
(To the Accuser Who Is God of this World.) NoP; TrGrPo; ViBoPo
Epilogue: "Well, when all is said and done." "Æ." MoBrPo
Epilogue: "What shall we do for Love these days?" Lascelles Abercrombie. *Fr.* Emblems of Love. MoBrPo; OBVV
Epilogue: "With heart at rest I climbed the citadel's." Baudelaire, *tr. fr. French by* Arthur Symons. AWP
Epilogue at Wallack's, An. John Elton Wayland. AA
Epilogue for a Masque of Purcell. Adrienne Rich. NePoEA; NYBP
Epilogue Spoken by Mrs. Boutell. Dryden. SeCV-2
(To the University of Oxford, 1674: Epilogue.) FaBoEn
Epilogue to a Book of Verse. Arthur Guiterman. InMe
Epilogue to a Human Drama. Stephen Spender. CMoP
Epilogue to "Asolando." Robert Browning. *See* Epilogue: "At the midnight in the silence of the sleep-time."
Epilogue to Lessing's Laocoön. Matthew Arnold. VLP
Epilogue to "Mithridates, King of Pontus." Dryden. OAEP
Epilogue to Rhymes and Rhythms. W. E. Henley. ViBoPo
Epilogue to the Breakfast-Table Series. Oliver Wendell Holmes. *Fr.* The Poet at the Breakfast Table. AA
Epilogue to the Outrider. Dorothy Livesay. CaP
Epilogue to the Satires [*or* 1738]. Pope. OAEL-1
Sels.
Power of Ridicule, The, *fr.* Dialogue II. NOBE
("Ask you what provocation I have had?") OBSV
(Defence of Satire.) NOEC
(Satire.) OBEC
"Spare then the person, and expose the vice," *fr.* Dialogue II. OBSV
Triumph of Vice, The, *fr.* Dialogue I. NOBE
("Virtue may choose the high or low degree.") OBSV
Epilogue to "The Sister," *sel.* Goldsmith.
"Lud! what a group the motley scene discloses!" OBSV
Epilogue to "Tyrannick Love." Dryden. SeCV-2
(Epilogue: "Hold! are you mad? you damned, confounded dog!") OAEP; ViBoPo
Epiphany. Eileen Duggan. ISi
Epiphany. Eileen Shanahan. NeIP
Epiphany. Christopher Smart. Hymns and Spiritual Songs, Hymn 3. NOCV
Epiphany, The. George Strong. GoYe
Epiphany: For the Artist. Elizabeth Sewell. EyDe
Epipsychidion. Shelley. EnRP
Sels.
"Let us become the overhanging day." OAEL-2
Seraph of Heaven. ISi
"Ship is floating in the harbour now, A." OBRV
"Spouse! Sister! Angel! Pilot of the Fate." ChER
"Thy wisdom speaks in me, and bids me dare." OAEL-2
True Love ("She met me, stranger"). LoBV
"True Love in this differs from gold and clay." OBNC
Episode. Cassiano Nunes, *tr. fr. Spanish by* E. A. Lacey. PeHV
Episode of a Night of May. Arthur Symons. *Fr.* Scènes de la Vie de Bohème. BrPo
Episode of the Cherry Tree. Mildred Weston. PV
Episode 17. William Carlos Williams. *Fr.* Paterson. OxBA
Epistemological Rag, The. Gray Burr. CoPo
Epistemologist, over a Brandy, Opining, The. Robert Sargent. AMV-80
Epistemology. Richard Wilbur. NePoEA; NoAm; NOBA; SUW
Epistle, An: "And may my humble dwelling stand." Matthew Green. *Fr.* The Spleen. LoBV
Epistle, An: "First, last and always dearest, closest, best." A. D. Hope. PoAu-2
Epistle, An: "Karshish, the picker-up of learning's crumbs." Robert Browning. *See* Epistle Containing the Strange Medical Experience of Karshish . . .
Epistle II: To a Socialist in London, *sel.* Robert Bridges.
"And what if all Nature ratify this merciless outrage?" FM
Epistle Answering to One That Asked to be Sealed of the Tribe of Ben, An. Ben Jonson. AnAnS-2; OAEP; SeCV-1
Epistle Containing the Strange Medical Experience of Karshish, the Arab Physician, An. Robert Browning. VLP
(Karshish, the Arab Physician, *abr.*) WGRP
Sels.
Karshish and Lazarus. GoBC
"So, the All-Great, were the All-Loving too." TRV
Epistle Dedicatory to Chapman's Translation of the Iliad, The, *sel.* George Chapman.
Poetry and Learning. OBS
Epistle from a Half-Pay Officer in the Country to His Friend in London, An. Richardson Pack. NOEC

Epistle from Mr. Pope, to Dr. Arbuthnot, An. Pope. *See* Epistle to Dr. Arbuthnot.
Epistle from Mrs. Yonge to Her Husband. Lady Mary Wortley Montagu. NoP
Epistle in Form of a Ballad to His Friends. Villon, *tr. fr. French by* Swinburne. AWP
Epistle of Condolence. Thomas Moore. OnYI
Epistle of Othea to Hector, The (A Lytil Bibell of Knyghthod), *sel.* Christine de Pisan, *tr. fr. French; adapted by* Joan Keefe.
"Phoebus, the goddess variant and changeable." PBWP
Epistle of Rosamond to King Henry the Second, The. Michael Drayton. *Fr.* England's Heroical Epistles. AnAnS-2
Epistle to a Desponding Sea-Man. Philip Freneau. MOS
Epistle to a Friend, to Persuade Him to the Wars, An. Ben Jonson. TEP
"Whole world here, leavened with madness, swells, The," *sel.* JCP
Epistle to a Lady, An. Mary Leapor. NOEC
Epistle to a Lady: Of the Characters of Women. Pope. *See* Moral Essays.
Epistle to a Young Friend. Burns. EBEV
(Letter to a Young Friend.) OHFP
Epistle to Augusta. Byron. EnRP
Epistle to Be Left in the Earth. Archibald MacLeish. CMoP; ImOP; MoAB; MoAmPo; NOBA; TrGrPo
Epistle to Davie, a Brother Poet. Burns. OBEC
Epistle to Dr. Arbuthnot. Pope. CABA; InPS; LoBV, *abr.;* NoP; OAEL-1; OAEP; PoEL-3
(Epistle from Mr. Pope to Dr. Arbuthnot, An.) NOEC
(To Dr. Arbuthnot, *abr.)* OxBoLi
Sels.
Apologia pro Vita Sua. NOBE
Atticus ("How did they fume, and stamp, and roar, and chafe!"). TW
Atticus ("Peace to all such! but were there one whose fires"). AWP; InPK; NOBE; OBEC; SeCePo; WHA
("Peace to all such!. . .") ViBoPo
"Bard whom pilf'red pastorals reknown, The." OBSV
Bufo ("Proud as Apollo on his forked hill"). OBEC; OBSV
"Shut, shut the door, good John!" HoPM
(Dire Dilemna, A.) WHA
Sporus. AWP; ChTr; NOBE; OBSV; TW
("Let Sporus tremble—'What? that thing of silk.' ") DBV; SCV
Verbal Critics. OBEC
("Pains, reading, study, are their just pretense.") PP
Why Did I Write ("Of all mad creatures if the learn'd are right"). OBEC
"Why did [*or* do] I write? what sin to me unknown." ChTr, *shorter sel.;* EBEV; FiP; ViBoPo
Epistle to Dr. Blacklock, *abr.* Burns. OBEC
Epistle to Elizabeth, Countess of Rutland, *sels.* Ben Jonson.
"Beautie, I know, is good, and bloud is more." FaBoEn
Power of Poets, The. WHA
"With you, I know, my offering will find grace." JCP
Epistle to George Keats, *sel.* Shelley.
"Should he upon an evening ramble fare." ChER
Epistle to Henry Wriothesley, Earl of Southampton. Samuel Daniel. EnRePo
Epistle to James Smith. Burns. BSV; OBEC
(To James Smith.) HoPM
Epistle to John Guthrie. Sydney Goodsir Smith. OxBS
Epistle to John Hamilton Reynolds. Keats. OBNC
"O that our dreamings all, of sleep or wake," *sel.* OAEL-2
Epistle to John Lapraik, an Old Scottish Bard. Burns. EnRP; OAEP
"I am nae poet, in a sense," *sel.* PP
Epistle to Lady Rutland, An. Ben Johnson. *See* Epistle to Elizabeth, Countess of Rutland.
Epistle to Miss [*or* Miss Teresa] Blount, on Her Leaving the Town after the Coronation. Pope. BoLoP; EBEV; NOBE; NOEC; NoP; PoEL-3; PPP
(To a Young Lady on Her Leaving the Town after the Coronation.) OBEC; SeCeV
Epistle to Mr. Murray. Byron. FaBoUs
Epistle to My Friend J. B., An. Robert Dodsley. NOEC
Epistle to Richard Boyle, Earl of Burlington, An. Pope. *See* Moral Essays.
Epistle to Robert Lloyd, Esq., An. William Cowper. FiP
Epistle to Robert Nugent, Esq. with a Picture of Doctor Swift in Old Age, An, *sel.* William Dunkin.
"Hibernia's Helicon is dry." NOEC
Epistle to Sir Edward Sackville, Now Earl of Dorset, An. Ben Jonson. NCEP
Epistle to Sir Richard Temple, *sel.* Pope.
"Wharton! the scorn and wonder of our days." DBV
(Wharton.) AWP
Epistle to Tammus, *sel.* J. B. Selkirk.
Border Burn, A. PoSH
Epistle to the Gentiles. Alfred Hayes. TrJP
Epistle to the President of the Scottish Society of Antiquaries: On Being Chosen a Correspondent Member. Alexander Geddes. OxBS
Epistle to the Rapalloan. Archibald MacLeish. PoA
Epistle to the Reader. Walker Gibson. PP
Epistle to the Right Hon. Charles James Fox, An, *sel.* Thomas Maurice.
"How cursed that country, how severe its doom." NOEC
Epistle to William Simpson, Ochiltree. Burns. *See* To William Simpson, Ochiltree.
Epistle Written in the Country to the Right Honourable the Lord Lovelace, An, *sel.* Soame Jenyns.
"In days, my Lord, when mother Time." OBSV
Epistles, *sel.* Horace, *tr. fr. Latin.*
To Fuscus Arustus, I, 10, *tr. by* Abraham Cowley. AWP
Epistles to His Friends in Town, *sel.* John Gilbert Cooper.
Temper of Aristippus, The. PBBP
Epistles to Mr. Pope, *sel.* Edward Young.
"These labouring wits, like paviours, mend our ways." OBSV
Epistolary Briefs to Proclus, *sel.* Jose I. de Diego Padró, *tr. fr. Spanish by* Julio Marzán.
"Friend Proclus, the world isn't a fantasy," I, II. InW
Epistolary Essay from M. G. to O. B. upon Their Mutual Poems, An. Earl of Rochester. APAS
Epistrophe. Amiri Baraka. CAD; NNP; PoNe
Epitaph: "As I was, so be ye." *Unknown.* TreFS
Epitaph, An: "As shining sand-drift." Margaret Sackville. HBMV
Epitaph, An: "Beneath this stone lies one good man; and when." W. H. Davies. ChMP
Epitaph: "Body, The/ of/ Benjamin Franklin." Benjamin Franklin. TRV
Epitaph, An: "Come knock your heads against this stone." Blake. TEP
Epitaph: "Daniel and Abigail." Miguel de Barrios, *tr. fr. Spanish.* TrJP
Epitaph: "Done to death by slanderous tongues." Shakespeare. *Fr.* Much Ado about Nothing, V, iii. CTC
(Claudio's Lament.) OBSC
Epitaph: "Dummer the shepherd sacrific'd." Cotton Mather. SCAP
Epitaph, An: "Enough; and leave the rest to fame." Andrew Marvell. LO; OBEV; PoPle
(Epitaph upon ———, An.) CaVP; LoBV
Epitaph, An: "Escaped the gloom of mortal life, a soul." James Beattie. BSV
Epitaph: "Even such is Time, which [*or* that] takes in trust." Sir Walter Ralegh. *See* Even Such Is Time.
Epitaph: "Fate to beauty still must give." Claudian, *tr. fr. Latin by* Howard Mumford Jones. AWP
Epitaph: "For this she starred her eyes with salt." Elinor Wylie. MoAmPo; SBG
Epitaph: "From out the stormy sea unto the shore." Azariah di Rossi, *tr. fr. Hebrew by* A. B. Rhine. TrJP
Epitaph: "Glassblower lies here at rest, A." J. B. Morton. FaBoEE
Epitaph: "He roamed half-round the world of woe." Aubrey Thomas De Vere. OBVV
Epitaph, An: "He worshipped at the altar of Romance." Colin Ellis. OxBTC
Epitaph: "Her grieving parents cradled here." Sylvia Townsend Warner. MoBrPo
Epitaph: "Here dead lie we because we did not choose." A. E. Housman. *See* Here Dead Lie We.
Epitaph: "Here—for they could not help but die." Philip Freneau. *Fr.* The Fading Rose. AA
Epitaph: "Here he lies moulding." Leslie Mellichamp. QQQ; ShM
Epitaph: "Here Johnson lies—a sage by all allow'd." William Cowper. LAuP
Epitaph: "Here lie I, Martin Elginbrodde." *Unknown, at. to* George Macdonald. WGRP
(At Aberdeen.) FaBoCo
(Elgin Cathedral Epitaph.) PoPle
(Epigram.) HBV-1
("Here lie I, Martin Elginbrod.") FaBoEE
Epitaph, An: "Here lie I, once a witty fair." Samuel Wesley. NOEC
Epitaph I: "Here lies a man, and still no man." *Unknown, tr. fr. Hebrew. Fr.* Duel with Verses over a Great Man. TrJP
Epitaph, An: "Here lies a most beautiful lady." Walter de la Mare. CoBMV; LiTB; LiTM; LoBV; MoAB; MoBrPo; MoVE; OAEP; OBEV; OBVV; ViBoPo
Epitaph: "Here lies a poet, briefly known as Hecht." Anthony Hecht. POL
Epitaph: "Here lies a poor woman who always was tired." *Unknown.* TreF
("Here lies a poor woman who was always tired.") FaBoEE
(On a Tired Housewife.) EvOK
Epitaph: "Here lies a simple Jew." Sholom Aleichem, *tr. fr. Yiddish by* Joseph Leftwich. TrJP
Epitaph: "Here lies I and my three daughters." *Unknown.* TreFT
("Here lies I and my three daughters.") FaBoEE; WhC

Epitaph: "Here lies John Hughes and Sarah Drew." Lady Mary Wortley Montagu. FaBoEE
Epitaph, An: "Here lies Nachshon, a man of great renown." Isaac Benjacob, *tr. fr. Hebrew by* Joseph Chotzner. TrJP
Epitaph: "Here lies Sir Tact, a diplomatic fellow." Timothy Steele. *See* Here Lies Sir Tact.
Epitaph: "Here lies the body of Richard Hind." Francis Jeffrey. OxBoLi
("Here lies the body of Richard Hind.") FaBoEE
(On Richard Hind.) FaBoCo
Epitaph: "Here lies the flesh that tried." Louise Driscoll. HBMV; WGRP
Epitaph: "Here lies the poet Wolker, lover of the world." Jiří Wolker, *tr. fr. Czech by* Karl W. Deutsch. WaaP
Epitaph: "Here lies the remains of great Senator Vrooman." Ambrose Bierce. DBV
Epitaph, An: "Here lieth under this marble ston." *Unknown.* MeEL
Epitaph: "Here, time concurring (and it does)." John Ciardi. BiP
Epitaph: "Hours before my death." Julio Marzán. InW
Epitaph: "I am old." Christopher Logue. OxBTC
Epitaph: "I, an unwedded wandering dame." Sylvia Townsend Warner. MoBrPo
Epitaph: "I never cared for Life: Life cared for me." Thomas Hardy. FaBoRV
("I never cared for Life: Life cared for me.") FaBoEE
Epitaph: "I, Richard Kent, beneath these stones." Sylvia Townsend Warner. MoBrPo
Epitaph: "If fruits are fed on any beast." J. M. Synge. *See* Epitaph after Reading Ronsard's Lines from Rabelais.
Epitaph: "Implacable angel, The/ Has shot his dart." Leone da Modena, *tr. fr. Hebrew.* TrJP
Epitaph: Inscription from Anticyra. *Unknown, tr. fr. Greek by* Richmond Lattimore. WaaP
Epitaph, An: Inscription on a Monument at Newstead Abbey. Byron. *See* Epitaph to a Dog.
Epitaph: "Insured for every accident." Richard Armour. ShM
Epitaph, An: "Interr'd beneath this marble stone." Matthew Prior. FaBoEE; OAEL-1; OBEC; OBSV; PoEL-3
Epitaph: Iohannis Sande. Thomas Bastard. FaBoEE
Epitaph: "It was for you that the mountains shook at Sinai." *Unknown.* TrJP
Epitaph: "John Bird, a laborer, lies here." Sylvia Townsend Warner. MoBrPo
Epitaph: "Like silver dew are the tears of love." A. E. Coppard. OBMV
Epitaph, An: "Like thee I once have stemm'd the sea of life." James Beattie. *See* Epitaph Intended for Himself, An.
Epitaph: "Lovely boy, thou art not dead." Francis Davison. OBSC
Epitaph, An: "Lovely young lady I mourn in my rhymes, A." George John Cayley. ELU; FiBHP; HBV-1
Epitaph: "Man who in his life trusts in this world, A." *Unknown.* TrJP
Epitaph: "Meek Francis lies here, friend, without stop or stay." Matthew Prior. FaBoEE
Epitaph: "Mr. Heath-Stubbs as you must understand." John Heath-Stubbs. NePoEA; OxBTC
Epitaph: "My brother is skull and skeleton now." William Montgomerie. OxBS; POL
Epitaph, An: "My name—my country—what are they to thee?" Paulus Silentarius, *tr. fr. Greek by* William Cowper. FaBoEE; OBVE
Epitaph: "Nature and Nature's laws lay hid in night." Pope. *See* Intended for Sir Isaac Newton.
Epitaph: "Nor practising virtue nor committing crime." Geoffrey Taylor. FaBoEE
Epitaph: "O mortal folk, you may behold and see." Stephen Hawes. *See* Epitaph of Grande Amoure, The.
Epitaph, An: On Elizabeth Chute. Ben Jonson. EnRePo
Epitaph: On Sir Walter Rawleigh at His Execution. *Unknown.* OBS
Epitaph: "One whom I knew, a student and a poet." Alex Comfort. MoBrPo; MOS
(Poem: "One whom I knew, a student and a poet.") SeCePo
Epitaph: "Or many things adulterate." Tristan Corbière, *tr. fr. French by* Joseph T. Shipley. AWP
Epitaph: "Posterity will ne'er survey." Byron. *See* Epitaph for Castelreagh, An.
Epitaph: "Remember man, that passeth by." *Unknown.* *See* Epitaph and a Reply, An.
Epitaph: "Roots of mankind are tangled in my hair, The." Wendy Rose. CDW
Epitaph: "See here, nice Death, to please his palate." *At. to* Pope. FaBoEE
Epitaph: "Serene descent, as a red leaf's descending." Sara Teasdale. PoA
Epitaph: "She was a high-class bitch and a dandy." Theodore Spencer. LiTA
Epitaph, An: "Shiftless and shy, gentle and kind and frail." J. C. Squire. HBMV
Epitaph: "Sir, you should [*or* shall] notice me: I am the Man." Lascelles Abercrombie. MoBrPo; ViBoPo
Epitaph: Snake River. Lance Henson. VoR
Epitaph: "Stavro's dead. A truant vine." Lawrence Durrell. FaBoCo
Epitaph: "Stone cries from the wall, The." *Unknown.* TrJP
Epitaph: "Stop, Christian passer-by!—Stop, child of God." Samuel Taylor Coleridge. EnRP; FiP; NOCV; NoP; OAEL-2; OAEP; OBRV
(Epitaph on Himself.) OxBoCh
(O, Lift One Thought.) CH
Epitaph: "This is the end of him." Amy Levy. TrJP
Epitaph, An: "This little vault, this narrow room." Thomas Carew. *See* Epitaph on the Lady Mary Villiers, An.
Epitaph: "Thou alive on earth, sweet boy." Francis Davison. OBSC
Epitaph: "Time and the World, whose magnitude and weight." Robert Southey. OBNC
Epitaph: "Time that bringes all things to light." Thomas Morton. SCAP
Epitaph: To the Four Husbands of Miss Ivy Saunders. *Unknown.* PV
Epitaph: "Tread softly; bid a solemn music sound." J. B. Morton. FaBoEE
Epitaph, An: "Under this sod and beneath these trees." *Unknown.* *See* On Samuel Pease.
Epitaph: "Underneath this marble stone." Abraham Cowley. *See* Epitaph of Pyramus and Thisbe.
Epitaph: "Underneath this wooden cross there lies." Karl Shapiro. *Fr.* Elegy for a Dead Soldier. OFD
Epitaph: "Warm summer sun shine kindly here." Robert Richardson. *See* Epitaph Placed on His Daughter's Tomb.
Epitaph: "We mourn the loss." Ambrose Bierce. DBV
Epitaph: "When I shall be without regret." J. V. Cunningham. ELU; InPK; PoCh
Epitaph: "When you perceive these stones are wet." Sir William Davenant. ACP
Epitaph: "Within this grave do lie." *Unknown.* *See* Within This Grave Do Lie.
Epitaph: "Wit's perfection, Beauty's wonder." Francis Davison. OBSC
Epitaph, The: "Write on my grave when I am dead." Katharine Tynan. WGRP
Epitaph after Reading Ronsard's Lines from Rabelais. J. M. Synge. FaBoEE
(Epitaph: "If fruits are fed on any beast.") PV
Epitaph and a Reply, An. *Unknown.* TreFS
(Epitaph: "Remember man, that passeth by.") TreFT
Epitaph. Cæcil. Boulstr. Lord Herbert of Cherbury. AnAnS-2; SeCP
Epitaph Ending in And, The. William Stafford. LCAP; NaP; NIP
Epitaph for a Bigot. Dorothy Vena Johnson. PoNe
Epitaph for a Cat. Margaret E. Bruner. PoLF
Epitaph for a Funny Fellow. Morris Bishop. FPL
Epitaph for a Godly Man's Tomb. Robert Wild. ChTr; FaBoEE; OxBoCh
Epitaph for a Horseman. Michael Hamburger. NePoEA-2
Epitaph for a Judge. Benedict Jeitteles, *tr. fr. Hebrew by* Joseph Chotzner. TrJP
Epitaph for a Lighthouse-Keeper's Horse. J. B. Morton. PV
Epitaph for a Man from Virginia City. Kenneth Porter. NePoAm-2
Epitaph for a Negro Woman. Owen Dodson. PoNe
Epitaph for a Postal Clerk. X. J. Kennedy. NIP; PCP; ShM
Epitaph for a Sailor Buried Ashore. Sir Charles G. D. Roberts. EtS
Epitaph for a Timid Lady. Frances Cornford. ELU
Epitaph for Any New Yorker. Christopher Morley. ShM
Epitaph for Bathsheba Whittier. *See* For a Little Girl Mourning Her Favorite Cat.
Epitaph for Castlereagh, An. Byron. DBV; NIP
(Epitaph: "Posterity will ne'er survey.") FaBoEE; TW
Epitaph for Erotion. Martial, *tr. fr. Latin by* James Michie.FaBoEE
Epitaph for G. B. Shaw. Max Beerbohm. FaBoEE
Epitaph for George Moore. Thomas Hardy. FaBoEE
Epitaph for Himself. Lord Herbert of Cherbury. AnAnS-2
Epitaph for James Smith. Burns. *See* On a Wag in Mauchline.
Epitaph for Jean Maillard. *Unknown, tr. fr. French.* PeHV
Epitaph for John and Richard. Karl Shapiro. TwAmPo
Epitaph for John Camden Hotten. G. A. Sala. DBV
Epitaph for Mr. Moses Levy. *Unknown.* TrJP
Epitaph for My Cat. Jean Garrigue. TAP
Epitaph for One Who Would Not Be Buried in Westminster Abbey. Pope. FaBoEE
Epitaph for Peter Stuyvesant. Henricus Selyns. NYP; SCAP
Epitaph for Sir Henry Lee. *Unknown.* FaBoEE
Epitaph for Someone or Other. J. V. Cunningham. NIP; OBAL
(Epigram: "Naked I came, naked I leave the scene.") VGW
Epitaph for the Poet V., *sels.* Arthur Davison Ficke. HBMV
"Beauty—what is it? A perfume without name," III.
"For Beauty kissed your lips when they were young," II.
"It is ordained,—or so Politian said," I.
"Peculiar ghost!—great and immortal ghost!" XVII.

Epitaph for the Race of Man, *sels.* Edna St. Vincent Millay.
"Here lies, and none to mourn him but the sea," I. MoPo
"Only the diamond and the diamond's dust," II. MoPo
"See where Capella with her golden kids," VI. CMoP; MoAB; MoAmPo
Epitaph for the Tomb of Adolfo Baez Bone. Ernesto Cardenal, *tr. fr. Spanish by* Janet Brof. POL
Epitaph for the Unknown Soldier. W. H. Auden. FaBoCo
Epitaph for William Pitt. Byron. FaBoEE
(Epigram: "With death doomed to grapple.") HBV-1
Epitaph, Found Somewhere in Space. Hugh Wilgus Ramsaur. TRV
Epitaph from a Yorkshire Churchyard. *Unknown.* DBV
("Here lies the mother of children seven," *sl. diff.*) WhC
Epitaph from Aberdeen. *Unknown. See* On an Aberdeen Favourite.
Epitaph from *The Great Gatsby.* F. Scott Fitzgerald. ELU
Epitaph in a Churchyard at Thetford, in Norfolk. *Unknown.* FaBoUs
Epitaph in Anticipation. Leonard Bacon. WhC
Epitaph in Christ Church, Bristol, on Thomas Turner, Twice Master of the Company of Bakers. Francis Jeffrey. OxBoLi
("Like to a baker's oven is the grave.") FaBoEE
Epitaph in Form of a Ballad, The. Villon, *tr. fr. French by* Swinburne. CTC
Epitaph in Obitum M.S., X° Maij, 1614. William Browne. *See* In Obitum M.S. . . .
Epitaph in St. Olave's [Church], Southwark, on Mr. Munday. *Unknown.* FaBoCo; OxBoLi
Epitaph in Sirmio. David Morton. PoLF
Epitaph Inscribed on a Small Piece of Marble. James Shirley. CavP
Epitaph Intended for Himself, An. James Beattie. HBV-2
(Epitaph, An: "Like thee I once have stemm'd the sea of life.") OBEV
Epitaph Intended for His Wife. Dryden. DBV; InMe
(Epigram: "Here lies my wife; here let her lie.") HBV-1
(Epitaph on His Wife.) TrGrPo; WhC
(Here Lies My Wife.) ShM
("Here lies my wife; here let her lie!") TreF
Epitaph Intended for Sir Isaac Newton. Pope. *See* Intended for Sir Isaac Newton.
Epitaph of a Faithful Man. Robert Mezey. ELU
Epitaph of a Stripper. William Jay Smith. AMV-80
Epitaph of Cleonicus. Theocritus, *tr. fr. Greek by* Charles Stuart Calverley. FaBoEE
Epitaph of Dionysia. *Unknown.* HBV-1; OBEV; OBVV
Epitaph of Eusthenes, The. Edward Cracroft Lefroy, *after the Greek of* Theocritus. *Fr.* Echoes from Theocritus. AWP; OBVV
Epitaph of [La] Grande Amoure, The. Stephen Hawes. *Fr.* The Pastime of Pleasure. ChTr; EBEV; FaBoRV; OBSC; SeCeV
(Epitaph, An: "O mortal folk, you may behold and see.") ACP; OBEV; TrGrPo
(Epitaphy of la Graunde Amoure.) FaBoEE
(His Epitaph.) GoBC
(O mortal folk, you may behold and see.") ViBoPo
Epitaph of Hipponax. Theocritus, *tr. fr. Greek by* Charles Stuart Calverley. FaBoEE
Epitaph of Maister Win Drowned in the Sea, An. George Turberville. FaBoEE
Epitaph of Nearchos. Ammianus, *tr. fr. Greek by* Dudley Fitts. WeW
Epitaph of Pyramus and Thisbe. Abraham Cowley. FaBoEE
(Epitaph: "Underneath this marble stone.") EnLoPo
Epitaph of Sarah Sexton. *Unknown.* TreFT
("Here lies the body of Sarah Sexton.") WhC
Epitaph of Sir Thomas Gravener, Knight, An. Sir Thomas Wyatt. EnRePo; OBSC; SiPS
Epitaph of the Death of Nicholas Grimald, An. Barnabe Googe. EnRePo
Epitaph on a Bombing Victim. Roy Fuller. NeBP
Epitaph on a Career Woman. William Cole. PV
Epitaph on a Child Killed by Procured Abortion. *Unknown.* NOEC
Epitaph on a Dentist. *Unknown. See* Dentist, A.
Epitaph on a Dormouse. *Unknown.* OxBChV
Epitaph on a Fir-Tree. Richard Murphy. FaBoTw
Epitaph on a Free but Tame Redbreast. William Cowper. PBBP
Epitaph on a Great Sleeper. Sir Aston Cokayne. FaBoEE
Epitaph on a Hare. William Cowper. FiP; FM; HAP; HBV-1; HBVY; HeIP; NOEC; NoP; PoEL-3; PoPle; SeCeV
Epitaph on a Jacobite. Macaulay. *See* Jacobite's Epitaph, A.
Epitaph on a Madman's Grave. Morris Gilbert. YaD
Epitaph on a Marf. *Unknown.* PV
Epitaph on a Party Girl. Richard Usborne. FaBoEE
Epitaph on a Pessimist. Thomas Hardy. FaBoEE; FF
Epitaph on a Robin Redbreast, An. Samuel Rogers. FaBoEE; FM; PBBP
Epitaph on a Schoolmaster. Burns. FaBoCo
("Here lie Willie M——hie's banes.") FaBoEE
Epitaph on a Soldier. Cyril Tourneur. *Fr.* The Atheist's Tragedy. ElL
Epitaph on a Talkative Old Maid. Benjamin Franklin. WhC
Epitaph on a Tuft-Hunter. Thomas Moore. FaBoCo; FaBoEE
Epitaph on a Tyrant. W. H. Auden. ELU; HeIP
Epitaph on a Vagabond. Alexander Gray. HBMV
Epitaph on a Waiter. David McCord. NIP; OBAL; PPJ
(On a Waiter.) WhC
Epitaph on a Warthog. J. B. Morton. PV
Epitaph on a Well-known Poet. Thomas Moore. *See* Epitaph on Robert Southey.
Epitaph on a Willing Girl. *At. to* Thomas Rowlandson. FaBoEE
Epitaph on a Worthy Clergyman. Benjamin Franklin. TRV
Epitaph on a Young Child. Ivor Gurney. FaBoEE
Epitaph on a Young Poet Who Died before Having Achieved Success. Amy Lowell. OBAL
Epitaph on Achilles. *Unknown, tr. fr. Greek by* William M. Hardinge. AWP
Epitaph on an Army of Mercenaries. A. E. Housman. BrPo; CMoP; CoBMV; MMA; MoAB; MoVE; NIP; NoAM; NOBE; OBEV; OBWP; OxBTC; PPP; PrIm; SaC; UnPo; ViBoPo; WaaP
Epitaph on an Engraver. Henry David Thoreau. EyDe
Epitaph on an Infant. Crinagoras, *tr. fr. Greek by* John William Burgon. AWP
Epitaph on an Irish Priest. *Unknown.* FaBoEE
Epitaph on an Unfortunate Artist. Robert Graves. FaBoEE; NOBL; WhC
Epitaph on Any Man. A. S. J. Tessimond. POL
Epitaph on Charles I. James Graham, Marquess of Montrose. *See* His Metrical Vow.
Epitaph on Charles II. Earl of Rochester. FaBoCo; FiBHP; HBV-1; TreFS; TrGrPo; WhC
("Here lies our Sovereign Lord, the King.") DBV
(King Charles II.) ViBoPo
Epitaph on Claudy Phillips, a Musician, An. Samuel Johnson. NOEC
Epitaph on Colonel Francis Chartres. John Arbuthnot. FaBoEE
(Colonel Chartres.) OBSV
Epitaph on Doctor Donne, Deane of Pauls, An. Richard Corbett. AnAnS-2
Epitaph on Dr. Johnson. Soame Jenyns. *See* Doctor Johnson.
Epitaph on Dr. Keene. Thomas Gray. FaBoEE
Epitaph on Dr. Keene's Wife. Thomas Gray. FaBoEE
Epitaph on Elizabeth, L. H. Ben Jonson. AnAnS-2; BiP; CABA; ElL; ELP; EnRePo; FaBoEE; HAP; HBV-2; HeIP; NIP; NoP; OBEV; OBS; SeCP; SeCV-1; ViBoPo; WHA
(Elizabeth L. H.) TreFT
Epitaph on Erotion. Leigh Hunt. OBRV
Epitaph on Floyd. *Unknown.* POL
Epitaph on Frederick, Prince of Wales. *Unknown. See* On Prince Frederick.
Epitaph on Himself ("Here sleeps at length poor Col, and without screaming"). Samuel Taylor Coleridge. FaBoEE
Epitaph on Himself ("Stop, Christian passer-by!—Stop, child of God"). Samuel Taylor Coleridge. *See* Epitaph: "Stop, Christian passer-by . . ."
Epitaph on Himself. Pope. FaBoEE
Epitaph on Himself. Matthew Prior. TreFS
(Epigram: "Nobles and heralds; by your leave.") HBV-1
(On Himself.) FaBoEE
(Prior's Epitaph.) TrGrPo
Epitaph on His Wife. Dryden. *See* Epitaph Intended for His Wife.
Epitaph on James Grieve, Laird of Boghead. Burns. *See* On James Grieve, Laird of Boghead, Tarbolton.
Epitaph on James Moore Smythe. Pope. FaBoEE
Epitaph on John Dove. Burns. FaBoCo
Epitaph on John Knott. *Unknown.* ChTr; FaBoEE; ShM
Epitaph on John Murray, 1777. *Unknown.* BSV
Epitaph on King Charles I. James Graham, Marquess of Montrose. *See* His Metrical Vow.
Epitaph on Lady Ossory's Bullfinch. Horace Walpole. *Fr.* Epitaphs on Two Piping-Bullfinches of Lady Ossory's. ChTr
Epitaph on Laurence Sterne. David Garrick. FaBoEE
Epitaph on M. H., An. Charles Cotton. EBEV; FaBoEE
Epitaph on Maria Wentworth. Thomas Carew. PoEL-3
Epitaph on Master Philip Gray, An. Ben Jonson. FaBoEE
Epitaph on Master Vincent Corbett, An. Ben Jonson. JCP
Epitaph on Mr. Robert Port. Charles Cotton. CavP
Epitaph on Mistress Mary Draper. Charles Cotton. CavP
Epitaph on Pegasus, a Limping Gay. Panormitanus, *tr. fr. Latin.* PeHV
Epitaph on Peter Robinson. Francis Jeffrey. *See* On Peter Robinson.
Epitaph on Prince Frederick. *Unknown. See* On Prince Frederick.
Epitaph on Prince Henry. Hugh Holland. FaBoEE
Epitaph on Robert Southey. Thomas Moore. FaBoCo; FaBoEE; PP
(Epitaph on a Well-known Poet.) DBV; InMe
Epitaph on S. P. [Salomon *or* Salathiel Pavy], a Child of Queen Elizabeth's Chapel. Ben Jonson. AnAnS-2; CABA; ElL; EnRePo; FaBoEn; GoBC; HBV-2; HeIP; HoPM; JCP; LoBV; MePo; NoP; OAEL-1; OAEP; OBEV; OBS; PoEL-2; PoPle; PPP; SeCP; SeCV-1; TrGrPo; UnPo; ViBoPo
(On Solomon Pavy, a Child of Queen Elizabeth's Chapel.) NOBE

Epitaph on Sir Edward Giles and His Wife. Robert Herrick. PoPle
Epitaph on Sir Isaac Newton. Pope. *See* Intended for Sir Isaac Newton.
Epitaph on Sir John Vanbrugh [Architect]. Abel Evans. *See* On Sir John Vanbrugh.
Epitaph on Sir Philip Sidney. *At. to* Fulke Greville *and also to* Sir Edward Dyer. LiTB; LoBV; OBSC
(Elegy on the Death of Sidney.) EnRePo
(Epitaph upon the Right Honorable Sir Philip Sidney, An.) Prf
Epitaph on Sir Philip Sidney. *At. to* Sir Walter Ralegh. SiPS
Epitaph on Sir Walter Pye. John Hoskyns. FaBoEE
Epitaph on the Admirable Dramatic Poet, W. Shakespeare, An. Milton. *See* On Shakespeare.
Epitaph on the Countess[e] Dowager of Pembroke. William Browne. *See* On the Countess Dowager of Pembroke.
Epitaph on the Duke of Buckingham. James Shirley. CavP
(On the Duke of Buckingham.) FaBoEE
Epitaph on the Duke of Grafton. Sir Fleetwood Shepherd. FaBoEE
Epitaph on the Earl of Leicester. Sir Walter Ralegh. EnRePo; SiPS
Epitaph on the Earl of Strafford. John Cleveland. CavP; FaBoEE; JCP; MePo; NOBE; OBS; SeCePo; TrGrPo
Epitaph on the Fart in the Parliament House. John Hoskyns. FaBoEE
Epitaph on the Favourite Dog of a Politician. Hilaire Belloc. OBSV
Epitaph on the Lady Mary Villiers ("The Lady Mary Villiers lies"). Thomas Carew. AnAnS-2; CaPo; CavP; FaBoEE; OAEP; OBEV; SeCV-1; ViBoPo
(On the Lady Mary Villiers.) NOBE
Epitaph on the Lady Mary Villiers, An ("This little vault, this narrow room"). Thomas Carew. SeCP
(Another.) CaPo
(Epitaph, An: "This little vault, this narrow room.") OBEV
(Other, An.) AnAnS-2; SeCV-1
Epitaph on the Late King of the Sandwich Isles. Winthrop Mackworth Praed. DBV; FiBHP
Epitaph on the Marchioness of Winchester, An. Milton. CavP; OBS
Epitaph on the Monument of Sir William Dyer at Colmworth, 1641. Lady Catherine Dyer. *Fr.* Sir William Dyer, Knight. BoLoP; EnLoPo; NIP
Epitaph on the Politician Himself. Hilaire Belloc. DBV; MoBrPo; OBSV; TreFT
("Here richly, with ridiculous display.") FaBoEE
(On a Politician.) PV; ShM; TW; WhC
Epitaph on the Proofreader of the Encyclopedia Britannica. Christopher Morley. ShM
Epitaph on the Secretary to the Muses. Jane Barker. FaBoCo
Epitaph on the Tomb of Sir Edward Giles and His Wife in the South Aisle of Dean Prior Church, Devon. Robert Herrick. QFR
Epitaph—on the Wife of Dr. Greenwood. Dr. Greenwood. FaBoUs
Epitaph on the World. Henry David Thoreau. FF; HeIP
Epitaph on Thomas Clere. Earl of Surrey. SiPS
(Norfolk Sprang Thee.) NCEP
("Norfolk sprang thee, Lambeth holds thee dead.") AAS; OBWP
Epitaph on True, Her Majesty's Dog, An. Matthew Prior. FM
Epitaph on Two Piping-Bullfinches of Lady Ossory's, Buried under a Rose-Bush in Her Garden. Horace Walpole. *See* Epitaphs on Two Piping-Bullfinches of Lady Ossory's . . .
Epitaph on Washington. *Unknown.* OHIP
Epitaph on William Hogarth. Samuel Johnson. EBEV
Epitaph on William Jones. *Unknown.* FaBoEE
Epitaph on William Whitehead. *Unknown.* FaBoEE
Epitaph Placed on His Daughter's Tomb. Robert Richardson, *ad. by* "Mark Twain." Tref
(Epitaph: "Warm summer sun shine kindly here.") PoLF
Epitaph to a Dog. Byron. BLPA; GDP
(Epitaph, An: Inscription on a Monument at Newstead Abbey, first part.) BoAnP
(Epitaph to a Newfoundland Dog.) TreFS
(Inscription on the Monument of a Newfoundland Dog.) TEP
Epitaph to Thomas Thetcher. *Unknown.* PoPle
Epitaph upon ———, An. Andrew Marvell. See Epitaph, An: "Enough; and leave the rest to fame."
Epitaph upon a Child, An ("Virgins promis'd when I died"). Robert Herrick. FaBoEE; SeCV-1
Epitaph upon a Child That Died ("Here she lies, a pretty bud"). Robert Herrick. *See* Upon a Child That Died.
Epitaph upon a Sober Matron, An. Robert Herrick. CaPo
Epitaph upon a Virgin, An. Robert Herrick. CaPo; FaBoEE; OxBoLi; PoEL-3; SeCV-1
Epitaph upon Husband and Wife Who [*or* Which] Died and Were Buried Together, An. Richard Crashaw. EBEV; LO; NOBE; OBEV; OBS; TreFS; TrGrPo
(Epitaph upon a Young Married Couple Dead and Buried Together, An.) ELP; FaBoEE; FaBoEn; NIP; OAEP; PAI; SeCePo; SeCP; WHA
Epitaph upon Mr. Ashton, a Conformable Citizen, An. Richard Crashaw. OBS
Epitaph upon My Dear Brother, Francis Beaumont, An. Sir John Beaumont. JCP
Epitaph upon That Profound and Learned Casuist, the Late Ordinary of Newgate, An. Thomas Brown. OBSV
Epitaph upon the Celebrated Claudy Philips, Musician, Who Died Very Poor, An. Samuel Johnson. OBEC
Epitaph upon the Right Honorable Sir Philip Sidney, An. *At. to* Fulke Greville *and to* Sir Edward Dyer. *See* Epitaph on Sir Philip Sidney.
Epitaphium Citharistriae. Victor Plarr. EnLoPo; HBMV; ViBoPo
(Stand Not Uttering Sedately.) PoRA
Epitaphium Meum. William Bradford. SCAP
Epitaphs (I-IX). Gabriello Chiabrera, *tr. fr. Italian by* Wordsworth. AWP
Epitaphs: For a Fickle Man. Mark Van Doren. ViBoPo
Epitaphs of the War, 1914-18. Kipling. BrPo; NoP; OBWP
Sels.
Batteries Out of Ammunition. MMA
Beginner, The. FaBoTw
Bridegroom, The. FaBoEE
Common Form. FaBoEE; FaBoTw; PV
Coward, The. FaBoEE; FaBoTw; OAEP
Dead Statesman, A. FaBoEE; OAEP
Drifter off Tarentum, A. FaBoEE; MMA; PoPle
Equality of Sacrifice. FaBoTw; OAEP
Refined Man, The. FaBoEE; FaBoTw; MMA
Salonikan Grave. OAEP
Son, A. FaBoEE
Epitaphs [*or* Epitaph] on Two Piping-Bullfinches of Lady Ossory's, Buried under a Rose-Bush in Her Garden. Horace Walpole. FaBoEE; NOEC
Epitaph on Lady Ossory's Bullfinch, *sel.* ChTr
Epitaphy of la Graunde Amoure. Stephen Hawes. *See* Epitaph of Grande Amoure, The.
Epithalamia. Thomas Lovell Beddoes. *See* Bridal Song to Amala.
Epithalamion: "Hark, hearer, hear what I do." Gerard Manley Hopkins. VLP
Epithalamion: "Look there! *The Lovers in the Flowers.*" Grace Schulman. FAZ
Epithalamion: "Our mound of earth dug up." Olga Broumas. LTB
Epithalamion: "Smile then, children, hand in hand." James Elroy Flecker. BrPo
Epithalamion: "These are the small hours when." Michael Longley. CIP
Epithalamion: "Ye learned sisters which have oftentimes." Spenser. AAS; BoLoP; CABA; EIL; EnRePo; HBV-1; InPS; MasP; NOBE; NoP; OAEL-1; OAEP; OBEV; OBSC; PoEL-1; SeCeV; TEP; ViBoPo
Sels.
"Hark how the minstrels gin to shrill aloud." WHA
"Now al is done; bring home the bride againe." FiP
"Wake, now my love, awake; for it is time." GBL
Who Is the Same, Which at My Window Peepes? NAs
Epithalamion Made at Lincolnes Inne. John Donne. OBS; SeCP
Epithalamion on the Lady Elizabeth and Count Palantine Being Married on St. Valentine's Day, An, *sel.* John Donne.
Hail, Bishop Valentine. ChTr
("Hail, Bishop Valentine, whose day this is.") OFD
Epithalamion Teratos. George Chapman. *Fr.* Hero and Leander. EIL; LoBV
Epithalamium: "Can the lover share his soul." Walter James Turner. OBMV
Epithalamium: "Come, virgin tapers of pure wax." Richard Crashaw. NOCV; ViBoPo, *sts.* 1-6
Epithalamium: "Crept side by side beyond the thresh." Vassar Miller. NePoEA
Epithalamium: "First a princess." John Ditsky. DFT
Epithalamium: "High in the organ loft with lilied hair." Edmund Gosse. OBVV
Epithalamium: "Hour is come, with pleasure crowned," *sel.* Johannes Secundus, *tr. fr. Latin by* George Ogle.
Wedding Night, The. UnTE
Epithalamium: "I saw two clouds at morning." John Gardiner Calking Brainard. *See* I Saw Two Clouds at Morning.
Epithalamium: "In the streets the crowds go about their business." Daniel Halpern. MAYP
Epithalamium: "Let mother Earth now deck herself in flowers." Sir Philip Sidney. *Fr.* Arcadia. SiPS
Epithalamium: "So you are married, girl. It makes me sad." Roy McFadden. NeIP
Epithalamium: "This body of my mother, pierced by me." Leo Kennedy. OBCV
Epithalamium: "Voice that breathed o'er Eden, The." John Keble. *See* Holy Matrimony.
Epithalamium for Cavorting Ghosts. Dachine Rainer. NePoAm-2

Epithalamium for Mary Stuart and the Dauphin of France, *abr.* George Buchanan, *tr. fr. Latin.* GoTS
Epithalamium upon the Marriage of Captain William Bedloe, An. Richard Duke. APAS
Epithalamy to Sir Thomas Southwell and His Lady, An. Robert Herrick. CaPo
Epoch ends, the world is still, The. Matthew Arnold. Bacchanalia; or, The New Age, II. OAEL-2
Epoch of a streetcar drawn by horses, The. Baby Pictures of Famous Dictators. Charles Simic. GeTw; WeW
Epochs. Emma Lazarus. SBG
Epode. Ben Jonson. SeCP; SeCV-1
Epodes, *sel.* Horace, *tr. fr. Latin.*
Country Life, II, *tr. by* Dryden. AWP
("Happy the Man whom bount'ous Gods allow," *tr. by* Abraham Cowley.) CavP
Epos. Harold Rosenberg. PoA
Eppie Morrie. *Unknown.* ESPB; OxBB
Eppur Si Muove? Robert Hillyer. GoYe
Equality, Father! Edith Bruck, *tr. fr. Italian by* Anita Barrows. VWA
Equality of Sacrifice. Kipling. *Fr.* Epitaphs of the War, 1914–18. FaBoTw; OAEP
("A. 'I was a Have.' B. 'I was a have-not.' ") NoP; OBWP
Equals. Louis Untermeyer. UnTE
Equation. Sir Herbert Read. BrPo
Equestrian fell from his horse, An. The Childhood of an Equestrian. Russell Edson. AmPA
Equestrienne. Joan Colby. PoDr
Equestrienne. Rachel Field. *Fr.* A Circus Garland. OBCA
(Girl on the Milk-White Horse, The.) SoPo
Equilibrists, The. John Crowe Ransom. AP; CMoP; CoBMV; HAP; LiTM; MoAB; MoPo; MoVE; NePA; NIP; NoAM; NOBA; OxBA; PPP; TAP
Equinoctial. Adeline D. T. Whitney. HBV-1
Equinox, The. Dubose Heyward. PoA
Equinox, The. Longfellow. *Fr.* Seaweed. EtS
Equinox. Gary Young. SUW
Equinoxial swore by the green leaves on the trees, trees. Little Phoebe. *Unknown.* FSW
Equipment. Paul Laurence Dunbar. TrPWD
'Er looked at me bunnet (I knows 'e ain't noo!). Her "Allowance!" Lillian Gard. SUMH
'Er name's Doreen. . .Well, spare me bloomin' days! The Intro. C. J. Dennis. WhC
Erased off the face of my earth, all that remains is a white space. House. Diana O Hehir. NPGG
Erasers are such handy things. Mistakes. George W. Swarberg. STF
Erce, Erce, Erce, mother of earth. Charms for Unfruitful Land. *Unknown, tr. by* Charles W. Kennedy. AnOE
Erd sould trymbill, the firmament sould schaik, The. Quod Dunbar to Kennedy. William Dunbar. OxBoLi
Ere famous Winthrops bones are laid to rest. Chelmsfords Fate. Benjamin Tompson. SCAP
Ere five score years have run their tedious rounds. A Prophecy. Arthur Lee. PAH
E're I forget the zenith of your love. To My Cosen Mrs. Ellinor Evins. George Alsop. SCAP
Ere last year's moon had left the sky. My Bird. "Fanny Forester." AA
Ere long they come, where that same wicked wight. The Cave of Despair [*or* To Be or Not to Be]. Spenser. *Fr.* The Faerie Queene. FaBoEn; NOBE; OAEL-1
Ere Murfreesboro's thunders rent the air. The Battle of Murfreesboro. Kinahan Cornwallis. PAH
Ere my heart beats too coldly and faintly. The Truants. Walter de la Mare. MoBrPo
Ere on my bed my limbs I lay. The Pains of Sleep [*or* A Child's Evening Prayer]. Samuel Taylor Coleridge. EnRP; NCEP; OAEP; OBNC; OBRV; OxBChV; SeCePo; SyP; TEP; TrPWD
Ere Sleep Comes Down to Soothe the Weary Eyes. Paul Laurence Dunbar. BALP; BANP; CDC; PoNe
Ere space exists, or earth, or sky. The Lord Is King. *Unknown, tr. by* Solomon Solis-Cohen. TrJP
Ere the beard of thistle sails. The Seasons. Thomas Holcroft. NOEC
Ere the cock has crowed. The Forsaken Girl. Randall Jarrell. OLR
Ere the long roll of the ages end. Fainne Gael an Lae. Alice Milligan. HBV-2
Ere the morn the East has crimsoned. Lines Suggested by the Fourteenth of February. Charles Stuart Calverley. InMe
Ere the steamer bore him Eastward, Sleary was engaged to marry. The Post That Fitted. Kipling. CenHV; HBV-2; OnMSP
Ere yet in Vergil I could scan or spell. "Hic Me, Pater Optime, Fessam Deseris." Lucy Catlin Robinson. AA
Ere yet the sun is high. The Iris. Gasetsu. TiPo
Ere yet your footsteps quit the place. Verses Addressed to a Friend, Just Leaving a Favourite Retirement. Samuel Henley. NOEC
Ere You Were Queen of Sheba. Sir Arthur Shipley. FaBoCo
Erected to the Memory of Mr. Jonathan Gill, Esq. *Unknown.* DBV
("Beneath this smooth stone by the bone of his bone.") FaBoEE
Eremites, The. Robert Graves. LiTB
Erev Shabbos. Marc Kaminsky. VWA
Erewhile, before the world was old. Jadis. Ernest Dowson. VLP
Eric. John Barford. PeHV
Eride, *sel.* Trumbull Stickney.
Now in the Palace Gardens, V. LiTA; NCEP; TwAmPo
E-ri-e, The ("We were forty miles from Albany"). *Unknown.* AS, *with music;* FSW
Erie Canal, The ("I've got a mule, her name is Sal"). William J. Allen. AmFN; AS, *with music;* BLSo, *with music;* FSW; TrAS, *with music*
Erige Cor Tuum ad Me in Caelum. Hilda Doolittle ("H. D."). AP; CMoP
Erin. *Unknown, tr. fr. Yoruba by* Ulli Beier. PBA
(Elephant, The [I].) TTY
Erin Go Braugh! *Unknown.* FSW
Erinna. Antipater, *tr. fr. Greek by* A. J. Butler. AWP
Erith, on the Thames. *Unknown.* FaBoPP; GBP
(Village of Erith, The.) ChTr; WSC
Erlinton. *Unknown.* ESPB (A *and* B *vers.*)
Erl-King, The. Goethe, *tr. fr. German by* Sir Walter Scott. AWP; OBVE; WSC
(Invisible King, The, *tr. by* Robert Bly.) NU
Ermine or blazonry, he knew them not. Andrew. Thomas William Parsons. AA
Ernest Dowson. John Hall Wheelock. HBMV
Ernest Liberal's Lament, The. Ernest Hemingway. *See* Earnest Liberal's Lament, The.
Ernest Maltravers, *sel.* Sir Edward Bulwer-Lytton.
Night and Love. HBV-1
Ernest was an elephant, a great big fellow. The Four Friends. A. A. Milne. TiPo
Eros. Robert Bridges. CMoP; LiTB; NBM; NOBE; PoEL-5; QFR; SeCeV
Eros. Emerson. FaBoBe; HBV-1
Eros D'Aute. Theodore Wratislaw. GBL
Eros Out of the Sea. Dilys Bennett Laing. PoA
Eros, pray discard your bow. Plea to Eros. *Unknown, tr. by* Louis Untermeyer. UnTE
Eros, thou yet behold'st me? Shakespeare. *Fr.* Antony and Cleopatra, IV, xiv. EBEV
Eros Turannos. E. A. Robinson. AP; CMoP; CoBMV; CrMA; GBL; HAP; LiTA; LiTM; MoAB; MoAmPo; MoPo; MoVE; NePA; NoAM; NOBA; NoP; OxBA; PoA; PPoe; QFR; TAP; TwAmPo
Erosion. Jorie Graham. MAYP
Erosion. E. J. Pratt. CaP
Erotic Suite, *sels.* José Luis Vega, *tr. fr. Spanish by* Julio Marzán. InW
"My love, like the vast majority."
"This poem is an erection."
Erotica Antiqua, *sel.* L. A. MacKay.
Propertian. PeCV
Erotion. Martial, *tr. fr. Latin by* Kirby Flower Smith. AWP
("Erotion rests here, in the/ Hastening shadows," *ad. by* Kenneth Rexroth.) NNaP
Erotion. Swinburne. PoEL-5
Errand Imperious, The. Edwin Markham. PAL; PGD
Errantry. Robert Fitzgerald. NYBP
Errata. Charles Simic. NNaP
Erris Coast, 1943. Hugh Connell. NeIP
Error Pursued. H. A. Pinkerton. NePoAm; QFR
Errore. Pier Giorgio Di Cicco. NOBC
Errors of Ecstasie, *sel.* George Darley.
"Ecstasie, rash production of the thoughts." OnYI
Erthe oute of erthe is wonderly wroghte. Earth out of Earth. *Unknown.* MeEL
Erthe Toc of Erthe. *Unknown.* HAP
Erubescent flax curls crisp and dry, The. Smoking Flax. Mary Josephine Benson. CaP
Erudite, solemn/ The pious bird. Rev Owl. A. M. Klein. TrJP
Es fällt ein Stern herunter. Heine, *tr. fr. German by* Richard Garnett. AWP
Es stehen unbeweglich. Heine, *tr. fr. German by* James Thomson. AWP; TrJP
Es war einmal. . .No, it's too heavy. Märchenbilder. John Ashbery. LCAP; NOBA
Esau. Leib Kwitko, *tr. fr. Yiddish by* Keith Bosley. VWA
Escalade. Arthur Symons. UnTE
Escalator, The. Alex Glasgow. OBET
Escapade, The. David Ignatow. PP
Escapade. Kenneth Leslie. EtS
Escape, An. Abu Nuwas, *tr. fr. Arabic by* E. Powys Mathers. ErPo

Escape. Robert Graves. BrPo; MoBrPo
Escape. Georgia Douglas Johnson. PoBA
Escape. Andrew McCord Jones. LFAC
Escape, The. Edwin Muir. WaP
Escape. Ilya Rubin, *tr. fr. Russian by* Linda Zisquit. VWA
Escape, The. William Stafford. NNaP
Escape, The. Mark Van Doren. MoAmPo
Escape. Elinor Wylie. LiTA; MoAmPo
Escape and Return. Elizabeth Jennings. NePoEA
Escape at Bedtime. Robert Louis Stevenson. HBVY; TiPo; TreFS; TrGrPo
Escape blossomed in the car. Vivisection. Gene Fowler. LFAC
Escape me?/ Never. Life in a Love [*or* Love's Pursuit]. Robert Browning. HBV-1; OAEP; OBNC; OBVV; TreFT; TrGrPo
Escape to Love, *sel.* Patrick MacDonogh.
"Alone and Godless, stopped by the sudden edge." BIrV
"Escaped the gloom of mortal life, a soul." An Epitaph. James Beattie. BSV
Escaping from the enemy's hand. The Escape. Edwin Muir. WaP
Escapist's Song. Theodore Spencer. POL
Eschatology. Morris Bishop. WhC
Ese!! Within your will-to-be culture. Pachuco Remembered. Tino Villanueva. FIA
Eshu, the God of Fate ("Eshu turns right into wrong"). *Yoruba Oral Tradition, tr. by* Ulli Beier. WTO
Eskimo Chant. *Unknown, tr. fr. Eskimo by* Knud Rasmussen. RFM; WHW
Eskimo, explorers state, The. The Immoral Arctic. Morris Bishop. FiBHP; WhC
Eskimo hunts, The. Al Capone in Alaska. Ishmael Reed. TW
Eskimo Occasion. Judith Rodriguez. CBAP
Eskimos in Manitoba. Recital. John Updike. OBAL
Esmeralda! Now we rest. Lines Written in Oregon. Vladimir Nabokov. NYBP
Esope, mine author, makis mentioun. *See* Aesop, mine author, makis mention.
Especially he loves. God Poem. Stanley Moss. VGW; VWA
Especially When the October Wind. Dylan Thomas. CABA; ChMP; LiTB; MoAB; MoBrPo; OAEP; OxBTC
(Poem: "Especially when the October wind.") NeBP
Esperanza. James Scully. LTB; NYP
Essay in Defense of the Movies. Walker Gibson. NePoAm
Essay on Criticism, An. Pope. CABA; PoEL-3
Sels.
"But most by numbers judge a poet's song," *fr.* Pt. II. FaBoUs; HAP; PP
(Poetical Numbers.) OBEC; SeCePo
(Sound and Sense.) NIP
"First follow Nature, and your judgment frame," *fr.* Pt. I. HAP; PP
(Nature and Art.) TreFT
"In wit, as nature, what affects our hearts," *fr.* Pt. II. HAP
Little Learning, A, *fr.* Pt. II. ChTr; LiTB; NOBE; OBEC; SeCePo
(Alps on Alps.) FaFP
("Little learning is a dangerous thing, A.") FPL; HAP; HoPM; PoLF; TreF; TrGrPo
"Of all the causes which conspire to blind." Pt. II. FaBoEn; NOEC; NoP; OAEP; PPoe
Pride, the Never-Failing Vice of Fools, *fr.* Pt. II. TreFT
"Some are bewildered in the maze of schools," *fr.* Pt. I. OBSV
"Some beauties yet no precepts can declare," *fr.* Pt. I. HAP
"Some ne'er advance a judgment of their own," *fr.* Pt. II. OBSV
"Such shameless bards we have; and yet 'tis true," *fr.* Pt. III. OBSV
" 'Tis hard to say, if greater want of skill," *fr.* Pt. I. FaBoEn; FiP; HAP; OAEL-1; OAEP; PP; WHA
" 'Tis with our judgments as our watches, none." ViBoPo
"True ease in writing comes from art, not chance," *fr.* Pt. II. HAP; PrIm; TrGrPo
(Sound and Sense.) SoSe; UnPo
"True wit is Nature to advantage dressed," *fr.* Pt. II. HAP
Essay on Lunch. Walker Gibson. NYBP
Essay on Man, An, *sels.* Pope.
"All are but parts of one stupendous whole," *fr.* Epistle I. WGRP
"Awake, my St. John! leave all meaner things," Epistle I. NoP; OAEP; PoEL-3
(Wild Garden, The.) PrIm, *ll.* 1-16
"Behold the child, by Nature's kindly law," *fr.* Epistle II. FaBoRV; POL
"Bliss of man (could pride that blessing find), The," *fr.* Epistle I. NOEC; NU
Faith, *fr.* Epistle III. WGRP
"Far as creation's ample range extends," *fr.* Epistle I. FM; ImOP, *fr.* I *and* II
"For forms of government let fools contest," *fr.* Epistle III. POL; ViBoPo
(Charity). OBEC
"Heav'n from all creatures hides the book of Fate," *fr.* Epistle I. ViBoPo
(Hope Springs Eternal.) OBEC
Henry St. John, Viscount Bolingbroke, *fr.* Epistle IV. OBEC
Honest Man, An, 2 *ll., fr.* Epistle IV. TreF
"Honor and shame from no condition rise," *fr.* Epistle IV. TrGrPo
Hope ("Hope springs eternal in the human breast"), 4 *ll., fr.* Epistle I. TreF
(Pleasure of Hope, The.) ACP
"Hope humbly then; with trembling pinions soar," *fr.* Epistle I. TrGrPo
"Know then thyself, presume not God to scan." Epistle II. BLPL, *ll.* 1-18; GOBC, *ll.* 1-18; LiTB, *fr.* II *and* IV; NOEC, *ll.* 1-18; NoP; OAEL-1, *ll.* 1-18; OBEC, *ll.* 1-18; PAI, *ll.* 1-18; PoEL-3; PPoe; SeCePo, *ll.* 1-18; TrGrPo, *ll.* 1-18; TRV, *ll.* 1-18; ViBoPo, *ll.* 1-18
(Know Thyself, *ll.* 1-18.) NOBE
(Man, *ll.* 1-18.) PrIm
(Paragon of Animals, The, *ll.* 1-18.) ACP
(Proper Study of Man, The, *ll.* 1-18.) TreFS
(Proper Study of Mankind, The, *ll.* 1-30.) FiP
(Second Epistle of the Essay on Man, The.) GoTL
Life's Poor Play, *fr.* Epistle II. SeCePo
"Lo, the poor Indian! whose untutor'd mind," *fr.* Epistle I. NU
"Nor think, in nature's state they blindly trod," *fr.* Epistle III. OAEL-1
"O sons of earth," *fr.* Epistle IV. TreFT
"Placed on this isthmus of a middle state," *ll.* 2-18, *fr.* Epistle II. WeW
"Presumptuous man! the reason wouldst thou find," *fr.* Epistle I. BiP
Riddle of the World, *fr.* Epistle II. FaFP
Soul's Calm Sunshine, The, *fr.* Epistle IV. FaBoRv
Vice, *fr.* Epistle II. ELU
"What would this Man? Now upward will he soar," *fr.* Epistle I. HeIP
"Whate'er the passion—knowledge, fame, or pelf," *fr.* Epistle II. TrGrPo
(Human Folly.) FiP
Whatever Is, Is Right, *fr.* Epistle I. OBEC
"What's Fame? a fancied life in others' breath," *fr.* Epistle IV. ViBoPo
"Who sees with equal eye, as God of all," *fr.* Epistle I. FaBoEn
Essay on Marriage, *sel.* Anne Finch.
"O, love, in your sweet name enough." FaBoTw
Essay on Memory, *sel.* Robert D. Fitzgerald.
"Rain in my ears: impatiently there raps." CBAP
Essay on Poetry, *sel.* John Sheffield, Duke of Buckingham and Normanby.
On Writing for the Stage. FaBoUs
Essay on Psychiatrists, *sel.* Robert Pinsky.
Their Speech, Compared with Wisdom and Poetry. PoA
Essay on Rime, *sels.* Karl Shapiro. PP
"But poets are name-proud craftsmen; Greeks and Jews."
"There is a general idiom to all rime."
Essay on Solitude, *sel.* Abraham Cowley.
"Hail, old patrician trees, so great and good!" ViBoPo
Essay on the Fleet Riding in the Downes, An. "J. D." CoMu
Essay on the Genius of Pope, The, *sel.* Charles Lloyd.
" 'Tis not so much these men more forms survey." OBRV
Essay on Translated Verse, An, *sel.* Earl of Roscommon.
"Each poet with a different talent writes." FaBoUs
Essay on Woman, An. Mary Leapor. NOEC
Essay upon Satire, An. John Sheffield, Duke of Buckingham and Normanby, *formerly at. to* Dryden. APAS
Essence. Samuel Greenberg. MoPo; NePA
Essence of existence, The. Chorus. Jack Kerouac. *Fr.* Mexico City Blues. NeAP
Essential oils—are wrung. Emily Dickinson. AmPP; AP; SBG
Essential poem at the center of things, The. A Primitive like an Orb. Wallace Stevens. NOBA
Essentials. Samuel Greenberg. LiTA
Essex Regiment March. George Edward Woodberry. PAH
Está Muy Caliente. George Bowering. MoCV
Estat ai en greu cossirier. Beatriz de Dia, *tr. fr. Provençal by* Paul Blackburn. ErPo
Estate and an earldom at seventy-four, An! Horace Walpole. FaBoEE
Estella, Estella, they're cooking up paella. Song in Praise of Paella. C. W. V. Wordsworth. FiBHP
Esther, *sels.* Wilfred Scawen Blunt.
"He who has once been happy is for aye." OBMV; OBNC; TrGrPo; ViBoPo
"When I hear laughter from a tavern door." NBM; OBMV; TrGrPo; ViBoPo
Esther. Fray Angelico Chavez. GoBC
Esther K. Comes to America: 1931. Jerome Rothenberg. NNaP
Esther's Tomcat. Ted Hughes. OxBC; PCat
Esthete in Harlem. Langston Hughes. BANP; BPo
Esthetic of Imitation, An. Donald Finkel. NePoEA
Esthétique du Mal Wallace Stevens. LiTM
Sels.
"He was at Naples writing letters home." CMoP; NOBA
"How red the rose that is the soldier's wound." CMoP; NOBA; WaP
(Soldier's Wound, The.) WaaP

"Life is a bitter aspic. We are not." CMoP
"Sun, in clownish yellow, but not a clown, The." NOBA
Esthonian Bridal Song. Johann Gottfried von Herder, *tr. fr. German by* W. Taylor. AWP
Estimable Mable. Gwendolyn Brooks. FB
Estranged. Walter de la Mare. FaBoEn
Estrich, thou feathered fool and easy prey. Lucasta's Fan, with a Looking-Glass in It. Richard Lovelace. CaPo
Estuarial Republic, The. Douglas Dunn. FaBoMo
Estuary. William Montgomerie.
Estuary, The. Ruth Pitter. MoVE
Estuary. Ted Walker. NYBP
Esyllt. Glyn Jones. DTC
Et Cetera. Earl of Rochester. UnTE
Et Cetera. Dee Walker. GoYe
Et in Arcadia Ego. W. H. Auden. CMoP
Et Incarnatus Est. William Langland. *Fr.* The Vision of Piers Plowman. NOBE
Et Mori Lucrum. John Lancaster Spalding. *Fr.* God and the Soul. AA
Et Nox Facta Est. Victor Hugo, *tr. fr. French by* Mary Ann Caws. NAWM-2
Et Quid Amabo Nisi Quod Aenigma Est. Stephen Sandy. NYBP
Et Sa Pauvre Chair. Alec Brock Stevenson. HBMV
État, *sel.* Anne-Marie Albiach, *tr. fr. French by* Paul Auster.
"Of the unended in the speed of." PBWP
Etched Away From. Paul Celan, *tr. fr. German by* Michael Hamburger. OBVE
Etching. W. E. Henley. In Hospital, XII. BrPo
Eternal. Agnes Foley Macdonald. CaP
Eternal Christmas. Elizabeth Stuart Phelps. PGD; TRV
Eternal City, The. A. R. Ammons. EyDe
Eternal Contour. Florida Watts Smyth. GoYe
Eternal Father, Strong to Save. William Whiting. FaPoR; MOS; NOCV; TreFS; VLP
(Hymn: "Eternal Fathers, strong to save.") NBM
Eternal Female groan'd, The! it was heard over all the earth. A Song of Liberty. Blake. EnRP
Eternal Feminine, The. Oliver Herford. TDH
Eternal gates' terrific porter lifted the northern bar, The. The Secrets of the Earth. Blake. NOBE
Eternal God, How They're Increased, *with music.* Cotton Mather. AH
Eternal God, maker of all. The Book. Henry Vaughan. JCP; SeCV-1
Eternal God omnipotent! The One. Invocation. Caelius Sedulius, *tr. by* George Sigerson. *Fr.* Carmen Paschale. OnYI
Eternal God, our life is but. A Prayer. "Yehoash," *tr. by* Isidore Goldstick. TrJP
Eternal God, Whose Power Upholds, *with music.* Henry Hallam Tweedy. AH
Eternal God Whose Searching Eye Doth Scan. Edwin McNeill Poteat. TrPWD
Eternal Goodness, The ("O friends! with whom my feet have trod"). Whittier. AA; OHFP; WGRP
Sels.
"And Thou, O Lord! by whom are seen." TrPWD
"I know not what the future hath." BLRP, *abr.;* NOCV; TreF
"I see the wrong that round me lies." TRV
Eternal Image, The. Ruth Pitter. MoBrPo; OxBTC
Eternal Jew, The. Jacob Cohen, *tr. fr. Hebrew by* I. M. Lask. TrJP
Eternal Justice, The. Anne Reeve Aldrich. AA
Eternal Kinship, The. Maurice E. Peloubet. GoYe
Eternal Life. Henry More. TRV
Eternal Light! Thomas Binney. NOCV; WGRP
Eternal Lord! Eased of a Cumbrous Load. Michelangelo, *tr. fr. Italian by* Wordsworth. TrPWD
Eternal Masculine. William Rose Benét. AWP; MoAmPo
Eternal Moment. "Katherine Hale." CaP
Eternal[l] Mover. Sir Henry Wotton. TrPWD, 4 *sts.*
(D. O. M.) OxBoCh
Eternal Power, of earth and air! The Doubter's Prayer. Anne Brontë. TrPWD; WGRP
Eternal Return, The. Robert Hillyer. NYBP
Eternal Return, The. Alan Loney. OCNZ
Eternal Reward, Eternal Pain. Sir Thomas More. *Fr.* The Twelve Weapons of Spiritual Battle. EnRePo
Eternal Road, The, *sel.* Franz Werfel, *tr. fr. German by* Ludwig Lewisohn.
Ye Sorrowers. TrJP
Eternal Ruler of the ceaseless round. Hymn. John W. Chadwick. TrPWD
Eternal Sabbath. Isaac Leibush Peretz, *tr. fr. Yiddish by* Joseph Leftwich. TrJP
Eternal spirit/ of dead dried. Black Lotus. Alicia Ley Johnson. NBP
Eternal Spirit of the chainless Mind! Sonnet on Chillon [*or* On the Castle of Chillon]. Byron. The Prisoner of Chillon, *intro. sonnet.* BeLS; EnRP; FiP; GTBS; GTBS-P; HBV-2; LiTB; LoBV; OAEP; OBRV; PoPl; SeCeV; TreFS; TrGrPo
Eternal Spirit, Source of Light, *with music.* Samuel Davies. AH
Eternal Spirit, you. A Prayer for My Son. Yvor Winters. CrMA; TrPWD
Eternal Spring, The. Milton. *Fr.* Paradise Lost, IV. GN
Eternal Time, that wastest without waste. To Time. "A. W." ElL
Eternal[l] Truth, almighty, infinite. Sonnet. Fulke Greville. *Fr.* Caelica. EnRePo; OBS; OxBoCh
Eternale Footeman's Tale, The. George Moor. BXAP
Eternall and all-working God, which wast. Michael Drayton. *Fr.* Noah's Floud. PoEL-2
Eternall Mover. Sir Henry Wotton. *See* Eternal Mover.
Eternities. Norman Mailer. NYBP
Eternity ("He who binds [*or* bends] to himself a joy"). Blake. *Fr.* Several Questions Answered. AWP; FaBoEE; LAuP; LoBV; NOBE; NoP; OBNC; TrGrPo
("He who binds to himself a joy.") EBEV
Eternity. Emily Dickinson. *See* On this wondrous sea.
Eternity. Robert Herrick. WHA
Eternity. Sir Thomas More. EnRePo
Eternity. Henry Vaughan. *See* World, The.
Eternity encountered on the stair. Chez Madame. Sam Harrison. NeIP
Eternity is like unto a ring. Time and Eternity. Bunyan. WiR
Eternity is passion, girl or boy. Whence Had They Come? W. B. Yeats. BoLoP
Eternity of Love Protested. Thomas Carew. MeLP; OBS
Eternity of Nature, The. John Clare. EBEV
Eternity, when I think thee. Quoniam Ego in Flagella Paratus Sum. William Habington. ACP
Eternity's Low Voice. Mark Van Doren. EaLo
Eternity's Speech against Time. Fulke Greville. *Fr.* Mustapha. JCP
Ethan Boldt. Roger Weingarten. AmPA
Ethelstan, *sel.* George Darley.
O'er the Wild Gannet's Bath. ChTr; PoEL-4
(Runilda's Chant.) OnYI
Ethereal minstrel! pilgrim of the sky! To a [*or* the] Skylark. Wordsworth. EnRP; FaFP; GTBS; GTBS-P; HBV-1; HBVY; OAEP; PBBP; TrGrPo
Ethick. Robert Bridges. *Fr.* The Testament of Beauty. OxBTC
Ethics. Linda Pastan. AMV-81
Ethics for Everyman. Roger Woddis. DBV; NOBL
Ethics put it well, The. The Magnanimous. Ellen de Young Kay. NePoEA
Ethinthus, Queen of Waters. Blake. *Fr.* Europe. ChTr
Ethiopia Saluting the Colors. Walt Whitman. PAH; PoNe
Ethnic Life, The. Daniel Halpern. AmPA
Ethnogenesis. Henry Timrod. AmPP; NOBA; OxBA
Etienne de Silhouette Cornelius J. Ter Maat. InPK
Etiolated flame is now abroad. Summer Lightning. Horatio Colony. TwAmPo
Etiquette. W. S. Gilbert. CenHV; FaBoCh; FaBoCo; FiBHP; VLP
Eton Boating Song. William Cory. ELP
Etosion achthos aroures ("Who goes there? God knows. I'm nobody. How should I answer?"). Robert Bridges. QFR
Etrick Forest is a fair forest[e]. The Outlaw Murray. *Unknown.* ESPB; OxBB
Etruscan Notebook, *sels.* Elena Clementelli, *tr. fr. Italian by* Ruth Feldman *and* Brian Swann. PBWP
"Cerveteri road."
"From gorge to gorge."
"Net rests on the water's surface, The."
Etruscan Tombs. Agnes Mary Frances Robinson. WHA
Etruscan Warrior's Head. Helen Rowe Henze. GoYe
Ettrick. Lady John Scott. BSV; WPE
Ettrick Forest in November. Sir Walter Scott. *See* November in Ettrick Forest.
Etude. Joseph Brodsky, *tr. fr. Russian by* Dimitry Pospielovsky *and* Keith Bosley. VWA
Etude for Voice and Hand. Gabriel Levin. VWA
Étude Géographique. Stoddard King. AmFN; BPAW; WhC
Étude Réaliste. Swinburne. GN; HBV-1
"Baby's feet, like sea-shells pink, A," I. FaPON; WeW
Etudes. Laurence W. Thomas. AMV-80
Euch, are you having your period? Alta. NMM
Euclid. Vachel Lindsay. Poems about the Moon, I. ImOP; TwAmPo; YaD
Euclid Alone Has Looked on Beauty Bare. Edna St. Vincent Millay. CMoP; HBMV; ImOP; MoAB; MoAmPo; MoVE; NoP; TAP
(Euclid Alone.) FaBV; FaFP
(Euclid Alone Has Looked.) WHA
(Sonnet: "Euclid alone has looked on beauty bare.") AWP
Euclid Avenue. Charles Simic. LCAP
Euclid devised the trap. The Sextant. A. M. Sullivan. GoBC

Eudaimon. Kathleen Raine. PBWP
Eugene Delacroix Says. Edward Dorn. NoAM
Eugene Onegin, *sel.* Pushkin, *tr. fr. Russian by* Walter Arndt.
"Now that he is in grave condition." NAWM-2
Eugenia, *sel.* George Chapman.
Presage of Storme. FaBoEn
Eugenia, young and fair and sweet. Charles Cotton. *Fr.* Old Tityrus to Eugenia. ViBoPo
Eugenio Pacelli. Francis Neilson. GoYe
Eugenist, The. Robert Graves. FaBoEE
Eugenius, thy son, who gaurds the Rock. Dedication. Pope Eugenius III, *tr. by* Raymond F. Roseliep. ISi
Eulalie. Poe. EvOK; Par
Eulogy for a Tough Guy. Daniel L. Klauck. LFAC
Eulogy for Alvin Frost. Audre Lorde. CNA
Eulogy for Hasdai ibn Shaprut. *Unknown, tr. fr. Hebrew by* Israel Abrahams. TrJP
Eulogy for Populations. Ron Welburn. PoBA
Eulogy to the Bow and Arrow. *Mongol Oral Tradition, tr. by* C. R. Bawden. WTO
Eumares. Asclepiades, *tr. fr. Greek by* Richard Garnett. AWP
Eumenides at Home, The. James Agate. BXAP
Eunica skornde me, when her I would have sweetly kist. Theocritus, *tr. fr. Greek.* Idylls, XX. OBVE
Eunice in the Evening. Gwendolyn Brooks. TiPo
Eunuch and the unicorn, The. The Primrose Bed. Robert Graves. TEP
Euphoria, Euphoria. Mark DeFoe. AMV-80
Eureka! Alfred Denis Godley. CenHV
Eureka. Ruth O. Maunders. AMV-80
Euridice Saved. Linda Gregg. NPGG
Euroclydon. Abbie Huston Evans. NePoAm
Europa. William Johnson Cory. NBM
Europa. William Plomer. MoBS
Europa. Stephen Henry Thayer. AA
Europa. Derek Walcott. NoP
Europa,/ your red-haired. For the West. Gary Snyder. NaP
Europe. John Ashbery. CoPo
Europe, *sel.* Blake.
Ethinthus, Queen of Waters. ChTr
Europe, *sels.* Louis Dudek.
"Commotion of these waves, however strong, cannot disturb, The." OBCV
"Ignorant present has scribbled over the past, The," XXXI. PeCV
"Sea retains such images, The," XCV. OBCV; PeCV
Europe and America. David Ignatow. AmFN; NNaP; UnPo
Europe lies in ruins: a black headline story. 1945. Sheila Cussons, *tr. by* Jack Cope *and* Uys Krige. PeSA
European Crimes. Charles Churchill. *Fr.* Gotham. NOEC
European Night, The. Stanislav Vinaver, *tr. fr. Serbo-Croat by* Vasa D. Mihailovich. VWA
European Shoe, The. Michael Benedikt. AmPA; ConAP; TwCP
Eurydice. Francis William Bourdillon. HBV-1
Eurydice. Hilda Doolittle ("H. D."). VGW
Eurydice. Linda Gregg. NPGG
Eurymachus's Fancy. Robert Greene. *Fr.* Francesco's Fortunes. OBSC
Eurynome. Jay Macpherson. NMP; OBCV; PV
Eurystheus, trembling, called me to the throne. Heracles. Yvor Winters. QFR; TwAmPo
Eutaw Springs. Philip Freneau. *See* To the Memory of the Brave Americans.
Euterpe; a Symmetric ("Euterpe, you must think us common queer"). David McCord. *Fr.* New Chitons for Old Gods. UnS
Euthymiae Raptus; or, The Teares of Peace, *sels.* George Chapman.
"And, now gives Time, her states description." PoEL-2
(Learning.) SeCePo
Poet Questions Peace, The. JCP
"Thus, by the way, to human loves interring." LoBV
Eutopia. Francis Turner Palgrave. EBVV; OBVV
Eutychides. E. A. Robinson, *after the Greek of* Lucilius. OBAL
Eva, I agree to love, among creation, all the creatures! Alfred de Vigny, *tr. by* Robert Bly. *Fr.* The Shepherd's House. NU
Evacuation of New York by the British. *Unknown.* PAH
Evadne. Hilda Doolittle ("H. D."). BoWoP
Evan just had the white birch lined up. Fear and Anger in the Mindless Universe. Hayden Carruth. NNaP
Evanescence. Frederic William Henry Myers. OBVV
Evanescence. Harriet Prescott Spofford. AA
Evangelical vicar in want. *See* Clergyman in want, A.
Evangeline. Longfellow. BeLS
Sels.
Church Scene, The. TreF
Embarkation, The. PAH
Evangeline in Acadie. AA
Finding of Gabriel, The. AA
Lakes of the Atchafalaya, The. PoEL-5
On the Atchafalaya. AA
Prelude: "This is the forest primeval. The murmuring pines and the hemlocks." TreF
(Primeval Forest, The.) WBLP
("This is the forest primeval. The murmuring pines and the hemlocks," *abr.*) SpRo
"They were approaching the region where reigns perpetual summer." FaBoEn
Evangeline. Norma E. Smith. CaP
Evangeline in Acadie. Longfellow. *Fr.* Evangeline. AA
Evangelist, The. Donald Davie. NePoEA
Evangelist, The. Bennie Lee Sinclair. TAT
Evangelist St. John my patron was, The. Newton's Statue. Wordsworth. *Fr.* The Prelude, III. FaBoRV; HAP
Evangelize! Henry Crocker. BLRP
Evans Country, The, *sels.* Kingsley Amis.
Aberdarcy: The Chaucer Road. NOBL
Aderdarcy: The Main Square. NOBL; OxBTC
Aldport (Mystery Tour). NOBL
(Terrible Beauty.) ErPo; NePoEA-2; PV
Brynbwrla. NOBL
Fforestfawr. NOBL
Langwell. NOBL; OxBC
Pendydd. NOBL
Evanthe's niplets are like sard. Niplets. *Unknown, tr. by* Wallace Rice. ErPo
Evaporation Poems. Kathleen Norris. IHMS
Evarra and His Gods. Kipling. MoBrPo
Evasion, An. Douglas Livingstone. PeSA
Evasion. Blanaid Salkeld. NeIP
Evasive souls, of whom the wise lose track. The Imaginative Life. Geoffrey Hill. NoAM
Eve. Arthur J. Bull. UnPo
Eve. Jakov Fichman, *tr. fr. Hebrew by* Robert Friend. VWA
Eve. David Gascoyne. GTBS-P
Eve. Oliver Herford. HBMV; OBAL; YaD
Eve. Ralph Hodgson. BrPo; CH; EvOK; HBV-2; LiTB; LiTM; MoAB; MoBrPo; OnMSP; SeCeV; TrCP; TrGrPo; UnPo
Eve. Milton. *Fr.* Paradise Lost, IX. OBS
("In bower and field he sought, where any tuft.") TEP
Eve. Christina Rossetti. CH; FM; GTBS-P; NBM; NIP; OxBoCh; PoEL-5; SeCeV
Eve, The. Howard Schwartz. VWA
Eve. Robert L. Wolf. HBMV
Eve. *Unknown. See* Eve's Lament.
Eve & her envy roving slammed me down. Gislebertus' Eve. John Berryman. LCAP
Eve in My Legend. Denis Devlin. IPY
Eve in Old Age. Rob Holland. NIP
Eve in Reflection. Jay Macpherson. OBCV
Eve is angel, though bone of bone. Waiting for Lilith. Jascha Kessler. VWA
Eve of Bunker Hill, The. Clinton Scollard. PAH
Eve of Crecy, The. William Morris. OBVV; VLP
Eve of St. Agnes, The. Keats. BeLS; CABA; ChER; DTo; EnRP; FiP, *abr.;* GoTL; HAP; HBV-2; HoPM; MaSP; NIP; NoP; OAEL-2; OAEP; OBNC; OBNV; OBRV; PoEL-4; PoLF; SeCeV; TEP; TreF; TrGrPo; WeW; WHA
"Out went the taper as she hurried in," *sel.* ViBoPo
Eve of Saint John, The. Sir Walter Scott. EnRP; PoEL-4
Eve of Saint Mark, The. Keats. CH; EnRP; OBRV; WHA
Eve of Waterloo, The. Byron. *See* Waterloo.
Eve of Waterloo, The. Thomas Hardy. *See* Before Waterloo.
Eve Penitent. Milton. *Fr.* Paradise Lost, X. OBS
Eve, smiling, pluck'd the apple, then. The Apple. Lady Margaret Sackville. OBVV
Eve-Song. Mary Gilmore. CBAP; PoAu-1
Eve Speaks to Adam ("With thee conversing I forget all time"). Milton. *Fr.* Paradise Lost, IV. ChTr; GBL
(Eve to Adam.) FaBoEn; TreFS; TrGrPo
("With thee conversing, I forget all time.") WiR
Eve, with her basket, was. Eve. Ralph Hodgson. BrPo; CH; EvOK; HBV-2; LiTB; LiTM; MoAB; MoBrPo; OnMSP; SeCeV; TrCP; TrGrPo; UnPo
Evelyn. Rossiter Johnson. AA
Evelyn Hope. Robert Browning. HBV-1; TrGrPo; VLP
Even a cloud. Even If. Rachel Fishman, *tr. by* Gabriel Preil *and* Howard Schwartz. VWA
Even a Pyrrhonist. A Lot of Night Music. Anthony Hecht. NIP; OxBC

Even after Confession. On a Catholic Childhood. Janet Campbell Hall. VoR
Even along the railway platform it was spring. We'll All Feel Gay. Winfield Townley Scott. MiAP
Even among the deformed. Beauty. Paul David Ashley. LFAC
Even as a child, of sorrow that we give. Pride of Youth. Dante Gabriel Rossetti. The House of Life, XXIV. FaBoEn; OBNC
Even as a lover, dreaming, unaware. Frederick Goddard Tuckerman. Sonnets, II, xiii. AP
Even as a young man. Once More Fields and Gardens. T'ao Ch'ien, *tr. by* Amy Lowell *and* Florence Ayscough. AWP
Even as children they were late sleepers. The Undead. Richard Wilbur. CAPP; CoAP; ConAP; OxBC
Even as I Hold You. Alice Walker. WeW
Even as love grows more, I write the less. Robert Hillyer. Sonnets, XVI. HBMV
Even as my hand to pen on paper lays. To His Lady, Who Had Vowed Virginity. Walter Davison. OBSC
Even as tender parents lovingly. The Child in the Street. John James Piatt. AA
Even as the day when it is yet at dawning. Canzone: Of His Love, with the Figure of a Sudden Storm. Prinzivalle Doria, *tr. by* Dante Gabriel Rossetti. AWP
Even as the others mock, thou mockest me. Dante, *tr. by* Dante Gabriel Rossetti. La Vita Nuova, VII. AWP
Even as the raven, the crow, and greedy kite. *Unknown.* PBBP
Even as the shadows of the statues lengthen. Mrs. Southern's Enemy. Sir Osbert Sitwell. ViBoPo
Even as the sun with purple-colour'd face. Venus and Adonis. Shakespeare. BeLS
Even as we kill. On the Birth of My Son, Malcolm Coltrane. Julius Lester. PoBA
Even as your progenitors ran. To a Race Horse at Ascot. Jennie M. Palen. PH
Even at its edge the lake is no miracle. Links. Ricardo Pau-Llosa. AMV-81
Even at sea the bodies of the unborn and the dead. The Changes. Robert Pinsky. NPGG
Even at their fairest still I love the less. A Dream of Flowers. Titus Munson Coan. AA
Even during War. Muriel Rukeyser. *Fr.* Letter to the Front. TrJP
Even for the wind there was no room. The Way the Bird Sat. Ray A. Young Bear. CDW; VoR
Even from the beach I could sense it. Attack of the Crab Monsters. Lawrence Raab. AmPA; NoP
Even from themselves they are a secret. The Close Clan. Mark Van Doren. GoYe
Even, I think, when you're bathing. A Bathing Girl. Johannes V. Jensen, *tr. by* Charles Wharton Stork. PoPl
Even If. Rachel Fishman, *tr. fr. Yiddish by* Gabriel Preil *and* Howard Schwartz. VWA
Even if I try not to ogle a boy in the street. Epigram. Strato. PeHV
Even if the geraniums are artificial. The Geraniums. Genevieve Taggard. VGW
Even if wars to come sleep small and warm. That Day. Mark Van Doren. WaP
Even in a light chop. Bait Shop. Thomas Reiter. WOLT
Even in bed I pose: desire may grow. Carnal Knowledge. Thom Gunn. BoLoP
Even in daylight, in murky waters. Feeling for Fish. Leonard Trawick. AMV-81
Even in death they prosper; even in the death. Necropolis. Karl Shapiro. MoAB; PoA
Even in my dreams/ I must no longer meet you. Lady Ise, *tr. fr. Japanese by* Etsuko Terasaki *and* Irma Brandeis. BoWoP
Even in my dreams you have denied yourself to me. To Kalon. Ezra Pound. PoA
Even in my village. Haiku. Kyorai, *tr. by* Lucien Stryk *and* Takashi Ikemoto. FAZ
Even in sleep my eyes are on the elements. An Astronomer's Journal. Jane Shore. PoA
Even in the moment of our earliest kiss. Edna St. Vincent Millay. VGW
Even in the time when as yet. The Wanderer. William Carlos Williams. TwAmPo
Even in the worst of times. Easter Flood. Brenda S. Stockwell. AMV-81
Even iron can put forth. Almond Blossom. D. H. Lawrence. FaBoPP
Even is come; and from the dark Park, hark. A Nocturnal Sketch. Thomas Hood. FaBoCo; FiBHP
Even like two little bank-dividing brooks. *See* Ev'n like two . . .
Even my dreams are hackneyed. Archetypes. Neal Bowers. AMV-81
Even now/ My thought is all of this gold-tinted king's daughter. Black Marigolds. Bilhana, *formerly at. to* Chauras, *tr. by* E. Powys Mathers. AWP; ErPo, *abr.*
Even now, mid-winter. The Ice Castle. Michael Harris. AMV-80
Even now she sometimes. Pomegranate. Gail N. Harada. BrSi
Even now the devastation is begun. Goldsmith. *Fr.* The Deserted Village. EBEV
Even now there are places where a thought might grow. A Disused Shed in Co. Wexford. Derek Mahon. CIP; OxBC
Even now this landscape is assembling. All Hallows. Louise Glück. AmPA; NU
Even now, when the long white hair. In the Fall. Alina Rivero. AMV-81
Even on clear nights, lead the most supple children. The Great Bear. John Hollander. LiTM; MP; NePoEA-2; NoAM; NYBP; TwCP
Even or odd, of all days in the year. Shakespeare. *Fr.* Romeo and Juliet. SCV
Even So. Dante Gabriel Rossetti. NOBE; OBNC; VLP
Even so deep in the jungle they were not safe. The Garden of Ships. Douglas Stewart. CBAP; PoAu-2
Even so distant, I can taste the grief. Deceptions. Philip Larkin. CABA; CMoP; ErPo; GTBS-P; NePoEA; NMP
"Even so" (the exulting Maiden said). Samuel Taylor Coleridge. *Fr.* The Destiny of Nations. ChER
Even Such Is Time. Sir Walter Ralegh. BLPL; ChTr; EIL; EnRePo; HAP; LiTB; PoRA; SeCeV; SiPS; TreF; WHA
(Author's Epitaph, Made by Himself [*or* Himselfe], The.) FaBoEn; OAEP; OxBoCh
(Conclusion, The.) EvOK; HBV-2; OBEV; WGRP
(Epitaph: "Even such is time, that [*or* which] takes in trust.") CTC; FaBoEE; NOBE; OBSC; TRV
(His Epitaph.) FaBoRV; TrGrPo
(Verses Found in His Bible.) PoPLe
(Verses Made the Night before He Dyed.) AAS
(Verses Written in His Bible.) ViBoPo
Even the Best. Gary Allan Kizer. LFAC
Even the dissident ones speak. America. John Newlove. NOBC
Even the morning is formal. The Morning Porches. Donald Hall. NePoAm-2
Even the sea dies, Lorca said at a weak moment. Guernica. James Lewisohn. LFAC
Even the sirens. The Sirens. Lou Lipsitz. LTB
Even the sky here in Connecticut has it. A Winter without Snow. J. D. McClatchy. FYAP
Even the sky is the colour of copper. Shetland, Hill Dawn. Robin Munro. PoSH
Even the spring water. The Cutting Edge. Philip Levine. NYBP
Even the sun-clouds this morning cannot manage such skirts. Poppies in October. Sylvia Plath. LCAP; NoAM
Even the sun, still warm. August/Fresno 1973. Roberta Spear. AmPA
Even the train is taller than those shacks. Homecoming. John Thompson. MAT
Even the unlived life within us. Like a Beach. Harvey Shapiro. VWA
Even the walls are flowing, even the ceiling. Variation on Heraclitus. Louis MacNeice. NoAM
Even There. Lyn Lifshin. IHMS
Even these stones I placed crudely once. The Little Fire in the Woods. Hayden Carruth. DiL
Even this is movement. Altars and Sacrifice. Jay Wright. FB
Even this late it happens. The Coming of Light. Mark Strand. PPJ
Even This Shall Pass Away. Theodore Tilton. BLPA; HBV-2; WGRP
(King's Ring, The.) TreFS
Even this suburb has overcome Death. Easter. Howard Nemerov. NoP
Even Though. John Stone. AMV-81
Even though he falls. The Chalk Angel. Dennis Schmitz. NPGG
Even though it's raining. Others. Harry Behn. SoPo; TiPo
Even though my hands/ are rough from much rice-pounding. *Unknown, tr. fr. Japanese by* Kenneth Yasuda. BoWoP
Even to the children/ on the disenchanted shore. The Blade of Grass Sings to the River. Leah Goldberg, *tr. by* Robert Friend. TrJP
Even weave of the canvas, The. Painted Passages. Gail N. Harada. BrSi
Even whilst I watch him I am remembering. To T. A. R. H. Stephen Spender. PeHV
Even with its own ax[e] to grind, sometimes. The Mind, Intractable Thing. Marianne Moore. LiTM; NYBP
Evenen in the Village. William Barnes. EBVV
Evening. Richard Aldington. MoBrPo; MOON; SeCePo
Evening, An. William Allingham. EnLoPo
Evening. Harry Behn. TiPo
Evening. Byron. *Fr.* Don Juan, III. TrGrPo
(Hesperus the Bringer.) AWP
Evening. John Clare. VLP
Evening. Charles Cotton. PoEL-3; WiR
(Evening Quatrains.) ChTr; LoBV

(Summer Evening.) TrGrPo
Evening. William Cowper. *See* Winter Evening.
Evening. Emily Dickinson. *See* Cricket sang, The.
Evening. George Washington Doane. *See* Evening Contemplation.
Evening. Hilda Doolittle ("H. D."). CMoP; FaBoMo; LoBV; VGW; WPE
Evening. Wendell Phillips Garrison. *Fr.* Post-Meridian. AA
Evening. John Keble. TrPWD, *abr.;* VLP
Evening. King D. Kuka. VoR
Evening. Itzik Manger, *tr. fr. Yiddish by* Miriam Waddington. VWA
Evening. Mary Matheson. CaP
Evening. Hugh McCrae. PoAu-1
Evening, An. Robert Mezey. NaP
Evening. Thomas Miller. OxBChV
Evening. Charles Sangster. CaP
Evening. Charles Simic. GeTw
Evening. Edith Sitwell. MoBS
Evening. James Stephens. MoBrPo
Evening. Tristan Tzara, *tr. fr. French by* Willis Barnstone *and* Matei Calinescu. VWA
Evening. Victor van Vriesland, *tr. fr. Dutch by* Adrian J. Barnouw. TrJP
Evening. James Wright. NOBA; NYBP; PrIm
Evening! A flight of pigeons in clear sky! The Flute; a Pastoral. José-Maria de Heredia, *tr. by* H. J. C. Grierson. AWP
Evening; an Elegy. Horatio Smith. BXAP
Evening, and Maidens. William Barnes. OBEV; OBVV
Evening and Morning in June, An. Gawin Douglas. *Fr.* Prologues to the Aeneid. BSV
Evening and Morning in Winter, An. Gawin Douglas. *Fr.* Prologues to the Aeneid. BSV
Evening, and the slender sugar tongs of a bird's small voice. Dinner Guest. Oscar Williams. TwAmPo
Evening: and we/ wait for a train to pass. Evening Song. John Matthias. AMV-81
Evening—another evening—and the lights flare. Thomas McGrath. Letter to an Imaginary Friend, Part Two, V, 2. NNaP
Evening, as slow thy placid shades descend. Sonnet. William Lisle Bowles. NOEC
Evening at the Farm. John Townsend Trowbridge. FaPON; GN
(Evening on the Farm.) MoShBr
Evening before Rain. L. A. G. Strong. OxBTC
Evening Bread. Jacob Glatstein, *tr. fr. Yiddish by* David G. Roskies *and* Hillel Schwartz. VWA
Evening by the Sea. Swinburne. FaBoPP; SyP
Evening came, a paw, to the gray hut by the river. Fall Journey. William Stafford. NaP; Str
Evening Ceremony; Dream for G. V. Wendy Rose. TWSS
Evening Cloud, The. John Wilson. HBV-1
Evening colours her amber breasts. Woman Made of Stars. Earle Thompson. STE
Evening comes. Freeze Tag. Gordon Henry. STE
Evening comes early, and soon discovers. Master's in the Garden Again. John Crowe Ransom. AP; NoAM
Evening comes, the fields are still, The. The First-born Star. Matthew Arnold. *Fr.* Bacchanalia. FaBoRV
Evening Contemplation. George Washington Doane. BLPA; BLPL; FaBoBe
(Evening.) AA; HBV-2
(Softly Now the Light of Day.) AH, *with music;* TreFS
Evening Dance of the Grey Flies. P. K. Page. NOBC
Evening Darkens Over, The. Robert Bridges. CMoP; HAP; NBM; PoEL-5
Evening Ebb. Robinson Jeffers. NoAM
Evening, ending, The. Guest Lecturer. Darwin T. Turner. BALP
Evening Falls, An. James Stephens. SUS
Evening falls on the smoky walls. Ballad of the Londoner. James Elroy Flecker. EnLoPo
Evening falls soon in the hills across the river. The White Eagle. Nan McDonald. PoAu-2
Evening falls, The. The sunset burns. On This Sea-Floor. Ralph Gustafson. PeCV
Evening Gleam, The. James Devaney. PoAu-1
Evening Harbour. Tom Paulin. AMV-81
Evening has brought its. Witnesses. W. S. Merwin. LCAP
Evening has brought the glow-worm to the green. Shepherd. Edmund Blunden. HBMV
Evening, here, and the gray garden. To One Far Away, Dancing. C. Stephen Finley. AMV-81
Evening Hymn. Sir Thomas Browne. *See* Colloquy with God, A.
Evening Hymn. William Henry Furness. AA; FaBoBe; HBV-2
(Light of Stars, The.) TrPWD
(Slowly, by God's Hand Unfurled, *with music.*) AH
Evening Hymn, An. Thomas Ken. OBS; OxBChV
Evening Hymn, *sel.* George Macdonald.
"O God, whose daylight leadeth down." TrPWD
Evening Hymn. Elizabeth Madox Roberts. TiPo
Evening Hymn in the Hovels. Francis Lauderdale Adams. OxBS
Evening in a Lab. Miroslav Holub, *tr. fr. Czech by* Stuart Friebert *and* Dana Hábová. SUW
Evening in Camp. Patricia Ledward. WaP
Evening in Gloucester Harbor. Epes Sargent. EtS
Evening in Paradise. Milton. *Fr.* Paradise Lost, IV. FaBoEn; GN; LoBV; NOBE
(Moon and the Nightingale, The.) ChTr; MOON
(Night Falls on Eden.) TreFS
Evening in Summer. Valentin Iremonger. *See* While the Summer Trees Were Crying.
Evening in the Sanitarium. Louise Bogan. FYAP; IHMS; MP; SBG; TwCP
Evening in the Suburbs. Stella Barnett. PV
Evening in the Walls. Jean Wahl, *tr. fr. French by* Charles Guenther. VWA
Evening in Tyringham Valley. Richard Watson Gilder. AA
Evening is clogged with gnats as the light fails. Alceste in the Wilderness. Anthony Hecht. ConAP; PoA
Evening is part of the jig-saw truth of her. Ode in Honour. Francis Scarfe. EAS
Evening Knell, The. John Fletcher. *See* Priest's Chant, The.
Evening lapses. No pity or pain, the badgered. From Government Buildings. Denis Devlin. IPY
Evening Meal in the Twentieth Century. John Holmes. MiAP
Evening Melody. Aubrey Thomas De Vere. GoBC; HBV-1
Evening Musicale. Phyllis McGinley. *See* Recipe for an Evening Musicale.
Evening of Ants, The. Gary Soto. NPGG
Evening of Russian Poetry, An. Vladimir Nabokov. NYBP
Evening of the Rose. Anthony Rudolf. VWA
Evening of the Visitation, The. Thomas Merton. ISi
Evening on Calais Beach. Wordsworth. *See* It Is a Beauteous Evening.
Evening on Howth Head. Eileen Brennan. NeIP
Evening on the Broads. Swinburne. TEP
Evening on the Farm. John Townsend Trowbridge. *See* Evening at the Farm.
Evening on the Harbor. Virginia Lyne Tunstall. HBMV
Evening Out, The. Ogden Nash. MoAmPo
Evening outdoors is only a larger lobby. One-Night Expensive Hotel. Ronald Everson. NOBC
Evening; Ponte al Mare, Pisa. Shelley. SyP
Evening Prayer. Edward Benlowes. *Fr.* Theophila. FaBoEn
Evening Prayer. Arthur Fitger, *tr. fr. German by* Jethro Bithell. AWP
Evening Prayer. Hermann Hagedorn. GoBC
Evening Prayer, An. Laura E. Kendall. BLRP
Evening Prayer, An ("Dear God, another day is done"). *Unknown.* STF
Evening Prayer ("Our Father, grant us to lie down in peace"). *Unknown, tr. fr. Hebrew by* Solomon Solis-Cohen. TrJP
Evening Primrose, The. John Clare. CH; TrGrPo
Evening Primrose, The. John Langhorne. OBEC
Evening Primrose, The. Dorothy Parker. InMe
Evening Quatrains. Charles Cotton. *See* Evening.
Evening red and morning gray. Weather Wisdom. *Unknown.* FaBoBe; FaBoUs; HBV-1; HBVY; OxNR; TreF
Evening Refrain. Sherod Santos. MAYP
Evening Revery, An, *sel.* Bryant.
"O thou great Movement of the Universe." AA
Evening Ride Jill Hoffman. PH
Evening Schoolboys. John Clare. GLGT
Evening Shade. John Leland. AmFP
(Day Is Past and Gone, The.) AH
Evening Song. Cecil Frances Alexander. OHIP
Evening Song. Kenneth Fearing. EAS
Evening Song. John Fletcher. *See* Priest's Chant, The.
Evening Song. Sidney Lanier. AP; TreFT; UnPo; WHA
Evening Song. John Matthias AMV-81
Evening Song. Jean Toomer. BPo; CDC
Evening Song of Senlin. Conrad Aiken. *Fr.* Senlin; a Biography. HBMV
Evening spread its rags of melancholy, The. The Wild Swan. D. S. Savage. NeBP
Evening Star. George Barker. ELU; ErPo; PoCh
Evening Star, The. Amy Carmichael. TRV
Evening Star, The. John Clare. *See* Hesperus.
Evening Star. Poe. AP
Evening Star, The. *Aborigine Oral Tradition, tr. by* R. M. Berndt. *Fr.* The Moon-Bone Cycle. WTO
Evening Star, enemy of lovers, why. Evening Star. George Barker. ELU; ErPo; PoCh
Evening star that in the vaulted skies, The. Verse Written in the Album of Mademoiselle. Pierre Dalcour, *tr. by* Langston Hughes. PoNe; TTY

Evening star that softly sheds, The. Refracted Lights. Celia Parker Wooley. WGRP
Evening Sun, The. Emily Brontë. CH
Evening Thought, An. Jupiter Hammon. PoNe
Evening traffic homeward burns. Before Disaster. Yvor Winters. HoPM; QFR
Evening Twilight. Baudelaire, *tr. fr. French by* Arthur Symons. SyP
Evening Twilight. Heine, *tr. fr. German by* John Todhunter. *Fr.* The North Sea. AWP
Evening Walk. Sonja Åkesson, *tr. fr. Swedish by* Joanna Bankier. WPOW
Evening Walk, An. William Stafford. NPAW
Evening Walk, An, *sels.* Wordsworth.
"Dear Brook, farewell! To-morrow's noon again." EnRP
Swans. OBEC
Evening was in the wood, louring with storm. Haunted. Siegfried Sassoon. CMoP
Evening-Watch, The. Henry Vaughan. AnAnS-1; NCEP
Evening Wind, The. Bryant. AA; AP
Evening without Angels. Wallace Stevens. MoPo; VGW
Evenings/ When the house is quiet. Setting the Table. Dorothy Aldis. FaPON; TiPo
Evening's barefoot monk. Evening. Itzik Manger, *tr. by* Miriam Waddington. VWA
Evenings below my window. Weldon Kees in Mexico, 1965. David Wojahn. MAYP
Evenings ever more willing lapse into my world's evening. Memoirs of a Turcoman Diplomat. Denis Devlin. IPY
Evenings I hear. A Plague of Starlings. Robert Hayden. HoAn
Evenings in Greece, *sel.* Thomas Moore.
The Two Streams, *fr.* First Evening. GoBC
Evening's Love, An, *sels.* Dryden.
Song: "After the pangs of a desperate lover," *fr.* II, i. FaBoEn
(After the Pangs [of a Desperate Lover].) ELP; OAEP; ViBoPo
(Love's Fancy.) ErPo
Song, A: "Calm was the even, and cleer was the sky [*or* skie]," *fr.* IV, i. CavP; SeCV-2
(Calm Was the Even [and Clear Was the Sky].) FF; OAEP
Song, A: "Celimena, of my heart," *fr.* V, i. CavP
(Damon and Celimena.) InvP
Song, A: "You charm'd me not with that fair face," *fr.* II, i. CaVP; SeCV-2
Evenings Songs John Vance Cheney. AA
Eveningsong. Ramona Wilson. VoR
Evensong. Conrad Aiken. HBMV
Even-Song, An. Sydney Dobell. OBVV
Evensong. Carleton Drewry. GoYe
Evensong. Peter Kane Dufault. AMV-80
Even-Song. George Herbert. AnAnS-1; FaBoEn
Evensong. C. S. Lewis. TrCP
Evensong. Judith Moffett. LTB
Evensong. Robert Louis Stevenson. TreFT; TrPWD; TRV
Evensong. George Tankervil. TRV
Evensong. Ridgely Torrence. HBV-1
Event, An. Edward Field. CoAP
Event, The. T. Sturge Moore. OBMV
Event. Sylvia Plath. NOBA
Event, An. Richard Wilbur. TwAmPo
Event worse than the omen, Th'; as his bride. The Death of Eurydice and Orpheus' Journey to Hell. Ovid, *tr. by* George Sandys. *Fr.* Metamorphoses. JCP
Eventide. Caroline Atherton Briggs Mason. TreFS
Events. George O'Neil. HBMV
Eventual Proteus. Margaret Atwood. MoCV
Ever and ever anon. The Road to the Bow. James David Corrothers. BANP
Ever as We Sailed. Shelley. *Fr.* The Revolt of Islam. SeCePo
Ever been kidnapped. Kidnap Poem. Nikki Giovanni. AmNP; BPo; InPK; NoAM; TAP
Ever before my face there went. Vain Finding. Walter de la Mare. BrPo
Ever charming, ever new. John Dyer. *Fr.* Grongar Hill. SeCePo
Ever-fixed Mark, An. Kingsley Amis. ErPo; NoAM; PeHV
Ever heard Bird. Mellowness and Flight. George Barlow. CNA
Ever let the fancy roam. Fancy [*or* The Realm of Fancy *or* To Fancy]. Keats. EnRP; GTBS; GTBS-P; HBV-2; LoBV; OBEV
Ever-living Church, The. Charles Wesley. STF
Ever myn happe is slack and slo in commyng. Petrarch, *tr. fr. Italian by* Sir Thomas Wyatt. OBVE
Ever On. *Unknown.* STF
Ever Since. Elizabeth J. Coatsworth. SiSoSe
Ever Since. Archibald MacLeish. NePA
Ever since boyhood it has been my joy. The Everlasting Mercy. J. C. Squire. BXAP
Ever since I realized there waz someone callt. No More Love Poems # 1. Ntozake Shange. BlSi
Ever since my daughters started to walk. The Green Tree. James Reiss. AmPA; DiL
Ever since our lunch of cheese. Dearest Man-in-the-Moon. Erica Jong. MOON
Ever since the great planes were murdered at the end of the gardens. Domus Caedet Arborem. Charlotte Mew. PBWP
Ever Since Uncle John Henry Been Dead, *with music. Unknown.* AS
Ever the green memory. Midway. John D. Engle, Jr. AMV-81
Ever-touring Englishmen, The. *Gond Oral Tradition, tr. by* V. Elwin *and* S. Hivale. WTO
Ever Watchful. Ta' Abbata Sharra, *tr. fr. Arabic by* W. G. Palgrave. AWP
Everglade. Anne Chernier. AMV-81
Evergreen. Ewart Milne. OxBI
Evergreen Cemetery. Alfred Purdy. MoCV
Evergreen shadow and the pale magnolia, The. Souls Lake. Robert Fitzgerald. MoPo; MP; TwCP
Everie bush new springing. *See* Every Bush New Springing.
Everlasting Arms, The. Bible, *O.T.* Psalms, XCI. *See* Mighty Fortress, A.
Everlasting Astronauts, The. Tom Buchan. BSV
Everlasting Contenders, The. Kenneth Patchen. CrMA; NaP
Everlasting Forests, The. Dahlia Ravikovitch, *tr. fr. Hebrew by* Chana Bloch. BoWoP
Everlasting Gospel, The, *sels.* Blake.
Epilogue: "I am sure this Jesus will not do." OBRV
"Jesus was sitting in Moses' chair." OxBoCh
"Vision of Christ that thou dost see, The." OBRV
"Was Jesus chaste? or did He." OBRV
Everlasting Love, The. Annie Johnson Flint. BLRP
Everlasting Mercy, The, *sels.* John Masefield.
"From '41 to '51." NoAM
"I did not think, I did not strive." TRV
"I opened the window wide and leaned." WGRP
"O Christ who holds the open gate." ILwL; TreFS; TRV
Everlasting Mercy, The, *parody.* J. C. Squire. BXAP
Everlasting Rest. Shakespeare. *See* Romeo's Last Words.
Everlasting universe of things, The. Mont Blanc. Shelley. EnRP; NIP; NoP; OAEL-2; PP; TEP
Everlasting Voices, The. W. B. Yeats. AWP
Everlastings, The. Norman Dubie. GeTw
Every afternoon. The Fire Breather, Mexico City. Jaime Jacinto. BrSi
Every afternoon at four. Quail Walk. Heather Ross Miller. BoAnP
"Every angel is terrible." Rilke Speaks of Angels. Susan Donnelly. PoDr
Every bar on The Block shut down. First Precinct Fourth Ward. Daniel Mark Epstein. TAT
Every branch big with it. Snow in the Suburbs. Thomas Hardy. BoNaP; CMoP; GoJo; MoAB; MoBrPo; OAEL-2; OBMV; OxBTC; PPP
Every Bush New Springing. *Unknown.* NCEP; PoEL-2
Every child who has gardening tools. Garden Lore. Juliana Horatia Ewing. OxBChV
Ev-er-y child who has the use. Some Geese [*or* Geese]. Oliver Herford. *Fr.* Child's Natural History. FiBHP; HBV-2; NA
Every Christian Born of God, *with music. Unknown, tr. fr. German.* AH
Every critic in the town. Critic and Poet. Robert Fuller Murray. DBV; POL
Every Day. *See also* Everyday.
Every Day. Ingeborg Bachmann, *tr. fr. German.* BoWoP, *tr. by* Christopher Middleton; PBWP, *tr. by* Michael Hamburger
Every day a wilderness—no. Dusting. Rita Dove. MAYP
Every day alone whittles me. Going In. Marge Piercy. DFF
Every-Day Characters, *sels.* Winthrop Mackworth Praed.
Belle of the Ball-Room, The. EnRP; FaBoCo; HBV-1; InMe
("Our love was like most other loves," 2 *sts.*) ViBoPo
Portrait of a Lady in the Exhibition of the Royal Academy. NBM; NOBL; PoEL-4
Vicar, The. EnRP; HBV-1; InMe; NBM; OBEV; OBNC; OBRV; OBVV; PoEL-4
Every day I meet the horses. Horses at Valley Store. Leslie Marmon Silko. VoR
Every day I peruse the box scores for hours. Baseball and Classicism. Tom Clark. LiSp
Every day I see from my window. Wild Oats. Norman MacCaig. OxBTC
Every day is a fresh beginning. New Every Morning. "Susan Coolidge." STF
Every day is Judgment Day. Judgment Day. John Oxenham. TRV
Every day now, since my wife told me to cease from writing poems. The Guest. Pentti Saarikoski, *tr. by* Anselm Hollo. PV
Every day our bodies separate. Villanelle. Marilyn Hacker. AmPA
Every Day Thanksgiving Day. Harriet Prescott Spofford. OHIP
Every day that their sky droops down. Moles. William Stafford. NYBP; RFM

Every day the dark blue sky of brother Van Gogh. The Sensitive Knife. Gerald Stern. DiL
Every day thou might lere. Remember the Day of Judgement. *Unknown.* MeEL
Every day, walking the city streets. The Nature of Jungles. W. R. Moses. NCSH
Every dwelling is a desolate hill. By the Pool. Allen Grossman. AMV-80
Every Earthly Creature. John Malcolm Brinnin. LiTA
Every evening Baby goes. Trot, Trot. Mary Frances Butts. HBV-1; HBVY
Every evening, down into the hardweed. Hardweed Path Going. A. R. Ammons. UnPo; VGW
Every few years,/ renewing its option. My Family's under Contract to Cancer. Greg Simison. AMV-80
Every game that Harvey plays. Harvey Always Wins. Jack Prelutsky. NTCP
Every hand is open to another's. As Long as the Heart Beats. Christine Zawadiwsky. AMV-81
Every Labor Day the two old guys trot out their flags. Labor Day. Gary Pacernick. TAT
Every lady in this [*or* the] land. Mother Goose. OxNR; PoPle
Every Land Is Exile. Claude Vigée, *tr. fr. French by* Anthony Rudolf. VWA
Every letter I write is. At Their Place. Paul Mariah. LFAC
Every Man. *See also* Everyman.
Every man has his sorrows; yet each still. Elegies, I. André Chénier, *tr. by* Arthur Symons. AWP
Every man in the world thinks his banner the best. Pat's Opinion of Flags. Fred Emerson Brooks. InPK
Every man should pride himself on something. Reflections of a Trout Fisherman. Andrew Demon. AMV-80
Every morning. Stafford in Kansas. James B. Hall. BXAP
Every morning at six o'clock, I go straight to my work. Everybody Works but Father. Charles W. McClintock. FSN; TreFS
Every morning from this home. The Heart to Carry On. Bertram Warr. PeCV
Every morning I break trail. Changeling VIII. Kristjana Gunnars. NOBC
Every morning I forget how it is. Poem. Charles Simic. NNaP
Every morning I get up/ Beautiful as the Goddess. Huang O, *tr. fr. Chinese by* Kenneth Rexroth *and* Ling Chung. BoWoP
Every morning I look. Where I Am Now. Harvey Shapiro. GP
Every morning I went to her charity and learned. To a Red-headed Do-good Waitress. Alan Dugan. CAPP
Every morning, in the dust. A Sparrow in the Dust. Ruth Domino, *tr. by* Daniel Hoffman *and* Jerre Mangione. BoWoP
Every morning lean thine arms while. Begin the Day with God. *Unknown.* TRV
Every morning she'd smear something brown. Man Arrested in Hacking Death Tells Police He Mistook Mother-in-Law for Raccoon. Susan Ludvigson. MAYP
Every morning the prisoner hears. The Prisoner. William Plomer. ChMP; PeSA
Every morning when the sun. This Happy Day. Harry Behn. TiPo
Every night from eve[n] till morn. To the Nightingale. Sir John Davies. *Fr.* Hymns of Astraea. OBSC; PBBP; TrGrPo
Every night I sleep. In the Trench. Leon Gellert. PoAu-1
Every night in the town. Shooting at the Moon. Kim Yo-sop, *tr. by* Ko Won. MOON
Every night my prayers I say. System. Robert Louis Stevenson. TEP
Every night when I went to bed. The Lament of the Unmarried Girl. Brian Merriman, *tr. by* Frank O'Connor. *Fr.* The Midnight Court. OBVE
Every Night When the Sun Goes In. *Unknown.* FSW; TrAS, *with music*
Every October millions of little fish come along the shore. Birds and Fishes. Robinson Jeffers. NoP
Every One. *See also* Everyone.
Every One to His Own Way. John Vance Cheney. AA
Every path a green lady. Four Songs from the Book of Samuel. Eli Mandel. MoCV
Every planet is a small plane. The Plane: Earth. Sun-Ra. PoBA
Every promised path ends in the Garden. On the Path. A. L. Strauss, *tr. by* Robert Friend. VWA
Every rose on the little tree. The Little Rose Tree. Rachel Field. FaPON; SUS; TiPo
Every Soul Is a Circus, *sel.* Vachel Lindsay.
Pontoon Bridge Miracle, The, IV. LoBV; NePA
Every stinking son of a bitch. Peace, So That. Greg Kuzma. InPK
Every sunday. Dirty Joke. D. L. Klauck. LTB
Every Sunday evening at seven o'clock. Street Preacher. Norman MacCaig. BSV
Every Sunday there's a throng. Westland Row. James Stephens. HBMV
Every Thing. *See also* Everything.
Every Thing. Harold Monro. MoBrPo
Every thread of summer is at last unwoven. Puella Parvula. Wallace Stevens. LCAP
Every Time I Climb a Tree. David McCord. NTCP; PDV; RHPC; SoPo; TiPo
Every time I come to town. Stop Kicking My Dog Around. *Unknown.* GDP
Every Time I Feel the Spirit. *Unknown.* FSW
(Ev'ry Time I Feel de Spirit, *with music.*) BoAn-1
Every time I nudge that spring. The Experiment with a Rat. Carl Rakosi. GP; POL
Every time I smell Lava soap it is 1948. The Story of Lava. David Allan Evans. Psk
Every time the bucks went clattering. Earthy Anecdote. Wallace Stevens. CMoP; GoJo; RFM
Every time we meet. Embroidery. Maria Jacobs. AMV-80
Every time you hear me sing this song. The Railroad Blues. *Unknown.* AmFP
Every towered city, every street. Exodus from a Renaissance Gallery. Ellen M. V. Acton. GoYe
Every valley drinks. Winter Rain. Christina Rossetti. BoNaP; WiR
Every waiting moment is a fold of sorrow. Low Tide. Lynette Roberts. NeBP
Every week of every season out of English ports go forth. An English Mother. Robert Underwood Johnson. HBV-2
Every year Emily Dickinson sent one friend. Accomplished Facts. Carl Sandburg. WHA
Every year without knowing it I have passed the day. For the Anniversary of My Death. W. S. Merwin. CAPP; CoAP; InPK; NaP; NOBA; PAI
Everybody but Me. Margaret Burroughs. BlSi; FB
Everybody else, then, going. Exeunt Omnes. Thomas Hardy. QFR
Everybody knew Clifton Cockerell was not half bright. The Beating. T. R. Hummer. MAYP
Everybody knows by now. Imperialist. A. R. Ammons. GP
Everybody loved Chick Lorimer in our town. Gone. Carl Sandburg. NOBA; TwAmPo
Everybody Loves Saturday Night. *Unknown.* FSW
Everybody Ought to Make a Change. *Unknown.* BluL
Everybody Says. Dorothy Aldis. FaPON; RHPC
Everybody stop and listen to my ditty. Prince of Wales' Marriage. *Unknown.* CoMu
Everybody wants to know why I sing the blues. Why I Sing the Blues. B. B. King. MAT
Everybody went to bat three times. Don Larsen's Perfect Game. Paul Goodman. LiSp
Everybody Works but Father. Charles W. McClintock. FSN, *with music;* TreFS
"Everybody Works but Father" as W. S. Gilbert Would Have Written It. Arthur G. Burgoyne. FiBHP
Everybody's Welcome, *with music.* *Unknown.* TrAS
Everyday. *See also* Every Day.
Everyday between classes intently over coffee in the Union. Academic Affair. Brenda S. Stockwell. AMV-80
Everyday Dirt. *Unknown.* FSW
Everyday I sit at a table. The August Second Syndrome Poem. J. A. Hines. LFAC
Everymaid. John Oxenham. TrCP
Everyman. *See also* Every Man.
Everyman. Siegfried Sassoon. MoBrPo
Everyman (*Old English Morality Play*). *Unknown.* OAEL-1; PoEL-1
Desertion of Beauty and Strength, The, *sel.* ACP
Everyman true to himself as Whitman—and that goes. Vincent O'Sullivan. Brother Jonathan, Brother Kafka, 31. OCNZ
Everyman's Library. John Ashbery. NoP
Everyone. *See also* Every One.
Everyone can see me standing in the center. Black Hawk in Hiding. George Keithley. NPGG
Everyone drinks Havdolah wine. Havdolah Wine. Miriam Ulinover, *tr. by* Seth L. Wolitz. VWA
Everyone grows younger; my thinning hair. Figures of Authority. Edward Watkins. NYBP
Everyone grumbled. The sky was grey [*or* gray]. Daddy Fell into the Pond. Alfred Noyes. FaPON; PDV; RHPC
Everyone in me is a bird. In Celebration of My Uterus. Anne Sexton. CAPP
Everyone is gone. Everyone. Blue. Christopher Gilbert. *Fr.* Beginning by Example. FYAP
Everyone knows he's blind as a bat. The Umpire. Walker Gibson. NePoAm
Everyone now is crowding everyone. Robert Lowell. *Fr.* Long Summer CAPP
Everyone Sang ("Everyone suddenly burst out singing"). Siegfried Sassoon.

BrPo; FaBV; GTBS-P; InvP; MoBrPo; NOBE; OBEV; OBWP; OxBTC; PoPl; PoSC; TrJP; WaP
Everyone sitting along with a sorrow. The Grief of Cafeterias. John Updike. PPJ
Everyone thinks I am poisonous. I am not. The Tarantula. Reed Whittemore. CoAP
Everyone writes of him, myself included. Gunfighter. Gerald Locklin. AMV-80
Everyone's going to ride tomorrow. Gabriel's Blues. Calvin Forbes. PoA
Everything. *See also* Every Thing.
Everything. Philip Levine. AMV-80
Everything. James Paul. HoAn
Everything described in this book. Light in the Open Air. Annie Dillard. SUW
Everything: Eloy, Arizona, 1956. Ai. AmPA; FF
Everything fell down. Fielding Error. Robert Paul Smith. CAD
Everything Has Its History. Phillis Levin. AMV-81
Everything has lasted till today. The Unknown Soldier. Alun Lewis. MoBrPo
Everything in Its Place. Arthur Guiterman. OBAL
Everything in the world has been photographed. Hold My Hand. Edmund Pennant. PoDr
Everything is black and gold. Black and Gold. Nancy Byrd Turner. SoPo; TiPo; YeAr
Everything is, once was not. Life after Death. Richard W. Thomas. PoBA
Everything is over and I'm feeling bad. *See* Ev'rything is over . . .
Everything Is Plundered. "Anna Akhmatova," *tr. fr. Russian by* Stanley Kunitz. WPOW
Everything Is Possible. Robert Pack. PPP
Everything is quiet in the garden. The Stone Garden. Richard Shelton. NPAW
Everything Is Round. Gabriela Mistral, *tr. fr. Spanish by* D. M. Pettinella. PBWP
Everything is round. Round. Rachel Boimwall, *tr. by* Gabriel Preil *and* Howard Schwartz. VWA
Everything is sexual at the beach. Concerning Unnatural Nature: An Inverted Form. Hollis Summers. ErPo
Everything is stopped. Stopped. Allen Polite. NNP
Everything Is Swimming. Stevie Smith. FaBoNo
Everything lives and nothing is dead. The Fugs. Edward Sanders. PoM
Everything shall be erased. Villa Sciarra: Rome. Christine Turner Curtis. GoYe
Everything That Acts Is Actual. Denise Levertov. NoAM
Everything that happens is the messsage. A Message from Space. William Stafford. SUW
Everything That Is. Daniel Berrigan. TwAmPo
Everything that lives has its own proper pride. Proper Pride. D. H. Lawrence. FaBoEE
Everything was bleak then, and. A History of Photography. Albert Goldbarth. MAYP
Everything was wrong; the local slaves wore smiles. Harpers Ferry. Selden Rodman. PoNe
Everything was yellow. The Painters. Judith Hemschemeyer. Psk
Everything we don't understand gathers. Orphan Boy, Fishing. Albert Goldbarth. WOLT
Everything will happen. Your friend. Love Poem. Lauris Edmond. OCNZ
Everything you own, Robert. Concerning Mme. Robert. Deems Taylor. UnTE
Everything's been different. The Birthday Child. Rose Fyleman. FaPON; SiSoSe
Everytime I leave you. Mother. Stephen Vincent. NeAC
Everywhere, everywhere, Christmas tonight! A Christmas Carol [*or* Christmas Everywhere]. Phillips Brooks. BLRP; FaFP; OHFP; OHIP; SoPo; WBLP
Everywhere, everywhere, following me. Camerados. Bayard Taylor. Par; UnPo
Everywhere in New York City there are factories. Factories. Edward Hirsch. AMV-81
Everywhere is far from somewhere else. Far from Somewhere. "Primus." WhC
Everywhere is our wilderness everywhere. George Barker. NeBP
Everywhere things have been taking place. Summer. Douglas Crase. NoP
Eve's Advice to the Children of Israel. Joachim Neugroschel. VWA
Eves Apologie. Emilia Lanier. BoWoP
Eve's Birth. Kim Chernin. VWA
Eve's Lament. *Unknown, tr. fr. Irish by* Kuno Meyer. OnYI
(Eve, *tr. by* Thomas MacDonagh.) BIrV
Eve's Song in the Garden. Lynn Gottlieb. VWA
Eve's tinted shadows slowly fill the fane. Sir Walter Scott at the Tomb of the Stuarts in St. Peter's. Richard Monckton Milnes. EBVV
Eve's Version. James Harrison. AMV-81
Evesong. Maureen Duffy. PeHV
Eviction, The. William Allingham. *Fr.* Laurence Bloomfield in Ireland BIrV
Eviction. Elizabeth Brewster. CaP
Eviction. Lucille Clifton. NTCP
(1st, The.) InPS
Evidence, The. Bible, *N.T.* Hebrews, XI: 1. TRV
Evidence. Arthur Kober. InMe
Evidence at the Witch Trials. James K. Baxter. OxBC
Evidence Read at the Trial of the Knave of Hearts. "Lewis Carroll." *Fr.* Alice's Adventures in Wonderland, *ch.* 12. FaBoNo; FaFP; GTBS-P; NBM; OxBoLi
(Silence in Court.) FaBoCo
Evil. Rimbaud, *tr. fr. French. Fr.* Eighteen-seventy. OBWP, *tr. by* Robert Lowell; WaaP, *tr. by* Norman Cameron
Evil Designs. Shakespeare. King Richard III, *fr.* I, i. TreF
(Hate the Idle Pleasures.) TrGrPo
Evil Devil Woman. *Unknown.* BluL
Evil does not go always. Lines for a Hard Time. Gena Ford. IHMS
Evil Eye, The. John Ciardi. MoBS; NAs
Evil-hearted Man. *Unknown.* FSW
Evil, if rightly understood. On the Origin of Evil. John Byrom. NOEC
Evil is here? That's work for us to do. Israel Zangwill. *Fr.* At the Worst. TRV
Evil Is No Black Thing. Sarah Webster Fabio. PoBA
"Evil Man, An!" Richard Beer-Hofmann, *tr. fr. German by* Ludwig Lewisohn. *Fr.* Der Graf von Charolais. TrJP
Evil Nigger Waits for Lightnin'. Amiri Baraka. NoAM; NOBA
Evil spirit, your beauty haunts me still, An. Sonnet. Michael Drayton. Idea, XX. AAS; EIL; GBL; HBV-1; LoBV; NOBE; OAEP; OBSC
"Evil thing is honor, An," once of old. George Edward Woodberry. Ideal Passion, XXVIII. HBMV
Evil was dangled in front of him like an apple. A Man of Sense. Richard Eberhart. MiAP
Evil World, An. *Unknown, tr. fr. Middle Irish by* Standish Hayes O'Grady. OnYI
Ev'n [*or* E'en *or* Even] like two little bank-dividing brooks [*or* brookes]. My Beloved Is Mine, and I Am His; He Feedeth among the Lillies [*or* Canticle]. Francis Quarles. *Fr.* Emblems. FaBoEn; HBV-2; LO; MeLP; MePo; NOBE; OBEV; OBS; TrGrPo
Evoe! Edith M. Thomas. HBV-2
Evolution. John Blight. CBAP
Evolution. Rochelle Owens. CoPo
Evolution. Langdon Smith. BeLS; BLPA; FaBoBe; FaFP; HBV-1; TreF; YaD
Evolution. May Swenson. TrGrPo
Evolution. John Banister Tabb. AA; HBV-2; PoPl; TreF
Evolution. Israel Zangwill. TrJP
Evolution from the Fish. Robert Bly. NoAM; NOBA
Evolution, though a good thing, has. Bathing with Father. Doug Fetherling. NeAC
Evolutionary Hymn. C. S. Lewis. NOBL
Ev'ry Saturday, Willie got his pay. The Bird on Nellie's Hat. Arthur J. Lamb. FSN
Ev'ry Time I Feel de Spirit *See* Every Time I Feel the Spirit. *Unknown.*
Ev'ry time I think about Jesus. Calvary. *Unknown.* BoAN-1
Ev'rything [*or* Everything] is over and I'm feeling bad. My Gal Sal. Paul Dresser. BLSo; FSN; TreFT
Ewes and lambs, loving the far hillplaces, The. Ad Limina. Joseph Campbell. BIrV
Ewing sweating. Patrick Ewing Takes a Foul Shot. Diane Ackerman. MAYP
Ex and Squarey. *Unknown.* ChTr
(Ex and Squarey, 1 *st.*) GBP
Ex-Basketball Player. John Updike. CTBA; LiSp; NYBP
"Ex Libris." Arthur Upson. HBV-2
Ex Maria Vergine. Norbert Engels. ISi
Ex Nihilo. David Gascoyne. *Fr.* Miserere. GTBS-P; NeBP
Ex Ore Infantium. Francis Thompson. FaBV; HBV-1; OBVV; OxBChV; SUS
(Child's Prayer, A.) HBVY; OHIP; TreFS
(Little Jesus.) PeD; TRV
Ex-Voto. Swinburne. MOS
Exaction. John Sweeney. TwAmPo
Exaltation. Franz Werfel, *tr. fr. German by* Edith Abercrombie Snow. TrJP
Examination, The. W. D. Snodgrass. CABA; CAPP; ConAP
Examination at the Womb-Door. Ted Hughes. NAs; OxBC
Examination of His Mistress' Perfections, The. Francis Beaumont. GoBC
Examination of Shakespeare, The. Walter Savage Landor. *See* Citation and Examination of William Shakespeare.
Examine the mirror closely, and your face. Sunday, July 14th; a Fine Day at the Baths. Julian Symons. WaP
Example, The. W. H. Davies. HBMV; MoBrPo; TrGrPo; WHA

Example of How a Daily Temporary Madness Can Help a Man Get the Job Done, An. John Stone. TAT
Exasperated, worn, you conjure a mansion. Desires of Men and Women. John Berryman. LiTM
Excavation for the new, The. Dedication for a Building. Alan Dugan. CAD; NYP
Excavator, explore rock from the great Ice Age. The Cave-Drawing. Vernon Watkins. LiTB
Exceeding sorrow/ Consumeth my sad heart! O Mors! Quam Amara Est Memoria Tua Homini Pacem Habenti in Substantiis Suis. Ernest Dowson. BrPo; OBMV
Exceeding tall, but built so well his height. House-Surgeon. W. E. Henley. In Hospital, XVI. BrPo
Excelente [*or* Excellent] Balade of Charitie, An. Thomas Chatterton. EBEV; EnRP; GoTL; LAuP; LiTB; NOEC; OBEC; SeCePo
Excellency of Christ. Giles Fletcher. *See* He Is a Path.
Excellent Balade of Charitie, An. Thomas Chatterton. *See* Excelente Balade . . .
Excellent Memory, An. Allen Curnow. OCNZ
Excellent New Ballad, Called the Brawny Bishop's Complaint, An. Arthur Mainwaring. APAS
Excellent New Ballad Called the Prince of Darkness, An. *Unknown.* APAS
Excellent New Ballad Giving a True Account of the Birth and Conception of a Late Famous Poem Called the Female Nine, An. Charles Sackville. APAS
Excellent New Song, Being the Intended Speech of a Famous Orator against Peace, An. Swift. APAS
Excellent New Song Called "Mat's Peace," An. Arthur Mainwaring. APAS
Excellent New Song on a Seditious Pamphlet, An. Swift. CoMu
Excellent New Song upon His Grace Our Good Lord Archbishop of Dublin, An. Swift. CoMu
Excellent Roman knives slip along the ribs. Robert Bly. *Fr.* The Teeth Mother Naked at Last. GP
Excellent work, my Hugh. The Beset Wife. Robert Farren. OxBI
Excelsior, *sel.* Emerson.
"Over his head were the maple buds." PeD
Excelsior. Longfellow. FaPON; FaPoR; HBV-2; HBVY; OBCA; OnMSP; PaPo; PrIm; SpRo; TreF; WBLP
Excelsior. *Unknown.* BXAP
Except for me, nobody remembers Clement Attlee. Clement Attlee. Michael Benedikt. InPS
Except I Love. Robert Parry. *Fr.* The Mirror of Knighthood. ElL
Except ourselves, we have no other prayer. Without Ceremony. Vassar Miller. CoPo; MoAmPo
Except the Lord build the house. Bible, *O.T.* Psalms, CXXVII. BiP; TreFT; TrJP; TRV
Except the Lord, That He for Us Had Been, *with music.* Henry Ainsworth. AH
Except under the cool shadows of pines. To a Wall of Flame in a Steel Mill, Syracuse, New York, 1969. Larry Levis. AMV-81; DiL; MAYP
Excepting the diner. Poem to Be Read at 3 A.M. Donald Justice. HoPM
Exceptional. Thelma Lewis. AMV-80
Excerpt from a Report to the Galactic Council. Robert Conquest. OxBC
Excerpts from the Notebook of the Poet of Santo Tomas. Richard Shelton. GP
Exchange, The. Samuel Taylor Coleridge. FiBHP; HBV-1; OAEP; WhC
Exchange. George Rostrevor Hamilton, *after the Greek of* Plato. FaBoEE
Exchange. Sister Mary Dorothy Ann. GoBC
Exchange. Dabney Stuart. HoPM
Exchange in greed the ungraceful signs. Thrust. The Violent Space. Etheridge Knight. BPo
Exchange of Hats, An. Stanley Moss. GP
Exchanges. Ernest Dowson. OBMV
Exchanges II, The. Robert Kelly. CoPo
Exchanging Glances. William Pitt Root. MAYP
Exciseman, The. Burns. *See* De'il's Awa wi' the Exciseman, The.
Excited, they sport high over our valley. Spring Hawks. Jim Thomas. AMV-81
Exclamation points surprise. Rain. Sister Mary Lucina. AMV-80
Exclusion. Emily Dickinson. *See* Soul selects her own society, The.
Exclusive Old Oyster, The. Laura A. Steel. TDH
Excursion, The. Tu Fu, *tr. fr. Chinese by* Amy Lowell *and* Florence Ayscough. AWP
Excursion, The, *sels.* Wordsworth.
Despondency Corrected, *fr.* IV. EnRP
"I have seen/ A curious child." OBRV; TreFT
("Curious child, who dwelt upon a tract, A," *shorter sel.*) WGRP
Discourse of the Wanderer, and an Evening Visit to the Lake, *fr.* IX. EnRP
"Diverging now (as if his quest had been)," *fr.* II. OBRV
Prospectus [*sel. fr.* The Recluse]. EnRP; NoP
("On man, on nature, and on human life.") OAEL-2, OBRV
Solitary, The, *fr.* II. EnRP
"Tenour which my life holds, The," *fr.* III. OBRV
Wanderer, The, I. EnRP, *abr.*
(Ruined Cottage, The, *diff. version.*) NoP; OAEL-2
"I see around me here." OBRV
(Wanderer Recalls the Past, The.) OBNC
"Such was the boy." OBRV
"Within the soul a faculty abides," *fr.* IV. OBRV
Excuse, The. Sir Walter Ralegh. AAS; SiPS
Excuse me if I don't weep. Funeral Song for Mamie Eisenhower. Nellie Wong. BrSi
Excuse me, isn't that you I see concealed underneath there. Thoughts. Michael Benedikt. ConAP
Excuse of Absence, An. Thomas Carew. CaPo; SeCP
Excuse Us, Animals in the Zoo. Annette Wynne. TiPo
Exeat. Stevie Smith. NoAM
Execration against Whores, An. John Webster. *Fr.* The White Devil, III, ii. TW
Execration upon Vulcan, An. Ben Jonson. AnAnS-2; SeCP
Execrators, The. David Galler. NMP
Execution, The. Alden Nowlan. PeCV
Execution. James A. Randall, Jr. BPo
Execution of Alice Holt. *Unknown.* OxBoLi
Execution of Cornelius Vane, The. Sir Herbert Read. BrPo; NoAM
Execution of King Charles, The. Andrew Marvell. PoRA
Execution of Lake Hutton, The. *Unknown.* OBET
Execution of Montrose, The. William Edmondstoune Aytoun. HBV-2; OnMSP
Executive. John Betjeman. NOBL
Executive's Death, The. Robert Bly. CoAP; NaP
Exeo in a spasm. Enueg I. Samuel Beckett. CIP
Exequies, The. Thomas Stanley. AnAnS-2; MeLP; OBS
Exequy, The. Henry King. AnAnS-2; CABA; FaBoEn; GBL; HAP; HBV-1; InvP; JCP; LoBV; MeLP; NoP; OBS; PoEL-2; PPoe; PrIm; QFR; SeCePo; SeCP; TEP
(Exequy on [*or* upon] His Wife.) BoLoP; NOBE; OBEV
(Exequy, The: To His Matchlesse Never to Be Forgotten Friend.) MePo
Sels.
"Accept, thou shrine of my dead saint." ViBoPo
"Dear loss! since thy untimely fate." LO; WHA
"Sleep on, my love, in thy cold bed." CH; PoPle; TrGrPo
Exequy, An. Peter Porter. OxBC
Exequy on [*or* upon] His Wife. Henry King. *See* Exequy, The.
Exequy: To Peter Allt. Kildare Dobbs. OBCV
Exercise. W. S. Merwin. NOBA
Exercise for the Left Hand. Constance Urdang. AMV-81
Exercise in a Meadow. Jean Elliot. GoYe
Exercise of Affection, The. Sir Robert Ayton. BSV
Exert thy voice, sweet harbinger of Spring! To the Nightingale. Countess of Winchilsea. SBG; WPE
Exeter Riddle, An. Gavin Ewart. OxBC
Exeunt. Richard Wilbur. BoNaP; ELU; HeIP; NCSH; PoLF; Psk; TwAmPo
Exeunt Omnes. Thomas Hardy. QFR
Exhausted now her sighs, and dry her tears. Walter Savage Landor. FaBoEE
Exhaustive experimentation. *Unknown.* DBV
Exhortation. Louise Bogan. QFR
Exhortation. Thomas Hastings. AA
Exhortation of a Father to His Children, The. Robert Smith. OxBChV
Exhortation: Summer, 1919. Claude McKay. CDC
Exhortation to Learn by Others' Trouble. Earl of Surrey. FaBoEE
("My Ratclif, when thy retchlesse youth offendes.") AAS
Exhortation to Prayer. William Cowper. NOCV
Exhortation to Prayer. Margaret Mercer. AA
Exigencies. Michael William Gilbert. AMV-80
Exile. Audrey Beecham. NeBP
Exile. Chana Bloch. GP
Exile. Ernest Dowson. BoLoP; BrPo
Exile. Donald Hall. NePA
Exile. George Rostrevor Hamilton, *after the Greek of* Isidoros of Aigai. FaBoEE
Exile, The. Larry Rubin. GoYe
Exile. Virna Sheard. PeCV
Exile. Joseph Stroud. NPGG
Exile. *Unknown, tr. fr. Irish by* Frank O'Connor. KiLC
Exile. Ellen Bryant Voigt. MAYP
Exile. Jennette Yeatman. GoYe
Exile/ by accident. Waiting for E. Gularis. Linda Pastan. SUW
Exile at Rest, The. John Pierpont. AA
Exile from God. John Hall Wheelock. GoBC; WGRP
Exile in Nigeria. Ezekiel Mphahlele. PBA

Exile of Erin. Thomas Campbell. HBV-2
Exiled. Edna St. Vincent Millay. EtS; MOS; PoRA
Exiled from places of honor about the Throne of Grace. Black Church on Sunday. Joseph M. Mosley, Jr. NBP
Exiled Heart, The. Maurice Lindsay. OxBS
Exiles. "Æ." BIrV; MoBrPo
Exiles, The. W. H. Auden. OxBTC
Exiles. William Hamilton Hayne. AA
Exile's Letter. Li Po, *tr. fr. Chinese by* Ezra Pound. CTC; FaBoMo; OxBA; SeCeV
Exile's Return, The. Robert Lowell. AmPP; AP; MiAP; NePA; OxBA
Exile's Reveries, The, *sel.* James Kennedy.
"Chased from my calling to this hackneyed trade." NOEC
Exile's Song, The. Robert Gilfillan. HBV-2
Existence. Sheila Moon. AMV-80
Existential. William Heyen. GeTw
Existentialism. Lloyd Frankenburg. FiBHP
Exit. Wilson MacDonald. CaP; ViBoPo
Exit. E. A. Robinson. MoAmPo
Exit from Eden, The. Milton. *See* Banishment, The.
Exit God. Gamaliel Bradford. HBMV; InMe
Exit Line. John Ciardi. WeW
Exit Lines. George Jonas. NeAC
Exit Molloy. Derek Mahon. POL
Exit, Pursued by a Bear. Ogden Nash. NYBP
Exit the fond, the familiar. Enter the strange. In a World of Change. Joseph Awad. AMV-80
Exit the ribald clown. Colombine. Hugh McCrae. PoAu-1
Exits and Entrances. Naomi Long Madgett. BlSi
Exodus, *sels.* Bible, *O.T.*
"Let us synge unto the Lorde, for he is become glorious," XV: 1-8, *tr. by* William Tyndale. OBVE
Ten Commandments, The. TreF (XX: 1-17); WBLP (XX: 3-17)
Then Sang Moses, XV: 1-18. TrJP
("Lord is a Man of War, The," 3-10.) WaaP
("Then sang Moses and the children of Israel this song.") OBWP
(Triumphal Chant, 1-13, 18.) TrGrPo
Exodus. George Oppen. GP
Exodus. Anita Endrezze Probst. CDW
Exodus. Harvey Shapiro. VWA
Exodus, *sel.* *Unknown, tr. fr. Anglo-Saxon by* Charles W. Kennedy.
Parting of the Red Sea, The. AnOE
Exodus, The (August 3, 1492). Emma Lazarus. *Fr.* By the Waters of Babylon. WPE
Exodus for Oregon. Joaquin Miller. BPAW
Exodus from a Renaissance Gallery. Ellen M. V. Acton. GoYe
Exodus from Egypt, The. Ezekielos of Alexandria, *tr. fr. Greek by* E. H. Gifford. TrJP
Exodus 1940. Alfred Wolfenstein, *tr. fr. German by* Erna Baber Rosenfeld. VWA
Exorcism. Oliver St. John Gogarty. AnIL
Exorcism, The. Theodore Roethke. NoAM
Expanded Want Ad, An. Brad Leithauser. MAYP
Expanded waters gather on the plain, The. The Flood. Ovid, *tr. by* Dryden. *Fr.* Metamorphoses, I. ChTr
Expanding in the chill. Cold-Weather Love. Ronald Everson. MoCV
Expanse of fields spreading out, The. Moving. Barbara Crooker. AMV-80
Expansive puppets percolate self-unction. The Canadian Authors Meet. F. R. Scott. NOBC; OBCV; WHC
Expect no thanks ever from anyone. Catullus, *tr. fr. Latin by* James Michie. DBV
Expect Nothing. Alice Walker. AmPA; FF
Expectancies: The Eleventh Hour. Karla M. Hammond. AMV-80
Expectans Expectavi. Charles Hamilton Sorley. FaBoCh; HBMV; WGRP
Expectant at the country gate the lantern. Ill. Bernard Spencer. NeBP
Expectant Father, The. Ai. GeTw
Expectant Mother. Penelope Shuttle. BrRo
Expectation, The. Frederick William Faber. *Fr.* Our Lady's Expectation. ACP
Expectation. Aliza Shenhar, *tr. fr. Hebrew by* Linda Zisquit. VWA
Expectation. Thomas Stanley. AnAnS-2; OBS
(Destiny.) LoBV
Expecting. Daniel J. Langton. AMV-81
Expecting no miracles, we walked. Outer Space, Inner Space. Gladys Cardiff. TWSS
Expecting to be put in a sack and dumped in a ditch. Nightmare. Edward Field. Str
Expedition to Wessagusset, The. Longfellow. *Fr.* The Courtship of Miles Standish. PAH
Expense of spirit in a waste of shame, The [*or* Th']. Sonnets, CXXIX. Shakespeare. AWP; BiP; CABA; EBEV; EnRePo; ErPo; GBL; HAP; HeIP; InPS; LiTB; LoBV; MasP; NIP; NOBE; NoP; OAEL-1; OBEV; OBSC; PAI; PPoe; PPP; QRF; SeCePo; SeCeV; TEP; TrGrPo; UnPo; ViBoPo; WeW; WHA
Expensive Wife, The. Judah ibn Sabbatai. *Fr.* The Gift of Judah the Woman-Hater. TrJP
Experience. Emerson. FPL; LiTA; PoEL-4; TAP
Experience. Lesbia Harford. CBAP; PoAu-1
Experience. Hugo von Hofmannsthal, *tr. fr. German by* John N. Miller. AMV-81
Experience. Aline Kilmer. HBMV
Experience. John Boyle O'Reilly. ACP; OBVV
Experience. Dorothy Parker. InMe; PoPl; WhC
Experience. James Simmons. BIrV; CIP
Experience, The. Edward Taylor. *Fr.* Preparatory Meditations: First Series, III. AmPP
Experience now doth show what God us taught before. On Edward Seymour, Duke of Somerset. *Unknown.* OBSC
Experience, though noon auctoritee. The Wife of Bath's Prologue [*or* The Prologue to the Wife of Bath's Tale]. Chaucer. *Fr.* The Canterbury Tales. OAEL-1; OxBoLi; PoEL-1
Experienced men, inured to city ways. John Gay.. *Fr.* Trivia; or, The Art of Walking the Streets of London, II.OAEL-1
Experienced wife, An. A Midwife's Story; Two. Anne Szumigalski. NOBC
Experiential Religion. Travis Du Priest. AMV-80
Experiment That Failed, The. John Logan. NU
Experiment with a Rat, The. Carl Rakosi. GP; POL
Expert. *Unknown.* TDH
Experts on Woman. Arthur Guiterman. InMe
Expiatory chapel, chains. Jardin de la Chapelle Expiatoire. Robert Finch. PeCV
Expiration, The. John Donne. EIL; MeLP; MePo; SeCP
Explain this if you can. Angler. Mark Vinz. WOLT
Explaining about the Dachshund. John Stone. NIP
Explaining to me that my mind. Friends Come. Lucille Clifton. GeTw
Explanation. William Barber. PeHV
Explanation. "Josh Billings." TreFT
Explanation. Geof Hewitt. NeAC
Explanation of America, An, *sel.* Robert Pinsky.
Serpent Knowledge. NPGG
Explanation of the Grasshopper, An. Vachel Lindsay. FaPON; SoPo
Explanation, on Coming Home Late. Richard Hughes. ELU
Explanations. Lucille Clifton. GeTw
Exploding before my very eyes. Peyote Vision. Lew Blockcolski. VoR
Exploration. Daniel Hoffman. CoAP; CoPo
Explorations. Louis MacNeice. ChMP; CoBMV
Explorations/ Bronchitis: The Rosario Beach House. Aleida Rodríguez, *tr. fr. Spanish by* Toni Empringham. FIA
Explorer, The. Kipling. WHA
Explorers, The. Margaret Atwood. CABA; MoCV
Explorers as Seen by the Natives. Doug Fetherling. NOBC
Explorers say that harebells rise. Ellesmereland I. Earle Birney. CABA
Explorers will come, The. The Explorers. Margaret Atwood. MoCV
Explosion, The. Philip Larkin. EBEV; FaBoMo; HAP; OxBC; SCV; WeW
Explosion of a bomb, The. Perhaps. Stephen Spender. NoAM
Expostulation, An. Isaac Bickerstaffe. FaBoCo; FiBHP; NIP; PV
Expostulation, The. Thomas Shadwell. *Fr.* The Squire of Alsatia. OAEP
Expostulation and Reply. Wordsworth. EnRP; HBV-1; OAEL-2; OAEP; OBRV
Exposure. Seamus Heaney. CIP; IPY
Exposure. Wilfred Owen. FaBoMo; InPS; MMA; MoVE; NoAM; OBWP; WaP
Expounding the Torah. Louis Zukofsky. VWA
Express. W. R. Rodgers. MoVE
Express, The. Stephen Spender. CMoP; GoJo; LiTM; MoAB; MoBrPo; MoVE; MP; NIP; NoAM; PoPl; RoGo; SeCeV; TwCP
Express Train. Karl Kraus, *tr. fr. German by* Albert Bloch. TrJP
Expression. Thom Gunn. OxBC
Expression. Isaac Rosenberg. MoBrPo
Expulsion from Paradise. Milton. *Fr.* Paradise Lost, XII. ChTr
Exquisite Lady. Mary Elizabeth Osborn. NePoAm-2
Exquisite Sonnet, The. J. C. Squire. HBMV
Exquisite stillness! What serenities. Don Juan's Address to the Sunset. Robert Nichols. OBMV
Exquisite torment, dainty Mrs. Hargreaves. Sapphics. D. B. Wyndham Lewis. NOBL
Exquisite wines and comestibles. Martial in London. Mortimer Collins. InMe
Exspecto Resurrectionem. Charlotte Mew. LO
Extasie, The. Abraham Cowley. AnAnS-2; SeCP
Extasie, The. John Donne. *See* Ecstasy, The.
Extempore Effusion Upon the Death of James Hogg. Wordsworth. EBEV; FaBoRV; FiP; NOBE; NoP; OAEL-2; OBRV; SCV

London, from Hampstead Heath, *sel.* FaBoPP
Extempore to Voltaire Criticising Milton. Edward Young. *See* Epigram on Voltaire.
Extempore Verses Intended to Allay the Violence of Party-Spirit. John Byrom. *See* Jacobite Toast.
Extempore Verses upon a Trial of Skill between the Two Great Masters of the Noble Science of Defence, Messrs. Figg and Sutton. John Byrom. OBEC
Extensions of Linear Mobility. Jeanine Hathaway. IHMS
Extermination. Richard D'Alton Williams. OnYI
Extermination of the Jews, The. Marvin Bell. VWA
External Element, The. David McFadden. NeAC
Extinct Birds. Judith Wright. PBWP
Extinct old ichthyosaurus, An. The Ichthyosaurus. *Unknown.* TDH
Extinct volcanoes are silent. Volcanoes. Bella Akhmadulina, *tr. by* W. H. Auden. PBWP
Extra Joyful Chorus for Those Who Have Read This Far, An. Robert Bly. EAS
Extract. Paul Bowles. PoA
Extract from Addresses to the Academy of Fine Ideas, An. Wallace Stevens. LiTA; LiTM
Extract from Memoirs. Howard Nemerov. OxBC
Extract the quint-essence. Francis Daniel Pastorius. SCAP
Extracts: From the Journal of Elisa Lynch. Maura Stanton. AmPA
Extraordinary Dog, The. Nancy Byrd Turner. TiPo
Extraordinary patience of things, The! Carmel Point. Robinson Jeffers. NoP
Extraordinary Will. Will Jackett. FaBoUs
Extras. Richard Burton. AA
Extravagant Drunkard's Wish, The. Edward Ward. NOEC
Extreme Unction. Ernest Dowson. ACP; MoBrPo; OAEL-2; OBMV; VLP
Extreme Unction in Pa. David Ray. AMV-81; FAZ
Extremes. James Whitcomb Riley. FaPON; HBVY
Extremum Tanain. Horace, *tr. fr. Latin by* Austin Dobson. Odes, III, 10. AWP
Exuberant, restless. West Lake. Kenneth O. Hanson. CoAP
Exultation is the going. Emily Dickinson. AP; CABA; NCEP
Exulting in his strength, he seems to dare. Virgil, *tr. by* Dryden. *Fr.* The Aeneid, XI. OBVE
Exxon man tugs his CATerpillar cap, The. Trout Fishing in Virginia. Michael Beirne McMahon. AMV-80
Eyam, *sel.* Anna Seward.
"In scenes paternal, not beheld through years." NOEC
Eyaya-eya./ I recognize/ A bit of song. I Should Be Ashamed. Uvlunuaq, *tr. fr. Eskimo.* WTO
Eye, The. Michael Benedikt. ConAP
Eye, The. Robert Herrick. CaPo
Eye, The. Robinson Jeffers. AP; CoBMV; CrMA; FaBoEn; LiTA; LiTM; NOBA; OxBA; WaP
Eye, The. Allen Tate. LiTA
Eye, The. Richard Wilbur. FiCP
Eye, The. Eithne Wilkins. NeBP
Eye and Tooth. Robert Lowell. CAPP
Eye can hardly pick them out, The. At Grass. Philip Larkin. HAP; NePoEA; OxBTC; WeW
Eye, dark, The. Hut Window. Paul Celan, *tr. by* Joachim Neugroschel. VWA
Eye drags all of winter, The. News Reel. David Ross. GoYe
Eye-flattering fortune, look thou never so fair. Fortune. Sir Thomas More. GoBC
Eye luminous, The. The Offender. Denise Levertov. NePoEA-2
Eye of God. Jim Tollerud. VoR
Eye of Humility, The. Kay Smith. OBCV
Eye of Love, The. George Moses Horton. BALP
Eye of the garden, queen of flowers. To the Rose. Sir John Davies. *Fr.* Hymns of Astraea. OBSC
Eye of this storm is not quiet, The. To a Gone Era. Irma McClaurin. BlSi
Eye opening is a mouth seeing, The. Eyesight II. Robert Duncan. EAS
Eye standing up eye lying down eye sitting. Making Feet and Hands. Benjamin Péret, *tr. by* David Gascoyne. EAS
Eye winker. *Unknown.* OxNR
Eye with the piercing eagle's fire, An. Thaddeus Stevens. Phoebe Cary. PAH
Eyeglasses. Tom Clark. ConAP
Eyeglasses, The. William Carlos Williams. NoAM
Eyeless labourer in the night, The. Woman to Man. Judith Wright. CBAP; PoAu-2; WPE
Eyelids fall, the star-charts, The. The Invention of Astronomy. William Matthews. POL
Eyelids glowing, some chill morning, The. Monet: "Les Nymphéas." W. D. Snodgrass. ConAP; CoAP
Eyelids meet, The. He'll catch a little nap. In the Smoking-Car. Richard Wilbur. ConAP; LiTM; MoAmPo
Eyelids of eve fall together at last, The. Before Waterloo [*or* The Eve of Waterloo]. Thomas Hardy. *Fr.* The Dynasts. MoAB; OAEL-2; OBWP
Eyes. W. H. Davies. BrPo; FM
Eyes. Walter de la Mare. BrPo
Eyes. Clarïsse Nicoidski, *tr. fr. Judezmo by* Stephen Levy. VWA
Eyes always open eyes. Eyewash. Niall Montgomery. EAS
Eyes and Tears. Andrew Marvell. MePo; NCEP
Eyes are lying again, posing, The. Pluck out. Self-Portrait. Robert Pack. CoPo
Eyes do not lie. Remainder. Frederika Blankner. GoYe
Eyes, Hide My Love. Samuel Daniel. *See* Secrecy.
Eyes like/ small field mice. Child Poem. Annette Arkeketa West. TWSS
Eyes like the morning star. The Colorado Trail. *Unknown.* AS; CoSo; FSW
Eyes of Cantonese Schoolmasters Remembered in Hong Kong, The. Willis Barnstone. GLGT
Eyes of Children at the Brink of the Sea's Grasp, The. Josephine Jacobsen. NePoAm-2
Eyes of despair, eyes of fire. Ophelia's Song. Marya Zaturenska. OLR
Eyes of Flesh, The. Sandra Hochman. NMM
Eyes of God, The. Hermann Hagedorn. HBMV
Eyes of men running, falling, screaming. *Unknown.* OBWP
Eyes of My Regret, The. Angelina Weld Grimkė. CDC
Eyes of Night-Time. Muriel Rukeyser. BoWoP; MiAP; NePA
Eyes of slain stag. In Some Seer's Cloud Car. Christopher Middleton. TwCP
Eyes of Texas, The. *Unknown.* FSW
Eyes of the pioneer woman are blue, The. The Pioneer Woman—in the North Country. Eunice Tietjens. AmFN
Eyes of twenty centuries, The. Judas Iscariot. Stephen Spender. MoAB; MoBrPo; NIP
Eyes open to a cry of pulleys, The. Love Calls Us to the Things of This World. Richard Wilbur. AmPP; CAPP; CMoP; HAP; HeIP; InPS; MoAmPo; NePA; NePoEA; NIP; NoAM; PoRA; PPP; SeCeV; TAP; TrGrPo; TwAmPo; UnPo; VGW
Eyes red, the lips blue, The. The Three Seamstresses. Isaac Leibush Peretz, *tr. by* Joseph Leftwich. TrJP
Eyes shut tight. Madness. Sachiko Yoshihara, *tr. by* James Kirkup *and* Shozo Tokunaga. BoWoP
Eyes, side-to-side. Directions. Onitsura, *tr. by* Harold G. Henderson. SoPo
Eyes So Tristful. Diego de Saldaña, *tr. fr. Spanish by* Longfellow. AWP
Eyes that drew from me such fervent praise, The. Petrarch, *tr. by* Edwin Morgan. Sonnets to Laura: To Laura in Death, XXIV. NAWM-1; PAI
Eyes that glass fear, though fear on furtive foot. A Hare. Walter de la Mare. EBEV
Eyes That Last I Saw in Tears. T. S. Eliot. NOBE; ViBoPo
Eyes that mock me sign the way, The. Bahnhofstrasse. James Joyce. NoAM
Eyes That Queenly Sit. Elizabeth Daryush. QFR
Eyes that weep for pity of the heart, The. Dante, *tr. by* Dante Gabriel Rossetti. La Vita Nuova, XIX. AWP; WGRP
Eyes, the Blood, The. David Meltzer. PoM; VWA
Eyesight II. Robert Duncan. EAS
Eyewash. Niall Montgomery. EAS
Eyewitness. Rodney Hall. PoAu-2
Eye-Witness. Ridgely Torrence. HBMV
Ez fer War. James Russell Lowell. *Fr.* The Biglow Papers. PPON
Ezekiel, *sels.* Bible, *O.T.*
Lamentation, XIX: 2-9. TrJP
Thy Mother Was like a Vine, XIX: 10-14. TrJP
Ezekiel. Laurence Binyon. ChMP
Ezekiel. A. N. Stencl, *tr. fr. Yiddish by* Joseph Leftwich. VWA
Ezekiel in the valley of Dry Bones. Ezekiel. Laurence Binyon. ChMP
Ezekiel Saw the Wheel. *Unknown.* AZ
(Ezekiel, You and Me, *with music, diff. vers.*) AS
('Zekial Saw de Wheel, *with music.*) BoAN-2
Ezra Pound. Robert Lowell. NoAM; NOBA
Ezra Pound (his fingers, bones). Postscript, on a Name. Stephen Ratcliffe. AMV-80
Ezra Shank. *Unknown.* ShM
Ezra, whom not with eye nor with ear have I ever. Epistle to the Rapalloan. Archibald MacLeish. PoA
Ezry. Archibald MacLeish. MoVE; NOBA

F

F Is the Fighting Firetruck. Phyllis McGinley. FaPON
Fr. All Around the Town.
Fa La La. *Unknown, at. to* John Hilton. *See* Madrigal: "My mistress frowns when she should play."
Fa, mi, fa, re, la, mi. *Unknown.* InPK
Fa saw the Forty-second. The Forty-second. *Unknown.* GBP
Fabien dei Franchi. Oscar Wilde. BrPo
Fable: "Bough will bend, the leaf will sometime fall, The." Mary Mills. NePoAm
Fable, A: "Dingy donkey, formal and unchanged, A." John Hookham Frere. FaBoCo
Fable, A: "In Aesop's tales an honest wretch we find." Matthew Prior. NoP
Fable: "Mountain and the squirrel, The." Emerson. AmPP; BiP; BLPL; FaBV; FaFP; FaPON; HBV-1; HBVY; InMe; LiTA; NePA; OBAL; OBCA; OnMSP; PoPl; TRV; YaD
(Mountain and the Squirrel, the.) BeLS; FaBoBe; GoJo; TreFT
Fable: "O the vines were golden, the birds were loud." Frederic Prokosch. WaP
Fable: "Once upon a time/ there was a lonely wolf." János Pilinszky, *tr. fr. Hungarian by* Ted Hughes *and* János Csokits. OBVE
Fable: "Pity the girl with crystal hair." Joan Aiken. WSC
Fable: "Tale is every time the same, The." Maurice James Craig. NeIP
Fable: "There is an inevitability." Norman Harris. NYBP
Fable: "Under a dung-cake." D. J. Opperman, *tr. fr. Afrikaans by* Jack Cope. PeSA
Fable for Critics, A, *sels.* James Russell Lowell.
Bryant. AP; NOBA; TAP
Cooper. AP; DBV; NOBA; OxBA; TAP
Emerson. AmPP; AP; NOBA; OxBA; TAP
("There comes Emerson first, whose rich words, every one.") PP
Hawthorne. AmPP; AP; NOBA; OxBA; TAP
Holmes. NOBA
Irving. TAP
Lowell. AmPP; AP; NOBA; OxBA; TAP
(On Himself.) AA
Poe and Longfellow. AmPP; AP; NOBA; OxBA
(Poe.) TAP
"There are truths you Americans need to be told." OBSV
To His Countrymen. AA
Whittier. AmPP; NOBA; OxBA
Fable Merchant, The. Charles Dobzynski, *tr. fr. French by* Charles Guenther. VWA
Fable of Midas, The. Swift. APAS
Fable of the Magnet and the Churn, The. W. S. Gilbert. *Fr.* Patience. FaPON; OnMSP
Fable of the Piece of Glass and the Piece of Ice, The. John Hookham Frere. OxBChV
Fable of the Speckled Cow. D. J. Opperman, *tr. fr. Afrikaans by* Jack Cope, Uys Krige, *and* Ruth Miller. PeSA
Fable of the Talented Mockingbird. Scott Bates. BoAnP
Fable of the War, A. Howard Nemerov. NePoEA; OBWP
Fable of the Water Merchants. Stephen Dixon. LTB
Fables, *sels.* John Gay.
Butterfly and the Snail, The. FM
Fox at the Point of Death, The. OBEC
Hare with Many Friends, The. HBV-1
Lion and the Cub, The. HBV-1
Turkey and the Ant, The. PBBP
Wild Boar and the Ram, The. FM; NOEC; PAI; PPON
Fabrication of Ancestors. Alan Dugan. NoAM
Fabulary Satire IV. Daryl Hine. NOBC
Fabulists, The. Kipling. ChMP
Fabulla, sweet virgin, you have learned your lesson too well. The Too Literal Pupil. Martial, *tr. by* Louis Untermeyer. UnTE
Fabullus I will treat you handsomely. Catullus, *tr. fr. Latin by* Richard Lovelace. OBVE
Fabulous Teamsters, The. Judith Johnson Sherwin. NYP
Fabulous Wizard of Oz, The. *Unknown.* QQQ; TDH
Façade, *sels.* Edith Sitwell.
Hornpipe. FaBoMo; GTBS-P; MoVE; OAEL-2; SeCePo
Sir Beelzebub. BoWoP; CoBMV; HoPM; MoAB; MoBrPo; OxBTC; PrIm
(When Sir Beelzebub.) FaBoMo
Waltz. OAEP
Face, A. Robert Browning. CTC
Face, The. Anthony Euwer. *See* As a Beauty I Am Not a Star.
Face, The. Karoniaktatie. STE
Face, The. Philip Levine. DiL
Face, A. Marianne Moore. PoCh
Face. Robert Morgan. GeTw
Face, The. Edwin Muir. ChMP; GTBS-P
Face, The. Lucien Stryk. GP
Face. Jean Toomer. CDC; NoP
Face against the Pane, The. Thomas Bailey Aldrich. TreFS
Face in a Mirror. Jack L. Anderson. LFAC
Face in the Mirror, The. Robert Graves. NoP; WeW
Face is quite smooth, The. Goethe's Death Mask. Linda Gregg. MAYP
Face Lift. Sylvia Plath. InPK
Face of all the world is changed, I think, The. Elizabeth Barrett Browning. Sonnets from the Portuguese, VII. CTC; HBV-1; OAEP; VLP
Face of Helen, The. Christopher Marlowe. *See* Was This the Face.
Face of Love, The. Ingrid Jonker, *tr. fr. Afrikaans by* Jack Cope. PeSA
Face of Poverty. Lucy Smith. NNP; PoNe
Face of the landscape is a mask, The. Mask. Stephen Spender. MoAB; MoBrPo
Face of the precipice is black with lovers, The. Salvador Dali [*or* In Defence of Humanism]. David Gascoyne. EAS; FaBoMo; OxBTC
Face of the Waters, The. Robert D. Fitzgerald. CBAP; PoAu-2
Face on the Daguerreotype. Norman Rosten. HoAn
Face on the Floor, The. Hugh D'Arcy. *See* Face upon the Floor, the.
Face-Paintings of the Caduveo Indians. William Dickey. FAZ
Face sings, alone, The. A Poem for Willie Best. Amiri Baraka. CAPP
Face that should content me wonders [*or* wonderous] well, A. Epigram. Thomas Wyatt. CTC; EnLoPo; OBSC
Face the Nation. Allen Ginsberg. *Fr.* Wichita Vortex Sutra. NaP
Face to Face. Frances Cochrane. HBV-1
Face to Face. Adrienne Rich. LiTM; NoP
Face to face in my chamber, my silent chamber, I saw her. Confessions. Elizabeth Barrett Browning. OBVV
Face to Face with Reality. John Oxenham. WBLP
Face upon [*or* on] the Floor, The. Hugh Antoine D'Arcy. BeLS; BLPA; FaBoBe; FaFP; FPL; HBV-2; PaPo; TreF; YaD
Faceless miner. For Laurence Jones. Gary Kizer. CTBA
Faces. Jack L. Anderson. LFAC
Faces. D. C. Berry. BXAP
Faces. John Ciardi. BiP; WeW
Faces. Walt Whitman. PoEL-5
Faces and the hands of her grandchildren, The. Belita. Alberto Ríos. LTB
Faces from a Bestiary. X. J. Kennedy. NePoEA-2
Faces in the Street. Henry Lawson. CBAP
Faces irresolute and unperplexed. In the National Gallery. Siegfried Sassoon. NoAM
Faces may alter, names can't change. Nathaniel Lee to Sir Roger L'Estrange. Nathaniel Lee. FaBoEE
Faces Seen Once. James Dickey. UnPo
Faces surround me that have no smell or color no time. Chain. Audre Lorde. BlSi
Faces, voices, yes of course. The House Remembers. Robert Francis. DFF
Facing a streetlight under batty moths. The Calculation. David Wagoner. NYBP
Facing the Chair. "Hugh MacDiarmid." FaBoMo
Facing the Gulf. Margaret L. Woods. *Fr.* The Return. HBMV
Facing the New Year. Mark Guy Pearse. BLRP
Facing the New Year. *Unknown.* PGD
Facing the sudden gulf, the silent. Facing the Gulf. Margaret L. Woods. *Fr.* The Return. HBMV
Facing West from California's Shore. Walt Whitman. MoAmPo; TAP
Facing you/ I am not jealous. Always. Pablo Neruda, *tr. by* Donald D. Walsh. OLR
Fact. Kenneth Rexroth. OBAL
Fact is, The. Some Me of Beauty. Carolyn M. Rodgers. CNA
Fact of this man having made, The. The Lift. Raymond Souster. POL
Faction, that ever dwells. Love and Fortune. Fulke Greville. *Fr.* Caelica. EnRePo; OBSC
Factories. Edward Hirsch. AMV-81
Factories, The. Margaret Widdemer. HBV-2
Factory, The. Olga Cabral. GP
Factory Girl, The. J. A. Phillips. SaC
Factory Girl, The. *Unknown.* FSW; SaC
Factory Girl's Come-All-Ye, The. *Unknown.* AmFP; OBAL
Factory Rainbow, A. Rose Saadi. SaC
Factory Windows Are Always Broken. Vachel Lindsay. CrMA; FaFP; LiTA; NePA; OBCA
Facts. "Lewis Carroll." FaBoUs
Facts. W. H. Davies. BrPo
Facts have no eyes. One must. Observation of Facts. Charles Tomlinson. NePoEA-2
Fade in the sound of summer music. Notes for a Movie Script. M. Carl Holman. AmNP; PoBA; PoNe

Faded boy in sallow clothes, A. Emily Dickinson. PoEL-5
Faded Face, The. Thomas Hardy. QFR
Faded Pictures. William Vaughn Moody. AP
Fading Beauty. Giambattista Marini, *tr. fr. Italian by* Samuel Daniel. AWP
Fading Beauty. *Unknown.* FaBoEE
Fading-Leaf and Fallen-Leaf. Richard Garnett. EBVV; OBVV
Fading light/ Dims the sight. Words for Army Bugle Calls: Taps. *Unknown.* TreF
Fading Rose, The, *sel.* Philip Freneau.
Epitaph: "Here—for they could not help but die." AA
Fading whistles outline our broken city, The. Poem from London, 1941. George Woodcock. NeBP
Faerie Queene, The, *sel.* Robin Blaser.
"Okay a nightingale." CoPo
Faerie Queene, The, *sels.* Spenser.
Address to Venus, *fr.* IV, 10, *tr. fr. the Latin of* Lucretius, *fr.* De Rerum Natura. AWP
(Prayer to Venus.) EIL
"And is there care in heaven? and is there love," *fr.* II, 8. NOCV; OAEL-1; OxBoCh
(Bright Squadrons, The.) GoBC
(Guardian Angels.) OBSC
Artegall and Radigund, *fr.* V, 5. OBSC
"At length nigh to the sea they drew," *fr.* V, 2. NoP
August, *fr.* VII, 7. GN
Autumn, *fr.* VII, 7. GN
"Ay me, how many perils doe unfold," *fr.* I, 8. OAEL-1
Balme, *fr.* I, 11. CH
Behold, O Man, *fr.* II, 6. EIL
Bower of Bliss, The, *fr.* II, 12. CH; FaBoEn; FiP; LoBV; OBSC; PoEL-1
("Eftsoones they heard a most melodious sound.") NOBE; SCV; ViBoPo
(Gather the Rose.) WHA
Britomart in the House of Busirane, *fr.* III, 11-12. FiP
Cave of Despair, The, *fr.* I, 9. LoBV, *longer sel.*; NOBE; OBNV. *longer sel.*
("Ere long they come, where that same wicked wight.") OAEL-1
(To Be or Not to Be.) FaBoEn
Cave of Mammon, The, II, 7. FiP, *sts.* 21-32; PoEL-1
("As pilot well expert in perilous wave.") OAEL-1
Cymochles and Phaedria, *fr.* II, 6. OBSC
Dame Nature, *fr.* VII, 7. PoEL-1
Dance of the Graces, The, *fr.* VI, 10. OBSC
(Dance, The.) TrGrPo
Death of the Dragon, The, *fr.* II, 11. WHA
Despair, *fr.* I, 9. SeCePo
(To Be or Not to Be.) FaBoEn
Dragon, The, *fr.* I, 11. SeCePo
Envy, *fr.* I, 4. TW
"Faire sir," quoth she, "be not displeased at all," *fr.* II, 6. MOS
Fight of the Red Cross Knight and the Heathen Sansjoy, The, *fr.* I, 5. FiP
("Noble heart that harbors virtuous thought, The.") ViBoPo
Garden of Adonis, *fr.* III, 6. NOBE; PoEL-1
Garden of Proserpina, The, *fr.* II, 7. ChTr
Gather the Rose ("The whiles some one did chant this lovely lay"), *fr.* II, 12. EIL
"Gentle knight was pricking on the plaine, A," *fr.* I, 1. EBEV; OAEL-1
(Red Cross Knight, The, 2 *sts.*) GoBC
Happy Isle, *fr.* IV, 10. OBSC
"Hard is the doubt, and difficult to deeme," *fr.* IV, 9. OAEL-1
"He there now does enjoy eternal rest," *fr.* I, 9. MOS
(Sleep after Toil.) ChTr
Hill of the Graces, *fr.* VI, 10. NOBE
House of Ate, The, *fr.* VI, 1. OBSC
House of Pride, The, *fr.* I, 4. WHA
House of Richesse, The, *fr.* II, 7. CH
"In such luxurious plentie of all pleasure," *fr.* IV, 10. OAEL-1
"It fortuned (as faire it then befell)," *fr.* I, 11. OAEL-1
Kinds of Trees to Plant, *fr.* I, 1. OHIP
Legend of Sir Guyon, The; or, Of Temperance, II, 12, *abr.* WHA
Legend of the Knight of the Red Cross, or of Holiness, The, I, 1-12. OAEP
(Invocation to the Faerie Queene.) FiP
("Lo! I the man, whose muse whilome did maske.") OAEL-1
"Like as a ship, that through the ocean wyde," *fr.* VI, 12. EtS; MOS
"Like as the tide that comes from th' ocean main," *fr.* IV, 3. HoPM
Malbecco and Hekkenore, *fr.* III, 9-10. NoP
"Mammon emovèd was with inward wrath," *fr.* II, 7. ViBoPo
Mask [*or* Masque] of Cupid, The, *fr.* III, 12. NOBE; OBSC; PoEL-1
Mask of Mutability, The, *fr.* VII, 7. OBSC
(Seasons, The.) GN
May, *fr.* VII, 7. GN
Mermaids, The, *fr.* II, 12. ChTr
Mutability ("For, all that from her springs, and is ybredde"), *fr.* VII, 7 *and* 8. FaBoEn
Mutability ("When these were past, thus gan the Titanesse"), *fr.* VII, 7 *and* 8. PoEL-1
Nature's Reply to Mutability, *fr.* VII, 7 *and* VIII, 1. NOBE
"Next to him was Neptune pictured," *fr.* III, 11. EtS
"Nought is on the earth more sacred or divine," *fr.* V, 7. OAEL-1
"Now, at the time that was before agreed," *fr.* VII, 7. OAEL-1
"Now strike your sailes, ye jolly mariners," *fr.* I, 12 *and* II, 6. EtS; MOS
"O what an endelesse worke have I in hand," *fr.* IV, 12. MOS
Old January, *fr.* VII, 7. YeAr
Pastoral, A: "From thence into the open fields he fled," *fr.* VI, 9. OBSC
Port after Stormie Seas, *fr.* I, 9. EtS
("What if some little paine the passage have.") CH; PoPle
Prince Arthur, *fr.* I, 7. OBSC
"Right well I wrote, most mighty soveraine," *fr.* II, *induction.* OAEL-1
Rivers Come to the Hall of Proteus for the Marriage of the Thames and the Medway, The, *fr.* IV, 2. FaBoPP
"Rugged forhead that with grave foresight, The," *fr.* IV, *proem.* OAEL-1
(Love.) OBSC
Sea Monsters, *fr.* II, 12. ChTr; FaBoEn
"So as they travelled, the drouping night," *fr.* IV, 5. OAEL-1
"So forth she comes, and to her coche does clyme," *fr.* I, 4. OAEL-1
"So oft as I with state of present time," *fr.* V, *proem.* OAEL-1
Song of Bliss, *fr.* II, 12. FF
("Whiles some one did chaunt this lovely lay, The.") OBVE
"Sudden upriseth from her stately palace," *fr.* I, 4. PPP
Summer, *br. sel. fr.* VII, 7. GN
Temple of Venus, The, *fr.* IV, 10. EIL; WHA
"Then said that royall Pere in sober wise," *fr.* I, 12. OAEL-1
"Thence forward by that painfull way they pas," *fr.* I, 10. OAEL-1
"There the most daintie Paradise on ground," *fr.* II, 12. EBEV
"They sate to meat, and Satyrane his chaunce," *fr.* III, 9. OAEL-1
"Tho when as chearelesse night ycovered had," *fr.* III, 12. OAEL-1
"Thus being entered, they behold around." OAEL-1
"Well may I weene, faire ladies, all this while," *fr.* III, 6. OAEL-1
"When I bethinke me on that speech whyleare," *fr.* VII, 8. OAEL-1; OxBoCh
"Who now does follow the foule Blatant Beast," *fr.* VI, 10. OAEL-1
Winter, *fr.* VII, 7. GN
Faerie's Child, The. Thomas Caulfield Irwin. OnYI
Faery Beam upon You, The. Ben Jonson. *Fr.* The Gypsies Metamorphosed. EBEV; TEP
(Faeries' Song, The.) SeCV-1
(Gipsy Song.) FaBoCh
(Patrico's Song.) LoBV
Faery Queen, The. Sir Walter Ralegh. *See* Vision upon This Conceit of the Faerie Queene, A.
Faëry Reaper, The. Robert Buchanan. OBVV
Faery Song. Keats. *See* Fairy Song.
Faery Song, A. W. B. Yeats. *See* Fairy Song.
Faeryes Farewell, The; or, God-a-Mercy Will. Richard Corbet. *See* Fairies' Farwell, The.
Faeryland. Robert Pinsky. MAYP
Faesulan Idyl. Walter Savage Landor. *See* Fiesolan Idyl, A.
Fag-End. Philip O'Connor. EAS
Faggots in Ancient Rome. Juvenal, *tr. fr. Latin. Fr.* The Satires, II. PeHV
Fagots blazed, the caldron's smoke, The. The Brewing of Soma. Whittier. PoEL-4
Faht's in there? What's in There? *Unknown.* CH
Failed Fathers. Lewis Turco. AMV-81
Failing Long Island light, The. Mother and Son. William Heyen. GeTw
Failing the Examination. Meng Chiao, *tr. fr. Chinese by* Stephen Owen. GLGT
Failure. Rupert Brooke. ILwL
Failure, A. C. Day Lewis. NOBE
Failure. Richmond Lattimore. PCP
Failure. E. L. Mayo. FAZ
Failure. Eithne Wilkins. NeBP
Failures. Arthur W. Upson. HBV-2; WGRP
Fain I Would. *Unknown.* EIL
Fain we ask Erinn. The Incantation. *At. to* Amergin, *tr. by* George Sigerson. OnYI
Fain would I be sleeping, dreaming. The Plaint of the Wife. *Unknown, tr. by* W. R. S. Ralston. AWP
Fain Would I Change That Note. *Unknown, at. to* Tobias Hume. EIL; ELP; OBS; PoEL-2; ViBoPo
(Devotion.) LiTB; OBEV
(No Other Choice.) EBEV; GBL; NOBE; TrGrPo
(Omnia Vincit.) GoBC
(Song.) HBV-1

Fain would I have a pretty thing. A Proper Song, Entitled: Fain Would I Have a Pretty Thing to Give unto My Lady. *Unknown.* CoMu; ElL; InvP; OAEP; ViBoPo
Fain would I kiss my Julia's dainty leg. Her Legs. Robert Herrick. SpRo
Fain would I ride with thee,/ Eivlin a rúin. Eileen Aroon. Carrol O'Daly, *tr. by* George Sigerson. OnYI
Fain Would I Wed a Fair Young Man. Thomas Campion. UnTE
Fain would I write, my mind ashamèd is. The Song of Mary the Mother of Christ. *At. to* Henry Walpole. ISi
Fain Would My Thoughts. John Austin. OxBoCh
Fainne Gael an Lae. Alice Milligan. HBV-2
Faint as a climate-changing bird that flies. Demeter and Persephone. Tennyson. VLP
Faint, faint and clear. The Wind-swept Wheat. "Madeline Bridges." AA
Faint Falls the Gentle Voice, *with music.* Henry Timrod. AH
Faint Heart. *See* Faintheart.
Faint Music. Walter de la Mare. FaBoCh
Faint shines the far moon. The Road. Nikolay Platonovich Ogarev, *tr. by* P. E. Matheson. AWP
Faint yet Pursuing. Coventry Patmore. The Unknown Eros, XXV. OxBoCh
Faint Heart. William James Linton. OBVV
Faint Heart. Rufinus, *tr. fr. Greek* by F. A. Wright. ErPo
Faintheart in a Railway Train. Thomas Hardy. CTC; EnLoPo
Faint heart wins not lady fair. Faint Heart. William James Linton. OBVV
Faintly and from Far Away. Vassar Miller. CoPo
Faintly as tolls the evening chime. A Canadian Boat Song. Thomas Moore. GoBC; HBV-1; OBRV
Faintly the ne'er-do-well. The Flute of the Lonely. Vachel Lindsay. CrMA
Fair/ Boy Christian Takes a Break. Jim Harrison. NoAM
Fair am I, mortals, as a stone-carved dream. La Beauté. Baudelaire, *tr. by* Lord Alfred Douglas. AWP
Fair Amazon of Heaven who tookst in hand. To Saint Margaret. Henry Constable. ACP; GoBC
Fair Amoret is gone astray. A Hue and Cry after Fair Amoret [*or* Amoret]. Congreve. NOEC; OBEC; OBEV; ViBoPo
Fair and bright assembly, A: never strode. Thomas Lovell Beddoes. *Fr.* Death's Jest Book, II, iii. CTC
Fair and Cruel, still in vain. Ode to Chloris. Charles Cotton. CavP
Fair and Fair. George Peele. *Fr.* The Arraignment of Paris. ElL; OBEV; ViBoPo
(Oenone and Paris.) NOBE
(Song of Oenone and Paris.) OBSC
Fair and Free Elections. *Unknown.* FSW
Fair, and Soft, and Gay, and Young. Robert Gould. UnTE
Fair and Unfair. Robert Francis. VGW
Fair angels pass'd by next in seemly bands. The Annunciation. Abraham Cowley. *Fr.* Davideis. OxBoCh
Fair Annie. *Unknown.* BSV; CH; ESPB (A, B, *and* E *vers.*); FaBoBa; HBV-2; OxBB; ViBoFo (A *and* C *vers.*)
Fair Annie an Sweet Willie. Lord Thomas and Fair Annet. *Unknown.* ESPB
Fair Annie had a costly bower. The Holy Nunnery. *Unknown.* BaBo; ESPB
Fair Annie of Lochyran. *Unknown.* *See* Lass of Lochroyan, The.
Fair are the flowers and the children, but their subtle suggestion is fairer. Indirection. Richard Realf. AA; HBV-2
Fair as the night, when all the astral fires. Love Sonnets, VIII. Charles Harpur. PoAu-1
Fair at Windgap, The. Austin Clarke. OnYI; OxBTC; SeCePo
Fair Beauty Bride, The. *Unknown.* AmFP
Fair below Helvellyn, The. Wordsworth. *Fr.* The Prelude, VII. FaBoPP
Fair blue sky, A. Breeze and Billow. Albert Durrant Watson. CaP
Fair by inheritance, whom born we see. Of the Nativity of the Lady Rich's Daughter. Henry Constable. OBSC
Fair Caroline, I wonder what. To C. F. H. on Her Christening-Day. Thomas Hardy. NAs
Fair Cassidy. *Unknown, tr. fr. Irish by* Donagh MacDonagh. BIrV
Fair Circassian, The. Richard Garnett. HBV-1; OBVV
Fair Cloris in a pig-stye lay. A Song to Cloris. Earl of Rochester. ErPo
Fair [*or* Fayre] copy of my Celia's face. To T. H., a Lady Resembling My Mistress. Thomas Carew. AnAnS-2; CaPo
Fair cousin mine! the golden days. Chivalry at a Discount. Edward Fitzgerald. HBV-1
Fair Cynthia, all the Homage that I may. Thoughts on the Sight of the Moon. Sarah Kemble Knight. SCAP
Fair Cynthia mounted on her sprightly pad. Cynthia on Horseback. Philip Ayres. EnLoPo
Fair daffodils [*or* Faire daffadills], we weep to see. To Daffodils. Robert Herrick. AnAnS-2; AWP; BoNaP; CaPo; ELP; EvOK; FaBoCh; FaBoEn; GN; GoJo; GTBS; GTBS-P; HBV-1; HBVY; InPS; JCP; LiTB; LoBV; NOBE; NoP; OAEP; OBEV; OBS; PoEL-3; PoRA; PPP; QFR; SeCeV; SeCP; SeCV-1; TrGrPo; UnPo; ViBoPo; WHA
Fair Damsel from London, The. *Unknown.* AmFP
Fair Danubie is praised for being wide. Rivers. Thomas Storer. ElL; FaBoCh
Fair Days; or, Dawns Deceitful. Robert Herrick. CaPo
Fair Ellen Irwin, when she sate. Ellen Irwin; or, The Braes of Kirtle. Wordsworth. PeD
Fair Ellender. *Unknown.* FSW
Fair England. Helen Gray Cone. AA
Fair Eve knelt close by the guarded gate. The Rose of Eden. Susan K. Phillips. BeLS
Fair Exchange, A. La Fontaine. UnTE
Fair eyes, sweet lips, dear heart, that foolish I. Astrophel and Stella, XLIII. Sir Philip Sidney. SiPS
Fair fa' your honest, sonsie face. Address to a Haggis. Burns. ViBoPo
Fair fields, proud Flora's vaunt, why is't you smile. Menaphon's Ditty. Robert Greene. *Fr.* Menaphon. OBSC
Fair Florella or the Jealous Lover. *Unknown.* *See* Florella; or, The Jealous Lover.
Fair flower of fifteen springs, that still. To His Young Mistress. Pierre de Ronsard, *tr. by* Andrew Lang. AWP
Fair Flower of Northumberland, The. *Unknown.* ESPB; OxBB
Fair flower, that dost so comely grow. The Wild Honeysuckle. Philip Freneau. AA; AmPP; AP; BLPL; HBV-1; LiTA; NOBA; OxBA; PoEL-4; PoLF; TAP; TrGrPo
Fair girl tripping out to meet her love, A. The Power of Interval. Lord De Tabley. VLP
Fair Golden Age! when milk was the only food. The Golden Age. Giovanni Battista Guarini, *tr. by* Sir Richard Fanshawe. *Fr.* Il Pastor Fido. OAEL-1; OBVE
Fair golden thoughts and lovely words. About Women. H. Phelps Putnam. TwAmPo
Fair Hebe. John West. HBV-1
Fair Helen. *Unknown.* *See* Helen of Kirconnell.
Fair Hills of Eiré, O, The. James Clarence Mangan. OBVV
Fair Hills of Ireland, The. *Unknown, tr. fr. Modern Irish by* Sir Samuel Ferguson. AnIV; FaBoPP; OBEV; OBVV; OnYI
Fair hope! our earlyer heav'n by thee. Richard Crashaw. *Fr.* M. Crashaw's Answer for Hope. FaBoEn
Fair Ines. Thomas Hood. EnRP; HBV-1; OBEV; OBRV; OBVV
Fair Iris and Her Swain. Dryden. *See* Song: "Fair Iris I love, and hourly I die."
"Fair is Alexis," I no sooner said. On Alexis. Plato, *tr. by* Thomas Stanley. AWP
Fair is each budding thing the garden shows. The Old-fashioned Garden. John Russell Hayes. AA
Fair is her body, bright her eye. Medieval Norman Song. *Unknown, tr. by* John Addington Symonds. AWP
Fair is my dove, my loved one. Marriage Song. Judah Halevi, *tr. by* Alice Lucas. TrJP
Fair Is My Love. Samuel Daniel. To Delia, VI. AAS; EnRePo; HBV-1; LiTB; NOBE; NoP; OAEP; OBSC; TEP; TrGrPo
(Beauty, Time and Love.) OBEV
(Sonnet: "Fair is my love, and cruel as she's fair.") ElL; HoPM; PoEL-2; ViBoPo
Fair Is My Love. Robert Greene. *See* Fair Is My Love for April's in Her Face.
Fair Is My Love. Shakespeare. *Fr.* The Passionate Pilgrim. ElL
Fair Is My Love for April's in Her Face. Robert Greene. *Fr.* Perimedes. HBV-1
(Fair Is My Love.) ElL
(Sonnet: "Fair is my love, for April's in her face.") ViBoPo
Fair [*or* Faire] is my love that feeds among the lilies. Fidessa, More Chaste than Kind, XXXVII. Bartholomew Griffin. ElL; ErPo; GBL; PoEL-2; TrGrPo; ViBoPo
Fair [*or* Fayre] is my love, when her fair golden heares. Amoretti, LXXXI. Spenser. ElL; NOP
Fair is not my face. A Woman Grows Soon Old. Larin Paraske, *tr. by* Jaakko A. Ahokas. PBWP
Fair is the hue of your mantle, Mary. The Mantle of Mary. Patrick O'Connor. ISi
Fair is the night, and fair the day. Song. William Morris. *Fr.* The Earthly Paradise: October. HBV-1
Fair Is the Rose. *Unknown.* ElL
Fair is the white star of twilight. The Heart's Friend. Mary Austin, *after Shoshone Indian.* BPAW
Fair Is the World. William Morris. FaBoRV
(Autumn on the Upper Thames.) FaBoPP
Fair Is Too Foul an Epithet. Christopher Marlowe. *Fr.* Tamburlaine the Great, Pt. I, Act V. LiTB
("Ah, fair Zenocrate, divine Zenocrate.") EBEV; PoEL-2; ViBoPo

Fair Isabel, poor simple Isabel! Isabella; or, The Pot of Basil. Keats. EnRP; ViBoPo
Fair Isabel sat in her bower door. Hind Etin. *Unknown.* OxBB
Fair Isabell of Rochroyall. *Unknown. See* Lass of Lochroyan, The.
Fair Janet. *Unknown.* ESPB (A *and* B *vers.*); OxBB, *with music*
Fair lady Isabel sits in her bower sewing. Lady Isabel and the Elf-Knight. *Unknown.* ESPB; FaBoBa; OAEP; ViBoFo
Fair [*or* Faire] lady, when you see the grace. To One Admiring Herself in a Looking Glass. Thomas Randolph. AnAnS-2; ViBoPo
Fair lady, will you travel. The Wooing of Etain. *Unknown, tr. by* John Montague. BIrV
Fair lady with the bandaged eye. Ode to Fortune. Fitz-Greene Halleck *and* Joseph Rodman Drake. *Fr.* The Croaker Papers. AA
Fair Lass of Islington, The. *Unknown. See* Lass of Islington, The.
Fair little girl sat under a tree, A. Good Night and Good Morning. Richard Monckton Milnes. OxBChV
Fair lovely maid, or if that title be. To the Fair Clarinda, Who Made Love to Me, Imagin'd More than Woman. Aphra Behn. SBG
Fair Lucy was sitting in her own cabin door. Lizie Wan. AmFP
Fair Lunacy! I see thee, with a crown. Mirthful Lunacy. Thomas Stoddart. *Fr.* The Death-Wake; or, Lunacy. OBNC
Fair Maid and the Sun, The. Arthur O'Shaughnessy. BeLS
Fair Maid by the Seashore, The. *Unknown.* BaBo
(Fair Maid by the Shore, The.) AmFP
Fair maid, had I not heard thy baby cries. To a Lofty Beauty, from Her Poor Kinsman. Hartley Coleridge. OBVV
Fair maid in a garden walking, A. A Sweetheart in the Army. *Unknown.* BaBo
Fair Maid of Amsterdam, The. *Unknown.* OxBoLi
(A-Roving.) FSW; ShS, *vers.* I, *with music*
(Maid of Amsterdam, *with music.*) AmSS
Fair Maid of the Exchange, *sel. Unknown, at. to* Thomas Heywood.
Ye Little Birds That Sit and Sing. ElL; ViBoPo
(Message, The.) HBV-1
Fair Maid of the West, The. *Unknown.* CoMu
Fair maid sat in her bower-door, A. The False Lover Won Back. *Unknown.* BaBo; ESPB
Fair Maiden. George Peele. *See* Song at the Well, The.
Fair maiden, fair maiden. Invocation to the Muse. Richard Hughes. MoBrPo
Fair maiden, white and red. A Voice [Speaks] from the Well. George Peele. *Fr.* The Old Wives' Tale. FaBoCh; NOBE; OBSC; OxBoLi
Fair Maiden, Who Is This Bairn? *Unknown.* ISi
Fair Margaret and Sweet William. *Unknown.* AmFP; ESPB (A *and* B *vers.*); OBET; OxBB, *with music;* ViBoFo
Fair Margret was a young ladye. Proud Margret [*or* Proud Lady Margaret]. *Unknown.* ESPB; OxBB
Fair Marjorie sat i her bower-door. Young Benjie. *Unknown.* ESPB
Fair Mary of Wallington. *Unknown.* ESPB (A *and* C *vers.*)
(Bonny Earl of Livingston, The.) OxBB
Fair Mary sat at her father's castle gate. Willie of Winsbury. *Unknown.* AmFP
Fair Morning, The. Jones Very. NOBA
Fair Mother Earth lay on her back last night. Ode to the Spirit of Earth in Autumn. George Meredith. TEP; VLP
Fair now is the springtide, now earth lies beholding. The Message of the March Wind. William Morris. OBNC; OBVV; WiR
Fair Nymph Scorning a Black Boy Courting Her, A. John Cleveland. AnAnS-2
Fair of face, full of pride. A Lyke-Wake Song. Swinburne. PAI
Fair, order'd lights (whose motion without noise). The Constellation. Henry Vaughan. SeCV-1
Fair Pamela came to town, The. Pamela in Town. Ellen Mackay Hutchinson Cortissoz. AA; HBV-1
Fair Penitent, The, *sel.* Nicholas Rowe.
Song: "Ah stay! ah turn! ah whither would you fly," *by* Congreve. LoBV; OBEC
Fair Phoebe and Her Dark-eyed Sailor. *Unknown.* AmFP
Fair Phyllis I saw sitting all alone. *Unknown.* GBL
Fair [*or* Faire] pledges of a fruitful tree. To Blossoms. Robert Herrick. BoNaP; CaPo; GTBS; GTBS-P; HBV-1; JCP; LoBV; OBEV; OBS; SeCP; SeCV-1
Fair princess of the spacious air. The Falcon. Richard Lovelace. CaPo; PB; PBBP
Fair rebel to thyself and time. The Revenge. Pierre de Ronsard, *tr. by* Thomas Stanley. AWP
Fair, Rich, and Young. Sir John Harington, *after the Latin of* Martial. ElL; NIP; PV; SeCePo
(Of a Fair Shrew.) FaBoEE
Fair rocks, goodly rivers, sweet woods, when shall I see peace? Echo. Sir Philip Sidney. *Fr.* Arcadia. SiPS
Fair Roslin Chapel, how divine. Roslin and Hawthornden. Henry van Dyke. AA
Fair Salamis, the billow's roar. Chorus. Sophocles, *tr. by* Winthrop Mackworth Praed. *Fr.* Ajax. AWP
Fair seed-time had my soul, and I grew up. Introduction—Childhood and School-Time [*or* On the Solitary Fells around Hawkshead]. Wordsworth. *Fr.* The Prelude, I. FaBoEn; FaBoPP; HAP; NOBE; NoP; OAEP; OBNC; OBRV; PoEL-4
Fair, shining mountains of my pilgrimage. The Brecon Beacons and the Black Mountains. Henry Vaughan. FaBoPP
Fair ship, that from the Italian shore. In Memoriam A. H. H., IX. Tennyson. PeHV
Fair Singer, The. Andrew Marvell. CavP; EnLoPo; MeLP; MePo; NOBE; NoP; PoEL-2; PoPle
Fair Sou-Chong-Tee, by a shimmering brook. Story of the Flowery Kingdom. James Branch Cabell. HBMV; OnMSP
Fair stands the wind again. Henley, July 4: 1914–1964. L. E. Sissman. PrIm
Fair star, new-risen to our wondering eyes. Bacchylides. George Meason Whicher. AA
Fair star of evening, splendour of the west. Composed by the Sea-Side, near Calais, August 1802. Wordsworth. EnRP; OAEP
Fair [*or* Faire] stood the wind for France. Agincourt [*or* The Ballad of Agincourt *or* To the Cambro-Britons]. Michael Drayton. BeLS; ElL; EnRePo; FaBoBe; FaBoCh; FaPoR; GN; GoTL; HBV-2; OAEP; OBEV; OBNV; OBS; OBWP; PoRA; PrIm; WHA
Fair Summer Droops. Thomas Nashe. *Fr.* Summer's Last Will and Testament. ElL; LoBV
(Waning Summer.) OBSC
Fair sun, if you would have me praise your light. Henry Constable. *Fr.* Diana. OBSC
Fair, sweet and young, receive a prize. A Song. Dryden. OBS
Fair Sylvia. *Unknown.* OBS
Fair, that you may truly know. To Amoret. Edmund Waller. SeCV-1
Fair the gift to Merlin given. Merlin's Apple-Trees. Thomas Love Peacock. *Fr.* The Misfortunes of Elphin. OBRV
Fair, the young acacia, thick with leaves. The Young Acacia. Hayyim Nahman Bialik, *tr. by* Helena Frank. TrJP
Fair these broad meads—these hoary woods are grand. Canadian Boat Song. *Unknown, at. to* John Galt *and also to* "Christopher North." BSV; GoTS; OxBS
Fair Thief, The. Charles Wyndham. HBV-1
Fair Thou Art. Mordecai ben Isaac, *tr. fr. Hebrew by* Herbert Loewe. TrJP
Fair-tinted cheeks, clear eyelids drawn. Cimabuella. Bayard Taylor. BXAP
Fair Tree! for thy delightful shade. The Tree. Countess of Winchilsea. OBEC
Fair Ursly, in a merry mood. Annibal Cruceius, *tr. fr. Latin.* FaBoEE
Fair Virgin/ Vestured with the sun! Ode to the Virgin. Petrarch, *tr. by* Helen Lee Peabody. *Fr.* Sonnets to Laura: To Laura in Death. ISi
Fair Virtue, the Mistress of Philarete, *sels.* George Wither.
Divided Heart, The. TrGrPo
Hence, Away, You Sirens, *also given in* Fidelia. ElL
Shall I Wasting in Despair, *also given in* Fidelia. ElL; LiTB; OBS; WHA
(Author's Resolution, The.) AWP; HBV-1; InMe; OBEV; TreFS
(Lover's Resolution, A.) BoLoP; NOBE
(Manly Heart, The.) FaBV; GTBS; GTBS-P
("Shall I, wasting in despair.") PoPle
(Sonnet: "Shall I, wasting in despair.") SeCV-1
(What Care I.) TrGrPo
Stolen Kiss, The. HBV-1
(Kiss, The.) UnTE
Fair Warning, A. E. L. Mayo. FAZ
Fair was the dawn, and but e'en now the skies. Fair Days; or, Dawns Deceitful. Robert Herrick. CaPo
Fair was this young wyf, and therwithal. Chaucer. *Fr.* The Canterbury Tales: The Miller's Tale. EBEV
Fair Weather. Dorothy Parker. SGB
Fair were our visions! Oh, they were as grand. In the Land Where We Were Dreaming. Daniel B. Lucas. PAH
Fair would I have a pretty thing. A Pretty Thing. *Unknown.* UnTE
Faire as unshaded Light; or as the Day. To the Queene, Entertain'd at Night by the Countesse of Anglesey. Sir William Davenant. FaBoEn; MeLP; MePo; OBS
Faire daffadills, we weep to see. *See* Fair daffodils. . .
Faire is my love that feeds among the lilies. *See* Fair is my love . . .
Faire lady when you see the grace. *See* Fair lady, when . . .
Faire pledges of a fruitfull Tree. *See* Fair pledges . . .
"Faire sir," quoth she, "be not displeasd at all." Spenser. *Fr.* The Faerie Queene, II, 6. MOS
Faire soule, how long shall veyles thy graces shroud? At Home in Heaven. Robert Southwell. AnAnS-1

Faire stood the wind for France. *See* Fair stood the wind . . .
Faire Virtue. *See* Fair Virtue . . .
Fairest action of our human life, The. Lady Elizabeth Carey. *Fr.* Mariam, IV. WPE
Fairest between Lincoln and Lindsey. *Unknown.* *See* When the Nightingale Sings.
Fairest day that ever yet has shone, The. The Lost. Jones Very. NOBA; QFR
Fairest Flower, The. John Audelay. OxBM
Fairest flower, all flowers excelling. To a Child Five Years Old. Nathaniel Cotton. OxBChV
Fairest isle, all isles excelling. Song of Venus. Dryden. *Fr.* King Arthur. LoBV; OxBoLi; PoEL-3; SeCeV
Fairest Lord Jesus. *Unknown, tr. fr. German.* TRV; WGRP
Fairest of Freedom's Daughters. Jeremiah Eames Rankin. PAH
Fairest of Her Days, The. *Unknown.* ElL
Fairest of morning lights appear. Psalm for Christmas Day. Thomas Pestel. OxBoCh
Fairest of stars, that with your persant light. Balade Simple. John Lydgate. GBL
Fairest of the fairest, rival of the rose. Mabel, in New Hampshire. James Thomas Fields. HBV-1
Fairest thing that shines below. Clad All in White. Abraham Cowley. *Fr.* The Mistress. SeCV-1
Fairfax, whose name in armes through Europe rings. On the Lord Gen. Fairfax at the Siege of Colchester. Milton. OBS
Fairground. W. H. Auden. NYBP
Fair-haired Girl, The. *Unknown, tr. fr. Modern Irish by* Sir Samuel Ferguson. OnYI
Fairies, The. William Allingham. AnIL; CH; ChTr; EvOK; FaBoCh; FaBoPP; FaBV; FaPON; HBV-1; HBVY; NOBE; OBEV; OBVV; OnMSP; OnYI; OxBChV; OxBI; PDV; PoPle; RHPC; RoGo; SUS; ViBoPo; WSC
(Fairy Folk, The.) GN; PaPo
(Up the Airy Mountain.) FaFP
Fairies. Hilda Conkling. TiPo; WSC
Fairies. Rose Fyleman. HBMV; HBVY; OxBChV; SoPo
Fairies, The. Robert Herrick. FaPON; OBS
Fairies, The. Patricia Hubbell. WSC
Fairies. Thomas Tickell. *Fr.* Kensington Garden. OBEC
Fairies Are Dancing All Over the World, The. Michael Rumaker. PeHV
Fairies break their dances, The. A. E. Housman. MoVE; NoAM
Fairies dance the livelong night, The. In the Moonlight. Norreys Jephson O'Conor. HBMV; SoPo; SUS
Fairies' Farewell, The. Richard Corbet. FaBoBa; FaBoCh, *abr.;* LiTB, *abr.;* NOBE; TrGrPo, *abr.;* ViBoPo, *abr.*
(Faeryes Farewell, The; or, God-a-Mercy Will.) SeCP
(Farewell, Rewards and Fairies.) LoBV; PoPle, *abr.*
(Farewell to the Fairies.) EvOK, *abr.;* HBV-1, *abr.;* HBVY, *abr.;* MoShBr, *abr.*
(Proper New Ballad Intituled the Faeryes Farewell, A.) AnAnS-2
(Proper New Ballad, A, Intituled the Fairies Farewell; or, God-a-Mercy Will.) OBS; OxBoLi
Fairies' Feast, The. Charles M. Doughty. CH
Fairies Have Never a Penny to Spend, The. Rose Fyleman. FaPON; HBMV; OxBoChV
Fairies in New Ross, The. *Unknown.* OnYI
Fairies' Lullaby, The. Shakespeare. *See* You Spotted Snakes.
Fairies of the Caldon-Low, The. Mary Howitt. BeLS; HBV-1; HBVY
Fairies' Shopping, The. Margaret Deland. HBVY
Fairweill. *Unknown.* OxBS
Fairy and the soul proceeded, The. The Magic Car Moved On. Shelley. *Fr.* Queen Mab. GN
Fairy Artist, The. Nellie M. Garabrant. PoPl
Fairy Blessing, The. Shakespeare. *See* Now the Hungry Lion Roars.
Fairy Book, The. Abbie Farwell Brown. HBV-1; HBVY
Fairy Book, The. Norman Gale. HBV-1; HBVY; OHIP
Fairy Dances. *Unknown.* *See* By the Moon.
Fairy Dawn. Joseph Rodman Drake. *Fr.* The Culprit Fay. GN
Fairy! Fairy! list and mark. The Fay's Crime. Joseph Rodman Drake. *Fr.* The Culprit Fay. GN
Fairy Fiddler, The. Nora Hopper. HBMV; ViBoPo
('Tis I Go Fiddling, Fiddling.) OxBI
Fairy Folk, The. William Allingham. *See* Fairies, The.
Fairy Folk, The. Robert N. Bird. HBV-1; HBVY
Fairy Godmothers. Eugene Lee-Hamilton. OBVV
Fairy Harpers, The. James B. Dollard. CaP
Fairy Host, The. *Unknown, tr. fr. Irish by* Alfred Perceval Graves. AnIV
Fairy in Armor, A. Joseph Rodman Drake. *Fr.* The Culprit Fay. FaPON
Fairy Lough, The. "Moira O'Neill." OBVV
Fairy Lover, The. Moireen Fox. AnIV
Fairy Lullaby ("You spotted snakes"). Shakespeare. *See* You Spotted Snakes.
Fairy Maimounè, The. John Moultrie. OBRV
Fairy Music. Francis Ledwidge. YeAr
Fairy Nurse, The. Edward Walsh. OnYI
Fairy Queen, The ("Come follow, follow me"). *Unknown.* PoPle
(Queen of Fairies, The.) ViBoPo
Fairy Ring, The. Andrew Young. ChTr
Fairy ring as round's the sun, A. Round Things. William Barnes. VLP
Fairy Ship, The. "Gabriel Setoun." PoPl
Fairy Song. Felicia Dorothea Hemans. HBVY
Fairy Song. Keats. FaPON; HBV-1
(Faery Song.) CH
Fairy Song, A. John Lyly. *See* Song by Fairies.
Fairy Song. Winthrop Mackworth Praed. SeCePo
Fairy Song. Thomas Randolph. *See* Song of Fairies Robbing an Orchard.
Fairy Song ("Come unto these yellow sands"). Shakespeare. *See* Ariel's Song: "Come unto these yellow sands."
Fairy Song ("Now the hungry lion roars"). Shakespeare. *See* Now the Hungry Lion Roars.
Fairy Song ("Now, until the break of day"). Shakespeare. *See* Now, Until the Break of Day.
Fairy Song ("Over hill, over dale"). Shakespeare. *See* Over Hill, over Dale.
Fairy Song ("Where the bee sucks"). Shakespeare. *See* Ariel's Song.
Fairy Song ("You spotted snakes with double tongue"). Shakespeare. *See* You Spotted Snakes.
Fairy Song. W. B. Yeats. *Fr.* The Land of Heart's Desire. MoBrPo; OnYI
("Wind blows out of the gates of the day, The.") ViBoPo
Fairy spirits of the breeze. Unwritten Poems. William Winter. AA
Fairy Story. Robert Penn Warren. *See* Treasure Hunt.
Fairy Tale, A. Kenneth MacKenzie. PoAu-2
Fairy Tale. John Frederick Nims. MiAP
Fairy Tale, A. Phyllis Thompson. DFT
Fairy Tale, A. Vitomil Zupan. DFT
Fairy Tales. Jane Flanders. DFT
Fairy Tales. Itzik Manger, *tr. fr. Yiddish by* Miriam Waddington. VWA
Fairy Temple, The; or, Oberon's Chapel. Robert Herrick. CaPo
Fairy Thorn, The. Sir Samuel Ferguson. AnIV; CH; OnMSP; OnYI; VLP
Fairy Thrall, The. May Byron. HBV-1; HBVY
Fairy Voyage, A. *Unknown.* SoPo
Fairy Went a-Marketing, A. Rose Fyleman. OxBChV; SoPo; SUS
Fairy Wings. Winifred Howard. SUS
Fairyland. Rabindranath Tagore. WSC
Fairy's Life, A. Shakespeare. *See* Ariel's Song: "Where the bee sucks, there suck I."
Fairy's Reply to Saturn, The. Thomas Hood. *Fr.* The Plea of the Midsummer Fairies. OBNC
Fairy's Wander-Song. Shakespeare. *See* Over Hill, over Dale.
Faith. Robert Browning. *Fr.* Paracelsus, V. TreFT
Faith. Ada Cambridge. PoAu-1
Faith. Elizabeth York Case, *wr. at. to* Edward Bulwer-Lytton. *See* There Is No Unbelief.
Faith. Preston Clark. HBMV
Faith. Victor J. Daley. PoAu-1
Faith. Marjorie Dunkels. PH
Faith. William Dean Howells. *See* What Shall It Profit?
Faith. Frances Anne Kemble. FaBoBe; HBV-2; OBVV
Faith. John Richard Moreland. OHIP
Faith. Ray Palmer. *See* My Faith Looks Up to Thee.
Faith. Pope. *Fr.* An Essay on Man. WGRP
Faith. Margaret E. Sangster. TRV
Faith. George Santayana. Sonnets, III. WGRP
Faith. John Banister Tabb. TRV; WGRP
Faith. Ella Wheeler Wilcox. BLRP; TRV
Faith. *Unknown.* TreFT
Faith. Whittier. TRV
Faith and Freedom. Wordsworth. *Fr.* It Is Not to Be Thought Of. GN
"Faith and Practice." John Balaban. GOA
Faith and Sight. Anna M. King. BLRP
Faith Came First, The. Sydney Carter. EBCP
Faith-Healer. *Unknown.* *See* Limerick: "There was a faith-healer of Deal."
Faith Healer Come to Rabun County. David Bottoms. TAT
Faith Healing. Philip Larkin. NoAM
Faith, Hope and Love. *Unknown.* BLRP
Faith, I Wish I Were a Leprechaun. Margaret Ritter. FaPON; TiPo
Faith is a fine invention. Emily Dickinson. AmPP; ELU; FaBV; NOBA; OxBA; TAP
Faith—is the pierless bridge. Emily Dickinson. AmPP
"Faith, måster, whither you will." Captain Car; or, Edom o Gordon. *Unknown.* ESPB
Faith of Abraham Lincoln, The. Abraham Lincoln, *arr. in verse by* Carl Sandburg. TRV

Faith of Our Fathers. Frederick W. Faber. TreFS
Faith on Trial, A, *sel.* George Meredith.
"Dream is the thought in the ghost, The." WGRP
Faith sees beyond the grave. Faith, Hope and Love. *Unknown.* BLRP
Faith shuts her eyes. Faith. Victor J. Daley. PoAu-1
Faith Trembling. "Madeline Bridges." AA
Faithful, The. Jane Cooper. NePoEA-2
Faithful Few, The. Chester E. Shuler. STF
Faithful Friend, The. William Cowper. FM
Faithful helm commands the keel, The. At Best. John Boyle O'Reilly. AA
Faithful Lover, The. Robert Pack. NePoEA
Faithful Shepherdess, The, *sels.* John Fletcher.
Come, Shepherds, Come! *fr.* I, iii. ElL; ErPo
God of Sheep, The, *fr.* V, v. ElL; FaBoCh
(To Pan.) TrGrPo
"Here be grapes, whose lusty blood," *fr.* I, i. ViBoPo
Hymn to Pan, *fr.* I, ii. NOBE; OBEV
(Sing His Praises.) ViBoPo
("Sing his praises that doth keep.") OBS
Priest's Chant, The, *fr.* II, i. OBS
(Evening Knell, The.) ElL
(Evening Song.) GN
(Folding the Flocks.) CH
River God, The ("I am this fountain's god"), *fr.* III, i. TrGrPo
River-God's Song, The ("Do not fear to put thy feet"), *fr.* III, i. FaPON; MoShBr
(Song: "Do not fear to put thy feet.") ElL; OBS
Satyr's Song ("See, the day begins to break"), *fr.* IV, iv. OBS
"Shall I stray/ In the middle air," *fr.* V, v. ViBoPo
"Thou divinest, fairest, brightest," *fr.* V, v. LO
(Satyr's Farewell, The.) OBS
(Satyr's Leave-taking, The.) LoBV
"Who hath restored my sense, given me new breath," *fr.* III, ii. LO
Faithful unto Death. Richard Handfield Titherington. PAH
Faithfully/We had covered the nasturiums. Mercy Killing. Kenneth Burke. TwAmPo
Faithfully Tinying at Twilight Voice. E. E. Cummings. NYBP
Faithless. Louis Lavater. PoAu-1
Faithless. *Unknown, tr. fr. Greek by* Louis Untermeyer. UnTE
"Faithless again!" I cry and she replies. Infatuated. *Unknown, tr. by* Louis Untermeyer. UnTE
Faithless familiars. November. Elizabeth Daryush. QFR
Faithless Nelly [*or* Nellie] Gray. Thomas Hood. BXAP; EnRP; FaBoCo; HBV-2; InMe; NA; NOBL; ShM; TreF; VLP
Faithless Sally Brown. Thomas Hood. HBV-2; NOBL; OBNV; TreFS
(Sally Brown.) FaBoCo
Faithless Shepherd, A. John Clare. VLP
Faithless Shepherdess, The. *Unknown. See* Unfaithful Shepherdess, The.
Faithless Wife, The. Federico García Lorca, *tr. fr. Spanish.* BoLoP, *tr. by* A. L. Lloyd; ErPo, *tr. by* Robert O'Brien
Faithlesse and fond mortality. Upon the Death of a Gentleman. Richard Crashaw. CavP
Faith's Difficulty. Theodore Maynard. TrPWD
Faith's Vista. Henry Abbey. AA
Falcon, The. Wilfrid Scawen Blunt. *See* To Manon, Comparing Her to a Falcon.
Falcon, The. Richard Lovelace. CaPo; PB; PBBP
Falcon, The. Richard Henry Stoddard. AA
Falcon, The. *Unknown. See* Corpus Christi Carol ("Lully, lullay, lully, lullay").
Falcon and the Dove, The. Sir Herbert Read. BrPo; FaBoMo
Falconer of God, The. William Rose Benét. HBMV; TreFT; WGRP
Falconers. Lady Luck. Ann Gottlieb. NMM
Falconry. Anne Wilkinson. MoCV; OBCV
Falkland at Newbury, 1643. Hugh Conway. EBVV
Fall, The. William Barnes. NBM; PoEL-4
Fall, The. Russell Edson. LCAP
Fall, The. Sir Richard Fanshawe, *after the Spanish of* Luis de Gongorá. *Fr.* Il Pastor Fido. MePo; OBS
(Great Favorit Beheaded, A.) OBVE
Fall. Aileen Fisher. YeAr
Fall. Robert Francis. VGW
Fall. Robert Hass. AmPA
Fall. Gabriela Melinescu, *tr. fr. Rumanian by* Michael Impey *and* Brian Swann. AMV-80
Fall, The. Milton. *Fr.* Paradise Lost, IX. PoEL-3
Fall, The. Kathleen Raine. MoPo
Fall, The. Alastair Reid. BSV
Fall, The. Earl of Rochester. EnLoPo; UnTE
Fall Again. H. R. Coursen. AMV-81
Fall Again, The. Howard Nemerov. ConAP
Fall Colors. Jerome Mazzaro. AMV-81
Fall Comes in Back-Country Vermont. Robert Penn Warren. NYBP; VGW
Fall Days. Marion Conger. SiSoSe
Fall Down. Calvin C. Hernton. CNA; PoBA
Fall eats its leaf from my hand, The: we are friends. Corona. Paul Celan, *tr. by* Joachim Neugroschel. VWA
Fall has come, clear as the eyes of chickens, The. Silence. Robert Bly. NaP
Fall In. Lincoln Kirstein. NoAM
Fall in Corrales. Richard Wilbur. CoPo
Fall in Long Island. Lake Success. Robert Conquest. OxBC
Fall Journey. William Stafford. NaP; Str
Fall, Leaves, Fall. Emily Brontë. CH; ELP; FaBoCh; FaBoRV; FaBV; LoBV; PoEL-5; TrGrPo
(Song.) NBM
Fall Letter. Dave Kelly. FAZ
Fall Lightly on Me. Roger Gaess. LTB
Fall 1961. Robert Lowell. OBWP; VGW
Fall now, my cold thoughts, frozen fall. Lament. Laurence Binyon. MoVE
Fall of deepbottom Arctic water, The. Time's Times Again. A. R. Ammons. SUW
Fall of Glomach. Andrew Young. PoSH
Fall of Hyperion, The, *sels.* Keats.
Dream, A, *fr.* I. OAEL-2; OBNC; OBRV
"Fanatics have their dreams, wherewith they weave," *fr.* I. EnRP
"None can usurp this height," *fr.* I. OBRV
Fall of J. W. Beane, The. Oliver Herford. OBAL
Fall of kings, The. Love of Nature. James Thomson. *Fr.* The Seasons: Autumn. OBEC
Fall of Leaves. D. S. Savage. PoA
Fall of Maubila, The. Thomas Dunn English. PAH
Fall of Princes, The, *sel.* John Lydgate.
"And semblably, though I go not upright," *fr.* Epilogue. OxBM
Fall of Richmond, The. Herman Melville. PAH
Fall of Rome, The. W. H. Auden. InPS; MAT; OAEL-2; OxBTC; UnPo
Fall of Tecumseh, The. *Unknown.* PAH
Fall of the Angels, The. Milton. *See* Satan as Rebel-Liberator.
Fall of the City, The, *sel.* Archibald MacLeish.
Voice of the Studio Announcer. HoPM
Fall of the House of Usher, The, *sel.* Poe.
Haunted Palace, The. AA; AP; BeLS; CH; ChTr; HBV-2; LiTA; NePA; NOBA; OBVV; OxBA; PoEL-4; PrIm; SyP; TAP; TreFS; TrGrPo; ViBoPo; WiR; WSC
Fall of the House of Usher, The. Reed Whittemore. GP; InPK
Fall of the Leaf, The. Henry David Thoreau. AP
Fall of the Plum Blossoms, The. Ranko, *tr. fr. Japanese.* TiPo
("I came to look, and lo.") SUS
Fall of the Year. Henry Ellison. OBVV
Fall, snow, and cease not! Flake by flake. Aubrey Thomas De Vere. *Fr.* A Year of Sorrow. ACP
Fall Song. Daniel David Moses. AMV-81
Fall that she turned fifty, The. The One Who Grew to Be a Wolf. Patricia Monaghan. PoDr
Fall To. Howard Jones. NBP
Fall which twisted love to lust, The. In Praise of Music in Time of Pestilence. Daryl Hine. OBCV
Fall Wind. William Stafford. PPJ
Fallen. Alice Corbin. SUMH
Fallen, The. Diana Gurney. SUMH
Fallen, The. Duncan Campbell Scott. TrPWD
Fallen Angels, The. Milton. *See* Satan Defiant.
Fallen as he is, this king of birds still seems. The Dead Eagle. Thomas Campbell. EnRP
Fallen flowers rise. Haiku. Moritake, *tr. by* Harold G. Henderson. SoSe
Fallen? How fallen? States and empires fall. On the Defeat of Henry Clay [*or* of a Great Man]. William Wilberforce Lord. AA; PAH
Fallen Leaves. Kathryn Munro Tupper. CaP
Fallen leaves are scattered by evening rain. Regretful Thoughts. Yü Hsüan-chi, *tr. by* Geoffrey Waters. BoWoP
Fallen Majesty. W. B. Yeats. PoA
Fallen Rain. Richard Watson Dixon. NBM
Fallen Star, The. George Darley. HBV-2; OBEV
Fallen Tower of Siloam, The. Robert Graves. WaP
Fallen Tree, The. Patrick Maybin. NeIP
Fallen Tree, The. Andrew Young. BoNaP
Fallen with autumn's falling leaf. On the Death of President Garfield. Oliver Wendell Holmes. PAH
Fallen Yew, A. Francis Thompson. BrPo; MoAB; MoBrPo
Fallen Zulu Commander, The. C. M. Van Den Heever, *tr. fr. Afrikaans by* Uys Krige *and* Jack Cope. PeSA
Falling. James Dickey. LCAP; NYBP
Falling. Bob Kaufman. PoBA

Falling Asleep. John Ciardi. DuDa
Falling Asleep. Siegfried Sassoon. MoBrPo; MoVE; OxBTC
Falling Asleep in a Garden. David Wagoner. AMV-81
Falling Asleep over the Aeneid. Robert Lowell. AP; CoBMV; CrMA; MoAmPo; NoAM; OxBA; TwAmPo
Falling Down to Bed. Nila NorthSun. STE
Falling flower, The. Haiku. Moritake, *tr. by* Babette Deutsch. SoSe
Falling in Love. Jon Anderson. MAYP
Falling in Love. David Perkins. NCSH
Falling in love with a mustache. Uneasy Rider. Diane Wakoski. NIP
Falling leaf and fading tree. Goodbye! George John Whyte-Melville. TreF
Falling leaf betrays the fawn, The. Late Autumn. A. M. Sullivan. GoBC
Falling Leaves, The. Margaret Postgate Cole. SUMH
Falling Moon. Roberta Hill. CDW
Falling of the Leaves, The. W. B. Yeats. VLP
Falling of the Snow, The. Raymond Souster. CaP
Falling Out. Helen Chasin. IHMS
Falling separate into the dark. Late at Night. William Stafford. POL; RFM
Falling Snow. *Unknown.* SoPo
Falling star, The. "Ping Hsin." *Fr.* Spring Waters. PBWP
Falling Star, The. Sara Teasdale. MoShBr; OBCA; PDV; SoPo; SUS; TiPo
Falling Upwards. David Shapiro. AMV-81
Fall'n, fall'n, a silent heap; her heroes all. John Dyer. *Fr.* The Ruins of Rome. OBEC
Fallow Deer at the Lonely House, The. Thomas Hardy. AWP; BoAnP; CH; CMoP; MoVE
Fallow Field, The. Julia Caroline Ripley Dorr. AA
Fallow fields, dark pewter sky. Winter Drive. James McAuley. PoA
Falls, The. F. D. Reeve. NYBP
Falls from her heaven the Moon, and stars sink burning. Moon-Bathers. John Freeman.
Falls of Glomach, The. Andrew Young. OxBS
Falltime. Carl Sandburg. PoA
Falmouth. W. E. Henley. *See* Home.
False Achitophel, The. Dryden. *See* Achitophel: The Earl of Shaftesbury.
False beauty who, although in semblance fair. Ballade to His Mistress. Villon, *tr. by* Norman Cameron. WeW
False Bride, The. *Unknown.* OBET
False Cadence. Bruce Berger. AMV-80
False Country of the Zoo. Jean Garrigue. LiTM; MP
False Dawn. Walter de la Mare. FaBoNo
False dawns. Hiawatha. Stephen Sandy. CoPo
False dreams, all false. Iliad. Humbert Wolfe. MoBrPo
False Enchantment. Jean Starr Untermeyer. MoAmPo
False Favorite's Downfall, The. *Unknown.* APAS
False Fox, The. *Unknown.* ChTr; GBP; OxBM
("False fox came into our croft, The.") PBBP
False Gallop of Analogies, A. Warham St. Leger. CenHV; FaBoCo; FiBHP; WhC
False Gods. Walter de la Mare. EaLo
False Heart, The. Hilaire Belloc. FaBoCh; FaBoEE; HBMV
(For False Heart.) MoBrPo
False Knight upon [*or* on] the Road, The. *Unknown.* AmFP; CH; EnSB; ESPB; GBP
(False Knight and the Wee Boy, The.) FaBoCh
(Fause Knicht upon the Road, The.) OxBoLi; OxBS
False life! a foil and no more. Quickness. Henry Vaughan. ELP; LoBV; MeLP; MePo; NOBE; NOCV; OBS; OxBoCh; SeCePo; SeCP; SeCV-1
False Love. *At. to* John Lilliat. OBSC
(Song: "When love on time and measure makes his ground.") ElL
("When love on time and measure makes his ground.") EBEV
False Love. Sir Walter Ralegh. *See* Farewell to False Love, A.
False love, and hast thou played me this. Sir Walter Scott. *Fr.* Waverley. ViBoPo
False Lover Won Back, The. *Unknown.* BaBo, *diff. vers.*; ESPB (A *and* B *vers.*)
(False Lover, The, *with music.*) OxBB
False Luve, and Hae Ye Played Me This? *Unknown.* BSV; GBP; POL
False Nancy. *Unknown.* AmFP
False Poets and True. Thomas Hood. HBV-2; PP
False Prophet. Emanuela O'Malley. AMV-81
False Security. John Betjeman. CMoP; NoP
False Sir John a wooing came. May Colven. *Unknown.* OxBB; TrGrPo
False Summer, The. Marya Zaturenska. CrMA
False Though She Be. Congreve. BoLoP; HBV-1; NOBE; OBEV
(Song: "False though she be to me and love.") EnLoPo; FaBoEn; NIP; OBEC; POL; ViBoPo
False True Love. *Unknown.* FSW
False world, good night. Since thou hast brought. To the World; a Farewell for a Gentlewoman, Virtuous and Noble. Ben Jonson. EnRePo; JCP; QFR; SeCP
False World, Thou Liest. Francis Quarles. Emblems, II, 5. SeCePo
(Vanity of the World, The, *abr.*) PPON
(Wilt Thou Set Thine Eyes upon That Which Is Not?) OBS
Falsehood. William Cartwright. OBEV
Falstaff's Lament over Prince Hal Become Henry V. Herman Melville. ViBoPo
Falstaff's Song. Edmund Clarence Stedman. AA; HBV-2
Fame. Robert Browning. PP; SoSe
Fame. Byron. *Fr.* Childe Harold's Pilgrimage. FiP
Fame. Eleanor Hollister Cantus. GoYe
Fame. Robert Herrick. FaBoEE
Fame. Walter Savage Landor. PV
("Ten thousand flakes about my window blow.") FaBoEE
Fame. Charlotte Mew. BrRo; PBWP; SBG
Fame. Sir Thomas More. EnRePo
Fame. Vern Rutsala. GP
Fame. John Banister Tabb. AA
Fame. *Unknown.* TreFT
Fame and Fortune. Michael Drayton. *Fr.* The Legend of Robert, Duke of Normandy. OBSC
Fame and Friendship. Austin Dobson. *See* Fame Is a Food That Dead Men Eat.
Fame I am called, marvel you nothing. Fame. Sir Thomas More. EnRePo
Fame is a fickle food. Emily Dickinson. TAP
Fame Is a Food That Dead Men Eat. Austin Dobson. HBV-2
(Fame and Friendship.) OBEV
Fame let thy trumpet sound. A Song. Joel Barlow. AmPP
Fame, like a wayward girl, will still be coy. Two Sonnets on Fame, I [*or* On Fame]. Keats. CABA; EnRP
Fame Makes Us Forward. Robert Herrick. CaPo
Fame, wisdom, love, and power were mine. All Is Vanity, Saith the Preacher. Byron. TrCP
Famed ship *California*, a ship of high renown, The. The Girls around Cape Horn. *Unknown.* AmFP
Fame's pillar here, at last, we set. The Pillar of Fame. Robert Herrick. AnAnS-2; CaPo; JCP; NIP; SeCP
Fames Plant takes Root from Vertue, grows thereby. Life and Death. Edward Benlowes. *Fr.* Theophila. FaBoEn
Familiar Epistle, A. Ann Murry. WPE
Familiar Epistle to J. B. Esq., A, *sels.* Robert Lloyd.
"Mark yon round parson, fat and sleek." OBSV
Public Schools. NOEC
Familiar Faces, Long Departed. Robert Hillyer. NYBP
Familiar Friends. James S. Tippett. SoPo; SUS
Familiar Letter to Several Correspondents, A. Oliver Wendell Holmes. FaBoUs; InMe
Familiar Lines. *Unknown.* FiBHP
Familiar, year by year, to the creaking wain. The Sower. Laurence Binyon. MMA
Familiarity Breeds Indifference. Martial, *tr. fr. Latin by* Louis Untermeyer. UnTE
Familie, The. George Herbert. AnAnS-1
Families, when a child is born. On the Birth of His Son. Su Tung-p'o, *tr. by* Arthur Waley. AWP; OBVE; OFD; PV; TRV
Family. Norman MacCaig. FF
Family. Josephine Miles. FYAP; GP; GrPl
Family ("The family is a little book"). *Unknown.* STF
Family, The ("Widdy-widdy-wurkey"). *Unknown, tr. fr. German by* Rose Fyleman. TiPo
Family Album, A. Alter Brody. VWA
Family Album. Lonny Kaneko. BrSi
Family Altar, The. Georgia B. Adams. STF
Family Cat, The. Roy Fuller. OxBC; TEP
Family Chronicle. Anselm Parlatore. SUW
Family Court. Ogden Nash. FiBHP
Family Cups. Steve Orlen. Str
Family 8. Lyn Lifshin. NeAC
Family Evening. Dan Huws. NYBP
Family Fool, The. W. S. Gilbert. *Fr.* Yeoman of the Guard. InMe
Family Fortunes. C. H. Sisson. OxBC
Family Goldschmitt, The. Henri Coulette. CoAP; FF
Family History. Wendy Bishop. AMV-81
Family is a little book, The. Family. *Unknown.* STF
Family Life. Allan M. Laing. FiBHP
Family Life. *Unknown.* DBV
Family Man, A. Maxine W. Kumin. IHMS; TAP
Family Matters. Günter Grass, *tr. fr. German by* Michael Hamburger. ELU
Family Meeting, The. Charles Sprague. HBV-2
Family of Eight, The. Abraham Reisen, *tr. fr. Yiddish by* Marcia Falk. VWA

Family of Nations, The. Willard Wattles.
Family Outing—A Celebration. Nicki Jackowska. BrRo
Family Photograph. Gerald Vizenor. VoR
Family Photograph 1939, A. James K. Baxter. OxBC
Family Plot. Sarah Singer. AMV–81
Family Poem. John Holloway. NMP
Family Portrait. Leonard Feeney. ISi
Family Portrait. Rebecca Hood-Adams. AMV–80
Family Portrait 1933. Peter Oresick. LTB
Family portrait not too stale to record, A. Father and Son: 1939. William Plomer. NoAM; PeSA
Family Prime. Mark Van Doren. VGW
Family Reunion. Jim Wayne Miller. Str
Family Reunion. Hollis Summers. GoYe
Family Romance. Larry Levis. MAYP
Family Screams. Hy Sobiloff. TwAmPo
Family story tells, and it was told true, The. Funnel. Anne Sexton. MoAmPo
Family Trees. Douglas Malloch. OHIP
Famine once we had. New England's Growth. William Bradford. PAH
Famine Song. *Unknown. See* Praties, The.
Famine Year, The. Lady Wilde. OnYI
Famous animals. Holiday Inn at Bemidji. Gerald Vizenor. STE
Famous Ballad of the Jubilee Cup, The. Sir Arthur Quiller-Couch. InMe; NA; WhC
"Famous bard, he comes, The! The vision nears!" Visiting Poet. John Frederick Nims. DBV; InPK; PV
Famous city of Boston. Hubbub in Hub. Laurence McKinney. WhC
Famous Fight at Malago, The; or, The Englishmen's Victory over the Spaniards. *Unknown.* CoMu
Famous Flower of Serving-Men, The; or, The Lady Turn'd Serving-Man. *Unknown.* ESPB; OBET; OxBB
Famous kingdom of the birds, The. Somewhere Is Such a Kingdom. John Crowe Ransom. CMoP; LiTA
Famous Light Brigade, The, *with music. Unknown.* ShS
Famous Outlaw Stops In for a Drink, The. David James. AMV–81
Famous painter, jealous of his wife, A. The Superfluous Saddle. La Fontaine. UnTE
Famous Poet. Ted Hughes. LiTM
Famous Sea-Fight, A. John Looke. CoMu
Famous Toast, A. Sheridan. *See* Let the Toast Pass.
Famously she descended, her red hair. A Recollection. John Peale Bishop. LiTA; TwAmPo
Fan, The, *sel.* John Gay.
"Rise, happy youth, this bright machine survey." ViBoPo
Fan. Walter Lew. BrSi
Fan, The. Edith Sitwell. HBMV
Fan-Piece, for Her Imperial Lord. Ezra Pound. MoAB
Fanaticism? No. Writing is exciting. Baseball and Writing. Marianne Moore. BoWoP; LiSp
Fanatics have their dreams, wherewith they weave. Keats. *Fr.* The Fall of Hyperion, I. EnRP; OAEL–2
Fancy. Robert Creeley. NOBA
Fancy. Keats. EnRP; LoBV; OBEV
(Realm of Fancy, The.) GTBS; GTBS–P
(To Fancy.) HBV–2
Fancy, A ("First shall the heavens want starry light"). Thomas Lodge. *Fr.* Rosalynde. EIL; LoBV; OBSC
(Lover's Protestation, A.) GoBC
(Love's Protestation.) ACP
Fancy, A ("When I admire the rose"). Thomas Lodge. *See* Rose, The.
Fancy. Shakespeare. *See* Tell Me Where Is Fancy Bred.
Fancy, A. *Unknown.* FaBoNo
Fancy, and I, last Evening walkt. To Amoret Gone from Him. Henry Vaughan. MeLP; OBS
Fancy Dress. Dorothea MacKellar. PoAu–1
Fancy Dress. Siegfried Sassoon. BrPo
Fancy, Farewell. Sir Edward Dyer. EnRePo
Fancy from Fontenelle, A. Austin Dobson. HBV–2; OBVV
Fancy halts my feet at the way-side well, A. The Way-Side Well. Joseph S. Cotter, Sr. CDC; PoNe
Fancy (quoth he), farewell, whose badge I long did bear. The Green Knight's Farewell to Fancy. George Gascoigne. EnRePo
Fancy, which that I have served long, The. The Restless Heart. Earl of Surrey. SiPS
Fancy's Knell. A. E. Housman. FaBoCh; OAEP; PoPle; PoRA
Fand Yields Cuchulain to Emer. *Unknown, tr. fr. Old Irish by* Sean O'Faolain. AnIL
Fandango. "Stanley Vestal." BPAW
Fane Wald I Luve. *At. to* John Clerk. OxBS
Fanfare for the Makers, A, *abr.* Louis MacNeice. NOBE
Fannie ("Fannie has the sweetest foot"). Thomas Bailey Aldrich. OBAL
Fanny. Anne Reeve Aldrich. HBV–1
Fanny, *sels.* Fritz-Greene Halleck.
"Fanny was younger once than she is now." CTC
"We owe the ancients something. You have read." OBAL
Fanny Foo-Foo was a Japanese girl. The Japanese Lovers. *Unknown.* BeLS; BLPA
Fanny! If in your arms my soul could slip. Keats to Fanny Brawne. Edgar Lee Masters. PoA
Fanny was younger once than she is now. Fitz-Greene Halleck. *Fr.* Fanny. CTC
Fanny's Removal in 1714. John Winstanley. NOEC
Fantasia. G. K. Chesterton. HBMV
Fantasia. Dorothy Livesay. MoCV; OBCV
Fantasia. Leonard Nathan. PPJ
Fantasia of a Fallen Gentleman on a Cold Bitter Night on the Embankment. T. E. Hulme. *See* Embankment, The.
Fantasia on a Wittelsbach Atmosphere. Siegfried Sassoon. MoVE
Fantasies of old age. Merced. Adrienne Rich. NOBA
Fantasy. Gwendolyn B. Bennett. BlSi; CDC
Fantasy in Purple. Langston Hughes. BANP; CDC
Fantasy of Little Waters, A. James Scully. NYBP
Fantasy Street. Andrew Glaze. NYP
Fantasy under the Moon. Emmanuel Boundzekei-Dongala, *tr. fr. French by* Gerald Moore *and* Ulli Beier. TTY
Fantoches. Paul Verlaine, *tr. fr. French by* Arthur Symons. AWP; OBMV
(Puppets.) SyP
Far above Cayuga's Waters *Unknown.* FSW
Far above the dome. It Pleases. Gary Snyder. TAT
Far across hill and dale. Plum Blossoms. Basho. SUS
Far and near, and now, from never. Beauty. Isaac Rosenberg. TrJP
Far and wide as the eye can wander. Peat Bog Soldiers. *Unknown.* FSW
Far and Wide She Went. Cædmon, *tr. fr. Anglo-Saxon. Fr.* Genesis. EtS
Far are the shades of Arabia. Arabia. Walter de la Mare. HBMV; WHA
Far as creation's ample range extends. Pope. *Fr.* An Essay on Man. FM; ImOP
Far as man can see,/ Comes the rain. Song of the Rain Chant. *Unknown, tr. by* Natalie Curtis. AWP
Far at [*or* in *or* to] sea and [to the] west of [*or* from] Spain. The Land of Cokaygne [*or* Cockaigne *or* Cockayne]. *Unknown, at. to* Friar Michael of Kildare. AnIL; BIrV, *tr. by* John Montague; OAEL–1, *paraphrased by* J. B. Trapp; OnYI, *mod. vers. by* Russell K. Alspach. *See also* Fer in see by west Spaygne.
Far away across the ocean. Ballad of Ho Chi Minh. Ewan MacColl. FSW
Far away and long ago. The Snare. Edward Davison. ViBoPo
Far away beyond the glamor of the city and its strife. The Picture That Is Turned toward the Wall. Charles Graham. TreF
Far away is one who now is sleeping. The Clock. Francis Scarfe. NeBP
Far away under us, they are mowing on the green steps. The Beholders. James Dickey. AP
Far back when I went zig-zagging. Orion. Adrienne Rich. NIP; NoAM; NoP; WPE
Far behind him crept blackness and flickering glimmer. The Song of the Spirits. Joseph Sheridan Le Fanu. *Fr.* The Legend of the Glaive. OnYI
Far beyond the sky-line, where the steamers go. Hot Weather in the Plains—India. E. H. Tipple. HBV–2
Far beyond the sunrise and the sunset rises. Plus Ultra. Swinburne. VLP
Far Country, The. Robert Greacen. NeIP
Far court opens for us all July, The. Prothalamion. Maxine W. Kumin. NYBP
Far Cry after a Close Call, A. Richard Howard. NYBP; UnPo
Far Cry from Africa, A. Derek Walcott. HeIP; NoAM; TTY; UnPo
Far Cry to Heaven, A. Edith M. Thomas. AA; WGRP
Far down the purple wood. The Constant Bridegrooms. Kenneth Patchen. CrMA; LiTM; NaP
"Far enough down is China," somebody said. Digging for China. Richard Wilbur. GoJo; GrPl; MP; NCSH; TwCP
Far faint protocols of Katherine's flute, The. Rehearsal. David Fisher. NPGG
Far, far away, beyond a hazy height. October in Tennessee. Walter Malone. AA
Far, far away, I know not where, I know not how. A Dream of November. Sir Edmund Gosse. SyP
Far, far down. City Afternoon. Barbara Howes. AmFN
Far far from gusty waves the children's faces. An Elementary School Classroom in a Slum. Stephen Spender. CoBMV; FaBoMo; FF; LiTB; MoAB; MoBrBo; MoPo; MP; NIP; OAEP; PPON; TrGrPo; TwCP; UnPo
Far, far from here. Cadmus and Harmonia [*or* The Song of Callicles]. Matthew Arnold. *Fr.* Empedocles on Etna, I, ii. FiP; GTBS–P; OBVV
Far, far from home they rode on their excursions. Two Englishmen. Douglas Stewart. CBAP

Far, far from the water's fall. Niagara Falls. Philip Parisi. FAZ
Far, far in the west. Far in the West. Douglas Fraser. PoSH
Far far the least of all, in want. The Prisoners. Stephen Spender. FaBoMo; MoAB; MoBrPo
Far, Far West, The. *Unknown.* CoSo
Far Field, The. Theodore Roethke. NoP; PrIm; SeCeV
Far from a cultural centre he was used. Sonnets from China, XIII. W. H. Auden. CMoP
Far from Africa: Four Poems. Margaret Danner. AmNP; NNP, *abr.*; PoBA
Garnishing the Aviary, I. BPo
Far from Our Friends, *with music.* Jeremy Belknap. AH
Far from our garden at the edge of a gulf. The Gulf. Denise Levertov. NNaP
Far from Somewhere. "Primus." WhC
Far from the deep roar of the Aegean main. Farewell. Plato, *tr. by* Charles Whibley. AWP
Far from the Heart of Culture. W. H. Auden. WaaP
Far from the loud sea beaches. A Visit from the Sea. Robert Louis Stevenson. FM; GN; MOS
Far from the Madding Crowd. Nixon Waterman. BLPA; FaBoBe (Vacation.) WBLP
Far from the parlour have your kitchen plac'd. William King. *Fr.* The Art of Cookery. FaBoUs
Far from the scent of the crocus. That's Life? Alan Bold. FF
Far from the sea and hard. The Life Not Given. David Habercom. AMV-81
Far from the sea in his grey later days. "Cap'n." Arthur Wallace Peach. EtS
Far from the tender tribe of boys remove. Tibullus. Odes, I, 4. PeHV
Far from the thronged luxurious town. On Honour. Bernard Mandeville. NOEC
Far from the trouble and toil of town. Old Man Platypus. A. B. Paterson. BoAnP
Far from the vulgar haunts of men. On the Same. Roy Campbell. OxBTC
Far from the waves that soothed. The Lonely Shell. Martha Eugenie Perry. CaP
Far from thy dearest self, the scope. To His Mistress in Absence. Tasso, *tr. by* Thomas Stanley. AWP
Far gone in weariness, in oblivion. Homer, *tr. by* Robert Fitzgerald. The Odyssey, VI. NAWM-1
Far greater numbers have been lost by hopes. Samuel Butler. FaBoEE
Far [*or* Farre] have I clamber'd [*or* clambred] in my mind. Hymn to Charity and Humility [*or* An Hymne in Honour of Those Two Despised Virtues]. Henry More. OBS; OxBoCh
Far have we come to this far spot of earth. Prometheus Bound. Aeschylus, *tr. by* Edith Hamilton. NAWM-1
Far I hear the bugle blow. The Day of Battle. A. E. Housman. A Shropshire Lad, LVI. OHIP; WaaP
Far in a Western Brookland. A. E. Housman. A Shropshire Lad, LII. AWP; NBM; OAEP; PoEL-5
Far in a wild, unknown to public view. The Hermit. Thomas Parnell. GoTL
Far in sea, west of Spain. *See* Far at sea and west of Spain.
Far in the country of Arden. Cassamen and Dowsabell [*or* Dowsabel *or* The Ballad of Dowsabell]. Michael Drayton. *Fr.* The Shepherd's Garland, Eclogue VIII. LoBV; OBSC; UnTE
Far in the grim Northwest beyond the lines. Temagami. Archibald Lampman. OBCV
Far in the Heavens my God retires. The Incomprehensible. Isaac Watts. WGRP
Far in the sea, to the west of Spain. *See* Far at sea and west of Spain.
Far in the West. Douglas Fraser. PoSH
Far in the woods my stealthy flute. The Magic Flute. W. D. Snodgrass. NYBP
Far inland/ go my sad thoughts. *Tr. fr. Eskimo by* Knud Rasmussen, *ad. by* Willis Barnstone. BoWoP
Far Land, The. John Hall Wheelock. WGRP
Far look in absorbed eyes, unaware, A. Magnets. Laurence Binyon. HBMV
Far moon maketh lovers wise, The. Moonlight. Walter de la Mare. EnLoPo
Far North, The. Terry Savoie. AMV-80
Far-off/ at the core of space. Swan. D. H. Lawrence. CMoP
Far off a lonely hound. The Hounds. John Freeman. OBMV
Far-off a young state rises, full of might. Farther. John James Piatt. AA
Far off, above the plain the summer dries. Second Air Force. Randall Jarrell. AP; CMoP; CoBMV; LiTM; WaP
Far off, far off, so faint against the sky. The Old Mountaineer. W. K. Holmes. PoSH
Far off, from the burned fields. Ashes. Philip Levine. AMV-80
Far-off mountains hide you from me, The. Absent Lover. *Unknown, tr. by* A. C. Jordan. PBA
Far off, the rumble of freight trains. The Trestle Bridge. Carolyne Wright. AMV-80
Far off the sea is grey and still as the sky. Week-End by the Sea. Edgar Lee Masters. MoAmPo
Far, oh, far is the Mango island. The Constant Cannibal Maiden. Wallace Irwin. OBAL
Far on its rocky knoll descried. Scenes from Carnac. Matthew Arnold. FaBoPP
Far on the desert ridges. Wind-Song. *Unknown, tr. fr. Hopi Indian by* Natalie Curtis. SUS
Far out across Carnarvon bay. The Welsh Sea. James Elroy Flecker. BrPo
Far out at sea it can be seen. Greed. Douglas Blazek. LTB
Far out beyond the city's lights, away from din and roar. The Country Store. *Unknown.* BLPA
Far out in the hush of the mountain land. The Emigrant's Child. Lyman H. Sproull. PoOW
Far out of sight forever stands the sea. The Slow Pacific Swell. Yvor Winters. HeIP; MOS; NoAM; NOBA; QFR
Far over the billows unresting forever. Thalatta. Willis Boyd Allen. EtS
Far over the misty mountains cold. J. R. R. Tolkien. *Fr.* The Hobbit. WSC
Far Rockaway. Delmore Schwartz. NoAM
Far sail shimmers, white and lonely, A. A Sail. Mikhail Lermontov, *tr. by* Avrahm Yarmolinsky. PoPl
Far Side of Introspection, The. Al Lee. CoAP
Far spread, below. The Story of Vinland. Sidney Lanier. *Fr.* The Psalm of the West. PAH
Far Sweeter than Honey. Abraham ibn Ezra, *tr. fr. Hebrew by* Israel Abrahams. TrJP
Far to sea, west from Spain. *See* Far at sea and west of Spain.
Far to the east I see them in my mind. The Wise Men. Edgar Bowers. NePoEA
Far to the left he saw the huts of men. East Anglian Fen. George Crabbe. *Fr.* Tales of the Hall: Delay Has Danger. FaBoPP
Far to the south, beyond the blue, there spreads. The Second Asgard. Matthew Arnold. *Fr.* Balder Dead. FiP
Far Trek. June Brady. QQQ; RHPC
Far Trumpets Blowing. Louis F. Benson. TRV
Far under the waves glide in, in rippling lines. From the Point. Paul Petrie. AMV-80
Far up the dim twilight fluttered. The Unknown God. "Æ." MoBrPo; WGRP
Far up the lonely mountain-side. A Georgia Volunteer. Mary Ashley Townsend. AA
Far voices/ and fretting leaves. Old Song. F. R. Scott. PeCV
Far West. A. J. M. Smith. PeCV
Fara Diddle Dyno. *Unknown.* ElL; FaBoCh; FaBoCo; LoBV
("A ha ha ha! this world doth passe.") PoEL-2
("Ha ha! ha! ha! This world doth pass.") FaBoNo; ViBoPo
(Idle Fyno.) ChTr
(Madrigal.) OxBoLi
Faraway hands are folded and folded. The Starry Night. George Starbuck. NYBP
Fare not abroad, O Soul, to win. Quo Vadis? Myles Connolly. TRV
Fare Thee Well. Byron. BLPA; EnRP; FaFP; FPL; HBV-1; OBNC; PoEL-4; TreFS
Fare Thee Well. Eli Siegel. GOA
Fare Thee Well Blues. *Unknown.* BluL
Fare wel [*or* Farewele] Advent! Christemas is cum [*or* come]. Farewell Advent. *At. to* James Ryman. MeEL; OxBM
Fare Well. Walter de la Mare. CoBMV; GTBS-P; MoVE; NOBE; OBEV
Fare Ye Well, My Darlin'. *Unknown. See* Fare You Well, My Darling.
Fare you well, green fields. A Prisoner for Life. *Unknown.* CoSo
Fare you well, my blue-eyed girl. Blue-eyed Girl. *Unknown.* AmFP
Fare You Well, My Darling. *Unknown.* AmFP
(Fare Ye Well, My Darlin', *with music, sl. diff. vers.*) OuSiCo
Fare you well, the Prince's Landing Stage. The Leaving of Liverpool. *Unknown.* ShS
Fareweel to a' our Scottish fame. Such a Parcel of Rogues in a Nation. Burns. OxBS
Fareweel ye dungeons dark and strong. MacPherson's Farewell. *Unknown.* FSW
Farewel dear babe, my heart's too much content. In Memory of My Dear Grand-Child Elizabeth Bradstreet. Anne Bradstreet. SCAP
Farewel, dear daughter Sara; now Thou'rt gone. In Saram. John Cotton. SCAP
Farewel to Worldly Joyes, A ("Farewel to unsubstantial joyes"). Anne Killigrew. BoWoP
Farewel ye guilded follies, pleasing troubles. *Unknown.* MeLP
Farewele! Advent, Christemas is come. *See* Fare wel Advent! Christemas is cum.

Farewell, A: "And if I did, what then?" George Gascoigne. *See* And If I Did What Then?
Farewell: "Far from the deep roar of the Aegean main." Plato, *tr. fr. Greek by* Charles Whibley. AWP
Farewell: "Farewell! if ever fondest prayer." Byron. *See* Farewell! If Ever Fondest Prayer.
Farewell: " 'Farewell to barn and stack and tree.' " A. E. Housman. *See* Farewell to Barn and Stack and Tree.
Farewell: "Farewell to the bushy clump close to the river." John Clare. NoP
Farewell, A: "Flow down, cold rivulet, to the sea." Tennyson. FaBoRV; HBV-2
Farewell, A: "Go fetch to me a pint o' wine." Burns. *See* Silver Tassie, The.
Farewell, The: "Gone, gone—sold and gone." Whittier. AA; AWP; PoNe
Farewell, A: "Good-bye!—no [*or* nay], do not grieve that it is over." Harriet Monroe. AA; HBMV; PoA
Farewell, A: "I go down from the hill in gladness." "Æ." AnIV; OBVV
Farewell, A: "I put thy hand aside, and turn away." "Madeline Bridges." AA
Farewell: "It is buried and done with." John Addington Symonds. OBVV
Farewell, The: "It was a' for our rightfu' king." Burns. BSV; CH; HBV-2; OBEV; PoPle; ViBoPo
(It was A' for Our Rightfu' King.) EnRP; GoTS; PoEL-4
Farewell: "Juliet, farewell. I would not be forgiven." Wilfrid Scawen Blunt. *Fr.* The Love Sonnets of Proteus. TrGrPo
Farewell: "Linden blossomed, the nightingale sang, The." Heine, *tr. fr. German by* John Todhunter. AWP
Farewell, The: "Methinks I draw but sickly breath." *Unknown.* OxBoCh
Farewell: "My boat goes west, yours east." Chao Li-hua, *tr. fr. Chinese by* J. P. Seaton. BoWoP
Farewell, A: "My cat was a southerner and a lady." Hildegarde Flanner. AMV-81
Farewell, A: "My fairest child, I have no song to give you." Charles Kingsley. BLPA; EBVV; GN; HBV-1; HBVY; OxBChV; TreF
Farewell, A: "My horse's feet beside the lake." Matthew Arnold. Switzerland, III. OAEP; VLP
Farewell: "Not soon shall I forget—a sheet." Katharine Tynan. CH
Farewell, A: "Oft have I mused, but now at length I find." Sir Philip Sidney. *Fr.* Certain Sonnets. EIL; GBL; NOBE; OBSC; SiPS
(Oft Have I Mused.) EnRePo
Farewell: "Shores of my native land." Isaac Toussaint L'Ouverture, *tr. fr. French by* Edna Worthley Underwood. TTY
Farewell, The: "Since fate commands me hence, and I." Thomas Stanley. CavP
Farewell: "Smell of death was in the air, The." John Press. PoRA
Farewell: "Tell them, O Sky-born, when I die." Harry Kemp. HBMV
Farewell: "Thou goest; to what distant place." John Addington Symonds. HBV-1
Farewell, A: "Thou wilt not look on me?" Alice Brown. HBV-1
Farewell, A: "Venus, take my votive glass." Matthew Prior. *See* Lady Who Offers Her Looking Glass to Venus, The.
Farewell: "What should I say." Sir Thomas Wyatt. GBL; GoBC; NOBE; OBSC
(Farewell, Unkist.) LoBV
(Revocation, A.) OBEV
("What should I say.") EnRePo; NoP; SiPS
("What shulde I saye.") PoEL-1
Farewell, A: "With all my will, but much against my heart." Coventry Patmore. *Fr.* The Unknown Eros. ACP; BoLoP; EnLoPo; FaBoEn; GTBS-P; HBV-1; NOBE; OBEV; OBNC; OBVV; PoEL-5; TrGrPo
Farewell: "You sang round-dance songs." Liz Sohappy Bahe. CDW
Farewell! a long farewell, to all my greatness! Cardinal Wolsey's Farewell [*or* Farewell to Greatness *or* Wolsey's Farewell to His Greatness]. Shakespeare *and probably* John Fletcher. *Fr.* King Henry VIII. LiTB; OHFP; TreF; TrGrPo
Farewell, a Welcome, A. Lisel Mueller. MOON
Farewell, adieu, that courtly life. Haltersick's Song [*or* Song]. John Pickering. *Fr.* Horestes. EIL; OBSC
Farewell Advent. *At. to* James Ryman. MeEL; OxBM
Farewell, all my welfare. Sir Thomas Wyatt. GBL; SiPS
Farewell and adieu to you, fair [*or* gay] Spanish Ladies. Spanish Ladies. *Unknown.* AmSS; FaBoCh
Farewell and Good. Denis Devlin. IPY
Farewell and Hail! Thomas Curtis Clark. PGD
Farewell Ballad of Poppies, A. Eva Brudne. VWA
Farewell, Bristolia's dingy piles of brick. Last Verses. Thomas Chatterton. TrGrPo
Farewell! But Whenever [You Welcome the Hour]. Thomas Moore. HBV-2; OAEP
(Long, Long Be My Heart with Such Memories Filled.) BLPL; FaBoBe
"Let Fate do her worst; there are relics of joy," *sel.* TreFT
Farewell Content. Shakespeare. *See* Othello's Farewell to His Career.
Farewell dear babe, my heart's too much content. In Memory of My Dear Grandchild Elizabeth Bradstreet [Who Deceased August, 1665, Being a Year and a Half Old]. Anne Bradstreet. AP; NOCV; WPE
Farewell, Dear Love! [Since Thou Wilt Needs Be Gone]. *Unknown.* EIL; OAEP; OBSC
Farewell, dear scenes, for ever closed to me. Lines Written upon [*or* on] a Window-Shutter at Weston. William Cowper. LAuP; NOEC
Farewell fair saint, may not the seas and wind. On His Mistresse Going to Sea. Thomas Cary. OBS
Farewell false friends, farewell ill wine. Farewell to England. *Unknown.* APAS
Farewell false love, the oracle of lies. A Farewell to False Love [*or* False Love]. Sir Walter Ralegh. BoLoP; EIL; OBSC; SiPS
Farewell, farewell! Before our prow. Charles Stuart Calverley. *Fr.* Dover to Munich. NOBL
"Farewell, farewell, my pretty maid." The True Lover's Farewell. *Unknown.* AS
Farewell—farewell to thee, Araby's daughter! The Peri's Lament for Hinda. Thomas Moore. *Fr.* Lalla Rookh. OBNC
Farewell for a While. Elizabeth Daryush. QFR
Farewell! for now a stormy morn and dark. Outward Bound. Edward Sydney Tylee. PAH
Farewell Frost; or, Welcome the Spring. Robert Herrick. CaPo
Farewell! I goe to sleep; but when. The Evening-Watch. Henry Vaughan. AnAnS-1; NCEP
Farewell! If Ever Fondest Prayer. Byron. EnRP; HBV-1; ViBoPo
(Farewell.) TrGrPo
Farewell in a Dream. Stephen Spender. MoAB; MoBrPo
Farewell, incomparable element. Hymn to Earth. Elinor Wylie. LiTM; MoAB; MoAmPo; MoPo; MoVE; NePA
Farewell, Life. Thomas Hood. EnRP
Farewell, Love, and all thy lawes [*or* laws] for ever. A Renouncing of Love [*or* The Lover Renounceth Love *or* Sonnet]. Sir Thomas Wyatt. AAS; FaBoEn; GBL; LiTB; OAEL-1; OAEP; SiPS; TrGrPo
Farewell Mercy, farewell thy piteous grace. Lament. John Lydgate. *Fr.* Court of Sapience. PoEL-1
Farewell my friend. Requiem. Martin T. O'Connor. AMV-80
Farewell, my more than fatherland! A Farewell to America. Richard Henry Wilde. AA
Farewell, my Muse! for, lo, there is no end. George Edward Woodberry. Ideal Passion, XLII. HBMV
Farewell, my Sweete, untill I come. To Chloris. Charles Cotton. CavP
Farewell, my tender brother. Think. Beatrice's Last Words. Shelley. *Fr.* The Cenci. FiP
Farewell, my Youth! for now we needs must part. Ave atque Vale. Rosamund Marriott Watson. HBV-1
Farewell, O Patrick Sarsfield. *Unknown. See* Farewell to Patrick Sarsfield.
Farewell, O Prince, farewell, O sorely tried! Theodor Herzl. Israel Zangwill. TrJP
Farewell of Clarimonde, The, *sel.* Ella Wheeler Wilcox.
"Adieu, Romauld! But thou canst not forget me." PeD
Farewell of the Attendant Spirit. Milton. *See* To the Ocean Now I Fly.
Farewell, old friend,we part at last. My Old Straw Hat. Eliza Cook. BrRo
Farewell, Old Year! Old and New. *Unknown.* BLRP
Farewell Patrick Sarsfield wherever you may roam. Patrick Sarsfield, Lord Lucan. *Unknown, tr. by* Frank O'Connor. KiLC
Farewell, Peace. *Unknown.* PAH
Farewell, Rewards and Fairies. Richard Corbet. *See* Fairies' Farewell, The.
"Farewell, Romance!" the Cave-men said. The King. Kipling. CABA; VLP
Farewell, sweet boy; complain not of my truth. Farewell to Cupid. Fulke Greville. *Fr.* Caelica. EnRePo; FaBoRV; GBL; NCEP; OBSC; QFR
Farewell, Sweet Dust. Elinor Wylie. LiTA
"Farewell, sweet Jane, for I must go across the flowing sea." Sweet Jane. *Unknown.* AmFP
Farewell, Sweet Mary. *Unknown.* AmFP
Farewell, the bell upon a ram's neck hung. Corydon's Farewell, on Sailing in the Late Expedition Fleet. *Unknown.* NOEC
Farewell the reign of cruelty. Sir Thomas Wyatt. SiPS
Farewell, This World. *Unknown.* MeEL, *abr.*; OxBM
(Cherry Fair, The.) FaBoRV
"This lyfe, I see, is but a cheyre feyre," *sel.* ChTr
Farewell! Thou art too dear [*or* deare] for my possessing. Sonnets, LXXXVII. Shakespeare. EBEV; EIL; GTBS; GTBS-P; InPS; InvP; LiTB; MasP; NOBE; OAEL-1; OAEP; OBEV; OBSC; PeHV; PoEL-2; QFR; TrGrPo; ViBoPo
Farewell, thou busy world, and may. The Retirement [*or* To Mr. Izaak Walton]. Charles Cotton. FaBoPP; HBV-1; OBS; ViBoPo
Farewell, thou child of my right hand, and joy. On My [*or* His] First Son[ne]. Ben Jonson. AnAnS-2; AWP; CABA; EBEV; EIL; EnRePo; FaBoEE; FaBoEn; FF; HAP; HeIP; HoPM; JCP; LiTB; LoBV; NIP;

NOBE; NoP; OAEL-1; OAEP; OBS; PoEL-2; PPoe; QFR; SeCP; SeCV-1; TEP; WeW
Farewell, thou fertile soil that Brutus first out found. Going towards Spain. Barnabe Googe. EnRePo
Farewell, Thou Minstrel Harp. Sir Walter Scott. *Fr.* The Lady of the Lake. OBNC
("Harp of the North, farewell! The hills grow dark.") OAEP; ViBoPo
Farewell thou thing, time-past so knowne, so deare. His Farewell to Sack. Robert Herrick. AnAnS-2; CaPo; OAEP; SeCP; SeCV-1
Farewell to a Fondling, A. Thomas Churchyard. ElL
Farewell to a Southern Melody, A. Huang O, *tr. fr. Chinese by* Kenneth Rexroth *and* Ling Chung. BoWoP
Farewell to Agassiz, A. Oliver Wendell Holmes. ImOP
Farewell to America, A. Richard Henry Wilde. AA
Farewell to an idea . . . A cabin stands. Wallace Stevens. *Fr.* The Auroras of Autumn. CMoP
Farewell to Anactoria. Sappho, *tr. fr. Greek by* Allen Tate. AWP
Farewell to Arms. George Peele. *See* His Golden Locks Time Hath to Silver Turned.
Farewell to Barn and Stack and Tree. A. E. Housman. *Fr.* A Shropshire Lad. CMoP; MoAB; MoBrPo; OAEP; SoSe; UnPo
Farewell to Bath. Lady Mary Wortley Montagu. WPE
Farewell to Cuba. Maria Gowen Brooks. AA
Farewell to Cupid. Fulke Greville. *Fr.* Caelica.
("Farewell, sweet boy; complain not of my truth.") EnRePo; FaBoRV; GBL; NCEP; OBSC; QFR
Farewell to Earth, *sel.* Lizzie Doten
"I would bear a love Platonic to the souls in earthly life." PeD
Farewell to England. *Unknown.* APAS
Farewell to English, A, *sel.* Michael Hartnett
"Gaelic is the conscience of our leaders." CIP
Farewell to Europe. William Pillen. VWA
Farewell to fair Alba, high house of the sun. Deirdre's Farewell to Alba. *Unknown, tr. by* Sir Samuel Ferguson. OnYI
Farewell to Fál, A. Gerald Nugent, *tr. fr. Late Middle Irish by* Padraic Pearse. OnYI
Farewell to False Love, A. Sir Walter Ralegh. BoLoP; ElL
(False Love.) OBSC; SiPS
Farewell to fields and butterflies. Garden-Song. James Branch Cabell. HBMV
Farewell to Follie [*or* Folly], *sel.* Robert Greene.
Maesia's Song. CTC; HBV-2; OBSC; UnPo
(Mind Content, A.) ElL; ViBoPo
(Poor Estate, The.) TrGrPo
Farewell to Greatness. Shakespeare. *See* Cardinal Wolsey's Farewell.
Farewell to Himself. The Bride. Ruth Comfort Mitchell. HBMV
Farewell to Ireland. *At. to* St. Columcille, *tr. fr. Irish by* Douglas Hyde. AWP
(Colum-Cille's Farewell to Ireland). AnIV
Farewell to Juliet ("I see you, Juliet, still, with your straw hat"). Wilfrid Scawen Blunt. *Fr.* The Love Sonnets of Proteus. BoLoP; EnLoPo; OxBTC
Farewell to Juliet ("Lame, impotent conclusion to youth's dreams"). Wilfrid Scawen Blunt. *Fr.* The Love Sonnets of Proteus. ViBoPo
Farewell to Kurdistan. Rosemary Tonks. OxBTC
Farewell to Lochaber, an' farewell my Jean. Lochaber No More. Allan Ramsay. HBV-1
Farewell to Love. John Donne. OAEL-1
Farewell to Love. Michael Drayton. *See* Idea: "Since there's no help. . ."
Farewell to Love. Sir John Suckling. CaPo
Farewell to My Mother. "Placido," *tr. fr. Spanish by* James Weldon Johnson. TTY
Farewell to Nancy. Burns. *See* Ae Fond Kiss.
Farewell to Narcissus. Robert Horan. NYBP
Farewell to New Zealand. Wynford Vaughan-Thomas. DBV; NOBL
Farewell to old England for ever [*or* the beautiful!]. Botany Bay. *Unknown.* FSW; PoAu-1
Farewell to Patrick Sarsfield [Earl of Lucan]. *Unknown, tr. fr. Irish by* James Clarence Mangan. AnIV; OxBI
(Farewell, O Patrick Sarsfield.) OnYI
(Patrick Sarsfield, Lord Lucan, *tr. by* Frank O'Connor.) KiLC
Farewell to Poetry. Goldsmith. *Fr.* The Deserted Village. OBEC
Farewell to Sir John Norris and Sir Francis Drake, A. George Peele. OBSC
Farewell to Sliev Morna. Lay of the Forlorn. George Darley. OnYI
Farewell to Summer. George Arnold. AA
Farewell to the bushy clump close to the river. Farewell. John Clare. NoP
Farewell to the caterpillars standing in minks. To Paul Eluard. Jorie Graham. AMV-80
Farewell to the Court. Sir Walter Ralegh. EnRePo; FaBoEn; OBSC; SiPS
Farewell to the Court, *sel.* Earl of Rochester.
"Tired with the noisome follies of the age." TrGrPo
Farewell to the Fairies. Richard Corbet. *See* Fairies' Farewell, The.
Farewell to the Farm. Robert Louis Stevenson. FaPON; TiPo
Farewell to the Highlands, farewell to the North. My Heart's in the Highlands. Burns. AWP; EnRP; FaFP
Farewell to the land where the clouds love to rest. Sir Walter Scott. *Fr.* Rob Roy. NBM
Farewell to the Moon, A. Ed Ochester. MOON
Farewell to the Muses. John Hamilton Reynolds. OBRV
Farewell to the Old Year. Eleanor Farjeon. SiSoSe
Farewell to the world, and to the night farewell. Chikamatsu Monzaemon. *Fr.* The Love Suicides at Sonezaki. DL
Farewell to the World of Richard Bishop. *Unknown.* CoMu
Farewell to Tobacco, A. Charles Lamb. NBM; OBRV; OxBoLi
Farewell to Town. Laurence Housman. HBMV
Farewell to Van Gogh. Charles Tomlinson. CMoP; GTBS-P; NMP
Farewell to Winnipeg. Roy Daniels. OBCV
Farewell to you, my own true love. The Leaving of Liverpool. *Unknown.* FSW
Farewell, too little and too lately known. To the Memory of Mr. Oldham. Dryden. AWP; CABA; EBEV; FaBoEn; FiP; HAP; HeIP; InPK; InPS; LoBV; NIP; NOBE; NoP; OAEL-1; OBS; PAI; PoEL-3; PP; PPoe; PPP; SeCeV; SeCeV-2; ViBoPo
Farewell, Ungrateful Traitor. Dryden. *Fr.* The Spanish Friar, V, i. BoLoP; ELP; EnLoPo; HAP; LiTB; NOBE; PoPle; ViBoPo
(Love's Despair.) ACP
(Song, A.) CavP; FaBoEn; FiP; OBS; SeCV-2
Farewell, Unkind! Farewell! to me, no more a father! *Unknown.* EnLoPo
Farewell, Unkist. Sir Thomas Wyatt. *See* Farewell: "What should I say."
Farewell Voyaging World! Conrad Aiken. NYBP
Farewell, whose like on earth I shall not find. In Memoriam—W. G. Ward. Tennyson. Valedictory, I. GoBC
Farewell with a Mischeife. George Gascoigne. AAS
Farewell World. Sir Philip Sidney. *See* Leave Me, O Love.
Farewell, ye blooming fields! ye cheerful plains! Michael Bruce. *Fr.* Elegy: To Spring. NOEC
Farewell, ye dungeons dark and strong. Macpherson's Farewell. Burns. BSV
Farewell you everlasting hills! I'm cast. Mans Fall, and Recovery. Henry Vaughan. AnAnS-1
Farewells from Paradise. Elizabeth Barrett Browning. OBEV; OBVV
Far-fetched and dear bought, as the proverb rehearses. A Singing Lesson. Swinburne. HBV-2
Farm, The. Donald Hall. LiTM
Farm, The. Vassar Miller. NCSH
Farm Boy after Summer. Robert Francis. NCSH
Farm boys wild to couple. The Sheep Child. James Dickey. CAPP; GP; NoAM; NOBA; Prf; TAP
Farm-brooks that come down to Rathfarnham. The Loss of Strength. Austin Clarke. IPY
Farm Child. R. S. Thomas. BoNaP; ChMP
Farm Gate. Uys Krige, *tr. fr. Afrikaans by* Uys Krige *and* Jack Cope. PeSA
Farm Hands, The. Dilys Laing. SaC
Farm Implements and Rutabagas in a Landscape. John Ashbery. CoAP; GP
Farm near Norman's Lane, The. Mary Finnin. PoAu-2
Farm on the Great Plains, The. William Stafford. HAP; PoCh; VGW
Farm on the Links, The. Rosamund Marriott Watson. OBVV
Farm Picture, A. Walt Whitman. InPS; PPoe
Farm Wife. Matt Field. AMV-81
Farm Wife. John Hanlon Mitchell. CaP
Farm-Woman's Winter, The. Thomas Hardy. VLP
Farmer. Liberty Hyde Bailey. YeAr
Farmer, The. "E." CBAP
Farmer. Padraic Fallon. OxBI
Farmer, The. A. P. Herbert. CenHV
Farmer, The. Fredegond Shove. MMA
Farmer, The. Terry Stokes. POL
Farmer. Lucien Stryk. FAZ
Farmer, The, *with music.* *Unknown.* AS
(Farmer Comes to Town, The, *with music.*) TrAS
(Farmer Is the Man, The.) FSW
Farmer and the Farmer's Wife, The. P. G. Hiebert. FiBHP
Farmer and the Shanty Boy, The. *Unknown.* AmFP
Farmer Comes to Town, The. *Unknown.* *See* Farmer, The.
Farmer Goes Beserk. Anne Elder. CBAP
Farmer had a daughter whose beauty ne'er was told, A. The Banks of Sweet Dundee. *Unknown.* AmFP
Farmer Is the Man, The. *Unknown.* *See* Farmer, The.
Farmer knew each time a friend went past, The. Hound on the Church Porch. Robert P. Tristram Coffin. GDP
Farmer lived in the north country, A. The Swan Swims So Bonny. *Unknown.* OBET
Farmer of Tilsbury Vale, The. Wordsworth. EBEV

Farmer once called his cow "Zephyr," A. Zephyr. *Unknown.* TDH
Farmer ploughs into the ground, The. Seed. Herman Charles Bosman. PeSA
Farmer Remembers the Somme, The. Vance Palmer. PoAu-1
Farmer say to de weevil, De. De Ballet of De Boll Weevil. *Unknown.* AS
Farmer went trotting upon his gray mare, A. Mother Goose. EvOK; HBVY; OxNR; TiPo
Farmer will never be happy again, The. The Farmer. A. P. Herbert. CenHV
Farmers. Thomas Lux. LCAP
Farmers. William Alexander Percy. WGRP
Farmers. Hortense Roberta Roberts. AMV-81
Farmer's Boy, The, *sels.* Robert Bloomfield.
"Again, the year's decline, midst storms and floods." OBRV
"Live, trifling incidents, and grace my song." OBRV
Moonlight . . . Scattered Clouds. OBNC
Summer. PBBP
Farmer's Boy, The ("The sun went down beyond yon hill"). *Unknown.* OBET
Farmer's Boy, A ("They strolled down the lane together"). *Unknown.* PoPle
Farmer's boy, starting to plough, A. "O-U-G-H-"; or, The Cross Farmer. D. S. Martin. TDH
Farmer's Bride, The. Charlotte Mew. BoLoP; ErPo; HBMV; MoAB; MoBrPo; OxBTC; SBG; TrGrPo; WPE
Farmer's clothes are soaked through and never dried, The. Ise Tayu, *tr. fr. Japanese by* Kenneth Rexroth *and* Ikuko Atsumi. WPOW
Farmer's Complaint, The, *orig. and mod. English prose.* *Unknown.* OxBM
Farmer's Curst Wife, The. *Unknown.* AmFP; BaBo (A *and* B *vers.*); ESPB (A *and* B *vers.*); ViBoFo
Farmer's eyes are dark, The; he speaks in song. On the Welsh Marches. Walter Stone. NYBP
Farmer's goose, who in the stubble, The. The Progress of Poetry. Swift. CABA; InvP; OnYI
Farmer's Ingle, The. Robert Fergusson. BSV
Farmer's Son So Sweet, A. *Unknown.* OBET
Farmer's Wife, The. Anne Sexton. HoPM; LiTM; NePoEA-2
Farmer's Wife and the Raven, The. John Gay. PBBP
Farmer's wife looked out of the dairy, The. The Rival. Sylvia Townsend Warner. MoAB; MoBrPo
Farmhouse lingers, though averse to square, The. A Brook in the City. Robert Frost. OxBA
Farmhouse skyline, draped with trees, The. Pastoral. Alan Creighton. CaP
Farmyard Song, A. *Unknown.* *See* Barnyard Song.
Farolita. Mei-Mei Berssenbrugge. BrSi
Farr off from these a slow and silent stream. The Place of the Damned. Milton. *Fr.* Paradise Lost, II. FaBoEn
Farragut. William Tuckey Meredith. AA; EtS; FaBoBe; HBV-2; HBVY; PAH
Farre have I clambred in my mind. *See* Far have I clamber'd in my mind.
Farrell O'Reilly. Oliver St. John Gogarty. OxBTC
Farther. John James Piatt. AA
Farther Along. *Unknown.* FSW
Farther and farther from the three Pa Roads. On New Year's Eve. Ts'uei T'u, *tr. by* Witter Bynner. OFD
Farther east it wouldn't be on the map. Midwest Town. Ruth Delong Peterson. AmFN
Farther he went the farther home grew, The. For the Grave of Daniel Boone. William Stafford. NoP; PAI; PoPl
Farther in the summer than the birds. Emily Dickinson. LiTA; PoEL-5; QFR
Farther than I have been. The Summit. Kathleen Raine. Beinn Naomh, IV. OxBS
Farthest from any war, unique in time. Hollywood. Karl Shapiro. LiTM; OxBA
Farwell, The ("Farwell, fond Love, under whose childish whipp"). Henry King. CavP
Farwell ungratefull traytor. *See* Farewell Ungrateful Traitor.
Fascination of What's Difficult, The. W. B. Yeats. BIrV; BrPo; PoEL-5
Fa'se Footrage. *Unknown.* *See* Fause Foodrage.
Fashion. Horace Twiss. BXAP
Fashion me strangely in the human mold. At 21. Eugene L. Belisle. AMV-81
Fashionable Heart, The. Jack Gilbert. NPGG
Fashions in Dogs. E. B. White. FiBHP; GDP
Fashions in the 70's. May Swenson. NYP
Fast Ball. Jonathan Williams. NeAP
Fast express for Gettysburg roared north, The. They Will Look for a Few Words. Nancy Byrd Turner. AmFN
Fast falls the snow, O lady mine. To F. C. Mortimer Collins. HBV-1; TreFS
Fasten the chamber! Bluebeard's Closet. Rose Terry Cooke. AA
Faster, faster,/ O Circe, Goddess. The Strayed Reveller. Matthew Arnold. LoBV; OAEL-2; VLP
Faster than fairies, faster than witches. From a Railway Carriage. Robert Louis Stevenson. FaPON; OxBChV; PDV; RHPC; TiPo
Faster than Light. *Unknown.* *See* Relativity.
Fastidious Serpent, The. Henry Johnstone. HBV-2; HBVY
Fastidious Yak, The. Oliver Herford. TDH
Fat black bucks in a wine-barrel room. The Congo. Vachel Lindsay. CMoP; FaFP; LiTA; MoAB; MoAmPo; NoAM; NOBA; OxBA; PoNe; PoRA; TAP; TreF; WHA
Fat Boy's Dream, The. Richard McCann. GrPl
Fat-buttocked Bushmen, The. Earnest A. Hooton. WhC
Fat Cat. John Ronan. AMV-81
Fat friar stroking golf balls, The. Walking along the Hudson. Donald Petersen. CoAP
Fat green frog sits by the pond. Grandfather Frog. Louise Seaman Bechtel. TiPo
Fat-kneed god! Feeder of mangy leopards! You Also, Gaius Valerius Catullus. Archibald MacLeish. NoAM; TAP
Fat lady came on, The. Landscape of the Vomiting Multitudes. Federico García Lorca, *tr. by* Ben Belitt. NYP
Fat Man, The. Vern Rutsala. DFF
Fat Man in the Mirror, The. Robert Lowell. PoA
Fat men go about the streets, The. Ballade of the Poetic Life. J. C. Squire. OBMV; WhC
Fat, pale proprietor, The. In an Arab Town. Susan Tichy. MAYP
Fat red barns lean east along Highway 109. Leaving Mendota, 1956. Lawrence Locke. GrPl
Fat sixty-year-old man woke me, A. "Hello." Birthday. John Ciardi. NAs
Fat torpedoes in bursting jackets. Fourth of July. Rachel Field. SiSoSe
Fat Tuesday. W. S. Di Piero. MAYP
Fat White Woman Speaks, The. G. K. Chesterton. SpRo
Fat women full of water. The Pueblo Women I Watched Get Down in Brooklyn. Wendy Rose. TWSS
Fatal Dream, The; or, The Unhappy Favourite. Emanuel Collins. NOEC
Fatal Love. Matthew Prior. FaBoCo
Fatal Mistake, A. Edward Lear. TDH
("There was an old man of Peru.") EBEV
Fatal Sisters, The. Thomas Gray, *after the Icelandic.* EnRP; LAuP; OAEP
Fatal Spell, The. Byron. *Fr.* Childe Harold's Pilgrimage, IV. OBNC
("Oh love! no habitant of earth thou art.") OAEL-2; ViBoPo
Fatal Wedding, The. W. H. Windom. TreFS
Fatales Poetae. Henry Parrot. FaBoEE
Fate. Louis James Block. AA
Fate. James Fenimore Cooper. HBMV
Fate. Susan Marr Spalding. AA; BLPA; HBV-1
Fate and the Younger Generation. D. H. Lawrence. OxBoLi; WhC
Fate gave the word, the arrow sped. A Mother's Lament for the Death of Her Son. Burns. HoPM
Fate hired me once to play a villain's part. Between the Acts. Stanley Kunitz. ELU
Fate! I Have Asked. Walter Savage Landor. ViBoPo
Fate, I will not ask for wealth or fame. The Higher Good. Theodore Parker. FaBoBe
Fate in Incognito. Michael Benedikt. OBAL
Fate Is Unfair. Don Marquis. *Fr.* Archy Does His Part. EvOK
Fate of Birds, The. Kenneth Seib. AMV-80
Fate of John Burgoyne, The. *Unknown.* PAH
Fate of King Dathi, The. Thomas Osborne Davis. OnYI
Fate of Narcissus, The. William Warner. *Fr.* Albion's England. OBSC
Fate of the Cabbage Rose, The. Wallace Irwin. FiBHP
Fate of the Oak, The. "Barry Cornwall." OHIP
Fate of the Prophets, The. Longfellow. *Fr.* Christus; a Mystery, Pt. I. WGRP
Fate on the left hand, and Death on the right. And Again. Humphrey Evans. BXAP
Fate struck the hour! Lincoln. Jane L. Hardy. OHIP
Fate to beauty still must give. Epitaph. Claudian, *tr. by* Howard Mumford Jones. AWP
Fates of Men. *Unknown, tr. fr. Anglo-Saxon by* Charles W. Kennedy. AnOE
Fates of the Apostles, *sel.* Cynewulf, *tr. fr. Anglo-Saxon by* Charles W. Kennedy.
"Now I pray the man who may love this lay." AnOE
Father. Rose Ausländer, *tr. fr. German by Ewald Osers. VWA*
Father. Paul Carroll. DiL; NeAP
Father. Arthur Davison Ficke. TrPWD
Father, The. Donald Finkel. CoPo; PAI
Father. Frances Frost. FaPON; SiSoSe; TiPo
Father. Margit Kaffka, *tr. fr. Hungarian by* Laura Schiff. PBWP
Father. Ted Kooser. Str
Father, The. Richmond Lattimore. EyDe; NePoAm-2
Father. Jean Lipkin. PeSA

Father. Myra Cohn Livingston. NTCP
Father. Robert Lowell. DiL
Father, The. Desmond O'Grady. NoAM
Father. Robert Pack. CoPo
Father. Lois Reiner. AMV-80
Father. Mildred Weston. PoSC
Father. John Wheelwright. DiL; UnPo
Father. Paul Zweig. DiL
Father/ I am not equal to the faith required. Confession. Lucille Clifton. GeTw
Father,/ one day longer on this earth than you. My Father, My Son. John Malcolm Brinnin. DiL; NYBP
Father/ You are the trunk. Psalm. Howard Schwartz. VWA
Father Abraham, *with music. Unknown.* BoAN-1
Father, and Bard revered! to whom I owe. Dedicatory Sonnet to S. T. Coleridge. Hartley Coleridge. OAEL-2
Father and Child. Gwen Harwood. CBAP; WPE
Father and His Children, The. *Unknown.* OxBChV
Father and I in the Woods. David McCord. SO
Father and I went down to camp. Yankee Doodle [*or* The Yankee's Return from Camp]. *Unknown, at. to* Edward Bangs *and also* Richard Shuckburg. AmFP; BLSo; FaFP; FaPON; HBV-2; OxBoLi; PAH; PAL; TrAS; TreF; YaD
Father and Mother. X. J. Kennedy. GrPl; RHPC
Father and Son. Richard Eberhart. DiL
Father and Son. F. R. Higgins. BIrV; OBMV; OxBI
Father and Son. David Ignatow. DiL
Father and Son. Stanley Kunitz. DiL; MP; NoAM; TwCP
Father and Son. Delmore Schwartz. DiL; LiTA
Father and Son. William Stafford. GP
Father and Son. Ronald Wallace. AMV-81
Father and Son: 1939. William Plomer. NoAM; PeSA
Father and Sons. Harvey Shapiro. FAZ
Father, be praised for a white jasmine. Consolation in July. Rayner Heppenstall. NeBP
Father being the loneliest word in the one language. John Berryman. *Fr.* Dream Songs. DiL
Father, between Thy strong hands Thou has bent. Prayer of a Teacher. Dorothy Littlewort. TrPWD
Father calls me William, sister calls me Will. Jest 'fore Christmas. Eugene Field. FaBV; FaFP; FaPON; FPL; HBV-1; HBVY; OHFP; PoLF; TreF
Father, chancing to chastise. Some Ruthless Rhymes, IV. Harry Graham. CenHV
Father Coyote. George Sterling. BPAW
Father Damien. John Banister Tabb. ACP
Father dead and mother dead. The Female Principle. A. D. Hope. OxBC
Father, Dear Father, Come Home with Me Now. Henry Clay Work. FSW; TreF
(Come Home, Father.) PaPo; YaD
Father Does His Best, A. E. B. White. WhC
Father Father Son and Son. Jon Swan. NYBP
Father, father, where are you going. The Little Boy Lost. Blake. *Fr.* Songs of Innocence. EnRP; LAuP; NoP; TiPo
Father Fisheye. Peter Balakian. MAYP
"Father Francisco! Father Francisco!" The Confessional. *Unknown, tr. by* Louis Untermeyer. UnTE
Father Grumble. *Unknown.* AmFP; BaBo; ViBoFo
(Old Man in the Wood.) FSW
(Old Man Who Lived in a Wood [*or* the Woods]. MoShBr, *sl. diff. vers.*; OnUR
Father has a workshop. The Workshop. Aileen Fisher. SoPo
Father, Hear the Prayer We Offer, *with music.* Love Maria Willis. AH
Father heard his children scream. The Stern Parent. Harry Graham. Some Ruthless Rhymes, I. CenHV; ChTr; TreFT
Father, here a temple in Thy name we build. Hymn of Dedication. Elizabeth E. Scantlebury. BLRP
Father, How Wide Thy Glories Shine. Charles Wesley. TrPWD; TRV
Father! I bless thy name that I do live. In Him We Live. Jones Very. OxBA
Father, I expect your eyes. Before the Mountain. Elizabeth Libbey. AmPA
Father, I have launched my bark. The Pilgrim. Emma C. Embury. OBCA
Father I have your rug. Melkon. David Kherdian. FAZ
Father, I lift my hands to Thee. Suppliant. Florence Earle Coates. TrPWD
Father, I loved you as a child, and still. The Mirror. Edgar Bowers. QFR
Father! I Own Thy Voice, *with music.* Samuel Wolcott. AH
Father, I scarcely dare to pray. A Last Prayer. Helen Hunt Jackson. AA; TrPWD; TRV
Father, I will not ask for wealth or fame. The Higher Good [*or* A New Year Prayer]. Theodore Parker. AA; HBV-2; PGD
Father! I'm hungered! give me bread. The Emigrant's Dying Child. G. W. Patton. BPAW
Father in Heaven ("For flowers that bloom about our feet"). *Unknown. See* Thanksgiving.
Father in heaven, after each lost day. Petrarch, *tr. fr. Italian by* Bernard Bergonzi. Sonnets to Laura: To Laura in Life, LXII. NAWM-1
Father in Heaven! from whom the simplest flower. A Prayer. Felicia Dorothea Hemans. TrPWD
Father in Heaven! humbly before thee. A Prayer for Peace. Edward Rowland Sill. TrPWD
Father in heaven, make me wise. A Father Speaks [*or* A Mother's Prayer]. *Unknown.* STF; TrPWD
Father in Tennessee, A. J. Edgar Simmons. TAT
Father, in Thy Mysterious Presence Kneeling, *with music.* Samuel Johnson. AH
(Prayer for Strength.) TRV
Father, in Thy starry tent. Rest in Peace. Wilfred J. Funk. PoLF
Father is, dedicatedly. Father. Lois Reiner. AMV-80
Father is hard to live with. Old Storm. David Phillips. NeAC
Father John's bread was made of rye. Rye Bread. William Stanley Braithwaite. CDC
Father Knows, The. "F. L. H." BLRP
Father Land and Mother Tongue. Samuel Lover. HBV-2
Father, lead me, day by day. A Child's Prayer. *Unknown.* BLRP
Father Malloy. Edgar Lee Masters. *Fr.* Spoon River Anthology. OxBA
Father Mapple's Hymn. Herman Melville. *Fr.* Moby Dick, *ch.* 9. EtS
(Ribs and Terrors, The.) EaLo; ViBoPo
(Whale, The.) PoPl; TrGrPo
Father Mat. Patrick Kavanagh. AnIL; CMoP
"In a meadow/ Beside the chapel three boys were playing football," *sel.* MoAB; NMP
Father Missouri takes his own. Foreclosure. Sterling A. Brown. PoBA; PoNe
Father Molloy. Samuel Lover. HBV-2
Father of all! in Death's relentless claim. Oliver Wendell Holmes. *Fr.* A Poem. TrPWD
Father of all! In every age. The Universal Prayer. Pope. BLPA; FaBoBe; FPL; GoBC; HBV-2; ILwL; NoP; OAEP; TreFT; WGRP
Father of Heaven, and him, by whom. The Litanie. John Donne. NOCV; PoEL-2
"Father of Jealousy, be thou accursed from the earth!" Blake. *Fr.* Visions of the Daughters of Albion. ViBoPo
"Father of lakes!" thy waters bend. Lake Superior. Samuel Griswold Goodrich. AA
Father of Life, with songs of wonder. Margaret L. Woods. *Fr.* The Return. TrPWD
Father of lights! what sunny [*or* sunnie] seed. Cock-crowing. Henry Vaughan. AnAnS-1; MePo; OAEL-1; PBBP; SeCV-1
Father of mercies, in Thy Word. O How Sweet Are Thy Words! Anne Steele. BLRP
Father of My Country, The. Diane Wakoski. NoAM; TAP
Father of the Man. Elizabeth Mabel Bryan. GoYe
Father of the Victim. Rae Ballard. AMV-80
Father of Women, A. Alice Meynell. BrRo; SBG; WPE
Father O'Flynn. Alfred Perceval Graves. HBV-2; OnYI
Father, on the first day on the Hunting Moon. The First Day of the Hunting Moon. Patricia Low. VGW
Father once said to his son, A. Punishment. *Unknown.* TDH
Father, part of his double interest. Holy Sonnets, XVI. John Donne. AnAnS-1; JCP; MasP; OBS
Father Poem. Joel Oppenheimer. PoM
Father raised words, The. Family. Norman MacCaig. FF
Father said that maybe. Tummy Ache. Aileen Fisher. SoPo
Father. . .—Say the *confiteor.*—I said it. The Confessor. G. G. Belli, *tr. by* Harold Norse. ErPo
Father Short came down the lane. *Unknown.* OxNR
Father, since always now the death to come. Sonnet for [*or* to] My Father. Donald Justice. DFF; DiL
Father, sitting on the side of your startled bed. D-Dawn. Margaret McGarvey. GoYe
Father Son and Holy Ghost. Audre Lorde. PoBa
Father Speaks, A. *Unknown.* STF
(Mother's Prayer, A, *at. to* Margaret E. Sangster.) TrPWD
Father Takes to the Road and Lets His Hair Down. Alan Chong Lau. BrSi
Father, Teach Me. Walter M. Lee. STF
Father, the visit/ was so unexpected. To My Father. Susannah Fried, *tr. by Anthony Rudolf. VWA*
Father, the Year Is Fallen. Audre Lorde. PoBA
Father, this year's jinx rides us apart. All My Pretty Ones. Anne Sexton. CoPo; NoAM
Father, through the dark that parts us. Ballad. Roy Fuller. ELU
Father, thy hand/ Hath reared. Bryant. *Fr.* A Forest Hymn. TrPWD

Father! Thy wonders do not singly stand. The Spirit Land. Jones Very. HAP
Father, thy word is past, man shall find grace. The Atonement. Milton. *Fr.* Paradise Lost, III. OBS
Father Time. Norman Ault. HBVY
Father to the Man. John Knight. EaLo
Father was and aye shall be, The. The Trinity. *Unknown.* ACP
Father, we come not as of old. Hymn. John W. Chadwick. TrPWD
Father, we thank Thee for the night. A Prayer. *Unknown.* SoPo
Father, who designs his babe a priest, The. William Cowper. *Fr.* Tirocinium; or, A Review of Schools. OBSV
Father, Who Mak'st Thy Suff'ring Sons, *with music.* Arthur C. Coxe. AH
Father, whom I knew well for forty years. The Gardener. John Hall Wheelock. DiL; NYBP; TwAmPo
Father, whom I murdered every night but one. Elegy for My Father. Howard Moss. CoAP; DiL; LiTM; NePoEA; VWA
Father! whose hard and cruel law. The Death of Grant. Ambrose Bierce. AA
Father William. "Lewis Carroll." *Fr.* Alice's Adventures in Wonderland, *ch.* 5. BiP; BXAP; FaBoNo; FaBoPa; FaPON; FiBHP; FPL; GoJo; HBV-1; HoPM; InMe; LiTB; PDV; PoLF; PoRA; RHPC; SpRo; TreF; TrGrPo
(You Are Old, Father William.) OxBChV; UnPo; WhC
(" 'You are old, Father William,' the young man said.") FaBoCo; NOBL; Par; TiPo
Father William ("You are old, Father William," the young man said,/ "And your nose has a look of surprise"). *Unknown.* NA
Fathered by March, the daffodils are here. Daffodils. Lizette Woodworth Reese. AA
Fatherland, The. James Russell Lowell. GN; HBV-2; HBVY; PGD; PoPl
Fatherland Song. Björnsterne Björnson, *tr. fr. Norwegian by* William Ellery Leonard. AWP
Fatherless and motherless. *Unknown.* GBP
Fatherless, 250 people. Verigin, Moving in Alone. John Newlove. NeAC
Fathers, The. John N. Morris. GP
Fathers, The. Edwin Muir. OxBS
Fathers, The. Benjamin Saltman. VWA
Fathers, The. Siegfried Sassoon. NoAM
Fathers: naked, you stand for their big faces. This Is a Poem for the Dead. Michael Ryan. AmPA; DiL
Fathers and Sons. *Unknown, tr. fr. Irish by* Frank O'Connor. KiLC
Father's Business, The. Edwin Markham. TRV
Father's Gold, The. *Unknown.* STF
Father's gone a-flailing. *Unknown.* OxNR
Father's Heart Is Touched, A. Samuel Hoffenstein. FiBHP
Father's locking up our house. When I Was Nine. Raymond Roseliep. FAZ
Father's Notes of Woe, A. Sir Walter Scott. *Fr.* The Lay of the Last Minstrel. OBNC
("Sweet Teviot! on thy silver tide.") OBRV
Father's Prayer, A. *Unknown.* STF
Father's Story. Elizabeth Madox Roberts. FaPON; PoSC
Father's Testament, A. Judah ibn Tibbon, *tr. fr. Hebrew by* Israel Abrahams. TrJP
Father's voice. William Stafford. RFM
Father's Whiskers. *Unknown.* FSW
Fathomless Is My Love. Kalola, *tr. fr. Hawaiian by* N. B. Emerson. WTO
Fathoms deep beneath the wave. Mermaids and Mermen [or Song of the Mermaids and Mermen]. Sir Walter Scott. *Fr.* The Pirate, *ch.* 16. EtS; WSC
Fath'r and I went down to camp. *See* Father and I went down. . .
Fatigue. Hilaire Belloc. FaBoCo; MoVE; NOBL; OxBTC; PV; TreFT
Fatigue, regrets. The lights. The Demon Lover. Adrienne Rich. IHMS
Fatigues. Richard Aldington. BrPo
Fatima. Tennyson. SeCePo; UnPo; UnTE
Fatness. Alan Ansen. CoAP
Fatted/ on herbs, swollen on crabapples. The Porcupine. Galway Kinnell. NaP; NOBA
Fattened sky, The. The Fifth Hell. Jerome Rothenberg. *Fr.* The Seven Hells of Jigoku Zoshi. NNaP
Fatty, Fatty, Boom-a-latty. *Unknown.* RHPC
Fault, The. Edward Lucie-Smith. NePoEA-2
Fault Is Not Mine, The. Walter Savage Landor. HBV-1
Faults, Male and Female. *Unknown.* DBV
Faun, The. Haniel Long. HBMV
Faun, The. Ezra Pound. FaBoCh; FaBoTw
Faun Sees Snow for the First Time, The. Richard Aldington. MoBrPo
Faun-taken. Rose O'Neill. HBMV
Faur Wid I Dee? J. C. Milne. PoSH
Fause Foodrage. *Unknown.* ESPB (A, B, *and* C *vers.*)
(Fa'se Footrage.) OxBB
Fause Knicht upon the Road, The. *Unknown.* *See* False Knight upon the Road, The.
Faust. John Ashbery. NoP; TwCP
Faust, *sels.* Goethe, *tr. fr. German.*
Chorus of the Archangels, The, 2 *versions, tr. by* Shelley. OBVE
Easter Chorus, *tr. by* Bayard Taylor. WGRP
(Christ Is Arisen, *diff. sel.*) TrCP
"Here stand I, ach, Philosophy." Pt. I, *tr. by* Louis MacNeice. NAWM-2
"Limits of the sphere of dream, The," *tr. by* Shelley. WSC
Lose This Day Loitering, *tr. by* John Anster. PoLF
Prologue in Heaven. AWP, *tr. by* Shelley; NAWM-2, *tr. by* Louis MacNeice
Soldier's Song, *tr. by* Bayard Taylor. AWP
"Stop playing with your melancholy," *tr. by* Walter Kaufman. DL
Faustina hath a spot upon her face. De Naevo in Facie Faustinae. Thomas Bastard. FaBoEE
Faustina hath the fairer face. *Unknown.* OBSC
Faustina, or Rock Roses. Elizabeth Bishop. FaBoMo; NMP
Faustine. Swinburne. BeLS; PeHV; UnTE, *abr.*
Faustine. Arthur Colton. AA
(Sometime It May Be.) HBV-1
Faust's Servant. Roy Fuller. OxBTC
Faustus Faces His Doom. Christopher Marlowe. *Fr.* Dr. Faustus. TreFT
Faustus Triumphant. Thom Gunn. FaBoMo
Fauxbourg, A. George Croly. OBRV
Favorite Grandson Braid. Phillip William George. VoR
Favour. Robert D. Fitzgerald. CBAP
Favourite Cat's Dying Soliloquy, A. Anna Seward. FM
Favourite pleasure hath it been with me, A. Wordsworth. *Fr.* The Prelude, IV. OBRV
Favourite Village, The, *sel.* James Hurdis.
"But most of all subdued, or fearful least." PBBP
Fawn in the Snow, The. William Rose Benét. MoAmPo
Fawnia. Robert Greene. *Fr.* Pandosto. HBV-1; OBEV; OBSC
(Ah, Were She Pitiful.) TrGrPo; ViBoPo
(In Praise of His Loving and Best-beloved Fawnia.) PoEL-2
Fawn's Foster-Mother. Robinson Jeffers. NoAm; NOBA
Fay Wray to the King. Judith Rechter. NMM
Fayned Fancy betweene the Spider and the Gowte, A, *sel.* Thomas Churchyard.
Old-Time Service. OBSC
Fayre copie of my Celia's face. *See* Fair copy of my Celia's face.
Fayre is my love, when her fayre golden heares. *See* Fair is my love, when. . .
Fay's Crime, The. Joseph Rodman Drake. *Fr.* The Culprit Fay. GN
Fay's Departure, The. Joseph Rodman Drake. *Fr.* The Culprit Fay. GN
(First Quest, The.) AA
Fay's Sentence, The. Joseph Rodman Drake. *Fr.* The Culprit Fay. AA; GN
Fe-Fi-Fo-Fum, *sel.* Dorothy Brown Thompson.
"I do like ogres." ShM
Fe [*or* Fee], fi, fo, fum. *Unknown.* EvOK; OxNR; ShM
Fear, The. Lascelles Abercrombie. OBMV
Fear. Aldo Camerino, *tr. fr. Italian by* Anita Barrows. VWA
Fear. Stephen Dobyns. AMV-80
Fear, A. Robert Francis. GP
Fear, The. Robert Frost. BeLS; TwAmPo
Fear. Anna Hajnal, *tr. fr. Hungarian by* Daniel Hoffman. BoWoP
Fear. Langdon Elwyn Mitchell. AA
Fear. Thomas Peacock. VoR
Fear. Alejandra Pizarnik, *tr. fr. Spanish by* Lynn Alvarez. AMV-80
Fear. Vittoria Aganoor Pompili, *tr. fr. Italian by* Brenda Webster. PBWP
Fear. Roger Stump. AMV-80
Fear. Dara Wier. MAYP
Fear and Anger in the Mindless Universe. Hayden Carruth. NNaP
Fear Death by Water. Richard Eberhart. AMV-81
Fear death?—to feel the fog in my throat. Prospice. Robert Browning. BiP; BLPL; DL; FaBoEn; FaBV; FiP; HBV-2; HBVY; LiTB; OAEP; OBVV; PoLF; PoRA; SeCeV; TreFS; TrCP; TrGrPo; TRV; VLP; WGRP
Fear, facing the New Year. Facing the New Year. Mark Guy Pearse. BLRP
Fear falls upon me on the moutain top. The Dog Child. Keaulumoku, *tr. fr. Hawaiian by* M. W. Beckwith. *Fr.* The Kumulipo; a Creation Chant. WTO
Fear Has Cast Out Love. Wilfrid Scawen Blunt. The Love Sonnets of Proteus, XXXVI. VLP
Fear, jealousy and murder are the same. Gamecock. James Dickey. HoPM; UnPo
Fear knocked at the door. Faith. *Unknown.* TreFT
Fear me, virgin whosoever. After the Pleasure Party. Herman Melville. PoEL-5

Fear no longer for the lone grey birds. End of the Flower World (A.D. 2300). Stanley Burnshaw. TrJP
Fear No More the Heat o' the Sun. Shakespeare. *Fr.* Cymbeline. AWP; CH; ChTr; EBEV; ElL; ELP; EnRePo; FaFP; FF; GBL; HAP; HelP; InPK; InPS; LiTB; LoBV; NoP; OAEP; PAI; PoPle; PoRA; PPoe; PrIm; QFR; RoGo; SCV; SeCeV; SoSe; TrGrPo; ViBoPo; WHA
(Dirge.) HBV-2; OAEL-1
(Dirge for Fidele.) NOBE
(Fidele.) GTBS; GTBS-P; OBEV
(Fidele's Dirge.) FaBoCh; OBSC
(Lament for Imogen.) TreF
(Lament of Guiderius and Arviragus.) FaBoEn
(Song: "Fear no more the heat o' the sun.") CTC; FiP; PoEL-2
Fear Not. J. Bullock. STF
Fear Not, Dear Love. Thomas Carew. UnTE
(Secrecy Protested [*or* Secresie Protested].) AnAnS-2; CaPo; OAEP; SeCP
Fear not, O little flock! the foe. Battle Hymn. Michael Altenburg, *tr. by* Catherine Winkworth. WGRP
Fear Not, Poor Weary One, *with music.* Thomas Cogswell Upham. AH
Fear not, shepherds, for I bring. Angel's Song. Charles Causley. OBCP
Fear not the atom in fission. Cradle Song. Samuel Hoffenstein. DBV
Fear of Bo-talee, The. N. Scott Momaday. STE
Fear of Death. John Ashbery. FaBoMo; TAP
Fear of Death, The. Lucretius, *tr. fr. Latin by* Dryden. *Fr.* De Rerum Natura, III. LoBV
Fear of Death, The. Shakespeare. *Fr.* Measure for Measure, III, i. TreFT
Fear of Death Confounds Me, The. William Dunbar. *See* Lament for the Makaris.
Fear of death disturbs me constantly, The. Prayer. Gabrielle de Coignard, *tr. by* Raymond Oliver. WPOW
Fear of Dying, The. John Holmes. MiAP
Fear of Flowers, The. John Clare. NBM; OBRV; SeCeV
Fear of Flying, The. Mona Van Duyn. NMM
Fear of poetry, The, is the/ fear. Reading Time: 1 Minute 26 Seconds. Muriel Rukeyser. MoPo; NePA; PBWP
Fear of the Earth. Alex Comfort. MoBrPo; NeBP
Fear of the Lord, The. Bible, *O.T.* Proverbs, I: 7. TrJP
Fear of Trembling, The. John Hollander. NePoEA
Fear Test: Integrity of Heroes. James Simmons. CIP
Fear the one who has sharp weapons. Song of the Lioness for Her Cub. *Tr. fr. Hottentot by* Thomas Hahn. BoWoP
Fear was about me. Hunger. *Tr. fr. Eskimo.* WTO
Feare No More. Shakespeare. *See* Fear No More the Heat o' the Sun.
Feare not (deare Love) that I'le reveale. *See* Fear Not, Dear Love.
Feare not, little flocke, for it is your fathers good pleasure to give you the kingdome. Bible, *N.T.* *Fr.* St. Luke. OBVE
Fearful Death. *Unknown.* MeEL
Fearful "had the root of the matter," bringing. Courage Means Running. William Empson. LiTB
Fearful of beauty, I always went. The Enamel Girl. Genevieve Taggard. HBMV; MoAmPo
Fearful Symmetry. Basil Bunting. PoA
Fearful the chamber's quiet; the veiled windows. A Development of Idiotcy. Ebenezer Jones. OBNC
Fearing that Albion should turn his back against the Divine Vision. Blake. *Fr.* Jerusalem. OAEL-2
Fearless, The. Mortimer J. Adler. PoA
Fears any one his bride lest she a virgin be not. Reasons for and against Marrying Widows. Henricus Selyns. SCAP
Fears in Solitude. Samuel Taylor Coleridge. EnRP; OBWP
Sels.
Looking Down on Nether Stowey. FaBoPP
O My Mother Isle ("O native Britain! O My Mother Isle!"). FaBoPP
"On the green sheep-track, up the healthy hill." OBNC
Feast, The. Robert Hass. GeTw
Feast. Edna St. Vincent Millay. WHA
Feast, The. David Wagoner. NePoEA-2
Feast and noon grew high, and sacrifice, The. Milton. *Fr.* Samson Agonistes. EBEV
Feast o' Saint [*or* St.] Stephen, The. Ruth Sawyer. OBCP; OHIP
Feast of All Saints, The. Elizabeth Smither. OCNZ
Feast of Blood, The. Joseph Fawcett. *Fr.* The Art of War. NOEC
Feast of Saint Brigid of Kildare, The. *At. to* St. Brigid, *tr. fr. Middle Irish by* Eugene O'Curry. OnYI
(I Should Like to Have a Great Pool of Ale, *tr. by* Kenneth Jackson.) AnIL
Feast of Stephen, The. Anthony Hecht. HAP; NoP
Feast of Stephen, The. Kevin Nichols. OBCP
Feast of the Monkeys, The. John Philip Sousa. OBAL
Feast of the Ram's Horn. Harvey Shapiro. VGW
Feast of the Snow, The. G. K. Chesterton. HBV-1
Feast-Time of the Year, The. *Unknown.* OHIP
Feast was over in Branksome tower, The. Sir Walter Scott. *Fr.* The Lay of the Last Minstrel, I. OBRV
Feast's begun, The/ And the wine is done. Water Song. Solomon ibn Gabirol, *tr. by* Israel Abrahams. TrJP
Feasts of Death, Feasts of Love. Stuart Z. Perkoff. NeAP
Feather, The. Lilian Bowes Lyon. ChMP
Feather, The. Vernon Watkins. FaBoTw; MoVE
Feather on feather. Snow in Spring. Ivy O. Eastwick. PDV
Feather or Fur. John Becker. FaPON; RHPC; TiPo
"Featherd fowl 's in your orchard, father, A." Brown Robin. *Unknown.* ESPB
Featherd songster chaunticleer, The. Bristowe Tragedie: or, The Dethe [*or* Death] of Syr Charles Bawdin. Thomas Chatterton. EnRP; OBEC; OxBB
Feathered Faith. *Unknown.* STF
Feathered Friends. Robert Peters. BXAP
Feathered thing of silver-grey and jade, The. Dollar Bill. John Frederick Nims. MiAP
Feathers and Moss. Jean Ingelow. SpRo
Feathers blacken against the sun. Manifest Destiny. Anita Endrezze Probst. CDW
Feathers in a fan, The. Man. Humbert Wolfe. MoBrPo
Feathers of Snow. *Unknown.* GBP
Feathers of the willow, The. Song [*or* Willow]. Richard Watson Dixon. BoNaP; CH; FaBoCh; GTBS-P; LoBV; NOBE; OBEV; OBNC; OBVV; YeAr
Feathers or Lead? James Broughton. NeAP
Feathers up fast, and steeples; then in clods. The Fountain. Donald Davie. GTBS-P; OxBTC
Feather's Weight, A. G. P. Lathrop. FaBoUs
Featherstone's Doom. Robert Stephen Hawker. OBNC
Feathery forests are blown back, frost rends, The. Winter. John Lyle Donaghy. BIrV
Featureless ghost under the wall cannot jerk out at us, The. Elegy for the Silent Voices and the Joiners of Everything. Kenneth Patchen. NaP
Features frozen in time. Family Portrait. Rebecca Hood-Adams. AMV-80
February. John Clare. *Fr.* The Shepherd's Calendar. NOBE; OBNC
(February; a Thaw, *sl. diff. vers.*) NCEP
February. John Heath-Stubbs. OBCP
February. W. S. Merwin. NNaP
February. Larry Moffi. AMV-80
February. D. S. Savage. NeBP
February. James Schuyler. NeAP
February. Frank Dempster Sherman. YeAr
February. Adeline D. T. Whitney. YeAr
February. Barbara Winder. PH
February. Francis Brett Young. HBMV; HBVY
February; a Thaw. John Clare. *See* February.
February Afternoon. Edward Thomas. NoAM
February brings despair. At the Nadir. Gerta Kennedy. PoPl
February 11, 1977. Frederick Morgan. AMV-80
February Evening in New York. Denise Levertov. InPS; NoAM
February, fortnights two. February. Frank Dempster Sherman. YeAr
February 14, 22 B.C. Franklin P. Adams. InMe
February Morning. King D. Kuka. VoR
February Park. Gerald Vizenor. VoR
February, Tall and Trim. Anna Neil Gilmore. YeAr
February Thaw. G. J. F. Dutton. PoSH
February; the Boy Breughel. Norman Dubie. LCAP
February 12, 1809. Gail Brook Burket. PGD
February 22. John Updike. GOA
February Twilight. Sara Teasdale. FaPON; OBCA; PDV; RHPC; SoPo; YeAr
February's Forgotten Mitts. Raymond Knister. NOBC
Fecht for Britain? Hoot awa! The Patriot. J. C. Milne. PoSH
Feckless Dinner Party, The. Walter de la Mare. FaBoTw
Fedele and Fortunio, *sel.* Anthony Munday, *ad. fr. the* Italian of Luigi Pasqualigo.
I Serve a Mistress. ElL
(Fedele's Song.) OBSC
("I serve a mistress whiter than snow.") HAP
Federal Constitution, The. William Milns. PAH
Federal Convention, The. *Unknown.* PAH
Fee, faw fum! bubble and squeak! Holy-Cros Day. Robert Browning. VLP
Fee, fi, fo, fum. *See* Fe, fi, fo, fum.
Feed. Raymond Knister. OBCV; PeCV
Feed/ Upon anticipation as you sow the seed. Harvest Time. Star Powers. GoYe
Feed Still Thyself. Sir Walter Ralegh. NCEP

Feede on my flocks securely. To His Flocks. *At. to* Henry Constable *and to* Henry Chettle. FM
Feede still thy selfe, thou fondling with beliefe. Feed Still Thyself. Sir Walter Ralegh. NCEP
Feeding, The. Joel Oppenheimer. NeAP
Feeding Ducks. Norman MacCaig. OxBS
Feeding the Fire. Donald Finkel. VWA
Feeding the Lions. Norman Jordan. BOLo; CTBA; NBP; PoBA
Feel for your bad fall how could I fail. A Sympathy, a Welcome. John Berryman. GrPl; NYBP
Feel free. To Bobby Seale. Lucille Clifton. CNA; PoBA
Feel like a Bird. May Swenson. TrGrPo
Feel Me. May Swenson. GP
Feel of that leather baby, The. Watching the Jets Lose to Buffalo at Shea. May Swenson. LiSp
Feel so low-down an' sad Lawd. Friendless Blues. Mercedes Gilbert. TrAS
Feel the sharpness. The Meeting. Ramona Wilson. VoR
Feeling, The. William Bronk. VGW
Feeling a pain in his breast, when he speaks. Ellas and the Statues. Gülten Akin, *tr. by* Nermin Menemencioglu. PBWP
Feeling all at once imprisoned, I stalk for the door. Fantasy Street. Andrew Glaze. NYP
Feeling for Fish. Leonard Trawick. AMV-81
Feeling Fucked Up. Etheridge Knight. GP; NNaP
Feeling it with me. Walking on Water. James Dickey. NePoEA-2
Feeling my face has the terrible shine of fish. Element. P. K. Page. MoCV; PeCV
Feeling sick, I take my morning walk. Autumn Song. Stephen Stepanchev. FAZ
Feeling That Way Too. Arthur Vogelsang. MAYP
Feeling the Quiet Strike. James Minor. WOLT
Feeling the urge my mother. Birth. Edith Bruck, *tr. by* Ruth Feldman *and* Brian Swann. BoWoP
Feeling the useless arm. Hospital Observation. Julian Symons. WaP
Feelings about Words. Mary O'Neill. RHPC
Feelings are perceived as vague as limbs in my dismembered past. At Eighty-seven. Dachine Rainer. NePoAm
Feelings go up into the air, The. Some Feelings. Michael Benedikt. ConAP
Feelings I don't have I don't have, The. To Women, as Far as I'm Concerned. D. H. Lawrence. InPS; WeW
Feels. J. C. Milne. PoSH
Feet. Mary Carolyn Davies. WGRP
Feet. "Harry." TiPo
Feet, a Sermon. James Paul. HoAn
Feet and faces tingle. Finland. Robert Graves. BrPo
Feet at their loveliest are like two hands. Conceit upon the Feet. William Zaranka. BXAP
"Feet just like ice" say. By Now. Ralph Salisbury. STE
Feet of Judas, The. George Marion McClellan. BANP; PoNe
Feet of morning the feet of noon and the feet of evening, The. The Domestic Stones (fragment). Hans Arp, *tr. by* David Gascoyne. EAS
Feigned Courage. Charles *and* Mary Lamb. GN; OxBChV
Feld, groes or goers, hus, doeg, dung. Returning to Roots of First Feeling. Robert Duncan. PoA
Felicia Ropps. Gelett Burgess. FaPON; TiPo
Felicity. Isaac Watts. OxBoCh
Feliks Skrzynecki. Peter Skrzynecki. CBAP
Félise. Swinburne. BeLS
Felix Randal. Gerard Manley Hopkins. BrPo; EBEV; EBVV; FaBoEn; FaBoMo; GTBS-P; HAP; InPS; LiTB; LiTM; MoAB; MoBrPo; MoPo; NoAM; NOBE; NoP; OAEP; OBEV; OBNC; PoPle; PoRA; PrIm; RoGo; SOTW; VLP; WeW
Felixstowe; or, The Last of Her Order. John Betjeman. OxBTC
Felled Plane Tree, The. Anna Hajnal, *tr. fr. Hungarian by* William Jay Smith. BoWoP
Feller I Know, A. Mary Austin. AmFN; FaPON
Feller isn't thinkin' mean, A. Out Fishin'. Edgar A. Guest. BLPL; PoLF
Fellow-Citizens. Verner von Heidenstam, *tr. fr. Swedish by* Charles Wharton Stork. PoPl
Fellow in a market-town, A. The Razor-Seller. "Peter Pindar." HBV-2; InMe
Fellow Named Hall, A. *Unknown. See* Limerick: "There was a young fellow named Hall."
Fellow, you have no flair for art, I fear. The Sitting Bard. Sir Owen Seaman. NOBL
Fellows in arms! whose bliss, whose chiefest good. Cato's Address to His Troops in Lybia. Lucan, *tr. by* Nicholas Rowe. *Fr.* Pharsalia, IX. OBEC
Fellows up in Personnel, The. The Perforated Spirit. Morris Bishop. FiBHP; QQQ
Fellowship. *Unknown.* BLPA
Felo de Se. Thomas Blackburn. OxBTC
Felo de Se. Richard Hughes. OBMV
Female bottom is a sight, The. Cudworth's Undergraduate Ode to a Bare Behind. John Ower. AMV-81
Female Frailty, *sel.* Philip Freneau.
Song of Thyrsis. AA; LiTA; ViBoPo
Female Friend, The. Cornelius Whur. FaBoCo
"Female genital, like the blank page anticipating the poem, The." Sentience. Sandra McPherson. PoA
Female giants, fauna of women. The Women of Rubens. Wislawa Szymborska, *tr. by* Celina Wieniewska. WPOW
Female God, The. Isaac Rosenberg. FaBoTw
Female hand puppet refuses to let the puppet master put, A. The Little Lady. Russell Edson. GP
Female Husband, Who Had Been Married to Another Female for Twenty-one Years, The. *Unknown.* CoMu
Female is fertile, and discipline, The. Praise for Sick Women. Gary Snyder. NeAP
Female of the Species, The. Kipling. BLPA; FPL; HBV-1; TreFS
Female Parricide, The. *Unknown.* APAS
Female Phaeton, The. Matthew Prior. HBV-1
Female Principle, The. A. D. Hope. OxBC
Female Rain. Laura Tohe. STE
Female Sailor, The. *Unknown.* OBET
Female Smuggler, The, *with music. Unknown.* AmSS
Female Warrior, The, *with music. Unknown.* ShS
Femina. Daphne Marlatt. NOBC
Feminine. H. C. Bunner. AA
Feminine Seal, The. Oliver Herford. TDH
Feminism, baby, feminism. Male Rage Poem. Pier Giorgio Di Cicco. NOBC
Femme et Chatte. Paul Verlaine, *tr. fr. French by* Arthur Symons. AWP; OBVE
Fen-Men of Lincolnshire's Holland, The. Michael Drayton. *Fr.* Polyolbion, Song XXV. FaBoPP
Fence, The. Heather McHugh. GeTw
Fence, A. Carl Sandburg. WeW
Fence beyond fence from breakfast. The Names of the Humble. Les A. Murray. CBAP
Fence or an Ambulance, A. Joseph Malins. BLPA
Fenceposts wear marshmallow hats, The. Snow [*or* On a Snowy Day]. Dorothy Aldis. PDV; TiPo
Fence Wire. James Dickey. NYBP; VGW
Fencing School. John Manifold. CBAP
Fer in see by west Spaygne. The Land of Cockayne. *Unknown.* OxBM. *See also* Far at sea and west of Spain.
Feral Pioneers, The. Ishmael Reed. PoBA; PoNe; UnPo
Ferdinand De Soto lies. The Distant Runners. Mark Van Doren. GOA; LiTA; LiTM; MoAmPo; NePA
Ferdinando and Elvira; or, The Gentle Pieman. W. S. Gilbert. FaBoCo; FaBoNo; FiBHP; NA
Fergus and the Druid. W. B. Yeats. VLP
Fergus Falling. Galway Kinnell. DiL
Fern. Ted Hughes. NYBP
Fern Hill. Dylan Thomas. BiP; CABA; ChMP; CMoP; CoBMV; EvOK; FaBoEn; FaBoPP; FaBV; FPL; GoJo; GTBS-P; HAP; HeIP; InPK; InPS; LiTB; LiTM; MasP; MoAB; MoBrPo; MoPo; MoVE; MP; NIP; NoAM; NOBE; NoP; OAEL-2; OAEP; OxBTC; PAI; PoLF; PoPl; PoRA; PPoe; PPP; RoGo; SoSe; TrGrPo; TwCP; ViBoPo; WeW
Fern House at Kew. Paul Dehn. ChMP
Fernando ("Fernando has a basketball"). Marci Ridlon. NTCP; RHPC
Ferns, The. Gene Baro. RHPC
Ferries ply like shuttles in a loom, The. This Is My Hour. Zoë Akins. HBV-1
Ferry, The. George Henry Boker. AA
Ferry Hinksey. Laurence Binyon. HBV-1
Ferry Me across the Water. Christina Rossetti. *Fr.* Sing-Song. BiP; ChTr; GoJo; OxBChV; PDV; SUS
(Ferryman, The.) SoPo
Ferry Ride, *sel.* Selma Robinson.
Bus Ride. FaPON
Ferry window frames a pop-art shovel, The. Debora Sleeping. William Logan. MAYP
Ferry-Boats. James S. Tippett. SoPo; SUS; TiPo
Ferryman, The. Christina Rossetti. *See* Ferry Me across the Water.
Fertile and rank and rich the coastal rains. Advent. William Everson. NeAP; TrCP
Fertile Muck, The. Irving Layton. NOBC; OBCV; PeCV
Fertile Valley of the Nile, The. Eve Merriam. IHMS
Festal Board, The. *Unknown.* BLPA; TreFS
Festal Song. William Pierson Merrill. *See* Rise Up, O Men of God.

Feste Burg Ist Unser Gott, Ein. Martin Luther. *See* Mighty Fortress Is Our God, A.
Feste's Song ("Come away, come away, Death"). Shakespeare. *See* Come Away, Come Away, Death.
Feste's Song ("O mistress mine, where are you roaming?"). Shakespeare. *See* O Mistress Mine, Where Are You Roaming?
Feste's Song ("When that I was, and a little tiny boy"). Shakespeare. *See* When That I Was, and a Little Tiny Boy.
Festival, The. Robert Eyres Landor. *Fr.* The Impious Feast. OBRV
Festival, The. Frederic Prokosch. LiTA; WaP
Festivals have I seen that were not names. Calais, August 15, 1802. Wordsworth. NAs
Festoons of Fishes. Alfred Kreymborg. HBMV
Festubert: The Old German Line. Edmund Blunden. MMA
Festus, *sel.* Philip James Bailey.
Proem: "Poetry is itself a thing of God." VLP
Fetch in the holly from the tree. Holly and Mistletoe. Eleanor Farjeon. PChr
Fetching Cows. Norman MacCaig. BoAnP; OxBC
Fetching the Wounded. Laurence Binyon. MMA
Fete, A. Larry Eigner. NeAP
Fete confused me, The. Guests played the part of gods. Sigismundo. Linda Gregg. AmPA
Fêtes, Fates. John Malcolm Brinnin. LiTA
Feuerzauber. Louis Untermeyer. TrJP
Feuilles d'Automne, *sels.* Victor Hugo, *tr. fr. French by* Francis Thompson.
Heard on the Mountain. AWP
Sunset, A. AWP
Fever, A. John Donne. OAEL-1
Fever. Thom Gunn. PeHV
Fever 103°. Sylvia Plath. CMoP; NMP; NoAM; NOBA; VGW
Fever, the clang in the beleaguered pumproom. A Curfew: December 13, 1981. Amy Clampitt. SUW
Fever Toy, The. Charles Wright. AmPA
Feverish room and that white bed, The. White Heliotrope. Arthur Symons. BoLoP; EBEV; InPS
Few beds are stonier than one shared by a sleeper. Bed Time. Peter Davison. UnPo
Few broken coughs . . . Then blood, a sobbing sigh! Nirvana. Ali S. Hilmi Törel. PeD
Few days after, A. Death of a Bird. Jon Silkin. NePoEA
Few days ago, A. A Wife Talks to Herself. Stephen Berg. NaP
Few days before you died, death, A. To a Pope. Pier Paolo Pasolini, *tr. by* James Kirkup. PeHV
Few ever came to help you speak or sell. Peter Dale. *Fr.* The Fragments. NOCV
Few Happy Matches. Isaac Watts. NOEC
Few have seen the King Selkie and few the grand. The Boar of Badenoch and the Sow of Atholl. Naomi Mitchison. PoSH
Few hours remain. Darkness is big, is surly. New Words for an Old Song. Babette Deutsch. NePoAm
Few, in the days of early youth. The World I Am Passing Through. Lydia Maria Child. AA; HBV-1
Few light flakes of snow, A. Kyoto: March. Gary Snyder. PPP
Few Lines to Fill up a Vacant Page, A. John Danforth. SCAP
Few men in any age have second sight. To a Reviewer Who Admired My Book. John Ciardi. OBAL
Few men of hero-mould. John Bright. Francis Barton Gummere. AA
Few miles from, A/ the Chugachimute. Chugachimute I Love the Name. Rochelle Owens. CoPo
Few Muddled Metaphors by a Moore-ose Melodist, A. Tom Hood. *See* Muddled Metaphors.
Few originals, but mighty. Primary. Abbie Huston Evans. GP
Few sashay, a few finagle, A. I Knew I'd Sing. Heather McHugh. GeTw
Few Things Can More Inflame. C. Day Lewis. OBMV
Few times back in the early fall, The. Measles. Kaye Starbird. RHPC
Few times only, then away, A. Night Song for a Woman. Al Purdy. NOBC
Few will acknowledge all they owe. Daniel Defoe. Walter Savage Landor. NCEP
Few year back and they told me Black, A. A Poem about Intelligence for My Brothers and Sisters. June Jordan. PAI
Fforestfawr. Kingsley Amis. *Fr.* The Evans Country. NOBL
Ffrom depth off sinn and from a diepe dispaire. *See* From depth of sin and from a deep despair.
Fhairshon swore a feud. The Massacre of the Macpherson. William Edmondstoune Aytoun. BXAP; CenHV; ChTr; FaBoCo
Fiametta. John Peale Bishop. LiTA; TwAmPo
Fiammetta. Boccaccio, *tr. fr. Italian by* Dante Gabriel Rossetti.
Of Fiammetta Singing. AWP; GoBC
Of His Last Sight of Fiammetta. AWP; GoBC
To Dante in Paradise, after Fiammetta's Death. AWP; GoBC
Fiascherino. Charles Tomlinson. NoAM
Fiat Lux. Lloyd Mifflin. AA
"Fiat!"—The flaming word. The Annunciation. John Banister Tabb. ISi
Fib Detected, A. Catullus, *tr. fr. Latin by* John Hookham Frere. AWP
("Varus, whom I chanced to meet.") OBVE
Fichtenbaum Steht Einsam, Ein. Heine, *tr. fr. German by* James Thomson. AWP
Fickle Hope. Harrison Smith Morris. AA
Fickle in the Arms of Spring. Susie Fry. AMV-81
Fickle One, The. Pablo Neruda, *tr. fr. Spanish by* Donald D. Walsh. FF; OLR
Fiction. Charles Sprague. *Fr.* Curiosity. AA
Fiction: A Message. Gavin Ewart. OxBC
Fiction and the Reading Public. Philip Larkin. NOBL; OBSV
Fiction of relationship, The. New Potatoes. Ken Belford. NeAC
Fiddlehead, The. David McFadden. NeAC
Fiddle-I-Fee. *Unknown.* AmFP
Fiddler, The. Martin Buber, *tr. fr. German by* Jawaid Awan. VWA
Fiddler, The. Edna Valentine Trapnell. HBMV
Fiddler and his wife, The. *Unknown.* OxNR
Fiddler Jones. Edgar Lee Masters. *Fr.* Spoon River Anthology. CMoP; LiTA; NoAM; OxBA; TAP; TrGrPo
Fiddler of Dooney, The. W. B. Yeats. EBVV; FaBoCh; HBV-2; OBVV; PoPle; TiPo
Fiddler settles in, The. Lament for the O'Neills. John Montague. CIP
Fiddler's Green. Theodore Goodridge Roberts. CaP
Fiddles were playing and playing, The. Across the Door. Padraic Colum. HBV-1
Fidele. William Collins. *See* Song from Shakespeare's "Cymbeline," A.
Fidele. Shakespeare. *See* Fear No More the Heat o' the Sun.
Fidele's Dirge. Shakespeare. *See* Fear No More the Heat o' the Sun.
Fidelia. George Wither. *See* Fair Virtue, the Mistress of Philarete.
Fidelis. Adelaide Anne Procter. BLPA; FaBoBe
Fidelities. Jean Valentine. NYP
Fidelity. Jerry Kass. AMV-80
Fidelity. Thomas Lodge. *See* Love Guards the Roses of Thy Lips.
Fidelity. Trumbull Stickney. LiTA; TwAmPo
Fidelity. Wordsworth. FM
Fidelity belongs in the Guinness Book of Records. Graffiti for Lovers. Joan Joffe Hall. AMV-80
Fidessa, More Chaste than Kind, *sels.* Bartholomew Griffin.
"Care-charmer sleepe, sweet ease in restles[s] miserie," XV. AAS; NIP
(Sleep.) OBSC
"Fair is my love that feeds among the lilies," XXXVII. GBL; ViBoPo
(Faire Is My Love.) PoEL-2
(My Love.) TrGrPo
(Sonnet: "Fair is my love that feeds among the lilies.") EIL; ErPo
"Fly [*or* Flye] to her heart; hover about her heart," XXIII. AAS
(Her Heart.) TrGrPo
"I have not spent the April of my time," XXXV. AAS
(Sonnet: "I have not spent the April of my time.") EIL
(Youth.) OBSC
"My ladies haire is threeds of beaten gold," XXXIX. AAS
Fie, Fie on Blind Fancy! Robert Greene. *Fr.* Greene's Groatsworth of Wit. EIL
(Lamilia's Song.) OBSC
Fie, fie upon her! Portrait of Cressida. Shakespeare. *Fr.* Troilus and Cressida, IV, v. TrGrPo
Fie! flattering Fortune, look thou never so fair. Lewis, the Lost Lover. Sir Thomas More. OBSC
Fie [*or* Fye], foolish earth, think[e] you the heaven wants glory. Love's Glory. Fulke Greville. *Fr.* Caelica. EnRePo; OBSC; PoEL-1
Fie on Eastern Luxury! ("Persicos odi"). Horace, *tr. fr. Latin by* Hartley Coleridge. Odes, I, 38. InPK
(Ad Ministram, *par. by* Thackeray.) HBV-2
("Dear Lucy, you know what my wish is.") OBVE
(Persicos Odi.) OBEV
("Ah child, no Persian—perfect art!" *tr. by* Gerard Manley Hopkins.) InPK; OBVE
("Persian pomps, boy, ever I renounce them," *tr. by* Christopher Smart.) OBVE
(Persicos Odi, *par. by* Franklin P. Adams.) HBMV
(Preference Declared, The, *tr. by* Eugene Field.) InPK
(Simplicity, *tr. by* William Cowper.) InPK
("Boy, I hate their empty shows.") OBVE
(Persian Fopperies.) AWP
Fie on sinful fantasy! Shakespeare. *Fr.* The Merry Wives of Windsor. ViBoPo
Fie, Pleasure, Fie! George Gascoigne. EIL; InvP
Fie, school of Patience, fie! Your lesson is. Astrophel and Stella, LVI. Sir Philip Sidney. SiPS

Fie upon hearts that burn with mutual fire. Against Fruition. Sir John Suckling. ErPo
Field. Susan Griffin. NPGG
Field, The. David Huddle. Str
Field, The. Douglas Lawder. PH
Field, The. Jean Valentine. LCAP
Field Ambulance in Retreat. May Sinclair. SUMH
Field and Forest. Randall Jarrell. LCAP; VGW
Field Day. W. R. Rodgers. BlrV
Field Flower, A. James Montgomery. HBV-1
Field-Glasses. Andrew Young. ChMP; GTBS-P
Field Full of Folk, The. William Langland. *See* Prologue: "In a summer season, when soft was the sun."
Field Hospital, The. Paul Muldoon. CIP
Field in sunshine is a field, A. Psalm of the Fruitful Field. A. M. Klein. Psalter of Avram Haktani, VIII. WHW
Fieldmouse, The. Cecil Frances Alexander. OxBChV
Field Mouse, The. "Fiona Macleod." FaPON; MoShBr
Fieldmouse, A/ crouches low. Robert Sund. BoAnP
Field mouse follows its own shadow, The. Snowfall; a Poem about Spring. James Wright. LCAP
Field of Autumn. Laurie Lee. LiTM; NCSH
Field of Folk, The. William Langland. *See* Prologue: "In a summer season, when soft was the sun."
Field of Glory, The. E. A. Robinson. HBV-2; MoAmPo
Field of golden wheat there grows, A. Harvest Song. Richard Dehmel, *tr. by* Ludwig Lewisohn. AWP
Field of Light, A. Theodore Roethke. LiTM; MP; TwCP
Field of Night, The. Miriam Waddington. VWA
Field of poetry ends here, The. The Dump. Greg Kuzma. PoA
Field of Talavera, The. Thomas Hardy. *Fr.* The Dynasts, Pt. II, Act IV, sc. iv. CMoP
Field of the Grounded Arms, The. Fitz-Greene Halleck. PoEL-4
Field of Waterloo, The. Thomas Hardy. *Fr.* The Dynasts. FaBoCh
(Chorus: "Yea, the coneys are scared by the thud of hoofs.") LoBV
(Chorus of the Years.) CMoP
Field-Path, The. Charles Swain. *See* Tripping down the Field-Path.
Field Sports. Pope. *Fr.* Windsor Forest. OBEC; SeCePo
("When milder autumn summer's heat succeeds.") PBBP
Field Sports, *sel.* William Somerville.
"When Autumn smiles, all beauteous in decay." FM
Field Trip. Gary Miranda. AMV-81
Field Work. Doug Cockrell. Psk
Fielding Error. Robert Paul Smith. CAD
Fieldmouse. *See* Field Mouse.
Fields Abroad with Spangled Flowers, The. *Unknown.* ChTr
Fields are black once more, The. Reading in Fall Rain. Robert Bly. GP; GrPl
Fields are chill, The; the sparse rain has stopped. Clearing at Dawn. Li Po, *tr. by* Arthur Waley. AWP
Fields are wrapped in silver snow, The. The Christmas Present. Patricia Hubbell. PDV
Fields at Evening. David Morton. HBMV
Fields close in on all sides, The. The Road of Birds. Harry Humes. AMV-80
Fields from Islington to Marybone, The. Blake. *Fr.* Jerusalem, II, Prologue. ChTr, *4 sts.*; OBNC; OBRV
Fields in fog, the low, dull resonance of morning, The. Early Meadow-Rue. Stanley Plumly. LCAP
Fields of Flanders, The. Edith Nesbit. SUMH
Field's Retention, The. José Y. Terán Jr. LFAC
Fields, Teruko-san, are threshed, The. A good. The Hibakusha's Letter (1955). David Mura. BrSi
Fields were silent, and the woodland drear, The. In the Dark. Mary Thacher Higginson. AA
Fields Where We Slept. Muriel Rukeyser. NNaP
Fiend, The. James Dickey. PPP
Fiend's Weather. Louise Bogan. MoVE
Fierce and brooding holocaust of faith, The. Two Poems on the Catholic Bavarians, I. Edgar Bowers. PoCh
Fierce is the flame on the vengeance of Erin. O'Neill's War Song. Michael Hogan. OnYI
Fierce is the wind tonight. The Viking Terror. *Unknown, tr. by* Fred Norris Robinson. AnIL; OnYI
Fierce luster of sun on sea, the gulls. The Purse—Seine. Paul Blackburn. CoPo
Fierce Mars I bid a glad farewell. New Mexico and Arizona. George Canterbury. PoOW
Fierce musical cries of a couple of sparrowhawks hunting on the headland, The. Birds. Robinson Jeffers. AP; CoBMV; TwAmPo; VGW
Fierce they drove on, impatient to destroy. Homer, *tr. by* Pope. *Fr.* The Iliad, XIII. OBVE
Fierce unrest seethes at the core, A. Unrest. Don Marquis. HBMV
Fierce wrath of Solomon. The Burning of the Temple. Isaac Rosenberg. FaBoMo; TrJP
Fiercely the battle raged and, sad to tell. Corporal. Ambrose Bierce. *Fr.* The Devil's Dictionary. DBV; OBAL
Fiery throb in every star, A. Elizabeth Barrett Browning. *Fr.* A Vision of Poets. PeD
Fiesolan Idyl, A. Walter Savage Landor. EnRP; OAEP
(Fæsulan Idyl.) OBRV; SeCePo
Fife and Drum. Dryden. *Fr.* A Song for St. Cecilia's Day, 1687. GN
Fife Tune. John Manifold. CBAP; FaFP; GoJo; LiTB; LiTM; WaaP; WaP
Fifine at the Fair, *sel.* Robert Browning.
"And so I somehow-nohow played." Par
Fifteen. William Stafford. CAD
Fifteen Boys, or Perhaps Even More. Bella Akhmadulina, *tr. fr. Russian by* Daniel Weissbort. WPOW
Fifteen churches lie here. At Dunwich. Anthony Thwaite. MoBS
Fifteen day of July, The. *See* Fifteenth day of July.
Fifteen Days of Judgement, The. Sebastian Evans. NBM
Fifteen foresters in the Braid alow. Johnie Cock. *Unknown.* ESPB
"Fifteen men on the dead man's chest." Derelict. Young E. Allison. BLPA; EtS; FaBoBe; FaFP; HBMV; OnMSP; TreFS
Fifteen Million Plastic Bags. Adrian Mitchell. OBSV; OxBTC
Fifteen nights I have lain awake and called you. Elegy for a Cricket. J. V. Cunningham. NoAM
Fifteen Ships on George's Banks. *Unknown.* AmFP; BaBo
Fifteen years ago/ I left this seacoast town. With Due Deference to Thomas Wolfe. Joanne Townsend. AMV-81
Fifteen years ago and twenty. To an Athlete Turned Poet. Peter Meinke. LiSp
Fifteen years ago I awoke. Above Machu Picchu, 129 Baker Street, San Francisco. Joseph Stroud. NPGG
Fifteen years ago, when soldiers. Graduation Day, 1965. Julio Marzán. InW
Fifteen years in the coal mine. Coal Diggin' Blues. *Unknown.* AmFP
Fifteen years up and her tongue's still flapping. Not Her, She Aint No Gypsy. Al Young. GP
Fifteenth [*or* Fifteen] day of July, The. Lord Willoughby [*or* Brave Lord Willoughby]. *Unknown.* CoMu; FaPoR
15th Raga: For Bela Lugosi. David Meltzer. *Fr.* Ragas. NeAP
Fifth and 94th. Stanley Plumly. NYP
Fifth Avenue Parade. Anthony Hecht. NYP
Fifth Choir of Angelicals. Cardinal Newman. *See* Chorus of Angels.
Fifth Day of the First Week, The, *sel.* Joshua Sylvester. *Fr.* Du Bartas: His Divine Weeks and Works.
"Pretty lark, climbing the welkin clear." PBBP
Fifth-Floor Window, The. Lola Ridge. WPE
Fifth from the north wall, The. The Cross of Gold. David Gray. AA
Fifth Hell, The. Jerome Rothenberg. *Fr.* The Seven Hells of Jigoku Zoshi. NNaP
Fifth Ode of Horace, The. Horace. *See* To Pyrrha.
Fifth of me's me, A. 80-Proof. A. R. Ammons. SUW
Fifth Season, The. Reg Saner. FYAP
Fifth Sense, The. Patricia Beer. MoBS
Fifth Sunday after Easter. Thomas Kinsella. NMP
Fifties, The. Ira Sadoff. AmPA
Fiftieth Birthday of Agassiz, The. Longfellow. ImOP
Fifty. Kenneth Rexroth. TAP
Fifty Faggots. Edward Thomas. BrPo; MoAB; MoBrPo
50-50. Langston Hughes. NoAM; NOBA
Fifty, not having expected to arrive here. Journey toward Evening. Phyllis McGinley. GoYe; NYBP
"Fifty stories more to fall." Rhyme of Rain. John Holmes. GrPl
Fifty times the rose has flower'd and faded. On the Jubilee of Queen Victoria. Tennyson. UnPo
Fifty today, old lad? Ode to Me. Kingsley Amis. NAs
Fifty wizards working in the wind. A Poem to Explain Everything about a Certain Day in Vermont. Genevieve Taggard. NYBP
Fifty Years. James Weldon Johnson. BANP
Fifty years and three. My Dad and Mam They Did Agree. *Unknown.* POL
Fifty Years Spent. Struthers Burt. HBMV
Fifty-one Tanka, *sel.* Izumi Shikibu, *tr. fr. Japanese by* Hiroaki Sato.
Love. LLLT
Fifty-seventh Street and Fifth. Alfred Corn. NYP
Fifty-two years ago. A Short History of the Teaching Profession. Sister Maura. AMV-80
Fig for those by law protected, A! Drinking Song. Burns. *Fr.* The Jolly Beggars. TrGrPo
Fig for St. Denis of France, A. St. Patrick of Ireland, My Dear! William Maginn. InMe

Fig-tree, a falling woolshed, a filled-in well, A. Mullabinda. David Rowbotham. CBAP; PoAu-2
Fight. *Unknown.* FaFP
Fight at Dajo, The. Alfred E. Wood. PAH
Fight at Nevadaville, The. *Unknown.* PoOW
Fight at [the] San Jacinto, The. John Williamson Palmer. AA; BPAW; HBV-2; PAH
Fight at Sumter, The. *Unknown.* PAH
Fight of Paso del Mar, The. Bayard Taylor. BeLS
Fight of the *Armstrong* Privateer, The. James Jeffrey Roche. PAH
Fight of the Red Cross Knight and the Heathen Sansjoy, The. Spenser. *Fr.* The Faerie Queene, I, 5. FiP
("Noble heart that harbours virtuous thought, The.") ViBoPo
Fight of the Year, The. Robert McGough. OBCP
Fight over the Body of Keitt, The. *Unknown.* PAH
"Fight the year out!" the war-lords said. A Fight to a Finish. S. Gertrude Ford. SUMH
Fight thou with shafts of silver, and o'ercome. Money Gets the Mastery. Robert Herrick. CaPo
Fight to a Finish, A. S. Gertrude Ford. SUMH
Fight was over, and the battle won, The. An Allegory. Barcroft Boake. CBAP
Fight your little fight, my boy. Don'ts. D. H. Lawrence. LiTB; LiTM; NoAM; OxBoLi
Fighter, The. Dave Etter. TAT
Fighter, The. S. E. Kiser. BLPA
Fighting Failure, The. Everard John Appleton. HBV-2; YaD
Fighting Her. David Phillips. NeAC
Fighting-Man, A. Joseph Campbell. OnYI
Fighting McGuire. William Percy French. CenHV
Fighting nature of the intellect, The. Vast Light. Richard Eberhart. CMoP; NMP
Fighting Race, The. Joseph I. C. Clarke. AA; BLPA; BLPL; HBV-2; OnYI; PAH; YaD
Fighting South of the Castle. *Unknown, tr. fr. Chinese by* Arthur Waley. AWP; WaaP
Fighting Téméraire, The. Sir Henry Newbolt. HBV-2
Fighting Words. Dorothy Parker. InMe
Fights, The. Milton Acorn. MoCV; NOBC
Figmental mannequin, Turk's-head for the trap. To the Eternal Feminine. Tristan Corbière, *tr. by* C. F. MacIntyre. ErPo
Figs. D. H. Lawrence. OAEL-2
Figs from Thistles. Edna St. Vincent Millay. FaBV; NoP; PoA
First Fig, *sel.* FaFP; FF; FPL; NoAm; PoLF; TAP
Figure and Ground. Elton Glaser. AMV-80
Figure for an Apocalypse. Thomas Merton. CrMA
Figure in the Carpet, The. James Camp. TW
Figured Wheel, The. Robert Pinsky. MAYP; NPGG
Figurehead, The. Léonie Adams. WPE
Figure-Head, The. Crosbie Garstin. EtS
Figurehead. Dorothy Paul. EtS
Figures, The. Robert Creeley. UnPo
Figures in a Ruined Ballroom. George Hitchcock. VGW
Figures in the fields against the sky! Poems. Antonio Machado, *tr. by* John Dos Passos. AWP
Figures of Authority. Edward Watkins. NYBP
Figures on the Frieze, The. Alastair Reid. ErPo; NYBP
Filaments of light. In the New Sun. Philip Levine. NNaP
Filbert, The. Robert Southey. FM
File-Hewer's Lamentation, The. Joseph Mather. NOEC
File into yellow candle light, fair choristers of King's. Sunday Morning, King's Cambridge. John Betjeman. EaLo
Filing-cabinet of human lives, A. Apartment House. Gerald Raftery. AmFN
Filipino Hombre, A, *with music.* *Unknown.* AS
Fill a Glass with Golden Wine. W. E. Henley. ViBoPo
Fill, fill the goblet full with sack! Song in a Siege. Robert Heath. CavP; OBS
Fill High the Bowl. John Keble. NOCV; OxBoCh
Fill, kind misses, fill the bowl. Heat. Anacreon, *tr. by* Abraham Cowley. UnTe
Fill the Bowl, Butler. *Unknown. See* How, Butler, How!
Fill the bowl with rosie wine. The Epicure [*or* The Epicure after Anacreon *or* Today Is Ours]. Abraham Cowley. CavP; HBV-2; OBS; SeCP; TrGrPo
Fill the Bumper Fair. Thomas Moore. HBV-2
Fill the piazza with blue water. Venetian Scene. Anne Ridler. NMP
Fill up your glass, O comrade true. The Pioneer. Eugene Field. BPAW; PoOW
Fill your dark glasses with water and toast. Rip-off #1: Hippie Capitalism. Geof Hewitt. NeAC
Filling an Order. John Townsend Trowbridge. OBAL
Filling her compact and delicious body. John Berryman. *Fr.* Dream Songs. BoLoP; CAPP; HAP; NoP; OBAL; WeW
Filling Station. Elizabeth Bishop. FaBoMo; HAP; NoP; NYBP; WeW
Filling Station. Edward Morin. SOTS
Filling the mind. The Clouds. William Carlos Williams. MoPo; VGW
Film, A. Albert Goldbarth. MAYP
Film Vermouth: Six o'Clock Show. Magda Portal, *tr. fr. Spanish by* Allan Francovich *and* Kathleen Weaver. PBWP
Filming a motion picture. Cut. David J. Feela. AMV-81
Fin de Siècle. Edmund Vance Cooke. BLPA
Fin de Siècle. Newton Mackintosh. NA
Fin God made Buchan flat and gweed. The Lairig. J. C. Milne. PoSH
Final Autumn. Josephine W. Johnson. NePA
Final Chorus. Archibald MacLeish. *Fr.* Panic. MoAmPo
Final Chorus, The. Shelley. *See* Chorus: "World's great age begins anew, The."
Final Curtain. Roger Woddis. FaBoPa
Final Cut, The. Vern Rutsala. AMV-81
Final Dirge. *Unknown. See* Lyke Wake Dirge, A.
Final end of all but purified souls, The. Your Animal. Gerald Stern. AMV-81
Final Fall, The. Alexandre L. Amprimoz. AMV-81
Final Green, The. Leah Bodine Drake. NePoAm
Final Hunger, The. Vassar Miller. LiTM
Final Inch, The. Emily Dickinson. *See* 'Twas like a maelstrom, with a notch.
Final Moments, The. E. J. Pratt. *Fr.* The Titanic. NOBC
Final Mystery, The. Sir Henry Newbolt. WGRP
Final Painting, The. Lee Harwood. EAS
Final Poem. Robert Bhain Campbell. MoPo; NePA
Final Prayer. Enheduanna, *tr. fr. Sumerian; ad. by* Aliki *and* Willis Barnstone. BoWoP
Final secret that two lovers shared, The. Speak This Kindly to Her. Robert Bagg. NePoAm-2
Final Soliloquy of the Interior Paramour. Wallace Stevens. HAP; LCAP
Final Soliloquy on a Randy Rooster (in a Key of Yellow). Robert Peters. BXAP
Final Struggle, The. Louis James Block. *Fr.* The New World. PAH
Final tiny gnash snapped strand from claw, A. Mus Ridiculus Non. Marie De L. Welch. BoAnP
Final Word, The. Dom Moraes. NePoEA-2
Finale. A. P. Herbert. *Fr.* Perseverance; or Half a Coronet. InMe
Finale. Christopher Marlowe. *See* End of Doctor Faustus, The.
Finale: Presto. Peter Davison. CoPo
Finality broods upon the things that pass. A Walk by the Charles. Adrienne Rich. NePoEA; NYBP
Finally. Vittoria Aganoor Pompili, *tr. fr. Italian by* Brenda Webster. PBWP
Finally, among the bottles shining. The Lady in the Barbershop. Raphael Rudnik. NYBP
Finally, brethren, whatsoever things are true. Think on These Things. Bible, *N.T.* *Fr.* Phillippians. TreFT
Finally, from your house there is no view. Water Island. Howard Moss. CoAP; MP; NePoEA-2; NYBP; Prf
Finally I heard. In What Manner the Body Is United with the Soule. Jorie Graham. NPGG
Finally retired pensionless. Big Momma. Don L. Lee. BPo; CNA
Finally, to forgo love is to kiss a leaf. Rescue the Dead. David Ignatow. ConAP; PrIm; VGW
Finally you will grow tired of it all. Gull Lake Reunion. Kelly Ivie. AMV-81
Financial Wisdom. *Unknown.* FaBoUs
Finch-notes and swallow-notes tell the new year. Spring Thoughts. Huang-fu Jan, *tr. by* Witter Bynner. OFD
Finches, The. Philip Murray. NePoAm
Finches, The. Thomas W. Shapcott. BoAnP; PoAu-2
Find. Josephine Miles. NoP; WPE
Find a good spot and sit there. How to Own Land. Susan Farley. AMV-80
Finder Found, The. Edwin Muir. PoA
Finders Keepers. Donald Finkel. VWA
Finding a Friend Home. Timothy Hamm. AMV-80
Finding a Poem. Eve Merriam. RFM
Finding a Teacher. W. S. Merwin. GLGT; NNaP
Finding an Old Newspaper in the Woods. Robert Morgan. WeW
Finding Francesca full of tears, I said. Obituary. Thomas William Parsons. AA; HBV-1; HBVY
Finding gold, *A* left. Exchange. George Rostrevor Hamilton, *after* Plato. FaBoEE
Finding is the first act. Emily Dickinson. AP; CABA; MoVE; NOBA
Finding of Gabriel, The. Longfellow. *Fr.* Evangeline. AA
Finding the Father. Robert Bly. DiL
Finding the Pistol. Gibbons Ruark. MAT

Finding Them Lost. Howard Moss. CoAP; NYBP
Finding those beams (which I must ever love). Absence. Sir Philip Sidney. SiPS
Finding You. Virginia Gilbert. IHMS
Fine! S. Omar Barker. BPAW
Fine, a Private Place, A. Diane Ackerman. MAYP
Fine Body. Josephine Clare. FAZ
Fine bright moon and thousands of stars, A! Night Piece. Mark Strand. NYP
Fine Clay. Winifred Shaw. PoAu-1
Fine Day, A. Michael Drayton. *Fr.* The Muses' Elysium. GN
(Lines: "Clear had the day been from the dawn.") LoBV
(Sixt Nimphall, The.) OBS
Fine delight that fathers thought, The; the strong. To R. B. Gerard Manley Hopkins. CMoP; CoBMV; GTBS-P; InvP; OAEL-2; VLP
Fine feelings under blockade! Cargoes just in from Kamschatka! Winter Coming On. Martin Bell, *after* Jules Laforgue. FaBoMo; OBVE; OxBTC
Fine fish to net. Ezra Pound, *after the Chinese.* OBVE
Fine game is grab-bag, a fine game to see, A! Grab-Bag. Helen Hunt Jackson. OBCA
Fine gold is here; yea, heavy yellow gold. The House of Colour. Francis Sherman. CaP
Fine Knacks for Ladies. *Unknown.* CH; EIL; EnRePo; HAP; LiTB; LoBV; NoP; QFR; ViBoPo
("Fine knacks for ladies, cheap, choice, brave and new.") EBEV; OBSC
(Peddler's Song, A.) OAEL-1
(Pedlar, A.) NOBE; OBEV; PoPle; WiR
Fine Madam Would-Be, wherefore should you fear. To Fine Lady Would-Be. Ben Jonson. FaBoEE; JCP; NoP
Fine merry franions. Going or Gone. Charles Lamb. BXAP
Fine Old English Gentleman, The. *Unknown.* CH; HBV-1
Fine Old English Gentleman, The; New Version. Charles Dickens. CoMu; FaBoBa; OBSV
Fine old wine and a fair young wife, A. Age and Youth. *Unknown, tr. by* Louis Untermeyer. UnTE
Fine rays of praise my asking rings from her. Bought. Francis Douglas Davison. NeBP
Fine times, babe, that summer on the dock. For Sue. Phil Hey. PPJ
Fine Work with Pitch and Copper. William Carlos Williams. OxBA
Fine Young Folly. William Habington. *Fr.* The Queen of Aragon. CavP; OBS
(Pretty Sport.) NOBE
(Song: "Fine young folly, though you were.") FaBoEn; MePo
Fineness of midnight. Midnight. Gabriela Mistral, *tr. by* David Garrison. BoWoP
Finesse be first, whose elegance deplores. Six Poets in Search of a Lawyer. Donald Hall. NYBP
Finger of Necessity. Coleman Barks. TW
Finger Points to the Moon, A. R. D. Laing. MOON
Fingernail Sunrise. Vernon Watkins. NYBP
Fingers. Uhuru. Mari Evans. CNA
Fingers aching, nails breaking. Rock Leader. Dave Barthgate. PoSH
Fingers in the Door. David Holbrook. NePoEA-2
Finigan's Wake. *Unknown. See* Finnegan's Wake.
Finis. Waring Cuney. AmNP; BANP
Finis. Walter Savage Landor. *See* On His Seventy-fifth Birthday.
Finis. Sir Henry Newbolt. TiPo
Finis. James Thomson. *Fr.* On the Death of Mr. William Aikman the Painter. BSV
(On the Death of a Particular Friend.) OBEV
(Verses Occasioned by the Death of Dr. Aikman.) OBEC
Finished at last, he escaped from that hideous. Christ's Descent into Hell. Rainer Maria Rilke, *tr. by* James Wright *and* Sarah Youngblood. Prf
Finished Course, The. St. Joseph of the Studium, *tr. fr. Latin by* John Mason Neale. WGRP
Finistére. Thomas Kinsella. IPY
Finisterra. Bayla Winters. AMV-81
Finite. Power Dalton. HBMV
Finite Reason. Dryden. *See* Reason and Revelation.
Finland. Robert Graves. BrPo
Finnair Fragment. Roald Hoffmann. SUW
Finnegans Wake, *sels.* James Joyce.
Ballad of Persse O'Reilly, The. FaBoBa; LiTB
Ondt and the Gracehoper, The. BIrV
Finnegan's Wake. *Unknown.* FaBoBa; FSW; TrAS, *with music*
(Finigan's Wake.) BLPA
Finnesburh Fragment, The. *Unknown, tr. fr. Anglo-Saxon by* Kevin Crossley-Holland. OBWP
Finnigin to Flannigan. Strickland W. Gillilan. FaBoBe; HBV-2; TreF; YaD
Fiorentina. Ernest Myers. OBVV
Fir Forest. Ethel Romig Fuller. PGD
Fir-Tree, The. Edith M. Thomas. OHIP
Fir-Tree of Bosnia, The. Dante Gabriel Rossetti. FaBoNo
Fir trees taper into twigs and wear, The. Firewood. John Clare. TrGrPo
Fire, The. William Burford. NePA
Fire. William Carpenter. Psk
Fire, The. Robert Creeley. NOBA
Fire, The. Robert Duncan. *Fr.* Passages. VGW
Fire. Joy Harjo. TWSS
Fire. Langston Hughes. NoAM; NOBA
Fire. Jose Emilio Pacheco, *tr. fr. Spanish by* Frederick Luciani. AMV-81
Fire, The. Sir Walter Scott. OBCP
Fire! *Unknown.* TDH
Fire. Dorothy Wellesley. OBMV
Fire a Simple Fire, A. Frederic Will. FAZ
Fire and Brimstone; or, The Destruction of Sodom, *sel.* George Lestey.
Lament of the Sodomites. PeHV
Fire and Ice. Robert Frost. AmPP; BiP; CABA; CMoP; CoBMV; FaBoEE; FaFP; FaPo; FF; FPL; HBMV; HeIP; HoPM; InPK; LiTA; LiTM; MoAB; MoAmPo; MoVE; NePA; NoAM; NOBA; OxBA; PAI; PoPl; PPP; PrIm; SoSe; TAP; TreFS; TrGrPo; TW; TwAmPo; ViBoPo; WHA
Fire and Ice. Michael Pettit. MAYP
Fire and sword cavort in her aging body. Cancer Patient. Jessica Powers. AMV-81
Fire and wild light of hope and doubt and fear. A Year's Burden [1870]. Swinburne. VLP
Fire at Alexandria, The. Theodore Weiss. CoPo; NoAM; PoA; TAP
Fire Breather, Mexico City, The. Jaime Jacinto. BrSi
Fire-Bringer, The, *sels.* William Vaughn Moody.
Of Wounds and Sore Defeat. HBV-2
Pandora Speaks. WGRP
(I Stood within the Heart of God, *with music.*) AH
Fire Burial. Edgar McInnis. CaP
Fire Burns Low, The. John Leax. TrCP
Fire darkens, the wood turns black, The. Song for the Sun That Disappeared behind the Rainclouds. *Unknown, tr. by* Ulli Beier. TTY
Fire Down Below. *Unknown.* FSW
Fire, fire. Song. Henry Bold. GBL
Fire! Fire! said [*or* says] the town crier. *Unknown.* GBP; OxNR
Fire, Hair, Meat and Bone. Fred Johnson. PoBA
Fire I praise was once perduring flame, The. Allen Tate. *Fr.* Sonnets of the Blood. PoA
Fire i' the Flint, The. Lucy Catlin Robinson. AA
Fire in leaf and grass, The. Living. Denise Levertov. VGW; WPE
Fire in My Meditation Burned, *with music.* Henry Ainsworth. AH
Fire in the heavens, and fire along the hills. Christopher Brennan. *Fr.* The Quest of Silence. CBAP; PoAu-1
Fire in the Snow, The. Vernon Watkins. LiTM; MoVE
Fire is out, and spent the warmth thereof, The. Dregs. Ernest Dowson. HBV-1; NCEP; OBMV; SeCePo
Fire is what's precious now. Carol. Alison Boodson. NeBP
Fire Island. Rita Mae Brown. IHMS
Fire Island. May Swenson. PoA; TAP
Fire Island pixie called "Mary," A. Limerick. *Unknown.* PeHV
Fire Island Poem. Diane Wakoski. BiP
Fire-kindled satellite. Napkin and Stone. Vernon Watkins. NYBP
Fire-mist and a planet, A. Each in His Own Tongue. William Herbert Carruth. BLPA; HBV-2; OHFP; TRV; WBLP; WGRP
Fire of Drift-Wood, The. Longfellow. AmPP; AP; BLPL; HBV-2; NOBA; NoP; OxBA; TAP
Fire of Frendraught, The. *Unknown.* ESPB (A *and* C *vers.*); OxBB, *with music;* ViBoFo
Fire of London, The. Dryden. *Fr.* Annus Mirabilis. ChTr; FaBoEn, *shorter sel.*
Fire of Love, The. Charles Sackville. UnTE
Fire of Meditation burns, The. A Præfatory Poem to the Little Book, Entituled, Christianus per Ignem. Nicholas Noyes. SCAP
Fire of our victims, The. The Knell. Muhammad Al-Fītūri, *tr. by* Samir M. Zoghby. TTY
Fire off the bells, ring out wild guns. Another Prince Is Born. Adrian Mitchell. NAs
Fire on the hearth is the woman's fire, The. Indian Song. Willard Johnson. BPAW
Fire on the Hills. Robinson Jeffers. CMoP
Fire Place, The. E. W. Mandel. OBCV
Fire-Queen. Ruth Fainlight. PoA
Fire rides calmly in the air. At War. Charles Madge. FaBoMo
Fire runs faster than emus, rams. Staying Ahead. Malcolm Glass. AMV-81; FAZ
Fire seven times tried this, The. Shakespeare. *Fr.* The Merchant of Venice, II, ix. CTC

Fire Ship, The. *Unknown.* AmSS, *with music*
(Fireship, The.) FSW
Fire. 10/78. Bart Plantenga. AMV-80
Fire that cancels all that is. Burning Love Letters. Howard Moss. DFF; HoPM
Fire, the dusky water lily edge on the horizon, The. To Helen Frankenthaler. Anne Cherner. PoDr
Fire the heather. "Adam Drinan." *Fr.* Men of the Rocks. OxBS
Fire: The People. Alfred Corn. MAYP
Fire threatens, The. Hyena's Song to her Children. *Unknown.* PeSA
Fire to see my wrongs for anger burneth, The. The Wronged Lover. Sir Philip Sidney. *Fr.* Arcadia. SiPS
Fire-Truck, A. Richard Wilbur. NCSH
Fire upon the hearth is low, The. In the Firelight. Eugene Field. AA
Fire was first. Genealogy. Donald Finkel. VWA
Fire was furry as a bear, The. Dark Song. Edith Sitwell. CMoP; FaBoTw; PBWP
"Fire, water, woman, are man's ruin!" A Dutch Proverb. Matthew Prior. FaBoEE; NOEC; POL
Fire, with well-dried logs supplied, The. The Fire. Sir Walter Scott. OBCP
Fireballs and thunder augment the wailing wind. The Ides of March. Roy Fuller. PoCh
Firebombing, The. James Dickey. CAPP; OBWP
Firebowl. Sydney Clouts. VWA
Firebrand. Harry Crosby. EAS
Fired Pot, The. Anna Wickham. FaBoTw; OxBTC
Fire-Dragon and the Treasure, The. *Unknown, tr. fr. Anglo-Saxon by* Charles W. Kennedy. *Fr.* Beowulf. AnOE
Fireflies. Edgar Fawcett. HBV-1
Fireflies. Aileen Fisher
Fireflies. Carolyn Hall. FaPON; HBMV; HBVY
Fireflies. "Fiona Macleod." *Fr.* Transcripts from Nature. FM
Fireflies, The, *sel.* Charles Mair.
"How dreamy-dark it is!" OBCV
Fireflies in the Garden. Robert Frost. RHPC
Firefly, The. Ogden Nash. FPL; WhC
Firefly. Elizabeth Madox Roberts. GoJo; NTCP; PDV; SUS; TiPo
Firefly. George Uba. BrSi
Firefly. Lillian Schulz Vanada. TiPo
("Fuzzy wuzzy, creepy crawly.") SoPo; SUS
Firefly, airplane, satellite, star. Back Yard, July Night. William Cole. BoNaP
Firefly light. Summer. Ramona Wilson. VoR
Firefly Lights His Lamp, The. *Unknown, tr. fr. Japanese.* SoPo
Firefly's flame, The. The Firefly. Ogden Nash. FPL; WhC
Firelight. E. A. Robinson. NoAM
Firelight. Whittier. *Fr.* Snow-bound. AA
("Shut in from all the world without.") OBCP
Firelight flickered on the age-old beams, The. At the Ship. R. P. Lister. FiBHP
Firelight in sunlight, silver-pale. The Marriage of Heaven and Earth. Howard Nemerov. NYBP
Fireman Save My Child. *Unknown.* *See* No More Booze.
Firemen, firemen! Help! X. J. Kennedy. RHPC
Fires, *sel.* W. W. Gibson.
Proem: "Snug in my easy chair." HBMV
Fires. William Heyen. MAYP
Fires in the dark you build; tall quivering flames. To a Very Wise Man. Siegfried Sassoon. BrPo
Fires of Driftwood. Isabel Ecclestone MacKay. CaP
Fireship, The. *Unknown.* *See* Fire Ship, The.
Fire Side, The; a Pastoral Soliloquy. Isaac Hawkins Browne. *Fr.* The Foundling Hospital for Wit. NOEC; OBEC
Firetail's Nest, The. John Clare. EnRP
Firewood. John Clare. TrGrPo
Fireworks. Babette Deutsch. NYBP; OFD
Fireworks. James Reeves. OnUR; PoSC
Fireworks. Valerie Worth. NTCP
Firm as young bones, fine as blown spume, still. Paradigm. Babette Deutsch. TrJP
Firm in the good brown earth. Planting a Tree. Nancy Byrd Turner. YeAr
Firm of Happiness, Limited, The. Norman Cameron. FaBoTw
Firm resolve of Silas Sharp, The. Patience. E. E. Nott-Bower. WhC
Firmament Displays on High, The. Barend Toerien, *tr. fr. Afrikaans by author.* PeSA
Firmament, with golden stars adorned, The. Resignation. *Unknown.* OBSC
Firmness. Anthony Hecht. OBAL; PV
1st, The. Lucille Clifton. InPS
First, The. Marya Mannes. *See* Canticles to Men.
First/ A far thud. Fireworks. Valerie Worth. NTCP
First/ it's not heat prostration. Woman par Excellence. Rochelle Owens. CoPo
First a monkey, then a man. Dawn of the Space Age. John Ciardi. OBAL
First a princess. Epithalamium. John Ditsky. DFT
First a sea: soft sand, muds, and marls. What Happened Here Before. Gary Snyder. PoM
First a word was fuzzy, and was nothing. Words. Richard Eberhart. NePA
First American Congress, The. Joel Barlow. PAH
First American Sailors, The. Wallace Rice. PAH
First and Last Man. Ralph McTell. OBET
First and Second Law. Michael Flanders. FaBoUs
First Anniversary, The. John Donne. *See* Anatomy of the World, An.
First, April, she with mellow showers. The Four Sweet Months [*or* July: The Succession of the Four Sweet Months]. Robert Herrick. FaPON; WiR; YeAr
First, are you our sort of a person? The Applicant. Sylvia Plath. MAT; NaP; NMM; NOBA; SBG; TwCP
First Aspen, *sel.* Lynn Strongin.
"Sensuous Latin poet, now I will go off with a thermos, A." IHMS
First, Best Country, The. Goldsmith. *Fr.* The Traveller. GN
First Birth, The. Rodney Jones. MAYP
First Blood. Jon Stallworthy. BoAnP; LiSp
First blow caught me sideways, my jaw, The. The Beating. Ann Stanford. WPE
First born of Chaos, who so fair didst come. Hymn: To Light. Abraham Cowley. MeLP; MePo; OBS; SeCV-1
First came the primrose. A Chanted Calendar [*or* The Procession of the Flowers]. Sydney Dobell. *Fr.* Balder. GN; HBV-1; HBVY; OBEV
First Canzone of the Convito, The. Dante, *tr. fr. Italian by* Shelley. OBVE
First Carolina Said-Song. A. R. Ammons. OBAL
First Christmas, The. Emilie Poulsson. OHIP
First Christmas, The. Bible, *N.T.* St. Luke, II. SoPo (8-16); TreFS (1-19)
("And there were in the same country shepherds," II: 8-14.) PChr
(Christmas Eve, II: 8-14.) SiSoSe
(Tidings of Great Joy, II: 8-14.) FaPON
First Citizen. James Jeffrey Roche. PGD
First clan of autumn, thistleball on a stem. Thistledown. James Merrill. UnPo
First cocks begin clearing the throat of morning, The. A Valley Where I Don't Belong. Marge Piercy. IHMS
First cold front came in, The. Winter's Onset from an Alienated Point of View. Alan Dugan. FF
First Cold Night of Autumn. John Stupp. AMV-81
First cold showers pour, The. The Monkey's Raincoat. Basho, *tr. by* Harold G. Henderson. SoPo
First come I. My name is Jowett. Henry Charles Beeching. *Fr.* Balliol Rhymes. CenHV; FaBoCo; FaBoEE; GLGT; NOBL; PoPle
First comes love and then comes marriage. Autograph Book/ Prophecy. Anne Halley. NMM
First Confession. X. J. Kennedy. ConAP; NCSH; NePoEA-2; NIP; PPP
First Corinthians, *sels.* Bible, *N.T.*
"But some one will ask, 'How are the dead raised?' " XV:35-57. DL
Love, XIII. TRV
"Now I would remind you, brethren," XV:1-8. DL
Though I Speak with the Tongues of Men and Angels, XIII: 1-13. BiP; LO; OAEL-1
(Greatest of These, The, *abr.*) TrGrPo
(St. Paul on Charity.) TreF
Ye Are the Temple of God, III: 16-17. TreFT
First Corncrake. John Hewitt. NeIP
First country to die was normal in the evening, The. The Last War. Kingsley Amis. OBSV; OxBC; SoSe
First cries were, The. Mother Poem. Joel Oppenheimer. PoM
First cut the gourds in slices, and then run. Recipe: Gourds. Nicander. FaBoUs
First Cycle of Love Poems (I-V). George Barker. MoPo
My Joy, My Jockey, My Gabriel, V. ErPo; MoBrPo
1st Dance—Making Things New—6 February 1964. Jackson MacLow. CoPo
First Dandelion, The. Walt Whitman. NePA
First Dark. Joyce Carol Oates. GeTw
First Day, The. Christina Rossetti. *Fr.* Monna Innominata. BLPL; BoLoP; FaBoBe; HBV-1; OLR
("I wish I could remember that first day.") GBL
First Day at School Michael Ivens. OxBTC
First day he had gone, The. A Space in the Air. Jon Silkin. NePoEA; TrJP
First day I shot dope, The. Summer Words of [*or* for] a Sistuh [*or* Sister] Addict. Sonia Sanchez. BlSi; BPo; UnPo
First day it rained we were glad, The. Flood. Irving Feldman. MP

First day. Jackie and I walking in leaves. Cruel Boys. Gary Soto. NPGG
First day of Christmas, The. The Twelve Days of Christmas. *Unknown.* AmFP; FaFP; OxNR; PChr; TreFT
First Day of Creation, The. Milton. *Fr.* Paradise Lost, VII. OxBoCh
First day of spring in the year ninety-three, The. Reynard the Fox. *Unknown.* OnYI
First Day of Teaching. Bonaro W. Overstreet. TrPWD
First Day of the Hunting Moon, The. Patricia Low. VGW
First day of this month I saw. Snowdrops. George MacBeth. OBCP
First day of Yole have we in mind, The. Sing We Yule. *Unknown.* MeEL
First Day Out, The. Thomas Reiter. WOLT
First day she passed up and down through the Heavens, The. Petrarch, *tr. by* J. M. Synge. *Fr.* Sonnets to Laura: To Laura in Death. OBMV
First-Day Thoughts. Whittier. AmPP; NoP; TrCP
First Days. Tuvia Ruebner, *tr. fr. Hebrew by* A. C. Jacobs. VWA
First day's night had come, The. Emily Dickinson. LiTA; LiTM; OxBA; WPOW
First Death. Donald Justice. FiCP
First Death in Nova Scotia. Elizabeth Bishop. CoAP; LCAP; NCSH; NOBA; NYBP
First Departure. Frances Frost. SiSoSe
First Division Marches, The. Grantland Rice. PAL; YaD
First draw the sea, that portion which between. Instructions to a Painter. Edmund Waller. APAS
First Dream, *sel.* Sister Juana Inés de la Cruz, *tr. fr. Spanish by* Samuel Beckett.
"But Venus first." BoWoP
First Elegy [for the Dead in Cyrenaica]. Hamish Henderson. ChMP; OxBS
First enters wearing the neon armour, The. Ten Types of Hospital Visitor. Charles Causley. OxBC
First (entitled to the place), The. Charles Churchill. *Fr.* The Duellist. OBSV
First Epistle of the First Book of Horace Imitated, The, *sel.* Pope.
"Well, if a King's a lion, at the least." OBSV
First Epistle of the Second Book of Horace [Imitated], *sels.* Pope.
Ideals of Satire, The. FiP
Poet's Use, The. OBEC
("Of little use the man you may suppose.") EBEV
First Families Move Over! Ogden Nash. FaBoCo
First Fathers, The. Robert Stephen Hawker. OBVV
First, feel, then feel, then. Young Soul. Amiri Baraka. BPo; CNA
First few days back at the Indian School, The. Cat or Stomp. Laura Tohe. STE
First Fig. Edna St. Vincent Millay. *Fr.* Figs from Thistles. FaFP; FF; FPL; NoAM; PoLF; TAP
First Fight. Then Fiddle. [Ply the Slipping String]. Gwendolyn Brooks. InPK; NIP; PoNe
First Flight. Daniel Hoffman. GrPl
First follow Nature, and your judgement frame. Nature and Art. Pope. *Fr.* An Essay on Criticism, I. HAP; PP; TreFT
First, for effusions due unto the dead. Upon His Sister-in-Law, Mistress Elizabeth Herrick. Robert Herrick. CaPo
First forget what time it is. Exercise. W. S. Merwin. NOBA
First Frost. Edwin Curran. HBMV
First frost, and on the windows snow. Our Strange and Lovable Weather. William Matthews. NPAW
First frost is weeks off, but the prudent man. Discretions of Alcibiades. Robert Pinsky. NPGG
First full moon of overgrown buffalo. America's Wounded Knee. Phillip William George. VoR
First Goodbye Letter, The. James Simmons. AMV-81
First Grade. Phillip William George. VoR
First gray smoke of daylight blurs, The. Sunrise. Rowena Bennett. TiPo
First Grief, The. Felicia Dorothea Hemans. *See* Child's First Grief, The.
First halt. They heard within a sugar patch. John Hunter-Duvar. *Fr.* The Emigration of the Fairies. CaP
First having read the book of myths. Diving into the Wreck. Adrienne Rich. HeIP; MOS; NIP; NoAM; NOBA; NoP
First he made the door, a walk. Four Pictures by Juan, Age 5. David McKain. PoDr
First hear the story of Kaspar the rosy-cheeked. Fräulein Reads Instructive Rhymes. Maxine W. Kumin. NYBP; Psk; SpRo
First Holes Are Fresh. Vivian Shipley. AMV-81
First hour was a word the color of dawn, The. Spring Morning—Sante Fe. Lynn Riggs. BPAW
First Hunt, The. Gordon Anderson. PPJ
First Hymn. John Gill. NeAC
First I am frosted. Mary Austin. *Fr.* Rhyming Riddles. TiPo
First I did take some squills, and fried them all. A Banquet. Sotades, *tr. by* Charles Duke Yonge. FaBoUs
First, I put my. The Power of Love He Wants Shih (Everything). Rochelle Owens. NMM
First, I saw a landscape fair. "Barry Cornwall." *Fr.* A Vision. OBRV
First I saw the white bear, then I saw the black. At the Zoo. Thackeray. NTCP; OxBChV
First Ice of Winter. Michael Shorb. AMV-81
First idea was not our own, The. Wallace Stevens. *Fr.* Notes toward a Supreme Fiction. NOBA
First I'll sing. Later, perhaps, I'll speak. The Condition. T. Carmi, *tr. by* Peter Everwine *and* Shula Starkman. VWA
First in a carriage. *Unknown.* OxNR
First in his pride the orient sun's display. Hilaire Belloc. FaBoEE
First in the fight, and first in the arms. Zollicoffer. Henry Lynden Flash. PAH
First in the North. The black sea-tangle[d] beaches. The Mythical Journey [*or* The Journey]. Edwin Muir. MoVE; NoAM; OxBS
First in the Pentathlon. Lucilius, *tr. fr. Greek by* Tom Dodge. LiSp
First Invasion of Ireland, The *Unknown, tr. fr. Irish by* John Montague. BIrV; NMP
First it was a pretty flower, dressed in pink and white. Riddle. Christina Rossetti. SoPo
First It Was Singing. Jon Silkin. NePoEA
First John, *sel.* Bible, *N.T.*
Brotherhood, II: 9-11; IV: 20-21. TreFT
First Joy. Vernon Watkins. ChMP
First king was Pharamond, The; after him came. Kings of France. Mary W. Lincoln. BLPA
First Kings, *sels.* Bible, *O.T.*
"And Hiram of Tyre sent his servants unto Solomon," V: 1-5, 11-14. EyDe
Solomon Judges between Two Women Disputing over a Child, III: 16-27. TreFT
First Kiss, The. Theodore Watts-Dunton. HBV-1
First Kiss of Love, The. Byron. HBV-1
First know, my friend, I do not mean. Matthew Green. *Fr.* The Spleen. NOEC
First lady of the throne room, The. The Restoration of Enheduanna to Her Former Station. Enheduanna, *tr. fr. Sumerian.* BoWoP
First, last and always dearest, closest, best. An Epistle. A. D. Hope. PoAu-2
First Lawcase, The. *Unknown, tr. fr. Irish by* John Montague. BIrV
First Law of Thermodynamics, The. First and Second Law. Michael Flanders. FaBoUs
First Lay of Gudrun, The. *Unknown, tr. fr. Old Norse by* William Morris *and* Eirikr Magnusson. *Fr.* The Elder Elda. AWP
First Lay of Gudrun: "Gudrun Laments over Sigurd," *sel.* OBVE
First Leaf, The. Howard Nemerov. TwAmPo
First Lesson. Philip Booth. BiP; LiSp; MP; TwCP
First Lesson, The. Thomas Reiter. WOLT
First Lessons in Musical Time. *Unknown.* FaBoUs
First, let me view what noxious nonsense reigns. Richard Savage. *Fr.* The Authors of the Town. OBSV
First Light. Thomas Kinsella. BIrV; CMoP; NoAM
First light of day in Mississippi. Birthday Poem. Al Young. NPGG
First Lord's Song, The. W. S. Gilbert. *Fr.* H. M. S. Pinafore. TreFS
(Sir Joseph's Song.) LiTB
First Love. Byron. *Fr.* Don Juan, I. OBRV
(". . . 'Tis sweet to hear/At midnight on the blue and moonlit deep," *shorter sel.*) ViBoPo
First Love. Charles Stuart Calverley. FiBHP; InMe
First Love. Thomas Campion. OxBoLi
("Silly boy, 'tis full moon yet, thy night as day shines clearly.") GBL
First Love. John Clare. BoLoP; ChTr; EnLoPo; GBL; HAP; NoP
(I Ne'er Was Struck.) ELP
First Love. Mary Dorcey. BrRo
First Love. Charles Gullans. NePoEA
First Love. Judith Hemschemeyer. Psk
First Love. Laurie Lee. ChMP
First Love. Sharon Olds. FYAP
First Love. *Unknown, tr. fr. Latin by* George F. Whicher. OLR
First love is first death. There is no other. The Sequel. Delmore Schwartz. LiTM
First Love Poem, The. Myra Glazer Schotz. VWA
First Maccabees, *sels.* Bible, Apocrypha.
Dirge, II: 8-14. TrJP
Great Mourning, I: 25-28. TrJP
Judas Maccabeus, III:1-9. TrJP
"Then they took whole stones according to the law," IV: 47-59. OFD
First, make a letter like a monument. The Book of Kells. Padraic Colum. BIrV
First Meditation. Theodore Roethke. *Fr.* Meditations of an Old Woman. AP; LCAP; NOBA
First Meeting, The. Lord Herbert of Cherbury. AnAnS-2
First Miracle. Genevieve Taggard. HBMV

First Monday Scottsboro Alabama. Tom Weatherly. PoBA
First month of his absence, The. Song. Alun Lewis. ChMP; DTC; LiTM; OBWP; WaaP
First morning it flew out of the fog, The. Waders and Swimmers. Stanley Plumly. GeTw
First morning of Three Mile Island: those first disquieting, uncertain, mystifying hours, The. Tar. C. K. Williams. GeTw
First mules in America, The. Ever Since. Elizabeth J. Coatsworth. SiSoSe
First, my father taught me to read poetry. To Hear My Head Roar. Henry Taylor. MAYP
First night, the first night, The. Carol for the Last Christmas Eve. Norman Nicholson. OBCP
First night when I came home, The. Our Goodman [*or* Four Nights Drunk *or* Three Nights Drunk]. *Unknown.* AmFP; OBAL; OuSiCo
First note, simple, The; the second note, distinct. Conrad Aiken. Preludes for Memnon; or, Preludes to Attitude, XXI. LiTA; TwAmPo
First Nowell [*or* Noel], The. *Unknown.* FSW; LiTB; PChr; TreFS; ViBoPo
First of All. Kenneth O. Hanson. GP
First of all her name was changed. Dream about Sunsets. Anabelle Hébert. GrPl
First of all it has to be anecdotal; ideas don't exist. The Canadian Prairies View of Literature. David Donnell. NOBC
"First of all, it's all true." The Creation: According to Coyote. Simon J. Ortiz. CDW
First of All My Dreams, The. E. E. Cummings. NYBP; VGW
First of April, some do say, The. All Fools' Day. *Unknown.* SiSoSe; SoPo
First of God by whom all grace is spread. Sources of Good Counsel. Peter Idley. OxBChV
First of My Lovers, The. Sydney Carter. OBET
First of the Emigrants, The, *with music.* *Unknown.* ShS
First of the undecoded messages read, The: "Popeye sits in thunder." Farm Implements and Rutabagas in a Landscape. John Ashbery. CoAP; GP
First One Drew Me, The. Rav Abraham Isaac Kook, *tr. fr. Hebrew by* Ben Zion Bokser. VWA
First or Last. Thomas Hardy. CMoP
First pale shoots, The. On a Picture of Your House. D. G. Jones. NOBC
First Party at Ken Kesey's with Hell's Angels. Allen Ginsberg. ConAP
First Pathways. Sidney Royse Lysaght. OBVV
First period, The: the epoch of thought. The Six Periods of Creation. *Maori Oral Tradition, tr. by* Richard Taylor. WTO
First person I loved, The. Coming Out. Jacqueline Lapidus. IHMS
First Philosopher's Song. Aldous Huxley. AWP; HBMV
First point is to love but one alone, The. The First Property. Sir Thomas More. *Fr.* The Twelve Properties or Conditions of a Lover. EnRePo
First Practice. Gary Gildner. AmPA; InPK; LiSp; Psk; TW
First Praise. William Carlos Williams. VGW
First Precinct Fourth Ward. Daniel Mark Epstein. TAT
First Pregnancy. Alta. NMM
First Prelude. Dream in Ohio; the Father. John Logan. *Fr.* Poem in Progress. LCAP
First Proclamation of Miles Standish, The. Margaret Junkin Preston. PAH; YaD
First Property, The. Sir Thomas More. *Fr.* The Twelve Properties or Conditions of a Lover. EnRePo
First Psalm, The. Bertolt Brecht, *tr. fr. German by* Robert Bly. NU
First Quest, The. Joseph Rodman Drake. *See* Fay's Departure, The.
First Rain. Zoë Akins. HBMV
First Rainfall. Alan P. Lightman. SUW
First Reader. Paris Leary. CoPo
First Reader, The. Winfield Townley Scott. PoA
First real job I had [*or* got] was delivering drugs, The. Getting Experience. Miller Williams. GP; TAT
First retainer, The. A Marriage. Robert Creeley. LiTM; NeAP
First Robin, The. Lilian Leveridge. CaP
First rose a low shore pastures green to the water. The Waving of a Hand. W. S. Merwin. DiL
First Samuel, *sels.* Bible, *O.T.*
David and Goliath, XVI, XVII: 1-51. TreFS
Hannah's Song of Thanksgiving, II: 1-10. AWP
(Hannah's Thanksgiving, II: 1-10.) BoWoP
(Song of Hannah, The, II, *ad. by* Michael Drayton.) TRCP
First Satire of the Second Book of Horace, The. Pope. OAEL-1; PPP
Sels.
Question of Libel, A. PrIm
"There are (I scarce can think it, but I am told)." OBSV
First, scattered rain on the Polish cities, The. 1 September 1939. John Berryman. NIP
First September day was blue and warm, The. The Artist on Penmaenmawr. Charles Tennyson-Turner. OBNC
1st September 1939. W.H. Auden. *See* September 1, 1939.
First shall the heaven[s] want starry light. A Fancy [*or* A Lover's (*or* Love's) Protestation]. Thomas Lodge. *Fr.* Rosalynde. ACP; ElL; GoBC; LoBV; OBSC
First Shaman Song. Gary Snyder. Myths and Texts: Hunting, I. NOBA
First she heard a sound. The Sound. Robert Kelly. PoM
First shot out of that sling, The. After Goliath. Kingsley Amis. NePoEA-2; NOBL; OxBTC; PoCh
First shot was fired to Wagnerian music, The. Laocoon. Don Gordon. WaaP
First Sight. Philip Larkin. BoNaP; NCSH; NTCP
First Sight of Her and After. Thomas Hardy. PoEL-5
First sign was your hair, The. I'm Just a Stranger Here, Heaven Is My Home. Carole Gregory Clemmons. PoBA
First Snow. Marie Louise Allen. RHPC; SoPo; TiPo
First Snow. Ivy O. Eastwick. TiPo
First Snow. Ted Kooser. GrPl
First Snow in Alsace. Richard Wilbur. AP; NoP; OBWP
First Snow of the Year, The. Mark Van Doren. NCSH
First Snow on an Airfield. John Ciardi. PoA
First snow was sleet, The. It swished heavily. Sleet. Norman MacCaig. OBCP
First Snowfall [*or* Snow-Fall], The. James Russell Lowell. AA; BLPA; BLPL; FaBoBe; HBV-1; TAP; TreF; WBLP
"Snow had begun in the gloaming, The," *sel.* FaPON; PoSC
First Solitude, The, *sels.* Luis de Góngora, *tr. fr. Spanish by* Edward Meryon Wilson.
River Compared to an Oratorical Sentence, The. OBVE
Wedding Feast, The. OBVE
Young Pilgrim Finds Refuge with the Goatherds, The. OBVE
First Song, The. Richard Burton. AA
First Song. Galway Kinnell. BiP; CTBA; GoJo; GrPl; LiTM; MP; NCSH; NePoAm; NoP; TwCP
First Song: "Doubt you to whom my Muse these notes intendeth." Sir Philip Sidney. *See* Astrophel and Stella: First Song.
First spasm became the continuous, The. Recluse. Aldo Camerino, *tr. by* Anita Barrows. VWA
First speaker said, The. "Paper Men to Air Hopes and Fears." Robert Francis. LCAP
First Spousal, The. Coventry Patmore. The Unknown Eros, II, ii. OBVV
First Spring Day, The. Christina Rossetti. WiR
First Spring Morning, The. Robert Bridges. BoNaP; YeAr
First stands the lofty Washington. Our Presidents. *Unknown.* BLPA
First Star. Dave Smith. AMV-81
First star shot up, The. Between Life and Death. Frantisek Gottlieb, *tr. by* Ewald Osers. VWA
First station off on a cold road to the country. The Chickadees. John Hay. NePoAm-2
First Step, The. Andrew Bice Saxton. AA
First Steps up Parnassus. Michael Drayton. *Fr.* To My Most Dearly Loved Henry Reynolds. NOBE
First strawberry, The. Original Strawberry. Nancy Willard. LCAP
First, suicide notes should be. Suicide. Alice Walker. FF
First Sun Day of the year. Tonight. Galway Kinnell. *Fr.* The Avenue Bearing the Initial of Christ into the New World. NaP
First Surf. Emanuel Di Pasquale. Str
First Swallow, The. Charlotte Smith. HBV-1
First Temptation, The. Milton. *Fr.* Paradise Regained, I. OxBoCh
First Test, The. Susan Fromberg Schaeffer. IHMS
First Thanksgiving, The. Jack Prelutsky. NTCP
First Thanksgiving, The. Clinton Scollard. PAH
First Thanksgiving, The. Nancy Byrd Turner. YeAr
First Thanksgiving Day, The. Alice Williams Brotherton. OHIP
First Thanksgiving Day, The. Margaret Junkin Preston. PAH
First Thanksgiving of All. Nancy Byrd Turner. FaPON; PAL; SiSoSe
First the bank-grass sags black. Salmon Fly Hatch on Yankee Jim Canyon of the Yellowstone. Greg Keeler. WOLT
First the falls, then the cave. Behind the Falls. William Stafford. RFM
First the heel. Lachlan Gorach's Rhyme. *Unknown.* PoPle
First the melody, clean and hard. How High the Moon. Lance Jeffers. CNA; PoBA
First, the middle, and the last, The. William Combe. *Fr.* Dr. Syntax in Search of the Picturesque. OBRV
First, the scene endlessly diminishes. Travelling Backward. Gene Baro. NYBP
First the soul of our house left, up the chimney. Tornado. William Stafford. NaP
First the tail begins to stiffen. Cow Pissing. Robert Morgan. GeTw
First the two eyes, which have the seeing power. Sight. Sir John Davies. LoBV
First, the two men stand pondering. Verona. James Wright. NNaP
First their eyes. Pulling Out. Lyn Lifshin. NeAC
First, then, soliloquies had need be few. On Writing for the Stage. John

Sheffield, Duke of Buckingham and Normanby. *Fr.* Essay on Poetry. FaBoUs
First there is the student. Ways of Loving. Theodore Weiss. GP
First there was putting hot-water bottles to it. Inevitable. John Betjeman. MoBrPo
First there was the lamb on knocking knees. Altarwise by Owl-Light, III. Dylan Thomas. CMoP
First there were those who died. Living among the Dead. William Matthews. GeTw
First, there's the Bible. The Hundred Best Books. Mostyn T. Pigott. InMe
First thing I saw in the morning, The. Mantova. James Wright. LCAP; NNaP
First thing, I think, is a keen sense, The. Juan Belmonte, Torero. Donald Finkel. NePoEA
First thing that I remember was Carlo tugging away, The. Asleep at the Switch. George Hoey. BeLS; PaPo
First Things. Lucienne Desnoues, *tr. fr. French by* Miller Williams. WPOW
First Things First. W. H. Auden. NePoAm-2; NYBP
First Three, The. Clinton Scollard. PAH
First Time, The. John Newlove. NeAC
First Time, The. Karl Shapiro. ErPo; VGW
First Time Ever I Saw Your Face, The. Ewan MacColl. FSW
First time he came to see me, The. Naomi (Omie) Wise. *Unknown.* BaBo
First Time He Kissed Me. Elizabeth Barrett Browning. Sonnets from the Portuguese, XXXVIII. BLPA; BLPL; CTC; FaBoBe; HBV-1; PoPl; ViBoPo
First time I ever saw a flying change. Flying Changes. Mary Wood. PH
First Time I Met You, The ("The first time I met the blues, mama, they came walking through the wood"). *Unknown.* BluL
First time I saw little Weevil he was on the western plain. The Ballet of the Boll Weevil. *Unknown.* ViBoFo
First time I seen my true love. Hard, Ain't It Hard. *Unknown.* FSW
First time I went to Frisco, I went up on a spree, The. Off to Sea Once More, *vers.* I. *Unknown.* ShS
First time I went to the fields alone, The. Strawberries. Judith Hemschemeyer. DFF
First time that the sun rose on thine oath, The. Elizabeth Barrett Browning. Sonnets from the Portuguese, XXXII. ViBoPo; WPE
First, to the feet, as they bear what you have grown to live in. Praise. William Matthews. AmPA
First to Throw a Stone. *Unknown.* STF
First Tooth, The. Charles *and* Mary Lamb. OxBChV; RHPC
First Tooth, The. William Brighty Rands. HBV-1; HBVY
First Travels of Max. John Crowe Ransom. MoAmPo
First truckload, The. Day of the Parade. Alan Chong Lau. BrSi
First Tuesday in the next October. An Auctioneer's Handbill. William Hall. FaBoUs
First, turn left at the Old Oraibi Bar. How to Get to New Mexico. John Brandi. TAT
First Vision, The. Tadhg Dall O'Huiginn, *tr. fr. Late Middle Irish by* the Earl of Longford. AnIL
"Vision of a Queen of Fairyland, A," *sel.* BIrV
First Voyage of John Cabot, The. Hezekiah Butterworth. PAH
First was Eve. Cain's Song. Donald Finkel. VWA
First was Fancy, like a lovely boy, The. The Masque of Cupid. Spenser. *Fr.* The Faerie Queene, III, 12. NOBE
First we saw of the high-tone tramp, The. Broncho versus Bicycle. John Wallace Crawford. BPAW
First Wedding in the World, The. Joel Rosenberg. VWA
First week the soil was clean, The. Digging for Indians. Gary Gildner. AmPA
First when Maggie was my care. Whistle o'er the Lave o't. Burns. BSV; OxBS
First whimper of the storm, The. A Local Storm. Donald Justice. NCSH
First wife floats in memory calmly, The. A Memory. Marvin Bell. GP
First William the Norman. *Unknown.* OxNR
First Winter. Gail N. Harada. BrSi
First Winter Storm. William Everson. NU
First Winter's Day. Dorothy Aldis. SoPo
First woman I loved, he said, The. Escapist's Song. Theodore Spencer. POL
First Woman's Lament. Brenda Chamberlain. *See* Lament: "My man is a bone ringed with weed."
First words spoken, The. Periods of Adjustment. Shawn Wong. BrSi
First World War. Kenneth Slade Alling. NePoAm
First you bite your fingernails. American Rhapsody. Kenneth Fearing. MoAmPo
First you must blow a bottle round your sleep. Directions for Dreamfishing. Martin Johnston. CBAP
First, you think they are dead. Lobsters in the Window. W. D. Snodgrass. BiP; BoAnP; HeIP; NCSH; NYBP; TAP
First young lady all around in town. Swing on the Corner. *Unknown.* TrAS
Firstborn, The. John Arthur Goodchild. HBV-1
Firstborn, The. Gary Soto. NPGG
Firstborn. Charles Wright. DiL
"Sugar dripping into your vein, The," *sel.* GP
Firstborn Land, The. Ingeborg Bachmann, *tr. fr. German by* Daniel Huws. BoWoP
First-born Star, The. Matthew Arnold. *Fr.* Bacchanalia. FaBoRV
Firste stok, fader of gentilesse, The. Gentilesse. Chaucer. AWP; OAEL-1
Firstfruits in 1812. Wallace Rice. PAH
Firstlings of grief, The. The Reapings. Theodore Weiss. NMP
Fisbo, *sel.* Robert Nichols.
"Talking of Ezra Pound and long-dead pantos." OBSV
Fish, The. Elizabeth Bishop. GoJo; HAP; HeIP; HoPM; InPK; LiTM; MiAP; MoAB; MoAmPo; MOS; NePA; NoAM; NOBA; NoP; NU; PAI; PoPl; TrGrPo; TwAmPo; ViBoPo; WeW
Fish, The. Rupert Brooke. FM; MOS
Fish, The. Ralph Gustafson. OBCV
Fish. Daniel Halpern. AmPA
Fish. Michael Hogan. GP
Fish. Larry Levis. AmPA
Fish, The. Marianne Moore. AmPP; MoAB; MoAmPo; MOS; MoVE; NoAM; OxBA; TwAmPo
Fish. Joe Rosenblatt. NOBC
Fish. W. W. E. Ross. MoCV; PeCV
Fish. Mario Satz, *tr. fr. Spanish by* Willis Barnstone. VWA
Fish. Shinkichi Takahashi, *tr. fr. Japanese by* Lucien Stryk. NU
Fish. Emily Townsend. NYBP
Fish. William Carlos Williams. NoAM
Fish. Sandra Witt. AMV-80
Fish and the Man, The. Leigh Hunt. *Fr.* The Fish, the Man, and the Spirit. RoGo
Fish Answers, A. Leigh Hunt. *Fr.* The Fish, the Man, and the Spirit. FiBHP
(Fish to Man.) MoShBr
Fish at Mass, The. *Unknown, tr. fr. Latin by* J. F. Webb. BIrV
Fish bones walked the waves off Hatteras. Cottonmouth Country. Louise Glück. CoAP; GeTw
Fish Come In Dancing, The. Kevin Roberts. WOLT
Fish Counter at Bonneville, The. William Stafford. AmFN
Fish Crier. Carl Sandburg. AmFN; OxBA
Fish dripping, A. Fish. W. W. E. Ross. MoCV; PeCV
Fish (fly-replete, in depth of June). Heaven. Rupert Brooke. BrPo; EBEV; HoPM; LiTB; LiTM; MoBrPo; NOBE; PoPle; PoRA; SeCeV; WGRP
Fish Food. John Wheelwright. LiTA; MOS; TwAmPo
Fish has laid her succulent eggs. Vicissitudes of the Creator. Archibald MacLeish. NePA
Fish has too many bones, The. The Old Men. Charles Reznikoff. DFF
Fish-Hawk, The. John Hall Wheelock. EtS; HBMV
Fish in River: "My house is not quiet, I am not loud." *Unknown, tr. fr. Anglo-Saxon by* Charles W. Kennedy. *Fr.* Riddles (Exeter Book). AnOE
Fish in the Unruffled Lakes. W. H. Auden. BoLoP; ChMP; CMoP; NoAM
(Song: "Fish in the unruffled lakes.") MoAB; MoBrPo
Fishmarket closed, the fishes gone into flesh, The. Galway Kinnell. *Fr.* The Avenue Bearing the Initial of Christ into the New World. ConAP; NaP; NMP
Fish of the sea couldn't come. How They Brought the Good News by Sea. Norma Farber. PChr
Fish Peddler and Cobbler. Kenneth Rexroth. NNaP
Fish Replies, A. Leigh Hunt. *Fr.* The Fish, the Man, and the Spirit. MOS; NOBL
Fish shop. Haiku. Basho, *tr. by* Lucien Stryk *and* Takashi Ikemoto. FAZ
Fish Sonata, The. Winfield Townley Scott. MP
Fish Story. Richard Armour. LiSp
Fish Story, A. Charles Fishman. WOLT
Fish Story. P. L. Jacobs. LFAC
Fish Story. B. Jo Kinnick. AMV-81
Fish, the Man, and the Spirit, The. Leigh Hunt. ChTr; EnRP; FM; HAP; MOS; NBM; NOBL; OBEV; PoEL-4; SeCePo; ViBoPo
Sels.
Fish and the Man, The. RoGo
Fish Answers, A. FiBHP
(Fish to Man.) MoShBr
Fish to Feed All Hunger, A. Sandra Alcosser. WOLT
Fish to Man. Leigh Hunt. *See* Fish Answers, A.
Fish took a notion, A. Tip-Toe Tail. Dixie Willson. NTCP
Fish Upstairs, The. William Dickey. Psk
Fishvendor, The. William Meredith. SaC

Fish wade, The/ through black jade. The Fish. Marianne Moore. MoAB; OxBA
Fish Will Swim as Before, The. Michael Spence. AMV-81
Fish with the Deep Smile, The. Margaret Wise Brown. PDV
Fisher, The. Roderic Quinn. CBAP; PoAu-1
Fisher Cat, The. Richard Eberhart. GrPl
Fisher, in your bright bark rowing. The Fisherman. *Unknown, tr. by* Anne Higginson Spicer. FaPON
Fisher-lad, A (no higher dares he look). Phineas Fletcher. Piscatorie Eclogues, III. SeCV-1
Fisher was casting his flies in a brook, A. The Microscopic Trout and the Machiavelian Fisherman. Guy Wetmore Carryl. WhC
Fisherman. Philip Booth. LiSp; WOLT
Fisherman, The. Abbie Farwell Brown. EtS; FaPON
Fisherman, The. George Bruce. BSV
Fisherman, The. Susan Fawcett. WOLT
Fisherman. Robert Francis. PPJ
Fisherman, The. Sam G. Harrison. AMV-80
Fisherman, The. Leonidas of Tarentum, *tr. fr. Greek by* Andrew Lang. AWP
Fisherman, The. Jay Macpherson. CABA; NOBC; PeCV
Fisherman, The. David McCord. PDV; TiPo
Fisherman, The. Dabney Stuart. LiSp
Fisherman, The. *Unknown, tr. fr. Portuguese by* Anne Higginson Spicer. FaPON
Fisherman, The. Will Wells. AMV-80
Fisherman, The. W. B. Yeats. BiP; CMoP; CoBMV; HAP; LiSp; NoAM
Fisherman Casts His Line into the Sea, The. Robert Holland. AMV-80
Fisherman goes out at dawn, The. The Fisherman. Abbie Farwell Brown. EtS; FaPON
Fisherman Writes a Letter to the Mermaid, The. Joan Aiken. WSC
Fisherman's Blunder off New Bedford, Massachusetts. Annemarie Ewing. NePoAm-2
Fisherman's Hymn, The. Alexander Wilson. AA; EtS
Fisherman's Luck. W. W. Gibson. EtS
Fisherman's Son. Charles Bruce. CaP
Fisherman's Song. *Unknown. See* We'll Go to Sea No More.
Fisherman's swapping a yarn for a yarn, The. The Flower-Boat. Robert Frost. PoA
Fisherman's Wife, The. Amy Lowell. BoWoP
Fisherman's Wife, The. Nora Mitchell. AMV-80
Fishermen. Basil Bunting. PoA
Fishermen. Stanley Moss. *See* Two Fishermen.
Fishermen. Gabriel Preil, *tr. fr. Hebrew by* Betsy Rosenberg. VWA
Fishermen, The. Theocritus, *tr. fr. Greek by* Charles Stuart Calverley. *Fr.* Idylls. AWP; OBVE
Fishermen, The. Whittier. EtS
Fishermen among the fireweed, The. By Rail through the Earthly Paradise, Perhaps Bedfordshire. Denise Levertov. NNaP
Fishermen at Ballyshannon. Limbo. Seamus Heaney. CIP; OxBC
Fishermen at Dawn. William Meissner. WOLT
Fishermen, Drowned beyond the West Coast. Vivian Smith. CBAP
Fishermen return with waterstars. Evening. Tristan Tzara, *tr. by* Willis Barnstone *and* Matei Calinescu. VWA
Fishermen say, when your catch is done, The. The Sea Wolf. Violet McDougal. FaPON
Fishermen will relate that in the South. The Lord of the Isle. Stefan George, *tr. by* Ludwig Lewisohn. AWP
Fishermen's Wives, The. Elaine Namanworth. AMV-80
Fisher's Apology, A. *Unknown, tr. fr. Latin by* Arthur Jonstone. GoTS
Fisher's Boy, The. Henry David Thoreau. AA; ChTr; MOS
Fisher's Life, The. *Unknown.* ChTr; EtS; GBP
Fisher's Widow, The. Arthur Symons. HBV-1
Fishes, The. *Unknown. See* Blow Ye Winds Westerly.
Fishes and the Poet's Hands, The. Frank Yerby. AmNP; PoNe
Fishes' Evening Song. Dahlov Ipcar. RHPC
Fishes swim in water clear. *Unknown.* OxNR
Fishin' Blues. Valentino Ramirez. AMV-81
Fishing. Philip Dow. WOLT
Fishing. Dorothy Wellesley. OBMV
Fishing, at Coot Shallows. Don Welch. WOLT
Fishing Blue Creek. Roy Scheele. PPJ
Fishing Blues. *Unknown.* BluL
Fishing boats have returned, The! Three Poems. "Ping Hsin." PBWP
Fishing Boats in Martigues. Roy Campbell. FaBoEE; FaBoPP
Fishing Drunk. Bob Mondy. WOLT
Fishing Fleet, The. Lincoln Colcord. HBMV
Fishing for sticklebacks, with rod and line. Sir Francis Burnand. PV
Fishing Harbour towards Evening. Richard Kell. CIP
Fishing in the Australian Alps. Ernest G. Moll. WhC
Fishing Lines. Donald M. Hassler. WOLT
Fishing on a Lake at Night. Robert Bly. LCAP
Fishing on a wide river from a boat. Supreme Death. Douglas Dunn. FaBoMo
Fishing Pole, The. Mary Carolyn Davies. FaPON
Fishing Season. Val Vallis. PoAu-2
Fishing Song. *Maori Oral Tradition, tr. by* A. Armstrong *and* R. Ngta. WTO
Fishing Song, A. William Brighty Rands. CenHV
Fishing the Big Hole. John Holbrook. WOLT
Fishing Village. Louis Dudek. *Fr.* Provincetown. MoCV
Fishing with Buddies. Gary Eddy. WOLT
Fishing with My Daughter in Miller's Meadow. Lucien Stryk. GP
Fish's Nightsong. Christian Morgenstern. WeW
Fisk is/ a/ negroid/ institution. Sharon Scott. JB
Fist, The ("The fist clenched round my heart"). Derek Walcott. LLLT
Fist Fight. Doug Cockrell. Psk
Fit of Rime [*or* Rhyme] against Rime [*or* Rhyme], A. Ben Jonson. AnAnS-2; InvP; MAT; OAEL-1; PoEL-2; PP; SeCP; SeCV-1; TEP
Fit of Something against Something, A. Alan Ansen. PP
Fit Only for Apollo. Francis Beaumont. *Fr.* Masque of the Inner Temple and Gray's Inne. ChTr
Fit theme for song, the sylvan maid. Madam Hickory. Wilbur Larremore. AA
Fitz Adam's Story. James Russell Lowell. AmPP
Five. Weldon Kees. PPP
Five-and-thirty black slaves. The Key-Board. Sir William Watson. HBV-2
Five Arabic Verses in Praise of Wine. *Unknown, tr. fr. Arabic by* Hartwig Hirschfeld. TrJP
Five Bells. Kenneth Slessor. CBAP; PoAu-2; PoRA; SeCePo
Five Birds Rise. William Hayward. NYBP
Five Carols for Christmastide, *sels.* Louise Imogen Guiney.
  "Ox and the Ass, The," V. ISi
  "Ox he openeth wide the Doore, The," I. ISi
    (Tryste Noel.) HBV-1; OBVV
  "Three without slumber ride from afar," III. ISi
  "Vines branching stilly," II. ISi; OBVV
    (Carol.) OBVV
.05. Ishmael Reed. InPK
"Five cents a glass!" Does anyone think. Price of a Drink. Josephine Pollard. PaPo
Five-Day Rain, The. Denise Levertov. NeAP
Five Days Old. Francis Webb. PoAu-2
Five Degrees South. Francis Brett Young. EtS
Five dollars a day is a white man's pay, way. A Dollar and a Half a Day. *Unknown.* TrAS
Five dollars, four dollars, three dollars, two. An Inheritance. Naomi Replansky. GP
Five Domestic Interiors. Vernon Scannell. OxBC
Five Dreams, The. John Woods. FiCP
Five Epigrams. J. V. Cunningham. UnTE
  Sels.
  And Now You're Ready Who While She Was Here. OBVE; TW
    (Epigram: "And now you're ready who while she was here.") ErPo
  "Bride loved old words, and found her pleasure marred." OBAL
  Epitaph for Someone or Other. NIP; OBAL
    (Epigram: "Naked I came, naked I leave the scene.") VGW
  "Lip was a man who used his head." OBAL; PV
    (Lip.) ErPo
Five Epigrams. Donald Hall. NePoAm-2
Five Eyes. Walter de la Mare. PCat
Five fearless knights of the first renown. The First American Sailors. Wallace Rice. PAH
515 Madison Avenue. Rhapsody. Frank O'Hara. NoAM; NYP
Five fives this year my years. The Conviction. J. M. Synge. SyP
Five for the Grace of Man. Winfield Townley Scott. VGW
5.40. The Bay View. After the office. Aberdarcy: The Chaucer Road. Kingsley Amis. *Fr.* The Evans Country. NOBL
Five geese deploy mysteriously. Bas-Relief. Carl Sandburg. CrMA
Five gleaming crows. In Air. Peter Clarke. PBA
Five Groups of Verse, *sels.* Charles Reznikoff.
  After I Had Worked All Day. PrIm
  "He was afraid to go through their grocery store." DiL
  Son with a Future, A. DiL
Five Hens, The. *Unknown.* GBP
    ("There was an old man who lived in Middle Row.") OxNR
Five Horses. May Swenson. PH
Five hours, (and who can do it less in?). The Lady's Dressing Room. Swift. ErPo; NCEP; NoP; TEP
Five hundred guests upon a summer's day. The View from Father's Porch. Celeste Turner Wright. Str
Five jolly rogues of a feather. Johnson's Ale. *Unknown.* FSW
Five Joys, The. *Unknown.* OxBM

Five Joys of Mary, The. *Unknown.* MeEL
Five Kernels of Corn. Hezekiah Butterworth. PAH
Five Little Chickens. *Unknown.* PDV
(Chickens, The.) FaPON; MoShBr
Five Little Fairies, The. Maud Burnham. HBVY
Five little monkeys/ Swinging from a tree. The Monkeys and the Crocodile. Laura E. Richards. FaPON; ShM; SoPo; SUS; TiPo
Five little pussy-cats, invited out to tea. The Cats' Tea-Party. Frederick E. Weatherly. TiPo
Five Little Sisters Walking in a Row. Kate Greenaway. MoShBr
Five Men against the Theme "My Name Is Red Hot. Yo Name Ain Doodley Squat." Gwendolyn Brooks. CNA
Five-Minute Orlando MacBeth, The. George MacBeth. NOBL
Five minutes, five minutes more, please! Bedtime. Eleanor Farjeon. SoPo; TiPo
Five oxen, grazing in a flowery mead. On a Seal. Plato, *tr. by* Thomas Stanley. AWP; FaBoEE
5 Poems. Robert Gray. CBAP
Five Poems about Poetry, *sels.* George Oppen.
From Virgil. NNaP
Gesture, The. NNaP
Five Poems for Dolls. Margaret Atwood. NIP
Five Reasons [for Drinking]. Henry Aldrich. *See* Reasons for Drinking.
Five Sense. Marvin Wyche, Jr. AmNP
Five Serpents. Charles Burgess. NePoAm-2
Five soldiers fixed by Mathew Brady's eye. Looking into History. Richard Wilbur. VGW
Five Stanzas on Perfection. George Jonas. PeCV
Five Students, The. Thomas Hardy. CMoP; GTBS-P; PoEL-5
Five summer days, five summer nights. The Bluefly. Robert Graves. CMoP; MoVe; NoAM; NYBP
Five Things White. Edward May. FaBoEE
5:30 A.M. Adrienne Rich. NMM; NOBA
5:32, The. Phyllis McGinley. *Fr.* I Know a Village. NMM; WPE
Five thousand souls are here, and all are bounded. Troopship in the Tropics. Alun Lewis. WaP
Five thousand years have fled, let us suppose. The Archaeologist of the Future. Leonard Bacon. WhC
Five times I howled. To a Captain in Sinai. Ada Aharoni. AMV-81
527 Cathedral Parkway. Rika Lesser. NYP
Five Unmistakable Marks, The. David Jones. In Parenthesis, VII. NoAM
Five Vignettes. Jean Toomer. BALP; PoBA
Five Visions of Captain Cook, *sel.* Kenneth Slessor.
"Flowers turned to stone! Not all the botany." PoAu-2
Five Voyages of Arnor, The. George Mackay Brown. NePoEA-2
Five Ways to Kill a Man. Edwin Brock. DL
Five Were Foolish, *with music.* Arthur J. Hodge. AH
Five Words for Joe Dunn on His 22nd Birthday. Jack Spicer. PoM
Five workmen hired here to shovel dirt. Workmen. Herbert Morris. NePoAm-2
Five years after Pastorius had written. Clausa Germanis Gallia. Millen Brand. GP
Five years ago we knew such ecstasies. Interim. Frank Ormsby. CIP
Five years have passed [*or* past]; five summers, with the length. Lines Composed a Few Miles above Tintern Abbey [on Revisiting the Banks of the Wye during a Tour, July 13, 1798]. Wordsworth. BiP; BLPL; CABA; ChER; EnRP; FaBoPP; FF; FiP; GoTL; HAP; HBV-2; HeIP; InPS; LiTB; LoBV; MasP; NIP; NoP; OAEL-2; OAEP; OBNC; OBRV; PoEL-4; PPP; PrIm; SeCePo; SeCeV; TEP; TreFS; TrGrPo; WHA
Five Years Old. Lysbeth Boyd Borie. SiSoSe
Five years since you died and I am. Letter to a Dead Father. Richard Shelton. DFF; GP
Fivesucked the features of my girl by glory. Nicholas Moore. PoA
Fix thy corporeal, and internal eye. Matthew Prior. *Fr.* Solomon on the Vanity of the World. FM
Fix'd were their habits; they arose betimes. Jonas Kindred's Household. George Crabbe. *Fr.* Tales: The Frank Courtship. FaBoEn
Fixer of Midnight. Reuel Denney. OBAL
Fixing to Die. *Unknown.* BluL
Fixture, A. May Swenson. NYBP
Flag, The. James Jeffrey Roche. PAH
Flag. Reg Saner. GP
Flag, The. Shelley Silverstein. PoSC
Flag Goes By, The. Henry Holcomb Bennett. FaBoBe; FaFP; FaPON; GN; HBV-2; HBVY; OHFP; PAL; PGD; SiSoSe; TreF; WBLP; YaD
Flag of the *Constellation,* The. Thomas Buchanan Read. EtS
Flag of the heroes who left us their glory. Union and Liberty. Oliver Wendell Holmes. OHIP
Flag Song. Lydia Avery Coonley Ward. YeAr
Flag Speaks, The. Emily Greene Balch. PGD
Flag We Fly, The. Aileen Fisher. YeAr
Flagpole Sitter, The. Donald Finkel. CoAP
Flags. Gwendolyn Brooks. AmNP
Flags of all sorts. Things We Dreamt We Died For. Marvin Bell. CoAP
Flags of war like storm-birds fly, The. The Battle Autumn of 1862. Whittier. PAH
Flail. Power Dalton. HBMV
Flake diamond of/ the sea. Larry Eigner. PoM
Flame at the core of the world. Song. Arthur Upson. HBV-1
Flame burns in the morning, A. Le Chariot. John Wieners. VGW
Flame-flower, day-torch, Mauna Loa. Lines to a Nasturtium. Anne Spencer. AmNP; CDC; PoNe
Flame-Heart. Claude McKay. AmNP; BALP; BANP; CDC; PoNe
Flame of God. Amy Carmichael. *See* Deliver Me.
Flame out, you glorious skies. The Dead Heroes. Isaac Rosenberg. MoBrPo
Flame went flitting through the wood, A. The Scarlet Tanager. Mary Augusta Mason. AA
Flames rising up, The. Dawn. David Shevin. VWA
Flaming Heart, The. Richard Crashaw. AnAnS-1; GoBC; LiTB; LoBV; OxBoCh; PoEL-2; SeCePo; SeCV-1; TEP; WHA
Sels.
"Live here, great heart; and love and dy and kill." OBS
"O Heart! the equal poise of love's both parts". TrGrPo
"O thou undaunted daughter of desires!" HAP
(Upon the Book and Picture of the Seraphical Saint Teresa.) NOBE; OBEV
"Well-meaning readers, you that come as friends." OAEL-1
Flaming Terrapin, The, *sel.* Roy Campbell.
"Maternal Earth stirs redly from beneath," I. MoBrPo
Flamingo, The. Lewis Gaylord Clark. NA
Flammonde. E. A. Robinson. AmPP; CMoP; LiTA; LiTM; NoAM; SeCeV
Flanagan got up on a Saturday morning. Lament for Barney Flanagan. James K. Baxter. NoP
Flanders Fields. Elizabeth Daryush. SUMH
Flanged, all bright colors—red, yellow, blue—the discs. Frisbee. Rolfe Humphries. GrPl
Flannan Isle. W. W. Gibson. CH; GoTL; MoVE; OBVV; PoRA
Flannery O'Connor. Dorothy Walters. IHMS; PoRA
Flap, flap, the captive bird in the cage. The Scholar in the Narrow Street. Tso Ssu, *tr. by* Arthur Waley. AWP
Flap my sole, bim bam! Bim Bam. Dorothy Rosenberg. PoNe
Flash. Stephen Todd Booker. LFAC
Flash, The. James Dickey. LCAP
Flash Crimson. Carl Sandburg. MoAmPo
Flash Frigate, The, *with music. Unknown.* AmSS
Flash Jack from Gundagai. *Unknown.* PoAu-1
Flash of light across the night, A. Ulric Dahlgren. Kate Brownlee Sherwood. PAH
Flash of lightning does not satisfy thirst, A. Modern Love Songs. Faarah Nuur, *tr. by* B. W. Andrzjewski *and* I. M. Lewis. TTY
Flashing of an arc that bright and briefly, The. Flying Fish. Katherine Kelley Taylor. EtS
Flashlight, A. Brain. Coleman Barks. PPJ
Flashlight beams and headlights. Opening the Seams. Stephen Lewandowski. WOLT
Flat on the bank I parted. The Trout. John Montague. BoAnP; IPY; NMP
Flat on the grey steel bulkhead arch her curves. Pin-up Girl. Louis O. Coxe. WaP
Flat One, A. W. D. Snodgrass. AP; CAPP; LiTM; NePoEA-2; PoCh
Flat River Girl, The. *Unknown. See* Jack Haggerty.
Flathead and Nez Perce Sin-ka-ha. William S. Lewis. BPAW
Flattered Flying Fish, The. E. V. Rieu. PDV; RHPC; ShM; SO
Flattery. Swift. *Fr.* Cadenus and Vanessa. TreFT
("'Tis an old maxim in the schools.") PV
Flaubert wanted to write a novel. Style. Howard Nemerov. NoAM
Flaunt of the sunshine I need not your bask! Song of Myself, XL. Walt Whitman. TrGrPo
Flavia's a name a deal too free. *Unknown.* FaBoEE
Flavia's a wit, has too much sense to pray. Characters of Women: Flavia, Atossa, and Cloe. Pope. *Fr.* Moral Essays, Epistle II. OBEC
Flavio Gonzales, 72, made jackhammer. The Moon Is a Diamond. Arthur Sze. AMV-81
Flavius, If Your Girl Friend. Catullus, *tr. fr. Latin by* Horace Gregory. ErPo
Flavor of vanilla drifts, A. Dark Romance. Lucha Corpi, *tr. by* Catherine Rodriguez-Nieto. WPOW
Flavor the speaking of this one. Not to Forget Miss Dickinson. Marshall Schacht. LiTM
Flaw in Paganism, The. Dorothy Parker. DBV
Flawless His Heart. James Russell Lowell. PAH
Flax. Ivan Bunin, *tr. fr. Russian by* Babette Deutsch *and* Avrahm Yarmolinsky. AWP

Flaxen-headed cow-boy, as simple as may be, A. Air. John O'Keefe. NOEC
Fle fro the pres and dwelle with sothefastnesse. *See* Flee from the press . . .
Flea, The. John Donne. AnAnS-1; BiP; BLPL; BoLoP; CABA; EBEV; FF; FM; HoPM; JCP; LiTB; MAT; MePo; NIP; OAEL-1; PAI; PoPle; PPoe; SCV; SeCP; SeCV-1; SoSe; TEP; TrGrPo
Flea, The. Roland Young. PoPl; RHPC; WhC
Flea and the Fly, The. *Unknown.* FaPON
("Flea and a fly [flew up] in a flue, A.") TiPo; WhC
(Fly and a Flea in a Flue, A.) RHPC
(Limerick: "Flea and a fly in a flue, A.") WhC
Flea Circus at Tivoli, The. Nancy Willard. HoAn
Flea flew by a bee, A. The bee. Combinations. Mary Ann Hoberman. *Fr.* Bugs. OBCA
Fleadh. Michael Longley. CIP
Fleas, The. Augustus De Morgan. *See* Great Fleas.
Fleche. Larry Eigner. VGW
Fled are the frosts, and now the fields appear. Farewell Frost; or, Welcome the Spring. Robert Herrick. CaPo
Fled are those times, when, in harmonious strains. Truth in Poetry. George Crabbe. *Fr.* The Village. OBEC
Fled is the blasted verdure of the fields. James Thomson. *Fr.* The Seasons: Autumn. OAEP
Fled is the swiftness of all the white-footed ones. Elegy. Joseph Auslander. TrJP
Fledgling Bard and the Poetry Society, The, *much abr.* George Reginald Margetson. BANP
Fledglings. Thomas Lake Harris. AA
Fledglings. William Meredith. GLGT
Fledglings have a language, The. Baby Talk. Anna Bird Stewart. RHPC
Flee from [*or* Fle fro] the press [*or* prees *or* pres] and dwelle with soothfastnesse [*or* sothefastnesse]. Balade de Bon [*or* Good] Conseyl [*or* Conseill *or* Truth]. Chaucer. ACP; AWP; GoBC; MeEL; NoP; OAEL-1; OxBM; TrGrPo; ViBoPo
Flee on Your Donkey. Anne Sexton. NYBP
Fleece, The, *sels.* John Dyer.
"Ah gentle shepherd, thine the lot to tend," *fr.* I. PoEL-3
Bedford Level, *fr.* II. FaBoPP
British Commerce, *fr.* IV. OBEC
English Weather, *fr.* I. OBEC
(English Fog, The.) TrGrPo
Happy Workhouse and the Good Effects of Industry, The, *fr.* III. NOEC
How to Shear Sheep, *fr.* II. FaBoUs
Nation's Wealth, A, *fr.* III. OBEC
Wool Trade, The, *fr.* III. OBEC; SeCePo
Fleeing from threatened flood, they sailed. The First Invasion of Ireland. *Unknown, tr. by* John Montague. BIrV; NMP
Fleet and fair. Gazelles and Unicorn. John Gray. *Fr.* The Long Road. ChTr
Fleet astronomer can bore, The. Vanity [*or* Vanitie]. George Herbert. MePo; NoP; SeCV-1
Fleet at Santiago, The. Charles E. Russell. PAH
Fleet ships encountering on the high seas. Good Ships. John Crowe Ransom. WeW
Fleet Street. Shane Leslie. OnYI
Fleet Street! Fleet Street! Fleet Street in the morning. A Song of Fleet Street. Alice Werner. HBV-2
Fleet with flags arrayed, A. A Ballad of the French Fleet. Longfellow. AA; HBV-2; PAH
Fleeting birds may soon in ocean swim, The. To Miss Laetitia Van Lewen. Constantia Grierson. WPE
Fleeting pomps of the world are like the green willow trees, The. Song of Nezahualcoyotl. *Unknown.* DL
Fleeting Return. Juan Ramon Jimenez, *ad. fr.* Spanish by William Moritz. AMV-80
Fleggit Bride, The. "Hugh MacDiarmid." OxBS
Flemish Madonna, A. Charles Wharton Stork. HBMV
Flemish Primitive. G. S. Fraser. BSV
Flesh. Mary Fullerton. PoAu-1
Flesh. Stan Rice. NPGG
Flesh and the Spirit, The. Anne Bradstreet. AmPP; AP; LiTA; NePA; NOBA; OxBA; SCAP; TAP
Flesh-Fly and the Bee, The. Coventry Patmore. FaBoEE
Flesh has a remarkable future. Flesh. Stan Rice. NPGG
Flesh, I Have Knocked at Many a Dusty Door. John Masefield. *Fr.* Sonnets ("Long, long ago"). LiTM
(Sonnet: "Flesh, I have knocked at many a dusty door.") MoBrPo; SeCePo
Flesh is sad alas, The! and all books I have read. Sea Breeze. Stéphane Mallarmé, *tr. by* Roger Fry. NAWM-2
Flesh is sad, alas, The! and all the books are read. Sea-Wind. Stéphane Mallarmé, *tr. by* Arthur Symons. AWP; SyP
Flesh-Scraper, The. Andrew Young. ELU
Fleshflower. William Pitt Root. GeTw
Fletcher, though some call it thy fault, that wit. Upon the Dramatick Poems of Mr. John Fletcher. William Cartwright. OBS
Fleur de Lys. Rayner Heppenstall. WaP
Fleur has fa'en, The. A Hint o' Snow. William Soutar. PoSH
Flicker, The. Lew Blockcolski. VoR
Flickering of incessant rain. John Gould Fletcher. Irradiations, II *or* V [VII]. MoAmPo; NePA; TwAmPo
Flies in the buttermilk, skip to my Lou. Skip to My Lou. *Unknown.* TrAS
Flies Love Me. Nuala Archer. AMV-81
Flight. Madison Cawein. AA
Flight, The. C. Day Lewis. *Fr.* A Time to Dance. MoVE
Flight. Helen Frazee-Bower. Two Married, III. HBMV
Flight, The. John Haines. EAS
Flight. Judith Hemschemeyer. PPJ
Flight. Barbara Howes. NYBP
Flight. George Johnston. WHW
Flight, The. Lloyd Mifflin. AA; HBV-2
Flight, The. Theodore Roethke. *Fr.* The Lost Son. TrGrPo
Flight. James Tate. InPK
Flight, The. Sara Teasdale. HBMV; WHA
Flight. Harold Vinal. FaPON
Flight. Ruth Whitman. SO
Flight 539. John Malcolm Brinnin. HoAn
Flight from the Convent, The. Theodore Tilton. AA
Flight in the Desert, The. William Everson. VGW
Flight into Egypt, The. W. H. Auden. *Fr.* For the Time Being; a Christmas Oratorio. OAEP; OxBA; SBVL
Flight into Egypt, The. Longfellow. *Fr.* Christus; a Mystery. OBVV
Flight into Egypt, The. Peter Quennell. LiTB; LiTM
Flight is but the praeparative. The Vision. Thomas Traherne. ILwL
Flight is the bird's value. Aesthetic. Norman Rosten. PoA
Flight of Apollo, The. Stanley Kunitz. MOON
Flight of Love, The. Shelley. *See* When the Lamp Is Shattered.
Flight of the Arrow, The. Richard Henry Stoddard. AA
Flight of the Birds, The. Edmund Clarence Stedman. GN
Flight of the Bucket, The. Kipling. BXAP
Flight of the Duchess, The. Robert Browning. VLP
Flight of the Earls, The, 1607, *sel.* Fearghal Og MacWard, *tr. fr. Irish by* the Earl of Longford.
"All Ireland's now one vessel's company." BIrV
Flight of the Earls, The. Aindrais MacMarcuis. *See* This Night Sees Ireland Desolate.
Flight of the Geese, The. Sir Charles G. D. Roberts. *Fr.* Songs of the Common Day. PeCV
Flight of the Goddess, The. Thomas Bailey Aldrich. HBV-2
Flight of the Heart, The. Dora Head Goodale. AA
Flight of the Roller Coaster. Raymond Souster. NOBC; PeCV; SO; WHW
Flight of the War-Eagle, The. Obadiah Cyrus Auringer. AA
Flight of Youth, The. Richard Henry Stoddard. AA; HBV-1
Flight Plan. Jane Merchant. RHPC
Flight-Sergeant Foster flattened Gloucester. Paul Dehn. *Fr.* A Leaden Treasury of English Verse. DBV; PV
Flight Shot, A. Maurice Thompson. AA
Flight songs the way they build their nests. The Burning of the Birds. Shirley Kaufman. GP
Flight 382. Doris Longman. AMV-81
Flight to Italy, *sel.* C. Day Lewis.
"Winged bull trundles to the wired perimeter, The." OxBTC
Flighting for Duck. William Empson. MoPo
Flights. Roger McDonald. CBAP
Fling forth the triple-colored flag to dare. The Need of the Hour. Edwin Markham. PAL
Fling Out the Banner! *with music.* George Washington Doane. AH
Fling this useless book away. Written in a Lady's Prayer Book. Earl of Rochester. BoLoP
Flint. Christina Rossetti. OxBChV; RHPC
("Emerald is as green as grass, An.") TiPo
Flint Hills, The. Lew Blockcolski. VoR
Flintlike, her feet struck. Hardcastle Crags [*or* Night Walk]. Sylvia Plath. GoYe; NYBP
Flip, clack! The windscreen wipers clear. Seven Rainy Months. William Plomer. OxBTC
Flip flop/ Flip flap. Fishes' Evening Song. Dahlov Ipcar. RHPC
Flippantly,/ In the cinemas past sleep. Before Dawn. Horace Hamilton. NYBP
Flirt, The. W. H. Davies. EnLoPo
Flirtation, The. Michael C. Blumenthal. AMV-81
Flitch of Dunmow, The. James Carnegie. HBV-2
Flitting, The, *sel.* John Clare.
"I've left my own old home of homes." OBRV

Flo was fond of Ebenezer. The Tides of Love. T. A. Daly. InMe; PoPl; WhC; YaD
Float up again. Celan. Asya, *tr. by* Gabriel Preil *and* Howard Schwartz. VWA
Floated in the cove. The Boat. Robert Kelly. CoPo
Floating, a floating, A. A Myth. Charles Kingsley. GN
Floating across the lake. Not Thinking of America. Judith Kroll. AmPA
Floating Bridge. *Unknown.* BluL
Floating Candles, The. Sydney Lea. MAYP
Floating, face up, on the open. Queer's Song. Richard Howard. *Fr.* Gaiety. ErPo
Floating finned and masked. Boundaries. Carrol B. Fleming. SUW
Floating Old Man, The. Edward Lear. *See* Limerick: "There was an old man in a boat."
Flock. Lance Henson. VoR
Flock at Evening, The. Odell Shepard. HBMV
Flock of birds, soaring, twisting, turning, A. Love Is. Ann Darr. GrPl
Flock of crows high from the Northland flies, A. Autumn. Detlev von Liliencron, *tr. by* Ludwig Lewisohn. AWP
Flock of Guinea Hens Seen from a Car, A. Eudora Welty. GrPl; NYBP; PrIm
Flock of merry singing-birds were sporting in the grove, A. The O'Lincon Family. Wilson Flagg. HBV-1; HBVY
Flock of scarlet birds, A. The Ocotillo in Bloom. Marilla Merrimar Guild. BPAW
Flock of sheep that leisurely pass by, A. To Sleep. Wordsworth. EnRP; GTBS; GTBS-P; HBV-2; OBRV; TrGrPo; ViBoPo
Flock of winds came winging [*or* flying] from the North, A. The Roaring Frost. Alice Meynell. EBVV; WPE
Flodden. Sir Walter Scott. *Fr.* Marmion. BSV
(Battle, The.) PoEL-4
Flodden Field. *Unknown.* ESPB
Flood, The. Charles G. Bell. GrPl
Flood. Mary Grant Charles. GoYe
Flood. Irving Feldman. MP
Flood. James Joyce. MoBrPo
Flood, The. Ewa Lipska, *tr. fr. Polish by* Peter Jay *and* Geri Lipschultz. VWA
Flood, The. Lev Mak, *tr. fr. Russian by* Neil Muhlberger *and* Marvin Misemer. VWA
Flood. Roger McGough. FF
Flood, The. Ovid, *tr. fr. Latin by* Dryden. *Fr.* Metamorphoses, I. ChTr
Flood, The. Andrew Young. ChMP
Flood didn't save me, The. The Flood. Ewa Lipska, *tr. by* Peter Jay *and* Geri Lipschultz. VWA
Flood of Years, The. Bryant. AA
Floodtide. Askia Muhammad Touré. PoBA; PoNe
Flood-tide below me! I see you face to face! Crossing Brooklyn Ferry. Walt Whitman. AmPP; AP; CABA; LiTA; NoAM; NOBA; NoP; NYP; TAP
Flood was down in the Wilga swamps, three feet over the mud, The. How the Fire Queen Crossed the Swamp. Will H. Ogilvie. PoAu-1
Flooded Mind. Norman MacCaig. OxBC
Flooding with a brilliant mist. To the Moon. Goethe, *tr. by* John Frederick Nims. MOON
Floods and gales. Et Cetera. Dee Walker. GoYe
Floods, by nature enemies to land, The. Ovid, *tr. by* Dryden. *Fr.* Metamorphoses, I. OBVE
Floods Clap Their Hands, The. Bible, *O.T.* Psalms, XCVIII. TrGrPo
(O Sing unto the Lord a New Song.) EaLo; TrJP
(Sing unto Jehovah.) BLRP
Floods of men. All the Spirit Powers Went to Their Dancing Place. Gary Snyder. UnPo
Floods of tears well from my deepest heart, The. Elegy. Immanuel di Roma, *tr. by* J. Chotzner. TrJP
Floods Swell around Me, Angry, Appalling, *with music.* Zachary Eddy. AH
Flood-Time on the Marshes. Evaleen Stein. AA
Flooer o the Gean. George Campbell Hay. OxBS
Floor. C. K. Williams. GeTw
Floor: Five. Stephen Vincent. *Fr.* Elevator Landscapes. NeAC
Floor: O. Stephen Vincent. *Fr.* Elevator Landscapes. NeAC
Floor and the Ceiling, The. William Jay Smith. GrPl; OBCA
Floor boards have a sour breath, The. Dust on Spring Street. Louis Grudin. NoP
Floor Is Dirty, The. Edward Field. *See* Dirty Floor, The.
Floor was muddy with the juice of peaches, The. Canning Time. Robert Morgan. Str
Floors are slippery with blood, The. The Dancers. Edith Sitwell. SUMH
Flora. Ray Fraser. NeAC
Floral Tribute. Sir Charles Jeffries. PoPle
Flora's Flower. *Unknown, tr. fr. Latin by* John Addington Symonds. UnTE
Flora's Lamentable Passion. *Unknown.* CoMu
Florella; or, The Jealous Lover. *Unknown.* AmFP
(Fair Florella or the Jealous Lover.) BaBo (A *and* B *vers.*)
(Jealous Lover, The.) ShS, *sl. diff. vers., with music;* ViBoFo
Florence. Elizabeth Barrett Browning. *Fr.* Aurora Leigh, VII. FaBoPP
Florence. Walter Savage Landor. SeCePo
Florence below was an abyss of lights of trembling sordidness. Night Character. Dino Campana, *tr. by* Frank Stewart. AMV-81
Florence MacCarthy's Farewell to His English Lover. Aubrey Thomas De Vere. NBM
Florence Vane. Philip Pendleton Cooke. AA; HBV-1
Florida. Dannie Abse. OxBC
Florida. Elizabeth Bishop. MP; TwCP
Florida. Carl Rakosi. TAP
Florida Road Workers. Langston Hughes. CTBA; MoAmPo
Floridian Museum of Art, A. Reed Whittemore. EyDe
Florin to the willing guard, A. The Rosy Bosom'd Hours. Coventry Patmore. EnLoPo
Florine. Thomas Campbell. BSV
Florio, one ev'ning, brisk, and gay. Epigram on Florio. John Winstanley. FaBoEE
Floris and Blauncheflour, *sel.* *Unknown.*
Lover's Stratagem, A. OxBM
Florist was told, cyclamen or azalea, The. Lines to Accompany Flowers for Eve. Carolyn Kizer. BoWoP
Florus, canst thou define that innate spark. To Mr. ———, an Unlettered Poet, on Genius Unimproved. Ann Yearsley. NOEC
Flos Lunae. Ernest Dowson. OBMV
Floss won't save you from an abyss. Emily Dickinson. LiTA; NePA
Flotsam and Jetsam. E. E. Cummings. NOBA; OBAL
Flour of England, fruit of Spain. Mother Goose. HBV-1; HBVY; OxNR
Flow down, cold rivulet, to the sea. A Farewell. Tennyson. FaBoRV; HBV-2
Flow Forth, Abundant Tears. *Unknown.* EnRePo
Flow Gently, Sweet Afton. Burns. *See* Afton Water.
Flow Not So Fast. *Unknown.* EnRePo; QFR; ViBoPo
Flow, O My Tears! *Unknown.* ElL
Flower, The. Robert Creeley. CAPP; PAI
Flower, The. Lee Wilson Dodd. HBMV
Flower, The. George Herbert. AnAnS-1; AWP; ELP; FaBoEn; FaBoRV; JCP; MePo; NIP; NOBE; NOCV; NoP; OBS; OxBoCh; PoEL-2; PPP; SeCP; SeCV-1
Flower, The. Samuel Speed. OxBoCh
Flower, The. Tennyson. HBV-2
Flower, The. Robert Penn Warren. PoPl
Flower and the Leaf, The, *sel.* Lady of the Arbour.
"And at the last I cast my mine eye aside." WPE
("And as I stood and cast aside mine eye.") PBBP
Flower-Boat, The. Robert Frost. PoA
Flower-Cart Man, The. Rachel Field. SiSoSe; SoPo
Flower Ensnarer of Psalms. Rossana Ombres, *tr. fr. Italian by* I. L. Salomon. BoWoP
Flower-fed Buffaloes, The. Vachel Lindsay. AmFN; BPAW; ChTr; CMoP; FaPON; GoJo; LoBV; MoAmPo; NOBA; OBCA; PPON; RFM; VGW
Flower for a Professor's Garden of Verses. Irwin Edman. DBV; InMe
Flower Given to My Daughter, A. James Joyce. OBMV; PoPl
Flower Herding on Mount Monadnock. Galway Kinnell. HeIP; LCAP; NaP; NOBA
(Flower Herding Pictures on Mount Monadnock.) ConAP
Flower—I never fancied, jewel—I profess you! Magical Nature. Robert Browning. VLP
Flower in the Crannied Wall. Tennyson. BoNaP; FaBV; FaFP; FaPON; InPK; LiTB; NIP; PoPl; TEP; TreFS; TrGrPo; TRV; WGRP
(Fragment.) BLPA; FPL
Flower Is Looking, A. Harold Monro. *Fr.* Strange Meetings. MoBrPo
Flower Market, The. Po Chü-i, *tr. fr. Chinese by* Arthur Waley. PPON
Flower of Beauty, The. George Darley. *See* Song: "Sweet in her green cell the flower of beauty slumbers."
Flower of Flame, The, *sel.* Robert Nichols.
"Before I woke I knew her gone." OBMV
Flower of Liberty, The. Oliver Wendell Holmes. HBVY
Flower of Love. Claude McKay. BALP
Flower of Mullein, A. Lizette Woodworth Reese. MoAmPo
Flower of Old Japan, The, *sel.* Alfred Noyes.
Epilogue: "Carol, every violet has." MoBrPo
Flower of the dust am I: for dust will flower. Clement Wood. Eagle Sonnets, VII. HBMV
Flower of the flock. On Sweet Killen Hill. Tom MacIntyre. CIP; NCSH
Flower of the medlar. A Pastoral. Théophile Marzials. HBV-1
Flower of the race, The. Gentlemen. Geoffrey Taylor. FaBoEE
Flower of the shining summer. The Pearly Everlasting. Ernest Fewster. CaP

Flower of this purple dye. Shakespeare. *Fr.* A Midsummer Night's Dream, III, ii. CTC
Flower of Virtue is the heart's content, The. Sonnet: Of Virtue. Folgore da San Geminiano, *tr. by* Dante Gabriel Rossetti. AWP
Flower of waves, A. Lady Ise, *tr. fr. Japanese by* Etsuko Terasaki *and* Irma Brandeis. BoWoP
Flower of youth, in the ancient frame. Judith. William Young. AA
Flower, that I hold in my hand. Tuberose. Louis James Block. AA
Flower that smiles to-day, The. Mutability. Shelley. EnRP; FaBoEn; HBV-2; NoP; OBNC; ViBoPo
Flower unblown, A: a book unread. The Year Ahead. Horatio Nelson Powers. WBLP
Flower Vendor, The. Luis Cabalquinto. BrSi
Flower was offered to me, A. My Pretty Rose Tree. Blake. *Fr.* Songs of Experience. BoLoP; LAuP
Flowering Bars, The. Charles Donnelly. CIP
Flowering Currant. Patrick MacDonogh. ErPo
Flowering Light of the Godhead, The, *sel.* Mechtild of Magdeburg, *tr. fr. German.*
"Ah dearest Love, for how long." ILwL
Flowering of the Rod, The, *sels.* Hilda Doolittle ("H. D.").
"Blue-geese, white-geese, you may say." NOBA
"It is no madness to say." FaBoMo
Flowering Urn, The. Laura Riding. LiTA
Flowering without End. Stefan Zweig, *tr. fr. German by* Eden Paul *and* Cedar Paul *Fr.* Jeremiah. TrJP
Flowers. Harry Behn. FaPON
Flowers. Roo Borson. NOBC
Flowers. *Gond Oral Tradition, tr. by* V. Elwin *and* S. Hivale. WTO
Flowers. Thomas Hood. HBV-1
Flowers, The. Kipling. OBVV
Flowers. Longfellow. HBV-1
Flowers. Stéphane Mallarmé, *tr. fr. French by* John Gray. SyP
Flowers, The. William Brighty Rands. OBVV
Flowers, The. Robert Louis Stevenson. FaPON
Flowers and Men. D. H. Lawrence. FaBoEE
Flowers Are a Silly Bunch. Arnold Spilka. RHPC
Flowers are dead, The. Scenery. Ted Joans. PoBA
Flowers by the Sea. William Carlos Williams. CMoP; GoJo; MoAB; MoAmPo; NoAM; SeCeV; TAP
Flowers do better here than peas and beans. All Things Are a Flowing. R. P. Blackmur. TwAmPo
Flowers for Luis Bunuel. Stuart Z. Perkoff. NeAP
Flowers for the Altar. Digby Mackworth Dolben. GoBC
Flowers for the Brave. Celia Thaxter. OHIP
Flowers for you, O Glory's son, war's prey! Unknown Soldier. Alta Booth Dunn. PGD
Flowers from the earth have arisen, The. Nature's Easter Music. Lucy Larcom. OHIP
Flowers get a darkening brilliance now, The. The Dying Garden. Howard Nemerov. Psk
Flowers hast thou in thyself, and foliage. Sonnet: To His Lady Joan, of Florence. Guido Cavalcanti, *tr. by* Dante Gabriel Rossetti. AWP
Flowers have fenced-in. The Clearing. Peter Everwine, *after the Nahuatl.* NNaP
Flowers I pass have eyes that look at me, The. Man in Harmony with Nature. Jones Very. AP
Flowers I Would Bring. Aubrey Thomas De Vere. HBV-1
Flowers in bud on the trees, The. On the Death of a New Born Child. Mei Yao Ch'en, *tr. by* Kenneth Rexroth. NaP
Flowers in the Valley. *Unknown.* OLR; OnMSP; OxBoLi
Flowers in the Ward. Shaw Neilson. CBAP
Flowers left thick at nightfall in the wood, The. In Memoriam (Easter, 1915). Edward Thomas. GTBS-P; NOBE; OBWP; OxBTC
Flower's Name, The. Robert Browning. Garden Fancies, I. CTC; HBV-1; VLP
Flowers nodding gaily, scent in air. A Duet. T. Sturge Moore. OBEV; OBVV
Flowers of Apollo, The. Hildegarde Flanner. HBMV
Flowers of Darkness. Frank Marshall Davis. AmNP; IDB; NoP; PoBA; PoNe
Flowers of Evil, The, *sel.* Baudelaire, *tr. fr. French by* Roy Campbell.
Ill Luck. PoPl
Flowers of Middle Summer. Shakespeare. *Fr.* The Winter's Tale, IV, iii. YeAr
(Flowers of Perdita, The.) FiP
("Here's flowers for you.") GBL
Flowers of mist and silence. Yucca in the Moonlight. Glen Ward Dresbach. BPAW
Flowers of Perdita, The. Shakespeare. *See* Flowers of Middle Summer.
Flowers of Politics, The, I ("This is the huge dream of us that we are heroes"). Michael McClure. NeAP
Flowers of Politics, The, II ("Only what is heroic and courageous moves our blood"). Michael McClure. NeAP
Flowers of Sion, *sel.* William Drummond of Hawthornden.
Angels, The. GN; HBV-1
(Angels for the Nativity of Our Lord, The.) OxBoCh
(Nativitie, The.) OBS
Flowers of the field, The. The Hawthorn Hath a Deathly Smell. Walter de la Mare. BrPo
Flowers of the Forest, The. Alison Rutherford Cockburn. BSV; OBEC
Flowers of the Forest, The; or, The Battle of Flodden. Jane Elliot. BSV; CH; FaBoCH; FaBoRV; GoTS; OBEC; OxBS; WPE
(Lament for Flodden A.) GTBS; GTBS-P; HBV-2; OBEV; PoPle; ViBoPo
Flowers shall hang upon the palls. Death. John Clare. GTBS-P
Flowers That Bloom in the Spring, The, *with music.* W. S. Gilbert. *Fr.* The Mikado. BLSo
Flowers—that have died upon my Sweet. A Song of Angiola in Heaven. Austin Dobson. HBV-2
Flowers that in thy garden rise, The. Song. Sir Henry Newbolt. FaBoTw
Flowers through the window. Nantucket. William Carlos Williams. HAP; OxBA; SOTW; TAP; WeW
Flowers turned to stone! Not all the botany. Kenneth Slessor. *Fr.* Five Visions of Captain Cook. PoAu-2
Flowers upon the rosemary spray, The. The Rosemary Spray. Luis de Góngora, *tr. by* E. Churton. AWP
Flowers upon your lips and hands. Love Poem. Maurice James Craig. NeIP
Flowing robe of words you weave, The. The Lethal Thought. Mary Boyd Wagner. GoYe
Flowing Summer, The, *sels.* Charles Bruce.
Attic, The. CaP
Dreaming Trout, The. CaP
Hayfield, The. CaP
Flown Soul, The. George Parsons Lathrop. AA
Flowrets—wreaths—thy banks along. To a Gentleman, Who Desired Proper Materials for a Monody. *Unknown.* NOEC
Floyd has died and few have sobb'd. Epitaph on Floyd. *Unknown.* POL
Fluent in all the languages dead or living. A Balanced Bait in Handy Pellet Form. Allen Curnow. OCNZ
Fluff from his lap robe hangs in a rift. The Train Out. Sydney Lea. MAYP
Flukum couldn't stand the strain. 2 Poems for Black Relocation Centers. Etheridge Knight. NNaP; NoAM
Flush and burn, your fever rose all night. Morning Song. Leon Stokesbury. AMV-80
Flush or Faunus. Elizabeth Barrett Browning. FM; NBM
Flush with the pond the lurid furnace burned. The Steam Threshing-Machine. Charles Tennyson-Turner. OBNC
Flushed with the hope of high desire. My Hero. Benjamin Brawley. BANP; PoNe
Flushing Meadows, 1939. Daniel Hoffman. CoPo
Flute, The. Joseph Russell Taylor. AA
Flute, The; a Pastoral. José-Maria de Heredia, *tr. fr. French by* H. J. C. Grierson. AWP
Flute Notes from a Reedy Pond. Sylvia Plath. FaBoMo
Flute of Daphnis, The. Edward Cracroft Lefroy, *after the Greek of* Theocritus. *Fr.* Echoes from Theocritus. AWP; OBVV
Flute of May, The. Harry Woodbourne. GoYe
Flute of the Lonely, The. Vachel Lindsay. CrMA
Flute Player. *Gond Oral Tradition, tr. by* V. Elwin *and* S. Hivale. WTO
Flute Players. Jean-Joseph Rabéarivelo, *tr. fr. French by* Langston Hughes. PBA
Flute-Priest Song for Rain, *sel.* Amy Lowell.
"Whistle under the water." UnS
Flute Song: "Hail, fathers, hail!" *Tr. fr. Hopi Indian by* Natalie Curtis. WTO
Flutesong willow winding weather. World War. Richard Eberhart. WaP
Flutes, and the harp on the plain. Home on the Range, February 1962. Edward Dorn. ConAP
Fluttering spread thy purple pinions. Lines by a Person of Quality. *At. to* Pope, *and to* Swift. InMe; NA
Flux. Richard Eberhart. Psk; VGW
Fly, The. Philip Ayres, *after the Spanish of* Quevedo. CavP; OBVE
Fly, The. Blake. *Fr.* Songs of Experience. FM; LAuP; TrGrPo
Fly, The. Walter de la Mare. OnUR; PoPle
Fly, The. Barnabe Googe. CH
(Once Musing as I Sat.) NoP
Fly. W. S. Merwin. NNaP
Fly, The. Ogden Nash. FaPON
Fly, The. Karl Shapiro. LiTM; MiAP; MoVE; NePA; NIP; NoAM; TW; TwAmPo
Fly about a Glass of Burnt Claret, A. Richard Lovelace. CaPo

Fly and a Flea in a Flue, A. *Unknown.* *See* Flea and the Fly, The.
Fly around My Blue-eyed Gal. *Unknown.* FSW
Fly away, away, swallow. Full Valleys. F. R. Scott. CaP
Fly away, fly away over the sea. Christina Rossetti. *Fr.* Sing-Song. SUS
Fly Caught in a Cobweb, A. Richard Lovelace. CaPo; SeCP
Fly down, Death: call me. Madboy's Song. Muriel Rukeyser. MoAmPo; TrJP
Fly, envious Time, till thou run out thy race. On Time. Milton. BLPL; CABA; LiTB; LoBV; MePo; OBEV; OBS; OxBoCh; SeCeV; TRV
Fly-fisherman in Wartime. Leonard Bacon. FYAP
Fly, fly, my friends! I have my death['s] wound—fly. Astrophel and Stella, XX. Sir Philip Sidney. OAEL-1; SiPS; TEP
Fly from the World. *Unknown.* NCEP
Fly Hence, Shadows. John Ford. *Fr.* The Lover's Melancholy. ViBoPo (Dawn.) OBEV
(Song: "Fly hence, shadows, that do keep.") LoBV
Fly hence those siren charms of wealth and pow'r. Naboth's Vineyard. John Caryll. APAS
Fly in December. Robert Wallace. NYBP
Fly is dying hard, The. Mayday. Ed Roberson. PoBA
Fly, Ladybug. Annette Burr Stowman. AMV-80
Fly, Love, That Art So Sprightly. *Unknown.* NCEP
Fly, Muse, thy wonted themes, nor longer seek. If Pope Had Written "Break, Break, Break" [*or* "Break, Break, Break"]. J. C. Squire. BXAP; CenHV; FaBoPa
Fly, Roadster, fly! Song for a Blue Roadster. Rachel Field. FaPON; TiPo
Fly [*or* Flye] That Flew into My Mistress's [*or* Mistris Her] Eye, A. Thomas Carew. AnAnS-2; CaPo
Fly, the fly, The. Oh the Toe-Test! Norma Farber. RHPC
Fly [*or* Flye] to her heart, hover about her heart. Her Heart. Bartholomew Griffin. *Fr.* Fidessa, More Chaste than Kind. AAS; TrGrPo
Fly to the desert, fly with me. Thomas Moore. *Fr.* Lalla Rookh. BIrV
"Fly to the mountain! Fly!" Conemaugh. Elizabeth Stuart Phelps Ward. PAH
Fly, white butterflies, out to sea. White Butterflies [*or* Envoi]. Swinburne. FaPON; GoJo; PDV; SUS; VLP
"Fly with me then to all's and the world's end." The World's End. William Empson. CoBMV; MoVE
Flycatchers. Robert Bridges. MoVE
Flye, flye, flye from the world, O fly, thou poor distrest. Fly from the World. *Unknown.* NCEP
Flye That Flew into My Mistris Her Eye, A. Thomas Carew. *See* Fly That Flew into My Mistress's Eye, A.
Flye to her heart, hover about her heart. *See* Fly to her heart . . .
Flyer's Fall. Wallace Stevens. CABA; MoAB
Flying. Henry Carlile. AMV-80
Flying. Kaye Starbird. PDV
Flying. J. M. Westrup. OnUR
Flying Blossoms. W. H. Davies. BrPo
Flying Bum, The: 1944. William Plomer. DTC
Flying Change, The. Henry Taylor. MAYP
Flying Changes. Mary Wood. PH
Flying Cloud, The. *Unknown.* AmFP; AmSS, *with music*; BaBo; OBET; ShS (2 *vers.*), *with music*); ViBoFo, *with music*
Flying Crooked. Robert Graves. FaBoMo; LiTM; MP; PCP; TwCP
Flying Crow. *Unknown.* BluL
Flying Deeper into the Century. Pier Giorgio Di Cicco. NOBC
Flying Dutchman, The. E. A. Robinson. MOS
Flying Dutchman, The. A. M. Sullivan. EtS
Flying Dutchman, The, *with music.* *Unknown.* ShS
Flying Fish, The. Jack Cope. PeSA
Flying Fish, The. John Gray. ChTr; LoBV
"Of the birds that fly in the farthest sea," II. OBNC
Flying Fish. J. Corson Miller. EtS
Flying Fish. Katherine Kelley Taylor. EtS
Flying Fox. Thomas W. Shapcott. CBAP
Flying Home from Utah. May Swenson. WPE
Flying Horse was in jail. The Urban Experience: Part Two. Lew Blockcolski. VoR
Flying in plane's rib. New York City. George Abbe. GoYe
Flying Inn, The, *sel.* G. K. Chesterton.
Wine and Water. ACP; CenHV; FaBoCo; FiBHP; GoBC; HBMV; InMe; MoBrPo; ViBoPo
Flying Islands of the Night, The, *sel.* James Whitcomb Riley.
Dwainie. AA
Flying Letters. Zerubavel Gilead, *tr. fr. Hebrew by* Dorothea Krook. VWA
Flying Noises. Thomas Lux. LCAP
Flying Scrolls, *sels.* Ralph Hodgson. FaBoTw
"Dust thou Art, but dust carefully."
Movement, she explained, would bring poetry to the rich, The."
Flying sea-bird mocked the floating dulse, The. The Sea-Weed. Elisabeth Cavazza Pullen. AA
Flying Tailor, The. James Hogg. BXAP; Par
Flying Trapeze, The. George Leybourne. *See* Man on the Flying Trapeze, The.
Flying Wheel, The. Katharine Tynan. WGRP
Flying word from here and there, A. The Master. E. A. Robinson. HBV-2; LiTA; LiTM; MoAB; MoAmPo; OHIP
Flyting o' Life and Daith, The. Hamish Henderson. OxBS
Fo' a yeah or mo' on this roof I'se layed. The Signal Fire. Aeschylus, *tr. by* Dallam Simpson. *Fr.* Agamemnon. CTC
Foal. Mary Britton Miller. PDV; PH
Foal. Vernon Watkins. OxBTC
Foam fluttered on the sea like birds' wings. Hills of Salt. Dahlia Ravikovitch, *tr. by* Chana Bloch. WPOW
Foamy with clouds like atole. Get Stuffed. Alurista, *tr. by* Toni Empringham. FIA
Fo'c'sle had gone under the creep, The. The Final Moments. E. J. Pratt. *Fr.* The Titanic. NOBC
Focus. Kathleen Norris. GP
Fod. *Unknown.* AmFP
Foe at the Gates, The. John Dickson Bruns. PAH
Foes to our race! if ever ye have known. Critics. George Crabbe. PP
Foetal Song. Joyce Carol Oates. IHMS; NAs
Foetus. Phyllis Haring. PeSA
Fog. Laurence Binyon. SyP
Fog, The. Robert P. Tristram Coffin. CrMA
Fog, The. W. H. Davies. TiPo
Fog. Kenneth Patchen. NaP
Fog ("The fog comes/ on little cat feet"). Carl Sandburg. AmPP; AP; FaBV; FaFP; FaPON; FPL; HBMV; HeIP; InPK; MoAB; MoAmPo; OBCA; PAI; PoPl; RHPC; SoPo; SoSe; SUS; TAP; TiPo
Fog and snow for New Year's greeting. Rhyming Prophecy for a New Year. Leonard Cooper. FaBoCo
Fog comes in with a big sound, The. The Sounding Fog. Susan Nichols Pulsifer. PDV
Fog Dream, The. Sandra M. Gilbert. PoA
Fog got him first. One, Two, Three. Samuel L. Albert. NePoAm-2
Fog is freezing on the trees and shrubs, The. White Dusk. Marion M. Boyd. HBMV
Fog 9/76. Richard Morris Dey. AMV-80
Fog over the base: the beams ranging. A Front. Randall Jarrell. OBWP; OxBC; VGW
Foggy, Foggy Dew. *Unknown.* AS, *with music;* DTC; FSW; GBP; LiTB; OxBoLi
(Foggy Dew, The.) CoMu; ELP; FSW, *diff. vers.*; OBET (*A and B vers.*); UnTE (2 *vers.*)
Foggy Mountain Top. *Unknown.* FSW
Fog-Horn. George Herbert Clarke. CaP
Fog-Horn. W. S. Merwin. NMP
Foghorns. Lilian Moore. RHPC
Fog-horns bellow across the fields of fog, The. Odalisque. Brian Coffey. CIP
Foghorns moaned, The. Foghorns. Lilian Moore. RHPC
Foil'd by our fellow-men, depress'd, outworn. Immortality. Matthew Arnold. FiP
Foiled Reaper, The. William Kean Seymour. HBMV
Foiled Sleep. "Marie Madelaine," *tr. fr. German by* Ferdinand E. Kappey. PeHV
Fold of my flesh. Sleep Close to Me. Gabriela Mistral, *tr. by* D. M. Pettinella. PBWP
Folded Flock, The. Wilfrid Meynell. GoBC; TrPWD
Folded Power. Gladys Cromwell. HBMV
Folded Skyscraper, A, *sel.* William Carlos Williams.
Hemmed-in Males. MAT; MoVE; PoRA
Folding a Shirt. Denise Levertov. NeBP
Folding and Unfolding, A. Welton Smith. PoNe
Folding chairs, a tennis bench. Liar Rumplestiltskin Loves. William Hathaway. *Fr.* Rumplestiltskin Poems. DFT
Folding the Flocks. John Fletcher. *See* Priest's Chant, The.
Folds of a White Dress/Shaft of Light. Deborah Keenan. PoDr
Foliage. Felicia Dorothea Hemans. OBRV
Foliage of Vision. James Merrill. MoPo; VGW
Folk Song: "At the boarding house where I live." *Unknown.* ShM
Folk-Song: "Back she came through the trembling dusk." Louis Untermeyer. HBV-1
Folk Tune. Esther Raab, *tr. fr. Hebrew by* Robert Friend *and* Shimon Sandbank. VWA
Folk Tune. Richard Wilbur. AmFN
Folk Who Live in Backward Town, The. Mary Ann Hoberman. OBCA; RHPC
Folk who lived in Shakespeare's day, The. Guilielmus Rex. Thomas Bailey Aldrich. AA
Folk Wisdom. Thomas Kinsella. TwCP

Folklore. Cyril Dabydeen. BrSi
Folks ain't got no right to censuah othah folks about dey habits. Accountability. Paul Laurence Dunbar. PoLF; YaD
Folks and Me. Lucile Crites. WBLP
Folks at home half the time are thinkin' about dirt, The. Soap, the Oppressor. Burges Johnson. PoLF
Folks, I Give You Science! Al Graham. WhC
Folks Need a Lot of Loving. Strickland Gillilan. TRV
(Need of Loving.) BLPA; WBLP
Folks, sex has never been. God Is a Masturbator. Gregory Corso. GP
Folks stopped by our place yestiddy 'bout dinner. All Things Being Equal. J. Lee Humphrey. AMV-81
Follies, The. Daniel Mark Epstein. MAYP
Follow. Thomas Campion. *See* Follow Thy Fair Sun.
Follow a shadow [*or* shaddow], it still flies you. That Women Are but Men's Shadows [*or* The Shadow *or* Women Men's Shadows]. Ben Jonson. ElL; FaBoEn; HBV-1; InPS; NOBE; OBEV; OBS; SeCP; ViBoPo; WBLP
Follow back from the gull's bright arc and the osprey's plunge. Water Ouzel. William H. Matchett. CoAP; NePoEA; NYBP; PoCh
Follow, follow. Thomas Campion. EnLoPo
Follow, follow me into the South. Ballad. Marjorie Allen Seiffert. HBMV
Follow Jesus. *Unknown.* STF
Follow Me. Longfellow. PGD
"Follow Me 'Ome." Kipling. OAEP
Follow my Bangalorey Man. *Unknown.* OxNR
Follow, poet, follow right. W. H. Auden. *Fr.* In Memory of W. B. Yeats. TRV
Follow the Gleam. Tennyson. *Fr.* Merlin and the Gleam, IX. TreFT
Follow the Leader ("Follow the leader away in a row"). Harry Behn. SoPo
Follow the Leader. Kathleen Fraser. RHPC
Follow the long snake. Desert River. Patricia Benton. GoYe
Follow the trickroutes. Auras on the Interstates. Gerald Vizenor. STE
Follow Thy Fair Sun [Unhappy Shadow]. Thomas Campion. ElL; ELP; EnLoPo; EnRePo; LiTB; LO; LoBV; NOBE; NoP; OAEP; OBSC; UnPo; ViBoPo
(Devotion.) OBEV
(Follow.) CH
(Followe Thy Faire Sunne.) AAS; Prf
(Song: "Follow thy fair[e] sun[ne], unhappy shadow[e].") PoEL-2; PoPle
Follow Your Saint [Follow with Accents Sweet]. Thomas Campion. AAS; EBEV; ElL; EnLoPo; EnRePo; FaBoEn; HAP; OAEL-1; OBSC; SeCePo; TrGrPo; ViBoPo
(Devotion.) NOBE; OBEV
Followe Thy Faire Sunne. Thomas Campion. *See* Follow Thy Fair Sun.
Followed the bird in the long forest where it cried. In Her Song She Is Alone. Jon Swan. NYBP
Follower. Michael Arvey. AMV-80
Follower. Seamus Heaney. IPY
Following across the moors a sound of bells. The Pansy and the Prayer-Book. Matilda Betham-Edwards. OBVV
Following forbidden streets. The Wraith-Friend. George Barker. OBMV
Following Van Gogh (Avignon, 1982). Marla Puziss. PoDr
Followis How Dumbar Wes Desyrd to Be ane Freir. William Dunbar. OAEP
Follows this a narrower bed. Bridal Couch. Donald J. Lloyd. NIP
Folly hath now turned out of door. Mandrake's Song. Thomas Lovell Beddoes. *Fr.* Death's Jest Book, I, i. NBM
Folly of Being Comforted, The. W. B. Yeats. AnIL; AnIV; BrPo; GBL; HeIP; VLP
Folly of Brown, The. W. S. Gilbert. InMe
Fond Affection, *with music. Unknown.* AS
Fond affection, hence, and leave me! Song. Robert Parry. *Fr.* The Mirror of Knighthood. ElL
Fond credos, wooden ecstasies! The Stranger. Adrienne Rich. CoPo
Fond Love, deliver up thy bow. Ode to Cupid. Charles Cotton. CavP
Fond man, Musophilus, that thus dost spend. Poet and Critic. Samuel Daniel. *Fr.* Musophilus; or, Defence of All Learning. OBSC
Fond man, that canst beleeve [*or* believe] her blood. Celia Bleeding, to the Surgeon. Thomas Carew. AnAnS-2; PeD; SeCP
Fond men! whose wretched care the life soon ending. Song. Phineas Fletcher. *Fr.* Brittain's Ida. ElL
Fond woman, which would'st have thy husband die. Jealosie [*or* Jealousy]. John Donne. Elegies, I. AnAnS-1; FF
Fond Youth. Samuel Rogers. *Fr.* Human Life. OBRV
Fondle me. Marrow of My Bone. Mari E. Evans. BPo
"Fondling," she saith, "since I have hemmed thee here." Shakespeare. *Fr.* Venus and Adonis. OAEL-1
Fondly, too curious Nature, to adorn. On the Marriage of a Beauteous Young Gentlewoman with an Ancient Man. Francis Beaumont. ViBoPo
Fone sayes, those mighty whiskers he do's weare. Upon Fone a School-master. Epigram. Robert Herrick. AnAnS-2
Font in the Forest, The. Léonie Adams. CrMA
Fontenoy. Thomas Osborne Davis. HBV-2; OnYI
Fontenoy. 1745. Emily Lawless. AnIV
Food. Victor M. Valle, *tr. fr. Spanish by* Toni Empringham. FIA
Food and Drink. Louis Untermeyer. MoAmPo
Food drops off a fork, The. Michael Silverton. POL
Food for a Cat. David Starr Jordan. TDH
Food for Fire, Food for Thought. Robert Duncan. NeAP
Food of Love, The. Shakespeare. *Fr.* Twelfth Night, I, i. TrGrPo
(Music.) TreFS
Food of the North. D. H. Lawrence. FaBoEE
Food Strike. Michael Hogan. GP
Fool, The. Padraic Pearse. OnYI
Fool—/ Killer lurks between the branches of every tree. The Book of Percival. Jack Spicer. CoPo
Fool, a fool, A!—I bet a fool i' the forest. A Cold Rendering. *Unknown.* BXAP
Fool, a fool, A! I met a fool i' the forest. Motley's the Only Wear [*or* A Worthy Fool]. Shakespeare. *Fr.* As You Like It, II, vii. TreFT; TrGrPo
Fool and False. *Unknown, tr. fr. Sanskrit by* Arthur W. Ryder. *Fr.* The Panchatantra. AWP
Fool and knave with different views, A. The Touch-Stone. Samuel Bishop. HBV-1
Fool by the Roadside, The. W. B. Yeats. MoVE
Fool hath said in his heart, The. Bible, *O.T.* Psalms, XIV. TrJP
Fool much bit by fleas put out the light, A. Richard Lovelace, *after the Greek of* Lucian. FaBoEE
Fool of Love, The. *Unknown, tr. fr. Russian by* Louis Untermeyer. UnTE
Fool of nature, stood with stupid eyes, The. The Power of Love. Dryden. *Fr.* Cymon and Iphigenia. OBS
Fool on the Hill, The. John Lennon *and* Paul McCartney. PPoe
Fool Song. Cornel Lengyel. GoYe
Fool, take up thy shaft again. Song. Thomas Stanley. EnLoPo
Fool there was and he made his prayer, A. The Vampire. Kipling. BLPA; BLPL; HBV-1
Fool there was, and she lowered her pride, A. A Woman's Answer to "The Vampire." Felicia Blake. BLPA
Fool, to put up four crosses at your door. Swift. FaBoEE
Fooled me once and you fooled me bad. All Night Long Fooling Me. *Unknown.* AmFP
Fooles, they are the onely nation. Ben Jonson. *See* Fools, They Are the Only Nation.
Foolish Child. *Unknown, tr. fr. Akan by* J. B. Danquah. PBA
Foolish I, why should I grieve. Of Maids' Inconstancy. Richard Brathwaite. *Fr.* A Strappado for the Devil. ElL
Foolish impatient apricot trees. Vegetable Destiny. Nina Cassian, *tr. by* Michael Impey *and* Brian Swann. PBWP
Foolish little maiden bought a foolish little bonnet, A. What the Choir Sang about the New Bonnet. M. T. Morrison. BLPA
Foolish man who boasts that he is able, The. Boastful Husbandman. *Unknown, tr. by* Louis Untermeyer. UnTE
Foolish men who accuse. She Proves the Inconsistency of the Desires and Criticism of Men Who Accuse Women of What They Themselves Cause. Sister Juana Inés de la Cruz, *tr. by* Aliki *and* Willis Barnstone. BoWoP
Foolish Miller, The. *Unknown.* UnTE
Foolish prater, what dost thou. The Swallow. Abraham Cowley. EBEV; FM; OBEV; PBBP
Foolish Proverb. *Unknown, tr. fr. Greek by* Louis Untermeyer. UnTE
Foolish rhythm turns in my idle head, A. A Tune. Arthur Symons. BoLoP; OBNC
Foolish useless man who had done nothing, A. Brummell at Calais. John Glassco. MoCV; PeCV
Foolish Woman, A. Bible, *O.T.* Proverbs, IX: 13-18. TrGrPo
Fools. Glenn Hardin. AMV-81
Fools. Ben Jonson. *See* Fools, They Are the Only Nation.
Fools' Adventure, The, *sel.* Lascelles Abercrombie.
Seeker, The. WGRP
Fool's Blues. *Unknown.* BluL
Fools Gaze at Painted Courts. Michael Drayton. *Fr.* Polyolbion: Nineteenth Song. ChTr
Fools in Love's College. John Lyly. *See* O Cupid! Monarch over Kings.
Fools of Forty-nine, The. *Unknown.* CoSo
Fool's Prayer, The. Edward Rowland Sill. AA; BeLS; FaBoBe; HBV-2; OHFP; OnMSP; PoLF; TreF; WBLP; WGRP
" 'Tis not by guilt the onward sweep," *sel.* TrPWD
Fool's Preferment, A, *sel.* Thomas Durfey.
I'll Sail upon the Dog-Star. FaBoCh; OxBoLi
Fool's Song. Thomas Holcroft. NOEC

Fools, They Are the Only Nation. Ben Jonson. *Fr.* Volpone. InvP
(Fools.) ElL
(Nano's Song.) LoBV; TrGrPo
(Song.) AnAnS-2
Foot in the stirrup, A. Indecision Means Flexibility. Elliot Abhau. PH
Foot of death has printed on my chest, The. The Shudder. Donald Hall. NYBP
Foot Race Song. *Unknown, tr. fr. Pima Indian by* Frank Russell. NU; OBVE
Foot Soldiers. John Banister Tabb. HBV-1; HBVY; OBAL
Football and Rowing—an Eclogue. Alfred Denis Godley. CenHV
Football Field: Evening. J. A. R. McKellar. LiSp
Football Game, A. Alice Van Eck. RHPC
Football Player, A. Edward Cracroft Lefroy. LiSp
Foot-folk, The. The Battle of Dunbar (1296). *Unknown.* OxBM
Foot-hills called us, green and sweet, The. On the Height. Eunice Tietjens. HBMV
Footnote. Anthony Delius. PeSA
Footnote to a Famous Lyric, A. Louise Imogen Guiney. AA
Footnote to a Gray Bird's Pause, A. James Cunningham. JB
Footnote to Enright's "Apocalypse." Martin Bell. FaBoMo
Footnote to Feynman. Jonathan V. Post. SUW
Footnote to History. Elizabeth J. Coatsworth. SiSoSe
Footnote to "Howl." Allen Ginsberg. CAPP
Footnote to Tennyson. Gerald Bullett. FiBHP
Footnote to the Lord's Prayer, *sel.* Kay Smith.
"Heaven which art in Heaven Our Father in Heaven." TrCP
Footnotes to "The Autobiography of Bertrand Russell," *sel.* Mona Van Duyn.
"This seems, in a world where love must take its chances," II. HAP
Footpath. Stella Ngatho. WPOW
Footpath Way, The. Katharine Tynan. HBV-1
Footpath would have been enough, A. The Entailed Farm. John Glassco. MoCV; NOBC
Footpaths Cross in the Rice Field. "Lin Ling," *tr. fr. Chinese by* Kenneth Rexroth *and* Ling Chung. PBWP
Footprints. Hamish Brown. PoSH
Footprints of the Heart-of-the-Daybreak, The! Heart-of-the-Daybreak. Eugène Marais, *tr. by* Uys Krige *and* Jack Cope. PeSA
Footprints on the Glacier. W. S. Merwin. NoAM
Footsteps. Hazel Hall. HBMV
Footsteps of a hundred years, The. The Founders of Ohio. William Henry Venable. PAH
Footsteps of Spring. Hayyim Nahman Bialik, *tr. fr. Hebrew by* Ruth Nevo. VWA
Footwear. May Justus. SoPo; YeAr
(Rain Has Silver Sandals, The.) RHPC
For a cap and bells our lives we pay. June Weather. James Russell Lowell. *Fr.* The Vision of Sir Launfal. AA
For a Child. Fannie Stearns Davis. FaPON
For a Child Expected. Anne Ridler. LiTM; MoVE; NeBP; SeCePo
For a Christening. Anne Ridler. MoPo
For a College Yearbook. J. V. Cunningham. NoAM
For a Coming Extinction. W. S. Merwin. NNaP
For a Copy of Theocritus. Austin Dobson. HBV-2
For a cough. Remedies. Gary Soto. Str
For a Daughter Gone Away. William Stafford. NPAW; SV
For a dawn moon, hard to hold its light. Failing the Examination. Meng Chiao, *tr. by* Stephen Owen. GLGT
For a day and a night Love sang to us, played with us. At Parting. Swinburne. HBV-1; ViBoPo
For a Dead Lady. E. A. Robinson. AP; CMoP; CoBMV; DL; FaBoEn; FYAP; HeIP; HoPM; InvP; LiTA; LiTM; MoAB; MoAmPo; NoAM; NOBA; OxBA; PoEL-5; PoRA; TreFT; TwAmPo; ViBoPo; WHA
For a Dewdrop. Eleanor Farjeon. HBVY
For a Far-out Friend. Gary Snyder. NeAP; PoM
For a Father. Anthony Cronin. FaBoTw
For a forehead: Kansas skies. Cosmogony. D. C. Berry. BXAP
For a Fountain. "Barry Cornwall." OBEV; OBVV
(Inscription for a Fountain.) OBRV
For a fresh start. Issa, *tr. fr. Japanese by* Nobuyuki Yuasa. *Fr.* Oraga Haru. OFD
For a Friend. Lyn Lifshin. NeAC
For a Friend. David Steingass. TW
For a Girl in Love. Florence Hynes Willette. GoBC
For a God that would smile like a child. Without More Weight. Giuseppe Ungaretti, *tr. by* Allen Mandelbaum. PoPl
For a good decade. The Drunk in the Furnace. W. S. Merwin. CAPP; LiTM; MAT; MP; NePoEA-2; NoAM; NoP; TwCP
For a Good Dog. Arthur Guiterman. GDP
For a Grotto. Mark Akenside. *See* Inscription for a Grotto.
For a Homecoming. Julia Randall. NMM
For a Lady I Know. Countee Cullen. Four Epitaphs, 4. CDC; HeIP; IDB; InPK; NIP; OBAL; PoNe; ShM; TAP
(Lady I Know, A.) MoAmPo; TRV
For a Lamb. Richard Eberhart. CMoP; LiTM; MiAP
For a Little Girl Mourning Her Favorite Cat. Whittier. POL
(Epitaph for Bathsheba.) PCat
For a Little Lady. Fred Saidy. InMe
For a living I pick apples. Identity Card. Susan Tichy. MAYP
For a long time, I was nailed to the pillory. The Pillory. Renée Vivien, *tr. by* Sandia Belgrade. PeHV
For a long time you looked stuffed. Lizard. Alan McLean. BoAnP
For a man that is almost blind. For Sore Eyes [*or* Mock Medicine]. *Unknown.* MeEL; OxBM
For a Man Who Learned to Swim When He Was Sixty. Diane Wakoski. FAZ
For a Marriage. Erica Jong. CTBA
For a Masseuse and Prostitute. Kenneth Rexroth. NNaP
For a minute, daughter, for an afternoon. The Prevention of Stacy Miller. Peter Miller. MoCV
For a Mocking Voice. Eleanor Farjeon. CH; TiPo
For a Moment. *Unknown, tr. fr. Burmese by* U Win Pe. PBWP
For a moment I saw a surging river. Impermanence. Lal Ded, *tr. fr. Kashmiri.* BoWoP
For a moment pause. The Mound. Thomas Hardy. OxBTC
For a moment, unaware. For a Moment. *Unknown, tr. by* U Win Pe. PBWP
For a Mouthy Woman. Countee Cullen. OBAL; PoBA; ShM
For a Musician. George Wither. *Fr.* Hallelujah. OBS
(To a Musician, *wr. at. to* William Austin.) OxBoCh
For a name unknown. Why. Bliss Carman. OBVV
For a Nativity. Lisel Mueller. NePoAm-2
For a Neighbor Girl. Yü Hsüan-chi. *See* Advice to a Neighbour Girl.
For a Patriot. Shakespeare. King Henry VIII, *fr.* III, ii. PGD
For a Pessimist. Countee Cullen. ShM
For a Picture Where a Queen Laments over the Tomb of a Slain Knight. Thomas Carew. CaPo
For a piece of the earth. The Earth Cycle Dream. Phillip Yellowhawk Minthorn. STE
For a Plaque on the Door of an Isolated House. William Stafford. FAZ
For a Poet. Countee Cullen. PoNe; TTY
For a Second Marriage. James Merrill. NePoEA
(Upon a Second Marriage.) NoP
For a second the word express appears. Capital. Heather McHugh. MAYP
For a Shetland Pony Brood Mare Who Died in Her Barren Year. Maxine W. Kumin. PH
For a Statue of Chaucer at Woodstock. Mark Akenside. SeCePo
For a Survivor of the Mesopotamian Campaign. Elizabeth Daryush. SUMH
For A' That and A' That, *parody.* Shirley Brooks. FaBoCo; NOBL; Par
(More Luck to Honest Poverty.) BXAP
For A' That an' A' That ("The bonniest lass that ye meet neist"). *At. to* Burns. CoMu; UnTE
For A' That and A' That ("Is there, for honest poverty"). Burns. CABA; FaBoBe; FaFP; FaPoR; HBV-2; HBVY; LAuP; LiTB; OAEL-1; OAEP; OHFP; TEP; WBLP
(Is There, for Honest Poverty.) EnRP; OBEC; TreF
(Man's a Man for A' That, A.) FSW; LoBV; MasP; OxBS; TrGrPo; ViBoPo
(Song: For A' That and A' That.) NOEC
For A' That and A' That, *parody. Unknown.* BXAP
For a thing done, repentance is no good. Sonnet: He Is Past All Help. Cecco Angiolieri da Siena, *tr. by* Dante Gabriel Rossetti. AWP
For a thousand years, you, African, suffered like a beast. Dawn in the Heart of Africa. Patrice Emery Lumumba. PBA; TTY
For "A Venetian Pastoral" by Giorgione. Dante Gabriel Rossetti. ViBoPo; VLP
For a Very Old Man, on the Death of His Wife. Jane Cooper. NePoEA-2
For a Virgin Lady. Countee Cullen. MoAmPo
For a Voice That Is Singing. Aldo Camerino, *tr. fr. Italian by* Anita Barrows. VWA
For a War Memorial. G. K. Chesterton. MMA
For a while there we had 25-inch Chinese peasant families. The Not-so-good Earth. Bruce Dawe. CBAP
For a Wife in Jizzen. Douglas Young. OxBS
For a Wine Festival. Vernon Watkins. OxBTC
For a Winnebago Brave. Joseph Bruchac. CDW
For a year, she walked past my window. Woman through the Window. Marcia Falk. VWA
For a Young South Dakota Man. Freya Manfred. TAT
For aa da scraimin stars at hing. Gallow Hill. William J. Tait. OxBS

For Adolf Eichmann. Primo Levi, *tr. fr. Italian by* Ruth Feldman *and* Brian Swann. VWA
For Adoration seasons change. Adoration. Christopher Smart. *Fr.* A Song to David. FaBoEn
For Alan Blanchard. John Oliver Simon. NeAC
For All Blasphemers. Stephen Vincent Benét. OxBA
For All in Pain. Amy Carmichael. TRV
For all life's beauties, and their beauteous growth. For Beauty, We Thank Thee [*or* We Thank Thee]. John Oxenham. BLRP; PGD
For All Mary Magdalenes. Desanka Maksimovic, *tr. fr. Croatian by* Vasa D. Mihailovich. WPOW
For All My Grandmothers. Beth Brant. STE
For All Sorts and Conditions. Norman Nicholson. EaLo
For, all that from her springs, and is ybredde. Mutability. Spenser. *Fr.* The Faerie Queene, VII. FaBoEn
For all that God in mercy sends. For Everything Give Thanks [*or* Give Thanks *or* Thanks for Everything]. Helen Isabella Tupper. BLRP; TreFT; WBLP
For all the beauties of the day. Grace at Evening. Edgar A. Guest. TrPWD
For all the gracious gifts in harvests fair. Thanksgiving Day. John Kendrick Bangs. TrPWD
For all the saints who from their labors rest. Funeral Hymn. William Walsham Howe. WGRP
For all the ungainly ones, the awkward, silent ones. The Power to Change Geography. Diana O Hehir. NPGG
For all the vision that took fire this night. Burning Bush. Martin Feinstein. TrJP
For all the wonders of this wondrous world. John Oxenham. *Fr.* A Te Deum of the Commonplace. PGD
For all things beautiful, and good, and true. Thanksgiving. John Oxenham. BLRP; WBLP
For All Things Black and Beautiful. Conrad Kent Rivers. CNA
For all those beaten, for the broken heads. Litany for Dictatorships. Stephen Vincent Benét. OxBA
For all Thy ministries. We Thank Thee [Lord]. John Oxenham. *Fr.* A Little Te Deum of the Commonplace. PGD; TRV; WBLP
For all true words that have been spoken. Thanksgiving. Margaret E. Sangster. TRV
For All We Have and Are. Kipling. FaPoR
For all your days prepare. Preparedness. Edwin Markham. FaFP; MoAmPo
For Allan, Who Wanted to See How I Wrote a Poem. Robert Frost. PChr
For Allen Ginsberg, Who Cut Off His Beard. Sanford Pinsker. AMV-80
For Alva Benson, and for All Those Who Have Learned to Speak. Joy Harjo. TWSS
For among My people are found wicked men. As Fowlers Lie in Wait. Bible, *O.T. Fr.* Jeremiah. TrJP
For Amy Lowell. Countee Cullen. PoA
For an Age of Plastics. Plymouth. Donald Davie. NePoEA-2
For "An Allegorical Dance of Women" by Andrea Mantegna. Dante Gabriel Rossetti. VLP
For an Autumn Festival, *sel.* Whittier.
Harvest Hymn. OHIP
("Once more the liberal year laughs out.") PGD
For an Early Retirement. Donald Hall. TW
For an Egyptian Boy, Died c. 700 B.C. Mary Baron. HoAn
For an Emigrant. Randall Jarrell. OxBA
For an Epitaph at Fiesole. Walter Savage Landor. FaBoEE; OBNC; OBRV
For an Eskimo. Annie Charlotte Dalton. CaP
For an Ex-Far East Prisoner of War. Charles Causley. OxBC
For an hour he wonders what the girl could be thinking. The White Skirt. Stephen Dobyns. MAYP
For an Obligate Parasite. Alan Dugan. TW
For an officer/ in the old Capital, fox fur. Ezra Pound, *after the Chinese.* OBVE
For an Old Friend. Norbert Krapf. AMV-81
For Andy Goodman—Michael Schwerner—and James Chaney. Margaret Walker. BPo
For Angela. Zack Gilbert. PoBA
For Angus MacLeod. Iain Crichton Smith. OxBS
For Ann Scott-Moncrieff. Edwin Muir. GTBS-P
For Anna. Irving Layton. NeAC
For Anne. Leonard Cohen. ELU; FF; PoCh
For Anne Gregory. W. B. Yeats. BiP; CMoP; DTC; FaFP; InPK; LiTM; LoBV; SeCeV; SOTW
For Anne, Who Doesn't Know. Gail Fox. IHMS
For Annie. Poe. AmPP; AP; BLPL; HBV-1; LiTA; LO; NePA; NOBA; OBEV; OBVV; OxBA; TreFS
For any golfer of resource. The Crow and the Nighthawk. Watson Kirkconnell. CaP
For Any Member of the Security Police. Josephine Jacobsen. NePoAm
For Artaud. Michael McClure. NeAP
For Arthur Gregor. Edward Field. FAZ
For at the window of my house. She of the Impudent Face. Bible, *O.T. Fr.* Proverbs. TrJP
For August, be your dwelling thirty towers. Sonnets of the Months: August [*or* August]. Folgore da San Geminiano, *tr. by* Dante Gabriel Rossetti. AWP; CTC
For authorities whose hopes. The Paper Nautilus. Marianne Moore. VGW
For Avi Killed in Lebanon. Mark Osaki. BrSi
For awhile I too was haunted by. Amnesiac. Mark Osaki. BrSi
For bards, like these, who neither sing nor say. On His Own Poetry. Charles Churchill. *Fr.* The Prophecy of Famine. NOEC
For beauty being the best of all we know. Robert Bridges. The Growth of Love, VIII. VLP
For Beauty kissed your lips when they were young. Arthur Davison Ficke. Epitaph for the Poet V., II. HBMV
For Beauty, We Thank Thee. John Oxenham. PGD
(We Thank Thee.) BLRP
For best work. Lorine Niedecker. VGW
For Bill. Geof Hewitt. NeAC
For Bill Hawkins, a Black Militant. William J. Harris. PoBA
For Black folks. The "Duke" and the "Count." Richard Fewell. AMV-81
For Black Poets Who Think of Suicide. Etheridge Knight. CNA; HeIP; PoBA
For blackmen. Blackmen: Who Make Morning. Angela Jackson. CNA
For Both of Us at Fisk. Sharon Scott. JB
For brave comportment, wit without offence. To His Honoured and Most Ingenious Friend, Master Charles Cotton. Robert Herrick. CaPo
For Britons, chief. British Commerce. James Thomson. *Fr.* Liberty, IV. OBEC
For Brother Malcolm. Edward S. Spriggs. CAD
For by forged letters he tried to accuse Parnell. William McGonagall. *Fr.* Richard Pigott, the Forger. PeD
For C. Philip Whalen. NeAP; VGW
For C. K. at His Christening. Daniel Lawrence Kelleher. NeIP
For Cal. James Cunningham. JB
For Carole. Diane Burns. TWSS
For certain he hath seen all perfectness. Dante, *tr. by* Dante Gabriel Rossetti. La Vita Nuova, XVII. AWP
For Charlie's Sake. John Williamson Palmer. HBV-1
For Chicle & Justina. Diana Bickston. LFAC
"For Christ's sweet sake, I beg an alms." James Russell Lowell. *Fr.* The Vision of Sir Launfal. WGRP
For City Spring. Stephen Vincent Benét. BXAP; PoPl
For Colored Girls Who Have Considered Suicide When the Rainbow Is Enuf, *sel.* Ntozake Shange.
"At 4:30 AM/ she rose." BoWoP
For Communion with God, *sel.* Thomas Shepherd.
"Alas, my God, that we should be." TrPWD
(Alas, My God, *longer sel.*) OxBoCh
For Cora Lightbody, R.N. John Glassco. PoA
For Crethis' store of tales and pleasant chat. Crethis. Callimachus, *tr. by* Richard Garnett. AWP
For Dan Berrigan. Etheridge Knight. NeAC
For Danny whistling slowly. Feed. Raymond Knister. OBCV; PeCV
For Daphne at Lone Lake. John Haines. NPAW
For David Shapiro. David Lehman. PoA
For dawn, wind. Crow Jane. Amiri Baraka. PoM
For days gold-bright. Song of Thanksgiving. John Richard Moreland. PGD
For days I have been walking around. Letter to a Friend in an Unknown Place. Anita Barrows. NMM
For days the east wind rids itself of rain. Handlining Tockers & Gizmos. Allen Planz. WOLT
For de Lawd. Lucille Clifton. CNA; PoBA; TAP; TwCP
For dear life some do. Portrait of an Artist. Barbara Howes. IHMS
For death must come, and change, and, though the loss. Immutabilis. Alice Learned Bunner. *Fr.* Vingtaine. AA
For dedy liif, my livy deth I wite. Come, Death—My Lady Is Dead. *At. to* Charles d'Orléans. MeEL
For deep deer-copse beneath Mount Han. Ezra Pound, *after the Chinese.* OBVE
For Deeper Life. Katharine Lee Bates. TrPWD
For Delphine. James Simmons. POL
For Demerara bound with cod she flies. Escapade. Kenneth Leslie. EtS
For do but note a wild and wanton herd. The Power of Music. Shakespeare. *Fr.* The Merchant of Venice, V, i. GN
For Dr. and Mrs. Dresser. Margaret Avison. MoCV; PeCV
For Doreen. Donald Davie. NMP
For Drum Hadley. Harold Littlebird. VoR
For E. C. J. Emmett Jarrett. NeAC

For E. J. P. Leonard Cohen. NoAM; NoP
For E. McC. Ezra Pound. LiSp
"For each man kills the thing he loves"—it's true. Eminent Critic. John Frederick Nims. TW
For Each of You. Audre Lorde. CNA
For Echo is the soul of the voice exerting itself in hollow places. The Instruments. Christopher Smart. WiR
For Edward Hicks. David Helwig. NOBC
For Edwin R. Embree. Owen Dodson. CNA
For Eleanor and Bill Monahan. William Carlos Williams. VGW
For Eleanor Boylan Talking with God. Anne Sexton. InPK
For Elizabeth Bishop. Sandra McPherson. GeTw; MAYP
For Elizabeth Madox Roberts. Janet Lewis. QFR
For England when with favoring gale. Heaving the Lead [*or* The Leadsman's Song *or* By the Deep Nine]. *At. to* J. [*or* W.] Pearce *and to* Charles Dibdin. ChTr; EtS; HBV-1
For Esther. Stanley Plumly. LCAP
For Eusi, Ayi Kwei and Gwen Brooks. Keorapetse Kgositsile. PoBA
For Evening. Sabine Baring-Gould. *See* Now the Day Is Over.
For Ever. *See* Forever.
For every bird there is this last migration. The Death of the Bird. A. D. Hope. PoAu-2
For Every Day. Frances Ridley Havergal. *See* Teacher's Prayer.
For every evil under the sun. Mother Goose. EvOK; HBV-1; HBVY; OxNR
For Every Last Batch When the Next One Comes Along. William Dickey. GP
For Every Man. Max I. Reich. STF
For every parcel I stoop down to seize. The Armful. Robert Frost. CMoP
For everyone. The Swimmer's Moment. Margaret Avison. NOBC
For Everything Give Thanks. Helen Isabella Tupper. TreFT
(Give Thanks.) BLRP
(Thanks for Everything.) WBLP
For everything there is a season. Bible, *O.T.* *Fr.* Ecclesiastes. DL
For Exmoor. Jean Ingelow. OBEV; OBVV
For eyes he waves greentipped. Slug in Woods. Earle Birney. CaP; NOBC; OBCV; PeCV
For False Heart. Hilaire Belloc. *See* False Heart, The.
For Fear. Robert Creeley. NoAM
For February Twelfth. Muriel M. Gessner. YeAr
For flowers that bloom about our feet. Thanksgiving [*or* Father in Heaven]. *Unknown, at. to* Emerson. SoPo; TreFT
For Forgiveness. John Donne. *See* Hymn to God the Father, A.
For forms of government let fools contest. Charity. Pope. *Fr.* An Essay on Man, Epistle III. OBEC; POL; ViBoPo
For forty years, for forty-one. This Dim and Ptolemaic Man. John Peale Bishop. CrMA; ImOP; LiTA; LiTM; NePA
For forty years I shunned the lust. For a Virgin Lady. Countee Cullen. MoAmPo
For four months the guards sabotaged. Getting Back to Work. Leon Baker. LFAC
For Fran. Philip Levine. FF; PoCh
For Freckle-faced Gerald. Etheridge Knight. BPo; LFAC; NeAC
For from my cradle you must know that I. Michael Drayton. *Fr.* To My Most Dearly Loved Friend, Henry Reynolds, Esq. PP
For Gabriel. Laya Firestone. VWA
For George Santayana. Robert Lowell. CMoP; VGW
For giving me desire. Desire. Thomas Traherne. LO; OxBoCh
For glowing autumn's brimming yield. We Thank Thee! Thomas Curtis Clark. PGD
For God, our God is a gallant foe. Ballad for Gloom. Ezra Pound. LiTM; MoAmPo; NePA; OBVV
For God so loved the world. Bible, *N.T.* *Fr.* St. John. LO
For God While Sleeping. Anne Sexton. CABA; CAPP; NePoEA-2
For Godsake [*or* God's sake] hold your tongue, and let me love. The Canonization. John Donne. AnAnS-1; BiP; BLPL; CABA; EIL; EnLoPo; HAP; JCP; LiTB; LoBV; MasP; MePo; NIP; NOBE; NoP; OAEL-1; OBS; PoEL-2; PPoe; PPP; SeCePo; SeCeV; SeCP; SeCV-1; TEP; TrGrPo; UnPo; UnTE; ViBoPo
For God's sake, let us sit upon the ground. Of the Death of Kings. Shakespeare. Richard II, *fr.* III, ii. ChTr; HoPM
For Good Luck. Juliana Horatia Ewing. FaPON
For government, though high, and low, and lower. Shakespeare. King Henry V, *fr.* I, ii. GN
For grace in me divined. Arbor Vitae. Siegfried Sassoon. PoPle
For Great Grandmother and Her Settlement House. Ann Darr. GP
For Guillaume Apollinaire. William Meredith. CoAP
For H. W. Fuller. Carolyn M. Rodgers. BPo
For Hani, Aged Five, That She Be Better Able to Distinguish a Villain. Gene Baro. NYBP
For He Had Great Possessions. Richard Middleton. HBV-1
For he was our puck, our miniature lar. Louis MacNeice. *Fr.* The Death of a Cat. PCat
For he was wounder amiabill. Squire Meldrum at Carrickfergus. Sir David Lindsay. *Fr.* The Historie of Squyer William Meldrum. OxBS
For Hekabë and the women of Ilion. Epigram. Plato, *tr. by* Peter Jay. PeHV
For her blood runs in my blood. Rachel. Rachel, *tr. by* N. N. VWA
For Her Brother. Al-Khansa. *See* Tumadir Al-Khansa for Her Brother.
For her gait, if she be walking. The Complete Lover [*or* Song]. William Browne. HBV-1; OBEV
For Her Heart Only. *Unknown.* EIL
For Her on the First Day Out. Robert Bagg. NePoAm-2
For Her Sake. Alastair Reid. PoPl
For here lies Juliet, and her beauty makes. Here Lies Juliet [*or* Thus with a Kiss I Die]. Shakespeare. *Fr.* Romeo and Juliet, V, iii. FaFP; TreFS; TrGrPo
For He's a Jolly Good Fellow. *Unknown.* BLSo, *with music*; FSW
For Hettie. Amiri Baraka. NeAP; NoAM; NOBA
For Hidden Mist Pavilion. Yü Hsüan-chi, *tr. fr. Chinese by* Geoffrey Waters. BoWoP
For him, it seems, everything was molten. Court-ladies flow in gentle streams. The Laughing Hyena, by Hokusai. D. J. Enright. MP; TwCP
For him, who, lost to ev'ry hope of life. Apology for Vagrants. John Langhorne. *Fr.* The Country Justice. OBEC
For him who sought his country's good. Washington's Monument. *Unknown.* OHIP; PAH
For his mind, I doe not care. Another Ladyes Exception Present at the Hearing. Ben Jonson. *Fr.* A Celebration of Charis. AnAnS-2; SeCP
For His Own Epitaph. Matthew Prior. *See* For My Own Monument.
For his religion it was fit. The Religion of Hudibras [*or* Sir Hudibras's Religion]. Samuel Butler. *Fr.* Hudibras. DBV; FaBoEn; InMe; LoBV; OBSV; ViBoPo
For His Wife, on Her Birthday. Charles Wesley. NOCV
For Hope. Richard Crashaw. LiTB; ViBoPo
(Answer for Hope.) MeLP
(M. Crashaw's Answer for Hope.) OBS; SeCV-1
(On Hope.) MePo; NoBE
"Fairhope! our earlyer heav'n by thee," *sel.* *FaBoEn*
For hours I've waited for the sun. Vigil. Michael Knoll. LFAC
For hours the princess would not play or sleep. The Yak. Virna Sheard. CaP; PeCV; WHW
For how long known this boundless wash of light. Summer Beach. Frances Cornford. BrRo; ChMP
For human nature Hope remains alone. Hope. Theognis, *tr. by* John Hookham Frere. AWP
For I am not without authority in my jeopardy. Christopher Smart. *Fr.* Jubilate Agno. LAuP; NCEP
For I bless the Prince of Peace and pray that all the guns may be nail'd up. Christopher Smart. *Fr.* Jubilate Agno. InPS
For I can snore like a bullhorn. After Making Love We Hear Footsteps. Galway Kinnell. DiL
For I Dipped [*or* Dipt] into the Future. Tennyson. *Fr.* Locksley Hall. PGD; PoLF; TRV
(Prophecy.) TreF; WBLP
For I Have Done a Good and Kindly Deed. Franz Werfel, *tr. fr. German by* Edith Abercrombie Snow. TrJP
For I have founde you folk faithful of speche. Alexander and the Gymnosophists. *Unknown.* OxBM
For I have learned. Wordworth. *Fr.* Lines Composed a Few Miles above Tintern Abbey. NU
For I have loved [*or* lov'd] the rural walk through lanes. Rural Sights and Sounds. William Cowper. *Fr.* The Task. EnRP; NOEC
For I inhabit a wood. Marban, a Hermit Speaks. *Unknown, tr. by* Michael Hartnett. BIrV; CIP
For I learn as the years roll onward. Lessons of the Year. *Unknown.* BLRP
For I say, through the grace given unto me. The Duties of Man. Bible, *N.T.* *Fr.* Romans. TreF
For I the ballad will repeat. Shakespeare. *Fr.* All's Well That Ends Well, I, iii. BiP; ViBoPo
For I Will Consider My Cat Jeoffry [*or* Jeoffrey]. Christopher Smart. *Fr.* Jubilate Agno. CTC; FM; HAP; HeIP; InPK; LAuP; NOEC; NoP; OAEL-1; PAI; PCat; PoEL-3; PPP; Prf; SCV; SeCeV; WeW
(My Cat Jeoffry.) ChTr; FaBoCh; LiTB; SeCePo; WiR
(Of Jeoffry, His Cat.) NU; PrIm
For I will consider my dog Poochkin. Jubilate Canis. Erica Jong. MAYP
For I would walk alone. Wordsworth. *Fr.* The Prelude, II. OBRV
"For if your boone be askeable." Thomas Cromwell. *Unknown.* ESPB
For I'm called Little Buttercup—dear Little Buttercup. Little Buttercup. W. S. Gilbert. *Fr.* H. M. S. Pinafore. TreFS
For in and out, above, about, below. Omar Khayyám, *tr. by* Edward FitzGerald. *Fr.* The Rubáiyát of Omar Khayyám of Naishápúr. TRV

For infants time is like a humming shell. O Dreams, O Destinations. C. Day Lewis. MoPo
For Inspiration. Michelangelo, *tr. fr. Italian by* Wordsworth. GoBC; WGRP
(To the Supreme Being.) AWP; TrPWD; TRV
For Instance. Robert McAlmon. PoA
For instance/ if the sea should break. If Something Should Happen. Lucille Clifton. MAT
For Isaac the ram. Bring Your Own Victim. Allen Curnow. OCNZ
For it is the day of the Lord's vengeance. God's Vengeance. Bible, *O.T. Fr.* Isaiah. FM
For Jack Chatham. Jared Carter. AMV-81
For James Baldwin. Kay Boyle. NMM
For James Dean. Frank O'Hara. NeAP; NNaP
For Jan. John Wieners. CoPo
For Jan, in Bar Maria. Carolyn Kizer. VGW
For Jane. Charles Bukowski. HoPM
For Jane Myers. Louise Glück. GeTw
For January I give you vests of skins. Sonnets of the Months: January. Folgore da San Geminiano, *tr. by* Dante Gabriel Rossetti. AWP
For Jean Vincent d'Abbadie, Baron St.-Castin. Alden Nowlan. NOBC
For Jeanette Piccard Ordained at 79. Renny Golden. AMV-80
For Jillian of Berry she dwells on a hill. Jillian of Berry [*or* Another Song]. Beaumont *and* Fletcher. *Fr.* The Knight of the Burning Pestle. ElL
For Jim, Easter Eve. Anne Spencer. AmNP; PoNe
For John Berryman, I. Robert Lowell. NOBA
For John Chappell. Gary Snyder. NNaP
For John Clare. John Ashbery. FYAP
For John Keats, Apostle of Beauty. Countee Cullen. Four Epitaphs, 2. CDC
For Johnny. John Pudney. OBWP
For July, in Siena, by the willow-tree. Sonnets of the Months: July. Folgore da San Geminiano, *tr. by* Dante Gabriel Rossetti. AWP
For Just Men Light Is Sown, *with music.* Michael Wigglesworth. AH
For K. R. on Her Sixtieth Birthday. Richard Wilbur. NoP
For Kai Snyder. Philip Whalen. PoM
For Kelley. Ken Belford. NeAC
For King, for Robert Kennedy. Robert Hayden. *Fr.* Words in the Mourning Time. CNA
For Kinte. Oliver La Grone. FB
For knighthood is not in the feats of war. The True Knight [*or* True Knighthood]. Stephen Hawes. *Fr.* The Pastime of Pleasure. ACP; OBEV; TrGrPo
For Kuo Hsiang. Yü Hsüan-chi, *tr. fr. Chinese by* Geoffrey Waters. BoWoP
For Laurence Jones. Gary Kizer. CTBA
For Leningrad, and My Jewish Ancestors. L. M. Rosenberg. AMV-81
For Lerida. David St. John. AmPA
For Life I Had Never Cared Greatly. Thomas Hardy. CMoP; HBMV; LiTM; NoAM
For life, with all it yields of joy and woe. Robert Browning. *Fr.* A Death in the Desert. TRV
For lighter, whiter skin in just ten days. Brainwashing Dramatized. Don Johnson. PoNe
For Little Boys Destined for Big Business. Samuel Hoffenstein. DBV
For Lo! My Jonah How He Slumped, *with music.* John Wilson. AH
For lo! the board with cups and spoons is crowned. Pope. *Fr.* The Rape of the Lock. ViBoPo
For, lo! the living God doth bare his arm. Democracy. Harriet Monroe. *Fr.* Commemoration Ode. AA
For lo! the sea that fleets about the land. The Dancing Sea. Sir John Davies. *Fr.* Orchestra. ChTr
For, Lo, the Winter Is Past. Bible, *O.T.* Song of Solomon, II: 10-13. TreF
("For, lo, the winter is past," II: 11-12.) PDV; SUS; TiPo
(Lo, the Winter Is Past, 11-13.) FaPON
(Winter Is Past, The, 11-12. SoPo; YeAr
For, Lord, the Crowded Cities Be. Rainer Maria Rilke, *tr. fr. German by* Ludwig Lewisohn. AWP; TrJP
For Love. Robert Creeley. ConAP; NOBA
For love he offered me his perfect world. Gift to a Jade. Anna Wickham. DBV; ELU
For love—I would. The Warning. Robert Creeley. NeAP; TAP; VGW
For love no time has she, or inclination. Soame Jenyns. *Fr.* The Modern Fine Lady. OBSV
For love of lovely words, and for the sake. Skerryvore. Robert Louis Stevenson. EyDe
For love one must risk. Love Song. Bob Zmuda. AMV-81
For love we all go. The People, the People. George Oppen. GP
For Lover Man, and All the Other Young Men Who Failed to Return from World War II. Mance Williams. NNP
For Love's sake, kiss[e] me once again[e]. Begging Another, on Colour of Mending the Former [*or* For Love's Sake]. Ben Jonson. *Fr.* A Celebration of Charis. AnAnS-2; OAEP; PoEL-2; SeCP; UnTE
For Lucas Cranach's Eve. Adelaide Crapsey. QFR
For lunch this noon, a mason jar full. Mason Jar. David Steinberg. AMV-81
For M. Bruce Williamson. NeIP
For M.S. Singing *Fruhlingsglaube* in 1945. Frances Cornford. BrRo
For Mabel: Pomo Basketmaker and Doctor. Wendy Rose. TWSS
For Mack C. Parker. Pauli Murray. PoBA
For maiden sweetness, and for strength of men. John Oxenham. *Fr.* A Little Te Deum of the Commonplace. TRV
For Malcolm: After Mecca. Gerald W. Barrax. CNA; OFD; PoBA
For Malcolm Who Walks in the Eyes of Our Children. Quincy Troupe. CNA; PoBA
For Malcolm X. Nanina Alba. PoBA
For Malcolm X. Margaret Walker. BPo; CNA; PoBA
For Malcolm's eyes, when they broke. A Poem for Black Hearts. Amiri Baraka. CAPP; IDB; PoBA; PoM; SOTW
For Man to Act. Thomas Traherne. *Fr.* Christian Ethics. OxBoCh
("For man to act as if his soul did see.") NOCV
For many blessings I to God upraise. Nature and the Child. John Lancaster Spalding. *Fr.* God and the Soul. AA
For many, many days together. Riding Together. William Morris. NOBE; OAEL-2
For many thousand ages. Es Stehen Unbeweglich. Heine, *tr. by* James Thomson. AWP; TrJP
For many unsuccessful years. Against Modesty in Love. Matthew Prior. ErPo
For Mao Tse-tung; a Meditation on Flies and Kings. Irving Layton. NOBC
For Maria. Cleopatra Mathis. MAYP
For Mariella, in Antrona. Tobey A. Simpson. AMV-80
For Mary. Kenneth Rexroth. PoPl
For Mary McLeod Bethune. Margaret Walker. PoNe
For Masturbation. Alan Dugan. CAPP; NoAM
For Mattie and Eternity. Sterling D. Plumpp. CNA
For Me and My Gal. Edgar Leslie *and* E. Ray Goetz. BLSo
For me, for me, two horses wait. The Wizard's Funeral. Richard Watson Dixon. ELP; LoBV; VLP
For me, I know nought; nothing I deny. Byron. *Fr.* Don Juan, XIV. OBRV
For me the jasmine buds unfold. The World Is Mine [*or* Song]. Florence Earle Coates. AA; HBV-1
For me, the naked and the nude. The Naked and the Nude. Robert Graves. NYBP; SoSe
For me the night still soughs. After an Eclipse of the Sun. Eugene Heimler, *tr. by* Peter Sherwood *and* Keith Bosley. VWA
For me there is no dismay. The Poet. C. Day Lewis. OxBI
For Mercy, Courage, Kindness, Mirth. A Song. Laurence Binyon. HBMV; MoBrPo
For Michael. Karen L. Mitchell. AMV-80
For Miriam. Marjorie Oludhe Macgoye. WPOW
For "Mr. Dudley," a Black Spy. James A. Emanuel. BPo
For modes of faith let graceless Zealots fight. Faith. Pope. *Fr.* An Essay on Man. WGRP
For months/ my books were stacked. February Park. Gerald Vizenor. VoR
For months now you've hated me. Love Letter. David Ray. TW
For more than sixty years he has been blind. War Blinded. Douglas Dunn. BSV; OBWP
For more years than I can remember. Our People. Teresa Anderson. LTB
For morning sun and evening dew. Thanksgiving. Arthur Ketchum. STF
For mother-love and father-care. We Thank Thee. *Unknown.* FaPON
For Muh' Dear. Carolyn M. Rodgers. CNA
For Mulatto. Raymond Ringo Fernandez. LFAC
For Murasaki. Josephine Jacobsen. FAZ
For Musia's Grandchildren. Irving Layton. NOBC
For Music. Byron. *See* Stanzas for Music.
For My Ancestors. Rolfe Humphries. PoRA
For My Brother. Owen Dodson. Poems for My Brother Kenneth, VII. BALP
("Sleep late with your dream.") IDB; PoBA; PoNe
For My Brother. Thomas Merton. TreFS
For My Brother and Sister Southwestern Indian Poets. Geary Hobson. STE
For My Brother Jesus. Irving Layton. NoP
For My Contemporaries. J. V. Cunningham. CoAP; PP
For My Daughter. Weldon Kees. CoAP
For My Daughter. Ronald Koertge. GP; Str
For My Daughter. Ed Ochester. Str
For My Father. Stephen Berg. DiL
For My Father. Rachel Field. InMe
For My Father. Paul Potts. FaBoTw
For My Father. Philip Schultz. DiL

For My Father. Philip Whalen. DiL
For My Father on His Birthday. Greg Kuzma. Str
For My Father: Two Poems. David Kherdian. GP
For my food. St. Ciaran and the Birds. Ciaran Carson. CIP
For My Funeral. A. E. Housman. CMoP; TrPWD; ViBoPo
For My Grandfather. Richard Robbins. AMV-81
For My Grandmother. Countee Cullen. Four Epitaphs, 1. CDC; MoAmPo; VGW
For My Grandmother, Bridgid [*or* Bridget] Halpin. Michael Hartnett. BIrV; CIP
For My Husband. Ellen Bryant Voigt. NoP
For My Lover, Returning to His Wife. Anne Sexton. IHMS; NMM; UnPo; WPE
For My Mother. Louise Glück. GeTw; UnPo
For My Mother. June Jordan. BoWoP; NMM
For My Mother. Iain Crichton Smith. OxBS
For My Mother, Feeling Useless. Paula Rankin. MAYP
For My Mother: Genevieve Jules Creeley. Robert Creeley. PoM
For My Own Monument. Matthew Prior. HBV-1; LoBV; OBEC; OBEV
(For His Own Epitaph.) FaBoEE
For my part, I never care. Tips Tongueless. Robert Herrick. CaPo
For my part, I'le not meddle with the cause. Homer, *tr. by* George Chapman. *Fr.* The Odyssey, XIV. CTC
For My People. Wendy Rose. CDW
For My People. Margaret Walker. AmNP; BALP; CNA; IDB; PoBA; PoNe
For my sister's sake. Hitomaro. *Fr.* Manyo Shu. AWP
For My Son. John Frederick Nims. MiAP
For My Son, Born during an Ice Storm. David Jauss. Str
For My Son, Noah, Ten Years Old. Robert Bly. DiL
For My Son on the Highways of His Mind. Maxine W. Kumin. MAT
For My Students, Returning to College. John Williams. NePoAm-2
For My Torturer, Lieutenant D——. Leila Djabali, *tr. fr. French by* Anita Barrows. WPOW
For My Twenty-fifth Birthday in Nineteen Forty-one. John Ciardi. WaP
For My Unborn and Wretched Children. A. B. Spellman. CNA; PoBA
For my unborn son. Two Poems, II. Robert J. Abrams. NNP
For My Wife. Steven Lautermilch. AMV-80
For My Wife. Julian Symons. NeBP; WaP
For Myself. J. A. Hines. LFAC
For Natalya Correia. Irving Layton. NeAC
For nations vague as weed. Nothing to Be Said. Philip Larkin. OxBTC
For Nature daily through her grand design. Frederick Goddard Tuckerman. Sonnets, I, xxvi. AP
For nearly fifty years I've been a cocky. Now I'm Easy. Eric Bogle. OBET
For New Year, Postumus, ten years ago. A Roman Thank-You Letter. Martial, *tr. by* James Michie. OBCP
For Nicholas, Born in September. Tod Perry. NYBP
For nine months. The Rite. Peter Dale. NAs
For No Clear Reason. Robert Creeley. VGW
For No Good Reason. Peter Redgrove. NMP
For no man wist who was best. The Round Table. Robert Mannyng. ACP
For No One. John Lennon *and* Paul McCartney. WTO
For noble minds, the worst of miseries. Poverty. Theognis, *tr. by* John Hookham Frere. AWP
For Nothing. Andrés Castro Ríos, *tr. fr. Spanish by* Julio Marzán. InW
For Nothing. Gary Snyder. NNaP
For Now. W. S. Merwin. CoPo; NaP
For now are wider ways, profounder tides. The Deeper Seas. Henry Bellamann. EtS
For now, love thou, I rede, Christ, as I thee tell. Richard Rolle. *Fr.* Love Is Life. ACP
For now the whetting of mind has stopped. Sleeping Beauty: August. Douglas Knight. DFT
For now too nigh/ The archangel stood, and from the other hill. Their Banishment. Milton. *Fr.* Paradise Lost, XII. SeCePo
For, O America, our country!—land. America. Arlo Bates. *Fr.* The Torch-Bearers. AA; PAL
For often my mammy has told. Air. Henry Brooke. *Fr.* Jack the Giant Queller; an Antique History. NOEC
For Once, Then, Something. Robert Frost. AP; NoAM; NOBA
For one carved instant as they flew. Sea Gulls. E. J. Pratt. EtS
For one long term, or e'er her trial came. Inscription for the Door of the Cell in Newgate Where Mrs. Brownrigg, the 'Prentice-Cide, Was Confined Previous to Her Execution [*or* Inscription]. George Canning *and* John Hookham Frere. FaBoCo; FaBoEE; Par
For One Moment. David Ignatow. NNaP
For one month afterwards the eye stays true. Departure. Kingsley Amis. NePoEA
For One Who Died Young. H. R. Hays. EAS
For one who says he feels. Petra von Morstein, *tr. fr. German by* Rosemarie Waldrop. BoWoP
For openers, the Federal Government. How to Change the U.S.A. Harry Edwards. NBP; TW
For other fruits my father was indifferent. My Father and the Fig Tree. Naomi Shihab Nye. GP
For others she may not be fair. Mother. Thomas Curtis Clark. PGD
For Our Lady. Sonia Sanchez. IHMS
For "Our Lady of the Rocks" by Leonardo da Vinci. Dante Gabriel Rossetti. VLP
("Our Lady of the Rocks.") OxBoCh
(Sonnets for Pictures: "Our Lady of the Rocks.") EBEV
For our own private reasons. Reasons. Thomas James. PoA
For Our Sakes. Oscar Wilde. PGD
For Our Soldiers Who Fell in Russia. Franco Fortini, *tr. fr. Italian by* Ruth Feldman. VWA
For Paddy Mac. Padraic Fallon. CIP
For parents, the only way. The Way of Pain. Wendell Berry. AMV-80
For Patrick, Aetat: LXX. John Betjeman. NAs
For Paul Laurence Dunbar. Countee Cullen. Four Epitaphs, 3. BALP; CDC
For people/ on trial. Perambulator Poems, II. David McCord. WhC
For Peter. Lee Gerlach. HoAn
For physic and farces his equal there scarce is. On Sir John Hill, M.D., Playwright [*or* David Garrick, the Actor, to Sir John Hill]. David Garrick. FaBoCo; FaBoEE; TreFT
For Pity, Pretty Eyes, Surcease. Thomas Lodge. ElL
(Armistice.) OBSC
For Poets. Al Young. CNA; DFF; PoBA; RFM
For Posterity. Kathleen Raine. NeBP
For printed instructions. No Holes Marred. Suzanne Douglass. QQQ; RHPC
For Prodigal Read Generous. E. E. Cummings. FaBoEE; NoAM
For rage and dignity no words compare. A Classical Quatrain. Paul Goodman. VGW
For Randie. Geof Hewitt. NeAC
For reading I can recommend. "Domaine Public." Geoffrey Hill. OxBC
For Real. Jayne Cortez. PoBA
For reasons any/ brigadier/ could tell. Irapuato. Earle Birney. NIP; PeCV
For Refugio Talamante. Ed Ochester. LTB
For Rhoda. Delmore Schwartz. *Fr.* The Repetitive Heart. MoAB; MoAmPo; MoVE; OxBA
(Calmly We Walk through This April's Day.) LiTM; PrIm
(Time Is the Fire.) LiTA
For right is right, since God is God. Right Is Right. Frederick William Faber. TRV; WBLP
For Righteousness' Sake. Whittier. PoEL-4
For rigorous teachers seized my youth. Matthew Arnold. *Fr.* Stanzas from the Grande Chartreuse. ViBoPo
For Robert Frost. Galway Kinnell. NOBA; VGW
"I saw you once on the TV," *sel.* PP
For Rosa Yen, Who Lived Here. Greg Pape. AmPA
For "Ruggiero and Angelica" by Ingres. Dante Gabriel Rossetti. VLP
For Sale. Robert Lowell. ConAP
For Sale. Shel Silverstein. CTBA
For Sale. *Unknown.* BPAW
For Sammy Younge. Charlie Cobb. PoBA
For Sapphires. Carolyn M. Rodgers. CNA
For Saturday. Christopher Smart. *Fr.* Hymns for the Amusement of Children. LAuP; NOEC
(Hymn for Saturday.) OxBChV
(Lark's Nest, A.) FaBoCh
For Saundra. Nikki Giovanni. BPo; TTY
For Scholars and Pupils. George Wither. OxBChV
For Scotland's and for freedom's right. Bruce and the Spider. Bernard Barton. BeLS
For seeing, a/ brightness within. A New Light. William Hawkins. MoCV
For seven long years I had declared my passion. The Cywdd to Morvydd. David ap Gwilim. NOEC
For seven years my mother has been visiting me. Visits. Daniel L. Klauck. LFAC
For several months. P.C. Plod versus the Dale St. Dog Strangler. Roger McGough. NoAM
For several weeks I have been reading. Expression. Thom Gunn. OxBC
"For shame!" cries Cypris as she sees. Indignant Protest. *Unknown, tr. by* Louis Untermeyer. UnTE
For shame! deny that thou bear'st love to any. Sonnets, X. Shakespeare. MasP
For shame, thou everlasting wooer. The Antiplatonick. John Cleveland. AnAnS-2; MePo; SeCP
For she is a vapour. Bible, Apocrypha (*Douay vers.*). *Fr.* Wisdom. ISi

For Sir John Vanbrugh, Architect. Abel Evans. *See* On Sir John Vanbrugh.
For sixty days and upwards. Vicksburg. Paul Hamilton Hayne. AA; PAH
For Sleep, or Death. Ruth Pitter. TrPWD
For Snow. Eleanor Farjeon. CH
For so long/ We looked into mirrors. Us. Julius Lester. PoBA
For Soldiers. Humphrey Gifford. CH; ElL
For Some Poets. Mae Jackson. BOLo; PoBA
For some strange reason, reading the yellow novel, one/ thinks of Greece. Seascape with Bookends Charles Edward Eaton. AMV-80
For some, the sea. Bathing Song. Anne Ridler. NYBP
For something out of sight. The Summons. James Dickey. LiSp
For Sore Eyes. *Unknown.* OxBM
(Mock Medicine.) MeEL
For Spring. D. G. Jones. NOBC
For Steph. Wendy Rose. CDW
For Stephen. Christopher Brookhouse. AMV-80
For Stephen Dixon. Zack Gilbert. PoBA
For Stephen Drawing Birds. Pattiann Rogers. MAYP
For Steve. Earle Birney. WaP
For stone that breaks the giant hold, for strength. David Homindae. Marjorie Stamm Rosenfeld. AMV-80
For such as you, I do believe. The Mother in the House. Hermann Hagedorn. HBMV; OHIP
For Sudek, this is sex. Instead of Features. Jim Moore. PoDr
For Sue. Phil Hey. PPJ
For Summer's bloom and Autumn's blight. Hymn. Josiah Gilbert Holland. *Fr.* Bitter-sweet. TrPWD
For Summer's Here. Ratcliffe Barnett. PoSH
For Sunday's play he never makes excuse. The Lout. John Clare. NBM
For sunlit hours and visions clear. Gratitude. Clyde McGee. BLRP
For that free Grace bringing us past terrible risks. Minnesota Thanksgiving. John Berryman. GOA
For That He Looked Not upon Her. George Gascoigne. ElL; NoP
For that I never knew you, I only learned to dread you. St. Roach. Muriel Rukeyser. GP
For that lovely face will fail. Thomas Carew. *Fr.* Persuasions to Love. ViBoPo
For the air is purified by prayer which is made aloud. Christopher Smart. *Fr.* Jubilate Agno. Prf
For the Altarpiece of the Roseau Valley Church, Saint Lucia. Derek Walcott. NoP
For the Anniversary of My Death. W. S. Merwin. CAPP; CoAP; InPK; NaP; NOBA; PAI
For the Baptist[e]. William Drummond of Hawthornden. BSV; GoTS; HBV-2; LoBV; OBS; OxBoCh
(Baptist, The.) TrGrPo
(Saint John [the] Baptist.) EaLo; GTBS; GTBS-P; NOBE; OBEV; TrCP
For the Barbers. Joel Oppenheimer. CoPo
For the Bed [*or* Beds] at Kelmscott. William Morris. *See* Inscription for an Old Bed.
For the Bicentenary of Isaac Watts. Norman Nicholson. EaLo
For the Book of Love. Jules Laforgue, *tr. fr. French by* Jethro Bithell. AWP; ErPo
For the bumps bangs and scratches of. Auto Mobile. A. R. Ammons. FF; InPK; OBAL
For the Candle Light. Angelina Weld Grimkė. BlSi; CDC; PoNe
For the Children. Thomas Peacock. VoR
For the Children. Gary Snyder. NoP; PAI
For the Children or the Grown-ups? *Unknown.* OBCP
For the Coming Year. Peter Everwine. OFD
For the Conjunction of Two Planets. Adrienne Rich. ImOP
For the Courtesan Ch'ing Lin. Wu Tsao, *tr. fr. Chinese by* Kenneth Rexroth *and* Ling Chung. WPOW
("On your slender body/ Your jade and coral girdle ornaments chime.") BoWoP
For the Crêche. G. K. Chesterton. *Fr.* Songs of Education. FaBoCo
For the Cultural Campaign. Chimedin Jigmed, *Mongol Oral Tradition, tr. by* C. R. Bawden. WTO
For the days when nothing happens. Thanksgiving. Margaret E. Sangster. BLRP
For the Death of Vince Lombardi. James Dickey. LiSp
For the Depressed. Julian Symons. WaP
For the dim regions whence my fathers came. Outcast. Claude McKay. AmNP; BALP; CABA; PoBA
For the doubling of flowers is the improvement of the gardners talent. Christopher Smart. *Fr.* Jubilate Agno. LAuP; NOEC
For the dream unfinished. Plain-Chant for America. Katherine Garrison Chapin. PAL
For the ERA Crusaders. X. J. Kennedy. SOTS
For the Earth God. *Unknown, tr. fr. Dahomean song by* Frances Herskovits. EaLo
For the Eating of Swine. Rodney Jones. MAYP
For the El Paso Weather Bureau. Peter Wild. MAT
For the Fallen. Laurence Binyon. NOBE; OBEV; OBWP; OxBTC
"They went with songs to the battle," *sel.* ViBoPo
For the Field. Eric Chock. BrSi
For the first Monday of my week. In the Cemetery of the Sun. Wilfred Watson. PeCV
For the first time. A Poem for Positive Thinkers. Barbara Mahone. PoBA
For the first time, on the road north of Tampico. Making a Fist. Naomi Shihab Nye. MAYP
For the first twenty yeares, since yesterday. The Computation. John Donne. OAEP
For the Fly-Leaf of a School-Book. Norman Cameron. OxBS
For the Fourth Birthday of My Daughter. George Barker. NAs
For the Gifts of the Spirit. Edward Rowland Sill. TrPWD
For the Girls 'cause They Know. Harold Littlebird. VoR
For the gladness here where the sun is shining at evening. Carl Sandburg. *Fr.* Our Prayer of Thanks. TRV
For the Goddess Too Well Known. Elsa Gidlow. PeHV
For the Grave of Daniel Boone. William Stafford. NoP; PAI; PoPl
For the Greek and Latin are not dead languages. Christopher Smart. *Fr.* Jubilate Agno. NCEP
For the Hearne [*or* Hern] and Duck. *Unknown.* NCEP; PBBP
For the heart, willing and not willing. The Clovers. Jean Garrigue. MoPo
For the Holy Family by Michelangelo. Dante Gabriel Rossetti. GoBC
For the Lady Olivia Porter; a Present upon a New Year's Day. Sir William Davenant. JCP; MeLP; MePo; OBS
For the last time Beowulf uttered his boast. Beowulf and Wiglaf Slay the Dragon. *Unknown, tr. by* Charles W. Kennedy. *Fr.* Beowulf. AnOE
For the Last Wolverine. James Dickey. LiSp
For the lifting up of mountains. Mountains. Lucy Larcom. WBLP
For the Lordes parte is his folke. Bible, *O.T.* Deuteronomy, XXXII: 9-15. OBVE
For the Lord's Day Evening. Isaac Watts. OxBChV
For the Lost Generation. Galway Kinnell. NePoAm; PAI; PPON
For the love of God is broader. There's a Wideness. Frederick William Faber. WBLP
For the Magdalene. William Drummond of Hawthornden. LoBV; PoEL-2
For the man I'd marry I picked a white flower. Alleys. Sandra McPherson. MAYP
For the Man Who Stole a Rose. Harley Elliott. FAZ
For the Market. Jane Mayhall. TAP
For the Marriage of Faustus and Helen. Hart Crane. AP; InPS; NePA; NoAM; NOBA
"Capped arbiter of beauty in this street," III. FaBoMo; LiTM
For the Marsh's Birthday. James Wright. NYBP
For the Master's Use. *Unknown.* BLRP
(Watered Lilies, The.) BLPA
For the Minority. Robert Peterson. NeAC
For the most part. Chances. Brenda S. Stockwell. AMV-81
For the New Railway Station in Rome. Richard Wilbur. NePoEA
For the New Union Dead in Alabama. Edward Dorn. PoM
For the New Year. Robert Creeley. NaP
For the New Year. Norman Nicholson. NeBP
For the Nightly Ascent of the Hunter Orion over a Forest Clearing. James Dickey. TwCP
For the Night-Mare. *Unknown.* OxBM
For the One Who Would Take Man's Life in His Hands. Delmore Schwartz. LiTA; LiTM; MiAP; MoAB; MoAmPo; MoVE; NePA; NoAM; VGW; WaP
For the Opening of the Hunting Season. Morris Bishop. BoAnP
For the Palace that lies desolate. We Sit Solitary. *Unknown.* TrJP
For the Passing of Groucho's Pursuer. John Hollander. *See* To the Lady Portrayed by Margaret Dumont.
For the past three days she had been wandering, and following. Charles Péguy, *tr. by* Julian Green. *Fr.* The Passion of Our Lady. ISi
"For the pleasures of the many." Variations, Calypso and Fugue on a Theme of Ella Wheeler Wilcox. John Ashbery. LCAP
For the poor body that I own. Garadh. Padraic Colum. OnYI
For the Queen Mother. John Betjeman. NAs
For the Rain It Raineth Every Day. Robert Graves. NYBP
For the Rebuilding of a House. Wendell Berry. EyDe
For the Record. Roy Blount, Jr. OBAL
For the Record. George Jonas. MoCV
For the rosebud's break of beauty. Lucy Larcom. *Fr.* A Thanksgiving. TrPWD
For the Running of the New York City Marathon. James Dickey. NYP
For the sake of a weathered gray city set high on a hill. Perugia. Amelia Josephine Burr. HBV-2
For the second shot. The Zen Archer. James Kirkup. EaLo
For the Sexes: The Gates of Paradise. Blake. LiTB; PoEL-4
For the Sin. *Unknown, tr. fr. Hebrew.* TrJP

For the Sisters of the Hôtel Dieu. A. M. Klein. SoSe; WHW
For the Sleepwalkers. Edward Hirsch. FYAP; MAYP
For the Slender Beech and the Sapling Oak. Thomas Love Peacock. *See* Song: "For the tender beech and the sapling oak."
For the sole edification. A Credo. Thackeray. HBV-2
For the spiritual musick is as follows. Christopher Smart. *Fr.* Jubilate Agno. NOEC
For the Stranger. Carolyn Forché. MAYP
For the Student Strikers. Richard Wilbur. GLGT; OxBC
For the Sun Declined, *sel.* Yitzhak Lamdan, *tr. fr. Hebrew by* Simon Halkin.
"Where am I, O awesome friend?" TrJP
For the sun that shone at the dawn of spring. A Song of Thanks. Edward Smyth Jones. BANP
For the tender [*or* slender] beech and the sapling oak. Song. Thomas Love Peacock. *Fr.* Maid Marian. EnRP; OHIP
For the Time Being; a Christmas Oratorio, *sels.* W. H. Auden.
Advent. OAEP; SBVL
At the Manger Mary Sings. EBCP; ILwL; SBVL
"Come to our well-run desert." TRV
Dialogue between Mary and Gabriel. ISi
Fugal-Chorus. LiTM; SeCeV
("Great is Caesar.") NePA
"He is the way." EaLo; SBVL
If on Account of the Political Situation. LiTA; WaP
"Led by the light of an unusual star. PChr
"Our Father, whose creative Will." ILwL; TrPWD
Vision of the Shepherds. SBVL
Well, So That Is That. OBCP
(After Christmas.) MoAB; MoBrPo
(Flight into Egypt, The.) OAEP; OxBA; SBVL
("Well, so that is that. Now we must dismantle the tree.") OAEL-2
For the Union: a young true-blue. Winslow Homer, Prisoners from the Front. Roger Blakely. PoDr
For the Union Dead. Robert Lowell. AmPP; CABA; CoAP; FYAP; HAP; HeIP; InPS; LCAP; LiTM; MP; NaP; NMP; NoAM; NOBA; NoP; OBWP; PPoe; PPP; SCV; SeCeV; TwCP; UnPo; WeW
For the wealth of pathless forests. A Thanksgiving. Lucy Larcom. OHIP
For the West. Gary Snyder. NaP
For "The Wine of Circe" by Edward Burne-Jones. Dante Gabriel Rossetti. VLP
For the woman/ African in ancestry. A Freedom Song for the Black Woman. Carole C. Gregory. BlSi
For the Word Is Flesh. Stanley Kunitz. DiL; VGW
For the Yiddish Singers in the Lakewood Hotels of My Childhood. Harvey Shapiro. VWA
For the Young Who Want To. Marge Piercy. Psk
For thee a crown of thorns I wear. Any Father to Any Son. Francis Burdett Money-Coutts. OBVV
For thee a stead was builded. The Grave. *Unknown.* ACP
For thee I shall not die. I Shall Not Die for Thee. *Unknown, tr. by* Douglas Hyde. AnIL; OxBI
For thee, little boy, will the earth pour forth gifts. Virgil, *tr. by* James Laughlin. *Fr.* Eclogue IV. PoPl
For thee, O dear dear country! Jerusalem [*or* Jerusalem the Golden]. Bernard of Cluny, *tr. by* John Mason Neale. *Fr.* De Contemptu Mundi. HBV-2; OBVV; VLP
For Them All. John Hall Wheelock. HBMV
For them, O God, who only worship Thee. William Wilberforce Lord. *Fr.* Worship. AA
For them the sun shines ever in full might. Life after Death. Pindar, *tr. by* Walter Headlam. EaLo
For there are two heavens, sweet. Two Heavens. Leigh Hunt. GN
For there is hope for a man. South Wind. Nathan Yonathan, *tr. by* Richard Flantz. VWA
For there is hope for a tree. Bible, *O.T.* Job, XIV: 7-17. DL
For they are dead. Respect for the Dead. Laura Riding. LiTA
For They Shall See God. Luci Shaw. TrCP
For they who fashion songs must live too close to pain. Weltschmerz. Frank Yerby. AmNP
For thirdly he works it upon stretch with the fore paws extended. Christopher Smart. *Fr.* Jubilate Agno. NCEP
For thirty year, come herrin'-time. The Skipper-Hermit. Hiram Rich. EtS
For this additional declaration. The Dissenters' Thanksgiving for the Late Declaration. *Unknown.* APAS
For this is not the road against which stand enemy lines. Piyyut for Rosh Hashana. Chaim Guri, *tr. by* Ruth Finer Mintz. OFD
For This Is Wisdom. "Laurence Hope." *Fr.* The Teak Forest. PoLF; TreFT
For this, Old Friend, we burn. In the Time of the Rose. John Savant. AMV-81
For this one/ You need a pocket dictionary. Did They Help Me at the State Hospital for the Criminally Insane? Mbembe Milton Smith. FAZ
For this peculiar tint that paints my house. My House. Claude McKay. CDC
"For this same night att [Bucklesfeildberry]." Little Musgrave and Lady Barnard. *Unknown.* ESPB
For this she starred her eyes with salt. Epitaph. Elinor Wylie. MoAmPo; SBG
For this the ancient stars were hurled. Evolution. Israel Zangwill. TrJP
For this your mother sweated in the cold. To Jesus on His Birthday. Edna St. Vincent Millay. TrCP; TrGrPo
For those my unbaptized rhymes. His Prayer for Absolution. Robert Herrick. AnAnS-2; OxBoCh; SeCV-1; TrPWD; TRV
For those that never know the light. The Children of the Night. E. A. Robinson. OxBA
For Those Who Died. Thomas Curtis Clark. PGD
For those who fell at Thermopylae. The Thermopylae Ode. Simonides, *tr. by* Richmond Lattimore. WaaP
For those who worship Thee there is no death. The Trees of Life. Jones Very. NOBA
For thou art with me here upon the banks. Wordsworth. *Fr.* Lines Composed a Few Miles above Tintern Abbey. Prf
For Though the Caves Were Rabbited. Henry David Thoreau. FaBoEn; PoEL-4
For though ye be true of your tongue and honestly earn. Good Works. William Langland, *mod. by* Donald Attwater. *Fr.* The Vision of Piers Plowman. NOCV
For thoughts that curve like winging birds. I Yield Thee Praise. Philip Jerome Cleveland. TrPWD; TRV
For three swift days. Gennady Trifonov, *tr. fr. Russian by* Simon Karlinsky. PeHV
For three years, out of key with his time. E. P. Ode pour l'Élection de Son Sépulcre. Ezra Pound. *Fr.* Hugh Selwyn Mauberley. AmPP; AP; CABA; CMoP; CoBMV; CrMA; FaBoEn; FaBoMo; HAP; InPS; LiTA; LiTM; MasP; MoAmPo; MoPo; MoVE; NePA; NoAM; NOBA; NoP; OxBA; PP; SeCeV; TAP; UnPo; VGW
For thus saith the Lord to the men of Judah and Jerusalem. Bible, *O.T.* Jeremiah, IV: 3-31. OBVE
For Tinkers Who Travel on Foot. Margaret Avison. NoAM
For to a torche or to a taper the Trinité is likened. The Trinity. William Langland. *Fr.* The Vision of Piers Plowman. OxBM
For to Admire. Kipling. MoBrPo
For Tom Numkena, Hopi/Spokane. Harold Littlebird. VoR
For Tony, Dougal, Mick, Bugs, Nick, *et al.* Dave Bathgate. PoSH
For Travelers Going Sidereal. Robert Frost. OBAL
For treuthe [*or* trewthe] telleth that love [*or* loue] is triacle to abate sinne [*or* of hevene]. The Incarnation. William Langland. *Fr.* The Vision of Piers Plowman. OBEV; PoEL-1
For twenty years/ she's spent her nights. The Telephone Operator. Pat-Therese Francis. AMV-80
For twenty years and more surviving after. Widows. Edgar Lee Masters. MoAmPo
For two days her lineage is in doubt. Life of a Queen. Lisel Mueller. GP
For Two Girls Setting Out in Life. Peter Viereck. MiAP
For two years I looked forward. Breakfast. Thom Gunn. OxBC
For *Under the Volcano.* Malcolm Lowry. NOBC
For us, born into a still. C. Day Lewis. Overtures to Death, VII. CMoP
For us like any other fugitive. Another Time. W. H. Auden. OxBA
For Us No Night Can Be Happier, *with music.* Nicolaus L. Zinzendorf, *tr. fr. German at. to* John Gambold. AH
For us, the dead, though young. The Unreturning. Clinton Scollard. PAH
For vacant song behold a shining theme! On Some Humming-Birds in a Glass Cage. Charles Tennyson Turner. FM
For Valour. May Herschel-Clarke. SUMH
For Walter Lowenfels. Wendy Rose. CDW
For want I will in woe I plain. Sir Thomas Wyatt. SiPS
For want of a nail. Mother Goose. FaBoBe; HBV-1; OxNR; TreFT
For wars his life and half a world away. A Lullaby. Randall Jarrell. OxBC
For We Are All Madwomen. Barbara Sweeney. AMV-81
For We Are Thy People. *Unknown.* TrJP
For we have thought the longer thoughts. Chapter Heading. Ernest Hemingway. PoA
For we the mighty mountain plains have trod. The Sacraments of Nature. Aubrey Thomas De Vere. ACP
For weeks and weeks the autumn world stood still. How One Winter Came in the Lake Region. Wilfred Campbell. CaP; NOBC; OBCV; PeCV
For weeks before it comes I feel excited, yet when it. Afterthought. Elizabeth Jennings. OBCP
For weeks, now months, the year in burden goes. Ninth Month. Robert Lowell. Marriage, *st.* 11. NAs
For weeks, of course, the phone still rang for you. One Year Later. Eric Torgerson. POL
For wha ere had a lealer luve. Brown Adam. *Unknown.* ESPB

For What as Easy. W. H. Auden. NoP
For what emperor. Bowl. Wallace Stevens. PAI
For what is Freedom, but the unfettered use. Samuel Taylor Coleridge. *Fr.* The Destiny of Nations. EnRP
For what the world admires I'll wish no more. The Resolve. Mary Lee, Lady Chudleigh. OBEC; WPE
For what to-morrow shall disclose. Quid Sit Futurum Cras Fuge Quaerere. Matthew Prior. FaBoEE
For what we owe to other days. Exit. E. A. Robinson. MoAmPo
For whatever is let go. May Song. Wendell Berry. AP
For when it dawn'd—they dropp'd their arms. Samuel Taylor Coleridge. *Fr.* The Rime of the Ancient Mariner. UnS
For when they meet, the tensile air. The Paradigm. Allen Tate. NOBA
For Whitman. Diane Wakoski. SUW
For who can longer hold? when every press. Prologue. John Oldham. *Fr.* Satires upon the Jesuits. SeCV-2
For whole nights—(don't ask how many). In an Alien Place. Leib Neidus, *tr. by* Ruth Whitman. VWA
"For Whom the Bell Tolls." Gavin Ewart. WaP
For whom the possessed sea littered, on both shores. Requiem for the Plantagenet Kings. Geoffrey Hill. NoAM
For why should we the busy soul believe. Sir John Davies. *Fr.* The Immortality of the Soul. ViBoPo
For why? the gaines doth seldome quitte the charge. George Gascoigne. AAS
For William Edward Burghardt Du Bois on His Eightieth Birthday. Bette Darcie Latimer. PoBA; PoNe
For Witches. Susan Sutheim. NMM
For X. Louis MacNeice. Trilogy for X, I. BoLoP; EnLoPo
("When clerks and navvies fondle.") ErPo
For Ye Shall Go Out with Joy. Bible, *O.T.* Isaiah, LV: 6-12. TreFT
For Years. Ralph J. Mills, Jr. AMV-80
For years he pried among the strata. A Geologist's Epitaph. Jane W. Stedman. WhC
For years I had not seen such a town. Reunion. Judith Herzberg, *tr. by* Shirley Kaufman. BoWoP
For years I have been a coal miner. A Coal Miner's Goodbye. *Unknown.* AmFP
For years I thought I knew, at the bottom of the dream. The Meeting. Louise Bogan. NePoAm-2; NYBP
For years I've heard. Poem. Robin Blaser. NeAP
For years I've lived with Breughel's painting. Proportions. Joseph Stroud. NPGG
For years I've read the books on how to. A Little Bow to Books on How To. Irwin Edman. WhC
For years I've watched the corners for signs. Blues for Benny Kid Paret. Dave Smith. LiSp
For years she smiled. The Metamorphosis of Aunt Jemima. William Childress. MAT
For years we collected arrowheads. Arrowheads. Leona Gom. AMV-81
For years we endured his insolence. Mask-Maker. Michael Jackson. OCNZ
For years we've had a little dog. Two Dogs Have I. Ogden Nash. GDP
For You. Carl Sandburg. MoAmPo
For you/ I will be a ghetto jew. The Genius. Leonard Cohen. MoCV
For You, Falling Asleep after a Quarrel. Diane Middlebrook. AMV-81
For you I have emptied the meaning. Louis Zukofsky. NoAM
For You, My Son. Horace Gregory. MoAmPo
For You, O Democracy. Walt Whitman. TrGrPo
For you Time past could not forget. Hymn to Proust. Gavin Ewart. NYBP
For you who are seeking to serve with your best. In His Service. Clarence E. Clar. STF
For Your Inferiority Complex. David O'Rourke. AMV-81
For Zbigniew Herbert, Summer, 1971, Los Angeles. Larry Levis. FYAP; LCAP
For Zion's Sake. Bible, *O.T.* Isaiah, LXII: 1-5. TrJP
For Zorro. Diana Bickston. LFAC
Foray of Con O'Donnell A.D. 1495, The, *sel.* Denis Florence MacCarthy.
"'Now, by Columba!' Con exclaimed." OnYI
Forbear, bold youth, all's heaven here. An Answer to Another [*or* To One] Persuading a Lady to Marriage. Katherine Philips. CavP; HAP; OBEV; WeW
Forbear this liquid fire, fly. A Fly about a Glass of Burnt Claret. Richard Lovelace. CaPo
Forbear, thou great good husband, little ant. The Ant. Richard Lovelace. CaPo
Forbearance. Emerson. AA; GN; HBV-2; HBVY; LiTA; TAP; TreFT; TrGrPo; ViBoPo; WGRP
Forbearance. Della Adams Leitner. STF
Forbidden, The. Phyllis Haring. PeSA
Forbidden Drink. Robert Lovett. WhC
Forbidden Lure, The. Fannie Stearns Davis. HBV-1
Force. Edward Rowland Sill. AA
Force. Derek Walcott. OxBC
Force. *Unknown.* FaBoUs
Force has the best of any argument. The Wolf and the Lamb. La Fontaine, *tr. by* Marianne Moore. NAWM-2
Force of Love, The. Samuel Jones. NOEC
Force That through the Green Fuse Drives the Flower, The. Dylan Thomas. BiP; BLPL; CABA; CMoP; CoBMV; EBEV; FaBoMo; ImOP; InPS; LiTB; LiTM; MoAB; MoBrPo; MoPo; MoVE; NIP; NoAM; NOBE; NoP; OAEP; OxBTC; PoPle; PPP; PrIm; SCV; TEP; UnPo; ViBoPo
(Poem.) NeBP
Forced Bridal, The. *Unknown.* PaPo
Forced March. Miklós Radnóti, *tr. fr. Hungarian by* Emery George. VWA
Forced Music, A. Robert Graves. MoBrPo
Force-feeding swans—let me tell. Farmers. Thomas Lux. LCAP
Forcing a Way. *Unknown.* NA
Ford Madox Ford. Robert Lowell. MP; OxBC; PoCh; TwCP
Ford o' Kabul River. Kipling. FaBoTw
Ford Pickup. David Allan Evans. PPJ
Fording the River. Seamus Deane. CIP
Fore-royal furled, I pause and I stand, The. Making Land. Thomas Fleming Day. EtS
Forebears. Monk Gibbon. NeIP
Foreboding, The. Robert Graves. ChMP; ELP; GBL; PoA
Foreboding. John Haines. ConAP
Foreboding. Hazel Hall. HBMV
Foreboding. Rainer Maria Rilke, *tr. fr. German by* Lori Weinstein. InPK
Foreboding sudden of untoward change. By the Conemaugh. Florence Earle Coates. PAH
Forecast. Josephine Miles. CrMA; NoAM
Forecasting the Economy. Edward Morin. SOTS
Foreclosure. Sterling A. Brown. PoBA; PoNe
Foreclosure. Mark Van Doren. CrMA
Forefather, The. Richard Burton. AA
Forefathers. Edmund Blunden. ChMP; NOBE; OBEV; OBMV; OxBTC
Forehead Dead-Ends Half-Way through the Poem. D. C. Berry. BXAP
Foreign Affairs. Stanley Kunitz. LiTM; NYBP; TwAmPo
Foreign Aid. Lionel Kearns. NOBC
Foreign Children. Robert Louis Stevenson. GoJo
Foreign Country, A. Natan Zach, *tr. fr. Hebrew by* Laya Firestone. VWA
Foreign Gate, The, *sels.* Sidney Keyes.
"Moon is a poor woman, The." OBWP
Were I to Mount beyond the Field, *fr.* V. MoPo
Foreign Land, The. Coventry Patmore. The Angel in the House, VI. HBV-1
(Woman.) OBVV
Foreign Lands. Robert Louis Stevenson. HBV-1; HBVY; SUS
Foreign Literature. Thackeray. FaBoNo
Foreign room, slab faces, dusty panes, A. The Rebel General. Chris Wallace-Crabbe. CBAP
Foreign Ruler, A. Walter Savage Landor. DBV; OBSV; TreFT; ViBoPo
(Foren Ruler, A.) PV
Foreign Soil. Dianne Hai-Jew. BrSi
Foreign Streets. Mary Crow. AMV-80
Foreign Student. Barbara B. Robinson. CTBA
Foreign Woman. Rosario Castellanos, *tr. fr. Spanish by* J. M. Cohen. WPOW
Foreigner Comes to Earth on Boston Common, A. Horace Gregory. EaLo
Foreigners at the Fair. Fred Emerson Brooks. OBAL
Foreman whacks him hard, The. Any Time, What May Hit You. T. R. Hummer. MAYP
Foreman's Wife, The. Jeff Tagami. BrSi
Foren Ruler, A. Walter Savage Landor. *See* Foreign Ruler, A.
Forenoon, The. Christopher Middleton. *Fr.* Herman Moon's Hourbook. NePoEA-2
Forenoon and afternoon and night. Life. Edward Rowland Sill. BLRP; TRV
Forensic Jocularities. The History of a Case Shortly Reported by a Master in Chancery. *Unknown.* OxBoLi
Forepledged. John Lancaster Spalding. AA
Forerunners. Emerson. AA; OBEV; OBVV; OxBA
Forerunners, The. George Herbert. AnAnS-1; JCP; MePo; NoP
Foreseen for so many years: these evils, this monstrous violence. May-June, 1940 [*or* Battle]. Robinson Jeffers. LiTA; LiTM; MoAB; MoAmPo; NePA; WaP
Foreseen in the vision of sages. America. Bayard Taylor. *Fr.* The National Ode, July 4, 1876. AA; PAL
Foresight. Lincoln Kirstein. NoAM; OBWP
Forest. Harriet Gray Blackwell. GoYe
Forest. Jean Garrigue. LiTM; NOBA
Forest Fire, The. Arthur W. Monroe. BPAW; PoOW

"Forest Folk," The. Strawberries mit Cream. Rochelle Owens. CoPo
Forest Hymn, A. Bryant. AA; AP; TAP
"Father, thy hand/ Hath reared," *sel.* TrPWD
Forest Leaves in Autumn, *sel.* John Keble.
November. OBEV; OBVV
(Red o'er the Forest.) OxBoCh
("Red o'er the forest glows the setting sun.") OBNC
Forest Maid, The. Bryant. *See* Oh Fairest of the Rural Maids.
Forest Meditation, A. Bernice Hall Legg. PGD
Forest nuns, who sheltered us and healed, The. The Krankenhaus of Leutkirch. Richmond Lattimore. NYBP
Forest rears on lifted arms, The. The Snake-Charmer. Thomas Gordon Hake. VLP
Forest so much fallen from what she was before, The. The Thirteenth Song. Michael Drayton. *Fr.* Polyolbion. SeCePo
Forest was fair and wide, The. Tristrem and the Hunters. *At. to* Thomas of Erceldoune. *Fr.* Sir Tristem. OxBS
Forest without Leaves, *sel.* John Haines.
"Coolness will come to their children, A." NPAW
Forester, The. *Unknown. See* I Have Been a Foster.
Forester's Song. A. E. Coppard. FaPON
Forest's afire, The! October's Song. Eleanor Farjeon. PoSC
Forests are branches of a tree lying down. Flying Home from Utah. May Swenson. WPE
Forests of Lithuania, The, *sel.* Donald Davie.
"But this, so feminine?" OxBTC
Forest's Queen, The. Philip Massinger. GoBC
"Forever." Charles Stuart Calverley. InMe; NOBL; WhC
Forever. Raymond Carver. GeTw
Forever. John Boyle O'Reilly. HBV-2; OnYI; WGRP
For Ever. William Caldwell Roscoe. *See* Parting.
Forever am I conscious, moving here. The Undiscovered Country. Thomas Bailey Aldrich. AA
Forever Ambrosia. Christopher Morley. OBAL
Forever and a Day. Thomas Bailey Aldrich. HBV-1
Forever Dead. Sappho, *tr. fr. Greek by* William Ellery Leonard. AWP
For ever, Fortune, wilt thou prove. To Fortune. James Thomson. GTBS; GTBS-P
Forever in My Dream and in My Morning Thought. Henry David Thoreau. PoEL-4
Forever, it comes from the head. Venom. James Dickey. PoA
For-ever Morning. Laura Riding. LiTA
Forever over now, forever, forever gone. The Cameo. Edna St. Vincent Millay. FYAP; LiTA; MoAmPo; UnPo; WPE
Forever the little thud of names, falling. Empty Dwelling Places. Kenneth Patchen. PoA
Forever; 'tis a single word! "Forever." Charles Stuart Calverley. InMe; NOBL; WhC
"For ever with the Lord!" At Home in Heaven. James Montgomery. HBV-2; VLP
Foreword to New Numbers. Christopher Logue. OxBTC
Forge, The. Oliver St. John Gogarty. AnIV
Forge me a tool, my Seamus. His Request. Owen Roe O'Sullivan, *tr. by* John Keefe. BIrV
Forget. John Donne. *See* Holy Sonnets: "If poisonous minerals, and if that tree."
Forget. *Unknown.* STF
Forget about It. Robert Currie. Str
Forget each kindness that you do as soon as you have done it. The Best Memory Course. *Unknown.* STF
Forget It. *Unknown.* PoLF; WBLP
Forget Me Not. Bob Kaufman. AmNP
Forget Not Yet [the Tried Intent]. Sir Thomas Wyatt. AAS; BiP; EIL; EnRePo; GoBC; HAP; HBV-1; NoP; OAEP; OBEV; SiPS
(Lover Beseecheth His Mistress Not to Forget His Steadfast Faith and True Intent, The.) LO; ViBoPo
(Steadfastness.) NOBE; OBSC
(Supplication, A.) GTBS; GTBS-P
Forget roadside crossings. How to See Deer. Philip Booth. Psk
Forget six counties overhung with smoke. Prologue: The Wanderers. William Morris. *Fr.* The Earthly Paradise. EBVV
Forget the dead, this time. There Are Children in the Dusk. Bertram Warr. PeCV
Forget the old year's sorrows, forget its lonely days. Forget. *Unknown.* STF
Forget the slander you have heard. Just Forget. Myrtle May Dryden. WBLP
Forget the time spent mining the rudiments of praise. Sketch for a Morning in Muncie, Indiana. G. E. Murray. MAYP
Forget Thee? John Moultrie. BLPA; FaBoBe
Forget thine anguish. Meditations. Solomon ibn Gabirol, *tr. by* Emma Lazarus. TrJP
Forget this rotten world; And unto thee. John Donne. *Fr.* Of the Progresse of the Soule. FaBoEn
Forget to mail my letter to my friend Death. Overdue Balance Sheet. Therese Plantier, *tr. by* Maxine *and* Judith Kumin. BoWoP
Forgettin'. "Moira O'Neill." HBV-1
Forgetting God. J. E. Harvey. STF
Forging of the Anchor, The. Sir Samuel Ferguson. HBV-1
Forgive!/ And tell me that sweet tale. Francis Burdett Money-Coutts. *Fr.* A Little Sequence. OBVV
Forgive and Forget. "Totius," *tr. fr. Afrikaans by* Anthony Delius. PeSA
Forgive, Lord, Have Mercy! *Tr. fr. Sanskrit* by Raimundo Panikkar. *Fr.* Vedic Hymns. ILwL
Forgive me, O Lord. Foul Water. Mordecai Temkin, *tr. by* Jeremy Garber. VWA
Forgive Me, Sire. Norman Cameron. FaBoEE; GTBS-P; OxBS
Forgive me that I pitch your praise too low. Apology for Understatement. John Wain. NePoEA-2; OxBTC
Forgive Me When I Whine. *Unknown.* STF
Forgive me, you whom they cast in a name. Prayer. Avraham Shlonsky, *tr. by* Francis Landy. VWA
Forgive, O Lord, My Little Jokes on Thee. Robert Frost. EaLo; LiTM
Forgive the hours spent listening to the radio [*or* to radios]. Looking at a Dead Wren in My Hand. Robert Bly. GP; NNaP
"Forgive them, for they know not what they do!" Abraham Lincoln. Edmund Clarence Stedman. PAH
Forgive Us, O Lord. T. S. Eliot. *Fr.* Murder in the Cathedral. EaLo
Forgive us, son of Amram, be not wroth. Epigram III. *Unknown. Fr.* Duel with Verses over a Great Man. TrJP
Forgiven A. A. Milne. SoPo
Forgiven Past, The. Laura Riding. NoAM; PBWP
Forgiveness. Elizabeth Sewell. EaLo
Forgiveness. Whittier. TrCP
Forgiveness Dream, The; Man from the Warsaw Ghetto. Jean Valentine. LCAP
Forgiveness Lane. Martha Dickinson Bianchi. AA
Forgiveness of Sins a Joy Unknown to Angels. Augustus Lucas Hillhouse. *See* Trembling before Thine Awful Throne.
Forgiving My Father. Lucille Clifton. GeTw
Forgotten City, The. William Carlos Williams. LiTA; NePA; PoPl
Forgotten Dead, I Salute You. Muriel Stuart. SUMH
Forgotten Dreams. Edward Silvera. PoNe
Forgotten Island, *sel.* Radclyffe Hall.
"As a lamp of fine crystal, wonderfully wrought." PeHV
Forgotten Man, The. Edwin Markham. BLPL; PoLF
Forgotten Rock, The. Richard Eberhart. NePA
Forgotten Star, The. Thomas Curtis Clark. PGD
Fork. Charles Simic. AmPA; GP; LCAP; PCP
Forlorn and glum the couples go. The Houses. Eden Phillpotts. OxBTC
Forlorn Saphira, with reclining head. Against Homosexuality. Thomas Gilbert. *Fr.* A View of the Town. In an Epistle to a Friend. NOEC
Form. Heather McHugh. GeTw
Form and Function of the Novel, The. Albert Goldbarth. GeTw
"Form Fours." Frank Sidgwick. WhC
Form is the woods: the beast. Poem. Jim Harrison. VGW
Form of Epitaph, A. Laurence Whistler. GTBS-P
Form of Passion, A. David McFadden. NOBC
Form of Women, A. Robert Creeley. CAPP; NaP
Form of youth without blemish, is not such the form divine, The? Song of My Soul. Ralph Chubb. PeHV
Form Rejection Letter. Philip Dacey. AmPA
Form Was the World. Maurice English. NYBP
Formal Application Donald W. Baker. FF; SoSe
Formal exercise for withered fingers, A. Old Fisherman with Guitar. George Mackay Brown. BSV; OxBC
Formal world relaxes her cold chain, The. Apology. Wordsworth. *Fr.* Sonnets upon the Punishment of Death. VLP
Formations. William Freedman. VWA
Forme of Prayer, A. Francis Quarles. MePo
Formed long ago, yet made today. Mother Goose. HBV-1; HBVY; OxNR
Former Age, The. Chaucer. OxBM
Former Barn Lot. Mark Van Doren. FaBV; MoAmPo; PoPl; PDV
Former Beauties. Thomas Hardy. At Casterbridge Fair, II. FaBoEn; NoAM; OBMV; OBNC
Former Life. Baudelaire, *tr fr. French by* Roy Campbell. NAWM-2
"Formerly a Slave." Herman Melville. PoNe; TAP
Forming Child Poems. Simon J. Ortiz. CDW
Forms, *sel.* Theodore Enslin.
"Things being what they are do not imply necessity," LXXVII. CoPo
Forms of Love, The. George Oppen. NNaP
Forms of the Earth at Abiquiu. N. Scott Momaday. CDW
Forsake me not thus, Adam, witness Heav'n. Eve Penitent. Milton. *Fr.* Paradise Lost, X. OBS

Forsaken. Zalman Schneour, *tr. fr. Yiddish by* Joseph Leftwich. TrJP
Forsaken, The. Duncan Campbell Scott. CaP; NOBC
"Once in the winter," *sel.* WHW
Forsaken ("He once did love with fond affection"). *Unknown.* AmFP
Forsaken ("O waly, waly up the bank"). *Unknown. See* Waly, Waly.
Forsaken Bride, The. *Unknown. See* Waly, Waly.
Forsaken Garden, A. Swinburne. EBEV; FaBoEn; FaBoPP; GTBS-P; HBV-1; LiTB; LoBV; NOBE; NoP; OAEL-2; OBNC; OBVV; TEP; VLP; WHA
Forsaken Girl, The. Randall Jarrell. OLR
Forsaken Maiden's Lament, A. *Unknown. See* He Is Far.
Forsaken Merman, The. Matthew Arnold. BeLS; EBEV; EtS; FaBoCh; FaPoR; FiP; GN; HBV-1; MOS; OAEP; OBNV; OBVV; PoPle; ViBoPo; VLP; WHA
Forsaken of all comforts but these two. Upone Tabacco. Sir Robert Aytoun. OxBS
"Forsaking all"—You mean. The Word. Margaret Avison. MoCV
Forsythia. Mary Ellen Solt. BoWoP
Forsythia Is the Color I Remember. Joseph Cherwinski. AMV-80
Fort Bowyer. Charles L. S. Jones. PAH
Fort by the oak trees there, The. The Fort of Rathangan. *At. to* Berchan. ChTr
Fort Duquesne. Florus B. Plimpton. PAH
Fort McHenry. *Unknown.* PAH
Fort of Rathangan, The. *At. to* Berchan, *tr. fr. Old Irish by* Kuno Meyer. CH; FaBoCh; OxBI; ChTr, *tr. unknown*
Fort Robinson. Ted Kooser. GP
Fort Wayne, Indiana 1964. Steven Lewis. TAT
Forth from Calais, at dawn of night, when sunset summer on autumn shone. A Channel Passage. Swinburne. VLP
Forth from the purple battlements he fared. Sir Eggnogg. Bayard Taylor. BXAP
Forth, to the alien gravity. The Launch. Alice Meynell. WPE
Forth went the candid man. The Candid Man. Stephen Crane. War Is Kind, IX. MoAmPo
Forthfaring. Winifred Howells. AA
Fortitude. *Somali Oral Tradition, tr. by* B. W. Andrzejewski *and* I. M. Lewis. WTO
Fortnight before Christmas Gypsies were everywhere, A. The Gypsy. Edward Thomas. HeIP; NoAM; NoP
Fortress, The. Anne Sexton. LiTM
Fortù, Fortù, my beloved one. The Englishman in Italy. Robert Browning. PoEL-5
Fortunate,/ Being articulate. Nocturne of the Self-evident Presence. Thomas MacGreevy. BIrV; CIP
Fortunate Fall, The. A. Alvarez. VWA
Fortunate Isles, The. Joaquin Miller. WGRP
Fortunate One, The. Harriet Monroe. AA
Fortunately for you I am resurrected in one piece, or nearly. The Child-Bride. Joyce Carol Oates. GeTw
Fortunatus Nimium. Robert Bridges. BrPo
(Nimium Fortunatus.) MoAB; MoBrPo
Fortune. Thomas Dekker. *Fr.* Old Fortunatus. OBSC
(Fortune and Virtue, *longer sel.*) GoTL
Fortune. Lawrence Ferlinghetti. *Fr.* A Coney Island of the Mind. CAD
Fortune. Charles Madge. FaBoMo
Fortune. Sir Thomas More. GoBC
Fortune. Sir Thomas Wyatt. OBSC
("Marvaill no more all tho.") AAS
("Marvel no more although.") OBSC
Fortune. *Unknown. See* Lady Fortune, The.
Fortune and Virtue. Thomas Dekker. *See* Fortune.
Fortune favours the brave, old proverbs say. Mr. Cromek to Mr. Stothard. Blake. FaBoEE
Fortune for Mirabel. Horace Gregory. TwAmPo
Fortune has brought me down—her wonted way. His Children. Hittan of Tayyi, *tr. by* Sir Charles Lyall. *Fr.* Hamasah. AWP
Fortune, in power imperious. Of Fortune, *abr.* Thomas Kyd. *Fr.* Cornelia. EIL
Fortune smiles, cry holy day! [*or* holiday]. Fortune [*or* Fortune and Virtue]. Thomas Dekker. *Fr.* Old Fortunatus. GoTL; OBSC
Fortune-Teller, A. Witter Bynner. HBMV
Fortune Teller, The. John Holmes. NePoAm-2
Fortunes of Men, The, *sel. Unknown, tr. fr. Anglo-Saxon.*
"Another shall hang from the gallows' height." PBBP
Fortunes of Nigel, The, *sel.* Sir Walter Scott.
" 'Twas when fleet Snowball's head was waxen gray." *fr. ch.* 15. NBM
Fortunes of War, The. *Unknown.* InPK; POL
Fortune's Treachery. Judah Halevi, *tr. fr. Hebrew by* Solomon Solis-Cohen. TrJP
Fortune's Wheel. Lord De Tabley. OBVV
Forty Days, *sel.* John Brooks Wheelwright.
Second Ascension of Christ, The. NOCV
48 Words for a Woman's Dance Song. Jerome Rothenberg. PoM
Forty-five Minutes from Broadway, *with music.* George M. Cohan. FSN
45 Pistol Blues. *Unknown.* BluL
Forty-five Years since the Fall of the Ch'ing Dynasty. Philip Whalen. *See* 10:X:57, 45 Years since the Fall . . .
Forty-gun frigate from Baltimore came, A. Paul Jones.ViBoFo
40—Love. Roger McGough. LiSp; NoAM
49 Stomp, The Lew Blockcolski. VoR
49th and 5th, December 13. Josephine Jacobsen. NYP
Forty Pounds of Blackberries Equals Thirteen Gallons of Wine. Robert D. Hoeft. AMV-80
Forty-second, The. *Unknown.* GBP
Forty Singing Seamen. Alfred Noyes. OnMSP
Forty-two years ago (to me if to no one else). Star-Gazer. Louis MacNeice. NoP
Forty Viziers saw I go. The Fair Circassian. Richard Garnett. HBV-1; OBVV
Forty Years Ago. *Unknown, at. to* A. J. Gault *and also to* Dill Armor Smith. HBV-1
(Twenty Years Ago.) BLPA
Forty years ago a saloon stood where the church is. The Last Farmer in Queens. Vickie Karp. NYP
Forty Years On. Edward Ernest Bowen. HBV-1
Forty Years Peace. Arye Sivan, *tr. fr. Hebrew by* Anthony Rudolf *and* Natan Zach. VWA
Forward. Edna Dean Proctor. HBV-2
Forward abrupt. Night and a Distant Church. Russell Atkins. PoBA
Forward lay sunlight silver on the sea. The Waterspout. William Hart-Smith. *Fr.* Christopher Columbus. PoAu-2
Forward rush by the lamp in the gloom, A. The Contretemps. Thomas Hardy. CMoP; LiTM
Forward, sons of the tribe! Tambourine Song for Soldiers Going into Battle. Hind bint Utba, *tr. by* Bridget Connelly *and* Deirdre Lashgari. WPOW
Forward! The crackling lashes send. The Wagon Train. Sam L. Simpson. BPAW
Forward, then, ye jades! Christopher Marlowe. *Fr.* Tamburlaine the Great. ViBoPo
Forward violet thus did I chide, The. Sonnets, XCIX. Shakespeare. OAEP; OBSC
Forward young woman, Miss Chaos, A. The Trumpeter. *Unknown.* CoMu
Forward youth that would appear, The. An Horatian Ode upon Cromwell's Return from Ireland. Andrew Marvell. AnAnS-1; EBEV; GTBS; GTBS-P; HAP; HBV-2; InPS; JCP; LoBV; MePo; NOBE; NoP; OAEL-1; OBEV; OBS; OBWP; PoEL-2; SeCP; SeCV-1
Fossil. E. D. Blodgett. NOBC
Fossil, The. John Lyle Donaghy. NeIP
Fossil Raindrops, The. Harriet Prescott Spofford. OBCA
Fossils, The. Galway Kinnell. NYBP
Fossils. James Stephens. OnYI
Fossils. Arthur Stewart. SUW
Fo'ty acres jes' fo' me! Freedom in Mah Soul. David Wadsworth Cannon, Jr. PoNe
Foul canker of fair virtuous action. To Detraction [I Present My Poesie]. John Marston. *Fr.* The Scourge of Villany. LoBV; OBSC; TW
Foul fa' the breast first treason bred in. Hobie Noble. *Unknown.* ESPB; OxBB; ViBoFo
Foul Shot. Edwin A. Hoey. RHPC
"Foul vermin they." Rats. Walter de la Mare. BoAnP
Foul Water. Mordecai Temkin, *tr. fr. Hebrew by* Jeremy Garber. VWA
Foules Rondel. Chaucer. *See* Now Welcome, Somer.
Found. Carol Muske. AmPA
Found. Sarah Taylor Shatford. PeD
Found a family, build a state. Fragments of a Lost Gnostic Poem of the Twelfth Century. Herman Melville. NOBA; NoP; PoEL-5; ViBoPo
Found dead a rat—no case could sure be harder. *Unknown.* FaBoEE
Found in a Storm. William Stafford. RFM
Found in the garden—dead in his beauty. The Burial of the Linnet. Juliana Horatia Ewing. OxBChV
Found myself seated by chance a few years ago. The Concept of Force. Robert Sargent. SUW
Found the songs first. Detective Work. Wendy Rose. TWSS
Foundation of American Industry, The. Donald Hall. GOA
Foundation waits, The (will rise). A Weekday. Larry Eigner. CoPo
Foundations. Henry van Dyke. TRV
Foundered Tram, The. Harold Monro. BrPo
Founder's Day. Robert Bridges. OBVV
Founders of Ohio, The. William Henry Venable. PAH
Founding Fathers, Nineteenth-Century Style. Robert Penn Warren. Promises, VIII. NoAM

Foundling Hospital for Wit, The, *sel.* Isaac Hawkins Browne.
Fire Side, The; a Pastoral Soliloquy. NOEC; OBEC
Fount there is, doth overfling, A. At the Fountain. Marcabrun, *tr. by* Harriet Waters Preston. AWP
Fountain, The. Donald Davie. GTBS-P; OxBTC
Fountain. Elizabeth Jennings. PoCh; WPE
Fountain, The Pavlos Liasides, *tr. by* Edmund Pennant. AMV-80
Fountain, The. James Russell Lowell. OBCA
Fountain, The. Mu'tamid, King of Seville, *tr. fr. Arabic by* Dulcie L. Smith. AWP
Fountain, The. A. J. M. Smith. CaP
Fountain, The. Wordsworth. EnRP; GTBS; GTBS-P; OBRV; SeCePo
Fountain, a Bottle, a Donkey's Ears and Some Books, A. Robert Frost. VGW
Fountain at the Tomb, The. Nicias, *tr. fr. Greek by* Charles Merivale. AWP
Fountain blows its breathless spray, The. John Gould Fletcher. Irradiations, VI. TwAmPo
Fountain, coolest fountain. Ballad of the Cool Fountain. *Unknown, tr. by* Edwin Honig. BoWoP
Fountain flows, but where the bowl, The. The Broken Bowl. Jones Very. AP
Fountain in the Park, The. Ed Haley. *See* While Strolling through the Park One Day.
Fountain of Fire whom all divide. I Seek Thee in the Heart Alone. Herbert Trench. WGRP
Fountain of forms! Life springs of unique being! Robert Duncan. *Fr.* A Set of Romantic Hymns. DiL
Fountain of Sweets! Eternal Dove! Whit Sunday. Joseph Beaumont. OxBoCh
Fountain of Tears, The. Arthur O'Shaughnessy. OBVV
Fountain of tears, river of grief. Christine de Pisan, *tr. fr. French by* Joanna Bankier. WPOW
Fountain of Youth, The. Hezekiah Butterworth. PAH
Fountains, The. W. R. Rodgers. MoVE; POL
Fountains ("Proud fountains, wave your plumes"). Sir Osbert Sitwell. MoBrPo
Fountains ("This night is pure and clear as thrice refinèd silver"). Sacheverell Sitwell. MoBrPo
Fountains and the garden, The. Song for Music. G. S. Fraser. ChMP
Fountains are dry and the roses over, The. The Manor Garden. Sylvia Plath. LCAP
Fountains mingle with the river, The. Love's Philosophy. Shelley. BLPA; BLPL; BoLoP; EnRP; FaBoBe; FaBV; GTBS; GTBS-P; HBV-1; HoPM; OAEP; OBRV; OLR; TreFT; TrGrPo; UnTE; ViBoPo
Fountains of fire, The. Henry Rago. *Fr.* A Sky of Late Summer. NMP
Fountains that frisk and sprinkle. Ballade Made in the Hot Weather [*or* Made in the Hot Weather]. W. E. Henley. GN; MoBrPo
Founts of Song, The. "Fiona Macleod." WGRP
Four, The. Geoffrey Grigson. WaP
Four Ages of Man, The. Anne Bradstreet. *See* Of the Four Ages of Man.
Four Ages of Man, The. W. B. Yeats. PAI; TrCP
Four and Eight. ffrida Wolfe. SiSoSe
Four-and-eighty years are o'er me. The Battle of Monmouth. Thomas Dunn English. PAH
4½ Point 5. Ed Lipman. LFAC
Four and twentieth day of May, The. The Swimming Lady; or, A Wanton Discovery. *Unknown.* ErPo; UnTE
Four and twenty bonny boys. Sir Hugh; or, The Jew's Daughter [*or* Hugh of Lincoln]. *Unknown.* CH; EnSB; ESPB; FaBoBa; OxBB; ViBoFo
Four-and-twenty Highland men. Eppie Morrie. *Unknown.* ESPB; OxBB
Four-and-twenty ladies fair. Bonny Baby Livingston. *Unknown.* ESPB
Four and Twenty Merulae. J. Moyr Smith. FaBoNo
Four and twenty noblemen they rode thro Banchory fair. Glenlogie; or, Jean o Bethelnie. *Unknown.* ESPB
Four and twenty nobles sits in the king's ha. Glenlogie; or, Jean o Bethelnie (B *vers.*). *Unknown.* ESPB
Four and twenty tailors. Mother Goose. GBP; OxNR
Four and twenty white bulls. *Unknown.* GBP
Four arms, two necks, one wreathing. Song. *Unknown.* ElL
Four Birds. *Unknown.* ChTr
("Robin and the wren, The.") PBBP
(Robin, Wren, Martin, Swallow.) GBP
Four Brothers. W. S. Di Piero. MAYP
Four Calls, The. Lydia Hadley. STF
Four Cardinal Times of Day, The. Rene Daumal, *tr. fr. French by* Jan Pallister. AMV-81
Four children on a rumbling cart. Tinker's Moon. Ewart Milne. OnYI
Four Choctaw Songs. Jim Barnes. STE
Four Christmas Carols, *sel.* *Unknown, tr. fr. Spanish by* Cheli Durán.
"How cold the snow." PChr
Four days the earth was rent and torn. Bombardment. Richard Aldington. MMA
Four Dears, The. Ebenezer Elliott. SaC
Four Deer, The. Mary Hoxie Jones. GoYe
Four Ducks on a Pond. William Allingham. OxBI; PoPle
(Memory, A.) HBVY; OBVV
Four Epigrams on the Naturalization Bill. John Byrom. NOBL
Four Epitaphs. Countee Cullen. AmNP; CDC; PoBA
Sels.
For a Lady I Know, 4. HeIP; IDB; InPK; NIP; OBAL; PoNe; ShM; TAP
(Lady I Know, A.) MoAmPo; TRV
For My Grandmother, 1. MoAmPo; VGW
For Paul Lawrence Dunbar, 3. BALP
Four Fawns. Barbara Howes. AMV-80
Four feet up, under the bruise-blue. Small Woman on Swallow Street. W. S. Merwin. ConAP; CoAP
Four fingers and a thumb. The Lesson. Beth Bentley. GLGT
Four for Sir John Davies. Theodore Roethke. AP; CoBMV; MoAmPo; NoAM; NOBE
Dance, The, I. CrMA; NePoAm
Four Friends, The. A. A. Milne. TiPo
Four Friends. Leo Ward. GoBC
IV from Childhood. Arthur Rimbaud, *tr. fr. French by* Louise Varèse. *Fr.* Illuminations. PoPl
Four gallant ships from England came. The Battle of Stonington on the Seaboard of Connecticut. Philip Freneau. PAH
Four gents up and swing Sally Goodin. Sally Goodin. *Unknown.* AmFP
Four Glimpses of Night. Frank Marshall Davis. AmNP; NoP; PoBA; PoNe
"Four good dogs dead in one night." Poisoned Lands. John Montague. NMP
Four great gates has the city of Damascus. Gates of Damascus. James Elroy Flecker. BrPo; HBMV
Four great walls have hemmed me in. Four Walls. Blanche Taylor Dickinson. CDC
Four Haiku. Richard Wright. NoAM
Haiku: "Balmy spring wind, A," *sel.* FAZ
Four Heads & How to Do Them. John Forbes. CBAP
Four hooves rang out and now are still. Early Waking. Léonie Adams. LiTM; MoVE
Four horsemen rode out from the heart of the range. The Bushrangers. Edward Harrington. PoAu-1
Four Horses, The. James Reeves. PH
Four hours the sun his high meridian throne. William Falconer. *Fr.* The Shipwreck, II. MOS
400-Meter Freestyle. Maxine W. Kumin. LiSp; SoSe
Four hundred urgent springs and ripened summers. Ronsard. Miriam Allen DeFord. HBMV
Four in the Morning. Edith Sitwell. NoAM
4 in 2 goes twice as fast. Crazy Arithmetic. D'Arcy Thompson. FaBoCo
Four insurgent generals, The. Los Cuatro Generales. *Unknown, tr. fr. Spanish.* FSW
Four Japanese Paintings, *sel.* Arthur Davison Ficke.
Wave Symphony, The. PoA
Four jays (I.) Avis. Ted Morison. AMV-81
Four-Leaf Clover. Ella Higginson. AA; FaPON; HBV-1
Four-legg'd Elder, The; or, A Horrible Relation of a Dog and an Elder's Maid. Sir John Birkenhead. CoMu
Four-legg'd Quaker, The. *Unknown.* CoMu
Four Legs, Two Legs, Three Legs. William Empson. MoPo
Four little children. The Lost Angel. Philip Levine. NOBA
Four Little Foxes. Lew Sarett. FaPON; PDV; PoSC; RFM; RHPC; YeAr
Four little girls. Birmingham Sunday. Langston Hughes. PoNe
Four Lovely Sisters ("Four lovely spinsters, sisters to a king"). C. A. Trypanis. ELU
Four Maries, The. *Unknown.* FSW
Four May Poems: "Be glaid, al ye that luvaris bene." *Unknown.* OxBS
Four May Poems: "Now in this mirthfull tyme of May." *Unknown.* OxBS
Four May Poems: "O Lusty May with Flora quene." *Unknown.* *See* Lusty May.
Four May Poems: "Quhen Flora had ourfret the firth." *Unknown.* *See* When Flora Had Ourfret the Firth.
Four men stood by the grave of a man. Alexander the Great. *Unknown.* CH
Four miles at a leap, over the dark hollow land. Health. Edward Thomas. SeCePo
Four Mountain Wolves. Leslie Silko. VoR
Four Nights Drunk. *Unknown.* *See* Our Goodman.
Four o'Clock Flower Blues. *Unknown.* AmFP
Four o'clock, four o'clock, four o'clock. Cow Time. Monica Shannon. SiSoSe
Four of, The/ them together. The Knot. Tom Clark. HoAn

Four of Them, The. Yehuda Karni, *tr. fr. Hebrew by* Jeremy Garbers. VWA
4 Part Geometry Lesson, A. Robin Blaser. NeAP
Four-Paws. Helen Parry Eden. HBMV
Four pelicans went over the house. Pelicans. Robinson Jeffers. FM; MoAmPo
Four Pence a Day. *Unknown. See* Fourpence a Day.
Four Pictures by Juan, Age 5. David McKain. PoDr
Four Poems for April. Louis Adeane. NeBP
Four Poems for Robin. Gary Snyder. NNaP; NoAM; NOBA; NoP; SOTW
Sels.
Autumn Morning in Shokoku-ji, An. HAP
Spring Night in Shokoku-ji, A. VGW
Four Poems for *The St. Louis Sporting News.* Jack Spicer. PoM
Four pointes, my will, or I hence departe. A Last Will and Testament. *Unknown.* MeEL
Four Prayers. *Unknown, tr. fr. Modern Irish by* Eleanor Hull. OnYI
I Lie Down with God, *sel.* AnIV
Four Preludes on Playthings of the Wind. Carl Sandburg. AP; CMoP; MoAB; MoAmPo; NePA; NOBA
Four Quartets, *sels.* T. S. Eliot.
Burnt Norton. CMoP; LiTM; MoAB; MoAmPo; MoPo; TwAmPo
"Words move, music moves," V. UnS; ViBoPo
Dry Salvages, The. CABA; LiTB; NoP; OxBA; SeCePo
"Lady, whose shrine stands on the promontory," IV. Isi
East Coker. ChMP; HAP; MoVE; NePA; PPP; VGW
Little Gidding. FaBoEn; FaBoMo; GTBS-P; NoAM; NOBA; NOBE; OAEL-2; OAEP; PrIm; SeCeV; TAP
"Ash on an old man's sleeve," II. FaBoTw
"We shall not cease from exploration," V. ImOP
Four Quartz Crystal Clocks. Marianne Moore. AmPP; ImOP; MP; TwCP
Four Questions Addressed to His Excellency, the Prime Minister. James P. Vaughn. AmNP
Four sails of the mill, The. Lubber Breeze. T. Sturge Moore. CH
Four Saints in Three Acts, *sel.* Gertrude Stein.
"Pigeons on the grass alas." CrMA; TAP
Four Seasons. Rowena Bennett. SiSoSe; TiPo
Four Seasons, The. Jack Prelutsky. RHPC
Four seasons fill the measure of the year. The Human Seasons. Keats. EnRP; FaFP; GTBS; GTBS-P; HBV-1; OBRV; WiR
Four Seasons of the Year, The. Anne Bradstreet. SCAP
Four sharp scythes sweeping—in concert keeping. A Day in Ireland. *Unknown, tr. by* Michael Cavanagh. AnIV
Four Sheets to the Wind and a One-Way Ticket to France. Conrad Kent Rivers. AmNP; *diff. version;* BPo; CABA, *diff. version;* IDB; NNP; PoBA; PoNe
4 sniffs & I'm high. Aether. Allen Ginsberg. CoPo
Four Songs from the Book of Samuel. Eli Mandel. MoCV
Four Spacious Skies. Susan Astor. AMV-80
Four Stanzas Written in Anxiety. George Jonas. MoCV
Four stiff-standers. *Unknown.* ChTr; GBP; OxNR, *diff. version*
Four straight brick walls, severely plain. The Quaker Graveyard. S. Weir Mitchell. AA
Four sweaters are woven upon me. Springer Mountain. James Dickey. CAPP
Four Sweet Months, The. Robert Herrick. WiR
(July: The Succession of the Four Sweet Months.) FaPON
(Succession of the Four Sweet Months, The.) YeAr
Four Tao philosophers as cedar waxwings. Waxwings. Robert Francis. LCAP; NU
.410 gauge pistol made from plumbing supplies, A. Pipe Dreams. Diana Bickston. LFAC
Four Things. Bible, *O.T.* Proverbs, XXX: 24-28. FaPON
Four Things. *Unknown.* TRV
Four Things. Henry van Dyke. AA; HBV-2; HBVY; PoLF; TreF; TRV
(Four Things to Do.) WBLP
Four things are white, the fifth exceeds the rest. Five Things White. Edward May. FaBoEE
Four Things Choctaw. Jim Barnes. STE
Four things in any land must dwell. Four Things. *Unknown.* TRV
Four Things Make Us Happy Here. Robert Herrick. CaPo
Four Things to Do. Henry van Dyke. *See* Four Things.
Four III. E. E. Cummings. FaBoMo
Four times the sun had risen and set; and now on the fifth day. The Embarkation. Longfellow. *Fr.* Evangeline. PAH
Four Translations from the English of Robert Hershon. Robert Hershon. NeAC
Four trees upon a solitary acre. Emily Dickinson. AP; PoEL-5
Four Walls. Blanche Taylor Dickinson. CDC
Four walls, a ceiling, and the baby grows. Baby. Joyce Carol Oates. GeTw
Four-way winds of the world have blown, The. Strike the Blow. *Unknown.* PAH
Four white heifers with sprawling hooves. The Orotava Road. Basil Bunting. NoAM
Four Winds, The. Shane Leslie. OnYI
Four Winds, The. Charles Henry Lüders. AA; HBV-1
Four Winds. Sara Teasdale. HBV-1
Four Wise Men on Edward II's Reign. *Unknown.* OxBM
Four Women. Nina Simone. MAT
Four-Word Lines. May Swenson. WPE
Four Years. Dinah Maria Mulock Craik. HBV-1
Four years ago, dear old ventriloquist. The Ventriloquist. Robert Huff. GP
Four years!—and didst thou stay above. Geist's Grave. Matthew Arnold. FM; HBV-1; TEP
"Four years," some say consolingly. "Oh well." The Lament of the Demobilised. Vera Brittain. SUMH
Four Years Were Mine at Princeton. John Peale Bishop. GLGT
Four young men, of a Monday morn. The Prize of the *Margaretta.* Will Carleton. PAH
Four Zoas, The. Blake. *See* Vala; or, The Four Zoas.
Fourpence [*or* Four Pence] a Day. *Unknown.* FSW; OBET
14 July 1956. Laurence Lerner. PeSA
Fourteen Men. Mary Gilmore. CBAP
1492. Emma Lazarus. WPE
Fourteen small broidered berries on the hem. What the Sonnet Is. Eugene Lee-Hamilton. HoPM; OBVV
Fourteen years old, learning the alphabet. The Reading Lesson. Richard Murphy. IPY
Fourteenth Birthday. Phyllis McGinley. NePoAm-2
Fourteenth of July had come, The. La Tricoteuse. George Walter Thornbury. BeLS
14th St/New York, *abr.* Patricia Jones. NYP
Fourth Act. Robinson Jeffers. LiTA; WaP
Fourth Book of Sibylline Oracles, The, *sel.* "The Jewish Sibyl," *tr. fr. Greek by* Bohn.
There Is a City. TrJP
Fourth Dance Poem. Gerald W. Barrax. PoBA
Fourth day came, but not a breath of air, The. Byron. *Fr.* Don Juan, II. ChER
Fourth Day's Battle, The. Dryden. *Fr.* Annus Mirabilis. OBS
Fourth Dimension, The. Leonard Nathan. AMV-81
Fourth Eglogue, The. George Wither. *Fr.* The Shepheards Hunting. SeCV-1
Fourth, eleventh, ninth, and sixth. The Months of the Year. *Unknown.* FaBoUs
Fourth Napoleon, *sel.* J. A. R. McKellar.
Love in a Cottage. PoAu-2
Fourth Ode to Persephone. Robert Kelly. The Book of Persephone, 16. PoM
Fourth of July. Marchette Chute. SiSoSe
Fourth of July. Rachel Field. SiSoSe
Fourth of July, The. John Pierpont. PAH; PAL; YeAr
4th of July. William Carlos Williams. PoA
Fourth of July in Maine. Robert Lowell. CAPP
Fourth of July Night. Dorothy Aldis. SiSoSe; TiPo
Fourth of July Night. Carl Sandburg. OFD
Fourth of July Song. Lois Lenski. SiSoSe
Fourth Option, The. Henry Rasof. AMV-80
Fourth Pearl, The: Temperance. Lady Diana Primrose. *Fr.* A Chain of Pearl. WPE
Fourth Song: "Only Joy! now here you are." Sir Philip Sidney. *See* Astrophel and Stella: Fourth Song.
Fourth Song the Night Nurse Sang. Robert Duncan. VGW
Fourth Station. Paul Claudel, *tr. fr. French by* Sister Mary David. ISi
Fourth Station. Padraic Colum. ISi
Fourth Station. William A. Donaghy. ISi
Fourth Station. Ruth Schaumann, *tr. fr. German by* William J. Brell. ISi
Fower-an-twenty Heilandmen. *Unknown.* FaBoNo
Fowler, The. W. W. Gibson. HBMV
Fowls [*or* Foweles] in the Frith. *Unknown.* HAP; NCEP
(I Live in Great Sorrow.) MeEL
Fowls of heaven, The. James Thomson. *Fr.* The Seasons: Winter. PBBP
Fowre muckle angels wi their trumpets, stalkin. Judgment Day. Robert Garioch, *after* Giuseppe Belli. OBVE
Fox. David Campbell. CBAP
Fox, The. John Clare. BoAnP
Fox, The. C. Day Lewis. BoAnP
Fox. Kenneth Rexroth. *Fr.* A Bestiary. NNaP
Fox, The. Marjorie Somers Scheuer. GoYe
Fox, The (*diff. versions*). *Unknown.* BaBo; FSW
("Fox jumped up one winter's night, A.") OxNR; PBBP
(Fox Went Out One Frosty Night, The.) BLPA

Fox and crow, their dirty business finished, The. Fabulary Satire IV. Daryl Hine. NOBC
Fox and the cat, as they travell'd one day, The. The Virtuous Fox and the Self-righteous Cat. John Cunningham. OnMSP
Fox and the Crow, The. La Fontaine, *tr. fr. French by* Marianne Moore. NAWM-2; OBVE; PPP
Fox and the Goose, The (" 'Pax vobis,' quod the fox"). *Unknown.* OxBM
Fox and the Grapes, The. La Fontaine, *tr. fr. French by* Marianne Moore. FM
Fox and the Hare, The. *Unknown.* OBET
Fox and the Wolf, The. *Unknown.* OxBM
Fox at the Point of Death, The. John Gay. *Fr.* Fables. OBEC
Fox at your neck and snakeskin on your feet, A. Leaving Something Behind. David Wagoner. CoAP
Fox Awakes, The. John Masefield. *Fr.* Reynard the Fox. MoVE
Fox came [*or* he came] lolloping, lolloping, The. Hunting Song. Donald Finkel. CoAP; MoBS; NCSH; NcPoEA
Fox came up by Stringer's Pound, The. Midnight. John Masefield. BrPo
Fox drags its wounded belly, The. January. R. S. Thomas. ELU
Foxfire. Nancy Willard. IHMS
Fox flees the farm in a red rogue dazzle. For Hani, Aged Five, That She Be Better Able to Distinguish a Villain. Gene Baro. NYBP
Fox gan out of the wode go, A. The Fox and the Wolf. *Unknown.* OxBM
Fox-Hunters, The. Ebenezer Elliott. TW
Fox, in heaven's trap that gleams, A. The Stars Go By. Lilian Bowes Lyon. ChMP
Fox, in life's extream decay, A. The Fox at the Point of Death. John Gay. *Fr.* Fables. OBEC
Fox is very clever, The. Fox. Kenneth Rexroth. *Fr.* A Bestiary. NNaP
Fox jumped up one winter's night, A. *Unknown.* OxNR; PBBP
Fox knew well, that before they tore him, The. John Masefield. *Fr.* Reynard the Fox. OBNV
Fox may steal your hens, sir, A. A Soldier and a Sailor [*or* Air]. John Gay. *Fr.* The Beggar's Opera, I, i. NOEC; TEP
Fox of Gascon, though some say of Norman descent, A. The Fox and the Grapes. La Fontaine, *tr. by* Marianne Moore. FM
Fox Rhyme, The. Ian Serraillier. ELU
Fox Who Watched for the Midnight Sun, The. Norman Dubie. LCAP; MAYP
Fox woman/ dances, string of blue beads. Second Skins—a Peyote Song. Joseph Bruchac. CDW
Foxes, The. Janet Frame. WPE
Foxglove by the cottage door, The. Four and Eight. ffrida Wolfe. SiSoSe
Foxgloves and Snow. Marion Angus. PoSH
Foxtail Pine. Gary Snyder. CoPo; NaP; NU
Fr Anselm Williams and Br Leander Neville. Elizabeth Smither. OCNZ
Fra Bank to Bank, Fra Wood to Wood I Rin. Mark Alexander Boyd. InPK; NoP; PPoe; QFR
(Cupid and Venus.) GoTS
(Sonet: "Fra bank [*or* banc] to bank [*or* banc], fra wood to wood I rin.") EBEV; LoBV; NCEP; OBEV; SeCeV
(Sonnet: "Fra banc to banc, fra wod to wod, I rin.") BSV; GBL; NOBE; OxBS
(Venus and Cupid.) HAP; Prf
Fra Lippo Lippi. Robert Browning. BiP; CTC; EBVV; NoP; OAEL-2; OAEP; TEP; ViBoPo; VLP
"I shall paint/ God in the midst," *sel.* Prf
Fra Pandolf, have you tried to reproduce. Technique. Burnham Eaton. GoYe
Fra whaur in fragrant wuds ye bide. Spring on the Ochils. J. Logie Robertson. OBVV
Frae great Apollo, poet say. The Poet's Wish; an Ode. Allan Ramsay, *after* Horace. OBEC; OBVE
Frae nirly, nippin', Eas'lan' breeze. Ille Terrarum. Robert Louis Stevenson. OxBS
Fragile blades of grass. "Ping Hsin," *tr. by* Kai-yu Hsu. *Fr.* The Stars. WPOW
Fragile splendour of the level sea, The. Mid-Ocean in War-Time. Joyce Kilmer. MOS
Fragment: "At her step the water-hen." Dante Gabriel Rossetti. FM
Fragment, A: "Boy stood on the burning deck, The/ His feet were covered with blisters." *Unknown.* FaBoPa
Fragment: "Breath of life imbued those few dim days, The." Jessie Fauset. CDC
Fragment: "Bury him deep. So damned a work should lie." Thomas Lovell Beddoes. *See* Bury Him Deep.
Fragment: "Cataract, whirling to the precipice, The." John Clare. BoNaP
Fragment, A: "Encinctured with a twine of leaves." Samuel Taylor Coleridge. *See* Fruit Plucker, The.
Fragment: "Flower in the crannied wall." Tennyson. *See* Flower in the Crannied Wall.
Fragment: "He that but once too nearly hears." Coventry Patmore. *See* Music of Forefended Spheres, The.
Fragment, A: "I cannot find my way to Nazareth." Yvor Winters. OBSV
Fragment: "I lived on this earth in an age." Miklós Radnóti, *tr. fr. Hungarian by* Steven Polgar, Stephen Berg, *and* S. J. Martin. VWA
Fragment: "I saw his round mouth's crimson deepen as it fell." Wilfred Owen. OAEL-2
Fragment: "I strayed about the deck, an hour, to-night." Rupert Brooke. BrPo
Fragment: "I walk'd [*or* walked] along a stream for pureness rare." Gervase Markham, *at. to* Christopher Marlowe. CTC; LoBV; OBSC
Fragment: "I would to Heaven that I were so much clay." Byron. *Fr.* Don Juan. CTC; FiP; NOBL; NoP; OAEL-2; OAEP; PrIm
Fragment, A: "In Cloe's chamber, she and I." John Bancks. NOEC
Fragment: "Language has not the power to speak what love indites." John Clare. FaBoEE; NBM; OAEL-2; PoEL-4
("Language has not the power to speak what love indites.") ELU; OBNC
Fragment: "Locke sank into a swoon." W. B. Yeats. NoAM
Fragment: "Mark you how the peacock's eye." Gerard Manley Hopkins. FM
Fragment: "Mountain summits sleep, glens, cliffs, and caves, The." Alcman, *tr. fr. Greek by* Thomas Campbell. AWP
Fragment: "No use/ being angry at the dead." Bruce Berlind. FAZ
Fragment, A: "Not a drum was heard, not a funeral note." *Unknown.* FaBoPa
Fragment: "Pity, Religion has so seldom found." William Cowper. WGRP
Fragment: Rain. Shelley. ChER
(Rain.) POL
Fragment: "Repeat that, repeat." Gerard Manley Hopkins. *See* Cuckoo, The.
Fragment: "Some pretty face remembered in our youth." John Clare. VLP
Fragment: "Spruce and limber yellow-hammer, The." Samuel Taylor Coleridge. FM
("Spruce and limber yellowhammer, The." PBBP)
Fragment: "There is a river clear and fair." Catherine Fanshawe. *See* Fragment in Imitation of Wordsworth.
Fragment: "There pipes the wood-lark, and the song thrush there." Thomas Gray. FM
Fragment: To the Moon. Shelley. *See* To the Moon.
Fragment, The: "Towards the evening of her splendid day." Hilaire Belloc. POL
Fragment: "Walk with thy fellow-creatures: note the hush." Henry Vaughan. TRV; WGRP
Fragment: "What is poetry? Is it a mosaic." Amy Lowell. WGRP
Fragment from "Clemo Uti—the Water Lilies." Ring Lardner. FiBHP
Fragment from the Elizabethans. W. Bridges-Adams. FaBoCo
Fragment in Imitation of Wordsworth. Catherine Fanshawe. FaBoNo; FaBoPa; HBV-1
(Fragment: "There is a river clear and fair.") Par
(Fragments.) BXAP
(Imitation of Wordsworth, An.) NA
Fragment of a Character. Thomas Moore. FaBoCo
Fragment of a Greek Tragedy. A. E. Housman. CenHV; FaBoNo; NOBL; Par; SpRo
Fragment of a Love Lament. *Unknown.* OxBM
Fragment of a Pastoral. Barry Schwabsky. AMV-80
Fragment of a Song. "Lewis Carroll." FaBoNo
Fragment of a Song on the Beautiful Wife of Dr. John Overall. *Unknown.* BoLoP
Fragment of a Sonnet. Pierre de Ronsard, *tr. fr. French by* Keats. AWP
("Nature withheld Cassandra in the skies.") OBVE
Fragment of an Agon. T. S. Eliot. LiTB
Fragment of an Anti-Papist Ballad. *Unknown.* CoMu
Fragment of an Ode to Maia [Written on May Day, 1818]. Keats. EnRP; OAEL-2; OAEP; OBEV; OBRV; PoEL-4
Fragment of Death. Villon. *See* Fragment on Death.
Fragment of Sappho. *Unknown, tr. fr. Greek by* Ambrose Philips. OBEC
Fragment on Death, A. Villon, *tr. fr. French by* Swinburne. CTC
(Fragment of Death.) AWP
Fragment 113: "Not honey,/ not the plunder of the bee." Hilda Doolittle ("H. D."). *See* Not Honey.
Fragment Reflection I. Doris Turner. JB
Fragment Thirty-six: "I know not what to do." Hilda Doolittle ("H. D."). CMoP; OxBA; VGW
Fragmenti. Ezra Pound. PoA
Fragments. John Cotton. AMV-80
Fragments, The, *sel.* Peter Dale.
"Few ever came to help you speak or sell." NOCV
Fragments. Catherine Fanshawe. *See* Fragment in Imitation of Wordsworth.
Fragments. W. B. Yeats. PrIm

Fragments Intended for the Dramas, *sel.* Thomas Lovell Beddoes.
Beautiful Night, A. ChER; LoBV
(Lines: "How lovely is the heaven of this night.") NBM
Fragments of a Lost Gnostic Poem of the Twelfth Century. Herman Melville. NOBA; NoP; PoEL-5; ViBoPo
Fragments of Ancient Poetry, Collected in the Highlands of Scotland, *sel.* James MacPherson.
"I sit by the mossy fountain; on the top of the hill of winds." NOEC
Fragments on Nature and Life, *sel.* Emerson.
Atom from Atom. ImOP
Fragments on the Poet and the Poetic Gift, *sel.* Emerson.
"If bright the sun, he tarries." PP
Fragmentum Petronius Arbiter, Translated. Petronius Arbiter. *See* Doing, a Filthy Pleasure Is, and Short.
Fragoletta. Swinburne. UnTE
Fragoletta, blessed one! Songs for Fragoletta. Richard Le Gallienne. HBV-1
Fragrance of the red lotus fades, The. Poem to the Tune of "Yi chian mei." Li Ch'ing-chao, *tr. by* Marsha Wagner. DWPOW
Fragrant prayer upon the air, A. A Poem to Be Said on Hearing the Birds Sing. Biddy Crummy, *tr. fr. Gaelic by* Douglas Hyde. AnIV; AWP; WTO
Fragrant silence filled the purple air, A. The Rosary, *abr.* Sister Maura. ISi
Fragrant the grasses of high Kane-hoa. Anklet Song. *Tr. fr. Hawaiian by* N. B. Emerson. WTO
Fragrant Thy Memories. "Judah," *tr. fr. Hebrew by* Herbert Loewe. TrJP
Frail as the leaves that quiver on the sprays. Homer, *tr. by* Samuel Johnson. *Fr.* The Iliad, VI. OBVE
Frail children of sorrow, dethroned by a hue. Hope. Georgia Douglas Johnson. CDC
Frail Life! in which, through mists of human breath. Life and Death. Sir William Davenant. *Fr.* The Christian's Reply to the Philosopher. OBS
Frail scorched grasses are ripped now, The. Drought. Oumar Ba, *tr. by* Kathleen Weaver. PBWP
Frail Sleep, that blowest by fresh banks. To Sleep. Percy MacKaye. HBMV
Frail sound of a tunic trailing, A. Poems. Antonio Machado, *tr. by* John Dos Passos. AWP
Frail the white rose and frail are. A Flower Given to My Daughter. James Joyce. OBMV; PoPl
Frail, wistful guardian of the broom. The Sweeper. Agnes Lee. HBMV; QFR
Frailty, The. Abraham Cowley. CavP
Frailty. George Herbert. NOCV; OxBoCh
Frailty and Hurtfulness of Beauty, The. Earl of Surrey. *See* Brittle Beauty.
Frailty of Beauty, The. "J. C." *Fr.* Alcilia. ElL
Frailty, Thy Name Is Woman. Shakespeare. *Fr.* Hamlet, I, i. TrGrPo
(Hamlet Broods over the Death of His Father.) TreFS
("O! that this too too solid flesh would melt.") SCV
Frainchman he don't lak to die in de fall. On Meesh-e-gan. *Unknown.* TrAS
Frame it. Everyone lies, you say. Portrait in Available Light. Sara Miles. NYP
Framed in her phoenix fire-screen, Edna Ward. Cottage Street, 1953. Richard Wilbur. FaBoMo
Framed in the cavernous fire-place sits a boy. An Old Thought. Charles Henry Luders. AA
Framed Photograph, A. Allen Curnow. *Fr.* Trees, Effigies, Moving Objects. OCNZ
Framer of the earth and sky. Hymn. St. Ambrose. TrCP
Framework-Knitters Lamentation, The. *Unknown.* CoMu
Framework-Knitters Petition, The. C. Briggs. CoMu
France. Goldsmith. *Fr.* The Traveller. OBEC
France; an Ode. Samuel Taylor Coleridge. EnRP; OAEP
France! It is I answering. Republic to Republic. Witter Bynner. PAH
France Blues. *Unknown.* BluL
France. Cradle and abstraction. Wildfire. Judit Tóth, *tr. by* Emery George. VWA
Francesca and Paolo. Dante, *tr. by* Byron. *Fr.* Divina Commedia: Inferno, V. TreFT
Francesco's Fortunes, *sels.* Robert Greene.
Eurymachus's Fancy. OBSC
Penitent Palmer's Ode, The. LoBV; OBSC
Francis Beaumont's Letter from the Country to Jonson. Francis Beaumont. *See* Mr. Francis Beaumont's Letter to Ben Johnson.
Francis, my brother, in the clear, wide morning. Boy Playing an Organ. Francis Sweeney. GoBC
Francisco Coronado rode forth with all his train. Quivíra. Arthur Guiterman. BPAW; PAH
Frangipanni. *Unknown.* NA
Frank Albert and Viola Benzena Owens. Ntozake Shange. BlSi
Frank Baker's my name, and a bachelor I am. Starving to Death on a Government Claim. *Unknown.* BPAW
Frank Courtship, The, *sels.* George Crabbe. *Fr.* Tales.
"Grave Jonas Kindred, Sybil Kindred's sire." OBRV
Jonas Kindred's Household. FaBoEn; OBNC, *longer sel.*
Frank Drummer. Edgar Lee Masters. *Fr.* Spoon River Anthology. NoAM
Frank James, the Roving Gambler. *Unknown.* AmFP
Frank Sinatra. Michael Waters. GeTw
Frank, wilt live handsomely? Trust not too far. Advice to My Best Brother, Colonel Francis Lovelace. Richard Lovelace. CaPo
Frankeleyn was in his compaignye, A. Chaucer. *Fr.* The Canterbury Tales: Prologue. ViBoPo
Frankenstein. Edward Field. FF
Frankenstein Gets His Man. Frank Carr. AmMo
Frankie and Johnny [*or* Johnnie]. *Unknown.* AmFP; BeLS; BiP, *2 versions*; BLSo, *with music*; FaFP; FF; FSW; InPK; NIP; NOBA; OxBoLi; TrAS; TreF; TrGrPo; UnPo; YaD
(Frankie.) BluL
(Frankie and Albert, *with music.*) AS; BaBo (A *and* B *vers.*); ViBoFo (A *and* B *vers.*)
(Frankie Blues, *with music.*) AS
(Josie, *with music.*) AS
Frankie Silvers. Frances Silvers. AmFP
Frankie's Trade. Kipling. EtS
Franklin D. Roosevelt's Back Again. *Unknown.* FSW
Franklin Hyde. Hilaire Belloc. FaBoUs
Franklin's Prologue, The. Chaucer. *Fr.* The Canterbury Tales. OAEL-1
Franklin's Tale, The. Chaucer. *Fr.* The Canterbury Tales. OAEL-1; OAEP
Frankly, I prefer the blue. Sentimental Lines to a Young Man Who Favors Pink Wallpaper While I Personally Lean to the Blue. Margaret Fishback. FiBHP
Franz Kafka had a nightmare. Kafka's Other Metamorphosis. Len Gasparini. NeAC
Frascati's. Aldous Huxley. ViBoPo
Frater Ave atque Vale. Tennyson. ChTr; EBVV; FaBoPP; GTBS-P; HAP; InPS; NoP
Fraternitas. Confucius, *tr. fr. Chinese by* Ezra Pound. *Fr.* Deer Sing. CTC; OBVE
Fraternity. Anne Reeve Aldrich. AA
Fraternity. John Banister Tabb. HBV-2
Frau Bauman, Frau Schmidt, and Frau Schwartze. Theodore Roethke. CoAP; InPK; MoAB; NePoAm; NoAM; NOBA; NYBP; SaC; TAP
Frau Doktor/ Mama Brundig. The Frog Prince. Anne Sexton. DFT
Fraud, a forger, and informer, too, A. A Bad Joke. Martial, *tr. by* Louis Untermeyer. UnTE
Fraudulent Days. Michael Benedikt. PoA
Fraudulent perhaps in that they gave. Swans. Lawrence Durrell. MoBrPo; SeCePo
Fräulein Reads Instructive Rhymes. Maxine W. Kumin. NYBP; Psk; SpRo
Fray began at the middle-gate, The. A Ballad of Orleans. Agnes Mary Frances Robinson. HBV-2
Freak is the other, The. Celebrating the Freak. Cynthia Macdonald. Psk
Freaks at Spurgin Road Field, The. Richard Hugo. LCAP
Freaks of Fashion. Christina Rossetti. FM
Freckles numberless as stars on my forehead. My Portrait. Moishe-Leib Halpern, *tr. by* Joseph Leftwich. TrJP
Fred. David McCord. TiPo
Fred Apollus at Fava's. Nicholas Moore. ErPo; NeBP
"Fred, where is north?" West-running Brook. Robert Frost. AP; BLPL; MoAB; MoAmPo; NOBA; NoP
Freddy. Dennis Lee. RHPC
Frederick Alexander Pott. Time's Fool. John Updike. DBV
Frederick Douglass. Sam Cornish. PoBA
Frederick Douglass. Paul Laurence Dunbar. BALP; PoBA
Frederick Douglass. Robert Hayden. AmNP; BiP; CNA; GOA; GP; HoAn; IDB; PoBA; PoNe; TTY
Frederick Douglass: 1817-1895. Langston Hughes. BPo
Fredericksburg. Thomas Bailey Aldrich. PAH
Fredome. John Barbour. *See* Freedom.
Free America. *At. to* Joseph Warren. FSW; PAH
Free are the Muses, and where freedom is. Breath on the Oat. Joseph Russell Taylor. HBV-2; PAH
Free at Last. *Unknown.* *See* I Thank God I'm Free at Las'.
Free Enterprise. Charles Stetler. GP
Free evening fades, outside the windows fastened with decorative iron grilles, The. Evening in the Sanitarium. Louise Bogan. FYAP; IHMS; MP; SBG; TwCP
Free Fall. Don Gordon. AMV-81
Free Fantasia on Japanese Themes. Amy Lowell. MoAmPo
Free, free, I would run until. Prison Break. Michael Hogan. GP
Free Grace. Charles Wesley. NOCV

Free I have my own self-reliance. I Drift in the Wind. Ingrid Jonker, *tr. by* Jack Cope. PeSA; WPOW
Free Kirk, The. Eighteen-forty-three. *Unknown.* FaBoCo
Free Little Bird. *Unknown.* AmFP; FSW
Free Nation, A. Edwin Markham. TRV
Free One, A. W. H. Auden. *See* Watch Any Day.
Free Parliament Litany, A. *Unknown.* OxBoLi
Free Silver. *Unknown.* AmFP
Free thinker! Do you think you are the only thinker. Golden Lines. Gérard de Nerval, *tr. by* Robert Bly. NU
Free Thoughts on Several Eminent Composers. Charles Lamb. DBV; FaBoCo; OBRV; OxBoLi
Free Will. Walter Clark. NCSH
Free Woman, The. Theodosia Garrison. HBMV
Free woman, A. At last free! *Tr. fr. Pali by* Willis Barnstone. BoWoP
Freeborn Man. Ewan MacColl. OBET
Freeborn Pindaric never does refuse. A Pindaric on the Grunting of a Hog. Samuel Wesley. NOBL
Freed dove flew to the Rajah's tower, The. The Dove of Dacca. Kipling. GN
Freedom. John Barbour. *Fr.* The Bruce. BSV; FaBoCh; GoTS; OBEV; TrGrPo
("A! fredome is a noble thing!") ViBoPo
(Fredome.) OxBS
Freedom. Joel Barlow. PAL
Freedom. J. Charles Green. LFAC
Freedom. Langston Hughes. PoBA
Freedom. Abraham ibn Ezra, *tr. fr. Hebrew by* Solomon Solis-Cohen. TrJP
Freedom. *Unknown.* PGD
Freedom; a Poem, Written in Time of Recess from the Rapacious Claws of Bailiffs, *sel.* Andrew Brice.
Poet's Terror at the Bailiffs of Exeter, The. NOEC
Freedom and dignity have reached us. Independence. *Somali Oral Tradition, tr. by* B. W. Andrzejewski *and* I. M. Lewis. WTO
Freedom and Love. Thomas Campbell. BSV; GTBS; GTBS-P
(Song: "How delicious is the winning.") HBV-1
Freedom called them—up they rose. The Gallant Fifty-one. Henry Lynden Flash. PAH
Freedom, farewell! Or so the soldiers say. Port of Embarkation. Randall Jarrell. MiAP
Freedom for the Mind. William Lloyd Garrison. AA; FaBoBe
Freedom I never saw in words. After Bombardment. John Pudney. WaP
Freedom in Mah Soul. David Wadsworth Cannon, Jr. PoNe
Freedom Is a Constant Struggle. *Unknown.* FSW
Freedom is a dream. Dark Testament. Pauli Murray. BlSi
Freedom is a hard-bought thing. Song of the Settlers. Jessamyn West. FaPON
Freedom is more than a word, more than the base coinage. The *Nabara.* C. Day Lewis. OBNV
Freedom, New Hampshire. Galway Kinnell. LCAP; NaP
Freedom of Love. André Breton, *tr. fr. French by* Edouard Roditi. EAS
Freedom of the Hills. Douglas Fraser. PoSH
Freedom of the Moon, The. Robert Frost. MOON
Freedom Song for the Black Woman, A. Carole C. Gregory. BlSi
Freedom will not come. Freedom. Langston Hughes. PoBA
Freedom's first champion in our fettered land! Garrison. Amos Bronson Alcott. AA
Freely Espousing. James Schuyler. NeAP; NoP
Freely, from a Song Sung by Jewish Women of Yemen. Stephen Levy. VWA
Freely the dead bracken breaks to your stride. Argenteuil County. Peter Dale Scott. MoCV
Freeman, I treat tonight, and treat your friends. The Invitation. Leonard Welsted. NOEC
Freemon Hawthorne. Melvin B. Tolson. FAZ
Freethinkers. Deborah Eibel. VWA
Freeze Tag. Gordon Henry. STE
Freight Boats. James S. Tippett. FaPON
Freight Train, The. Rowena Bastin Bennett. PDV
Freight Train. *Unknown.* FSW
Freight train rolls, A. The Journey. Henry Johnson. LFAC
Freighter. Bruce Ruddick. CaP
Freighter, gay with rust, The. Jews at Haifa. Randall Jarrell. MoAmPo
Freighting from Wilcox to Globe. *Unknown.* AmFP; CoSo
Freiheit (Freedom). Karl Ernst *and* Peter Daniel, *tr. fr. German.* FSW
Freind! for your epitaphs I'm griev'd. Epigram on One Who Made Long Epitaphs. Pope. FaBoEE
French. Osbert Lancaster. *Fr.* Afternoons with Baedeker. FaBoCo; NOBL
French and Russian they matter not. A Chant of Hate against England. Ernst Lissauer, *tr. by* Barbara Henderson. HBV-2
French and the Spanish Guerrillas, The. Wordsworth. WaaP
(Sonnet: French and the Spanish Guerrillas, The.) ChER
French bus halts on the Plateau of Antiques, The. A Visit to Van Gogh. Charles Causley. PoCh
French Clock. Hortense Flexner. HBMV
French clocks struck two-thirty, and above, The. Under the Arc de Triomphe: October 17. Marilyn Hacker. PoA
French Cookery. Thomas Moore. *Fr.* The Fudge Family in Paris. OBRV
French, The, 1870-1871. *Unknown.* FaBoEE
French government, The—or maybe it was the English—placed. Birds in the Night. Luis Cernuda, *tr. by* Erskine Lane. PeHV
French guns roll continuously, The. The Iron Music. Ford Madox Ford. HBMV
French Lisette; a Ballad of Maida Vale. William Plomer. ErPo
French Mood, The. Abo Stoltzenberg, *tr. fr. Yiddish by* Gabriel Preil *and* Howard Schwartz. VWA
French Peasants. Monk Gibbon. NeIP; OxBI
French Revolution, The, *sel.* Blake.
Louis XVI. ChER
French Revolution as It Appeared to Enthusiasts at Its Commencement, The. Wordsworth. *See* Residence in France (Continued).
Frenchman's Ball, The, *with music.* *Unknown.* OuSiCo
Frenchmen sin in lechery. Robert Mannyng. *Fr.* Handlyng Synne. DBV
Frend, farly nocht; na caus is to complene. Gavin Douglas. *Fr.* Prologues to the Aeneid. OxBoCh
Frenzy. George Crabbe. *Fr.* Sir Eustace Grey. NOBE
Frequency of bumping, The. There Are in Such Moments. David I. Silverstein. AMV-80
Frère Jacques (Brother John). *Unknown, tr. fr. French.* FSW
Frere ther was, a wantowne and a merye, A. Chaucer. *Fr.* The Canterbury Tales: Prologue. BiP
Fresco-Sonnets to Christian Sethe. Heine, *tr. fr. German by* John Todhunter. AWP
Frescoes for Mr. Rockefeller's City. Archibald MacLeish. UnPo
Sels.
Burying Ground by the Ties, III. GOA; MoAmPo
Landscape as a Nude, I. AmPP; CMoP
Frescoes that crumble, marbles bullet-scarred. The Fault. Edward Lucie-Smith. NePoEA-2
Fresh Air. Kenneth Koch. CAPP; NeAP; NNaP; NoAM; PP
Fresh Air, The. Harold Monro. CH
Fresh bread on the table, pregnant, whole, A. Evening Bread. Jacob Glatstein, *tr. by* David G. Roskies *and* Hillel Schwartz. VWA
Fresh, bright bloom of the daffodils, The. April Fantasie. Ellen Mackay Hutchinson Cortissoz. AA
Fresh Cheese and Cream. Robert Herrick. UnTE
Fresh clad from heaven in robes of white. In My Own Album. Charles Lamb. OBRV
Fresh day cracks, goat's milkspurt. Six-forty-two Farm Commune Struggle Poem. Jay Leifer. MAT
Fresh from the dewy hill, the merry year. Song. Blake. EnRP
Fresh I'm cum fra Sandgate Street. Do Li A. *Unknown.* GBP
Fresh in the flush light gleam. The Sorrow of Unicume. Sir Herbert Read. BrPo; ChMP
Fresh light from a morning sky blocked through clouds. Light. Carol Coates. CaP
Fresh Morning, A. J. C. Squire. WhC
Fresh morning gusts have blown away all fear. Sonnet. Keats. EnRP
Fresh News from the Past. Marvin Bell. LCAP
Fresh Paint. Boris Pasternak, *tr. fr. Russian by* Babette Deutsch. PoPl; TrJP
Fresh palms for the Old Dominion! The Battle of Charlestown. Henry Howard Brownell. PAH
Fresh Spring. Elizabeth Daryush. QFR
Fresh Spring, the Herald of Love's Mighty King. Amoretti, LXX. Spenser. AWP; CABA; ChTr; ElL; FaBoEn; FF; HAP; HBV-1; NoP; OBEV; OBSC; SeCeV; ViBoPo
(Fresh Spring, the Herald.) LiTB
Fresh Start, The. Anna Wickham. ViBoPo
Fresh strewings allow. The Peter-Penny. Robert Herrick. CaPo
Fresh were the breathings of the nightborn gale. Wild Nature. Charles Newton. *Fr.* Stanzas. NOEC
Freshet springs from woodland cleft, The. Postscript to Die Schöne Müllerin. R. P. Lister. POL
Freshmen. Barry Spacks. NYBP
Fret not thyself because of evil doers. Bible, *O.T.* Psalm XXXVII, 1-4, 7. TreFT
Fretful ladybirds complain, The. The Ladybirds. Edward Lucie-Smith. BoAnP
Freud: Dying in London, He Recalls the Smoke of His Cigar Beginning to Sing. James Schevill. TAP
Friar and the Fair Maid, The. *Unknown.* *See* As I Lay Musing.
Friar and the Nun, The. *Unknown.* GBP

Friar Complains, A. *Unknown.* MeEL
(Friars' Retort, The.) OxBM
Friar in the Well, The. *Unknown.* *See* As I Lay Musing.
Friar Laurence's Cell. Shakespeare. *Fr.* Romeo and Juliet, II, vi. GoBC
Friar Lubin. Clement Marot, *tr. fr. French by* Longfellow. AWP; DBV
Friar of Orders Gray, The. John O'Keefe. OnYI; OxBI
Friar of Orders Gray [*or* Grey], The. *Unknown.* ACP; GoBC; HBV-2; NOEC; OBEC
Friar of Orders Grey, The. Dante Gabriel Rossetti. *See* Old Song Ended, An.
Friar of Orders Grey, The. Shakespeare. *See* How Should I Your True Love Know.
Friars. William Langland. *Fr.* The Vision of Piers Plowman. PPON
Friars' Enormities. *Unknown.* MeEL
Friars' Retort, The. *Unknown.* *See* Friar Complains, A.
Friday came and the circus was there. The Circus. Elizabeth Madox Roberts. FaPON; SoPo
Friday Evening. Julio Marzán. InW
Friday in Berkeley. Untitled I. Ishmael Reed. CNA
Friday Night. Kendrick Smithyman. OCNZ
Friday Night after Bathing. Stephen Levy. VWA
Friday night's dream on a Saturday told. Mother Goose. HBVY; TreF
Friday the Thirteenth. Allen Ginsberg. NNaP
Friday. Wet Dusk. Christopher Logue. OxBTC
Fridays, when I draw my pension. Betjeman at the Post Office. Stanley J. Sharpless. FaBoPa
Friend. Gwendolyn Brooks. CNA
Friend, A. Lionel Johnson. HBV-2
Friend, The. Marge Piercy. NMM
Friend, A. Marguerite Power. FaBoCo; FaFP
Friend, A. Santob de Carrion. *Fr.* Proverbios Morales. TrJP
Friend, A. W. D. Snodgrass. MAT
Friend!/ Poor, foolish blossom! Beauty. Peter Hille, *tr. by* Jethro Bithell. AWP
Friend/ Savior/ woman. Redemption. Stanley Cooperman. AMV-80
Friend Advises Me to Stop Drinking, A. Mei Yao Ch'en, *tr. fr. Chinese by* Kenneth Rexroth. HoPM
Friend and Lover. "Madeline Bridges." AA; HBV-1
Friend calls us, A. Six Years. Alice Bloch. PeHV
Friend Cato. Anna Wickham. MoBrPo
Friend Col and I, both full of whim. David Garrick. FaBoEE
Friend, coming in a friendly wise. If Any Be Pleased to Walk into My Poor Garden. Francis Daniel Pastorius. SCAP
Friend, don't be angry. Mirabai, *tr. fr. Hindi by* Willis Barnstone *and* Usha Nilsson. BoWoP
Friend drops me at Indian Cemetary, A. The Hemingway Syndrome. Adrian C. Louis. STE
Friend Hedylus' cloak is a sight to behold. Epigram: On Hedylus. Martial. PeHV
Friend, how can I meet my lord? Mirabai, *tr. fr, Hindi by* Willis Barnstone *and* Usha Nilsson. BoWoP
Friend, if the mute and shrouded dead. Love and Death. Catullus, *tr. by* H. W. Garrod. AWP
Friend in the Garden, A. Juliana Horatia Ewing. FaPON; OxBChV
Friend of Humanity and the Knife-Grinder, The. George Canning *and* John Hookham Frere. BXAP; FaBoCo; HBV-1; Par
(Knife-Grinder, The.) InMe
(Sapphics.) NOEC; OBEC
Friend of mine was married to a scold, A. All's Well That Ends Well. *Unknown.* FaFP
Friend of Ronsard, Nashe and Beaumont. On a Birthday. J. M. Synge. ChTr; GBL; OBMV
Friend of the Family, A. Louis Simpson. NNaP
Friend of the Fourth Decade, The. James Merrill. NYBP
Friend of the wise! and Teacher of the Good! To William Wordsworth. Samuel Taylor Coleridge. EnRP; OAEL-2
Friend of Two, A. Wilbur D. Nesbit. PoLF
Friend, on this scaffold Thomas More lies dead. Epigram. J. V. Cunningham. InPK; NePoAm
Friend, Ortho of Syracuse gives thee this charge. Ortho's Epitaph. Theocritus, *tr. by* Charles Stuart Calverley. FaBoEE
Friend Proclus, the world isn't a fantasy. Epistolary Briefs to Proclus. José I. de Diego Padró, *tr. by* Julio Marzán. InW
Friend sparrow, do not eat, I pray. Basho, *tr. fr. Japanese by* Curtis Hidden Page. AWP
Friend, though thy soul should burn thee, yet be still. The Truth. Archibald Lampman. CaP
Friend, when I think of your delicate feminine face. On the Death of an Acquaintance. Oscar Williams. *Fr.* Variations on a Theme. LiTA; NePA
Friend Who Just Stands By, The. B. Y. Williams. PoLF
Friend Who Never Came. William Stafford. FAZ
Friend, whose unnatural early death. An Elegy. David Gascoyne. FaBoTw; MP; TwCP
Friend writes me from the temperate zone, A. Termites. Charles G. Bell. NePoAm-2
Friend, you are grieved that I should go. Creeds. Karle Wilson Baker. HBMV; WGRP
Friend, you seem thoughtful. I not wonder much. A Sea Dialogue. Oliver Wendell Holmes. EtS; MOS; OBAL
Friendless and faint, with martyred steps and slow. Calvary. E. A. Robinson. MoAmPo; OFD; TreFS; WGRP
Friendless Blues, *with music.* Mercedes Gilbert. TrAS
Friendly Address, A. Thomas Hood. PoEL-4
Friendly Beasts, The. *Unknown.* FaPON; OnMSP; PChr; PoSC; SiSoSe; SoPo
Friendly cow all red and white, The. The Cow. Robert Louis Stevenson. BrPo; FaPON; FM; NTCP; OxBChV; SoPo; SUS; TiPo
Friendly Game of Football, A. Edward Dyson. CBAP
Friends. John Ashbery. LCAP
Friends. Abbie Farwell Brown. HBV-1; HBVY
Friends. Ray Durem. PoBA
Friends. Mary Goose. STE
Friends. A. E. Housman. SeCePo
Friends. Lionel Johnson. GoBC
Friends. E. V. Lucas. HBV-2
Friends. William Stafford. PPJ
Friends. W. B. Yeats. NoAM
Friends!/ I came not here to talk. Rienzi to the Romans. Mary R. Mitford. TreFS
Friends,/ you are lucky you can talk. Vidya, *tr. fr. Sanskrit by* Willis Barnstone. BoWoP
Friends and loves we have none, nor wealth, nor blest abode. The Seekers. John Masefield. HBV-2; WGRP
Friends Beyond. Thomas Hardy. CoBMV; EBVV; FaBoRV; GTBS-P; OBEV; OBVV; VLP
Friend's Burial, The. Whittier. OBVV
Friends Come. Lucille Clifton. GeTw
Friends Departed. Henry Vaughan. *See* They Are All Gone into the World of Light.
Friend's Greeting, A. Edgar A. Guest. BLPA; BLPL
Friends, my heart is half aweary. The Old Times Were the Best. James Whitcomb Riley. FaFP
Friends of the Muse, to you of right belong. The Strong Heroic Line. Oliver Wendell Holmes. AA
Friend's Passing, A. Barclay Sheaks. AMV-80
Friends, Romans, countrymen, lend me your ears. Antony's Oration [over Caesar's Body *or* I Come to Bury Caesar *or* Mark Antony addresses the Mob]. Shakespeare. *Fr.* Julius Caesar. FaPoR; LiTB; PoPl; TreF; TrGrPo; WHA
Friends said: about eight o'clock they used to come. Reports of Midsummer Girls. Richmond Lattimore. PCP
Friends, whom she lookt at blandly from her couch. William Savage Landor. *Fr.* Pericles and Aspasia: Myrtis. OBRV
Friendship. Robert Blair. *Fr.* The Grave. OBEC
Friendship. Hartley Coleridge. *See* To a Friend.
Friendship. Dinah Maria Mulock Craik. BLPA
Friendship. Katherine Mansfield. PeHV
Friendship, The. Robert Mezey. NaP
Friendship. Sadi, *tr. fr. Persian by* L. Cranmer-Byng. *Fr.* The Gulistan. AWP
Friendship. Shel Silverstein. NTCP
Friendship. Lucien Stryk. GP
Friendship Game, The. Pier Giorgio Di Cicco. AMV-81
Friendship in Perfection. Andrew Michael Ramsay. NOEC
Friendship is constant in all other things. Beauty Is a Witch. Shakespeare. *Fr.* Much Ado about Nothing, II, i. TrGrPo
Friendship Is Love without His Wings. Byron. TreFT
Friendship, like love, is but a name. The Hare with Many Friends. John Gay. *Fr.* Fables. HBV-1
Friendship's Mystery [to My Dearest Lucasia]. Katherine Philips. PeHV; ViBoPo
Frieze, A. John Peale Bishop. MoPo
Frigate Jones, the Pussyfooter. Kenneth Burke. OBAL
Frigate Pelican, The. Marianne Moore. InvP
Frightened/ by the sound of my own voice. Lawrence Ferlinghetti. *Fr.* A Coney Island of the Mind. NoAM; TAP
Frightened Face. Marion Strobel. HBMV
Frightened Flier Goes North, The. Judith Kazantzis. BrRo
Frightened Flower. William J. Harris. BOLo
Frightened Man, The. Louise Bogan. SBG
Frightened Ploughman, The. John Clare. PoEL-4
Frightening. Claudia Lewis. RHPC
Frigid and sweet her parting face. Emily Dickinson. PeHV
Fringed Gentian. Emily Dickinson. *See* God made a little gentian.

Fringed Gentians. Amy Lowell. FaPON
Fringèd vallance of your eyes advance, The. Song. Thomas Shadwell. ViBoPo
Fringed with coral, floored with lava. Christmas Island. Katharine Lee Bates. HBMV; HBVY
Fringes, The. Harris Lenowitz. VWA
Fringilla Melodia, The. Henry Beck Hirst. AA
Fringing cypress forests dim. Sassafras. Samuel Minturn Peck. AA
Frisbee. Rolfe Humphries. GrPl
Frisco, Denver, Memphis. My Own Brand. Art Cuelho. TAT
'Frisco Town. *Unknown.* BluL
Frisco Whistle Blues. *Unknown.* BluL
Frisco's Defi. H. S. Hooper. BPAW
Frisky as a lambkin. The Lovable Child. Emilie Poulsson. HBV-1; HBVY
Frithiof's Saga, *sels.* Esaias Tegner, *tr. fr. Swedish by* Longfellow.
Frithiof's Farewell. AWP
Frithiof's Homestead. AWP
Frog, The. Hilaire Belloc. FaBoBe; FaBV; FaPON; FiBHP; GoJo; HBV-2; InMe; MoShBr; NA; NTCP; OxBChV; RHPC
Frog, The. *Unknown.* MoShBr; NTCP; TreFT; WhC; YaD
Frog and the Crow, The. *Unknown.* GBP
Frog and the Golden Ball, The. Robert Graves. DFT; NoP
Frog and the Mouse, The. *Unknown.* *See* Frog Went a-Courtin'.
Frog embryos spin, The. Neural Folds. Lucille Day. SUW
Frog He Would a-Wooing Go, A. *Unknown.* *See* Frog Went a-Courtin'.
Frog Hunting. Peter Cooley. MAYP
Frog lay in the step-child's bed, The. The Wooing Frog. James Reeves. SO
Frog Prince, The. Robert Pack. DFT
Frog Prince. Phoebe Pettingell. DFT
Frog Prince, The. Anne Sexton. DFT
Frog Prince, The. Stevie Smith. DFT; HAP
Frog under you, A. The Wife. Denise Levertov. ErPo
Frog Went a-Courtin'. *Unknown.* BLPA; TrAS, *with music*
(Frog and the Mouse, The, *diff. vers.*) WiR
(Frog He Would a-Wooing Go, A, *diff. vers.*) OnMSP; OxNR
(Froggie Went a-Courting.) AmFP; BLSo, *with music;* FSW
(Mister Frog Went a-Courting, *with music.*) AS
Frog went walking one fine day, A. The Frog and the Mouse. *Unknown.* WiR
Frog Who Would Be an Ox, The. La Fontaine, *tr. fr. French by* Marianne Moore. NAWM-2
Frog will serenade, The. Serenade. Alan Britt. FAZ
Froggles. Don Marquis. *Fr.* Savage Portraits. HBMV
Frogs. Norman MacCaig. BoAnP
Frogs. Louis Simpson. BoAnP; InPS
Frogs and the serpents each had a football team, The. Cheers. Eve Merriam. LiSp
Frogs jump. Jump or Jiggle. Evelyn Beyer. SoPo; TiPo
Frogs' Singing-School, The. E. T. Carbell. SoPo
Frogs sit more solid. Frogs. Norman MacCaig. BoAnP
Frogs time out of mind, The. Aesop's Fable of the Frogs. La Fontaine, *tr. by* John Hookman Frere. OBVE
Frolic. "Æ." FaPON; MoBrPo
Frolic, A. Robert Herrick. FaBoEE
Frolic Mariners of Devon, The. William Browne. *Fr.* Britannia's Pastorals, II, Song III. ChTr
Frolic[k]some Farmer, The. *Unknown.* CoMu; UnTE
Frolicsome Parson Outwitted, The. *Unknown.* CoMu
From. Richard Terrill. AMV-81
From a Birch. P. Wolny. DFF
From a branch/ The bird called. The Bird. Max Michelson. TrJP
From a Brother Dreaming in the Rye. James Cunningham. JB
From a Bus. Malaika Ayo Wangara. NBP
From a Car-Window. Ruth Guthrie Harding. HBMV
From a Cheerful Alphabet. John Updike. FaBoCo
From a Childhood. Rainer Maria Rilke, *tr. fr. German by* C. F. MacIntyre. TrJP
From a Churchyard in Wales. *Unknown.* *See* This Spot.
From a city window, 'way up high. Motor Cars. Rowena Bennett. FaPON; SoPo; TiPo
From a Connecticut Newspaper. Levi Rockwell. FaBoUs
From a Correct Address in a Suburb of a Major City. Helen Sorrells. PAI; WPE
From a Diary. Frederick Morgan. NYP
From a distance, I watch. Practical Concerns. William J. Harris. PoBA
From a Full Heart. A. A. Milne. InMe
From a granite rib of rock off Viareggio. Off Viareggio. Kenneth Pitchford. CoPo
From a green sack on a green hill. Here and There. Jon Stallworthy. NoAM
From a high mountain I see how the banks of a river. The Banks of a River. Abraham Sutskever, *tr. by* Ruth Whitman. VWA
From a hillslope I look on the wet fields flattening before me. Daphne. Claire McAllister. TwAmPo
From a Hint in the Minor Poets. Samuel Wesley. OBEC
From a Lavatory Wall. *Unknown.* FaBoEE
From a Letter from Lesbia. Dorothy Parker. DBV
From a Litany. Mark Strand. PPP
From a London Bookshop. *Unknown.* FaBoUs
From a magician's midnight sleeve. Late Air. Elizabeth Bishop. PoPl
From a Marriage Broker's Card, 1776. *Unknown.* FaBoUs
From a Munster vale they brought her. The Dying Girl. Richard D'Alton Williams. OnYI
From a Museum Man's Album. John Hewitt. OxBTC
From a place I came. Two Invocations of Death, II. Kathleen Raine. OxBTC
From a poverty-shadowed life. Imagined Happiness. Erik Axel Karlfeldt, *tr. by* Charles Wharton Stork. PoPl
From a Printed Bill, Fixed in the Beak of One in a Group of Five Stuffed Owls in the Shop Window of a Bird Stuffer, at Richmond, Yorkshire. *Unknown.* FaBoUs
From a Railway Carriage. Robert Louis Stevenson. FaPON; OxBChV; PDV; RHPC; TiPo
From a Rise of Land to the Sea. Roald Hoffmann. SUW
From a ruler that's a curse. The Litany. Charles Cotton. OBSV
From a Street Corner. Eleanor Hammond. HBMV
From a Survivor. Adrienne Rich. GP; PAI
From a Tobacco Wrapper. *Unknown.* FaBoUs
From a Trench. Maud Anna Bell. SUMH
From a Venetian Sequence. Adèle Naudé. PeSA
From a Very Little Sphinx. Edna St. Vincent Millay. OBAL
From "A Vigo-Street Eclogue." Sir Owen Seaman. WhC
From a village up the Hudson. The Dark Girl Dressed in Blue. *Unknown.* BeLS
From a vision red with war I awoke and saw the Prince of Peace. The New Day. Fenton Johnson. BANP
From a Window in Princes Street. W. E. Henley. EBVV
From a Woman to a Greedy Lover. Norman Cameron. Three Love Poems, I. ELU; FaBoEE; GTBS-P
From a wreck of tree in the wash of night. Speak with the Sun. David Campbell. SeCePo
From across the stream, on the side of the opposite hill. Not Seeing Is Believing. Paul Petrie. TAP
From Age to Age They Gather, *with music.* Frederick Lucian Hosmer. AH
From all my ancestors. Greeting Descendants. A. G. Sobin. FAZ
From all my lame defeats and oh! much more. The Apologist's Evening Prayer. C. S. Lewis. TrCP
From All Peoples, *sel.* Nathan Alterman, *tr. fr. Hebrew by* Simon Halkin.
"When our children cried in the shadow of the gallows." TrJP
From All That Dwell below the Skies. Isaac Watts. EBCP; TRV
From all the jails the boys and girls. Emily Dickinson. GLGT
From All These Events. Stephen Spender. LiTB
From almost naught to almost all I flee. On the Calculus. J. V. Cunningham. QFR
From America. James M. Whitfield. BPo
From an Asylum; Kathy Chattle to Her Mother, Ruth Arbeiter. Anne Stevenson. BrRo
From an Irish-Latin Macaronic. Geoffrey Taylor. NeIP
From an Old House in America. Adrienne Rich. NNaP
From an old man. Dusk. Ken Belford. NeAC
From an old photo. The Chauffeur of Lilacs. George Hitchcock. GP
From ancient Edens long forgot. A White-Throat Sings. Walter Prichard Eaton. HBMV
From Ancient Fangs. Peter Viereck. LiTA; MiAP
From Another Room. Gregory Corso. NeAP
From Arranmore the weary miles I've come. Mavrone. Arthur Guiterman. BXAP; FiBHP; InMe; SpRo
From Battle Clamour. Samuele Romanelli, *tr. fr. Hebrew by* Nina Davis Salaman. TrJP
From behind the Bars, *sel.* Fadwa Tuqan, *tr. fr. Arabic by* Hatem Hossaini.
From the Diary of ——. WPOW
From being anxious, or secure. John Donne. *Fr.* The Litany. OxBoCh
From Belsen a crate of gold teeth. Riddle. William Heyen. GP
From Bethlehem Blown. Mary Sinton Leitch. PGD
From Bethlehem to Calvary. Meredith Nicholson. PGD
From Beyond. Lucia Trent. PGD
From beyond the wooded island. Stenka Razin. *Unknown, tr. fr. Russian.* FSW
From bill to breast a snake. Swan. Edward Lowbury. GTBS-P
From blacked-out streets. Crystal Night. Denise Levertov. *Fr.* During the Eichmann Trial. NMP
From body's self the body. Body's Freedom. Helen Neville. NePA

From Braddon's penniless subornation. A New Litany in the Year 1684. *Unknown.* APAS
From breasts/ Of Africland. Africland. Oliver LaGrone. FB
From British novels a thrill I get. Britannia Rules of Orthography. "Firth." InMe; WhC
From Brooklyn over the Brooklyn Bridge, on this fine morning. Invitation to Miss Marianne Moore. Elizabeth Bishop. MoVE; TwAmPo
From Bulgaria thick, wild cannon pounding rolls. Picture Postcards. Miklós Radnóti, *tr. by* Emery George. VWA
From Burton the Anatomist. Maurice James Craig. NeIP
From buses beached like an invasion fleet. Port Authority Terminal: 9 A.M. Monday. Chad Walsh. PPON
From Calpe's rock, with loss of leg. The Soldier That Has Seen Service. *Unknown.* NOEC
From camp to camp, through the foul womb of night. Before Agincourt. Shakespeare. *Fr.* King Henry V, *prologue to* Act IV. ChTr
From cavities of bones. From the Cavities of Bones. Patricia Parker. BlSi
From Childhood's Hour. Poe. NePA; PoEL-4
From Citron-Bower. Hilda Doolittle ("H. D."). AP
From Clee to heaven the beacon burns. 1887. A. E. Housman. CoBMV; FaPoR; NIP; PrIm; UnPo; VLP
From Colony to Nation. Irving Layton. CABA; NOBC
From Countless Hearts, *with music.* Gail Brook Burket. AH
From Country to Town. Hartley Coleridge. *See* 'Tis Strange to Me.
From Creature to Ghost. Pauline Hanson. TAP
From dark the striped muscles sprang. "God's First Creature Was Light." Winifred Welles. ImOP
From darkness/ I go onto the road/ of darkness. Izumi Shikibu, *tr. fr. Japanese by* Willis Barnstone. BoWoP
("From darkness/ Into the path of darkness," *tr. by* Edwin A. Cranston.) PBWP
From darkness into darkness. Hoot Owl Shift. Robert Stricklin. AMV-80
From dawn to dark they stood. "Our Left." Francis Orrery Ticknor. PAH
From day to day/ The calcium in our cells grows less and less. Leningrad: 1943. Vera Inber, *tr. by* Dorothea Prall Radin *and* Alexander Kaun. *Fr.* The Pulkovo Meridian. WaaP
From deep sleep. Nightmare. James A. Emanuel. BPo
From [*or* Ffrom] depth of sin and from a deep despair. Psalm CXXX, *par. by* Sir Thomas Wyatt. NOCV; OBVE
From Disciple to Master. Monk Gibbon. AnIV
From dollars to T-shirts. World's Fare. Charles Stetler. GP
From Drogheda all along the coast, the Irish sea. Back to Dublin. R. A. D. Ford. CaP; MoCV
From Dublin soon to London spread. Swift. *Fr.* Verses on the Death of Doctor Swift. ViBoPo; WHA
From dusk till dawn the livelong night. Betsy's Battle Flag. Minna Irving. PAH
From Dust I rise. Thomas Traherne. *Fr.* The Salutation. FaBoEn
From earliest schooldays. Natural History. Laura Fargas. SUW
From east and south the holy clan. The Bishop of Rum-ti-Foo. W. S. Gilbert. CenHV
From Eastertide to Eastertide. A Ballad of a Nun. John Davidson. BeLS; HBMV; MoBrPo; OnMSP
From England to California I went. Roll, *Julia,* Roll. *Unknown.* ShS
From eve to morn, from morn to parting night. On His Own Agamemnon and Iphigeneia. Walter Savage Landor. OBRV
From every quarter came the night confounding. Burial at Sea. E. J. Pratt. *Fr.* The *Roosevelt* and the *Antinoe.* CaP
From fair Jamaica's fertile plains. Lines. "Ada." BlSi
From fairest creatures we desire increase. Sonnets, I. Shakespeare. CTC; FaBoEn; LiTB; MasP; OAEP; OBSC; TrGrPo
From falsehood and error. A Prayer. Digby Mackworth Dolben. GoBC
From Far Away. Delmira Agustini, *tr. fr. Spanish by* D. M. Pettinella. PBWP
From Far Away. William Morris. OHIP
From far away. Waking on a Greyhound. Gordon Henry. STE
From far away, from far away. My Letter. Grace Denio Litchfield. AA
From far away we come to you. From Far Away. William Morris. OHIP
From Far, from Eve and Morning. A. E. Housman. A Shropshire Lad, XXXII. CMoP; HAP; HeIP; MoBrPo; NBM; NoP; PoEL-5; PrIm
From far she watched his wanderings, and sighed. Seven Sad Sonnets, IV. Mary Aldis. HBMV
From far she's come, and very old. Age in Youth. Trumbull Stickney. NCEP
"From fear to fear, successively betrayed." Reflection from Rochester. William Empson. PoA
From Feathers to Iron, *sels.* C. Day Lewis.
Now She Is like the White Tree-Rose. CMoP; FaBoTw; MoBrPo
"Now the full-throated daffodils." ViBoPo
Though Bodies Are Apart. NAs
From Fortune's frowns and change removed. Old Damon's Pastoral. Thomas Lodge. OBSC
From '41 to '51. John Masefield. *Fr.* The Everlasting Mercy. NoAM
From Four Lakes' Days. Richard Eberhart. MiAP
From France, desponding and betray'd. On the British Invasion. Philip Freneau. PAH
From frozen climes, and endless tracts of snow. A Winter-Piece [*or* To the Earl of Dorset]. Ambrose Philips. LoBV; NOEC; OBEC; SeCePo
From gallery-grave and the hunt of a wren-king. W. H. Auden. *Fr.* Thanksgiving for a Habitat. EyDe
From garden to garden, ridge to ridge. John Muir. RFM
From Garvey's Farm: Seneca, Wisconsin. Ed Hoeppner. AMV-80
From Generation to Generation. William Dean Howells. AA
From Generation to Generation. Sir Henry Newbolt. FaBoTw
From Gestures to the Dead. John Wheelwright. MoVE
From ghoulies and ghosties. Litany for Halloween [*or* Ghoulies and Ghosties *or* Things That Go Bump in the Night]. *Unknown.* NTCP; OFD; PoSC; ShM; SiSoSe; SoPo; WSC
From giant oaks, that wave their branches dark. Vegetable Loves. Erasmus Darwin. *Fr.* The Botanic Garden: The Loves of the Plants. OBEC; SeCePo
From Gloucester Out. Edward Dorn. CoPo; NoAM; NOBA; PoM
From God's lofty City/ my Lady looks down. Lady of Lidice. Fray Angelico Chavez. ISi
From gods of other men, fastidious heart. False Gods. Walter de la Mare. EaLo
From going always over bars his glance. The Panther. Rainer Maria Rilke, *tr. by* Paul Engle. PoPl
From golden dawn to purple dusk. The March of Humanity. J. Corson Miller. HBMV
From gorge to gorge. Elena Clementelli, *tr. by* Ruth Feldman and Brian Swann. *Fr.* Etruscan Notebook. PBWP
From Government Buildings. Denis Devlin. IPY
From Grant's grave Galena. Old Dubuque. Dave Etter. AmFN
From Greenland to Iceland. *Unknown.* FaFP
From Greenland's Icy Mountains. Reginald Heber. FaPoR; HBV-2; TreF; VLP; WGRP
From groves of spice. Cradle Song. Sarojini Naidu. FaPON
From Halifax station a bully there came. Halifax Station. *Unknown.* PAH
From harmony, from heavenly [*or* heav'nly] harmony. A Song for St. Cecilia's Day, 1687. Dryden. AWP; BiP; CABA; FaBoEn; GoBC; GTBS; GTBS-P; HAP; HBV-2; InPS; LiTB; MasP; OAEL-1; OAEP; OBEV; PoEL-3; PPP; SeCV-2; TEP; TreFT; TrGrPo; UnS, *abr.*
From Heals and Harrods come her lovely bridegrooms. Made in Heaven. Peter Porter. PPON
From heart through mind into image. The Past. William Oandasan. STE
From Heart to Heart, *with music.* William Channing Gannett. AH
(Stream of Faith, The.) WGRP
From Heaven High I Come to You. *At. to* Martin Luther, *tr. fr. German.* PChr
From heaven his spirit came, and robed in clay. The Soul of Dante. Michelangelo, *tr. by* John Addington Symonds. GoBC
From Heaven's Gate to Hampstead Heath. The Ballad of Hampstead Heath. James Elroy Flecker. MoBrPo
From heaven's high embrasure. A Frosty Morning. John Davidson. VLP
From heavy dreams fair Helen rose. William and Helen. Sir Walter Scott. EnRP; OAEP
From her bed's high and odoriferous roome. Homer, *tr. by* George Chapman. *Fr.* The Odyssey, IV. CTC
From her pool in the muddy shallows. Pregnant Teenager on the Beach. Mary Balazs. AMV-80
From Heraclitus. Alan Dugan. PoA
From here, boulders are pebbles. Looking Down a Hill. A. R. Thompson. PoSH
From here through tunnelled gloom the track. The Railway Junction. Walter de la Mare. ChMP; OxBTC
From Here to There. Rachel Korn, *tr. fr. Yiddish by* Seymour Mayne *and* Rivka Augenfeld. VWA
From here to there/ To Washington Square. *Unknown.* OxNR
From high windows. Shabbat Morning. Bradley R. Strahan. AMV-81
From his brimstone bed at break of day. The Devil's Thoughts [*or* The Devil's Walk]. Robert Southey *and* Samuel Taylor Coleridge. FaBoCo; OBSV; OxBoLi; PV
From his garden bed our Lord. The Harvesting of the Roses. Menahem ben Jacob. TrJP
From his library in Surrey. Nothing Sacred. Roger Woddis. NOBL
From his pouch he took his colors. Longfellow. *Fr.* The Song of Hiawatha. EyDe
From his shoulder Hiawatha. Hiawatha's Photographing. "Lewis Carroll." BXAP; CenHV; FaBoCo; FaBoPa; FiBHP; NOBL; SpRo
From his small city Columbus. Voyage. Josephine Miles. LiTM

From his wanderings far to eastward. Longfellow. *Fr.* The Song of Hiawatha. GOA
From hollows of a tree. Fable of the Speckled Cow. D. J. Opperman, *tr. by* Jack Cope, Uys Krige, *and* Ruth Miller. PeSA
From holy flower to holy flower. The Study of a Spider. Lord De Tabley. VLP
From Holy, Holy, Holy ones. The Lancashire Puritane. *Unknown.* CoMu
From hoofbeat to chug-chug to roar of jet. Progress. Suzanne Douglass. QQQ
From hunting whores and haunting play. A Letter to Lord Middleton. Sir George Etherege. CavP
From immaculate construction to half death. The Man from the Top of the Mind. David Wagoner. NePoEA-2
From inland ledges I had dreamed this bay. At the Battery Sea-Wall. Clifford James Laube. GoYe
From inside nothing is plausible. Late Autumn Walk. J. D. McClatchy. AMV-80
From inside the bird a dream hums itself out and turns. These Horses Came. Ray A. Young Bear. CDW
From its dancers circulates among the other/dancers. The Dance. Robert Duncan. NeAP
From ivory towers they come. Soul. Austin Black. NBP
From Java, Sumatra, and old Cathay. A Ship Comes In. Oliver Jenkins. EtS
From Jerusalem: A First Poem. Gabriel Preil, *tr. fr. Hebrew by* Robert Friend. VWA
From keel to fighting top, I love. Manila Bay. Arthur Hale. PAH
From Killybegs to Ardara is seven Irish miles. A Road of Ireland. Charles L. O'Donnell. HBMV
From Le Havre. Charles G. Bell. NePoAm
From learned Florence, long time rich in fame. The Earl of Surrey to Geraldine. Michael Drayton. OBSC
From left to right, she leads the eye. Myth on Mediterranean Beach: Aphrodite as Logos. Robert Penn Warren. HAP; WeW
From Lewis, Monsieur Gérard came. Yankee Doodle's Expedition to Rhode Island. *Unknown.* PAH
From Life. Lazer Eichenrand, *tr. fr. Yiddish by* Gabriel Preil *and* Howard Schwartz. VWA
From Life. Brian Hooker. HBV-1
From life's grim nightmare he is now released. Jacob Epstein. *Unknown.* FaBoCo
From Lois in London. Angela McCabe. AmPA
From loud sound and still chance. Baroque Comment. Louise Bogan. CrMA
From low to high doth dissolution climb. Mutability. Wordsworth. *Fr.* Ecclesiastical Sonnets. CABA; EBEV; EnRP; HeIP; InPK; LiTB; NOBE; NoP; OAEL-2; OBEV; OBRV; PoEL-4; PrIm; SeCeV
From many a field with patriot blood imbrued. Decoration Day. George Hurlbut Barbour. OHIP
From Matlock Bath's half-timbered station. Matlock Bath. John Betjeman. NYBP
From mental mists to purge a nation's eyes. George Canning *and* John Hookham Frere. *Fr.* New Morality. NOEC
From Mexico there's just come a strange new decree. De Mexico Ha Venido. *Unknown.* TrAS
From mighty wrongs to petty perfidy. Fame. Byron. *Fr.* Childe Harold's Pilgrimage. FiP
From Mistra: A Prospect. Ted Higgs. AMV-80
From Mobberley on a bright morning, on a snow-white pure-bred mare. The Wizard of Alderley Edge. Peter Coe. OBET
From moccasins to shoes. First Grade. Phillip William George. VoR
From Montauk Point. Walt Whitman. RFM
From moonwater, from mirror mist, a slender porcelain. Gift Hour. Maria Banus, *tr. by* Willis Barnstone *and* Matei Calinescu. BoWoP; VWA
From morn to [*or* till] midnight, all day through. Expectans Expectavi. Charles Hamilton Sorley. FaBoCh; HBMV; WGRP
From Mount Nebo. Karl Wolfskehl, *tr. fr. German by* Erna Baber Rosenfeld. VWA
From mountains covered deep with snow. Chipeta's Ride. John W. Taylor. PoOW
From My Arm-Chair. Longfellow. BLPA
From my city bed in the dawn. SF. Earnest Leverett. QQQ
From my couch I rise, afire. Fire and Ice. Michael Pettit. MAYP
From My Diary, July 1914. Wilfred Owen. CoBMV; FaBoMo; LiTM; MoAB; MoBrPo
From my father's head I sprung. Athene's Song. Eavan Boland. CIP
From my first city bed in the dawn I see a raccoon. Science Fiction. Reed Whittemore. GP
From my front wheels the scared rabbits. Iowa, June. Michael Dennis Browne. AmPA
From my grief on Fál's proud plain I sleep. Geoffrey Keating, *tr. by* Padraic Pearse. *Fr.* My Grief on Fál's Proud Plain. OnYI
From my head this bubble labeled "Love." Look. William Stafford. FAZ
From My High Love. Kenneth Patchen. MoAmPo
From my hill I look down on the freeway and over. All the Way from There to Here. Jack Gilbert. NPGG
From My Lai the Thunder Went West. Richard Ryan. CIP
From my mother, the antique mirror. Heritage. Linda Hogan. TWSS
From My Mother's Home. Leah Goldberg. *See* My Mother's House.
From my mother's sleep I fell into the State. The Death of the Ball Turret Gunner. Randall Jarrell. AP; BiP; CMoP; CoBMV; ELU; FF; HAP; HoPM; InPK; LCAP; LiTM; MiAP; MoAmPo; NAs; NIP; NMP; NoAM; NOBA; NoP; OBWP; OxBA; PAI; PoPl; PPP; PrIm; SeCeV; SoSe; TAP; UnPo; VGW; WaaP; WaP
From my personal album. For Malcolm X. Nanina Alba. PoBA
From My Rural Pen. T. S. Watt. FiBHP
From My Thought. Daniel Smythe. GoYe
From my wind-blown book I look. Spring. W. R. Rodgers. AnIL
From My Window. Mary Elizabeth Coleridge. OBNC
From My Window. C. K. Williams. SV
From my window, facing South. The Autumn House. George M. Brady. OnYI
From my years young in dayes of youth. Epitaphium Meum. William Bradford. SCAP
From mysteries of the Past. To the Modern Man. John Hall Wheelock. HBMV
From near the sea, like Whitman my great predecessor, I call. Ode: Salute to the French Negro Poets. Frank O'Hara. NeAP; NNaP; PoM; PoNe
From noise of scare-fires rest ye free. The Bellman. Robert Herrick. CaPo; CH; PoPle
From Now On. *Unknown.* BluL
From now on kill America out of your mind. Millions Are Learning How [*or* Lyric]. James Agee. GOA; PoPl
From Number Nine, Penwiper Mews. Edward Gorey. *See* Number Nine, Penwiper Mews.
From Oberon, in fairy land. Robin Goodfellow. *Unknown.* FaBoCh; ViBoPo
From off a hill whose concave wombe reworded. A Lover's Complaint. Shakespeare. NCEP
From off his pointed head flies Herr Schmidt's hat. End of the World. Jakov van Hoddis, *tr. by* Edouard Roditi. VWA
From old Fort Walla Walla and the Klickitats. In the Oregon Country. William Stafford. AmFN
From One of Case's Pill-Boxes. John Case. FaBoUs
From one shaft at Cleator Moor. Cleator Moor. Norman Nicholson. FaBoTw; NeBP
From One Who Stays. Amy Lowell. BoWoP
From Orford Ness to Shingle Street. Dawn on the East Coast. Alun Lewis. OBWP
From Our Album. Lawson Fusao Inada. AmPA
From our hidden places. The Others. "Seumas O'Sullivan." AnIV; HBMV; OxBI
From our loves, heat and light are taught to twine. Mutual Love. William Hammond. JCP
From our low seat beside the fire. The Call. Charlotte Mew. ChMP
From Our Master. Whittier. WGRP
From out a book into my lap. A Withered Rose. "Yehoash," *tr. by* Isidore Goldstick. TrJP
From out Cologne there came three kings. The Three Kings. Eugene Field. GN
From out his castle on the sand. The Sea-King. L. Frank Tooker. EtS
From out my deep, wide-bosomed West. Rejoice. Joaquin Miller. PAH
From out of a wood did a cuckoo fly. The Birds. *Unknown.* PChr
From out of our/ dwellings have I heard. Desert Stone. Miriam Waddington. VWA
From out of the North-land his leaguer he led. Saint Leger. Clinton Scollard. PAH
From out the dragging vastness of the sea. Convalescence. Amy Lowell. SUMH
From out the South the genial breezes sigh. The Mother. *Unknown, tr. by* George Barrow. OHIP
From out the stormy sea unto the shore. Epitaph. Azariah di Rossi, *tr. by* A. B. Rhine. TrJP
From Paumanok Starting I Fly like a Bird. Walt Whitman. GOA
From Pembroke's princely dome, where mimic Art. Sonnet: Written after Seeing Wilton-House. Thomas Warton, the Younger. OBEC
From Pent-up Aching Rivers. Walt Whitman. AP; BoLoP; CABA; NOBA; ViBoPo
From pitch and catch. Fungo. Stanley Plumly. AmPA
From plains that reel to southward, dim. Heat. Archibald Lampman. CaP; NOBC; OBCV; PeCV
From Plane to Plane. Robert Frost. MoAmPo
From pleasure of the bed. The Chambermaid's Second Song. W. B. Yeats. ErPo

From plum-tree and cherry. Flowering Currant. Patrick MacDonogh. ErPo
From point A a wind is blowing to point B. After the Broken Arm. Ron Padgett. ConAP; EAS
From Potomac to Merrimac. Edward Everett Hale. PAH
From prayer that asks that I may be. Deliver Me [*or* Flame of God]. Amy Carmichael. STF
From prehistoric distance, beyond clocks. Street Fight. Harold Monro. FaBoTw
"From public noise and factious strife." To a Young Gentlemen in Love; a Tale. Matthew Prior. TEP
From Romany to Rome. Wallace Irwin. HBV-1
From Rome, for More Public Fountains in New York City. Alan Dugan. NYP; Prf
From Russian Hill. Ina Coolbrith. BPAW
From St. Luke's Hospital. Madeleine L'Engle. CTBA
From Sand Creek, *sel.* Simon J. Ortiz.
"At the Salvation Army." STE
From Santiago, spurning the morrow. The Destroyer of Destroyers. Wallace Rice. PAH
From Sappho to myself, consider the fate of women. Pro Femina, I. Carolyn Kizer. NMM
From Sappho's Death: Three Pictures by Gustave Moreau. T. Sturge Moore. SyP
From scars where kestrels hover. Missing. W. H. Auden. OxBTC
From Sebek's dark waters. Canopic Jar. Rika Lesser. MAYP
From seeing and seeing the seeing has become so exhausted. The Panther. Rainer Maria Rilke, *tr. by* Robert Bly. NU
From Sex, This Sea. D. G. Jones. NOBC
From shadows of rich oaks outpeer. The Pike. Edmund Blunden. LiTM; MoVE
From shores of Senegal, from Lake Omandaba. O My Swallows! Ernst Toller, *tr. by* Ashley Dukes. TrJP
From six o'clock I traversed to and fro. Verses to Miss ———. J. Wilde. NOEC
From Skye, Early Autumn. M. L. Michal. PoSH
From Soil Somehow the Poet's Word. Kenneth Leslie. OBCV
From some sweet home, the morning train. The School Girl. William Henry Venable. AA
From something in the trees. For the New Year. Robert Creeley. NaP
From stainless steel basins of water. The Operation. W. D. Snodgrass. InPK; TAP
From Stirling Castle we had seen. Yarrow Unvisited. Wordsworth. EnRP; GTBS; GTBS-P; HBV-2; PoRA
From Stone to Steel ("From stone to bronze, from bronze to steel"). E. J. Pratt. NoP; PeCV
From such old boards. "Dangerous Condition": Sign on Inner-City House. Russell Atkins. CNA
From summer and the wheel-shaped city. Washington Cathedral. Karl Shapiro. MiAP
From Sunset to Star Rise. Christina Rossetti. SBG
From Susquehanna's farthest springs. The Indian Student; or, Force of Nature. Philip Freneau. OxBA
From that blest bed the hero came. Andrew Marvell. *Fr.* Upon Appleton House, to My Lord Fairfax. JCP
From that first flash when awful Love took flame. Sonnet IV. Louise Labé, *tr. by* Willis Barnstone. BoWoP
From that first night. Izumi Shikibu, *tr. fr. Japanese by* Edwin A. Cranston. PBWP
From that high apple-tree, my love. The Apple Tree. James K. Baxter. OxBC
From that last acre on oblivion's heap. Edna St. Vincent Millay Exhorts Little Boy Blue. Louis Untermeyer. *Fr.* Mother Goose Up-to-Date. MoAmPo
From that they found most lovely, most abhorred. Beginning. Alden Nowlan. NeAC; NOBC
From the afterbirth of your bitterness. As All Things Pass. Diana Bickston. LFAC
From the Antique. Christina Rossetti. EnLoPo
From the Arabic; an Imitation. Shelley. HBV-1; OBEV
From the back it looks like a porch. For Esther. Stanley Plumly. LCAP
From the balcony you watched her walking. Memory, a Small Brown Bird. Rich Ives. AMV-81
From the Ballad of Evil. N. P. Van Wyk Louw, *tr. fr. Afrikaans by* Anthony Delius. PeSA
From the Ballad of Two-Gun Freddy. Walter R. Brooks. SoPo
From the bathing machine came a din. Edward Gorey. OBAL
From the Batter's Box. David K. Harford. AMV-80
From the besieged Ardea all in post. The Rape of Lucrece. Shakespeare. BeLS
From the Brothers Grimm to Sister Sexton to Mother Goose; One Transmogrification. David Cummings. BXAP
From the *Caledonian Mercury.* Gavin Wilson. FaBoUs
From the cassowary's beak come streaks of light. Morning at Arnheim. William Jay Smith. NePoEA
From the Cavities of Bones. Patricia Parker. BlSi
From the center of the room to the center. Fish. Mario Satz, *tr. by* Willis Barnstone. VWA
From the center of the Sea of Tranquility. The Planet. Josephine Jacobsen. GP
"From the colour the nature." Ezra Pound. Cantos, XC. VGW
From the commandant's quarters on Westchester height. Aaron Burr's Wooing. Edmund Clarence Stedman. PAH
From the Commonwealth. Sandra Maria Esteves. LTB
From the confusion of estranging years. For Elizabeth Madox Roberts. Janet Lewis. QFR
From the converts in Uganda. Grass on the Prayer Path. *Unknown.* PeD
From the Country to the City. Elizabeth Bishop. CrMA; NYP
From the Crag. Mani Leib, *tr. fr. Yiddish by* David G. Roskies *and* Hillel Schwartz. VWA
From the crowded belfry calling. Bega. Majorie Pickthall. CaP
From the dark mood's control. The Recovery. Edmund Blunden. MoBrPo
From the dark Stygian banks I come. Marvell's Ghost. John Ayloffe. APAS
From the Dark Tower. Countee Cullen. BALP; BANP; BPo; CDC; IDB; LiTM; PoBA; PoNe
From the dark woods that breathe of fallen showers. The Zebras. Roy Campbell. LiTB; MoBrPo; PoPle; PrIm; ViBoPo
From the dark yard by the sheep barn the cock crowed. The Henyard Round. Donald Hall. Psk
From the Day-Book of a Forgotten Prince. Jean Starr Untermeyer. HBMV
From the deepest part of a dream the escaped. Doorway to Time in Three Voices. Luis Palés Matos, *tr. by* Rachel Benson. InW
From the depth of the dreamy decline of the dawn through a notable nimbus of nebulous moonshine. Nephelidia. Swinburne. *Fr.* The Heptalogia. BXAP; FaBoCo; FaBoNo; FaBoPa; HBV-1; HoPM; InMe; NA; OAEP; Par; SpRo
From the Depths. Otakar Fischer, *tr. fr. Czech.* VWA
From the desert I come to thee. Bedouin Song. Bayard Taylor. AA; FaBoBe; HBV-1; PaPo; TreFT
From the Diary of ——. Fadwa Tuqan, *tr. fr. Arabic by* Hatem Hossaini. *Fr.* From behind the Bars. WPOW
From the dire monument of thy black room. Calling Lucasta from Her Retirement. Richard Lovelace. CaPo
From the Domain of Arnheim. Edwin Morgan. BSV
From the drear North, a cold and cheerless land, our fathers sprang. The Heritage. Edward Bliss Reed. EtS
From the drear wastes of unfulfilled desire. Disappointment. Thomas Stephens Collier. AA
From the dull confines of the drooping West. His Return to London. Robert Herrick. AnAnS-2; CaPo; FaBoPP; FF
From the Dust. Elaine Dallman. VWA
From the elm-tree's topmost bough. Robin's Come. William Warner Caldwell. HBVY
From the Embassy. Robert Graves. PoA
From the far-off Rocky Mountains, where they meet the eastern hills. The Gathering on the Plains. William T. Butler. PoOW
From the field behind our house, a low howling. Back Country. Joyce Carol Oates. Psk
From the first cry. First It Was Singing. Jon Silkin. NePoEA
From the first light we fear falling. Hotel Fire: New Orleans. Paul Ruffin. AMV-81
From the first shock of leaves their alliance. Park Poem. Paul Blackburn. CoPo
From the Flats. Sidney Lanier. NePA; NOBA; OxBA
From the forests and highlands. Hymn of Pan. Shelley. EnRP; FaBoCh; HBV-2; OAEP; OBEV; OBRV; PoEL-4; SeCeV
From the four corners of the earth. Carl Sandburg. *Fr.* The People, Yes, Sec. 1. CMoP
From the frantic weather into his creaking tomb. His Necessary Darkness. Nancy Sullivan. TAP
From the German of Uhland. James Weldon Johnson. CDC
From the gray woods they come, on silent feet. The Dancers. Babette Deutsch. HBMV
From the great Atlantic Ocean, to the wide Pacific shore. Wabash Cannonball. *Unknown.* BLSo; TreFT
From the Greek Anthology. L. A. G. Strong. WhC
("Bill Jupp lies 'ere, aged sixty year"). DBV
From the Greek of Moschus. Moschus. *See* Ocean, The.
From the Grove Press. Anthony Hecht. OBAL
From the Gulf. Will H. Ogilvie. PoAu-1
From the hag [*or* hagg] and hungry [*or* hungrie] goblin. Tom o' [*or* a] Bedlam's Song [*or* Roaring Mad Tom *or* Loving Mad Tom]. *Unknown.*

ChTr; EBEV; EnSB; EvOK; HAP; HBV-2; InvP; LiTB; MOON; NOBE; OAEL-1; OxBoLi; PoEL-2; SeCeV; TrGrPo; ViBoPo; WeW; WiR
From the half/ Of the sky. The Approach of the Storm. *Tr. by* Frances Densmore. OBVE
From the Halls of Montezuma. The Marines' Hymn [*or* Song]. *Unknown.* BLSo; PAL; TreF; YaD
From the Harbor Hill. Gustav Kobbé. HBV-1
From the Hazel Bough. Earle Birney. HeIP; NIP
From the Head. Louis Zukofsky. VWA
From the heart of a flower. Leave It to Me Blues. Joel Oppenheimer. CoPo; VGW
From the heart of the mighty mountains strong-souled for my fate I came. The Song of the Colorado. Sharlot M. Hall. HBV-2
From the high deck of Santa Fe's El Capitan. A Siding near Chillicothe. Richmond Lattimore. AmFN
From the high terrace porch I watch the dawn. On a View of Pasadena from the Hills. Yvor Winters. QFR
From the Highest Camp. Thom Gunn. MP; TwCP
From the hodge porridge. The Farmer's Wife. Anne Sexton. HoPM; LiTM; NePoEA-2
From the hold of this ship. Mediterranean. Israel Pincas, *tr. by* A. C. Jacobs. VWA
From the House of Yemanjá. Audre Lorde. NoP
From the Ice Age. Barbara Bloom. AMV-81
From the icy niche where men placed you. Death Sonnet I. Gabriela Mistral, *tr. by* David Garrison. BoWoP
From the immense hemicycle, from the blue fire of the earth. The Tree of Death. Claude Vigée, *tr. by* J. R. Le Master *and* Kenneth L. Beaudoin. VWA
From the Joke Shop. Roy Fuller. OxBC
From the Journals of the Frog Prince. Susan Mitchell. DFT; NIP
From the land of refuge. Week-Seek. Jim Tollerud. VoR
From the laurel's fairest bough. The Battle of Valparaiso. *Unknown.* PAH
From the lone shieling of the misty island. The Misty Island. *Unknown.* PoSH
From the madding crowd they stand apart. The V-A-S-E. James Jeffrey Roche. HBV-1
From the misty shores of midnight, touched with splendors of the moon. Tennyson. Henry van Dyke. AA
From the mountains we come. Warrior Nation Trilogy. Lance Henson. VoR
From the mouth of the Harlem Gallery. Lamda. Melvin B. Tolson. PoNe
From the Night of Forebeing. Francis Thompson. OBVV
From the North Saskatchewan. Eli Mandel. NOBC
From the north-west a cloud has come up. Prince Sumiya. *Mongol Oral Tradition, tr. by* C. R. Bawden. WTO
From the obscurity of the past, we saw. Nat Turner. Samuel Allen. CNA; FB
From the old slave shack I chose my lady. Trellie. Lance Jeffers. CNA; FB
From the oracular archives and the parchment. Altarwise by Owl-Light, IX. Dylan Thomas. CMoP; NoAM
From the Other Shore. William Pitt Root. MAYP
From the Parthenon I Learn. Willard Wattles. HBMV
From the Pentlands, *sel.* John Buchan.
Leap in the Smoke. PoSH
From the place where I was sitting. El Gusano. Irving Layton. PeCV
From the Point. Paul Petrie. AMV-80
From the Prison House. Adrienne Rich. NNaP
From the private ease of Mother's womb. Baby Song. Thom Gunn. NAs
From the Provinces. Norman Rosten. HoAn
From the Rain Down. Rhina P. Espaillat. GoYe
From the Rain Forest. Desirée Flynn. BrRo
From the ravine pours silent angry darkness. From the Diary of ——. Fadwa Tuqan, *tr. by* Hatem Hossaini. *Fr.* From behind the Bars. WPOW
From the Righteous Man Even the Wild Beasts Run Away. David Bromwich. PoA
From the Rio Grande's waters to the icy lakes of Maine. Buena Vista. Albert Pike. PAH
From the rodeo's mazy stalls. The Bumper Sticker on His Pickup Said. Eldon Ray Fox. LiSp
From the Roof. Denise Levertov. NoP
From the sad eaves the drip-drop of the rain! Desolate. Sydney Dobell. NBM; OBNC
From the shieling that stands by the lone mountain river. War Song of O'Driscol. Gerald Griffin. OnYI
From the slopes of the mountain. Clear Bright. Li Ch'ing-chao, *tr. by* Kenneth Rexroth. BoWoP
From the small life that loves with tooth and nail. Coventry Patmore. FaBoEE
From the soft dyke-road, crooked and waggon-worn. Haying. John Frederic Herbin. CaP; PeCV
From the starry heav'ns descending. Christmas Carol. J. R. Newell. BLRP
From the Station House. Galway Kinnell. *Fr.* The Avenue Bearing the Initial of Christ into the New World. NMP
From the sustaining air. Larry Eigner. PoM
From the tattered banana tree after months of waiting. Banana. Charles G. Bell. ErPo; NePoAm-2
From the tawny light. Everything That Acts Is Actual. Denise Levertov. NoAM
From the thick cover of unknowingness. On the Curve-Edge. Abbie Huston Evans. NYBP
From the thin slats of the Venetian blinds. Underwood. Howard Moss. MP; NePA; NePoEA-2; PP; TwCP
From the time of our old Revolution. That Things Are No Worse, Sire. Helen Hunt Jackson. OHIP
From the top of a bridge. The River Is a Piece of Sky. John Ciardi. PDV; PoPl; SoPo
From the tragic-est novels at Mudie's. Dora versus Rose. Austin Dobson. NOBL
From the Turkish. Byron. HBV-1
From the unoiled wheels of a bicycle. Listening. Douglas Dunn. BSV
From the uttermost part of the earth. I Waste Away. Bible, *O.T. Fr.* Isaiah. TrJP
From the veranda I watch the jetsam. Turista. Mark Osaki. BrSi
From the very first coming down. The Letter. W. H. Auden. FaBoTw; NoAM
From the Wash the Laundress Sends. A. E. Housman. InPK; NoAM
From the Wave. Thom Gunn. NoP
From the Welsh of Aneirin. Henry Vaughan. FaBoRV
From the wind I get/ the predicate of plants. Saved. Maria Teresa Horta, *tr. by* Suzette Macedo. PBWP
From the Window Down. Louis O. Coxe. NYBP
From the window I can see the corner of a gutter. The Gutter. Franco Fortini, *tr. by* Ruth Feldman. VWA
From the window of my grandfather's. Late Gothic. Phyllis Gotlieb. NOBC
From the Window of the Beverly Wilshire Hotel. Michael McClure. EAS
From the window of your sister's house. For Daphne at Lone Lake. John Haines. NPAW
From the winter's grey despair. Ave, Caesar! W. E. Henley. In Hospital, XIV. BrPo
From the years. Things Kept. William Dickey. NYBP
From Thee to Thee. Solomon ibn Gabirol, *tr. fr. Hebrew by* Israel Abrahams. EaLo; TrJP
From their folded mates they wander far. Black Sheep. Richard Burton. AA; HBV-2
From thence into the open fields he fled. A Pastoral. Spenser. *Fr.* The Faerie Queene, VI, 9. OBSC
From these bare trees. Chinese Winter. F. R. Higgins. BIrV
From these hie hilles as when a spring doth fall. Comparison of Love to a Streame Falling from the Alpes. Sir Thomas Wyatt. FaBoEn
From these sights/ Take one,—that ancient festival, the Fair. Wordsworth. *Fr.* The Prelude, VII. HAP
From this beach I want to make a poem. Beachhead Preachment. Ahmos Zu-Bolton. AMV-81
From this far, late-come country that still keeps. Gordon Childe. David Martin. PoAu-2
From this high place all things flow. Watershed. Robert Penn Warren. PoA
From this hospital bed. The Injury. William Carlos Williams. AP
From this hundred-terraced height. The Centennial Meditation of Columbia. Sidney Lanier. PAH
From this low-lying valley, oh, how sweet. Two Points of View. Lucian B. Watkins. BANP
From this sheer tower, as from time's parapet. New York. John Hall Wheelock. NYP
From this swaying city. Birthday Poem from Venice. Patricia Beer. OxBC
From This There's No Returning. Jean Garrigue. TwAmPo
From this tower room above the wall. Cups of Illusion. Henry Bellamann. HBMV
From this valley they say you are going. Red River Valley. *Unknown.* AS; BLSo; BPAW; CoSo; FaBoBe; FaFP; FSW; TrAS; TreFS
From thorax of storms the voices of verbs. George Barker. *Fr.* Pacific Sonnets. LiTM; MasP; MOS; WaP
From thy fair face I learn, O my loved lord. Michelangelo, *tr. fr. Italian by* John Addington Symonds. PeHV
From Titian's "Bacchanal" in the Prado at Madrid. T. Sturge Moore. QFR
From Tomorrow On. *Unknown, tr. fr. Yiddish by* Joseph Leftwich. TrJP
From Travancore to Tripoli. Ballad of the Oedipus Complex. Lawrence Durrell. FaBoCo

From Trollope's Journal. Elizabeth Bishop. GOA
From troubles of the world. Ducks. Frederick William Harvey. OnUR
From Tuscan came my lady's worthy race. Description and Praise of His Love Geraldine. Earl of Surrey. AAS; OAEP; SiPS
From 22 I see my first 8 weren't. 22 Miles. José Angel Gutiérrez. FIA
From twenty yards I saw my old love. Art and Reality. James Simmons. CIP
From twigs of visionary boughs. Prophet and Fool. Louis Golding. HBMV
From unremembered ages we. Chorus of Spirits. Shelley. *Fr.* Prometheus Unbound, I. LoBV
From up my own sleeve I came. The Magician. Bin Ramke. MAYP
From V. C. (a Gentleman of Verona). Gavin Ewart. OxBC
From Venice Was That Afternoon. Jean Garrigue. LiTA; NOBA
From Virgil. George Oppen. *Fr.* Five Poems about Poetry. NNaP
From Virgin's womb this day did spring. A Carol for Christmas Day. Francis Kinwelmersh. SBVL
From Water-Tower Hill to the brick prison. Point Shirley. Sylvia Plath. NIP; NoP
From way down south on the Rio Grande. Down South on the Rio Grande. *Unknown.* CoSo
From what did man fall? The Passion of Christ. Denis Devlin. IPY
From what dripping cell, through what fairy glen. A Drunkard to His Bottle. Joseph Sheridan Le Fanu. OnYI
From what great sleep. Watts. Alvin Saxon. PoBA
From what proud star I know not, but I found. The Giant Puffball. Edmund Blunden. FaBoTw
From whence arrived the praying mantis? The Praying Mantis. Ogden Nash. PV
From whence cometh song? Song. Theodore Roethke. NCSH
From Whence Doth This Union Arise? *with music.* Thomas Baldwin. AH
From where dark clouds of curling smoke arise. Susanna Blamire. *Fr.* Stoklewath; or, The Cumbrian Village. NOEC
From where I live, from windows on four sides. Juniper. Robert Francis. VGW
From where I sit, I see. Viewpoint. George Scarbrough. AMV-81
From where I sit, I see the stars. Midnight. Archibald Lampman. OBCV; PeCv
From where I stand now. 12 October. Myra Cohn Livingston. NTCP; RHPC
From where I stand the sheep stand still. Sheep. Robert Francis. LCAP
From Which War. Phillip Yellowhawk Minthorn. STE
From Whitehall Stairs, whence oft with distant view. Whitehall Stairs. Aaron Hill. NOEC
From Whitsuntide to Whitsuntide. A Ballad of a Bun. Sir Owen Seaman. CenHV
From Wibbleton to Wobbleton is fifteen miles. *Unknown.* OxNR
From Wicklow to the throb of dawn. Sea Dawn. Francis Hackett. AnIV
From William Tyndale to John Frith. Edgar Bowers. NePoEA; QFR
From winter-sleep. Ladybug's Christmas. Norma Farber. PChr
From within/ Slight rain seems to purr. Rain on a Cottage Roof. Freda Laughton. OnYI
From witty men and mad. The Poet. Thomas Randolph. POL
From Wynyard's Gap the livelong day. A Trampwoman's Tragedy. Thomas Hardy. BeLS; HBMV; MoVE; OBNC; OBNV; VLP
From year to year I shall return. Among High Hills. William Soutar. PoSH
From yon black clump of wheat that grows. The Lark's Nest. John Clare. PBBP
From yonder wood, make blue-eyed Eve proceed. Progress of Evening. Walter Savage Landor. OBNC
From Yorktown on the fourth of May. The Gallant Fighting "Joe." James Stevenson. PAH
From you, Beethoven, Bach, Mozart. Dead Musicians. Siegfried Sassoon. BrPo
From you have I [*or* I have] been absent in the spring. Sonnets, XCVIII. Shakespeare. AWP; ChTr; EBEV; EIL; LiTB; NOBE; OBEV; OBSC; PoPle; TEP; ViBoPo
From you, Ianthe, little troubles pass. Ianthe's Troubles. Walter Savage Landor. *Fr.* Ianthe. GBL; NOBE; OBEV; OBNC; TrGrPo; ViBoPo
From you, Rose, I do not like. Rondeau for You. Mário de Andrade, *tr. by* John Nist. TTY
From your eyes I thought. Silences; a Dream of Governments. Jean Valentine. LCAP
From your high bridge wave and wail. Prayer. Lev Mak, *tr. by* Dan Jaffe. VWA
Fronleichnam. D. H. Lawrence. GBL
Front, A. Randall Jarrell. OBWP; OxBC; VGW
Front Street. Howard Moss. NYBP
Frontier, The. John Hewitt. BIrV
Frontispiece. May Swenson. CoAP; NePoEA; WPE
Frost. Stella Benson. OxBTC
Frost. W. H. Davies. BoNaP
Frost, The. Hannah Flagg Gould. BLPA; HBV-1; HBVY
Frost. John Hewitt. NeIP
Frost. George Johnston. WHW
Frost. E. J. Pratt. WHW
Frost. Edith M. Thomas. AA
Frost and snow, frost and snow. Ariel. David Campbell. CBAP; PoAu-2
Frost at Midnight. Samuel Taylor Coleridge. CABA; EBEV; EnRP; FaBoEn; FiP; GLGT; HAP; LoBV; NAs; NOBE; NoP; OAEL-2; OAEP; OBNC; OBRV; PoEL-4; PPP; PrIm
Silent Icicles, The, *sel.* FaBoRV
Frost at Night. James Thomson. *Fr.* The Seasons: Winter. OBEC
Frost breaks across the dawn. Fall Again. H. R. Coursen. AMV-81
Frost called to water "Halt!" Hard Frost. Andrew Young. BoNaP; MoVE
Frost flowers on the window glass. A Valentine. Eleanor Hammond. TiPo; YeAr
Frost has sealed. Tree in December. Melville Cane. MoAmPo
Frost Heaves. Michael Dorris. AMV-80
Frost is tight upon the land. Now in the Time of This Mortal Life. Norman Nicholson. NeBP
Frost-locked all the winter. Spring. Christina Rossetti. OBNC
Frost looked forth, one still, clear night, The. The Frost. Hannah Flagg Gould. BLPA; HBV-1; HBVY
Frost moved up the window-pane, The. Frost. E. J. Pratt. WHW
Frost on my window. Frost. George Johnston. WHW
Frost on the Flower. Shakespeare. *Fr.* Romeo and Juliet, IV, v. FaBoRV
Frost performs its secret ministry, The. Frost at Midnight. Samuel Taylor Coleridge. CABA; EBEV; EnRP; FaBoEn; FiP; GLGT; HAP; LoBV; NAs; NOBE; NoP; OAEL-2; OAEP; OBNC; OBRV; PoEL-4; PPP; PrIm
Frost shall freeze; fire melt wood. Maxims (Exeter Book). *Unknown, tr. by* Charles W. Kennedy. AnOE
Frost Spirit, The. Whittier. HBV-1
Frost Warning. Ron McFarland. AMV-81
Frosted over with cold flakes. First Winter's Day. Dorothy Aldis. SoPo
Frosted Pane, The. Sir Charles G. D. Roberts. HBV-1
Frosty Christmas Eve, A. Noel; Christmas Eve, 1913. Robert Bridges. LiTB; MoVE; NOCV; OBCP; OxBoCh; PoEL-5
Frosty Day, A. Lord De Tabley. LoBV
Frosty Morning, A. William Cowper. *See* Winter Morning Walk, The.
Frosty Morning, A. John Davidson. VLP
Frosty Night, A. Robert Graves. CH; MoAB; MoBrPo; MoBS; OxBTC
Frosty, the bite of the autumn air. Blessing the Hounds. Mary Winter. GoYe
Froude informs the Scottish youth. A Hymn on Froude and Kingsley. William Stubbs. CenHV; FaBoEE
Froward Maymond ("A froward knave plainly to descrive"). John Lydgate. OxBM
Frowardness of the Elect in the Work of Conversion, The. Edward Taylor. SCAP
Frowned the Laird on the Lord: "So, red-handed I catch thee?" Muckle-Mouth Meg. Robert Browning. HBV-1
Frowning, the mountain stronghold stood. The Lost Colors. Elizabeth Stuart Phelps Ward. AA; HBV-2; HBVY
Frozen Fire. Floris Clarke McLaren. CaP
Frozen Girl, The. *Unknown.* *See* Young Charlottie.
Frozen Hands. Joseph Bruchac. CDW
Frozen Heart, The. Robert Herrick. CavP
Frozen Hero, The. Thomas H. Vance. NYBP
Frozen lemonade, frozen limas. Shopping. Jane Chance Nitzche. AMV-80
Frozen Logger, The. *Unknown.* BPAW (*At. to* James Stevens); FSW; OBAL
Frozen Ocean, The. Viola Meynell. CH
Frozen, rotting, dark leaves. Scene from a Dream. Janet Campbell Hale. STE
Frozen Zone, The; or Julia Disdainful. Robert Herrick. CaPo
Frugal snail, with forecast of repose, The. The Housekeeper [*or* The Snail]. Vincent Bourne, *tr. by* Charles Lamb. GN; HBV-1; MoShBr; PoLF
Fruit breaks on the summer mouth. The Garden. George M. Brady. NeIP
Fruit of all the service that I serve, The. Epigram. Sir Thomas Wyatt. SiPS
Fruit of Loneliness. Mary Sarton. PoA
Fruit of the Flower. Countee Cullen. PoLF
Fruit of the orchard is over-ripe, Elaine, The. Lancelot. Arna Bontemps. CDC
Fruit of the Tree, The. David Wagoner. NYBP
Fruit on the trees is aging fast, The. Words to a Song. Agnes Nemes Nagy, *tr. by* Bruce Berlind. BoWoP
Fruit Plucker, The. Samuel Taylor Coleridge. CH; SeCeV
(Fragment, A.) OBNC

(In a Moonlight Wilderness.) FaBoCh
Fruit Rancher, The. Lloyd Roberts. CaP
Fruit that was atop the shelf, The. Till the Sea Runs Dry. *Malay Oral Tradition, tr. by* R. J. Wilkinson. WTO
Fruit-tree's branch by very wealth, The. The Penalty of Virtue. *Unknown, tr. by* Arthur W. Ryder. *Fr.* The Panchatantra. AWP
Fruit white and lustrous as a pearl. The Lychee. Wang I, *tr. by* Arthur Waley. FaBoCh
Fruitful earth drinks up the rain. All Things Drink. Thomas Stanley. AWP
Fruitionless. Ina Coolbrith. AA
Fruits of War, The, *sel.* George Gascoigne.
"Conference among ourselves we called, A." OBWP
Fruits you give me are more savory than others, The. Marguerite Burnat-Provins, *tr. fr. French by* Cassia Borman. BoWoP
Frustrate. Louis Untermeyer. HBMV; InMe; YaD
Frustrated Male. Hughes Mearns. *Fr.* Later Antigonishes. InMe
Frustration. Elizabeth Daryush. QFR
Frustration. Dorothy Parker. DBV
Frutta di Mare. Geoffrey Scott. ChTr; EtS; OBMV
Fryar was walking in Exeter-Street, A. The Crafty Miss of London; or, The Fryar Well Fitted. *Unknown.* CoMu; OxBB
Frying Pan Skillet Blues. *Unknown.* BluL
Frying Trout while Drunk. Lynn Emanuel. MAYP
Fuchsia Hedges in Connacht. Padraic Colum. GoBC
Fudge Family in Paris, The, *sels.* Thomas Moore.
"After dreaming some hours of the land of Cockaigne." BIrV
"At length, my Lord, I have the bliss." OBSV
French Cookery. OBRV
Miss Biddy Fudge to Miss Dorothy. NBM
Fugal-Chorus ("Great is Caesar"). W. H. Auden. *Fr.* For the Time Being. LiTM; NePA; SeCeV
Fugato (Coda.) Gad Hollander. VWA
Fugitive, The. Alice Meynell. NOCV
Fugitive Slaves, The. Jones Very. AP; TAP
Fugitive Slave's Apostrophe to the North Star, The. John Pierpont. AA
Fugs, The. Edward Sanders. PoM
Fugue. Constance Carrier. GoYe
Fugue. Howard Nemerov. TAP
Fugue. Kathleen Spivack. AMV-80
Fugue of Death. Paul Celan, *tr. fr. German by* Christopher Middleton. OBVE
(Death Fugue.) TrJP, *tr. by* Clement Greenberg; VWA, *tr. by* Joachim Neugroschel
Führer Bunker, The, *sel.* W. D. Snodgrass.
Dr. Joseph Goebbels. TW
Fuimus Fumus. Joshua Sylvester. FaBoEE
Fulani Cattle. John Pepper Clark. PBA
Fulfill, O gracious God, to-day. Pentecost. Adelbert Sumpter Coats. TrPWD
Fulfillment. Helene Johnson. CDC; PoNe
Fulfillment. Vassar Miller. NePoEA-2
Fulfillment. William A. Muhlenberg. WGRP
Fulfilment. Elsa Barker. *Fr.* The Spirit and the Bride. HBMV
Fulfilment. Louis V. Ledoux. HBMV
Fulfilment. Robert Nichols. HBMV
Full and True Account of a Horrid and Barbarous Robbery, A. *sel.* John Byrom.
"Dear Martin Folkes, dear scholar, brother, friend." NOBL
Full be the year, abundant be the grain. Ezra Pound, *after the Chinese.* OBVE
Full clear and bright the Christmas night range. Christmas Rede. Jane Barlow. OBVV
Full cloves, The. A Shallot. Richard Wilbur. GP
Full Consciousness. Juan Ramón Jiménez, *tr. fr. Spanish by* Robert Bly. NU
Full Cycle. John White Chadwick. PAH
Full days come striding with measured, The. Concerning the Awakening of My Soul. Henriette Roland-Holst, *tr. by* Jonathan Crewe. WPOW
Full Fathom Five. Sylvia Plath. MOS
Full fathom five thy father lies. June Mercer Langfield. FaBoPa
Full fathom [*or* fadom] five thy father lies. Ariel's Song [*or* A Sea Dirge]. Shakespeare. *Fr.* The Tempest, I, ii. AWP; BiP; ChTr; EBEV; EIL; ELP; EtS; EvOK; FaBoCh; FaBoEn; GN; GoJo; GTBS; GTBS-P; HAP; HBV-2; HeIP; HoPM; InPK; InPS; LiTB; LoBV; MOS; NOBE; NoP; OAEP; OBEV; OBSC; PAI; PoEL-2; PoPle; PoRA; PPoe; SeCePo; SeCeV; TEP; TreFT; TrGrPo; ViBoPo; WHA
Full forty days he pass'd, whether on hill. The First Temptation. Milton. *Fr.* Paradise Regained, I. OxBoCh
Full happy is the man who comes at last. The Year's End. Timothy Cole. HBV-1
Full Heart, The. Robert Nichols. BoNaP; HBMV
Full in her glory, she as Tirzah fair. The Prophet Jeremiah and the Personification of Israel. *At. to* Eleazar ben Kalir, *tr. by* Nina Davis Salaman. TrJP
Full knee-deep lies the winter snow. The Death of the Old Year. Tennyson. HBV-1; PoSC
Full life, sweet rest, great love that cannot cease. Four Friends. Leo Ward. GoBC
Full many a dreary hour have I past. To My Brother George. Keats. EnRP
Full many a gem of purest ray serene. A "Prize" Poem. Shirley Brooks. FaBoCo; FaBoNo
Full many a glorious morning have I seen. Sonnets, XXXIII. Shakespeare. AWP; EBEV; EIL; FaBoEn; FaFP; HAP; HBV-1; LiTB; LoBV; NoP; OAEL-1; OAEP; OBSC; PoRA; PPP; SeCePo; SeCeV; TEP; TreFS; TrGrPo; ViBoPo; WeW
Full many a project that never was hatched. Humpty Dumpty. Adeline D. T. Whitney. HBV-2
Full many are the centuries since the days. Assurance. Ida Norton Munson. PGD
Full many lift and sing. Negro Poets. Charles Bertram Johnson. BANP
Full many sing to me and thee. The Barren Shore. Coventry Patmore. GBL
Full Moon. Walter de la Mare. BoNaP; TiPo
Full Moon. Robert Graves. FaBoEn; NOBE
Full Moon. Robert Hayden. BPo
Full Moon. Galway Kinnell. NePoAm-2
Full Moon. V. Sackville-West. MoShBr
Full Moon. Sappho, *tr. fr. Greek by* William Ellery Leonard. AWP
Full Moon. Elinor Wylie. CrMA; MoAB; MoAmPo; SBG; VGW
Full Moon and Little Frieda. Ted Hughes. OxBC
Full Moon at Tierz; before the Storming of Huesca. John Cornford. OBWP
Full moon easterly rising, furious, The. A Love Story. Robert Graves. CMoP; FaBoTw; LiTB; MoVE
Full moon half way up the sky, The. Gulls. E. A. Muir. NCSH
Full moon hung above the sea, The. The Play. Charles Otis Judkins. PeD
Full Moon in Malta. Asphodel. BrRo
Full moon is partly hidden by cloud, The. A Fable of the War. Howard Nemerov. NePoEA; OBWP
Full moon is so fierce that I can count the, The. Europa. Derek Walcott. NoP
Full Moon; New Guinea. Karl Shapiro. MiAP
Full moon on the Colosseum, The. Colosseum. Harold Norse. TrJP
Full moon. Our Narragansett gales subside. John Berryman. *Fr.* Dream Songs. CoAP
Full moon rising on the waters of my heart. Evening Song. Jean Toomer. BPo; CDC
Full Moon; Santa Barbara. Sara Teasdale. OBCA
Full night. The moon has yet to rise. Sodom. Herman Melville. Clarel, XXXVI. AmPP
Full nineteen centuries have passed since then. A Call to Pentecost. Inez M. Tyler. BLRP
Full of her long white arms and milky skin. The Equilibrists. John Crowe Ransom. AP; CMoP; CoBMV; HAP; LiTM; MoAB; MoPo; MoVE; NePA; NIP; NoAM; NOBA; OxBA; PPP; TAP
Full of oatmeal. Miss Norma Jean Pugh. Mary O'Neill. RHPC
Full of rebellion, I would die. Nature. George Herbert. OAEP
Full of superstition. The New Notebook. Maria Banus, *tr. by* Laura Schiff *and* Dana Beldiman. PBWP
Full of the Moon. Karla Kuskin. PDV
Full oft beside some gorgeous fane. The Mother. Sara Coleridge. OBVV
Full oft of old the islands changed their name. Epitaph on an Infant. Crinagoras, *tr. by* John William Burgon. AWP
Full often as I rove by path or stile. Wind on the Corn. Charles Tennyson Turner. EBVV
Full, ripe apple, a pear and banana. Rainer Maria Rilke, *tr. by* Christopher Hawthorne. *Fr.* Sonnets to Orpheus. SOTW
Full Sea Rolls and Thunders, The. W. E. Henley. EtS
Full Valleys. F. R. Scott. CaP
Full Well I Know. Hartley Coleridge. NCEP
Full well I know that she is there. Stanzas in Meditation. Gertrude Stein. PoA
Full well it may be seen. Sir Thomas Wyatt. SiPS
Full well, my gentle sir, I know. To an Artful Theatre Manager. Lorenzo da Ponte, *tr. by* John Mazzinghi. *Fr.* Il Capriccio Dramatico. TrJP
Full year since, I took this eager city, A. An Irishman in Coventry. John Hewitt. BIrV; CIP
Fuller and Warren. *Unknown, at.* to Moses Whitecotton. AmFP; BeLS; CoSo, *with music*; ViBoFo
Fully imagined, I suppose. For My Father on His Birthday. Greg Kuzma. Str
Fulness of life and power of feeling. Matthew Arnold. *Fr.* Empedocles on Etna. OAEP

Fum and Hum, the Two Birds of Royalty. Thomas Moore. OBSV
Fun in a Garret. Emma C. Dowd. SUS; TiPo
Fun with Fishing. Eunice Tietjens. FaPON
Function Room, The. Patrice Phillips. MAT
Fundament Is Shifted, The. Abbie Huston Evans. NYBP
Fundamental Project of Technology, The. Galway Kinnell. SUW; SV
Funebrial Reflections. Ogden Nash. *See* Among the Anthropophagi.
Funeral. Murray Bennett. GoYe
Funeral, The. Walter de la Mare. CMoP; MoVE
Funeral [*or* Funerall], The. John Donne. AnAnS-1; AWP; BiP; BoLoP; CABA; EBEV; EnLoPo; EnRePo; HeIP; LO; MeLP; NoP; OAEL-1; OBEV; OBS; PoEL-2; PoPle; PoRA; SeCP; SeCV-1
Funeral, The. Norman Dubie. MAYP
Funeral, The. "M. J.," *tr. fr. Polish by* A. Glanz-Leyeless. TrJP
Funeral. Bert Meyer. PCP
Funeral, The. Stephen Spender. CMoP; MoAB; MoBrPo; NoAM
Funeral. Joanna Thompson. AMV-81
Funeral at Ansley. Don Welch. GP; TAT
Funeral Elegy on the Death of His Very Good Friend, Mr. Michael Drayton. Sir Aston Cokayne. OBS
Funeral Elogy, upon . . . Mrs. Anne Bradstreet, A. John Norton. SCAP
Funeral Games for Anchises, The: Entellus. Virgil, *tr. fr. Latin by* Rolfe Humphries. *Fr.* The Aeneid, V. LiSp
Funeral Games for Patroclus, The: The Boastful Boxer. Homer, *tr. fr. Greek by* Ennis Rees. *Fr.* The Iliad, XXIII. LiSp
Funeral Games for Patroclus, The: Wrestling to a Draw. Homer, *tr. fr. Greek by* Ennis Rees. *Fr.* The Iliad, XXIII. LiSp
Funeral gent led us, The. Choosing Coffins. Raymond Souster. MoCV
Funeral Home, The. Robert Mezey. *See* In the Environs of the Funeral Home.
Funeral Hymn. William Walsham Howe. WGRP
Funeral Lament (Kommos) from Epiros. *Tr. fr. Modern Greek by* Elene Kolb. BoWoP
Funeral Notices. Alfonsina Storni, *tr. fr. Spanish by* Dorothy Scott Loos. AMV-81
Funeral of Martin Luther King, Jr., The. Nikki Giovanni. AmNP; BOLo; BPo
Funeral of Napoleon I. Sir John H. Hagarty. CaP
Funeral of Philip Sparrow, The, *abr.* John Skelton. *Fr.* Phyllyp Sparowe. ACP
Funeral of Rufino Contreras. Ruth Wildes Schuler. SOTS
Funeral of Time, The. Henry Beck Hirst. AA
Funeral Oration, A. David Wright. MP
Funeral Oration for a Mouse. Alan Dugan. AP; HAP; NoAM; PPP
Funeral Parlor, The. Henry Johnson. LFAC
Funeral Poem. Amiri Baraka. CNA
Funeral Pyre, The. *Unknown, tr. fr. Anglo-Saxon by* Charles W. Kennedy. *Fr.* Beowulf. AnOE
Funeral [*or* Funerall] Rites of the Rose, The. Robert Herrick. AnAnS-2; CABA; CaPo; OBEV
Funeral Song. Fletcher *and* Shakespeare. *Fr.* The Two Noble Kinsmen, I, v. ChTr; OBS
(Dirge of the Three Queens.) OBEV
(Urns and Odours Bring Away!) EIL
Funeral Song ("Now we are left out"). *Unknown, tr. fr. Sotho by* Dan Kunene *and* Jack Cope. PeSA
Funeral Song for Mamie Eisenhower. Nellie Wong. BrSi
Funeral [*or* Funerall] stone, A. To Laurels. Robert Herrick. CaPo; SeCV-1
Funerall, The. John Donne. *See* Funeral, The.
Funerall Rites of the Rose, The. Robert Herrick. *See* Funeral Rites of the Rose, The.
Funerall Song, A ("Come to me, grief, for ever"). *Unknown.* CH
Fungo. Stanley Plumly. AmPA
Funiculi, Funicula. Luigi Denza. TreFT
Funky Football. Ruby C. Saunders. BlSi
Funnel. Anne Sexton. MoAmPo
Funnels, The. Christian Morgenstern, *tr. fr. German by* Geoffrey Grigson. FaBoNo
Funny Fantasies Are Never So Real as Oldstyle. Lawrence Ferlinghetti. *Fr.* A Coney Island of the Mind. ErPo
Funny, how Felicia Ropps. Felicia Ropps. Gelett Burgess. FaPON; TiPo
Funny Joke, A. Leon Stokesbury. MAYP
Funny old lady named Borgia, A. Limerick. *Unknown.* WhC
Funny Old Man and His Wife, The. *Unknown, at. to* D'Arcy W. Thompson. OnUR; SoPo; SUS
Funny (or not so). The Artist. Stewart Brisby. LFAC
Funny Rigs of Good and Tender-hearted Masters. *Unknown.* OBET
Funny the Way Different Cars Start. Dorothy W. Baruch. FaPON
Funny thing is that he's reading a paper, The. The Sandwich Man. Ron Padgett. ConAP
Furies sink upon their iron beds, The. Pope. *Fr.* Ode on St. Cecilia's Day. FaBoCo
Furious prisoner of the womb, The. An Argument—of the Passion of Christ. Thomas Merton. CrMA
Furius, Aurelius, bound to Catullus. Catullus, *tr. fr. Latin by* Horace Gregory. NAWM-1
Furl that Banner, for 'tis weary. The Conquered Banner. Abram Joseph Ryan. AA; HBV-2; PAH; TreF
Furlough in heart and hand, the soldier at last walks. No Furlough. Stephen Stepanchev. WaP
Furnace for a life that's done. End of the War in Merida. Anthony Ostroff. FAZ
Furnace is of stone and clay, A. The Fire Place. E. W. Mandel. OBCV
Furnace of Colors, The. Vernon Watkins. NYBP
Furnace tolls the knell of falling steam, The. Elegy Written in a Country Coal-Bin. Christopher Morley. OBAL
Furnished Lives. Jon Silkin. NePoEA-2; NMP; NoAM
Furnished Room, The. James Merrill. NOBA
Furnished room beyond the stinging of, A. Good-bye for a Long Time. Roy Fuller. NeBP
Furniture. Chana Bloch. GP
Furniture. Phyllis Harris. NYBP
Furniture: humble, dependent. Judith Wright. Habitat, IV. CBAP
Furniture of a Woman's Mind, The. Swift. PPoe
Furniture of the Poem, The. Dennis Saleh. NeAC
Furred magnificence, the precious stones, The. Epiphany: For the Artist. Elizabeth Sewell. EyDe
Furry Bear. A. A. Milne. SoPo; TiPo
Further Advantages of Learning. Kenneth Rexroth. TAP
Further Fables for Our Time, *sel.* James Thurber.
Morals. FaBV
Further in summer than the birds. Emily Dickinson. AmPP; AP; NOBA; NoP
Further Instructions. Vincent O'Sullivan. OCNZ
Further Instructions. Ezra Pound. MP; TwCP
("Come, my songs, let us express our baser passions.") PoA
Further it comes, The. Country-Western Music. Ted Kooser. TAT
Further Language from Truthful James. Bret Harte. FaBoCo; NOBL
(Truthful James.) CenHV
Further Notice. Philip Whalen. PoM; VGW
Furtive lights that herald dawn, The. Dawn amid Scotch Firs. "Fiona Macleod." SyP
Fury against the Moslems at Uhud. Hind bint Utba, *tr. fr. Arabic by* Bridget Connelly *and* Deirdre Lashgari. WPOW
Fury of Aerial Bombardment, The. Richard Eberhart. BiP; CMoP; FaBoMo; FF; FYAP; HeIP; HoPM; InPK; LiTA; LiTM; MiAP; MP; NIP; NMP; NoAM; NoP; OBWP; PAI; PrIm; TAP; TwCP; UnPo; VGW; WaP
Fury of Flowers and Worms, The. Anne Sexton. BoWoP
Fury of Hating Eyes, The. Anne Sexton. TW
Fury of taunt was followed by fury of blow, The. E. J. Pratt. *Fr.* Brébeuf and His Brethren. PeCV
Fury Said to a Mouse. "Lewis Carroll." *Fr.* Alice's Adventures in Wonderland, *ch* 3. NoP
(Mouse's Tale, The.) FaBoNo
Fury this Friday broke through my wall, The. In Memory of a Friend. George Barker. OxBTC
Fury's Field. Cecil Bodker, *tr. fr. Danish by* Nadia Christensen. PBWP
Fuscara; or, The Bee Errant. John Cleveland. AnAnS-2
Fuscus is free, and hath the world at will. In Fuscum. Sir John Davies. FaBoEE
Fust Banjo, De. Irwin Russell. *Fr.* Christmas Night in the Quarters. AA; BLPA; HBV-2
Futile to chide the stinging shower. Perspectives. Dudley Randall. AmNP
Futility. Wilfred Owen. ChMP; CMoP; CoBMV; FaBoMo; GTBS-P; MMA; MoAB; MoBrPo; NoAM; NoP; OAEP; OBWP; PAI; SeCePo; TrGrPo
Future, The. Matthew Arnold. OAEP
Future, The. Michael Benedikt. SUW
Future, The. George Frederick Cameron. OBCV
Future, The. James Oppenheim. TrJP
Future, The. Edward Rowland Sill. HBV-2
Future, The. Vahan Tekeyan, *tr. fr. Armenian by* James Russell. AMV-81
Future and the Ancestor, The. Andrée Chedid, *tr. fr. French by* Samuel Hazo *and* Mirène Ghossein. WPOW
Future Blues. *Unknown.* BluL
Future Generation. Nila NorthSun. STE
Future is for tomorrow, The. Anna Gréki, *tr. fr. French by* Mildred P. Mortimer. WPOW
Future is withdrawn again, The. The Future. Michael Benedikt. SUW
Future lies, The/ With those whose eyes. The Goal and the Way. John Oxenham. PGD

Future Phenomenon, The. Stéphane Mallarmé, *tr. fr. French by* George Moore. SyP
Future smiles again, The. The Future. Vahan Tekeyan, *tr. by* James Russell. AMV-81
Fuzzy fellow without feet, A. Emily Dickinson. TAP
Fuzzy-Wuzzy. Kipling. BrPo; HBV-2; MoBrPo; TrGrPo
Fuzzy wuzzy, creepy crawly. Firefly. Lillian Schulz Vanada. SoPo; SUS; TiPo
Fuzzy Wuzzy Was a Bear. *Unknown.* NTCP
Fy let us a to the bridal. The Blythsome Bridal. *Unknown, at. to* Frances Sempill. GBP
Fye foolish earth, thinke you the heaven wants glory. *See* Fie, foolish earth, think you the heaven wants glory.

G

G. Hilaire Belloc. FiBHP
G is a grumbler gruff. A Grumbler Gruff. Oliver Herford. TDH
G Is for Gustave. Isabel Frances Bellows. TDH
G. K. Chesterton. Humbert Wolfe. TrJP
G. K. Chesterton on His Birth. A. E. Housman. FaBoNo
G. M. B. Donald Davie. OxBC
G stands for Gnu, whose weapons of defense. The Gnu. Hilaire Belloc. BoAnP; FaBoNo
G. Wilson humbly as before. From the *Caledonian Mercury*. Gavin Wilson. FaBoUs
Gaa-a-Muna, a Mountain Flower. Harold Littlebird. VoR
Gaberlunzie Man, The. *Unknown.* BSV; EnSB; GoTS; OxBB, *with music;* OxBS
"Gables are not burning, The." The Finnesburn Fragment. *Unknown, tr. by* Kevin Crossley-Holland. OBWP
Gabriel. Adrienne Rich. VGW
Gabriel. Willard Wattles. HBMV
Gabriel, from Hevene-King. The Annunciation. *Unknown.* MeEL; OxBM
Gabriel Meets Satan. Milton. *Fr.* Paradise Lost, IV. LoBV
Gabriel Preil, the Grand Duke of New York. The Grand Duke of New York. Dan Pagis, *tr. by* Robert Friend. VWA
Gabriel's Blues. Calvin Forbes. PoA
Gadoshkibos. Diane Burns. STE
Gae bring my guid auld harp ance mair. Scotland Yet. Henry Scott Riddell. HBV-2
Gaelic bard they praise who in fourteen adjectives, A. The Ancient Speech. Kathleen Raine. *Fr.* Eileann Chanaidh. PoSH
Gaelic Christmas, A. Liam P. Clancy. ISi
Gaelic is the conscience of our leaders. Michael Hartnett. *Fr.* A Farewell to English. CIP
Gaelic Litany to Our Lady, The. *Unknown, tr. fr. Old Irish by* Eugene O'Curry. ISi
Gaeltacht. Pearse Hutchinson. BIrV
Gaeta from wool and weaving first began. In Gaetam. Thomas Bastard. FaBoEE
Gaffer Gray. Thomas Holcroft. HBV-2; NOEC
Gaggle of Geese, a Pride of Lions, A. John Moore. DuDa
Gaiety, *sel.* Richard Howard.
Queer's Song. ErPo
Gaiety of Descendants. Douglas Newton. NeBP
Gaiety of three winds is a game of green, The. White Goat, White Ram. W. S. Merwin. NePoEA; TwAmPo
Gaily bedight,/ A gallant knight. Eldorado. Poe. AmPP; AP; AWP; FaBoBe; FaBoCh; FPL; HBV-2; NePA; NOBA; NoP; OxBA; PAI; TAP; WiR
Gaily I Lived. *Unknown.* ELU
Gaily into Ruislip Gardens. Middlesex. John Betjeman. OxBTC
Gaily the Troubadour, *with music.* Thomas Haynes Bayly. BLSo
Gain without gladness. Liadain. *Unknown, tr. by* Frank O'Connor. KiLC; WPOW
Gal I Left behind Me, The. *Unknown.* BPAW; CoSo, *with music;* FSW
Galante Garden: I ("Spring morning"). Juan Ramón Jiménez, *tr. fr. Spanish by* H. R. Hays. PoPl
Galante Garden: II ("There was no one. The water—no one?"). Juan Ramón Jiménez, *tr. from Spanish by* H. R. Hays. WSC
Galatea Again. Genevieve Taggard. WHA
Galatea and Pygmalion. Robert Graves. PAI
Galathea, *sel.* John Lyly.
Cupid's Indictment. ElL
(Song of Diana's Nymphs, A.) OBSC
Gale had passed, but chilling was the air, The. Circumstance without Pomp. John Kendall. WhC
Gale in April. Robinson Jeffers. MoAB; MoAmPo
Gale of August, '27, The, *with music.* George Swinamer. ShS
Galileo Galilei. William Jay Smith. PoCh
Gallant Château. Wallace Stevens. MoAB; MoAmPo
Gallant Fifty-one, The. Henry Lynden Flash. PAH
Gallant Fighting "Joe," The. James Stevenson. PAH
Gallant foeman in the fight, A. Robert E. Lee. Julia Ward Howe. PAH
Gallant Highwayman, The. James De Mille. WHW
Gallant laird of Lamington, The. Katharine Jaffray. *Unknown.* ESPB
Gallant Youth, who may have gained, The. Yarrow Revisited. Wordsworth. EnRP; VLP
Gallantry. Keith Douglas. OBWP
Gallants attend, and hear a friend. The Battle of the Kegs [*or* British Valor Displayed]. Francis Hopkinson. OBAL; PAH
Gallathea. John Lyly. *See* Galathea.
Galleons in sea-pomp sails. An Armada of Thirty Whales. Daniel G. Hoffman. NePa
Gallery of My Heart. King D. Kuka. VoR
Gallery Shepherds. Patricia Beer. OxBC
Gallery, The. Andrew Marvell. AnAnS-1; MeLP; NoP; OBS
Galley, The. Sir Thomas Wyatt. OBSC
Galley of Count Arnaldos, The. Longfellow. *See* Secret of the Sea, The.
Galley-Slave, The. Kipling. BrPo
Galley Slave, The, *sel.* *Unknown.*
"How fortune deceives! I had pleasure in tow." PeD
Galliass, The. Walter de la Mare. FaBoTw
Gallop apace, you fiery-footed steeds. Shakespeare. *Fr.* Romeo and Juliet, III, ii. GBL
Gallop, Gallop to a Rhyme. Monica Shannon. SiSoSe
Gallop of Fire, A. Marie E. J. Pitt. PoAu-1
Galloping. Cordelia Chitty. PH
Galloping away to the farthest pasture. Dexter. Joan Byers Grayston. PH
Galloping Cat, The. Stevie Smith. BrRo
Galloping collection of boards, The. Somewhere. Robert Creeley. NoAM
Gallow Hill. William J. Tait. OxBS
Galloway Shore, The. Sydney Tremayne. BSV
Gallows, The. Edward Thomas. ChMP; FM; InPS; LiTB; MoAB; MoBrPo; NoAM; PAI; UnPo
Gallows and Cross. J. E. H. MacDonald. CaP
Gallows in my garden, people say, The. A Ballade of Suicide. G. K. Chesterton. FiBHP; HBV-1; InMe
Gallows Pole, The. *Unknown.* *See* Maid Freed from the Gallows, The.
Gallows Tree, The. Frederick Robert Higgins. OnYI
Galoshes. Rhoda W. Bacmeister. NTCP; SoPo; TiPo
Galveston with a seawall. Wasn't That a Mighty Storm? *Unknown.* AmFP
Galway. Donagh MacDonagh. NeIP
Galway. Louis MacNeice. OxBI
Galway. Mary Devenport O'Neill. NeIP; OxBI
Galway called out of sleep. Galway. Donagh MacDonagh. NeIP
Galway is a blackguard place. Clonakilty. *Unknown.* FaBoEE
Galway Races. *Unknown.* OxBoLi
Gamarra is a dainty steed. The Blood Horse. "Barry Cornwall." GN; HBV-1
Gambler, The ("Gambler's life I do admire, du-da, du-da"). *Unknown.* AmFP
Gambler, The ("Good morning Mister Railroad man"). *Unknown.* FSW
Gambler, The ("My father was a gambler"). *Unknown.* ViBoFo
Gamblers, The. Anthony Delius. PeSA
Gambler's Blues. *Unknown.* *See* St. James Infirmary.
Gambler's life I do admire, du-da, du-da. The Gambler. *Unknown.* AmFP
Gambler's Repentance, The. Gerald, Baron of Offaly. AnIV
Gamblers they. Farmers. Hortense Roberta Roberts. AMV-81
Gambling. Royall Tyler. TAP
Gamboling Man, The, *with music.* *Unknown.* AS
Game, The. Walker Gibson. NePoAm-2
Game at Salzburg, A. Randall Jarrell. MiAP; NoAM
Game called kick the can, which used to last about a month, A. We Used to Play. Don Welch. Psk
Game of Chance, A. Howard Moss. PoA
Game of Chess, A. T. S. Eliot. *Fr.* The Waste Land. SCV
Game of Consequences, A. Paul Dehn. ErPo; FiBHP; NOBL
Game of Cricket, The. Hilaire Belloc. DBV; FiBHP
Game of Dice, A. *Unknown, tr. fr. Greek by* Louis Untermeyer. UnTE
Game of Glass, A. Alastair Reid. NePoEA; PoCh
Game of Life, The. John Godfrey Saxe. BLPA; BLPL
Game out of Hand. Allison Ross. GoYe
Game Resumed. Richmond Lattimore. LiSp; NYBP
Gamecock. James Dickey. HoPM; UnPo
Games. Sandra McPherson. LCAP
Gamesters All. DuBose Heyward. HBMV
Gamma rays weep through my body. The Amish. William Doreski. SOTS
Gammer Gurton's Needle, *sel.* *At. to* William Stevenson *and also to* John Still

Back and Side Go Bare, Go Bare. HeIP; InvP; LiTB; OAEP; ViBoPo
(Drinking Song.) WiR, *at. to* John Still
(In Praise of Ale.) TrGrPo
(Jolly Good Ale and Old.) HBV-2; NoP; OBEV; SeCeV
(Of Jolly Good Ale and Old.) ElL
(Song of Ale, A.) OBSC
Gamorra is a dainty steed. The Blood Horse. "Barry Cornwall." PH
Gampta, my little grey sister. The Desert Lark. Eugène Marias, *tr. by* Uys Krige *and* Jack Cope. PeSA
Gane were but the winter cauld. Gone Were but the Winter Cold. Allan Cunningham. CH
Gang of labourers on the piled wet timber, A. Morning Work. D. H. Lawrence. MoAB; MoBrPo
Gang wanted to give Oedipus Rex a going away present, The. Oedipus. Josephine Miles. WPE
Ganga. Thomas Blackburn. MoBS
Gangan my lane amang the caulkstane alps. Ice-Flumes Owregie Their Ladies. Douglas Young. SeCePo
Ganges, The. Norman Dubie. LCAP
Gangrel Rymour and the Pairdon of Sanct Anne, The, *sel.* Sydney Goodsir Smith, *after the French of* Tristan Corbière.
"But ae braithless note." OBVE
Gangrene. Philip Levine. VGW
Gangster's Death, The. Ishmael Reed. PoBA
Ganymede. William Plomer. PeHV
Ganymede and Helen. *Unknown, tr. fr. Latin.* PeHV
Gaol Song, The. *Unknown.* GBP
Gap in the Cedar, The. Roy Scheele. Psk
Gar, The. Charles G. Bell. AmFN
Garadh. Padraic Colum. OnYI
Garage Sale. Karl Shapiro. Psk
García Lorca. Louis Dudek. MoCV; NOBC
Garcia Lorca. In Memory of Garcia Lorca. Eldon Grier. PeCV
Garcia Lorca Murdered in Granada. John Manifold. CBAP
Garcon! You—you. The Hero of the Commune. Margaret Junkin Preston. AA
Garden, The. Joseph Beaumont. JCP; OBS; OxBoCh
Garden, The. George M. Brady. NeIP
Garden, The, *sel.* Abraham Cowley
Great Diocletian. ChTr
Garden, The, *sel.* William Cowper. *Fr.* The Task, III.
"I was a stricken deer, that left the herd." EnRP; FaBoRV; OAEP; OxBoCh; PAI
(Stricken Deer, The.) FiP; LoBV
Garden, The. Digby Mackworth Dolben. GoBC
Garden, The. Hilda Doolittle ("H. D."). LiTA; TwAmPo
Heat, *sel.* AP; CMoP; HeIP; InPK; MoAmPo; NoAM; OxBA; PrIM; TAP; UnPo; WHA
Garden, The. Caroline Giltinan. HBMV
Garden, The. Louise Glück. AmPA; FiCP
Garden, The. Susan Griffin. *Fr.* Woman and Nature. NPGG
Garden, The. Nicholas Grimald. OAEL-1
Garden, The ("How vainly men themselves amaze"). Andrew Marvell. AWP; BIP; BLPL; CABA; FaBoEn; HAP; HBV-1; InPS; InvP; JCP; LiTB; LoBV; MasP; MeLP; MePo; NIP; NOBE; NoP; OAEL-1; OAEP; OBS; PoEL-2; PoLF; PoPle; PoRA; PPoe; PPP; QFR; SeCePo; SeCeV; SeCP; SeCV-1; TrGrPo; TEP; ViBoPo
(Thoughts in a Garden.) GTBS; GTBS-P; OBEV; TreFT
Sels.
"What wondrous life is this I lead!" BoNaP; CH; ChTr
"When we have run our passion's heat." WHA
Garden, A ("See how the flowers, as at parade"). Andrew Marvell. *Fr.* Upon Appleton House. HBV-1; OBEV
(Garden at Appleton House, The.) PoPle
(Garden of Appleton House, The, *longer sel.*) NOBE
("See how the flowers, as at parade.") TrGrPo
Garden, The. Rose Parkwood. WGRP
Garden, The. Ezra Pound. AWP; CABA; HeIP; LiTA; MoAB; MoAmPo; MP; NIP; NoP; PPP; SOTW; TwCP
Garden, The. James Shirley. CavP; OBS
Garden, The. Marvin Solomon. NePoAm
Garden, The. Mark Strand. GeTw
Garden, The. Jones Very. AP; OxBA; TAP
Garden, The. Robert Penn Warren. PoA
Garden, The. Oscar Wilde. *See* Le Jardin.
Garden and Cradle. Eugene Field. AA
Garden at Appleton House, The. Andrew Marvell. *See* Garden, A ("See how the flowers, as at parade").
Garden at St. John's, The. May Swenson. NePoEA; PoPl
Garden beds I wandered by, The. A Conservative. Charlotte Perkins Gilman. AA; HBV-1
Garden bower in bower, A. God's Mother. Laurence Housman. ISi
Garden by the Sea, A. William Morris. *Fr.* The Life and Death of Jason, IV. NOBE; OAEL-2; OBNC; PoEL-5
(I Know a Little Garden-Close.) CH; ViBoPo
(Nymph's Song to Hylas, The.) HBV-1; OBEV
Garden called Gethsemane, The. Gethsemene. Kipling. FaBoTw
Garden cannot move, The. Mortally. James Kirkup. NeBP
Garden Fancies. Robert Browning. VLP
Sels.
Flower's Name, The, I. CTC; HBV-1
Sibrandus Schafnaburgensis, II. CTC; EBVV; TEP
Garden flew round with the angel, The. The Pleasures of Merely Circulating. Wallace Stevens. LiTA; MAT; OBAL
Garden Hose, The. Beatrice Janosco. NTCP; POL
Garden in September, The. Robert Bridges. PoPle
Garden is a lovesome thing, God wot, A! My Garden. Thomas Edward Brown. BLPL; EBCP; FaBV; HBV-1; HBVY; InPK; OBEV; OBVV; PeD; PoLF; TreF; TRV; WBLP; WGRP
Garden is a *lovesome* thing, A? What rot! My Garden. J. A. Lindon. DBV; InPK; POL
Garden is only for you, The. It is a shell. The Center of the Garden. Ann Stanford. AMV-80
Garden is very quiet tonight, The. Dusk Song. William H. A. Moore. BANP
Garden-Lion. Evelyn Hayes. ChTr
Garden Lore. Juliana Horatia Ewing. OxBChV
Garden Lyric, A. Frederick Locker-Lampson. HBV-1; PeD
Garden of Adonis, The. Spenser. *Fr.* The Faerie Queene, III, 6. NOBE; PoEL-1
Garden of Amour, The. Guillaume de Lorris, *tr. fr. French by* Chaucer. *Fr.* The Romance of the Rose. PoEL-1
Garden of Appleton House, The. Andrew Marvell. *See* Garden, A ("See how the flowers, as at parade").
Garden of Cymodoce, The, *sel.* Swinburne.
Sark. FaBoPP
Garden of Earthly Delights, The. Charles Simic. NoP
Garden of God, The. "Æ." WGRP
Garden of Love, The. Blake. *Fr.* Songs of Experience. AWP; CABA; EnLoPo; EnRP; FaBV; GBL; HAP; LAuP; LiTB; LO; LoBV; MAT; NIP; NoP; OAEP; PAI; PPoe; SeCeV; SoSe; TEP; ViBoPo
Garden of mouthings, A. Purple, scarlet-speckled, black. The Beekeeper's Daughter. Sylvia Plath. IHMS
Garden of my soul grows duller, The. The Unfading. "Marie Madelaine," *tr. by* Ferdinand E. Kappey. PeHV
Garden of Proserpina, The. Spenser. *Fr.* The Faerie Queene, II, 7. ChTr
Garden of Proserpine, The. Swinburne. AWP; BLPA; BLPL; FaBoRV; FaBV; FaPoR; HAP; HBV-2; LiTB; NOBE; NoP; OAEP; OBNC; PoEL-5; PoPl; PoPle; PoRA; SeCePo; SeCeV; TreFT; TrGrPo; ViBoPo; VLP; WHA
Sels.
"Here, where the world is quiet." SCV
Proserpine. ChTr
("Pale, beyond porch and portal.") FaBoEn
Garden of Shadow, The. Ernest Dowson. FaBoEn; HBV-1; OBNC
Garden of Ships, The. Douglas Stewart. CBAP; PoAu-2
Garden of Shushan! Before the Feast of Shushan. Anne Spencer. BlSi; BANP
Garden of Situations, A. Jack Anderson. PoA
Garden of the Holy Souls, The. Eleanor Hamilton King. *Fr.* Hours of the Passion. ACP
Garden Party, The. Hilaire Belloc. DTC; MoVE
Garden Party, The. Donald Davie. NePoEA
Garden Party. Mary Mills. NePoAm
Garden Party. Sir Herbert Read. BrPo
Garden Puzzle. Gray Burr. CoPo
Garden Seat, The. Thomas Hardy. GoJo; HAP
Garden-Song. James Branch Cabell. HBMV
Garden Song, A. Austin Dobson. BoNaP; HBV-1; LoBV; OBEV; OBNC; OBVV
Garden Song, A. Thomas Moore. *See* Child's Song.
Garden That I Love, The. Florence L. Henderson. HBV-2
Garden Where There Is No Winter, The. Louis James Block. AA
Garden within was shaded, The. Thisbe. Helen Gray Cone. AA
Garden Year, The. Sara Coleridge. FaBoBe; HBV-1; HBVY; TreFT
("January brings the snow." TiPo
(Months, The.) OxBChV; RHPC
Gardener, The. Evelyn Eaton. GoYe
Gardener. Emerson. *Fr.* Quatrains. OxBA
Gardener, The. Laurence Housman. TrPWD
Gardener, The. Sidney Keyes. ChMP; MoAB; MoBrPo
Gardener, The. Robert Louis Stevenson. HBV-1; HBVY; TreFS
Gardener, The. Arthur Symons. BoNaP

Gardener, The, *sels.* Rabindranath Tagore.
In the Dusky Path of a Dream. OBMV
Yellow Bird Sings, The. OBMV
Gardener, The. *Unknown.* BaBo; ESPB; GBP
Gardener, The. John Hall Wheelock. DiL; NYBP; TwAmPo
Gardener does not love to talk, The. The Gardener. Robert Louis Stevenson. HBV-1; HBVY; TreFS
Gardener in his old brown hands, The. The Gardener. Arthur Symons. BoNaP
Gardener Janus Catches a Naiad. Edith Sitwell. MoAB; MoBrPo
Gardener of Eden and Gethsemane. Unearth. Alfred Barrett. GoBC
Gardener stands in his bower-door, The. The Gardener. *Unknown.* BaBo; ESPB
Gardener to His God, The. Mona Van Duyn. TrCP; UnPo; WPE
Gardeners. David Ignatow. PCPC
Gardener's Cat, The. Patrick R. Chalmers. HBMV; HBVY
Gardener's rule applies to youth and age, The. An Adage. H. J. Byron. FaBoUs
Gardener's Song, The. "Lewis Carroll." *See* Mad Gardener's Song, The.
Gardens Are All My Heart. Eve Triem. GoYe
Garden's grillwork gate, The. Plainness. Jorge Luis Borges, *tr. by* Norman Thomas Di Giovanni. NYBP
Gardens No Emblems. Donald Davie. LiTM; NePoEA-2; OAEL-2
Gardens of Alcinous, The ("Close to the gates a spacious garden lies"). Homer, *tr. fr. Greek by* Pope. *Fr.* The Odyssey, VII. OAEL-1; OBVE
Gardens of Alcinous, The ("Without the hall and close upon the gate"). Homer, *tr. fr. Greek by* George Chapman. *Fr.* The Odyssey, VII. OAEL-1; OBVE
Gardens of Proserpine, The. Turner Cassity. PoA
Gardens of the Sea, The. George Sterling. EtS
Garden's quit with me, The: as yesterday. The Garden. Joseph Beaumont. JCP; OxBoCh; OBS
Gardin was, by mesuring, The. The Garden of Amour. Guillaume de Lorris, *tr. by* Chaucer. *Fr.* The Romance of the Rose. PoEL-1
Garfield's Ride at Chickamauga. Hezekiah Butterworth. PAH
Gargantua, *sel.* Rabelais, *tr. by* Sir Thomas Urquhart.
Inscription above the Entrance to the Abbey of Theleme. FaBoRV
Gargoyle. Thomas Rabbitt. MAYP
Gargoyle. Carl Sandburg. NoAM; NOBA
Garibaldi Hymn, The. Luigi Mercantini, *tr. fr. Italian.* WBLP
Garland and the Girdle, The. Michelangelo, *tr. fr. Italian by* John Addington Symonds. AWP
Garland for a Propagandist. Ted Pauker. NOBL
Garland for a Storyteller. Jessie Farnham. GoYe
Garland for Heliodora, A. Meleager, *tr. fr. Greek by* "Christopher North." AWP
Garland of Recital Programs, A. Franklin P. Adams. InMe
Garland of roses, whether you come. Martial, *tr. fr. Latin by* James Michie. FaBoEE
Garland Sunday. Padraic Colum. GoYe
Garlande [*or* Garlands] of Laurell, The, *sels.* John Skelton.
To Maystres Jane Blenner-Haiset. AAS
To Mistress [*or* Maystres] Isabell Pennell. AAS; NAs; NOBE; OAEP; OBEV; OBSC; OxBoLi; PoEL-1; SeCeV; TrGrPo; ViBoPo
(In Praise of Isabell Pennell.) CH
To Mistress [*or* Maystres] Margaret Hussey. AAS; EBEV; EnLoPo; GoBC; GoJo; HBV-1; HeIP; HoPM; LoBV; NOBE; NoP; OAEL-1; OAEP; OBEV; OBSC; PoEL-1; PoRA; PPoe; PPP; SCV; TreFT; TrGrPo
To Mistress Gertrude Statham. OAEP
To Mistress Margaret Tilney. MeEL
To Mistress Margery Wentworth. EBEV; EnLoPo; EnRePo; LoBV; NOBE; OAEL-1; OBEV; OBSC; TrGrPo
To My Lady Mirriel Howard. LoBV
Garlands fade that Spring so lately wove, The. Sonnet Written at the Close of Spring [*or* Elegiac Sonnet]. Charlotte Smith. FaBoEn; OBEC
Garlic. Marvin Bell. GP
Garlic, The. Bert Meyers. VWA
Garlic. Justin Richardson. PV
Garlic's taste is briefest pleasure. Garlic. Justin Richardson. PV
Garment of Good Ladies, The. Robert Henryson. ACP
(Garmont of Gude Ladies, The.) GoTS
Garments of inattention, oh mere items. Teaching Swift to Young Ladies. William Dickey. PoA
Garnishing the Aviary. Margaret Danner. Far from Africa, I. BPo
Garret, The. Pierre Jean de Béranger, *tr. fr. French by* Thackeray. HBV-1
Garret, The. Ezra Pound. PoPl; SOTW
Garrison. Amos Bronson Alcott. AA
Garrison Town. Emanuel Litvinoff. WaP
Garrulous old man who once had owned, The. Under the Casuarina. Elizabeth Riddell. PoAu-2
Garryowen. *Unknown.* OnYI
Gary Gotow. George Uba. BrSi
Gas and Hot Air. Morris Bishop. OBAL
Gas from a Burner. James Joyce. DBV; TW
Gas Lamp. Willis Barnstone. VWA
Gas-lamps abandoned by the night burn on. Baudelaire in Brussels. Anthony Cronin. BIrV
Gas ring's hoarse exhaling wheeze, The. Twinings Orange Pekoe. Judith Moffett. PoA
Gas was on in the Institute, The. A Shropshire Lad. John Betjeman. MoBS
Gasbags. *Unknown.* NOBL
(Lines by an Old Fogy.) DBV
Gasco; or, The Toad. Günter Grass, *tr. fr. German by* Jerome Rothenberg. ELU
Gascoigne's Good Morrow. George Gascoigne. AAS; EnRePo; NOCV
Gascoigne's [*or* Gascoygnes] Good-Night. George Gascoigne. AAS; NOCV
Gascoigne's Lullaby [*or* Lullabie]. George Gascoigne. *See* Lullaby of a Lover, The.
"Common speech is, spend and God will send, The," III. EnRePo
"In haste, post haste, when first my wandering mind," IV. AAS; EnRePo
Gascoigne's Memories, *sels.* George Gascoigne.
"Vain excess of flattering fortune's gifts, The," II. EnRePo
Gascoigne's Passion. George Gascoigne. *See* Passion of a Lover, The.
Gascoigne's Praise of His Mistress. George Gascoigne. EnRePo
Gascoigne's Woodmanship. George Gascoigne. AAS; EnRePo; QFR
Gascon Punished, The ("A Gascon, being heard one day to swear"). La Fontaine, *tr. fr. French.* UnTE
Gascoygnes Good Night. George Gascoigne. *See* Gascoigne's Good-Night.
Gash, The. William Everson. GP
Gasholders, russet among fields. Geoffrey Hill. Mercian Hymns, VII. HAP; NoP
Gasoline makes game scarce. Written on the Stub of the First Paycheck. William Stafford. *Fr.* The Move to California. InPK
Gaspara Stampa. William Rose Benét. HBMV
Gassed going between classes. Witness. Josephine Miles. GP
Gassing the woodchucks didn't turn out right. Woodchucks. Maxine W. Kumin. HoPM; NIP
Gastric. "C. T." PeD
Gastrology, *sel.* Archestratus, *tr. fr. Greek by* Isaac D'Israeli.
"I write these precepts for immortal Greece." FaBoUs
Gate, The. Yasmeen Jamal. LFAC
Gate. David McAleavey. SUW
Gate, The. Edwin Muir. CMoP; LiTM
Gate at the End of Things, The. *Unknown.* BLPA
Gate of the Year, The, *sel.* M. Louise Haskins.
"And I said to the man who stood at the gate of the year." TreFS; TRV
Gate was open, The; the fence under the aspens, fallen. Mountain Corral. Helen Sorrells. WPE
Gates. Ted Kooser. GP
Gates. Sister Mary Madeleva. GoBC
Gates, The, *sel.* Muriel Rukeyser.
Church of Galilee, The. GP
Gates and Doors. Joyce Kilmer. HBV-1; HBVY
Gates are open on the road, The. The Seekers. Charles Hamilton Sorley. WGRP
Gates clanged and they walked you into jail, The. The Conscientious Objector. Karl Shapiro. OxBA
Gates fly open with a pretty sound, The. Under the Hill. Daryl Hine. MoCV
Gates of Damascus. James Elroy Flecker. BrPo; HBMV
Gates of Dreamland, The. "Æ." *See* Carrowmore.
Gates of Paradise, The, *sel.* Blake.
Epilogue: "Truly, my Satan, thou art but a dunce." CABA; HAP; OAEL-2; OBNC; WeW
(Epilogue: To the Accuser Who Is God of This World.) FaBoEn
(To the Accuser Who Is the God of This World.) NoP; TrGrPo; ViBoPo
Gates of the Year, The. John Mervin Hull. STF
Gate's Open, The. John Blight. CBAP
Gateway, The. A. D. Hope. BoLoP; ErPo; UnTE
Gateway to the Sea, A—St. Andrews. George Bruce. BSV
Gather all kindreds of this boundless realm. The Poet. Cornelius Mathews. AA
Gather for festival. Hilda Doolittle ("H. D."). Songs from Cyprus, I. MoAmPo
Gather kittens while you may. Song. Oliver Herford. SpRo
Gather the Rose ("Eftsoones they heard a most melodious sound"). Spenser. *See* Bower of Bliss, The.
Gather the Rose ("The whiles some one did chant this lovely lay"). Spenser. *See* Song of Bliss.
Gather while you may. Rose. Kathleen Raine. WPE
Gather ye bank-notes while ye may. Election Time. *Unknown.* FaBoPa

Gather, ye brave sons of Ukadi Awaka! Moon Song. Chuba Nweke. PBA
Gather Ye Rosebuds. Laurence Fowler. BXAP
Gather ye rose-buds while ye may. To the Virgins, to Make Much of Time. Robert Herrick. AnAnS-2; AWP; BLPA; BoLoP; CABA; CaPo; CavP; ChTr; ELP; EnLoPo; ErPo; FaBoEn; FaBV; FaFP; FF; FPL; GBL; GTBS; GTBS-P; HAP; HeIP; HBV-1; InMe; InPK; InPS; JCP; LiTB; LoBV; MasP; NIP; NOBE; NoP; OAEL-1; OAEP; OBEV; OBS; OLR; PAI; PoEL-3; PoPl, PPoe; PrIm; QFR; SCV; SeCeV; SeCP; SeCV-1; SoSe; SpRo; TEP; TreFS; TrGrPo; ViBoPo; WHA
Gather Ye Roses. Robert Louis Stevenson. TreFT
Gather ye soap-suds while ye may. Counsel to Girls. Archibald Stodart-Walker. *Fr.* The Moxford Book of English Verse. CenHV
Gathered at the River. Denise Levertov. SV
Gathered in inter-admiration. When the Five Prominent Poets. Josephine Jacobsen. TAP
Gathered under leaded/ skies. Manomin. Phyllis Wolf. STE
Gathering, The. E. J. Pratt. *Fr.* Towards the Last Spike. MoCV; OBCV
Gathering, The. Sir Walter Scott. *Fr.* The Lady of the Lake. OBNC
("Time rolls his ceaseless course. The race of yore," *shorter sel.*) ViBoPo
Gathering, The. Herbert B. Swett. PAH
Gathering, The. Dwayne Thorpe. AMV-81
Gathering Leaves. Robert Frost. VGW
Gathering of things, boxed against, A. Moving Day. Lewis B. Horne. HoAn
Gathering on the Plains, The. William T. Butler. PoOW
Gathering Song of Donald the Black [*or* Donuil Dhu]. Sir Walter Scott. *See* Pibroch.
Gathering the bloom of all the fairest boys that be. Epigram. Strato, *tr. by* Sydney Oswald. PeHV
Gathering the Bones Together. Gregory Orr. AmPA; GeTw; Psk
Gathering the Sparks Howard Schwartz. VWA
Gatigwanasti, Ayunini, Suate. Owl and Rooster. Gladys Cardiff. STE
Gatineaus, The. James Wreford Watson. CaP
Gaudeamus Igitur. *Unknown, tr. fr. Latin by* John Addington Symonds. *Fr.* Carmina Burana. GLGT; HBV-2
Gauger walked with willing foot, The. A Song of the Road. Robert Louis Stevenson. BrPo
Gauley Bridge. Muriel Rukeyser. NNaP
Gauley Bridge is a good town for Negroes. George Robinson: Blues. Muriel Rukeyser. NNaP
Gauls Sacrifice, The. C. M. Doughty. *Fr.* The Dawn in Britain. FaBoTw
Gaunt brown walls, The. Interior. W. E. Henley. In Hospital, III. BrPo
Gaunt in gloom. Nightpiece. James Joyce. NoAM; PoA; SyP
Gaunt in the midst of the prairie. Chicago. John Boyle O'Reilly. PAH
Gaunt kept house with her child for the old man. Montana Fifty Years Ago. J. V. Cunningham. Prf
Gaunt, rueful knight, on raw-boned, shambling hack. Don Quixote. Craven Langstroth Betts. AA
Gaunt thing, The. Babylon Revisited. Amiri Baraka. BPo; NoAM; TW
Gautama in the Deer Park at Benares. Kenneth Patchen. NaP
Gave me things I. Swallow the Lake. Clarence Major. PoBA
Gave proof through the night. Poem to My Sister, Ethel Ennis, Who Sang "The Star-spangled Banner" at the Second Inauguration of Richard Milhous Nixon. June Jordan. TAP
Gawain and the Lady of the Castle, *orig. and mod. English prose. Unknown. Fr.* Sir Gawain and the Green Knight. OxBM
("Thus laykes this lorde by lunde-wodes eves.") EBEV
Gawayn spurred on, and he picked out a path. Sir Gawayn Goes to Receive His Return Blow from the Green Knight. *Unknown. Fr.* Sir Gawain and the Green Knight. FaBoPP
Gay, The. "Æ." OBMV
Gay and audacious crime glints in his eyes. In the Vices. Donald Evans. HBMV
Gay belles of fashion may boast of excelling, The. The Needle. Samuel Woodworth. GN; HBV-2
Gay Boys. James Kirkup. PeHV
Gay citizen, myself, and thoughtful friend. More Sonnets at Christmas, IV. Allen Tate. LiTA; LiTM; NePA
Gay Epiphany. James Mitchell. PeHV
Gay, gay, gay, gay. Remember the Day of Judgement. *Unknown.* MeEL
Gay go up and gay go down. The Bells of London [*or* London Bells]. *Unknown.* ChTr; EvOK; HBV-1; HBVY; LiTB; OxBoLi; OxNR; PoPle; PoRA
Gay Goshawk [*or* Goss-Hawk], The. *Unknown, at. to* Anna Gordon Brown. ESPB (A *and* E *vers.*); GN; HBV-2; OxBB, *with music;* WPE
Gay, guiltless pair. The Winged Worshippers. Charles Sprague. AA; HBV-2
Gay hussars, The—I love them all. Song of the Vivandière. Heine, *tr. by* Louis Untermeyer. UnTE
Gay jolly cowboy is up with the sun, The. *Unknown.* CoSo
Gay little Dandelion. Little Dandelion. Helen Barron Bostwick. HBV-1; HBVY
Gay little Girl-of-the-Diving-Tank. At the Carnival. Anne Spencer. BANP; BlSi; CDC; NoAM; PoNe
Gay Old Hag, The. *Unknown.* BIrV
Gay raftsmen, oh where are they, The? The Raftsmen. *Unknown.* FSW
Gay sea-plants familiar were to her, The. Sea-nurtured. Jean Ingelow. EtS
Gaze North-east. *Unknown, tr. fr. Irish by* John Montague. BIrV
Gaze not on Swans, in whose soft breast. Beauty Extoll'd [*or* On His Mistress]. *Unknown, at. to* Henry Noel and to William Strode. ChTr; ELP; OBS; PoEL-2
Gaze not on thy beauties pride. Good Counsel [*or* Counsell] to a Young Maid [*or* Song]. Thomas Carew. AnAnS-2; CaPo; CavP; ErPo; OBS
Gaze Not on Youth. *Unknown.* NCEP
Gazelle, A. Richard Henry Stoddard. AA
Gazelle Calf, The. D. H. Lawrence. OxBTC
Gazelles and Unicorn. John Gray. *Fr.* The Long Road. ChTr
Gazelles, The. T. Sturge Moore. BrPo; OBMV
Gazeteer of Newfoundland. Michael Harrington. CaP
Gazing upon him now, severe and dead. Edna St. Vincent Millay. SBG
Gean Trees, The. Violet Jacob. PoSH
Gebir, *sels.* Walter Savage Landor.
"But Gebir when he heard of her approach," *fr.* I. OBRV
"Long awaited day at last arrived, The," *fr.* VII. OBRV
Masar, *fr.* V. LoBV
("Once a fair city, courted then by Kings," *shorter sel.*) OBRV
Sea-Nymph's Parting, The. FaBoEn
Tamar's Wrestling, *fr.* I. EnRP
(Shepherd and the Nymph, The.) OBNC
Gee, but I Want to Go Home. *Unknown.* FSW
Gee, but it's tough to be broke, kid. I Can't Give You Anything but Love. Dorothy Fields. BLSo
Gee Ho, Dobin. *Unknown.* CoMu
Gee I Like to Think of Dead. E. E. Cummings. HoPM
Gee, Officer Krupke. Stephen Sondheim. OBAL
Gee-up Dar, Mules. Edwin Ford Piper. YaD
Gee up, Neddy, to the fair. *Unknown.* OxNR
Geeandess. William Cole. PV
Geese. Oliver Herford. *See* Some Geese.
Geese, The. Hyam Plutzik. BiP
Geese fly off, but sometimes they don't take, The. Owning a Dead Man. Marcia Southwick. AMV-80; MAYP
Geese in the pond are drifting, five. Wandsworth Common. David Bromwich. PoA
Geiger, geiger, ticking slow. Paul Dehn. SpRo
Geisha. Gary Gildner. GP; POL
Geist's Grave. Matthew Arnold. FM; HBV-1; TEP
Gellatley's Song to the Deerhounds. Sir Walter Scott. *See* Hie Away.
Gellius, what reason can you give why those ruddy lips of yours. Catullus, *tr. fr. Latin.* PeHV
Gem and the Flower, The. Pope. *Fr.* Moral Essays, Epistle I. OBEC
Gem of all isthmuses and isles that lie. Sirmio. Catullus, *tr. by* Charles Stuart Calverley. AWP
Gem of the crimson-colour'd Even. To the Evening Star. Thomas Campbell. GTBS; GTBS-P; OBNC
Gemini and Virgo. Charles Stuart Calverley. WhC
"And, if you asked of him to say," *sel.* FiBHP
Gemini Elegy. Margaret Gibson. MAYP
Gemini Jones. Willard R. Espy. FaBoUs
Gemlike Flame, The. R. P. Lister. DBV; FiBHP
Gemmed with white daisies was the great green world. To Tony (Aged 3). Marjorie Wilson. SUMH
Gems and jewels let them heap. In a Garret. Herman Melville. OBAL
Gemwood. Marvin Bell. FiCP; LCAP
Gender of a Latin Noun, The. Memorial Lines on the Gender of Latin Substantives. Benjamin Hall Kennedy. FaBoUs
Genealogical Reflection. Ogden Nash. OBAL
Genealogy. Donald Finkel. VWA
Genealogy. Frank Lamont Phillips. AmNP
Genealogy. Eléni Vakaló, *tr. fr. Modern Greek by* Paul Merchant. PBWP
General, The. Siegfried Sassoon. BrPo; CMoP; DBV; ELU; FaBV; FiBHP; LiTM; MMA; MoVE; OBWP; OxBoLi; OxBTC; TW
General Armstrong, The. *Unknown.* PAH
General Communion, A. Alice Meynell. NOCV; WPE
General dashed along the road, The. The General's Death. Joseph O'Connor. AA
General Eclipse, The. John Cleveland. AnAnS-2
General Elliott, The. Robert Graves. DBV
General Howe's Letter. *Unknown.* PAH
General John. W. S. Gilbert. NA
General Joseph Warren's Address. John Pierpont. *See* Warren's Address at Bunker Hill.
General Ludd's Triumph. *Unknown.* OBET
General Prologue. Chaucer. *See* Canterbury Tales, The: Prologue.

General Public, The. Stephen Vincent Benét. GLGT
General requires a portrait, The. On a Portrait by Copley. Arthur Freeman. DBV
General Secretary's feet whispered over the red carpet, The. Anteroom: Geneva. Denis Devlin. CIP
General Store. Rachel Field. SoPo; SUS
General Summary, A. Kipling. HBV-1
General William Booth Enters into Heaven. Vachel Lindsay. AmPP; CMoP; HBV-2; LiTA; LiTM; MoAB; MoAmPo; MoPo; NoAM; NOBA; OxBA; PoA; SeCeV; TAP; TreFS; TrGrPo; WGRP
Generalities. Robert Conquest. OxBC
Generalization. Joseph Capp. *See* Man Is a Fool.
General's Death, The. Joseph O'Connor. AA
Generation before me departed too soon, The. Generations. Moishe Steingart, *tr. by* Gabriel Preil. VWA
Generation Gap, The. Ruby C. Saunders. BlSi
Generation Gap Bronwen Wallace. AMV-80
Generations. Joseph Awad. AMV-81
Generations, The. George M. Brady. OnYI
Generations. Robert Clark. PoAu-2
Generations. Judy Dothard Simmons. CNA
Generations. Moishe Steingart, *tr. fr. Yiddish by* Gabriel Preil. VWA
Generosity. *Unknown, tr. fr. Irish by* Frank O'Connor. KiLC
"Generosity of her love provides, The." The Grand Guignols of Love. Michael Benedikt. AmPA
Generous Creed, A. Elizabeth Stuart Phelps. WGRP
Generous man will not deny, The. An Elegy on the Late King of Patagonia. St. John Emile Clavering Hankin. CenHV
Generous Years, The. Stephen Spender. PoCh
Genesis, *sels.* Bible, *O.T.*
Adam and Eve, II: 7-III: 23. TreFT
"And God saw that the wickedness of man was great," VI: 5-9. NAWM-1
"And the Lord God planted a garden eastward in Eden," II: 8-22. OAEL-1
"And the whole earth was of one language, and of one speech," X: 1-9. EyDe; NAWM-1
"And there came two angels to Sodom even," XIX: 1-38. HoPM
"In the beginning God created the heaven and the earth." ImOP (I: 1-31); NAWM-1 (I-IV)
(Creation, The, I: 1-II: 3.) TreF
"I will put enmities/ Between thee and the woman," III: 15, *Douay vers.* ISi
"Joseph, being seventeen years old, was feeding the flock with his brethren," XXXVII-XLVI, *abr.* NAWM-1
"See, the smell of my sone is as the smell of a feld," XXVII: 27-29, *tr. by* William Tyndale. OBVE
Genesis, *sels.* Caedmon, *tr. fr. Anglo-Saxon.*
Approach of Pharaoh, The, *tr. by* C. W. Kennedy. ACP; WaaP
Far and Wide She Went. EtS
Noah's Flood, *tr. by* C.W. Kennedy. AnOE
"Son of Lamech let a black raven, The." PBBP
Temptation and Fall of Man, The, *tr. by* C. W. Kennedy. AnOE
Genesis. Brian Higgins. FaBoTw
Genesis Geoffrey Hill. HAP; NePoEA; OAEL-2; OxBC
Genesis. John Hall Ingham. AA
Genesis. Lotte Kramer. VWA
Genesis, *sel.* Delmore Schwartz.
You Are a Jew! TrJP
Genesis. Jules Alan Wein. TrJP
Genesis, Exo, Levi, Num, Deutero, Joshua, Judges. Memoria Technica for the Books of the Bible. *Unknown.* FaBoUs
Genesis of Butterflies, The. Victor Hugo, *tr. fr. French by* Andrew Lang. AWP
Genesis of Vowels. James Broughton. CrMA
Geneva. Alastair Reid. NYBP
Genia, The. Ann Stanford. WSC
Genial Grimalkin, The. J. G. Francis. TDH
Genitori. David Ray. TW
Genius, The. Leonard Cohen. MoCV
Genius. R. J. P. Hewison. FaFP
Genius. Louis Saunders Perkins. PeHV
Genius. Edward Lucas White. AA; WGRP
Genius in Beauty. Dante Gabriel Rossetti. The House of Life, XVIII. OAEP
Genius Loci. Margaret L. Woods. HBV-2; OBEV; OBVV
Genius Loci of the Morning. Doug Fetherling. NeAC
Genius of ancient Greece! whose faithful steps. Invocation to the Genius of Greece. Mark Akenside. *Fr.* The Pleasures of Imagination, I. OBEC
Genius of Death, The. George Croly. HBV-2
Genji caught a gray bird, fluttering. Journeys. Gary Snyder. NU
Genocide. Nora Dauenhauer. TWSS
Genocide/ castrated nation. An Irish Blessing. Joan Murray. LTB
Gen'ral, The! one of those brave old commanders. The Old General. Sir Charles Hanbury Williams. *Fr.* Isabella. OBEC
Genteel, elegant once, the place has seen hard times. Gramercy Park Hotel. David Smith. NYP
Genteel in personage. A Maiden's Ideal of a Husband. Henry Carey. *Fr.* The Contrivances. HBV-1
Gentian sleeps in waters, The. Symphony in Blue. Raymond F. Roseliep. ISi
Gentian weaves her fringes, The. Emily Dickinson. PoRA
Gentilesse. Chaucer. AWP; OAEL-1
Gentill butler, bell ami. Fill the Bowl, Butler! *Unknown.* MeEL
Gentle Alice Brown. W. S. Gilbert. FaBoCo; FiBHP; InMe; NA
Gentle and generous, brave-hearted, kind. The Comfort of the Trees. Richard Watson Gilder. PAH
Gentle and smiling as before. The Wheel. Robert Hayden. BPo
Gentle at last, and as clean as ever. Grandfather in the Old Men's Home W. S. Merwin. ConAP; LiTM
Gentle Check, The. Joseph Beaumont. PBBP
Gentle Cock, The. *Unknown. See* I Have a Gentle Cock.
Gentle Craft, The, *sels.* Thomas Deloney.
Song: "Primrose in the green forest, The." TiPo; ViBoPo
Would God That It Were Holiday! ElL
Gentle Echo on Woman, A. Swift. FaBoCo; FiBHP; NU; OLR; OnYI
Gentle footsteps on the sand. The Crows. Maria Valli. CBAP
Gentle Heart, A: Two. Judith Johnson Sherwin. BoWoP
Gentle Hill, The. Salvatore Quasimodo, *tr. fr. Italian by* Allen Mandelbaum. PoPl
Gentle hunter. Leopard. *Yoruba Oral Tradition, tr. by* Ulli Beier. WTO
Gentle Jane once chanced to sit. The Swift Bullets. Carolyn Wells. ShM
Gentle Jesus [Meek and Mild]. Charles Wesley. OxBChV; OxBoCh; TreFS
Gentle knight was pricking on the plain, A. The Red-Cross Knight. Spenser. *Fr.* The Faerie Queene, I, 1. EBEV; OAEL-1; GoBC
Gentle lady, do not sing. James Joyce. Chamber Music, XXVIII. OLR
Gentle Mary, noble maiden, give us help! Prayer to the Virgin. *Unknown, tr. by* John Strachan *and* Kuno Meyer. OnYI
Gentle milk jug blue and white, The. The Milk Jug. Oliver Herford. HBMV; HBVY
"Gentle, modest little flower." To Phoebe. W. S. Gilbert. InMe; OLR
Gentle Name. Selma Robinson. MoShBr
Gentle Nymphs, Be Not Refusing. William Browne. *Fr.* Britannia's Pastorals. ElL; ViBoPo
Gentle of hand, the Dean of St. Patrick's guided. A Sermon on Swift. Austin Clarke. BIrV; IPY
Gentle Park, A. Moss Herbert. GoYe
Gentle River, Gentle River. *Unknown, tr. fr. Spanish by* Thomas Percy. AWP
Gentle Shepherd, The, *sels.* Allan Ramsay.
Dainty Sang, A. OBEC
(Jocky Said to Jeany.) BSV
My Peggy. GN
(Sang: "My Peggy is a young thing.") LoBV; OBEC
Gentle Snorer, The. Mona Van Duyn. NePA
Gentle sounds rise up to me. From Mount Nebo. Karl Wolfskehl, *tr. by* Erna Baber Rosenfeld. VWA
Gentle thought there is will often start, A. Dante, *tr. by* Dante Gabriel Rossetti. La Vita Nuova, XXVI. AWP
Gentle Wind, A. Fu Hsüan, *tr. fr. Chinese by* Arthur Waley. AWP
"Gentle youth, forbear." Hero Feels the Shaft of Love. Christopher Marlowe. *Fr.* Hero and Leander. GBL
Gentled Beast, The. Dilys Laing. PH
Gentleman, The. Menahem ben Judah Lonzano, *tr. fr. Hebrew by* A. B. Rhine. TrJP
Gentleman cam oure the sea, A. The Cruel Brother. *Unknown.* ESPB
Gentleman in hunting rode astray, A. The Beggar Woman. William King. NOEC
Gentleman of Fifty Soliloquizes, A. Don Marquis. HBMV
Gentleman of the Old School, A. Austin Dobson. HBV-1
Gentlemen. Geoffrey Taylor. FaBoEE
Gentlemen and Ladies, I pray you lend an ear. Colonel Sharp. *Unknown.* BaBo
Gentlemen, as we take our seats. The Rehearsal. Horace Gregory. VGW
"Gentlemen, look on this wonder." The Adhesive Autopsy of Walt Whitman. Jonathan Williams. PoM
Gentleness of rain was in the wind, The. Fragment: Rain. Shelley. ChER; POL
Gentlest Lady, The. Dorothy Parker. ISi
Gentlest of women, put your weapons by. Lay Your Arms Aside. Pierce Ferriter, *tr. by* Eilean Ni Chuilleanain. BIrV
Gentlest poet, with free thoughts endowed, The. Suggested by a Picture of the Bird of Paradise. Wordsworth. VLP
Gently dip, but not too deep. The Song at the Well [*or* Celanta at the Well

of Life *or* The Voice from the Well]. George Peele. *Fr.* The Old Wives' Tale. ChTr; ELP; FaBoEn; InPS; LoBV; SeCeV
Gently! Gently! Gently! The Ocean Is like a Wreath. Kuapakaa, *tr. fr. Hawaiian.* WTO
Gently I stir a white feather fan. In the Mountains on a Summer Day. Li Po, *tr. by* Arthur Waley. AWP
Gently I wave the visible world away. The Absinthe-Drinker. Arthur Symons. BrPo; FaBoTw
Gently Johnny, My Jingalo. *Unknown.* FSW, *diff. vers.*; OBET; UnTE
Gently, Lord, oh, gently lead us. In Sorrow. Thomas Hastings. AA; HBV-2
Gently, years, gently! Ralph Hodgson. POL
Gently!—gently!—down!—down! Chorus of Spirits. George Darley. *Fr.* Sylvia; or, The May Queen. OnYI
Geoffrey Chaucer. E. C. Bentley. *Fr.* Clerihews. PV
Geographers. Alexander Barclay. *Fr.* The Ship of Fools. ACP
Geographers, The. Karl Shapiro. OxBA
Geography. G. K. Chesterton. *Fr.* Songs of Education. HBMV; OBSV
Geography, *sels.* Michael Dransfield.
"In the forest, in unexplored," III. CBAP
"Sky ceases. There is only," VI. CBAP
Geography. Eleanor Farjeon. FaPON
Geography. Kenneth Koch. NoAM
Geography; a Song. Howard Moss. CAD; PV
Geological Faults. Barbara Unger. AMV-81
Geologist's Epitaph, A. Jane W. Stedman. WhC
Geo-Politics. Alvaro Cardona-Hine. PoDr
Geordie. *Unknown.* AmFP; BaBo (A, B, *and* C *vers.*); ESPB (A *and* D vers.); FaBoBa; FSW; OBET; OxBB, *with music*
George. Hilaire Belloc. FiBHP
George. Dudley Randall. BPo; ConAP; NoAM
George Allen. *Unknown.* AmFP
(Engine 143.) FSW
George Aloe and the *Sweepstake,* The. *Unknown.* BaBo; ESPB; ViBoFo
George and Martha Washington. Picture People. Rowena Bennett. YeAr
George Britton, *with music. Unknown.* CoSo
George Collins. *Unknown.* FSW
George Collins came home last Saturday night. Lady Alice. *Unknown.* AmFP
George Collins drove home one cold winter night. George Collins. FSW
George Crabbe. E. A. Robinson. AP; BLPL; CMoP; CoBMV; LiTA; LiTM; MoAB; MoAmPo; MoVE; NePA; NOBA; NoP; OxBA; PoEL-5; PP; TAP
George-Hector. The Emancipation of George-Hector (a Colored Turtle). Mari Evans. AmNP
George Hirst. E. C. Bentley. *Fr.* Clerihews. PoPle
George lives in an apartment and. Radiator Lions. Dorothy Aldis. SoPo
George Ridler's Oven. *Unknown.* OBET
George Robinson: Blues. Muriel Rukeyser. NNaP
George Sand. Dorothy Parker. FiBHP
George Simic. Charles Simic. DiL
George I—Star of Brunswick. Thackeray. *Fr.* The Georges. FaBoEE
George the First was always reckoned. The Georges. Walter Savage Landor. ChTr; DBV; FaBoCo; FaBoEE; FiBHP; NIP; OBSV
George IV. Thackeray. *Fr.* The Georges. FaBoEE
George the Fourth in Ireland. Byron. OBRV
George the Fourth, the son of Third, the grandson of the Second. Lines on the Succession of the Kings of England (Reversed). *Unknown.* FaBoUs
George II. Thackeray. *Fr.* The Georges. FaBoEE
George the Third. E. C. Bentley. *Fr.* Clerihews. DBV; FaBoCo; FiBHP; NOBL; OxBoLi; PV
George the Third. Byron. *Fr.* The Vision of Judgement. FiP; TW
George III. Thackeray. *Fr.* The Georges. FaBoEE
George III and the Sailor. "Peter Pindar." *Fr.* The Royal Tour, and Weymouth Amusements. NOEC
George III said with a smile. *Unknown.* FaBoUs
George III Visits Whitbread's Brewery. "Peter. Pindar." *Fr.* Instructions to a Celebrated Laureat. NOEC
George the Third's Soliloquy. Philip Freneau. NOBA
George Washington. Rosemary *and* Stephen Vincent Benét. FaPON
George Washington. John Hall Ingham. AA; OHIP; PAH; PAL
George Washington. Shelley Silverstein. PoSC
George Washington. James S. Tippett. YeAr
George Washington. *Unknown.* OHIP
George Washington Goes to a Girlie Movie. Aram Boyajian. NeAC
George Washington is tops with me. George Washington. Shelley Silverstein. PoSC
George Washington, the farmer. George Washington. James S. Tippett. YeAr
George Washington, your name is on my lips. Patriotic Poem. Diane Wakoski. OFD; VGW
George Whalen, *with music. Unknown. See* Whalen's Fate.
Georges Bank. Julia Older. WOLT
Georges, The. Walter Savage Landor. ChTr; DBV; FaBoEE; FiBHP; NIP; OBSV
(On the Four Georges.) FaBoCo
Georges, The (I-IV). Thackeray. FaBoEE
Georgia Boy, *with music. Unknown.* OuSiCo
Georgia Dusk. Jean Toomer. AmNP; BPo; CDC; NoAM; NoP; PoBA
Georgia Land, *with music. Unknown.* OuSiCo
Georgia Towns. Daniel Whitehead Hicky. AmFN
Georgia Volunteer, A. Mary Ashley Townsend. AA
Georgiad, The, *sels.* Roy Campbell.
"Hail, mediocrity, beneath whose spell." MoBrPo
"Next him Jack Squire through his own tear-drops splashes." OxBTC
Georgian Spring. Roy Campbell. OBSV
Georgics, *sels.* Virgil, *tr. fr. Latin.*
Care of Bees, The, *fr.* IV, *tr. by* Dryden. FaBoUs
"Observe the daily circle of the sun," *fr.* I, *tr. by* Dryden. FaBoUs
Prelude: "What makes a plenteous harvest," *fr.* I, *tr. by* Dryden. AWP
We Have Paid Enough Long Since in Our Own Blood, *tr. by* Richmond Lattimore. WaaP
Georgie Porgie. Franklin P. Adams. HBMV
Georgie Porgie, pudding and pie. Mother Goose. OxNR
Georgie Wedlock. *Unknown.* AmFP
Gerald kissed me when he left. Another Cynical Variation. "Helen." InMe
Geraldine's Daughter, The. Egan O'Rahilly, *tr. fr. Modern Irish by* James Clarence Mangan. AnIL; OnYI
Geranium, houseleek, laid in oblong beds. Poem. John Gray. SyP
Geranium, The. Theodore Roethke. CoAP; UnPo; WeW
Geranium, The. Sheridan. BoLoP; ErPo; UnTE
Geraniums, The. Genevieve Taggard. VGW
Gerbil Who Got Away, The. Judith C. Root. AMV-81
Gerda, My Husband's Wife. Eve Triem. GP
Geriatric Whore, The. Pete Winslow. PV
Germ, The. Ogden Nash. CenHV; MoShBr
German Fatherland, The. Ernst Moritz Arndt, *tr. fr. German.* HBV-2
German Legion, The. Sydney Dobell. PeD
German Shepherd. Myra Cohn Livingston. RFM
German submarines were an idea we watched. The Home Front. Marvin Bell. GP
Germanic. Crossing. Anthony Barnett. VWA
Germans in Greek, The. Porson on German Scholarship. Richard Porson. FaBoCo; FaBoEE
Germans live in Germany, The. Home. J. H. Goring. MoShBr
Germans rub it on, The. The Stones of Sleep. E. L. Mayo. FAZ
Germinal. "Æ." BIrV; MoBrPo; OBEV; OBMV
Germination. Arlene Stone. VWA
Geron and Histor. Sir Philip Sidney. *Fr.* Arcadia. SiPS
Geronimo. Ernest McGaffey. AA; BPAW; PAH
Geronimo: Old Man Lives On. Ronald James Dessus. LFAC
Gerontion. T. S. Eliot. AmPP; AP; CABA; ChMP; CMoP; CoBMV; EBEV; FaBoEn; GTBS-P; HAP; InPS; LiTA; LiTM; LoBV; MoPo; NePA; NoAM; NOBA; OAEL-2; OAEP; OxBA; PAI; PPP; SBVL; SeCePo; SeCeV; TAP; TwAmPo
Gertie Green made eyes at me. Serve Her Right. John Barford. PeHV
Gertrude and Gulielma, sister-twins. Elegy in Six Sonnets. Frederick Goddard Tuckerman. *Fr.* Sonnets. AP; HAP; QFR
Gertrude Stein at Snails Bay. Peter Porter. OxBC
Gertrude's Prayer. Kipling. FaBoEn
Gervais. Margaret Adelaide Wilson. SUMH
Gest of Robyn Hode, A. *Unknown.* ESPB; OxBB
Gesture. Donald Finkel. InPK
Gesture, The. Elizabeth Libbey. WeW
Gesture, The. George Oppen. *Fr.* Five Poems about Poetry. NNaP
Gesture. Winifred Welles. HBMV
Gesture by a Lady with an Assumed Name, A. James Wright. ConAP; LiTM
Gesture the gesture the gesture the gesture, The. Michael McClure. *Fr.* Hymn to St. Geryon. NeAP
Get a Transfer. *Unknown.* BLPA; WBLP
Get away, they're all gone. Chops Are Flyin. Stanley Crouch. NBP
"Get down, get down, lovin' Henry," she cried [*or* said]. Young Hunting [*or* Loving Henry]. *Unknown.* AmFP; BaBo
Get Hence Foule Griefe. Sir Philip Sidney. *Fr.* Arcadia. PoEL-1
(Contentment.) SiPS
Get Into the Boosting Business. *Unknown.* WBLP
Get it right or let it alone. Morals. James Thurber. *Fr.* Further Fables for Our Time. FaBV
Get on Board, Little Children. *Unknown. See* Gospel Train, The.
Get on, expecting the worst—a mount like a statue. The Trail Horse. David Wagoner. PH
"Get out of my way!" Roosters. Elizabeth J. Coatsworth. SO

Get place and wealth; if possible, with grace. Ambition. Pope. DBV
Get ready your money and come to me. *Unknown.* OxNR
Get Somebody Else. Paul Laurence Dunbar. BLRP; TRV
(Too Busy.) WBLP
Get Stuffed. Alurista, *tr. fr. Spanish by* Toni Empringham. FIA
Get the Gasworks. David Ignatow. InPK; InPS
"Get the verb right." About Motion Pictures. Ann Darr. GrPl
Get Thee behind Me, Satan. Lee Hays, Millard Lampell, *and* Pete Seeger. FSW
Get thee glass eyes. Shakespeare. *Fr.* King Lear. DBV
Get thee to the mountains. Birthing: 2000. Pancho Aguila. LFAC
Get them new. Jeans. J. V. Brummels. GP
Get Up. Philip Levine. NYP
Get Up! Joseph Skipsey. InPK; VLP
Get Up and Bar the Door. *Unknown.* AmFP; BaBo; BiP; BSV; EnSB; ESPB (A *and* B *vers.*); FaBoBa; GoTS; HeIP; NoP (A *vers.*); OnMSP; OxBS; PDV; TrGrPo; ViBoPo
Get Up, Blues. James A. Emanuel. AmNP; BOLo; PoBA
Get Up, Get Up. *Unknown.* FiBHP; NTCP
Get up, get up for shame, the blooming morn. Corinna's Going a-Maying. Robert Herrick. AnAnS-2; BiP; BoNaP; CABA; CaPo; GN; HAP; HBV-1; JCP; NIP; NOBE; NoP; OAEL-1; OAEP; OBEV; OBS; PoEL-3; PoPle; PPP; PrIm; SeCeV; SeCP; SeCV-1; TEP; TreFT; TrGrPo; WHA
"Get up, get up, pretty Polly," he says. Pretty Polly. *Unknown.* UnTE
Get up, get up, you lazy-head. Get Up, Get Up. *Unknown.* FiBHP; NTCP
"Get up, our Anna dear, from the weary spinning wheel." The Fairy Thorn. Sir Samuel Ferguson. AnIV; CH; OnMSP; OnYI; VLP
"Get up!" the caller calls, "Get up!" Get Up! Joseph Skipsey. InPK; VLP
Get up under a mule. The Mule. Coleman Barks. POL
Get You Gone. Sir Charles Sedley. ELP
Get your tongue. Poem. Ted Kooser. POL
Gethsemane. Arna Bontemps. CDC
Gethsemane. Kipling. FaBoTw
Gethsemane. William B. Tappan. *See* 'Tis Midnight and on Olive's Brow.
Gettin' Born. Anthony Euwer. PoPl; WhC
Getting a Job. Paul Blackburn. NYP
Getting a Poem in the Rain. Dick Lourie. NeAC
Getting Across. Carter Revard. VoR
Getting at the Root of the Matter. Henry Taylor. BXAP
Getting Back. Dorothy Brown Thompson. SiSoSe
Getting Back to Work. Leon Baker. LFAC
Getting By on Honesty. Stephen E. Smith. AMV-80
Getting Down to Get Over. June Jordan. TAP
Getting Drunk with Daughter. Robert Huff. NePoEA-2
Getting Experience. Miller Williams. GP; TAT
Getting Inside the Miracle. Luci Shaw. TrCP
Getting Loaded. Jim Thomas. AMV-80
Getting Lost in Nazi Germany. Marvin Bell. VWA
Getting Older Here. Barbara Hauk. AMV-80
Getting On. Stephen Sandy. CAD
Getting Out. J. J. Maloney. LFAC
Getting Out. Cleopatra Mathis. MAYP
Getting Out of Bed. Eleanor Farjeon. SiSoSe
Getting Serious. Gary Soto. NPGG
Getting the Mail. Galway Kinnell. UnPo
Getting Through. Maxine W. Kumin. SUW
Getting Through. James Merrill. NYBP
Getting through with the world. Approach to a City. William Carlos Williams. CAD; PoRA
Getting tired of sleeping in this: : low down lonesome cE-Ell. Prison Cell Blues. *Unknown.* BluL
Getting Under. Alan P. Lightman. AMV-81
Getting Up. Stephen Dobyns. MAYP
Gettysburg. James Jeffrey Roche. PAH
Gettysburg. Edmund Clarence Stedman. PAH
Gettysburg Ode, The, *sel.* Bayard Taylor.
Lincoln at Gettysburg. PAH
("After the eyes that looked, the lips that spake.") OHIP
Geve place, ye lovers, here before. Earl of Surrey. *See* Give Place, Ye Lovers.
Ghaisties. Robert Garioch. NeBP
Ghaists, The; a Kirk-Yard Eclogue. Robert Fergusson. OxBS
Ghastly, ghoulish, grinning skull. To a Skull. Joshua Henry Jones. BANP
Ghazal. Philip Dow. NPGG
Ghazal: Japanese Paintbrush. Randy Mott. PoDr
Ghazal XII. Mirza Ghalib, *tr. fr. Urdu by* W. S. Merwin *and* Aijaz Ahmad. LLLT
Ghazals, *sels.* Jim Harrison.
"After the 'invitation' by the preacher she collapsed in the." NoAM
"Dog, the lightning frightened us, dark house and both of us." InPS
"He sings from the bottom of a well but she can hear him up." NoAM
"I imagined her dead, killed by some local maniac who." InPS
"She climbed the ladder looking over the wall at the party." InPS
Ghazals: Homage to Ghalib, *sel.* Adrienne Rich.
"When your sperm enters me, it is altered." CABA
Ghazel of Absence, A. Gerrit Lansing. CoPo
Gheluvelt. Robert Bridges. BrPo
Ghetto Lovesong—Migration. Carole Gregory Clemmons. NBP; NMM
(Migration.) PoBA
Ghetto Summer School. Douglas Worth. FF
Ghetto Twilight. Alter Brody. VWA
Ghillies and shepherds are shouting Bravo. Macinnes's Mountain Patrol. Tom Patey. PoSH
Ghost, The, *sel.* Charles Churchill.
"Pomposo (insolent and loud"). OBSV
Ghost, The. Hilary Corke. NYBP
Ghost, The. W. H. Davies. BrPo
Ghost, The. Walter de la Mare. BrPo; ChMP; CMoP; ELP; EnLoPo; HBMV; LiTM; MoAB; MoBrPo; MoVE; NOBE; OAEL-2; OAEP; OxBTC
Ghost, The. Robert Lowell, *after the Latin of* Sextus Propertius. MoVE; PoA
Ghost. Christian Morgenstern, *tr. fr. German by* W. D. Snodgrass *and* Lore Segal. WSC
Ghost, The. ——— O'Brien. NOEC
Ghost. John V. A. Weaver. HBMV
Ghost Boy. Mark Van Doren. SO
Ghost-Flowers. Mary Thacher Higginson. AA; WeW
Ghost-grey the fall of night. A Robin. Walter de la Mare. ChTr; CMoP; FaBoRV; PB
Ghost House. Robert Frost. WSC
Ghost in the Cellarage, The. John Heath-Stubbs. NeBP
Ghost in the Martini, The. Anthony Hecht. OxBC
Ghost is someone, A: death has left a hole. The Ghost. Robert Lowell, *after* Sextus Propertius. MoVE; PoA
Ghost Night. Lizette Woodworth Reese. HBMV
Ghost of a Ghost, The. Brad Leithauser. MAYP
Ghost of a little white kitten, The. The Little Cat Angel. Leontine Stanfield. BLPA
Ghost of a mouldy larder is one thing, A: whiskery bread. Corposant. Peter Redgrove. NePoEA-2; OxBTC
Ghost of an Education, The. James Michie. NYBP
Ghost of another comes to visit and we hold, The. The Dance. Mark Strand. GeTw
Ghost of Ninon would be sorry now, The. Veteran Sirens. E. A. Robinson. NoAM; NOBA; QFR; SoSe
Ghost of Patroclus, The. Homer, *tr. fr. Greek by* Pope. *Fr.* The Iliad, XXII. PeHV
Ghost of the Buffaloes, The. Vachel Lindsay. *See* Ghosts of the Buffaloes, The.
Ghost of the Cargo Boat, The. Pablo Neruda, *tr. fr. Spanish by* Donald D. Walsh. WSC
Ghost Pet. Horatio Colony. GoYe
Ghost Poem Five. Mary Norbert Körte. IHMS
Ghost Story. Dylan Thomas. OBCP
Ghost That Jim Saw, The. Bret Harte. ShM
Ghost, that loved a lady fair, A. The Phantom-Wooer. Thomas Lovell Beddoes. EnRP; OBRV; TrGrPo; ViBoPo; WiR
Ghostesses. *Unknown.* ChTr
Ghostly Crew, The, 2 *versions, with music. Unknown.* ShS
Ghostly Father, The. Peter Redgrove. MoBS; NePoEA-2
Ghostly Gladness. Richard Rolle of Hampole. HAP
Ghostly Story. Milton Acorn. NeAC
Ghostly Tree. Léonie Adams. MoAB; MoAmPo
Ghosts. Harry Behn. RHPC
Ghosts. Elizabeth Jennings. NePoEA-2; PPJ
Ghosts, The. Longfellow. *Fr.* The Song of Hiawatha. LoBV
Ghosts. Ethna MacCarthy. NeIP
Ghosts. Richard Kendall Munkittrick. AA
Ghosts. Alastair Reid. NYBP
Ghosts are attacking me, crowding up from. The Poet Haunted. Wendy Rose. TWSS
Ghost's Leavetaking, The. Sylvia Plath. NePoEA-2
Ghosts of flowers went sailing, The. Changelings. Mary Thacher Higginson. AA
Ghosts of the Buffaloes, The. Vachel Lindsay. MoAmPo; NePA
(Ghost of the Buffaloes, The.) BPAW
Ghost's Song, The. *Unknown.* *See* Cauld Lad of Hilton, The.
Ghosts' Stories. Alastair Reid. NePoEA-2
Ghosts there must be with me in this old house. Solitude. Walter de la Mare. CMoP; FaBoEn

Ghosts: they conjure. Translations. Wing Tek Lum. BrSi
Ghoul, The. Jack Prelutsky. OBCA
Ghoul Care. Ralph Hodgson. MoBrPo
Ghoulies and Ghosties. *Unknown. See* Litany for Halloween.
Ghoulish Old Fellow in Kent, A. Morris Bishop. ShM
Ghouls, The. Helen Hamilton. SUMH
Ghyrlond of the Blessed Virgin Marie, The. Ben Jonson. ISi
Giant brontosaurus, The. Brontosaurus. Gail Kredenser. RHPC
Giant came to me when I was young, A. The Lost Genius. John James Piatt. AA
Giant Decorative Dahlia. Molly Holden. OxBTC
Giant Norway spruce from Podunk, The. December. James Schuyler. NoAM
Giant-Power from earth's remotest caves, The. Steam Power. Erasmus Darwin. *Fr.* The Botanic Garden. NOEC
Giant Puffball, The. Edmund Blunden. FaBoTw
Giant sparkler,/ Lights of the river. "A 4." Louis Zukofsky. *Fr.* "A." VGW
Giant Squid of Tsurai, The. Kirk Robertson. GP
Giant Thunder. James Reeves. BoNaP; DuDa
Giant Tortoise, The. Edward Lucie-Smith. BoAnP
(“Giant tortoise had a look, The.”) POL
Giant wink in a clown's cheek, The. Phaeton. Eli Mandel. PeCV
Giantess. Baudelaire, *tr. fr. French.* ErPo, *tr. by* Karl Shapiro; OBVE, *tr. by* Roy Campbell
Giant's Tomb in Georgian Bay. "Katherine Hale." CaP
Giardino Pubblico. Sir Osbert Sitwell. ChMP
Gibberish. Mary Elizabeth Coleridge. MoVE
Gibbs, *sel.* Muriel Rukeyser.
"It was much later in his life he rose." ImOP
Gibraltar. Wilfrid Scawen Blunt. ACP; HBV-2; OBEV; OBVV
Gibraltar. Richard Chenevix Trench. OBRV; OBVV
Giddy lark reacheth the steepy air, The. The Lark. *Unknown.* PBBP
Gideon at the Well. Geoffrey Hill. NePoEA
"Gie corn to my horse, mither." The Mother's Malison; or, Clyde's Water. *Unknown.* ESPB
Gi'e me a lass with a lump of land. Lass with a Lump of Land. Allan Ramsay. NOEC
Gie the Lass her Fairin'. Burns. CoMu; ErPo
Gife Langour. Lord Darnley. OxBS
Giffen's Debt. Kipling. VLP
Gift, The. "Æ." HBMV
Gift, The. John Ciardi. BiP; LiTM; MP; NMP
Gift. Leonard Cohen. NoAM; SoSe
Gift, The. Robert Creeley. NOBA
Gift, The. Ann Darr. PAI
Gift. Carol Feeeman. *See* Christmas Morning I.
Gift, The. Louise Glück. GP
Gift. Judith Hemschemeyer. PCP
Gift, The. Dick Lourie. NeAC
Gift, The. Ed Ochester. DFF; GP; Psk
Gift, The. Ann Stanford. GP
Gift, The. *Unknown.* PGD
Gift, The. William Carlos Williams. NePoAm-2; PoPl
Gift from Kenya. May Miller. BlSi
Gift from the cold and silent past! The Norsemen. Whittier. PAH
Gift Hour. Maria Banus, *tr. fr. Rumanian by* Willis Barnstone *and* Matei Calinescu. BoWoP; VWA
Gift of a Mirror to a Lady. David Wagoner. NePoAm-2
Gift of a Skull, The. John Skelton. *See* Upon a Dead Man's Head.
Gift of God, The. E. A. Robinson. AP; CoBMV; MoAB; MoAmPo; OxBA; TwAmPo
Gift of God, A. *Unknown.* STF
Gift of Gravity, The. Wendell Berry. GeTw
Gift of Great Value, A. Robert Creeley. LCAP; NaP
Gift of Judah the Woman-Hater, The, *sel.* Judah ibn Sabbatai.
Expensive Wife, The. TrJP
Gift of Sight. Robert Graves. PCP
Gift of Song, The. Anthony Hecht. NYBP
Gift of Speech, The. Sadi, *tr. fr. Persian by* L. Cranmer-Byng. *Fr.* The Gulistan. AWP
Gift of Water, The. Hamlin Garland. AA; BPAW
Gift Outright, The. Robert Frost. AmFN; AmPP; AP; CMoP; CoBMV; FaBoEn; GOA; LiTM; MoAB; MoAmPo; NoAM; NOBA; NoP; OxBA; PAL; PPP; SeCeV; WaP
Gift to a Jade. Anna Wickham. DBV; ELU
Gift to Be Simple, The. Howard Moss. ImOP; MP; Psk; TwCP
Gift with the Wrappings Off. Mary Elizabeth Counselman. RHPC
Gifts. Mary Elizabeth Coleridge. PBWP
Gifts, The. John Heath-Stubbs. OxBC
Gifts. Emma Lazarus. TrJP; WGRP
Gifts, The. Charles Levendosky. TAT
Gifts. Chauncey R. Piety. PGD
Gifts. Karen Snow. FYAP
Gifts. Leon Stokesbury. GP
Gifts. James Thomson ("B. V."). Sunday up the River, XV. HBV-1; OBEV; OBVV; TreF
Gifts of God, The. George Herbert. *See* Pulley, The.
Gifts of God, The. Jones Very. AA
Gifts of Rain. Seamus Heaney. IPY
Gifts Return'd, The. Walter Savage Landor. OBVV
Gifts that to our breasts we fold, The. Recompense. Nixon Waterman. HBV-2
Gig at Big Al's. Heather McHugh. GeTw
Gigantic beauty of a stallion, fresh and responsive to my caresses, A. The Stallion. Walt Whitman. *Fr.* Song of Myself, XXXII. PDV; PH
Gigantic mass, the hard material, The. Shore Leave Lorry. Roy Fuller. NoAM
Gigha. W. S. Graham. NeBP
Gil Brenton. *Unknown.* ESPB; OxBB
Gil Morrice, *with music. Unknown.* OxBB
Gil, the Toreador. Charles Henry Webb. AA
Gilbertian Recipe for a Politician. J. A. Lindon. DBV
Gilbertus Glanvil, whose heart was a hard as an anvil. *Tr. fr. Latin by* Matthew Prior. FaBoEE
Gildas a Latin "History of Britain's Conquest" wrote. Principal British Writers. Edward B. Goodwin. FaBoUs
Gilded Boys, The. Felice Picano. PeHV
Gilderoy. *Unknown.* OBET
(My Handsome Gilderoy.) CH
Giles Collin he said to his mother one day. Lady Alice (C *vers.*). *Unknown.* ESPB
Giles Collins he said to his old mother. Lady Alice (B *vers.*). *Unknown.* ESPB
Giles Corey. Lucy Larcom. PAH
Giles Corey of the Salem Farms, *sels.* Longfellow.
Prologue: "Delusions of the days that once have been." PAH
Trial, The. PAH
Giles Corey was a wizzard strong. Giles Corey. Lucy Larcom. PAH
Giles Johnson, Ph.D. Frank Marshall Davis. BPo; PoBA
Gilgamesh. *Unknown. See* Epic of Gilgamesh, The.
Gilk. Don Marquis. *Fr.* Savage Portraits. HBMV
Gill Boy. Dennis Schmitz. NPGG
Gill Morice stood in stable-door. Childe Maurice. *Unknown.* ESPB; ViBoFo
Gilliflower of Gold, The. William Morris. WHA
Gilly Silly Jarter. *Unknown.* OxNR
Gimboling. Isabella Gardner. ErPo
Gimel. Stuart Z. Perkoff. VWA
Gimme Dat Ol'-Time Religion, *with music. Unknown.* BoAN-1
(Give Me That Old Time Religion.) FSW
Gimme de Banjo, *with music. Unknown.* ShS
Gimme the ball, Willie is saying. Charge. Christopher Gilbert. MAYP
Gimme Yo' Han', *with music. Unknown.* BoAN-2
Gin a body meet a body. Comin' thro' the Rye. Burns. FaFP; FSW; LiTB; TreF; WBLP.
Gin a body meet a body. Rigid Body Sings [*or* In Memory of Edward Wilson]. James Clerk Maxwell. BXAP; FaBoCo; FaBoPa; Par; SpRo; WhC
Gin by Pailfuls. Sir Walter Scott. ChTr
Gin I Were a Doo. *Unknown.* GBP
Gin I were on my milkwhite steed. The Bents and Broom. *Unknown.* OxBB
Gin the Goodwife Stint. Basil Bunting. CTC; TW
Gin ye hae'd corneich airth an' time. To His Coy Mistress, *parody.* Gerry Hamill. BXAP
Gineral B. is a sensible man. *See* Guvener B. is a sensible man.
Ginevra. Samuel Rogers. BeLS; PoLF
Ginevra, *sel.* Shelley.
"She is still, she is cold." ChER
Ginger Bread Mama. Doughtry Long. BPo; PoBA
Gingerbread House, The. John Ower. AMV-80; DFT
Gingham dog and the calico cat, The. The Duel. Eugene Field. BeLS; CenHV; FaBoBe; FaFP; FaPON; FPL; HBV-1; HBVY; MoShBr; OBAL; OBCA; OHFP; OnMSP; PoLF; PoPl; PoRA; RHPC; SoPo; TreF; TiPo
Gingilee. Moishe-Leib Halpern, *tr. fr. Yiddish by* Joseph Leftwich. TrJP
Ginkgoes in Fall. Howard Nemerov. GP
Ginsberg had insight. Matrix III. Ed Lipman. LFAC
Gioconda. Thomas McGreevy. OnYI
Giorno dei Morti. D. H. Lawrence. BrPo; FaBoRV; NOBE; SeCePo
Giotto, I have not found. To Giotto. Wesley Trimpi. NePoEA
Giotto's Campanile. Guy Butler. PeSA
Giotto's Tower. Longfellow. EyDe

Giovanni da Fiesole on the Sublime; or, Fra Angelico's "Last Judgment." Richard Howard. Prf
"Giovinette, Che Fate All'Amore." Lorenzo da Ponte, *tr. fr. Italian by* Natalie MacFarren. *Fr.* Don Giovanni. TrJP
Gipsies. *See also* Gypsies.
Gipsies ("The gipsies seek wide sheltering woods again"). John Clare. ChTr
Gipsies ("The snow falls deep; the forest lies alone"). John Clare. CH; NBM; PoEL-4
(Gipsy Camp, The.) ChTr
(Gypsies.) NoP; PrIm
Gipsies, The. "Richard Scrace." CaP
Gipsies came to lord Cassilis' gate, The. *See* Gypsies they came to my lord Cassilis' yett, The.
Gipsies came to our good lord's gate, The. *See* Gypsies came to our good lords gate, The.
Gipsies lit their fires by the chalk-pit gate anew, The. The Idlers. Edmund Blunden. CH
Gipsies seek wide sheltering woods again, The. Gipsies. John Clare. ChTr
Gipsy Camp, The. John Clare. *See* Gipsies ("The snow falls deep").
Gipsy Girl, The. Ralph Hodgson. MoBrPo
Gipsy Jane. William Brighty Rands. FaPON
(Gypsy Jane.) SoPo; TiPo
Gipsy Laddie, The. *Unknown. See* Wraggle Taggle Gipsies, The.
Gipsy of the sea. Stormpetrel. Richard Murphy. IPY
Gipsy Queen. John Alexander Chapman. OBEV
Gipsy Song. Ben Jonson. *See* Faery Beam upon You.
Gipsy Trail, The. Kipling. HBV-1; PoRA
Gipsy's Warning, The. *Unknown.* BeLS
Giraffe, The, *sel.* Nikolai Gumilev, *tr. fr. Russian by* C. M. Bowra.
"Listen:/ There roams, far away, by the waters of Clead." FaPON
Giraffe. Stanley Plumly. AmPA
Giraffe, The. Marvin Solomon. NePoAm-2
Giraffe and the Woman, The. Laura E. Richards. PDV
Giraffe and Tree. W. J. Turner. CH; GrPl
Giraffe. *Unknown, tr. fr. Hottentot.* PeSA
Giraffes, The. Roy Fuller. ChMP; NeBP; NoAM
Girandole. Dorothy Donnelly. NYBP
Gird up thy loins now like a man. Out of the Whirlwind. Bible, *O.T. Fr.* Job. AWP
Girl, A. Babette Deutsch. HBMV
Girl. Dom Moraes. NePoEA-2
Girl, A. Ezra Pound. MoAB; MoAmPo
Girl. A. W. Purdy. NoAM
Girl at the Seaside. Richard Murphy. BIrV; NMP
Girl Athletes. Haniel Long. HBMV
Girl awaiting her lover is not more still with fear, A. Night Alert. Alison Boodson. NeBP
Girl Combs Her Hair, A. Kimiko Hahn. BrSi
Girl he married, The. The Good Woman. Crystal MacLean. FAZ
Girl Held without Bail. Margaret Walker. BPo; CNA; PoBA
Girl Help. Janet Lewis. HeIP; QFR
Girl hustles her islands of pure flesh, The. For Jan. John Wieners. CoPo
Girl I Call Alma, The. Linda Gregg. AmPA; NPGG
Girl I Left behind Me, The ("Break and trail home"). *Unknown.* AmFP
Girl I Left behind Me, The ("The dames of France are fond and free"). *Unknown, at. to* Thomas Osborne Davis. AmSS, *with music;* FaBoBe; FaFP; HBV-1; OnYI; TreF
Girl I Left behind Me, The ("I'm lonesome since I cross'd the hill"). *Unknown.* BLSo, *with music*; FSW; OBET
Girl I Left behind Me, The ("My parents raised me tenderly"). *Unknown.* AmFP
Girl I Love, The. *Unknown, tr. fr. Modern Irish by* Jeremiah Joseph Callanan. OnYI
Girl I Took to the Cocktail Party, The. Trevor Williams. FiBHP
Girl in a Black Bikini. Allan Brown. AMV-80
Girl in a grey frock. A Grey Frock. Zinaida Hippius, *tr. by* Temira Pachmuss. PBWP
Girl in a Library, A. Randall Jarrell. NoAM; NOBA; NoP
Girl in a Nightgown. Wallace Stevens. OxBA
Girl in a White Coat. John Malcolm Brinnin. SaC
Girl in a Window, A. James Wright. ErPo
Girl in Front of the Bank. Robert Wallace. DFF
Girl in the Foreign Movie, The. Patricia Goedicke. FAZ
Girl in the lane, The. Mother Goose. OxNR
Girl in the sand, The. Nude Kneeling in Sand. John Logan. ErPo
Girl in the tea shop, The. The Tea Shop. Ezra Pound. HeIP
Girl in the Willow Tree, The. Carolyn Maisel. IHMS
Girl in trousers wheeling a red baby, The. Metamorphoses. Roy Fuller. OxBTC
Girl in White. Stephen Dobyns. MAYP
Girl is twirling a parasol, A. Snapshot. John Fuller. NePoEA-2
Girl of Constant Sorrow. Sara Ogan Gunning. FSW
Girl of Pompeii, A. Edward Sandford Martin. AA; HBV-1
Girl of the Future, feared of all. A Dresscessional. Carolyn Wells. WBLP
Girl of the musing mouth. Statuette: Late Minoan. C. Day Lewis. OxBI
Girl of the Red Mouth. Martin MacDermott. HBV-1; OnYI
Girl of three cows don't crow! Showing Off. *Unknown, tr. by* Frank O'Connor. KiLC
Girl on the Greenbriar Shore, The. *Unknown.* FSW
Girl on the Milk-white Horse, The. Rachel Field. *See* Equestrienne.
Girl Powdering Her Neck. Cathy Song. MAYP
Girl Sitting Alone at Party. Donald Justice. DFF
Girl Takes Her Place among the Mothers, The. Marya Zaturenska. HBMV
Girl, The/The Girlie Magazine. Pat Gray. AMV-81
Girl to Soldier on Leave. Isaac Rosenberg. MMA
Girl to Woman. Nixeon Civille Handy. AMV-80
Girl today, dreaming, A. Auf dem Wasser zu Singen. Stephen Spender. EnLoPo
Girl Walking. Charles G. Bell. ErPo; NePoAm-2
Girl, when rejecting me you never guessed. To a Jilt. Martin Armstrong. FaBoEE
Girl who felt my stare and raised her eyes, The. The Invisible Man. T. S. Matthews. POL
Girl Who Had Borne Too Much, The. John Woods. GP
Girl Who Learned to Sing in Crow, The. Paul Mariani. GeTw
Girl with Doves. Stephen Gray. PeSA
Girl with 18 Nightgowns, The. Gregory Orr. POL
Girl with Long Dark Hair. Stephen Gray. PeSA
Girl with the beautiful legs, The. The Tides. Paul Blackburn. PoM
Girl with the Green Skirt. Dana Naone. CDW
Girl with the theater hat, The. The Theater Hat. Carolyn Wells. TDH
Girl Writing Her English Paper, The. Robert Wallace. Psk
Girl, your young loveliness. White Swan. A. Glanz-Leyeles, *tr. by* Keith Bosley. VWA
Girls. Pablo Neruda, *tr. fr. Spanish by* Donald D. Walsh. OLR
Girls. Kenneth Rosen. AmPA
Girls, The. Siasconset Song. Philip Booth. NePoAm
Girls and boys, come out to play. Mother Goose. TiPo
Girls are simply the prettiest things. My Cat and I. Roger McGough. OxBTC; POL
Girls around Cape Horn, The. *Unknown.* AmFP
Girls, at bows, string concentric blooms. On the College Archery Range. Robert Wallace. LiSp
Girls, brighter than wine, are clothed and naked, The. Night Club. F. R. Scott. NOBC
Girls Can, Too! Lee Bennett Hopkins. RHPC
Girl's far treble, muted to the heat, The. Milkmaid. Laurie Lee. BoLoP; ChMP; FaBoTw
Girls from Home. Abraham Reisen, *tr. fr. Yiddish by* Keith Bosley. VWA
Girls in Their Seasons. Derek Mahon. BoLoP
Girl's Lamentation, The, *sl. abr.* William Allingham. SeCePo
Girl's Mood, A. Lizette Woodworth Reese. HBMV
Girls' Names. Eleanor Farjeon. SUS; TiPo
Girls on mopeds rode to Fécamp parties. The Musical Orchard. Douglas Dunn. FaBoMo
Girls on Saddleless Horses. R. G. Vliet. PH
Girls on the Yueh River. Li Po, *tr. fr. Chinese.* ChTr
Girls scream. School's Out. W. H. Davies. OBMV
Girl's Song, A. Katharine Tynan. OnYI; SUMH
Girl's Song. *Unknown, tr. fr. Taitok by* Willard Trask. LLLT
Girl's Song. Marya Zaturenska. OLR
Girls today in society, The. Brush Up Your Shakespeare. Cole Porter. OBAL
Girls' Voices. Brendan Gill. POL
Girls wake, stretch, and pad up to the door, The. Apartment Cats. Thom Gunn. GrPl
Girls with fat thighs and no breasts. Before Bed. Keith Waldrop. InPK
Girls Working in Banks. Karl Shapiro. WeW
Girod Street Cemetery: New Orleans. Harry Morris. GoYe
Girt in dark growths, yet glimmering with one star. Sleepless Dreams. Dante Gabriel Rossetti. The House of Life XXXIX. OAEP
Girt in my guiltless gown, as I sit here and sew. A Woman's Answer. *At. to* the Earl of Surrey. SiPS
Girt Woak Tree That's in the Dell, The. William Barnes. HBV-1
(Oak-Tree, The.) OBVV
Girt wold house o' mossy stuone, The. The Old House. William Barnes. OBVV
Girtonian Funeral, A. *Unknown.* FaBoCo; Par
Gislebertus' Eve. John Berryman. LCAP
Gisli, the Chieftain, *sel.* Isabella Valancy Crawford.
Song of the Arrow, The. OBCV; PeCV
Git Along Down to Town. *Unknown.* AmFP
Git Along Little Dogies. *Unknown.* BPAW; FSW; MoShBr
(As I Walked Out.) BPAW

(Whoopee Ti Yi To, Git Along Little Dogies.) AS, *with music;* CoSo, *with music;* FaPON; TiPo; TreF
Git on Board, Little Chillen. *Unknown.* *See* Gospel Train, The.
Git yer [*or* yo'] little sage hens ready. At a Cowboy Dance. James Barton Adams. BPAW; HBV-2; PoOW
Gita Govinda, The, *sels.* Jayadeva, *tr. fr. Sanskrit.*
Hymn to Vishnu, *tr. by* Sir Edwin Arnold. AWP
"Sandal and garment of yellow and lotus garlands upon his body of blue," *tr. by* George Keyt. ErPo
Gitanjali, *sels.* Rabindranath Tagore.
Day after Day, LXXVI. OBMV
"Day was when I did not keep myself in readiness, The," XLIII. ILwL
"Have you not heard his silent steps?" XLV WGRP
"Here is thy footstool and there rest they feet," X-XI. WGRP
I Have Got My Leave. OBMV
If It Is Not My Portion, LXXIX. OBMV
On the Slope of the Desolate River, LXIV. OBMV
Thou Art the Sky, LXVII. OBMV
"Thou hast made me endless, such is thy pleasure," I. ILwL
Gittin'-up Hollers. *Unknown.* CoSo
Giuseppe, da barber, ees greata for "mash." Mia Carlotta. T. A. Daly. InMe; TreFS; WhC
Giv but to things their tru esteem. Right Apprehension. Thomas Traherne. PoEL-2
Give a man a horse he can ride. Gifts. James Thomson ("B. V."). Sunday up the River, XV. HBV-1; OBEV; OBVV; TreF
Give a man his. Wait for Me. Robert Creeley. NOBA; PPP
Give a Rouse. Robert Browning. Cavalier Tunes, II. HBV-2; OAEP
Give a rouse, then, in the Maytime. A Stein Song. Richard Hovey. *Fr.* Spring. HBV-2
Give All to Love. Emerson. AmPP; AP; AWP; FaBoEn; FaFP; FPL; HBV-1; LiTA; NePA; NOBA; OBEV; OBVV; OxBA; PoEL-4; PoLF; TreFS; TrGrPo; TAP; ViBoPo
Give as you would if an angel. How to Give. *Unknown.* BLRP
Give attention to my ditty and I'll not keep you long. My Grandfather's Days. *Unknown.* OBET
Give Beauty All Her Right. Thomas Campion. AAS; OBSC; ViBoPo
(Beauty Is Not Bound.) TrGrPo
Give ear my children to my words. John Rogers' Exhortation to His Children. *Unknown.* *Fr.* The New England Primer. OBCA
Give Ear, O God, to My Loud Cry, *with music.* Thomas Prince. AH
Give Ear, O Heavens, to That Which I Declare, *with music.* Henry Ainsworth. AH
Give ear to my prayer, O God. Bible, *O.T.* Psalms, LV. AWP
Give ear, ye British hearts of gold. Rodney's Glory. Owen Roe O'Sullivan. OnYI
Give Ear, Ye Heavens. Bible, *O. T.* Deuteronomy, XXXII: 1-43. TrJP
Give ear you lusty gallants. A Famous Sea-Fight. John Looke. CoMu
Give freely to the friend thou hast. Koina ta ton Philon. John Addington Symonds. OBVV
Give God thy heart. Motto for a Sundial. *Unknown.* FaBoEE
Give greatly of your grunts, O pig. Hymn to Joy. Julia Cunningham. PChr
Give her but a least excuse to love me! Song. Robert Browning. *Fr.* Pippa Passes. ViBoPo
Give him the darkest inch your shelf allows. George Crabbe. E. A. Robinson. AP; BLPL; CMoP; CoBMV; LiTA; LiTM; MoAB; MoAmPo; MoVE; NePA; NOBA; NoP; OxBA; PoEL-5; PP; TAP
Give honor and love for evermore. Peter Cooper. Joaquin Miller. AA
Give honour unto Luke Evangelist. Saint Luke the Painter. Dante Gabriel Rossetti. The House of Life, LXXIV. GoBC; VLP
Give Love To-Day. Ethel Talbot. HBV-1
Give Lucinda pearl nor stone. To the New Year. Thomas Carew. CaPo
Give me a boy whose tender skin. Epigram. Martial, *tr. by* Brian Hill. PeHV
Give me a chair. Song of the Poor Man. *Unknown, tr. by* Anselm Hollo. TTY
Give me a color. America. Wendy Rose. CDW
Give me a death like Buddha's, let me fall. Prayer. Stanley Moss. GP; POL
"Give me a fillet, Love," quoth I. Love and Life. Julie Mathilde Lippmann. AA; HBV-1
Give me a girle [*or* girlie] (if one I needs must meet). Women. William Cartwright. ELU; ErPo
Give me [*or* us] a good digestion, Lord, and also something to digest. An Ancient Prayer. Thomas H. B. Webb. BLPA; FaBoBe; STF; TreFS
Give me a heart where no impure. To Castara. William Habington. AnAnS-2
Give me a home in the far, far West. The Far, Far West. *Unknown.* CoSo
Give Me a Kiss [from Those Sweet Lips of Thine]. *Unknown.* InvP
Give me a man that is not dull. His Desire. Robert Herrick. CABA; OAEP
Give me a race that is run in a breath. The Hundred-Yard Dash. William Lindsey. AA
Give me a royal niche—it is my due. George III. Thackeray. *Fr.* The Georges. FaBoEE
Give me a spirit that on life's rough sea. The Master Spirit. George Chapman. *Fr.* The Conspiracy of Charles, Duke of Byron. EtS; ViBoPo
Give me a spoon of oleo, Ma. Domestic Science. *Unknown.* WBLP
Give me a thrill, says the reader. Fiction and the Reading Public. Philip Larkin. NOBL; OBSV
Give Me Ale. *Unknown.* *See* In Praise of Ale.
"Give me but two brigades," said Hooker. The Battle of Lookout Mountain. George Henry Boker. PAH
Give Me Five. William J. Harris. CNA
Give me, give me Buriano. Bacchus's Opinion of Wine, and Other Beverages. Francesco Redi, *tr. by* Leigh Hunt. *Fr.* Bacchus in Tuscany. AWP; OBVE
Give me hunger. At a Window. Carl Sandburg. FaBoBe; HBMV; TrPWD
Give me, in this inconstant ebb and flow. Seaward Bound. Alice Brown. TrPWD
Give Me Jesus. *Unknown.* BoAN-1, *with music;* BPo
Give me kisses! Do not stay. To Lesbia. John Godfrey Saxe. HBV-1; UnTE
Give Me Leave. "A. W." TrGrPo
(Petition to Have Her Leave to Die.) OBSC
Give Me More Love. Thomas Carew. *See* Mediocrity in Love Rejected.
Give Me My Infant Now. Te-whaka-io-roa, *tr. fr. Maori by* John White. NAs; WTO
Give me, my love, that billing kiss. The Kiss. Thomas Moore. EnLoPo
Give me my robe, put on my crown; I have. Death of Cleopatra. Shakespeare. *Fr.* Antony and Cleopatra, V, ii. FaBoRV; FiP; TreFS; TrGrPo
Give Me My Scallop-Shell of Quiet. Sir Walter Ralegh. *See* Passionate Man's Pilgrimage, The.
Give me my scallop shell of quiet; let me go. Theme and Variations. W. P. Ker. PoSH
Give Me My Work. George Whetstone. ElL
Give me no mansions ivory white. The Desire. Katharine Tynan. HBV-1
Give Me Not Tears: Despair. Rose Hawthorne Lathrop. AA
Give Me Not Tears: Joy. Rose Hawthorne Lathrop. AA
Give me, O friend, the secret of thy heart. Rosa Rosarum. Agnes Mary Frances Robinson. HBMV
Give me, O indulgent Fate! The Petition for an Absolute Retreat. Countess of Winchilsea. OBEC; PoEL-3; SBG; TrGrPo; WPE
Give me of every language, first my vigorous English. The English Language. William Wetmore Story. GN
Give me one kiss. To Dianeme. Robert Herrick. CaPo; FaBoBe
Give me something to eat. Poor Crow! Mary Mapes Dodge. OBCA
Give me sweet nectar in a kiss. *Unknown.* FaBoEE
Give me that man that dares bestride. His Cavalier. Robert Herrick. CaPo; GoJo
Give Me That Old Time Religion. *Unknown.* *See* Gimme Dat Ol'-Time Religion.
Give me the avowed, the erect, the manly foe. The Candid Friend. George Canning. TreFS; TreFT
Give me the dance of your boughs, O Tree. Song to a Tree. Edwin Markham. FaPON
Give me the darkest corner of a cloud. Sonnet. R. W. Dixon. LO
Give me the Daulian bird and Locrian Arsinoë. From V. C. (a Gentleman of Verona). Gavin Ewart. OxBC
Give me the hills and wide water. The Hills and the Sea. Wilfred Campbell. CaP
Give me the hills, that echo silence back. The Silent Ranges. Stephen Moylan Bird. HBMV
Give me the lowest place; not that I dare. The Lowest Place. Christina Rossetti. TrPWD
Give me the merchants of the Indian mines. Mine Argosy from Alexandria. Christopher Marlowe. *Fr.* The Jew of Malta, I, i. ChTr
Give Me the Old. Robert Hinckley Messinger. *See* Winter Wish, A.
Give me the plains—the barren and sun-beaten plains! The Plains. Maynard Dixon. BPAW
Give me the priest these graces shall possess. The Priest of Christ. Thomas Ken. TRV
Give me the right of way. Irish. Paul Celan, *tr. by* Michael Hamburger. OBVE
Give me the room whose every nook. The Library. Frank Dempster Sherman. AA
"Give me the salt spray in my face." What the Red-haired Bo'sun Said. Charles H. Souter. PoAu-1
Give Me the Splendid Silent Sun. Walt Whitman. AA; BoNaP; FaPON; HAP; MoAmPo; NOBA; NYP

Give me the sunlight and the sea. Sunlight and Sea. Alfred Noyes. MOS
Give me the wretched refuse of your teams: pitchers with sore elbows. Amurrika! Philip Appleman. BXAP
Give me this day a faith not personal. More Sonnets at Christmas, III. Allen Tate. LiTA; LiTM; NePA; SBVL; WaP
Give Me Three Grains of Corn, Mother. Amelia Blandford Edwards. AS, *with music;* BLPA
Give Me Thy Heart. Adelaide Anne Procter. ACP; GoBC
Give me to die unwitting of the day. Mors Benefica. Edmund Clarence Stedman. AA
Give me truths. Blight. Emerson. AP; NoP; NOBA
Give me white paper! Columbus. Edward Everett Hale. PAH
Give me work to do. A Prayer. *Unknown.* PGD
"Give me your bark, O Birch-tree!" Hiawatha's Canoe. Longfellow. *Fr.* The Song of Hiawatha. OHIP
Give me your hand old Revolutionary. The Centenarian's Story. Walt Whitman. CTC
Give me your pardon, sir. I have done you wrong. Shakespeare. *Fr.* Hamlet, V, ii. DL
Give money me, take friendship whoso list. Of Money. Barnabe Googe. ElL; EnRePo; FF; NoP
Give My Heart a Song. Anna M. Gilleland. STF
Give My Regards to Broadway, *with music.* George M. Cohan. BLSo; FSN
Give No White Flower. Brenda Chamberlain. NeIP
Give Our Conscience Light. Aline B. Carter. TrPWD
Give over seeking bastard joy. Exhortation. Louise Bogan. QFR
Give over to high things the fervent thought. To Lovers of Earth: Fair Warning. Countee Cullen. CDC
Give pardon, blessèd soul, to my bold cries. On the Death of Sir Philip Sidney [*or* To Sir Philip Sidney's Soul]. Henry Constable. ElL; GoBC; OBEV; OBSC; SeCePo
Give patient eare to something I man saye. Admonition to Montgomerie. James I, King of England. OxBS
Give Peace in These Our Days, O Lord, *with music.* Edmund Grindal. AH
Give Peace, O God, the Nations Cry, *with music.* John W. Norris. AH
Give pensions to the learned pig. Blake. FaBoEE
Give place all ye that doth rejoice. Sir Thomas Wyatt. SiPS
Give Place, Ye Lovers. Earl of Surrey. EnRePo; SiPS
("Geve place, ye lovers, here before.") AAS
(His Incomparable Lady.) OBSC
(Praise of His Love, Wherein He Reproveth Them That Compare Their Ladies with His, A.) ElL; WHA
Give place, you ladies, and be gone! A Praise of His Lady. *At. to* John Heywood. ElL; HBV-1; OBEV; OBSC; ViBoPo
Give store of days, good Jove, give length of years. Juvenal, *tr. by* Henry Vaughan. *Fr.* Satires, X. OBSV
Give Thanks. Helen Isabella Tupper. *See* For Everything Give Thanks.
Give thanks, O heart, for the high souls. Edwin Markham. *Fr.* Conscripts of the Dream. PGD
Give the mourning doves any sun. The Ruined Motel. Reginald Gibbons. MAYP
Give the sounds of the curved mated phonographs. Three Found Poems. George Hitchcock. OBAL
Give them my regards when you go to the school reunion. More of a Corpse than a Woman. Muriel Rukeyser. NMM
Give Them the Flowers Now. *Unknown.* WBLP
Give to me the life I love. The Vagabond. Robert Louis Stevenson. BrPo; HBV-1; HBVY; TreFT; ViBoPo
Give to the Living. Ida Goldsmith Morris. WBLP
Give to the Winds Thy Fears. Paul Gerhardt, *tr. fr. German by* John Wesley. TRV
(Courage.) WGRP
Give unto the Lord, O ye mighty. Bible, *O.T.* Psalms, XXIX. AWP
Give us a good digestion, Lord. *See* Give me a good digestion, Lord . . .
"Give us a song!" the soldiers cried. The Song of the Camp. Bayard Taylor. AA; BeLS; GN; HBV-2; HBVY; WBLP
Give us a virile Christ for these rough days! A Virile Christ. Rex Boundy. TRV; WGRP
Give us a watchword for the hour. Evangelize! Henry Crocker. BLRP
Give us a wrack or two, Good Lard. The Wreckers' Prayer. Theodore Goodridge Roberts. OBCV; PeCV
Give us another poem, he said. Prelude. Patrick Kavanagh. IPY; NoAM
Give Us Sober Men. Walter E. Isenhour. STF
"Give Us This Day Our Daily Bread." Maltbie D. Babcock. TRV
Give Us This Day Our Daily Day. Robert J. Levy. AMV-81
Give Way. Donald Finkel. NePoEA-2
Give Way! Charlotte Perkins Gilman. WGRP
Give way to the man coming at you. Give Way. Donald Finkel. NePoEA-2
Give Way, Ye Gates. Theodore Roethke. CMoP; NMP
Giveaway, The. Phyllis McGinley. PoRA
Given, not lent. Unto Us a Son Is Given. Alice Meynell. EBCP
Given Note, The. Seamus Heaney. NCSH
Given the morning, its rush of flowers. Machupuchare. What the Mountain Said. Shaking the Dead Bones, Christmas Eve, 1974. Joseph Stroud. NPGG
Given the seriousness of these affairs. Textile Mills and Prison Reform. George Rachow. LFAC
Given this light. Ostia Antica. Anthony Hecht. NePA
Giver of bliss and pain, of song and prayer. Epilogue. William Alexander Percy. TrPWD
Giver of Life, The. *Unknown, tr. fr. Dahomean song by* Frances Herskovits. EaLo
Giving and Taking. James Kirkup. EaLo
Giving oneself to the dentist or doctor who is a good one. The Kind of Act Of. Robert Creeley. NeAP
Giving Thanks. Bible, *O.T.* Psalm C: 4. BLRP
Giving the Moon a New Chance. Terry Stokes. MOON
Giving Up Butterflies. Geraldine Kudaka. BrSi
Giving Up on the Shore. Gabriel Preil, *tr. fr. Hebrew by* Gabriel Levin. VWA
Gizzard and some ruby inner parts, A. A Lament. Margaret Avison. HAP
Glabrous girl and hispid boy, The. Male and Female. W. Craddle. WhC
Glaciers pushed, The. The Ronan Robe Series. Jaune Quick-To-See-Smith. TWSS
Glad and Blithe Might Ye Be. *Unknown.* SBVL
(Hymn of the Incarnation, A.) MeEL
Glad, but not flush'd with gladness. Swinburne. *Fr.* Before the Mirror. OBEV
Glad Christmas comes, and every hearth. December. John Clare. OBCP
Glad Day. W. Graham Robertson. HBV-1
Glad Day. Louis Untermeyer. TrJP
Glad Earth. Ella C. Forbes. YeAr
Glad harvest greets us, The; brave toiler for bread. Song of the Harvest. Henry Stevenson Washburn. OHIP
Glad that I live am I. A Little Song of Life. Lizette Woodworth Reese. FaPON; HBMV; OBCA; TiPo; TreFT
Glad tidings we bring of peace on earth. Shalom Chaverim. *Unknown.* FSW
Glad youth had come thy sixteenth year to crown. Epigram. Ausonius. PeHV
Gladdest spaniel who prancing brings the ball, The. Dog Alice. Harold Witt. BoAnP
Glade, The. Robert Kelly. The Book of Persephone, 18. PoM
Gladioli for My Mother. Harriet Bernstein. AMV-81
Gladness of Nature, The. Bryant. HBV-1; HBVY
Gladness of the May, The. Wordsworth. YeAr
Gladstone. Julian Symons. WaP
Gladstone gave his name to the gladstone bag. Christopher Reid. POL
Gladstone was still respected. Yeux Glauques. Ezra Pound. *Fr.* Hugh Selwyn Mauberley. MoAmPo
Glamour of the end attic, the smell of old, The. Perdita. Louis MacNeice. PoA
Glance, The. George Herbert. AnAnS-1
Glance at the Album, A. Gray Burr. CoPo
Glanced down at Shannon from the sky-way. Irish-American Dignitary. Austin Clarke. BlrV
Glanmore Sonnets, *sels.* Seamus Heaney.
"I dreamt we slept in a moss in Donegal," X. NoP
"This evening the cuckoo and the corncrake," III. IPY
"Thunderlight on the split logs: big raindrops," VII. IPY
"Vowels plowed into other: opened ground," I. NoP
Glasgerion. *Unknown.* ESPB (A *and* B *vers.*); OxBB; ViBoFo
Glasgow, *sel.* John Mayne.
"Hail, Glasgow! famed for ilka thing." BSV
Glasgow. Alexander Scott. BSV
Glasgow Peggie. *Unknown.* BaBo; ESPB
Glasgow Schoolboys, Running Backwards. Douglas Dunn. OxBC
Glasgow Street. William Montgomerie. OxBS
Glass. Robert Francis. DFF; PP
Glass. Brendan Galvin. LTB
Glass. Takako Uchino Lento. BoWoP
Glass. W. S. Merwin. EAS
Glass antique, 'twixt thee and Nell. Nell Gwynne's Looking-Glass. Laman Blanchard. HBV-1
Glass Bubbles, The. Samuel Greenberg. LiTA; NePA
Glass Dialectic. Howard Nemerov. WaP
Glass Door, The. Robert Watson. GP
Glass Eaters, The. George Jonas. NeAC
Glass falls lower, The. Sad Green. Sylvia Townsend Warner. MoBrPo
Glass had been falling all the afternoon, The. Storm Warnings. Adrienne Rich. NIP
Glass I've wanted to live. Through You. Edwin Honig. TAP

Glass of Beer, A. James Stephens, *after the Irish of* David O'Bruaidar. CMoP; DBV; DTC; FaBoCo; FiBHP; NCSH; NoAM; OBMV; OxBTC; SeCePo; TreFT; TW; WhC
(Righteous Anger.) AnIV; MoAB; MoBrPo; PoPl
Glass of Pure Water, The, *sel.* "Hugh MacDiarmid."
"Hold a glass of pure water to the eye of the sun!" BSV
Glass of Water, The. Wallace Stevens. AP; CABA; CoBMV; MoAB; MoAmPo; MoPo; OxBA; TAP
Glass on the picture from the Bible, The. Darkening Hotel Room. Alfred Corn. MAYP
Glass, out of deep and out of desperate want. Upon Glass: Epigram. Robert Herrick. JCP
Glass Town, The. Alastair Reid. NYBP
Glass was the street. Emily Dickinson. OxBA
Glass World. Dorothy Donnelly. NCSH
Glass Blower, The. James Scully. MP; NYBP; TwCP
Glassblower lies here at rest, A. Epitaph. J. B. Morton. FaBoEE
Glassed with cold sleep and dazzled by the moon. Train Journey. Judith Wright. PBWP
Glasses are raised, the voices drift into laughter, The. Pub. Julian Symons. LiTB; WaP
Glaucopis. Richard Hughes. OBMV
Glaucous-Gull's Death, The. Daniel James O'Sullivan. NeIP
Glaukos, why is it you and I are honored beyond all men. Sarpedon to Glaukos. Homer, *tr. by* Richmond Lattimore. *Fr.* The Iliad. WaaP
Glaze of ice glistens in the manure, A. The Kiss. Robert Pack. AMV-81
Glazed day crumbles to its fall, The. Provincetown, Mass. Harvey Shapiro. PoA
Glazier, The. Stéphane Mallarmé, *tr. fr. French by* Keith Bosley. OBVE
Glazunoviana. John Ashbery. LCAP
Gleaming in silver are the hills! Washed in Silver. James Stephens. ELU; MOON
Gleaner, The. Jane Taylor. OxBChV
Glee for Winter, A. Alfred Domett. HBV-1
Glee—The Ghosts. Thomas Love Peacock. *Fr.* Melincourt. ViBoPo
Glen Lough. Geoffrey Grigson. FaBoPP
Glen of Silence, The. "Hugh MacDiarmid." CMoP; NeBP
Glen Pean. Dennis Rixon. PoSH
Glen Rosa. William Jeffrey. PoSH
Glenara. Thomas Campbell. HBV-2
Glenaradale. Walter Chalmers Smith. OBEV; OBVV
Glenarm. John Lyle Donaghy. NeIP
Glenaveril, *sel.* "Owen Meredith."
Tears. EBVV
Glencoe. G. K. Chesterton. PoSH
Glencoe. Douglas Stewart. CBAP
Glenfinlas; or, Lord Ronald's Coronach. Sir Walter Scott. GoTL
Glengormley. Derek Mahon. CIP
Glenkindie. William Bell Scott. HBV-2
Glenkindie was ance a harper gude. Glasgerion. *Unknown.* ESPB
Glenlogie; or, Jean o Bethelnie, *diff. versions. Unknown.* ESPB (A *and* B *vers.*); GN; HBV-1
Glenn Miller and I were heroes. Chorus. Jack Kerouac. *Fr.* Mexico City Blues. NeAP
Glenn Miller's music is a trunk. Carmen Valle, *tr. fr. Spanish by* Julio Marzán. InW
Glenpool. Annette Arkeketa West. TWSS
Glens, The. John Hewitt. NeIP
Glide Soft, Ye Silver Floods. William Browne. *Fr.* Britannia's Pastorals. ElL
Glimpse, A. Frances Cornford. OBMV
Glimpse. Pearl Cleage Lomax. PoBA
Glimpse, A. Walt Whitman. AmPP; NePA; OxBA; PeHV; PPP
Glimpse of a once-loved face, The. What Do They Say. Gary Snyder. NNaP
Glimpse of the Body Shop, A. Stephen Berg. NaP
Glimpse through an interstice caught, A. A Glimpse. Walt Whitman. AmPP; NePA; OxBA; PeHV
Glimpsed world, halfway through the film, A. The Malice of Innocence. Denise Levertov. NNaP
Glimpses. Roy Helton. HBMV
Glimpses #xii, *sel.* Lawrence McGaugh.
"Old man walks to me, The." BOLo
Glion?—Ah, twenty years, it cuts. Obermann Once More. Matthew Arnold. PoEL-5
Glittering, adroit, the Sicilian wonder. Death and Empedocles 444 B.C. Horace Gregory. PoA
Glittering high in the midnight sky the starry rockets soar. Dewey and His Men. Wallace Rice. PAH
Glittering leaves of the rhododendrons, The. Green Symphony. John Gould Fletcher. MoAmPo; MoVE
Glittering rises in flocks, The. The Approaches. W. S. Merwin. NOBA; Prf
Glittering roofs are still with frost, The; each worn. A January Morning. Archibald Lampman. OBCV
Gloaming. Robert Adger Bowen. HBV-1
Gloat, glittering talmudist. Talmudist. Stanley Burnshaw. VWA
Globe, a paper of the Tories, The. A Suggestion Made by the Posters of the *Globe.* J. E. Thorold Rogers. FaBoEE
Gloire de Dijon. D. H. Lawrence. BrPo; CMoP; ELP; EnLoPo; ErPo; GBL; NoAM; OAEP; PAI
Gloom of death is on the raven's wing, The. The Raven. E. A. Robinson, *after* Nicarchus. AWP; FaBoEE; OBAL
Glooms of the live-oaks, beautiful-braided and woven. The Marshes of Glynn. Sidney Lanier. AA; AmPP; AP; HBV-1; LiTA; NePA; NOBA; OxBA; PrIm; TreFT; WGRP; WHA
Gloomy and dark art thou, O chief of the mighty Omahas. To the Driving Cloud. Longfellow. ChTr; FaBoEn; FaBoRV; PoEL-5
Gloomy Cathedral, A. Paris. Gertrud Kolmar, *tr. by* David Kipp. PBWP
Gloomy grammarians in golden gowns. Of [*or* On] the Manner of Addressing Clouds. Wallace Stevens. PoA; QFR
Gloomy hulls, in armour grim, The. The *Temeraire.* Herman Melville. WaaP
Gloomy night before us flies, The. Jefferson and Liberty. *Unknown.* FSW; TrAS
Gloomy night embraced the place. The Shepherds' Hymn. Richard Crashaw. *Fr.* In the Holy Nativity of Our Lord God. NOBE; ViBoPo
Gloomy Night of Sadness, The, *with music. Unknown.* AH
Gloomy thought, Ben Bulben, A. The Deserted Mountain. *Unknown, tr. by* John Montague. BIrV
Gloria in Excelsis. *Unknown.* WGRP
"Gloria Patri," The. John Heywood. ACP
Glories of Our Blood and State, The. James Shirley. *Fr.* The Contention of Ajax and Ulysses. CaVP; ChTr; FaBoRV; HAP; InvP; JCP; NoP; OBS; PoPle; PoRA; PPP; TrGrPo; ViBoPo; WaaP
(Death the Leveller.) BLPL; FaPoR; FF; GTBS; GTBS-P; LiTB; LoBV; NOBE; OBEV; PPON; SeCeV; UnPo
(Death's Final Conquest.) HBV-2
(Dirge, A.) ACP; AWP; OAEL-1; PoEL-2; TreFT
(Of Death.) WHA
(Our Blood and State.) GoBC
(Song.) FaBoEn
Glories of the world sink down in gloom, The. Sic Transit. Joseph Mary Plunkett. ACP
Glories of the world struck me, made me aria, once, The. John Berryman. Dream Songs, XXVI. NaP
Glories, Pleasures. John Ford. *Fr.* The Broken Heart, V, iii. ViBoPo
(Dirge: "Glories, pleasures, pomps, delights, and ease.") LoBV
(Song, A: "Glories, pleasures, pomps, delights, and ease.") OBS
Glorious Game, The. Richard Burton. HBMV
Glorious it is/ to see long-haired winter caribou. *Tr. fr. Eskimo. Fr.* Song of Caribou, Musk Oxen, Women, and Men Who Would Be Manly. RFM
Glorious it is to see/ The caribou flocking down from the forests. Song of Caribou, Musk Oxen, Women, and Men Who Would Be Manly. *Tr. fr. Eskimo.* WTO
Glorious sun went blushing to his bed, The. Michael Drayton. Idea's Mirrour, XXV. OBSC
Glorious the day when in arms at Assunpink. Assunpink and Princeton. Thomas Dunn English. PAH
Glorious the sun in mid career. Christopher Smart. *Fr.* A Song to David. FaBoCh
Glorious Things of Thee Are Spoken. John Newton. NOCV; WGRP
(Zion, or the City of God.) NOEC
Glorious Twelfth, The. Robert Greacen. NeIP
Glorious Victory of Navarino, The! *Unknown.* CoMu
Glorious Virgin, heavenly vision. O Virgin. *Tr. fr. Gaelic by* Douglas Hyde. WTO
Glory. Marianne Moore. NYBP
(Carnegie Hall: Rescued.) NYP
Glory. Harvey Shapiro. POL
Glory, The. Edward Thomas. OxBTC
Glory, *with music.* Joseph Wise. AH
Glory and honor and fame and everlasting laudation. Sherman. Richard Watson Gilder. AA
Glory and loveliness have pass'd away. To Leigh Hunt, Esq. [*or* Dedication: To Leigh Hunt, Esq. *or* Dedication to Leigh Hunt]. Keats. EnRP; OBNC; ViBoPo
Glory be to God for dappled things. Pied Beauty. Gerard Manley Hopkins. AWP; BiP; BrPo; CABA; CMoP; CoBMV; EaLo; EBCP; EBVV; FaBoEn; FaBoMo; FaFP; GoJo; GTBS-P; HAP; HeIP; HoPM; InPK; InPS; InvP; LiTB; LiTM; MoAB; MoBrPo; MoVE; NIP; NoAM; NOBE; NoP; OAEL-2; OAEP; OBEV; OBMV; OBNC; PAI; PoPl;

PoRA; PPP; PrIm; SCV; SoSe; SOTW; TEP; TreFS; TrGrPo; TRV; ViBoPo; VLP; WeW
Glory be to God on high. The Incarnation. Charles Wesley. NOCV
Glory be to God on high, and on earth peace, good-will towards men. Gloria in Excelsis. *Unknown.* WGRP
Glory, Glory to the Sun. John Alford. HBMV
Glory Hallelujah! or, John Brown's Body. *Unknown, at. to* Charles Sprague Hall. *See* John Brown's Body.
Glory of and Grace in the Church Set Out, The. Edward Taylor. *Fr.* God's Determinations. AmPP; AP
Glory of Early Rising, The. Frank Sidgwick. WhC
Glory of God in Creation, The. Thomas Moore. OHIP
(Thou Art, O God, *abr.*) TrPWD
Glory of God, The. Bible, *O.T.* Psalms, XIX. *See* Heavens Declare the Glory of God, The.
Glory of Hanalei is its heavy rain, The. Alfred Alohikea, *tr. fr. Hawaiian by* S. H. Elbert *and* N. Mahoe. WTO
Glory of Him who moveth all that is, The. Dante, *tr. by* Laurence Binyon. Divina Commedia: Paradiso. NAWM-1
Glory of Lincoln, The. Thomas Curtis Clark. PGD
Glory of Love is brightest when the glory of self is dim, The. The True Apostolate. Ruby T. Weyburn. BLRP
Glory of Nature, The. Frederick Tennyson. OBNC
Glory of soundless heaven, wheel of stars. Valediction. John Hall Wheelock. NePoAm
Glory of the beauty of the morning, The. The Glory. Edward Thomas. OxBTC
Glory of the Day Was in Her Face, The. James Weldon Johnson. BANP; CDC; IDB; PoBA
Glory of the Garden, The. Kipling. EBCP
Glory of the sunset and the night, The. Youth. Preston Clark. HBMV
Glory of Toil, The. Edna Dean Proctor. PGD
Glory of warrior, glory of orator, glory of song. Wages. Tennyson. OAEP
Glory of Women. Siegfried Sassoon. MMA; OBWP
Glory Road, De. Clement Wood. HBMV; YaD
Glory to God and to God's Mother chaste. Sonnet: To Dante Alighieri (He Commends the Work of Dante's Life). Giovanni Quirino, *tr. by* Dante Gabriel Rossetti. AWP
Glory to Osiris, the Prince of Everlastingness. He Singeth a Hymn to Osiris, the Lord of Eternity. *Unknown, tr. by* Robert Hillyer. *Fr.* Book of the Dead. AWP
Glory to Thee, My God, This Night. Thomas Ken. NOCV
Glory to you, oh pain, sorrow unending! The Grey-eyed King. "Anna Akhmatova," *tr. by* Robert Tracy. PBWP
Glory Trail, The. Charles Badger Clark, Jr. BPAW; PH
Gloss. Padraic Fiacc. CIP
Gloss. David McCord. OBAL
Gloucester Harbor. Elizabeth Stuart Phelps Ward. AA
Gloucester Moors. William Vaughn Moody. AP; HBV-2; NOBA; OxBA; TreFT; WHA
"This earth is not the steadfast place," *sel.* WGRP
Gloucestershire Wassail. *Unknown.* OBET
Glove, The. Harold Bond. NYBP
Glove, The. Andrew Greig. BSV
Glove, The. Ben Jonson. *Fr.* Cynthia's Revels. ElL
("Thou more than most sweet glove.") GBL
Glove and the Lions, The. Leigh Hunt. BeLS; FaPON; GN; HBV-1; HBVY; TreF; WBLP
Glove Glue. Ken Belford. NeAC
Glow and beauty of the stars, The. Sappho, *tr. fr. Greek by* Willis Barnstone. BoWoP
Glow and the glory are plighted, The. A Nice Correspondent. Frederick Locker-Lampson. HBV-1
Glow, little glow-worm, fly of fire. The Glow-Worm. Johnny Mercer. OBAL
Glow of purples at set of sun, A. Desert Bloom. Gertrude Thomas Arnold. BPAW
Glow of the restaurant is faked, the dream, The. Reality. Raymond Souster. CaP
Glow-Worm, The. Johnny Mercer. OBAL
Glow Worm, *with music.* Lila Cayley Robinson. BLSo
Glow-Worm, The. Edward Shanks. WHA
Glow-Worm, The. Charlotte Smith. FM
Glowworm in a garden prayed, A. A Very Minor Poet Speaks. Isabel Valle. BLPA
Glow-worm-like the daisies peer. Summer. John Davidson. BoNaP
Gluggity Glug. George Colman. *Fr.* The Myrtle and the Vine. HBV-2
Glunk!/ I toss my heels up to my head. Oiseaurie. Margaret Widdemer. BXAP
Gluskap's Hound. T. G. Roberts. WHW
Glut on the Market, A. Patrick Kavanagh. *See* Pegasus.
Glutton, The. Robert Graves. CMoP; TW
Glutton, The. William Langland. *See* Glutton in the Tavern.
Glutton, The. John Oakman. OxBChV
Glutton, The. Karl Shapiro. DFF
Glutton in the Tavern. William Langland. *Fr.* The Vision of Piers Plowman. OxBM
(Glutton, The.) ACP
Glycine's Song. Samuel Taylor Coleridge. *Fr.* Zapolya. CH; OBEV; PoPL
(Song: "Sunny shaft did I behold, A.") PBBP; PoSC
Glyph. *Unknown, tr. fr. Washoe-Paiute by* Mary Austin. LiTA
Gnarled black limbs poke. Village in Snowstorm. Norbert Krapf. FAZ
Gnarled Riverina Gum-Tree, A. Ernest G. Moll. PoAu-2
Gnarly and bent and deaf's a pos'. Zeke. L. A. G. Strong. MoBrPo
Gnat, The. Joseph Beaumont. FM; LoBV; OBS
Gnat, be my messenger, and fly. To a Gnat. *Unknown, tr. by* Louis Untermeyer. UnTE
Gnat on My Paper. Richard Eberhart. DFF
Gnat-Psalm. Ted Hughes. NoAM
Gnawing the Breast. Sandra McPherson. LCAP
Gnome. Samuel Beckett. BIrV
Gnome, The. Harry Behn. FaPON; PDV; SoPo; TiPo
Gnome Matter. Carolyn Wells. TDH
Gnomes, The. Beth Bentley. SaC
Gnomic Verses. Blake. *Poems indexed separately by titles and first lines.*
Gnosis. Christopher Pearse Cranch. HBV-2
(Stanza from an Early Poem.) AA
(Thought.) WGRP
Gnostics on Trial. Linda Gregg. AMV-80; NPGG
Gnostology. Sam Hamill. AMV-81
Gnôthi seautón—and is this the prime. Self-Knowledge. Samuel Taylor Coleridge. SeCePo
Gnu, The. Hilaire Belloc. BoAnP
("G stands for Gnu, whose weapons of defence.") FaBoNo
Gnu up at the zoo, The. Elegy. John Hall Wheelock. NYBP
Gnu Wooing, The. Burges Johnson. HBVY
Go Ahead; Goodbye; Good Luck; and Watch Out. William Bronk. GP
Go and ask Robin to bring the girls over. Vision by Sweetwater. John Crowe Ransom. AP; CMoP; CoBMV; CrMA; FaBoMo; MoAB; NOBA; OxBA
Go and Catch a Falling Star. John Donne. *See* Song: "Go and catch a falling star."
Go and dig my grave both long and narrow. Dig My Grave. *Unknown.* AmFP; OuSiCo
Go and lose your way one night. Ahasuerus. Joseph Roth, *tr. by* Erna Baber Rosenfeld. VWA
Go and spy on the sheep. The Good Shepherd. Keidrych Rhys. NeBP
Go and tell Aunt Nancy. The Old Grey Goose. *Unknown.* ChTr
"Go ask Papa," the maiden said. Proposal. *Unknown.* TreFS
Go back, dark blood, to the springs from which you came. The Dream and the Blood. Louis Untermeyer. UnTE
Go back now; pause to mark. Horizon Thong. George Abbe. GoYe
Go back, old Devil and look up on your shelf. Old Devil. *Unknown.* BluL
Go Back to the Country. *Unknown.* BluL
Go bet, peny, go bet, go! Penny Is a Hardy Knight. *Unknown.* OxBM
Go bow thy head in gentle spite. To a Lily. James Matthew Legaré. AA
Go boy, and thy good mistress tell. Macbeth. Horace *and* James Smith. BXAP
"Go break to the needy charity's bread." How Long Shall I Give? *Unknown.* BLRP
Go Bring Me Back My Blue-eyed Boy, *with music.* *Unknown.* AS
"Go Bring Me," Said the Dying Fair, *with music.* William Hunter. AH
"Go bring the captive, he shall die." Ortiz. Hezekiah Butterworth. PAH
Go By. Tennyson. *See* Come Not, When I Am Dead.
Go call a careful painter, let him show. Of the French Kings Nativity. Benjamin Harris. SCAP
Go count the stars! Counting. Fenton Johnson. AmNP
Go, daughters of Zion. The Death of Tammuz. Saul Tchernichowsky, *tr. by* L. V. Snowman. TrJP
Go dig a hole in the meadow. Darling Cora. *Unknown.* TrAS
Go Down Death. James Weldon Johnson. AmNP; DL; PoBA; TRV
Go Down, Moses. *Unknown.* BoAN-1, *with music;* BPo; EaLo; EBCP; FSW; NOBA; TrAS, *with music;* TreF
(When Israel Was in Egypt's Land.) AH, *with music*
Go Down, Old [*or* Ol'] Hannah, *diff. versions.* *Unknown.* AmFP; OuSiCo, *with music;* TTY
Go down to hell. This end is good to see. A Dead King. Swinburne. VLP
"Go down to the zoo," Rodin told Rilke. "Go and take a look." Further Instructions. Vincent O'Sullivan. OCNZ
Go Down, You Little Red Rising Sun, *with music.* *Unknown.* OuSiCo
Go Down You Murderers. Ewan MacColl. FSW
Go, dumb-born book. Envoi. Ezra Pound. *Fr.* Hugh Selwyn Mauberley. CTC; HAP; MoAB; MoAmPo; NePA; OxBA; SeCeV; UnPo; VGW
Go Far; Come Near. Walter de la Mare. CoBMV

Go fetch to me a pint o'wine. The Silver Tassie. Burns. BSV; GTBS; GTBS-P; HBV-1; NOBE; OBEC; OBEV; PoPle; ViBoPo
Go, flaunting Rose! The Aesthete to the Rose. *Unknown.* BXAP
Go Fly a Saucer. David McCord. ImOP
"I've seen one flying saucer. Only when," *sel.* FaPON
Go, for they call you, Shepherd, from the hill. The Scholar-Gipsy. Matthew Arnold. CABA; ChTr; EBEV; EBVV; FaBoEn; FaBoPP; FiP; GoTL; HAP; HBV-2; HeIP; LoBV; MasP; NOBE; NoP; OAEL-2; OAEP; OBEV; OBNC; OBVV; PoEL-5; PoPle; SeCeV; TEP; ViBoPo; VLP
Go, Forget Me. Charles Wolfe. HBV-1
Go forth and weep. The Death of Tammuz. Shaul Tchernichovsky, *tr. by* Mark Elliot Shapiro. VWA
"Go Forward." "A. R. G." BLRP
Go friendly, go lovely, go naked. Jealousy. Stephen Vincent. NeAC
Go from me: I am one of those who fall. Mystic and Cavalier. Lionel Johnson. MoBrPo; SeCePo; VLP
Go from me, summer friends, and tarry not. From Sunset to Star Rise. Christina Rossetti. SBG
Go from Me [Yet I Feel That I Shall Stand]. Elizabeth Barrett Browning. Sonnets from the Portuguese, VI. BLPL; HBV-1; OBEV; OBVV; TreFS; TrGrPo; ViBoPo
"Go get me some of your father's gold." Pretty Polly. *Unknown.* AS
Go Get the Ax [*or* Axe], *with music. Unknown.* AS; TrAS
Go get the third johnny head and touch it north. Sis Joe. *Unknown.* OuSiCo
Go, go, queint folies, sugred sin. Idle Verse. Henry Vaughan. OAEP
Go, grieving rimes of mine, to that hard stone. Petrarch, *tr. by* Morris Bishop. Sonnets to Laura: To Laura in Death, LX. NAWM-1
Go [*or* Goe], happy Rose, and, interwove [*or* enterwove]. To the Rose; a Song. Robert Herrick. HBV-1; OBS; SeCP
Go, happy rose, and wreathe my dear friend's brow. Epigram: Go, Happy Rose. Martial, tr. by Brian Hill. PeHV
Go, Hart. *Unknown. See* Go, Heart, unto the Lamp of Licht.
Go Heart, Hurt with Adversity. *Unknown.* MeEL; OxBM
Go, Heart, unto the Lamp of Licht. *Unknown.* BSV; GoTS
(Go, Hart.) OxBS
Go Home. Janet Reed McFatter. GrPl
Go [*or* Goe]! hunt the whiter ermine, and present. For the Lady Olivia Porter; a Present upon a New Year's Day. Sir William Davenant. JCP; MeLP; MePo; OBS
Go I must; when I am gone. To His Tomb-Maker. Robert Herrick. SeCV-1
Go, I will shut the windows. Alienation. Harry Kemp. HBMV
Go, ill-sped book, and whisper to her or. John Berryman. BoLoP
Go inside a stone. Stone. Charles Simic. NU
Go, let the fatted calf be killed. The Welcome. Abraham Cowley. *Fr.* The Mistress. BoLoP; SeCV-1
Go, let us go my friends, go home. Home. *Zulu Oral Tradition, tr. by* H. Tracey. WTO
Go, litel book [*or* bok], go litel myn tragedye [*or* tregedie]. The Envoy. Chaucer. *Fr.* Troilus and Criseyde. FiP; OAEL-1; OxBM; ViBoPo
Go! little bill, and command me hertely. She Saw Me in Church. *Unknown.* MeEL
Go! little bill, and do me recommende. A Love Letter. *Unknown.* MeEL
Go, Little Book. Robert Louis Stevenson. *See* Envoy: "Go, little book, and wish to all."
Go, little book, and leave me still in doubt. Epilogue to a Book of Verse. Arthur Guiterman. InMe
Go, little book, and wish to all. Envoy [*or* Wishes *or* Go Little Book]. Robert Louis Stevenson. HBV-2; MoBrPo; OBEV; OBVV; TreFT
Go, Little Book. Chaucer. *See* Envoy, The: "Go, litel book, go litel myn tregedie."
Go, little quair. L'Envoy: To His Book. John Skelton. EnRePo
Go, lovely boy! to yonder tow'r. Verses Written during the War, 1756-1763. Thomas Osbert Mordaunt. OBEC
Go [*or* Goe], Lovely Rose. Edmund Waller. AWP; BoLoP; CTC; EnLoPo; FF; GTBS; GTBS-P; HAP; HBV-1; HeIP; InPK; NOBE; OAEP; OBEV; OLR: PAI; PoPle; PoRA; SeCeV; TEP; TreFS; TrGrPo; UnPo; ViBoPo; WeW; WHA
(Song: "Go [*or* Goe] lovely rose.") AnAnS-2; CABA; CavP; ELP; FaBoEn; GBL; GoJo; JCP; LoBV; MePo; NIP; NoP; OAEL-1; OBS; PoEL-3; PPoe; PrIm; SeCP; SeCV-1
Go, loving woodbine, clip with lovely grace. On a Pair of Garters. Sir John Davies. SiPS
Go, my flock, go get you hence. Sir Philip Sidney. Astrophel and Stella, Ninth Song. SiPS
Go, my songs, seek your praise from the young and from the intolerant. Ité. Erza Pound. HAP; MoAB; MoAmPo; PP; TwAmPo
Go, my songs, to the lonely and the unsatisfied. Commission. Ezra Pound. BoLoP; MP; NIP; TwCP
Go, Nightly Cares. *Unknown.* EnRePo
Go not, happy day. Tennyson. *Fr.* Maud, Pt. 1, XVII. EBVV; OBVV
Go not to the hills of Erinn. The Wind on the Hills. Dora Sigerson Shorter. HBMV
Go not too frequently thy friends to see. Advice to Bores. Abraham ibn Chasdai, *tr. by* J. Chotzner. TrJP
Go not too near a house of rose. Emily Dickinson. MoAB; MoAmPo
Go Now, My Song. Andrew Young. ChTr
Go on, brave heros, you whose merits claim. An Ironical Encomium. *Unknown.* APAS
Go on, thou noisy one! Praise of a Train. *Zulu Oral Tradition, tr. by* B. W. Vilakazi. WTO
Go out, good ships, across the tide. Ships. Nancy Byrd Turner. SoPo; SUS
Go out with a small flashlight and a star chart. Things to Do around a Ship at Sea. Gary Snyder. CAPP
Go patter to lubbers and swabs, do ye see. Poor Jack. Charles Dibdin. BeLS; HBV-1
Go, perjured man, and if thou e'er return. The Curse; a Song. Robert Herrick. CaPo
Go, Piteous Heart. John Skelton. *See* Unfriendly Fortune.
Go, Ploughman, Plough. Joseph Campbell. HBMV
Go pretty child and bear this flower. To His Saviour, a Child; a Present, by a Child [*or* A Child's Present]. Robert Herrick. OHIP; OxBChV; OxBoCh; SeCP; TrCP
Go, roads, to the four quarters of our quiet distance. The Evening of the Visitation. Thomas Merton. ISi
Go, Rose, and in her golden hair. To a Rose. Frank Dempster Sherman. AA
Go, rose, my Chloe's bosom grace. Love's Emblem. John Clare. NIP
Go Round. Laura Chester. NPGG
Go, Sad Complaint. Charles d'Orléans. MeEL
Go sad or sweet or riotous with beer. The Old Women. George Mackay Brown. NePoEA-2; OxBS
Go saddle up my milk-white steed. Geordie. *Unknown.* BaBo
Go, said old Lyce, senseless lover, go. Lyce. William Walsh. BoLoP
Go seeker, if you will, throughout the land. Burning in the Night. Thomas Wolfe. AmFN
Go, Silly Worm. Joshua Sylvester. *See* Omnia Somnia.
Go Sleep, Ma Honey. Edward D. Barker. AA
Go Slow. Langston Hughes. LiTM
Go [*or* Goe], smiling souls [*or* soules], your new-built cages break. To the Infant Martyrs. Richard Crashaw. NoP; PAI; SeCV-1
Go [*or* Goe], solitary wood, and henceforth be. On the Death of a Nightingale. Thomas Randolph. AnAnS-2; PBBP
Go, Songs. Francis Thompson. *See* Envoy: "Go, songs, for ended is our brief, sweet play."
Go, Soul [*or* Goe soule], the body's guest. The Lie. Sir Walter Ralegh. AAS; ChTr; CTC; EBEV; EnRePo; HAP; HBV-2; InvP; LiTB; MasP; NOBE; NoP; OAEP; OBSC; PoEL-2; PPoe; PPON; QFR; SCV; SeCeV; SiPS; TEP; TreFT; TrGrPo; ViBoPo; WGRP
Go soule, go sweetest soule for ever blest. Ariosto, *tr. by* Sir John Harington. *Fr.* Orlando Furioso, XXIX. OBVE
Go, speed the stars of thought. Intellect. Emerson. GLGT
"Go steal your father's weight in gold." Lady Isabel and the Elf-Knight. *Unknown.* ViBoFo
Go, swallow, and tell, now that the summer is dying. Cwmrhydyceirw Elegiacs. Vernon Watkins. PoA
Go Take the World. Jay Macpherson. MoCV; OBCV
Go talk with those who are rumored to be unlike you. For the Student Strikers. Richard Wilbur. GLGT; OxBC
Go Tell. *Unknown. See* Go Tell It on the Mountain.
Go tell Amynta gentle swain. A Song. Dryden. *Fr.* Sylvoe. CavP
Go tell at Sparta, traveler passing by. On the Spartan Dead at Thermopylae. Simonides. WeW
Go tell Aunt Rhody [*or* Nancy]. The Old Gray Goose. *Unknown.* AmFP; FSW; GBP
Go tell her to make me a cambric shirt. The Cambric Shirt. *Unknown.* FSW
Go tell him to clear me one acre of ground. The Elfin Knight. *Unknown.* AmFP; WSC
Go Tell It on the Mountain. *Unknown.* FSW
(Go Tell.) EBCP
Go tell the king: the daedal. The Last Utterance of the Delphic Oracle. *Tr. fr. Greek by* Kenneth Rexroth. OBVE
Go tell the Spartans, thou that passest by. Thermopylae [*or* Inscription to Spartans Dead at Thermopylae]. Simonides, *tr. by* William Lisle Bowles. AWP; OBVE; OBWP; TreF
Go ter sleep, go ter sleep. Go to Sleepy. *Unknown.* TrAS
Go, Then. Edith Bruck, *tr. fr. Italian by* Anita Barrows. VWA
Go then, my dove, but now no longer mine. Cotton Mather. SCAP
Go thou and seek the house of prayer! Written on a Sunday Morning. Robert Southey. OBEC

Go thou forth, my book, though late. To His Book. Robert Herrick. CaPo
Go thou thy way, and I go mine. Mizpah. Julia A. Baker. BLPA; FaBoBe
Go Thou to Rome. Shelley. *Fr.* Adonais. ChTr
(Grave of Keats, The.) FaBoPP
Go through the gates with closed eyes. Close Your Eyes! Arna Bontemps. AmNP; CDC; FB; PoBA; PoNe
Go Throw Them Out. Moishe Leib Halpern, *tr. fr. Yiddish by* Ruth Whitman. VWA
Go thy way, eat thy bread with joy, and drink thy wine with a merry heart. Live Joyfully. Bible, *O.T.* *Fr.* Ecclesiastes. TreFS
Go to Bed. *Unknown.* ChTr
("Go to bed first.") GBP; OxNR
Go to bed late. *Unknown.* OxNR
Go to bed, Tom. *Unknown.* OxNR
Go to dark Gethsemane. Christ Our Example in Suffering. James Montgomery. HBV-2
Go to him, ah, go to him, and lift your eyes aglow to him. To Her—Unspoken. Amelia Josephine Burr. HBV-1
"Go to jail. Go directly to jail. Do not pass Go. Do not collect $200.00." The Book of Merlin. Jack Spicer. CoPo
Go to Old Ireland. *Unknown.* AmFP
Go to sleep, go to sleepy. All the Pretty Little Horses. *Unknown.* AmFP
Go to sleep, my little oaf. Mamma Sings. Samuel Hoffenstein. DBV
Go to sleep, my son. Crabe dans Calalou. *Unknown.* OuSiCo
Go to sleep you weary hobo. Hobo's Lullaby. Goebel Reeves. FSW
Go to sleep—though of course you will not. A Goodnight. William Carlos Williams. MoAmPo; MoAB
Go to Sleepy, *with music.* *Unknown.* AS; TrAS
Go to the Ant. Bible, *O.T.* Proverbs, VI: 6-11. FaPON; TreFT
(Go to the Ant, Thou Sluggard.) TrJP
(Reproof, A.) TrGrPo
"Go to the Ant." Stanley J. Sharpless. NOBL
Go to the Shine That's on a Tree. Richard Eberhart. UnS
Go to the western gate, Luke Havergal. Luke Havergal. E. A. Robinson. AA; AmPP; AP; AWP; CoBMV; CrMA; GBL; LiTA; LiTM; MoAB; MoAmPo; MoPo; MOVE; NePA; NoAM; NOBA; PoEL-5; QFR; TreFT; UnPo
Go way, Eadie, you dirty dog. Eadie. *Unknown.* OuSiCo
Go 'way, fiddle! folks is tired o' hearin' you a-squawkin'. De Fust Banjo. Irwin Russell. *Fr.* Christmas Night in the Quarters. AA; BLPA; HBV-2
Go 'Way f'om Mah Window, *with music.* *Unknown.* AS
Go 'way from dat window, "My Honey, My Love." Song to the Runaway Slave. *Unknown.* BPo
Go when the morning shineth. Secret Prayer. John Cross Belle. STF
Go Where Glory Waits Thee. Thomas Moore. OBNC; TreFS
Go where we will, at ev'ry time and place. Charles Churchill. *Fr.* The Times. PeHV
Go with your tauntings, go. Song. John Clare. OBRV
"Go ye into the highways." Compel Them to Come In. Leonard Dodd. BLRP
Go you, O winds that blow from north to south. Sonnet. Alexander Craig. ElL
Goal and the Way, The. John Oxenham. PGD
Goal of Intellectual Man, The. Richard Eberhart. MoPo
Goat, The. Umberto Saba, *tr. fr. Italian by* Anita Barrows. VWA
Goat, The. *Unknown.* BLPL; OnUR; PoLF
(Bill Groggin's Goat.) FSW
Goat, The. Roland Young. BoAnP; WhC
Goat Dance. Ron Loewinsohn. GP
Goat Paths, The. James Stephens. AnIV; AWP; CH; GoJo; LiTB; OxBI; UnPo; WHA
Goat was nibbling on a vine, A. The Vine and the Goat. Aesop, *tr. by* William Ellery Leonard. AWP
Goat-Woman Dares. Judith Mountain Leaf Volborth. TWSS
Goatherd, The. Grace Hazard Conkling. TiPo
Goat-herd follows his flock, The. Juan Quintana. Alice Corbin. BPAW; HBMV
Goat's-Leaf. Marie de France, *tr. fr. Old French by* Aline Allard. PBWP
(Honeysuckle [Chevrefoil], *tr. by* Patricia Terry.) BoWoP
Goblin, The. Rose Fyleman. NTCP; TiPo
Goblin Feet. J. R. R. Tolkien. FaPON
Goblin Goose, The. *Unknown.* FaBoPa
Goblin has a wider mouth, The. How to Tell Goblins from Elves. Monica Shannon. FaPON; RHPC; TiPo
Goblin lives in our house, in our house, in our house, A. The Goblin. Rose Fyleman. NTCP; TiPo
Goblin marked his monarch well, The. The Fay's Departure [*or* The First Quest]. Joseph Rodman Drake. *Fr.* The Culprit Fay. AA; GN
Goblin Market. Christina Rossetti. DTo; EBEV; GoTL; OAEP; OBNV; SBG; VLP
Sels.
"Laughed every goblin." BrPo
Laura and Lizzie Asleep. PeHV
Goblinade, A. Florence Page Jaques. TiPo
Goblins on the doorstep. This Is Halloween. Dorothy Brown Thompson. RHPC; TiPo; YeAr
Goblin's Song, The. James Telfer. ChTr
God. Gamaliel Bradford. TRV; WGRP
God. Alphonse de Lamartine, *tr. fr. French.* ILwL
God, *sel.* Alexander McLachlan.
"Hail, Thou great mysterious Being!" CaP
God. Isaac Rosenberg. MoPo; VWA
God. Boris Slutsky, *tr. fr. Russian by* Dimitry Pospielovsky *and* Keith Bosley. VWA
God. John Banister Tabb. TreFT
God. *At. to* James Cowden Wallace. *See* God the Omniscient.
God!/ glad I'm black. Blue Black. Bloke Modisane. PBA
God—/they fear you, they hold you so. Testimony. Carolyn M. Rodgers. BPo
God, a man at Yale, adopted a monkey. Monkey. Josephine Miles. LiTM
God above, for man's delight, The. A New Ballade of the Marigolde. William Forrest. CoMu
God almighty's colly cow. The Ladybird. *Unknown.* GBP
God, although this life is but a wraith. Prayer. Louis Untermeyer. WGRP
God and I in space alone. Illusion. Ella Wheeler Wilcox. WGRP
God and Man. Samuel Hazo. ELU
God and man, though in this amphitheatre. Sonnet. William Alabaster. SBVL
God and Nature. Musa Moris Farhi. VWA
God and Saint [*or* Sanct] Peter was gangand be the way. How the First Hielandman [of God] Was Made. *Unknown.* FaBoCo; GBP; OBSV
God and the devil in these letters. The Postman's Bell Is Answered Everywhere. Horace Gregory. MoAmPo; MoVE; NYBP
God and the devil still are wrangling. For a Mouthy Woman. Countee Cullen. OBAL; PoBA; ShM
God and the Soldier. *Unknown.* TreFS
God and the Soul, *sels.* John Lancaster Spalding.
At the Ninth Hour. AA
Et Mori Lucrum. AA
Nature and the Child. AA
Starry Host, The. AA; HBV-2
Void Between, The. AA
God and the Strong Ones. Margaret Widdemer. HBMV
God and Yet a Man, A? *Unknown.* HAP
(Wit Wonders.) MeEL
God appears, and God is Light. Blake. *Fr.* Auguries of Innocence. TRV
God! ask me not to record your wonders. Scholfield Huxley. Edgar Lee Masters. *Fr.* Spoon River Anthology. LiTA; MoPo; TrPWD
God bade the birds break not the silent spell. The Thrush. Laura Benét. HBMV
God banish from your house. Benediction. Stanley Kunitz. VGW
God be here, God be there. *Unknown.* OxNR
God Be in My Head. *Unknown.* *Fr.* Sarum Primer. EaLo; OxBoCh; TRV
(God with Us.) TreFT
(Hymnus: "God be in my hede.") ChTr; FaBoRV
God be merciful unto us, and bless us. Let the Nations Be Glad. Bible, *O.T.* Psalms, LXVII. FaPON
God be praised. Working with God. "George Eliot." *Fr.* Stradivarius. TRV
God be with the night that's gone! The Vanished Night. Niall MacMurray, *tr. by* Frank O'Connor. KiLC
God be with thee, my beloved,—God be with thee! A Valediction. Elizabeth Barrett Browning. HBV-1
God be with trewthe wher he be! Truth. *Unknown.* OxBM
God be with you in the Springtime. Through the Year. Julian S. Cutler. BLPA
God be with You till We Meet Again. Jeremiah E. Rankin. AH, *with music;* TreFS
God, bless all little boys who look like Puck. Blessing on Little Boys. Arthur Guiterman. TrPWD
God bless all policemen. Goodbat Nightman. Roger McGough. NoAM
God Bless America. Irving Berlin. BLSo, *with music;* TreFT
God Bless America. John Fuller. OBSV
God bless Henry. He lived like a rat. John Berryman. *Fr.* Dream Songs. CAPP
God bless my little kitchen. A Kitchen Prayer. M. Peterson. STF
God bless our country's emblem. Our Country's Emblem. *Unknown.* WBLP
God bless our good and gracious King. Impromptu on Charles II. Earl of Rochester. FaBoEE; InPK; NIP; NOBL; OBSV; PAI
God bless our meat. *Unknown.* OxNR
God bless pawnbrokers! Pawnbrokers. Marguerite Wilkinson. HBMV

God bless the craft of Clanranald. Birlinn Chlann-Raghnaill. Alexander MacDonald, *tr. by* "Hugh MacDiarmid." GoTS
God bless the field and bless the furrow. The Robin's Song. C. Lovat Fraser. MoShBr
God bless the King!—I mean the Faith's Defender. A Jacobite Toast [*or* Extempore Verses *or* A Toast *or* Epigram]. John Byrom. FaBoCo; FaBoEE; HBV-1; NOBL; OBEC; ViBoPo
"God bless the man who first invented sleep!" Early Rising. John Godfrey Saxe. BLPL; HBV-2; InMe; PoLF; WhC
God bless the master of this house,/ The mistress also. Christmas Carol [*or* A Grace *or* Souling Song]. *Unknown.* MoShBr; OBET; OHIP; OxNR; SiSoSe; TiPo
God bless the master of this house, and all that are therein. The Singers in the Snow. *Unknown.* OHIP
God bless thee and keep thee thro' the coming days. A New Year's Wish. "J. H. S." BLRP
God bless this food, and bless us all. *Unknown.* BLRP
God bless this house from thatch to floor. *Unknown.* OxNR
God Bless You, Dear, To-Day! John Bennett. AA; HBV-1
God braced me with His firm hand. The Tool of Fate. "Yehoash," *tr. by* Isidore Goldstick. TrJP
God breathe a blessing on. Bestiary. A. M. Klein. OBCV
God broke into my house last night. Scapegoat. W. R. Rodgers. CIP
God broke the years to hours and days. As Thy Days So Shall Thy Strength Be. "George Klingle." BLRP; TRV
God broke upon this upturned field; trees. Body of a Rook. David Wevill. MoCV
God! but this rain-sweet greenness shakes the heart. Soon with the Lilac Fades Another Spring. Patrick MacDonogh. OxBI
God called the nearest angels who dwell with Him above. The Two Angels. Whittier. AA
God Cares. Helen Annis Casterline. BLRP
God Cares. "Marianne Farningham." BLRP
(He Careth.) WBLP
God conceived the world, that was poetry. God's Work. Charlotte Cushman. TreFT
God decided he was tired. Budgie Finds His Voice. Wendy Cope. FaBoPa
God Does Do Such Wonderful Things! Angela Morgan. TRV
God Doeth All Things Well. *Unknown.* STF
God Don't Like It, *with music.* *Unknown.* OuSiCo
God Don't Never Change. *Unknown.* BluL
God don't want no coward soldiers. God's Goin' to Set This World on Fire. *Unknown.* AS
God doth dwell in men, from th' blessed seats, A. In Consort to Wednesday, Jan. 1st. 1701. Richard Henchman. SCAP
God dreamed—the suns sprang flaming into space. Creation. Ambrose Bierce. AA
God dwells alone, The. Deserted Shrine. Avner Treinin, *tr. by* A. C. Jacobs. VWA
God Everywhere. Abraham ibn Ezra, *tr. fr. Hebrew by* "D. E. de L." TrJP
God exists, though he doesn't exist. Phallus. Shiraishi Kazuko, *tr. by* Ikuko Atsumi. BoWoP
God Fashioned the Ship of the World Carefully. Stephen Crane. The Black Riders, VI. MOS
God from His Throne with Piercing Eye, *with music.* Joseph Steward. AH
God gave His children memory. Roses in December. G. A. Studdert-Kennedy. BLPA
God gave my son in trust to me. My Son. James D. Hughes. BLPA
God gave the pig. Ode of Lament. Randolph Jeck. WhC
God, give me speech, in mercy touch my lips. The Unutterable Beauty. G. A. Studdert-Kennedy. TrPWD
God, give me sympathy and sense. A Prayer. Margaret Bailey. TRV
God Give to Men ("God give the yellow man"). Arna Bontemps. BANP; BPo; CDC; PoNE
God, Give Us Men! Josiah Gilbert Holland. BLPA; PAL; TreF; WBLP
(Wanted.) TrPWD; TRV
God give you faith this coming year! Invocation for the New Year. Margaret D. Armstrong. STF
"God give you peace!" Your happy lay. Joculator Domini. Sister Mary John Frederick. GoBC
God gives them sleep on ground, on straw. Roger Williams. SCAP
God gives to you another year. The New Year. *Unknown.* STF
God gives us joy that we might give. Life's Joy. *Unknown.* STF
God, God!/ With a child's voice I cry. Elizabeth Barrett Browning. *Fr.* The Soul's Travelling. ILwL
God, God, be lenient her first night there. Prayer for a Very New Angel. Violet Alleyn Storey. BLPA; TreFS
God grant that I may never be. Prayer in April. Sara Henderson Hay. TrPWD
God grant thee thine own wish, and grant thee mine. John Donne, *after* Gazaeus. OBVE
God granted, God denies. Frustration. Elizabeth Daryush. QFR
God 'graves His cryptic script with inexorable pen. Palimpsest. Hyman Edelestein. CaP
God has a brown voice. For Eleanor Boylan Talking with God. Anne Sexton. InPK
God has His best things for the few. His Best. Albert Benjamin Simpson. STF
God has His times: No power of man. On Time with God. C. D. Nutter. STF
God has no end of material. Little Things. *Unknown.* STF
God Has Pity on Kindergarten Children. Yehuda Amichai, *tr. fr. Hebrew by* Stephen Mitchell. VWA
God Has Spoken. Paul Verlaine, *tr. fr. French by* John Gray. *Fr.* Sagesse. SyP
God Hasn't Made Room. Mririda n'Ait Attik, *tr. fr. French version by* Daniel Halpern *and* Paula Paley. PBWP
God hath been patient long. In eons past. The Harvest Waits. Lloyd Mifflin. HBV-2
God hath not promised. What God Hath [*or* Has] Promised! Annie Johnson Flint. BLRP; STF; TRV; WBLP
God hath two wings, which He doth ever move. Mercy and Love. Robert Herrick. SeCV-1
God, He called John while he was a-writin'. John Was a-Writin'. *Unknown.* OuSiCo
God He rejects all prayers that are sleight. Prayers Must Have Poise. Robert Herrick. LiTB
God help the homeless ones who lack this night. Midnight. Margaret E. Sangster. TRV
God, how I envy you these great oak roots. A Jew Walks in Westminster Abbey. Aubrey Hodes. TrJP
God, How I Hate You. Arthur Graeme West. MMA
God! How I Long for You. Kenneth Mackenzie. CBAP
God! how they plague his life, the three damned sisters. The Little Brother. James Reeves. DTC; OxBTC
God, I am travelling out to death's sea. Valley of the Shadow. John Galsworthy. OHIP; TrPWD
God I had forgotten how. New York—Albany. Lawrence Ferlinghetti. PoCh
God I love thee in Thy robe of roses. Zebaoth. Else Lasker-Schüler, *tr. by* Jethro Bithell. TrJP
God if he isn't is. Phallic Root. Shiraishi Kazuko. WPOW
God, if this were enough. If This Were Faith. Robert Louis Stevenson. BrPo; OBNC; TrPWD; WGRP
God, in His infinite wisdom. Acceptance. Langston Hughes. NePoAm-2
God in the Nation's Life. *Unknown.* BLRP; WBLP
God in Whom We Trust, The. *Unknown.* STF
God in Wrath, A. Stephen Crane. The Black Riders, XIX. TAP
God is a distant, stately lover. Emily Dickinson. SoSe
God Is a Masturbator. Gregory Corso. GP
God is a proposition. Third Enemy Speaks. C. Day Lewis. *Fr.* The Magnetic Mountain. EaLo
God is a screwball. From the Batter's Box. David K. Harford. AMV-80
God Is at the Anvil. Lew Sarett. HBMV; TRV; WGRP
God Is Faithful. Frances Ridley Havergal. BLRP
God is great and God is good. *Unknown.* BLRP
God Is Here Again. Charles Angoff. AMV-80
God Is in Every Tomorrow. Laura A. Barter Snow. BLRP; STF
God is indeed a jealous God. Emily Dickinson. NOBA
God, is it sinful if I feel. A Prayer. Mary Dixon Thayer. HBMV; TrPWD
God, Is, Like, Scissors. José Garcia Villa. EaLo
God Is Love. Sir John Bowring. FaBoBe
God is love. Then by inversion. History of Ideas. J. V. Cunningham. NIP
God, The, is near, and/ difficult to grasp. Patmos. David Gascoyne, *after* Friedrich Hölderlin. OBVE
God is never sure He has found. Walking the Wilderness. William Stafford. NaP
God Is Nigh. *Unknown.* TRV
God is no botcher, but when God wrought you two. On Botching. John Heywood. FaBoCo; FaBoEE
God Is Not Dumb. James Russell Lowell. *Fr.* Bibliolaters. WGRP
God is our refuge and strength, a very present help in trouble. Bible, *O.T.* Psalms, XLVI. AWP; TreFT; TrGrPo; TRV; WGRP
God is praise and glory. Psalm of Battle. *Unknown.* *Fr.* The Thousand and One Nights. AWP
God is shaping the great future of the islands of the sea. The Islands of the Sea. George Edward Woodberry. PAH
God is still glorified. Building in Stone. Sylvia Townsend Warner. MoBrPo
God is the Most High. Muhammedan Call to Prayer. Bilal, *tr. by* Raoul Abdul. TTY
God is the Old Repair Man. The Old Repair Man. Fenton Johnson. AmNP

God Is There. Walter E. Isenhour. STF
God Is with Me. Oswald J. Smith. STF
God Is Working His Purpose Out. A. C. Ainger. BLRP; FaPoR
God, keep all claw-denned alligators. Prayer for Reptiles. Patricia Hubbell. PDV
God Keep You. "Madeline Bridges." AA
God keep you safe, my little love. My Little Love. Charles B. Hawley. HBV-1
God knew what lay before us. The Best for Us. Olive H. Burnett. STF
God Knoweth Best. *Unknown.* WBLP
(Your Father Knoweth.) BLRP
God knows how many nights upon her bed. Old Maid. John U. Nicolson. HBMV
God knows it, I am with you. To a Republican Friend, 1848. Matthew Arnold. VLP
God knows, not I, the reason why. Faith. Margaret E. Sangster. TRV
God Knows the Answer. F. B. Whitney. STF
God knows what beat him down into that deadland. At the Entrance. Douglas Stewart. CBAP
God Knows What He's About. *Unknown.* STF
God lay dead in heaven. Stephen Crane. The Black Riders, LXVII. AmPP
God Leads the Way. Cleanthes, *tr. fr. Greek by* C. C. Martindale. EaLo
God let never soe old a man. Old Robin of Portingale. *Unknown.* ESPB
God, listen through my words to the beating of my heart. Prayer. Marguerite Harmon Bro. TrPWD
God love you. A Poem for the Old Man. John Wieners. NeAP
God love you now, if no one else will ever. Ode for the American Dead in Korea. Thomas McGrath. NePoEA; PoPl; VGW
God Lyaeus, Ever Young. John Fletcher. *Fr.* The Tragedy of Valentinian, V, viii. OBEV; ViBoPo
God made a little gentian. Emily Dickinson. FaBV
(Fringed Gentian.) AA
God Made a Trance. *Unknown.* OBET
God made a wonderful mother. A Wonderful Mother. Pat O'Reilly. BLPA
God made bees, and bees made honey. Old Lesson. *Unknown.* TreFT
God made Him birds in a pleasant humor. The Making of Birds. Katharine Tynan. HBMV; OxBI
God made my lady lovely to behold. How My Songs of Her Began. Philip Bourke Marston. HBV-1
God made my mother on an April day. My Mother. Francis Ledwidge. HBMV; OHIP
God made the bees. Mother Goose. SaC
God Made the Country. William Cowper. *Fr.* The Task, I. FiP; PoEL-3
(Town and Country.) FaBoEn
God made the wicked grocer. The Song against Grocers. G. K. Chesterton. CenHV; DBV; FaBoCo
God-Maker, Man, The. Don Marquis. HBV-2; WGRP
God Makes a Path. Roger Williams. PAH; TRV; WGRP
God makes not good men wantons, but doth bring. Good Men Afflicted Most. Robert Herrick. LiTB
God makes sech nights, all white an' still. The Courtin'. James Russell Lowell. *Fr.* The Biglow Papers. AA; AmPP; BeLS; HBV-1; InMe; NOBA; OBAL; OBVV; TreFS
God meant me to be hungry. God's Will. Mildred Howells. HBV-2
God Moves in a Mysterious Way. William Cowper. *See* Light Shining Out of Darkness.
God Moves on the Water, *with music.* *Unknown.* OuSiCo
God of Abraham, of Isaac, and of Jacob. *Unknown, tr. fr. Yiddish by* Olga Marx. TrJP
God of all power and might. Cecil Arthur Spring-Rice. *Fr.* In Memoriam, A. C. M. L. TrPWD
God of Bethel Heard Her Cries, The, *with music.* Richard Allen. AH
God of Comfort, The. *Unknown.* STF
God of Galaxies, The. Mark Van Doren. ImOP
God of grave nights. A Chant Out of Doors. Marguerite Wilkinson. TrPWD
God of light and blossom. Prayer. James P. Mousley. GoYe
God of love among the silent flowers, A. The Moment of the Rose. Dunstan Thompson. LiTA
God of love my Shepherd is, The. The Twenty-third Psalm. George Herbert. EBCP
God of Mercy. Kadia Molodowsky, *tr. fr. Yiddish by* Irving Howe. WPOW
God of Might, God of Right. *Unknown.* TrJP
God of Music dwelleth out of doors, The. Music. Edith M. Thomas. HBV-2
God of my father discovered at midnight. Oya. Audre Lorde. CNA
God of My Life! Benjamin Colman. *See* Hymn of Praise on a Recovery from Sickness, A.
God of Our Fathers, *with music.* Melancthon W. Stryker. AH
God of Our Fathers, Bless This Our Land, *with music.* John Henry Hopkins, Jr.. AH
God of our fathers, known of old. Recessional. Kipling. AWP; BLPA; BLPL; BLRP; BrPo; CABA; FaBV; FaFP; FaPo; FaPoR; GN; HBV-2; HBVY; LiTB; MoBrPo; NOBE; NoP; OAEP; OBEV; OBNC; OBVV; OHFP; TreF; TrGrPo; TRV; UnPo; ViBoPo; VLP; WBLP; WGRP; WHA
God of Our Fathers, Whose Almighty Hand, *with music.* Daniel C. Roberts. AH
(National Hymn.) PAL
God of our lives, O hear our prayer. Reconsecration. Dorothy Gould. PGD
God of Peace, in Peace Preserve Us, *with music.* Ernst W. Olson. AH
God of Sheep, The. John Fletcher. *Fr.* The Faithful Shepherdess. ElL; FaBoCh
(To Pan.) TrGrPo
God of Summer—I have seen. Touring. David Morton. TrPWD
God of the Earth, the Sky, the Sea. Samuel Longfellow. TRV
(God, Through All and in You All.) TrPWD
God of the Granite and the Rose! Elizabeth Doten. *Fr.* Reconciliation. TrPWD
God of the Living, The. John Ellerton. WGRP
God of the Nations. Walter Russell Bowie. AH, *with music;* TrPWD
God of the Nations, Near and Far, *with music.* John Haynes Holmes. AH
God of the Prophets! Bless the Prophets' Sons, *with music.* Denis Wortman. AH
God of the seasons, hear my parting prayer. The Old Year's Prayer. Minna Irving. PGD
God of the sky. Small Song. Luci Shaw. EBCP
God of the Strong, God of the Weak. Richard Watson Gilder. *See* Hymn: "God of the strong . . ."
God of the vineyard's royal store. The Husbandman. Frances Beatrice Taylor. CaP
God of the World. Israel Najara, *tr. fr. Hebrew by* Israel Abrahams. TrJP
God of the World, Thy Glories Shine, *with music.* Sewall Sylvester Cutting. AH
God of us who kill our kind! A Prayer of the Peoples. Percy MacKaye. TrPWD, 3 *sts.*; WGRP
God of Visions. Emily Brontë. *See* Plead for Me.
God of War, The. Aeschylus, *tr. fr. Greek. Fr.* Agamemnon. PPON
God of war, money changer of dead bodies, The. Aeschylus, *tr. by* Richmond Lattimore. *Fr.* Agamemnon. WaaP
God Once Commanded Us, A. Leah Goldberg, *tr. fr. Hebrew by* Robert Friend. VWA
God only knows what he'd been doing. Painting or sewing? Parish. Norman Dubie. MAYP
God Our Father. Frederick William Faber. *See* Come to Jesus.
God Our Help. *Unknown.* OxBoCh
God Our Refuge. Richard Chenevix Trench. EBCP; OxBoCh; TreFT
(If There Had Anywhere Appeared.) TrPWD
God, patient of beginnings. A Prayer for the New Year. Violet Alleyn Storey. TrPWD
God pity all the brave who go. God's Pity. Louise Driscoll. WGRP
God Pity Him. *Unknown.* STF
God Poem. Stanley Moss. VGW; VWA
God pours for me His draught divine. Thanks from Earth to Heaven. John Hall Wheelock. HBMV
God Prays. Angela Morgan. WGRP
God prosper long our Gracious King. An Ode for the New Year. *At. to* John Gay. OxBoLi
God prosper long our noble king. Chevy Chase [*or* The Hunting of the Cheviot]. *Unknown.* BaBo; ESPB; FaBoBa; GN; HBV-2; OAEP; OBET; ViBoFo
God Provides. Bible, *N.T.* St. Matthew, VI: 26-34. BLRP
God Replies. Bible, *O.T. Fr.* Job. *See* Then the Lord Answered.
God rest that Jewy woman. Song for the Clatter-Bones. F. R. Higgins. AnIL; LiTB; OBMV; OnYI; OxBI
God Rest Ye, Merry Gentlemen. Dinah Maria Mulock Craik. GN; OHIP
God Rest You Merry, Gentlemen. *Unknown.* FaFP; FSW; HBV-1; HBVY; LiTB; TreFS; ViBoPo
God rest you, merry Innocents. A Carol for Children. Ogden Nash. EaLo
God rest you, rest you, rest you, Ireland's dead! To the Dead of '98. Lionel Johnson. HBV-2
God Said, "I Made a Man." José Garcia Villa. TwAmPo
God Save Elizabeth! Francis Turner Palgrave. HBV-2
God save great George our King. God Save the King. *Unknown, at. to* Henry Carey. OBEC; PeD
God Save Great Thomas Paine. Jospeh Mather. NOEC
God Save Ireland. Timothy Daniel Sullivan. OnYI
God save our gracious King. God Save the King. *Unknown, at. to* Henry Carey. HBV-2; TreFS; WBLP
God Save Our President. Francis DeHaes Janvier. PAH; PAL

God Save the Flag. Oliver Wendell Holmes. FaFP; OHFP
God Save the King ("God save our gracious King"). *Unknown, at. to* Henry Carey. HBV-2, 3 *sts.*; TreFS; WBLP, 3 *sts.*
(God Save the King ["God save great George our King"].) OBEC; PeD
God save the King, that King that sav'd the land. Benjamin Harris. SCAP
God Save the Nation. Theodore Tilton. AA
God Save the People. Ebenezer Elliott. *See* When Wilt Thou Save the People?
God Save the Plough. Lydia Huntley Sigourney. OBAL
God save the Rights of Man! Ode. Philip Freneau. AP; GOA
God Scatters Beauty. Walter Savage Landor. EnRP
("God scatters beauty as he scatters flowers.") FaBoEE
God-seeking. Sir William Watson. WGRP
God Send Easter. Lucille Clifton. CNA
God send the Devil is a gentleman. The Knight Fallen on Evil Days. Elinor Wylie. MoAmPo
God send us a little home. A Prayer for a Little Home. Florence Bone. BLPA; FaBoBe; FaFP; TreFT
God Send Us Men, *sel.* Frederick J. Gillman.
"God send us men with hearts ablaze." TRV
God send us peace, and keep red strife away. At Fredericksburg. John Boyle O'Reilly. PAH
God sent us wit to banish far. Peace in the World. John Galsworthy. PoLF
God Set Us Here, *with music.* Nicasius de Sille, *tr. fr. Dutch.* AH
God Sour the Milk of the Knacking Wench. Alden Nowlan. MoCV; PeCV
God spake three times and saved Van Elsen's soul. Van Elsen. Frederick George Scott. HBV-2
God Speed the Plough! *Unknown.* OxBM
God spoke in a dream. Argument against Metaphor. Gad Hollander. VWA
God spoke once in the dark; dead sound. The Precision. Yvor Winters. EAS
God spoke once that made your girdle fall, The. Daphne. Selden Rodman. PoNe
God strengthen me to bear myself. The Battle Within [*or* Who Shall Deliver Me?]. Christina Rossetti. OxBoCh; TRV
God Supreme! To Thee We Pray, *with music.* Penina Moise *and* Edward N. Calisch. AH
God That Doest Wondrously. Moses ibn Ezra, *tr. fr. Hebrew by* Solomon Solis-Cohen. TrJP
God, that mad'st her well regard her. Dieu Qu'il la Fait. Charles d'Orléans, *tr. by* Ezra Pound. AWP
God the Architect. Harry Kemp. HBMV; TRV; WGRP
(To God, the Architect.) TrPWD
God, the Artist. Angela Morgan. BLPA
God the Omniscient. *At. to* James Cowden Wallace, *also at. to* John A. Wallace. BLRP
(God.) WGRP
(Prayer Moves the Hand That Moves the World.) STF
God, the Port of Peace. John Walton. OxBM
God, thou great symmetry. Envoi. Anna Wickham. MoBrPo
God, though this life is but a wraith. Prayer. Louis Untermeyer. MoAmPo; TrJP
God thought to give the sweetest thing. The Gift. *Unknown.* PGD
God, Through All and in You All. Samuel Longfellow. *See* God of the Earth, the Sky, the Sea.
God to Be First Served. Robert Herrick. OxBChV
God, to get the clay that stayed me. William Baylebridge. Life's Testament, XIII. PoAu-1
God to Man. *Fr.* The Talmud. TrJP
God to Thee We Humbly Bow, *with music.* George H. Boker. AH
God, to whom we look up blindly. Bayard Taylor. *Fr.* The Poet's Journal. TrPWD
God told Noah about the rainbow sign. Lining Track. *Unknown.* AmFP
God tried to teach Crow how to talk. Crow's First Lesson. Ted Hughes. InPS; NoAM
God Wants a Man. *Unknown.* BLRP
God wants our best. He in the far-off ages. What Shall We Render. *Unknown.* BLRP
God Was in Christ. Bible, *N.T.* Second Corinthians, V: 18-21. TRV
God, we don't like to complain. Caliban in the Coal Mines. Louis Untermeyer. HBV-2; MoAmPo; PDV; PoPl; TreFS; TrJP; TRV
God, what a day it is to be abroad! Out-of-Doors. Robert Whitaker. TrPWD
God, what a world, if men in street and mart. True Brotherhood. Ella Wheeler Wilcox. WBLP
God! What mockery is this life of ours! The Mockery of Life. Wilfrid Scawen Blunt. The Love Sonnets of Proteus, LXXIV. VLP
God, when you thought of a pine tree. God, the Artist. Angela Morgan. BLPA
God who created me. Prayers [*or* A Boy's Prayer]. Henry Charles Beeching. GN; OBEV; OBVV
God, who devisedst man who then devised. Prayer for the Age. Myron H. Broomell. TrPWD
God who fled down with a standard yard, The. William Empson. *Fr.* Bacchus. PoA
God who formed the mountains great. All Nature Has a Voice to Tell. James Gilchrist Lawson. BLRP
God who had such heart for us, The. The Cool Gold Wines of Paradise. Robert Farren. AnIV; SeCePo
God, Who Hath Made the Daisies. E. P. Hood. OHIP
God, who made man out of dust. The Continuing City. Laurence Housman. WGRP
God who made New Hampshire, The. Emerson. *Fr.* Ode Inscribed to W. H. Channing. ViBoPo
God who mounts the winged winds, The. Homer, *tr. by* Pope. *Fr.* The Odyssey, V. OBVE
God, who touchest earth with beauty. The Camp Hymn [*or* A Prayer-Poem]. Mary S. Edgar. BLRP; TRV
God, Whom Shall I Compare to Thee? Judah Halevi, *tr. fr. Hebrew by* Alice Lucas. TrJP
God whose goodness filleth every clime, The. Racine, *tr. by* Charles Randolph. *Fr.* Athalie. WGRP
God, whose kindly hand doth sow. Francis Ledwidge. *Fr.* A Dream of Artemis. TrPWD
God, why have you ruined me. Job's Ancient Lament. Owen Dodson. FB
God will have all, or none; serve Him, or fall. Neutrality Loathsome. Robert Herrick. LiTB; NoP
God will never fail us. God Is Faithful. Frances Ridley Havergal. BLRP
God will not let my field lie fallow. The Ploughman. Karle Wilson Baker. WGRP
God wills no man a slave. The man most meek. Washington. James Jeffrey Roche. PAH
God with a Roll of Honour in His hand. The Investiture. Siegfried Sassoon. NoAM
God with His million cares. Dawn and Dark. Norman Gale. HBV-1
God with Us. *Unknown.* *See* God Be in My Head.
God would come, the god would go, The. Man Is God's Nature. Richard Eberhart. EaLo
God would not let the spheric Lights accost. Hugh Stuart Boyd. Elizabeth Barrett Browning. VLP
God, you could grow to love it. Ecclesiastes. Derek Mahon. BIrV; CIP
God, You Have Been Too Good to Me. Charles Wharton Stork. TrPWD; WGRP
Godamighty Drag, *with music.* *Unknown.* OuSiCo
Goddess, The. Denise Levertov. AP; LiTM; NeAP; NOBA; PoCh; PoM
Goddess. Judith Johnson Sherwin. BoWoP
Goddess azure-mantled and aureoled. Our Lady. Robert Bridges. ISi
Goddess Fortune be praised (on her toothed wheel), The. The Unpredicted. John Heath-Stubbs. BoLoP; OxBC
Goddess of poetry. To the Moon. Yvor Winters. HeIP
Goddess of rhyme, that didst inspire. An Epithalamium upon the Marriage of Captain William Bedloe. Richard Duke. APAS
Goddess of threads gladly. *Tr. fr. Icelandic by* George Johnston. *Fr.* The Saga of Gisli. OBVE
Goddess or ghost, you say, by shuddering. To a Scottish Poet. G. S. Fraser. BSV
Goddesse bade the nymphs remove, The. *Unknown, tr. fr. Latin by* Thomas Stanley. *Fr.* Venus Vigils. OBVE
Goddesse, I do love a girle. A Short Hymne to Venus. Robert Herrick. CavP
Goddis sonne is borne. A Cause for Wonder. *Unknown.* MeEL
Goddwyn, *sel.* Thomas Chatterton.
Ode to Liberty. TrGrPo
Gode sire, pray ich thee. I Am from Ireland. *Unknown.* MeEL
Godfrey Gordon Gustavus Gore. William Brighty Rands. FaPON; HBVY; TiPo
(Reformation of Godfrey Gore, The.) HBV-1
Godfrey of Bulloigne; or, The Recoverie of Jerusalem, *sels.* Tasso, *tr. fr. Italian by* Edward Fairfax.
"Joyous birds, hid under greenewood shade, The," *fr.* XVI. OBVE
Pluto's Council. OBSC
Prayer Brings Rain, A. OBSC
"Sweet Armida tooke this charge on hand, The," *fr.* IV. OBVE
Godiva. D. C. Berry. BXAP
Godiva. Tennyson. BeLS; HBV-2
Godlike beneath his grave divinities. The Druid. John Banister Tabb. AA
Godly and the Ungodly, The. Bible, *O.T.* Psalms, I. TreF
("Blessed is the man that walketh not in the counsel of the ungodly.") AWP; BiP
(Tree and the Chaff, The.) WGRP
Godly Casuistry. Samuel Butler. *Fr.* Hudibras, II, 2. OBS

Godly Dream, A, *sels.* Elizabeth Melvill, Lady Culross. WPE
"I looked down and saw a pit most black."
"Into that pit when I did enter in."
"Then up I rose, and made no more delay."
"This pit is Hell where through thou now must go."
"Weary I was, and thought to sit at rest."
Godly Girzie. Burns. CoMu; ErPo; UnTE
Godmother. Phyllis B. Morden. RHPC; SoPo
Godmother. Dorothy Parker. PoRA
Gododdin, The, *sels.* Aneirin, *tr. fr. Welsh.*
"Men went to Gododdin, laughter-loving," *tr. by* Joseph P. Clancy. OBWP
"To Cattraeth's vale in glitt'ring row," *tr. by* Thomas Gray. OBVE
Godolphin Horne. Hilaire Belloc. CenHV; DTC; FaBoCo
Gods, The. Dennis Lee. NOBC
Gods, The. W. S. Merwin. NaP
God's-Acre. Longfellow. HBV-2
God's a-Gwinter Trouble de Water, *with music.* *Unknown.* BoAN-2
(Wade in the Water.) FSW
Gods and furies now depart. On Reading the *Metamorphoses.* George Garrett. NePoAm-2
God's angry man, His crotchety scholar. The Thunderer. Phyllis McGinley. EaLo
Gods are happy, The. The Strayed Reveller to Ulysses. Matthew Arnold. OBEV
Gods Are Mighty, The. N. P. Van Wyk Louw, *tr. fr. Afrikaans by* Jack Cope. PeSA
God's blessing lead us, help us! *At. to* St. Colman, *tr. by* Whitley Stokes *and* John Strachan. *Fr.* Hymn against Pestilence. OnYI
God's Blessing on Munster. *At. to* St. Patrick, *tr. fr. Old Irish by* Whitley Stokes. OnYI
God's Call. *Unknown.* STF
God's Character. Gerard Manley Hopkins. LiTB
Gods chase/ Round vase. Ode on a Grecian Urn Summarized. Desmond Skirrow. NIP; NOBL
God's child in Christ adopted—Christ my all. My Baptismal Birthday. Samuel Taylor Coleridge. NOCV
God's Controversy with New-England. Michael Wigglesworth. SCAP
God's Dark. John Martin. PoLF
God's Determinations, *sels.* Edward Taylor.
Christ's Reply. PoEL-3
Glory of and Grace in the Church Set Out, The. AmPP; AP
God's Selecting Love in the Decree. PoEL-3
Joy of Church Fellowship Rightly Attended, The. AmPP; AP; OxBA; SCAP
(In Heaven Soaring Up.) AH, *with music*
Preface, The: "Infinity, when all things it beheld." AmPP; AP; HAP; NOBA; OxBA; SCAP
Soul's Groan to Christ for Succour, The. PAI; PoEL-3
God's Dominion and Decrees. Isaac Watts. OBEC
God's Eye Is on the Sparrow. Bertha Meyer. STF
"God's First Creature Was Light." Winifred Welles. ImOP
God's Funeral. Thomas Hardy. WGRP
God's Garden. Richard Burton. TRV; WGRP
God's Gifts. Jakov de Haan, *tr. fr. Dutch by* David Soetendorp. VWA
God's Glory. Bible, *O.T.* Psalms, XIX. *See* Heavens Declare the Glory of God, The.
God's Goin' to Set This World on Fire (A *and* B *vers., with music*). *Unknown.* AS
God's Goodness. C. D. Martin. WBLP
God's Grandeur. Gerard Manley Hopkins. AWP; BiP; BLPL; BrPo; CABA; CMoP; EBCP; EBVV; FaFP; FF; HAP; ILwL; InPK; InvP; LiTM; LoBV; MoAB; MoBrPo; MoPo; MoVE; NoAM; NOBE; NoP; OAEL-2; OBNC; OxBoCh; PAI; PPP; PrIm; SeCeV; SoSe; SOTW; TEP; TrCP; TreFT; TrGrPo; UnPo; VLP; WeW
God's Harp. Gustav Falke, *tr. fr. German by* Ludwig Lewisohn. AWP
Gods have heard me, Lyce, The. Revenge! Horace, *tr. by* Louis Untermeyer. Odes, IV, 13. AWP
Gods Have Heard My Vows, The. *Unknown.* EnRePo
Gods have taken alien shapes upon them, The. Exiles. "Æ." BIrV; MoBrPo
God's head for a paperweight, A. The Desk. Cid Corman. VGW
Gods i am pent in a cockroach. The Wail of Archy. Don Marquis. *Fr.* Archy and Mehitabel. FiBHP
God's Ideal Mother. Cora M. Pinkham. STF
God's in His Heaven: He never issues. Ninth Philosopher's Song. Aldous Huxley. ViBoPo
Gods in Vietnam. Eugene Redmond. NBP; PoBA
Gods it is I ask to release me from this watch, The. Agamemnon. Aeschylus, *tr. by* Louis MacNeice. NAWM-1
God's Judgment [*or* Judgement] on a Wicked Bishop. Robert Southey. EnRP; HBV-1; HBVY; OBRV; OnMSP
(Bishop Hatto.) ChTr; OBNV
(Bishop Hatto and the Rats.) PaPO
God's Key. *Unknown.* STF
God's Language. Ruth Fainlight. VWA
God's Little Mountain. Geoffrey Hill. NePoEA
God's Love. *Unknown.* BLRP
God's Mercy. William Langland, *mod. by* Donald Attwater. *Fr.* The Vision of Piers Plowman. NOCV
God's Mother. Laurence Housman. ISi
Gods Must Not Know Us, The. Linda Gregg. NPGG
Gods of Africa regard me, The. Distance. Anthony Delius. PeSA
Gods of Hellas, gods of Hellas. The Dead Pan. Elizabeth Barrett Browning. VLP
Gods of the Copybook Headings, The. Kipling. FaPoR; OHFP; OxBTC; OBSV; TW
Gods of the Earth Beneath, The. Edmund Blunden. BrPo
God's Pay. *Unknown.* STF
God's Pity. Louise Driscoll. WGRP
God's pity on poor kings. Poor Kings. W. H. Davies. HBV-2
God's plan had a hopeful beginning. Limerick. *Unknown.* NIP
God's Plans. Mary Riley Smith. BLRP
God's Plans. *Unknown.* BLRP
God's Precepts Perfect. Bible, *O.T.* Psalms, XIX: 7-9. BLRP
God's Presence Makes My Heaven. Oswald J. Smith. STF
God's Promises. *Unknown.* BLRP
God's Residence. Emily Dickinson. *See* Who has not found the heaven below.
God's rod doth watch while men do sleep; and then. Temptation. Robert Herrick. LiTB
God's Rule. Bible, *O.T. Fr.* Isaiah. *See* Peaceable Kingdom, The.
God's Saints. Henry Vaughan. TRV
God's Selecting Love in the Decree. Edward Taylor. *Fr.* God's Determinations. PoEL-3
God's spice I was, and pounding was my due. The Martyrdom of Mary, Queen of Scots. Robert Southwell. ACP
God's Sunshine. John Oxenham. WBLP
Gods, The! The Gods! D. H. Lawrence. CMoP
God's Trails Lead Home. John R. Clements. BLRP
God's Treasure. "A. M. N." STF
God's Vengeance. Bible, *O.T.* Isaiah, XXXIV: 8-15. FM
God's Virtue. Barnabe Barnes. *See* World's Bright Comforter, The.
Gods, what a sun! I think the world's aglow. A Summer Day in Old Sicily. Edward Cracroft Lefroy. *Fr.* Echoes from Theocritus. OBVV
God's Will. Charles E. Guthrie. BLRP
God's Will. Mildred Howells. HBV-2
God's Will. Alice Nevin. BLRP
God's Will for Us. *Unknown.* BLRP; WBLP
(God's Will for You and Me.) SoSe
God's will in me. God's Will. Alice Nevin. BLRP
God's Will Is Best. Thelma Curtis. STF
God's Will Is Best. *Unknown.* BLRP
God's will is better than our will. God's Will Is Best. Thelma Curtis. STF
Gods! with what pride I see the titled slave. Charles Churchill. *Fr.* The Author. OBSV
God's Word. John Clifford. *See* Anvil of God's Word, The.
God's Work. Charlotte Cushman. TreFT
God's World. Mildred Keeling. BLRP
God's World. Edna St. Vincent Millay. BLPL; CMoP; FaBoBe; FaBV; HBV-1; MoAmPo; PoPl; PoSC; TrCP
Godspeed. Harriet Prescott Spofford. EtS
Goe and Catche a Falling Starre. John Donne. *See* Song: "Go and catch a falling star."
Goe happy rose, and enterwove. *See* Go, happy Rose, and, interwove.
Goe! hunt the whiter ermine! and present. *See* Go! hunt the whiter ermine, and present.
Goe little book, and once a week shake hands. Ad Librum. Samuel Danforth, Jr. SCAP
Goe lovely Rose. *See* Go Lovely Rose.
Goe now; and with some daring drugg. Temperance or the Cheap Physitian upon the Translation of Lessius. Richard Crashaw. SeCV-1
Goe, pale-fac't paper, to my Deare. The Letter. John Tatham. CavP
Goe smiling soules, your new built cages breake. *See* Go, smiling souls, your new-built cages break.
Goe solitary wood, and henceforth be. *See* Go, solitary wood . . .
Goe soule, the bodies guest. *See* Go, Soul, the body's guest.
Goe stop the swift-wing'd moments in their flight. Elegie. William Habington. AnAnS-2
Goe thou gentle whispering wind. A Prayer to the Wind. Thomas Carew. AnAnS-2
Goes through the mud. *Unknown.* OxNR
Goethe and Frederika. Henry Sidgwick. HBV-1
Goethe in Weimar sleeps, and Greece. Memorial Verses. Matthew Arnold. CABA; FiP; HBV-2; OAEL-2; OAEP; PP; VLP

Goethe said that 'twixt embraces. Not Lotte. Katherine Hoskins. ErPo
Goethe's Death Mask. Linda Gregg. MAYP
Goff, The; an Heroi-comical Poem, *sel.* Thomas Mathison.
Victory on the Last Green. NOEC
Gofongo, The. Spike Milligan. AmMo
Goin' Back T'morrer. Hamlin Garland. OBAL
Goin' 'cross the Mountain. *Unknown.* AmFP
Goin' down the road, Lawd. Bound No'th Blues. Langston Hughes. AmNP; BiP
Goin' down to Cripple Creek, goin' at a run. Cripple Creek. *Unknown.* AmFP
Goin' down to the delta. Mississippi Blues. *Unknown.* AmFP
Goin' Down to Town, *with music. Unknown.* AS
Goin' up State Street, comin' down Main. Take a Whiff on Me. *Unknown.* NOBA
Goin' up the River, *with music. Unknown.* TrAS
Going. Peter Everwine. NNaP
Going, The. Thomas Hardy. EBEV; ELP; LiTB; NOBE; PAI; UnPo
Going. Robert Kelly. CoPo
Going. Philip Larkin. CMoP
Going abruptly into a starry night. Starlight. William Meredith. NePoEA
Going a-Maying. Robert Herrick. *See* Corinna's Going a-Maying.
Going and Staying. Thomas Hardy. CMoP; NoAM
Going a-Nutting. Edmund Clarence Stedman. GN
Going Away. Howard Nemerov. DFF
Going Away. Ann Stanford. GP; PH
Going Away Blues. *Unknown.* BluL
Going Back. Salvatore Quasimodo, *tr. fr. Italian by* Rina Ferrarelli. AMV-81
Going Back. George Rachow. LFAC
Going Back Again. "Owen Meredith." EvOK; FiBHP
(Check to Song.) FaBoCo
Going Down Hill on a Bicycle. Henry Charles Beeching. HBV-1; HBVY; OBEV; OBVV
Going Down the Mountain. Valentin Iremonger. NeIP
(Descending.) EnLoPo
Going down the old way. Song. Margaret Widdemer. HBMV
Going down to town. Lynchburg Town. *Unknown.* OuSiCo
Going for Water. Robert Frost. HBMV
Going from us at last. The Escape. Mark Van Doren. MoAmPo
Going Home. Maurice Kenny. STE
Going home by lamplight across Boston Common. A Revivalist in Boston. Adrienne Rich. EaLo
Going Home, 1945, *sel.* L. E. Sissman.
"My father casts a stone whose ripples ride." DiL
Going Home with Jesus. Walter E. Isenhour. STF
Going In. Marge Piercy. DFF
Going In to Dinner. Edward Shanks. OBMV; OxBTC
Going into Breeches. Charles *and* Mary Lamb. OxBChV
Going my way of old. Marriage. W. W. Gibson. HBV-1
Going on six thousand years. After Six Thousand Years. Victor Hugo, *tr. by* Selden Rodman. WaaP
Going or Gone. Charles Lamb. BXAP
Going out, those bold days. Autumn. W. R. Rodgers. NeBP
Going the Rounds; a Sort of Love Poem. Anthony Hecht. BoLoP
Going, the wild things of our land. The Passing of the Buffalo. Hamlin Garland. BPAW
Going Through. Bruce P. Woodford. MAT
Going through Changes. Jean Tepperman. NMM
Going thru cases and cases. The Sculptors. Alfred Purdy. PeCV
Going To and Fro and Walking Up and Down, *sel.* Charles Reznikoff.
Autobiography: Hollywood. VWA
Going to Bed. Marchette Chute. PDV
Going to Bed. John Donne. Elegies, XIX. AnAnS-1; EBEV; GBL; LiTB; PPP
(Elegie [*or* Elegy]: Going to Bed.) EnRePo; MePo.
(Elegie XIX: To His Mistris Going to Bed.) SeCP
(To His Mistress [*or* Mistris] Going to Bed.) BoLoP; ErPo; JCP; NoP; OAEL-1; TEP; UnTE
Going to Boston. *Unknown.* FSW
Going to Church. Coventry Patmore. *Fr.* The Angel in the House. LoBV
Going to Germany. *Unknown.* BluL
Going to Hell. *Unknown.* OxBM
Going to Mass by the heavenly mercy. Mary Hynes. Anthony Raftery, *tr. by* Frank O'Connor. KiLC
Going to Mass Last Sunday. Donagh MacDonagh. BIrV; NeIP; OxBI
Going to Moscow. Lauris Edmond. OCNZ
Going to Norway. Jack Anderson. GP
Going to Press. Judith Moffett. AMV-80
Going to Remake This World. James Welch. CDW
Going to School. Karl Shapiro. TrJP
Going to School in France or America. Tom Clark. ConAP
Going to sing about Emily. Microcosmos, XXV. Nigel Heseltine. NeBP
Going to sleep, I cross my hands on my chest. Death. William Knott. EAS
Going to Sleep in the Country. Howard Moss. DFF; PoCh
Going to the Dogs. *Unknown.* TreFS
Going to the North. Stanislaw Wygodski, *tr. fr. Polish by* Isaac Komem. VWA
Going to the Warres. Richard Lovelace. *See* To Lucasta, Going to the Wars.
Going to the Water. Geary Hobson. STE
Going to Town. Linda Hogan. TWSS
Going to Town. Fred Lape. PH
Going Too Far. Mildred Howells. OnMSP; TiPo
Going towards Spain. Barnabe Googe. EnRePo
Going Up. John Travers Moore. RHPC
Going Up and Down. Jim Daniels. AMV-81
Going up for the jump shot. The Poet Tries to Turn In His Jock. David Hilton. LiSp
Going up the river, or down, their tuneless look. Barges on the Hudson. Babette Deutsch. WPE
Going up through the hill called the vineyard. The Vineyard. W. S. Merwin. NNaP
Going Up to London. Nancy Byrd Turner. HBMV
Going Uptown to Visit Miriam. Victor Hernandez Cruz. FF; MAT; NYP
Going—to—her! Emily Dickinson. PeHV
Golagros and Gawane, *sel. Unknown.*
"Thai passit in thare pilgramage." OxBS
Gol-darned Wheel, The, *with music. Unknown.* CoSo
Gold. Donald Hall. ConAP; InPS
Gold. Thomas Hood. WBLP
Gold. Glyn Jones. NeBP
Gold,/ Silver. *Unknown.* OxNR
Gold and all this werdis win. Crucified to the World. *Unknown.* MeEL
Gold and Black. Michael Ondaatje. NoP
Gold-armoured ghost from the Roman road, The. The Youth with Red-gold Hair. Edith Sitwell. FaBoTw; MoVE
Gold as an infant's humming dream. Long Summer. Laurie Lee. BoNaP
Gold Coast Customs, *sel.* Edith Sitwell.
"One fantee wave." OBMV
Gold-coloured skin of my Lebanese friends, The. A Trip to Four or Five Towns. John Logan. CoAP; ConAP; NNaP
Gold Country; Hotel Leger, Mokelumne Hill, Revisited, The. Joseph Stroud. NPGG
Gold Factory, The. William Hathaway. *Fr.* Rumplestiltskin Poems. DFT
Gold! Gold! Gold! Gold! Gold. Thomas Hood. WBLP
"Gold is for the mistress—silver for the maid." Cold Iron. Kipling. OnMSP
Gold Is the Son of Zeus: Neither Moth nor Worm May Gnaw It. "Michael Field." OBMV
Gold I've none, for use or show. Lyric[k] for Legacies. Robert Herrick. FaBoRV; JCP; OBS
Gold Leaves. G. K. Chesterton. OxBTC
Gold locks, and black locks. The Barber's. Walter de la Mare. GoJo; SoPo; SUS
Gold mountain men said, The. Chinatown Talking Story. Kitty Tsui. BrSi
Gold Nest, The. Robert Wallace. PPJ
Gold of a ripe oat straw, gold of a southwest moon. Falltime. Carl Sandburg. PoA
Gold of heaven, The. Love. Tom Dent. NNP
Gold on her head, and gold on her feet. The Eve of Crecy. William Morris. OBVV; VLP
Gold or iv'ry's not intended. Horace, *tr. by* Christopher Smart. Odes, II, 18. OBVE
Gold, red and green flies. Near Dusk. Joseph Auslander. FaPON
Gold savours well, though it be got. Isabella Whitney. *Fr.* A Sweet Nosegay, or Pleasant Posy. WPE
Gold-Seekers, The. Hamlin Garland. AA; FaBoBe; YaD
Gold Seekers, The. Marion Muir Richardson. PoOW
Gold Seeker's Song, The. *Unknown.* PoOW
Gold tane from the kings harbengers. Robin Hood and Queen Katherine. *Unknown.* ESPB
Gold That Fell on Danae. Horatio Colony. TwAmPo
Gold-tinted Dragon, The. Karla Kuskin. SoPo
Gold Tooth Blues. Tennessee Williams. OBAL
Gold will not buy this voyage. Looking for a Country under Its Original Name. Colleen J. McElroy. BlSi
Gold wings across the sea! The Song of Jehane du Castel Beau [*or* Song]. William Morris. *Fr.* Golden Wings. ChTr; LoBV
Golda. Adrienne Wolfert. AMV-80
Goldbrown upon the sated flood. Flood. James Joyce. MoBrPo
Golden Age, The. Ernest Francisco Fenollosa. AA

Golden Age, The. Giovanni Battista Guarini, *tr. fr. Italian by* Sir Richard Fanshawe. *Fr.* Il Pastor Fido. OAEL-1
("Fair Golden Age! when milk was th' onely food.") OBVE
Golden Age, The, *sel.* Thomas Heywood.
Hymn to Diana. ElL
Golden Age, The. Ovid, *tr. fr. Latin by* Arthur Golding. *Fr.* Metamorphoses, I. OAEL-1
Golden Age, The. Tasso. *See* Pastoral, A: "Oh happy golden age."
Golden Age, The. *Unknown.* APAS
Golden Age is come, The. The Newmarket Song. *Unknown.* APAS
Golden age was when the world was young, The. Fulke Greville. *Fr.* Caelica. OAEL-1
Golden as your singing-note. Amber Beads. Audrey Alexandra Brown. CaP
Golden bee a-cometh, A. A Merry Bee. Joseph Skipsey. OBVV
Golden Bird, The. Rex Ingamells. PoAu-2
Golden Bough. Helen Hoyt. HBMV
Golden Bough. Elinor Wylie. MoAmPo; PBWP
Golden bridle of Bellerephon. The Fourth Pearl: Temperance. Lady Diana Primrose. *Fr.* A Chain of Pearl. WPE
Golden Calf. Norman MacCaig. OxBS
Golden Carol, The. *Unknown.* OHIP
Golden casket I designed, A. Epigram. John Swanwick Drennan. BIrV
Golden cloud slept for her pleasure, A. The Mountain. Mikhail Yuryevich Lermontov, *tr. by* Max Eastman. AWP
Golden cradle under you, and you young, A. He Meditates on the Life of a Rich Man. Douglas Hyde, *tr. by* Lady Gregory. OBMV
Golden crocus reaches up, The. The Crocus. Walter Crane. RHPC; SoPo
Golden eagle swooped out of the sky, The. Salmon Drowns Eagle. Malcolm Lowry. MoCV; OBCV
Golden Echo, The. Gerard Manley Hopkins. *See* Leaden Echo and the Golden Echo, The.
Golden Fish, The. George Arnold. HBV-1
Golden Fleece, The. Oscar Williams. PoA
Golden flie one shew'd to me, A. Upon a Flie. Robert Herrick. FM
Golden Gate: The Teacher. Lilyan S. Mastrolia. AMV-80
Golden Gates. *Unknown.* ShM
Golden gates of Sleep unbar, The. A Bridal Song. Shelley. OBRV
Golden gift that nature did thee give, The. Earl of Surrey. AAS; SiPS
Golden gilliflower to-day, A. The Gilliflower of Gold. William Morris. WHA
Golden girl/ in a golden gown. College Formal: Renaissance Casino. Langston Hughes. BALP
Golden globe incontinent, The. Midsummer Day in France. Alexander Hume. *Fr.* Of the Day Estivall. FaBoPP
Golden Glove, The. *Unknown.* AmFP
Golden goats with lapis eyes. Panegyric. Harris Lenowitz. VWA
Golden Grain. Helen M. Wright. PH
Golden Gullies of the Palmer, The. *Unknown.* PoAu-1
Golden hair that Gulla wears, The. Bought Locks. Martial, *tr. by* Sir John Harington. AWP
Golden head by golden head. Laura and Lizzie Asleep. Christina Rossetti. *Fr.* Goblin Market. PeHV
Golden Heart, The. Witter Bynner. HBMV
Golden Hour, The. Thomas Moore. *Fr.* Lalla Rookh. OBNC
Golden Journey to Samarkand, The. James Elroy Flecker. FaBoRV; HBMV
Sels.
"And how beguile you? Death has no repose," II. OxBTC
Epilogue: "Away, for we are ready to a man!" NOBE
Prologue: "We who with songs beguile your pilgrimage." BrPo; FaPoR; GoJo; OBMV; OxBTC
Golden Legend, The, *sel.* Longfellow.
"This is indeed the blessed Mary's Land." ISi
Golden lemon is not made, The. A Song for the Spanish Anarchists. Sir Herbert Read. ChMP
Golden Lines. Gérard de Nerval, *tr. fr. French by* Robert Bly. NU
Golden Lot, A. Joseph Skipsey. VLP
("In the coal-pit, or the factory.") SaC
Golden Mean, The. Horace. *See* To Licinius.
Golden Mean, The. Earl of Surrey, *after* Horace. SiPS
("Of thy lyfe, Thomas, this compasse well mark.") OBVE
Golden Mile-Stone, The. Longfellow. PoEL-5
Golden Month, The. Marion Doyle. YeAr
Golden Moonrise. William Stanley Braithwaite. PoBA
Golden Oldie. Paul Mariani. GeTw
Golden one is gone from the banquets, The. Epigram. Hilda Doolittle ("H. D."). PoA
Golden-Robin's Nest, The. John White Chadwick. AA
Golden Rod, The. Frank Dempster Sherman. FaPON
Golden rose the house, in the portal I saw. Apparuit. Ezra Pound. TwAmPo
Golden Rule, The. James Wells. STF
Golden Sea-Otter, The. Wakarpa, *tr. by* Arthur Waley. *Fr.* Kutune Shirka (The Ainu Epic). WTO
Golden Shower, The, *sel.* Roy Campbell.
"Here, where relumed by changing seasons, burn." OxBTC
Golden Silence. Christina Rossetti. NBM
Golden Slippers. James A. Bland. *See* Oh, Dem Golden Slippers!
Golden Slumbers [Kiss Your Eyes]. Thomas Dekker *and others. Fr.* The Pleasant Comedy of Patient Grissel. CH; ELP; HBV-1; ViBoPo
(Cradle Song, A: "Golden slumbers kiss your eyes.") OBSC; OxBChV; TrGrPo
(Lullaby: "Golden slumbers kiss your eyes.") ElL; LoBV
Golden spider of the sky, The. Solar Myth. Genevieve Taggard. MoAmPo
Golden spring redeems the withered year, The. Robert Hillyer. Sonnets, II. HBMV
Golden Spurs. Virginia Scott Miner. SiSoSe
Golden Spurs, The. *Unknown, tr. fr. Greek by* Louis Untermeyer. UnTE
Golden Stallion, The. Paul Thompson. BPAW
Golden State. Frank Bidart. DiL
Golden Stockings. Oliver St. John Gogarty. OxBI
Golden strand that weaves through tapestry, A. The Father's Gold. *Unknown.* STF
Golden sun is garish, The. Rain. Frances Shaw. HBMV
Golden sun that brings the day, The. In Praise of the Sun. "A. W." CTC; OBSC
Golden [*or* Goldyn] Targe, The. William Dunbar. BSV; OxBS
Sels.
"O reverend Chaucere, rose of rethoris all." PP
Poet's Dream, The. PoEL-1
("Right as the star of day began to shine," *shorter sel.*) PBBP
Golden through the golden morning. The Return. Eleanor Rodgers Cox. PAH
Golden Vanity, The. *Unknown.* BaBo (C *vers.*) CH; ELP; FaBoCh; FSW; OBET; PoPle; ViBoFo; WiR
(Golden Vanitie, The.) EnSB
(Low-down, Lonesome Low, The, *with music, diff. vers.*) OuSiCo
(Sir Walter Raleigh Sailing in the Lowlands, *diff. vers.*) OxBoLi
(Sweet Trinity, The, A *and* B *vers.*) AmFP; BaBo; ESPB
Golden Wedding, The. David Gray. FaBoBe; HBV-1
Golden Wings. William Morris. OBNC; WHA
Sels.
Ancient Castle, An. SeCePo
("Midways of a walled garden.") ChTr
Song of Jehane du Castel Beau, The. ChTr
(Song: "Gold wings across the sea!") LoBV
Golden, within this golden hive. Danaë. Barbara Howes. WPE
Goldenhair. James Joyce. Chamber Music, V. ChTr; HBMV
Goldenhair. Sir John Waller. PeHV
Goldenrod. Elaine Goodale Eastman. HBV-1
Goldenrod [*or* Golden-rod] is yellow, The. September [Days Are Here]. Helen Hunt Jackson. FaPON; FPL; GoJo; OBCA; PoLF; TiPo; YeAR
Goldfinches, The. Richard Jago. PBBP
Goldfinches. Keats. *Fr.* I Stood Tip-Toe. GN
("Sometimes goldfinches one by one will drop.") PBBP
Goldfish, The. Audrey Alexandra Brown. CaP
Goldfish. Harold Monro. BrPo
Goldfish. Howard Nemerov. BoAnP
Goldfish on the Writing Desk. Max Brod, *tr. fr. German by* Babette Deutsch *and* Avram Yarmolinsky. TrJP
Goldfish Wife, The. Sandra Hochman. NYBP; UnPo
Goldsmith's Wife, The. *Unknown, tr. fr. Irish by* Frank O'Connor. KiLC
Goldyn Targe, The. William Dunbar. *See* Golden Targe, The.
Golem, The. Shlomo Reich, *tr. fr. French by* Mira Reich. VWA
Golf Ball. John Delaney. AMV-81
Golf Links, The. Sarah N. Cleghorn. FaFP; InMe; PAI; PoPl; PPON
(Golf Links Lie So Near the Mill, The.) HBMV; PoLF
(Quatrain.) NIP
Golfers. Irving Layton. CABA
Golfers. John Updike. LiSp
Golfer's Rubaiyat, The. H. W. Boynton. BXAP
Golgotha. X. J. Kennedy. NYBP
Golgotha Is a Mountain. Arna Bontemps. AmNP; CDC; PoNe
Golgotha's journey is an ancient way. Crucifixion. Hugh O. Isbell. PGD
Goliath and David. Louis Untermeyer. TrJP
Goliath of Gath. Phillis Wheatley. BALP
Goliathus goliathus, the one banana. The Zoo. Gilbert Sorrentino. NeAP
Goll's Parting with His Wife. *Unknown, tr. fr. Early Modern Irish by* Eoin MacNeill. AnIL
Golly, How Truth Will Out. Ogden Nash. LiTA; MoAmPo
Gombeen, The. Joseph Campbell. BIrV
Gondibert, *sels.* Sir William Davenant.
"By what bold passion am I rudely led," *fr.* I, 3. FaBoEn; OBS

"Of all the Lombards, by their Trophies knowne," *fr.* I, i. SeCV-1
Praise and Prayer, *fr.* II, vi. GoBC; OBEV
Gondoliers, The, *sels.* W. S. Gilbert.
Duke of Plaza-Toro, The. FaPON; FiBHP
Grand Inquisitor's Song, The. OnMSP
There Lived a King. FiBHP; PoPle; WhC
(King Goodheart.) InMe
Gone. Mary Elizabeth Coleridge. HBV-2; OBEV; OBNC; OBVV
Gone. Walter de la Mare. GoJo
Gone, A. Larry Eigner. NeAP
Gone. Ralph Pomeroy. DFF
Gone. Carl Sandburg. NOBA; TwAmPo
Gone. Joanna Thompson. AMV-80
Gone are the coloured princes, gone echo, gone laughter. The Ruin. Richard Hughes. OBMV
Gone Are the Days. Norman MacCaig. OxBC
Gone are the days when my heart was young and gay. Old Black Joe. Stephen Collins Foster. FaFP; PSoN; TreFS
Gone are the drab monosyllabic days. Tilth. Robert Graves. FaBoEE; OBSV
Gone are the games we played all night. Mahsati, *tr. fr. Farsi by* Deirdre Lashgari. WPOW
Gone are the sensuous stars, and manifold. Chaucer. Benjamin Brawley. BANP
Gone are those three, those sisters rare. The Three Sisters. Arthur Davison Ficke. HBV-1
Gone Boy. Langston Hughes. NePoAm-2
Gone Dead Train, The. *Unknown.* BluL
Gone down in the flood, and gone out in the flame! The Sinking of the *Merrimac.* Lucy Larcom. PAH
Gone—faded out of the story, the sea-faring friend I remember? Pasa Thalassa Thalassa. E. A. Robinson. EtS; MOS
Gone Fishing. Mark Sanders. WOLT
Gone! Gone! Forever Gone. Gerald Griffin. OnYI
Gone, gone—sold and gone. The Farewell. Whittier. AA; AWP; PoNe
Gone, I say, and walk from church. The Truth the Dead Know. Anne Sexton. MoAmPo; NePoEA-2; NIP; NoAM; PBWP; TAP
Gone in the Wind. James Clarence Mangan, *after the German of* Friedrich Rückert. ACP; GoBC; OBVV; OnYI; OxBI; SeCePo
Gone is the city, gone the day. The Right Kind of People. Edwin Markham. BLPA; FPL
Gone Is the Sleepgiver. Penelope Shuttle. BrRo
Gone Is Youth. Salamah, Son of Jandal, *tr. fr. Arabic by* Sir Charles Lyall. *Fr.* The Mufaddaliyat. AWP
Gone, my white tangible angel falling. Four Poems for April, IV. Louis Adeane. NeBP
Gone now the baby's nurse. Home after Three Months Away. Robert Lowell. NoP
Gone she is a long, long way. Upon a Maid. Robert Herrick. CaPo
Gone the three ancient ladies. Frau Bauman, Frau Schmidt, and Frau Schwartze. Theodore Roethke. CoAP; InPK; MoAB; NePoAm; NoAM; NOBA; NYBP; SaC; TAP
Gone were but the winter. Spring Quiet. Christina Rossetti. BoNaP; CH; GTBS-P; LoBV; PoEL-5; WPE
Gone Were But the Winter Cold. Allan Cunningham. *See* Spring of the Year, The.
Gone while your tastes were keen to you. For E. McC. Ezra Pound. LiSp
Gone Years, The. Alice Fulton. Str
"Goneys an' gullies an' all o' the birds o' the sea." Sea-Change. John Masefield. FaBoTW; MOS; OBMV
Gonna dig my grave both long and narrow. Dig My Grave. *Unknown.* FSW
Gonna Lay My Head Down on Some Railroad Line. *Unknown.* AmFP
Gonna sit around for a while. I Don't Know. *Unknown.* BluL
Goober Peas. *Unknown.* FSW; PSoN, *with music*
Good Advice. Lady Mary Wortley Montagu. POL
("Be plain in dress and sober in your diet.") FaBoEE
Good afternoon, Sir Smasham Uppe! Sir Smasham Uppe. E. V. Rieu. RHPC
Good aged Bale, that with thy hoary hairs. To Doctor Bale. Barnabe Googe. EnRePo
Good and Bad. James Stephens. MoBrPo
Good and Bad. Unknown, *at. to* Edward Wallis Hoch. *See* Charity.
Good and bad and right and wrong. Good and Bad. James Stephens. MoBrPo
Good and Bad Children. Robert Louis Stevenson. EBVV; FaBoCh; FaFP; HBV-1; HBVY; NBM; OxBChV; TreF
Good and Bad Luck. John Milton Hay. *See* Good Luck and Bad.
Good and Bad Wives. *Unknown.* CoMu
Good and Clever. Elizabeth Wordsworth. OxBTC
Good, and great God, can I not think[e] of thee. To Heaven. Ben Jonson. AnAnS-2; EnRePo; HAP; ILwL; JCP; LiTB; LoBV; NOCV; OBS; OxBoCh; PPoe; QFR; SeCeV; SeCP; TrPWD; UnPo
Good and great God! How should I fear. No Coming to God without Christ. Robert Herrick. EBCP; OxBoCh; TRV
Good bailiff of my farm, that snug domain. Horace, *tr. fr. Latin by* John Conington. OBVE
Good, better, best. *Unknown.* OxNR
Good Bishop, A. *Unknown, tr. fr. German by* William Taylor. WGRP
Good Bishop Valentine. Eleanor Farjeon. PoSC
Good Boy, The, *with music. Unknown.* AS
Good Breasts, The. Willis Barnstone. VWA
Good brother Philip, I have borne you long. Astrophel and Stella, LXXXIII. Sir Philip Sidney. PBBP; SiPS
Good-by and Keep Cold. Robert Frost. CMoP
Goodby Betty, Don't Remember Me. E. E. Cummings. CMoP
Good-by er Howdy-do. James Whitcomb Riley. CTC
Goodby girls, I'm goin' to Boston. Going to Boston. *Unknown.* FSW
Good-by [*or* Goodbye], good-by to summer! Robin Redbreast. William Allingham. FaBoBe; HBV-1; HBVY; MoShBr; OxBChV; PBBP
Good-by Liza Jane. *Unknown. See* Goodbye 'Liza Jane.
Good-by My Winter Suit. N. M. Bodecker. RHPC
Good-by: nay, do not grieve that it is over. *See* Good-bye!—no, do not grieve . . .
Good-by, Old Paint. *Unknown. See* Old Paint.
Good-by, Steer. Robert V. Carr. BPAW
Good-by, the tears are in my eyes. Rondel. Villon, *tr. by* Andrew Lang. AWP
Good-by to my pals of the prairie. The Dying Cowboy of Rim Rock Ranch. *Unknown.* CoSo
Goodbye. Bella Akhmadulina, *tr. fr. Russian by* Barbara Einzig. BoWoP
Goodbye. Chana Bloch. MAYP
Good-Bye. Walter de la Mare. FaBoEn; NoP
Good-bye. Emerson. FaFP; HBV-2; LiTA; TAP; TreF
("Good-bye, proud world!") WGRP
Goodbye. Galway Kinnell. Str
Goodbye. William Knott. EAS
Goodbye. Alun Lewis. BoLoP; OBWP; OxBTC
Goodbye. Sherod Santos. MAYP
Goodbye! George John Whyte-Melville. TreF
Good-bye,/ try to stay awake now you're dead. Book of the Dead, Prayer 14. Mei Berssenbrugge. GP
Goodbye/ Until such time as bobolinks do dine. To Janet. Ralph Pomeroy. NYBP
Good-bye, Brother, *with music. Unknown.* AS
Goodbye cigar. A Sort of Elegy. Blanche Farley. SOTS
Goodbye David Tamunoemi West. Margaret Danner. BPo
Good-bye, divisions of people. Leaving. Linda Hogan. TWSS
Good-bye, Fare You Well, *with music. Unknown.* AmSS
Good-bye for a Long Time. Roy Fuller. NeBP
Goodbye, goodbye to summer! *See* Good-by, good-by to summer!
Goodbye "Hello." Philip Dow. NPGG
Goodbye, lady in Bangor, who sent me. The Correspondence School Instructor Says Goodbye to His Poetry Students. Galway Kinnell. NOBA; NoP; TAP
Goodbye, Little Bonnie, Goodbye. *Unknown.* FSW
(Little Bonny, *with music.*) OuSiCo
Goodbye, Little Bonny Blue Eyes. *Unknown.* AmFP
Goodbye [*or* Good-By] 'Liza Jane. *Unknown.* AS, *with music;* FSW
Good-bye My Fancy! Walt Whitman. AP; FaFP; LiTA; PrIm; TAP
Good Bye, My Lady Love, *with music.* Joseph E. Howard. FSN
Goodbye, My Lover, Goodbye. *Unknown.* FSW
Goodbye Nkrumah. Diane di Prima. PoM
Good-bye! [*or* Good-by]—no [*or* nay], do not grieve that it is over. A Farewell. Harriet Monroe. AA; HBMV; PoA
Goodbye Now, or, Pardon My Gauntlet. Ogden Nash. FiBHP
Goodbye Old Paint. *Unknown. See* Old Paint.
Goodbye pale cold inconstant. A Farewell, a Welcome. Lisel Mueller. MOON
Good-bye, proud world! I'm going home. Good-bye. Emerson. FaFP; HBV-2; LiTA; TAP; TreF; WGRP
"Good-bye," said the river, "I'm going downstream." Howard Nemerov. WeW
Goodbye, Sally. James Simmons. BIrV
Goodbye to Regal. Daniel Huws. NYBP
Goodbye to Serpents. James Dickey. NYBP
Goodbye to the Aegean. On the Athenian Dead at Ecbatana. Plato, *tr. by* Ralph Gladstone. PoPl
Good-bye to the Mezzogiorno. W. H. Auden. OxBTC
Goodbye, Winter. Prognosis. Louis MacNeice. CMoP; NOBE; OxBI
"Good-bye," you said, and your voice was an echo. Tak for Sidst. Babette Deutsch. PoA

Goodbyes and griefs come here to join the world. Railway Station. John Hay. WaP
Good children, refuse not these lessons to learn. A Schoolmaster's Admonition. *Unknown.* OxBChV
Good christian Reader judge me not. God's Controversy with New-England. Michael Wigglesworth. SCAP
Good Christians. Robert Herrick. LiTB
Good Christians all attend unto my ditty. A Ballad of the Strange and Wonderful Storm of Hail. *Unknown.* CoMu
Good Christians all, both great and small. The Avondale Mine Disaster. *Unknown.* AmFP; BaBo; ViBoFo
Good Company. Karle Wilson Baker. FaPON; HBV-1; WGRP
Good Company. Henry VIII, King of England. *See* Pastime.
Good Company. *Unknown.* OBET
Good Company, Fine Houses. John Newlove. PeCV
Good Counsel. James I, King of Scotland. ACP
Good Counsel to a Young Maid. Thomas Carew. AnAnS-2; CavP; ErPo
(Good Counsell to a Young Maid.) OBS
(Song: Good Counsel to a Young Maid.) CaPo
Good Creatures, Do You Love Your Lives. A. E. Housman. TW
Good dame looked from her cottage, The. The Leak in the Dike. Phoebe Cary. FaFP; FaPON; PaPo; TreF
Good dame Mercy with dame Charite, The. The Seven Deadly Sins. Stephen Hawes. *Fr.* The Pastime of Pleasure. PoEL-1
Good Day, The. Henry Howarth Bashford. HBV-2
Good day, good day. In Honour of Christmas. *Unknown.* MeEL
Good days/ I'm out. Perambulator Poems, VII. David McCord. WhC
Good day's work, two contracts made, A. Between a Contractor and His Wife. *Unknown.* NOEC
Good Dream, The. Denise Levertov. NNaP
"Good Egg"—her favorite words. Mac. Mark Vinz. Str
Good English Hospitality. Blake. *Fr.* An Island in the Moon. CoMu
(Mayors, The.) CH
Good evening, here is the news. The Bridge. Derek Walcott. NYP
Good Fairies have trooped off one by one, The. Christenings. Peter Porter. NAs
Good father, I have sent for you because. The Merry Little Maid and Wicked Little Monk. *Unknown.* ErPo
Good Father John O'Hart. The Priest of Coloony [*or* The Ballad of Father O'Hart]. Yeats. OnYI; VLP
Good flat earth . . . and not so very high, The. Two Mountains Men Have Climbed. Pauline Starkweather. GoYe
Good folk [*or* folke], for gold or hire [*or* hyre]. The Crier. Michael Drayton. EIL; InvP; OAEP; PoEL-2; WhC
Good Folks at the Camp Meeting, The. William Kloefkorn. *Fr.* Loony. GP
Good folks ever will have their way. The Doctor's Story. Will M. Carleton. BLPA
Good for Nothing Man, *sels.* Kenneth Pitchford.
Blues Ballad. CoPo
Jacqueline Gray. CoPo
Onion Skin, The. CoPo
Pickup in Tony's Hashhouse. CoPo; ErPo
Young Buck's Sunday Blues. CoPo
Good Fortune. Heine, *tr. fr. German by* Louis Untermeyer. BLPA
Good Fortune, when I hailed her recently. Epigram. J. V. Cunningham. PV
Good Frend, *sel.* Hilda Doolittle ("H. D.").
"Time has an end, they say." NOBA
Good frend for Jesus sake forbeare. Inscription on Stone over Shakespeare's Grave. *Unknown.* TreFS
Good Friday. Arlene De Bevoise. AMV-81
Good Friday. John Frederick Nims. TW
Good Friday. Christina Rossetti. OFD; PoEL-5; TRV
Good Friday. A. J. M. Smith. CaP
Good Friday ("Christ made a trance"). *Unknown.* ChTr
Good Friday and the Present Crucifixion. Vincent Buckley. CBAP
Good Friday Evening. Christina Rossetti. PGD
Good Friday in My Heart. Mary Elizabeth Coleridge. PGD
Good Friday. Somewhere a death. Good Friday and the Present Crucifixion. Vincent Buckley. CBAP
Good Friday was the day. The Martyr. Herman Melville. PoEL-5; TAP; TrGrPo
Good Friday [*or* Goodfriday], 1613. Riding Westward. John Donne. AnAnS-1; EnRePo; JCP; MeLP; MePo; NOCV; NoP; OAEL-1; OBS; OxBoCh; PoEL-2; PPP; SeCP; SeCV-1; TEP
Good Gad! who's this? What's this, my son? The Democratic Barber; or, Country Gentleman's Surprise. John Parrish. NOEC
Good God! and can it be that such a nook. The Milking Shed. John Clare. VLP
Good God of scholar, simpleton, and sage! Grace. Johnstone G. Patrick. TrPWD
Good God, What a Night That Was. Petronius Arbiter, *tr. fr. Latin by* Kenneth Rexroth. BoLoP; ErPo
Good Gossips Mine. *Unknown.* OxBM
Good gray [*or* grey] guardians of art, The. Museum Piece. Richard Wilbur. CMoP; ConAP; FaBoMo; MiAP; NePA; NIP; NoP; PoPl; TAP
Good Grease. Mary TallMountain. STE; TWSS
Good Great Man, The. Samuel Taylor Coleridge. HBV-2
(Complaint.) WhC
Good heaven [*or* Heav'n], I thank thee since it was designed [*or* design'd]. On Myself [*or* Myselfe]. Countess of Winchilsea. SBG; TrGrPo
Good Hour, The. Louise Driscoll. HBMV
Good house, and ground whereon, A. The Salt Garden. Howard Nemerov. NePoEA
Good Humor Man, The. Phyllis McGinley. MoShBr
Good in graves as heavenly seed are sown, The. The Christmas Reply to the Phylosopher. Sir William Davenant. MeLP
Good Inn, The. Herman Knickerbocker Vielé. *Fr.* The Inn of the Silver Moon. HBV-1
Good intent of God became the Christ, The. The Christ. John Oxenham. TRV
Good is an orchard, the saint saith. Of an Orchard. Katharine Tynan. GoBC; HBV-1; OBVV; WGRP
Good Joan, The. Lizette Woodworth Reese. FaPON; MoShBr
Good Junipero, the Padre. Discovery of San Francisco Bay. Richard Edward White. PAH
Good King Wenceslas. *Unknown, tr. fr. Latin by* John Mason Neale. FSW; HBV-2; HBVY; OHIP; OnMSP; TreFS
Good ladies, ye that have your pleasure in exile. The Lady Again Complains. Earl of Surrey. SiPS
Good Lady/ I have corn and beets. A Negro Peddler's Song. Fenton Johnson. AmNP
Good Lawd Know My Name, De. Frank L. Stanton. WBLP
Good Life, A. Robert Watson. AMV-81
Good little boys should never say. Politeness. Elizabeth Turner. HBV-1; HBVY
Good-looking, I'll never stoop for you. Mahsati, *tr. fr. Farsi by* Deirdre Lashgari. WPOW
Good Lord, behold this dreadfull enemy. The Souls Groan to Christ for Succour. Edward Taylor. *Fr.* God's Determinations. PAI; PoEL-3
Good Lord gave, the Lord has taken from me, The. The Mother's Prayer. Dora Sigerson Shorter. HBV-1
Good Lord Graeme is to Carlisle gane. Graeme and Bewick. *Unknown.* EnSB
Good Lord Nelson had a swollen gland, The. A Ballad of the Good Lord Nelson. Lawrence Durrell. ErPo; LiTM
"Good lord of the land, will you stay thane." Lord Maxwell's Last Goodnight. *Unknown.* ESPB; OxBB
Good Luck and Bad ("Good luck is the gayest of all gay girls"). John Milton Hay, *after the German of* Heine. FaBoEE
(Good and Bad Luck.) InMe; OBAL
Good luck to the milkman. The Milkman. "Seumas O'Sullivan." SUS
Good Man, The. *Fr.* The Talmud. TrJP
Good Man in Hell, The. Edwin Muir. MoBrPo; TW
Good man was there [*or* ther] of religion [*or* religioun], A. The Poor [*or* Poure] Parson [*or* Persoun]. Chaucer. *Fr.* The Canterbury Tales: Prologue. ACP; GoBC; NOCV; PAI; WGRP
Good manners may in seven words be found. Of Courtesy. Arthur Guiterman. TiPo
Good Master and Mistress. *Unknown.* EvOK
Good master, you and I were born. A Decanter of Madeira, Aged 86, to George Bancroft, Aged 86. S. Weir Mitchell. AA; ViBoPo
Good Memory. Sotero Rivera-Avilés, *tr. fr. Spanish by* Julio Marzán. InW
Good Men Afflicted Most. Robert Herrick. LiTB
Good men and true! in this house who dwell. The Croppy Boy. William B. McBurney. OnYI
Good Moolly Cow, The. Eliza Lee Follen. OBCA
Good morn t'ye, John. How b'ye? how b'ye? Eclogue: The Common a-Took In. William Barnes. VLP
Good Mornin', Blues. *Unknown.* InPK
(Good Morning Blues.) FSW
(I Got the Blues.) TTY
Good Morning. Muriel Sipe. SoPo; SUS; TiPo
Good Morning. Mark Van Doren. DuDa
Good morning, Algernon: Good morning, Percy. On Mundane Acquaintances. Hilaire Belloc. ELU; FaBoEE; FiBHP; MoVE; OxBTC
Good Morning America, *sel.* Carl Sandburg.
"Now it's Uncle Sam sitting on top of the world," XIV. OFD
Good Morning Blues. *Unknown.* *See* Good Mornin', Blues.
Good morning captain. Mule Skinner Blues. *Unknown.* FSW
Good morning, daddy! Dream Boogie. Langston Hughes. AmPP
Good morning, Father Francis. *Unknown.* OxNR

"Good morning; good morning!" the General said. The General. Siegfried Sassoon. BrPo; CMoP; DBV; ELU; FaBV; FiBHP; LiTM; MMA; MoVE; OBWP; OxBoLi; OxBTC; TW
Good morning, Judge what may be my fine. Judge Harsh Blues. *Unknown.* BluL
Good morning, Life—and all. A Greeting. W. H. Davies. MoBrPo
Good Morning Love! Paul Blackburn. NMP; NoAM
Good morning Mister Railroad man. The Gambler. *Unknown.* FSW
Good morning, Mistress and Master. *Unknown.* OxNR
Good morning to the great trees. Good Morning. Mark Van Doren. DuDa
Good morning to You, Almighty God. Kaddish. Levi Yitzhok, *tr. by* Joseph Leftwich. TrJP
Good morning to you, Lord of the world! Invocation. Levi Isaac of Berditshev, *tr. by* Olga Marx. EaLo
Goodmorning with Light. John Ciardi. WaP
Good Morrow, The. John Donne. AnAnS-1; AWP; BiP; BoLoP; CABA; EBEV; ElL; EnLoPo; EnRePo; FaBoBe; FaBoEn; FABV; FF; FPL; HBV-1; HoPM; InPS; InvP; JCP; LiTB; LoBV; MeLP; MePo; NIP; NoP; OAEL-1; OBS; OLR; PoEL-2; PoPle; PoRA; PPP; SCV; SeCeV; SeCP; SeCV-1; SoSe; TEP; TreFT; TrGrPo; UnTE; ViBoPo
Good Morrow. Thomas Heywood. *See* Pack, Clouds, Away.
"Good morrow, my lord!" in the sky alone. Sir Lark and King Sun; a Parable. George Macdonald. *Fr.* Adela Cathcart. GN; HBV-1; HBVY
Good morrow, 'tis St. Valentine's day. Song. Shakespeare. *Fr.* Hamlet, IV, v. SiSoSe
Good morrow to the day so fair. The Mad Maid's Song. Robert Herrick. AWP; CaPo; CH; EnLoPo; LoBV; OAEL-1; OBEV; SeCV-1; TrGrPo; ViBoPo; WiR
Good morrow to thy sable beak. The Blackcock. Joanna Baillie. PBBP
Good morrow to you, Valentine. *Unknown.* OxNR
Good Mr. Fortune, A.R.A. The Imperfect Artist. George Rostrevor Hamilton. DBV
Good Mr. Peeps or Peps or Pips. The Gospel of Mr. Pepys. Christopher Morley. InMe
Good Muse, rock me asleep. To His Muse. Nicholas Breton. OBSC
Good my king, in your garden close. The King's Ballad. Joyce Kilmer. HBV-1
Good Name, A. Shakespeare. *Fr.* Othello, III, iii. FaFP; TreFS
Good name is better than precious oil [*or* ointment], A. The Better Path. Bible, *O.T.* *Fr.* Ecclesiastes. TreFS; TrJP
Good-natur'd Man, The, *sel.* Samuel Johnson.
Prologue: "Prest by the load of life, the weary mind," *by* Goldsmith. LoBV
"Good-nature" is thy sterling name. Loveliness. Christopher Smart. Hymns for the Amusement of Children, 14. NOCV
Good neighbor, tell me why that sound. The Neighbors of Bethlehem. *Unknown, tr. fr. French.* OHIP
Good neighbors, dear, be cautious. Allalu Mo Wauleen. *Unknown.* AnIV
Good neighbour, why do you look awry? A Song. *Unknown.* TW
Good News. *Unknown.* FSW
Good News from New-England. *At. to* Edward Johnson. SCAP
"With hearts revived in conceit, new land and trees they eye," *sel.* GOA
Good news. It seems he loved them after all. A Song about Major Eatherly. John Wain. OxBTC
Good-Night. Hester A. Benedict. HBV-1
Goodnight. John Ciardi. OBAL
Good Night. Thomas Hood. SiSoSe; SoPo
Good Night. Victor Hugo, *tr. fr. French.* FaPON; SiSoSe; SoPo; SUS; TiPo
Good-Night. S. Weir Mitchell. HBV-1
Good Night. John Nichol. OBVV
Good Night. Dorothy Mason Pierce. SiSoSe
Good Night, A. Frances Quarles. OBS; TrGrPo
Good-Night. Shelley. HBV-1; ViBoPo
Good-Night. Jane Taylor. HBV-1; HBVY
Good-Night. Edward Thomas. NoP
Goodnight, A. William Carlos Williams. MoAB; MoAmPo
Good night,/ Sleep tight. Night Blessing. *Unknown.* HBVY
Good-night? ah! no; the hour is ill. Good-Night. Shelley. HBV-1; ViBoPo
Good Night and Good Morning. Richard Monckton Milnes. OxBChV
Goodnight and goodbye to the life whose signs denote us. In Harbour. Swinburne. VLP
Good Night, at last. Envoy. Robert Duncan. *Fr.* Passages. VGW
Good Night, Babette! Austin Dobson. HBV-1; OBVV
Good night, big world. Back to the Ghetto. Jacob Glatstein, *tr. by* Joseph Leftwich. TrJP
Good-night, dear friend! I say good-night to thee. Good-Night. Hester A. Benedict. HBV-1
Good-night; ensured release. Parta Quies [*or* Alta Quies]. A. E. Housman. NOBE; TEP; SeCeV
Good night for the fireplace to be, A. The Heat in the Room. Weldon Kees. EAS
Good night, God bless you. *Unknown.* OxNR
Good night! Good night!/ Far flies the light. Good Night. Victor Hugo. FaPON; SiSoSe; SoPo; SUS; TiPo
Good-night. Good-night. Ah, good the night. Good-Night. S. Weir Mitchell. HBV-1
Good night, good rest. Ah! neither be my share. A Night Watch. *Unknown.* *Fr.* The Passionate Pilgrim, XIV. OBSC
Good-night! I have to say good-night. Palabras Cariñosas. Thomas Bailey Aldrich. AA; HBV-1
Goodnight Ladies. *Unknown.* FSW
Good night, my love, good night! Good Night. John Nichol. OBVV
Good night, my love, may gentle rest. Ode. Charles Cotton. ViBoPo
Good night, my two little cloud ladies. For the Girls 'cause They Know. Harold Littlebird. VoR
Good-Night, or Blessing, The. Robert Herrick. CaPo
Good night, sweet repose. *Unknown.* OxNR
Goodnight to the Season! Winthrop Mackworth Praed. InvP; NOBE; NOBL; OBNC; OxBoLi; PoEL-4
Good night to the Year Academic. A Grouchy Good Night to the Academic Year. Ted Pauker. NOBL
Good night to thee, Fair Goddess. Sunset Song. *Tr. by* N. Barnes. WTO
"Good Night, Willie Lee, I'll See You in the Morning." Alice Walker. WeW
Good oars, for Arnold's sake. Pax Paganica. Louise Imogen Guiney. AA
Good of the Chaplain to enter Lone Bay. Billy in the Darbies. Herman Melville. *Fr.* Billy Budd, Foretopman. HAP; LoBV; NCEP; NOBA; OxBoLi; PoEL-5
Good old Mother Fairie. To Mother Fairie. Alice Cary. OBCA
Good Old Rebel, The. Innes Randolph. *See* Rebel, The.
Good Parson, The. Chaucer. *See* Poor Parson, The.
Good people: What? Will you of all be bereft? A Ballad on the Times. Henry Hall. APAS
Good people all, I pray attend. The New-fashioned Farmer. *Unknown.* OBET
Good people all, of every sort. An Elegy on the Death of a Mad Dog. Goldsmith. *Fr.* The Vicar of Wakefield. BeLS; BLPA; FaBoBe; FaBoCh; FaBoCo; FaFP; FPL; GDP; GN; HBV-2; HBVY; LauP; NA; NOEC; OAEP; OBEC; OBNV; PoPle; RoGo; ShM; TEP; TreF
Good people all, with one accord. An Elegy on That [*or* the] Glory of Her Sex, Mrs. Mary Blaize [*or* Mrs. Mary Blaize *or* Elegy on Mrs. Mary Blaize]. Goldsmith. FaBoCo; FaBoNo; HBV-2; InMe; LAuP; NA; OAEP; OBEC; OnYI; TreFT; WhC
Good people attend now, and I will declare. Man's Amazement. *Unknown.* CoMu
Good people, come and listen, a sad story I will tell. The Gale of August, '27. George Swinamer. ShS
Good people come buy. A New Song of an Orange. *Unknown.* CoMu
Good people draw near as you pass along. Alphabetical Song on the Corn Law Bill. *Unknown.* OxBoLi
Good people, give attention, a story you shall hear. Lord Delamere. *Unknown.* ESPB
Good people give attention and listen unto me. The Carpet-Weavers' Lament. *Unknown.* OBET
Good people give attention who now around me stand. The Female Sailor. *Unknown.* OBET
Good people, I pray now attend to my muse. The Lord Chancellours Villanies Discovered; or, His Rise and Fall in the Four Last Years. *Unknown.* CoMu
Good people, what, will you of all be bereft. A Ballad on the Taxes. Edward Ward. OxBoLi; PPON
Good Play, A. Robert Louis Stevenson. FaPON; MoShBr; TiPo
Good reader! if you e'er have seen. Nonsense. Thomas Moore. FaBoEE; InMe; NA
Good reason thou allow. Of the Clock and the Cock. George Turberville. EnRePo
Good Reasons. Keith Preston. WhC
Good repute is water carried in a sieve. Lalleswari, *tr. fr. Kashmiri by* George Grierson; *ad. by* Deirdre Lashgari. WPOW
Good Resolution, A. Roy Campbell. OBSV
Good Rich Man, The. G. K. Chesterton. DTC
Good Riddance to Bad Rubbish O at Last. Paul Goodman. TW
Good St. Paul and Vincent Peale. A Saint . . . He Ain't. E. Y. Harburg. DBV
Good Samaritan, The. Bible, *N.T.* St. Luke, X: 25-37. TreF
Good Shepherd, The. Bible, *N.T.* St. John, X: 7-18. TreFS
Good Shepherd, The. Keidrych Rhys, *tr. fr. Welsh.* NeBP
Good Ships. John Crowe Ransom. WeW

Good sir, if you will shew the best of your skill. How to Choose a Wife. *Unknown.* FaBoUs
Good sir, whose powers are these? Shakespeare. *Fr.* Hamlet, IV, i. WaaP
Good sirs, be civil, can one man, d'ye think. The Answer of Mr. Waller's Painter to His Many New Advisers. *Unknown.* APAS
Good Sportsmanship. Richard Armour. LiSp
Good Start, A. Larry Moffi. AMV-81
Good stout tankard at a Rhineland inn, A. Der Heilige Mantel von Aachen. Benjamin Francis Musser. ISi
Good Susan, Be as Secret as You Can. *Unknown.* ErPo
Good sword and a trusty hand, A! The Song of the Western Men. Robert Stephen Hawker. EnRP; EvOK; FaPoR; GoBC; HBV-2; OBNC; OBRV; OBVV; PaPo; RoGo
Good Thanksgiving, A. Annie Douglas Green Robinson. PoLF
Good Thing, A. Ray Mathew. CBAP
Good Thinking. *Unknown.* TDH
Good Tidings of Great Joy to All People. James Montgomery. *See* Angels, from the Realms of Glory.
Good Time Coming, The. Charles Mackay. PaPo; VLP
Good Times. Lucille Clifton. AmNP; AmPA; BPo; CNA; FF; GrPl; InPS; NCSH; PAI; PoBA; TAP; TwCP
Good Times and No Bread. Reginald Lockett. CNA
Good toll-gate keeper, kindle a light! Halt and Parley. George Herbert Clarke. CaP
Good Town, The. Edwin Muir. CMoP
Good Tradition, The. *Unknown, tr. fr. Early Modern Irish by* Robin Flower. AnIL
Good Weather. Giuseppe Gioachino Belli, *tr. fr. Italian by* Miller Williams. AMV-81
"Good weather for hay." Vermont Conversation. Patricia Hubbell. CTBA
Good Wif [*or* Wyf] was ther of biside [*or* bisyde] Bathe, A. The Wife of Bath. Chaucer. *Fr.* The Canterbury Tales: Prologue. BiP; EBEV; InPS; OxBM; PPoe; TrGrPo; ViBoPo
Good Wife, The. Bible, *O.T.* Proverbs, XXXI: 10-31. TrGrPo
Good Will to Men—Christmas Greetings in Six Languages. Dorothy Brown Thompson. OBCP
Good wine maketh good blood. Logic. *Unknown.* FaBoUs
Good Wish. *Unknown, tr. fr. Gaelic by* Alexander Carmichael. FaBoCh
Good Woman, The. Crystal MacLean. FAZ
Good wood. Food for Fire, Food for Thought. Robert Duncan. NeAP
Good Works. William Langland, *mod. by* Donald Attwater. *Fr.* The Vision of Piers Plowman. NOCV
Good Wyf was ther of bisyde Bathe, A. *See* Good Wif was ther of biside Bathe, A.
Good, your worship, cast your eyes. The Maunding Soldier; or, The Fruits of Warre Is Beggery. Martin Parker. CoMu; WaaP
Goodbat Nightman. Roger McGough. NoAM
Goodby. *See* Good-by.
Goodbye. *See* Good-bye.
Goode friend for Iesus sake forbeare. Inscription in a Library. W. G. Wendell. WhC
Goodfriday, 1613. Riding Westward. John Donne. *See* Good Friday, 1613. Riding Westward.
Goodly Child, A. *Unknown.* OxBChV
Goodly host one day was mine, A. Mine Host of "The Golden Apple." Thomas Westwood. GN; OHIP
Goodman's Sauce. *Unknown.* FaBoUs
Goodnight. *See* Good Night.
Goods She Can Carry, The: Canticle of Her Basket Made of Reeds. Gibbons Ruark. MAYP
Goodwill, Inc. Dennis Schmitz. AmPA
Goody Blake and Harry Gill, *sel.* Wordsworth.
"Oh! what's the matter? what's the matter?" Par
Goody Bull and her daughter together fell out. The World Turned Upside Down. *Unknown.* PAH
Goody O'Grumpity. Carol Ryrie Brink. FaPON
Googs, The. Don Marquis. *Fr.* Savage Portraits. HBMV
Goops they lick their fingers, The. Table Manners. Gelett Burgess. OBCA; RHPC
Goose. Richard Emil Braun. NoAM
Goose, affected, empty, vain, A. Edward Moore. *Fr.* The Goose and the Swans. PBBP
Goose and Gander. *Unknown.* *See* Gray Goose and Gander.
Goose and the Gander, The. *Unknown.* GBP
Goose and the Swans, The, *sel.* Edward Moore.
"Goose, affected, empty, vain, A." PBBP
Goose Fish, The. Howard Nemerov. CMoP; HeIP; InPK; LiTM; NePoEA; NoAM; NIP; NMP; NoP
Goose Girl, The. Dorothy Roberts. CaP
Goose Pond. Stanley Kunitz. PoA
Goose that laid the golden egg, The. Ars Poetica. X. J. Kennedy. ErPo; NIP; PP; PV
Goose that on our Ock's green shore, The. Goodman's Sauce. *Unknown.* FaBoUs
Gooseberries. Stephen Berg. NaP
Gooseberries. Peter Wild. DFF; GP
Goosepimples. Coleman Barks. PV
Goosey, goosey gander,/ Who stands yonder? *Unknown.* OxNR
Goosey Goosey Gander—by Various Authors. William Percy French. CenHV
Goosey, goosey, gander, where [*or* whither] shall I wander? Mother Goose. HBV-1; OxNR; PBBP
Gopher remarked to the Prairie Dog, The. The Prairie Dog. Arthur Guiterman. BPAW
Gorbo and Batte. Michael Drayton. *Fr.* The Shepherd's Garland, Eclogue IX. LoBV
("Gorbo, as thou cam'st this way.") ViBoPo
(Ninth Eclogue, The.) OAEP
(Sheepheard's Daffadil, The.) FaBoEn
(Shepherd's Daffodil, The.) ElL
Gordion Knot, The. Thomas Tomkis. *Fr.* Lingua. ElL
Gordian Knot, The. *Unknown.* UnTE
Gordon Childe. David Martin. PoAu-2
Gorg, a Detective Story. B. P. Nichol. NOBC
Gorgio Lad. Amelia Josephine Burr. HBMV
Gorilla, The. Baxter Hathaway. HoAn
Gorilla at Twenty Nine Years, The. J. D. Reed. NeAC
Gorilla lay on his back, The. Au Jardin des Plantes. John Wain. NePoEA-2; OxBTC
Gormley's Laments, *sel.* Gormley, *tr. fr. Irish by* Joan Keefe.
"I have loved thirty by three." PBWP
Gorse is yellow on the heath, The. The First Swallow. Charlotte Smith. HBV-1
Goshawk, The. John Haines. GP
Gospel According to St. John. Bible, *N.T.* *See* St. John.
Gospel According to St. Luke. Bible, *N.T.* *See* St. Luke.
Gospel According to St. Mark. Bible, *N.T.* *See* St. Mark.
Gospel According to St. Matthew. Bible, *N.T.* *See* St. Matthew.
Gospel According to You, The. *Unknown.* BLRP; STF
Gospel of Labor, The. Henry van Dyke. TRV; WBLP; WGRP
Gospel of Mr. Pepys, The. Christopher Morley. InMe
Gospel of Peace, The. James Jeffrey Roche. PAH
Gospel Train, The. *Unknown.* BLSo, *with music;* TrAS, *with music*
(Get on Board, Little Children.) FSW
(Git on Board, Little Chillen.) BoAN-1, *with music;* BPo
Gosport Tragedy, The. *Unknown.* AmFP; BaBo (A *and* B *vers.*)
(Pretty Polly.) AmFP, 2 *vers.*
Gossamer, The. Charlotte Smith. ViBoPo
Gossip, The. Daniel Halpern. SO
Gossip grows like weeds. Hitomaro, *tr. fr. Japanese by* Kenneth Rexroth. OLR
Got a little bitty mama, and a big mama too. Big Woman. *Unknown.* BluL
"Got any boys?" the Marshal said. The Puzzled Census Taker. John Godfrey Saxe. HBV-2
Got Dem Blues, *with music.* *Unknown.* AS
Got me a special place. Martin Luther King. Myra Cohn Livingston. RHPC
Got my hands on the gospel plow. Keep Your Hands on That Plow. *Unknown.* OuSiCo
Got the Blues, Can't Be Satisfied. *Unknown.* BluL
Got three womens: yellow, brown and black. Three Women Blues. *Unknown.* BluL
Got to pull this timber 'fore the sun goes down. Timber (Jerry the Mule). *Unknown.* FSW
Got up and dressed up. Chorus. Jack Kerouac. *Fr.* Mexico City Blues. NeAP
Got up one morning, went out to plow. Tee Roo. *Unknown.* OuSiCo
Got up this morning/ The blues, walking like a man. Preaching Blues. *Unknown.* BluL
Got your note today and I'm glad you wrote. A Letter to Peter. Fay Chiang. BrSi
Gotham, *sels.* Charles Churchill.
European Crimes. NOEC
Poet as King of Gotham, The. NOEC
Gothic church, A. At one end of an aisle. A Crucifix. Paul Verlaine, *tr. by* John Gray. *Fr.* Amour. SyP
Gothic Dusk, The. Frederic Prokosch. PoA
Gothic Landscape. Irving Layton. TrJP
Gothic looks solemn, The. On Oxford. Keats. Par
"Gotta' Smoke?" William Franklin. LFAC
Gourd Dancer, The. N. Scott Momaday. CDW; STE
Gourd has still its bitter leaves, The. I Wait My Lord. *Unknown, tr. by* Helen Waddell. *Fr.* Shi King. AWP

Gourmand, The. Harry Graham. FaBoPa
Gourmet's Love-Song, The. P. G. Wodehouse. NOBL
Gouty Merchant and the Stranger, The. Horace Smith. BeLS
Government! Tuta Nihoniho, *tr. fr. Maori by* A. Armstrong. WTO
Government gave Simeon Clay, The. And/Or. Clarence Day. WhC
Government Injunction. Josephine Miles. PoNe
Governor your husband lived so long, The. John Berryman. *Fr.* Homage to Mistress Bradstreet. MoVE; NoAM; NOBA; TwAmPo
Gowa! Gowa! Crow's Ditty. *Unknown.* GBP
Gowan glitters on the sward, The. The Trysting Bush. Joanna Baillie. WPE
Gowk, The. William Soutar. BSV; GoTS; NeBP
Gown, The. Mary Carolyn Davies. HBMV
Gown which I do use to wear, The. Robert Southwell. *Fr.* The Image of Death. ViBoPo
Grab-Bag. Helen Hunt Jackson. OBCA
Grace. Emerson. AmPP; NoP; TrPWD
Grace. George Herbert. JCP; SeCV-1
Grace. Johnstone G. Patrick. TrPWD
Grace, A. Thomas Tiplady. TrPWD; TRV
Grace, A. *Unknown. See* Christmas Carol: "God bless the master of this house."
Grace. Richard Wilbur. LiTA
Grace after Dinner. Burns. FaBoEE
Grace after Meals. *Unknown, tr. fr. Hebrew by* Alice Lucas. TrJP
Grace at Evening. Edgar A. Guest. TrPWD
Grace at Evening. Edwin McNeill Poteat. TrPWD; TRV
Grace at the Atlanta Fox. Turner Cassity. NIP
Grace before Meat. Robert Herrick. *See* Grace for a Child.
Grace before Sleep. Sara Teasdale. TrPWD
Grace comes only after the long study of choice. Prelude. Traise Yamamoto. BrSi
Grace Darling. *Unknown.* OBET
Grace for a Child. Robert Herrick. AWP; FaPON; InPS; LoBV; MoShBr; OAEP; TrGrPo; ViBoPo
(Another Grace for a Child.) AnAnS-2; CABA; CavP; EBCP; GoJo; HeIP; InPK; InvP; OBS; OxBChV; OxBoCh; SeCV-1
(Child's Grace, A.) Ealo; FaBoCh; LiTB; OBEV; SeCeV; TreFs
(Grace before Meat.) ChTr
(Two Graces, I.) PoPle
Grace for Children ("What God gives, and what we take"). Robert Herrick. EBCP; OxBChV; OxBoCh
(Two Graces, II.) PoPle
Grace for Gardens. Louise Driscoll. TrPWD
Grace for Theology. William Langland. *Fr.* The Vision of Piers Plowman. GoBC
Grace full of grace, though in these verses here. Henry Constable. *Fr.* Diana. OBSC
Grace-Note, The. Denise Levertov. ConAP
Grace of Cynthia's Maidenhood, The. Vinnie-Marie D'Ambrosio. IHMS
Grace of the Way, *sel.* Francis Thompson.
"Now of that vision I, bereaven." MoAB; MoBrPo
Grace of the Word immaculate. Raziel. Yvan Goll, *tr. by* Anthony Rudolf. VWA
Grace that never can be told. All Needs Met. J. H. Sammis. BLRP
Grace, thou source of each perfection. Epiphany. Christopher Smart. Hymns and Spiritual Songs, Hymn 3. NOCV
Grace to Be Said at the Supermarket. Howard Nemerov. SoSe
Graceful Acacia. Walter Savage Landor. PoEL-4
Graceful and sure with youth, the skaters glide. The Skaters. John Williams. LiSp; NePoAm-2
Graceful as acorus or lotus flower. Aliter. Confucius, *tr. by* Ezra Pound. *Fr.* Songs of Ch'en. CTC
Graceful Bastion, The. William Carlos Williams. NYBP
Gracefullest leaper, the dappled fox-cub. Young Reynard. George Meredith. HoPM
Gracey Nugent. Austin Clarke, *tr. fr. Irish.* CIP
Gracie. Faye Kicknosway. GeTw; NMM
Gracious Goodness. Marge Piercy. BoAnP; HoAn; Psk
Gracious Lady:/ Simple as when I asked your aid before. Prayer to the Virgin of Chartres. Henry Adams. GoBC; ISi
Gracious Mother of our Redeemer, for ever abiding. Alma Redemptoris Mater. *At. to* Hermanus Contractus, *tr. by* Winfred Douglas. ISi
Gracious Saviour, We Adore Thee, *with music.* Sewall Sylvester Cutting. AH
Gracious Spirit o'er this earth presides, A. Wordsworth. *Fr.* The Prelude, V. OBRV
Gracious Time, The. Shakespeare. *See* Christmas.
Gracius and Gay. *Unknown.* SeCePo
Grackle, The. Ogden Nash. DBV; PV
Gradatim. Josiah Gilbert Holland. FaFP; HBV-2; HBVY; OHFP; TreFS; WGRP
Gradual bud and bloom and seedfall speeded up. July 4th. May Swenson. PoA
Gradually growing fur. Traveling North. John Woods. POL
Graduate, The. Charles Stetler. GP
Graduation Day, 1965. Julio Marzán. InW
Graecinus, I blame you. Yours that memorable remark. Ovid, *tr. by* Guy Lee. Amores, II, 10. NAWM-1
Graecinus (well I wot) thou told'st me once. Ovid, *tr. by* Christopher Marlowe. Amores, II, 10. EBEV
Graeme and Bewick. *Unknown. See* Bewick and Graham.
Graf von Charolais, Der, *sel.* Richard Beer-Hofmann, *tr. fr. German by* Ludwig Lewisohn.
"Evil Man, An!" TrJP
Graffiti. Edward Field. CABA; CoPo
Graffiti for Lovers. Joan Joffe Hall. AMV-80
Graffiti in a University Restroom: "Killing People Is Easier than Writing Poetry." Jim Mitsui. BrSi
Grafted Tongue, A. John Montague. BIrV; CIP
Graham Bell and the Photophone. G. F. Montgomery. SUW
Grail, The. Sidney Keyes. FaBoTw
Grain Elevator. A. M. Klein. CaP
Grain of Moonlight, A. Asya, *tr. fr. Yiddish by* Gabriel Preil *and* Howard Schwartz. VWA
Grain of Rice, A. F. R. Scott. PeCV
Grain of Salt, A. Wallace Irwin. HBV-2; WhC
Grains of snow ride down here as bits. Letter from a Black Soldier. Bill Anderson. VGW
Gramercy, Death, as you've my love to win. Sonnet: He Argues His Case with Death. Cecco Angiolieri da Siena, *tr. by* Dante Gabriel Rossetti. AWP
Gramercy Park Hotel. David Smith. NYP
Gramma thinks about her grandchildren. The Way and the Way Things Are. Nila NorthSun. GP
Grammar, A. Andrei Codrescu. EAS
Grammar commences with a 5-line curse. Palladas, *tr. fr. Greek by* Tony Harrison. OBVE
Grammar in a Nutshell. *Unknown.* HBVY; TreFS
(Grammar in Rhyme.) HBV-1
(Parts of Speech, The.) FaBoUS
Grammar Lesson. Linda Pastan. Psk
Grammar-Rules. Sir Philip Sidney. Astrophel and Stella, LXIII. FaBoUs
("O grammar-rules, O now your virtues show.") SiPS
Grammarian's Funeral, A. Robert Browning. HBV-2; LoBV; OAEP; VLP; WGRP
Grammer's Shoes. William Barnes. EBVV
Gramophone, The. James Reaney. CaP
Gramophone Tunes. Eva Dobell. SUMH
Grampa Schuler. Ruth Suckow. HBMV
Gramps held the rooster. Killing the Rooster. Sheryl L. Nelms. Str
Grand Abacus. John Ashbery. EAS; PoA
Grand attempt some Amazonian dames, A. On a Fortification at Boston Begun by Women. Benjamin Tompson. GOA; PAH; SCAP
Grand Canyon, The. James Merrill. TAP
Grand Chorus of Birds. Aristophanes. *See* Chorus of Birds.
Grand Conversation on Brave Nelson. *Unknown.* OBET
Grand Duke of New York, The. Dan Pagis, *tr. fr. Hebrew by* Robert Friend. VWA
Grand Finale. Irving Layton. NOBC
Grand Guignols of Love, The. Michael Benedikt. AmPA
Grand Hotel, Calcutta. Layle Silbert. AMV-81
Grand Inquisitor's Song, The. W. S. Gilbert. *Fr.* The Gondoliers. OnMSP
Grand Match, The. Moira O'Neill. HBMV
Grand old Duke of York, The. Mother Goose. SoPo; TiPo
Grand Opening of the People's Theatre. O. J. Goldrick. PoOW
Grand Rapids. Julia A. Moore. OBAL
Grand Rapids Cricket Club, *sel.* Julia A. Moore.
"Brave Kelso, he's considered great." PeD
Grand road from the mountain goes shining to the sea, The. The Little Waves of Breffny. Eva Gore-Booth. AnIV; HBV-2; HBVY; OnYI
Grand Ronde Valley, The. Ella Higginson. AA
Grand Street and the Bowery. David Ghitelman. FAZ
Grandad, I didn't burn it, I. Legacy. Gena Ford. IHMS
Grand-dad, they say you're old and frail. A Child to His Sick Grandfather. Joanna Baillie. NOEC
Granddaddy longlegs did twilight, The. Ohio Valley Swains. James Wright. NNaP
Grandest writer of late ages, The. Distribution of Honours for Literature. Walter Savage Landor. FaBoEE
Grandeur of Ghosts. Siegfried Sassoon. MoBrPo; OBMV
Grandeur of this earthly round, The. Plato to Theon. Philip Freneau. AA
Grandeurs of the crazy man alone, The. Theodore Roethke. POL
Grandfa' Grig/ Had a pig. *Unknown.* OxNR

Grandfather. Willis Barnstone. VWA
Grandfather. George Bowering. NOBC
Grandfather. Mary Joan Coleman. AMV-80
Grandfather. Michael S. Harper. FiCP; GeTw; LCAP; TAP
Grandfather. Lance Henson. CDW
Grandfather. Derek Mahon. OxBC
Grandfather. Joseph Stroud. NPGG
Grandfather, bring me down. Getting Under. Alan P. Lightman. AMV-81
Grandfather Frog. Louise Seaman Bechtel. TiPo
Grandfather has three sparks. Akawense. Phyllis Wolf. STE
Grandfather I never knew, The. The Admiral's Daughter. E. G. Burrows. HoAn
Grandfather in the Old Men's Home. W. S. Merwin. ConAP; LiTM
"Grandfather" in Winter. Frederick Feirstein. NYP
Grandfather never went to school. Legacy II. Leroy V. Quintana. GP
Grandfather Poem, A. William J. Harris. CNA; PoBA
Grandfather puts down his tea-glass. A Night in Odessa. Louis Simpson. NNaP
Grandfather showed me how stars grow in apples. How Stars and Hearts Grow in Apples. Virginia Elson. AMV-81
Grandfather, sleepless in a room upstairs. John Berryman. *Fr.* The Black Book. VGW
Grandfather Watt's Private Fourth ("Grandfather Watts used to tell us boys"). H. C. Bunner. PoSC; TiPo
Grandfather, we come to you now. Yahrzeit. Susan Fromberg Schaeffer. VWA
Grandfather wrote from Valley Forge. Prophecy in Flame. Frances Minturn Howard. AmFN
Grandfather Yoneh. Emily Borenstein. AMV-81
Grandfathers. Michael Castro. VWA
Grandfathers, The. Donald Justice. NCSH
(After a Line by John Peale Bishop.) PoCh
Grandfathers. Dennis Shady. LFAC
Grandfather's Clock. Henry Clay Work. BLPA; BLSo, *with music*; FaFP; FSW; PSoN, *with music*; TreF
Grandfather's Heaven. Naomi Shihab Nye. Str
Grandiloquent Goat, The. Carolyn Wells. MoShBr
Grandma and the children left at night. My Polish Grandma. Edward Field. Prf
Grandma didn't snore. Eclipse. William Carson Fagg. LFAC
Grandma Fire. Charles G. Ballard. VoR
Grandma lit the stove. History. Gary Soto. GP
Grandma said never tell a lie because. The Difference between a Lie and the Truth. Ronald James Dessus. LFAC
Grandma Shorba and the Pure in Heart. Freya Manfred. FAZ
Grandma sleeps with. Medicine. Alice Walker. NMM; PAI
Grandma told me all about it. The Minuet. Mary Mapes Dodge. OHFP
Grandmamma's Birthday. Hilaire Belloc. DBV; ELU; FiBHP; PoPl
Grandma's Advice. *Unknown.* *See* My Grandmother Green.
Grandma's Lost Balance. Sydney Dayre. OBCA
Grandmither, Think Not I Forget. Willa Cather. HBV-1; WPE
Grandmother. Paula Gunn Allen. STE; TWSS
Grandmother, The. Wendell Berry. DFF; GP; SaC
Grandmother. Henry Carlile. DFF; GP
Grandmother. John Paul Minarik. LFAC
Grandmother. Ray A. Young Bear. STE
Grandmother and Grandson. W. S. Merwin. NePoEA-2
Grandmother Came Down to Visit Us, The. Joseph Bruchac. CDW
Grandmother, I dreamed of you again. The Visit. Phillip William George. VoR
Grandmother Jackson. David Jackson. OBCP
Grandmother Poems. Marilyn Chin. BrSi
Grandmother, Rocking. Eve Merriam. GrPl; PCP
Grandmother Sleeps. Liz Sohappy Bahe. CDW
Grandmother Watching at Her Window. W. S. Merwin. PrIm; VGW
Grandmothers, The. Mary Oliver. WPE
Grandmother's Apple Pies. Bruce Weston Munro. PeD
Grandmother's love. Love Necessitates. Eugene Redmond. CNA
Grandmother's mother: her age, I guess. Dorothy Q. Oliver Wendell Holmes. AA; AP; HBV-1; InMe; NOBA; TreFS
Grandmother's Old Armchair. *Unknown.* BLPA
Grandmother's Story of Bunker-Hill Battle. Oliver Wendell Holmes. PAH
Grandmothers who wring the necks. Classic Ballroom Dances. Charles Simic. GeTw; LCAP
Grandpa Bear. Susan Eisenberg. AMV-81
Grandpa Bear's Lullaby. Jane Yolen. RHPC
Grandpa died on his vacation. Poor Grandpa. R. C. O'Brien. ShM
Grandpa Dropped His Glasses. Leroy F. Jackson. RHPC
Grandpa, I saw you die in the Indian hospital at Pawnee. Hartico. Anna Walters. VoR
Grandpa Is Ashamed. Ogden Nash. PV
Grandpapa ("Grandpapa fell down a drain"). Harry Graham. RHPC; WhC
Grandparents. Robert Lowell. LiTM
Grandpa's .45. W. M. Ransom. CDW
Grandpa's Picture. Paul Ruffin. Str
Grandser. Abbie Farwell Brown. HBMV
Grandson, The. James Scully. NYBP
Grandson Is a Hoticeberg, A. Margaret Danner. BlSi; CNA; FB
Grania. *Unknown, tr. fr. Irish by* Frank O'Connor. KiLC
Granite—/ a granite slab. Charlton Heston. Elliot Fried. AMV-80
Granite and Cypress. Robinson Jeffers. AmPP
Granite and marble. Homage to Paul Mellon, I. M. Pei, Their Gallery, and Washington City. William Meredith. EyDe
Granite and Steel. Marianne Moore. NYBP
Granite cliff on either shore, A. The Brooklyn Bridge. Edna Dean Proctor. PAH
Granite Mountain, The. Lew Sarett. HBMV
Granma's Words. Ted D. Palmanteer. STE
Granny and I with dear Dadu. A Very Odd Fish. D'Arcy Wentworth Thompson. OxBChV
Granny Crack. James Reaney. NOBC
"Granny, I saw a witch go by." Halloween. Marie A. Lawson. SiSoSe; TiPo
Granpa,/ he was a warrior. Pass It On Grandson. Ted D. Palmanteer. STE
Grant a canoe that shall be swift as a fish! Prayer on Making a Canoe. *Tr. by* N. B. Emerson. WTO
Grant at Appomattox. Gertrude Claytor. GoYe
Grant Heaven could once have given us liberty. Predestination and Free Will. Dryden. *Fr.* The State of Innocence. NOCV
Grant it, Father. Petition. Eleanor Slater. TrPWD
Grant, Lord, that through the printed page. Call to Conflict. *Unknown.* STF
Grant me, dear Lord, the alchemy of toil. Suppliant. Alan Sullivan. CaP
Grant me sweet Christ the grace to find. The Hermitage. *Unknown, at. to* St. Monchan of Lemanaghan in Offaly, *tr. by* Frank O'Connor. KiLC
Grant me the great and solemn breath withdrawn. Invocation and Prelude. Stefan George, *tr. by* Ludwig Lewisohn. AWP
Grant me to share the common, human lot. The Common Lot. Adelbert Sumpter Coats. TrPWD
Grant, O regal in bounty, a subtle and delicate largess. Hymn to the Sea. Sir William Watson. EtS
Grant us the knowledge that we need. Henry van Dyke. *Fr.* The Builders. TrPWD
Grant Wood's American Landscape. Winfield Townley Scott. GOA
Granted that what we summon is absurd. T. R. Donald Hall. PoA
Granted that you write verse. The Romancing Poet. Helen Hamilton. SUMH
Granted, we die for good. Table Talk. Wallace Stevens. NoP
Grape Daiquiri. Tina Koyama. BrSi
Grape-gathering. Abraham Shlonsky, *tr. fr. Hebrew by* I. M. Lask. TrJP
Grape is my mulatto mother. Wino. Ted Hughes. NoAM
Grape is ripened, tilled the field, The. Quiet. Giuseppe Ungaretti, *tr. by* Allen Mandelbaum. PoPl
Grapes. Sister Maris Stella. GoBC
Grapes. *Unknown, tr. fr. Greek by* Alma Strettell. AWP
Grapes hang purple. Taste of Purple. Leland B. Jacobs. RHPC
Grapes Making. Léonie Adams. FYAP; MoVE; NePA; UnPo
Grapes of Wrath, The. Christopher Morley. WhC
Grapevine, The. Zoe Kincaid Brockman. GoYe
Grape-Vine Swing, The. William Gilmore Simms. HBV-1
"Graphemics," *sels.* Jack Spicer. VGW
"Like a scared rabbit running over and," 1.
"Love is not mocked whatever use," 10.
"Walden Pond/ All those noxious gases rising from it," 7.
Grasmere Sonnets. David Wright. NoAM
Grasping with opposite hand the side of his pram. Outside the Supermarket. Roy Fuller. OxBC
Grass, The. George Bowering. MoCV
Grass. Alfred Corn. MAYP
Grass, The. Emily Dickinson. *See* Grass so little has to do, The.
Grass. John Holmes. MiAP
Grass. Carl Sandburg. AWP; BLPL; FaBV; MoAB; MoAmPo; MoVE; NoAM; NOBA; NoP; OBWP; OHFP; OxBA; PoLF; PoPl; TrGrPo; WaaP; WHA
Grass. Mary Morison Webster. PeSA
Grass. Walt Whitman. Song of Myself, VI. BLPL; NePA
("Child, A, said, *What is the grass?*") NoP; TrGrPo
(Leaves of Grass, *fr.* VI *and* XX.) AA
Grass afield wears silver thatch. A Frosty Day. Lord De Tabley. LoBV
Grass, Alas, The. Dick Emmons. QQQ

Grass bends, The: blades crack from a wind. Camping Out on Rainy Mountain. Jim Barnes. CDW
Grass caught in willow tells the flood's height. Briggflatts, IV. Basil Bunting. FaBoMo; NoAM
Grass clutches at the dark dirt with finger holds. Grassroots. Carl Sandburg. RFM
Grass cuts our feet as we wend our way, The. The Young Prince and the Young Princess. John Ashbery. ConAP
Grass Fingers. Angelina Weld Grimké. CDC
Grass fire swooped like a red wolf pack, The. The Wrangler Kid. *Unknown.* BPAW
Grass gave way, and suddenly, The. Watercress & Ice. Chase Twichell. MAYP
Grass, Grass. George Bowering. NeAC
Grass-green and aspen-green. Variables of Green. Robert Graves. FaBoEE
Grass grows long in the meadow, The. July Meadow. Louise Driscoll. YeAr
Grass hath such a simple faith, The. Grass. Mary Morison Webster. PeSA
Grass hung wet on Rydal banks, The. With Wordsworth at Rydal. James Thomas Fields. AA
Grass Is a Reasonable Colour, The. John Newlove. NeAC
Grass is green, The/ The sky is blue. Spring Song of a Super-Blake. Louis Untermeyer. HBMV
Grass is half-covered with snow, The. Snowfall in the Afternoon. Robert Bly. CAPP; EAS; NMP; NOBA
Grass is short and newly yellow-green, The. Return to Lane's Island. William H. Matchett. PoPl
Grass is so green that, The. Green Grass and Sea. George Woodcock. AMV-81
Grass is very green, my friend, The. A Unison. William Carlos Williams. NOBA; SeCeV
Grass of fifty Aprils hath waved green, The. On the Proposal to Erect a Monument in England to Lord Byron. Emma Lazarus. AA
Grass of levity. An Inscription. *Unknown.* ElL
Grass on the Cliff. Robinson Jeffers. *Fr.* The Trumpet. PoA
Grass on the Mountain, The. *Unknown, tr. fr. Paiute Indian by* Mary Austin. AmFN; AWP; FaPON: GOA
Grass on the Prayer Path. *Unknown.* PeD
Grass people bow, The. To Turn Back. John Haines. BoNaP; ConAP
Grass resurrects to mask, to strangle. The Distant Fury of Battle. Geoffrey Hill. NoP
Grass singed and low. Chickory. Zerubavel Gal'ed. TrJP
Grass so little has to do, The. Emily Dickinson. HBVY
(Grass, The.) FaPON; GN
Grass that is under me now, The. The Dying Lover. Richard Henry Stoddard. HBV-1
Grass was the green of parades when we'd leave, The. Leaving One of the State Parks after a Family Outing. Elizabeth Macklin. AMV-81
Grasse-Hopper, The. Sir John Denham. AnAnS-2
Grasse-Hopper, The. Richard Lovelace. *See* Grasshopper, The.
Grasse: The Olive Trees. Richard Wilbur. NOBA; NoAM; NYBP
Grasses. Ralph J. Mills, Jr. FAZ
Grasses are clothed, The. Divine Abundance. *Unknown.* BLRP
Grasses green of sweet content, The. Arthur Hugh Clough. VLP
Grasshopper, The. Abraham Cowley, *after the Greek of* Anacreon. AWP; FM; HBV-1; HBVY; OAEL-1; OBVE; SeCV-1; WiR
Grasshopper, The. Richard Lovelace. CaPo; EBEV; JCP; LoBV; NOBE; NoP; OAEL-1; OBEV; OBS; PPP; SeCePo; SeCV-1
(Grasse-Hopper, The.) FaBoEn; MeLP; MePo
Grasshopper, The. David McCord. GrPl
Grasshopper, The. Thomas Stanley, *after the Greek of* Anacreon. OBVE
Grasshopper, A. Richard Wilbur. HAP; HoPM; WeW
Grasshopper and the Ant, The. La Fontaine, *tr. fr. French by* Marianne Moore. NAWM-2
Grasshopper and the Elephant, The. *Unknown. See* Way Down South.
Grasshopper Green. *Unknown.* FaPON; HBVY; SoPo
Grasshopper, the Grasshopper, The. An Explanation of the Grasshopper. Vachel Lindsay. FaPON; SoPo
Grasshopper thrice-happy! who. The Grasshopper. Thomas Stanley, *after the Greek of* Anacreon. OBVE
Grasshopper, your fairy [*or* tiny] song. Earth. John Hall Wheelock. HBMV; LiTA; MoAmPo
Grasshoppers/ Chirping in the sleeves. Kawai Chigetsu-ni, *tr. fr. Japanese by* Kenneth Rexroth *and* Ikuko Atsumi. WPOW
Grasshoppers beware. The Cropdusting. William Zaranka. BXAP
Grasshoppers four a-fiddling went. Rilloby-Rill. Sir Henry Newbolt. HBVY
Grasshopper's Song, The. Hayyim Nahman Bialik, *tr. fr. Hebrew by* Jessie Sampter. FaPON
Grassroots. Carl Sandburg. RFM
Gratiana Dancing [*or* Dauncing] and Singing. Richard Lovelace. AnAnS-2; CaPo; CavP; JCP; LoBV; MeLP; MePo; OAEP; OBEV, 2 *sts.*; OBS; SeCV-1
Gratitude. William Cornish. *See* Pleasure It Is.
Gratitude. Louise Glück. HeIP
Gratitude. Annette Lynch. FF
Gratitude. Clyde McGee. BLRP
Gratitude. Christopher Smart. *Fr.* Hymns for the Amusement of Children. LAuP; NOEC
Gratitude for Work. John Oxenham. PGD
Gratitude to Mother Earth, sailing through night and day. Prayer for the Great Family. Gary Snyder. HAP; OFD
Gratulatory to Mr. Ben Johnson for His Adopting of Him to Be His Son, A. Thomas Randolph. AnAnS-2; JCP; OBS
Grauballe Man, The. Seamus Heaney. CIP
Grave, The, *sels.* Robert Blair.
Friendship. OBEC
"See yonder hallowed fane, the pious work." ViBoPo
(Church and Church-Yard at Night.) OBEC
"While [*or* Whilst] some affect the sun, and some the shade." EnRP; NOEC
Grave, The. John Lyle Donaghy. NeLP
Grave, A. Marianne Moore. CABA; CMoP; CrMA; FaBoEn; HAP; HeIP; InPK; LiTA; MoPo; MOS; MoVE; NoAM; NOBA; PPoe; SeCeV; TAP; UnPo; WPE; WeW
Grave, A. John Richard Moreland. HBMV
Grave, The. Saul Tchernichowsky. *See* Grave in Ukraine, A.
Grave, The ("For thee a stead was builded"). *Unknown, tr. fr. Anglo-Saxon.* ACP
Grave, The ("When the turf is thy tower"). *Unknown.* ChTr
Grave, The. Yvor Winters. MoVE; NoAM
Grave and the Rose, The. Victor Hugo, *tr. fr. French by* Andrew Lang. AWP
Grave at Cassino. Noah Stern, *tr. fr. Hebrew by* Harold Schimmel. VWA
Grave came to him, at his wish, before, The. Dr. Donne. Kenneth Slade Alling. NePoAm
Grave charge in Mayfair bathroom case. Headline History. William Plomer. FaBoCo
Grave Clothes. Karen Swenson. AMV-80
Grave House of Commons, by hook or by crook, The. A Ballad, November 1680, Made upon Casting the Bill against the Duke of York. *Unknown.* APAS
Grave in Hollywood Cemetery, Richmond, A. Margaret Junkin Preston. AA
Grave in Ukraine, A. Saul Tchernichowsky, *tr. fr. Hebrew by* L. V. Snowman. TrJP
(Grave, The, *tr. by* Robert Mezey *and* Shula Starkman.) VWA
Grave Jonas Kindred, Sybil Kindred's sire. George Crabbe. *Fr.* Tales: The Frank Courtship. OBRV
Grave of Alexander Hamilton is in Trinity yard, The. Trinity Place. Carl Sandburg. NYP
Grave of Hipponax, The. Edward Cracroft Lefroy, *after the Greek of* Theocritus. *Fr.* Echoes from Theocritus. AWP
Grave of Keats, The. Shelley. *See* Go Thou to Rome.
Grave of King Arthur, The. Thomas Warton. EnRP; GoTL
Grave of Love, The. Thomas Love Peacock. CH; HBV-1
(Beneath the Cypress Shade.) EnRP; OBRV
Grave of Rury, The. Thomas W. H. Rolleston. AnIL; AnIV; OnYI
Grave physician, used to write for fees, A. Upon the Author of the "Satire against Wit." Sir Charles Sedley. APAS
Grave said to the Rose, The. The Grave and the Rose. Victor Hugo, *tr. by* Andrew Lang. AWP
Grave seems only six feet deep, A. A Grave. John Richard Moreland. HBMV
Grave-Tree, The. Bliss Carman. CaP
Grave wise man that had a great rich lady, A. Of an Heroical Answer of a Great Roman Lady to Her Husband. Sir John Harington. BoLoP; ErPo
Gravedigger, The. Bliss Carman. BoNaP
Gravel. Paul Mariah. LFAC
Gravel-Pit Field, The. David Gascoyne. NeBP
Gravelly Run. A. R. Ammons. CoAP; PoA; Prf
Graven Thoughts. Sir Philip Sidney. *Fr.* Arcadia. SiPS
Graves Are Made to Waltz On. Peter Viereck. PoA
Graves at Elkhorn. Richard Hugo. UnPo
Grave's Cherub, The. Sydney Clouts. PeSA
Graves grow deeper, The. The Dead. Mark Strand. HeIP
Graves in Queens. Richard Hugo. NYP
Graves of a Household, The. Felicia Dorothea Hemans. FaPoR; HBV-2; VLP; WBLP; WPE
Graves of Infants. John Clare. OBVV

Graves! Where in dust are laid our dearest hopes! Vigilantius, or a Servant of the Lord Found Ready. Cotton Mather. SCAP
Gravestones. Floyd C. Stuart. AMV-80
Gravestones. Vernon Watkins. ChMP; TEP
Graveyard, The. Hayyim Nahman Bialik, *tr. fr. Hebrew by Bertha Beinkinstadt. TrJP*
Graveyard, The. Jane Cooper. NePoEA-2
Graveyard. Robert P. Tristram Coffin. AmFN
Grave-Yard, The. Jones Very. NOBA
Graveyard by the Sea. Thomas Lux. LCAP
Graveyard in Queens, A. John Montague. IPY
Graveyard is wet, The. All Songs. B. Sanford Page. AMV-81
Graveyard Rabbit, The. Frank Lebby Stanton. AA
Graveyard Road, The. Tom McKeown. HoAn
Gravities. Seamus Heaney. NoAM
Gray. *See also* Grey.
Gray and dingy house in Meudon. House in Meudon. Margarita Aliger, *tr. by* Elaine Feinstein. VWA
Gray as a government holiday. Easter Monday. Michael McFee. AMV-80
Gray [*or* Grey] as a mouse. Oliphaunt. J. R. R. Tolkien. AmMo; RHPC
Gray-blue shadows lift. Starlight Scope Myopia. Yusef Komunyakaa. MAYP
Gray brick, ash, hand-bent railings, steps so big. Cumberland Station. Dave Smith. MAYP
Gray Days. Joanne Lawlor. AMV-80
Gray despair. The Old Mare. Elizabeth J. Coatsworth. MoAmPo
Gray distance hid each shining sail. Jubilate. George Arnold. EtS
Gray-eyed huntress in whose hair. Hymn to Artemis, the Destroyer. Marya Zaturenska. MOON
Gray financier in a thin black auto, A. Dead Snake. William Jay Smith. NePoAm-2
Gray fur collars on a steel limb. Golgotha. X. J. Kennedy. NYBP
Gray Glove. Roo Borson. NOBC
Gray Goose, The. *Unknown.* FSW
Gray [*or* Grey] Goose and Gander. *Unknown.* GBP; OxBoLi; OxNR; PBBP
(Goose and Gander.) ChTr
Gray grassy hill, A. Prairie Spring. Edwina Fallis. SUS
Gray, gray [*or* Grey, grey] is Abbey Asaroe, by Ballyshanny town. Abbey Asaroe. William Allingham. OnYI; OxBI
Gray [*or* Grey] haunted eyes, absent-mindedly glaring. The Face in the Mirror. Robert Graves. NoP; WeW
Gray Hills Taught Me Patience, The, *with music.* Allen Eastman Cross. AH
Gray maidservant lets me in, A. Matinees. James Merrill. NOBA; Prf
Gray Mare, The. *Unknown.* AmFP
Gray mist wolf. Four Mountain Wolves. Leslie Marmon Silko. VoR
Gray Oak Twilight, The. James C. Kilgore. SOTS
Gray old Owl could scarce believe his eyes, The. The Last Violet. Oliver Herford. OHIP
Gray owl sing fum de chimbly top, De. A Plantation Ditty. Frank L. Stanton. AA; HBV-2
Gray Plume, The. Francis Carlin. HBMV
Gray sea and the long black land, The. *See* Grey sea . . .
Gray Shore. James Rorty. EtS
Gray Silk Twisting. Patrick Lane. NeAC
Gray smoke rose from the morning ground. Actual Vision of Morning's Extrusion. Alan Dugan. PPP
Gray Squirrel, The. Humbert Wolfe. GoJo; MoBrPo
Gray steel, cloud-shadow-stained. Watch the Lights Fade. Robinson Jeffers. CMoP; NoAM; NOBA
Gray Swan, The. Alice Cary. BeLS; GN
Gray swept the angry waves. How the *Cumberland* Went Down. S. Weir Mitchell. PAH
Gray the vacant circle of the sea, The. Bermuda Suite. Winfield Townley Scott. MiAP
Gray Thrums. Clara Doty Bates. OBCA
Gray tide flows and flounders in the rocks, The. At Sainte-Marguerite. Trumbull Stickney. LiTA; MoVE; NCEP; OxBA; TwAmPo
Gray tiled roof, A. Seeds of Lead. Amir Gilboa, *tr. by* Stephen Mitchell. VWA
Gray waves rock against the gray skyline, The. When Nature Hath Betrayed the Heart That Loved Her. Sophie Jewett. AA
Gray Weather. Robinson Jeffers. CMoP; NoAM
Gray Whale. For a Coming Extinction. W. S. Merwin. NNaP
Gray whales are going south, The: I see their fountains. Ocean. Robinson Jeffers. AP; CoBMV
Grazing Locomotives. Archibald MacLeish. PPJ
Greasy oysters on friday nights. Cycles, Cycles. Suzanne Berger Rioff. NMM
Greasy sky-line where the grey, A. The Sailor. Goodridge MacDonald. CaP
Greasy Spoon Blues. Len Gasparini. NeAC
Great, A. E. E. Cummings. NYBP
Great A, little a. Mother Goose. OxNR
Great A was alarmed at B's bad behaviour. Alphabet. *Unknown.* FaBoUs; OxNR
Great Adventure, The. Henry David Thoreau. HBV-2; OBVV
Great Adventurer, The. *Unknown. See* Love Will Find Out the Way.
Great Alexander sailing was from his true course turned. The Speaking Tree. Muriel Rukeyser. VGW
Great All in All, that art my rest, my home. Francis Quarles. *Fr.* Emblems. TrPWD
Great Amazon of God behold your bread. For Mary McLeod Bethune. Margaret Walker. PoNe
Great American Bum, The. *Unknown.* FSW
Great and glorious thing it is, A. Arithmetic on the Frontier. Kipling. OBWP; VLP
Great Auk's Ghost, The. Ralph Hodgson. MoShBr; PoPl; PoPle; PV; RHPC; ShM; WhC
Great-Aunt Rebecca. Elizabeth Brewster. NOBC
Great Aunts of My Childhood, The. Alice Fulton. Str
Great Bacchus: From the Greek. Matthew Prior. FaBoCo
Great Bear, The. John Hollander. LiTM; MP; NePoEA-2; NoAM; NYBP; TwCP
Great Bear Lake Meditations, The, *sels.* J. Michael Yates.
"Again and again I go away from you." HoPM
"I persist in a little fabric between me and the world." NOBC
"*Legend*: The god in the sun made two men." HoPM
"Wolves say to the dogs, The." HoPM
Great beasts rumble and sway, The. Under the Shawl. Rose Drachler. VWA
Great Bell Roland, The. Theodore Tilton. PAH
Great blue ceremony of the air, The. Mary and the Bramble. Lascelles Abercrombie. OBMV
Great Blue Heron, The. Carolyn Kizer. CoAP; NePoEA-2; WPE
Great brass bell of austerity. Sousa. Edward Dorn. CoPo
Great Breath, The. "Æ." MoBrPo; OBEV; OBMV; OxBI; WGRP; WHA
Great Brown Owl, The. Jane Euphemia Browne. OxBChV
Great Canzon, The. Kenneth Rexroth. NoAM
Great Central Railway, Sheffield Victoria to Banbury. John Betjeman. NYBP
Great Charles, among the holy gifts of grace. An Epigram to King Charles for an Hundred Pounds He Sent Me in My Sickness. Ben Jonson. OAEP
Great Churches. *Unknown.* STF
Great Commandment, The. Bible, *N.T.* St. Matthew, XXII: 34-40. TreFT
Great, creaking worm. The Elevated Train. James S. Tippett. SUS
Great Creator from His Work Returned, The. Milton. *Fr.* Paradise Lost, VII. TreFT
Great cry, A, went up from the stockyards and slaughterhouses. The Delicate, Plummeting Bodies. Stephen Dobyns. FYAP
Great cup tumbled, ringing like a bell, The. The Grail. Sidney Keyes. FaBoTw
Great Day ("Great day! Great day, de righteous marchin' "), *with music. Unknown.* BoAN-2
Great Day ("One of these mornings bright and fair"). *Unknown.* FSW
Great Day ("The chariot rode on the mountain top"). *Unknown.* FSW
Great Day, The. W. B. Yeats. BIrV; CMoP; FF
Great Depression, The. Patricia Goedicke. GP
Great Despair of the London Whigs, The. *Unknown.* APAS
Great Destiny the Commissary of God. The Progress of the Soul. John Donne. OxBoCh
Great Diocletian. Abraham Cowley. *Fr.* The Garden. ChTr
Great Discovery, The. Eleanor Farjeon. PoSC
Great Divide, The. Lew Sarett. HBMV
Great dream stinks like a whale gone aground, The. Why the Soup Tastes like the Daily News. Marge Piercy. MAT
Great Duke of Wellington, The. E. C. Bentley. *Fr.* Clerihews. CenHV
Great Emperor Otto, The. E. C. Bentley. *Fr.* Clerihews. PV
Great-enough both accepts and subdues. Phenomena. Robinson Jeffers. NoAM; NOBA; OxBA
Great eucalypti, black amid the flame. The Grave. Yvor Winters. MoVE; NoAM
Great events, we often find. The Power of Littles. *Unknown.* TreFT
Great Farewells, The. Amanda Benjamin Hall. GoYe
Great Farm. Philip Booth. PoPl
"Great father Alighier, if from the skies." To Dante. Vittorio Alfieri, *tr. by* Lorna De' Lucchi. AWP
Great Favorit Beheaded, A. Sir Richard Fanshawe. *See* Fall, The.
Great fear is expected to flash, The. Shrouds and Away. Alfred G. Bailey. PeCV
Great Figure, The. William Carlos Williams. NoAM; QFR
Great Fire, The. Dryden. *Fr.* Annus Mirabilis. FiP

Great fish's eyes never shut, The. Rosario Castellanos, *tr. fr. Spanish by* Willis Barnstone. BoWoP
Great Fleas ("Great fleas have little fleas"). Augustus De Morgan. BXAP; WhC
(Fleas, The.) FaBoCo
(On Fleas.) TreFS
Great folks are of a finer mould. Epigram on Scolding. Swift. FaBoEE
Great fool, The. Work Song. Raymond Mazisi Kunene, *tr. by* D. K. Rycroft. WTO
Great Fortune is an hungry thing. Chorus. Aeschylus, *tr. by* Gilbert Murray. *Fr.* Agamemnon. AWP
Great Fountains, The. Anne Hébert, *tr. fr. French by* Willis Barnstone. BoWoP
Great Freight, The. Ingeborg Bachmann, *tr. fr. German by* Bill Crisman. PBWP
Great freight truck, A. Gary Snyder. *Fr.* Hitch Haiku. InPK
Great Friend. Henry David Thoreau. PoEL-4
Great Frost, The. John Gay. *Fr.* Trivia; or, The Art of Walking the Streets of London. OBEC; SeCePo
Great Garret, or 100 Wheels, The. James McMichael. AmPA
Great Gawd, I'm Feelin' Bad, *with music. Unknown.* AS
Great Getting Up Morning. *Unknown.* FSW
Great Giver of the open hand. *Unknown, tr. by* Eleanor Hull. *Fr.* Four Prayers. OnYI
Great God, attend while Zion sings. Isaac Watts. AmFP
Great God, How Frail a Thing Is Man, *with music.* Mather Byles. AH
Great God, how short's mans time; each minute speaks. Meditations for July 19, 1666. Philip Pain. SCAP
Great God, I Ask Thee for No Meaner Pelf. Henry David Thoreau. *See* My Prayer.
Great God, let all my tuneful pow'rs. Ottiwell Heginbothom. AmFP
Great God of Hope, how green Thy trees. Hope. Amy Carmichael. TRV
Great God of Nations, now to Thee. Hymn of Gratitude. *Unknown.* BLRP
Great God Pan, The. Elizabeth Barrett Browning. *See* Musical Instrument, A.
Great God Paused among Men. Daniel Berrigan. MAT
Great God, Preserver of All Things, *with music.* Francis Daniel Pastorius. AH
Great God, that bowest sky and star. Hymn for the Church Militant. G. K. Chesterton. OxBoCh
Great God, the Followers of Thy Son, *with music.* Henry Ware, Jr. AH
Great God, Thou giver of all good. *Unknown.* BLRP
Great God, Thy Works, *with music.* Mather Byles. AH
Great God: within whose simple essence. To God the Father. Henry Constable. GoBC
Great Goddesse to whose throne in Cynthian fires. The Shadow of Night. George Chapman. NCEP; PoEL-2
Great gold apples of night, The. People. D. H. Lawrence. BrPo
Great, good and just, could I but rate. His Metrical Vow [*or* Epitaph on Charles I *or* Epitaph on King Charles I *or* Lines on the Execution of King Charles I]. James Graham, Marquess of Montrose. BSV; GOTS; NOBE; OBS; OxBS; ViBoPo
Great-Granddad, *with music. Unknown.* CoSo
Great-Grandma. Carol Shields. Str
Greatgrandma's bending to pluck some vegetable. Recipe. Albert Goldbarth. VWA
Great-Grandmother, The. Robert Graves. DTC
Great-grandmother talks by the hour to me. Irish Grandmother. Katherine Edelman. AmFN; SiSoSe
Great-great Grandma, Don't Sleep in Your Treehouse Tonight. X. J. Kennedy. GrPl
Great grief came over me. Aleqaajik, *tr. fr. Eskimo.* WTO
Great Guest Comes In, The. Edwin Markham. WBLP
Great guns of England, they listen mile on mile, The. Lord Dunsany. Songs from an Evil Wood, III. HBV-2
Great-Heart. Kipling. HBV-2
Great heart, who taught thee so to dye? Epitaph: On Sir Walter Rawleigh at His Execution. *Unknown.* OBS
Great-hearted Christ, importunate and mild. Invocation. Chad Walsh. *Fr.* The Psalm of Christ. TrCP
Great Heav'n! how frail thy creature man is made! Love and Reason. Matthew Prior. *Fr.* Solomon. OBEC
Great House, The. Edwin Muir. EyDe
Great Hunger, The, *sels.* Patrick Kavanagh.
"April, and no one able to calculate." IPY
"Clay is the word and clay is the flesh." IPY; NoAM; OxBTC
"He gave himself another year." BIrV
"Health and wealth and love he too dreamed of in May." MoAB
"Maguire is not afraid of death, the Church will light him a candle." CIP
"Poor Paddy Maguire, a fourteen-hour day." IPY
Great-in-counsels made her this reply, The. Ulysses Leaves the Nymph Calypso. Homer, *tr. by* George Chapman. *Fr.* Odyssey, V. JCP
Great is Caesar: He has conquered Seven Kingdoms. Fugal Chorus. W. H. Auden. *Fr.* For the Time Being. LiTM; NePA; SeCeV
Great is my envy of you, earth, in your greed. Petrarch, *tr. by.* Edwin Morgan. Sonnets to Laura: To Laura in Death, XXXII. NAWM-1
Great is the folly of a feeble braine. Satire XII: The Love-sicke Poet. Joseph Hall. *Fr.* Virgidemiarum. EBEV; FaBoEn
Great is the likeness of those beauteous two. Morphine. Heine, *tr. by* Ernst Feise. NAWM-2
Great is the sun, and wide he goes. Summer Sun. Robert Louis Stevenson. MoBrPo
Great is the tumult of men's anger grown. From Bethlehem Blown. Mary Sinton Leitch. PGD
Great is thy worke in Wildernesse, Oh man. Mr. Eliot Pastor of the Church of Christ at Roxbury. Edward Johnson. SCAP
Great Jack of Lent, clad in a robe of air. A Copy of Non Sequitors. *Unknown.* FaBoNo
Great Jehovah speaks to us, The. The Old Testament [*or* Names and Order of the Books of the Old Testament]. Thomas Russell. BLPA; TreFS
Great Jehova's working word effecting wondrously, The. Good News from New-England. Edward Johnson. SCAP
Great king, the sovereign [*or* sov'raigne] ruler of this land. To His Late Majesty Concerning the True Form of English Poetry. Sir John Beaumont. JCP; OBS
"Great lady, were you Helen long ago?" Helen—Old. Isabel Ecclestone MacKay. CaP
Great Lakes of Canada, The. Gordon Perry. FaBoUs
Great Lakes Suite, The. James Reaney. WHW
Great land and a wide land was the east land, A. Who Are They? *Unknown, tr. by* D. G. Brinton. NIP
Great Lord of All, Whose Work of Love, *with music.* Jacob Duché. AH
Great Lover, The. Rupert Brooke. BrPo; FaFP; FPL; HoPM; LiTB; LiTM; MoBrPo; PoRA; TreF; TrGrPo; WaP
Great [*or* Greate] Macedon, that out of Persia chased, The. In Praise of Wyatt's Psalms. Earl of Surrey. AAS; SiPS
Great Magicians, The. C. Day Lewis. EaLo
Great Man, A. Goldsmith. NA
Great Man. B. S. Johnson. ELU
Great Man, The. Eunice Tietjens. WGRP
Great many gentlemen take great delight, A. Bold Reynard the Fox. *Unknown.* OBET
Great melech lies waking over Judah, The. Saul. Else Lasker-Schüler, *tr. by* Joachim Neugroschel. VWA
Great Men Have Been among Us. Wordsworth. EnRP; PoEL-4
(England, 1802, III.) HBV-2; OBEV
Great Merchant, Dives Pragmaticus, Cries His Wares, The, *sel.* Thomas Newbery.
"What lack you, sir? What seek you? What will you buy?" OxBChV
Great Misgiving, The. Sir William Watson. HBV-2; OBVV
Great Moth, The. Robert Gittings. OxBTC
Great Mourning. Bible, Apocrypha. First Maccabees, I: 25-28. TrJP
Great Nature clothes the soul, which is but thin. The Soul's Garment. Margaret Cavendish, Duchess of Newcastle. OxBoCh; SeCePo; WPE
Great Nature Is an Army Gay. Richard Watson Gilder. HBV-1
Great Nebula in Andromeda, The. Hugh Seidman. AmPA
Great Ocean! strongest of creation's sons. Ocean. Robert Pollok. EtS
Great one, austere. Prayer before Work. May Sarton. SaC
Great Overdog, The,/ That heavenly beast. Canis Major. Robert Frost. *Fr.* A Sky Pair. MoAB; MoAmPo
Great Pacific railway, The. The Railroad Cars Are Coming. *Unknown.* AmFN; AS; BPAW; FaPON
Great Panjandrum, The [Himself]. Samuel Foote. FaBoCh; FaBoCo; MoShBr; Par; PoLF; WhC
Great Pelides, stretch'd along the shore. The Ghost of Patroclus. Homer, *tr. by* Pope. *Fr.* The Iliad, XXII. PeHV
Great philosopher did choke, A. Samuel Butler. FaBoEE
Great Physician, The. Sadi, *tr. fr. Persian by* Sir Edwin Arnold. *Fr.* The Bustan. AWP
Great Poet, The. Linda King. GP
Great poets are not in the language but in business, The. Poetry Paper. Andrei Codrescu. EAS
Great Powers Conference. Edith Lovejoy Pierce. PGD
Great Prince of heaven, begotten of that King. To God the Son. Henry Constable. OBSC
Great princes have great playthings. Playthings. William Cowper. WaaP
Great River, The. Henry van Dyke. TrPWD
Great Round-up, The. *Unknown.* BPAW; CoSo
Great Sad One, The. Uri Zvi Greenberg, *tr. fr. Hebrew by* Robert Mezey *and* Ben Zion Gold. VWA
Great Santa Barbara Oil Disaster Or, The. Conyus. AmPA

Great Sassacus fled from the eastern shores. Death Song. Alonzo Lewis. PAH
Great Scarf of Birds, The. John Updike. NYBP
Great Sea, The. Uvavnuk, *tr. fr. Eskimo by* Knud Rasmussen. NU
(Song of Joy.) WTO
(Woman Shaman's Song, A, *tr. ad. by* Tom Lowenstein.) WPOW
Great ship spreads her wings, her plumes are flying, The. Godspeed. Harriet Prescott Spofford. EtS
Great Silkie of Sule Skerry [*or* Skerrie], The. *Unknown.* ChTr; ESPB; FaBoBa; FaBoCh; FSW; GBP; MAT; MOS; ViBoFo (A *vers.;* B *vers., with music*)
(Grey Selchie of Sule Skerry, The, *with music.*) OxBB
(Silkie o' Sule Skerrie, The.) EtS
Great Sir, having just had the good luck to catch. Copy of an Intercepted Despatch from His Excellency Don Strepitoso Diabolo. Thomas Moore. NBM; OBSV
Great sir, our poor hearts were ready to burst. The Humble Address. *Unknown.* APAS
Great Society, The. Robert Bly. CAD; NoAM; NYP; PAI
Great soul, to all brave souls akin. The Star. Marion Couthouy Smith. PAH
Great South Land, The, *sel.* Rex Ingamells.
"'They made impudent inspection of our coast.'" CBAP
Great Sovereign of the earth and sea. Europa. Stephen Henry Thayer. AA
Great Spaces. Howard Moss. TwCP
Great Speckled Bird, The. *Unknown.* FSW
Great Spirit of the speeding spheres. Hymn. John Haynes Holmes. TrPWD
Great spirits now on earth are sojourning. Addressed to Haydon. Keats. EnRP; OBNC
Great star has fallen into my lap, A. Reconciliation. Else Lasker-Schüler, *tr. by* Robert Alter. PBWP
Great Statue of the General Du Puy, The. Wallace Stevens. *Fr.* Notes toward a Supreme Fiction. LiTA
Great, still shape, alone, A. Ireland. John James Piatt. AA
Great stone hearth has gone, The. Fire. Dorothy Wellesley. OBMV
Great Strafford! worthy of that name, though all. On the Earl of Strafford's Trial and Death. John Denham. LoBV
Great streets of silence led away. Emily Dickinson. NOCV
Great Summons, The. Ch'ü Yüan, *tr. fr. Chinese by* Arthur Waley. AWP
Great sun has changed itself into a pumpkin moon, The. Goodbye. Sherod Santos. MAYP
Great sun sinks behind the town, The. To an Ungentle Critic. Robert Graves. HBMV; InMe
Great Swamp Fight, The. Caroline Hazard. PAH
Great swart cheek and the gleam of tears, A. The Washer-Woman. Otto Leland Bohanan. BANP
Great Sword Bearer, The, only knows just when He'll wound my heart—not I. The Conclusion of the Whole Matter. Ridgely Torrence. *Fr.* The House of a Hundred Lights. HBV-2
Great tempest rages on the Plain of Ler, A. Song of the Sea. *At. to* Rumann MacColmain, *tr. by* Kuno Meyer. OnYI
Great Things. Blake. *Fr.* Gnomic Verses. PV
("Great things are done when men and mountains meet.") TrGrPo
Great Things. Thomas Hardy. GTBS-P; MoVE; NOBE; TreFT
Great things are done when men and mountains meet. Great Things. Blake. *Fr.* Gnomic Verses. PV; TrGrPo
Great thoughts in crude, unshapely verse set forth. On Reading. Thomas Bailey Aldrich. AA
Great thrushes have not appeared this year, The. The Unremarkable Year. Roy Fuller. OxBC
Great tiger, The. Folk Tune. Esther Raab, *tr. by* Robert Friend *and* Shiman Sandbank. VWA
Great Time, A. W. H. Davies. LiTB; MoBrPo; MoVE; WHA
Great *Titanic.* *Unknown.* AmFP
Great Tom. Richard Corbet. OxBoLi
Great truths are dearly bought. The common truth. How We Learn. Horatius Bonar. HBV-2
Great unequal conflict past, The. Occasioned by General Washington's Arrival in Philadelphia, on His Way to His Residence in Virginia. Philip Freneau. PAH
Great Venus, Queene of beautie and of grace. Address [*or* Prayer] to Venus. Lucretius, *tr. by* Spenser. *Fr.* De Rerum Natura *and fr.* The Faerie Queene. AWP; EIL
Great Victory, The. R. V. Gilbert. BLRP
Great Virginian, The. James Russell Lowell. *Fr.* Under the Old Elm. PGD
("Never to see a nation born.") GOA
Great Voices, The. Charles Timothy Brooks. HBV-2
Great Wager, The. G. A. Studdert-Kennedy. TrCP
Great War, The. Vernon Scannell. OBWP
Great Wave, The: *Hokusai.* Donald Finkel. PoPl
Great Wave off Kanagwa, The. Constance Egemo. PoDr
Great Wheel, The. "Hugh MacDiarmid." OxBS
Great, wide, beautiful, wonderful World. The Wonderful World [*or* The Child's World *or* The World]. William Brighty Rands. FaPON; HBV-1; HBVY; OBVV; OHIP; OxBChV; TiPo; TreFT
Great wind blowing, raging sea, A. Comforted. Amy Carmichael. TRV
Great wind sweeps, A. Wild Weather. Katharine Lee Bates. PGD
Great winds may blow now. Knocking at the Door. John Freeman. HBMV
Great without pomp, without ambition brave. Tribute to Washington. *Unknown.* OHIP
Great woe, fire & war come on me. Epigram. Skythinos, *tr. by* Thomas Meyer. PeHV
Great wrought-iron gates have been, The. Twilight at the Zoo. Alex Rodger. NCSH
Great Yahweh fingered through His Bible. Apocrypha. X. J. Kennedy. PV
Great you call Demosthenes. Self-Portrait. Moses Mendelssohn. TrJP
Great Zeus, beset by love and lechery. Matter of Taste. *Unknown, tr. by* Louis Untermeyer. UnTE
Greate Macedon that out of Persy chased, The. *See* Great Macedon, that out of Persia chased, The.
Greater Cats, The. V. Sackville-West. OBMV; PoPle
("Greater cats with golden eyes, The.") LO
Greater Country, The. Grace V. Watkins. AMV-80
Greater Friendship Baptist Church, The. Carole C. Gregory. BlSi
Greater, he called them, than Homer or Chaucer. The Men of Sudbury. Carlos Baker. GOA
Greater Love. Wilfred Owen. BrPo; CMoP; EnLoPo; FaBoMo; FaBoRV; FaFP; GTBS-P; LiTB; LiTM; LO; MasP; MoAB; MoBrPo; NoAM; OAEP; SeCeV; ViBoPo; WaaP; WaP
Greater Love Hath No Man. Bible, *N.T.* St. John, XV: 13-16. TreFT
Greater masters of the commonplace, The. Staff-Nurse: Old Style. W. E. Henley. In Hospital, VIII. BrPo
Greater Music, The. Theodore Weiss. NePoAm-2
Greater than memory of Achilles or Ulysses. The Wallabout Martyrs. Walt Whitman. GOA
Greater Trial, The. Countess of Winchilsea. TrGrPo
Greater world is water, The. The Tower. Mark Van Doren. MoPo
Greatest Battle That Ever Was Fought, The. Joaquin Miller. TreF
Greatest bore is boredom, The. *Unknown.* CenHV
Greatest in many things, in some the least. On a Distinguished Politician. J. E. Thorold Rogers. FaBoEE
Greatest of These, The. Bible, *N.T.* *Fr.* First Corinthians. *See* Though I Speak with the Tongues of Men and Angels.
Greatest of virtues is humility. Against Women's Fashions. John Lydgate. ACP
Greatest Person in the Universe, The. Daniel L. Marsh. BLRP
Greatest poem ever known, The. To a Child. Christopher Morley. HBMV
Greatest saints and sinners have been made, The. Samuel Butler. FaBoEE
Greatly shining,/ The autumn moon floats in the thin sky. Wind and Silver. Amy Lowell. BoWoP; HelP; MoAmPo; MOON; PAI
Greatness. *Unknown.* OBS
Grecian Muse, to earth who bore, The. California. Thomas Lake Morris. AA
Greece. Byron. *Fr.* Childe Harold's Pilgrimage, II. OBRV
Greece was; Greece is no more. "The White City." Richard Watson Gilder. PAH
Greed. Douglas Blazek. LTB
Greed, *sel.* Diane Wakoski.
Turtle, The. NoAM
Greed Song, The. Albert Goldbarth. AMV-80
Greedy hawk with sudden sight of lure, The. *Unknown.* PBBP
Greedy Jane. *Unknown.* HBVY; OxBChV
Greedy Richard. Jane Taylor. OxBChV
Greedy small Lassie once said, A. Too Much. *Unknown.* TDH
Greedy the People, The. E. E. Cummings. SoSe
Greek Architecture. Herman Melville. NoP
Greek Athlete, The. Euripides, *tr. fr. Greek by* Tom Dodge. LiSp
Greek Epigram. Ezra Pound. MoAB; MoAmPo
Greek Excavations. Bernard Spencer. ChMP
Greek Room, The. James W. Thompson. BPo
Greek ship, A/ Sails on the sea. The Couple. Sandra Hochman. CTBA; NYBP
Greek Transfiguration. Kimon Friar. HoAn
Greeks, The. Tom Clark. PoA
Greeks' chieftains, all irked with the war, The. Virgil, *tr. by* the Earl of Surrey. *Fr.* The Aeneid, II. OAEL-1
Greeks dismay'd, confus'd disperse or fall, The. Homer, *tr. by* Pope. Fr. The Iliad, XV. OBVE

Greeks were wrong who said our eyes have rays, The. Lamarck Elaborated. Richard Wilbur. AP; NePoEA
Green. William Barnes. VLP
Green. Walter de la Mare. FaBoNo
Green. John Gray, *after the French of* Paul Verlaine. SyP
Green. D. H. Lawrence. ELU; GBL; MoBrPo; PoA
Green Afternoon, The. Henry Rago. VGW
Green and growing thorn-tree, A. Forgive and Forget. "Totius," *tr. by* Anthony Delius. PeSA
Green and Pleasant Land, A. John Peale Bishop. PoPl
Green and silent spot, amid the hills, A. Fears in Solitude. Samuel Taylor Coleridge. EnRP; OBWP
Green and the Black, The. Anthony Bailey. NYBP
Green and Yellow. *Unknown.* OBET
Green Apples. Dudley Randall. FB
Green are the tussocks of the marsh-grass springing. Yellow. Kenton Kilmer. GoYe
Green arsenic smeared on an egg-white cloth. L'Art, 1910. Ezra Pound. HeIP; OxBA
Green as a seedling the one lane shines. City Traffic. Eve Merriam. PDV
Green Autumn Stubble, The. *Unknown, tr. fr. Irish by* Patrick Browne. OxBI; WTO
Green be the turf above thee. On the Death of Joseph Rodman Drake. Fitz-Greene Halleck. AA; BLPA; HBV-2; OBVV; PAH; PoEL-4; TreFS
Green Bed, The. *Unknown.* AmFP
Green blood fresh pulsing through the trees. April and Dying. Anne Reeve Aldrich. AA
Green-blue ground, The. On Gay Wallpaper. William Carlos Williams. MoAB; MoAmPo; TAP
Green, blue, yellow, and red. The One. Patrick Kavanagh. MoBrPo
Green Briar Shore, The. *Unknown.* AmFP
Green Broom. *Unknown. See* Broom, Green Broom.
Green Buddhas/ On the fruit stand. Watermelons. Charles Simic. OBAL; PPJ
Green Candles. Humbert Wolfe. HBMV; MoBrPo; RHPC; SO
Green catalpa tree has turned, The. April Inventory. W. D. Snodgrass. AP; BiP; CABA; CAPP; CoAP; HAP; LiTM; MP; NePoEA; NoAM; NoP; PAI; PoPl; PPoe; TAP; TwCP
Green cheese, yellow laces. *Unknown.* OxNR
Green cocklEburs, The. Haiku. Richard Wright. FAZ
Green Corn. *Unknown.* FSW
Green Corn Dance, The. Alice Corbin. BPAW
Green Dryad's Plea, The. Thomas Hood. *Fr.* The Plea of the Midsummer Fairies. OBNC
Green elm with the one great bough of gold, The. October. Edward Thomas. ChMP; MoVE; NoAM
Green enravishment of human life. Sister Juana Inés de la Cruz, *tr. fr. Spanish by* Samuel Beckett *and* Octavio Paz. WPOW
Green Estaminet, The. A. P. Herbert. HBMV
Green Eye, The. James Merrill. PoA
Green Eye of the Yellow God, The. J. Milton Hayes. BLPA; PaPo
Green-eyed Care. Old Cat Care. Richard Hughes. OBMV
Green Family, The. Colleen Thibaudeau. NOBC
Green Fields of England. Arthur Hugh Clough. OAEP
Green fields, The. The green fields. The Poetry Reading. Bill Manhire. OCNZ
Green Frog at Roadstead, Wisconsin. James Schevill. TAP
Green Frogs. David Rigsbee. AMV-81
Green gardens in Laventie! Home Thoughts in Laventie. Edward Wyndham Tennant. HBMV
Green-Gown, The. *Unknown.* CoMu
Green grape, and you refused me. Brief Autumnal. *Unknown, tr. by* Dudley Fitts. PAI; WeW
Green Grass. *Unknown.* CH; GBP; OxBoLi
("A dis, a dis, a green grass.") OxNR; PoPle
Green Grass and Sea. George Woodcock. AMV-81
Green Grass and White Milk. Winifred Welles. TiPo
Green Grass Growing. Patrick Evans. NeBP
Green Grass Growing All Around, The. *Unknown.* HBVY; MoShBr
(Green Grass Grew All Around, The, *diff. version.*) FSW
Green grass growing upward splits the concrete pavement. Green Grass Growing. Patrick Evans. NeBP
Green, Green Is El Aghir. Norman Cameron. MoBS; OBWP; OxBTC
(El Aghir.) FaBoTw
Green grew the reeds and pale they were. Symbols. Vance Thompson. AA
Green Grow the Lilacs. *Unknown.* FSW; TreFT
Green Grow the Rashes. Burns. CoMu, *diff. vers.*; CTC; ErPo, *diff. vers.*; FaFP; NoP; ViBoPo; WHA
(Green Grow the Rashes, O.) EnRP; FSW; HBV-1; LAuP; LiTB; OAEL-1; OBEC; PPoe; PPP; SeCePo; UnTE
(Green Grows the Rashes.) GBP, *diff. vers.*
(Song: Green Grow the Rashes.) AWP
Green Grow the Rushes O. *Unknown. See* Carol of the Numbers.
Green Groweth the Holly. Henry VIII, King of England. *See* As the Holly Groweth Green.
Green Grows the Rashes. Burns. *See* Green Grow the Rashes.
Green Haven Halls. Charles Culhane. LFAC
Green Hills of Africa, The. Roy Fuller. NoP
Green hobgoblin, A. A Goblinade. Florence Page Jaques. TiPo
Green Horse, The. Bin Ramke. MAYP
Green, humped, wrinkled hills, The: with such a look. The Green Hills of Africa. Roy Fuller. NoP
Green Hunters, The. Florence M. Wilson. AnIV
Green I love you green. Sleepwalkers' Ballad. Federico García Lorca, *tr. by* John Frederick Nims. WeW
Green Ice. Vivienne Finch. BrRo
Green, in the wizard arms. The Banshee. John Todhunter. OnYI
Green Inn, The. Theodosia Garrison. HBMV
Green iridescent flies. Sleeping Beauty. Jane Shore. DFT
Green is go. Yellow. David McCord. RHPC
Green is the color of everything. One West Coast. Al Young. NPGG
Green is the night, green kindled and apparelled. The Candle, a Saint. Wallace Stevens. PoRA
Green is the plane-tree in the square. A London Plane-Tree. Amy Levy. OBVV
Green Island. William Logan. MAYP
Green Isle of Lovers, The. Robert Charles Sands. AA
Green Jade Plum Trees in Spring. Ou-yang Hsiu, *tr. fr. Chinese by* Kenneth Rexroth. NaP
Green Knight's Farewell to Fancy, The. George Gascoigne. EnRePo
Green lady, green lady, come doon for thy tea. *Unknown.* GBP
Green Lake, The. Michael Roberts. ChMP
Green lamp flares on the table, The. This Life. Rita Dove. AmPA
Green lane now I traverse, where it goes, The. John Clare. *Fr.* Summer Images. OBRV
Green lawn/ a picket fence. Once. Alice Walker. BlSi; PoBA
Green Leaf, The. Louis Zukofsky. CoPo
("Green leaf that will outlast the winter.") VGW
Green level of lily leaves, A. To Paint a Water Lily. Ted Hughes. PP
Green Light. Kenneth Fearing. VGW
Green light floods the city square, The. Sunken Evening [in Trafalgar Square]. Laurie Lee. LiTM; NYBP
Green Linnet, The. Wordsworth. EnRP; GTBS; GTBS-P; HBV-1; PBBP
Green little boy in a green little way, A. Verdancy. *Unknown.* ShM
Green Little Shamrock of Ireland, The. Andrew Cherry. HBV-2
Green little vaulter in the sunny grass. To the Grasshopper and the Cricket. Leigh Hunt. EnRP; GN; HBV-1; OBNC
Green mistletoe! Winter. Walter de la Mare. ChTr; MoVE; YeAr
Green morning of indolence one hedge beyond, A. Morning in the Park. John Ciardi. MiAP
Green Mossy Banks of the Lee, The. *Unknown.* OBET
Green Moth. Winifred Welles. FaPON; TiPo
Green Mountain Boy. Florida Watts Smyth. GoYe
Green Mountain Boys, The. Bryant. PAH; PoPl
Green mwold on zummer bars do show. Tokens. William Barnes. NBM; PoEL-4; VLP
Green of the cedars is unlike, The. Poem for Good Friday. D. G. Jones. PeCV
Green Pastures. Dick Allen. AMV-80
Green Place, A. William Jay Smith. GrPl
Green Plumes of Royal Palms, *with music.* LeRoy V. Brant. AH
Green points on the shrub. An Elegy for D. H. Lawrence. William Carlos Williams. NoAM
Green Rain. Dorothy Livesay. NIP; NOBC
Green Rain. Mary Webb. BoNaP; CH; FaPON
Green Red Brown and White. May Swenson. VGW
Green Refrain, A. Avraham Huss, *tr. fr. Hebrew by* Mark Elliott Shapiro. VWA
Green River. Bryant. AP; NOBA; OxBA
Green River, The. Lord Alfred Douglas. HBMV; OBEV; OBVV
Green road lies this way, The. El Camino Verde. Paul Blackburn. CoPo
Green Roads, The. Edward Thomas. FaBoPP; NoAM
Green rushes with red shoots. Plucking the Rushes. *Tr. fr. Chinese by* Arthur Waley. BoLoP; OBVE; OLR
Green rustlings, more-than-regal charities. Royal Palm. Hart Crane. AP; CMoP; MoAB; MoAmPo; NoAM; NoP; TrGrPo
Green screen door, The. How About. Sheryl L. Nelms. Str
Green-shadowed people sit, or walk in rings. Spring. Philip Larkin. MoBrPo
Green Shepherd, The. Louis Simpson. MP; NePoEA; NIP; NoAM; NYBP
Green shingles of rest homes unfold revealing, The. The United States Prepare for the Permanent Revolution. George Hitchcock. EAS

Green shutters, shut your shutters! Windyridge. John Betjeman. *Fr.* Beside the Seaside. OxBTC
Green-Sickness Beauty, The. Lord Herbert of Cherbury. AnAnS-2
Green sky underfoot, A. Moss. Nancy Willard. HoAn
Green Slates. Thomas Hardy. FaBoPP
Green Sleeves ("Green sleeves and tartan ties"). *Unknown.* GBP
Green Snake, when I hung you round my neck. To the Snake. Denise Levertov. AmPP; LiTM; NePoEA-2; NMM; PAI; PoA
Green snakes in the mulch pile note, The. Neighbors. Charles Malam. AMV-80
Green Song. Philip Booth. BoNaP
Green spires of the forest, The. A Forest Meditation. Bernice Hall Legg. PGD
Green Spring receiveth. The Great Summons. Ch'ü Yüan, *tr. by* Arthur Waley. AWP
Green Spring tide has risen, until its crest, The. Spring in England. Charles Buxton Going. HBMV
Green star Sirius. Winter Dawn. D. H. Lawrence. BrPo
Green Stems. Margaret Wise Brown. RHPC
Green Sussex. Tennyson. *Fr.* Prologue to General Hamley. FaBoPP
Green Symphony. John Gould Fletcher. MoAmPo; MoVE
Green the drawn curtains, the walls. Three Women. Lauris Edmond. OCNZ
Green Things Growing. Dinah Maria Mulock Craik. FaFP; GN; HBV-1; HBVY; OHIP
Green Train, The. E. V. Rieu. SO
Green Tree, The. James Reiss. AmPA; DiL
Green Valley. Dorothy Vena Johnson. PoNe
Green Valley, The. Sylvia Townsend Warner. MoBrPo
Green! What a world of green! My startled soul. June Rapture. Angela Morgan. HBMV
Green Willow, The. *Unknown.* OBSC
(Complaint of a Lover Forsaken of His Love, The.) CoMu
Green Willow, Green Willow. *Unknown.* AmFP
Green willows are for girls to study under. Heresy for a Class-Room. Rolfe Humphries. GLGT
Green World Two. Miriam Waddington. PeCV
Greenback Dollar, The. *Unknown.* AmFP
Greener Grass. Frank Steele. Psk
Greene's Farewell to Folly, *sel.* Robert Greene.
Song: "Sweet are the thoughts that savour of content." PoEL-2
Greene's Groatsworth of Wit, *sels.* Robert Greene.
Fie, Fie on Blind Fancy! ElL
(Lamilia's Song.) OBSC
Palinode, A. OBSC
Greene's Mourning Garment, *sels.* Robert Greene.
Hexametra Alexis in Laudem Rosamundi. ElL; GBL; PoEL-2
Shepherd's Wife's Song, The. ElL; HAP; HBV-1; LoBV; OBSC; ViBoPo
Greene's Vision, *sel.* Robert Greene.
Description of Sir Geoffrey Chaucer, The. CTC; OBSC
(Sir Geoffrey Chaucer.) FaBoCh
Greenhouse, The. James Merrill. TwAmPo
Green-house is my summer seat, The. The Faithful Friend. William Cowper. FM
Greenland Whale Fishery, The (*diff. versions*). *Unknown.* AmFP; BaBo; OBET; OuSiCo, *with music*; ViBoFo, *with music*
(Greenland Fisheries.) FSW
(Greenland Whale, The.) GBP
(Whale, The.) AmSS, *with music*; ChTr
Greenness. Angelina Weld Grimké. CDC
Greenock. John Davidson. *Fr.* A Ballad in Blank Verse of the Making of a Poet. BSV
Greens. David Ray. VGW
Greens, *with music. Unknown.* AS
Greensleeves. *Unknown.* BLSo, *with music;* FSW; UnTE
(Lady Greensleeves.) GBL; PoEL-2
(New Courtly Sonnet of the Lady Greensleeves.) ElL; FaBoCh; OAEP; OBSC
Greenwich Avenue. James Schuyler. NYP
Greenwich Observatory. Sidney Keyes. MoAB; MoBrPo
Greenwood fawn at the hidden brook, The. Song for the Greenwood Fawn. I. L. Salomon. GoYe
Greer County, *with music. Unknown.* CoSo
Greet the bights that gave me shelter. The Old Fisherman. George Campbell Hay. BSV
Greeting, A. W. H. Davies. MoBrPo
Greeting. Ella Young. AnIV
Greeting Descendants. A. G. Sobin. FAZ
Greeting from a Distance. Hans Sahl, *tr. fr. German by* Erna Baber Rosenfeld. VWA
Greeting from England. *Unknown.* PAH
Greeting of the Roses, The. Hamlin Garland. AA
Gregory Griggs. Laura E. Richards. OxNR; SoPo
Grenada. Mikhail Arkadyevich Svetlov, *tr. fr. Russian by* Alexander Kaun. WaaP
Grenadier. A. E. Housman. OBMV; OBWP
Grenadier, The. *Unknown.* GBP
("Who comes here?/ A grenadier.") OxNR
Grenadiers of Austria are proper men and tall, The. Cremona. Sir Arthur Conan Doyle. HBV-2
Grendel. *Unknown, tr. fr. Anglo-Saxon by* Burton Raffel. *Fr.* Beowulf. NU
Grene groweth the holy. Love Ever Green. Henry VIII, King of England. MeEL
Gresford Disaster, The. *Unknown.* GBP; OBET
Gretel in Darkness. Louise Glück. AmPA; DFT; GP
Grevus is my sorow. Unkindness Has Killed Me. *Unknown.* MeEL
Grew in Hades. The Creation. *Maori Oral Tradition, tr. by* Richard Taylor. WTO
Grey. *See also* Gray.
Grey as a guinea-fowl is the rain. Two Kitchen Songs. Edith Sitwell. CMoP
Grey as a mouse. *See* Gray as a mouse.
Grey brick upon brick. Dublin. Louis MacNeice. CIP; FaBoPP; OxBI; OxBTC
Grey Cock, The; or, Saw You My Father? *Unknown.* BaBo (A *and* B *vers.*); ELP; ESPB; FaBoBa; OBET
Grey countries and grim empires pass away. Morning in the North-West. Arthur Stringer. CaP
Grey day left the dusk in doubt, The. Winter Night. Robert Fitzgerald. PoPl
Grey Eye Weeping, A. Egan O'Rahilly, *tr. fr. Modern Irish by* Frank O'Connor. AnIL; KiLC; OBMV; OxBI
Grey-eyed King, The. "Anna Akhmatova," *tr. fr. Russian by* Robert Tracy. PBWP
Grey flies, fragile, slender-winged and slender-legged. Evening Dance of the Grey Flies. P. K. Page. NOBC
Grey friar, The. Cloisters. Anthony Barnett. VWA
Grey Frock, A. Zinaida Hippius, *tr. fr. Russian by* Temira Pachmuss. PBWP
Grey Funnel Line, The. Cyril Tawney. OBET
Grey Galloway. Thomas S. Cairncross. PoSH
Grey gaunt days dividing us in twain, The. The Minute before Meeting. Thomas Hardy. VLP
Grey girl who had not been singing stopped, The. New Year's Eve. John Berryman. LiTM; NMP
Grey goose and gander. *See* Gray Goose and Gander.
Grey grass in the early winter, The. The Stallion. Alan Porter. PH
Grey-green stretch of sandy grass, The. At Dieppe: Grey and Green. Arthur Symons. FaBoPP; SyP
Grey, grey is Abbey Asaroe, by Belashanny town. *See* Gray, gray is . . .
Grey Hair, The. Judah Halevi, *tr. fr. Hebrew by* J. Chotzner. TrJP
Grey haunted eyes, absent-mindedly glaring. *See* Gray haunted eyes . . .
Grey Him. Paul Mariah. LFAC
Grey Horse, The. James Reeves. PH
"Grey Horse Troop," The. Robert W. Chambers. HBV-2; PAH
Grey in the sky and blue against the trees. Journey. Sam Harrison. NeIP
Grey is the color of time. Morning Song. Charlotte DeClue. STE; TWSS
Grey Linnet, The. James McCarroll. CaP
Grey, low ceiling, sough of sea wind along forest. The Lairdless Place. Kate Rennie Archer. GoYe
Grey October. "The Critics." OBET
Grey o'er the pallid links, haggard and forsaken. The Farm on the Links. Rosamund Marriott Watson. OBVV
Grey Ones, The. Louis MacNeice. CMoP
Grey over Riddrie the clouds piled up. King Billy. Edwin Morgan. BSV
Grey psychopath in her season, The. Cat. Joe Rosenblatt. NOBC
Grey [*or* Gray] sea and the long black land, The. Meeting at Night. Robert Browning. AWP; BoLoP; ELP; FaBoEn; FaBV; FF; FiP; GBL; HBV-1; HeIP; InPS; InVP; MOS; NOBE; OAEP; OBEV; OBNC; OLR; PAI; PoPl; PoPle; PoRA; SCV; SeCePo; SoSe; TreFT; TrGrPo; UnPo; ViBoPo; VLP; WEW
Grey Selchie of Sule Skerry, The. *Unknown. See* Great Silkie of Sule Skerry, The.
Grey sheep came, The. I ran. The Exorcism. Theodore Roethke. NoAM
Grey water tanks in grey mist. Bayonne Turnpike to Tuscarora. Allen Ginsberg. NNaP
Grey winter hath gone like a wearisome guest. September in Australia. Henry Clarence Kendall. OBVV; PoAu-1
Grey Wolf, The. Arthur Symons. BrPo; FaBoTw
Grey Woman. Gladys Cardiff. CDW; TWSS
Greyer than the tide below, the tower. Homage to Jack Yeats. Thomas McGreevy. OBMV
Greyport Legend, A. Bret Harte. EtS; GN; MOS
Greystone Cottage. Richard Hugo. NPAW

Grief. Wendell Berry. GeTw
Grief. Elizabeth Barrett Browning. FPL; HBV-2; HeIP; InPK; LoBV; OBEV; OBNC; OBVV; PoLF; SBG; TrGrPo; VLP; WPE
Grief, The. Rainer Maria Rilke, *tr. fr. German by* Steven Lautermilch. AMV-81
Grief/ o grief/ grief for ever. Alarum. Urszula Koziol, *tr. by* Czeslaw Milosz. WPOW
Grief and God. Stephen Phillips. WGRP
Grief, find the words, for thou hast made my brain. Astrophel and Stella, XCIV. Sir Philip Sidney. SiPS
Grief for her absent master in her wrought. The Dog. Frederick William Faber. FM
Grief hath been known to turn the young head gray. The Young Gray Head. Caroline Bowles Southey. BeLS
Grief of a Girl's Heart, The. *Unknown. See* Donal Oge: Grief of a Girl's Heart.
Grief of Cafeterias, The. John Updike. PPJ
Grief of Love, The. *Unknown, tr. fr. Arabic by* Wilfrid Scawen Blunt. AWP
Grief of Our Genitals, The. Henry Carlile. GP
Grief Plucked Me Out of Sleep. Jill King. PeSA
Grief Streams Down My Chest. Lance Jeffers. PoBA
Grief that is but feigning, The. The Valley of Vain Verses. Henry van Dyke. HBV-2
Griefs of Women, The. David R. Slavitt. BXAP
Griesly Wife, The. John Manifold. MoBrPo; MoBS
Grievance. Amy Lowell. ViBoPo
Grievance, A. James Kenneth Stephen. BXAP; FaBoPa; HBV-1; Par
Grieve Not for Beauty ("Grieve not for the invisible, transported brow"). Witter Bynner. PoA
Grieve Not for Me. *Unknown.* ShM
Grieve Not, Ladies. Anna Hempstead Branch. FaFP; HBV-1
Grieve Not the Holy Spirit. George Herbert. AnAnS-1
Grieve not too much, my Albius, since Glycera is no longer. It Always Happens. Horace, *tr. by* Thomas Charles Baring. UnTE
Grievous folly shames my sixtieth year, A. Hafiz, *tr. by* Richard Le Gallienne. Odes, IV. AWP
Griffin calls to come and kiss him goodnight. Bearhug. Michael Ondaatje. PPJ
"Grill me some bones," said the Cobbler. At the Keyhole. Walter de la Mare. DTC; MoAB; MoBrPo
Grim death took little Jerry. *Unknown.* WhC
Grim in my little black coat as the sleazy beetle. Tom, Tom, the Piper's Son. John Crowe Ransom. ViBoPo
Grim monarch! see, deprived of vital breath. To a Lady on the Death of Her Husband. Phillis Wheatley. TAP
Grim visor'd cavalier! Rides silently mischance. Le Chevalier Malheur. Paul Verlaine, *tr. by* John Gray. *Fr.* Sagesse. SyP
Grim was fishere swithe good. Havelok at Grimsby and Lincoln. *Unknown. Fr.* Havelok. OxBM
Grinder, who serenely grindest. Lines on Hearing the Organ. Charles Stuart Calverley. CenHV; FaBoCo; FiBHP; InMe; NBM; NOBL
Grinders, The; or, The Saddle on the Right Horse. *Unknown.* GBP
Grinding Vibrato. Jayne Cortez. BlSi
Grinding yoke from Israel's neck he tore, The. Eulogy for Hasdai ibn Shaprut. *Unknown, tr. by* Israel Abrahams. TrJP
Grinning, the foreman asked them for a vote. In the Jury Room. Hodding Carter. MAT
Grip, The. Brendan Kennelly. CIP
Grisaille with a Spot of Red. Samuel Yellen. NePoAm-2
Griselda's dead, and so's her patience. Patient Griselda. Chaucer, *mod. by* Edward Hodnett. *Fr.* The Canterbury Tales: The Clerk's Tale. PoRA
Grizzel Grimme. *Unknown.* FaBoEE
Grizzly. Bret Harte. AA; BPAW
Grizzly Bear. Mary Austin. BPAW; FaPON; GoJo; OnUR; PDV; SoPo; TiPo
Grizzly Bear. *Unknown.* FSW
Grizzly Bear is huge and wild, The. Infant Innocence. A. E. Housman. CenHV; ChTr; DTC; FaBoCh; FaBoCo; FaFP; LiTB; OxBoLi
Groan of earth in labor pain, A. San Francisco Falling. Edwin Markham. BPAW
Groaning Board, The. "Pink." InMe
Groans of love, The. Coloratura. Geoff Page. AMV-81
Groans of nature in this nether world, The. William Cowper. *Fr.* The Task, VI. NoP
"Grob! Grob," goes the raven peering from his rift. Cypress Grove. Austin Clarke. IPY
Grog-an'-Grumble Steeplechase. Henry Lawson. PH
Groggy fighter on his knees, The. Athletes. Walker Gibson. LiSp
Groined by deep glens and walled along the west. The Glens. John Hewitt. NeIP
Groins, for his fleshly burglary of late. Upon Groins: Epigram. Robert Herrick. CaPo
Grongar Hill. John Dyer. ChTr; EnRP; FaBoPP; GoTL; LAuP; LoBV; NOEC; NoP; OBEC; PoEL-3
Sels.
"Below me Trees unnumber'd rise." FaBoEn
"Ever charming, ever new." SeCePo
"O may I with myself agree." TrGrPo
"Old castles on the cliff arise." ViBoPo
Groom's Lament, The. Robert Peterson. NeAC
Groping along the tunnel, step by step. The Rear-Guard. Siegfried Sassoon. MoBrPo; NoAM; OBWP; WaP
Groping back to bed after a piss. Sad Steps. Philip Larkin. NoP
"Gross, Coarse, Hideous" (Police Description of My Pictures). D. H. Lawrence. FaBoEE
Gross sun squats above, The. Song. Dom Moraes. NePoEA-2
Grotesque. Amy Lowell. BoWoP
Grotesque ("Dr. Newman with the crooked pince-nez"). Robert Graves. DTC
Grotesque ("Sir John addressed the Snake-god in his temple"). Robert Graves. DTC
Grotesque, jumping out. Sky Diver. Adrien Stoutenburg. LiSp
Grotesque Love-Letter, A. *Unknown.* MeEL
Grotesque, the line of trees, pronged. Outside. Phyllis Beauvais. IHMS
Grotesques. Robert Graves. CMoP
Sels.
"Dr. Newman with the crooked pince-nez." DTC
"Sir John addressed the Snake-god in his temple." DTC
Grotesques, *sel.* Don Marquis.
"Was it fancy, sweet nurse." FiBHP
Grotto, The. Ray Fraser. NeAC
Grotto, The. Francis Scarfe. NeBP; PoA
Grouchy Good Night to the Academic Year, A. Ted Pauker. NOBL
Ground beneath my feet is cracked, The. Day Twenty-three. Victor Coleman. NOBC
Ground for the Floor. *Unknown.* OBET
Ground Hog. *See* Groundhog.
Ground is white with snow, The. Resolution. Ted Berrigan. OFD
Ground of contradictions, where motif, A. The Cemetery Is. Audrey McGaffin. NePoAm-2
Ground Swell. G. Stanley Koehler. NePoAm-2
Ground-Swell, The. E. J. Pratt. CaP
Ground twitches and the noble head, The. The Second Coming. Dannie Abse. NMP; NoAM
Groundhog, The. Richard Eberhart. CABA; CMoP; DTC; FaBoMo; FaFP; LiTA; LiTM; MasP; MiAP; MoAB; MoAmPo; MoPo; MoVE; NePA; NoAM; NoP; NU; PAI; PPoe; SeCeV; TAP; TwAmPo; UnPo; WaP
Groundhog, The. Luci Shaw. TrCP
Ground Hog [*or* Groundhog]. *Unknown.* FSW; TrAS, *with music*
Ground Hog Day. Lilian Moore. RHPC
Ground Hog Day. Marnie Pomeroy. PoSC
Groundhog Foreshadowed, The. Steven Sher. AMV-80
Groundhog is, at best, a simple soul, The. The Groundhog. Luci Shaw. TrCP
Ground Hog sleeps. Ground Hog Day. Lilian Moore. RHPC
Groundhog we dumped in the woods, The. Middle Age. Paula Rankin. MAYP
Group of jolly cowboys, discussing plans at ease, A. When the Work's All Done This Fall. *Unknown.* AS; BPAW; CoSo; FSW
Groups of Me. State Prison 4:00 P.M. Thomas G. Nickens. LFAC
Grove, The. Edwin Muir. LiTM; MoPo
Grove and Building. Edgar Bowers. NePoEA
Grove beyond the Barley, The. Alden Nowlan. MoCV
Grover Cleveland. Joel Benton. PAH
Groves are down, The. Gary Snyder. Myths and Texts: Logging, XIV. NaP
Groves of Blarney, The. Richard Alfred Millikin. FaBoPP; HBV-2; OnYI, *with add. verse by* Francis Sylvester Mahoney; OxBI; OxBoLi
Groves of Eden, vanished now so long, The. Pope. *Fr.* Windsor Forest. OAEL-1; OBEC
Groves were God's first temples, The. A Forest Hymn. Bryant. AA; AP; TAP
Grow old along with me! Rabbi Ben Ezra. Robert Browning. BLPL; FaBV; FaFP; FiP; HBV-1; MasP; OAEP; OBNC; OBVV; PoPl; TEP; TreFT; TRV; WGRP
Grow weary if you will, let me be sad. Lesbia. Richard Aldington. PoLF
Growing Gray. Austin Dobson. HBV-1
Growing in Grace. Jack Clemo. NOCV
Growing in the vale. Christina Rossetti. *Fr.* Sing-Song. TiPo
Growing need to be moving around it to see it, The. A View of the Brooklyn Bridge. William Meredith. MoVE
Growing Old. Matthew Arnold. FaFP; FiP; HBV-1; OAEL-2; PoEL-5; VLP

Growing Old. Byron. *Fr.* Don Juan, I. NOBE
("But now at thirty years my hair is grey.") SCV
Growing Old. Douglas Fraser. PoSH
Growing Old. Rose Henderson. RHPC
Growing Old. Walter Learned. HBV-1
Growing Old. *Unknown, tr. fr. Irish by* Frank O'Connor. ErPo; KiLC
(Autumn.) OBMV
Growing Old. Rollin J. Wells. TreFT; WBLP
Growing Old. Ella Wheeler Wilcox. *See* Interlude.
Growing old but not retiring. Ever On. *Unknown.* STF
Growing Older. R. G. Wells. BLPA
Growing Smiles. *Unknown.* PoLF
Growing Together. Joyce Carol Oates. IHMS
Growing Up. Harry Behn. PDV; RHPC; SiSoSe; SoPo
Growing Up. Linda Gregg. NPGG
Growing Wild. Jim Wayne Miller. GP
Growltiger's Last Stand. T. S. Eliot. FaBoCh; OBCA; PoPle; RoGo
"Grown men"/ those kids pissing into a clay bank. Cardrona Valley. Ian Wedde. OCNZ
Grown old in love from seven till seven times seven. Blake. FaBoEE; OAEL-2
Grown sick of war, and war's alarms. On the British King's Speech. Philip Freneau. PAH
Grown-up. Edna St. Vincent Millay. NoAM; PAI
Grownups. William Wise. TiPo
Growth can sit there from. Regenesis. Ron Welburn. NBP
Growth of Heptarchy we trace, The. Edward B. Goodwin. *Fr.* English History in Rhyme, or a Rhyming Epitome of the History of England, from B.C. 55 to A.D. 1872. FaBoUs
Growth of Love, The, *sels.* Robert Bridges
"For beauty being the best of all we know," VIII. VLP
"I will be what God made me, nor protest," LXII. VLP
"Man that sees by chance his picture, made, A," XXXIX. NoAM
O Weary Pilgrims, XXIII. MoAB; MoBrPo
"Spring hath her own bright days of calm and peace," XXIV. VLP
"They that in play can do the thing they would," I. NoAM
"Whole world now is but the minister, The," III. VLP
Gr-r-r—there go, my heart's abhorrence! Soliloquy of the Spanish Cloister. Robert Browning. CABA; DTo; FaBoCo; InPK; LiTB; NIP; NOBL; NoP; OAEL-2; OAEP; PAI; SeCeV; TEP; TrGrPo; TW
Grub Street Recessional, A. Christopher Morley. InMe
Grudges mend and wear and turn in winter. Household. Laura Jensen. LCAP
Gruesome. Roger McGough. AmMo
Gruesome ghoul, the grisly ghoul, The. The Ghoul. Jack Prelutsky. OBCA
Grumble Family, The. *Unknown.* WBLP
Grumbler Gruff, A. Oliver Herford. TDH
Grunion. Myra Cohn Livingston. RFM
Grunion. Wendy Rose. CDW
Gryll/ Had his fill. Gryll's State. Roy Blount, Jr. OBAL
Gryll eates, but ne're sayes grace; to speak the troth. Upon Gryll. Robert Herrick. AnAnS-2
Gryll Grange, *sel.* Thomas Love Peacock.
Love and Age. HBV-1; OBEV; OBNC; PoPle; ViBoPo
Gryll's State. Roy Blount, Jr. OBAL
Guadalajara Hospital. Ai. MAYP
Guadalupe, W.I. Nicolás Guillén, *tr. fr. Spanish by* Anselm Hollo. TTY
Guantanamera. Jose Marti, *ad. fr. Spanish by* Pete Seeger *and* Hector Angulo. FSW
Guard. Michael C. Martin. WaP
Guard at the Binh Thuy Bridge, The. John Balaban. FYAP
Guard has a right to despair, The. He stands by God. In Galleries. Randall Jarrell. EyDe
Guard of the Sepulcher, A. Edwin Markham. WGRP
Guard Thy Tongue. Alice M. Barr. STF
Guarded Wound, The. Adelaide Crapsey. WPE
Guardian Angel, The. Robert Browning. GoBC; HBV-2
Guardian Angel. Cardinal Newman. GoBC
Guardian Angels. Spenser. *Fr.* The Faerie Queene, II, 8. OBSC
("And is there care in heaven? and is there love?") NOCV; OAEL-1; OxBoCh
(Bright Squadrons, The.) GoBC
Guardians, The. Geoffrey Hill. NePoEA-2; NoP
Guarding the doors of the Hispanic Society. The Spanish Lions. Phyllis McGinley. NYBP
Gubbinal. Wallace Stevens. SOTW
Gude and Godlie Ballatis, The, *sel.* *Unknown.* Till Christ. OxBS
Gude Lord Graeme is to Carlisle gane. The Bewick and the Graeme. *Unknown.* OxBB
Gude Lord Scroop's to the huntin gane. Hughie Grame. *Unknown.* ESPB
Gude Wallace. *Unknown.* ESPB (A *and* G *vers.*)
Gudrun of old days. The First Lay of Gudrun. *Unknown, tr. by* William Morris *and* Eirikr Magnusson. *Fr.* The Elder Edda. AWP
Guerdon, The. John James Piatt. AA
Guerdon of the Sun, The. George Sterling. HBMV
Guernica. James Lewisohn. LFAC
Guerrilla Handbook, A. Amiri Baraka. PoBA
Guess what I have gone and done. My Invention. Shel Silverstein. PV; QQQ
Guess who is this creature. A Song to the Wind. Taliessin, *tr. by* A. P. Graves. FaBoCh
Guessed you but how I loved you, watched your smile. To W. J. M. "G. G." PeHV
Guessing. *Unknown, tr. fr. Burmese by* U Win Pe. PBWP
Guest, The. Wendell Berry. AP
Guest. D. J. Enright. OxBC
Guest, The. Harriet McEwen Kimball. AA
Guest. E. A. Lacey. PeHV
Guest, The. Pentti Saarikoski, *tr. fr. Finnish by* Anselm Hollo. PV
Guest, The. *Unknown.* EaLo; EBCP; GoBC; OBS; OxBoCh; TrCP
(Coming of the King, The.) TrGrPo
(Guests.) EvOK
(Preparations.) NOBE; OBEV; PoPle
(Royal Guest, A.) CH
(Yet If His Majesty, Our Sovereign Lord.) FaBoCh; NoP; PoRA; ViBoPo
Guest for whom I did not care, A. Lines Scratched in Wet Cement. Ethel Jacobson. ShM
Guest Lecturer. Darwin T. Turner. BALP
Guests. *Unknown.* *See* Guest, The.
Guests, The. Louis Zukofsky. CoPo
Guests in their summer colors have fled, The. The Last Picnic. Stanley Kunitz. NoAM
Guid day now, bonnie Robin. Robin Redbreast's Testament. *Unknown.* GBP
Guid-Mornin to Your Majesty! Burns. *Fr.* A Dream. NAs
Guidance. Cardinal Newman. *See* Pillar of the Cloud, The.
Guide, The Arthur Gregor. GP
Guide and Friend. *Unknown.* BLRP
Guide me, O thou great Jehovah. The Christian Pilgrim's Hymn [*or* The Divine Hand]. William Williams. BLRP; WGRP
Guide to Familiar American Incest, A, *sel.* Dennis Saleh.
Inventing a Family. NeAC
Guide to Jerusalem. Dennis Silk. VWA
Guide to the Ruins. Howard Nemerov. EyDe
Guide to the Symphony. Weldon Kees. VGW
Guided Missiles Experimental Range. Robert Conquest. OxBC
Guido, I would that Lapo, thou, and I. Sonnet: To Guido Cavalcanti [*or* Sonnet: Dante Alighieri to Guido Cavalcanti]. Dante, *tr. by* Shelley. AWP; OBVE
Guidwife when your guidman's from home. Could You Do That? Burns. UnTE
Guild's Signal. Bret Harte. PaPo
Guilielmus Rex. Thomas Bailey Aldrich. AA
Guilt and Sorrow, *sel.* Wordsworth.
Salisbury Plain and Stonehenge. FaBoPP
Guilt unavowed is guilt in its extreme. Error Pursued. H. A. Pinkerton. NePoAm
Guilty. Marguerite Wilkinson. TRV
Guilty have fewer dreams, The. Solutions. David Barton. AMV-81
"Guilty or Not Guilty?" *Unknown.* BeLS; BLPA
Guinea. Jacques Roumain, *tr. fr. French by* Langston Hughes. TTY
Guinea-Pig, The. *Unknown.* NA
(Guinea-Pig Song, A.) OxBChV
("There was a little guinea-pig.") OxNR
Guinevere, *sel.* Tennyson.
"I made them lay their hands in mine and swear." TRV
Guitar. Federico García Lorca, *tr. fr. Spanish by* Keith Waldrop. InPK
Guitar. David St. John. MAYP
Guitarist Tunes Up, The. Frances Cornford. ELU; SoSe
Gulbeyaz. Byron. *Fr.* Don Juan, V. PoEL-4
Gulf, The. Denise Levertov. NNaP
Gulf, The. Derek Walcott. NoP
Gulf Stream, The. Henry Bellamann. EtS
Gulf Stream. "Susan Coolidge." AA; EtS
Gulf-Weed. Cornelius George Fenner. EtS
Gulfs of blue air, two lochs like spectacles. High Up on Suilven. Norman MacCaig. PoSH
Gulistan, The, *sels.* Sadi, *tr. fr. Persian.*
Alas! *tr. by* L. Cranmer-Byng. AWP
Courage, *tr. by* Sir Edwin Arnold. AWP
Friendship, *tr. by* L. Cranmer-Byng. AWP
Gift of Speech, The, *tr. by* L. Cranmer-Byng. AWP

He Hath No Parallel, *tr. by* L. Cranmer-Byng. AWP
Help, *tr. by* Sir Edwin Arnold. AWP
Hyacinths to Feed Thy Soul. BLPA; BLPL; FaBoBe; TRV
Love's Last Resource, *tr. by* L. Cranmer-Byng. AWP
Mesnevi, *tr. by* L. Cranmer-Byng. AWP
On the Deception of Appearances, *tr. by* L. Cranmer-Byng. AWP
Sooth-Sayer, The, *tr. by* Sir Edwin Arnold. AWP
Take the Crust, *tr. by* L. Cranmer-Byng. AWP
Wealth, *tr. by* Sir Edwin Arnold. AWP
Gull. William Jay Smith. TiPo
Gull, ballast of its wings. Stabilities. Anne Stevenson. NCSH
Gull Decoy, The, *with music.* Larry Gorman. ShS
Gull Goes Up, A. Léonie Adams. WHA
Gull, it is said, The. Nakasuk, *tr. fr. Eskimo.* WTO
Gull Lake Reunion. Kelly Ivie. AMV-81
Gull Lake set in the rolling prairie. At Gull Lake; August, 1810. Duncan Campbell Scott. NOBC; OBCV
Gull shall whistle in his wake, the blind wave break in fire, The. The Voortrekker. Kipling. HBV-1
Gull, up close, A. Seagulls. John Updike. Psk
Gulling Sonnets, *sel.* Sir John Davies.
Gulling Sonnet, A, I. ElL
Gulliver. Sylvia Plath. NOBA
Gulls. Barbara Howes. BoAnP
Gulls. E. A. Muir. NCSH
Gulls. William Carlos Williams. FaBoEn; NoP; OxBA; TwAmPo
Gulls and Dreams. Lionel Stevenson. CaP
Gulls in an äery morrice. W. E. Henley. PBBP
Gulls spiral high above. Dayley Island. Frederick Seidel. CoPo
Gulls, that live by the water and hang around docks. Random Reflections on a Cloudless Sunday. John Hall Wheelock. NePoAm
Gulls when they fly move in a liquid arc. A Gull Goes Up. Léonie Adams. WHA
Gumble. Michael Dugan. RHPC
Gun full swing the swimmer catapults and cracks, The. 400-Meter Freestyle. Maxine W. Kumin. LiSp; SoSe
Gun Teams. Gilbert Frankau. OxBTC
Gun, the trap, the axe are borne, The. Revenge of the Hunted. R. A. D. Ford. LiSp; MoCV
Gunfighter. Gerald Locklin. AMV-80
Gunga. Rachel Field. *Fr.* A Circus Garland. OBCA
(Elephant, The.) SoPo
Gunga Din. Kipling. BrPo; EBVV; FaFP; FPL; HBV-2; LiTB; MoBrPo; OnMSP; PoPl; TreF; VLP
Gunner. Randall Jarrell. OFD; PAI
Gunner, The. Francis Webb. CBAP
Gunpowder Plot, The. *Unknown.* FaBoUs
("Please to remember.") OxNR
Guns. Ronald Crowe. AMV-81
Guns. John Woods. GP
Guns are hushed, The. On every field once flowing. The Rear Guard. Irene Fowler Brown. PAH
Guns in the Grass, The. Thomas Frost. PAH
Guns know what is what, but underneath, The. Memories of a Lost War. Louis Simpson. NePoAm; OBWP; VGW
Guns spell money's ultimate reason, The. Ultima Ratio Regum. Stephen Spender. CMoP; FaFP; LiTB; LiTM; OAEL-2; OBWP; SeCePo; WaaP; WaP
Gunslinger, *sels.* Edward Dorn.
"I met in Mesilla." NoAM
Idle Visitation, An. NOBA
Gup, Scot! John Skelton. OxBoLi
Gus: The Theatre Cat. T. S. Eliot. CenHV; OBCA; OxBTC
Gus the Greek is a short-order cook. Greasy Spoon Blues. Len Gasparini. NeAC
Gustavo said. What the Rooster Does before Mounting. Cyn Zarco. BrSi
Gusts of the sun race on the approaching sea. Of Thomas Traherne and the Pebble Outside. Sydney Clouts. VWA
Gusty and raw was the morning, a fog hung over the seas. The Fight of Paso del Mar. Bayard Taylor. BeLS
Gut eats all day, and lechers all the night. On Gut. Ben Jonson. AnAnS-2; JCP; NoP
Guthlac, *sel.* Cynewulf, *tr. fr. Anglo-Saxon.*
Death of Saint Guthlac. ACP
Gutter, The. Franco Fortini, *tr. fr. Italian by* Ruth Feldman. VWA
Guttural Muse, The. Seamus Heaney. NoP
Guvener [*or* Gineral] B. is a sensible man. What Mr. Robinson Thinks. James Russell Lowell. The Biglow Papers, 1st Series, No. III. AA; AmPP; HBV-1; InMe; PAH; YaD
Guy. Emerson. NOBA
Guy asked two jays at St. Louis, A. Two Jays at St. Louis. Ferdinand G. Christgau. TDH
Guy Mannering, *sels.* Sir Walter Scott.
Nativity Chant, The. ChTr; FaBoCh; NAs
Twist Ye, Twine Ye! Even So, *fr. ch.* 4. EnRP
Wasted, Weary, Wherefore Stay, *fr. ch.* 27. EnRP
Guyana. Fern Pankratz Ruth. AMV-80
Guys and Dolls. Frank Loesser. OBAL
Gwalia Deserta, *sel.* Idris Davies.
"O what can you give me?" DTC
G'way an' quit dat noise, Miss Lucy. When Malindy Sings. Paul Laurence Dunbar. PoBA; PoNe
Gwendoline. Bayard Taylor. BXAP
Gwendolyn Brooks. Don L. Lee. NoAM
Gwine to Alabamy, *with music.* *Unknown.* TrAS
Gwine to Run All Night; or, De Camptown Races. Stephen Collins Foster. *See* Camptown Races, The.
Gwine Up, *with music.* *Unknown.* BoAN-1
Gwineter Ride Up in de Chariot Soon-a in de Mornin', *with music.* *Unknown.* BoAN-2
Gwinter Sing All Along de Way, *with music.* *Unknown.* BoAN-1
Gyang ower by Rothiemurchus whan the snaw lies thick. Rothiemurchus. Colin Lamont. PoSH
Gyges' ring they bear about them still, A. Lovers How They Come and Part. Robert Herrick. GBL; OxBoLi; PoEL-3
Gymnasiad, The, or Boxing Match, *sel.* Paul Whitehead.
"As when two monarchs of the brindled breed." NOEC
Gypsies. *See also* Gipsies.
Gypsies. John Clare. *See* Gipsies ("The snow falls deep; the forest lies alone").
Gypsies. John Langhorne. *Fr.* The Country Justice. NOEC
Gypsies. Alden Nowlan. NeAC
Gypsies [*or* Gipsies] came to our good lord's gate, The. The Gypsy [*or* Gipsy] Laddie. *Unknown.* BSV; ESPB; HAP
Gypsies came to our Lord's yett, The. Johny Faa. *Unknown.* OxBB
Gypsies carry sacks of walnuts out of the groves, The. Coleridge Crossing the Plain of Jars; 1833. Norman Dubie. LCAP
Gypsies in the Wood. *Unknown.* DTC; OxBoLi
("My mother said.") OxNR; PoPle
Gypsies Metamorphosed, *sels.* Ben Jonson.
All Your Fortunes We Can Tell Ye. ChTr
Faery Beam upon You, The. EBEV; TEP
(Faeries' Song, The.) SeCV-1
(Gypsy Song.) FaBoCh
(Patrico's Song.) LoBV
Gypsies passed her little gate, The. The Dreamers. Theodosia Garrison. HBMV
Gypsies' Road, The. Dora Sigerson Shorter. OBVV
Gypsies [*or* Gipsies] they came to [my] Lord Cassilis' yett [*or* gate], The. The Gypsy Laddie [*or* Jackie Faa *or* Johnny Faa]. ChTr; EnSB; ESPB; FaBoBa; ViBoFo
Gypsy. Josephine Miles. NoAM
Gypsy, The. Edward Thomas. HeIP; NoAM; NoP
Gypsy, a gypsy, A. Being Gypsy. Barbara Young. SoPo
Gypsy Bible, The. Julian Tuwim, *tr. fr. Polish by* Isaac Komem. VWA
Gypsy Countess, The. *Unknown.* OBET; PoPle
Gypsy Davy, The. *Unknown.* AmFP; AS, *with music*
(Gypsy Davey, *ad. by* Woody Guthrie.) FSW
Gypsy Girl, The. Henry Alford. HBV-1
Gypsy-Heart. Katharine Lee Bates. HBMV
Gypsy Jane. William Brighty Rands. *See* Gipsy Jane.
Gypsy Laddie, The. *Unknown.* *See* Wraggle Taggle Gipsies, The.
Gypsy Love Song, *with music.* Harry B. Smith. FSN
Gypsy-race my pity rarely move, The. Gypsies. John Langhorne. *Fr.* The Country Justice. NOEC
Gypsy Rover, The. *Unknown.* FSW
Gypsy woman told my mother, The. Hoochie Coochie. *Unknown.* BluL
Gyre's Galax. Norman Henry Pritchard II. PoBA
Gyres, The. W. B. Yeats. GTBS-P; HAP; NoAM

H

H. Baptisme ("Since, Lord, to thee/A narrow way and little gate"). George Herbert. *See* Holy Baptism.
H. Communion, The ("Not in rich furniture or fine aray"). George Herbert. AnAnS-1
H.M.S. *Hero.* Michael Roberts. OxBTC
H. M. S. Pinafore, *sels.* W. S. Gilbert.
Englishman, The. NOBL
First Lord's Song, The. TreFS
I Am the Captain of the Pinafore. TreFT

I Am the Monarch of the Sea. TreFT
Little Buttercup. TreFS
Sir Joseph's Song. LiTB
H. Rap Brown. Henry Blakely. CNA
H. S. Beeney Auction Sales. David R. Pichaske. AMV-81
H. Scriptures, The. George Herbert. AnAnS-1
H. Scriptures. Henry Vaughan. AnAnS-1
H—— [*or* H(ome)], thou return'st from Thames, whose Naiads long. An Ode on the Popular Superstitions of the Highlands of Scotland. William Collins. EnRP; LAuP; NOEC; OAEL-1; OAEP; OBEC
H was an indigent Hen. Limerick. Bruce Porter. NA
Ha! are there wood-ghosts in this solitude. La Belle Sauvage. John Hunter-Duvar. *Fr.* De Roberval. OBCV
Ha ha! ha ha! This world doth pass. Fara Diddle Dyno [*or* Madrigal]. *Unknown.* EIL; FaBoCh; FaBoCo; FaBaNo; LoBV; OxBoLi; ViBoPo
Ha Ha This-a-Way. Leadbelly (Huddie Ledbetter). FSW
Ha! Original Sin. Ogden Nash. FaBoCo
Ha! sir, I have seen you sniffing and snoozling. The Faun. Ezra Pound. FaBoCh; FaBoTw
Ha! Steward, how are you, my old boy? How to Tell Bad News. *Unknown.* TreF
Ha' we lost the goodliest fere o' all. Ballad of the Goodly Fere. Ezra Pound. CMoP; HBV-2; LiTA; LiTM; MoAB; MoAmPo; MoBS; NePA; NoAM; OFD; PoRA; TrCP; TrGrPo
Ha! whare ye gaun, ye crowlin' ferlie! To a Louse [on Seeing One on a Lady's Bonnet at Church]. Burns. BLPA; EnRP; FaFP; LiTB; InvP; NOEC; OAEP; OxBS; PrIm; SeCeV; TreF; ViBoPo
Haar in Princes Street. Alexander Scott. BSV
Haarlem Heights. Arthur Guiterman. PAH
Habakkuk. Edouard Roditi. VWA
Habana. Julian Bond. NNP
Habeas Corpus. Helen Hunt Jackson. AA; WGRP
Habeas Corpus Blues, The. Conrad Aiken. NYBP
Habit of Perfection, The. Gerard Manley Hopkins. ACP; BrPo; CoBMV; LiTB; MoAB; MoBrPo; NoAM; NoP; OAEP; OBEV; OBMV; PoPle; PoRA; TrGrPo; ViBoPo; VLP
"Elected Silence, sing to me," *sel.* UnS
Habitat, *sels.* Judith Wright.
"Charity lotteries for dream houses, The," VI. CBAP
"Furniture: humble, dependent," IV. CBAP
Habitation. Margaret Atwood. BoWoP
Habitations. Hilaire Belloc. PV
Habits of the Hippopotamus. Arthur Guiterman. BoAnP; FaBV; FiBHP; OBCA; OnUR; RHPC; TiPo
Habitue. Helen Frith Stickney. GoYe
Habla Usted Español? James Reiss. AmPA
Hack and Hew. Bliss Carman. CaP; HBV-2
Had a great ride boss. Artists Shouldnt Have Offspring. Don Marquis. *Fr.* Archys Life of Mehitabel. CrMA
Had a Little Fight in Mexico, *with music.* *Unknown.* OuSiCo
Had a piece of pie an' I had a piece of puddin'. Sally Goodin. *Unknown.* FSW
Had Cain been Scot, God would have changed his doom. On Scotland. John Cleveland. DBV; PV
Had Cowley ne'er spoke, Killigrew ne'er writ. Sir John Denham. FaBoEE
Had everyone Suum. To the Archbishop of Tuam. *Unknown.* FaBoEE
Had Gadyaa Kid, a Kid. *Unknown, tr. fr. Hebrew.* TrJP
Had hardly happened. The Victory of the Battle of Wounded Knee. Tom Parson. SOTS
"Had he and I but met." The Man He Killed. Thomas Hardy. BrPo; CMoP; CoBMV; DL; FaFP; FF; HAP; HeIP; InPS; LiTB; LiTM; MoAB; MoBrPo; NIP; OBWP; PAI; PoPl; TreF; WaaP; WeW; WHA
Had he but spar'd his Tongue and Pen. Swift. *Fr.* Verses On the Death of Dr. Swift. FaBoEn
Had I a Golden Pound. Francis Ledwidge. AnIV
Had I a heart for falsehood fram'd. Song. Sheridan. *Fr.* The Duenna, I. HBV-1; OBEC
Had I a voice of steel to tune my song. Christ's Triumph after Death. Giles Fletcher. *Fr.* Christ's Victory and Triumph, IV. LoBV
Had I been mindful of my high descent. Hadewijch, *tr. fr. Dutch by* Frans van Rosevelt. PBWP
Had I but lived a hundred years ago. At Lulworth Cove a Century Back. Thomas Hardy. ChMP
Had I but plenty of money, money enough and to spare. Up at a Villa—Down in the City. Robert Browning. FaBoPP; GTBS-P; HBV-1; NOBE; PoRA; PPP; SeCeV
Had I but strength enough, and time. Charles Robinson. BXAP
Had I but the torrent's might. The Death of Hoel. Thomas Gray. NOEC
Had I concealed my love. Love Song. Elinor Wylie. BLPL
Had I lived till now. Poem for the Year Twenty Twenty. Al Lee. AmPA
Had I my wish I would distend my guts. The Extravagant Drunkard's Wish. Edward Ward. NOEC
Had I not cradled you in my arms. Pocahontas to Her English Husband, John Rolfe. Paula Gunn Allen. STE
Had I not seen him by a swerve of eye. Heron in Swamp. Frances Minturn Howard. GoYe
Had I that haze of streaming blue. In Phæacia. James Elroy Flecker. HBMV
Had I the Choice. Walt Whitman. PP; SoSe
Had I the heavens' embroidered cloths. Aedh [*or* He] Wishes for the Cloths of Heaven. W. B. Yeats. CMoP; MoBrPo; NoAM; OBEV; OBVV; OLR; SOTW
Had I the power. The Queen's Song. James Elroy Flecker. BrPo; HBV-2
Had I the power/ To cast a bell. A Bell. Clinton Scollard. AA
Had Lucan hid the truth to please the time. To the Translator of Lucan's Pharsalia (1614). Sir Walter Ralegh. SiPS
Had me a cat, the cat pleased me. Fiddle-I-Fee. *Unknown.* AmFP
Had mournful Ovid been to Brent condemned. William Diaper. *Fr.* Brent; a Poem to Thomas Palmer Esq. OBSV
Had perfect pitch. Aunt Melissa. R. T. Smith. Str
Had Sacharissa liv'd when Mortals made. At Penshurst [Another]. Edmund Waller. AnAnS-2; OAEL-1; SeCV-1
Had she come all the way for this. The Haystack in the Floods. William Morris. BeLS; CABA; EBEV; EBVV; HAP; LoBV; NBM; NoP; OAEL-2; OAEP; OBNC; OBNV; PoEL-5; PoRA; SeCeV; VLP; WeW; WHA
Had Sorrow Ever Fitter Place. Samuel Daniel. *Fr.* Hymn's Triumph. EIL (Sorrow.) OBSC
Had there been peace there never had been riven. Dedication. Drummond Allison. FaBoTw
Had this effulgence disappeared. Composed upon an Evening of Extraordinary Splendour and Beauty. Wordsworth. EnRP; OAEL-2
"Had we a king," said Wallace then. Gude Wallace. *Unknown.* ESPB
Had we but world enough, and time. To His Coy Mistress. Andrew Marvell. AnAnS-1; AWP; BiP; BoLoP; CABA; CavP; EBEV; ELP; EnLoPo; ErPo; FaBoEn; FaBV; FaFP; FF; FPL; GBL; HAP; HBV-1; HeIP; HoPM; InPK; InPS; InvP; JCP; LiTB; LoBV; MasP; MAT; MeLP; MePo; NIP; NOBE; NoP; OAEL-1; OAEP; OBEV; OBS; PAI; PoEl-2; PoLF; PoPl; PoPle; PoRA; PPoe; PPP; PrIm; SCV; SeCePo; SeCeV; SeCP; SeCV-1; SoSe; TEP; TreFT; TrGrPo; UnPo; UnTE; ViBoPo; WeW; WHA
Had we but world enough, and time. To His Coy Mistress. Stanley J. Sharpless. BXAP
Had we two met, blythe-hearted Burns. Walter Savage Landor. FaBoEE
Hadad, *sel.* James Abraham Hillhouse.
Demon-Lover, The. AA
Hadn't heard of the atom bomb. The Seals in Penobscot Bay. Daniel Hoffman. MP; TwCP
Hadn't I been. Distance. Robert Creeley. CoPo
Hadrian's Address to His Soul When Dying. Emperor Hadrian, *tr. fr. Latin by* Byron. OBVE
(Adriani Morientis ad Animam Suam, *tr. by* Matthew Prior.) OBVE
(Emperor Hadrian to His Soul, The, *tr. by* Stevie Smith.) OBVE
(Emperor Hadrian's Dying Address to His Soul, *tr. unknown.*) TreFT
("My little soul, my vagrant charmer," *tr. by* J. V. Cunningham.) OBVE
(To His Soul, *tr. by* Elinor Wylie.) PoPl
Hae ye ivver been at Elsdon? At Elsdon. George Chatt. FaBoPP
Hae ye smelt the tang o heather. Wine o Living. Matt Marshall. PoSH
"Haec Olim Meminisse Iuvabit." Deems Taylor. InMe
Haemorrhage. Padraic Fiacc. CIP
Hag, The ("The hag is astride"). Robert Herrick. CaPo; FaBoCh; PoSC; WiR; WSC
Hag, The ("The staff is now greased"). Robert Herrick. CaPo; FaBoCh; PoSC; WiR; WSC
Hag and the Slavies, The. La Fontaine, *tr. fr. French by* Edward Marsh. AWP; OBVE
Hag of Beare, The. *Unknown, tr. fr. Irish by* John Montague. BIrV; CIP; PBWP, *abr.;* OBVE, *tr. by* Lady Gregory
(Old Woman of Beare, The.) AnIL, *tr. by* Frank O'Connor; KiLC, *tr. by* Frank O'Connor; OnYI, *abr., tr. by* Kuno Meyer
(Old Woman of Beare Regrets Lost Youth, The, *tr. by* Frank O'Connor.) OBMV
(Woman of Beare, The, *tr. by* Stephen Gwynn.) AnIV
Hag-ridden. Robert Graves. BIrV
Hagar. Francis Lauderdale Adams. OxBS
Hagar. Elisabeth Eybers, *tr. fr. Afrikaans by author.* PeSA
Hagar and Ishmael. Else Lasker-Schüler, *tr. fr. German.* BoWoP, *tr. by* Rosemarie Waldrop; VWA, *tr. by* Joachim Neugroschel
Hagar to Ishmael. Deborah Eibel. VWA
Haggadah. A. M. Klein. TrJP
Hagiograph. Rayner Heppenstall. NeBP
Hai. Stuart Z. Perkoff. VWA
Hai! daughter of the Thundercloud. Dance-Song of the Lightning. *Unknown.* PeSA

Haidée ("It was the cooling hour, just when the rounded"). Byron. *Fr.* Don Juan, II. OBRV
(Haidée and Don Juan.) OBNC
("It was the cooling hour, just when the rounded.") ViBoPo
Haidee ("One of the two, according to your choice"). Byron. *Fr.* Don Juan, IV. SeCePo
Haifa. Dovid Knut, *tr. fr. Russian by* Daniel Weissbort. VWA
Haiku: "August heat." Gerald Vizenor. VoR
Haiku: "Autumn's bright moon." Kaga no Chiyo, *tr. fr. Japanese by* R. H. Blyth. PBWP
Haiku: "Balmy spring wind, A." Richard Wright. FAZ
Haiku: "Bitter morning, A." J. W. Hackett. BoAnP
Haiku: "Coming from the woods." Richard Wright. FAZ
Haiku: "Crow flew so fast, The." Richard Wright. FAZ
Haiku: "Dew of the rouge-flower, The." Kaga no Chiyo, *tr. fr. Japanese by* R. H. Blyth. PBWP
Haiku: "Dog's violent sneeze, The." Richard Wright. FAZ
Haiku: "Eastern guard tower." Etheridge Knight. BPo; NeAC; NoAM; TAP
Haiku: "Empty sickbed, An." Richard Wright. FAZ
Haiku: "Even in my village." Kyorai, *tr. fr. Japanese by* Lucien Stryk *and* Takashi Ikemoto. FAZ
Haiku: "Falling flower, A." Moritake, *tr. fr. Japanese by* Babette Deutsch. SoSe
(Haiku: "Fallen flowers rise," *tr. by* Harold G. Henderson.) SoSe
Haiku: "Fish shop." Basho, *tr. fr. Japanese by* Lucien Stryk *and* Takashi Ikemoto. FAZ
Haiku: "Green cockleburs, The." Richard Wright. FAZ
Haiku: "Halo of the moon, The." Buson, *tr. fr. Japanese.* MOON
Haiku: "I would like a bell." Richard Wright. FAZ
Haiku: "Just enough of rain." Richard Wright. FAZ
Haiku: "Lightning gleam, A." Basho, *tr. fr. Japanese by* Harold G. Henderson. SoSe
(Haiku: "Lightning flashes, The!" *tr. by* Earl Miner.) SoSe
Haiku: "Moor:/ point my horse." Basho, *tr. fr. Japanese by* Lucien Stryk *and* Takashi Ikemoto. FAZ
Haiku: "No need to cling." Joso, *tr. fr. Japanese by* Lucien Stryk *and* Takashi Ikemoto. FAZ
Haiku: "Plum-viewing." Buson, *tr. fr. Japanese by* Lucien Stryk *and* Takashi Ikemoto. FAZ
Haiku: "Seaweed/ between rocks." Kito, *tr. fr. Japanese by* Lucien Stryk *and* Takashi Ikemoto. FAZ
Haiku: "Spring rain." Kaga no Chiyo, *tr. fr. Japanese by* R. H. Blyth. PBWP
Haiku: "These branches." Joso, *tr. fr. Japanese by* Lucien Stryk *and* Takashi Ikemoto. FAZ
Haiku: "Things long forgotten." Masaoka Shiki, *tr. fr. Japanese by* Lucien Stryk *and* Takashi Ikemoto. FAZ
Haiku: "Why is the hail so wild." Richard Wright. FAZ
Haiku: "Winter rain at night." Richard Wright. FAZ
Haiku Ambulance. Richard Brautigan. InPK
Haiku, for Cinnamon. Lillie D. Chaffin. PH
Haiku, you ku, he. The Traditional Grammarian as Poet. Ted Hipple. POL
Hail, aged God who lookest on thy Father. He Prayeth for Ink and Palette That He May Write. *Unknown, tr. by* Robert Hillyer. *Fr.* Book of the Dead. AWP
Hail and beware the dead who will talk life until you are blue/ in the face. A Newly Discovered "Homeric" Hymn. Charles Olson. NeAP; NoAM; PoM
Hail and Farewell. Anne Higginson Spicer. HBMV
Hail and farewell! Lo, I am the last of a glorious fleet of sail. The Last Gloucesterman. Gordon Grant. EtS
Hail be thou, Mary, maiden bright. The Five Joys. *Unknown.* OxBM
Hail, beauteous Dian, queen of shades. Hymn to Diana. Thomas Heywood. *Fr.* The Golden Age. EIL
Hail, beauteous stranger of the grove [*or* wood]! To the Cuckoo. Michael Bruce, *revised by* John Logan. BSV; HBV-1; NOEC; OBEC; OBEV; PBBP; ViBoPo
Hail, Bishop Valentine. John Donne. *Fr.* An Epithalamion on the Lady Elizabeth and Count Palatine Being Married on St. Valentine's Day. ChTr
("Hail, Bishop Valentine, whose day this is.") OFD
Hail, blessed Virgin, full of heavenly grace. On the Infancy of Our Saviour. Francis Quarles. OBS; OxBoCh; SeCePo
Hail, blissfulest maiden. On the Annunciation. *Unknown, tr. by* Shane Leslie. ISi
Hail, bright morning beam! The Dream. Francis Burdett Money-Coutts. OBVV
Hail, Columbia. Joseph Hopkinson. AA; BLSo, *with music;* FaBoBe; FaFP; PAH; PAL; TreFS; YaD
Hail, Comly and Clene. *Unknown. Fr.* The Second Shepherd's Play. NAs
(Haylle, Comly and Clene.) OBEV; OxBoli
(Shepherds at Bethlehem, The.) ChTr
Hail, Dionysos. Dudley Randall. BPo
Hail, door, to husband and to father dear! Dialogue with a Door. Catullus, *tr. by* John Nott. UnTE
Hail, ever-pleasing Solitude! Hymn on Solitude. James Thomson. NOEC
Hail, Fair Morning. *Unknown, tr. fr. Late Middle Irish by* Standish Hayes O'Grady. *Fr.* The Life of St. Cellach of Killala. OnYI
Hail, Father! whose creating call. Hymn to God the Father. Samuel Wesley. OxBoCh
Hail, fathers, hail! Flute Song. *Tr. fr. Hopi Indian by* Natalie Curtis. WTO
Hail, favour'd casement!—where the sight. William Combe. *Fr.* Dr. Syntax in Search of the Picturesque. OBRV
Hail, Freedom! thy bright crest. New National Hymn. Francis Marion Crawford. PAH
Hail, Glasgow! famed for ilka thing. John Mayne. *Fr.* Glasgow. BSV
Hail, glorious edifice, stupendous work! Loyal Effusion. Horace Smith *and* James Smith. OBRV
Hail, God revived in glory! Hymn to Horus. Mathilde Blind. OBVV
Hail, great Apollo! guide my feeble pen. The British Lyon Roused. Stephen Tilden. PAH
Hail, guest! We ask not what thou art. America Greets an Alien. *Unknown.* PAL; PGD
Hail! Hail! Hail! A Dance Chant. *Unknown, tr. by* E. S. Parker. WGRP
Hail, hail to thy blessed name, O Mary. Salutation. Zerea Jacob, *tr. by* F. Baetman. ISi
Hail, happy bride, for thou art truly blest! On the Death of Mrs. Bowes. Lady Mary Wortley Montagu. BoWoP
Hail, happy Britain, Freedom's blest retreat. "Prophecy." Gulian Verplanck. PAH
Hail, happy day, when, smiling like the morn. To the Right Honourable William, Earl of Dartmouth. Phillis Wheatley. AmPP; SBG
Hail, happy lot of the laborious man. Poverty, in Imitation of Milton. Samuel Jones. NOEC
Hail happy William, thou art strangely great. A Panegyric. *Unknown.* APAS
Hail hi'roglyphick state machin. Daniel Defoe. *Fr.* A Hymn to the Pillory. NCEP
Hail! Ho! A Sea-Song from the Shore. James Whitcomb Riley. TiPo
Hail, Holy Land. Thomas Tillam. *See* Uppon the First Sight of New England, June 29, 1638.
Hail, holy Lead!—of human feuds the great. Ambrose Bierce. *Fr.* The Devil's Dictionary. OBAL
Hail, Holy Light. Milton. *Fr.* Paradise Lost, III. FiP; LoBV; WHA
("Hail, holy light, offspring of Heaven first-born.") OAEL-1; OAEP; SCV; ViBoPo
(Holy Light.) NOBE
(Hymn to Light.) FaBoEn
(Light.) LiTB; OBEV; OBS
Hail, Jesus' Virgin-Mother ever Blest. Votive Ode. Erasmus, *tr. by* J. T. Walford. ISi
Hail! King I thee call. A Lyric from a Play. *Unknown.* MeEL
Hail, Maiden Root. Caelius Sedulius, *tr. fr. Latin by* Raymond F. Roseliep. *Fr.* Carmen Paschale. ISi
Hail Mary!/ Ich am sary. *Unknown.* OxBM
Hail Mary, full of grace, it once was said. An Epigram to the Queen Then Lying In. Ben Jonson. SBVL
Hail, mediocrity, beneath whose spell. Roy Campbell. *Fr.* The Georgiad. MoBrPo
Hail mer-/ry, tricky, and clandestine. Ode to Pornography. Jack Anderson. PoA
Hail, mildly pleasing solitude. Hymn on Solitude. James Thomson. OBEC
Hail! Mother-Maid, unmatched since time was born. Salutations: To Mary, Virgin. *Unknown, tr. by* Raymond F. Roseliep. ISi
Hail, Mother of the Savior. Adam of Saint Victor, *tr. fr. Latin by* Digby S. Wrangham. ISi
Hail, Muse! et caetera.—We left Juan sleeping. Byron. *Fr.* Don Juan, III. OAEL-2
Hail native Language, that by sinews weak. Milton. *Fr.* At a Vacation Exercise in the College [Part Latin, Part English]. JCP; OBS; PP
Hail, O most worthy in all the world! Advent Lyrics, IX. *Unknown, tr. by* Charles W. Kennedy. *Fr.* Christ 1. AnOE
Hail O ye seven pupils. On a School-Teacher. *Unknown, tr. by* Dudley Fitts. GLGT
Hail, Oh Hail to the King, *with music.* Beatrice Quickenden. AH
Hail, old October, bright and chill. Old October. Thomas Constable. HBV-1
Hail, old patrician trees, so great and good! Of Solitude [*or* Essay on Solitude]. Abraham Cowley. OBS; ViBoPo

Hail Our Incarnate God! *with music.* William Duke. AH
Hail, pious days! thou most propitious time. On the Sentence Passed by the House of Lords on Dr. Sacheverell. *Unknown.* APAS
Hail sacred shades! cool, leavy house! Upon the Priory Grove, His Usual Retirement. Henry Vaughan. FaBoPP
Hail Saint Michael with thy longe spere! *See* Hail, St. Michael with the long spear!
Hail[e], sister springs! Saint Mary Magdalene; or, The Weeper. Richard Crashaw. AnAnS-1; MeLP; MePo; OAEL-1; OBEV; SeCP; SeCV-1; ViBoPo
Hail sons of generous valor. To the Defenders of New Orleans. Joseph Rodman Drake. PAH
Hail Sovereign Queen of secrets, who hast power. Shakespeare, *and* John Fletcher. *Fr.* The Two Noble Kinsmen. PoEL-2
Hail, St. Michael with the [*or* thy] long spear! A Satire on the People of Kildare [*or* An Irish Satire]. *Unknown, at. to* Friar Michael of Kildare, *mod. vers. by* St. John Seymour. OnYI; OxBM
Hail, Star of the Sea. Star of the Sea. Richard Webb Sullivan. ISi
Hail [*or* Haile *or* Hale] sterne superne! Hail in eterne. Ballad of Our Lady [*or* A Hymn to Mary]. William Dunbar. ACP; MeEL; OxBS
Hail, sword of Carroll! Oft hast thou been in the great woof of war. The Song of Carroll's Sword. *At. to* Dallan MacMore, *tr. by* Kuno Meyer. OnYI
Hail, Sympathy! thy soft idea brings. William Lisle Bowles. Byron. *Fr.* English Bards and Scotch Reviewers. OBNC
Hail! the Glorious Golden City. Felix Adler. AH, *with music;* WGRP
Hail then ye daring few! who proudly soar. The Air Balloon. Henry James Pye. *Fr.* Aerophorion. NOEC
Hail, thou Great God in thy Boat. He Embarketh in the Boat of Ra. *Unknown, tr. by* Robert Hillyer. *Fr.* Book of the Dead. AWP
Hail, Thou great mysterious Being! Alexander McLachlan. *Fr.* God. CaP
Hail thou most sacred venerable thing! Hymn to Darkness. John Norris. MePo; OBS; OxBoCh
Hail thou, my native soil! thou blessed plot. The Frolic Mariners of Devon. William Browne. *Fr.* Britannia's Pastorals, II, Song III. ChTr
Hail, thou who shinest from the moon. He Establisheth His Triumph. *Unknown, tr. by* Robert Hillyer. *Fr.* Book of the Dead. AWP
Hail to Hobson! Hail to Hobson! hail to all the valiant set! The Men of the *Merrimac.* Clinton Scollard. PAH
Hail to the Brightness of Zion's Glad Morning, *with music.* Thomas Hastings. AH
(Latter Day, The.) AA
Hail to the Chief Who in Triumph Advances! Sir Walter Scott. *Fr.* The Lady of the Lake, II. EnRP
(Boat Song.) OAEP; PoEL-4
Hail to the Headlong! the Headlong Ap-Headlong! Chorus. Thomas Love Peacock. *Fr.* Headlong Hall. OBRV
Hail to the Joyous Day, *with music.* Royall Tyler. AH
Hail to the land whereon we tread. New England. James Gates Percival. AA
Hail to the Queen, *with music. Unknown.* AH
Hail to the Sabbath Day, *with music.* Stephen Greenleaf Bulfinch. AH
Hail to the Town of Limerick. Langford Reed. TDH
Hail to thee. The Carnation. Paul Hannigan. POL
Hail to thee, beautiful, mighty, and golden! Deirdre's Song at Sunrise. Sister Maura. CaP
Hail to Thee, Blithe Owl. Ring Lardner. OBAL
Hail to thee, blithe roadster! To a Bicycle. *Unknown.* BXAP
Hail to thee, blithe Spirit! To a Skylark [*or* Ode to a Skylark]. Shelley. BoAnP; EnRP; FaBoBe; FaBV; FaFP; FaPON; FPL; GN; GTBS; GTBS-P; HAP; HBV-1; HBVY; InPS; InvP; LiTB; LoBV; NOBE; NoP; OAEL-2; OAEP; OBEV; OBNC; OBRV; OHFP; PB; PBBP; PoLF; RoGo; TEP; TreFS; TrGrPo; WHA
Hail to thee, gallant foe. Cervera. Bertrand Shadwell. PAH
Hail to thee, our Savior's mother! Hail, Mother of the Savior. Adam of Saint Victor, *tr. by* Digby S. Wrangham. ISi
Hail, Tranquil Hour of Closing Day, *with music.* Leonard Bacon. AH
Hail Wedded Love! Jay Macpherson. MoCV
Hail wedded love, mysterious law, true source. Their Wedded Love. Milton. *Fr.* Paradise Lost, IV. BiP; OBS; SeCePo
Haile from the dead, or from eternity. Lines on a Purple Cap Received as a Present from My Brother. George Alsop. SCAP
Haile gracefull morning of eternall Daye. William Alabaster. AnAnS-1
Haile great Redeemer, man, and God, all haile. A Hymne to Our Saviour on the Crosse. George Chapman. PoEL-2
Haile, sister springs. *See* Hail, sister springs.
Haile! sterne superne. *See* Hail, sterne superne.
Haile wedded love, mysterious law, true source. *See* Hail wedded love . . .
Haill! Quene of Heven and steren of blis. A Little Hymn to Mary. *Unknown.* MeEL
Haill warld waited, The. Problems. Alexander Scott. FF
Hailstorm in June 1831, The. John Clare. VLP
Hain't no use to weep, hain't no use to moan. Down in the Lonesome Garden. *Unknown.* BPo
Hair. Remy de Gourmont, *tr. fr. French by* Jethro Bithell. AWP; ErPo
Hair. Maxine Silverman. VWA
Hair—/ silver-gray. Face. Jean Toomer. CDC; NoP
Hair—braided chestnut. Portrait in Georgia. Jean Toomer. NoP
Hair is heaven's water flowing eerily over us. Hair Poem. William Knott. EAS
Hair long, cheekbones high. Three Dreams. James Michie. NePoEA-2
Hair ornament of the sun, The. Mitsuhashi Takajo, *tr. fr. Japanese by* Kenneth Rexroth *and* Ikuko Atsumi. BoWoP
Hair Poem. William Knott. EAS
Hair splayed on the pillow. I think: a Kyoto comb's the thing. Biting Through. Traise Yamamoto. BrSi
Hair-Tonic Bottle, The. Ben King. OBAL
Haircut. William Packard. CAD
Haircut. Karl Shapiro. MoPo; MoVE; MP; TwCP
Hairdresser, The. David Hopes. AMV-81
Hair-dressing. Louis Untermeyer. UnTE
Hairless and worse than leathery, the skin. Corrib: An Emblem. Donald Davie. PoCh
Hairless beast in old clothes. Citizen. Louis Grudin. NePA
Hairnet covered her head, A. For All My Grandmothers. Beth Brant. STE
Hairs in My Nose, The. Aram Boyajian. NeAC
Hair's-Breadth, The. Nicholas Moore. NeBP
Hairy Dog, The. Herbert Asquith. FaPON; PDV; RHPC; SoPo; SUS; TiPo
Hairy was here. News from the Cabin. May Swenson. NMP; NYBP
Haitian Suite. Gregory Orr. MAYP
Hakluyt Unpurchased. Franklin McDuffee. EtS
Halcyon, *sel.* Hilda Doolittle ("H. D.").
"I'm not here." MoAmPo
Halcyon Days. Jim Barnes. CDW
Halcyon Days. Walt Whitman. NePA; OxBA
Halcyon's Nest, The. Giles Fletcher. *Fr.* Christ's Victory and Triumph. FaBoPP
Hale, sterne superne! *See* Hail, sterne superne!
Haleluiah; or, Britan's Second Remembrancer. George Wither. *See* Hallelujah; or, Britain's Second Remembrancer.
Half. Hawley Truax. NYBP
Half a bar, half a bar. The Village Choir. *Unknown.* FaBoPa
Half a dozen white loaves lie. The Loaves. Ronald Everson. WHW
Half a league, half a league. The Charge of the Light Brigade. Tennyson. BeLS; BLPA; FaBoBe; FaBV; FaFP; FaPo; FaPON; FaPoR; FPL; GN; HBV-2; HBVY; NIP; OBWP; OHFP; PaPo; PoPl; PrIm; TEP; TreF; WBLP
Half a mile from the shining sea. A Song of Degrees. W. P. Ker. PoSH
Half awake in my Sunday nap. Three Green Windows. Anne Sexton. NYBP
Half-bent Man. Richard Eberhart. NYBP
Half Black, Half Blacker. Sterling Plumpp. PoBA
Half-blown Rose, The. Samuel Daniel. *Fr.* To Delia. SeCePo
Halfbreed Chronicles; Isamu. Wendy Rose. TWSS
Half-Breed Girl, The. Duncan Campbell Scott. CaP
Half close your eyelids, loosen your hair. Aedh [*or* He] Thinks of Those Who Have Spoken Evil of His Beloved. W. B. Yeats. CTC; ELU; NoAM; VLP
"Half-cracked" to Higginson, living. "I Am in Danger—Sir." Adrienne Rich. NOBA
Half Door, The. "Seumas O'Sullivan." AnIV
Half-door, hall door. Purgatory. W. B. Yeats. CMoP
Half doun the hill, whaur fa's the linn. The Gowk. William Soutar. BSV; GoTS; NeBP
Half-drying rocks in shades of gray. Bog. Leen Volwerk. PoSH
Half-heard. Christopher Koch. PoAu-2
Half-hidden by trees, the sheer roof of the barn. The Barn. Stephen Spender. CMoP
Half-hidden in a graveyard. The Stranger. Walter de la Mare. BrPo; MoVE; OxBTC
Half-holiday for the burial, A. Of course, they punish. Black Spring. Robert Lowell. NaP
Half Hours with the Classics. H. J. DeBurgh. InMe
Half in the dim light from the hall. To ———. William Stanley Braithwaite. BALP; PoBA
Half-Light. Jean Percival Waddell. CaP
Halflives. Daniel Hoffman. SOTS
Half loving-kindliness and half disdain. To My Cat. Rosamund Marriott Watson. PCat
Half-Mast. Lloyd Mifflin. PAH
Half-mile long jetty. Nantucket/Mussels/October. Stephen Lewandowski. WOLT

Half Moon. Federico García Lorca, *tr. fr. Spanish by* W. S. Merwin. RFM
Half Moon Shows a Face of Plaintive Sweetness, The. Christina Rossetti. MOON
Half-moon slides by clumsily, as if on tracks, The. Canal Street, Chicago. Clyde Fixmer. TAT
Half-moons of her calves eclipse, The. Notes on a Girl. Peter Kane Dufault. ErPo
Half my friends are dead. Sea Canes. Derek Walcott. HeIP
Half of a clasping of the hands. Half. Hawley Truax. NYBP
Half of death. In Prague. Paul Celan, *tr. by* Joachim Neugroschel. VWA
Half of his/ body hung in. Spirits. Victor Hernandez Cruz. PoBA; WSC
Half of Life. Friedrich Hölderlin, *tr. fr. German by* James Blair Leishman. OBVE
Half of me died at Bapaume. Despair. Olive E. Lindsay. SUMH
Half of me is beautiful. Lilith. Ruth Feldman. VWA
Half of my life is gone, and I have let. Mezzo Cammin. Longfellow. FPL; NoP; TAP
Half of our borders, rivers and mountains were gone. In the Home of the Scholar Wu Su-chiang. Wu Tsao, *tr. by* Kenneth Rexroth *and* Ling Chung. BoWoP; WPOW
Half Past Four, October. Anna Hajnal, *tr. fr. Hungarian by* Daniel Hoffman. BoWoP
Half past nine—high time for supper. In Praise of Cocoa, Cupid's Nightcap. Stanley J. Sharpless. ErPo; FiBHP
Half-past three in the morning! Louise on the Door-Step. Charles Mackay. EBVV
Half seeing and half smelling a scrap. Existential. William Heyen. GeTw
Half-shut doors through which we heard that music, The. Multitudes Turn in Darkness. Conrad Aiken. PoA
Half Sigh. *Unknown, tr. by* Miriam Koshland. PBA
Half spirit, the older. The Jest. Austin Clarke. BIrV
Half squatter, half tenant (no rent). Manuelzinho. Elizabeth Bishop. NYBP
Half the time they munched the grass, and all the time they lay. Cows. James Reeves. NTCP; PoSC
Half the year has hot nights, like this. Elegies for the Hot Season. Sandra McPherson. AmPA
Half-Tide Ledge. R. P. Blackmur. MOS; TwAmPo
Halfway. Maxine W. Kumin. GoYe
Halfway across a bridge one night. The Swerve. William Stafford. GP
Half-way across the racing river. Midstream. D. J. Enright. OxBC
Half way between the house and the barn. Death on the Farm. Cary Waterman. GP
Halfway Down. A. A. Milne. FaPON; SO; TiPo
Half-way, for One Commandment Broken. A. E. Housman. PeHV
Halfway up the Hemlock valley turnpike. Emilia. Sarah N. Cleghorn. HBV-1
Half-world's width divides us, The; where she sits. Divided. David Gray. AA
Halibut Cove Harvest. Kenneth Leslie. CaP; NOBC
Halidon Hill. Laurence Minot. OxBM
Halieutica, *sels.* William Diaper, *after the Greek of* Oppian.
"Lamprey, glowing with uncommon fires, The." OBVE
"Shelly crawlers each returning year, The." FM
"Strange the formation of the eely race." OBVE
(Eels and Tortoises.) NOEC
"When pleasing heat, and fragrant blooms inspire." BXAP; PeD
"When they in throngs a safe retirement seek." OBVE
Halifax Station. *Unknown.* PAH
Hall of Ocean Life. John Hollander. PoA
Hallelu-u-u, Hallelu, O, my Lord. Death Come to My House He Didn't Stay Long. *Unknown.* BoAN-2
Halleluja!/ What sound is this across the dark. A Christmas Eve Choral. Bliss Carman. ISi
Hallelujah. Bible, *O.T.* Psalms, CXLVI. TrJP
Hallelujah! A. E. Housman. FiBHP; PV; ShM
(On the Death of a Female Officer of the Salvation Army.) FaBoNo
Hallelujah! *with music.* *Unknown.* BoAN-1
Hallelujah./ Praise the Lord, O my soul. Hallelujah. Bible, *O.T.* Psalms, CXLVI. TrJP
Hallelujah./ Praise ye the Lord from the heavens. Praise Ye the Lord. Bible, *O.T.* Psalms, CXLVIII. TrJP
Hallelujah; a Sestina. Robert Francis. PoCh
Hallelujah, Bum Again. *Unknown.* *See* Hallelujah, I'm a Bum.
Hallelujah I'm a Bum ("I read in the news, the President said"). Barbara Dane *and* Irwin Silber. FSW
Hallelujah, I'm a Bum ("Oh why don't you work"). *Unknown.* AS, *with music;* FSW; TrAS, *with music*
(Hallelujah, Bum Again.) GBP
"Oh why don't you work," *sel.* SaC
Hallelujah, I'm a-Travelin'. Harry Raymond. FSW
Hallelujah! kneel and sing. Bible, *O.T., paraphrased by* Christopher Smart. Psalms, CXLVIII. OBVE
Hallelujah; or, Britain's Second Remembrancer, *sels.* George Wither.
For a Musician. OBS
(To a Musician, *wr. at. to* William Austin.) OxBoCh
Hymne I: Generall Invitation to Praise God, A. SeCV-1
Hymn L: Rocking Hymn, A. SeCV-1
(Lullaby, A, *wr. at. to* William Austin.) OxBoCh
(Rocking Hymn, A.) OxBChV
Hallelujah! Praise the Lord, *with music.* Edwin Francis Hatfield. AH
"Hallelujah!" was the only observation. Hallelujah! [*or* On the Death of a Female Officer of the Salvation Army]. A. E. Housman. FaBoNo; FiBHP; PV; ShM
Halleluyah I'm a Bum. *Unknown.* *See* Hallelujah, I'm a Bum.
Hallo My Fancy. William Cleland. CH; OxBoLi
Halloo to man, the pleasuring, lording creature. So, Man? Gene Derwood. NePA
Hallow days o Yule are come, The. The Wife of Usher's Well. *Unknown.* ESPB
Hallow-Fair. Robert Fergusson. OxBS
Hallow the threshold, crown the posts anew! On the Queen's Return from the Low Countries. William Cartwright. MePo; OBEV
Hallowed be the Ordainer of/ the world! A Little Prayer. Paul Goodman. LiTA
Hallowed be the Sabbaoth. Epitaph in St. Olave's, Southwark, on Mr. Munday. *Unknown.* FaBoCo; OxBoLi
Hallowed be Thy name—Halleluiah! The Human Cry. Tennyson. ILwL
Hallowed Ground. Thomas Campbell. BLPA; HBV-2
Hallowed Places. Alice Freeman Palmer. HBV-1
Hallowe'en. Harry Behn. FaPON; PDV; PoSC; SiSoSe; TiPo; YeAr
Halloween, *abr.* Burns. OBEC
Hallowe'en. Frances Frost. TiPo
Halloween. Marie A. Lawson. SiSoSe; TiPo
Halloween. Myra Cohn Livingston. OFD
Hallowe'en. John Mayne. HBV-2
Halloween. Marnie Pomeroy. PoSC
Halloween Concert. Aileen Fisher. SiSoSe
Hallowe'en Indignation Meeting. Margaret Fishback. PoSC
Hallowe'en 1971. Michael Dennis Browne. AmPA
Halloween Witches. Felice Holman. WSC
Halls of fame are open wide, The. Fame. *Unknown.* TreFT
Hallucination, I. Arthur Symons. SyP
Hallway stairs, reserved for my emotions. Masochistic Tendencies. Carolyn Baxter. LFAC
Halo. Ralph Nixon Currey. PeSA
Halo, A. Ralph Salisbury. FAZ
Halo of the moon, The. Haiku. Buson. MOON
Halt, The. Josephine Miles. ELU
Halt and Parley. George Herbert Clarke. CaP
Halt in the desert where I have in mind, A. Hugh Maxton. *Fr.* Mastrim; a Meditation. CIP
Halt looks into the eyes of the halt and looks away, The. The Halt. Josephine Miles. ELU
Halt! Shoulder arms! Recover! As you were! Sonnet to Britain. William Edmonstoune Aytoun. FaBoCo
Halted against the shade of a last hill. Spring Offensive. Wilfred Owen. BrPo; GTBS-P; LiTB; MoVE
Haltersick's Song. John Pickering. *Fr.* Horestes. OBSC
(Song: "Farewell, adieu, that court-like life!") EIL
Ham and eggs, Lord, pork and beans. I Got to Roll. *Unknown.* OuSiCo
Ham Hound Crave. *Unknown.* BluL
Hamadryad, The. Walter Savage Landor. *Fr.* The Hellenics. EnRP
Hamasah, *sel.* Hittan of Tayyi, *tr. fr. Arabic by* Sir Charles Lyall.
His Children. ASP
Hamatreya. Emerson. AmPP; AP; FaBoEn; HeIP; MAT; NOBA; NoP; OxBA; PoEL-4; PrIm; SeCeV; TAP
Hambone and the Heart, The. Edith Sitwell. OBMV
Hambone Blues. *Unknown.* BluL
Hame came our goodman. Our Goodman. *Unknown.* BaBo; ESPB; ViBoFo
Hame, Hame, Hame. Allan Cunningham. BSV; CH; HBV-2; OBEV; OBRV
(Loyalty, *abr.*) GN
Hamelin Town's in Brunswick. The Pied Piper of Hamelin. Robert Browning. BeLS; BiP; BLPL; FaBoBe; FaBoCh; FaFP; FaPo; GN; HBV-1; HBVY; OBNV; OxBChV
Hamewith. Sydney Goodsir Smith. BSV
Hamilton Greene. Edgar Lee Masters. *Fr.* Spoon River Anthology. NoAM; OxBA; PAI
"Hamlet." Emmett Jarrett. NeAC
Hamlet, *sels.* Shakespeare.
"Angels and ministers of grace defend us!" *fr.* I, iv. EBEV

Bird of Dawning, *fr.* I, i. FaBoRV
Death of Hamlet, *fr.* V, ii. FiP
(I Am Dead, Horatio.) FaBoRV
Frailty, Thy Name Is Woman, *fr.* I, ii. TrGrPo
(Hamlet Broods over the Death of His Father.) TreFS
"Give me your pardon, sir. I have done you wrong," *fr.* V, ii. DL
"Good sir, whose powers are these?" *fr.* IV, i. WaaP
Gracious Time, The, *fr.* I, i. GN
(Christmas.) ChTr
("Some say that ever 'gainst that season comes.") OFD; PCHr
Hamlet's Instructions to the Players, *fr.* III, ii. TreFS
"How all occasions do inform against me," *fr.* IV, iv. BiP; HoPM
Man ("What a piece of work is a man!") *fr.* II, ii. TreF
"O! that this too too solid flesh would melt," *fr.* I, ii. SCV
"O, what a rogue and peasant slave am I," *fr.* II, ii. TreFT
Ophelia's Death, *fr.* V, i. ChTr
Ophelia's Songs, *fr.* IV, v.
And Will He [*or* A'] Not Come Again? PoEL-2; ViBoPo
(Ophelia's Songs, 2.) TrGrPo
"He is dead and gone, lady." LO
How Should I Your True Love Know. EBEV; EnLoPo; LiTB; PoRA; QFR; ViBoPo
(Friar of Orders Grey, The.) GoBC
(Ophelia's Song.) ChTr; GBL; OBSC
(Ophelia's Songs, 1.) TrGrPo
(Song: "How should I your true love know?") CH
Tomorrow Is Saint Valentine's Day. EnLoPo; OFD; PV; ViBoPo
(Ophelia's Song.) UnTE
(Saint Valentine's Day.) LiTB
(Song: "Tomorrow is [*or* Good morrow,' tis] Saint Valentine's Day.") FaPON; NTCP; SiSoSe
Polonius' Advice to Laertes, *fr.* I, iii. OHFP; PoPl
("And these few precepts in thy memory.") MasP
(Polonius' Advice to His Son.) TreF
(Polonius to Laertes.) GN
(This Above All.) TrGrPo; TRV, 3 *11.*
(To Thine Own Self Be True.) FaFP; LiTB
"Rugged Pyrrhus, he whose sable arm, The," *fr.* II, ii. Par
"To be, or not to be, that is the question," *fr.* III, i. BiP; FaFP; FF; FiP; HoPM; LiTB; MasP; PAI; PoPl; TreFT; TrGrPo; WHA
(Hamlet Contemplates Suicide.) TreF
(Hamlet's Soliloquy.) WBLP
(Soliloquy from "Hamlet.") OHFP
"What ceremony else?" *fr.* V, i. EBEV
"What man dost thou dig it for?" *fr.* V, i. DL
Witching Time of Night, The, *fr.* III, ii. TreFT
Hamlet. Stanley J. Sharpless. BXAP
Hamlet's Soliloquy Imitated. Richard Jago. FaBoCo; FaBoPa
("To print, or not to print—that is the question.") BXAP
Hammam Name, The. James Elroy Flecker. BrPo; PeHV
Hammer. Erica Funkhouser. AMV-81
Hammer, The,/ struck my nail. Almanac. May Swenson. NYBP
Hammer and Anvil. Samuel Valentine Cole. PoLF
Hammer keeps a-ring-in' on somebody's coffin, The. Way Over in the New Buryin' Groun'. *Unknown.* AS
Hammer Man, *with music.* *Unknown.* AS
Hammer me, let me see. Another Cross. Stephen Gardner. AMV-80
Hammer, Ring. *Unknown.* AmFP
Hammerin' Hank. D. Roger Martin. SOTS
Hammers, The. Ralph Hodgson. GoJo; MoBrPo; NOBE; OxBTC
Hammers and Anvil. John Clifford. *See* Anvil of God's Word, The.
Hammerstroke and. The Murdered Girl Is Found on a Bridge. Jane Hayman. NYBP
Hampstead; the Horse Chestnut Trees. Thom Gunn. NoP
Hampton Court. Pope. *Fr.* The Rape of the Lock. FaBoPP
Hanabi-ko (Koko). Wendy Rose. TWSS
Ha'nacker Mill. Hilaire Belloc. FaPoR; HBMV; MoBrPo; OxBTC
Hand, The. Brian Fawcett. NOBC
Hand, The. Ebenezer Jones. OBVV
Hand, The. Howard Moss. TAP
Hand. Edouard Roditi. EAS
Hand, A. Bernard Spencer. NeBP
Hand, The. R. S. Thomas. NOCV; OxBC
Hand a shade of moonlight on the pillow, The. Non Ti Fidar. Louis Zukofsky. VGW
Hand and Foot, The. Jones Very. AP; NePA; OxBA; PoEL-4; QFR; TAP
Hand at Callow Hill Farm, The. Charles Tomlinson. NePoEA-2
Hand by Hand We Shall Us Take. *Unknown.* OxBM; SBVL
Hand-clapping Rhyme. *Unknown.* NTCP
Hand goes up, The. Country Greeting. Frank Steele. Psk
Hand in hand, they are marching. The Children. Mark Vinz. DFF; GP
Hand is not always extremity enough, The. Hammer. Erica Funkhouser. AMV-81
Hand Me Down My Walking Cane. *Unknown, ad. by* James Morehead. FSW
Hand-Mirror, A. Walt Whitman. OxBA; TW
Hand of art here torpid lies, The. Epitaph on William Hogarth. Samuel Johnson. EBEV
Hand of Lincoln, The. Edmund Clarence Stedman. AA; OHIP; PGD
Hand of the copper boy pours tea. Café Tableau. May Swenson. ErPo
Hand Saw. Erica Funkhouser. AMV-81
Hand that aches for the pitchfork heft, The. Work. Robert Penn Warren. *Fr.* Boy's Will, Joyful Labor without Pay, and Harvest Home. SaC
Hand That Held It, The. W. G. Elmslie. TRV
Hand That Rocks the Cradle Is the Hand That Rules the World, The. William Ross Wallace. BLPL; FaFP; PoLF; TreF; WBLP
"Hand that rocks the cradle, The"—but there is no such hand. The Modern Baby. William Croswell Doane. BLPA; YaD
Hand that rounded Peter's dome, The. Emerson. *Fr.* The Problem. EyDe
Hand That Signed the Paper Felled a City, The. Dylan Thomas. MoAB; MoBrPo; MoPo; NoAM; NOBE; NoP; OBWP; SeCePo; TrGrPo; WaP
Hand that swept the sounding lyre, The. On a Dead Poet. Frances Sargent Osgood. AA
Hand trembling towards hand; the amazing. Sonnet Reversed. Rupert Brooke. NOBL
Handball Players at Brighton Beach, The. Irving Feldman. NYP
Handbook of Versification. Gilbert Sorrentino. PoA
Handcart Song, The. *Unknown.* AmFP
Handful came to Seicheprey, A. Seicheprey. *Unknown.* PAH
Handful here, that once was Mary's earth, The. Her Epitaph. Thomas William Parsons. AA; HBV-2
Handful of Ashes. Ilya Rubin, *tr. fr. Russian by* Linda Zisquit. VWA
Handful of Dust, A. James Oppenheim. TrJP
Handful of old men walking down the village street, A. Memorial Day. Theodosia Garrison. OHIP; PoSC
Handful of Small Secret Stones, A. Chris Bursk. AMV-81
Handfuls. Carl Sandburg. AP
Handicapped. Daniel Berrigan. FAZ
Handiwork of God, The. *Unknown.* *See* Nature's Creed.
Handlining Tockers & Gizmos. Allen Planz. WOLT
Handlyng Synne, *sels.* Robert Mannyng.
Dancers of Colbek, The. OxBM
"Frenchmen sin in lechery." DBV
Handmaid of Religion, The. Edgell Rickword. OBSV
Hands. Dorothy Aldis. SUS
Hands, The. Anthony Euwer. *Fr.* The Limeratomy. HBMV
Hands. Donald Finkel. CoAP; MAT
Hands, The. Tony Harrison. FaBoTw
Hands. Robinson Jeffers. GOA
Hands, The. Denise Levertov. NeAP; PoM
Hands, The. Daniel David Moses. AMV-80
Hands-across-the-Sea Poem, The. J. C. Squire. HBMV
Hands and lit faces eddy to a line. The Night Journey. Rupert Brooke. BrPo
Hands are being plated, The; they'll be brass. Clock without Hands. John Frederick Nims. PoA
Hands clenched under my shawl. "Anna Akhmatova," *tr. fr. Russian by* Robert Tracy. PBWP
Hands, do what you're bid. The Balloon of the Mind. W. B. Yeats. POL
Hands down, you were my favorite. Dear Mrs. McKinney of the Sixth Grade. David Kherdian. GLGT
Hands folded like napkins in my lap. Robert Peterson. NeAC
Hands must touch and handle many things, The. The New Man. Jones Very. AP; NOBA
Hands of beggars peddle cigarets, The. Cante Hondo. Ellen de Young Kay. NePoEA
Hands of Christ, The. His Hands. John Richard Moreland. TRV
Hands that eased my mother's labor drew, The. Rhyme for the Child as a Wet Dog. Judith Johnson Sherwin. TAP
Hands they were made to assist, The. The Hands. Anthony Euwer. *Fr.* The Limeratomy. HBMV
Hands Up. Anthony Rudolf. VWA
Hands upon hands. Pleading Voices. Shalom Katav, *tr. by* Yoffee Berkovitz. VWA
Hands were yours, the arms were yours, The. Elegy for My Father. Mark Strand. DiL; GeTw; LCAP; UnPo
Handsel Ring, The. George Houghton. AA
Handsome Cabin Boy, The. *Unknown.* FSW
Handsome friend, charming and kind. Beatrice de Die, *tr. fr. Provençal by* Meg Bogin. WPOW
Handsome? I hardly know. Her profile's fine. A Countrywoman of Mine. Elaine Goodale Eastman. AA
Handsome Molly. *Unknown.* FSW

Handsome one, white-black checkered son of the water. The Muscovy Drake. E. A. S. Lesoro, *tr. by* Dan Kunene *and* Jack Cope. PeSA
Handsome Young Airman, The. *Unknown. See* Dying Airman, The.
Handsome young gent down in Fla., A. A Helpful Nurse. *Unknown.* TDH
Handwriting on the Wall, The. Knowles Shaw. BLPA
Handwriting on the Wall. *Unknown.* AmFP
Handy Andy, *sel.* Samuel Lover.
Widow Machree. HBV-2
Handy dandy. *Unknown.* OxNR
Handy Guide, A. *Unknown.* TDH
Handy high and handy low. So Handy. *Unknown.* ShS
Handy Spandy, Jack-a-dandy. Mother Goose. SoPo
Handyman. Homer Phillips. QQQ
Hang a small bugle cap on, as big as a crown. The Beau's Receipt for a Lady's Dress. *Unknown.* CoMu
Hang at my hand as I write now. Verses for a First Birthday. George Barker. MoAB; MoBrPo
Hang down your head Tom Dooley. Tom Dooley. *Unknown.* FSW
Hang garlands on the bathroom door. The Bath. R. C. Lehmann. GDP
Hang-Glider's Daughter, The. Marilyn Hacker. MAYP
Hang it all, Ezra Pound, there is only the one sestina! Sestina. Donald Hall. NePoEA
Hang it all, Robert Browning. Ezra Pound. Cantos, II. AmPP; CoBMV; HAP; MoAB; MoAmPo; NePA; NoAM; NOBA; OxBA; PoA; TwAmPo
Hang It on the Wall. *Unknown.* BluL
Hang Me, O Hang Me, and I'll Be Dead and Gone. *Unknown.* AmFP
Hang on! Cling on! No matter what they say. Keep Your Grit. *Unknown.* STF
Hang out our banners on the outward walls. Shakespeare. *Fr.* Macbeth, V, v. EBEV
Hang Out the Flags. James S. Tippett. SiSoSe
Hang out your cloth, and let the trumpet sound. The Character of a Trimmer. *Unknown.* APAS
Hang sorrow, cast away care. Song. *Unknown.* OBS
Hang thee, vile North Easter. Another Ode to the North-East Wind. *Unknown.* Par
Hang to Your Grit! Louis A. Thayer. WBLP
Hang Up the Baby's Stocking! *Unknown.* OBCP
Hang up those dull, and envious fooles. Another. In Defence of Their Inconstancie. Ben Jonson. SeCP
Hang up your weaponed wit. J. V. Cunningham. QFR
Hang your serious songs. Sipsop's Song. Blake. *Fr.* An Island in the Moon. FaBoNo
Hanged man, please grow wild and luminous. To Her Dead Mate, Montana, 1966. Elizabeth Libbey. AmPA
Hanging, The. J. E. H. MacDonald. OBCV
Hanging/ out under the bridge. Getting Across. Carter Revard. VoR
Hanging Fire. Audre Lorde. NIP; NoP
Hanging from fresh trees. Lemons, Lemons. Al Young. HeIP
Hanging from the beam. The Portent. Herman Melville. AmPP; AP; NOBA; NoP; OBWP; OxBA; PoEL-5; PrIm; TAP; WiR
Hanging from the branches of a green/ willow tree. Lady Ise, *tr. fr. Japanese by* Willis Barnstone. BoWoP
Hanging Johnny. *Unknown.* AmSS, *with music;* FSW; GBP; ShS, *with music*
Hanging of Sam Archer, The. *Unknown.* AmFP
Hanging of the Crane, The, *sel.* Longfellow.
New Household, A. GN
Hanging on the wall, an iron face watches me. The Mask. Irma McClaurin. BlSi
Hanging on the walls. Gallery of My Heart. King D. Kuka. VoR
Hanging Out the Linen Clothes, *with music. Unknown.* AS
Hanging Scroll. Gerald Stern. PoDr
Hangman. Ai. AmPA
Hangman. *Unknown. See* Maid Freed from the Gallows, The.
Hangman's Love Song, The. Stanley Moss. VGW
Hangman's Tree. Lillian Zellhoefer White. AmFN
Hangover. Philip H. Rhinelander. WhC
Hangover Cure. Alexis, *tr. fr. Greek.* FaBoUs
Hangover Cure. Amphis, *tr. fr. Greek.* FaBoUs
Hangover Cure. Nicochares, *tr. fr. Greek.* FaBoUs
Hangs./ whipped/ blood. Biography. Amiri Baraka. TAP
Hangs, a fat gun-barrel. Trout. Seamus Heaney. CIP
Hangsaman. *Unknown. See* Maid Freed from the Gallows, The.
Hangtown Girls. *Unknown.* FSW
Hannah Bantry. *Unknown.* OxNR
Hannah Binding Shoes. Lucy Larcom. GN; HBV-1
Hannah Dustin. Louis O. Coxe. TwAmPo
Hannah's Song of Thanksgiving. Bible, *O.T.* First Samuel, II: 1-10. AWP
(Hannah's Thanksgiving.) BoWoP
Hannibal. Juvenal, *tr. fr.* Latin. *Fr.* Satires, X.
Tr. by William Gifford. OBVE
Tr. by Robert Lowell. OBVE
Tr. by Henry Vaughan. OBVE
Hans Beimler. Ernst Busch, *tr. fr. German.* FSW
Hans Breitmann's Party [*or* Barty]. Charles Godfrey Leland. CenHV; FaBoCo; HBV-2; NOBL; OBAL
Hans Christian Andersen in Central Park. Hy Sobiloff. PoPl
Hansel and Gretel Return. David Ray. DFT
Hansom Cabbies. Wilfrid Thorley. HBMV
Han'som, stranger? Yes, she's purty, an' ez peart ez she kin be. The Engineer's Story. Eugene J. Hall. PaPo
Hanukah. Jakov de Haan, *tr. fr. Dutch by* David Soetendorp. VWA
Hanukkah Hymn. *Unknown.* TreFT
Hap. Thomas Hardy. AWP; CABA; CMoP; CoBMV; EaLo; EBVV; MoBrPo; NIP; NoAM; NoP; OAEL-2; OAEP; PPON; PPP; TEP; VLP
Hap which Paris had as due for his desert, The. Gascoigne's Praise of His Mistress. George Gascoigne. EnRePo
Happened like this: it was hot as hell. The Death of the Craneman. Alfred Hayes. LiTA; NCSH; WaP
Happening. Edwin Honig. NePA
Happening In. Mark Sanders. WOLT
Happie is he, that from all businesse cleere. *See* Happy is he that from all business clear.
Happier, I would surely be. The Unfortunate Male. Kalonymos ben Kalonymos, *tr. by* J. Chotzner. *Fr.* The Touchstone. TrJP
Happiest Day, the Happiest Hour, The. Poe. AmPP; NePA; OxBA
(Happiest Day, The.) LiTA
Happiest Heart, The. John Vance Cheney. AA; HBV-2; HBVY; TreFS; WGRP
Happiness. William Dickey. Psk
Happiness. Louise Glück. MAYP
Happiness. Horace, *par. by* Dryden. *See* Happy the Man.
Happiness. Walter Isenhour. STF
Happiness. Priscilla Leonard. BLPA
Happiness. A. A. Milne. TiPo
Happiness. Carl Sandburg. OxBA
Happiness amidst Troubles. Immanuel di Roma, *tr. fr. Italian by* J. Chotzner. TrJP
Happiness an Art. Edward Young. *See* Art of Happiness, The.
Happiness Dependent on Ourselves. Goldsmith. *Fr.* The Traveller. OBEC
Happiness doesn't have any songs. Pain. Edith Södergran, *tr. by* Samuel Charters. WPOW
Happiness Found, *sel.* Augustus M. Toplady.
"Lord, it is not Life to live." TrPWD
Happiness is like a crystal. Happiness. Priscilla Leonard. BLPA
Happiness Makes Up in Height for What It Lacks in Length. Robert Frost. MoAB; MoAmPo; MoPo
Happiness of 6 A.M. Harvey Shapiro. NYBP
Happy are men who yet before they are killed. Insensibility. Wilfred Owen. ChMP; CMoP; FaBoTw; InPS; LiTB; LiTM; MMA; MoAB; OAEP; OBWP; OxBTC; SeCeV; WaP
Happy are they and charmed in life. Memorial: On the Slain at Chickamauga. Herman Melville. AA
Happy Are Those Who Have Died. Charles Péguy, *tr. fr. French by* Jessie Degen *and* Richard Eberhart. WaaP
Happy are you, whom Quantock overlooks. William Diaper. *Fr.* Brent; a Poem to Thomas Palmer Esq. FaBoPP; NOEC; OBSV
Happy at 40. Peter Meinke. GP
Happy Beggarman, The. *Unknown.* OnYI
Happy Bird, The. John Clare. PBBP
Happy bit hame this auld world would be, A. We Are Brethren A'. Robert Nicoll. HBV-2
Happy Britannia. James Thomson. *Fr.* The Seasons: Summer. OBEC; SeCePo
(Britannia.) FaBoPP
Happy choristers of air. A Pastoral[l] Hymn[e]. John Hall. MeLP; OBS; OxBoCh; TrPWD
Happy Christmas, A. Frances Ridley Havergal. BLRP
Happy Countryman, The. Nicholas Breton. *See* Shepherd and Shepherdess.
Happy Day (or Independence Day). James Cunningham. JB
Happy Day Will Soon Appear, The, *with music. Unknown.* AH
Happy Death. John Freeman. HBMV
Happy Endings. Gail White. DFT
Happy Family, The. John Ciardi. DuDa
Happy He. *Unknown.* ElL
Happy he whose eyes have view'd. Boethius, *tr. by* Samuel Johnson. *Fr.* The Consolation of Philosophy, III, 12. OBVE
Happy Heart, The. Thomas Dekker. *See* Sweet Content.
Happy Hen, The. James Agee. ErPo
Happy Husbandman, The; or, Country Innocence. *Unknown.* CoMu
Happy Hyena, The. Carolyn Wells. TDH

Happy insect, what can be. The Grasshopper. Abraham Cowley, *after the Greek of* Anacreon. AWP; FM; HBV-1; HBVY; OAEL-1; OBVE; SeCV-1; WiR
Happy Insensibility. Keats. *See* In a Drear-nighted December.
Happy [*or* Happie] is he that from all business clear. The Praises of a Country Life. Ben Jonson. OBVE; SeCP
Happy Is the Country Life. *Unknown.* OBS
Happy Is the Man. Bible, *O.T.* Psalms, I. TrJP
Happy Is the Man That Findeth Wisdom. Bible, *O.T.* Proverbs, III. TreF (11–18); TrJP (13–18)
Happy is the man that hath not walked. Happy Is the Man. Bible, *O.T.* Psalms, I. TrJP
Happy is the man who loves the woods and waters. Beatus Vir. Richard Le Gallienne. HBMV; OHIP
Happy is the man whom Thou hast set apart. Psalm. "Yehoash," *tr. by* Isidore Goldstick. TrJP
Happy Isle, The. Spenser. *Fr.* The Faerie Queene, IV, 10. OBSC
Happy Life of a Country Parson, The. Pope. BXAP
Happy Life, The. Martial, *tr. fr. Latin.* NOBE, *tr. by* Earl of Surrey; OBVE, *tr. by* Sir Richard Fanshawe; SiPS, *tr. by* Earl of Surrey
("Marshall, the thinges for to attayne," *tr. by* Earl of Surrey.) OBVE
(Martial's Quiet Life, *tr. by* Earl of Surrey.) OBSC
(Means to Attain Happy Life, The, *tr. by* Earl of Surrey.) ElL; EnRePo; FaBoEE; HBV-2; OBEV; ViBoPo
("My friend, the things that do attain," *tr. by* Earl of Surrey.) CABA; NoP
(Things That Cause a Quiet Life, The, *tr. by* Earl of Surrey.) TrGrPo
("Things that make the happier life, are these, The," *tr. by* Ben Jonson.) FaBoEE; OBVE
("Would you, my friend, in little room express," *tr. by* Elijah Fenton.) OBVE
Happy Life, The, *sel.* William Thompson.
"Book, a friend, a song, a glass, A." ViBoPo
Happy Life, The. Sir Henry Wotton. *See* Character of a Happy Life, The.
Happy Lifetime to You. Franklin P. Adams. InMe
Happy Man, A. Carphyllides, *tr. fr. Greek by* E. A. Robinson. AWP
Happy Man, The. G. K. Chesterton. EBCP
Happy men that lose their heads, The. Fantasia. G. K. Chesterton. HBMV
Happy Miner, The. *Unknown.* CoSo
Happy mortal, who these treasures shares, The. The Island of the Blest. Pindar, *tr. by* Gilbert West. *Fr.* Olympian Ode II. OBEC
Happy Myrtillo. Henry Carey. SeCePo
Happy New Year, A, *sels.* W. H. Auden. OBSV
"Colonel from Cheltenham stopped everyone, A."
"Cry went through me like a stab of a knife, A."
"Doctors attended behind each chair."
"In corduroy trousers and seedy black coats."
"On a lorry the centre of a gaping crowd."
Happy New Year, Anyway. Joanna Cole. NTCP
Happy New Year! Happy New Year! *Unknown.* PoSC
Happy Night, The. John Sheffield, Duke of Buckinghamshire. UnTE
Happy Night, The. J. C. Squire. HBMV
Happy Nightingale, The. *Unknown.* OxBChV
Happy Pair, The, *sel.* Sir Charles Sedley.
Marriage and Money. OBSV
Happy people die whole, they are all dissolved in a moment. Post Mortem. Robinson Jeffers. MoAmPo; MoPo; TrGrPo
Happy Poem, The. Thomas Brush. LTB
Happy road that brought me here, The. Shankill. Eileen Shanahan. NeIP
Happy, Saviour, Would I Be, *with music.* Edwin H. Nevin. AH
Happy Sheep, The. Wilfred Thorley. SoPo
Happy Song-sparrow, that on woodland side. The Fringilla Melodia. Henry Beck Hirst. AA
Happy Swain, The. Ambrose Philips. EnLoPo
Happy That First White Age When We. Boethius, *tr. fr. Latin by* Henry Vaughan. *Fr.* The Consolation of Philosophy. OBVE; PAI
(Metrum V.) PPON
Happy the dead! Consolation in War. Lewis Mumford. NYBP
Happy the feeling from the bosom thrown. Sonnet: To ——. Wordsworth. ChER
Happy the hare at morning, for she cannot read. The Cultural Presupposition. W. H. Auden. CABA; PAI
Happy the Man. Horace, *par. by* Dryden. *Fr.* Odes, III, 29. FaPoR
(Happiness.) TreF
Happy the man, who free as air. The Widower. Royall Tyler. OBAL
Happy the man, who his whole time doth bound. The Old Man of Verona. Claudian, *tr. by* Abraham Cowley. AWP; OBVE
Happy the man who in his pot contains. The Suet Dumpling. *Unknown.* BXAP
Happy the man, who on the mountain-side. After Reading Homer. Digby Mackworth Dolben. GoBC
Happy the man who, safe on shore. The Hurricane. Philip Freneau. AP; MOS; TAP
Happy the man, who void of cares and strife. The Splendid Shilling. John Phillips. BXAP; NOEC; OAEL-1; Par
Happy the Man whom bount'ous Gods allow. Horace, *tr. by* Abraham Cowley. Epodes, II. CavP
Happy the man whose wish and care. Ode on Solitude [*or* The Contented Man *or* The Quiet Life *or* Solitude]. Pope. AWP; FaFp; FiP; GoBC; GTBS; GTBS-P; HBV-1; HBVY; HeIP; InMe; InvP; NIP; OAEP; OBEC; PAI; PoPl; PoPle; PoRA; PPoe; Prf; SeCeV; TEP; TreFS; TrGrPo; ViBoPo
Happy the moment when we are seated in the Palace. Jalal al-Din Rumi, *tr. fr. Persian.* ILwL
Happy the nations of the moral North! Donna Julia. Byron. *Fr.* Don Juan, I. PoEL-4
Happy the savage of those early times. European Crimes. Charles Churchill. *Fr.* Gotham. NOEC
Happy the stark bare wood on the hill of Bree! The Triad of Things Not Decreed. Alice Furlong. AnIV
Happy they who die for the earth which also dies. Happy Are Those Who Have Died. Charles Péguy, *tr. by* Jessie Degen *and* Richard Eberhart. WaaP
Happy those early days [*or* dayes]! when I. The Retreat[e]. Henry Vaughan. AnAnS-1; AWP; BLPL; CABA; FaBoEn; FF; GTBS; GTBS-P; HAP; HBV-1; HeIP; InPS; InvP; JCP; LiTB; LoBV; MeLP; MePo; NIP; NOBE; NOCV; NoP; OAEL-1; OAEP; OBEV; OBS; PoEL-2; PoPle; PoRA; PPP; SBVL; SeCePo; SeCeV; SeCP; SeCV-1; TreFT; TrGrPo; ViBoPo; WHA
Happy Thought. Robert Louis Stevenson. FaBoBe; HBV-1; HBVY; OxBChV; RHPC; TiPo; TreFS
Happy, thrice happy times in silver age! Desiderium. Phineas Fletcher. *Fr.* The Purple Island, I. OBS
Happy Too Much. Boethius, *tr. fr. Latin by* Elizabeth I, Queen of England. *Fr.* The Consolation of Philosophy. CTC
Happy Tree, The. Gerald Gould. WGRP
Happy trifles, can ye bear. Sent to Miss Bell H——, with a Pair of Buckles. John Cunningham. FaBoUs
Happy View, A. C. Day Lewis. CMoP
Happy Wanderer, The. Percy Addleshaw. OBVV
Happy Warrior, The. Sir Herbert Read. MMA
Happy Warrior, The. Wordsworth. OHFP
Happy Were He. Earl of Essex. ElL
(Content.) OBSC
Happy whitethroat on the sweeing bough, The. The Happy Bird. John Clare. PBBP
Happy who like Ulysses, or that lord. Heureux Qui, comme Ulysse, A Fait un Beau Voyage. Joachim du Bellay, *tr. by* G. K. Chesterton. AWP
Happy Workhouse and the Good Effects of Industry, The. John Dyer. *Fr.* The Fleece, III. NOEC
Happy ye leaves! when as those lily hands. Amoretti, I. Spenser. AAS; EBEV; LoBV; NIP; OAEL-1
Happy: yea, happy for ever and aye! Fulfilment. Louis V. Ledoux. HBMV
Happy Youth, that shalt possesse. To My Cousin (C.R.) Marrying My Lady (A.). Thomas Carew. AnAnS-2; SeCP
Happy's the man whose pleasant labours with the lark. The Ploughman, in Imitation of Milton. Samuel Jones. NOEC
Harald, the Agnostic Ale-loving Old Shepherd Enemy of the Whisky-drinking Ploughmen and Harvesters, Walks over the Sabbath Hill to the Shearing. George Mackay Brown. NePoEA-2
Harangue on the Death of Hayyim Nahman Bialik. César Tiempo, *tr. fr. Spanish by* Donald Devenish Walsh. TrJP
Harbingers. Basho, *tr. fr. Japanese by* Harold G. Henderson. PoPl
Harbingers are come, The. See, see their mark. The Forerunners. George Herbert. AnAnS-1; JCP; MePo; NoP
Harbor. Nancy Price. IHMS
Harbor, The. Carl Sandburg. NCSH; PoPl; TAP
Harbor at Seattle, The. Robert Hass. NPGG
Harbor Dawn, The. Hart Crane. *Fr.* The Bridge: Powhatan's Daughter. MoPo; NePA; NYP; OxBA
Harbor wears a look of space, The. Little Steamboat. Oscar Williams. PoPl
Hard, Ain't It Hard. *Unknown.* FSW
Hard aport! Now close to shore sail! Adrian Block's Song. Edward Everett Hale. PAH
Hard as hurdle arms, with a broth of goldish flue. Harry Ploughman. Gerard Manley Hopkins. FaBoMo
Hard brown bug, maybe a beetle, A. He Faces the Second Winter. Philip Levine. *Fr.* Sierra Kid. PoA
Hard by the Indian lodges, where the bush. The Corn Husker. Pauline Johnson. CaP

Hard by the lilied Nile I saw. Thomas Lovell Beddoes. *Fr.* The Last Man. FM
Hard changes, The: concrete cracks and sprouts. Power Failure. Josephine Jacobsen. FAZ
Hard coming we had of it, A. The Poets. David Wevill. PP
Hard con, A. Mask of Stone. Henry Johnson. LFAC
Hard Country. Philip Booth. CoAP
Hard Daddy. Langston Hughes. BANP
Hard-edged buildings; cloudless blue enamel. Fifty-seventh and Fifth. Alfred Corn. NYP
Hard Frost. Andrew Young. BoNaP; MoVE
Hard Heart of Mine, *with music.* Henry Alline. AH
Hard, heavy, slow, dark. The Ikons. James K. Baxter. OCNZ
Hard helmets and high boots. Daredevil. Kirby Congdon. PeHV
Hard is my fate, thus to want bread. Between an Unemployed Artist and His Wife. *Unknown.* NOEC
Hard is the doubt, and difficult to deeme. Spenser. *Fr.* The Faerie Queene, IV, 9. OAEL-1
Hard Is the Fortune of All Womankind. *Unknown.* FSW
Hard is the stone, but harder still. The Image-Maker. Oliver St. John Gogarty. OBEV; OBMV; PoRA
Hard it is, very hard. The Choice of the Cross. Dorothy L. Sayers. *Fr.* The Devil to Pay. TrCP
Hard Journey, A. Yes. Hayden Carruth. VGW
Hard knowledge to come by. The Music of the Spheres. Marvin Bell. PoA
Hard Lovers, The. George Dillon. PoA
Hard luck poppa, a-countin' his toes. Brown's Ferry Blues. *Unknown.* FSW
Hard old grey eyes, no pity. The Rancher. Keith Wilson. GP
Hard on a high flower comes the sun. The Energy of Light. John Hay. NePoAm-2
Hard Questions. Margaret Tsuda. RFM
Hard Rock Returns to Prison from the Hospital for the Criminal Insane. Etheridge Knight. ConAP; LFAC; NIP; NNaP; NoAM; TAP; UnPo
Hard sand breaks, The. Hermes of the Ways. Hilda Doolittle ("H. D."). LiTA; WPE
Hard Strain in a Delicate Place. Janet Sylvester. MAYP
Hard Time Killin' Floor Blues. *Unknown.* BluL
Hard Times ("Come listen a while"). *Unknown.* AmFP
Hard Times, but Carrying On. Dave Smith. TAT
Hard times here every, where you go. Hard Time Killin' Floor Blues. *Unknown.* BluL
Hard Times in the Country, *with music. Unknown.* OuSiCo
Hard tin bird was my lover, A. Weathercock. Elizabeth Jennings. NePoEA
Hard to Bear. Tudor Jenks. OBCA
Hard Traveling. Woody Guthrie. FSW
Hard Way to Learn. James Hearst. AMV-80
Hardcastle Crags. Sylvia Plath. GoYe
(Night Walk.) NYBP
Harden Now Thy Tired Heart. Thomas Campion. NCEP
("Harden now thy tyred hart with more then flinty rage.") AAS; OBVE
Harder lesson, to learn continence, A. Cymochles and Phaedria. Spenser. *Fr.* The Faerie Queene, II, 6. OBSC
Harder Task, The. *Unknown.* BLRP
Harder time is coming, A. The Respite. Ingeborg Bachmann, *tr. by* Michael Hamburger. WPOW
Hardest headlands, The,/ Gravel down. La Rose des Vents. Richard Wilbur. MiAP
Hardest work I ever did, The. Bile Them Cabbage Down. *Unknown.* AmFP
Hardly a Man Is Now Alive. Ring Lardner. OBAL
Hardly a shot from the gate we storm'd. Badminton. Sir Alfred Comyn Lyall. *Fr.* Studies at Delhi. OBVV
Hardly spring, with ice. Chiyo, *tr. fr. Japanese by* David Ray. BoWoP
Hardness Scale, The. Joyce Peseroff. LLLT
Hardon ("Get One Today"). Ian Wedde. OCNZ
Hardship of Accounting, The. Robert Frost. FaBoCh; FaBoCo; FaFP; OBAL; WhC
Hardweed Path Going. A. R. Ammons. UnPo; VGW
Hard-working Miner, The ("The hard-working miners"). *Unknown.* AmFP
Hard-working Miner, The ("To the hard-working miner"). *Unknown.* AmFP
Hardy's Plymouth. Geoffrey Grigson. FaBoPP
Hare, A. Walter de la Mare. EBEV; TiPo
Hare. Molly Holden. TEP
Hare, The. *Unknown. See* By a Forest.
Hare and the Pig, The. L. J. Bridgman. RHPC
Hare and the Tortoise, The. Ian Serraillier. SO
Hare-hunting. William Somervile. *Fr.* The Chase. NOEC; OBEC
Hare in Winter. Marge Piercy. NeAC
Hare with Many Friends, The. John Gay. *Fr.* Fables. HBV-1
Harebells in June. Annette Wynne. SUS
Harelip Mary. Ronald Koertge. GP
Hares on the Mountain. *Unknown.* ErPo; OBET; UnTE
Hari helps his people. Mirabai, *tr. fr. Hindi by* Willis Barnstone *and* Usha Nilsson. BoWoP
Hari, look at me a while. Mirabai, *tr. fr. Hindi by* Willis Barnstone *and* Usha Nilsson. BoWoP
Hark. John Webster. *See* Hark, Now Everything Is Still.
Hark! . . ./ What booming. Arcana Sylvarum. Charles De Kay. AA
Hark! ah, the nightingale. Philomela. Matthew Arnold. HBV-1; OAEL-2; OAEP; OBEV; PBBP; PPP; SeCeV; UnPo; VLP; WHA
Hark, All Ye Lovely Saints. *Unknown.* OAEL-1
Hark, All You Ladies. Thomas Campion. ElL
(Hark, All You Ladies That Do Sleep.) OAEP
("Harke, al you ladies that do sleep.") AAS; EBEV; PoEL-2
(In the Dark What the Day Doth Forbid.) UnTE
(Proserpina.) OBSC
Hark, and Hear My Trumpet Sounding, *with music. Unknown.* AH
Hark at the lips of this pink whorl of shell. A Quatrain. Frank Dempster Sherman. AA
Hark! do I hear again the roar. Columbus Dying. Edna Dean Proctor. PAH
Hark! from the tombs a doleful sound. Plenary. *Unknown.* AmFP
Hark! from yon covert, where those tow'ring oaks. Hare-hunting. William Somervile. *Fr.* The Chase. NOEC; OBEC
Hark! from yon high grey Downs the tremulous musical sheep-bells. Above the Medway. A. J. Munby. *Fr.* The Vales of the Medway. FaBoPP
Hark, happy lovers, hark! A Kiss. William Drummond of Hawthornden. ElL
Hark, hark!/ Bow-wow. Song: Hark, Hark! Shakespeare. *Fr.* The Tempest. SoSe
Hark! hark! down the century's long reaching slope. Yorktown Centennial Lyric. Paul Hamilton Hayne. PAH
Hark! hark! that pig—that pig! the hideous note. Ode to a Pig while His Nose Was Being Bored. Robert Southey. NOBL
Hark, hark, the dogs do bark. Mother Goose. GBP; HBVY; OxNR; TiPo
Hark! Hark! the Lark. Shakespeare. *Fr.* Cymbeline, II, iii. AWP; CH; ChTr; EnRePo; FaBoCh; FaBV; FaFP; FaPON; HBV-1; HeIP; LiTB; LoBV; NIP; NoP; PrIm; SeCeV; TreF; TrGrPo; ViBoPo; WHA
(Aubade.) OBEV
(Morning Song, A.) GN
(Song: "Hark! hark! the lark at heaven's gate sings.") ElL; FiP
(Song to Imogen.) OBSC
Hark! Hark! with Harps of Gold, *with music.* Edwin Hubbell Chapin. AH
Hark, hearer, hear what I do. Epithalamion. Gerard Manley Hopkins. VLP
Hark, how chimes the Passing Bell. The Passing Bell. James Shirley. ACP
Hark, how my Celia, with the choice. Celia Singing. Thomas Carew. OAEP
Hark, how the birds do sing. Man's Medley. George Herbert. ViBoPo
Hark how the lyrick choristers o' th' wood. To Clarastella on St. Valentines Day Morning. Robert Heath. OBS
Hark how the minstrels gin to shrill aloud. Spenser. *Fr.* Epithalamion. WHA
Hark [*or* Heark] how the Mower Damon sung. Damon the Mower. Andrew Marvell. AnAnS-1; JCP; OAEL-1
Hark, how the Passing Bell. Upon a Passing Bell. Thomas Washbourne. FaBoRV
Hark, I hear the bells of Westgate. Westgate-on-Sea. John Betjeman. OxBoLi
Hark I hear the cannons roar. A Carrouse to the Emperor, the Royal Pole, and the Much-wronged Duke of Lorrain. *Unknown.* CoMu
Hark! I hear the tramp of thousands. The Reveille. Bret Harte. GN; HBV-2; OHIP; PAH; PAL
Hark! in the still night. Who goes there? Sixteen Dead Men. Dora Sigerson Shorter. ACP; OnYI
Hark! My Beloved! Bible, *O.T.* The Song of Solomon, II: 8-13. TrJP
Hark, my Flora! Love doth call us. A Song of Dalliance. William Cartwright. ErPo; JCP
Hark, My Soul. John Austin. OxBoCh
Hark, my soul! it is the Lord. Lovest Thou Me? William Cowper. HBV-2; OBEC
Hark [*or* Hearke], Now Everything Is Still. John Webster. *Fr.* The Duchess of Malfi, IV, ii. ElL; HAP; InPS; LoBV; NoP; OBS; QFR; SeCePo; ViBoPo
(Hark.) CH
(Shrouding of the Duchess of Malfi, The.) NOBE; OBEV
(Summons to Execution.) FaBoEn
Hark! O hark, you guilty trees. Orpheus to Woods. Richard Lovelace. CaPo

Hark! one saith: "Proclaim!" All Flesh Is Grass. Bible, *O.T.* *Fr.* Isaiah. TrJP
Hark, reader! wilt be learn'd i' th' wars? To My Truly Valiant, Learned Friend, Who in His Book Resolved the Art Gladiatory into the Mathematics. Richard Lovelace. CaPo; PoEL-3
Hark! she is call'd, the parting hour [*or* houre] is come. In [*or* On] the Glorious Assumption of Our Blessed Lady [*or* On the Assumption]. Richard Crashaw. AnAnS-1; ISi; LoBV; OBS
Hark! She is calling to her cat. The Cat. Richard Church. BoAnP; PCat
Hark, the bonny Christchurch bells! Christchurch Bells. *Unknown.* OBET
Hark! the cock crows, and yon bright star. The New Year. Charles Cotton. GoTL; OBS
Hark! the cock proclaims the morning. St. Matthias. Christopher Smart. *Fr.* Hymns and Spiritual Songs. LAuP
Hark! the flow of the four rivers. Farewells from Paradise. Elizabeth Barrett Browning. OBEV; OBVV
Hark! the Herald Angels Sing. Charles Wesley. FSW; SBVL; TreFS
(Nativity, The.) BLRP
Hark the herald angels sing/ Beecham's pills are just the thing. Sir Thomas Beecham. PV
Hark, the herald angels sing/ Glory to the newborn thing. Paul Dehn. *Fr.* A Leaden Treasury of English Verse. DBV; PV
Hark the herald angels sing/ "Mrs. Simpson's pinched our King." Abdication Street Song. *Unknown.* PV
Hark! the herald angels sing/ timidly. Dean Inge [*or* On Dean Inge]. Humbert Wolfe. ChTr; FaBoEE
Hark! the Mavis. Burns. *See* Ca' the Yowes.
Hark the sound of holy voices, chanting at the crystal sea. All Saints' Day, Nov. 1. Christopher Wordsworth. VLP
Hark! the Vesper Hymn Is Stealing. Thomas Moore. EnRP
Hark! They cry! I hear by that. Yolp, Yolp, Yolp, Yolp. *Unknown.* ElL
Hark! through the quiet evening air, their song. Emma Lazarus. *Fr.* In Memoriam Rev. J. J. Lyons. SBG
Hark! 'tis freedom that calls, come, patriots, awake! A Song. *Unknown.* PAH
Hark! 'Tis the Saviour of Mankind, *with music.* John Murray. AH
Hark! 'tis the twanging horn o'er yonder bridge. The Winter Evening [*or* The Post-Boy]. William Cowper. The Task, IV. FiP; OAEP; SeCePo
Hark! 'tis the voice of the mountain. The Battle of Eutaw. William Gilmore Simms. PAH
Hark to that happy shout!—the school-house door. Evening Schoolboys. John Clare. GLGT
Hark to the rumble of the earthquake god! Ruaumoko—the Earthquake God. Mohi Turei, *tr. by* A. Armstrong. WTO
Hark to the story of poor Romeo! Romeo and Juliet. Fred Newton Scott. InMe
Hark to the story of Willie the Weeper. Willie [*or* Willy] the Weeper. *Unknown.* GBP; TrAS
Hark to the thrush gurgling in yonder tree! The Thrush. Alfred Austin. TEP
Hark to the whimper of the sea-gull. The Sea-Gull. Ogden Nash. FaFP; FPL; MOS; NePA
Hark, ye sighing sons of sorrow. The Mouldering Vine. *Unknown.* AmFP
Hark you such sound as quivers? Kings will hear. November. Mahlon Leonard Fisher. HBV-1
Hark! Young Democracy from sleep. Bernard O'Dowd. *Fr.* Young Democracy. PoAu-1
Harke, Al You Ladies That Do Sleep. Thomas Campion. *See* Hark, All You Ladies.
Harlackenden, among these men of note Christ hath thee seated. Among These Troopes of Christs Souldiers, Came. . .Mr. Roger Harlackenden. Edward Johnson. SCAP
Harlaw. Sir Walter Scott. *Fr.* The Antiquary. BSV, *abr.*
("Herring loves the merry moonlight, The," 1 *st.*) FaBoCh; PoPle
(Red Harlaw.) OxBB
Harlem. Jean Brierre, *tr. fr. French by* John F. Matheus. TTY
Harlem ("Here on the edge of hell"). Langston Hughes. CAD; PPP
(Puzzled.) UnPo
Harlem ("What happens to a dream deferred"). Langston Hughes. *Fr.* Lenox Avenue Mural. AmNP; AmPP; BiP; CABA; HeIP; HoPM; InPS; NoP; PoNe
(Dream Deferred.) FF; InPK; LiTM; PoBA; PPP; SoSe
(Harlem [A Dream Deferred].) NIP
Harlem Dancer, The. Claude McKay. BALP; BANP; BPo; FF; NoAM; TAP
Harlem dud. For "Mr. Dudley," a Black Spy. James A. Emanuel. BPo
Harlem Freeze Frame. Lebert Bethune. PoBA
Harlem Gallery, *sels.* Melvin B. Tolson.
Birth of John Henry, The. BPo
("Night John Henry is born an ax, The.") TTY
Sea-Turtle and the Shark, The. PoBA
Harlem Gallery: From the Inside. Larry Neal. BPo
Harlem in January. Julia Fields. CAD; CNA
Harlem is vicious. Return of the Native. Amiri Baraka. BPo
Harlem, Montana; Just Off the Reservation. James Welch. CDW; GP; STE
Harlem Riot, 1943. Pauli Murray. PoBA
Harlem Shadows. Claude McKay. AmPP; BANP; PoNe
Harlem Sounds: Hallelujah Corner. William Browne. AmNP
Harlem Sweeties. Langston Hughes. CABA; LiTM; NoP; PoNe; TTY
Harlequin of Dreams, The. Sidney Lanier. AA; AP
Harlot, The. Hamish Brown. PoSH
Harlot's Catch. Robert Nichols. ErPo; FaBoTu
Harlot's House, The. Oscar Wilde. EBVV; InPK; MoBrPo; SyP
Harmless Streets. Tess Gallagher. LTB
Harmonica Man. P. Wolny. PCP
Harmonie du Soir. Baudelaire, *tr. fr. French by* Lord Alfred Douglas. AWP
Harmonious Heedlessness of Little Boy Blue, The. Guy Wetmore Carryl. BoAnP
Harnet and the Bittle, a Wiltshire Tale, The ("A harnet zet in a hollur tree"). J. Y. Akerman. ChTr
Haro! Haro! The Appeal to Harold. H. C. Bunner. AA
Harold at Two Years Old. Frederick W. H. Myers. HBMV
Harold Bates, who lives next door. Neighbors. "Lennox." DBV; InMe
Harold the Dauntless, *sel.* Sir Walter Scott.
'Tis Merry in Greenwood. FaPON; OHIP
Harold the Valiant. Mary Elizabeth DeWitt Stebbins. AA
Harold's Song: Rosabelle. Sir Walter Scott. *See* Rosabelle.
Haroun Al-Rachid for Heart's-Life. *Unknown, tr. fr. Arabic by* E. Powys Mathers. *Fr.* The Thousand and One Nights. AWP
Haroun, the Caliph, through the sunlit street. Power. Thomas Stephens Collier. AA
Haroun's Favorite Song. *Unknown, tr. fr. Arabic by* E. Powys Mathers. *Fr.* The Thousand and One Nights. AWP
Harp, The. Bruce Weigl. MAYP
Harp and flute and violin, throbbing through the night. The Hired Man on Horseback. Eugene Manlove Rhodes. BPAW
Harp in the Rigging. Hamish Maclaren. EtS
Harp of Alfred, The. G. K. Chesterton. *Fr.* The Ballad of the White Horse. MoVE
Harp of David, The. Jacob Cohen, *tr. fr. Hebrew by* Sholom J. Kahn. TrJP
Harp of David, The. "Yehoash," *tr. fr. Yiddish by* Alter Brody. TrJP
Harp of Renfrewshire, The. Douglas Dunn. BSV
Harp of Sorrow, The. Ethel Clifford. HBV-2; WGRP
Harp of the North, farewell! The hills grow dark. Farewell, Thou Minstrel Harp. Sir Walter Scott. *Fr.* The Lady of the Lake, VI. OAEP; OBNC; ViBoPo
Harp of the North! that mouldering long hast hung. The Chase. Sir Walter Scott. *Fr.* The Lady of the Lake, I. EnRP; OAEP; ViBoPo
Harp Song of the Dane Women. Kipling. *Fr.* Puck of Pook's Hill. FaBoEn; HAP; OAEP; OBNC; PoRA; SeCePo
Harp That Once through Tara's Halls, The. Thomas Moore. ACP; AnIL; BLPL; EnRP; FaPoR; FSW; GN; OAEP; OBNC; OnYI; OxBI; PoLF; RoGo; TreF; ViBoPo
Harpalus' Complaint [of Phillida's Love]. *Unknown.* OBSC; ViBoPo
Harper, The. Thomas Campbell. NCEP
(Irish Harper and His Dog, The.) CH
Harper, The. *Unknown, tr. fr. Early Modern Irish by* Frank O'Connor. AnIL; KiLC
Harpers Ferry. Selden Rodman. PoNe
Harpkin. *Unknown.* GBP
Harps Hung Up in Babylon. Arthur Colton. WGRP
Harried we were, and spent. The Waradgery Tribe. Mary Gilmore. PoAu-1
Harriet. Audre Lorde. BlSi
Harriet. Robert Lowell. NoP
"Unaccustomed ripeness in the wood, An," *sel.* CAPP
Harriet Beecher Stowe. Paul Laurence Dunbar. BPo
Harriet Simper Has Her Day. John Trumbull. *Fr.* The Progress of Dulness. AmPP
Harriet there was always somebody calling us crazy. Harriet. Audre Lorde. BlSi
Harriet Tubman. Margaret Walker. PoNe
Harrington Barn Dance, The. *Unknown.* CoSo
Harrow Grave in Flanders, A. Robert Offley Ashburton. HBV-2
Harrowing of Hell, The. *Unknown.* ACP
Harry Carey's General Reply, to the Libelling Gentry, Who Are Angry at His Welfare. Henry Carey. HBV-2
Harry Dunne, 2 *vers., with music.* *Unknown.* ShS
Harry Lorrequer, *sel.* Charles Lever.
Pope He Leads a Happy Life, The. HBV-2
Harry Parry. *Unknown.* GBP; OxNR
Harry Pearce. David Campbell. PoAu-2
Harry Ploughman. Gerard Manley Hopkins. FaBoMo
H——y P——tt. *Unknown.* CoMu

Harry Semen. "Hugh MacDiarmid." NoAM
Harry, whose tuneful and well-measured song. To Mr. H. Lawes on His Airs. Milton. AWP; LoBV; NoP; OBS
Harry Wilmans. Edgar Lee Masters. *Fr.* Spoon River Anthology. PPON
Harry, you know at night. To-Night. Edward Thomas. PoPle
Harsh bray and hollow, The. Two Kitchen Songs. Edith Sitwell. CMoP
Harsh Climate. Charles Simic. LCAP
Harsh cry the crows. The Solitary. Nietzsche, *tr. by* Ludwig Lewisohn. AWP
Hart Crane. Robert Creeley. AP
Hart Crane. Julian Symons. PoA
Hart he loves the high wood, The. Mother Goose. FaBoCh; GBP; OxNR
Hart-Leap Well. Wordsworth. BeLS
Hartico. Anna Walters. VoR
Hart's Castle. Gavin Douglas. *Fr.* King Hart. PoEL-1
Harvest, The. William Aberg. LFAC
Harvest. Ellen Mackay Hutchinson Cortissoz. AA; HBV-1
Harvest. Eva Gore-Booth. HBMV
Harvest. Jeannette Maino. AMV-80
Harvest. Thomas Nashe. *Fr.* Summer's Last Will and Testament. OBSC
Harvest. Gene Shuford. GoYe
Harvest. Edith Sitwell. CoBMV; OAEP
Harvest and Consecration. Elizabeth Jennings. NePoEA-2
Harvest Dawn Is Near, The, *with music.* George Burgess. AH
Harvest Home. Henry Alford. WGRP
Harvest Home. Dryden. *Fr.* King Arthur. PrIm
(Song: "Your hay it is mow'd, and your corn is reap'd.") SeCV-2
Harvest Home. Arthur Guiterman. RHPC; YeAr
Harvest Home. Frederick Tennyson. OBVV
Harvest-Home. Theocritus, *tr. fr. Greek by* Charles Stuart Calverley. *Fr.* Idylls. AWP
Harvest Hymn. Whittier. *Fr.* For an Autumn Festival. OHIP
("Once more the liberal year laughs out.") PGD
Harvest Moon, The. Longfellow. AP; GN
Harvest of the Sea, The. John McCrae. EtS
Harvest of the Sea. Máire Mhac an tSaoi. PBWP
Harvest of Time, The. Harold Trowbridge Pulsifer. HBMV
Harvest Poem. David Fisher. NPGG
Harvest Song. Joseph Campbell. OFD
Harvest Song. Richard Dehmel, *tr. fr. German by* Ludwig Lewisohn. AWP
Harvest Song. Ludwig Heinrich Christoph Hölty, *tr. fr. German by* Charles T. Brooks. AWP
Harvest Song. Jean Toomer. NoP
Harvest Time. Star Powers. GoYe
Harvest Time. G. A. Watermeyer, *tr. fr. Afrikaans by* Guy Butler, Uys Krige, *and* Jack Cope. PeSA
Harvest to Seduce, A. Melville Cane. NYBP
Harvest Waits, The. Lloyd Mifflin. HBV-2
Harvester, The. Terry Lawrence. AMV-80
Harvester's Song. George Peele. *Fr.* The Old Wives' Tale. TrGrPo
Harvesting. Selma Robinson. InMe
Harvesting of the Roses, The. Menahem ben Jacob, *tr. fr. Hebrew.* TrJP
Harvesting Wheat for the Public Share. Li Chü, *tr. fr. Chinese by* Kenneth Rexroth *and* Ling Chung. BoWoP; PBWP
Harvey Always Wins. Jack Prelutsky. NTCP
Harvey Logan, *with music. Unknown.* OuSiCo
Has a gold tooth, sits long hours. Black Bourgeoisie. Amiri Baraka. BPo
Has a love of adventure, a promise of gold. The Whaleman's Song. *Unknown.* EtS
Has a problem he is too old. The Wolfman. Greg Kuzma. GP
Has any one seen my fair. Cressid. Nora Perry. AA
Has Any One Supposed It Lucky to Be Born? Walt Whitman. *Fr.* Song of Myself. NAs
Has anybody seen my Mopser? The Bandog. Walter de la Mare. BrPo; EvOK; TiPo
Has anybody seen my mouse? Missing. A. A. Milne. MoShBr; PDV
Has auld Kilmarnock seen the dell? Tam Samson's Elegy. Burns. PoEL-4
Has backpacked to the low shoals of Lake James. Suppose a Man. R. T. Smith. WOLT
Has Been. Alice F. Worsley. AMV-80
Has he tempered the viol's wood. Ezra Pound. *Fr.* Cantos, LXXXI. HAP
Has never written me a letter himself. He. Ronald Koertge. Str
Has not altered. Spenser's Ireland. Marianne Moore. LiTA; LiTM; MasP; NePA; NoAM; NOBA; OxBA; TAP
Has not the night been as a drunken rose. The Drunken Rose. Amarou, *tr. by* E. Powys Mathers. AWP
Has someone seen Christ in you today? Christ in You. *Unknown.* STF
Has Sorrow Thy Young Days Shaded? Thomas Moore. OxBI
Has summer come without the rose. Song. Arthur O'Shaughnessy. HBV-1
"Has the Marquis La Fayette." A New Song. Joseph Stansbury. PAH
Has there any old fellow got mixed with the boys? The Boys. Oliver Wendell Holmes. HBV-1; WBLP
Has thrust his nose under every board. Ego. Robert Siegel. GeTw; PoA
Hasbrouck and the Rose. H. Phelps Putnam. MoVE; OxBA; TwAmPo; ViBoPo
Haschish, The. Whittier. OBAL
Hasidic Jew from Sadagora. Rose Ausländer, *tr. fr. German by* Ewald Osers. VWA
Hasidim Dance. Nelly Sachs, *tr. fr. German by* Keith Bosley. VWA
Haskell. Witter Bynner. GLGT
Hassan, *sels.* James Elroy Flecker.
Hassan's Serenade, *fr.* I, ii. OBEV
War Song of the Saracens, The, *fr.* III, iii. FaBV; MoBrPo; OBVV; WHA
Hast thou a charm to stay the morning-star. Hymn before Sunrise, in the Vale of Chamouni. Samuel Taylor Coleridge. EnRP; HBV-1; OAEP; OxBoCh; WGRP
Hast thou a cunning instrument of play. Preparation. Thomas Edward Brown. OBEV; OBVV
Hast thou a heritage. In Shadow. Caroline Hazard. GoBC
Hast thou a lamp, a little lamp. The Lamp. Sarah Pratt McLean Greene. AA
Hast thou given the horse strength? The Horse. Bible, *O.T. Fr.* Job. ChTr; FaPON; TrGrPo
Hast Thou Heard It, O My Brother, *with music.* Theodore Chickering Williams. AH
Hast Thou Heard the Nightingale? Richard Watson Gilder. AA
Hast thou named all the birds without a gun? Forbearance. Emerson. AA; GN; HBV-2; HBVY; LiTA; TAP; TreFT; TrGrPo; ViBoPo; WGRP
Hast thou not known? They That Wait upon the Lord [*or* Power from God]. Bible, *O.T. Fr.* Isaiah. TreFt; TRV
Hast Thou Not Seen an Aged Rifted Tower. Hartley Coleridge. EnRP
"Hast thou ony greencloth." Robin Hood's End. *Unknown.* GoTL
Hast thou seen reversed the prophet's miracle. Frederick Goddard Tuckerman. *Fr.* Sonnets. NOBA
"Hast thou seen that lordly castle." The Castle by the Sea. Ludwig Uhland, *tr. by* Longfellow. AWP
Hast thou seen the down i' th' air. A Song to a Lute [*or* A Song]. Sir John Suckling. AnAnS-2; CaPo; EnLoPo; TrGrPo
Hast thou then survived. Wordsworth. *Fr.* Address to My Infant Daughter. EvOK; Par
Haste, haste my verses with your sharpened teeth. Unto the Breach. Andrea Poliziano, *tr. by* John Addington Symonds. PeHV
Haste thee, Nymph, and bring with thee. Mirth, with Thee I Mean to Live. Milton. *Fr.* L'Allegro. FaBV; GN
Haste to the Wedding. Alex Comfort. ErPo
Haste, ye purple gleams of light. An African Song. Thomas Chatterton. LoBV
Hasten on your childhood to the hour when white. Poem. Pablo Picasso, *tr. by* David Gascoyne. EAS
Hastening on, the wanderer strode. The Wanderer. "Yehoash," *tr. by* Isidore Goldstick. TrJP
Hastin Dot Klish, just Navajo. Saddle. William Haskel Simpson. BPAW
Hastings Mill. Cecily Fox-Smith. HBV-1
Hasty Pudding, The. Joel Barlow. AmPP; AP; OBAL, *abr.*; TAP
"Ye Alps audacious, thro' the Heavens that rise," I. NOBA; OxBA
Hasty sin of the young after a dance, The. Living in Sin. Austin Clarke. ELU
Hat Bar. Mildred Weston. FiBHP
Hatch, The. Norma Faber. SO
Hatched in a rasping darkness of dry sand. Letter IV. William Empson. LiTB
Hate! Pavel Antokolsky, *tr. fr. Russian by* Babette Deutsch. TrJP
Hate. James Stephens. MoAB; MoBrPo; OBVV
Hate and Debate Rome through the World Hath Spread. Sir John Harington. TW
(In Roman.) PV
Hate, be a faithful prop, and find. Hate! Pavel Antokolsky, *tr. by* Babette Deutsch. TrJP
Hate in the world's hand. A Proud Lady. Elinor Wylie. SBG
Hate is only one of many responses. Poem. Frank O'Hara. NeAP; SOTW
Hate me or love, I care not, as I pass. The Unicorn. Ruth Pitter. MoBrPo; MoVE
Hate only will I love. Love and Hate. *Unknown, tr. by* Frank O'Connor. KiLC; TW
Hate-Song, A. Shelley. EnLoPo
Hate the Idle Pleasures. Shakespeare. *See* Evil Designs.
Hate Whom Ye List. Sir Thomas Wyatt. EnRePo
("Hate whom ye list, for I care not.") SiPS
Hated dog sits, The. In Memory of the Moon (A Killing). Charlotte DeClue. STE; TWSS
Hater he came and sat by a ditch, A. A Hate-Song. Shelley. EnLoPo

Hath any loved you well, down there. Song from "Chartivel" [*or* Sarrazine's Song to Her Dead Lover]. Marie de France, *tr. by* Arthur O'Shaughnessy. *Fr.* Chartivel. AWP; EnLoPo; HBV-1; WPOW
Hath God, who freely gave you his own Son. To the Rev'd Mr. Jno. Sparhawk on the Birth of his Son. Samuel Sewall. SCAP
Hath not the dark stream closed above thy head. The Tears of the Poplars. Edith M. Thomas. AA
Hath not the morning dawned with added light? Ethnogenesis; Written during the Meeting of the First Southern Congress, at Montgomery, February, 1861. Henry Timrod. AmPP; NOBA; OxBA
Hath the rude laugh of Boreas frighted thee. To a Mayflower. William E. Marshall. CaP
Hath this world, without me wrought. Questionings. Samuel Johnson. HBV-2
Hatikvah—a Song of Hope. Naphtali Herz Imber, *tr. fr. Hebrew by* Henry Snowman. TrJP
Hating Your Life. John N. Morris. CABA
Hatred. Gwendolyn B. Bennett. AmNP; BANP; BlSi; CDC; PoBA
Hatred, The. Cincinnati. Cid Corman. GP
Hatred and greed and pride shall die. He Shall Speak Peace. Thomas Curtis Clark. WBLP
Hatred and Vengeance, My Eternal Portion. William Cowper. *See* Lines Written during a Period of Insanity.
Hatred of Men with Black Hair. Robert Bly. NaP; TW
Hats. R. H. W. Dillard. GP
Hats off!/ Along the street there comes. The Flag Goes By. Henry Holcomb Bennett. FaBoBe; FaFP; FaPON; GN; HBV-2; HBVY; OHFP; PAL; PGD; SiSoSe; TreF; WBLP; YaD
Hatshepsut, old girl, old friend. Sister Pharaoh. Ruth Whitman. MAT
Hattage. A. P. Herbert. FiBHP
Hatteras Calling. Conrad Aiken. BoNaP; NoAM; NOBA; TAP
Hatters, The. Nan McDonald. PoAu-2
Hauf-Roads up Schiehallion. Donald Campbell. PoSH
Haughty eagle bird, of birds the best, The. My Love Is Past. Thomas Watson. PBBP
Haughty lion, from his burning sand, A. The Lion and the Wave. William Allingham. FM
Haughty Snail-King, The. Vachel Lindsay. SO
Haughty they said he was, at first, severe. Whom We Revere. James Russell Lowell. *Fr.* Under the Old Elm. PGD
Haul Away Joe. *Unknown.* AmSS, *with music;* FSW; ShS, 2 *vers., with music*
Haul Away, My Rosy. *Unknown.* AmFP; OuSiCo, *with music*
Haul on the Bowline. *Unknown.* AmSS, *with music;* FSW; ShS, *with music*
Haul on the rope. Make the high bell lean. To the Bell-Ringer. Robert Farren. OnYI
Haul up the flag, you mourners. Elegy for Two Banjos. Karl Shapiro. LiTA; TrJP; WaP
Haulage. E. E. Nott-Bower. WhC
Haunched like a faun, he hooed. Metamorphosis. Sylvia Plath. PoA
Haunt him, Mona! Haunt him, demon sister! The Brother-in-Law. Larry Rubin. GP; TW
Haunted. Siegfried Sassoon. CMoP
Haunted Country. Robinson Jeffers. OxBA
Haunted Garden, The. Henry Treece. NeBP
Haunted House, The. Robert Graves. OxBI
Haunted House, The. Thomas Hood. EBEV; SeCePo; WiR
Haunted House. Valerie Worth. WSC
Haunted Oak, The. Paul Laurence Dunbar. BANP; UnPo
Haunted Odysseus: The Last Testament. Horace Gregory. MoVE
Haunted Oven, The. X. J. Kennedy. WSC
Haunted Palace, The. Poe. *Fr.* The Fall of the House of Usher. AA; AP; BeLS; CH; ChTr; HBV-2; LiTA; NePA; NOBA; OBVV; OxBA; PoEL-4; PrIm; SyP; TAP; TreFS; TrGrPo; ViBoPo; WiR; WSC
Haunter, The. Thomas Hardy. ChMP; NOBE; PoPle; QFR
Haunting, The. Irving Layton. NeAC
Haunts me the lugubrious shape. Half-bent Man. Richard Eberhart. NYBP
Haunts of the Halcyon, The. Charles Henry Luders. AA
Havana Dreams. Langston Hughes. PoNe
Havdolah. Susan Litwack. VWA
Havdolah Wine. Miriam Ulinover, *tr. fr. Yiddish by* Seth L. Wolitz. VWA
Have-at a Venture. *Unknown.* CoMu; ErPo
Have Courage, My Boy, to Say No! L. M. Hilton. STF; WTO
Have dark Egyptians stolen Thee away. Eugene Lee-Hamilton. Mimma Bella, I. HBV-1
Have dinosaurs come back again? Highway Construction. Carol Earle Chapin. QQQ
Have done with care, my hearts! aboard amain. A Farewell to Sir John Norris and Sir Francis Drake. George Peele. OBSC
Have done, you men and women all! The Animals in the Ark. *Unknown.* *Fr.* The Deluge. ChTr; GBP
Have fair fallen, O fair, fair have fallen, so dear. Henry Purcell. Gerard Manley Hopkins. TEP; VLP
Have Faith. Edward Carpenter. WGRP
Have Faith in God. Joe Budzynski. STF
Have Gentlemen perhaps forgotten this? A Poet Speaks from the Visitors' Gallery. Archibald MacLeish. NYBP
Have, have ye no regard, all ye. His Saviour's Words, Going to the Cross. Robert Herrick. NOCV
Have I a hundred years since or. John Landless Leads the Caravan. Iwan Goll, *tr. by* William Carlos Williams. TrJP
Have I a wife? Bedam I have! The Brewer's Man. L. A. G. Strong. DBV; DTC; ELU; FaBoCo; FiBHP; WhC
Have I caught my heavenly jewel. Stella Sleeping. Sir Philip Sidney. Astrophel and Stella, Second Song. SiPS
Have I Done My Best for Jesus? Edwin Young. STF
Have I ever been other? Exercise for the Left Hand. Constance Urdang. AMV-81
Have I Found Her? *Unknown.* ElL; EnRePo
Have I Got Dogs! William Cole. GDP
Have I nocht made ane honest shift. Sir David Lyndsay. *Fr.* Ane Satire of the Three Estaitis. GoTS
Have I not blessed thee? Then go forth; nor fear. To His Book. Robert Herrick. CaPo
Have I spent all my life turning. Simon and the Tarantula. James Wright. NNaP
Have I spoken too much or not enough of love? Epilogue. Richard Aldington. BrPo
Have I the power to bid the frost not melt. To Barba. Edward May. FaBoEE
Have I, this moment, led thee from the beach. Walter Savage Landor. GBL
Have I told you the name of a lady? Have You Seen the Lady? John Philip Sousa. OBAL
Have learned to burn my hands with fire. Breaking Ground in Me. Tom Kryss. NeAC
Have little care that Life is brief. Envoy. Bliss Carman. HBV-2
"Have mercy, god!" and on the dune sun-curs'd. Dead on the Desert. Harrison Conrard. BPAW
Have no accidents. They loop. Bats. George MacBeth. NoAM
Have patience; it is fit that in this wise. Sorrow. George Santayana. WGRP
Have pity on us, Power just and severe. Prayer. John Hall Wheelock. EaLo; NePoAm
Have pity, pity, friends, have pity on me. Epistle in Form of a Ballad to His Friends. Villon, *tr. by* Swinburne. AWP
Have the poets left a single spot for a patch to be sewn? Mu'allaqa. Antar, *tr. by* A. J. Arberry. TTY
Have the swallows come? The Swallows. Patric Dickinson. ChMP
Have thou no other gods but me. The Ten Commandments. *Unknown.* FaBoUs; OxBChV
Have We Not Seen Thy Shining Garment's Hem. Amy Carmichael. TRV
Have ye beheld (with much delight). Upon the Nipples of Julia's Breast. Robert Herrick. CaPo; ErPo; UnTE; ViBoPo
"Have ye founded your thrones and altars, then." James Russell Lowell. *Fr.* A Parable. PGD
Have ye left the greenwood lone? Fairy Song. Felicia Dorothea Hemans. HBVY
Have ye seen the morning sky. The Happy Swain. Ambrose Philips. EnLoPo
Have ye seen the would-be-not-humble dandy. The Road to Zoagli. Max Beerbohm. FaBoNo
Have you a gold cup. The Question. Robert Duncan. NeAP
Have you any gooseberry wine. Mazilla and Mazura. *Unknown.* ChTr
Have you any room for Jesus. Room for Jesus. Barbara H. Staples. STF
Have you any work for a tinker, Mistris. *Unknown.* OBS
Have You Been at Carrick? *Unknown, tr. fr. Irish by* Edward Walsh. AnIV; BIrV
Have you been at sea on a windy day. A Windy Day. Winifred Howard. FaPON
Have you been to that country where the gold. Mignon. Goethe, *tr. by* Robert Bly. NU
"Have you been with the King to Rome." The Palatine. Willa Cather. HBMV
Have you cast your net out over the world? Questions and Answers. Doris Muhringer, *tr. by* Beth Bjorklund. AMV-80
Have you come to the Red Sea place in your life. At the Place of the Sea [*or* The Red Sea Place in Your Life]. Annie Johnson Flint. BLPA; BLRP; STF
Have you committed all to God? Our Times Are in His Hands. Mary D. Freeze. STF
Have you dug the spill. Harlem Sweeties. Langston Hughes. CABA; LiTM; NoP; PoNe; TTY

Have you ever gone visiting for a weekend of ravelry. Tallyho-Hum. Ogden Nash. PH
Have You Ever Had a Witch Bloom like a Highway. Richard Brautigan. InPK
Have you ever heard of the Sugar-Plum Tree? The Sugar-Plum Tree. Eugene Field. FaFP; HBV-1; HBVY; OxBChV; SoPo; TreF
Have you ever heard that a tailor was ill? The Tailor. Joseph Leftwich. TrJP
Have you ever heard the wind go "Yooooo?" The Night Wind. Eugene Field. FaPON
Have you ever in your life seen a Possum play possum? Opossum. William Jay Smith. TiPo
Have you ever sat by the railroad track. Empties Coming Back. Angelo De Ponciano. BLPA
Have You Ever Seen? *Unknown.* RHPC
Have you ever seen the moon. Have You Seen It. Lula Lowe Weeden. CDC
Have you ever smelled summer? That Was Summer. Marci Ridlon. NTCP
Have you ever took a trip, baby, on the Mobile Line. France Blues. *Unknown.* BluL
Have you ever tried to get along. The Other Person's Place. Donald H. Hover. STF
Have you ever woke up with them. Bullfrog Blues. *Unknown.* BluL
Have you forgotten yet? Aftermath. Siegfried Sassoon. BrPo; MoBrPo; TrJP; ViBoPo; WaP
Have you gazed on naked grandeur, where there's nothing else to gaze on. The Call of the Wild. Robert W. Service. CaP
Have you got a brook in your little heart. Emily Dickinson. FaBV
Have you had a kindness shown? Pass It On. Henry K. Burton. BLRP
Have you had your tonsils out? The New Neighbor. Rose Fyleman. SoPo; TiPo
Have you heard about that bully. The Bully Song. Charles E. Trevathan. BLSo
Have you heard of one Humpty Dumpty. The Ballad of Persse O'Reilly. James Joyce. *Fr.* Finnegans Wake. FaBoBa; LiTB
Have you heard of our fighting Twenty-first. The Dash for the Colors. Frederick G. Webb. BeLS
Have you heard of the dreadful fate. The Ashtabula Disaster. Julia Moore. EvOK; OBAL
Have you heard of the manly turning taken. The Day of Inverlochy. Iain Lom. GoTS
Have you heard of the quaint people. Strawberries in November. Shaw Neilson. PoAu-1
Have you heard of the terrible family They. They Say. Ella Wheeler Wilcox. WBLP
Have you heard of the wonderful one-hoss shay. The Deacon's Masterpiece; or, The Wonderful "One-Hoss Shay." Oliver Wendell Holmes. *Fr.* The Autocrat of the Breakfast Table. AmPP; AP; BeLS; FaBoBe; FaFP; FaPo; FPL; HBV-1; HBVY; InMe; LiTA; MoShBr; NePA; NOBA; OBAL; OBCA; OHFP; OxBA; PaPo; PoLF; PoRA; TAP; TreF; WBLP; YaD
Have you heard the blinking toad. The Song of the Toad. John Burroughs. FaPON
Have you heard the Master's call? The Master's Call. Oswald J. Smith. STF
Have you heard the story that gossips tell. John Burns of Gettysburg. Bret Harte. HBV-2; OHIP; PAH; PAL
Have you heard the tale of the aloe plant. The Aloe Plant. Henry Harbaugh. BLPA
Have you heard? The troubles. Sulpicia, *tr. fr. Latin by* Aliki *and* Willis Barnstone. BoWoP
Have you hearkened the eagle scream over the sea? The Irish Hurrah. Thomas Osborne Davis. OnYI
Have you listened for the things I have left out? Unsaid. A. R. Ammons. NOBA
Have you lived long, sir, in these parts? An Interview. K. W. Grandsen. OxBTC
Have You Lost Faith? *Unknown.* WBLP
Have you met Miss Mabel Green. If It Looks like Jelly, Shakes like Jelly, It Must Be Gel-a-tine. *Unknown.* BluL
Have you no eyes for me? The Intruder. Marya Zaturenska. OLR
Have you no weathervane? Straws. Elizabeth J. Coatsworth. AmFN
Have you not fallen asleep to strong men's rowing. The Rowers. Laura Benét. GoYe
Have you not heard his silent steps? Rabindranath Tagore. *Fr.* Gitanjali. WGRP
Have you not heard the poets tell. Baby Bell. Thomas Bailey Aldrich. HBV-1
Have you not in a chimney seen. A Description of Maidenhead. Earl of Rochester. NOBL; UnTE
Have you not noted, in some family. The Birth-Bond. Dante Gabriel Rossetti. The House of Life, XV. HBV-1; OAEP
Have You Noted the White Areas. Carlyle Reedy. PPJ
Have you noticed. Angels. Anne Szumigalski. NOBC
Have you noticed the docile appeal. Letter from a State Hospital. Frank Mundorf. GoYe
Have you noticed the little shadow? Les Jours Gigantesques/The Titanic Days. Kathleen Fraser. NPGG
Have you observ'd the wench in the street. *Unknown.* OBS
Have you seen an apple orchard in the spring? An Apple Orchard in the Spring. William Martin. GN
Have you seen but a bright lily grow. So White, So Soft, So Sweet [*or* So Sweet Is She]. Ben Jonson. *Fr.* A Celebration of Charis: The Triumph of Charis. FaBoCh; GN; TrGrPo; UnTE
"Have you seen Hugh?" The King of Connacht. *Unknown, tr. by* Frank O'Connor. KiLC
Have You Seen It. Lula Lowe Weeden. CDC
Have you seen me at all. Before the Thaw. John Gill. NeAC
Have you seen the Hidebehind? The Hidebehind. Michael Rosen. AmMo
Have You Seen the Lady? John Philip Sousa. OBAL
Have you sometimes, calm, silent let your tread aspirant rise. Heard on the Mountain. Victor Hugo, *tr. by* Francis Thompson. *Fr.* Feuilles d'Automne. AWP
Have You Thanked a Green Plant Today. Don Anderson. QQQ
Have you time for a story. Charity Overcoming Envy. Marianne Moore. NYBP
Have You Watched the Fairies? Rose Fyleman. SoPo; TiPo
Havelok, *sel.* *Unknown.*
  Havelok at Grimsby and Lincoln. OxBM
Haven. Donald Jeffrey Hayes. AmNP; PoNe
Haven and last refuge of my pain, The. Three Poems, II. Michelangelo, *tr. by* George Santayana. AWP
Haven't been to one in almost three years. Powwow 79, Durango. Paula Gunn Allen. STE
Haven't I said that part of having intercourse. Leslie Scalapino. *Fr.* Hmmmm. NPGG
Haven't you wondered. Doesn't It Seem to You. Gevorg Emin, *tr. by* Martin Robbins. AMV-81
Having a fine new suit. Apologue. Tony Connor. BoLoP
Having a Wonderful Time. D. B. Wyndham Lewis. FiBHP
Having attained success in business. Robert Whitmore. Frank Marshall Davis. BPo; NoP; PoBA; PoNe
Having banged the piano too hard. The Fish Sonata. Winfield Townley Scott. MP
Having been tenant long to a rich lord. Redemption. George Herbert. AnAnS-1; CABA; EaLo; EBCP; FF; HAP; InPS; JCP; LiTB; MeLP; MePo; NoP; NOBE; NOCV; OBS; PAI; SCV; SeCeV; SeCP; SeCV-1; SoSe; TEP; TrCP; WeW
Having bitten on life like a sharp apple. Aubade. Louis MacNeice. NIP; ViBoPo
Having come to this place. This Place in the Ways. Muriel Rukeyser. MiAP
Having come under the baleful, red influence of Mars. Apollo 113. Diderik Finne. AMV-80
Having confused me. A Voice from the Roses. Maxine W. Kumin. NMM
Having crowded once onto the threshold of mortality. Divinities. W. S. Merwin. PoA
Having Eaten Breakfast. D. C. Berry. BXAP
Having enough plowshares. Bucolic. W. S. Merwin. NMP
Having heard the instruction. One Modern Poet. Carl Sandburg. OBAL
"Having her under me," the man said, "in bed, and remembering." Leslie Scalapino. *Fr.* Hmmmm. NPGG
Having hooded my face with hair. The Sibyl's Song. Michele Roberts. BrRo
Having inherited a vigorous mind. My Descendants. W. B. Yeats. *Fr.* Meditations in Time of Civil War, IV. LiTB
Having interred her infant-birth. An Ode, upon a Question Moved, Whether Love Should Continue Forever? Lord Herbert of Cherbury. AnAnS-2; JCP; MeLP; MePo; NOBE; OBS; SeCP
Having invented a new Holocaust. U.S. 1946 King's X. Robert Frost. NIP
Having known war and peace. Turning Fifty. Judith Wright. NAs
Having learned to play the guitar. On Learning to Play the Guitar. Ray Fraser. NeAC
Having left hard [*or* solid] ground behind. The Insular Celts. Ciaran Carson. BIrV; CIP
Having little kids around, they say, is truly bliss. Did You? William Cole. RHPC
Having lived a Coney Island life. A Coney Island Life. James L. Weil. AmFN
Having lost my leather purse. My Son. Ruth Stone. WPE

Having Lost My Sons, I Confront the Wreckage of the Moon: Christmas, 1960. James Wright. CoAP
Having met as older graduate student and emigrant-prof. When a Body. Gene Dawson. AMV-80
Having never read or wanted to. Below Bald Mountain. Janice Townley Moore. AMV-80
Having No Ear. Donald Davie. AMV-81
Having no father anymore, having got up. The Homecoming of Emma Lazarus. Galway Kinnell. NaP
Having no past, I invent one. Album. Carol Papenhausen. AMV-81
Having put yourself on the way. Spirits, Dancing. Arthur Gregor. NYBP; VGW
Having read and written myself almost to sleep, I stretch. Under the Sign of Moth. David Wagoner. AMV-81
Having Read Books. Heather McHugh. GeTw
Having read the inscriptions. Wang Peng's Recommendation for Improving the People. Paul Eldridge. ShM
Having Replaced Love with Food and Drink. Diane Wakoski. NAs
Having scrubbed away the gray sweat. Old Michael. George M. Brady. NeIP
Having so rich a treasury, so fine a hoard. The Daisy. Marya Zaturenska. GrPl; MoAmPo
Having split up the chaparral. The Wide Land. A. R. Ammons. TwCP
Having squandered my years to follow that wake beyond the elm. Mystery. Claire McAllister. TwAmPo
Having taken her slowly by surprise. A Pause for Breath. Ted Hughes. NYBP
Having this day my horse, my hand, my lance. Astrophel and Stella, XLI. Sir Philip Sidney. EnRePo; HAP; OAEP; OBSC; SiPS
Having unbuckled themselves. Mount Saint Helens/ Loowit; an Indian Woman's Song. Wendy Rose. TWSS
Having used every subterfuge. A Renewal. James Merrill. PoPl
Having written several poems which I will not publish. Baedeker for Metaphysicians. Brian Higgins. FaBoTw
Hawaii Dantesca. Charles Wright. LCAP
Hawk, The. Raymond Knister. OBCV
Hawk, The. W. B. Yeats. PoA
Hawk and Snake. Leslie Silko. VoR
Hawk free of jess. Elegy for a Diver. Philip Booth. LiSp
Hawk Is a Woman. Hildegarde Flanner. WPE
Hawk Nailed to a Barn Door. Peter Blue Cloud. VoR
Hawk Roosting. Ted Hughes. CMoP; GTBS-P; HAP; HeIP; LiTM; MP; NePoEA-2; NMP; OxBTC; PB; PPP; TwCP; UnPo
Hawk with heavy-lidded eyes, The. The Last Summer. Vivian Smith. PoAu-2
Hawkbit, The. Sir Charles G. D. Roberts. HBV-1
Hawking for the Partridge. Thomas Ravenscroft. NCEP; OxBoLi
Hawks. James Stephens. HBMV
Hawk's Eyes. Yvor Winters. PoA
Hawk's Way. Ted Olson. HoPM
Haworth Churchyard, *sel.* Matthew Arnold.
"Where, behind Keighley, the road." FaBoPP
Hawthorn, The. *Unknown.* ChTr; GBP; OxBM
Hawthorn apples turn red years stumble. Lines from a Misplaced Person. Jeanne Hill. FAZ
Hawthorn Dyke. Swinburne. VLP
Hawthorn Hath a Deathly Smell, The. Walter de la Mare. BrPo
Hawthorn Hedge, The. Judith Wright. PoAu-2; WPE
Hawthorn morning moving, The. Renewal by Her Element. Denis Devlin. CIP
Hawthorn Tree, The. Willa Cather. HBMV
Hawthorne. Amos Bronson Alcott. AA
Hawthorne. Longfellow. NCEP; PoEL-5
Hawthorne. James Russell Lowell. *Fr.* A Fable for Critics. AmPP; AP; NOBA; OxBA; TAP
Hawthorne Garland, A. Richard Harter Fogle. NIP; OBAL
Hay Appeareth, The. Bible, *O.T.* Proverbs, XXVII: 25. FaPON
Hay, Ay, Hay, Ay. *Unknown.* SBVL
(Now Is Yule Come.) OxBM
Hay for the Horses. Gary Snyder. ConAP; CTBA; GrPl; InPS; NaP
Hay, hay, by this day. A Schoolboy's Complaint [*or* The Scholar Complains]. *Unknown.* MeEL; OxBM
Hay Hotel, The. Oliver St. John Gogarty. BIrV
Hay, house-dust, or the fur from cats. Allergy. Walker Gibson. NePoAm
Hay is for horses. *Unknown.* OxNR
Hay! now [*or* nou] the day dawis [*or* dauis]. *See* Hey! now the day dawis.
Hay Scuttle. Robert Morgan. MAYP
Hay-Time; or, The Constant Lovers. A Pastoral. Josiah Relph. NOEC
Haydn; the Horn. Daniel Berrigan. TwAmPo
Hayeswater Boat, The, *sel.* Matthew Arnold.
Hayeswater. FaBoPP
Hayfield, The. Charles Bruce. *Fr.* The Flowing Summer. CaP
Haying. John Frederic Herbin. CaP; PeCV
Hayle holy-land wherein our holy lord. Uppon the First Sight of New England, June 29, 1638. Thomas Tillam. GOA; SCAP
Haylle, Comly and Clene. *Unknown. See* Hail, Comly and Clene.
Haymakers, Rakers. Thomas Dekker. *Fr.* The Sun's Darling. ELP; ViBoPo
(Country Glee.) OBSC
Haymaking. Edward Thomas. BrPo; MoAB; MoBrPo; SeCePo
Hayseed, The. Arthur L. Kellog. FSW
Hayseed, *with music. Unknown.* AS
Hayseed. Theodore Weiss. TwAmPo
Haystack, The. Andrew Young. POL
Haystack in the Floods, The. William Morris. BeLS; CABA; EBEV; EBVV; HAP; LoBV; NBM; NoP; OAEL-2; OAEP; OBNC; OBNV; PoEL-5; PoRA; SeCeV; VLP; WeW; WHA
Haywood. Harold LaMont Otey. LFAC
Hazardous Occupations. Carl Sandburg. SaC
Hazard's friend Elliot is homosexual. Wholesome. William Meredith. TAP
Haze. Henry David Thoreau. *Fr.* A Week on the Concord and Merrimack Rivers. HeIP; NoP; PoPl
(Woof of the Sun, Ethereal Gauze.) AP; TAP; ViBoPo
Haze, and out of it we appear. Eagle Squadron. Vern Rutsala. AMV-80
Haze, char, and the weather of All Souls'. In the Elegy Season. Richard Wilbur. InPK; MoAB; NePoEA; NYBP
Haze is on the lake, A; the dipping grasses. August, at an Upstairs Window. Harold McCurdy. AMV-80
Haze upon the meadow, The. What Is Winter? Edmund Blunden. ChMP
Hazlitt Sups. Katharine Day Little. GoYe
Hazy day in Puerto Rico, A. The Last Flight of the Great Wallenda. Barbara Helfgott Hyett. AMV-80
He. John Ashbery. SOTW
He. Lawrence Ferlinghetti. NeAP; PoM
He. Ronald Koertge. Str
He. Stanley Kunitz. CrMA; VGW
He/ and she, A. A Pair. May Swenson. RFM
He Abjures Love. Thomas Hardy. OBNC
He accepts the circle, speech and so. Anne-Marie Albiach, *tr. fr. French by* Keith Waldrop. BoWoP
He adored the desk, its brown-oak inlaid with ebony. Geoffrey Hill. Mercian Hymns, X. HAP; NoP
He all that time among the sewers of Troy. Troy. Edwin Muir. CMoP
He always comes on market days. The Balloon Man. Rose Fyleman. SoPo; SUS
He always has something to grumble about. A Chip on His Shoulder. *Unknown.* BLPA; WBLP
He always was one for a jeer and a jest. Epitaph for a Funny Fellow. Morris Bishop. FPL
He and a gentle Pardoner rode together. Chaucer, *mod. version by* Nevill Coghill. *Fr.* The Canterbury Tales: Prologue. BiP
He and his, unwashed all winter. The Native. W. S. Merwin. NePoEA-2; PoRA
He and I. Dante Gabriel Rossetti. The House of Life, XCVIII. NBM
He and She. Sir Edwin Arnold. BLPA
He and She. Eugene Fitch Ware. PoLF; YaD
He Approacheth the Hall of Judgment. *Unknown, tr. fr. Egyptian by* Robert Hillyer. *Fr.* Book of the Dead. AWP
He arrived at the funeral parlor. The Funeral Parlor. Henry Johnson. LFAC
He as O, A. E. E. Cummings. InPS
He ascended from a lonely crag in winter. On the Death of Karl Barth. Jack Clemo. NOCV
He Asked about the Quality. C. P. Cavafy, *tr. fr. Greek by* Edmund Keeley *and* Philip Sherrard. PeHV
He Asketh Absolution of God. *Unknown, tr. fr. Egyptian by* Robert Hillyer. *Fr.* Book of the Dead. AWP
He ate and drank the precious words. Emily Dickinson. AA; AP
He awoke this morning from a strange dream. Chief Leschi of the Nisqually. Duane Niatum. CDW; STE
He bare him up, he bare him down. The Corpus Christi Carol [*or* The Falcon *or* Lully, Lulley, Lully, Lulley *or* Over Yonder's a Park]. *Unknown.* ACP; BaBo; HAP; LoBV; MeEL; ViBoPo
He behind the straight plough stands. Ploughman at the Plough. Louis Golding. HBMV; OHIP
He Biddeth Osiris to Arise from the Dead. *Unknown, tr. fr. Egyptian by* Robert Hillyer. *Fr.* Book of the Dead. AWP
He blinks upon the hearth-rug. On a Cat, Ageing. Sir Alexander Gray. BSV
He breathes into my earpiece late at night. The Obscene Caller. Cheri Fein. TW
"He Bringeth Them unto Their Desired Haven." Lewis Frank Tooker. HBV-2

He brought a Grecian queen, whose youth and freshness. Portrait of Helen. Shakespeare. *Fr.* Troilus and Cressida, II, ii, *and* IV, i. TrGrPo
He brought a light so she could see. Strains of Sight. Robert Duncan. CMoP; NMP
He brought a lily white. To His Mother. John Banister Tabb. *Fr.* The Child. AA
He built a mud-wall'd hovel, where he kept. George Crabbe. *Fr.* The Borough, Letter XXII. SaC
He built no temple, yet the farthest sea. The Man Christ. Therese Lindsey. TRV
He built right on the top of the land. Where She Was Not Born. Yvonne. CNA
He by no means flies straight at petunia. The Bee and the Petunia. Katherine Hoskins. ErPo
He calleth to me out of Seir, Watchman, what of the night? Watchman, What of the Night? Bible, *O.T.* *Fr.* Isaiah. AWP
He calls: no answer from his folks. The Carpenter's Real Anguish. Stephen Gardner. AMV-81
He calls you in his wedding coat. The Wedding Coat. Harriet Rose. BrRo
He came/ striding. A Legend of Paul Bunyan. Arthur S. Bourinot. AmFN; FaPON
He came/ When the 60's went from flowers to flames. Who Needs Charlie Manson? Raymond Thompson. LFAC
He came, a youth, singing in the dawn. Paul Laurence Dunbar. James David Corrothers. BANP; PoNe
He came all so still. A Carol [*or* An Ancient Christmas Carol]. *Unknown.* HBV-1; HBVY; OHIP; PChr
He came and took me by the hand. The Mystery. Ralph Hodgson. CH; HBV-2; MoAB; MoBrPo; WGRP
He came apart in the open. Martin's Blues. Michael S. Harper. CNA; PoBA
He came back and shot. He shot him. When he came. Incident. Amiri Baraka. NoAM
He came down the old road. Ghost Boy. Mark Van Doren. SO
He came from hills to comfortable plains. The Mountaineer. Robert Nathan. TrJP
He came from Malta; and Eumelus says. A [*or* The] Maltese Dog. Tymnes, *tr. by* Edmund Blunden. FaBoCh; FaBoEE; GDP; TiPo
He came from the North, and his words were few. The Man of the North Countrie. Thomas D'Arcy McGee. OnYI
He came in silvern armor, trimmed with black. Sonnet. Gwendolyn B. Bennett. AmNP; CDC; PoBA; PoNe
He came into the world with showers Assuming the Name of Any Next Child. John Tagliabue. AMV-80
He came not as the princes born to rule. Lincoln. Clyde Walton Hill. PGD
He came not in the red dawn. The Adventurer. Odell Shepard. HBMV
He came to be The Light. It Was Not Strange. Esther Lloyd Hagg. PGD
He came to call me back from death. Eurydice. Francis William Bourdillon. HBV-1
He came to his love's window at the dead of the night. The Little Drummer. *Unknown.* AmFP
"He came to me in his swift course." *Unknown, tr. by* J. G. O'Keefe. *Fr.* Sweeney the Mad. OnYI
He came to my desk with a quivering lip. A [*or* The] New Leaf. Kathleen Wheeler. BLRP; PGD; STF; WBLP
He came to shut. Eichmann. Douglas Blazek. LTB
He came to the desert of London town. William Blake. James Thomson ("B.V.") HBV-2; OAEP; OBVV
He came to us every other summer. The Missionary Visits Our Church in Scranton. Jay Parini. MAYP
He Came to Visit Me. Martin Seymour-Smith. FaBoTw
He Came Too Late. Elizabeth Bogart. AA
He Came Unlook'd For. Sara Coleridge. *Fr.* Phantasmion. OBRV (Song: "He came unlook'd for, undesir'd.") OBVV
He came with roses in his mouth. Joy o' Living. Amanda Benjamin Hall. HBMV
He can hear the owl's flight in daylight. Blind Man. Michael Hamburger. NePoEA-2
He cannot help it that his only eye. The Photographer Whose Shutter Died. Williiam Meissner. PoDr
He Cares. Owen C. Salway. STF
He Careth. "Marianne Farningham." *See* God Cares.
He carries shadows in his face like caves. On the Apparition of Oneself. William Burford. PoA
He carved the red deer and the bull. In the Caves of Auvergne. W. J. Turner. HBMV
He caught his chisel, hastened to his bench. The Death of Azron. Alice Wellington Rollins. AA
He ceased; and Satan stayed not to reply. Satan [*or* Satan Views the World]. Milton. *Fr.* Paradise Lost, II. SeCePo; WHA
He chants a boy-chant. The Grace of Cynthia's Maidenhood. Vinnie-Marie D'Ambrosio. IHMS
He Charges Her to Lay Aside Her Weapons. Pierce Ferriter, *tr. fr. Late Middle Irish by* the Earl of Longford. AnIL; OnYI
"He chases shadows," sneered the British tars. The First Voyage of John Cabot. Hezekiah Butterworth. PAH
He clasps the crag with crooked hands. The Eagle. Tennyson. CABA; CH; FaBoCh; FaPON; FF; FiP; FM; GN; GoJo; GTBS-P; HBV-1; HeIP; InPK; NoP; NTCP; OAEL-2; OAEP; PAI; PB; PBBP; PDV; PoPle; PPoe; PrIm; RHPC; SeCePo; SeCeV; SUS; SyP; TreFT; TrGrPo; UnPo; WiR
He climbed to the top. Fergus Falling. Galway Kinnell. DiL
He climbs its ladder, twisted. DNA Lab. Michael Spence. SOTS
He climbs the stair. Waterchew! Gregory Corso. VGW
He collects used words. The Word Man. Larry Moffi. AMV-80
He Comes Among. George Barker. OBMV
He comes down to the shadow. Heron. Ted Walker. NYBP
He comes from afar. Air Traveler. Lillian Morrison. RHPC
He comes from the house as lightning flickers in the sky. Love and Music. *Gond Oral Tradition, tr. by* V. Elwin *and* S. Hivale. WTO
He comes,—he comes,—the Frost Spirit comes! You may trace his footsteps now. The Frost Spirit. Whittier. HBV-1
He comes in the night! He comes in the night! Santa Claus. *Unknown.* HBVY
He comes in the spring. Shaman. Erika Mumford. PoDr
He comes, the happy warrior. Sinfonia Eroica. Alice Archer James. AA
He comes, the old one, his shabby cap askew. Old Man with a Mowing Machine. May Carleton Lord. GoYe
He comes, the pest and terror of the yard. Summer. Robert Bloomfield. *Fr.* The Farmer's Boy. PBBP
He comes through the door. The Assassin's Fatal Error. Lawrence Raab. AmPA
He comes unknown and heard and stands there. Man into a Churchyard. Bernard Gutteridge. EAS
He comes with herald clouds of dust. Superior Nonsense Verses. *Unknown.* NA
He comes with western winds, with evening's wandering airs. Emily Brontë. *Fr.* The Prisoner. ELP
He Cometh. Judah Halevi, *tr. fr. Hebrew by* Emma Lazarus. TrJP
He Cometh Forth into the Day. *Unknown, tr. fr. Egyptian by* Robert Hillyer. *Fr.* Book of the Dead. AWP
He cometh, O bliss! He Cometh. Judah Halevi, *tr. by* Emma Lazarus. TrJP
He Comforts Himself. Christopher Morley. *Fr.* Translations from the Chinese. EvOK
He Commandeth a Fair Wind. *Unknown, tr. fr. Egyptian by* Robert Hillyer. *Fr.* Book of the Dead. AWP
He compares his beloved to a snake. Microcosmos, VII. Nigel Heseltine. NeBP
He Complains to Bishop Hartgar of Thirst. Sedulius Scottus. *See* Nunc Viridant Segetes.
He cooked cornbread. Ned Christie. Robert J. Conley. STE
He Could Have Found His Way. Kathleen Dalziel. PoAu-1
He could hit a blade of grass with his spear. A Skilful Spearman! *Tr. fr. Hawaiian.* WTO
He could not die when trees were green. The Dying Child. John Clare. EnRP; NCEP; TrGrPo
He could see the little lake. The Lake. James Stephens. MoBrPo
He could sing sweetly on a string. Orpheus. Elizabeth Madox Roberts. MoAmPo
He couldn't hear their roar. Drowned Sailor. Neufville Shaw. CaP
He cradled his head in those hands. Morning. Alberto Ríos. MAYP
He crawls along the mountain walls. On the Heights. Lucius Harwood Foote. AA
He crawls to the edge of the foaming creek. Meeting the Mountains. Gary Snyder. NoAM; TAP
He cried aloud to God: "The men below." Genius. Edward Lucas White. AA; WGRP
He crouches, and buries his face on his knees,/ And hides in the dark of his hair. The Last of His Tribe. Henry Kendall. CBAP; PoAu-1
He cut a sappy sucker from the muckle rodden-tree. The Whistle. Charles Murray. GoTS; OxBS
He cuts down the lakes so they appear straight. He. John Ashbery. SOTW
He debated whether. Arthur Ridgewood, M.D. Frank Marshall Davis. BPo
He deemed his task a solemn one. Priest and Pagan. Albert Durrant Watson. CaP
He Defendeth His Heart against the Destroyer. *Unknown, tr. fr. Egyptian by* Robert Hillyer. *Fr.* Book of the Dead. AWP
He did not come/ A gnostic. Incarnation Poem. John Leax. TrCP

He did not come to woo U Nu. Just Dropped In. William Cole. FiBHP; GoJo; POL; PoPl
He Did Not Know. Harry Kemp. WGRP
He did not wear his scarlet coat. The Ballad of Reading Gaol. Oscar Wilde. BeLS; BrPo; DTo; HBV-2; MoBrPo; NOBE; OAEL-2; OBMV; OBNC; OBNV; OnYI; TreF
He did not wear his swallow tail. The Gourmand. Harry Graham. FaBoPa
He didn't know much music. The Mocking-Bird. Frank Lebby Stanton. AA
He didn't know why he nursed the white man back to. Tonto. Ronald Koertge. GP
"He Didn't Oughter." A. P. Herbert. FiBHP
He didn't want to do it with skill. Lion & Honeycomb. Howard Nemerov. PP
He died for me, my Saviour, He. It Was for Me. Eva Gray. STF
He died in attempting to swallow. The Death of Polybius Jubb. Roy Campbell. WhC
"He died," saith the cross, "my very name." The Cross and the Tomb. Annie Johnson Flint. STF
He "Digesteth Harde Yron." Marianne Moore. CMoP; NoAM
He dines alone surrounded by reflections. Witch Doctor. Robert Hayden. AmNP; MAT; NoAM; PAI
He disagrees with Simone de Beauvoir. His Plans for Old Age. William Meredith. TAP
He disappeared in the dead of winter. In Memory of W. B. Yeats. W. H. Auden. CABA; CMoP; CoBMV; FaFP; HAP; HeIP; HoPM; LiTB; LiTM; MasP; MoAB; MoBrPo; MoVE; NePA; NoAM; NOBE; OAEL-2; OAEP; OxBTC; PAI; PP; PPoe; PPP; PrIm; TrGrPo; UnPo; ViBoPo; WeW
He discovers himself on an old airfield. The Old Pilot. Donald Hall. LCAP
He does not die that can bequeathe. Duncton Hill. Hilaire Belloc. GoBC
He does not hear the struck string. Music God. Mark Van Doren. UnS
He does not lead me year by year. Step by Step. Barbara C. Ryberg. STF
He does not lounge with the old men. For William Edward Burghardt Dubois on His Eightieth Birthday. Bette Darcie Latimer. PoNe
He does not think that I haunt here nightly. The Haunter. Thomas Hardy. ChMP; NOBE; PoPle; QFR
He doesn't know when it was that the last door closed. After Some Day of Decision. Reed Whittemore. NePoEA
He doesn't like it, of course. His Body. Sandra McPherson. AmPA; GeTw; GP
He Doeth All Things Well. Anne Brontë. TRV
He doeth well who doeth good. Best of All. *Unknown.* WBLP
He Done His Level Best. "Mark Twain." BPAW
He drank strong waters and his speech was coarse. Kipling. *Fr.* Plain Tales from the Hills. PV
He dreamed first. Adam's Dying. Ridgely Torrence. FYAP
He dreamed of lovely women as he slept. Undergraduate. Merrill Moore. ErPo
He dreamt that he saw the buffalant. A Quadrupedremian Song. Tom Hood. AmMo; FaBoNo
He drew a circle that shut me out. Outwitted. Edwin Markham. BLPA; ELU; FPL; MoAmPo; TreFT; TRV
He drew hundreds of women. Beauty and Sadness. Cathy Song. MAYP
He drives onto the grassy shoulder and unfastens. Earth Walk. William Meredith. MAT
He drove to Terre Haute. Looking for a Home. Bert Stern. FAZ
He drowsed and was aware of silence heaped. The Death-Bed. Siegfried Sassoon. LiTM; MMA; MoVE; PoPle
He dumped her in the wheelbarrow. Wheelbarrow. Eleanor Farjeon. FiBHP
He dwelt among "Apartments let." Jacob. Phoebe Cary. InMe; OBAL
He eats of the fruits of the great Speckle. Real Life. Ted Berrigan. NoAM
He Embarketh in the Boat of Ra. *Unknown, tr. fr. Egyptian by* Robert Hillyer. *Fr.* Book of the Dead. AWP
He ended; and midst those who heard were some. March. William Morris. *Fr.* The Earthly Paradise. VLP
He ended; and thus Adam last reply'd. The Retreat from Paradise. Milton. *Fr.* Paradise Lost, XII. HeIP; PoEL-3
He ended, nor the Argicide refus'd. Homer, *tr. by* William Cowper. *Fr.* The Odyssey, V. OBVE
He entered with the authority of politeness. The Southerner. Karl Shapiro. NYBP; PoNe
He Entereth the House of the Goddess Hathor. *Unknown, tr. fr. Egyptian by* Robert Hillyer. *Fr.* Book of the Dead. AWP
He Establisheth His Triumph. *Unknown, tr. fr. Egyptian by* Robert Hillyer. *Fr.* Book of the Dead. AWP
He expects the old names to return. Mail Call. John Bensko. MAYP
He Faces the Second Winter. Philip Levine. *Fr.* Sierra Kid. PoA
He fears the tiger standing in his way. The Drunkard. Philip Levine. NePoEA-2
He feels small as he awakens. The Awakening. Robert Creeley. NeAP
He Fell among Thieves. Sir Henry Newbolt. EBVV; FaPoR; HBV-2; HBVY; OBEV; OBVV; OBWP; OnMSP; OxBTC
He fell from the roof. News. Louis Dudek. *Fr.* Provincetown. MoCV
He fell in victory's fierce pursuit. The General Elliott. Robert Graves. DBV
He fell off the wheel of souls. DOA in Dulse. Diane Burns. STE
He finished his speech in a/ gruesome way. Introducing a Madman. Keith Waldrop. TW
He first deceased; she for a little tried. Upon the Death of Sir Albert Morton's Wife. Sir Henry Wotton. AnAnS-2; BoLoP; EnLoPo; FaBoEE; NIP; NOP; OBEV; OBS; PoPle; SeCP; TreFT; TrGrPo; ViBoPo; WeW
He Fishes with His Father's Ghost. Lewis Nordan. AMV-81
He floats down the Seine. Body Fished from the Seine. Gregory Corso. GP
He followed me up and he followed me down. Lady Isabel and the Elf Knight (Pretty Polly). *Unknown.* AmFP
He found a formula for drawing comic rabbits. Epitaph on an Unfortunate Artist. Robert Graves. FaBoEE; NOBL; WhC
He found a Woman in the cave. Thalaba and the Magic Thread. Robert Southey. SeCePo
He found her by the ocean's moaning verge. Modern Love, XLIX. George Meredith. HBV-1; LoAS; NoP; OAEL-2; OAEP
He from the wind-bitten North with ship and companions descended. A Drifter off Tarentum. Kipling. *Fr.* Epitaphs of the War. FaBoEE; MMA; PoPle
He fumbles at your soul. Emily Dickinson. NOCV
He gathered cherry-stones, and carved them quaintly. An Art Master. John Boyle O'Reilly. AA
He gave her some kind of elixir. A Mean Trick. *Unknown.* TDH
He gave himself another year. Patrick Kavanagh. *Fr.* The Great Hunger. BIrV
He Gave Himself for Me. *Unknown.* STF
He gave his card. How many times have I. Contact. Dorothy Livesay. CaP
He gave his life upon the cross. His Garments. Esther Lloyd Hagg. PGD
He gave silver shoes to the rabbit. Blake Leads a Walk on the Milky Way. Nancy Willard. OBCA
"He gave the little wealth he had." Swift. *Fr.* On the Death of Doctor Swift. ViBoPo
He gave the solid rail a hateful kick. The Egg and the Machine. Robert Frost. CABA; MoAmPo
He gave us all a good-bye cheerily. Messmates. Sir Henry Newbolt. CH; EBVV; HBV-1
He gets mostly dead sage and thornbush. Prospero on the Mountain Gathering Wood. Jack Gilbert. NPGG
He gives to me His wondrous grace. This Blessed Christ of Calvary. *Unknown.* STF
He Giveth More [Grace]. Annie Johnson Flint. BLRP; STF; TRV; WBLP
He goes regularly to the taverna. The Twenty-fifth Year of His Life. C. P. Cavafy, *tr. by* Edmund Keeley *and* Philip Sherrard. PeHV
He grew where waves ride nine feet high. In Memoriam: Roy Campbell. Ralph Nixon Currey. PeSA
He had a falcon on his wrist. Love Me, Love My Dog. Isabella Valancy Crawford. WHW
He had a many-coloured glance like flowers. Edward James. *Fr.* Carmina Amico. PeHV
He had awaited me. A Meeting. Daniel Hoffman. CoPo
He had been coming a very long time. For Malcolm Who Walks in the Eyes of Our Children. Quincy Troupe. CNA; PoBA
He had been falling in the abyss some four thousand years. Et Nox Facta Est. Victor Hugo, *tr. by* Mary Ann Caws. NAWM-2
He had been long t'wards Mathematicks. Sir Sidrophel, the Conjuror [*or* Portrait of Sidrophel]. Samuel Butler. *Fr.* Hudibras. FaBoEn; PoEL-3
He had been singing—but I had not heard his voice. The Quiet Singer. Charles Hanson Towne. HBV-2
He had been stuttering, by the edge. Hart Crane. Robert Creeley. AP
He had done for her all that a man could. I Will Write. Robert Graves. PCP
He had driven half the night. Hay for the Horses. Gary Snyder. ConAP; CTBA; GrPl; InPS; NaP
He had fought for the wrong causes. Suicide. Louis MacNeice. DTC
He had got, finally. A Poem for Speculative Hipsters. Amiri Baraka. NoAM; NOBA
He had habits, my grandfather. Zeyde. Roberta Metz. AMV-81
He had his beer. *Unknown.* WhC
He had hitched a chicken to a cart. The Prophylactic. Russell Edson. GP

He had in his hand a red plant. Meeting by the Gjulika Meadow. Geoffrey Grigson. WaP
He had lived for the sorrow of numbers. Two Sorrows. David St. John. SUW
He had need of a way. Being Somebody. Edwin Honig. TAP
He had no friend. About to Die. *Gond Oral Tradition, tr. by* V. Elwin *and* S. Hivale. WTO
He had no heart for war, its ways and means. A Volunteer. Helen Parry Eden. SUMH
He had no past and he certainly. Pity Ascending with the Fog. James Tate. NoAM
He had not reckoned on a visitor. Death Was a Woman. Sydney King Russell. GoYe
He had played for his lordship's levee. The Child-Musician. Austin Dobson. GN
He had red hair. A Boy Thirteen. Jeff Irish. DL
He Had Served Eighty Masters. Lesbia Harford. PoAu-1
He had shag hair and a boutique. How to Swing Those Obbligatos Around. Alice Fulton. LTB
He had smiled at us. Maximus, to Gloucester, Letter 19. Charles Olson. *Fr.* The Maximus Poems. CMoP
He had studied in private years ago. Artichoke. Henry Taylor. MAYP
He hands/ down the gift. The Gift. Robert Creeley. NOBA
He hangs between his wings outspread. The Eagle. Andrew Young. ELU; PoSH
He has a drooping winged moustache. Texas Types—"The Bad Man." William Lawrence Chittenden. PoOW
He has annihilated the enemies! War Song. *Zulu Oral Tradition, tr. by* D. K. Rycroft. WTO
He has built himself a cottage in the wood. A Cottage in the Wood. Russell Edson. LCAP
He has, by his wife's reckoning, failed so often. Trying. Leonard Nathan. Str
He has come back at last, the boy with the inky fingers. Self-congratulatory Ode on Mr. Auden's Election to the Professorship of Poetry at Oxford. Ronald Mason. FaBoPa
He has come the way of the fighting men and fought by the rules of the Game. The Fighting Failure. Everard Jack Appleton. HBV-2; YaD
He has come to report himself. The Missing Person. Donald Justice. NYBP
He has come to such a pitch. Lines for an Eminent Poet and Critic. Patric Dickinson. PV
He has conned the lesson now. Fairy Song. Winthrop Mackworth Praed. SeCePo
He has drawn you one character, though, that is new. James Fenimore Cooper. James Russell Lowell. *Fr.* A Fable for Critics. DBV
He Has Fallen from the Height of His Love. Wilfrid Scawen Blunt. *Fr.* The Love Sonnets of Proteus. ViBoPo
He has grown in love. Of an Old Con. George Mosby, Jr. LFAC
He has hanged himself—the Sun. November. F. W. Harvey. OxBTC
He has never heard of tides. German Shepherd. Myra Cohn Livingston. RFM
He has not woo'd, but he has lost his heart. A Country Dance. Charles Tennyson Turner. VLP
He has observed the golden rule. Blake. *Fr.* Gnomic Verses. PV; TrGrPo
He has only to pass by a tree moodily walking head down. The Fiend. James Dickey. PPP
He has solved it—Life's wonderful problem. Laurels and Immortelles. *Unknown.* BLPA
He has sprouted; he has burgeoned. Inanna's Song. *Unknown, tr. by* Diane Wolkstein *and* Samuel Noah Kramer. LLLT
He has the sign. Portrait of Malcolm X. Etheridge Knight. CNA; PoBA
He has two antennae. Gnat on My Paper. Richard Eberhart. DFF
He hasn't gone to work. The Poem Circling Hamtramck, Michigan All Night in Search of You. Philip Levine. NNaP
He hated them all one by one but wanted to show them. A Teacher. Reed Whittemore. GLGT; NCSH
He Hath No Parallel. Sadi, *tr. fr. Persian by* L. Cranmer-Byng. *Fr.* The Gulistan. AWP
He hath no place to rest his head. Judaeus Errans. Louis Golding. TrJP
He heard, and dreamed the night-wind on. Muse-haunted. Hugh McCrae. PoAu-1
He heard them in the silence of the night. Airman, R.F.C. Agnes Grozier Herbertson. SUMH
He Hears the Bugle at Killarney. Tennyson. *See* Splendor Falls, The.
He Hears the Cry of the Sedge. W. B. Yeats. OxBTC
(Aedh Hears the Cry of the Sedge.) VLP
He hears the summer at a distance. Vanishing Point. Peter Cooley. AmPA
He Hears with Gladdened Heart the Thunder. Robert Louis Stevenson. TreFT
He Held Radical Light. A. R. Ammons. NoAM
He held the lamp of Truth that day. The Hand That Held It. W. G. Elmslie. TRV
He hides his heart. Sightings I. Jerome Rothenberg. CoPo
He Hides within the Lily, *with music.* William Channing Gannett. AH
(Consider the Lilies.) WGRP
He hie fie finger. The Man. Robert Creeley. OBAL
He Holdeth Fast to the Memory of His Identity. *Unknown, tr. fr. Egyptian by* Robert Hillyer. *Fr.* Book of the Dead. AWP
He hovers at the back door. The Real Muse. Fred Muratori. AMV-81
He huffs from the north. March Wind. Maud E. Uschold. YeAr
He hunches into his fur coat. Wolf Dream. Edward Lense. AMV-81
He imagines her. The Modes of Vallejo Street, San Diego, Los Angeles, 3. Hugh Seidman. UnPo
He invented a rainbow but lightning struck it. Bushed. Earle Birney. MoCV; NOBC; NoP; OBCV; PeCV
He is a bad sleeper and it is a joy to me. A Bad Sleeper. Paul Verlaine, *tr. by* François Pirou. PeHV
He is a bird round which a trap closes. The Holy Man. *Unknown, tr. by* Whitley Stokes *and* John Strachan. *Fr.* The Devil's Tribute to Moling. OnYI
He is a heart. A Love Song. *Unknown, tr. by* Myles Dillon. AnIL
He Is a Path. Giles Fletcher. *Fr.* Christ's Victory and Triumph. TRV
(Excellency of Christ.) WGRP
He is a tower unleaning. But how will he not break. Vaunting Oak. John Crowe Ransom. OxBA; VGW
He is all male. The Defiant One. Alice Morrey Bailey. AMV-80
He is always right. The Interrogator. Elizabeth Jennings. WPE
He is always standing there. My Policeman. Rose Fyleman. SoPo; TiPo
He is an Englishman! The Englishman. W. S. Gilbert. *Fr.* H. M. S. Pinafore. NOBL
He is as salt. Salt. Lucille Clifton. GP
He is aware of a simple fire. A Fire a Simple Fire. Frederic Will. FAZ
He Is Coming. Gladys M. Gearhart. STF
He is coming, my long-desired lord. The River of Heaven. *Unknown, tr. by* Lafcadio Hearn. *Fr.* Manyo Shu. AWP
He is crying there near the toilet. Outburst from a Little Face. John Woods. GP
He is daily with us, loving, loving, loving. "Daily with You." Annie Johnson Flint. BLRP
He is dead and gone, lady. Shakespeare. *Fr.* Hamlet, IV, v. LO
He is dead, the beautiful youth. Killed at the Ford. Longfellow. AP; OHIP
He Is Declared True of Word. *Unknown, tr. fr. Egyptian by* Robert Hillyer. *Fr.* Book of the Dead. AWP
He Is Far. *Unknown.* OAEL-1; OxBM
(Forsaken Maiden's Lament, A.) SeCePo
He is firm and strong. Oriki Erinle. *Unknown, tr. by* Ulli Beier. PBA; TTY
He is found with the homeless dogs. Kid. Robert Hayden. CAD; NCSH
He is gone on the mountain. Coronach. Sir Walter Scott. *Fr.* The Lady of the Lake, III. BSV; CH; EnRP; GTBS; GTBS-P; HBV-2; OAEP; OBRV; OHIP; TreFS; TrGrPo; ViBoPo; WHA; WiR
He is having his hair cut he is only. Haircut. William Packard. CAD
He is just plain drunk. "I Am a Sioux Brave," He Said in Minneapolis. James Wright. ELU
He is leading his grandfather under the sun to market. Niño Leading an Old Man to Market. Leonard Nathan. CTBA; NCSH
He Is like the Lotus. *Unknown, tr. fr. Egyptian by* Robert Hillyer. *Fr.* Book of the Dead. AWP; EaLo
(Death as a Lotus Flower, *tr. by* Ulli Beier.) TTY
He Is like the Serpent Saka. *Unknown, tr. fr. Egyptian by* Robert Hillyer. *Fr.* Book of the Dead. AWP
He is made one with Nature: there is heard. Shelley. *Fr.* Adonais. WGRP
He is making love with his wife on the roof. The Roof of the World. Michael Dennis Browne. AmPA
He is more than a hero. Sappho, *tr. fr. Greek by* Mary Barnard. PBWP
He is murdered upright in the day. Vaticide. Myron O'Higgins. IDB; PoBA
He Is My Countryman. Antoni Slonimski, *tr. fr. Polish by* Frances Notley. TrJP
He is my God, who maketh all things perfect. Whatsoever Hath Been Made, God Made. Dadu. ILwL
He is my love/ my sweet nutgrove. *Unknown, tr. fr. Irish by* Michael Hartnett. BIrV
He is no friend who in thine hour of pride. Friendship. Sadi, *tr. by* L. Cranmer-Byng. *Fr.* The Gulistan. AWP
He is no one I really know. Piccola Commedia. Richard Wilbur. GP
He is not a brother to me. The Brother. Semion Yakovlevich Nadson, *tr. by* H. Badanes. TrJP
He Is Not Dead. James Whitcomb Riley. *See* Away.
He is not dead nor liveth. The Buried Child. Dorothy Wellesley. *Fr.* Deserted House: Epilogue. DTC; OBMV

He is not ded that somtyme hath a fall. Sir Thomas Wyatt. AAS; OBVE
He is not here, the old sun. No Possum, No Sop, No Taters. Wallace Stevens. MoVE; OxBA; TAP; VGW
He is not John the gardener. A Friend in the Garden. Juliana Horatia Ewing. FaPON; OxBChV
He is not the wise man, who comes. The Imbecile. Donald Finkel. NePoEA-2
He is old, two weeks to eighty. Blue Sparks in Dark Closets. Richard Snyder. Psk
He is older than the naval side of British history. Chief Petty Officer. Charles Causley. OxBTC
He is one of the prophets come back. He. Lawrence Ferlinghetti. NeAP; PoM
"He Is Our Peace." Molly Anderson Haley. PGD
He is patient. Obatala, the Creator. *Yoruba Oral Tradition, tr. by* Ulli Beier. WTO
He is quick, thinking in clear images. In Broken Images. Robert Graves. PPoe
He is Shaka the unshakable. Shaka, King of the Zulus. *Unknown, tr. by* A. C. Jordan. PBA; TTY
He is sleeping, soundly sleeping. "A Departed Friend." Julia A. Moore. FiBHP
He is so small, he does not know. Six Weeks Old. Christopher Morley. RHPC
He is stark mad, who ever says. The Broken Heart. John Donne. EBEV
He is that fallen lance that lies as hurled. A Soldier. Robert Frost. MoPo; NePA; OFD; SeCeV; WaaP; WaP
He is the bow, firm. Telemachus and the Bow. Randall Colaizzi. AMV-81
He is the despots' Despot. All must bide. The Dance of Death. Austin Dobson. HBV-2
He is the happy wanderer who goes. The Happy Wanderer. Percy Addleshaw. OBVV
He Is the Lonely Greateness. Madeleine Caron Rock. CH
He is the pond's old father, its brain. The Snapper. William Heyen. AmPA; MAYP; PCP
He is the primal rock. Gray, wise, and old. Nation. Mendel Naigreshel, *tr. by* Joachim Neugroschel. VWA
He Is the Way. W. H. Auden. *Fr.* For the Time Being; a Christmas Oratorio. EaLo; SBVL
He is to weet a melancholy carle. A Portrait [*or* Spenserian Stanzas on Charles Armitage Brown]. Keats. BXAP; InMe
He is very busy with his looking. Young Heroes. Gwendolyn Brooks. BPo
He is walking in the road. A Conceited Man. *Gond Oral Tradition, tr. by* V. Elwin *and* S. Hivale. WTO
He is wasted now. Dylan, Who Is Dead. Samuel Allen. PoBA
He isn't all Indian. Our Hired Man (And His Daughter, Too). Monica Shannon. FaPON
He Jests at Scars [That Never Felt a Wound]. Shakespeare. *Fr.* Romeo and Juliet, II, ii. LiTB; MasP; PAI; TreF
(Living Juliet, The.) TrGrPo
He jumped me while I was asleep. Assailant. John Raven. BPo
He jumped, seeing an island like a hand. Hart Crane. Julian Symons. PoA
He keeps the valley like this with his heart. Prospero without His Magic. Jack Gilbert. NPGG
He [*or* When he] killed the noble Mudjokivis. The Modern Hiawatha. George A. Strong. *Fr.* The Song of Milkanwatha. BXAP; FaBoCo; FaBoPa; FaFP; FaPON; FiBHP; HBV-1; InMe; MoShBr; NA; Par; RHPC; SpRo; TreFS; WhC; YaD
He Kindleth a Fire. *Unknown, tr. fr. Egyptian by* Robert Hillyer. *Fr.* Book of the Dead. AWP
He knelt beside her pillow, in the dead watch of the night. Asleep. William Winter. AA
He knelt, the Savior knelt and prayed. The Agony in the Garden. Felicia Dorothea Hemans. TrCP
He knew how Roman legions looked, for he. The Fog. Robert P. Tristram Coffin. CrMA
He knew what I wanted. O Dirty Bird Yr Gizzard's Too Big & Full of Sand. James Koller. PoM
"He Knoweth Not That the Dead Are Thine." Mary Elizabeth Coleridge. ELU; OBNC
He Knoweth the Souls of the East. *Unknown, tr. fr. Egyptian by* Robert Hillyer. *Fr.* Book of the Dead. AWP
He Knoweth the Souls of the West. *Unknown, tr. fr. Egyptian by* Robert Hillyer. *Fr.* Book of the Dead. AWP
He knows celebrities. . .or else he lies. Froggles. Don Marquis. *Fr.* Savage Portraits. HBMV
He knows, He loves, He cares. The Best Choice. *Unknown.* STF
He knows he must explain this. The Modes of Vallejo Street, San Diego, Los Angeles, 9. Hugh Seidman. UnPo
He knows not bit nor bridle, his nostrils are flaming. The Neighing North. Annie Charlotte Dalton. CaP
He Knows the Way. *Unknown.* STF
He knows when shadows come my way. Because He Was Tempted. *Unknown.* STF
He larved ond he larved on he merd such a nauses. The Ondt and the Gracehoper. James Joyce. *Fr.* Finnegans Wake. BIrV
He laughed derision when his foes. Heart-Hurt. *Unknown.* TreFT
He Laughed Last. Francis Whiting Hatch. WhC
He lay, and those who watched him were amazed. The Sprig of Lime. Robert Nichols. GTBS-P
He lay in the middle of the world, and twitcht. John Berryman. *Fr.* Dream Songs. NoP
He lay in's armour; as if that had been. A Soldier's Death. Cyril Tourneur. *Fr.* The Atheist's Tragedy. SeCePo
He lay on the bed, thinking. The Man on the Bed. Debora Greger. MAYP
He Leadeth Me. *Unknown, at. to* H. H. Barry. *See* On the Twenty-third Psalm.
He Leadeth Me. Joseph H. Gilmore. AH, *with music;* BLRP; WBLP; WGRP
He leads us on. Through the Maze. *Unknown.* BLRP
He Leads Us Still. Arthur Guiterman. OHIP
He leaned. Treaty-Trip from Shulus Reservation. Patrick Lane. NeAC
He leans forward in his chair. The Gesture. Elizabeth Libbey. WeW
He leant at the door. The Unfrocked Priest. Joseph Campbell. AnIL; OnYI
He leaped. With none to hinder. Empedocles. George Meredith. VLP
He leaves unplowed his furrow. Here's to the Ranger! *Unknown.* CoSo
He led his five senses into dreams. When Father Slept. James Anderson. AMV-80
He led me out to water, as you may understand. The Messenger Song. *At. to* John Calhoun. ShS
He left his hose, his Hannah, and his love. To the Memory of a Young Man. *Unknown.* WhC
He left his pants upon a chair. The Mistake [*or* Epigram: The Mistake]. Thoedore Roethke. NePoAm-2; NIP; UnTE
He left me exposed on a hill of woman, my mother. Oedipus at San Francisco. Donald Finkel. CoPo
He left the kitchen. Dory Miller. Sam Cornish. CNA
He left the office where he'd been given. He Asked about the Quality. C. P. Cavafy, *tr. by* Edmund Keeley *and* Philip Sherrard. PeHV
He left two children, who for virtue, wit. Of Sir Philip Sidney Sir John Beaumont. GoBC
He lies/ Beside me. On Death and Love. Janet Campbell Hale. VoR
He lies in state. Dirge. Austin Clarke. CIP
He lies low in the levelled sand. At the Grave of Walker. Joaquin Miller. AA
He lies upon his bed. Archibald MacLeish. *Fr.* Einstein. ImOP
He lifted up, among the actuaries. So Long? Stevens. John Berryman *Fr.* Dream Songs. HAP; NOBA
He lifts his hopeful eyes at each new tread. Lost Dog. Frances Rodman. GDP
He liked best watching TV. The Artist. Peter Meinke. PoDr
He Liked the Dead. Malcolm Lowry. OxBTC
He lists them. Yahrzeit. Dan Jaffe. VWA
He Lived amidst th' Untrodden Ways. Hartley Coleridge. FaBoCo; Par
(On Wordsworth.) FaBoPa; FiBHP
(Wordsworth Unvisited.) NOBL
He lived apart, sometimes in a cave in the mountains. Shaman. Will Inman. GP
He lived at Dingle Bank—he did. At Dingle Bank [*or* Dingle Bank]. Edward Lear. FaBoNo; WhC
He lived in a cave by the seas. Double Ballade of Primitive Man. Andrew Lang *and* Edward Burnett Tylor. CenHV
He lived in that past Georgian day. A Gentleman of the Old School. Austin Dobson. HBV-1
He lived one hundred and five. *Unknown.* WhC
He lives among a dog. The Child. Donald Hall. NCSH; NePoEA-2
He Lives! He Lives to Bless! Dorothy Conant Stroud. STF
He lives in the outer land. Blood Marksman and Kureldei the Marksman. *Tatar (Turkic) Oral Tradition, tr. fr. German and Russian versions by* Norman Cohn. WTO
He Lives Long Who Lives Well. Thomas Randolph. WBLP
He lives on edge throughout his days. Hare. Molly Holden. TEP
He lives out. The Giant Squid of Tsurai. Kirk Robertson. GP
He lives unsociable, aloof. The Liftman. H. A. C. Evans. POL
He lives, who last night flopped from a log. Burning. Galway Kinnell. CoAP
He lives within the hollow wood. The Charcoal-Burner. Sir Edmund Gosse. OBVV
He Liveth Long Who Liveth Well. Horatius Bonar. HBV-2; HBVY

He longs to open his arms, we can see that. My Father's Heart. Stuart Friebert. Str
He looked about six or seven, only much too thin. The Forgiveness Dream; Man from the Warsaw Ghetto. Jean Valentine. LCAP
He looks at the white square. Nikos Painting. Kenneth O. Hanson. FAZ
He looks down to watch the river twist. Gargoyle. Thomas Rabbitt. MAYP
He looks like a fat little old man. Dead Seal. Alfred Purdy. MoCV; NoAM
He look't and saw what numbers numberless. The Parthians. Milton. *Fr.* Paradise Regained, III. OBS
He loved her, having felt his love begin. The Contrast. Helen Gray Cone. AA
He loved his cabin: there. Salt Water Story. Richard Hugo. NoP
He loved the brook's soft sound. The Peasant Poet. John Clare. OAEL-2; OBNC; WGRP
He loved three things in life. "Anna Akhmatova," *tr. fr. Russian by* Barbara Einzig. BoWoP
He Loves and He Rides Away. Sydney Dobell. OBNC
He loves me. *Unknown.* OxNR
He loves not well whose love is bold. My [*or* The] Queen. William Winter. AA; HBV-1
He lumbers from the bed like a. The Great Poet. Linda King. GP
He lying spilt like water from a bowl. Poem. Alison Boodson. ErPo; NeBP
He made his master to cutte his hore. Ipomadon Plays the Fool at Court. *Unknown. Fr.* Ipomadon. OxBM
He made no history, even. Elegy for a Countryman. Padraic Fallon. NeIP
He Made the Night. Lloyd Mifflin. HBV-1
He made them and He called them good. Address to the Crown. Charles L. O'Donnell. GoBC
He Made Us Free. Maurice Francis Egan. AA
He makes himself comfortable. 1st Dance—Making Things New—6 February 1964. Jackson MacLow. CoPo
He makes sweet music who, in serious lines. Sir John Beaumont. *Fr.* To His Late Majesty, Concerning the True Form of English Poetry. PP
He Maketh Himself One with Osiris. *Unknown, tr. fr. Egyptian by* Robert Hillyer. *Fr.* Book of the Dead. AWP
He Maketh Himself One with the God Ra. *Unknown, tr. fr. Egyptian by* Robert Hillyer. *Fr.* Book of the Dead. AWP
He Maketh Himself One with the Only God, Whose Limbs Are the Many Gods. *Unknown, tr. fr. Egyptian by* Robert Hillyer. *Fr.* Book of the Dead. AWP
He Maketh No Mistake. A. M. Overton. STF
He marched away with a blithe young score of him. He Went for a Soldier. Ruth Comfort Mitchell. SUMH
He May Be Envied, Who with Tranquil Breast. Charlotte Smith. SBG
He may be six kinds of a liar. Loyalty. Berton Braley. BLPA
He Meditates on the Life of a Rich Man. Douglas Hyde, *tr. fr. Irish by* Lady Gregory. OBMV
He met a lady. From the Hazel Bough. Earle Birney. HeIP
He Met Her at the Green Horse. Peter Levi. NePoEA-2
He might have won the highest guerdon that heaven to earth can give. Saturninus. Katherine Eleanor Conway. AA
He mightn't have had wherewith to buy. Last Mathematician. Hyman Edelestein. CaP
He motions me over with a question. Kidnaper. Tess Gallagher. AmPA
He moved among blocked facades. Yiddish Poet. A. C. Jacobs. VWA
He must be hardly twenty-two. And yet. The Next Table. C. P. Cavafy, *tr. by* John Mavrogordato. PeHV
He must not laugh at his own wheeze. The Humorist. Keith Preston. EvOK; HBMV; WhC
He never acted well by man or woman. George IV. Thackeray. *Fr.* The Georges. FaBoEE
He never completed his History of Ephesus. On a Certain Scholar. W. Craddle. WhC
He Never Expected Much. Thomas Hardy. NAs; NoAM; OxBTC; SCV
He never felt twice the same about the flecked river. This Solitude of Cataracts. Wallace Stevens. LCAP
He never gave me a chance to speak. After the Quarrel. Adam Lindsay Gordon. OBVV
He never heard of Newton's law. The Rigger. Washington Jay McCormick. WhC
He never lives to tell. Calenture. Alastair Reid. NYBP; PrIm
He never made the dive—not while I watched. The Springboard. Louis MacNeice. ChMP; PoA
He Never Smiled Again. Felicia Dorothea Hemans. HBV-2
He never spoke a word to me. Simon the Cyrenian Speaks. Countee Cullen. AmNP; BPo; HAP; MoAmPo; TrCP; TTY
He never used to notice me. The Policeman. Marjorie Seymour Watts. TiPo
He Never Will Forget. "M. G. H." STF
He no longer marvels at stars. The Specialist. Anne S. Perlman. SUW
He nothing common did or mean. King Charles on [*or* upon] the Scaffold. Andrew Marvell. *Fr.* An Horatian Ode upon Cromwell's Return from Ireland. ChTr; FaBoRV
He observes. He has a great black notebook. The Observer. David C. Yates. AMV-81
He, of his gentleness. In the Wilderness. Robert Graves. EaLo; OxBI
He often would ask us. The Choirmaster's Burial. Thomas Hardy. DTC
He once did love with fond affection. Forsaken. *Unknown.* AmFP
He opened the car door. There was a low rumble. The Meeting. Nicki Jackowska. BrRo
He opens his eyes with a cry of delight. A Child's Christmas Day. *Unknown.* OBCP
He Overcometh the Serpent of Evil in the Name of Ra. *Unknown, tr. fr. Egyptian by* Robert Hillyer. *Fr.* Book of the Dead. AWP
He Paid Me Seven. *Unknown.* BPo
He painted the mountain over and over again. Dearest Reader. Michael Palmer. NPGG
He passed by with another. Ballad. Gabriela Mistral, *tr. by* Doris Dana. OLR
He paused on the sill of a door ajar. The Newcomer's Wife. Thomas Hardy. BoLoP; OxBTC
He paused: the listening dames again. Sir Walter Scott. *Fr.* The Lay of the Last Minstrel, IV. OBRV
He picks up what he thinks is/ a road map. My Father; October 1942. William Stafford. DiL; NaP
He places his hand on her head as a hand placed against pain. Rain. Haim Guri, *tr. by* Mark Elliott Shapiro. VWA
He planked down sixpence and he took his drink. Henry Turnbull. W. W. Gibson. ELU; FaBoTw
He played by the river when he was young. Washington. Nancy Byrd Turner. FaPON; RHPC; SoPo; TiPo; YeAr
He posed her, naked. The Photographer's Wife. Janet Beeler. AMV-81
He Praises Her Hair. *Unknown, tr. fr. Late Middle Irish by* the Earl of Longford. AnIL
He Praises His Wife When She Has Left [*or* Had Gone from] Him. *Unknown, tr. fr. Late Middle Irish by* Robin Flower. AnIL; OxBI
He praises me, and I praise Him. Ibn al-Arabi, *tr. fr. Arabic.* ILwL
He Praises the Trees. *Unknown, tr. fr. Irish by* Robin Skelton. BIrV
He prayed for patience; Care and Sorrow came. His Answer. Clara Ann Thompson. BlSi
He Prayeth Best. Samuel Taylor Coleridge. *Fr.* The Rime of the Ancient Mariner VII. FaPON, 1 *st.*
("He prayeth best, who loveth best.") TRV, 1 *st.*
He Prayeth for Ink and Palette That He May Write. *Unknown, tr. fr. Egyptian by* Robert Hillyer. *Fr.* Book of the Dead. AWP
He preached upon "Breadth" till it argued him narrow. Emily Dickinson. AmPP; AP; CABA; NOCV
He preaches to the crowd that power is lent. Vox Populi. Dryden. *Fr.* The Medal. NOBE
He preferr'd Hanover to England. George I—Star of Brunswick. Thackeray. *Fr.* The Georges. FaBoEE
He promised to meet me at Linstead Market. Linstead Market. *Unknown.* FSW
He proposed to me on the Ferris wheel. Arches and Shadows. Annie Dillard. CTBA
He pushes behind the words. Waiting. Robert Creeley. VGW
He put away his tiny pipe. Spring Cricket. Frances Rodman. FaPON; SiSoSe
He put his acorn helmet on. A Fairy in Armor. Joseph Rodman Drake. *Fr.* The Culprit Fay. FaPON
He puts footnotes on the paintings. The Perfectionist. Bernice Fleisher. PoDr
He Puts Me to Rest. David Ignatow. VGW
He quickly arms him for the field. Pigwiggin Arms Himself [*or* The Arming of Pigwiggen]. Michael Drayton. *Fr.* Nymphidia; or, The Court of Fairy. GN; MoShBr
He Raise a Poor Lazarus, *with music.* *Unknown.* AH
He ran right out of the woods to me. The Story of the Baby Squirrel. Dorothy Aldis. TiPo
He ran the course and as he ran he grew. Innocence. Thom Gunn. LiTM; NePoEA-2; NoAM
He reaches Weymouthtreads the Esplanade. The Royal Tour, *abr.* "Peter Pindar." OxBoLi
He realized that night how much he was in their power. The Movies. Jack Gilbert. NPGG
He received from some thoughtful relations. The Pleasing Gift. *Unknown.* TDH
He Records a Little Song for a Smoking Girl. James Whitehead. GP
He Remembers Forgotten Beauty. W. B. Yeats. CTC; LLLT
(Michael Robartes Remembers Forgotten Beauty.) BrPo
He Renounceth All the Effects of Love. Thomas, Lord Vaux. EnRePo

He replied to his own question, and with the unmannered. A Meditation on John Constable. Charles Tomlinson. NePoEA-2
He Resigns. John Berryman. WeW
He Resolves to Say No More. Thomas Hardy. TEP
He rested in the cool, that traveller. The African Tramp. Geoffrey Haresnape. PeSA
He Revisits Cambridge. In Memoriam A. H. H., LXXXVII. Tennyson. FaBoPP
He rides about the ranks, and strives t'inspire. Richard III's Speech. Sir John Beaumont. *Fr.* Bosworth Field. JCP
He rides at their head. The College Colonel. Herman Melville. AA; OBWP
He rises and begins to round. The Lark Ascending. George Meredith. LoBV; OAEP; PBBP; WiR
He riseth up early in the morning. The Mighty Hunter. J. B. Worley. PoLF
He roam'd half-round the world of woe. Epitaph. Aubrey Thomas De Vere. OBVV
He roars in the swamp. The Alligator. Beatrice Ravenel. WPE
He rocked the boat. Ezra Shank. *Unknown.* ShM
He rode forth armed: breast-plate and crest. A Romance. Chester Kallman. PoA
He rose at dawn and, fired with hope. The Sailor Boy. Tennyson. MOS
He rose like a sleepwalker just. Dürer's Piece of Turf. Norbert Krapf. PoDr
He rose up on his dying bed. Hope. Langston Hughes. OBAL
He rubbed his eyes and wound the silver horn. Little Boy Blue. John Crowe Ransom. LiTM; TwAmPo
He runs before the wise men: He. He. Stanley Kunitz. CrMA; VGW
He Said. Jean Valentine. TAP
He said:/ "Let's stay here." Party Piece. Brian Patten. BoLoP
He said: I am a parson, but I take. Fishing in the Australian Alps. Ernest G. Moll. WhC
He Said: "If in His Image I Was Made." Trumbull Stickney. LiTA; TwAmPo
He said an old poet, meaning himself. Testing Ground. Karla M. Hammond. AMV-81
He said he had been a soldier. Dorothy Wordsworth. SaC
He said he was tired and sore all day. Uncle Mells and the Witches' Tree. Elizabeth Madox Roberts. WSC
He said he would be back and we'd drink wine together. Waiting for Icarus. Muriel Rukeyser. NNaP
He Said, Lying There. Alta. GP
He Said That He Was Not Our Brother. John Banim. OnYI
He Said the Facts. Merrill Moore. CrMA
He said: The road you are going will lead you to Hate. The Road to Hate. Patrick Kavanagh. TW
He said: "The shadows darken down." Ballad. May Kendall. HBV-1
He said to Patancala Kapya and to the students. *Tr. by* Raimundo Panikkar. *Fr.* Upanishads. ILwL
He said, unreal the buffalo is standing. Unreal the Buffalo Is Standing. *Unknown.* GOA
He sang/ How the swan blanched forever. Owl's Song. Ted Hughes. PAI
He sang above the vineyards of the world. The Singing Man. Josephine Preston Peabody. HBV-2
He sang an old song. The Kilkenny Boy. Eileen Shanahan. NeIP
He sang of God—the mighty source. The Catholic Amen. Christopher Smart. *Fr.* A Song to David. GoBC; TRV
He sang of joy; whate'er he knew of sadness. A Hero. Florence Earle Coates. OHIP
He sang of life, serenely sweet. The Poet. Paul Laurence Dunbar. BPo
He sang one song and died—no more but that. The Singer of One Song. Henry Augustin Beers. AA
He sang the airs of olden times. The Blind Psalmist. Elizabeth Clementine Kinney. AA
He sat above it, watching it recede. Utrillo's World. John Glassco. PeCV
He sat alone upon an ash-heap by. Love. Nicholas Moore. ErPo
He sat at the Algonquin, smoking a cigar. At the Algonquin. Howard Moss. Psk
He sat at the foot of my bed. Father and Son. Ronald Wallace. AMV-81
He sat by a fire of seven-fold heat. The Refiner's Fire. *Unknown.* BLRP
He sat in a wheeled chair, waiting for dark. Disabled. Wilfred Owen. BiP; BrPo; CMoP; FF; InPS; LiTM; MMA; NIP; NoAM; OxBTC; WaP
He sat in the cool morning. The New Warden. Jimmy Santiago Baca. LFAC
He sat on a boulder, his miniature. The Lizard. Ruth Lechlitner. AMV-81
He sat upon the rolling deck. Sailor. Langston Hughes. PoA
He saw a lawyer killing a viper. Richard Porson. *Fr.* The Devil's Thoughts. DBV
He saw, abandoned to the sand. The Trail beside the River Platte. William Heyen. GOA
He saw beneath the bughouse wall. Solo for Bent Spoon. Donald Finkel. NePoEA-2
He Saw Far in the Concave Green of the Sea. Keats. *Fr.* Endymion, III. EtS
He saw her from the bottom of the stairs. Home Burial. Robert Frost. AP; CoBMV; PrIm; TAP; TwAmPo
He saw his white walls shining in the sun. Lambro's Return. Byron. *Fr.* Don Juan, III. OBRV
He saw it clearly and clairvoyant bright. Blueprint. D. B. Steinman. GoYe
He saw it last of all before they herded in the steerage. Teresina's Face. Margaret Widdemer. HBMV
He saw the grey on black, and that. Rothko. James Moore. AMV-81
He saw the portrait of his enemy, offered. The Enemy's Portrait. Thomas Hardy. EyDe; TW
He says he doesn't feel like working today. My Erotic Double. John Ashbery. LCAP
He says he wrote by moonlight. Katharyn Machan Aal. AMV-81
He says, *My reign is in peace,* so slays. A Foreign [*or* Foren] Ruler. Walter Savage Landor. DBV; OBSV; PV; TreFT; ViBoPo
He says that woman speaks with nature. Prologue. Susan Griffin. *Fr.* Woman and Nature. NPGG
He scanned it, staggered, dropped the loop. Emily Dickinson. PoEL-5
He scans the world with calm and fearless eyes. The New Negro. James Edward McCall. CDC
He scarce had ceased when the superior Fiend. Satan and the Fallen Angels. Milton. *Fr.* Paradise Lost, I. LiTB; OBS; SeCePo
He seemed to know the harbour. The Shark. E. J. Pratt. NOBC; WHW
He Sees His Beloved. James I, King of Scotland. *Fr.* The Kingis Quair. PoEL-1
("Bewailing in my chambers thus alone.") BSV
(Coming of Love, The.) GOTS
He sees the gentle stir of birth. If Birth Persists. Matthew Arnold. *Fr.* Resignation. FaBoRV
He sees the rosy apples cling like flowers to the bough. The Fruit Rancher. Lloyd Roberts. CaP
He sees them pass. Once. Eric N. Batterham. CH
He Sees Through Stone. Etheridge Knight. BALP; ConAP; LFAC; NBP; NNaP; PoBA
He seized me round the waist and kissed my throat. Charleston in the 1860s. Adrienne Rich. CoAP
He sells door to door. Salesman. Ruth Roston. AMV-80
He sent us letters, which we read. The Summer Story. John Lehmann. MP
He served his God so faithfully and well. On a Puritan. Hilaire Belloc. FaBoEE
He served his master well from youth to age. Old Stephen. Charles Tennyson-Turner. EBVV
He set out and kept hunting. The Hunter. Frank O'Hara. NNaP
He set out snares. Poultry. Diana Der Hovanessian. GrPl
He shall not hear the bittern cry. Lament for Thomas MacDonagh. Francis Ledwidge. AnIV; BIrV; OnYI; OxBI
He Shall Speak Peace. Thomas Curtis Clark. WBLP
He Shall Speak Peace unto the Nations. Lila V. Walters. WBLP
He Shot at Lee Wing. *Unknown.* ShM
He shuddered briefly and stared down the long valley. The Return of Robinson Jeffers. Robert Hass. AmPA
He shudders . . . feeling on the shaven spot. Electrocution. Lola Ridge. WPE
He Singeth a Hymn to Osiris, the Lord of Eternity. *Unknown, tr. fr. Egyptian by* Robert Hillyer. *Fr.* Book of the Dead. AWP
He Singeth in the Underworld. *Unknown, tr. fr. Egyptian by* Robert Hillyer. *Fr.* Book of the Dead. AWP
He sings from the bottom of a well but she can hear him up. Jim Harrison. *Fr.* Ghazals. NoAM
He sings in the courtyard, snuggling in his tatters. Jewboy. Julian Tuwim, *tr. by* Isaac Komem. VWA
He sipped at a weak hock and seltzer. The Arrest of Oscar Wilde at the Cadogan Hotel. John Betjeman. CMoP; DTC; EBEV; InvP; MoBrPo; NoAM; NoP; OxBTC
He sits/ among his drums. A Portrait of Rudy. James Cunningham. CNA
He sits above the clang and dust of Time. The Sovereign Poet. Sir William Watson. WGRP
He sits at the bar in the Alhambra. Simple. Naomi Long Madgett. FB; PoBA
He sits in a deckchair reading Colette. Villa Thermidor. George Hitchcock. GP
He sits in silence on his porch at night. An Old Habitant. Frank Oliver Call. CaP

He sits over the glimmering coal. The Old Age Pensioner. Joseph Campbell. AnIL
He sleeps at last—a hero of his race. A Dead Soldier. George Edgar Montgomery. AA
He sleeps on the top of a mast. The Unbeliever. Elizabeth Bishop. LiTA; NoAM
He slid out of the skin, leaving it. Summer. Diane Wakoski. VGW
He slides the cut paper out. The Paper Cutter. David Ignatow. CTBA
He slowly paced his distance off, and turned. The High Jump. *Unknown.* LiSp
He slumbers well and has a right to slumber. The Poet to the Sleeping Saki. Goethe, *tr. by* John Weiss. PeHV
He snuggles his fingers. After Winter. Sterling A. Brown. PoBA; PoNe
He sought the sea; His footsteps press the dry. Christ Quiets the Tempest. Caelius Sedulius, *tr. by* George Sigerson. *Fr.* Carmen Paschale. OnYI
He speaks not well who doth his time deplore. The Heroic Age. Richard Watson Gilder. AA; OHIP
He speaks of voyages. Tour Guide: La Maison des Esclaves. Melvin Dixon. LTB
He spoke, and Sohrab kindled at his taunts. Sohrab's Death. Matthew Arnold. *Fr.* Sohrab and Rustum. WHA
He spoke; and Sohrab smiled on him, and took/ The spear. The Death of Sohrab. Matthew Arnold. *Fr.* Sohrab and Rustum. FiP
He spoke, and spoke in many periods. Fishing Lines. Donald M. Hassler. WOLT
He spoke of undying love. The Talker. Benjamin Appel. TrJP
He sported round the watery world. Jonah and the Whale. Viola Meynell. EtS
He Sports by Himself. Susan Miles. BXAP
He Standeth at the Door. Arthur Cleveland Coxe. *See* In the Silent Midnight Watches.
He stands in the door. Dried Fruit. Philip Dow. BXAP
He stared at ruin. Ruin stared straight back. John Berryman. *Fr.* Dream Songs. CAPP
He stares upward at a monstrous face. The Pieta, Rhenish, 14th C., The Cloisters. Mona Van Duyn. Prf
He startles awake. His eyes are full of white light. The Hermit Wakes to Bird Sounds. Maxine W. Kumin. GrPl; Psk
He stayed, and was imprisoned in possession. Sonnets from China, IV. W. H. Auden. CMoP
He steps down from the dark train, blinking; stares. Ten Days Leave. W. D. Snodgrass. MoAmPo; Psk; UnPo
He stood a moment at the edge. Life or Death. Glenn Ward Dresbach. *Fr.* In Western Mountains. HBMV
He stood, a worn-out City clerk. Peace. Charles Stuart Calverley. EBVV; NBM; WhC
He stood alone within the spacious square. James Thomson ("B. V."). The City of Dreadful Night, IV. WiR
He stood among a crowd at Drumahair [*or* Dromahair]. The Man Who Dreamed of Faeryland. W. B. Yeats. CMoP; NoAM; NoP; OAEP; PoPle
He stood and call'd/ His legions, angel forms, who lay intranced. The Summons [*or* Satan's Legions and the Beech Leaves of the Casentino]. Milton. *Fr.* Paradise Lost, I. FaBoPP; WHA
He stood, and heard the steeple. Eight o'Clock. A. E. Housman. BrPo; CABA; CMoP; InPK; LoBV; MoAB; MoBrPo; NoAM; NoP; PAI; SoSe; TrGrPo
He stood before the Sanhedrim. Religion and Doctrine. John Hay. WGRP
He stood in the pulpit. The Pastor. William C. Summers. STF
He stood on his head by the wild seashore. His Mother-in-Law. Walter Parke. FiBHP
He stood up in our khaki with the poise. Gee-up Dar, Mules. Edwin Ford Piper. YaD
He stood upon the coast of County Clare. St Enda. Laurence Lerner. PeSA
He stoops above the clumsy snare. The Snare. Patrick MacDonogh. NeIP
He stoops down, and crawls on hands and knees. Soil Searcher. J. Joyce. CTBA
He stopped on the irreproachable sidewalk. Elysee. Larry Eigner. VGW
He strides across the grassy corn. The Scarecrow. Andrew Young. BSV; FaBoTw
He stripped five of our women. What Pablo Picasso Did in "Les Demoiselles d'Avignon." John Robert Colombo. PeCV
He strode along the chapel aisle. Sabbath Reflection. Denis Wrafter. NeIP
He stumbled all morning through the market. Below Mount T'ui K'oy, Home of the Gods, Todos Santos Cuchumatán, Guatemalan Highlands. Joseph Stroud. NPGG
He stumbled home from Clifden fair. High and Low. James H. Cousins. HBMV; OnYI; OxBI
He stumbles silver-haired among his bees. The Veteran. Edmund Blunden. BrPo
He swings down like the flourish of a pen. Skier. Robert Francis. LiSp; NCSH; RFM
He switched on the electric light and laughed. Intimate Supper. Peter Redgrove. FaBoMo; OxBC
He takes the long review of things. To a Certain Most Certainly Certain Critic. David McCord. OBAL
He talked, and as he talked. The Story-Teller. Mark Van Doren. CTBA
He talked of Delhi brothels half the night. Long Tom. W. W. Gibson. OxBTC
He talks and talks. Like Ripples on the Water. *Gond Oral Tradition, tr. by* V. Elwin *and* S. Hivale. WTO
He taught Math at the Ecole Centrale. Salomon. Pierre Morhange, *tr. by* Edouard Roditi. VWA
He taught me hands. The Dutchman. Don Welch. WOLT
He teeters along the crumbling top. The Fall. Alastair Reid. BSV
He tells many bad things. Young Training. Lawrence McGaugh. PoBA
He tells me in Bangkok he's robbed. Baby Villon. Philip Levine. CoAP; NaP
He tells you when you've got on too much lipstick. The Perfect Husband. Ogden Nash. DFF; FaBoUs
He that but once too nearly hears. The Music of Forefended Spheres [*or* Fragment]. Coventry Patmore. *Fr.* The Victories of Love, I, ii. FaBoRV; NBM
He that can trace a ship making her way. The Heart Is Deep. Roger Wolcott. SCAP
He that dwelleth in the secret place of the most High. A Mighty Fortress [*or* The Everlasting Arms]. Bible, *O.T.* Psalms, XCI. AWP; TrGrPo; WGRP
He that fights and runs away. *Unknown.* TreF
He that from dust of worldly tumults flies. Of True Liberty. Sir John Beaumont. OBS
He that had come that morning. Ballad of John Cable and Three Gentlemen. W. S. Merwin. CoAP; NePoEA; NOBA
He that has and a little tiny wit. Shakespeare. *Fr.* King Lear, III, ii. ViBoPo
He that has grown to wisdom hurries not. Sonnet: Of Moderation and Tolerance. Guido Guinicelli, *tr. by* Dante Gabriel Rossetti. AWP
He that has sail'd upon the dark blue sea. Byron. *Fr.* Childe Harold's Pilgrimage, II. MOS
He that has seen a great oak dry and dead. Joachim du Bellay, *tr. by* Spenser. *Fr.* Ruins of Rome. FaBoPP
He that hath no mistress, must not wear a favour. *Unknown.* GBL
He that hath set his headlong heart. Boethius, *tr. by* Helen Waddell. *Fr.* The Consolation of Philosophy. NAWM-1
He that hath such acuteness, and such wit. On Mr. Francis Beaumont (Then Newly Dead). Richard Corbet. OBS
He that intends to take a wife. The Wife-Hater. *Unknown.* CoMu
He that is by Mooni now. Mooni. Henry Clarence Kendall. OBEV; OBVV
He that is down needs fear no fall. The Shepherd Boy Sings in the Valley of Humiliation [*or* Enough! *or* A Song of Low Degree *or* The Song of the Shepherd in the Valley of Humiliation]. Bunyan. *Fr.* The Pilgrim's Progress. BLRP; CavP; EaLo; EBCP; EBEV; GN; HBV-2; HBVY; NOBE; OBEV; OBS; OxBoCh; STF; TRV; WGRP
He that is in the battle slain. Fight. *Unknown.* FaFP
He That Is Slow to Anger. Bible, *O.T.* Proverbs, XVI: 32. FaPON
He that is weary, let him sit. Employment. George Herbert. JCP; OBS; OxBoCh; SeCP; TEP
He that lies at the stock. Rock, Ball, Fiddle. *Unknown.* CH; OxBoLi; OxNR
He That Loves. Sir Philip Sidney. ErPo
He That Loves a Rosy Cheek. Thomas Carew. *See* Disdain Returned.
He That Loves a Rosy Cheek. Heinrich von Rugge, *tr. fr. German by* Jethro Bithell. AWP
He that loves and fears to try. He That Loves. Sir Philip Sidney. ErPo
He That Ne'er Learns His ABC. *Unknown.* GBP; GLGT
He That Never Read a Line. *Unknown, tr. fr. Old Irish by* Robin Flower. AnIL
He that of such a height hath built his mind. To the Lady Margaret, Countess of Cumberland. Samuel Daniel. LoBV; OBSC
He that only rules by terror. The Captain. Tennyson. MOS
He that owns wealth, in mountain, wold, or waste. Wealth. Sadi, *tr. by* Sir Edwin Arnold. *Fr.* The Gulistan. AWP
He That Regards the Precious Things of Earth. Moses ibn Ezra, *tr. fr. Hebrew by* Solomon Solis-Cohen. *Fr.* The World's Illusion. TrJP
He that saith he is in the light, and hateth his brother. Brotherhood. Bible, *N.T.* *Fr.* First John. TreFT
He that to God's law doth cling. Freedom. Abraham ibn Ezra, *tr. by* Solomon Solis-Cohen. TrJP

He that will be a lover in every wise. Three Things Jeame Lacks. *Unknown.* MeEL
He that will court a Wench that is coy. Song. *Unknown.* ErPo
He that will not love must be. Not to Love. Robert Herrick. CaPo; OAEP
He that will not reason is a bigot. Reason. *Unknown.* TreF
He that will thrive must rise at five. *See* He that would thrive . . .
He that would live for aye. *Unknown.* FaBoUs
He that would the daughter win. *Unknown.* FaBoUs
He that would [*or* will] thrive must rise at five. Rules of Behavior [*or* Proverb]. *Unknown.* FaBoUs; HBV-1; HBVY; OxNR
He the Beloved, *sel.* Qorratu'l-Ayn, *tr. fr. Farsi by* Deirdre Lashgari. "Cupbearer, O victorious Falcon, come!" WPOW
He, the indiscreet agent. Doves. Joachim Neugroschel. VWA
He there does now enjoy eternal rest. Sleep after Toil. Spenser. *Fr.* The Faerie Queene, I, 9. ChTr; MOS
He Thinks of His Past Greatness When a Part of the Constellations of Heaven. W. B. Yeats. DTC; OAEP; PoEL-5
He Thinks of Those Who Have Spoken Evil of His Beloved. W. B. Yeats. *See* Aedh Thinks of Those Who Have Spoken Evil of His Beloved.
He thought he kept the universe alone. The Most of It. Robert Frost. BiP; CABA; CrMA; HAP; MoPo; NePA; NoP; NU; PPoe; WeW
He thought he saw a buffalo [*or* a banker's clerk *or* an elephant]. The Mad Gardener's Song. "Lewis Carroll." *Fr.* Sylvie and Bruno. BLPL; EvOK; FaBoCo; FaBoNo; FiBHP; HBV-2; HBVY; NA; NBM; OnUR; OxBChV; TreFS; WiR
He thought if he could surround himself with quotations. That Man in Manhattan. Shannon Keith Kelley. AMV-80
He threw the shroud about his head. John Donne's Statue. John Peale Bishop. EyDe
He thrust his joy against the weight of the sea. The Surfer. Judith Wright. WPE
He told himself and he told his wife. The Riddle. Ralph Hodgson. PoPl; WhC
He told his life story to Mrs. Courtly. Autumn. Stevie Smith. ELU
He Told Me His Name Was Sitting Bull. Joy Harjo. TAT
He told me, you'll end up. Marriage. Marea Gordett. AMV-81
He told the barmaid he had things to do. Dodona's Oaks Were Still. Patrick MacDonogh. NeIP
He too has an eternal part to play. The Historical Judas. Howard Nemerov. NoP
He too must with me wash his body, though. An Anniversary of Death. John Wieners. PoM
He took a thousand islands and he didn't lose a man. Dewey in Manila Bay. R. V. Risley. PAH
He took castle and towns; he cut short limbs and lives. Thomas Love Peacock. *Fr.* Crotchet Castle. DBV; PV
He Took Her. Tom Masson. OBAL
He took her fancy when he came. What He Took. *Unknown.* CoMu
He took her one day. A Fine, a Private Place. Diane Ackerman. MAYP
He took his wig off, with his sleeve. The Clown: He Dances in the Clearing by Night. Ramon Guthrie. NMP
He took the great bunch of letters and kissed it! To the Postmaster General. Peter Redgrove. AMV-81
He took the great harp wearily. The Songs of Guthrum and Alfred. G. K. Chesterton. *Fr.* The Ballad of the White Horse. HBV-2
He took the quaint cup in unpractised hands. Poor Fool. Evan V. Shute. CaP
He took three big gulps. Big Man. Mason Jordan Mason. PoNe
He touches, and the wheel of time goes round. Hurdy-Gurdy Man in Winter. Vernon Watkins. NYBP
He tried to convince us, but his billiard ball. My Physics Teacher. David Wagoner. SUW
He Tries out the Concords Gently. Edward Bagritsky, *tr. fr. Russian by* C. M. Bowra. TrJP
He turned his field into a meeting-place. W. H. Auden. In Time Of War, VIII. PoPl; SCV
He turns his truck on its side. Long Lonely Lover of the Highway. Frederic Will. AMV-81
He turns to you, measly immortal page. Page. Sandra McPherson. PoA
He Understands the Great Cruelty of Death. Petrarch, *prose tr. fr. Italian by* J. M. Synge. Sonnets to Laura: To Laura in Death, XLVII. BIrV
He unto whom thou art so partial. Post-Obits and the Poets. Martial, *tr. by* Byron. AWP; FaBoEE; NIP; OBVE
He used me today. The Gardener. Evelyn Eaton. GoYe
He used to come here till he donned gold braid. To a Tyrant. Joseph Brodsky, *tr. by* Alan Myers. VWA
He used to dream of things he'd do. The Dreamer. Thomas Nunan. WBLP
He usually managed to be there when. Because He Liked to Be at Home. Kenneth Patchen. NaP
He Waiata mo Te Kare. James K. Baxter. OCNZ
He wakens from the clover rick. The Sun-Witch to the Sun. George Howe. NYBP
He wakes in a new world and wears new eyes. Reformed Drunkard Vernon Scannell. AMV-80
He wakes; speak to him. Shakespeare. *Fr.* King Lear. SCV
He wakes to a confused dream of boats, gulls. Murphy in Manchester. John Montague. NMP
He walked through the woods. The Walk. W. W. E. Ross. PeCV
He walked up and down the street 'till the shoes fell off his feet. Tramp, Tramp, Tramp, Keep on a-Tramping. *Unknown.* AS
He Walketh by Day. *Unknown, tr. fr. Egyptian by* Robert Hillyer. *Fr.* Book of the Dead. AWP
He Walks in Peace. *Unknown, tr. fr. Chinese. Fr.* Tao Teh King. TRV
He walks still upright from the root. The Hewel, or Woodpecker. Andrew Marvell. *Fr.* Upon Appleton House. ChTr
He walks, the enchanter, on his sea of glass. Antichrist. Edwin Muir. EaLo
He wanted/ a pickup truck. Julio. Kell Robertson. TAT
He Was. Richard Wilbur. NCSH; SaC
He was a big man, says the size of his shoes. Abandoned Farmhouse. Ted Kooser. DFF; GP
He was a big two-fisted brute. Bucko-Mate. Samuel Schierloh. GoYe
He was a braids-and-shades dog soldier. Another Dying Chieftain. Rayna Green. TWSS
He Was a Friend of Mine. *Unknown.* FSW
He was a gash an' faithful tyke. Luath. Burns. GDP
He was a good man. Wake Cry. Waring Cuney. BANP
He was a man and a friend always. My Ramblin' Boy. Tom Paxton. FSW
He was a man as hot as whiskey. Andrew Jackson. Martha Keller. AmFN
He was a mighty hunter in his youth. The White Cat of Trenarren. A. L. Rowse. OxBTC; PCat
He was a rat and she was a rat. The Two Rats [*or* What Became of Them?]. *Unknown.* OBCA; OxBChV; PoPle
He was a reprobate I grant. The Deceased. Keith Douglas. FaBoTw
He was a singer caroling in dark. Countee Cullen. Eugene T. Maleska. PoNe
He was afraid to go through their grocery store. Charles Reznikoff. *Fr.* Five Groups of Verse. DiL
He was as loyal as them all—and more. Peeping Tom. Francis Hope. ErPo
He was as old as old could be. Danny Murphy. James Stephens. OnUR; RoGo
He was at Naples writing letters home. Esthétique du Mal. Wallace Stevens. CMoP; LiTM; NOBA
He was born in Alabama. Of De Witt Williams on His Way to Lincoln Cemetery. Gwendolyn Brooks. CAPP; NoAM; NOBA
He was born in Deutschland, as you would suspect. The Progress of Faust. Karl Shapiro. MoAB; MP; NYBP
He was called tractor. Tractor. John L. Sellers. LFAC
He Was Formidable. Robert Penn Warren. LiSp
He was found by the Bureau of Statistics to be. The Unknown Citizen. W. H. Auden. BiP; CABA; ChMP; FF; HeIP; InPK; LiTA; LiTM; MoAB; NePA; NIP; NOBL; NYBP; OBSV; PAI; PoRA; PPON; SoSe; TreFT; UnPo
He was going to be all that a mortal should be—Tomorrow. Do It Now. *Unknown.* STF
He was hauled-hung. Lynched. Stephen Todd Booker. LFAC
He was impoverished, possessing a full island. Castaway. John Nerber. PoA
He was in logic[k] a great critic[k]. The Metaphysical Sectarian [*or* Hudibras, the Presbyterian Knight *or* Portrait of Hudibras *or* Presbyterian Knight and Independent Squire *or* Sir Hudibras, His Passing Worth]. Samuel Butler. *Fr.* Hudibras. FaBoCo; MeLP; OBS; OxBoLi; PoEL-3
He was in love with Truth and knew her near. Walt Whitman. Harrison Smith Morris. AA
He was just a boy, as I could see. An Incident. Mary H. J. Henderson. SUMH
He was just a lonely cowboy. Cowboy Jack. *Unknown.* CoSo
He was just a young aviator. Lindbergh. *Unknown.* AmFP
He was just back. Vietnam. Clarence Major. PoBA
He was like the Lord drunk. Alcoholic. F. D. Reeve. NYBP
He was lodging above in Coom. The 'Mergency Man. J. M. Synge. PoPle
He was lost!—not a shade of doubt of that. Little Lost Pup. Arthur Guiterman. TreFS
He was no good. Somewhere. Black Jess. Peter Kane Dufault. NYBP
He was not bad, as emperors go, not really. Apology for Domitian [*or* Two Pieces after Suetonius]. Robert Penn Warren. NOBA; PAI
He was not only friend and my lover. Second Woman's Lament. Brenda Chamberlain. NeIP
He Was Not Willing. Lucy R. Meyer. STF

He was now alone. The lovers had wandered across. Poet and Goldsmith. Vernon Watkins. PoCh
He was of stature tall. Wordsworth. *Fr.* The Prelude, IV. SyP
He was once a tiny, helpless thing. Aaron Nicholas, Almost Ten. Janet Campbell Hale. VoR
He was one who followed. Sailor Man. H. Sewall Bailey. EtS
He was only a common puncher, such as the punchers were. Panhandle Cob. *Unknown.* CoSo
He was only a lavender cowboy. The Lavender Cowboy. Harold Hersey. BPAW; CoSo; FSW
He was protuberant behind, before. Johnson on Pope. David Ferry. PP
He was reading late, at Richard's, down in Maine. Henry's Understanding. John Berryman. NoAM; NOBA
He was really her favorite. In Spite of His Dangling Pronoun. Lyn Lifshin. IHMS
He was serving a life sentence. Mule-Train. John L. Sellers. LFAC
He was sitting there on a stone. Elderberry Flute Song. Peter Blue Cloud. STE
He was six years old, just six that day. A Little Boy's Vain Regret. Edith M. Thomas. AA
He was so compounded. Remembering Him. Joe Reccardi. AMV-80
He was still Uncle. The Empress Brand Trim: Ruby Reminisces. Sherley Anne Williams. BlSi
He was the best postilion. The Postilion Has Been Struck by Lightning. Patricia Beer. OxBC
He was the doctor up to Combe. Coroner's Jury. L. A. G. Strong. OxBTC
He was the last. Truly the last. The Butterfly. Pavel Friedmann, *tr. by* Dennis Silk. VWA
He was the slave of Ambition. The Mills of the Gods. *Unknown.* BLPA; FPL
He was the Word that spake it. The Sacrament. John Donne. TRV
He was the youngest son of a strange brood. Otto. Theodore Roethke. DiL
He was their servant (some say he was blind). Sonnets from China, VII. W. H. Auden. CMoP
He was, through boyhood's storm and shower. A Dedication. G. K. Chesterton. FiBHP
He was weak, and I was strong—then. Emily Dickinson. PeD
He was wounded and he fell in the midst of hoarse shouting. Fallen. Alice Corbin. SUMH
He wasn't handsome or young or even clever, but oh. On Don Juan del Norte, Not Don Juan Tenorio del Sur. Alan Dugan. ErPo
He wasn't my grandpa but we. Grandpa Bear. Susan Eisenberg. AMV-81
He watched the spring come like a gentle maid. To One Who Died in Autumn. Virginia McCormick. HBMV
He watched the stars and noted birds in flight. Sonnets from China, VI. W. H. Auden. CMoP
He watched with all his organs of concern. Poem. W. H. Auden. PoA
He wears a beard to let us see that he is pure within. Sanctimony. *Malay Oral Tradition, tr. by*R. J. Wilkinson. WTO
He Went for a Soldier. Ruth Comfort Mitchell. SUMH
He went into a grey day. For One Who Died Young. H. R. Hays. EAS
He went into his harvest barn. The Farmer. "E." CBAP
He went out to their glorious. The Summons. James Laughlin. LiTA
He went so blithely on the way. The Blithe Mask. Dollett Fuguet. TRV
He went there. Poem of the Conscripted Warrior. "Rui Nogar," *tr. by* Dorothy Guedes *and* Philippa Rumsey. TTY
He went to fix the awning. Fixer of Midnight. Reuel Denney. OBAL
He went to Harvard in a tank. Considering the Death of John Wayne. Louis Phillips. SOTS
He went to the wood and caught it. Riddle. *Unknown.* GBP; OxNR
He whistled soft whistlings I knew were for me. In the Park. Helen Hoyt. HBMV
He whittled scallops for a hardy thatch. The Thatcher. Brendan Kennelly. CIP
He who ascends to mountain-tops shall find. The Isolation of Genius. Byron. WBLP
He who becomes his contrary. Shekhina and the Kiddushim. Edouard Roditi. VWA
He who binds [*or* bends] to himself [*or* himself to] a joy. Eternity. Blake. *Fr.* Several Questions Answered. AWP; EBEV; FaBoEE; LAuP; LoBV; NOBE; NoP; OBNC; TrGrPo
He who but yesterday would roam. Epitaph for a Sailor Buried Ashore. Sir Charles G. D. Roberts. EtS
He who crosses a park in great and flourishing Havana. Central Park *Some People (3 P.M.).* Nancy Morejón. PBWP
He who did most, shall bear most; the strongest shall stand the most weak. Robert Browning. *Fr.* Saul. TRV
He who died at Azan sends. After Death in Arabia. Sir Edwin Arnold. HBV-2; WGRP
He who died on Calvary. A Thought. Margaret E. Sangster. TRV
He who first met the Highlands' swelling blue. The Highlands' Swelling Blue. Byron. *Fr.* The Island. OBRV
He Who Forsakes the Clerkly Life. *Unknown, tr. fr. Late Middle Irish by* Standish Hayes O'Grady. *Fr.* The Life of St. Cellach of Killala. OnYI
He who has a thousand friends has not a friend to spare. Make Friends. Ali Ben Abu Taleb. TRV
He Who Has Lost All. David Diop, *tr. fr. French by* Anne Atik. TTY
He who has lost soul's liberty. Soul's Liberty. Anna Wickham. MoBrPo
He who has made his reckoning with life. Boethius, *tr. by* Helen Waddell. *Fr.* The Consolation of Philosophy. NAWM-1
He who has never known hunger. Elizabeth J. Coatsworth. TiPo
He who has no hands. Orator. Emerson. *Fr.* Quatrains. OxBA
He who has once been happy is for aye. With Esther. Wilfrid Scawen Blunt. *Fr.* Esther. OBEV; OBMV; OBNC; OBVV; TrGrPo; ViBoPo
He who has rolled his pants up to his knee. Crossing a Creek. Herbert Clark Johnson. PoNe
He who has seen the wild tornado sweep. Isaac Clason. *Fr.* Don Juan. PeD
He who has toiled and bought for himself books. Proverbs. Samuel Ha-Nagid, *tr. by* Israel Abrahams. TrJP
He who hath led will lead. Guide and Friend. *Unknown.* BLRP
He Who Hath Loved. Walter Malone. AA
He who hath never warred with misery. Epistle to Henry Wriothesley, Earl of Southampton. Samuel Daniel. EnRePo
He who hung on Calvary's tree. Wondrous Son of God. Berniece Goertz. STF
He who in his pocket hath no money. Epigram. *Unknown.* HBV-1
He who is my master. The "Word" of a Watch-Dog. Sandag, *tr. by* C. R. Bawden. WTO
He Who Knows ("He who knows not and knows not that he knows not"). *Unknown, tr. fr. Arabic.* BLPA
(Arabian Proverb.) TreF
He who knows not what thing is Paradise. Three Ballate, II. Angelo Poliziano, *tr. by* John Addington Symonds. AWP
He who learns may feed on lies. Dedication for a Book of Criticism. Yvor Winters. GLGT
He, who navigated with success. Death of a Young Son by Drowning. Margaret Atwood. BoWoP; NOBC
He who of Rankine sang, lies stiff and dead. Lines on the Author's Death. Burns. PV
He, who once was my brother, is dead by his own hand. Justice Is Reason Enough. Diane Wakoski. AmPA; CoPo
He who plants a tree. Plant a Tree. Lucy Larcom. HBVY; OHFP; PGD; WBLP
He who saved Ankoma Oh nature. Prelude to Akwasidae. *Unknown, tr. by* Halim El-Dabh. TTY
He who sits from day to day. Lines on a Bill of Mortality, 1790 [*or* On a Similar Occasion for the Year 1790]. William Cowper. NOCV; OxBoCh
He who stole my virginity/ is the same man. Silabhattarika, *tr. fr. Sanskrit by* W. S. Merwin *and* J. Moussaieff Masson. WPOW
He who wants to hear good rhyme. Aucassin and Nicolette. *Unknown, tr. by* Edward Francis Moyer *and* Carey DeWitt Eldridge. NAWM-1
He Who was bodiless, having heard the bidding secretly in his soul. The Akathistos Hymn. *Unknown, tr. by* Vincent McNabb. ISi
He who would acclaim Cleanness in becoming style. "The Pearl Poet," *tr. fr. Middle English by* Brian Stone. *Fr.* Cleanness. NOCV
He who would climb the heights of tone. Behold This Dreamer. Elizabeth Bartlett. NePoAm-2
He who would echo Horace' lays. Horace. John Osborne Sargent. AA
He who would valiant be. *See* Who would true valour see.
He who writ this, not without pains and thought. Prologue to "Secret-Love; or, The Maiden-Queen." Dryden. SeCV-2
He Whom a Dream Hath Possessed. Shaemas O'Sheel. AnIV; HBV-2; HBVY; TRV; WGRP
He whose active thoughts disdain. Loves Heretick. Thomas Stanley. CavP
"He Will Give Them Back." "George Klingle." BLRP
He will go over and tell the king. Over the Wall: Berlin, May 1975. C. H. Sisson. OxBC
He will have turned. Old Story. Lance Henson. VoR
He will insist on. The Bath. Joel Oppenheimer. NeAP
He will know me when we meet, his blade. The Mugger. Robert Pack. GP
He will not come, and still I wait. A Little Boy in the Morning. Francis Ledwidge. OnYI
He will not see the East catch fire again. A Cock Crowing in a Poulterer's Shop. John Ferguson. BoAnP
He will silently plan for thee. God's Plans. *Unknown.* BLRP
He will sit at the bare table, reading a dictionary. Time of Waiting. Geoffrey Dutton. CBAP
He will watch the hawk with an indifferent eye. Discovered in Mid-Ocean [*or* Icarus]. Stephen Spender. MoBrPo; NoAM; PrIm

He wings a slow and watched flight. The Vulture of the Plains. Hamlin Garland. BPAW
He Wishes for the Cloths of Heaven. W. B. Yeats. *See* Aedh Wishes for the Cloths of Heaven.
He with body waged a fight. The Four Ages of Man. W. B. Yeats. PAI; TrCP
He withdrew his hand slowly. Open Heart. Michael Salcman. AMV-80
He wore a piece of purple towel. Hep-Cat. John L. Sellers. LFAC
He wore his coffin for a hat. For a Pessimist. Countee Cullen. ShM
He works/ stone to. Rock Painting. Carroll Arnett. VoR
He worshipped at the altar of Romance. An Epitaph. Colin Ellis. OxBTC
He would burn his books and gladly die. An Aged Writer. Roy McFadden. NeIP
He would declare and could himself believe. Never Again Would Birds' Song Be the Same. Robert Frost. CrMA; FYAP; HAP; InPK; NIP; NoAM; NoP; VGW
He would drink by himself. Casualty. Seamus Heaney. IPY
He Would Have His Lady Sing. Digby Mackworth Dolben. EBEV; GoBC
He Would Not Stay for Me; and Who Can Wonder? A. E. Housman. PeHV
He writes again. Friendship. Lucien Stryk. GP
He writes from the provinces: It is. Reply to the Provinces. Galway Kinnell. NYBP
He wrote a final poem down. Then died. Lecture Note: Elizabethan Period. Geoffrey Grigson. PV
He wrote upon his heart. Inscription. Donald Jeffrey Hayes. CDC
He wrought at one great work for years. A Ballad of Heaven. John Davidson. BeLS
He yelled at me in Greek. John Berryman. *Fr.* Dream Songs. FYAP
He yelled *count finished!* The machinery. A Typical 6:00 P.M. in the Fun House. Daniel Berrigan. LFAC
Head, The. Padraic Fallon. CIP
Head, A. James Schuyler. NoAM; PoM
Head and Bottle. Edward Thomas. BrPo
Head and the feet keep warm, The. *Unknown.* FaBoUs
Head bumper. *Unknown.* OxNR
Head Couples. William H. Matchett. NYBP
Head in a cloud Moses stands. Moses. Sydney Tremayne. OxBS
Head Is a Paltry Matter, The. Pier Giorgio Di Cicco. NOBC
Head Itself. Laura Riding. PoA
Head like a snake, a neck like a drake, A. How a Good Greyhound Is Shaped. *Unknown.* BoAnP
Head of Medusa. Marya Zaturenska. MoAmPo
Head of the congregation here stands at the head, The. The Poem on the Jews. Avot Yeshurun, *tr. by* Harold Schimmel. VWA
Head or Tail, A—which does he lack? The Hippo. Theodore Roethke. VGW
Head pure, sinless quite of brain or soul, A. Burns. FaBoEE
Head That Once Was Crowned with Thorns, The. Thomas Kelly. TRV
Head the ship for England! Homeward Bound. William Allingham. FaBoBe; HBV-1; HBVY
Head thrusts in as for the view, A. All Revelation. Robert Frost. CABA; MoPo; NePA
Head tilts back, like a heavy leaf, the eyes sew shut, The. Infant. Diana O Hehir. NPGG
Heading for Eugene. Lorenza Schmidt. FIA
Headland. Brewster Ghiselin. PoA
Headless Phantoms, The. *Unknown, tr. fr. Early Modern Irish by* Eoin MacNeill. AnIL
Headless squirrel, some blood, A. A Day Begins. Denise Levertov. DFF; NaP
Headless, without an arm, a figure leans. On a Cast from an Antique. George Pellew. AA
Headlights bounce off. The Black Bottom Bootlegger. Esther M. Leiper. TAT
Headlights show that the old, The. Fall Song. Daniel David Moses. AMV-81
Headline History. William Plomer. FaBoCo
Headlong Hall, *sels.* Thomas Love Peacock.
Chorus: "Hail to the Headlong! the Headlong Ap-Headlong!" OBRV
In His Last Binn Sir Peter Lies. EnRP
(Song.) OBRV; ViBoPo
Headrock. Brian Coffey. CIP
Heads, impenetrable, The. Oxen: Ploughing at Fiesole. Charles Tomlinson. OxBTC
Heads of strong old age are beautiful, The. Promise of Peace. Robinson Jeffers. AP; CoBMV; LiTA; LiTM; MoAB; MoAmPo; NePA
Headsong. Joseph Bennett. NePA
Head-Stone, The. William Barnes. *See* Readen ov a Head-Stwone.
Headstone, like a petrified congregation, The. In the Old Jewish Cemetery, Prague, 1970. Edward Lowbury. VWA
Headstones are thin, The; the trees are thick. The Cows near the Graveyard. Howard Nelson. NU
Healed of My Hurt. Herman Melville. AmPP
Healer, The, *sel.* Whittier.
"So stood the holy Christ." PGD
Healing. Charlotte DeClue. TWSS
Healing. Abraham Reisen, *tr. fr. Yiddish by* Joseph Leftwich. TrJP
Healing Arnica. Simples. Gladys Cardiff. TWSS
Healing of the Leper, The. Vernon Watkins. FaBoTw
Healing Song. *Tr. fr. Papago Indian by* Frances Densmore. OBVE
Healing the Wound. Heine, *tr. fr. German by* Louis Untermeyer. UnTE
Health. Stewart Parker. CIP
Health, A. Edward Coote Pinkney. AA; HBV-1; TreFS
Health. Edward Thomas. SeCePo
Health and Fitness. J. B. Morton. FaBoCo
Health and wealth and love he too dreamed of in May. Patrick Kavanagh. *Fr.* The Great Hunger. MoAB
Health at the Ford, A. Robert Cameron Rogers. AA; FaBoBe
Health Counsel. Sir John Harington. TreFT
("Use three physicians' skill: first, Dr. Quiet.") FaBoUs
Health enough to make work a pleasure. A Wish for the New Year. Phillips Brooks. STF
Health Food. *Unknown.* FaBoUs
Health from the lover of the country, me. To Fuscus Aristus. Horace, *tr. by* Abraham Cowley. Epistles I, 10. AWP
Health! I seek thee; dost thou love. Robert Bloomfield. *Fr.* Shooter's Hill. OBNC
Health is the first good lent to men. Four Things Make Us Happy Here. Robert Herrick. CaPo
Health of Body Dependent on Soul. Jones Very. WGRP
Health to great Gloucester [*or* Gloster]—from a man unknown. The Dedication [to the Sermons]. Charles Churchill. OBSV; QFR
Health to the Maxwels' veteran Chief! To Terraughty, on His Birth-Day. Burns. NAs
Health to the Tackers, A. *Unknown.* APAS
Health unto His Majesty, A. Jeremy Savile. ChTr
Heap cassia, sandal-buds and stripes. Song. Robert Browning. *Fr.* Paracelsus. OBEV; OBRV; WHA
Heap high the board with plenteous cheer and gather to the feast. Thanksgiving. Alice Williams Brotherton. PGD
Heap high the farmer's wintry hoard. The Corn-Song. Whittier. GN; OHIP
Heap of Rags, The. W. H. Davies. BrPo
Heap On More Wood! Sir Walter Scott. *See* Christmas in the Olden Time.
Hear a word, a word in season, for the day is drawing nigh. All for the Cause. William Morris. VLP
Hear! hear! Lilian's Song. George Darley. OBNC
Hear, Hear, O Ye Nations, *with music.* Frederick Lucian Hosmer. AH
Hear how selection was the efficient cause. Darwin on Species. *Unknown.* FaBoUs
Hear, Lord, hear. The Leper Cleansed. John Collop. TrGrPo
Hear me/ don't you hear me. Tambourine. James Cunningham. JB
Hear me as if thy eares had palate, Jack. An Ode in the Praise of Sack. *Unknown.* OBS
Hear me, great ones of Uruk. *Unknown.* *Fr.* The Epic of Gilgamesh. DL
Hear me, Melissus; I will tell you a dream. The Terror by Night. Giacomo Leopardi, *tr. by* John Heath-Stubbs. MOON
Hear me, my warriors; my heart is sick and sad. War. Chief Joseph. PGD
Hear me [*or* Heare mee], O God! A Hymn to God the Father. Ben Jonson. AnAnS-2; EBCP; EnRePo; GoBC; MePo; NoP; OBS; OxBoCh; SeCP; SeCV-1; TrCP; TrPWD
Hear me, whom I betrayed. Envoi. J. V. Cunningham. VGW
Hear me, ye smokeless skies and grass-green earth. Charles Mair. *Fr.* The Last Bison. NOBC
Hear Me Yet. *Unknown.* ElL
Hear my petition you, God who do not exist. The Atheist's Prayer. Miguel de Unamuno. ILwL
Hear my prayer, O Lord, and let my cry come unto thee. Bible, *O.T.* Psalms, CII. BiP
Hear my voice, birds of war! Ojibwa War Songs. *Unknown, tr. by* H. H. Schoolcraft. AWP
Hear, nature, hear; dear goddess, hear! King Lear Condemns His Daughter [*or* Lear's Curse on Goneril]. Shakespeare. *Fr.* King Lear, I, iv. TreFT; TW
Hear now a curious dream I dreamed last night. My Dream. Christina Rossetti. BrRo; VLP
Hear now, O Soul, the last command of all. The Final Mystery. Sir Henry Newbolt. WGRP
Hear now this fairy legend of old Greece. James Russell Lowell. *Fr.* Rhœcus. AA
Hear, O Israel! André Spire, *tr. fr. French by* Stanley Burnshaw. TrJP; VWA

Hear, O Israel. Shema Yisrael. *Unknown.* TrJP
Hear, O Israel, Jehovah, the Lord our God is one. Israel. Israel Zangwill. TrJP
Hear, O Israel, the commandments of life. The Path of Wisdom. Bible, Apocrypha. *Fr.* Baruch. TrJP
Hear, O Lord, my loud cry. The Serenity of Faith. Bible, *O.T.* Psalms, XXVII: 7-14. BLRP
Hear, O Self-Giver, infinite as good. Thysia, XXXVII. Morton Luce. HBV-1
Hear, sweet spirit, hear the spell. A Voice Sings [*or* An Invocation]. Samuel Taylor Coleridge. *Fr.* Remorse. CH; OAEP; ViBoPo
Hear the fluter with his flute. The Amateur Flute. *Unknown.* BXAP; Par; SpRo
Hear the legend of the Admen. The Legend of the Admen. Everett W. Lord. BLPA
Hear the mellow wedding bells. Poe. *Fr.* The Bells. PoPl
Hear the sledges with the bells. The Bells. Poe. AA; FaFP; FaPON; FPL; GN; HBV-2; LiTA; NePA; OBAL; OBCA; OHFP; PoLF; SpRo; TAP; TreF; WBLP
Hear the sound. Listen. Charles Patterson. NBP
Hear the Voice of the Bard (*Introd. to* Songs of Experience). Blake. EBEV; ELP; NOBE; NU; OBEC
(Bard, The.) TRV; WGRP
(Hear the Voice.) OBEV
(Introduction: "Hear the voice of the bard!") CABA; EnRP; HAP; InPS; LAuP; LoBV; NOEC; NoP; OAEL-2; OAEP; PoEL-4; TEP
(Poet's Voice, The.) ChTr
Hear the Word of the Lord. Bible, *O.T.* Isaiah, I: 10-23. TrJP
Hear the word that Jesus spake. A Lost Word of Jesus. Henry van Dyke. TrCP; WGRP
Hear this and tremble, all. Upon My Lord Chief Justice's Election of My Lady Anne Wentworth for His Mistress. Thomas Carew. CaPo
Hear this, O ye that would swallow the needy. O Ye That Would Swallow the Needy. Bible, *O.T. Fr.* Amos. TrJP
Hear through the morning drums and trumpets sounding. Jackson at New Orleans. Wallace Rice. PAH
Hear what Claudius suffered: When his wife knew he was asleep. Juvenal, *tr. by* Hubert Creekmore. *Fr.* The Sixth Satire. ErPo
Hear, ye children, the instruction of a father. The Legacy. Bible, *O.T. Fr.* Proverbs. TrJP
Hear [*or* Heare], Ye Ladies [That Despise]. John Fletcher. *Fr.* The Tragedy of Valentinian. ElL; ELP; NOBE: OAEP; OBEV; ViBoPo
(Mighty Love.) TrGrPo
(Power of Love, The.) HEV-1; UnTE
(Song.) PoEL-2
Hear, ye virgins, and I'll teach. To Virgins. Robert Herrick. CaPo; UnTE; ViBoPo
. . .heard him gladly. Waldere I. *Unknown, tr. by* Charles W. Kennedy. AnOE
Heard in a Violent Ward. Theodore Roethke. NoAM
Heard in the Cougate. Robert Garioch. OxBTC
Heard on the Mountain. Victor Hugo, *tr. fr. French by* Francis Thompson. *Fr.* Feuilles d'Automne. AWP
Heard ye eer of the silly blind harper. The Lochmaben Harper. *Unknown.* ESPB
Heard ye how the bold McClellan. How McClellan Took Manassas. *Unknown.* PAH
Heard ye that thrilling word. Dirge for Ashby. Margaret Junkin Preston. PAH
Heard ye the thunder of battle. Trafalgar. Francis Turner Palgrave. BeLS; FaBoBe
Heare mee, O God! *See* Hear me, O God!
Heare ye Ladies that despise. *See* Hear, Ye Ladies.
Hearing a sound that may be thy return. Hildegarde Flanner. *Fr.* Sonnets in Quaker Language. WPE
Hearing him, the birds came in a crowd. Saint Francis and the Birds. Roy McFadden. OxBI
Hearing how tourists, dazed with reverence. Aldport (Mystery Tour) [*or* Terrible Beauty]. Kingsley Amis. *Fr.* The Evans Country. ErPo; NePoEA; NOBL; PV
Hearing I ask from the holy races. Voluspo. *Unknown, tr. by* Henry Adams Bellows. *Fr.* The Elder Edda. AWP
Hearing James Brown at Café des Nattes (Sidi-bou-Saïd, Tunisia). Richard A. Long. AmNP
Hearing Men Shout at Night on MacDougal Street. Robert Bly. CAD
Hearing of Harvests Rotting in the Valleys. W. H. Auden. MoAB; MoBrPo
(Paysage Moralisé.) LiTB; OAEL-2; UnPo
Hearing of the End of the War. Richard Tillinghast. MAYP
Hearing of you, I never lost a brother. Stepping Outside. Tess Gallagher. AmPA
Hearing one saga, we enact the next. Remembering the 'Thirties. Donald Davie. NePoEA; OxBTC; PP
Hearing our voices raised. Looking On. Anthony Thwaite. NePoEA-2
Hearing Russian Spoken. Donald Davie. GTBS-P; NePoEA-2
Hearing the Wind at Night. May Swenson. BoNaP
Hearing your words, and not a word among them. Edna St. Vincent Millay. CMoP; NoAM; VGW
Heark how she laughs aloud. Lucasta Laughing. Richard Lovelace. PoEL-3
Heark how the Mower Damon sung. *See* Hark how the Mower Damon sung.
Hearke, Now Every Thing Is Still. John Webster. *See* Hark, Now Everything Is Still.
Hearken all ye, 'tis the feast o' Saint Stephen. The Feast o' Saint Stephen. Ruth Sawyer. OBCP
Hearken, Lady Betty, hearken. Christopher Anstey. *Fr.* The New Bath Guide. NOEC
Hearken?—now the hermit bee. The Quiet Enemy. Walter de la Mare. BrPo
Hearken the stirring story. The Fall of Maubila. Thomas Dunn English. PAH
Hearken, thou craggy ocean pyramid! To Ailsa Rock [*or* Sonnet to Ailsa Rock]. Keats. EnRP; MOS; OBNC
Hearken to me, gentlemen. King Estmere. *Unknown.* ESPB; OBNV; OxBB
Hears Not My Phillis, How the Birds. Sir Charles Sedley. CavP
(Phillis [*or* Phyllis] Knotting.) NOBE; OBS
(Song.) EnLoPo; SeCV-2
Hearse Song, The. *Unknown.* AS (A *and* B *vers., with music*); DTC; FSW; OxBoLi
Hearse was the oven of the crematory, The. The Funeral. "M. J.," *tr. by* A. Glanz-Leyeless. TrJP
Hears't thou, my soul, what serious things. Dies Irae [*or* The Day of Judgment]. Thomas of Celano, *tr. by* Richard Crashaw. AWP; OBVE
Heart, The. Stephen Crane. *See* In the Desert.
Heart, The. David Ignatow. VWA
Heart. Joan LaBombard. PPJ
Heart, The. Harvey Shapiro. HoPM
Heart, The. Jacob Steinberg, *tr. fr. Hebrew by* Harry H. Fein. TrJP
Heart, The, *sels.* Francis Thompson.
All's Vast. MoAB; MoBrPo
(Correlated Greatness.) GTBS-P
("O nothing, in this corporal earth of man.") OBMV
"Heart you hold too small and local thing, The." OBMV
Heart and Mind. Edith Sitwell. ChMP; MoPo; MP; OAEP; OxBTC; TwCP
Heart and service to you proffer'd, The. Sir Thomas Wyatt. SiPS
Heart asks pleasure first, The. Emily Dickinson. AmPP; AP; CMoP; MoAB; MoAmPo; NOBA; NoP; OxBA; PPP; PrIM; SBG; TrGrPo; WPE
Heart Burial. Geoffrey Grigson. POL
Heart Exchange. Sir Philip Sidney. *See* My True Love Hath My Heart.
Heart Flies Up, Erratic as a Kite, The. Delmore Schwartz. PoA
Heart for All Her Children. Albert J. Hebert, Jr. ISi
Heart free, hand free. Sic Vita. William Stanley Braithwaite. BANP
Heart goes out ahead, The. Poem of the Mother. Myra Sklarew. AMV-80; Str
Heart Has Its Reasons, The. Felice Picano. PeHV
Heart Has Its Reasons, The. *Unknown.* GoBC
Heart has need of some deceit, The. Only the Polished Skeleton. Countee Cullen. PrIm; VGW
Heart-Hurt. *Unknown.* TreFT
Heart is a snail, The. Catalogue. Hilde Domin, *tr. by* Tudor Morris. VWA
Heart Is Deep, The. Roger Wolcott. SCAP
Heart leaps with the pride of their story, The. The Fleet at Santiago. Charles E. Russell. PAH
Heart Mountain Japanese Relocation Camp, The: 30 Years Later. Charles Levendosky. TAT
Heart must always come again to home. The Heart's Wild Geese. Henry Treece. WaP
Heart of a Girl Is a Wonderful Thing, The. *Unknown.* BLPA
Heart of a Woman, The. Georgia Douglas Johnson. BANP; BlSi; CDC; PoLF; PoNe
Heart of All the Scene, The. Emerson. *Fr.* Woodnotes, I. AA
Heart of Herakles, The. Kenneth Rexroth. *Fr.* The Lights in the Sky Are Stars. NU
Heart of man is encumbered, The. A Child's Christmas without Jean Cocteau. David Fisher. NPGG
Heart of Midlothian, The, *sel.* Sir Walter Scott.
Proud Maisie, *fr. ch.* 38. BSV; CH; ChTr; EnRP; FF; GoTS; HBV-1; InPK; LoBV; NBM; OAEL-2; OAEP; OBEV; OBRV; OxBS; PoEL-4; SeCePo; SeCeV; TEP; TrGrPo; UnPo
(Madge Wildfire Sings.) OBNC

(Madge Wildfire's Death Song.) HAP
(Madge Wildfire's Song.) NOBE
(Pride of Youth, The.) GTBS; GTBS-P
("Proud Maisie is in the wood.") FaBoCh; PBBP
Heart of My Heart. *Unknown.* HBV-1
Heart of my heart, the world is young. Unity. Alfred Noyes. HBV-1
Heart of Oak. David Garrick. HBV-2; NOEC; OBEC; OxBoLi
Heart of Oak. Charles Henry Luders. AA
Heart of the city. The Market. Gary Snyder. CoPo
Heart-of-the-Daybreak. Eugène Marais, *tr. fr. Afrikaans by* Uys Krige *and* Jack Cope. PeSA
Heart of the heartless world. Huesca [*or* To Margot Heinemann]. John Cornford. BoLoP; ChMP; OBWP; OxBTC
Heart of the rulers is sick, The, and the high-priest covers his head. A Song in Time of Revolution 1860. Swinburne. VLP
Heart of the soft, wild rose. Two Questions. William Stanley Braithwaite. BALP
Heart of the Tree, The. H. C. Bunner. OHFP; OHIP; PGD
Heart of the Woods. Wesley Curtright. GoSl; PoNe
Heart of the World, The. Nahman of Bratzlav, *tr. fr. Yiddish by* Joseph Leftwich. TrJP
Heart of Thomas Hardy, The. John Betjeman. TW
Heart on the Hill, The. Petrarch, *tr. fr. Italian by* C. B. Cayley. Sonnets to Laura: To Laura in Life, CCV. AWP
Heart oppress'd with desperate thought. Sir Thomas Wyatt. SiPS
Heart soars up like a bird, The. The Flight of the Heart. Dora Head Goodale. AA
Heart Specialist. Elias Lieberman. ImOP
Heart-summoned. Jesse Stuart. GoYe
Heart, that hideous bear, The. Falling in Love. David Perkins. NCSH
Heart That Weeps, A. Oswald J. Smith. STF
Heart that's been broken, A. Maureen Owen. LLLT
Heart to Carry On, The. Bertram Warr. PeCV
Heart to Praise Thee, A. George Herbert. TRV
Heart, we will forget him! Emily Dickinson. AA; LLLT; OLR; ViBoPo
Heart you hold too small and local thing, The. Francis Thompson. *Fr.* The Heart. OBMV
Heartbreak Camp. Roy Campbell. OxBTC
Heartbreak Road. Helen Gray Cone. HBMV
Hearth. Peggy Bacon. FaPON
Hearth and Home. Stoddard King. OBAL
Hearth of Urien, The. Llywarch the Aged, *tr. fr. Welsh by* William Barnes. ChTr
Hearth Song. Robert Underwood Johnson. YeAr
Hearthside Story. X. J. Kennedy. CoPo
Hearthstone. Harold Monro. OBMV
Heart's Abysses, The. Walter Savage Landor. FaBoEE; OBSV
Hearts and Flowers, *with music.* Mary D. Brine. FSN
Hearts are pumping, The—feel!—the air. Air Shaft. Ian Healy. *Fr.* Poems from the Coalfields. PoAu-2
Heart's Compass. Dante Gabriel Rossetti. The House of Life, XXVII. WHA
Heart's Content. *Unknown.* HBV-2; PoLF
Hearts-Ease. Walter Savage Landor. EnRP
Heart's Friend, The. Mary Austin, *after Shoshone Indian.* BPAW
Hearts good and true. Written in a Little Lady's Little Album. Frederick William Faber. HBV-1; HBVY
Heart's Haven. Dante Gabriel Rossetti. The House of Life, XXII. OAEP
Heart's Hope. Dante Gabriel Rossetti. The House of Life, V. HBV-1
Hearts, like doors, will ope with ease. Rules of Behavior. *Unknown.* HBV-1; HBVY; OxNR
Heart's Low Door, The. Susan Mitchell. HBMV
Heart's Music. *Unknown, at. to* Thomas Campion. OBEV
("Tune thy musicke to thy hart.") AAS
Heart's Needle. W. D. Snodgrass. CAPP; CoPo
Sels.
"Child of my winter born," I. ConAP
(Child of My Winter.) MoAmPo
"Easter has come around," VI. ConAP; NePoEA; NMP
"Here in the scuffled dust," VII. NCSH; NePoEA; NMP
"I thumped on you the best I could," VIII. NePoEA; NoAM;
"Late April and you are three; today," II. NePoEA
"No one can tell you why," IV. ConAP; NePoEA
"Vicious winter finally yields, The," X. NePoEA
"Winter again and it is snowing," V. AP
Heart's Proof, The. James Buckham. BLRP; WBLP
Heart's Summer, The. Epes Sargent. AA
Hearts Were Made to Give Away. Annette Wynne. TiPo
Heart's Wild Geese, The. Henry Treece. WaP
Heartsearch. Evelyn K. Gibson. STF
Heartstring. Blessed wood. Copacetic Mingus. Yusef Komunyakaa. MAYP
Hearty Cook, A. Roy Blount, Jr. TDH
Heat. Anacreon, *tr. fr. Greek by* Abraham Cowley. UnTE
Heat. Hilda Doolittle ("H.D."). The Garden, II. AP; CMoP; HeIP; InPK; MoAmPo; NoAM; OxBA; PrIm; TAP; UnPo; WHA
Heat. Archibald Lampman. CaP; NOBC; OBCV; PeCV
Heat. Kenneth Mackenzie. CBAP; PoAu-2
Heat acrost the desert was a-swimmin' in the sun, The. Waring of Sonora-Town. Henry Herbert Knibbs. BPAW
Heat in the Room, The. Weldon Kees. EAS
Heat is past that did me fret, The. A Farewell to a Fondling. Thomas Churchyard. ElL
Heat uncovers the window and attic-fan, The. Looking for My Old Indian Grandmother in the Summer Heat of 1980. Diane Glancy. STE
Heath, The. Thomas Boyd. OnYI
Heathen Are Come into Thine Inheritance, The. Bible, *O.T.* Psalms, LXXIX. TrJP
Heathen Chinee, The. Bret Harte. *See* Plain Language from Truthful James ("Which I wish to remark").
Heathen Hymn, A, *sel.* Lewis Morris.
"I praise Thee not, with impious pride." TrPWD
Heathen named Min, passing by, A. Tra-La-Larceny. Oliver Herford. TDH
Heathen Pass-ee, The, *parody.* A. C. Hilton. CenHV; FaBoCo; NOBL
Heather, The. Neil Munro. OBVV
Heather was blooming, the meadows were mawn, The. Hunting Song. Burns. PBBP
Heat's on, dead wind shoots up, The. John Garfield. Nicholas Christopher. MAYP; NYP
Heat's on the hooker, The. Translations from the English. George Starbuck. VGW
Heautontimoroumenos. Baudelaire, *tr. fr. French by* Naomi Lewis. NAWM-2
Heave at the windlass!—Heave O, cheerly, men! Windlass Song. William Allingham. GN
Heave Away, 2 *versions, with music. Unknown.* ShS
Heave Away ("Heave away, heave away! I'd rather court a yellow gal"), *with music. Unknown.* AS; TrAS
Heave away, Rio! Rio Grande, *vers.* I. *Unknown.* ShS
Heaven. Martha Dickinson Bianchi. AA; HBV-1
Heaven. Rupert Brooke. BrPo; EBEV; HoPM; LiTB; LiTM; MoBrPo; NOBE; PoPle; PoRA; SeCeV; WGRP
Heaven. George Herbert. AnAnS-1; SeCP; TrCP; TrGrPo
Heaven. Langston Hughes. NOBA; TiPo
(Heaven, Heaven, Heaven Is the Place, *longer version, with music.*) AH
Heaven. Philip Levine. LCAP; NaP
Heaven. Milton. *Fr.* Paradise Lost, III. OBS
Heaven. Gary Soto. NPGG
Heaven ("Heaven is closed"). *Unknown, par. fr. German by* Louis Untermeyer. UnTE
Heaven ("Think of —/ Stepping on shore"). *Unknown.* PoLF
Heaven. Isaac Watts. *See* Prospect of Heaven Makes Death Easy, A.
Heaven above is softer blue. Possession. *Unknown.* BLRP; TRV
Heaven and Earth. James I, King of England. ChTr
(Sonnet: "Azured vault, the crystal circles bright, The.") ElL; MOON; SeCePo
Heaven and earth, and all that hear me plain. A Protest. Sir Thomas Wyatt. OBSC; SiPS
Heaven and Hell. James Kenneth Stephen. CenHV
Heaven and Hell. *Unknown, tr. fr. Eskimo by* Edward Field. DL
Heaven, from thy endless goodness, send prosperous life. This Royal Infant. Shakespeare. King Henry VIII, *fr.* V, iv. NAs
"Heaven hath no rage like love to hatred turned." Congreve. *Fr.* The Mourning Bride, III, viii TreF
Heaven-Haven. Gerard Manley Hopkins. ACP; BrPo; FaBoEn; GoBC; HeIP; LoBV; MoAB; MoBrPo; MOS; NoAM; NOBE; NOCV; OAEP; OBEV; OBNC; PAI; SoSe; SOTW; TrGrPo; ViBoPo; VLP
Heaven, Heaven, Heaven Is the Place. Langston Hughes. *See* Heaven.
Heaven is/ The place where. Heaven. Langston Hughes. NOBA; TiPo
Heaven is a fine place, a fine place entirely. In a Low Rocking-Chair. Helen Coale Crew. HBMV
Heaven is closed, proclaims the preacher. Heaven. *Unknown, par. fr. German by* Louis Untermeyer. UnTE
Heaven Is Heaven. Christina Rossetti. YeAr
Heaven Is Here, *with music.* John G. Adams. AH
Heaven is in my hand, and I. A Blackbird Suddenly. Joseph Auslander. TiPo
Heaven is lovelier than the stars. Driftwood. Trumbull Stickney. HBV-2
Heaven is mirrored, Love, deep in thine eyes. Aidenn. Katrina Trask. AA
"Heaven Is Not Far." Christina Rossetti. OxBoCh
Heaven is not reached [*or* gained] at [*or* by] a single bound. Gradatim. Josiah Gilbert Holland. FaFP; HBV-2; HBVY; OHFP; TreFS; WGRP

Heaven is open every day. The Way to Heaven. Charles Goodrich Whiting. AA
Heaven is what I cannot reach. Emily Dickinson. NOCV
Heaven, O Lord, I Cannot Lose. Edna Dean Proctor. AA
Heaven of Animals, The. James Dickey. AP; CAPP; CoAP; HeIP; LiTM; NCSH; NoAM; NOBA; TAP
Heaven Overarches Earth and Sea. Christina Rossetti. HBV-2
Heaven shall forgive you bridge at dawn. Ballade d'une Grande Dame. G. K. Chesterton. OxBoLi
Heaven, the earth, and all the liquid mayne, The. Virgil, *tr. by* Sir Walter Ralegh. *Fr.* The Aeneid, VI. OBVE
Heaven which art in Heaven Our Father in Heaven. Kay Smith. *Fr.* Footnote to the Lord's Prayer. TrCP
Heaven, which man's generations draws. Epilogue. Francis Thompson. *Fr.* A Judgment in Heaven. MoAB; MoBrPo
Heaven Will Protect the Working Girl. Edgar Smith. FaFP; TreF
"You may tempt the upper classes," *sel.* FiBHP
Heaven won't have to do with its multitudes. The Saints. Robert Creeley. NMP
Heavenly Aeroplane, The. *Unknown.* NOCV
Heavenly Archer, bend thy bow. Dust to Dust. Walter de la Mare. TrPWD
Heavenly Banquet, The. *At. to* St. Brigid, *tr. fr. Middle Irish by* Sean O'Faolain. OnYI
Heavenly bay, ringed round with cliffs and moors, The. In Guernsey. Swinburne. VLP
Heavenly City, The. Stevie Smith. FaBoTw
Heavenly City, The. *Unknown. See* New Jerusalem, The.
Heavenly Eloquence. Samuel Daniel. *See* English Poetry.
Heavenly Evil, holy One. Hymn to Evil. Louis Ginsberg. PoA
Heavenly Father, bless this food. *Unknown.* BLRP
"Heavenly Father," take to thee. Emily Dickinson. ILwL; PoEL-5
Heavenly Foreigner, The, *sel.* Denis Devlin.
"Spires, firm on their monster feet rose light and thin, The." CIP
Heavenly Grass. Tennessee Williams. PoPl
Heavenly Jerusalem, The. Giles Fletcher. *Fr.* Christ's Victory and Triumph. OxBoCh
Heavenly Jerusalem, Jerusalem of the Earth. Leah Goldberg, *tr. fr. Hebrew by* Robert Friend. VWA
Heavenly Pilot, The. Comac, *tr. fr. Old Irish by* George Sigerson. *Fr.* Book of Leinster. OnYI
Heavenly Stranger, The. Ada Blenkhorn. BLRP
Heavenly Tree Grows Downward, The. Gerrit Lansing. CoPo
Heavenly Vision. William Billings. AmFP
Heavens, The. Bible, *O.T.* Psalms, XIX. *See* Heavens Declare the Glory of God, The.
Heavens Above and the Law Within, The. Bible, *O.T.* Psalms, XIX. *See* Heavens Declare the Glory of God, The.
Heavens Are Our Riddle, The. Herbert Bates. AA
Heavens are wrath, The—the thunders rattling peal. Written in a Thunder Storm July 15th 1841. John Clare. VLP
Heavens bright lamp, shine forth some of thy light. George Alsop. SCAP
Heavens Declare the Glory of God, The. Bible, *O.T.* Psalms, XIX.
FaPON (1-4); TreF
(Glory of God, The.) TrJP
(God's Glory.) TrGrPo
(Heavens, The, 1-4.) ChTr
(Heavens Above and the Law Within, The, *Moulton, Modern Reader's Bible.*) WGRP
("Heavens doe declare, The," *Bay Psalm Book.*) SCAP
(Nineteenth Psalm.) BLRP; TRV; WBLP
(Psalm XIX.) AWP; BiP; NAWM-1; OBVE
Heavens Declare Thy Glory, Lord! Isaac Watts. TreFT
Heavens Do Declare, The, *with music.* *Unknown.* AH
Heavens doe declare, The. Bible, *O.T.* Psalms, XIX. SCAP
Heavens first in tune I'll set, The. Love Sets Order in the Elements. Thomas Nabbes. *Fr.* Microcosmus. UnS
Heaven's Last Best Work. Pope. *Fr.* Moral Essays, Epistle II. OBEC
Heaven's Magnificence. William August Muhlenberg. AA
Heaven's mercy shines, wonders and glorys meet. The Mercies of the Year. John Danforth. SCAP
Heaven's power is infinite; earth, air, and sea. Baucis and Philemon. Ovid, *tr. by.* Dryden. *Fr.* Metamorphoses, VIII. OAEL-1
Heaven's Queene. Sir Walter Ralegh. MOON
Heavens themselves, the planets, and this center, The. Order and Degree. Shakespeare. *Fr.* Troilus and Cressida, I, iii. ImOP; NIP; PAI
Heavens! what a goodly prospect spreads around. Happy Britannia. James Thomson. *Fr.* The Seasons: Summer. FaBoPP; OBEC; SeCePo
Heavenward. Lady Nairne. HBV-2
Heaviest Cross of All, The. Katherine Eleanor Conway. AA
Heaving Roses of the Hedge Are Stirred, The. Richard Watson Dixon. CH
(Winter Will Follow.) GTBS-P
Heaving the Lead. *At. to* J. [*or* W.] Pearce *and to* Charles Dibdin.
(By the Deep Nine.) ChTr
(Leadsman's Song, The.) HBV-1
Heaving the Lead Line. *Unknown.* AmFP
Heav'n Boun' Soldier, *with music.* *Unknown.* BoAN-1
Heav'n from all creatures hides the book of fate. Hope Springs Eternal. Pope. *Fr.* Essay on Man, Epistle I. OBEC; ViBoPo
Heavnly frame sets forth the fame, The. Bible, *O.T.* Psalms, XIX, *paraphrased by* Sir Philip Sidney. OBVE
Heavy Bear Who Goes with Me, The. Delmore Schwartz. The Repetitive Heart, IX. CrMA; LiTA; LiTM; MiAP; MoPo; MoVE; MP; NePA; NIP; NoAM; NOBA; TAP; TrJP; TwCP; UnPo
Heavy glacier and the terrifying Alps, The. Long Lines. Paul Goodman. NMP; VGW
Heavy hangs the raindrop. The Two Children [*or* A. E.]. Emily Brontë. NBM; PoEL-5
Heavy-hearted. Judah al-Harizi, *tr. fr. Hebrew.* TrJP
Heavy, heavy, hangs my head. The Sad Child's Song. Mark Van Doren. SO
Heavy Heavy Heavy. John Malcolm Brinnin. NYBP
Heavy, heavy, heavy, hand and heart. Tenebrae. Denise Levertov. CABA; NoP
Heavy heavy lies over our head. Game out of Hand. Allison Ross. GoYe
Heavy, Heavy—What Hangs Over? Kenneth Burke. POL
Heavy mist, A. A muffled sea. Atheling Grange; or, The Apotheosis of Lotte Nussbaum. William Plomer. OBNV
Heavy mists have crept away, The. Mark. Ernest McGaffey. AA
Heavy smells of Spring, The. Jack. Louis Golding. TrJP
Heavy sounds are over-sweet, The. City-Storm. Harold Monro. MoBrPo
Heavy umbrellas, The. Crocus Night. James Schuyler. PoM
Heavy with salt, and warm. The Equinox. Dubose Heyward. PoA
Heavyweight champ of Seattle, The. *Unknown.* OBAL
Hebe. James Russell Lowell. AA; HBV-1
Hebrew Lesson. Max Brod, *tr. fr. German.* AMV-80
Hebrew Letters in the Trees. J. Rutherford Willems. VWA
Hebrew Melodies, *sel.* Heine, *tr. fr. German by* Charles Godfrey Leland.
By the Waters of Babylon. TrJP
Hebrew nation did not write it, The. Blake. OAEL-2
Hebrew of Your Poets, Zion, The. Charles Reznikoff. VGW; VWA
Hebrew Script. Tali Loewenthal. VWA
Hebrew Sibyl, The. Ruth Fainlight. VWA
Hebrews, *sel.* Bible, *N.T.*
Evidence, The, XI: 1. TRV
Hebrews. James Oppenheim. TrJP
Hecatomb to His Mistress, The. John Cleveland. AnAnS-2
Hecatompathia; or, Passionate Century of Love, *sels.* Thomas Watson.
Come, Gentle Death! ElL
Here Lieth Love. ElL
(Love's Grave.) OBSC
"Some that reporte great Alexanders life." AAS
"Speake gentle heart, where is thy dwelling place?" AAS
Time. FaBoRV; OBSC
Hector. Valentin Iremonger. CIP; NeIP; OxBI
Hector and Andromache. Homer, *tr. fr. Greek by* Pope. *Fr.* The Iliad, VI. OBEC
Hector Protector was dressed all in green. Mother Goose. HBV-1; HBVY; MoShBr; OxNR
Hector, the captain bronzed, from simple fight. Geoffrey Scott. *Fr.* The Skaian Gate. OBMV
Hector the Collector. Shel Silverstein. CTBA
Hector the Dog. Kate Barnes. GDP
He'd become completely degraded. His erotic tendencies. Days of 1896. C. P. Cavafy, *tr. by* Edmund Keeley *and* Philip Sherrard. PeHV
He'd been sitting in the café since ten-thirty. Two Young Men, 23 to 24 Years Old. C. P. Cavafy, *tr. by* Edmund Keeley *and* Philip Sherrard. PeHV
He'd found some lumber from an old fence rotting. Boy with a Hammer. Russell Hoban. PCP
He'd had enough of lying in the furze. The Ghostly Father. Peter Redgrove. MoBS; NePoEA-2
He'd have the best, and that was none too good. Tombstones in the Starlight: The Very Rich Man. Dorothy Parker. NIP
He'd Nothing but His Violin. Mary Kyle Dallas. AA, *abr.;* HBV-1
He'd play, after the bawdy songs and blues. When de Saints Go Ma'chin' Home. Sterling A. Brown. AmNP
He'd rent the horse and it sounding like it had asthma. The Horse. Faye Kicknosway. GeTw
He'd take a human life as soon as he would take a drink. A Tough Cuss from Bitter Creek. James Barton Adams. PoOW
Hedge before me, one behind, A. *Unknown, tr. fr. Irish by* Flann O'Brien. BIrV
Hedge Life. James Dickey. LCAP

Hedge of trees surrounds me, A. The Scribe. *Unknown, tr. fr. Old Irish.* AnIL, *tr. by* Kuno Meyer; OnYI, *tr. by* Whitley Stokes *and* John Strachan
Hedgehog, The. J. J. Bell. RHPC
Hedgehog, The. John Clare. SeCeV
Hedgehog. Paul Muldoon. BIrV
Hedgehog hides beneath the rotten hedge, The. The Hedgehog. John Clare. SeCeV
Hedgehog sleeps beneath the hedge, The. The Hedgehog. J. J. Bell. RHPC
Hedgerows are wiser than I, The. Easter Thought. Leo Cox. CaP
Hedges Freaked with Snow. Robert Graves. OxBTC
Hee That Loves a Rosie Cheeke. Thomas Carew. *See* Disdain Returned.
Hee that would write an Epitaph for thee. An Epitaph on Doctor Donne, Deane of Pauls. Richard Corbett. AnAnS-2
Heed the old oracles. The Undersong. Emerson. *Fr.* Woodnotes. AA
Heedless o' My Love. William Barnes. GBL
Heedless she strayed from note to note. The Waiting Chords. Stephen Henry Thayer. AA
Hegel. Amiri Baraka. CoPo
Heicht o the biggins is happit in rauchens o haar, The. Haar in Princes Street. Alexander Scott. BSV
Heifer Clambers Up, A. Gary Snyder. NoAM; NOBA
Heigh! brother mine, art a-waking or a-sleeping. Les Belles Roses sans Mercie. Arthur Shearly Cripps. OBVV
Heigh ho! daisies and buttercups. Seven Times Four [*or* Maternity]. Jean Ingelow. *Fr.* Songs of Seven. HBV-1; OHIP
Heigh ho! my heart is low. *Unknown.* OxNR
Heigh-ho on a Winter Afternoon. Donald Davie. NePoEA-2; OxBTC
Heigho! the lark and the owl! Shelley. *Fr.* Charles the First, sc. v. PBBP
Heigh-ho, what shall a shepheard doe. James Shirley. *Fr.* The Triumph of Beautie Song. ErPo
Heigh in the hevynnis figure circulere. The Kingis Quair, *abr.* James I, King of Scotland. OxBS
Height of the Ridiculous, The. Oliver Wendell Holmes. AA; FaFP; FiBHP; FPL; HBV-2; MoShBr; OBAL; OBCA; PoPl; TreFT; WhC; YaD
Heights, The. Helen Frazee-Bower. Two Married, I. HBMV
Heights, The. Longfellow. *Fr.* The Ladder of St. Augustine. TreF
Heimkehr, Die, *sels.* Heine, *tr. fr. German by* Ezra Pound. AWP
"Mutilated choir boys, The."
"Tell me where thy lovely love is."
"This delightful young man."
Heine's mother was a monster. A Century Piece for Poor Heine. John Logan. NNaP
Heinrich Heine. Ludwig Lewisohn. TrJP
Heir and Serf. Don Marquis. HBMV
Heir of Linne, The. *Unknown.* BaBo; ESPB (A *and* B *vers.*)
Heir of Vironi, The, *sel.* Isaac Pocock.
Song: "Oh! say not woman's love is bought." HBV-1
Heir to Several Yesterdays. Parham J. Kelley. AMV-80
Heir to the office of a man not dead. A Miltonic Sonnet for Mr. Johnson on His Refusal of Peter Hurd's Official Portrait. Richard Wilbur. CAPP; TW
Heiress and Architect. Thomas Hardy. VLP
Heirloom. Leonard Cohen. NOBC
Heirloom. A. M. Klein. NIP; NOBC; OBCV; PeCV; TrJP
Hekatompathia; or, Passionate Century of Love. Thomas Watson. *See* Hecatompathia.
Hektor to Andromache. Homer, *tr. fr. Greek by* Richmond Lattimore. *Fr.* The Iliad, VI. WaaP
Hélas! Oscar Wilde. AnIV; BrPo; MoBrPo; TEP; UnTE; VLP
Helbatrawss, The. Kingsley Amis. NOBL
Held between wars. Käthe Kollwitz. Muriel Rukeyser. NMM
Held on the slightest of bamboo poles. Ode to the Chinese Paper Snake. Richard Eberhardt. CrMA
Helen. "Susan Coolidge." AA
Helen. Hilda Doolittle ("H. D."). BoWoP; LiTM; MoAmPo; MoVE; NOBA; NoP; PAI; SBG; TAP; TW
Helen. Mary Ann Lamb. OBRV
Helen. Christopher Marlowe. *See* Was This the Face.
Helen. Paul Valéry, *tr. fr. French by* Robert Lowell. OBVE
(Helen, the Sad Queen, *tr. by* Joseph T. Shipley.) AWP
Helen. Edward A. U. Valentine. AA
Helen and Corythos. Walter Savage Landor. *Fr.* Corythos. LoBV
Helen Grown Old. Janet Lewis. QFR
Helen, had I known yesterday. Release. D. H. Lawrence. CMoP
Helen Hunt Jackson. Ina Coolbrith. AA
Helen in Egypt, *sels.* Hilda Doolittle ("H. D.").
"Alas, my brothers." NOBA
"Another shout from the wharves." NOBA
"Thetis is the moon-goddess." MOON
Helen Keller. Edmund Clarence Stedman. AA
Helen, my cousin, says she still has the scar. Helen's Scar. Alden Nowlan. Str
Helen of Kirconnell [*or* Kirkconnell]. *Unknown.* AWP; BSV; CH; ELP; GoTS; HBV-1; LiTB; LoBV; OBEV; PoPle; SeCeV; TreFT
(Fair Helen.) FaFP; GTBS; GTBS-P; ViBoPo
("I wish I were where Helen lies.") LO
Helen of Troy. Christopher Marlowe. *See* Was This the Face.
Helen of Troy. Shakespeare. *Fr.* Troilus and Cressida, IV, i. TreFT
Helen—Old. Isabel Ecclestone MacKay. CaP
Helen, the Sad Queen. Paul Valéry. *See* Helen.
Helen, thy beauty is to me. To Helen. Poe. AA; AmPP; AP; AWP; BoLoP; CABA; CH; ChTr; FaBoBe; FaBoEn; FaBV; FaFP; FaPo; FPL; GBL; HAP; HBV-1; HBVY; HeIP; HoPM; InPS; InvP; LiTA; LoBV; NePA; NIP; NOBA; NoP; OBEV; OBRV; OBVV; OxBA; PAI; PoEL-4; PoLF; PoRA; PrIM; SeCeV; TAP; TreF; TrGrPo; ViBoPo; WeW; WHA
Helena and Hermia. Shakespeare. *Fr.* A Midsummer Night's Dream, III, ii. GN
Helena Embarks for Palestine. Cynewulf, *tr. fr. Anglo-Saxon by* Charles W. Kennedy. *Fr.* Elene. AnOE
Helen's Lamentation. Homer, *tr. fr. Greek by* Congreve. *Fr.* The Iliad, XXIV. OBVE
Helen's lips are drifting dust. Love Triumphant. Frederic Lawrence Knowles. HBV-1; TreFT
Helen's lips, as drifting dust. Consolation. Arthur Guiterman. BXAP
Helen's Scar. Alden Nowlan. Str
Helicon. John Hollander. NoAM
Heliodore. Andrew Lang. OBVV
Heliodore. J. D. Logan. CaP
Heliogabalus. John Hollander. OBAL
Heliotrope. Harry Thurston Peck. AA; HBV-1
Hell. Abraham Cowley. *Fr.* Davideis. OxBoCh
Hell. Milton. *Fr.* Paradise Lost, II. OBS
Hell. *Tr. from Gaelic by* Douglas Hyde. WTO
Hell and Heaven. *Unknown.* OxBoLi
Hell-bound Train, The. *Unknown.* BeLS; BLPA; BPAW; CoSo, *with music*
Hell freezing over. To keep sane. Mandelstam. David Young. AmPA
Hell Gate. A. E. Housman. NoAM; UnPo
Hell Hath No Fury. Charles Bukowski. GP
Hell in Texas. *Unknown.* BLPA; BPAW; CoSo, *with music*
Hell is a city much like London. Shelley. *Fr.* Peter Bell the Third. OBSV
Hell is a red barn on a hill. The Curse. Robert Francis. TW
"Hell" said the Devil, as it might have been. Reborn. Kingsley Amis. OxBC
Hell whose rains and cold appal. Hell. *Tr. from Gaelic by* Douglas Hyde. WTO
Hellas, *sels.* Shelley.
Chorus: "World's great age begins anew, The." EBEV; FaBoEn; HAP; HBV-2; LoBV; NOBE; NoP; OAEL-2; OAEP; OBRV; PoEL-4; SeCeV; TEP
(Final Chorus, The.) SeCePo
(Hellas.) ChTr; OBEV
(World's Great Age [Begins Anew], The.) FiP; HeIP
Chorus: "World's on worlds are rolling ever." NoP; OAEP; TEP
(Worlds on Worlds.) HeIP
Hellenics, The, *sels.* Walter Savage Landor.
Hamadryad, The. EnRP
Iphigeneia and Agamemnon. BeLS
(Iphigenia.) EnRP
On the Hellenics. EnRP
(Proem to Hellenics.) ViBoPo
Ternissa! You Are Fled. LoBV; PoEL-4; SeCeV
(On Ternissa's Death.) ELP
(Ternissa.) FaBoEn; NOBE; OBNC
Hellhound on My Trail. *Unknown.* BluL
Hello. John Berryman. NAs
Hello. Gregory Corso. PoM
Hello! Louise Ayres Garnett. SiSoSe
Hello dar, Miss Melerlee! Miss Melerlee. John Wesley Holloway. BANP; PoNe
Hello, Girls, *with music.* *Unknown.* AS
Hello, Hello. William Matthews. PCP
"Hello, hello, hello, sir." Jump-Rope Rhyme. *Unknown.* NTCP
"Hello" his first word. Ian Wedde. Earthly: Sonnets for Carlos, 53. OCNZ
Hello, Ma [*or* My] Baby. Joseph E. Howard *and* Ida Emerson. BLSo, *with music*; FSN, *with music*; FSW
Hello, Sister. Mark Saylor. AMV-80
Hello, Somebody, *with music.* *Unknown.* ShS
Hello There. Brian S. Salome. BXAP
Hello there, Biscuit! You're a better-looking broad. Hello. John Berryman. NAs

Hello there, Walt! To Walt Whitman. Tom MacInnes. CaP
Hell's Bells. Margaret Fishback. ShM
Hell's Pavement. John Masefield. BrPo
Hellvellyn. Sir Walter Scott. FM; TEP
Helmet, The. Philip Levine. LCAP
Helmet and rifle, pack and overcoat. The Battle. Louis Simpson. OBWP
Helmeted, booted, numbered, horsed, and always at a distance. Polo Match. John Ciardi. LiSp
Helmets, The; a Fragment. Thomas Penrose. NOEC
Helmsman, The. Hilda Doolittle ("H. D."). CMoP; OxBA
Helmsman, The; an Ode. J. V. Cunningham. MoVE
Help! X. J. Kennedy. RHPC
Help. Sadi, *tr. fr. Persian by* Sir Edwin Arnold. *Fr.* The Gulistan. AWP
Help from History. William Stafford. AMV-81
Help, Good Shepherd. Ruth Pitter. OxBoCh
Help Is on the Way. Herbert Scott. GP
Help, Lord, because the Godly Man, *with music.* Francis Rous. AH
Help[e] me! help[e] me! now I call. To His Mistresses. Robert Herrick. CaPo; ErPo; SeCP; UnTE
Help me now. Song. Emmett Jarrett. NeAC
Help me to help your life. Letter to P. Robert Friend. NYBP
Help me to hold the Vision Undefiled. The Scribe's Prayer. Arthur Guiterman. TrPWD
Help Me to Seek. Sir Thomas Wyatt. FF; InvP
("Helpe me to seke for I lost it there.") AAS
(Rondeau.) SiPS
Help Thy Servant, *with music.* Andrew Broaddus. AH
Help Us to Live. John Keble. TRV
Help Wanted. Franklin Waldheim. BLPA
Helped the cook pick a chicken. Some Modern Good Turns. Dennis Dibben. FAZ
Helpful Nurse, A. *Unknown.* TDH
Helping Hand, A. Georgia B. Adams. STF
Helping the Handicapped. Emily Dickinson. *See* If I can stop one heart from breaking.
Helpless am I indeed. "Laborers Together with God." Lucy Alice Perkins. BLRP
Helpmate. Henry Chapin. FAZ
Hem and Haw. Bliss Carman. HBV-1
Hem of His Garment, The. Anna Elizabeth Hamilton. TrPWD
He-man, the sea-man, The. Pickup in Tony's Hashhouse. Kenneth Pitchford. *Fr.* Good for Nothing Man. CoPo; ErPo
Hematite Lake. James Galvin. AMV-80
Hemingway House in Key West, The. Philip Schultz. MAYP
Hemingway Syndrome, The. Adrian C. Louis. STE
Hemlock Mountain. Sarah N. Cleghorn. HBV-1
Hemmed-in Males. William Carlos Williams. *Fr.* A Folded Skyscraper. MAT; MoVE; PoRA
Hemorrhage, The. Stanley Kunitz. NYP; WaP
Hen, The. Lord Alfred Douglas. RHPC
Hen, The. Oliver Herford. NA
Hen and the Carp, The. Ian Serraillier. OnUR
Hen and the Oriole, The. Don Marquis. *Fr.* Archy and Mehitabel. EvOK; FiBHP
Hen: Cock, cock, I have la-a-a-yd. Hen and Cock. *Unknown.* GBP
Hen Dying. Alasdair MacLean. BoAnP
Hen Flower, The. Galway Kinnell. NNaP
Hen is a ferocious fowl, The. The Hen. Lord Alfred Douglas. RHPC
Hen remarked to the mooley cow, The. Art. *Unknown.* BLPA
Hen the turuf is thi tuur. *Unknown.* SeCePo
Hen under Bay-Tree. Ruth Pitter. OxBTC
Hen Woman. Thomas Kinsella. CIP; IPY
Hence, All You Vain Delights. John Fletcher. *See* Melancholy.
Hence away, nor dare intrude! Inscription on a Grot. Samuel Rogers. *Fr.* The Pleasures of Memory. OBEC
Hence, Away, You Sirens! George Wither. *Fr.* Fidelia. EIL
Hence Cupid! with your cheating toys. Against Love. Katherine Philips. BoWoP; SBG; WPE
Hence, flames and darts! ye amorous sighs, hence! The Honeymoon. Henry Luttrell. *Fr.* Advice to Julia. OBRV
Hence, Hairt, with Her That Must Depairt. Alexander Scott. BSV
(Bequest of His Heart, A.) OBEV
Hence, hence, profane; soft silence let us have. A Dirge upon the Death of the Right Valiant Lord, Bernard Stuart. Robert Herrick. SeCV-1
Hence, hence unhallowed ears and hearts more hard. The Argument of Democritus Platonissans, or the Infinitie of Worlds. Henry More. SeCV-2
Hence, loath'd vulgarity. Fashion. Horace Twiss. BXAP
Hence, loathèd Melancholy. L'Allegro. Milton. AWP; CABA; FaFP; FiP; GTBS; GTBS-P; HAP; HBV-2; HoPM; JCP; LiTB; LoBV; MasP; NoP; OAEL-1; OBEV; OBS; PPP; SeCePo; SeCeV; TEP; TreFS; TrGrPo; ViBoPo; WHA
Hence prophane grim man, nor dare. To Death, Castara Being Sicke. William Habington. AnAnS-2
Hence, rude Winter! crabbed old fellow. A Glee for Winter. Alfred Domett. HBV-1
Hence These Rimes. Bert Leston Taylor. FiBHP
Hence, vain deluding joys. Il Penseroso. Milton. AWP; CABA; FiP; GTBS; GTBS-P; HAP; HBV-2; HoPM; JCP; LiTB; MasP; NoP; OAEL-1; OBEV; OBS; PPP; SeCeV; TEP; TrGrPo; ViBoPo; WHA
Hence, ye profane! I hate you all. The Profane. Horace, *tr. by* Abraham Cowley. Odes, III, 1. AWP; OBVE
Henceforth, from the Mind. Louise Bogan. LiTA; MoPo; MoVE; NePA; QFR; WPE
Henceforth I will not set my love. Sir Arthur Gorges. GBL
Henchman, The. Whittier. HBV-1; OBEV; OBVV
Hendecasyllabics. Swinburne. FaBoRV; SyP; VLP
Hendecasyllabics. Tennyson. EBEV; FaBoCo; NOBL; VLP
("O you chorus of indolent reviewers.") PV
Hendecasyllables, help! Come to my call. Catullus, *tr. fr. Latin by* James Michie. DBV
Hengest Cyning. Jorge Luis Borges, *tr. fr. Spanish by* Norman Thomas di Giovanni. NYBP
Henley, July 4: 1914-1964. L. E. Sissman. PrIm
Henpecked Husband, A. *Unknown.* OxBM
Henri was suited to appraise the arts. A Portrait of Henry III. Théodore Agrippa d'Aubigné. *Fr.* Les Tragiques. PeHV
Henry Adams. W. H. Auden. OBAL
Henry and King Pedro, clasping. The Death of Don Pedro. *Unknown, tr. by* John Gibson Lockhart. AWP
Henry and Mary. Robert Graves. BrPo; GoJo; SO
(Henry Was a Worthy King.) MoShBr
Henry before Agincourt: October 25, 1415. John Lydgate. CH
Henry C. Calhoun. Edgar Lee Masters. *Fr.* Spoon River Anthology. LiTA; LiTM
Henry VIII. Shakespeare. *See* King Henry VIII.
Henry VIII. *Unknown.* FaBoUs
Henry V. Shakespeare. *See* King Henry V.
Henry V at Harfleur. Shakespeare. *See* Once More unto the Breach.
Henry V before Agincourt. Shakespeare. King Henry V, *fr.* IV, iii. FaPoR
(St. Crispin's Day.) FF
Henry Fifth's Address to His Soldiers. Shakespeare. *See* Once More unto the Breach.
Henry V's Conquest of France. *Unknown.* *See* King Henry Fifth's Conquest of France.
Henry IV, Pt. I. Shakespeare. *See* King Henry IV, Pt. I.
Henry IV, Pt. II. Shakespeare. *See* King Henry IV, Pt. II.
Henry got me with child. Amanda Barker. Edgar Lee Masters. *Fr.* Spoon River Anthology. NoAM
Henry Green. *Unknown.* BaBo
(Mary Wyatt and Henry Green, *with 3 add. sts.*) AmFP
Henry hates the world. What the world to Henry. John Berryman. Dream Songs, LXXIV. NaP
Henry Hudson's Quest. Burton Egbert Stevenson. HBV-2; PAH; PAL
Henry in Ireland to Bill underground. An Elegy for W.C.W., the Lovely Man. John Berryman. *Fr.* Dream Songs. NoP
Henry James. Robert Louis Stevenson. OBNC
Henry James/ (Whatever his other claims). Jacobean. Clifton Fadiman. FiBHP
Henry James at Newport. Weldon Kees. PoA
Henry K. Sawyer. *Unknown.* AmFP
Henry King [Who Chewed Bits of String]. Hilaire Belloc. CenHV; DTC; FaBoNo; FaBoUs; HBMV; ShM
Henry Martin [*or* Martyn]. *Unknown.* BaBo; ESPB (A *and* E *vers.*); FSW; ViBoFo (A *vers.;* B *vers., with music*)
Henry Miller: A Writer. Carol Lem. AMV-80
Henry My Son. *Unknown.* OBET
Henry Purcell. Gerard Manley Hopkins. TEP; VLP
Henry St. John, Viscount Bolingbroke. Pope. *Fr.* An Essay on Man, Epistle IV. OBEC
Henry VI, Pt. I. Shakespeare. *See* King Henry VI, Pt. I.
Henry VI, Pt. III. Shakespeare. *See* King Henry VI, Pt. III.
Henry the Second keepeth (with much care). The Epistle of Rosamond to King Henry the Second. Michael Drayton. *Fr.* England's Heroical Epistles. AnAnS-2
Henry to Rosamond. Michael Drayton. *See* King Henry to Rosamond.
Henry Turnbull. W. W. Gibson. ELU; FaBoTw
Henry Wadsworth Longfellow. Austin Dobson. HBV-2
Henry Ward Beecher. *At. to* Oliver Wendell Holmes. *See* Limerick: "Reverend Henry Ward Beecher, The."
Henry Ward Beecher. Charles Henry Phelps. AA
Henry Was a Worthy King. Robert Graves. *See* Henry and Mary.
Henry was every morning fed. The Boy and the Snake. Charles *and* Mary Lamb. OxBChV

Henry's Confession. John Berryman. *Fr.* Dream Songs. LCAP; NoAM; TwCP
Henry's Lament. Samuel Daniel. *Fr.* The Complaint of Rosamond. OBSC
Henry's mind grew blacker the more he thought. John Berryman. *Fr.* Dream Songs. FaBoMo; NOBA
Henry's pelt was put on sundry walls. John Berryman. *Fr.* Dream Songs. NoAM
Henry's Secret. Dorothy Kilner. OxBChV
Henry's Understanding. John Berryman. NoAM; NOBA
Hens. Alden Nowlan. POL
Hens, The. Elizabeth Madox Roberts. FaPON; GoJo; HBMV; OBCA; PDV; SoPo; TiPo
Hens, The. James S. Tippett. SUS
Hen's Nest. John Clare. PBBP
Henyard Round, The. Donald Hall. Psk
Hep-Cat. John L. Sellers. LFAC
Hep-Cat Chung, 'ware my town. Confucius, *tr. by* Ezra Pound. *Fr.* Songs of Cheng. CTC
Heptalogia, The, *sels.* Swinburne.
Higher Pantheism in a Nutshell, The. BXAP; FaBoNo; HBV-1; NA; Par; SpRo
John Jones. NA; OAEP
(At the Piano.) FaBoNo
Nephelidia. BXAP; FaBoCo; FaBoNo; FaBoPa; HBV-1; HoPM, *first sixteen lines*; InMe; NA; OAEP; Par; SpRo
Sonnet for a Picture. BXAP; FaBoNo; OAEL-2; OAEP
Her/ strong/ white/ legs. Romp. Dave Etter. WeW
Her, a Statue. Thomas Stoddart. OBNC
Her absorption, close to total, was. The End of My Sister's Guggenheim. John Malcolm Brinnin. GLGT
Her aged hands are worn with works of love. To One Being Old. Langdon Elwyn Mitchell. AA
Her "Allowance!" Lillian Gard. SUMH
Her angel looked upon God's face. The Eternal Image. Ruth Pitter. MoBrPo; OxBTC
Her Answer. John Bennett. AA; BLPA
Her Application to Elysium. Kathleen Norris. IHMS
Her Apron through the Trees. Roger Weingarten. AmPA
Her arms across her breast she laid. The Beggar Maid. Tennyson. BeLS; HBV-1; OnMSP
Her arms are gravelled at the undertow. Airport. Martin Johnston. CBAP
Her arms pinned back, impaled against the night. Jacob and the Angel. Stephen Mitchell. VWA
Her Beauty. Max Plowman. HBMV
Her Birthday. Harold Witt. AMV-80
Her blue dress lightly. The Dress. Christopher Middleton. NMP
Her body dances in my dream, and my body. A Foreign Country. Natan Zach, *tr. by* Laya Firestone. VWA
Her body is not so white as. Queen-Ann's-Lace. William Carlos Williams. AmPP; AP; BLPL; MoAB; MoAmPo; NoAM; NOBA; NoP; PrIm; TAP
Her body is pouchy. The Old Nudists. Joan Colby. AMV-80
Her breast is cold; her hands how faint and wan! Virtue. Walter de la Mare. MMA
Her breast is fit for pearls. Emily Dickinson. PeHV
Her Careful Distinct Sex Whose Sharp Lips Comb. E. E. Cummings. ErPo
Her casement like a watchful eye. Balder's Wife. Alice Cary. AA
Her chair drawn to the door. The Laundress. Thomas Kinsella. IPY
Her chariot ready straight is made. The Queen's Chariot. Michael Drayton. *Fr.* Nymphidia. OBS
Her chaunging lookes no colour longe can holde. Seneca, *tr. by* John Studley. *Fr.* Medea, IV. OBVE
Her cheeks are hot, her cheeks are white. Bianca, I. Arthur Symons. UnTE; VLP
Her cheeks were white, her eyes were wild. The Sea. W. H. Davies. FaBoTw
Her Commendation. Francis Davison. OBSC
(Madrigal: "Some there are as fair to see to.") ElL
Her cruel hands go in and out. A Maiden and Her Hair. W. H. Davies. BrPo
Her curving bosom images. Bodily Beauty. George Rostrevor Hamilton. HBMV
Her Dairy. Peter Newell. NA
Her Dancing Days. Anna Adams. BrRo
Her day out from the workhouse-ward, she stands. The Ice. W. W. Gibson. OxBTC
Her Dead Brother. Robert Lowell. NePoEA
Her Dilemma. Thomas Hardy. BrPo
Her dimpled cheeks are pale. A Southern Girl. Samuel Minturn Peck. AA
Her drooping wrist, her arm. Piano Recital. Babette Deutsch. NePoAm
Her Dwarf. George P. Elliott. MAT
Her Dwelling-Place. Ada Foster Murray. HBV-1
Her Epitaph. Thomas William Parsons. AA; HBV-2
Her Eyes. John Crowe Ransom. LiTM; NePA; OBAL; PoPl
Her eyes are like forget-me-nots. To a Little Girl. Gustav Kobbé. HBV-1
Her eyes are velvet, soft and fine. My Poker Girl. Tom Masson. OBAL
Her Eyes Are Wild. Wordsworth. NAs
Her eyes be like the violets. Anne. Lizette Woodworth Reese. AA
Her eyes? Dark pools of deepest shade. Portrait. George Leonard Allen. CDC
Her Eyes Don't Shine like Diamonds, *with music.* David Marion. FSN
Her eyes have seen the monoliths of kings. Oblivion. George Sterling. *Fr.* Three Sonnets on Oblivion. HBV-2
Her eyes long hollowed out to pits of shadow. The Worshiper. Vassar Miller. NePoEA-2
Her eyes that might be filled with wishes. Thenot Protests. "C. N. S." InMe.
Her eyes the glow-worm lend thee. The Night-Piece, to Julia. Robert Herrick. AnAnS-2; CaPo; CH; ELP; HBV-1; InvP; JCP; LiTB; LoBV; NoP; OAEL-1; OAEP; OBEV; OSB; PoEL-3; PoPle; PoRA; SeCeV; SeCP; SeCV-1; TEP; TreFT; UnTE; WHA
Her eyes were gentle; her voice was for soft singing. An Old Woman Remembers. Sterling A. Brown. CNA; PoBA
Her face has made my life most proud and glad. Sonnet: Of His Lady's Face. Jacopo da Lentino, *tr. by* Dante Gabriel Rossetti. AWP
Her face her tongue her wit. *At. to* Sir Arthur Gorges. GBL
Her face is a scrubbed glove. Clinic: Examination. Audrey Conard. AMV-80
Her face like a rain-beaten stone on the day she rolled off. Elegy. Theodore Roethke. CTBA; DFF; NCSH
Her face turned sour. Sensibility. Louis Simpson. GP
Her face was in a bed of hair. Emily Dickinson. NU
Her face was like sad things: was like the lights. A Stranger. Lionel Johnson. VLP
Her face was very fair to see. Our Sister. Horatio Nelson Powers. HBV-1
Her face wrinkles out like tree rings in a cut-off stump. The Old Peasant Woman at the Monastery of Zagorsk. James Schevill. NMP
Her failing spirits with derisive glee. Helen and Corythos. Walter Savage Landor. *Fr.* Corythos. LoBV
Her fair eyes, if they could see. Written in My Lady Speke's Singing-Book. Edmund Waller. CavP
Her Fairness, Wedded to a Star. Edward J. O'Brien. FaBoBe; HBMV
Her Faith. Hilaire Belloc. *See* Because My Faltering Feet.
Her Fancy Ball, *abr.* Thomas Hood. *Fr.* Miss Kilmansegg and Her Precious Leg. VLP
Her father loved me; oft invited me. Othello's Defense. Shakespeare. *Fr.* Othello, I, iii. EBEV; SCV; TreF
Her Favorites. Mattie Lee Hausgen. PoPl
Her feet beneath her petticoat. The Bride. Sir John Suckling. *Fr.* A Ballad upon a Wedding. TrGrPo
Her fingers shame the ivory keys. Amy Wentworth. Whittier. BeLS
Her flesh sticks to my hands, something held. Meeting Anais Nin's Elena. Gene Frumkin. AMV-81
Her gait detached from the moving throng. The Beautiful Negress. Ruth Pitter. MoVE
Her gentle limbs did she undress. Christabel and Geraldine. Samuel Taylor Coleridge. *Fr.* Christabel. PeHV
Her Gifts. Dante Gabriel Rossetti. The House of Life, XXXI. HBV-1; VLP
Her Going. Shirley Kaufman. PCP
Her grandmother called her from the playground. Legacies. Nikki Giovanni. CTBA
Her grieving parents cradled here. Epitaph. Sylvia Townsend Warner. MoBrPo
Her Hair. Baudelaire, *tr. fr. French by* Doreen Bell. NAWM-2
Her Hair. Sir Robert Chester. *Fr.* Love's Martyr. ElL
Her hair has a sweet smell of girlhood under his face. Enigma. Richard Murphy. CIP
Her hair the net of golden wire. So Fast Entangled. *Unknown.* TrGrPo
Her hair upgathered thus behind the neck. Doric. Anghelos Sikelianos, *tr. by* Edmund Keeley *and* Philip Sherrard. ErPo
Her hair was a waving bronze and her eyes. Disappointment. John Boyle O'Reilly. ACP; OnYI
Her hair was tawny with gold, her eyes with purple were dark. A Court Lady. Elizabeth Barrett Browning. BeLS; HBV-2
Her hand a goblet bore for him. The Two. Hugo von Hofmannsthal, *tr. by* Ludwig Lewisohn. AWP
Her hand in my hand. Dunce Song 6. Mark Van Doren. DuDa
Her hand that holds. Jesus Drum. Pearl Cleage Lomax. CNA
Her hand which touched my hand she moved away. On a Hand. Hilaire Belloc. ELU
Her hands are cold; her face is white. Under the Violets. Oliver Wendell Holmes. *Fr.* The Professor at the Breakfast Table. AA

Her hands have much/ Of Christlike touch. Mother—a Portrait. Ethel Romig Fuller. PGD
Her health is good. She owns to forty-one. Occupation: Housewife. Phyllis McGinley. *Fr.* I Know a Village. DBV; WPE
Her Heards Be Thousand Fishes. Spenser. *Fr.* Colin Clout's Come Home Again. ChTr
Her Heart. Bartholomew Griffin. *Fr.* Fidessa, More Chaste than Kind. TrGrPo
("Flye to her heart, hover about her heart.") AAS
Her heart is like her garden. My Mother's Garden. Alice E. Allen. BLPA; BLPL; FaBoBe
Her Horoscope. Mary Ashley Townsend. AA
Her house is become like a man dishonored. Dirge. Bible, Apocrypha. *Fr.* First Maccabees. TrJP
Her Husband. Ted Hughes. OxBC
Her imaginary playmate was a grown-up. Cinderella. Randall Jarrell. DFT; LCAP
Her Irish maids could never spoon out mush. Mary Winslow. Robert Lowell. MiAP; MoVE; PPP
Her iron beats. Domestic Scene. Michael Hartnett. BIrV
Her ivory hands on the ivory keys. In the Gold Room. Oscar Wilde. SyP
Her Kind. Anne Sexton. CoAP; FF; HeIP; LiTM; MP; PPP; TAP; TwAmPo; TwCP; WPOW
Her—"last poems." Emily Dickinson. SBG
Her laughter was infectious; so, some found. The Ecstasies of Dialectic. Howard Nemerov. TwAmPo
Her Legs. Robert Herrick. SpRo
Her Letter. Bret Harte. HBV-1; PoLF
Her life is in the marble! yet a fall. Her, a Statue. Thomas Stoddart. OBNC
Her Lips Are Copper Wire. Jean Toomer. NoAM
Her lips blue from tasting, her eyes so blue. Among Blackberries. Michael Waters. GeTw
Her lips' remark was: "Oh, you kid!" Servant Girl and Grocer's Boy. Joyce Kilmer. YaD
Her lips they are redder than coral. *Unknown.* FaBoCo
Her lips were so near. In Explanation. Walter Learned. AA; HBV-1
Her little face is like a walnut shell. Visitor. W. E. Henley. In Hospital, XX. BrPo
Her long with ardent look his eye pursu'd. Milton. *Fr.* Paradise Lost, IX. UnPo
Her Longing. Theodore Roethke. NU
Her love is like an island. My Mother's Love. *Unknown.* STF
Her love is true I know. True Love. Waring Cuney. CDC
Her Love Poem. Lucille Clifton. GP
Her loveliness stirred my circumstances. Moved by Her Music. Richard Gillman. NePoAm-2
Her lute hangs shadowed in the apple-tree. A Sea-Spell. Dante Gabriel Rossetti. SyP; VLP; WSC
Her Man Described by Her Owne Dictamen. Ben Jonson. *Fr.* A Celebration of Charis. AnAnS-2; SeCP
Her Merriment. W. H. Davies. EnLoPo
Her mind lives in a quiet room. Interior. Dorothy Parker. SBG
Her Mother. Alice Cary. OHIP
Her mother died when she was young. Kemp Owyne. *Unknown.* EnSB; ESPB; SeCeV; ViBoFo
Her mother watched her closely, yet one day. The Surprise. *Unknown, tr. by* Louis Untermeyer. UnTE
Her mother's old and can't help herself. Keno. Dara Wier. MAYP
Her Mouth. Richard Aldington. BrPo
Her mouth an O. The Poetess Kō Ōgimi. Helen Chasin. NMM
Her mouth is a crushed flower. Her Mouth. Richard Aldington. BrPo
Her mouth is as fragrant as a vine. Cleopatra. Swinburne. BeLS
Her mouth is filled with silver pins. Watching My Daughter Sew. Katharine Privett. AMV-81
Her Music. Martha Dickinson Bianchi. AA
Her Name. Walter Savage Landor. *See* Well I Remember.
Her name, Melissa, means she is a bee. Melissa. *Unknown, tr. by* Louis Untermeyer. UnTE
Her name was Ate, mother of debate. The House of Ate. Spenser. *Fr.* The Faerie Queene, IV, 1. OBSC
Her name was Marian Claribel Lee. The Ballad of Sir Brian and the Three Wishes. Newman Levy. FiBHP
"Her Pa committed suicide." Such a Pleasant Familee. Wallace Irwin. ShM
Her Passing. William Drummond of Hawthornden. *See* Madrigal: "Beauty and the life, The."
Her patience is infinite. The Problems of a Writing Teacher. David Ray. NePoEA-2
Her Pedigree. Arthur Davison Ficke. Sonnets of a Portrait Painter, IX. HBMV
Her Picture. Ellen Mackay Hutchinson Cortissoz. AA
Her Polka Dots. Peter Newell. NA
Her Praises. Anthony Scoloker. EIL
Her pretty feet. Upon Her Feet. Robert Herrick. CaPo; ViBoPo
Her Rambling. Thomas Lodge. *Fr.* The Life and Death of William Longbeard. LoBV; OBSC
Her red cloth is like the lightning. Red Beauty. *Gond Oral Tradition, tr. by* V. Elwin *and* S. Hivale. WTO
Her red pump tapping, her ankle-length gown slit at the knee. Mrs. Applebaum's Sunday Dance Class. Philip Schultz. AMV-81; MAYP
Her Reply. Sir Walter Ralegh. *See* Nymph's Reply to the Shepherd, The.
Her Rival for Aziza. *Unknown, tr. fr. Arabic by* E. Powys Mathers. *Fr.* The Thousand and One Nights. AWP
Her Sacred Bower. Thomas Campion. *See* Where She Her Sacred Bower Adorns.
Her sails are strong and yellow as the sand. The Clipper. Thomas Fleming Day. EtS
Her scarf *à la* Bardot. Twice Shy. Seamus Heaney. NCSH; TwCP
Her seas and mountains made. The Weaving of the Wing. Ralph Hodgson. BrPo
Her sense of humor has no gold stop. Telephonist. Janet Frame. WPE
Her Shadow. Elisabeth Cavazza Pullen. AA
Her sight is short, she comes quite near. Jenny Wren. W. H. Davies. MoBrPo
Her Sister. Moira O'Neill. OxBTC
Her smiling eyes in the glass. Calculating Female. Jill Hellyer. POL
Her soul is a select district. Paysage Choisi. Francis Sparshott. MoCV
Her stiffening captor lies in wait. Mercedes, Her Aloneness. Colette Inez. IHMS
Her Story. Naomi Long Madgett. IHMS; PoBA
Her Strong Enchantments Failing. A. E. Housman. FaBoTw; MAT; NOBE; OAEL-2
Her suffering ended with the day. A Death-Bed. James Aldrich. AA; HBV-2
Her sweet weight on my heart a night. Emily Dickinson. PeHV
Her talk was all of woodland things. The Wife from Fairyland. Richard Le Gallienne. HBV-1
Her thin puny little body. Clinic Day. Jo Barnes. BrRo
Her thoughts are like a flock of butterflies. From Life. Brian Hooker. HBV-1
Her touch heals. Sarah: Cherokee Doctor. Wendy Rose. STE
Her Triumph. Ben Jonson. *See* Triumph of Charis, The.
Her True Body. Jerred Metz. VWA
Her veil was artificial flowers and leaves. Christopher Marlowe. *Fr.* Hero and Leander. HoPM
Her voice did quiver as we parted. On Fanny Godwin. Shelley. ChER; FaBoEn; OBNC
Her voice was cold as a bill collector's. The Price of Paper. Lawrence Russ. AMV-81
Her voice was like the song of birds. A Child. Richard Watson Gilder. AA
Her Way. William Rose Benét. HBMV
Her ways were gentle while a babe. Elizabeth Oakes Smith. *Fr.* The Sinless Child. AA
Her Whole Life Is an Epigram. Blake. FaBoEE; InPK; NIP; OAEL-2; PV (Character, A.) OxBoLi
Her Window. Richard Leigh. CavP
Her Words. Anna Hempstead Branch. FaPON
Her world is all aware. She reads. For Her Sake. Alastair Reid. PoPl
Her wraithful turnings and her soft answers head me off. Soft Answers. Robert Bagg. FF; UnTE
Her young employers, having got in late. A Summer Morning. Richard Wilbur. FaBoMo
Hera, Hung from the Sky. Carolyn Kizer. NMM; WPE
Heracles. Yvor Winters. QFR; TwAmPo
Heraclitus. William Johnson Cory, *paraphrased fr. the Greek of* Callimachus. AWP; EBVV; ELU; FaBoEE; FaPoR; HBV-2; InPK; NOBE; OBEV; OBNC; OBVV; PeHV; PoRA; SeCePo; TreF; ViBoPo; VLP
Heraclitus in the West. Charles G. Bell. NePoAm
Herald Crane, The. Hamlin Garland. HBV-1
Heralded into a belly swelling bladder bloating banquet. On Meeting the Clergy of the Holy Catholic Church in Osaka. Joy Kogawa. BrSi
Heralds of Christ, *with music.* Laura S. Copenhaver. AH
Herb-Leech, The. Joseph Campbell. AnIL; OnYI
Herbert Glerbett. Jack Prelutsky. RHPC
Herbert Street Revisited. John Montague. CIP; IPY
Herbert White. Frank Bidart. AmPA
Herbivorous Thoreau, The. Alimentary. Clifton Fadiman. PV
Herbs in the Attic. Marilyn Nelson Waniek. AMV-81; MAYP
Hercules Furens, *sel.* Seneca, *tr. fr. Latin by* Jasper Heywood.
"Let oken club now strike, and poast of might," *fr.* IV. OBVE
Hercules Oetaetus, *sel.* Seneca, *tr. fr. Latin by* John Studley.
"Let other mount aloft, let other sore," *fr.* II. OBVE

Herd, The. Frances Cornford. FM
Herd Boy, The. Haniel Long. HBMV
Herd Boy, The. Lu Yu, *tr. fr. Chinese by* Arthur Waley. ChTr
Herdmen, The. *Unknown, at to* William Byrd. *See* Quiet Life, The.
Herds, The. W. S. Merwin. NaP; NYBP
Herdsman. Michael Pettit. MAYP
Herdsmen, The. Theocritus, *tr. fr. Greek by* Charles Stuart Calverley. *Fr.* Idylls. AWP
Here. Marvin Bell. AmPA
Here. Robert Creeley. NOBA
Here. Philip Larkin. CMoP
Here. R. S. Thomas. GTBS-P
Here. Hat Bar. Mildred Weston. FiBHP
Here/ High on the hill. Song of the Hill. Edith Lodge. GoYe
Here/ With my beer/ I sit. Beer. George Arnold. AA; OBAL; TreFT
Here a little child I stand. Grace for a Child [*or* Another Grace for a Child *or* A Child's Grace *or* Grace before Meat]. Robert Herrick. AnAnS-2; AWP; CABA; CavP; ChTr; EaLo; EBCP; FaBoCh; FaPON; GoJo; HeIP; InPK; InPS; InvP; LiTB; LoBV; MoShBr; OAEP; OBEV; OBS; OxBChV; OxBoCh; PoPle; SeCeV; SeCV-1; TreFS; TrGrPo; ViBoPo
Here a Nit-Wit Lies. Patrick Barrington. WhC
Here a pretty baby lies. Upon a Child. Robert Herrick. LoBV; OBEV; OBS; SeCV-1; TrGrPo
Here, a sheer hulk, lies poor Tom Bowling. Tom Bowling [*or* Poor Tom]. Charles Dibdin. AmSS; EtS; HBV-1; NOEC; OBEC; OxBoLi
Here a solemn [*or* solemne] fast we keep[e]. An Epitaph upon a Virgin. Robert Herrick. CaPo; FaBoEE; OxBoLi; PoEL-3; SeCV-1
Here a wandering seaweed. Anti-Nostalgia. Henryk Grynberg, *tr. by* Isaac Komem. VWA
Here, above,/ cracks in the buildings are filled with battered moonlight. The Man-Moth. Elizabeth Bishop. LiTA; LiTM; MAT; MiAP; MoAB; MoAmPo; NoAM; NOBA; NYP; PoCh; PPP
Here again (she said) is March the third. March the 3rd. Edward Thomas. NAs
Here am I, a shape under a cedar. Sitting in the Woods: A Contemplation. W. R. Moses. NCSH
Here am I, little jumping Joan. Mother Goose. NTCP; OxNR; TiPo
Here am I now cast down. Ex Nihilo. David Gascoyne. *Fr.* Miserere. GTBS-P; NeBP
Here am I, this carrot eating. In Common. Gene Derwood. NePA; PoPl
Here among long-discarded cassocks. Diary of a Church Mouse. John Betjeman. OxBTC
Here Ananias lies because he lied. F. W. MacVeagh. WhC
Here and Now. Catherine Cater. AmNP; PoNe
Here and Now. Philip Levine. PoA; VWA
Here and There. Jon Stallworthy. NoAM
Here are/ blue teapot. Components. Roger McDonald. CBAP
Here are cakes for thy body. The Other World. *Unknown, tr. by* Robert Hillyer. *Fr.* Book of the Dead. AWP
Here are fine gifts, children. Sappho, *tr. fr. Greek by* Willis Barnstone. BoWoP
Here, are five letters in this blessed Name. The Ghyrlond of the Blessed Virgin Marie. Ben Jonson. ISi
Here are no signs of festival. African Christmas. John Press. OBCP
Here are old trees, tall oaks, and gnarled pines. The Antiquity of Freedom. Bryant. AA; AP
Here are sweet peas, on tiptoe for a flight. Sweet Peas. Keats. GN
Here are the lady's knives and forks. *Unknown.* OxNR
Here are the ragged towers of vines. The Labourer in the Vineyard. Stephen Spender. NeBP
Here are the Schubert *Lieder.* Now begin. For M.S. Singing *Fruhlingsglaube* in 1945. Frances Cornford. BrRo
Here are weeds about his mouth. Wide Empty Landscape with a Death in the Foreground. N. Scott Momaday. CDW
Here, as a bare, unlichened wall, the Castle front goes up. At Ferns Castle. Padraic Colum. NePoAm
Here as I sit by the Jumna bank. The Hindu Ascetic. Sir Alfred Comyn Lyall. *Fr.* Studies at Delhi. OBVV
Here, as in a painting, yellow noon burns [*or* noon burns yellow]. Natalya Gorbanyevskaya, *tr. fr. Russian by* Daniel Weissbort. BoWoP; PBWP
Here, at last, is the fever. A Day in My Union Suit. Michael Pettit. MAYP
Here at right of the entrance this bronze head. A Bronze Head. W. B. Yeats. LiTB
Here, at the airport, waiting. At the Airport. John Malcolm Brinnin. MoAB
Here, at the beginning of the new season. Meditation on the BMT. Paul Blackburn. CoPo
Here at the center of the turning year. New Year. Stephen Spender. AWP
Here at the country inn. The Forefather. Richard Burton. AA
Here at the roots of the mountains. Rapids at Night. Duncan Campbell Scott. CaP
Here at the seashore they use the clouds over & over. Rhode Island. William Meredith. NoP
Here at the Vespasian-Carlton, it's just one. Boom! Howard Nemerov. LiTM; MP; NIP
Here at the village crossing. The Call. Daniel Corkery. OnYI
Here at the wayside station, as many a morning. The Wayside Station. Edwin Muir. FaBoTw; MoVE
Here at this sudden age of mine. An Autumn Walk. Witter Bynner. GoYe
Here Awa', There Awa'. *Unknown.* OBS
Here Be Dragons. Ginny Friedlander. AMV-80
Here be grapes, whose lusty blood. John Fletcher. *Fr.* The Faithful Shepherdess. ViBoPo
Here be rural graces, sylvan places. Wild Cherry Tree. Edmund Blunden. BrPo
Here be woods as green. John Fletcher. *Fr.* The Faithful Shepherdess. ViBoPo
Here beside dwelleth. The Magician and the Baron's Daughter. *Unknown.* MeEL
Here beside my Paris fire, I sit alone and ponder. Retrospect. Agnes Mary Frances Robinson. OBVV
Here between lunch and teatime, and days and hours between. Lines to Dr. Ditmars. Kenneth Allan Robinson. ImOP
Here blew winter once with the snowstorms spurning. The Enchanted Heart. Edward Davison. HBMV
Here bring your purple and gold. Flowers for the Brave. Celia Thaxter. OHIP
Here busy and yet innocent lyes dead. On the Death of a Monkey. Thomas Heyrick. FM; MePo
Here, but Unable to Answer. Richard Hugo. DiL
Here by the grey north sea. A Northern Vigil. Bliss Carman. OBEV; OBVV; PeCV
Here by the moorway you returned. Your Last Drive. Thomas Hardy. OBNC
Here, by the shore, a carven figure shows. The Living Statue. *Unknown, tr. by* Louis Untermeyer. UnTE
Here, by the shore, we go out each morning. Diving for Pearls. Traise Yamamoto. BrSi
Here, Caelia, for thy sake I part. To the Mutable Fair. Edmund Waller. AnAnS-2; SeCP
Here, Charmian, take my bracelets. Cleopatra. William Wetmore Story. AA
Here Cleita sleeps. You ask her life and race? The Monument of Cleita. Edward Cracroft Lefroy. *Fr.* Echoes from Theocritus. AWP
Here clove the keels of centuries ago. The Salt Flats. Sir Charles G. D. Roberts. CaP
Here come real stars to fill the upper skies. Fireflies in the Garden. Robert Frost. RHPC
Here Come Three Merchants a-Riding, *with music.* *Unknown.* TrAS
(Ransi-Tansi-Tay ["Here come three dukes a-riding"].) PoPle
Here comes a girl so damned shapely. Girl Walking. Charles G. Bell. ErPo; NePoAm-2
Here Comes a Lusty Wooer. *Unknown.* CH; OxNR
Here comes another, bumping over the sage. Tumbleweed. David Wagoner. BoNaP
Here comes Kate Summers who, for gold. The Bird of Paradise. W. H. Davies. BrPo; MoVE
Here comes my lady with her little baby. *Unknown.* OxNR
Here comes Old Man Adkins with a battle-ax. Coal Loadin' Blues. *Unknown.* AmFP
Here comes the elephant. The Elephant. Herbert Asquith. SoPo; SUS; TiPo
Here comes the Marshal. The Proclamation. Longfellow. *Fr.* John Endicott. PAH
Here comes the shadow not looking where it is going. Sire. W. S. Merwin. CoAP; NaP; VGW
Here continueth to rot. Epitaph on Colonel Francis Chartres. John Arbuthnot. FaBoEE; OBSV
Here costive many minutes did I strain. Privy-Love for My Landlady. George Farewell. NOEC
Here cursing swearing Burton lies. Burns. FaBoEE
Here, Cyprian, is my jeweled looking-glass. To Aphrodite; with a Mirror. Aline Kilmer. HBMV
Here Dead Lie We. A. E. Housman. FPL; OAEL-2; PoLF
(Epitaph.) MoVE
("Here dead lie we because we did not choose.") ELU; FaBoEE; NoP; OAEP
Here deare Iöas lies. Iöas' Epitaph. William Drummond of Hawthornden. PoEL-2
Here Delia's buried at fourscore. Hildebrand Jacob. FaBoEE
Here did sway the eltrot flow'rs. Times o' Year. William Barnes. BoNaP
Here do I put my name for to betraye. *Unknown.* FaBoUs

Here dock and tare. In the Grave No Flower. Edna St. Vincent Millay. CrMA
Here doth Dionysia lie. Epitaph of Dionysia. *Unknown.* HBV-1; OBEV; OBVV
Here down my wearied limbs I'll lay. On Himself. Robert Herrick. CaPo
Here enter not vile bigots, hypocrites. Inscription above the Entrance to the Abbey of Theleme. Rabelais, *tr. by* Sir Thomas Urquhart. *Fr.* Gargantua. FaBoRV
Here envy and lying/ Held me enclosed. On Leaving Prison. Luis de Léon. ILwL
Here even experts can. Ragoût Fin de Siècle (with Reference to Certain Cafés). Erich Kästner, *tr. by* Walter Kaufman. ErPo; PeHV
Here, ever since you went abroad. What News. Walter Savage Landor. BoLoP
Here falls no light of sun nor stars. Richard Hovey. *Fr.* Taliesin. AA
Here first the day does break. Her Window. Richard Leigh. CavP
Here, five feet deep, lies on his back. On the Astrologer and Almanac Maker, John Partridge. Swift. FaBoEE
Here Followeth the Songe of the Death of Mr. Thewlis. *Unknown.* CoMu
Here Follows Some Verses upon the Burning of Our House. Anne Bradstreet. *See* Some Verses upon the Burning of Our House, July 10th, 1666.
Here for a little we pause. Benicasim. Sylvia Townsend Warner. OBWP
Here—for they could not help but die. Epitaph. Philip Freneau. *Fr.* The Fading Rose. AA
Here from the brow of the hill I look. The Old Mill. Thomas Dunn English. AA
Here from the start, from our first days, look. The Tally Stick. Jarold Ramsey. NIP
Here further up the mountain slope. The Birthplace. Robert Frost. EyDe; OFD
Here goes a man of seventy-four. Seventy-four and Twenty. Thomas Hardy. WhC
Here goes a poor old chimney sweeper. The Chimney Sweeper. *Unknown.* AmFP
Here halt we our march, and pitch our tent. The Green Mountain Boys. Bryant. PAH
Here has my salient faith annealed me. Key West. Hart Crane. CMoP
Here Have I Been These One and Twenty Years. Arthur Hugh Clough. NAs
Here he lets go the struggling imp, to clutch. Shakespeare. Thomas Hood. *Fr.* The Plea of the Midsummer Fairies. OBRV
Here he lies moulding. Epitaph. Leslie Mellichamp. QQQ; ShM
Here, here are our enjoyments done. Lucasia, Rosania and Orinda Parting at a Fountain, July 1663. Katherine Philips. PeHV
Here, here I live with what my board. His Content in the Country. Robert Herrick. CaPo; SeCV-1; TEP
Here, here, oh here Eurydice. Orpheus to Beasts. Richard Lovelace. CaPo
Here, hold this glove (this milk-white cheveril glove). Sonnet. Richard Barnfield. Sonnets, XIV. PeHV
Here, houses close their sleepy window eyes. Arizona Village. Robert Stiles Davieau. AmFN
Here Huntington's ashes long have lain. Ambrose Bierce. DBV
Here I Am. Abraham Sutskever, *tr. fr. Yiddish by* Joseph Leftwich. TrJP
Here I am,/ Novice of many years. Two Roads, Etc. Dorothy Walters. IHMS
Here I am, an industry without chimneys. The Perfection of Dentistry. Marvin Bell. AmPA; CoAP
Here I am, an old man in a dry month. Gerontion. T. S. Eliot. AmPP; AP; CABA; ChMP; CMoP; CoBMV; EBEV; FaBoEn; GTBS-P; HAP; InPS; LiTA; LiTM; LoBV; MoPo; NePA; NoAM; NOBA; OAEL-2; OAEP; OxBA; PAI; PPP; SBVL; SeCePo; SeCeV; TAP; TwAmPo
Here I am and forth I must. Prayer for the Journey. *Unknown.* OxBM
Here I am, seated, with all my words. Silence Concerning an Ancient Stone. Rosario Castellanos, *tr. by* George D. Schade. PBWP
Here I am, sprouted to my full height. Here I Am. Abraham Sutskever, *tr. by* Joseph Leftwich. TrJP
Here I am, troubling the dream coast. In California. Louis Simpson. NoAM
Here I am whole, I know. Herdsman. Michael Pettit. MAYP
Here I am with my rabbits. *Unknown.* OxNR
Here I come creeping, creeping everywhere. The Voice of the Grass. Sarah Roberts Boyle. AA; HBV-1; HBVY
Here I drone in this human hive. The Landlubber's Chantey. James Stuart. HBMV
Here I go again. Starting from San Francisco. Lawrence Ferlinghetti. BiP; CAPP
Here I go again. Away. Lucien Stryk. GP
Here I go drawing pictures again. Chasing the Paper-Shamans. Wendy Rose. TWSS
Here I lie asleep. The Absence. Denise Levertov. NaP
Here I lie at [*or* outside] the chancel door. On Elizabeth Ireland [*or* Outside the Chancel Door]. *Unknown.* FaBoEE; ShM
Here I lie for the last time. Epitaph on an Irish Priest. *Unknown.* FaBoEE
Here I lie outside the chancel door. *See* Here I lie at the chancel door.
Here I ligg, Sydney Slugabed Godless Smith. Under the Eildon Tree. Sydney Goodsir Smith. OxBS
Here I myself might likewise die. Poetry Perpetuates the Poet. Robert Herrick. FaBoEE
Here I sit. Bad Morning. Langston Hughes. OBAL
Here I Sit Alone. *Unknown.* OxBoCh
Here I sit in my infested cubicle. Theresa Greenwood. CTBA
Here I sit on Buttermilk Hill. Buttermilk Hill. *Unknown.* FSW
Here I slept with my face turned. Prospect Beach. Lou Lipsitz. VGW
Here I stand. The Climber Surveys His Mountain. Hugh Ouston. PoSH
Here I stand/ Humble, with outstretched arms. Hymn to the Air Spirit. *Tr. fr. Eskimo.* WTO
Here I will rest beside this hill. Contentment. Lawrence E. Estes. AMV-80
Here I'm supposed to be a great poet. 3:16 and One Half. Charles Bukowski. GP
Here in a crumbled corner of the wall. The Church Mouse. Gerald Bullett. BoAnP
Here in a distant place I hold my tongue. Egan O Rahilly. *Unknown, tr. by* James Stephens. EBEV; NoAM; OBMV; SeCePo
Here, in a field. In a Field. Robert Pack. MAT; NePoEA-2
Here in a quiet and dusty room they lie. The Seed Shop. Muriel Stuart. BoNaP; GoTS
Here, in huge cauldrons, the rough mass they stow. The Iron Industry in Birmingham. Richard Jago. *Fr.* Edge-Hill; or, The Rural Prospect Delineated and Moralised. NOEC
Here in Kansas is a school. Haskell. Witter Bynner. GLGT
Here in Katmandu. Donald Justice. CoAP; ConAP; HeIP; LiSp; NIP; RFM
Here, in late spring, the summer is on us already. Hot Afternoons Have Been in West 15th Street. Paul Blackburn. VGW
Here in my careful garden I have nourished. Two Gardens. Arlene De Bevoise. AMV-80
Here in my curving hands I cup. This Quiet Dust. John Hall Wheelock. MoAmPo; WHA
Here in my hands a small cold-chisel. The Little Chisel. N. P. Van Wyk Louw, *tr. by* Jack Cope *and* Uys Krige. PeSA
Here in my head, the home that is left for you. Burning the Letters. Randall Jarrell. MiAP; MoAB; MoAmPo
Here, in my parents' home. Visit. Vic Coccimiglio. Str
Here, in my rude log cabin. The Battle of New Orleans. Thomas Dunn English. PAH
Here, in my snug little fire-lit chamber. Alone by the Hearth. George Arnold. HBV-1
Here in my vaster pools, as white as snow or milk. Lincolnshire's Holland Speaks of Her Waterfowl. Michael Drayton. *Fr.* Polyolbion, Song XXV. FaBoPP
Here in Nantucket does the tiny soul. Phenomenal Survivals of Death in Nantucket. Louise Glück. AmPA
Here in our aging district the wood pigeon lives with us. All Morning. Theodore Roethke. NaP
Here in our cloud we talk. Quiet Town. William Stafford. MAT
Here, in the/ book. The Book of Mysteries. Anthony Barnett. VWA
Here in the Cloisters a fourth dimension evolves. The Cloisters. Samuel Yellen. NePoAm
Here in the cool and book-infested den. Ulysses' Library. David Daiches. PoA
Here in the country's heart. The Country Faith. Norman Gale. HBV-1; OBEV; OBVV; WGRP
Here in the dark, O heart. Second Best. Rupert Brooke. MoBrPo; OBVV
Here in the dark what ghostly figures press! In Tesla's Laboratory. Robert Underwood Johnson. AA
Here, in the darkness, where this plaster saint. Madeleine in Church. Charlotte Mew. SBG
Here in the dim and the almost dark and the warmth of the truth. The Riding Stable in Winter. John Tagliabue. PH
Here, in the field, last year. Compensation. Gerald Gould. HBMV
Here in the green scooped valley I walk to and fro. The Green Valley. Sylvia Townsend Warner. MoBrPo
Here, in the hidden palm of the Pajaro Valley. Stonehouse. Jeff Tagami. BrSi
Here in the marshland, past the battered bridge. A Harrow Grave in Flanders. Robert Offley Ashburton. HBV-2
Here in the midnight, where the dark mainland and island. Night Hymns on Lake Nipigon. Duncan Campbell Scott. OBCV
Here, in the most Unchristian basement. The Men's Room in the College Chapel. W. D. Snodgrass. GP; MoAmPo; PPP; TW

Here in the newspaper—the wreck of the East Bound. It's Here in The. Russell Atkins. AmNP; PoBA
Here, in the night, I'm staring. Dino Campana and the Bear. Edward Hirsch. MAYP
Here in the North, our houses and their appointments. How Was Your Trip to L.A.? Philip Whalen. TAT
Here in the open cockpit. Lispy Bails Out. David Barker. GP
Here in the pine shade is the nest of night. Night and the Pines. Duncan Campbell Scott. OBCV
Here, in the sand, where someone laid him down. Cruciform. Winifred Welles. LO; NYBP
Here in the Scuffled Dust. W. D. Snodgrass. Heart's Needle, VII. NCSH; NePoEA; NIP; NMP
Here in the self is all that man can know. Sonnet. John Masefield. *Fr.* Lollingdon Downs. AWP
Here in the uplands. Scotland. Alexander Gray. BSV; GoTS; OxBS
Here, in the withered arbor, like the arrested wind. Statue and Birds. Louise Bogan. EyDe; MoAB; MoAmPo
Here in their health and youth they're sitting down. Schoolgirl on Speech-Day in the Open Air. Iain Crichton Smith. NePoEA-2
Here in this bleak city of Rochester. Sestina d'Inverno. Anthony Hecht. NoP
Here in this car is surcease from a thousand dead. Surcease. Patrick Lane. NeAC
Here in this dim, dull, double-bedded room. Children: Private Ward. W. E. Henley. In Hospital, XVIII. BrPo
Here in this great house in the barrack square. The Hambone and the Heart. Edith Sitwell. OBMV
Here in this inland garden. Alien. Archibald MacLeish. EtS
Here in this leafy place. Before Sedan. Austin Dobson. TreFS
Here, in This Little Bay. Coventry Patmore. *See* Magna Est Veritas.
Here in this narrow room there is no light. Prothalamium. A. J. M. Smith. CaP
Here in this room where first we met. As She Feared It Would Be. Lilla Cabot Perry. Meeting after Long Absence, I. AA
Here in this sequestered close. A Garden Song. Austin Dobson. BoNaP; HBV-1; LoBV; OBEV; OBNC; OBVV
Here in this simple house his presence clings. House in Springfield. Gail Brook Burket. PGD
Here in this world/ I won't live. Izumi Shikibu, *tr. fr. Japanese by* Willis Barnstone. BoWoP
Here in veins of metal and glass. The Dead Sea. Henryk Grynberg, *tr. by* Isaac Komem. VWA
Here is a beetle as black as my hat. E. S. Goodwill. BXAP
Here is a child who is leaning over a paper. The Mirror. John N. Morris. PoA
Here is a child who presses his head to the ground. The Windows. W. S. Merwin. DFF
Here is a coast; here is a harbour. Arrival at Santos. Elizabeth Bishop. OxBC
Here is a cup left empty in their. Broken Home. William Stafford. NNaP
Here is a face that says half-past seven. Clocks. Carl Sandburg. CrMA
Here is a family so little famous. Photograph in a Stockholm Newspaper for March 13, 1910. Don Coles. NOBC
Here is a famous world. There Is No Place to Hide. Gwendolyn MacEwen. *Fr.* The T. E. Lawrence Poems. NOBC
Here is a fat animal, a bear. Self-Portrait, as a Bear. Donald Hall. SO
Here is a fountain of Christ's blood. Our Saviour's Love. *Unknown.* OBET
Here is a place that is no place. Madhouse [*or* The Patient: Rockland County Sanitarium]. Calvin C. Hernton. IDB; NNP; PoBA; PoNe
Here is a poem for the two of us to play. The Newly Pressed Suit. Roger McGough. NoAM
Here is a rarity. Know Thyself. Kenneth Burke. OBAL
Here is a room with heavy-footed chairs. The Nature of an Action. Thom Gunn. NePoEA
Here is a ship you made. The Ship. J. F. Hendry. NeBP
Here Is a Song, *with music.* John Peck. AH
Here is a symbol in which. Rock and Hawk. Robinson Jeffers. MoVE; NoAM; NOBA; OxBA
Here Is a Toast That I Want to Drink. Walter Lathrop. PoLF
Here is a world which slowed the hands of time. Okefenokee Swamp. Daniel Whitehead Hicky. AmFN
Here is an apple. Like your little breast. Apple Offering. *Unknown, tr. by* Louis Untermeyer. UnTE
Here is another poem in a picture. Untitled. Daryl Hine. NoAM; TwCP
Here is cruel Frederick, see! Cruel Frederick. Heinrich Hoffmann, *tr. fr. German.* SpRo
Here is cruel Psamtek, see. The Story of Cruel Psamtek. *Unknown.* NA
Here is dominion for peace. Country Reverie. Carol Coates. CaP
Here is fresh matter, poet. Church and State. W. B. Yeats. CMoP
"Here is Honor, the dying knight." The Soul Speaks. Edward H. Pfeiffer. HBMV
Here is how I eat a fish. Eating Fish. George Johnston. WHW
Here is Israel. Pictures at an Exhibition. Nathan Rosenbaum. GoYe
Here is Joe Blow the poet. On Being Asked for a Peace Poem. Howard Nemerov. OxBC
Here is Kit Logan with her love-child come. Kit Logan and Lady Helen. Robert Graves. HBMV
Here is Klito's little shack. Kenneth Rexroth, *after the Greek of* Leonidas. NNaP
Here is my foot, so small it cannot walk. In Jail. Juan Antonio Corretjer, *tr. by* Julio Marzán. InW
Here is no golden-crowned, celestial queen. A Flemish Madonna. Charles Wharton Stork. HBMV
Here is no peace, although the air has fainted. Innocent Landscape. Elinor Wylie. OxBA
Here is no shadow but cloudshadow and nightshadow. Hide in the Heart. Lloyd Frankenberg. LiTA
Here is one leaf already gone from green. The First Leaf. Howard Nemerov. TwAmPo
Here is that far, deep country I've. Magic Lantern. William Stafford. FAZ
Here Is the Abattoir Where. Michael Smith. CIP
Here is the ancient floor. The Self-Unseeing. Thomas Hardy. EBEV; FaBoEn; HAP; MoBrPo; NOBE; OBNC; PrIm; VLP; WeW
Here is the church, and here is the steeple. *Unknown.* OxNR
Here is the crab tree. The Crab Tree. Oliver St. John Gogarty. AnIL; OxBI
Here is the Dog. Since time began. The Dog. Oliver Herford. FaBV
Here is the fern's frond, unfurling a gesture. Fern. Ted Hughes. NYBP
Here is the fix: an hour of time crossed over. Despair in Seascape. Richmond Lattimore. TwAmPo
Here is the foreign cliff and the fabled sea. On a Picture by Michele Da Verona, of Arion as a Boy Riding upon a Dolphin. Anne Ridler. PoA
Here is the long-bided hour: the labor of years is accomplished. Work. Pushkin, *tr. by* Babette Deutsch *and* Avrahm Yarmolinsky. AWP
Here is the place. Looking for Maimonides: Tiberias. Shirley Kaufman. VWA
Here is the place; right over the hill. Telling the Bees. Whittier. AP; AWP; BLPL; HBV-1; NOBA; TAP
Here Is the Place Where Loveliness Keeps House. Madison Cawein. HBV-1
Here is the reply made by Benny. Raisin Bread. Lee Blair. TDH
Here is the same familiar land. Thoughts upon a Walk with Natalie, My Niece, at Houghton Farm. Harold Trowbridge Pulsifer. HBMV
Here is the soundless cypress on the lawn. The Nightingale near the House. Harold Monro. HBMV; MoBrPo
Here is the spinner, the orb weaver. The Orb Weaver. Robert Francis. PPON
Here is the story. Freddy. Dennis Lee. RHPC
Here is the stream again under the rainbow. Tchicaya U Tam'si, *tr. by* E. S. Yntema. *Fr.* Debout. PBA
Here Is the Tale. Anthony C. Deane. InMe; NA
(Jack and Jill—as Kipling Might Have Written It.) CenHV; FaBoPa
Here is the tale of Carrousel. The Ballad of a Barber. Aubrey Beardsley. PAI; SyP
Here is the train to Glasgow. The Train to Glasgow. Wilma Horsburgh. OnUR
Here is the way the white man's heaven felt. On a Picture by Pippin, Called "The Den." Selden Rodman. PoNe
Here is the Will of Cathaeir Mor. The Testament of Cathaeir Mor. *Unknown, tr. by* James Clarence Mangan. *Fr.* Book of Rights. OnYI
Here is the yoke, with arrow and share near by. The Laborer. José-Maria de Heredia, *tr. by* Wilfrid Thorley. AWP
Here is this transport. Scrawled in Pencil in a Sealed Railway Car. Dan Pagis, *tr. by* Anthony Rudolf. VWA
Here is thy footstool and there rest thy feet. Rabindranath Tagore. Gitanjali, X-XI. WGRP
Here Is Wine. Keats. *Fr.* Endymion, II. OBRV
Here it begins, the day we shall not forget. Bidean Nam Bian. A. M. Dobson. PoSH
Here it comes! Frightening. Claudia Lewis. RHPC
Here, it is never enough. February. Larry Moffi. AMV-80
Here it speaks. The Diary of Amanda McFadden. Linda Hogan. TWSS
Here it's harvest. Dust. Love. Jorie Graham. NPGG
Here its like that. Blue Tanganyika. Lebert Bethune. PoBA
Here I've got you, Philip Desmond, standing in the market-place. In the Market-Place. John Francis O'Donnell. *Fr.* Limmerich Towne. NBM
Here Jack and Tom Are Paired with Moll and Meg. George Meredith. Modern Love, XVIII. InvP; PoEL-5
(Sonnet XVIII: "Here Jack and Tom are paired with Moll and Meg.") NBM

Here Johnson lies—a sage by all allow'd. Epitaph. William Cowper. LAuP
Here Keats and Shelley heard. Piazza di Spagna. Willard M. Grimes. GoYe
Here lapped in hallowed slumber Saon lies. Saon of Acanthus. Callimachus, *tr. by* J. A. Symonds. AWP; TRV
Here lay a fair fat land. Culbin Sands. Andrew Young. GTBS-P; OxBS; OxBTC
Here let me rest me feet! Reverie of a Mum. Nancy Keesing. CBAP
Here let my Lord hang up his conquering lance. The Celestial City. Giles Fletcher. *Fr.* Christ's Victory and Triumph, IV. OBS
Here let the brows be bared. At the Tomb of Washington. Clinton Scollard. OHIP
Here lie Ciardi's pearly bones. Elegy Just in Case. John Ciardi. MiAP; MP; TwAmPo; TwCP
Here lie I, Martin Elginbrodde. Epitaph [*or* At Aberdeen *or* Epigram]. *Unknown, at. to* George Macdonald. FaBoCo; FaBoEE; HBV-1; PoPle; WGRP
Here lie I, once a witty fair. An Epitaph. Samuel Wesley. NOEC
Here lie I, Timon. Timon's Epitaph. Shakespeare, *after* Callimachus. *Fr.* Timon of Athens, V, iv. AWP
Here lie my husbands One Two Three. Epitaph: To the Four Husbands of Miss Ivy Saunders. *Unknown.* PV
Here lie my old bones: my vexation now ends. Messenger Mounsey. FaBoEE
Here lie the banes o' Tammy Messer. Tammy Messer. *Unknown.* FaBoEE
Here lie the bones of Elizabeth Charlotte. *See* Here lies the body of Elizabeth Charlotte.
Here lie the relics of a martyred knight. On Sir John Fenwick. Henry Hall. APAS
Here lie the remains of Thomas Wood*hen.* On Thomas Woodcock. *Unknown.* WhC
Here lie two poor lovers, who had the mishap. Three Epitaphs on John Hewet and Sarah Drew, III. Pope. NIP
Here lie Willie Michie's [*or* M——hie's] banes. Epitaph on a Schoolmaster. Burns. FaBoCo; FaBoEE
Here Lies. . . Stevie Smith. PoA
Here lies/ A bully. Tombstone. Lucia M. *and* James L. Hymes, Jr. RHPC
Here lies a bard, Hipponax—honored name! The Grave of Hipponax. Edward Cracroft Lefroy. *Fr.* Echoes from Theocritus. AWP
Here lies a bard, let epitaphs be true. My Epitaph. H. J. Daniel. FaBoEE
Here lies a clerk who half his life had spent. The Volunteer. Herbert Asquith. MMA; OBWP; OxBTC
Here lies a Doctor of Divinity. On a Doctor of Divinity. Richard Porson. FaBoCo; FaBoEE
Here lies a dog: may every dog that dies. Epitaph on the Favourite Dog of a Politician. Hilaire Belloc. OBSV
Here lies a frigid man whom men deplore. A Man Whom Men Deplore. Alfred Kreymborg. HBMV
Here lies a great and mighty King. The King's Epitaph [*or* Epigram]. Earl of Rochester. CavP; SeCePo. *See also* Here lies our Sovereign Lord the King.
Here lies a great sleeper, as everybody knows. Epitaph on a Great Sleeper. Sir Aston Cokayne. FaBoEE
Here Lies a Lady. John Crowe Ransom. AWP; CMoP; CoBMV; EvOK; HAP; HBMV; InvP; LiTM; MoAB; MoAmPo; NoAM; PoRA; TAP; TwAmPo; VGW
Here lies a little bird. On a Little Bird. Martin Armstrong. CH
Here lies a man, and still no man. Epitaph I. *Unknown. Fr.* Duel with Verses over a Great Man. TrJP
Here lies a man much wronged in his hopes. On a Rope Maker Hanged. William Browne. CavP
Here lies a man who was killed by lightning. At Great Torrington, Devon. *Unknown.* FaBoCo; FaBoEE; ShM
Here lies a most beautiful lady. An Epitaph. Walter de la Mare. CoBMV; LiTB; LiTM; LoBV; MoAB; MoBrPo; MoVE; OAEP; OBEV; OBVV; ViBoPo
Here lies a peer. Epitaph on the Duke of Grafton. Sir Fleetwood Shepherd. FaBoEE
Here lies a piece of Christ; a star in dust. An Epitaph for a Godly Man's Tomb. Robert Wild. ChTr; FaBoEE; OxBoCh
Here lies a poet, briefly known as Hecht. Epitaph. Anthony Hecht. POL
Here lies a poet—where's the great surprise! "Z. Z." FaBoEE
Here lies a poet who would not write. Here Lies. . . Stevie Smith. PoA
Here lies a poor woman who always was tired. Epitaph [*or* On a Tired Housewife]. *Unknown.* EvOK; FaBoEE; TreF
Here Lies a Prisoner. Charlotte Mew. MoBrPo
Here lies a shoemaker whose knife and hammer. At His Father's Grave. John Ormond. FaBoTw
Here lies a simple Jew. Epitaph. Sholom Aleichem, *tr. by* Joseph Leftwich. TrJP
Here lies a woman—known to me, and you. R.I.P. "Jan Struther." InMe
Here lies, and none to mourn him but the sea. Edna St. Vincent Millay. Epitaph for the Race of Man, XVIII. MoPo
Here Lies Bill. Oliver Herford. WhC
Here lies Boghead among the dead. On [*or* Epitaph on] James Grieve, Laird of Boghead, Tarbolton. Burns. DBV; TW
Here lies, but seven years old, our little maid. Afraid. Walter de la Mare. WeW
Here lies Cock Robbin dead and cold. *See* Who killed Cock Robin?
Here lies David Garrick, describe me [*or* him] who can. David Garrick. Goldsmith. *Fr.* Retaliation. DBV; NOEC; OBEC; SeCeV
Here lies Dr. Keene, the good Bishop of Chester. Epitaph on Dr. Keene. Thomas Gray. FaBoEE
Here lies Factotum Ned at last. Fragment of a Character. Thomas Moore. FaBoCo
Here lies father and mother and sister and I. In a Staffordshire Churchyard. *Unknown.* PoPle; WhC
Here lies Fred. On Prince Frederick [*or* Epitaph on Prince Frederick]. *Unknown.* DBV; FaBoCo; FaBoEE; NOBL; OxBoLi; TreFS; WhC
Here lies free from blood and slaughter. In Memory of Captain Underwood Who Was Drowned. *Unknown.* FaBoEE
Here lies hee, whom the Tyrants rage. Epitaph on Mr. Robert Port. Charles Cotton. CavP
Here lies Hilaire Belloc, who. Hilaire Belloc. Humbert Wolfe. FaBoEE
Here lies I and my three daughters. Epitaph. *Unknown.* FaBoEE; TreFT; WhC
Here lies I, no wonder I'm dead. *Unknown.* FaBoEE
Here lies in death, who living always lied. On Rÿneveld, an Unpopular Dutch Judge. *Unknown.* FaBoEE
Here lies intombed/ Beneath these bricks. Epitaph on a Willing Girl. *At. to* Thomas Rowlandson. FaBoEE
Here lies John Auricular. *Unknown.* WhC
Here lies John Bun. John Bun. *Unknown.* FaBoCo; PoPle; ShM; WhC
Here lies John Coil. John Coil. *Unknown.* ShM
Here lies John Hill, a man of skill. *Unknown.* WhC
Here lies John Hughes and Sarah Drew. Epitaph. Lady Mary Wortley Montagu. FaBoEE
Here lies John Knott. Epitaph on John Knott. *Unknown.* ChTr; FaBoEE; OAEP; OBS; SeCV-1; ShM
Here lies John Trot, the friend of all mankind. Blake. FaBoEE
Here lies Johnny Cuncapod. *Unknown.* WhC
Here lies Johnny Pidgeon. Epitaph on John Dove. Burns. FaBoCo
Here lies Jonson [*or* lyes Johnson] with the rest. Upon Ben Jonson [*or* Johnson]. Robert Herrick. CaPo; FaBoEE; NoP; OAEP; OBS; SeCV-1
Here lies Judge A——, he's done with legal tort. Epitaph for a Judge. Benedict Jeitteles, *tr. by* Joseph Chotzner. TrJP
Here Lies Juliet. Shakespeare. *Fr.* Romeo and Juliet, V, iii. FaFP; TreFS (Thus with a Kiss I Die.) TrGrPo
Here lies Landor. Walter Savage Landor. FaBoEE
Here lies Lester Moore. At Boot Hill in Tombstone, Arizona. *Unknown.* ShM
Here lies Lord Coningsby—be civil. Lord Coningsby's Epitaph. Pope. FaBoEE
Here lies magnanimous Humility. Upon the Tomb of the Most Reverend Mr. John Cotton. Benjamin Woodbridge. SCAP
Here lies Mary, the wife of John Ford. At Potterne, Wiltshire. *Unknown.* DBV; FaBoCo
Here lies Mistress Keene the Bishop of Chester. Epitaph on Dr. Keene's Wife. Thomas Gray. FaBoEE
Here lies Mr. Chesterton. G. K. Chesterton. Humbert Wolfe. TrJP
Here lies my dear wife, a sad slattern and a shrew. *Unknown.* FaBoEE
Here lies my gude and gracious Auntie. *Unknown.* WhC
Here lies my poor wife, much lamented. *Unknown.* FaBoEE
Here lies my poor wife, without bed or blanket. *Unknown.* FaBoEE
Here Lies My Wife. Dryden. *See* Epitaph Intended for His Wife.
Here lies my wife. Susannah Prout. Walter de la Mare. FaBoEE
Here lies my wife. At Leeds. *Unknown.* FaBoCo; PV; WhC
Here lies my wife. Eternal peace. Epigram. J. V. Cunningham. NePoAm; NIP; OBAL
Here lies my wife: here let her lie! Epitaph Intended for [*or* on] His Wife. Dryden. DBV; HBV-1; InMe; ShM; TreF; TrGrPo; WhC
Here lies Nachshon, a man of great renown. An Epitaph. Isaac Benjacob, *tr. by* Joseph Chotzner. TrJP
Here lies, neatly wrapped in sod. *See* Here lies wrapped up tight in sod.
Here lies New Critic who would fox us. J. V. Cunningham. *Fr.* Three Epigrams. MoAmPo; OBAL
Here lies Nolly Goldsmith, for shortness call'd Noll. On Oliver Goldsmith. David Garrick. FaBoEE
Here lies old Forty-five Per Cent. Old Forty-five Per Cent. *Unknown.* FaBoEE
Here lies old Hobson, Death hath broke his girt. On the University Carrier

[Who Sickn'd in the Time of His Vacancy]. Milton. EBEV; FaBoCh; FaBoEE; MePo; PoPle; PrIm; SaC
Here lies old Jones. *Unknown.* WhC
Here lies one blown out of breath. Merideth. *Unknown.* WhC
Here lies one box within another. *Unknown.* WhC
Here lies one who for medicine would not give. *Unknown.* WhC
Here lies our good Edmund, whose genius was such. Edmund Burke. Goldsmith. *Fr.* Retaliation. DBV; FaBoEE; InvP; NOEC; OBEC; SeCeV
Here lies our Sovereign Lord the King. Epitaph on Charles II [*or* King Charles II]. Earl of Rochester. DBV; FaBoCo; FiBHP; HBV-1; TreFS; TrGrPo; ViBoPo; WhC
Here lies Piron—a man of no position. Alexis Piron, *tr. fr. French.* FaBoEE
Here lies poor Burton. A Brewer. *Unknown.* FaBoCo; WhC
Here lies poor [*or* Sam] Johnson. Reader! have a care. Doctor Johnson. Soame Jenyns. ELU; FaBoEE; OBSV
Here lies poor Ned Pardon, from misery freed. On a Bookseller. Goldsmith. PV
Here lies poor stingy Timmy Wyatt. *Unknown.* WhC
Here lies resting, out of breath. Little Elegy. X. J. Kennedy. CoAP; ConAP; ELU; GoJo; HoPM; NCSH
Here lies returned to clay. *Unknown.* WhC
Here lies Robert Trollope. On a Newcastle Architect. *Unknown.* WhC
Here lies Sam Johnson: Reader have a care. *See* Here lies poor Johnson . . .
Here lies Sir John Plumpudding of the Grange. *Unknown.* FaBoEE
Here Lies Sir Tact. Timothy Steele. TW
(Epitaph: "Here lies Sir Tact, a diplomatic fellow.") InPK
Here lies Sprawlings, a quarterback. Caught in the Pocket. William D. Barney. LiSp
Here lies that poet, buried in the night. On a Poet. Henry Parrot. FaBoEE
Here lies the author of the "Apparition." An Author's Epitaph. Written by Himself. Abel Evans. FaBoEE
Here lies the best and worst of fate. Epitaph on the Duke of Buckingham. James Shirley. CavP; FaBoEE
Here lies the body of Andrew Gear. Andrew Gear of Sunderland. *Unknown.* FaBoCo
Here lies the body of Ann Mann. *Unknown.* WhC
Here lies the body of Anna. In Memory of Anna Hopewell. *Unknown.* ShM
Here lies the body of Cassie O'Lang! Cassie O'Lang. *Unknown.* ShM
Here lies the body of Daniel Saul. *Unknown.* FaBoEE
Here lies the body of Edith Bone. On Myself. Edith Bone. FaBoEE
Here lies [*or* lie] the body [*or* bones] of Elizabeth Charlotte. On an Aberdeen Favourite [*or* Epitaph from Aberdeen]. *Unknown.* DBV; FaBoEE; FaBoPP
Here lies the body of Henry Round. *Unknown.* WhC
Here lies the body of Jonathan Near. *Unknown.* WhC
Here lies the body of Jonathan Stout. *Unknown.* WhC
Here lies the body of Mary Anne Lowder. Mary Anne Lowder. *Unknown.* WhC
Here lies the body of Richard Hind. Epitaph [*or* On Richard Hind]. Francis Jeffrey. FaBoCo; FaBoEE; OxBoLi
Here lies the body of Sarah Sexton. Epitaph of Sarah Sexton. *Unknown.* TreFT; WhC
Here lies the body of Sir John Guise. *Unknown.* FaBoEE
Here lies the body of this world. Epitaph on the World. Henry David Thoreau. FF; HeIP
Here lies the body of W. W. On William Wilson, Tailor. *Unknown.* FaBoEE
Here lies the body of William Jones. Epitaph on William Jones. *Unknown.* FaBoEE
Here lies the bones of Elizabeth Charlotte. *See* Here lies the body of Elizabeth Charlotte.
Here lies the corpse of Doctor Chard. *Unknown.* FaBoEE
Here lies the corpse of William Prynne. On William Prynne. Samuel Butler. FaBoEE
Here lies the Devil—ask no other name. On a Lord. Samuel Taylor Coleridge. FaBoCo; FiBHP; PV
Here lies the flesh that tried. Epitaph. Louise Driscoll. HBMV; WGRP
Here lies the good old knight Sir Harry. Epitaph for Sir Henry Lee. *Unknown.* FaBoEE
Here lies the great. False marble, where? *Unknown.* FaBoEE
Here lies the lighthouse-keeper's horse. Epitaph for a Lighthouse-Keeper's Horse. J. B. Morton. PV
Here lies, the Lord have mercy upon her. Upon One of the Maids of Honour to Queen Elizabeth. John Hoskyns. FaBoEE
Here lies the man Richard. *Unknown.* WhC
Here lies the man that madly slain. John Hoskyns. FaBoEE
Here lies the man who in life. On a Contentious Companion. John Hoskyns. FaBoEE
Here lies the man who stripp'd Sin bare. Ebenezer Elliot. FaBoEE
Here lies the mother of children five [*or* seven]. Epitaph from a Yorkshire Churchyard. *Unknown.* DBV; WhC
Here lies the noble Warrior that never blunted sword. Epitaph on the Earl of Leicester. Sir Walter Ralegh. EnRePo; SiPS
Here lies the poet, deaf and dumb. Lines for a Dead Poet. David Ferry. PP
Here lies the poet Wolker, lover of the world. Epitaph. Jiří Wolker, *tr. by* Karl W. Deutsch. WaaP
Here lies the preacher, judge and poet, Peter. On Peter Robinson [*or* Epitaph on Peter Robinson]. Francis Jeffrey. DBV; FaBoCo; FaBoEE; OxBoli; WhC
Here lies the remains of great Senator Vrooman. Epitaph. Ambrose Bierce. DBV
Here lies the Reverend Jonathan Doe. On the Reverend Jonathan Doe. *Unknown.* ChTr; FaBoEE
Here lies the street of the three balls. To an Avenue Sport. Helen Johnson Collins. PoNe
Here lies the stripper stripped, disrobed for good. Epitaph of a Stripper. William Jay Smith. AMV-80
Here lies Thomas Logge—a Rascally Dogge. Thomas Logge. Walter de la Mare. FaBoEE
Here lies Timocreon: Lord, what a mess. Timocreon. Simonides, *tr. by* H. W. Garrod. DBV
Here lies [*or* lyes], to each her parents' ruth. On My First Daughter. Ben Jonson. AnAnS-2; EBEV; EnRePo; FaBoEE; HoPM; JCP; LoBV; NOBE; NoP; OBS; SeCP; SeCV-1; TEP
Here lies what had not birth, nor shape, nor frame. Epitaph on James Moore Smythe. Pope. FaBoEE
Here lies, whom hound did ne'er pursue. Epitaph on a Hare. William Cowper. FiP; FM; HAP; HBV-1; HBVY; HeIP; NOEC; NoP; PoEL-3; PoPle; SeCeV
Here lies Will Smith—and, what's something rarish. On Will Smith. *Unknown.* FaBoCo
Here lies wise and valiant dust. Epitaph on the Earl of Strafford. John Cleveland. CavP; FaBoEE; JCP; MePo; NOBE; OBS; SeCePo; TrGrPo
Here lies with Death auld Grizzel Grimme. Grizzel Grimme. *Unknown.* FaBoEE
Here lies, within his tomb, so calm. On the Clerk of a Country Parish. William Shenstone. FaBoEE
Here lies wrapped up in forty thousand towels. On Queen Caroline's Deathbed. Pope. TW
Here lies wrapped up tight [*or* neatly wrapped] in sod. Epitaph for a Postal Clerk. X. J. Kennedy. NIP; PCP; ShM
Here lieth Hercules the Second. John Baynham's Epitaph. Thomas Dermody. OnYI
Here lieth John Cruker, a maker of bellows. The Bellows Maker of Oxford. John Hoskyns. FaBoEE
Here Lieth Love. Thomas Watson. *Fr.* Hecatompathia. ElL
(Love's Grave.) OBSC
Here lieth one, who did most truly prove. On the Oxford Carrier. Milton. NA
"Here lieth One whose name was writ on water!" On Keats. Shelley. FaBoEE
Here lieth the worthy warrior/ Who never bloodied sword. On the Earl of Leicester. *Unknown.* FaBoEE
Here lieth Thom Nick's body. Upon a Fool. John Hoskyns. FaBoEE
Here lieth under this marble ston. An Epitaph. *Unknown.* MeEL
Here lith the fresshe flowr of Plantagenet. On the Death of Elizabeth, Queen of Henry VII, and Mother of Henry VIII. *Unknown.* FaBoRV
Here lived the soul enchanted. Poe's Cottage at Fordham. John Henry Boner. AA
Here lives a man, who, by relation. Written over a Gate. John Sheffield. NIP
Here living and the stone. Duomo, Milan. Raymond Henri. View of the Cathedral, II. EyDe
Here Lockyer lyes interred, enough his Name. Advertising Epitaph: On One Lockyer, Inventor of a Patent Medicine. *Unknown.* FaBoUs
Here, Lord, Retired, I Bow in Prayer, *with music.* Matthew Bolles. AH
Here luxury's the common lot. The light. Grasse: The Olive Trees. Richard Wilbur. NoAM; NOBA; NYBP
Here lyes Johnson with the rest. *See* Here lies Jonson with the rest.
Here lyes to each her parents ruth. *See* Here lies to each . . .
Here lyeth he, who was born and cried. On One That Lived Ingloriously. John Hoskyns, *after* Simonides. FaBoEE
Here majestic mountains tower. In the Canadian Rockies. Virginia Shearer Hopper. AMV-80
Here malice, rapine, accident, conspire. Samuel Johnson. *Fr.* London. DBV
Here may the band, that now in triumph shines. The Heavenly Jerusalem. Giles Fletcher. *Fr.* Christ's Victory and Triumph. OxBoCh
Here meet together the prefiguring day. The Passover in the Holy Family. Dante Gabriel Rossetti. GoBC

Here 'mid these leafy walls. Woodland Worship. Ethelwyn Wetherald. CaP
Here might we live in . . . not quite peace, but relative. Fragment of a Pastoral. Barry Schwabsky. AMV-80
Here, mower, take my shiners bright. The Recruiting Sergeant. *Unknown.* OBET
Here must wee rest; and where else should wee rest? A Serious and a Curious Night-Meditation. Thomas Traherne. SeCP
Here, Nancy, let me take your hand. To a Child [With a Copy of the Author's "Hansel and Gretel"]. Norreys Jephson O'Conor. DFT; HBMV
Here Nature holds as in a hollowed hand. The Skylark's Nest. R. H. Long. PoAu-1
Here, newness is all. Or almost all. And like. Day Begins at Governor's Square Mall. Leon Stokesbury. MAYP
Here! No sweetness trips so well as here. Bird Song. John Hay. NePoAm-2
Here not the flags, the rhythmic. Neutrality. Sidney Keyes. MoAB; MoBrPo
Here nothing warns. Dante Gabriel Rossetti. *Fr.* Jenny. NBM
Here now once more I lie. Tenth Renunion. Edward Steese. GoYe
Here, O lily-white lady mine. The Handsel Ring. George Houghton. AA
Here, O my Lord, I see Thee face to face. Horatius Bonar. *Fr.* This Do in Remembrance of Me. TrPWD
Here often, when a child, I lay reclined. Lines. Tennyson. CABA; FaBoPP; PAI
Here on the earth's brink. The Fiddler. Martin Buber, *tr. by* Jawaid Awan. VWA
Here on the edge of hell. Harlem [*or* Puzzled]. Langston Hughes. CAD; PPP; UnPo
Here on the heich hill. Stanes. Duncan Glen. PoSH
Here on the mellow hill. Autumn Scene. Basil Dowling. BoNaP
Here, on this earth soft. As in the Land of Darkness. Robert Miklitsch. AMV-80
Here on this open, ancient book. Diary of a Raccoon. Gertrude Ryder Bennett. GoYe
Here on your bed I have. January. Deborah Godin. AMV-80
Here once the evenings sobbed. The Pear-Tree. Iwan Goll, *tr. by* Babette Deutsch *and* Avram Yarmolinsky. TrJP
Here, or not many feet from hence. Certain True Woords Spoken Concerning One Benet Corbett after Her Death. Richard Corbett. AnAnS-2; SeCP
Here Pause: The Poet Claims at Least This Praise. Wordsworth. EnRP
Here penned within the human fold. The Human Fold. Edwin Muir. LiTM
Here Pilate's Court is. The Stations of the Cross. Padraic Colum. GoBC
Here ploughshares rot and farmers. Garrison Town. Emanuel Litvinoff. WaP
Here poise, like flowers on flowers, the butterflies. At the Grave of Champernowne. John Albee. HBV-2
Here rage the furies that have shaped the world. Land's End. Stanton A. Coblentz. BPAW; EtS
Here redbuds like momentary trees. Locus. Robert Hayden. FYAP
Here rest in peace the bones of Henry Reece. A History of Peace. Robert Graves. HBMV
Here rest the relics of a friend below. Tray's Epitaph. "Peter Pindar." TreFS
Here Reynolds is laid, and to tell you my mind. Sir Joshua Reynolds. Goldsmith. *Fr.* Retaliation. FaBoEE; NOEC; OBEC; SeCePo
Here [*or* How] richly, with ridiculous display. Epitaph on the Politician Himself [*or* On a Politician]. Hilaire Belloc. DBV; FaBoEE; MoBrPo; OBSV; PV; SLM; TreFT; TW; WhC
Here room and kingly silence keep. By the Pacific Ocean. Joaquin Miller. AA
Here shall remain all tears for lovely things. To Song. Thomas S. Jones, Jr. HBV-2
Here She Is. Mary Britton Miller. TiPo
Here she lies, a pretty bud. Upon a Child That Died [*or* Epitaph upon a Child That Died]. Robert Herrick. CaPo; CavP; CH; InPK; NoP; OBEV; PAI; SeCV-1
Here she lies (in bed of spice). Upon a Maid. Robert Herrick. CaPo; ChTr; FaBoCh; FaBoEE; OxBoLi
Here She Stands. Jean-Joseph Rabéarivelo, *tr. fr. French by* Miriam Koshland. PBA
Here she was wont to go, and here, and here! Aeglamour's Lament. Ben Jonson. *Fr.* The Sad Shepherd. CH
Here sit a shepherd and a shepherdess. The Green Shepherd. Louis Simpson. MP; NePoEA; NIP; NoAM; NYBP
Here sits the Lord Mayor. Mother Goose. HBV-1; HBVY; OxNR
Here, six years old, by Destiny's crime. Epitaph for Erotion. Martial, *tr. by* James Michie. FaBoEE
Here Skugg lies snug. Benjamin Franklin. WhC
Here sleeps at length poor Col, and without screaming. Epitaph on Himself. Samuel Taylor Coleridge. FaBoEE
Here sleeps in peace a Hampshire Grenadier. Epitaph to Thomas Thetcher. *Unknown.* PoPle
Here something stubborn comes. Seed Leaves. Richard Wilbur. BoNaP; NCSH
Here sown to dust lies one that drave. A Dead Warrior. Laurence Housman. HBMV
Here sparrows build upon the trees. My Early Home. John Clare. HBV-2; PoLF
Here stand I, ach, Philosophy. Goethe, *tr. by* Louis MacNeice. Faust, Pt. I. NAWM-2
Here stand I, for whores as great. *Unknown.* FaBoEE
Here stands a good old apple tree. Apple Wassail. *Unknown.* OBET
Here stillness sounds like echoes in a tomb. In a Museum. Babette Deutsch. HBMV
Here stood a lofty church—there is a steeple. Pleasant Delusion of a Sumpteous Citty. Sarah Kemble Knight. SCAP
Here stood Hypocrisy, in sober brown. Timothy Dwight. *Fr.* The Triumph of Infidelity. NOCV
Here take my picture; though I bid farewell. His Picture [*or* Elegie: His Picture]. John Donne. Elegies, V. EnRePo; FaBoEn; MeLP; MePo; NoP; OBS
Here tame boys fly down the long light of halls. To a Visiting Poet in a College Dormitory. Carolyn Kizer. PoA
Here the big stars roll down. Spoken through Glass. Eithne Wilkins. NeBP
Here the crow starves, here the patient stag. Rannoch, by Glencoe. T. S. Eliot. Landscapes, IV. BiP; FaBoEn; FaBoPP; PoSH
Here the delicate dance of silence. Woodtown Manor. John Montague. IPY
Here the eye is inevitably cast. Sakhara. R. A. D. Ford. NOBC
Here the foot prints stop. After Twenty Years. Fadwa Tuquan, *tr. fr. Arabic.* PBWP
Here the Frailest Leaves of Me. Walt Whitman. AP
Here the hangman stops his cart. The Carpenter's Son. A. E. Housman. A Shropshire Lad, XLVII. CoBMV; MoAB; MoBrPo; SpRo
Here the hills are earth's bones. Asian Desert. Dorothy Wellesley. OBMV
Here the horse-mushrooms make a fairy ring. The Fairy Ring. Andrew Young. ChTr
Here the human past is dim and feeble and alien to us. Haunted Country. Robinson Jeffers. OxBA
Here the jack-hammer jabs into the ocean. Colloquy in Black Rock. Robert Lowell. AP; CAPP; CoBMV; MiAP; MoAB; MoAmPo; NoAM
Here the Messiah lives. Encounter in Safed. Moshe Yungman, *tr. by* Gabriel Preil *and* Howard Schwartz. VWA
Here the oceans twain have waited. Panama. James Jeffrey Roche. PAH
Here the round begins again. A Traveller. J. R. Rowland. CBAP
Here the rude clamour of the sportsman's joy. James Thomson. *Fr.* The Seasons: Autumn. PBBP
Here the scanted daisy glows. Flanders Fields. Elizabeth Daryush. SUMH
Here the Stem Rises. Daniel Berrigan. TwAmPo
Here the young lover, on his elbow raised. The Corner of the Field. Frances Cornford. ELU
Here, then, we stand, on the Canadian shore. John Hunter-Duvar. *Fr.* De Roberval. CaP
Here they all come to die. The Country of a Thousand Years of Peace. James Merrill. PoCh
Here they are. The soft eyes open. The Heaven of Animals. James Dickey. AP; CAPP; CoAP; HeIP; LiTM; NCSH; NoAM; NOBA; TAP
Here they are. Think of it. Women Open Cautiously. Deborah Lee. BrSi
Here they come. The Trash Men. Charles Bukowski. NoP
Here they lie mottled to the ground unseen. Partidges. John Masefield. LiSp; OxBTC
Here they went with smock and crook. Forefathers. Edmund Blunden. ChMP; NOBE; OBEV; OBMV; OxBTC
Here those of us who really understand. Manhattan. Osbert Lancaster. *Fr.* Afternoons with Baedeker. NOBL
Here through our little world of outward sense. Eternal Moment. "Katherine Hale." CaP
Here, time concurring (and it does). Epitaph. John Ciardi. BiP
Here time unfastens knot and strap. Glen Rosa. William Jeffrey. PoSH
Here to the leisured side of life. The Lamplighter. "Seumas O'Sullivan." BIrV; OxBI
Here, too, like in Jerusalem. The Jews. Mieczyslaw Jastrun, *tr. by* Isaac Komem. VWA
Here tradesmen, 'tis plain, at no roguery stop. London Adulterations. *Unknown.* OBET
Here under leafy bowers. Under Leafy Bowers. Judah al-Harizi. TrJP
Here under the radiant rays of the sun. Facing the Chair. "Hugh MacDiarmid." FaBoMo

Here under this sod and under these trees. Solomon Pease. *Unknown.* WhC
Here war is harmless like a monument. W. H. Auden. Sonnets from China, XII. OBWP
Here was raised. The Plain of Adoration. *Unknown, tr. by* John Montague. BIrV
Here was the autumn orchard where now stand. Autumn Orchard. Catherine Haydon Jacobs. AMV-80
Here was the sound of water falling only. The Owl. Robert Penn Warren. MoAmPo
Here we are, all, by day; by night we're hurled. Dreams. Robert Herrick. CaPo; HAP
Here we are, all dressed up to honor death! At the Funeral of Great-Aunt Mary. Robert Bly. Str
"Here we are at the river" I said to no one. The Gift. Dick Lourie. NeAC
Here we are, if you have any more. Thomas Middleton. *Fr.* The Changeling, V, iii. PoEL-2
Here we are, picking the first fern-shoots. Song of the Bowmen of Shu. Ezra Pound, *after the Chinese.* OBVE
Here we bring new water. A New Year Carol [*or* New Year's Water *or* The New Year]. *Unknown.* CH; GBP; OBCP; OFD; OxBoLi; POL; PoSC
Here we broached the Christmas barrel. The House of Hospitalities. Thomas Hardy. NoAM
Here we can observe the superior mirages. Traveller's Guide to Antarctica. Adrien Stoutenburg. NYBP
Here we come a-caroling. *Unknown.* FaPON
Here we come again, again, and here we come again! The Children's Carol. Eleanor Farjeon. PChr; RHPC
Here We Come a-Piping. *Unknown.* CH; PoPle; SiSoSe; TiPo
Here We Come a-Wassailing. *Unknown.* *See* Wassail Song.
Here we come gathering nuts an' may. Nuts an' May. *Unknown.* EvOK
Here we dance Looby Loo. *See* Here We Go Looby Loo.
Here we go around this ring. Marriage. *Unknown.* AmFP
Here we go dancing jingo-ring. *Unknown.* OxNR
Here we go in a flung festoon. Road-Song of the Bandar-Log. Kipling. *Fr.* The Jungle Book. OAEP
Here We Go Looby Loo. *Unknown.* FSW
(Looby Loo ["Here we dance Looby Loo"].) SoPo
Here we go round ring by ring. *Unknown.* OxNR
Here we go the jingo-ring. The Merry-ma-Tanzie. *Unknown.* GBP
Here we halt our march, and pitch our tent. The Green Mountain Boys. Bryant. PoPl
Here we have thirst. An Egyptian Pulled Glass Bottle in the Shape of a Fish. Marianne Moore. PBWP
Here We March All Around in a Ring. *Unknown.* AmFP
"Here we stan' on the Constitution, by thunder!" The Debate in the Sennit. James Russell Lowell. *Fr.* The Biglow Papers. HBV-1; PAH
Here we will rest us, under these. The Flight into Egypt. Longfellow. *Fr.* Christus; a Mystery. OBVV
Here were planes. But everything else was gone. Wendling. Coman Leavenworth. Norfolk Memorials, III. LiTA
Here, west of winter, lies the ample flower. Prayer for This Day. Hildegarde Flanner. TrPWD
Here, when precipitate Spring with one light bound. *See* Here, where precipitate Spring . . .
Here Where Coltrane Is. Michael S. Harper. CNA; PoBA
Here, where fecundity of Babel frames. Babylon and Sion (Goa and Lisbon). Luis de Camoes, *tr. by* Richard Garnett. AWP
Here where I watch the dew. Hymn to Dispel Hatred at Midnight. Yvor Winters. TW
Here, where my father lies under the ornamental plum. Churchyard of St. Mary Magdalene, Old Milton. John Heath-Stubbs. NePoEA
Here where no increase is. Supplication. Josephine Johnson. TrPWD
Here where our Lord once laid his head. Upon the Holy Sepulchre. Richard Crashaw. FaBoEE
Here, where [*or* when] precipitate Spring with one light bound. A Fiesolan Idyl [*or* Fæsulan Idyl]. Walter Savage Landor. EnRP; OAEP; OBRV; SeCePo
Here, where relumed by changing seasons, burn. Roy Campbell. *Fr.* The Golden Shower. OxBTC
Here, where summer slips. The Red and the Green. Anne Wilkinson. MoCV
Here, where the baby paddles in the gutter. Lean Street. G. S. Fraser. NeBP; OxBS
Here, where the breath of the scented-gorse floats through the sun-stained air. Breton Afternoon. Ernest Dowson. OBNC
Here where the fields lie lonely and untended. A Deserted Home. Sidney Royse Lysaght. CH
Here, where the night is clear as sea-water. Lament for a Sailor. Paul Dehn. WaP
Here, where the pale grass struggles with each wind. A Decayed Monastery. Thomas Dermody. OnYI
Here where the parrots come down. Thomas and Charlie. Peter Wild. AmPA
Here, where the red man swept the leaves away. Frederick Goddard Tuckerman. *Fr.* Sonnets. NOBA; TAP
Here where the river is naming itself. The Sixth Day. Betty Adcock. LiSp
Here where the river is slender and small. The Dipper. Phoebe Hesketh. PoSH
Here, where the taut wave hangs. Life's Circumnavigators. W. R. Rodgers. AnIV; GTBS-P; OxBI
Here where the wind is always north-north-east. New England. E. A. Robinson. CABA; FaBoEn; GOA; HeIP; MoAB; MoAmPo; MoVE; NOBA; NoP; OxBA; TAP; WhC
Here where the wind skins Drumochter. Drumochter. Anne B. Murray. PoSH
Here, where the world is quiet. The Garden of Proserpine. Swinburne. AWP; BLPA; BLPL; FaBoRV; FaBV; FaPoR; HAP; HBV-2; LiTB; NOBE; NoP; OAEP; OBNC; PoEL-5; PoPl; PoPle; PoRA; SCV; SeCePo; SeCeV; TreFT; TrGrPo; ViBoPo; VLP; WHA
Here where tides come and go. Tides. Will H. Blackwell. AMV-80
Here, where Vespasian's legions struck the sands. Embarcation. Thomas Hardy. BrPo; OBWP
Here where we are, wrapped in the afternoon. Obligations. Jane Cooper. NePoEA-2
Here where you left me alone. Letter from Slough Pond. Isabella Gardner. ELU
Here X. lies dead, but God's forgiving. J. E. Thorold Rogers. FaBoEE
Here you are. The Well-intentioned Question. Wendy Rose. STE; TWSS
Here! You sons of the men. English Thornton. Edgar Lee Masters. *Fr.* Spoon River Anthology. OxBA
Hereabouts the signs are good. Midsummer. Thomas Kinsella. IPY
Hereafter. Harriet Prescott Spofford. HBV-1
Heredity. Thomas Bailey Aldrich. AA
Heredity. Arthur Guiterman. OBAL
Heredity. Thomas Hardy. CTC; EBEV; ImOP
Heredity. Lydia Avery Coonley Ward. HBV-2
Herefor and therefor and therefor I cam. This Pretty Woman. *Unknown.* OxBM
Here's A, B, and C. A Learned Song. *Unknown.* *Fr.* Mother Goose's Melody. FaBoUs
Here's a body—there's a bed! Good Night. Thomas Hood. SiSoSe; SoPo
Here's a clean year. A New Year. Mary Carolyn Davies. YeAr
"Here's a fine bag of meat." Bags of Meat. Thomas Hardy. BoAnP; FM
Here's a hand to the boy who has courage. Our Heroes. Phoebe Cary. BLPA
Here's a health to the blacksmith, the best of all fellows. The Blacksmith's Song. *Unknown.* GBP
Here's a health to the Tackers, my boys. A Health to the Tackers. *Unknown.* APAS
Here's a Health to Them That's Awa'. Burns. HBV-2
Here's a health unto His Majesty. A Health unto His Majesty. Jeremy Savile. ChTr
Here's a hotel where even the stairs. Hot Springs. Earle Birney. OxBC
Here's a land where all are equal. Creede. Cy Warman. BPAW; PoOW
Here's a large one for the lady. The Broom Squire's Song. *Unknown.* OxNR
Here's a little mouse) and. Four III. E. E. Cummings. FaBoMo
Here's a mellow cup of tea, golden tea! The Poets at Tea, VII. Barry Pain. Par
Here's a poor widow from Babylon. *Unknown.* OxNR
Here's a song. Scel Lem Duib. *Unknown, tr. by* Flann O'Brien. BIrV; OxBI
Here's a song of praise for a beautiful world. The Beautiful World. W. L. Childress. OHIP
Here's Abbey Way: here are the rooms. The Chrysanthemum Show. C. Day Lewis. MoVE
Here's an adventure! What awaits. On Opening a New Book. Abbie Farwell Brown. YeAr
Here's an example from/ A butterfly. The Example. W. H. Davies. HBMV; MoBrPo; TrGrPo; WHA
Here's an old lady, almost ninety-one. Two Old Ladies. Siegfried Sassoon. OxBTC
Here's another day, dear. Glad Day. W. Graham Robertson. HBV-1
Here's Cooper, who's written six volumes to show. Cooper. James Russell Lowell. *Fr.* A Fable for Critics. AP; NOBA; OxBA; TAP
Here's Finiky Hawkes. "Black Your Honour's Shoes?" *Unknown.* OxNR
Here's flowers for you. Flowers of Middle Summer [*or* The Flowers of Perdita]. Shakespeare. *Fr.* The Winter's Tale, IV, iii. FiP; GBL; YeAr
Here's fourteen pills for thirteen pence. From One of Case's Pill-Boxes. John Case. FaBoUs
Here's good wind, here's sweet wind. Song of the Full Catch. Constance Lindsay Skinner. CaP

Here's one in whom Nature feared—faint at such vying. Cardinal Bembo's Epitaph on Raphael. Thomas Hardy, *after* Pietro Bembo. EyDe; FaBoEE
Here's pretty conduct, Hugh O'Rourke. To Tomas [*or* Tomaus] Costello at the Wars. Tomas O'Higgins, *tr. by* Frank O'Connor. AnIV; KiLC
Here's shade and comfort by this towering tree. Christmas 1942. Eric Irvin. PoAu-2
Here's string o' wild geese. *Unknown.* PBBP
Here's Sulky Sue. Mother Goose. OxNR
Here's sweet little Sarah Samantha. Sarah Samantha. *Unknown.* TDH
Here's the bus now. All aboard please. Three Fitts. Stewart Parker. CIP
Here's the garden she walked across. The Flower's Name. Robert Browning. Garden Fancies, I. CTC; HBV-1; VLP
Here's the mail, sort it quick. A Sure Sign. Nancy Byrd Turner. SoPo; TiPo
Here's the mould of a musical bird long passed from light. In a Museum. Thomas Hardy. UnS
Here's the spot. Look around you. Above on the height. Caldwell of Springfield. Bret Harte. PAH
Here's the Tender Coming. *Unknown.* GBP
(Press-Gang, The.) ChTr
Here's to good old Boston. *See* And this is good old Boston.
Here's to "La Canadienne"! Vive la Canadienne. *Tr. fr. French.* FSW
Here's to New Haven and Boston. To New Haven and Boston. Walter Foster Angell. TreFS
Here's to nick and nora charles. A Toast. Charles Stetler. GP
Here's to the blood, in his mettle and pride. The Cock of the Game. *Unknown.* OBET
Here's to the Maiden. Sheridan. *See* Let the Toast Pass.
Here's to the man who invented stairs. Stairs. Oliver Herford. FiBHP; InMe; WhC
Here's to the man with the leather lung. My Candidate. Norman H. Crowell. YaD
Here's to the men who lose! To the Men Who Lose. George L. Scarborough. BLPA
Here's to the Ranger! *Unknown.* CoSo
Here's to the Red of it. A Toast To the Flag. John Jay Daly. PAL; PoLF
Here's to the town of New Haven. On the Democracy of Yale [*or* To New Haven]. Frederick Scheetz Jones. HBV-1; TreFS; WhC; YaD
Here's to the year that's awa'! The Year That's Awa'. John Dunlop. HBV-2
Here's to thee, old apple tree. *Unknown.* OxNR
Here's to ye absent lords, may they. A Toast. *Unknown.* WhC
Here's to you and here's to me. A Toast. *Unknown.* PV
Here's to your eyes. Toast. Frank Horne. BANP; PoNe
Here's tropic flora. Hotel Lobby. Mildred Weston. WhC
Here's two or three jolly boys. *Unknown.* OxNR
Here's what I think. The Clock. Felice Holman. GrPl
Here's witts extraction morall and divine. One Presenting a Rare Book to Madame Hull. John Saffin. SCAP
Heresy for a Class-Room. Rolfe Humphries. GLGT
Heretic, The. Bliss Carman. WGRP
Heretics All. Hilaire Belloc. ACP
Heretic's Tragedy, The. Robert Browning. OAEL-2
Hereto I come to view a voiceless ghost. After a Journey. Thomas Hardy. ChMP; CMoP; DTC; EBEV; ELP; EnLoPo; FaBoEn; FaBoPP; GBL; GTBS-P; MoVE; OBNC; OxBTC; PoEL-5
Heretse! Baboon. *Unknown.* PeSA
Heriot's Ford. Kipling. PoRA
Heritage. Gwendolyn B. Bennett. AmNP; BANP; BlSi; PoBA
Heritage. Countee Cullen. AmNP; BALP; BANP; BPo; MoAmPo; NoAM; NoP; PoBA; TTY
What Is Africa to Me? *sel.* FaBV
Heritage. Mary Gilmore. CBAP
Heritage. Linda Hogan. TWSS
Heritage, The. James Russell Lowell. HBV-1; HBVY
Heritage, The. Edward Bliss Reed. EtS
Heritage. Augustus Young. CIP
Heritage of hopes and fears, An. The Soul. Madison Cawein. AA
Herkens to my tale that I shall here shewe. Marvels. *Unknown.* OxBM
Herm whose length measured degrees of heat, The. William Empson. *Fr.* Bacchus. PoA
Herman Altman. Edgar Lee Masters. *Fr.* Spoon River Anthology. OxBA
Herman Melville. Conrad Aiken. NoAM; NOBA; TAP
Herman Melville. W. H. Auden. LiTA; NePA; OAEP; OxBA
Herman Moon's Hourbook, *sels.* Christopher Middleton. NePoEA-2
Abasis.
Ant Sun, The.
Forenoon, The.
Ode on Contemplating Clapham Junction.
Pointed Boots.
Waterloo Bridge.
Hermann Ludwig Ferdinand Von Helmholtz ("Hermann Helmholtz said the/ problem"). Peter Meinke. SUW
Hermaphrodite fairy of Kew, A. Limerick. *Unknown.* PeHV
Hermaphrodite's Song, The. Lorna Mitchell. BrRo
Hermaphroditus. Swinburne. SyP; TEP; VLP
Hermaphroditus, a delight, a. Ovid, Meet a Metamorphodite. Jonathan Williams. PoM
Hermes came to me in a dream. I said. Sappho, *tr. fr. Greek by* Willis Barnstone. BoWoP
Hermes, god/ of crossed sticks. Prayer to Hermes. Robert Creeley. PoM
Hermes of the Ways. Hilda Doolittle ("H. D."). LiTA; WPE
Hermetic Bird. Philip Lamantia. VGW
Hermione. "Barry Cornwall." OBVV
Hermit. David Baker. AMV-80
Hermit, The. W. H. Davies. BrPo; MoBrPo
Hermit, The. Daniel Halpern. AMV-80
Hermit, The. Hsü Pên, *tr. fr. Chinese by* Henry H. Hart. RFM
Hermit, The. Howard Moss. NePoAm
Hermit, The. Thomas Parnell. GoTL
Hermit, The. *At. to* Sir Walter Ralegh. *See* Like to a Hermit Poor.
Hermit Cackleberry Brown, on Human Vanity, The. Jonathan Williams. OBAL; PoM
Hermit Has a Visitor, The. Maxine W. Kumin. BoWoP
Hermit Hoar. Samuel Johnson. PV; ViBoPo
(Idyll: "Hermit hoar, in solemn cell.") NOBL
(Imitation of the Style of ****.) FaBoCo
Hermit Picks Berries, The. Maxine W. Kumin. RFM
Hermit Wakes to Bird Sounds, The. Maxine W. Kumin. GrPl; Psk
Hermitage, The. *Unknown, at to* St. Manchan of Lemanaghan in Offaly, *tr. fr. Irish by* Frank O'Connor. KiLC
Hermit's Song, A. *Unknown.* *See* Wish of Manchin of Liath, The.
Hermotimus. William Edmondstoune Aytoun. OBVV
Hern flew east, the hern flew west, The. *See* Heron flew east, the heron flew west, The.
Herndon. S. Weir Mitchell. PAH
Hero, A. Florence Earle Coates. OHIP
Hero, The. Robert Graves. PCP
Hero, The. Leroy F. Jackson. SiSoSe
Hero, The. Marianne Moore. *Fr.* Part of a Novel, Part of a Poem, Part of a Play. CMoP; NOBA; OxBA; PoA; TwAmPo
Hero, The. Robert Nicoll. HBV-2
Hero, The. Siegfried Sassoon. OBWP
Hero, The. Roger Woddis. FaBoPa
Hero and Leander, *sels.* Thomas Hood. EnRP
Death of Leander, The.
Scylla's Lament.
Hero and Leander. Christopher Marlowe. (First *and* Second Sestiads), *completed by* George Chapman. AAS (First *and* Second Sestiads); CABA (First *and* Second Sestiads); NoP (First and Second Sestiads); OBSC (First *and* Second Sestiads)
Sels.
"Amorous Leander, beautiful and young," *fr.* First Sestiad. Marlow. PeHV
Amorous Neptune, *fr.* Second Sestiad. Marlowe. NOBE
"And now the sun that through the horizon peeps," *fr.* Second Sestiad. Marlowe. OAEL-1
Bridal Song, *fr.* Fifth Sestiad. Chapman. NOBE; OBEV
(Song: "O Come, soft rest of cares, come Night.") ViBoPo
"By this, Leander, being near the land," *fr.* Second Sestiad. Marlowe. EBEV; ErPo
Epithalamion Teratos, *fr.* Fifth Sestiad. Chapman. ElL; LoBV
(Wedding of Alcmane and Mya, The.) OBSC
"Her veil was artificial flowers and leaves," *fr.* First Sestiad. Marlowe. HoPM
Hero Feels the Shaft of Love, *fr.* First Sestiad. Marlowe. GBL
Hero the Fair[e], *fr.* First Sestiad. Marlowe. FaBoEn; WHA
It Lies Not in Our Power to Love or Hate, *fr.* First Sestiad. Marlowe. TrGrPo; WHA
(Love at First Sight.) FaBoEn; TreFT
(Who Ever Loved, That Loved Not at First Sight?) BLPL; FaFP; LiTB
"Leander to the envious light," *fr.* Third Sestiad, *argument.* Chapman. OAEL-1
"New light gives new directions, fortunes new," *fr.* Third Sestiad. Chapman. OAEL-1
"Now from Leander's place she rose, and found," *fr.* Fourth Sestiad. Chapman. EBEV
"On Hellespont, guilty of true love's blood," *fr.* First Sestiad. Marlowe. LoBV; OAEL-1; OAEP; PoEL-2; SeCePo; TEP
"On this feast day, O cursèd day and hour," *fr.* First Sestiad. Marlowe. ViBoPo
(Love at First Sight.) NOBE
Repentance, *fr.* Third Sestiad. Chapman. OBSC

"She stay'd not for her robes, but straight arose," *fr.* Second Sestiad. Marlowe. UnTE
Hero and Leander. Joseph S. Newman. FiBHP
Hero Entombed I. Peter Quennell. LiTB
Hero Feels the Shaft of Love. Christopher Marlowe. *Fr.* Hero and Leander. GBL
Hero first thought it, The. Truth. "Æ." AnIL; MoBrPo
Hero in the Land of Dough, A. Robert Clairmont. WhC
Hero of Bridgewater, The. Charles L. S. Jones. PAH
Hero of the Commune, The. Margaret Junkin Preston. AA
Hero Song. Robert Duncan. CrMA
Hero the Fair[e]. Christopher Marlowe. *Fr.* Hero and Leander. FaBoEn; WHA
Herod sitting on his throne. The Children's Ghosts. Winifred M. Letts. HBMV
Hérodiade. Stéphane Mallarmé, *tr. fr. French by* Arthur Symons.
"To mine own self I am a wilderness." SyP
Heroes. Robert Creeley. NOBA; NoP; PPP
Heroes. Edna Dean Proctor. HBV-2
Heroes, The. Louis Simpson. NePoAm; OBWP
Heroes. Walt Whitman. *Fr.* Song of Myself, XXXIII *and* XXXV. AA
("I understand the large hearts of heroes," *fr.* XXXIII.) InPS
Heroes, and Kings! your distance keep. Epitaph for One Who Would Not Be Buried in Westminster Abbey. Pope. FaBoEE
Heroes of the Strip. Sheila Cudahy. TAT
Heroes paused upon the plain, The. The Byrnies. Thom Gunn. NePoEA-2; NoAM; OxBTC
Heroes screamed from my fingertips. Bard. Gavin Bantock. FaBoTw
Heroic Age, The. Richard Watson Gilder. AA; OHIP
Heroic Good, target for which the young. Faint yet Pursuing. Coventry Patmore. The Unknown Eros, XXV. OxBoCh
Heroic Heart. Charles Donnelly. CIP
Heroic soul, in homely garb half hid. Lincoln. John Townsend Trowbridge. PGD
Heroic Vengeance. Milton. *Fr.* Samson Agonistes. OBS
Heroides, *sel.* Ovid, *tr. fr Latin by* George Turberville.
"To Paris that was once her owne though now it be not so." OBVE
Heroique Stanzas, Consecrated to the Glorious Memory of His Most Serene and Renowned Highnesse, Oliver, Late Lord Protector of This Common-Wealth. Dryden. SeCV-2
Heroism. Emerson. ViBoPo
Heron. Philip Booth. NePoEA; PPJ; Psk; WOLT
Heron, The. John Lyle Donaghy. NeIP
Heron, The. Edward Hovell-Thurlow. HBV-1
Heron, The. Philip Murray. BoAnP
Heron. Stanley Plumly. AmPA
Heron, The. Theodore Roethke. BoAnP; MiAP; PDV; RFM
Heron, The. *Unknown.* EnSB
(Corpus Christi Carol, The) GBP
(Knight in the Bower, The) ChTr
Heron. Ted Walker. NYBP
Heron, The. Vernon Watkins. ChMP; GTBS-P; MP; TwCP; UnPo
Heron [*or* Hern] flew east, the heron [*or* hern] flew west, The. The Heron [*or* The Knight in the Bower *or* The Corpus Christi Carol]. *Unknown.* ChTr; EnSB; GBP
Heron in Swamp. Frances Minturn Howard. GoYe
Heron is harsh with despair. Song. Brenda Chamberlain. NeBP; NeIP
Heron makes a cross, The. Turtle Mountain Reservation. Louise Erdrich. TWSS
Heron stands in water where the swamp, The. The Heron. Theodore Roethke. BoAnP; MiAP; PDV; RFM
Heron Weather. Douglas Crase. NoP
Herons. Robin Blaser. NeAP
Herons, The. Francis Ledwidge. ACP; OnYI; OxBI
(Ardan Mór.) AnIV; AWP
Herons. *Unknown, tr. fr. Japanese.* SUS
Heron's Bay. Martin Galvin. AMV-81
Hero's daughter, Leinster's loveliest! All Gold. *Unknown, tr. by* Frank O'Connor. KiLC
Herrick's Julia. Helen Bevington. BXAP; SpRo
Herring. Kenneth Rexroth. *Fr.* A Bestiary. HoPM
Herring and ling! The Red Herring. *Unknown.* FaBoNo
Herring is prolific, The. Herring. Kenneth Rexroth. *Fr.* A Bestiary. HoPM
Herring Loves the Merry Moonlight, The. Sir Walter Scott. *See* Harlaw.
Herring-run was over, The. The long days. The Hayfield. Charles Bruce. *Fr.* The Flowing Summer. CaP
Herring Weir, The. Sir Charles G. D. Roberts. *Fr.* Songs of the Common Day. NOBC; PeCV
Herrings. Swift. *Fr.* Verses for Fruitwomen. AnIV; OnYI
Herself. John Holmes. HoPM; MiAP
Herself a Rose Who Bore the Rose. Christina Rossetti. ISi
Herself listening to herself, having no name. Herself. John Holmes. MiAP
Hershey Kiss. Patti Renner-Tana. SOTS
Hertha. Swinburne. OAEL-2; OAEP; VLP
Hertza. Benjamin Fondane, *tr. fr. French by* Matei Calinescu *and* Willis Barnstone. VWA
Hervé Riel. Robert Browning. BeLS; FaBoBe; GN; HBV-2; HBVY; MOS; OnMSP
Hervordshir, shild and spere. The Shires. *Unknown.* OxBM
He's a Fool. *Unknown.* FSW
He's a fool that marries at Yule. A Scottish Proverb. *Unknown.* FaBoUs
He's a little dog, with a stubby tail, and a moth-eaten coat of tan. Bum. W. Dayton Wedgefarth. BLPA
He's a little man with a corporation who can say. The Beak. Elizabeth Smither. OCNZ
He's an old grey horse, with his head bowed sadly. The Old Whim Horse. Edward Dyson. CBAP
He's asleep, or dead, numb with wind. The Rattlesnake. Robert Wrigley. AMV-80
He's bought a bed and a table too. Mary Ann. Joseph Tabrar. PV
He's Coming. Mark Van Doren. FaBV
He's dead/ the dog won't have to. Death. William Carlos Williams. OxBA; VGW
He's dead. Into the vault and out. Lying in State. Adrian Mitchell. ELU
He's Doing Natural Life. Conyus. PoBA
He's gone, and all our plans. To His Love. Ivor Gurney. MMA; OBWP
He's gone, and Fate admits of no return. Epitaph on the Secretary to the Muses. Jane Barker. FaBoCo
He's Gone Away. *Unknown.* AS, *with music;* FSW; TrAS; *with music*
He's gone, I am now sad and lonely. My Johnny. *Unknown.* OBET
He's gone to school, wee Hughie. Wee Hughie. Elizabeth Shane. HBMV
He's Got the Whole World in His Hands. *Unknown.* BLSo, *with music;* FSW
He's half Creek, half plains. It's the Same at Four A.M. Joy Harjo. TWSS
He's helping me now—this moment. This Moment. Annie Johnson Flint. BLRP
He's Jus' de Same Today. *Unknown. See* Just the Same Today.
He's lost him completely. And he now tries to find. In Despair. C. P. Cavafy, *tr. by* Edmund Keeley *and* Philip Sherrard. PeHV
He's my doll! A Kiss. *Unknown, tr. by* Frank O'Connor. KiLC
He's neither Chinese. A Buddhist Priest. Ho Xuan Huong, *tr. by* Nguyen Ngoc Bich. PBWP
He's nothing much but fur. A Kitten. Eleanor Farjeon. TiPo
He's on my front porch rapping. The Businessman of Alicante. Philip Levine. NaP
He's out stuck in a bird's craw. Gary Snyder. Myths and Texts: Burning, IV. NaP
He's shy Buck McLeish says. Buying the Dog. Michael Ondaatje. Str
He's slight and old and sits up timidly. Old Man of Tennessee. John Hay. NePoAm-2
He's so vulnerable. That complexion. Fish Story. P. L. Jacobs. LFAC
He's struttin' sho ernuff. De Drum Majah. Ray Garfield Dandridge. BANP
He's such a wanderer in his thoughts. The Wanderer. Amanda Benjamin Hall. HBMV
He's the man—we all recognize. Man Asleep in the Desert. Thomas Lux. LCAP
He's up early for breakfast. David in April. Betty Booker. PPJ
Hesiod, 1908. Alexander Mair. GoTS
Hesitant door chain, The. Into Blackness Softly. Mari Evans. PoBA
Hesitating Ode. Miklos Radnoti, *tr. fr. Hungarian by* Steven Polgar, Stephen Berg, *and* S. J. Marks. LLLT
Hesitation Blues. *Unknown.* FSW
Hesperia. Swinburne. OBNC; OBVV
Hesperides, The. Tennyson. OAEL-2; SyP
Hesperos, you bring home all the bright dawn disperses. Sappho, *tr. fr. Greek by* Willis Barnstone. BoWoP
Hesperus. John Clare. EBVV; FaBoRV; GTBS-P; OAEL-2
(Evening Star, The.) ChTr
Hesperus' Hymn to Cynthia [*or* Hesperus' Song]. Ben Jonson. *See* Hymn to Diana.
Hesperus the Bringer. Byron. *See* Evening.
Hesperus! the day is gone. Hesperus [*or* The Evening Star]. John Clare. ChTr; EBVV; FaBoRV; GTBS-P; OAEL-2
Hester. Charles Lamb. EnRP; GTBS; GTBS-P; HBV-2; LoBV; OBEV; OBRV
Hester MacDonagh. Jeannette Slocomb Edwards. GoYe
Hetero-sex is best for the man of a serious turn of mind. Epigram. Marcus Argentarius, *tr. by* Fleur Adcock. PeHV
Heterodoxy, A. Lord Dunsany. OnYI
Heth. Carlos Montemayer, *tr. fr. Spanish by* Nigel Grant Sylvester. AMV-81

"Heureux Qui comme Ulysse." John Manifold. WaaP; WaP
Heureux Qui, comme Ulysse, A Fait un Beau Voyage. Joachim du Bellay, *tr. by* G. K. Chesterton. *Fr.* Regrets. AWP
Hev ye seen owt o' maw bonnie lad. Maw Bonnie Lad. *Unknown.* GBP
Hewel, or Woodpecker, The. Andrew Marvell. *Fr.* Upon Appleton House. ChTr
Hex on the Mexican X, A. David McCord. FiBHP
Hexameter and Pentameter. *Unknown.* ChTr; FaBoNo
Hexametra Alexis in Laudem Rosamundi. Robert Greene. *Fr.* Greene's Mourning Garment. EIL; GBL; PoEL-2
Hey Betty Martin. *Unknown.* AS, *with music;* FSW
Hey, boys, joint ahead. Track-lining Song. *Unknown.* AmFP
Hey, Bug! Lilian Moore. RHPC
"Hey C-9758." Inside a Prison Cell at Count Time. Daniel L. Klauck. LFAC
Hey, Coolidge boy. Brooklyn Bridge. Vladimir Mayakovsky, *tr. by* Vladimir Markov *and* Merrill Sparks. NYP
Hey daddy/ hey daddy/ don't let me cry in vain. Oh Ambulance Man. *Unknown.* BluL
Hey Derry Derry. Thomas Dekker. *See* Cold's the Wind.
Hey diddle diddle/ And hey diddle dan! *Unknown.* OxNR
Hey [*or* High *or* Sing hey], diddle, diddle,/ The cat and the fiddle. Mother Goose. FaBoBe; FaFP; HBV-1; HBVY; HoPM; OxBoL; OxNR; SoPo; TiPo
Hey diddle diddle/ The physicists fiddle. Paul Dehn. *Fr.* Rhymes for a Modern Nursery. FiBHP
Hey diddle diddle, the cat and the fiddle,/ bombers come with the moon. Maturity. J. Elgar Owen. WaP
Hey diddle dinkety, poppety, pet. Mother Goose. GBP; OxNR
Hey diddle dout,/ My candle's out. *Unknown.* OxNR
Hey ding a ding. *Unknown.* OxNR
Hey, dorolot, dorolot! *Unknown.* OxNR
"Hey, down a down!" did Dian sing. A Nymph's Disdain of Love. *Unknown.* EIL
Hey Fella Would You Mind Holding This Piano a Moment. William J. Harris. GP
Hey girl, how long you been here? Motown/Smokey Robinson. Jessica Hagedorn. BrSi
Hey! hey! by this day! The Unhappy Schoolboy. *Unknown.* OxBChV
Hey, hey, hey, hey/ I will have the whetstone. I Will Have the Whetstone. *Unknown.* FaBoNo; GBP
Hey, hey Jane, Jane. Jane, Jane. *Unknown.* FSW
Hey-ho Knave; a Catch. *Unknown.* GBP
Hey, Ho, Nobody Home. *Unknown.* FSW
Hey, how!/ Sely men, God helpe you! An Old Man and His Wife. *Unknown.* OxBM
Hey-How for Hallowe'en. *Unknown.* FaBoCh
(Witches, The.) ChTr
Hey, Joe! Cigarette! Cioccolat'! Cigarette for the Bambino. Gavin Ewart. WaP
Hey, Johnnie Cope, are ye wauking yet? Johnnie Cope. Adam Skirving. OxBS
Hey, Krup! Mellow Groove Grave Elegy. Michael C. Ford. SOTS
Hey, laddie, hark, to the merry, merry lark. The Sky-Lark's Song. John Bennett. *Fr.* Master Sky-Lark. AA
Hey, little yellow boy. From a Bus. Malaika Ayo Wangara. NBP
Hey, mama/ Tell me what have I. Awful Fix. *Unknown.* BluL
Hey, Mister Tambourine Man, play a song for me. Mister Tambourine Man. Bob Dylan. NIP
Hey moonface. Only a Little Litter. Myra Cohn Livingston. QQQ
Hey, my kitten, my kitten. Mother Goose. OxNR
Hey, my lad, ho, my lad! Welcome to the New Year. Eleanor Farjeon. YeAr
Hey! My Pony! Eleonor Farjeon. FaPON
Hey, Neruda! Hey, Ritsos! Two Communist Poets. Irving Layton. AMV-81
Hey, Nonny! Charles Kingsley. *See* Dolcino to Margaret.
Hey Nonny No! *Unknown.* CH; ChTr; EBEV; EIL; LoBU; OBEV; TrGrPo; ViBoPo
(Round, A.) FaBoCh
Hey! now, now, now. Welcome! Our Messiah. *Unknown.* MeEL
Hey! now [*or* Hay! nou] the day dawis [*or* dauis]. The Night Is Near Gone [*or* The Nicht Is Neir Gane]. Alexander Montgomerie. BSV; CH; GoTS; OBEV; OxBS
Hey Robin. Joseph Skipsey. EBVV
Hey, sidewalk pacers. Just for One Day. Lillian Morrison. RHPC
Hey! the little postman. The Postman. Laura E. Richards. SoPo; TiPo
Hey there poleece. Poem to a Nigger Cop. Bobb Hamilton. TTY
Hey, this little kid gets roller skates. 74th Street. Myra Cohn Livingston. CTBA
"Hey, troly loly lo, maid, whither go you?" Pastourelle. *Unknown.* OBSC
Hey, Wully Wine. *Unknown.* CH
Hey, young bride! Teasing Song. Princess Magogo, *tr. by* D. K. Rycroft. WTO
Hi, Hi, Curlywig. *Unknown.* PoPle
"Hi!" said the blackbird, sitting on a chair. The Birds' Courting Song. *Unknown.* TrAS
"Hi," said the little leatherwing bat. Leatherwing Bat. *Unknown.* FSW
Hi! we shout with voice ecstatic. Roundel in the Rain. *Unknown.* FiBHP
Hialmar Speaks to the Raven. Leconte de Lisle, *tr. fr. French by* James Elroy Flecker. AWP; SyP
Hiatus. Margaret Avison. HAP
Hiawatha. Stephen Sandy. CoPo
Hiawatha Revisited. George A. Strong. *See* Modern Hiawatha, The.
Hiawatha's Canoe. Longfellow. *Fr.* The Song of Hiawatha. OHIP
Hiawatha's Childhood. Longfellow. *Fr.* The Song of Hiawatha, III. FaBV; FaPON; OHFP; TiPo; TreF; WBLP
("By the shores of Gitche Gumee.") SpRo
Hiawatha's Photographing. "Lewis Carroll." BXAP; CenHV; FaBoCo; FaBoPa; FiBHP; NOBL; SpRo
Hiawatha's Wooing. Longfellow. *Fr.* The Song of Hiawatha, X. BeLS; TreFS
Hibakusha's Letter (1955), The. David Mura. BrSi
Hibernia. Stuart Howard-Jones. DBV; NOBL
Hibernia's Helicon is dry. William Dunkin. *Fr.* An Epistle to Robert Nugent, Esq. with a Picture of Doctor Swift in Old Age. NOEC
Hibiscus on the Sleeping Shores. Wallace Stevens. InPS
Hibou et Minou allèrent à la mer. Le Hibou et la Poussiquette. Francis Steegmuller. NYBP
Hiboux, Les. Baudelaire, *tr. fr. French by* Arthur Symons. AWP
Hic, Hoc, the Carrion Crow. *Unknown.* OxBoLi
Hic Jacet. Louise Chandler Moulton. AA
Hic jacet Tom Shorthose. *Unknown.* FaBoEE
Hic liber ad me pertinet. Robert Barclay. FaBoUs
Hic liber est meus. To the Borrower of This Book. Samuel Showell, Jr. FaBoUs
"Hic Me, Pater Optime, Fessam Deseris." Lucy Catlin Robinson. AA
"Hic Vir, Hic Est." Charles Stuart Calverley. NBM; OxBoLi
Hicche-Hykeres Tale, The. W. F. N. Watson. BXAP
Hick-a-more, Hack-a-more. Mother Goose. OxNR
Hickenthrift and Hickenloop. X. J. Kennedy. WSC
Hickety pickety i sillickety [*or* i-silicity]. *Unknown.* GBP; OxNR
Hickety, pickety, my black hen. *See* Higgledy, Piggledy. . .
Hickok rests by Calamity Jane. Lay of the Last Frontier. Harold Hersey. PoOW
Hickory, dickory, dock. Mother Goose. FaBoBe; FaFP; HBV-1; HBVY; OxNR; PoPl; SoPo; TiPo
Hickory Stick Hierarchy. Len G. Selle. AMV-80
Hickup, hickup, go away. Charm: Hiccups. *Unknown.* FaBoUs
Hid by the august foliage and fruit. To a Chameleon. Marianne Moore. GoYe; PoPl
Hid in a maze of quaintly-fashioned things. A Wedgewood Bowl. Frances Beatrice Taylor. CaP
Hidden Bow. Mordecai Temkin, *tr. fr. Hebrew by* Jeremy Garber. VWA
Hidden far somewhere trembling with. The Mountain That Got Little. William Stafford. FAZ
Hidden Flame. Dryden. *See* Song: "I feed a flame within, which so torments me."
Hidden immortal. Near a Waterfall at Ryumon. Lady Ise, *tr. by* Etsuko Terasaki *and* Irma Brandeis. BoWoP
Hidden in wonder and snow, or sudden with summer. Laurentian Shield. F. R. Scott. NOBC; OBCV
Hidden Line, The. Joseph Addison Alexander. *See* Doomed Man, The.
Hidden lovers' woes. His Own True Wife. Wolfram von Eschenbach, *tr. by* Jethro Bithell. AWP
Hidden strength, A. Chastity. Milton. *Fr.* Comus. OBS
Hidden Valley. E. G. Burrows. HoAn
Hidden Weaver, The. Odell Shepard. WGRP
Hide [*or* Hyd], Absalon [*or* Absolon], thy gilte tresses clear [*or* clere]. Balade [*or* A Lady without Paragon]. Chaucer. *Fr.* The Legend of Good Women: Prologue. AWP; ChTr; EBEV; FiP; GBL; HAP; LoBV; MeEl; NOBE; OAEL-1; OBEV; OxBM; SeCeV
Hide and Seek. Robert Graves. NTCP
Hide and Seek. Dan Pagis, *tr. fr. Hebrew by* Bernhard Frank. AMV-81
Hide, happy damask, from the stars. Serenade. Henry Timrod. HBV-1
Hide in the Heart. Lloyd Frankenberg. LiTA
Hide not, hide not. The Rousing Canoe Song. Hermia Harris Fraser. CaP; WHW
Hide not thy love and myne shal bee. Pure Simple Love. Aurelian Townshend. AnAnS-2; SeCP
Hide of My Mother, The. Edward Dorn. NeAP
Hide, Oh, Hide Those Hills of Snow. John Fletcher, *and others.* *Fr.* The Bloody Brother, V, ii. ViBoPo

Hide this one night thy crescent, kindly Moon. To the Moon. Pierre de Ronsard, *tr. by* Andrew Lang. AWP
Hide Thou Me. *Unknown.* AmFP
Hidebehind, The. Michael Rosen. AmMo
Hidesong. Aig Higo. TTY
Hiding. Dorothy Aldis. FaPON; SoPo; SUS; TiPo
Hiding in the/ cucumber garden. Vidya, *tr. fr. Sanskrit by* W. S. Merwin *and* J. Moussaieff Masson. WPOW
Hiding in the church of an abandoned stone. Confession to J. Edgar Hoover. James Wright. CAPP; ConAP
Hiding Place. Richard Armour. NIP
Hiding tuft, a green-barked yew-tree, A. The Hermit's Song. *Unknown, tr. by* Frank O'Connor. KiLC
Hie Away. Sir Walter Scott. *Fr.* Waverley, *ch.* 12. MoShBr; ViBoPo
(Gellatley's Song to the Deerhounds.) OBRV
(Hie Away, Hie Away.) EnRP; TiPo
Hie, hie, says Anthony. Mother Goose. OxNR
Hie prudence, and wirking mervelous, The. The Preiching of the Swallow. Robert Henryson. OxBS
Hie to the market, Jenny come trot. *Unknown.* OxNR
Hie upon Hielands [*or* High up on highland *or* High upon Highlands]. Bonnie [*or* Bonny] George [*or* James] Campbell. *Unknown.* AmFP; AWP; BaBo; BSV; CH; ELP; EnRP; ESPB; FaBoBa; GBP; GoTS; HBV-2; NoP; OxBB; OxBoLi; PoPle; ViBoPo
Hieland Laddie. *Unknown.* FSW
Hiems. Shakespeare. *Fr.* Love's Labour's Lost. *See* When Icicles Hang by the Wall.
Hierarchie of the Blessed Angles, *sel.* Thomas Heywood.
"I sought thee round about, O thou my God!" WGRP
(Search for God, The.) OxBoCh, *abr.*
Hieroglyph. Paul Auster. VWA
Hieroglyphic. Myra Sklarew. SUW
Hierusalem, My Happy Home. *Unknown.* *See* New Jerusalem, The.
Higgledy-piggledy/ Andrea Doria. Last Words. John Hollander. OBAL; PV
Higgledy-piggledy,/ Benjamin Harrison. Historical Reflections. John Hollander. DBV; NIP; OBAL
Higgledy-piggledy/ Dorothy Richardson. The Lower Criticism. John Hollander. DBV; PV
Higgledy-piggledy/ Franklin D. Roosevelt. Danish Wit. John Hollander. PV
Higgledy, piggledy [*or* Higamus hogamus]/ Gloria Vanderbilt. Poor Kid. William Cole. OBAL; PV
Higgledy-piggledy/ Heliogabalus. Heliogabalus. John Hollander. OBAL
Higgledy-piggledy/ John Simon Guggenheim. No Foundation. John Hollander. OBAL
Higgledy-piggledy/ Josephine Bonaparte. Appearance and Reality. John Hollander. OBAL
Higgledy-piggledy/ Ludwig van Beethoven. Wrath. John Hollander. PV
Higgledy-piggledy/ Ludwig van Beethoven. E. William Seaman. PV; WeW
Higgledy-piggledy/ Mme. de Maintenon. Firmness. Anthony Hecht. OBAL; PV
Higgledy-piggledy/ President Jefferson. Twilight's Last Gleaming. Arthur W. Monks. OFD
Higgledy-piggledy/ Ralph Waldo Emerson. From the Grove Press. Anthony Hecht. OBAL
Higgledy-piggledy/ Thomas A. Edison. Progress. Sally Belfrage. PV
Higgledy-piggledy/ Thomas Stearns Eliot. Vice. Anthony Hecht. OBAL
Higgledy-Piggledy here we lie. *Unknown.* OxNR
Higgledy, piggledy [*or* Higgleby, Piggleby *or* Hickety, pickety], my black [*or* fat] hen. Mother Goose. FaBoBe; HBV-1; OxNR; PBBP; SoPo; TiPo
Higgledy, piggledy! see how they run! Kate Greenaway. TiPo
Higglety, Pigglety, Pop! Samuel Goodrich. OxNR; RHPC
High/ in your room. The Belongings. Theodore Enslin. CoPo
High above all a cloth of state was spred. The House of Pride. Spenser. *Fr.* The Faerie Queene, I, 4. WHA
High above hate I dwell. Sanctuary. Louise Imogen Guiney. AA
High above Suilven an eagle soars. Assynt. Alan Gilchrist. PoSH
High adventure. Maps. Dorothy Brown Thompson. RHPC; TiPo
High amid/ gothic rocks the altar stands. Sub Specie Aeternitatis. Robert Hayden. AmPP
High and inscrutable the old man stood. The Death of Haidée. Byron. *Fr.* Don Juan, IV. WHA
High and Low. James H. Cousins. HBMV; OnYI; OxBI
High and Low. John Banister Tabb. TDH
High and mighty lord of Glendare, The. The Cricket's Story. Emma Huntington Nason. HBV-1; HBVY
High and proud on the barnyard fence. Chanticleer. John Farrar. SoPo; TiPo
High and solemn mountains guard Rioupéroux. Rioupéroux. James Elroy Flecker. OBEV; OBVV
High are the mountains and low is the plain. When Billy the Kid Rides Again. S. Omar Barker. BPAW
High Barbaree, The. Laura E. Richards. SoPo; SUS
High Barbaree, The. *Unknown.* AmSS, *with music*; FSW; OuSiCo, *with music;* ViBoFo, *with music*
(High Barbary.) BaBo
(Wild Barbaree; The.) AmFP
High bare field, brown from the plough, and borne, A. The Potato Harvest. Sir Charles G. D. Roberts. CaP; NOBC
High-born Helen, round your dwelling. Helen. Mary Ann Lamb. OBRV
High Bridge above the Tagus River at Toledo, The. William Carlos Williams. CTC
High cockalorum diddledum! Direct Song. Eve Merriam. UnTE
High-cool/ 2. James Cunningham. JB
High diddle diddle/ The cat and the fiddle. *See* Hey! diddle, diddle . . . .
High diddle ding, did you hear the bells ring? *Unknown.* OxNR
High ding a ding, and ho ding a ding. The Parliament Soldiers. *Unknown.* GBP
High Diver. Robert Francis. LiSp; NePoAm
High Fidelity. Thom Gunn. PoA
High Field—First Day of Winter. Gary Eddy. AMV-80
High Flight. John Gillespie Magee, Jr. FaFP; FaPON; PGD; TreFS; TRV
High Germany. Edward Shanks. OBMV
High Germany. *Unknown.* FSW; OBET; WaaP
High grace, the dower of queens; and therewithal. Her Gifts. Dante Gabriel Rossetti. The House of Life, XXXI. HBV-1; VLP
High grew the snow beneath the low-hung sky. The Axe of the Pioneer. Isabella Valancy Crawford. CaP
High, high and far away. Buzzard. Michael Daugherty. PoSH
High, high in the branches. The Ferns. Gene Baro. RHPC
High Hills, The. Ivor Gurney. FaBoPP
High in the breathless hall the minstrel sate. Song at the Feast of Brougham Castle. Wordsworth. EnRP
High in the jacaranda shines the gilded thread. The 90th Year. Denise Levertov. FiCP
High in the mountains of Soviet Armenia. Out of the Deepness. William (Haywood) Jackson. AMV-81
High in the organ-loft with lilied hair. Epithalamium. Sir Edmund Gosse. OBVV
High in the pine-tree. The Turtle-Doves' Nest. *Unknown.* HBVY
High in the woodland, on the mountain-side. The Ant-Heap. A. C. Benson. EBVV
High Island. Richard Murphy. CIP
High Jump, The. *Unknown.* LiSp
High-Life Low-Down. Justin Richardson. PV
High-loping Cowboy, The. Curley W. Fletcher. BPAW
High-lying, sea-blown stretches of green turf. The Beds of Fleur-de-Lys. Charlotte Perkins Gilman. AA
High Midnight was garlanding her head, The. Moonlight. Jacques Tahureau, *tr. by* Andrew Lang. AWP
High o'er his moldering castle walls. A Voice from the Invisible World. Goethe, *tr. by* James Clarence Mangan. AWP
High o'er the Hills, *with music.* William Walker. AH
High o'er the Poop the Audacious Seas Aspire. William Falconer. EtS
High on a banyan tree in a row. Monkey. William Jay Smith. TiPo
High on a mountain's highest ridge. Wordsworth. *Fr.* The Thorn. Par
High on a ridge of tiles. Poem. Maurice James Craig. BoAnP; NeIP
High on a rough and dismal crag. The Miner's Lament. "Mark Twain." BPAW
High on a throne of royal state, which far. Milton. *Fr.* Paradise Lost, II. NIP; OAEP
High on Ben Alder on wintery night. Night Expedition from Ben Alder Cottage. Roger A. Redfern. PoSH
High on his figured couch beyond the waves. Theseus and Ariadne. Robert Graves. HAP
High on his stockroom ladder like a dunce. Playboy. Richard Wilbur. FF; NoAM; NOBA; NoP; WeW
High on the bold, gray granite shelf. The Stationed Scout. Lyman H. Sproull. PoOW
High on the Hog. Julia Fields. CNA
High on the mountain of sunrise where standeth the Temple of Sebek. He Knoweth the Souls of the West. *Unknown, tr. by* Robert Hillyer. *Fr.* Book of the Dead. AWP
High on the thrilling strand he dances. Tightrope Walker. Vernon Scannell. NCSH
High over Mecca Allah's prophet's corpse. Dissatisfaction with Metaphysics. William Empson. CMoP
High-pitched waves of glory. Mahalia. Michael S. Harper. FAZ
High Place, A. Eithne Wilkins. NeBP
High-placed above me the branches quiver. The Lost. *Malay Oral Tradition, tr. by* R. J. Wilkinson *and* R. O. Winstedt. WTO
High Plains Harvest. Bruce Morton. AMV-81

High poetry and low. Wallace Stevens. PoA
High Price Blues. *Unknown.* BluL
High-priced jeans, the new car, The—she got what. A Teen-Ager. W. D. Snodgrass. TW
High Priest, The. *Unknown, tr. fr. Hebrew by* Arthur Davis. TrJP
High Priests of telescopes and cyclotrons, The. Ode to Terminus. W. H. Auden. HAP
High Renaissance. George Starbuck. OBAL
High-riding kites appear to range quite freely. Gravities. Seamus Heaney. NoAM
High School Band, The. Reed Whittemore. GLGT; NCSH
High sheriff been here, The. Big Rock Jail. *Unknown.* BluL
High Sheriff Blues. *Unknown.* BluL
High-speed metal snake switches its tail, A. The Chief of the West, Darkling. David Knight. MoCV
High-spirited friend. The Noble Balm. Ben Jonson. OBEV
High stretched upon the swinging yard. Disguises. Thomas Edward Brown. VLP; WGRP
High Summer. Guy Rotella. AMV-80
High Summer on the Mountains. Idris Davies. OxBTC
High summer's sheen upon all things. The Web. Theodore Weiss. CoAP; NoAM
High the vanes of Shrewsbury gleam. The Welsh Marches. A. E. Housman. FaBoTw
High there in our grove the little birds. In the Morning All Over. William Stafford. FAZ
High Tide. Jean Starr Untermeyer. MoAmPo
High Tide at Gettysburg, The. Will Henry Thompson. AA; BeLS; BLPA; FaBoBe; HBV-2; PAH; PAL; PaPo; TreFS
High Tide on the Coast of Lincolnshire, The (1571). Jean Ingelow. BeLS; EBVV; FaBoPP; GN; HBV-2; NBM; OBVV; OnMSP; PaPo
High-toned Old Christian Woman, A. Wallace Stevens. AP; CMoP; CoBMV; MoVE; NoAM; NOBA; PPP; TAP
High-toned Old Fascist Gentleman, A. William Zaranka. BXAP
High towered the palace and its massive pile. Palace of the Gnomes. Maria Gowen Brooks. *Fr.* Zophiël. AA
High towers the grass where once we'd meet and wander. Parting. *Malay Oral Tradition, tr. by* R. J. Wilkinson *and* R. O. Winstedt. WTO
High trees grieve like the sea's water, The. In Wicklow. Rhoda Coghill. NeIP
High up among the mountains, through a lovely grove of cedars. Bears. Arthur Guiterman. PoRA
High up, birches have a homely aspect. Stopping by Shadows. Robin Fulton. PoSH
High up, I/ see deer circle. On Foinaven. Donald G. Saunders. PoSH
High up in the courts of heaven today. A Little Dog-Angel. Norah M. Holland. PoLF
High up on highland. *See* Hie upon Hielands.
High Up on Suilven. Norman MacCaig. PoSH
High upon Highlands. *See* Hie upon Hielands.
High upon the gallows tree swung the noble-hearted three. God Save Ireland. Timothy Daniel Sullivan. OnYI
High walls and huge the body may confine. Freedom for the Mind. William Lloyd Garrison. AA; FaBoBe
High walls . . . of stones. Aran Islands. Irving Layton. NeAC
High Water Everywhere: 1 ("The back water done rose around Sumner, now"). *Unknown.* BluL
High Water Everywhere: 2 ("Back water at Blytheville"). *Unknown.* BluL
High Wheat Country. Elijah L. Jacobs. AmFN
High Wind, The. *Unknown. See* Wind, The.
High Wind at the Battery. Ralph Pomeroy. NYBP
High wind. . .They turn their backs to it, and push. Glasgow Schoolboys, Running Backwards. Douglas Dunn. OxBC
High Windows. Philip Larkin. FaBoMo
High Wonders. Naomi Marks. BXAP
High-yellow of my heart, with breasts like tangerines. The Peasant Declares His Love. Emile Roumer, *tr. by* John Peale Bishop. ErPo; TTY
Higher ("The shadows of night were a-comin' down swift"). *Unknown.* FiBHP; SpRo
Higher Calling, The. W. M. Czamanske. STF
Higher Catechism, The. Sam Walter Foss. WGRP
Higher Empiricism, The. Francis C. Golffing. PoA
Higher Good, The. Theodore Parker. AA; FaBoBe; HBV-2
(New Year Prayer, A.) PGD
Higher Pantheism, The. Tennyson. HBV-2; SpRo; TRV; VLP; WGRP
Higher Pantheism in a Nutshell, The, *parody.* Swinburne. *Fr.* The Heptalogia. BXAP; FaBoNo; HBV-1; NA; Par; SpRo
Higher than a house,/ Higher than a tree. Mother Goose. OxNR; SoPo; TiPo
Higher than gull's nests, higher than children go. Rock Climbing. Jane Cooper. NMM
Higher than heaven they sit. The Hope of the World. Sir William Watson. WGRP
Highest Divinity. *Unknown, tr. fr. Hebrew by* Israel Zangwill. TrJP
Highest of Immortals bright. Indra, the Supreme God. *Unknown, tr. by* Romesh Dutt. *Fr.* The Rig-Veda. AWP
Highland Cattle, *sel.* Dinah Maria Mulock Craik.
"Down the wintry mountain." GN
Highland Glen near Loch Ericht, A. Arthur Hugh Clough. *Fr.* The Bothie of Tober-na-Vuolich, III. FaBoPP
("There is a stream, I name not its name.") BoNaP; VLP
Highland Harry Back Again. *At. to* Burns. EBEV
Highland Laddie, *with music.* *Unknown.* ShS
Highland Loves. Rennie McOwan. PoSH
Highland Mary. Burns. AWP; EnRP; GTBS; GTBS-P; HBV-1; OAEP; OBEC; OBEV; TreFS; TrGrPo; ViBoPo; WBLP
Highland Shooting Lodge. Maurice Lindsay. PoSH
Highland Tinker, The. *Unknown.* CoMu
Highlandmen hae a' come down, The. The Lady of Arngosk. *Unknown.* ESPB
Highlands of Hudson! ye saw them pass. The Storming of Stony Point. Arthur Guiterman. PAH
Highlands' swelling blue, The. Byron. *Fr.* The Island. OBRV
Highroad's barren scar, A. Autumn Dawn. Antonio Machado, *tr. by* Jean Rogers Longland. PoPl
Highty, tighty, paradighty, clothed in green. Riddle. *Unknown.* ChTr; OxNR
Highway, The. Louise Driscoll. HBV-1
Highway, The. William Channing Gannett. WGRP
Highway, The. W. S. Merwin. PoA
Highway Blues. *Unknown.* BluL
Highway Construction. Carol Earle Chapin. QQQ
Highway forever draws away, The. Lily. Rosanna Warren. MAYP
Highway Patrol Stops Me, Going Too Slow. Robert Peterson. NeAC
Highway, since you my chief Parnassus be. Astrophel and Stella, LXXXIV. Sir Philip Sidney. EIL; EnRePo; LiTB; OAEP; OBEV; OBSC; SiPS
Highway turnpike thruway mall. A Charm for Our Time. Eve Merriam. QQQ
Highwayman, The. Alfred Noyes. BeLS; FaBV; FaFP; FaPON, *abr.;* FPL; HBV-2; HBVY; OBNV; OHFP; PoLF; TreFS
Highwaymen, The. John Gay. *Fr.* The Beggar's Opera. WiR
Hiking. Joseph Bruchac. CDW
Hiking a levee through the salt marsh. Wings and Seeds. Sandra McPherson. GeTw
Hiking Up Hieizan with Alam Lau/Buddha's Birthday 1974. Garret Kaoru Hongo. BrSi
Hilaire Belloc. Humbert Wolfe. FaBoEE
Hilas, o Hilas, why sit we mute. Chloris and Hilas. Made to a Saraban. Edmund Waller. SeCV-1
Hill, The. Rupert Brooke. HBV-1; MoBrPo; OxBTC; ViBoPo
Hill, The. Robert Creeley. ConAP; NoAM
Hill, A. Anthony Hecht. CoAP; NYBP
Hill, The. Horace Holley. WGRP
Hill, The. Edgar Lee Masters. *Fr.* Spoon River Anthology. CMoP; FYAP; LiTA; LiTM; NePA; NoAM; NOBA; OxBA; SeCeV; TAP; ViBoPo
Hill above the Mine, The. Malcolm Cowley. PoPl; SaC
Hill Burns, The. Nan Shepherd. PoSH
Hill Farmer Speaks, The. R. S. Thomas. GTBS-P
Hill full, a hole full, A. Mother Goose. SoPo; TiPo
Hill Hunger. John Foster West. TAT
Hill Love. James Macmillan. PoSH
Hill of Intrusion, The. W. S. Graham. NePoEA
Hill of the Graces, The. Spenser. *Fr.* The Faerie Queene, VI, 10. NOBE
Hill of Zion yields, The. Mount Zion. *Unknown.* AmFP
Hill People. Harriet Gray Blackwell. AmFN
Hill Pines Were Sighing, The. Robert Bridges. OAEP
Hill Summit, The. Dante Gabriel Rossetti. The House of Life, LXX. NOP; VLP
Hill was higher every year, The. Model T. Adrien Stoutenburg. CTBA
Hill Wife, The. Robert Frost. CMoP; HAP; LiTM; NoP
Sels.
House Fear. VGW; WSC
Impulse, The. HoPM; NePA; NoAM
Loneliness. FaBoEn; VGW
Hill-billy, hill-billy come to buy. Pedlar. Confucius, *tr. by* Ezra Pound. *Fr.* Wei Wind. CTC; OBVE
Hillcrest. E. A. Robinson. AP; CoBMV; FaBoEn; MoAB; OxBA; PPoe
Hillman Looks Back, The. Rennie McOwan. PoSH
Hills, The. Frances Cornford. MoBrPo
Hills, The. Julian Grenfell. HBV-1
Hills. Arthur Guiterman. HBVY
Hills. Robin Munro. PoSH

Hills and rivers of the lowland country, The. A Protest in the Sixth Year of Ch'ien Fu. Ts'ao Sung, *tr. by* Arthur Waley. FaBV
Hills and the Sea, The. Wilfred Campbell. CaP
Hills are calling me from care and reason, The. Bright Abandon. Tessa Sweazy Webb. GoYe
Hills are high in Caribou, The. The Yellow Witch of Caribou. Clyde Robertson. BPAW; PoOW
Hills are stark, their outlines hard with frost, The. Aviemore. Janet Waller. PoSH
Hills are white, but not with snow, The. An Orchard at Avignon. Agnes Mary Frances Robinson. HBV-1
Hills are wroth, The; the stones have scored you bitterly. To a Young Girl Leaving the Hill Country. Arna Bontemps. CDC
Hills Brothers Coffee. Luci Tapahonso. STE
Hills moved. I watched their shadows. Beetle on the Shasta Daylight. Shirley Kaufman. NYBP; WPE
Hills o' My Heart. "Ethna Carbery." HBV-2
Hills of Cualann, The. Joseph Campbell. AnIV
Hills of God, The. A. A. Buist. PoSH
Hills of God, Break Forth in Singing, *with music.* John Wright Buckham. AH
Hills of Pomeroy, The. Ewart Milne. NeIP
Hills of Rest, The. Albert Bigelow Paine. HBV-2; WGRP
Hills of Salt. Dahlia Ravikovitch, *tr. fr. Hebrew by* Chana Bloch. WPOW
Hills of Sewanee, The. George Marion McClellan. BANP
Hills of the Middle Distance. Archie Mitchell. PoSH
Hills of *Tsa la gi,* The. Robert J. Conley. STE
Hills of Zion, The. The Four of Them. Yehuda Karni, *tr. by* Jeremy Garber. VWA
Hills picking up the/ moonlight like. Nina Cassian, *tr. fr. Rumanian by* Stavros Deligiorgis. BoWoP
Hills shall miss him, The—while the pines. The Dead Prospector. Arthur Chapman. BPAW
Hills step off into whiteness, The. Sheep in Fog. Sylvia Plath. LCAP; NaP
Hills turn hugely in their sleep, The. Robert Hillyer. *Fr.* Prothalamion. MoAmPo
Hills yet hills, and still the yellow town, The. Naples Again. Arthur Freeman. NYBP
Hillside. Alexander Craig. PoAu-2
Hillside Farmer, A. John Farrar. HBMV
Hillside Pause. Catharine Morris Wright. GoYe
Hillside Thaw, A. Robert Frost. CMoP
Hillsides were of rushing, silvered water, The. Gioconda. Thomas McGreevy. OnYI
Hillstones pebbles and boulders. Mountain Sculpture. James Will. PoSH
Hilo, Hanakahi, rain rustling lehua. *Tr. fr. Hawaiian by* S. H. Elbert *and* N. Mahoe. WTO
Him Evermore I Behold. Longfellow. TRV
Him the Almighty Power. Satan Defiant [*or* The Fallen Angels]. Milton. *Fr.* Paradise Lost, I. FaBoEn; WHA
Himself, *sel.* Edwin John Ellis.
"At Golgotha I stood alone." OBMV
Himself. Daniel Hoffman. AMV-80
Himself is all he'll talk about to you. The Egotist. H. A. C. Evans. POL
Hind, The. Sir Thomas Wyatt. *See* Whoso List to Hunt.
Hind and the Panther, The, *sels.* Dryden.
"But, gratious God, how well dost thou provide," *fr.* I. TrPWD
(Church's Testimony, The.) ACP
Catholic Church, The, *fr.* II. OBS
Church of England, The, *fr.* I. OBS
Conversion, *fr.* III. ACP
(Worldly Vanity.) FiP
"Dame, said the Panther, times are mended well," II. PoEL-3
King James II, *fr.* III. ACP
"Milk white Hind, immortal and unchang'd, A," *fr.* I. SeCV-2
(Churches of Rome and of England, The, *much abr.*) ACP
"One evening, while the cooler shade she sought," *fr.* I. PoEL-3
"Portly Prince, and goodly to the sight, A," *fr.* III. OBSV
Presbyterians, The, *fr.* I. OBS
Private Judgement Condemned, *fr.* I. OBS
(Confessio Fidei.) NOBE
(Prayer, A: "What weight of ancient witness can prevail.") FiP
"To this the Panther, with a scornful smile," *fr.* III. SeCV-2
Hind Etin. *Unknown.* ESPB (A *and* B *vers.*); OxBB
Hind Horn *(diff. versions). Unknown.* AmFP; ESPB (A *and* G *vers.*); ViBoFo
(Hynde [*or* Hynd] Horn.) GN; OxBB, *with music*
Hind, knocked sprawling by my shot, The. Death of a Hind. Alasdair Maclean. PoSH
Hindoo died, A; a happy thing to do. Paradise; a Hindoo Legend. George Birdseye. DBV; HBV-1
Hindoo, The: He Doesn't Hurt a Fly or a Spider Either. A. K. Ramanujan. OxBC
Hinds of Kerry, The. William S. Wabnitz. GoYe
Hindu Ascetic, The. Sir Alfred Comyn Lyall. *Fr.* Studies at Delhi. OBVV
Hinge, The. Sheila Cowing. AMV-81
Hinky Dinky [Parlee-Voo]. *See* Mademoiselle from Armentières.
Hint from Herrick, A. Thomas Bailey Aldrich. HBV-2
Hint from Voiture. William Shenstone. EnLoPo
Hint o' Snow, A. William Soutar. PoSH
Hint to the Wise, A. Pringle Barret. HBVY
Hinted Wish, A. Martial, *tr. fr. Latin by* Francis Lewis. AWP
Hints on Pronunciation for Foreigners. *Unknown.* FaBoUs
Hinty, minty, cuty, corn. Counting-out Rhymes. *Unknown.* FaPON
Hinx! minx!/ The old witch winks! Children's Runes and Omens. *Unknown.* MAT; OxNR
Hip-deep in swamp I watch. Trout Fishing; a Sign. Richard Behm. WOLT
Hip Shakin' Strut. *Unknown.* BluL
Hippety hop to the barber shop. Mother Goose. SoPo; TiPo
Hippity Hop to Bed. Leroy F. Jackson. TiPo
Hippo, The. Theodore Roethke. VGW
Hippo decided one day, A. Ballet. *Unknown.* TDH
Hippodromania; or, Whiffs from the Pipe, *sel.* Adam Lindsay Gordon.
"Rest, and be thankful! On the verge." CBAP
Hippolytus. Euripides, *tr. fr. Greek by* Rex Warner. NAWM-1
Sels.
No More, O My Spirit, *tr. by* Hilda Doolittle ("H. D."). AWP
O for the Wings of a Dove, *tr. by* Gilbert Murray. AWP
Hippolytus Temporizes. Hilda Doolittle ("H. D."). SBG
Hippopotamothalamion. John Hall Wheelock. FiBHP; FYAP; NePoAm-2
Hippopotamus, The. Hilaire Belloc. FaBoNo; FiBHP; InPK; PoPl; WhC
("I shoot the hippopotamus.") CenHV
Hippopotamus. Joanna Cole. NTCP
Hippopotamus, The. Georgia Roberts Durston. TiPo
Hippopotamus, The. T. S. Eliot. AWP; HoPM; LiTB; OBMV; PAI; PoPl; VGW
Hippopotamus, The. Oliver Herford. NA
Hippopotamus, The. Ogden Nash. FaBV; OnUR
Hippopotamus, The. Jack Prelutsky. RHPC
Hippopotamus had a bride, A. Hippopotamothalamion. John Hall Wheelock. FiBHP; FYAP; NePoAm-2
Hippopotamus is strong, The. Habits of the Hippopotamus. Arthur Guiterman. BoAnP; FaBV; FiBHP; OBCA; OnUR; RHPC; TiPo
Hipporhinostricow. Spike Milligan. AmMo
Hir bowgy cheekes been as softe as clay. A Description of His Ugly Lady. Thomas Hoccleve. MeEL
Hiraeth in N.W.3. Wynford Vaughan-Thomas. NOBL
"Hiram, I think the sump is backing up." Mending Sump. Kenneth Koch. BXAP; HeIP; InPK; NeAP; NoAM; PV
Hiram Powers' "Greek Slave." Elizabeth Barrett Browning. SBG; VLP
Hired Man on Horseback, The. Eugene Manlove Rhodes. BPAW
Hired Man's Way, The. John Kendrick Bangs. OBCA
Hiroshige. Mark M. Perlberg. NYBP
Hiroshima. Margaret Rockwell. PPON
Hiroshima Exit. Joy Kogawa. BrSi
His/ name was. A Marriage. Anthony Barnett. VWA
His Age, Dedicated to His Peculiar Friend, Master John Wickes, under the Name of Posthumus. Robert Herrick. CaPo; SeCP
His age drawn out behind him to be watched. Old Man. Elizabeth Jennings. NePoEA-2
His aging widow dreams of youth. Memorial Service. Ursula Vaughan Williams. POL
His Answer. Clara Ann Thompson. BlSi
His are the generous days that balance. The Generous Years. Stephen Spender. PoCh
His Are the Thousand Sparkling Rills. Frances Alexander. OxBI
His art is eccentricity, his aim. Pitcher. Robert Francis. LiSp; NePoAm; PP; SoSe; WeW
His artificial feet calumped in holy rhythm. Deacon Morgan. Naomi Long Madgett. BlSi
His Banner over Me. Gerald Massey. HBV-2; WGRP
His bark/ The daring mariner shall urge far o'er. Prophecy. Luigi Pulci. *Fr.* Il Morgante Maggiore. PAH
His being gone is a gift to my people. Wulf and Eadwacer. *Unknown, tr. by* Willis Barnstone *and* Elene Kolb. BoWoP
His Being Was in Her Alone. Sir Philip Sidney. ELP; PAI
His Best. Albert Benjamin Simpson. STF
His bicycle stood at the window-sill. A Constable Calls. Seamus Heaney. IPY
His blood on my arm is warm as a bird. Prayer for Messiah. Leonard Cohen. OBCV
His Body. Sandra McPherson. AmPA; GeTw; GP

His body is smashed. The Crucifix. Sir Herbert Read. BrPo
His body lies interred within this mould. Epitaph on a Soldier. Cyril Tourneur. *Fr.* The Atheist's Tragedy. ElL
His body lies upon the shore. Richard Somers. Barrett Eastman. AA
His Books. Robert Southey. OBEV
His bridle hung around the post. Horse. Elizabeth Madox Roberts. PH; TiPo
His broad-brimmed hat pushed back with careless air. Vaquero. Joaquin Miller. AA; BPAW
His brother after dinner. Uncle Bull-Boy. June Jordan. PoBA
His brother said that pain was what he knew. Traction: November 22, 1963. Howard Moss. AmFN
His brow spreads large and placid, and his eye. "The Chief." W. E. Henley. In Hospital, XV. BrPo
His Camel. Alqamah, *tr. fr. Arabic by* Sir Charles Lyall. *Fr.* The Mufaddaliyat. AWP
His car was worth a thousand pounds and more. One Poet Visits Another. W. H. Davies. DTC; TW
His care-free swagger was a fine invention. Sonnets from China, V. W. H. Auden. CMoP
His case inspires interest. A Man of Words. John Ashbery. PoA
His castrating wife is at the controls. Blue Max. Harvey Shapiro. GP
His Cavalier. Robert Herrick. CaPo; GoJo
His cedar paddle, scented, red. The Lily Bed. Isabella Valancy Crawford. PeCV
His Charge to Julia at His Death. Robert Herrick. SeCV-1
His cherished woods are mute. The stream glides down. At Chappaqua. Joel Benton. AA
His Children. Hittan of Tayyi, *tr. fr. Arabic by* Sir Charles Lyall. *Fr.* Hamasah. AWP
His chosen comrades thought at school. What Then? W. B. Yeats. CMoP
His classic studies made a little puzzle. Don Juan's Education. Byron. *Fr.* Don Juan. WHA
His cock is big and red when I am there. Lines. Paul Goodman. PeHV
His comb was redder than the fine coral. Chaucer. *Fr.* The Canterbury Tales: The Nun's Priest's Tale. PBBP
His compassionate face, slightly wan. On the Street. C. P. Cavafy, *tr. by* Rae Dalven. BoLoP
His Confession. "The Archpoet," *tr. fr. Latin by* Helen Waddell. NAWM-1
His Content in the Country. Robert Herrick. CaPo; SeCV-1
("Here, here I live with what my board.") TEP
His corpse owre a' the city lies. The Dead Liebknecht. "Hugh MacDiarmid," *after the German of* Rudolf Leonhard. OBVE
His Creed. Robert Herrick. SeCeV
His cry was always sad. Taught to Be Polite. Virginia Brady Young. AMV-81
His daughter Charlotte said to Mr. Brontë. Sampler from Haworth. Frances Minturn Howard. WPE
His delicate fingers, moving among the roses. The Utopia of Lord Mayor Howard. Randolph Stow. PoAu-2
His Desire. Robert Herrick. CABA; OAEP
His desires, growing. Black Man's Feast. Sarah Webster Fabio. PoBA;. PoNe
His Discourse with Cupid. Ben Jonson. *Fr.* A Celebration of Charis. AnAnS-2; SeCP
His Dream of the Sky-Land: A Farewell Poem, *sel.* Li Po, *tr. fr. Chinese by* Shigeyoshi Obata.
"Seafarers tell of the Eastern Isle of Bliss, The." WSC
His echoing axe the settler swung. The Settler. Alfred Billings Street. AA; FaBoBe; PAH
His Ejaculation to God. Robert Herrick. SeCV-1
His Elegy. Chidiock Tichborne. *See* Elegy: "My prime of youth is but a frost of cares."
His Epitaph. Stephen Hawes. *See* Epitaph of Grande Amoure, The.
His Epitaph. Walter Savage Landor. OBVV
His Epitaph. Sir Walter Ralegh. *See* Even Such Is Time.
His Excellency General Washington. Phillis Wheatley. *See* To His Excellency, General Washington.
His Excuse for Loving. Ben Jonson. *Fr.* A Celebration of Charis. AnAnS-2; EnRePo; JCP; PoEL-2; QFR; SeCP; SeCV-1
His eyes are closed. They are closed. His eyes are closed. The Mummy. Vernon Watkins. MoPo; NeBP
His eyes are green and his nose is brown. The King of the Hobbledygoblins. Laura E. Richards. OBCA
His eyes are quickened so with grief. Lost Love. Robert Graves. AWP; CH; ChMP;FaBoCh; MoAB; MoBrPo; NoP
His eyes can be quite old and stern. Father. Mildred Weston. PoSC
His eyes grow hot, his words grow wild. The Wise Woman. Louis Untermeyer. HBMV
His eyes saw all things in the symmetry. Coleridge. Aubrey Thomas De Vere. GoBC
His eyes were once blue and pure. Hard Times, but Carrying On. Dave Smith. TAT
His Face. Florence Earle Coates. OHIP
His face is pale and shrunk, his shining hair. November Sun. Elizabeth Daryush. PBWP
His face is truly of the Roman mould. A Character. Charlotte Fiske Bates. AA
"His face shone" she said. A Death. Elizabeth Jennings. NMP
His face was blue, on his fingers. Mourning and Melancholia. A. Alvarez. VWA
His face was glad as dawn to me. Shule, Agrah! "Fiona Macleod." OBVV
His face was the oddest that ever was seen. The Strange Man. *Unknown.* FaPON
His falchion flashed along the Nile. The Exile at Rest. John Pierpont. AA
His Farewell to His Unkind and Unconstant Mistress. Francis Davison. ElL; OBSC
His Fare-well to Sack. Robert Herrick. AnAnS-2; CaPo; OAEP; SeCP; SeCV-1
His father gave him a box of truisms. The Truisms. Louis MacNeice. NOBE; OBSV
His father said: Marry her. She's had a hard life. The Chosen—Kalgoorlie, 1894. Fay Zwicky. VWA
His feet were shod with music and had wings. Milton. Lloyd Mifflin. AA
His figure's not noted for grace. The Wild Boarder. Kenyon Cox. TDH
His finger resembled. The Accident. Len Gasparini. NeAC
His fingers wake, and flutter; up the bed. Conscious. Wilfred Owen. MMA
His first day they asked. Arbeit Macht Frei. Dennis Schmitz. NPGG
His flaggy wings when forth he did display. The Dragon. Spenser. *Fr.* The Faerie Queene. SeCePo
His flesh/ fish underwater. The Death of the Epileptic Poet Yesenin. Aram Boyajian. NeAC
His footprints have failed us. Dead in the Sierras. Joaquin Miller. AA; BPAW
His fourscore years and five. Whittier. Margaret E. Sangster. AA
His friend the watchman was still awake. A Leave-Taking. Arno Holz, *tr. by* Jethro Bithell. AWP
His friends went off and left Him dead. The Resurrection. Jonathan Henderson Brooks. AmNP; CDC; PoNe
His fur resembles waves. Lynx. Ben Howard. GrPl
His Further Resolution. *Unknown.* HBV-1
His Garments. Esther Lloyd Hagg. PGD
His gentle heart shows through. Manong Benny. Virginia Cerenio. BrSi
His Gift and Mine. *Unknown.* BLRP
His gimpy leg was testimony to/ some other surgeon's art. Old Doc. Mark Vinz. Psk
His Golden Lock[e]s [Time Hath to Silver Turned]. George Peele. *Fr.* Polyhymnia. ElL; EnRePo; FaBoRV; HeIP; LoBV; NoP; PPoe; ViBoPo; WHA
(Farewell to Arms, A.) HBV-1; NIP; NOBE; OBEV; OBWP; PoPle; PoRA
(Old Knight, The.) ChTr; OBSC; TrGrPo
(Sonet, A: "His golden lockes, Time hath to silver turn'd.") FaBoEn; PoEL-2
(Sonnet, A: "His golden locks time hath to silver turned.") ELP; InPS
His Grace! impossible! what dead! A Satirical [*or* Satyrical] Elegy on the Death of a Late Famous General, 1722. Swift. CABA; FF; HoPM; NIP; NoP; OBSV; PoEL-3; SeCeV
His Grace of Marlborough, legends say. Tradition of Conquest. Sarah Morgan Bryan Piatt. AA
His graceful swag blocks catch the eye. The Destruction of Bulfinch's House. Stephen Sandy. CoPo
His Grange, or Private Wealth. Robert Herrick. AnAnS-2; CaPo; FM; GoJo; OAEP; SeCV-1
His green eyes on the homestead of another man. The Snake. Andrew Suknaski. NOBC
His haire was blacke, and in small curls did twine. Christ's Victorie on Earth. Giles Fletcher. *Fr.* Christ's Victorie and Triumph. SeCV-1
His hand came out of the east. Homer, *tr. by* Christopher Logue. *Fr.* The Iliad, XVI. OBVE
His Hand Shall Cover Us. Isaac ben Samuel of Dampière, *tr. fr. Hebrew by* Nina Davis Salaman. TrJP
His hand was a puppet, more wood than flesh. The Doctor Rebuilds a Hand. Gary Young. AMV-80; SUW
His Hands. John Richard Moreland. TRV
His hands were talented for intricate transactions. With a Posthumous Medal. John Malcolm Brinnin. SaC
His hat is rammed on. Near the School for Handicapped Children. Thomas W. Shapcott. CBAP
His hatbrim's full Copernican ellipse. The Portrait of Prince Henry. Sydney Clouts. VWA

His head is tiny because he has few brains. Whippet. Prudence Andrew. GDP
His head like a fist rooted in his abdomen. The Agents. Robert Conquest. EAS
His head split in four parts. Promenade. David Ignatow. TrJP
His headstone said. The Funeral of Martin Luther King, Jr. Nikki Giovanni. AmNP; BOLo; BPo
His heart, to me, was a place of palaces and pinnacles and shining towers. I Have Been through the Gates. Charlotte Mew. MoAB; MoBrPo; TrGrPo
His heart was in his garden; but his brain. Frederick Goddard Tuckerman. Sonnets, II, vii. AP
His heart was light, and all the living day. Canadian Farmer. Genevieve Bartole. CaP
His Heart Was True to Poll. Francis Cowley Burnand. HBV-2
His Helplessness. John Berryman. *Fr.* Dream Songs. NoP
His high-boned, young face is so brown. White Pass Ski Patrol. John Logan. BiP; CAPP
His Highness's Dog. Pope. *See* Epigram Engraved on the Collar of a Dog Given to His Royal Highness.
His Hirsute Suit. Frank Sidgwick. WhC
His holly hair, his berry eye are here. Nativity. W. R. Rodgers. NeBP
His home a speck in a vast Universe. Microcosm. Bertram Dobell. OBVV
His home is on the heights; to him. The Poet. Edwin Markham. WGRP
His Hope or Sheet-Anchor. Robert Herrick. CaPo
His hope undone, now raves the impious king. The Slaughter of the Innocents by Order of King Herod. Caelius Sedulius, *tr. by* George Sigerson. *Fr.* Carmen Paschale. OnYI
His hottest love and most delight. The Happy Hen. James Agee. ErPo
His house is a haven where fingers dare. Heart Specialist. Elias Lieberman. ImOP
His Immortality. Thomas Hardy. CMoP; PoPle
His Incomparable Lady. Earl of Surrey. *See* Give Place, Ye Lovers.
His iron-frame, long deem'd so ably plann'd. Watt's Improvements to the Steam Engine. Thomas Baker. *Fr.* The Steam Engine; or, The Power of Flame. FaBoUs
His job was. Branches Back Into. Ken Belford. NeAC
His kiss a bristling. Against Winter. Elaine Feinstein. VWA
His Lachrimae or Mirth, Turn'd to Mourning. Robert Herrick. SeCV-1
His Lady's Cruelty. Sir Philip Sidney. *See* Astrophel and Stella: Sonnets, XXXI.
His Lady's Death. Pierre de Ronsard, *tr. fr. French by* Andrew Lang. AWP
His Lady's Eyes. Fulke Greville. *See* You Little Stars That Live in Skies.
His Lady's Hand. Sir Thomas Wyatt. *See* O Goodly Hand.
His Lady's Might. Philippe Desportes. *See* Conquest.
His Lady's Tomb. Pierre de Ronsard, *tr. fr. French by* Andrew Lang. AWP
His lamp, his bow, and quiver laid aside. Cupid Turned Plowman [*or* Cupid a Plowman]. Moschus, *tr. by* Matthew Prior. AWP; OBVE
His landlocked dreams were rainbow-tides that ran. Old Voyager. Walter Blackstock. GoYe
His last days linger in that low attic. The Old Jockey. F. R. Higgins. AnIV; OBMV; OxBI; OxBTC
His Last Sonnet. Keats. *See* Bright Star, Would I Were Steadfast as Thou Art!
His Last Week. Elinor Lennen. PGD
His Late Wife's Wedding-Ring. George Crabbe. *See* Marriage Ring, A.
His Legs Ran About. Ted Hughes. LLLT
His Letanie, to the Holy Spirit. Robert Herrick. *See* His Litany to the Holy Spirit.
His life frightened him. The sun in the sky. Fear. Stephen Dobyns. AMV-80
His life is in the body of the living. The Soul and Body of John Brown. Muriel Rukeyser. MoAmPo
His Life Is Ours. Dorothy Conant Stroud. STF
His Litany to the Holy Spirit. Robert Herrick. BLPL; DTC; ELP; HBV-2; JCP; OAEP; OxBoCh; PoLF; QFR; SeCePo; TeP
(His Letanie, to the Holy Spirit.) AnAnS-2; OBS; SeCV-1
(Litany, The: "In the hour of my distress.") ILwL
(Litany to the Holy Spirit.) OBEV; PoPle, *abr.*
His Living Monument. Minna Irving. PGD
His locks were wild, and wild his eye. Taking Long Views. May Kendall. CenHV
His logic unperturbed, exacting new. Metaphysician. Robert Fitzgerald. PoA
His lordship's steed. Riding. William Allingham. OxBChV
His Lunch Bucket. Doug Cockrell. Psk
His lungs heaving all day in a sulphur mist. Black Money. Tess Gallagher. GeTw; LTB
His Majesty. Theron Brown. AA
His malice was a pimple down his good. Three around the Old Gentleman. John Berryman. AP
His mansion in the pool. Emily Dickinson. OBAL
His Metrical Prayer. James Graham, Marquess of Montrose. *See* On Himself, upon Hearing What Was His Sentence.
His Metrical Vow [on the Death of King Charles I]. James Graham, Marquess of Montrose. OxBS; ViBoPo
(Epitaph on Charles I.) NOBE
(Epitaph on King Charles I.) OBS
(Lines on the Execution of King Charles I.) BSV; GoTS
His mither sings to the bairnie Christ. O Jesu Parvule. "Hugh MacDiarmid." BSV
His most kind sister all his secrets knew. Repentance. George Chapman. *Fr.* Hero and Leander, Third Sestiad. OBSC
His mother dear, Cupid offended late. Astrophel and Stella, XVII. Sir Philip Sidney. SiPS
His Mother in Her Hood of Blue. Lizette Woodworth Reese. ISi; OHIP
His Mother-in-Law. Walter Parke. FiBHP
His mother loved him. All the world of man. His Mother's Love. Noah Stern, *tr. by* Harold Schimmel. VWA
His Mother's Joy. John White Chadwick. AA
His Mother's Love. Noah Stern, *tr. fr. Hebrew by* Harold Schimmel. VWA
His Mother's Service to Our Lady. Villon, *tr. fr. French by* Dante Gabriel Rossetti. AWP; CTC; ISi
His Mother's Wedding Ring. George Crabbe. *See* Marriage Ring, A.
His mouth babbling under the earphones. Boy in the Lamont Poetry Room, Harvard. D. G. Jones. PeCV
His murderers met. Their consciences were free. Easter Eve. James Branch Cabell. HBMV
His Muse Speakes to Him. William Habington. AnAnS-2
His naked skin clothed in the torrid mist. The Serf. Roy Campbell. GTBS-P; LiTB; MoBrPo; OBMV
His Name at the Top. *Unknown.* STF
His name is/ Rubin. Rubin. Charles Cooper. PoBA
His name it is Pedro-Pablo-Ignacio-Juan-/ Francesco García y Gabaldon. A Feller I Know. Mary Austin. AmFN; FaPON
His name, they told me afterwards, was Able. In Memory of My Uncle Timothy. Alastair Reid. NePoEA-2
His name was Chance, Jack Chance, he said. Ballad of a Strange Thing. H. Phelps Putnam. MoVE; OxBA
His native sea-washed isle. Sea-Distances. Alfred Noyes. MOS
His Necessary Darkness. Nancy Sullivan. TAP
His nose is short and scrubby. My Dog. Marchette Chute. FaPON; PDV; SoPo; TiPo
His Own Epitaph. John Gay. *See* My Own Epitaph.
His Own Epitaph. Robert Herrick. CaPo
His Own Epitaph, When He Was Sick. John Hoskyns. FaBoEE
His Own True Wife. Wolfram von Eschenbach, *tr. fr. German by* Jethro Bithell. AWP
His pads furring the scarp's rime. The Snow-Leopard. Randall Jarrell. LiTM; MoPo; MP; TwCP
His palms are black with India ink. Scrimshaw. Michael Hogan. LFAC
His paper propped against the electric toaster. Daniel at Breakfast. Phyllis McGinley. OBSV
His Parting from Her. John Donne. Elegies, XII. EBEV
(Elegie: His Parting from Her.) OBS
His Petition to Queen Anne of Denmark (1618). Sir Walter Ralegh. SiPS
His Picture. John Donne. Elegies, V. NoP
(Elegie: His Picture.) FaBoEn; MePo; OBS
(Elegie [*or* Elegy] V: His Picture.) EnRePo; MeLP
His Pilgrimage. Sir Walter Ralegh. *See* Passionate Man's Pilgrimage, The.
His place, as he sat and as he thought, was not. A Quiet Normal Life. Wallace Stevens. LCAP
His place is before, not in, the National Gallery. London Pavement Artist. James Schevill. TAP
His Plan. *Unknown.* STF
His Plan for Me. Martha Snell Nicholson. STF
His Plans for Old Age. William Meredith. TAP
His plumage is dun. Jailbird. Vernon Scannell. OxBC
His poems, yellow, torn and fading. Langston Hughes. Lew Blockcolski. VoR
His Poetry His Pillar. Robert Herrick. CaPo; JCP; LoBV; QFR
(His Poetrie His Pillar.) AnAnS-2; FaBoEn; OBS; SeCP
"His policy," do you say? Mr. Johnson's Policy of Reconstruction. Charles Graham Halpine. PAH
His Prayer for Absolution. Robert Herrick. AnAnS-2; OxBoCh; SeCV-1; TrPWD; TRV
His Prayer to Ben Jonson [*or* Johnson]. Robert Herrick. AnAnS-2; CaPo; CavP; JCP; NoP; OAEP; OBS; OxBoLi; PP; SeCeV; SeCV-1; TrGrPo
His Presence. Dale Schulz. STF
His Presence Came like Sunrise. Ralph S. Cushman. *See* Secret, The.
His pride/ Had cast him out from Heaven. Satan. Milton. *Fr.* Paradise Lost, I. PPoe; TreFT; TrGrPo
His proper name was Peter Sweet. The Reformed Pirate. Theodore Goodridge Roberts. WHW

His Quest. Lewis Frank Tooker. AA
His radiant fingers so adorning. Dawn. George B. Logan, Jr. HBV-1
His Remedie for Love. Michael Drayton. *Fr.* Idea. AAS
His Request. Owen Roe O'Sullivan, *tr. fr. Irish by* Joan Keefe. BIrV
His Request to Julia. Robert Herrick. CaPo; OBS
His Return[e] to London. Robert Herrick. AnAnS-2; CaPo; FaBoPP; FF
His Reward. Sir Thomas Wyatt. *See* With Serving Still.
His role is to invert the fairy tale. Psychiatrist. Peter DeVries. OBAL
His sad brown bulk rears patient as the hills. A Bull. Babette Deutsch. BoAnP; LiSp
His Sailing from Julia. Robert Herrick. PoEL-3
His Saviour's Words, Going to the Cross. Robert Herrick. NOCV
His science has progressed past stone. The Spider. Loren Eiseley. SUW
His self-conceit's so swollen by inflation. Positive, a Coxcomb. William Plomer. POL
His shadow monstrous on the palace wall. Oedipus. Thomas Blackburn. FaBoTw
His Shield. Marianne Moore. DTC; LiTM; NePA; TwAmPo
His shoulder did I hold. Any Saint. Francis Thompson. MoBrPo
His Side/ Her Side. Jeffrey Skinner. AMV-81
His sister named Lucy O'Finner. "Lewis Carroll." FaBoNo
His Sleep. Constance Urdang. AMV-81
His Son. Callimachus, *tr. fr. Greek by* G. B. Grundy. AWP
His songs were a little phrase. Of [*or* On] a Poet Patriot. Thomas MacDonagh. AnIV; HBMV; OnYI; OxBI
His soul extracted from the public sink. The Scurrilous Scribe. Philip Freneau. AA
His soul to God! on a battle-psalm! Albert Sidney Johnston. Francis Orrery Ticknor. PAH
His sovereignty is o'er my gathered throng. His Sovereignty. Kalonymos ben Moses of Lucca, *tr. by* Nina Davis Salaman. TrJP
His speckled pastures dipped to meet the beach. Biography. Charles Bruce. CaP
His speculation he regretted. I Want a Tenant; a Satire. John O'Keefe. NOEC
His spirit in smoke ascended to high heaven. The Lynching. Claude McKay. BALP; BANP; IDB; PoBA
His spirit went into the television. When Daddy Died. Duane Ackerson. POL
His Statement of the Case. James Herbert Morse. AA
His stature was not very tall. The Description of Sir Geoffrey Chaucer. Robert Greene. *Fr.* Greene's Vision. CTC; FaBoCh; OBSC
His sullen kinsmen, by the winter sea. Santa Claus. Dom Moraes. NoAM
His Swans. Geoffrey Grigson. FaBoRV
His Sweetheart Slain. *Unknown.* OxBM
His tail is remarkably long. The Kangarooster. Kenyon Cox. TiPo
His Task—And Ours. Dorothy Gould. PGD
His Tears to Thamasis [*or* Thamesis]. Robert Herrick. FaBoPP; OAEP
His teeth are white as curds. The Arrow of Desire. *Gond Oral Tradition, tr. by* V. Elwin *and* S. Hivale. WTO
His thesis was crystals. Waiting. Judith Skillman. SUW
His Throne Is with the Outcast. James Russell Lowell. TrCP
His tongue was touched with sacred fire. Henry Ward Beecher. Charles Henry Phelps. AA
His triumphs of a moment done. On the Departure of the British from Charleston. Philip Freneau. PAH
His trousers are torn, rolled up to the knee. The Teacher Sees a Boy. Margaret Morningstar. STF
His trousers are wind. Song to a Lover. *Tr. fr. Amharic (Ethiopia) by* Willis Barnstone. BoWoP
His tundra'd mind sprouts leaflets. Senile. Pat Folk. PCP
His Uncle came on Franklin Hyde. Franklin Hyde. Hilaire Belloc. FaBoUs
His villa in the mountains was made over. Teahouse. Nicholas Rinaldi. AMV-81
His was the first corpse I had ever seen. My Wicked Uncle. Derek Mahon. OxBC
His way in farming all men knew. At Marshfield. William Cleaver Wilkinson. *Fr.* Webster; an Ode. AA
His well shaped ears were chestnut brown and they. The Huckster's Horse. Julia Hurd Strong. GoYe
His wet fur, velvet-smooth, was sleek as reeds. Otters. William Hart-Smith. BoAnP
His whiskers didn't come, his mustache is gone. A Mustacheless Bard. J. Gordon Coogler. OBAL
His Wife. Shirley Kaufman. LCAP
His Wife. Rachel, *tr. fr. Hebrew by* Sholom J. Kahn. WPOW
His Wife's Wedding Ring. George Crabbe. *See* Marriage Ring, A.
His wild heart beats with painful sobs. The Happy Warrior. Sir Herbert Read. MMA
His Will Be Done. Annie Johnson Flint. BLRP
His Winding-Sheet. Robert Herrick. CaPo; HBV-2; OBEV
His window is over the factory flume. Widow Brown's Christmas. John Townsend Trowbridge. BeLS
His Wisdom. Nicholas Breton. *Fr.* The Strange Fortunes of Two Excellent Princes. OBSC
(I Would Thou Wert Not Fair [or I Were Wise].) EIL; InvP
His Wish to God. Robert Herrick. AnAnS-2; OxBoCh
His words were magic and his heart was true. Uncle Ananias. E. A. Robinson. MoAmPo; NePA; NIP
His work is done, his toil is o'er. Faithful unto Death. Richard Handfield Titherington. PAH
His work well done, the leader stepped aside. First Citizen. James Jeffrey Roche. PGD
Hist?. . ./ Through the corridor's echoes. Clinical. W. E. Henley. In Hospital, XI. BrPo
Hist, but a word, fair and soft! Master Hugues of Saxe-Gotha. Robert Browning. OAEL-2
Hist Whist. E. E. Cummings. OFD; RHPC; SO
Historic Moment, An. William J. Harris. BOLo
Historic Time. Robert Eyres Landor. *Fr.* The Impious Feast. OBRV
Historical Incidents. Clarence Day. InMe
Historical Judas, The. Howard Nemerov. NoP
Historical Museum, Manitoulin Island. Lisel Mueller. PoA
Historical Poem, An. *Unknown.* APAS
Historical Reflections. John Hollander. DBV; NIP; OBAL
Historie of Squyer William Meldrum, The, *sel.* Sir David Lindsay.
Squire Meldrum at Carrickfergus. OxBS
History. G. K. Chesterton. *Fr.* Songs of Education. OBSV
History. Robert Fitzgerald. FYAP; MoVE
History. Robert Francis. LCAP
History. Jorie Graham. NPGG
History. Arthur Gregor. TAP
History. D. H. Lawrence. BrPo
History. James Liddy, *tr. fr. Irish.* CIP
History. Myra Cohn Livingston. RHPC
History. Robert Lowell. TAP
History. Gary Soto. GP
History. Paul Tanaquil. HBMV
History. Robert Penn Warren. NoAM
History, A. John Williams. NePoAm-2
History among the Rocks. Robert Penn Warren. *Fr.* Kentucky Mountain Farm. GOA; MoAmPo; MoVE
History and Abstraction. Thomas Lux. AmPA
History has to live with what was here. History. Robert Lowell. TAP
History Lesson. Mark Van Doren. NYBP
History Lesson for My Son. Ted Kooser. POL
History: Madness. Stan Rice. NPGG
History of a Literary Movement. Howard Nemerov. NePoEA; PP
History of Arizona, The: How It Was Made and Who Made It. Charles O. Brown. BPAW
History of blacklife is put down in the motions, The. The Sound of Afroamerican History Chapt I. S. E. Anderson. PoBA
History of Civilization, A. Albert Goldbarth. MAYP
History of Education. David McCord. NIP; OBAL; WhC
History of human-kind to trace, The. Thomas Hood. *Fr.* A Black Job VLP
History of Ideas. J. V. Cunningham. NIP
History of Insipids, The. John Freke. APAS
History of Lesbianism, A. Judy Grahn. PeHV
History of Love, A. William Carlos Williams. VGW
History of My Heart. Robert Pinsky. NPGG
History of Peace, A. Robert Graves. HBMV
History of Photography, A. Albert Goldbarth. MAYP
History of Prince Edward Island, The. Larry Gorman. ShS
History of the city, The. Always Modern Times. Bradford Stark. LTB
History of the Flood, The. John Heath-Stubbs. MoBS; OxBTC
History of the Modern World. Stanton A. Coblentz. PGD
History of the Pets, A. David Huddle. PPJ
History of the U.S., The. Winifred Sackville Stoner. TreF; YaD
History of the World as Pictures, The. Nancy Sullivan. CoPo
History of Truth, The. W. H. Auden. FaBoMo
History of World Languages. D. J. Enright. OxBC
History she (Zelda) said stops here. Inside History. Angela McCabe. AmPA
History, the angel, was stirred. Northern Ireland: Two Comments. Seamus Deane. CIP
History to the historian. History. Robert Francis. LCAP
Hit at the Times, A. A. O. McGrew. PoOW
Hit me! Jab me! Third Degree. Langston Hughes. BPo
Hit Tune. *Unknown.* TDH
Hit wes upon a Scere-thorsday that ure loverd aros. Judas. *Unknown.* ESPB; ViBoFo

Hitch Haiku. Gary Snyder. LCAP
Sels.
"After weeks of watching the roof leak." InPK
"Drinking hot saké." InPK
"Great freight truck, A." InPK
"Over the Mindanao Deep." InPK
"They didn't hire him." InPK
Hitch up my buggy, saddle up my black mare. I'm a Stranger Here. *Unknown.* OuSiCo
Hitchhiker, The. Ai. GeTw
Hitchhiker. Jack Marshall. NYBP
Hither, Strephon, Chloe, Phyllis. A Woodland Revel. Clarence Urmy. HBMV
Hither thou com'st: the busy [*or* busie] wind all night. The Bird [*or* To a Bird after a Storm]. Henry Vaughan. AnAnS-1; FM; LoBV; OBEV; PoEL-2; SeCV-1; TRV
Hither We Come, Our Dearest Lord, *with music.* Enoch W. Freeman. AH
Hither, where tangled thickets of the acacia. The Babiaantje. F. T. Prince. ChMP; MoBrPo
Hitherto and Henceforth. Annie Johnson Flint. BLRP
Hitherto Hath the Lord Helped. *Unknown.* BLRP
Hitherto the Lord hath helped us. Hitherto and Henceforth. Annie Johnson Flint. BLRP
Hitler, frothy-mouth, wooden-head. *Tr. fr. Maori by* Barry Mitcalfe. WTO
Hit's a mighty fur ways up de Far'well Lane. My Honey, My Love. Joel Chandler Harris. *Fr.* Uncle Remus and His Friends. AA; FaBoBe
Hitty Pitty within the wall. *Unknown.* OxNR
Hm Hm my Lord! Hm. Po' Mourner's Got a Home at Las'. *Unknown.* BoAN-2
Hmmmm, *sels.* Leslie Scalapino. NPGG
"As Rimbaud said, I thought today sitting in the library."
Epilogue: Anemone.
"Haven't I said that part of having intercourse."
"Having her under me," the man said, "in bed, and remembering."
"How can I help myself, as one woman said to me about wanting."
"How was I to know that the woman, seated next to me on the bus."
Seeing the Scenery.
"So I decided watching an old woman like her, who could rise so easily."
"We put our heads into the window of a car which was passing."
"Woman who had been dressed by someone, in the same way that, A."
Ho. Al Young. GP; NPGG
Ho, a song by the fire! Dartmouth Winter-Song. Richard Hovey. AA
Ho, all you cats in all the street. Cat's Meat. Harold Monro. OBMV
Ho, boys, ho! for California, O! The Banks of Sacramento. *Unknown.* AS
Ho! brother [*or* broder] Teague, dost hear the [*or* de] decree. Lilli Burlero [*or* Lilliburlero *or* A New Song]. Thomas, Lord Wharton. APAS; CoMu; FSW; OxBoLi; ViBoFo
Ho, Brother Teig. *Unknown.* GBP
Ho! burnish well, ye cunning hands. Song of the Mariner's Needle. C. R. Clarke. EtS
Ho! City of the gay! The Return of Napoleon from St. Helena. Lydia Huntley Sigourney. AA
Ho! Cupid calls, come Lovers, come. Cupids Call. James Shirley. ErPo
Ho, Everyone That Thirsteth. A. E. Housman. OAEL-2
Ho! for Pike's Peak, where gold is found. Song for the Pike's Peaker. "Syntax." PoOW
Ho, for taxis green or blue. Taxis. Rachel Field. FaPON; SoPo; TiPo
Ho! for the blades of Harden! The Blades of Harden. Will H. Ogilvie. *Fr.* Whaup o' the Reed. GoTS
Ho, for the Pirate Don Durk of Dowdee! The Pirate Don Durk of Dowdee. Mildred Plew Meigs. OnUR; PDV; SoPo; TiPo
Ho, giant! This is I! The Bean-Stalk. Edna St. Vincent Millay. WSC
Ho! he exclaim'd, King George of England standeth in judgement! The Absolvers. Robert Southey. *Fr.* A Vision of Judgement. EnRP
Ho! Ho! The fine fellow. Camden Magpie. Hugh McCrae. PoAu-1
Ho! Ho! Yes! Yes! It's very all well. Ballade of Soporific Absorption. J. C. Squire. InMe
"Ho!" laughs the Winter. March. Arthur Guiterman. YeAr
Ho, let her rip—with her royal clew a-quiver. In the Trades. C. Fox Smith. EtS
Ho, Moeris! whether on thy way so fast? Lycidas and Moeris. Virgil, *tr. by* Dryden. Eclogues, IX. AWP
Ho, my comrades, see the signal. Hold the Fort. Philip Paul Bliss. FSW
Ho! Persephone brings flowers, to them. The Old Men. Irving Feldman. MP; TwCP
Ho! pony. Down the lonely road. Army Correspondent's Last Ride. George Alfred Townsend. AA
Ho, pretty page, with the dimpled chin. The Age of Wisdom. Thackeray. *Fr.* Rebecca and Rowena. HBV-1; WhC
"Ho!" quod the knight, "Good sir, namore of this." The Nun's Priest's Prologue. Chaucer. *Fr.* The Canterbury Tales. OAEL-1
"Ho, Rose!" quoth the stout Miles Standish. The First Proclamation of Miles Standish. Margaret Junkin Preston. PAH; YaD
"Ho, sailor of the sea!" "How's My Boy?" Sidney Dobell. CH; EtS; GN; HBV-1; OHIP
Ho! See the fleet foot hosts of men. Roddy M'Corley. *Unknown.* FSW
"Ho, there! Fisherman, hold your hand!" The Second Mate. Fitz-James O'Brien. AA
Ho! Westward Ho! *with music.* Ossian E. Dodge. BLSo
"Ho! why dost thou shiver and shake." Gaffer Gray. Thomas Holcroft. HBV-2; NOEC
Ho, woodsmen of the mountain-side! A Cry to Arms. Henry Timrod. PAH
Ho! Ye Sun, Moon, Stars. *Unknown, tr. fr. Omaha Indian.* PrIm
Hoarded Grapes. *Unknown, tr. fr. Greek by* Louis Untermeyer. UnTE
Hoary mountains seem gray and old, The. At Timber Line. Frank H. Mayer. PoOW
Hob Gobbling's Song. James Russell Lowell. OBCA
Hob, shoe, hob; hob, shoe, hob. *Unknown.* OxNR
Hob upon a Holiday ("Hob yawned three times and rubbed his eyes"). *Unknown.* NOEC
Hobbes clearly proves that every creature. Critics. Swift. *Fr.* On Poetry; a Rhapsody. HAP; OBEC; PP; SCV; SeCePo
Hobbes, 1651. John Hollander. NoAM
Hobbit, The, *sel.* J. R. R. Tolkien.
"Far over the misty mountains cold." WSC
Hobie Noble. *Unknown.* ESPB; ViBoFo
Hobnelia seated in a dreary Vale. Thursday; or, The Spell. John Gay. *Fr.* The Shepherd's Week. PoEL-3
Hoboes in, The. Things of the Spirit. Mason Jordan Mason. PoNe
Hobo's Lullaby. Goebel Reeves. FSW
Hobson and His Men. Robert Loveman. PAH
Hobson-Jobson children were enamoured of the sciences, The. Ed and Sid and Bernard. Edward MacDuff. QQQ
Hobthrush, The. *Unknown.* GBP
Hoc Cygno Vinces. Henry Hawkins. ACP
Hoc Est Corpus. Alex Comfort. LiTB; LiTM
Hoccleve's Humorous Praise of His Lady. Thomas Hoccleve. OAEP
(Description of His Ugly Lady, A, *shorter vers.*) MeEL
Hoccleve's Lament for Chaucer and Gower. Thomas Hoccleve. *See* Lament for Chaucer and Gower.
Hock-Cart, or Harvest Home, The. Robert Herrick. AnAnS-2; CaPo; EBEV; JCP; OAEP; OBS; SeCP; SeCV-1
"Come sons of Summer, by whose toil," *sel.* ViBoPo
Hocus Pocus. Eat with Care. *Unknown.* FaBoUs
Hoddley, poddley, puddle and fogs. *Unknown.* FaBoNo; OxNR
Hoddy doddy. *Unknown.* OxNR
Hoelderlin's Old Age. Stephen Spender. NoAM
Hog at the Manger. Norma Farber. PChr
Hog butcher for the world. Chicago. Carl Sandburg. AmPP; AP; BiP; BLPL; CMoP; FaBV; HBMV; LiTM; MoAB; MoAmPo; MoVE; NePA; NoAM; NOBA; NoP; OxBA; PoA; PoPl; TAP; TreF; UnPo; VGW; ViBoPo; YaD
Hog-calling. Roy Blount, Jr. TDH
Hog-calling Competition. Morris Bishop. RHPC; TDH
Hog Drovers. *Unknown.* AmFP
Hog-Eye, *with music.* *Unknown.* AS
Hog-Eye Man, The, *with music.* *Unknown.* AS
Hog Meat. Daniel Webster Davis. BANP
Hog Rogues on the Harricane, *with music.* *Unknown.* OuSiCo
Hogamus, Higamus. *Unknown.* ELU
Hogarth. Charles Churchill. DBV
Hogger on his death-bed lay, A. The Dying Hogger. *Unknown.* AS
Hoggie dead, A! a hoggie dead! a hoggie dead! *Unknown.* PBBP
Hogwash. Robert Francis. LCAP
Hogyn. *Unknown.* GBP
Hohenlinden. Thomas Campbell. BeLS; CH; ChTr; EnRP; FaBoCh; FaBoRV; FaPoR; GN; GTBS; GTBS-P; HBV-2; NOBE; OBNC; OBRV; OBWP; OnMSP; RoGo; TreF; WaaP; WBLP; WHA
(Battle of Hohenlinden, The.) PaPo
Hoise up the sail, cried they who understand. A Sea-Voyage from Tenby to Bristol. Katherine Philips. SBG; WPE
Hoist up and I could lean over, A. The Bull Moses. Ted Hughes. NoP
Hokey, pokey, whisky, thum. *Unknown.* OxNR
Hokkaido. Jim Trifilio. FAZ
Hokku: In the Falling Snow. Richard Wright. IDB
Hokku Poems. Richard Wright. AmNP; PoBA
"In the falling snow," *sel.* IDB
Hokusai's Wave. Olga Cabral. PoDr
Hol' de Win' Don't Let It Blow, *with music.* *Unknown.* BoAN-2
"Hold." Patrick R. Chalmers. HBV-1
Hold a glass of pure water to the eye of the sun! "Hugh MacDiarmid." *Fr.* The Glass of Pure Water. BSV

Hold! are you mad? you damn'd, confounded dog! Epilogue to "Tyrannick Love." Dryden. OAEP; SeCV-2; ViBoPo
Hold Back Thy Hours. Beaumont *and* Fletcher. *See* Bridal Song ("Hold back thy hours").
Hold fast to dreams. Dreams. Langston Hughes. RHPC
Hold Fast Your Dreams. Louise Driscoll. BLPA; FaBoBe; FaPON; FPL; HBMV; SoPo; TiPo
Hold, furious youth—better thy heat assuage. The Best Time for Conception. Claude Quillet, *tr. by* George Sewell. *Fr.* Callipaedia; or, The Art of Getting Beautiful Children. FaBoUs
Hold hard, Ned! Lift me down once more, and lay me in the shade. The Sick Stockrider. Adam Lindsay Gordon. CBAP; OBVV; PoAu-1
Hold her softly, not for long. At a Child's Baptism. Vassar Miller. GoJo
Hold, hold it tight. Song for a Girl on Her First Menstruation. *Tr. fr. Papuan by* Joe Prentuo. BoWoP
Hold it up sternly—see this it sends back, (who is it? is it you?). A Hand-Mirror. Walt Whitman. OxBA; TW
Hold My Hand. Edmund Pennant. PoDr
Hold my rooster, hold my hen. Precious Things. *Unknown.* TTY
Hold On. *Unknown.* FSW
(Mary Wore Three Links of Chain.) AS, *with music*
Hold out yo' light you heav'n boun' soldier. Heav'n Boun' Soldier. *Unknown.* BoAN-1
Hold suffering on a tight leash. Desert. Agnes Gergely, *tr. by* Emery George. VWA
Hold the Fort. Philip Paul Bliss. FSW
Hold the Fort. *Unknown.* FSW
Hold the Wind. *Unknown.* GBP
Hold up your head. *Unknown.* OxNR
"Hold your hand, Lord Judge," she says. The Maid Freed from the Gallows. *Unknown.* ESPB
Holding a beggar's child. Meditation. Toyohiko Kagawa. TRV
Holding black whips. Thoughts of Chairman Mao. David Young. AmPA
Holding Hands. Lenore M. Link. FaPON; MoShBr; NTCP; RHPC; SoPo
Holding its huge life open to the sky. To My Friends. Stephen Berg. NaP; NYBP
Holding On. Richard Jackson. AMV-80
Holding our knives. The Wharf, May 1978. Carolyn Foster Segal. WOLT
Holding the distance up before his face. The Traveller. W. H. Auden. SyP
Holding the Mirror Up to Nature. Howard Nemerov. PoA
Holding the naked body I had bought. A Bought Embrace. G. S. Fraser. WaP
Holding the Sky. William Stafford. RFM
Hole in the Floor, A. Richard Wilbur. NoAM; NOBA; SoSe
Hole in the head where the bullet, The. On a Very Young, Very Dead Soldier. Richard Gillman. NePoAm
Hole in the right front pocket, A. The Challenge. Calvin Murry. LFAC
Hole in the Sea, The. Marvin Bell. NYBP
Holes, The. Stephen Berg. NaP; NYBP
Holes in my arms. For Real. Jayne Cortez. PoBA
Holes in the floor of the barn loft, The. Hay Scuttle. Robert Morgan. MAYP
Holes in the Sky, *sel.* Louis MacNeice.
"And man is a spirit." TRV
Holiday. John Davidson. OBVV
Holiday. Horace, *tr. fr. Latin by* Louis Untermeyer. Odes, III, 28. AWP
Holiday. Henry Dawson Lowry. OBVV
Holiday, A. Lizette Woodworth Reese. AA
Holiday at Hampton Court. John Davidson. EBVV
Holiday in Reality. Wallace Stevens. NePA; OxBA
Holiday Inn at Bemidji. Gerald Vizenor. STE
Holiday Task, A. Gilbert Abbot à Beckett. NA
Holidays. Eva Mylonas, *tr. fr. Modern Greek by* Kimon Friar. BoWoP
Holiness[e] on the head. Aaron. George Herbert. MeLP; MePo; OAEL-1; OAEP; OBS
Holland, that scarce deserves the name of land. The Character of Holland. Andrew Marvell. ChTr; NOBL; OBSV
Hollandaise. Sharon Bryan. MAYP
Hollin, Green Hollin. *Unknown.* GBP
Holloe Menn, The. Harrison Everard. BXAP
Hollow eyes of shock remain, The. Two Years Later. John Wieners. CoPo; PoM
Hollow-feeling, empty of sleep and as yet unbreakfasted. Morning. Harry Fainlight. POL
Hollow Flute, The. Avner Strauss. VWA
Hollow Land, The, *sel.* William Morris.
"Christ keep the Hollow Land." ChTr
(Song.) NBM; PoEL-5
Hollow Men, The. T. S. Eliot. AP; BiP; CoBMV; InPS; LiTA; LiTM; MoAB; MoAmPo; OAEL-2; OBMV; PoPl; TwAmPo
Hollow reed against his lips, A. The Reed-Player. Archibald MacLeish. HBMV
Hollow Thesaurus, The. Roger McDonald. CBAP
Hollow Tree, A. Robert Bly. GP; NNaP
Hollow winds begin to blow, The. Signs of Rain. Edward Jenner. BLPA; BoNaP; FaBoUs
Holly, The. Walter de la Mare. CMoP
Holly, The. Henry VIII, King of England. *See* As the Holly Groweth Green.
Holly against Ivy. *Unknown. See* Holly Beareth Berries.
Holly and Ivy ("Holly standeth [*or* Holy stond] in the hall"). *Unknown.* MeEL
(Holly and His Merry Men.) OxBM
(Nay, Ivy, Nay.) CH
Holly and Ivy ("Holver and Hivy [*or* Holly and Ivy] made a gret [*or* great] party"). *Unknown.* OxBM
(Carol in Praise of the Holly and Ivy.) OHIP
Holly and Mistletoe. Eleanor Farjeon. PChr
Holly and the Ivy, The ("The holly and the ivy,/ When they are both full grown"). *Unknown.* CH; ChTr; ELP; FSW; GBP; OBET; OFD; OxBoCh; PChr
Holly Beareth Berries, *abr. Unknown.* PBBP
(Holly against Ivy: "Holy bereth beries.") MeEL
Holly Bough, The. Charles MacKay. OBVV
Holly Tree, The. Robert Southey. EnRP; HBV-1
Hollyhock, A. Frank Dempster Sherman. AA
Hollyhocks, The. Craven Langstroth Betts. AA
Hollyhocks are ten feet tall, The. Wet Summer. May Williams Ward. GoYe
Holly's up, the house is all bright, The. The Christmas Tree. Peter Cornelius. PChr
Hollywood. Don Blanding. YaD
Hollywood. Karl Shapiro. LiTM; OxBA
Hollywood. . .Hollywood. . .sh/ Fabulous Follywood. Hollywood. Don Blanding. YaD
Hollywood Park Race Track is thirty miles. Please. Ronald Koertge. GP
Holmes. James Russell Lowell. *Fr.* A Fable for Critics. NOBA
Holocaust 1944. Anne Ranasinghe. VWA
Holstein cows parked. Black and White. Tom Schmidt. NeAC
Holstenwall. Sidney Keyes. FaBoTw
Holver and Hivy made a gret party. Holly and Ivy. *Unknown.* OxBM
Holy angels and blest. A Christmas Cradlesong. Lope de Vega, *tr. by* George Ticknor. PoPl
Holy angels, in envy I cast no sigh. Gaspara Stampa, *tr. fr. Italian by* J. Vitiello. BoWoP
Holy Baptism[e]. George Herbert. HBV-2; PoEL-2
(H. Baptisme.) SeCV-1
Holy bereth beris. Holly against Ivy. *Unknown.* MeEL
Holy Bible, Book Divine. John Burton. BLRP; WBLP
Holy boy, The. Children of Love. Harold Monro. MoBrPo
Holy City, The. Frederic Edward Weatherly. BLRP; WBLP
Holy Communion, The. Henry Vaughan. AnAnS-1
Holy Cross. *Unknown. See* Steadfast Cross.
Holy-Cross Day. Robert Browning. VLP
Holy Fair, The. Burns. EnRP; LAuP; OAEP; OBSV
Holy Family. Muriel Rukeyser. MoAmPo
Holy Father, Great Creator, *with music.* Alexander V. Griswold. AH
Holy Field, The. Henry Hart Milman. OxBoCh
Holy Ghost, *with music. Unknown.* OuSiCo
Holy God, We Praise Thy Name. Clarence Walworth. AH, *with music;* TreFT
Holy Grail, The, *sel.* Jack Spicer.
Book of Gawain, The. PoM
Holy Hill, A. "Æ." AWP
Holy, Holy, Holy. Reginald Heber. HBV-2; OHIP; TreFT; VLP
(Thrice Holy.) WGRP
Holy! Holy! Holy! Holy! Holy! Holy! Footnote to Howl. Allen Ginsberg. CAPP
Holy Innocents, The. Robert Lowell. ConAP; InvP; MoAB; MoAmPo; NePoEA; OBCP; OxBC; SBVL
Holy Innocents. Christina Rossetti. HBV-1; HBVY
Holy Jesus, Thou art born. Dedication. Victoria Saffelle Johnson. GoBC; TrPWD
Holy Land of Walsingham, The. Benjamin Francis Musser. ISi
Holy Land of Walsinghame, The. *Unknown, sometimes at. to* Sir Walter Ralegh. *See* As You Came from the Holy Land.
Holy Light. Milton. *See* Hail, Holy Light.
Holy Longing, The. Goethe, *tr. fr. German by* Robert Bly. NU
Holy Man, The. *Unknown, tr. fr. Old Irish by* Whitley Stokes *and* John Strachan. *Fr.* The Devil's Tribute to Moling. OnYI
Holy man, ungird your gabardeen. Rest. Roots. Seymour Mayne. NOBC
Holy Matrimony. John Keble. HBV-1; VLP
(Epithalamium.) NOCV
Holy men. Freethinkers Deborah Eibel. VWA

Holy monks, concealed from men, The. St. Philip in Himself. Cardinal Newman. GoBC
Holy Nativity of Our Lord God, The. Richard Crashaw. *See* In the Holy Nativity of Our Lord God.
Holy Night. Nathaniel A. Benson. CaP
Holy Night. Lucille Clifton. GeTw
Holy Nunnery, The. *Unknown.* BaBo; ESPB
Holy of England! since my light is short. On First Entering Westminster Abbey. Louise Imogen Guiney. AA
Holy of Holies, The. G. K. Chesterton. TRV; WGRP
Holy Office, The. James Joyce. FaBoTw; NoAM; OxBTC
Holy Ones, the Young Ones, The. Chayyim Zeldis. TrJP
Holy Order. J. B. Boothroyd. FiBHP
Holy Poems (I-III). George Barker. MoPo
Holy Poet, I have heard. John Hall Wheelock. *Fr.* Thanks from Earth to Heaven. TrPWD
Holy-Rood come forth and shield. The Old Wives Prayer. Robert Herrick. SeCV-1
Holy Rose, The. Vyacheslav Ivanov, *tr. fr. Russian by* Babette Deutsch *and* Avrahm Yarmolinsky. AWP
Holy Satyr. Hilda Doolittle ("H. D."). MoAmPo
Holy Scripture, Writ Divine. From a London Bookshop. *Unknown.* FaBoUs
Holy Sonnets. John Donne. AnAnS-1; MasP
Sels.
"As due by many titles I resign[e]," II. JCP; MePo; OBS
"At the round earths imagined corners, blow," VII. AnAnS-1; BLPL; CABA; EaLo; EBEV; EnRePo; FaBoEn; FaBoRV; HAP; HeIP; InPS; JCP; LiTB; LoBV; MasP; MeLP; MePo; NOBE; NoP; OAEL-1; OAEP; OBS; OxBoCh; PAI; PoEL-2; PoPle; PPoe; PPP; QFR; SeCeV; SeCP; SeCV-1; TEP; TreFT; ViBoPo
(Blow Your Trumpets.) ChTr
(Teach Me How to Repent.) EBCP
"Batter my heart, three person'd God; for you," XIV. BiP; BLPL; CABA; EaLo; EBEV; EnRePo; FaFP; FF; GoBC; HAP; HeIP; HoPM; ILWL; InPK; InPS; JCP; LiTB; MeLP; MePo; NIP; NOBE; NoP; OAEL-1; OAEP; OBS; OxBoCh; PAI; PoEL-2; PPoe; PPP; PrIm; SeCePo; SeCeV; SeCP; SeCV-1; SoSe; TEP; TrCP; TreFT; TrGrPo; TrPWD
"Death be not proud, though some have called thee," X. BiP; CABA; ChTr; DL; EIL; EnRePo; FaBoEn; FaBoRV; FaBV; FaFP; FF; FPL; GoBC; HAP; HBV-2; HeIP; InvP; JCP; LiTB; LoBV; MeLP; MePo; NIP; NOBE; NoP; OAEL-1; OAEP; OBS; PAI; PoEL-2; PoRA; PPoe; PPP; PrIm; SCV; SeCeV; SeCP; SeCV-1; TEP; TrCP; TreFS; TrGrPo; TRV; ViBoPo; WeW; WHA
(Death.) OBEV; PPON
(On Death.) EBCP
"Father, part of his double interest," XVI. JCP; OBS
"I am a little world made cunningly," V. CABA; EnRePo; NIP; NoP; OBS; OxBoCh; SeCP; TEP
"If faithful soules be alike glorifi'd," VIII. OBS
"If poisonous [*or* poysonous] mineral[l]s, and if that tree," IX. BiP; CABA; EBEV; EnRePo; JCP; LiTB; MePo; NoP; OAEL-1; OBS; PoEL-2; PPP; SeCP; UnPo
(Forget.) WHA
"O might those sigh[e]s and tear[e]s returne againe," III. BiP; OBS
"Oh my black[e] soule! now thou art summoned," IV. EBEV; JCP; OAEL-1; OBS; TEP
"Oh, to vex me, contraries [*or* contraryes] meet in one," XIX. OAEL-1; PoEL-2
(Devout Fits.) SeCePo
"Show me dear[e] Christ, thy spouse, so bright and clear," XVIII. MeLP; NoP; OAEP; OBS
"Since she whom I lov'd hath paid [*or* payd] her last debt," XVII. JCP; MePo; OAEP
"Spit in my face you Jew[e]s, and pierce my side," IX. JCP; OBS; OxBoCh
"This is my play's [*or* playes] last scene, here heavens appoint," VI. EBEV; JCP; LoBV; MeLP; MePO; NIP; OAEP; OBS; OxBoCh; PAI; SeCP; TEP
"Thou hast made me, and shall thy work[e] decay?" I. EBEV; EnRePo; FaBoEn; MasP; MeLP; NOBE; NOCV; NoP; OAEP; OBS; OxBoCh; PoEL-2; SeCP; TEP
(Sonnet.) AnAnS-1; FaBoEn
"What if this present were the world's last night?" XIII. EBEV; HeIP; InPS; JCP; LiTB; MeLP; NOCV; OAEP; OBS; SeCeV; TEP
"Why are we[e] by all creatures waited on?" XII. CABA; JCP; NOCV; OBS; PoEL-2; TrCP
"Wilt thou love God, as he thee! then digest," XV. JCP; OBS; TrCP
Holy Spirit, Faithful Guide, *with music.* Marcus Morris Wells. AH
Holy Spirit, Lead Me. *Unknown.* STF
Holy Spirit, Lord of light. Hymn to the Holy Spirit. Stephen Langton. TrCP
Holy Spirit, Truth Divine, *with music.* Samuel Longfellow. AH
Holy Spring. Dylan Thomas. WaP
Holy stillness, beautiful and deep, A. A Summer Noon at Sea. Epes Sargent. EtS
Holy stond in the hall. Holly and Ivy. *Unknown.* MeEL
"Holy Supper is kept, indeed, The." James Russell Lowell. *Fr.* The Vision of Sir Launfal. TRV
Holy Thursday ("Is this a holy thing to see"). Blake. *Fr.* Songs of Experience. EnRP; FF; InPS; LAuP; NoEC: NoP; OAEL-2; OAEP; TEP
Holy Thursday (" 'Twas on a Holy Thursday"). Blake. *Fr.* Songs of Innocence. CH; EnRP; HBV-1; InPS; LAuP; NOBE; NOEC; NoP; OAEL-2; OAEP; OBEC; OFD; SCV; TEP; TrCP
Holy Thursday. Charles Wright. GeTw
Holy Tide, The. Frederick Tennyson. OBEV; OBVV
Holy Transportations, *sel.* Charles Fitz-Geffry.
Take Frankincense, O God. ChTr
Holy virtue of living, the soul's delight, The. A Hymn of Form. Gordon Bottomley. BrPo
Holy Was Demeter Walking th' Corn Furrow. Edward Sanders. PoM
Holy water come and bring. The Spell. Robert Herrick. CaPo; WSC
Holy Well, The. *Unknown.* BaBo; FaBoCh; GBP; NOCV; OBET; OxBoCh
Holy Willie's Prayer. Burns. BSV; EBEV; EnRP; GoTS; InPS; LAuP; NOEC; NoP; OAEL-1; OBSV; OxBoLi; OxBS; PoEL-4; PPP; TW; ViBoPo
Holyday. Emily Brontë. *See* Little While, Little While, A.
Holyhead, Sept. 25th, 1727. Swift. BIrV
Homage. Gilbert Highet. *See* Homage to Ezra Pound.
Homage. Gustave Kahn, *tr. fr. French by* Jethro Bithell. TrJP
Homage. R. J. Schoeck. GoYe
Homage and Lament for Ezra Pound in Captivity. Robert Duncan. NOBA
Homage of War. Bruce Williamson. NeIP
Homage to a Government. Philip Larkin. EBEV
Homage to Arthur Waley. Weldon Kees. NaP
Homage to Carracci. Tom Disch. PoA
Homage to Chagall. Duane Niatum. CDW
Homage to change that scatters the poppy seed. Rondeau. Ronald Bottrall. MoVE
Homage to David Smith. John Haines. LCAP
Homage to Diana. Sir Walter Ralegh. *See* Diana.
Homage to Edward Hopper. Emery George. HoAn
Homage to Elvis, Homage to the Fathers. Bruce Weigl. MAYP
Homage to Ezra Pound. Gilbert Highet. Par
(Homage.) BXAP
Homage to Ghosts. Jean Garrigue. TwAmPo
Homage to Hart Crane. Peter Balakian. MAYP
Homage to Hieronymus Bosch. Thomas MacGreevy. BIrV; EAS; OnYI
Homage to Jack Yeats. Thomas MacGreevy. OBMV
Homage to Marcel Proust. Thomas MacGreevy. CIP
Homage to Marian Pyszko. Richard Snyder. SOTS
Homage to Mistress Bradstreet. John Berryman. TwAmPo
Sels.
"Governor your husband lived so long, The." MoVE; NoAM; NOBA
"I trundle the bodies, on the iron bars." NOBA
"O all your ages at the mercy of my loves." NOBA
"So squeezed, wince you I scream? I love you & hate." FF
"When by me in the dusk my child sits down." CrMA
"Winters close, Springs open, no child stirs, The." NAs; NoAM
Homage to Our Leaders. Julian Symons. NeBP
Homage to Paul Mellon, I. M. Pei, Their Gallery, and Washington City. William Meredith. EyDe
Homage to René Magritte. George Melly. EAS
Homage to Robert Bresson. Jon Anderson. MAYP
Homage to Sextus Propertius, *sels.* Ezra Pound.
"Me happy, night, night full of brightness." ErPo; InvP; VGW
"Now if ever it is time to cleanse Helicon." CrMA; VGW
"Shades of Callimachus, Coan ghosts of Philetas." CMoP; HAP; MoAB; MoVE; NoAM; NOBA; OBVE; OxBA; PP
"When, when, and whenever death closes our eyelids." MoAB; NoAM; OBMV; PoA
"Who, who will be the next man to entrust his girl to a friend?" FaBoMo; NoAM
Homage to Texas. Robert Graves. LiTB
Homage to the British Museum. William Empson. CMoP; FaBoMo; LiTM; MoAB; MoBrPo
Homage to the Empress of the Blues. Robert Hayden. CABA; CNA; LCAP; PoBA; PoNe
Homage to the New World. Michael Harper. LCAP
Homage to the Philosopher. Babette Deutsch. ImOP; TrJP
Homage to the Weather. Michael Hamburger. NMP
Homage to thee, O Ra, at thy tremendous rising! The Dead Man Ariseth

and Singeth a Hymn to the Sun. *Unknown, tr. by* Robert Hillyer. *Fr.* Book of the Dead. AWP
Homage to Theodore Dreiser on the Centennial of His Birth, *sel.* Robert Penn Warren.
"Who is the ugly one slump-slopping down the street?" GP
Homage to William Cowper. Donald Davie. NePoEA
Homage to Wren. Louis MacNeice. EyDe
Home, The. Susan Axelrod. NMM
Home. Joseph Beaumont. *See* House and Home.
Home. Robert V. Carr. BPAW
Home. Stephen Chalmers. HBMV
Home. Sam Cornish. CNA
Home. Robert Frost. *Fr.* The Death of the Hired Man. TRV
(Home Defined.) TreF
Home. W. W. Gibson. HBMV
Home. J. H. Goring. MoShBr
Home. Dora Greenwell. HBV-1
Home. Edgar A. Guest. BLPA; BLPL; FaBoBe; NIP; OBAL; OHFP; TreF; YaD
Home. Verner von Heidenstam, *tr. fr. Swedish by* Charles Wharton Stork. PoPl
Home. W. E. Henley. GN; HBV-2; PoLF
(Falmouth.) MoBrPo; MOS
Home. Steve Kowit. AMV-81
Home. Martha Snell Nicholson. STF
Home. Edward Rowland Sill. HBV-2
Home. Hollis Summers. SOTS
Home, The. Rabindranath Tagore. GoJo
Home. *Unknown.* HBV-2
Home. Henry van Dyke. STF
Home. *Zulu Oral Tradition, tr. by* H. Tracey. WTO
Home/ oh/ home. Africa. Lucille Clifton. CNA
Home/ where my/ ground. Home. Sam Cornish. CNA
Home after Three Months Away. Robert Lowell. NoP
Home Again. Susan Petrykewycz. AMV-81
Home again? Spendthrift. I. A. Richards. PoPl
Home Alone These Last Hours of the Afternoon, Dusk Now, the Sabbath Setting In, I Sit Back, and These Words Start Welling Up in Me. Stephen Levy. VWA
Home at Grasmere. Wordsworth. *See* Recluse, The.
Home at Last. G. K. Chesterton. TRV; WGRP
Home! at the word, what blissful visions rise. Home, Sweet Home, with Variations. H. C. Bunner. CenHV; InMe; OBAL
Home-bound ship stood out to sea, The. The Mystery of Cro-a-tàn. Margaret Junkin Preston. PAH
Home, Boys, Home. *Unknown.* FSW
Home Burial. Robert Frost. AP; CoBMV; PrIm; TAP; TwAmPo
Home came our goodman [*or* the old man]. Our Goodman. *Unknown.* UnTE; ViBoFo
Home comes a lad with the bonnie hair. The Pipes o' Gordon's Men. J. Scott Glasgow. HBV-2
Home Cooking Cafe. Greg Field. FAZ; PPJ
Home, Dearie, Home, *with music. Unknown.* AmSS
Home Defined. Robert Frost. *See* Home.
Home Fire, The. Orrick Johns. HBMV
Home for Thanksgiving. W. S. Merwin. NoAM
Home from Guatemala, back at the Waldorf. Arrival at the Waldorf. Wallace Stevens. NYP; PP
Home from his morning task the swain retreats. Summer. James Thomson. *Fr.* The Seasons. FM
Home from the observatory. Stella. Charles Henry Crandall. AA
Home Front, The. Marvin Bell. GP
Home, home the horizon far and clear. At Night [*or* To W. M.]. Alice Meynell. CH; GoBC; HBV-1; OBVV
Home, home—where's my baby's home? Anne Hutchinson's Exile. Edward Everett Hale. PAH
Home in Indianapolis. Richard Pflum. AMV-80
Home in That Rock. *Unknown.* FSW
Home is more than just four walls. Hearth and Home. Stoddard King. OBAL
Home is mysterious: a place to die, a place to breed. Destinations. Josephine Jacobsen. WPE
Home Is So Sad. Philip Larkin. NoP
Home is the place where, when you have to go there. Home [*or* Home Defined]. Robert Frost. *Fr.* The Death of the Hired Man. TreF; TRV
Home Is the Sailor. Phyllis McGinley. DBV
Home Is Where There Is One to Love Us. Charles Swain. BLPA; BLPL; FaBoBe
Home Leave. Barbara Howes. MP; TwCP
Home Movies. Carter Revard. VoR
Home No More Home to Me. Robert Louis Stevenson. CH
Home of Aphrodite, The. Euripides, *tr. fr. Greek by* Gilbert Murray. *Fr.* Bacchae. AWP
Home of the Naiads, The. John Armstrong. *Fr.* The Art of Preserving Health, II. OBEC
Home of the Percys' high-born race. Alnwick Castle. Fitz-Greene Halleck. AA
Home of the Soul. Ellen H. Gates. BLRP
Home on the Range, A. *Unknown.* BLSo, *with music;* BPAW; CoSo (A *and* B vers., *with music*); FaBoBe; FSW; TreFS
(Oh, Give Me a Home Where the Buffalo Roam.) FeFP
Home on the Range, February 1962. Edward Dorn. ConAP
Home Place, The. Robert Currie. PPJ
Home Prayer, A. *Unknown, at. to* Cecily Halleck. *See* Lord of All Pots and Pans and Things.
Home Revisited: Midnight. John Ciardi. NYBP
Home should have a wife, a cat, A. The Curtain Poem. Edwin Brock. NMP
Home Song. Longfellow. GN
(Song: "Stay, stay at home, my heart, and rest.") HBV-2
Home, Sweet Home. John Howard Payne. *Fr.* Clari, the Maid of Milan. AA; BLPA; BLSo, *with music;* FaBoBe; FaFP; FSW; HBV-2; PaPo; PSoN, *with music;* TreF; WBLP
Home, Sweet Home ("We were lying on a prairie on Slaughter's ranch one night"). *Unknown.* CoSo
Home, Sweet Home, with Variations, *parody.* H. C. Bunner. BXAP; CenHV; InMe; OBAL
Home they brought her sailor son. The Recognition. Frederick William Sawyer. HBV-1
Home They Brought Her Warrior Dead. Tennyson. *Fr.* The Princess. HBV-1; TreFS; TrGrPo
(Song: "Home they brought her warrior dead."). OAEP
H(ome), thou returnest from Thames, whose Naiads long. *See* H——, thou return'st from Thames, whose Naiads long.
Home Thoughts. Odell Shepard. HBMV
Home Thoughts from Abroad. Robert Browning. AWP; BoNaP; EBVV; FaBoBe; FaBoEn; FaBV; FaFP; FaPON; FaPoR; FiP; FPL; HBV-1; HBVY; HeIP; LiTB; NOBE; NoP; OAEP; OBEV; OBNC; OBVV; PoLF; PoRA; PrIm; SeCeV; TEP; TreF; TrGrPo; WHA
(April in England.) GN
Home Thoughts from Abroad, *parody. Unknown.* Par
Home-Thoughts from France. Isaac Rosenberg. MMA
Home Thoughts, from the Sea. Robert Browning. AWP; EBVV; FaBoCh; FiP; MOS; NOBE; OAEP; OBAL; OBEV; OBVV
Home Thoughts in Laventie. Edward Wyndham Tennant. HBMV
Home Winner, The. Gene Lindberg. PoOW
Home without a Bible, A, *abr.* Charles D. Meigs. WBLP
Home! You're Where It's Warm Inside. Jack Prelutsky. RHPC
Home-coming. Léonie Adams. HBMV; MoAmPo
Homecoming. Bruce Dawe. CBAP
Home-Coming. Albert Ehrenstein, *tr. fr. German by* Babette Deutsch *and* Avram Yarmolinsky. TrJP
Homecoming. Stefan George, *tr. fr. German by* Peter Viereck. AMV-8
Home-coming. Isobel Hume. HBMV
Homecoming. Anna Margolin, *tr. fr. Yiddish by* Keith Bosley. VWA
Homecoming. Sonia Sanchez. PoBA
Homecoming. Karl Shapiro. MiAP
Homecoming. Wislawa Szymborska, *tr. fr. Polish by* Benjamin Sher. AMV-81
Homecoming. John Thompson. MAT
Homecoming. *Unknown.* AnIV
Homecoming. Peter Viereck. CoAP
Homecoming. Theodore Weiss. TwAmPo
Homecoming Blues. Vassar Miller. GP
Homecoming Celebration. Rosemary Catacalos. AMV-80
Homecoming in Storm. Bernice L. Kenyon. EtS
Homecoming—Massachusetts. John Ciardi. NYBP
Homecoming of Emma Lazarus, The. Galway Kinnell. NaP
Homecoming of the Sheep, The. Francis Ledwidge. HBMV
Homecoming Singer, The. Jay Wright. PoBA
Homeland, The. Hugh Reginald Haweis. BLRP
Homeless, The. Joan Joffe Hall. AMV-81
Homeless!/ The Living Bread. Despised and Rejected. Katharine Lee Bates. TrCP
Homeless Blues. *Unknown.* BluL
Homely Meats. John Davies of Hereford. *See* Author Loving These Homely Meats, The.
Homeowners unite. The Firebombing. James Dickey. CAPP; OBWP
Homer. Albert Ehrenstein, *tr. fr. German by* Babette Deutsch *and* Avram Yarmolinsky. TrJP
Homer was a vinous Greek who loved the flowing bottle. Chantey of Notorious Bibbers. Henry Morton Robinson. InMe

Homer was poor. His scholars live at ease. Epigram. J. V. Cunningham. VGW
Homeric Hymns, *sels.* *Unknown, tr. fr. Greek.*
Homeric Hymn to Neptune, *tr. by* George Chapman. EtS
Hymn to Athena, *tr. by* Shelley. AWP
Hymn to Castor and Pollux, *tr. by* Shelley. AWP
Hymn to Earth the Mother of All, *tr. by* Shelley. AWP
Hymn to Mercury, *abr., tr. by* Shelley. OBVE
Hymn to Selene, *tr. by* Shelley. AWP
Homeric Unity. Andrew Lang. HBV-2
Homes, The. Anne Pitkin. AMV-80
Home's not merely four square walls. Home Is Where There Is One to Love Us. Charles Swain. BLPA; BLPL; FaBoBe
Homes of England, The. Felicia Dorothea Hemans. FaPoR; PaPo; SBG; WPE
Homes of the Cliff Dwellers. Stanley Wood. PoOW
Homes where children live exude a pleasant rumpledness. Where Children Live. Naomi Shihab Nye. MAYP
Homesick. Else Lasker-Schüler, *tr. fr. German by* Michael Hamburger. PBWP
(Homesickness, *tr. by* Joachim Neugroschel.) VWA
Homesick? and yet your country walks. To Henry Vaughan. A. J. M. Smith. OBCV
Homesick Blues. Langston Hughes. CDC; MoAmPo; PoPl
Homesick Song. William Haskel Simpson. BPAW
Home-Sickness. Charlotte Brontë. GLGT
Home-Sickness. Justinus Kerner, *tr. fr. German by* James Clarence Mangan. AWP
Home-Sickness. Hedwig Lachmann, *tr. fr. German by* Jethro Bithell. TrJP
Homesickness. Else Lasker-Schüler. *See* Homesick.
Homestead—Winter Morning. Mary Ballard Duryee. GoYe
Hometown. Luis Cabalquinto. BrSi
Hometown Piece for Messrs. Alston and Reese. Marianne Moore. OBAL
Homeward Bound, The. Bill Adams. EtS
Homeward Bound. William Allingham. FaBoBe; HBV-1; HBVY
Homeward Bound, *sels.* Heine, *tr. fr. German.*
And When I Lamented, *tr. by* Emma Lazarus. TrJP
Dearest Friend, Thou Art in Love, *tr. by* Emma Lazarus. TrJP
Du bist wie eine Blume, *tr. by* Kate Freiligrath Kroeker. AWP
I, a Most Wretched Atlas, *tr. by* Emma Lazarus. TrJP
Mortal, Sneer Not at the Devil, *tr. by* Emma Lazarus. TrJP
Thou Hast Diamonds, *tr. by* Emma Lazarus. TrJP
"Thou seemest like a flower," *tr. by* Emma Lazarus. TrJP
Homeward Bound. D. H. Rogers. EtS
Homeward Bound. Robert Southey. *See* She Comes Majestic with Her Swelling Sails.
Homeward Bound. L. Frank Tooker. EtS
Homeward Bound. *Unknown.* AmSS, *with music;* ShS, 3 *vers., with music*
Homeward Bound. George Edward Woodberry. Wild Eden, XXV. AA
Homeward bound and ready for sea. Canso Strait. *Unknown.* ShS
Homeward Journey, The. L. Aaronson. TrJP
Homework. Russell Hoban. RHPC
Homework. Jane Yolen. RHPC
Homework for Annabelle. Phyllis McGinley. GLGT
Homework sits on top of Sunday, squashing Sunday flat. Homework. Russell Hoban. RHPC
Homing. Arna Bontemps. CDC
Homing. P. C. Bowman. AMV-81
Homing, The. John Jerome Rooney. AA
Homing. Reg Saner. NPAW
Homing Heart, The. Daniel Henderson. HBMV
Homing Pigeons. Ted Walker. NYBP
Hominization. Miroslav Holub, *tr. fr. Czech by* David Young *and* Dana Háová. SUW
Homo Factus Est. Digby Mackworth Dolben. *See* Come to Me, Beloved.
Homo Sapiens. Earl of Rochester. *Fr.* A Satire against Mankind. NOBE
Homosexual Sonnets. Kenneth Pitchford. GP
Homosexuality. Frank O'Hara. NYP; PeHV; PoA; TAP
Homunculus et la Belle Étoile. Wallace Stevens. MoAB; MoAmPo
Honeeeeeeeey, I'm all out and down. All Out and Down. *Unknown.* BluL
Honest Abe Lincoln. Max Shulman. OBAL
Honest Fame. Pope. *Fr.* The Temple of Fame. OBEC
Honest Man, An. Pope. Essay on Man, 2 *ll. fr.* Epistle IV. TreF
Honest regular work Dick Daring gave up. A Shining Night; or, Dick Daring, the Poacher. *Unknown.* CoMu
Honest Stradivari made me. The Violin's Complaint. William Roscoe Thayer. AA
Honest Whore, The, *sel.* Thomas Dekker.
"Patience, my lord! why, 'tis the soul of peace." ViBoPo
Honest, Wouldn't You? *Unknown.* WBLP
Honestly I wish I were dead! Sappho, *tr. fr. Greek by* Willis Barnstone. BoWoP
Honesty. Horatius Bonar. *See* Be True.
Honesty. Sir Thomas Wyatt. *See* Throughout the World.
Honesty at a Fire. J. C. Squire. FiBHP
Honesty, little slut, must you insist. To the Contemporary Muse. Edgar Bowers. ELU
Honey/ When de man. Sister Lou. Sterling A. Brown. AmNP; PoBA; PoNe
Honey and Sherry and little Bashaw. Golden Grain. Helen M. Wright. PH
Honey and water. Medieval Christ Speaks on a Spanish Sculpture of Himself. Rochelle Owens. CoPo
Honey Bee, The. Don Marquis. BoAnP; FPL; PoPl; WhC
Honey Bee. Lucy Fitch Perkins. SUS
Honey bee is sad and cross, The. The Honey Bee. Don Marquis. BoAnP; FPL; PoPl; WhC
Honey Dripping from the Comb. James Whitcomb Riley. AA
Honey-flowers to the honey-comb. Chimes. Dante Gabriel Rossetti. OBNC
Honey from the Lion. Leah Bodine Drake. NePoAm
Honey Lamb, The. Jonathan Williams. PoM
Honey-Mead. *Unknown, tr. fr. Anglo-Saxon by* Charles W. Kennedy. *Fr.* Riddles (Exeter Book). AnOE
Honey mist on a day of frost in a dark oak wood, A. The Cooleen. Douglas Hyde. OBVV
Honey people murder mercy U.S.A. In Memoriam: Martin Luther King, Jr. June Jordan. PoBA
Honey, pepper, leaf-green limes. Jamaica Market. Agnes Maxwell-Hall. TTY
Honey, see dat jay-bird dah. Settin' on de Fence. *Unknown.* WBLP
Honey, Take a Whiff on Me. *Unknown.* OxBoLi
Honey, trus' der Lawd a bit, an' doan foghit to smile! Trus' an' Smile. B. Y. Williams. BLRP
Honey, you been gone all day that you may make whoopee all night. Whoopee Blues. *Unknown.* BluL
Honeyed by time. The Wooden Chamber. Anne Hébert, *tr. by* Birgit Swenson. WPOW
Honeyflowing moon is on every madman's tongue, The. Moonlight. Guillaume Apollinaire, *tr. by* William Meredith. MOON
Honeymoon. Samuel L. Albert. GoYe
Honeymoon, The. Henry Luttrell. *Fr.* Advice to Julia. OBRV
Honeystain/ the rhetoricians of blackness. The Anti-Semanticist. Everett Hoagland. BPo
Honeysuckle. James Paul. HoAn
Honeysuckle, The. Dante Gabriel Rossetti. SyP
Honeysuckle (Chevrefoil). Marie de France. *See* Goat's-Leaf.
Honeysuckle, nightshade. Poem for L. C. Peter Klappert. AmPA
"Honeysuckle Was the Saddest Odor of All, I Think." Thadious M. Davis. BlSi
Hongo Store 29 Miles Volcano Hilo, Hawaii, The. Garrett Kaoru Hongo. MAYP
Honi Soit Qui Mal Y Pense. Ian Young. PeHV
Honky. Charles Cooper. PoBA
Honour. Abraham Cowley. BoLoP
Honor a going thing, goldfinch, corporation, tree. Mechanism. A. R. Ammons. HAP
Honor and Desert. Coventry Patmore. *Fr.* The Angel in the House, II. HBV-1
Honor and shame from no condition rise. Pope. *Fr.* An Essay on Man. TrGrPo
Honor and truth and manhood. Things That Endure. Ted Olson. WBLP
Honour Dishonoured. Wilfrid Scawen Blunt. OBMV
Honor in chief, our oath is to uphold. Chorus Primus: Wise Counsellors. Fulke Greville. *Fr.* Mustapha. OBS
Honour is flashed off exploit, so we say. In Honour of St. Alphonsus Rodriguez. Gerard Manley Hopkins. EBEV; VLP
Honour is so sublime perfection. To the Countesse of Bedford. John Donne. MeLP
Honor of God and man is not on, The. Trees Once Walked and Stood. Joshua Tan Pai, *tr. by* Yishai Tobin. VWA
Honour, riches, marriage—blessing. Shakespeare. *Fr.* The Tempest, IV, i. PoPle
Honour the leaves, and the leaves of life. The Holy Well (Sweet Jesus). *Unknown.* BaBo
Honour thy parents; but good manners call. God to Be First Served. Robert Herrick. OxBChV
Honour with Age. Walter Kennedy. OxBS
Honourable Entertainment Given to the Queen's Majesty in Progress at Elvetham, 1591, The, *sels.* Nicholas Breton, *and others.*
Phillida and Coridon. Nicholas Breton. HBV-1; OBEV; UnTE; ViBoPo
(Pastoral, A.) TrGrPo
(Phyllida and Corydon.) EIL; OAEP; SeCePo
(Ploughman's Song, The.) FaBoEn; NOBE; OBSC

With Fragrant Flowers We Strew the Way. Thomas Watson. EIL
(Ditty of the Six Virgins, The.) OBSC
Hon. Mr. Sucklethumbkin's Story. "Thomas Ingoldsby." *Fr.* The Ingoldsby Legends. OBRV
Honorable the City Clerk, The: Dear Sir. Letter to the City Clerk. Frederick A. Wright. FaFP
Honoured I lived e'erwhile with honoured men. Honour Dishonoured. Wilfrid Scawen Blunt. OBMV
Honours that the people give always, The. The Thespians at Thermopylae. Norman Cameron. ChMP; GTBS-P
Hoo-Kee hear me. Blackfoot Sin-ka-ha. William S. Lewis. BPAW
Hoo, Suffolk. *Unknown.* GBP
Hoochie Coochie. *Unknown.* BluL
Hood. C. K. Williams. InPK
Hooded Crow, The. Rennie McOwan. PoSH
Hooded reptile, in his guile, The. The Serpent. Joseph Langland. MP
Hoofer, The. A. K. Redwing. VoR
Hook for Leviathan, A. Norman Cameron. ChMP
Hooked on the Magic Muscle. Linda King. GP
Hookerlumps in the Love Canal. William Sylvester. SOTS
Hooker's Across! George Henry Boker. PAH
Hooking the Rainbow. Tama Baldwin. WOLT
Hoop, a rolling O, oh those have power, A. Ode on Zero. Phoebe Pettingell. PoA
Hoopoe. George Darley. *Fr.* Nepenthe. OBNC
("Solitary wayfarer!") OBRV; PBBP
Hoosen Johnny. *Unknown.* AS, *with music;* FaPON; FSW
Hoot Owl Shift. Robert Stricklin. AMV-80
Hooter wakes me up to face the day again, The. Unaccompanied. Harvey Andrews. OBET
Hop Garden, The, *sels.* Christopher Smart.
Hops along the Medway. FaBoPP
How to Cure Hops and Prepare Them for Sale. FaBoUs
Hop hop, thump thump. Stevie Smith. *Fr.* The Dedicated Dancing Bull and the Water Maid. WPE
Hop-poles stand in cones, The. The Midnight Skaters. Edmund Blunden. FaBoTw; GoJo; GTBS-P; MoBrPo; NOBE
Hop, Skip, and Jump. Gary Snyder. LCAP
Hop Up, My Ladies. *Unknown. See* Uncle Joe.
Hope. Kenneth L. Anderson. AMV-80
Hope. William Lisle Bowles. EnRP
Hope. Gamaliel Bradford. HBMV
Hope. Emily Brontë. NoP
Hope. Amy Carmichael. TRV
Hope, *sel.* William Cowper.
"Though clasp'd and cradled in his nurse's arms." PoEL-3
Hope. William Dickey. GDP; POL
Hope. Sir Richard Fanshawe. *Fr.* Il Pastor Fido. OBS
Hope. Goldsmith. *Fr.* The Captivity; an Oratorio, II. OBEC; TreFT
Hope. George Herbert. PoEL-2; WeW
Hope. William Dean Howells. AA; MOS
Hope. Langston Hughes. OBAL; OBCA
Hope. Randall Jarrell. MoAB; MoAmPo
Hope. Georgia Douglas Johnson. CDC
Hope. Anna Blake Mezquida. TRV
Hope. Frank O'Connor, *tr. fr. Irish.* CIP
Hope ("Hope springs eternal in the human breast"). Pope. *Fr.* An Essay on Man, Epistle I. TreF
(Pleasure of Hope, The.) ACP
Hope. F. D. Reeve. PoA
Hope. Edith Södergran, *tr. fr. Swedish by* Jaakko O. Ahokas. PBWP
Hope. Phillips Stewart. CaP
Hope. Theognis, *tr. fr. Greek by* John Hookham Frere. AWP
Hope and Despair. Lascelles Abercrombie. HBV-2; OBMV
Hope and Faith. Isaac Leibush Peretz, *tr. fr. Yiddish by* Henry Goodman. TrJP
Hope and Fear. Swinburne. FaBoBe; HBV-2
Hope and Joy. Christina Rossetti. OxBChV
Hope, art thou true, or dost thou flatter me? Astrophel and Stella, LXVII. Sir Philip Sidney. SiPS
Hope Evermore and Believe. Arthur Hugh Clough. WGRP
Hope humbly then; with trembling pinions soar. Pope. *Fr.* An Essay on Man. TrGrPo
Hope I dreamed of was a dream, The. Mirage. Christina Rossetti. BoLoP; LLLT; PoRA
Hope is a crushed stalk. Dark Testament. Pauli Murray. AmNP
Hope is like a harebell trembling from its birth. Comparisons. Christina Rossetti. OxBChV
Hope is the thing with feathers. Emily Dickinson. AmPP; BLPL; MoAB; MoAmPo; MoShBr; NOBA; OxBA; SBG; TAP
Hope, is this thy hand. Fickle Hope. Harrison Smith Morris. AA
Hope, like a gleaming taper's light. Hope. Goldsmith. *Fr.* The Captivity; an Oratorio, II. TreFT
Hope, like the hyaena [*or* hyena], coming to be old. Henry Constable. *Fr.* Diana. EnLoPo; OBSC
Hope! Not distant is the Springtime. Hope and Faith. Isaac Leibush Peretz, *tr. by* Henry Goodman. TrJP
Hope of Our Hearts. Sir Edward Denny. STF
Hope of the World, The. Sir William Watson. WGRP
Hope Springs Eternal ("Heav'n from all creatures hides the book of fate"). Pope. *Fr.* An Essay on Man, Epistle I. OBEC
("Heav'n from all creatures hides the book of fate.") ViBoPo
Hope springs eternal in the human breast. Hope [*or* The Pleasure of Hope]. Pope. *Fr.* An Essay on Man, Epistle I. ACP; TreF, 4 *ll.*
Hope was but a timid friend. Hope. Emily Brontë. NoP
Hope we not in this life only. Not in Vain. *Unknown.* BLRP
Hope, whose weak being ruined is. Against Hope [*or* On Hope]. Abraham Cowley. *Fr.* The Mistress. LiTB; MeLP; MePo; NOBE; OBS; SeCV-1
Hopeless Desire Soon Withers and Dies. "A. W." OBSC
Hopelessly handcuffed to a mysterious butterfly. A Lost Mohican Visits Hell's Kitchen. A. K. Redwing. VoR
Hopes, The. Dieter Fringell, *tr. fr. German by* A. Leslie Willson. AMV-80
Hopes grimly banished from the heart. Exiles. William Hamilton Hayne. AA
Hope's Song. Francis Carlin. HBMV
Hopi Lament. Charles Beghtol. BPAW
Hopi Prayer. Charles Beghtol. BPAW
Hopi Prayer, A. Harrison Conrad. BPAW
Hopi Woman. Lillian White Spencer. BPAW
Hoping all the time. *Unknown, tr. by* Arthur Waley. *Fr.* Kokin Shu. AWP
Hoping this night my true love to see. *Unknown.* FaBoUs
Hopper's "Nighthawks" (1942). Ira Sadoff. PoDr
Hoppity. A. A. Milne. FaBV; NTCP; TiPo
Hops. Boris Pasternak, *tr. fr. Russian by* Jon Stallworthy *and* Peter France. BoLoP
Hops along the Medway. Christopher Smart. *Fr.* The Hop Garden. FaBoPP
Hop't She. *Unknown.* GBP
("Pie sat on a pear tree, A," *sl. diff. vers.*) PBBP
Hora Christi. Alice Brown. HBV-2; TrPWD; WGRP
Horace. John Osborne Sargent. AA
Horace, Book V, Ode III. Charles Larcom Graves. CenHV
Horace, for whom I entertain. Two Garden Scenes. Charles Burgess. NePoAm-2
Horace Kephart. Robert Morgan. MAYP
Horace Paraphrased. Isaac Watts. LoBV
Horace the Wise. Morrie Ryskind, *after the Latin of* Horace. HBMV
Horae Canonicae, *sel.* W. H. Auden.
Lauds. TrCP
Nones. CoBMV
Prime. CMoP
Vespers. FaBoMo
Sext. SaC
H-óran ó a vee-ó. A Complaint about Exile. Máiri MacLeod, *tr. by* Joan Keefe. PBWP
Horas Tempestatis Quoque Enumero: The Sundial. John Hollander. NePoEA
Horat. Ode 29. Book 3. Paraphras'd in Pindarique Verse. Dryden. *See* To Maecenas.
Horatian Epode to the Duchess of Malfi. Allen Tate. FaBoMo
Horatian Ode. Joseph Warren Beach. PoA
Horatian Ode upon Cromwel[l]'s Return from Ireland, An. Andrew Marvell. AnAnS-1; EBEV; GTBS; GTBS-P; HAP; HBV-2; InPS; JCP; LoBV; MePo; NOBE; NoP; OAEL-1; OBEV; OBS; OBWP; PoEL-2; SeCP; SeCV-1
Sels.
King Charles upon [*or* on] the Scaffold. ChTr; FaBoRV
"So restless Cromwell could not cease." ViBoPo
Horatian Variation. Leonard Bacon. NYBP
Horatians, The. W. H. Auden. NYBP
Horatio Alger Uses Scag. Amiri Baraka. GP
Horatio, of ideal courage vain. Feigned Courage. Charles *and* Mary Lamb. GN; OxBChV
Horatius [at the Bridge]. Macaulay. *Fr.* Lays of Ancient Rome. BeLS; FaBoCh, *abr.*; FaFP; FaPoR; HBV-2; HBVY; OBNV, *abr.*; OBWP; OHFP, *abr.*; PoLF; TreF
(" 'Horatius,' quoth the Consul.") VLP
Horch, horch, die Bell am Backdoor ringt! Morning Song. Kurt M. Stein. FiBHP
Horestes, *sel.* John Pickering.
Haltersick's Song. OBSC
(Song: "Farewell, adieu, that court-like life!") EIL
Horizon is Definitely Speaking, The. Diana Chang. BrSi

Horizon of Holland, The. Ian Hamilton Finlay. InPK
Horizon Thong. George Abbe. GoYe
Horizon without Landscape. Tom Lowenstein. VWA
Horizontal in a deckchair on the bleak ward [*or* Horizontal on a deckchair in the Ward]. Ezra Pound. Robert Lowell. NoAM; NOBA
Horizontal World. Thomas Saunders. CaP
Horn, The. Léonie Adams. MoAB; MoAmPo
Horn. James Hayford. NePoAm-2
Horn, The. James Reaney. OBCV; PeCV
Horn, The. James Reeves. SO
Horn: "Time was when I was weapon and warrior." *Unknown, tr. fr. Anglo-Saxon by* Charles W. Kennedy. *Fr.* Riddles (Exeter Book). AnOE
Horn and Hardart is closing. Samurai and Hustlers. Joe Johnson. CNA
Horn Blow, The. Jeff Tagami. BrSi
Horn, Mouth, Pit, Fire. William Dickey. AMV-81
Horned Lizard. Charles Molesworth. GrPl
Hornets occasionally build their nests near roads. Homer, *tr. by* Christopher Logue. *Fr.* The Iliad, XVI. OBVE
Hornless hart carries off the harem, The. The Royal Stag. "Hugh MacDiarmid." FaBoMo
Hornpipe. Edith Sitwell. *Fr.* Façade. FaBoMo; GTBS-P; MoVE; OAEL-2; SeCePo
Hornpout. Presott Evarts, Jr. WOLT
Horns [*or* Hornes] to bulls wise Nature lends. Beauty. Thomas Stanley, *after the Greek of* Anacreon. AWP; OBVE
Horns weaving an adagio disclose. Symphony. Alfred Dorn. AMV-80
Horny-Goloch, The. *Unknown.* AmMo
("Horny-goloch is an awesome beast, The"). FaBoCh
Horologium, *sel. Unknown, tr. fr. Greek by* G. R. Woodward.
Mother of God, The. ISi
Horoscope. J. V. Cunningham. NePoAm
Horribeloved Klaubautermann. Klabauterwife's Letter. Christian Morgenstern, *tr. by* W. D. Snodgrass *and* Lore Segal. WSC
Horrible crime was committed, A. Pearl Bryan. *Unknown.* AmFP
Horrible Decree, The, *sel.* Charles Wesley.
"Sinners, abhor the Fiend." NOCV
Horrible Things. Roy Fuller. OnUR
Horrid Voice of Science, The. Vachel Lindsay. PoA
Horror. Peter Baum, *tr. fr. German by* Jethro Bithell. AWP
Horror. Henry Treece. EAS
Horror Comic. Robert Conquest. OxBTC
Horror Movie. Howard Moss. NePoEA-2
Hors d'Oeuvre. Deems Taylor, *tr. fr. French.* UnTE
Horse. Gerard Benson. PH
Horse, The. Bible, *O.T.* Job, XXXIX. FaPON (19-21; 24-25); TrGrPo (19-25)
(Hast Thou Given the Horse Strength? XXXIX: 19-25.) ChTr
Horse. Randy Blasing. PH
Horse, The. A. E. Coppard. BoAnP
Horse, The. José María Eguren, *tr. fr. Spanish by* Cheli Durán. WSC
Horse. Louise Glück. MAYP
Horse. Jim Harrison. BoAnP; PH
Horse, The. Faye Kicknosway. GeTw
Horse, The. Philip Levine. CoAP
Horse, The. W. S. Merwin. GP
Horse, The. Francis Ponge, *tr. fr. French by* Beth Archer. NU
Horse. Kenneth Rexroth. *Fr.* A Bestiary. NNaP
Horse. Elizabeth Madox Roberts. PH; TiPo
Horse, The. Naomi Royde-Smith. FaBoCo; FiBHP
("I know two things about the horse.") CenHV
Horse, The. Shakespeare. King Henry V, *fr.* III, vii. PH
Horse, The. Shel Silverstein. PH
Horse and a flea and three blind mice, A. Whoops! *Unknown.* FaFP; NTCP; RHPC
Horse and hattock. The Witch's Broomstick Spell. *Unknown.* ChTr; GBP
Horse and His Rider, The. Joanna Baillie. NOEC
Horse and mule live thirty years, The. Liquor and Longevity. *Unknown.* FPL; WhC
Horse & Rider. Wey Robinson. BXAP; WhC
Horse and the Mule, The. John Huddlestone Wynne. OxBChV
Horse and the Whip, The. Eliezer Steinbarg, *tr. fr. Yiddish by* Curt Leviant. VWA
Horse breaks glass, A. Horses. Myra Von Riedemann. OBCV
Horse can't pull while kicking, A. Horse Sense. *Unknown.* BLPA; TreFT; WBLP
Horse-Chestnut Time. Kaye Starbird. PDV
Horse Chestnut Tree, The. Richard Eberhart. CMoP; CrMA; LiTIM; MoAB; MoAmPo; NePA; NePoAm; PoPl
Horse-Girl. Henry Petroski. PH
Horse Graveyard. Fred Lape. PH
Horse, head-swinging, The. February. Barbara Winder. PH
Horse, huge. Inviolable. Daniel Hoffman. GrPl
Horse I am, whom bit, A. The Trojan Horse. William Drummond of Hawthornden. EyDe
Horse in a Field. Walter de la Mare. HBMV
Horse in the Drugstore, The. Tess Gallagher. AmPA
Horse is Lorca's word, fierce as wind. Weed. Robert Hass. MAYP
Horse, Lord Epsom did bestride, A. Lord Epsom. Hilaire Belloc. PH
Horse Named Bill, A. *Unknown.* AS, *with music;* FSW
Horse of poetry nibbles, The. The Invitation. Donagh MacDonagh. OnYI
Horse Sense. *Unknown.* BLPA; TreFT; WBLP
Horse Show, The. William Carlos Williams. CMoP; NOBA; TAP; VGW
Horse Show at Midnight, The. Henry Taylor. PH
Horse skin; hessian or hard hot silk. Horse. Gerard Benson. PH
Horse Thief, The. William Rose Benét. BPAW; HBMV; MoAmPo; OnMSP
Horse Trader's Song, The. *Unknown.* AmFP
Horse would tire, A. Elizabeth J. Coatsworth. TiPo
Horse Wrangler, The, *with music. Unknown.* CoSo
Horseman, The. Walter de la Mare. GoJo; RHPC; SoPo; SUS; TiPo
Horseman on the Skyline, The. Henry Lawson. CBAP
Horseman riding, A. Woodcut. R. N. D. Wilson. OxBI
Horsemen, The. Gene Baro. NePoEA-2
Horses. Richard Armour. PoPl; WhC
Horses. Robert Dana. PH
Horses, The. Ted Hughes. NoAM; PH
Horses. Kipling. BoAnP; POL
(Thrown Away.) PH
Horses, The. Maxine W. Kumin. DuDa
Horses. Louis MacNeice. PH
Horses, The ("Barely a twelvemonth after"). Edwin Muir. CMoP; HAP; MoBrPo; NMP; NoAM; NOBE; OAEL-2; OxBTC; PPoe; TEP; WeW
Horses ("Those lumbering horses in the steady plough"). Edwin Muir. CMoP; FaBaCh; MoVE; OAEL-2; PoPle; SeCePo
Horses. Myra von Riedemann. OBCV
Horses. Dorothy Wellesley. ChMP; OBMV; OxBTC
Horses/ Are no longer used in the Armed Forces. War Horses. William Cole. PH
Horses Aboard. Thomas Hardy. BoAnP; FM
Horses and Men in the Rain. Carl Sandburg. PoLF
Horses are going away, The. Going Away. Ann Stanford. GP; PH
Horses at Valley Stores. Leslie Silko. VoR
Horses Chawin' Hay. Hamlin Garland. OBAL
Horses Graze. Gwendolyn Brooks. CNA; GP
Horses in front of me. Merry-go-round. Mark Van Doren. SO
Horses in horsecloths stand in a row. Horses Aboard. Thomas Hardy. BoAnP; FM
Horses of earth. Horses. Robert Dana. PH
Horses of Marini, The. Tania Van Zyl. PeSA
Horses of the sea, The. Christina Rossetti. *Fr.* Sing-Song. FaPON; GoJo; NTCP; SUS
Horses of the sea, The; remember. On a Horse Carved in Wood. Donald Hall. EyDe
Horses on the Camargue. Roy Campbell. GTBS-P; PeSA; PoPle; SeCePo
Horses out of their brains bored all, The. Flying Noises. Thomas Lux. LCAP
Horses, the pigs, The. Familiar Friends. James S. Tippett. SoPo; SUS
Horses were ready, the rails were down, The. Where the Pelican Builds. Mary Hannay Foott. PoAu-1
Horsey Gap. *Unknown.* FaBoPP; GBP
Hos Ego Versiculos. Francis Quarles. *Fr.* Argalus and Parthenia. OBS. *See also* Man's Mortality, *sl. diff. vers. at. to* Simon Wastell, *fr.* Microbiblion.
(Like as the Damask Rose.) LoBV
Hosanna. Thomas Traherne. PoEL-2; SeCV-2
Hosanna—musick is divine. Psalm CXLVII: "Praise ye the Lord." Christopher Smart. NOCV
Hosanna to Christ. Isaac Watts. NOCV
Hose and Iron. Greg Kuzma. MAT
Hospital, The. Patrick Kavanagh. BIrV; CIP
Hospital. G. C. Millard. PeSA
Hospital, A. Alfred Noyes. PoPl
Hospital. Karl Shapiro. VGW
Hospital floors give away, The. Sister Rose. Richard Martin. AMV-81
Hospital for Defectives. Thomas Blackburn. GTBS-P; OxBTC
Hospital for sick and needy Jews, A. The New Jewish Hospital at Hamburg. Heine, *tr. by* Charles Godfrey Leland. TrJP
Hospital Observation. Julian Symons. WaP
Hospital/ Poem. Sonia Sanchez. BPo; PoBA
Hospital Prison Ship, The. Philip Freneau. *Fr.* The British Prison Ship. AmPP
Hospital, The—Retrospections. Kenneth Mackenzie. CBAP
Hospital Visitor, The. Alys Fane Trotter. SUMH
Hospital Waiting-Room, The. W. H. Davies. BrPo

Hospital Window, The. James Dickey. BiP; CoPo; DiL; HeIP
Hospitality in Ancient Ireland. *Unknown, tr. fr. Middle Irish by* Kuno Meyer. OnYI
Hossolalia. Mildred Luton. PH
Host is riding from Knocknarea, The. The Hosting of the Sidhe. W. B. Yeats. NoAM
Host of the Air, The. W. B. Yeats. BrPo; CH; OnYI; SeCeV
Hostage and His Takers, The. Sharon Olds. SOTS
Hostess' Daughter, The. Ludwig Uhland, *tr. fr. German by* Margarete Münsterberg. AWP
Hostia. Irving Layton. PV
Hosting of the Sidhe, The. W. B. Yeats. NoAM
Hosts, The. George M. Brady. NeIP
Hosts, The. W. S. Merwin. GP
Hosts of Faery, The. *Unknown, tr. fr. Middle Irish by* Kuno Meyer. OnYI
Hosts of Gods do not know my origin, The. The One. *Tr. fr. Sanskrit by* Raimundo Panikkar. *Fr.* Bhagavadgita. ILwL
Hot Afternoons Have Been in West 15th Street. Paul Blackburn. VGW
Hot cross buns, hot cross buns!/ One a penny poker. *Unknown.* OxNR
Hot cross buns! Hot-cross buns!/ One a penny, two a penny. Mother Goose. OxNR; SoPo
Hot Day and Human Nature, The. Gordon Johnston. AMV-81
Hot Day at the Races. Tom Raworth. EAS
Hot Flame of My Grief, The. Moses ibn Ezra, *tr. fr. Hebrew by* Solomon Solis-Cohen. TrJP
Hot in June a narrow winged. A Nameless One. Margaret Avison. HeIP; NOBC
Hot Ir'n! S. Omar Barker. PoOW
Hot Line. Louella Dunann. QQQ; RHPC
Hot mice feeding in red, The. Paul Klee. John Haines. LCAP
Hot midsummer night on Water Street, A. Hot Night on Water Street. Louis Simpson. MP; TwCP
"Hot night makes us keep our bedroom windows open, The." "To Speak of Woe That Is in Marriage." Robert Lowell. CAPP; NoAM
Hot night of the ramparts. Embrace the Blade. Joyce Mansour, *tr. by* Carol Cosman. PBWP
Hot Night on Water Street. Louis Simpson. MP; TwCP
Hot nights I slept with you, The. For Maria. Cleopatra Mathis. MAYP
Hot September sun shone down on the wide and peaceful bay, The. The Wide Open Spaces. Oscar H. Lear. InMe
Hot Springs. Earle Birney. OxBC
Hot Stuff. Edward Botwood. PAH
Hot sun [*or* sunne], cool[e] fire, tempered with sweet air[e]. Bethsabe's Song [*or* Bethsabe Bathing]. George Peele. *Fr.* David and Bethsabe. ElL; EnRePo; GBL; LoBV; NOBE; NoP; OBSC; OxBoLi; PoEL-2; SeCeV; TEP; TrGrPo
Hot through Troy's ruin Menelaus broke. Menelaus and Helen. Rupert Brooke. SeCePo
Hot Time in the Old Town, A. Joe Hayden. FSN, *with music;* YaD (There'll Be a Hot Time.) BLSo
Hot Weather in the Plains—India. E. H. Tipple. HBV-2
Hot-Weather Song, A. Don Marquis. HBMV; WhC; YaD
Hotel. Adam Wazyk, *tr. fr. Polish by* Isaac Komem. VWA
Hotel Continental. William Jay Smith. WaP
Hotel de l'Univers et Portugal. James Merrill. MoAB; NePoAm; NePoEA-2; PoA
Hotel Fire: New Orleans. Paul Ruffin. AMV-81
Hotel in Paris. Dennis Trudell. PoA
Hotel Lobby. Mildred Weston. WhC
Hotel Paradiso e Commerciale. John Malcolm Brinnin. HoAn; MP; NoAM; NYBP; PoCh; TwCP
Hotel Peine Forte et Dure in Santa Monica, The. John Carey's Second Song. Thomas McGrath. FAZ
Hotel register claims this used to be an exciting town, The. Jefferson, Texas. Naomi Shihab. TAT
Hotel Sierra. David St. John. MAYP
Hôtel Transylvanie. Frank O'Hara. NoAP; PoM
Hotels. David Donnell. AMV-81
Hotten/ Rotten. Epitaph for John Camden Hotten. G. A. Sala. DBV
Hottentot, The. Thomas Pringle. OBRV
Hottest Brand Goin'. *Unknown.* BluL
Houdini. Eli Mandel. NIP; NOBC
Hound, The. Babette Deutsch. HBMV
Hound, The. Robert Francis. SoSe
Hound, The. Sidney Lanier. *Fr.* The Jaquerie. AA; GDP
Hound, The/ Could never be called refined. The Angry Poet. Frank O'Connor, *tr. fr. Irish.* CIP
Hound of Heaven, The. Francis Thompson. ACP; BLPL; BrPo; FaBV; FaFP; GoBC; GoTL; HBV-2; IlwL; LiTB; LiTM; LoBV; MasP; MoAB; MoBrPo; OAEP; OBMV; OxBoCh; PoEL-5; SeCePo; SeCeV; TrGrPo; TRV; ViBoPo; VLP; WGRP; WHA
"I fled Him, down the nights and down the days," *sel.* TreF
Hound on the Church Porch. Robert P. Tristram Coffin. GDP
Hound Voice. W. B. Yeats. SyP
Hound was cuffed, the hound was kicked, The. The Hound. Sidney Lanier. *Fr.* The Jacquerie. AA; GDP
Hounded Lovers, The. William Carlos Williams. NYBP; TrGrPo
Hounded slave that flags in the race, leans by the fence, The. The Wounded Person. Walt Whitman. *Fr.* Song of Myself. PoNe
Hounds, The. Patric Dickinson. ChMP
Hounds, The. John Freeman. OBMV
Hounds are all out, and the morning does peep, The. The Huntsman's Rouse. Henry Carey. SeCePo
Hounds charging from one wall to another. Insomnia. Joyce Carol Oates. DFF
Hounds of Spring, The. Swinburne. *See* When the Hounds of Spring.
Hounds of the Soul, The. Louis Ginsberg. TrJP
Hounds sleep well, The. It is not they who stir the fox. With Hands like Leaves. James Still. GrPl
Hounds, The. The great man's dream. The stone. The Hounds. Patric Dickinson. ChMP
Hounslow Heath. *Unknown.* APAS
Hour, The. Uri Zvi Greenberg, *tr. fr. Hebrew by* Robert Mezey *and* Ben Zion Gold. VWA
Hour after hour the cards were fairly shuffled. Whist. Eugene Fitch Ware. PoLF
Hour at last come round, The. The Dying Gaul. Desmond O'Grady. BIrV
"Hour gets later, the times get worse, The." Preliminary Poem. John Heath-Stubbs. OxBC
"Hour is late, The," the shepherds said. The Shepherd Left Behind. Mildred Plew Meigs. TrCP
Hour is very weary, as before sleep, The. The Hour. Uri Zvi Greenberg, *tr. by* Robert Mezey *and* Ben Zion Gold. VWA
Hour of Death, The. Felicia Dorothea Hemans. HBV-2; LoBV; OBNC
Hour of Feeling, The. Louis Simpson. FiCP
Hour of Magic, The. W. H. Davies. MoBrPo
Hour of Peaceful Rest, The. William Bingham Tappan. AA; HBV-2 (There Is an Hour of Peaceful Rest, *with music.*) AH
Hour of Prayer, The. Georgia B. Adams. STF
Hour of Prayer, The. Charlotte Elliott. STF
Hour of Prayer, The. Albert L. Hoy. AMV-80
Hour of sight, The. Still Life. Kathleen Raine. NeBP
Hour ten he rose, ten-sworded, every finger. Timoshenko. Sidney Keyes. OBWP
Hour told by the owl and the moon, The. Lament for Better or Worse. Gene Baro. NePoEA-2
Hour was on us, The; where the man? Lincoln. John Vance Cheney. OHIP
Hour with Thee, An. Sir Walter Scott. BoLoP
Hour-Glass, The. Robert Herrick. CaPo
Hour-Glass [*or* Hourglass], The. Ben Jonson. BLPL; EnLoPo; EnRePo; LiTB; NIP; OAEL-1; SeCP
Hourglass, The, *sel.* Weldon Kees.
"Crew is changed, the stone's face notched in darkness, The." NYP
Hour Glass, The. Edward Quillinan. OBRV
Hour-glass whispers to the lion's roar, The. Our Bias. W. H. Auden. NoAM; NoP
Hourly I Die. Dryden. *See* Song: "Fair Iris I love, and hourly I die."
Hours, The. John Peale Bishop. MoVE; OxBA
Hours, The. Norman Dubie. GeTw
Hours, The. Susan Tichy. MAYP
Hours after fate had brot us 2gether in. She Employed the Familiar "Tu" Form. Doug Fetherling. NeAC
Hours before dawn we were woken by the quake. Aubade. William Empson. FaBoMo; FaBoTw; LiTB; OxBTC
Hours before my death. Epitaph. Julio Marzán. InW
Hours I spent with thee, dear heart, The. The Rosary. Robert Cameron Rogers. AA; BLSo; FaBoBe; FSN; HBV-1; TreF; WBLP
Hours late and afraid to go in. Lantern. Gary Soto. Str
Hours of a Bridge, The. W. S. Merwin. LCAP
Hours of Idleness. Byron. EvOK (Tear, The.) Par
Hours of Sleepy Night, The. Thomas Campion. *Fr.* The Mountebank's Mask. ElL (Dismissal.) OBSC
Hours of the Passion, *sel.* Eleanor Hamilton King.
Garden of the Holy Souls, The. ACP
Hours of the Passion, The. *Unknown.* MeEL
Hours of the Passion, *sel.* William of Shoreham.
"At Prime Jesus was y-led." ACP
Hours Rise Up Putting Off Stars and It Is, The. E. E. Cummings. CAD; OxBA (Impression.) MoAmPo

House, The. George Bowering. NOBC
House. Robert Browning. OAEP; PP
House, The. Robert Creeley. CoPo
House, The. T. Walking Eagle Marietta. LFAC
House, The. Paula Nelson. GoYe
House. Diana O Hehir. NPGG
House, The. Winfield Townley Scott. MiAP
House, The. Tania Van Zyl. PeSA
House, The. William Carlos Williams. VGW
House across the Way, The. Ralph Hodgson. FaBoTw
House All Pictures, A. Emery George. AMV-81
House and Grounds, A. Leigh Hunt. OBRV
House and hollow; village and valley-side. Winter Encounters. Charles Tomlinson. LiTM
House and Home. Joseph Beaumont. OBS
House and Home. Victor Hugo, *tr. fr. French.* TRV
House and Shutter. Lewis Turco. PoPl
House and the Road, The. Josephine Preston Peabody. TreFT
House Beautiful, The. Robert Louis Stevenson. NOBE
House Blessing, A. William Cartwright. *Fr.* The Ordinary. ChTr
(Saint Francis and Saint Benedight). EaLo
House Blessing. Arthur Guiterman. TiPo; TrPWD
House-Builders, The. Kamala Das. PBWP
House by the Side of the Road, The. Sam Walter Foss. BLPA; BLPL; FaBoBe; FaFP; HBV-2; HBVY; OHFP; TreF; TRV; WBLP; WGRP
House by the Tracks, A. Dave Etter. TAT
House Carpenter, The. *Unknown. See* Demon Lover, The.
House Carpenter's Wife, The. *Unknown. See* Demon Lover, The.
House catch on fire and ain't no water 'round. Southern Blues. *Unknown.* BluL
House dawned, The. Reconciliation. David Rosenmann-Taub, *tr. by* Charles Guenther. VWA
House Divided, A. Michael Ondaatje. MoCV
House Dog's Grave, The. Robinson Jeffers. GDP
House Fear. Robert Frost. *Fr.* The Hill Wife. VGW; WSC
House. For Sale. Leonard Clark. RHPC
House full, a hole full, A. *Unknown.* OxNR
House full, yard full. Riddle. *Unknown.* NTCP
House Guest. Elizabeth Bishop. NCSH; NYBP; TAP
House had gone to bring again, The. The Need of Being Versed in Country Things. Robert Frost. FaBoEn; NoAM; NOBA; OxBA; UnPo
House-hunting. David Wagoner. DFF
House I Go to in My Dream, The. George Barker. OnUR
House in Broad Street, red brick, with nine rooms, The. The Things. Conrad Aiken. HAP; WeW
House in Denver. Thomas Hornsby Ferril. AmFN
House in Meudon. Margarita Aliger, *tr. fr. Russian by* Elaine Feinstein. VWA
House in St. Petersburg. Stanley Burnshaw. VWA
House in Springfield. Gail Brook Burket. PGD
House in Taos, A. Langston Hughes. CDC
House in the Green Well, The. John Hall Wheelock. MoAmPo
House in the Wood, The. Randall Jarrell. LCAP
House Is an Enigma. Laura Jensen. LCAP
House is built of logs and stone, A. House and Home. Victor Hugo. TRV
House is crammed, The: tier beyond tier they grin. "Blighters." Siegfried Sassoon. CMoP; FaBoTw; MMA; MoVE; NoAM
House is filled, The. The last heartthrob. Near the Ocean. Robert Lowell. NOBA
House is inhabited by squirrels, The. The Abandoned House. Patricia Hubbell. WSC
House is so quiet now, The. The Vacuum. Howard Nemerov. NePoEA; NIP
House is yours, The. The House. William Carlos Williams. VGW
House leaks and leans, The. The Ancestors. John Peale Bishop. PoA
House lies vacant now, forbear to knock, The. Miser. Gordon LeClaire. CaP
House lifts off, The. Down below. Night Flight. Ruth Daigon. AMV-81
House my earthly parent left, The. The Cottage. Jones Very. OxBA
House Next Door, The. Douglas Dunn. OxBC
House o' the Mirror, The. Helen Adam. MAT; NMM
House of a Hundred Lights, The, *sel.* Ridgely Torrence.
Conclusion of the Whole Matter, The. HBV-2
House of Ate, The. Spenser. *Fr.* The Faerie Queene, IV, 1. OBSC
House of Broken Swords, The, *sel.* William Hervey Woods.
Prayer of Beaten Men, The. HBV-2
House of cards, A. Christina Rossetti. *Fr.* Sing-Song. PoPl
House of Christmas, The. G. K. Chesterton. GoBC; HBV-1; HBVY; MoBrPo
House of Colour, The. Francis Sherman. CaP
House of Desire, The. Sherley Anne Williams. BlSi
House of Dust, The, *sel.* Conrad Aiken.
Portrait of One Dead. HBMV; WHA
House of Falling Leaves, The. William Stanley Braithwaite. PoLF; PoNe
House of Fame, The, *sels.* Chaucer. OxBM
Eagle Converses with Chaucer, The.
Jove's Eagle Carries Chaucer into Space.
House of Fire. Theodore Weiss. CoPo
House of five fires, you never raised me. In the Longhouse, Oneida Museum. Roberta Hill Whiteman. STE
House of God, The. A. D. Hope. OxBC
House of Hospitalities, The. Thomas Hardy. NoAM
House of Life, The *sels.* Dante Gabriel Rossetti.
Ardour and Memory, LXIV. OAEL-2
Autumn Idleness, LXIX. GBL; OAEL-2
Barren Spring, LXXXIII. EBVV; FaBoEn; NoP; OAEL-2; OBNC; PoEL-5; VLP
Birth-Bond, The, XV. HBV-1; OAEP
Body's Beauty, LXXVIII. HBV-1; OAEL-2; TrGrPo; VLP
(Lilith.) PoEL-5
Bridal Birth, II. OAEP
Choice, The, LXXI-LXXIII. HBV-2; OBVV; ViBoPo
"Eat thou and drink," LXXI. WHA
"Think thou and act," LXXIII. GTBS-P; OBEV; WHA
Dark Glass, The, XXXIV. HBV-1
Day of Love, A, XVI. VLP
Death-in-Love, XLVIII. SyP; VLP
Genius in Beauty, XVIII. OAEP
He and I, XCVIII. NBM
Heart's Compass, XXVII. WHA
Heart's Haven, XXII. OAEP
Heart's Hope, V. HBV-1
Her Gifts, XXXI. HBV-1; VLP
Hill Summit, The, LXX. NoP; VLP
Inclusiveness, LXIII. NBM; NCEP; SyP; VLP
Kiss, The, VI. VLP
(What Smouldering Senses.) UnTE
Landmark, The, LXVII. NBM
Life-in-Love, XXXVI. HAP; VLP
Lost Days, LXXXVI. GoBC; NCEP; OAEP; WHA
Lost on Both Sides, XCI. NoP; SeCePo; VLP
Love-Sweetness, XXI. OAEP
Lovers' Walk, The, XII. OAEP
Love's Last Gift, LIX. VLP
Lovesight, IV. EBVV; FaBoEn; GTBS-P; HBV-1; OAEP; OBNC; OBVV; TrGrPo; ViBoPo; VLP; WHA
Mid-Rapture, XXVI. BLPL; FaBoBe; HBV-1; OAEP
Not as These, LXXV. VLP
Nuptial Sleep, VI (A). EBVV: LoBV; VLP
One Hope, The, CI. HBV-2; OAEL-2; VLP
Portrait, The, X. VLP
Pride of Youth, XXIV. FaBoEn; OBNC
Saint Luke the Painter, LXXIV. GoBC; VLP
Severed Selves, XL. BoLoP; SyP
Silent Noon, XIX. HAP; HBV-1; NoP; OAEP; OBNC; PoEL-5; TrGrPo; VLP; WHA
Sleepless Dreams, XXXIX. OAEP
Song-Throe, The, LXI. VLP
Soul's Beauty, LXXVII. OAEP; OBEV; OBVV; VLP
Superscription, A, XCVII. EBVV; FaBoEn; GTBS-P; HBV-1; NoP; OAEL-2; OBNC; PoEL-5; SeCePo; VLP; WHA
Through Death to Love, XLI. SyP
Transfigured Life, LX. VLP
Vain Virtues, LXXXV. HBV-2; VLP
Vase of Life, The, XCV. SyP
Willowwood, XLIX-LII. OAEL-2; OAEP; VLP
"I sat with Love upon a woodside well," XLIX. HBV-1; PoEL-5; WHA
Without Her, LIII. GBL; NCEP; OBNC; PoEL-5; ViBoPo; VLP
Youth's Antiphony, XIII. VLP
Youth's Spring-Tribute, XIV. VLP
House of Lords, The. W. S. Gilbert. *See* House of Peers, The.
House of Madam Juju, The. Kanai Mieko, *tr. fr. Japanese by* Christopher Drake. BoWoP
House of Night, The, *sels.* Philip Freneau.
"By some sad means, when Reason holds no sway." PoEL-4
Death. AP
Death's Epitaph, *br. sel.* AA
House of Pain, The. Florence Earle Coates. HBV-2
House of Peers, The. W. S. Gilbert. *Fr.* Iolanthe. InMe
(House of Lords, The.) TrGrPo
House of Pride, The. Spenser. *Fr.* The Faerie Queene, I, 4. WHA
House of Readers, A. Jim Wayne Miller. GP; PPJ

House of Richesse, The. Spenser. *Fr.* The Faerie Queene, II, 7. CH
House of sleepers, A—I, alone unblest. Insomnia. Edith M. Thomas. AA
House of the Living. Claude Vigée, *tr. fr. French by* Henry Braun. VWA
House of the Mouse, The. Lucy Sprague Mitchell. NTCP; SoPo; TiPo
House of the Rising Sun. *Unknown.* FSW
(Rising Sun Blues, The, *with music.*) OuSiCo
House of the Trees, The. Ethelwyn Wetherald. CaP
House of Wisdom, The. Bible, *O.T.* Proverbs, IX: 1-6. TrGrPo
House on Buder Street, The. Gary Gildner. TAP
House on fire, A! We stumbled over the snow. Houses Burning; Quebec. Patrick Anderson. NOBC
House on the Hill, The. E. A. Robinson. AA; FaPON; GoJo; HBMV; MoAmPo; PrIm; TreFT; TrGrPo; WHA
House Plants. David McFadden. NOBC
House Poem. Jane Cooper. AMV-81
House Remembers, The. Robert Francis. DFF
House ringed round with trees and in the trees, A. Asylum. John Freeman. OBMV
House silent. In the Old House. Joan Aiken. WSC
House-snake dwells here still, The. The Closed World. Denise Levertov. NoP
Housesnake's made her nest in the woodshed, A. This Cold Nothing Else. Dara Wier. MAYP
House-Surgeon. W. E. Henley. In Hospital, XVI. BrPo
House That Jack Built, The. *Unknown.* FaBoBe; OxBoLi; OxNR; SoPo
House That Was, The. Laurence Binyon. MoBrPo
House-Top, The. Herman Melville. AP; LiTA; NCEP; NOBA; NYP; Prf
House was empty and, The. Music in an Empty House. Hugh Sykes Davies. EAS
House Was Quiet and the World Was Calm, The. Wallace Stevens. HAP; NoP; VGW
House was shaken by a rising wind, The. Brainstorm. Howard Nemerov. HAP; NCSH; NoAM
House where every, A. Louis Zukofsky. *Fr.* Light. NoAM
House where I was born, The. The Doves. Katharine Tynan. AnIV; AWP
House with coarse stuccoed, The. The House. Tania Van Zyl. PeSA
House with Nobody in It, The. Joyce Kilmer. BLPA; BLPL
House, you are done. Consecration of the House. W. S. Fairbridge. PoAu-2
Houseboats of brass. Dear Country Cousin. E. G. Burrows. HoAn
Housecleaner, The. Gail White. AMV-80
Household. Laura Jensen. LCAP
Household Remedies. *Unknown.* OBET
Householder, The. Robert Browning. LO
Housekeeper, The. Vincent Bourne, *tr. fr. Latin by* Charles Lamb. GN; HBV-1; PoLF
(Snail, The.) MoShBr
Houseless Downs, The. George Ferebe. *Fr.* The Shepherds' Song, Sung before Queen Anne, on the Wiltshire Downs, 11 June 1613. FaBoPP
House-Mates. Leon Gellert. CBAP
Houseplant. Felicity Napier. BrRo
Houses. Aileen Fisher. NTCP; SoPo
Houses. Donald Justice. EyDe; PPJ
(Poem: "Time and the weather wear away.") PoA
Houses, The. Eden Phillpotts. OxBTC
Houses, an embassy, the hospital. Days of 1964. James Merrill. CoAP
Houses and rooms are full of perfumes, the shelves are crowded with perfumes. Song of Myself, II. Walt Whitman. TrGrPo; UnPo
Houses are faces. Houses. Aileen Fisher. NTCP; SoPo
Houses are haunted, The. Disillusionment of Ten O'Clock. Wallace Stevens. CMoP; CrMA; FF; InPK; InPS; NIP; OxBA; PAI; PPoe; SOTW
Houses are swaying, swimming in gray light. Homecoming. Anna Margolin, *tr. by* Keith Bosley. VWA
Houses Burning; Quebec. Patrick Anderson. NOBC
Houses, churches, mixed together. A Description of London. John Bancks. NOEC
"Houses I dreamed and drew alive come now," he said. Architect. Louise Townsend Nicholl. EyDe
Houses of men are on fire, The. The Seventh Hell. Jerome Rothenberg. CoPo; NMP
Houses, Past and Present. Eli Bachar, *tr. fr. Hebrew by* Jeremy Garber. VWA
Housewife, The. Catherine Cate Coblentz. BLRP; TrPWD; TRV
Housewife. Josephine Miles. PCP
Housewife. Susan Fromberg Schaeffer. IHMS
Housewife. Anne Sexton. NMM
Housewife, A. *Unknown.* TDH
Housewife on her drying-green, A. The Drying-Green. Douglas Dunn. BSV
Housewifery. Edward Taylor. *See* Huswifery.
Housewife's Lament, The. *Unknown.* FSW; MAT
Housewife's Letter: To Mary. Anne Halley. NMM
Housewife's Prayer, The. Blanche Mary Kelly. GoBC
Housework. Amanda Berenguer, *tr. fr. Spanish by* Priscilla Joslin. WPOW
Housework. William Matthews. NPAW
Housing Shortage. Naomi Replansky. NMM
Housing Starts. Peter Davison. EyDe
Houston and Bowery, 1981. Diane Burns. TWSS
Houston Street, N. Y. Carolyn Baxter. LFAC
Hovering and huge, dark, formless sway, The. The Virgin Mary. Edgar Bowers. NePoEA; QFR
How. S. J. Marks. NYBP
How? Abraham Sutskever, *tr. fr. Yiddish by* Ruth Whitman. VWA
How? *Unknown.* STF
How/ Then,/ Distinguish. Query. Mildred Weston. POL
How a Girl Got Her Chinese Name. Nellie Wong. WPOW
How a Girl Was Too Reckless of Grammar [by Far]. Guy Wetmore Carryl. FiBHP; OBAL
How a Good Greyhound Is Shaped. *Unknown.* BoAnP
How About. Sheryl L. Nelms. Str
How all men wrongly death to dignify. The Wisdom of Old Jelly Roll. A. J. M. Smith. PeCV
How all occasions do inform against me. Shakespeare. *Fr.* Hamlet, IV, iv. BiP; HoPM
How am I held within a tranquil shell. The Woman with Child. Freda Laughton. OnYI
How am I hitched. Suffering. Albert Ehrenstein, *tr. by* Babette Deutsch. TrJP
How Amiable Are Thy Tabernacles! Bryant. *See* Dedication: "Thou, whose unmeasured temple stands."
How amiable are thy tabernacles, O Lord of hosts! Bible, *O.T.* Psalms, LXXXIV. TRV
How and When and Where and Why. Phyllis Gotlieb. WHW
How and with what will you fill. How? Abraham Sutskever, *tr. by* Ruth Whitman. VWA
How Annandale Went Out. E. A. Robinson. AP; CoBMV; HBMV; MoAB; MoAmPo; NoAM; NOBA
How are our Spirituall Gamesters slipt away? An Elegy upon the Death of That Holy Man of God Mr. John Allen. Edward Taylor. PoEL-3
How are songs begot and bred? Songs. Richard Henry Stoddard. AA
How Are the Mighty Fallen. Bible, *O.T.* Second Samuel, I: 19-27. WaaP
How Are Thy Servants Blest. Joseph Addison. OxBoCh
(Ode: "How are thy servants blest, O Lord.") OBEC; TrPWD
How Are You? Arthur Guiterman. WhC
(Of Tact.) MoShBr
How Are You, Dear World, This Morning? Horace Traubel. TrJP
How, as a spider's web is spun. To Jessie's Dancing Feet. William De Lancey Ellwanger. AA
How badly and how beautifully she speaks. A Bagatelle. James Reeves. POL
How bald that microscope was. V. D. Clinic. Adrien Stoutenburg. GP
"How bare! How all the lion-desert lies." Macrinus against Trees. "Michael Field." WPE
How Beastly the Bourgeois Is. D. H. Lawrence. ChTr; LiTM; NoAM; OBSV; PAI; TW
How beauteous is the bond. The Peau de Chagrin of State Street. Oliver Wendell Holmes. AP
How beautiful and calm how crimson pale. The Spirit Craft. Charles Ballard. VoR
How beautiful! from his blue throne on high. The Ocean. George D. Prentice. EtS
How beautiful is genius when combined. Sacred Poetry. John Wilson. WBLP
How beautiful is night! Night. Robert Southey. GN
How beautiful is the flag. Que Bonita Bandera. *Tr. fr. Spanish.* FSW
How beautiful is the rain! Rain in Summer. Longfellow. GN
How beautiful it was, that one bright day. Hawthorne. Longfellow. NCEP; PoEL-5
How beautiful the Earth is still. Anticipation. Emily Brontë. OBNC
How beautiful their feet. Martin Tupper. *Fr.* The Train of Religion. FaBoCo
How beautiful this hill of fern swells on! Stanzas from "Child Harold" [*or* In Epping Forest]. John Clare. *Fr.* Child Harold. FaBoPP; OBNC
How beautiful to live as thou didst live! Tennyson. Florence Earle Coates. AA
How Beautiful upon the Mountains. Bible, *O.T.* Isaiah, LII: 7-10. TrJP
How Beautiful You Are: 3. Elaine Edelman. IHMS
How, best of kings, dost thou a scepter beare! To King James. Ben Jonson. OAEP
How Big Was Alexander? Elijah Jones. BLPA
How blessed is he, who leads a country life. To My Honour'd Kinsman, John Driden, of Chesterton. Dryden. OBS

How blessed [*or* blest] was the created state. The Fall. Earl of Rochester. EnLoPo; UnTE
How blessèd were Judean hills. Noel. Gail Brook Burket. PGD
How blest art thou, canst love the countrey, Wroth. To Sir Robert Wroth. Ben Jonson. SeCV-1
How blest is he, who for his country dies. To the Earl of Oxford, Late Lord Treasurer. Swift, *after the Latin of* Horace. OBVE
How blest the maid whose heart—yet free. The Three Cottage Girls. Wordsworth. HBV-1
How blest was the created state. *See* How blessed was the created state.
How blest would be Ierne's isle. Written in Ireland. Mary Alcock. NOEC
How blowsy the trees are today. June Song. Abby Rosenthal. AMV-81
"How brent is your brow, my Lady Elspat!" Lady Elspat. *Unknown.* ESPB
How bright on the blue. The Kite. Harry Behn. FaPON; TiPo
How brim-full of nothing's the life of a beau! The Life of a Beau. James Miller. OBEC
How busie are the sonnes of men? Roger Williams. GOA; SCAP
How, Butler, How! *Unknown.* ViBoPo
(Fill the Bowl, Butler.) MeEL; OxBM
How calm and proud that lady, Nefertiti, walked. Lady and Crocodile. Charles Burgess. NePoAm-2
How calm, how beautiful, comes on. The Golden Hour. Thomas Moore. *Fr.* Lalla Rookh. OBNC
How calmly cows move to the milking sheds. The Herd. Frances Cornford. FM
How Came She to Such Poppy-Breath? Judith Mountain Leaf Volborth. TWSS
"How came that blood on thy coat-lap?" The Dead Brother. *Unknown.* EnSB
How can a flower stand out. Botany Lesson. F. D. Reeve. AMV-80
How can a girl with such a big belly be so desirable? Mrs. Loewinsohn &c. Ron Loewinsohn. NeAP
How can a long-used body reconstrue. Canticles to Men [*or* The First]. Marya Mannes. AMV-80; FAZ
How can he dare to cross me. Slug. Gwen Head. GP
How can I begin to thank. A Life of T. S. Eliot. Michael Frayn. FaBoPa
How can I call out? How can I shout? At Night. Bella Akhmadulina, *tr. by* Daniel Halpern *and* Albert Todd. BoWoP
How can I care whether you sigh for me. Song: How Can I Care? Robert Graves. GBL
How can I choose but love, and follow her. Another on Her. Robert Herrick. SpRo
How can I climb the Mount of Purgatory? Cato. C. H. Sisson. NOCV
How can I help myself, as one woman said to me about wanting. Leslie Scalapino. *Fr.* Hmmmm. NPGG
How Can I Keep from Singing? Robert Lowry. FSW
"What though my joys and comforts die?" *sel.* TRV
How Can I Keep My Maidenhead. Burns. ErPo; UnTE
How can I regret my life. The Signal. David Ignatow. NNaP
How Can I See You, Love. David Vogel, *tr. fr. Hebrew by* A. C. Jacobs. VWA
How can I sing light-souled and fancy-free. Two Lyrics, II. Lorenzo de' Medici, *tr. by* John Addington Symonds. AWP
How Can I Smile? Florence B. Hodgdon. BLRP
How can I sustain. Private Pain in Time of Trouble. Kathleen Spivack. AmPA
How can I tell you. How. S. J. Marks. NYBP
How can I, that girl standing there. Politics. W. B. Yeats. CMoP; FF; HeIP; InPS; OxBTC; POL; SCV
How can I then return in happy plight. Sonnets, XXVIII. Shakespeare. OBSC
How can I turn this wheel that turns my life. The Wheel. Edwin Muir. NoAM
How can I, who cannot control. Blind Steersmen. Francis Ernest Kobina Parkes. PBA
How can it be that I forget. Recollection. Anne Reeve Aldrich. AA
How Can Man Die Better. Tyrtaeus, *tr. fr. Greek by* T. F. Higham. WaaP
How can one e'er be sure. Lady Horikawa, *tr. by* Curtis Hidden Page. *Fr.* Hyaku-Nin-Isshu. AWP
How can one tell what Love may be about. Psychoanalysis. Gavin Ewart. NYBP
How can our minds and bodies be. Grace before Sleep. Sara Teasdale. TrPWD
How can snow sifting so fine. Snow. John Kelleher. ELU
How can that tree but withered be. Song. *Unknown.* EIL
How can the heart for sea and stone. On a Memory of Beauty. G. S. Fraser. NeBP
How Can the Heart Forget Her? Walter Davison. *See* At Her Fair Hands.
How can the tree but waste and wither away. No Pleasure without Some Pain [*or* Death in Life]. Thomas, Lord Vaux. EIL; EnRePo; OBSC
How can they go on, you see them. Another Academy. Charles Bukowski. TAT
How can they write or paint. Observations in a Cornish Teashop. Kenneth Rexroth. OBAL
How can this boyish and uplifted face. Michelangelo: "The Creation of Adam." Gregory Djanikian. AMV-81
How can we find? how can we rest? Thoughts on the Shape of the Human Body. Rupert Brooke. BrPo
How can we justify a life. For Tony, Dougal, Mick, Bugs, Nick et Al. Dave Bathgate. PoSH
How can we stand the soup? Getting a Job. Paul Blackburn. NYP
How Can You? Maxine Stevens. STF
How can you believe in it. Friday Night. Kendrick Smithyman. OCNZ
How can you comfort the suffering. How Can You? Maxine Stevens. STF
"How can you, friend?" the Swedish say. How Do You Do? H. Bedford Jones. WBLP
How can you live, how exist. The Likeness. Arthur Gregor. VGW
How can you look at the Neva. "Anna Akhmatova," *tr. fr. Russian by* Stanley Kunitz *and* Max Hayward. BoWoP
How can you set to the table a-dining? The Lost Baby. *Unknown.* AmFP
How can you stand it. The Last Song. Joy Harjo. TAT; TWSS
How carefully she does her mouth. Artist. Ernestine Mercer. InMe
How changed is here each spot man makes or fills! Thyrsis. Matthew Arnold. FaBoPP; FiP; NOBE; NoP; OAEP; OBEV; OBNC; OBVV; VLP
How close the white-ranked crosses stand. Armistice. Charles Buxton Going. HBMV
How cold are thy baths, Apollo! Jugurtha. Longfellow. AA; AP
How cold the snow. *Unknown.* *Fr.* Four Christmas Carols. PChr
How Collingbourne Was Cruelly Executed for Making a Foolish Rhyme. William Baldwin. NCEP
How Come? David Ignatow. CAD; NYP
How come nobody is being bombed today? All Quiet. David Ignatow. ConAP
How comely glisten the rounded cheeks. Fatness. Alan Ansen. CoAP
How comes this [*or* that] blood on thy shirt sleeve [*or* all over your shirt]? Edward. *Unknown.* HoPM; ViBoFo
How cool beneath this stone the soft moss lies. Epitaph for a Negro Woman. Owen Dodson. PoNe
How cool the cattle seem! Cattle. *Unknown.* SoPo
How Copernicus Stopped the Sun. R. H. W. Dillard. SUW
How could her dim eyes. Recollection. Duane Big Eagle. STE
"How could I cheat those lips of their true food?" J. W. Scholl. *Fr.* The Poet's Prothalamion. PeD
How could I know. The Dance Called David. Theodore Weiss. CoPo
How could I love you more? Prelude. Richard Aldington. BrPo
How could nothing turn so gold? Message at Sunset for Bishop Berkeley. Heather McHugh. GeTw
How could they think women a recreation? Don Giovanni on His Way to Hell II. Jack Gilbert. NMP; NPGG
How Could We, Beforehand, Live in Quiet. Nikolai Gumilev, *tr. fr. Russian by* Jeannette Eyre. WaaP
How could you be so happy, now some thousand years. Note to Wang Wei. John Berryman. NYBP
How could you dream mere body's eloquence. A Prophecy. Christopher Levenson. ErPo
How courteous is the Japanese. The Japanese. Ogden Nash. DBV; InMe; WhC
How crowded is the heavenly House of Light. For Those Who Died. Thomas Curtis Clark. PGD
How cursed that country, how severe its doom. Thomas Maurice. *Fr.* An Epistle to the Right Hon. Charles James Fox. NOEC
How cute is our kitchen. A Man about the Kitchen. Rodney Hobson. QQQ
How Cyrus Laid the Cable. John Godfrey Saxe. PAH
How dare one say it? The Unexpressed. Walt Whitman. NePA; PP
How dare we deem that in this age. Empires. Francis Burdett Money-Coutts. OBVV
How dared you die before me? It was not. Elegy for Former Students. Virginia Scott Miner. AMV-81
How dark to my mind are the scenes of my childhood. The Old, Filthy Beer Pail. Katie V. Hall. InPK; PeD
How Daur Ye Call Me Owlet Face. Burns. PoPle
("How daur ye ca' me 'Howlet-face.") FaBoEE
How dear to my heart are the grand politicians. The Old Hokum Buncombe. Robert E. Sherwood. InMe
How dear to my [*or* this *or* the] heart are the scenes of my childhood. The Old Oaken Bucket [*or* The Bucket]. Samuel Woodworth. AA; BLPA; BLSo; FaBoBe; FaFP; FaPON; FPL; FSW; HBV-1; PaPo; PSoN; TreF; WBLP
How dear to my heart is the old village drugstore. The Hair-Tonic Bottle. Ben King. OBAL

How dear to my heart was the old-fashioned hurler. The Old-fashioned Pitcher. George E. Phair. SoSe
How dear to this heart are the scenes of my childhood. *See* How dear to my heart are the scenes of my childhood.
How Death Came. *Unknown, tr. fr. Hottentot by* W. H. I. Bleek. PeSA; TTY
How Death Comes. *Unknown.* MeEL
How deep is his duplicity who in a flash. High Diver. Robert Francis. LiSp; NePoAm
How delicious is the winning. Freedom and Love [*or* Song]. Thomas Campbell. BSV; GTBS; GTBS-P; HBV-1
How delightful, at sunset, to loosen the boat! The Excursion. Tu Fu, *tr. by* Amy Lowell *and* Florence Ayscough. AWP
How delightful to meet Mr. Hodgson! Lines to Ralph Hodgson, Esqre. T. S. Eliot. OBAL
How delightful to see. Sheep Shearing. *Unknown.* OBET
How desolate! Solitude. Thomas Traherne. OBS
How did a great Red-tailed Hawk. The Dead by the Side of the Road. Gary Snyder. HAP
How did he die/ O if I told you. The Gangster's Death. Ishmael Reed. PoBA
How Did He Get Here? H. Leivick, *tr. fr. Yiddish by* Ruth Whitman. VWA
How did it come ungathered all the sheaved throng, The. Failure. Richmond Lattimore. PCP
How did it happen that we quarreled? Words! Words! Jessie Fauset. CDC
How did the Devil come? When first attack? Norfolk. John Betjeman. ChMP
How did the party go in Portman Square? Juliet. Hilaire Belloc. BaLoP; ELU; EnLoPo
How did they fume, and stamp, and roar, and chafe. Atticus. Pope. *Fr.* Epistle to Dr. Arbuthnot. InPK; TW
How did they kill my grandmother? How They Killed My Grandmother. Boris Slutsky, *tr. by* Daniel Weissbort. VWA
How did you come to me, my sweet? To a Child Who Inquires. Olga Petrova. BLPA
How Did You Die? Edmund Vance Cooke. BLPA; OHFP; PeD
How did you feel, you libertarians. Jacob Godbey. Edgar Lee Masters. *Fr.* Spoon River Anthology. LiTA
"How did you know her?" Story from Russian Author. Peter Redgrove. NePoEA-2
How did your father come down at Lodore? The Cataract at Lodore. Helen Bevington. SpRo
How Different! Ebenezer Elliott. EBEV
How do I enter the silence of stones. Mona Sa'udi, *tr. fr. Arabic by* Kamal Boullata. WPOW
How do I feel. Second Nature. Diana Chang. BrSi
How do I love thee? Let me count the ways. Sonnets from the Portuguese, XLIII. Elizabeth Barrett Browning. BoLoP; CTC; EBVV; FaBoBe; FaBV; FaFP; FF; FPL; HBV-1; HeIP; HoPM; InPS; LiTB; NIP; NoP; OAEP; OLR; PoLF; PoPl; PoRA; TEP; TreF; TrGrPo; TRV; UnPo; ViBiPo; WHA; WPE
How do I love you? Song. Irene Rutherford McLeod. HBV-1
How do robins build their nests? What Robin Told. George Cooper. FaPON; TiPo
How do they do it, the ones who make love. Sex without Love. Sharon Olds. MAYP
How do we know, by the bank-high river. The Last Lap. Kipling. OxBTC
How Do You Do? H. Bedford Jones. WBLP
How Do You Do? *Unknown. See* Misty-Moisty Was the Morn.
How do you do? Sure You Can Ask Me a Personal Question. Diane Burns. STE
"How do you do?" Will asked of me. Lines on a Certain Friend's Remarkable Faculty for Swift Generalization. Max Beerbohm. PV
How do you know it is time to bloom. Creative Force. Maude Miner Hadden. GoYe
How do you know that May has come. May-Day at Sea. John F. Finerty. EtS
How do you know that the pilgrim track. The Year's Awakening. Thomas Hardy. CMoP; OxBTC
How do you like to go up in a swing. The Swing. Robert Louis Stevenson. FaBoBe; FaFP; GoJo; NTCP; PDV; SoPo; SUS; TEP; TiPo; TreF
How Do You Live? *Unknown.* STF
How do you make bread talk, this old treasure all wrapped. Bread Is Born. Anne Hébert, *tr. by* Maxine W. Kumin. BoWoP
How do you recognize death? Minor Elegy. Henriqueta Lisboa, *tr. by* Willis Barnstone *and* Nelson Cerqueira. BoWoP
How Do You Spell "Missile"?: Preliminary Instructions in the Nuclear Age. George Uba. BrSi
How do you think I began in the world? The Sow Took the Measles. *Unknown.* FSW
How does a person get to be a capable liar? Golly, How Truth Will Out. Ogden Nash. LiTA; MoAmPo
How does it happen, tell me. Judge Somers. Edgar Lee Masters. *Fr.* Spoon River Anthology. FaBoEE; OBSV
How does it help me if, with flawless art. Elegy XXIII. Louise Labé, *tr. by* Raymond Oliver. WPOW
How does it know. The Seed. Aileen Fisher. OnUR
How does my royal lord? How fares your Majesty? Shakespeare. *Fr.* King Lear, IV, vii. Prf
"How does the water/ Come down at Lodore?" The Cataract of Lodore. Robert Southey. GN; HBV-1; OxBChV; SpRo; TEP; TreFS; WBLP
How does your little toe. Meetings and Absences. Roy Fuller. OnUR
How does your patient, doctor? A Mind Diseased. Shakespeare. *Fr.* Macbeth, V, iii. TreFT
How dost thou wear and weary out thy days. Chorus. Samuel Daniel. *Fr.* The Tragedie of Philotas. OBSC
How doth the city sit solitary, that was full of people! The Misery of Jerusalem. Bible, *O.T.* *Fr.* Lamentations. AWP
How Doth the Little Busy Bee. Isaac Watts. FaPON; HBV-1; HBVY; HoPM; TreF
(Against Idleness and Mischief.) NOEC; OBEC; OxBChV; PaPo; Par; SpRo
(Little Busy Bee.) SoPo
How Doth the Little Crocodile. "Lewis Carroll." *Fr.* Alice's Adventures in Wonderland, *ch.* 2. FaBoCh; FaBoCo; FaBoEE; FaBoNo; FaFP; FaPON; MoShBr; NIP; NOBL; Par; ShM; SoPo; SpRo; TiPo; TreFS; WhC
(Crocodile, The.) HoPM; RHPC; TrGrPo
How dreamy-dark it is! Charles Mair. *Fr.* The Fireflies. OBCV
How dull and how insensible a beast. An Essay upon Satire. John Sheffield, Duke of Buckingham and Normanby. APAS
How Easily Men's Cheeks Are Hot. Verner von Heidenstam, *tr. fr. Swedish by* Charles Wharton Stork. PoPl
How easily the ripe grain. The Widow. W. S. Merwin. NYBP; UnPo; VGW
How easy 'tis to sail with wind and tide! The Medal Reversed. Elkanah Settle. APAS
How Einstein Started It Up Again. R. H. W. Dillard. SUW
How empty seems the town now you are gone! From One Who Stays. Amy Lowell. BoWoP
How erring oft the judgment in its hate. The English Fog [*or* English Weather]. John Dyer. *Fr.* The Fleece. OBEC; TrGrPo
How everything gets tamed. Mountain, Fire, Thornbush. Harvey Shapiro. VGW
How Everything Happens. May Swenson. HAP; RFM
How fades that native breath. Sweets That Die. Langdon Elwyn Mitchell. AA
How fair a flower is sown. Coventry Patmore. FaBoEE
How fair is San Francisco Bay. San Francisco Bay. Joaquin Miller. BPAW
How fair is youth that flies so fast! Then be happy, ye who may. Triumph of Bacchus and Ariadne. Lorenzo de' Medici, *tr. by* Richard Aldington. *Fr.* Carnival Songs. CTC
How falls it, oriole, thou hast come to fly. To an Oriole. Edgar Fawcett. HBV-1
How Far? Vassar Miller. CoPo
How far are they deceived who hope in vain. Ephelia to Bajazet. Sir George Etherege. APAS
How far friends are! They forget you. Friends. William Stafford. PPJ
How Far Is It Called to the Grave? *Unknown.* BLPA
"How far is it to Babylon?" The Road to Babylon. Margaret Adelaide Wilson. HBMV
How Far Is It to Bethlehem? Frances Chesterton. HBMV; HBVY; PChr
"How far is it to Bethlehem Town?" How Far to Bethlehem? Madeleine Sweeny Miller. BLPA; FPL
How far is it to peace, the piper sighed. Our Lady Peace. Mark Van Doren. WaP
How far is it to you by foot? How Far? Vassar Miller. CoPo
"How far is St. Helena from a little child at play?" A St. Helena Lullaby. Kipling. EBEV; FaBoCh; MoVE; OAEP; OBMV; PoEL-5
How far they throw their cheer, their gracious glow. At Christmastide. Laura Simmons. PGD
How Far to Bethlehem? Madeleine Sweeny Miller. BLPA; FPL
"How fared you when you mortal were?" After. Ralph Hodgson. MoBrPo
"How farest thou?" quod he to me. The Eagle Converses with Chaucer. Chaucer. *Fr.* The House of Fame. OxBM
How fashionably sad my early poems are! About My Poems. Donald Justice. PoA
How fell sage Helen? through a swain like thee. A Countryman's Wooing. Theocritus, *tr. by* Charles Stuart Calverley. ErPo
How felt the land in every part. Washington's Vow. Whittier. OHIP

How fever'd is the [*or* that] man, who cannot look. Two Sonnets on Fame, II [*or* On Fame]. Keats. EnRP; NCEP

"How few," the Muse in plaintive accents cries. Erasmus Darwin. *Fr.* The Temple of Nature; or, The Origin of Society, IV. FM

How fierce in its loyalties the beat of the heart. Coronary Thrombosis. William Price Turner. OxBS

How fierce was I when I did see. Upon Julia Washing Herself in the River. Robert Herrick. CaPo

How Firm a Foundation. "K.," *perhaps* Robert Keene, *sometimes at. to* George Keith. TreFT; WGRP

How first we met do you still remember? Brussels and Oxford. William Hurrell Mallock. EBVV

How Five and Twenty Shillings Were Expended in a Week. *Unknown.* OBET

How fleet is air! how many things have breath. William King. *Fr.* Mully of Mountown. FM

How fond are men of rule and place. The Lion and the Cub. John Gay. *Fr.* Fables. HBV-1

How foolish men on expeditions go! On Riding to See Dean Swift in the Mist of the Morning. Alexander Pope *and* Thomas Parnell. FaBoEE

How foolishly I loved. Poema Morale. Charles Gullans. NePoEA

"How fortune deceives! I had pleasure in tow." *Unknown. Fr.* The Galley Slave. PeD

How frail. Niagara. Adelaide Crapsey. PAI

How fresh, O Lord, how sweet and clean. The Flower. George Herbert. AnAnS-1; AWP; ELP; FaBoEn; FaBoRV; JCP; MePo; NIP; NOBE; NOCV; NoP; OBS; OxBoCh; PoEL-2; PPP; SeCP; SeCV-1

How funny you are today New York. Steps. Frank O'Hara. CAPP; ConAP

How gay those bulks that tattered. Ship Bottom. Richmond Lattimore. NePoAm-2

How Gentle God's Commands. Philip Doddridge. TRV

How gently sings my soul and whets its wings. Laurence Dakin. *Fr.* Tancred, III, i. CaP

How glad I am that I was bound apprentice. For Patrick, Aetat: LXX. John Betjeman. NAs

How Glorious Are the Morning Stars, *with music.* Benjamin Keach. AH

How glorious is the hour of secret prayer. The Hour of Prayer. Albert L. Hoy. AMV-80

How Glorious Is Thy Name. Bible, *O.T.* Psalms, VIII. TrJP

How glows each patriot bosom that boasts a Yankee heart. The *United States* and *Macedonian. Unknown.* PAH

How God speeds the tax-bribed plough. Drone *v.* Worker. Ebenezer Elliott. NBM; OBSV

How Goes the Night? *Unknown, tr. fr. Chinese by* Helen Waddell. *Fr.* Shi King. AWP

How good to hear your voice again. The Priest Rediscovers His Psalm-Book. *Unknown, tr. by* Frank O'Connor. KiLC

How good to lie a little while. Friends. Abbie Farwell Brown. HBV-1; HBVY

How good we imagine it would be. Light Morning Snow, We Wait for a Warmer Season. John Garmon. AMV-80

How goodly are thy tents, O Jacob [*or* the tentes of Jacob]. Balaam's Blessing. Bible, *O.T. Fr.* Numbers. OBVE; TrGrPo

How Goodly Is Thy House, *with music.* Henry S. Jacobs. AH

How! gossip mine, gossip mine. Good Gossips Mine. *Unknown.* OxBM

How Grand and How Bright. *Unknown.* GBP

How grandly glow the bays. On the Death of Francis Thompson. Alfred Noyes. OBVV

How Gray the Rain. Elizabeth J. Coatsworth. SoPo; TiPo

How Great My Grief. Thomas Hardy. BrPo

How Great unto the Living Seem the Dead! Charles Heavysege. CaP (Dead, The.) NOBC

How green the earth, how blue the sky. The Settlers. Laurence Housman. HBV-2; OBVV

How happy a thing were a wedding. On Marriage [*or* The Bachelor's Song]. Thomas Flatman. ELU; EnLoPo; FaBoUs; FiBHP; NOBL; WhC

How happy could I be with either. Air XXXV. John Gay. *Fr.* The Beggar's Opera. ViBoPo

How happy I can be with my love away! The Absence. Sylvia Townsend Warner. MoBrPo

How happy in his low degree. Country Life. Horace, *tr. by* Dryden. *Fr.* Epodes. AWP

How happy is he born and taught. The Character of a Happy Life [*or* The Happy Life]. Sir Henry Wotton. AnAnS-2; EIL; FaPoR; GTBS; GTBS-P; HBV-2; HBVY; LiTB; NOBE; OBEV; OBS; TreF; TrGrPo; ViBoPo; WGRP

How happy is the blameless vestal's lot! Eloisa [*or* The Vestal]. Pope. *Fr.* Eloisa to Abelard. ACP; OBEC

How happy is the little stone. Emily Dickinson. NePA

How Happy the Little Birds. *Unknown, tr. fr. Modern Irish by* Padraic Pearse. OnYI

How Happy the Lover. Dryden. *Fr.* King Arthur. LoBV; ViBoPo

How Happy the Man. *Unknown.* OBET

How happy the red. Parable: November. Stephen Tapscott. FAZ

How happy were my days, till now. Song. Isaac Bickerstaffe. *Fr.* Love in a Village. OBEC

How hard for unaccustomed feet. In the Time of Trouble. Leslie Savage Clark. TrPWD

How hard I tried to be hard. The Sentimentalist. Edward Field. PPJ

How hard is my fortune. The Convict of Clonmel [*or* Clonmala]. *Unknown, tr. by* Jeremiah Joseph Callanan. AnIL; AnIV; NBM; OnYI; OxBI

How hard it is for the river here to re-enter. Wanting a Child. Jorie Graham. MAYP

How hard it is, we say. Clothes Maketh the Man. Theodore Weiss. NoAM

How hard one has to labor at it. Being Natural. Carl Rakosi. GP

How hard the years dies: no frost yet. Intercession in Late October. Robert Graves. MoAB

How Hardly I Conceal'd My Tears. Anne Wharton. CavP

How has kind Heav'n adorn'd the happy land. Italy and Britain. Joseph Addison. *Fr.* A Letter from Italy. OBEC

How hath the oppressor ceased! Downfall of the Tyrant. Bible, *O.T. Fr.* Isaiah. TrGrPo

How have I bin religious? what strange good. To Fletcher Reviv'd. Richard Lovelace. OBS

How have I laboured? Ortus. Ezra Pound. LiTA; NePA

How he advanced, with a white fillet twisted. The Lyre Player. Stefan George, *tr. by* Carol North Valhope *and* Ernst Morowitz. PeHV

How He Saved St. Michael's. Mary A. P. Stansbury. BLPA

How He Saw Her. Ben Jonson. *Fr.* A Celebration of Charis. AnAnS-2; EnRePo; OAEP; QFR; SeCP; SeCV-1

How he survived them they could never understand. The Jew Wrecked in the German Cell [*or* The Diaspora]. W. H. Auden. LiTA; WaP

How he thought. Drop the Wires. Hugh Seidman. AmPA

How, hey! It is none les. A Henpecked Husband. *Unknown.* OxBM

How High the Moon. Lance Jeffers. CNA; PoBA

How high the night clouds that pass over us. Night Clouds. Tom McKeown. HoAn

How high Thou art! our songs can own. The Mediator. Elizabeth Barrett Browning. TrPWD

How history repeats itself. Can't. Harriet Prescott Spofford. PAH

How Homer Should Have Written the Iliad. Edwin Meade Robinson. *Fr.* Limericised Classics. HBMV

"How, how," he said. "Friend Chang," I said. The Chinese Nightingale. Vachel Lindsay. HBMV; MoAmPo; NePA

How I Brought the Good News from Aix to Ghent (or Vice Versa). R. J. Yeatman *and* W. C. Sellar. BXAP; FaBoPa; FiBHP; OnMSP; SpRo; WhC

How I Came to Be a Graduate Student. Wendy Rose. STE

How I doe love thee, Beaumont, and thy Muse. To Francis Beaumont. Ben Jonson. OAEP; OBS

How I Escaped from the Labyrinth. Philip Dacey. POL; PPJ

How I forsook/ Elias and Pisa after, and betook. Giovanni Battista Guarini, *tr. by* Sir Richard Fanshawe. *Fr.* Il Pastor Fido. AWP

How I go courting a charming beauty bright. Charming Beauty Bright. *Unknown.* AmFP

How I Got Ovah. Carolyn M. Rodgers. CNA

How I loved him. Courtship. Diana O Hehir. NPGG

How I loved one like you when I was little. Slug. Theodore Roethke. CABA

How I loved those old movies. Old Movies. John Cotton. FF

How I Was Her Kitchen-Boy. Gunter Grass, *tr. fr. German by* Betty Falkenberg. AMV-81

How I wish I had known/ beforehand of this journey. *Tr. fr. Japanese by* Kenneth Yasuda. BoWoP

How I wish I were able to say what I think. Gertrude Stein. *Fr.* Stanzas in Meditation. PBWP

How I wish I. The Value of Pi. *Unknown.* FaBoUs

How I wish the Argo had never reached the land. Medea. Euripides, *tr. by* Rex Warner. NAWM-1

How I'd Have It. John Stone. AMV-81

How ill doth he deserve a Lovers name. Eternity of Love Protested. Thomas Carew. MeLP; OBS

How impotent a deity am I! Sir Samuel Garth. *Fr.* The Dispensary. OBSV

How in Heaven's name did Columbus get over. Columbus. Arthur Hugh Clough. AmFN; PoSC

How Infinite Are Thy Ways. William Force Stead. *Fr.* Uriel. OBMV ("I thought the night without a sound was falling.") TrPWD

How innocent their lives look. Photos of a Salt Mine. P. K. Page. NOBC

How is it I can eat bread here and cut meat. Evening Meal in the Twentieth Century. John Holmes. MiAP

How is it now? Questions [2]. Donald Hall. FF

How is it proved? The Great Wager. G. A. Studdert-Kennedy. TrCP
How is it that I am so careless here. Meditation 62. Philip Pain. NOBA
How is it with another woman? An Attempt at Jealousy. Marina Tsvetaeva, *tr. by* Robert Perelman *and* Aleksandar Petrov. WPOW
How is man parcell'd out! how ev'ry hour. The Tempest. Henry Vaughan. AnAnS-1
"How is she?" I asked. Lily, Lois & Flaubert; the Site of Loss. Kathleen Fraser. NPGG
How is 't, my Soul, that thou giv'st eyes their sight. To My Soul. Phineas Fletcher. OxBoCh
How Is the Gold Become Dim. Bible, *O.T.* Lamentations, IV: 1-5. ChTr
How it feels to be touching. We Become New. Marge Piercy. TAP
How It Goes On. Maxine W. Kumin. FAZ; FiCP
How It Is. Uri Zvi Greenberg, *tr. fr. Hebrew by* Robert Mezey *and* Ben Zion Gold. VWA
How it is I returned. Childhood. Sherod Santos. AMV-81
How it responds with its heart. For a Voice That Is Singing. Aldo Camerino, *tr. by* Anita Barrows. VWA
How it sits, like a muddle. Jealousy. Rachel de Vries. AMV-81
How It Strikes a Contemporary. Robert Browning. CTC; GTBS-P; OAEL-2; PP; VLP
How Jack Found That Beans May Go Back on a Chap. Guy Wetmore Carryl. HoPM
How joyous his neigh! Song of the Horse. *Unknown, tr. by* Natalie Curtis. AWP
How joyously the young sea-mew. The Sea-Mew. Elizabeth Barrett Browning. HBV-1; VLP
How kind, how secretly, the sun. The Garden. Robert Penn Warren. PoA
How large unto the tiny fly. The Fly. Walter de la Mare. OnUR; PoPle
How late the assassins ply their trade tonight. Nausea. E. L. Mayo. MiAP
How! Liberty of Conscience! that's a change. Dr. Wild's Ghost. *Unknown.* APAS
How life and death in Thee. To Our Blessed Lord upon the Choice of His Sepulchre [*or* Upon Our Saviour's Tomb Wherein Never Man Was Laid]. Richard Crashaw. ACP; OAEL-1
How like a marriage is the season of clouds. Cloud Country. James Merrill. NePoEA
How like a well-kept garden is your soul. Moonlight. Paul Verlaine, *tr. by* John Gray. SyP
How like a Winter hath my absence been[e]. Sonnets, XCVII. Shakespeare. AWP; CABA; ElL; EnLoPo; EnRePo; FaBoEn; GTBS; GTBS-P; NOBE; OAEL-1; OBEV; OBSC; PoRA; TEP; TrGrPo
How like an angel came I down. Wonder. Thomas Traherne. AnAnS-1; CH; HAP; LiTB; LoBV; NoP; PPoe; SeCePo; SeCeV; SeCP; SeCV-2; TrGrPo; WHA
How like the leper, with his own sad cry. The Buoy-Bell. Charles Tennyson Turner. EtS
How Like You This? Sir Thomas Wyatt. *See* Lover-Showeth How He Is Forsaken of Such as He Sometime Enjoyed, The.
How Lil[l]ies Came White. Robert Herrick. AnAnS-2; CaPo
How little does history manage to tell? Lessons in History. Robert Penn Warren. AMV-80
How long ago Hector took off his plume. Parting in Wartime. Frances Cornford. NIP
How long ago she planted the hawthorn hedge. The Hawthorn Hedge. Judith Wright. PoAu-2; WPE
How long ago we dreamed. Carol of the Three Kings. W. S. Merwin. PChr
How long, dear Savior, O how long. Isaac Watts. AmFP
How long, great God, how long must I. The Aspiration. John Norris. LoBV; OxBoCh
"How Long Hast Thou Been a Gravemaker?" David Perkins. NCSH
How long have you been living here? The Arkansas Traveller. Mose Case. PSoN
How long, how long must I regret? The Lost Tribe. Ruth Pitter. WPOW
How long I pleaded I can never guess. Long Pursuit. *Unknown, tr. by* Louis Untermeyer. UnTE
How long it seems since that mild April night. Seaward. Celia Thaxter. AA
How long I've loved thee, and how well. Love's Wisdom. Margaret Deland. AA
How Long, Jehovah? *with music.* Henry Ainsworth. AH
How long must we two hide the burning gaze. United. Paulus Silentiarius, *tr. by* W. H. D. Rouse. AWP
How long, O lion, hast thou fleshless lain? The Lion's Skeleton. Charles Tennyson Turner. FM; NBM; VLP
How long, O Lord, shall I forgotten be? Bible, *O.T.* Psalms, XIII, *paraphrased by* Sir Philip Sidney. OBVE
How long, O sister, how long. The Bells at Midnight. Thomas Bailey Aldrich. PAH
"How long shall fortune faile me now." The Earl of Westmoreland. *Unknown.* ESPB
How long shall I endure without reply. The Medal of John Bays; a Satire against Folly and Knavery. Thomas Shadwell. APAS
How Long Shall I Give? *Unknown.* BLRP
How long shall I pine for love? Pining for Love. Francis Beaumont. POL
"How long shall man be nature's fool?" Man cries. The Sakiyeh. Mathilde Blind. SBG
How long shall this like dying life endure. Amoretti, XXV. Spenser. EnRePo
How long shall you and I be bound. Water Whirligigs. D. J. Opperman, *tr. by* Jack Cope *and* Uys Krige. PeSA
How long she waited for her executioner! Head of Medusa. Marya Zaturenska. MoAmPo
How long this giant hugged and spanned. Windmill on the Cape. William Vincent Sieller. GoYe
How Long This Night Is. *Unknown. See* Merry It Is.
How long this way: that everywhere. Red Sea. James Agee. *Fr.* Two Songs on the Economy of Abundance. MoAmPo
How long until the war's end sets you free? Longing. "Michael Lewis." *Fr.* Cherry Blossoms. UnTE
How long will it last? Lady Horikawa, *tr. fr. Japanese by* Kenneth Rexroth *and* Ikuko Atsumi. WPOW
How long will these graves go on? Graves in Queens. Richard Hugo. NYP
How long will you remain a boy? Meditation. Carl Rakosi. VWA
How long, young men, unsoldiered, disregarding. A Call to Action. Callinus, *tr. by* T. F. Higham. WaaP
How look'd your love, sweet Shepherd, yestereven. The Orchard by the Shore; a Pastoral. Elinor Sweetman. OBVV
How lost is the little fox at the borders of night. Night of Wind. Frances M. Frost. FaPON; TiPo
How lovely are the tombs of the dead nymphs. Panope. Edith Sitwell. MoAB; MoBrPo
How lovely are thy dwellings fair! Psalm LXXXIV. Milton. TrPWD
How lovely are Thy tabernacles. Bible, *O.T.* Psalm LXXXIV: 1-5. TrJP
How lovely is the heaven of this night. A Beautiful Night [*or* Lines]. Thomas Lovell Beddoes. ChER; LoBV; NBM
How lovely is the sound of oars at night. Boats at Night. Edward Shanks. CH
How lovely it was, after the official fright. The Phenomenon. Karl Shapiro. CMoP; NMP; NYBP
How lovely the elder brother's. Brothers. Gerard Manley Hopkins. OAEP
How Low Is the Lowing Herd. Walt Kelly. FiBHP
How low when angels fall their black descent. The Promise in Disturbance. George Meredith. VLP
How lush, how loose, the uninhibited squash is. Squash in Blossom. Robert Francis. FYAP
How many a thing which we cast to the ground. Modern Love, XLI. George Meredith. HBV-1
How many a time have I. Swimming. Byron. *Fr.* The Two Foscari. GN
How Many Bards Gild the Lapses of Time! Keats. EnRP
How many bullets does it take. Death in Yorkville. Langston Hughes. PoBA
How many buttons are missing today! Nobody Knows but Mother. Mary Morrison. BLPA
How many dawns, chill from his rippling rest. To Brooklyn Bridge [*or* Proem]. Hart Crane. *Fr.* The Bridge. AmPP; AP; BLPL; CABA; CMoP; CoBMV; CrMA; EyDe; FaBoEn; HAP; HeIP; InPS; LiTA; LiTM; MoAB; MoAmPo; MoPo; NePA; NoAM; NOBA; NoP; NYP; OxBA; PoPl; PrIm; SeCeV; TAP; WeW
How many days has my baby to play? Mother Goose. OxNR; TiPo
How many doors will this man open. Death. Roy Fuller. NoAM
How many equal with the Argive queen. The Power of Poets. Ben Jonson. *Fr.* Epistle to Elizabeth, Countess of Rutland. WHA
How many evenings in the arbor by the river. Li Ch'ing-chao, *tr. fr. Chinese by* Eugene Eoyang. BoWoP
How many fires. George Reavey. EAS
How Many Heavens. Edith Sitwell. TrCP
How many humble hearts have dipped. To a Post-Office Inkwell. Christopher Morley. PoLF
How many kisses do I ask? To Anne. William Stirling-Maxwell. HBV-1
How many kisses, Lesbia, you ask. Ad Lesbiam. Catullus, *tr. by* Niall Sheridan. OxBI
How many lives, made beautiful and sweet. Giotto's Tower. Longfellow. EyDe
How many men are killed by Power, by Power. Sejanus. Juvenal, *tr. by* Robert Lowell. *Fr.* Satires, X. OBVE
How many miles to Babylon [*or* Barley-Bridge]? Mother Goose. FaBoCh; GBP; MoShBr; OxBoLi; OxNR
How many million Aprils came. Blue Squills. Sara Teasdale. HBMV
How many moments must (amazing each). E. E. Cummings. PoA
How many morning suns have kissed this glass? Kitchen Window. Ruth N. Ebberts. AMV-80

How many names for what bees see? The Letters of a Name. Colette Inez. AMV-81
How Many New Years Have Grown Old. *Unknown.* ElL
How Many Nights. Galway Kinnell. MAT; NaP
How many of the body's health complain. Soul-Sickness. Jones Very. AP
How many paltry, foolish, painted things. Michael Drayton. Idea, VI. AAS; ElL; EnLoPo; EnRePo; GBL; HAP; HBV-1; HeIP; LoBV; NIP; NoP; OAEL-1; OBSC; PrIm; TEP
"How many pounds does the baby weigh." Weighing the Baby. Ethel Lynn Beers. HBV-1
How Many Seconds in a Minute? Christina Rossetti. SiSoSe
How many skies does the earth hold? Ourobouros. Jorge Plescoff, *tr. by* Yishai Tobin. VWA
How many strive to force a way. Forcing a Way. *Unknown.* NA
How many summers, love. The Poet's Song to His Wife. "Barry Cornwall." HBV-1
How many thousand of my poorest subjects. The Cares of Majesty [*or* O Gentle Sleep *or* Soliloquy on Sleep]. Shakespeare. King Henry IV, Pt. II, *fr.* III, *i.* FaBoRV; FiP; LiTB; TreF
How many thousands never heard the name. Samuel Daniel. *Fr.* Musophilus. PP
How many times, Death. O All Down within the Pretty Meadow. Kenneth Patchen. WeW
How Many Times Do I Love Thee, Dear? Thomas Lovell Beddoes. *See* Song: "How many times do I love thee, dear?"
How many times must I tell. My Angel. Philip Levine. AMV-81
How many times these low feet staggered. Emily Dickinson. AmPP; AP; CABA; HAP; PoEL-5; WeW
How Many Ways. John Masefield. *Fr.* Sonnets ("Long long ago"). LiTB ("How many ways, how many times.") WGRP
How many wise men and heroes. To the Tune "The River Is Red." Ch'iu Chin, *tr. by* Kenneth Rexroth *and* Ling Chung. BoWoP; PBWP
How Marigolds Came Yellow. Robert Herrick. ChTr
How marvellous and fair a thing. Springtime in Cookham Dean. Cecil Roberts. HBMV
How McClellan Took Manassas. *Unknown.* PAH
How McDougal Topped the Score. Thomas E. Spencer. PoAu-1
How memory cuts away the years. Autumn. Jean Starr Untermeyer. HBMV; MoAmPo
How mighty a wizard. Z Is for Zoroaster. Eleanor Farjeon. WSC
How mobile is the bed on these. Rain. Vladimir Nabokov. GrPl
How monarchs die is easily explained. On a Royal Demise. Thomas Hood. FiBHP; PV
How Morning Glories Could Bloom at Dusk. Jorie Graham. NPGG
How most unnatural-seeming, yet how proper. Sirocco at Deyá. Robert Graves. MoVE
How most unworthy, echoing in mine ears. Frederick Goddard Tuckerman. Sonnets, II, xii. AP
How mournful seems, in broken dreams. Not Lost, but Gone Before. Caroline Elizabeth Sarah Norton. BLRP; PaPo; WBLP
How much are they deceived who vainly strive. Love and Jealousy. William Walsh. BoLoP
How Much Earth. Philip Levine. NNaP
How much living have you done? The Poet Speaks. Georgia Douglas Johnson. AmNP
How Much Longer? Robert Mezey. OBWP
How Much Longer Will I Be Able to Inhabit the Divine Sepulcher. John Ashbery. NeAP; NoAM; PoM
How much more. The Process. Robert Kelly. CoPo
How much of me is sandwiches radio beer? Lonesome in the Country. Al Young. MAT; NPGG
How much, preventing God, how much I owe. Grace. Emerson. AmPP; NoP; TrPWD
How much the heart may bear, and yet not break! Endurance. Elizabeth Akers Allen. HBV-2
How much we pay to say, "*Je suis.*" Samuel Hoffenstein. *Fr.* As the Crow Flies. WhC
How much wood would a woodchuck chuck? If a Woodchuck Would Chuck. *Unknown.* FaPON; TiPo
How Music's Made. Dilys Laing. ELU
How must you be now, old woman. Words to Remind Me of Grandmother. Andrés Castro Ríos, *tr. by* Julio Marzán. InW
How mutable is every thing that here. Meditation 29. Philip Pain. *Fr.* Meditations for July 26, 1666. NOBA; SCAP
How My Father Died. Nissim Ezekiel. VWA
How My Songs of Her Began. Philip Bourke Marston. HBV-1
How my thoughts betray me! A Prayer for Recollection. *Unknown, tr. by* Frank O'Connor. KiLC
How near me came the hand of Death. A Widow's Hymn. George Wither. LO; OBEV
How nice to be a local swan. Sitting Pretty. Margaret Fishback. PoLF
How Night Falls in the Courtyard. Christine Rimmer. AMV-80
How No Age Is Content [with His Own Estate]. Earl of Surrey. *See* Laid in My Quiet Bed.
How no shoe fit them. My Mother's Feet. Stanley Plumly. GeTw
How now could body-soul's symbol be this. The White Rat. Marguerite Young. MoPo
How now, spirit! whither wander you? Shakespeare. *Fr.* A Midsummer Night's Dream. GN
How odd/ Of God. The Chosen People. W. N. Ewer. DBV; FaBoEE
How of the Virgin Mother shall I sing? Ennodius, *tr. fr. Latin. Fr.* Hymnus Sanctae Mariae. ISi
How oft against the sunset sky or moon. Wild Geese. Frederick Peterson. HBV-1; HBVY
How oft am I for rhyme to seek? Ben Jonson. *Fr.* To Dr. Delaney. PP
How oft amid the heaped and bedded hay. Written in July, 1824. Mary Russell Mitford.
How Oft Has the Banshee Cried. Thomas Moore. AnIV; AWP
How oft have I, my dere and cruell foe. Sir Thomas Wyatt. AAS
How oft I dream of childhood days, of tricks we used to play. Rosie Nell. *Unknown.* AS
How oft I prayed to hold her in my arms. Faint Heart. Rufinus, *tr. by* F. A. Wright. ErPo
How oft when men are at the point of death. Romeo's Last Words. Shakespeare. *Fr.* Romeo and Juliet, V, iii. DL; FiP
How oft, when pressed to marriage, have I said. Pope. *Fr.* Eloisa to Abelard. ViBoPo
How oft, when thou, my music, music play'st. Sonnets, CXXVIII. Shakespeare. ElL
How Often. Ben King. HBV-1
How often does a man need to see a woman? The Word Made Flesh. W. J. Turner. OBMV
How often have I started out. Inspiration. Robert W. Service. WeW
How often have my tears. In Allusion to the French Song. Richard Lovelace. CaPo
How often in the summer-tide. Across the Field to Anne. Richard Burton. HBV-1
How often in the years that close. A Meditation. Herman Melville. GOA
How often should we think of this, that we. Meditations for August 1, 1666. Philip Pain. SCAP
How often, when life's summer day. Walter Savage Landor. FaBoEE
How Old Are You? H. S. Fritsch. PoLF
How Old Brown Took Harper's Ferry. Edmund Clarence Stedman. HBV-2; OnMSP; PAH; PoNe
How Old Is My Heart. Christopher Brennan. *Fr.* The Wanderer. PoAu-1
How old may Phillis [*or* Phyllis] be, you ask. Phillis's [*or* Phyllis's] Age. Matthew Prior. EnLoPo; FaBoEE
How old was Mary out of whom you cast. Charlotte Mew. *Fr.* Madeleine in Church. LO; MoAB; MoBrPo
How Old's the Moon? *Unknown, tr. fr. Japanese by* Graehme Wilson. MOON
How on Solemn Fields of Space. Elizabeth Daryush. NOCV
How One-Thumb Willie Got His Name. John L. Sellers. LFAC
How One Winter Came in the Lake Region. Wilfred Campbell. CaP; NOBC; OBCV; PeCV
How Our Forefather Got His Wife. Eda Lou Walton. BPAW
How our good king does Papists hate. Satire on Old Rowley. *Unknown.* APAS
How Paddy Stole the Rope. *Unknown.* BLPA
How pitiful are little folk. Creeds. Willard Wattles. HBMV
How pitiful is her sleep. In Memory of Kathleen. Kenneth Patchen. MoAmPo
How placid, how divinely sweet. Meandering Wye. Robert Bloomfield. *Fr.* The Banks of Wye. OBNC
How placidly shine/ The river, the spring, and the sun. Rosalía de Castro, *tr. fr. Galician by* Benjamin M. Woodbridge, Jr. PBWP
How Pleasant Is This Flowery Plain. *Unknown.* OBS
How pleasant it is that always. Song. Florence Smith. BLPA
How Pleasant It Is to Have Money. Arthur Hugh Clough. *See* As I Sat at the Café.
How Pleasant to Know Mr. Lear. Edward Lear. ChTr; EBEV; FaBoCo; FiBHP; HAP; NOBE; NOBL; NoP; PAI; SpRo; VLP; WeW; WhC
(By Way of Preface.) GTBS-P; InPS; InvP; NBM; OxBoLi; PoEL-5
(Lines to a Young Lady.) InMe; NA
(Self-Portrait of the Laureate of Nonsense.) FaBoCh
How pleased within my native bowers. Song: The Landskip [*or* The Landscape]. William Shenstone. OBEC; SeCePo
How poor, how rich, how abject, how august. Edward Young. *Fr.* The Complaint; or, Night Thoughts, I. OAEL-1
How precise it seems, like a doll house. Housework. William Matthews. NPAW
How prone we are to sin, how sweet were made. And Forgive Us Our Trespasses. Aphra Behn. EBEV

How pure the hearts of lovers as they walk. Prothalamium. May Sarton. NePoAm
How quickly the dandelions. Americana XVII: A Reminder of William Carlos Williams. Carl Rakosi. InPS
How quiet is the morning in the hills! Morning in the Hills. Bliss Carman. NOBC
How quiet the day is. The Leaf. John Williams. NePoAm-2
How quietly in ruined state. Aix-La-Chappelle, 1945. Edgar Bowers. NePoEA
How rare to be born a human being! Gary Snyder. Myths and Texts: Hunting, XVI. CAPP; NaP
How Red the Rose That Is the Soldier's Wound. Wallace Stevens. *Fr.* Esthétique du Mal. CMoP; NOBA; WaP
(Soldier's Wound, The.) Waap
How rewarding to know Mr. Smith. Mr. Smith (with Nods to Mr. Lear and Mr. Eliot). William Jay Smith. FiBHP; SpRo
How rich and pleasing thou, my Julia, art. To Julia. Robert Herrick. CaPo
How rich, O Lord! how fresh thy visits are. Unprofitablenes. Henry Vaughan. AnAnS-1; SeCV-1
How rich the wave, in front, imprest. Lines Written near Richmond, upon Thames, at Evening. Wordsworth. OBEC
How rich we were, to know them, exiles. Priest Lake. William Stafford. PoA
How richly, with ridiculous display. *See* Here, richly, with ridiculous display.
How Roses Came Red. Robert Herrick. CaPo; CavP; ChTr; SoSe
How sad if, by some strange new law. Suppose. Anne Reeve Aldrich. HBV-1
How sad it must be. A Poem for My Father. Sonia Sanchez. BPo; IHMS
How sad the note of that funereal drum. On the Death of Commodore Oliver H. Perry. John G. C. Brainard. PAH
How safe, methinks, and strong, behind. After Floods on the Wharfe. Andrew Marvell. *Fr.* Upon Appleton House. FaBoPP
How say that by law we may torture and chase. She's Free! Frances E. W. Harper. BlSi
How see you Echo? When she calls I see. Echo. Viscountess Grey of Fallodon. CH
How seldom, friend! a good great man inherits. The Good Great Man [*or* Complaint]. Samuel Taylor Coleridge. HBV-2; WhC
How Shall a Man Fore-doomed. Hartley Coleridge. Three Sonnets, II. NCEP
"How shall I a habit break?" A Builder's Lesson. John Boyle O'Reilly. PoLF
How shall I address Thee, O God? how shall I praise Thee? *Unknown. Fr.* Nanak and the Sikhs. WGRP
How shall I array my love? The Question. Frederick Goddard Tuckerman. AP
"How shall I be a poet?" Poeta Fit, Non Nascitur. "Lewis Carroll." FaBoNo; NBM; OBSV
How shall I begin my song. Songs for the Four Parts of the Night. Owl Woman (Juana Manwell), *tr. by* Frances Densmore. PBWP
How shall I forsake wisdom? In Praise of Wisdom. Solomon ibn Gabirol, *tr. by* Solomon Solis-Cohen. TrJP
How shall I guard my soul so that it be. The Song of Love. Rainer Maria Rilke, *tr. by* Ludwig Lewisohn. AWP
How shall I keep April. Foreboding. Hazel Hall. HBMV
How shall I know if my love lose his youth. Epigram. Strato, *tr. by* Sydney Oswald. PeHV
How shall I name you, immortal, mild, proud shadows? W. B. Yeats. NU
How shall I plead my cause, when you, my judge. Cleopatra and Antony. Dryden. *Fr.* All for Love. FiP
How shall I report. The Commendations of Mistress Jane Scrope. John Skelton. *Fr.* Phyllyp Sparrowe. OBSC; ViBoPo
How shall I speak of doom, and ours in special. Tales from a Family Album. Donald Justice. NePoEA-2; TwAmPo
How shall I still mankind's good will retrieve. August, Graf von Platen. Sonnets to Karl Theodore German, XXII. PeHV
How shall I tell the measure of my love? Thysia, XLV. Morton Luce. HBV-1
How shall I tell the torments of that hour. The Author Consults a Critic and Sells His Manuscript. Francis Hawling. *Fr.* The Signal; or, A Satire against Modesty. NOEC
How shall I withhold my soul so that. Lovesong. Rainer Maria Rilke, *tr. by* M. D. Herter Norton. OLR
How shall my tongue expresse that hallow'd fire. Francis Quarles. Emblems, V, 11. AnAnS-1
How shall the bayonet and bomb. Design for Peace. Janet Norris Bangs. PGD
How shall the river learn. Max Schmitt in a Single Scull. Richmond Lattimore. EyDe; NePoAm-2
How shall the wine be drunk, or the woman known? A Voice from under the Table. Richard Wilbur. AmPP; HAP; NePoEA; NOBA; SeCeV
How shall we adorn. Angle of Geese. N. Scott Momaday. CDW; QFR
How Shall We Honor Them? Edwin Markham. PGD
How shall we know it is the last good-by? The Last Good-by. Louise Chandler Moulton. AA
How Shall We Mourn You Who Are Killed and Wasted. Charles Reznikoff. InPK
How shall we please this age? If in a song. To Nysus. Sir Charles Sedley. FaBoEE; OBSV
How shall we praise the magnificence of the dead. Tetélestai. Conrad Aiken. LiTA; LiTM; MoAB; MoAmPo; PrIm
How Shall We Rise to Greet the Dawn? Sir Osbert Sitwell. WGRP
How shall we speak of Canada. W. L. M. K. F. R. Scott. NOBC
How shall we summon you? Hymn to Chance. H. Phelps Putnam. TwAmPo
How shall we tell an angel. Angels. Gertrude Hall. AA
How She Resolved to Act. Merrill Moore. MoAmPo
How shocking the stocking that matches the pink. Color Blind. Carol Paine. PV
How Should I Be So Pleasant. Sir Thomas Wyatt. LoBV; SiPS
(Betrayal.) OBSC
How should I describe you—eternal. Koala. Alan Ross. BoAnP
How should I find speech. Person, or a Hymn on and to the Holy Ghost. Margaret Avison. PeCV
How should I love my best? Madrigal. Lord Herbert of Cherbury. AnAnS-2; PoEL-2; SeCP; ViBoPo
How should I praise thee, Lord! how should my rymes. The Temper. George Herbert. AnAnS-1; MePo; NOCV; NoP; OBS; OxBoCh; PoEL-2; WHA
How Should I Rule Me? *Unknown.* OxBM
How Should I Your True Love Know. Shakespeare. *Fr.* Hamlet, IV, v. EBEV; EnLoPo; LiTB; PoRA; QFR; ViBoPo
(Friar of Orders Grey, The.) GoBC
(Ophelia's Song.) ChTr; GBL; OBSC; TrGrPo
(Song.) CH
How should I your true love know. An Old Song Ended [*or* The Friar of Orders Grey]. Dante Gabriel Rossetti. BoLoP; EBVV; GoBC
How should the world be luckier if this house. Upon a House Shaken by the Land Agitation. W. B. Yeats. CMoP
How shril are silent tears! when sin got head. Admission. Henry Vaughan. AnAnS-1
How sick I get. Father. Paul Carroll. DiL; NeAP
How silent comes the water round that bend. Minnows. Keats. GN
How silly that soldier is pointing his gun at the wood. Russians. Keith Douglass. OxBTC
How silly were those sages heretofore. Samuel Butler. *Fr.* Satire upon the Licentious Age of Charles II. NOBL
How Singular. Tom Hood. FaBoNo
How singular some old words are! Singular Singulars, Peculiar Plurals. Willard R. Espy. FaBoUs
How Sleep the Brave. William Collins. GN; HBV-2; HBVY; NOBE; OBEV; TreF
(Ode: "How sleep the brave, who sink to rest.") ELP; LoBV; OAEP; ViBoPo
(Ode Written in 1746.) GTBS; GTBS-P; TrGrPo; WHA
(Ode, Written in the Beginning of the Year 1746.) AWP; EnRP; HAP; HeIP; LAuP; NOEC; NoP; OBEC; PAI; PoEL-3; SeCeV
(Sleep of the Brave, The.) OHIP
How sleep the brave who sink to rest. On a Watchman Asleep at Midnight. James Thomas Fields. CenHV
How slight a thing may set one's fancy drifting. Honey Dripping from the Comb. James Whitcomb Riley. AA
How slow they are awakening, these trees. Plain Fare. Daryl Hine. CoAP
How slow time moves when torment stops the clock! The Conclusion. Delmore Shwartz. TwAmPo
How slowly creeps the hand of Time. The Churchyard. Robert Buchanan. HBV-2
How slowly learns the child at school. Citizenship; Form 8889512, Sub-Section Q. G. K. Chesterton. OxBoLi
How Slowly Time, the Loathsome Snail. Heine, *tr. fr. German by* Ernst Feise. NAWM-2
How small a tooth hath mined the season's heart! Frost. Edith M. Thomas. AA
How Small Is Man. John Stuart Blackie. PoSH
How smooth that lake expands its ample breast! Stanzas. Anne Radcliffe. WPE
How soon doth man decay! Mortification. George Herbert. AnAnS-1; MePo; OAEP; SeCP; ViBoPo
How Soon Hath Time [the Subtle Thief of Youth]. Milton. CABA; FF; HeIP; InPS; LiTB; NAs; OAEP; PAI; PPoe; SeCePo; SeCeV
(On His Having arrived at the Age of Twenty-three.) AWP; PrIm; TrGrPo
(On His 24th Birthday.) FaBoEn

(On His Twenty-third Birthday.) FiP
(Sonnet: "How soon hath time, the subtle thief of youth.") LoBV; OAEL-1; OBS; TRV; ViBoPo
(Sonnet: On His Having Arrived to the Age of Twenty-three.) HBV-1
How sound are ye sleeping, comrades. Bitter Question. Arthur R. Macdougall, Jr. PGD
How splendid in the morning glows. Hassan's Serenade. James Elroy Flecker. *Fr.* Hassan. OBEV
How spoke the king, in his crucial hour victorious? King of the Belgians. Marion Couthouy Smith. PAH
How Stands the Glass Around? *Unknown, at. to* James Wolfe. *See* Why, Soldiers, Why?
How Stars and Hearts Grow in Apples. Virginia Elson. AMV-81
How startling to find the portraits of the gods. Mythological Sonnet XVI. Roy Fuller. ErPo
How stately stand yon pines upon the hill. Spring to Winter [*or* In Suffolk]. George Crabbe. *Fr.* The Ancient Mansion. ChTr; FaBoPP
How still he stands as mists begin to move. The Guard at the Binh Thuy Bridge. John Balaban. FYAP
How still, how happy! These [*or* Those] are words. Emily Brontë. OBNC; VLP
How still, how very still the air is. The Unwilling Guest; an Urban Dialogue. Horace Gregory. CrMA
How still it is here in the woods. Solitude. Archibald Lampman. BoNaP; OBCV; PeCV
How still the day is, and the air how bright! By the Wood. Robert Nichols. ChMP; HBMV; MMA
How Still the Hawk. Charles Tomlinson. LiTM
How still the morning of the hallowed day! Sunday Morning. James Grahame. OBRV
How still the room is! But a while ago. In Death. Mary Emily Bradley. AA
How still the sea! behold; how calm the sky! Pastoral Landscape. Ambrose Philips. *Fr.* Pastorals. OBEC
How still this quiet cornfield is to-night. August, 1914. John Masefield. HBV-2
How straight it flew, how long it flew. Seaside Golf. John Betjeman. LiSp; PoPl
How strange at night [*or* it is] to wake. Night and Sleep [*or* The Shadow of Night]. Coventry Patmore. CH; EBVV
How strange is Love; I am not one. The Gourmet's Love-Song. P. G. Wodehouse. NOBL
How Strange It Is. Claudia Lewis. RHPC
How strange it is to wake. *See* How strange at night to wake.
How strange it seems! These Hebrews in their graves. The Jewish Cemetery at Newport. Longfellow. AmPP; AP; HAP; HeIP; HoPM; NOBA; NoP; OxBA; PPON; TAP
How strange the pride of many Irishmen! The New Style. David O'Bruadair, *tr. by* John Montague. BIrV
How strange the sculptures that adorn these towers! Longfellow. Divina Commedia, II. GoBC; NePA; SeCeV
How strange to awake in a city. Hearing Men Shout at Night on MacDougal Street. Robert Bly. CAD
How strange to think of giving up all ambition! Watering the Horse. Robert Bly. NaP; NCSH
How strangely this sun reminds me of my love! Stephen Spender. PeHV
How strong does my passion flow. On Her Loving Two Equally. Aphra Behn. SBG
How struts my love my cavalier. Cock-a-Hoop. Isabella Gardner. WPE
How subtle-secret is your smile! Oscar Wilde. *Fr.* The Sphinx. MoBrPo; UnTE
How sweet and lovely dost thou make the shame. Sonnets, XCV. Shakespeare. MasP; TrGrPo
How sweet and silent is the place. A Communion Hymn. Alice Freeman Palmer. TrPWD
How Sweet I Roamed from Field to Field. Blake. *See* Song: "How sweet I roam'd from field to field."
How sweet is harmless solitude! Solitude. Mary Mollineux. CavP
How Sweet Is the Language of Love, *with music.* Oliver Holden. AH
How sweet is the shepherd's sweet lot. The Shepherd. Blake. *Fr.* Songs of Innocence. EnRP; HBV-1; LoBV; OBEC; TiPo
How sweet it is, at first approach of morn. Oliver Goldsmith, the Younger. *Fr.* The Rising Village. OBCV
How sweet the answer Echo makes. Echo [*or* Echoes]. Thomas Moore. ELP; GoBC; GTBS; GTBS-P; OxBI
How sweet the harmonies of afternoon. The Blackbird. Frederick Tennyson. HBV-1
How sweet the moon is climbing heaven's hill! Moonlight. Edward Moxon. OBRV
How Sweet the Moonlight Sleeps. Shakespeare. *Fr.* The Merchant of Venice, V, i. FaBoRV; TreFS; TrGrPo
(Moonlight.) OHFP
How Sweet the Name of Jesus Sounds. John Newton. *See* Name of Jesus, The.
How sweet the silent backward tracings! Memories. Walt Whitman. PCP
How sweet the tuneful bells' responsive peal! Sonnet: At Ostend [*or* The Bells of Ostend]. William Lisle Bowles. EnRP; NOEC; OBEC
How Sweet Thy Precious Gift of Rest. Menahem ben Makhir of Ratisbon, *tr. fr. Hebrew by* Herbert Loewe. TrJP
How sweet, to see the dells so shady. An Englishman with an Atlas; or, America the Unpronounceable. Morris Bishop. GOA
How sweet to wear a shape of snow. Duck in Central Park. Frances Higginson Savage. GoYe
How sweet, when weary, dropping on a bank. Summer. John Clare. BoNaP
How sweetly did the moments glide. The Cottager's Complaint, on the Intended Bill for Enclosing Sutton-Coldfield. John Freeth. NOEC; OBET
How sweetly doth My Master sound! My Master! The Odour. George Herbert. AnAnS-1; OBS
How sweetly on the autumn scene. The Hawkbit. Sir Charles G. D. Roberts. HBV-1
How sweetly on the wood-girt town. Pentucket. Whittier. PAH
How sweetly sings this stream. Laurence Dakin. *Fr.* Pyramus and Thisbe, III, iii. CaP
How swift along the winding way. Upon Boys Diverting Themselves in the River. Thomas Foxton. OxBChV
How tenderly the evening creeps between. Evening. Hugh McCrae. PoAu-1
How terrible their trust, the little leaves. April, 1942. Mark Van Doren. WaP
How thankful I am. Demonstration. Margaret Finefrock. AMV-80
How that vast heaven intitled First is rolled. Sonnet. William Drummond of Hawthornden. EIL
How the blithe lark runs up the golden stair. The Skylark. Frederick Tennyson. GN; HBV-1
How the *Cumberland* Went Down. S. Weir Mitchell. PAH
How the days went. Now That I Am Forever with Child. Audre Lorde. PoBA
How the Death of a City Is Never More than the Sum of the Deaths of Those Who Inhabit Its Spaces. Victor Coleman. NOBC
How the Doughty Duke of Albany like a Coward Knight Ran Away Shamefully, *sel.* John Skelton.
"O ye wretched Scots." OBSV
How the elements solidify! Event. Sylvia Plath. NOBA
How the Fire Queen Crossed the Swamp. Will H. Ogilvie. PoAu-1
How the First Hielandman [of God] Was Made. *Unknown.* FaBoCo; GBP; OBSV
How the Flowers Grow. "Gabriel Setoun." SoPo
How the Great Guest Came. Edwin Markham. BeLS; BLPA; BLPL
How the greenest of wheat rang gold at his birth! For My Son. John Frederick Nims. MiAP
How the Helpmate of Blue-Beard Made Free with a Door. Guy Wetmore Carryl. InMe
How the Hen Sold Her Eggs to the Stingy Priest. Nancy Willard. LCAP
How the Invalids Make Love. Susan Feldman. AmPA
How the Joy of It Was Used Up Long Ago. Linda Gregg. NPGG
How the kerosene outlasted. David Martinson. *Fr.* Nineteen Sections from a Twenty Acre Poem. TAT
How the Laws of Physics Love Chocolate! Reg Saner. GP
How the Leaves Came Down. "Susan Coolidge." HBV-1; HBVY
How the light breaks when it does. Observation. Derk Wynand. AMV-80
How the Little Kite Learned to Fly. *Unknown, at. to* Katharine Pyle. HBV-1; HBVY
How the Money Rolls In. *Unknown.* TreFT
(My Sister She Works in a Laundry, *with music.*) AS
How the mountains talked together. A Farewell to Agassiz. Oliver Wendell Holmes. ImOP
How the place has grown. I hardly recognize it. Are You Just Back for a Visit or Are You Going to Stay? Francis Coleman Rosenberger. AMV-81
How the Ploughman Learned His Paternoster. *Unknown.* OxBM
How the red road stretched before us, mile on mile. Independence. Nancy Cato. PoAu-2; WPE
How the river cools your blood is something you can't explain. Autobiography, Chapter XVII: Floating the Big Piney. Jim Barnes. STE
How the Sky Begins to Fall. Joan Colby. AMV-81
How the splendour of these veils and of this dress. Phaedra. Osip Mandelstam, *tr. by* James Greene. OBVE
How the waters closed above him. Emily Dickinson. DL; PoEL-5
How the Women Will Stop War. Aristophanes, *tr. fr. Greek by* B. B. Rogers. *Fr.* Lysistrata. WaaP

How then shall man so order life that when his tale of years is told. Sir Richard Francis Burton. *Fr.* The Kasidah, IX. HBV-2
How there is anything so old. Dinosaur Tracks in Beit Zayit. Shirley Kaufman. FiCP
How they are provided for upon the earth. Beginners. Walt Whitman. AA
How They Brought the Good News by Sea. Norma Farber. PChr
How They Brought the Good News from Ghent to Aix. Robert Browning. BeLS; BLPL; FaBoBe; FaFP; FaPoR; GN; HBV-2; HBVY; HoPM; PaPo; RoGo; SpRo; TreF
How They Came from the Blue Snows. Arnold Kenseth. PPON
How they came into the world. A History of Lesbianism. Judy Grahn. PeHV
How They Do It. J. C. Squire *See* Little Commodore, The; *and* Poor Old Man, The.
How They Killed My Grandmother. Boris Slutsky, *tr. fr. Russian by* Daniel Weissbort. VWA
How They Made the Golem. John Robert Colombo. MoCV
How thin and sharp is the moon tonight. Winter Moon. Langston Hughes. DuDa; RHPC
How Things Fall. Donald Finkel. VWA
How things grow upright. Against Gravity. Edith E. Cutting. AMV-80
How this woman came by the courage, how she got. John Berryman. *Fr.* Dream Songs. TAP
How this year of years do I best see. May Trees in a Storm. Geoffrey Grigson. GBL
How those loose rocks got piled up here like this. 18,000 Feet. Ed Roberson. PoNe
How Time Consumeth All Earthly Things. Thomas Proctor *See* Proper Sonnet, How Time Consumeth All Earthly Things, A.
How time reverses. For My Contemporaries. J. V. Cunningham. CoAP; PP
How to Amuse a Stone. Richard Shelton. AMV-80
How to Be Happy. *Unknown.* BLPA
How to Be Old. May Swenson. MAT; UnPo
How to behold what cannot be held? Giovanni da Fiesole on the Sublime; or, Fra Angelico's "Last Judgment." Richard Howard. Prf
How to Build a Ha-ha. William Mason. *Fr.* The English Garden. FaBoUs
How to Catch Trout. Thomas Barker. *Fr.* The Art of Angling. FaBoUs
How to Catch Unicorns. William Rose Benét. HBMV
How to Catch Wasps. John Philips. *Fr.* Cyder. FaBoUs
How to Change the U.S.A. Harry Edwards, *arr. in verse by* Walter Lowenfels. NBP; TW
How to Choose a Horse. *Unknown.* FaBoUs
How to Choose a Wife. *Unknown.* FaBoUs
How to Conceive Boys. Claude Quillet, *tr. fr. Latin by* George Sewell. *Fr.* Callipaedia; or, The Art of Getting Beautiful Children. FaBoUs
How to Cure Hops and Prepare Them for Sale. Christopher Smart. *Fr.* The Hop-Garden. FaBoUs
How to Eat Alone. Daniel Halpern. MAYP
How to explain that on the day. Irreconcilables. Arthur Gregor. NYBP
How to Exterminate Rats. James Grainger. *Fr.* The Sugar-Cane. FaBoUs
How to Fertilize Soil. James Grainger. *See* Compost.
How to Fertilize Soil. John Scott. *Fr.* Amoebaean Eclogues, II. FaBoUs
How to Find Your Way Home. Mario Petaccia. LFAC
How to Fly by Standing Still, *sel.* James K. Baxter.
"They bring me in two eggs and a slice of bacon," 3. OCNZ
How to Get On in Society. John Betjeman. NOBL; OBSV; OxBTC
How to Get There. Bonnie Nims. RHPC
How to Get There. Frank O'Hara. NoP
How to Get to New Mexico. John Brandi. TAT
How to Give. *Unknown.* BLRP
How to Go and Forget. Edwin Markham. HBMV
How to Grow Cucumbers. William Cowper. *Fr.* The Task, III. FaBoUs
How to Hide Jesus. Steve Turner. EBCP
How to Keep Accounts. *Unknown.* FaBoUs
How to keep—is there any any, is there none such. The Leaden Echo and the Golden Echo. Gerard Manley Hopkins. BrPo; CMoP; CoBMV; DTC; FaFP; GTBS-P; LiTB; LiTM; LoBV; MasP; MoAB; MoBrPo; MoVE; OAEP; OBMV; OBNC; SOTW
How to Kill. Keith Douglas. ChMP; FaBoMo; NOBE
How to Measure a Cat. Louis Johnson. OCNZ
How to Meditate. Jack Kerouac. PoM
How to Murder Your Best Friend. Diana O Hehir. NPGG
How to Own Land. Susan Farley. AMV-80
How to Paint a Perfect Christmas. Miroslav Holub, *tr. fr. Czech by* George Theiner *and* Ian Milner. OBCP
How to Reach the Moon Marsha Pomerantz. VWA
How to See Deer. Philip Booth. Psk
How to Shear Sheep. John Dyer. *Fr.* The Fleece, II. FaBoUs
How to Start a War. Phyllis McGinley. DBV; OBSV
How to Swing Those Obbligatos Around. Alice Fulton. LTB
How to Tell Bad News. *Unknown.* TreF
How to Tell Goblins from Elves. Monica Shannon. FaPON; RHPC; TiPo
How to Tell Juan Don from Another. Gardner E. Lewis. FiBHP
How to Tell the Top of a Hill. John Ciardi. SoPo
How To Tell the Wild Animals. Carolyn Wells. FaFP; FaPON; FiBHP; HBVY; TiPo
How to the invisible. Elementary Cosmogony. Charles Simic. NNaP
How to the Singer Comes the Song? Richard Watson Gilder. WGRP
How to Treat Elves. Morris Bishop. DBV; FiBHP; OBAL; OBCA; PoPl
How to Walk in a Crowd. Robert Hershon. FF
How to win her. A Serious Poem. Ernest Walsh. ErPo
How to Write a Letter. Elizabeth Turner. MoShBr; OxBChV
How to Write a Poem about the Sky. Leslie Marmon Silko. NoP
How totally unpredictable we are to one another. Robert Sward. POL
How Tuesday Began. Kathleen Fraser. CTBA; NYBP
How uneasy is his life. The Joys of Marriage. Charles Cotton. InMe
How unhappy (though unmarried) is an uncle who, bereft. Horace, Book V, Ode III. Charles Larcom Graves. CenHV
How unpleasant to meet Mr. Eliot! Lines for Cuscuscaraway and Mirza Murad Ali Beg. T. S. Eliot. FiBHP; OBAL; PoPl; SpRo
How vainly men themselves amaze. The Garden [*or* Thoughts in a Garden]. Andrew Marvell. AnAnS-1; AWP; BiP; BLPL; CABA; FaBoEn; GTBS; GTBS-P; HAP; HBV-1; InPS; InvP; JCP; LiTB; LoBV; MasP; MeLP; MePo; NIP; NOBE; NoP; OAEL-1; OAEP; OBEV; OBS; PoEL-2; PoLF; PoPle; PoRA; PPoe; PPP; QFR; SeCePo; SeCeV; SeCP; SeCV-1; TEP; TreFT; TrGrPo; ViBoPo
How vastly pleasing is my tale. Blessings on Doneraile. Patrick O'Kelly. OnYI
How very modern once they were. The Modernists. Tom MacInnes. CaP
How very sad it is to think. Poor Brother. *Unknown.* NA
How Violets Came Blue. Robert Herrick. CaPo
How warm this woodland wild Recess! Recollections of Love. Samuel Taylor Coleridge. ChER
How was I to know that the woman seated next to me on the bus. Leslie Scalapino. *Fr.* Hmmmm. NPGG
How was November's melancholy endear'd to me. Robert Bridges. *Fr.* The Testament of Beauty. MoVE
How was this I did not see. The Faded Face. Thomas Hardy. QFR
How was thy mother a lioness. Lamentation. Bible, *O.T.* *Fr.* Ezekiel. TrJP
How Was Your Trip to L.A.? Philip Whalen. TAT
How wasteful, as they say, is Nature. Love. Walker Gibson. NePoAm-2
How We Beat the Favourite. Adam Lindsay Gordon. CBAP
How We Became a Nation. Harriet Prescott Spofford. PAH
How We Built a Church at Ashcroft. Jack Leahy. PoOW
How We Burned the *Philadelphia.* Barrett Eastman. PAH
How we desire desire! Joy of surcease. Epigram. J. V. Cunningham. VGW
How We Drove the Trotter. W. T. Goodge. PH
How we envy their not caring. The Card-Players. David Ray. VGW
How We Heard the Name. Alan Dugan. CoAP; NMP; NoAM
How We Learn. Horatius Bonar. HBV-2
How well (dear Brother) art thou called Stone? To My Reverend Dear Brother, M. Samuel Stone. John Cotton. SCAP
How Well for the Birds. *Unknown, tr. fr. Irish by* Frank O'Connor. KiLC ("How well for the birds that can rise in their flight.") WTO
How well her name an army doth present. Ana(Mary-Army)gram. George Herbert. CABA; OAEL-1
How well I know what I mean to do. By the Fire-Side. Robert Browning. EBVV; OAEL-2; VLP
How well I remember those days of danger. The Road to Pengya. Tu Fu, *tr. by* Rewi Alley *and* Edward Field. Prf
How well my eyes remember the dim path! Elegy: The Summer-House on the Mound. Robert Bridges. GoTL
How well you served me above ground. Spirit's Song. Louise Bogan. NYBP
"How will he hear the bell at school." Mutterings over the Crib of a Deaf Child. James Wright. LCAP; PoPl
How will I think of you. December 21st. Jean Valentine. LCAP
How Will You Call Me, Brother. Mari Evans. BlSi
How will you cross the autumn mountain alone? Princess Oku, *tr. fr. Japanese by* Willis Barnstone. BoWoP
How will you manage. Princess Daihaku. *Fr.* Manyo Shu. AWP
How will you your Christmas keep? Keeping Christmas. Eleanor Farjeon. OBCP
How wisely Nature did decree. Eyes and Tears. Andrew Marvell. MePo; NCEP
How wonderful you were, so pious and holy. Sabbath. Jakov de Haan, *tr. by* David Soetendorp. VWA
How would it be if you took yourself off. Landscape with Tractor. Henry Taylor. MAYP

How you dazzle my mind, panarchaic grandeur. Rebecca. Joseph Eliyia, *tr. by* Rae Dalven. VWA
How You Get Born. Erica Jong. UnPo
How you go along all day. Strange. Kirby Doyle. NeAP
How young I was. Old Age. *Gond Oral Tradition, tr. by* V. Elwin *and* S. Hivale. WTO
Howard. A. A. Milne. *See* Young Puppy, The.
Howard Lamson. Edgar Lee Masters. *Fr.* The New Spoon River. ViBoPo
Howdy, Honey, Howdy! Paul Laurence Dunbar. PoLF
However dry and windless. Bamboo. William Plomer. PeSA
However gracefully/ the spare leaves of the fig tree. Casa d'Amunt. Alastair Reid. NePoEA
However it came, this great house has gone done. The Great House. Edwin Muir. EyDe
However the battle is ended. An Inspiration. Ella Wheeler Wilcox. WGRP
However they talk, whatever they say. Motto. *Unknown.* TiPo
However we wrangled with Britain awhile. Literary Importation. Philip Freneau. TAP
Howie gave sentence of slaughter. The Desertion of the Women and Seals. George Mackay Brown. OxBC
Howl. Allen Ginsberg. AmPP; CAPP; PoM
Sels.
"I saw the best minds of my generation destroyed by madness," I. InPS, *ll.* 1-30; NaP; NeAP; NIP; NoAM; NoP; SOTW, *abr.;* TAP
"What sphinx of cement and aluminum bashed open their skulls," II. NeAP; PoCh; SOTW, *abr.;* TAP
Howling of Wolves, The. Ted Hughes. OxBTC
Howling storm is brewing, A. The Storm. Heine, *tr. by* Louis Untermeyer. AWP
How's My Boy? Sydney Dobell. CH; EtS; GN; HBV-1; OHIP
"How's your father?" came the whisper. Conversational. *Unknown.* FiBHP
Hub for the Universe, A. Walt Whitman. Song of Myself, XLVIII. FaFP
("I have said that the soul is not more than the body.") TrGrPo
Hubbard is dead, the old plumber. Elegy for Alfred Hubbard. Tony Connor. SoSe
Hubbub in Hub. Laurence McKinney. WhC
Hubert Horatio Humphrey (1911-1978). Martin Galvin. SOTS
Hubert's Museum. Louis Simpson. OxBC
Huck Finn at Ninety, Dying in a Chicago Boarding House Room. James Schevill. TAP
Huckleberry, Gooseberry, Raspberry Pie. Clyde Watson. RHPC
Huckleberry Hunting, *with music. Unknown.* ShS
Hucksters haggle in the mart, The. For a War Memorial. G. K. Chesterton. MMA
Huckster's Horse, The. Julia Hurd Strong. GoYe
Hudibras, *sels.* Samuel Butler.
Art of Love, The (" 'Tis true, no lover has that power"), *fr.*I, 1. FaBoEn
"Egyptians say, the Sun has twice, The," *fr.* II, 3. ImOP
Godly Casuistry ("The sun had long since in the lap"), *fr.* II, 2. OBS
Hudibras the Sectarian ("Besides he was a shrewd Philosopher"), *fr.* I, 1. SeCePo
"In mathematicks he was greater," *fr.* I, 1. ImOP; NOBL
Independent Squire ("A squire he had whose name was Ralph"), *fr.* I, 1. NOBE
Metaphysical Sectarian, The ("He was in logick a great critic"), *fr.* I, 1. MeLP
(Hudibras, the Presbyterian Knight, *abr.*) OxBoLi
(Portrait of Hudibras.) PoEL-3
(Presbyterian Knight and Independent Squire, *abr.*) OBS
(Sir Hudibras, His Passing Worth.) FaBoCo
Presbyterian Church Government ("Synods are whelps of the Inquisition"), *fr.* I, 3. OBS
Presbyterian Knight, *fr.* I, 1. NOBE
("When civil dudgeon first grew high.") OAEL-1; ViBoPo
("When civil fury first grew high.") EBEV; SeCV-2
"Question then, to state it first, The," *fr.* I, 3. NOBL
"Quoth he, my faith as adamantine," *fr.* II, 1. OBSV
"Quoth he, to bid me not to love," *fr.* II, 1. NOBL
Religion of Hudibras, The, *fr.* I, 1. DBV; InMe
("For his religion it was fit.") LoBV; OBSV; ViBoPo
(Sir Hudibras's Religion.) FaBoEn
Sidrophel, the Rosicrucian Conjurer ("This said, he turned about his steed"), *fr.* II, 3. OxBoLi
"Sir Hudibras, his passing worth," *fr.* I, Argument. EBEV; OAEL-1; SeCV-2
Sir Sidrophel, the Conjurer ("He had been long t'wards Mathematicks"), *fr.* II, 3. FaBoEn
(Portrait of Sidrophel.) PoEL-3
"Some were for setting up a king," *fr.* III, 2. EBEV
"There is a tall long-sided dame," *fr.* II, 1. OBSV
"This place (quoth she) they say's enchanted," *fr.* II, 1. NOBL
"This sturdy squire, he had, as well," *fr.* I, 1. ViBoPo
"What makes a knave a child of God," *fr.* III, 1. NOBL; OBSV
Hudibras and Milton Reconciled. William Somervile. NOEC
Hudson Ferry. James Schuyler. NYP
Hudson Hornet. William W. Cook. AMV-80
Hue and Cry after Blood and Money, A. *Unknown.* APAS
Hue and Cry after Cupid, The, *sel.* Ben Jonson.
Beauties, Have Ye Seen This Toy. OAEP
(Cupid.) InMe
(Venus' Runaway.) HBV-1
Hue and Cry after Fair Amoret, A. Congreve. NOEC; OBEC; OBEV
(Amoret.) ViBoPo
Hues of the rich unfolding morn. Morning. John Keble. OBRV
Huesca. John Cornford. BoLoP; ChMP
(To Margot Heinemann.) OBWP; OxBTC
Huey. Etheridge Knight. NNaP
Huff the talbot and our cat Tib. The Wars of the Roses. *Unknown.* GBP
Huffy Henry hid the day. John Berryman. *Fr.* Dream Songs. CAPP; NoP
Hug me closer, closer, mother. Little Bessie. *Unknown.* AmFP
Hug Me Tight. John Kendall. WhC
Hug o' War. Shel Silverstein. NTCP; RHPC
Huge and alert, irascible yet strong. A Toast to Our Native Land. Robert Bridges. PAH; PAL
Huge commentators grace my learned shelves. James Bramston. *Fr.* The Man of Taste. FaBoCo
Huge-headed oak. He Praises the Trees. *Unknown, tr. by* Robin Skelton. BIrV
Huge hippopotamus hasn't a hair, The. The Hippopotamus. Jack Prelutsky. RHPC
Huge Leviathan, The. Spenser. *Fr.* Visions of the World's Vanity. ChTr
Huge, perfect creatures move across the screen. Bijou. Vern Rutsala. DFF
Huge red-buttressed mesa over yonder, The. Rain in the Desert. John Gould Fletcher. Arizona Poems, VI. BPAW; NCSH
Huge shoe mounts up from the horizon, A. The Wounded Breakfast. Russell Edson. LCAP
Huge through the darkened street. The Dray. Laurence Binyon. SyP
Huge upon the hazy plain. Grazing Locomotives. Archibald MacLeish. PPJ
Huge wound in my head began to heal, The. The Wound. Thom Gunn. NePoEA
Hugging the ground by the lilac tree. Man and Beast. Clifford Dyment. BoAnP
Hugging the Jukebox. Naomi Shihab Nye. MAYP
Hugh Maguire. Eochy O'Hussey, *tr. fr. Late Middle Irish by* Frank O'Connor. AnIL; KiLC
Hugh of Lincoln. *Unknown. See* Sir Hugh; or, The Jew's Daughter.
Hugh Selwyn Mauberley. (Life and Contacts). Ezra Pound. AmPP; AP; CABA; CMoP, *complete with* Mauberley; CoBMV; InPS; LiTA; LiTM, *complete with* Mauberley; MasP; MoPo; NoAM, *complete with* Mauberley; NOBA, *complete with* Mauberley; NoP; TAP
Sels.
"Age demanded an image, The," II. HAP; MoAmPo; VGW
"Beneath the sagging roof," X. MoAmPo
Brennhaum. MoAmPo
E. P. Ode pour l'Election de Son Sepulchre. CrMA; FaBoEn; HAP; MoAmPo; MoVE; NePA; PP; SeCeV; VGW
("For three years, out of key with his time.") OxBA; UnPo
(Pour l'Election de Son Sepulchre, I-V.) FaBoMo
Envoi (1919). CTC; HAP; SeCeV; UnPo; VGW
(Envoi: "Go, dumb-born book.") MoAB; MoAmPo; NePA; OxBA
Medallion. SeCeV
Mr. Nixon. MoAmPo
"Siena Mi Fe'; Disfecemi Maremma." MoAmPo
"Tea-rose tea-gown, etc., The." III. MoAmPo; NOBE
"There died a myriad," V. DBV; FF; MoAmPo; NIP; NOBE; PAI; WaaP
"These fought in any case," IV. FF; HeIP; MoAmPo; NOBE; OBWP; PPoe; VGW; WaaP
Yeux Glaques. MoAmPo
Hugh Spencer's Feats in France. *Unknown.* ESPB (A *and* B *vers.*)
Hugh Stuart Boyd. Elizabeth Barrett Browning. VLP
Hughie at the Inn. Elinor Wylie. NYBP; WPE
Hughie Grame. *Unknown.* ESPB (A *and* C *vers.*)
(Hughie Graham.) OxBB, *with music*
Hughley Steeple. A. E. Housman. A Shropshire Lad, LXI. FaBoPP
Huguenot, A. Mary Elizabeth Coleridge. OBVV
Hullabaloo Belay. *Unknown.* FSW
"Hullo!" S. W. Foss. PaPo
Hull's Surrender. *Unknown.* PAH
Humaine Cares. Nathaniel Wanley. OBS

Human Abstract, The. Blake. *Fr.* Songs of Experience. BiP; EnRP; LAuP; NOEC; OAEL-2; PoEL-4; PPP
Human Animal, The. Jane Mayhall. TAP
Human Being Is a Lonely Creature, The. Richard Eberhart. NePoAm
Human contours are so easily lost, The. The Human Form Divine. Kathleen Raine. WPE
Human Cry, The. Tennyson. ILwL
Human Debasement; a Fragment. Edward Rushton. NOEC
Human Dilemma. Jim Rosemergy. AMV-80
Human face becoming locked insect face. Richard Hunt's Arachne. Robert Hayden. FB
Human Fold, The. Edwin Muir. LiTM
Human Folly. Pope. *Fr.* An Essay on Man, Epistle II. FiP
("Whate'er the passion—knowledge, fame, or pelf.") TrGrPo
Human Form Divine, The. Kathleen Raine. WPE
Human Frailty. William Cowper. HBV-2
Human Geography. Gloria Fuertes, *tr. fr. Spanish by* Willis Barnstone. BoWoP
Human Geography. Ruth Whitman. AMV-80
Human Greatness. Edwin Barclay. PBA
Human hand lying on my hand, The. A Hand. Bernard Spencer. NeBP
Human Happiness. Dryden. *Fr.* The Indian Emperor, IV, i. FiP
Human Image, The, *sel.* Blake.
London ("There souls of men are bought and sold"). ChTr
Human Instinct, A. Christopher Morley. *Fr.* Translations from the Chinese. EvOK
Human Life. Aubrey Thomas De Vere. HBV-1; OnYI
Human Life. Matthew Prior. FaBoEE
Human Life, *sels.* Samuel Rogers.
Another and the Same. OBNC
Fond Youth. OBRV
Man's Going Hence. OBNC
Human Life; on the Denial of Immortality. Samuel Taylor Coleridge. ChER
Human Mind, The. Ai Shih-te, *tr. fr. Chinese by* William C. White. TrJP
Human Needs. *Unknown.* POL
Human Outlook, The. John Addington Symonds. *See* These Things Shall Be.
Human Plan, The. Charles Henry Crandall. AA
Human race is going to the cemetery, The. Etel Adnan. *Fr.* The Beirut-Hell Express. WPOW
Human Races, The. R. P. Lister. FiBHP
Human Relations. Emmett Jarrett. NeAC
Human Relations. C. H. Sisson. POL; TW
Human Seasons, The. Keats. EnRP; FaFP; GTBS; GTBS-P; HBV-1; OBRV; WiR
Human Soul. René Maran, *tr. fr. French by* Mercer Cook. TTY
Human Things. Howard Nemerov. BoNaP
Human Touch, The. Spencer Michael Free. BLPA; FaBoBe
Human Tragedy, The, *sel.* Alfred Austin.
"When with staid mothers' milk and sunshine warmed." FaBoCo
Humane Thought. Rebecca McCann. YaD
Humanities Course. John Updike. GLGT
Humanities 5 section man, The. Whom Do You Visualize as Your Reader? Linda Pastan. PPJ
Humanities Lecture. William Stafford. GLGT; NNaP
Humanity. Richard Watson Dixon. OBVV
Humanity of Europe, The. Spring Death. Russell Marano. AMV-81
Humble Address, The. *Unknown.* APAS
Humble-Bee, The. Emerson. AA; FM; GN; HBV-1; HBVY; NOBA; OxBA
"Burly dozing humble-bee," *sel.* FaPON
Humble boon was soon obtain'd, The. Sir Walter Scott. *Fr.* The Lay of the Last Minstrel. OBRV
Humble Petition of Bruar Water to the Noble Duke of Athole, The, *sel.* Burns.
"Sober laverock, warbling wild, The." PBBP
Humble Petition of Poor Ben to the Best of Monarchs, Masters, Men, King Charles, The. Ben Jonson. PP
Humble Service. Lillian G. Heard. STF
Humble springs of stately Plimouth Beach, The. Upon the Springs Issuing out from the Foot of Plimouth Beach. Samuel Sewall. SCAP
Humble Springs of Stately Sandwich Beach, The. Samuel Sewall. SCAP
Humble Wish, An; off Porto-Sancto, March 29, 1779, *sel.* Edward Thompson.
"I've served my country nine and twenty years." NOEC
Humble Yo'Self de Bell Done Ring, *with music.* *Unknown.* BoAN-2
Humbly resolving to pray that God. Sleeping on Fists. Alberto Ríos. DiL
Humbug Steamship Companies. *Unknown.* BPAW
Humiliation Revisited. Nova Trimble Ashley. AMV-80
Humility. Marie Luise Kaschnitz, *tr. fr. German by* Michael Hamburger. WPOW
Humming bee purrs softly o'er his flower, The. The Cricket. Frederick Goddard Tuckerman. FM; NOBA; QFR
Hummingbird, A. Emily Dickinson. *See* Route of evanescence, A.
Hummingbird, The. Michael Flanders. RHPC
Humming Bird, The. Harry Hibbard Kemp. FaPON; HBMV
Humming-Bird. D. H. Lawrence. CMoP; InPS; LiTB; LiTM; PPP; SeCePo
Hummingbird. Harold Littlebird. VoR
Hummingbird. Marge Piercy. GeTw
Hummingbird, he has no song, The. The Hummingbird. Michael Flanders. RHPC
Humorist, The. Keith Preston. EvOK; HBMV; WhC
Humorless, hundreds of trunks gray in the blue expanse. Leafless Trees, Chickahominy Swamp. Dave Smith. MAYP
Humorous Ant, The. Oliver Herford. TDH
Humorous Verse. Abu Dolama, *tr. fr. Arabic by* Raoul Abdul. TTY
Humour Out of Breath, *sel.* John Day.
Ditty, A: "Peace, peace, peace, make no noise." ElL
Humours of Donnybrook Fair, The. Charles O'Flaherty. OnYI
Humours of Donnybrook Fair, The. *Unknown.* OnYI
Humours of the King's Bench Prison, a Ballad, The. Leonard Howard. NOEC
Hump, The. Kipling. *See* Camel's Hump, The.
Hump-backed and rugged, blue on blue. For My Father. Rachel Field. InMe
Humphrey Hardfeature's Descriptions of Cast-Iron Inventions. *Unknown.* OBET
Humps are lumps. Lumps. Judith Thurman. RHPC
Humpty Dumpty. Adeline D. T. Whitney. HBV-2
Humpty Dumpty sat on a wall. Mother Goose. FaBoBe; HBV-1; HBVY; OxBoLi; OxNR
Humpty Dumpty sat on the wall. Mother Goose (circa 2054). Irene Sekula. QQQ; ShM
Humpty Dumpty's Song [*or* Recitation]. "Lewis Carroll." *Fr.* Through the Looking Glass. ChTr; FaBoCo; FaBoNo; FiBHP; GTBS-P; NBM; OnMSP; OxBChV; OxBoLi
("In winter, when the fields are white.") EBEV
Hunc, Said He. *Unknown.* *See* Lady Who Loved a Swine, The.
Hunchback, The. John Peale Bishop. PoA
Hunchback in the Park, The. Dylan Thomas. EBEV; FaBoTw; MoAB; MoBrPo; MP; NoP; PrIm; TwCP
Hunchback on the corner, with gum and shoelaces, The. Pursuit. Robert Penn Warren. CrMA; HAP; LiTA; MoAmPo; MoPo; MP; NePA; PPP; TwAmPo; TwCP
Hunchbacked/ by his heart. The Life. Philip Dow. AmPA
Hunchbacked and corrected. Ken Belford. NeAC
Hunchèd camels of the night, The. An Arab Love-Song. Francis Thompson. AWP; MoAB; MoBrPo
Hunched forward under rain. Man Holding Boy. Melvin Dixon. LTB
Hunder pipers canna blaw, A. Calvinist Sang. Alexander Scott. OxBS
Hundred Best Books, The. Mostyn T. Pigott. InMe
Hundred buffalo, A. Bone Yard. Jim Barnes. CDW
Hundred Collars, A. Robert Frost. YaD
Hundred-dollar cats, the sixty, The. Pet Shop. Robert Sward. ELU
Hundred-gated Thebes. George Darley. *Fr.* Nepenthe. NOBE
Hundred mares, all white, A! their manes. The Mares of the Camargue. Frédéric Mistral, *tr. by* George Meredith. *Fr.* Mirèio. AWP; PoPl
Hundred strange things, A. Ghost Night. Lizette Woodworth Reese. HBMV
Hundred-sunned Phenix. George Darley. *See* O Blest Unfabled Incense Tree.
Hundred thousand Northmen, A. Wait for the Wagon. *Unknown.* PAH
Hundred thousand welcomes, thou Body of the Lord, A. *Tr. from Gaelic by* Douglas Hyde. WTO
Hundred wings are dropt as soft as one, A. On Startling Some Pigeons. Charles Tennyson Turner. PB
Hundred-Yard Dash, The. William Lindsey. AA
Hundred Years Ago, A, *with music.* *Unknown.* AS
Hundred Years from Now, A. Mary A. Ford. BLPA
Hundred years from now, dear heart, A. In a Rose Garden. John Bennett. BLPA; FaBoBe; HBV-1
Hundred years is a very long time, A. A Hundred Years Ago. *Unknown.* AS
Hundred Years to Come, A. Hiram Ladd Spencer, *wr. at. to* William Goldsmith Brown. HBV-2
Hundreds of migrating hawks are roosting in the hedgerows. Driving into Enid. Michael Van Walleghen. FYAP
Hundreds of stars in the pretty sky. Only One Mother [*or* Only One *or* Our Mother]. George Cooper. AA; FaPON; OHIP; SiSoSe
Hundreth Good Poyntes of Husbandry, A, *sel.* Thomas Tusser.
"When harvest is done all thing placed and set." FaBoUs
Hung be the heavens with black, yield day to night! A King Is Dead. Shakespeare. King Henry VI, Pt. I, *fr.* I, i. ChTr

Hung between stretched wings, the sea bird sat. Carmarthen Bar. John Malcolm Brinnin. HoAn
Hung between thief and thief. Improperia. Francis Sparshott. MoCV
Hung from a stone branch of city wall. Beware the Months of Fire. Patrick Lane. NeAC
Hunger. Laurence Binyon. OxBTC
Hunger. Arthur Rimbaud, *tr. fr. French by* Edgell Rickword. AWP
Hunger. Charles Simic. NNaP
Hunger. Gaspara Stampa, *tr. fr. Italian by* Brenda Webster. WPOW
Hunger. *Tr. fr.* Eskimo. WTO
Hunger. *Unknown, tr. fr. Yoruba by* Ulli Beier. PBA; TTY
Hunger, and sultry heat, and nipping blast. The French and the Spanish Guerrillas [*or* Sonnet]. Wordsworth. ChER; WaaP
Hunger and Thirst. Robert Penn Warren. PoA
Hunger crawls into you. Hunger in New York City. Simon Ortiz. MAYP
Hunger for Me Alta. GP
Hunger in New York City. Simon Ortiz. MAYP
Hunger is a/ Poet's bread. Poet's Bread. Sister Mary Philip. GoBC
Hunger is beating me. *Yoruba Oral Tradition, tr. by* Ulli Beier *and* B. Gbadamosi. WTO
Hunger makes a person climb up to the ceiling. Hunger. *Unknown, tr. by* Ulli Beier. PBA; TTY
Hunger makes a person lie down. *Yoruba Oral Tradition*, tr. by Ulli Beier. WTO
Hunger Moon. Jane Cooper. CABA
Hunger Striker. William Franklin. LFAC
Hungering on the gray plain of its birth. A Lion Named Passion. John Hollander. NePoEA-2
Hungry and thirsty we break these stones in the heat of the sun. The Roadmenders' Song. *Gond Oral Tradition*, tr. by V. Elwin *and* S. Hivale. WTO
Hungry Black Child, The. Adam David Miller. PoBA
Hungry cancer will not let him rest, A. A Thorn Forever in the Breast. Countee Cullen. BiP
Hungry fox went out one night, A. The Fox. *Unknown.* BaBo
Hungry Grass, The. Donagh MacDonagh. BIrV; NeIP; OxBI
Hungry, hungry are we. Raggedy. *Unknown.* FSW
"Hungry winter, this winter." To Hell with It. Frank O'Hara. NeAP
Hunkie Tunkie. *Unknown.* BluL
Hunt, The. Walter de la Mare. BoAnP
Hunt, The. Daniel Halpern. LiSp
Hunt. Melvin Walker La Follette. NePoEA
Hunt, The. Pope. *Fr.* Windsor Forest. NIP
Hunt, The. Harriet Prescott Spofford. AA
Hunt, The. *Unknown.* CoMu
Hunt, hunt again. If you do not find it, you. Treasure Hunt [*or* Fairy Story]. Robert Penn Warren. NoP; NYBP
Hunt in the Black Forest, A. Randall Jarrell. CoAP; LCAP
Hunt Is Up, The. *Unknown.* CH; GBP
Hunt is up, the hunt is up, The. The Song of the Hunt. John Bennett. *Fr.* Master Sky-Lark. AA
Hunt not, fish not, shoot not. Bishop Blomfield's First Charge to His Clergy. *At. to* Sydney Smith. FaBoEE
Hunt of Sliabh Truim, The, *sel. Unknown, tr. fr. Late Middle Irish.*
"One day that we mustered on Sliabh Truim." OnYI
Hunt of the Poem, The. Richard Behm. AMV-80
Hunt was up, the hunt was up, The. The Capture of Edwin Alonzo Boyd. Peter Miller. MoCV
Hunted City, The, *sel.* Kenneth Patchen.
"Little hill climbs up to the village and puts its green hands, The." NaP
Hunter, The. Ogden Nash. EvOK; LiSp; PPJ
Hunter, The. Frank O'Hara. NNaP
Hunter, The. Raymond Souster. NOBC
Hunter, The. W. J. Turner. HBMV
Hunter, The. Eleanor Glenn Wallis. NePoAm-2
Hunter crouches in his blind, The. The Hunter. Ogden Nash. EvOK; LiSp; PPJ
Hunter Named Shephard, A. *Unknown.* TDH
Hunter of the Prairies, The. Bryant. AA; LiSp
Hunter Sees What Is There, The. Edgar Jackson. LFAC
Hunter Trials. John Betjeman. FiBHP; PH
Hunters are back from beating the winter's face, The. The Woman Thing. Audre Lorde. BlSi; NMM
Hunters in the Snow: Brueghel. Joseph Langland. LiTM; NePoEA
Hunters in the Snow, The. William Carlos Williams. Pictures from Brueghel, III. LCAP
Hunter's Moon. Stephen Sandy. NYBP
Hunter's Morning. Harold Littlebird. STE
Hunters of Kentucky, The. Samuel Woodworth. BLSo, *with music*; FSW; PAH; TrAS, *with music*
(Hunters of Kentucky, The; or, Half Horse and Half Alligator, *with music.*) AS
Hunters of the Deer, The. Dale Zieroth. NOBC
Hunter's Prayer. *Unknown, tr. fr. Hottentot.* PeSA
Hunters search out every mountain hollow, Epicydes. The One Who Runs Away. Callimachus, *tr. by* Tom Dodge. LiSp
Hunter's Song, The. "Barry Cornwall." GN
Hunter's Song. Sir Walter Scott. *Fr.* The Lady of the Lake, IV. NBM
(Toils Are Pitched, The) EnRP
Hunters went out with guns, The. Good Grease. Mary TallMountain. STE; TWSS
Hunters were oot on a Scottish hill. The Day of the Crucifixion. "Hugh MacDiarmid." PV
Hunting. Gary Snyder. *Fr.* Myths and Texts. CoPo
Sels.
"All beaded with dew," VII. NaP
"Birds in a whirl, drift to the rooftops," III. NaP
First Shaman Song, I. NOBA
"How rare to be born a human being!" XVI. CAPP; NaP
"Out the Greywolf valley," XII. NaP
"Swallow-shell that eases birth, The," IV. NaP
This Poem Is for Bear, VI. NOBA; NU
("Bear down under the cliff, A.") NaP
This Poem Is for Deer, VIII. CAPP; NOBA
(" 'I dance on all the mountains.' ") NaP
Hunting. "Yehoash," *tr. fr. Yiddish by* Isidore Goldstick. TrJP
Hunting at Dusk. Doug Cockrell. Str
Hunting Civil War Relics at Nimblewill Creek. James Dickey. ConAP; GOA
Hunting for Blueberries. Thomas James. AmPA
Hunting my cat along the evening brook. Night Heron. Frances Frost. RHPC
Hunting of Cupid, The, *sels.* George Peele.
Song of Coridon and Melampus. OBSC
What Thing Is Love. EIL; ELP; EnRePo; NOBE; OAEP; SeCePo; UnTE
(Love.) OBSC
Hunting of the Cheviot, The. *Unknown. See* Chevy Chase.
Hunting of the Gods, The. *Unknown.* OxBoLi
Hunting of the Hare, The. Margaret Cavendish, Duchess of Newcastle. FM
Hunting of the Snark, The. "Lewis Carroll." FaBoNo; FiBHP, *much abr.;* MasP; NA, *much abr.;* OnMSP; OBNC; OBNV; PoEL-5
Sels.
Baker's Tale, The. EBEV
Landing, The. WhC
Hunting Pheasants in a Cornfield. Robert Bly. ConAP
Hunting Season. W. H. Auden. LiSp
Hunting season. Long Hair. Gary Snyder. NOBA
Hunting Song. Burns. PBBP
Hunting Song. Henry Fielding. *See* A-Hunting We Will Go.
Hunting Song. Donald Finkel. CoAP; MoBS; NePoEA; NCSH
Hunting-Song. Richard Hovey. *Fr.* King Arthur. HBV-1
Hunting Song. Sir Walter Scott. *Fr.* The Lay of the Last Minstrel. EnRP; EvOK; GN; GTBS; GTBS-P; OAEP; TrGrPo; WiR
Hunting-Song. *Unknown, tr. fr. Navaho Indian by* Natalie Curtis. AWP; PAI
Hunting Song. Paul Whitehead. *Fr.* Apollo and Daphne. OBEC; OxBoLi
Hunting them, a man must sweat, bear. The Lilies. Wendell Berry. GeTw
Hunting tribes of air and earth, The. Man the Enemy of Man. Sir Walter Scott. *Fr.* Rokeby. WBLP
Hunting with My Father. Tom Absher. AMV-80
Huntress, The. George Johnston. WHW
Huntsman, The. John Wheelwright. CrMA
Huntsman, What Quarry? Edna St. Vincent Millay. LiSp
Huntsman's Rouse, The. Henry Carey. SeCePo
Huntsmen, The. Walter de la Mare. CenHV; DuDa; HBMV; PH; SiSoSe; TiPo
Hurdy-Gurdy Man in Winter. Vernon Watkins. NYBP
Hurl down the nerve-gnarled body hurtling head. The Final Hunger. Vassar Miller. LiTM
Hurled back, defeated, like a child I sought. Earthborn. Peter McArthur. CaP
Hurly, hurly, roon the table. *Unknown. Fr.* Two Graces. FaBoCh
Hurlygush. Maurice Lindsay. BSV; OxBS
Huron, The. Ruth Herschberger. WPE
Huron Carol, The. Jesse Edgar Middleton. *See* Jesous Ahatonhia.
Hurrah for revolution and more cannon-shot! The Great Day. W. B. Yeats. BIrV; CMoP; FF
Hurrah for the choice of the nation! Lincoln and Liberty. *At. to* F. A. Simpson *and to* Jesse Hutchinson. AS; FSW; TrAS
Hurrah for the Lachlan. The Shearer's Song. *Unknown.* PoAu-1
Hurrah! the seaward breezes. The Fishermen. Whittier. EtS
Hurrahing in Harvest. Gerard Manley Hopkins. BiP; BoNaP; BrPo; ChTr; CMoP; EBCP; FaBoPP; InvP; LO; MoAB; MoBrPo; MoPo; MoVE; VLP

Hurray, hurray, the jade's away. The Witch o' Fife. James Hogg. BSV
Hurricane, The. Hart Crane. AP; CMoP; CoBMV; MoAB; MoAmPo; OxBA; TrCP
Hurricane, The. Philip Freneau. AP; MOS; TAP
Hurricane. Archibald MacLeish. NCSH
Hurricane, The. Luis Palés Matos, *tr. fr. Spanish by* Alida Malkus. FaPON
Hurrier, The. Harold Monro. MoBrPo
Hurry Me Nymphs. George Darley. *Fr.* Nepenthe. NBM
Hurry of the Spirits, in a Fever and Nervous Disorders, The. Isaac Watts. NOEC
Hurry On, My Weary Soul, *with music.* *Unknown.* AH
Hurry the baby as fast as you can. Making a Man. Nixon Waterman. BLPA
Hurry to bless the hands that play. The Players Ask for a Blessing on the Psalteries and Themselves. W. B. Yeats. VLP
Hurry, worry, unwary. Old Amusement Park. Marianne Moore. NYBP
Hurrying Away from the Earth. Robert Bly. NaP; PoA
Hurrying Brook, The. Edmund Blunden. BoNaP
Hurrying thru eternity. After the Cries of the Birds. Lawrence Ferlinghetti. CAPP
Hurt./ U worried abt a. To All Sisters. Sonia Sanchez. PoBA
Hurt Hawks. Robinson Jeffers. AmPP; AP; CMoP; CoBMV; FYAP; LiTA; LiTM; MoAB; MoAmPo; MoVE; NoAM; NOBA; NoP; OxBA; PAI; PrIm; TAP; UnPo
Hurt No Living Thing. Christina Rossetti. *Fr.* Sing-Song. FaPON; FM; PDV; RHPC; SiSoSe; SoPo
Hurt of Love, The. George Macdonald. TrCP
Hurt people crawl as if they. These Days. William Stafford. NNaP
Hurtful Habits. Edward Lear. *See* Limerick: "There was an old person whose habits."
Hurting. Vi Gale. GP
Hurtled under the lover-sundering river. Traveling Boy. William Meredith. NoAM
Husband, The. Donald Finkel. ELU
Husband and Heathen. Sam Walter Foss. OBAL
Husband Betrayed. John Crowe Ransom. TwAmPo
Husband! thou dull unpitied miscreant. Against Marriage. *Unknown.* DBV
Husband with No Courage in Him, The. *Unknown.* FSW
Husbandman, The. Frances Beatrice Taylor. CaP
Husbandman and Serving-Man, The. *Unknown.* OBET
Husbandry, *sel.* Sir Anthony Fitzherbert.
Memorial Verses for Travellers. FaBoUs
Husbandry. William Hammond. JCP
Husbands and Wives. Miriam Hershenson. NTCP
Husbands and Wives. *Unknown, tr. fr. Greek by* Louis Untermeyer. UnTE
Husband's Lament, The. Brian Merriman, *tr. fr. Modern Irish by* Frank O'Connor. *Fr.* The Midnight Court. OBVE
Husband's Message, The. *Unknown, tr. fr. Anglo-Saxon by* Charles W. Kennedy. AnOE
Husbands would never go whoring. Husbands and Wives. *Unknown, tr. by* Louis Untermeyer. UnTE
Hush. David St. John. DiL; LCAP; MAYP
Hush!/ With sudden gush. Overflow. John Banister Tabb. HBV-1
Hush and Baloo. *Unknown.* GBP
Hush! Did you hear. Chopin Prelude. Eleanor Norton. HBMV
Hush dove the summer. Lullaby. Miriam Waddington. CaP
Hush had fallen on the birds, A. The Young Calves. Robert P. Tristram Coffin. TiPo
Hush! hear you how the night wind keens around the craggy reek? A Lay of the Famine. *Unknown.* OnYI
Hush Honey. Ruby C. Saunders. BlSi
Hush, Hush. Mani Leib, *tr. fr. Yiddish by* Joseph Leftwich. TrJP
Hush, hush,/ Nobody cares! Now We Are Sick. J. B. Morton. FaBoPa; PV; SpRo
Hush, hush, do not speak. Hush, Hush. Mani Leib, *tr. by* Joseph Leftwich. TrJP
Hush, Hush, New House in Charlotte. E. M. Schorb. AMV-81
Hush is over all the teeming lists, A. Frederick Douglass. Paul Laurence Dunbar. BALP; PoBA
Hush Little Baby. *Unknown.* BLSo, *with music*; FSW
(Hush Li'l' Baby, *with music.*) OuSiCo
("Hush, little baby, don't say a word.") OxNR
(Mocking Bird, The.) AmFP
Hush! lullaby, my baby, nor mix thy tears with mine. The Mother's Lullaby. John Clare. NAs
Hush, lullay. Lullaby. Léonie Adams. MoAB; MoAmPo
Hush, my baby, do not cry. *Unknown.* OxNR
Hush! my dear, lie still and slumber. A Cradle Hymn [*or* A Cradle Song]. Isaac Watts. EBCP; HBV-1; LoBV; OBEC; OBEV; OxBChV; OxBoCh; PoEL-3; SBVL; SoPo; SUS; TreFS
Hush! not a whisper! Oars, be still! The Coracle Fishers. Robert Bloomfield. *Fr.* The Banks of Wye. OBNC
Hush now, my little one, and sleep. Christmas Lullaby. Ulrich Troubetzkoy. YeAr
"Hush! oh ye billows." Hymn. Joseph Sheridan Le Fanu. OnYI
Hush, Suzanne! The Mouse in the Wainscot. Ian Serraillier. PDV
Hush thee, my babby. *Unknown.* OxNR
Hush Thee, Princeling, *with music.* Anna Elizabeth Bennett. AH
Hush up, baby,/ Don't say a word. The Mocking Bird. *Unknown.* AmFP
Hush, woman, do not speak to me! The Tryst after Death. *Unknown, tr. by* Kuno Meyer. OnYI
Hush! Yo' mouth. Hush Honey. Ruby C. Saunders. BlSi
Hush your prayers, 'tis no saintly soul. Requiem. Conal O'Riordan. HBV-2
Hush-a-ba birdie [*or* burdie], croon, croon. *Unknown.* GBP; OxNR
Hush-a-baa, baby/ Dinna mak' a din. *Unknown.* OxNR
Hushaby[e],/ Don't you cry. All the Pretty Little Horses. *Unknown.* FSW; OxBoLi
Hush-a-by, baby. Italian Lullaby. *Unknown.* FaPON
Hush-a-bye a baa lamb. *Unknown.* OxNR
Hush-a-bye, baby/ The beggar shan't have 'ee. *Unknown.* OxNR
Hush-a-bye, baby, on the tree-top. *See* Rock-a-bye baby, on the tree top.
Hush-a-bye, baby, they're gone to milk. *Unknown.* OxNR
Hush'd Be the Camps To-Day. Walt Whitman. OHIP
Hush'd is each busy shout. Prelude. A. C. Benson. OBVV
Hushed are the pigeons cooing low. The Christmas Silence. Margaret Deland. OHIP
Hushed by the Hands of Sleep. Angelina Weld Grimké. CDC
Hushed, cruel, amber-eyed. Pumas. George Sterling. BPAW
Hushed to inaudible sound the deepening rain. The Lyre-Bird. Roland Robinson. PoAu-2
Husheen the herons are crying. Lullaby. "Seumas O'Sullivan." OnYI
Hushie ba, burdie beeton. *Unknown.* OxNR
Hushing of the Wye, The. Tennyson. *See* In Memoriam A. H. H.: "Danube to the Severn gave, The."
Husky Hi. Rose Fyleman. TiPo
Hustle and Grin. *Unknown.* WBLP
Hustler, The. *Unknown.* TW
Huswifery. Edward Taylor. AP; EaLo; EBCP; FaBV; NOBA; OxBA; SaC; SCAP; TAP
(Housewifery.) LiTA; NePA; NIP; NoP
Hut. G. J. F. Dutton. PoSH
Hut, and a tree, A. Diogenes. Max Eastman. HBV-2
Hut in the bush of bark or rusty tin, The. The Hatters. Nan McDonald. PoAu-2
Hut Window. Paul Celan, *tr. fr. German by* Joachim Neugroschel. VWA
Huts that stand like plaited baskets. Village and Factory. Alexander Bezymensky, *tr. by* Babette Deutsch. TrJP
Huxley Hall. John Betjeman. OBSV
Huzza for our liberty, boys. Terrapin War. *Unknown.* PAH
Huzza Huzza for Admiral Byrd. Admiral Byrd. Ogden Nash. InMe; YaD
Huzza, my Jo Bunkers! no taxes we'll pay. A Radical Song of 1786. St. John Honeywood. PAH
Hwaet! A dream came to me. The Dream of the Rood. *Unknown, tr. by* Michael Alexander. NOCV
Hy-Brasail—the Isle of the Blest. Gerald Griffin. *See* O Brazil, the Isle of the Blest.
Hyacinths to Feed Thy Soul. Sadi, *tr. fr. Persian.* *Fr.* The Gulistan. BLPA; BLPL; FaBoBe; TRV
Hyaenas, The. Kipling. OBSV
Hyaku-Nin-Isshu, *sels.* *Tr. fr. Japanese by* Curtis Hidden Page. AWP
"Day will soon be gone, The," Fujiwara no Michinobu.
"How can one e'er be sure," Lady Horikawa.
"I would that even now," Princess Shoku.
"Like a great rock, far out at sea." Lady Sanuki.
Hyd, Absolon, thy gilte tresses clere. *See* Hide, Absalon, thy gilte tresses clear.
Hyder Iddle. *Unknown.* NA; OxNR
Hydraulic Ram, The. Charles Tennyson Turner. NBM
Hydrogen Dog and the Cobalt Cat, The. Frederick Winsor. *Fr.* The Space Child's Mother Goose. QQQ; ShM
Hydrographic Report. Frances Frost. EtS
Hye Nonny Nonny Noe. *Unknown.* FaBoCo; NOBL
Hyena. Carol Muske. AmPA
Hyena ("My father came in the darkness"). *Unknown, tr. by* George Economou. TTY
Hyena ("You who make your escape from the tumult"). *Unknown, tr. fr. Hottentot.* PeSA
Hyena's Song to Her Children. *Unknown, tr. fr. Hottentot.* PeSA
Hygienist, in your dental chair. Ode to a Dental Hygienist. Earnest A. Hooton. FiBHP; WhC
Hyla Brook. Robert Frost. BoNaP; TwAmPo

Hylas. Propertius, *tr. fr. Latin by* F. A. Wright. Elegies, I, 20. AWP
Hylas, the world's perceptual scene. Equation. Sir Herbert Read. BrPo
Hymen, *sel.* Hilda Doolittle ("H. D.").
"Never more will the wind." CTC; TrGrPo; ViBoPo
Hymenaei, *sel.* Ben Jonson.
Angel Describes Truth, An. OBS
Hymeneal, *sel.* Catullus, *tr. fr. Latin by* James Michie.
"Unmuzzle the broad joke." PeHV
Hymeneal Song on the Nuptials of the Lady Anne Wentworth and the Lord Lovelace, An. Thomas Carew. CaPo
Hymeneall Dialogue, An. Thomas Carew. AnAnS-2; SeCP
Hymen's Triumph, *sels.* Samuel Daniel.
Constancy. OBSC
Early Love. ErPo
Love Is a Sickness. ELP; LoBV; NOBE; OAEP; OBEV; PoEL-2; TreFS; ViBoPo
(Love.) ElL; OBSC
(Song: "Love is a sickness full of woes.") HBV-1
Secrecy. OBSC; OLR
(Eyes, Hide My Love.) ElL
Sorrow. OBSC
(Had Sorrow Ever Fitter Place.) Ell
Hymettus' bees are out on filmy wing. The Sunflower to the Sun. Mary Elizabeth DeWitt Stebbins. AA
Hymmnn. Allen Ginsberg. NOBA
Hymn: "Abide with me; fast falls the eventide." Henry Francis Lyte *See* Abide with Me.
Hymn: "At morn, at noon, at twilight dim." Poe. ISi
Hymn: "Brightest and best of the sons of the morning." Reginald Heber. *See* Brightest and Best of the Sons of the Morning.
Hymn: "Church's Restoration, The." John Betjeman. FaBoPa
Hymn: Crucifixus pro Nobis. Patrick Carey. OxBoCh
Hymn: "Dear Lord, Whose serving-maiden." Josephine Preston Peabody. TrPWD
Hymn: "Drop, drop, slow tears." Phineas Fletcher. ElL; LoBV
(Drop, Drop, Slow Tears.) NOBE
(Hymne, An: "Drop, drop, slow tears.") OBS
(Litany, A.) OBEV; OxBoCh
Hymn: "Eternal Father, strong to save." William Whiting. *See* Eternal Father, Strong to Save.
Hymn: "Eternal Ruler of the ceaseless round." John W. Chadwick. TrPWD
Hymn: "Father, we come not as of old." John W. Chadwick. TrPWD
Hymn: "For Summer's bloom and Autumn's blight." Josiah Gilbert Holland. *Fr.* Bitter-sweet. TrPWD
Hymn: "Framer of the earth and sky." St. Ambrose, *tr. fr. Latin.* TrCP
Hymn: "God of the strong, God of the weak," *abr.* Richard Watson Gilder. TrPWD
(God of the Strong, God of the Weak, *with music, abr.*) AH
Hymn: "Great Spirit of the speeding spheres." John Haynes Holmes. TrPWD
Hymn: " 'Hush! oh ye billows.' " Joseph Sheridan Le Fanu. OnYI
Hymn, A: "Hymn of glory let us sing, A." The Venerable Bede, *tr. fr. Latin by* Elizabeth Charles. WGRP
Hymn: "I know if I find you I will have to leave the earth." A. R. Ammons. ConAP
Hymn, The: "It was the winter wild." Milton. *See* Hymn on the Morning of Christ's Nativity.
Hymn, A: "Lead gently, Lord, and slow." Paul Laurence Dunbar. *See* Hymn, A, after Reading "Lead, Kindly Light."
Hymn: "Lord, by whose breath all souls and seeds are living." Andrew Young. EaLo
Hymn: "Lord, when the wise men came from far[r]." Sidney Godolphin. HAP; JCP; MeLP; MePo; NOCV; OBS
(Wise Men and Shepherds.) BLPL; NOBE; OxBoCh
Hymn: "Lord, with glowing heart I'd praise thee." Francis Scott Key. TrPWD
Hymn: "Mighty fortress is our God, A." Martin Luther. *See* Mighty Fortress Is Our God, A.
Hymn: "My God, I love thee, not because." St. Francis Xavier, *tr. fr. Latin.* WGRP
Hymn: Nativity of Our Lord and Saviour Jesus Christ, The. Christopher Smart. *See* Nativity of Our Lord and Saviour Jesus Christ, The.
Hymn: "New every morning is thy love." John Keble. *See* Morning Hymn.
Hymn: "Now the day is over." Sabine Baring-Gould. *See* Now the Day Is Over.
Hymn: "Now we must praise heaven-kingdom's Guardian." Caedmon, *tr. fr. Anglo-Saxon.* TrCP
(Hymn: "Now we should praise Heaven-kingdom's guard," *tr. by* D. K. Fry.) PAI
Hymn: "O Christ, the glorious Crown." Philip Howard. ACP
Hymn, A: "O fly, my soul! What hangs upon." James Shirley. *See* O Fly My Soul.
Hymn, A: "O God of earth and altar." G. K. Chesterton. HBMV; TreFT; TrPWD
(Prayer.) WGRP
Hymn: "O thou who camest from above." Charles Wesley. *See* O Thou Who Camest from Above.
Hymn: "Queen and huntress, chaste and fair." Ben Jonson. *See* Hymn to Diana.
Hymn L: Rocking Hymn, A. George Wither. *Fr.* Hallelujah; or, Britain's Second Remembrancer. SeCV-1
(Lullaby, A, *wr. at. to* William Austin.) OxBoCh
(Rocking Hymn, A.) OxBChV
Hymn: St. Philip and St. James. Christopher Smart. *See* St. Philip and St. James.
Hymn: "Since without Thee we do no good." Elizabeth Barrett Browning. TrPWD
Hymn: "Sing, my tongue, the Saviour's glory." St. Thomas Aquinas, *tr. fr. Latin.* WGRP
Hymn: "Slant of sun on dull brown walls, A." Stephen Crane. *See* Slant of Sun . . .
Hymn: "Some sort of fire leaped out of the dirty and poor and merciless city." Otto Orban, *tr. fr. Hungarian by* Emery George. VWA
Hymn: "Spacious firmament on high, The." Joseph Addison. *See* Spacious Firmament on High, The.
Hymn: "There's a wideness in God's mercy." Frederick William Faber. NBM
Hymn: "Thou God of all, whose presence dwells." John Haynes Holmes. TrPWD
Hymn: "Thou hidden love of God, whose height." John Wesley. NOEC; OBEC
Hymn: To Light. Abraham Cowley. MeLP; OBS
Hymn: "When all thy mercies, O my God." Joseph Addison. *See* When All Thy Mercies.
Hymn: "When by the marbled lake I lie and listen." Wathen Mark Wilks Call. OBVV
Hymn: "When storms arise." Paul Laurence Dunbar. TrPWD; TRV
Hymn, A: "Wilt thou forgive that sin where I begun." John Donne. *See* Hymn to God the Father, A.
Hymn: "Words of hymns abruptly plod, The." Louise Townsend Nicholl. EaLo
Hymn: "Ye golden Lamps of Heav'n, farewel." Philip Doddridge. *See* "Ye Golden Lamps of Heaven."
Hymn about a Spoonful of Soup, A. Jozef Wittlin, *tr. fr. Polish by* Isaac Komem. VWA
Hymn, A, after Reading "Lead, Kindly Light." Paul Laurence Dunbar. TRV
(Hymn, A: "Lead gently, Lord, and slow.") TrPWD
Hymn against Pestilence, *sel. At. to* St. Colman, *tr. fr. Old Irish by* Whitley Stokes *and* John Strachan.
"God's blessing lead us, help us!" OnYI
Hymn before Sunrise, in the Vale of Chamouni[x]. Samuel Taylor Coleridge. EnRP; HBV-1; OAEP; OxBoCh; WGRP
Hymn for a Household. Daniel Henderson. HBMV
Hymn for Atonement Day. Judah Halevi, *tr. fr. Hebrew by* Solomon Solis-Cohen. TrJP
Hymn for Canada, A. Albert Durrant Watson. CaP
Hymn for Christmas. Felicia Dorothea Hemans. GN
Hymn for Christmas Day, A. John Byrom. NOCV; OBEC; PoEL-3; SBVL
Hymn for Easter Morn. John Mason Neale. *See* Light's Glittering Morn.
Hymn for Lanie Poo, *sel.* Amiri Baraka.
Each Morning. IDB; NNP; PoBA
Hymn for Laudes; Feast of Our Lady, Help of Christians. *Unknown, tr. fr. Latin by* Sister Maura. ISi
Hymn for Laudes; Feast of Our Lady of Good Counsel. *Unknown, tr. fr. Latin by* Sister Maura. ISi
Hymn for Nations. *Unknown.* FSW
Hymn for Saturday. Christopher Smart. *See* For Saturday.
Hymn for Second Vespers; Feast of the Apparition of Our Lady of Lourdes. *Unknown, tr. fr. Latin by* Raymond F. Roseliep. ISi
Hymn for St. John's Eve. *Unknown, tr. fr. Latin by* Dryden. AWP
Hymn for the Church Militant. G. K. Chesterton. OxBoCh
Hymn for the Close of the Week. Peter Abelard, *tr. fr. Latin.* TrCP
Hymn for the Dedication of a Church. Andrews Norton. AA
Hymn for the Eve of the New Year. Abraham Gerondi, *tr. fr. Hebrew by* Solomon Solis-Cohen. TrJP
Hymn for the Feast of the Annunciation. Aubrey Thomas De Vere. ISi
Hymn for the Slain in Battle. William Stanley Braithwaite. BALP
Hymn from the French of Lamartine, *sel.* Whittier.
"O Thou who bidst the torrent flow." TrPWD
Hymn in Adoration of the Blessed Sacrament. Richard Crashaw. *See* Hymn of Saint Thomas in Adoration of the Blessed Sacrament, The.
Hymn in Columbus Circle. Stephen Vincent Benét. OBAL

Hymn in Praise of Neptune, A. Thomas Campion. *See* In Praise of Neptune.
Hymn of Apollo. Shelley. EnRP; HBV-1; OAEL-2; OAEP; OBRV
Hymn of Dedication. Elizabeth E. Scantlebury. BLRP
Hymn of Form, A. Gordon Bottomley. BrPo
Hymn of glory let us sing, A. A Hymn. The Venerable Bede, *tr. by* Elizabeth Charles. WGRP
Hymn of Gratitude. *Unknown.* BLRP
Hymn of Hate, The. Joseph Dana Miller. PGD
Hymn of Heavenly Beauty, An, *sel.* Spenser.
"But whoso may, thrice happy man him hold." WGRP
Hymn of Joy. Henry van Dyke. TRV
Hymn of Labor. Henry van Dyke. TRV
(Jesus, Thou Divine Companion.) AH
Hymn of Man. Swinburne. VLP
Hymn of Nature, A. Robert Bridges. YeAr
Hymn of Pan. Shelley. EnRP; FaBoCh; HBV-2; OAEP; OBEV; OBRV; PoEL-4; SeCeV
Hymn of Praise on a Recovery from Sickness, A. Benjamin Colman. SCAP
(God of My Life! *with music.*) AH
Hymn of Saint Thomas in Adoration of the Blessed Sacrament, The. Richard Crashaw. OBS
(Hymn in Adoration of the Blessed Sacrament.) MeLP
Hymn of Sivaite Puritans. *Unknown.* WGRP
Hymn of Thanksgiving, A. Wilbur Dick Nesbit. OHIP
Hymn of the Alamo. Reuben M. Potter. BPAW
Hymn of the Earth. William Ellery Channing. AA
Hymn of the Incarnation, A. *Unknown. See* Glad and Blithe Might Ye Be.
Hymn of the Moravian Nuns of Bethlehem. Longfellow. PAH
Hymn of the Nativity. Richard Crashaw. *See* In the Holy Nativity of Our Lord God.
Hymn of the Resurrection, A. William Dunbar. *See* Done Is a Battle.
Hymn of the Sea, A. Bryant. MOS
Hymn of the West. Edmund Clarence Stedman. HBV-2; PAH
(Hymn to the West.) TrPWD
Hymn of the World Without. Bible, *O. T. (Moulton, Modern Readers' Bible).* Psalms, CIV. WGRP
(Psalm CIV.) NAWM-1; OHIP, *abr.;* TrJP
Hymn of Touch, A. Gordon Bottomley. BrPo
Hymn of Trust. Oliver Wendell Holmes. *Fr.* The Professor at the Breakfast Table, *ch.* 11. AA; TrPWD
(O Love Divine, That Stooped to Share, *with music.*) AH
Hymn of Trust, A. Nettie M. Sargent. BLRP
Hymn of Unity. *Unknown, tr. fr. Hebrew by* H. M. Adler. TrJP
Hymn of Victory: Thutmose III. Amon-Re, *tr. fr. Egyptian by* James Henry Breasted. WaaP
Hymn of Weeping. Amittai ben Shefatiah, *tr. fr. Hebrew by* Nina Davis Salaman. TrJP
Hymn on Froude and Kingsley, A. William Stubbs. FaBoEE
("Froude informs the Scottish youth.") CenHV
Hymn on Solitude. James Thomson. NOEC; OBEC
Hymn on the Morning of Christ's Nativity. Milton. *Fr.* On the Morning of Christ's Nativity. NOBE; OBEV
(Hymn, The: "It was the winter wild.") WHA, *abr.*
(On the Morning of Christ's Nativity.) FiP
Hymn [*or* Hymne] on the Nativity [*or* Nativitie] of My Saviour, A. Ben Jonson. SBVL; SeCV-1; TrCP
Hymn on the Omnipresence, An. John Byrom. TrPWD
Hymn on the Seasons, A. James Thomson. *Fr.* The Seasons. EnRP; LAuP; OxBoCh
Hymn Sung as by the Shepherds, A. Richard Crashaw. *See* Shepherd's Hymn, The.
Hymn Sung at the Completion of the Concord Monument April 19, 1836. Emerson. *See* Concord Hymn.
Hymn to Adversity. Thomas Gray. EnRP; GTBS; GTBS-P; OBEC
Hymn to Amen Ra, the Sun God. *Unknown, tr. fr. Egyptian by* Frank Lloyd Griffith. WGRP
Hymn to Artemis, the Destroyer. Marya Zaturenska. MOON
Hymn to Athena. *Unknown, tr. fr. Greek by* Shelley. *Fr.* Homeric Hymns. AWP
Hymn to Bacchus, A. Robert Herrick. JCP
Hymn to Castor and Pollux. *Unknown, tr. fr. Greek by* Shelley. *Fr.* Homeric Hymns. AWP
Hymn to Chance. H. Phelps Putnam. TwAmPo
Hymn to Charity and Humility. Henry More. OxBoCh
(Hymne in Honour of Those Two Despised Virtues, Charitie and Humilitie, An.) OBS
Hymn [*or* Hymne] to Christ, at the Author's Last Going into Germany, A. John Donne. AnAnS-1; EBEV; EnRePo; FaBoEn; JCP; LiTB; MeLP; MePo; OAEP; OBS; OxBoCh; SeCV-1; ViBoPo
Dark Churches, *sel.* FaBoRV
Hymn to Colour. George Meredith. OBNC
Hymn to Comus. Ben Jonson. *Fr.* Pleasure Reconciled to Virtue. ElL; OAEP
(Hymn to the Belly.) SeCePo
Hymn to Contentment, A. Thomas Parnell. NOEC; OBEC
Hymn to Cynthia. Ben Jonson. *See* Hymn to Diana.
Hymn to Darkness. John Norris. MePo; OBS; OxBoCh
Hymn to Diana. Catullus, *tr. fr. Latin by* Richard Claverhouse Jebb. AWP
Hymn to Diana. Thomas Heywood. *Fr.* The Golden Age. ElL
Hymn to Diana. Ben Jonson. *Fr.* Cynthia's Revels, V, vi. AWP; CH; ChTr; ElL; EnRePo; GTBS; GTBS-P; HAP; MOON; NOBE; OBEV; OBS; PoPle; PoRA; QFR; SeCP; TrGrPo; WHA; WiR
(Hesperus' Hymn to Cynthia.) JCP; LoBV; SeCV-1
(Hesperus' Song.) GN
(Hymn [*or* Hymne], The: "Queen[e] and huntress, chaste, and fair.") AnAnS-2; PoEL-2; ViBoPo
(Hymn to Cynthia.) PrIm; SeCePo
("Queen[e] and huntress[e], chaste and fair.") CABA; HeIP; NoP; OAEL-1; OAEP
(Song: To Cynthia.) HBV-1
Hymn to Dispel Hatred at Midnight. Yvor Winters. TW
Hymn to Earth. Elinor Wylie. LiTM; MoAB; MoAmPo; MoPo; MoVE; NePA
Hymn to Earth the Mother of All. *Unknown, tr. fr. Greek by* Shelley. *Fr.* Homeric Hymns. AWP
Hymn to Evil. Louis Ginsberg. PoA
Hymn to God in Time of Stress, A. Max Eastman. TrPWD
Hymn [*or* Hymne] to God My God, in My Sickness[e]. John Donne. AnAnS-1; CABA; ChTr; DTC; EBEV; EnRePo; FaBoEn; GoBC; HeIP; LoBV; MasP; MeLP; MePo; NIP; NoP; OAEL-1; OAEP; OBS; OxBoCh; PoEL-2; PPP; SeCP; SeCV-1; TrPWD, *abr.*
Hymn [*or* Hymne] to God the Father, A. John Donne. AWP; BiP; EaLo; EBCP; EBEV; EnRePo; GoBC; HAP; HBV-2; InPK; JCP; LiTB; LoBV; MeLP; MePo; OAEL-1; OBS; OxBoCh; PAI; PoEL-2; PoRA; PPoe; SCV; SeCeV; SeCP; SeCV-1; TreFT; TrGrPo; TrPWD; ViBoPo
(For Forgiveness.) WGRP
(Hymn: "Wilt Thou forgive that sin where I begun.") NOBE
(To Christ.) AnAnS-1
Hymn to God the Father, A. Ben Jonson. AnAnS-1; EBCP; EnRePo; GoBC; MePo; NoP; OBS; OxBoCh; SeCP; SeCV-1; TrCP; TrPWD
Hymn to God the Father. Samuel Wesley. OxBoCh
Hymn to Her Unknown. W. J. Turner. OBMV
Hymn to Horus. Mathilde Blind. OBVV
Hymn to Intellectual Beauty. Shelley. BiP; BLPL; EnRP; HAP; HeIP; NoP; OAEL-2; OAEP; OBNC; OBRV
Hymn to Jesus, A. Richard of Caistre. MeEL
Hymn to Joy. Julia Cunningham. PChr
Hymn to Light. Milton. *See* Hail, Holy Light.
Hymn to Light. Abraham Cowley. MePo; SeCV-1
Hymn to Love. Lascelles Abercrombie. *Fr.* Emblems of Love. OBEV; OBVV
Hymn to Marduk, *sels. Unknown, tr. fr. Assyrian.* WGRP
"O Marduk, lord of countries, terrible one."
"O Mighty, powerful, strong one of Ashur."
Hymn to Mary, A. William Dunbar. *See* Ballad of Our Lady.
Hymn to Mary, A. *Unknown. See* Hymn to the Virgin, A.
Hymn to Moloch. Ralph Hodgson. HBMV; OxBTC
Hymn to My God in a Night of My Late Sicknesse, A. Sir Henry Wotton. AnAnS-2; MeLP; MePo; OBS
Hymn to Night. Melville Cane. MoAmPo
Hymn to Night, A. Max Michelson. TrJP
Hymn to Pan. Keats. *Fr.* Endymion, I. ChER; OBRV; PoEL-4
Hymn to Pan. John Fletcher. *Fr.* The Faithful Shepherdess, I, ii. NOBE; OBEV
(Sing His Praises.) ViBoPo
("Sing his praises that doth keep.") OBS
Hymn to Priapus. D. H. Lawrence. CMoP; CoBMV; MoAB; OBMV
Hymn to Proserpine. Swinburne. EBVV; OAEL-2; OAEP; OBNC; OBVV; PoEL-5; SeCeV; TEP; VLP
"I have lived long enough, having seen one thing, that love hath an end," *sel.* WHA
Hymn to Proust. Gavin Ewart. NYBP
Hymn to St. Geryon, *sel.* Michael McClure.
"Gesture the gesture the gesture the gesture, The." NeAP
Hymn to St. Teresa. Richard Crashaw. *See* Hymn to the Name and Honour of the Admirable Saint Teresa, A.
Hymn to Science. Mark Akenside. PoEL-3
Hymn to Selene. *Unknown, tr. fr. Greek by* Shelley. *Fr.* Homeric Hymns. AWP
Hymn to the Air Spirit. *Tr. fr. Eskimo.* WTO
Hymn to the Belly. Ben Jonson. *See* Hymn to Comus.
Hymn to the Creation. Joseph Addison. *See* Spacious Firmament on High, The.

Hymn to the Cross, A. *Unknown.* MeEL
Hymn to the Evening, An. Phillis Wheatley. WPE
Hymn to the Fallen. *Unknown, at. to* Chu Yuan, *tr. fr. Chinese by* Arthur Waley. OBWP
(Battle, The, *sl. diff. vers.*) WaaP
Hymn to the Holy Spirit. Stephen Langton. TrCP
Hymn to the Holy Spirit. Richard Wilton. OxBoCh
Hymn to the Morning, An. Phillis Wheatley. TAP
Hymn to the Name and Honour [*or* Honor] of the Admirable Saint[e] T[h]eresa, A. Richard Crashaw. FaBoEn; JCP; LoBV; NOBE; NOP; OAEP; OBEV; OBS; PoEL-2; SeCV-1, *abr.*
(Hymn to St. Teresa.) ACP; EBEV; MeLP; MePo; OxBoCh; WGRP
(In Memory of the vertuous and Learned Lady Madre de Teresa.) AnAnS-1
"Love, thou are absolute sole lord," *sel.* HAP
Hymn to the Night. Longfellow. AA; AP; BLPL; HBV-1; HBVY; LoBV; NePA; NOBA; OxBA; TAP; TreFS; TrGrPo; ViBoPo; WHA
Hymn to the Pillory, A, *sels.* Daniel Defoe.
"Hail hi'roglyphick state machin." NCEP
"Next bring some lawyers to thy bar." DBV
Hymn to the Sea, A. Richard Henry Stoddard. EtS
Hymn to the Sea. Sir William Watson. EtS
Hymn to the Spirit of Nature. Shelley. *See* Life of Life.
Hymn to the Sun, The. Akhenaton, *tr. fr. Egyptian by* J. E. Manchip White. TTY
Hymn to the Sun. C. M. Doughty. *Fr.* The Dawn in Britain. FaBoTw
Hymn to the Sun. William Alexander Percy. TrPWD
Hymn to the Sun. Michael Roberts. FaBoCh; OxBTC
Hymn to the Sunrise. *Unknown.* NA
Hymn to the Supreme Being on Recovery from a Dangerous Fit of Illness, *sel.* Christopher Smart.
"But, O immortals! What had I to plead." NOEC
Hymn to the Virgin. Sir Walter Scott. *Fr.* The Lady of the Lake, III. EnRP; GoBC
(Ave Maria.) ISi
Hymn to the Virgin, A. *Unknown.* OBEV
(Hymn to Mary, A.) MeEL
(In Praise of Mary.) NOBE
(Of One That Is so Fair and Bright.) HAP; ISi; OxBM
(Song to the Virgin, A.) SeCePo
Hymn to the Virgin. *At. to* William of Shoreham. OxBM
(Song to Mary, A.) MeEL
Hymn to the Virgin Mary. Conal O'Riordan, *tr. fr. Gaelic by* Eleanor Hull. ISi
Hymn to the West. Edmund Clarence Stedman. *See* Hymn of the West.
Hymn to the Winds. Joachim du Bellay, *tr. fr. French by* Andrew Lang. AWP
Hymn to Tsui-Xgoa. *Unknown, tr. fr. Hottentot.* PeSA
Hymn to Venus, The, *sels.* *Unknown, formerly at. to* Homer; *tr. fr. Greek by* Congreve.
"Among the springs which flow from Ida's head." OBVE
"But when the golden-thron'd Aurora made." OBVE
Hymn to Vishnu. Jayadeva, *tr. fr. Sanskrit by* Sir Edwin Arnold. *Fr.* The Gita Govinda. AWP
Hymn to Zeus. Aeschylus, *tr. fr. Greek by* Gilbert Murray. *Fr.* Agamemnon. WGRP
Hymn to Zeus. Cleanthes, *tr. fr. Greek.* ILWL, *tr. by* James Adam; WGRP, *tr. by* Edward Hayes Plumptre
Hymn Written after Jeremiah Preached to Me in a Dream. Owen Dodson. AmNP
Hymn Written for the Two Hundredth Anniversary of the Old South Church, Beverly, Massachusetts. Lucy Larcom. OHIP
Hymn Written in Windsor Forest, A. Pope. *See* Lines Written in Windsor Forest.
Hymnal: "Bringer of sun, arrower of evening, star-begetter and moon-riser." Harold Vinal. TrPWD
Hymne, An: "Drop, drop, slow tears." Phineas Fletcher. *See* Hymn: "Drop, drop, slow tears."
Hymne I: Generall Invitation to Praise God, A. George Wither. *Fr.* Haleluiah; or, Britain's Second Remembrancer. SeCV-1
Hymne: "Queene and Huntresse, chaste, and faire." Ben Jonson. *See* Hymn to Diana.
Hymne for the Epiphanie, A. Richard Crashaw. *See* In the Glorious Epiphanie of Our Lord God.
Hymne in Honour of Beautie, An, *sel.* Spenser.
Beauty. OBSC
(Soul Is Form, *abr.*) GoBC
Hymne in Honour of Those Two Despised Virtues, Charitie and Humilitie, An. Henry More. *See* Hymn to Charity and Humility.
Hymne in Prayse of Neptune, A. Thomas Campion. *See* In Praise of Neptune.
Hymne of the Ascension, An. William Drummond of Hawthornden. OBS
Hymne of the Nativity, Sung as by the Shepheards, An. Richard Crashaw. *See* In the Holy Nativity of Our Lord God.
Hymne on the Nativitie of My Saviour, A. Ben Jonson. *See* Hymn on the Nativity of My Saviour.
Hymne to Christ, at the Authors Last Going Into Germany, A. John Donne. *See* Hymn to Christ . . .
Hymne to God My God, in My Sicknesse. John Donne. *See* Hymn to God My God, in My Sickness.
Hymne to God the Father, A. John Donne. *See* Hymn to God the Father, A.
Hymne to God the Father, A. Ben Jonson. *See* Hymn to God the Father, A.
Hymne to Our Saviour on the Crosse, A. George Chapman. PoEL-2
Hymnes on Teresa. Richard Crashaw. *See* Apology for the Foregoing Hymn, An.
Hymns and Spiritual Songs, *sels.* Christopher Smart.
Ascension of Our Lord Jesus Christ, XIV. NOCV
Epiphany, III. NOCV
Nativity of Our Lord and Saviour Jesus Christ, The, XXXII. EBEV; HAP; LAuP; LoBV; NOBE; NOCV; PoEL-3; SBVL
(Christmas Day, *sts.* 6-9.) ChTr; OBCP
(Hymn.) NAs; NoEC
St. Mark, XII. LAuP
St. Matthias, VIII. LAuP
St. Philip and St. James, XIII. LoBV, *shorter vers.;* NOCV; NOEC
(Spring, *shorter vers.*) OBEC
Hymns for the Amusement of Children, *sels.* Christopher Smart.
Elegance, XIII. NOCV
For Saturday, XXXIII. LAuP; NOEC
(Hymn for Saturday.) OxBChV
(Lark's Nest, A.) FaBoCh
Gratitude, XXII. LAuP; NOEC
Long-Suffering of God, XXIX. LAuP; NOCV
Loveliness, XIV. NOCV
Mirth, XXV. LAuP; OxBChV
Moderation, IX. NOCV
Mutual Subjection, XXVI. NOCV
(Consideration for Others.) OxBChV
Taste, XV. NOCV
Hymns of Astraea, *sels.* Sir John Davies.
Of Astraea. TrGrPo
To the Nightingale. OBSC; PBBP; TrGrPo
To the Rose. OBSC
To the Spring. EIL
Hymns of the Marshes, *sel.* Sidney Lanier.
Sunrise. AA; PoEL-5
Hymns to the Night, *sel.* "Novalis," *prose poem version tr. fr German by* Robert Bly.
Second Hymn to the Night, The. NU
Hymnus: "God be in my hede." *Unknown.* *See* God Be in My Head.
Hymnus in Noctem. George Chapman. *Fr.* The Shadow of Night. PoEL-2
Hymnus Sanctae Mariae, *sel.* Ennodius, *tr. fr. Latin.*
How of the Virgin Mother Shall I Sing? ISi
Hynde [*or* Hynd] Horn. *Unknown.* *See* Hind Horn.
Hypatia, *sel.* Elizabeth Tollet.
"What cruel laws depress the female kind." NOEC
Hyperbole! Can't you arise. Prose for Des Esseintes. Donald Davie, *after* Mallarmé. OBVE
Hyperion; a Fragment. Keats. EnRP; OAEL-2
Sels.
"Apollo then,/ With sudden scrutiny and gloomless eyes," *fr.* III. OBRV
"As when, upon a trancéd summer-night," *fr.* I. ViBoPo
"But one of the whole mammoth-brood still kept," *fr.* I. OBRV
"Deep in the shady sadness of a vale," *fr.* I. ChER; FaBoEn; FiP; OAEP; OBRV; PoEL-4
(Saturn.) LOBV; OBNC; TrGrPo
Den of the Titans, The, *fr.* II. WHA
Hyperion and Saturn, *fr.* II. SeCePo
"Just at the self-same beat of Time's wide wings," *fr.* II. OBRV
(Bruised Titans, The.) OBNC
"O leave them, Muse! O leave them to their woes," *fr.* III. ViBoPo
Recollection of the Stone Circle near Keswick, A, *fr.* II. FaBoPP
Hypnopompic Poem. William Cole. POL
Hypochondriacus. Charles Lamb. BXAP
Hypocrisy will serve as well. Samuel Butler. FaBoEE
Hypocrite, The. John Caryll. APAS
Hypocrite, The. Kalonymos ben Kalonymos, *tr. fr. Hebrew by* J. Chotzner. *Fr.* The Touchstone. TrJP
Hypocrite Auteur. Archibald MacLeish. AmPP; MoVE; NePA
Hypocrite is strange of race, A. The Hypocrite. Kalonymos ben Kalonymos, *tr. by* J. Chotzner. *Fr.* The Touchstone. TrJP

Hypocrite Swift. Louise Bogan. PoA; SBG
Hypocrite Women. Denise Levertov. CAPP; MAT; NMM; PoM
Hypocrites shed tears. On Watching Politicians Perform at Martin Luther King's Funeral. Etheridge Knight. NNaP
Hypodermic Release. Del Corey. AMV-81
Hypsithilla, ask me over. An Invitation to an Invitation. Catullus, *tr. by* Gardner E. Lewis. ErPo
Hysteria. Chu Shu-chen, *tr. fr. Chinese by* Kenneth Rexroth. NaP

I

I. E. E. Cummings. NYBP
"I." Louis Golding. TrJP
I/ am going to rise. Vive Noir! Mari Evans. BOLo; IHMS; PoBA
I,/ at one time. The Self-Hatred of Don L. Lee. Don L. Lee. BPo
I/ Have Arrived. Status Symbol. Mari Evans. IDB
I/ heard de preachin' of de Elder. I Heard de Preachin' of de Word o' God. *Unknown.* BoAN-2
I/ is the total black, being spoken. Coal. Audre Lorde. BlSi; NoP; PoBA
I/ love/ you so. Chocolate Chocolate. Arnold Adoff. RHPC
I/ never/ guessed any. I. E. E. Cummings. NYBP
I/ never liked/ white folks. Alice Walker. *Fr.* Once. PoBA
I. . ./One. . ./ I smelt the weird Atlantic. Finistère. Thomas Kinsella. IPY
I/ saw/ the/ dragonfly. By a Rich Fast Moving Stream. John Tagliabue. ELU
I/ seek/ integration. The New Integrationist. Don L. Lee. BOLo
I;/ Thou. The Little Poem of Life. John Oxenham. TRV
"I/ Through/ Blue/ Sky/ Fly." The Aeronaut to His Lady. Frank Sidgwick. WhC
I/ want you/ to listen. Kenneth Patchen. *Fr.* The Journal of Albion Moonlight. NaP
I/ was five/ when/ mom and dad got married. Black Sketches. Don L. Lee. NeAC
I/ wonder why/ some. Tom Poole. BOLo
I, ——— A. B. do declare. Tax Return. *Unknown.* FaBoUs
I, a blue wolf. The "Word" of a Wolf Encircled by the Hunt. Sandag, *tr. by* C. R. Bawden. WTO
I, a boat with a bony keel. A Dentist's Window. James K. Baxter. OxBC
I, a Most Wretched Atlas. Heine, *tr. fr. German by* Emma Lazarus. *Fr.* Homeward Bound. TrJP
I, a princess, king-descended, decked with jewels, gilded, drest. A Royal Princess. Christina Rossetti. BrRo
I, a slave, chained to an oar of poem. Stoic. Lawrence Durrell. NYBP
I a tender young maid have been courted by many. My Thing Is My Own. *Unknown.* CoMu
I abdicate my daily self that bled. Vita Nuova. Stanley Kunitz. VGW
I abhor the slimy kiss. Kisses Loathesome. Robert Herrick. CaPo
I abide and abide and better abide. Sonnet. Sir Thomas Wyatt. BoLoP; EnLoPo; SiPS
I Accept. Harold Trowbridge Pulsifer. HBMV
I 'ad no education, and my pile. A Ballade of Any Father to Any Son. J. C. Squire. WhC
I address you only. Letter to My Mother. Dom Moraes. NoAM
I admire the driven, those who rise from choice. Cinema at the Lighthouse. Henri Coulette. *Fr.* The War of the Secret Agents. NePoEA-2
I adore you as much as the vault of night. Baudelaire, *tr. fr. French by* Anthony Hartley. NAWM-2
I adore you darling. Complaint. Rufinus Domesticus, *tr. by* Dudley Fitts. OLR
I advise rest; the farmhouse. To a Print of Queen Victoria. James K. Baxter. OxBC
I advocate a semi-revolution. A Semi-Revolution. Robert Frost. LiTM
I affirm. Perambulator Poems, III. David McCord. WhC
I ain't afeard uv snakes, or toads, or bugs, or worms, or mice. Seein' Things. Eugene Field. HBV-1; HBVY; TreF
I ain't gonna tell no body 34 have done for me-e-e. 34 Blues. *Unknown.* BluL
I ain't got no father. Poor Lonesome Cowboy. *Unknown.* CoSo; TiPo
I ain't never been to heaven but Ah been told. Swing Low, Sweet Chariot. *Unknown.* GBP
I ain't never loved but three womens in my life. Back Gnawing Blues. *Unknown.* BluL
I almost caught the bentwood chair. Urban Ode. Sandra McPherson. MAYP
I almost know you now. You are your name. Eight Lines for a Script Girl. George Jonas. NeAC
I almost ruined the stew and where. The Pigs for Circe in May. Joanne Kyger. PoM
I, Alphonso, live and learn. Alphonso of Castile. Emerson. AP; NOBA
I always choose the plainest food. In Praise of Water-Gruel. Matthew Green. *Fr.* The Spleen. FaBoUs
I always eat peas with honey. *See* I Eat My Peas with Honey.
I always hope Father is going to play. Newspaper. Aileen Fisher. SoPo
I always like summer. Knoxville, Tennessee. Nikki Giovanni. AmNP; BlSi; BOLo; BPo; CNA; InPS; PoBA; SO
I always liked to go to bed. A Song for My Mother—Her Stories. Anna Hempstead Branch. OHIP
I always loved this solitary hill. L'Infinito. Giacomo Leopardi, *tr. by* Lorna De' Lucchi. AWP
I always loved to call my lady Rose. Madrigal. *Unknown.* ElL
I always remember your beautiful flowers. Pad, Pad. Stevie Smith. ELU
I always say I won't go back to the mountains. Sourdough Mountain Lookout. Philip Whalen. NeAP; PoM
I always see, I don't know why. The Knowledgeable Child. L. A. G. Strong. OBMV
I always shout when Grandma comes. Afternoon with Grandmother. Barbara A. Huff. FaPON
I always think of a coffin's quiet. A Poem for a Poet. Audre Lorde. NMM
"I always think that when I see you you." Estimable Mable. Gwendolyn Brooks. FB
I always thought that. Surfaces. David Madden. AMV-80
I always wanted a red balloon. Tragedy. Jill Spargur. BLPA
I always was afraid of Somes's Pond. Atavism. Elinor Wylie. HBMV; PoA; SBG
I Am. John Clare. EBCP; EBEV; EBVV; EnRP; FaBoEn; GTBS-P; HAP; LiTB; NBM; NOBE; NoP; OAEL-2; OBNC; PoEL-4; PoPl; Prf; PrIm; TrGrPo; VLP; WHA
(I Am: Yet What I Am Who Cares or Knows?) InvP
(Written in Northampton County Asylum.) OBEV; OBVV; ViBoPo
I Am. Hilda Conkling. FaPON; TiPo
I am—/ Excuse me, I was—the Alamo. Last Fall of the Alamo. "O. Henry." BPAW
I am/ look/ ing at. You Too? Me Too—Why Not? Soda Pop. Robert Hollander. NIP
I am a babe of royalty. Royal Education. Winthrop Mackworth Praed. OBSV
I am a black Pierrot. A Black Pierrot. Langston Hughes. OLR
I Am a Black Woman. Mari Evans. CNA; NMM; PAI
I am a bold cowboy, from Midland I came. The Lovesick Cowboy. *Unknown.* CoSo
I am a bonded highwayman, Cole Younger is my name. *See* I am a highway bandit man, Cole Younger is my name.
I Am a Book I neither Wrote nor Read. Delmore Schwartz. TAP
I am a boy. A Young David: Birmingham. Helen Morgan Brooks. PoNe
I am a bridge. Golden Gate: The Teacher. Lilyan S. Mastrolia. AMV-80
I Am a Brisk and Sprightly Lad. *Unknown.* AmSS
I am a broken-hearted milkman, in grief I'm arrayed. Polly Perkins. *Unknown.* DTC; ELP; OxBoLi
I am a bunch of red roses. *Turkish Love Songs, tr. by* Reza Baraheni *and* Zahra-Soltan Shokoohtaezeh. BoWoP
I am a camel in all the sand. Camel. Alan Brownjohn. RHPC
I am a child/ of six generations here. The Sequence of Generations. Hayim Be'er, *tr. by* Stephen Mitchell. VWA
I am a circus dancer. A Circus Dancer. Celia Dropkin, *tr. by* Howard Schwartz. VWA
I am a composite being. I Am the Flag. Lawrence M. Jones. PAL; PGD
I am a cowboy by my trade. A Wild Rattling Cowboy. *Unknown.* CoSo
I Am a Cowboy in the Boat of Ra. Ishmael Reed. InPK; NBP; NoP; PoBA; PrIm
I am a crazy woman with a painted face. I Light Your Streets. Meridel LeSueur. GP
I Am a Dangerous Woman. Joy Harjo. TWSS
I am a dispossessed Ontario wood. Silverthorn Bush. Robert Finch. NOBC
I am a downright Country-man, both faithful (aye) and true. The Downright Country-Man; or, The Faithful Dairy Maid. *Unknown.* CoMu
I am a faire maide, if my glasse doe not flatter. The Wooing Maid. Martin Parker. CoMu
I am a feather on [*or* in] the bright sky. The Delight Song of Tsoai-Talee. N. Scott Momaday. CDW; GrPl; STE
I am a flag by distant space surrounded. Foreboding. Rainer Maria Rilke, *tr. by* Lori Weinstein. InPK
I am a fool, I can no good. Love. *Unknown.* OxBM
I am a friar of orders gray. The Friar of Orders Gray. John O'Keefe. OnYI; OxBI
I am a frightful monster. Be a Monster. Roy Fuller. AmMo
I am a frog. The Frog Prince. Stevie Smith. DFT; HAP
I am a gentleman in a dustcoat trying. Piazza Piece. John Crowe Ransom. AP; BoLoP; CoBMV; ErPo; HeIP; MoAB; MoAmPo; MoVE; NoAM; NOBA; NoP; OxBA; PAI; SoSe; TAP; TreFT; TrGrPo

I am a girl of constant sorrow. Girl of Constant Sorrow. Sara Ogan Gunning. FSW
I am a goddess of the ambrosial courts. Artemis Prologizes. Robert Browning. LoBV
I am a hand weaver to my trade. The Weaver and the Factory Maid. *Unknown.* OBET
I am a highway bandit man [*or* bonded highwayman], Cole Younger is my name. Cole Younger. *Unknown.* AmFP; FSW
I Am a Horse. Hans Arp, *tr. fr. French by* Harriet Watts. FaBoNo
I Am a Jew. David Martin. VWA
I am a jolly soldier. Bunker's Hill, or the Soldier's Lamentation. John Freeth. NOEC
I am a jolly young fellow. The Jolly Driver. *Unknown.* CoMu; UnTE
I am a jovial collier lad, as blithe as blithe can be. Down in a Coal Mine. J. B. Geoghegan. AmFP; TreFS
I am a jovial marriner, our calling is well known. The Jovial Marriner; or, The Sea-Man's Renown. John Playford. CoMu
I am a kind of farthing dip. A Portrait. Robert Louis Stevenson. SeCePo
I Am a King. I. Z. Rimon, *tr. fr. Hebrew by* Shlomo Vinner *and* Howard Schwartz. VWA
I am a king's daughter, you a king's wife. A Letter to Her Mother. Eristi-Aya, *tr. fr. Akkadian by* Willis Barnstone. BoWoP
I am a lady. Small Sad Song. Alastair Reid. NYBP
I am a lamp, a lamp that is out. She Warns Him. Frances Cornford. EnLoPo
I Am a Leaf. Yehuda Amichai, *tr. fr. Hebrew by* Shlomo Vinner *and* Howard Schwartz. VWA
I am a lioness. 'Aisha bint Ahmad al-Qurtubiyya, *tr. fr. Arabic by* Elene Margot Kolb. WPOW
I am a little boy. Feet. "Harry." TiPo
I am a Little Church (No Great Cathedral). E. E. Cummings. NePoAm-2
I am a little world made cunningly. John Donne. Holy Sonnets, V. AnAnS-1; CABA; EnRePo; MasP; NIP; NoP; OBS; SeCP; TEP
I am a lone, unfathered chick. Orphan Born. Robert Jones Burdette. OBAL
I am a man now. Here. R. S. Thomas. GTBS-P
I am a man of constant sorrow. Man of Constant Sorrow. *Unknown.* FSW
I am a man of few beliefs. Thespian in Jerusalem. Myra Glazer Schotz. VWA
I am a man of war and might. A Soldier. Sir John Suckling. SeCV-1
I am a man with no ambitions. The Advantages of Learning. Martial, *tr. by* Kenneth Rexroth. ErPo
I am a miner. The light burns blue. Nick and the Candlestick. Sylvia Plath. CAPP; CoAP; LCAP; PBWP
I am a Mormon bishop and I will tell you what I know. The Mormon Bishop's Lament. *Unknown.* CoSo
I am a most superior person. Henry Charles Beeching. *Fr.* The Masque of Balliol. CenHV
I am a native of the land of Erin. A Convict's Lament on the Death of Captain Logan. *Unknown.* PoAu-1
I Am a Negro. Muhammad Al-Fituri, *tr. fr. Arabic by* Halim El-Dabh. TTY
I Am a Parcel of Vain Strivings Tied. Henry David Thoreau. AP; FaBoEn; NOBA; NoP; PoEL-4; TAP
(Sic Vita.) AmPP; NePA; OxBA
I am a part of all that I have met. Tennyson. *Fr.* Ulysses. TRV
I Am a Peach Tree. Li Po, *tr. fr. Chinese by* Shigeyoshi Obata. OLR
I am a peevish student, I. Melancholia. *Unknown.* NA
I Am a Pilgrim. *Unknown.* FSW
I am a poet of the Hudson River, and the heights above it. America, America! Delmore Schwartz. NYP
"I am a poor girl, and my fortune is bad." The Wagoner's Lad. *Unknown.* BaBo
I am a poor lad and my fortune is bad. Limbo. *Unknown.* OBET
I am a poor old man, come listen to my song. When This Old Hat Was New. *Unknown.* OBET
I am a poor prisoner condemned to die. The Execution of Luke Hutton. *Unknown.* OBET
I am [*or* I'm just] a poor wayfaring stranger. Poor Wayfaring Stranger. *Unknown.* AmFP; BLSo; FSW; OuSiCo; TrAS
I am a poor workman as rich as a Jew. Contentment; or, The Happy Workman's Song. John Byrom. OBEC
I am a pretty wench. *Unknown.* OxNR
I am a quiet gentleman. The Tired Man. Anna Wickham. HBMV; ViBoPo
I am a reaper whose muscles set at sundown. All my oats are cradled. Harvest Song. Jean Toomer. NoP
I am a reek and a rambling one. The Reek and the Rambling Blade. *Unknown.* OuSiCo
I am a rich widow, I live all alone. The Rich Widow. *Unknown.* AmFP
I am a river. No More. Carl Clark. JB
I am a roving cowboy off from the Western plains. The Black Tail Range. *Unknown.* CoSo
I am a roving gambler, I've gambled all around. The Roving Gambler [*or* Roving Gambler Blues]. *Unknown.* AS; FSW; TrAS
I am a roving shanty boy, love to sing and dance. The Roving Shanty Boy. *Unknown.* AmFP
I am a roving traveler and go from town to town. The Gamboling Man. *Unknown.* AS
I am a sea-shell flung. Frutta di Mare. Geoffrey Scott. ChTr; EtS; OBMV
I am a senseless thing, with a hey, with a hey. A New Ballad, to an Old Tune, Called, I Am the Duke of Norfolk, etc. *Unknown.* APAS
I am a shoemaker by my trade. The Shoemaker. *Unknown.* TrAS
I am a sincere man. José Martí, *tr. by* Seymour Resnick. *Fr.* Simple Verses. TTY
"I Am a Sioux Brave," He Said in Minneapolis. James Wright. ELU
I am a skinny girl. The Skinny Girl. Anne Hébert, *tr. by* Willis Barnstone. BoWoP
I am a sleeping body. Ark Apprehensive. Jay Macpherson. *Fr.* The Ark. NOBC
I am a soldier blithe and gay. The Rambling Soldier. *Unknown.* OBET
I am a soul in the world: in. The Invention of Comics. Amiri Baraka. AmNP; CAPP; PoBA
I am a stag: of seven tines. The Alphabet Calendar of Amergin [*or* Song of Amergin]. *Unknown, tr. by* Robert Graves. BIrV; MOON
I am a stranger. The Jewish Woman. Gertrud Kolmar, *tr by* Henry A. Smith. VWA
I am a stranger in the land. Death. *Unknown.* BLPA; FPL
I am a sundial, and I make a botch. On a Sundial. Hilaire Belloc. FaBoEE; PV; QQQ
I am a sundial. Ordinary words. Hilaire Belloc. FaBoEE
I am a sundial, turned the wrong way round. Hilaire Belloc. FaBoEE; POL
I am a thief. Listen. Jessica Hagedorn. WPOW
I am a tongue for beauty. Not a day. Clement Wood. Eagle Sonnets, XIX. HBMV
I am a trombone. By the chinaberry tree. New Orleans. Hayden Carruth. AmFN
I am a vaquero by trade. Pinto. *Unknown.* CoSo
I am a very mature person. A Decision. Edith Södergran. PBWP
I am a very old pussy. An Old Cat's Confessions. Christopher Pearse Cranch. OBCA
I am a very personable man. A New Shakespeare. Andrew Lang. CenHV
I Am a Victim of the Telephone. Allen Ginsberg. GP; NYP
I am a wandering, bitter shade. What's in a Name? Helen F. More. PAH
I am a wandering cowboy, from ranch to ranch I roam. The Wandering Cowboy. *Unknown.* CoSo
I am a weaver by my trade. Wil the Merry Weaver, and Charity the Chamber-Maid; or, A Brisk Encounter between a Youngman and His Love. *Unknown.* CoMu
I am a white falcon, hurrah! The Falcon. Richard Henry Stoddard. AA
I am a widow, robed in black, alone. Christine de Pisan, *tr. fr. French by* Willis Barnstone. BoWoP
I am a wild and wicked youth. The Rambling Boy. *Unknown.* OBET
I Am a Wild Young Irish Boy, *with music. Unknown.* ShS
I Am a Woman, *sel.* Akhtar Amiri, *tr. fr. Farsi by* Fereshte Mahamadi. "My home is the mountain." WPOW
I am a woman and my poems. The Practice of Magical Evocation. Diane di Prima. PoM
I am a woman—therefore I may not. A Woman's Thought. Richard Watson Gilder. HBV-1
I am a wonder. I vary my voice. Riddle: Jay: *Higora. Unknown.* PBBP
I am a young dairy maid, buxom and tight. The Buxom Young Dairy Maid. *Unknown.* OBET
I am a young executive. No cuffs than mine are cleaner. Executive. John Betjeman. NOBL
I am a young girl. Motet. *Unknown, tr. by* Carol Cosman. PBWP
I am a young girl, gay. *Unknown, tr. fr. French by* Willis Barnstone. BoWoP
I am a young jolly brisk sailor. Tarpauling Jacket. *Unknown.* DTC; OxBoLi
I am a youthful lady, my troubles they are great. Victory. *Unknown.* CoMu
I am abandoning my vessel. In Distress. David Wagoner. SUW
I am adrift in a desert where too much sun. Desert Shipwreck. Barbara Leslie Jordan. GoYe
I am afraid. *Unknown, tr. fr. Eskimo.* WSC
I am afraid I may be Ilia. Fear. Anna Hajnal, *tr. by* Daniel Hoffman. BoWoP
I am afraid of being crushed in the pincers. Sometimes. Greg Kuzma. Psk
I am afraid of silence. The Voice. Sister Maris Stella. GoBC
I am afraid to own a body. Emily Dickinson. LiTA
I am alert to these letters in extraordinary numbers. Bordering Manuscript. James Applewhite. PoA

I am alive at night. Moon Song, Woman Song. Anne Sexton. MOON; PPP
I am alive—I guess. Emily Dickinson. NOBA
I am all bent to glean the golden ore. Madrigal: To His Lady Selvaggia Vergiolesi; Likening His Love to a Search for Gold. Cino da Pistoia, *tr. by* Dante Gabriel Rossetti. AWP
I am all Thine, Belovèd, for. Exchange. Sister Mary Dorothy Ann. GoBC
I am all things. Some Magic. James Koller. PoM
I Am Almost Asleep. Eldon Grier. MoCV; PV
I am alone. A Dog. Charlotte Zolotow. GDP
I am already quite scarce. For years. The Last Ones. Dan Pagis, *tr. by* Stephen Mitchell. VWA
I am always aware of my mother. Mother. Nagase Kiyoko, *tr. by* Kenneth Roxroth *and* Ikuke Atsumi. BoWoP
I am Ambassador of Otherwhere. From the Embassy. Robert Graves. PoA
I Am an American. Elias Lieberman. FaPON; PAL; PoLF; TreFT
I am an ancient jest! Ballade of the Primitive Jest. Andrew Lang. HBV-1
I am an ancient reluctant conscript. Old Timers. Carl Sandburg. NoAM; YaD
I am an Eskimo. Magic Word. Edgar Jackson. LFAC
"I am an owl of orders gray." The Song of the Owl. Richard Kendall Munkittrick. OBCA
I am an unadventurous man. De Gustibus. St. John Emile Clavering Hankin. CenHV; LiSp
"I am an urn of anger," cried the bull. The Bull. Freda Laughton. NeIP
I am Andrew Cecil Bradley. Cecil Arthur Spring-Rice. *Fr.* The Masque of Balliol. CenHV
I am anxious after praise. Egoism. W. Craddle. FiBHP; WhC
I am approaching. Past dry. Loot. Thom Gunn. ErPo; NePoEA-2
I am as awful as my brother War. Peace. Eleanor Farjeon. SUMH
"I am as brown as brown can be." The [Bonny] Brown Girl. *Unknown.* BaBo; ELP; ESPB; OBET; OxBB
I am as I am and so will I be. Sir Thomas Wyatt. SiPS
I Am as Light as Any Roe. *Unknown. See* Woman Is a Worthy Thing, A.
I am as tired as fencewire. Gone Fishing. Mark Sanders. WOLT
I am at Deep Well where the spirit-trees. Roland Robinson. *Fr.* Deep Well. CBAP
I am back from up the country—very sorry that I went. Up the Country. Henry Lawson. CBAP
I am beautiful, O mortals! like a dream of stone. Beauty. Baudelaire, *tr. by* Elaine Marks. NAWM-2
I am become a frightful bloody murtherer. Fragment from the Elizabethans. W. Bridges-Adams. FaBoCo
I am become a shell of delicate alleys. Airliner. Francis Webb. CBAP
I am becoming a god! Everything Is Possible. Robert Pack. PPP
I am beside you, now. The Shadow's Song. Yvor Winters. POL
I am bewildered still and teased by elves. Tricksters. William Rose Benét. HBMV
I am black and I have seen black hands. I Have Seen Black Hands. Richard Wright. NoAM; PoBA
I am blessed with my location. The Lost Pictures. Hollis Summers. HoPM
I am blessing two, not one. The Time of Creation Has Come. *Yoruba Oral Tradition, tr. by* Ulli Beier. WTO
I am blood of your ancient blood, bone of your fragile bone. To the Jews in Poland. Jozef Wittlin, *tr. by* Isaac Komen. VWA
I am Branson; Nature's laws. Henry Charles Beeching, *and* John Bowyer Nichols. *Fr.* Balliol Rhymes. FaBoEE
I am broke and hungry. Broke and Hungry. *Unknown.* BluL
I am broken by the tumult of the years. Old Joyce. Seán Jennett. NeIP
I am brooding over a nest of red plums and ruby plums. Still Life. Betsy Bering. PoDr
I am but a little woman. Kivkarjuk, *tr. fr. Eskimo.* WTO
I am but clay in thy hands; but thou art the all-loving artist. I in Thee, and Thou in Me. Christopher Pearse Cranch. HBV-2
I am called by name of man. *Unknown.* GBP
I Am Called Childhood. Sir Thomas More. NCEP
(Childhood.) EnRePo
(Pageant Verses.) AAS
I am caught in the new power. Custer Must Have Learned to Dance. Elizabeth Woody. STE
I am caught up in her. Woman. Jane Chambers. IHMS
I Am Cherry Alive. Delmore Schwartz. RHPC
I Am Christmas. *Unknown.* OxBM
I am come home again. Home-coming. Isobel Hume. HBMV
I am come into my garden, my sister, my spouse. Bible, *O.T. Fr.* The Song of Solomon. OBVE
I am come to make thy tomb. John Webster. *Fr.* The Duchess of Malfi. ChTr
I am concerned because my mind. Ballade to My Psychoanalyst. Kenneth Lillington. FiBHP
I am confident. More Truth and Light. John Robinson. TRV
I am confirm'd a woman can. Verses. Sir John Suckling. CavP
I am content, I do not care. Careless Content. John Byrom. HBV-2; NOEC; OBEC
I am content with latticed sights. Late Winter. Hazel Hall. HBMV
I am contented by remembrances. James Branch Cabell. Retractions, II. HBMV
I am Count Orlo come to day farewell. Orlo's Valediction. Jon Manchip White. NePoEA
I am custodian of close things. When Senses Fled. John Woods. CoPo
I am dangerous. Scissor-Man. George MacBeth. FaBoMo
I Am Dark and Fair to See. *Unknown.* UnTE
I Am Dead, Horatio. Shakespeare. *Fr.* Hamlet, V, ii. FaBoRV
(Death of Hamlet.) FiP
I am desolate. Love's Despair. Diarmad O'Curnain, *tr. by* George Sigerson. OnYI; OxBI
I Am Disquieted When I See Many Hills. Hyam Plutzik. VGW
I am dressed in my old grey running suit. The Work-out. Geoffrey Movius. MAT
I am driven mad with the printed word. Am Driven Mad. Allen Polite. NNP
I am driving; it is dusk; Minnesota. Driving toward the Lac Qui Parle River. Robert Bly. ConAP; LCAP; NaP; NCSH; NoP
I am drunk of the pot. I, Lessimus, of Salt Lake City. Robert Peters. BXAP
I am dying, Egypt, dying. Antony to [*or* and] Cleopatra. William Haines Lytle. AA; BeLS; BLPA; FaPo; HBV-2; TreF
I am dying, Egypt, dying. Death of Antony. Shakespeare. *Fr.* Antony and Cleopatra, IV, xv. FiP
I am Edgar, an Eskimo. Self-Portrait. Edgar Jackson. LFAC
I am enamored, and yet not so much. Sonnet: He Will Not Be Too Deeply in Love. Cecco Angiolieri da Siena, *tr. by* Dante Gabriel Rossetti. AWP
I am entrenched. Winter. Samuel Menashe. GrPl
I am Eve, great Adam's wife. Eve's Lament [*or* Eve]. *Unknown, tr. by* Kuno Meyer. BIrV; OnYI
I am far frae my hame, an' I'm weary often whiles. My Ain Countree. Mary Lee Demarest. HBV-2
I am featly-tripping Lee. Henry Charles Beeching. *Fr.* Balliol Rhymes. CenHV; FaBoEE; GLGT
I am fevered with the sunset. The Sea Gypsy [*or* Gipsy]. Richard Hovey. EtS; FaPON; HBV-1; HBVY; PDV; TreFS
I am filled with joy. Dead Man's Song, Dreamed by One Who Is Alive. Paulinaoq, *tr. fr. Eskimo.* WTO
I am filled with the sorrow of all things seen. Euridice Saved. Linda Gregg. NPGG
I am fish. Fish. Emily Townsend. NYBP
I am fixed in waiting. Sagimusume: The White Heron Maiden. Jonny Kyoko Sullivan. WPOW
I Am Forsaken. *Unknown.* OxBM
I am four monkeys. The Tree. Alfred Kreymborg. HBMV; PoPl
I am fourteen. Hanging Fire. Audre Lorde. NoP; NIP
I Am from Ireland. *Unknown. See* Irish Dancer, The.
I am from Ireland. Dispossessed Poet. Monk Gibbon. OnYI
I am full of grief, and the tear runs from my eye. Five Arabic Verses in Praise of Wine. *Unknown, tr. by* Hartwig Hirschfeld. TrJP
I Am Fur from My Sweetheart. *Unknown.* CoSo
I am furious with myself. Elsa Tio, *tr. fr. Spanish by* Willis Barnstone. BoWoP
I am gai. I am poet. I dvell. Vers Nonsensiques. George Du Maurier. HBV-2
"I am Gaspar. I have brought frankincense." The Three Kings. Rubén Darío, *tr. by* Lysander Kemp. PChr
I am glad daylong for the gift of song. Rhapsody. William Stanley Braithwaite. AmNP; BALP; BANP
I am glad I met you on the edge. A Childhood. Stephen Spender. NeBP
I am glad of that other life. The Dark. William Heyen. EyDe
I am going blind. Perhaps. Lucille Clifton. GeTw
I am going home with Jesus. Going Home with Jesus. Walter E. Isenhour. STF
I am going out West, partner. Po' Laz'us. *Unknown.* OuSiCo
I am going to carry my bed into New York City tonight. 96 Vandam. Gerald Stern. NYP
I Am Going to Sleep (Suicide Poem). Alfonsina Storni, *tr. fr. Spanish by* Aliki *and* Willis Barnstone. BoWoP
I Am Goya. Andrei Voznesensky. OBWP
I am greeting you, Mayor of Lagos. Mayor of Lagos. *Yoruba Oral Tradition, tr. by* Ulli Beier. WTO
I Am Ham Melanite. William Millett. GoYe
I am he as you are he as you are me and we are all together. I Am the Walrus. John Lennon *and* Paul McCartney. PPoe

I Am He That Aches with Love. Walt Whitman. *Fr.* Song of Myself. LLLT
I Am He That Walks with the Tender and Growing Night. Walt Whitman. *Fr.* Song of Myself. ChTr
"I am he who bursts the guarded gate." Boast of Masopha. Z. D. Mangoaela. PeSA
I am hearing the shape of the rain. In the Mountain Tent. James Dickey. CAPP
I Am Here. Robert Mezey. VWA
I am here again/ pox marks have obscured my dimples. I Would Be a Painter Most of All. Len Chandler. NBP
I am here again. Making an Impression. William (Haywood) Jackson. AMV-80
I am here, I have traversed the Tomb. He Cometh Forth into the Day. *Unknown, tr. by* Robert Hillyer. *Fr.* Book of the Dead. AWP
I am here only. Ayohu Kanogisdi. Carroll Arnett. STE
I am here with my beautiful bountiful downy womanful child. At a Summer Hotel. Isabella Gardner. GrPl
I am Hermes. I stand in the crossroads by a windy. Anyte, *tr. fr. Greek by* Willis Barnstone. BoWoP
I am his Highness' dog at Kew. Epigram Engraved on the Collar of a Dog Given [*or* Which I Gave] to His Royal Highness [*or* Engraved on the Collar . . .]. Pope. CABA; ChTr; FaBoCo; FaBoEE; FM; HBV-1; InPK; LiTB; NOEC; NTCP; OxBoLi; PAI; PoPle; RHPC; SeCeV; SoSe; TreFS; WhC
I am holding this turquoise. The Serenity in Stones. Simon J. Ortiz. CDW
I am home in heaven, dear ones. Safely Home. *Unknown.* STF
I am Huxley, blond and merry. John Bowyer Buchanan Nichols. *Fr.* Balliol Rhymes. CenHV
I am I, old Father Fisheye that begat the ocean, the worm. The End. Allen Ginsberg. ConAP
I am immortal! I know it! I feel it! Dryad Song. Margaret Fuller. WGRP
I am in a desert. Bushed. Barry McKinnon. NOBC
"I Am in Danger—Sir." Adrienne Rich. NOBA
I am in love with high far-seeing places. View from Heights. Arthur Davison Ficke. Sonnets of a Portrait Painter, XIII. HBMV
I am in love with the laughing sickness. Zizi's Lament. Gregory Corso. NeAP; VGW
I am in love with the sea, but I do not trust her yet. The Sea-Captain. Gerald Gould. EtS
I am in my Eskimo-hunting-song mood. Eskimo Occasion. Judith Rodriguez. CBAP
I am in prison for trying to swindle the/ Keepsake Corporation. The Keepsake Corporation. David Fisher. NPGG
I am in the old room across from the synagogue. The Old Room. W. S. Merwin. NYBP
I am in the tub with my body. To My Body. Nancy Sullivan. TAP
I am inside someone. An Agony. As Now. Amiri Baraka. AmPP; BALP; BPo; LiTM; PPP
I am interested in the logic of secrets, how it has always moved me. La Reproduction Interdite/Not to Be Reproduced. Kathleen Fraser. NPGG
I Am Ireland. Padraic Pearse, *tr. fr. Irish by* Lady Gregory. OBMV
I am jealous: I am true. My Share of the World. Alice Furlong. HBV-1; OBVV
I am Jesu that cum to fight. Undo Your Heart. *Unknown.* MeEL
I am just a weary pilgrim. When the Saints Come Marching In. Edward C. Redding. BLSo
I am just on my way tomb. Oracle. E. L. Mayo. MiAP
I am just seventeen years and five months old. Robert Browning. The Ring and the Book, VII. OAEP
I am just two and two, I am warm, I am cold. A Riddle. William Cowper. HBV-1
I am Lake Superior. The Great Lakes Suite. James Reaney. WHW
I am leading a quiet life. Autobiography. Sonja Akesson, *tr. by* Ingrid Claréus. BoWoP
I am learning how to make a horse go left. New Skills. Naomi Shihab Nye. PH
I Am like a Book. David Rokeah, *tr. fr. Hebrew by* Robert Mezey. VWA
I am like a field/ waiting. Like a Field Waiting. Raquel Chalfi, *tr. by* Myra Glazer Schotz. VWA
I am like a flag unfurled in space. Presaging. Rainer Maria Rilke, *tr. by* Jessie Lemont. AWP; TrJP
I am like a jackfruit on the tree. The Jackfruit. Ho Xuan Huong, *tr. by* Nguyen Ngoc Bich. PBWP
I am like a slip of comet. Gerard Manley Hopkins. VLP
I am like bound because of Abraham's knife. Microcosmos, LVI. Nigel Heseltine. NeBP
I am listening here in Rome. A Song for the Ragged Schools of London. Elizabeth Barrett Browning. SBG
I am living more alone now than I did. The Last Chapter. Walter de la Mare. CMoP; MoBrPo
I Am Lonely. "George Eliot." *Fr.* The Spanish Gypsy. GN; HBV-1
I am lonely. Poem for Some Black Women. Carolyn M. Rodgers. BlSi
I Am Long Weaned. William Everson. NMP
I am looking at trees. Trees. W. S. Merwin. GP; PPJ
I am looking for a past. The Journey. David Ignatow. Psk
I am looking for nests. News from Detroit. Judith Minty. SOTS
I am looking rather seedy now while holding down my claim. The Little Old Sod Shanty [on My Claim]. *Unknown.* AS; BPAW; CoSo; FSW
I am lost in hot fits. Air. Amiri Baraka. SOTW
"I am Lot's pillar, caught in turning." Columns and Caryatids. Carolyn Kizer. WPE
I am lying face up on a raft. Dream. David Ignatow. VWA
I am made to sow the thistle for wheat, the nettle for a nourishing dainty. The Price of Experience. Blake. *Fr.* Vala; or, The Four Zoas. EnRP; Prf
I am making soup. Recipe: Sausage. Axionicus. FaBoUs
I am Miss Stein. Gertrude Stein at Snails Bay. Peter Porter. OxBC
I am monarch of all I survey. Verses Supposed to Be Written by Alexander Selkirk during His Solitary Abode on [*or* in] the Island of Juan Fernandez [*or* The Solitude of Alexander Selkirk *or* Alexander Selkirk *or* The Monarch *or* Verses]. William Cowper. FiP; FPL; GTBS; GTBS-P; HBV-2; LiTB; NOEC; PoEL-3; PoLF; RoGo; TreFS
I am my ancient self. The Pilgrim. Richard Wightman. WGRP
I Am My Beloved's. Bible, *O.T.* The Song of Solomon, VII: 11-14. TrJP
I Am My Beloved's, and His Desire Is towards Me. Francis Quarles. *See* Like to the Arctic Needle.
I am my lover's and he desires me. Bible, *O.T.* *Fr.* The Song of Solomon, *ad. by* Willis Barnstone. BoWoP
I am my mammie's ae bairn. I'm Owre Young to Marry Yet. Burns. UnTE
I am my own. As I Am My Father's. Rose Drachler. VWA
I am my prison. Conundrum. Carl Clark. JB
I am nae poet, in a sense. Burns. *Fr.* Epistle to J. Lapraik. PP
I Am New York City. Jayne Cortez. BoWoP
I am no brazen face to hale the Lord. Rabbi Yom-Tob of Mayence Petitions His God. A. M. Klein. TrJP
I am no Norseman, come to plunder. On Devenish Island. Frank Ormsby. CIP
I am no shepherd of a child's surmises. Montana Pastoral. J. V. Cunningham. MAT; MoAmPo; PrIm; VGW
I Am No Subject unto Fate. *Unknown.* OBS
I am no worshiper, but a member. Poem for David Janssen. R. T. Smith. AMV-81
I am nobody/ A red sinking autumn sun. Hokku Poems. Richard Wright. AmNP; PoBA
I Am Not a Camera. W. H. Auden. EyDe
I am not a flower of song. Ghazal XII. Mirza Ghalib, *tr. by* W. S. Merwin *and* Aijaz Ahmad. LLLT
I am not a handsome man. Eclipse. Ed Roberson. PoNe
I am not a metaphor or symbol. The Distant Drum. Calvin C. Hernton. BOLo; CTBA; FF; NNP; TTY
I am not a painter, I am a poet. Why I Am Not a Painter. Frank O'Hara. ConAP; HoAn; NeAP; NoAM; NOBA; PoM
I am not afraid in April. White Fear. Winifred Welles. HBMV
I am not ambitious at all. The Ballade of the Incompetent Ballade-Monger. James Kenneth Stephen. VLP
"I am not as these are," the poet saith. Not as These. Dante Gabriel Rossetti. The House of Life, LXXV. VLP
I am not blind. For Steph. Wendy Rose. CDW
I Am Not Bound to Win. Abraham Lincoln. TRV
I am not bred and born New Englander. Late Comer. Fanny de Groot Hastings. GoYe
I am not concern'd to know. True Riches. Isaac Watts. OBEC
I am not cousin to thinking brain. Cousins. Paula B. Cullen. AMV-81
I am not gay by your definition. Explanation. William Barber. PeHV
I am not going to invite you. Blond. Joseph de Roche. HeIP
I am not Mahomet. E. C. Bentley. *Fr.* Clerihews. NOBL
I am not of those fierce, wild wills. My Political Faith. George Frederick Cameron. PeCV
I am not one who much or oft delight. Personal Talk. Wordsworth. CABA; EnRP; NOBE
I am not physically perfect. Ella of the Cinders. Mary Blake French Crouch. DFT
I am not poor, but I am proud. Thought. Emerson. AmPP
I am not resigned to the shutting away of loving hearts. Dirge without Music. Edna St. Vincent Millay. CMoP; DL; LiTA; LO; NePA; NoAM; PPON; SBG; TrGrPo
I am not strong till Thou has clasped my hand. Freedom. *Unknown.* PGD
I am not sure if I knew the truth. Youth. "Laurence Hope." WeW
I am not sure that earth is round. Certainty Enough. Amelia Josephine Burr. HBMV

I am not surprised. On a Clear Day I Can See Forever. Alex Kuo. BrSi
I am not surprised. Waking Up. Tom Schmidt. GP
"I am not treacherous, callous, jealous, superstitious." A Face. Marianne Moore. PoCh
I am not what I was yesterday. The Butterfly. Alice Archer James. AA
I am not yet born; O hear me. Prayer before Birth. Louis MacNeice. GTBS-P; LiTB; MP; NAs; OAEP; TwCP
I am not you. Africa's Plea. Roland Tombekai Dempster. PBA; TTY
I am not your God. African Easter. Abioseh Nicol. PBA
"I Am Not Yours." Sara Teasdale. VGW
I am now so weary with waiting. Gaspara Stampa, *tr. fr. Italian by* Harold M. Priest. WPOW
"I Am of Ireland." W. B. Yeats. CMoP; LiTB; OnYI
I Am of Ireland. *Unknown. See* Irish Dancer, The.
I am of little worth and poor, apart. Song of Loneliness. Judah Halevi, *tr. by* Nina Davis Salaman. TrJP
I am of Shropshire, my shins be sharp. A Shropshire Lad. *Unknown.* ChTr
I Am of the Earth. Anna Walters. VoR
I am of the family of the universe, and with all of us together. In No Way. David Ignatow. AMV-81
I am of this world. On the Death of Emperor Tenji. *Unknown, tr. fr. Japanese by* Geoffrey Bownas *and* Anthony Thwaite. BoWoP
I am off down the road. Goblin Feet. J. R. R. Tolkien. FaPON
I am Ojistoh, I am she, the wife. Ojistoh. Pauline E. Johnson. NOBC
I am old. Epitaph. Christopher Logue. OxBTC
I am old and blind! Milton's Prayer for [*or* of] Patience. Elizabeth Lloyd Howell. AA; TRV; WGRP
I am one of a band of outlaws, Cole Younger is my name. Cole Younger. *Unknown.* BeLS
I am one of those troubled hearts. Human Soul. René Maran, *tr. by* Mercer Cook. TTY
I am only one. Lend a Hand. Edward Everett Hale. TRV
I am, outside. Incredible panic rules. John Berryman. Dream Songs, XLVI. CAPP; NaP
"I am Pancho Villa," says the truck. Pancho Villa. Lou Lipsitz. NCSH
I am peopled by women. A Folding and Unfolding. Welton Smith. PoNe
I am picking wild grapes last year. The Winemaker's Beat-étude. Alfred Purdy. MoCV
I am poor and old and blind. Belisarius. Longfellow. PoEL-5; WiR
I am poor brother Lippo, by your leave! Fra Lippo Lippi. Robert Browning. BiP; CTC; EBVV; NoP; OAEL-2; OAEP; TEP; ViBoPo; VLP
I am pretty wench. Plaint. *Unknown.* OxNR
I am provoked. Epigram. Strato, *tr. by* W. G. Shepherd. PeHV
I am Prytherch. Forgive me. I don't know. Invasion on the Farm. R. S. Thomas. POL
I am put high over all others in the city today. Killers. Carl Sandburg. MoVE
I am Queen Anne, of whom 'tis said. Queen Anne. *Unknown.* ChTr
I am quite sure he thinks that I am God. Bishop Doane on His Dog. George Washington Doane. BLPA; FaBoBe
I Am Raftery [*or* Rafferty]. Anthony Raftery, *tr. fr. Modern Irish by* Douglas Hyde. AnIL (*tr. by* James Stephens); AnIV; AWP; OnYI (*incl. tr. by* James Stephens); SeCePo
I Am Raftery ("I am Raftery, hesitant and confused"). Derek Mahon. CIP; OxBC
I am rather tall and stately. *Unknown. Fr.* Balliol Rhymes. FaBoEE
I am reading Li Po. The T.V. is on. Growing Up. Linda Gregg. NPGG
I am reading. The Distant Orgasm. James Tate. AmPA
I am remembering in the long ago. The Dream of the Rood. *Unknown.* ACP
I am reminded, by the tan man who wings. The Elevator Man Adheres to Form. Margaret Danner. PoBA; PoNe
I am reminded of the vestment. I'm Not Here / Never Was. Constanta Buzea, *tr. by* Stavros Deligiorgis. BoWoP
I am riding on a limited express, one of the crack trains of the nation. Limited. Carl Sandburg. HAP; MoAB; MoAmPo; OxBA
I am rooted in the wall. Snapdragon. Cardinal Newman. GoBC
I Am Rose. Gertrude Stein. NePA; OBCA; RHPC; TrJP
I am Saint John on Patmos of my heart. Holy Poems (I-III). George Barker. MoPo
I am saved, but is self buried? Saved, But. *Unknown.* STF
I am saying goodbye to the trees. A Departure. Derek Mahon. CIP
I am scorned by patterns which hold. Moon at Three A.M. Lance Henson. CDW
I am silver and exact. I have no preconceptions. Mirror. Sylvia Plath. HAP; NYBP; PAI
I Am Sitting Here. Yehuda Amichai, *tr. fr. Hebrew by* Ruth Nevo. VWA
I am sitting here. The Poor Girl's Meditation. *Unknown, tr. by* Padraic Colum. BIrV; OBMV; OLR
I am sitting in Mike's Place trying to figure out. One Thousand Fearful Words for Fidel Castro. Lawrence Ferlinghetti. CoPo; VGW
I am sitting. The Muddy Puddle. Dennis Lee. RHPC
I am sleepy, I'm tired, and I'm hungry and dry. What's Wrong, Little Blonde. *Unknown.* OuSiCo
I am slow as the world. I am very patient. Three Women. Sylvia Plath. NAs
I am slowly dying, water evaporating. George Bowering. *Fr.* Summer Solstice. NOBC
I am smoking Camels and crying. The Clouds. Arthur Vogelsang. MAYP
I am so empty and so incomplete. Fulfilment. Elsa Barker. *Fr.* The Spirit and the Bride. HBMV
I Am So Far from Pitying Thee. *Unknown.* NCEP
I am so fragile this morning. The U.S. Coast and Geodetic Survey Ship *Pioneer.* Robert Hershon. NeAC
I Am So Glad and Very. E. E. Cummings. CMoP
I am so little and grey. The Prayer of the Mouse. Carmen Bernos de Gasztold. PDV
I am so lonely, I am so blue. Somebody's Sweetheart I Want to Be. Will D. Cobb. FSN
I am so old a king that I remember. The Old King. John Heath-Stubbs. NePoEA
I am so out of love through poverty. Sonnet: Of Why He Would Be a Scullion. Cecco Angiolieri da Siena, *tr. by* Dante Gabriel Rossetti. AWP
I am so passing rich in poverty. Sonnet: He Jests Concerning His Poverty. Bartolomeo di Sant' Angelo, *tr. by* Dante Gabriel Rossetti. AWP
I am so tired and weary. Supplication. Joseph Seamon Cotter, Jr. BANP; CDC; PoNe
I am sorry I seldom speak I. Awkward Goodbyes. Vassar Miller. FAZ
I am sorry to speak of death again. Poetics against the Angel of Death. Phyllis Webb. MoCV; NOBC
I am soul in the world: in. The Invention of Comics. Amiri Baraka. LiTM
I am standing on the threshold of eternity at last. On the Threshold. *Unknown.* BLPA
I am standing upon the seashore. The Ship. *Unknown.* PoLF
I am still bitter about the last place we stayed. Codicil. Ruth Stone. BoWoP
I am still hurt, Plin. A Letter for Allhallows. Peter Kane Dufault. NYBP
I Am Stone of Many Colors. Tauhindauli. STE
I am stuffing this bolster. Slipping Out of Intensive Care. Florence Trefethen. AMV-80
I Am Sure of It. Jimmy Santiago Baca. LFAC
I am sure this Jesus will not do. Epilogue. Blake. *Fr.* The Everlasting Gospel. OBRV
I am surprised to find today. The Professor Waking. James Tate. FF
I am surprised to see. Letter Written on a Ferry [while] Crossing Long Island Sound. Anne Sexton. CoAP; MP; NYBP; TwCP
I am surrounded by armies, I have sent them word. Note in Lieu of a Suicide. Donald Finkel. CoPo
I am tall and rather stately. *Unknown. Fr.* Balliol Rhymes. NOBL
I am telling you a number of half-conditioned ideas. Sunday Evening. Barbara Guest. NeAP
I am telling you this. Blue Ruth: America. Michael S. Harper. PoBA
I am ten and no one I love has died. Deborah Lee. Yvonne. CNA
I am Tex Ritter. I am not Eldridge Cleaver. The Skyjacker. Stan Rice. NPGG
I am that binge you need. Tango. Elena Jordana, *tr. by* Kathrine Jason. AMV-80
I am that Dido which thou here do'st see. Decimus Magnus Ausonius, *tr. fr. Latin by* Sir Walter Ralegh. OBVE
I am that man who with a luminous look. Brevities. Siegfried Sassoon. PoLF
I am that man with helmet made of thorn. For an Ex-Far East Prisoner of War. Charles Causley. OxBC
I am that serpent-haunted cave. The Pythoness. Kathleen Raine. MoBrPo; ViBoPo
I am that which began. Hertha. Swinburne. OAEL-2; OAEP; VLP
I am that woman whose works are good. Sovereign Queen. Padeshah Khatun, *tr. by* Deirdre Lashgari. WPOW
I am the American heartbreak. American Heartbreak. Langston Hughes. AmPP; BPo; CABA; LiTM
I am the ancient Apple-Queen. Pomona. William Morris. WiR
I Am the Autumn. Itzig Manger, *tr. fr. Yiddish by* Joseph Leftwich. TrJP
I Am the Beginning. Isaiah Shembe, *tr. fr. Zulu by* G. C. Oosthuizen. WTO
I am the bird of the wayside. Prelude. Christine Ama Ata Aidoo. PBWP
I am the black centipede, the rusher with a black nose. Praises of the Train. Demetrius Segooa. PeSA
I Am the Blood. Isaac Rosenberg. MoBrPo
I am the blue! I come from the lower world. Helen. Paul Valéry, *tr. by* Robert Lowell. OBVE

I am the boy perched in the high. Haitian Suite. Gregory Orr. MAYP
I Am the Bread of Life. Bible, *N.T.* St. John, VI: 35-40. TreFS
I am the captain of my soul. An Awful Responsibility. Keith Preston. PoPl; WhC
I Am the Captain of the Pinafore. W. S. Gilbert. *Fr.* H.M.S. Pinafore. TreFT
I Am the Cat. Leila Usher. BLPA
I am the cat of cats. I am. The Cat of Cats [*or* Kitty: What She Thinks of Herself]. William Brighty Rands. MoShBr; OxBChV; RHPC
I am the chaunt-rann of a Singer. The Poet. Padraic Fiacc. CIP; NeIP
I am the child of the Yangtse running. Child of the World. Edna L. S. Barker. GoYe
I am the crazy woman. Birthright. Geraldine Kudaka. BrSi
I am the dancer of the wood. The Spirit of the Birch. Arthur Ketchum. OHIP
I am the Dark Cavalier; I am the Last Lover. The Dark Cavalier. Margaret Widdemer. HBMV
I am the darker brother. I, Too, Sing America. Langston Hughes. PoLF
I am the Dean, and this is Mrs. Liddell. *Unknown.* *Fr.* Balliol Rhymes. FaBoEE
I am the Dean of Christ Church, Sir. Cecil Arthur Spring-Rice. *Fr.* Balliol Rhymes. CenHV; FaBoCo; FaBoEE; NOBL
I am the dog world's best detective. The Bloodhound. Edward Anthony. GDP
I Am the Door. Richard Crashaw. OAEP
I Am the Duke of Norfolk. *Unknown.* GBP
I am the family face. Heredity. Thomas Hardy. CTC; EBEV; ImOP
I am the farmer, stripped of love. The Hill Farmer Speaks. R. S. Thomas. GTBS-P
I am the first that ever lov'd. Love Speaks at Last. Lord Herbert of Cherbury. AnAnS-2
I Am the Flag. Lawrence M. Jones. PAL; PGD
I am the flower of the field. Bible, *O.T. (Douay vers.).* *Fr.* The Song of Solomon. ISi
I am the flute of Daphnis. On this wall. The Flute of Daphnis. Edward Cracroft Lefroy. *Fr.* Echoes from Theocritus. AWP; OBVV
I am the ghost of Shadwell Stair. Shadwell Stair. Wilfred Owen. FaBoTw
I Am the Gilly of Christ. Joseph Campbell. AnIL; OnYI
I am the god of things that burrow and creep. The Gods of the Earth Beneath. Edmund Blunden. BrPo
I am the great Professor Jowett. *Unknown.* FiBHP; PV
I am the inland man. Midwestern Man. Paul Giandi. AMV-81
I am the key that parts the gates of Fame. Death. Florence Earle Coates. HBV-2
I am the lamp that Flaccus gave his love. Faithless. *Unknown, tr. by* Louis Untermeyer. UnTE
I Am the Little Irish Boy. Henry David Thoreau. NAs
I am the little man who smokes & smokes. John Berryman. Dream Songs, XX. WeW
I am the Lord of Light, the self-begotten Youth. He Maketh Himself One with the God Ra. *Unknown, tr. by* Robert Hillyer. *Fr.* Book of the Dead. AWP
I Am the Lord, *with music.* Alexander Mack, *tr. fr. German by* Sheema Z. Buehne. AH
I am the magical mouse. The Magical Mouse. Kenneth Patchen. SO
I am the maiden in bronze set over the tomb of Midas. Cleobulus' Epitaph. Simonides, *tr. by* Richmond Lattimore. PoPl
I am the man crouched behind a bush. The Rapist. Stephen Dunn. POL
I am the man that hath seen affliction. Affliction. Bible, *O.T.* *Fr.* Lamentations. TrJP
I am the man who. The Carpenter. Michael Perkins. POL
I Am the Monarch of the Sea. W. S. Gilbert. *Fr.* H.M.S. Pinafore. TreFT
I am the mother of fair love. Bible, Apochrypha *(Douay vers.).* *Fr.* Ecclesiasticus. ISi
I am the mother of sorrows. The Paradox. Paul Laurence Dunbar. CABA; PoBA
I Am the Mountainy Singer. Joseph Campbell. AnIL; GoBC; HBMV; MoBrPo
I am the Muse who sung alway. Solution. Emerson. OBAL
I am the New Year, and I come to you pure and unstained. The New Year. J. D. Templeton. PGD
I am the old one here. Desert Tortoise. Byrd Baylor. RHPC
I Am the One. Thomas Hardy. OxBTC
I am the one who looks the other way. The Bystander. Rosemary Dobson. CBAP
I Am the Only Being Whose Doom. Emily Brontë. MAT; NCEP; TW; ViBoPo, 2 *sts.*; VLP
I am the only living thing. The Stallion. Boynton Merrill, Jr. PH
I am the only me I am. Me I Am! Jack Prelutsky. RHPC
I Am the People, the Mob. Carl Sandburg. AmPP; OxBA; TAP
I am the poet of the body and I am the poet of the soul. Song of Myself, XXI [*or* Leaves of Grass, XXI]. Walt Whitman. BiP; SeCeV; TrGrPo; WeW
I am the Prince in the Field. He Maketh Himself One with Osiris. *Unknown, tr. by* Robert Hillyer. *Fr.* Book of the Dead. AWP
I am the Prince. Envoi. Charles Causley. FF
I am the pure lotus. He Is like the Lotus [*or* Death as a Lotus Flower]. *Unknown, tr. by* Robert Hillyer. *Fr.* Book of the Dead. AWP; EaLo; TTY, *tr. by* Ulli Beier
I am the pure, the true of word, triumphant. He Defendeth His Heart against the Destroyer. *Unknown, tr. by* Robert Hillyer. *Fr.* Book of the Dead. AWP
I am the pure traveler. He Entereth the House of the Goddess Hathor. *Unknown, tr. by* Robert Hillyer. *Fr.* Book of the Dead. AWP
I am the reality of things that seem. Poetry. Ella Heath. HBV-2; WGRP
I am the Reaper. W. E. Henley. Echoes, V. OBNC
"I Am the Resurrection and the Life," Saith the Lord! Robert Stephen Hawker. GoBC
I am the rooftree and the keel. Tapestry Trees. William Morris. BoNaP; FaPON; OHIP
I am the rose of Sharon, and the lily of the valleys. Bible, *O.T.* *Fr.* The Song of Solomon, II. BiP; BoLoP; ChTr; FF; GBL; LLLT; OBVE; OLR
I am the ruined queen. Dido: Swarming. Kathleen Spivack. PoA
I am the saint at prayer on the terrace like the. Childhood, IV. Rimbaud, *tr. by* Louise Varèse. *Fr.* Illuminations. PoPl
"I am the sea." Poetry Is. Bruce Bennett. AMV-81
I am the serpent, fat with years. He Is like the Serpent Saka. *Unknown, tr. by* Robert Hillyer. *Fr.* Book of the Dead. AWP
I am the seventh son of the son. Malcolm X—an Autobiography. Larry Neal. AmNP; BPo
I am the shadow in the shadow of the wicker. Home Revisited: Midnight. John Ciardi. NYBP
I am the sister of him. Little. Dorothy Aldis. FaPON; NTCP; SUS; TiPo
I am the smoke king. The Song of the Smoke. W. E. B. DuBois. PoBA; UnPo
I am the sorrow in the wheat fields. Ellen Bass. NMM
I am the spirit astir. Autochthon. Sir Charles G. D. Roberts. CaP
I am the spirit of the morning sea. Ode. Richard Watson Gilder. AA
I am the stage, impassive, mute and cold. Nature. Alfred de Vigny, *tr. by* Margaret Jourdain. AWP
I am the terrour of the sea. On the Crocodile. Thomas Heyrick. FM
I am the tomb of Crethon; here you read. The Tomb of Crethon. Leonidas of Tarentum, *tr. by* John Hermann Merivale. AWP
I am the torch, she saith, and what to me. Modern Beauty. Arthur Symons. HBV-1
I am the toy-maker; I have brought from the town. The Toy-Maker. Padraic Colum. SaC
I am the true vine, and my Father is the husbandman. Bible, *N.T.* *Fr.* St. John. OBVE
I am the trumpet blown by time. The Trumpet. Ilya Ehrenburg, *tr. by* Y. Hornstein. TrJP
I am the Turquoise Woman's son. The War God's Horse Song. *Unknown, tr. by* Dane Coolidge *and* Mary Roberts Coolidge. LiTA
I am the very model of a modern college president. The Very Model of a Modern College President, *parody.* Harold A. Larrabee. WhC
I am the very model [*or* pattern] of a modern Major-General. The Modern Major-General [*or* Major General's Song]. W. S. Gilbert. *Fr.* The Pirates of Penzance. FaPo; InMe; NBM; NOBL; NoP
I am the Virgin; from this granite ledge. The Wayside Virgin. Langdon Elwyn Mitchell. AA
I Am the Walrus. John Lennon *and* Paul McCartney. PPoe
"I Am the Way." Alice Meynell. ACP; EBCP; OBMV; TRV
I Am the Wind. Zoë Akins. HBV-1
I am the wind which breathes upon the sea. The Mystery. *At. to* Amergin, *tr. by* Douglas Hyde. OnYI; OxBI
I am the woman of the principal fountain. Shaman. Maria Sabina, *tr. by* Henry Munn. WPOW
I am the woman who sits by the river. Let Us Gather at the River. Marge Piercy. GeTw
I am the woman you see in Bloomingdale's. Ordinary Women I. Marilyn Hacker. LTB
I am the woman-drawer. The Song of the Woman-Drawer. Mary Gilmore. PoAu-1
I am thinking of tents and tentage, tents through the ages. Thinking of Tents. Reed Whittemore. TAP
I am thinking tonight of the days that are gone. The Plain Golden Band, 2 *vers.* *At. to* Joe Scott. ShS
I am third in a line of murderers. Shooting Gallery. Martin Galvin. AMV-80
I am 32 years old. Writ on the Eve of My 32nd Birthday. Gregory Corso. NAs

I am this fountain's god. The River God. John Fletcher. *Fr.* The Faithful Shepherdess. TrGrPo
I am thy fugitive, thy votary. To the Lord Love. "Michael Field." OBMV
I am Thy grass, O Lord! Trust. Lizette Woodworth Reese. AA
"I am thy soul, Nikoptis. I have watched." The Tomb of Akr Çaar. Ezra Pound. TwAmPo
I am tired of cursing the Bishop. Crazy Jane on the Mountain. W. B. Yeats. CMoP
I am tired of looking at you through this glass. The Flirtation. Michael C. Blumenthal. AMV-81
I am tired of planning and toiling. The Cry of the [*or* a] Dreamer. John Boyle O'Reilly. BLPA; OnYI; TreFS
"I am tired of this barn!" said the colt. The Barn. Elizabeth J. Coatsworth. OBCP; SoPo
I am tired of work; I am tired of building up somebody else's civilization. Tired. Fenton Johnson. BANP; IDB; PAI; PoBA; PoLF; PoNe; TTY
I am to follow her. There is much grace. George Meredith. Modern Love, XLII. ViBoPo
I am to my honey what marijuana is. Skirt Dance. Ishmael Reed. FF
I am told, sir, you're keeping an eye on your wife. The Careful Husband. *Unknown, tr. by* the Earl of Longford. OnYI; OxBI
I am too angry to sleep beside you. Love Letter Postmarked Van Beethoven. Diane Wakoski. BiP
I am too near to be dreamt of by him. Wislawa Szymborska, *tr. fr. Polish by* Czeslaw Milosz. BoWoP; PBWP
I am too near, too clear a thing for you. A Flower of Mullein. Lizette Woodworth Reese. MoAmPo
I am too young to grow a beard. Street Song. Thom Gunn. HeIP; NoP; OxBC
I am trying/ to learn to walk again. Walk. Frank Horne. BPo
I am trying to imagine. Re-forming the Crystal. Adrienne Rich. TAP
I am trying to pry open your casket. Dear Reader. James Tate. EAS
I Am 25. Gregory Corso. CoPo
I am 25 years old. My Poem. Nikki Giovanni. AmNP; BOLo; BPo; PoBA
I am two fools [*or* fooles], I know. The Triple Fool. John Donne. GBL; OAEP; PP
I am type of singleness. Artemis. Dulcie Deamer. PoAu-1
"I am unable," yonder beggar cries. A Lame Beggar. John Donne. FF
I am undone. Today, Prison Won. Jessica Scarbrough. LFAC
I am unhappy that I am not God. He Puts Me to Rest. David Ignatow. VGW
I am unjust, but I can strive for justice. Why I Voted the Socialist Ticket. Vachel Lindsay. MoAmPo
I am valued by men, fetched from afar. Honey-Mead. *Unknown, tr. by* Charles W. Kennedy. *Fr.* Riddles (Exeter Book). AnOE
I am very fond of the little ribs of women. Vincent McHugh. *Fr.* Talking to Myself. ErPo
I Am Waiting. Lawrence Ferlinghetti. *Fr.* Oral Messages. CAPP
"I am waiting for my case to come up," *sel.* GOA; PoPl
I am waiting for. A Black Poetry Day. Alicia Loy Johnson. BOLo
I am waiting for the dawning. Waiting for the Dawning. *Unknown.* BLRP
I am walking as fast as I can. Foreign Streets. Mary Crow. AMV-80
I am walking rapidly through striations of light and dark. I Dream I'm the Death of Orpheus. Adrienne Rich. NMM; NoAM
I am walking the U.S. Lost Contact. Sylvia Wheeler. FAZ
I am warm. The Promise. Johari M. Kunjufu. BlSi
I am watching them churn the last milk. The Mad Yak. Gregory Corso. CoPo; NoAM
I am wearing absent-minded red. Spots of Blood. Phyllis Webb. NOBC
I am weary of lying within the chase. Ballade de Marguerite. *Unknown, tr. by* Oscar Wilde. AWP
I Am Weary of Straying, *with music.* Sarah E. York. AH
I am weary of the Garden. Said the Rose. George H. Miles. BLPA
I am weary of these times and their dull burden. Quid Restat. Lucius Beebe. RFM
I am weaving a song of waters. Song. Gwendolyn B. Bennett. BlSi
I Am What You Make Me. Franklin K. Lane. PGD
I am who the trail took. Exploration. Daniel Hoffman. CoAP; CoPo
I am willowy boughs. I Am. Hilda Conkling. FaPON; TiPo
"I Am with Thee." Ernest Bourner Allen. BLRP
I Am with Those. Ingrid Jonker, *tr. fr. Afrikaans by* Jack Cope *and* William Plomer. BoWoP
I am within as white as snow. Riddle. *Unknown.* ChTr; GBP
I am wondering how I could have changed her blood. Marlow and Nancy. Sandra McPherson. AmPA
I am writing to you in answer to your letter. The Connection. Daniil Kharms, *tr. by* George Gibian. FaBoNo
I am yesterday, to-day and to-morrow. He Walketh by Day. *Unknown, tr. by* Robert Hillyer. *Fr.* Book of the Dead. AWP
I Am: Yet What I Am Who Cares or Knows? John Clare. *See* I Am.
I am your big trimmer. The Big Trimmer. Ronald P. Tanaka. BrSi
I Am Your Loaf, Lord. David Ross. GoYe
I am your mother, your mother's mother. Jalal ud-Din Rumi, *tr. fr. Persian by* Elizabeth Daryush. OBVE
I am your noble savage. First and Last Man. Ralph McTell. OBET
I am yours and you are mine so. Michael Silverton. POL
I am yours, you are mine. Frau Ava, *tr. fr. German by* Willis Barnstone. BoWoP
I amna' fou' sae muckle as tired—deid dune. Sic Transit Gloria Scotia. "Hugh MacDiarmid." CMoP
I, an old woman in the light of the sun. An Old Woman. Edith Sitwell. CoBMV; MoPo
I, an old woman whose heart is like the Sun. Harvest. Edith Sitwell. CoBMV; OAEP
I, an unwedded wandering dame. Epitaph. Sylvia Townsend Warner. MoBrPo
I and my cousin Wildair met. Praise-God Barebones. Ellen Mackay Hutchinson Cortissoz. AA
I and my sisters three. Victorian Song. John Farrar. GoYe
I and my white Pangur. The Monk and His Pet Cat. *Unknown.* CH; OnYI
I and Pangur Bán, my cat. Pangur Bán. *Unknown, tr. by* Robin Flower. AnIL; FaBoCh; OnYI; OxBI
I and the other intruders. Of Objects Considered as Fortresses in a Baleful Place. Hyam Plutzik. VGW
I, Angelo, obese, black-garmented. Angelo Orders His Dinner. Bayard Taylor. BXAP; Par
I approach with such. Something. Robert Creeley. NaP
I argue/ that where the body is concerned. Saddle and Cell. The Three Marias, *tr. by* Helen R. Lane. BoWoP
I arise from dreams of thee. The Indian Serenade [*or* Lines to an Indian Air]. Shelley. AWL; BLPL; EnRP; FaBoBe; FiP; GTBS; GTBS-P; HBV-1; HoPM; LiTB; LoBV; OAEP; OBEV; OBRV; PoPl; TreF; TrGrPo; UnTE; ViBoPo
I arise to-day. The Deer's Cry [*or* St. Patrick's Breastplate]. *At. to* St. Patrick. AnIL, *tr. by* Whitley Stokes, John Strachan, *and* Kuno Meyer; AnIV, *tr. by* Kuno Meyer; OnYI, *tr. by* Whitley Stokes, John Strachan, *and* Kuno Meyer; WGRP
I, Arnor the red poet, made. The Five Voyages of Arnor. George Mackay Brown. NePoEA-2
I arose early and stepped outside. February Morning. King D. Kuka. VoR
I arose swiftly that night, for I heard a knock at my door. The Future. James Oppenheim. TrJP
I arrive. Song for My Father. Jessica Hagedorn. BrSi
I arrive/ Langston. Do Nothing till You Hear from Me. David Henderson. CNA; PoBA
I arrive where an unknown earth is under my feet. Landfall. *Maori Oral Tradition, tr. by* A. S. Thomson. WTO
I ask but one thing of you, only one. To a Friend. Amy Lowell. FPL; PoLF
I ask but right: let her that caught me late. Ovid, *tr. by* Christopher Marlowe. Amores, I, 3. EBEV
I ask for the strength to follow through my life. Time of Day. Selden Rodman. PoA
I ask good things that I detest. Prayer. Robert Louis Stevenson. TrPWD
I ask no kind return of love. Prayer for Indifference. Fanny Greville. OBEV
I ask not how thy suffering came. Fraternity. Anne Reeve Aldrich. AA
I ask not that my bed of death. A Wish. Matthew Arnold. HBV-2
I ask Thee not to withhold grief. A Morning Prayer. Betty Perpetuo. STF
I ask thy aid, O potent rum! Resentments Composed because of the Clamor of Town Topers Outside My Apartment. Sarah Kemble Knight. SCAP
I ask, who will buy a poem? Who Will Buy a Poem? Mahon O'Heffernan, *tr. by* Kenneth Jackson. AnIL
I ask you this. Prayer. Langston Hughes. CDC; EaLo
I ask'd if I got sick and died, would you. A Question. J. M. Synge. OBVV
I Asked a Thief. Blake. NoP; SeCeV
(Angel, The.) LiTB
("I asked a thief to steal me a peach.") CABA; LAuP; OBNC; ViBoPo
I asked for just a crumb of bread. More than We Ask. Faith Wells. BLRP
I Asked for Peace. Digby Mackworth Dolben. EBCP; OxBoCh
(Requests.) TrPWD
I asked [God] for strength, that I might achieve. Prayer of an Unknown Confederate Soldier [*or* Prayer Answered]. *Unknown.* STF; TreFT
I asked her, "Is Aladdin's lamp." The Sorceress! Vachel Lindsay. PDV; WSC
I asked her why she didn't. Girl with Long Dark Hair. Stephen Gray. PeSA
I asked if I got sick and died, would you. A Question. J. M. Synge. ELU; MoBrPo; OBMV; OxBI; OxBTC; PAI

I asked if I should pray. Mohini Chatterjee. W. B. Yeats. NoAM
I asked my dear friend, Orator Prigg. Orator Prigg. Blake. OBSV
I Asked My Fair, One Happy Day. Gotthold Ephraim Lessing, *ad. fr. German by* Samuel Taylor Coleridge. HBV-1
I asked my love to go with me. Banks of the Ohio. *Unknown.* FSW
I Asked My Mother. *Unknown.* MoShBr; RHPC
("I asked my mother for fifty [*or* fifteen] cents.") FaFP; OxBoLi; TiPo
I asked my parents. Going to Norway. Jack Anderson. GP
I asked no other thing. Emily Dickinson. NOBA; OxBA
I asked of Time to tell me where was Love. Love. Jones Very. AP
I asked professors who teach the meaning of life. Happiness. Carl Sandburg. OxBA
I asked the heaven of stars. Night Song at Amalfi. Sara Teasdale. MoAmPo
I asked the holly, "What is your life if . . . ?" Trees. Ted Hughes. NYBP
I Asked the Little Boy Who Cannot See. *Unknown.* OnUR
I asked the Lord that I might grow. My Prayer. *Unknown.* STF
I asked the Master for a motto sweet. God's Will. Charles E. Guthrie. BLRP
I asked the roses as they grew. Transformed. D. Weston Gates. STF
I asked thee oft what poets thou hast read. Upon the Same (Detractor). Robert Herrick. CaPo
I assume the grievous penitence. The Purple Blemish. Pär Lagerkvist, *tr. by* Lennart Bruce. AMV-81
I at my window sit, and see. Autumn. *Unknown.* NOEC
I ate at Ostendorff's, and saw a dame. Traümerei at Ostendorff's. William Laird. HBMV
I ate my fill of army bread. The Air Sentry. Patrick Barrington. CenHV
I attach no importance to life. The Spectral Attitudes. André Breton, *tr. by* David Gascoyne. EAS
I attended school and I liked the place. Values in Use. Marianne Moore. NePoAm-2
I attended the burial of all my rosy feelings. Transaction. A. R. Ammons. PoA
I await his coming. Guessing. *Unknown, tr. by* U Win Pe. PBWP
I awaken to a flow of night. Voyage. Donald G. H. Schramm. AMV-81
I awakened to dryness and the ferns were dead. The Tragedy of Leaves. Charles Bukowski. HoPM
I awoke hot, startled in daylight, calling. Mother. Philip Dow. NPGG
I awoke in profuse sweat, arms aching. Hag-ridden. Robert Graves. BIrV
I awoke in the Midsummer not to call night, in the white and the walk of the morning. Moonrise. Gerard Manley Hopkins. FaBoPP; MoAB; MoBrPo; MOON; SeCePo
I awoke only to hear the dull clobbing of the wind. Night Shore. Barry O. Higgs. PeSA
I Awoke with the Room Cold. Marge Piercy. NeAC
"I baited bears and prayed." Testimonies. Weldon Kees. NYP
I banked the five in the side. Kelly. Robert Hershon. NeAC
I bargained with life for a penny. My Wage. Jessie B. Rittenhouse. BLPA
I bear an unseen burden constantly. The Burden of Love. "Owen Innsley." AA
I bear, in sign of love. Francis Andrewes. *Fr.* Shepherdess' Valentine. OFD
I Been a Bad, Bad Girl, *with music. Unknown.* OuSiCo
I been 'buked an' I been scorned. Hell and Heaven. *Unknown.* OxBoLi
I been drifting and rolling along the road. Rolling Log Blues. *Unknown.* BluL
I been ridin' fer cattle the most of my life. The High-loping Cowboy. Curley W. Fletcher. BPAW
I been scarred and battered. Still Here. Langston Hughes. BPo
I been t'inkin' 'bout de preachah; whut he said de othah night. Philosophy. Paul Laurence Dunbar. BPo
I Been Treated Wrong. *Unknown.* BluL
I been walking all day and all night too. No Job Blues. *Unknown.* BluL
I before E. *Unknown.* FaBoUs
I beg my bones to be good but. The Poet. Lucille Clifton. DFF; GP
I beg the pardon of these flowers. With Lilacs. Charles Henry Crandall. AA
I beg you come tonight and dine. The Menu. Thomas Bailey Aldrich. HBV-2
I began in Ohio. Stages on a Journey Westward. James Wright. CABA; LCAP; NaP
I begin through the grass once again to be bound to the Lord. Reconciliation. "Æ." OBMV; OxBI; TrCP
I begin to get like a guy in the movies—I eat. Vincent O'Sullivan. Brother Jonathan, Brother Kafka, 15. OCNZ
I begin with the hills. This House. Ray A. Young Bear. CDW
I begin with words of air but delightful ones. Sappho, *tr. fr Greek by* Bill Zavatsky. POL
I beheld, and lo a great multitude, which no man could number. Heavenly Vision. William Billings. AmFP
I beheld her, on a day. How He Saw Her. Ben Jonson. *Fr.* A Celebration of Charis [in Ten Lyrick Peeces, II]. AnAnS-2; EnRePo; OAEP; QFR; SeCP; SeCV-1
I, Being Born a Woman and Distressed. Edna St. Vincent Millay. BoLoP; NoP; SGB
(Sonnet: "I, being born a woman and distressed.") ErPo
I Believe. J. B. Lawrence. BLRP
I Believe. Saul Tchernichowsky, *tr. fr. Hebrew by* Reginald V. Feldman. TrJP
I believe a leaf of grass is no less than the journeywork of the stars. Walt Whitman. Song of Myself, XXXI. InPS; PDV; SeCeV; TiPo; TrGrPo; TRV
I believe if I should die. Creed. Mary Ashley Townsend. BLPA; FaBoBe
I Believe I'll Dust My Broom. *Unknown.* BluL
I believe in human kindness. A Creed. Norman McLeod. WGRP
I believe in the brook as it wanders. Nature's Creed [*or* The Handiwork of God]. *Unknown.* OHIP; TRV
I believe in the fitness of surprises. Waiting. Liz Stout. AMV-81
I believe in the flesh and the appetites. Walt Whitman. Song of Myself, XXIV. Prf
I believe in the ultimate justice of Fate. Credo. Georgia Douglas Johnson. BALP; PoBA
I believe in this stalled magnificence. The Snowbound City. John Haines. EAS
I believe in you my soul. Walt Whitman. Song of Myself, V. BiP; Prf
I believe it! 'tis Thou, God, that givest, 'tis I who receive. Robert Browning. *Fr.* Saul. ILwL
I believe that if I had my sweet woman's heart in my hand. Drive Away Blues. *Unknown.* BluL
I believe the will of God prevails. The Faith of Abraham Lincoln. Abraham Lincoln, *arr. in verse by* Carl Sandburg. TRV
I believe we came together. Past Time. Harvey Shapiro. POL
I bend above the moving stream. Solitude and the Lily. Richard Henry Horne. OBVV
I bend over an old hollow cottonwood stump. A Hollow Tree. Robert Bly. GP; NNaP
I Bended unto Me. Thomas Edward Brown. NTCP; PeD; PoSC
I bent in the deep of night. The Pedigree. Thomas Hardy. CoBMV
I bent my ears to a lily's cup. Mother Love. Janie Alford. PGD
I bent unto the ground. The Voice of God. James Stephens. WGRP
I bespeak words. Introduction. Clere Parsons. FaBoTw
I bet God understands about givin up five. Yasmeen Jamal. LFAC
"I bet I can hold my breath." One-Upmanship. Miriam Chaikin. NTCP
I Bind My Heart. Lauchlan MacLean Watt. TRV
I bind the Soul that fathered me. The Hanging. J. E. H. MacDonald. OBCV
I bind unto myself to-day. St. Patrick's Breastplate [*or* The Breastplate of St. Patrick]. *At. to* St. Patrick. FaBoCh, *tr. by* Frances Alexander; OxBI, *tr. by* Frances Alexander; TRV
I blame Myrtis. Korinna, *tr. fr. Greek by* John Dillion. PBWP
"I bleed by the black stream." Haemorrhage. Padraic Fiacc. CIP
I bless[e] Thee, Lord, because I grow. Paradise. George Herbert. OAEL-1; SeCP; TrGrPo
I Bless Thee, Lord, for Sorrows Sent, *with music.* Samuel Johnson. AH
I blow ashes into the hearth. Sutra Blues; or, This Pain Is Bliss. Jody Aliesan. LTB
I Blow My Pipes. Hugh McCrae. PoAu-1
I bought a shop on Dizengoff. Buying a Shop on Dizengoff. Erez Biton, *tr. by* Judith Katz. VWA
I break my smooth, full loaf of warm white bread. Whatsoever I Do. Mary Louise Hector. GoBC
I Break the Sky. Owen Dodson. PoBA
I breathe into you. The Sinew of Our Dreams. Edgar Jackson. LFAC
I breathe (sweet Ghib:) [*or* sweet Gib,] the temperate ayre [*or* air] of Wrest. To my Friend G.N. from Wrest. Thomas Carew. AnAnS-2; CaPo
I breathed enough to take the trick. Emily Dickinson. NoAM
I breathed upon the aluminum microphone-stand a body's length away. Thus Crosslegged on Round Pillow Sat in Space. Allen Ginsberg. NNaP
I bring fresh showers for the thirsting flowers. The Cloud. Shelley. BLPL; ChER; EnRP; FaPON; GN; HBV-1; ImOP; LiTB; NoP; OAEP; OBRV; OHFP; PoEL-4; SeCeV; TreF; TrGrPo; ViBoPo
I bring myself back from the streets that open like long. Home for Thanksgiving. W. S. Merwin. NoAM
I bring ye love. Question. What will love do? Upon Love, by Way of Question and Answer. Robert Herrick. CaPo
I bring you a goat. Hroswitha von Gandersheim, *tr. by* Patrick Diehl. *Fr.* Paphnutius. WPOW
I bring you all my olden days. To-Day. Benjamin R. C. Low. HBV-1
I bring you the scent of the earth on my body. The Faun. Haniel Long. HBMV
I bring you with reverent hands. A Poet to His Beloved. W. B. Yeats. BrPo

I brocht my love a cherry. Auld Sang. William Soutar. OxBS
I broider the world upon a loom. The Loom of Dreams. Arthur Symons. VLP
I broke bread. Under the Williamsburg Bridge. Galway Kinnell. NYP
I broke my heart because of you, my dear. Literary Love. Harry Kemp. HBMV
I broke one day a slender stem. A Spray of Honeysuckle. Mary Emily Bradley. AA
I brush the spider webs from the dismantled sky. Housework. Amanda Berenguer, *tr. by* Priscilla Joslin. WPOW
I built a chimney for a comrade old. Two at a Fireside. Edwin Markham. TRV
I Built My Hut. T'ao Yuan-ming. *See* Two Drinking Songs.
I built my soul a lordly pleasure-house. The Palace of Art. Tennyson. OAEP; VLP
I buried Mama in her wedding dress. She Didn't Even Wave. Ai. MAYP
I Buried the Year. W. Luff. STF
I buried you deeper last night. To a Persistent Phantom. Frank Horne. AmNP; BANP; CDC
I Burn for England with a Living Flame. Gervase Stewart. WaaP
(Poem: "I burn for England with a living flame.") WaP
I burn no incense, hang no wreath. Votive Song. Edward Coate Pinkney. AA
I burne, and cruell you, in vaine. Song: To My Mistris, I Burning in Love. Thomas Carew. AnAnS-2; SeCP
"I burned, I wept, I sang; I burn, sing, weep again." Gaspara Stampa. William Rose Benét. HBMV
I Burned My Candle at Both Ends. Samuel Hoffenstein. ELU; FiBHP
I burned my life that I might find. The Alchemist. Louise Bogan. AWP; LLLT; MoAmPo
I bury my dreams well, under. Awakening. David Robinson. AMV-81
I buyed me a little dog. Little Brown Dog. *Unknown.* FSW
I Call and I Call. Robert Herrick. ChTr
I call everyone. The Fat Man. Vern Rutsala. DFF
I call my years back, I, grown old. The Days. Theodosia Garrison. HBMV
I call that parent rash and wild. The Velvet Hand. Phyllis McGinley. TreFT
I Call the Old Time Back. Whittier. ViBoPo
I call up words that he may write them down. Demands of the Muse. Vernon Watkins. PoA
I called him to come in. Evening. James Wright. NOBA; NYBP; PrIm
I called my mother in 1979. Collect Calls. Diana Bickston. LFAC
I called out of mine affliction. Jonah's Prayer. Bible, *O.T. Fr.* Jonah. TrJP
I called to gray squirrel. Conversation. Anne Robinson. SUS
I called to the wind. Kyorai, *tr. fr. Japanese by* Harry Behn. WSC
I called today, Peter, and you were away. The Thermal Stair. W. S. Graham. FaBoMo
I called your moon-dried name. Nuflo de Olano (Who Sailed with Balboa). Antar S. K. Mberi. LTB
I came/ in the blinding sweep. To Mother. Frank Horne. *Fr.* Letters Found near a Suicide. BPo
I came, a scooped out woman. Desert March. Gerda Norvig. VWA
I came across her browsing on a slope. Cow Dance. Bruce Beaver. PoAu-2
I Came a-Riding. Reinmar von Zweter, *tr. fr. German by* Jethro Bithell. AWP
I came as a shadow. Nocturne Varial. Lewis Alexander. PoBA; PoNe
I came back to where we killed the deer. Ben Alder 1963-1977. Des Hannigan. PoSH
I came before the water. Mussel Hunter at Rock Harbor. Sylvia Plath. NYBP
I came from Alabama wid my banjo on my knee. *See* I come from Alabama . . .
I came from England into France. The Journey into France. *Unknown.* CoMu; FaBoBa
I came from far for thee. "This Do in Remembrance of Me." *Unknown.* STF
I came from ole Kentucky. Jim Crow. Thomas D. Rice. VLP
I came from ole Virginny. Maple Leaf Rag. Sydney Brown. BLSo
I Came from Salem City. *Unknown. See* I Come from Salem City.
I came from somewhere. Poem of the Future Citizen. José Craveirinha, *tr. by* Dorothy Guedes *and* Philippa Rumsey. TTY
I came here with a young girl. The Cemetery at Academy, California. Philip Levine. NYBP
I came home the other night as drunk as I could be. Four Nights Drunk. *Unknown.* FSW
I came, I saw, and was undone. The Thraldome. Abraham Cowley. *Fr.* The Mistress. SeCV-1
I came into the City and none knew me. An Upper Chamber. Frances Bannerman. HBV-2; OBEV
I came out a winner. O Realm Bejewelled. Forugh Farrokhzad, *tr. by* Jascha Kessler *and* Amin Banani. WPOW
I came then to the city of my brethren. The Shore of Life. Robert Fitzgerald. VGW
I came to a field. Pastoral. Charles Simic. NNaP
I came to a great door. The Beast. Theodore Roethke. SO
I Came to Jesus. George White. STF
I came to look, and lo! The Fall of the Plum Blossoms. Ranko. TiPo
I came to see you in the spring. Remembering Apple Times. John T. Hitchner. AMV-80
I came to the crowded Inn of Earth. The Inn of Earth. Sara Teasdale. LiTA
I came to the door of the House of Love. Song. Alfred Noyes. HBV-1
I Came to the New World Empty-handed. Hildegarde Hoyt Swift. AmFN
I Came to This Country in 1865, *with music. Unknown.* OuSiCo
I came to you with a greeting. Morning Song. Afanasi Afanasievich Fet, *tr. by* Max Eastman. AWP
I came too late to the hills: they were swept bare. The Wilderness. Kathleen Raine. BoWoP; PoSH; WPE
I came upon a child of God. Woodstock. Joni Mitchell. NIP
I came upon it unaware. Honey from the Lion. Leah Bodine Drake. NePoAm
I came upon them by a strip of sea. The Net Menders. Brian Vrepont. PoAu-2
I can afford to discriminate. The Discriminator. Vernon Scannell. OxBC
I can almost see. On the Rouge. Raymond Souster. NOBC
I can change my-/ self more easily. Margaret Atwood. NeAC
I can clear a beach or swimming pool without. Stereo. Don L. Lee. AmNP; POL
I can close my eyes and see Him. The Last Day. Lola Derosier. STF
I can feel the tug. Punishment. Seamus Heaney. NoP
I Can Fly. Felice Holman. NTCP; RHPC
I can get through a doorway without any key. The Wind. James Reeves. RHPC
I can give myself to her. Yosano Akiko, *tr. fr. Japanese by* Kenneth Rexroth *and* Ikuko Atsumi. WPOW
I can imagine, in some otherworld. Humming-Bird. D. H. Lawrence. CMoP; InPS; LiTB; LiTM; PPP; SeCePo
I can imagine quite easily ending up. Plains. W. H. Auden. NePA
I can look through muddy water. Dry Land Blues. *Unknown.* BluL
I can love both fair and brown. The Indifferent. John Donne. AnAnS-1; BiP; BoLoP; CABA; OAEP; SeCV-1; TEP; UnTE
I can make out the rigging of a schooner. North Haven. Elizabeth Bishop. PAI
"I" Can Never Be a Great Man, An. Stephen Spender. OBMV
I can no longer live in Amsterdam, he writes. Return to Prinsengracht. Janice Blue-Swartz. AMV-81
I can only say I have waited for you. Time of Waiting in Amsterdam. Ingrid Jonker, *tr. by* Jack Cope *and* William Plomer. BoWoP
I can preserve your letters, not your love. Ceremony. Vassar Miller. NePoEA
I can prove who I am. I draw my wallet like. Plexus and Nexus. Judson Jerome. AMV-81
I can remember. I can remember. The Boy Actor. Noel Coward. OxBTC
I can remember looking cross-lots from. House in Denver. Thomas Hornsby Ferril. AmFN
I can remember lying. Sunday Funnies. Anne Keiter. DFF
I can remember our sorrow, I can remember our laughter. Memory. Helen Hoyt. PoLF
I can remember the fine image. Morning Fog. Quinton Duval. AMV-81
I can remember when there were trees. When There Were Trees. Nancy Willard. HoAn
I can see by your eyes. Juanita, Wife of Manuelito. Simon Ortiz. MAYP
I can see him. The Last Democrat. D. J. Enright. NMP
I can see him now. My Grandfather Was a Quantum Physicist. Duane Big Eagle. STE
I can see outside the gold wings without birds. The Clear Air of October. Robert Bly. NaP; NoAM
I can shake the wild hay, and wet seed sticks to my hand. Stalks of Wild Hay. H. L. Davis. PoA
I can sing of myself a true song. *Unknown, tr. by* L. Iddings. The Seafarer, Pt. I. PoRA
I can support it no longer. Flower Herding [Pictures] on Mount Monadnock. Galway Kinnell. ConAP; HeIP; LCAP; NaP; NOBA
I can sweep a broom. Trash. Earl Gene Box. LFAC
I can take the wildest bronco in the tough old woolly West. The Gol-darned Wheel. *Unknown.* CoSo
I can tell by the way the trees beat, after. The Man Watching. Rainer Maria Rilke, *tr. by* Robert Bly. NU
I Can Tell by the Way You Smell. *Unknown.* BluL
I can tell my dog. Pistol Slapper Blues. *Unknown.* BluL

I can tell you about this, sure enough. The Discovery of Tradition. Lawson Fusao Inada. LTB
I can tell you. How I Got Ovah. Carolyn M. Rodgers. CNA
I can wade grief. Emily Dickinson. NOBA
I canna tell what has come ower me. Ich Weiss Nicht Was Soll es Bedeuten. Heine, *tr. by* Alexander Macmillan. AWP
I cannot acclaim you. From the Depths. Otakar Fischer, *tr. fr. Czech.* VWA
I cannot always feel His greatness. The Great Man. Eunice Tietjens. WGRP
I cannot be hurt anymore. Image. Henry Dumas. BOLo
I Cannot Believe That I Am of Wind. Samuel Greenberg. LiTA
I cannot believe them old, nor believe them dead. Lost Companions. Helen Bryant. AMV-80
I cannot bring a world quite round. Wallace Stevens. The Man with the Blue Guitar, II. CMoP
I cannot brook thy gaze, belovèd bird. Mother Carey's Chicken. Theodore Watts-Dunton. OBVV
I cannot but ask, in the park and the streets. Arthur Hugh Clough. *Fr.* Spectator ab Extra, III. NBM; OxBoLi
I cannot, but God can. Not I, but God. Annie Johnson Flint. STF
I cannot call you as lovely as you were. Reunion. Paul Dehn. PV
I cannot change as others do. Constancy. Earl of Rochester. CavP; HBV-1; OBEV; OBS
I cannot choose but I think upon the time. Brother and Sister. "George Eliot." GN
I can not do it alone. Jesus and I. Dan Crawford. BLRP; TRV
I cannot dry my eyes when I think of the distant time. Microcosmos, LVII. Nigel Heseltine. NeBP
I cannot eat but little meat. Jolly Good Ale and Old [*or* In Praise of Ale]. *At. to* William Stevenson. *Fr.* Gammer Gurton's Needle. HBV-2; OBEV; SeCeV; TrGrPo
I cannot explain the sadness. The Loreley. Heine, *tr. by* Aaron Kramer. WSC
I cannot find my way; there is no star. Credo. E. A. Robinson. AmPP; AP; CMoP; LiTM; MoAmPo; NePA; OxBA; TAP; TrCP; TreFT; WGRP
I cannot find my way to Nazareth. A Fragment. Yvor Winters. OBSV
I cannot find thee! Still on restless pinion. The Quest [*or* Who by Searching Can Find Out God?]. Eliza Scudder. TrPWD; WGRP
I cannot follow them into their world of death. Chrysothemis. Henry Reed. MoVE
I cannot forget/ The sight of that straight young neck. Kevin Barry. Terence Ward. OnYI
I cannot forget my jo. A Poor French Sailor's Scottish Sweetheart. William Johnson Cory. EBVV
I cannot get to my love if I should dee. The Waters of Tyne. *Unknown.* GBP
I cannot give you the Metropolitan Tower. Parting Gift. Elinor Wylie. OxBA
I cannot guess her face or form. Mater Desiderata. Winthrop Mackworth Praed. OBVV
I cannot hear thy voice with others' ears. To the Canary Bird. Jones Very. AP
I cannot hold my peace, John Keats. To John Keats, Poet, at Springtime. Countee Cullen. BANP; CDC
I cannot live with you. Emily Dickinson. AmPP; AP; MAT; MoAB; MoAmPo; NOBA; NoP; OxBA; PoEL-5; PPoe; SBG
I cannot look above and see. The Clouds. William Croswell. AA
I cannot make him dead! My Child. John Pierpont. AA; HBV-1
I cannot move. Malcolm. Welton Smith. BPo
I cannot ope mine eyes. Mattens. George Herbert. AnAnS-1; TrPWD
I cannot praise the Doctor's eyes. On Hearing a Lady Praise a Certain Rev. Doctor's Eyes. George Outram. DBV; EBVV; TreFT
I cannot praise Thee. By his instrument. Shall the Dead Praise Thee? George Macdonald. TrCP
I cannot pray, as Christians use to pray. Credo. "Seumas O'Sullivan." OnYI
I cannot put the Presence by, of Him, the Crucified. The Voice of Christmas. Harry Kemp. HBV-2
"I cannot quite remember . . . There were five." The Messages. W. W. Gibson. OHIP
I cannot reach it; and my striving eye. Childhood. Henry Vaughan. OxBoCh
I cannot rival Helen's face. Compensation. Virgina Maughan Kammeyer. AMV-80
I cannot say, and I will not say. Away [*or* He Is Not Dead]. James Whitcomb Riley. BLPA; BLRP; FPL; TreFT; TRV; WGRP
I cannot say. Amen. F. G. Browning. BLRP
I cannot see fairies. Fairies. Hilda Conkling. TiPo; WSC
I cannot see how in time it will be possible to look at. The Altarpiece Finished. John Hollander. NoAM
I cannot see the features right. Tennyson. In Memoriam A. H. H., LXX. LiTB; PoEL-5
I cannot see the short, white curls. The Dumb World. W. H. Davies. OxBTC
I cannot see your face. A Sprig of Rosemary. Amy Lowell. PeHV
I Cannot Sing the Old Songs. Charlotte Alington Barnard. TreF
I cannot sleepe, my eyes ill neighbouring lids. John Marston. *Fr.* The Malcontent. PoEL-2
I cannot sleep;the beautiful Lynnhaven. The River. Mary Sinton Leitch. HBMV
I cannot spare water or wine. Mithridates. Emerson. AP; NOBA
I cannot speak to crowds. This I Can Do. H. T. Lefevre. STF
I cannot stand the man who wears. Ringless. Diane Wakoski. Prf
I cannot take these poor. Said the Innkeeper. Myles Connolly. TRV
I cannot tell, not I, why she. Poem. Walter Savage Landor. GBL; OAEL-2
I cannot tell who loves the skeleton. La Bella Bona Roba. Richard Lovelace. CaPo; CavP; EBEV; OAEL-1; PoEL-3; SeCP
I cannot tell you how I love. Post-Impressionism. Bert Leston Taylor. HBMV; InMe
I cannot tell you how it was. May. Christina Rossetti. GBL
I cannot think of them as dead. My Dead. Frederick Lucian Hosmer. WGRP
I cannot think or reason. Comrades of the Cross. Willard Wattles. HBMV
I cannot think that you have gone away. To My Father. Iris Tree. HBMV
I cannot turn from Jesus. I Turn to Jesus. Oswald J. Smith. STF
I Cannot Wash My Eye without an Eyecup. *Unknown.* PV
I cannot worry. Dusk. Marcia Southwick. MAYP
I can't appease Ashimbabbar, the moon god An. Crimes of Lugalanne. Enheduanna, *tr. fr. Sumerian.* BoWoP
I can't be talkin' of love, dear. Song. Esther Mathews. FaFP; NePA
I can't break with the Dark One. Mirabai, *tr. fr. Hindi by* Willis Barnstone *and* Usha Nilsson. BoWoP
I can't do it often. Your Woods. Margaret Holley. AMV-80
I can't fall asleep. Falling Asleep. Ian Seraillier. DuDa
I Can't Feel at Home in This World Anymore. *Unknown.* FSW
I Can't Figure You Out. Elliot Fried. AMV-81
I can't forget. Piazza di Spagna, Early Morning. Richard Wilbur. GrPl; InPS; VGW
I can't get 'em up, I can't get 'em up. Words for Army Bugle Calls: Reveille. *Unknown.* TreF
I can't get him out of my mind, out of my mind. John Berryman. *Fr.* Dream Songs. NoP
I Can't Give You Anything but Love, *with music.* Dorothy Fields. BLSo
I can't go there. Yesterday. Carol Lee Sanchez. TWSS
I can't guarantee my name for posterity. As Yet. Vicente Rodríguez Nietzche, *tr. by* Julio Marzán. InW
I Can't Have a Martini, Dear, but You Take One. Ogden Nash. PoRA
I Can't Help but Wonder Where I'm Bound. Tom Paxton. FSW
I can't hold it, keep it. Lake. R. A. Simpson. CBAP
I can't hold you and I can't leave you. Sister Juana Inés de la Cruz, *tr. fr. Spanish by* Judith Thurman. PBWP
I can't live in this world. Further Notice. Philip Whalen. PoM; VGW
I can't read any more of this Rich Critical Prose. John Berryman. *Fr.* Dream Songs. CAPP
I can't sleep tonight, can you? Gooseberries. Stephen Berg. NaP
I can't stand it, said the old man. In the End. Peter Everwine, *after* Natan Sach. NNaP
I can't stand Willy wet-leg. Willy Wet-Leg. D. H. Lawrence. CMoP; TW
I can't talk. Give Me Five. William J. Harris. CNA
I Can't Think What He Sees in Her. A. P. Herbert. FiBHP
I can't understand it. Kind. A. R. Ammons. NoP; PrIm
I care not a curse though from birth he inherit. The Worker. Gerald Massey. EBVV
I Care Not for These Ladies. Thomas Campion. AAS; CABA; ErPo; HAP; NIP; NoP; OAEP; OBSC; ViBoPo
(Amarillis.) HBV-1
(Amaryllis.) ElL
(When We Court and Kiss.) UnTE
I care not, fortune, what you me deny. Indifference to Fortune. James Thomson. *Fr.* The Castle of Indolence. OBEC
I care not what the sailors say. Crazy Jane Reproved. W. B. Yeats. CMoP
I Carried Statues. Agnes Nemes Nagy, *tr. fr. Hungarian by* Bruce Berlind. BoWoP
I carried two things around in my mind. Three Things. May Sarton. AMV-80
I carry it on my keychain, which itself. The Ring. Diane Wakoski. PoA
"I carry my death within me." My Death. A. J. M. Smith. OBCV
I carry my keys like a weapon. To Nowhere. David Ignatow. CAD; NCSH

I carry the ground-hog along by the tail. The Hunter. Raymond Souster. NOBC
I carry three passengers on a nightly journey. The Trip. Emmett Jarrett. NeAC
I carry you in a glass jar. The Doll. Gregory Orr. AmPA
I Carry Your Heart with Me (I Carry It In. E. E. Cummings. TAP
I carve my first head. Then I carve another. Hallowe'en 1971. Michael Dennis Browne. AmPA
I cast from me the medications. Loneliness. Franz Werfel, *tr. by* Edith Abercrombie Snow. TrJP
I cast these lyric offerings at your feet. Sonnets to Miranda, V. Sir William Watson. HBV-1
I catch myself drifting. Harbor. Nancy Price. IHMS
I catch the movement of his lips. Marina Tsvetayeva, *tr. by* Paul Schmidt. *Fr.* The Daughter of Jairus. BoWoP
I Catcha da Plenty of Feesh, *with music. Unknown.* AS; TrAS
I Caught a Fish. Bertram Murray. OnUR
I caught a tremendous fish. The Fish. Elizabeth Bishop. GoJo; HAP; HeIP; HoPM; InPK; LiTM; MiAP; MoAB; MoAmPo; MOS; NePA; NoAM; NOBA; NoP; NU; PAI; PoPl; TrGrPo; TwAmPo; ViBoPo; WeW
I caught the American bull. Buffalo. Henry Dumas. PoBA
I Caught This Morning at Dawning. Dennis Neagle. AMV-80
I caught this morning morning's minion. The Windhover. Gerard Manley Hopkins. ACP; BiP; BrPo; CABA; CMoP; CoBMV; EaLo; EBCP; EBVV; FaBoEn; GTBS-P; HAP; InPK; InPS; InvP; LiTB; LiTM; LoBV; MoAB; MoBrPo; MoPo; MoVE; NIP; NoAM; NOBE; NoP; OAEL-2; OAEP; OBNC; PAI; PBBP; PoEL-5; PoPl; PoPle; PoRA; PPoe; PPP; PrIm; SCV; SeCeV; SyP; TEP; TreFT; UnPo; VLP; WeW
I caught you grazing on my knee. To a Flea in a Glass of Water. D. A. Greig. PeSA
I caught you, sir, having a look at her. Once in Love with Amy. Frank Loesser. BLSo
I cease not from desire till my desire. Hafiz, *tr. by* Gertrude Lowthian Bell. Odes, IX. AWP
I celebrate myself, and sing myself. Song of Myself. Walt Whitman. AA; AmPP; AP; BiP; BLPL; FaBoBe; LiTA; MoAmPo; NePA; NOBA; NoP; OxBA; PP; SOTW; TAP; TrGrPo; ViBoPo; WHA
I celebrate Rhegion, Italy's tip, licked by. Epigram. *Unknown, tr. by* Peter Jay. PeHV
I celebrate the personality of Jack! Jack and Jill. Charles Battell Loomis. BXAP
I chanced upon a new book yesterday. To Edward Fitzgerald. Robert Browning. DBV; TW
I chanced upon an early walk to spy. The Orchard and the Heath. George Meredith. OBNC
I, Chang P'ing-tzu, had traversed the Nine Wilds and seen their wonders. The Bones of Chuang Tzu. Chang Heng, *tr. by* Arthur Waley. AWP
I Change. Witter Bynner. HBMV
I change, and so do women too. Written on a Looking-Glass [*or* Epigram]. *Unknown.* FaBoEE; HBV-1
I charge you, lady young and fair. He Charges Her to Lay Aside Her Weapons. Pierce Ferriter, *tr. by* the Earl of Longford. AnIL; OnYI
I charge you, O winds of the West, O. Mathilde Blind. *Fr.* Love in Exile. TrJP
I charm thy life. Kehama's Curse. Robert Southey. *Fr.* The Curse of Kehama. LoBV; OBNC; OBRV
I choose at random, knowing less and less. An Old Atheist Pauses by the Sea. Thomas Kinsella. ELU; PAI
I choose not to walk among ghosts. Antigone VI. Herbert Martin. PoBA
"I choosed my love at the bonny yates of Gight." Geordie. *Unknown.* BaBo
I chopped down the house that you had been saving to live in next summer. Variations on a Theme by William Carlos Williams. Kenneth Koch. BXAP; CAPP; FF; NIP; NoP; PoM; PV; SpRo
I circled on leather paws. The Return. Theodore Roethke. PoA
I claim the right of knowing whom I serve. Manhood. Oliver Wendell Holmes. *Fr.* Wind-Clouds and Star-Drifts. AP
I clasp in the hot pit and bed. Memorial Couplets for the Dying Ego. George Barker. EBEV
I climb the Barra half-hill. View. Robin Munro. PoSH
I climb the black rock mountain. Where Mountain Lion Lay [*or* Laid] Down with Deer. Leslie Marmon Silko. STE; VoR; WPOW
I climb the hill: from end to end. Tennyson. In Memoriam A. H. H., C. EBVV; PoEL-5
I climb the tower of Ste. Anne des Monts. The Bell of Ste. Anne Des Monts. Leo Cox. CaP
I climb to the tower-top and lean upon broken stone. I See Phantoms of Hatred and of the Heart's Fullness and of the Coming Emptiness. W. B. Yeats. *Fr.* Meditations in Time of Civil War, VII. LiTB
I climb'd a hill, whose Summit crown'd with wood. An Essay on the Fleet Riding in the Downes. "J. D." CoMu
I climb'd [*or* climbed] the dark brow of the mighty Hellvellyn. Hellvellyn. Sir Walter Scott. FM; TEP
I climbed a [*or* the] hill as light fell short. The Song of Honour. Ralph Hodgson. LiTB; MoBrPo
I climbed into the chinaberry. The Evening of Ants. Gary Soto. NPGG
I climbed the stair in Antwerp church. Antwerp and Bruges. Dante Gabriel Rossetti. VLP
I climbed through woods in the hour-before-dawn dark. The Horses. Ted Hughes. NoAM; PH
I climbed towards you on a ray of moonlight. Fantasy under the Moon. Emmanuel Boundzekei-Dongala, *tr. by* Gerald Moore *and* Ulli Beier. TTY
I climbed up on the merry-go-round. Merry-go-round. Dorothy Walter Baruch. SoPo; SUS; TiPo
I clink my castanet. A Starling's Spring Rondel. James Cousins. HBV-1; HBVY
I clip coupons from magazines. Yachting in Arkansas. Craig Weeden. AMV-80
I clipped and the brown petals. Boundaries. Roberta Spear. MAYP
I Close Her Eyes. Heine, *tr. fr. German by* Louis Untermeyer. UnTE
I closed another chapter. My Book of Life. Frances Humphrey. STF
I closed my ears with stinging bugs. Elegy for a Puritan Conscience. Alan Dugan. CAPP; NoAM
I closed my eyes as I sat in the jet. Day Flight. Jack Davis. CBAP
I Closed My Eyes To-Day and Saw. William Force Stead. OBMV
I Closed My Shutters Fast Last Night. Georgia Douglas Johnson. PoNe
I comaunde alle the ratones that are here aboute. Rats Away! *Unknown.* OxBM
I come/ from a long line. My Elbow Ancestry. Larry Mollin. NeAC
I come/ to the White Painted Woman. Puberty Rite Dance Song (Traditional). *Tr. fr. Apache Indian by* Willis Barnstone. BoWoP
I come alone. To surprise you. Visit. James Welch. AmPA
I come among the peoples like a shadow. Hunger. Laurence Binyon. OxBTC
I Come and Stand at Every Door. Nazim Hikmet. FSW
I come back to cold lights. Revisiting the Field. Walter Pavlich. AMV-81
I come back to the cottage in. Only Years. Kenneth Rexroth. TAP
I come back to the geography of it. Letter 27. Charles Olson. *Fr.* The Maximus Poems. CoPo; NOBA
I come dis night to sing an' pray. Oh, Yes! Oh, Yes! Wait 'til I Git on My Robe. *Unknown.* BoAN-2
I come down against stones lightly. Fossils. Arthur Stewart. SUW
I come from a wet land. For My Brother and Sister Southwestern Indian Poets. Geary Hobson. STE
I come [*or* came] from Alabama with [*or* wid] my banjo on my knee. Oh! [*or* O!] Susanna. Stephen Collins Foster. BLSo; FaFP; FSW; OBAL; PSoN; TrAS; TreF
I come from far away. I have forgotten my country. Foreign Woman. Rosario Castellanos, *tr. by* J. M. Cohen. WPOW
I come from farm folk. Radiation Leak. Jody Aliesan. LTB
I come from haunts of coot and hern. The Brook [*or* The Brook's Song]. Tennyson. BoNaP; FaBoBe; FaBV; FaFP; FaPON; GN; GoJo; HBV-1; HBVY; PoPle; TreF
I come from nothing, but from where. A Song of Derivations. Alice Meynell. WGRP
I Come from Salem City, *with music. Unknown.* AmSS
(I Came from Salem City.) AmFP
I come from Salem County. Cowboy Song. Charles Causley. NePoEA; PoRA
I come from the city of Boston. Boston. John Collins Bossidy. FaBoCo; FaBoEE; OBAL (*At. to* Samuel C. Bushnell); OxBoLi (*At. to* Samuel C. Bushnell)
I come from woods enchaunted. Dream Song. Richard Middleton. HBV-1
I come home from you through the early light of spring. Adrienne Rich. *Fr.* Twenty-one Love Poems. BoWoP
I Come Home Wanting to Touch Everywhere. Stephen Dunn. AMV-81
I come more softly than a bird. Snow. Mary Austin. *Fr.* Rhyming Riddles. BoNaP; GrPl; SoPo; TiPo
I come of a mighty race. Hebrews. James Oppenheim. TrJP
I come of the seed of the people, the people that sorrow. The Rebel. Padraic Pearse. OnYI
I come out of a California orange grove. Smudging. Diane Wakoski. AmPA; PrIm
I come sailing through the Indian Ocean. To a Foreign Friend. Leonard Natham. GP
I Come to Bury Caesar. Sydney Justin Harris. PoA
I Come to Bury Caesar. Shakespeare. *See* Antony's Oration.
I come to my kitchen. Of Pardons, Presidents, and Whiskey Labels. Richard Snyder. SOTS
I Come to Supplicate. Simeon ben Isaac ben Abun of Mainz, *tr. fr. Hebrew by* Nina Davis Salaman. TrJP

I come to tell you that my son is dead. The Prince. Edgar Bowers. ConAP
I come to the garden alone. In the Garden. C. Austin Miles. TreFT
I come to thee, O God long since forgot. Before the Statue of Apollo. Saul Tchernichowsky, *tr. by* L. V. Snowman. TrJP
I come to town the other night. Old Dan Tucker. Daniel Decatur Emmett. BLSo; PSoN; TrAS
I come to work as well as play. The March Wind. *Unknown.* RHPC
I come to you with the vertigoes of the source. Yvonne Caroutch, *tr. fr. French by* David Cloutier. BoWoP
"I, Conscience, know this Mother-Wit me it taught." The Age of Reason. William Langland, *mod. by* Donald Attwater. *Fr.* The Vision of Piers Plowman. NOCV
I Consider the Tree. Martin Buber, *tr. fr. German by* Howard Schwartz. VWA
I could bring you jewels—had I a mind to. Emily Dickinson. TAP
I could divide a leaf. Propositions. Phyllis Webb. MoCV
I could draw its map by heart. Amor Loci. W. H. Auden. NOCV
I could have a job, but am too lazy to choose it. Lazy Man's Song. Po Chü-i, *tr. by* Arthur Waley. OBVE
I could have painted pictures like that youth's. Pictor Ignotus. Robert Browning. CTC; TEP; VLP
I could have said makes love. Behind That Wall My Roommate Fucks His Girl. Geof Hewitt. NeAC; POL
I could have stemmed misfortune's tide. The Wife. Anna Peyre Dinnies. AA
I could have wept and howled. Song of the Unloved. *Unknown, tr. by* Jack Cope *and* Dan Kunene. PeSA
I could kill you right now. Lobo. Charles Lillard. NOBC
I could look at. Joy. Robert Creeley. PPP
I could lose an eyelid and see forever. Checking the Firing. R. T. Smith. AMV-80
I could love her with a love so warm. The World Is a Mighty Ogre. Fenton Johnson. AmNP
I could love thee till I die. The Platonic Lady. Earl of Rochester. UnTE
I could make you songs. Song. Dorothy Dow. HBMV
I could not choose but gaze; a fascination. Shelley. *Fr.* The Revolt of Islam. ChER
I could not dig: I dared not rob. A Dead Statesman. Kipling. *Fr.* Epitaphs of the War. FaBoEE; OAEP
I could not, ever and anon, forbear. The Solitary. Wordsworth. *Fr.* The Excursion, II. EnRP
I could not hope/ to touch the sky. Sappho, *tr. fr. Greek by* Willis Barnstone. BoWoP
I could not look on Death, which being known. The Coward. Kipling. *Fr.* Epitaphs of the War. FaBoEE; FaBoTw; OAEP
I could not name a single blessing. Neither Shadow of Turning. Jack Clemo. NOCV
I could not see You with my eyes. Sight and Insight. Eleanor Slater. TrPWD
I could not sleep/ For the sea was so smooth. Walrus Hunting. Aua, *tr. fr. Eskimo.* WTO
I Could Not Sleep for Thinking of the Sky. John Masefield. Lollingdon Downs, V. ChMP; LiTM
I Could Not though I Would. George Gascoigne. PoEL-1
I could replace. Earth Psalm. Denise Levertov. PPP
I could resign that eye of blue. Abnegation [*or* To Cloe]. Martial, *tr. by* Thomas Moore. AWP; UnTE
I could see bruises or shadows. My Grandfather Dying. Ted Kooser. Str
I could take the Harlem night. Juke Box Love Song. Langston Hughes. GrPl; IDB; OLR; PoBA
I could wish to be dead! The Tragic Mary Queen of Scots, II. "Michael Field." OBMV
I Couldn't Hear Nobody Pray. *Unknown.* BoAN-1, *with music*; FSW
I couldn't touch a stop and turn a screw. Thirty Bob a Week. John Davidson. BSV; EBEV; EBVV; FaBoTw; FaFP; InPS; LiTB; NBM; NoAM; NOBE; OAEL-2; OBNC; OxBS; OxBTC; VLP
I could've spent my life banging young chicks. Expecting. Daniel J. Langton. AMV-81
I count black-lipped. Come Back Blues. Michael S. Harper. PoBA
I Count My Time by Times That I Meet Thee. Richard Watson Gilder. AA
I counted them, and now I look through the door. My Father's Ghost. David Wagoner. Str
I, country-born an' bred, know where to find. Spring. James Russell Lowell. *Fr.* The Biglow Papers. FaBV
I courted pretty Polly the livelong night. Pretty Polly. *Unknown.* FSW; OuSiCo
I crave an ampler, worthier sphere. Anno 1829. Heine, *tr. by* Charles Stuart Calverley. AWP; OBVE
I crave, dear Lord. Ike Walton's Prayer. James Whitcomb Riley. AA
I craved for flash of eye and sword. Dreams. Israel Zangwill. TrJP
I crawl up the couch leg feeling. Whose Scene? Ruth Stone. BoWoP
I cried unto God with my voice, even unto God with my voice. Bible, *O.T.* Psalms, LXXVII. AWP
I cross a weedy meadow. Thistle, Yarrow, Clover. Kenneth Porter. NePoAm
I cross'd pynot [*or* crossed the pynot], an't' pynot cross'd me. Against the Magpie. GBP; PBBP
I crossed over the county line. Crossing the County Line. Elizabeth Randall-Mills. GoYe
I crossed the furze-grown table-land. Dartmoor. Coventry Patmore. NBM
I crossed the gangway in the winter's raining. Stowaway. Bill Adams. EtS
I crossed the pynot. *See* I cross'd pynot, an't' pynot cross'd me.
I crouch over my radio. Speech. Henry Taylor. MAT
I cry I cry. No Categories! Stevie Smith. NoP
I Cry, Love! Love! Theodore Roethke. LCAP; MoVE
I cry out to find something elsewhat is it? A Person, a Mexican. Lorri Martinez. LFAC
I cry out war to those who spend their utmost. Stormy Nights. Robert Louis Stevenson. BrPo
I cry to be broken open. Multiplicity. Eleanor Berry. AMV-80
I cry to the mountains; I cry to the sea. We Whom the Dead Have Not Forgiven. Sara Bard Field. PGD
I Cry to You as I Pass Your Windows. Christopher Brennan. *Fr.* The Wanderer. PoAu-1
I Cry Your Mercy. Keats. *See* To Fanny.
I curse my bearing, childhood, youth. J. M. Synge. FaBoEE
I cursed the puddle when I found. The Puddle. Eden Phillpotts. HBMV
I curst thee oft, I pity now thy case. Astrophel and Stella, XLVI. Sir Philip Sidney. SiPS
I cut in two/ A long November night. Hwang Chin-i, *tr. fr. Korean by* Peter H. Lee. PBWP
I, Cynisca, who descend from Spartan kings. Cynisca. *Unknown, tr. by* Tom Dodge. LiSp
"I dance on all the mountains." This Poem Is for Deer. Gary Snyder. *Fr.* Myths and Texts: Hunting. CAPP; NaP; NOBA
I Danced before I Had Two Feet. Max Dunn. PoAu-2
I danced in the morning. Lord of the Dance. Sydney Carter. OBET
I dare but sing of you in such a strain. Sonnets to Miranda, III. Sir William Watson. HBV-1
I dare not ask a kiss. To Electra. Robert Herrick. BLPL; CaPo; CavP; HoPM; HBV-1; LoBV; OBEV; OBS; SeCV-1
I dare not ask your very all. Your Tears. Edwin Markham. HBMV
I Dare Not Pray to Thee. Maurice Baring. TrPWD
I dare not think that thou art by, to stand. Infinity. Philip Henry Savage. AA
I daresay that's the custom in your church. Bagman O'Reilly's Curse. Les A. Murray. TW
I, dark in light, exposed. Milton. *Fr.* Samson Agonistes. TrGrPo
I dedicate this poem. Daughters. Astra. BrRo
I delight in the prime of a boy of twelve. Epigram. Strato, *tr. by* Thomas Meyer. PeHV
I delight in this naethingness. De Profundis. "Hugh MacDiarmid." SeCePo
I demand a thatched house. The Poet's Request. *Unknown, tr. by* John Montague. BIrV
I denounce those who are normal. J'Accuse. Peter Klappert. AMV-81
I descended in the evening to the fountain. Saul's Song of Love. Saul Tchernichowsky, *tr. by* Robert Friend. VWA
I desire that my body be. When I Am Dead. George MacBeth. OxBTC
I despise my friends more than you. To an Enemy. Maxwell Bodenheim. TrJP
I destroyed the first cat we had. Catastrophe. Edwin Brock. NMP
I did but look and love awhile. The Enchantment. Thomas Otway. HBV-1; OBEV; ViBoPo
I Did But Prompt the Age. Milton. NoP
(On the Same.) SeCeV
I did not come to kiss her for she was kiss herself. All of Her. Samuel L. Albert. NePoAm-2
I did not cry at all. Song of the Captured Woman. James Devaney. PoAu-1
I did not cut myself this hollow reed. It Is the Reed. Sister Maris Stella. GoBC
I did not know she'd take it so. Under the Mistletoe. Countee Cullen. PChr
I Did Not Know the Truth of Growing Trees. Delmore Schwartz. LiTM
I did not know where you kept your heart. A "Case of Assault." Lydia Stephanou, *tr. by* Kimon Friar. BoWoP
I did not know you then. The Blinded Soldier to His Love. Alfred Noyes. PoPl
I did not know you. Celan. Anthony Barnett. VWA
I did not live until this time. To My Excellent Lucasia, on Our Friendship. Katherine Philips. CavP; MeLP; OBS; PeHV; SBG; WPE; WPOW

I did not look upon her eyes. Penumbra. Dante Gabriel Rossetti. VLP
I Did Not Lose My Heart in Summer's Even. A. E. Housman. LiTM
I did not make the conditions of my life whereby. Desire. Kathleen Raine. MoPo
I did not question anything. Finite. Power Dalton. HBMV
I did not see the frigate Constitution. Resurrection. R. P. Blackmur. PoA
I did not see the iris move. A Matter of Life and Death. Anne Ridler. MP
I did not see the pachyderms. The Circus. E. B. White. InMe
I did not think, I did not strive. John Masefield. *Fr.* The Everlasting Mercy. TRV
I did not think that I should find them there. The Clerks. E. A. Robinson. AA; CABA; MoAB; MoAmPo; MoVE; PoEL-5
I did not want to be old Mr. Uncle Dog; the Poet at 9. Robert Sward. CoAP; CoPo; PrIm; VGW
I did not want to die. I wanted you. Sacco Writes to His Son. Alun Lewis. DTC
I did not want to go. Speaking: The Hero. Felix Pollak. CTBA
I did not want to grow, but quick-fingered memories. The Tower. Dan Pagis, *tr. by* Stephen Mitchell. VWA
I Didn't Find Light by Accident. Hayyim Nahman Bialik, *tr. fr. Hebrew by* Ruth Nevo. VWA
I didn't get much sleep last night. Underwear. Lawrence Ferlinghetti. CoPo; OBAL
I Didn't Know My Soul. Avraham Ben-Yitzhak, *tr. fr. Hebrew by* A. C. Jacobs. VWA
I didn't make you know how glad I was. A Servant to Servants. Robert Frost. CMoP
I didn't mind the bosses' pistol-whipping. Notes on the Post-Industrial Revolution. Edward Morin. FAZ
I didn't want this, not. Marina Tsvetayeva, *tr. by* Elaine Feinstein *and* Angela Livingstone. *Fr.* The Poem of the End. OBVE
I didn't want to walk through remote control doors. Long Parenthesis, The. Roberta Hill. TWSS
I die/ If I but spy. Upon Julia. Ernest Radford. BXAP
I die; but when the grave shall press. Emily Brontë. TEP
I die for Your holy word without regret. Elegy. Antonio Enriquez Gomez. TrJP
I died for beauty—but was scarce. Emily Dickinson. AP; AWP; BLPL; BoWoP; FaFP; LiTA; LiTM; MasP; MoAB; MoAmPo; MoVE; NCEP; NOBA; NoP; PAI; SBG; TreFT; TwAmPo; WHA
I died; they wrapped me in a shroud. A Dream of Death. "Owen Innsley." AA
I Died True. Beaumont *and* Fletcher. *See* Aspatia's Song.
I died with the first blow and was buried. Autobiography. Dan Pagis, *tr. by* Robert Friend. VWA
I dig in the soft earth all. The Negatives. Philip Levine. NePoEA-2
I dim my eyes (to shut them could be cataclysmic). Birthday on Deathrow. Harold LaMont Otey. LFAC
I dined with a friend in the East, one day. The Sunbeam. *Unknown.* NA
I dined with Demetrius last night. Epigram. Automedon. PeHV
I disapprove even of eloquent/ Myrtis. Corinna, *tr. fr. Greek by* Richmond Lattimore. WPOW
I do affirm that thou hast saved the race. Delay. Charlotte Fiske Bates. AA
I do be thinking God must laugh. Boys. Winifred M. Letts. HBMV
I do be thinking, lassie, of the old days now. The Shoogy-Shoo. Winthrop Packard. HBV-1
I do believ. Thomas Traherne. *Fr.* Solitude. FaBoEn
I do believe that die I must. His Creed. Robert Herrick. SeCeV
I do confess, in many a sigh. Lying. Thomas Moore. FiBHP
I do confess thou'rt smooth and fair. To His Forsaken Mistress [*or* Inconstancy Reproved]. Sir Robert Ayton. BSV; ElL; ErPo; GBL; HBV-1; OBEV; OBS; SeCePo
I do like ogres. Dorothy Brown Thompson. *Fr.* Fe-Fi-Fo-Fum. ShM
I do not always know what lies before me. God Doeth All Things Well. *Unknown.* STF
I do not ask. A Preacher's Prayer. *Unknown.* STF
I do not ask for love, ah! no. Lethe. Georgia Douglas Johnson. CDC
I do not ask—for you are fair. The Complaisant Swain. Ovid, *tr. by* F. A. Wright. Amores, III, 14. AWP
I do not ask, Oh Lord, that life may be. Per Pacem ad Lucem. Adelaide Anne Procter. TrPWD
I do not ask that God will keep all storms away. The All-sufficient Christ. Bernice W. Lubke. BLRP
I Do Not Ask Thee, Lord. *Unknown.* BLRP
I do not ask Thee, Lord, for outward sign. Jesus Himself. Henry Burton. BLRP
I do not ask Thee straightway to appear. Supplication. Edith Lovejoy Pierce. TrPWD
I do not believe in a God. Lost Word. Jean Burden. AMV-80
I do not believe this room. A Game of Glass. Alastair Reid. NePoEA; PoCh
I do not care for kisses. 'Tis a debt. The Pleasures of Love. Wilfrid Scawen Blunt. HBV-1
I do not count the hours I spend. Waldeinsamkeit. Emerson. AP; HBV-1; NOBA; WGRP
I do not fear to lay my body down. Exile from God. John Hall Wheelock. GoBC; WGRP
I do not fear to tread the path that those I love long since have trod. My Creed. Jeanette Gilder. WGRP
I do not go, my dear, to storm. On Going to the Wars. Earle Birney. WaP
I do not grudge them; Lord, I do not grudge. The Mother. Padraic Pearse. OnYI
I do not have faith in those. Free Fall. Don Gordon. AMV-81
I do not hold with him who thinks. Thoughts on the Cosmos. Franklin P. Adams. HBMV
I do not know/ if you were taught. The Book Rises Out of the Fire. Edmond Jabès, *tr. by* Rosemarie Waldrop. VWA
I do not know/ In what strange far off earth. Holocaust 1944. Anne Ranasinghe. VWA
I do not know, I cannot see. Confidence. *Unknown.* BLRP
I do not know if the world has lied. What I'm Doing Here. Leonard Cohen. PeCV
I do not know much about gods; but I think that the river. The Dry Salvages. T. S. Eliot. *Fr.* Four Quartets. CABA; LiTB; NoP; OxBA; SeCePo
I do not know what haunts me. Loreley. Heine, *tr. by* Ernst Feise. NAWM-2
I do not know what next may come. The Best for Me. *Unknown.* STF
I do not know why. It is not only. The Double Tree. Winfield Townley Scott. PoPl
I do not lack for Jack or Joan. Me. Hughes Mearns. *Fr.* Later Antigonishes. InMe
I do not like my state of mind. Symptom Recital. Dorothy Parker. SBG
I do not like the other sort. An Ulsterman. "Lynn Doyle." OnYI
I do not like the way you slide. Soft-boiled Egg [*or* Egg Thoughts.]. Russell Hoban. NTCP; RHPC
I do not like thee, Doctor Fell. *See* I do not love thee, Doctor Fell.
I do not look for love that is a dream. Christina Rossetti. GBL
I Do Not Love Thee. Caroline Elizabeth Sarah Norton. HBV-1; OBEV
I do not love [*or* like] thee, Doctor Fell. Doctor Fell [*or* Non Amo Te]. Thomas Brown, *after the Latin of* Martial. AWP; ChTr; DBV; FaBoCo; FaBoEE; FaFP; ImOP; MoShBr; NIP; OBVE; OxNR; TreFT; WhC
I do not love thee!—no! I do not love thee! I Do Not Love Thee. Caroline Elizabeth Sarah Norton. HBV-1
I Do Not Love to See Your Beauty Fire. John Hall Wheelock. HBMV
I do not love to wed. The Poet Loves a Mistress, but Not to Marry. Robert Herrick. CaPo; CavP; ErPo
I do not need a springtime. Morning Song. Henry Blakely. CNA
I do not need the skies'/ Pomp. All Flesh. Francis Thompson. BrPo
I do not own an inch of land. A Strip of Blue. Lucy Larcom. AA; HBV-1; WGRP
I do not pity the old men, fumbling after. Pity. Babette Deutsch. WHA
I do not pray for peace nor ease. Prayer for Pain. John G. Neihardt. HBV-2; TrPWD; WGRP
I do not remember the day you disappeared. Elegy for My Father. Robert Louthan. AMV-80
I do not say this. Your Need Is Greater than Mine. Theodore Enslin. CoPo
I do not see the sense of my toil putting thoughts in a dying tongue. Sorley Maclean. Dain do Eimhir, LV. NeBP
I do not see you. A Jewish Child Prays to Jesus. Ilse Blumenthal-Weiss, *tr. by* Erna Baber Rosenfeld. VWA
I do not sleep at night. Night-Piece. Raymond Richard Patterson. CAD; PoBA; WSC
I do not thank Thee, Lord. Thanks Be to God. Janie Alford. PGD
I do not think Grandmother or Grandfather. Favorite Grandson Braid. Phillip William George. VoR
I do not think of you lying in the wet clay. In Memory of My Mother. Patrick Kavanagh. CIP; NoAM
I do not think that skies and meadows are. Reciprocity. John Drinkwater. PoA
I do not think the ending can be right. But That Is Another Story. Donald Justice. CoAP; NePoEA-2
I do not think we can save them. The Children. William Heyen. GeTw; GP
I do not understand the world, father. On the Subject of Poetry. W. S. Merwin. PAI; PP
I do not understand. In Memoriam II. Franco Fortini, *tr. by* Ruth Feldman. VWA
I do not understand. The Unknown. E. O. Laughlin. BLPA

I do not visit his grave. He is not there. Peachstone. Dannie Abse. OxBC
I do not want. My Definition of Poetry. Douglas Blazek. LTB
I do not want a gaping crowd. When I Am Dead. James Edward Wilson. PoLF
I do not want a plain box, I want a sarcophagus. Last Words. Sylvia Plath. FYAP
I do not want only. Poem. Colleen Thibaudeau. NOBC
I do not want to be reflective any more. Wolves. Louis MacNeice. NoAM; OxBTC
I do not want to be your weeping woman. Poem. Alison Boodson. NeBP
I do not want to pour out my heart any more. Marcus Aurelius. C. H. Sisson. OxBC
I do not want to stand. My Own Hallelujahs. Zack Gilbert. PoBA
I do not want to turn away. Two Poems, I. Robert J. Abrams. NNP
I do not want your praises later on. May 1506 (Christopher Columbus Speaking). Winfield Townley Scott. GOA
I do not waste what is wild. Empty Kettle. Louis (LittleCoon) Oliver. STE
I do not wish to know. After the Persian. Louise Bogan. NePoAm; NYBP
I do not wish to report on Medusa directly, this variation of her/ writhing. Medusa's Hair Was Snakes. Was Thought, Split Inward. Kathleen Fraser. NPGG
I do seem to zee Grammer as she did use. Grammer's Shoes. William Barnes. EBVV
I do tricks in order to know. With My Crowbar Key. William Stafford. ConAP
I do veel vor ye, Thomas, vor I be afear'd. Dobbin Dead. William Barnes. VLP
I do what I have to. Leah. Shirley Kaufman. VWA
I doe but name thee Pembroke, and I find. To William Earle of Pembroke. Ben Jonson. SeCP
I Done Done What Ya' Tol' Me to Do, *with music.* *Unknown.* BoAN-1
I Done Got So Thirsty That My Mouth Waters at the Thought of Rain. Patricia Jones. BlSi
I done lose all-a my money. Frying Pan Skillet Blues. *Unknown.* BluL
I done try go to church, I done go for court. One Wife for One Man. Frank Aig-Imoukhuede. PBA
I don't/ pity this man, I love him. Vanzetti. Charles Buckmaster. CBAP
I don't appwove this hawid waw. Swell's Soliloquy. *Unknown.* FiBHP
I don't ask you to tell me the great truths. Words to My Mother. Alfonsina Storni, *tr. by* Marion Hodapp *and* Mary Crow. AMV-80
I don't believe in ristercrats. My Sort o' Man. Paul Laurence Dunbar. AmNP
I don't care for women. Epigram. *Unknown.* PeHV
I don't care if you're married I still love you. Big Fun. Diane Burns. STE; TWSS
I Don't Care, *with music.* Jean Lenox. FSN
I don't dream anymore about arthritic spiders. Succubi. John Newlove. NeAC
I don't give a $\sqrt{D^2}$. A Radical Creed. Gelett Burgess. FaBoNo
I don't go much on religion. Little Breeches. John Hay. AA; BeLS; FaBoBe; HBV-2; PaPo; TreFS
I Don't Have No Bunny Tail on My Behind. Alta. GP; TW
I Don't Have the Energy. Artie Gold. NOBC
"I Don't Hear Any Melody Breathing I Hear." John Gill. NeAC
I Don't Know. *Unknown.* BluL
I don't know about anything sometimes. Between Me and Anyone Who Can Understand. Sharon Scott. JB
I don't know about you, whiteman all dressed in black. For Dan Berrigan. Etheridge Knight. NeAC
I don't know any greatest treat. The Parterre. E. Harriet Palmer. FaBoCo; NA; NOBL
I don't know anyone more lonely. Singles. Michael Waters. GeTw; MAYP
I don't know but it might have been. News That Stays News. Paul Mariani. GeTw
I don't know how he came. Ossawatomie. Carl Sandburg. CMoP; OxBA
I don't know how it was. Mystery. "Yehoash," *tr. by* Marie Syrkin. TrJP
I don't know if he is rare on these northern lakes. The Pelican. Greg Kuzma. AmPA
I Don't Know if Mount Zion. Abba Kovner, *tr. fr. Hebrew by* Shirley Kaufman. VWA
I don't know my real name I don't know when I was born. I Been Treated Wrong. *Unknown.* BluL
I don't know politics but I know the names. An Introduction. Kamala Das. WPOW
I don't know somehow it seems sufficient. Gravelly Run. A. R. Ammons. CoAP; PoA; Prf
I don't know the language. Homesick [*or* Homesickness]. Else Lasker-Schüler, *tr. fr. German.* PBWP; VWA
I don't know the species, but this one has been. I Point Out a Bird. Quinton Duval. FAZ
I don't know what I'm looking at. Focus. Kathleen Norris. GP
I don't know what to think of the years in New York. Homosexual Sonnets. Kenneth Pitchford. GP
I don't know what you think you're doing. To an Adolescent Weeping Willow. Marvin Bell. DiL
I don't know whether the gray deer knows. The Deer. Asya, *tr. by* Gabriel Preil *and* Howard Schwartz. VWA
I don't know who they are. The Pointed People. Rachel Field. FaPON; WSC
I don't know. A Poem against Rats. Fred Levinson. AmPA
I Don't Let the Girls Worry My Mind. *Unknown.* AmFP
I Don't Like Beetles. Rose Fyleman. OxBChV
I Don't Like No Railroad Man. *Unknown.* AS, *with music*; OuSiCo
"I don't like the look of little Fan, mother." Little Fan. James Reeves. SO
I Don't Like You. Kit Wright. OnUR
I don't look back: God knows the fruitless efforts. We See Jesus. Annie Johnson Flint. BLRP
I don't make them name it. I Show the Daffodils to the Retarded Kids. Constance Sharp. DFF
I don't mind eels. The Eel. Ogden Nash. FaBV; FaPON; NTCP
I don't operate often. When I do. John Berryman. Dream Songs, LXVII. NaP
I don't pretend to drink. A Welcome for Etheridge. James Cunningham. JB
I don't remember anything of then, down there around the magnolias. Ode to Michael Goldberg's Birth and Other Births. Frank O'Hara. NAs; NeAP
I don't remember the name of the story. The Mystery of the Caves. Michael Waters. GeTw; MAYP
I don't sleep. All night. Mirabai, *tr. fr. Hindi by* Willis Barnstone *and* Usha Nilsson. BoWoP
I don't think it important. The Beast Section. Welton Smith. PoBA
I don't wanna march in the infantry. I Just Wanna Stay Home. Irwin Silber. FSW
I don't want a dog that is wee and effeminate. Dog Wanted. Margaret Mackprang Mackay. GDP
I Don't Want Any More Visitors. Ingrid Jonker, *tr. fr. Afrikaans by* Ingrid Jonker. PeSA
I don't want no woman if her hair ain't no longer'n mine. Short Haired Woman. *Unknown.* BluL
I don't want none of your weevily wheat. Weevily Wheat. *Unknown.* FSW; TrAS
I Don't Want to Be a Gambler, *with music.* *Unknown.* AS
I don't want to be a nun. *Unknown, tr. fr. Spanish by* Willis Barnstone. BoWoP
I don't want to be sheltered here. For the Yiddish Singers in the Lakewood Hotels of My Childhood. Harvey Shapiro. VWA
I don't want to boast. Vindication. Daniil Kharms, *tr. by* George Gibian. FaBoNo
I Don't Want to Get Adjusted. *Unknown.* FSW
I don't want to open my eyes again. Sleep. Del Marie Rogers. LTB
I Don't Want to Play in Your Yard. Philip Wingate. FSN, *with music*; TreFT
I don't want your greenback dollar. The Greenback Dollar. *Unknown.* AmFP
I Don't Want Your Millions Mister. Jim Garland. FSW
I dote the baple buds are swellig. Kerchoo! Margaret Fishback. PoSC
I Doubt a Lovely Thing Is Dead. Neil Tracy. CaP
I doubt if ten men in all Tilbury Town. E. A. Robinson. *Fr.* Captain Craig. PoEL-5
I doubt if the wind in your boots. Stiles. John Pudney. NYBP
I doubt if you knew. The Rescue. John Logan. CoAP; NYBP
I doubt life is fulfilled, or love let go. Dichterliebe. Robert Klein Engler. AMV-81
I doubt not God is good, well-meaning, kind. Yet Do I Marvel. Countee Cullen. AmNP; BANP; BPo; CDC; FF; IDB; NoAM; PoBA; PoNe; TAP; TTY
I drag a boat over the ocean. Lal Ded, *tr. fr. Kashmiri by* Willis Barnstone. BoWoP
I dragged my feet through desert gloom. The Prophet. Pushkin, *tr. by* Babette Deutsch. WGRP
I drank,/ my arteries filled with fat. Organ Transplant. J. D. Reed. POL
I drank at every vine. Feast. Edna St. Vincent Millay. WHA
I drank cool water from the fountain. The Raisin. James Wright. TAP
I drank up two glasses of hot tea and milk. Tuesday. Zishe Landau, *tr. by* Ruth Whitman. VWA
I draw a deep breath. Remembering. Akjartoq, *tr. fr. Eskimo.* WTO
I draw your outline. After Spending All Day at the National Museum of Art. Alan Britt. FAZ

I dreaded that first robin, so. Emily Dickinson. AmPP; AP; HAP; MoAmPo
I Dream a World. Langston Hughes. AmNP
I Dream I'm the Death of Orpheus. Adrienne Rich. NMM; NoAM
I dream my love goes riding out. Song for a Dancer. Kenneth Rexroth. TAP
I dream my mother. Generation Gap. Bronwen Wallace. AMV-80
I dream now of green places. In the Third Year of War. Henry Treece. WaP
I dream of a rose-red tree. Women and Roses. Robert Browning. ViBoPo
I dream of Jeanie with the light brown hair. Jeanie with the Light Brown Hair. Stephen Collins Foster. BLSo; FaFP; FSW; TrAS; TReF
I dream of journeys repeatedly. The Far Field. Theodore Roethke. NoP; PrIm; SeCeV
I dream of Serenity. I'm a Dreamer. Kattie M. Cumbo. BlSi
I dream of the birth of the child. Creation of the Child. Susan Litwack. VWA
I dream of whales. I feel upon my skin. The Suicides. George MacBeth. NoAM
I dream'd I walk'd, in raptures high. T. Baker. *Fr.* The Steam-Engine. BXAP
I Dream'd in a Dream. Walt Whitman. AP
I dream'd that as I wander'd by the way. *See* I dreamed that, as I wandered by the way.
I dream'd that I walk'd in Italy. Going Back Again [*or* Check to Song]. "Owen Meredith." EvOK; FaBoCo; FiBHP
I dream'd this mortal part of mine. *See* I dreamed this mortal part of mine.
I dream'd we both were in a bed. *See* I dreamed we both were in a bed.
I dreamed a dream last night, when all was still. Reality. Angela Morgan. WGRP
I dreamed a dream next Tuesday week. My Dream. *Unknown.* NA
I dreamed a dream the other night, when everything was still. Prospecting Dream. *Unknown.* AmFP
I dreamed a dreary dream this night. The Braes of Yarrow. *Unknown.* ESPB; OxBB; ViBoFo
I dreamed all my fortitude screamed. Letter across Doubt and Distance. M. Carl Holman. AmNP; PoNe
I dreamed (God pity babes at play). In Time of War. Lesbia Thanet. SUMH
I dreamed I held/ A sword against my flesh. Lady Kasa, *tr. fr. Japanese by* Kenneth Rexroth. BoWoP; WPOW
I dreamed I lay in a little gray boat. Waking. Katherine Pyle. OBCA
I Dreamed I Moved among the Elysian Fields. Edna St. Vincent Millay. NoP
I dreamed I passed a doorway. The Unknown Beloved. John Hall Wheelock. HBMV
I dreamed I saw a little brook. A Vision of Children. Thomas Ashe. EBVV
I dreamed I saw Joe Hill last night. Joe Hill. Alfred Hayes. UnPo
I dreamed I saw that ancient Irish queen. Chivalry. "Æ." ViBoPo
I dreamed I saw the crescent moon. *Unknown.* POL
I dreamed I stood upon a little hill. Two Loves. Lord Alfred Douglas. PeHV
I dreamed I was a barber; and there went. The Barber. John Gray. SyP
I dreamed I was a cave-boy. The Cave-Boy. Laura E. Richards. FaPON
I dreamed I was digging a grave. Immortality. Ai. MAYP
I dreamed kind Jesus fouled the big-gun gears. Soldier's Dream. Wilfred Owen. ILwL
I dreamed last night I dreamed, and in that sleep. Le Rêve. Edgar Bowers. ConAP
I Dreamed Last Night of My True Love, *with music. Unknown.* AS
I Dreamed My Love. *Unknown.* UnTE
I dreamed my love came in my sleep. Lowlands, *vers. I. Unknown.* AmSS
I dreamed my love lay in her bed. I Dreamed My Love. *Unknown.* UnTE
I dreamed of a shark following us two. Sharks. Dick Lourie. NeAC
I dreamed of him last night, I saw his face. The Dead Poet. Lord Alfred Douglas. HBMV; PeHV; ViBoPo
I dreamed of my true love last night. Locks and Bolts. *Unknown.* FSW
I dreamed of Ted Williams. Dream of a Baseball Star. Gregory Corso. NoAM; VGW
I dreamed of war-heroes, of wounded war-heroes. The Heroes. Louis Simpson. NePoAm; OBWP
I dreamed one night I came. A Heterodoxy. Lord Dunsany. OnYI
I dreamed [*or* dream'd] that, as I wandered by the way. The Question [*or* A Dream of the Unknown]. Shelley. CH; EnRP; FiP; GTBS; GTBS-P; HBV-1; OBEV; OBRV; PoPle
I dreamed [*or* dreamt] a dream the other night. Lowlands. *Unknown.* ChTr; FSW; OxBoLi
I dreamed that/ the gentiles crucified Mozart. Mozart. Jacob Glatstein, *tr. by* Ruth Whitman. VWA
I dreamed that, buried in my fellow clay. The Dream. *Unknown.* NOEC
I dreamed that dead, and meditating. The Weed. Elizabeth Bishop. MoPo
I Dreamed That in a City Dark as Paris. Louis Simpson. CoAP; NePoEA
I dreamed that one had died in a strange place. A Dream of Death. W. B. Yeats. GBL
I dreamed that someone's coming. Someone like No One Else. Forugh Farrokhzad, *tr. by* Deirdre Lashgari. WPOW
I dreamed that when I died a jukebox played. Death of a Jazz Musician. William Jay Smith. NePoAm-2
I dreamed the Fairies wanted me. Crab-Apple. Ethel Talbot. TiPo
I dreamed there was an Emperor Antony. Cleopatra's Lament. Shakespeare. *Fr.* Antony and Cleopatra, V, ii. UnPo
I dreamed there would be spring no more. In Memoriam A. H. H., LXIX. Tennyson. NOBE
I dreamed [*or* dream'd] this mortal part of mine. The Vine. Robert Herrick. CaPo; CavP; ErPo; NoP; UnTE
I dreamed two spirits came—one dusk as night. The Two Spirits. James Benjamin Kenyon. AA
I dreamed [*or* dream'd] we both were in bed. The Vision [to Electra]. Robert Herrick. SeCP; UnTE
I dreamed you were my child, and I had come. The Dream. Paul Petrie. TAP
I dreamt a dream the other night. *See* I dreamed a dream the other night.
I dreamt a dream; till morning light. Arthur Hugh Clough. *Fr.* Dipsychus, Pt. I, sc. v. OAEP
I dreamt a dream! what can it mean? The Angel. Blake. *Fr.* Songs of Experience. CH; EnRP; LAuP
I dreamt her sensual proportions. The Death of Venus. Robert Creeley. NOBA
I dreamt I came to a kind inn. A Kind Inn. George Dillon. GoYe
I dreamt I climbed to a high, high plain. The Pitcher. Yüan Chen, *tr. by* Arthur Waley. AWP
I Dreamt I Dwelt in Marble Halls. Alfred Bunn. *Fr.* The Bohemian Girl. TreFS
I dreamt I dwelt in marble halls. The Palace of Humbug. "Lewis Carroll." FaBoNo
I dreamt I saw great Venus by me stand. A Dream of Venus. Bion, *tr. by* Leigh Hunt. AWP
I dreamt. I saw three ladies in a tree. The Three Ladies. Robert Creeley. NeAP
I dreamt I was in love again. The One before the Last. Rupert Brooke. OBVV
I dreamt it! such a funny thing. What the Prince of I Dreamt. Henry Cholmondeley-Pennell. NA
I dreamt last night. For No Clear Reason. Robert Creeley. VGW
I dreamt last night of you, John-John. John-John. Thomas MacDonagh. AnIV; AWP; HBMV; OnYI; OxBI
I dreamt (no "dream" awake—a dream indeed). In Sleep. Alice Meynell. BrRo
I dreamt of the old house. To My Sister. Olga Berggolts, *tr. by* Daniel Weissbort. BoWoP
I dreamt that I was God Himself. Ezra Pound, *after the German of* Heine. FaBoEE
I dreamt we slept in a moss in Donegal. Seamus Heaney. Glanmore Sonnets, X. NoP
I dressed my father in his little clothes. The Boat. Robert Pack. CoAP; DiL; NePoEA-2
I drew it from its china tomb. A Dead Letter. Austin Dobson. HBV-1
I drew the blind on Christmas Morn. Red Sky at Morning. Gilbert Thomas. LO; TreFS
I Drift in the Wind. Ingrid Jonker, *tr. fr. Afrikaans by* Jack Cope. PeSA; WPOW
I drift to another time and space when jazz listens to my moods. All That Jazz. Yasmeen Jamal. LFAC
I drink of the ale of Southwark, I drink of the ale of Chepe. The Maltworm's Madrigal. Austin Dobson. HBV-2
I drink to forget, but whenever I think. Alan Bold. POL
I drink to your glory my god. The Scorner. Felix TchiKaya U'Tamsi, *tr. by* Gerald Moore *and* Ulli Beier. TTY
I drink, wherever I go, to the charms. Gracey Nugent. Austin Clarke, *tr. fr. Irish.* CIP
I drive my car to supermarket. Superman. John Updike. LiSp
I drive Westward. Tumble and loco weed. To What Strangers, What Welcome. J. V. Cunningham. NoAM
I dropped my pen;—and listened to the wind. Sonnet: Composed while the Author Was Engaged in Writing a Tract Occasioned by the Convention of Cintra. Wordsworth. ChER
I dropped my sail and dried my dropping seines. Mass at Dawn. Roy Campbell. PeSA
I dropped my wad. Spoon River Anthology. Edwin Meade Robinson. Limericised Classics, V. HBMV
I drove to Little Hunger promontory. Little Hunger. Richard Murphy. BIrV

I drove up to the graveyard, which. The Soul Longs to Return Whence It Came. Richard Eberhart. CMoP
I du believe in Freedom's cause. The Candidate's Creed. James Russell Lowell. *Fr.* The Biglow Papers. YaD
I dug a grave under an oak-tree. Amy Lowell. *Fr.* Dreams in War Time. BoWoP
I dug and dug amongst the snow. Christina Rossetti. FaBoEE
I dug, beneath the cypress shade. The Grave of Love [*or* Beneath the Cypress Shade]. Thomas Love Peacock. CH; EnRP; HBV-1; OBRV
I dug in with all the spirit of spring. Knowing. Mary Coghill. BrRo
I dwell/ In a dark small cell. The Genia. Ann Stanford. WSC
I dwell alone—I dwell alone, alone. Autumn. Christina Rossetti. BrRo
I dwell apart. The Hermit. Hsü Pên, *tr. by* Henry H. Hart. RFM
I dwell in a lonely house I know. Ghost House. Robert Frost. WSC
I dwell in Grace's court. Content and Rich. Robert Southwell. OBSC
I dwell in Possibility. Emily Dickinson. AP; NIP; NoAM; NOBA; OxBA; PP
I dwell in this leaky Western castle. Dowager. John Montague. IPY
I dwell on the misty steppe. The "Word" of an Antelope Caught in a Trap. Sandag, *tr. by* C. R. Bawden. WTO
I dwelt alone. Eulalie. Poe. EvOK; Par
I dwelt in a city enchanted. The City of Prague. William Jeffery Prowse. CenHV
I eagerly await your miniature, wish the artist would hurry. Letter to My Wife. Keidrych Rhys. WaP
I eat my cereal with a sliced peach. Getting a Poem in the Rain. Dick Lourie. NeAC
I Eat My Peas with Honey. *Unknown.* CenHV; EvOK; NTCP; OnUR; RHPC
(Peas.) FaBoUs; FaPON
(Peas and Honey.) PoPle
I eat noodles with the Emperor's brother. Just a Few Scenes from an Autobiography. John Tagliabue. FAZ
I eat what I wish. Cat's Menu. Richard Shaw. RHPC
I edged back against the night. High Tide. Jean Starr Untermeyer. MoAmPo
I embrace these shoulders and I look. Étude. Joseph Brodsky, *tr. by* Dimitry Pospielovsky *and* Keith Bosley. VWA
I embraced the summer dawn. Dawn. Arthur Rimbaud, *tr. by* Enid Rhodes Peschal. *Fr.* Illuminations. SOTW
I employ the blind mandolin player. A Music. Wendell Berry. VGW
I empty myself of the names of others. I empty my pockets. The Remains. Mark Strand. NYBP; PPP
I encountered the crowd returning from amusements. Resolution of Dependence. George Barker. FaBoTw; LiTB; LiTM
I enter and as I enter all is abandoned. Microcosmos, I. Nigel Heseltine. NeBP
I enter, and I see thee in the gloom. Longfellow. Divina Commedia, III. GoBC; NePA
I Enter by the Darkened Door. Jenny King. BXAP
I enter, jingling hindu temple bells, deodorant ears. Allen Ginsberg Blesses a Bride and Groom [*or* Blessing a Bride and Groom]; a Wedding Night Poem. Robert Peters. BXAP; GP
I Entreat You, Alfred Tennyson. Walter Savage Landor. OAEP
(To Alfred Tennyson.) FaBoUs; POL
I entrust my all to you, Aurelius. Catullus, *tr. fr. Latin.* PeHV
I envy e'en the fly its gleams of joy. Written in Prison. John Clare. OAEL-2
I envy every flower that blows. A Lover's Envy. Henry van Dyke. HBV-1
I envy not Endymion now no more. Sonnet. William Alexander, Earl of Stirling. *Fr.* Aurora. EIL
I envy not in any moods. In Memoriam A. H. H., XXVII [*or* Lost Love]. Tennyson. FaBoEn; HBV-2; LiTB; OBNC; PeHV; TreFS
I envy not the lark his song divine. Invention. Sir William Watson. HBV-2
I envy not the sun. Aspiration. John Banister Tabb. LO
I envy seas, whereon he rides. Emily Dickinson. OLR
I envy the silence. Sounding. David Jauss. Str
I, even I, am he who knoweth the roads. De Aegypto. Ezra Pound. VGW
I even I know the Eastern Gate of Heaven. He Knoweth the Souls of the East. *Unknown, tr. by* Robert Hillyer. *Fr.* Book of the Dead. AWP
I exchange eyes with the Mad Queen. Vision. Harry Crosby. EAS
I exist in a real world—made real by death and dying. Lamentation. Harold LaMont Otey. LFAC
I exist that I may say. Document. Tuvia Ruebner, *tr. by* Harold Schimmel. VWA
I Expected My Skin and My Blood to Ripen. Wendy Rose. TWSS; WPOW
I expected this face but did not predict it. Elijah Speaking. Doug Fetherling. NOBC
I fasted three canonical hours. The Maiden's Plight. Brian Merriman, *tr. by* Frank O'Connor. *Fr.* The Midnight Court. BIrV
I fear, I fear the rarity. Death by Rarity. Marguerite Young. LiTA
I fear no earthly powers. On Himself. Robert Herrick. CaPo
I Fear No Power a Woman Wields. Ernest McGaffey. AA; HBV-1
I fear that appearances are worshipped throughout France. The Rat and the Elephant. La Fontaine, *tr. by* Marianne Moore. OBVE
I fear that I shall never make. Poet-Tree. Earle Birney. OxBC
I fear that Puck is dead—it is so long. The Death of Puck. Eugene Lee-Hamilton. HBMV; OBVV
I Fear Thy Kisses, Gentle Maiden. Shelley. GTBS; GTBS-P; HBV-1
(To ———.) ViBoPo
I fear to love thee, Sweet, because. To Olivia. Francis Thompson. MoBrPo
I fear to me such fortune be assign'd. Sonnet. William Drummond of Hawthornden. NCEP
I fear you letters. The Aleph Bet. Fay Lipshitz. VWA
I feared the darkness as a boy. The Dark. Roy Fuller. DuDa
I Feed a Flame Within. Dryden. *See* Song: "I feed a flame within . . ."
I feel a breath from other planets blowing. Rapture. Stefan George, *tr. by* Ludwig Lewisohn. AWP
I feel a poem in my heart to-night. Embryo. Mary Ashley Townsend. AA; HBV-2
I feel an apparition. Wallace Stevens, *after the French of* Jean Le Roy. OBVE
I Feel I Am. John Clare. SeCePo
(John Clare.) OAEL-2
I feel I know what you have worked through, you. For John Berryman. Robert Lowell. NOBA
I feel it when the game is done. Footnote to Tennyson. Gerald Bullett. FiBHP
I Feel like My Time Ain't Long ("I feel like"), *with music. Unknown.* BoAN-2
I Feel like My Time Ain't Long ("Oh, de hearse keep a-rollin"), *with music. Unknown.* OuSiCo
I feel my face being bitten by the tides. The Knowledge That Comes through Experience. Jane Cooper. NMM
I feel my heart melting. Dusk. Gabriela Mistral, *tr. by* David Garrison. BoWoP
I feel my stomach. Not-Knowing. Dawn Hinshaw. AMV-81
I feel myself like the flame. The Candle Flame. Janet Lewis. CrMA
I feel, O Laudanum, thy power divine. In Praise of Laudanum. William Harrison. NOEC
I feel remorse for all that time has done. Love's Remorse. Edwin Muir. OxBTC
I feel ridiculous. Put Down. Léon Damas, *tr. by* Seth L. Wolitz. TTY
I feel so awful blue. Teasing; or, I Was Only, Only Teasing You. Cecil Mack. FSN
I feel so exceedingly lazy. A Hot-Weather Song. Don Marquis. HBMV; WhC; YaD
I feel so lonesome you can hear me when I moan. Terraplane Blues. *Unknown.* BluL
I feel the breath of the summer night. A Summer Night. Elizabeth Stoddard. AA
I feel the spring far off, far off. Spring in War-Time. Sara Teasdale. OHIP; SUMH
I feel the stubborn humming. Swift Floods. Kata Szidónia Petröczi, *tr. by* Laura Schiff. WPOW
I feel towards God just as a woman might. Spiritual Passion. George Barlow. OBVV
I feel your steps in the hall. Karin Boye, *tr. by* Nadia Christensen. *Fr.* A Dedication. PBWP
I fell in the battle of Ashdod. Since Then. Yehuda Amichai, *tr. by* Shlomo Vinner *and* Howard Schwartz. VWA
I felt a cleavage [*or* cleaving] in my mind. Emily Dickinson. NOBA; OxBA
I felt a funeral, in my brain. Emily Dickinson. AmPP; AP; BoWoP; CABA; CMoP; LiTA; MasP; NOBA; NoP; OxBA; PBWP; PoEL-5; PoRA; SCV; TAP; TwAmPo
I felt a spirit of love begin to stir. Dante, *tr. by* Dante Gabriel Rossetti. La Vita Nuova, XV. AWP
I felt my heart beat like an engine high in the air. Depression. Robert Bly. NaP
I felt no pain when they cut it off. Child with Six Fingers. Carol Muske. AmPA
I felt no tremor and I caught no sounds. The White Dust. W. W. Gibson. MoBrPo
I felt the lurch and halt of her heart. Lightning. D. H. Lawrence. CMoP; MoAB; MoBrPo; UnTE
I felt the wind soft from the land of souls. Olives and Mountains. Elizabeth Barrett Browning. *Fr.* Aurora Leigh, VII. FaBoPP
I felt the world a-spinning on its nave. The Last Journey. John Davidson. *Fr.* The Testament of John Davidson. BSV; GoTS
I fight a battle every day. The Fighter. S. E. Kiser. BLPA
I Fights Mit Sigel! Grant P. Robinson. BLPA
I figure her. Takes All Kinds. R. P. Dickey. POL

I figured/ anything anybody. Mrs. Sadie Grindstaff, Weaver and Factotum. Jonathan Williams. OBAL
I fill this cup to one made up of loveliness alone. A Health. Edward Coote Pinkney. AA; HBV-1; TreFS
I finally found a way of using the tree. The Beckett Kit. Linda Gregg. AmPA
I finally ran into me one night. And Then What? Dave Kelly. POL
I find him in the garden. Staked tomato-plants are what. Early Discoveries. David Malouf. CBAP
I find it normal, passing these great frontiers. Manchouli. William Empson. CoBMV
I find my love fishing. Ezra Pound *and* Noel Stock, *fr. Egyptian hieroglyphics.* BoWoP; PBWP
I find [*or* fynde] no peace, and all my war is done. Description of the Contrarious Passions in a Lover. Petrarch, *tr. by* Sir Thomas Wyatt. Sonnets to Laura: To Laura in Life, CIV. AAS; AWP; FF; LiTB; OAEL-1; OAEP; OBVE; PPoe; SiPS; TrGrPo
I find the door standing open. Entering the Room. Roger Pfingston. PoDr
I finish the *Times.* Shut eyes. My head. Commuter's Entry in a Connecticut Diary. Robert Penn Warren. AMV-81
I first adventure, with foolhardy might. Prologue. Joseph Hall. *Fr.* Virgidemiarum. ViBoPo
I first tasted under Apollo's lips. Evadne. Hilda Doolittle ("H. D."). BoWoP
I first would have him understand. On His Garden Book. Francis Daniel Pastorius. SCAP
I fixe mine eye on thine, and there. Witchcraft by a Picture. John Donne. EyDe
I fled Him, down the nights and down the days. The Hound of Heaven. Francis Thompson. ACP; BLPL; BrPo; FaBV; FaFP; GoBC; GoTL; HBV-2; ILwL; LiTB; LiTM; LoBV; MasP; MoAB; MoBrPo; OAEP; OBMV; OxBoCh; PoEL-5; SeCePo; SeCeV; TreF; TrGrPo; TRV; ViBoPo; VLP; WGRP; WHA
I flee the city, temples, and each place. Sonnet XVII. Louise Labé, *tr. by* Willis Barnstone. BoWoP
I flew my kite. Kite. David McCord. PDV
I Flung Me Round Him. Roden Noel. *Fr.* The Water-Nymph and the Boy. HBV-2; OBVV
I flung my soul to the air like a falcon flying. The Falconer of God. William Rose Benét. HBMV; TreFT; WGRP
I Flung Up My Arm Half from Sleep. Tram Combs. MP
I follow from my window down. From the Window Down. Louis O. Coxe. NYBP
I follow October, that yogi. Follower. Michael Arvey. AMV-80
I follow the deer through shadows. Deer Hunt, Salt Lake Valley. Helen Handley. GrPl
I follow the scent of a woman. Dancing the Shout to the True Gospel; or, The Song Movement Sisters Don't Want Me to Sing. Rita Mae Brown. NMM; PeHV
I Followed a Path. Patricia Parker. BlSi
I followed her to the station, with her suitcase in my hand. Love in Vain. Robert Johnson. UnPo
I followed once a fleet and mighty serpent. Lines. Thomas Lovell Beddoes. NBM
I followed where they led. His Throne Is with the Outcast. James Russell Lowell. TrCP
I forget everything. I forget faces. The Keeper. William Carpenter. Psk
I forgot my Lord in the summertime. Forgetting God. J. E. Harvey. STF
I forgotten who. Bumi. Amiri Baraka. PoBA
I found a/ hummingbird. The Container. Cid Corman. VGW
I found a ball of grass among the hay. Mouse's Nest. John Clare. ChTr; InPK; LiTB; LoBV; PAI; SeCeV; VLP
I found a dimpled spider, fat and white. Design. Robert Frost. AP: BLPL; CABA; CMoP; CoBMV; CrMA: HeIP; InPK; InPS; NIP; NoAM; NOBA; NoP; PAI; PPP; PrIm; SeCeV; SoSe; TAP
I found a flower in the wood. Wood Flower. Richard Le Gallienne. HBMV
I found a garden of thyme and thrift. The Perfect Garden. Winifred Robertson. PoSH
I Found a Horseshoe, *with music. Unknown.* AS
I found a house at Florence on the hill. Florence. Elizabeth Barrett Browning. *Fr.* Aurora Leigh, VII. FaBoPP
I found a little beetle, so that Beetle was his name. Forgiven. A. A. Milne. SoP
I found a pigeon's skull on the machair. Perfect. "Hugh MacDiarmid." NeBP
I found a torrent falling in a glen. The Torrent. E. A. Robinson. NePA
I found a yellow flower in the grass. A Summer Sanctuary. John Hall Ingham. AA
I found another baby scorpion today. Playing House. Jack Gilbert. NPGG
I found at daybreak yester morn. Medieval Norman Song. *Unknown, tr. by* John Addington Symonds. AWP
I Found God. Mary Afton Thacker. TRV
I Found Her Out There. Thomas Hardy. CH; CMoP; LO; MoVE; NoAM; NOBE; OAEL-2; PAI; PoEL-5
I found him in the guard-room at the Base. Lamentations. Siegfried Sassoon. OBSV
"I found him in the shining of the stars." Arthur's Disillusionment. Tennyson. *Fr.* Idylls of the King. TreFS
I found him openly wearing her token. A Conquest. Walter Herries Pollock. OBVV
I found his wool face, I went away. Reading Walt Whitman. Calvin Forbes. PoBA
I found in dreams a place of wind and flowers. A Ballad of Life. Swinburne. HBV-1
I found in Innisfail the fair. Aldfrid's Itinerary through Ireland. *Unknown, tr. by* James Clarence Mangan. OnYI
I found in Munster, unfettered of any. *Unknown, tr. by* James Clarence Mangan. *Fr.* Aldfrid's Itinerary through Ireland. BIrV
I found it in a legendary land. On Discovering a Butterfly. Vladimir Nabokov. NYBP
I found it in the bottom drawer. The Manual. Larry Rubin. GP
I found my son fallen. Windfall. Joel Arsenault. AMV-81
I found myself one day. The Hatch. Norma Faber. SO
I found myself one day all, all alone. Three Ballate, I. Angelo Poliziano, *tr. by* John Addington Symonds. AWP
I found no beauty on the mountain heights. Beauty. Joel Elias Springarn. HBMV
I found ten kinds of wild flowers growing. Late October. Sara Teasdale. PoSC; YeAr
I found that ivory image there. Crazy Jane Grown Old Looks at the Dancers. W. B. Yeats. CMoP; EBEV
I found the black bones one day in a trunk. Playing the Bones. Elizabeth Brewster. AMV-81
I found the phrase [*or* words] to every thought. Emily Dickinson. AA; AmPP
"I found the place last winter." Eric's voice. The Dreaming Trout. Charles Bruce. *Fr.* The Flowing Summer. CaP
I found the preserves in the cellar. Preserves. Michael Waters. GeTw
I found the words to every thought. *See* I found the phrase to every thought.
I found Thee in my heart, O Lord. Edward Dowden. *Fr.* New Hymns for Solitude. TrPWD
I found them there today. Mementos, II. W. D. Snodgrass. NePoEA-2
I found this photograph. Returning to the Town Where We Used to Live. Susan Musgrave. NOBC
I found this salamander. Samuel. Bobbi Katz. RHPC
I found you in a newspaper. Idea of a Swimmer. Jean-Richard Bloch, *tr. by* "S. P." TrJP
I found you on a rainy morning. Nansen. Gary Snyder. InPS
I found your Horace with the writing in it. On First Looking into Loeb's Horace. Lawrence Durrell. FaBoMo; LiTM
I, François Villon, ta'en at last. Would I Be Shrived? John D. Swain. BLPA
I freeze, I freeze, and nothing dwels. The Frozen Heart. Robert Herrick. CavP
I fynde no peace and all my warr is done. *See* I find no peace . . .
I gaed to spend a week in Fife. The Annuity. George Outram. HBV-2
I galloped on a scarlet filly. Absalom. Zerubavel Gilead, *tr. by* Dorothea Krook. VWA
I gat your letter, winsome Willie. To [*or* Epistle to] William Simpson, Ochiltree. Burns. BSV; OxBS
I gather clay and work it with my fingers. Shaman. Esther M. Leiper. AMV-81
I gather thyme upon the sunny hills. Immalee. Christina Rossetti. BoNaP
I gathered marble Venus in my arms. A Parable for Poetasters. Oliver St. John Gogarty. WhC
I gathered mosses in Easedale. Dorothy Wordsworth. SaC
I Gave Her Cakes; I Gave Her Ale. *Unknown.* TreFS
(Cakes and Ale.) FaFP
I gave my life to learning how to live. Postscript. Sandra Hochman. NMM
I gave my love a cherry without a [*or* that had no] stone. The Riddle Song [*or* Captain Wedderburn's Courtship]. *Unknown.* BLSo; FSW; ViBoFo
I gave myself to him. Emily Dickinson. FaBV
I gave to Hope a watch of mine: but he. Hope. George Herbert. PoEL-2; WeW
I gave you immortality and what did you give me? Sorley Maclean. Dain do Eimhir, XIX. NeBP
I gaze out a hundred windows. Lied in Crete. Alvaro Mutis. AMV-80
I gaze upon the beauty of the stars. The Beauty of the Stars. Moses ibn Ezra, *tr. by* Solomon Solis-Cohen. TrJP

I gaze, where August's sunbeam falls. Newark Abbey. Thomas Love Peacock. NOBE; OBNC
I gaze with grief upon our generation. A Thought. Mikhail Yuryevich Lermontov, *tr. by* Max Eastman. AWP
I gazed, and lo! Afar and near. Battle of Somerset. Cornelius C. Cullen. PAH
I gazed upon the cloudless moon. Emily Brontë. ChTr; MOON
I gazed upon the glorious sky. June. Bryant. AA; HBV-2
I Gazed Within. Emily Brontë. ViBoPo
I gently touched her hand: she gave. I Pressed Her Rebel Lips. *Unknown.* BoLoP; ErPo
I get a cinder in my eye. Walking. Frank O'Hara. TAT
I get into my blue wolf-car. Morning. Marjorie Saiser. AMV-80
I get my degree. Lawd, Dese Colored Chillum. Ruby C. Saunders. BlSi
I get up. I am sick of/ Rouging my cheeks. Morning. Chu Shu-chen, *tr. by* Kenneth Rexroth. BoWoP
I give and bequeath. Extraordinary Will. Will Jackett. FaBoUs
I give more praise to Troy's redoubt. On Troy. Oliver St. John Gogarty. WhC
I Give My Soldier Boy a Blade. William Maginn. HBV-2; PAH
I give my word on it. There is no way. Still and All. Burns Singer. NePoEA-2; OxBS
I give rest to clear words. A Dawn of Jaffa Pigeons. Eli Bachar, *tr. by* Jeremy Garber. VWA
I give thee thanks, Adonai! My Soul in the Bundle of Life. *Unknown, tr. by* E. Margaret Rowley. *Fr.* The Dead Sea Scrolls. TrJP
I give thee treasures hour by hour. Then. Rose Terry Cooke. HBV-1
I give you a house of snow. The Dove of New Snow. Vachel Lindsay. MoAmPo
I give you horses for your games in May. Sonnets of the Months: May. Folgore da San Geminiano, *tr. by* Dante Gabriel Rossetti. AWP
I give you meadow-lands in April, fair. Sonnets of the Months: April. Folgore da San Geminiano, *tr. by* Dante Gabriel Rossetti. AWP
I give you my hand. Microcosmos, VIII. Nigel Heseltine. NeBP
I give you now Professor Twist. The Purist. Ogden Nash. DBV; FiBHP; GoJo; MoAmPo; MoShBr; OBCA; PV; ShM; TreFT
I Give You Thanks My God. Bernard Dadié, *tr. fr. French by* Donatus Ibe Nwoga. TTY
I give you the end of a golden string. To the Christians [*or* Epigraph]. Blake. *Fr.* Jerusalem. EnRP; OBNC; OBRV; WGRP
I give you the rain, its long hollow. Around You, Your House. William Stafford. NPAW
I give you this Bible and more to take. Inscription on the Flyleaf of a Bible. Dannie Abse. TrJP
I glance from humble toil and see. Kitchen Window. J. E. H. MacDonald. CaP
I gnarled me where the spinster tree. Waterwall Blues. Howard Moss. MoPo; NePA
I go/ through Sunday's tunnel, hushed and deep. How to Get There. Bonnie Nims. RHPC
I go/ towards the trumpets of light. Tammuz. Nathan Alterman, *tr. by* Robert Friend. VWA
I go a long way back to find that bent tree. Bent Tree. Peter Serchuk. AMV-80
I go about dumbfoundedly, and show a dullard's glance. The Glorious Game. Richard Burton. HBMV
I go back again. Hawk and Snake. Leslie Silko. VoR
I go back ways to hurl rooftops. In My Mind. Norman MacCaig. OxBC
I Go by Road. Catulle Mendès, *tr. fr. French by* Alice Meynell. AWP; TrJP
I go digging for clams once every two or three years. Clamming. Reed Whittemore. NYBP; TAP
I go down from the hill in gladness. A Farewell. "Æ." AnIV
I go down to Dupont Street. Chinatown Chant. Tom MacInnes. CaP
I go in under foliage. In Rain. Wendell Berry. GeTw
I go inland each afternoon. The Harvester. Terry Lawrence. AMV-80
I go North to cold, to home, to Kinnaird. Kinnaird Head. George Bruce. BSV; NeBP
I go one step forward. Student. Cheng Min, *tr. by* Kenneth Rexroth *and* Ling Ching. PBWP
I go out of darkness/ Onto a road of darkness. Izumi Shikibu, *tr. fr. Japanese by* Kenneth Rexroth. WPOW
I go out to totem street. Knock on Wood. Henry Dumas. CNA; PoBA
I go separately. Santa Fe Trail. Barbara Guest. NeAP; PoM
I go through hollyhocks. Las Trampas U.S.A. Charles Tomlinson. TwCP
I go to concert, party, ball. My Rival. Kipling. OxBTC
I go to knit two clans together. The Wedding of the Clans. Aubrey Thomas De Vere. AnIL
I go to say goodbye to the Cailleach. The Wild Dog Rose. John Montague. BIrV; CIP; IPY
I go to school. Why Do You Want to Suffer Less. David Fisher. NPGG
I go to the Turkish shop, buy a bun. The Turkish Bakery. *Unknown, tr. by* Peter H. Lee. PBWP
I Go to Whiskey Bars. Raymond Thompson. LFAC
I go with earth, experiencing light. Time in the Sun. Louise Townsend Nicholl. NePoAm-2
I got a friend named Percy. Percy/ 68. Glenn Myles. NBP
I got a gal/ She's got a baker's shop. High Price Blues. *Unknown.* BluL
I got a gal and she loves me. Cripple Creek. *Unknown.* FSW
I Got a Gal at the Head of the Holler, *with music. Unknown.* AS
I Got a Home in-a Dat Rock. *Unknown.* BoAN-1, *with music;* BPo
I Got a Letter from Jesus, *with music. Unknown.* AS
I got a letter from my home. Sporting Life Blues. *Unknown.* FSW
I got a robe, you got a robe. All God's Chillun Got Wings. *Unknown.* BoAN-1; TreFS
I got a shoe, you got a shoe. All God's Children Got Shoes. *Unknown.* FSW
I got a valentine from Timmy. Valentine. Shelley Silverstein. PoSC; RHPC
I got a woman in West Helena, Arkansas. West Helena Blues. *Unknown.* BluL
I got an old tom cat. Tom Cat Blues. *Unknown.* FSW
I got cold feet in Columbus. Cold Feet in Columbus. William Heath. TAT
"I got her in the Black Bull." Elegy XIII. Sydney Goodsir Smith. *Fr.* Under the Eildon Tree. BSV
I got me flowers to straw [*or* strew] Thy way. George Herbert. *Fr.* Easter. CH; FaBoCh; FaBoEn; NOBE; OBEV; OBS; OHIP; TrGrPo; TRV
I got one good look. Coon Song. A. R. Ammons. NoAM; NOBA
I got out of bed twice, took down boxes and. Last Night There Was a Cricket in Our Closet. Leroy V. Quintana. GP
I got pocketed behind 7X-3824. Ambition. Morris Bishop. AmFN
I got so I could hear his name. Emily Dickinson. CMoP
I Got So Old. *Unknown.* BluL
I got stones in my passway. Stones in My Passway. *Unknown.* BluL
I Got the Blues. *Unknown. See* Good Mornin', Blues.
I got the blues for my baby. My Crime. *Unknown.* BluL
I got those little white schoolhouse blues. Little White Schoolhouse Blues. Florence Becker Lennon. PoNe
I got to Kansas City on a Frid'y. Kansas City. Oscar Hammerstein II. OBAL
I Got to Roll, *with music. Unknown.* OuSiCo
I got up in the night. The Riverman. Elizabeth Bishop. NYBP
I got up one mornin' jes' 'bout four o'clock. Stagolee. *Unknown.* BaBo; ViBoFo
I got up this morning. I Got So Old. *Unknown.* BluL
I got up this morning and meant to be good. The Wrong Start. Marchette Chute. RHPC
I gotta/ buy me a new. Après le Bain. William Carlos Williams. OBAL
I grab a slice of moon. Toward Tenses Two Moons. George Rachow. LFAC
I grant indeed that fields and flocks have charms. Rural Life [*or* Truth in Poetry]. George Crabbe. *Fr.* The Village. NOBE; SeCePo
I grazed the green as I fell. Summer. P. K. Page. PeCV
I greet my love with wine and gladsome lay. Sabbath, My Love. Judah Halevi, *tr. by* Solomon Solis-Cohen. TrJP
I greet thee, my Redeemer sure. Salutation to Jesus Christ. John Calvin. WGRP
I greet you, son, with joy and winter rue. Muse in Late November. Jonathan Henderson Brooks. PoNe
I grew/ for you. The Strong Bond. Juana de Ibarbourou, *tr. by* Linda Scheer. PBWP
I grew out of a vicious, viscous swamp. A Reed. Osip Mandelstam, *tr. by* James Greene. VWA
I grew up bent over. Prodigy. Charles Simic. GeTw
I grieve about my fellow-men. Wednesday. "Elspeth." WhC
I grieve and dare not show my discontent. On Monsieur's Departure. Elizabeth I, Queen of England. WPE
I grieve for my second daughter. Written on Seeing the Flowers, and Remembering My Daughter. Kao Ch'i. DL
I grieve to think of you alone. Prescience. Donald Jeffrey Hayes. PoNe
I grieve when I think on the dear happy days of my youth. Draherin O Machree. *Unknown.* AnIV
I Grieved for Buonaparté. Wordsworth. EnRP
I grow. Survivor. Judy Dothard Simmons. CNA
I grow a white rose. José Martí, *tr. by* Seymour Resnick. *Fr.* Simple Verses. TTY
I grow accustomed to a new disguise. Journal. John Ciardi. PoA
I grow old, old. Little Red Riding Hood. Olga Broumas. DFT
I grow old under an intensity. Mirror. James Merrill. CoAP; NePoEA-2; TwAmPo
I grow together everywhere. Mandelstam. Richard Burns. VWA
I guess because it was Key West. Meeting the Reincarnation Analyst. Gary Gildner. AmPA
I guess it is ever green. Evergreen Cemetery. Alfred Purdy. MoCV

I guess there is a garden named. The Mirror Perilous. Alan Dugan. LiTM; MP; TwCP
I guess you love me now. Songs of Divorce. Jane Green, *tr. by* Frances Densmore. WPOW
I. H. B. William Winter. AA
I had/ a dream of women, dark. A Dream of Women. Carolyn Maisel. IHMS
I had a beginning but shall have no end. Stone Angel. Anne Ridler. EaLo
I Had a Black Man. *Unknown.* OxBoLi
I had a brother in the infantry. Put My Name Down. Irwin Silber. FSW
I had a cat and the cat pleased me. Barnyard Song [*or* A Farmyard Song]. *Unknown.* OxNR; SoPo; TrAS
I had a chair at every hearth. The Lamentation of the Old Pensioner [*or* The Old Pensioner]. W. B. Yeats. InPK; NoAM; VLP; WeW
I had a dog/ Whose name was Buff. *Unknown.* OxNR
I had [*or* Well, I had] a dog and his name was Blue. Old Blue. *Unknown.* FSW; GDP
I had a dog like a love. Penny Trumpet. Raphael Rudnik. MAT; NYBP
I had a donkey. Faith. Marjorie Dunkels. PH
I had a donkey, that was all right. The Donkey. Theodore Roethke. GrPl; OBCA
I Had a Dove [and the Sweet Dove Died]. Keats. CH; FM
(Dove, The.) HBV-2
(Song: "I had a dove, and the sweet dove died.") FaPON; PBBP
I had a dream. A wondrous thing. Spring and Death. Gerard Manley Hopkins. BrPo; SyP
I had a dream last night. I dreamed. Andre. Gwendolyn Brooks. TiPo
I had a dream three walls stood up wherein a raven bird. Anger's Freeing Power. Stevie Smith. OxBC
I had a dream, which was not all a dream. Darkness. Byron. EnRP; LiTB; OAEL-2; OAEP; PoEL-4; TEP
I had a duck and the young duck died. A. Stodart-Walker. FM
I Had a Duck-billed Platypus. Patrick Barrington. CenHV; FiBHP
I had a feeling in my neck. Mumps. Elizabeth Madox Roberts. FaPON; SoPo
I had a friend: or thought I had a friend. The Mantis Friend. Vincent McHugh. NePoAm-2
I Had a Future. Patrick Kavanagh. BIrV; NoAM
I had a good teacher. Education. Don L. Lee. AmNP; BALP
I had a heart as good as gold. The Golden Heart. Witter Bynner. HBMV
I Had a Hippopotamus. Patrick Barrington. CenHV
I had a horse, his name was Bill. A Horse Named Bill. *Unknown.* FSW
I had a little bird. The Orphan's Song. Sydney Dobell. CH; ELP; OBNC
I had a little chamber in the house. Elizabeth Barrett Browning. *Fr.* Aurora Leigh, I. FaBoPP
I had a little cow. *Unknown.* OxNR
I had a little dog and his name was Blue Bell. *Unknown.* OxNR
I had a little hobby horse, it was well shod. Mother Goose. OxNR
I had a little horse, his name was Dappled Grey. *Unknown.* OxNR
I had a little husband. Mother Goose. EvOK; FaFP; HBV-1; HBVY; OxNR
I had a little moppet. Mother Goose. OxNR
I had a little nag. *Unknown.* OxNR
I had a little nut-tree; nothing would it bear. Mother Goose. CH; GBP; MoShBr; OxBoLi; OxNR; SoPo
I Had a Little Pig. *Unknown.* RHPC
I had a little pony. Mother Goose. OxNR; PH; SoPo; TiPo
I had a little sorrow. The Penitent. Edna St. Vincent Millay. YaD
I had a live joy once and pampered her. Joy's Treachery. Wilfrid Scawen Blunt. The Love Sonnets of Proteus, XVII. VLP
I had a lovely bottle, bottle-blue. One Man's Goose; or, Poetry Redefined. George Starbuck. PP
I had a Mother who read to me. The Reading Mother. Strickland Gillilan. BLPA
I had a penny. Market Square. A. A. Milne. TiPo
I Had a Rooster. *Unknown.* FSW
I had a silver penny. Nursery Rhyme of Innocence and Experience. Charles Causley. GoJo
I had a sudden vision in the night. The Ladder. Leonora Speyer. HBMV
"I had a true love but she left me." The Quaker's Wooing. *Unknown.* AS
I had a true love, if ever a girl had one. The Tri-colored Ribbon. Peadar Kearney. OnYI
I had a true-love, none so dear. Fortune's Wheel. Lord De Tabley. OBVV
I had a vision when the night was late. The Vision of Sin. Tennyson. OAEL-2; VLP
I Had a Wife. *Unknown.* FSW
I had always been told. The Crippler. Danny Siegel. VWA
I had ambition, by which sin. Ambition. W. H. Davies. MoBrPo; TrGrPo
I had an uncle once who kept a rock in his pocket. I've Got a Home in That Rock. Raymond Patterson. FF; PoBA; PoNe
I had as lief be embraced by the porter at the hotel. Two Figures in Dense Violet Light. Wallace Stevens. MoAB; MoAmPo
I had awakened early. Second Ode to Persephone. Robert Kelly. The Book of Persephone, 9. PoM
I had become callous like most. On the Death of Lisa Lyman. Della Burt. BlSi
I had been hungry, all the years. Emily Dickinson. LiTA; LiTM; MoAmPo; SBG
I had been sitting for days. Long Distance. Dana Naone. CDW
I had been watching the child appear. Bedtime. Hillel Schwartz. AMV-81
I Had But Fifty Cents. *Unknown.* BeLS; BLPA; TreF
I had come to the house, in a cave of trees. Medusa. Louise Bogan. AWP; BoWoP; HoPM; MoAB; MoAmPo; MoPo; MoVE; NoP; PAI; WPE
I had eight birds hatcht in one nest. In Reference to Her Children, 23 June, 1656. Anne Bradstreet. BoWoP; SBG; TAP
I had expected. To Stephen Spender. Timothy Corsellis. WaP
I had finished my dinner. An Easy Decision. Kenneth Patchen. CTBA
I had forgotten how to pray. When I Had Need of Him. S. E. Kiser. BLRP
I had four brothers over the sea. The Tokens of Love. *Unknown.* GBP
I had gone broke, and got set to come back. Epigram. J. V. Cunningham. MoAmPo; NePoAm; PV; QFR
I had gone fruitless and defenceless, Lady. A Nun to Mary, Virgin. Sister Mary St. Virginia. ISi
I had heard/ before, of an. Mr. Brodsky. Charles Tomlinson. NoAM; OxBC
I had long known the diverse tastes of the wood. Gift of Sight. Robert Graves. PCP
I had my birth where stars were born. My Birth. Minot Judson Savage. AA; WGRP
I had my papers, but I was running. Dark in the Reich of the Blond. William Heyen. MAYP
I had never heard of the whiteness. The Poem. David Schloss. PoA
I had no God but these. Christ and the Pagan. John Banister Tabb. TrCP
I had no mother. Eve's Song in the Garden. Lynn Gottlieb. VWA
I had no thought of violets of late. Sonnet. Alice Dunbar Nelson. BANP; BlSi; CDC; PoBA; PoNe
I had no time to hate, because. Emily Dickinson. FPL; PoLF
I had no voice. Lilith's Child. Edward Francisco. DL
I had not been there before where the vagina opens. The First Birth. Rodney Jones. MAYP
I had not fastened my sash over my gown. Tzu Yeh, *tr. fr. Chinese by* Kenneth Rexroth *and* Ling Chung. WPOW
I had not minded walls. Emily Dickinson. AWP; CABA
I had not seen my son's dear face. San Lorenzo Giustiniani's Mother. Alice Meynell. HBV-2
I had not thought to have unlockt my lips. Temperance and Virginity. Milton. *Fr.* Comus. OBS
I had often, cowled in the slumberous heavy air. Dürer; Innsbruck, 1495. "Ern Malley." CBAP
I had over-prepared the event. Villanelle: The Psychological Hour. Ezra Pound. CTC
I had seen, as dawn was breaking. La Nuit Blanche. Kipling. MoBrPo
I had so little. The Toy. Cid Corman. GP
I had soaked the old house. Zimmer and His Turtle Sink the House. Paul Zimmer. Psk
I had the blues/ Last night. Never Let Your Left Hand Know. *Unknown.* BluL
I had the nicest Christmas list. His Name at the Top. *Unknown.* STF
"I had this dream." My Dream. Lew Blockcolski. VoR
I had thought I would need him. Packing In with a Man. Judith McCombs. LTB
I had thought of putting an/ altar. Prayer. Isabella Maria Brown. NNP; PoNe
I had thought of the bear in his lair as fiercely free. Part of the Darkness. Isabella Gardner. BoAnP
I had three friends. Three Friends. *Unknown, tr. by* Ulli Beier. BoWoP; PBA
I had time and a shovel. I began to dig. In the Hole. John Ciardi. HoAn
I Had to Be Secret. Mark Van Doren. SO
I had to kick their law into their teeth in order to save them. Negro Hero. Gwendolyn Brooks. CAPP
I had to laugh. Montana Wives. Gwendolen Haste. AmFN
I had two pigeons bright and gay. *Unknown.* OxNR; PBBP
I had walked life's way with an easy tread. I Met the Master. *Unknown.* BLRP; PoLF; STF
I had walked since dawn and lay down to rest on a bare hillside. Vulture. Robinson Jeffers. BoAnP; NOBA; NoP
I had wanted a daughter. Mothers of Sons. Lesley Saunders. BrRo
I had watched the ascension and decline of the moon. Walter James Turner. *Fr.* The Seven Days of the Sun. OBMV
I had watched these trees get gradually bigger. The Ravine. James Applewhite. AMV-80

I had written him a letter which I had, for want of better. Clancy of the Overflow. A. B. Paterson. PoAu-1
I had written to Aunt Maud. Waste [*or* Aunt Maud]. Harry Graham. FaBoCo; MoShBr; ShM
I Hae a Wife o' My Ain. Burns. LAuP
I hae seen great anes and sat in great ha's. My Ain Fireside. Elizabeth Hamilton. FaBoBe; HBV-2
I haf von funny leedle poy. Yawcob Strauss. Charles Follen Adams. PaPo
I hail from high in the alkali. When West Comes East. Carey Ford. InMe
I hailed me a woman from the street. My Madonna. Robert W. Service. BLPA
I hailed the bus and I went for a ride. Bus Ride. Selma Robinson. *Fr.* Ferry Ride. FaPON
I hang by my heels from the sky. Hera, Hung from the Sky. Carolyn Kizer. NMM; WPE
I happen to be a veteran. The Significance of a Veteran's Day. Simon J. Ortiz. GP
I happened once upon a time. James Hatley. *Unknown.* ESPB
"I hardly ever ope my lips," one cries. Epigram. Richard Garnett. HBV-1
I hardly suppose I know anybody who wouldn't rather be a success than a failure. Kindly Unhitch That Star, Buddy. Ogden Nash. LiTA; PoPl
I hate. What Literature Needs. John A. Holmes. InMe
I hate a prologue to a story. The Duke of Benevento. Sir John Henry Moore. OBEC
I hate and love./ And if you ask me why. Catullus, *tr. fr. Latin by* Horace Gregory. NAWM-1
I hate and love. Why? You may ask but. Odi et Amo. Catullus, *tr. by* Ezra Pound. CTC; OBVE
I hate and love, wouldst thou the reason know? Catullus, *tr. fr. Latin by* Richard Lovelace. OBVE
I hate, and yet I love thee too. To Lesbia. Catullus, *tr. by* Abraham Cowley. PoPl
I Hate Harry. Miriam Chaikin. RHPC
I Hate Men. Cole Porter. DBV
"I hate my verses, every line, every word." Love the Wild Swan. Robinson Jeffers. HeIP; InPS; MoAmPo; TW; TwAmPo
"I hate successful people," you declare. What's Hard. Laurence Lerner. NePoEA-2
I Hate That Drum's Discordant Sound. John Scott of Amwell. NIP; PAI; TW
(Drum, The.) NOBE; OBEC; OBWP; ViBoPo
(Ode: "I hate that drum's discordant sound.") NOEC
(Retort on the Foregoing.) OBEV; PPON
I hate the dreadful hollow behind the little wood. Maud. Tennyson. OAEP; VLP
I hate the man who builds his name. The Poet and the Rose. John Gay. TEP
I hate thee, Death! Mors, Morituri Te Salutamus. Francis Burdett Money-Coutts. OBVV
I hate these phrases: Of power absolute. Joshua Sylvester, *after the French of* Guy du Faur de Pibrac. FaBoEE
I hate to be a kicker. Explanation. "Josh Billings." TreFT
I [*or* Ah] hate to see de ev'nin' sun go down. Saint Louis Blues. W. C. Handy. BLSo; FF
I Hate to See You Clad. Paul Verlaine, *tr. fr. French by* Louis Untermeyer. UnTE
I hate to sing your hackneyed birds. A Panegyric on Geese. Francis S. Mahony. OnYI
I hate to spend the night. Thanks Just the Same. *Unknown.* PoLF
"I hates to think of dyin'," says the skipper to the mate. The Worried Skipper. Wallace Irwin. BLPA
I Haue a Yong Suster. *Unknown. See* I Have a Young Sister.
I Haunt the Hills That Overlook the Sea. John Davidson. *Fr.* The Testament of a Man Forbid. BSV
I Have a Big Favour to Ask You, Brothers. Zishe Landau, *tr. fr. Yiddish by* Ruth Whitman. VWA
I Have a Blue Piano. Else Lasker-Schüler, *tr. fr. German by* Ralph Manheim. TrJP
I have a bookcase, which is what. Shake, Mulleary and Go-ethe. H. C. Bunner. FiBHP; InMe
I have a bottle and a pen. Thoughts from a Bottle. Carl Clark. JB
I have a bowl of paper whites. Window Ledge in the Atom Age. E. B. White. OBAL
I have a boy of five years old. Anecdote for Fathers. Wordsworth. EnRP
I have a dog. Notice. David McCord. SoPo
I have a dog of Blenheim birth. My Dog Dash. John Ruskin. FM
I have a dream bone. The Hollow Flute. Avner Strauss. VWA
I have a fairy by my side. My Fairy. "Lewis Carroll." FaBoNo
I have a feeling. The Nets on the Andrea Doria. Karen G. Tepfer. AMV-81
I have a feeling for those ships. The Stone Fleet. Herman Melville. EtS
I have a feeling that my boat. Oceans. Juan Ramón Jiménez, *tr. by* Robert Bly. NU
I have a fifth of therapy. Interview with Doctor Drink. J. V. Cunningham. NMP; TW; VGW
I Have a Friend. Anne Spencer. CDC
I have a friend. My Friend. Samuel Allen. FB
I have a friend, she says. The Cross-eyed Lover. Donald Finkel. Prf
I have a friend so kind and true. My Friend. Marjorie Lorene Buster. STF
I have a friend who would give a price for those long fingers all of one length. Snakes, Mongooses, Snake-Charmers and the Like. Marianne Moore. CMoP
I have a funny Airedale dog. My Airedale Dog. W. L. Mason. SoPo
I have a garden here, shaped. Letter from an Institution: III. Michael Ryan. AmPA
I have a garden of my own. Child's Song [*or* A Garden Song]. Thomas Moore. BoNaP; GoBC; OxBI; SUS; ViBoPo
I Have a Gentle Cock [*or* Gentil Cok]. *Unknown.* EBEV; HAP; NCEP; NOBE; NoP; OxBM; PBBP; SeCePo; ViBoPo
(Cockerel.) GBP
(Gentle Cock, The.) OxBoLi
(I Have a Noble Cock.) MeEL
I have a golden ball. Rune of Riches. Florence Converse. SUS
I Have a Goodly Heritage. Bible, *O.T.* Psalms, XVI: 5-9. TreFT
I have a grief. Agitato ma Non Troppo. John Crowe Ransom. OxBA
I have a jolly shilling, a lovely jolly shilling. The Jolly Shilling. *Unknown.* OBET
I have a king who does not speak. Emily Dickinson. TwAmPo
I have a life of my own. Maxine W. Kumin. *Fr.* Song for Seven Parts of the Body. POL
I have a life that did not become. Easter Morning. A. R. Ammons. NoP
I have a little bed. My Bed. Lucy Sprague Mitchell. SoPo
I have a little home amidst the city's din. The Complacent Cliff-Dweller. Margaret Fishback. PoLF
I have a little inward light, which still. The Inward Light. Henry Septimus Sutton. WGRP
I have a little kinsman. The Discoverer. Edmund Clarence Stedman. AA; HBV-1
I have a little pussy. Catkin [*or* Little Gray Pussy]. *Unknown.* SoPo; TiPo
I have a little shadow that goes in and out with me. My Shadow. Robert Louis Stevenson. FaBoBe; FaBV; FaPON; HBV-1; HBVY; OnUR; OxBChV; PDV; SoPo; TEP; TiPo; TreF
I have a little sister, they call her Peep-Peep. Mother Goose. OxNR; TiPo
I have a little valentine. My Valentine. Kitty Parsons. SoPo
I have a little windmill on my head. Sliding Trombone. Georges Ribemont-Dessaignes, *tr. by* David Gascoyne. EAS
"I have a Love I love too well." The Sacrilege. Thomas Hardy. DTo
I have a love is Heven-King. The Love of God. John Audelay. OxBM
I have a mistress, for perfections rare. A Devout Lover. Thomas Randolph. HBV-1; HoPM; OBEV
I have a name, a little name. The Pet Name. Elizabeth Barrett Browning. HBV-1
I Have a New Garden. *Unknown.* MeEL
(Pear-Tree, The.) GBP
I Have a Noble Cock. *Unknown. See* I Have a Gentle Cock.
I have a notion that the world is round. John Wain. *Fr.* A Boisterous Poem about Poetry. PP
I have a picture in my room in which. Intaglio. Henri Coulette. NePoEA; PoCh
I Have a Place. Lily A. De Young. AMV-80
I have a pretty little flow'r. Francis Daniel Pastorius. SCAP
I have a proved, unerring Guide. The Unerring Guide. Anna Shipton. BLRP
I have a reason. Madness does have limits. Logic. Calvin Murry. LFAC
I Have a Rendezvous with Death. Alan Seeger. BLPA; DL; FaBV; FaFP; HBV-2; OHFP; PoPl; TreF; ViBoPo; WaP
(Rendezvous, The.) FaPoR; WGRP
I Have a Rendezvous with Life. Countee Cullen. CDC
I have a river in my mind. Six o'Clock. Owen Dodson. PoNe
I Have a Roof. Ada Jackson. TrPWD
I have a room whereinto no one enters. Memory. Christina Rossetti. OBNC
I have a secret place to go. Keziah. Gwendolyn Brooks. RHPC
"I have a ship in the North Countrie." The Sweet Trinity; or, The Golden Vanity. *Unknown.* BaBo; OBET
I have a smiling face, she said. The Mask. Elizabeth Barrett Browning. OBNC; OBVV
I have a story fit to tell. The Strong Swimmer. William Rose Benét. PoNe
I have a suit of new clothes in this happy new year. "When I Think of the Hungry People." O-Shi-O. TRV
I have a terrible fear of being an animal. César Vallejo, *tr. fr. Spanish by* Robert Bly. EAS

I have a thousand pictures of the sea. Muna Lee. Sonnets, IV. HBMV
I have a tree, a graft of love. Arbor Amoris. Villon, *tr. by* Andrew Lang. AWP
I have a vague remembrance. The Challenge. Longfellow. AP
I have a white cat whose name is Moon. Moon. William Jay Smith. PDV
I have a wide, friendly face. Zimmer Envying Elephants. Paul Zimmer. GP
I have a young love. The Sailor. Sylvia Townsend Warner. OBMV
I Have a Young Sister. *Unknown.* CH; MeEL; NoP; OAEL-1; OxBM
(I Haue [*or* Have] a Yong Suster.) InPS; PoEL-1; SeCeV
("I have a young suster.") EBEV
(Love without Longing.) OxBoLi
(Tokens of Love, The.) GBP
I have abjured the flesh, and I. Two against One. *Unknown, tr. by* Louis Untermeyer. UnTE
I have achieved. That which the lonely man. The Seeker. Lascelles Abercrombie. *Fr.* The Fools' Adventure. WGRP
I have, alas, no taste. Taste. John Updike. AMV-81
I have all/ my mother's habits. Mother's Habits. Nikki Giovanni. BlSi
I have all the sudden quietness. A Wintering Moon. R. Wayne Hardy. LFAC
I have allowed myself. For Masturbation. Alan Dugan. CAPP; NoAM
I Have Always Found It So. Birdie Bell. BLRP
I Have Always Heard of These Old Men. *Unknown.* AmFP
I have always known. The Way It Is. Gloria Oden. CNA; IHMS
I have always loved the word *guitar.* Guitar. David St. John. MAYP
I have an arrow that will find its mark. Emerson. WhC
I Have an Orchard. Christopher Marlowe *and* Thomas Nashe. *Fr.* The Tragedy of Dido, IV, v. ChTr
I have an uncle I don't like. Manners. Mariana Griswold Van Rensselaer. FaPON; HBMV; HBVY; RHPC
I have an understanding with the hills. After Sunset. Grace Hazard Conkling. HBMV
I Have Approached. Alan Paton. PeSA
I have appropriated the windy twittering of aspen leaves. Plunder. A. R. Ammons. NoAM
I have arranged a final test. The Test. Rachel McAlpine. OCNZ
I have assumed a conscious sociability. Garden Party. Sir Herbert Read. BrPo
I have awakened. Reading Sign. Jack L. Anderson. LFAC
I have awakened from the unknowing to the knowing. For William Edward Burghardt Du Bois on His Eightieth Birthday. Bette Darcie Latimer. PoBA
I have baptized thee Withy, because of thy slender limbs. To ———? Richard Dehmel, *tr. by* Jethro Bithell. AWP
I have become without desire. Twoborn. Rokwaho. STE
I have been/ Three separate times, in war. James Harold Manning. *Fr.* What Is Truth? CaP
I have been a/ way so long. Homecoming. Sonia Sanchez. PoBA
I have been a censor for fifteen months. Censorship. Arthur Waley. OxBTC; WaP
I Have Been a Foster. *Unknown.* FaBoRV; GBP
(Forester, The.) OxBM
("I have been a foster long and many day.") EBEV
I have been abus'd of late. The Scolding Wives Vindication; or, An Answer to the Cuckold's Complaint. *Unknown.* CoMu
I have been busy writing a terribly critical. Notes on a Certain Terribly Critical Piece. Reed Whittemore. PP
I have been cherish'd and forgiven. Lines. Hartley Coleridge. PoEL-4
I have been counselled. The Part of Fortune. Ann Sanfedele. AMV-81
I have been cruel to a fat pigeon. Fly. W. S. Merwin. NNaP
I have been dreaming all a summer day. Dreams. Victor J. Daley. PoAu-1
I have been figuring that in a way. The Time Is Today. John Farrar. GoYe
I have been given a horn. The Messiah-Blower. Paul Goodman. FAZ
I have been here before. Sudden Light. Dante Gabriel Rossetti. BoLoP; CTC; ELP; FaBoEn; FPL; LO; LoBV; NBM; NOBE; NoP; OAEL-2; OAEP; OBNC; PoLF; TrGrPo; VLP
I have been here. Dispersed in meditation. Agnosco Veteris Vestigia Flammae. J. V. Cunningham. QFR; TwAmPo; VGW
I have been in a marine aquarium and I have seen. The Marine Aquarium. Louis Dudek. *Fr.* Atlantis. MoCV
I have been in love, and in debt, and in drink. Drinking Song. Alexander Brome. PoPle
"I have been in the hills all day." Levavi Oculos. Marion Campbell. PoSH
I have been in this bar. The Man Who Married Magdalene: Variation on a Theme by Louis Simpson. Anthony Hecht. CoPo
I have been introduced to death in bookshops. Thinking of Bookshops. James Liddy. CIP
I have been my arm. Margo Taft. NMM
I have been one acquainted with the night. Acquainted with the Night. Robert Frost. AP; ChTr; CMoP; CoBMV; FPL; HAP; LiTM; MoAmPo; MP; NePA; NoAM; NOBA; PDV; PoLF; PPP; SoSe; TAP; TwCP; VGW; WeW
I have been profligate of happiness. To Olive. Lord Alfred Douglas. OBEV; OBVV
I have been seeing his face everywhere, the face of a former lover. The Lover. Robert Duncan. PeHV
I have been so great a lover. The Great Lover. Rupert Brooke. BrPo; FaFP; FPL; HoPM; LiTB; LiTM; MoBrPo; PoRA; TreF; TrGrPo; WaP
I have been so misused by chaste men with one wife. Ship near Shoals. Anna Wickham. HBMV
I have been standing at the edge. 3 a.m. in New York. Jean Valentine. NYP
I have been sure of three things all my life. Clement Wood. Eagle Sonnets, III. HBMV
I have been there. On Looking at an Old Climbing Photograph. Douglas Fraser. PoSH
I have been there again, and seen the backs. Again. Jon Stallworthy. OxBC
I Have Been Through the Gates. Charlotte Mew. MoAB; MoBrPo; TrGrPo
I have been through the valley of weeping. The God of Comfort. *Unknown.* STF
I have been treading on leaves all day until I am autumn-tired. A Leaf-Treader. Robert Frost. MoAmPo
I have been walking today. Furnished Lives. Jon Silkin. NePoEA-2; NMP; NoAM
I have been walking under the sky in the moonlight. Academic Moon. Helen Bevington. GLGT
I have been warned. It is more than thirty years since I wrote. But I Am Growing Old and Indolent. Robinson Jeffers. AP; NoAM; NOBA; TAP
I have been wondering. A Letter. Anthony Hecht. NYBP; OxBC
I have been young, and now am not too old. Report on Experience. Edmund Blunden. FaBoEn; FaBoTw; GTBS-P; LO; NOBE; OBMV; OBWP
"I have beene all day looking after." The Witches' Song. Ben Jonson. CH
I have begun to die. The Sentry. Alun Lewis. DTC
I have believed too long in one thing. March Weather. Jon Swan. NYBP
I have borne the anguish of love, which ask me not to describe. Hafiz, *tr. by* John Hindley. Odes, XI. AWP
I Have Bowed before the Sun. Anna Lee Walters. WPOW
I have brought berries on a grape-leaf. Keepsake from Quinault. Dorothy Alyea. GoYe
I have brought the wine. This Is My Love for You. Grace Fallow Norton. HBV-1
I have buried her under a stone. The Stationmaster's Lament. Jerome Rothenberg. CoPo
I have but one story. Summer Is Gone. *Unknown, tr. by* Sean O'Faolain. AnIL; PoPl
I Have Cared for You, Moon. Grace Hazard Conkling. HBMV
I have carried for five years. The Return. Jon Silkin. NePoEA-2
I have carried it with me each day: that morning I took. A Morning. Mark Strand. GeTw
I have carried my pillow to the windowsill. Summer near the River. Carolyn Kizer. CoAP; VGW
I have climbed into silence trying for clear air. Recuerdo. Paula Gunn Allen. STE
I have come again, gentlemen and ladies. Spring Song. Theodore Spencer. TwAmPo
I have come all this way. Ways of Day. Robert Penn Warren. *Fr.* Notes on a Life to Be Lived. NoAM
I have come at last to the short. The Great Canzon. Kenneth Rexroth. NoAM
I have come back again. The Return of the Native. Harley Matthews. PoAu-2
I have come back to Princeton three days in a row. Hanging Scroll. Gerald Stern. PoDr
I have come down to the garden. At the Place of the Roman Baths. "Richard Scrace." CaP
I have come far enough. A Form of Women. Robert Creeley. CAPP; NaP
I have come far to have found nothing. Three Tiny Songs. Cid Corman. HoAn; VGW
I have come to catch birds. The Bird Catcher. *Unknown, tr. by* Ulli Beier. TTY
I have come to rely. Birds and Roses Are Birds and Roses. William Heyen. GeTw
I have come to the borders of sleep. Lights Out. Edward Thomas. BrPo; MMA; NOBE
I Have Come to the Conclusion. Nelle Fertig. FF

I have come to where the world drops off. Visit to a Hospital. Jean Valentine Chace. GoYe
I have come to you, Babi Yar. Babi Yar. Lev Ozerov, *tr. by* Daniel Weissbort. VWA
I have come upon the visage again. Wood Floor Dreams. Lance Henson. VoR
I have consider'd it; and find. The Resolve. Henry Vaughan. AnAnS-1; NCEP
I have consider'd it, and finde. The Reprisall [*or* The Second Thanksgiving]. George Herbert. AnAnS-1; OAEP
I have continued to seek her. The Constant Lover. Louis Simpson. NYBP
I have courage and hardihood. Besieged. Zalman Schneour, *tr. by* Joseph Leftwich. TrJP
I have crouched in your kivas by night. Taos Drums. William Haskel Simpson. BPAW
I Have Cut an Eagle. James Koller. PoM
I have desired to go. Heaven-Haven. Gerard Manley Hopkins. ACP; BrPo; FaBoEn; GoBC; HeIP; LoBV; MoAB; MoBrPo; MOS; NoAM; NOBE; NOCV; OAEP; OBEV; OBNC; PAI; SoSe; SOTW; TrGrPo; ViBoPo; VLP
I have discovered a country. Connais-Tu le Pays? Richard Shelton. NYBP
I have discovered finally to-day. The Silent Pool. Harold Monro. BrPo
I have discovered that most of. January Morning. William Carlos Williams. InPS; SOTW
I have done all I could. The Tree and the Lady. Thomas Hardy. MoAB; MoBrPo
I have done it again. Lady Lazarus. Sylvia Plath. CAPP; ConAP; InPK; MAT; NaP; NIP; NoAM; NOBA; NoP; PPoe; PrIm; TAP; VGW
I have done my bit of carving. The Old Figurehead Carver. H. A. Cody. EtS
I have done one braver thing. The Undertaking. John Donne. MePo; NOBE
I have done the deed. Didst thou not hear a noise? Macbeth Does Murder Sleep. Shakespeare. *Fr.* Macbeth, II, ii. EBEV; FiP
I have done what I could but you avoid me. My Life by Somebody Else. Mark Strand. GP
I have done with being judged. Robert Browning. *Fr.* The Ring and the Book, VI. OAEP
I have dreamt it again: standing suddenly still. Wormwood. Thomas Kinsella. CIP
I have drifted in silence. Imitations Based on the American. Frank Polite. BXAP
I have driven North after midnight, machined. Poem for My Thirty-second Birthday. John Ciardi. MiAP
I have drunk ale from the Country of the Young. He Thinks of His Past Greatness When a Part of the Constellations of Heaven. W. B. Yeats. DTC; OAEP; PoEL-5
I have eaten/ the plums. This Is Just to Say. William Carlos Williams. FF; GoJo; HoPM; InPK; InPS; NIP; NOBA; NoP; PAI; RHPC; SOTW; SpRo; TAP
I have eaten the city. Manhattan. H. R. Hays. EAS
I have eaten your bread and salt. Prelude to "Departmental Ditties." Kipling. VLP
I have entreated care to cut the thread. Dan Bartholmew's Dolorous Discourses. George Gascoigne. EnRePo
I have escaped from the two acre rolled garden. If It Would All Please Hurry. James Tate. MAYP
I Have Exhausted the Delighted Range. Michael Hartnett. CIP
I have fallen in love with American names. American Names. Stephen Vincent Benét. AmFN; GOA; OBAL; OxBA; TreFT; YaD
I have fastened everything within a black cloak. The Assignation. Juana de Ibarbourou, *tr. by* Brian Swann. PBWP
I have fathered. Father Poem. Joel Oppenheimer. PoM
I have felt it as they've said. Larry Eigner. PoM
"I have finished another year," said God. New Year's Eve. Thomas Hardy. MoBrPo; NoAM
I Have Folded My Sorrows. Bob Kaufman. AmNP; PoBA
I have followed you model. Ode to a Model. Vladimir Nabokov. OBAL; PoPl
I have forgotten you as one forgets at dawning. Words. Helen Morgan Brooks. NNP; PoNe
I have forsworn it while I life. The Wake at the Well. *Unknown.* GBP
I Have Fought the Good Fight, *with music.* Jared B. Waterbury. AH
I have found a way to capture color. The Indian. Thomas Reed. AMV-81
I have found, my dear Miss Ware, a new way of coloring the glass. The Stained Glass Man. Cynthia Macdonald. FiCP
I have found out a gift for my Erin. A Pastoral Ballad by John Bull. Thomas Moore. BIrV; OBSV
I have found out a gig-gig-gift for my fuf-fuf-fair. An Invitation to the Zoological Gardens. *Unknown.* BoAnP
I have four loves, four loves are mine. My Estate. John Drinkwater. HBMV
I have gathered luss/ At the wane of the moon. The Herb-Leech. Joseph Campbell. AnIL; OnYI
I have gone back in boyish wonderment. Return. Sterling A. Brown. BALP; CDC
I have gone down to the ground. 4 1/2 Point 5. Ed Lipman. LFAC
I have gone far from my beloved ones. Jerusalem the Dismembered. Uri Zvi Greenberg, *tr. by* Charles A. Cowen. *Fr.* Jerusalem. TrJP
I have gone out, a possessed witch. Her Kind. Anne Sexton. CoAP; FF; HeIP; LiTM; MP; PPP; TAP; TwAmPo; TwCP; WPOW
I have gone past all those times when the poets. In Memory of Leopardi. James Wright. NaP
I have good news to bring and that is why I sing. The Old Gospel Ship. *Unknown.* FSW
I have got a new-born sister. Choosing a Name. Mary Lamb. HBV-1; OxBChV
I Have Got My Leave. Rabindranath Tagore. *Fr.* Gitanjali. OBMV
I Have Got to Stop Loving You. Ai. GeTw
I have great need that the Saint grant help. Cynewulf, *tr. by* Charles W. Kennedy. *Fr.* Juliana. AnOE
I have grete marvel of a brid. Fragment of a Love Lament. *Unknown.* OxBM
I have grown old. The Old Man's Song. *Tr. fr. Eskimo.* WTO
I have grown past hate and bitterness. Nationality. Mary Gilmore. CBAP; PoAu-1
I have grown used to the retreat of seasons. Lady Anne Bathing. Anthony Delius. PeSA
I have had courage to accuse. The Crowning Gift. Gladys Cromwell. HBMV
I have had enough of women, and enough of love. Wanderer's Song. Arthur Symons. ViBoPo
I have had not one word from her. Sappho, *tr. fr. Greek by* Mary Barnard. PeHV
I have had playmates, I have had companions. The Old Familiar Faces. Charles Lamb. AWP; BLPA; FaBoBe; FaFP; FaPoR; FPL; GTBS; GTBS-P; HBV-1; NBM; NOBE; OBEV; OBRV; PoPl; TreF; ViBoPo
I have had to learn the simplest things. Maximus, to Himself. Charles Olson. *Fr.* The Maximus Poems. CMoP; NeAP; NMP; NOBA; PoM; VGW
I have had to stop answering yes and no. Diseases of the Moon. Doug Fetherling. NeAC
I Have Heard. *Unknown.* FiBHP
I have heard/ He does not bestow horses for poems. A Miserly Patron. *Unknown, tr. by* Myles Dillon. AnIL
I have heard echoes and seen visions of you. Jerked Heartstrings in Town. Emily B. C. Jones. HBMV
I have heard how in Ohio. Coal for Mike. Bertolt Brecht, *tr. by* H. R. Hays. PoPl
I have heard ingenuous Indians say. Roger Williams. SCAP
I have heard of fish. The Sun. Anne Sexton. NYBP; PBWP
I have heard of this destruction. The Letter. Charles Reznikoff. VWA
"I have heard," said a maid of Montclair. Opportunity's Knock. Morris Bishop. TDH
I have heard some jealous women say. Romantic. George Garrett. HoPM
I have heard talk of bold Robin Hood. Robin Hood's Golden Prize. *Unknown.* ESPB
I have heard tell somewhere. The Old Dog in the Ruins of the Graves at Arles. James Wright. NNaP
I have heard that hysterical women say. Lapis Lazuli. W. B. Yeats. ChMP; CMoP; CoBMV; DTC; FaBoMo; FaBoTw; FF; InPK; InPS; LiTB; LiTM; MAT; MoPo; MoVE; NoAM; NOBE; NoP; OAEL-2; OAEP; PP; PPoe; TEP
I have heard the pigeons of the Seven Woods. In the Seven Woods. W. B. Yeats. CMoP; LoBV; NoAM
I have heard the stirring chorus. I Have Heard. *Unknown.* FiBHP
I have heard your voice floating, royal and real. To Dinah Washington. Etheridge Knight. PoBA
I have hopped, when properly wound up, the whole length. The Tin Frog. Russell Hoban. RHPC
I have humped my bluey in all the States. My Old Black Billy. Edward Harrington. PoAu-1
I have hunted the first ice. First Ice of Winter. Michael Shorb. AMV-81
I have imagined all this. The Sleeping. Lynn Emanuel. MAYP
I have in my hand here a brown bottle. The Bottle. Al Levine. GrPl
I have in my house. My House. Jane W. Krows. SoPo
I have inherited the universe! Ode to Joy. Michael McClure. GP
I have it in my heart to serve God so. Sonnet: Of His Lady in Heaven. Jacopo da Lentino, *tr. by* Dante Gabriel Rossetti. AWP
I have just come down from my father. The Hospital Window. James Dickey. BiP; CoPo; DiL; HeIP

"I have just come from the salt, salt sea." The House Carpenter. *Unknown.* AS
I have just flown 1100 miles from Australia. Christchurch, N. Z. Earle Birney. OxBC
I have just realized the leaves. Us. Jiri Wyatt. LTB
I have just seen a [most] beautiful thing. The Black Finger. Angelina Weld Grimké. AmNP; PoBA
I have killed the moth flying around. Moth-Terror. Benjamin De Casseres. TrJP
I have known it from the beginning. Aristophanes' Symposium. Rita Mae Brown. IHMS
I have known nights rain-washed and crystal-clear. Wisdom. Frank Yerby. AmNP
I have known one bound to a bed by wrist and ankle. The Choice. Hilary Corke. MP; NYBP
I have known the inexorable sadness of pencils. Dolor. Theodore Roethke. AmPP; AP; BiP; CABA; CMoP; CoBMV; HeIP; HoPM; InPK; InPS; LiTM; MoVE; NMP; NoAM; PoA; PPON
I have known the silence of the stars and of the sea. Silence. Edgar Lee Masters. MoAmPo
I have known the strange nurses of Kindness. But I Do Not Need Kindness. Gregory Corso. CoPo; NeAP
I have known two worlds. T. S. Eliot. *Fr.* The Rock. OxBoCh
I have known what it is to love. Love. Darwin T. Turner. BALP
I Have Labored Sore. *Unknown.* WeW
I have lain in the sun. Fortunatus Nimium [*or* Nimium Fortunatus]. Robert Bridges. BrPo; MoAB; MoBrPo
I have learned. Wordsworth. *Fr.* Tintern Abbey. TRV
I have learned sloppiness from an old sow. For the Eating of Swine. Rodney Jones. MAYP
I have learned the wondrous secret. Abiding. A. B. Simpson. STF
I have learned to go back and walk around. Time-Travel. Sharon Olds. AMV-80
I have led a good life, full of peace and quiet. The Good Boy. *Unknown.* AS
I have led her home, my love, my only friend. Tennyson. *Fr.* Maud. ChER; EBVV; ELP; FiP; PoEL-5
I have left a basket of dates. The Little Sister of the Prophet. Marjorie Pickthall. HBV-2
I Have Lighted the Candles, Mary. Kenneth Patchen. TrCP
I have lived and died. The Edge. James K. Bowen. AMV-80
I have lived and I have loved. Vixi. *At. to* Charles Mackay. HBV-2
I have lived in important places, times. Epic. Patrick Kavanagh. BIrV; CIP; IPY; OxBI
I Have Lived Long Enough. Shakespeare. *Fr.* Macbeth, V, iii. TrGrPo
I have lived long enough, having seen one thing, that love hath an end. Hymn to Proserpine. Swinburne. EBVV; OAEL-2; OAEP; OBNC; OBVV; PoEL-5; SeCeV; TEP; VLP; WHA
I have looked at this photograph. Rescue. Dabney Stuart. NYBP
I have lost, and lately, these. Upon the Loss[e] of His Mistresses. Robert Herrick. AnAnS-2; CaPo; OAEP; SeCV-1
I have lost her, I know. Mother. Daniel Lawrence Kelleher. NeIP
"I have lost my portmanteau." The Bishop and His Portmanteau. *Unknown.* DBV
I Have Lost My Shoes. Constantino Suasnavar, *tr. fr. Spanish by* Muna Lee. FaPON
I have loved colors, and not flowers. Amends to Nature. Arthur Symons. HBMV
I have loved coming by the back roads. Rural Route. R. T. Smith. AMV-81
I Have Loved England. Alice Duer Miller. *Fr.* The White Cliffs. BLPL; PoLF
I Have Loved Flowers. Robert Bridges. GoJo; MoAB; MoBrPo (Song: "I have loved flowers that fade.") VLP
I have loved large cities, capitals of the world. The Master City. Rose J. Orente. GoYe
I have loved so many violent loves. Declaration at Forty. Judson Crews. UnTE
I have loved thirty by three. Gormley, *tr. by* Joan Keefe. *Fr.* Gormley's Laments. PBWP
I have loved to-night; from love's last bordering steep. The Happy Night. J. C. Squire. HBMV
I have lucky teeth. I'm Lucky. Charlotte Mandel. AMV-81
I have lyric aspiration. The Curse of Faint Praise. Irwin Edman. InMe
I have made a sirventes against the city of Toulouse. Sirventes. Paul Blackburn. NeAP; PoM
I have made tales in verse, but this man made. The Waggon-Maker. John Masefield. EBEV
I have marked, as on the heather now I strayed. As on the Heather. Reinmar von Hagenau, *tr. by* Jethro Bithell. AWP
I have met them at close of day. Easter, 1916. W. B. Yeats. BrPo; CABA; ChMP; CMoP; CoBMV; FaBoMo; FaPoR; HAP; InPS; LiTM; MoAB; NIP; NoAM; NOBE; NoP; OAEL-2; OBWP; OxBI; OxBTC; PPoe; PPP; SeCeV
I have mislaid the torment and the fear. Success. William Empson. OxBTC
I have more memories than if I had lived a thousand years. Spleen LXXVI. Baudelaire, *tr. by* Anthony Hecht. NAWM-2
I have moved to Dublin to have it out with you. John Berryman. NoAM
I have my heart on my fist. The Tomb of the Kings. Anne Hébert, *tr. by* Kathleen Weaver. PBWP
I have my piety too, which could. An Epitaph on Master Vincent Corbett. Ben Jonson. JCP
"I have my verses, every line, every word." Love the Wild Swan. Robinson Jeffers. MoAB
I have named you queen. The Queen. Pablo Neruda, *tr. by* Donald D. Walsh. OLR
I have never been on the cloudy slopes of Olympus. The Valley of Men. Uri Zvi Greenberg, *tr. by* Robert Mezey *and* Ben Gold Zion. VWA
I have never beheld you, O pawky Scot. Who Taught Caddies to Count? or, A Burnt Golfer Fears the Child. Ogden Nash. LiSp
I have never seen him, this invisible member of the panel, this thirteenth juror. The People vs. the People. Kenneth Fearing. MoAmPo
I have never seen that beast. Rhinoceros. Adrien Stoutenburg. BoAnP
I have never seen the place where I was born. Birthplace. Tahereh Saffarzadeh, *tr. by* Deirdre Lashgari. WPOW
I have never seen volcanoes. Emily Dickinson. PoEL-5
I have new shoes in the Fall-time. New Shoes. Alice Wilkins. SUS; TiPo
I have no ale. The Muse. W. H. Davies. BrPo
I have no brother,—they who meet me now. Thy Brother's Blood. Jones Very. AP; NOBA; PoEL-4; QFR; TAP
I have no care for systematic theology. Eschatology. Morris Bishop. WhC
I have no chill despondence that I am. Farewell to the Muses. John Hamilton Reynolds. OBRV
I have no desire to live, but I am afraid of death. Ts'ai Yen, *tr. by* Kenneth Rexroth *and* Ling Chung. Eighteen Verses Sung to a Tatar Reed Whistle, XI. WPOW
I have no dog, but it must be. My Dog. John Kendrick Bangs. BLPA; BLPL; FaBoBe
I have no embroidered headband. Sappho, *tr. fr. Greek by* Willis Barnstone. BoWoP
I have no folded flock to show. The Battle-Flag of Sigurd. Dora Greenwell. OBVV
I have no more a golden store. The Merry Jovial Beggar. Peter Casey, *tr. by* Douglas Hyde. WTO
"I have no name." Infant Joy. Blake. *Fr.* Songs of Innocence. FaPON; GoJo; HBV-1; HBVY; LAuP; LoBV; NAs; PoLF; SiSoSe; TEP; ViBoPo
I have no news of the animals. The Animals. Charles Simic. GeTw
I Have No Pain. *Unknown.* FaBoCo
I Have No Strength for Mine. Joanne Kyger. PoM
I have no wife. To the Old Masters. Wing Tek Lum. BrSi
I have no wings, but yet I fly. Mary Austin. *Fr.* Rhyming Riddles. SoPo; TiPo
I have no wit, no words, no tears. A Better Resurrection. Christina Rossetti. EBCP; HBV-2; OxBoCh; TrPWD; VLP
I have no word to match with its white wonder. Of Wounds. Sister Mary Madeleva. ISi
I have not been as Joshua when he fought. Three Helpers in Battle. Mary Elizabeth Coleridge. EaLo
"I have not come here to talk." The Beggar on the Beach. Horace Gregory. NMP
I have not ever seen my father's grave. Father Son and Holy Ghost. Audre Lorde. PoBA
I have not gathered gold. To Death. Padraic Pearse, *tr. by* Thomas MacDonagh. AnIV
I have not gone like a pilgrim. The Tourist. Garret Keizer. AMV-81
I have not known a quieter thing than ships. Ships in Harbour. David Morton. EtS
I Have Not Lingered in European Monasteries. Leonard Cohen. NOBC
I have not loved the world, nor the world me. The Poet and the World. Bryon. *Fr.* Childe Harold's Pilgrimage. OBRV; SeCePo
I have not needed you for thirteen years. Father. Robert Pack. CoPo
I have not seen your writing. The Letter. Patricia Beer. OxBC
I have not so much emulated the birds that musically sing. To Soar in Freedom and in Fullness of Power. Walt Whitman. RFM
"I have not sought Thee, I have not found Thee." Love Is Stronger than Death. Christina Rossetti. LO
I have not spent the April of my time. Sonnet [*or* Youth]. Bartholomew Griffin. Fidessa, More Chaste than Kind, XXXV. AAS; EIL; OBSC
I have not the purity. Light. Jon Silkin. NoAM
I have not told my garden yet. Emily Dickinson. AA
I have not used my darkness well. Squall. Stanley Moss. CoAP

I have not where to lay my head. Mountain Song. Harriet Monroe. HBV-2
I have not written my poem. The Experiment That Failed. John Logan. NU
I have not yet begun to relate. Lune Concrete. Raymond Federman. MOON
I have nothing new to ask of you. Another Year Come. W. S. Merwin. NYBP; OFD; PAI; PCP
I have observed the learned astronomer. For Whitman. Diane Wakoski. SUW
I have oft wondred, why thou didst elect. Madam Gabrina, or the Ill-favourd Choice. Henry King. CavP
"I have often been told," said the horse. The Thoroughbred Horse. Oliver Herford. TDH
I have often wisht to love; what shall I do? The Request. Abraham Cowley. AnAnS-2
I have packed away your clothes. Relics. Suzanne Gegna. AMV-81
I have poured my dreams in the pot's dim womb. Peter Titheradge. Teatime Variations: After W. B. Yeats. FaBoPa
I have praised many loved ones in my song. Mother. Theresa Helburn. FaPON; HBV-1; OHIP
I have properly spoken. A Poem for Anton Schmidt. William Pillen. VWA
I have put my days and dreams out of mind. Swinburne. *Fr.* The Triumph of Time. ViBoPo
I have received jewels of conspicuous beauty. Egan O'Rahilly, *tr. by* P. S. Dinneen *and* T. O'Donoghue. *Fr.* On a Pair of Shoes Presented to Him. OnYI
I have renounced already that hope. I renounce the sudden Whole. Spring Song. Rayner Heppenstall. NeBP
I have risen from your body. The Onion. John Thompson. NOBC
I have robbed the garrulous streets. For the Goddess Too Well Known. Elsa Gidlow. PeHV
I have said I will marry the moon. The One-eyed Bridegroom. Constance Urdang. MOON
I have said that the soul is not more than the body. A Hub for the Universe. Walt Whitman. Song of Myself, XLVIII. FaFP; TrGrPo
I Have Seen. Kathleen McCracken. AMV-80
I have seen/ A curious child. Wordsworth. *Fr.* The Excursion, IV. OBRV; TreFT
I have seen a gum-tree. Flesh. Mary Fullerton. PoAu-1
I have seen a lovely thing. Blight. Arna Bontemps. BANP; CDC
I have seen all the words that are done under the sun. All Is Vanity. Bible, *O.T. Fr.* Ecclesiastes. TRV
I have seen an old street weeping. La Rue de la Montagne Sainte-Gènevième. Dorothy Dudley. HBMV
I Have Seen Black Hands. Richard Wright. NoAM; PoBA
I have seen bus depots. Reflecting on the Aging-Process. Robert Peters. BXAP
I have seen faces of want. The Songs of Maximus, V. Charles Olson. *Fr.* The Maximus Poems. PAI
I have seen flowers come in stony places. An Epilogue. John Masefield. FaBoEE; OxBTC
I have seen her, wonderful! This Version of Love. Dorothy Hewett. CBAP
I Have Seen Higher, Holier Things than These. Arthur Hugh Clough. OAEP
I have seen in the Virginia forest. Apparition. John Peale Bishop. MoVE
I have seen mannequins. W. J. Turner. *Fr.* The Seven Days of the Sun. OBMV
I have seen, O desolate one, the voice has its tower. Bell Tower. Léonie Adams. MoAB; MoAmPo; PoPl
I have seen old ships sail like swans asleep. The Old Ships. James Elroy Flecker. BrPo; CH; EtS; EvOK; FaBoRV; MoBrPo; MOS; MoVE; OBMV; PoPle; PoRA; RoGo; WHA
I have seen Our Lady in Ireland, being carried in procession in May. Heart for All Her Children. Albert J. Hebert, Jr. ISi
I have seen some good friends. Because San Quentin Killed Two More Today. Ed Lipman. LFAC
I have seen tall chimneys without smoke. Drought [*or* Soliloquy]. Frederick E. Laight. CaP; OBCV
I have seen the Birds of Paradise. The Birds of Paradise. John Peale Bishop. GoJo
I have seen the hardened innocence. Repetition. Wyatt Prunty. AMV-81
I have seen the light coming up over the town, like ash. Overture to Strangers. Phyllis Haring. PeSA
I have seen the poets of the West. That Poem. Juan Sáez Burgos, *tr. by* Julio Marzán. InW
I Have Seen the Robins Fall. Louis Dudek. CaP
I have seen the sea in many moods. The Sea. Ken Noyle. MOS
I have seen the smallest minds of my generation. Problem in Social Geometry—the Inverted Square! Ray Durem. NBP; PoBA
I have seen the soft light flicker. Message from Ohanapecosh Glacier. W. M. Ransom. CDW
I have seen the white horsemen riding to hell. Apocalypse and Resurrection. John Bayliss. EAS
I have seen the young Negroes and Puerto Ricans. A Documentary on Airplane Glue. David Henderson. MAT
I have seen them at many hours. Moths. Julia Fields. *Fr.* Poems: Birmingham 1962-1964. PoBA; PoNe
I have seen you suffer in the midst of winters. Harlem. Jean Brierre, *tr. by* John F. Matheus. TTY
I have seen your feet gilded by morning. Metamorphoses of M. John Peale Bishop. ErPo
I have seldom loved more than one thing at a time. My Love for All Things Warm and Breathing. William Kloefkorn. AMV-81
I Have Set My Heart So High. *Unknown.* OAEL-1; OxBM
I have set out to follow the day. The Cry of Generations. Mordechai Husid, *tr. by* Seymour Mayne *and* Rivka Augenfeld. VWA
I have settled down. Sleepless on a Summer Night. Umberto Saba, *tr. by* Keith Bosley. VWA
I have ships that went to sea. Ships at Sea. Barry Gray. EtS
I have shut my little sister in from life and light. The Factories. Margaret Widdemer. HBV-2
I have so many faults myself. What I See in Me. *Unknown.* STF
I have so much faith in you. I believe. To Trust. Antonia Pozzi, *tr. by* Lynne Lawner. PBWP
I Have Some Friends before Me Gone, *with music. Unknown.* AH
I have something for you to laugh at, Cato. Catullus, *tr. fr. Latin.* PeHV
I have sometimes thought. The Teacher to Heloise (After Waddell). Daniel Burke. AMV-81
I have sought long with steadfastness. Sir Thomas Wyatt. EnRePo; SiPS
I have sown beside all waters in my day. A Black Man Talks of Reaping. Arna Bontemps. AmNP; BANP; BPo; CDC; FB; IDB; PoBA; PoNe
I have sown upon the fields. The Idle Flowers. Robert Bridges. BoNaP; ChTr
I have spoken to a goat. The Goat. Umberto Saba, *tr. by* Anita Barrows. VWA
I have spot-resistant trousers. Summer Song. W. W. Watt. FiBHP; QQQ
I have stopped scrubbing his shirts a moment. Milton's Wife on Her Twenty-third Birthday. Jane Conant-Bissell. AMV-80
I have struggled all day with a thought like a wild noble horse. Wild Horse. Elder Olson. GrPl
I have studied the tight curls on the back of your neck. Movement Song. Audre Lorde. CNA
I have sung, to deceive the evil-sounding clock of time. Jean Cocteau, *tr. by* Wallace Fowlie. *Fr.* Plain Song. PoPl
I have sunk to the cold weary depths of despair! Mourning. Josephine Van Fossan. STF
I have sworn ten thousand times. Kenneth Rexroth, *after the Greek of* Palladas. NNaP
I have taken that vow. The Red-haired Man's Wife. James Stephens. HBMV; MoBrPo; OBVV
I have taken the woman of beauty. The Bear's Song. *Unknown, tr. by* Constance Lindsay Skinner. AWP; BPAW
I have taken up the dulcimer again. Widow to Her Son. R. T. Smith. Str
I have the greatest fun at night. The Quilt. Mary Effie Lee Newsome. CDC
I have these words you sent me. Long-Distance. Carol Burns. AMV-81
I have this bulging belly because. The Pot-bellied Anachronism. Ann Darr. GP
I have this deal of death about my hands. Blood. Ray Bremser. NeAP
I have this to say, if I can say it. Before Sentence Is Passed. R. P. Blackmur. LiTA
I have thought long this wild wet night that brought no rest. A Sleepless Night. Egan O'Rahilly, *tr. by* Frank O'Connor. AnIL; KiLC
I have thought of beaches, fields. Bundles. Carl Sandburg. MoAmPo
I have threatened Theology a thousand times over. Grace for Theology. William Langland. *Fr.* The Vision of Piers Plowman. GoBC
I have three candles in my room. Candle-lighting Song. Arthur Ketchum. HBMV
I Have Three Daughters. Ruth Stone. NMM
I have thrown wide my window. Midnight. Michael Roberts. OBMV
I Have to Have It. Dorothy Aldis. SoPo
I have to live with myself, and so. Myself. Edgar A. Guest. BLPA; BLPL
I have to stop answering yes and no. Diseases of the Moon. Doug Fetherling. POL
I have to take my little brother. Lil' Bro'. Karama Fufuka. RHPC
I have to thank God I'm a woman. The Affinity. Anna Wickham. HBMV
I have told you. Tenth Symphony. John Ashbery. NOBA
I have told you in another poem, whether you've read it or not. My Burial Place. Robinson Jeffers. AP
I have tongues in secret places—no one. Tongues. Sharon Berg. AMV-80

I have tossed hours upon the tides of fever. Bout with Burning. Vassar Miller. LiTM; MoAmPo; NePoEA
I have touched her liquid fur. The Angora. Jim Gerard. AMV-80
I have travell'd this wide world over. Old Rosin the Beau. *Unknown.* PSoN
I have travelled sometime up and down our coast. Gazeteer of Newfoundland. Michael Harrington. CaP
I have trod this path a hundred times. The Miracle. Emerson. FM
I have turned to the landscape because men disappoint me. The Ram's Horn. John Hewitt. BIrV
I Have Twelve Oxen. *Unknown.* ChTr; GBP
(Twelve Oxen, The.) CH
I have two dashing, prancing steeds. Steeds. Paul Hiebert. WHW
I have two friends—two glorious friends—two better could not be. The Two Friends. Charles Godfrey Leland. AA
I have two sons and a son-in-law. The Frenchman's Ball. *Unknown.* OuSiCo
I have two sparrows white as snow. Michael Drayton. *Fr.* The Muses' Elysium: The Second Nymphal. PBBP
"I have two wives." Mohammed Ibrahim Speaks. Martha Beidler. FF
I have walked a great while over the snow. The Witch. Mary Elizabeth Coleridge. BrRo; NCEP; WPE
I have walked always in a veil. Imprisoned. Eunice Tietjens. HBMV
I have walked and prayed for this young child an hour. W. B. Yeats. *Fr.* A Prayer for My Daughter. ViBoPo
I have walked through many lives. The Layers. Stanley Kunitz. AMV-80
I have wanted other things more than lovers. Monody to the Sound of Zithers. Kay Boyle. PoA
I have watched a thousand days. Salonikan Grave. Kipling. *Fr.* Epitaphs of the War, 1914-18. OAEP
I have watched you. Saying Goodbye. Suzanne Juhasz. IHMS
I have watched you dancing. Theme Brown Girl. Elton Hill. NBP
I have watched your fingers drum. The Hand. Howard Moss. TAP
I have wept a million tears. The Man to the Angel. "Æ." OBVV
I have wept with the spring storm. After the Persian. Louise Bogan. PoA
I have wished a bird would fly away. A Minor Bird. Robert Frost. CMoP; PB
I have with fishing-rod and line. The Wounded Hawk. Herbert Palmer. FaBoTw
I have worshipped in churches and chapels. At My Mother's Knee. *Unknown.* STF
I have wrapped my dreams in a silken cloth. For a Poet. Countee Cullen. PoNe; TTY
I have written high school teachers down savants. Chant Royal from a Copydesk. Rufus Terral. InMe
I have wrought these words together out of a wryed existence. The Wife's Complaint. *Unknown, tr. by* Michael Alexander. BoLoP
I have xeroxed my navel. Certified Copy. Ann Deagon. NIP
I have your lewd letter received. Skelton Laureate, Defender, against Lusty Garnesche, Well-beseen Christopher, Challenger. John Skelton. TW
I haven't got a cent. Penny Whistle Blues. E. H. L. Island. InMe
I haven't sung your praise. To My Country. "Rahel." PBWP
I Hear a River. Trumbull Stickney. NCEP
I hear a sound, like music through the gale. The Last Longhorn's Farewell. John P. Sjolander. BPAW
I hear a sudden cry of pain! The Snare. James Stephens. CH; CMoP; HBMV; OxBI; PDV; TiPo
I Hear a Voice. H. Leivick, *tr. fr. Yiddish by* David G. Roskies. VWA
I hear a whisper in the heated air. Ceylon. A. Hugh Fisher. HBV-2
I hear a whistling. Emmett Till. James A. Emanuel. CNA; NIP; PoBA
I hear a young girl singing. Beside the Blackwater. Norreys Jephson O'Conor. HBMV
I hear again the tread of war go thundering through the land. Albert Sidney Johnston. Kate Brownlee Sherwood. PAH
I Hear America Griping. Morris Bishop. AmFN; QQQ
I Hear America Singing. Walt Whitman. AmFN; AWP; FaBoBe; FaBV; FaFP; FaPON; FF; FPL; HAP; LiTA; MoAmPo; PAL; PDV; PoPl; PoSC; SaC; TreFS; TrGrPo; WeW; YaD
I Hear an Army [Charging upon the Land]. James Joyce. Chamber Music, XXXVI. AnIV; AWP; InPK; LiTM; MoBrPo; NoAM; NOBE; OxBI; OxBTC; PoRA; PrIm; SyP; ViBoPo
I hear and behold God in every object, yet understand God not in the least. Walt Whitman. *Fr.* Song of Myself. WGRP
I Hear and See Not Strips of Cloth Alone. Walt Whitman. WaaP
I hear enormous noises in the night. March Winds. Cecil Francis Lloyd. CaP
I hear in my brain all New England echoing down around me. New England Suite. Charles Philbrick. TwAmPo
I hear in my heart, I hear in its ominous pulses. The Wild Ride. Louise Imogen Guiney. AA; HBV-2
I hear it in the river first. Spring Sequence. Judith Minty. AMV-80
"I Hear It Said." Barbara Young. BLPA
I Hear It Was Charged against Me. Walt Whitman. LiTA; MoAmPo; PPP
I hear leaves drinking rain. The Rain. W. H. Davies. OxBTC; TiPo
I hear many voices. To Adhiambo. Gabriel Okara. PBA
I hear my mother whose hips have/ broadened. Violets for Mother. Lonny Kaneko. BrSi
I hear some say, "This man is not in love!" Michael Drayton. Idea XXIV. OAEP; TrGrPo
I hear that Andromeda. Sappho, *tr. fr. Greek by* Mary Barnard. PBWP
I hear that Lycoris has buried. Martial, *tr. fr. Latin.* DBV
I hear the autumn winds blow down the sky. The Widow. Mariana B. Davenport. AMV-80
I hear the beat. The Talking Drums. Kojo Gyinaye Kyei. PBA
I hear the doctor's loud success. Waiting for the Doctor. Colette Inez. IHMS
I hear the engine pounding. The Ways of Trains. Elizabeth J. Coatsworth. SoPo; TiPo
I hear the halting footsteps of a lass. Harlem Shadows. Claude McKay. AmPP; BANP; PoNe
I hear the low wind wash the softening snow. The Flight of the Geese. Sir Charles G. D. Roberts. *Fr.* Songs of the Common Day. PeCV
I hear the man downstairs slapping the hell out of his stupid wife again. The .38. Ted Joans. NNP; WeW
I hear the noise about thy keel. Tennyson. In Memoriam A. H. H., X. EBVV
I hear the robins singing in the rain. On a Gloomy Easter. Alice Freeman Palmer. OHIP
I hear the shadowy horses, their long manes a-shake. Michael Robartes Bids His Beloved Be at Peace [*or* The Shadowy Horses]. W. B. Yeats. BrPo; NoAM; SyP
I hear the sound of affliction. They are weeping. How It Is. Uri Zvi Greenberg, *tr. by* Robert Mezey *and* Ben Zion Gold. VWA
I hear the voice of the bells. My New Year Prayer. *Unknown.* STF
I Hear the Wave. *Unknown, tr. fr. Middle Irish by* Eugene O'Curry. OnYI
I hear the wind a-blowing. Mad Song. Hester Sigerson. AnIV
I hear their signal alert. Keys. Glen Rockwell. AMV-81
I hear them. . .the crickets. Owl. Rokwaho. STE
I hear voices praising Tshombe, and the Portuguese. Hatred of Men with Black Hair. Robert Bly. NaP; TW
I hear you call. The Call of the River Nun. Gabriel Okara. PBA
I hear you, little bird. Joy of the Morning. Edwin Markham. AA; FaPON; HBV-2
I hear you, little spirit, in the bushes. To Puck. Beatrice Llewellyn Thomas. HBMV
I Hear You've Let Go. Rosario Ferre, *tr. fr. Spanish by* Willis Barnstone. BoWoP
I heard a/ couple of fleas. Archy, the Cockroach, Speaks. Don Marquis. *Fr.* Certain Maxims of Archy. FaPON
I heard a bird at break of day. Overtones. William Alexander Percy. HBMV; HBVY
I heard a bird at dawn. The Rivals. James Stephens. FaPON; InvP; MoVE; NoAM; OBEV; OBMV; PoPl
I Heard a Bird Sing. Oliver Herford. NTCP; PDV; PoLF; RHPC; SiSoSe; SoPo; YeAr
I heard a brooklet gushing. Whither? Wilhelm Müller, *tr. by* Longfellow. AWP
I heard a clash, and a cry. Middle Ages. Siegfried Sassoon. SO
I heard a cow low, a bonnie cow low. The Queen of Elfland's Nourrice [*or* Elfan's Nourice]. *Unknown.* ESPB; FaBoCh
I heard a cry in the night from a far-flung host. Memorial Day. William E. Brooks. PAL; PGD
I heard a fly buzz—when I died. Emily Dickinson. AmPP; AP; BoWoP; CABA; CMoP; DL; FF; HAP; HoPM; InPK; LiTA; LiTM; MasP; MoAB; MoAmPo; MoVE; NePA; NoAM; NOBA; NoP; OxBA; PAI; PoRA; PPP; SCV; SeCeV; SOTW; TAP; TwAmPo; WeW
I heard a herald's note announce the coming of a king. Rex Mundi. David Gascoyne. ChMP
I heard a horseman. The Horseman. Walter de la Mare. GoJo; RHPC; SoPo; SUS; TiPo
I Heard a Linnet Courting. Robert Bridges. BrPo; LiTB; LiTM; OBMV
(Linnet, The.) OBEV
I heard a mouse. The Mouse. Elizabeth J. Coatsworth. FaPON; MoShBr; OBCA; SoPo; SUS; TiPo
I Heard a Noise and Wishèd for a Sight. *Unknown.* EBEV; EnRePo; HAP; InvP
(Shadow, A.) EIL
(Shadow and Substance.) OAEL-1
I heard a red-winged black-bird singing. A June Day. Sara Teasdale. YeAr
I Heard a Soldier. Herbert Trench. CH; HBV-1
I heard a thousand blended notes. Lines Written in Early Spring. Wordsworth. EnRP; FPL; GTBS; GTBS-P; HBV-1; OAEL-2; OAEP; OBRV; PAI; PoLF; TreFT; TRV

I heard a voice at evening softly say. Day by Day. Julia Harris May. BLRP
I heard a voice that cried, "Make way for those who died!" The March. J. C. Squire. HBMV; OHIP; PoSC
I heard a woman's voice that wailed. In Ruin Reconciled. Aubrey Thomas De Vere. BIrV
I Heard a Young Man Saying. Julia Fields. NNP
I heard an ancient sound: a cock that crew. Daybreak. Frances Cornford. FM
I heard an angel speak last night. A Curse for a Nation. Elizabeth Barrett Browning. SBG; WPE; WPOW
I heard an ignorant crow call, "Life is now." Old Snapshot. Ronald Everson. MoCV
I heard an old farm-wife. The Son. Ridgely Torrence. HBMV; InvP; WHA
I heard Andrew Jackson say, as he closed his Virgil. Andrew Jackson's Speech. Robert Bly. ConAP
I Heard Christ Sing. "Hugh MacDiarmid." NoAM
I Heard de Preachin' of de Word o' God, *with music. Unknown.* BoAN-2
I heard from Rémon, Rémon. Rémon. *Unknown.* TrAS
I heard him faintly, far away. The Corn Crake. James H. Cousins. BoAnP; OnYI
"I heard him fall. He's lying." The Secret. Lonny Kaneko. BrSi
I heard how, to the beat of some quick tune. The Dancer. Sadi, *tr. by* Sir Edwin Arnold. *Fr.* The Bustan. AWP
I Heard Immanuel Singing. Vachel Lindsay. HAP
I heard in the night the pigeons. No Child. Padraic Colum. OBMV
I heard men saying, Leave hope and praying. The Voice of Toil. William Morris. HBV-2
I heard my ancient sea-blood say. A Life. George Edward Woodberry. EtS
I heard my love was going to Yang-chou. *Tr. fr. Chinese by* Arthur Waley. *Fr.* Tzu Yeh Songs. BoWoP
I heard my loved published in church. The False Bride. *Unknown.* OBET
I heard no sound where I stood. The Sleeping House. Tennyson. *Fr.* Maud. FaBoEn; OBNC
I heard of a man. Poem. Leonard Cohen. ELU
I heard of gold at Sutter's Mill. When I Went Off to Prospect. *Unknown.* AmFP
I heard one who said: "Verily." Cassandra. E. A. Robinson. CMoP; LiTA; LiTM; NePA; NoAM; OxBA; PPON; SeCeV
I heard, or seemed to hear, the chiding Sea. Sea-Shore. Emerson. EtS; LiTA; MOS; OxBA
I heard the bells across the trees. Victory Bells. Grace Hazard Conkling. HBV-2; PAH
I heard the bells of Bethlehem ring. The Birds of Bethlehem. Richard Watson Gilder. AA
I Heard the Bells on Christmas Day. Longfellow. *See* Christmas Bells.
I heard the carping [*or* herde a carpyng] of a clerk. Robyn and Gandeleyn. *Unknown.* EnSB; ESPB; OxBB; OxBM
I heard the dogs howl in the moonlight night. A [*or* The] Dream. William Allingham. BIrV; OxBI
I heard the front door close. After a Death. Gregory Orr. GeTw
I heard the happy lark exult. Inst., Ult., and Prox. A. P. Herbert. FaBoUs
I heard the hymn of being sound. Ralph Hodgson. *Fr.* The Song of Honor. LO
I heard the old, old men say. The Old Men Admiring Themselves in the Water. W. B. Yeats. CMoP; FaBoCh; GoJo; PCP
I Heard the Old Song. B. W. Vilakazi, *tr. fr. Zulu.* PeSA
I heard the Poor Old Woman say. Lament for the Poets: 1916. Francis Ledwidge. AnIV; AWP; OnYI; OxBI
I heard the sea murmur in my ears. One Goes with Me along the Shore. Manfred Winkler, *tr. by* Mary Zilzer. VWA
I heard the sighing of the reeds. In Ireland: By the Pool at the Third Rosses. Arthur Symons. FaBoPP; OBNC; VLP
I heard the song of breath. A Song of Breath. Stephen Vincent Benét. MoVE
I heard the songs. The Songs. *Tr. fr. Zuni Indian by* K. Kennedy. WTO
I heard the sparrows shouting "Eat, eat." In the Night Fields. W. S. Merwin. AP; PoCh
I heard the trailing garments of the night. Hymn to the Night. Longfellow. AA; AP; BLPL; HBV-1; HBVY; LoBV; NePA; NOBA; OxBA; TAP; TreFS; TrGrPo; ViBoPo; WHA
I heard the virgins sigh, I saw the sleeke. Obsequies to the Lady Anne Hay. Thomas Carew. AnAnS-2
I heard the voice of Jesus say. The Voice from Galilee. Horatius Bonar. HBV-2
I heard the wild beasts in the wood complain. Mundus Morosus [*or* The World Morose]. Frederick William Faber. ACP; NBM; OBVV
I heard the wild geese flying. Wild Geese. Elinor Chipp. FaPON; HBMV; TiPo
I heard the wind coming. Hearing the Wind at Night. May Swenson. BoNaP
I heard them in their sadness say. Dust. "Æ." HBMV; WGRP
I heard them say, "Her hands are hard as stone." Her Beauty. Max Plowman. HBMV
I heard this morning. Summer 1970. Lindiwe Mabuza. WPOW
I heard—'twas on a morning, but when it was and where. Singing Water. Rudolph Chambers Lehmann. HBMV
I heard two workers say, "This chaos/ Will soon be ended." Idiom of the Hero. Wallace Stevens. OxBA
I Heard You Solemn-sweet Pipes of the Organ. Walt Whitman. NePA; OxBA
I heare the whistling plough-man all day long. On the Plough-Man. Francis Quarles. OBS
I hedge rebellious grasses in. The Stranger. Daniel Henderson. HBMV
"I heeard da ole folks talkin' in our house da other night." Why Adam Sinned. Alex Rogers. BANP
I held a jewel in my fingers. Emily Dickinson. WHA
I Held a Lamb. Kim Worthington. SoPo; TiPo
I Held a Shelley Manuscript. Gregory Corso. VGW
I held Europe in my hand. Yonder. Richard Eberhart. GOA
I held her hand, the pledge of bliss. The Test. Walter Savage Landor. HBV-1
I held it truth, with him who sings. In Memoriam A. H. H., I. Tennyson. EBVV; HBV-2; LiTB; NoP; OBNC
I held on her neck. Doe. Philip Dow. NPGG
I held you. Eventual Proteus. Margaret Atwood. MoCV
I herde a carpyng of a clerk. *See* I heard the carping of a clerk.
I Hereby Swear That to Uphold Your House. Elinor Wylie. *Fr.* One Person. NePA
(Sonnet: "I hereby swear that to uphold your house.") LiTA; MoAB; OxBA
(Sonnet from "One Person.") MoAmPo
I, Hermes, have been set up. Anyte, *tr. fr. Greek by* Kenneth Rexroth. OBVE
I hesitate to write about the spring. The Faithful Lover. Robert Pack. NePoEA
I hid my heart. The Robber. Ivy O. Eastwick. SiSoSe
I hid my heart in a nest of roses. A Ballad of Dreamland. Swinburne. HBV-1
I Hid My Love. John Clare. *See* Secret Love.
I hid the peppermint. I Had to Be Secret. Mark Van Doren. SO
I Hid You. Miklós Radnóti, *tr. fr. Hungarian by* Steven Polgar, Stephen Berg, *and* S. J. Marks. LLLT; VWA
I hit my wife and went out and saw. The Winter Moon. Tagaki Kyozo, *tr. by* James Kirkup *and* Nakamo Michio. LLLT
I hoard a little spring of secret tears. On Shooting a Swallow in Early Youth. Charles Tennyson Turner. FM
I hoe and I plow. Farmer. Liberty Hyde Bailey. YeAr
I Hoed and Trenched and Weeded. A. E. Housman. A Shropshire Lad, LXIII. LiTM; MoBrPo; TrGrPo; UnPo; VLP; WeW
I hold a letter in my hand. A Poem for the Meeting of the American Medical Association. Oliver Wendell Holmes. PoEL-5
I hold a newspaper, reading. Fish. Shinkichi Takahashi, *tr. by* Lucien Stryk. NU
I Hold Him Happiest. Menander, *tr. fr. Greek.* TreFT
I hold him, verily, of mean emprise. Canzone: He Perceives His Rashness in Love, but Has No Choice. Guido Guinicelli, *tr. by* Dante Gabriel Rossetti. AWP
I hold him wise and wel y-taught. Bear a Horn and Blow It Not. *Unknown.* OxBM
I hold in my hands. Look Closely. Morton Marcus. FF
I hold it good—as who shall hold it bad? Columbia's Agony. "Orpheus C. Kerr." OBAL
I hold my daughter up to the firelight. Lilly's Song. Evan Zimroth. AMV-81
I hold my honey and I store my bread. My Dreams, My Works, Must Wait till after Hell. Gwendolyn Brooks. NoP
I hold no dream of fortune vast. Success. Edgar A. Guest. TreF
I hold that Christian grace abounds. My Creed. Alice Cary. WGRP
I hold that when a person dies. A Creed. John Masefield. HBMV; WGRP
I hold you at last in my hand. The Butterfly. Alice Freeman Palmer. HBV-1
I hope he doesn't see me walking past his bed. Letter. Alexander Bergman. TrJP
I Hope I Don't Have You Next Semester, But. Edwin S. Godsey. HoPM
I hope the old Romans. Ancient History. Arthur Guiterman. OBCA
I hope there is a resurrection day. Resurrection. Harry Kemp. HBV-2
I hope when I am dead that I shall lie. Oblivion. Jessie Redmond Fauset. BANP; PoNe

I hope when you're yourself and twice my age. Metaphor for My Son. John Holmes. MiAP
I hoped/ —the night came anyway. Conjugation of the Verb, "To Hope." Lou Lipsitz. FiCP
I hoped that with the brave and strong. He Doeth All Things Well. Anne Brontë. TRV
I hoped to see the sun today, but ice. On the Edge. Frank Dwyer. AMV-81
I hung my verses in the wind. The Test. Emerson. AA; OBAL; PP
I hunt. Photographer. Philip Booth. EyDe
I, Icarus. Alden Nowlan. NCSH
I idle stand that I may find employ. The Idler. Jones Very. AA; HBV-2
I imagine him still with heavy brow. Beethoven's Death Mask. Stephen Spender. OxBTC
I imagine the time of our meeting. Forms of the Earth at Abiquiu. N. Scott Momaday. CDW
I imagine this [*or* the] midnight moment's forest. The Thought-Fox. Ted Hughes. FaBoMo; HeIP; NCSH; NePoEA-2; NoAM; NoP; NYBP; SCV
I imagined her dead, killed by some local maniac who. Jim Harrison. *Fr.* Ghazals. InPS
I imagined the bombs and fighters. Air Raid. Peter Wild. Psk
I implore thy pity, Thou, the unique, I adore. De Profundis Clamavi. Baudelaire, *tr. by* Arthur Symons. SyP
I, in My Intricate Image. Dylan Thomas. EAS; LiTB
I in Thee, and Thou in Me. Christopher Pearse Cranch. HBV-2
I in these flowery meads would be. The Angler's Wish. Izaac Walton. *Fr.* The Compleat Angler. HBV-1
I inherited forty acres from my father. Cooney Potter. Edgar Lee Masters. *Fr.* Spoon River Anthology. CTBA; SaC
I intended an ode. Urceus Exit [*or* Triolet]. Austin Dobson. *Fr.* Rose-Leaves. HBV-1; OBEV; PoPle
I invite you, child, to dance. You come. I bow my blond head. Song for a Dance. Abraham Sutskever, *tr. by* Ruth Whitman. VWA
I invited Mozart to dinner. The Dinner. Gregory Orr. POL
I invoke the land of Ireland. Invocation to Ireland [*or* Aimirgin's Invocation]. *At. to* Amergin, *tr. by* R. A. S. Macalister *and* Eoin MacNeill. AnIV; OnYI
I is for Ignorant Ida. Ignorant Ida. Isabel Frances Bellows. TDH
I is the ghost of Stevey Fizzlegig. The Ghost. ——— O'Brien. NOEC
I jabbed a jack-knife in my thumb. My Sore Thumb. Burges Johnson. HBVY
I jes' don' know ef de kohn'll grow. De Good Lawd Know My Name. Frank L. Stanton. WBLP
I Jocky Bell o'Braikenbrow lyes under this stane. On Jocky Bell. *Unknown.* FaBoEE
I journeyed on a winter's day. Jane Smith. Kipling. HBV-1; SpRo
I joy, deare Mother, when I view. The British Church. George Herbert. AnAnS-1
I joy not in no earthly bliss. The Quiet Mind. *Unknown.* OBSC
I jump with terror seeing him. Modes of Pleasure. Thom Gunn. PeHV; PPP
I just came by the prison door. Pray Remember the Poor. Christopher Smart. NOEC
I just said I didn't know. Parachutes, My Love, Could Carry Us Higher. Barbara Guest. NeAP
I just thought. Postcard to a Foetus. Kirk Robertson. GP
I just turned a pan. Another Day. Isabella Maria Brown. PoNe
I Just Walk Around, Around, Around. Moishe Kulbak, *tr. fr. Yiddish by* Ruth Whitman. VWA
I Just Wanna Stay Home. Irwin Silber. FSW
I just want to get back to Birmingham. Third Alley Blues. *Unknown.* BluL
I keep feeling all space as my image. Poem. Sanders Russell. EAS
I keep him waiting, tuck in the curtains. Planning the Perfect Evening. Rita Dove. MAYP
I keep my parents in a garden. Eden Is a Zoo. Margaret Atwood. WPE
I keep pushing this. The Prophets. Richard Shelton. NYBP
I keep seeing your car in the streets. The Little Brother Poem. Naomi Shihab Nye. Str
I keep thinking of you standing in Korea, in the courtyard. Solitary. Sharon Olds. SOTS
I Keep Three Wishes Ready. Annette Wynne. PDV; SoPo
I Keep to Myself Such Measures. Robert Creeley. NoAM
I keep walking around myself, mouth open with amazement. Immoral. James Oppenheim. HBV-2
I ken these islands each inhabited. Harry Semen. "Hugh MacDiarmid." NoAM
I kenning through astronomy divine. Meditation VIII. Edward Taylor. *Fr.* Preparatory Meditations, First Series. AmPP; AP; LiTA; NOBA; NoP; OxBA; PoEL-3; SCAP; TAP
I kept my answers small and kept them near. Answers. Elizabeth Jennings. NePoEA; OxBTC
I kept neat my virginity. Song. Glyn Jones. NeBP
I kept the house on the corner of Linden and Pineapple Streets. Birdie McReynolds. Samuel Hoffenstein. BXAP
I kicked an Edinbro dug-luver's dug. Nemo Canem Impune Lacessit. Robert Garioch. BSV
I killed them, but they would not die. The Immortals. Isaac Rosenberg. FaBoTw; MMA; TrJP
I kiss my hand to you. To the Lighted Lady Window. Marguerite Wilkinson. ISi
I kiss you good-bye, my darling. D. H. Lawrence. *Fr.* The Virgin Mother. ViBoPo
I kissed a kiss in youth. Scintilla. William Stanley Braithwaite. AmNP; BANP; CDC
I kissed my darling at the Zoo. The Prodigy. A. P. Herbert. EvOK
I Kissed Pa Twice after His Death. Mattie J. Peterson. PeD
I kissed them in fancy as I came. Two Lips. Thomas Hardy. BoLoP
I Kissed You. *Unknown.* BLPA
I kneel not now to pray that Thou. A Prayer. Harry Kemp. HBV-2; WGRP
I knew a black beetle, who lived down a drain. Christopher Morley. Nursery Rhymes for the Tender-hearted, IV. HBMV; YaD
I knew a boora clownish card. The Folly of Brown. W. S. Gilbert. InMe
I Knew a Boy with Hair like Gold. Melvin Walker La Follette. NePoEA-2
I Knew a Cappadocian. A. E. Housman. FiBHP
I knew a man, he was my chum. Trench Poets. Edgell Rickword. DBV
I knew a man who used to say. The Statesman. Hilaire Belloc. NOBE
I knew a man with a terrible obsession. Myth. Ned O'Gorman. TwAmPo
I knew a most superior camper. The Bunyip and the Whistling Kettle. John Manifold. LiTB; PoAu-2; WaP
I knew a much-loved mariner. "He Bringeth Them unto Their Desired Haven." Lewis Frank Tooker. HBV-2
I knew a simple soldier boy. Suicide in [the] Trenches. Siegfried Sassoon. BrPo; MMA
I Knew a Woman [Lovely in Her Bones]. Theodore Roethke. AmPP; BiP; BoLoP; CABA; ErPo; HAP; HeIP; HoPM; InPK; LiTM; MAT; MoAmPo; MP; NePA; NePoAm-2; NIP; NoAM; NOBA; NoP; PPoe; PrIm; SeCeV; SoSe; TAP; TwAmPo; TwCP; UnPo; UnTE (Poem.) TrGrPo
I knew an old lady. Antique Shop. Carl Carmer. FaPON
I knew her first as food and warmth and rest. My Mother. Amelia Josephine Burr. HBMV
I knew his house by the poplar-trees. Norah. Zoë Akins. HBV-1
I Knew I'd Sing. Heather McHugh. GeTw
I knew like a song your vows weren't strong. Mahsati, *tr. fr. Farsi by* Deirdre Lashgari. WPOW
I knew not 'twas so dire a crime. Last Words. Emily Brontë. WPE
I knew once,/ In your embrace. Poem about Waking. David Ferry. NePoAm-2
I knew she lay above me. The White Jessamine. John Banister Tabb. HBV-2
I knew that you were coming, June, I knew that you were coming! June. Douglas Malloch. YeAr
I knew the dignity of the words. My Grandfather's Funeral. James Applewhite. TAT
I knew the man. I see him, as he stands. Lincoln. George Henry Boker. OHIP
I knew the town from nightmares. Christmas at Vail: On Staying Indoors. Pat Monaghan. AMV-80
I knew you forever and you were always old. Some Foreign Letters. Anne Sexton. MoAmPo; PoCh
I knew you long before great motors buzzed. Big Thompson Canon. Jean Milne Gower. PoOW
I knock again and try [again] the key. A Pagan Reinvokes the Twenty-third Psalm. Robert Wolf. HBMV; TrPWD
I Know. Elsa Barker. HBMV
I Know. Verda Group. STF
I know/ I saw/ a spooky witch. October Magic. Myra Cohn Livingston. PDV
I know/ Not these my hands. Amaze. Adelaide Crapsey. QFR
I know/ that when a grumbling old woman. Superstition. Minji Karibo. WPOW
I know/ Where the wind flowers blow! Song from "April." Irene Rutherford McLeod. SUS
I know a bank where [*or* whereon] the wild thyme blows. A Violet Bank [*or* Where the Wild Thyme Blows]. Shakespeare. *Fr.* A Midsummer Night's Dream, II, i. BoNaP; FaPON; PoPle; TrGrPo
I know a barber. Edward Anthony. TiPo
I know a barn in Breckenridge on the Blue. Old Men on the Blue. Thomas Hornsby Ferril. PoOW

I know a boy who went to meet the morning. Morning. Dorothy Hamilton Gallagher. SiSoSe
I know a city on a hill, a mountain's castled crown. Assisi. Alfred Noyes. GoBC
I know a flower of beauty rare. The Lay of the Captive Count. Goethe, *tr. by* James Clarence Mangan. AWP
I Know a Flower So Fair and Fine, *with music.* Nicolai F. S. Grundtvig, *tr. fr. Norwegian by* Olav Lee. AH
I know a funny litle man. Mr. Nobody. *Unknown.* FaPON; HBVY
I know a girl. The Canal Bank. James Stephens. GrPl
I know a girl with teeth of pearl. Wouldn't You Like to Know. John Godfrey Saxe. HBV-1
I know a green grass path that leaves the field. The Green River. Lord Alfred Douglas. HBMV; OBEV; OBVV
I know a house made of mud & wattles. The Songs of Maximus, IV. Charles Olson. *Fr.* The Maximus Poems. PAI
I know a Jew fish crier down on Maxwell Street. Fish Crier. Carl Sandburg. AmFN; OxBA
I Know a Lady. Joyce Carol Thomas. CNA
I know a little cupboard. The Cupboard. Walter de la Mare. FaPON; NTCP; SoPo; TiPo
I Know a Little Garden-Close. William Morris. *See* Garden by the Sea, A.
I know a little garden path. A Hint to the Wise. Pringle Barret. HBVY
I know a little island. Aloha. William Griffith. HBMV
I know a little language of my cat, tho Dante says. Robert Duncan. *Fr.* Dante. PoM
I know a little man both ept and ert. Gloss. David McCord. OBAL
I know a little what it is like, once here at high tide. Seaweeds. Sandra McPherson. AmPA; PoA
I Know a Lovely Lady Who Is Dead. Struthers Burt. HBMV
I Know a Man. Robert Creeley. CAPP; ConAP; CoPo; InPK; InPS; MAT; NOBA; PoM; PPP
I Know a Man. Peggy Steele. PPJ
I know a mount, the gracious sun perceives. Rudel to the Lady of Tripoli. Robert Browning. LoBV
I know a mountain, lone it lies. The Granite Mountain. Lew Sarett. HBMV
I Know a Name! *Unknown.* BLRP
I know a place/ that's oh, so green. A Boy's Place. Rose Burgunder. PDV
I know a place all fennel-green and fine. A Green Place. William Jay Smith. GrPl
I know a place, in the ivy on a tree. The Bird's Nest. John Drinkwater. EvOK; PDV; SoPo
I know a place where summer strives. Emily Dickinson. NePA
I know a place where the sun is like gold. Four-Leaf Clover. Ella Higginson. AA; FaPON; HBV-1
I know a renegade hotel. Traveler's Rest. Ogden Nash. DBV; InMe
I know a road that leads from town. The Road to the Pool. Grace Hazard Conkling. HBMV
I know a secret, such a one. The Serf's Secret. William Vaughn Moody. HBV-1
I know a soul that is steeped in sin. I Know a Name! *Unknown.* BLRP
I know a spot where Love delights to dream. A Sacred Grove. Edward Cracroft Lefroy. *Fr.* Echoes from Theocritus. AWP
I know a story, fairer, dimmer, sadder. My Babes in the Wood. Sarah Morgan Bryan Piatt. AA
I know a tavern in the town. Table for One. John Holmes. WhC
I know a thing that's most uncommon. *See* I know the thing that's most uncommon.
I know a town tormented by the sea. Galway. Mary Davenport O'Neill. NeIP; OxBI
I Know a Village, *sels.* Phyllis McGinley.
5:32, The. NMM; WPE
Occupation: Housewife. DBV; WPE
I know a wasted place high in the Alps. Two Poems on the Catholoic Bavarians, II. Edgar Bowers. PoCh
I know a way. The Song in the Dell. Charles Edward Carryl. AA
I know a young girl who can speak. A Warning. Mary A. Webber. TDH
I know a young lady's high-piled ashen hair. His Helplessness. John Berryman. *Fr.* Dream Songs. NoP
I know, although when looks meet. Crazy Jane and Jack the Journeyman. W. B. Yeats. CMoP
I know an ice handler who wears a flannel shirt. Ice Handler. Carl Sandburg. OxBA
I know an old lady who swallowed a fly. The Old Lady Who Swallowed a Fly. *Unknown.* ShM
I know, as my life grows older. Whatever Is—Is Best. Ella Wheeler Wilcox. BLPA; TreFS
I know but will not tell. Elegy. Alan Dugan. AP; CAPP; DiL
I Know de Lord's Laid His Hands on Me, *with music.* *Unknown.* BoAN-2
I Know de Moonlight. *Unknown.* BPo
I know derisive men and women. Aboriginal Sin. John Hay. NePoAm-2
I know four winds with names like some strange tune. Weather Words. David McCord. ImOP
I Know He Is Real. *Unknown.* STF
I know her story-telling eye. The Eye of Love. George Moses Horton. BALP
I know him;/ He'll give no horse for a poem. *Unknown, tr. fr. Irish by* Vivian Mercier. BIrV
I know him, February's thrush. The Thrush in February. George Meredith. OBNC
I know him now, not now to know demanding. Nunc Scio, Quid Sit Amor. L. A. Mackay. OBCV
I know how it would be . . . a rainy moon. After Storm. David Morton. HBMV
I know how to hold. How to Go and Forget. Edwin Markham. HBMV
I know I am/ The Negro Problem. Dinner Guest: Me. Langston Hughes. BPo
I know I am but summer to your heart. Sonnet. Edna St. Vincent Millay. HBMV
I know I change. Daguerreotype Taken in Old Age. Margaret Atwood. BoWoP
I know I have a lot of faults. Let Me Look at Me. Bessie June Martin. STF
I know I have the best of time and space. Walt Whitman. Song of Myself, XLVI. BiP
I know, I know—though the evidence. Blow, West Wind. Robert Penn Warren. *Fr.* Notes on a Life to Be Lived. NoAM
I know I look the kind of dolt. To a Junior Waiter. A. P. Herbert. FiBHP
I know if I find you I will have to leave the earth. Hymn. A. R. Ammons. ConAP
I Know I'm Not Sufficiently Obscure. Ray Durem. BPo; PoBA
I know it is my sinne, which locks thine eares. Church-Lock and Key. George Herbert. AnAnS-1
I know it must be winter (though I sleep). Winter Sleep. Edith M. Thomas. AA
I know it will not ease the smart. Edith and Harold. Arthur Gray Butler. OBVV
I know I've got a job. The Working Man. Gregory Donovan. AMV-81
I know, Justine, you speak me fair. Justine, You Love Me Not! John Godfrey Saxe. HBV-1
I know lots of men who are in love. I Never Even Suggested It. Ogden Nash. FiBHP; FPL; PoLF
I know monks masturbate at night. The Earnest Liberal's Lament. Ernest Hemingway. OBAL; OBSV
I Know Moonlight, *with music.* *Unknown.* AS
I Know Moonrise. *Unknown.* UnPo
I know my body's of so frail a kind. Man [*or* Which Is a Proud, and Yet a Wretched Thing *or* I Know Myself a Man]. Sir John Davies. *Fr.* Nosce Teipsum. ChTr; EIL; WHA
I Know My Love. *Unknown.* AnIV; FSW
I Know My Soul. Claude McKay. BPo
I know my soul hath power to know all things. Man. Sir John Davies. *Fr.* Nosce Teipsum. OBEV
I Know Myself a Man. Sir John Davies. *See* Man.
I know not but in every leaf. Fraternity. John Banister Tabb. HBV-2
I know not by what methods rare. Prayer. Eliza M. Hickok. BLRP; STF
I know not how it may be with others. Old Furniture. Thomas Hardy. MoVE; OxBTC
I Know Not How That Bethlehem's Babe, *with music.* Harry Webb Farrington. AH
(Our Christ.) STF; TRV
I know not how to speak to thee, girl (damselle?). Love Song. Reed Whittemore. AmFN
I know not if from uncreated spheres. Three Poems, I. Michelangelo, *tr. by* George Santayana. AWP
I know not if I love her overmuch. Sonnets after the Italian. Richard Watson Gilder. HBV-1
I know not of what we ponder'd. Companions. Charles Stuart Calverley. FaBoCo; HBV-1; NA; NOBL
I know not Seville. Seville. L. D'O. Walters. HBMV
I know not that the men of old. The Men of Old. Richard Monckton Milnes. OBEV; OBVV
I know not too well how I found my way home in the night. Robert Browning. *Fr.* Saul. LoBV
I know not what my health will be. I Know. Verda Group. STF
I know not what shall [*or* will] befall me: God hangs a mist o'er my eyes. Mary Gardiner Brainard. *Fr.* Not Knowing. AA; TRV
I know not what spell is o'er me. Lorelei. Heine, *tr. by* Emma Lazarus. TrJP
I know not what the future hath. Whittier. *Fr.* The Eternal Goodness. BLRP; NOCV; TreF
I know not what to do. Fragment Thirty-six. Hilda Doolittle ("H. D."). CMoP; OxBA; VGW

I know not what will befall me: God hangs a mist o'er my eyes. *See* I know not what shall befall me.
I know not when this tiresome man. The Sundowner. Shaw Neilson. CBAP; PoAu-1
I know not where my steps may lead. He Knows the Way. *Unknown.* STF
I Know Not Where the Road Will Lead, *with music.* Evelyn Atwater Cummins. AH
I Know Not Whether I Am Proud. Walter Savage Landor. EnRP
I know not who thou art, oh lovely one! To the Lady in the Chemisette with Black Buttons. Nathaniel Parker Willis. OBAL
I know not why, but even to me. A Trifle. Henry Timrod. HBV-1
I know not why I yearn for thee again. Dreams of the Sea. W. H. Davies. EtS
I know not why my soul is rack'd. Changed. Charles Stuart Calverley. FiBHP
I know not why or whence he came. The Deserter. Joseph S. Cotter, Jr. CDC
I know now. I Thought It Was Tangiers I Wanted. Langston Hughes. PoNe
I know seven mice. Edward Anthony. *Fr.* Oddity Land. TiPo
I know, Sister, that solitude. To a Severe Nun. Thomas Merton. CoPo
I know some lonely houses off the road. Emily Dickinson. MoAB; MoAmPo; OxBA; PoRA; SO; WSC
I Know Something Good about You. Louis C. Shimon. BLPA
I Know That All beneath the Moon Decays. William Drummond of Hawthornden. BSV
(Sonnet: "I know that all beneath the moon decays.") JCP
I know that any weed can tell. Song. Louis Ginsberg. TrJP
I know that face! Daphne. Bliss Carman. OBCV
I know that He exists. Emily Dickinson. AmPP
I Know That I Am a Great Sinner. Purohit. OBMV
I Know That I Must Die Soon. Else Lasker-Schüler, *tr. fr. German by* Ralph Manheim. TrJP
I know that I shall meet my fate. An Irish Airman Foresees His Death. W. B. Yeats. CABA; CoBMV; FaBoCh; FaBoMo; GoJo; GTBS-P; HeIP; HoPM; LiTM; MMA; MoAB; MoBrPo; NoAM; NOBE; NoP; OBMV; OBWP; PoPl; PPP; SCV; TrGrPo; WaaP; WaP; WeW
I know that if thou please thou canst provide. George Wither. *Fr.* Brittan's Remembrancer. SeCV-1
I know that life is Jason. The Golden Fleece. Oscar Williams. PoA
I know that mind. ESP. Carter Revard. VoR
I Know That My Redeemer Lives. Charles Wesley. TreFS
I know that my Redeemer liveth—but out of the depths of time. The Redeemer. "Fiona Macleod." WGRP
I know that the sun rising. Pindar's Revenge. Edward Sanders. PoM
I know that these poor rags of womanhood. Afterwards. "Violet Fane." HBV-2; OBVV
I know that this my crying, like the crying. Night. Hayyim Nahman Bialik, *tr. by* Maurice Samuel. AWP
I know that what our neighbours call *longueurs.* Byron. *Fr.* Don Juan, II. OBSV
I know the bottom, she says. I know it with my great tap root. Elm [*or* The Elm Speaks]. Sylvia Plath. NoAM; NOBA; NoP; NYBP
I know the gun. The Foreman's Wife. Jeff Tagami. BrSi
I know the injured pride of sleep. Night and Morning. Austin Clarke. AnIL; CIP; IPY; MoAB; NeIP; NoAM
I know the man. The Man Who Dreamt He Was Turquoise. Wendy Rose. TWSS
I know the mind that feels indeed the fire. William Cowper. *Fr.* Table Talk. PP
I know the night is near at hand. Vespers. S. Weir Mitchell. WGRP
I know the reputation/ of the idle ways. Lady Kii, *tr. fr. Japanese by* Kenneth Rexroth *and* Ikuko Atsumi. WPOW
I know the story, how. Life Story. J. Kates. AMV-81
I know the [*or* a] thing that's most uncommon. On a Certain Lady at Court. Pope. HBV-1; NOBE; NOEC; OAEP; OBEC; OBEV; PoPle; TrGrPo
I know the ways [*or* wayes] of learning: both the head. The Pearl. George Herbert. AnAnS-1; EBEV; FaBoEn; HAP; JCP; MePo; NOCV; OAEL-1; OxBoCh; PoEL-2; SeCP; SeCV-1
I know there are some fools that care. The Deformed Mistress. Sir John Suckling. BXAP; ErPo
I know there is a worm in the human heart. John Clare. Jon Anderson. AmPA
I know there is someone. Poem to Be Read and Sung. César Vallejo, *tr. by* James Wright *and* Robert Bly. EAS
I know this road like the back of my hand. Ballad of the Three Coins. Vernon Watkins. NoAM
I know those tits. Matisse Tits. David Barker. GP
I know 'tis sordid, and 'tis low. The Frailty. Abraham Cowley. CavP
I know two things about the horse. The Horse. Naomi Royde-Smith. CenHV; FaBoCo; FiBHP
I know two women. The Wife. Robert Creeley. AP; VGW
I know very well, goddess, she is not beautiful. Calypso's Island. Archibald MacLeish. MoAB; NoP
I know very well what I'd rather be. Rathers. Mary Austin. FaPON
I know what I feel like. Changing. Mary Ann Hoberman. RHPC
I know what the caged bird feels, alas! Sympathy. Paul Laurence Dunbar. AmNP; CDC; IDB; PoBA; PoNe
"I know what you're going to say," she said. Candor. H. C. Bunner. HBV-1
I know when the sun is in China. Moonlight. Joy Harjo. TWSS
I know, where Hampshire fronts the Wight. "Hold." Patrick R. Chalmers. HBV-1
I Know Where I'm Going. *Unknown.* AnIV; ELP; FSW; GBP; MoShBr; OBET; OLR; OnYI; ViBoPo; WTO
I know why, getting up in the cold dawn. To a Daughter with Artistic Talent. Peter Meinke. Psk
I know why lilies ring their bells. Secret. Esther Hull Doolittle. YeAr
I know, within my mouth, for bashful fear. Love's Despair. Richard Lynch. *Fr.* Diella. EIL
I know you got some good apples. Big Apple Blues. *Unknown.* BluL
I Know You Rider. *Unknown.* FSW
I know you: solitary griefs. The Precept of Silence. Lionel Johnson. HBV-2; MoBrPo; ViBoPo; VLP
I knowed a man, which he lived in Jones. Thar's More in the Man than Thar Is in the Land. Sidney Lanier. AP; NOBA
I knows a gal that you don't know. Li'l Liza Jane. *Unknown.* BLSo
I Korinna am here to sing the courage. Korinna, *tr. fr. Greek by* Willis Barnstone. BoWoP
I lack the braver mind. Confession of Faith. Elinor Wylie. MoAmPo; SBG
I laid me down beside the sea. Lassitude. Mathilde Blind. SBG
I laid me down upon a bank. Blake. EnLoPo; GBL; ViBoPo
I laid me down upon the shore. Preëxistence. Frances Cornford. HBMV
I laid my haffet on Elfer Hill. Elfer Hill. *Unknown, tr. by* Robert Jamieson. AWP
I laid my wife beneath this stone. *Unknown.* WhC
I Lais, once an arrow. Kenneth Rexroth, *after the Greek of* Sekundos. NNaP
I laks yo' kin' of lovin'. Long Gone. Sterling A. Brown. BALP; BANP; BPo; CDC
I landed on Iona's holy isle. Iona. Frederick Tennyson. GoBC
I lang hae thought, my youthfu' friend. Epistle [*or* Letter] to a Young Friend. Burns. EBEV; OHFP
I lately lived in quiet ease. Love Is like a Dizziness. James Hogg. HBV-1; InMe
I lately lost a preposition. The Naughty Preposition. Morris Bishop. FiBHP; NYBP; PV
I lately saw, what now I sing. The Sparrow and Diamond. Matthew Green. FM; PBBP
I Lately Vowed, but 'Twas in Haste. John Oldmixon. HBV-1
(Song: "I lately vow'd, but 'twas in haste.") POL
I laugh and sing, but cannot tell. To Lucasta. Richard Lovelace. OBS
I laugh at each dull bore, taste's parasite. Fresco-Sonnets to Christian Sethe. Heine, *tr. by* John Todhunter. AWP
I laughed at sweethearts I met at schools. My Heart Stood Still. Lorenz Hart. BLSo
I laughed at the lovers I passed. Terenure. Blanaid Salkeld. NeIP
I laughed when the dawn was a-peepin'. The Night Herder. Charles Badger Clark, Jr. BPAW
I laved my hands. Lost for a Rose's Sake. *Unknown, tr. by* Andrew Lang. AWP
I lay among the ferns. Among the Ferns. Edward Carpenter. WGRP
I lay and speculated on the impact of a bullet. Terror. Thomas O'Brien. NeIP
I lay at the edge of a well. The Underground Stream. James Dickey. NOBA
I lay down. Children of Night. Richard Shelton. FiCP
I lay down to sleep only to find I can't. Prison Walls—Red Brick Crevices. Terri Meyette Wilkins. LFAC
I lay down with my love and there was song. Armorial. Ralph Gustafson. MoCV; PeCV
I lay i' the bosom of the sun. Palabras Grandiosas. Bayard Taylor. OBAL
I lay in my tent at mid-day. The Crossing at Fredericksburg. George Henry Boker. PAH
I lay in silence, dead. A woman came. Another Way. Ambrose Bierce. AA
I lay me down, but down is deep. Nap. Mark Van Doren. TwAmPo
I lay me down to sleep. In the Hospital. Mary Woolsey Howland. HBV-2
I Lay My Lute beside Thy Door. Clarence Urmy. HBMV
I lay on Delos of the Cyclades. The Ship. Lloyd Mifflin. AA
I lay quietly listening to some musical rabbi. Night Poem in an Abandoned Music Room. William Pillen. VWA

I lay upon the summer grass. The Oracle. Arthur Davison Ficke. HBV-1
I lay waiting. Bog Queen. Seamus Heaney. PAI
I lay with my heart under me. Cicada. Adrien Stoutenburg. NYBP; RFM
I leaf through the flat plains. Poem from "The Revolution." Ilya Rubin, *tr. by* Linda Zisquit. VWA
I lean on a lighthouse rock. Girl at the Seaside. Richard Murphy. BIrV; NMP
I leaned out of window, I smelt the white clover. Seven Times Three—Love. Jean Ingelow. *Fr.* Songs of Seven. PoLF
I leant [*or* leaned] upon a coppice gate. The Darkling Thrush. Thomas Hardy. BrPo; CMoP; CoBMV; EBVV; EvOK; FaFP; FPL; HAP; HBMV; InPS; LiTB; LiTM; MasP; MoAB; MoBrPo; MoPo; NIP; NoAM; NOBE; NoP; OAEL-2; OAEP; OBEV; OBNC; OBVV; PAI; PBBP; PPP; RoGo; SeCeV; SoSe; TEP; TreFT; TrGrPo; UnPo; VLP; WaP
I learn, as the years roll onward. Life's Lessons. *Unknown.* BLRP; FPL; PoLF; STF
I learned in my credulous youth. Why, Some of My Best Friends Are Women. Phyllis McGinley. NMM
I learned to ride with the Colonel. Riding. Florence Grossman. PH
I learned two things. Riding Lesson. Henry Taylor. PH
I learnt the collects and the catechism. Elizabeth Barrett Browning. *Fr.* Aurora Leigh. TEP
I leave behind me the elm-shadowed square. Outward Bound. Thomas Bailey Aldrich. AA; EtS
I leave here I'm gonna catch that M and O. M & O Blues. *Unknown.* BluL
I leave Mortality, and things below. The Extasie. Abraham Cowley. AnAnS-2; SeCP
I leave my heart in the doorway. Thank You for the Valentine. Diane Wakoski. HoPM
I leave their fields. The Long Night Home. Charles F. Gordon. NBP
I Leave Tonight from Euston. *Unknown.* PoSH
I leave with unreverted eye the towers. Florence. Walter Savage Landor. SeCePo
I leave you in your garden. To Yvor Winters, 1955. Thom Gunn. GTBS-P
I Left. Tuvia Ruebner, *tr. fr. Hebrew by* Betsy Rosenberg. VWA
I left a lei, Lady. Lady of Peace. Fray Angelico Chavez. ISi
I left my hills. Izumi Shikibu, *tr. fr. Japanese by* Willis Barnstone. BoWoP
I left my prayers and the kneeling pilgrims. Fair Cassidy. *Unknown, tr. by* Donagh MacDonagh. BIrV
I left my temporary home and set off. I Left. Tuvia Ruebner, *tr. by* Betsy Rosenberg. VWA
I left old Lake Chemo a long way behind me. Lake Chemo. James Wilton Rowe. AmFP
I left the farm I loved. I went. Exile. George Rostrevor Hamilton, *after* Isidoros of Aigai. FaBoEE
I left the streets of Galway town. The Tramp's Song. Mary Devenport O'Neill. AnIV
I left the valley, no longer heard. Anabasis. Rodney Nelson. AMV-81
I left thee last, a child at heart. Rosalind's Scroll. Elizabeth Barrett Browning. *Fr.* The Poet's Vow. HBV-1
I left thee with a courage high. J. C. Squire. *Fr.* My Father's Cot. BXAP
I, Lessimus, of Salt Lake City. Robert Peters. BXAP
I let him find, but never what he sought. Epitaph on Any Man. A. S. J. Tessimond. POL
I let my soul drift with the thistledown. Soul-Drift. Mathilde Blind. SBG
I let the incense grow cold. Li Ch'ing-chao, *tr. fr. Chinese by* Kenneth Rexroth. BoWoP
I lie down & take off my body. Losing the Straight Way. Ian Wedde. OCNZ
I Lie Down with God. *Unknown, tr. fr. Modern Irish by* Eleanor Hull. *Fr.* Four Prayers. AnIV; OnYI
I lie for a long time on my left side and my right side. Dead Color. Charles Wright. LCAP
I lie here beside you. Mount Gilboa. Malka Heifetz Tussman, *tr. by* Marcia Falk. PBWP
I lie in darkness, as the dead shades gather. Lament. Matangi Hauroa, *tr. by* Barry Mitcalfe. WTO
I lie in the hay. Swallow Tails. Tom Robinson. FaPON
I lie in wait. It is the in-between. Expectancies: The Eleventh Hour. Karla M. Hammond. AMV-80
I Lie on the Chilled Stones of the Great Wall. Stephen Shu Ning Liu. BrSi
I lie under the crust of the night singing. Pregnant Woman. Ingrid Jonker, *tr. by* Jack Cope *and* Uys Krige. PeSA
I lie under your hand—a cur. Dog. Ingrid Jonker, *tr. by* Jack Cope *and* William Plomer. PBWP
I lie upon my bed and hear and see. The Largest Life. Archibald Lampman. CaP
I lift mine eyes, and all the windows blaze. Longfellow. Divina Commedia, V. GoBC; NePA; SeCeV
I lift my eyes, but I cannot see. A Seeker in the Night. Florence Earle Coates. TrPWD
I Lift My Eyes Up to the Hills, *with music.* Cotton Mather. AH
I lift my head from lowly bed. Moschatel. Daniel James O'Sullivan. NeIP
I Lift My Heart to Thee, *with music.* Thomas Sternhold. AH
I lift my heart to Thee, O God. Thankful Heart. F. W. Davis. STF
I lift my songs. Battle Song. Macuilxochitl, *tr. by* Miguel León-Portilla; *English vers. by* Catherine Rodriquez-Nieto. WPOW
I lift the Lord on high. Père Lalement. Marjorie Pickthall. CaP; NOBC; OBCV; PeCV
I lift these hands with iron fetters banded. South Carolina to the States of the North. Paul Hamilton Hayne. PAH
I lift this sumach-bough with crimson flare. Torch-Light in Autumn. John James Piatt. AA
I lifted my eyes to the sky. Twilight Thoughts in Israel. Melech Ravitch, *tr. by* Seymour Levitan. VWA
I Light Your Streets. Meridel Le Sueur. GP
I like/ the feel of your pulsating fibers. Love Poem. Yuri Kageyama. BrSi
I like a church; I like a cowl. The Problem. Emerson. AA; AmPP; AP; AWP; HBV-2; LiTA; NePA; NOBA; NoP; OxBA; TAP; WGRP
I like a look of agony. Emily Dickinson. AP; InPS; NCEP; NoP; TAP
I like a man around. Hooked on the Magic Muscle. Linda King. GP
I like a road that leads away to prospects white and fair. The Best Road of All. Charles Hanson Towne. HBMV
I, like a slow, morose and shabby fatalist. The Elephant to the Girl in Bertram Mills' Circus. Anthony Cronin. CIP
I Like Americans. Nancy Boyd. YaD
I like best. Of Man and Nature. Horace Mungin. BOLo
I like coffee, I like tea. *Unknown.* FaFP
I like days. December. Aileen Fisher. SiSoSe
I like her gentle hand that sometimes strays. Sonnets after the Italian. Richard Watson Gilder. HBV-1
I Like Housecleaning. Dorothy Brown Thompson. FaPON
I like it here just fine. Girl Held without Bail. Margaret Walker. BPo; CNA; PoBA
I Like It When It's Mizzly. Aileen Fisher. PDV
I Like Little Pussy. Jane Taylor. FaBoBe; HBV-1; HBVY
(I Love Little Pussy.) FaPON; OxNR; SoPo; TiPo
(Pussy.) OxBChV
I like movies because. Why I Like Movies. Patricia Jones. BISi
I Like My Body When It Is with Your Body. E. E. Cummings. *Fr.* Sonnets—Actualities. BoLoP; ErPo; LLLT; UnTE; VGW
I like my fingers. Mark's Fingers. Mary O'Neill. RHPC
I like not lady-slippers. Tiger-Lilies. Thomas Bailey Aldrich. GN
I like not tears in tune, nor will [*or* do] I prize. On the Memory [*or* Upon the Death] of Mr. Edward King, Drowned in the Irish Seas. John Cleveland. AnAnS-2; HAP; OAEL-1; OBS; SeCP
I like rust on a nail. And the Same Words. David Ignatow. NNaP
I like that ancient Saxon phrase, which calls. God's-Acre. Longfellow. HBV-2
I like the clouds. Summer Sky. Ruth McKee Gordon. TiPo
I like the fall. The Mist and All. Dixie Willson. FaPON; SoPo; YeAr
I like the hunting of the hare. The Old Squire. Wilfrid Scawen Blunt. FaPoR; HBV-1; OBEV; OBVV
I like the man who faces what he must. The Inevitable. Sarah Knowles Bolton. AA; WGRP
I like the park best at evening, on a cool day. The Park at Evening. Leslie Norris. DuDa
I like the story of the circus waif. The Road. Herbert Morris. NePoAm-2
I like the streets of New York City, where I was born. Autobiography: Hollywood. Charles Reznikoff. *Fr.* Going To and Fro and Walking Up and Down. VWA
I like the town on rainy nights. Rainy Nights. Irene Thompson. RHPC
I like the way that the world is made. Contentment. Burges Johnson. GDP
I like the whistle of trains at night. Trains at Night. Frances M. Frost. TiPo
I like the wind. Wind Secrets. Diane Wakoski. AmPA
I like the woods. Autumn Woods. James S. Tippett. SUS; TiPo
I like them pale, fair or honey-skinned. Epigram. Strato. PeHV
I like to find. Pleasures. Denise Levertov. AP; CAPP; NeAP; NoAM; NOBA
I like to fish. The Big One. Luis Cabalquinto. BrSi
I like to go to the stable after supper. White Cat. Raymond Knister. WHW
I like to look for bridges. Bridges. Rhoda W. Bacmeister. SoPo
I like to move. There's such a feeling. Moving. Eunice Tietjens. TiPo
I like to picture it this way. How Copernicus Stopped the Sun. R. H. W. Dillard. SUW
I Like to Quote. Mitchell D. Follansbee. PoPl; WhC
I like to ride in my uncle's plane. Flying. Kaye Starbird. PDV
I like to see/ The spotted clown. The Clown. Dorothy Aldis. PDV

I like to see a thunder storm. Rhyme. Elizabeth J. Coatsworth. RHPC
I like to see it lap the miles. Emily Dickinson. AP; BoWoP; CABA; FaBV; FaPON; InPK; LiTA; LiTM; MoAB; MoAmPo; MoShBr; MoVE; NOBA; OBAL; OBCA; OxBA; PDV; PrIm; SoSe
I like to see the bay filled up with boats. Fear Death by Water. Richard Eberhart. AMV-81
I Like to Sing Also. John Updike. FiBHP
I like to think (and/ the sooner the better!). All Watched Over by Machines of Loving Grace. Richard Brautigan. MAT
I Like to Think of Harriet Tubman. Susan Griffin. NMM
I like to think of you as brown and tall. The Wind on the Downs. Marian Allen. SUMH
I like to think one day. To This Hill Again. James Macmillan. PoSH
I like to toss him up and down. My Cats. Stevie Smith. FaBoNo
I like to walk/ And hear the black crows talk. Crows. David McCord. PDV; RFM; TiPo
I like wrestling with Herbie because. Wrestling. Kathleen Fraser. RHPC
I like you, Mrs. Fry! I like your name! A Friendly Address. Thomas Hood. PoEL-4
I liked to walk in the river meadows. The Midnight Court. Bryan Merryman, *tr. by* Frank O'Connor. KiLC
I likes a woman. Preference. Langston Hughes. NOBA
I linger, knowing you are eager (having seen). Eurydice. Linda Gregg. NPGG
I 'listed at home for a lancer. Lancer. A. E. Housman. MoBrPo; OBWP
I listen, and the mountain lakes. Maybe Alone on My Bike. William Stafford. NYBP
I listen for him through the rain. At Daybreak. Siegfried Sassoon. PeHV
I listen to my parent's language. When Father Came Home for Lunch. Jim Mitsui. BrSi
I listen to this. Look Back. Carroll Arnett. STE
I listened, there was not a sound to hear. Full Moon; Santa Barbara. Sara Teasdale. OBCA
I listened to the foliage grow at night. What I Did Last Summer. Ron Ikan. AMV-80
I listened to the man and he. Psychometrist. James Stephens. NoAM
I listened to the Phantom by Ontario's shore. The Poet. Walt Whitman. *Fr.* By Blue Ontario's Shore. MoAmPo
I little know or care. Forever and a Day. Thomas Bailey Aldrich. HBV-1
I live at a distance. The Hermit. Daniel Halpern. AMV-80
I live but in the present,—where art thou? Today. Jones Very. TAP
I live for the good of my nation. Old Rosin, the Beau. *Unknown.* BLSo; CoSo; FSW
I live for those who love me. What I Live For [*or* My Aim]. George Linnaeus Banks. BLPA; FaBoBe; TreFS; WBLP
"I live here: 'Wessex' is my name." A Popular Personage at Home. Thomas Hardy. FM
I live, I die, I burn myself and drown. Sonnet VIII. Louise Labé, *tr. by* Willis Barnstone. BoWoP
I live in a beautiful place, a city. New York. Edward Field. NYP
I live in a room named East. Suddenly. Robin Blaser. PoM
I live in a stone house high in the mountains. Tequila. Elizabeth Spires. MAYP
I Live in Great Sorrow. *Unknown. See* Fowls in the Frith.
I live in hope some day to see. A Bird in the Bush. Lord Kennet. PV
I live in my wooden legs and O. Where I Live in This Honorable House of the Laurel Tree. Anne Sexton. TwAmPo
I live in this house, walls being plastered. Keep Me Still, for I Do Not Want to Dream. Larry Eigner. NeAP
I live invisible (in my whole sky). Too Bright a Day. Norman MacCaig. GTBS-P
I live my father's old age. My Father. Abraham Chalfi, *tr. by* Shlomo Vinner *and* Howard Schwartz. VWA
I live my life in growing orbits. Rainer Maria Rilke, *tr. fr. German by* Robert Bly. NU
I Live Not Where I Love. *Unknown.* OBET
I live on this depraved and lonely cliff. Vittoria da Colonna, *tr. fr. Italian by* Willis Barnstone. BoWoP
I live only to do Thy will. *At. to* Ansari of Herat. ILwL
I Live up Here. W. S. Merwin. CAPP
I live where darkness/ is not. Mukta Bai, *tr. fr. Marathi by* Willis Barnstone. BoWoP
I live without inhabiting/ Myself. St. John of the Cross, *tr. by* Roy Campbell. *Fr.* Coplas about the Soul Which Suffers with Impatience to See God. OBVE
I lived a life without love, and saw the being. The Mirage. Oscar Williams. CrMA; LiTM; NePA
I lived alone as happy as Larry. The Husband's Lament. Brian Merriman, *tr. by* Frank O'Connor. *Fr.* The Midnight Court. OBVE
I lived among great houses. The Statesman's Holiday. W. B. Yeats. CMoP; OxBTC
I lived here nearly 5 years before I could. Chicago Poem. Lew Welch. NeAP; PoM
I lived in a dry well. Wells. Donald Hall. NMP
I Lived in a Town, *with music. Unknown.* TrAS
I lived in a very special room once. I Have a Place. Lily A. De Young. AMV-80
I lived in a wood for a number of years. Ground for the Floor. *Unknown.* OBET
I lived in the first century of world wars. Poem (I Lived in the First Century). Muriel Rukeyser. UnPo
I lived my days apart. A Mystic as Soldier. Siegfried Sassoon. WGRP
I lived on this earth in an age. Fragment. Miklós Radnóti, *tr. by* Steven Polgar *and* Stephen Berg *and* S. J. Marks. VWA
I lived to tell the truth, and truth was wrong. Laocoon. Donald Hall. NePoAm-2
"I lived with Mr. Punch, they said my name was Judy." Variations. Randall Jarrell. MiAP; VGW
I lived with visions for my company. Elizabeth Barrett Browning. Sonnets from the Portuguese, XXVI. OAEP
I loathe, abhor, detest, despise. Dried Apple Pies. *Unknown.* BLPA
I loathe [*or* lothe] that I did love. The Aged Lover Renounceth Love [*or* The Image of Death]. Thomas, Lord Vaux. EIL; EnRePo; GoTL; OAEL-1; OAEP; OBSC; PoEL-1
I loathe the very thought of her. Morning Star. James J. Galvin. ISi
I loed you for yir kindness. The Deean Tractorman, Clear. Edith Anne Robertson. OxBS
I loitered weeping with my bride for gladness. James Agee. *Fr.* Lyrics. MoAmPo; PoPl
I long had rack'd my brains to find. A New Simile in the Manner of Swift. Goldsmith. LAuP
I long not now, a little while at least. Protest. Countee Cullen. CDC
I long to be the wanton breeze. Lovesick. *Unknown, tr. by* Louis Untermeyer. UnTE
I long to know/ How my dear mistress fares. George Chapman. *Fr.* Bussy d'Ambois. ViBoPo
I long to talk[e] with some old lover's ghost. Love's Deity [*or* Deitie]. John Donne. AnAnS-1; AWP; EIL; EnRePo; GBL; LiTB; MePo; OAEP; SeCePo; SeCP; SeCV-1; WHA
I longed to love a full-boughed beech. The Ivy-Wife. Thomas Hardy. VLP
I look across the table and think. Incident. Norman MacCaig. FF
"I look and smell," Aunt Sponge declared, "as lovely as a rose!" Aunt Sponge and Aunt Spiker. Roald Dahl. RHPC
I Look at My Hand. Angel González, *tr. fr. Spanish by* Joel Hancock. AMV-81
I look at the cousin. Slow Waker. Thom Gunn. Str
I look at the crisp golden-threaded hair. Canzone: His Portrait of His Lady, Angiola of Verona. Fazio degli Uberti, *tr. by* Dante Gabriel Rossetti. AWP
I look at the swaling sunset. In Trouble and Shame. D. H. Lawrence. OBMV
I look down the mountainside. Just below my window. In a Mountain Cabin in Norway. Robert Bly. RFM
I look for the way. Poetics. A. R. Ammons. NoP
I Look into My Glass. Thomas Hardy. BrPo; CABA; EBEV; FaBoTw; HAP; NOBE; NoP; PoPle; PrIm; SCV; VLP; WeW
I look into the henyard. The Darkling Chicken. Robert Peters. BXAP
I Look into the Stars. Jane Draper. HBMV
I look on kingship in high pines. Exile. Jennette Yeatman. GoYe
I look onto an alley here. A Day for Anne Frank. C. K. Williams. GeTw
I look out at the white sleet covering the still streets. Sleet Storm on the Merritt Parkway. Robert Bly. ConAP; NOBA
I look out into the Yonder. Last Call. Langston Hughes. NePoAm-2
I look out the window: spring is coming. To Robert Lowell and Osip Mandelstam. Frederick Seidel. AMV-81
I look over my own shoulder. The Zen of Housework. Al Zolynas. LTB
I look to Thee in ev'ry need. The Christian Life. Samuel Longfellow. WGRP
I look upon the world—and she resembles a garden. The End of Man Is Death. Moses ibn Ezra, *tr. by* Solomon Solis-Cohen. TrJP
I look upon thy happy face. To a Child. George Edgar Montgomery. AA
I look. You look. Over. R. S. Thomas. FF
I looked across and beyond the churned-up lake. A Dream. Hugh Connell. NeIP
I looked and I saw. Who but the Lord? Langston Hughes. BPo
I Looked and Saw History Caught. A. B. Spellman. NBP
I looked and saw your eyes. Three Shadows. Dante Gabriel Rossetti. HBV-1; ViBoPo
I looked down and saw a pit most black. Elizabeth Melvill, Lady Culross. *Fr.* A Godly Dream. WPE
I looked far back into other years, and lo, in bright array. Mary, Queen of Scots. Henry Glassford Bell. BeLS; BLPA; FaBoBe

I Looked for a Sounding-Board. Henriette Roland-Holst, *tr. fr. Dutch by* Jonathan Crewe. WPOW
I looked for that which is not, nor can be. A Pause of Thought. Christina Rossetti. FaBoEn; NOBE; OBNC
I looked from the hall to the top of the stair. Talking Nothin'. *Unknown.* FSW
I looked from the stair-well. Karamazov. Ben Belitt. DiL
I looked in my heart while the wild swans went over. Wild Swans. Edna St. Vincent Millay. CMoP; MoAmPo; PBWP; UnPo
I looked in the first glass. The Three Mirrors. Edwin Muir. NoAM
I Looked in the Mirror. Beatrice Schenk de Regniers. PDV
I looked into a lake and saw a forest. Playmates. Lillian Everts. GoYe
I looked into my body. X-Ray. Leonora Speyer. ImOP
I looked into my heart to write. Summer Song. George Barker. ChMP
I looked like Abraham Lincoln. Elliott Hawkins. Edgar Lee Masters. *Fr.* Spoon River Anthology. OxBA
I looked on that prophetic land. Presences Perfected. Siegfried Sassoon. MoBrPo
I looked one night, and there Semiramis. A Look into the Gulf. Edwin Markham. AA
I looked out into the morning. James Thomson ("B. V."). *Fr.* Sunday up the River. OAEP; ViBoPo
I looked over Jordan and [*or* an'] what did I see. Swing Low, Sweet Chariot. *Unknown.* AmFN; BLSo; FaPON; UnPo
I looked to find a man who walked with God. Enoch. Jones Very. HAP
I looked to find Spring's early flowers. The Lament of the Flowers. Jones Very. NOBA; OxBA
I Looked Up from My Writing. Thomas Hardy. MMA
I looked upon the dreary waste. The Message of the Bells. Thomas Curtis Clark. PGD
I looked upon the earth: it was a floor. Our Lady in the Middle Ages. Frederick William Faber. ACP; ISi
I, Lord, of All Mortals! *Malay Oral Tradition, tr. by* R. O. Winstedt. WTO
I lost my eyes in the blacksmith shop. The Blind Fiddler. *Unknown.* FSW
I lost my mare in Lincoln Lane. *Unknown.* OxNR
I lost my pardner, what'll I do? Skip to My Lou. *Unknown.* AmFP
I Lost the Love of Heaven. John Clare. *See* Vision, A.
I lothe that I did love. *See* I loathe that I did love.
I Lov'd Thee Once. Sir Robert Ayton. OBS
I Love. Stevie Smith. FaBoCo
I Love a Flower. Robert Nichols. ChMP
I Love a Flower. *At. to* Thomas Phillipps. MeEL
(Roses.) OxBM
I Love a Hill. Ralph Hodgson. BrPo
I love a lass as fair as ere was seen. Of a Mistress. Sir Aston Cokayne. CavP
I love a prayer-book. A Girl's Mood. Lizette Woodworth Reese. HBMV
I love Adam. He is brave of heart. Eve. Jakov Fishman, *tr. by* Robert Friend. VWA
I Love All Beauteous Things. Robert Bridges. BrPo; CMoP; EBEV; HBMV; HBVY; TrCP
(To L. B. C. L. M.) OAEP; ViBoPo
I love all waves and lovely water in motion. Five Degrees South. Francis Brett Young. EtS
I love and fear him. Lady Kasa, *tr. fr. Japanese by* Kenneth Rexroth. BoWoP
I love and hate. Ah! never ask why so! Catullus, *tr. fr. Latin by* Walter Savage Landor. OBVE
I love, and he loves me again. A Nymph's Secret. Ben Jonson. OBEV
I love and worship thee in that thy ways. Madonna Natura. "Fiona Macleod." WGRP
I love as though I were not born to die. Samis Idyll. Dachine Rainer. NePoAm
I love at early morn, from new-mown swath. Summer Images. John Clare. ChTr
I love breasts, hard. Breasts. Charles Simic. NNaP
I Love But Thee. Heine, *tr. fr. German by* Louis Untermeyer. AWP
I love contemplating—apart. Napoleon and the British Sailor. Thomas Campbell. BeLS
I love crows. Crows. William Witherup. PCP; POL
I love daffodils. Spring Song. Hilda Conkling. PoSC
I love him not; but shew no reason can. Antipathy. Rowland Watkyns, *after* Martial. FaBoEE
I love him wisely if I love him well. John Gambril Nicholson. *Fr.* A Chaplet of Southernwood. PeHV
"I love, I love and whom love ye?" I Love a Flower [*or* Roses]. *At. to* Thomas Phillipps. MeEL; OxBM
I love it! I love it! And who shall dare. The Old Arm-Chair. Eliza Cook. BrRo; InPK; PaPo; WBLP
I Love Life, *with music.* Irwin M. Cassel. BLSo
I Love Little Pussy. Jane Taylor. *See* I Like Little Pussy.
I love, loved, and so doth she. Sir Thomas Wyatt. SiPS
I love my friend—but love my ease. The Citizen and the Red Lion of Brentford. Christopher Smart. NCEP
I love my God, but with no love of mine. Adoration [*or* By Thy Life I Live]. Mme Guyon. STF; TRV; WGRP
I Love My Jean. Burns. *See* Of A' the Airts.
I Love My Jesus Quite Alone, *with music. At. to* Johannes Kelpius, *tr. fr. German by* Christopher Witt. AH
I love my lady; she is very fair. My Beautiful Lady. Thomas Woolner. OBVV
I love my lady's eyes. Song. Robert Bridges. VLP
I Love My Life, but Not Too Well. Harriet Monroe. HBV-1
I love my little son, and yet when he was ill. The Two Parents. "Hugh MacDiarmid." FaBoTw; OxBTC
I Love My Love. Helen Adam. NeAP; NMM; WPOW
I Love My Love in the Morning. Gerald Griffin. ACP; GoBC; OnYI
I love my love with a v. Gertrude Stein. *Fr.* Before the Flowers of Friendship Faded Faded. PeHV
I love my prairies, they are mine. My Prairies. Hamlin Garland. FaPON
I love my work and my children. God. Ovid in the Third Reich. Geoffrey Hill. FaBoMo; NoAM; POL
I love noodles. Give me oodles. Oodles of Noodles. Lucia *and* James L. Hymes, Jr. RHPC
I love not Colorado. Westward Ho. *Unknown.* CoSo
I love not thy perfections. When I hear. Depreciating Her Beauty. Wilfrid Scawen Blunt. The Love Sonnets of Proteus, VI. OBMV
I love Octopussy, his arms are so long. The Octopussycat. Kenyon Cox. FaPON; SoPo; TiPo
I love old gardens best. A Charleston Garden. Henry Bellamann. PoLF
I love old mothers—mothers with white hair. Dear Old Mothers. Charles S. Ross. PGD
I Love Old Women. William Kloefkorn. AMV-80
I love sea words. Sea Words. Mary Sinton Leitch. EtS
I love sixpence, jolly little sixpence. Mother Goose. OxNR
I love snow and all the forms. Shelley. TiPo
I Love Somebody. *Unknown.* AmFP
I love the church that Jesus bought. Not on Sunday Night. *Unknown.* STF
I love the country air. Mother Pin a Rose on Me. David Lewis, Paul Schindler, *and* Bob Adams. FSN
I love the days of long ago. My Africa. Michael Dei-Anang. PBA
I love the English country scene. I Love. Stevie Smith. FaBoCo
I love the evenings, passionless and fair, I love the evens. A Sunset. Victor Hugo, *tr. by* Francis Thompson. *Fr.* Feuilles d'Automne. AWP
I love the hoss from hoof to head. The Kentucky Thoroughbred. James Whitcomb Riley. ELU
I Love the Lord, *with music. Unknown.* AH
I love the luminous poison of the moon. A Sapphic Dream. George Moore. SyP
I love the old melodious lays. Poem. Whittier. AA; AP; HBV-2; NePA; NoP; OxBA; TAP
"I love the sea because it has drowned me." Sea Shanty. Clifford Dyment. POL
I love the secret place of prayer. The Secret Place of Prayer. Georgia B. Adams. STF
I love the sound of the horn in the deep, dim woodland. The Sound of the Horn. Alfred de Vigny, *tr. by* Wilfred Thorley. AWP
I love the stony pasture. The Deserted Pasture. Bliss Carman. HBV-1
I love the stream flowing endlessly. Robert Bly Finds Something in New Jersey. Carol Poster. BXAP
I Love the Woods. Leib Neidus, *tr. fr. Yiddish by* Keith Bosley. VWA
I love thee and I love thee not. The Reason Why. Thomas Lovell Beddoes. OBRV
I love thee, Betty. *Unknown.* OxNR
I love thee, Mary, and thou lovest me. The Chemist to His Love. *Unknown.* InMe; QQQ
I love thee when thy swelling buds appear. The Tree. Jones Very. GN; HBV-1; OHIP; PoSC
I love this boy, not for his beauty only. F. W. Soodley. PeHV
I love this byre. Shadows are kindly here. The Innkeeper's Wife. Clive Sansom. OBCP
I love this little house because. Motto for a Dog House. Arthur Guiterman. GDP
I love this white and slender body. This White and Slender Body. Heine, *tr. by* Louis Untermeyer. UnTE
I Love Thy Kingdom, Lord, *with music.* Timothy Dwight. AH
(Love to the Church.) AA; HBV-2
I love Thy Word, O God. The Word of God. J. Harold Gwynne. STF
I love to hear the little bird. The Bird. Samuel Hoffenstein. FiBHP; PV
I love to hear thine earnest voice. To an Insect. Oliver Wendell Holmes. HBV-1; HBVY; TreF
I love to listen to men in bars. Frank Sinatra. Michael Waters. GeTw

I love to peep out on a summer's morn. Summer Morning. John Clare. PoSC
I love to rise in a summer morn. The Schoolboy. Blake. *Fr.* Songs of Experience. BoNaP; CH; FaBoCh; GLGT
I love to see boards lying on the ground in early spring. Old Boards. Robert Bly. CAPP; NaP
I love to see the little stars. The Oneness of the Philosopher with Nature. G. K. Chesterton. FaBoNo
I love to see the old heath's withered brake. Emmonsail's Heath in Winter. John Clare. FaBoEn; PoEL-4
I love to see those loving and beloved. Lonely Love. Edmund Blunden. OxBTC
I love to see, when leaves depart. Autumn. Roy Campbell. GTBS-P; MoBrPo; OBMV; OxBTC
I Love to Steal Awhile Away, *with music.* Phoebe Hinsdale Brown. AH
(Private Devotion.) AA
I Love to Tell the Story. Katherine Hankey. TreFT
I love to think of things I hate. The Complete Misanthropist. Morris Bishop. FiBHP; FPL; TW
I love to think this fragrant air. Winds of Eros. "Æ." HBMV
I Love What Is Not. Manfred Winkler, *tr. fr. Hebrew by* Mary Zilzer. VWA
I Love You. *Unknown.* RHPC
I Love You. Ella Wheeler Wilcox. BLPA; FaBoBe; FPL
I love you,/ Not only for what you are. Love. *At. to* Roy Croft. BLPA; FaBoBe; TreFT; TRV
I love you and the rosebush. Armando Uribe, *tr. fr. Spanish by* Miller Williams. HoPM
I love you as a sheriff searches for a walnut. To You. Kenneth Koch. CAPP
I love you as a stranded ship the beach. Enigma. Kenneth Burke. TwAmPo
I love you, baby, I ain't gonna lie. When Things Go Wrong with You. *Unknown.* FSW
I love you, because in my thousand and one nights. Love without Love. Luis Lloréns Torres, *tr. by* Julio Marzán. InW
I love you better than I love my race. Charles Mair. *Fr.* Tecumseh. NOBC
I love you first because your face is fair. V-Letter. Karl Shapiro. AP; CoBMV; MiAP; NoAM; NYBP; TrJP; WaP
I love you for your brownness. To a Dark Girl. Gwendolyn B. Bennett. BANP; BlSi; CDC; PoBA
I love you ginger bread mama. Ginger Bread Mama. Doughtry Long. BPo; PoBA
I love you, great new Titan! Soldier: Twentieth Century. Isaac Rosenberg. ChMP; MMA
"I love you, Horowitz," he said, and blew his nose. Love in Brooklyn. John Wakeman. AMV-81; SoSe
I love you, I like you. Love. William Jay Smith. RHPC
I love you, Mrs. Acorn. Would your husband mind. Song. Kath Fraser. PeHV
I love you more than the gilder his gilding. Token. Peggy Bacon. PV
"I love you, Mother," said little John. Which Loved Best? "Joy Allison." OHIP; WBLP
"I love you, my Lord!" Triolet. Paul T. Gilbert. PV
I love you, not because I love the guillotine. Ode to Freedom. Aaron Zeitlin, *tr. by* Keith Bosley. VWA
I love you, rotten. Medlars and Sorb-Apples. D. H. Lawrence. OAEL-2
"I love you, sweet: how can you ever learn." Youth's Antiphony. Dante Gabriel Rossetti. The House of Life, XIII. VLP
I love you—Titan lover. Girl to Soldier on Leave. Isaac Rosenberg. MMA
I Love You Truly. Carrie Jacobs Bond. BLSo, *with music*; FSN, *with music*; TreFS
I love you well, my steel-white dagger. Dagger. Mikhail Yuryevich Lermontov, *tr. by* Max Eastman. AWP
"I love you," you said between two mouthfuls of pudding. A Considered Reply to a Child. Jonathan Price. BoLoP
I love you! You say, "I don't believe you." Words Words Words. Marilyn Krysl. AMV-80
I love your hands. Your Hands. Angelina Weld Grimké. CDC; PoBA
I love your lips when they're wet with wine. I Love You. Ella Wheeler Wilcox. BLPA; FaBoBe; FPL
I loved/ secretly. *Unknown, tr. fr. Latin by* Willis Barnstone. *Fr.* Carmina Burana. BoWoP
I loved a child of this countrie. *Unknown.* GBL; PBWP
I Loved a Lass. George Wither. CH; HBV-1; NOBE; OBEV; PoPle; UnTE
(Love Sonnet, A.) ElL; FaBoPP; GBL; OBS; ViBoPo
I loved her for that she was beautiful. My Lady. Philip James Bailey. OBVV
I loved her, one/ Not learned, save in gracious household ways. Tennyson. *Fr.* The Princess. PGD
I loved her softness, her warm human smell. The Lion's Bride. Gwen Harwood. BoWoP
I loved him not; and yet, now he is gone. The Maid's Lament. Walter Savage Landor. *Fr.* The Citation and Examination of William Shakespeare. HBV-1; OBEV; OBNC; OBRV; OBVV
I loved him three storms ere he loved me again. Love's Flight. Else Lasker-Schüler, *tr. by* Jethro Bithell. TrJP
I loved my friend. Poem. Langston Hughes. DFF; NTCP
I loved my lord, my black-haired lord, my young love. The Magnet. Ruth Stone. MoAmPo; NePA
I Loved Thee. Robert, Earl Nugent. *See* Epigram: "I loved thee beautiful and kind."
I Loved Thee, Atthis, in the Long Ago. Bliss Carman. CaP
I loved thee beautiful and kind. Epigram. Robert, Earl Nugent. FiBHP; NOEC
I loved thee ere I loved a woman, Love. To Art. Dante Gabriel Rossetti. POL
I loved thee long and dearly. Florence Vane. Philip Pendleton Cooke. AA; HBV-1
I Loved Thee Once. Sir Robert Aytoun. ViBoPo
(On a Woman's Inconstancy.) ElL
(To an Inconstant.) HBV-1
(To an Inconstant Mistress.) BSV
(To an Inconstant One.) OBEV; QFR
I loved thee, though I told thee not. The Secret. John Clare. GBL
I loved to talk of home. Pacific Epitaphs. Dudley Randall. NoAM
I Loved You Once. Pushkin, *tr. fr. Russian by* Dudley Randall. AmNP
("I loved you; even now I may confess," *tr. by* Reginald Mainwaring Hewitt.) BoLoP
I loved you, so I drew these tides of men into my hands. To S. A. T. E. Lawrence. PeHV
I, Lysidus, equestrian, offer these. The Golden Spurs. *Unknown, tr. by* Louis Untermeyer. UnTE
I. M. H. Maurice Baring. ACP
I. M.—R. T. Hamilton Bruce. W. E. Henley. *See* Invictus.
I machine-gunned tourists. Disillusionment. Claribel Alegria, *tr. by* Darwin Flakoll. AMV-80
I made a footing in the wall. Byron. *Fr.* The Prisoner of Chillon. OBRV
I made a loaf of bread. The White Bird. Roy McFadden. NeIP
I made a pilgrimage to find the God. Revelation. Edwin Markham. WGRP
I made a posy [*or* posie], while the day ran by. Life. George Herbert. AnAnS-1; FaBoRV; HBV-2; JCP; LiTB; MeLP; MePo; NoP; OBS; PoPle; SeCeV; SeCP; SeCV-1
I made a song and placed it far, near God. Fugato (Coda). Gad Hollander. VWA
I made a song for my dear love's delight. A Song's Worth. Susan Marr Spalding. AA
I made another garden, yea. Song. Arthur O'Shaughnessy. HBV-1; OBEV; OBVV
I made god upon god. Hilda Doolittle ("H. D."). *Fr.* Pygmalion. WGRP
I made my fire of little sticks. Little Sticks. Eric Rolls. PoAu-2
I made my song a coat. A Coat. W. B. Yeats. CABA; CMoP; LiTM; NoAM; PoEL-5
I made myself as a tree. March Hares. Andrew Young. MoVE
I made peanut butter sandwiches. The Runaway. Bobbi Katz. RHPC
I made the cross myself whose weight. A Little Parable. Anne Reeve Aldrich. AA; HBV-2
I made the Muses sick. The Death of the Gods; an Ode Written in Imitation of Pindar. L. Ker. NOEC
I made them lay their hands in mine and swear. Tennyson. *Fr.* Guinevere. TRV
I made up my mind for to change my way. The Trail to Mexico. *Unknown.* AmFP; CoSo
I made up my mind in the early morn. Trail to Mexico. *Unknown.* FSW
I, Maister Andro Kennedy. The Testament of Mr. Andro Kennedy. William Dunbar. OxBS
I make a pact with you, Walt Whitman. A Pact. Ezra Pound. AmPP; ELU; LiTA; NePA; NoAM; NOBA; OxBA; PAI; PoPl; TAP
I make a simple assertion. Working with Tools. A. R. Ammons. NoAM
I make a trip to each clock in the apartment. Two Mornings and Two Evenings. Elizabeth Bishop. PoA
I make all the poetic pauses. Dana Naone. CDW
I make man's ancient food. Bread. Nancy Keesing. PoAu-2
I make my shroud but no one knows. Song. Adelaide Crapsey. HBV-2
I make no question of your right to go. Muna Lee. Sonnets, III. HBMV
I make this dirge for you Miss Mary Binning I miss you. Dirge. *Unknown, tr. by* Armand Schwerner BoWoP
I make this song about me full sadly. The Wife's Lament. *Unknown, tr. fr. Anglo-Saxon.* WPE

I make this song sadly about myself. The Wife's Lament. *Tr. fr. Anglo-Saxon by* Willis Barnstone *and* Elene Kolb. BoWoP
I make you sightsee the sheer walls. To an Alcoholic. Sandra McPherson. MAYP
I marked all kindred powers the heart finds fair. Love Enthroned. Dante Gabriel Rossetti. The House of Life, I. OBNC
I marked the slow withdrawal of the year. In Memorabilia Mortis. Francis Sherman. CaP
I married a man of the Croydon class. Nervous Prostration. Anna Wickham. TW
I Married in My Youth a Wife. J. V. Cunningham. MoAmPo; TW (Epigram: "I married in my youth a wife.") PV
I married me a wife in the month of June. Risselty-Rosselty. *Unknown.* FSW
I marry'd a wife of late. Keep a Good Tongue in Your Head. Martin Parker. CoMu
I Marvel at the Ways of God. E. B. White. WhC
I marvel not Bassanio was so bold. Portia. Oscar Wilde. BrPo
I marvell'd why a simple child. Only Seven. Henry S. Leigh. BXAP; HBV-1; SpRo
I mastered the easy one first. Swallowing. Harold Bond. AMV-81
I, Maximus of Gloucester, to You. Charles Olson. *Fr.* The Maximus Poems. LiTM; NoAM; NOBA; PoM
I may be dead to-morrow, uncaressed. For the Book of Love. Jules Laforgue, *tr. by* Jethro Bithell. AWP; ErPo
I may be fast, I may be loose. Apologia. Herbert Farjeon. PV
I may be smelly and I may be old. The River God. Stevie Smith. BrRo; FaBoNo; FaBoTw; PBWP
I May, I Might, I Must. Marianne Moore. ELU; FF; OBAL
I may never be as clever as my neighbor down the street. Dad's Greatest Job. *Unknown.* STF
I may not touch the hand I saw. A Separation. William Johnson Cory. OBNC
I may not venture to your door. I Send Our Lady. Sister Mary Thérèse. ISi
I mean/ if I didn't know. Discovering. Sharon Scott. JB
I mean/ the fiddleheads have forced their babies. May 10th. Maxine W. Kumin. BoNaP; NYBP; RFM
I mean, I'm a no shoes hillbilly an' home. Gracie. Faye Kicknosway. GeTw; NMM
I mean not to defend the scapes of any. Apology for Loose Behavior. Ovid, *tr. by* Christopher Marlowe. Amores, II, 4. UnTE
I mean to penetrate the particular. The Medium IV: Sights. Carl Rakosi. InPS
I meant to do my work today. Called Away. Richard Le Gallienne. SoPo; SUS; TiPo
I meant to have but modest needs. Emily Dickinson. BiP
I Meant to Tell You. Sean Haldane. POL
I measure every grief I meet. Emily Dickinson. MoAB; MoAmPo
I measured myself by the wall in the garden. Day Dreams, or Ten Years Old. Margaret Johnson. BLPA
I meditate long. She. Manfred Winkler, *tr. by* Mary Zilzer. VWA
I meditate upon a swallow's flight. Coole Park, 1929. W. B. Yeats. OAEL-2; OBMV; OxBI
I meet Mother on the street. Poem. Lennart Bruce. POL
I meet you in an evil time. An Eclogue for Christmas. Louis MacNeice. FaBoMo; MoPo; MoVE; NoAM; OBMV
I member we went to the hospital that day. The Killing of the Birds. Shirley Williams. BoWoP
I mend the fyre and beikit me about. Robert Henryson. *Fr.* The Testament of Cresseid. EBEV
I met a Californian who would. Robert Frost. *Fr.* New Hampshire. DBV
I met a child upon the moor. On the Moor. Cale Young Rice. HBV-1
I met a cracksman coming down the Strand. Theodore Martin. *Fr.* The Thieves' Anthology. FaBoPa
I met a girl from Derrygrave. A New Song. Seamus Heaney. FaBoTw
I met a lady/ on a lazy street. From the Hazel Bough. Earle Birney. NIP
I met a little Elf-man, once. The Little Elf [*or* Elfman]. John Kendrick Bangs. AA; FaBoBe; HBV-1; HBVY; NTCP; OBCA; OnUR; PDV; SoPo; TiPo
I met a little girl in Knoxville. Knoxville Girl. *Unknown.* FSW
I Met a Man. Hughes Mearns. *See* Little Man Who Wasn't There, The.
I met a man as I went walking. Puppy and I. A. A. Milne. FaPON; OnUR; PDV; SoPo; TiPo
I met a man in an onion bed. The Man in the Onion Bed. John Ciardi. SO
I met a man in older lands. On the Safe Side. Lord Dunsany. OxBI
I met a man in South Street, tall. Cutty Sark. Hart Crane. *Fr.* The Bridge. FaBoMo
I met a man the other day. The Counselor. Dorothy Parker. InMe
I met a man with a triple-chin. The Man Who Sang the Sillies. John Ciardi. OBCA
I met a ragged man. The Song. Theodore Roethke. AP; CrMA
I met a seer. The Book of Wisdom. Stephen Crane. *Fr.* The Black Riders. HoPM; MoAmPo
I met a strange woman. C Is for Charms. Eleanor Farjeon. WSC
I met a toad. Warty Bliggens, the Toad. Don Marquis. *Fr.* Archy and Mehitabel. FiBHP
I met a traveler [*or* traveller] from an antique land. Ozymandias [*or* Ozymandias of Egypt *or* Sonnet: Ozymandias]. Shelley. AWP; BeLS; BiP; CABA; CH; DL; EnRP; FaBoBe; FaBoCh; FaBoEn; FaBoRV; FaFP; FaPo; FaPoR; FF; FiP; FPL; GTBS; GTBS-P; HAP; HBV-2; HBVY; HeIP; HoPM; InPK; LoBV; NIP; NOBE; NoP; OAEL-2; OAEP; OBNC; PAI; PoLF; PoPle; PoRA; PrIM; RoGo; SCV; SeCeV; SoSe; SpRo; TEP; TreF; TrGrPo; WeW; WHA
I met a traveller from an antique land. Ozymandias Revisited. Morris Bishop. BXAP; SpRo
I met an adolescent kitten on Lexington Ave. Eastside Chick with Drive. Albert Spector. CTBA
I met an elf-man in the woods. How to Treat Elves. Morris Bishop. DBV; FiBHP; OBAL; OBCA; PoPl
I met an honest man today. Alien. William Price Turner. OxBS
I Met at Eve. Walter de la Mare. HBMV
I met ayont the cairney. Empty Vessel. "Hugh MacDiarmid." BSV; FaBoTW; NoP; OxBS
I Met by Chance. Heine, *tr. fr. German by* John Todhunter. AWP
I met Death—he was a sportsman—on Cole's/ Island. Cole's Island. Charles Olson. *Fr.* The Maximus Poems. PoM
I met four guinea hens today. Life. Alfred Kreymborg. ELU
I met God in the morning. The Secret [*or* His Presence Came like Sunrise]. Ralph Spaulding Cushman. BLRP; STF; TRV
I met her as a blossom on a stem. The Dream. Theodore Roethke. LLLT; MoVE; NIP; NoP; NYBP; UnPo
I Met Her in the Garden Where the Praties Grow, *with music.* *Unknown.* AS
I met her on the Umbrian Hills. The Lady Poverty. Evelyn Underhill. HBV-2
I met him again, he was trudging along. I Fights Mit Sigel! Grant P. Robinson. BLPA
I met him in Venezuela. Venezuela. *Unknown.* FSW
I met in Mesilla. Edward Dorn. *Fr.* Gunslinger. NoAM
I met Louisa in the shade. Louisa. Wordsworth. EnRP; GBL
I met Musette/ In the water-closet. Vague Lyric by G. M. Max Beerbohm. FaBoEE
I met my preacher the other day. Scandalize My Name. *Unknown.* FSW
I Met My Solitude. Naomi Replansky. BrRo
I met Poetry, an old prostitute walking. Moral Story II. David Wright. ChMP; PeSA
I met the Bishop on the road. Crazy Jane Talks with the Bishop. W. B. Yeats. BoLoP; CABA; CMoP; CoBMV; EBEV; ErPo; InPK; NoAM; NoP; OAEL-2; OAEP; PAI; PPP
I met the boss; he wanted me to go. On the Trail to Idaho. *Unknown.* CoSo
I met the boy from Donegal, sez I, "Come here a minute." Sheskinbeg. Elizabeth Shane. HBMV
I met the Love-Talker one eve in the glen. The Love-Talker. "Ethna Carbery." AnIV; CH; OnYI; OxBI; WPE
I Met the Master. *Unknown.* BLRP; PoLF; STF
I met the yawning of my appetite. The North of Wales. Herbert Morris. NePoAm-2
I Met This Guy Who Died. Gregory Corso. NAs; Psk
I met three children on the road. The Three Children near Clonmel. Eileen Shanahan. OnYI; OxBI
I met with a country lass. The Thankful Country Lass; or, The Jolly Batchelor Kindly Entertained. *Unknown.* CoMu
I met with a jovial girl. The Roaring Lad and the Ranting Lass; or, A Merry Couple Madly Met. *Unknown.* CoMu
I met with Death in his country. Lord Dunsany. Songs from an Evil Wood, IV. HBV-2
I met with the girls coming from afar off. Love-Song of the Water Carriers. *Unknown.* PeSA
I mid the hills was born. Harold the Valiant. Mary Elizabeth DeWitt Stebbins. AA
I might have resented. Being Sad. Orban Veli Kanik, *tr. by* Talat Sait Halman. LLLT
I might have touched you where you lay. Quarrel. Jean McDougall. GoBC
I might not, if I could. Lines by a Medium. *Unknown.* NA
I might—unhappy word—oh me, I might. Astrophel and Stella, XXXIII. Sir Philip Sidney. OAEL-1; OBSC; SiPS
I mind as 'ow the night afore that show. The Chances. Wilfred Owen. MMA; OxBTC
I mind, love, how it ever was this way. Bed-Time. Ralph M. Jones. HBMV

I mind me in the days departed. The Deserted Garden. Elizabeth Barrett Browning. HBV-1
I mind, when I dream at nicht. The Gean Trees. Violet Jacob. PoSH
I Minded God, *with music.* Henry Ainsworth. AH
I mingle with your bones. The One Lost. Isaac Rosenberg. MoBrPo
I miss the peace and quiet of Chicago. Poem after Apollinaire. Ira Sadoff. AmPA
I miss the sun. Especially this winter. Turner's Sunrise. Helen Bevington. EyDe
I missed him when the sun began to bend. Lost and Found. George Macdonald. TRV; WGRP
I Missed His Book, but I Read His Name. John Updike. OBAL
I mock thee not, though I by thee am mocked. To Flaxman. Blake. FaBoEE; OxBoLi
I mourn "Patroclus," whilst I praise. My Last Terrier. John Halsham. HBV-1
I move amid your throng, I watch you hold. Sonnets to Miranda, VI. Sir William Watson. HBV-1
I move among my pots and pans. Trimming the Sails. Vassar Miller. NMM
I move back by shortcut. The World. Vern Rutsala. Psk
I move on feeling and have learned to distrust those who don't. Poem of Angela Yvonne Davis. Nikki Giovanni. PoBA
I move the curtain back. After I Have Voted. Laura Jensen. AmPA
I Move the Meeting Be Adjourned. Nicanor Parra, *tr. fr. Spanish by* Miller Williams. *Fr.* Manifesto. HoPM
I Move to Random Consolations. William Heyen. AmPA
I moved like a double agent among the big concepts. England's Difficulty. Seamus Heaney. CIP
I moved, to keep the moon. On Aesthetics, More or Less. Peter Kane Dufault. NYBP
I moved to the window to wait for somebody. A Suicide. Tom Kryss. NeAC
I Mun Be Married a Sunday. Nicholas Udall. *Fr.* Ralph Roister Doister. EIL
I Murder Hate by Field or Flood. Burns. NCEP
I Muriel stood at the altar-table. Don Baty, the Draft Register. Muriel Rukeyser. NNaP
I Muse Not. Francis Davison. TW
I must/ Not trust. Anacreontic. Robert Herrick. CaPo
I Must and I Will Get Married, *with music.* *Unknown.* TrAS
I must be dreaming through the days. Experience. Lesbia Harford. CBAP; PoAu-1
"I must be going, no longer staying." The Grey Cock. *Unknown.* ELP; OBET
I must be mad, or very tired. Meeting-House Hill. Amy Lowell. MoAmPo; OxBA; PoRA; SBG
I must complain, yet doe enjoy my love. Thomas Campion. AAS
I must confess that often I'm. *Time* like an Ever-rolling Stream. P. G. Wodehouse. FiBHP
I must depart, but like to his last breath. Parted Souls. Lord Herbert of Cherbury. AnAnS-2; SeCP
"I must eat an apple," said Link. An Apple a Day. Lee Blair. TDH
I must explain why it is that at night, in my own house. Still Life. Reed Whittemore. CoAP; ConAP
I must go back to winter. Two Decisions. Vernon Watkins. OxBTC
I must go down to the seas again, to the lonely sea and the sky. Sea Fever. John Masefield. EtS; FaBoBe; FaBV; FaPON; FaPoR; FPL; HBV-1; HBVY; MoAB; MoBrPo; MOS; OBVV; OHFP; OxBTC; PDV; PoLF; PoPl; TiPo; TreF; TrGrPo; WHA
I must go down to the seas again, where the billows romp and reel. Sea-Chill. Arthur Guiterman. BXAP; FaBoPa; MOS
I must go. I must gather my few things. Listening to Her. Natan Zach, *tr. by* Laya Firestone. VWA
I Must Go Walk the Wood So Wild. *Unknown.* MeEL; NCEP
(Wood So Wild, The.) WiR
I must have been mistaken. The Trick Is Consciousness. Paula Gunn Allen. TWSS
I must have passed the crest a while ago. The Long Hill. Sara Teasdale. HBMV; LiTA; MoAmPo; PoPl
I must have wanton poets, pleasant wits. Christopher Marlowe. *Fr.* Edward the Second. ViBoPo
I must, I will have gin!—that skillet take. Strip Me Naked, or Royal Gin for Ever; a Picture. *Unknown.* NOEC
I must lie down with them all soon and sleep. Thomas Kinsella. *Fr.* Nightwalker. BIrV
I must not gaze at them although. The Barrier. Claude McKay. BANP
I must not grieve my Love, whose eyes would read. To Delia, XLVIII. Samuel Daniel. EIL; HBV-1; OBEV; PoPle
I must not think of thee; and, tired yet strong. Renouncement. Alice Meynell. BoLoP; HBV-1; MoBrPo; NOBE; OBEV; OBMV; OBNC; OBVV; TreFT; ViBoPo; WPE
I must not throw upon the floor. The Crust of Bread. *Unknown.* HBV-1; HBVY
I must possess you utterly. Possession. Richard Aldington. MoBrPo
I must remember. Shelley Silverstein. PoSC
I must remember to dismiss. Nature Study, after Dufy. Helen Bevington. NYBP
I must tell you. The Grass. George Bowering. MoCV
I must tell you. Young Sycamore. William Carlos Williams. TAP
I must wait for a stranger to knock on my door. Elegy. David Ignatow. NNaP
I, my dear, was born to-day. On My Birthday, July 21. Matthew Prior. OBEV
I myself saw furious with blood. Aeneas at Washington. Allen Tate. AP; FYAP; LiTA; MoPo; MoVE; NePA; NoAM; NOBA; OxBA
I nail Picasso's girl with a mirror. Notes from an Analyst's Couch. Anita Endrezze Probst. CDW
I, named by the tribe, am no rabbi. Axioms. Gad Hollander. VWA
I need/ No world more spacious than the region here. Greenock. John Davidson. *Fr.* A Ballad in Blank Verse of the Making of a Poet. BSV
I need a little stick when I. I Have to Have It. Dorothy Aldis. SoPo
I need a strength to keep me true. My Need. *Unknown.* STF
I Need No Sky. Witter Bynner. EaLo
I Need Not Go. Thomas Hardy. DTC; NOBE; OBEV; OBVV; OxBTC
I need not shout my faith. Thrice eloquent. Silence. Charles Hanson Towne. TRV; WGRP
I need not your needles. *Unknown.* OxNR
I need only fall asleep/ to return. Ana Blandiana, *tr. fr. Rumanian by* Stavros Deligiorgis. BoWoP
I need so much the quiet of your love. At Nightfall. Charles Hanson Towne. BLPA; FaBoBe
I ne'er could any lustre see. Air. Sheridan. *Fr.* The Duenna. HBV-1; NOEC
I Ne'er Was Struck. John Clare. *See* First Love.
I never asked for more than thou hast given. G. Lowes Dickinson. PeHV
I never asked you to be perfect—did I? The Imperfect Lover. Siegfried Sassoon. BrPo
I never believed that in my broken life. Ts'ai Yen, *tr. by* Kenneth Rexroth *and* Ling Chung. Eighteen Verses Sung to a Tatar Reed Whistle, XIII. BoWoP; WPOW
I never bought a young gazelle. 'Twas Ever Thus. *Unknown.* BXAP
I never build a song by night or day. My Comrade. Edwin Markham. AA
"I never can do it," the little kite said. How the Little Kite Learned to Fly. *Unknown.* HBV-1; HBVY
I never cared for Life: Life cared for me. Epitaph. Thomas Hardy. FaBoEE; FaBoRV
I never cast a flower away. Partings. Maria Jane Jewsbury. OxBChV
I never crossed your threshold with a grief. The Closed Door. Theodosia Garrison. BLPA
I never cut my neighbor's throat. Guilty. Marguerite Wilkinson. TRV
I never did on cleft Parnassus dream. Prologue to the First Satire. Persius, *tr. by* Dryden. AWP
I never drank of Aganippe well. Astrophel and Stella, LXXIV. Sir Philip Sidney. CABA; EnRePo; HeIP; OBSC; SiPS
I never even hear. Whistles. Rachel Field. TiPo
I Never Even Suggested It. Ogden Nash. FiBHP; FPL; LiTA; PoLF
I never felt so much. A Birthday. Edwin Muir. BSV; NAs
I never gave a lock of hair away. Sonnets from the Portuguese, XVIII. Elizabeth Barrett Browning. EBVV; HAP; HBV-1
I never got a telegram before. Telegram. William Wise. TiPo
I never had a barrel of money. Poor Man Blues. *Unknown.* FSW
I never had a happier time. One Saturday. "Marian Douglas." AA
I Never Had a Piece of Toast. James Payn. CenHV; FaBoPa
I never have got the bearings quite. The Flag. James Jeffrey Roche. PAH
I never have seen the snow so white. Christmas Birthday. Grace Ellen Glaubitz. SiSoSe
I never hear that one is dead. Emily Dickinson. MoVE
I never hear the word "escape." Emily Dickinson. CMoP; NCEP; NOBA
"I never hurt maid in all my time." *Unknown.* *Fr.* Robin Hood's Death. ViBoPo
I Never Knew. Glenn E. Wagoner. STF
I never knew how words were vain. Rain. Kenneth Slade Alling. HBMV
I never knew the earth had so much gold. Feuerzauber. Louis Untermeyer. TrJP
I never knew what real peace meant. I Never Knew. Glenn E. Wagoner. STF
I never know. When All the World Is Full of Snow. N. M. Bodecker. RHPC
I never learned the names. Santa Caterina. Myra Glazer Schotz. VWA
I never let you come to the games. I never. Basketball. Stephen Vincent. LiSp; NeAC
I never like the fellow's plan. The Down-Pullers. Walter E. Isenhour. STF
I never look at himself. Mirror Images. Laurel Speer. AMV-80

I never look upon the sea. Aunt Zillah Speaks. Herbert Palmer. FaBoTw
I never lost as much but twice. Emily Dickinson. AP; BLPL; MoAB; MoAmPo; NOBA; NoP; TAP
I never loved a dear gazelle. Tèma con Variazióni. "Lewis Carroll." FaBoNo; SpRo
I never loved your plains. Hills. Arthur Guiterman. HBVY
I never muse upon my lady's grace. George Edward Woodberry. Ideal Passion, XXV. HBMV
"I never nursed a dear gazelle." Thomas Moore. *Fr.* Lalla Rookh. SpRo
I never played for you. You'd have thrown. For the Death of Vince Lombardi. James Dickey. LiSp
I never plucked—a bumblebee. *Unknown.* WeW
I never prayed for Dryads, to haunt the woods again. An Invocation. William Johnson Cory. HBV-2; OBVV
I never quite saw fairy-folk. Very Nearly. Queenie Scott-Hopper. FaPON; SoPo
I never read of any enforceable regulation. Because Sometimes You Can't Always Be So. Kenneth Patchen. NaP
I never reared a young gazelle. 'Twas Ever Thus. Henry S. Leigh. FaBoCo; FaBoPa; HBV-1; SpRo
I never said I loved you, John. "No, Thank You, John." Christina Rossetti. TEP
I Never Saw a Man in a Negligee. Alta. GP
I never saw a moor. Emily Dickinson. AA; AP; EBCP; EvOK; FaFP; FaPON; FPL; GN; GP; HBV-2; HeIP; LiTA; LiTM; MoAB; MoAmPo; NePA; PoLF; PoPl; TAP; TreF; TrGrPo; TRV; WGRP
I never saw a purple cow. The Purple Cow. Gelett Burgess. CenHV; FaBoCo; FaBoNo; FaFP; FaPON; FiBHP; FPL; GrPl; HBV-2; HBVY; NA; NePA; NTCP; OBAL; OBCA; PDV; PoLF; PoPl; RHPC; SoPo; TiPo; TreFS; YaD
I never saw a wild thing. Self-Pity. D. H. Lawrence. BoAnP; OxBTC
I never saw any point. Alan Dugan. GP
I never saw more frogs. One of the Many Days. Norman MacCaig. PoSH
I never saw my father old. A Celebration. May Sarton. NePoAm-2
I never saw my father's father's face. Grandfather Yoneh. Emily Borenstein. AMV-81
I never saw the morning till to-day. Chariots. Witter Bynner. HBMV
I Never Saw the Train. Jean Roberts. AMV-80
I never saw you madam, lay [*or* sawe my Ladye laye] apart. The Cornet [*or* Complaint That His Ladie after She Knew of His Love Kept Her Face Alway Hidden from Him]. Earl of Surrey. AAS; OBSC; PoEL-1; SiPS
I never see the colored boats of night. The Age of Sheen. Dorothy Hughes. NYBP
I never see the newsboys run. Fleet Street. Shane Leslie. OnYI
I never see the red rose crown the year. Sonnet. John Masefield. *Fr.* Sonnets ("Long, long ago"). GoYe
I never see upon a hill. Symbols. John Richard Moreland. PGD
I never set my two eyes on a head was so fine as your head. A Translation from Walter von der Vogelweide. Walter von der Vogelweide, *tr. by* J. M. Synge. MoBrPo
I Never Shall Love the Snow Again. Robert Bridges. BrPo; CH; CMoP; FaBV; OAEP
I never speak a word. Mary Austin. *Fr.* Rhyming Riddles. TiPo
I never swung a staff and deep, oh deep. Roy Daniells. *Fr.* Deeper into the Forest. PeCV
I never thought that my love would leave me. Love Is Teasing. *Unknown.* OBET
I never thought that youth would go. Youth. Jessie B. Rittenhouse. HBMV
I never told you. What They Do to You in Distant Places. Marvin Bell. Psk
I never wanted to be a star. On Earth. Forugh Farrokhzad, *tr. by* Girdhard Tikku. BoWoP
I never will complain of my dear husband, Mrs. Henn. "He Didn't Oughter." A. P. Herbert. FiBHP
I Never Will Marry. *Unknown.* FSW
I never would 'ave done it if I'd known what it would be. Mules. C. Fox-Smith. BoAnP
I never would have remembered your name. Jimmy Bruder on Quincey Street. Carol Artman Montgomery. AMV-81
I newly had your little house erected. To My Lady Rogers, the Authors Wives Mother, How Doctor Sherwood Commended Her House in Bathe. Sir John Harington. EyDe
I no longer want to meet. For a Young South Dakota Man. Freya Manfred. TAT
I notified the Chasm Inspector about. A Chasm. Michael Silverton. PV
I, now at Carthage. He, shot dead at Rome. *Vale* from Carthage. Peter Viereck. LiTM; MiAP; MoAmPo
I now mean to be serious;—it is time. Lady Adeline Amundeville. Byron. Don Juan, XIII. PoEL-4
I now remembered slowly how I came. The Journey. Yvor Winters. MoVE
I now solicit not the Muses nine. William Woty. *Fr.* A Mock Invocation to Genius. NOEC
I now think[e], Love is rather deaf[e], then blind. My Picture Left in Scotland. Ben Jonson. AnAnS-2; EnRePo; MePo; PoEL-2; QFR; SeCP; SeCV-1
I now will throw myself down. A Dialogue. David Ignatow. NNaP
I nursed it in my bosom while it lived. Memory. Christina Rossetti. OBNC
I objurgate the centipede. The Centipede. Ogden Nash. FaPON
I observe: "Our sentimental friend the moon!" Conversation Galante. T. S. Eliot. HBMV
I, Oedipus, the club-foot, made to stumble. Oedipus. Edwin Muir. CMoP
I of my Spenser quite bereft. Book-Lender's Lament. *Unknown.* FaBoUs
I offer my back to the silken net. An Allegory. David Ignatow. VGW
I offer wrong to my beloved Saint. Caelica, XVIII. Fulke Greville. NCEP
I offer you the chance to forgive your wounds. Song from the Maker of Totems. Duane Niatum. STE
I oft have heard of Lydford law. Lydford Journey. William Browne. CavP
I oft stand in the snow at dawn. Don Marquis. *Fr.* To a Lost Sweetheart. FiBHP
I often dream of Auschwitz now. Dreams of Auschwitz. Boris Slutsky, *tr. by* Daniel Weissbort. VWA
I often have been told. The *Constitution* and the *Guerrière*. *Unknown.* PAH
I often have to wonder. Snoring. Aileen Fisher. SoPo
I often say my prayers. Do I Really Pray? John Burton. STF
I often sit and wish that I. A Kite. *Unknown.* SoPo; TiPo
I often think how once we used in summer fields to play. The Little Factory Girl to a More Fortunate Playmate. *Unknown.* SaC
I often wander on the beach. The Old Swimmer. Christopher Morley. LiSp
I Often Want to Let My Lines Go. Leib Neidus, *tr. fr. Yiddish by* Ruth Whitman. VWA
I often wish I were a King. If I Were King. A. A. Milne. OnUR
I often wonder as the fairy-story. The Lucky Marriage. Thomas Blackburn. GTBS-P
I often wonder if the race should die. On the Persistence of Humanity. G. S. Fraser. BSV
I on my horse, and Love on me, doth try. Astrophel and Stella, XLIX. Sir Philip Sidney. NoP; OAEL-1; SiPS
I once believed a single line. For E. J. P. Leonard Cohen. NoAM; NoP
I once broke evening bread with the brown-faced, white-smiled Prince of Siam. Words of Oblivion and Peace. Gabriel Preil, *tr. by* Robert Friend. VWA
I once conjectur'd that those tygers hard. Seaconk or Rehoboths Fate. Benjamin Tompson. SCAP
I once did an hour-long TV show reading. Osip Mandelshtam. Irving Layton. NeAC
I once did court a damsel most beautiful and bright. A Lover's Lament. *Unknown.* AmFP
I once did know a Turkish man. Ben Allah Achmet; or, The Fatal Tum. W. S. Gilbert. VLP
I once dressed up and went to town. Devilish Mary. *Unknown.* FSW
I once had a gal and I loved her well. When I Was a Brave Cowboy. *Unknown.* CoSo
I once had a sweet little doll, dears. The Lost Doll [*or* Song]. Charles Kingsley. *Fr.* The Water Babies. FaPON; MoShBr; OxBChV; PaPo; SoPo; TiPo
I once had money and a friend. Money and a Friend. *Unknown.* BLPA
I once knew a fellow named Arthur McBride. Arthur McBride. GBP; OBET
I once knew a lass and I loved her to [*or* I've oft heard her] tell. So I Let Her Go. *Unknown.* AmFP
I once knew a little girl, a charming beauty bright. The Rejected Lover. *Unknown.* AmFP
I Once Knew a Man. Lucille Clifton. GeTw
I once knowed an ole Sexion Boss but he done been laid low. The Old Section Boss. *Unknown.* BPo
I once lov'd a boy, and a bonny, bonny boy. *Unknown.* WTO
I Once Loved a Young Man. *Unknown.* AmFP
I once loved a young man as dear as my life. I'm Going to Georgia. *Unknown.* AmFP
I once may see when yeares shall wreck my wrong. Samuel Daniel. *Fr.* To Delia. AAS
I once spent an evening in a village. The Man Upright. Thomas MacDonagh. BIrV
I once thought that snowflakes were feathers. Snowflakes. Marchette Chute. PDV
I once was a bold fellow and went with a team. The Carter. *Unknown.* OBET
I Once Was a Maid. Burns. *Fr.* The Jolly Beggars. OxBoLi; UnTE

I once was a Pirate what sailed the 'igh seas. Cat Morgan Introduces Himself. T. S. Eliot. NOBL
I once was a seaman stout and bold. Jolly Soldier. *Unknown.* AmFP; OFD
I once was a tool of oppression. The Hayseed. Arthur L. Kellog. FSW
I once was happy, when, while yet a child. Charlotte Smith. *Fr.* Beachy Head. WPE
I once was in service. Rosemary Lane. *Unknown.* OBET
I once wrote a letter as follows. The Invoice. Robert Creeley. VGW
I Only Am Escaped Alone to Tell Thee. Howard Nemerov. CoAP; HeIP; NePA; NoAM
I only dreamed that high cliff we were on. With Kathy at Wisdom. Richard Hugo. FAZ
I only knew one poet in my life. How It Strikes a Contemporary. Robert Browning. CTC; GTBS-P; OAEL-2; PP; VLP
I only know that I was there. Ante-natal Dream. Patrick Kavanagh. NAs
I open an anthology. On the Dates of Poets. Michael L. Johnson. AMV-80
I open my eyes. A Factory Rainbow. Rose Saadi. SaC
I open the door and walk in. Pop. David McFadden. NeAC
I opened my door to this nutty witch. I've been suicidal. After Reading Sylvia Plath. Alta. IHMS
I opened the window wide and leaned. John Masefield. *Fr.* The Everlasting Mercy. WGRP
I ordered this, this clean wood box. The Arrival of the Bee Box. Sylvia Plath. FaBoMo; NaP
I Ought to Weep. *Unknown.* MeEL
I Ovid poet of my wantonnesse. Ovid, *tr. by* Christopher Marlowe. Amores, II, 1. OBVE
I owe nothing to winter. My Winter Past. Eldon Grier. NOBC
I owe you an apology. A Question of Form and Content. Jon Stallworthy. OxBC
I own John Graydon's place. John Graydon. Wilson MacDonald. CaP
I owned a slope full of stones. The Stones. Wendell Berry. GP
I pace the sounding sea-beach and behold. Milton. Longfellow. AA; AmPP; AP; AWP; NePA; NoP; TAP; TrGrPo
I paced alone on the road across the field. The Home. Rabindranath Tagore. GoJo
I pack the mirrors again and again. Invitation of the Mirrors. Tom McKeown. AMV-81
I paid a man at Martinmas. The Plowman. Burns. UnTE
I Paint What I See. E. B. White. NYBP
I paint you this. Troopship for France, War II. George Bogin. FAZ
I painted a picture—green sky—and showed it to my mother. Accomplishments. Cynthia MacDonald. DFF; GP
I painted her a gushing thing. Disillusioned [*or* My Fancy]. "Lewis Carroll." CenHV; FaBoCo
I painted my eyes with black antimony. Love Song. *Tr. fr. Bagirmi by* H. Gaden. BoWoP
I painted on the roof of a skyscraper. People Who Must. Carl Sandburg. PDV
I painted the mailbox. That was fun. Painting the Gate. May Swenson. WeW
I paints and paints. Shirley Brooks. CenHV
I park the car because I'm happy. Now. Christopher Gilbert. MAYP
I park the car half in the ditch and switch off and sit. Stealing Trout. Ted Hughes. NYBP
I parted from my life last night. On the Death of His Wife. Muireadach O'Dalaigh, *tr. by* Frank O'Connor. BIrV; CIP
I Pass a Lighted Window. Clement Wood. HBMV
I pass my days among the quiet places. Hallowed Places. Alice Freeman Palmer. HBV-1
I passed a tomb among green shades. Her Rival for Aziza. *Unknown, tr. by* E. Powys Mathers. *Fr.* The Thousand and One Nights. AWP
I passed along the water's edge below the humid trees. The [*or* An] Indian upon God. W. B. Yeats. MoBrPo; WGRP
I passed beside the reverend walls. *See* I past beside the reverend walls.
I passed between the bell and the glass. 49th and 5th, December 13. Josephine Jacobsen. NYP
I passed by a garden, a little Dutch garden. A Little Dutch Garden. Harriet Whitney Durbin. AA
I passed by the beach. Yamabe no Akahito, *tr. fr. Japanese by* Kenneth Rexroth. HoPM
I passed by the house of the young man who loves me. Love Song. *Unknown, tr. by* J. E. Manchip White. TTY
I passed Olympus in the night. Tourist. Mark Van Doren. NePoAm-2
I passèd through a garden green. Verbum Caro Factum Est. *Unknown.* SBVL
I passed through the gates of the city. Life and Nature. Archibald Lampman. PeCV
I past [*or* passed] beside the reverend walls. He Revisits Cambridge. In Memoriam A. H. H., LXXXVII. Tennyson. EBVV; FaBoPP
I pause not now to speak of Raleigh's dreams. John Smith's Approach to Jamestown. James Barron Hope. PAH
I paused in a garden alley of cypress and rose, resembling Paradise. Last Things. Kathleen Raine. NYBP
I paused last eve beside the blacksmith's door. *See* Last eve I passed beside a blacksmith's door.
I peeled bits of straw and I got switches too. Bits of Straw [*or* Song]. John Clare. VLP; WiR
I peeped through the window. *Unknown.* OxNR
I perceive the cow's slightly. Life in the Country. Michael Silverton. ELU
I persist in a little fabric between me and the world. J. Michael Yates. *Fr.* The Great Bear Lake Meditations. NOBC
I pick up the *World Herald* and turn. Robert Lowell Is Dead. Patrick Worth Gray. SOTS
I picked up a leaf. Les Etiquettes Jaunes. Frank O'Hara. CAPP
I picked up the clod. The Clod. Edwin Curran. HBMV
I picture her there in the quaint old room. Dreaming in the Trenches. William Gordon McCabe. AA
I picture it as coming. Divorce. Kate Jennings. AMV-80
I pitched my day's leazings in Crimmercrock Lane. The Dark-eyed Gentleman. Thomas Hardy. MoAB; MoBrPo; UnPo; VLP
I place myself at the edge of thy Grace. *Tr. from Gaelic by* Douglas Hyde. WTO
I place these numbed wrists to the pane. Nightmare Begins Responsibility. Michael S. Harper. DiL; GeTw; LCAP; TAP
I place two cups beside each other. Family Cups. Steve Orlen. Str
I placed/ my hand. Misunderstanding. Irving Layton. PV
I placed a jar in Tennessee. Anecdote of the Jar. Wallace Stevens. AmPP; AP; CMoP; CoBMV; HeIP; HoPM; InPK; LiTA; MoAB; MoAmPo; MoVE; NePA; NIP; NoAM; NOBA; NoP; OxBA; PAI; PoA; PPP; PrIm; SOTW; TAP; UnPo
I placed my dream in a boat. Song. Cecilia Meireles, *tr. by* Eloah F. Giacomelli. WPOW
I planned to have a border of lavender. Paul Goodman. VGW
I plant corn four years. Corn-Planter. Maurice Kenny. STE
"I play a spade.—Such strange new faces." Arrivals at a Watering-Place. Winthrop Mackworth Praed. NOBL
"I play for Seasons; not Eternities!" Modern Love, XIII. George Meredith. FaBoEn; OBNC
I play it cool. Motto. Langston Hughes. PoBA; PoNe
I play pool. I aim toward the faces. Games. Sandra McPherson. LCAP
I play the Masonic Funeral March. Birmingham. Julia Fields. *Fr.* Poems: Birmingham 1962-1964. PoBA; PoNe
I play your furies back to me at night. High Fidelity. Thom Gunn. PoA
I played a game of baseball, I belong to Casey's Nine. Slide, Kelly, Slide. J. W. Kelly. FaFP; TreFS
I played I was two polar bears. The Bear Hunt. Margaret Widdemer. FaPON
I Played on the Grass with Mary. Ernest Walsh. ErPo
I played with you 'mid cowslips blowing. Love and Age. Thomas Love Peacock. *Fr.* Gryll Grange. HBV-1; OBEV; OBNC; PoPle; ViBoPo
I pledge myself through thick and thin. Tory Pledges. Thomas Moore. FaBoCo; OBSV
I pluck the white hibiscus. Mr. A. E. Housman on the Olympic Games. E. V. Knox. WhC
I plucked a honeysuckle where. The Honeysuckle. Dante Gabriel Rossetti. SyP
I plucked a throstle from the throat of God. The Thrush. Timothy Corsellis. WaaP; WaP
I plucked my soul out of its secret place. I Know My Soul. Claude McKay. BPo
I plucked pink blossoms from mine apple-tree. An Apple Gathering. Christina Rossetti. OBNC; OLR
I ply with all the cunning of my art. The Craftsman. Marcus B. Christian. PoNe
I Point Out a Bird. Quinton Duval. FAZ
I ponder how He died, despairing once. Before an Old Painting of the Crucifixion. N. Scott Momaday. QFR
I pop my whip, I bring the blood. Ox-driving Song. *Unknown.* OuSiCo
I praise a snakeskin or a stone. Snakeskin and Stone. Keith Douglas. NePoEA
I praise God's mankind in an old woman. Lines: I Praise God's Mankind in an Old Woman. Wilfred Watson. NOBC
I praise the disk of the rising sun. Vidya, *tr. by* Daniel H. H. Ingalls. *Fr.* The Sun. PBWP; WPOW
I praise the Frenchman, his remark was shrewd. Retirement. William Cowper. BLPA
I praise Thee not, with impious pride. Lewis Morris. *Fr.* A Heathen Hymn. TrPWD
I pray attend unto this Jest. The Fair Maid of the West. *Unknown.* CoMu
I pray for memory. Turtle. Robert Lowell. LCAP

I pray! My little body and whole span. Supplication of the Black Aberdeen. Kipling. BLPA
I pray not for the joy that knows. A Prayer. Marion Franklin Ham. TrPWD
"I pray," said Rolfe, "a word." Ungar and Rolfe. Herman Melville. *Fr.* Clarel. OxBA
I pray that the great world's flowering stay as it is. The Gardener to His God. Mona Van Duyn. TrCP; UnPo; WPE
I pray the prayer the Easterners do. Salaam Alaikum. *Unknown.* PoLF
I pray thee, Dante, shouldst thou meet with Love. To Dante Alighieri: He Mistrusts the Love of Lapo Gianni. Guido Cavalcanti, *tr. by* Dante Gabriel Rossetti. AWP
I Pray Thee Leave, Love Me No More. Michael Drayton. *See* To His Coy Love.
I pray thee Nymph Penaeis stay, I chase not as a fo. Ovid, *tr. by* Arthur Golding. *Fr.* Metamorphoses, I. OBVE
I pray Thee O Lord. A Prayer. Juljan Tuwim, *tr. by* Wanda Dynowska. TrJP
I Pray You. Thomas Moore. *Fr.* Odes to Nea. OBNC; OBRV
I pray you all give your audience. Everyman. *Unknown.* OAEL-1; PoEL-1
I pray you all with one thought. Amend Me. *Unknown.* OxBM
"I pray you, cum kiss me." My Little Pretty Mopsy. *Unknown.* OxBM
I pray you, let us roam no more. I Pray You. Thomas Moore. *Fr.* Odes to Nea. OBNC; OBRV
I pray you, M, to me be trew. Letter to "M." *Unknown.* OxBM
I pray you, what's asleep? As the Day Breaks. Ernest McGaffey. AA
I prayed for strength, and then I lost awhile. The Answered Prayer. Annie Johnson Flint. STF
I preached as never sure to preach again. Richard Baxter. *Fr.* Love Breathing Thanks and Praise. TRV
I press [*or* presse] not to the quire, nor dare I greet. To My Worthy Friend Master George Sands [*or* Sandys], on His Translation of the Psalms. Thomas Carew. AnAnS-2; CaPo; JCP; MeLP; MePo; OBS; SeCV-1
I Pressed Her Rebel Lips. *Unknown.* ErPo
("I gently touched her hand: she gave.") BoLoP
I prithee [*or* prethee] let my heart alone. Song. Thomas Stanley. AnAnS-2; ViBoPo
I prithee send me back my heart. Song. *At. to* Henry Hughes *and also to* Sir John Suckling. HBV-1; JCP; ViBoPo
I Promessi Sposi. Cid Corman. HoAn
I Promise Nothing. A. E. Housman. PPP
I promise to make you more alive than you've ever been. Ordeal. Nina Cassian, *tr. by* Michael Imply *and* Brian Swann. PBWP
I promise you by the harsh funeral. Burns Singer. Sonnets for a Dying Man, XLVIII. NePoEA-2
I promised once if I got hold of. Written in a Copy of Swift's Poems, for Wayne Burns. James Wright. NOBA
I promised Sylvia to be true. Song: I Promised Sylvia [*or* Song]. Earl of Rochester. CavP; SeCePo
I propose to you. The Statue. Robert Creeley. LCAP
I pull out of the depths of the earth. Etnairis Rivera, *tr. fr. Spanish by* Julio Marzán. InW
I put my hand all in her own. Gently Johnny, My Jingalo. *Unknown.* FSW
I put my hand upon [*or* on] her toe. Gently, Johnny My Jingalo. *Unknown.* OBET; UnTE
I put my hat upon my head. A Second Stanza for Dr. Johnson. Donald Hall. FiBHP; ShM
I put my hat upon my head. Ballad. Samuel Johnson. NOBL
I put my hat upon my head, *parody.* F. A. V. Madden. BXAP
I put my hat upon my head, *parody.* Ian Sainsbury. BXAP
I put my hat upon my head, *parody.* Zan Stirling. BXAP
I put my hat upon my head, *parody.* Peter Veale. BXAP
I put those things there.—See them burn. The Song of the Demented Priest. John Berryman. MoPo
I put thy hand aside, and turn away. A Farewell. "Madeline Bridges." AA
I quarreled with kings till the Sabbath. Song of the Sabbath. Kadia Molodowsky, *tr. by* Jean Valentine. PBWP; WPOW
I quarreled with my brother. The Quarrel. Eleanor Farjeon. FaPON
I question not God's means or ways. God Knows the Answer. F. B. Whitney. STF
"I quite realized," said Columbus. E. C. Bentley. *Fr.* Clerihews. FiBHP
I raced west away from the dawn. Thaba Bosio. S. D. R. Sutu, *tr. by* Dan Kunene *and* Jack Cope. PeSA
I, Rainey Betha, 22. Plaint. Charles Henri Ford. EAS; MoVE; PPON
I raise my cup and invite. Moon, Flowers, Man. Su Tung-p'o, *tr. by* Kenneth Rexroth. NaP
I raise the curtains and go out. Alone. Chu Shu-chen, *tr. by* Kenneth Rexroth. BoWoP
I raised a dog and his name was Blue. Old Blue. *Unknown.* OuSiCo
I Raised a Great Hullabaloo. *Unknown.* PDV; RHPC
I raised my eyes aloft, and I beheld. Dante. *Fr.* Divina Commedia: Paradiso. TRV
I ran along the yellow sand. Pete at the Seashore. Don Marquis. GDP
I ran for a catch. Coulson Kernahan. CenHV
I ran from the prison house but they captured me. The Prison House. Alan Paton. PeSA
I ran onto Mehitabel again. The Old Trouper. Don Marquis. *Fr.* Archy and Mehitabel. FaBoCo
I ran out in the morning, when the air was clean and new. Autumn Morning at Cambridge. Frances Cornford. HBMV; MoVE; OBVV; PoRA
I ran to the church. Journey Back to Christmas. Gwen Dunn. OBCP
I ran until lips tripped over. Escape. Ilya Rubin, *tr. by* Linda Zisquit. VWA
I ran up and grabbed your arm, the way a man. At the Washing of My Son. David Ray. DiL
I ran upon life unknowing, without or science or art. Tennyson. FaBoEE
I rang them up, while touring Timbuctoo. To Someone Who Insisted I Look Up Someone. X. J. Kennedy. PV
I rasp like a sick dog. Theodore Roethke. POL
I reach from pain. Reuben, Reuben. Michael S. Harper. GeTw
I reach the marble-streeted town. The Marble-streeted Town. Thomas Hardy. FaBoPP
I reached that waterhole, its mud designed. Roland Robinson. *Fr.* The Wanderer. CBAP
I reached the highest place in Spoon River. Henry C. Calhoun. Edgar Lee Masters. *Fr.* Spoon River Anthology. LiTA; LiTM
I Read a Tight-fisted Poem Once. Nancy Woods. RFM
I read about the Blaskets and Dunquin. J. M. Synge. FaBoEE
I read an impatient man. To a Western Bard Still a Whoop and a Holler Away from English Poetry. William Meredith. PP
I read in the news, the President said. Hallelujah I'm a Bum. Barbara Dane *and* Irwin Silber. FSW
I read it in the restroom, in pink nail polish. You're Sorry, Your Mother Is Crazy, & I'm a Chinese Shiksa. Deborah Lee. BrSi
I read last night of the Grand Review. A Second Review of the Grand Army. Bret Harte. HBV-2; PAH
I read last night with many pauses. Troy. Robin Flower. SeCePo
I read my sentence steadily. Emily Dickinson. NePA; NoAM; QFR
I read of a thousand killed. A Thousand Killed. Bernard Spencer. OBWP
I read once more this care-worn, patient face. On a Picture of Lincoln. John Vance Cheney. PGD
I read or write, I teach or wonder what is truth. Apologia pro Vita Sua. Sedulius Scottus, *tr. by* Helen Waddell. BIrV
I read somewhere that a swan, snow-white. The Watch of a Swan. Sarah Morgan Bryan Piatt. AA
I read the marble-lettered name. A Grave in Hollywood Cemetery, Richmond. Margaret Junkin Preston. AA
I read the news today, oh boy. A Day in the Life. John Lennon *and* Paul McCartney. PPoe
I read with him at Hopkins, substituting. Robert Lowell. Richard O'Connell. AMV-81
I read with varying degrees. Edna St. Vincent Millay. *Fr.* Journal. ImOP
I read your testimony and I thought. John Beecher. *Fr.* To Alexander Meiklejohn. GOA
I reade in ancient times of yore. The Map of Mock-Begger Hall. *Unknown.* CoMu
I really do not like that cat. What Could It Be? William Cole. BoAnP
"I really take it very kind." Domestic Asides; or, Truth in Parentheses. Thomas Hood. EnRP
I reason, earth is short. Emily Dickinson. TAP
I recall, before the banks. By the Bridge. Ted Walker. NYBP
I reckon—when I count at all. Emily Dickinson. MoAmPo; PP
I recognized him by his skips and hops. Pan and the Cherries. Paul Fort, *tr. by* Jethro Bithell. AWP
I recognized you because when I saw the print. Juan Ramón Jiménez, *tr. fr. Spanish by* H. R. Hays. OLR
I recollect a nurse call'd [*or* called] Ann. A Terrible Infant. Frederick Locker-Lampson. FiBHP; HBV-1; InMe; TreFS; WhC
I recollect in early life. My First Love. Harry Graham. FiBHP
I recommend for plain dis-ease. Convalescence, VII. David McCord. WhC
I refuse the breakage. Model. A. R. Ammons. FAZ
I regretted the arrival of my death. What Profit? Immanuel di Roma, *tr. by* J. Chotzner. TrJP
I Remember. Thomas Hood. CH
I Remember. Mae Jackson. BOLo; CNA; PoBA
I Remember. Ricardo Sánchez, *tr. fr. Spanish by* Toni Empringham. FIA
I Remember. Stevie Smith. BoLoP; BoWoP; InPK; OxBC
I remember a dim evening in Kishinyov. A Woman from the Book of Genesis. Dovid Knut, *tr. by* John Glad. VWA
I remember a dug-out we dug in the backyard as children. Reflections upon

a Recurrent Suggestion by Civil Defense Authorities That I Build a Bombshelter in My Backyard. Reed Whittemore. PoCh
I remember a house where all were good. In the Valley of the Elwy. Gerard Manley Hopkins. NOCV; ViBoPo
I remember a strong old man. I Remember. Ricardo Sánchez, *tr. by* Toni Empringham. FIA
I remember, as if it were yesterday. One and One. C. Day Lewis. OAEP
I remember at times. Scholar II. Seamus Deane. CIP
I remember . . . (at what hour of the day). The Agonizing Memory. Pierre Louys. *Fr.* Chansons de Bilitis. PeHV
I remember back in hi school. The Art of Enforced Deprivation. Alta. GP
I remember coming up. Breath. Reginald Gibbons. MAYP
I remember distinctly the tired tumult of my urges. Journey to a Parallel. Bruce McM. Wright. PoNe
I Remember Galileo. Gerald Stern. FYAP
I remember gestures of infants. To Drink. Gabriela Mistral, *tr. by* Gunda Kaiser. NU
I remember God as an eccentric millionaire. Quite Apart from the Holy Ghost. Adrian Mitchell. OBSV
I remember hiding in the hall closet. Light under the Door. Marilyn Waniek. MAYP
I remember how I came here. Winter Evening Poem. Laura Jensen. LCAP
I remember how, long ago, I found. Crystals like Blood. "Hugh MacDiarmid." HAP; InPS; NoP
I Remember How She Sang. Rob Penny. CNA; PoBA
I remember how we stood. The Last Corn Shock. Glenn Ward Dresbach. FaPON
I Remember, I Remember. Thomas Hood. BLPA; ELP; EnRP; FaBoBe; FaBV; FaFP; FaPoR; FaPON; FPL; HBV-1; LiTB; NOBE; OBRV; PoEL-4; TreF
(I Remember.) CH
(Past and Present.) GTBS; GTBS-P; TRV
I Remember, I Remember. Philip Larkin. FaBoPP; NOBL
I remember it well; 'twas a morn dull and gray. Macdonald's Raid. Paul Hamilton Hayne. PAH
I remember little. October Hill. R. Wayne Hardy. LFAC
I remember long veils of green rain. Green Rain. Dorothy Livesay. NIP; NOBC
I remember Longwood. Blind Adolphus. Angela McCabe. AmPA
I remember mother. Down Home. Randolph Outlaw. LFAC
I remember my father. To My Son, Not Yet Born. William Virgil Davis. AMV-81
I remember my first gun. Two Childhood Memories. Al Zolynas. LTB
I remember my mother, the day that we met. For the Crêche. G. K. Chesterton. *Fr.* Songs of Education. FaBoCo
I remember my mother's Aunt Rebecca. Great-Aunt Rebecca. Elizabeth Brewster. NOBC
I remember not knowing. Puberty. Jon Wallace. AMV-80
I remember now how first I knew what death was. Original Sin. Alexander Laing. NYBP
I remember one September/ On one Friday night. Billy Lyons and Stack O'Lee. *Unknown.* BluL
I remember one September,/ Storm winds swept the town. Mighty Day. *Unknown.* FSW
I remember or remember hearing. Once upon a Great Holiday. Anne Wilkinson. WHW
I remember partly. Southwest Passage. Dudley Fitts. PoA
I remember rooms that have had their part. Rooms. Charlotte Mew. PBWP
I remember that before. Flying Letters. Zerubavel Gilead, *tr. by* Dorothea Krook. VWA
I remember the August afternoon. August Afternoon. Nancy Remaly. CTBA
I remember the day/ Mama called me in from. Rice and Rose Bowl Blues. Diane Mei Lin Mark. BrSi
I remember the day I arrived. Doubting. Louis Simpson. NNaP
I remember the dread with which I at a quarter past four. False Security. John Betjeman. CMoP; NoP
I remember the evening. The Swarming Bees. James Laughlin. VGW
I remember the feel of a hammer. Elegy. Robert Winner. DiL.
I remember the forehead born. Uncle. Philip Levine. NNaP
I remember the Indian Hospital. Birthplace. Duane Big Eagle. STE
I remember the last red rose. 3 A.M. Lauris Edmond. OCNZ
I remember the neckcurls, limp and damp as tendrils. Elegy for Jane. Theodore Roethke. AmPP; AP; BiP; CoAP; FF; GLGT; HAP; InPK; InPS; LiTM; MoAB; MoAmPo; MP; NePA; NoP; PAI; PPoe; TAP; TwAmPo; TwCP; WeW
I remember the night. Somebody Call. Carolyn M. Rodgers. JB
I remember the Roman Emperor, one of the cruellest of them. Exeat. Stevie Smith. NoAM
I remember the time. A Little Girl's Dream World. Della Burt. BlSi
I remember them, man and wife, in their little car. Couple. Walter Stone. NYBP
I remember, they sent. Corpse-bearing. Thomas Ashe. EBVV
I remember Wednesday was the day. Two Lean Cats. Myron O'Higgins. PoBA; PoNe
I remember when a Sunday friend and I. Letter to My Mother. Anita Skeen. IHMS
I remember when the unicorns. The Days of the Unicorns. Phyllis Webb. NOBC
I remember you in young peaches like jade. Elegy for the Wife of a Friend. Yü Hsüan-chi, *tr. by* Geoffrey Waters. BoWoP
I remember, you tell me, a daughter, a love, as high as my kneecap. Shore. Diana O Hehir. NPGG
I remembered today. Phil. Ted Kooser. AMV-81
I remove a red cement slab in the dead of night. What I Have Done. Gerard Malanga. FAZ
I renounce the blindness of the magazines. A Prayer to Escape from the Market Place. James Wright. NaP
I reside at Table Mountain and my name is Truthful James. The Society upon the Stanislaus [*or* Plain Language from Truthful James]. Bret Harte. AA; BeLS; BPAW; FaBoCo; HBV-2; InMe; OBAL
I resign! Song of Resignation. Yehuda Amichai, *tr. by* Assia Gutmann. NYBP
I resist/ my banker. Fire Island Poem. Diane Wakoski. BiP
I rest with Thee, O Jesus. *Unknown, tr. by* Eleanor Hull. *Fr.* Four Prayers. OnYI
I retain your image on incandescent microfilm. Artificial Death, II. Elizabeth Ann James. SOTS
I retrace your path in my bare feet. Letter from a Wife. S. Carolyn Reese. PoNe
I return the bitterness. Transformation. Lewis Alexander. CDC; PoNe
I Return unto Zion. Bible, *O.T.* Zechariah, VIII: 3-5. TrJP
I returned, and saw under the sun. Bible, *O.T.* Ecclesiastes, IX: 11-12. Prf
I, Richard Kent, beneath these stones. Epitaph. Sylvia Townsend Warner. MoBrPo
I ride/ the "A" train. Riding the "A." May Swenson. CAD
I Ride an Old Paint. *Unknown.* AmFP; AS, *with music;* FSW; TrAS, *with music*
I ride into town. The Famous Outlaw Stops In for a Drink. David James. AMV-81
I ride through a dark, dark land by night. Ichabod! The Glory Has Departed. Ludwig Uhland, *tr. by* James Clarence Mangan. AWP
I ride through Queens. An Invitation to Madison County. Jay Wright. PoBA
I rise at 2 a.m. these mornings, to. The Feral Pioneers. Ishmael Reed. PoBA; PoNe; UnPo
I rise in the dawn, and I kneel and blow. The Song of the Old Mother. W. B. Yeats. AnIV; MoBrPo
"I rise on Sugar-loaf Mountain." Molasses River. Richard Kendall Munkittrick. OBCA
I rise up from rest. Morning Prayer. Aua, *tr. fr. Eskimo.* WTO
I 'rived in the camp, and all I could see. Burn's Log Camp. *Unknown.* ShS
I rode a dream motorcycle. The Dream Motorcycle. Pete Winslow. PV
I rode a line on the open range. The Old Cowboy. *Unknown.* CoSo
I rode in Montana and Old Idaho. Up the Trail. *Unknown.* CoSo
I rode my horse to the hostel gate. Both Less and More. Richard Watson Dixon. LoBV
I rode one evening with Count Maddalo. Julian and Maddalo. Shelley. OAEL-2, *abr.*
I Rode Southern, I Rode L. & N. *Unknown.* AmFP
I rode till I reached the House of Wealth. Rest Only in the Grave. James Clarence Mangan. BIrV
I rode to church last Sunday. My Love She Passed Me By. *Unknown.* AmFP
I Rode with My Darling. Stevie Smith. BrRo
I rode with my mother and father. Triad. Donald Foster. AMV-80
I rose at night, and visited. The Unborn. Thomas Hardy. CMoP
I rose betimes to go I knew not where. The Poor Man's Province. John Wright. NOEC
I rose in joy at the pinking sheared sky. Shattered Sabbath. Roberta B. Goldstein. AMV-81
I rose up when the battle was dead. Comrades. Laurence Housman. HBV-2
I rush to the newspapers. The News & the Weather. Rika Lesser. MAYP
I rush to your dwelling. Pursuit. Juljan Tuwim, *tr. by* Watson Kirkconnell. TrJP
I sagh Him with flesh al bi-spred: He cam from Est. *See* I saw him with flesh all bespred. . .
I said:/ Now will the poets sing. Scottsboro, Too, Is Worth Its Song. Countee Cullen. PoBA

I said, Ah! what shall I write? A, a, a, Domine Deus. David Jones. FaBoTw; NOCV
I said, I like our bodies clean. Friday Night after Bathing. Stephen Levy. VWA
I said, "I will find God," and forth, I went. Seeking God. Edward Dowden. WGRP
I said, "I will take heed to my ways." Lord, Make Me to Know Mine End. Bible, *O.T.* Psalms, XXXIX. TrJP
I said I would have my fling. The Price He Paid. Ella Wheeler Wilcox. WBLP
I said I'd get her a towel and ran. Girls. Kenneth Rosen. AmPA
I said, in drunken pride of youth and you. Challenge. Sterling A. Brown. CDC
I said, "Let me walk in the fields." Obedience [*or* What Christ Said]. George Macdonald. BLRP; HBV-2; TreFT; TRV; WGRP
I said: "My heart, now let us sing a song." A Wedding Song. John White Chadwick. AA
I said sometimes with tears. Samuel Crossman. OxBoCh
"I," said the duck, "I call it fun." Who Likes the Rain? Clara Doty Bates. TiPo
I said: "The moon is obviously a boat." Nocturnal Landscape. Malcolm Cowley. PoA
I said the word "spatial," and in it. Space Fiction. Norman MacCaig. TEP
I said—Then, dearest, since 'tis so. The Last Ride Together. Robert Browning. BoLoP; FiP; HBV-1; LiTB; OAEP; OBEV; OBVV; PoEL-5; UnPo; VLP; WHA
I Said, This Misery Must End. Christopher Brennan. *Fr.* Pauca Mea. PoAu-1
I said to Death: "Supposing it were true." Dancing Partners. Philip Child. CaP
I said to Heart, "How goes it?" Heart replied. The [*or* For] False Heart. Hilaire Belloc. FaBoCh; FaBoEE; HBMV; MoBrPo
I said to heaven that glowed above. Hafiz, *tr. by* Emerson. Odes, XII. AWP
I said to Lettice, our sister Lettice. Lettice. Dinah Maria Mulock Craik. HBV-1
I Said to Love. Thomas Hardy. GBL; NoAM
I said to my baby. Same in Blues. Langston Hughes. *Fr.* Lenox Avenue Mural. InPS
I Said to My Heart. Charles Mordaunt, Earl of Peterborough. NOEC (Chloe.) OBEC
I said to myself one morning. Waking. Annie Higgins. ELU
I said to Sorrow's awful storm. The Soul's Defiance. Lavinia Stoddard. AA
I said, when the word came, "She will break." Of Little Faith. Harold T. Pulsifer. EtS
I said, "Why should a pyramid." The Innovator. Stephen Vincent Benét. EyDe
I said: "Within the garden trimly bordered." Inspiration. E. V. Knox. CenHV
"I said, 'You're right!' At last they've found." Asylum. David R. Clark. PPON
I sail over the ocean blue. I Catcha da Plenty of Feesh. *Unknown.* AS; TrAS
I sailed in my dreams to the Land of Night. Fantasy. Gwendolyn B. Bennett. BlSi; CDC
I sang as one. The Conflict. C. Day Lewis. LiTB; LiTM; MoAB; MoBrPo; NoP
I sang the songs of red revenge. Homer. Albert Ehrenstein, *tr. by* Babette Deutsch *and* Avram Yarmolinsky. TrJP
I sank past bitten leaves. Cicada. John Haines. NPAW
I sat all morning in the college sick bay. Mid-Term Break. Seamus Heaney. NCSH; NoP
I sat alone with my conscience. Conscience. Charles William Stubbs. BLPA
I Sat among the Green Leaves. Marjorie Pickthall. HBMV
I sat at my loom in silence. The Weaver. *Unknown.* BLRP
I sat before my glass one day. The Other Side of a Mirror. Mary Elizabeth Coleridge. BoWoP
I sat behind the glowing grate, fresh heaped. A Meditation on Rhode Island Coal. Bryant. TAP
I sat beside the red stock route. Harry Pearce. David Campbell. PoAu-2
I sat beside the streamlet. Remember or Forget. Hamilton Aidé. HBV-1
I sat by a stream in a. Classic. A. R. Ammons. NOBA
I sat by the granite pillar, and sunlight fell. Commemoration. Sir Henry Newbolt. FaBoTw; OBVV
I sat here this morning, detached, summoning up, I think. The Deviator. Bertram Warr. OBCV
I sat in the cold limbs of a tree. The Man in the Tree. Mark Strand. EAS
I sat in the school of sorrow. The School of Sorrow. Harold Hamilton. BLRP
I Sat Me Weary on a Pillar's Base. James Thomson ("B. V."). The City of Dreadful Night, XX. BSV; NBM; OAEP
I sat next [to] the Duchess at tea. Limerick. *Unknown.* NIP; SoSe
I sat on the Dogana's steps. Cantos, III. Ezra Pound. TAP
I sat wi' my love, and I drank wi' my love. *Unknown.* GBP
I sat with Doris, the shepherd maiden. Doris; a Pastoral. Arthur Joseph Munby. HBV-1
I sat with her, and spoke right goldenly. The Lady of Life. Tom Kettle. ACP
I sat with John Brown. That night moonlight framed. Narrative. Russell Atkins. PoBA
I sat with Love upon a woodside well. Willowwood. Dante Gabriel Rossetti. The House of Life, XLIX. HBV-1; OAEL-2; OAEP; PoEL-5; VLP; WHA
I sat with one I love last night. Last Night. George Darley. HBV-1; OnYI
I saunter by the shore and lose myself. A Hymn to the Sea. Richard Henry Stoddard. EtS
I saw/ a specialist a cook. To the Heart. Tadeusz Rozewicz, *tr. by* Victor Contoski. POL
I saw,/ With a catch of the breath and the heart's uplifting. A War Film. Teresa Hooley. SUMH
I saw/ Your hands on my lips like blind needles. Pirouette. Audre Lorde. NNP
I saw a bee, I saw a flower. The Bee-Orchis. Andrew Young. ChTr
I saw a boy with eager eye. The Two Boys. Mary Lamb. OBRV
I saw a bus marked Xanadu. Thoughts. Roy Davis. WhC
I Saw a Chapel All of Gold. Blake. CABA; EnRP; LAuP; LiTB
I saw a cottage in the sky. Friends. John Ashbery. LCAP
I saw a dead man's finer part. His Immortality. Thomas Hardy. CMoP; PoPle
I saw a donkey. The Donkey. *Unknown.* RHPC
I saw a doo flee our the dam. *Unknown.* GBP
I saw a fair maiden. A Lullaby of the Nativity [*or* Lullay Mine Liking]. *Unknown.* MeEL; SBVL
I saw a famous man eating soup. Soup. Carl Sandburg. NOBA; OBCA
I Saw a Fish-Pond All on Fire. *Unknown.* ChTr; GBP; NOBL; OxNR
I saw a fly within a bead. The Amber Bead [*or* A Trapped Fly]. Robert Herrick. CaPo; ChTr; WiR
I saw a frieze on whitest marble drawn. Ecstasy. W. J. Turner. CH
I saw a gardener with a watering can. The Progress of Poetry. "Christopher Caudwell." OxBTC
I Saw a Ghost. Joan Boilleau. TiPo
I saw a gnome. The Gnome. Harry Behn. FaPON; PDV; SoPo; TiPo
I saw a hawk devour a screaming bird. Hawk Is a Woman. Hildegarde Flanner. WPE
I saw a herd of the wild red deer. Caenlochan. Helen B. Cruickshank. PoSH
I saw a holly sprig brought from a hurst. A Vision of the World's Instability. Richard Verstegan. ElL
I saw a hunchback climb over a hill. The Hunchback. John Peale Bishop. PoA
I Saw a Jolly Hunter. Charles Causley. BoAnP; OnUR
"I saw a light," Columbus said. Light in the Darkness. Aileen Fisher. YeAr
I Saw a Little Girl I Hate. Arnold Spilka. RHPC
I saw a little snail. Little Snail. Hilda Conkling. TiPo
I saw a little squirrel. A Little Squirrel. *Unknown.* TiPo
I saw a little tailor sitting stitch, stitch, stitching. Tailor. Eleanor Farjeon. OxBChV
I saw a maid sit on a bank. *See* I sawe a mayd. . .
I Saw a maiden. *Unknown.* ISi
I Saw a Man. Stephen Crane. *See* I Saw a Man Pursuing the Horizon.
I saw a man, by some accounted wise. Erastus Wolcott Ellsworth. *Fr.* What Is the Use? AA
I saw a man come down to the furious sea. The Antagonist. David Ferry. NePoAm-2
I Saw a Man Pursuing the Horizon. Stephen Crane. The Black Riders, XXIV. AmPP; FF; HoPM; LiTA; LiTM; MAT; MoAmPo; NePA; NOBA
I saw a man whose face was white as snow. The Uninfected. E. L. Mayo. MiAP
I saw a Monk of Charlemaine. The Monk. Blake. *Fr.* Jerusalem. EnRP; LoBV; OBRV
I saw a mouth jeering. Gargoyle. Carl Sandburg. NoAM; NOBA
I Saw a New World. William Brighty Rands. NBM
I saw a pale tree, the leafless boughs—but two. Ecstasy. Hélène Swarth, *tr. by* Jonathan Crewe. WPOW
I Saw a Peacock [with a Fiery Tail]. *Unknown.* CH; ChTr; FaBoCh; GBP; ImOP; OxBoLi; OxNR; PoPle
I saw a people rise before the sun. Yom Kippur. Israel Zangwill. TrJP

I Saw a Phoenix in the Wood Alone. Spenser. *Fr.* The Visions of Petrarch. ChTr
I saw a picture once by Angelo. An Unpraised Picture. Richard Burton. AA
I saw a proud, mysterious cat. The Mysterious Cat. Vachel Lindsay. ChTr; FaPON; GoJo; OBCA; SoPo; TiPo
I saw a querulous old man, the tobacconist of Eighth Street. The Tobacconist of Eighth Street. Richard Eberhart. MiAP; NYP
I saw a shadow on the ground. The Sky. Elizabeth Madox Roberts. MoAmPo
I saw a ship a-sailing. Mother Goose. FaBoBe; HBV-1; HBVY; MoShBr; NTCP; OxNR; SoPo; TiPo
I saw a ship a-sailing. The Fairy Ship. "Gabriel Setoun." PoPl
I saw a ship a-sailing, a-sailing, a-sailing. An Old Song Re-sung. John Masefield. EvOK; LiTB
I saw a ship of martial build. The Berg. Herman Melville. AmPP; AP; InPK; LiTA; NOBA; NoP; PoEL-5; TAP
I saw a sickly cellar plant. The Incentive. Sarah N. Cleghorn. HBMV
I saw a silvery creature scurrying. Riddle 29: The Moon and the Sun. *Unknown, tr. by* Burton Raffel. GoJo
I saw a slowly stepping train. God's Funeral. Thomas Hardy. WGRP
I saw a snail. Little Snail. Hilda Conkling. FaPON
I Saw a Stable. Mary Elizabeth Coleridge. EBCP; OBCP; OxBoCh; PChr; TRV
I saw a star slide down the sky. The Falling Star. Sara Teasdale. MoShBr; OBCA; PDV; SoPo; SUS; TiPo
I saw a staring virgin stand. Two Songs from a Play, I. W. B. Yeats. *Fr.* The Resurrection. CABA; CMoP; CoBMV; FaBoTw; HAP; LiTB; MoPo; NOBE; NoP; OAEL-2; PPoe; PPP; PrIm; SeCeV
I saw a sweet and silly sight. O Jesu Parvule. *Unknown.* ISi
I saw a thing, and stopped to wonder. The Pine Bough. Richard Aldridge. NePoAm; PoSC
I saw a tiny pebble fall. What Price. Lulu Minerva Schultz. GoYe
I saw a tree that was greater than all the others. Edith Södergran, *tr. fr. Swedish by* Jaakko A. Ahokas. PBWP
I saw a very strange fairy tale. A Fairy Tale. Vitomil Zupan. DFT
I saw a vision yesternight. To the State of Love; or, The Senses' Festival. John Cleveland. AnAnS-2; MePo; PeD
I saw a vulture in the sky. Life and Death. W. J. Turner. FaBoTw
I saw a woman in a green field. Alex Comfort. *Fr.* The Postures of Love. NeBP
I saw a worm, with many a fold. Psyche. Jones Very. AP
I saw a young snake glide. Snake. Theodore Roethke. NOBA; NYBP; PoPl; RFM
I saw a youth and maiden on a lonely city street. Take Back Your Gold. Louis W. Pritzkow. FSN; TreF
I saw about her spotless wrist. Upon a Black Twist, Rounding the Arm of the Countess of Carlisle. Robert Herrick. CaPo
I saw an aged beggar in my walk. The Old Cumberland Beggar. Wordsworth. EnRP; LaA
"I saw an elephant walking down the road." April Fool. Elizabeth J. Coatsworth. YeAr
I saw an old black man walk down the road. Black Soul of the Land. Lance Jeffers. FB
I saw, and trembled for the day. A Warning. Coventry Patmore. EnLoPo
I saw autumn today . . . incipiently, on the sunset. Entry September 6. Walter Benton. *Fr.* This Is My Beloved. UnTE
I saw between a shadow and a bough. The Ungathered Apples. James Wright. ErPo
I saw Butch. 224 Stoop. Victor Hernandez Cruz. BOLo
I saw by looking in his eyes. The Wandering Jew. Robert Bridges. QFR
I saw cold thunder in the grass. Herons. Robin Blaser. NeAP
I saw dawn creep across the sky. A Summer Morning. Rachel Field. PDV; SoPo; SUS; TiPo
I saw death this afternoon lurking near the tennis courts. Near the Base Line. Samuel L. Albert. NePoAm-2
I saw each soul as light, each single body. Night of Souls. Ann Stanford. WPE
I saw Esau sawing wood. *Unknown.* FaBoNo
I Saw Eternity. Louise Bogan. LiTA
I saw eternity the other night. The World [*or* Eternity]. Henry Vaughan. AnAnS-1; AWP; CABA; EBEV; FaBoEn; FaBV; GoTL; HAP; HBV-2; HeIP; ILwL; ImOP, 1 *st.*; JCP; LiTB; LoBV; MasP; MePo; NOBE; NOCV; OAEL-1; OAEP; OBEV; OBS; OxBoCh; PoEL-2; PPoe; PPP; SeCeV; SeCP; SeCV-1; TEP; TrCP; TreFS; TrGrPo; ViBoPo; WGRP
I saw fair[e] Chloris walk alone. On Chloris [*or* a Gentlewoman] Walking in the Snow [*or* Chloris in the Snow]. William Strode. ELP; HBV-1; JCP; NOBE; OAEL-1; OBEV; OBS
I saw five birds all in a cage. Riddle. *Unknown.* GBP
I Saw from the Beach. Thomas Moore. OBNC; OxBI
I saw, from yonder silent cave. The Two Streams. Thomas Moore. *Fr.* Evenings in Greece, First Evening. GoBC
I Saw God ("I saw God bare his soul one day"). William L. Stidger. PGD
I saw God! Do you doubt it? What Thomas [an Buile] Said in a Pub. James Stephens. CMoP; MoAB; MoBrPo; NoAM; PAI; PoRA; TrGrPo; WGRP
I Saw God Wash the World. William L. Stidger. BLPA; TRV
I saw green banks of daffodil. E. Wyndham Tennant. TiPo
I saw her amid the dunghill debris. Tinker's Wife. Patrick Kavanagh. CIP; NoAM
I saw her crop a rose. Where She Told Her Love. John Clare. VLP
I saw her first abreast the Boston Light. The *William P. Frye.* Jeanne Robert Foster. PAH
I saw her first in gleams. The Spirit's Odyssey. M. Krishnamurti. PeD
I saw her on the bridal night. The Forced Bridal. *Unknown.* PaPo
I saw her once, one little while, and then no more. And Then No More. Friedrich Rückert, *tr. by* James Clarence Mangan. AnIV; BIrV; BLPA
I saw her scan her sacred scroll. Alma Mater's Roll. Edward Everett Hale. AA
I saw him a squat man with red hair. Off Brighton Pier. Alan Ross. OBWP
I saw him beat the surges under him. Shakespeare. *Fr.* The Tempest, II, i. MOS
I saw him dead, a leaden slumber lies [*or* lyes]. Cromwell Dead. Andrew Marvell. *Fr.* A Poem upon the Death of Oliver Cromwell [*or* His Late Highness the Lord Protector]. ChTr; JCP; OBS; ViBoPo
I saw him forging link by link his chain. The Slave. Jones Very. AP; TAP
I saw him in the Airstrip Gardens. Betjeman, 1984. Charles Causley. FaBoCo; NOBL; OxBTC
I saw him lying there—my father—with eyes. The Addict. Larry Rubin. GoYe
I saw him naked on a hill. The Shepherd Boy. Edward J. O'Brien. HBMV
I saw him once before. The Last Leaf. Oliver Wendell Holmes. AA; AmPP; AP; FaBoBe; FaPON; HBV-1; OBVV; PoLF; SeCeV; TreF; WBLP
I saw [*or* sagh] Him with flesh all bespred—He came from East. The Coming of Christ [*or* Christ's Coming]. *Unknown.* ACP; OxBM
I saw his back. Wallace Stevens Gives a Reading. Harriet Zinnes. AMV-81
I saw his round mouth's crimson deepen as it fell. Fragment. Wilfred Owen. OAEL-2
I saw, I saw the lovely child. Evanescence. Frederic William Henry Myers. OBVV
I saw in dream a dapper mannikin. Im Traum sah ich ein Männchen klein und putzig. Heine, *tr. by* Sir Theodore Martin. AWP
I Saw in Louisiana a Live-Oak Growing. Walt Whitman. AP; AWP; InPK; LiTA; MAT; NePA; NoAM; NOBA; NoP; OxBA; PrIm
I saw in the East a sign, a sign. Blues Ballad. Kenneth Pitchford. *Fr.* Good for Nothing Man. CoPo
I saw it all, Polly, how when you had call'd for sop. Poor Poll. Robert Bridges. EBEV; MoPo; OxBoLi; OxBTC
I saw it in an empty window. In an Empty Window. Ray Fraser. NeAC
I saw it light the cactus sky. Back Again from Yucca Flats. Reeve Spencer Kelley. AmFN
I saw it once where myriad works adorn. On a Sculptured Head of the Christ. Mahlon Leonard Fisher. HBV-2
I saw it settle like a stain. Death's-Head Moth. Stanley Roger Green. BSV
I saw magic on a green country road. Sonnet. Michael Hartnett. BIrV
I Saw My Darling. Frederick Morgan. UnPo
I saw my daughter. When I Came to Israel. Bert Meyers. AMV-80; VWA
I saw my face. Jew. Pierre Morhange, *tr. by* Edouard Roditi. VWA
I Saw My Father. E. L. Mayo. MiAP
I saw my grandmother grow weak. First Death. Donald Justice. FiCP
I Saw My Lady Weep. *Unknown.* EIL; ELP; EnLoPo; HBV-1; LiTB; OBSC; TrGrPo; ViBoPo
(My Lady's Tears.) EBEV; NOBE; OBEV
I Saw My Life as Whitest Flame. Christopher Brennan. *Fr.* Towards the Source. PoAu-1
I saw my love, younger than primroses. In a Wood. E. J. Scovell. GBL
I saw my scattered hopes upon the floor. The Phallic Symbol. Nicholas Moore. NeBP
I saw my soul at rest upon a day. Sestina. Swinburne. VLP
I saw myself leaving. Reflections. Carl Gardner. NNP; PoBA
I saw new worlds beneath the water lie [*or* ly]. On Leaping over the Moon. Thomas Traherne. LiTB; LoBV; MOON; SeCV-2
I saw no doctor, but, feeling queer inside. *Unknown, tr. fr. Greek by* Humbert Wolfe. ShM; WhC
I saw no way—the heavens were stitched. Emily Dickinson. AP; BoWoP
I saw old Autumn in the misty morn. Autumn [*or* Ode to Autumn]. Thomas Hood. BLPL; HBV-1; LiTB; OAEL-2; OBEV; OBNC; OBRV; PoEL-4; UnPo; ViBoPo; VLP
I saw old Duchesses with their young loves. Vanity. Anna Wickham. FaBoTw

I saw on earth another light. The Light from Within. Jones Very. WGRP
I saw on the slant hill a putrid lamb. For a Lamb. Richard Eberhart. CMoP; LiTM; MiAP
I saw on the snow. Merry Christmas. Aileen Fisher. RHPC
I Saw One Hanging. *Unknown.* STF
I saw one hung upon a cross. Gallows and Cross. J. E. H. MacDonald. CaP
I saw, one sultry night above a swamp. Fireflies. Edgar Fawcett. HBV-1
I saw only the edge. A Glance at the Album. Gray Burr. CoPo
I saw that country in a dream. Wilderness Theme. Ian Mudie. PoAu-2
I saw that guy in Oklahoma. A Scholder Indian Poem. Joy Harjo. TWSS
I saw the archangels in my apple-tree last night. The Apple-Tree. Nancy Campbell. AnIV
I saw the best minds of my generation. Squeal. Louis Simpson. BXAP; FiBHP; Par; UnPo
I saw the best minds of my generation destroyed by madness, starving hysterical naked. Howl. Allen Ginsberg. AmPP; CAPP; InPS; NaP; NeAP; NIP; NoAM; NoP; PoM; SOTW; TAP
I saw the black trees leaning. Trees and Evening Sky. N. Scott Momaday. CDW
I saw the bodies of earth's men. The Navigators. W. J. Turner. OBMV
I saw the city's towers on a luminous pale-gray sky. Winter-Solitude. Archibald Lampman. PeCV
I Saw the Clouds. Hervey White. HBV-2
I saw the Connaught Rangers when they were passing by. The Connaught Rangers. Winifred M. Letts. HBMV
I saw the Conquerors riding by. The Conquerors. Harry Kemp. HBV-2
I saw the constellated matin choir. Prelude. Edmund Clarence Stedman. AA
I saw the day's white rapture. Song. Charles Hanson Towne. HBV-1
I saw the dead/ dying a second time. The Pulverized Screen. Edmond Jabes, *tr. by* Anthony Rudolf. VWA
I saw the Devil walking down the lane. The Devil's Bag. James Stephens. WSC
I saw the festivities in the streets. Mulberry Street. Ruth Herschberger. HoAn
I saw the first pear. Orchard. Hilda Doolittle ("H. D."). CMoP; LiTA; LiTM; MoAmPo; OxBA
I saw the fog grow thick. The Fog. W. H. Davies. TiPo
I saw the fox, his red tail beating. Gone. Joanna Thompson. AMV-80
I saw the garden where my aunt had died. The Entertainment of War. Roy Fisher. FaBoMo
I saw the ghostesses. Ghostesses. *Unknown.* ChTr
I saw the human millions as the sand. Sydney Dobell. *Fr.* Sonnets on the War. VLP
I saw the Lord Christ tonight. Inasmuch! William E. Brooks. PGD
I saw the lovely arch. The Rainbow. Walter de la Mare. SoPo; TiPo
I saw the Master of the Sun. He stood. The Sun God. Aubrey Thomas De Vere. ACP; OBVV
I saw the midlands. Kisses in the Train. D. H. Lawrence. MoAB; MoBrPo
I saw the moon/ One windy night. Flying. J. M. Westrup. OnUR
I saw the object of my pining thought. Sonnet. Thomas Watson. ElL
I saw the old Chinese men standing. Some Painful Butterflies Pass Through. Tess Gallagher. MAYP
I saw the old man pause, then turn his head. The Old Conservative. L. Frank Tooker. EtS
I saw the people climbing up the street. Zeppelins. Nancy Cunard. SUMH
I saw the ramparts of my native land. Sonnet: Death Warnings. Francisco de Quevedo y Villegas, *tr. by* John Masefield. AWP
I saw the roofs of Elfin Town. Elfin Town. Rachel Field. WSC
I saw the salt. Ode to Salt. Pablo Neruda, *tr. by* Robert Bly. NU
I saw the shapes that stood upon the clouds. London Nightfall. John Gould Fletcher. MoAmPo
I saw the shepherd fold the sheep. The Folded Flock. Wilfrid Meynell. GoBC; TrPWD
I saw the silver morning mist. The Dead Horse. Cecília Meireles, *tr. by* James Merrill. PBWP
I saw the sky descending, black and white. Where the Rainbow Ends. Robert Lowell. AP; CoBMV; MoAB; MoAmPo; NePoEA; TrGrPo
I saw the Son of God go by. The Question. Rachel Annand Taylor. HBV-2
I saw the spiders marching through the air. Mr. Edwards and the Spider. Robert Lowell. AP; CABA; CAPP; CMoP; CoAP; FaBoMo; HeIP; InPS; LiTM; MoAB; MoPo; MoVE; MP; NePoEA; NOBA; NoP; SeCeV; SoSe; TwCP
I saw the spires of Oxford. The Spires of Oxford. Winifred M. Letts. FaFP; HBV-2; OHFP; OnYI; PoLF; PoRA; TreF; WGRP
I saw the spot where our first parents dwelt. The Garden. Jones Very. AP; OxBA; TAP
I saw the sunlit vale, and the pastoral fairy-tale. The Sunlit Vale. Edmund Blunden. ChMP; MoVE
I saw the throng, so deeply separate. A General Communion. Alice Meynell. NOCV; WPE
I saw the twinkle of white feet. Hebe. James Russell Lowell. AA; HBV-1
I saw the two starlings. The Manoeuvre. William Carlos Williams. PCP
I Saw the Vision of Armies. Walt Whitman. WaaP
I Saw the Wind Today. Padraic Colum. GoJo; SUS (Wind, The.) PDV; RoGo
I Saw Thee. Ray Palmer. HBV-2
I saw thee, child, one summer's day. Emily Brontë. VLP
I saw thee once, and nought discerned. The Discovery. Cardinal Newman. OBRV
I saw thee start and quake. In a Dream. J. M. Synge. SyP
I saw thee when, as twilight fell. I Saw Thee. Ray Palmer. HBV-2
I saw them at games every. Seven Mexican Children. Tom Schmidt. NeAC
I saw them chase the gipsies. The Gipsies. "Richard Scrace." CaP
I saw them coming in the eyeless day. And the Dead. Sean Jennett. NeBP
I Saw Them Lynch. Carole Freeman. NMM; PoBA
I saw them walk that lane again. On Seeing Swift in Laracor. Brinsley MacNamara. AnIV; OxBI
I saw these dreamers of dreams go by. The Gold-Seekers. Hamlin Garland. AA; FaBoBe; YaD
I saw this eve the wandering sun. Prodigals. Charles L. O'Donnell. HBMV
I saw this much from the window. The Gap in the Cedar. Roy Scheele. Psk
I saw three Cupids (so I dream'd). The Kites. Coventry Patmore. *Fr.* The Angel in the House. VLP
I Saw Three Ships ("As I sat under a sycamore tree"). *Unknown. See* As I Sat under a Sycamore Tree.
I saw three ships come sailing by. Mother Goose. OxNR
I Saw Three Ships Come Sailing In. *Unknown.* BLPA; EBCP; FSW; OxBoCh
I saw three withered women limp across. The Private Meeting Place. James Wright. NYBP
I saw thy beauty in its high estate. To a Magnolia Flower in the Garden of the Armenian Convent at Venice. S. Weir Mitchell. AA
I saw—'twas in a dream, the other night. Montefiore. Ambrose Bierce. AA
I Saw Two Clouds at Morning. John Gardiner Calkins Brainard. HBV-1 (Epithalamium.) AA
I saw two trees embracing. All That Time. May Swenson. FF
I saw where in the shroud did lurk. On an Infant Dying as Soon as Born. Charles Lamb. GTBS; GTBS-P; OBEV; OBRV
I saw with open eyes. Stupidity Street. Ralph Hodgson. BrPo; CH; HBV-2; LiTM; MoAB; MoBrPo; OxBTC; PDV; SiSoSe; TreFS
I saw you/ on my walk last. Glimpse. Pearl Cleage Lomax. PoBA
I saw you/ peeking out thru the flower pots. As the World Turns. Larry Mollin. NeAC
I saw you die. Murdered Little Bird. *Unknown.* FiBHP
I saw you once on the TV. Galway Kinnell. *Fr.* For Robert Frost. PP
"I saw you take his kiss!" " 'Tis true." The Kiss. Coventry Patmore. The Angel in the House, II, viii. BoLoP; EnLoPo; FiBHP; OBVV; PoPle
I saw you toss the kites on high. The Wind. Robert Louis Stevenson. GN; HBVY; SoPo; SUS; TiPo
I saw you walking. At Long Last. Lindsay Patterson. CNA
I saw your hinee. *Unknown.* PV
I sawe a mayd sitte on a bank. The Carelesse Nurse Mayd. Thomas Hood. FaBoNo; VLP
I Say. Malka Heifetz Tussman, *tr. fr. Yiddish by* Marcia Falk. VWA
I say I woke up this morning, baby so dark I couldn't hardly see. Y M & V Blues. *Unknown.* BluL
I Say I'll Seek Her. Thomas Hardy. QFR
I say it to comfort me over and over. The Cynic. Theodosia Garrison. HBMV
I say it under the rose. Thalia. Thomas Bailey Aldrich. AA; HBV-1; InMe
I say no more for Clavering. Clavering. E. A. Robinson. CrMA; HBMV; OxBA
I say now, Fernando, that on that day. Hibiscus on the Sleeping Shores. Wallace Stevens. InPS
"I say, stranger." Between the Walls of the Valley. Elisabeth Peck. AmFN
I say that I think for myself, but what is this Self of mine. Heir and Serf. Don Marquis. HBMV
I say the pulpit (in the sober use). William Cowper. *Fr.* The Task. TRV
I say the Rock Island Line is a mighty good road. Rock Island Line. *Unknown.* FSW
I say the women don't sleep right. Explanation. Geof Hewitt. NeAC

I say things to myself. Phraseology. Jayne Cortez. BlSi
I say this evening we'll all get drunk. Suction's Anthem. Blake. *Fr.* An Island in the Moon. FaBoNo
I say to the Almighty. I Say. Malka Heifetz Tussman, *tr. by* Marcia Falk. VWA
I say to the lead. Poem without a Title. Charles Simic. GP; NNaP
I say to thee, do thou repeat. The Kingdom of God. Richard Chenevix Trench. WBLP
I say what Lindbergh's father. Maps for a Son Are Drawn as You Go. Samuel Hazo. AMV-81
I, says the buzzard. From Virgil. George Oppen. *Fr.* Five Poems about Poetry. NNaP
I scarce believe [*or* beleeve] my love to be so pure. Love's Growth. John Donne. AnAnS-1; JCP; MePo; NoP; SeCV-1
I scarcely think. The Zoo. Humbert Wolfe. MoShBr
I Scattered My Sighs to the Wind. Hayyim Nahman Bailik, *tr. fr. Hebrew by* Naomi Nir. VWA
I scooped up the moon. The Moon. Ryuho. SoPo
I scream/ You scream. *Unknown.* FaBoNo
I Scream You Scream. Don McKay. NOBC
I scrub the floor. The Clorox Kid. Kirk Robertson. GP
I scuff/ my feet along. Sulk. Felice Holman. RHPC
I search for familiar hair. Out of Body. Janice Townley More. AMV-81
I search the room with all my mind. Officers' Mess (1916). Harold Monro. BrPo
I see a beautiful gigantic swimmer swimming naked through the eddies of the sea. The Beautiful Swimmer. Walt Whitman. PeHV
I see a farmer walking by himself. The Farmer. Fredegond Shove. MMA
I see a great round wonder rolling through space. Walt Whitman. *Fr.* Salut au Monde! SUS
I see a man who is dull. *Tr. fr. Arabic by* Willis Barnstone. BoWoP
I see a tiny fluttering form. The Southern Snow-Bird. William Hamilton Hayne. AA
I see all this new matter of the snow. New Forms. Peter Redgrove. NMP
I see around me here. The Wanderer Recalls the Past. Wordsworth. *Fr.* The Excursion. OBNC; OBRV
I see at last our great Lamorna Cove. Lamorna Cove. W. H. Davies. BrPo
I see before me now a traveling army halting. Bivouac on a Mountain Side. Walt Whitman. AA; AP; ChTr; OxBA; PAL; PoLF
I see before me the gladiator lie. The Dying Gladiator. Byron. *Fr.* Childe Harold's Pilgrimage, IV. NOBE
I see black dragons mount the sky. Shapes and Signs. James Clarence Mangan. OnYI
I see bodies in the morning kneel. Shirley Kaufman. BoWoP
I See God. *Unknown.* STF
I see her against the pearl sky of Dublin. My Mother's Sister. C. Day Lewis. OxBTC
I see her in the festal warmth to-night. Ursula. Robert Underwood Johnson. HBV-1
I see her seventeen. Arizona Highways. James Welch. CDW
"I see herrin'."—I hear the glad cry. With the Herring Fishers. "Hugh MacDiarmid." BSV; LiTM
I see him old, trapped in a burly house. A Pauper. Allen Tate. LiTM
I See His Blood upon the Rose. Joseph Mary Plunkett. GoBC; HBMV; OnYI; OxBI; PoLF; TRV; WGRP
I see in his last preached and printed booke. On John Donne's Book of Poems. John Marriot. CH
I see it. Song for the Dead, III. *Unknown, tr. by* Frances S. Herskovits. TTY
I see I've come a pilgrimage. I didn't. The *Weepers Tower* in Amsterdam. Paul Goodman. VGW
I See My Plaint. *At. to* John Harington. ElL
I see no bird arise. My Sun-killed Tree. Marguerite Harris. GoYe
I see no equivalents. The Poet at Night-Fall. Glenway Wescott. PoA
I See Phantoms of Hatred and of the Heart's Fullness and of the Coming Emptiness. W. B. Yeats. Meditations in Time of Civil War, VII. LiTB
I see that chance hath chosen me. Sir Thomas Wyatt. SiPS
I see that there it is on the beach. Memorial Service for the Invasion Beach Where the Vacation in the Flesh Is Over. Alan Dugan. MP; NMP; TwCP
I see that wreath which doth the wearer arm. To My Dead Friend Ben: Johnson. Henry King. AnAnS-2; SeCP
I see that you're a poetry lover, sweet Diane. Sweet Diane. George Barlow. CNA
I See the Boys of Summer. Dylan Thomas. LiTB
I see the children running out of school. The Poet Laments the Coming of Old Age. Edith Sitwell. NoAM
I see the cloud-born squadrons of the gale. A Storm in the Distance. Paul Hamilton Hayne. AA
"I see the dawn e'en now begin to peer." Popular Songs of Tuscany. *Unknown, tr. by* John Addington Symonds. AWP
I see the golden hunter go. Bliss Carman. Songs of the Sea-Children, LIV. OBCV
I see the horses and the sad streets. The Eye. Allen Tate. LiTA
I see the house. My heart thyself contain! Astrophel and Stella, LXXXV. Sir Philip Sidney. SiPS
I see the map of summer, lying still. Movies for the Home. Howard Moss. NePoEA-2; NYBP
I See the Moon. *Unknown.* GBP, *diff. version*; NTCP; OxNR; SoPo; TiPo
I see the mosquito kneeling on the soft underside of my arm. The Mosquito. Rodney Jones. MAYP
I see the sparrow bones folded in their thin shoes. The Fathers. Benjamin Saltman. VWA
I see the star-lights quiver. The Flight from the Convent. Theodore Tilton. AA
I see the sun. Sometimes on My Way Back Down to the Block. Victor Hernandez Cruz. BOLo
I see the thin bell-ringer standing at corners. The Jew at Christmas Eve. Karl Shapiro. VGW
I see the use, and know my blood [*or* bloud]. The Storm. Henry Vaughan. AnAnS-1; FaBoPP
I see the wealthy miller yet. The Miller's Daughter. Tennyson. VLP
I see the wrong that round me lies. Whittier. *Fr.* The Eternal Goodness. TRV
I see the young bride move among. George Barker. *Fr.* The True Confession of George Barker. ErPo
I see thee ever in my dreams. The Karamanian Exile. James Clarence Mangan. OBVV
I see Thee in the distant blue. God. John Banister Tabb. TreFT
I see thee pine like her in golden story. Coleridge. Theodore Watts-Dunton. HBV-2; OBVV
I see thee still! thou art not dead. A Remembrance. Willis Gaylord Clarke. AA
I see them/ Puerto Ricans. You're Nothing but a Spanish Colored Kid. Felipe Luciano. PoBA
I see them a mother and daughter. On the Bridge of Athlone; a Prophecy. Donagh MacDonagh. OxBI
I see them, crowd on crowd they walk the earth. The Dead. Jones Very. AA; AP; HAP; NOBA; OxBA; TAP
I see them go through the slums at night. Grand Street and the Bowery. David Ghitelman. FAZ
I see them nightly in my sleep. The Eyes of God. Hermann Hagedorn. HBMV
I see them working in old rectories. The Country Clergy. R. S. Thomas. GTBS-P; OxBTC
I see they worked you over. What you in for? Coming of Age in the County Jail. Carter Revard. VoR
I see weapons. James Gerard. Paul D. Shiplett. LFAC
I see why the touched needle scents about. Mysteries Revealed after Death. John Reynolds. *Fr.* Death's Vision. NOEC
I see you. Letters from Kazuko (Kyoto, Japan—Summer 1980). Alan Chong Lau. BrSi
I see you, a child. The Album. C. Day Lewis. ChMP; EnLoPo; FaBoEn; OxBI; OxBTC
I see you, brothers and sisters, Randall, John. A Paragraph. Hayden Carruth. FAZ
I see you did not try to save. Passing the Graveyard. Andrew Young. DTC
I see you displaced, condensed, within my dream. Dream. Josephine Miles. PoA
I see you in her bed. The Lovemaker. Robert Mezey. NePoEA-2
I see you in the silver. Arctic Tern in a Museum. Effie Lee Newsome. PoNe
I see you, Juliet, still, with your straw hat. Farewell to Juliet. Wilfrid Scawen Blunt. *Fr.* The Love Sonnets of Proteus. BoLoP; EnLoPo; OxBTC
I see you sitting. Matmiya. Mary TallMountain. WTSS
I see you with my inner eye. Greeting from a Distance. Hans Sahl, *tr. by* Erna Baber Rosenfield. VWA
I see you, you're twelve. Player. Stephen Dunning. FAZ
I see'd her in de springtime. She Hugged Me and Kissed Me. *Unknown.* BPo
I seed 'im squattin' there. Jis' Knowin'. Thomas G. Nickens. LFAC
I seek mercy. For All Mary Magdalenes. Desanka Maksimovic, *tr. by* Vasa D. Mihailovich. WPOW
I Seek Thee in the Heart Alone. Herbert Trench. WGRP
I seen a dunce of a poet once, a-writin' a little book. Gelett Burgess. *Fr.* The Protest of the Illiterate. FiBHP
I seize the sphery harp. I strike the strings. Enitharmon's Song. Blake. *Fr.* Vala. ChTr

I sell the best brandy and sherry. O'Tuomy's Drinking Song. John O'Tuomy, *tr. by* John O'Daly. OnYI
I send a garland to my love. The Lover's Posy. Rufinus, *tr. by* W. H. D. Rouse. AWP
I send, I send here my supremest kiss. His Tears to Thamesis. Robert Herrick. FaBoPP; OAEP
I send my heart up to thee, all my heart. Robert Browning. *Fr.* In a Gondola. ViBoPo
I send my poisoned candies through the mail. End of the Affair. Geoffrey Grigson. GBL
I Send Our Lady. Sister Mary Thérèse. ISi
I send thee a shell from the ocean beach. With a Nantucket Shell. Charles Henry Webb. AA
I send thee myrrh, not that thou mayest be. Not of Itself but Thee. *Unknown, tr. by* Richard Garnett. AWP
I send you here a sort of allegory. To ———: With the Following Poem. Tennyson. *Introd. poem to* The Palace of Art. VLP
I send you here a wreath of blossoms blown. Roses. Pierre de Ronsard, *tr. by* Andrew Lang. AWP
I send you perfume fresh as dew. Perfume. *Unknown, tr. by* Louis Untermeyer. UnTE
I send your own words back. Lines to a Friend in Trouble. W. S. Di Piero. MAYP
I sense that I may someday be assailed. Arcady Revisited. Robert Funge. AMV-80
I sent a letter to my love. George Barker. *Fr.* The True Confession of George Baker. FaBoTw
I sent for Radcliffe [*or* Ratcliffe]; was so ill. The Remedy Worse than the Disease. Matthew Prior. FaBoEE; HBV-1; TrGrPo
I Sent My Brown Jug Downtown. *Unknown.* FSW
I sent my Collie to the wash. Nonsense Quatrains. Gelett Burgess. CenHV
I sent my love two roses—one. The White Flag. John Hay. HBV-1
I sent my mother copies of my poems in print. Poems. Gary Gildner. Psk
I sent you this bluebird of the name of Joe. Happiness. William Dickey. Psk
I Serve a Mistress. Anthony Munday, *ad. fr. the Italian of* Luigi Pasqualigo. *Fr.* Fedele and Fortunio. EIL
(Fedele's Song.) OBSC
("I serve a mistress whiter than the snow.") HAP
I Served in a Great Cause. Horace L. Traubel. AA
I served my time in the Black Ball Line. Blow, Boys, Blow, *vers.* IV. *Unknown.* ShS
I set a charm upon your hurrying breath. A Marriage Charm. Nora Hopper. HBV-1
I set a jumpy mouse trap. A Change of Heart. Valine Hobbs. SiSoSe
I Set Aside. Mary Morison Webster. PeSA
I set forth hopeful—cotton-blossom Lal. Lalleswari, *tr. fr. Kashmiri by* George Grierson; *ad. by* Deirdre Lashgari. WPOW
I set my heart to sing of leaves. Anticipation. Lord De Tabley. ELP
I set this down. Magister, can it be? Memory of a Scholar. Richmond Lattimore. GLGT
I shake my hair in the wind of morning. Triumph of Love. John Hall Wheelock. MoAmPo
I shall always come to find you here. Orpheus. J. F. Hendry. NeBP
"I shall arise." For centuries. Resurgam. *Unknown.* WGRP
I shall be beautiful when you come back. Transformation. Jessie B. Rittenhouse. HBMV
I shall be capricious, I shall have a whim. A Man's Woman. Mary Carolyn Davies. PoLF
"I shall be careful to say nothing at all." How She Resolved to Act. Merrill Moore. MoAmPo
I Shall Be Loved as Quiet Things. Karle Wilson Baker. HBMV
I Shall Be Married on Monday Morning. *Unknown.* ErPo
I shall be quite content. Growing Old. Douglas Fraser. PoSH
I shall be shapen. A Pair of Lovers. Jeanne Robert Foster. HBMV
I shall beat you without rage. Heautontimoroumenos. Baudelaire, *tr. by* Naomi Lewis. NAWM-2
I shall begin by learning to throw. Formal Application. Donald W. Baker. FF; SoSe
I shall come back in ways I think you'll know. Unregenerate. Jacqueline Embry. HBMV
I shall come back to die. In This Dark House. Edward Davison. OBMV
I shall come this way again. Auf Wiedersehen. Donald Jeffrey Hayes. CDC
I shall cry God to give me a broken foot. Flash Crimson. Carl Sandburg. MoAmPo
I shall dance, I shall have hope. Dance Hymn. Isaiah Shembe, *tr. by* B. G. M. Sundkler. WTO
I shall die, but that is all that I shall do for Death. Conscientious Objector. Edna St. Vincent Millay. WPOW
I Shall Forget You Presently, My Dear. Edna St. Vincent Millay. TAP
I shall gather myself into myself again. The Crystal Gazer. Sara Teasdale. MoAmPo
I shall give you five words for your birthday. Five Words for Joe Dunn on His 22nd Birthday. Jack Spicer. PoM
I shall go among red faces and virile voices. Cattle Show. "Hugh MacDiarmid." BSV; FaBoMo; GoTS; HAP; MoBrPo; OBMV; OxBTC
I shall go as my father went. The Tenancy. Mary Gilmore. CBAP; PoAu-1
I shall go away. And the birds will still be there. The Conclusive Voyage. Juan Ramón Jiménez, *tr. by* H. R. Hays. PoPl
I Shall Go Back. Edna St. Vincent Millay. MoAmPo; NePA; UnPo
I shall go down from the stark, gray-stone towers. Refuge. Hervey Allen. HBMV
I shall go forth one day to joust with death. The Last Tourney. Frederic F. Van de Water. HBMV
I shall go on the gypsies' road. The Gypsies' Road. Dora Sigerson Shorter. OBVV
I shall go out as all men go. I Accept. Harold Trowbridge Pulsifer. HBMV
I shall go out when the light comes in. Death at Daybreak. Anne Reeve Aldrich. AA
I shall go to Mamre's oaks. Abraham. Eisig Silberschlag. VWA
I shall hate you. Hatred. Gwendolyn B. Bennett. AmNP; BANP; BlSi; CDC; PoBA
I shall have a gold room. Chanson d'Or. Ann Hamilton. HBMV
I shall have pearls blacker than caviar. Capriccio. Babette Deutsch. HBMV
I shall have three grey poplar trees above me when I sleep. The Three Poplars. Philip Francis Little. OxBI
I shall know why—when time is over. Emily Dickinson. NoAM; NOCV
I Shall Laugh Purely. Robinson Jeffers. CrMA; LiTA; LiTM; WaP
I shall leave tonight from Euston. I Leave Tonight from Euston. *Unknown.* PoSH
I shall lie hidden in a hut. Prophecy. Elinor Wylie. BLPL; BoWoP; PrIm; VGW
I shall make a song like your hair. Secret. Gwendolyn B. Bennett. BlSi; CDC
I shall make a song of the Queen of Crete. The Queen of Crete. John Grimes. HBMV
I shall make offering in a new basket of marsh-grass. Intervals. Beatrice Ravenel. HBMV
I shall never forget my mother's voice singing. Now That Can Never Be Done. Sister Maris Stella. GoBC
I shall never get you put together entirely. The Colossus. Sylvia Plath. CAPP; LiTM; MP; NePoEA-2; NoAM; NOBA; NoP; TAP
I Shall Never Go. A. J. Hovde. AMV-80
I Shall Not Be Afraid. Aline Kilmer. HBMV
I shall not call for help until they coffin me. Last Lines. Egan O'Rahilly, *tr. by* Frank O'Connor. KiLC
I Shall Not Care. Sara Teasdale. HBV-1; MoAmPo; PoPl; TrGrPo; UnPo
I Shall Not Cry Return. Ellen M. H. Gates. HBV-1
I Shall Not Die for Thee. *Unknown, tr. fr. Modern Irish by* Douglas Hyde. AnIL; OxBI; CTC, *tr. by* Padraic Colum
(I Shall Not Die, *tr. by* Frank O'Connor.) KiLC
(O Woman, Shapely as the Swan, *tr. by* Padraic Colum.) BIrV
I shall not get my poem done. Poet Songs. Karle Wilson Baker. HBMV
I shall not lie to you any more. The Modern Woman to Her Lover. Margaret Widdemer. HBMV
I shall not linger in that draughty square. French. Osbert Lancaster. *Fr.* Afternoons with Baedeker. FaBoCo; NOBL
I Shall Not Pass Again This Way ("The bread that bringeth strength I want to give"). *Unknown.* BLRP; TreF; WBLP
I Shall Not Pass This Way Again ("Through this toilsome world, alas!"). *Unknown.* BLPA; FPL; TreFS
I Shall Not Pass This Way Again. Eva Rose York. FaFP; OHFP; WBLP
I shall not regard my swelled head as a sign of real glory. Aimé Césaire, *tr. by* Emile Snyders. *Fr.* Return to My Native Land. TTY
I shall not see the faces of my friends. The Dying Reservist. Maurice Baring. HBV-2
I Shall Not Want: In Deserts Wild, *with music.* Charles F. Deems. AH
I Shall Not Weep. Belle MacDiarmid Ritchey. HBMV
I shall not wonder more, then. Change. Raymond Knister. CaP; OBCV; PeCV
I shall note first/ the ones I loved. The Chronicler. Alexander Bergman. TrJP
I shall paint/ God in the midst. Robert Browning. *Fr.* Fra Lippo Lippi. Prf
I shall rot here, with those whom in their day. In Death Divided. Thomas Hardy. DTC
I shall say, Lord, "Is it music, is it morning." Resurgam. Marjorie Pickthall. OBCV; TrCP

I shall say what inordinate love is. Inordinate Love. *Unknown.* EBEV; MeEL
I shall see justice done. Witch. Patricia Beer. OxBC
I shall slough my self as a snake its skin. "I." Louis Golding. TrJP
I shall steal upon her. Chanson Naïve. John McClure. HBMV
I shall walk down the road. Death. Maxwell Bodenheim. TrJP
I shall wear laughter on my lips. Hope. Anna Blake Mezquida. TRV
I Shall Weep. Peretz Hirshbein, *tr. fr. Yiddish by* Joseph Leftwich. TrJP
I shall write of the old men I knew. In These Dissenting Times. Alice Walker. PoBA
I shave my face, comb my hair. Getting Serious. Gary Soto. NPGG
I shipped, d'ye see, in a Revenue sloop. The Darned Mounseer. W. S. Gilbert. *Fr.* Ruddigore. NOBL
I shipped on board of a Liverpool liner. Sally Brown. *Unknown.* AmFP
I shipped on board of th' *Ebenezer.* The *Ebenezer.* *Unknown.* ShS
I shiver, Spirit fierce and bold. At the Grave of Burns. Wordsworth. EnRP
I shoot the hippopotamus. The Hippopotamus. Hilaire Belloc. CenHV; FaBoNo; FiBHP; InPK; PoPl; WhC
I shop in the streets of my hometown with/ my family. Bruce Beaver. Letters to Live Poets, II. CBAP
I shot a rocket in the air. Enough. Tom Masson. OBAL
I shot an arrow into the air. A Shot at Random. D. B. Wyndham Lewis. FaBoCo; FaFP; FiBHP
I shot an arrow into the air. The Arrow and the Song. Longfellow. AA; FaFP; HBV-2; HBVY; PoPl; TreF
I shot an otter because I had a gun. The Shooting. Robert Pack. CoPo
I shot my friend to save my country's life. The Body Politic. Donald Hall. MP; NePoEA
I Should Be Ashamed. Uvlunuaq, *tr. fr. Eskimo.* WTO
I should grieve to desperation. Anacreon to the Sophist. "B. H." InMe
I should have been a gypsy child. Heir to Several Yesterdays. Parham J. Kelley. AMV-80
I should have been too glad, I see. Emily Dickinson. NOCV
I should have cut my life. Eviction. Elizabeth Brewster. CaP
I should have seen the sign: "Fresh paint." Fresh Paint. Boris Pasternak, *tr. by* Babette Deutsch. PoPl; TrJP
I should have thought. At Baia. Hilda Doolittle ("H. D."). LiTA; NOBA; TwAmPo
I should like a great lake of ale. The Feast of Saint Brigid of Kildare. *At. to* St. Brigid, *tr. by* Eugene O'Curry. OnYI
"I should like," said the vase from the china-store. The Toys Talk of the World. Katherine Pyle. OBCA
"I should like to buy you a birthday present," said Billy to Betsy Jane. Betsy Jane's Sixth Birthday. Alfred Noyes. SiSoSe
I should like to creep. A Mona Lisa. Angelina Weld Grimké. BlSi; CDC
I Should Like to Have a Great Pool of Ale. *At. to* St. Bridget. *See* Feast of Saint Brigid of Kildare, The.
I should like to rise and go. Travel. Robert Louis Stevenson. BrPo; FaBoCh; FaPON; MoShBr; TiPo
I should like to see that country's tiled bedrooms. Keeping Their World Large. Marianne Moore. WaP
I should pray but my soul is stopt. At the Ocean's Verge. Ralph Gustafson. OBCV
I should rather say one prayer to the Mother of God. Preference. Daniel Sargent. ISi
I shout my words above the blowing wind. I Sing America Now! Jesse Stuart. AmFN
I shouted day and night. Let Zulu Be Heard. Isaiah Shembe, *tr. by* G. C. Oosthuizen. WTO
I Show the Daffodils to the Retarded Kids. Constance Sharp. DFF
I shudder thinking. The Cold Irish Earth. Knute Skinner. InPK
I shut the door on the racket. Shoe Shop. Barton Sutter. SoSe
I sicken of men's company. The Green Inn. Theodosia Garrison. HBMV
I sieze the sphery harp. I strike the strings. Enitharmon Revives with Los. Blake. *Fr.* Vala; or, The Four Zoas. OBNC
I Sigh, As Sure to Wear the Fruit. *Unknown.* NCEP
I sigh for the heavenly country. The Heavenly City. Stevie Smith. FaBoTw
I Sigh When I Sing ("I sike al when I singe"). *Unknown.* OxBM
(Crucifixion, The.) MeEL
I sing a song of sixpence, and of rye. An Ode. Anthony C. Deane. NOBL
I sing a song reluctantly. Comtesse de Die, *tr. fr. Provençal by* Carol Cosman *and* Howard Bloch. PBWP
I sing a theme deserving praise. The Manchester Ship Canal. *Unknown.* OBET
I sing a woeful ditty. A Ballad Called the Haymarket Hectors. *Unknown.* APAS
I Sing America Now! Jesse Stuart. AmFN
I Sing an Old Song. Oscar Williams. LiTM; NePA
I sing her worth and praises hy. A Description. Lord Herbert of Cherbury. AnAnS-2; SeCP
I sing no longer of the skies. The Song of the King's Minstrel. Richard Middleton. HBV-1
I Sing No New Songs. Frank Marshall Davis. PoBA; PoNe
I sing no song. I spin instead. Spider. Norma Farber. PChr
I sing not of the draper's praise, nor yet of William Wood. An Excellent New Song upon His Grace Our Good Lord Archbishop of Dublin. Swift. CoMu
I sing of a frigate, a frigate of fame. The Flash Frigate. *Unknown.* AmSS
I sing of a hero, unsung, unrecorded. Crispus Attucks McCoy. Sterling A. Brown. BPo
I Sing of a Maiden. *Unknown.* CABA; CH; EBEV; ELP; FaBoCh; FF; InPS; ISi; LiTB; MeEL; NOBE; NOCV; NoP; OAEL-1; OxBM; PoEL-1; SBVL; SCV; SeCeV; TreFS; TrGrPo; ViBoPo
(Carol: "I sing of a maiden.") OBEV; OxBoCh
(Carol to Our Lady, A.) GOBC
(I Sing of a Maiden That Is Makeless.) InPK
(I Sing [*or* Syng] of a Mayden.) HAP; OAEP
(Maiden Makeles, The.) ChTr
(Maiden That Is Makeless, A.) OFD
(Two Carols to Our Lady, I.) ACP
I sing of a woman and summer. Canto Cantare Cantavi Cantatum. Rita Mae Brown. PeHV
I sing of arms and of a man. The Aeneid. Virgil, *tr. by* Allen Mandelbaum. NAWM-1
I sing of autumn and the falling fruit. Ship of Death. D. H. Lawrence. DTC; MoAB; MoBrPo; ViBoPo
I sing of brooks, of blossom[e]s, birds, and bowers. The Argument of His Book. Robert Herrick. AnAnS-2; CaPo; EBEV; HAP; HBV-2; HeIP; InvP; JCP; NoP; OAEL-1; OAEP; OBS; PoEL-3; PoPle; PoRA; SeCePo; SeCeV; SeCP; SeCV-1; TEP; TrGrPo; ViBoPo; WHA
I sing of George Augustus Chadd. The Ballad of Private Chadd. A. A. Milne. CenHV
I sing of ghosts and people under ground. The End. Mark Van Doren. ViBoPo
I sing of men and angels, and the days. Ebenezer Elliott. *Fr.* Spirits and Men. OBRV
I sing of myself, a sorrowful woman. Wife's Lament. *Unknown, tr. by* Kemp Malone. PBWP
I sing of news, and all those vapid sheets. George Crabbe. *Fr.* The Newspaper. PPON
I Sing of Olaf Glad and Big. E. E. Cummings. HeIP; LiTM; NoAM; NOBA; NoP; OBSV; OBWP; VGW
(I Sing of Olaf.) LiTA; NePA; PPON; WaP
I Sing of Shine. Etheridge Knight. BPo
(Dark Prophesy: I Sing of Shine.) GP
I sing of slum scabs on city faces. Today. Margaret Walker. FB
I sing of sweepers, frequent in thy streets. The Sweepers. William Whitehead. NOEC
I sing of the Good Samaritan. The Song of the Good Samaritan. Vernon Watkins. LiTM
I sing th' adventures of mine worthy wights. The Poem. Thomas Morton. SCAP
I sing the birth was born tonight. A Hymn [*or* Hymne] on the Nativity [*or* Nativitie] of My Saviour. Ben Jonson. SBVL; SeCV-1; TrCP
I Sing the Body Electric. Walt Whitman. CTC; MasP
Sels.
"O my body! I dare not desert the likes of you in other men and women, nor the likes of the parts of you." ErPo
"This is the female form." ErPo
I sing the furious battles of the spheres. Ad Johannuelem Leporem, Lepidissimum, Carmen Heroicum. *Unknown.* FaBoNo
I sing the glorious Power with azure eyes. Hymn to Athena. *Unknown, tr. by* Shelley. *Fr.* Homeric Hymns. AWP
I sing the hymn of the conquered, who fell in the battle of life. Io Victis! William Wetmore Story. AA; HBV-2; WGRP
I sing the Man, by Heav'ns peculiar grace. A Poem on Elijahs Translation. Benjamin Colman. SCAP
I Sing the Mighty Power of God. Isaac Watts. TRV
I sing the Name which none can say. To the Name above Every Name, the Name of Jesus, a Hymn [*or* On the Name of Jesus]. Richard Crashaw. AnAnS-1; SeCV-1
I sing the praise of honored wars. Soldier's Song. *Unknown.* WiR
I sing the simplest flower. Karl Shapiro. Six Religious Lyrics, I. CMoP
I sing the sofa. I who lately sang. The Sofa. William Cowper. *Fr.* The Task. LAuP; OAEP
I sing the song of a new Dawn waking. Song of the New World. Angela Morgan. HBMV; HBVY
I sing the song of the sleeping wife. Sing Song. Robert Creeley. NMP
I sing the tree is a heron. Merce of Egypt. Charles Olson. NoP
I sing the uplift and the up-welling. Jehovah. Israel Zangwill. WGRP
I, singularly moved. Winter. Coventry Patmore. The Unknown Eros, I, iii. FaBoRV; LO; NOBE; OBNC

I sink into a rare luminous blindness. Blindness. Delmira Agustini, *tr. by* D. M. Pettinella. PBWP
I sink my soft butt in an easy chair. News. Marnie Pomeroy. POL
I sip the dregs, my tongue. Willows. Laura Schreiber. AMV-81
I sit alone late at night. An Extra Joyful Chorus for Those Who Have Read This Far. Robert Bly. EAS
I sit among the hoary trees. The Lizard. Edwin Markham. BPAW
I Sit and Look Out. Walt Whitman. CABA; CTBA; OxBA; PAI; PPON; TAP
("I sit and look out upon all the sorrows of the world.") TRV
I Sit and Sew. Alice Dunbar Nelson. BlSi; CDC; WPOW
I Sit and Wait for Beauty. Mae V. Cowdery. BlSi
I sit at a gold table with my girl. At the Altar. Robert Lowell. Between the Porch and the Altar, IV. InPK; InPS
I sit at home and sew. Needle Travel. Margaret French Patton. HBMV
I sit at the top of the tree. Crow Resting. Edward Pygge. BXAP; FaBoPa
I sit beneath the throne of Allah! I, Lord, of All Mortals! *Malay Oral Tradition, tr. by* R. O. Winstedt. WTO
I sit beside my peaceful hearth. The Due of the Dead. Thackeray. OBWP
I sit beside old retired Italians. Park. David Ignatow. Psk
I sit by the mossy fountain; on the top of the hill of winds. James MacPherson. *Fr.* Fragments of Ancient Poetry, Collected in the Highlands of Scotland. NOEC
I sit by the window, reading a book. With a Book at Twilight. Jakov Steinberg, *tr. by* Mark Elliott Shapiro. VWA
I sit clumsy in my flesh, my legs. The Cigarette Poem. Faye Kicknosway. IHMS
I sit down at a table and open a book of poems. Library. Louis Jenkins. NU
I sit here at the window. Poetry and Thoughts on Same. Franklin P. Adams. HBMV
I sit here with the wind is in my hair. To Helen of Troy (N.Y.) Peter Viereck. WeW
I sit in a huge auditorium. The Return. Dennis Saleh. NeAC
I sit in a roadside diner. September 1, 1965. Paris Leary. CoPo
I sit in an office at 244 Madison Avenue. Spring Comes to Murray Hill. Ogden Nash. FiBHP
I sit in my garden among the roses. Prisoners. Nancy Barr Mavity. HBMV
I sit in one of the dives. September 1, 1939. W. H. Auden. CMoP; CoBMV; FaBoEn; LiTA; MasP; MoAB; MoBrPo; MoVE; NePA; OAEP; OxBA; PrIm; SeCeV; WaP
I sit in the dusk. I am all alone. Tableau at Twilight. Ogden Nash. FiBHP
I sit in the top of the wood, my eyes closed. Hawk Roosting. Ted Hughes. CMoP; GTBS-P; HAP; HeIP; LiTM; MP; NePoEA-2; NMP; OxBTC; PB; PPP; TwCP; UnPo
I sit musing, ten minutes from the Jap. A Letter for Marian. Thomas McGrath. VGW
I sit on a hard bench in the park. Spot-Check at Fifty. Vernon Scannell. NAs
I sit on the back platform of the train. The Train Butcher. Thomas Hornsby Ferril. GoYe
I sit on the edge. The Piano. Frank Davey. NOBC
I sit on the ground. Place-of-Many-Swans. Charlotte DeClue. STE; TWSS
I sit on the surge called ten stories tall. The Seesaw. Oscar Williams. LiTA
I sit thinking of a rowing-boat I saw. The Waiting-Room. Robin Fulton. PoA
I sit waiting for one of two kinds of miracle. Incanto. Stan Rice. NPGG
I Sit with My Dolls. *Unknown, tr. fr. Yiddish by* Joseph Leftwich. TrJP
I sit with my toes in the brook. *Unknown.* FaBoNo
I sit with you at the window. Barnabooth Enters Russia. Paul Hoover. AMV-81
I sit within my room and joy to find. The Presence. Jones Very. HAP
I slam the door. Outside I find the day. John Nobody. Dom Moraes. NoAM
I Sleep, but My Heart Waketh. Bible, *O.T.* The Song of Solomon, V: 2-16; VI: 1-3. TrJP
("I sleep but my heart is awake," *shorter sel., ad. by* Willis Barnstone.) BoWoP
I sleep in your arms. In Your Arms. Miklós Radnóti, *tr. by* Steven Polgar *and* Stephen Berg *and* S. J. Marks. VWA
I sleep with/ my feet in the fire. Cinderella Liberated. Anne Hussey. DFT
I sleep with thee, and wake with thee. To Mary: I Sleep with Thee, and Wake with Thee. John Clare. EnLoPo; GBL
I slept and dreamed that life was Beauty. Duty [*or* Beauty and Duty]. Ellen S. Hooper. BLPA; HBV-2; TreFS
I slept in a sleepy field. Airship. Hy Sobiloff. NePA
I slept in an old homestead by the sea. Chimney Swallows. Horatio Nelson Powers. HBV-1
I slept under rhododendron. Four Poems for Robin. Gary Snyder. NNaP; NoAM; NOBA; NoP; SOTW
I slump in the bucket seat. Twink Drives Back, in a Bad Mood, from a Party in Massachusetts. George Amabile. NYBP
I smacked you in the mouth for no good reason. Icicle. David Huddle. Str
I smile sometimes, although my grief[e] be great. The Passion of a Lover [*or* Gascoigne's Passion]. George Gascoigne. EnRePo; NCEP
I So Liked Spring. Charlotte Mew. OxBTC
I somersault just like a clown. Somersault. Dorothy Aldis. SoPo
I sometimes sleep with other girls. Cavalier Lyric. James Simmons. InPK; POL
I sometimes think I'd rather crow. To Be or Not to Be. *Unknown.* FaBoCo; FaFP; MoShBr; RHPC
I sometimes think that never blows so red. Omar Khayyám, *tr. by* Edward Fitzgerald. *Fr.* The Rubáiyát of Omar Khayyám. LO
I sought a theme and sought for it in vain. The Circus Animals' Desertion. W. B. Yeats. BiP; CMoP; FaBoMo; FaBoTw; LiTB; MAT; NIP; NoAM; NOBE; NoP; OAEL-2; OAEP; OxBTC; PAI; PP; PrIm; TEP
I Sought All Over the World. John Tagliabue. Psk
I sought for Peace, but could not find. Peace. Samuel Speed. OxBoCh
I sought for the greatness. America Is Great Because. *At. to* Alexis de Tocqueville. TreFT
I sought Him in a great cathedral, dim. Search. Anne Marriott. TRV
I sought his love in sun and stars. The Search. Thomas Curtis Clarke. WGRP
I sought, I found, she asked me what I would. Rachel Speght. *Fr.* A Dream. WPE
I Sought My Soul. *Unknown.* TreFT; TRV
I Sought the Lord. *Unknown.* TRV
I sought Thee round about, O Thou my God. The Search for God. Thomas Heywood. *Fr.* Hierarchie of the Blessed Angels. OxBoCh; WGRP
I sought to hear the voice of God. The Voice of God. Louis I. Newman. TreF
I Sought with Eager Hand. Allan Dowling. ErPo
I Sowed the Seeds of Love. *Unknown. See* Seeds of Love, The.
I span and Eve span. Eve-Song. Mary Gilmore. CBAP; PoAu-1
I speak for each no-tonguéd tree. Sidney Lanier. *Fr.* The Symphony. ViBoPo
I speak for Erin. The Muse of Amergin. *Unknown, tr. by* John Montague. BIrV
I Speak, I Say, I Talk. Arnold L. Shapiro. GrPl
I speak of that great house. Beyond the Hunting Woods. Donald Justice. ConAP; NCSH; NePoEA; NYBP; PoPl
I speak of that lady I heard last night. The Lady's Complaint. John Heath-Stubbs. MP; TwCP
I speak of the history of the world. Plain Song Talk. Richard Eberhart. PoA
I speak this poem now with grave and level voice. Immortal Autumn. Archibald MacLeish. AP; BiP; CMoP; CoBMV; LiTA; MoAB; MoAmPo; TrGrPo
I speak with a proud tongue of the people who were. Slainthe! [*or* Dedication]. Patrick MacGill. AnIV; OnYI
I spent a nicht amang the cognoscenti. I Was Fair Beat. Robert Garioch. OxBTC
I spent a night turning in bed. The Whip. Robert Creeley. NaP; NeAP; NoAM; PoM
I spent the day in a heavenly way. Katharine. Heine, *tr. by* Louis Untermeyer. UnTE
I spied a bear/ On the drifting floe. Bear Hunting. Aua, *tr. fr. Eskimo.* WTO
I spied a very small brown duck. Duck-chasing. Galway Kinnell. MP; NMP; TwCP; VGW
I spied beside the garden bed. In the Garden. Ernest Crosby. HBV-1; HBVY
I spied John Mouldy in his cellar. John Mouldy. Walter de la Mare. NCSH; OxBChV; PoPle
I splash—I flop. The Lesson. Jane W. Krows. SoPo
I spoiled the day. A Wasted Day. Frances Cornford. HBMV; MoBrPo
I spoke a word. Influence. John Oxenham. STF
I spoke the sea, that reaches green. Gray Shore. James Rorty. EtS
I spoke with a tangle-haired forester from Saskatchewan. A Summing Up. Gabriel Preil, *tr. by* Jeremy Garber. VWA
I spoke without caring. Investigation. Julia Vinograd. IHMS
I spot the hills. Theme in Yellow. Carl Sandburg. TiPo; YeAr
I sprang to the rollocks and Jorrocks and me. How I Brought the Good News from Aix to Ghent (or Vice Versa). R. J. Yeatman *and* W. C. Sellar. BXAP; FaBoPa; FiBHP; OnMSP; SpRo; Whc
I sprang to the stirrup, and Joris, and he. How They Brought the Good

News from Ghent to Aix. Robert Browning. BeLS; BLPL; FaBoBe; FaFP; FaPoR; GN; HBV-2; HBVY; HoPM; PaPo; RoGo; SpRo; TreF
I Spread Out unto Thee My Hands, *with music.* Henry Ainsworth. AH
I staid the night for shelter at a farm. *See* I stayed the night. . .
I stand amid the roar. Poe. *Fr.* A Dream within a Dream. ChTr
I stand and listen, head bowed. Self-employed. David Ignatow. NNaP
I stand as on some mighty eagle's beak. From Montauk Point. Walt Whitman. RFM
I stand at the window. Period Piece. Bruce Berlind. FAZ
I stand before the window that opens. Street Kid. Duane Niatum. STE
I stand before your cage to make my sketch. Artist and Ape. Gordden Link. GoYe
I stand below the gun tower. The Ritual. Paul David Ashley. LFAC
I Stand Corrected. Margaret Fishback. PoPl; WhC
I stand here by my window every night. Beyond the Wall. J. J. Maloney. LFAC
I stand high in the belfry tower. On the Tower. Annette von Droste-Hülshoff, *tr. by* James Edward Tobin. PBWP; WPOW
I stand in front of the tree. Pre-Positions. Jose Isaacson, *tr. by* Yishai Tobin. VWA
I stand in my door and look over the low field[s] of Drynam. The Widow of Drynam. Patrick MacDonogh. NeIP; OnYI; OxBI
I stand in the dark light in the dark street. Birthplace Revisited. Gregory Corso. CAD; NeAP; PoM; VGW
I stand in the late sun. The Reply. Philip Levine. PoA
I stand knee-deep in the ocean. Ancestry. Louis Daniel Brodsky. AMV-81
I stand most humbly. Wisdom. Langston Hughes. TiPo
I stand on slenderness all fresh and fair. A Cut Flower. Karl Shapiro. BoNaP; HAP; WeW
I stand on the deck of a small boat as rain sends bright daggers. The Island of Rhum. Roy Ferguson. PoSH
I stand on the mark beside the shore. The Runaway Slave at Pilgrim's Point. Elizabeth Barrett Browning. BrRo; PoNe; SBG
I stand on the porch. Exchanging Glances. William Pitt Root. MAYP
I stand there slapping a house. The Apprentice Painter. Jack Myers. AmPA
I stand upon the summit of my life [*or* years]. Thalatta! Thalatta! Joseph Brownlee Brown. AA; HBV-2
I stand upon the threshold of two years. Backward—Forward. *Unknown.* BLRP
I stand within the stony, arid town. The City Tree. Isabella Valancy Crawford. CaP
I stand within the willowing shadows of Memp-ch-ton. On Hearing the Marsh Bird's Water Cry. Duane Niatum. CDW
I star in the loam. Deadsong. Don Domanski. NOBC
I stare into the dark of night to see. On the Night Express to Madrid. Lora Dunetz. AMV-81
I stared at the printed words. Printed Words. Liz Sohappy Bahe. CDW
I start awake at night afraid of death. Sonnet 21. Paul Goodman. VGW
I start out for a walk at last after weeks at the desk. After Long Busyness. Robert Bly. PoA
I started early, took my dog. Emily Dickinson. AmPP; HAP; InPK; LiTM; MOS; NCEP; PoEL-5; SBG; WeW
(By the Sea.) LiTA
I started on the trail of June twenty-third. The Lone Star Trail. *Unknown.* AS
I started out with Maw and Paw. The Bank of the Arkansaw. *Unknown.* OuSiCo
I started picking up the stones. Apologia pro Vita Sua. A. R. Ammons. NOBA
I stay;/ But it isn't as if. An Empty Threat. Robert Frost. RFM
I stay clear. I Have No Strength for Mine. Joanne Kyger. PoM
I stayed in jail and worked for thirty long days. Nashville Stonewall Blues. *Unknown.* BluL
I stayed [*or* staid] the night for shelter at a farm. The Witch of Coös. Robert Frost. *Fr.* Two Witches. AP; CMoP; CoBMV; LiTM; MoAB; NePA; NoAM; NOBA; SeCeV; ViBoPo
I steal across the sodden floor. The Dream House. Marjorie Allen Seiffert. HBMV
I step around a gate of bushes. Cold Water. Donald Hall. NCSH
I step into my heart and there I meet. John Davidson. *Fr.* Thirty Bob a Week. ELU
I stepped from plank to plank. Emily Dickinson. AP; CMoP; NOBA; NOCV
I stepped on the black winter seeds. Seeds. Thurmond Snyder. NNP
I stick my tongue in you. Gray Silk Twisting. Patrick Lane. NeAC
I still bear in mind the picture of the globe. The Philosophic Apology. Samuel Greenberg. MoPo; NePA
I still have a sister in Guang Dung. The Landlord's Wife. Marilyn Chin. BrSi
I still have some money. In Terror of Hospital Bills. James Wright. GP
I Stole Brass. *Unknown.* ChTr
I stole forth dimly in the dripping pause. Moon Compasses. Robert Frost. MOON; MoVE
I stole the prince and I brought him here. The Grand Inquisitor's Song. W. S. Gilbert. *Fr.* The Gondoliers. OnMSP
I stole through the dungeons, while everyone slept. Alternative Endings to an Unwritten Ballad. Paul Dehn. FiBHP
I stood above the sown and generous sea. The Morality of Poetry. James Wright. PP
I stood among the wanting many. Just Making It. Richard Thomas. PoNe
I stood and leant upon the mast. The Voyage. Heine, *tr. by* John Todhunter. AWP
I stood and saw my mistress dance. On Her Dancing. James Shirley. PoPle
I stood and watched him dig one hole all day. Robert Frost's Left-leaning *Trespassers Will Be Shot* Sign. William Zaranka. BXAP
I stood aside to let the cows. Man and Cows. Andrew Young. EBEV
I stood at eve, as the sun went down, by a grave where a woman lies. 'Ostler Joe. George R. Sims. BeLS; BLPA; HBV-2; TreF
"I stood at the back of the shop, my dear." At the Draper's. Thomas Hardy. *Fr.* Satires of Circumstance. MoAB; MoBrPo
I stood beside a hill. February Twilight. Sara Teasdale. FaPON; OBCA; PDV; RHPC; SoPo; YeAr
I stood between two mirrors when you died. Elegy. William Jay Smith. NePoEA
I stood by Honor and the Dean. Sahara. Coventry Patmore. *Fr.* The Angel in the House. EBVV
I stood by the old fort's crumbling wall. Sutter's Fort, Sacramento. Lucius Harwood Foote. BPAW
I stood by the river where the flesh of our world. In Bed with a River. George Bradley. AMV-80
I stood in a meadow. Green Valley. Dorothy Vena Johnson. PoNe
I Stood in Jerusalem. Zelda, *tr. fr. Hebrew by* Marcia Falk. VWA
I stood in my mother's kitchen. Ants. Katharyn Machan Aal. AMV-80
I stood in the gloom of a spacious room. Awake, My Lute! C. S. Lewis. CenHV; FaBoNo
I stood in the ride, and the glamour. My Woodcock. Patrick Reginald Chalmers. CenHV
I stood in Venice on the Bridge of Sighs. Venice [*or* On the Bridge of Sighs]. Byron. Childe Harold's Pilgrimage, IV. EnRP, *abr.*; FaBoPP, 4 *sts.*; HBV-2, 4 *sts.*; OAEP, *abr.*; OBRV, 9 *sts.*; ViBoPo, 3 *sts.*
I stood on a roof top and they wove their cage. On the Pilots Who Destroyed Germany in the Spring of 1945. Stephen Spender. NeBP
I stood on the Atlantic ocean, on the wide Pacific shore. The Wabash Cannonball. *Unknown.* FSW
I stood on the bridge at midnight. *Unknown.* FaFP
I stood on the bridge at midnight. The Bridge. Longfellow. HBV-2; TreF
I stood one day beside a blacksmith's door. *See* Last eve I passed beside a blacksmith's door.
I stood still and was a tree amid the wood. The Tree. Ezra Pound. CMoP; TwAmPo
I Stood Tiptoe [upon a Little Hill]. Keats. EnRP; FaPON
(Sigh of Silence, The.) GN
"Sometimes goldfinches one by one will drop," *sel.* PBBP
(Goldfinches.) GN
I Stood upon a High Place. Stephen Crane. The Black Riders, IX. LiTA; NePA
I stood upon a shore, a pleasant shore. The Shell's Song. Keats. EtS
I stood watching the great hulk of desire. Coming Back. Linda Gregg. NPGG
I stood where real estate, measured in always smaller and more precious. Dana Point. Brewster Ghiselin. AMV-81
I Stood with the Dead. Siegfried Sassoon. ChMP
I stood with three comrades in Parliament Square. Armistice Day. Charles Causley. OBWP
I stood within the City disinterred. At Pompeii. Shelley. *Fr.* Ode to Naples. FaBoPP
I stood within the cypress gloom. Implora Pace. Charles Lotin Hildreth. AA
I Stood within the Heart of God, *with music.* William Vaughn Moody. *Fr.* The Fire Bringer. AH
(Pandora Speaks.) WGRP
I stoop to gather a seabird's feather. The Feather. Vernon Watkins. FaBoTw; MoVE
I stooped to the silent Earth and lifted a handful of her dust. A Handful of Dust. James Oppenheim. TrJP
I stopped deep. African in Louisiana. Kojo Gyinaye Kyei. PBA
I stopped in a sidestreet surplus shop, just south of Yorkville. The Cot. Grover Amen. NYBP; NYP
I stopped to pick up the bagel. The Bagel. David Ignatow. ConAP; FF; TwCP

I strayed about the deck, an hour, to-night. Fragment. Rupert Brooke. BrPo
I strayed, all alone, where the Autumn. A Rose in October. James Whitcomb Riley. OBAL
I strayed along the strand with mussels strewn. Along the Strand. Alfred Mombert, *tr. by* Jethro Bithell. TrJP
I Stroll. Peter Redgrove. NePoEA-2
I strolled across/ An open field. The Waking. Theodore Roethke. RFM
I strolled beside the shining sea. The Cumberbunce. Paul West. NA
I strove with all, for all were worth my strife. Epitaph for G. B. Shaw. Max Beerbohm. FaBoEE
I strove with none, for none was worth my strife. On His Seventy-fifth Birthday [*or* Dying Speech of an Old Philosopher *or* Envoi *or* Finis *or* The End]. Walter Savage Landor. *Fr.* The Last Fruit off an Old Tree. AWP; BLPL; ChTr; EBEV; EnRP; FaBoEE; FaBoEn; FaPoR; GLGT; GTBS-P; HBV-2; HeIP; LiTB; NOBE; NoP; OAEL-2; OAEP; OBEV; OBNC; OBVV; SeCePo; SeCeV; TreF; TrGrPo; ViBoPo; VLP; WHA
I struck for what I deemed the right. After the Battle. George Sylvester Viereck. GoYe
I struck the board, and cried [*or* cry'd]: No more. The Collar. George Herbert. AnAnS-1; AWP; BiP; BLPL; CABA; EaLo; EBEV; FaBoEn; HAP; HBV-2; HeIP; InPS; JCP; LiTB; LoBV; MasP; MeLP; MePo; NIP; NOBE; NOCV; NoP; OAEL-1; OAEP; OBS; OxBoCh; PAI; PoEL-2; PoPle; PoRA; PPoe; PPP; SCV; SeCePo; SeCeV; SeCP; SeCV-1; TEP; TrGrPo; ViBoPo; WeW; WHA
I struck the trail in seventy-nine. The Gal I Left behind Me. *Unknown.* BPAW; CoSo; FSW
I struck tomorrow square in the face. Hidesong. Aig Higo. TTY
I studied my tables over and over. A Mortifying Mistake. Anna Maria Pratt. AA; HBV-1
I study out a dark similitude. The Swan. Theodore Roethke. VGW
I study the lives on a leaf: the little. The Minimal. Theodore Roethke. BiP; NoAM; NOBA
I Substitute for the Dead Lecturer. Amiri Baraka. NOBA
I suddenly saw I was wrang when I felt. Deep-Sea Fishing. "Hugh MacDiarmid." SeCePo
I suffered so much from printer's errors. The Author's Epitaph. *Unknown.* FiBHP
I summon to the winding ancient stair. A Dialogue of Self and Soul. W. B. Yeats. CABA; CMoP; FaBoMo; LiTB; LiTM; MasP; MoBrPo; NoAM; OAEP
I sundry see, for beauty's gloss. That He Findeth Others as Fair, but Not So Faithful as His Friend. George Turberville. ElL
I supped where bloomed the red rose. Supper. Walter de la Mare. NYBP
I suppose even molecules are driven to distraction. Swing One, Swing All. George Bradley. AMV-80
I Suppose Her Mother Told Her. Francine Corcos. AMV-80
I suppose it's because we're on foot I'm reminded. Kyran's Christening. Alden Nowlan. NeAC
I supposed I knew my Bible. Read the Bible Through. Amos R. Wells. STF
I suspect. Blue Stones. Larry Levis. DiL
I suspect he knew that trunks are metaphors. Houdini. Eli Mandel. NIP; NOBC
I swam the Huron of love, and am not ashamed. The Huron. Ruth Herschberger. WPE
I swear by what the sages spoke. Crazy Bill to the Bishop. Robert Peters. BXAP
I swear I ain't done what Richard. Say Hello to John. Sherley Anne Williams. BlSi
I swear I begin to see the meaning of these things. Walt Whitman. *Fr.* By Blue Ontario's Shore. InPS
I swear to the Lord. The Black Man Speaks. Langston Hughes. TreFT
I sweep the street and lift me hat. The Old Man at the Crossing. L. A. G. Strong. OBMV
I swim in darkness, swim. Arrivals and Departures. Melvin Walker La Follette. CoPo
I swing up on the sideboard of the old car. Almost Grown. Ai. MAYP
I switch on the light. Crickets tick. Sleep in the Heat. Laura Jensen. AmPA
I swore I would go back. O Lyric Love. Winfield Townley Scott. VGW
I swore to stab the sonnet with my pen. Karl Shapiro. *Fr.* White-haired Lover. PoA
I swung and swung at empty air. The Abominable Baseball Bat. X. J. Kennedy. WSC
I Syng of a Mayden. *Unknown. See* I Sing of a Maiden.
I take as my theme, "The Independent Woman." Pro Femina, II. Carolyn Kizer. MAT; NMM
I Take 'Em and Like 'Em. Margaret Fishback. PoPl; WhC
I take four devils with me when I ride. Poem. Gervase Stewart. WaP
I take him down upon the beach. Son and Surf. Julia Hurd Strong. GoYe
I take it he doesn't think at all. The Pike. John Bruce. LiSp
I take it you already know. Hints on Pronunciation for Foreigners. *Unknown.* FaBoUs
I take my Aunt out in her pram. My Aunt. Peggy Wood. POL
I take my chaperon to the play. The Chaperon. H. C. Bunner. AA; HBV-1
I take my old clothes out of the cupboard and deck. My Best Clothes. Eli Netser, *tr. by* Bernhard Frank. AMV-81
I take my son outside. What I Tell Him. Simon J. Ortiz. CDW
I take my son to visit in the distant. Sons. Don Polson. AMV-81
I take no books, nor I read no papers. The Gull Decoy. Larry Gorman. ShS
I take off my shirt, I show you. Taking Off My Clothes. Carolyn Forché. AmPA
I take the dogs into. La Bagarède. Galway Kinnell. NYBP
I take the twist-about, empty street. The Rendezvous. Bernard Spencer. GTBS-P
I Take Thee Life. Margot Ruddock. OBMV
I take their hands. They. R. S. Thomas. OxBTC
I take what never can be taken. The Poet. Haniel Long. HBMV
I take you as I take the moon rising. Death. Charles Wright. FiCP
I take you looking at the statue. The Statue. Kenneth Allott. EAS
I takes and I paints. Poem by a Perfectly Furious Academician. *Unknown.* FiBHP
I takes up for my colored men. The Generation Gap. Ruby C. Saunders. BlSi
I talk through my mouth with many tongues. Riddle: Nightingale. *Unknown.* PBBP
I talk to my inner lover, and I say, why such rush? The Radiance. Kabir, *tr. by* Robert Bly. LLLT
I Talk to You. John Newlove. PeCV
I talked one midnight with the jolly ghost. All in a Garden Green. W. E. Henley. OBMV
I talked to old Lem. Old Lem. Sterling A. Brown. BPo; FB; IDB; PoBA; PoNe; TTY
I tarry in days shaped like the high staired street. A Birthday Memorial to Seventh Street. Audre Lorde. CNA
I taste a draught beer never brewed. Emily's Haunted Housman. David Cummings. BXAP
I taste a liquor never brewed. Emily Dickinson. AmPP; AP; CABA; CMoP; FaBV; FF; HeIP; LiTA; LiTM; MoAmPo; NePA; NOBA; NoP; OxBA; PoEL-5; SBG; SeCeV; SoSe; TAP; TreFS; WPE
(Little Tippler, The.) EvOK
I taught myself to live simply and wisely. "Anna Akhmatova," *tr. fr. Russian by* Richard McKane. PBWP
I taught the talented. Sappho, *tr. fr. Greek by* Mary Barnard. GLGT
I teach how we cheat the young. A 4 Part Geometry Lesson. Robin Blaser. NeAP
I teach in a high school. The Wrong Kind of Insurance. John Ashbery. NYP
I teach-a da bird an' I blow-a da ring. The Educated Love Bird. Peter Newell. FiBHP
I tell him *eat your dinner*. Einstein's Father. D. L. Klauck. LTB
I tell him how it used to be in Paguate. Harold Littlebird. *Fr.* After the Pow-Wow. STE
I tell my friend in California. California, This Is Minnesota Speaking. Stephen Dunn. GP
I tell my secret? No indeed, not I. Winter: My Secret. Christina Rossetti. BrRo; TEP
I Tell of Another Young Death. Cesar Tiempo, *tr. fr. Spanish by* Donald Devenish Walsh. TrJP
I tell thee, Dick, where I have been. A Ballad upon a Wedding. Sir John Suckling. AnAnS-2; CABA; CaPo; CavP; CoMu; EBEV; FaBoBa; HBV-1; InvP; JCP; LoBV; NoP; OBS; Par; SeCeV; SeCP; SeCV-1; UnTE; ViBoPo
I tell Therese. Therese. Alden Nowlan. NeAC
I tell words that talk in trees, this hill. Pot Shot. Padraic Fallon. CIP
I tell ye, Sue, it ain't no use! Goin' Back T'morrer. Hamlin Garland. OBAL
I tell yeh whut! The chankin'. Horses Chawin' Hay. Hamlin Garland. OBAL
I tell you, hopeless grief is passionless. Grief. Elizabeth Barrett Browning. FPL; HBV-2; HeIP; InPK; LoBV; OBEV; OBNC; OBVV; PoLF; SBG; TrGrPo; VLP; WPE
I tell you how dat hypocrite do. That Hypocrite. *Unknown.* BPo
I tell you, Lesbia, life is love. Catullus to Lesbia. James Reeves. ErPo
I tell you that I see her still. I Only Am Escaped Alone to Tell Thee. Howard Nemerov. CoAP; HeIP; NePA; NoAM
I Thank God I'm Free at Las'. *Unknown.* BoAN-2, *with music*; BPo; TAP
(Free at Last.) FSW
I thank thee and I praise thee, O thou radiant grace. Thanksgiving. "Yehoash," *tr. by* Isidore Goldstick. TrJP
I Thank Thee, Lord. *Unknown.* BLRP; WBLP

I Thank You God. E. E. Cummings. *See* I Thank You God for Most This Amazing.
I thank you, God,/ that swallows know their way. Thanksgiving. Louise Driscoll. YeAr
I Thank You God for Most This Amazing. E. E. Cummings. BiP; EaLo; ILwL; MoAB; TAP
(I Thank You God.) TrCP
I that had found the way so smooth. The Return. Jessie Fauset. CDC
I that have beene a lover, and could shew it. A Sonnet, to the Noble Lady, the Lady Mary Worth. Ben Jonson. AnAnS-2
I that in heill wes [*or* health was] and gladnes[s]. Lament for the Makaris [*or* The Fear of Death Confounds Me *or* Timor Mortis Conturbat Me]. William Dunbar. ACP; BSV; ChTr; EBEV; FaBoRV; GoTS; HAP; MeEL; NOBE; NoP; OAEL-1; OAEP; OBEV; OxBS; PoEL-1; PP; ViBoPo
I that lived ever about you. English Girl. *Unknown, tr. by* E. Powys Mathers. OBMV
I that tremble at your feet. The Missive. Sir Edmund Gosse. HBV-1
I that whilom lived secure. A Testament. *Unknown.* OBSC
I' the how-dumb-deid o the cauld hairst nicht. The Eemis-Stane. "Hugh MacDiarmid." BSV; NeBP
I, the old woman of Beare. The Old Woman of Beare [Regrets Lost Youth]. *Unknown, tr. by* Frank O'Connor. AnIL; KiLC; OBMV
I, the poet William Yeats. To Be Carved on a Stone at Thoor Ballylee. W. B. Yeats. FaBoEE; NoAM; NoP
I thee advise. To One That Had Little Wit. George Turberville. EnRePo
I, then, will not restrain my mouth. Let Me Alone. Bible, *O.T. Fr.* Job. PPON
I, therefore, will begin. Soul of the age! Ben Jonson. *Fr.* To the Memory of My Beloved Mr. William Shakespeare. NOBE
I think a time will come when you will understand. For My Father. Paul Potts. FaBoTw
I think about where I'd really like to be. Delaying Tactics. Christopher Wiseman. AMV-81
I think all this is somewhere in myself. The Room. W. S. Merwin. NaP; NOBA
I think before they saw me the giraffes. The Giraffes. Roy Fuller. ChMP; NeBP; NoAM
I think between my cradle-bars. Ballade of Faith. Tom MacInnes. CaP
I Think Continually of Those Who Were Truly Great. Stephen Spender. ChTr; CMoP; EaLo; FaBoEn; HAP; LiTB; LiTM; MoAB; MoBrPo; NOBE; NoP; OAEL-2; OAEP; OxBTC; PAI; PoPl; PoRA; PP; TreFT; TrGrPo; ViBoPo; WaP
I think flowers can see. Thoughts of a Little Girl. María Enriqueta, *tr. by* Emma Gutiérrez Suárez. FaPON
I think God sang when He had made. The Star. Beatrice Redpath. CaP
I think God took the fragrance of a flower. Mothers. *Unknown.* PGD
I think he had not heard of the far towns. St. John Baptist. Arthur O'Shaughnessy. HBV-2
I think he sits at that strange table. At It. R. S. Thomas. OxBC
I think I am becoming. Interior Monologue 666. Tom Marshall. NOBC
I think I could live at seventy miles an hour. Nostalgia for 70. Jim Wayne Miller. AMV-81
I Think I Could Turn and Live with Animals. Walt Whitman. *Fr.* Song of Myself. HAP; NU; PDV; TrGrPo; WeW; WGRP
(Animals.) FaFP; NePA; PAI; POL; PoPl; PPON
(Beasts, The.) HBV-2; OBVV
I think I grow tensions. The Flower. Robert Creeley. CAPP; PAI
I think I hear the angels sing. Shew! Fly Don't Bother Me. *At. to* Billy Reeves, *and to* T. Brigham Bishop. PSoN
I think I heard the belle. The Old Lady's Lament for Her Youth. Villon, *tr. by* Robert Lowell. BoLoP
I Think I Know No Finer Things than Dogs. Hally Carrington Brent. BLPA
I think I like this room. Picture of Little Letters. John Koethe. AMV-81
I think I remember this moorland. We Have Been Here Before. Morris Bishop. EvOK; FiBHP; InMe; NYBP; WhC
I think I see her sitting bowed and black. Oriflamme. Jessie Redmond Fauset. BANP; BlSi; PoBA
I Think I See Him There. Waring Cuney. CDC
I think I shall live for a while a bit gamely. The Poet Loves from Afar. Desmond O'Grady. NoAM
I think I sing that little song. Union Man. Albert Morgan. AmFP
I think I smell smoke. Il Janitoro. George Ade. OBAL
"I think I want some pies this morning." Greedy Richard. Jane Taylor. OxBChV
I think I will learn some beautiful language, useless for commercial. Intention to Escape from Him. Edna St. Vincent Millay. SBG
I think if I should cross the room. The Room's Width. Elizabeth Stuart Phelps Ward. AA
I think if you had loved me when I wanted. Success. Rupert Brooke. OxBTC
I think I'll get a paper. Nerves. "Sagittarius." OxBTC
"I think I'm going to die," I tried to say. Finale: Presto. Peter Davison. CoPo
I think it better that in times like these. On Being Asked for a War Poem. W. B. Yeats. MoVE; NIP; OBWP; PP
I think it is all light at the end; I think it is air. The Quilt. Larry Levis. MAYP
I think it is in Virginia, that place. Low Fields and Light. W. S. Merwin. ConAP; LCAP
I think it is over, over. In Harbor. Paul Hamilton Hayne. AA; HBV-2
I think it's worth it today. Souster. Ray Fraser. NeAC
I think mice/ Are rather nice. Mice. Rose Fyleman. EvOK; FaPON; NTCP; PDV; RHPC; SoPo; SUS; TiPo
I think not on the state, nor am concerned. Upon the Double Murther of King Charles I. Katherine Philips. SBG
I think now of latitudes solitary, Asian, and velvet. In a Valley of this Restless Mind. Ewart Milne. NeIP
I think Odysseus, as he dies, forgets. Odysseus Dying. Sheila Wingfield. OxBI
I think of a flower that no eye has ever seen. Beauty. Laurence Binyon. MoBrPo
I think of all the things at school. Johnny's Hist'ry Lesson. Nixon Waterman. FPL; PoLF
I think of corner shots, the ball. Day and Night Handball. Stephen Dunn. AmPA; LiSp
I think of God. The Hairs in My Nose. Aram Boyajian. NeAC
I think of him/ Who lives south of the big sea. *Unknown, tr. fr. Chinese by* Wai-lim Yip. BoWoP
I Think of Him as One Who Fights. Anna Hempstead Branch. HBMV
I Think of Housman Who Said the Poem Is a Morbid Secretion, like the Pearl. Judith Kroll. UnPo
I think of my name, Julia Grahm. Waiting for Winter. George Keithley. NPGG
I think of my wife, and I think of Lot. Marriage Couplet. William Cole. OBAL
I Think of Oblivion. Yehuda Amichai, *tr. fr. Hebrew by* Ruth Nevo. VWA
I think of the Celts as rather a whining lady. The Celts. Stevie Smith. NoP
I think of the starved foreign children. The Last Bite. Richard Frost. AMV-80
I think of the things that might have been and were not. Things That Might Have Been. Jorge Luis Borges, *tr. by* Alastair Reid. AMV-80
I think of the tribes: the women prized for fatness. The Tribes. Roy Fuller. LiTM
I think of the unknowing art my watching made. Voyeur. John Edward Hardy. ErPo
I think of things like the shadow of a branch. The Shadow of a Branch. Edith Marcombe Shiffert. WPE
I think of you writing that poem. Patty Hearst Hoists the Carbine. Sibyl James. SOTS
I think oft times as night draws nigh. Are All the Children In? *Unknown.* STF
I think, old bone, the world's not with us much. To William Wordsworth from Virginia. Julia Randall. NMM; WPE
I think some saint of Eirinn wandering far. Fuchsia Hedges in Connacht. Padraic Colum. GoBC
I Think Sometimes. Michael Hartnett. CIP
I think sometimes. Blue Waves. David St. John. MAYP
I think that I am drawing to an end. The Poets at Tea, II. Barry Pain. Par
I think that I live in a street. For the Record. George Jonas. MoCV
I think that I shall never make. In a Garden. Donald G. Babcock. NePoAm
I think that I shall never see/A billboard. Song of the Open Road. Ogden Nash. FaBoCo; FPL; OBAL; PPJ; TreFS; WhC
I think that I shall never see/ A poem. Trees. Joyce Kilmer. BLPA; FaBoBe; FaFP; FaPON; FPL; HBV-1; HBVY; OHFP; TreF; WBLP; WGRP
I think that I shall never ski. Winter Trees. Conrad Diekmann. LiSp
I think that is some faery spirit strewed. The Salesman. Robert Mezey. NePoEA
I think that look of Christ might seem to say. The Meaning of the Look. Elizabeth Barrett Browning. TrCP; TRV
I think that man hath made no beauteous thing. To Melody. George Leonard Allen. CDC
I think that Mary Magdalene. Mary Magdalene. Leonora Speyer. HBMV
I think that night's our balance. Suite to Fathers. Jim Harrison. AmPA; DiL
I think that we retain of our dead friends. Remembrance. John Henry Boner. AA
I think that what he gave us most was pride. Thanksgiving, 1963. Molly Kazan. TreFT

I think the dead are tender. Shall we kiss? She. Theodore Roethke. BoLoP; ErPo; NIP
I think the fairies to my christening came. Fairy Godmothers. Eugene Lee-Hamilton. OBVV
I think the gentle soul of him. Ilicet. Theodosia Garrison. PoLF
I think the Lord on his axe-chopped cross. James K. Baxter. Autumn Testament, 29. OCNZ
I Think the New Teacher's a Queer. Perry Brass. PeHV
I think the thing you call Renown. Winthrop Mackworth Praed. *Fr.* The Chaunt of the Brazen Head. OBSV
I think they had no pattern. Beside the Line of Elephants. Edna Becker. RHPC
I think thou waitest, Love, beyond the gate. The Lonely Road. Kenneth Rand. HBV-1
"I think," thought Sam Butler. English Liberal. Geoffrey Taylor. FaBoEE
I think when Judas' mother heard. Judas Iscariot. Countee Cullen. PoLF
I think you have to be Catholic to be a nurse. Modern American Nursing. Lucy Hricz. AMV-80
I thirst, but not as once I did. My Soul Thirsts for God. William Cowper. TrCP
I thirst for God, to Him my soul aspires. The Living God. Abraham ibn Ezra, *tr. by* Alice Lucas. TrJP
I thirst for violins, as drunkards thirst. Ideal and Reality. Joseph Campbell. BIrV
I thought a horse was "Gee!" and "Whoa!" Learner. J. A. Lindon. PH
I thought, beloved, to have brought to you. The Gift. "Æ." HBMV
I thought he was dumb. Tortoise Shout. D. H. Lawrence. LiTM; NoAM
I thought I had found a swan. Epilogue. Denise Levertov. LLLT
I thought I heard a knock on the door. Rispetti: On the Death of a Child. Paul Heyse, *tr. by* E. H. Mueller. PoPl
I thought I heard the old man say. Leave Her, Johnny. *Unknown.* FSW
I thought I saw an angel flying low. Nocturne at Bethesda. Arna Bontemps. AmNP; BALP; BANP; CDC; PoNe
I Thought I Saw Stars. R. P. Lister. PV
I thought I saw white clouds, but no! Lilies. Shiko. SUS; TiPo
I thought I was so tough. Tamer and Hawk. Thom Gunn. FaBoTw; NePoEA
I thought I woke: the midnight sun. Stanzas. Paul Goodman. PoA
I thought I'd win the spelling bee. Bananananananananana. William Cole. RHPC
I Thought It Was Tangiers I Wanted. Langston Hughes. PoNe
I Thought Joy Went by Me. Willard Wattles. HBMV
I thought Love lived in the hot sunshine. Where to Seek Love. Blake. *Fr.* William Bond. TRV
I thought of cards along the mantelpiece. December Fragments. Richmond Lattimore. PChr
I thought of Chatterton, the marvellous Boy. We Poets in Our Youth. Wordsworth. *Fr.* Resolution and Independence. FaBoRV
I thought of Thee, my partner and my guide. After-Thought. Wordsworth. The River Duddon, XXXIV. EnRP; FaBoEn; FaBoPP; FaBoRV; NOBE; OAEP; OBEV; OBNC; OBRV; SeCePo
I thought once how Theocritus had sung. Sonnets from the Portuguese, I. Elizabeth Barrett Browning. EBVV; GBL; HBV-1; NOBE; NoP; OAEP; OBEV; OBNC; TreFT; ViBoPo; WPE
I thought one spring, just for fun. The Tenderfoot. *Unknown.* FSW
I thought she was white. Old Indian Trick. Rayna Green. TWSS
I thought Silver must have snaked logs. Silver. A. R. Ammons. NoP
I thought that I could follow Him. There Was No Room on the Cross. *Unknown.* GoBC
I thought that Love had been a boy. *Unknown.* EnLoPo
I thought the dawn would flush to sudden glory. Mountain Vigil. Douglas Fraser. PoSH
I thought the earth. Sleeping in the Forest. Mary Oliver. NU
I thought the night without a sound was falling. How Infinite Are Thy Ways. William Force Stead. *Fr.* Uriel. OBMV; TrPWD
I thought the sun breaking through Sangre de Cristo. Two Horses. Joy Harjo. TWSS
I thought the winner had been found. Brooklynese Champion. Margaret Fishback. WhC
I Thought There Were Limits. Douglas G. Jones. MoCV
I thought they'd be strangers aroun' me. The Curate's Kindness. Thomas Hardy. CoBMV
I thought to die that night in the solitude. The Edge. Lola Ridge. OnYI
I thought you loved me. *Zulu Oral Tradition, tr. by* H. Tracey. WTO
"I thought you loved me." "No, it was only fun." In the Orchard. Muriel Stuart. ErPo; FF; OxBTC
I threw a penny in the air. *Unknown.* CenHV
I threw the inside of my gizzard out, splashing. Zimmer Drunk and Alone, Dreaming of Old Football Games. Paul Zimmer. MAT
I, through all chances that are given to mortals. To Ausonius. Paulinus of Nola, *tr. by* Helen Waddell. PeHV
I throw off all the ceremony. Yom Kippur. Eric Chaet. VWA
I throw open the door. April Fourth. Robert Mezey. NaP
I throw things away. Old Bibles. Marilyn Waniek. MAYP
I thumped on you the best I could. Heart's Needle, VIII. W. D. Snodgrass. NePoEA; NoAM
I, thy servant, full of sighs, cry unto thee. Penitential Psalm. *Unknown.* WGRP
I tink I hear my brudder say. Stars Begin to Fall. *Unknown.* AA
"I to my home shall be going." The Parting of Hector and Andromache. Homer, *tr. by* William B. Smith *and* Walter Miller. *Fr.* The Iliad, VI. TreFS
I to My Perils. A. E. Housman. ViBoPo; WeW
I to the hills lift up mine eyes. Psalm 121. *Unknown. Fr.* The Bay Psalm Book. OBCA
I to the Hills Will Lift Mine Eyes, *with music.* Francis Rous. AH
I to the Lord from My Distress, *with music. Unknown.* AH
I told him a tale that I adore. Andrew's Bedtime Story. Ian Serraillier. DuDa
I Told Jesus. Sterling Plumpp. PoBA
I told my captain that old Maude was dead. Captain Captain. *Unknown.* BluL
I told my son. Saul's Progress. Harvey Shapiro. DiL
I told myself in singing words. As It Was. Lilla Cabot Perry. Meeting after Long Absence, II. AA
I told the Sun that I was glad. The Sun. John Drinkwater. FaPON; NTCP; SoPo; TiPo
I, Too. Langston Hughes. AmNP; CDC; FF; HeIP
(Epilogue: "I, too, sing America.") BALP; VGW
(I, Too, Sing America.) IDB; PoBA; PoLF; PoNe
I too/ once lived/ in the country. Pachuta, Mississippi/ A Memoir. Al Young. TAT
I, too, dislike it: there are things that are important beyond all this fiddle. Poetry. Marianne Moore. AmPP; AP; BiP; BLPL; BoWoP; CABA; CMoP; CoBMV; FF; HAP; HeIP; LiTA; LiTM; MoAB; MoAmPo; NePA; NIP; NoAM; NOBA; NoP; OxBA; PAI; PP; SeCeV; TAP; TreFT; TwAmPo; UnPo; ViBoPo
I, too, have plucked a stalk of grass. Letters to Walt Whitman, V. Ronald Johnson. VGW
I, Too, Know What I Am Not. Bob Kaufman. NBP
I, too, saw God through mud. Apologia pro Poemate Meo. Wilfred Owen. ChMP; CoBMV; FaBoRV; LiTM; MoAB; MoBrPo
I, Too, Sing America. Langston Hughes. *See* I, Too.
I too was a little child once. Epilogue. Joseph Eliyia, *tr. by* Rae Dalven. VWA
I too was born out of a lion's mouth. Let Heroes Account to Love. Alan Dugan. NoAM
I took/ a coney island of the mind. Clickety-Clack. Paul Blackburn. NoAM
I Took a Bow and Arrow. John Ciardi. EvOK
I took a day to search for God. Vestigia. Bliss Carman. CaP; WGRP
I Took a Hansom on To-Day. W. E. Henley. HBV-1
I took a piece of plastic clay. Sculpture. *Unknown.* BLPL; PoLF
I took a piece of the rare cloth of Ch'i. A Present from the Emperor's New Concubine. Lady Pan, *tr. by* Kenneth Rexroth. BoWoP
I took away three pictures. Sandhill People. Carl Sandburg. CMoP
I took her dainty eyes, as well. Villanelle of His Lady's Treasures. Ernest Dowson. HBV-1
I took leave of my beloved one evening: how I wish. At Taliq, *tr. fr. Arabic by* A. R. Nykl. PeHV
I took money and bought flowering trees. Planting Flowers on the Eastern Embankment. Po Chü-i, *tr. by* Arthur Waley. BoNaP
I took my cat apart. The Secret in the Cat. May Swenson. DFF; GP; PAI
I took my girl to a fancy ball. I Had But Fifty Cents. *Unknown.* BeLS; BLPA; TreF
I took my girlfriend to your last poetry reading. Short Order. Charles Bukowski. HoPM
I took my heart in my hand. Twice. Christina Rossetti. GBL; NOBE; OBEV; OBNC; OBVV; TrCP; ViBoPo; VLP
I took my oath I would inquire. The Inquest. W. H. Davies. DTC; GTBS-P; NOBE; OxBTC
I took my power in my hand. Emily Dickinson. NePA
I took my watch beside the rose. Anne Wilkinson. *Fr.* Nature Be Damned. PeCV
I took off down the town's disaster route. Soliloquy in a Motel. Walker Gibson. GrPl
I took one small breath to lift her. The Minyan. Jack Myers. VWA
I took the embankment path. An Advancement of Learning. Seamus Heaney. NCSH
I took you to the clinic today. Physical for My Son. Barbara Smith. AMV-80
I tossed my friend a wreath of roses, wet. Gifts. Mary Elizabeth Coleridge. PBWP

I touch and recollect. Tiresias' Lament. Ellen de Young Kay. NePoEA
I touch you in the night, whose gift was you. The Science of the Night. Stanley Kunitz. MoAmPo; MP; TwCP; UnTE
I touch your face. Poems of Night. Galway Kinnell. NaP
I touched a shining mote of sand. Lyric. Philip Child. CaP
I touched the flesh with my eyes. Fish. Joe Rosenblatt. NOBC
I touched the nothingness of air once. I Read a Tight-fisted Poem Once. Nancy Woods. RFM
I traded a girl. Trader. Jim Harrison. NoAM
I trail and trail along with the mountain range. My Indian Girl. Ali Sedat Hilmi Törel. PeD
I tramped the pavements, cursing God. Comrade Jesus. Ralph Cheyney. PGD
I travel in a train. I Am a Horse. Hans Arp, *tr. by* Harriet Watts. FaBoNo
I travel through thin jails of rain. Patrol. Ralph Pomeroy. CoPo
I travel'd thro' a land of men. The Mental Traveller. Blake. EnRP; LAuP; MasP; OAEL-2; PoEL-4
I Traveled among Unknown Men. Wordsworth. *Fr.* Lucy. AWP; EnRP; FaBV; GTBS; GTBS-P; HBV-1; OAEL-2; OAEP; OBEV; OBRV; TrGrPo
(Lucy.) OBNC
I traveled [*or* travell'd] on, seeing the hill, where lay. The Pilgrimage. George Herbert. AnAnS-1; ChTr; FaBoRV; PAI
I traveled to the ocean. Prayer to the Pacific. Leslie Silko. CDW; NoP; VoR
I Traveled with Them. Mu'tamid, King of Seville, *tr. fr. Arabic by* J. B. Trend. AWP
I travelled the land from Leap to Corbally. The Volatile Kerryman. Owen Roe O'Sullivan, *tr. by* Sean O'Riada. BIrV
I traversed a dominion. Mute Opinion. Thomas Hardy. CMoP
I tread on many autumns here. Walking in Beech Leaves. Andrew Young. MoVE
I tread the dark and my steps are silent. Brightness as a Poignant Light. David Ignatow. DiL
I tried but I could not remember my dream. The Hills of Pomeroy. Ewart Milne. NeIP
I tried each thing, only some were immortal and free. As One Put Drunk into the Packet-Boat. John Ashbery. HAP
I tried to live by bread alone. Satisfied. Edgar Cooper Mason. BLRP
I tried to live small. Housing Shortage. Naomi Replansky. NMM
I tried to save those glorious jacarandas. Mrs. Asquith Tries to Save the Jacarandas. Harold Witt. AMV-81
I tried to tell her. Offspring. Naomi Long Madgett. FB
I tripped along a narrow way. Forthfaring. Winifred Howells. AA
"I trow that gude ending." Bruce Consults His Men. John Barbour. *Fr.* The Bruce. GoTS
I trundle the bodies, on the iron bars. John Berryman. *Fr.* Homage to Mistress Bradstreet. NOBA
I trust I have not wasted breath. In Memoriam A. H. H., CXX. Tennyson. ImOP; SeCePo
I, trusting that the truly sweet. A Retrospect. Coventry Patmore. VLP
I try to knead and spin, but my life is low the while. In Leinster [*or* Song]. Louise Imogen Guiney. AA; GoBC; HBV-2; OBVV
"I try to look hard-boiled, but I." Early Morning. Morris Bishop. PV
I Try to Waken and Greet the World Once Again. James Wright. InPS
I turn my steps where the lonely road. In Dark Hour. Seumas MacManus. WGRP
I turn the page and read. At the British Museum. Richard Aldington. MoBrPo
I Turn to Jesus. Oswald J. Smith. STF
I turn to you. To the Divine Neighbor. Judah Leib Teller, *tr. by* Gabriel Preil *and* Howard Schwartz. VWA
I turn you out of doors. Alain Chartier, *tr. fr. French by* Edward Lucie-Smith. BoLoP
I turned an ancient poet's book. Home. Henry van Dyke. STF
I turned and gave my strength to woman. Two Generations. L. A. G. Strong. OBMV
I turned aside into the trees, among the shadows. In the Garden of the Turkish Consulate. Pinhas Sadeh, *tr. by* Harris Lenowitz. VWA
I turned my back when in the pot they tossed. Walthena. Elisabeth Peck. AmFN
I turned to speak to God. Not All There. Robert Frost. FaBoCo
I turned to the parlor in panic. Frustrate. Louis Untermeyer. HBMV; InMe; YaD
I turned upon the world an inward eye. The Meeting. Jocelyn Hollis. AMV-80
I twist your arm. A Deux. William Wood. ELU
I understand the large hearts of heroes. Heroes. Walt Whitman. *Fr.* Song of Myself. AA; InPS
I understand the ties that are between us. The Summing Up. James Simmons. POL
I understand you well enough, John Donne. A Letter to John Donne. C. H. Sisson. NOCV
I upon the first creation. Gratitude. Christopher Smart. *Fr.* Hymns for the Amusement of Children. LAuP; NOEC
I use no colors, just number threes. Drawing Wildflowers. Jorie Graham. NPGG
I used to be a drill man. Drill Man Blues. George Sizemore. AmFP; WTO
I used to be a radical. The Radical in the Alligator Shirt. Lou Lipsitz. AMV-80
I used to believe I wouldn't live past 16. Fan. Walter Lew. BrSi
I used to curse the wind and rain. Cursing and Blessing. "Michael Lewis." *Fr.* Cherry Blossoms. UnTE
I used to dream militant. Revolutionary Dreams. Nikki Giovanni. CNA; GP
I used to fall. My Heart Belongs to Daddy. Cole Porter. OBAL
I used to have an old grey horse. Goin' Down to Town. *Unknown.* AS
I used to laugh silently as I watched him. Someone Gave Him Some Plastic Flowers Once. Dennis Shady. LFAC
I used to lie on my back, imagining. Childhood. Maura Stanton. MAYP
I used to live on Cottonwood and owned a little farm. A Mormon Immigrant Song. *At. to* George A. Hicks. CoSo
I used to live on mountain top. Old Joe Clarke. *Unknown.* TrAS
I used to look at with disgust. Falling Down to Bed. Nila NorthSun. STE
I Used to Love My Garden. C. P. Sawyer. FaBoCo
I used to see her daily, we would lie. Mental Health. Elliot Fried. GP
I used to see her in the door. Paul. James Wright. NePoEA; PoPl
I used to tell you, "Frances, we grow old." Kenneth Rexroth, *after the Latin of* Ausonius. NNaP
I used to think that grown-up people chose. Childhood. Frances Cornford. OxBTC
I used to walk on solid gr'und. To a Sea Eagle. "Hugh MacDiarmid." MoBrPo
I used to walk the morning stream. Walk. Brian Merriman, *tr. by* Brendan Behan. *Fr.* The Midnight Court. BIrV
I used to watch you, sleeping. Kathleen Raine. *Fr.* My Mother's Birthday. NAs
I used to wonder. Border Line. Langston Hughes. PoCh
I Used to Wrap My White Doll Up In. Mae Jackson. BOLo; PoBA
I usta wonder who i'd be. Adulthood. Nikki Giovanni. NMM
I uster own the Double D. Cyclone Blues. *Unknown.* CoSo
I venture to suggest that I. An Election Address. James Kenneth Stephen. NBM
I verse a settler's tale of olden times. Charles Harpur. *Fr.* The Creek of the Four Graves. CBAP
I view the backless rooms. The Doll House. Darlene Button Kitzman. AMV-81
I Vision God. *Unknown.* TTY
I vow'd unvarying faith, and she. Constancy [Rewarded]. Coventry Patmore. *Fr.* The Angel in the House. OBVV; VLP
I wad ha'e gi'en him my lips tae kiss. Mary's Song. Marion Angus. BSV
I wadna gi'e my ain wife. My Ain Wife. Alexander Laing. HBV-1
I wage not any feud with Death. In Memoriam A. H. H., LXXXII. Tennyson. LiTB; PPON
I wait and watch: before my eyes. The Waiting. Whittier. WGRP
I wait for her who restores my fingertips. Song of Expectancy. George Hitchcock. EAS
I wait for his foot fall. Earth Trembles Waiting. Blanche Shoemaker Wagstaff. PoLF
I wait for wonder, or the weather's turn. Absent Creation. D. S. Savage. NeBP
I Wait My Lord. *Unknown, tr. fr. Chinese by* Helen Waddell. *Fr.* Shi King. AWP
I wait to tangle fear around my hand. Night along the Mackinac Bridge. Roberta Hill. CDW; STE
I wait, with those that rest. Ark to Noah. Jay Macpherson. *Fr.* The Ark. NOBC; PoA
I waited and worked/ To win myself leisure. Koheleth. Louis Untermeyer. TrJP
I waited for the train at Coventry. Godiva. Tennyson. HBV-2
I wake and feel the city trembling. Lines Written near San Francisco. Louis Simpson. CABA
I Wake and Feel the Fell of Dark, Not Day. Gerard Manley Hopkins. BrPo; CMoP; CoBMV; GTBS-P; HAP; LiTB; NoAM; NOBE; NOCV; NoP; OAEL-2; OAEP; PAI; PoEL-5; PoPle; PPoe; PPP; SCV; SeCeV; TW; VLP
(Terrible Sonnets, The, III.) MoPo
I wake and hear it raining. Morning Worship. Mark Van Doren. NePoAm-2; TwAmPo
I wake before the clock begins the day. Waking Early. R. L. Barth. AMV-81
I wake, but before I know it it is done. Aging. Randall Jarrell. PoA

I wake despondent. Morning. Tove Ditlevsen, *tr. by* Nadia Christensen. PBWP
I wake from my nightsweats to build up the fire. Voices in the Winter. Ken McCullough. LTB
I wake in a dark flat. Afterlives. Derek Mahon. CIP
I wake in the morning early. Singing-Time. Rose Fyleman. SiSoSe; TiPo
I wake in the night. Middle of the Way. Galway Kinnell. NU
I wake in the night with such uncertain gladness. The Girl Takes Her Place among the Mothers. Marya Zaturenska. HBMV
I wake late and leave. A Cardinal. W. D. Snodgrass. PP
I Wake, My Friend, I. Faye Kicknosway. IHMS
I wake to find myself lying in an open field. Robert Bly Says Something Too. Henry Taylor. BXAP
I wake to see the morning. Morning and Myself. Nia Francisco. STE
I wake to sleep, and take my waking slow. The Waking. Theodore Roethke. AmPP; AP; BiP; CoAP; CoBMV; CrMA; HAP; HeIP; InPS; LiTM; MoAmPo; MP; NIP; NoAM; NOBA; NoP; PoPl; PPP; PrIm; SeCeV; SoSe; TAP; TwCP; WeW
I wake up early while you sleep. Going to Town. Linda Hogan. TWSS
I wake up first and with a sense of. Genius Loci of the Morning. Doug Fetherling. NeAC
I wake up in the bed my grandmother died in. Stove. Philip Booth. FYAP
I waked; the sun was in the sky. On Waking from a Dreamless Sleep. Annie Fields. AA
I wakened on my hot, hard bed. The Watch. Frances Cornford. DTC; HBMV; HeIP; InPK; MoBrPo; OxBTC
I Wakened to a Calling. Delmore Schwartz. PoPl
I wakened to love and music; coaxed from the shelter. One Morning. Vassar Miller. AMV-80
I walk/ between the cobblestones. Peripatetic. Robert Lima. AMV-81
I walk a road—an ancient, trodden way. Another While. Morris Rosenfeld. TrJP
I walk along the bustling streets. Girls from Home. Abraham Reisen, *tr. by* Keith Bosley. VWA
I walk and I wonder. Spring. Isaac Rosenberg. TrJP
I walk at dawn across the hollow hills. Poem. Ruthven Todd. EAS
I walk back. Getting the Mail. Galway Kinnell. UnPo
I walk behind you, hand. Days of 1956. Robin Magowan. EAS
I walk [*or* walked] beside the prisoners to the road. A Camp in the Prussian Forest. Randall Jarrell. AP; CMoP; MiAP; MoAmPo; NMP; OBWP; OxBC
I walk down a long. A Poem for Museum Goers. John Wieners. NeAP
I walk down the garden paths. Patterns. Amy Lowell. AWP; BoWoP; DL; FaFP; FPL; HBV-1; LiTA; MoAmPo; NePA; OnMSP; OxBA; TreFS; TrGrPo
I walk down the narrow. The Man in the Mirror. Mark Strand. NYBP
I walk downhill, slow. Roll Call: A Land of Old Folk and Children. Isaac J. Black. CNA
I walk, I trust, with open eyes. Love's Reality. Coventry Patmore. *Fr.* The Angel in the House. VLP
I walk in loneliness through the greenwood. *Unknown, tr. fr. French by* Willis Barnstone. BoWoP
I walk in nature still alone. Great Friend. Henry David Thoreau. PoEL-4
I walk in the old street. Louis Zukofsky. VGW
I walk into your house, a friend. A Friend. W. D. Snodgrass. MAT
I walk Main Street, a pelican. Small Town: The Friendly. Stephen Dunn. POL
I walk my paint-box suburb. The clear air. Edinburgh Spring. Norman MacCaig. NMP
I walk on grass as soft as wool. An Old Woman Laments in Spring-Time. Edith Sitwell. ViBoPo
I Walk on the River at Dawn. Joanne Hart. PoDr
I walk on the waste-ground for no good reason. For No Good Reason. Peter Redgrove. NMP
I walk on two legs. A Riddle. Cynthia Ozick. VWA
I walk the alleys trampled through the wheat. Sensation. Arthur Rimbaud, *tr. by* John Gray. SyP
I walk the dusty ways of life. The Troubadour of God. Charles Wharton Stork. WGRP
I walk the purple carpet into your eye. Inside Out. Diane Wakoski. CoAP; NYBP
I walk the tightrope of the heart. Acrobat. Edward Watkins. AMV-80
I walk through the long schoolroom questioning. Among School Children. W. B. Yeats. AnIL; BLPL; CABA; ChMP; CMoP; CoBMV; FaBoEn; GTBS-P; HAP; LiTB; LiTM; MoAB; MoBrPo; MoVE; NIP; NoAM; NOBE; NoP; OAEL-2; OAEP; OxBTC; PrIm; PPoe; PPP; SeCeV; TrGrPo; WeW
I walk upon the rocky shore. My Mother. Josephine Rice Creelman. OHIP
I walk'd along a stream for pureness rare. *See* I walked along a stream . . .
I walk'd in the lonesome evening. Song. William Allingham. EnLoPo
I walked a mile with Pleasure. Along the Road. Robert Browning Hamilton. BLPA; BLPL; TreFS
I walked abroad in [*or* on] a snowy day. Soft Snow. Blake. FF; SoSe; TEP
I walked all the way from East St. Louis. East St. Louis Blues. *Unknown.* AmFP
I walked [*or* walk'd] along a stream for pureness rare. A Fragment. Gervase Markham, *at. to* Christopher Marlowe. CTC; LoBV; OBSC
I walked beside the evening sea. Ebb and Flow. George William Curtis. AA; HBV-2
I walked beside the prisoners to the road. *See* I walk beside . . .
I walked entranced/ Through a land of Morn. King Cahal Mór of the Wine-red Hand [*or* A Vision of Connaught in the Thirteenth Century]. James Clarence Mangan. AnIL; AnIV; GoBC
I walked in loamy Wessex lanes, afar. The Pity of It. Thomas Hardy. CMoP; LiTM; WaP
I walked into a loge in the Teatro Melisso. Pound at Spoleto. Lawrence Ferlinghetti. PoM
I walked into a moon of gold last night. One Night. Millicent Sutherland. SUMH
I walked my fastest down the twilight street. Apparition. John Erskine. HBMV
I walked on the banks of the tincan banana dock. Sunflower Sutra. Allen Ginsberg. AmPP; CoAP; MAT; NeAP; NOBA
I walked one day on a lonely road. No Greater Love. *Unknown.* STF
I Walked Out to the Graveyard to See the Dead. Richard Eberhart. MiAP; MoPo
I walked over the grave of Henry James. Richard Eberhart. VGW
I walked the mountains. Microcosmos, XLIII. Nigel Heseltine. NeBP
I Walked [*or* Walkt] the Other Day [to Spend My Hour]. Henry Vaughan. AnAnS-1; FaBoEn; JCP; MePo; OBS; OxBoCh
I walked through Ballinderry in the spring-time. Lament for [the Death of] Thomas Davis. Sir Samuel Ferguson. AnIV; BIrV; NBM; OnYI; OxBI
I walked through the woodland meadows. The Bird with a Broken Wing. Hezekiah Butterworth. WBLP
I walked, when love was gone. A Breath of Air. James Wright. NOBA; PoPl
I walked where in their talking graves. At the British War Cemetery, Bayeux. Charles Causley. OBWP; OxBC
I walked with a flower. Earth, Sky. Sydney Clouts. PeSA
I walked with Maisie long years back. The Ballad of Camden Town. James Elroy Flecker. HBV-1
I walked with my reason out beside the sea: we were together. Sorley Maclean. Dain do Eimhir, XXII. NeBP
I walked with you as far as the graineries beside the gates. Songs for a Three-String Guitar. Léopold Sédar-Senghor, *tr. by* Miriam Koshland. PBA
I walked with you this eleventh in the coppice. November Poppies. Hilary Corke. NYBP
I walkit air, I walkit late. Scrievin. Alexander Scott. BSV
I Walkt the Other Day. Henry Vaughan. *See* I Walked the Other Day.
I wander aimless, to and fro. Aimless. Louis Palagyi, *tr. by* Watson Kirkconnell. TrJP
I wander all night in my vision. The Sleepers. Walt Whitman. AmPP
I wander by the edge. He [*or* Aedh] Hears the Cry of the Sedge. W. B. Yeats. OxBTC; VLP
I wander down on Clinton street south of Polk. Clinton South of Polk. Carl Sandburg. AmFN
I wander on as in a dream. Love Me, and the World Is Mine. David Reed, Jr. TreFT
I wander through a crowd of women. At Piccadilly Circus. Vivian de Sola Pinto. OBMV
I wander through [*or* thro'] each chartered [*or* charter'd] street. London. Blake. *Fr.* Songs of Experience. AWP; CABA; ChER; ChTr; EnRP; FaBoEn; FaBoPP; FF; HAP; HeIP; InPK; InPS; LAuP; LiTB; MAT; NIP; NOBE; NOEC; NoP; OAEL-2; OBNC; PAI; PoEL-4; PPON; PrIm; SCV; SeCePo; SeCeV; TEP; UnPo; ViBoPo; WeW
I wandered angry as a cloud. Paul Dehn. SpRo
I wandered by the brookside. The Brookside. Richard Monckton Milnes. HBV-1; TreFS
I Wandered Lonely as a Cloud. Wordsworth. BoNaP; CABA; EnRP; FaBoPP; HBV-1; HBVY; InPK; LoBV; MasP; NoP; OAEL-2; OAEP; OBRV; PAI; PoPl; PoRA; RoGo; SpRo; SUS; TEP; UnPo; ViBoPo; WHA
(Daffodils,[The].) BLPA; FaBoBe; FaBV; FaFP; FaPON; FiP; FPL; GN; GoJo; GTBS; GTBS-P; LiTB; NOBE; OBEV; OBNC; OHFP; SCV; SeCeV; TreF; TrGrPo; WBLP
I wandered on through field and fold. The Ploughman. Gilbert Thomas. HBMV
I wandered out awhile agone. The Divided Heart. George Wither. *Fr.* Fair Virtue, the Mistress of Philarete TrGrPo

I wandered [*or* wander'd] today to the hill, Maggie. When You and I Were Young, Maggie. George W. Johnson. BLSo; FSW; PSoN; TreF
I wandered up an autumn loaning. The Hills of God. A. A. Buist. PoSH
I wandered up to Beaucourt; I took the river track. Beaucourt Revisited. A. P. Herbert. MMA
I wandering went/ Among the haunts and dwellings of mankind. Shelley. *Fr.* Prometheus Unbound, III. FiP
I want/ a love to hold. Defense Rests. Vassar Miller. MoAmPo
I want/ to make a myth of you. Love Poem. Rosemary Aubert. AMV–80
I Want a Girl. Will Dillon *and* Harry Von Tilzer. TreFS
I want a good lover. What Do You Want? John Newlove. NOBC
I want a hero: an uncommon want. Don Juan, I. Byron. EnRP; NoP; OAEL–2, *abr.*; OAEP, *abr.*
I want a job as a low cloud. Job Hunting. Tom Hennen. GP
I want a little witch cat. Witch Cat. Rowena Bennett. SiSoSe
I Want a Tenant; a Satire. John O'Keefe. NOEC
I want a typewriter. In Despair He Orders a New Typewriter. Elder Olson. AMV–81
I want all you women to listen to my tale of woe. Death Sting Me Blues. *Unknown.* BluL
I want free life and I want fresh air. Lasca. Frank Desprez. BeLS; BLPA; BPAW; FaBoBe; TreF
I Want God's Heab'n to Be Mine, *with music. Unknown.* BoAN–2
I want it to be clear for us. On My Stand. Sharon Scott. JB
I want my buddies and all my friends. Dupree. *Unknown.* ViBoFo
I want nothing but your fire-side now. Hearthstone. Harold Monro. OBMV
I want something suited to my special needs. Needs. A. R. Ammons. NIP; OBAL
I want the New Year's opening days. A Prayer for the New Year. *Unknown.* BLRP
I want to apologize. Getting Through. Maxine W. Kumin. SUW
I Want to Be a Cowboy. *Unknown.* BPAW
I want to be a white horse! Three Presidents. Robert Bly. LCAP
I want to be buried in an anonymous crater inside the moon. Unholy Missions. Bob Kaufman. CNA; TTY
I want to be in a garden with my love. *Tr. fr. Arabic by* Willis Barnstone. BoWoP
I Want to Be Married and Cannot Tell How. *Unknown.* OnYI
I want to be near this mild unforgiving man. Father. Paul Zweig. DiL
"I want to be new," said the duckling. The New Duckling. Alfred Noyes. FaPON
I want to be ready. Walk in Jerusalem, Just [*or* Jus'] like John. *Unknown.* BoAn–2; FSW
I want to be still as a quiet hill. Be Still. Betsy W. Kline. STF
I want to be with my love in a garden. *Tr. fr. Arabic by* Willis Barnstone. BoWoP
I want to dance. The Deepest Bow. Marie Takvan, *tr. by* Harold P. Hansen. AMV–81
I Want to Die Easy When I Die, *with music. Unknown.* BoAN–2
I want to die in the saddle. An enemy of civilization. Drinking Song. Jim Harrison. WOLT
I Want to Die While You Love Me. Georgia Douglas Johnson. AmNP; BANP; BlSi; CDC
I want to drown in good-salt water. Says Something Too. Samuel Hoffenstein. BXAP
"I want to fight you," he said in a Belfast accent. Experience. James Simmons. BIrV; CIP
I want to flee to the frozen north when cliques who prattle. Faggots in Ancient Rome. Juvenal. *Fr.* The Satires, II. PeHV
I want to forget my manners. Hope. Edith Södergran, *tr. by* Jaakko A. Ahokas. PBWP
"I want to get away somewhere and re-read Proust." Problems of a Journalist. Weldon Kees. NaP; NYP
I want to give my babies to the moon. Giving the Moon a New Chance. Terry Stokes. MOON
I want to give you a spoonful of hot soup. A Hymn about a Spoonful of Soup. Jozef Wittlin, *tr. by* Isaac Komem. VWA
I want to give you words. Words. Ulálume González De Leon, *tr. by* Sara Nelson. AMV–81
I want to go home and I ain't got sufficient. Bad Luck Blues. *Unknown.* BluL
I Want to Know. John Drinkwater. FaPON
I want to know the unity in all things. Ballad. A. R. Ammons. GP
I want to know why when I'm late. I Want to Know. John Drinkwater. FaPON
I want to lament the princess who was killed. In Memory, 1978. Judith Kazantzis. BrRo
I want to live in an old adobe house on the outskirts of Santa Fe. Prospectus. Albert Huffstickler. AMV–81
I Want To One Morning. Gordon Turner. AMV–80
I want to remember the fallen palm. Oblivion. Ellis Ayitey Komey. PBA
I want to see it face to face. Nothing. Charles Simic. NNaP
I want to see the slim palm trees. Heritage. Gwendolyn B. Bennett. AmNP; BANP; BlSi; PoBA
I want to speak to you while I can. I Am Here. Robert Mezey. VWA
I Want to Tell You. Sandra Hochman. GP
I want to tell you of a trip I did take. George Britton. *Unknown.* CoSo
I want to travel the common road. The Common Road. Silas H. Perkins. BLPA; FaBoBe
I want to understand the steep thing. Climbing You. Erica Jong. PoA
I Want to Write a Jewish Poem. Gary Pacernick. VWA
I want to write a poem. Noises. Fred Johnson. CNA
I Want You. Arthur L. Gillom. BLPA; FaBoBe
I want you to see me in it. The White Dress. Roberta Spear. MAYP
I want you when the shades of eve are falling. I Want You. Arthur L. Gillom. BLPA; FaBoBe
I wanta say just gotta say something. Beautiful Black Men. Nikki Giovanni. BPo; NMM
I wanted a rib sandwich. Rib Sandwich. William J. Harris. CNA
I wanted a rifle for Christmas. Presents. Marchette Chute. EvOK; SiSoSe
I wanted her to stop. Woman Guard. Pancho Aguila. LFAC
I wanted my name. A Poem for Ed "Whitey" Ford. Jonathan Holden. MAYP
I wanted so ably. The World. Robert Creeley. NaP; NoAM; NoP
I wanted the gold, and I sought it. The Spell of the Yukon. Robert W. Service. BLPA; BLPL; FaBoBe; FaFP; PoPl; TreF
I wanted this morning to bring you a gift of roses. The Roses of Sa'adi. Marceline Desbordes-Valmore, *tr. by* Barbara Howes. BoWoP
I wanted to be a cauliflower. The Cauliflower. John Haines. GP; InPK
I wanted to be a nature poet. "Honeysuckle Was the Saddest Odor of All, I Think." Thadious M. Davis. BlSi
I wanted to be sure to reach you. To the Harbormaster. Frank O'Hara. CoAP; MOS; PoM
I wanted to bring you this Jap iris. For C. Philip Whalen. NeAP; VGW
I Wanted to Die in the Desert. *Unknown.* BPAW; CoSo
I wanted to give him some gift. To Evan. Richard Eberhart. DFF
I wanted to harness and go. Baroness Mu Impeded in Her Wish to Help Famine Victims in Wei. Confucius, *tr. by* Ezra Pound. *Fr.* Yung Wind. CTC
I wanted to know my mother when she sat. Leroy. Amiri Baraka. BPo; PoBA
I wanted to see you,/ thighs showing. Leila Miccolis, *tr. fr. Portuguese by* Willis Barnstone *and* Nelson Cerqueira. BoWoP
I wanted to take a walk. Walking Past Paul Blackburn's Apt. on 7th St. Diane Wakoski. TAP
I wanted to write. For Saundra. Nikki Giovanni. BPo; TTY
I wanted you to hear that song, she told me. Poem for Pat. Paula Gunn Allen. TWSS
I wanted you when skies were red. Unanswered. Martha Dickinson Bianchi. AA
I war against the folly that is War. The New Mars. Florence Earle Coates. PGD
I warmed both hands before the fire of Life. Envoi. D. B. Wyndham Lewis. FiBHP
I warn, like the one drop of rain. The Voice of the Void. George Parsons Lathrop. AA
"I warn ye all, ye gay ladies." Child Waters. *Unknown.* ESPB
I warned the parents, you know. Father to the Man. John Knight. EaLo
I was/ the girl of the chain letter. Love Song. Anne Sexton. NCSH
I was a bachelor, I lived by myself. The Weaver. *Unknown.* AS
I was a boy when I heard three red words. Threes. Carl Sandburg. CMoP; OxBA; PoLF
I Was a Brook. Sara Coleridge. *Fr.* Phantasmion. OBRV
I Was a Bustlemaker Once, Girls. Patrick Barrington. PoPle; WhC
I was a child and overwhelmed: Mozart. The Corner Knot. Robert Graves. NYBP
I was a dreamer: I dreamed. The Dream-Teller. Padraic Gregory. HBMV; OnYI
I was a girl waiting by the roadside for my boyfriend to come. The Elwha River. Gary Snyder. NoAM
I was a goddess ere the marble found me. A Statue in a Garden. Agnes Lee. HBMV
I was a high-born gentleman. Gypsy Davy. *Unknown.* AS
I was a humble clerk. The African Trader's Complaint. Dennis C. Osadebay. PBA
I was a joke at dinners; aye, any would-be wit. Revenge to Come. Propertius, *tr. by* Kirby Flower Smith. Elegies, III, 25. AWP
I Was a Labourer. Sean Jennett. *Fr.* Cycle: Seven War Poems. OnYI
I was a lady of high renown. Jamie [*or* Lord] Douglas. *Unknown.* ESPB; OxBB; ViBoFo; WHA
I was a laughing child. Travelling Song. Thomas McGrath. FAZ
I was a leather skinned harridan. Granny Crack. James Reaney. NOBC
I was a lover of turkey and holly. Carol. Anne Wilkinson. OBCV

I was a mere boy in a stone-cutter's shop. Abraham. Delmore Schwartz. VWA
I was a peasant girl from Germany. Elsa Wertman. Edgar Lee Masters. *Fr.* Spoon River Anthology. NoAM; OxBA; PAI
I was a poor groom of thy stable, king. Shakespeare. King Richard II, *fr.* V, v. PoPle
I was a quack, and there are men who say. Advertising Epitaph: On a Quack. *Unknown.* FaBoUs
I was a Roman soldier in my prime. A Guard of the Sepulcher. Edwin Markham. WGRP
I was a squanderer once of love and days. Conservative. Harold Witt. AMV-80
I Was a Stricken Deer, That Left the Herd. William Cowper. *Fr.* The Task. EnRP; FaBoRV; OAEP; OxBoCh; PAI
(Stricken Deer, The.) FiP; LoBV
I was a traveller then upon the moor. Wordsworth. *Fr.* Resolution and Independence. SpRo
I was a wandering sheep. Lost but Found. Horatius Bonar. HBV-2
I was a woman always liked spangles. Sleep, Madame, Sleep. Annemarie Ewing. NePoAm
I was a young maid truly. The Sandgate Girl's Lamentation. *Unknown.* CoMu; ELP
I was about to go, and said so. Loneliness. Brooks Jenkins. CTBA
I was all night at this. Putting On My Shoes I Hear the Floor Cry Out beneath Me. Michael Heffernan. BXAP
I was alone once, waiting. For the Marsh's Birthday. James Wright. NYBP
I was already. Three Shades of Light on the Windowsill. Susan Griffin. NPGG
I was altered in the placenta. The Dead Poet. Al Purdy. NOBC
I was always a lover of ladies' hands! Your Hands. Ernest Dowson. UnTE
I was always called in early for dinner. Don't Forget. Stephen Berg. PoA
I was always fascinated. Alma Villanueva. WPOW
I was angry with my cow. The Cry of the Child. William Zaranka. BXAP
I was angry with my friend. A Poison Tree. Blake. *Fr.* Songs of Experience. AWP; CABA; EnRP; FaFP; HAP; HoPM; LAuP; LiTB; NoP; OAEP; PAI; PoEL-4; PPoe; PPP; SCV; SoSe; TreFS; TrGrPo; TW; WeW
I was asking for something specific and perfect for my city. Mannahatta. Walt Whitman. AA; EyDe; GOA; HBV-2; MoAmPo; NYP
"I was bat seven year alld." *See* "I was but seven year auld."
I was beautiful when we came into Egypt. Sarai. Joseph Sherman. VWA
I was born/ In spittin distance. Mountain Born. Marcia Inzer Bost. AMV-80
I Was Born about [*or* Almost] Ten Thousand Years Ago. *Unknown.* AS, *with music*; FSW
I was born [*or* borned] and raised in East Virginia. East Virginia. *Unknown.* FSW; OuSiCo
I Was Born at a Place of Pines. Geoffrey Lehmann. *Fr.* Ross's Poems. CBAP
I was born conscious, I can't remember. Rino's Song. Lynne Lawner. IHMS
I was born for deep-sea faring. A Son of the Sea. Bliss Carman. EtS
I was born in a bad slum. Plot Improbable, Character Unsympathetic. Elder Olson. NePA
I was born in a time of peace. Ts'ai Yen, *tr. by* Kenneth Rexroth *and* Ling Chung. *Fr.* Eighteen Verses Sung to a Tatar Reed Whistle. BoWoP; PBWP; WPOW
I was born in Belfast between the mountain and the gantries. Carrickfergus. Louis MacNeice. AnIL; FaBoPP; NoAM; OnYI
I was [*or* Oh I was] born in Boston [city], a city you all know well. The Boston Burglar. *Unknown.* AmFP; CoSo; FSW
I was born in Bristol, and it is possible. Family Fortunes. C. H. Sisson. OxBC
I was born in Cologne. Winter in Another Country. Ai. AMV-81
I was born in Illinois. My Fathers Came from Kentucky. Vachel Lindsay. AmFN; HBMV
I was born in the city. Greener Grass. Frank Steele. Psk
I was born in the congo. Ego Tripping. Nikki Giovanni. NoAM; Psk
I was born in the desert. New Minglewood Blues. *Unknown.* BluL
I was born in the month of the bull. Brooding Likeness. Louise Glück. MAYP
I was born in the town of Boston. The Boston Burglar. *Unknown.* ViBoFo
I was born long ago. Beans, Bacon and Gravy. *Unknown.* FSW
I was born on a street named Joy. Lines on His Birthday. John Logan. CAPP
I was born the year of the loon. Chronicles: Number Three. Mei Berssenbrugge. GP
I Was Born upon Thy Bank, River. Henry David Thoreau. ELU; PoEL-4
I was born with a song in my tongue. Ars. Marina Tsvetayeva, *tr. by* Willis Barnstone *and* Edward Brown. BoWoP
I was borned and raised in east Virginia. *See* I was born and raised in East Virginia.
I was broke and out of a job in the city of London. Paddy, Get Back. *Unknown.* AmFP; AmSS; ShS
I was brought up in a rampart. The Stolen Fifer. Padraic Fiacc. NeIP
I was brought up in Sheffield, all of a high degree. The Sheffield 'Prentice. *Unknown.* AmFP
I was buried near this dyke. Blake. FaBoEE
"I was but [*or* bat] seven year auld [*or* alld]." The Laily Worm and the Machrel of the Sea. *Unknown.* ChTr; ESPB; InvP; LoBV; OxBB; PoEL-1
I was carried to a font. Dithyramb in Retrospect. Peter Hopegood. PoAu-2
I was combing some long hair coming out of a tree. In the Forest. Russell Edson. LCAP
I was conceived in the summer of Nineteen Eighteen. True Confessional. Lawrence Ferlinghetti. NAs
I was considering how. Impressions, Number III. E. E. Cummings. UnPo
I was content with the pseudonym. Encounter. Vassar Miller. GP
I was cut in two. The Married Man. Robert Phillips. GeTw
I was dead and I wanted peace. A Grammar. Andrei Codrescu. EAS
I was descending from the mountains of sleep. Afternoon Sleep. Robert Bly. NaP
I was down and I cried. Tin Cup Blues. *Unknown.* BluL
I was drawn to look at an apartment. The Empty Apartment. Aaron Zeitlin, *tr. by* Ruth Whitman. VWA
I was easy, a somnambulist, as I climbed. On Pali Lookout. Stephen Shu Ning Liu. BrSi
I was eighteen when I came in these gates. Words from Hell. David Helwig. NOBC
I Was Fair Beat. Robert Garioch. OxBTC
I was far forward on the plain, the burning swamp. The Little Girl with Bands on Her Teeth. Genevieve Taggard. VGW
I was fishing in the abandoned reservoir. Quinnapoxet. Stanley Kunitz. DiL
I was 5 years old. New York City—1935. Gregory Corso. Psk
I was forced to take. A Catch-22 Test. John L. Sellers. LFAC
I was foretold that on a certain day. Sonnet XX. Louise Labé, *tr. by* Willis Barnstone. BoWoP
I was foretold, your rebell [*or* rebel] sex. A Deposition from Love. Thomas Carew. AnAnS-2; CaPo; CavP; MeLP; OAEP; OBS
I was frightened, for a wind. The Secret. James Stephens. WSC
I was glad when they said unto me. Bible, *O.T.* Psalms, CXXII. TRV
I was going to make a boat. But That Was Yesterday. Aileen Fisher. SoPo
I was going to say something. Ancestor. Thomas Kinsella. BIrV
I was hangin' round town just a spendin' my time. The Strawberry Roan. *Unknown.* FSW
I was in Margate last July, I walked upon the pier. Misadventures at Margate. "Thomas Ingoldsby." *Fr.* The Ingoldsby Legends. HBV-2
I was in the Harbor. Resolution. "Wiolar." InMe
I was in the lane and saw the car pass. A and B. C. H. Sisson. OxBC
I was in Vegas. Celibate and able. Vegas. J. V. Cunningham. DBV; PV
I was just turned twenty-one. Harry Wilmans. Edgar Lee Masters. *Fr.* Spoon River Anthology. PPON
I was leavin' the Blue Dog on the run. Indigo Pete's J. B. Henry Herbert Knibbs. BPAW
I was led into captivity by the bitch business. Money. C. H. Sisson. POL
I was lying still in a field one day. Zhenya Gay. TiPo
I Was Made Erect and Lone. Henry David Thoreau. FaBoEn; PoEL-4
I Was Made of This and This. Gertrude Robison Ross. HBMV
I was milking in the meadow when I heard the Banshee keening. The Warnings. Alice Furlong. AnIV
I was myself blown. For My People. Wendy Rose. CDW
I was never the light lad. The Spawn of Slums. James W. Thompson. BPo
I was never there. A Young Deer/Dust. Hemda Roth, *tr. by* Myra Glazer Schotz. VWA
I was not born to Helicon, nor dare. A Gratulatory to Mr. Ben. Johnson for His Adopting of Him to Be His Son. Thomas Randolph. AnAnS-2; JCP; OBS
I was not meant to stand in a sea-edge garden. Figurehead. Dorothy Paul. EtS
I was not ready for this world. Bargain. Ruth Stone. GP
I was not sorrowful, I could not weep. Spleen. Ernest Dowson. BrPo; MoBrPo; NCEP; SyP
I was not train'd in Academic bowers. Written at Cambridge. Charles Lamb. EnRP; OBRV
I was of delicate mind. I stepped aside for my needs. The Refined Man. Kipling. *Fr.* Epitaphs of the War. FaBoEE; FaBoTw; MMA
I was on a tower in the midst of the stars. Lightning of the Abyss. Jules Laforgue, *tr. by* Vernon Watkins. SyP

I was on the drive in sixty [*or* Eighty], working under Silver Jack. Silver Jack [*or* Silver Jack's Religion]. John P. Jones. BPAW; CoSo
I was out in the country one beautiful night. The Widow's Old Broom. *Unknown.* AmFP
I was out walking an' a-ramblin' one day. The Wild Rippling Water. *Unknown.* CoSo
I was over in Aberdeen on my way to New Orleans. Aberdeen, Mississippi Blues. *Unknown.* BluL
I was playing golf that day. *Unknown.* FiBHP; PV
I was playing with my hoop along the road. The Turn of the Road. James Stephens. SO; WSC
I was raised up in Louisville, a town you all knew well. Frank James, the Roving Gambler. *Unknown.* AmFP
I was round and small like a pearl. *Unknown.* GBP
I was run over by the truth one day. To Whom It May Concern. Adrian Mitchell. OBWP
I was running back when I heard him call. Ballad for the Unknown Soldier. Allan Taylor. OBET
I was sat in the church of their Lord. Microcosmos, XXXV. Nigel Heseltine. NeBP
I was sent in to see her. Tear. Thomas Kinsella. IPY
I was seventy-seven, come August. The Little Old Lady in Lavender Silk. Dorothy Parker. InMe; YaD
I was sick. Jesus Was Crucified or: It Must Be Deep. Carolyn M. Rodgers. BlSi; PoBA
I Was Sick and in Prison. Jones Very. NOBA
I was sitting in mcsorley's. E. E. Cummings. NoAM
I was sitting in my study. Papa's Letter. *Unknown.* WeW
I was sitting in the sitting room. Gruesome. Roger McGough. AmMo
I was six when I first saw kittens drown. The Early Purges. Seamus Heaney. NCSH
I was sixteen, a freshman, a former Catholic buddhist. Rissem. Sandra M. Gilbert. AMV-81
I was sixteen years of age. Song Ballet. *Unknown.* AmFP
I was sleeping. A Translation From. Fred Levinson. AmPA
I was sleepless, I was awake all night. Sleepless. Al-Khansa, *tr. fr. Arabic by* Willis Barnstone. BoWoP
I was so chill, and overworn, and sad. Song. Anna Wickham. MoBrPo
I was so sick last night I. Morning After. Langston Hughes. NoAM
I was spawned from the glacier. The Iceberg. Sir Charles G. D. Roberts. CaP
I was speaking to the librarians. After the Speech to the Librarians. David Wagoner. NPAW
I was standing by the window. Can the Circle Be Unbroken? *Unknown.* FSW
I was standing by the window yesterday morning. The Letter Edged in Black. *Unknown.* FSW
I was standing in a crap game doing no harm, Baby! You've Been a Good Old Wagon, but You've Done Broke Down. Ben Harney. OBAL
I was stung by a man-of-war. The Lesson. Larry Rubin. GoYe
I was takin' off my bonnet. Darwinism in the Kitchen. *Unknown.* FiBHP
I was taught prayer as a child, to bend the knee. Prayer at Dawn. Diarmuid O'Shea, *tr. by* Frank O'Connor. KiLC
I was the chief of the race—he had stricken my father dead. The Voyage of Maeldune. Tennyson. PoEL-5
I Was the Child. Valerie S. Warren. Str
I was the choice of many old men when I was young. The Old Wife. Rolly Kent. FF
I was the clumsy child. Apples. Michael Waters. GeTw
I was the father. The Settlers. Judith Hemschemeyer. SO
I was the first fruits of the battle of Missionary Ridge. Knowlt Hoheimer. Edgar Lee Masters. *Fr.* Spoon River Anthology. OxBA
I was the first made woman. I first wept. Lilith. Allen Grossman. VWA
I was the last passenger of the day. The Bus. Leonard Cohen. CAD; HeIP
I was the moon. Dead. Rhoda Coghill. OnYI
I was the Moor Moraima. A Lovely Young Moor. *Unknown, tr. by* Willis Barnstone. BoWoP
I was the only child of Frances Harris of Virginia. Hamilton Greene. Edgar Lee Masters. *Fr.* Spoon River Anthology. NoAM; OxBA; PAI
I was the patriarch of the shining land. John Sutter. Yvor Winters. MoAmPo; MoVE; NoAM; NOBA; PoPl; QFR
I was the staunchest of our fleet. The Derelict. Kipling. BrPo
I was the third man running in a race. The Service. Burges Johnson. HBMV
I was there and I remember the brown brocade. In Memory of V. R. Lang. Mac Hammond. PoA
"I was thinking, Mother, of that poor old horse." Reserved. Walter de la Mare. GTBS-P
I was thinking of a son. Menstruation at Forty. Anne Sexton. CAPP
I was thirsty. Epigram. Meleager, *tr. by* Sydney Oswald. PeHV
I was three and already. Passing It On. Reg Saner. GP
I was thy neighbour once, thou rugged pile! Elegiac Stanzas Suggested by a Picture of Peele Castle, in a Storm [Painted by Sir George Beaumont]. Wordsworth. ChER; EnRP; FaBoPP; GTBS; GTBS-P; HBV-2; NoP; OAEL-2; OAEP; OBNC; OBRV
I was tired of being a woman. Consorting with Angels. Anne Sexton. NMM
I was traveling fast. Highway Blues. *Unknown.* BluL
I was traveling through South Americas. Travelin' Blues. *Unknown.* BluL
I was upon the high and blessed mound. Sonnet: Of the Grave of Selvaggia, on the Monte della Sambuca. Cino da Pistoia, *tr. by* Dante Gabriel Rossetti. AWP
I was walking a mile. Tennyson. *Fr.* Maud, IX. EBVV
I was walking along, reciting the Lord's Prayer. The Orange Tree. Ellen Pearce. IHMS
I was walking along the Sea of Galilee. Walking along the Sea of Galilee. Dovid Knut, *tr. by* John Glad. VWA
I was walking down by the old/ Santee. Second Carolina Said-Song. A. R. Ammons. OBAL
I was walking downtown. The Man in Black. Mark Strand. EAS
I was walking in a government warehouse. Fifteen Million Plastic Bags. Adrian Mitchell. OBSV; OxBTC
I was watching the great God dance. Ellora. Leonard Nathan. GP
"I was with Grant," the stranger said. The Aged Stranger. Bret Harte. AA; AmFN; TreFS
I was wrapped in black. Us. Anne Sexton. CAPP
I was writing a trenta-sei for the boat-people. An Apology for a Lost Classicism. John Ciardi. AMV-81
I was wrong, quite wrong. Soliloquy II. Richard Aldington. BrPo; MMA
I was wrought of walnut blocks and rolled rod steel. The Springfield Calibre Fifty. Joseph Mills Hanson. PoOW
I was yesterday in Ben Dorain and in her precincts. Last Leave of the Hills. Duncan Ban MacIntyre. GoTS
I was young./ A hundred yards off. Wheel Turning on the Hub of the Sun. William Pitt Root. MAYP
I was young/ when I foreswore. A Deposition by John Wilmot. Vincent McHugh. ErPo
I washed my face in water. Riddle. *Unknown.* ChTr; GBP
I wasn't born here man. Man I Thought You Was Talking Another Language That Day. Victor Hernandez Cruz. BOLo
I wasn't getting anywhere. Impressionist. Heather McHugh. MAYP
I Wasn't No Mary Ellen. Linda King. GP
I Waste Away. Bible, *O.T.* Isaiah, XXIV: 16-20. TrJP
I waste my teeming age. I do not know. Abishag. Jakov Fichman, *tr. by* Robert Friend. VWA
I watch, across the loch. Above Inverkirkaig. Norman MacCraig. PoSH
I watch airplanes land. Bright Winter Morning. Chris Klein. AMV-81
I watch beside you in your silent room. Thysia, VII. Morton Luce. HBV-1
I watch her fingers where they prance. Enigma. Hugh McCrae. PoAu-1
I watch her in the corner there. Arachne. Rose Terry Cooke. AA
I watch my concern for the world, how it changes. What Form the World Has. William Bronk. AMV-80
I watch the TV close its bleary eye. Sleeping Alone. Kurt J. Fickert. AMV-80
I watch the battle in the orange-grove. The Rout of San Romano. Jon Manchip White. NePoEA
I watch the calligraphy of shadows. Philodendron. Helen Armstead Johnson. AmNP
I watch the curious hastened trait of twilight. Sadness, Glass, Theory. Roy Fuller. WaP
I watch the doctors walking with the nurses to and fro. The Memory. Lord Dunsany. OxBI
I watch the dung-cart stumble by. In December. Andrew Young. SeCePo
I watch the farmers in their fields. Farmers. William Alexander Percy. WGRP
I watch the Indians dancing to help the young corn at Taos pueblo. New Mexico [*or* Mexican] Mountain. Robinson Jeffers. GOA; InPS; NoAM
I watch the jocks come out in the post parade. My Style. Charles Bukowski. AMV-81
I watch the leaves that flutter in the wind. Leaves at My Window. John James Piatt. AA
I watch the orderly stack the day's dead. Guadalajara Hospital. Ai. MAYP
I watch the roses float. Requiem. Stephen Vincent. NeAC
I watch them on the drill field, the awkward and the grave. The Drill. Harry Brown. WaaP
I watched a blackbird on a budding sycamore. Thomas Hardy. PB
I watched a laughing cloud. Evening. King D. Kuka. VoR
I watched a man in a cafe fold a slice of bread. In a Cafe. Richard Brautigan. PCP
I watched a rosebud very long. Symbols. Christina Rossetti. VLP

I watched an armory combing its bronze bricks. Poem. Frank O'Hara. NoP
I watched last night the rising moon, upon a foreign strand. The Moon behind the Hill. *Unknown.* WTO
I watched old squatting chimpanzee: he traced. Sporting Acquaintances. Siegfried Sassoon. OxBTC
I watched the Captains. Captain of the Years. Arthur R. Macdougall, Jr. TRV
I watched the hills drink the last color of light. Thought's End. Léonie Adams. MoAB; MoAmPo
I watched the house, and barked agreeably, and. Sudden Assertion. Kenneth Leslie. BoAnP; GDP; POL
I watched the Lady Caroline. Lovelocks. Walter de la Mare. MoVE
I watched the moon around the house. Emily Dickinson. MOON
I watched the new moon fly. The Golden Bird. Rex Ingamells. PoAu-2
I watched the rain amaze me again that water. Two Poems Based on Fact. Frank J. Lepkowski. AMV-81
I watched the sea for hours blind with sun. Sonnet. Winfield Townley Scott. MiAP
I watched the seeds come down this afternoon. At a Country Hotel. Howard Nemerov. PoRA
I watched thee when the foe was at our side. Love and Death. Byron. EBEV; NOBE
I watched them as thay raised their voices to the sky. T. Walking Eagle Marietta. LFAC
I watched them once, at dusk, on television, run. Salmon. Jorie Graham. MAYP
I watched them playing there upon the sand. The Castle. Sidney Alexander. PoNe
I watched them tearing a building down. Which Are You? *Unknown.* FPL; PoLF
I watched two. Last May. Carroll Arnett. STE
I watched you grow old. Poem for My Father. Annette Arkeketa West. TWSS
I watches me climb. First Flight. Daniel Hoffman. GrPl
I watcht as the flung screen door. The Envies. George Bowering. NOBC
I wear a cobra's black bonnet. Godiva. D. C. Berry. BXAP
I Wear a Crimson Cloak To-Night. Lois Seyster Montross. HBMV
I wear a snow-white rose today. Love's Tribute. Lorena W. Sturgeon. PGD
I weave my blanket red. The Marriage Dance. Eda Lou Walton, *after Blackfoot Indian.* BPAW
I weave the night, I cross the weft with stars. In the Flight of the Blue Heron: To Montezuma. Anita Endrezze Probst. CDW
I Weep. Angelina Weld Grimké. CDC
I weep a sight which was not seen. Doom-devoted. Louis Golding. HBMV
I weep, but with no bitterness I weep. Souvenir. Alfred de Musset, *tr. by* George Santayana. AWP
I weep for Adonais—he is dead! Adonais; an Elegy on the Death of John Keats. Shelley. CABA; ChER; EBEV; EnRP; FiP; GoTL; HBV-2; HoPM; LoBV; MasP; NoP; OAEL-2; OAEP; OBRV; PoEL-4; TrGrPo; ViBoPo; WHA
I weep for my loved one. Song of Despair. Rangiaho, *tr. fr. Maori by* Barry Mitcalfe. WTO
I weep those dead lips, white and dry. Linen Bands. Vance Thompson. AA
I weep when the gay are around me. Mary and Her Dead Canary. Alexander Kerr. InPK
I weigh 486 lbs on Jupiter. A Letter to Ron Silliman on the Back of a Map of the Solar System. Dennis Schmitz. LCAP
I weigh not fortune's frown or smile. A Contented Mind. Joshua Sylvester. HBV-2
I welcome the anonymity of the middle years. Letters to Live Poets, XIX. Bruce Beaver. CBAP
I welcomed the Spring in romantic Chungking. Lyric to Spring. Joseph W. Stilwell. DBV; OBAL
I well remember how the race began. On Becoming Man. R. P. Lister. PV
I Wende to Dede. *Unknown. See* I Went to Death.
I went a roaming, maidens, one bright day. Three Ballate, III. Angelo Poliziano, *tr. by* John Addington Symonds. AWP
I went across the pasture lot. The Cornfield. Elizabeth Madox Roberts. GoJo; SUS
I went a-riding, a-riding. Texas. Amy Lowell. AmFN; BPAW
I went a-sailing with my deer. A Tail of the See. Elizabeth T. Corbett. OBCA
I went away last August. Eat-It-All Elaine. Kaye Starbird. PDV; RHPC
I went back an old-time lane. In the Fall o' Year. Thomas S. Jones, Jr. HBV-1
I went by the Druid stone. The Shadow on the Stone. Thomas Hardy. QFR
I went down by Cascadilla. Cascadilla Falls. A. R. Ammons. NIP; NOBA
I went down in Death Valley. Death Valley Blues. *Unknown.* BluL
I Went Down into the Desert to Meet Elijah. Vachel Lindsay. WGRP
I went down the lane to buy a penny whistle. Hi, Hi, Curlywig. *Unknown.* PoPle
I went down to malcolmland. Half Black, Half Blacker. Sterling Plumpp. PoBA
I went down to Saint James this morning. St. James Infirmary. *Unknown.* AmFP
I Went Down to the Depot, *with music.* *Unknown.* AS
I went down to the river, poor boy. Bow Down Your Head and Cry. *Unknown.* CoSo; WTO
I went down to the shouting sea. Sand-between-the-Toes. A. A. Milne. TiPo
I went for a walk over the dunes again this morning. Corsons Inlet. A. R. Ammons. CoAP; NoAM; NOBA; NoP; PPP
I went into a public-'ouse to get a pint o' beer. Tommy. Kipling. BrPo; CABA; EBEV; FaBV; FaPoR; MoBrPo; NoP; OBWP; OxBTC; TreFS
I went into my garden to gather some herbs. A Ditty. Bertha Jacobs, *tr. by* Jonathan Crewe. WPOW
I went into my grandmother's garden/ And there I found a farden. *Unknown.* OxNR
I went into my grandmother's garden,/ And there I found a farthing. *Unknown.* OxNR
I went into the chandler's shop some candles for to buy. The Chandler's Wife. *Unknown.* FSW
I Went into the Maverick Bar. Gary Snyder. MAT
I went into the stable, to see what I could see. Old Wichet. *Unknown.* GBP
I went on Friday afternoons. Au Tombeau de Mon Père. Ronald McCuaig. PoAu-2
I went out alone to gather rocks. Prostration. David Semah, *tr. by* Yoffee Berkovitz. VWA
I went out at daybreak and stood on Primrose Hill. Birds Waking. W. S. Merwin. NOBA
I Went Out into the Garden. Moses ibn Ezra, *tr. fr. Hebrew by* Solomon Solis-Cohen. TrJP
I went out only once with my bow last year. Hunter's Morning. Harold Littlebird. STE
I went out to the city streets. The Hero. Roger Woddis. FaBoPa
I went out to the farthest meadow. Love Is a Terrible Thing. Grace Fallow Norton. HBV-1
I went out to the hazel wood. The Song of Wandering Aengus. W. B. Yeats. BrPo; CABA; CH; CMoP; FaBoCh; GoJo; MAT; MoAB; MoBrPo; PoEL-5; PoRA; SOTW; TiPo; VLP; WSC
I went soft. Impotence. Arthur Winfield Knight. SOTS
I went to a foreign land to work for money. Sure a Poor Man. *Tr. fr. Hawaiian by* M. K. Pukui *and* A. L. Korn. WTO
I went to bat for the Lady Chatte. A Lass in Wonderland. Francis Reginald. MoCV
I went to court last night. Puck Goes to Court. Fenton Johnson. CDC
"I went to dances when I carried you." To My Mother. Edwin Brock. NMP
I Went to Death. *Unknown.* FaBoRV; OxBM
(I Wende to Dede.) HAP
I went to dig a grave for Love. Love's Change. Anne Reeve Aldrich. AA
I went to Frankfort, and got drunk. Epigram on an Academic Visit to the Continent [*or* Porson's Visit to the Continent]. Richard Porson. FaBoCo; FaBoEE; OxBoLi; PV; WhC
I went to heaven. Emily Dickinson. FaBV; NePA
I went to her who loveth me no more. Enchainment [*or* Song]. Arthur O'Shaughnessy. HBV-1; OBNC
I went to ma daddy. Hard Daddy. Langston Hughes. BANP
I went to Noke. *Unknown.* GBP; OxNR
I went to San Francisco. Trip: San Francisco. Langston Hughes. AmFN
I went to school. Class of 19——. Frederick Dec. PCP
I went to see "Ane Tryall of Hereticks." And They Were Richt. Robert Garioch. BSV
I Went to See Irving Babbitt. Richard Eberhart. GLGT; OBAL
I went to seek for Christ. The Search. James Russell Lowell. TRV
I went to sleep smiling. Prescience. Margaret Widdemer. HBMV
I went to someone's dinner and a play. Moan in the Form of a Ballade. Maurice Baring. WhC
I went to Strasbourg, where I got drunk. On a German Tour. Richard Porson. FiBHP. *See also* I went to Frankfort, and got drunk.
I went to the animal fair. Animal Fair. *Unknown.* AS; BLPA; FaBoBe; FPL; MoShBr; NTCP; PoPle; RHPC; SoPo; YaD
I went to the Captain with my hat in my hand. Take This Hammer. *Unknown.* OuSiCo
I Went to the City. Kenneth Patchen. PoPl
I went to the dances at Chandlerville. Lucinda Matlock. Edgar Lee

Masters. *Fr.* Spoon River Anthology. CMoP; FaBV; FF; HAP; LiTA; LiTM; MoAmPo; MoVE; NoAM; NOBA; OxBA
I went to the fields with the leisure I got. The Frightened Ploughman. John Clare. PoEL-4
I went to the Garden of Love. The Garden of Love. Blake. *Fr.* Songs of Experience. AWP; CABA; EnLoPo; EnRP; FaBV; GBL; HAP; LAuP; LiTB; LO; LoBV; MAT; NIP; NoP; OAEP; PAI; PPoe; SeCeV; SoSe; TEP; ViBoPo
I went to the Hotel Broog. A Difference of Zoos. Gregory Corso. VGW
I went to the park. The Balloon. Karla Kuskin. PDV
I went to the river: couldn't get across. Keep It Clean. *Unknown.* BluL
I went to the sea. *Unknown.* PBBP
I went to the toad that lies under the wall. *Unknown.* OxNR
I went to the valley. Lucille Clifton. CNA; TAT
I went to the Wood of Flowers. The Wood of Flowers. James Stephens. PDV
I went to turn the grass once after one. The Tuft of Flowers. Robert Frost. AP; AWP; CoBMV; GoYe; HBV-2; HBVY; LiTA; MoAB; MoAmPo; OxBA; SeCeV
I went to worship in a house of God. Prayer in a Country Church. Ruth B. Van Dusen. TrPWD
I went up to London Town. Devilish Mary. *Unknown.* OuSiCo
I went up to Moses and said to him. Moses. Amir Gilboa, *tr. by* Stephen Mitchell. VWA
I went up to the light of truth as if into a chariot. To Truth. *Unknown, tr. by* J. Rendel Harris. *Fr.* Solomon. WGRP
I went uptown last Saturday night. Blue Monday. *Unknown.* AmFP
I went visiting Miss Melinda. Strawberry Jam. May Justus. FaPON
I wept a tear. Tears for Sale. Leonora Speyer. HBMV
I Wept as I Lay Dreaming. Heine, *tr. fr. German by* John Todhunter. AWP
I whispered, "I am too young." Brown Penny. W. B. Yeats. BoLoP; CMoP; ELP; FaBoCh; LLLT; OLR
I whispered my great sorrow. The Sedges. "Seumas O'Sullivan." AnIV
I, who a decade past had lived recluse. A Lawn-Tennisonian Idyll. *Unknown.* FaBoPa
I, who all my life had hurried. Epitaph for Any New Yorker. Christopher Morley. ShM
I who am dead a thousand years/ And wrote this sweet archaic song. To a Poet a Thousand Years Hence. James Elroy Flecker. ChTr; FaBoRV; HBV-2; MoBrPo; PoRA
I who am dead a thousand years/ And wrote this crabbed post-classic screed. To a Poet a Thousand Years Hence. John Heath-Stubbs. OxBC
I who am nothing, and this tissue. Hoc Est Corpus. Alex Comfort. LiTB; LiTM
I who am street-known am also street knowing. Investigator. Miriam Waddington. CaP
I who by day am function of the light. Motto for a Sun Dial. J. V. Cunningham. InPK; VGW
I, who cut off my sorrows. Akazome Emon, *tr. fr. Japanese by* Kenneth Rexroth *and* Ikuko Atsumi. BoWoP; WPOW
I who employ a poet's tongue. Timid Lover. Countee Cullen. BANP
I, Who Fade with the Lilacs. William Griffith. HBMV
I Who Had Been Afraid. Sister Maris Stella. GoBC
I who have favour'd many, come to be. To the Most Learned, Wise, and Arch-Antiquary, M. John Selden. Robert Herrick. SeCV-1
I, who have lost the stars, the sod. On a Subway Express. Chester Firkins. YaD
I who have walked splay-footed in hobnailed boots. Imaginary Correspondence, *parody.* Frank Sidgwick. WhC
I who love you bring. Song. Theodore Spencer. TwAmPo
I who was driven mad and cast out. The Hebrew Sibyl. Ruth Fainlight. VWA
I who write here came here to find. Found. Sarah Taylor Shatford. PeD
I whom thou seest with horyloge in hand. Time. Sir Thomas More. EnRePo
"I Will Accept." Christina Rossetti. OxBoCh
I will accomplish that and this. In After Days. George Frederick Cameron. CaP
I will always love you. Poem. Frank O'Hara. LLLT
I will always miss the feeling. Poem for Viet Nam. Ray A. Young Bear. STE
I will arise and go now, and go to Innisfree. The Lake Isle of Innisfree. W. B. Yeats. BrPo; CMoP; CoBMV; FaBoPP; FaBV; FaFP; FaPON; FaPoR; FPL; HBV-1; InPS; LiTM; MoAB; MoBrPo; NoAM; NOBE; NoP; OAEP; OBEV; OBVV; OnYI; OxBTC; PAI; PoPl; PoRA; PrIm; RoGo; TEP; TreF; TrGrPo; VLP; WeW; WHA
I will arise and go now, and go to Inverness. The Cockney of the North. Harry Graham. CenHV
I will arise, and leave these haggard realms. The Prodigal Son. Arthur Symons. BrPo
I will attempt the Capel track. Ante Mortem. Syd Scroggie. PoSH
I Will Be. E. E. Cummings. VGW
I will be a lion. Wild Beasts. Evaleen Stein. SoPo
I will be exacting before the closing. Song of the Closing Service. Aliza Shenhar, *tr. by* Linda Zisquit. VWA
I will be patient while my Lord. Cinderella. Ruby C. Saunders. BlSi
I will be the gladdest thing. Afternoon on a Hill. Edna St. Vincent Millay. FaPON; GrPl; NTCP; OBCA; OxBA; PDV; SoPo
I will be what God made me, nor protest. Robert Bridges. The Growth of Love, LXII. VLP
I will begin to delineate the green family. The Green Family. Colleen Thibaudeau. NOBC
I Will Believe. William H. Roberts. BLRP
I Will Bow and Be Simple. *Unknown.* EaLo
I will call you. My Friend the Wind. King D. Kuka. VoR
I will carry my coat and not put on my belt. *Tr. fr. Chinese by* Arthur Waley. *Fr.* Tzu Yeh Songs. BoWoP
I will confront these shows of the day and night! Walt Whitman. *Fr.* By Blue Ontario's Shore, XVIII. InPS
I will consider the outnumbering dead. Merlin. Geoffrey Hill. POL
I will drink, I will gamble, I will play wild again. O-Bar Cowboy. *Unknown.* CoSo
I will drink to your health, sweet Amy. To Amy. J. Gordon. Coogler. OBAL
I Will Enjoy Thee Now. Thomas Carew. *See* Rapture, A.
I will exchange a city for a sunset. Barter. Marie Blake. PoPl
I will fling wide the windows of my soul. Robert Hillyer. Sonnets, XII. HBMV
I will found a habitation by the water. Unearthing. Betsy Rosenberg. VWA
I Will Go Away. Zvi Shargel, *tr. fr. Yiddish by* Gabriel Preil *and* Howard Schwartz. VWA
I will go back to the great sweet mother. Stanzas [*or* The Return *or* The Sea]. Swinburne. *Fr.* The Triumph of Time. EtS; HBV-1; OAEP; TrGrPo
I will go down to the sea again. Sea Song. Norah Holland. CaP
I will go for a walk before. Around the Block. Keith Waldrop. AMV-80
I Will Go into the Ghetto. Charles Reznikoff. VGW
I will go out and hear the strain. Macquarie Place. Robert D. Fitzgerald. PoAu-2
I will go walking on Eighth Street. Eighth Street West. Rachel Field. SiSoSe
I Will Go with My Father a-Ploughing. Joseph Campbell. AnIL; FaPON; GoBC; OFD; OnYI; SiSoSe; TiPo
I will go with the first air of morning. Fishing. Dorothy Wellesley. OBMV
I will grieve alone. In Response to a Rumor That the Oldest Whorehouse in Wheeling, West Virginia, Has Been Condemned. James Wright. CAPP; CoAP; NNaP; TW
I will haunt these States. A Vow. Allen Ginsberg. OBWP
I will have all my beds blown up, not stuft. Ben Jonson. *Fr.* The Alchemist, II, i. EBEV
I will have an image. Larry Eigner. CoPo
I will have one built/ Like Pompey's theatre. John Day. *Fr.* The Parliament of Bees. ViBoPo
I Will Have the Whetstone. *Unknown.* FaBoNo; GBP
I will have to accept women. This Form of Life Needs Sex. Allen Ginsberg. NNaP
I will hold beauty as a shield against despair. Beauty as a Shield. Elsie Robinson. BLPA
I will install windows in my dream. Windows. Mordechai Husid, *tr. by* Seymour Mayne *and* Rivka Augenfeld. VWA
I will keep the fire of hope ever burning on the altar of my soul. Realization. Anandan Acharya. WGRP
I will leave the dust of the City street and the noise of the busy town. The Vagrant. Pauline Slender. HBMV
I Will Lift Up Mine Eyes unto the Hills. Bible, *O.T.* Psalms, CXXI. AWP; FaPON; ILwL; TreF; TRV
(Pilgrim's Song, The, *Moulton, Modern Reader's Bible.*) WGRP
(Song of Trust, A.) TrGrPo
I will live in Ringsend. Ringsend. Oliver St. John Gogarty. AnIL; OBMV; OxBTC
I will look with detachment. On Being Head of the English Department. Pinkie Gordon Lane. BlSi
I will lose you. It is written. The Sweater. Gregory Orr. PPJ
I will make known the eagle's nature. The Nature of the Eagle. *Unknown. Fr.* The Bestiary. PBBP
I will make love. *Unknown, tr. fr. Spanish by* Willis Barnstone. BoWoP
I will make you brooches and toys for your delight. Romance [*or* My Valentine]. Robert Louis Stevenson. BLPL; BrPo; BSV; EBVV; FaPON; GoTS; GrPl; HBV-1; MoBrPo; OBEV; OBVV; OFD; PoSC; SiSoSe; TrGrPo
I will my collection of hats. An Exchange of Hats. Stanley Moss. GP

"I will never eate nor drinke," Robin Hood said. Robin Hood's Death. *Unknown.* ESPB
I will never more deceive you. You Naughty, Naughty Men. T. Kennick. BLSo
I will no longer kiss. On Himself. Robert Herrick. CaPo
I will not be inhabited. The Turtle's Belly. Ellen Pearce. IHMS
I will not be reduced to what I am. Five Stanzas on Perfection. George Jonas. PeCV
I will not break the tryst, my dear. A Tryst. Louise Chandler Moulton. HBV-1
I will not change my horse with any that treads. The Horse. Shakespeare. King Henry V, *fr.* III, vi. PH
I will not doubt, though all my ships at sea. Faith. Ella Wheeler Wilcox. BLRP; TRV
I will not have the mad Clytie. Flowers. Thomas Hood. HBV-1
I will not have you think me less. A Jewish Poet Counsels a King. Santob de Carrion. *Fr.* Consejos y Documentos al Rey Dom Pedro. TrJP
I will not kiss you country fashion. A Calvinist in Love. Jack R. Clemo. ChMP
I Will Not Let Thee Go. Robert Bridges. BeLS; BLPL; CMoP; CoBMV; EnLoPo; FaBoBe; OBNC
I will not play at tug o' war. Hug o' War. Shel Silverstein. NTCP; RHPC
I will not rail or grieve when torpid eld. Sonnet—Age. Richard Garnett. OBVV
I will not say to you, "This is the Way; walk in it." To My Son. *Unknown.* PoLF
I will not shut me from my kind. In Memoriam A. H. H., CVIII. Tennyson. SBVL
I will not tell her that she's fair. A Song. Matthew Coppinger. CavP
I will not toy with it nor bend an inch. The White City. Claude McKay. BPo; NoAM; TAP; TW
I will not walk on that road again. The Goshawk. John Haines. GP
I will not weep, for 'twere as great a sin. An Elegy. Henry King. AnAnS-2
I will now address myself to the problem of writing. A Week of Doodle. Reed Whittemore. NePoEA
I will paint her as I see her. A Portrait. Elizabeth Barrett Browning. GN; HBV-1
I will pluck from my tree a cherry-blossom wand. The Cherry-Blossom Wand. Anna Wickham. MoBrPo
I will praise Christopher Smart. To Christopher Smart. Joseph Stroud. NPGG
I will praise thee, O Lord, with my whole heart. I Will Sing Praise. Bible, *O.T.* Psalms, IX. FaPON
I will put enmities/ Between thee and the woman. Bible, *O.T. (Douay vers.). Fr.* Genesis. ISi
"I will put upon you the Telephone Curse," said the witch. The Witch of East Seventy-second Street. Morris Bishop. NYBP; NYP
I will reach into the grab-bag of unconscious things. Private Pantomime. Ruth Stone. PoA
I will read a few of these to see if they exist. The Theory of the Flower. Michael Palmer. NPGG
I will remember you on Bloom Street. Bloom Street. Angela McCabe. AmPA
I will repudiate the lie. "If a Man Die." John Richard Moreland. PGD
I will rise. Wine Bowl. Hilda Doolittle ("H. D."). NoP
I will rise, I will go from the places that are dark with passion and pain. Seaward. George Edward Woodberry. Wild Eden, XLI. AA
I will row my boat on Muckross Lake. The Wings of Love. James H. Cousins. AnIV
I will sing a song,/ A song that is strong. My Breath. Orpingalik, *tr. by* K. Rasmussen. WTO
I will sing a song of battle. The Song of Chess. *At. to* Abraham ibn Ezra, *tr. by* Nina Davis Salaman. TrJP
I will sing, if ye will hearken. The Laird o' Logie. *Unknown.* CH; ESPB
I will sing no more songs! O'Bruadair. David O'Bruadair, *tr. by* James Stephens. BIrV; OxBI
I Will Sing Praise. Bible, *O.T.* Psalms, IX. FaPON
I will sing unto the Lord, for he hath triumphed gloriously. Triumphal Chant. Bible, *O.T. Fr.* Exodus. TrGrPo
I will sing unto the Lord, for He is highly exalted. Then Sang Moses. Bible, *O.T. Fr.* Exodus. TrJP
I will sing you a song. Streets of Cairo; or, The Poor Little Country Maid. James Thornton. FSN
I will sing you a song of that beautiful land. Home of the Soul. Ellen H. Gates. BLRP
I will sleep. December. Ron Padgett. EAS
I will speak about women of letters, for I'm in the racket. Pro Femina, III. Carolyn Kizer. MAT; NMM
I will speak of your deeds. An Oration, Entitled "Old, Old, Old, Old Andrew Jackson." Vachel Lindsay. YaD
I will take nails. Eclipse. Tomaz Salamun, *tr. by* Michael Scammel *and* Veno Taufer. VWA
I will teach you my townspeople. Tract. William Carlos Williams. AP; BiP; BLPL; CoBMV; DL; FF; LiTA; LiTM; MoAB; MoAmPo; MP; NePA; NoAM; NOBA; PAI; TAP; TrGrPo; TwAmPo; TwCP; VGW
I will teach you to become American, my students. Notes for a Lecture. David Ignatow. NNaP
I will tell you of a fellow. Common Bill. *Unknown.* AS; FSW
I will tell you of a gallant soldier. The Soldier's Wooing. *Unknown.* AmFP
I will track you down the years. Quest. Naomi Long Madgett. BPo
I Will Turn Your Money Green. *Unknown.* BluL
I will twine and will mingle my raven black hair. Wildwood Flower. *Unknown.* BLSo; FSW
I will visit/Unknown woman. Spirit Song. *Tr. fr. Eskimo.* WTO
I Will Write. Robert Graves. PCP
I will write a sketch of my early life. The Author's Early Life. Julia A. Moore. PeD
I Will Write Songs against You. Charles Reznikoff. VGW
I, Willie Wastle. *Unknown.* OxNR
I Wish. Nancy Byrd Turner. SiSoSe
I wish a cricket in a wicker boat. A Japanese Birthday Wish. Thomas Burnett Swann. GoYe
I wish all the/ mandragona. Blue Funk. Joel Oppenheimer. NeAP
I wish, because the sweetness of your passing. Wild Wishes. Ethel M. Hewitt. HBV-1
I wish he were the Polar Star in Heaven. Anchises. Blanaid Salkeld. OxBI
I wish, how I wish, that I had a little house. The Shiny Little House. Nancy M. Hayes. SUS
I wish I could lend a coat. Akahito. *Fr.* Manyo Shu. AWP
I Wish I Could Meet the Man That Knows. John Ciardi. RHPC
I wish I could remember the [*or* that] first day. The First Day. Christina Rossetti. *Fr.* Monna Innominata. BLPL; BoLoP; FaBoBe; GBL; HBV-1; OLR
I wish I could tell it—how wondrous is He. I Know He Is Real. *Unknown.* STF
I wish I had a great big ball. Bouncing Ball. Sara Ruth Watson. SoPo
I wish I had a man any man. Chiaroscuro. Carole Bergé. ErPo
I wish I had a nickel. Round and Round Hitler's Grave. *Unknown.* FSW
I wish I had been born beside a river. The Upper Canadian. James Reaney. NOBC
I wish I had the voice of Homer. Cancer's a Funny Thing. J. B. S. Haldane. OxBTC
I wish I knew geography—for what would tell me why. Lines on a Mysterious Occurrence. Alfred Denis Godley. CenHV
I wish I knew the names of all the stars. Stars. Alden Nowlan. POL
I wish I lived in a caravan. The Peddler's [*or* Pedlar's] Caravan. William Brighty Rands. HBV-1; HBVY; OxBChV; SoPo
I wish I loved the human race. The Wishes of an Elderly Man. Sir Walter Alexander Raleigh. CenHV; DBV; FaBoCh; FaBoCo; FaBoEE; FiBHP; FPL; NOBL; PV; WhC
I wish I owned a Dior dress. Reflections at Dawn. Phyllis McGinley. FiBHP; NOBL
I Wish I Was a Little Bird, *with music. Unknown.* AS
I Wish I Was a Mole in the Ground. *Unknown.* AmFP
I wish I was an apple, a-hangin' on a [*or* in the] tree. Cindy. *Unknown.* TrAS; TreFS
I Wish I Was [*or* Were] by That Dim Lake. Thomas Moore. GoBC; NBM; PoEL-4
I wish I was in the [*or* de] land of [*or* ob] cotton. Dixie. Daniel Decatur Emmett. BLSo; FaFP; FaPON; FSW; HBV-2; PSoN; TrAS; TreF; TrGrPo; YaD
I Wish I Was Single Again. *Unknown. See* I Wish I Were Single Again.
I Wish I Were. *Unknown.* FaFP; OxBoLi
("I wish I were a/ Elephantiaphus.") FaBoNo
I wish I were as in the years of old. Tiresias. Tennyson. VLP
I Wish I Were by That Dim Lake. Thomas Moore. *See* I Wish I Was by That Dim Lake.
I wish I were close. Yamabe no Akahito. HoPM; OLR
I wish I were in the Dutchman's Hall. Lowlands, *vers. III. Unknown.* AmSS
I Wish I Were [*or* Was] Single Again. *Unknown.* AmFP, 2 *versions*; AS; FSW
(Oh, I Wish I Were Single Again, *diff. vers.*) AmFP
I wish I were the little key. A Child's Wish. Abram Joseph Ryan. AA
I wish I were where Helen lies. Helen of Kirconnell [*or* Fair Helen]. *Unknown.* AWP; BSV; CH; ELP; FaFP; GoTS; GTBS; GTBS-P; HBV-1; LiTB; LO; LoBV; OBEV; PoPle; SeCeV; TreFT; ViBoPo
I Wish, I Wish. *Unknown.* OBET
I Wish My Tongue Were a Quiver. L. A. MacKay. *Fr.* The Ill-tempered Lover. TW
("I wish my tongue were a quiver the size of a huge cask.") CaP; OBCV

I wish not Thasos rich in mines. Mimnermus Incert. Walter Savage Landor. PoEL-4
I wish not to lie here. Iona; the Graves of the Kings. Robinson Jeffers. PrIm
I wish, O son of the Living God. The Wish of Manchin of Liath [*or* The Hermit's Song]. *Unknown.* AnIL, *tr. by* Kenneth Jackson; OnYI, *tr. by* Kuno Meyer
I wish she would not ask me if I love the kitten more than her. Concerning Love. Josephine Preston Peabody. WhC
I wish sometimes, although a worthlesse thing. Licia, XII. Giles Fletcher the Elder. AAS
I wish that Easter eggs would do. If Easter Eggs Would Hatch. Douglas Malloch. SoPo
I wish that I could get in line. They Don't Speak English in Paris. Ogden Nash. OBAL
I wish that I could have my wish to-night. Shakespeare. Henry Ames Blood. AA
I Wish That My Room Had a Floor. Gelett Burgess. FiBHP; InvP; OBCA (Limerick: "I wish that my room had a floor.") CenHV; NA; WhC (Nonsense Verses.) HBV-2
I wish that there were some wonderful place. The Land of Beginning Again. Louisa Fletcher. BLPA
I wish that when you died last May. May and Death. Robert Browning. FaBoRV; NOBE
I wish the Prince had left me where he found me. The Sleeper. Sara Henderson Hay. DFT
I wish the rent. Little Lyric (of Great Importance). Langston Hughes. OBAL
I wish there were a touch of these boats about my life. Boat Poem. Bernard Spencer. FaBoTw; OxBTC
I wish they would hurry up their trip to Mars. A Projection. Reed Whittemore. NePoEA
"I wish to buy a dog," she said. On Buying a Dog. Edgar Klauber. GDP; NTCP
I wish to God my child was born. Lullaby. *Unknown.* AmFP
I wish to make a positive statement. Peace. George Jonas. NeAC
I wish to make my sermon brief. Praise of Little Women. Juan Ruiz, Archpriest of Hita, *tr. by* Longfellow. AWP
I wish to paint my eyes. Willis Barnstone, *fr. Egyptian hieroglyphics.* BoWoP
"I wish, when summer's drawing near about the end of May." I Wish. Nancy Byrd Turner. SiSoSe
I wish you all that pen and ink. Thanksgiving Wishes. Arthur Guiterman. PoSC
I wish you for your birthday as you are. Moving In. Karl Shapiro. NAs
I wish you triumphs that are yours already. For Marianne Moore's Birthday. Kay Boyle. NMM
I wish you were a pleasant wren. Child's Talk in April. Christina Rossetti. GN
I wish you were not flying, and I wish. For a Homecoming. Julia Randall. NMM
I wish you would come. Izumi Shikubu, *tr. fr. Japanese by* Willis Barnstone. BoWoP
I wish you'd speak to Mary, Nurse. The Game of Cricket. Hilaire Belloc. DBV; FiBHP
I wish your breast was made of glass. The Lover's Lament. *Unknown.* AS
I wished you awake for the bird song. Bird Song. Betsy Rosenberg. VWA
I wish't I was a mole in the ground. Mole in the Ground. *Unknown.* FSW
I wist not what to wish, yet sure thought I. Anne Bradstreet. *Fr.* Contemplations. PBWP
I with the morning's love have oft made sport. Sunrise on the Sea. Shakespeare. *Fr.* A Midsummer Night's Dream, III, ii. ChTr
I with uncovered head. James Russell Lowell. *Fr.* Ode Recited at the Harvard Commemoration. OHIP
I, with whose colors [*or* colours] Myra dressed [*or* dress'd] her head. Myra [*or* To Myra]. Fulke Greville. Caelica, XXII. EIL; EnRePo; GBL; HAP; InVP; LiTB; LoBV; NOBE; OBEV; OBSC; PoPle; QFR; ViBoPo
I woke/ Just about daybreak and fell back. Poems to a Brown Cricket. James Wright. NaP; NYBP
I woke at three; for I was bid. Going to Church. Coventry Patmore. *Fr.* The Angel in the House. LoBV
I woke before the day, when the night bird. Thomas Iron-Eyes. Marnie Walsh. WPOW
I woke by first light in a wood. Sestina. Donald Justice. NePoEA
I woke from death and dreaming. A Shepherd's Coat. Lilian Bowes Lyon. ChMP
I Woke Up. Revenge. A. Poulin, Jr. TW
I woke up/ shook off the street. Rip the Apple Seller Awakes; or, After 50 Years, the Great Depression (1929-79) Reawakens. Duane Ackerson. SOTS
I woke up at night and my language was gone. Nothingness. Aharon Amir, *tr. fr. Hebrew.* VWA
I woke up this mornin'. Sylvester's Dying Bed. Langston Hughes. NoAM; UnPo
I woke up this mornin'. Empty Bed Blues. Bessie Smith. OBAL; UnPo
I woke up this mornin' 'bout four o'clock. Casey Jones. *Unknown.* ViBoFo
I woke up this mornin' with the blues all round my bed. Good Mornin', Blues [*or* I Got the Blues]. *Unknown.* InPK; TTY
I woke up this morning feeling around for my shoes. Walking Blues. *Unknown.* BluL
I woke up this morning, four o'clock. Kassie Jones. *Unknown.* BluL
I woke up this morning my good gal was gone. No No Blues. *Unknown.* BluL
I woke up this morning with the blues all 'round my bed. You'll Never Miss Your Jelly. *Unknown.* BluL
I woke up with morning yawning in my mouth. Dawn. Louis Dudek. PeCV
I wold fain be a clarke. The Scholar Complains. *Unknown.* MeEL
I wolde witen of sum wis wight. The World an Illusion. *Unknown.* MeEL
I, Woman. Irma McClaurin. BlSi
I won a noble fame. Sir Marmaduke's Musings. Theodore Tilton. AA
I won the prize essay at school. John Horace Burleson. Edgar Lee Masters. *Fr.* Spoon River Anthology. CrMA
I wonder about/ the brother. Come On Home. Sharon Scott. JB
I wonder about the trees. The Sound of [the] Trees. Robert Frost. NoAM; OxBA; TwAmPo
I Wonder as I Wander. *Unknown, arr. by* John Jacob Niles. EaLo; PChr
I wonder as into bed I creep. Sweet Dreams. Ogden Nash. OnUR
I wonder, by my troth, what thou and I. The Good-Morrow. John Donne. AnAnS-1; AWP; BiP; BoLoP; CABA; EBEV; EIL; EnLoPo; EnRePo; FaBoBe; FaBoEn; FaBV; FF; FPL; HBV-1; HoPM; InPS; InvP; JCP; LiTB; LoBV; MeLP; MePo; NIP; NoP; OAEL-1; OBS; OLR; PoEL-2; PoPle; PoRA; PPP; SCV; SeCeV; SeCP; SeCV-1; SoSe; TEP; TreFT; TrGrPo; UnTE; ViBoPo
I wonder, dear, if you had been. A Conjecture. Charles Francis Richardson. AA
I wonder do you feel to-day. Two in the Campagna. Robert Browning. EBEV; EBVV; ELP; FaBoEn; GTBS-P; HBV-1; NOBE; NoP; OAEL-2; OAEP; OBNC; PoEL-5; SeCePo; SeCeV; TrGrPo; VLP; WHA
I wonder, have I giv'n my best to Jesus. Have I Done My Best for Jesus? Edwin Young. STF
I wonder how it happens. I Change. Witter Bynner. HBMV
I wonder how many old men last winter. The Minneapolis Poem. James Wright. FYAP; NoAM; UnPo
I Wonder How Many People in This City. Leonard Cohen. CAD; ELU
I Wonder How My Home Is. *Tr. fr. Tewa Indian by* H. J. Spinden. WTO
I wonder how the organist. The Organist. George W. Stevens. BLPA
I wonder if Christ had a little black dog. The Little Black Dog. Elizabeth Gardner Reynolds. PoLF
I wonder if his appetite was good? Byron. *Fr.* Don Juan, V. OAEL-2
I wonder if in that far isle. Braddan Vicarage. Thomas Edward Brown. FaBoPP
I wonder if, sunning in Eden's vales. Ballade of the Ancient Wheeze. Nate Salsbury *and* Newman Levy. InMe
I wonder if the elephant. Pete at the Zoo. Gwendolyn Brooks. PDV
I wonder if the engine. Engine. James S. Tippett. SoPo; SUS
I wonder if the old cow died or not. The Question. W. W. Gibson. MMA
I wonder if the sap is stirring yet. The First Spring Day. Christina Rossetti. WiR
I wonder if they like it—being trees? Tree Feelings. Charlotte Perkins Stetson. PGD
I wonder if they sleep better here. Graveyard by the Sea. Thomas Lux. LCAP
I wonder if, when Galatea woke. A Question. Edna Livingston. GoYe
I wonder in what Isle of Bliss. A Ballad of Dead Ladies. Justin Huntly M'Carthy. *Fr.* If I Were King, *ch.* 9. HBV-1
I wonder: is there no way for us to meet again. Wallada, *tr. fr. Arabic by* A. R. Nykl. PBWP
I wonder, James, through the whole history. To His Friend ———. Henry Vaughan. PP
I wonder poet, can you take it. The Muse to an Unknown Poet. Paul Potts. FaBoTw
I wonder, since we are both travelling out. The Travelling Out. Lucile Adler. IHMS; NYBP
I wonder sometimes if the soldiers lying. Song for the Heroes. Alex Comfort. MoBrPo; NeBP
I Wonder What Became of Rand, McNally. Newman Levy. InMe; WhC
I Wonder What It Feels Like to Be Drowned? Robert Graves. BrPo; MoBrPo
I wonder what the clover thinks. A Song of Clover. Helen Hunt Jackson. GN

I wonder what to mean by sanctuary, if a real or. Triphammer Bridge. A. R. Ammons. NOBA
I wonder where it could of went to. Legend. John V. A. Weaver. AmFN; YaD
I wonder whether the girls are mad. William Bond. Blake. NECP; OxBB
I wonder who is haunting the little snug café. At the Lavender Lantern. Charles Divine. HBMV
I wonder why. Tom Poole. NBP
I wonder why I am living at this time. The Revenant. Robert Siegel. GeTw
I wonder will he be gentle. The Young Bride's Dream. Rhoda Coghill. OxBI
I wondered if the others felt. The Search Party. William Matthews. GeTw
I won't be my father's Jack. Mother Goose. OxNR
"I won't go with you. I want to stay with Grandpa!" My Last Afternoon with Uncle Devereux Winslow. Robert Lowell. NoP; VGW
I won't say much for the sea. On the Coast near Sausalito. Robert Hass. WOLT
I won't slide down that metal. Sisyphus Angers the Gods of Condescension. Calvin Murry. LFAC
I work all day, and get half drunk at night. Aubade. Philip Larkin. SoSe
I work all day long for you, until the sun go down. *Unknown.* WTO
I work like a pump in my own sweat. Song of the Farmworker. T. R. Jahns. AMV-80
I work or play, as I think best. Emancipation. *Unknown.* BLPA; FPL
I work to music on the radio. The Campus. David Posner. NYBP
I worked all the winter. Tired as I Can Be. *Unknown.* BluL
I worked for a woman. Madam and Her Madam. Langston Hughes. BALP
I worked with all aurora at my loom. Archne. Richard Foerster. AMV-80
I worship the greatest first. Hippolytus Temporizes. Hilda Doolittle ("H. D."). SBG
I Worship Thee, O Holy Ghost, *with music.* William F. Warren. AH
I worshipped, when my veins were fresh. William Baylebridge. *Fr.* Life's Testament, VI. PoAu-1
I wot full well that beauty cannot last. To His Friend, Promising That Though Her Beauty Fade, Yet His Love Shall Last. George Turberville. CTC; OBSC
I would adore doing it over. A Plan to Live My Life Again. Diana O Hehir. NPGG
I would ask of you, my darling. Will You Love Me When I'm Old? *Unknown.* BLPA; BLPL; FaBoBe
I Would Be a Painter Most of All. Len Chandler. NBP
I would be dismal with all the fine pearls of the crown of a king. To a Blue Flower. Shaw Neilson. PoAu-1
I would be ignorant as the dawn. The Dawn. W. B. Yeats. MoVE
I would be married, but I'd have no wife. On Marriage. Richard Crashaw. FaBoEE
I Would Be True. Howard Arnold Walter. *See* My Creed.
I would be wandering in distant fields. In Bondage. Claude McKay. PoBA
I would be with the wind. Theodore Roethke. POL
I would bear a love Platonic to the souls in earthly life. Lizzie Doten. *Fr.* Farewell to Earth. PeD
I would despise myself if I had the strength for it. The Cost of Pretending. Peter Davison. TW
I would exorcise you like some common demon. That Is Not Indifference. Howard G. Hanson. AMV-81
I would follow Jesus. Follow Jesus. *Unknown.* STF
I would go around biting my nails. Salvador Villanueva, *tr. fr. Spanish by* Julio Marzán. InW
"I would go up to the gates of hell with a friend." The Utmost in Friendship. John E. McCann. TreFT
I would have gone; God bade me stay. Weary in Well-doing. Christina Rossetti. SeCePo; TrPWD
I would have loved you then. What Music. Joy Harjo. TWSS
I would have spared you this, Prytherch. Too Late. R. S. Thomas. NMP
I would I had been island-born. A Ballade of Islands. Lucy Catlin Robinson. AA
I would I had some flowers o'th' spring that might. Shakespeare. *Fr.* The Winter's Tale, IV, iii. PoPle
I would I had something to do—or to think! All in the Downs. Tom Hood. CenHV
I would I had thrust my hands of flesh. Edmund Pollard. Edgar Lee Masters. *Fr.* Spoon River Anthology. ErPo
I would I had thy courage, dear. To Manon, on Her Lightheartedness. Wilfrid Scawen Blunt. *Fr.* The Love Sonnets of Proteus. NBM
I Would I Might Forget That I Am I. George Santayana. AWP
I would I were a bird so free. Popular Songs of Tuscany. *Unknown, tr. by* John Addington Symonds. AWP
I Would I Were Actaeon. *Unknown, at. to* ——Bewe. EIL (Actaeon.) OBSC
I would, if I could. Mother Goose. OxNR
I would immortalize these nymphs: so bright. L'Après-Midi d'un Faune. Stéphane Mallarmé, *tr. by* Aldous Huxley. AWP
I would in rich and golden coloured raine. Thomas Lodge, *after* Pierre de Ronsard. Phillis, XXXIV. AAS
I would kiss the whole length of the rich black locks that grace thy neck. The Kiss. Pierre Louÿs, *tr. by* Horace M. Brown. *Fr.* The Songs of Bilitis. UnTE
I would lie low—the ground on which men tread. The Earth. Jones Very. OxBA
I would like/ to make. Oh—Yeah. Sharon Scott. JB
I would like a bell. Haiku. Richard Wright. FAZ
I would like all things to be free of me. Proof. Brendan Kennelly. CIP
I would like my love to die. Samuel Beckett, *tr. fr. French.* BIrV; CIP
I would like to be as mobile as my mind. Evaporation Poems. Kathleen Norris. IHMS
I would like to bury. The Fury of Hating Eyes. Anne Sexton. TW
I would like to dive. The Diver. W. W. E. Ross. NOBC; OBCV; PeCV; WHW
I would like to give you. Unposted Birthday Card. Norman MacCaig. NAs
I would like to have the men of Heaven. The Heavenly Banquet. *At. to* St. Brigid, *tr. by* Sean O'Faolain. OnYI
I would like to more than touch you everywhere. More Than. Susan Fitzpatrick. AMV-80
I would like to remind/ the management. The Music Crept by Us. Leonard Cohen. FF
I would like to scream but there is no one to hear. Setting/ Slow Drag. Carolyn Rodgers. JB
I would like to think. Art. Hjalmar Flax, *tr. by* Julio Marzán. InW
I would like to visit my Grandfather. Moose Lake State Hospital. Dennis Shady. LFAC
I would like to watch you sleeping. Variation on the Word *Sleep.* Margaret Atwood. NOBC
I Would Like You for a Comrade. Edward Abbott Parry. OxBChV
I would live all my life in nonchalance and insouciance. Introspective Reflection. Ogden Nash. WhC
I would live for a day and a night. The Song-Maker. Anna Wickham. MoBrPo
I would make a list against the evil days. A Ballade-Catalogue of Lovely Things. Richard Le Gallienne. HBMV
I would make songs for you. Songs. Babette Deutsch. HBMV
I would make you. Petition for a Miracle. David Morton. *Fr.* Boke of Two Ladies. ISi
I would not alter thy cold eyes. Flos Lunae. Ernest Dowson. OBMV
I Would Not Ask. Grace E. Troy. STF
I would not ask Thee that my days. A Prayer for Faith. Alfred Norris. BLRP
I would not ask Thee why. I Would Not Ask. Grace E. Troy. STF
I would not be a servingman to carry the cloke-bag still. Merrythought's Song. Beaumont *and* Fletcher. *Fr.* The Knight of the Burning Pestle, IV, i. OBS
I would not be the moon, the sickly thing. In Dispraise of the Moon. Mary Elizabeth Coleridge. BoNaP; CH; MOON; NBM
I would not feign a single sigh. Song. John Clare. GBL
I would not give my Irish wife. The Irish Wife. Thomas D'Arcy McGee. HBV-1
I would not have a god come in. Mastery. Sara Teasdale. HBV-2; WGRP
I Would Not Live Alway. William Augustus Muhlenberg. AA; AH, with music; HBV-2
I would not marry a blacksmith. Soldier Boy for Me. *Unknown.* AmFP
I would not meek in dire rebuttal. Pride and Hesitation. Cerise Farallon. UnTE
I would not paint—a picture. Emily Dickinson. NOBA
I would not tell them why I had smashed the window. "In This House, There Shall Be No Idols." Carolyn M. Rodgers. JB
I would not want, I think, a higher intelligence, one. Erosion. Jorie Graham. MAYP
I would not wish to sit. Between Two Prisoners. James Dickey. AP
I would play, plucking flowers by the gate. Two Letters from Chang-kan. Li Po, *tr. by* Shigeyoshi Obata. OLR
I would prefer to live quietly in silks. Running through Sleep. Kathleen Norris. IHMS
I would rather be buried/ in some cypress grove. Cypress Grove Blues. *Unknown.* BluL
I would rather have one little rose. Kindness during Life. *Unknown.* STF
I would rather ruffle leaves. Summer Lightning. T. Sturge Moore. BrPo; SyP
I would rather sleep. The Weaver. Lisel Mueller. AMV-81
I would say a band. Retreat. Martha Collins. AMV-80
"I would," says Fox, "a tax devise." Epigram. Sheridan. HBV-1

I would set all things whatsoever front to back. Wyndham Lewis. *Fr.* One-Way Song. CTC
I would sleep until the mottled jaguar dawn. Auditory Hallucinations. Joyce Mansour, *tr. by* Carol Cosman. PBWP
I would tell a marvelous vision. The Dream of the Cross. *Unknown, tr. by* Sally Purcell. EBEV
I would that all men my hard case might know. Behold the Deeds! H. C. Bunner. HBV-2; InMe
I would that even now. Princess Shoku, *tr. by* Curtis Hidden Page. *Fr.* Hyaku-Nin-Isshu. AWP
I would that folk forgot me quite. Tess's Lament. Thomas Hardy. FaBoTw; TEP
I would the gift I offer here. Dedication: "I would the gift I offer here." Whittier. *Fr.* Songs of Labor. OxBA
I Would Thou Wert Not Fair [*or* I Were Wise]. Nicholas Breton. *See* His Wisdom.
I would to God, that mine old age might have. His Wish to God. Robert Herrick. AnAnS-2; OxBoCh
I would to heaven that I were so much clay. Fragment. Byron. *Fr.* Don Juan. CTC; FiP; NOBL; NoP; OAEL-2; OAEP; PrIm
I would unto my fair restore. Of Joan's Youth. Louise Imogen Guiney. AA; HBV-1
I would worry less if she sang. If She Sang. Gerald W. Barrax. CNA
I would worship if I could. Great Spaces. Howard Moss. TwCP
I wouldn't coax the plant if I were you. Woman with Flower. Naomi Long Madgett. AmNP; FB
I wouldn't marry a bachelor. Old Maid's Song. *Unknown.* AmFP
I wouldn't question the kisses you may offer. For Nothing. Andrés Castro Ríos, *tr. by* Julio Marzán. InW
I write about a silly ass. Hero and Leander. Joseph S. Newman. FiBHP
I write. He sits beside my chair. A New Poet. William Canton. HBV-1
I write, Honora, on the sparkling sand! Elegy Written at the Sea-Side, and Addressed to Miss Honoria Sneyd. Anna Seward. PeHV
I write my name as one. An Autograph. Whittier. AA
I write of a cemetery, of the. Funeral at Ansley. Don Welch. GP; TAT
I Write Poems. Gloria Fuertes, *tr. fr. Spanish by* Philip Levine. WPOW
I write these precepts for immortal Greece. Archestratus, *tr. by* Isaac D'Israeli. *Fr.* Gastrology. FaBoUs
I write this poem. For Musia's Grandchildren. Irving Layton. NOBC
I write to make you suffer. Ann-Marie Kegels, *tr. fr. French by* Willis Barnstone. BoWoP
I wrote him out a check. Country Cemetery. Freda Newton Bunner. AMV-80
I wrote some lines once on a time. The Height of the Ridiculous. Oliver Wendell Holmes. AA; FaFP; FiBHP; FPL; HBV-2; MoShBr; OBAL; OBCA; PoPl; TreFT; WhC; YaD
I wrote the postcard to you and went out. Getting Through. James Merrill. NYBP
I wrung my hands under my dark veil. "Anna Akhmatova," *tr. fr. Russian by* Max Hayward *and* Stanley Kunitz. BoLoP
I wus mighty good-lookin' when I wus young. 'Späcially Jim. Bessie Morgan. HBV-2
I years had been from home. Emily Dickinson. BLPL; NOBA; OxBA; PoRA
I yield, dear enemy, nor know. La Belle Ennemie. Thomas Stanley. CavP
I Yield Thee Praise. Philip Jerome Cleveland. TrPWD; TRV
I you assure. To Mistress Margaret Tilney. John Skelton. *Fr.* The Garlande of Laurell. MeEL
I zot awhile, wi' eyelids down. The Zun a-Lighten Eyes a-Shut. William Barnes. VLP
Iambic Feet Considered as Honorable Scars. William Meredith. PoA
Iambicum Trimetrum. Spenser. BoLoP; EBEV; EIL; OBEV; PoEL-1
(Iambica.) OxBoLi
Ianthe, *sels.* Walter Savage Landor.
"Do you remember me? or are you proud?" EnRP; OBNC; ViBoPo
(Ianthe's Question.) OBEV
"Ianthe! you resolve [*or* are called] to cross the sea!" OBNC; OBVV
(Absence.) EnRP; OBRV
(Ianthe.) OBVV
Ianthe's Troubles. GBL; NOBE; ViBoPo
("From you, Ianthe, little troubles pass.") OBNC; TrGrPo
(Ianthe.) OBEV
"Mild is the parting year, and sweet." EnLoPo; TrGrPo
"My hopes retire; my wishes as before." GBL; OBNC
"Past ruin'd Ilion Helen lives." CTC; ELP; EnLoPo; EnRP; GBL; HAP; HelP; LoBV; NoP; OAEP; OBNC; OBRV; POL; PoRA; TreFT; TrGrPo; ViBoPo; WeW
(Ianthe.) FaBoEn; LiTB; PoEL-4
(Passed Ruin'd Ilion.) AWP
(To Ianthe.) NOBE; VLP
(Verse: "Past ruin'd Ilion . . .") HBV-2; OBEV
"Proud word you never spoke, but you will speak." EnLoPo; GBL; OBEV; ViBoPo
"Remain, ah not in youth alone." HAP; OAEP; OBNC
"Thou hast not rais'd, Ianthe, such desire." GBL
"Well I remember how you smiled." HAP; LoBV; OBNC; TrGrPo; ViBoPo
(Her Name.) OBVV
(Ianthe.) FaBoEn
"When Helen first saw wrinkles in her face." EnLoPo
"Ye walls! sole witnesses of happy sighs." EnLoPo
Ibadan. John Pepper Clark. CAD
Ibant Obscuræ. Thomas Edward Brown. OBNC
Ibby Damsel. *Unknown.* AmFP
Iberian! palter no more! To Spain—a Last Word. Edith M. Thomas. PAH
Ibikunle! the Lord of his Quarters. Praise of Ibikunle. *Yoruba Oral Tradition, tr. by* B. Awe. WTO
IBM Hired Her. W. J. J. Gordon. QQQ
Ibycus. John Heath-Stubbs. PoCh
Icarus. Ronald Bottrall. GTBS-P
Icarus. Valentin Iremonger. BIrV; CIP; NeIP; OnYI; OxBI
Icarus. Harry Lyman Koopman. AA
Icarus. Stephen Spender. *See* Discovered in Mid-Ocean.
Icarus. *Unknown. See* Love Winged My Hopes.
Ice. Ai. FYAP
Ice. Dorothy Aldis. SUS; TiPo
Ice. Jack Driscoll. AMV-80
Ice, The. W. W. Gibson. OxBTC
Ice. Sir Charles G. D. Roberts. BoNaP; OBCV; RHPC; WHW
Ice. Stephen Spender. FaBoMo; GTBS-P; SeCePo
Ice age is here, The. Attention. Adrienne Rich. TAP
Ice and Fire. Sir Edward Sherburne. CavP
Ice berglets, poked down. Finnair Fragment. Roald Hoffmann. SUW
Ice built, ice bound, and ice bounded. Alaska. Joaquin Miller. PAH
Ice cannot shiver in the cold. Howard Lamson. Edgar Lee Masters. *Fr.* The New Spoon River. ViBoPo
Ice Castle, The. Michael Harris. AMV-80
Ice Cream. Peter Wild. Psk
Ice Cream in Paradise. Robert Hollander. AMV-80
Ice-Cream Man, The. Rachel Field. FaPON; SiSoSe; SoPo
Ice-Cream Wars, The. John Ashbery. PoA
Ice Dragons. Diane Ackerman. SUW
Ice Eagle, The. Diane Wakoski. InPS
Ice-fishing House, The: Long Lake, Minnesota. Michael S. Harper. TAT
Ice-Floes, The. E. J. Pratt. CaP
Ice flow cut this valley, The. The Ice Has Spoken. Denis Rixson. PoSH
Ice-Flumes Owregie Their Ladies. Douglas Young. SeCePo
Ice Handler. Carl Sandburg. OxBA
Ice has been cracking all day. Spring. Michael Hogan. LFAC; TAT
Ice Has Spoken, The. Denis Rixson. PoSH
Ice here and there a hand's-breadth, thin. The First Day Out. Thomas Reiter. WOLT
Ice Horses. Joy Harjo. TWSS
Ice King, The. A. B. Demille. WHW
Ice of heroic heart seals plasmic soil. Heroic Heart. Charles Donnelly. CIP
Ice-Skaters. Elder Olson. LiSp
Ice Skin, The. James Dickey. NYBP
Ice tinkled in glasses. Blues and Bitterness. Lerone Bennett, Jr. FF; NNP; PoBA
Iceberg, The. Sir Charles G. D. Roberts. CaP
Icebergs. William Prescott Foster. EtS
Iced with a vanilla. A Meeting of Cultures. Donald Davie. OxBC
Icehouse in Summer, The. Howard Nemerov. NoAM
Iceland First Seen. William Morris. VLP
Ich Am of Irlonde. *Unknown. See* Irish Dancer, The.
Ich herde men upon mold make muche mone. The Farmer's Complaint. *Unknown.* OxBM
Ich sterbe. . .Life ebbs with an easy flow. The End of a War. Sir Herbert Read. OBMV; WaP
Ich was in one sumere dale. Owl against Nightingale. *Unknown. Fr.* The Owl and the Nightingale. OxBM
Ich Weiss Nicht Was Soll es Bedeuten. Heine, *tr. fr. German by* Alexander Macmillan. AWP
"Ich wünscht', ich wäre ein Vöglein." The Bird. Louis Simpson. NePoEA-2
Ichabod. Whittier. AA; AP; HBV-1; LiTA; NOBA; OxBA; PAH; PoEL-4; TAP
Ichabod! The Glory Has Departed. Ludwig Uhland, *tr. fr. German by* James Clarence Mangan. AWP
Icham of Irlaunde. *Unknown. See* Irish Dancer, The.

Ich'ot a burde in a bowr as breyl so bright. Annot and John. *Unknown.* OxBM
Ichot a burde in boure bryht. Blow, Northern Wind. *Unknown.* OBEV; OxBM
Ichthycide. Joe Rosenblatt. NOBC
Ichthyosaurus, The. *Unknown.* TDH
Icicle. David Huddle. Str
Ickle ockle, blue bockle. *Unknown.* OxNR
Icon. Mark Osaki. BrSi
Icons. Miriam Waddington. NOBC
Icos. Charles Tomlinson. GTBS-P
Icosasphere, The. Marianne Moore. ImOP
Icy, empty dawn cracks in the fields, The. Pacifists. George Woodcock. NOBC
Icy evil that struck his father down, The. El-Hajj Malik El-Shabazz. Robert Hayden. CNA; PoBA
I'd a dream to-night. Mater Dolorosa. William Barnes. CH; HBV-1; NOBE; OBEV
I'd Be a Butterfly. Thomas Haynes Bayly. HBV-1
I'd been on duty from two till four. Stand-to: Good Friday Morning. Siegfried Sassoon. FaBoTw
I'd build a house with windows. Skycoast. Samuel Hazo. GrPl
I'd draw all this into a fine element,—a color. The Rug. Michael McClure. NeAP
I'd fill up the house with guests this minute. A Revel. Donagh MacDonagh. NeIP
I'd have no flowers. How I'd Have It. John Stone. AMV-81
I'd Have You, Quoth He. *Unknown.* ErPo; FF
I'd Leave. Andrew Lang. FaPON
I'd like a different dog. Dogs and Weather. Winifred Welles. FaPON; TiPo
I'd like a little/ Of that nourishing victual. *Unknown.* FaFP
I'd like to/ pull. The Intelligent Sheepman and the New Cars. William Carlos Williams. NePoAm-2; OBAL
I'd like to be a dentist with a plate upon the door. The Dentist. Rose Fyleman. SoPo; TiPo
I'd Like to Be a Lighthouse. Rachel Field. PDV; SoPo
I'd like to be a worm. Zhenya Gay. TiPo
I'd like to be the sort of friend that you have been to me. A Friend's Greeting. Edgar A. Guest. BLPA; BLPL
I'd like to hear a sermon done. S.P.C.A. Sermon. Stuart Hemsley. FiBHP
I'd like to hear the bees again. The Grass, Alas. Dick Emmons. QQQ
I'd like to live with you. Marina Tsvetayeva, *tr. fr. Russian by* Paul Schmidt. BoWoP
I'd Like to Mark Myself. Milton Acorn. NeAC
I'd like to run like a rabbit in hops. Rabbit. Tom Robinson. FaPON
I'd Love to Be a Fairy's Child. Robert Graves. FaPON; HBVY; PDV; SoPo
I'd much rather sit there in the sun. Song. Ruth Krauss. RHPC; SO
I'd never dare to walk across. The Invisible Bridge. Gelett Burgess. NA; TreFT
I'd oft heard tell of this Sledburn fair. Sledburn Fair. *Unknown.* CH
I'd often seen before. The Sheaf. Andrew Young. ChTr
I'd rather be the devil/ to be that woman's ma-a-an. Devil Got My Woman. *Unknown.* BluL
I'd rather be the devil/ oh rather be the devil. Evil Devil Woman. *Unknown.* BluL
I'd rather have fingers than toes. On Digital Extremities [*or* Nonsense Verses]. Gelett Burgess. FaPON; HBV-2; HBVY
I'd rather have habits than clothes. Limerick. Gelett Burgess. NA
I'd rather have the thought of you. Choice. Angela Morgan. PoLF
I'd rather hear a rattler rattle. The Bloody Injians. *Unknown.* CoSo
I'd rather lie on a rye-grass bed. The Water-Hole. Charles Erskine Scott Wood. BPAW
I'd rather listen to a flute. Samuel Hoffenstein. FiBHP; POL
I'd rather see a sermon than to hear it any day. How Do You Live? *Unknown.* STF
I'd "read" three hours. Both notes and text. A Dialogue from Plato. Austin Dobson. HBV-1
I'd run about/ on the desert. *Tr. fr. Papago Indian by* Ruth Underhill. BoWoP
I'd sit inside the abandoned shack all morning. About a Year after He Got Married He Would Sit Alone in an Abandoned Shack in a Cotton Field Enjoying Himself. James Whitehead. GP
I'd smoke in the freezer. Shoplifters. Maura Stanton. MAYP
I'd walk her home after work. New York, Summer. Jack Gilbert. NPGG
I'd wandered all over the country. The Old Settler's Song. Francis Henry. BPAW
I'd Want Her Eyes to Fill with Wonder. Kenneth Patchen. LLLT
I'd wave the gnats away and try. Crew Practice on Lake Bled, in Jugoslavia. James Scully. NYBP
I'd weave a wreath for those who fought. Through Fire in Mobile Bay. *Unknown.* PAH
I'd wed you without herds, without money, or rich array. Cashel of Munster. *At. to* William English, *tr. by* Sir Samuel Ferguson. AnIV; BIrV; GBL; OBEV; OBVV; OnYI; OxBI
Ida Red. *Unknown.* FSW
Ida, Sweet as Apple Cider. Eddie Leonard. BLSo, *with music*; FSN, *with music*; TreFT
Idaho. *Unknown.* BPAW (*At. to* Frank French); GBP
Idaho Jack. *At. to* Jack H. Lee. BPAW
Idbury bells are ringing. Country Thought. Sylvia Townsend Warner. MoBrPo
Idea, *sels.* Michael Drayton.
  "As other men, so I myself do muse," IX. JCP
  "Bright star of beauty! on whose eyelids sit," IV. HBV-1
  "Calling to my mind [*or* minde] since first my love begun," LI. EnRePo; NOBE; OBSC; PoEL-2
  "Cupid, I hate thee, which I'd have thee know," XLVIII. LO
  "Deare [*or* Dear], why should you command [*or* commaund] me to my rest," XXXVII. AAS; HBV-1; NOBE; OAEP; OBSC; PoEL-2; ViBoPo
  (Night and Day.) LiTB
  (Sonnet: "Dear [*or* Deere], why should you command me to my rest.") ElL; FaBoEn
  "Evil [*or* Evill] spirit, your beauty, haunts me still, An," XX. AAS; ElL; GBL; HBV-1; LoBV; NOBE; OAEP; OBSC
  "How many paltry, foolish, painted things," VI. AAS; EnLoPo; EnRePo; GBL; HAP; HBV-1 (XLII); HeIP; NIP; NoP; OAEL-1; OBSC; PrIm; TEP
  (Sonnet: "How many paltry . . .") ElL; LoBV
  "I hear some say, this man is not in love," XXIV. OAEP; TrGrPo
  "If he, from heaven that filched the living fire," XIV. AAS; NoP; TEP
  "Into these loves, who but for passion looks," *introd. sonnet.* HBV-1; NoP; ViBoPo
  (To the Reader of These Sonnets.) AAS; EnRePo
  "My heart the anvil where my thoughts do beat," XL (*also given as XLIV in* Idea's Mirrour). HBV-1
  "Nothing but no and I, and I and no," V. GBL; PoEL-2
  "Since there's [*or* ther's] no help[e], come let us kiss[e] and part," LXI. AAS; AWP; BoLoP; CABA; EnLoPo; EnRePo; GBL; HAP; HBV-1; HeIP; InPK; InPS; JCP; NOBE; NoP; OAEL-1; OAEP; OBSC; PAI; PoEL-2; PoPle; PPoe; PrIm; SeCePo; SoSe; TEP; TrGrPo; ViBoPo; WHA
  (Come, Let Us Kiss and Part.) TreFS
  (Farewell to Love.) BLPL
  (Love's Farewell.) GTBS; GTBS-P
  (Parting, The.) LiTB; OBEV; SCV; SeCeV
  (Sonnet: "Since there's no help . . .") ElL; FaBoEn; LoBV
  "Since to obtaine thee, nothing me will sted," XV.
  (His Remedie for Love.) AAS
  Sonnet to the Critic, XXXI. LoBV
  "Stay, speedy [*or* Sweet] time; behold, before thou pass," XVII (*also given as VII in* Idea's Mirrour). EnRePo; OBSC
  "There's nothing grieves me, but that age should haste," VIII. AAS; OAEL-1
  "To nothing fitter can I thee compare," X. ElL; OBSC; TrGrPo; ViBoPo
  "Truce, gentle love, a parley now I crave," LXIII. NoP
  "When conquering love did first my heart assail," XXIX. OAEP
  "When first I ended, then I first began," LXII (*also given as L in* Idea's Mirrour). TrGrPo
  "Whilst thus my pen strives to eternize thee," XLIV. AAS; OBSC; ViBoPo
  "Why should your fair eyes with such sovereign grace," XLIII. OBSC
  "Witlesse gallant, a young wench that woo'd, A," XXI. AAS
  "You [*or* You're] not alone when you are still alone," XI. PoEL-2; TrGrPo
Idea of a Swimmer. Jean-Richard Bloch, *tr. fr. French by* "S. P." TrJP
Idea of Ancestry, The. Etheridge Knight. BALP; BPo; CNA; ConAP; LFAC; NIP; NNaP; PoBA; PPoe; SV
Idea of Entropy at Maenporth Beach, The. Peter Redgrove. FaBoMo
Idea of justice may be precious, An. Ode. Frank O'Hara. NeAP
Idea of Order at Key West, The. Wallace Stevens. AP; CMoP; CoBMV; FF; HAP; HeIP; MoAB; MoAmPo; MoPo; MOS; NIP; NoAM; NOBA; NoP; OxBA; PP; PPP; PrIm; SeCeV; TAP
Idea of Trust, The. Thom Gunn. Psk
Ideal, The. Baudelaire, *tr. fr. French by* Arthur Symons. SyP
Ideal. Padraic Pearse, *tr. fr. Modern Irish by* Thomas MacDonagh. AnIV; AWP; OnYI
Ideal, The. Francis Saltus Saltus. AA
Ideal and Reality. Joseph Campbell. BIrV
Ideal Angels. John Robert Colombo. MoCV
Ideal Husband to His Wife, The. Sam Walter Foss. InMe
Ideal Landscape. Adrienne Rich. NoAM

Ideal Passion, *sels.* George Edward Woodberry. HBMV
"Between my eyes and hers so thin the screen," XXXVII.
" 'Evil thing is honor, An,' once of old," XXVIII.
"Farewell, my Muse! for, lo, there is no end," XLII.
"I never muse upon my lady's grace," XXV.
"Immortal Love, too high for my possessing," XL.
"In what a glorious substance did they dream," XXVI.
"Oh, how with brightness hath Love filled my way," XXX.
"Why, Love, beneath the fields of asphodel," XXXIII.
Idealism. Ronald Arbuthnott Knox. FaBoCo; PoPle
(Limerick: "There once was a man who said 'God.' ") NOBL
("There once was a man who said, 'God.' ") OxBoLi
Ideals of Satire, The. Pope. *Fr.* First Epistle of the Second Book of Horace. FiP
Idea's Mirrour, *sels.* Michael Drayton.
"Black pitchy night, companion of my woe," XLV. LoBV; OBSC
"Cupid, dumb idol, peevish saint of love," XXVI. EnRePo
"Glorious sun went blushing to his bed, The," XXV. OBSC
"If chaste and pure devotion of my youth," XXXVIII. OBSC; ViBoPo
"My fair, look from those turrets of thine eyes," XXXIV. OBSC
"My heart, imprisoned in a hopeless isle," XXII. OBSC
"My heart the anvil where my thoughts do beat," XLIV (*also given as XL in* Idea). HBV-1
"Read here (sweet maid) the story of my woe," I. OBSC
"Stay speedy time; behold, before thou pass," VII (*also given as XVII in* Idea). EnRePo
"Sweet secrecy, what tongue can tell thy worth?" XLVI. ViBoPo
"Three sorts of serpents do resemble thee," XXX. EnRePo
"When first I ended, then I first begun," L (*also given as LXII in* Idea). TrGrPo
Identification in Belfast (I.R.A. Bombing). Robert Lowell. OxBC
Identities. Al Young. NPGG
Identity. Thomas Bailey Aldrich. AA
Identity. Robert Friend. GP; VWA
Identity. Elizabeth Jennings. NePoEA
Identity. Sister Mary Helen. GoBC
Identity Card. Susan Tichy. MAYP
Identity, known or unknown, survives. Indecision. Helen Pinkerton. QFR
Ides of March, The. Roy Fuller. PoCh
Idiom of the Hero. Wallace Stevens. OxBA
Idiot, The. John Ashbery. *Fr.* Two Sonnets. VGW
Idiot, The. Adèle Naudé. PeSA
Idiot, The. Dudley Randall. BPo
Idiot. Allen Tate. FaBoMo; LiTA; TwAmPo
Idiot, The. Keith Wilson. Psk
Idiot Boy. Rowland M. Hill. AMV-81
Idiot Boy, The. Wordsworth. OBNV
Idiot greens the meadows with his eyes, The. Idiot. Allen Tate. FaBoMo; LiTA; TwAmPo
Idle Charon. Eugene Lee-Hamilton. OBVV
Idle Chatter. Charles Cooper. BOLo
Idle chatter, rising like a fountain, The. Lèse-Majesté. Herbert S. Gorman. HBMV
Idle cuckoo, having made a feast, The. On the Cuckoo. Francis Quarles. PBBP
Idle dayseye, the laborious wheel, The. O. Richard Wilbur. LiTA; MoPo
Idle Flowers, The. Robert Bridges. BoNaP; ChTr
Idle Fyno. *Unknown. See* Fara Diddle Dyno.
Idle Life I Lead, The. Robert Bridges. LiTM
Idle poet, here and there, An. The Revelation. Coventry Patmore. *Fr.* The Angel in the House. EnLoPo; GBL; GTBS-P; HAP; NBM; OBNC: ViBoPo
Idle Verse. Henry Vaughan. OAEP
Idle Visitation, An. Edward Dorn. *Fr.* Gunslinger. NOBA
Idle Words. Walter Savage Landor. OBSV
Idleness. S. Weir Mitchell. AA
Idler, The. Elizabeth Jennings. NePoEA
Idler, The. Jones Very. AA; HBV-2
Idler with a wand for a walking stick, An. Batyushkov. Osip Mandelstam, *tr. by* W. S. Merwin *and* Clarence Brown. OBVE
Idlers, The. Edmund Blunden. CH
Idler's Calender, An, *sel.* Wilfrid Scawen Blunt.
January: Cover Shooting. VLP
Idleset: "Ill's the airt o the Word the day." Thurso Berwick. OxBS
Idling pivot of the frigate bird, The. Man o' War Bird. Derek Walcott. TTY
Idling through the mean space dozing. Choice. A. R. Ammons. PAI
Idly in the sun. Meridian. Brewster Ghiselin. AMV-80
Idly she yawned, and threw her heavy hair. Sonnet. George Moore. ErPo
Idol, The. Louise Driscoll. HBMV
Idolatry. Arna Bontemps. AmNP; PoNe
Idols. Richard Burton. TrPWD
Idol's Eye, The, *sel.* Harry B. Smith.
Tattooed Man, The. InMe
Idyl: "And my young sweetheart sat at board with me." Alfred Mombert, *tr. fr. German by* Ludwig Lewisohn. AWP
Idyll: "At noon the sun puffed up, outsize." Francis Webb. PoAu-2
Idyl, An: "Come down, O maid, from yonder mountain height." Tennyson. *See* Come Down, O Maid.
Idyll: "Hermit hoar, in solemn cell." Samuel Johnson. *See* Hermit Hoar.
Idyll: "In Switzerland one idle day." Hugh Macnaghten. HBMV
Idyl: Sunrise. Henrietta Cordelia Ray. BlSi
Idyl: Sunset. Henrietta Cordelia Ray. BlSi
Idyl in Idleness, An. Robert Pack. NePoEA
Idyll of the Rose. Ausonius, *tr. fr. Latin by* John Addington Symonds. AWP
Idylls, *sels.* Theocritus, *tr. fr. Greek.*
"Amorous shepherd lov'd a charming boy, An," XXIII, *tr. by* Thomas Creech. PeHV
"And so an easier life our Cyclops drew," XI, *tr. by* Elizabeth Barrett Browning. OBVE
(Cyclops, The.) AWP
Death of Daphnis, The, I, *tr. by* Charles Stuart Calverley. AWP
Enchantment, The, II, *tr. by* Thomas Creech. CTC; OBVE
(Incantation, The, *tr. by* Charles Stuart Calverley.) AWP
"Eunica skornde me, when her I would have sweetly kist," XX, *tr. unknown.* OBVE
Fishermen, The, XXI, *tr. by* Charles Stuart Calverley. AWP; OBVE
Harvest-Home, VII, *tr. by* Charles Stuart Calverley. AWP
Herdsmen, The, IV, *tr. by* Charles Stuart Calverley. AWP
"Shepheard Paris bore the Spartan bride, The," XXVII, *tr. by* Dryden. OBVE
"Wine, friend, and truth, the proverb says, agree," XXVI, *tr. by* Thomas Creech. PeHV
Idylls of the King, *sels.* Tennyson.
Balin and Balan.
Vivien's Song ("But now the wholesome music of the wood"). OAEL-2
Coming of Arthur, The.
Merlin's Riddling. FaBoRV
Dedication: "These to His Memory—since he held them dear." CABA;VLP
Gareth and Lynette.
To the Queen ("O loyal to the royal in thyself"). VLP
Geraint and Enid.
Enid's Song. FaBoRV
Holy Grail, The.
Lancelot and the Grail. GoBC
Percivale's Quest. OAEL-2
Lancelot and Elaine.
Song of Love and Death, The. OBNC
(Elaine's Song.) FaBoEn
Last Tournament, The.
"As the crest of some slow-arching wave." FaBoPP
Tristram's Song. FaBoRV
Merlin and Vivien.
In Love, If Love Be Love. CABA; TrGrPo
(All in All.) LiTB; TRV
("In Love, if Love be Love, if Love be ours.") PoEL-5
(Vivien's Song.) FaBoEn; OBNC
Passing of Arthur, The. OBNC
(Morte d'Arthur, *incorporated in the* Idylls *with changes, as* The Passing of Arthur.) DL; FiP; OAEL-2; VLP
"And answer made King Arthur, breathing hard." EBEV
"And slowly answered Arthur from the barge." FaBoEn
Arthur's Disillusionment. TreFS
But Now Farewell. FaBoRV
Prayer ("Pray for my soul. More things are wrought by prayer"). TreF; WGRP
Iesu. George Herbert. *See* Jesu.
Iesu, swete sone dere! *See* Jesu, sweete sone dear.
If. Franklin P. Adams. OBAL
If. John Kendrick Bangs. OBCA
If. Mortimer Collins. FiBHP; HBV-1; Par
If. Rebecca Foresman. WBLP
If. William Dean Howells. AA
If. Kipling. BLPA; FaBoBe; FaFP; FaPoR; FPL; HBV-2; HBVY; OHFP; OxBChV; OxBTC; PaPo; TreF; WBLP
If. Patrick Lane. NOBC
If. James Jeffrey Roche. HBV-1
If. *Unknown.* NA
If/ ice shall melt. If Ice. W. W. E. Ross. NOBC; OBCV
If a clear fountain still keeping a sad course. The Duke's Song. Sidney Wroth, Countess of Montgomery. *Fr.* Urania Mary. WPE

If a daughter you have, she's the plague of your life. Sheridan. *Fr.* The Duenna. DBV
If a gate stands open long enough. Gates. Ted Kooser. GP
If a good man were ever housed in Hell. The Good Man in Hell. Edwin Muir. MoBrPo; TW
If a Maid Be Fair. Laura Goodman Salverson. CaP
If a man can find rich consolation, remembering his good deeds. Catullus, *tr. fr. Latin by* Horace Gregory. NAWM-1
"If a Man Die." John Richard Moreland. PGD
If a man with a shovel came down the road. The Diggers. W. S. Merwin. EAS
If a man would be a soldier, he'd expect, of course, to fight. A Little Rhyme and a Little Reason. Henry Anstadt. BLRP
If a person conceives an opinion. Poeta Loquitur. Swinburne. OAEL-2
If a task is once begun. Always Finish [*or* Perseverance]. *Unknown.* BLPA; FaBoBe; TreFT WBLP
If a Woodchuck Would Chuck. *Unknown.* FaPON
("How much wood would a woodchuck chuck?") TiPo
If after kirk ye bide a wee. An Angel Unawares. *Unknown.* BLRP; TRV
"If, after obtaining Buddhahood, anyone in my land." Gary Snyder. Myths and Texts: Burning, X. NaP
If after rude and boisterous seas. The Plaudite, or End of Life. Robert Herrick. CaPo
If again in the spring. Seeing the Plum Blossoms by the River. Lady Ise, *tr. by* Etsuko Terasaki *and* Irma Brandeis. BoWoP
If (aged Charon), when my life shall end. Licia, XLI. Giles Fletcher the Elder. ES
If Ah evah git to glory, an' Ah hop to mek it thoo. Black Mammies. John Wesley Holloway. BANP
If all a top physicist knows. After Reading a Child's Guide to Modern Physics. W. H. Auden. NYBP
If all be true that I do think. Reasons for Drinking [*or* A Catch *or* The Five Reasons]. Henry Aldrich. FaBoCo; FaBoEE; FF; InMe; InvP; OBS; TreFT; YaD
If all my days were summer, could I know. Revelation. Warren F. Cook. BLRP
If all the answer's to be the Sinai sort. Golden Calf. Norman MacCaig. OxBS
If all the good people were clever. Good and Clever. Elizabeth Wordsworth. OxBTC
If all the harm that women have done. A Thought. James Kenneth Stephen. FiBHP
If all the land were apple-pie. If. *Unknown.* NA
If All the Pens That Ever Poets Held. Christopher Marlowe. *Fr.* Tamburlaine the Great, Pt. I, Act V, sc. ii. ChTr; TrGrPo
If all the seas were one sea. Mother Goose. OnUR; OxNR; SoPo
If all the ships I have at sea. My Ships. Ella Wheeler Wilcox. PoLF
If All the Skies [Were Sunshine]. Henry van Dyke. WBLP; WGRP
If All the Thermo-nuclear Warheads. Kenneth Burke. QQQ
If all the trees in all the woods were men. Cacoëthes Scribendi. Oliver Wendell Holmes. AA
If all the verse what I have wrote. Archys Autobiography. Don Marquis. *Fr.* Archys Life of Mehitabel. CrMA
If All the Voices of Men. Horace L. Traubel. AA
If all the women in the town were bundled up together. The Agricultural Irish Girl. *Unknown.* OnYI
If all the world and love were young. The Nymph's Reply to the [Passionate] Shepherd [*or* Answer to Marlowe *or* Her Reply *or* The Nymph's Reply *or* Reply to Marlowe's "The Passionate Shepherd to His Love"]. Sir Walter Ralegh. AAS; BiP; BoLoP; CABA; CTC; EIL; FaBoPa; FF; HAP; HBV-1; HeIP; HoPM; LiTB; LoBV; NIP; NOBE; NoP; OAEL-1; OAEP; OBEV; OBSC; OLR; PAI; PPP; SeCePo; SeCeV; SiPS; TreFS; TrGrPo; ViBoPo; WeW; WHA
If all the world were [*or* was] apple-pie. Mother Goose. FaFP; HBV-1; HBVY; SoPo
If All the World Were [*or* Was] Paper. *Unknown.* FaBoCo; FaBoNo; GBP; LoBV; NTCP; OxNR; PoPle
If amorous faith, a heart of guileless ways. Signs of Love. Petrarch, *tr. by* C. B. Cayley. AWP
If an eagle be imprisoned. America. Henry Dumas. BOLo; PoBA
If an unkind word appears. On File. John Kendrick Bangs. WBLP
If angels sung a Savior's birth. *At. to* John Stephenson. AmFP
If, antique hateful bird. The Raven. Adrienne Rich. NePoEA-2
If any ask why there's no great She-Poet. Dedication of the Cook. Anna Wickham. MoBrPo
If Any Be Pleased to Walk into My Poor Garden. Francis Daniel Pastorius. SCAP
If any flower that here is grown. Inscription in a Garden. George Gascoigne. OBSC; TrGrPo
If any God should say. Rebirth. Kipling. LoBV; OBNC
If any have a stone to shy. The Pebble. Elinor Wylie. MoAmPo
If any man would know the very cause. Sonnet: He Is Out of Heart with His Time. Guerzo di Montecanti, *tr. by* Dante Gabriel Rossetti. AWP
If any mourn us in the workshop, say. Batteries Out of Ammunition. Kipling. *Fr.* Epitaphs of the War. MMA
If any question why we died. Common Form. Kipling. *Fr.* Epitaphs of the War. FaBoEE; FaBoTw; PV
If any wench Venus's girdle wear. Song. John Gay. *Fr.* The Beggar's Opera. PoEL-3
If any would portray thee. Before the Ikon of the Mother of God. Constantine of Rhodes, *tr. by* G. R. Woodward. ISi
If anybody ask ye who I am. Child of God. *Unknown.* FSW
If anybody comes to I. On Dr. Lettsom. *Unknown.* FaBoEE
If anyone long for a musical song. The Wanton Trick [*or* 'Tis but a Wanton Trick]. *Unknown.* CoMu; UnTE
If apples were pears. To My Valentine. *Unknown.* SoPo
If art and industry should doe as much. New English Canaan; Prologue. Thomas Morton. SCAP
If as a flowre doth spread and die. Employment. George Herbert. SeCV-1
If as the windes and waters here below. The Storm. George Herbert. AnAnS-1
If, as well may happen. Read Me, Please! Robert Graves. NYBP
If asked the day that this man dies. At a Loss. James L. Weil. GoYe
If at your coming princes disappear. Comets and Princes. Samuel Johnson. FaBoEE
If aught can teach us aught, Affliction's looks. Affliction. Sir John Davies. *Fr.* Nosce Teipsum. NOBE; OBSC
If aught I may have said or done. An Evening Prayer. Laura E. Kendall. BLRP
If aught [*or* ought] of oaten stop, or pastoral song. Ode to Evening. William Collins. AWP; CABA; EBEV; EnRP; FaBoBe; FaBoEn; GTBS; GTBS-P; HAP; HBV-1; LAuP; LiTB; LoBV; MasP; NOBE; NOEC; NoP; OAEL-1; OAEP; OBEC; OBEV; PoEL-3; PPP; SeCePo; SeCeV; TreFT; TrGrPo; ViBoPo; WHA
If aught of simple song have power to touch. The Birthday Crown. William Alexander. OBVV
If aught that stumbles in my speech. Abstemia. Gelett Burgess. NA
If babies could speak they'd tell mother or nurse. Bringing Up Babies. Roy Fuller. RHPC
If bees stay at home. Weather Wisdom. *Unknown.* HBVY; OxNR; TreF
If, before being earth, the thought of sound. Anticipation. Joseph Tusiani. GoYe
If Bet bedecks herself with gems, bestirs herself when bid. Why Not? *Unknown.* WhC
If Bethlehem were here today. Christmas Morning. Elizabeth Madox Roberts. MoAmPo; PChr; PoSC; SUS
If Birds That neither Sow nor Reap, *with music.* Roger Williams. AH
If Birth Persists. Matthew Arnold. *Fr.* Resignation. FaBoRV
If Blood Is Black Then Spirit Neglects My Unborn Son. Conrad Kent Rivers. PoBA
If blossoms could blossom. To Be Sung. Peter Viereck. FaBV
If body were not Art. Open Poetry Reading. Jesús Papoleto Meléndez. AMV-81
If bright the sun, he tarries. Emerson. *Fr.* Fragments on the Poet and the Poetic Gift. PP
If but One Year. *Unknown.* STF
If but some vengeful god would call to me. Hap. Thomas Hardy. AWP; CABA; CMoP; CoBMV; EaLo; EBVV; MoBrPo; NIP; NoAM; NoP; OAEL-2; OAEP; PPON; PPP; TEP; VLP
If by Dull Rhymes Our English Must Be Chained. Keats. *See* On the Sonnet.
If by your art, my dearest father, you have. Shakespeare. *Fr.* The Tempest, I, ii. MOS
"If Candlemas be fine and clear." At Candlemas. Charles Causley. OBCP
If Candlemas Day be dry and fair. *Unknown.* PoSC
If Candlemas Day be fair and bright. *Unknown.* FaBoUs; PoSC
If care do cause men cry, why do not I complain. Earl of Surrey. SiPS
If chance assign'd. Sir Thomas Wyatt. SiPS
If chaste and pure devotion of my youth. Michael Drayton. Idea's Mirrour, XXXVIII. OBSC; ViBoPo
If Christ were here to-night, and saw me tired. Margaret E. Sangster. TRV
If come into this world again I must. Dew on a Dusty Heart. Jean Starr Untermeyer. MoAmPo
If "compression is the first grace of style." To a Snail. Marianne Moore. CMoP; FaBoMo
If Cynthia Be a Queen. Sir Walter Ralegh. SiPS
If Dante mourns, there wheresoe'er he be. To One Who Had Censured His Public Exposition of Dante. Boccaccio, *tr. by* Dante Gabriel Rossetti. *Fr.* Sonnets. AWP; GoBC
If dead, we cease to be; if total gloom. Human Life; on the Denial of Immortality. Samuel Taylor Coleridge. ChER
If deare Anthea, my hard fate it be. To Anthea. Robert Herrick. OBS

If death is what he seeks in life he fails. The Malefic Surgeon. Gerrit Lansing. CoPo
If death were truly conquered, there would be. Death. L. E. Jones. POL
If desire is absence—the wind. Learning to Live without You. Susan Wood. AMV-81
If Doughty Deeds. Robert Graham. BSV; GoTS; OBEV
(Cavalier's Song.) HBV-1
("If doughty deads my lady please.") GTBS; GTBS-P
(O Tell Me How to Woo Thee.) OBEC
If down his throat a man should choose. An Unsuspected Fact. Edward Cannon. NA
If, dumb too long, the drooping Muse hath stayed. To the Earl of Warwick, on the Death of Mr. Addison. Thomas Tickell. HBV-2; NOEC; OBEC
If earthward you could wing your flight. England Expects? Sir Owen Seaman. NOBL
If Easter Be Not True. Henry H. Barstow. BLRP; PGD; TRV
If Easter Eggs Would Hatch. Douglas Malloch. SoPo
If echoes from the fitful past. Abstrosophy. Gelett Burgess. CenHV; NA
If e'er in thy sight I found favour, Apollo. The Poet's Prayer. *Unknown.* OBSV
If ever a garden was [a] Gethsemane. For Jim, Easter Eve. Anne Spencer. AmNP; PoNe
If ever a sailor was fond of good sport. Jack's Fidelity. Charles Dibdin. EtS
If ever against this easy blue and silver. Interruption. Robert Graves. LiTB; LiTM
If ever chance or choice thy footsteps lead. The Flying Tailor. James Hogg. BXAP; Par
If Ever Hapless Woman Had a Cause. Countess of Pembroke. WPE
If ever happiness hath lodg'd with man. Consummate Happiness. Wordsworth. *Fr.* The Prelude, IV. OBNC
If ever I had dreamed of my dead name. Sonnet to My Friend, with an Identity Disc. Wilfred Owen. PeHV
If Ever I Marry, I'll Marry a Maid. *Unknown.* ElL
If ever I should condescend to prose. Poetical Commandments [*or* Poet's Credo]. Byron. *Fr.* Don Juan, I. FiP; OBRV; OxBoLi; SeCePo
"If ever I walk to church to wed." The Satin Shoes. Thomas Hardy. CoBMV
If ever man might him avaunt. Sir Thomas Wyatt. SiPS
If ever mercy move you murder me. To the Mercy Killers. Dudley Randall. DL
If ever round our domicile you chance to be a-wandering. "Everybody Works but Father" as W. S. Gilbert Would Have Written It. Arthur G. Burgoyne. FiBHP
If ever Sorrow spoke from soul that loves. Sonnet. Henry Constable. *Fr.* Diana. ElL
If ever the sun had thought to pass this way. Dark Corner. Graham Hough. NMP
If ever there is something nice. Five Years Old. Lysbeth Boyd Borie. SiSoSe
If ever there lived a Yankee lad. Darius Green and His Flying-Machine. John Townsend Trowbridge. BeLS; BLPL; FaBoBe; HBV-2; HBVY; InMe; MoShBr; OBAL; OBCA; OxBChV; PoLF; YaD
If ever two were one, then surely we. To My Dear and Loving Husband. Anne Bradstreet. AmPP; AP; BLPL; BoWoP; FF; HAP; HeIP; NePA; NOBA; NOC[illegible]; OxBA; PoEL-3; PoLF; PrIm; SBG; SCAP; TAP; WeW; WPE
If ever you go to Dolgelley. The Dolgelley Hotel. Thomas Hughes. CenHV; FaBoCo
If Ever You Go to Dublin Town. Patrick Kavanagh. AnIL; CIP; CMoP; IPY; NMP
If ever you go to the North Countree. Edenhall. "Susan Coolidge." OBCA
If ever you should follow. Belden Hollow. Leslie Nelson Jennings. GoYe
If ever you should go by chance. How To Tell the Wild Animals. Carolyn Wells. FaFP; FaPON; FiBHP; HBVY; TiPo
If ever your spirits are damp, low. A Drinking Song. *Unknown.* FaBoUs
If Everything Happens That Can't Be Done. E. E. Cummings. SoSe; WeW
If external action is effete. The Past Is the Present. Marianne Moore. PP
If faithfull soules be alike glorifi'd. John Donne. Holy Sonnets, VIII. AnAnS-1; MasP; OBS
If fancy [*or* fansy] would favor. Sir Thomas Wyatt. AAS; SiPS
If Fathers Knew but How to Leave. *Unknown.* ElL
If fired upon, he cannot fire. Telephone Lineman. Ernest Kroll. AMV-81
If flowers want to grow. The City. David Ignatow. PCP
If for a woman I would die. A Song. Countess of Winchilsea. ViBoPo
If Frequently to Mass. Christine de Pisan, *tr. fr. French by* J. G. Legge. PoPl
If from the earth we came, it was an earth. Anatomy of Monotony. Wallace Stevens. BiP
If from the public way you turn your steps. Michael [a Pastoral Poem]. Wordsworth. EnRP; GoTL; OAEL-2; OAEP; WHA
If fruits are fed on any beast. Epitaph after Reading Ronsard's Lines from Rabelais [*or* Epitaph]. J. M. Synge. FaBoEE; PV
If girls were as charming after the fact as before it. Andante, ma Non Assai. Rufinus, *tr. by* Dudley Fitts. ErPo
If God ever had intended. Man Has No Smokestack. *Unknown.* STF
If God Exists. Ewa Lipska, *tr. fr. Polish by* Peter Jay *and* Geri Lipshultz. VWA
If God has been good enough to give you a poet. Let Them Alone. Robinson Jeffers. AP
If God kept a terrarium. W. J. Turner. *Fr.* The Seven Days of the Sun. OBMV
If Gray Had Had to Write His Elegy in the Cemetery of Spoon River Instead of in That of Stoke Poges. J. C. Squire. FaBoPa; WhC
(Elegy in the Cemetery of Spoon River Instead of in That of Stoke Pages.) BXAP
If grief come early. First or Last. Thomas Hardy. CMoP
If grief for grief can touch thee. The Appeal. Emily Brontë. EnLoPo; LoBV; OBNC
If Hamlet would betray. Midrash on Hamlet. Francis Landy. VWA
If He be truly Christ. Second Seeing. Louis Golding. WGRP
If he chanced to spit, it was whole basketsful of goldfinches. Shrovetide's Countenance. Rabelais, *tr. by* Sir Thomas Urquhart. FaBoNo
If he does not look at her face. The Circumcision. Linda Zisquit. VWa
If he from heaven that filched the living fire. Idea, XIV. Michael Drayton. AAS; NoP; TEP
If he is held in love. Joyful Prophecy. Vassar Miller. CoPo
If He Let Us Go Now. Shirley Williams. BoWoP
If he that erst the form so lively drew. Earl of Surrey. SiPS
If health and strength permit thee, don't refuse. Choosing a Wet-Nurse. M. Saint-Marthe. *Fr.* Paedotrophiae; or, The Art of Bringing Up Children. FaBoUs
If heaven were to do again. The Peaceful Shepherd. Robert Frost. *Fr.* A Sky Pair. MoAB; MoAmPo
If heav'n the grateful liberty would give. The Choice. John Pomfret. NOEC; OBEC
If He'd Be a Buckaroo, *with music. Unknown.* OuSiCo
If her neck is. Parallel Texts. Robert Kelly. CoPo
If here and now be but a timely span. Here and Now. Catherine Cater. AmNP; PoNe
If homely virtues draw from me a tune. Envoy. James Weldon Johnson. TrPWD
If hope grew on a bush. Hope and Joy. Christina Rossetti. OxBChV
If hours be years the twain are blest. At a Hasty Wedding. Thomas Hardy. VLP
If humility and purity be not in the heart. T. S. Eliot. *Fr.* The Rock. TiPo
If hungry, Lord, I need bread. In Harbor. Lizette Woodworth Reese. TrPWD
If I am amazed by anybody. Nothing but Image. Jody Swilky. AMV-81
If I am proud, you surely know. Called Proud. Walter Savage Landor. GBL
If I ask why/ You need not reply. The Question Is Proof. Elizabeth Bartlett. NePoAm-2
If I bring back. For My Unborn and Wretched Children. A. B. Spellman. CNA; PoBA
If I But Knew. Amy E. Leigh. AA
If I can do some good today. My Daily Prayer. Grenville Kleiser. BLRP
If I can find this place near-abandoned. Jersey Bait Shack. Peter Balakian. MAYP
If I can stop one heart from breaking. Emily Dickinson. AH, *with music;* FPL; OHFP; PoLF; TreF; TRV
If I consider/ My body like the fields. Lady Ise, *tr. fr. Japanese by* Donald Keene. WPOW
If I could believe that death. Gaspara Stampa. *tr. fr. Italian by* Lynne Lawner. PBWP
If I could choose a role. The Guide. Arthur Gregor. GP
If I could choose my paradise. No and Yes. Thomas Ashe. HBV-1
If I could come again to that dear place. John Masefield. *Fr.* Sonnets. ("Long long ago"). HBV-2
If I could drive steel like John Henry. Drivin' Steel. *Unknown.* AS
If I could get within this changing I. John Masefield. *Fr.* Sonnets ("Long long ago"). WGRP
If I could go on kissing your honeyed eyes. Catullus, *tr. fr. Latin.* PeHV
If I Could Grasp a Wave from the Great Sea. John Richard Moreland. EtS
If I could have/ Two things in one. Moriturus. Edna St. Vincent Millay. LiTA
If I could hide in the woods. O, Beautiful They Move. William Pillen. VWA
If I could I surely would. Pharoah's Army Got Drownded [*or* Oh, Mary Don't You Weep]. *Unknown.* AS; FSW
If I could, I'd write. Housewife's Letter: To Mary. Anne Halley. NMM

If I could know that here about. Evelyn. Rossiter Johnson. AA
If I could linger on his lovely chest. Sonnet XIII. Louise Labé, *tr. by* Aliki *and* Willis Barnstone. BoWoP
If I Could Meet God. Dennis Schmitz. NPGG
If I Could Only Live at the Pitch That Is near Madness. Richard Eberhart. FF; LiTM; MAT; MiAP; MoAB; PoPl
If I could paint you, friend, as you stand there. A Football-Player. Edward Cracroft Lefroy. LiSp
If I could reach you now, in any way. Letter to a Mute. Thomas James. AmPA
If I could rise and see my father young. Art of the Sonnet: XXXIII. Gil Orlovitz. DiL
If I could see a little fish. On the Bridge. Kate Greenaway. RHPC
If I Could Shut the Gate [against My Thoughts]. *Unknown.* ElL; HBV-2; LoBV; NOCV; OxBoCh
If I could smell smells with my ears. Curious Something. Winifred Welles. TiPo
If I could stand, gel, goldenly. Come Michaelmas. A. Newberry Choyce. HBMV
If I could start my life again. The Child's Dream. Susan Ludvigson. AMV-80; MAYP
If I Could Tell You. W. H. Auden. *See* Villanelle: "Time can say nothing but I told you so."
If I could tell you. Impasse. Langston Hughes. LiTM
If I Could Touch. William Stanley Braithwaite. BALP
If I Could Trust Mine Own Self. Christina Rossetti. EBCP
If I Could Walk Out into the Cold Country. Elizabeth Brewster. NOBC
If I dare pray for one. A Prayer. Vernon Watkins. PoPl
If I deny my kinship to a man. A Gentle Park. Moss Herbert. GoYe
If I describe my house. The House. George Bowering. NOBC
If I did come of set intent. To Archinus. Callimachus, *tr. by* F. A. Wright. AWP
If I Die a Railroad Man, *with music. Unknown.* AS
If I die, don't take me to the cemetery. Life-Hook. Juana de Ibarbourou, *tr. by* Marti Moody. WPOW
If I die here in a strange land. Song of a Man about to Die in a Strange Land. *Unknown.* DL
If I don't bring you. The Couple. Joel Oppenheimer. CoPo
If I don't drive around the park. Observation. Dorothy Parker. *Fr.* Some Beautiful Letters. FiBHP; InMe
If I drink water while this doth last. Chorus. Thomas Love Peacock. *Fr.* Crotchet Castle. ViBoPo
If I eat one more piece of pie, I'll die! Pie Problem. Shel Silverstein. RHPC
If I entreat this lady that all grace. Sonnet: To a Friend Who Does Not Pity His Love. Guido Cavalcanti, *tr. by* Dante Gabriel Rossetti. AWP
If I Felt Less. Morris Wintchevsky, *tr. fr. Yiddish by* Joseph Leftwich. TrJP
If I Forget Thee. Emanuel Litvinoff. TrJP; VWA
If I forget thee not, New York. A Curse. Irving Feldman. TW
If I found the iron kettle. Choosing a Death. Alberta Turner. LCAP
If I freely may discover. Song. Ben Jonson. *Fr.* The Poetaster, II, ii. AnAnS-2: ElL
If I Go Not, Pray Not, Give Not. *Unknown.* STF
If I go to see the play. Old Stuff. Bert Leston Taylor. HBMV
If I Got My Ticket, Can I Ride? *with music. Unknown.* OuSiCo
If I had a creature's mouth. Suppositions. Margherita Faulkner. AMV-80
If I had a donkey that wouldn't go. *Unknown.* OxNR
If I had a farm, an' no need to be beggin' my bread. The Beggar. H. L. Doak. HBMV
If I Had a Firecracker. Shelley Silverstein. PoSC
If I had a hundred dollars to spend. The Animal Store. Rachel Field. PDV; SoPo; TiPo
If I had a little wife. *Unknown.* OxNR
If I had a nickel. .05. Ishmael Reed. InPK
If I had a shiny gun. Frustration. Dorothy Parker. DBV
If I had a son! A little child. Barren. Rachel, *tr. by* L. V. Snowman. TrJP
If I had a spoon. Clouds. Dorothy Aldis. SoPo
If I had a trunk like a big elephant. If. John Kendrick Bangs. OBCA
If I had a-listened what my mother said. Prison Moan. *Unknown.* OuSiCo
If I had [*or* I'd] as much money as I could spend. Mother Goose. FaFP; HBV-1; OxNR
If I had been a heathen. The Song of the Strange Ascetic. G. K. Chesterton. HBMV
If I had but one year to live. If but One Year. *Unknown.* STF
If I Had but Two Little Wings. Samuel Taylor Coleridge. CH; OHIP (Something Childish, but Very Natural.) OBRV
If I had chosen thee, thou shouldst have been. To Manon, as to His Choice of Her [*or* As to His Choice of Her]. Wilfrid Scawen Blunt. The Love Sonnets of Proteus, VIII. HBV-1; ViBoPo
If I had just one penny. Choice. John Farrar. SiSoSe
If I Had Known. Mary Carolyn Davies. BLPA
If I had known in the morning. Our Own. Margaret E. Sangster. BLPA
If I had known what trouble you were bearing. If I Had Known. Mary Carolyn Davies. BLPA
If I had lightly given at the first. A Lodging for the Night. Elinor Wylie. ErPo
If I Had My Way. *Unknown.* BluL
If I had never known your face at all. Sonnets to Miranda, VIII. Sir William Watson. FaBoBe; HBV-1
If I had only loved your flesh. Song. V. Sackville-West. HBMV
If I had peace to sit and sing. The Singer. Anna Wickham. HBMV; MoBrPo
If I Had Ridden Horses. Theodore Maynard. HBMV
If I had sight enough. The Flesh-Scraper. Andrew Young. ELU
If I had thought thou couldst have died. To Mary. Charles Wolfe. HBV-1; LO; OBEV; OBRV; ViBoPo
If I had trained a gull I'd send it off to Boothbay Harbor. A Ghazel of Absence. Gerrit Lansing. CoPo
If I had wings like Noah's dove. *See* Ef I had wings . . .
If I had wit for to indite. A Secret. *Unknown.* OBSC
If I had won my Wendy. Luck. Evan V. Shute. CaP
If I have any taste, it is hardly. Hunger. Arthur Rimbaud, *tr. by* Edgell Rickword. AWP
If I have complained I hope I have done with it. The Gods. W. S. Merwin. NaP
If I have erred or run a course unfit. To the Right Worthy Knight Sir Fulke Greville. Samuel Daniel. EnRePo
If I have faltered more or less. The Celestial Surgeon. Robert Louis Stevenson. BrPo; EBCP; EBVV; HBV-2; HBVY; MoBrPo; TreFS; TrGrPo; TrPWD; TRV; ViBoPo; WGRP
If I Have Lifted Up Mine Eyes to Admire. Amos N. Wilder. TrPWD
If I Have Made, My Lady, Intricate. E. E. Cummings. CMoP; FaBV; NOBA; PoRA
If I have run my course and seek the pearls. The Marathon Runner. Fenton Johnson. CDC
If I have since done evil in my life. The Sinner-Saint. Wilfrid Scawen Blunt. ACP
If I Have Sinn'd in Act. Hartley Coleridge. NCEP
If I have wounded any soul to-day. My Evening Prayer. Charles H. Gabriel. BLPA; FaBoBe
If I Have Wronged You. Trumbull Stickney. NCEP
"If I hold my breath and do not speak." Ganga. Thomas Blackburn. MoBS
If I hope that Death is a pass. From Skye, Early Autumn. M. L. Michal. PoSH
If I kiss Anthea's breast. Love Perfumes All Parts. Robert Herrick. UnTE
If I knew you and you knew me. At Church Next Sunday. *Unknown.* BLRP
If I knew you and you knew me. To Know All Is to Forgive All. Nixon Waterman. BLPA; TreFT
If I knocked in this dead night. Threshold. Edmund Blunden. HBMV
If I lay waste and wither up with doubt. What Shall it Profit? [*or* Faith]. William Dean Howells. AA; WGRP
If I leave all for thee, wilt thou exchange. Elizabeth Barrett Browning. Sonnets from the Portuguese, XXXV. ViBoPo
If I, like Solomon. O to Be a Dragon. Marianne Moore. CTC; GoYe; PoPl
If I live [*or* grow] to be old, for I find I go down. The Old Man's Wish. Walter Pope. CoMu; OBS
If I make the lashes dark. Before the World Was Made. W. B. Yeats. GTBS-P
If I make up this leaf. Two Pictures of a Leaf. Marvin Bell. LCAP
"If I may trust your love," she cried. Tantalus—Texas [*or* The Llano Estacado]. *Unknown, at. to* Joaquin Miller. CoSo, HBV-1
If I Might Choose. John Anster. OnYI
If I might guess, then guess I would. Dorcas. George Macdonald. OBVV
If I might only love my God and die! If Only. Christina Rossetti. EBCP; OxBoCh; TrCP
If I must go, let it be easy, slow. Improvisation on an Old Theme. Dorothy Livesay. CaP
If I must of my senses lose. Prayer. Theodore Roethke. MP; TwCP
If I needed brandy alone. On Drinking and a New Moon through the Window. Keith Wilson. GP
If I Only Was the Fellow. Will S. Adkin. BLPA
If I painted, I'd paint landscapes. Landscapes. Richard Hugo. GP
If I profane with my unworthiest hand. Shakespeare. *Fr.* Romeo and Juliet, II, v. BiP; SoSe
If I reach out. The Balcony Poems. Douglas Smith. AMV-81
If I really, really trust Him. A Question. *Unknown.* BLRP
If I rest for a moment near The Equestrian. Music. Frank O'Hara. NoP; NYP
If I Ride This Train. Joe Johnson. PoBA
If I said, "Little wives." The Wives. Donald Hall. CoAP

If I say to you "Come, Ponto, want some meat?" My Dog Ponto. Edgar Lee Masters. FM
If I shall ever win the home in heaven. Daniel Gray. Josiah Gilbert Holland. AA; HBV-2
If I should die. Emily Dickinson. MoAB
If I Should Die. Ben King. *See* If I Should Die Tonight.
If I should die and leave you here a while. Turn Again to Life. Mary Lee Hall. BLPL; PoLF
If I Should Die before I Wake. Robert Mezey. *See* Bedtime Story, A.
If I should die, think only this of me. The Soldier. Rupert Brooke. *Fr.* 1914. BrPo; FaBoEn; FaBV; FaFP; FaPoR; FF; FPL; HBV-2; HeIP; LiTB; LiTM; MoBrPo; MoVE; NIP; NOBE; OBEV; OBWP; OxBTC; PoA; PoLF; PoPl; PoRA; TEP; TreF; TrGrPo; ViBoPo; WaP; WHA
If I Should Die Tonight. Ben King. BLPL; FiBHP; HBV-1; InMe; OBAL; PoLF; TreFS; YaD
(If I Should Die.) OBAL
If I Should Die Tonight. Arabella Eugenia Smith. BLPA; HBV-2; TreF
If I Should Ever by Chance. Edward Thomas. FaBoCh; GoJo; HBMV; MoAB; MoBrPo; MoShBr; OBMV; OxBChV
If I should ever need to reach your heart. Understanding. Pauline E. Soroka. PoLF
If I should go away. Postscript for Gweno. Alun Lewis. BoLoP; GTBS-P
If I should labor through daylight and dark. Philosophy. Dorothy Parker. InMe
If I should paint thy portrait, mother dear. My Mother. Bertha Nolan. PGD
If I should pamphleteer twenty years against royalists. To the Ghost of John Milton. Carl Sandburg. PP
If I should pass the tomb of Jonah. Losers. Carl Sandburg. CMoP; HBMV; MoAB; MoAmPo; MoVE; NoAM; TrGrPo
If I should round the corner quickly. The Mythos of Samuel Huntsman. Hyam Plutzik. LiTM
If I Should Sleep with a Lady Called Death. E. E. Cummings. BoLoP; VGW
If I should touch her she would shriek and weeping. Secretary. Ted Hughes. ErPo; InPK
If I shouldn't be alive. Emily Dickinson. FM; TwAmPo
If I sing because I must. Signature. Hannah Kahn. IHMS
If I speak of love you'll think I am like everyone else. Love. Izumi Shikibu, *tr. by* Hiroaki Sato. *Fr.* Fifty-one Tanka. LLLT
If I Stand in My Window. Lucille Clifton. BPo
If I stay quiet, I am always praying. The Scholar's Wife. Susan Mernit. VWA
If I stoop. Faith. Robert Browning. *Fr.* Paracelsus, V. TreFT
If I think myself. The Insidious Dr. Fu Man Chu. Amiri Baraka. CoPo
If I think of a horse wandering about sleeplessly. Night. Robert Bly. NaP
If I told you a rookie. Poker Poem. Michael Pettit. AMV-80
If I want to go to pieces. Occupational Hazards. David Young. FiCP
If I was drawn here from a distant place. To ——— in Church. Alan Seeger. HBV-1
If I was on some foggy mountain top. Foggy Mountain Top. *Unknown.* FSW
If I Went Away. Desmond O'Grady, *tr. fr. Irish.* CIP
If I were a bear. Furry Bear. A. A. Milne. SoPo; TiPo
If I were a Cassowary. Samuel Wilberforce. CenHV
(Impromptu.) FaBoNo
If I were a chipmunk. No Escape. Harriet L. Delafield. GoYe
If I were a cinnamon peeler. The Cinnamon Peeler. Michael Ondaatje. NOBC
If I were a cloud in heaven. Lise. Rose Terry Cooke. AA
If I Were a Pilgrim Child. Rowena Bennett. YeAr
If I Were a Queen. Christina Rossetti. SiSoSe
If I Were a Voice. Charles Mackay. TreF
"If I were a woman," he said. Whore. Linda King. GP
If I were asked to play the part. If I Were on the Stage; or, Kiss Me Again. Henry Blossom. FSN
If I were called in. Water. Philip Larkin. FaBoMo
If I Were Dead. Coventry Patmore. The Unknown Eros, I, 14. ACP; GoBC; HBV-1
If I were dead, and, in my place. A Song to Amoret. Henry Vaughan. HBV-1; ViBoPo
If I were dead in the Desert—as you would like me to be. To a Depraved Lying Woman. Sorley Maclean. NeBP
"If I were dead, you'd sometimes say, 'Poor Child!'" If I Were Dead. Coventry Patmore. *Fr.* The Unknown Eros. ACP; GoBC; HBV-1
If I were fierce, and bald, and short of breath. Base Details. Siegfried Sassoon. DBV; FF; HeIP; MMA; MoBrPo; NIP; SoSe
If I were fire, I'd burn the world away. Sonnet: Of All He Would Do. Cecco Angiolieri da Siena, *tr. by* Dante Gabriel Rossetti. AWP
If I were God, up in the sky. A Child's Thought. Bertha Moore. PaPo
If I were hanged on the highest hill. Mother o' Mine. *Fr.* The Light That Failed. Kipling. FaFP; TRV; WBLP
If I were in a fairy tale. The Duck. Edith King. HBVY
If I were just a fairy small. A Fairy Voyage. *Unknown.* SoPo
If I Were King, *sels.* Justin Huntly M'Carthy.
Ballad of Dead Ladies, A, *fr. ch.* 9, *par. fr. the French of* Villon. HBV-1
If I Were King ("All French folk, whereso'er ye be"), *fr. ch.* 2, *par. fr. the French of* Villon. HBV-1.
If I Were King ("If I were king—ah, love, if I were king"), *introd. poem, par. fr. the French of* Villon. FaFP; PoLF; TreF
If I Were King. A. A. Milne. OnUR
If I were King of France, that noble fine land. The Heather. Neil Munro. OBVV
If I were less the man, I might have kept. Two Sonnets for a Lost Love, II. Samuel A. DeWitt. GoYe
If I were Lord of Tartary. Tartary. Walter de la Mare. HBMV; OxBChV
If I were mild, and I were sweet. Dilemma. Dorothy Parker. InMe
If I Were Old. Will H. Ogilvie. PoSH
If I Were on the Stage. Henry Blossom. *See* Kiss Me Again.
If I were only dafter. Witter Bynner. Spectra: Opus 6. InPK
If I were rich what would I do? Why Tomas [*or* Thomas] Cam Was Grumpy. James Stephens. CMoP; WhC
If I were Sophocles, brave with truth. Kaire. Richard Eberhart. NoAM
If I were stone dead and buried under. Felo de Se. Richard Hughes. OBMV
If I were the kind of man I want. Broads. David R. Slavitt. BXAP
If I were the Prime Minister of Britain. I Don't Like You. Kit Wright. OnUR
If I Were Tickled by the Rub of Love. Dylan Thomas. FF
If I were to see. Grandmother. Ray A. Young Bear. STE
If I were to tell of our labours, our hard lodging. Aeschylus, *tr. by* Louis MacNeice. *Fr.* Agamemnon. WaaP
If I were told that I must die to-morrow. When. "Susan Coolidge." HBV-2
If I were very sure. The Coup de Grace. Edward Rowland Sill. AA
If I were well-to-do. Birthday. D. H. Lawrence. NAs
If I when [*or* If when] my wife is sleeping. Danse Russe. William Carlos Williams. CMoP; InPK; InPS; NOBA; NoP; PPP; TAP
If I, who only sing, in other ways. The New Physician. Stephen Chalmers. HBMV
If Ice. W. W. E. Ross. NOBC; OBCV
If I'd a-known my captain was blind, Darlin', Darlin'. Darlin'. *Unknown.* FSW
If I'd as much money/ As I could tell. *Unknown.* OxNR
If I'd as much money as I could spend. *See* If I had as much money as I could spend.
If ("If all the land were apple-pie"). *Unknown.* NA
If "ifs" and "ands." Proverb. *Unknown.* FaBoBe; HBV-1
If, in an odd angle of the hutment. Eighth Air Force. Randall Jarrell. FF; MiAP; MoVE; NoAM; NOBA; NoP; OBWP; PoCh
If in Beginning Twilight. E. E. Cummings. NYBP
If in his study he [*or* Hammon] hath so much care. Antiquary. John Donne. EBEV; FF; InPK; NIP
If in some far-off, future day. Epitaph for a Cat. Margaret E. Bruner. PoLF
If in that secret place. Barter. Margaret Widdemer. HBMV; WGRP
If in that Syrian garden, ages slain. Easter Hymn. A. E. Housman. CABA; ChMP; EaLo; EBEV; MoAB; OAEP; OFD; SeCeV
If in the fight my arm was strong. The Warrior to His Dead Bride. Adelaide Anne Procter. OBVV
If, in the month of dark December. Written after Swimming from Sestos to Abydos. Byron. InMe; LiSp; MOS; NoP; OBRV
If, in the silent mind of One all-pure. In Utrumque Paratus. Matthew Arnold. OAEP; OBNC; PoEL-5; VLP
If in the World There Be More Woe. Sir Thomas Wyatt. EIL; SiPS
(Disdain.) TrGrPo
(Treizaine.) OBSC
If, in well-bred society, ("hear! hear!"). Nathaniel Parker Willis. *Fr.* The Lady Jane; a Humorous Novel in Rhyme. OBAL
If injured monarchs may their cause explore. A Dialogue between King William and the Late King James on the Banks of the Boyne. Charles Blount. APAS
If it/ Were lighter touch. The Guarded Wound. Adelaide Crapsey. WPE
If it ain't simply this, what is it? Keep Talking. Philip Levine. WeW
If It All Went Up in Smoke. George Oppen. VWA
If It Be Destined. Petrarch, *tr. fr. Italian by* Edward Fitzgerald. Sonnets to Laura: To Laura in Life, XI. AWP
If it be pleasant to look on, stalled in the packed *serai.* Certain Maxims of Hafiz. Kipling. HBV-1
If It Comes. Philip Booth. NCSH
If it do come to pass. Shakespeare. *Fr.* As You Like It, II, v. ViBoPo
If it form the one landscape that looks as bad. Quicksands. William Zaranka. BXAP
If it form the one landscape that we, the inconstant ones. In Praise of

Limestone. W. H. Auden. CABA; CMoP (1973 ed.); CoBMV; FYAP; HAP; MoAB; MoVE; NEPA; NoAM; NoP; OAEL-2; PPP
If It Is Not My Portion. Rabindranath Tagore. *Fr.* Gitanjali. OBMV
If it is only for the taking off. In Praise of Clothes. Erica Jong. MAYP
If it is true that we no longer seek. The Fear of Trembling. John Hollander. NePoEA
If it is you, there/ in the light boat on the pond. Lady Ise, *tr. fr. Japanese by* Etsuko Terasaki *and* Irma Brandeis. BoWoP
If It Looks like Jelly, Shakes like Jelly, It Must Be Gel-a-tine. *Unknown.* BluL
If it must be; if it must be, O God! Sonnet. David Gray. *Fr.* In the Shadows. BSV; OxBS
If It Offend Thee. Horace Gregory. NMP
If it should come to this. A Prospect of Death. Andrew Young. DTC
If it wasn't for me and the likes of me. Madeline at Jefferson Market Night Court. Margaret McGovern. WhC
If it were done when 'tis done, then 'twere well. Vaulting Ambition [*or* The Murder Pact]. Shakespeare. *Fr.* Macbeth, I, vii. FiP; UnPo; WHA
If it were not for the voice. Nakatsukasa, *tr. by* Arthur Waley. *Fr.* Shui Shu. AWP
If it were real/ Perhaps I'd understand it. Ono no Komachi, *tr. fr. Japanese by* Rob Swigart. WPOW
If it were set anywhere else but so. Head Itself. Laura Riding. PoA
If It Would All Please Hurry. James Tate. MAYP
If it would walk at all. Shadow to Shadow. Hervey Allen. HBMV
If Italy is a boot. Italian Woman. Diane Wakoski. GrPl
If It's Ever Spring Again. Thomas Hardy. OxBTC
If it's love, and if, as you say, it's ridiculous. Love's Fool. John Rosenthal. AMV-81
If it's rice-grain, say it's rice-grain. The Lover's Prayer. *Malay Oral Tradition, tr. by* R. J. Wilkinson *and* R. O. Winstedt. WTO
If I've a babe in town, Babe. Belle. *Unknown.* OuSiCo
If, Jerusalem, I Ever Should Forget Thee. Heine, *tr. fr. German by* Margaret Armour. TrJP
If Jesus Came to Your House. *Unknown.* STF
If Jesus Christ is a man. The Song of a Heathen. Richard Watson Gilder. AA; TRV; WGRP
If Justice Moved. Bettie M. Sellers. TW
If life be as a flame that death doth kill. A Rhyme of Life. Charles Warren Stoddard. HBV-2
If life be time that here is spent. Of the Loss of Time. John Hoskyns. FaBoEE
If life were never bitter. If. Mortimer Collins. FiBHP; HBV-1; Par
If Life's a Lousy Picture, Why Not Leave before the End. Roger McGough. OxBTC
If life's pleasures cheer thee. Our Rock. Francis Scott Key. STF
If little mice have birthdays. Birthday Cake. Aileen Fisher. PDV
If livelihood by knowledge were endowed. Mesnevi. Sadi, *tr. by* L. Cranmer-Byng. *Fr.* The Gulistan. AWP
If, Lord, Thy Love for Me Is Strong. St. Theresa of Avila, *tr. fr. Spanish by* Arthur Symons. AWP; PBWP
If love be life, I long to die. Dispraise of Love, and Lovers' Follies. "A. W." EiL; HBV-1; LO; OBSC; TrGrPo
If Love, for Love of Long Time Had. John Heywood. EIL
If love is the greatest reality. Into Their True Gentleness. Pearse Hutchinson. CIP
If love is what would make one offer himself. Coming and Going. Louis Johnson. OCNZ
If love were but a little thing. Song. Florence Earle Coates. HBMV
If Love Were Jester at the Court of Death. Frederic Lawrence Knowles. HBV-2
If love were what the rose is. A Match. Swinburne. ELP; HBV-1; OBVV
If Love's a Yoke. D. C. Berry. AMV-81
If Luther's day expand to Darwin's year. Epilogue. Herman Melville. *Fr.* Clarel. AP; ImOP
If Man Him Bethought. *Unknown.* OxBM
If Man, That Angel of Bright Conciousness. Conrad Aiken. NePA
If Mary came would Mary. A Penitent Considers Another Coming of Mary. Gwendolyn Brooks. NoAM; PChr
If Mary goes far out to sea. Stately Verse. *Unknown.* FaPON; TiPo
If meat the gods give, I the steam. Steam in Sacrifice. Robert Herrick. CaPo
If medals were ordained for drinks. To a Boon Companion. Oliver St. John Gogarty. OBMV
If memory were only in the head. Fine Body. Josephine Clare. FAZ
If men be judged wise. Epigram. Joseph Solomon del Medigo. TrJP
If men may credit give to true reported fames. In Praise of a Gentlewoman. George Gascoigne. EnRePo
If Michael, leader of God's host. The Rose of Peace. W. B. Yeats. OBVV
If mine eyes can speak to do hearty errand. Sapphics. Sir Philip Sidney. *Fr.* Arcadia. SiPS
If mine eyes do e're declare. The Soul. Abraham Cowley. AnAnS-2
If Music [*or* Musique] and Sweet Poetry [*or* Poetrie] Agree. Richard Barnfield. *See* To His Friend Master R. L., in Praise of Music and Poetry.
If Music be the food of love, play on. The Food of Love [*or* Music]. Shakespeare. *Fr.* Twelfth Night, I, i. TreFS; TrGrPo
If my bark sink. Emily Dickinson. TRV
If my best wines mislike thy taste. Quits. Thomas Bailey Aldrich. AA
If, My Darling. Philip Larkin. EBEV; LiTM
If my face could only promise that its color would remain. Face to Face. Frances Cochrane. HBV-1
If my garden oak spares one bare ledge. Creed. Anne Spencer. CDC
If My Hands Were Mute. Manfred Winkler, *tr. fr. Hebrew by* Mary Zilzer. VWA
If My Head Hurt a Hair's Foot. Dylan Thomas. NoAM
If my mother had never been the protected child. House in St. Petersburg. Stanley Burnshaw. VWA
If my nipples were to drip milk. Sappho, *tr. fr. Greek by* Willis Barnstone. BoWoP
If my peculiar pulchritude in Paris seemed to please. An Intermezzo for the Fourth Act. William Allen White. InMe
If, my religion safe, I durst embrace. To Sir Henrie Savile [upon His Translation of Tacitus]. Ben Jonson. OBS; SeCV-1
If my torch goes out it will be dark. Search. Claribel Alegria, *tr. by* Aliki *and* Willis Barnstone. BoWoP
If my vain soul needs blows and bitter losses. Ella Wheeler Wilcox. *Fr.* The Christian's New-Year Prayer. TrPWD
If Nancy Hanks/ Came back as a ghost. Nancy Hanks. Rosemary *and* Stephen Vincent Benét. FaBV; FaPON; NTCP; PoPl; SiSoSe; TiPo
If nature prompts you, or if friends persuade. William Whitehead. *Fr.* A Charge to the Poets. OBSV
If Nature says to you. The Daily Grind. Fenton Johnson. AmNP
If neither brass, nor marble, can withstand. The Power of Time [*or* Shall I Repine]. Swift. FaBoEE; NCEP; PV
If night takes the form of a whale and. Isabel Fraire, *tr. fr. Spanish by* Thomas Hoeksema. BoWoP
If nine times you your bridegroom kiss. The Tithe: To The Bride. Robert Herrick. CaPo
If no love is, O God, what fele I so. Song of Troylus. Chaucer, *after* Petrarch. *Fr.* Troilus and Criseyde. AWP; FF; OAEL-1
If No One Ever Marries Me. Laurence Alma-Tadema. OxBChV; RHPC
If no one sees you, friend. Poem about Your Face. Nathan Alterman, *tr. by* Ruth Nevo. VWA
If none but you in the world today. The Gospel According to You. *Unknown.* STF
If Not. H. A. C. Evans. FaBoPa
If not birds. Blind Panorama of New York. Federico García Lorca, *tr. by* Ben Belitt. NYP
If not for the man. Binding Arbitration. Robert Wrigley. SOTS
If not necessary, is essential. Love. Anne Stevenson. NCSH
If now thou seest me a wreck, worn out and minished of sight. Old Age. Al-Aswad, Son of Ya'fur, *tr. by* Sir Charles Lyall. *Fr.* The Mufaddaliyat. AWP
If now you cannot hear me, it is because. The Barricades. Denise Levertov. NeBP
If, O Maecenas, versed in lore antique. Horace, *tr. fr. Latin by* Sir Theodore Martin. OBVE
If of a beetle you'd make game. "Oh That My Love Were in My Arms." *Malay Oral Tradition, tr. by* R. J. Wilkinson *and* R. O. Winstedt. WTO
If of thy mortal goods thou art bereft. Hyacinths to Feed Thy Soul. Sadi. *Fr.* The Gulistan. BLPA; BLPL; FaBoBe; TRV
If, on Account of the Political Situation. W. H. Auden. *Fr.* For the Time Being. LiTA; WaP
If on my theme I rightly think. Why I Drink. Henry Aldrich. NIP; WhC
If on the Book itself we cast our view. The Scriptures. Dryden. *Fr.* Religio Laici. OBS
If once I could gather in song. Song. W. W. Gibson. OBVV
If Once You Have Slept on an Island. Rachel Field. RHPC
If one could have that little head of hers. A Face. Robert Browning. CTC
If one could only be certain beyond all question. The Anti-Symbolist. Sidney Keyes. MoPo
If one should bring me this report. Of One Dead. Tennyson. In Memoriam A. H. H., XIV. LiTB
If one should tell them what's clearly seen. Crumbs or the Loaf. Robinson Jeffers. CMoP
If Only. Christina Rossetti. EBCP; OxBoCh; TrCP
If only/ The heart had a lid. Swahili Love Song. *Unknown, tr. by* Jan Knappert. LLLT
If only I could love. Before the Dive. Elizabeth Kempf. AMV-81
If only I could send you one small slice. Letter from the Vieux Carre. Ethel Green Russell. GoYe
If only I'd quit fooling round with rhyme. Epistle to the Reader. Walker Gibson. PP

If only in dreams may man be fully blest. The First Kiss. Theodore Watts-Dunton. HBV-1
If only Mr. Roosevelt. E. C. Bentley. *Fr.* Clerihews. CenHV
If only once for every perjured oath. Barine, the Incorrigible. Horace, *tr. by* Louis Untermeyer. Odes, II, 8. UnTE
If only once the chariot of the Morn. The Glory of Nature. Frederick Tennyson. OBNC
If only the brown leaf were gold. Generosity. *Unknown, tr. by* Frank O'Connor. KiLC
If Only the Dreams Abide. Clinton Scollard. HBV-2
If only the phantom would stop reappearing! Faust. John Ashbery. NoP; TwCP
If Only We Understood. *Unknown.* STF
If only, when one heard. *Unknown, tr. by* Arthur Waley. *Fr.* Kokin Shu. AWP
If orange chiffon sadness. Orange Chiffon. Jayne Cortez. BlSi
If origin had lived in these birds. Daybreak. Phillip Yellowhawk Minthorn. STE
If Orpheus' voice [*or* voyce] had force to breathe such music's love. Sir Philip Sidney. Astrophel and Stella, Third Song. PoEL-1; SiPS
If ought of oaten stop, or pastoral song. *See* If aught of oaten stop, or pastoral song.
If out of a dire suspicion. Wet Hair: If Now His Mother Should Come. Robert Penn Warren. *Fr.* Penological Study: Southern Exposure. NoAM
If parting be decreed for the two of us. Parting. Judah Halevi, *tr. by* Nina Davis Salaman. AWP; TrJP
If people ask me. Politeness. A. A. Milne. PoPl
If people came to know where my king's palace is, it would vanish into air. Fairyland. Rabindranath Tagore. WSC
If Pigs Could Fly. James Reeves. OnUR
If Pliny, Lord High Treasurer of all. Painture. Richard Lovelace. CaPo
If poisonous [*or* poysonous] mineral[l]s, and if that tree. Holy Sonnets, IX. John Donne. AnAnS-1; BiP; CABA; EBEV; EnRePo; JCP; LiTB; MasP; MePo; NoP; OAEL-1; OBS; PoEL-2; PPP; SeCP; UnPo; WHA
If poor (you say) she drains her husband's purse. Chaucer, *mod. version by* Pope. *Fr.* The Canterbury Tales: The Wife of Bath's Prologue. OBSV
If Pope Had Written "Break, Break, Break." J. C. Squire. CenHV; FaBoPa ("Break, Break, Break.") BXAP
If poverty be a title to poetry, I am sure nobody can dispute mine. *Fr.* The Beggar's Opera. John Gay. OAEL-1
If questioning could make us wise. Because She Would Ask Me Why I Loved Her. Christopher Brennan. CBAP
If radio's slim fingers can pluck a melody. Proof. Ethel Romig Fuller. TRV
If recollecting were forgetting. Emily Dickinson. AA
If religion was a thing that money could buy. All My Trials. *Unknown.* FSW
If rest is sweet at shut of day. A Roundel of Rest. Arthur Symons. HBV-2
If rightly tuneful bards decide. Amoret. Mark Akenside. HBV-1; OBEV
If Rome so great, and in her wisest age. To Edward Allen (Alleyne). Ben Jonson. OAEP; OBS
If Sackvile, all that have the power to doe. An Epistle to Sir Edward Sackville, now Earl of Dorset. Ben Jonson. NCEP
If sadly thinking, with spirits sinking. The Deserter's Lamentation [*or* The Deserter *or* Let Us Be Merry before We Go]. John Philpot Curran. AnIV; FaBoRV; SeCePo; ViBoPo
If St. Paul be fair and clear. *Unknown.* FaBoUs
If seasons all were summers. The Farm-Woman's Winter. Thomas Hardy. VLP
If seen by many minds at once your image. By the Lake. Lawrence Durrell. *Fr.* Eight Aspects of Melissa. NeBP
If she asks why the sun. To Jann, in Her Absence. C. J. Driver. PeSA
If She Be Made of White and Red. Herbert P. Horne. HBV-1
If she be made of white and red. Shakespeare. *Fr.* Love's Labour's Lost, I, ii. CTC
If she be not as kind as fair. Song. Sir George Etherege. *Fr.* The Comical Revenge; or, Love in a Tub. CavP
If She but Knew. Arthur O'Shaughnessy. HBV-1
If she had been beautiful, even. Of a Woman, Dead Young. Dorothy Parker. SBG
If she had someplace to run to, she would run. Couple. Mary Swope. AMV-81
If She Sang. Gerald W. Barrax. CNA
If she should die (as well suspect we may). Upon Thought Castara May Die. William Habington. *Fr.* Castara. ACP
If Sleep and Death be truly one. In Memoriam A. H. H, XLIII. Tennyson. OBNC
If sloth or negligence the task forbear. Tartar. Solyman Brown. *Fr.* Dentologia; a Poem on the Diseases of the Teeth and Their Proper Remedies. FaBoUs
If snow falls on the far field. Mother's Song. *Unknown, tr. by* Willis Barnstone. BoWoP
If so be a toad be laid. A Charme, or an Allay for Love. Robert Herrick. FaBoCh; FaBoUs
If so it hap, this of-spring of my care. Samuel Daniel. To Delia, III. AAS
If So the Man You Are, *sels.* D. B. Wyndham Lewis. OBSV
"Am I too dangerous, that no man can let."
"I'm no He-man you know, I'm not a He."
"You now solicit a few enemy thrusts."
If some boy were to come to me by night. Guest. E. A. Lacey. PeHV
If Some Grim Tragedy. Ninna May Smith. HBMV
If some nosey body asks "well." Poem for a "Divorced" Daughter. Horace Coleman. LTB
If someone asks you. Mitchell Donian. PoSC
If someone insults you. Autant En Emporte le Vent. Marguerite de Navarre, *tr. by* Aline Allard. PBWP
If someone said, Escape. Longface Mahoney Discusses Heaven. Horace Gregory. VGW
If Someone, Something, somehow (as Man dreams). A Musical Critic Anticipates Eternity. Siegfried Sassoon. UnS
If someone was walking across. A Confession. Robert Mezey. AmPA; NaP
If Something Should Happen. Lucille Clifton. MAT
If sometimes strangeness seems on me to fall. The New House. Joseph Easton McDougall. CaP
If Spirits Walk. Sophie Jewett. AA; HBV-1
If spring should rise like a heron. A Mirage. Ruth Setterberg. AMV-80
If Still They Live. Edith M. Thomas. *Fr.* The Inverted Torch. AA
If strange things happen where she is. On Portents. Robert Graves. FaBoMo
If Suddenly a Clod of Earth. Harold Monro. *Fr.* Strange Meetings. MoBrPo
If suddenly, wonderfully, glittering among the leaves. The Daily Manna. Sara Henderson Hay. GoYe
If sunlight fell like snowflakes. Sunflakes. Frank Asch. NTCP
If the autumn would. Winter Is Another Country. Archibald MacLeish. NCSH
If the Birds Knew. John Ashbery. PoA
If the Black Frog Will Not Ring. Ed Roberson. PoBA
If the butterfly courted the bee. Topsy-turvy World. William Brighty Rands. OxBChV
If the compass of his mind. Specialist. Theodore Roethke. PV
If the day looks kinder gloomy. Just Keep on Keepin' On [*or* Just Try This]. *Unknown.* STF; WBLP
If the deep wood is haunted, it is I. Nocturne. Robert Hillyer. FYAP
If the fat butcher thinks he slays. Mutton. *Unknown.* BXAP
If the First of July be rainy weather. *Unknown.* FaBoUs
If the great outside system—species and stars—proceeds. Across Space and Time. Charles Olson. PoM
If the Heart Be Homeless. Annemarie Ewing. NePoAm-2
If the Heart of a Man. John Gay. *Fr.* The Beggar's Opera, II, i. ELP; HeIP
("If the heart of a man is depress with cares.") EnLoPo
(Would You Have a Young Virgin?) TEP
If the hill overlooking our city has always been known. Vespers. W. H. Auden. FaBoMo
If the lady hath any loveliness, let it die. Blackberry Winter. John Crowe Ransom. OxBA; PoRA
If the lost word is lost, if the spent word is spent. T. S. Eliot. *Fr.* Ash-Wednesday. OxBoCh
If the maiden coughs immediately after. J. H. Thomas. BXAP
If the Man Who Turnips Cries. Samuel Johnson. WhC
(Burlesque [of Lope de Vega].) FaBoCo; FaFP
(Burlesque Translation of Lines from Lope de Vega's "Arcadia.") EBEV
(Epigram.) HBV-1; NOBL
("If a man who turnips cries.") OxNR
(If the Man.) TreFT
(Turnip Crier, The.) PoPle
(Turnip Seller, The.) EvOK
"If the mist comes down, just sit still." Weather Rhymes. Hamish Brown. PoSH
If the moon shines/ On the black pines. What Night Would It Be? John Ciardi. PDV
If the moon smiled, she would resemble you. The Rival. Sylvia Plath. PAI
If the oak is out before the ash. *Unknown.* OxNR
If the Owl Calls Again. John Haines. BoAnP; BoNaP; CoAP; ConAP; HeIP; LCAP; NCSH; NU
If the picture ever moved at all. Grandpa's Picture. Paul Ruffin. Str
If the power of the word is anything, America. Diane DiPrima. Revolutionary Letter 40. GP
If the quick spirits in your eye. Persuasions [*or* Perswasions] to Enjoy [*or* Song: Perswasions to Enjoy *or* Persuasions to Joy; a Song]. Thomas

Carew. AnAnS-1; CaPo; HBV-1; MePo; NOBE; OBEV; SeCP; SeCV-1
If the red slayer think he slays. Brahma. Emerson. AA; AmPP; AP; AWP; BiP; EaLo; HAP; HBV-2; ILwL; LiTA; NePA; NoP; NOBA; OBEV; OBVV; OxBA; PAI; PoRA; SeCeV; TAP; TreF; TrGrPo; UnPo; ViBoPo; WGRP; WHA
If the robin sings in the bush. *Unknown.* PBBP
If the scorn of your bright eyne. Song. Shakespeare. *Fr.* As You Like It, IV, iii. CTC
If the shack get raided ain't no body run. Charlie Cherry. *Unknown.* BluL
If the sons of company directors and judges' private daughters. Palaces of Gold. Leon Rosselson. OBET
If the speed is open. A Piano. Gertrude Stein. *Fr.* Tender Buttons. PBWP
"If the spray-bead gem be won." Joseph Rodman Drake. *Fr.* The Culprit Fay. GN
If the Stars Should Fall. Samuel Allen. IDB; NNP; PoBA
If the sudden tidings came. The World's Justice. Emma Lazarus. HBV-2
If the sun low down in the West, my friend. A Lady to a Lover. Roden Noel. OBVV
If the table was empty before. Silent Movies. Pedro Juan Pietri. InW
If the things of earth must pass. If Only the Dreams Abide. Clinton Scollard. HBV-2
If the time ever came. Poem for Ben Barney. Leslie Silko. CDW; VoR
If the truth were but known, when she came at last. Lady Godiva. Edward Shanks. HBMV
If the twenty-fourth of August be fair and clear. *Unknown.* FaBoUs
If the unfortunate fate engulfing me. Farewell to My Mother. "Placido," *tr. by* James Weldon Johnson. TTY
If the whole of Paris is not quite wholly mine. The Enigmatic Traveler. Byron Vazakas. AMV-80
If the wild bowler thinks he bowls. Brahma. Andrew Lang. BXAP; CenHV; FaBoCo; NOBL
If the woman in the purple petticoat. Give No White Flower. Brenda Chamberlain. NeIP
If the year is meditating a suitable gift. Request to a Year. Judith Wright. CBAP
If There Are Any Heavens. E. E. Cummings. DFF; MoAB; MoAmPo
If there are wild men. In Iceland. Howard McCord. GP
If there be graveyards in the heart. God Bless You, Dear, To-Day! John Bennett. AA; HBV-1
If their bee nothing new, but that which is. Sonnets, LIX. Shakespeare. FaBoEn
If there be some weaker one. Whittier. *Fr.* Andrew Rykman's Prayer. TRV
If There Be Sorrow. Mari Evans. NNP; PoNe
If there exists a hell—the case is clear. To Sir Toby. Philip Freneau. AP; NoP; TAP
If There Had Anywhere Appeared. Richard Chenevix Trench. *See* God Our Refuge.
If there is a man white as marble. Metaphor as Degeneration. Wallace Stevens. LCAP
If There Is a Perchance. Thomas McAfee. AMV-81
If there is no change in the ocean. No Change in Me. *Unknown.* AmFP
If there must be a god in the house, must be. Less and Less Human, O Savage Spirit. Wallace Stevens. VGW
If there was only a road there. The Blue West. Dahlia Ravikovich, *tr. by* Chana Bloch. PBWP
If there were an open way. On One Condition. Charles Madge. EAS
If there were dreams to sell. Dream-Pedlary. Thomas Lovell Beddoes. CH; EnRP; FaBoBe; HAP; LiTB; LoBV; NOBE; OBEV; OBNC; OBRV; OBVV; PoEL-4; TreFS; TrGrPo; ViBoPo; WiR
If there were no past, but specious present only. Speculative Evening. Marguerite Young. LiTA
If there were, oh! an Hellespont of cream. The Author Loving These Homely Meats [*or* Homely Meats *or* Buttered Pippin-Pies]. John Davies of Hereford. *Fr.* The Scourge of Folly. ChTr; ElL; FaBoCh; FaBoNo
If there were sound, the slapping. Tall Tale God. Mark Van Doren. CrMA
If there's a fox, he said, I'll whistle the beggar. Mahony's Mountain. Douglas Stewart. PoAu-2; SeCePo
If there's a wind, we get it. Lobster Cove Shindig. Lillian Morrison. BoNaP
If there's no wick within the lamp. And Tomorrow Wend Our Ways. *Malay Oral Tradition, tr. by* R. J. Wilkinson *and* R. O. Winstedt. WTO
If there's one who often falters. First to Throw a Stone. *Unknown.* STF
If These Endure. Lilith Lorraine. PGD
If they ask, who here doth lie. Epitaph on Sir Walter Pye. John Hoskyns. FaBoEE
If they had cursed the man. A Part-Sequence for Change. Robert Duncan. VGW
If they hint, O Musician, the piece that you played. The Ballad of Imitation. Austin Dobson. HBV-1
If They Honoured Me, Giving Me Their Gifts. "Michael Field." OBMV
If they made any noise in forming. Sinkholes. Janet Reed McFatter. GrPl
If they say my furred cloak. Chanson. Pernette du Guillet, *tr. by* Joan Keefe *and* Richard Terdiman. PBWP
If They Spoke. Mark Van Doren. ImOP
If they true bailiffs be, who for the law maintaining. On Mercenary and Unjust Bailiffs. Henricus Selyns. SCAP
If they wanted freedom. Eeva-Liisa Manner, *tr. by* Jaakko A. Ahokas. *Fr.* Cambrian. PBWP
If they'd been summoned to worship the God of wine, or Pan, or to visit the Queen of Love. Lysistrata. Aristophanes, *tr. by* Charles T. Murphy. NAWM-1
If this ain't the Holy Ghost, I don't know. Holy Ghost. *Unknown.* OuSiCo
If this air were to speak to you. Your Air of My Air. Hugo Margenat, *tr. by* Julio Marzán. InW
If This Be All. Anne Brontë. TrPWD
If this be love, to draw[e] a weary [*or* wearie] breath. To Delia, IX. Samuel Daniel. AAS; GBL; OBSC; TrGrPo
If this brain's over-tempered. I've Tasted My Blood. Milton Acorn. MoCV; NOBC
If this bright lily. A Song at Easter. Charles Hanson Towne. BLRP
If this comes creased and creased again and soiled. Pocket Poem. Ted Kooser. PPJ
If this country were a sea (that is solid rock). Pennines in April. Ted Hughes. PPP
If this divine quiet. Calm. Aldo Camerino, *tr. by* Anita Barrows. VWA
If this is peace, this dead and leaden thing. Dead Fires. Jessie Redmond Fauset. BANP; PoNe
If this is soccer. Late Game. B. H. Fairchild. AMV-81
If this is what we've all been. The Happy Poem. Thomas Brush. LTB
If this life-saving rock should fail. On Middleton Edge. Andrew Young. ELU
If This Little World To-Night. Oliver Herford. *Fr.* The Bashful Earthquake. ShM
(Proem.) AA
If this our little life is but a day. A Sonnet to Heavenly Beauty. Joachim du Bellay, *tr. by* Andrew Lang. AWP; CTC
If this pale rose offend your sight. On Presenting to a Lady a White Rose and a Red on the Tenth of June. William Somervile. OBEC
If this uncertain age in which we dwell. The Lesson for Today. Robert Frost. LiTA; LiTM; NePA; WaP
If this was our battle, if these were our ends. To a President. Witter Bynner. OBAL
If This Were Faith. Robert Louis Stevenson. BrPo; OBNC; TrPWD; WGRP
If this world's friends might see but once. The Seed Growing Secretly. Henry Vaughan. AnAnS-1; OxBoCh; SeCV-1
If thou a reason dost desire to know. To Cynthia: On Her Embraces. Sir Francis Kynaston. GBL; NCEP
If thou art sleeping, maiden. Song. Gil Vicente, *tr. by* Longfellow. AWP
If thou beest he; but O how fall'n! how chang'd. Milton. *Fr.* Paradise Lost, I. SCV
If thou be'st ice, I do admire. The Miracle. Sir John Suckling. CaPo
If thou canst fashion no excuse. To His Friend J. H. Alexander Brome. CavP
If thou canst wake with me, forget to eate. John Ford. *Fr.* The Lover's Melancholy, IV, ii. PoEL-2
If thou didst feed on western plains of yore. To a Goose [*or* Gosse]. Robert Southey. BXAP; FM; NOBL
If thou dislik'st the piece thou light'st on first. To the Sour[e] Reader. Robert Herrick. AnAnS-2; NoP; OAEP; SeCP
If thou hast squander'd years to grave a gem. A Charge. Herbert Trench. HBV-2; OBEV; OBVV
If thou hast wisdom, hear me, Celia. Ben Jonson. *Fr.* Volpone, III, vii. ViBoPo
If thou in surety safe wilt sit. Look or You Leap [*or* The Lookers-On]. Jasper Heywood. ACP; ElL
If Thou Indeed Derive Thy Light from Heaven. Wordsworth. EnRP; OBRV; TrCP; VLP
If thou must love me, let it be for naught [*or* nought]. Sonnets from the Portuguese, XIV. Elizabeth Barrett Browning. CTC; FaFP; HBV-1; HeIP; LiTB; NOBE; OBEV; OBNC; OBVV; TreFS; TrGrPo; UnPo; ViBoPo; WHA; WPE
If Thou, O God, the Christ didst leave. Prayer of a Modern Thomas. Edward Shillito. PGD
If thou of fortune be bereft. Not by Bread Alone. *Unknown, tr. by* James Terry White. PoLF; TreFT
If thou seekest the dread throne of God on earth. On Our Lady of Blachernae. *Unknown, tr. by* Shane Leslie. ISi

If thou serve a lord of prise. A Warning to Those Who Serve Lords. *Unknown.* MeEL
If thou shouldst bid thy friend farewell. Counsel. Mary Evelyn Moore Davis. HBV-2
If thou shouldst ever come by choice or chance. Ginevra. Samuel Rogers. BeLS; PoLF
If thou survive my well-contented day. Sonnets, XXXII. Shakespeare. EIL; GTBS; GTBS-P; HBV-1; OBSC; PP
If Thou Wert by My Side, My Love. Reginald Heber. HBV-1
If thou wert lying cold and still and white. Reconciliation. Caroline Atherton Briggs Mason. AA
If thou wilt come and dwell with me at home. Daphnis to Ganymede. Richard Barnfield. *Fr.* The Affectionate Shepherd. EIL
If Thou Wilt Ease Thine Heart. Thomas Lovell Beddoes. *See* Dirge: If Thou Wilt Ease Thine Heart.
If Thou Wilt Hear, *with music.* John Grave. AH
If thou wilt love me, thou shalt be my boy. Richard Barnfield. *Fr.* The Affectionate Shepherd. PBBP
If Thou Wilt Mighty Be. Sir Thomas Wyatt. EnRePo
("If thou wilt mighty be, flee from the rage.") SiPS
If thou wouldest roses scent. Francis Daniel Pastorius. SCAP
If thou wouldst have me speak, Lord, give me speech. The Preacher's Prayer. George Macdonald. TRV
If Thou Wouldst Know. Hayyim Nahman Bialik, *tr. fr. Hebrew by* Harry H. Fein. TrJP
If thou wouldst learne, not knowing how, to pray. A Forme of Prayer. Francis Quarles. MePo
If thou would'st stand on Etna's burning brow. Our Traveller. Henry Cholmondeley-Pennell. InMe
If thou would'st view fair Melrose aright. Melrose Abbey [*or* Sir William of Deloraine at the Wizard's Tomb]. Sir Walter Scott. *Fr.* The Lay of the Last Minstrel, II. FaBoPP; OBNC; OBRV; SeCePo
If through my perjured lips Thy voice may speak. A Prayer for a Preacher. Edward Shillito. TrPWD
If through the eyes the heart speaks clear and true. Waiting in Faith. Michelangelo. ILwL
If thy sad heart, pining for human love. Sarah Helen Whitman. Sonnet (From the Series Relating to Edgar Allan Poe), VI. AA
"If thy wife is small bend down to her &." Ian Wedde. Earthly: Sonnets for Carlos, 9. OCNZ
If tired of trees I seek again mankind. The Vantage Point. Robert Frost. CoBMV; OxBA
If to be absent were to be. To Lucasta, [on] Going beyond the Seas [*or* To Lucasta]. Richard Lovelace. AnAnS-2; CaPo; FaBoEn; GTBS; GTBS-P; HBV-1; LiTB; LoBV; MeLP; MOS; OAEP; OBEV; OBS; PoPle; SeCP; SeCV-1; TreFT; ViBoPo
If to demands of others I agree. Resolving Doubts. William Dickey. ErPo
If to Die. Myrtle Romilu. BLRP
If to the Pump Room in the morn we go. *Unknown.* *Fr.* The Diseases of Bath; a Satire. NOEC
If to your twilight land of dream. In Memoriam—Leo: A Yellow Cat. Margaret Sherwood. BLPA
If (touched by love's own secret) we, like homing. E. E. Cummings. PoA
If 'Trane had only seen. Poem No. 21. Doughtry Long. CNA
If trees were tall and grasses short. By the Babe Unborn. G. K. Chesterton. NAs
If true that notion, which but few contest. *Unknown.* FaBoEE
If 'twere the time of lilies. To the Lady Radegunde, with Violets. Venantius Fortunatus, *tr. by* Helen Waddell. NAWM-1
If waker care, if sodayne pale coulor. Sir Thomas Wyatt. AAS
If wandering in a wizard's car. To Helen. Winthrop Mackworth Praed. HBV-1
If we are truly free, and live in a free country. Turning Away from Lies. Robert Bly. LCAP
If we, as we are, are dust, and dust, as it will, rises. Snow. Charles Wright. LCAP
If We Believed in God. Jessie Wiseman Gibbs. BLRP
If We Break Faith. Joseph Auslander. TRV
If We Cannot Live as People. Charles Lynch. CNA; PoBA
If we could get the hang of it entirely. Entirely. Louis MacNeice. CMoP; LiTB
If we could push ajar the gates of life. God's Plans. Mary Riley Smith. BLRP
If We Didn't Have Birthdays. "Dr. Seuss." RHPC
If We Didn't Have to Eat. Nixon Waterman. OBAL
"Life would be an easy matter," *sel.* FiBHP
If we dreamed that we loved her aforetime. To San Francisco. S. J. Alexander. PAH
If we gave unto the living as we lavish on the dead. Give to the Living. Ida Goldsmith Morris. WBLP
If we had dope for an excuse, or love. In Memory of My First Chapatis. Diane di Prima. PoM
If we had lived on that long-gone day. Crucifixion. Mrs. Roy L. Peifer. STF
If we hate the rush hour subways. One Year to Life on the Grand Central Shuttle. Audre Lorde. CNA
If We Knew. May Riley Smith. BLPA
If we lay bound upon the wheel of change. Sir Edwin Arnold. *Fr.* The Light of Asia, VIII. VLP
If We Must Die. Claude McKay. AmNP; AmPP; BALP; BANP; BPo; CABA; FaBV; IDB; NoAM; PoBA; PoNe; PPP; TTY; UnPo
If we must part. A Valediction. Ernest Dowson. BoLoP
If we must stand alone. As Rocks Rooted. Howard G. Hanson. AMV-80
If we shadows have offended. Epilogue. Shakespeare. *Fr.* A Midsummer Night's Dream, V, ii. OBSC
If we shall live, we live. Meeting. Christina Rossetti. GBL
If we square a lump of pemmican. Scientific Proof. J. W. Foley. QQQ
If we stayed with each other long enough. The River Again and Again. Linda Gregg. NPGG
If we're to be anywhere at all. The Torch. Greg Forker. LFAC
If what began (look far and wide) will end. Conclusion. John Frederick Nims. PoA
If what heals can bless. Come Green Again. Winfield Townley Scott. PoPl
If what I find I do not love. Resignation. Santob de Carrion, *tr. by* George Ticknor. TrJP
If what we fought for seems not worth the fighting. Lines for the Hour. Hamilton Fish Armstrong. HBMV
If what you want is jobs. Revolutionary Letter # 9. Diane Di Prima. IHMS
If when Don Cupid's dart. Love's Offence. Sir John Suckling. CaPo
If When I Die. William Fowler. EIL
If, when I kneel to pray. Prayer. Charles Francis Richardson. AA
If when my wife is sleeping. *See* If I when my wife is sleeping.
If when the sun at noone displayes. A Beautifull Mistress. Thomas Carew. OBS
If when the wind blows. Daniel Webster's Horses. Elizabeth J. Coatsworth. AmFN; MoAmPo; OBCA; PH
If, whittler and dumper, gross carver. The Arc Inside and Out. A. R. Ammons. NoAM; NoP
If wine and musick have the pow'r. A Song. Matthew Prior. LoBV
If wisdom, as it seems it is. Epigram. J. V. Cunningham. QFR
If wisdom's height is only disenchantment. A Word to the Wise. Caroline Duer. AA
If wishes were horses. Mother Goose. FaBoBe; HBV-1; OxNR
If wit or honesty cou'd save. An Epitaph on True, Her Majesty's Dog. Matthew Prior. FM
If with complaint the pain might be express'd. Sir Thomas Wyatt. SiPS
If with light head erect I sing. Inspiration. Henry David Thoreau. AA; BLPL; FaBoBe; HBV-2; WGRP, *abr.*
If with pleasure you are viewing any work a man is doing. Do It Now. Berton Braley. BLPA; FaFP; WBLP
If Women Could Be Fair. Edward de Vere, Earl of Oxford. EIL; OAEP (Renunciation, A.) GTBS; GTBS-P; HBV-1
If wrath embitter the sweet mouth of song. Apologia. Swinburne. VLP
If ye fear to be affrighted. A Charm. Robert Herrick. ChTr
If ye will with Mab find grace. The Fairies. Robert Herrick. FaPON; OBS
If yet I have not all thy love. Lovers' Infiniteness[e]. John Donne. AnAnS-1; EIL; FaBoEn; LiTB; MeLP; OAEL-1; OBS; PoEL-2; SeCP; SeCV-1
If yet there be a few that take delight. Prologue. Dryden. *Fr.* The Loyal General (*by* Nahum Tate). SeCV-2
If yet thine Eyes (Great Henry) may endure. The Epistle of Rosamond to King Henry the Second. Michael Drayton. AnAnS-2
If yo' brother done you wrong. You Fight On. *Unknown.* AS
If You. Robert Creeley. NeAP; NoAM; NOBA
If you all will shut your trap. The Tramp. Joe Hill. FSW
If you are/ in Spain. Drowning in Spain. Tom Schmidt. NeAC
If you are a delicate man. A Warning. Alexander Nicolson. PoSH
If you are a gentleman. *Unknown.* OxNR
If you are a revolutionary. The Reactionary Poet. Ishmael Reed. CNA
If you are bound to till a soil where farms. A Letter from the Country. Howard Baker. TwAmPo
If you are determined and wishful to go. Railroad to Hell. *Unknown.* VLP
If You Are Fire. Isaac Rosenberg. ChMP
If you are merry sing away. Mirth. Christopher Smart. *Fr.* Hymns for the Amusement of Children. LAuP; OxBChV
If you are on the Gloomy Line. Get a Transfer. *Unknown.* BLPA; WBLP
If you are still alive when you read this. Goodbye. William Knott. EAS
If you are tempted to reveal. Three Gates. Beth Day, *after the* Arabian. BLPA; TreFS

If you ask for the cause of our national flaws. Eureka! Alfred Denis Godley. CenHV
If you ask me whence the story. Goosey Goosey Gander—by Various Authors (Longfellow's Version). William Percy French. CenHV
If you be that May Margaret. May Margaret. Théophile Marzials. HBV-1
If you become a nun, dear. The Nun. Leigh Hunt. HBV-1; InMe; OBRV; OBVV
If You But Knew. *Unknown.* BLPA; FaBoBe
If You Can Hear My Hooves. Harold Littlebird. STE; VoR
If you can keep your head when all about you. If. Kipling. BLPA; FaBoBe; FaFP; FaPoR; FPL; HBV-2; HBVY; OHFP; OxBChV; OxBTC; PaPo; TreF; WBLP
If you can lie, Torquatus, when you take. Horace, *tr. fr. Latin by* John Conington. OBVE
If you can make life brighter. Humble Service. Lillian G. Heard. STF
If you cannot on the ocean. Your Mission. Ellen M. H. Gates. BLPA; BLRP; TreFT
If you cannot speak like angels. Something You Can Do. *Unknown.* STF
If you can't be a pine on the top of the hill. Be the Best of Whatever You Are. Douglas Malloch. BLPA; YaD
If You Can't Eat You Got To. E. E. Cummings. CMoP; PrIm
If you can't trim your sails to suit the weather. If Not. H. A. C. Evans. FaBoPa
If you c'n keep alive when li'l bleeders. A London Sparrow's If. J. A. Lindon. BoAnP
If You Come Back. Jack Cope. PeSA
If you come here and it is barely fall. At Pont-Aven, Gauguin's Last Home in France. Andrew Grossbardt. AMV-81
If you come my way that is. Poem from Llanybri. Lynette Roberts. NeBP
If You Come Softly. Audre Lorde. AmNP
If you could bring her glories back! Babylon. Ralph Hodgson. BrPo; HBMV
If you could crowd them into forty lines! Limitations. Siegfried Sassoon. MoBrPo
If you could see, fair brother, how dead beat. Prolonged Sonnet: When the Troops Were Returning from Milan [*or* When the Troops Were Returning from Milan]. Niccolò degli Albizzi, *tr. by* Dante Gabriel Rossetti. AWP; OBVE; WaaP
If you desire to paralyze. The Better Way. Walter Leaf. FaBoCo
If you do love, as well as I. The Thought. Lord Herbert of Cherbury. AnAnS-2; InvP; LoBV
"If you do love me weel, Willie." Fair Janet. *Unknown.* ESPB
If you do not shake the bottle. On Tomato Ketchup. *Unknown.* FaBoUs
If you don't know [how], why pretend? To the Tune "Red Embroidered Shoes." Huang O, *tr. by* Kenneth Rexroth *and* Ling Chung. PBWP; WPOW
If you don't know the kind of person I am. A Ritual to Read to Each Other. William Stafford. NePA
If you don't like my apples. *Unknown.* GBP; OxBoLi
If you don't quit monkeying with my Lulu. Lulu. *Unknown.* CoSo
If you evah go to Houston. Midnight Special. *Unknown.* AS
If you ever, ever, ever meet a grizzly bear. Grizzly Bear. Mary Austin. BPAW; FaPON; GoJo; OnUR; PDV; SoPo; TiPo
If you ever get there. Going. Robert Kelly. CoPo
If you for orders, and a gown design. John Oldham. *Fr.* A Satyr Address'd to a Friend That Is About to Leave the University, and Come Abroad in the World. OBS
If you give me your attention, I will tell you what I am. The Disagreeable Man. W. S. Gilbert. FiBHP
If you go away,/ why should I adorn myself? *Tr. fr. Japanese by* Kenneth Yasuda. BoWoP
If you go over desert and mountain. The Fountain of Tears. Arthur O'Shaughnessy. OBVV
If you had asked of me. The Idol. Louise Driscoll. HBMV
If You Had Known. Thomas Hardy. FaBoRV; GBL
If you had lived in that more stately time. Sonnets to Miranda, II. Sir William Watson. HBV-1
If You Happy Would Be, *with music.* Abraham Fernández. AH
If you hate the British Army, clap your hands. Ballymurphy. *Unknown.* FSW
If You Have a Friend. *Unknown.* FaFP
(Say It Now.) BLPA; WBLP
If you have a thing to do. Do It Right. Samuel O. Buckner. WBLP
If you have climbed a laden apple tree. Afternoon in a Tree. Sister Maris Stella. GoBC
If you have ever, like me. Please Excuse Typing. J. B. Boothroyd. FiBHP
If you have forgotten water-lilies floating. Water-Lilies. Sara Teasdale. MoAmPo
If you have formed a circle to go into. To God. Blake. OAEL-2
If you have lost the radio beam, then guide yourself by the sun or the stars. Any Man's Advice to His Son. Kenneth Fearing. CMoP
If you have no time. Izumi Shikibu, *tr. fr. Japanese by* Willis Barnstone. BoWoP
If you have revisited the town, thin Shade. To a Shade. W. B. Yeats. AnIL; LiTB; PoEL-5
If you haven't any ideas. Deny Yourself. Christopher Morley. YaD
If you haven't made noise enough to warn him, singing, shouting. Meeting a Bear. David Wagoner. HAP
If you hear a kind word spoken. Tell Him So. *Unknown.* BLPA; BLPL; WBLP
If you hear rustling in the straw. David Philips. BXAP
If You Hear That a Thousand People Love You. Guadalupe de Saavedra. PAI
If you hold a blue rock to your ear. Why Stone Does Not Sing by Itself. Anita Endrezze-Danielson. STE
If you iron tonic need. Dietary Advice. *Unknown.* FaBoUs
If you know about the Babylonian Jews. Straus Park. Gerald Stern. NYP
If you listen, I'll sing you a sweet little song. My Wild Irish Rose. Chauncey Olcott. BLSo; FSN; FSW; TreFT
If you live where I come from. Excerpts from the Notebook of the Poet of Santo Tomas. Richard Shelton. GP
If you look out from some high, high window. Sweet Loving Friendship. Peter Bellamy. OBET
If you love God, take your mirror between your hands and look. Song. Mahmud Djellaladin Pasha, *tr. by* E. Powys Mathers. ErPo
If you love me. Izumi Shikibu, *tr. fr. Japanese by* Willis Barnstone. BoWoP
If you love me, as I love you. Samuel Hoffenstein. FiBHP
If you must crack it. Easter Egg. Alan Kieffaber. AMV-80
If you must draw mere beauty. Design for a Stream-lined Sunrise. Sister Mary Madeleva. GoBC
If you never do anything for anyone else. The Immoral Proposition. Robert Creeley. LiTM; NeAP; PoM
If you, O Aynabo, my fleet and fiery horse. Battle Pledge. *Somali Oral Tradition, tr. by* M. Laurence. WTO
If you plant grain. A Robin's Poem. Nikki Giovanni. AmNP
If you really care for me. *Unknown, tr. fr. Spanish by* Willis Barnstone. BoWoP
If You Saw a Negro Lady. June Jordan. IHMS; NMM
If you see a tall fellow ahead of a [*or* the] crowd. Forget It. *Unknown.* PoLF; WBLP
If you see my mother, partner, tell her pray for me. Mack Maze. WTO
If you see someone beautiful. Epigram. Adaios, *tr. by* Alistair Elliot. PeHV
If You See This Man. Thomas Lux. AmPA
If you shortened many a road and put a halo. Raftery's Dialogue with the Whiskey. Padraic Fallon. DTC
If you should go before me, dear, walk slowly. Walk Slowly. Adelaide Love. BLPA
If You Should Lightly. Trumbull Stickney. NCEP
If you should look for this place after a handful of lifetimes. Tor House. Robinson Jeffers. LoBV
If you should meet a crocodile. *Unknown.* OnUR; PDV; SoPo
If you should see a man. The Truth [*or* Voice in the Crowd]. Ted Joans. AmNP; BOLo; TTY
If You Should Tire of Loving Me. Margaret Widdemer. HBMV
If you sit down at set of sun. Count That Day Lost [*or* At Set of Sun]. "George Eliot." PoPl; TreFT; TRV
If you smoke a cigarette. A Cigarette. *Mongol Oral Tradition, tr. by* C. R. Bawden. WTO
If you spin me around until I'm so dizzy. Six of Cups. Diane Wakoski. CoPo
If you stay to school dinners. *Unknown.* WTO
If you stop caressing me. My True Memory. Asya, *tr. by* Gabriel Preil *and* Howard Schwartz. VWA
If you strike a thorn or rose. Keep a-Goin'. Frank L. Stanton. FaFP; OHFP; WBLP
If you take the moon in your hands. The Moon in Your Hands. Hilda Doolittle ("H. D."). BoWoP; NYBP
If you tell them something truthful. Father and Sons. Harvey Shapiro. FAZ
If you, that have grown old, were the first dead. The New Faces. W. B. Yeats. GTBS-P; MoVE
If you think you are beaten, you are. Thinking [*or* The Man Who Thinks He Can]. Walter D. Wintle. PoLF; SoSe; WBLP
If you wake at midnight, and hear a horse's feet. A Smuggler's Song. Kipling. *Fr.* Puck of Pook's Hill. OxBChV; PoPle
If you walked past the lot on any good Sunday. The Wrecker Driver Foresees Your Death. David Baker. MAYP
If you wander far enough. Oh No. Robert Creeley. HeIP; InPK; NaP
If you want a great revival. Pray, Christian, Pray! *Unknown.* STF
If you want higher wages let me tell you what to do. Talking Union. Lee Hays, Millard Lampell, *and* Pete Seeger. FSW
If you want my apartment, sleep in it. Rent. Jane Cooper. FYAP; TAP

If you want to drive wrinkles from belly and brow. Eating Song. Sir Walter Ralegh. WhC
If you want to find the sergeant. The Old Battalion. *Unknown.* OBET
If you want to get to heaven, let me tell you what to do. Talking Blues. *Unknown.* FSW
If You Want to Go a-Courting, *with music.* *Unknown.* TrAS
If you want to go to heaven. The Blood-strained Banders. *Unknown.* AmFP; OuSiCo
If You Want to Go to Heben. *Unknown.* GBP
If you want to have the kind of a church. It Isn't the Church—It's You. *Unknown.* BLPA; WBLP
If you want to know where the privates were. Where They Were. *Unknown.* AS
If you want to live in the country. The Power of Maples. Gerald Stern. NU
If you want to live in the kind of a town. It Isn't the Town, It's You. R. W. Glover. BLPA
If you want to work in the kind of a church. It's You. L. A. McDonald. STF
If you want to write me a letter. Si Me Quieres Escribir (If You Want to Write Me). *Unknown, tr. fr. Spanish.* FSW
If you watch. This Evening, without Blinking. Pattiann Rogers. AMV-80
If you were a Chinese born in America, who would you believe. A Chinaman's Chance. Marilyn Chin. BrSi
If you were an owl. That's What We'd Do. Mary Mapes Dodge. OBCA
If you were busy being kind. If. Rebecca Foresman. WBLP
If you were coming in the Fall. Emily Dickinson. AmPP; AP; NOBA; OxBA; PoRA
If you were exchanged in the cradle and/ your real mother died. A Story That Could Be True. William Stafford. NTCP
If you were going to get a pet. If You. Robert Creeley. NeAP; NoAM
If You Were Here. Philip Bourke Marston. HBV-1
If you were just in keeping our pact of love. Wallāda, *tr. fr. Arabic by* A. R. Nykl. PBWP
If you were only one inch tall, you'd ride a worm to school. One Inch Tall. Shel Silverstein. OBCA
If you were queen of bloaters. A Catch. Tom Hood. CenHV
If you were so innocent. Survival in a Stone Maze. George Rachow. LFAC
If you were twenty-seven. Heaven. Philip Levine. LCAP; NaP
If You Will. Josephine Miles. GP
If you will come on such a day. The Gardener. Sidney Keyes. ChMP; MoAB; MoBrPo
If you will listen a while I will sing you a song. Jim Fisk. *Unknown.* ViBoFo
If you will tell me why the fen. I May, I Might, I Must. Marianne Moore. ELU; FF; OBAL
If you wish to live for ever. *Unknown.* FaBoUs
If you wish to pull a cork. Lilliputian's Beer Song. Septimus Winner. OBAL
If you would happy company win. Titmouse. Walter de la Mare. BrPo
If you would have dark themes and high-flown words. Insights. Catherine Davis. NePoEA
If you would know the love which I you bear. Sir John Davies. *Fr.* Sonnets to Philomel. SiPS
If you would learn. The Antiquary. Joseph Campbell. OxBTC
If you would run. For the Running of the New York City Marathon. James Dickey. NYP
If you would work one small miracle. Prison. Paul David Ashley. LFAC
If you your lips would keep from slips. Our Lips and Ears. *Unknown.* BLPA; TreF; WBLP
If you'd have me go on loving you. Ezra Pound. *Fr.* Impressions of François-Marie Arouet (de Voltaire). MoAB
If you'd rather not to kiss then say so then. Rebuff. Samuel L. Albert. NePoAm-2
If you'll come gather round me, I'll sing you a song. Lone Driftin' Riders. *Unknown.* CoSo
If you'll listen a while, I'll sing you a song. Jim Fisk. *Unknown.* AS
If you'll listen awhile I'll sing you a song. The Road to Cook's Peak. *Unknown.* CoSo
If your brother has a burden. A Helping Hand. Georgia B. Adams. STF
If your friend has got a heart. Your Friend. *Unknown.* TreFT
If your man gets personal. Traveling Riverside Blues. *Unknown.* BluL
If you're anxious for to shine in the high aesthetic line as a man of culture rare. Bunthorne's Song: The Aesthete. W. S. Gilbert. *Fr.* Patience. EBVV; FiBHP; LiTB; NBM; OAEL-2; VLP
If You're Ever Going to Love Me. *Unknown.* BLPA
If you're in London, Will'um, then I take it you're en route. To William Allen White. Edna Ferber. InMe
If you're longing for fun or enjoyment. Duffy's Hotel. *Unknown.* ShS
If you're not home, where. Numbers, Letters. Amiri Baraka. BPo; NOBA
If you're so out of love with happiness. John Oldham. *Fr.* A Satire Addressed to a Friend. OBSV
If You're the Man You Ought to Be. Walter E. Isenhour. STF
If you're Volunteer Artist or Athlete, or if you defend the Home. "Form Fours." Frank Sidgwick. WhC
If you've ever been in a car. Stun. James Schuyler. MAT
If you've ever been one. Misnomer. Eve Merriam. RHPC
If you've got a job to do. Do It Now! *Unknown.* BLPA; FaFP; WBLP
If You've Never. Elsie M. Fowler. SoPo
Ifa divination was performed for Tiger. Tiger. *Yoruba Oral Tradition, tr. by* B. King. WTO
Ifa speaks in parables. *Yoruba Oral Tradition, tr. by* J. A. Adedîji. WTO
Ignorance of Death. William Empson. CMoP; CoBMV; LiTM; NoAM
Ignorance of Man, The. James Merrick. OxBoCh
Ignorant dawn of William Butler Yeats, The. We Love You the Way You Are. David McFadden. NeAC
Ignorant Ida. Isabel Frances Bellows. TDH
Ignorant, in the sense. Death of an Irishwoman. Michael Hartnett. CIP
Ignorant men, who disclaim. Sister Juana Inés de la Cruz, *tr. by* Judith Thurman. *Fr.* A Satirical Romance. PBWP
Ignorant present has scribbled over the past, The. Louis Dudek. Europe, XXXI. PeCV
Ignorant two, we glide. On Minding One's Own Business. James Wright. PoPl
Ignore dull days; forget the showers. Lesson from a Sun-Dial. *Unknown.* TiPo
Ignotum per Ignotius, or a Furious Hodge-Podge of Nonsense; a Pindaric. *Unknown.* NOEC
Ignu. Allen Ginsberg. NaP
Ijajee's Story. Charlotte DeClue. STE; TWSS
Ike Walton's Prayer. James Whitcomb Riley. AA
Ikons, The. James K. Baxter. OCNZ
"Il Est Cocule Chef de Gare!" H. S. Mackintosh. WhC
I'l gaze no more on her bewitching face. Murdering Beauty. Thomas Carew. OAEP
Il Insonio Insonado, *sel.* Nathaniel Whiting.
 Office of Poetry, The. OBS
Il Janitoro. George Ade. OBAL
Il Morgante Maggiore, *sel.* Luigi Pulci, *tr. fr. Italian by* Byron.
 Appeal for Illumination, Canto I, ii. ISi
Il Pastor Fido, *sels.* Sir Richard Fanshawe, *after the Italian of* Giovanni Battista Guarini.
 "Fair Golden Age! When milk was th' onely food." OBVE
  (Golden Age, The.) OAEL-1
 Fall, The. MePo; OBS
  (Great Favorit Beheaded, A.) OBVE
 Hope. OBS
 "How I forsook." AWP
 "Learn women all from this housewifery." OBVE
 Now War Is All the World About. LoBV
  (Ode on His Majesty's Proclamation.) NOBE
  (Ode, upon Occasion of His Majesties Proclamation in the Year 1630, An.) MePo; OBS
 Of Beauty. BoLoP
  (Beauty.) GBL
 "Our beauty is to us that which to men." OBVE
 Rose, A. CavP; HBV-1; OBEV; OBS; PoEL-2; SeCePo
  (Rose of Life, The.) AWP
 "Well may that kisse be sweet that's giv'n t' a sleek." OBVE
Il Penseroso. Milton. AWP; CABA; FiP; GTBS; GTBS-P; HAP; HBV-2; HoPM; JCP; LiTB; MasP; NoP; OAEL-1; OBEV; OBS; PPP; SeCeV; TEP; TrGrPo; ViBoPo; WHA
 "Sweet bird that shunn'st the noise of folly," *sel.* CH
Il Piccolo Rifiuto. Louis MacNiece. CMoP
Il pleut doucement sur la ville. Paul Verlaine, *tr. fr. French by* Ernest Dowson. AWP; BrPo
 ("Tears fall within my heart," *tr. by* Ernest Dowson.) SyP
 ("Tears in my heart that weeps," *tr. by* Arthur Symons.) SyP
Ile [*or* I'l] gaze no more on her bewitching face. Song: Murdring Beautie [*or* Murdering Beauty]. Thomas Carew. AnAnS-2; OAEP; SeCP
Ile give thee leave my love, in beauties field. Earl of Stirling. Aurora, XXVI. OxBS
Ile sooth his plots: and strow my hate with smiles. George Chapman. *Fr.* Bussy D'Ambois, IV, ii. PoEL-2
I'le tell you a tale of my love and I. *See* I'll tell you a tale . . .
Ilex Tree, The. Agnes Lee. PoA
Iliad, The, *much abr.* Homer, *tr. fr. Greek by* Robert Fitzgerald. NAWM-1
 Sels.
 Achilles Shows Himself in the Battle by the Ships, *fr.* XVIII, *tr. by* George Chapman. OBS
 Achilles to Lycaon, *fr.* XXI, *tr. by* Richmond Lattimore. WaaP

"Achilles with wild fury in his heart," *fr.* XXII, *tr. by* Robert Fitzgerald. OBWP
"Ajax the swift swerv'd never from the side," *fr.* XIII, *tr. by* William Cowper. OBVE
"All grave old men, and souldiers they had bene, but for age," *fr.* III, *tr. by* George Chapman. OBVE
"And as in winter time when Jove his cold-sharpe Javelines throwes," *fr.* XII, *tr. by* George Chapman. OBVE
"And as when with the West-wind's flawes the sea thrusts up her waves," *fr.* IV, *tr. by* George Chapman. OBVE
"And now was Paris come/ From his high towres," *fr.* VI, *tr. by* George Chapman. OBVE
"And when they came together in one place," *fr.* IV, *tr. by* Tennyson. OBVE
Andromache's Lamentation, *fr.* XXIV, *tr. by* Congreve. OBVE
"As when an architect some palace wall," *fr.* XVI, *tr. by* William Cowper. OBVE
"As when devouring flames some forest seize," *fr.* II, *tr. by* William Cowper. OBVE
"As when of frequent bees," *fr.* II, *tr. by* George Chapman. OBVE
"As when the winds, ascending by degrees," *fr.* IV, *tr. by* Pope. OBVE
"At her departure his disdain return'd," *fr.* I, *tr. by* Dryden. OBVE
"At this th' impatient hero sowrly smil'd," *fr.* I, *tr. by* Dryden. OBVE
"Big with great purposes and proud, they sat," *fr.* VIII, *tr. by* William Cowper. OBVE
"But ere sterne conflict mixt both strengths, faire Paris stept before," *fr.* III, *tr. by* George Chapman. OBVE
"But now, no longer deaf to honour's call," *fr.* VI, *tr. by* Pope. OBVE
Death of Hector, The, *fr.* XXII, *tr. by* George Chapman. OBS
"Embodied close, the lab'ring Grecian train," *fr.* V, *tr. by* Pope. OBVE
"Fierce they drove on, impatient to destroy," *fr.* XIII, *tr. by* Pope. OBVE
"Frail as the leaves that quiver on the sprays," *fr.* VI, *tr. by* Samuel Johnson. OBVE
Funeral Games for Patroclus, The: The Boastful Boxer, *fr.* XXIII, *tr. by* Ennis Rees. LiSp
Funeral Games for Patroclus, The: Wrestling to a Draw, *fr.* XXIII, *tr. by* Ennis Rees. LiSp
Ghost of Patroclus, The, *fr.* XXIII, *tr. fr. Greek by* Pope. PeHV
"Greeks dismay'd, confus'd disperse or fall, The," *fr.* XV, *tr. by* Pope. OBVE
Helen's Lamentation, *fr.* XXIV, *tr. by* Congreve. OBVE
"His hand came out of the east," *fr.* XVI, *tr. by* Christopher Logue. OBVE
"Hornets occasionally build their nests near roads," *fr.* XVI, *tr. by* Christopher Logue. OBVE
"Like leaves on trees, the race of man is found," *fr.* VI, *tr. by* Pope. OBVE
"Meanwhile Achilles, plung'd," *fr.* I, *tr. by* Edward, Earl of Derby. PoPl
"Meanwhile the troops beneath Patroclus' care," *fr.* XVI, *tr. by* Pope. OBVE
Nestor, *fr.* XXIII, *tr. by* Ennis Rees. LiSp
Night Encampment outside Troy, *fr.* VIII, *tr. by* Tennyson. RoGo
(Trojans outside the Walls, The, *tr. by* George Chapman.) OBVE
"Nor lingered Paris in the lofty house," *fr.* VI, *tr. by* Tennyson. OBVE
"Nor long the trench or lofty walls oppose," *fr.* XII, *tr. by* Pope. OBVE
"Now front to front the hostile armies stand," *fr.* III, *tr. by* Pope. OBVE
"Now side by side, with like unweary'd care," *fr.* XIII, *tr. by* Pope. OBVE
"Now when the solemn rites of pray'r were past," *fr.* I, *tr. by* Dryden. OBVE
"Now, when twelve days complete had run their race," *fr.* I, *tr. by* George Chapman. OBVE
"Oileus by his brother's side stood close," *fr.* XIII, *tr. by* George Chapman. OBVE
Parting of Hector and Andromache, The, *fr.* VI, *tr. by* William B. Smith *and* Walter Miller. TreFS
(Hector and Andromache, *tr. by* Pope.) OBEC
(Hector to Andromache, *tr. by* Richmond Lattimore.) WaaP
("She, with his sight made breathless haste to meet him," *tr. by* George Chapman.) ViBoPo
Patroclus' Body Saved, *fr.* XVII, *tr. by* E. R. Dodds. WaaP
Priam and Achilles, *fr.* XXIV, *tr. by* George Chapman. OBS *tr. by* Pope. OBEC
Pyre of Patroclus, The, *fr.* XXIII, *tr. by* Pope. OBEC
Sarpedon to Glaukos, *fr.* XII, *tr. by* Richmond Lattimore. WaaP
(Sarpedon's Speech, *shorter sel., tr. by* George Chapman.) OBS
("Thus to Glaucus spake/ Divine Sarpedon," *tr. by* Sir John Denham.) OBVE
"So Hector spake; the Trojans roared applause," *fr.* VIII, *tr. by* Tennyson. OBVE
"So saying, light-foot Iris passed away," *fr.* XVIII, *tr. by* Tennyson. OBVE
"Son of Enops, Thestor next he smote, The," *fr.* XVI, *tr. by* William Cowper. OBVE
"Their ardour kindles all the Grecian pow'rs," *fr.* XII, *tr. by* Pope. OBVE
"Their ground they stil made good," *fr.* V, *tr. by* George Chapman. OBVE
"Then first he form'd th' immense and solid shield," *fr.* XVIII, *tr. by* Pope. OBVE
"Then rising in his rage above the shores," *fr.* XXI, *tr. by* Pope. OBVE
"There sate the seniors of the Trojan race," *fr.* III, *tr. by* Pope. OBVE
"This said, he reacht to take his sonne," *fr.* VI, *tr. by* George Chapman. OBVE
"This speech all Troyans did applaud," *fr.* VIII, *tr. by* George Chapman. OBVE
"Thus at the panting dove a falcon flies," *fr.* XXII, *tr. by* Pope. OBVE
"Troops exulting sate in order round, The," *fr.* VIII, *tr. by* Pope. OBVE
"Unweary'd watch their list'ning leaders keep, Th'," *fr.* X, *tr. by* Pope. OBVE
"Why boast we, Glaucus! our extended reign," *fr.* XII, *tr. by* Pope. OBVE
" 'Why dost thou so explore,' " *fr.* VI *tr. by* George Chapman. OBVE
"Wrath of Peleus son, O muse, resound, The," Invocation, *tr. by* Dryden. OBVE
Iliad. Humbert Wolfe. MoBrPo
Ilicet. Theodosia Garrison. PoLF
Ilion, Ilion. Tennyson. LoBV
Ilkla Moor. *Unknown.* FaBoPP
(Ilkley Moor Baht 'At.) FSW
Ill. Bernard Spencer. NeBP
I'll act out a weird dream. Marie-Francoise Prager, *tr. fr. French by* Willis Barnstone *and* Elene Kolb. BoWoP
Ill-advised, An/ And foolish thing. Episode of the Cherry Tree. Mildred Weston. PV
Ill-advised, in these parts, to shout. The Dam, Glen Garry. Robert Symmens. PoSH
I'll always dress in black and rave. Christine de Pisan, *tr. fr. French by* Willis Barnstone. BoWoP
I'll ask for a red rose blossoming in the snow. The Princess. Sara Henderson Hay. DFT
I'll Aye Ca' in by Yon Town. Burns. BSV
I'll be an otter, and I'll let you swim. River-Mates. Padraic Colum. AnIV; AWP
I'll Be Fourteen Next Sunday. *Unknown.* AmFP; OLR
I'll be going home today. Bunky Boy Bunky Boy Who's My Little Bunky Boy. Larry Mollin. NeAC
I'll be the strongest amid you. The Strongest. "Yehoash," *tr. by* Marie Syrkin. TrJP
I'll Be Your Epitaph. Leonora Speyer. HBMV
I'll believe then that you are dead. Then I'll Believe. B. W. Vilakazi, *tr. by* Jack Cope. PeSA
I'll build a house of arrogance. Haven. Donald Jeffrey Hayes. AmNP; PoNe
I'll Build My House. Amanda Benjamin Hall. HBMV
Ill busi'd man! why should'st thou take such care. My Midnight Meditation. Henry King. MePo; OBS
I'll buy you a tartan bonnet. *Unknown.* OxNR
I'll call thy frown a headsman, passing grim. To My Lady. George Henry Boker. *Fr.* Sonnets. AA
I'll carry you off. Fragment of an Agon. T. S. Eliot. LiTB
I'll Come to Thee. Robert Herrick. UnTE
(To Electra.) CaPo
I'll come to thee in all those shapes. To Electra. Robert Herrick. CaPo
I'll come when thou art saddest. Emily Brontë. VLP
I'll do what the raids suggest. A Boy. John Ashbery. DiL; NeAP
I'll eat when I'm hungry, I'll drink when I'm dry. Rye Whisky. *Unknown.* CoSo; OxBoLi
"Ill fares the land to hastening ills a prey." On Vital Statistics. Hilaire Belloc. POL
Ill fares the land, to hastening ills a prey. The Common Man. Goldsmith. *Fr.* The Deserted Village. OBSV; TreFT; TRV
I'll find me a spruce. Christmas Tree. Aileen Fisher. PDV
I'll Find My Self-Belief. Jacob Glatstein, *tr. fr. Yiddish by* Ruth Whitman. VWA
I'll frame, my Heliodora! a garland for thy hair. A Garland for Heliodora. Meleager, *tr. by* "Christopher North." AWP
I'll Give My Love a Light and Friendly Kiss, *with music. Unknown.* OuSiCo
"I'll give to you a paper of pins." Paper of Pins. *Unknown.* AmFP; BLSo; FSW
I'll give you the weight of my hands. Tonight When You Leave. Gayle Elen Harvey. AMV-81
I'll go into the bedroom silently and lie down between the bridegroom and the bride. Love Poem on Theme by Whitman. Allen Ginsberg. CAPP; NaP
I'll go, said I, to the woods and hills. The Apostate. A. E. Coppard. OBMV
I'll go up on the mountain top. Liza Jane [*or* Mountain Top]. *Unknown.* AS

I'll go where You want me to go, dear Lord. Think It Over. *Unknown.* STF
I'll Go with Her Blues. *Unknown.* BluL
I'll greet the sun once more. Once More. Forugh Farrokhzad, *tr. by* Jascha Kessler *and* Amin Banani. BoWoP
I'll Have a Collier for My Sweetheart. William Oliver. WTO
I'll have you by the short and curly hair. Catullus, *tr. fr. Latin by* James Michie. PeHV
I'll just take my greenery. No Mixed Green Salad for Me, Thanks. Georgie Starbuck Galbraith. QQQ
I'll keep your shirt white. *Turkish Death Songs, tr. by* Reza Baraheni *and* Zahra-Soltan Shokoohtaezeh. BoWoP
Ill lay he long, upon this last return. John Berryman. *Fr.* Dream Songs. TAP
I'll lay you five hundred pounds. The Broomfield Hill. *Unknown.* AmFP
I'll lick these screwfaced torches all night long. Fat Tuesday. W. S. Di Piero. MAYP
Ill Luck. Baudelaire, *tr. fr. French by* Roy Campbell. *Fr.* The Flowers of Evil. PoPl
Ill Met by Zenith. Ogden Nash. NYBP
I'll Never Get Drunk Any More. *Unknown.* OnYI
I'll Never Love Thee More. James Graham, Marquess of Montrose. GBL; HBV-1; NOBE; OBEV; PoPle
"I'll never reach forty," my mother would say. She'd Say. Frank Davey. NOBC
I'll Never Use Tobacco. *Unknown.* FaBoUs
I'll not forget the warm blue night when my bold girl. A Thing Remembered. *Unknown, tr. by* E. Powys Mathers. ErPo
I'll Not Marry at All. *Unknown.* AmFP
I'll not touch wood nor, fingers crossed. Favour. Robert D. Fitzgerald. CBAP
I'll not weep that thou art going to leave me. Stanzas. Emily Brontë. LoBV; WPE
Ill Omens. Thomas Moore. PoEL-4
I'll prop her, I swear, ankle, butt and chin. The Nude on the Bathroom Wall. Gena Ford. IHMS
I'll Remember You, Love, in My Prayers. *Unknown.* BLPA; FaBoBe
(When the Curtains of Night Are Pinned Back, *with music.*) AS
I'll rest me in this sheltered bower. The Arbour. Anne Brontë. EBVV
I'll Sail upon the Dog-Star. Thomas Durfey. *Fr.* A Fool's Preferment. FaBoCh; OxBoLi
Ill sat to be with the calm, The. Essentials. Samuel Greenberg. LiTA
I'll sing of heroes, and of kings. Love. Abraham Cowley, *after the Greek of* Anacreon. AWP; OBVE
I'll sing of Hildebrand Montrose. I'll Strike You with a Feather. Arthur Lloyd. VLP
I'll sing you a good old song. The Fine Old English Gentleman. *Unknown.* CH; HBV-1
I'll sing you a new ballad, and I'll warrant it first-rate. The Fine Old English Gentleman; New Version. Charles Dickens. CoMu; FaBoBa; OBSV
I'll sing you a song/ Nine verses long. *Unknown.* OxNR
I'll sing you a song/ The days are long. *Unknown.* OxNR
I'll sing you a song about two true lovers. William Taylor. *Unknown.* OBET
I'll sing you a song and it'll be a sad one. *See* I'll sing you a song, though it may be a sad one.
I'll sing you a song and it's not very long. Young Man Who Wouldn't Hoe Corn. *Unknown.* FSW
I'll sing you a song, not very long. His Heart Was True to Poll. Francis Cowley Burnand. HBV-2
I'll sing you a song of a schooner of fame. The Loss of the *Druid.* *Unknown.* ShS
I'll sing you a song of Peace and Love. Whack Fol the Diddle. Peadar Kearney. FiBHP; OnYI
I'll sing you a song of the world and its ways. Six Feet of Earth. *Unknown.* BLPA
I'll sing you a song that has often been sung. Brigham Young. *Unknown.* CoSo
I'll sing you a song, though it may be a sad one [*or* and it'll be a sad one]. Sioux Indians. *Unknown.* AmFP; CoSo
I'll sing you a true song of Billy the Kid. Billy the Kid. *Unknown.* BPAW; CoSo; FaBoBe; FSW
I'll sing you one-O [*or* twelve O]. Carol of the Numbers [*or* The Dilly Song *or* Green Grow the Rushes]. *Unknown.* AmFP; FSW; GBP; OBET; OxBoLi
I'll sit down again, Steve, with your shy ghost. For Steve. Earle Birney. WaP
I'll Strike You with a Feather. Arthur Lloyd. VLP
I'll Take You Home Again, Kathleen. Thomas P. Westendorf. FSW; PSoN, *with music*; TreF
I'll teach my sons. My Sons. Ron Loewinsohn. DFF; NeAP
I'll tell all you skinners. Pete Orman. *Unknown.* BPAW
I'll tell my own daddy. *Unknown.* OxNR
I'll tell thee everything I can. The White Knight's Song [*or* The Aged Aged Man *or* A-Sitting on a Gate *or* Ways and Means *or* The White Knight's Ballad]. "Lewis Carroll." *Fr.* Through the Looking-Glass. BXAP; FaBoCh; FaBoCo; FaBoNo; FaBoPa; FiBHP; HAP; InPS; InvP; NA; NOBE; NOBL; NoP; OAEL-2; OxBChV; Par; PoRA; SpRo; VLP
I'll tell you a story/ About Jack a Nory. Mother Goose. HBV-1; OxNR
I'll tell you a story, a story anon. King John and the Bishop. *Unknown.* ESPB
I'll tell you a story about Omie Wise. Omie Wise. *Unknown.* FSW
I'll tell you a story of a row in the town. Erin Go Braugh! *Unknown.* FSW
I'll tell you a story that will thrill you, I know. Pattonio, the Pride of the Plain. *Unknown.* CoSo
I'll tell you a story that's not in Tom Moore. Please to Ring the Belle. Thomas Hood. HBV-2
I'll [*or* I'le] tell you a tale of my love and I. The Shepherd [*or* Shepheard] and the Milkmaid. *Unknown.* CoMu; UnTE
I'll tell you everything, I give you my word! "Shatnes" or Uncleanliness. Eliezer Steinberg, *tr. by* Seth L. Wolitz. VWA
I'll tell you how the leaves came down. How the Leaves Came Down. "Susan Coolidge." HBV-1; HBVY
I'll tell you how the sun rose. Emily Dickinson. AmPP; AP; FaBV; MoShBr; PDV; PoEL-5; SiSoSe; SUS; TAP; TreFS
I'll tell you of a come-lye young lady fair. Fair Phoebe and Her Dark-eyed Sailor. *Unknown.* AmFP
I'll tell you of a wild Colloina boy. The Wild Colloina Boy. *Unknown.* AmFP
I'll tell you the story of Jimmy Jet. Jimmy Jet and His TV Set. Shel Silverstein. CTBA; OBCA; RHPC
I'll Tell You What a Flapper Is. Anne Hobson Freeman. GrPl
"I'll tell you what a tank is." There's Nothing Polite about a Tank. John Paul Minarik. LFAC
I'll tell you what I heard that day. Upon the Hill before Centreville. George Henry Boker. PAH
I'll tell you why I'm afraid of the dark. Dark. Eloise Klein Healy. AMV-80
Ill-tempered Lover, The, *sel.* L. A. Mackay.
"I wish my tongue were a quiver the size of a huge cask." OBCV
(I Wish My Tongue Were a Quiver.) TW
I'll twine white violets and the myrtle green. Meleager, *tr. fr. Greek by* Goldwin Smith. NIP
"I'll wager, I'll wager, I'll wager with you." The Broomfield Hill. *Unknown.* ESPB
I'll wake you and shake you. To the Laggards. Joseph Bovshover, *tr. by* Joseph Bovshover. TrJP
I'll Wear a Shamrock. Mary Carolyn Davies. SiSoSe; YeAr
I'll Wear Me a Cotton Dress. *Unknown.* BPo
Ill Wind, The. Jay Macpherson. MoCV
I'll write a poem, then sink to dreams. Count William's Escapade. Guillaume de Poitiers, *tr. by* Hubert Creekmore. ErPo
I'll write, because I'll give. To Critics. Robert Herrick. CaPo; PV
I'll write no more of love, but now repent. On Himself. Robert Herrick. CaPo
I'll write no more verses—plague take 'em! Those Flapjacks of Brown's. Bert Leston Taylor. OBAL
Illa iuventus, that is so nise. Fearful Death. *Unknown.* MeEL
Ille Terrarum. Robert Louis Stevenson. OxBS
Illegitimate Things. William Carlos Williams. MoAB; MoAmPo
Illi Morituri. Mary Morison Webster. PeSA
Illicit. D. H. Lawrence. *See* On the Balcony.
Illiterate, The. William Meredith. NoP
Ill's the airt o the Word the day. Idleset. Thurso Berwick. OxBS
Illumination, The. Stanley Kunitz. GP; TAP
Illumination and Ecstasy. *Tr. fr. Arabic, at. to* Baba Kuhi of Shiraz. ILwL
Illumination for Victories in Mexico. Grace Greenwood. PAH
Illuminations, *sels.* Arthur Rimbaud, *tr. fr. French.*
After the Flood, *tr. by* Enid Rhodes Peschal. SOTW
Childhood. ("This idol with black eyes and yellow hair"), *tr. by* T. Sturge Moore. SyP
Dawn, *tr. by* Enid Rhodes Peschal. SOTW
IV from Childhood, *tr. by* Louise Varèse. PoPl
Lice Seekers, The. *tr. by* Kenneth Koch *and* Georges Guy. SOTW
Royalty, *tr. by* Enid Rhodes Peschal. SOTW
Illusion. Sir Edmund Gosse. SyP
Illusion. Ella Wheeler Wilcox. WGRP
Illusion forms before us like a grove. The Triumph of Death. Barbara Howes. MoAmPo; NePoAm-2
Illusions, The: they fit like an iron lung, and. Memorandum/ The Accountant's Notebook. Kathleen Norris. OBAL
Illustration, The/ is nothing to you without the application. To a Steam

Roller. Marianne Moore. BoWoP; CMoP; FaBoMo; MoAB; MoAmPo; OxBA; PP; VGW
Illustration, The—a Footnote. Denise Levertov. PoA
Illustrious Ancestors. Denise Levertov. AmPP; NoAM; NOBA; VGW
Illustrious Holland! hard would be his lot. Byron. *Fr.* English Bards and Scotch Reviewers. OBRV; OBSV
Illustrious monarch of Iberia's soil. Columbus to Ferdinand. Philip Freneau. OBCA; PAH
Illustrious One, in whom death is the vagrom wound. Singing Death. Stan Rice. FYAP
Illyrian woodlands, echoing falls. To E.L., on His Travels in Greece. Tennyson. SeCePo
Illyria's hair fell down. The Oracular Portcullis. James Reaney. ErPo; PeCV
I'm/ lost. Supermarket. Felice Holman. QQQ
I'm a Baby. Cid Corman. GP
I'm a blizzard from the Brazos on a tear, hear me hoot. The Bad Man from the Brazos. *Unknown.* CoSo
I'm a broken-hearted Gardener, and don't know what to do. The Broken-hearted Gardener. *Unknown.* ChTr; GBP
I'm a Decent Boy from Ireland, *with music. Unknown.* ShS
I'm a decent boy just landed. No Irish Need Apply. *Unknown.* FSW; WTO
I'm a Dreamer. Kattie M. Cumbo. BlSi
I'm a fashionable beau, just turn'd out the newest go. The Dandy O. *Unknown.* CoMu
I'm a freeborn man of the travelling people. Freeborn Man. Ewan MacColl. OBET
I'm a gay puncher, fresh from the Pecos Flat. The Pecos Puncher. *Unknown.* CoSo
I'm a gay tra, la, la. Swiss Air. Bret Harte. NA
I'm a grandchild of the gods. The Complaint of New Amsterdam. Jacob Steendam. PAH
I'm a gwine [*or* I'm-a goin'] to tell you bout de comin' ob [*or* of] de Saviour. In Dat Great Gittin'-up Mornin'. *Unknown.* AA; BoAN-2
I'm a happy miner, I love to sing and dance. The Happy Miner. *Unknown.* CoSo
I'm a heartbroken raftsman, from Greenville I came. Jack Haggerty. AmFP; ViBoPo
I'm a howler from the prairies of the West. The Desperado. *Unknown.* CoSo; TreFS
I'm a lean dog, a keen dog, a wild dog, and lone. Lone Dog. Irene Rutherford McLeod. FaPON; GDP; PDV; RHPC; TiPo
I'm a little butterfly. *Unknown.* OxNR
I'm a little Hindoo. *Unknown.* FaFP
I'm a lonely bullwhacker. The Bullwhacker. *Unknown.* CoSo
I'm a peevish old man with a penny-whistle. Beggar's Serenade. John Heath-Stubbs. BoLoP; ErPo; NeBP
I'm a pig, I'm a seagull. The Animals. Stephen Berg. NaP
I'm a poor cotton weaver as many one knows. The Poor Cotton Weaver [*or* Jone o' Grinfield]. *Unknown.* OBET; VLP
I'm a poor little girl. The Wagoner's Lad. *Unknown.* AmFP
I'm a poor lonesome cowboy. Poor Lonesome Cowboy. *Unknown.* AS
I'm a rambler and a gambler. Rambling Gambler. *Unknown.* CoSo
I'm a rambling wretch of poverty, from Tip'ry town I came. The Son of a Gambolier. *Unknown.* AS
I'm a riddle in nine syllables. Metaphors. Sylvia Plath. HeIP; InPK; SoSe
I'm a Rollin', *with music. Unknown.* BoAN-1
I'm a Roman Jew and I've been Roman. A Roman Roman. Crescenzo del Monte, *tr. by* Barbara Garvin. VWA
I'm a six foot t'ree from Brooklyn. Situation Normal. Hank Chernick. WhC
I'm a snake doctor man. Snake Doctor Blues. *Unknown.* BluL
I'm a Soldier in the Army of the Lord. *Unknown.* AmFP
I'm a stable cat, a working cat. The Stable Cat. Leslie Norris. PChr
I'm a strange contradiction; I'm new and I'm old. A Book [*or* A Riddle]. Hannah More. GN; PoSC
I'm a strange creature, for I satisfy women. Riddle. *Unknown, tr. by* Kevin Crossley-Holland. PV
I'm a Stranger Here ("Ain't it hard to stumble"). *Unknown.* FSW
I'm a Stranger Here. ("Hitch up my buggy, saddle my black mare"), *with music. Unknown.* OuSiCo
I'm a stranger here just blowed in your town. Doggin' Me Around Blues. *Unknown.* BluL
I'm a stranger in your city, [and] my name is Paddy [*or* Patty] Flynn. Portland County Jail. *Unknown.* AS; FSW
I'm a tiger in the rain. Sad Day in Berlin. Sarah Kirsch, *tr. by* Gerda Mayer. PBWP
I'm a walking down the track. 900 Miles. *Unknown.* FSW
I'm a weaver, a Calton weaver. The Calton Weaver. *Unknown.* FSW
I'm a young lad, Jack Rollins by name. Blooming Sally. *Unknown.* OBET
I'm a young married man that is tired of [*or* in] life. Cod Liver Oil [*or* Ile]. *Unknown.* FSW; OuSiCo
I'm a-goin' to tell you 'bout the comin' of a new day. Great Getting Up Morning. *Unknown.* FSW
I'm Agoing to Lay Down My Sword, *with music. Unknown.* AH
I'm Alabama bound. Alabama Bound. *Unknown.* FSW
I'm a-layin' around, just spendin' muh time. The Strawberry Roan. Curley W. Fletcher. BPAW
I'm all alone in this world, she said. 50—50. Langston Hughes. NoAM; NOBA
I'm Alone in the Evening. Michael Rosen. RHPC
I'm always/ most surprised. Justice. Petra von Morstein, *tr. by* Rosemarie Waldrop. BoWoP
I'm always told to hurry up. Going to Bed. Marchette Chute. PDV
I'm an Old Cowhand. Johnny Mercer. OBAL
I'm as free a little bird as I can be. Free Little Bird. *Unknown.* AmFP; FSW
I'm as mild-mannered as can be. The Popular Wobbly. T-Bone Slim. FSW
I'm at the edge. Here Be Dragons. Ginny Friedlander. AMV-80
I'm a-tellin' you the truth and not lying nor joking. Cheyenne. *Unknown.* CoSo
I'm beginning to lose patience. W. H. Auden. PV
I'm beginning to understand that man in old boots. Beginning to Understand. Ruth Stone. GP
I'm Black and Blue. Heine, *tr. fr. German by* John Todhunter. AWP
I'm bored to extinction with Harrison. Lim'ricks and Puns. *Unknown.* TDH
I'm bound to follow the long-horn cows. The Lone Star Trail. *Unknown.* CoSo
I'm by myself. Up in the Pine. Nancy Dingman Watson. RHPC
I'm called by the name of a man. *Unknown.* OxNR; PBBP
I'm Captain Jinks of the Horse Marines. Captain Jinks. *Unknown, at. to* T. Maclagan *or* William Horace Lingard. BLPA; BLSO; FaFP; FSW; TreF
I'm ceded, I've stopped being theirs. Emily Dickinson. SBG; ViBoPo; WPOW
I'm cold in hand can't get nothing here. No Woman No Nickel. *Unknown.* BluL
I'm comin' back and haunt you, don't you fret. Ghost. John V. A. Weaver. HBMV
I'm Coming I'm Coming. Edgar Jackson. Three Songs, II. LFAC
"I'm corrupt," he said to me in the French. The Corrupt Man in the French Pub. Brian Higgins. OxBTC
I'm cross with god who has wrecked this generation. John Berryman. *Fr.* Dream Songs. FaBoMo
I'm dead drunk this morning, daddy. Dead Drunk Blues. *Unknown.* BluL
I'm determined to be an old maid. I'll Marry Not at All. *Unknown.* AmFP
I'm discontented with homes that are rented. Tea for Two. Irving Caesar. BLSo
I'm displaying here my authentic Yankee ignorance. Wreathmakertraining. Karl Patten. FAZ
I'm down, good Fate, you've won the race. Thrown. Ralph Hodgson. HBMV
I'm dreaming now of Hally [*or* Hallie], sweet Hally, sweet Hally. Listen to the Mocking-Bird. Septimus Winner. BLSO; FSW; PSoN; TrAS; TreFT
I'm driving my car back to you filled. The Furniture of the Poem. Dennis Saleh. NeAC
I'm eating alone lately. Things of Late. David Phillips. NeAC
I'm far frae my hame, an' I'm weary aftenwhiles. My Ain Countree. Mary Lee Demarest. TRV; WGRP
I'm flagging to South Carolina. Long Distance Moan. *Unknown.* BluL
I'm folding up my little dreams. My Little Dreams. Georgia Douglas Johnson. BANP; BlSi; CDC; PoNe
I'm fonder of carats than carrots. I Take 'Em and Like 'Em. Margaret Fishback. PoPl; WhC
I'm frigid when I wear see thru negligees. I Never Saw a Man in a Negligee. Alta. GP
I'm full of everything I do not want. Sonnet: Of the 20th of June 1291. Cecco Angiolieri da Siena, *tr. by* Dante Gabriel Rossetti. AWP
I'm getting old and feeble and I cannot work no more. The Old Miner's Refrain. *Unknown.* AmFP
I'm Glad. *Unknown.* HBVY
(Cheerfulness.) TreFT
("I'm glad the sky is painted blue.") RHPC; SoPo; WhC
I'm glad I am living this morning. God's World. Mildred Keeling. BLRP
I'm glad I walk'd. How fresh the meadows look. Walking to the Mail. Tennyson. VLP
I'm glad our house is a little house. Song for a Little House. Christopher Morley. FaPON; TreF

I'm glad that I/ Live near a park. The Park. James A. Tippett. SUS; TiPo
I'm glad that I am born to die. Shout for Joy. *Unknown.* AmFP
I'm glad the sky is painted blue. I'm Glad [*or* Cheerfulness]. *Unknown.* HBVY; RHPC; SoPo; TreFT; WhC
I'm goin' away baby take me seven long months to ride. Big Chief Blues. *Unknown.* BluL
I'm goin' away for to stay a little while. He's Gone Away. *Unknown.* AS; FSW; TrAS
I'm Goin' [*or* Going] down This Road Feelin' [*or* Feeling] Bad. *Unknown.* FSW; TrAS, *with music*
I'm goin' downtown, gonna get me a sack of flour. Keep My Skillet Good and Greasy. *Unknown.* FSW
I'm goin' get up in the morning. I Believe I'll Dust My Broom. *Unknown.* BluL
I'm goin' out West, down on the Rio Grande. Alice B. *Unknown.* AS
I'm goin' where them chilly winds don' [*or* won't] blow, darlin' baby. Chilly Winds. *Unknown.* OuSiCo; TrAS
I'm going away. Going Away Blues. *Unknown.* BluL
I'm going away for to leave you, love. The Storms Are on the Ocean. *Unknown.* FSW
I'm going back where I come f'm. Old Dog Blue. *Unknown.* BluL
"I'm going down," she said, tying her yellow scarf. Going down the Mountain [*or* Descending] . Valentin Iremonger. EnLoPo; NeIP
I'm Going down This Road Feeling Bad. *Unknown.* *See* I'm Goin' down This Road Feelin' Bad.
I'm going home/ friends, sit down. That's No Way to Get Along. *Unknown.* BluL
I'm going out to clean the pasture spring. The Pasture. Robert Frost. BiP; BLPL; CMoP; FaPON; GoJo; MoAB; MoAmPo; MoShBr; NOBA; OxBA; PDV; PoPl; SoPo; SUS; TiPo; ViBoPo
I'm going out to dine at Gray's. Ballade of Hell and of Mrs. Roebeck. Hilaire Belloc. MoVE
I'm going over to 3rd Alley lord, but I'm gonna carry my 45. 45 Pistol Blues. *Unknown.* BluL
I'm going softly all my years in wisdom if in pain. Babylon. Viola Taylor. HBV-1
I'm going to be just like you, Ma. A Dance for Ma Rainey. Al Young. NBP
I'm going to break out. Carmen Valle, *tr. fr. Spanish by* Julio Marzán. InW
I'm going to California. Bina Mossman, *tr. fr. Hawaiian by* S.H. Elbert *and* N. Mahoe. WTO
I'm Going to Georgia. *Unknown.* AmFP
I'm going to Germany—I'll be back some day. Going to Germany. *Unknown.* BluL
I'm going to leave old Texas now. The Texas Song. *Unknown.* CoSo
I'm Going to Rocky Island. *Unknown.* AmFP
I'm going to sing you a brand new song. The Other Side of Jordan. *Unknown.* FSW
I'm going to the North on the left rail. Going to the North. Stanislaw Wygodski, *tr. by* Isaac Komem. VWA
I'm going to write a novel, hey. An Ode. John Updike. FiBHP
I'm go'n' to [*or* gonna] lay down my sword and shield. Ain' Go'n' to Study War No Mo' [*or* Study War No More]. *Unknown.* AS; FSW
I'm gonna get up in the morning do like Buddy Brown. 98 Degree Blues. *Unknown.* BluL
I'm Gonna Move to the Outskirts of Town. *Unknown.* BluL
I'm Gonna Run to the City of Refuge. *Unknown.* BluL
I'm gonna stay around this town. 'Tain't Nobody's Business. *Unknown.* BluL
I'm gonna tell you a story 'bout grizzly bear. Grizzly Bear. *Unknown.* FSW
I'm gonna walk the Streets of Glory. Streets of Glory. *Unknown.* FSW
I'm grateful, really grateful. Sulpicia, *tr. fr. Latin by* John Dillon. PBWP
I'm growin auld, I'm growin' cauld. The Spell o' the Hills. Douglas Fraser. PoSH
"I'm growing old, I've sixty years." Carcassonne. Gustave Nadaud, *tr. by* John R. Thompson. BLPA; FaBoBe; HBV-1
I'm gwine to Alabamy, oh. Gwine to Alabamy. *Unknown.* TrAS
I'm Gwine Up to Heab'n Anyhow, *with music.* *Unknown.* BoAN-2
I'm Happiest When Most Away. Emily Brontë. SeCePo
I'm happy, Kerouac, your madman Allen's. Malest Cornifici Tuo Catullo. Allen Ginsberg. NeAP
I'm having an affair with Hamlet. "Hamlet." Emmett Jarrett. NeAC
I'm Here. David Ignatow. GP
I'm Here. Theodore Roethke. *Fr.* Meditations of an Old Woman. CoAP; NYBP
I'm here, on the dark porch, restyled in my mother's chair. Sitting at Night on the Front Porch. Charles Wright. LCAP
I'm hiding, I'm hiding. Hiding. Dorothy Aldis. FaPON; SoPo; SUS; TiPo
I'm Honest Abe. Honest Abe Lincoln. Max Shulman. OBAL
I'm Hungry! Jack Prelutsky. RHPC
I'm in a nice bit of trouble, I confess. Waiting at the Church; or, My Wife Won't Let Me. Fred W. Leigh. FSN
I'm in a 10der mood today. O I C. *Unknown.* WhC
I'm in New York covered by a layer of soap foam. How Come? David Ignatow. CAD; NYP
I'm in trouble. Bubble Gum. Nina Payne. RHPC
I'm jilted, forsaken, outwitted. The Jilted Nymph. Thomas Campbell. EnLoPo
I'm just a poor wayfaring stranger. *See* I am a poor wayfaring stranger.
I'm Just a Stranger Here, Heaven Is My Home. Carole Gregory Clemmons. PoBA
I'm just like an old rooster. Looking Up at Down. *Unknown.* BluL
"I'm King of the cabbages green." Old King Cabbage. Richard Kendall Munkittrick. OBCA
I'm king of the road! I gather. His Majesty. Theron Brown. AA
I'm Leery of Firms with Easy Terms. C. S. Jennison. QQQ
I'm like a skiff on the ocean tost. John Gay. EnLoPo
I'm like the king of a rain-country, rich. Spleen LXXVII. Baudelaire, *tr. by* Robert Lowell. NAWM-2
I'm lonesome since I cross'd [*or* crossed] the hill. The Girl I Left behind Me. *Unknown.* BLSo; FSW; OBET
I'm longing for the forest. Home. Verner von Heidenstam, *tr. by* Charles Wharton Stork. PoPl
I'm looking at your lofty head/ Away up in the air. Pikes [*or* Pike's] Peak. *Unknown.* BPAW; PoOW
I'm looking funny in my eye, and I. Fixing to Die. *Unknown.* BluL
I'm looking mighty seedy while holding down my claim. Little Old Sod Shanty. *Unknown.* AmFP
I'm looking through the paintings of Arthur Dove. Studies from Life. Martha Dickey. FAZ
I'm lost in my name. Theodore Roethke. POL
I'm Lucky. Charlotte Mandel. AMV-81
I'm made in sport by Nature. On an Indian Tomineois, the Least of Birds. Thomas Heyrick. FM
I'm makin' a road. Florida Road Workers. Langston Hughes. CTBA; MoAmPo
I'm melted down into a black ooze. In a Remote Cloister Bordering the Empyrean. Joel Sloman. VGW
I'm middle-aged. Political Activist Living Alone. Pat Arrowsmith. BrRo
I'm mighty glad to see you, Mrs. Curtis. The Transparent Man. Anthony Hecht. FYAP
I'm more afraid of those I love than dying. A Letter Catches Up with Me. Eric Chaet. VWA
I'm nine years old! an' you can't guess how much I weigh, I bet. The Little Hunchback. James Whitcomb Riley. PeD
"I'm 92," Joe said. Tom Weber. CTBA
I'm no He-man you know, I'm not a He. D. B. Wyndham Lewis. *Fr.* If So the Man You Are. OBSV
I'm no longer the bitter girl. Love Which Frees. Gloria Fuertes, *tr. by* Philip Levine. WPOW
I'm nobody! Who are you? Emily Dickinson. AmPP; BoWoP; NCEP; NOBA; OBCA; PDV; PoPl; RHPC; SBG; SO; TAP; TreFS; WHA; WPE; YaD
I'm none of yer London gentry. Sall. Inez Quilter. SUMH
I'm Not a Single Man. Thomas Hood. HBV-1
I'm not alone. Interior. Joseph Milbauer, *tr. by* Edouard Roditi. VWA
I'm not here. Hilda Doolittle ("H. D."). *Fr.* Halcyon. MoAmPo
I'm Not Here / Never Was. Constanta Buzea, *tr. fr. Rumanian by* Stavros Deligiorgis. BoWoP
I'm not ready, I shout. Urgency. Betsy Sholl. AMV-80
I'm Not Really Lazy. Arnold Spilka. RHPC
I'm Not Rich. Joseph Rolnik, *tr. fr. Yiddish by* Keith Bosley. VWA
I'm not sure there will be walls. Portrait by Alice Neel. Aaron Kramer. EyDe
I'm not without you. The Place of O. Ray A. Young Bear. VoR
I'm now arriv'd the soul desired port. Edmund Davie 1682; Annagram. Benjamin Tompson. SCAP
I'm O'er [*or* Owre] Young to Marry Yet. Burns. UnTE; ViBoPo
"I'm old." Old Botany Bay. Mary Gilmore. PoAu-1
I'm on My Way to Canaan, *with music.* *Unknown.* AH
I'm on my way to Freedom land. *Unknown.* FWS
I'm Only a Broken-down Miner. *Unknown.* AmFP
I'm only a consumer, and it really doesn't matter. Cheer for the Consumer. Nixon Waterman. OBAL
I'm only a little sparrow. The Sparrow's Song. *Unknown.* STF
I'm only a merchant of time. The Fable Merchant. Charles Dobzynski, *tr. by* Charles Guenther. VWA
I'm only a poor little mouse, ma'am. The Mouse. Laura E. Richards. OBCA
I'm out to find the new, the modern school. The Fledgling Bard and the Poetry Society, *much abr.* George Reginald Margetson. BANP
I'm Owre Young to Marry Yet. Burns. *See* I'm O'er Young to Marry Yet.

I'm persistent as the pink locust. The Pink Locust. William Carlos Williams. PP
I'm quiet as an old leather belt lapped snakewise. Quiet. Brian Swann. AmPA
I'm quite the opposite of my clever master. Faust's Servant. Roy Fuller. OxBTC
I'm ready. Sleep. M.R. Doty. AMV-80
I'm red pepper in a shaker. Sugar in the Cane. Tennessee Williams. OBAL
I'm regressing. Regressing. Franz Douskey. LTB
"I'm rich,"/ said/ Irish. Eternities. Norman Mailer. NYBP
I'm ridin' tonight round the dam bed-ground. Up the Trail. *Unknown.* CoSo
I'm riding on that new river train. New River Train. *Unknown.* FSW
I'm running from myself down this percolating highway. Percolating Highway. Michael Castro. VWA
I'm Sad. Forugh Farrokhzad, *tr. fr. Persian by* Reza Baraheni. BoWoP
I'm Sad and I'm Lonely. *Unknown.* AS, *with music*; FSW; TrAS, *with music*
I'm scared a lonely. Never see my son. Dream Songs, XL. John Berryman. CoAP
I'm Seventeen Come Sunday. *Unknown.* UnTE
I'm shouting/ I'm singing. Spring. Karla Kuskin. PDV; RHPC
I'm sick of love; O let me lie. To Sycamores. Robert Herrick. CaPo
I'm sick of you hypocrites babbling about gods! The Sanctimonious Poets. Friedrich Hölderlin, *tr. by* Robert Bly. NU
I'm sister and brotherless. Remember Way Back. *Unknown.* BluL
I'm sittin' on the stile, Mary. Lament of the Irish Emigrant. Helen Selina Sheridan. HBV-1; OBVV
I'm sitting alone by the fire. Her Letter. Bret Harte. HBV-1; PoLF
I'm sitting down here wondering would a, would a matchbox hold my clothes. Packin' Trunk Blues. *Unknown.* BluL
I'm sitting in the living room. Sonic Boom. John Updike. QQQ
I'm sitting on the grass by the roadside. The Wheel Change. Bertolt Brecht, *tr. by* Eric Bentley. ELU
I'm Smith of Stoke, aged sixty-odd. Epitaph on a Pessimist. Thomas Hardy. FaBoEE; FF
I'm Sneaky Bill, I'm terrible mean and vicious. Sneaky Bill. William Cole. RHPC
I'm so glad good whiskey have made it through. More Good Whiskey Blues. *Unknown.* BluL
I'm so sorry for old Adam. Old Adam. *Unknown.* AS
I'm so sorry I got happy too late. Now Look What Happened. Molly Peacock. MAYP
I'm so tired of being a Jew, an Arab. Nationalism. Harry Rosolenko. AMV-80
I'm Soaked Through with You. Rachel Korn, *tr. fr. Yiddish by* Ruth Whitman. VWA
I'm sorry but we can't go to the immersions tonight. The Ganges. Norman Dubie. LCAP
I'm sorry for the old wharves. The Old Wharves. Rachel Field. SoPo
I'm sorry to say my dear wife is a dreamer. Be Off! Stevie Smith. OxBC
I'm speaking again. Speaking. Michael Ryan. AmPA
I'm speaking from the half. To You on the Broken Iceberg. Tess Gallagher. GP
I'm speeding west somewhere in the top of Ohio or Indiana. Drive Imagining. Arthur Vogelsang. MAYP
I'm spending my nights in the flop house. Soup Song. Maurice Sugar. FSW
I'm starting to feel good. A Letter from the Hotel. Aliki Barnstone. FAZ
I'm such a quiet little ghost. The Superstitious Ghost. Arthur Guiterman. ShM
I'm sure every word that you say is absurd. A Woman's Reason. Gelett Burgess. FaBoNo
"I'm tell j'you what, these sheeps beezness." The Sheep Beezness. S. Omar Barker. BPAW
I'm Thankful That My Life Doth Not Deceive. Henry David Thoreau. PoEL-4
I'm thankful that the sun and moon. Gasbags [*or* Lines by an Old Fogy]. *Unknown.* DBV; NOBL
I'm that distinguished twice-born hero. The Death of Digenes Akritas. John Heath-Stubbs. NePoEA
I'm the bloke that's trained to sit behind the public stamp machines. A Song of the GPO. Gerry Hamill. NOBL
I'm the gardener today. Lawn-Mower. Dorothy W. Baruch. SoPo; SUS
I'm the great Sir William Anson. *Unknown. Fr.* Balliol Rhymes. FaBoEE
I'm the kid that's all the candy. The Yankee Doodle Boy. George M. Cohan. BLSo; FSN
I'm the king of the castle. King of the Castle. *Unknown.* OxNR
I'm the man, the very fat man. The Man That Waters the Workers' Beer. Paddy Ryan. FSW
I'm the Police Cop Man, I Am. Margaret Morrison. SoPo
I'm the snow on mountains. *Turkish Death Songs, tr. by* Reza Baraheni *and* Zahra-Soltan Shokoohtaezeh. BoWoP
"I'm the sort of girl." Nausicäa. Irving Layton. ErPo
I'm the sub-average male *Time* reader. The Sub-average *Time* Reader. Ernest Wittenberg. FiBHP
I'm thirty years old. Paris by Night. Gustave Kahn, *tr. by* Edouard Roditi. VWA
I'm three I'm balancing. This Is My Death-Dream. Ralph Salisbury. STE
I'm Through with You. *Unknown.* WTO
I'm tired of keeping my eyes. The Woman Driving the Country Squire. David Dayton. AMV-81
I'm tired of Love: I'm still more tired of Rhyme. Fatigue. Hilaire Belloc. FaBoCo; MoVE; NOBL; OxBTC; PV; TreFT
I'm tired of murdering children. (End) of Summer (1966). William Knott. EAS
I'm tired of symbols, of laws divine. To My Generation. Benyamin Galai, *tr. by* Jacob Sonntag. TrJP
I'm tired of trying to think. Existentialism. Lloyd Frankenburg. FiBHP
"I'm tired—oh, tired of books," said Jack. The Bookworm. Walter de la Mare. TiPo
I'm told that certain insect wives. Insect Wives. Rudolph Altrocchi. WhC
I'm touched that you, my one disciple. From the Provinces. Norman Rosten. HoAn
Im Traum sah ich ein Männchen klein und putzig. Heine, *tr. fr. German by* Sir Theodore Martin. AWP
I'm travellin' down the Castlereagh, and I'm a station-hand. A Bushman's Song. A. B. Paterson. PoAu-1
I'm trav'ling to my grave. The Traveler. *Unknown.* AmFP
I'm Troubled in Mind, *with music. Unknown.* BoAN-1
I'm up against the wall. The Wall. William Hawkins. MoCV
I'm upset you are upset. Jill. R. D. Laing. WeW
"I'm very drowsy," said the Bear. Hard to Bear. Tudor Jenks. OBCA
I'm very, very glad indeed. The Centipede. Samuel Hopkins Adams. InMe
I'm wearin' [*or* wearing] awa', John [*or* Jean]. The Land o' the Leal. Lady Nairne. GTBS; GTBS-P; HBV-2; OBEV; OxBS; WBLP; WGRP
I'm weary o' the rose as o' my brain. The Great Wheel. "Hugh MacDiarmid." OxBS
I'm weary of towns, it seems a'most a pity. Tired of Towns. Andrew Lang. EBVV
I'm wife; I've finished that. Emily Dickinson. CMoP; ViBoPo
I'm wild and woolly. Cowboy. *Unknown.* ChTr
I'm with you and you're with me and. Marching to Pretoria. *Unknown.* FSW
I'm woken up. Central Heating System. Stephen Spender. GrPl
I'm Worried Now but I Won't Be Worried Long, *with music. Unknown.* OuSiCo
I'm writing just after an encounter. Whatever You Say Say Nothing. Seamus Heaney. OBWP; OxBC
I'm yours, dearest, as are the winter towns. Marceline, to Her Husband. Elizabeth Libbey. AmPA
Image. Anna de Noailles, *tr. fr. French by* Carol Cosman. PBWP
Image. Henry Dumas. BOLo
Image, The. Roy Fuller. ChMP; GTBS-P; OxBTC
Image, The. Richard Hughes. OBMV
Image. T. E. Hulme. InPK; OxBTC
Image, The/ the pawnees. The Pride. John Newlove. MoCV; NOBC
Image comes, An. Laser. A. R. Ammons. NOBA
Image comes down to live as fact, and turns. The Shadowgraphs. Richmond Lattimore. NYBP
Image dance of change, An. Conclusion. Siegfried Sassoon. MoBrPo
Image from Beckett, An. Derek Mahon. CIP
Image in a Lilac Tree. Terence Tiller. NeBP
Image in a Mirror. Mae Winkler Goodman. GoYe
Image in the bulb-ringed mirror. Mask. Elizabeth Cox. GoYe
Image in the Mirror. Peggy Susberry Kenner. JB
Image o' God, The. Joe Corrie. OxBS
Image of City. Lance Henson. VoR
Image of Death, The. Thomas, Lord Vaux. *See* Aged Lover Renounceth Love, The.
Image of Death, The, *sel.* Robert Southwell.
"Gown which I do use to wear, The." ViBoPo
Image of Delight, The. William Ellery Leonard. HBMV
Image of earth, The. The Year of Winter. Tauhindauli. STE
Image of God, The. Francesco de Aldana, *tr. fr. Spanish by* Longfellow. WGRP
Image of Lethe, An. The Coming of War; Actaeon. Ezra Pound. CMoP; PoA
Image the images the great games therefore the locked. The Book of Job and a Draft of a Poem to Praise the Paths of the Living. George Oppen. NNaP
Image-Maker, The. Oliver St. John Gogarty. OBEV; OBMV; PoRA

Image-Nation (the Poēsis). Robin Blaser. PoM
Image-Nation 13 (the Telephone). Robin Blaser. PoM
Image-Nation 3. Robin Blaser. PoM
Imageries of dreams reveal a gracious age. The Age of a Dream. Lionel Johnson. OBMV
Images. Richard Aldington. MoBrPo; PoA
Images. Alastair Campbell. MOON
Images. Kathleen Raine. NYBP
Images. Richard Schaukal, *tr. fr. German by* Ludwig Lewisohn. AWP
Images break upon a sad day, The. Gladstone. Julian Symons. WaP
Images drip down my back like sweat. On the Morning of the Third Night above Nisqually. W. M. Ransom. CDW; NU
Images leap with him from branch to branch. A Poet at Twenty. Donald Hall. EAS
Images of Angels. P. K. Page. MoCV
Images of beauty and of destruction. Sgoran Dhu. Nan Shepherd. PoSH
Images of J—— assail him. The Bus Trip. Joel Oppenheimer. NeAP
Images! Venerable as Druidical trees. George Barker. *Fr.* In Memory of David Archer. FaBoMo
Imaginary Correspondence, *parody.* Frank Sidgwick. WhC
Imaginary Elegies, I-IV. Jack Spicer. NeAP
Imaginary Iceberg, The. Elizabeth Bishop. LiTM; MoAB; MoAmPo; MoVE
Imaginary man, go. Here is your passport. Instructions for Crossing the Border. Dan Pagis, *tr. by* Stephen Mitchell. VWA
Imagination. Shakespeare. *See* Lunatic, the Lover, and the Poet, The.
Imagination ("Imagination—here the Power so called"). Wordsworth. *Fr.* The Prelude, VI. FiP
Imagination. John Davidson. *Fr.* New Year's Eve. MoBrPo
Imagination and Taste, How Impaired and Restored. Wordsworth. *See* Prelude, The.
Imagination of Necessity, The. Andrei Codrescu. EAS
Imaginative Life, The. Geoffrey Hill. NoAM
Imagine: a Town. Daphne Marlatt. *Fr.* Steveston. NOBC
Imagine a town where no one walks the streets. Hopper's "Nighthawks" (1942). Ira Sadoff. PoDr
Imagine a world of people whose motto is. Ronald James Dessus. LFAC
Imagine father that you had a brother were. Landscape with Next of Kin. Olga Broumas. BoWoP
Imagine Grass. Knute Skinner. GP
Imagine it, a Sophocles complete. The Fire at Alexandria. Theodore Weiss. CoPo; NoAM; PoA; TAP
Imagine lamenting our longing, no. Cradle Song. Yona Wallach, *tr. by* Leonore Gordon. VWA
Imagine my surprise when. Unplanned Design. Neal Bowers. AMV-80
Imagine that any mind ever *thought* a red geranium! Red Geranium and Godly Mignonette. D. H. Lawrence. GTBS-P
Imagine that July morning: Cape Henry and Virginia. The Tempest. William Jay Smith. MoAmPo
Imagine the lake behind your house. Fear. Roger Stump. AMV-80
Imagine the princess' surprise. The Frog Prince (A Speculation on Grimm's Fairy Tale). Robert Pack. DFT
Imagine the shivers on the cold metal. An Old Polish Lesson. Deanna Louise Pickard. AMV-81
Imagine the South. George Woodcock. MoCV; NeBP; NOBC
Imagine them as they were first conceived. Images of Angels. Patricia K. Page. MoCV
Imagine what it would have been like. Supreme Fiction. Howard Winn. SOTS
Imagine what Mrs. Haessler would say. Dance of the Abakweta. Margaret Danner. PoNe
Imagine your old bow father. Concertmaster. Richard Burgin. AMV-81
Imagined Happiness. Erik Axel Karlfeldt, *tr. fr. Swedish by* Charles Wharton Stork. PoPl
Imagining How It Would Be to Be Dead. Richard Eberhart. LiTA
Imbecile, The. Donald Finkel. NePoEA-2
(Im)C-A-T(mo). E.E. Cummings. HAP
Imitated from the Persian. Robert Southey. *See* Lord, Who Art Merciful as Well as Just.
Imitation of Chaucer. Pope. FaBoPa; Par
Imitation of Christ, *sels.* Thomas à Kempis, *tr. fr. Latin.* TreF
Man Proposes, *fr.* I, 19.
Of Love of Silence and of Solitude.
Imitation of Horace, *sel.* Dryden.
Happiness. TreF
Imitation of Julia A. Moore. "Mark Twain." OBAL
Imitation of Martial, Book II Ep. 105, An. "Captain H——." NOEC
Imitation of Robert Browning. James Kenneth Stephen. *See* Sincere Flattery of R. B.
Imitation of Spenser. Keats. EnRP
(Morning.) GN
Imitation of the Style of * * * *. Samuel Johnson. *See* Hermit Hoar.
Imitation of Walt Whitman. James Kenneth Stephen. *See* Sincere Flattery of W. W. (Americanus).
Imitation of Wordsworth, An. Catherine M. Fanshawe. *See* Fragment in Imitation of Wordsworth.
Imitations Based on the American. Frank Polite. BXAP
Immaculate Conception, The. John Banister Tabb. ISi
Immaculate Palm. Joseph Joel Keith. ISi
Immalee. Christina Rossetti. BoNaP
Immanence. Richard Hovey. TRV; WGRP
Immanent. Walter de la Mare. PoA
Immeasurable haze. To the Holy Spirit. Yvor Winters. MoAmPo; MoVE; QFR; VGW
Immeasurable sadness! Sadness. Tennyson. FaBoEE
Immense hope, and forbearance, The. Spring Day. John Ashbery. NOBA
Immense room as quiet, An. The Penn Central Station at Beacon, N.Y. Ed Ochester. TAT
Immensitie cloysterd in thy deare wombe. *See* Immensity cloistered in thy dear womb.
Immensity. Gerald Stern. AMV-80
Immensity [*or* Immensitie] cloistered [*or* cloysterd] in thy dear [*or* deare] womb [*or* wombe]. Nativity [*or* Nativitie]. John Donne. *Fr.* La Corona. AnAnS-1; OBS; SBVL
Immensity of music seizes me like the Sea, The! The Music. Baudelaire, *tr. by* Arthur Symons. SyP
Immersed in night, my senses sharpen, hear. Porch. Alden Nowlan. NeAC
Immigrants. Robert Frost. GOA
Immigrants. Stanley Nelson. AMV-81
Immigrants. Nancy Byrd Turner. AmFN
Immigration Act of 1924, The. Laureen Mar. BrSi
Immoderate Death that wouldst not once confer. On the Death of the Lord Treasurer. *Unknown.* FaBoEE
Immolated. Herman Melville. ViBoPo
Immolation. Robert Farren. OnYI
Immoral. James Oppenheim. HBV-2
Immoral Arctic, The. Morris Bishop. FiBHP; WhC
Immoral Proposition, The. Robert Creeley. LiTM; NeAP; PoM
Immorality, An. Ezra Pound. CMoP; GoJo; GrPl; HBV-1; LiTM; MoAB; MoAmPo; NePA; NOBA; OBAL; OLR; PoPl
Immortal, The. Blake. *Fr.* The Book of Los, *ch.* 2. LiTB; LoBV
Immortal, The. Majorie Pickthall. CaP
Immortal. Sara Teasdale. WGRP
Immortal. Mark Van Doren. MoAmPo
Immortal Autumn. Archibald MacLeish. AP; BiP; CMoP; CoBMV; LiTA; MoAB; MoAmPo; TrGrPo
Immortal clothing I put on. The Transfiguration. Robert Herrick. CaPo
Immortal Flowers. Wallace Rice. AA
Immortal Hate. Milton. *Fr.* Paradise Lost, I. NOBE
Immortal Imogen, crowned queen above. The Two Swans. Thomas Hood. CH
Immortal is an ample word. Emily Dickinson. NOCV
Immortal Israel. Judah Halevi, *tr. fr. Hebrew by* Solomon Solis-Cohen. TrJP
Immortal Longings. Shakespeare. *See* Death of Cleopatra.
Immortal[l] love, autho[u]r of this great frame. Love. George Herbert. AnAnS-1; HoPM; SeCV-1
Immortal Love, Forever Full. Whittier. AH, *with music*
(From Our Master.) WGRP
(Our Master.) BLRP, 4 *sts.*; TRV; WBLP, 4 *sts.*
Immortal Love, too high for my possessing. George Edward Woodberry. Ideal Passion, XL. HBMV
Immortal Mind, The. Byron. WGRP
Immortal Nature. Erasmus Darwin. *Fr.* The Botanic Garden. OBEC
Immortal Newton never spoke. On Mr. Nash's Present of His Own Picture at Full Length. Earl of Chesterfield. NOEC
Immortal Part, The. A. E. Housman. A Shropshire Lad, XLIII. MasP; MoBrPo; UnPo; VLP
Immortal spirit hath no bars, The. Dawn. Frederick George Scott. CaP; PoPl
Immortal stood frozen amidst, The. The Immortal. Blake. *Fr.* The Book of Los, *ch.* 2. LiTB; LoBV
Immortalis. David Morton. HBV-2
Immortality. "Æ." AnIV; AWP; OBMV; WGRP
Immortality. Ai. MAYP
Immortality. Matthew Arnold. FiP
Immortality. Bible, *O. T. (Moulton, Modern Reader's Bible).Fr.* Job. *See* Man That Is Born of a Woman.
Immortality. Richard Henry Dana. AA; WGRP
Immortality. Emily Dickinson. *See* It is an honorable thought.
Immortality. Samuel Greenberg. LiTA
Immortality. Arthur Sherburne Hardy. AA
Immortality. Frank Horne. BANP
Immortality. Joseph Jefferson. BLPA

Immortality. Susan L. Mitchell. OnYI
Immortality. Nicolai Maksimovich Minsky, *tr. fr. Russian by* Babette Deutsch. TrJP
Immortality. Lizette Woodworth Reese. AA; HBMV; HBVY
Immortality. Sir Philip Sidney. *See* Who Hath His Fancy Pleased.
Immortality of the Soul, The, *sel.* Sir John Davies.
"For why should we the busy soul believe." ViBoPo
Immortality of Verse, The. Horace, *tr. fr. Latin by* Pope. Odes, IV, 9. AWP
Immortall love, authour of this great frame. *See* Immortal love, author of this great frame.
Immortals, The. Isaac Rosenberg. FaBoTw; MMA; TrJP
Immutabilis. Alice Learned Bunner. *Fr.* Vingtaine. AA
Imogen. Sir Henry Newbolt. HBMV
Impartial Inspection, The. *Unknown.* APAS
Impartial Law enrolled a name, The. My Name and I. Robert Graves. NoAM; NYBP
Impasse. Langston Hughes. LiTM
Impasto or washes as a rule. Irish Poetry. Michael Longley. CIP
Impatient all the foggy day for night. Fever. Thom Gunn. PeHV
Impatient as we were for all of them to join us. The Bungalows. John Ashbery. CoAP
Impatient with cripples, foreigners, children. Il Piccolo Rifiuto. Louis MacNeice. CMoP
Impatient with the enigmatic, Al Capone. Suite for Celery and Blind Date. Philip Dow. BXAP
Impatiently she tampered with the locks. Bluebeard's Wife. Daryl Hine. NoAM
Impenitentia Ultima. Ernest Dowson. BrPo; HBV-1
Imperator Victus. Hart Crane. OxBA
Imperceptively the world became haunted by her white dress. The White Dress. Marya Zaturenska. MoAmPo; TwAmPo
Impercipient, The. Thomas Hardy. EBVV; OAEP; PrIm; TrGrPo; ViBoPo; WGRP
Imperfect Artist, The. George Rostrevor Hamilton. DBV
Imperfect Enjoyment, The. Earl of Rochester. BoLoP; ErPo; UnTE
Imperfect enough once for all at thirty. Last Things, Black Pines at 4 a.m. Robert Lowell. NOBA
Imperfect Lover, The. Siegfried Sassoon. BrPo
Imperfect Sestina. Phyllis Webb. NOBC
Imperial Adam. A. D. Hope. CBAP; ErPo; HAP; NoAM; NoP; UnTE
Imperial boy had fallen in his pride, The. My Fatherland. William Cranston Lawton. AA
Imperial consort of the fairy king, The. The Wild Duck's Nest [*or* Sonnet: The Wild Duck's Nest]. Wordsworth. ChER; FM
Imperial Man. James Russell Lowell. *Fr.* Under the Old Elm. PGD
Imperial Thumbprint. Tom Weatherly. PoBA
Imperialist. A. R. Ammons. GP
Imperious Muse, your arrows ever strike. Japanese Beetles. X. J. Kennedy. HoAn; OBAL
Imperiously he leaps, he neighs, he bounds. Shakespeare. *Fr.* Venus and Adonis. BoAnP
Impermanence. Lal Ded, *tr. fr. Kashmiri by* Willis Barnstone. BoWoP
Impersonal the aim. Night of Battle. Yvor Winters. PoA
Impetuous Samuel. Harry Graham. NA
Impiety, *sel.* Helene Magaret.
"Lord, I have not time to pray." TrPWD
Impious Feast, The, *sels.* Robert Eyres Landor. OBRV
Babylon.
Festival, The.
Historic Time.
Jew's Home, The.
Nineveh.
Sleep.
Implacable angel, The/ Has shot his dart. Epitaph. Leone da Modena. TrJP
Implacable, unmerciful, fulfilled. Eric. John Barford. PeHV
Implacable woman. The Land. Dorothy Livesay. *Fr.* The Colour of God's Face. PeCV
Implausible/ that my lifting the receiver. Dial Tone. Felix Pollak. PPJ
Implicated generations made, The. Celtic Cross. Norman MacCaig. OxBS
Implicit Faith. Aubrey Thomas De Vere. May Carols, Pt. II, 64. GoBC
Implora Pace. Charles Lotin Hildreth. AA
Imploring Mecca. Be-Bop Boys. Langston Hughes. OBAL
Importance of Mirrors, The. Helga Sandburg. IHMS
Importance of Personal Relationships, The. Bill Manhire. OCNZ
Importance of Poetry, or the Coming Forth from Eternity into Time, The. Hyam Plutzick. PP
"Important is the nation's health." The Double Standard. Franklin P. Adams. OBAL
Important Statement. Patrick Kavanagh. PoCh
Important thing is not, The. Is. Patrick Kavanagh. FaBoTw
Importer, An. Robert Frost. FaBoCo
Importune Me No More. Elizabeth I, Queen of England. *See* When I Was Fair and Young.
Impossibilities to His Friend. Robert Herrick. OLR
Impossibility, The. Coventry Patmore. *Fr.* The Angel in the House, I, i. VLP
Impossible Dream, The, *with music* Joe Darion. BLSo
Impossible the years have fled away so fast! The Mice at the Door. Vincent McHugh. NePoAm-2
Impossible to call a lamb a lambkin. Gone Are the Days. Norman MacCaig. OxBC
Impossible to Trust Women. *Unknown.* MeEL
Imposture, The, *sels.* James Shirley.
O Fly My Soul, *fr.* II, ii. OBS; OxBoCh
(Hymn, A: "O fly, my soul!") GoBC
(Song of Nuns, A.) ACP
Piping Peace. ACP; LoBV; NOBE
(Song: "You virgins that did late despair.") PoEL-2
(You Virgins.) ViBoPo
Impotence. Marvin Bell. AmPA
Impotence. Arthur Winfield Knight. SOTS
Impotent Lover, The. Ovid. *See* Shameful Impotence.
Imprecation against Foes and Sorcerers, An. *Unknown, tr. fr. Sanskrit by* A. A. MacDonnell. WSC
Impression. E. E. Cummings. *See* Hours Rise Up . . .
Impression. Sir Edmund Gosse. HBV-1
Impression. Arthur Symons. SyP
Impression de Nuit; London. Lord Alfred Douglas. OBEV; OBVV
Impression de Paris. Oscar Wilde. SyP
Impression du Matin. Oscar Wilde. BrPo; CABA; EBVV; MoBrPo; SyP; VLP
Impression Japonais. Oscar Wilde. SyP
Impression which this seal shall make, The. Sent to a Lady, with a Seal. Robert Lloyd. FaBoUs
Impressionist. Heather McHugh. MAYP
Impressions, *sels.* Oscar Wilde.
La Fuite de la Lune. SyP
La Mer. SyP; VLP
Le Jardin ("The lily's withered chalice falls"). SeCePo; SyP
(Garden, The.) PoRA
Les Silhouettes. BrPo; EBVV; MOS; SyP
"Sea is flecked with bars of grey, The." MOS
Impressions, Number III. E. E. Cummings. UnPo
Impressions of François-Marie Arouet (de Voltaire), *sel.* Ezra Pound.
"If you'd have me go on loving you." MoAB
Impressions of My Father, *sel.* Marcia Masters.
Country Ways, I. GoYe
Imprimis he was "broke." Thereafter left. Giffen's Debt. Kipling. VLP
Imprimis, there's a table blotted. An Inventory of the Furniture of a Collegian's Chamber. John Winstanley. OBSV
Imprimis—My departed shade I trust. Mira's Will. Mary Leapor. NOEC
Imprisoned. Eunice Tietjens. HBMV
Imprisoned in the marble block. Sleeping Beauty. Elinor Wylie. DFT
Imprisoned Soul, The. Walt Whitman. *See* Last Invocation, The.
Imprisoned, The. Robert Fitzgerald. MP; TwCP
Imprisoned winds slumber within their caves, Th'. On the Dark, Still, Dry, Warm Weather Occasionally Happening in the Winter Months. Gilbert White. NOEC
Impromptu. Thomas Gray. *See* On Lord Holland's Seat near Margate, Kent.
Impromptu. *Unknown, wr. at. to* Benjamin Franklin. *See* Jack and Roger.
Impromptu. Samuel Wilberforce. *See* If I Were a Cassowary.
Impromptu on Charles II. Earl of Rochester. ChTr; InPK; NIP; NOBL; OBSV; PAI
("God bless our good and gracious king.") FaBoEE
Improperia. Francis Sparshott. MoCV
Improved Binoculars, The. Irving Layton. NOBC
Improved Farm Land. Carl Sandburg. RFM
Improvisation on an Old Theme. Dorothy Livesay. CaP
Improvisations: Light and Snow, *sel.* Conrad Aiken.
"When I was a boy, and saw bright rows of icicles." BoNaP
Improvisations on Aesop. Anthony Hecht. OBAL
Improvising. Louise Townsend Nicholl. NePoAm-2
Impulse, The. Robert Frost. *Fr.* The Hill Wife. HoPM; NePA; NoAM
Impulse of October, The. W. R. Moses. NCSH
In a Bar near Shibuya Station, Tokyo. Paul Engle. AmFN; CAD
In a basement just off Saint-Michel. 104 Boulevard Saint-Germain. Kenneth Pitchford. NYBP
In a Bath Teashop. John Betjeman. ELU; EnLoPo
In a Boat. Hilaire Belloc. ISi
In a book the life of the turtle dove. The Nature of the Turtle Dove. *Unknown. Fr.* The Bestiary. PBBP

In a bookstore on the East Side. Burning Oneself In. Adrienne Rich. NYP
In a borrowed field they dig in their feet. Women's Tug of War at Lough Arrow. Tess Gallagher. MAYP
In a bowl to sea went wise men three. The Wise Men of Gotham. Thomas Love Peacock. BXAP; FaBoNo
In a branch of [a] willow hid. To a Caty-did. Philip Freneau. AA; TAP
In a Cafe. Richard Brautigan. PCP
In a Café. Rosemary Dobson. CBAP
In a cafe under a lazy fan. Country Nun. Geoff Page. CBAP
In a Cathedral City. Thomas Hardy. EnLoPo; FaBoPP
In a cavern, in a canyon. Paul Dehn. *Fr.* Rhymes for a Modern Nursery. FiBHP; PV; ShM
In a cavern [*or* cabin], in a canyon. Oh, My Darling Clementine. *Unknown, at. to* Percy Montross. AmFP; BLSo; FaBoBe; FaFP; FSW; OBAL; PSoN; TreF
In a cell I am bunked. Martial, *tr. fr. Latin.* DBV
In a certain crypt-like courtroom. When Nobody Prays. Merl A. Clapper. STF
In a chariot of light from the regions of day. Liberty Tree. Thomas Paine. PAH
In a Child's Album. Wordsworth. *See* to a Child.
In a Chinese window. Elephants from the Sea. Ian Young. NeAC
In a chirche ther I con knel. Deo Gracias. *Unknown.* OxBM
In a church which is furnished with mullion and gable. All Saints'. Edmund Yates. HBV-1
In a Churchyard. Richard Wilbur. HeIP
In a City Square. Eleanor Glenn Wallis. NePoAm-2
In a climate where. Intuition. Anthony Delius. PeSA
In a Closed Universe. James Hayford. NePoAm-2
In a coffee house at 3 am. My Son and I. Philip Levine. DiL; FAZ; GP; NYP
In a coign of the cliff between lowland and highland. A Forsaken Garden. Swinburne. EBEV; FaBoEn; FaBoPP; GTBS-P; HBV-1; LiTB; LoBV; NOBE; NoP; OAEL-2; OBNC; OBVV; TEP; VLP; WHA
In a cold glade sacred to nothing. Tales Told of the Fathers. John Hollander. DiL
In a cool curving world he lies. The Fish. Rupert Brooke. FM; MOS
In a Copy of Browning. Bliss Carman. HBMV
In a Copy of Omar Khayyám. James Russell Lowell. AA
In a corner. Dissembler. Charles Shaw. GoYe
In a corner of blue sky. Daily Wages. Amrita Pritam, *tr. by author and* Charles Brasch. PBWP
In a Corner of Eden. Peter Levi. NePoEA-2
In a cottage embosom'd within a deep shade. Blue Ey'd Mary. *Unknown.* CoMu
In a cottage in Fife. Mother Goose. OxNR
In a Country Cemetery in Iowa. Ted Kooser. DFF
In a Country Church. R. S. Thomas. FaBoMo
In a country without saints or shrines. The Springs. Wendell Berry. GP
In a crosshatched 16th-century print. Note from an Exhibition. Albert Goldbarth. AMV-81
In a dark, dark wood, there was a dark, dark house. The Dark House. *Unknown.* NTCP
In a dark, silent, shady grove. Et Cetera. Earl of Rochester. UnTE
In a Dark Time. Theodore Roethke. EaLo; HAP; HeIP; MAT; MoAmPo; NoAM; NOBA; NoP; NYBP; PPP; TAP
In a days-and-nights ghetto. In a Ghetto. Jacob Glatstein, *tr. by* Ruth Whitman. VWA
In a dead tree. The Horse. W. S. Merwin. GP
In a Desert Town. Lionel Stevenson. AmFN
In a dingy kitchen/ Facing a Ghetto backyard. Lamentations. Alter Brody. TrJP; VWA
In a Double Rainbow. Harold Littlebird. VoR
In a Dream. David Ignatow. GP; PoA
In a Dream. J. M. Synge. SyP
In a dream I open the door. The Fat Boy's Dream. Richard McCann. GrPl
In a dream I returned to the river of bees. The River of Bees. W. S. Merwin. HeIP; LCAP
In a dream I saw a beautiful island. Island of Night. Galway Kinnell. NePoAm
In a Dream Ship's Hold. Suzanne Bernhardt. VWA
In a Drear-nighted December. Keats. CH; ELP; EnRP; NOBE; PoPle; TEP
(December.) GN
(Happy Insensibility.) GTBS; GTBS-P
(In Drear-nighted December.) OAEL-2; PAI
(Stanzas: "In a drear-nighted December.") ChER; HBV-2; OBEV; OBNC; OBRV
In a factory building there are wheels and gearings. Our Father's Hand. Annie Johnson Flint. BLRP
In a far land upon a day. The Riding of the Kings. Eleanor Farjeon. YeAr
In a fashionable suburb of Santa Barbara. In Montecito. Randall Jarrell. CoAP; MAT; NoP; NYBP; VGW
In a few moments. The Death of a Negro Poet. Conrad Kent Rivers. BPo
In a Field. Robert Pack. MAT; NePoEA-2
In a field. Keeping Things Whole. Mark Strand. CoAP; HeIP; LCAP; NoAM; PPP; TAP
In a field of swaying grain. Death Seed. Ricarda Huch, *tr. by* Susan C. Strong. PBWP
In a frith as I can fare fremede. The Lady in the Wood. *Unknown.* OxBM
In a frosty sunset. Winter: East Anglia. Edmund Blunden. LiSp; OxBTC
In a Garden. Donald G. Babcock. NePoAm
In a Garden. Elizabeth Jennings. NOCV
In a garden of shining sea-weed. The Sea Princess. Katharine Pyle. SoPo
In a garden shady this holy lady. Song for St. Cecilia's Day. W. H. Auden. FaBoTw; MP; TwCP
In a garden where the whitethorn spreads her leaves. Alba Innominata. *Unknown, tr. by* Ezra Pound. AWP
In a Garret. Elizabeth Akers Allen. AA
In a Garret. Herman Melville. OBAL
In a gay jar upon his shoulder. The Amphora. Fyodor Sologub, *tr. by* Babette Deutsch *and* Avrahm Yarmolinsky. AWP
In a Ghetto. Jacob Glatstein, *tr. fr. Yiddish by* Ruth Whitman. VWA
In a Glass-Window for Inconstancy. Lord Herbert of Cherbury. AnAnS-2; SeCP
In a glorius garden grene. The Lily-White Rose. *Unknown.* MeEL
In a Gondola. Robert Browning. OBEV; OBVV
Sels.
"I send my heart up to thee, all my heart." ViBoPo
"Moth's kiss, first, The!" BoLoP; GBL; UnTE
(Song: "Moth's kiss, first, The!") TrGrPo
"Past we glide, and past, and past!" PeD
In a goodly night, as in my bede I laye. Waking Alone. *Unknown.* MeEL
In a gorge titanic. Ula Masondo's Dream. William Plomer. MoBS
In a Grave-Yard. William Stanley Braithwaite. PoBA
In a green place lanced through. The Blue Heron. Theodore Goodridge Roberts. CaP; NOBC; OBCV; PeCV
In a grove most rich of shade. Astrophel and Stella: Eighth Song. Sir Philip Sidney. OAEP; OBSC; SiPS
In a gym in Spanish Harlem. To a Fighter Killed in the Ring. Lou Lipsitz. LiSp
In a harbour grene aslepe whereas I lay. *See* In a herber green . . .
In a Hard Intellectual Light. Richard Eberhart. CMoP; LiTM; MoVE
In a heavy bowl two pears. Sadness and Still Life. Bin Ramke. MAYP
In a herber [*or* a harbour *or* an arbour] green [*or* grene], asleep [*or* aslepe] whereas [*or* where as *or* where] I lay. In Youth Is Pleasure [*or* Of Youth He Singeth *or* In an Arbour Green *or* Youth]. Robert Wever. *Fr.* Lusty Juventus. ChTr; EIL; ELP; GBL; NOBE; OBEV; OBSC
In a high-fashion journal for queers. Limerick. *Unknown.* PeHV
In a hole of the heel of an old brown stocking. Stocking Fairy. Winifred Welles. FaPON; SoPo; TiPo
In a Hotel Writing-Room. John Cowper Powys. OxBTC
In a house born of the brown earth. An Adobe House. Witter Bynner. BPAW
In a hundred places in North Dakota. Something Is Dying Here. Thomas McGrath. TAT
In a Hundred Years. *At. to* Elizabeth Doten. BLPA
In a hut of mud and fire. Gautama in the Deer Park at Benares. Kenneth Patchen. NaP
In a Liberal Arts Building. Ruth Stone. TwAmPo
In a London Schoolroom. James Kirkup. GLGT
In a lonely, frozen park. Sentimental Conversations. Paul Verlaine, *tr. by* Lloyd Alexander. WSC
In a loose robe of tinsel forth [*or* tynsell foorth] she came. Corinna Bathes [*or* Natures Naked Jem]. George Chapman. *Fr.* Ovid's Banquet of Sense. FaBoEn; OBSC
In a lovely garden, filled with fair and blooming flowers. The Mission of the Flowers. Frances E. W. Harper. BlSi
In a Lovely Garden Walking. Ludwig Uhland, *tr. fr. German by* George MacDonald. AWP
In a Low Rocking-Chair. Helen Coale Crew. HBMV
In a Maple Wood. Pat Schneider. AMV-81
In a Meadow. John Swinnerton Phillimore. OBEV; OBVV
In a meadow/ Beside the chapel three boys were playing football. Father Mat. Patrick Kavanagh. AnIL; CMoP; MoAB; NMP
In a mean abode in [*or* on] the Shankill Road. The Ballad of William Bloat [*or* Belfast Linen]. *Unknown.* DBV; NOBL; WTO
In a Mexican mission bells toll no mark. Going Back. George Rachow. LFAC
In a Mirror. Marcia Stubbs. MAT
In a Mist. Al Young. AMV-80

In a month all those frozen waterfalls. Modern Love. Gerald Stern. AMV-80
In a Moonlight Wilderness. Samuel Taylor Coleridge. *See* Fruit Plucker, The.
In a Moonlit Hermit's Cabin. Allen Ginsberg. MOON
In a Motion. Laura Chester. NPGG
In a Mountain Cabin in Norway. Robert Bly. RFM
In a Museum. Babette Deutsch. HBMV
In a Museum. Thomas Hardy. UnS
In a Museum Cabinet. May Swenson. WSC
In a museum here I saw a Celtic swordblade. The Celt in Me. Keith Wilson. GP
In a museum, I ask. Tutankhamen. William Dickey. Psk
In a Museum in the Capital. William Stafford. LCAP
In a museum we find them. Ice Dragons. Diane Ackerman. SUW
In a Music-Hall. John Davidson. EBVV
In a nation of one hundred fine, mob-hearted, lynching, relenting, repenting millions. Bryan, Bryan, Bryan, Bryan. Vachel Lindsay. CMoP; CrMA; LiTA; OxBA; OxBoLi
In a net of mist the moon depends on the wood. Spring Song. George Brandon Saul. GoYe
In a Night. Ann Marie Savage. AMV-81
In a nook. In May. J. M. Synge. MoBrPo
In a noon-tide of a sumers day. Turn Again. *Unknown.* OxBM
In a one-button gray wool sweater. Harmonica Man. P. Wolny. PCP
In a Parlor Containing a Table. Galway Kinnell. ELU
In a phone booth. Of Human Bondage. Miller Williams. NYP
In a pine tree. I Try to Waken and Greet the World Once Again. James Wright. InPS
In a place of worhip I know, they made a strange mosaic. The Wall. Ludvik Askenazy, *tr. fr. Czech.* VWA
In a place where hunchbacks and old women. The Sleeping Beauty. E. L. Mayo. DFT
In a plain pleasant cottage, conveniently neat. The Miller. John Cunningham. OBEC
In a plume of sky firelight. Night Teeth. Peter Brett. AMV-80
In a Poem. Robert Frost. PP
In a Prominent Bar in Secaucus [One Day]. X. J. Kennedy. ConAP; FYAP; HoAn; HoPM; NIP; OBAL; PoCh; PPP; UnTE
In a Province. F. T. Prince. MoVE
In a quiet water'd [*or* watered] land, a land of roses. The Dead at Clonmacnois [*or* Clonmacnoise]. Angus O'Gillan, *tr. by* Thomas William Rolleston. AnIL; AnIV; FaBoPP; HBV-2; OBEV; OBMV; OBVV; OnYI; OxBI
In a Railway Compartment. John Fuller. NePoEA-2
In a real city, from a real house. The Noodle-Vendor's Flute. D. J. Enright. NoP
In a red winter hat blue. Self-Portrait, I. William Carlos Williams. *Fr.* Pictures from Brueghel. LCAP
In a Remote Cloister Bordering the Empyrean. Joel Sloman. VGW
In a Restaurant, 1917. Eleanour Norton. SUMH
In a Roman tram, where the famous Roman mob. The Thief. Stanley Kunitz. MoAmPo; VGW
In a Rose Garden. John Bennett. BLPA; FaBoBe; HBV-1
In a salt ring of moonlight. Moorings. Norman MacCaig. OxBTC
In a Season of Unemployment. Margaret Avison. MoCV; NOBC
In a semi-circle we toed the line chalked round the master's. The Wanderer. Seamus Heaney. CIP
In a sense. Life. Artie Gold. NOBC
In a shady nook one moonlit night. The Leprahaun. Robert Dwyer Joyce. OnYI
In a shoe box stuffed in an old nylon stocking. The Meadow Mouse. Theodore Roethke. HeIP; InPK; NaP; PAI; PPoe; SeCeV
In a Shoreham Garden. Laurence Lerner. NePoEA-2
In a sick shade of spruce, moss-webbed, rock-fed. As It Looked Then. E. A. Robinson. CMoP; NePA; NoAM
In a small theodolite of paper. Soluble Noughts and Crosses; or, California, Here I Come. Roger Roughton. EAS
In a small throaty soprano. Songs My Mother Taught Me. David Wagoner. Str
In a small wheelbarrow. A Cathedral. Stanislav Vinaver, *tr. by* Vasa D. Mihailovich. VWA
In a snug little cot lived a fat little mouse. The Country Mouse and the City Mouse. Richard Scrafton Sharpe. OxBChV
In a snug little court as I stood t'other day. The Pleasing Constraint. Aristaenetus, *tr. by* Sheridan *and* Nathaniel Brassey Halhed. ErPo
In a solitude of the sea. The Convergence of the Twain (Lines on the Loss of the *Titanic*). Thomas Hardy. BiP; BrPo; CoBMV; FaBoTw; HeIP; InPK; LiTB; LiTM; MoAB; MoBrPo; MoPo; MOS; MoVE; NoAm; NoP; OAEL-2; OAEP; OxBTC; PAI; PrIm; SeCeV; TEP
In a somer seson [*or* summer season], whan softe [*or* whenne softe *or* when soft] was the sonne [*or* sun]. Prologue [*or* The Field of Folk *or* The Field Full of Folk *or* On Malverne Hilles, the Place of Piers Plowman's Vision]. William Langland. *Fr.* The Vision of Piers Plowman. EBVV; FaBoPP; OAEL-1; OxBM; PoEL-1
In a Southern garden Lucinda sits. The Bones of Incontention. Robert David Cohen. NYBP
In a spathe of silence. The Messenger. Frances Horovitz. BrRo
In a Spring Still Not Written Of. Robert Wallace. BoNaP; PP
In a stable of boats I lie still. The Lifeguard. James Dickey. CoPo; LiSp; NoP; NYBP
In a Staffordshire Churchyard. *Unknown.* PoPle; WhC
In a stately hall at Brentford, when the English June was green. The Last Meeting of Pocahontas and the Great Captain. Margaret Junkin Preston. PAH
In a Station of the Metro. Ezra Pound. AmPP; CABA; CAD; HAP; HeIP; InPK; MoAB; MoAmPo; NIP; NOAM; NOBA; NoP; OxBA; PAI; TAP; UnPo; VGW; WeW
In a storm after the storm. Spring Sunday on Quaker Street. Tom Bass. FAZ
In a summer season, when soft was the sun. *See* In a somer seson, whan softe was the sonne.
In a Surrealist Year. Lawrence Ferlinghetti. *Fr.* A Coney Island of the Mind. PAI; PPON
In a tabernacle of a toure [*or* tower] Quia Amore Langueo. *Unknown.* ACP; MeEL
In a tangled, scented hollow. Sleep. Lewis Frank Tooker. AA
In a tea-garden overhanging Rotha. Grasmere Sonnets. David Wright. NoAM
In a temple at Kioto in far-away Japan. The Three Wise Monkeys. Florence Boyce Davis. WBLP
In a throng,/ A festal company. Wordsworth. *Fr.* The Prelude, IV. EBEV; OBRV
In a Time of Pestilence. Thomas Nashe. *See* Adieu, Farewell Earth's Bliss.
In a time of summer's day. Revertere. *Unknown.* PBBP
In a Town Garden. Donald Mattam. ELU; FiBHP
In a Train. Robert Bly. CAPP; NaP; POL
In a tree at the edge of the clearing. On Falling Asleep to Birdsong. William Meredith. PoCh
In a U-Haul North of Damascus. David Bottoms. FYAP; MAYP
In a V.A.D. Pantry. Alberta Vickridge. SUMH
In a valley, centuries ago. The Petrified Fern. Mary Bolles Branch. AA; HBV-2
In a Valley of This Restless Mind. Ewart Milne. NeIP
In a valley of this restless [*or* restles] mind. Quia Amore Langueo. *Unknown.* LO; OBEV
In a Vermont bedroom closet. A Record Stride. Robert Frost. NePA
In a Warm Bath. Carl Rakosi. TAP
In a wee cot hoose far across the muir. Kate Dalrymple. *Unknown.* GBP
In a week of perpetual rain. The Tray. Thomas Cole. NePoAm
In a weird, forlorn voice. The President Slumming. James Tate. OBAL
In a while they rose and went out aimlessly riding. Merlin Enthralled. Richard Wilbur. CMoP; NePoEA; NYBP
In a white gully among fungus red. Native Born. Eve Langley. PoAu-2; WPE
In a wild moraine of forgotten books. The Old School List. James Kenneth Stephen. CenHV
In a Wine Cellar. Victor J. Daley. PoAu-1
In a Wood. Thomas Hardy. OAEP; OBNC; PAI; PoPl; VLP
In a Wood. E. J. Scovell. GBL
In a Wood Clearing. Wilson MacDonald. CaP
In a wood they call the Rouge Bouquet. Rouge Bouquet. Joyce Kilmer. HBV-2; PAH; PoPl; TreFS
In a wooden room, surrounded by lights and/ Faces. The Killing. George MacBeth. FaBoMo
In a world of battlefields there came. When the Dead Men Die. Rose O'Neill. HBMV
In a World of Change. Joseph Awad. AMV-80
In a world of orange serenity. The Lacemaker (Vermeer). Anne Marx. GoYe
In Absentia. Alastair Mackie. BSV
In Adam's fall/ We sinned all. An ABC. *Unknown.* *Fr.* The New England Primer. GBP; OBCA
In Aesop's tales an honest wretch we find. A Fable. Matthew Prior. NoP
In After Days. George Frederick Cameron. CaP
In After Days. Austin Dobson. HBV-2; OBEV; OBVV; TreFS
In after times when strength or courage fail. Buffel's Kop. Roy Campbell. ChMP; PeSA
In after years, when you look back upon. The Window. Francis Scarfe. NeBP
In Agrigentum, earlier in Olympia. Empedocles on Etna. H. B. Mallalieu. PoA
In Agypt's land contaygious to the Nile. Pharao's Daughter. Michael Moran. BIrV

In Air. Peter Clarke. PBA
In all humanity, we crave. The Commons' Petition to Charles II. Earl of Rochester. FaBoCo
In all my Emma's beauties blest. Emma. Goldsmith. OnYI
In All the Argosy of Your Bright Hair. Dunstan Thompson. WaP
In All the Days of My Childhood. Russell Edson. AmPA
In all the Eastern hemisphere. The Fall of J. W. Beane. Oliver Herford. OBAL
In all the good Greek of Plato. Survey of Literature. John Crowe Ransom. FaBoCh; LiTA; MP; OBAL; TAP; TwCP; VGW
In all the land, range up, range down. Langley Lane. Robert Buchanan. HBV-2
In All the Magic of Christmas-Tide, *with music.* John Jacob Niles. AH
In all the midwest. Early June. R. P. Dickey. TAT
In all the towns and cities fair. Thomas Winterbottom Hance. W. S. Gilbert. InMe
In All These Acts. William Everson. NoP
In all these rotten shops, in all this broken furniture. The Dancing. Gerald Stern. DiL
In All These Turning Lights I Find No Clue. Maxwell Anderson. *Fr.* Winterset. TreFT
In all those stories the hero. Heroes. Robert Creeley. NOBA; NoP; PPP
IN) all those who got. E. E. Cummings. FaBoEE
In all thy humors, whether grave or mellow. Temperament. Martial, *tr. by* Joseph Addison. AWP; ELU
In Allusion to the French Song. Richard Lovelace. CaPo
In amaze. Ode to Quinbus Flestrin. Pope. OAEP
"In America," began. The Student. Marianne Moore. MP; TwCP
In among the silver birches winding ways of tarmac wander. Indoor Games near Newbury. John Betjeman. MoVE
In Ampezzo ("In days of summer let me go"). Trumbull Stickney. TwAmPo
In Ampezzo ("Only once more and not again—the larches.") Trumbull Stickney. CrMA; NCEP; TwAmPo
In Amsterdam there dwells [*or* dwelt *or* lived] a maid. The [Fair] Maid of Amsterdam [*or* A-Roving]. *Unknown.* AmSS; FSW; OxBoLi; ShS (*vers.* I)
In an age of fops and toys. Voluntaries [*or* So Nigh Is Grandeur]. Emerson. FPL; HBVY; LiTA; PoLF; TreFS
In an Album. James Russell Lowell. OBAL
In an Alien Place. Leib Neidus, *tr. fr. Yiddish by* Ruth Whitman. VWA
In an Arab Town. Susan Tichy. MAYP
In an Arbour Green. Robert Weever. *See* In Youth Is Pleasure.
In an Artist's Studio. Christina Rossetti. NoP; OAEP; PAI
In an Autumn Wood. William Alexander Percy. HBMV
In an elegy for a musician. An Elegy for Bob Marley. William Matthews. MAYP
In an Empty Field at Night. Gregory Orr. PAI
In an Empty Window. Ray Fraser. NeAC
In an envelope marked. Personal. Langston Hughes. AmNP; NOBA; PoNe
In an exciting world of love-bites, nipple-nipping. The Lovesleep. Gavin Ewart. OxBC
In an Hour the Sun. Ray Freed. WOLT
In an Indian ditch lies. The World's Last Unnamed Poem. A. K. Redwing. VoR
In an instant, by instinct, I apprehended. An Act. Kenneth Rosen. AmPA
In an Iridescent Time. Ruth Stone. MoAmPo; PoPl; TwAmPo
In an oak there liv'd an owl. The Owl in the Oak. *Unknown.* FaBoNo
In an ocean, 'way out yonder. The Dinkey-Bird. Eugene Field. AA; AmMo; HBVY; NA; TreFS
In an old and ashen island. Sappho's Tomb. Arthur Stringer. CaP
In an old book at even as I read. "Ex Libris." Arthur Upson. HBV-2
In an old chamber softly lit. During a Chorale by César Franck. Witter Bynner. HBMV
In an old, dark house. Fly in December. Robert Wallace. NYBP
In an Old House. Spencer Brown. NYBP
In an Old Nursery. Patrick R. Chalmers. HBMV
In an Old Orchard. Peter Kane Dufault. NYBP
In an orchard a little fountain flows. Song of the Ill-Married. *Unknown, tr. by* Patricia Terry. BoWoP
In an upper room at midnight. The Love Feast. W. H. Auden. ErPo
In ancient China under rule of Shang. Myths. D. L. Klauck. LTB
In ancient days there lived a Turk. Kafoozalum. *Unknown.* BeLS; BLPA
In ancient Egypt. The Fertile Valley of the Nile. Eve Merriam. IHMS
In ancient times, as story tells. Baucis and Philemon; Imitated from the Eighth Book of Ovid. Swift. GN; GoTL; NOEC; OAEL-1; OBEC
In ancient times e'er peace with lenient smile. Danebury. *Unknown.* PeHV
In ancient times, no matter where. Little Britain. *Unknown.* NOEC
In ancient times—'twas no great loss. On a Nomination to the Legion of Honour. *Unknown.* FaBoEE
In and Out. L. E. Sissman. NYBP
Severance of Connections, 1946, *sel.* TwCP
In and out the bushes, up the ivy. The Chipmunk's Day [*or* Song]. Randall Jarrell. BoAnP; NCSH; OBCA; PDV; RHPC
In anguish we uplift. War Song. John Davidson. NBM; OBNC
In animalcules, Muse display. The Animalcule, a Tale. Richard Savage. PeD
In another country, black poplars shake themselves over a pond. The North Country. D. H. Lawrence. OAEP
In another world, there may be utterances. No Such Thing. Marcia Southwick. AMV-81
In Answer of an Elegiacall Letter upon the Death of the King of Sweden. Thomas Carew. AnAnS-2
In Answer to a Lady Who Advised Retirement. Lady Mary Wortley Montagu. OBEC
(Answer to a Lady Advising Me to Retirement, An.) TEP
In Answer to a Question. Wilfrid Scawen Blunt. *Fr.* The Love Sonnets of Proteus. ViBoPo
In Answer to Your Query. Naomi Lazard. GP
In Antarctica drooping their little shoulders. The View from Here. William Stafford. ELU; RFM
In any hour the singers with mouths of gold. Two Musics. Norman McCaig. NeBP
In any medium except that of verse. Wyndham Lewis. *Fr.* One-Way Song. PP
In Apia Bay. Sir Charles G. D. Roberts. PAH
In Aprell and in May. Besse Bunting. *Unknown.* MeEL
In April. Ethelwyn Wetherald. CaP
In April we will pierce his body. Letters to a Stranger. Thomas James. AmPA
In April, when raining is sunlight. Great Farm. Philip Booth. PoPl
In Aprile at the hicht of noon. On Seein an Aik-Tree Sprent Wi Galls. Robert Garioch. OxBS
In Aprill the koocoo can sing her song by rote. The Koocoo. *Unknown.* GBP
In Arabia's book of fable. Princess Sabbath. Heine, *tr. by* Charles Godfrey Leland. TrJP
In Arcadia. Lawrence Durrell. MoBrPo
In Arcady. Cosmo Monkhouse. OBVV
In Arden. Charles Tomlinson. OxBC
In Arizona/ (how many years in the mountains). Louis Zukofsky. NoAM
In Armorik, that called is Britayne. The Franklin's Tale. Chaucer. *Fr.* The Canterbury Tales. OAEL-1
In arrogance and vanity. Only One King. John Richard Moreland. PGD
In Assisi. Michael Blumenthal. MAYP
In Auchtermuchty there dwelt ane man. The Wife of Auchtermuchty. *Unknown.* BSV; GoTS
In August. William Dean Howells. GN
In Autumn. Jon Anderson. AmPA
In Autumn. Barbara Howes. LiSp
In autumn/ the rich all over the world. The Suicides of the Rich. Victor Contoski. FAZ
In autumn down the beechwood path. Beech Leaves. James Reeves. OnUR
In autumn, the bats. The Bat. Roberta Spear. AmPA; MAYP
In Autumpne, whan the sonne in vyrgyne. The Bowge of Courte. John Skelton. AAS
In Baalbec there were lovers. The Passing Flower. Harry Kemp. HBMV
In back of our town. Gasco; or, The Toad. Günter Grass, *tr. by* Jerome Rothenberg. ELU
In Back of the Real. Allen Ginsberg. AmPP; HeIP; InPK
In Bacon see the culminating prime. Sir Francis Bacon. Ambrose Bierce. DBV
In Baltimore there lived a boy. The Boy Who Laughed at Santa Claus. Ogden Nash. CenHV
In Barracks. Siegfried Sassoon. FaBoTw
In battle-line of sombre gray. The Spirit of the *Maine.* Tudor Jenks. AA; PAH
In Bed. Myra Sklarew. AMV-81
In bed./ My hand on Mark's bare chest. At Rochdale. Ian Young. NeAC
In bed/ with my friend's young brother. A Sugar-Candy Bird. Ian Young. NeAC
In bed, dull man? Upon My Lord Brohall's Wedding. Sir John Suckling. CaPo
In bed I muse on Tenier's boors. The Bench of Boors. Herman Melville. OBAL
In bed we laugh, in bed we cry. Translation of Lines by Benserade. Samuel Johnson. CABA; FaBoEE
In Bed with a River. George Bradley. AMV-80

In bed with the stranger who had picked him up. A Bride. Harry Fainlight. BoLoP
In Belgrade, the windows of the tourist. Endurance. Carolyn Forché. SV
In Bertram's Garden. Donald Justice. BoLoP; ErPo; InPK; NePoEA; VGW
In Between the Curve. Barbara Bacon. AMV-80
In Beverley town a maid did dwell. The Beverley Maid and the Tinker. *Unknown.* CoMu
In Black Chasms. Leslie Norris. WSC
In black core of night, it explodes. African Dream. Bob Kaufman. AmNP; PoBA
In Blanco County. Russell T. Fowler. AMV-80
In Bloemfontein. Alan Ross. BoLoP
In blows the loitering air of spring. Spring Air. Gene Derwood. FaFP
In Blue. D. C. Berry. BXAP
In Bodenstown Churchyard there is a green grave. Tone's Grave. Thomas Osborne Davis. OnYI
In Bodleian and Harleian/ Lurk ambushes of grace.. Our Lady of the Libraries. Sister Mary Ignatius. ISi
In bodnie (bonnie), bright and fair Scotland, where bluebells they did grow. The Paisley Officer, *vers.* II. *Unknown.* ShS
In Bohemia. Arthur Symons. *See* City Nights: In Bohemia.
In Bondage. Claude McKay. PoBA
In bower and field he sought, where any tuft. Eve. Milton. *Fr.* Paradise Lost, IX. OBS; TEP
In boxes lined with faded satin. Pawnshop Window. R. H. Grenville. GoYe
In, boy; go first. You houseless poverty. Poor Naked Wretches. Shakespeare. *Fr.* King Lear, III, iii. PPON
In Breughel's great picture, The Kermess. The Dance. William Carlos Williams. AmPP; CMoP; GoJo; GrPl; HAP; HeIP; InPK; LiTM; NCSH; NIP; NoAm; NOBA; NoP; OxBA; PAI; POL; PrIm; SoSe; TAP; WeW
In bright morning sunlight, the horse appears pink. The Triangular Field. Stephen Dobyns. MAYP
In Britain's isles, as Heylyn notes. Matthew Prior. *Fr.* Alma; or, The Progress of the Mind. NOEC
In Brittany. Charles Weekes. OnYI
In Broad Street building (on a winter night). The Gouty Merchant and the Stranger. Horace Smith. BeLS
In Broken Images. Robert Graves. PPoe
In Brunton Town. *Unknown.* BaBo
(Bruton Town, *diff. vers.*) EnSB
"In Buckinghamshire hedgerows." The Icosasphere. Marianne Moore. ImOP
In Burgundy, beyond Auxerre. Sheep in the Rain. James Wright. AMV-80
In Cabin'd Ships at Sea. Walt Whitman. MOS
In Cagliostro's mirror the magician keeps all his women. Picasso's Women. Olga Cabral. PoDr
In California. Louis Simpson. NoAM
In California/ ankle-high animals occupy the tablelands. Report from California. Lois Moyles. NYBP
In calm and cool and silence, once again. First-Day Thoughts. Whittier. AmPP; NoP; TrCP
In calm fellowship they sleep. In a Grave-Yard. William Stanley Braithwaite. PoBA
In came her sister. Lady Maisry. *Unknown.* ESPB
In Camus Fields. L. A. G. Strong. DBV
In canary grass insects. Ethan Boldt. Roger Weingarten. AmPA
In candent ire the solar splendor flames. Aestivation [*or* Intramural Aestivation]. Oliver Wendell Holmes. *Fr.* The Autocrat of the Breakfast Table. ChTr; FaBoNo; InMe; NA; NOBL; OBAL; WhC
In Canterbury Cathedral. E. W. Oldenburg. EBCP
In Carmel Bay the people say. Abalone. *Unknown.* AS
In Caroline, whar I was born. Walk, Jaw-Bone. S. S. Steele. TrAS
In Carrowdore Churchyard. Derek Mahon. CIP
In Cavan of little lakes. A Song of Freedom. Alice Milligan. AnIV; OnYI
In Cawsand Bay lying, with the Blue Peter flying. Cawsand Bay. *Unknown.* PoPle
In Celebration. Ellen Bass. NMM
In Celebration of My Uterus. Anne Sexton. CAPP
In Celia's face a question did arise. Lips and Eyes. Giovan Battista Marino, *tr. by* Thomas Carew. OBVE
In Cemeteries. D. J. Enright. OxBC
In Chagall's Village. Rose Ausländer, *tr. fr. German by* Ewald Osers. VWA
In Chapman's day poets had to write about Gods. On First Looking into Chapman's Homer II. Peter Peterson. BXAP
In chariot like an hibiscus flower at his side. Confucius, *tr. by* Ezra Pound. *Fr.* Songs of Cheng. CTC
In Cherbourg Roads the pirate lay. The Eagle and Vulture. Thomas Buchanan Read. PAH
In Chester town there lived. A Brisk Young Widow. *Unknown.* OBET
In Childbed. Thomas Hardy. NAs
In childhood, when with eager eyes. The Trance of Time. John Henry Newman. OxBoCh
In childhood you think. Thanksgiving. John N. Morris. OFD
In childhood's unsuspicious hours. Epicurean. William James Linton. EBVV
In China they have ghost chairs. Once and Future. Diana Chang. BrSi
In Christ there is no East or [*or* nor] West. No East or West [*or* All One in Christ *or* In Christ]. John Oxenham. BLRP; STF; TRV
In Chu hai, dead machine guns lie frozen in the sun. Chrome Babies Eating Chocolate Snowmen in the Moonlight. A. K. Redwing. VoR
In Church. Thomas Hardy. *Fr.* Satires of Circumstance, II. DTC; MoAB; MoBrPo; SCV
In church he never felt the. The Man Who Invented Las Vegas. Gerald Costanzo. TAT
In church your grandsire cut his throat. On an Upright Judge. Swift. DBV
In cinemas we sought. Sing, Brothers, Sing! W. R. Rodgers. MoAB; MoBrPo
In Cipres springes [*or* Cyprus springs] (wheras [*or* whereas] dame Venus dwelt). Earl of Surrey. AAS; SiPS
In City Streets. Ada Smith. HBV-1
In Clementina's Artless Mien. Walter Savage Landor. *See* Of Clementina.
In Cloe's chamber, she and I. A Fragment. John Bancks. NOEC
In Clonmel Parish Churchyard. Sarah Morgan Bryan Piatt. AA
In Cnidus born, the consort I became. By Heraclides. *Unknown, tr. by* William Cowper. OBVE
In cock-wattle sunset or grey. Nostalgia. Louis MacNeice. OnYI
In Cold Hell, in Thicket. Charles Olson. PoM
In cold November. The News Stand. Daniel Berrigan. CAD
In Cold Storm Light. Leslie Marmon Silko. NoP; VoR
In college once I climbed the tree. Sickle Pears. Owen Dodson. AmNP
In college when a second language was required. Learning to Speak. Melvin Wilk. AMV-81
In Cologne, a town of monks and bones. Cologne. Samuel Taylor Coleridge. PV
In Columbus, Ohio. John Matthias. AMV-80
In Come de Animuls Two by Two. *Unknown.* GBP
In comes the captain's daughter, the captain of the yeos. The Boys of Wexford. *Unknown.* ELP
In coming down to Manchester to gain my liberty. The Soldier's Farewell to Manchester. *Unknown.* CoMu
In coming to the feast I found. The Horn. Léonie Adams. MoAB; MoAmPo
In Commendation of George Gascoigne's Steel Glass. Sir Walter Ralegh. SiPS
(Walter Rawley of the Middle Temple, in Commendation of Steele Glasse.) AAS
In Commendation of Music. William Strode. ELP; OBEV
In Common. Gene Derwood. NePA; PoPl
In companies or lone. The Knitters. Padraic Colum. SaC
In Computers. Alan P. Lightman. SUW
In concord then they set up hasty ways. Freighter. Bruce Ruddick. CaP
In Conjunction. Charles Madge. NeBP
In Consort to Wednesday, Jan. 1st. 1701. Richard Henchman. SCAP
In Cool, Green Haunts. Mahlon Leonard Fisher. WeW
In Cordoba the Caliph's Gardens. Cordoba. Asher Mendelssohn. VWA
In corduroy trousers and seedy black coats. W. H. Auden. *Fr.* A Happy New Year. OBSV
In costly sheen and gaudy cloak array'd. The Bull Fight. Byron. *Fr.* Childe Harold's Pilgrimage, I. LiSp
In countries where no birds are alive. For Edwin R. Embree. Owen Dodson. CNA
In Country Sleep. Dylan Thomas. LiTB
In court to serve decked with fresh array. The Courtier's Life. Sir Thomas Wyatt. FaBoEE
In crimson flood, wave thousands to his tomb. John Danforth. *Fr.* Pindarick Elegy upon the Renowned Mr. Samuel Willard. PeD
In Crisis. Lawrence Durrell. LiTM
In cruelty you greater are. To Francelia. Thomas Duffett. CavP
In crystal towers [*or* towns] and turrets richly set. Content [*or* Song]. Geffrey Whitney. ACP; ElL
In Cumberland city, as you shall all hear. Villkins and His Dinah. *Unknown.* BaBo
In Cupid's school whoe'er would take degree. Ovid, *tr. by* Dryden. *Fr.* The Art of Love. UnTE
In Cyprus springs—whereas dame Venus dwelt. Earl of Surrey. *See* In Cipres springes . . .
In Danger from the Outer World. Robert Bly. CAPP
In Dark Hour. Seumas MacManus. WGRP
In dark sockets. Jars. Paul Raboff. VWA

In darkest hours, in nights so drear. With Thee. Cora M. Pinkham. STF
In Dat Great Gittin'-up Mornin'. *Unknown.* AA; BoAN-2, *with music*
In daylight, even. The Countershadow. Philip Booth. NYBP
In days long gone God spake unto our sires. The Call. Thomas Curtis Clark. PGD
In days, my Lord, when mother Time. Soame Jenyns. *Fr.* An Epistle Written in the Country to the Right Honourable the Lord Lovelace. OBSV
In days of ease, when now the weary sword. The Court of Charles II. Pope. *Fr.* To Augustus. OBEC
In Days of New. Elizabeth Bartlett. AMV-81
In days of old,/ So I've been told. The Feast of the Monkeys. John Philip Sousa. OBAL
In days of old, those far off times. The Toad. Robert S. Oliver. RHPC
In days of old, when Englishmen were—men. Italian Opera. James Miller. OBEC
In days of old when Spenser sang. Ballade of the Goth. Sir Walter Raleigh. WhC
In days of peace my fellow-men. From a Full Heart. A. A. Milne. InMe
In days of summer let me go In Ampezzo. Trumbull Stickney. TwAmPo
In days when Albion's seamen knew. Sea-Birds. Fray Angelico Chavez. ISi
In de dead of night I sometimes. The Old Cabin. Paul Laurence Dunbar. PoLF
In de ebening by de moonlight when his darkie's work was over. In the Evening by the Moonlight. James A. Bland. TreFS
In de Lord, in de Lord. My Soul's Been Anchored in de Lord. *Unknown.* BoAN-2
In de Vinter Time, *with music. Unknown.* AS
In Dead Air, under Furious Sun. William Hathaway. *Fr.* Rumplestiltskin Poems. DFT
In Deadly Fear. Blake. *Fr.* Jerusalem. SeCePo
In Dear Detail, by Ideal Light. William Stafford. NaP
In dear old New York it's remarkable. The Streets of New York. Henry Blossom. FSN
In Death. Mary Emily Bradley. AA
In Death Divided. Thomas Hardy. DTC
In death the dead remember their spirit. Funeral Poem. Amiri Baraka. CNA
In Death's Field. Al-Khansa, *tr. fr. Arabic by* Willis Barnstone. BoWoP
In Debtor's Yard the stones are hard. Oscar Wilde. *Fr.* The Ballad of Reading Gaol. ViBoPo
In December. Andrew Young. SeCePo
In December predawn. The Fisherman's Wife. Nora Mitchell. AMV-80
In December, when the days draw to be short. Little John Nobody. *Unknown.* OxBoLi
In Defence of Humanism. David Gascoyne. *See* Salvador Dali.
In Defense of Black Poets. Conrad Kent Rivers. BOLo; BPo
In Defense of Felons. Robert Mezey. NePoEA
In Defense of Metaphysics. Charles Tomlinson. MoBrPo
In Defense of Satire. Sir Carr Scroope. APAS
In Defense of Superficiality. Elder Olson. NYBP
In deference to the cloud parade. The Cloud Parade. Laura Jensen. LCAP
In Defiance to the Dutch. *Unknown.* APAS
In desolation, here a lost world lies. Epitaph, Found Somewhere in Space. Hugh Wilgus Ramsaur. TRV
In Despair. C. P. Cavafy, *tr. fr. Greek by* Edmund Keeley *and* Philip Sherrard. PeHV
In despair at not being able to rival the creations of God. Hymn to Her Unknown. W. J. Turner. OBMV
In Despair He Orders a New Typewriter. Elder Olson. AMV-81
In Dessexshire as It Befel. *Unknown.* GBP
In desultory walk through orchard grounds. Prelude. Wordsworth. VLP
In Detroit, I walk out Woodward Avenue. R. R. Cuscaden. POL
In dim green depths rot ingot-laden ships. Sunken Gold. Eugene Lee-Hamilton. EtS; NCEP
In Discreet Splendor. A. L. Strauss, *tr. fr. Hebrew by* Robert Friend. VWA
In Disguise. Joseph Rolnik, *tr. fr. Yiddish by* Keith Bosley. VWA
In Dispraise of Poetry. Jack Gilbert. PP
In Dispraise of the Moon. Mary Elizabeth Coleridge. BoNaP; CH; MOON; NBM
In Distress. David Wagoner. SUW
In Distrust of Merits. Marianne Moore. AP; CoBMV; EaLo; LiTA; LiTM; MoAB; MoAmPo; NePA; OBWP; OxBA; SeCeV; TreFT; TrGrPo; ViBoPo; WaaP; WaP
In Dives' Dive. Robert Frost. VGW
In Domrèmy a maid. The Maid of Arc. Gordon Bottomley. GoTL
In Dream. J. M. Synge. SyP
In dream I saw two Jews that met by chance. Moses and Jesus. Israel Zangwill. TrJP
In Dream: The Privacy of Sequence. Ray A. Young Bear. CDW
In dream the waterfall. The Practice of Absence. Robert Friend. VWA
In dreams a dark château. The Dark Château. Walter de la Mare. BrPo
In dreams I see the Dromedary still. The Dromedary. A. Y. Campbell. HBMV
In dreams my life came toward me. American Dreams. Louis Simpson. GP
In Dreamy Swoon. George Darley. *Fr.* Nepenthe. OBNC
("Over a bloomy land, untrod.") OBRV
In Drear-nighted December. Keats. *See* In a Drear-nighted December.
In Dresden, in the square one day. The Violinist. Archibald Lampman. CaP
In drooping leaves of the plane. August. Laurence Binyon. SyP
In Dublin town I was brought up, a city of great fame. Bold Jack Donahue. *Unknown.* FSW
In Dublin's fair city, where [the] girls are so pretty. Cockles and Mussels. *Unknown.* ELP; FSW; OnYI
In Dublin's fair city. Dublin Doggerel. Richard Conniff. DBV
In due course of course you will [all] be issued with. Unarmed Combat. Henry Reed. Lessons of the War, III. HeIP; LiTB
In Due Season. W. H. Auden. Prf
In due season the amphibious crocodile. Amphibious Crocodile. John Crowe Ransom. OBAL
In due time bridges collapse, handsome people get. In the Palms of Ancient Bodhisattvas. John Tagliabue. AMV-81
In Dulci Jubilo. *Unknown, tr. fr. German by* John Wedderburn. ChTr
In each mans heart that doth begin. Loves World. Sir John Suckling. SeCV-1
In Earliest Spring. William Dean Howells. *See* Earliest Spring.
In early days/ If kings were made by men. Human Debasement; a Fragment. Edward Rushton. NOEC
In early fall, along the Salt Fork. 61. Charlotte DeClue. TWSS
In early March, before the lark. The Missel-Thrush's Nest. John Clare. VLP
In early morning twilight, raw and chill. The Eviction. William Allingham. *Fr.* Laurence Bloomfield in Ireland. BIrV
In early snow. Road. W. S. Merwin. PPJ
In Early Spring. Alice Meynell. HBV-1
In early summer moonlight I have strayed. The Sedge-Warbler. Ralph Hodgson. PB
In early winter before the first snow. An Elegy. E. J. Scovell. ChMP
In early youth's unclouded scene. Thirty-eight. Charlotte Smith. SBG; WPOW
In Earthen Vessels. Whittier. BLRP; TRV
In Egypt. Paul Celan, *tr. fr. German by* Joachim Neugroschel. VWA
In Egypt they worshiped me. I Am the Cat. Leila Usher. BLPA
In Egypt's sandy silence, all alone. On a Stupendous Leg of Granite, Discovered Standing by Itself in the Deserts of Egypt, with the Inscription Inserted Below. Horatio H. Smith. PrIm
In eighteen hundred and eighty nine. Obituary. Conrad Aiken. OBAL
In eighteen hundred and forty-five. Greenland Whale Fishery. *Unknown.* OuSiCo
In eighteen hundred and forty one, I put my corduroy breeches on. Pat Works on the Railway. *Unknown.* FSW; TrAS
In eighteen hundred and sixty-one. The *Alabama, vers.* II. *Unknown.* ShS
In 1855. State School. Paul D. Shiplett. LFAC
In 1876/ The Cooper & Bailey Great London Circus. The Cooper & Bailey Great London Circus. Robert Hershon. MAT
In 1867. White Bear. Susan Griffin. GP
In either mood, to bless or curse. Doom. Arthur O'Shaughnessy. OBVV
In elder times an ancient custom 'twas. Swearing. Henry Fitzsimon. ACP
In elderis dayis, as Esope can declair. The Taill of the Foxe, That Begylit the Wolf, in the Schadow of the Mone. Robert Henryson. OxBS
In England rivers all are males. On the American Rivers. James Smith. FaBoUs
In England's Green & (a Garland and a Clyster). Jonathan Williams. CoPo
In enterprise of martial kind. The Duke of Plaza-Toro. W. S. Gilbert. *Fr.* The Gondoliers. FaPON; FiBHP
In Epping Forest. John Clare. *See* Stanzas from "Child Harold."
In Eternum. Sir Thomas Wyatt. NOBE
("In eternum I was ons determed.") AAS; SiPS
In ethics class so many years ago. Ethics. Linda Pastan. AMV-81
In Europe, you can't move without going down into history. In the Yukon. Ralph Gustafson. MoCV
In Evening Air. Theodore Roethke. NYBP; TAP
In every church, in every clime. The Faithful Few. Chester E. Shuler. STF
In every city I want to listen: people. Berkeley, Madison, Ann Arbor, Kent. William Stafford. SOTS
In every direction from here. Delphine. Teresa Anderson. LTB
In every dream thy lovely features rise. Sonnet. William Barnes. BoLoP
In every leaf that crowns the plain. Faith. John Richard Moreland. OHIP
In every line a supple beauty. A Likeness. Willa Cather. HBMV

In every old lady I chance to meet. Old Ladies. Will Allen Dromgoole. WeW
In every place ye may well see. What Women Are Not. *Unknown.* MeEl
In every seed to breathe the flower. Faith. John Banister Tabb. TRV; WGRP
In every solemn tree the wind. Love Song from New England. Winifred Welles. HBMV
In Every Thing Give Thanks. *Unknown.* STF
In every trembling bud and bloom. An Easter Canticle. Charles Hanson Towne. OHIP; TrPWD
In every war, strange legends circulate. Philippine Madonna. Louise Crenshaw Ray. ISi
In evil hour did Pope's declining age. On the Edition of Mr. Pope's Works with a Commentary and Notes. Thomas Edwards. TW
"In Evil Long I Took Delight." John Newton. OxBoCh
In evrich mart that stands on British ground. The School-Mistress. William Shenstone. NOEC
In ev'ry thought, in ev'ry wish I own. Joseph Howe. *Fr.* Acadia. CaP
In ev'ry town where Thamis rolls his tide. The Alley; an Imitation of Spenser. Pope. NOEC
In Exile. Emma Lazarus. SBG
In Explanation. Walter Learned. AA; HBV-1
In Extremis. Margaret Fishback. FiBHP
In Extremis. Geroge Sterling. HBV-2
In fair Worcester City and in Worcestershire. The Gosport Tragedy. *Unknown.* BaBo
In faith, good Histor, long is your delay. Geron and Histor. Sir Philip Sidney. *Fr.* Arcadia. SiPS
In faith, I do[e] not love thee with mine eyes. Sonnets, CXLI. Shakespeare. PoEL-2; TrGrPo
In faith I wot not what to say. Sir Thomas Wyatt. SiPS
In faith methinks it is no right. Resignation. Sir Thomas Wyatt. OBSC
In faith thou shalt haue mine. Robin Hood Rescuing Three Squires. *Unknown.* ESPB
In fall when we went the roads. Fear. Dara Wier. MAYP
In fallow college days, Tom Harland. The Ballad of Lager Bier. Edmund Clarence Stedman. OBAL
In far forests' leafy twilight, now is stealing gray dawn's shy light. Music of the Dawn. Virginia Bioren Harrison. HBV-1
In Fargo, North Dakota, a man. To Flood Stage Again. James Wright. NOBA; Prf
In fashion as a snow-white rose, lay then. The Saints in Glory. Dante, *tr. by* Henry F. Cary. *Fr.* Divina Commedia: Paradiso. WGRP
In Favor of One's Time. Frank O'Hara. NeAP; PoA
In fear of the rich mouth. The Frightened Man. Louise Bogan. SBG
In February. Henry Simpson. HBV-1
In February. John Addington Symonds. YeAr
In February I give you gallant sport. Sonnets of the Months: February. Folgore da San Geminiano, *tr. by* Dante Gabriel Rossetti. AWP
In February there are days. When. Dorothy Aldis. RHPC; SiSoSe
In February when few gusty flakes. Ground Hog Day. Marnie Pomeroy. PoSC
In fellowship Religion has its founts. George Meredith. *Fr.* The Test of Manhood. WGRP
In Festubert. Edmund Blunden. OBMV
In fiction tales we keep performing. The Collies. Edward Anthony. GDP
In Fields of Summer. Galway Kinnell. BoNaP; RFM; VGW
In '59 Pike's Peakers were a sight. The Pike's Peakers. Lawrence N. Greenleaf. PoOW
In Fine, Transparent Words. David Vogel, *tr. fr. Hebrew by* A. C. Jacobs. VWA
In fire-script. Thou Shalt Not. Malka Heifitz Tussman, *tr. by* Marcia Falk. VWA
In First People's sky there is no moon. Raven/Moon. Anita Endrezze Probst. VoR
In five-score summers! All new eyes. 1967. Thomas Hardy. NoAM
In Flanders Fields. John McCrae. BLPA; CaP; FaBV; FaFP; FaPo; FaPoR; FPL; HBV-2; NOBC; OBCV; OBWP; OHFP; PAL; PeCV; PGD; PoPl; SiSoSe; TreF; ViBoPo
In Flanders Fields. *Unknown, ad. fr.* John D. Mccrae. WBLP
In Flanders Fields the cannons boom. Another Reply to "In Flanders Fields." J. A. Armstrong. BLPA; PAL
In Flanders Now. Edna Jaques. CaP
In Flanders once there was a company. The Pardoner's Tale. Chaucer, *mod. version by* Nevill Coghill. *Fr.* The Canterbury Tales. BiP
In Flaunders [*or* Flandres] whilom [*or* whylom] was a compaignye [*or* companye]. The Pardoner's Tale. Chaucer. *Fr.* The Canterbury Tales. FiP; HAP; NoP; OAEL-1; PoEL-1
In Flavia's eyes is every grace. On Miss Eleanor Ambrose, a Celebrated Beauty in Dublin. Earl of Chesterfield. FaBoEE
In flight in escape. Nelly Sachs, *tr. fr. German by* Arthur Wensinger. BoWoP
In flowed at once a gay embroidered race. A Young Traveller Is Presented to the Goddess Dulness. Pope. The Dunciad, IV, i. NOEC
In fond delusion once I left thy side. A Sonnet to My Mother. Heine, *tr. by* Emma Lazarus. TrJP
In Fond du Lac, Bronxville, Butte, Chicago. Last Year's Discussion: The Nobel Russian. Phyllis McGinley. FaBoEE
In Foreign Parts. Laura E. Richards. HBV-2; HBVY
In forgiving mood, this sultry July afternoon. Goodbye to Regal. Daniel Huws. NYBP
In form and feature, face and limb. The Twins. Henry Sambrooke Leigh. CenHV; FaPON; HBV-2; HBVY; PoPl; RHPC; ShM; TiPo
In former days my father and mother. Cuckoo. *Unknown, tr. by* Charles W. Kennedy. *Fr.* Riddles (Exeter Book). AnOE
In former days we'd both agree. Bhartrihari, *tr. fr. Sanskrit by* John Brough. BoLoP
In former times, when Israel's ancient creed. Absolute and Abitofhell. Ronald Arbuthnott Knox. CenHV; FaBoCo
In fourteen hundred and ninety-two. Christopher Columbus. Franklin P. Adams. InMe
In fourteen hundred and ninety-two. Christofo Columbo. *Unknown.* AmSS
In fourteen hundred and ninety-two. Moosehead Lake. *Unknown.* OuSiCo
In fourteen hundred ninety-two, Columbus sailed the ocean blue. The History of the U.S. Winifred Sackville Stoner. TreF; YaD
In fragrant Dixie's arms. Church Burning: Mississippi. James A. Emanuel. PoBA; PoNe
In France. Frances Cornford. HBMV
In France, the men who for their desperate ends. Wordsworth. *Fr.* The Prelude, X. OBRV
In Francum. Sir John Davies. FaBoEE
In Freedom's War, of "Thirty Years" and more. Enfant perdu. Heine, *tr. by* Lord Houghton. AWP
In Front of a Poster of Garibaldi. Stanley Moss. DiL
In front of our mouths, wherever we swim. Goldfish on the Writing Desk. Max Brod, *tr. by* Babette Deutsch *and* Avram Yarmolinsky. TrJP
In Front of the Landscape. Thomas Hardy. OBNC
In front of the mighty washing machine. The Small Lady. Stevie Smith. TEP
In Front of the Seine, Recalling the Río de la Plata. Silvina Ocampo, *tr. fr. Spanish by* Jason Weiss. AMV-80
In front of the sombre mountains. On the Balcony [*or* Illicit]. D. H. Lawrence. BrPo; GBL; PoA
In front the awful Alpine track. Stanzas in Memory of the Author of "Obermann." Matthew Arnold. VLP
In front the horse's rump bright as a lantern. Sleighride. Patrick Anderson. CaP; OBCV
In full glare of sunlight I came here, man-tall but thin. The Roundhouse Voices. Dave Smith. AMV-80; GeTw; LiSp; MAYP
In Fur. William Stafford. RFM
In Fury and Terror. The Storm. Elizabeth J. Coatsworth. OBCA
In Fuscum. Sir John Davies. FaBoEE
In Gaetam. Thomas Bastard. FaBoEE
In Galilee. Mary Frances Butts. AA
In Galleries. Randall Jarrell. EyDe
In Galloway. Andrew Greig. BSV
In gayer hours, when high my fancy ran [*or* run]. The Bastard's Lot. Richard Savage. *Fr.* The Bastard. NOEC; OBEC; OBSV
In Genesis, the world was made. Old Testament Contents. *Unknown.* BLPA
In Genoa the superb O'Connell dies. The Dead Tribune. Denis Florence MacCarthy. ACP
In Glasgow, in 'Eighty-four. In a Music-Hall. John Davidson. EBVV
In Glencullen. J. M. Synge. ELU; FM; OBMV; OxBI
In gloomy eyes there wells no tear. The Silesian Weavers. Heine, *tr. by* Aaron Kramer. NAWM-2
In go-cart so tiny. Kate Greenaway. FaPON; TiPo
In God's Eternal Studios. Paul Shivell. *Fr.* The Studios Photographic. HBV-2
In God's Eternity, *with music.* Hosea Ballou I. AH
In going to my naked bed, as one that would have slept. Amantium Irae [Amoris Redintegratio]. Richard Edwards. EIL; HBV-2; LoBV; OBEV; OBSC
In gold sandals. Sappho, *tr. fr. Greek by* Willis Barnstone. BoWoP
In Golden Gate Park That Day. Lawrence Ferlinghetti. *Fr.* A Coney Island of the Mind. NoAM; PAI
In golden winters one misses them most. California Dead. G. E. Murray. MAYP
In Good King Charles's Golden Days. *Unknown.* *See* Vicar of Bray, The.
In good old Benjamin Franklin's time. The Truth about B. F. Albert Stillman. InMe
In good old colony times. Old Colony Times. *Unknown.* BLSo

In good old Stalin's early days. Garland for a Propagandist. Ted Pauker. NOBL
In good old times, which means, you know. Verses Intended to Go with a Posset Dish to My Dear Little Goddaughter, 1889. James Russell Lowell. AP
In Gosport of late a young damsel did dwell. The Gosport Tragedy. *Unknown.* AmFP
In Goya's Greatest Scenes [We Seem to See]. Lawrence Ferlinghetti. *Fr.* A Coney Island of the Mind. FF; HeIP; LiTM; NeAP; NMP; NoAM; PoM; TAP
In grade school I wondered. Zimmer in Grade School. Paul Zimmer. GP
In Grandfather's Glasses. Patricia Peters. Str
In graves where drips the winter rain. The Song of the Graves. *Unknown, tr. by* Ernest Rhys. *Fr.* The Black Book of Carmarthen. OBMV
In green Caledonia they ne'er were two lovers. Burns and His Highland Mary. *Unknown.* ShS
In Green Old Gardens. "Violet Fane." HBV-1
In grey April when the bud rounded. The Flute of May. Harry Woodbourne. GoYe
In grey-haired Celia's withered arms. A Paraphrase from the French. Matthew Prior. OxBoLi
In grimy winter dusk. Stop. Richard Wilbur. LCAP
In-Group. Lionel Kearns. PeCV
In groves of green trees. Black Students. Julia Fields. NBP
In Guernsey. Swinburne. VLP
In Hades. Anna Callender Brackett. AA
In haist ga hy thee to sum hoill. John Rolland. *Fr.* The Seven Seages. OxBS
In Hampton Beach, the airs of March were bland. The Attack. Thomas Buchanan Read. PAH
In Hans' old mill his three black cats. Five Eyes. Walter de la Mare. PCat
In Harbor. Paul Hamilton Hayne. AA; HBV-2
In Harbor. Lizette Woodworth Reese. TrPWD
In Harbour. Swinburne. VLP
In hard/ country. Hard Country. Philip Booth. CoAP
In Hardin County, 1809. Lulu E. Thompson. PoSC
In Hardwood Groves. Robert Frost. HAP
In Harmony with Nature. Matthew Arnold. OAEP
In Hässelby. Evening Walk. Sonja Åkesson, *tr. by* Joanna Bankier. WPOW
In haste, post haste, when first my wandering mind. Gascoigne's Memories, IV. George Gascoigne. AAS; EnRePo
In health, they do abuse. *Unknown.* FaBoUs
In hearts too young for enmity there lies the way. Disarm the Hearts. Ethel Blair Jordan. PGD
In Heaven/ Some little blades of grass. The Blades of Grass. Stephen Crane. *Fr.* The Black Riders. MoAmPo; PoPl; TreFT
In Heaven a spirit doth dwell. Israfel. Poe. AA; AmPP; AP; AWP; BLPL; HBV-2; LiTA; NePA; NOBA; OxBA; PoEL-4; TAP; TreFS; WHA
In Heaven, I Suppose, Lie Down Together. C. Day Lewis. MoPo
In heaven queene is she among the spheares. Heaven's Queene. Sir Walter Ralegh. MOON
In Heaven Soaring Up. Edward Taylor. *See* Joy of Church Fellowship Rightly Attended, The.
In heaven there is a star I call my own. Irene Rutherford McLeod. *Fr.* Sonnets. HBMV
In heaven, too. Heard in a Violent Ward. Theodore Roethke. NoAM
In heaven-high musings and many. The Strength of Fate. Euripides, *tr. by* A. E. Housman. *Fr.* Alcestis. AWP
In Heavenly Realms of Hellas Dwelt. E. E. Cummings. NOBA; OBSV
In Heavy Mind. James Agee. MoAmPo
In Hebrew "In the beginning." From the Head. Louis Zukofsky. VWA
In her boudoir, the young lady—unacquainted with grief. *Tr. fr. Chinese by* Arthur Waley. OBVE
In her coffin, satin-shirred. A Poor Relation. Audrey McGaffin. NePoAm-2
In her fair cheeks two pits do lie. A Song. Thomas Carew. UnTE
In her first passion woman loves her lover. Byron. *Fr.* Don Juan, III. ErPo; UnTE
In her gnarled sleep it/ begins. The Cherry Tree. Thom Gunn. Psk
In her hands she holds. The Man She Called Honey, and Married. Alberto Ríos. MAYP
In her own isle's remotest grove. The Temple of Venus. Soame Jenyns. NOEC
In Her Praise. Robert Graves. BIrV
In her room at the prow of the house. The Writer. Richard Wilbur. OxBC; Str
In her room she is/ small and adrift. The Death of the Sailor's Wife. Fred Barton. AMV-80
In Her Song She Is Alone. Jon Swan. NYBP
In here/ the gods have lost all their words. Isolation Cell Poem. J. Charles Green. LFAC
In High Places. Harriet Monroe. PoA
In highest way of heaven the sun did ride. Astrophel and Stella, XXII. Sir Philip Sidney. OBSC; SiPS
In Him. James Vila Blake. WGRP
In Him. Annie Johnson Flint. BLRP; TRV
In him inexplicably mixed appeared. Byron. Lara, XVII-XIX. OAEL-2
In Him We Live. Jones Very. OxBA
In his chamber, weak and dying. Longfellow. *Fr.* The Norman Baron. PeD
In his chamber, weak and dying. A Strike among the Poets. *Unknown.* FaBoCo; FiBHP; PP
In his dream Jacob was in a wilderness. Jacob. Charles Reznikoff. VWA
In his father's face flying. Icarus. Ronald Botrall. GTBS-P
In His hands I leave tomorrow. Tomorrow. Della Adams Leitner. STF
In his landscapes silence is eloquent. Homage to Edward Hopper. Emery George. HoAn
In His Last Binn Sir Peter Lies. Thomas Love Peacock. *Fr.* Headlong Hall. EnRP
(Song: "In his last bin[n] Sir Peter lies.") OBRV; ViBoPo
In his low-ceilinged oaken room. The Silent Room. Kingsley Amis. OxBC
In his malodorous brain what slugs and mire. God. Isaac Rosenberg. MoPo; VWA
In his old gusty garden of the North. Robert Louis Stevenson. Lizette Woodworth Reese. HBV-2
In his own image the Creator made. On Man. Walter Savage Landor. NBM; OBNC; OBRV
In his sea lit/ distance, the pitcher winding. The Double Play. Robert Wallace. LiSp; PP
In His Service. Clarence E. Clar. STF
In His Steps. Katharine Lee Bates. PGD
In his still corner Rocky takes the count. On a Boxer. X. J. Kennedy. PPJ
In his tall senatorial. The Drum; the Narrative of the Demon of Tedworth. Edith Sitwell. FaBoTw
In his travels, the elephant. Elephant. David McFadden. WHW
In His Utter Wretchedness. John Audelay. MeEL
(Dread of Death.) OxBM
In Hoc Signo. Godfrey Fox Bradby. TRV
In holly hedges starving birds. Christmas Eve. John Davidson. OHIP
In holy books, in church, I hear curses. The Morning of the Red-tailed Hawk. Bettie M. Sellers. AMV-80
In honnour of this heghe fest, of custume yere by yere. A Lover's New Year's Gift. John Lydgate. PoEL-1
In Honour of Christmas. *Unknown.* MeEL
In Honour of St. Alphonsus Rodriguez. Gerard Manley Hopkins. EBEV; VLP
In Honour of Taffy Topaz. Christopher Morley. TiPo
In Honour of That High and Mighty Princess Queen Elizabeth of Happy Memory. Anne Bradstreet. SBG
In Honour of the City of London. William Dunbar. *See* To the City of London.
In Hospital. James Elroy Flecker. OxBTC
In Hospital. W. E. Henley. BrPo
Sels.
Apparition, XXV. TrGrPo
Before, IV. MoBrPo; VLP
Casualty, XIII. VLP
Romance. PAH
Staff Nurse: New Style, X. NBM
Vigil, VII. LOBV
Waiting, II. NBM; VLP
In Hospital: Poona, I ("Last night I did not fight for sleep"). Alun Lewis. DTC; NeBP; SeCePo
In Hospital: Poona, II ("The sun has sucked and beat the encircling hills"). Alun Lewis. DTC
In Hotels Public and Private. Ralph Pomeroy. CoPo
In Humbleness. Daniel G. Hoffman. NePA
In Iceland. Howard McCord. GP
In Imitation of Anacreon. Matthew Prior. *See* On Critics.
In Imitation of Pope. Isaac Hawkins Browne. *Fr.* A Pipe of Tobacco. OBEC
("Blest leaf! whose aromatic gales dispense.") BXAP; Par
In Imitation of Young. Isaac Hawkins Browne. *Fr.* A Pipe of Tobacco. OBEC
In Immemoriam. "Cuthbert Bede." NA
In Impressions of Hawk Feathers Willow Leaves Shadow. Elizabeth Woody. STE
In India. Karl Shapiro. NYBP
In Ionia whence sprang old poets' fame. Phoebe on Latmus. Michael Drayton. *Fr.* Endimion and Phoebe. OBSC

In Ireland, *sel.* Arthur Symons.
By the Pool at the Third Rosses, II. FaBoPP; OBNC; VLP
In Ireland they were put in foundling homes. Orphans. David Ray. FiCP
In Islington for the moment I reside. Important Statement. Patrick Kavanagh. PoCh
In Italy, where this sort of thing can occur. A Hill. Anthony Hecht. CoAP; NYBP
In its absence it has become beautiful. The Glove. Harold Bond. NYBP
In its going down, the moon. Poem. Robert Hogg. MoCV
In its own way rising to crest by me, the day. Fall Lightly on Me. Roger Gaess. LTB
In Its Place. Carol Stager. AMV-80
In its tenth year we realize. Bring the War Home. William Matthews. GeTw
In Jail. Juan Antonio Corretjer, *tr. fr. Spanish by* Julio Marzán. InW
In James Street. Thirty Childbirths. Millen Brand. AMV-80
In January, 1962. Ted Kooser. Psk
In Japanese,/ two characters combine. Definitions of the Word *Gout.* Tina Koyama. BrSi
In jealously of cause and pride of plan. Autonomous. Mark Van Doren. LiTA
In Jersey City where I did dwell. The Butcher Boy. *Unknown.* AmFP
In Jerusalem Are Women. Arye Sivan, *tr. fr. Hebrew by* David Shevin. VWA
In Josef Koudelka's photograph, untitled & with no date. Sensationalism. Larry Levis. MAYP
In Judgment of the Leaf. Kenneth Patchen. VGW
In July month, ae bonny morn. My Winsome Dear. Robert Fergusson. *Fr.* Leith Races. SeCePo
In july of 19 somethin. With All Deliberate Speed. Don L. Lee. JB
In jumping and tumbling. Tumbling. *Unknown.* OxBChV
In June. Nora Perry. YeAr
In June, amid the golden fields. The Groundhog. Richard Eberhart. CABA; CMoP; DTC; FaBoMo; FaFP; LiTA; LiTM; MasP; MiAP; MoAB; MoAmPo; MoPo; MoVE; NePA; NoAM; NoP; NU; PAI; PPoe; SeCeV; TAP; TwAmPo; UnPo; WaP
In June and Gentle Oven. Anne Wilkinson. MoCV; NOBC; PeCV
In June I give you a close-wooded fell. Sonnets of the Months: June. Folgore da San Geminiano, *tr. by* Dante Gabriel Rossetti. AWP
In June the bush we call. The Victors. Denise Levertov. NoP
In June the early signs. For a Christening. Anne Ridler. MoPo
In just-/ Spring when the world is mud. E. E. Cummings. Chansons Inocentes, I. AmPP; CAD; FaBV; FaPON; HeIP; InPK; MoAB; MoAmPo; MoShBr; NCSH; NIP; NoP; PrIm; SoSe; WeW
In Kansas. *Unknown.* FSW
In Katam. Sir John Davies. *See* Kate Being Pleased.
In Kensington Gardens. Arthur Symons. EnLoPo
In Kerem Abraham. Tabernacle of Peace. Hayim Be'er, *tr. by* Stephen Mitchell. VWA
In Kerry. J. M. Synge. FaBoPP; GBL; MoBrPo
In kirtle of myrtle the goose girl goes. The Goose Girl. Dorothy Roberts. CaP
In kohl mines and estaminets of gold. The Vole. Marvin Solomon. NePoAm-2
In Köhln [*or* Köln], a town of monks and bones. Cologne. Samuel Taylor Coleridge. DBV; FaBoEE; HBV-1; InMe; TW; WhC
In kraals of slanting shade the herd. Buffalo. Charles Eglington. PeSA
In Lady Lusher's drawing-room, where float the strains of Brahms. The Martyred Democrat. C. J. Dennis. CBAP
In lands I never saw, they say. Emily Dickinson. NePA
In Lantana Street's mid-morning. At the Nature-Strip. Judith Rodriguez. CBAP
In late winter/ I sometimes glimpse bits of steam. The Bear. Galway Kinnell. CoAP; NNaP; RFM; VGW
In Laughter. Ted Hughes. InPS
In Leinster. Louise Imogen Guiney. AA; OBVV
(Song: "I try to knead and spin, but my life is low the while.") GoBC; HBV-2
In Leonardo's painting, she studies. The Annunciation. Margot Kriel. PoDr
In letters large upon the frame. What's In a Name? R. K. Munkittrick. InMe
In Librum. Sir John Davies. FaBoEE
In Lieu. Louis MacNeice. CMoP
In life three ghostly friars were we. Glee—The Ghosts. Thomas Love Peacock. *Fr.* Melincourt. ViBoPo
In Life's Stable. Kadya Molodovsky, *tr. fr. Yiddish by* Ruth Whitman. VWA
In like a Lion. Geof Hewitt. PPJ
In Lincolnshire, a village full of tongues. On Looking at Stubb's Anatomy of the Horse. Edward Lucie-Smith. NePoEA-2
In Lithuania, on the Neman. The Little House in Lithuania. Samuel Marshak, *tr. by* Daniel Weissbort. VWA
In Little Hands. Mani Leib, *tr. fr. Yiddish by* Keith Bosley. VWA
In Little Rock the people bear. The Chicago "Defender" Sends a Man to Little Rock. Gwendolyn Brooks. AmNP; PoBA
In Liverpool there liv'd a man. The Big Five-Gallon Jar. *Unknown.* ShS
In London at Bessborough Gardens. Conrad. Antoni Slonimski, *tr. by* Isaac Komem. VWA
In London city was Bicham born. Young Beichan. *Unknown.* ESPB; FaBoBa; ViBoFo
In London City where I once did dwell, there's where I got my learning. Barbara [*or* Barbra] Allen. *Unknown.* AS; BeLS
In London I never know what to be at. Country and Town. Charles Morris. NOEC
In London, September 1802. Wordsworth. *See* Written in London, September, 1802.
In London there I was bent. London Lickpenny [*or* Lackpenny]. *Unknown.* ChTr; CoMu; FaBoPP; OBSV
In London town where I did dwell. The Butcher Boy. *Unknown.* ViBoFo
In London was young Beichan born. Young Beichan and Susie Pye. *Unknown.* HBV-2; OnMSP
In loneliness or grief, I treasure yet my friendship with Ben A'an. In Praise of Ben Avon. Brenda G. Macrow. PoSH
In lonely watches night by night. Requiescant. Frederick George Scott. OHIP
In Long Valley the Finns. Washrags. Vern Rutsala. GP
In loopy links the canker crawls. Indifference. *Unknown.* NA
In Lord Carpenter's Country. Barry O. Higgs. PeSA
In Louisiana. Albert Bigelow Paine. AA; AmFN
In Love. David Wevill. MoCV
In Love, at Stonehenge. Coventry Patmore. *Fr.* The Angel in the House. FaBoPP
In Love for Long. Edwin Muir. BoLoP; LiTM; MoBrPo
In Love, if Love Be Love. Tennyson. *Fr.* Idylls of the King: Merlin and Vivien. CABA; PoEL-5; TrGrPo
(All in All.) LiTB; TRV
(Vivien's Song.) FaBoEn; OBNC
In love they wore themselves in a green embrace. Adolescence. P. K. Page. CaP; OBCV
In love to be sure what disasters we meet. The Lover's Arithmetic. *Unknown.* OxBoLi
In Love with the Bears. Greg Kuzma. NYBP
In Love with You. Kenneth Koch. CAPP
In loving, each one hath free choice. Isabella Whitney. *Fr.* A Sweet Nosegay or Pleasant Posy. WPE
In lower orders up to the mammal. The Membrane. Mei-mei Berssenbrugge. LTB
In lowly dale, fast by a river's side. The Land of Indolence [*or* Enchanted Ground]. James Thomson. *Fr.* The Castle of Indolence, Canto I. BSV; EnRP; NOEC; OBEC; SeCePo; ViBoPo
In Lucas, Kansas. Jonathan Williams. FAZ
In lungs fresh like honeycomb. Indian. Laura Jensen. AmPA
In Lythe Strathdon. Charles Murray. PoSH
In Madrid's outlying trenches. Hans Beimler. Ernst Busch, *tr. fr. German.* FSW
In Maidstone Gaol, I am lamenting. Farewell to the World of Richard Bishop. *Unknown.* CoMu
In man, ambition is the common'st thing. Ambition. Robert Herrick. CaPO
In Manchester Square. Alice Meynell. SBG
In many forms we try. The Bohemian Hymn. Emerson. WGRP
In many places here and. Fate Is Unfair. Don Marquis. *Fr.* Archy Does His Part. EvOK
In marble walls [*or* halls] as white as milk. Mother Goose. ChTr; GBP; HBV-1; HBVY; OxNR; PoPle
In March. Philip Martin. PoAu-2
In March and April, thereabout. Alison. *Unknown.* HAP
In March birds couple, a new birth. From the Welsh of Henry Vaughan. Aneirin [*or* The Leaves Come Again]. FaBoEE; FaBoRV
In March come the March winds. The March Winds. George Washington Wright Houghton. YeAr
In March I dreamed of mud. From the Journals of the Frog Prince. Susan Mitchell. DFT; NIP
In March I give you plenteous fisheries. Sonnets of the Months: March. Folgore da San Geminiano, *tr. by* Dante Gabriel Rossetti. AWP
In March, kites bite the wind. Paper Dragons. Susan Alton Schmeltz. RHPC
In March the seed. Mater Dei. Padraic Fallon. NOCV
In March, the small river. Love Poem: The Dispossessed. T. R. Hummer. MAYP
In March, when the earth begins. Wires. Lee Bassett. SOTS

In Marion, the honey locust trees are falling. Two Poems about President Harding. James Wright. CoAP; NoAM
In martial sports I had my cunning tried. Astrophel and Stella, LIII. Sir Philip Sidney. SiPS
In mathematic[k]s he was greater. Samuel Butler. *Fr.* Hudibras, I, i. ImOP; NOBL
In Mather's Magnalia Christi. The Phantom Ship. Longfellow. EtS
In matters of commerce the fault of the Dutch. A Political Despatch [*or* Epigram: The Dutch *or* The Dutch]. George Canning. DBV; FaBoCo; OxBoLi
In May. W. H. Davies. OBVV
In May. J. M. Synge. MoBrPo
In May. Blue Tropic. Luis Cabalquinto. BrSi
In May, approaching the city, I. The Ritualists. William Carlos Williams. NYBP
In May, the sun climbs. May. John Stevens Wade. AMV-80
In May, when sea-winds pierced our solitudes. The Rhodora [On Being Asked Whence Is the Flower]. Emerson. AA; AmPP; AP; AWP; BoNaP; FaBV; FaFP; GN; HBV-1; HBVY; HelP; LiTA; NOBA; NoP; OHFP; OxBA; SeCeV; TAP; TreFS; TrGrPo; TRV; WHA
In May, when sea-winds pierced our solitudes. Variation on a Line by Emerson. W. S. Merwin. NePA
In Me, Past, Present, Future Meet. Siegfried Sassoon. OBEV
In me (the worm) clearly. Hilda Doolittle ("H. D."). *Fr.* The Walls Do Not Fall. NoAM
In me there is a vast and lonely place. Zora Cross. Love Sonnets, XLIX. CBAP
In Measure Time We'll Row, *with music. Unknown.* ShS
In melancholic fancy. Hallo My Fancy. William Cleland. CH; OxBoLi
In mellowy orchards, rich and ripe. The Snitterjipe. James Reeves. AmMo
In Memorabilia Mortis. Francis Sherman. CaP
In Memorial. J. Gordon Coogler. OBAL
In Memoriam. "Max Adeler." DTC; FaBoCo
In Memoriam. Padraig de Brun. WTO
In Memoriam I ("You used to ask me once what was wrong"). Franco Fortini, *tr. fr. Italian by* Ruth Feldman. VWA
In Memoriam II ("I do not understand"). Franco Fortini, *tr. fr. Italian by* Ruth Feldman. VWA
In Memoriam. Dave Gingell. PoSH
In Memoriam. Ada Jackson. PGD
In Memoriam. Richard Monckton Milnes. HBV-2
In Memoriam, A. C. M. L., *sel.* Cecil Arthur Spring-Rice.
"God of all power and might." TrPWD
In Memoriam: A. C., R. J. O., K. S. John Betjeman. NYBP
In Memoriam A. H. H. Tennyson. EBVV, *abr.*; OAEL-2, *abr.*; OAEP, *abr.*; VLP
Sels.
"Again at Christmas did we weave," LXXVIII. PChr
"And all is well, though faith and form," CXXVII. HBV-2
"And, star and system rolling past," *fr.* Epilogue. ImOP
"Are God and Nature then at strife," *fr.* LV. TRV
"As sometimes in a dead man's face," LXXIV. LiTB
"Be near me when my light is low," L. ELP; HAP; NOCV; NoP; PoEL-5; SCV
(Be Near Me.) LiTB
"By night we linger'd [*or* lingered] on the lawn," XCV. HAP; LoBV; NoP; OBNC; PoEL-5
"Calm is the morn without a sound," XI. EBEV; ELP; FaBoEn; FaBoRV; FiP; NOBE; NoP; OBNC; PoEL-5; SeCeV; TrGrPo
(Calm Is the Morn.) ChTr; LiTB
(Lincolnshire Wolds and Lincolnshire Sea.) FaBoPP
"Contemplate all this work of Time," CXVIII. FF; SeCeV
"Danube to the Severn gave, The," XIX. FF; GTBS-P; LoBV; NoP
(Hushing of the Wye, The.) FaBoPP
"Dark house, by which once more I stand," VII. EBEV; FaBoEn; GTBS-P; HAP; InPK; NOBE; NoP; OBNC; PeHV; PoEL-5; PPoe; SCV; SeCeV; UnPo
(Dark House.) LiTB
"Dip down upon the northern shore," LXXXIII. ViBoPo
(Spring.) HBV-1
"Doors, where my heart was used to beat," CXIX. NoP; OBNC; PoEL-5; SCV
"Fair ship, that from the Italian shore," IX. PeHV
"I cannot see the features right," LXX. LiTB; PoEL-5
"I climb the hill: from end to end," C. PoEL-5
"I dreamed there would be spring no more," LXIX. NOBE
"I envy not in any moods," XXVII. FaBoEn; HBV-2; LiTB; OBNC; PeHV
(Lost Love.) TreFS
"I held it truth, with him who sings," I. HBV-2; NoP; OBNC
(I Held it Truth.) LiTB
"I past [*or* passed] beside the reverend walls," LXXXVII.
(He Revisits Cambridge.) FaBoPP
"I trust I have not wasted breath," CXX. ImOP; SeCePo
"I wage not any feud with death," LXXXII. LiTB; PPON
"I will not shut me from my kind," CVIII. SBVL
"If one should bring me this report," XIV.
(Of One Dead.) LiTB
"If sleep and death be truly one," XLIII. OBNC
"It is the day when he was born," CVII. SBVL
"Lo, as a dove when up she springs," XII. LoBV
"Love is and was my lord and king," CXXVI. HBV-2; NOBE; NOCV; OBEV; OBNC; SeCeV
(My Lord and King.) ChTr
"Man, that with me trod, The," *fr.* Epilogue. TRV
"My own dim life should teach me this," XXXIV. SeCePo
"Now fades the last long streak of snow," CXV. FaBoEn; FaBoRV; GTBS-P; NOBE; OBNC; SeCeV; ViBoPo
(Spring.) HBV-1; TreFT
"O days and hours, your work is this," CXVII. HBV-2
"O living will that shalt endure," CXXXI. FaBoBe; HBV-2
(Prayer, The: "O living will that shalt endure.") WGRP
"O sorrow, cruel fellowship," III. HAP
"O[h] yet we trust that somehow good," LIV. BiP; EaLo; HBV-2; LoBV; NoP; OBNC; SeCeV; TrGrPo; TRV
(Larger Hope, The.) TreFS; WGRP
(Oh Yet We Trust.) LiTB
"Old warder of these buried bones," XXXIX. PoEL-5
"Old yew, which graspest at the stones," II. ELP; FaBoEn; GTBS-P; NOBE; NoP; OBNC; PAI; PoEL-5; SeCeV; UnPo
"On that last night before we went," CIII. PoEL-5
"One writes, that 'other friends remain,'" VI. PoEL-5
"Our little systems have their day," *fr.* Proem. TRV
"Path by which we twain did go, The," XXII. SCV
"Perplext in faith, but pure in deeds," *fr.* XCVI. TRV
"Ring out, wild bells, to the wild sky," CVI. FiP, 7 *sts.*; HBV-2; PGD; SBVL; SeCeV; TrGrPo; TRV
(Ring Out the Old, Ring In the New.) WBLP
(Ring Out, Wild Bells.) BLPL; FaFP; FaPON, 2 *sts.*; FaPoR; LiTB; OFD; TiPo, 2 *sts.*; TreF; WiR, 7 *sts., incl.* 2 *sts. fr.* CV
"Risest thou thus, dim dawn, again," LXXII. OBNC; PoEL-5
"Sad Hesper o'er the buried sun," CXXI. NoP
"'So careful of the type?' but no," LVI. FF; HAP; HBV-2; LoBV; NoP; OBNC; SeCeV
"So many worlds, so much to do," LXXIII. HBV-2
"Strong Son of God, immortal love," Proem. HAP; HBV-2; LiTB; SeCeV; TreF; TrGrPo; TrPWD; TRV; WGRP; WHA
(Strong Son of God.) EaLo; OxBoCh; TrCP
"Tears of the widower, when he sees," XIII. PeHV
"That which we dare invoke to bless," CXXIV. NOCV; WGRP
"There rolls the deep where grew the tree," CXXIII. HAP; NOBE; SeCePo; SeCeV
(There Rolls the Deep.) FaBoRV
"Tho' truths in manhood darkly join," XXXVI.
(Word, The.) GoBC
"Thy voice is on the rolling air," CXXX. HBV-2; NoP; PeHV; TRV
"Till now the doubtful dusk reveal'd," *fr.* XCV. GTBS-P
"Time draws near the birth of Christ, The," XXVIII. FaBoRV; NOCV; PChr; PGD
"Time draws near the birth of Christ, The," CIV. SBVL
"To-night the winds begin to rise," XV. BiP; FaBoEn; GTBS-P; NOBE; OBNC; PoEL-5
(To-night the Winds Begin.) LiTB
"Tonight ungather'd [*or* ungathered] let us leave," CV. SBVL
"Unwatch'd [*or* unwatched], the garden bough shall sway," CI. ELP; GTBS-P; OBNC; PoEL-5; PoPle; SCV; SeCeV
(Somersby, Lincolnshire; after Leaving the Refectory.) FaBoPP
"We leave the well-beloved place," CII. PoEL-5
"What hope is here for modern rhyme," LXXVII. PP
"What words are these have fallen from me," XVI. EBEV
"When on my bed the moonlight falls," LXVII. LoBV; NoP; SeCePo; SeCeV
"When rosy plumelets tuft the larch," XCI. FaBoEn; OBNC; ViBoPo
"Wild bird, whose warble, liquid sweet," LXXXVIII. NoP; PBBP
"Wish, that of the living whole, The," LV. HAP; HBV-2; LoBV; NoP; OBNC; PAI; SeCeV
"Witch-elms that counterchange the floor," LXXXIX. OBNC
"Yet if some voice that man could trust," XXXV. ViBoPo
"You say, but with no touch of scorn," XCVI. NOCV
(Doubt.) WGRP
"Yule-clog sparkled keen with frost, The," *fr.* LXXVIII. TRV
In Memoriam (Easter, 1915). Edward Thomas. GTBS-P; NOBE; OBWP; OxBTC

In Memoriam I, Elizabeth at Twenty. Richard Weber. ErPo
In Memoriam II, Elizabeth in Italy. Richard Weber. *See* Elizabeth in Italy.
In Memoriam: Ernst Toller. W. H. Auden. NYBP
In Memoriam F. A. S. Robert Louis Stevenson. BrPo
In Memoriam: Francis Ledwidge. Norreys Jephson O'Conor. HBMV
In Memoriam; Ingvald Bjorndal and His Comrade. Malcolm Lowry. OBCV
In Memoriam: John Davidson. Ronald Campbell Macfie. GoTS
In Memoriam—Leo: A Yellow Cat. Margaret Sherwood. BLPA
In Memoriam: Margaritae Sorori. W. E. Henley. *See* Margaritae Sorori.
In Memoriam: Martin Luther King, Jr. June Jordan. PoBA
In Memoriam Paul Celan. Gad Hollander. VWA
In Memoriam, Private D. Sutherland. Ewart Alan Mackintosh. BSV
In Memoriam: Rev. J. J. Lyons, *sel.* Emma Lazarus.
"Hark! through the quiet evening air, their song." SBG
In Memoriam: Roy Campbell. Ralph Nixon Currey. PeSA
In Memoriam S. C. W., V. C. Charles Sorley. MMA
In Memoriam S. L. Akintola. David Knight. MoCV
In Memoriam—W. G. Ward. Tennyson. Valedictory, I. GoBC
In Memory, *sel.* Lionel Johnson.
"Ah! fair face gone from sight." FaBoEn; OBNC; PoEL-5
In Memory. Katha Pollitt. MAYP
In Memory, 1978. Judith Kazantzis. BrRo
In Memory of a Friend. George Barker. OxBTC
In Memory of Ann Jones. Dylan Thomas. *See* After the Funeral.
In Memory of Anna Hopewell. *Unknown.* ShM
In Memory of Arthur Winslow. Robert Lowell. AP; MiAP
Death from Cancer, *sel.* MP; TwCP
In Memory of "Barry Cornwall." Swinburne. HBV-2
In Memory of Basil, Marquess of Dufferin and Ava. John Betjeman. OBWP
In Memory of Bryan Lathrop. Edgar Lee Masters. PoA
In Memory of Captain Underwood Who Was Drowned. *Unknown.* FaBoEE
In Memory of Colonel Charles Young. Countee Cullen. PoBA
In Memory of Con and Eva Gore-Booth. W. B. Yeats. *See* In Memory of Eva Gore-Booth and Con Markiewicz.
In Memory of David Archer, *sel.* George Barker.
"Images! Venerable as Druidical trees." FaBoMo
In Memory of Edward Wilson. James Clerk Maxwell. *See* Rigid Body Sings.
In Memory of Eva Gore-Booth and Con Markiewicz. W. B. Yeats. CABA; MoAB; NoAM; OAEL-2; OBMV; OxBTC
(In Memory of Con and Eva Gore-Booth.) OxBI
In Memory of Francois Rabelais. Yunna Moritz, *tr. fr. Russian by* Elaine Feinstein. VWA
In Memory of G. K. Chesterton. Walter de la Mare. GoBC
In Memory of García Lorca. Eldon Grier. PeCV
In Memory of General Grant. Henry Abbey. AA
In Memory of George Whitby, Architect. John Betjeman. EyDe
In Memory of James T. Fields. Whittier. OBVV
In Memory of Jane Fraser [*or* Frazer]. Geoffrey Hill. NePoEA; NoAM; OxBTC
In Memory of John Lothrop Motley. Bryant. AA
In Memory of Kathleen. Kenneth Patchen. MoAmPo
In Memory of Leopardi. James Wright. NaP
In memory of Maggie. On a Monument in France Which Marks the Last Resting Place of an Army Mule. *Unknown.* ShM
In Memory of Major Robert Gregory. W. B. Yeats. AnIL; EBEV; OAEL-2; OAEP
In Memory of My Arab Grandmother. Evelyn Arcad Zerbe. WPOW
In Memory of My Dear Grandchild [Anne Bradstreet]. Anne Bradstreet. BoWoP; TrCP
In Memory of My Dear Grandchild Elizabeth Bradstreet, [Who Deceased August, 1665, Being a Year and a Half Old]. Anne Bradstreet. AP; NOVC; SCAP; WPE
In Memory of My Father. James Agee. DiL
In Memory of My Feelings. Frank O'Hara. NeAP; PoM
In Memory of My First Chapatis. Diane di Prima. PoM
In Memory of My Mother. Patrick Kavanagh. BIrV; CIP; NoAM
In Memory of My Uncle Timothy. Alastair Reid. NePoEA-2
In Memory of Radio. Amiri Baraka. NeAP; NIP; NoP; PoM
In Memory of Sigmund Freud. W. H. Auden. CoBMV; HAP; LiTB; OAEL-2; OxBA
In Memory of the Circus Ship *Euzkera*, [Wrecked in the Caribbean Sea, 1 September 1948]. Walker Gibson. NCSH; NePoAm
In Memory of the Moon (A Killing). Charlotte DeClue. STE; TWSS
In Memory of the Utah Stars. William Matthews. GeTw; MAYP; NPAW; Psk
In Memory of the Vertuous and Learned Lady Madre de Teresa. Richard Crashaw. *See* Hymn to the Name and Honour of the Admirable Saint Teresa, A.
In Memory of Two Sons. Russell Stellwagon. STF
In Memory of V.R. Lang. Mac Hammond. PoA
In Memory of W. B. Yeats. W. H. Auden. CABA; CMoP; CoBMV; FaFP; HAP; HeIP; HoPM; LiTB; LiTM; MasP; MoAB; MoBrPo; MoVE; NePA; NoAM; NOBE; OAEL-2; OAEP; OxBTC; PAI; PP; PPoe; PPP; PrIm; TrGrPo; UnPo; ViBoPo; WeW
Sels.
"Earth, receive an honoured guest." ChMP; ChTr; FaBoRV; FaBoTw (4 *sts.*)
"Follow, poet, follow right." TRV
"In the nightmare of the dark." TRV
In Memory of Walter Savage Landor. Swinburne. HBV-2; PoEL-5
In Memphis—in Tennessee. On the Birth of a Black/Baby/Boy. Etheridge Knight. DiL
In Men Whom Men Condemn as Ill. Joaquin Miller. *Fr.* Byron. HBV-2; PoLF; TreFT
In Mercy, Lord, Incline Thine Ear, *with music.* Isaac M. Wise. AH
In Merioneth, over the sad moor. Dead. Lionel Johnson. BrPo; FaBoEn; OBNC; PoEL-5
In merry old England, it once was a rule. On the New Laureate. *Unknown.* FaBoCo
In merry Scotland, in merry Scotland. Henry Martyn. *Unknown.* BaBo; ESPB
In mery May, quhen medis springis. Prologue to the Avowis of Alexander. John Barbour. *Fr.* The Buik of Alexander. OxBS
In Mexico. Evaleen Stein. AA
In Mexico women have hands strong enough. In the Small Boats of Their Hands. Pamela Kircher. AMV-80
In mid-river we join the ancient force. Baptism. Dale Zieroth. NOBC
In midst of this city celestial. The Celestial City. Giles Fletcher, the Younger. *Fr.* Christ's Victory and Triumph, IV. NOBE
In midst of woods or pleasant grove. The Blackbird. *Unknown.* ElL
In Mind. Denise Levertov. InPS; NMM
In minds pure glasse when I my selfe behold. Sonnet. William Drummond of Hawthornden. OBS
In Misery's darkest cavern known. Samuel Johnson. *Fr.* On the Death of Mr. Robert Levet, a Practiser in Physic. ViBoPo
In Missing. Ray A. Young Bear. CDW
In Mississippi/ balloons of hunger. No New Music. Stanley Crouch. PoBA
In Missoula, Montana, where the townsfolk water. Pendant Watch. Madeline DeFrees. NMM
In Misty Blue. Laurence Binyon. HBMV
In mole-blue indolence the sun. The Jungle. Alun Lewis. MoPo
In Montana. Washington Jay McCormick. WhC
In Montecito. Randall Jarrell. CoAP; MAT; NoP; NYBP; VGW
In Mornigan's park there is a deer. The Crescent Moon [*or* Riddle]. *Unknown.* ChTr; GBP; MOON
In morning light my damson show'd [*or* showed]. The Plum Tree by the House. Oliver St. John Gogarty. OBEV; PoRA
In Mortem Venerabilis Andreae Prout Carmen. Francis Sylvester Mahony. NBM
In Moses' hand 'twas but a rod. What Is That in Thine Hand? Eva Gray. STF
In moss-prankt dells which the sunbeams flatter. Lovers, and a Reflection. Charles Stuart Calverley. FaBaPo; FaBoCo; NA; SpRo; VLP; WhC
In most cases. Who Makes the Journey. Cathy Song. BrSi
In most things I did as my father had done. George II. Thackeray. *Fr.* The Georges. FaBoEE
In mothers womb thy fingers did me mak. A Thankful Acknowledgment of God's Providence. John Cotton. SCAP
In Mountjoy jail one Monday morning. Kevin Barry: Died for Ireland, 1st November, 1920. *Unknown.* FaBoBa
In moving-slow he has no peer. The Sloth. Theodore Roethke. FiBHP; NEPA; NePoAm; OBAL; OBCA; RHPC
In Moynihan's meadow. The Grip. Brendan Kennelly. CIP
In Murasaki's time. Tale of Genji. Hugh Seidman. AmPA
In my bed at night. Bible, *O.T.* *Fr.* The Song of Solomon, *ad. by* Willis Barnstone. BoWoP
In my beginning is my end. In succession. East Coker. T. S. Eliot. *Fr.* Four Quartets. ChMP; HAP; MOVE; NePA; PPP; VGW
In my boat that goes. Saigyo Hoshi, *tr. fr. Japanese by* Arthur Waley. AWP
In my cave lives a solitary rat. Chez-Nous. A. G. Austin. PoAu-2
In my collection, the words are, we use. Elegy. Alan Loney. OCNZ
In My Craft or Sullen Art. Dylan Thomas. BoLoP; ChMP; CMoP; GTBS-P; HAP; HeIP; InvP; LiTM; MAT; NeBP; NIP; NoAM; NoP; OAEP; PAI; PP; WeW
In my dream by Henry James there is a sentence. My Dreams by Henry James. Michael Ryan. SV
In my dream, Joey, both of us were alive. Cuba. Lawrence Kearney. AMV-81
In my dream the brooding child. The Child. George Keithley. NPGG

In my dreams I always speak Spanish. Sueños. James Reiss. FiCP
In my dreams I hear my tribe. Then and Now. Kath Walker. IHMS
In My Dreams I Searched for You. *Gond Oral Tradition, tr. by* V. Elwin *and* S. Hivale. WTO
In my dreams we are always together. Dedication. Richard Stull. AMV-81
In my dry cell. The Riven Quarry. Gloria C. Oden. PoBA
In my father's brickyard. Clay and Water. Sandra Hochman. Str
In My Father's House, *with music. Unknown.* AS
In my father's house are many cobwebs. Portrait of the Artist as an Old Man. Michael Dransfield. CBAP
In my fingers the world can be grasped. Seismograph. Ephraim Auerbach, *tr. by* Howard Schwartz. VWA
In My First Hard Springtime. James Welch. AmPA; CDW
In my grandmother's house there was always chicken soup. A Story about Chicken Soup. Louis Simpson. LCAP; NMP; NNaP; NoAM; TAP
In my heart's depth. Akazome Emon, *tr. fr. Japanese by* Kenneth Rexroth *and* Ikuko Atsumi. WPOW
In my house I keep green books. The Plants. Michael Dennis Browne. GP
In my land there are no distinctions. Poem for the Young White Man Who Asked Me How I, an Intelligent, Well-read Person, Could Believe in the War between Races. Lorna Dee Cervantes. WPOW
In My Lifetime. James Welch. CDW; STE
In My Merry Oldsmobile, *with music.* Vincent Bryan. FSN
In My Mind. Norman MacCaig. OxBC
In my mind you stand with creel. Along South Inlet. Greg Kuzma. WOLT
In my most spectacular, technicolored dream. Zimmer's Hard Dream. Paul Zimmer. GP
In My New Clothing. Basho, *tr. fr. Japanese.* SoPo
In My Own Album. Charles Lamb. OBRV
In my own shire, if I was sad. A. E. Housman. A Shropshire Lad, XLI. BrPo
In my own twentieth century. Natalya Gorbanyevskaya, *tr. fr. Russian by* Daniel Weissbort. PBWP
In My Place. Esther Archibald. STF
In my prison cell I sit, thinking Mother, dear, of you. Tramp! Tramp! Tramp! George F. Root. BLSo
In my room, the world is beyond my understanding. Of the Surface of Things. Wallace Stevens. ELU
In my rudyard-kipling-simple years I read. The Thrifty Elephant. John Holmes. NYBP
In my shanks. Reb Hanina. Paul Raboff. VWA
In my sleep I was fain of their fellowship, fain. Sunrise. Sidney Lanier. *Fr.* Hymns of the Marshes. AA; PoEL-5
In my stone eyes I see. What Riddle Asked the Sphinx. Archibald MacLeish. HoPM
In My Thirtieth Year. Archibald MacLeish. *See* L'An Trentiesme de Mon Eage.
In my thirtieth year of life/ when I had drunk down all my disgrace. The Testament. Villon, *tr. by* Galway Kinnell. NAWM-1
In my young days I drank a/ Lot of wine. A Friend Advises Me to Stop Drinking. Mei Yao-ch'en, *tr. fr. Chinese by* Kenneth Rexroth. HoPM
In my younger years. Dreams. Nikki Giovanni. CNA; PoBA
In my youth the growls. Tennyson. FaBoEE
In my youth's summer I did sing of one. The Wandering Outlaw. Byron. *Fr.* Childe Harold's Pilgrimage. FiP
In Mysterious Ways. Faye Kicknosway. GeTw
In Nakedness. Marnie Pomeroy. ErPo
In nature apt to like, when I did see. Astrophel and Stella, XVI. Sir Philip Sidney. SiPS
In Nature There Is neither Right nor Left nor Wrong. Randall Jarrell. OxBC
In "nature" there's no choice. Beyond the End. Denise Levertov. NeAP; VGW
In natures peeces still I see. A Divine Mistris. Thomas Carew. AnAnS-2
In Neglect. Robert Frost. VGW
In Nets of Golden Wires. *Unknown.* EnRePo
In New Hampshire's green paradise this June. Sonnet to Seabrook. David Ray. AMV-80
In New Ross. Valentin Iremonger. NeIP
In New South Wales, as I plainly see. William Forster. *Fr.* The Devil and the Governor. CBAP; PoAu-1
In New York I got drunk, to tell the truth. John Logan. *Fr.* A Trip to Four or Five Towns. NMP
In New York, it is said. A Place (Any Place) to Transcend All Places. William Carlos Williams. NYP
In Newbern Tennessee he lies awake. The Wake. Wyatt Prunty. AMV-80
In night, when colors [*or* colours] all to black[e] are cast. Fulke Greville. *Fr.* Caelica. AAS; EnRePo; OAEL-1; QFR
In 1915 my grandfather's. Grandfather. Michael S. Harper. FiCP; GeTw; LCAP; TAP
In 1945, when the keepers cried kaput. The Gift. John Ciardi. BiP; LiTM; MP; NMP
In nineteen hundred and twenty-two. Mr. Vachel Lindsay Discovers Radio. Samuel Hoffenstein. BXAP
In nineteen hundred they preferred. Upper Family. Maxwell Bodenheim. OBAL
In 1910 a royal princess. English. Osbert Lancaster. *Fr.* Afternoons with Baedeker. FaBoCo; NOBL
In nineteen-thirty-four I spent July. 1934. Donald Hall. PoPl
In 1939 the skylark had nothing to say to me. The Ninth of July. John Hollander. CoAP
In no country. No Offence. D. J. Enright. OxBTC
In No Strange Land. Francis Thompson. *See* Kingdom of God, The.
In No Way. David Ignatow. AMV-81
In no way that I chose to go. The Snow. Clifford Dyment. MoVE
In North Great George's Street. "Seumas O'Sullivan." BIrV
In Northern seas there roams a fish called a K'un. The P'eng That Was a K'un. Chuang Tzu, *at. to* Lao-tse, *tr. by* Robert Graves. AmMo
In Norway land[s] there lived a maid. The Grey Selchie [*or* Great Silkie] of Sule Skerry. *Unknown.* OxBB; ViBoFo
In Nottamun Town not a soul would look up. Nottamun Town. *Unknown.* FaBoNo; NCEP; OxBoLi
In Nottingham there lives a jolly tanner. Robin Hood and the Tanner. *Unknown.* ESPB
In November. Anne Reeve Aldrich. AA
In November. Archibald Lampman. NOBC; OBCV
In November, in the days to remember the dead. St. Malachy. Thomas Merton. CoPo; VGW
In numbers, and but these few. An Ode on the Birth of Our Saviour. Robert Herrick. GN; SBVL
In Obitum M. S., X° Maij [*or* Maii], 1614. William Browne. EIL; FaBoBEE; JCP; NOBE; SeCeV
(Epitaph in Obitum M. S., X° Maij, 1614. OBEV; OBS
In Obitum Promi. Henry Parrot. FaBoCo
In Obtuse Angle's Study. Blake. *Fr.* An Island in the Moon. FaBoNo
In Ocean's wide domains. The Witnesses. Longfellow. GOA
In October. Bliss Carman. YeAr
In October. Michael Hamburger. NePoEA
In October. October. Maurice Sendak. RHPC
In October at midnight in the olive groves. Thoughts from Abroad. Patrick Maybin. NeIP
In October of the year. Ox Cart Man. Donald Hall. FYAP; LCAP
In October the pregnant woman walked by the river. In October. Michael Hamburger. NePoEA
In Ohio. James Wright. NNaP
In Ohio, where these things happen. The Breathers. James Reiss. AmPA
In Oklahoma an old man died, long ago. Elf Night. Ron Rogers. STE
In old commercial Boston down on Milk Street. Gas Lamp. Willis Barnstone. VWA
In old Kentuck in de arternoon. Clare de Kitchen. *Unknown.* BLPA
In Old Tucson. Charles Beghtol. BPAW
In Old Tucson. Harrison Conrard. BPAW
In Old Tucson. Sharlot M. Hall. BPAW
In One Battle. Amiri Baraka. BPo
In 100% surefire arsenic. Shake'nbake Ballad. Peter van Toorn. NOBC
In one of London's most exclusive haunts. After Bourlon Wood. Helen Dircks. SUMH
In one of these excursions, travelling then. The Climb to Snowdon [*or* The Snowdon Sunrise]. Wordsworth. *Fr.* The Prelude, XIV. EBEV; FaBoPP; FaBoRV
In one of Watteau's pencil sketches. Nude. Daniel Halpern. MAYP
In One Place. Robert Wallace. Psk
In one room of the house. The Eve. Howard Schwartz. VWA
In only thee, my timid, fleet gazelle. The Timid Gazelle. Kasmuneh. TrJP
In Orange, tree-plague has struck the mile-long groves. Greased. Orange County Plague: Scenes. Laurence Lieberman. CoPo
In Orangeburg My Brothers Did. A. B. Spellman. BPo; PoBA
In Orbit. Henry Taylor. BXAP
In orchard under the hawthorne. Vergier. *Unknown, tr. by* Ezra Pound. GBL
In Order To. Kenneth Patchen. NaP
In order to perfect all readers. Wall, Cave, and Pillar Statements, after Asôka. Alan Dugan. CoAP
In Orknay. William Fowler. GoTS; OxBS
In other men we faults can spy. The Turkey and the Ant. John Gay. *Fr.* Fables. PBBP
In Our Boat. Dinah Maria Mulock Craik. HBV-1
In our cabin we eat breaded oysters and fries. Marriage. Raymond Carver. GeTw
In our Country, in our Country. The Merry Hay-Makers; [or, Pleasant

Pastime between the Young-Men and Maids, in the Pleasant Meadows]. *Unknown.* CoMu; ErPo
In our Durham County I am sorry for to say. The Durham Lock-out. *Unknown.* CoMu
In our fields, fallow and burdened, in grass and furrow. Christopher Fry. *Fr.* The Boy with a Cart. LiTB
In our house every floor was a wailing wall. My Guardian Angel Stein. Philip Schultz. MAYP
In our Museum galleries. The Burden of Nineveh. Dante Gabriel Rossetti. OAEP
In our museum—we always go there on Sundays. Family Matters. Günter Grass, *tr. by* Michael Hamburger. ELU
In our old shipwrecked days there was an hour. Love Dies. George Meredith. Modern Love, XVI. BoLoP; HBV-1; SeCePo; WHA
In our smoke house. Shelby County, Ohio. November 1974. G. E. Murray. FAZ
In Our Time. Michael Roberts. WaP
In our town, people live in rows. The Fired Pot. Anna Wickham. FaBoTw; OxBTC
In Oxford City. *Unknown.* OBET
In Oxford there lived a merchant by trade. The Crafty Farmer. *Unknown.* AmFP
In Oxford town the faggots they piled. Latimer's Light. *Unknown.* TRV
In Paco town and in Paco tower. The Ballad of Paco Town. Clinton Scollard. PAH
In pain she bore the son who her embrace. Elegy. Moses ibn Ezra, *tr. by* Solomon Solis-Cohen. TrJP
In pairs/ as if to illustrate their sisterhood. For the Sisters of the Hôtel Dieu. A. M. Klein. SoSe; WHW
In Panelled Rooms. Ruth Herschberger. LiTA
In paper case. Epitaph on a Dormouse. *Unknown.* OxBChV
In Paradise. Arlo Bates. AA
In Parenthesis, *sels.* David Jones.
"And the place of their waiting a long burrow." FaBoMo
"But sweet sister death has gone debauched today and stalks." OBWP
Five Unmistakable Marks, The. NoAM
King Pellam's Launde. NoAM; OAEL-2
"You can hear the silence of it." FaBoMo
In Paris. Thomas MacDonagh. OnYI
In part these nightly terrors to dispel. Moonlight . . . Scattered Clouds. Robert Bloomfield. *Fr.* The Farmer's Boy. OBNC
In parts, through prospects scattered far and near. Birmingham and Wolverhampton. James Woodhouse. *Fr.* The Life and Lucubrations of Crispinus Scriblerus. NOEC
In paschall feast, the end of ancient rite. Of the Blessed Sacrament of the Altar. Robert Southwell. GoBC
In Passing. Roy Helton. HBMV
In Passing. Gerald Jonas. GrPl
In Passing. J. Barrie Shepherd. AMV-81
In passing with my mind. The Right of Way. William Carlos Williams. MoVE
In pasture where the leaf and wood. The Quest. James Wright. NYBP
In "pastures green"? Not always; sometimes He. On the Twenty-third Psalm [*or* He Leadeth Me]. *Unknown.* BLRP; TRV
In Paths Untrodden. Walt Whitman. AP; NePA; NOBA; OxBA
In Patterdale. Wordsworth. *Fr.* The Prelude, I. FaBoRV
In peace, Love tunes the shepherd's reed. Sir Walter Scott. *Fr.* The Lay of the Last Minstrel. ViBoPo
In Peblis town sum tyme, as I heard tell. *At. to* John Reid of Stobo. *Fr.* The Thre Prestis of Peblis. OxBS
In Pennsylvania; it's sort of like losing. Another Night on the Porch Swing. Cathleen Quirk. NMM
In Peterborough Churchyard. Paulus Silentiarius, *tr. fr. Greek.* NOBL
("Reader, pass on, nor idly waste your time.") FaBoEE
("Reader, pass on!—don't waste your time.") WhC
In petticoat of green. Of Phyllis [*or* Phyllis]. William Drummond of Hawthornden. EIL; GN; HBV-1
In Phæacia. James Elroy Flecker. HBMV
In Piam Memoriam. Geoffrey Hill. NePoEA-2; OxBC
In Pilgrim Life Our Rest, *with music.* Edwin Sandys. AH
In pious times, e'r [*or* ere] priest-craft did begin. Absalom and Achitophel, Pt. I. Dryden. HAP; NoP; OAEL-1; OAEP; SeCV-2
In Piranezi's rarer prints. Prelusive. Herman Melville. Clarel, XXXV. AmPP
In pity for man's darkening thought. Two Songs from a Play, II. W. B. Yeats. *Fr.* The Resurrection. CABA; CMoP; CoBMV; FaBoTw; HAP; LiTB; MoPo; NOBE; NoP; OAEL-2; PPoe; PPP; PrIm; SeCeV
In Place of a Curse. John Ciardi. HoAn
In placid hours well-pleased we dream. Art. Herman Melville. AmPP; AP; NOBA; ViBoPo
In Plague Time. Thomas Nashe. *See* Adieu, Farewell Earth's Bliss.
In Pleasant Lands Have Fallen the Lines, *with music.* James Flint. AH
In Plymouth Town there lived a maid. A-roving. *Unknown.* UnTE
In Populated. Lucille Clifton. GeTw
In Portugal, 1912. Alice Meynell. NOCV; OxBoCh
In Postures That Call. Oscar Williams. WaP
In Prague. Paul Celan, *tr. fr. German by* Joachim Neugroschel. VWA
In Praise of a Beggar's Life. "A. W." EIL; TrGrPo
(Play, Beggars, Play!) WHA
(Song in Praise of a Beggar's Life, A.) OBSC
In Praise of a Gentlewoman. George Gascoigne. EnRePo
In Praise of a Guilty Conscience. Wislawa Szymborska, *tr. fr. Polish by* Grazyna Drabik *and* Austin Flint. AMV-81
In Praise of Aed. *Unknown, tr. fr. Old Irish by* Robin Flower. AnIL
In Praise of Ale ("I cannot eat but little meat"). *Unknown, at. to* William Stevenson. *See* Back and Side Go Bare, Go Bare.
In Praise of Ale ("Whenas the chill sirocco [*or* Charoko] blow[e]s.") *Unknown, at. to* Thomas Bonham. FaBoCh; OBS; ViBoPo
(Give Me Ale.) HBV-2
(Pipe and Can II.) OBEV
In Praise of Antonioni. Stephen Holden. NYBP
In Praise of Ben Avon. Brenda G. Macrow. PoSH
In Praise of Beverly. Stephen Orlen. GP; MAYP
In Praise of Blur. G. Sharat Chandra. FAZ
In Praise of Clothes. Erica Jong. MAYP
In Praise of Cocoa, Cupid's Nightcap. Stanley J. Sharpless. ErPo; FiBHP
In Praise of Commonplace. Sir Owen Seaman. InMe
In Praise of Country Life. Robert Chamberlain. CavP
In Praise of Creation. Elizabeth Jennings. PAI
In Praise of His Daphnis. Sir John Wotton. EIL
In Praise of His Lady. Matthew Grove. *Fr.* Pelops and Hippodamia. EIL
In Praise of His Love. Sir John Wotton. EIL
In Praise of His Loving and Best-beloved Fawnia. Robert Greene. *See* Fawnia.
In Praise of Isabel Pennell. John Skelton. *See* To Mistress Isabel Pennell.
In Praise of Ivy. *Unknown.* *See* Ivy, Chief of Trees.
In Praise of Laudanum. William Harrison. NOEC
In Praise of Limestone. W. H. Auden. CABA; CMoP; CoBMV; FYAP; HAP; MoAB; MoVE; NePA; NoAM; NoP; OAEL-2; PPP
In praise of little children I will say. Laus Infantium. William Canton. HBV-1
In Praise of Llamas. Arthur Guiterman. FiBHP
In Praise of Mary ("Edi be thu, Hevene Quene"). *Unknown.* *See* Queen of Heaven.
In Praise of Mary ("Of one that is so fair and bright"). *Unknown.* *See* Hymn to the Virgin.
In Praise of May. *At. to* Fionn MacCunhaill, *tr. fr. Old Irish by* T. W. Rolleston. AnIV
(Song of Finn, *tr. by* John O'Donovan.) OnYI
In Praise of Music in Time of Pestilence. Daryl Hine. OBCV
In Praise of Neptune. Thomas Campion. BoNaP; NOBE; WiR
(Hymn[e] in Praise [*or* Prayse] of Neptune, A.) EtS; MOS; OBEV
(Neptune.) OBSC
In Praise of Old Women. Marya Fiamengo. WPOW
In Praise of Robert Penn Warren. David Lehman. AMV-81
In Praise of the Sun. "A. W." CTC; OBSC
In Praise of Virginity. Hroswitha, *tr. fr. Latin by* John Dillon. PBWP
In Praise of Water-Gruel. Matthew Green. *Fr.* The Spleen. FaBoUs
In Praise of Winchester. *Unknown.* OxBM
In Praise of Wisdom. Solomon ibn Gabirol, *tr. fr. Hebrew by* Solomon Solis-Cohen. TrJP
In Praise of Wyatt's Psalms. Earl of Surrey. SiPS
(Greate Macedon that out of Persy chased, The.") AAS
In pride of May. *Unknown.* OBSC
In Prison. William Morris. NBM
In prison you put on your clothes. Rehabilitative Report: We Can Still Laugh. Daniel Berrigan. LFAC
In Prize. Cicely Fox Smith. WhC
In Procession. Robert Graves. MP; TwCP
In Progress. Christina Rossetti. BoWoP; WPE
In Prospect Street, outside the Splendid Bar. Sweeney to Mrs. Porter in the Spring. L. E. Sissman. NYBP
In Puna's fragrant glades. Puna's Fragrant Glades. Princess Lili'u-o-ka-lani, *tr. fr. Hawaiian by* S. H. Elbert *and* N. Mahoe. WTO
In purest song one plays the constant fool. Infirmity. Theodore Roethke. CoAP; NYBP
In Puritan New England a year had passed away. The First Thanksgiving Day. Alice Williams Brotherton. OHIP
In Pusseyville, where pussies live. Cats and Dogs. Howard Moss. OBAL
In pyntarris. *Unknown.* WhC
In Queen Victoria's early days. The New Vicar of Bray. Colin Ellis. NOBL
In quietness and confidence. A Hymn of Trust. Nettie M. Sargent. BLRP
In Railway Halls. Stephen Spender. FaBoMo

In Rain. Wendell Berry. GeTw
In rain-forest Chiapas, at the table of Chang. Two Families. Charles G. Bell. FAZ
In rain or shine; in heat or snow. Pushcart Row. Rachel Field. SoPo
In Rama. George Alfred Townsend. AA
In Random Fields of Impulse and Repose. Jeanine Hathaway. AMV-81
In Rattlesnake Gulch of the Skihootch Range. The Ballad of Pug-nosed Lil. Robert H. Fletcher. BPAW
In re Solomon Warshawer. A. M. Klein. MoCV
In readin' the story of early days, it's a cause of much personal pain. The Mule-Skinners. *At. to* John Caldwell. BPAW
In Reading Gaol by Reading Town. Oscar Wilde. *Fr.* The Ballad of Reading Gaol. FaFP; LiTB; PoPl
In Rebellion. J. M. Synge. SyP
In red wool jacket and earflaps. The Week-End Indian. Anita Endrezze Probst. VoR
In Reference to Her Children, 23 June, 1656. Anne Bradstreet. BoWoP; SBG; TAP
In Respect of the Elderly. Thomas Peacock. VoR
In Respectful Memory of Mr. Yarker, *sel.* John Close.
"And have we lost another friend?" FaBoCo
In Response to a Rumor That the Oldest Whorehouse in Wheeling, West Virginia, Has Been Condemned. James Wright. CAPP; CoAP; NNaP; TW
In Response to Executive Order 9066: All Americans of Japanese Descent Must Report to Relocation Centers. Dwight Okita. BrSi
In restaurants we argue. They Eat Out. Margaret Atwood. NeAC; NoP
In revel and carousing. Theodosia Burr: The Wrecker's Story. John Williamson Palmer. PAH
In Richard's days, when lost his pastur'd plain. The Country Justice. John Langhorne. LaA
In right I have no power to live. The Soul's Bitter Cry. *Unknown.* WGRP
In Roman. Sir John Harington. *See* Hate and Debate Rome through the World Hath Spread.
In Romney Marsh. John Davidson. BSV; EBVV; FaBoPP; GoTS; OBVV; OxBTC; PoPle; ViBoPo
In rooms of stone. Abandoned Copper Refinery. Dan Gillespie. TAT
In rosy-fingered dawn they go. Jersey Cattle. R. N. Currey. OxBTC
In round round rooms of our wanderings. Hiroshima Exit. Joy Kogawa. BrSi
In Ruin Reconciled. Aubrey Thomas De Vere. BIrV
In ruling well what guerdon? Life runs low. The Two Old Kings. Lord De Tabley. OBEV; OBVV
In Sabbath quiet, a street. The Grace-Note. Denise Levertov. ConAP
In sable weeds the beaux and belles appear. The Mourners. Bevil Higgons. APAS
In sad and ashy weeds I sigh. Elegy on the Death of Her Husband. Anne Howard, Duchess of Arundel. WPE
In Salem. Lucille Clifton. AmPA; PAI
In Salem seasick spindrift drifts or skips. Salem. Robert Lowell. CABA; NePoEA
In San Juan I wonder how my home is. I Wonder How My Home Is. *Tr. fr. Tewa Indian by* H. J. Spinden. WTO
In Santa Maria del Popolo. Thom Gunn. CMoP; FaBoMo; GTBS-P; NePoEA-2; NMP; OxBC; QFR
In Saram. John Cotton. SCAP
In Saturday Market, there's eggs a-plenty. Saturday Market. Charlotte Mew. *Fr.* Saturday Market. FaPON
In Saturn's reign, at Nature's early birth. Juvenal, *tr. by* Dryden. *Fr.* Satires, VI. OAEL-1; OBSV; OBVE
In Scarlet town, where I was born [*or* bound]. Barbara Allen [*or* Barb'ra Allen *or* Bonny Barbara Allan *or* Barbara Allen's Cruelty]. *Unknown.* BLSo; BSV; ESPB; FaFP; FSW; HBV-2; OBEV; TreF; TrGrPo; ViBoFo; ViBoPo
In scenery I like flat country. Passing Remark. William Stafford. GP
In scenes paternal, not beheld through years. Anna Seward. *Fr.* Eyam. NOEC
In schomer, when the leves spryng. Robin Hood and the Potter. *Unknown.* ESPB
In School-Days. Whittier. AA; BLPA; FaBoBe; FPL; GLGT; OBCA; OxBChV; PoPl; TreF
"Still sits the schoolhouse by the road, *sel.*" FaPON
In Scorching Time. Alex Stevens. AMV-81
In Scotia so fair, 'tis a custom they say. To Lydia, with a Coloured Egg, on Easter Monday. John Jones. FaBoUs
In Scotland there was a babie born. Hind Horn. *Unknown.* ESPB; ViBoFo
In Scotland town where I was borned. Hind Horn. *Unknown.* AmFP
In Scotland, where the porridge grows. Of the Stalking of the Stag. Sir Owen Seaman. CenHV
In seaboard town there was a merchant. In Brunton Town. *Unknown.* BaBo
In sea-cold Lyonesse. Sunk Lyonesse. Walter de la Mare. CoBMV; FaBoCh; LiTM
In Search of a Short Poem for My Grandmother. Louise Hardeman. AMV-81
In Search of the Picturesque. William Combe. *Fr.* Dr. Syntax in Search of the Picturesque. OBRV
In secreit place, this hindir nicht. The Man of Valour to His Fair Lady. William Dunbar. MeEL
In secret/ be quiet say nothing. Poem. Pablo Picasso, *tr. by* David Gascoyne. EAS
In secret place where once I stood. The Flesh and the Spirit. Anne Bradstreet. AmPP; AP; LiTA; NePA; NOBA; OxBA; SCAP; TAP
In seed time learn, in harvest teach, in winter enjoy. Blake. *Fr.* The Marriage of Heaven and Hell. FF
In se'enteen hunder'n [*or* hunder an'] forty-nine. On Andrew Turner. Burns. DBV; PV
In sensuous coil. Kings. *Unknown, tr. by* Arthur W. Ryder. *Fr.* The Panchatantra. AWP
In Sepia. Jon Anderson. PoA
In September she appeared. Foreign Student. Barbara B. Robinson. CTBA
In Service. Winifred M. Letts. HBMV
In seventeen hundred and forty-four. The Kilruddery Hunt. Thomas Mozeen. BIrV
In seventeen hundred and seventy-five. The Bombardment of Bristol. *Unknown.* PAH
In shades we live, in shades we die. Amanda's Complaint. Philip Freneau. AP
In Shadow. Hart Crane. NOBA; TwAmPo
In Shadow. Caroline Hazard. GoBC
In shadowy calm the boat. Hope. Phillips Stewart. CaP
In shadowy formation they rise. The Raiders. Marian Allen. SUMH
In Shaka's days we lived well. Those Were the Days. *Zulu Oral Tradition, tr. by* H. Tracey. WTO
In Shame and Humiliation. James Wright. CAPP
In shantung suits we whites are cool. The Devil-Dancers. William Plomer. PeSA
In shaping the snow into blossoms. "Ping Hsin," *tr. fr. Chinese by* Kai-yu Hsu. *Fr.* Spring Waters. BoWoP; WPOW
In shards the sylvan vases lie. The Ravaged Villa. Herman Melville. AP; CTC; NOBA; PoEL-5
In Sherwood lived stout Robin Hood. *Unknown.* OBSC
In shining groups, each stem a pearly ray. Ghost-Flowers. Mary Thacher Higginson. AA; WeW
In Siberia's wastes. Siberia. James Clarence Mangan. BIrV; NBM; RoGo
In Sickness [Written Soon after the Author's Coming to Live in Ireland, upon the Queen's Death, October 1714]. Swift. NOEC; OBEC
In signe of favor stedfast still. To His Darrest Freind. John Steward of Baldynneis. OxBS
In silence I lie. Buddha's Death Day: February 15, 1815. Issa, *tr. by* Nobuyuki Yuasa. *Fr.* Oraga Haru. OFD
In silence I must take my seat. Table Rules for Little Folk[s]. *Unknown.* FaBoUs; OxBChV
In silent gaze the tuneful choir among. Stanzas to Mr. Bentley. Thomas Gray. NoP
In silent night, when rest I took. Some Verses upon the Burning of Our House, July 10th, 1666 [*or* Here Follow[e]s Some Verses . . .]. Anne Bradstreet. AP; BoWoP; NOBA; NoP; OxBA; PAI; SCAP; SGB; TAP; WPE
In simmer, whan aa sorts foregether. Embro to the Ploy. Robert Garioch. OxBS
In simpler verse than triolets. An Old-fashioned Poet. Ada Foster Murray. HBV-2
In sixteen hundred and sixty-six. *Unknown.* FaBoUs
In Sleep. Richard Burton. AA
In Sleep. Alice Meynell. BrRo
In sleep he hunches away from me. His Sleep. Constance Urdang. AMV-81
In sleep when an old man's body is no longer aware of its boundaries. A Journey through the Moonlight. Russell Edson. LCAP
In Sligo the country was soft; there were turkeys. County Sligo [*or* Sligo and Mayo]. Louis MacNeice. FaBoPP; OnYI
In slow procession. Knockmany. Richard Ryan. CIP
In slow procession, one by one, silently. From Far Away. Delmira Agustini, *tr. by* D. M. Pettinella. PBWP
In slow recuperative hours. David McCord. Convalescence, V. WhC
In slumbers of midnight the sailor-boy lay. The Mariner's Dream. William Dimond. BeLS; HBV-1
In small backyards old men's long underwear. The Patricians. Douglas Dunn. OxBC
In Small Townlands. Seamus Heaney. CIP; NoAM

In smoky outhouses of the court of love. In the Queen's Room. Norman Cameron. Three Love Poems, II. GTBS-P; OxBTC
In snorts of wind, the tawny meadow. Runaway. Kim Kurt. NePoAm-2
In sober mornings, doe [*or* do] not thou reherse [*or* rehearse]. When He Would Have His Verses Read. Robert Herrick. CaPo; NOBE; OAEP; OBS; SeCV-1
In Soho's square mile of unoriginal sin. After the Release of Ezra Pound. Daniel Abse. NMP
In solemn conclave vow and swear. Constitution for a League of Nations. Arthur Guiterman. InMe
In solitary august, like a story. Passage of an August. Eithne Wilkins. NeBP
In Solitary Confinement, Sea Point Police Cells. C. J. Driver. PeSA
In Some Seer's Cloud Car. Christopher Middleton. TwCP
In some unused lagoon, some nameless bay. The Dismantled Ship. Walt Whitman. AmPP; CABA; MOS; NoAM; NoP; OxBA
In some versions of the universe the stars. Stars. Howard Moss. HoAn
In Some Way or Other the Lord Will Provide, *with music.* Mrs. M. A. W. Cook. AH
In somebody's shoes. A Halo. Ralph Salisbury. FAZ
In somer, when the shawes be sheyne. Robin Hood and the Monk [*or* Robyn Hode and the Munke]. *Unknown.* CH; ESPB; FaBoBa; OBEV; OxBB; ViBoFo; ViBoPo. *See also* In summer, when the shaws be sheen.
In something you have written in school, you say. Serpent Knowledge. Robert Pinsky. *Fr.* An Explanation of America. NPGG
In Sorrow. Thomas Hastings. AA; HBV-2
In sour seasons, in diff-/icult wind. Dislike of Tasks. Richmond Lattimore. SaC
In South Australia, I was born. South Australia. *Unknown.* FSW
In South Oregon the Klamath play. The Woyi. Lew Blockcolski. VoR
In Space-Time Aware. Abbie Huston Evans. GP
In Spain. Emily Lawless. AnIV
In Spain. Sir Thomas Wyatt. *See* Tagus, Farewell.
In Spain: Drinking Song. Emily Lawless. AnIV
In Spain, where the courtly Castilian hidalgo twangs lightly. Carmen. Newman Levy. FiBHP
In Spanish he whispers there is no time left. The Visitor. Carolyn Forché. FYAP
In speaking of a person's faults. Be Careful What You Say. Joseph Kronthal. STF
In spite of all the learned have said. The Indian Burying Ground. Philip Freneau. AA; AmPP; AP; HAP; HBV-2; HeIP; LiTA; NePA; NOBA; NoP; OxBA; PoEL-4; PoLF; PoPl; TAP
In spite of all the solemn-hearted fools. The Joy of Love. Allan Dowling. ErPo
In Spite of All This Much Needed Thunder. Zack Gilbert. PoNe
In spite of cold and chills. Daffodils. Kikurio. SoPo; SUS; TiPo
In Spite of His Dangling Pronoun. Lyn Lifshin. IHMS
In spite of mid-winter, the air is risen. Thaw. T. Alan Broughton. AMV-81
In spite of my sad financial state. I'm Leery of Firms with Easy Terms. C. S. Jennison. QQQ
In spite of Rice, in spite of Wheat. Epigram on the Poor of Boston Being Employed in Paving the Streets, 1774. *Unknown.* PAH
In Spite of Sorrow. Adoniram Judson. TRV
In spots/ it is warm enough. Ken Belford. NeAC
In spring I look gay. *Unknown.* OxNR
In spring if there are dogs they will bark. Ballade of Sayings. W. S. Merwin. NNaP
In spring the sheep are driven over the mountain. Sheep Country. Margaret Pond. BPAW
In spring we tried with sharpened spade to dig. Harvest. Jeannette Maino. AMV-80
In spring when everything. Desire. Isaac de Botton, *tr. by* Stephen Levy. VWA
In spring when maple buds are red. Daylight Saving Time. Phyllis McGinley. RHPC
In Springtime. Kipling. BrPo
In springtime when the leaves are young. Seasons. Christina Rossetti. YeAr
In Staffordshire I was born. The Posy of Thyme. *Unknown.* OBET
In Stamford, at the edge of town, a giant statue stands. The Best Line Yet. Edward Allen. InPK; POL
In State, *sel.* Forceythe Willson.
"O Keeper of the Sacred Key." AA
In stature, the Manlet was dwarfish. The Manlet [*or* The Little Man That Had a Little Gun]. "Lewis Carroll." BXAP; FaBoNo; Par
In stillness, I wait. Softly, White and Pure. Dorothy R. Fulton. AMV-80
In stone settlements when the moon is stone. Peter Levi. EBEV
In streets, among the rocks of time and weather. The Mountains. Louis Dudek. CaP
In strenuous hope I wrought. Vesica Piscis. Coventry Patmore. VLP
In Such a Night. Shakespeare. *Fr.* The Merchant of Venice, V, i. ChTr; FiP; WHA
In such a night, when every louder wind. A Nocturnal Reverie. Countess of Winchilsea. EBEV; FaBoEn; GoTL; LoBV; NOEC; NoP; OBEC; PBWP; PoEL-3; SBG; SeCePo; WPE
In such a place. Pond. Fredrick Zydek. AMV-81
In such an armor he may rise and raid. Bronzeville Man with a Belt in the Back. Gwendolyn Brooks. IDB; POBA
In such luxurious plentie of all pleasure. Spenser. *Fr.* The Faerie Queene, IV, 10. OAEL-1
In Suffolk. George Crabbe. *See* Spring to Winter.
In Summer. Trumbull Stickney. NCEP
In Summer. Charles Hanson Towne. HBMV
In Summer. *Unknown. See* Robin Hood and the Monk.
In summer-colored dresses, six young girls. Baptism. Alden Nowlan. POL
In summer elms are made for me. Dilemma of the Elm. Genevieve Taggard. MoAmPo
In summer I am very glad. Playgrounds. Laurence Alma-Tadema. HBV-1; HBVY
In Summer, in the open air. Summer Sabbath. Jessie E. Sampter. TrJP
In summer time, when leaves grew green and birds were singing. King Edward the Fourth and a Tanner of Tamworth. *Unknown.* BaBo; ESPB
In summer time when leaves grow green/ And birds sit on the tree. Under the Greenwood Tree. *Unknown.* GBP
In summer time, when leaves grow green/ Down a down a down. Robin Hood and the Tinker. *Unknown.* ESPB
In summer time, when leaves grow green and flowers are fresh and gay. Robin Hood and the Curtal Friar. *Unknown.* ESPB
In summertime, when leaves grow green, when they doe grow both green and long. The Noble Fisherman; or, Robin Hood's Preferment. *Unknown.* ESPB
In summer, when the days were long. Summer Days. Wathen Mark Wilks Call. EBVV
In summer, when the grass is thick, if mother has the time. The Fairy Book. Norman Gale. HBV-1; HBVY; OHIP
In summer when the hills are blond. January. Geoffrey Dutton. PoAu-2
In summer, when the shaws be sheen. Robin Hood and the Monk, *abr. Unknown.* OBNV. *See also* In somer, when the shawes be sheyne.
In Summer's Heat. Ovid, *tr. fr. Latin by* Christopher Marlowe. Amores, I, 5. UnTE
(Corinnae Concubitus.) GBL
(Elegy to His Mistress.) ErPo
("In summer's heat[e] and mid-time of the day.") BoLoP; EBEV; OBVE
(Ovid's Fifth Elegy.) NCEP
In summer's mellow midnight. The Night Wind. Emily Brontë. ChER; ChTr; EBVV; NCEP; OAEP; RoGo; TEP; VLP
In summertime on Bredon. Bredon Hill. A. E. Housman. A Shropshire Lad, XXI. BrPo; EBVV; FaBoPP; MoAB; MoBrPo; SoSe; TreF; VLP; WHA
In sunburnt parks where Sundays lie. Cobb Would Have Caught It. Robert Fitzgerald. GrPl; HAP; InvP; MP; TwCP; WeW
In sunlight on the Avenue. Galway Kinnell. *Fr.* The Avenue Bearing the Initial of Christ into the New World. NMP
In sunlight raindrops look like dew. A Battle of Similes. *Malay Oral Tradition, tr. by* R. J. Wilkinson *and* R. O. Winstedt. WTO
In sunny girlhood's vernal life. A Portrait. Joseph Ashby-Sterry. HBV-1
In Sweet Communion. John Newton. TRV
In Switzerland lang syne befell. The Ballant o' the Laird's Bath. Douglas Young. BSV
In Switzerland one idle day. Idyll. Hugh Macnaghten. HBMV
In Sylvia Plath Country. Erica Jong. IHMS
In t' other hundred, o'er yon swarthy moor. The Country Curate. Henry Taylor. NOEC
In taking of my lonely walk on a cold and wintry day. The Collier Lad's Lament. *Unknown.* OBET
In talking. To a Lady Holding the Floor. Mildred Weston. FiBHP
In Tall Grass. Carl Sandburg. PoA
In tangled wreaths, in clustered gleaming stars. Yellow Jessamine. Constance Fenimore Woolson. AA; HBV-1
In tattered old slippers that toast at the bars. The Cane-bottomed [*or* Cane-bottom'd] Chair. Thackeray. HBV-2; PaPo
In Taurus was the sun and flowery Spring. Ganymede and Helen. *Unknown.* PeHV
In tears to her mother poor Harriet came. The Disappointment. Jane Taylor. FaBoUs
In Teesdale. Andrew Young. FaBoPP
In temporary pain. The New God. Witter Bynner. *Fr.* The New World. WGRP
In Temptation. Charles Wesley. *See* Jesus, Lover of My Soul.
In tender May when the sweet laugh of Christ. The Puritan. Karl Shapiro. MoAmPo

In Tenebris. Thomas Hardy. FaBoEn; LiTB; NOBE; NoP; PrIm; SeCePo
Sels.
"There have been times when I well might have passed and the ending have come," III. OAEL-2
"When the clouds' swoln bosoms echo back the shouts of the many and strong," II. BrPo; CMoP; LiTM; NoAM; OxBTC; VLP
"Wintertime nighs," I. OAEL-2; OAEP; TreFS
In Tennessee once the heart of the campfire glowed. Recollection Long Ago: Sad Music. Robert Penn Warren. SV
In Terror of Hospital Bills. James Wright. GP
In terror the aches. Shechem. David Shevin. VWA
In Tesla's Laboratory. Robert Underwood Johnson. AA
In Texas Grass. Quincy Troupe. PoBA
In Thankfull Remembrance for My Dear Husband's Safe Arrivall Sept. 3, 1662. Anne Bradstreet. TrPWD
In that ago when being was believing. The History of Truth. W. H. Auden. FaBoMo
In that ancient time—in eternity. Words Spoken by Pasternak during a Bombing. Bella Akhmadulina, *tr. by* Jean Valentine *and* Olga Carlisle. BoWoP
In that bad year and city of your birth. For an Emigrant. Randall Jarrell. OxBA
In that building, long and low. The Ropewalk. Longfellow. AP
In that country of thresholds we move like vandals. Papermill Graveyard. Ben Belitt. NYBP
In that country the animals. The Animals in That Country. Margaret Atwood. NoP
In That Dark Cave. Shel Silverstein. ELU
In that dark world the only light. Tick Picking in the Quetico. Don Johnson. MAYP
In that day I had hoped for a pair of boots to guard my feet on the terrible trek. My Head on My Shoulders. Jeremy Ingalls. GoYe
In that desolate land and lone. The Revenge of Rain-in-the-Face. Longfellow. BPAW; PAH
In That Dim Monument Where Tybalt Lies. Arthur Davison Ficke. HBMV
In that fair land where slope and plain. The Maiden of the Smile. Alfred Austin. TEP
In that hotel my life. The Illumination. Stanley Kunitz. GP; TAP
In that hour when the heat of day no more. Dante, *tr. by* Laurence Binyon. Divina Commedia: Purgatorio, XIX. NAWM-1
In that I have so greatly failed thee, Lord. So Little and So Much. John Oxenham. BLRP
In that instant. An Image from Beckett. Derek Mahon. CIP
In that land all is and nothing's ought. Neither Here nor There. W. R. Rodgers. LiTB; LiTM; MoAB; MoBrPo; NeBP; ViBoPo
In that lost Caucasian garden. The Naming of the Beasts. Francis Sparshott. NOBC
In that new world toward which our feet are set. Compensation. Celia Thaxter. HBV-1
In that November off Tehuantepec. Sea Surface Full of Clouds. Wallace Stevens. AmPP; AP; CMoP; CoBMV; MoAB; MoAmPo; MOS; TwAmPo; VGW
In that, O Queen of queens, thy birth was free. To Our Blessed Lady. Henry Constable. ACP; GoBC; ISi; OBSC
In that photograph of the child and her mother there is a side space. Silence. Susan Griffin. *Fr.* Woman and Nature. NPGG
In that Poussin the clouds are like golden tea. Poussin. Louis MacNeice. EyDe
In that rapacious littoral now slaked by sea. Shore Birds. Vi Gale. GoYe
In that same gardin all the goodly flowres. The Garden of Adonis. Spenser. The Faerie Queene, III, 6. NOBE
In that so sudden summer storm they tried. Summer Storm. Louis Simpson. ErPo; OxBC
In that soft mid-land where the breezes bear. Rodney's Ride. *Unknown.* PAH
In that sore hour around thy bed there stood. Deliverance. William James Dawson. OBVV
In that town, nothing is sane but the sea. Beads from Blackpool. Anne Ridler. NMP
In that town were hard spaces. Town I Left. Helen Sorrells. IHMS
In that tribe the priests are chosen. Finders Keepers. Donald Finkel. VWA
In the/ In the Quarter. Cultural Exchange. Langston Hughes. PoNe
In the afternoon on the thirteenth. Crazy Movie. Gregorio Barrios, *tr. by* Toni Empringham. FIA
In the afternoon, while the wind. Views from the High Camp. W. S. Merwin. ConAP
In the air there are no coral-/ Reefs or ambergris. A Song. Duncan Campbell Scott. PeCV
In the America of the dream. The Lonesome Dream. Lisel Mueller. CoAP
In the American dream it is customarily deleted. The Bush on Mount Venus. Donald Finkel. CoPo
In the *Analects* Confucius says. Portoncini dei Morti. Daniel Halpern. MAYP
In the ancient town of Bruges. The Belfry of Bruges. Longfellow. HBV-2
In the Annals of Tacitus. Philip Murray. NePoAm
In the Aztec design God crowds. Ultimate Problems. William Stafford. NU
In the Backs. Frances Cornford. BrRo
In the backyard of the world. Hide and Seek. Dan Pagis, *tr. by* Bernhard Frank. AMV-81
In the bad old days a bewigged old Squire. Wigs and Beards. Robert Graves. NOBL
In the Badlands. David Wagoner. UnPo
In the Baggage Coach Ahead. Gussie L. Davis. FSN, *with music*; TreFS
In the Baggage Room at Greyhound. Allen Ginsberg. NaP; NoP
In the Balance. *Unknown, tr. fr. Latin by* George F. Whicher. *Fr.* Carmina Burana. OLR
In the Bar. Robert Vander Molen. TAT
In the barn the tenant cock. Day; a Pastoral [*or* Morning]. John Cunningham. NOEC; OBEC
In the Barrio. Alurista, *tr. fr. Spanish by* Toni Empringham. FIA
In the basement beneath my consciousness. The Basement Watch. Thomas Tolnay. AMV-80
In the basement by the furnace lies. The New Calf. James Hearst. TAT
In the basement my mother tended. Translations. Patricia Y. Ikeda. BrSi
In the Bay. Arthur Symons. *Fr.* Amorix Exsul. PBBP
In the Bayou. Don Marquis. AmFN
In the Bazaars of Hyderabad. Sarojini Naidu. FaPON
In the Beach House. Anne Sexton. PPP
In the Beginning. Rachel Fishman, *tr. fr. Yiddish by* Gabriel Levin. VWA
In the Beginning. Daniel G. Hoffman. PP
In the Beginning. Harriet Monroe. AA
In the Beginning. Jenny Lind Porter. GoYe
In the Beginning. Valerie Sinason. BrRo
In the beginning. Testament. Lucille Clifton. GeTw
In the beginning arose the Golden Germ. To the One God. *Tr. fr. Sanskrit by* Raimundo Panikkar. *Fr.* Vedic Hymns. ILwL
In the beginning, at every step, he turned. The Sickness of Adam. Karl Shapiro. *Fr.* Adam and Eve. AP; CoBMV; MoAB
In the beginning God Created the heaven and the earth. The Creation. Bible, *O.T.* *Fr.* Genesis. ImOP; NAWM-1; TreF
In the beginning God created the world. Waste and void. T. S. Eliot. *Fr.* The Rock, VII. OxBoCh
In the beginning I stood by the window. Windows in Providence. Aliki Barnstone. BoWoP
In the beginning the Great Spirit gave the prairie rare gifts. The Western Trail. Robert V. Carr. PoOW
In the beginning, there was nought. Creation. Alfred Noyes. GoBC; OBVV
In the beginning there were transports. Genesis. Jules Alan Wein. TrJP
In the Beginning Was a Word. Robert Graves. PoA
In the beginning was the air. Memory Air. Charles Dobzynski, *tr. by* Anita Barrows. VWA
In the Beginning Was the Bird. Henry Treece. LiTB; WaP
In the Beginning Was the Word. Bible, *N.T.* St. John, I: 1-17. TreF (Word, The, I:1-5.) TrGrPo
In the beginning, we had to deny you. Face on the Daguerreotype. Norman Rosten. HoAn
In the beginning, when green came on the pasture. In the Beginning. Jenny Lind Porter. GoYe
In the beginning, your name was never mentioned. *Unknown.* ILwL
In the bell toll of a clang. Salt. Ruth Stone. NMM
In the bend of your mouth soft murder. Lion. May Swenson. LiTM; SoSe
In the big-flaked sugar-snow. Maple Feast. Frances Frost. SiSoSe
In the black forest. Song of the Trees of the Black Forest. Edmond Jabes, *tr. by* Anthony Rudolf. VWA
In the black furrow of a field. The Hare. Walter de la Mare. TiPo
In the black winter morning. Bereft. Thomas Hardy. BoLoP; NoAM
In the Bleak Mid-Winter. Christina Rossetti. *See* Christmas Carol, A: "In the bleak mid-winter."
In the blossom-land Japan. An Old Song. "Yehoash," *tr. by* Marie Syrkin. AWP
In the bloud of Adam death was taken. Charm: Bleeding. *Unknown.* FaBoUs
In the blue distance. Nelly Sachs, *tr. by German by* Ruth *and* Matthew Mead. BoWoP
In the blue dusk. Canadice Lake. Bob Mondy. WOLT
In the blue eye of the medievalist there is a cart in the road. Another November. Stanley Plumly. LCAP

In the blue hubbub of the same-through-wealth sky. Geography. Kenneth Koch. NoAM
In the blue night. Pine Tree Tops. Gary Snyder. NOBA; Prf
In the blue winter of 1812. Johann Gaertner (1793–1887). Gary Gildner. FAZ
In the blurring low-blood-pressure. The Judgment. Kathleen Spivack. BoWoP
In the book of the iron angels there is nothing. Of the Beloved Caravan. Conny Hannes Meyer, *tr. by* Herbert Kuhner. VWA
In the *Boston Sunday Herald* just three lines. To an American Poet Just Dead. Richard Wilbur. NoP
In the bowl of buildings alias the back yard. Milk at the Bottom of the Sea. Oscar Williams. LiTA; MoPo
In the boys' room at Macon Elementary. The Naming. Terry Hummer. AMV-81
In the bramble bush shelley slowly eats a lark's heart. Hot Day at the Races. Tom Raworth. EAS
In the Breeze. Boris Pasternak, *tr. fr. Russian by* C. M. Bowra. TrJP
In the bright bay of your morning, O God. Prayer. Claire Goll, *tr. by* Babette Deutsch *and* Avram Yarmolinsky. TrJP
In the bright broad Swiss glare I stand listening. Recessional. Thomas MacGreevy. CIP
In the broken light, in owl weather. Colloquy. Weldon Kees. NaP; NYBP
In the buffalo's skull. Vihio Images. Judith Mountain Leaf Volborth. TWSS
In the burgeoning age of Arnaut when for God and man to be. A Fit of Something against Something. Alan Ansen. PP
In the Cabinet. Shlomo Vinner, *tr. fr. Hebrew by* Laya Firestone *and* Howard Schwartz. VWA
In the Cafe. Roo Borson. PPJ
In the Cage. Robert Lowell. FF; NOBA; SyP
In the Canadian Rockies. Virginia Shearer Hopper. AMV-80
In the cantina. At the Cantina. Gary Soto. MAYP
In the Canyon of Echo, there's a railroad begun. Echo Canyon. *Unknown.* AmFP
In the Carolinas. Wallace Stevens. VGW
In the Carpenter's Shop. Sara Teasdale. HBMV
In the Case of Lobsters. Petra von Morstein, *tr. fr. German by* Rosemarie Waldrop. BoWoP
In the castle of my soul. Walter Rauschenbusch. *Fr.* The Postern Gate. TRV
In the Catacombs. Harlan Hoge Ballard. YaD
In the Cathedral. Patricia Beer. OxBC
In the Cathedral Close. Edward Dowden. EBVV; NBM; OBVV; OxBI
In the cathedral the acolytes are praying. The Habeas Corpus Blues. Conrad Aiken. NYBP
In the cave with a long-ago flare. Painters. Muriel Rukeyser. EyDe
In the Caves of Auvergne. W. J. Turner. HBMV
In the Cellars. Jiri Gold, *tr. fr. Czech by* Jaroslav Kotan *and* Daniel Weissbort. VWA
In the cellars of old churches frightened mouths. Buildings. Daniela Gioseffi. FAZ
In the cemetery of Lodz. Mother. Julian Tuwim, *tr. by* Isaac Komem. VWA
In the Cemetery of the Sun. Wilfred Watson. PeCV
In the censer the coals are high. Final Prayer. Enheduanna, *tr. fr. Sumerian.* BoWoP
In the center my grandfather sits. Family Portrait 1933. Peter Oresick. LTB
In the center of a harsh and spectrumed city. Outside. Audre Lorde. NIP
In the center of the field a Lamb. At Christmas. Robert Duncan. NoAM
In the central terminal rain pouring. Spring in the Old World. Philip Levine. FAZ
In the centre of the poster, Napoleon. A Poster of Our Dazzling Victory at Saarbrucken. Arthur Rimbaud, *tr. by* Robert Lowell. *Fr.* Eighteen-seventy. OBWP
In the chaos of the autumn sun. The Smell of Old Newspapers Is Always Stronger after Sleeping in the Sun. Mike Lowery. Psk
In the chapel. Territory. Susan Wood-Thompson. AMV-81
In the cheap room. Episode. Cassiano Nunes, *tr. by* E. A. Lacey. PeHV
In the Cheviots. Maurice Lindsay. PoSH
In the Children's Hospital. "Hugh MacDiarmid." NoP; PAI
In the Children's Hospital. Tennyson. HBV-1
In the chorus of memories a blessing in disguise. Declension. Stephen Sandy. PoA
In the Churchyard. Eleanor Ross Taylor. UnPo
In the Churchyard at Cambridge. Longfellow. AmPP; AP; PoEL-5; TAP
In the City. Israel Zangwill. WGRP
In the City of Bogotá. Greg Pape. MAYP
In the city of Marseilles, there lived a beautiful lady. The Lowly Peasant. *Unknown, tr. by* Rina Benmayor. PBWP
In the city of St. Francis they have taken down the statue of St. Francis. Afterwards, They Shall Dance. Bob Kaufman. PoNe; TwCP; VGW
In the clear light that confuses everything. The Laurel Tree. Louis Simpson. NNaP
In the clearing stands. Missionaries in the Jungle. Linda Piper. BlSi
In the cliff over the frog pond. The Fossils. Galway Kinnell. NYBP
In the close covert of a grove. The Geranium. Sheridan. BoLoP; ErPo; UnTE
In the Coach, *sel.* Thomas Edward Brown.
Conjergal Rights. VLP
In the coal-pit, or the factory. A Golden Lot. Joseph Skipsey. SaC; VLP
In the coiled shell sounds Ocean's distant roar. The Tutelage. Robert Mowry Bell. AA
In the cold/ and half light. November. Samuel S. Turner. AMV-80
In the cold, cold parlor. First Death in Nova Scotia. Elizabeth Bishop. CoAP; LCAP; NCSH; NOBA; NYBP
In the cold months. Trout. Norman Hindley. WOLT
In the cold October night-time. The Boatman's Song. Thomas Hardy. *Fr.* The Dynasts. WaaP
In the cold orange light we stared across. At the Firth of Lorne. Iain Crichton Smith. BSV
In the common day I find a common fact. Everything Has Its History. Phillis Levin. AMV-81
In the concrete cells of the hatchery. Winter Trout. James Dickey. LiSp
In the cool evening the master. A Plum. Mani Leib, *tr. by* David G. Roskies *and* Hillel Schwartz. VWA
In the cool, impersonal room. The Egoist Dead. Elizabeth Brewster. CaP
In the Cool of the Evening. Alfred Noyes. HBV-1
In the cool waters of the river. Woman. Valente Goenha Malangatana, *tr. by* Dorothy Guedes *and* Philippa Rumsey. PBA; TTY
In the copper marsh. Heron. Philip Booth. NePoEA; PPJ; Psk; WOLT
In the Corn Land. Quentin R. Howard. TAT
In the corner a violet jug the bells the folds of paper. Poem. Pablo Picasso, *tr. by* David Gascoyne. EAS
In the corner the fire made a place. Two Women. Tania Van Zyl. PeSA
In the cot beside the water. The German Legion. Sydney Dobell. PeD
In the county of Essex there lived a squire. The Wandering Shepherdess. *Unknown.* OBET
In the County Tyrone, in [*or* near] the town of Dungannon. The Old [*or* Ould] Orange Flute. *Unknown.* FaBoBa; FSW; GBP; OxBoLi; WTO
In the Courts of Evil/ Borgias dine. Saint Francis Borgia; or, A Refutation for Heredity. Phyllis McGinley. NePoAm-2
In the Courtyard. Miriam Ulinover, *tr. fr. Yiddish by* Seth L. Wolitz. VWA
In the cowslip pips [*or* peeps] I lie. Clock-a-Clay [*or* Clock-o'-Clay]. John Clare. EBVV; FaPON; LiTB; LoBV; NBM; OAEL-2; OBNC; PoEL-5; SeCeV; TrGrPo; VLP; WHA
In the cream gilded cabin of his steam yacht. Mr. Nixon. Erza Pound. *Fr.* Hugh Selwyn Mauberley. MoAmPo
In the crimson of the morning, in the whiteness of the noon. The Coming of His Feet. Lyman W. Allen. BLPA
In the cross field. Out West. Gary Snyder. NNaP
In the Cross of Christ I Glory. Sir John Bowring. HBV-2; WGRP
In the crowd's multitudinous mind. Crucifixion. Eva Gore Booth. WGRP
In the Crypted Way. Thomas Hardy. *See* In the Vaulted Way.
In the custom of the Jews. The Unveiling. Suzanne Bernhardt. VWA
In the daisied lap of summer. The Season's Lovers. Miriam Waddington. MoCV; OBCV; PeCV
In the Dark. George Arnold. HBV-2
In the Dark. Francis Louisa Bushnell. AA
In the Dark. Mary Thacher Higginson. AA
In the Dark. Sophie Jewett. TrPWD
In the dark/ each sits alone. Train. Ken Smith. EAS
In the dark aisles of Bruckner's symphonies. Bruckner. James Camp. MAT
In the dark and narrow street. When the Night and Morning Meet. Dora Greenwell. EBVV
In the dark and peace of my final bed. Little Pagan Rain Song. Frances Shaw. HBMV
In the dark at first, we see things in their sleep. Girandole. Dorothy Donnelly. NYBP
In the dark caverns of the night. Poem. Henry Treece. NeBP
In the dark church of music. Vivaldi. Delmore Schwartz. NYBP
In the Dark, in the Dew. Mary Newmarch Prescott. HBV-1
In the dark night where none could ever spy. Wasted Night. *Unknown, tr. by* Louis Untermeyer. UnTE
In the Dark None Dainty. Robert Herrick. CaPo; ELU; PoPle
In the dark of night. The Mailman. Victor Contoski. GP
In the dark pathways of his Gothic mind. Sketch. "Seumas O'Sullivan." AnIV
In the Dark What the Day Doth Forbid. Thomas Campion. *See* Hark, All You Ladies.

In the dark womb where I began. C. L. M. [*or* To His Mother]. John Masefield. HBV-1; LiTM; MoBrPo; OBVV; OxBTC
In the darkening church. Rufus Prays. L. A. G. Strong. MoBrPo
In the darkness/ of the house of the white brother. Indian School. Norman H. Russell. MAT
In the darkness deep. The Song of the Turnkey. Harry Bache Smith. AA
In the darkness east of Chicago. A Valedictory to Standard Oil of Indiana. David Wagoner. NYBP
In the darkness he sings of the dawning. The Poet. Mary Sinton Leitch. HBMV
In the dating bar, the potted ferns lean down. A History of Civilization. Albert Goldbarth. MAYP
In the Dawn. Odell Shepard. WGRP
In the dawn of breaking day. With Him. Julia E. Martin. STF
In the days before the high tide. A Sea Song. Digby Mackworth Dolben. EBVV
In the days of Caesar Augustus. Christmas Day; the Family Sitting. John Meade Falkner. NOCV; OxBTC
In the Days of Crinoline. Thomas Hardy. WhC
In the days of my season of salad. A Song of Renunciation. Sir Owen Seaman. CenHV
In the Days of Old. Thomas Love Peacock. *Fr.* Crotchet Castle. HBV-1
In the Days of Old Rameses, *with music. Unknown.* AS
In the Days of Rin-Tin-Tin. Daniel Hoffman. CoPo
In the days that tried our fathers. The Rejected "National Hymns." "Orpheus C. Kerr." OBAL
In the days when everyone said. Meantime. Heather McHugh. GeTw
In the daytime/ I walk in the South Bronx. Change of Venue. Jill Clockadale. AMV-80
In the Dead of the Night. Norman Dubie. AmPA
In the dead of winter, when. Mockingbird in Winter. Ernest Kroll. AMV-80
In the dead park a bench sprawls drunkenly. End of the Season on a Stormy Day—Oban. Iain Crichton Smith. NePoEA-2
In the Dean's porch a nest of clay. In the Cathedral Close. Edward Dowden. EBVV; NBM; OBVV; OxBI
In the Deep Channel. William Stafford. NaP
In the Deep Museum. Anne Sexton. MoAmPo; Prf
In the deep shadow of the porch. Bind-Weed. "Susan Coolidge." GN
In the deep sphagnum moss. Accommodation. Anselm Parlatore. SUW
In the depths of the Greyhound Terminal. In the Baggage Room at Greyhound. Allen Ginsberg. NaP; NoP
In the Desert. Stephen Crane. The Black Riders, III. FaBoEE; LiTM; NOBA; PAI; TAP
(Four Poems, I.) CrMA
(Heart, The.) HoPM; InPK; MoAmPo; TW
In the deserted, moon-blanch'd street. A Summer Night. Matthew Arnold. OAEP; SeCePo; SeCeV
In the deserted village, sunken down. The Deserted Village. Robin Hyde. WPE
In the desolate depths of a perilous place. The Bogeyman. Jack Prelutsky. RHPC
In the Dials. W. E. Henley. BrPo
In the diaphanous fall of your gown. Unter der Linde. George Ellenbogen. AMV-81
In the dim and distant ages, in the half-forgotten days. A Soldier of Weight. John Kendall. WhC
In the Distance. H. L. Van Brunt. FAZ
In the Distress upon Me, *with music.* Henry Ainsworth. AH
In the Dock. Walter de la Mare. ChMP; LiTM
In the Dome Car of the "Canadian." Sid Marty. NOBC
In the dome of my sires as the clear moonbeam falls. Newstead Abbey. Byron. ChER
In the Doorway. Robert Browning. *Fr.* James Lee's Wife. NCEP
In the Dordogne. John Peale Bishop. OBWP; VGW
In the downhill of life, when I find I'm declining. Tomorrow. John Collins. GTBS; GTBS-P; HBV-1; TreFT
In the dragoon's ride from out the north. A Bold Dragoon. *Unknown.* OBET
In the dream, in the charmed dream we are flying. The Eye of Humility. Kay Smith. OBCV
In the Dream of the Body. David Keller. AMV-80
In the drinking-well. Aunt Eliza. Harry Graham. ChTr; DBV; FaFP; NA; WhC
In the Dry Riverbed. Zelda, *tr. fr. Hebrew by* Marcia Falk. VWA
In the Due Honor of the Author Master Robert Norton. John Smith. SCAP
In the Dumps. *Unknown.* FaBoCo; NA
("We are all in the dumps.") OxNR
(We're All in the Dumps.) FaBoNo; GBP
In the dungeon-crypts idly did I stray. The Prisoner. Emily Brontë. OAEP
In the dusk of the evening. Old Mountain Road. Charles Simic. FYAP
In the dusk the path. Izumi Shikibu, *tr. fr. Japanese by* Kenneth Rexroth. WPOW
In the Dusky Path of a Dream. Rabindranath Tagore. *Fr.* The Gardener. OBMV
In the dust are my father's beautiful hands. At Night. Richard Eberhart. Str
In the early days in our own wild way we hurried the time along. The Ruin of Bobtail Bend. James Barton Adams. PoOW
In the early morning/ when the light and the sea smell come stumbling in. In Solitary Confinement, Sea Point Police Cells. C. J. Driver. PeSA
In the early morning I saw. A Test of Competence. Greg Forker. LFAC
In the early morning, past the shut houses. Scroppo's Dog. May Swenson. GDP
In the early white of a February morning, the snow clings. Poem for John My Brother. William Aberg. LFAC
In the earnest path of duty. Poem. Charlotte Forten. BlSi
In the earth—the earth—thou shalt be laid. Warning and Reply. Emily Brontë. OBVV; OxBI; WPE
In the East, in the East is my heart. My Heart Is in the East. Judah Halevi. TrJP
In the echo of my deaths. Fear. Alejandra Pizarnik, *tr. by* Lynn Alvarez. AMV-80
In the Egypt of my night. Locusts of Silence. Seymour Mayne. VWA
In the Egyptian Museum. Janet Lewis. NYBP; QFR
In the elbow of a macaroni. A Blue Jeaned Rock Queen in Search of Happiness on a Blind Thursday at 1/3 Speed and Crying. A. K. Redwing. VoR
In the Elegy Season. Richard Wilbur. InPK; MoAB; NePoEA; NYBP
In the Emptied Rest Home. Bella Akhmadulina, *tr. fr. Russian by* Jean Valentine *and* Olga Carlisle. BoWoP
In the empty lot—a place. The Wild. Wendell Berry. VGW
In the encyclopedia. Fact. Kenneth Rexroth. OBAL
In the End. Peter Everwine, *after* Natan Sach. NNaP
In the End of Days. Bible, *O.T.* Isaiah II: 2-4. TrJP
In the end of the sabbath, as it began to dawn. Easter Morning. Bible, *N.T. Fr.* St. Matthew. TreF
In the end you are tired of those places. Locations. Jim Harrison. AmPA
In the Environs of the Funeral Home. Robert Mezey. NePoEA
(Funeral Home, The.) LiTM
In the Evening. Thomas Hardy. ImOP
In the evening/ haze darkening on the hills. Another Night in the Ruins. Galway Kinnell. CoAP
In the evening/ my griefs come to me. Old Woman. Linda Pastan. FiCP
In the Evening by the Moonlight. James A. Bland. FSW; PSoN, *with music*; TreFS
In the evening from my window. *Unknown.* SUS
In the evening I would sit. Edna St. Vincent Millay. *Fr.* Journal. SaC
In the evening, just before. For Mary. Kenneth Rexroth. PoPl
In the evening of a brightly. Greenwich Avenue. James Schuyler. NYP
In the evening the dusk. The Poet Is Dead. William Everson. NoP
In the evening there is a snail. Talking to the Mule. Laura Jensen. AmPA
In the evening there were flocks of nighthawks. September 2. Wendell Berry. PoA
In the evening when I sit alone a-dreaming. Sweet Adeline. Richard H. Gerard. FSN; FSW; TreFT
In the evening, when the world knew he was dead. In the Evening. Thomas Hardy. ImOP
In the eye of seafaring man. The Winds of Change. Charles Ballard. VoR
In the factories at eight in the morning. With Schoolchildren. Willis Barnstone. GLGT
In the fair days when God. To Victor Hugo. Swinburne. OBVV
In the fair fields of suburban. Decks. Robert Phillips. GeTw; NYP
In the Fall, *sel.* "Hugh MacDiarmid."
"Let the only consistency." FaBoMo
In the Fall. Alina Rivero. AMV-81
In the fall, I believe again in poetry. Still. Aila Meriluoto, *tr. by* Jaakko A. Ahokas. PBWP
In the Fall o' Year. Thomas S. Jones, Jr. HBV-1
In the fall, rain of the happy tears returns. Whatever Comes. William Stafford. NPAW
In the Falling Deer's Mouth. Michael Levien. PoRA
In the falling snow. Hokku: In the Falling Snow. Richard Wright. *Fr.* Hokku Poems. AmNP; IDB; PoBA
In the fall-out of daisies on the rockland. Absent Daughter. Barend Toerien, *tr. by author..* PeSA
In the family drinking well. Sister Nell. *Unknown.* FaPON
In the far corner. The Blackbird. Humbert Wolfe. FaPON; GoJo; GrPl; HBMV; HBVY; RHPC; SUS; TiPo
In the Far Years. Wilson MacDonald. CaP
In the few warm weeks. A Christmas Message. Gavin Ewart. FaBoMo
In the Field. Phyllis Janik. IHMS

In the Field. Richard Wilbur. NYBP
In the Field Forever. Robert Wallace. PPJ
In the Fields. Charlotte Mew. BoNaP; MoAB; MoBrPo
In the fields, the silos open their mouths. Hangman. Ai. AmPA
In the Firelight. Eugene Field. AA
In the First Cave. Seymour Mayne. VWA
In the First House. Joseph Joel Keith. GoYe
In the First Place of My Life. Ray A. Young Bear. STE
In the first place, the slow sloth labors. Three-toed Sloth. Dorothy Donnelly. HoAn
In the first rank of these did Zimri stand. Zimri. Dryden. *Fr.* Absalom and Achitophel, Pt. I. HAP; SeCePo; ViBoPo
In the first ruder age, when love was wild. Love's Force. Thomas Carew. CaPo
In the first taxi he was alone, tra-la. The Taxis. Louis MacNeice. OxBTC
In the first year of freedom's second dawn. George III. Byron. *Fr.* The Vision of Judgment. TW
In the first year of the last disgrace. News of the World II. George Barker. DTC; FaBoTw; LiTB
In the Fishing Village. Sheila Nickerson. WOLT
In the flash of that explosion. Wedding Day at Nagasaki. Rodney Hall. CBAP
In the fleece of your flesh. The Moment before Conception. Eve Merriam. UnTE
In the Fleeting Hand of Time. Gregory Corso. NAs
In the Flight of the Blue Heron: To Montezuma. Anita Endrezze Probst. CDW
In the Flowering Season. Michael Roberts. FaBoTw
In the foil-and-pastel tea room. Non-Euclidean Elegy. John Frederick Nims. MoVE
In the footsteps of the walking air. Kenneth Patchen. EAS
In the Ford plant. The Foundation of American Industry. Donald Hall. GOA
In the Forest. George Bowering. NOBC
In the Forest. Russell Edson. LCAP
In the Forest. Pinhas Sadeh, *tr. fr. Hebrew by* Harris Lenowitz. VWA
In the Forest. Oscar Wilde. SyP
In the forest, in unexplored. Michael Dransfield. Geography, III. CBAP
In the forest of noyous hevynesse. Lost. Charles d'Orléans. OxBM
In the forest there. The King of Sunshine. Michael Silverton. PV
In the forties and fifties it seemed like everytime. Train Blues. Paul Zimmer. PPJ
In the furrows of the world. Nation. Charlie Cobb. PoBA
In the Garden. Ernest Crosby. HBV-1; HBVY
In the Garden. Emily Dickinson. *See* Bird came down the walk, A.
In the Garden. Richard Eberhart. NePoAm-2
In the Garden. C. Austin Miles. TreFT
In the Garden. Tom Schmidt. NeAC
In the Garden. *Unknown.* SoSe
("In the garden there strayed.") LO
In the Garden at Swainston. Tennyson. OBEV; OBNC; OBVV; VLP
(Valedictory, II.) GoBC
In the Garden City Café with its murals on the wall. Huxley Hall. John Betjeman. OBSV
In the garden of death, where the singers whose names are deathless. In Memory of "Barry Cornwall." Swinburne. HBV-2
In the Garden of Eden, planted by God. Trees. Bliss Carman. OHIP
In the Garden of the Lord. Helen Keller. TRV; WGRP
In the Garden of the Turkish Consulate. Pinhas Sadeh, *tr. fr. Hebrew by* Harris Lenowitz. VWA
In the garden. Summer's end. Evening. On a bench. Verses Written on Sand. Melech Ravitch, *tr. by* Seymour Mayne *and* Rivka Augenfeld. VWA
In the garden there strayed. In the Garden. *Unknown.* LO; SoSe
In the Garden: Villa Cleobolus. Lawrence Durrell. ChMP
In the garret under the sloping eaves. The Wedding Gift. Minna Irving. BLPA
In the gathering dew. Lady Sagami, *tr. fr. Japanese by* Willis Barnstone. BoWoP
In the gathering gloom they lie. Terror. "Yehoash," *tr. by* Isidore Goldstick. TrJP
In the Gazebo. Philip Appleman. BXAP
In the Ghetto. Hugo Sonnenschein, *tr. fr. German by* Edouard Roditi. VWA
In the ghetto of my mouth. The Golem. Shlomo Reich, *tr. by* Mira Reich. VWA
In the glittering collection of paste diamonds one in particular ranks very high. Oh, Stop Being Thankful All over the Place. Ogden Nash. NePA
In the Gloaming. James C. Bayles. NA
In the Gloaming ("In the gloaming to be roaming"). Charles Stuart Calverley, *parody.* BXAP; InMe; NOBL
In the Gloaming ("In the gloaming, oh, my darling"). Meta Orred. BLSo, *with music*; FaFP; FSW; TreF
In the gloom of mighty cities. The Commonwealth of Toil. Ralph Chaplin. FSW
In the gloom of whiteness. Snow. Edward Thomas. FaBoTw; MoVE
In the gloomy ocean bed. The *Kearsarge.* James Jeffrey Roche. AA; PAH
In the Glorious Assumption of Our Blessed Lady. Richard Crashaw. LoBV
(On the Glorious Assumption of Our Blessed Lady.) ISi; OBS
(On the Assumption.) AnAnS-1
In the Glorious Epiphanie of Our Lord God. Richard Crashaw. PoEL-2
(Hymne for the Epiphanie, A.) AnAnS-1
In the glow of early morning. Christ Is Coming. W. Macomber. STF
In the Gold Mines. B. W. Vilakazi. TTY
(On the Gold Mines.) PeSA
In the Gold Room. Oscar Wilde. SyP
In the golden air, the risky autumn. Piazzas. Barbara Guest. NeAP
In the golden glade the chestnuts are fallen all. North Wind in October. Robert Bridges. VLP
In the golden twilight the rain. The Terrace in the Snow. Su Tung-p'o, *tr. by* Kenneth Rexroth. NaP
In the Good Old Summertime. Ren Shields. BLSo, *with music*; FSN, *with music*; FSW; TreF
In the Grass. Annette von Droste-Hulshoff, *tr. fr. German by* James Edward Tobin. PBWP
In the Grass. Hamlin Garland. AA
In the Grave No Flower. Edna St. Vincent Millay. CrMA
In the gray dawning across the white lake. Wild March. Constance Fenimore Woolson. YeAr
In the gray evening. The Garden Hose. Beatrice Janosco. POL
In the great gardens, after bright spring rain. The Innocent Spring. Edith Sitwell. *Fr.* The Sleeping Beauty. NOBE; OxBTC
In the Great House, and in the House of Fire. He Holdeth Fast to the Memory of His Identity. *Unknown, tr. by* Robert Hillyer. *Fr.* Book of the Dead. AWP
In the great night my heart will go out. Owl Woman's Death Song. *Tr. fr. Papago Indian by* Ruth Underhill. BoWoP
In the great place the great house is gone from. Slave Quarters. James Dickey. CAPP; NYBP
In the great world—which, being interpreted. Byron. *Fr.* Don Juan, XI. OxBoLi
In the green hedge tall and thick. June in Wiltshire. Geoffrey Grigson. WaP
In the green light of water, like the day. The Swans. Edith Sitwell. CMoP; MoVE; WPE
In the greenest growth of the Maytime. An Interlude. Swinburne. ViBoPo
In the greenest of our valleys. The Haunted Palace. Poe. *Fr.* The Fall of the House of Usher. AA; AP; BeLS; CH; ChTr; HBV-2; LiTA; NePA; NOBA; OBVV; OxBA; PoEL-4; PrIm; SyP; TAP; TreFS; TrGrPo; ViBoPo; WiR; WSC
In the greenhouse lives a wren. *Unknown.* OxNR
In the grey beginning of years, in the twilight of things that began. Hymn of Man. Swinburne. VLP
In the grey evening. The Garden Hose. Beatrice Janosco. NTCP
In the grey wastes of dread. Horses on the Camargue. Roy Campbell. GTBS-P; PeSA; PoPle; SeCePo
In the groined alcoves of an ancient tower. The Second Volume. Robert Mowry Bell. AA
In the grooved earth the old grapple. Confrontations of March. H. C. Dillow. AMV-80
In the groves of Africa from their natural wonder. An African Elegy. Robert Duncan. NoAM
In the growing haste of the world must this thing be. Sails. George Sterling. EtS
In the Half Light of Holding and Giving. John Wieners. CoPo
In the Half-Point Time of Night. Ann Menebroker. AMV-80
In the hall-grounds, by evening-gloom concealed. The Hydraulic Ram. Charles Tennyson Turner. NBM
In the hallway. Derelict. Henry Johnson. LFAC
In the Hamptons. John N. Morris. NYP
In the happier years gone by me. February 14, 22 B.C. Franklin P. Adams. InMe
In the harbor of Askalon. Light of Judea. Claude Vigée, *tr. fr. French.* VWA
In the harbour, in the island, in the Spanish Seas. Trade Winds. John Masefield. FaBoCh; OBMV
In the hazy shape of my mind. Squall. John Moore. NCSH
In the Heart of Contemplation. C. Day Lewis. MoPo; MP
In the heart of the Hills of Life, I know. My Springs. Sidney Lanier. UnPo
In the heart of the hills the rain unabated. *Malay Oral Tradition, tr. by* R. J. Wilkinson *and* R. O. Winstedt. WTO
In the Heartland. Mark Vinz. GP

In the heat-locked room. As a Child Seeing a Cardinal. John Gill. NeAC
In the heat of the day a funnel cloud. For the El Paso Weather Bureau. Peter Wild. MAT
In the Hedgeback. "Hugh MacDiarmid." BSV; NeBP
In the Hellgate Wind. Madeline DeFrees. NYP
In the Henry James Country. William Abrahams. WaP
In the heydays of 'forty-five. For George Santayana. Robert Lowell. CMoP; VGW
In the high jungle where Assam meets Tibet. Moschus Moschiferus A. D. Hope. CBAP; GrPl
In the high places lo! there is no light. Lighten Our Darkness. Lord Alfred Douglas. HBMV
In the high seat, before-dawn dark. Why Log Truck Drivers Rise Earlier than Students of Zen. Gary Snyder. NNaP; SOTW
In the Highlands. Robert Louis Stevenson. BSV; FaBV; GoTS; HBV-1; OBEV; OBVV; OxBS; PoSH
(“In the highlands, in the country places.") BrPo; FaBoCh
In the Hole. John Ciardi. HoAn
In the Holy Nativity of Our Lord God. Richard Crashaw. CABA; PoEL-2; SBVL; SeCeV; SeCV-1
(Holy Nativity, The.) WGRP
(Hymn [*or* Hymne] of the Nativity, An.) AnAnS-1; HAP; MeLP; MePo; OBS
(Nativity, The.) OxBoCh
Sels.
Shepherds' Hymn, The. NOBE
("Gloomy night embraced the place.") ViBoPo
Shepherd's Hymn, The ("We saw Thee in Thy balmy nest"). ACP; TrGrPo, 3 *sts.*
(Hymn Sung as by the Shepherd, A.) GoBC
(Verses from the Shepherd's Hymn.) OBEV
In the Home of the Scholar Wu Su-chiang. Wu Tsao, *tr. fr. Chinese by* Kenneth Rexroth *and* Ling Chung. BoWoP; WPow
In the Hospital. Arthur Guiterman. WGRP
In the Hospital. Mary Woolsey Howland. HBV-2
In the Hospital. Laura Jensen. AmPA
In the Hospital of the Holy Physician. Nancy Willard. IHMS
In the hot valley of the never was. The Last Campaign. Geoffrey Lehmann. PoAu-2
In the hotel room, on tour. Tennis. Nina Nyhart. AMV-81
In the hour of death, after this life's whim. Dominus Illuminatio Mea. Richard Doddridge Blackmore. OBEV; OBVV; TreFS
In the hour of Fresno. California #2. Victor Hernández Cruz. TAT
In the hour [*or* houre] of my distress [*or* distresse]. His Litany [*or* Letanie] to the Holy Spirit. Robert Herrick. AnAnS-2; BLPL; DTC; ELP; HBV-2; ILwL; JCP; OAEP; OBEV; OBS; OxBoCh; PoLF; PoPle; QFR; SeCePo; SeCV-1; TEP
In the Hours of Darkness. James Flexner. FaPON
In the house/ of Mr. and Mrs. Spouse. Teevee. Eve Merriam. QQQ
In the House of Idiedaily. Bliss Carman. OBVV
In the House of the Dying. Jane Cooper. NMM
In the house of the hangman. The Hangman's Love Song. Stanley Moss. VGW
In the House of the Judge. Dave Smith. MAYP
In the house with the tortoise chair. Poem to Ease Birth. *Unknown, tr. by* Anselm Hollo. BoWoP
In the huge, rectangular room, the ceiling. My Mother, Who Came from China, Where She Never Saw Snow. Laureen Mar. WPOW
In the huge, wide-open, sleeping eye of the mountain. The Bear. Ted Hughes. FaBoMo
In the human cities, never again to. Despisals. Muriel Rukeyser. NMM; Prf
In the hungry kitchen. Kitchen Poem. Francis Scarfe. EAS
In the Huon Valley. James McAuley. CBAP
In the inn they had no room. Easter, Day of Christ Eternal. Maurice Moore. STF
In the Inner City. Lucille Clifton. CNA; HeIP
In the innermost cavern of labyrinths. Educational Music or Erosion. William H. Schubert. AMV-81
In the Interstices. Ruth Stone. ErPo
In the Isle of Dogs. John Davidson. OBNC; VLP
In the jolly, jolly spring. What the Toys Are Thinking. ffrida Wolfe. TiPo
In the Jury Room. Hodding Carter. MAT
In the kitchen/ making dishes with a brush. A Plea to My Sister. James Cunningham. JB
In the kitchen of the old house, late. In the Old House. Donald Hall. NePoEA-2
In the kosher meat market. This One Is about the Others. Dan Jaffe. FAZ
In the laboratory waiting room. Through a Glass Eye, Lightly. Carolyn Kizer. BoWoP
In the Ladies' Room at the Bus Terminal. William Zaranka. BXAP
In the Lake Country. Kay Wissinger. AMV-80
In the lamplight falling. Night. Peter Everwine. NNaP
In the land of dwarfs. Forugh Farrokhzad, *tr. fr. Persian by* Girdhard Tikku. BoWoP
In the land of God. Cecil County. Ron Welburn. PoBA
In the land of Tao-chou. The People of Tao-chou. Po Chü-i, *tr. by* Arthur Waley. ChTr
In the land of turkeys in turkey weather. Dance of the Macabre Mice. Wallace Stevens. CMoP; NePA; NOBA; OxBA; SeCeV
In the Land Where We Were Dreaming. Daniel B. Lucas. PAH
In the last bar on the way to your wild game. Nine Charms against the Hunter. David Wagoner. TW
In the last days. Apocalypse. Francis Ernest Kobina Parkes. PBA
In the Last Flicker of the Sinking Sun. Peretz Markish, *tr. fr. Yiddish by* Keith Bosley. VWA
In the last letter that I had from France. Easter Monday. Eleanor Farjeon. SUMH
In the last storm, when hawks. The Epitaph Ending in And. William Stafford. LCAP; NaP; NIP
In the last village before the frontier. The Republic 1939. James Liddy. CIP
In the late winter. The Bear. Galway Kinnell. TAP
In the Library. Elizabeth Brewster. OBCV
In the Library. Michael Patrick Hearn. NTCP
In the Library. Ed Ochester. Psk
In the licorice fields at Pontefract. The Licorice Fields at Pontefract. John Betjeman. CMoP; NMP
In the life we live [*or* lead] together every paradise is lost. Against Botticelli. Robert Hass. AmPA; NPGG
In the light beneath the leafage. A Shot in the Park. William Plomer. MP
In the light of the moon. Love Song. Hayim Be'er, *tr. by* Stephen Mitchell. VWA
In the light of the moon, by the side of the water. My Daughter Louise. Homer Greene. HBV-1
In the Lilac-Rain. Edith M. Thomas. HBV-2
In the lips' flare. Bridges and Tunnels. Beth Bentley. EyDe
In the Local Museum. Walter de la Mare. HAP
In the lonesome latter years. The Promissory Note. Bayard Taylor. BXAP; HBV-1; Par; SpRo
In the long journey out of the self. Journey to the Interior. Theodore Roethke. CABA; LCAP; NYBP; VGW
In the long, sleepless watches of the night. The Cross of Snow. Longfellow. AP; HeIP; NOBA; OxBA; TAP
In the long summer days when I was four. Shells. Medb Mahony. AMV-80
In the Longhouse, Oneida Museum. Roberta Hill Whiteman. STE
In the loud waking world I come and go. Nihil Humani Alienum. Titus Munson Coan. AA
In the low house, whose thick lights. Lady Day. Padraic Fallon. NeIP
In the lower lands of day. Before Sunset. Swinburne. VLP
In the Lybian desert I. Modo and Alciphron. Sylvia Townsend Warner. MoBrPo
In the Madison Zoo. Roberta Hill. CDW
In the Madness of Love. Gary Soto. NPGG
In the magnets of computers will. In Computers. Alan P. Lightman. SUW
In the mandrill. The Mandrill. Conrad Aiken. RHPC
In the manger of course were cows and the Child Himself. Pig. Anthony Hecht. OxBC
In the maple-sugar bush. March. Elizabeth J. Coatsworth. YeAr
In the Marble Quarry. James Dickey. AmFN; NoP
In the market, in the cloister—only God I saw. Illumination and Ecstasy. *Tr. fr. Arabic, at. to* Baba Kuhi of Shiraz. ILwL
In the Market-Place. John Francis O'Donnell. *Fr.* Limmerich Towne. NBM
In the marvelling quiet of morning. World Enough. Jeanine Hathaway. AMV-80
In the Matter of Two Men. James David Corrothers. BANP
In the merry month of June, when the roses were in bloom. Little Ball of Yarn. *Unknown.* FSW
In the merry month [*or* merrie moneth] of May. Phyllida and Corydon [*or* A Pastoral *or* The Ploughman's Song]. Nicholas Breton. *Fr.* The Honourable Entertainment Given to the Queen's Majesty in Progress at Elvetham, 1591. EIL; FaBoEn; HBV-1; NOBE; OAEP; OBEV; OBSC; SeCePo; TrGrPo; UnTE; ViBoPo
In the merry month of May. The Sound of the Drum. *Unknown.* OBET
In the merry month of May from my home I started. The Rocky Road to Dublin. *Unknown.* FaBoBa
In the Middle of August. Edward Hirsch. MAYP
In the middle of the harbour. Derek Walcott. *Fr.* A Sea-Chantey. TTY
In the middle of the night. In Childbed. Thomas Hardy. NAs

In the middle of the night he started up. Silver Wedding. Ralph Hodgson. HBMV; OxBTC; TrGrPo
In the middle of the night in the next room. The Cell of Himself. Arthur Freeman. TwCP
In the middle of the sea lies an island. Minotaur. Robert Fisher. AmMo
In the middle of this life's journey. An American Takes a Walk. Reed Whittemore. MoVE
In the midmost of ocean. The Sea. Lloyd Frankenberg. MOS
In the midst of my garden. The Palm Tree. Abd-ar-Rahman I, *tr. by* J. B. Trend. AWP
In the midst of words your wordless image. The Heart. Harvey Shapiro. HoPM
In the Mines. John Swett. BPAW
In the Mirror. Elizabeth Fleming. OnUR
In the monethe of Maye when mirthes been fele. The Poacher. *Unknown. Fr.* The Parlement of the Thre Ages. OxBM
In the month of Beaver. Ts'eekkaayah. Mary TallMountain. STE; TWSS
In the Month of Green Fire. Sophie Himmell. GoYe
In the month of the long decline of roses. Hendecasyllabics. Swinburne. FaBoRV; SyP; VLP
In the Moonlight. Thomas Hardy. NoAM
In the Moonlight. Norreys Jephson O'Conor. HBMV; SoPo; SUS
In the moonlight. Anecdote of the Prince of Peacocks. Wallace Stevens. SOTW
"In the moonlight evening." By Moonlight. *Unknown, tr. by* Louis Untermeyer. UnTE
In the moonlit room your face. Clair de Lune. Arthur Symons. SyP
In the Morgue. Israel Zangwill. TrJP
In the Morning. Jayne Cortez. BlSi
In the Morning. Paul Laurence Dunbar. BPo
In the Morning All Over. William Stafford. FAZ
In the morning I went out with my bow. Ambulance Call. Lorrie Goldensohn. AMV-81
In the Morning I Will Pray, *with music.* William Henry Furness. AH
In the morning in the blue snow. Annual Gaiety. Wallace Stevens. MoAB; MoAmPo
In the morning, in the dark. The Night Hunt. Thomas MacDonagh. GDP; OxBI; RoGo
In the Morning, in the Morning. A. E. Housman. InPK
In the morning light a line. The Morning Light. Louis Simpson. NNaP; NoAM
In the morning rain. Rainy Morning. Sotero Rivera-Avilés, *tr. by* Julio Marzán. InW
In the morning the city. City [San Francisco]. Langston Hughes. AmFN; FaPON; PDV; RHPC
In the morning the hawk and the sun flew up together. Night and the Child. Judith Wright. SeCePo
In the morning the shadow of the old city falls. Shadow of the Old City. Yehuda Amichai, *tr. by* Shirley Kaufman. VWA
In the morning there is bacon. Camping at Thunder Bay. David Fedo. AMV-81
In the morning, very early. Barefoot Days. Rachel Field. FaPON; YeAr
In the Motel. X. J. Kennedy. RHPC; Str
In the Mountain Tent. James Dickey. CAPP
In the mountain where you are unworshiped. Inanna and Ebih. Enheduanna, *tr. fr. Sumerian.* BoWoP
In the Mountains. Edgar Jackson. Three Songs, I. LFAC
In the Mountains, *sel.* Robert Penn Warren.
Skiers. LiSp
In the mountains. First Cold Night of Autumn. John Stupp. AMV-81
In the mountains. The Guests. Louis Zukofsky. CoPo
In the mountains o' the west. The Maid o' the West. John Clare. OAEL-2
In the Mountains on a Summer Day. Li Po, *tr. fr. Chinese by* Arthur Waley. AWP
In the mountains, there is more than slate. Blue Ridge. Elizabeth Hodges. AMV-81
In the Mourning Time. Robert Hayden. BPo
In the mud of the Cambrian main. A Ballade of Evolution. Grant Allen. EBVV
In the Museum. Isabella Gardner. ELU; NYBP
In the Museum Art School at night the men. Life Study. Stephen Orlen. MAYP
In the museum of antiquities. Glory. Harvey Shapiro. POL
In the mustardseed sun. Poem on His Birthday. Dylan Thomas. NAs; SeCeV
In the Naked Bed, in Plato's Cave. Delmore Schwartz. LiTA; LiTM; MiAP; MoAB; MoAmPo; MoVE; NoAM; NOBA; NePA; PoA; TwAmPo; VGW
In the name of Allah, the Merciful the Compassionate! Love Charm. *Malay Oral Tradition, tr. by* R. O. Winstedt. WTO
In the name of God, the merciful, the compassionate! Of Iron Am I. *Malay Oral Tradition, tr. by* W. W. Skeat. WTO
In the Name of Jesus Christ. Claudia Cranston. HBMV
In the Name of Our Sons. Dorothy Gould. PGD
In the name of the Eternal. Inscriptions at the City of Brass. *Unknown, tr. by* E. Powys Mathers. *Fr.* The Thousand and One Nights. AWP
In the National Gallery. Siegfried Sassoon. NoAM
In the Nativity of Our Lord. Richard Crashaw. *See* In the Holy Nativity of Our Lord God.
In the nativity of time. Love in the First Age: To Chloris. Sir John Denham. AnAnS-2
In the nativity of time. Love Made in the First Age: To Chloris. Richard Lovelace. CaPo; CavP; JCP; OAEL-1; SeCP
In the negro gardens negro birds. To Eliza, Duchess of Dorset. Joseph Bennett. LiTA; NePA
In the new city of marble and bright stone. The Unknown Soldier. Conrad Aiken. *Fr.* The Soldier. WaaP; WaP
In the New Sun. Philip Levine. NNaP
In the Night. Elizabeth Jennings. MP; NePoEA; NYBP
In the Night. Elizabeth Madox Roberts. WSC
In the Night. James Stephens. OBMV
In the Night. *Unknown.* NA
("Night was growing old, The.") FaBoNo
In the night/ Gray, heavy clouds muffled the valleys. The Peaks. Stephen Crane. War Is Kind, XVIII. AA; HBV-1; WGRP
In the Night Fields. W. S. Merwin. AP; PoCh
In the night I get up and walk. Skylights. Tess Gallagher. MAYP
In the night in the train pulling out of the city. Among Commuters. Jon Swan. NYP
In the night my great swamp-willow fell. Who Guessed Amiss the Riddle of the Sphinx. James Merrill. TwAmPo
In the Night of the Full Moon. Carl Busse, *tr. fr. German by* Jethro Bithell. AWP
In the night the agile mole. The Unfortunate Mole. Mary Kennedy. GoYe
In the night the man could hear the wind walking. Harvest. Gene Shuford. GoYe
In the night there was a murder in the street. Of Autumn. Veronica Porumbacu, *tr. by* Willis Barnstone *and* Matei Calinescu. BoWoP; VWA
In the Night Watches. Sir Charles G. D. Roberts. PeCV
In the nightmare of the dark. W. H. Auden. *Fr.* In Memory of W. B. Yeats. TRV
In the nook of a wood—where a pool freshed with dew. The Stranger. Walter de la Mare. OAEP
In the north the cloud flower blossoms. The Cloud-Flower Lullaby. *Tr. fr. Tewa Indian by* H. J. Spinden. WTO
In the northern hemisphere. Kangaroo. D. H. Lawrence. EBEV; InPS; MoVE; OxBTC
In the novels I shall never write. The Right to Life. John N. Morris. AMV-80
In the numb time when foam froze. All That Is, and Can Delight. Robert Farren. OxBI
In the ocean there's a very sad turtle. Jack Kerouac. *Fr.* Mexico City Blues. PoM
In the old back streets o' Pimlico. The Rambling Sailor. Charlotte Mew. HBMV; PoRA
In the Old Churchyard at Fredericksburg. Frederick Wadsworth Loring. AA
In the Old City. Yehuda Amichai, *tr. fr. Hebrew by* Laya Firestone *and* Howard Schwartz. VWA
In the Old City. Jacob Fichman, *tr. fr. Hebrew by* Sholom J. Kahn. TrJP
In the old colony days, in Plymouth the land of the Pilgrims. The Courtship of Miles Standish. Longfellow. BeLS; TreFS
In the old days (a custom laid aside). Abraham Davenport. Whittier. AmPP; NoP
In the old days the white gates swung. Pastoral. Clifford Dyment. MoVE
In the old days when we were kids. Roger and Me. Anne Le Dressay. AMV-81
In the old days with married women's stockings. The Libertine. Louis MacNeice. DTC; NoAM
In the Old Guerilla War. Linda Pastan. TW
In the Old House. Joan Aiken. WSC
In the Old House. Donald Hall. NePoEA-2
In the Old Jewish Cemetery, Prague, 1970. Edward Lowbury. VWA
In the old, lonely park all white with frost. Sentimental Colloquy. Paul Verlaine, *tr. by* Alan Conder. LO
In the old, old days when the West was young. The Texas Ranger. Margie B. Boswell. BPAW
In the old part of the cemetery. Circa 1814. David Staudt. AMV-80
In the old photograph, my sister and I. Quills. Charlotte Gafford. AMV-81

In the old photograph the two of us. Marginal Music. R. K. Meiners. AMV-81
In the "Old South." Whittier. AA
In the olive darkness of the sally-trees. The Bull. Judith Wright. GrPl; PoAu-2
In the one cool room of the house. Developing a Wife. Andrew Taylor. CBAP
In the one state of ours that is a shire. To the Right Person. Robert Frost. GLGT
In the one-two domestic goose one-two one-two step. Henry Beissel. *Fr.* New Wings for Icarus. MoCV
In the only free. In the Ladies' Room at the Bus Terminal. William Zaranka. BXAP
In the open-faced river. Giving Up on the Shore. Gabriel Preil, *tr. by* Gabriel Levin. VWA
In the Open Fields. Hugo Sonnenschein, *tr. fr. German by* Edouard Roditi. VWA
In the Operating Room. Alden Nowlan. NOBC
In the Orchard. Robert Friend. GP
In the Orchard. Ibsen, *tr. fr. Norwegian by* Sir Edmund Gosse. AWP
In the Orchard. James Stephens. RoGo; SO; WSC
In the Orchard. Muriel Stuart. ErPo; FF; OxBTC
In the Orchard. Swinburne, *after the Provençal.* BoLoP; UnTE
In the orchestra the fixed stars. Round Dance, and Canticle. Robert Kelly. CoPo
In the Oregon Country. William Stafford. AmFN
In the other gardens. Autumn Fires. Robert Louis Stevenson. SUS; TiPo; YeAr
In the Outhouse. Mitsuye Yamada. *Fr.* Camp Notes. WPOW
In the outlying districts where we know something. Everyman's Library. John Ashbery. NoP
In the painkilling cold that wrapped. Snow. David Wevill. MoCV
In the painting. Up against the Wall. D. C. Berry. BXAP
In the pale mauve twilight, streaked with orange. Evensong. Conrad Aiken. HBMV
In the palm. A Guerrilla Handbook. Amiri Baraka. PoBA
In the Palms of Ancient Bodhisattvas. John Tagliabue. AMV-81
In the Pantry. "Hugh MacDiarmid." NoAM
In the Paralelo a one-legged. Entered in the Minutes. Louis MacNeice. LiTB
In the Park. Gwen Harwood. CBAP
In the Park. Helen Hoyt. HBMV
In the park I saw a stranger. Interrupted Romance. *Unknown, tr. by* Louis Untermeyer. UnTE
In the parlour of the shanty where the lives have all gone wrong. Will Yer Write It Down for Me? Henry Lawson. CBAP
In the Past. Trumbull Stickney. NOBA; OxBA
In the Pauper's Turnip-Field. Herman Melville. PoEL-5
In the pause. Wallflower to a Moonbeam. Louis Untermeyer. BXAP
In the peninsula all is velvet and rich. The Eyes of Cantonese Schoolmasters Remembered in Hong Kong. Willis Barnstone. GLGT
In the Person of Woman Kind. Ben Jonson. NIP; SeCP; SeCV-1
In the photograph he stands alone. Chinese Camp, Kamloops (circa 1883). Andrew Suknaski. NOBC
In the picture the people stroll and stroll all day. Public Holiday: Paris. Joyce Horner. GoYe
In the pinch of time, facing. Victorian Grandmother. Margo Lockwood. Psk
In the Pines. *Unknown.* AmFP
In the Pines (Where Did You Sleep Last Night?). Leadbelly (Huddie Ledbetter). FSW
"In the Pink." Siegfried Sassoon. CMoP
In the place where. Judy Grahn. *Fr.* Edward the Dyke and Other Poems. PeHV
In the place where the fight was. Where the Fight Was. Alice Corbin, *after the Chippewa Indian.* BPAW
In the Planetarium. Siv Cedering Fox. LTB
In the Plaza We Walk. Nephtalí De León. FIA
In the pleasant pastime of temple viewing. Manners. Edith Marcombe Shiffert. WPE
In the Pocket. James Dickey. LiSp
In the poet's vigorous fifties. Confidential. Winfield Townley Scott. ELU
In the pond in the park. Water Picture. May Swenson. BoNaP
In the pond of our new garden. Visiting Hour. Stewart Conn. BSV
In the Poppy Field. James Stephens. PoRA
In the portraits he sits cross-legged on a mat. The Last Frontier. John Thomas. GP
In the prison cell I sit. Tramp! Tramp! Tramp! or, The Prisoner's Hope. George Frederick Root. FSW; PSoN; TreFS
In the Prison Pen. Herman Melville. PoEL-5; TAP
In the Proscenium. Gene Derwood. LiTA
(War's Clown in the Proscenium.) NePA
In the Public Garden. Marianne Moore. NOBA
In the Public Gardens. John Betjeman. NYBP
In the pure soul, although it sing or pray. Eternal Christmas. Elizabeth Stuart Phelps. PGD; TRV
In the purple light, heavy with redwood, the slopes drop seaward. Apology for Bad Dreams. Robinson Jeffers. AmPP; AP; CoBMV; LiTA; MoAB; MoAmPo; NOBA; OxBA; SeCeV; TwAmPo
In the pushcart market, on Sunday. Galway Kinnell. *Fr.* The Avenue Bearing the Initial of Christ into the New World. NaP; NMP
In the quarter of the Negroes. Cultural Exchange. Langston Hughes. BPo; PoBA
In the Queen's Room. Norman Cameron. Three Love Poems, II. GTBS-P; OxBTC
In the quiet before cockcrow when the cricket's. Dear Men and Women. John Hall Wheelock. NYBP; Prf
In the rain that has passed by. Lost City. Ingrid Jonker, *tr. by* Jack Cope *and* Ruth Miller. PeSA
In the rain, the naked old father is dancing, he will get wet. Natural History. Robert Penn Warren. FF
In the rain's push and the wind's hand. From My Thought. Daniel Smythe. GoYe
In the rat race he won by a whisker. Lifelines. Gavin Ewart. EAS
In the Ravine. W. W. E. Ross. PeCV
In the reading room in the New York Public Library. Reading Room, The New York Public Library. Richard Eberhart. GP; NYP
In the red water. New Spring. Juan Ramón Jiménez, *tr. by* H. R. Hays. OLR
In the Redwood Forest. Ralph Pomeroy. CoPo
In the region where the roses always bloom. Ida, Sweet as Apple Cider. Eddie Leonard. BLSo; FSN; TreFT
In the Restaurant. Thomas Hardy. *Fr.* Satires of Circumstance. MoAB; MoBrPo
In the ribs of an ugly school building. Three Brown Girls Singing. M. Carl Holman. NIP
In the Ringwood. Thomas Kinsella. CMoP; NMP; OxBI
In the riprap. Mussels. Mary Oliver. NU
In the Room. James Thompson. OBVV
In the Round. Theodore Weiss. NMP
In the Royal City spring is almost over. The Flower Market. Po Chü-i, *tr. by* Arthur Waley. PPON
In the Rude Age. Earl of Surrey. NCEP
(Another Tribute to Wyatt.) SiPS
("In the rude age when scyence was not so rife.") AAS
In the Rue Monsieur le Prince. Song for "Buvez les Vins du Postillion"—Advt. Jean Garrigue. TAP
In the Rut. Hamish Brown. PoSH
In the sad cafes that are our lives. Cafes. Robert B. Smith. LFAC
In the sad Southwest, in the mystical Sunland. Homes of the Cliff Dwellers. Stanley Wood. PoOW
In the sad spirit. To the Unknown Light. Edward Shanks. TrPWD
In the salt terror of the stormy sea. The City of the Soul. Lord Alfred Douglas. HBMV
In the sand I grew, by the rocky sea-wall. The Husband's Message. *Unknown, tr. by* Charles W. Kennedy. AnOE
In the Santa Clara Valley, far away and far away. On the Great Plateau. Edith Wyatt. HBMV
In the scented bud of the morning—O. The Daisies. James Stephens. AnIV; AWP
In the sea, Biscayne, there prinks. Homunculus et la Belle Étoile. Wallace Stevens. MoAB; MoAmPo
In the Sea of Tears. Naomi Replansky. BrRo; GP
In the sea-port of Saint Malo 'twas a smiling morn in May. Jacques Cartier. Thomas D'Arcy McGee. CaP
In the Season of Wolves and Names. Mariève Rugo. AMV-80
In the Secret House. Christopher Middleton. FaBoMo
In the Selkirks. Duncan Campbell Scott. CaP
In the Seminole darkness of your singing eyes. Poem to a Redskin. Wendy Rose. CDW
In the Seraglio. David R. Slavitt. ErPo; PeHV
In the Servants' Quarters. Thomas Hardy. MoAB; MoBrPo
In the Seven Woods. W. B. Yeats. CMoP; LoBV; NoAM
In the shabby cafeteria on the lower east side. Circumstance. Laurie Stroblas. AMV-80
In the shabby train no seat is vacant. The Refugees. Randall Jarrell. MoAB; MoAmPo
In the Shade of the Old Apple Tree. Harry H. Williams. FSN, *with music*; TreFT
In the shadow of Old South Church the turn of spring is. A Foreigner Comes to Earth on Boston Common. Horace Gregory. EaLo
In the Shadow of the Valley of Death. Abu al-Qasim al-Shabbi, *tr. fr. Arabic by* Mounah A. Khouri. DL

In the Shadows, *sel.* David Gray.
Sonnet I: "If it must be; if it must be, O God!" BSV; OxBS
In the Shadowy Whatnot Corner. Robert Silliman Hillyer. NePoAm
In the shaking of a sieve the refuse remaineth. The Test of Men. Bible, Apocrypha. Ecclesiasticus, XXVI: 5-8. TrJP
In the shape of this night, in the still fall of snow, Father. At the New Year. Kenneth Patchen. LiTM
In the sheltered garden, pale beneath the moon. Pierrot Goes to War. Gabrielle Elliot. SUMH
In the Shire of Phestos hard by Cnossus dwelt of yore. Ovid, *tr. by* Arthur Golding. *Fr.* Metamorphoses, IX. PeHV
In the shoppes. Gemwood. Marvin Bell. FiCP; LCAP
In the shower not ten minutes ago and blind from the vinegar rinse. Under the Umbrella of Blood. William Pitt Root. GeTw
In the Shreve High football stadium. Autumn Begins in Martins Ferry, Ohio. James Wright. CAPP; InPS; NaP; POL
In the shut drawer, even now, they rave and grieve. Packet of Letters. Louise Bogan. GrPl; PCP
In the Silence. Stephany Fuller. BPo
In the silence that falls on my spirit. My Father's Voice in Prayer. May Hastings Nottage. BLRP
In the silence that prolongs the span. Black Jackets. Thom Gunn. HeIP; MP; TwCP
In the Silent Midnight Watches. Arthur Cleveland Coxe. AH, *with music* (He Standeth at the Door.) HBV-2
In the Silent Night. Isaac Leibush Peretz, *tr. fr. Yiddish by* Joseph Leftwich. TrJP
In the silent ridges of a late. On the Edge of a Safe Sleep. Teresa D. Cader. AMV-81
In the Silks. Diane Ackerman. MAYP
In the Sitting Room of the Opera. Criss E. Cannady. PoDr
In the six-acre field. Lost. Millen Brand. NYBP
In the sixth grade they gave us a belgian nun. Pedagogy. Gerald Locklin. GP
In the sky. How Strange It Is. Claudia Lewis. RHPC
In the sky, clearest blue. Rosalía de Castro, *tr. fr. Galician by* Benjamin M. Woodbridge, Jr. PBWP
In the sky the bright stars glittered. When I Saw Sweet Nelly Home [*or* Seeing Nellie Home]. Francis Kyle. FSW; PSoN
In the sky there is a moon and stars. Proportion. Amy Lowell. BoWoP
In the sleepy forest where the bluebells. The Awakening of Dermuid. Austin Clarke. *Fr.* The Vengeance of Finn. AnIV
In the slow lapse of unrecorded afternoon. No Answer. Laurence Whistler. MoVE
In the small beauty of the forest. Psalm. George Oppen. NNaP
In the Small Boats of Their Hands. Pamela Kircher. AMV-80
In the small New England places. Graveyard. Robert P. Tristram Coffin. AmFN
In the smoke-blue cabaret. Ecclesiastes. Morris Bishop. HBMV
In the Smoking-Car. Richard Wilbur. ConAP; LiTM; MoAmPo
In the Snack-Bar. Edwin Morgan. FF
In the Snake Park. William Plomer. NoAM; NYBP; OxBTC
In the Snowfall. Gwerfyl Mechain, *tr. fr. Welsh by* Willis Barnstone. BoWoP
In the soft dark night. Fireflies. Aileen Fisher. SoPo
In the soft Finnish summer they become. Ode to the Finnish Dead. Chad Walsh. HoAn
In the sorrow and the terror of the nations. The Mother. Nettie Palmer. PoAu-1
In the Soul Hour. Robert Mezey. AmPA; NaP
In the South be drooping trees. Chou and the South. *Unknown, at. to* Confucius, *tr. by* Ezra Pound. *Fr.* Shi King. CTC
In the south, sleeping against. Legacy. Amiri Baraka. NoAM; NOBA; PoBA
In the southern land many birds sing. The South. Wang Chien, *tr. by* Arthur Waley. AWP
In the southern village the boy who minds the ox. The Herd Boy. Lu Yu, *tr. by* Arthur Waley. ChTr
In the space of time. Ashkelon. Anthony Rudolf. VWA
In the Sprightly Month of May. Sir John Vanbrugh. *Fr.* Aesop. UnTE
In the Spring. William Barnes. GBL
In the Spring. Meleager, *tr. fr. Greek by* Andrew Lang. AWP
In the Spring ("In the spring a fuller crimson comes upon the robin's breast"). Tennyson. *Fr.* Locksley Hall. BoNaP
In the spring, by the big shuck-pile. Burning the Cat. W. S. Merwin. NIP
In the spring twilight, in the colour'd twilight. An Even-Song. Sydney Dobell. OBVV
In the spring woods, how good it is to see. Aspects of the World like Coral Reefs. William Bronk. VGW
In the square of a lighted window. Observation of a Bee. Leah Goldberg, *tr. by* Stephen Mitchell. WPOW
In the squdgy river. The Hippopotamus. Georgia Roberts Durston. TiPo
In the stagnant pride of an outworn race. Santiago. Thomas A. Janvier. PAH
In the state of old Kentucky. The Death of Samuel Adams. *Unknown.* AmFP
In the States. Robert Louis Stevenson. BrPo
In the steadying breadth of day. Poem for My Dead Husband. Sheila Roberts. AMV-80
In the steel room. Birth. George Ella Lyon. Str
In the still air the music lies unheard. The Master's Touch. Horatius Bonar. HBV-2; TrPWD
In the still of an island evening. Island Moment. Ian Hamilton Finlay. NMP
In the still room, a scholar frowns in thought. The Company of Scholars. Helen Bevington. GLGT
In the Still, Star-lit Night. Elizabeth Stoddard. AA
In the stillness. Expectant Mother. Penelope Shuttle. BrRo
In the stony night move the stars' white mouths. Alex Comfort. *Fr.* The Postures of Love. NeBP
In the strange city of life. Nostalgia. Walter de la Mare. CoBMV; LiTM
In the strange house. The Messenger. Jean Valentine. LCAP
In the Stravinsky book by Lillian Libman. Reading in the Night. Roy Fuller. OxBC
In the Street. Shaw Neilson. CBAP
In the street two children sharpen. East Bronx. David Ignatow. ConAP
In the streetcar conductor's uniform. Portrait: The Freedom Fighter. George Jonas. NeAC; NOBC
In the Streets of Catania. Roger Casement. AnIV
In the streets the crowds go about their business. Epithalamium. Daniel Halpern. MAYP
In the stump of the old tree, where the heart has rotted out. Poem. Hugh Sykes Davies. EAS
In the Suburbs. Louis Simpson. ELU; MAT
"In the Subway." Juan Ramón Jiménéz, *tr. fr. Spanish by* Robert Bly. NYP
In the summer even. Ballad. Harriet Prescott Spofford. HBV-1
In the summer heat and fever crackling. The Boy; or, Son of Rip-off. Malcolm Glass. BXAP
In the summer I live so. Winter Saint. A. R. Ammons. TW
In the Summer of Sixty. *Unknown.* CoSo; PoOW
In the summer of the first year of Chia-yu (A.D. 1056). The Cicada. Ou-yang Hsiu, *tr. by* Arthur Waley. AWP
In the sunny orchard closes. In the Orchard. Ibsen, *tr. by* Sir Edmund Gosse. AWP
In the Surgery. J. M. Ditta. AMV-80
In the surround of snow-touched mountains. A Circle Begins. Harold Littlebird. STE
In the swamp in secluded recesses. Walt Whitman. *Fr.* When Lilacs Last in the Dooryard Bloom'd. RFM
In the Sweet Bye-and-Bye [*or* In the Sweet By and By]. Sanford Fillmore Bennett. FSW; TreFT
(Sweet By and By.) PSoN
(There's a Land That Is Fairer than Day, *with music.*) AH
In the sweet shire of Cardigan. Simon Lee [the Old Huntsman]. Wordsworth. EnRP; GTBS; GTBS-P
In the Tail of the Scorpion. Genevieve Taggard. VGW
In the tall quiet pines of Washington. For Tom Numkena, Hopi/Spokane. Harold Littlebird. VoR
In the Tank. Thom Gunn. NoAM
In the Taxidermist's Shop. Siv Cedering. AMV-81
In the third-class seat sat the journeying boy. Midnight on the Great Western. Thomas Hardy. CH; CoBMV; NOBE
In the third day of May. The Boy and the Mantle. *Unknown.* ESPB; OxBB
In the third month, a sudden flow of blood. The Vow. Anthony Hecht. ConAP; NePoEA; PoCh; Prf
In the Third Year of War. Henry Treece. WaP
In the thirtieth year of life. J. V. Cunningham. POL
In the tides of the warm south wind it lay. Verazzano. Hezekiah. Butterworth. PAH
In the time of old sin without sadness. Variations on [*or* of] an Air: After [Algernon Charles] Swinburne. G. K. Chesterton. FaBoPa; NOBL; Par
In the Time of Revolution, *sels.* Julius Lester. PoBA
"It cannot be/ reasoned with," V.
"One needs a lyric poet in these," IV.
"One needs a lyric poet in this, " VI.
In the Time of the Rose. John Savant. AMV-81
In the Time of Trouble. Leslie Savage Clark. TrPWD
In the time of wild roses. Bab-Lock-Hythe. Laurence Binyon. MoVE
In the time when herbs and flowers. Caelica and Philocell. Fulke Greville. *Fr.* Caelica. OBSC
In the time when swan and swan. Waratah. Roland Robinson. PoAu-2
In the Town. *Unknown, tr. fr. French by* Eleanor Farjeon. OBCP; PChr

In the town by the sea I walked. Dragging the Main. David Ray. TAT
In the town of Athy one Jeremy Lanigan. Lanigan's Ball. *Unknown.* OxBoLi
In the town of Odessa. Dvonya. Louis Simpson. NNaP; NOBA
In the town of Springhill, Nova Scotia. Ballad of Springhill (The Springhill Mine Disaster). Ewan MacColl *and* Peggy Seeger. FSW
In the town where I was born. Yellow Submarine. John Lennon *and* Paul McCartney. PPoe
In the Trades. C. Fox Smith. EtS
In the Train. Arthur Symons. *See* City Nights: In the Train.
In the Train. James Thomson ("B. V."). *Fr.* Sunday at Hampstead. OBEV
("As we rush, as we rush in the train.") ViBoPo
In the Tree House at Night. James Dickey. NoP
In the Tree-Top. Lucy Larcom. OBCA
In the Trench. Leon Gellert. PoAu-1
In the Trenches. Richard Aldington. MMA
In the Tub We Soak Our Skin. Edward Newman Horn. ELU
In the tunnel/ Light is haloed. The Dark Scent of Prayer. Rose Drachler. VWA
In the tunnel of woods, as the road. Last Things. William Meredith. NoAM
In the Turkish Ward. Peter Balakian. MAYP
In the turret's great glass dome, the apparition, death. Siegfried. Randall Jarrell. MiAP
In the twentieth century. Machine Out of the God. Thomas E. Sanders. AMV-81
In the Twentieth Century of My Trespass on Earth. Galway Kinnell. *Fr.* The Dead Shall Be Raised Incorruptible. GP; TW
In the Twilight. James Russell Lowell. AA; HBV-1
In the 2 A.M. Club, a working man's bar. Robert Peterson. NeAC
In the unbelievable days. After Her Death. Anne Stevenson. HoAn
In the unnavigable dusk, when. Owl. Peter Kane Dufault. NYBP
In the vacant lot behind the hospital. Night Blooming Flowers. Katha Pollitt. MAYP
In the vacant lots. Song of Degrees. Paul Auster. VWA
In the vale [*or* vaile] of restless mind [*or* mynd]. Quia Amore Langueo. *Unknown.* NOBE, *tr. by* Helen Gardner; NOCV, *tr. by* Helen Gardner; OxBM; OxBoCh; PoEL-1
In the Valley of Cauteretz. Tennyson. BoLoP; NOBE; OBVV; VLP
In the Valley of the Elwy. Gerard Manley Hopkins. NOCV; ViBoPo
In the valley of the Pegnitz, where across broad meadowlands. Nuremberg. Longfellow. AmPP; HBV-2
In the Van Gogh Room. Traise Yamamoto. BrSi
In the Vaulted Way. Thomas Hardy. BoLoP; OLR
(In the Crypted Way.) VLP
In the vegetarian guest-house. The Flying Bum: 1944. William Plomer. DTC
In the very earliest time. Magic Words. *Unknown, tr. fr. Eskimo.* NU
In the very early morning when the light was low. The Interpreter. Orrick Johns. HBMV
In the vestibule behind the church I saw the parson. Parson's Pleasure. Barry O. Higgs. PeSA
In the Vices. Donald Evans. HBMV
In the village churchyard she lies. In the Churchyard at Cambridge. Longfellow. AmPP; AP; PoEL-5; TAP
In the village it must be a clear night with the light of a red. The Everlastings. Norman Dubie. GeTw
In the village of the dead. First Shaman Song. Gary Snyder. Myths and Texts: Hunting, I. CoPo; NOBA
In the village squares. The Unemployed. LeVan Roberts. PGD
In the village the children. Then. Gary Gildner. FiCP
In the violet country. Dont Tell Bad Dreams Says Tita's Mother. John Oliver Simon. NeAC
In the Virginia lowlands I was born. Lowlands, *vers.* II. *Unknown.* ShS
In the visions of sailors. Between Rivers and Seas. Lance Henson. VoR
In the Waiting Room. Elizabeth Bishop. HeIP; LCAP; NOBA; Prf
In the wake of the yellow sunset one pale star. The Wykhamist. Nora Griffiths. SUMH
In the waking night. The Cage. David Gascoyne. EAS
In the warm rods of your ears. Elegy for 41 Whales Beached in Florence, Ore., June, 1979. Linda Bierds. AMV-81
In the water cave, below the root. Howard Nemerov. *Fr.* The Scales of the Eyes. NoAM
In the wax works of Nature they strike. Note. Anthony Euwer. *Fr.* The Limeratomy. HBMV
In the Web. E. L. Mayo. MiAP
In the Week When Christmas Comes. Eleanor Farjeon. PChr; SiSoSe
In the West/ circles a wheel. Wandering Chorus. B. Alquit, *tr. by* Howard Schwartz. VWA
In the wet dusk silver-sweet. A Memory of Earth. "Æ." OBVV
In the white-flowered hawthorn brake. Song from "Ogier the Dane." William Morris. *Fr.* The Earthly Paradise. OAEP; ViBoPo
In the White Giant's Thigh. Dylan Thomas. LiTB
In the white moonlight, where the willow waves. The Graveyard Rabbit. Frank Lebby Stanton. AA
In the white of noon-day's brightness the city seems blotted out. In the Old City. Jacob Fichman, *tr. by* Sholom J. Kahn. TrJP
In the wicked afternoon. Abracadabra. Dorothy Livesay. WHW
In the Wide Awe and Wisdom of the Night. Sir Charles G. D. Roberts. CaP
In the wild autumn weather, when the rain was on the sea. Love and Death. Rosa Mulholland. HBV-1
In the wild October night-time, when the wind raved round the land. The Night of Trafalgar [*or* Trafalgar]. Thomas Hardy. *Fr.* The Dynasts, Pt. I, Act V, *sc.* vii. CH; ChTr; FaBoCh; MoBrPo; MOS; OBMV
In the Wilderness. Robert Graves. CH; EaLo; MoAB; MoBrPo; OxBI; SeCePo
In the Wilderness. Edith Lovejoy Pierce. TrPWD
In the windmill of evening. The Windmill of Evening. Shlomo Reich, *tr. by* Mira Reich. VWA
In the window of a grange. Love and Honour. Fulke Greville. *Fr.* Caelica. OBSC
In the Wind's Eye. R. P. Blackmur. Scarabs for the Living, II. CrMA
In the winter, in the winter. The Organ Grinders' Garden. Mildred Plew Meigs. SoPo
In the Winter of My Thirty-eighth Year. W. S. Merwin. NOBA
In the winter the rabbits match their pelts to the earth. White Season. Frances M. Frost. FaPON; TiPo
In the wintertime. Toe'osh; a Laguna Coyote Story. Leslie Silko. CDW; STE; VoR
In the winter time we go. White Fields. James Stephens. BoNaP; FaPON; MoShBr; PoSC; SiSoSe; SoPo; SUS
In the winter when the wet lanes hissed and sucked. Microcosmos, XXXIII. Nigel Heseltine. NeBP
In the wood that dissolves in spark and flame. Fire. Jose Emilio Pacheco, *tr. by* Frederick Luciani. AMV-81
In the Woods. Frederick George Scott. CaP
In the woods I came on an old friend fishing. Finding a Teacher. W. S. Merwin. GLGT; NNaP
In the woods my master went. Ballad of Trees and the Master. Sidney Lanier. TreFT
In the woods the fox is no more timorous. Autumnal. Horatio Colony. TwAmPo
In the woodyard were green and dry. The Rick of Green Wood. Edward Dorn. NeAP; PoM
In the Workhouse: Christmas Day. George R. Sims. *See* Christmas Day in the Workhouse.
In the world are millions and millions of men, and each man. Angel and Stone. Howard Nemerov. NYBP
In the world which He has created. Hymmnn. Allen Ginsberg. NOBA
In the world's mighty gall'ry of pictures. A Picture from Life's Other Side. *Unknown.* FSW
In the worst inn's worst room, with mat half-hung. The Duke of Buckingham [*or* The Death of Buckingham]. Pope. *Fr.* Moral Essays, Epistle III. FiP; NOBE; OBEC
In the Wrack[e]s [*or* Wrecks] of Walsingham. *Unknown.* *See* Lament for the Priory of Walsingham, A.
In the wrath of the lips that assail us. Stigmata. Charles Warren Stoddard. TrPWD
In the yard choking. Without Names. Jeff Tagami. BrSi
In the Year 1945 an Original Child Was Born. Thomas Merton. *Fr.* Original Child Bomb. NAs
In the year 1910—and I give the date without uncertainty. Versos de Montalgo. *Unknown, pr. tr. by* Frank J. Dobie. AS
In the year ninety-eight, when our troubles were great. The Cow Ate the Piper. *Unknown.* GBP
In the Year of Many Conversions and the Private Soul. John Ciardi. MiAP
In the year of one thousand seven hundred and ninety eight. Dunlavin Green. *Unknown.* FaBoBa
In the Year of Two Thousand. Menke Katz. AMV-81
In the year since Jesus died for men. The Siege of Corinth. Byron. GoTL
In the years about twenty. An Irish Love-Song. Robert Underwood Johnson. HBV-1
In the years of her age the most beautiful. Petrarch, *tr. by* J. M. Synge. *Fr.* Sonnets to Laura: To Laura in Death. OBMV
In the Yellow Light of Brooklyn. Al Lee. NYP
In the youth of summer. The Hills of Cualann. Joseph Campbell. AnIV
In the Yucca Land. Madge Morris. BPAW
In the Yukon. Ralph Gustafson. MoCV
In the zero of the night, in the lipping hour. The Approach to Thebes. Stanley Kunitz. PoA
In the zócalo. Three Portraits. George Hitchcock. VGW
In thee, thou valiant man of Persia. The Overreacher. Christopher Marlowe. *Fr.* Tamburlaine the Great, Pt. I, Act I. NIP

In their congealed light. Through Binoculars. Charles Tomlinson. OAEL-2
In their long/ Arabesque, wings ferrying the steady. Gulls. Barbara Howes. BoAnP
In their own way, by their own lights. Meditations for a Savage Child. Adrienne Rich. LCAP
In their ragged regimentals. Carmen Bellicosum. Guy Humphreys McMaster. AA; GN; HBV-2; PAH; PAL
In their religion they are so unev'n. Daniel Defoe. *Fr.* The True-born Englishman, Pt. II. OBSV
In their small, queer houses. Ant-Hills. "Marian Douglas." OBCA
In them days/ they won't hardly no way to know if. First Carolina Said-Song. A. R. Ammons. OBAL
In these ambiguous photos, their faces gaze. A Nisei Picnic. David Mura. BrSi
In these cold evenings, when the rain. Fear of the Earth. Alex Comfort. MoBrPo; NeBP
In these days of indigestion. Some Little Bug. Roy Atwell. PoLF; ShM
In these deep solitudes and awful cells. Eloïsa to Abelard. Pope. LoBV; OAEP; PoEL-3; TEP
In These Dissenting Times. Alice Walker. PoBA
In these drear wastes of sea-born land, these wilds where none may dwell but He. Sir Richard Francis Burton. *Fr.* The Kasidah, II. HBV-2
In these firm ranks a load slips from his soul. The Young Recruit. Arthur Davison Ficke. ELU
In these miraculous Catalan streets, yellow. Survivors. Elaine Feinstein. VWA
In these ohias light depends. Above the Falls at Waimea. Don Johnson. MAYP
In these, our first. Theresa. John Pass. AMV-81
In these restrained and careful times. Impression. Sir Edmund Gosse. HBV-1
In Thine Arms. Oliver Wendell Holmes. TRV
In Thine Own Heart. "Angelus Silesius," *tr. fr. German.* TRV
In things a moderation keep. Moderation. Robert Herrick. FaBoEE
In 'thirty-nine, in Poland. Children's Crusade 1939. Bertolt Brecht, *tr. by* Michael Hamburger. MoBS
In this Aegean island of white fire. Greek Transfiguration. Kimon Friar. HoAn
In this air. One of the Regiment. Douglas Le Pan. CaP
In this ancient parable. The Town Rat and the Country Rat. La Fontaine, *tr. by* Marianne Moore. NAWM-2
In this beloved marble view. On the Bust of Helen by Canova. Byron. EyDe
In this book I see your face and in your face. Frontispiece. May Swenson. CoAP; NePoEA; WPE
In this buff-gray cliff. Sandstone. Anne Marriott. CaP
In this café Durruti. The Midget. Philip Levine. NaP; NoAM
In This City. Alan Brownjohn. CAD
In this city how many masters are clouds. Amsterdam. Jean Garrigue. TAP
In this city I loved you, where light. Chicago. Galway Kinnell. NePoAm
In this city, perhaps a street. In This City. Alan Brownjohn. CAD
In this cold monument lies one. An Epitaph on M. H. Charles Cotton. EBEV; FaBoEE
In this cold room. Samuel Hearne in Wintertime. John Newlove. NOBC
In this congealit season sharp and chill. An Evening and Morning in Winter. Gawin Douglas. *Fr.* Prologues to the Aeneid. BSV
In this cool corner where dark stars of ivy. Destroying Angel. Hilary Corke. NYBP
In this country I planted not one seed. Sailing from the United States. Stanley Moss. VGW
In this country there is neither measure nor balance. Two Campers in Cloud Country. Sylvia Plath. NYBP
In This Dark House. Edward Davison. OBMV
In This Deep Darkness ("In this deep heavy darkness"). Natan Zach, *tr. fr. Hebrew by* Peter Everwine *and* Shula Starkman. VWA
In this desolation. The Soldier. Uys Krige, *tr. by author* PeSA
In this exploded diagram of my heart, the large. Starship. David McAleavey. AMV-81
In this factory, here the axe-grinders. University Curriculum. William Price Turner. OxBS; POL
In this fair niche above the unslumbering sea. A Singer Asleep. Thomas Hardy. OAEP
In this fair stranger's eyes of grey. Absence. Matthew Arnold. Switzerland, VI. OAEP
In this falling of seasons. Burning against the Wind. Judith Minty. GeTw
In this glass palace are flowers in golden baskets. The Lovers. Conrad Aiken. AP; NYBP
In this green chest is laid away. On a Fair Woman. Francis Burdett Money-Coutts. OBVV
In this green month when resurrected flowers. Memorial Wreath. Dudley Randall. CNA; IDB; NNP; PoBA; PoNe
In this green world budged by the round shoulder. Merits of Laughter and Lust. Eli Mandel. PeCV
In this high pasturage, the Blunden time. The Archaeological Picnic. John Betjeman. EnLoPo
In this house, she said, in this high second storey. Under. J. C. Squire. FaBoTw
"In This House, There Shall Be No Idols." Carolyn M. Rodgers. JB
In this imperfect, gloomy scene. The Female Friend. Cornelius Whur. FaBoCo
In this ink blot, there are two lions. Rorschach. Laura Fargas. SUW
In this kind of weather. Changes around the Bay. Michael Palmer. NPGG
In This Life. Robert Mezey. SUW
"In this life/ Of error, ignorance, and strife." Shelley. *Fr.* The Sensitive Plant: Conclusion. LO
In this little urn[e] is laid. Upon Prue [*or* Prew], His Maid. Robert Herrick. CaPo; CavP; InPk; JCP; NoP; OAEP; PAI; SeCV-1
In this little vault she lyes. Upon a Wife That Dyed Mad with Jealousie. Robert Herrick. CavP
In this lone, open glade I lie. Lines Written in Kensington Gardens. Matthew Arnold. FaBoPP; NIP
In this meadow starred with spring. Morning Glory. Siegfried Sassoon. TrCP
In this merry morn of May. Medieval Norman Song. *Unknown, tr. by* John Addington Symonds. AWP
In this my green world. What There Is. Kenneth Patchen. LLLT
In this nation. Of Being Numerous #24. George Oppen. *Fr.* Of Being Numerous. GOA
In this our English coast much blessed blood is shed. A Song of Four Priests Who Suffered Death at Lancaster. *Unknown.* ACP
In this picture/ Custer is wearing. Custer 2. Alison Baker. FAZ
In this poem the bear shambles in. The Bear That Came to the Wedding. Howard McCord. GP
In this quiet town, it is odd to discover. In New Ross. Valentin Iremonger. NeIP
In This River. Valentin Iremonger. NeIP
In this road that I must take. Journey. Roy Daniells. MoCV
In this room, holding hands. All Day We've Longed for Night. Sarah Webster Fabio. BlSi
In this sad place. The Haunted Garden. Henry Treece. NeBP
In this secluded shrine. To a Wood-Violet. John Banister Tabb. HBV-1
In this small character is sent. Upon a Braid of Hair in a Heart. Henry King. EnLoPo
In this squalid, dirty dooryard. The Pear Tree. Edna St. Vincent Millay. MoAmPo
In this stoned and. Definition of Nature. Eugene Redmond. PoBA
In this sweet book, the treasury of wit. To His Lady. Sir John Davies. SiPS
In this the hour of new reckonings! This Hour. Oliver La Grone. NNP; PoNe
In this Theayter they has plays. An Old Woman, Outside the Abbey Theater. L. A. G. Strong. DBV; FiBHP; MoBrPo
In this town, in the blurred and snowy dawn. Geneva. Alastair Reid. NYBP
In this vintage season, when the skies are full of movement. I Didn't Know My Soul. Avraham Ben-Yitzhak, *tr. by* A. C. Jacobs. VWA
In this woman the earth speaks. Earth and Fire. Wendell Berry. FF; GP
In this world. Flannery O'Connor. Dorothy Walters. IHMS
In this world of toil and trouble. I Don't Want to Get Adjusted. *Unknown.* FSW
In this world (the Isle of Dreams). The White Island; or, The Place of the Blest [*or* Blessed]. Robert Herrick. AnAnS-2; ChTr; HBV-2; JCP; NoP; OAEL-1; OBS; OxBoCh; WiR
In this worlds raging sea. Regrat. William Drummond of Hawthornden. PoEL-2
In th'olde dayes of the Kyng Arthour. The Wife of Bath's Tale. Chaucer. *Fr.* The Canterbury Tales. OAEL-1; ViBoPo
In Thorney Moor Woods in Nottinghamshire. The Nottinghamshire Poacher. *Unknown.* OBET
In those days/ When civilization kicked us in the face. The Vultures. David Diop, *tr. by* Ulli Beier. PBA; TTY
In those fields haunted by fear. Three Barrows Down. Jocelyn Brooke. ChMP
In those old days which poets say were golden. Beer. Charles Stuart Calverley. BXAP; CenHV; FaBoCo
In those twelve days let us be glad. The New Dial. *Unknown.* OBET
In those two silent moments, when we stand. Revision. Eileen Newton. SUMH
In those years when our sense, desire and wit. Caelica, XCVI. Fulke Greville. NOCV

In through every lattice-bar/ Where the trellis gapes ajar. Annunciation Night. Abby Maria Hemenway. *Fr.* Mary of Nazareth. ISi
In thy coach of state. A Crowned Poet. Anne Reeve Aldrich. AA
In thy fair domain. Landscape. William Mason. *Fr.* The English Garden, I. OBEC
In Thy garden, in Thy garden, though the rain. The Garden of the Holy Souls. Eleanor Hamilton King. *Fr.* Hours of the Passion. ACP
In tight pants, tight skirts. The Young Ones, Flip Side. James A. Emanuel. PCP
In Tilbury Town did Old King Cole. Old King Cole. E. A. Robinson. HBV-1
In till this tyme that I of tell. Macbeth. Andrew of Wyntoun. OxBS
In Time. Robert Graves. FaBoEE
In Time. Kathleen Raine. NeBP; WPE
In time all undertakings are made good. In Time. Robert Graves. FaBoEE
In Time like Air. May Sarton. NYBP
In Time like Glass. W. J. Turner. MoBrPo; OBMV
In Time of Crisis. Raymond R. Patterson. *See* You Are the Brave.
In Time of Gold. Hilda Doolittle ("H. D."). PoA
In Time of Grief. Lizette Woodworth Reese. AA
In Time of Need. William Stafford. UnPo
In Time of Need. Katharine Tynan. TrPWD
In Time of Pestilence [*or* Plague]. Thomas Nashe. *See* Adieu, Farewell Earth's Bliss.
In Time of Silver Rain. Langston Hughes. SoPo; TiPo
In time of sorrow one should be. Thought for the Winter Season. Mary Elizabeth Osborn. NePoAm
In Time of "The Breaking of Nations." Thomas Hardy. BoLoP; CMoP; CoBMV; EBEV; HAP; LiTB; LiTM; LoBV; MMA; MoAB; MoBrPo; NoAM; NoP; NOBE; OAEL-2; OAEP; OBEV; OBWP; POL; PPP; QFR; SeCeV; TreF; WeW
In Time of War, *sel.* W. H. Auden.
"He turned his field into a meeting-place," VIII. PoPl; SCV
In Time of War. Lesbia Thanet. SUMH
In time of yore when shepherds dwelt. Olden Love-making. Nicholas Breton. OBSC
In time the snowman always dies. Thaw. Walker Gibson. ELU; NePoAm
In time [*or* tyme] the strong and stately [*or* statelie] turrets fall. Licia, XXVIII. Giles Fletcher the Elder. AAS; EBEV; NIP; OBSC
In time to come, if such a crime should be. To Maecenas. Horace, *tr. by* Thomas Flatman. OBVE
In time we rode that trail. Thanksgiving at Snake Butte. James Welch. STE
In time we see that silver drops. Doralicia's Song. Robert Greene. *Fr.* Arbasto. LoBV; OBSC
In Time's concatenation and/ Carnal conventicle. After Night Flight. Robert Penn Warren. Mortmain, I. DiL; NOBA; PoCh; Prf
In times like these, when widows, orphans weep. To a Friend in Love during the Riots. William Parsons. NOEC
In times o'ergrown with rust and ignorance. Priestcraft and Private Judgement. Dryden. *Fr.* Religio Laici. OBS
In times of calm or hurricane, in days of sun or shower. The Dog Parade. Arthur Guiterman. BoAnP; GDP
In times of old, when time was young. Vanbrug's House. Swift. PP
In times when princes canceled nature's law. Tarquin and Tullia. Arthur Mainwaring. APAS
In to thir dirk [*or* dark] and drublie dayis. Meditation in Winter [*or* Meditatioun in Wyntir]. William Dunbar. BSV; NCEP; OxBS; SeCePo
In Tolouse or Ankara, in Hungary or Scotland. All. Antoni Slonimski, *tr. by* Wanda Dynowska. TrJP
In Tommy Morton's byre. Birth. Craig Raine. *Fr.* Anno Domini. NAs
In tottering row, like shadows, silently. By the Sea. Richard Watson Dixon. OBNC
In town, in the foodshop, men are making sandwiches. Big Sheep Knocks You About. Sharon Bryan. MAYP
In Tribute. Vernal House. CaP
In Troop 51 in those days. Robert's Rules of Order. Robert Peterson. FAZ
In tropical climes there are certain times of day. Mad Dogs and Englishmen. Noel Coward. CenHV; FiBHP; NOBL; WhC
In troth, I do myself persuade. Love Enthroned. Richard Lovelace. CaPo
In Trouble and Shame. D. H. Lawrence. OBMV
In Trust. Mary Mapes Dodge. SiSoSe
In truth how glorious was the High Priest. The High Priest. *Unknown, tr. by* Arthur Davis. TrJP
In truth, O Love, with what a boyish kind. Sonnet. Sir Philip Sidney. Astrophel and Stella, XI. ElL; InvP; SiPS
In Tuaim Inbhir here I find. The Ivy Crest. *Unknown, tr. by* Robin Flower. AnIL
In Tupelo, Mississippi. The Tupelo Destruction. *Unknown.* AmFP
In Tuscany, the vintage season reigns. The Vintage. Belle Cooper. GoBC
In twice five years the "greatest living poet." Contemporary Poets. Byron. *Fr.* Don Juan, XI. OBRV
In tyme the strong and statelie turrets fall. *See* In time the strong and stately turrets fall.
In unexperienced infancy. Shadows in the Water. Thomas Traherne. HAP; LiTB; MePo; NoP; OAEL-1; OBS; PoEL-2; SeCP
In unplowed Maine he sought the lumberers' gang. Emerson. *Fr.* Woodnotes I. TAP
In us and into us and ours. For Eusi, Ayi Kwei and Gwen Brooks. Keorapetse Kgositsile. PoBA
In using there are always two. Song of the Fucked Duck. Marge Piercy. BoWoP; NMM
In Utrumque Paratus. Matthew Arnold. OAEP; OBNC; PoEL-5; VLP
In vacant corners, on the hamlet waste. How to Fertilize Soil. John Scott. *Fr.* Amoebaean Eclogues, II. FaBoUs
In Vain. Rose Terry Cooke. AA
In vain/ They shook their garments. Irony of God. Eva Warner. TrCP
In vain, dear Madam, yes, in vain you strive. An Epistle to a Lady. Mary Leapor. NOEC
In vain did Heav'n its miracles produce. A Poem on England's Happiness. *Unknown.* APAS
In Vain Earth Decks Herself. Moses ibn Ezra, *tr. fr. Hebrew by* Solomon Solis-Cohen. *Fr.* The World's Illusion. TrJP
In vain her veins incised—jagged boulders. Spokane Falls. Philip William George. VoR
In vain I look around. To the Memory of a Lady, *abr.* George Lyttelton. OBEC
In vain, in vain—the all-composing hour. The Triumph of Dullness [*or* Chaos *or* The Reign of Chaos]. Pope. *Fr.* The Dunciad. EBEV; FiP; LoBV; NOBE; NOEC; NoP; SCV; ViBoPo
In Vain, Mine Eyes. Sir Philip Sidney. *Fr.* Arcadia. SiPS
In vain, poor nymph, to please our youthful sight. An Elegy, to an Old Beauty. Thomas Parnell. NOEC
In vain the cords and axes were prepared. William Falconer. *Fr.* The Shipwreck, III. OBEC
In vain to me the smiling mornings shine. Sonnet on the Death of Mr. Richard West. Thomas Gray. EnRP; LAuP; NOBE; NOEC; NoP; OAEP; OBEC; PeHV; PoEL-3; SeCePo; TrGrPo; ViBoPo
In vain was I born. Nezalhualcoyotl. ILwL
In vain we call old notions fudge. Stealing [*or* International Copyright]. James Russell Lowell. AA; PV; TreF
In vain you tell your parting lover. Song. Matthew Prior. HBV-1
In vain your bangles cast. Abiku. Wole Soyinka. PBA
In vaine faire sorceresse, thy eyes speake charmes. To a Wanton. William Habington. AnAnS-2; SeCP
In valleys green and still. A. E. Housman. *Fr.* Last Poems. BrPo; FaBoTw; OAEL-2; OAEP; SCV
In Vienna there are ten young girls. Little Viennese Waltz. Federico García Lorca, *tr. by* William B. Logan. SOTW
In Vinculis, *sel.* Wilfrid Scawen Blunt.
Deeds That Might Have Been, The. TrGrPo
In Virgyne the sweltrie sun gan sheene. An Excelente Balade of Charitie. Thomas Chatterton. EnRP; EBEV; GoTL; LAuP; LiTB; NOEC; OBEC; SeCePo
In Vistas of Stone. Abo Stoltzenberg, *tr. fr. Yiddish by* Gabriel Preil *and* Howard Schwartz. VWA
In Wakefield there lives a jolly pinder. The Jolly Pinder of Wakefield. *Unknown.* ESPB
In War. Mason Jordan Mason. PoNe
In warm war-sun they erupt. Mules. Ted Walker. NYBP
In Waste Places. James Stephens. MoAB; MoBrPo; MoVE
(Waste Places, The.) HBV-2
In water nothing is mean. The fugitive. Patience. Elaine Feinstein. BrRo
In waves of heat. August. Roy Scheele. PPJ
In Weather. Robert Hass. AmPA; GeTw
In Wee-John-Boo the bellies of bloodhounds. Orange Jews. Ted Berrigan *and* Ron Padgett. EAS
In Western Mountains, *sel.* Glenn Ward Dresbach.
Life or Death. HBMV
In western skies. Idyl: Sunset. Henrietta Cordelia Ray. BlSi
In Westminster Abbey. Francis Beaumont. *See* On the Tombs in Westminster Abbey
In Westminster Abbey. John Betjeman. CMoP; DBV; FaBoCo; InPK; NIP; NOBL; OAEL-2; OBSV
In Westminster not long ago. The Ratcatcher's Daughter. *Unknown.* ChTr; GBP; OxBoLi
In wet green midspring, midnight and the wind. Mrs. Walpurga. Muriel Rukeyser. NMM
In wet May, in the months of change. An Exequy. Peter Porter. OxBC
In what a glorious substance did they dream. George Edward Woodberry. Ideal Passion, XXVI. HBMV

In what a silence princes pass away. On the Death of a Prince; a Meditation. Thomas Philipott. JCP
In what a strange bewilderment do we. Morn. Helen Hunt Jackson. AA
In what at least. 18 West 11th Street. James Merrill. NYP
In what estate so ever I be. *See* In what state that ever I be.
In what finite tendon dost thou rise? Spirituality. Samuel Greenberg. LiTA
In What Manner the Body Is United with the Soule. Jorie Graham. NPGG
In What Manner the Soule Is United to the Body. Sir John Davies. *Fr.* Nosce Teipsum. LiTB; PoEL-2
(Soul and the Body, The.) CTC; NOBE; OBSC
In what order or what degree. Be True to Your Condition in Life. John Audelay. MeEL
In what state that [*or* estate so] ever I be. The Sparrow-Hawk's Complaint [*or* Timor Mortis]. *Unknown.* FF; NoP; OxBM; PBBP
In what torn ship soever I embark. A Hymn to Christ, at the Author's Last Going into Germany. John Donne. AnAnS-1; EBEV; EnRePo; FaBoEn: JCP; LiTB; MeLP; MePo; OAEP; OBS; OxBoCh; SeCV-1; ViBoPo
In where the smoke runs black against the snow. Spring Offensive, 1941. Maurice Biggs. PoAu-2
In which I live hurtles airless a razor's slash. The Present Tense. Joyce Carol Oates. AMV-81
In Which She Satisfies a Fear with the Rhetoric of Tears. Sister Juana Ines de la Cruz, *tr. fr. Spanish by* Aliki *and* Willis Barnstone. BoWoP
("This evening, my love, even as I spoke vainly," *tr. by* Judith Thurman.) PBWP
In White Tie. David Huddle. Str
In whitest hour of pain the iron air. Prayer in Time of War. Henry Treece. WaP
In whose will is our peace? Thou happiness. Epigram. J. V. Cunningham. QFR; VGW
In Wicklow. Rhoda Coghill. NeIP
In wildest woods, on treetop shelves. The Darkling Elves. Jack Prelutsky. RHPC
In Windsor Castle. Earl of Surrey. NOBE; OBSC; SeCePo
(Prisoned in Windsor, He Recounteth His Pleasure There Passed.) FaBoEn; OAEP
("So crewell [*or* cruell] prison, how[e] could betyde [*or* betide], alas.") AAS; SiPS
(So Cruel Prison.) EnRePo; HAP; NoP
In windy June, the prairie grasses bow. Missouri Town. John Palen. AMV-80
In Winter. Paul Blackburn. NYP
In Winter. C. H. Bretherton. InMe
In Winter. Michael Ryan. MAYP
In Winter. Arthur Symons. BrPo
In Winter. Robert Wallace. BoNaP
In winter I get up at night. Bed in Summer. Robert Louis Stevenson. GoJo; OxBChV; PoPl; TreFT
In winter in my room. Emily Dickinson. AmPP; AP; BiP; ErPo; LiTA; NoAM; NOBA; OxBA; SeCeV; TwAmPo
In Winter in the Woods Alone. Robert Frost. HeIP
In winter, strangeness stained the fields. Somewhere Farm. Guy Rotella. AMV-81
In winter twilight on a side street. Ghostly Story. Milton Acorn. NeAC
In winter two kinds of fields on the hills. Prosser. Raymond Carver. GeTw
In winter when people pay a call. Visitors. Harry Behn. SoPo
In winter, when the fields are white. Humpty Dumpty's Song [*or* Recitation]. "Lewis Carroll." *Fr.* Through the Looking-Glass. ChTr; EBEV; FaBoCo; FaBoNo; FiBHP; GTBS-P; NBM; OnMSP; OxBChV; OxBoLi
In winter when the nights are long. The Beggar Wind. Mary Austin. BoNaP
In winter when the rain rain'd cauld. Tak' Your Auld Cloak about Ye. *Unknown.* OxBS
In winter's just return, when Boreas gan his reign. Earl of Surrey. AAS; SiPS
In wintertime I have such fun. Quoits. Mary Effie Lee Newsome. CDC
In Wintry Midnight, o'er a Stormy Main. Petrarch, *tr. fr. Italian by* William Barnes. ChTr
In wiser days, my darling rosebud, blown. To My Daughter Betty, the Gift of God. Thomas M. Kettle. HBMV; OnYI
In wishing nothing we enjoy still most. Human Happiness. Dryden. *Fr.* The Indian Emperor, IV, i. FiP
In wit, as nature, what affects our hearts. Pope. *Fr.* An Essay on Criticism. HAP
In wonderment I walk to music pouring. Undersong. Mark Van Doren. PoCh
In wonted walks, since wonted fancies change. Sir Philip Sidney. CABA; PoEL-1
In woods so long time bare. Cuckoo! Hilaire Belloc. MoVE
In woods still winter bare. Shadbush. Christina Rainsford. GoYe
In Worcester, Massachusetts. In the Waiting Room. Elizabeth Bishop. HeIP; LCAP; NOBA; Prf
In Word and Will I am a friend to you. On Himself. William Oldys. FaBoEE
In wrath and grief away the Paynims fly. *Unknown, tr. by*Dorothy L. Sayers. *Fr.* The Song of Roland. OBWP
In wrestling I was pinned first. First in the Pentathlon. Lucilius, *tr. by* Tom Dodge. LiSp
In Wyoming,/ plain as far as my eye can see. Other Women's Children. Mary Nelson Waniek. AMV-80
In Xanadu did Kubla Khan. Kubla Khan. Samuel Taylor Coleridge. AWP; BiP; CABA; CH; ChER; ChTr; ELP; EnRP; EyDe; FaBoBe; FaBoCh; FaBoEn; FaBV; FaFP; FF: FiP; FPL; GN; GoJo; HAP; HBV-2; HeIP; HoPM; InPK; InPS; InvP; LiTB; LoBV; MasP; MAT; NIP; NOBE; NoP; OAEL-2; OAEP; OBEV; OBNC; OBRV; PAI; PoEL-4; PoPl; PoRA; PP; PPoe; PrIm; RoGo; SCV; SeCeV; SoSe; SyP; TEP; TreFS; TrGrPo; UnPo; ViBoPo; WeW; WHA; WSC
In Yad Vashem, where all vows are renewed. Hands Up. Anthony Rudolf. VWA
In yellow meadows I take no delight. Sir Thomas Browne. FaBoEE
In yon hollow Damon lies. In Arcady. Cosmo Monkhouse. OBVV
In yonder grave a Druid lies. Ode Occasioned by [*or* on] the Death of Mr. Thomson. William Collins. LAuP; NOEC; OBEC; SeCePo
In yonder marble hero's shade. Italian. Osbert Lancaster. *Fr.* Afternoons with Baedeker. FaBoCo
In Your Arms. Miklós Radnóti, *tr. fr. Hungarian by* Steven Polgar, Stephen Berg, *and* S. J. Marks. VWA
In Your Arrogance. Lynne Lawner. ErPo
In Your Bad Dream. Richard Hugo. LCAP
In your daily round of duties. The Golden Rule. James Wells. STF
In your ears my song. You Laughed and Laughed and Laughed. Gabriel Okara. PBA
In your face I sometimes see. To My Little Son. Julia Johnson Davis. HBMV
In your hesitant moments, remember Cornford and Fox. They Live. Randall Swingler. WaP
In your next letter I wish you'd say. Letter to N. Y. Elizabeth Bishop. MP; NoP; NYP; TwCP
In your presence I rediscovered my name. Your Presence. David Diop, *tr. by* Ulli Beier. PBA
In your quiet hand I touch. The Survivors. Miriam Waddington. VWA
In your scarred, peeling crib you lay neglected. The Sleeping Beauty. Sara de Ford. DFT
In your silk robe I hate to see you clad. I Hate to See You Clad. Paul Verlaine, *tr. by* Louis Untermeyer. UnTE
In your watercolor, Nely Silvínová. Robert Mezey. *Fr.* Theresienstadt Poems. NaP; VWA
In your words. Prologue. Lazer Eichenrand, *tr. by* Gabriel Preil *and* Howard Schwartz. VWA
In Youth. Evaleen Stein. AA
In youth from rock to rock I went. To the Daisy. Wordsworth. EnRP
In youth, gay scenes attract our eyes. The Vanity of Existence. Philip Freneau. AmPP; AP
In youth I frowned. Old Woman's Song. Thomas Cole. NePoAm-2
In youth I served my time. Retirement. *Unknown, tr. by* Frank O'Connor. ErPo; KiLC
In Youth Is Pleasure. Robert Wever. *Fr.* Lusty Juventus. ChTr; NOBE; OBEV
("In a herber green, asleep whereas I lay.") GBL
(In an Arbour Green.) ELP
(Of Youth He Singeth.) EIL
(Youth.) OBSC
In youth's spring it was my lot. The Lake. Poe. OBRV
In zummertide, I took my road. Sheep in the Sheade. William Barnes. FM
Inability to Depict an Eagle. Richard Eberhart. GOA
Inadequate Aqua Extremis. Ruth M. Walsh. QQQ
Inanna and An. Enheduanna, *tr. fr. Sumerian; ad. by* Aliki *and* Willis Barnstone. BoWoP
Inanna and Ebih. Enheduanna, *tr. fr. Sumerian; ad. by* Aliki *and* Willis Barnstone. BoWoP
Inanna and Enlil. Enheduanna, *tr. fr. Sumerian; ad. by* Aliki *and* Willis Barnstone. BoWoP
Inanna and Ishkur. Enheduanna, *tr. fr. Sumerian; ad. by* Aliki *and* Willis Barnstone. BoWoP
Inanna and the Anunna. Enheduanna, *tr. fr. Sumerian; ad. by* Aliki *and* Willis Barnstone. BoWoP
Inanna and the City of Uruk. Enheduanna, *tr. fr. Sumerian; ad. by* Aliki *and* Willis Barnstone. BoWoP
Inanna and the Divine Essences. Enheduanna, *tr. fr. Sumerian; ad. by* Aliki *and* Willis Barnstone. BoWoP

Inanna Exalted, *sel.* Enheduanna, *tr. fr. Sumerian.*
"O lady of all truths bright light going forth," *tr. by* Anne Draffkorn Kilmer, *based on text by* W. W. Hallo *and* J. J. A. van Dijk. WPOW
Inanna's Song. *Unknown, tr. fr. Sumerian by* Diane Wolkstein *and* Samuel Noah Kramer. LLLT
Inapprehensiveness. Robert Browning. VLP
Inasmuch! William E. Brooks. PGD
Inaudible move day and night. Silence. John Lancaster Spalding. AA
Incandescence. Lucille Clifton. GeTw
Incantation, The. *At. to* Amergin, *tr. fr. Old Irish by* George Sigerson. OnYI
Incantation, An. Byron. *Fr.* Manfred, I. OBRV
Incantation, The. Theocritus, *tr. fr. Greek by* Charles Stuart Calverley. *Fr.* Idylls. AWP
Incantation to Get Rid of a Sometime Friend. Emanuel diPasquale. TW
Incantation to Oedipus. Dryden. *Fr.* Oedipus, III, i. OFD; WSC (Spell, A.) WiR
Incanto. Stan Rice. NPGG
Incarnate for our marriage you appeared. The Marriage. Yvor Winters. MoVE; QFR
Incarnate Love. Wilbur Fisk Tillett. BLRP
Incarnatio Est Maximum Donum Dei. William Alabaster. MePo (Sonnet: "Like as the fountain of all light created.") SBVL
Incarnation, The. William Langland. *Fr.* The Vision of Piers Plowman. PoEL-1
("For trewthe telleth that loue is triacle of hevene.") OBEV
Incarnation, The. Charles Wesley. NOCV
Incarnation and Passion, The. Henry Vaughan. TrCP
Incarnation Poem. John Leax. TrCP
Incendiary. Vernon Scannell. OxBC
Incense. Louise Townsend Nicholl. NePoAm-2
Incense, and flesh of swine, and this year's grain. To Phidyle. Horace, *tr. by* Austin Dobson. Odes, III, 23. AWP
Incense of the Lucky Virgin. Robert Hayden. AmPP
Incentive, The. Sarah N. Cleghorn. HBMV
Incentive, The. Martial, *tr. fr. Latin by* Louis Untermeyer. UnTE
Incentive/ born in ancient. On Riots. Cy Leslie. NBP
Inchcape Rock, The. Robert Southey. BeLS; ChTr; FaBoBe; GN; HBV-1; HBVY; OBNV; OBRV; PaPo; PoPle; TreFS
Incident. Amiri Baraka. NoAM
Incident. Countee Cullen. BiP; BPo; CABA; CDC; CTBA; FF; IDB; NoAM; NTCP; OBCA; PoBA; PoNe; SoSe; VGW
Incident, An. Mary H. J. Henderson. SUMH
Incident, An. Douglas Le Pan. MoCV; PeCV
Incident. Norman MacCaig. FF
Incident. Harvey Shapiro. FAZ
Incident, An. Frederick Tennyson. GoBC
Incident at Mossel Bay. Mary Balazs. AMV-81
Incident Characteristic of a Favourite Dog. Wordsworth. FM
Incident Here and There, An. Hilda Doolittle ("H. D."). *Fr.* The Walls Do Not Fall. CrMA; NoAM; OBWP
Incident in a Rose Garden. Donald Justice. NCSH
Incident in the Early Life of Ebenezer Jones, Poet, 1828, An. John Betjeman. CMoP; NoAM
Incident of the French Camp. Robert Browning. BeLS; FaPo; FaPoR; GN; HBV-2; HBVY; OBWP; RoGo; TreF; TrGrPo
Incident on a Front Not Far from Castel di Sangro. Harry Brown. NYBP
Incident on a Journey. Thom Gunn. NePoEA
Incidental Pieces to a Walk. James Cunningham. JB
Incidents in Playfair House. Nicholas Moore. ErPo; NeBP
Incidents in the Life of My Uncle Arly. Edward Lear. FaBoNo; FPL; MoShBr; NA; NBM; OAEL-2; OxBoLi; TrGrPo; WhC
Incipit Vita Nova. William Morton Payne. AA
Incline Thine ear, O God. Therefore, We Thank Thee, God. Reuben Grossman, *tr. by* L. V. Snowman. TrJP
Inclusions. Elizabeth Barrett Browning. HBV-1; OBVV; UnTE
Inclusiveness. Dante Gabriel Rossetti. The House of Life, LXIII. NBM; NCEP; SyP; VLP
Incognita. Austin Dobson. CenHV; EBVV
Incognita of Raphael. William Allen Butler. AA
Incognitos of masquerading moons. Festoons of Fishes. Alfred Kreymborg. HBMV
Income taxes. Taxes. Don L. Lee. BOLo
Incomprehensible, The. Isaac Watts. WGRP
Incomprehensible/ O Masterfate and mystery. Sanctus. David Gascoyne. *Fr.* Miserere. NeBP
Inconclusive Evening, An. Frances Bellerby. FaBoTw
Inconsistencies. Michelle Roberts. LFAC
Inconsistent. Mark Van Doren. ELU
Inconstancy Reproved. Sir Robert Ayton. *See* To His Forsaken Mistress.
Inconvenience, An. John Raven. BPo
Incorrigible Music, An. Allen Curnow. OCNZ
Incorrigible one, still groping with your eyes. Thought and the Poet. Peter Yates. ChMP
Increasing moonlight drifts across my bed, The. Fredericksburg. Thomas Bailey Aldrich. PAH
Incredible Yachts, The. Philip Booth. GP
Incrusted in his island home that lies beyond the sea. The Neutral British Gentleman. "Orpheus C. Kerr." OBAL
Incubation, The. Al Zolynas. LTB
Indecision. Helen Pinkerton. QFR
Indecision Means Flexibility. Elliot Abhau. PH
Indeed I must confess. Platonic[k] Love. Abraham Cowley. *Fr.* The Mistress. NoP; SeCV-1
Indeed Indeed, I Cannot Tell. Henry David Thoreau. TW
Indeed indeed it is growing very sultry. The Cubical Domes. David Gascoyne. EAS
Indeed, it will soon be over, I shall be done. Intimations of Mortality. Stanley Kunitz. MoAmPo
Indeed, my Caelia, 'tis in vain. Song. Sir John Henry Moore. LO; OBEC
Indeed, Sir Peter, I could wish, I own. On Clergymen Preaching Politics. John Byrom. SeCePo
Indeed this very love which is my boast. Sonnets from the Portuguese, XII. Elizabeth Barrett Browning. HBV-1
Indelicate is he who loathes. Epidermal Macabre. Theodore Roethke. NoAM; TW
Independence. Nancy Cato. PoAu-2; WPE
Independence. Adebayo Faleti, *tr. fr. Yoruba by* Bakare Gbadamosi *and* Ulli Beier. PBA
Independence. Roy McFadden. OxBI
Independence. Guy Mason. CaP
Independence. Tobias Smollett. OBEC
Independence. *Somali Oral Tradition, tr. by* B. W. Andrzejewski *and* I. M. Lewis. WTO
Independence. Henry David Thoreau. TreFS
Independence Bell—July 4, 1776. *Unknown.* BLPA; FaBoBe; FPL; PAL (Liberty and Independence.) TreFS
Independence Day. Wendell Berry. OFD
Independence Day. William Jay Smith. MP; TwCP
Independence Day. Royall Tyler. PAH
Independent, The. Phyllis McGinley. FaBoEE
Independent Squire. Samuel Butler. *Fr.* Hudibras, I, 1. NOBE
India. Florence Earle Coates. AA
India. W. J. Turner. MoBrPo; PDV
India Guide, The; or, Journal of a Voyage to the East Indies in 1780, *sel.* Sir George Dallas.
Miss Emily Brittle Sails for India. NOEC
Indian. Jeanne Doriot. AMV-81
Indian. Laura Jensen. AmPA
Indian, The. Thomas Reed. AMV-81
Indian America. Mah-do-ge Tohee. STE
Indian at the Burial-Place of His Fathers, An. Bryant. HeIP
Indian Blood. Mary TallMountain. STE; TWSS
Indian Burying Ground, The. Philip Freneau. AA; AmPP; AP; HAP; HBV-2; HeIP; LiTA; NePA; NOBA; NoP; OxBA; PoEL-4; PoLF; PoPl; TAP
Indian Camp. Janet Reed McFatter. GrPl
Indian chief who, fam'd of yore, The. The Prophecy of King Tammany. Philip Freneau. GOA
Indian Children. Annette Wynne. SoPo; SUS; TiPo
Indian Children Speak. Juanita Bell. PAI
Indian Convert, The. Philip Freneau. TAP
Indian Dance. Frederick Niven. CaP
Indian Death. Alice Corbin. BPAW
Indian Death. Eda Lou Walton. BPAW
Indian Education. Adrian C. Louis. STE
Indian Elephant, The. C. J. Kaberry. FiBHP
Indian Emperor, The, *sels.* Dryden.
Ah, Fading Joy, *fr.* IV, iii. ChTr; FiP; LoBV; OAEP; TreFT; ViBoPo (Song: "Ah, fading joy, how quickly art Thou past?") FaBoEn; NoP
Human Happiness, *fr.* IV, i. FiP
Indian Ghost Dance and War, The. W. H. Prather. PoOW
Indian Graveyard, The. Ramona Weeks. TAT
Indian Guys at the Bar. Simon J. Ortiz. STE
Indian Hunter, The. Eliza Cook. BLPA
Indian Lass, The. *Unknown.* OBET
Indian Love Song. Lew Blockcolski. VoR
Indian Macho. Louis (LittleCoon) Oliver. STE
Indian Maid, The; Demararie, Oct. 27, 1781. Edward Thompson. NOEC
Indian Mother about to Destroy Her Child, An. James Montgomery. PaPo
Indian Mounds. Angela Peace. AMV-80
Indian Names. Lydia Huntley Sigourney. AmFN; FaPON; GOA; HBV-2; PAH; PoLF; OBCA
Indian Night Tableau. Hyman Edelestein. CaP

Indian Painting, Probably Paiute, in a Cave near Madras, Oregon. Jarold Ramsey. TAT
Indian Pipe and Moccasin Flower. Arthur Guiterman. SUS
Indian Prayer. Chief Joseph Strongwolf. TRV
Indian Princess, The. The Pet Deer. James Tate. EAS
Indian Queen, The, *sel.* Sir Robert Howard *and* John Dryden.
"Poor mortals that are clogged with earth below." TEP
Indian Reservation: Caughnawaga. A. M. Klein. LiTM; NOBC; NoP; OBCV
Indian Rock, Bainbridge Island, Washington. Duane Niatum. CDW
Indian School. Norman H. Russell. MAT
Indian Serenade, The. Shelley. AWP; BLPL; EnRP; HoPM; LiTB; LoBV; OAEP; OBEV; OBRV; PoPl; TreF; TrGrPo; UnTE; ViBoPo
(Lines to an Indian Air.) FaBoBe; FiP; GTBS; GTBS-P; HBV-1
Indian Sky. Alfred Kreymborg. BPAW
Indian Song. Willard Johnson. BPAW
Indian Song, An. W. B. Yeats. VLP
Indian Song: Survival. Leslie Silko. CDW; VoR
Indian Student, The; or, Force of Nature. Philip Freneau. OxBA
Indian Summer. Gray Burr. AMV-80
Indian Summer. Wilfred Campbell. CaP; NOBC; OBCV; PoPl; WHW
Indian Summer. Emily Dickinson. *See* These are the days when birds come back.
Indian Summer. A. S. Draper. YeAr
Indian Summer. Barbara Howes. IHMS
Indian Summer. William Ellery Leonard. *Fr.* Two Lives. HBMV
Indian Summer. Susanna Moodie. CaP
Indian Summer. John Banister Tabb. AA
Indian Summer Day on the Prairie, An. Vachel Lindsay. BPAW; RFM; SoPo
Indian Summer Here, You in Honolulu. Donald Johnson. AMV-80
Indian Summer is with us now. Indian Summer. A. S. Draper. YeAr
Indian Summer: Montana, 1956. W. M. Ransom. CDW
Indian Summer, 1927. Anne Hussey. AMV-81
Indian Summer: Vermont. Anne Stevenson. NCSH
Indian to His Love, The. W. B. Yeats. VLP
Indian upon God, The. W. B. Yeats. MoBrPo; WGRP
Indian war was over, The. The Captive's Hymn. Edna Dean Proctor. PAH
Indian weed [now] withered quite, The. A Religious Use of Tobacco [*or* Pipe and Can]. *Unknown, at. to* Robert Wisdome. EIL; HBV-2; OBEV; OBS
Indian, who lived at Muskingum, remote, An. The Indian Convert. Philip Freneau. TAP
Indian Woman's Death-Song. Felicia Dorothea Hemans. SBG
Indian Women Are Listening, The; to the Nuke Devils. Wendy Rose. TWSS
Indiana. Hart Crane. *Fr.* The Bridge: Powhatan's Daughter. TwAmPo
Indiana: no blustering summit or coarse gorge. Midwest. John Frederick Nims. MoVE; PoPl
Indians. John Fandel. AmFN; NYBP
Indians. Charles Sprague. GN
Indians at the Guthrie. Gerald Vizenor. STE; VoR
Indians chant and dance about, The. Not a Cloud in the Sky. Richard Armour. WhC
Indians Come Down from Mixco, The. Miguel Angel Asturias, *tr. fr. Spanish by* Donald Devenish Walsh. FaPON
Indians count of men as dogs, The. Roger Williams. SCAP
Indian's Grave, The. George J. Mountain. CaP
Indians have mostly gone, The. Like Ghosts of Eagles. Robert Francis. GOA; LCAP
Indians on Alcatraz, The. Paul Muldoon. CIP
Indians prize not English gold, The. Roger Williams. SCAP
Indians stole fair Annie, The. Fair Annie. *Unknown.* ViBoFo
Indian's Welcome to the Pilgrim Fathers, The. Lydia Huntley Sigourney. AA
Indications and tally of time, The. Walt Whitman. *Fr.* Song of the Answerer. PP
Indictment, The, *abr.* Frederick Fanning Ayer. PeD
Indifference. Harry Graham. DBV
Indifference, The. Sir Charles Sedley. SeCV-2
Indifference. G. A. Studdert-Kennedy. EBCP; PGD; TrCP; TRV
Indifference ("In loopy links the canker crawls"). *Unknown.* NA
Indifference to Fortune. James Thomson. *Fr.* The Castle of Indolence. OBEC
Indifferent, The. Francis Beaumont. EIL; HBV-1
Indifferent, The. John Donne. AnAnS-1; BiP; BoLoP; CABA; OAEP; SeCV-1; TEP; UnTE
Indifferent, but indifferent-pshaw! he doth it not. Sir Walter Scott. *Fr.* The Monastery. NBM
Indigestion of the Vampire, The. W. S. Merwin. NaP
Indignant at the fumbling wits, the obscure spite. Paudeen. W. B. Yeats. HAP; InPS; PoEL-5
Indignant Protest. *Unknown, tr. fr. Greek by* Louis Untermeyer. UnTE
Indignation Dinner, An. James David Corrothers. BANP; PoNe
Indigo, chartreuse, tangerine, lillipop. Resort. Kendrick Smithyman. OCNZ
Indigo Glass in the Grass, The. Wallace Stevens. PoA
Indigo, magenta, color of ghee. Whitebeard on Videotape. James Merrill. NoP
Indigo Pete's J. B. Henry Herbert Knibbs. BPAW
Indirection. Richard Realf. AA; HBV-2
Individualist Speaks, The. Louis MacNeice. MoVE; OBMV
Indolence. Robert Bridges. BrPo; VLP
Indolence. Vernon Watkins. FaBoTw
Indolent, The. Paul Verlaine, *tr. fr. French by* Arthur Symons. SyP
Indolent Gardener, The. Mary Kennedy. BoNaP
Indomitable, The. Carl Rakosi. GP
Indoor Games near Newbury. John Betjeman. MoVE
Indoors. George Johnston. PoA
Indra, the Supreme God. *Unknown, tr. fr. Sanskrit by* Romesh Dutt. *Fr.* The Rig-Veda. AWP
Induction to "A Mirror for Magistrates." Thomas Sackville. *Fr.* A Mirror [*or* Mirour] for Magistrates. AAS; OBSC
(Complaint of Henry Duke of Buckingham, The.) PoEL-1
Sels.
Midnight ("Midnight was come . . ."). CH
Sleep ("By him lay heavy Sleep . . ."). WHA
Troy ("But Troy, alas . . ."). SeCePo
Vision of Sorrow ("But how can I describe . . ."). LoBV
Vision of War, A ("Lastlie stode warre . . ."). FaBoEn
(Shield of War, The.) NOBE
Winter ("Wrathful winter, 'proaching on apace, The . . ."). EIL; SeCePo
Indulge thy smiling scorn, if smiling still. The Fish Turns into a Man, and Then into a Spirit, and Again Speaks. Leigh Hunt. *Fr.* The Fish, the Man, and the Spirit. MOS; NOBL
Indulgences. Michael Hogan. AMV-80
Indulgent giants burned to crisp. Lavish Kindness. Elinor Wylie. CrMA
Indulgent Nature on each kind bestows. On Dr. Evans Cutting Down a Row of Trees. *Unknown.* FaBoEE
Industrial Evils. Joseph Cottle. *Fr.* Malvern Hills. NOEC
Industrious, unfatigued in faction's cause. The Character of a Certain Whig. William Shippen. APAS
Inebriates. Philip Brasfield. LFAC
Inebriety. George Crabbe. BXAP
Ineffable Dou, The. Sydney Goodsir Smith. OxBS
Inefficacious Egg, The. Roy Bishop. HBMV
Inert he lies on the saltgold sand. The Sunbather. Vernon Watkins. MoPo; MoVE
Inert in his chair. Drugged. Walter de la Mare. BrPo
Inertia. Kirti Chaudhari, *tr. fr. Hindi by* Leonard Nathan. WPOW
Inertia. Vivienne Finch. BrRo
Inertia. Audrey McGaffin. NePoAm
Inevitable. John Betjeman. MoBrPo
Inevitable, The. Sarah Knowles Bolton. AA; WGRP
Inexhaustible. Israel Zangwill. TrJP
Inexorable. William Drummond of Hawthornden. *See* Madrigal: "My thoughts hold mortal strife."
Inextinguishable Blaze. Charles Wesley. *See* O Thou Who Camest from Above.
Infallibility. Thomas Stephens Collier. AA
Infant. Diana O Hehir. NPGG
Infant Diseases and Their Treatment. M. Saint-Marthe, *tr. fr. French. Fr.* Paedotrophiae; or, The Art of Bringing Up Children. FaBoUs
Infant Innocence. A. E. Housman. ChTr; DTC; FaBoCh; FaBoCo; FaBoNo, *sl. diff.*; FaFP; LiTB; NOBL, *sl. diff.*; OxBoLi; WhC, *sl. diff.*
("Grizzly Bear is huge and wild, The.") CenHV
Infant Joy. Blake. *Fr.* Songs of Innocence. FaPON; GoJo; HBV-1; HBVY; LAuP; LoBV; NAs; PoLF; SiSoSe; TEP; ViBoPo
Infant Noah. Vernon Watkins. NeBP
Infant she played in the shadow. Anne and the Peacock. Noel Welch. FF
Infant Song. Charles Causley. NAs; OxBC
Infant Sorrow. Blake. *Fr.* Songs of Experience. FaBoEn; InPS; LAuP; NAs; OBNC; PAI; PoEL-4; PoPle
Infant Spring. Fredegond Shove. HBMV
Infantryman, An. Edmund Blunden. ViBoPo
Infants' gravemounds are steps of angels, where. Graves of Infants. John Clare. OBVV
Infants of Summer. Lennox Raphael. NBP
Infatuated. *Unknown, tr. fr. Greek by* Louis Untermeyer. UnTE
Inferno. Dante. *See* Divina Commedia.
Inferno: A New Circle. Frank Ormsby. CIP
Infida's Song. Robert Greene. *Fr.* Never Too Late. OBSC

Infidel Reclaimed, The. Edward Young. *Fr.* The Complaint; or, Night Thoughts on Life, Death and Immortality, VII. NOEC
Infidelity. Olga Berggolts, *tr. fr. Russian by* Daniel Weissbort. BoWoP
Infidelity. Louis Untermeyer. TrJP
Infinite, The. John Boyle O'Reilly. OnYI
Infinite consanguinity it bears. Hart Crane. Voyages, III. MoPo; MoVE
Infinite grief! amazing woe! Look on Him Whom They Pierced, and Mourn. Isaac Watts. NOCV
Infinite orderliness of the natural world, The. The Spiral. John Holmes. MiAP
Infinite power essenciall, The. Mary, Queen of Heaven. *Unknown.* MeEL
Infinite Power, eternal Lord. The Comparison and Complaint. Isaac Watts. TrPWD
Infinite Truth and Might! whose love. Thy Name We Bless and Magnify. John Power. BLRP
Infinite weariness comes into the faces of the old tenements, An. Ghetto Twilight. Alter Brody. VWA
"Infinite," The. Word horrible! at feud. Legem Tuam Dilexi. Coventry Patmore. The Unknown Eros, X. NBM; OxBoCh; PoEL-5
Infinito, L'. Giacomo Leopardi, *tr. fr. Italian by* Lorna De' Lucchi. AWP
Infinity. Philip Henry Savage. AA
Infinity. Walt Whitman. *Fr.* Song of Myself, XLIV-XLV. AA
Infinity, when all things it beheld. The Preface. Edward Taylor. *Fr.* God's Determinations. AmPP; AP; HAP; NOBA; OxBA; SCAP
Infir Taris. *Unknown.* ChTr; OxNR
Infirmity. Theodore Roethke. CoAP; NYBP
Inflamed Disciple, The. Arthur Kramer. InMe
Inflammable Woman, The. James K. Baxter. OxBC
Inflatable Globe, The. Theodore Spencer. LiTA; NePA; WaP
Inflated boys, when clergymen are odd. Memorandum for Minos. Richard Kell. ELU
Inflation. Charles O. Hartman. PoA
Inflictis. Archibald Stodart-Walker. *Fr.* The Moxford Book of English Verse. CenHV
Influence. John Oxenham. STF
Influence of Local Attachment, The, *sel.* Richard Polwhele.
  Visit to the Author's Paternal Seat, A. NOEC
Influence of Natural Objects. Wordsworth. *Fr.* The Prelude, I. AWP; LoBV; OBRV
Influence of Time on Grief. William Lisle Bowles. *See* Time and Grief.
Informer, art thou in the tree. On the Meetings of the Scotch Covenanters. *Unknown.* FaBoEE
Informing Spirit, The. Emerson. AWP
Infusorial earthmounds of the Upper Amazon, The. Lost Explorer. Edmund Pennant. GoYe
Ingenious Little Old Man, The. John Bennett. FaPON
Ingenious Raconteur. Renée Haynes. PV
Ingestion. Barry McDonald. POL
Ingle-Side, The. Hew Ainslee. HBV-2
Inglorious friend! most confident I am. Sonnet to a Clam. John Godfrey Saxe. BoAnP
Ingmar Bergman's "Seventh Seal." Robert Duncan. NMP
Ingoldsby Legends, The, *sels.* "Thomas Ingoldsby."
  "But to see now how strangely things sometimes turn out." *Fr.* Lay of St. Gengulphus. VLP
  Cynotaph, The. FM
  Hon. Mr. Sucklethumbkin's Story. OBRV
  Jackdaw of Rheims, The. FaBoCo; HBV-2; OBNV; OnMSP; PaPo; VLP
  Misadventures at Margate. HBV-2
  Not a Sou [*or* Sous] Had He Got. *Fr.* The Cynotaph. FaBoCo; HBV-1
  St. Cuthbert Intervenes. NBM
Ingrateful[l] Beauty Threatened. Thomas Carew. AnAnS-2; CaPo; HBV-1; InvP; MeLP; OBEV; OBS; SeCP; SeCV-1
Ingratitude. Francis Thynne. PBBP
Ingratitude, how deadly is the smart. Sonnet. Anna Seward. NOEC
Inhabitants of old Jerusalem, The. The Popish Plot. Dryden. *Fr.* Absolom and Achitophel. ACP
Inhabited Emptiness, An. Jiri Gold, *tr. fr. Czech by* Jaroslav Kotan *and* Daniel Weissbort. VWA
Inheritance. Mary Thacher Higginson. AA
Inheritance, An. Naomi Replansky. GP
Inheritance. *Unknown, tr. fr. Irish by* Frank O'Connor. DBV; KiLC; TW
Inheritors, The. Gary Geddes. NOBC
Inheritors, The. Dorothy Livesay. CaP
Inhuman Henry. A. E. Housman. FiBHP
Inimitably quick. Static Autumn. Yvor Winters. PoA
Inis Fal. Egan O'Rahilly, *tr. fr. Irish by* James Stephens. BIrV; OBMV
Inisgallun. Darrell Figgis. OnYI
Initial. Arthur Boyars. NePoEA-2
Initial Response. Katherine Soniat. AMV-80
Initials. Michael S. Glaser. AMV-81
Initiate, The. W. S. Merwin. NNaP
Initiation. Jayne Cortez. PoBA
Initiation. Rainer Maria Rilke, *tr. fr. German by* C. F. MacIntyre. TrJP
Injian Ocean sets an' smiles, The. For to Admire. Kipling. MoBrPo
Injured Maple. Ronald Everson. NOBC
Injured Moon, The. Baudelaire, *tr. fr. French by* Robert Lowell. MOGN
Injured Stuart line is gone, The. On Seeing the Royal Palace at Stirling in Ruins. Burns. DBV
Injury, The. William Carlos Williams. AP
Ink runs from the corners of my mouth. Eating Poetry. Mark Strand. GrPl; MAT; NoAM; PPP; TAP
Inland,/ far inland go my thoughts. Song of the Rejected Woman. Kibkarjuk, *tr. by* Knud Rasmussen; *tr. into English by* Tom Lowenstein. WPOW
Inland City. John Crowe Ransom. CMoP
Inland Lighthouse, The. James McMichael. AmPA
Inland Passages, *sel.* Wendell Berry.
  Long Hunter, The. GP
Inland, within a hollow Vale, I stood. Near Dover, September 1802 [*or* Sonnet: September, 1802 *or* September 1802; Near Dover]. Wordsworth. ChER; EnRP; OAEP
Inn of Care, The. Samuel Waddington. OBVV
Inn of Earth, The. Sara Teasdale. LiTA
Inn of the Silver Moon, The, *sel.* Herman Knickerbocker Viele.
  Good Inn, The. HBV-1
Inn That Missed Its Chance, The. Amos Russel Wells. TrCP
Innate Helium. Robert Frost. ImOP
Inner Brother. Stephen Stepanchev. WaP
Inner-City Lullaby. Russell Atkins. CNA
Inner cry, An. The Wind Carries Me Free. Dennis Shady. LFAC
Inner greet. Greenberg said it. Columbus. Muriel Rukeyser. GOA
Inner Light, The. Frederic William Henry Myers. *Fr.* Saint Paul. HBV-2; WGRP
Inner Man, The. Plato, *tr. fr. Greek.* PoPl
Inner Part, The. Louis Simpson. InPS
Inner Silence, The. Harriet Monroe. HBMV
Inner Temple Masque, The, *sels.* William Browne
  Sirens' Song, The. EtS; NOBE; OBEV; PoPle
    (Song of the Sirens.) ElL
    (Song of the Syrens.) ChTR; OBS
    ("Steer hither, steer your wingèd pines.") ViBoPo
    (Syrens' Song, The.) GBL
  "Son of Erebus and Night." ViBoPo
Inner Vision, The. Wordsworth. GTBS; GTBS-P; HBV-2
    (Most Sweet It Is with Unuplifted Eyes.) EnRP; VLP
Inniskeen Road: July Evening. Patrick Kavanagh. IPY; NoAM; NoP
Innkeeper's Wife, The. Clive Sansom. OBCP
Innocence. George S. Chappell. YaD
Innocence, The. Robert Creeley. NeAP; NoAM
Innocence. Thom Gunn. LiTM; NePoEA-2; NoAM
Innocence. Norman MacCaig. NMP
Innocence. James Scully. LTB
Innocence. Anne Spencer. CDC
Innocence. Thomas Traherne. AnAnS-1
Innocence of her, The. The Innocent Breasts. Joel Oppenheimer. PoM
Innocent, The. Gene Derwood. NePA; WaP
Innocent Breasts, The. Joel Oppenheimer. PoM
Innocent country girl going to town, An. Advice to Country Girls. *Unknown, tr. by* Louis Untermeyer. UnTE
Innocent Country-Maid's Delight, The; or, A Description of the Lives of the Lasses of London. *Unknown.* CoMu
Innocent decision: to enjoy. Triple Feature. Denise Levertov. FF; NoP
Innocent eyes not ours. All Things Wait upon Thee. Christina Rossetti. GN
Innocent Gazer, The. John, Lord Cutts. CavP
Innocent Landscape. Elinor Wylie. OxBA
Innocent Play. Isaac Watts. NOEC
Innocent spirits, bright, immaculate ghosts. From Generation to Generation. William Dean Howells. AA
Innocent Spring, The. Edith Sitwell. *Fr.* The Sleeping Beauty. NOBE
    ("In the great gardens, after bright spring rain.") OxBTC
Innocent, sweet Day is dead, The. Night and Day. Sidney Lanier. AA
Innocents, The. Jay Macpherson. OBCV
Innocent's Song. Charles Causley. GTBS-P; OBCP
Innominatus. Sir Walter Scott. *See* Breathes There the Man.
Innovator, The. Stephen Vincent Benét. EyDe
Innumerable Beauties, thou white haire. Sonnet. Lord Herbert of Cherbury. PoEL-2
Innumerable Christ, The. "Hugh MacDiarmid." EaLo; EBEV; NoP; OxBS
Inordinate Love. *Unknown.* EBEV; MeEL
Inquest, The. W. H. Davies. DTC; GTBS-P; NOBE; OxBTC
Inquietude. Pauli Murray. BlSi
Inquisitive Leopard, The. Oliver Herford. TDH

Inquisitors, The. Robinson Jeffers. MoAmPo
Insatiableness. Thomas Traherne. OxBoCh
Insatiate, The. Johannes Secundus, *tr. fr. Latin by* John Nott. *Fr.* Basia. UnTE
"Insatiate brute, whose teeth abuse. The Small Silver-coloured Bookworm. Thomas Parnell. OnYI
Inscape. Susan Litwack. VWA
Inscribed in Melrose Abbey. *Unknown.* FaBoEE; FaBoRV
Inscribed upon a Rock. Wordsworth. SyP
Inscription: "Eagle, stooping from yon snow-blown peaks, The." Whittier. GOA
Inscription: "For one long term, or e'er her trial came." George Canning *and* John Hookham Frere. FaBoCo; FaBoEE; Par
(Inscription for the Door of the Cell in Newgate Where Mrs. Brownrigg, the 'Prentice-cide, Was Confined Previous to Her Execution.) Par
Inscription, An: "Grass of levity." *Unknown.* EIL
Inscription: "He wrote upon his heart." Donald Jeffrey Hayes. CDC
Inscription: "It is not hard to tell of a rose." Ann Hamilton. HBMV
Inscription, An: "Over the sheer rocks over the gorges." Stanislav Vinaver, *tr. fr. Serbo-Croat by* Vasa D. Mihailovich. VWA
Inscription, The: "Sealed with the seal of Life, thy soul and mine." Elsa Barker. *Fr.* The Spirit and the Bride. HBMV
Inscription: "Whoe'er thou art whose path in summer lies." Mark Akenside. NOEC
Inscription: "Ye powers unseen, to whom the bards of Greece." Mark Akenside. OBEC
Inscription above the Entrance to the Abbey of Theleme. Rabelais, *tr. fr. French by* Sir Thomas Urquhart. *Fr.* Gargantua. FaBoRV
Inscription at Mount Vernon. *Unknown.* OHIP
(Washington.) OFD
Inscription by the Sea, An. E. A. Robinson, *after the Greek of* Glaucus. AWP; ChTr; ELU; FaBoEE
Inscription for a Fountain. "Barry Cornwall." *See* For a Fountain.
Inscription for a Fountain on a Heath. Samuel Taylor Coleridge. OAEP
Inscription for a Grotto. Mark Akenside. NOEC; OBEC; PoEL-3
(For a Grotto.) SeCePo
Inscription for a Headstone. Austin Clarke. BIrV; CIP
Inscription for a Mirror in a Deserted Dwelling. William Rose Benét. MoAmPo
Inscription for a Portrait of Dante. Boccaccio, *tr. fr. Italian by* Dante Gabriel Rossetti. *Fr.* Sonnets. AWP; GoBC (*in* A Tribute to Dante)
Inscription for a Tablet on the Banks of a Stream. Robert Southey. OBEC
Inscription for a Wayside Spring. Frances Cornford. BrRo
Inscription for an Old Bed. William Morris. OBEV; OBVV; WiR
(For the Bed [*or* Beds] at Kelmscott.) FaBoRV; NBM; PoEL-5
(Lines for a Bed at Kelmscott Manor.) CH
Inscription for Arthur Rackham's Rip Van Winkle. James Elroy Flecker. BrPo
Inscription for Marye's Heights, Fredericksburg. Herman Melville. UnPo
Inscription for the Door of the Cell in Newgate Where Mrs. Brownrigg, the 'Prentice-cide, Was Confined Previous to Her Execution. George Canning *and* John Hookham Frere. *See* Inscription: "For one long term, or e'er her trial came."
Inscription for the Entrance to a Wood. Bryant. AmPP; AP; BiP; OxBA; TAP
Inscription for the Sign of *The Jolly Barber,* with a Razor in One Hand, and a Pot of Beer in the Other, *sel.* Swift.
"Roam not from pole to pole, but enter here." FaBoUs
Inscription for the Tank. James Wright. TwCP
Inscription in a Book. Gilean Douglas. AMV-81
Inscription in a Garden. George Gascoigne. OBSC; TrGrPo
Inscription in a Hermitage. Thomas Warton, the Younger. HBV-1
Inscription in a Library. W. G. Wendell. WhC
Inscription on a Chemise. *Unknown, tr. fr. Arabic by* E. Powys Mathers. *Fr.* The Thousand and One Nights. ErPo
Inscription on a Grot. Samuel Rogers. *Fr.* The Pleasures of Memory. OBEC
Inscription on an Ancient Bell. *Unknown, tr. fr. Latin by* Fr. Bridgett. ISi
Inscription on Stone over Shakespeare's Grave. *Unknown.* TreFS
Inscription on the Cross. Bible, *N.T.* St. John, XIX: 19-22. TreFT
Inscription on the Flyleaf of a Bible. Dannie Abse. TrJP
Inscription on the Monument of a Newfoundland Dog. Byron. *See* Epitaph to a Dog.
Inscription on the Tombe of the Lady Mary Wentworth, The. Thomas Carew. *See* Maria Wentworth.
Inscription to Spartans Dead at Thermopylae. Simonides of Ceos. *See* On the Spartan Dead at Thermopylae.
Inscriptions at the City of Brass. *Unknown, tr. fr. Arabic by* E. Powys Mathers. *Fr.* The Thousand and One Nights. AWP; WaaP
Inscriptions for the Caledonian Canal. Robert Southey. NBM
Inscriptions on Greek tombstones intrigued him. Ronald Wyn. Robert Bagg. MP; TwAmPo
Insect is really not built too well, The. Brief Reflection on the Insect. Miroslav Holub, *tr. by* Stuart Friebert *and* Dana Hóbová. SUW
Insect Kitchen, The. Nicki Jackowska. BrRo
Insect or blossom? Fragile, fairy thing. The Mariposa Lily. Ina Coolbrith. AA; BPAW
Insect Shuffle Method, The. Gary Tapp. AMV-80
Insect Wives. Rudolph Altrocchi. WhC
Insects. Isidor Schneider. TrJP
Insects, The. Nancy Willard. LCAP
Insensibility. Wilfred Owen. ChMP; CMoP; FaBoTw; InPS; LiTB; LiTM; MMA; MoAB; OAEP; OBWP; OxBTC; SeCeV; WaP
Inseparable. Philip Bourke Marston. BoLoP
Inseparable from the fire. Coda. William Carlos Williams. NOBA
Inside/ the voices of the boys. Inside, Outside, and Beyond. John Ratti. AMV-80
Inside a cave in a narrow canyon near Tassajara. Hands. Robinson Jeffers. GOA
Inside a Prison Cell at Count Time. Daniel L. Klauck. LFAC
Inside and Out. Robert Phillips. GeTw
Inside Chance, The. Marge Piercy. LTB
Inside every widow. Portrait of a Widow. Avner Strauss. VWA
Inside History. Angela McCabe. AmPA
Inside its zig-zag lines the little camp is asleep. The Magazine Fort, Phoenix Park, Dublin. William Wilkins. SeCePo
Inside many of us. Rumpelstiltskin. Anne Sexton. DFT
Inside my father's close. My Father's Close. *Unknown, tr. by* Dante Gabriel Rossetti. AWP
Inside of a whirlpool, The. Warning. John Ciardi. PDV
Inside of King's College Chapel, Cambridge. Wordsworth. Ecclesiastical Sonnets, XLIII. EnRP; GoBC; OAEP; OBNC; OBRV: OxBoCh
(Within King's College Chapel, Cambridge.) GTBS; GTBS-P
Inside or out, the key is pain. It holds. Hospital. Karl Shapiro. VGW
Inside Out. Diane Wakoski. CoAP; NYBP
Inside, Outside, and Beyond. John Ratti. AMV-80
Inside that figure rides opaque malice. The Picador Bit. Bink Noll. LiSp
Inside the brain they are holding a mass funeral for the dead brain cells. The Brain Cells. Donald Hall. TAP
Inside the Cave. Geoffrey Grigson. FaBoPP
Inside the child. Night Watch. Margo Magid. NMM
Inside the coconut is Katerina's baby. A Coconut for Katerina. Sandra McPherson. FiCP; LCAP
Inside the fog that encloses the trees. Trees Lose Parts of Themselves Inside a Circle of Fog. Francis Ponge, *tr. by* Robert Bly. NU
Inside the light of a three-way lamp. The Fire Burns Low. John Leax. TrCP
Inside the River. James Dickey. PoA
Inside the tower not a broken tower two. Image-Nation (the Poësis). Robin Blaser. PoM
Inside the Tulip. George Bowering. MoCV
Inside the veins there are navies setting forth. Waking from Sleep. Robert Bly. CAPP; EAS; InPS; NoAM; NOBA; NoP
Inside this clay jug there are canyons and pine mountains. The Clay Jug. Kabir, *ad. by* Robert Bly. NU
Inside this green cafeteria, a woman in blue. Sunlight in a Cafeteria. Criss E. Cannady. PoDr
Inside this northern summer's fold. Siena. Swinburne. VLP
Inside this shell. What Is Lived. Carmen Valle, *tr. by* Julio Marzán. InW
Inside this street scene frozen in its frame. West Fifty-seventh Street. Byron Vazakas. FAZ
Insidious Dr. Fu Man Chu, The. Amiri Baraka. CoPo
Insight. Mary Goose. STE
Insight. Lionel Kearns. PeCV
Insights. Catherine Davis. NePoEA; QFR
Insistently through sleep—a tide of voices. The Harbor Dawn. Hart Crane. *Fr.* The Bridge: Powhatan's Daughter. MoPo; NePa; NYP; OxBA
Insomnia. Elizabeth Bishop. LLLT
Insomnia. Ethna MacCarthy. NeIP
Insomnia. Joyce Carol Oates. DFF
Insomnia. Marge Piercy. DFF
Insomnia. John Banister Tabb. TrPWD
Insomnia. Edith M. Thomas. AA
Insomnia, *sel.* Marina Tsvetayeva, *tr. fr.* Russian by Elaine Feinstein *and* Angela Livingstone.
"Black as the centre of an eye, the centre, a blackness." PBWP
Insomnia. Elizabeth Zelvin. AMV-80
Insomnia the Gem of the Ocean. John Updike. DFF; QQQ
Insomniac Poem. Ron Loewinsohn. NeAP
Insomniac Sleeps Well for Once and, The. Hayden Carruth. NNaP
Insomniacs, The. Adrienne Rich. NYBP
Insomuch, Bassa, as I never saw. Epigram. Martial. PeHV
Inspection. Wilfred Owen. WaP
Inspection, The. Frederick B. Watt. CaP

Inspector of stairs is on the stairs. Walk-up. W. W. Merwin. CoPo
Inspiration. Mary Fullerton. PoAu-1
Inspiration. W. W. Gibson. WGRP
Inspiration. Samuel Johnson. AA; HBV-2; TrPWD; WGRP
(Life of Ages, Richly Poured, *with music.*) AH
Inspiration. E. V. Knox. CenHV
Inspiration, The. James Montgomery. *Fr.* The West Indies. PAH
Inspiration. Robert W. Service. WeW
Inspiration. John Banister Tabb. WGRP
Inspiration. Henry David Thoreau. AmPP; AA; AP; BLPL; EBCP; FaBoBe; HBV-2; NOBA; OxBA
"If with light head erect I sing," *br. sel.* WGRP
Inspiration. *Unknown, tr. by* J. Rendel Harris. *Fr.* Solomon, VI. WGRP
Inspiration, An. Ella Wheeler Wilcox. WGRP
Inspirations. William James Dawson. WGRP
Inspire our sons to seek their man-shadows. If We Cannot Live People as People. Charles Lynch. CNA; PoBA
Inst., Ult., and Prox. A. P. Herbert. FaBoUs
Instalment, The, *sel.* Edward Young.
"Since Brunswick's smile has authoris'd my muse." FaBoCo
Instamatic. Edwin Morgan. FF
Instance, An. Alastair Reid. PP
Instans Tyrannus. Robert Browning. EBEV
Instant released, it spins, The. Playing Catch. Keith Moul. AMV-80
Instant splendour, the swung bells that speak, The. Prothalamion. Terence Tiller. NeBP
Instantaneous ("Instantaneously!"). Vivian Ayers. NNP
Instead of a Journey. Michael Hamburger. NYBP
Instead of being sad and hurt. Forbearance. Della Adams Leitner. STF
Instead of blushing cherry hue. Allan M. Laing. PV
Instead of cabbage, acorns boil to-morrow. Hangover Cure. Nicochares. FaBoUs
Instead of Features. Jim Moore. PoDr
Instead of Incense (Blessed Lord) if wee. Nathaniel Wanley. *Fr.* Royal Presents. TrPWD
Instead of loving your enemies, treat your friends a little better. Ed Howe. YaD
Instead of Neat Inclosures. Robert Herrick. *Fr.* An Ode of the Birth of Our Saviour. ChTr
Instead of the Puritans landing on Plymouth Rock. Thoughts for St. Stephen. Christopher Morley. ShM; WhC
Instead of you, I choose the blood. The Unwanted. Mary Gordon. IHMS
Instinctively, unwittingly. Love Poem. Janet Lewis. QFR
Instructed in love. Ingeborg Bachmann, *tr. fr. German by* Daniel Huws. *Fr.* Songs in Flight. WPOW
Instruction from Bly. Cynthia Macdonald. NMM
Instruction Manual, The. John Ashbery. HAP; NeAP; NoAM; NOBA; PoM; SOTW; WeW
Instruction sore long time I bore. Charles Kingsley. CenHV
Instructions. Anita Skeen. IHMS
Instructions for a Park. Brad Walker. AMV-80; AMV-81
Instructions for Crossing the Border. Dan Pagis, *tr. fr. Hebrew by* Stephen Mitchell. VWA
Instructions for the Messiah. Myra Sklarew. VWA
Instructions of King Cormac, The, *sel.* *Unknown, tr. fr. Irish by* Kuno Meyer.
" 'O Cormac, grandson of Conn,' said Carbery." BIrV
Instructions to a Celebrated Laureat, *sel.* "Peter Pindar."
George III Visits Whitbread's Brewery. NOEC
Instructions to a Painter. Edmund Waller. APAS
Instructions to a Princess. Ishmael Reed. CNA; PoBA
Instructor said, The. Theme for English B. Langston Hughes. BALP; NoAM; NOBA; NoP
Instrument, The. Kathleen Raine. PoA
Instruments, The. Christopher Smart. WiR
Insufficient Vengeance. Martial, *tr. fr. Latin by* Louis Untermeyer. UnTE
Insular Celts, The. Ciaran Carson. BIrV; CIP, *revised version*
Insult, The. Robert Layzer. NePoEA
Insulting Beauty. Earl of Rochester. CavP
Insured for every accident. Epitaph. Richard Armour. ShM
Insusceptibles, The. Adrienne Rich. ConAP; HeIP; InPK
Intaglio. Henri Coulette. NePoEA; PoCh
Integer Vitae. Thomas Campion. *See* Man of Life Upright.
Intellect. Emerson. GLGT
Intellect of man is forced to choose, The. The Choice. W. B. Yeats. CMoP; NoAM; OxBTC
Intellectual, The. Karl Shapiro. CMoP
Intellectuals, The. Dudley Randall. PoBA
Intelligent Sheepman and the New Cars, The. William Carlos Williams. NePoAm-2; OBAL
Intend the impossible, he sd. Conversations from the Nightmare. Carol Lee Sanchez. TWSS
Intended for Sir Isaac Newton. Pope. InPK; OAEP; WeW
(Epitaph.) SeCeV; TreFT
(Epitaph Intended for Sir Isaac Newton.) FaBoEn; ImOP
(Epitaph on Sir Isaac Newton.) FiP; ViBoPo
("Nature, and Nature's laws, lay hid in night.") FaBoCo; FaBoEE; QQQ
Intense and terrible beauty, how has our race with the frail naked nerves. Gale in April. Robinson Jeffers. MoAB; MoAmPo
Intention to Escape from Him. Edna St. Vincent Millay. SBG
Inter, mitzy, titzy, tool. *Unknown.* OxNR
Inter Sodales. W. E. Henley. HBV-2
Intercession in Late October. Robert Graves. MoAB
Intercessor, An. *Unknown.* STF
Intercessors. Austin Clarke. CMoP; NMP
Interests of a black man in a cellar, The. Black Tambourine. Hart Crane. AP; CoBMV; NoAM; OxBA; PPP; TAP
Interim. Clarissa Scott Delany. CDC; PoNe
Interim. Frank Ormsby. CIP
Interior. Padraic Colum. MoBrPo
Interior. W. E. Henley. In Hospital, III. BrPo
Interior. Joseph Milbauer, *tr. fr. French by* Edouard Roditi. VWA
Interior. Dorothy Parker. SBG
Interior Landscape. Gloria Fuertes, *tr. fr. Spanish by* Willis Barnstone. BoWoP
Interior Monologue 666. Tom Marshall. NOBC
Interior with Mme. Vuillard and Son. Kathleen Fraser. NPGG
Interlude, An. John Peale Bishop. LiTA
Interlude, An. Robert Duncan. CMoP
Interlude. W. E. Henley. In Hospital, XVII. BrPo
Interlude. Walter Savage Landor. GTBS-P
Interlude. Theodore Roethke. MiAP
Interlude. Karl Shapiro. DFF; MoVE
Interlude. Edith Sitwell. MoAB; MoBrPo
Interlude. Welton Smith. PoBA
Interlude, An. Swinburne. ViBoPo
Interlude. Ella Wheeler Wilcox. HBV-2
(Growing Old.) BLPA; FPL
Interlude: The Casement. Christopher Brennan. PoAu-1
Intermezzo. Robert Silliman Hillyer. NePoAm
Intermezzo for the Fourth Act, An. William Allen White. InMe
Intermezzo: Pastoral, *sel.* Arthur Symons.
At Glan-y-Wern, IV. VLP
Interminable ocean lay beneath, The. Sunrise at Sea. Edwin Atherstone. EtS
Intermission, Please! Irwin Edman. WhC
Internal Cerberus, whose griping fangs. Conscience. Sir Edward Sherburne. ACP
Internal Firesides. Mathilde Blind. FM
Internal Injuries. Robert Penn Warren. NYP
International Brigade Arrives at Madrid, The. Pablo Neruda, *tr. fr. Spanish by* Angel Flores. WaaP
International Brigade Dead. Thomas O'Brien. NeIP
International Chainpoem. *Unknown.* EAS
International Conference. Colin Ellis. FaBoEE
International Copyright. James Russell Lowell. *See* Stealing.
International Episode, An. Caroline Duer. AA; PAH
International Hymn. George Huntington. PoLF
International Motherhood Assoc. M. L. Hester. AMV-81
Internationale, The. Eugene Potter *and* Pierre Degeyter. FSW
Interplanetary Limericks. Al Graham. QQQ
Interpreter, The. Orrick Johns. HBMV
Interpreters, The. D. J. Enright. PP
Interpreters, The. Swinburne. PoEL-5
Interracial. Georgia Douglas Johnson. PoNe; TTY
Interred [*or* Interr'd] beneath this marble stone. An Epitaph. Matthew Prior. FaBoEE; OAEL-1; OBEC; OBSV; PoEL-3
Interrogation, The. Edwin Muir. CMoP; LiTB; SeCePo
Interrogations, The. Michael Knoll. LFAC
Interrogator, The. Elizabeth Jennings. WPE
Interrupted, The. Josephine Jacobsen. GP
Interrupted Romance. *Unknown, tr. fr. Russian by* Louis Untermeyer. UnTE
Interruption. Robert Graves. LiTB; LiTM
Intersection. Florence Dolgorukov. AMV-80
Interval. Joseph Auslander. FYAP
Interval with Fire. Dorothy Livesay. CaP
Intervals. Beatrice Ravenel. HBMV
Interview, An. Philip Brasfield. LFAC
Interview, An. K. W. Grandsen. OxBTC
Interview. Sara Henderson Hay. DFT; OBCA
Interview. Laurence Lieberman. AMV-81
Interview. Dorothy Parker. *Fr.* Some Beautiful Letters. InMe

Interview near Florence, An. Samuel Rogers. *Fr.* Italy. OBNC
Interview with a Tourist. Margaret Atwood. IHMS
Interview with Doctor Drink. J. V. Cunningham. NMP; TW; VGW
Intery, mintery, cutery corn. Mother Goose. OxNR; TiPo
Intil the pit-mirk nicht we northwart sail. Arctic Convoy. J. K. Annand. OxBS
Intimacy. Al Young. NPGG
Intimate Associations. Baudelaire, *tr. fr. French by* Robert Bly. NU
Intimate friend of the Czar was I, An. Shootin' with Rasputin. *Unknown.* FSW
Intimate Parnassus. Patrick Kavanagh. MoBrPo
Intimate Supper. Peter Redgrove. FaBoMo; OxBC
Intimates. D. H. Lawrence. BoLoP
Intimations. Alma Johanna Koenig, *tr. fr. German by* Edouard Roditi. VWA
Intimations of Immortality. Wordsworth. *See* Ode: Intimations of Immortality. . .
Intimations of Mortality. Stanley Kunitz. MoAmPo
Intimations of Sublimity. Wordsworth. *Fr.* The Prelude, II. OBNC
Into a forest. Otsuji, *tr. fr. Japanese by* Harry Behn. WSC
Into a gentle wildness and confusion. Sea Side. Robert Graves. MoPo
Into a little close of mine I went Two Lyrics, I. Lorenzo de' Medici, *tr. by* John Addington Symonds. AWP
Into a sweet May morning. John of Hazelgreen. *Unknown.* BaBo; ESPB; ViBoFo
Into a ward of the whitewashed walls. Somebody's Darling. Marie La Coste. BLPA; HBV-2; TreF; UnPo; WBLP
Into a world where children shriek like suns. On a Child Who Lived One Minute. X. J. Kennedy. DFF; HoAn; HoPM; NYBP
Into & At. Edmund Pennant. SOTS
Into azure cloudland searching. To My Distant Beloved. Alois Jeitteles, *tr. by* the Reverend Dr. Troutbeck. TrJP
Into Battle. Julian Grenfell. FaPoR; HBV-2; LoBV; MMA; OBEV; OBMV; OBWP; OxBTC; WaaP
Into Blackness Softly. Mari Evans. PoBA
Into Hell's cave stepped a new guest. Arrival in Hell. Ricarda Huch, *tr. by* Susan C. Strong. PBWP
Into her mother's bedroom to wash the ballooning body. Jessie Mitchell's Mother. Gwendolyn Brooks. BoWoP; NAs; NMM
Into love and out again. Theory. Dorothy Parker. SBG
Into my empty head there come. Morning Swim. Maxine W. Kumin. LiSp; WPE
Into my eyes he loving looked. The Mirror. Judah Halevi, *tr. by* Emma Lazarus. TrJP
Into My Heart an Air That Kills. A. E. Housman. A Shropshire Lad, XL. ChTr; CMoP; EBEV; EvOK; GoJo; LiTB; LiTM; MasP; MoAB; MoBrPo; NoAM; NOBE; OAEL-2; OAEP; OxBTC; POL; ViBoPo
(Yon Far Country.) SeCePo
Into my heart's treasury. The Coin. Sara Teasdale. HBMV; TiPo
Into my room to-night came June. June Night. Hazel Hall. HBMV
Into our empty room. Their Party, Our House. Jon Swan. NYBP
Into Slumbers. John Fletcher. *See* Care-charming Sleep.
Into Suburbia between eight and nine. Three-handed Fugue. Phyllis Gotlieb. NOBC
Into that pit. Burning Shit at An Khe. Bruce Weigl. MAYP
Into that pit when I did enter in. Elizabeth Melvill, Lady Culross. *Fr.* A Godly Dream. WPE
Into the bit-flaked sugar-snow. Maple Feast. Frances Frost. RHPC
Into the Book. Martin Grossman. VWA
Into the bosom of the one great sea. The Unity of God. Panatattu. WGRP
Into the caverns of the sea. Joy Enough. Barrett Eastman. AA
"Into the core of Nature." True Enough: To the Physicist (1820). Goethe, *tr. by* Michael Hamburger. SUW
Into the crucible of life. Onwardness. Doris Hedges. CaP
Into the Dark. Paul Monette. AmPA
Into the Devil tavern. The Three Troopers. George Walter Thornbury. BeLS; HBV-2
Into the dusk and snow. A Traveller. *Unknown.* WGRP
Into the endless dark. City Lights. Rachel Field. FaPON; PDV; RHPC
Into the fire. Goat-Woman Dares. Judith Mountain Leaf Volborth. TWSS
Into the frenzy of falling bodies. Buster Keaton. Michael McFee. AMV-81
Into the furnace let me go alone. Baptism. Claude McKay. PoNe
Into the Future. Harold Witt. SOTS
Into the Glacier. John Haines. CoAP
Into the gray March light. March Light. Ralph J. Mills, Jr. AMV-81
Into the inmost temple thus I came. The Temple of Venus. Spenser. *Fr.* The Faerie Queene, IV, 10. WHA
Into the lonely park all frozen fast. Colloque Sentimental [*or* Sentimental Conversation]. Paul Verlaine, *tr. by* Ernest Dowson. BrPo; SyP
Into the night. The Inland Lighthouse. James McMichael. AmPA
Into the Noiseless Country. Thomas William Parsons. AA
Into the pool of silence our tears made. The Ancient Couple on Lu Mountain. Mark Van Doren. VGW
Into the quiet of this room. The Room. William Soutar. EBEV
Into the Salient. Edmund Blunden. ViBoPo
Into the scented woods we'll go. Green Rain. Mary Webb. BoNaP; CH; FaPON
Into the shadow Kunai-mai-pa Mo. Kunai-mai-pa Mo. Ethel Anderson. PoAu-2
Into the Silent Land! Song of the Silent Land. Johann Gaudenz von Salis-Seewis, *tr. by* Longfellow. AWP; HBV-2
Into the silent places. The Old Year and the New. Annie Johnson Flint. BLRP
Into the silver night. Revelation. Sir Edmund Gosse. OBEV
Into the skies, one summer's day. The Thought. William Brighty Rands. OBEV; OBVV
Into the slain tons of needles. By Canoe through the Fir Forest. James Dickey. NYBP
Into the sunshine. The Fountain. James Russell Lowell. OBCA
Into the thick of the fight he went, pallid and sick and wan. Wheeler at Santiago. James Lindsay Gordon. PAH
Into the topaz the crystalline signals. Towards a City That Sings. June Jordan. NYP
Into the town of Conemaugh. The Man Who Rode to Conemaugh. John Eliot Bowen. PAH
Into the Twilight. W. B. Yeats. HBV-2
Into the west of the waters on the living ocean's foam. Homeward Bound. George Edward Woodberry. Wild Eden, XXV. AA
Into the Wind. Winfield Townley Scott. NMP
Into the Woods My Master Went. Sidney Lanier. *See* Ballad of Trees and the Master, A.
Into the World and Out ("Into the world he looked with sweet surprise"). Sarah M. B. Piatt. HBV-1
Into Their True Gentleness. Pearse Hutchinson. CIP
Into these loves, who but for passion looks [*or* lookes]. To the Reader of These Sonnets. Michael Drayton. Idea, *introd.* AAS; EnRePo; HBV-1; NoP; ViBoPo
Into thir inmost bower. Milton. *Fr.* Paradise Lost, IV. FF
Into what fictive worlds can imagination. The Horatians. W. H. Auden. NYBP
Into whose ear the deeds are spoken. The only. History. Jorie Graham. NPGG
Into your arms I came. To the Anxious Mother. Valente Malangatana, *tr. by* Dorothy Guedes *and* Philippa Rumsey. PBA
Intolerably sad, profound. Before the Anæsthetic; or, A Real Fright. John Betjeman. EBCP; SeCePo
Intoxicated Rat, The. *Unknown.* FSW
Intramural Aestivation, or Summer in Town, by a Teacher of Latin. Oliver Wendell Holmes. *See* Aestivation.
Intra-Political. Margaret Avison. MoCV
Intreat [*or* Entreat] Me Not to Leave Thee. Bible, *O.T.* Ruth, I: 16-17. TreF; TRV
("And Ruth said, Intreat me not to leave thee.") FF; Lo; PoPl
(Ruth to Naomi.) TrGrPo
Intrepid Ricardo, The. E. C. Bentley. *Fr.* Clerihews. CenHV
Intro, The. C. J. Dennis. WhC
Introducing a Madman. Keith Waldrop. TW
Introduction, The: "Did I, my lines intend for publick view." Countess of Winchilsea. SBG; WPOW
Introduction: "Hear the voice of the bard!" Blake. *See* Hear the Voice of the Bard.
Introduction: "I bespeak words." Clere Parsons. FaBoTw
Introduction, An: "I don't know politics but I know the names." Kamala Das. WPOW
Introduction: "Piping down the valleys wild." Blake. *See* Piping Down the Valleys Wild.
Introduction: "Romance, who loves to nod and sing." Poe. *See* Romance.
Introduction: "Should you ask me, whence these stories?" Longfellow. *Fr.* The Song of Hiawatha. NOBA
Introduction: " 'Twas late in my long journey, when I had clomb to where." Robert Bridges. *Fr.* The Testament of Beauty. MoVE
Introduction and Anecdotes. "Peter Pindar." *Fr.* Bozzy and Piozzi. PoEL-3
Introduction—Childhood and School-Time. Wordsworth. *See* On the Solitary Fells.
Introduction of a refrain, The. 'Twixt Cup and Lip. Mark Hollis. FiBHP
Introduction of the Shopping Cart. Gerald Costanzo. MAYP
Introduction to Dogs, An. Ogden Nash. MoShBr
Introduction to the Man of Law's Prologue. Chaucer. *Fr.* The Canterbury Tales. FiP
Introspective Reflection. Ogden Nash. WhC

Introversion. Evelyn Underhill. WGRP
Intruder. Susan Feldman. AmPA
Intruder, The. Carolyn Kizer. BoWoP; GP; NePoEA-2
Intruder, The. James Reeves. OnUR; PDV
Intruder, The. Marya Zaturenska. OLR
Intuition. Anthony Delius. PeSA
Intuitive guilt and the sun's harsh light. On the Seventh Anniversary of the Death of My Father. Robert Pack. NePoEA
Inundation, The. Howard Sergeant. EAS
Invaders, The. John Haines. TAT
Invalid. Audrey McGaffin. NePoAm-2
Invariably when wine redeems the sight. The Wine Menagerie. Hart Crane. AP; NoAM; NOBA; OxBA; VGW
Invasion Exercise on the Poultry Farm. John Betjeman. NOBL
Invasion from Dutchland is all the discourse, An. All Shams. *Unknown.* APAS
Invasion North. Richard Hugo. GP
Invasion on the Farm. R. S. Thomas. POL
Invasion Song. *Unknown.* PoOW
Invasion Weather. Douglas Newton. NeBP
Invective against Ibis, *sel* Ovid, *tr. fr. Latin by* Thomas Underdowne.
"While Thracians shal with arrowes war, Iaziges with bowe." OBVE
Invective against the Wicked of the World, An, *sel.* Nicholas Breton.
"Let but a fellow in a fox-furred gown." ViBoPo
Invented a Person. Lenore G. Marshall. GoYe
Inventing a Family. Dennis Saleh. *Fr.* A Guide to Familiar American Incest. NeAC
Inventing a story with grass. A Birth. James Dickey. NOBA
Invention. Sir William Watson. HBV-2
Invention begs from door to door in the indescribable darkness. Kissing Natalia. Eldon Grier. NOBC
Invention of Astronomy, The. William Matthews. POL
Invention of Comics, The. Amiri Baraka. AmNP; CAPP; LiTM; PoBA
Invention of Fire, The. Andrew Taylor. CBAP
Invention of New Jersey, The. Jack Anderson. InPS; TAT; TW
Invention of the Telephone, The. Peter Klappert. AmPA; PPJ
Invention of Zero, The. Constance Urdang. VWA
Inventions. Samuel Butler. PV
Inventor of the geodesic domes. Air. Philip Dow. BXAP
Inventor's Wife, The. E. R. Corbett. PoLF
Inventory, in Answer to the Usual Mandate Sent by a Surveyor of the Taxes, Requiring a Return of the Number of Horses, Servants, Carriages, etc., Kept, The. Burns. FaBoUs
Inventory of the Furniture of a Collegian's Chamber, An. John Winstanley. OBSV
Inverberg. J. F. Hendry. NeBP
Inverey cam doun Deeside, whistlin and playin. The Baron of Brackley. *Unknown.* ESPB
Inverse Ratio. *Unknown.* WhC
Inversnaid. Gerard Manley Hopkins. ACP; BLPL; BrPo; CABA; CMoP; FaBoPP; GTBS-P; InPK; LiTB; LiTM; LoBV; MoAB; MoBrPo; NoAM; OAEL-2; PoRA; PoSH; UnPo
Inverted exclamation point. The Heart Mountain Japanese Relocation Camp: 30 Years Later. Charles Levendosky. TAT
Inverted Torch, The, *sels.* Edith M. Thomas. AA
If Still They Live.
Tell Me.
When in the First Great Hour.
Will It Be So?
Investigation. Julia Vinograd. IHMS
Investigator. Miriam Waddington. CaP
Investiture, The. Siegfried Sassoon. NoAM
Investment, The. Robert Frost. CMoP; OxBA
Investor's Soliloquy. Kenneth Ward. FaFP; FPL
Invictus. W. E. Henley. Echoes IV. BLPA; FaBoBe; FaBV; FaFP; FaPo; FaPoR; FPL; HBV-2; HBVY; HoPM; LiTB; MoBrPo; OBEV; OBMV; OBVV; OHFP; PoPl; TEP; TreF; TrGrPo; WGRP; WHA
(Echoes.) LoBV
(I. M.—R. T. Hamilton Bruce.) ViBoPo; VLP
("Out of the night that covers me.") NOBE; OBNC
Inviolable. Daniel Hoffman. GrPl
Invisible, The. Richard Watson Gilder. WGRP
Invisible Bride, The. Edwin Markham. HBV-1
Invisible Bridge, The. Gelett Burgess. NA; TreFT
Invisible hand, An. Sierra. Alfonsina Storni, *tr. by* Rachel Benson. PBWP
Invisible, indivisible spirit. Hilda Doolittle ("H. D."). *Fr.* Tribute to the Angels. BoWoP
Invisible King, The. Goethe. *See* Erl-King, The.
Invisible Landscape. Charles Wright. LCAP
Invisible Man, The. T. S. Matthews. POL
Invisible Playmate, The. Margaret Widdemer. FaPON
Invisible Trumpets Blowing. E. J. Pratt. *Fr.* Brébeuf and His Brethren. CaP
Invisible Woman, The. Robin Morgan. IHMS; NMM
Invitation. Harry Behn. FaPON; SoPo
Invitation. Victor Contoski. PV
Invitation, The. George Herbert. AnAnS-1
Invitation, The. Robert Herrick. CaPo; OAEP
Invitation. Solomon ibn Gabirol, *tr. fr. Hebrew by* Israel Zangwill. TrJP
Invitation, The. Donagh MacDonagh. OnYI
Invitation. *Malay Oral Tradition, tr. by* R. J. Wilkinson *and* R. O. Winstedt. WTO
Invitation, The. Shelley. GTBS; GTBS-P; OBEV
(Invitation, to Jane, The.) CH
(To Jane: The Invitation.) HBV-1; OBRV; SeCeV
Invitation, The. *Unknown.* OxBoCh
Invitation, The. Leonard Welsted. NOEC
Invitation au Festin. Aelfrida Tillyard. SUMH
Invitation of the Mirrors. Tom McKeown. AMV-81
Invitation Standing. Paul Blackburn. VGW
Invitation to a Mistress. *Unknown, tr. fr. Latin by* George F. Whicher. UnTE
Invitation to a Spirit. *Malay Oral Tradition, tr. by* W. W. Skeat. WTO
Invitation to an Invitation, An. Catullus, *tr. fr. Latin by* Gardner E. Lewis. ErPo
Invitation to Dalliance. *Unknown.* FaBoEE
Invitation to Eternity. John Clare. NCEP; PoEL-4
(Invite to Eternity.) NBM; OAEL-2; OBNC
Invitation to Hsiao Ch'u-shih. Po Chü-i, *tr. fr. Chinese by* Arthur Waley. OBVE
Invitation, to Jane, The. Shelley. *See* Invitation, The.
Invitation to Juno. William Empson. CMoP; FaBoMo
Invitation to Lubberland, An. *Unknown.* FaBoNo; GBP
Invitation to Madison County, An. Jay Wright. PoBA
Invitation to Miss Marianne Moore. Elizabeth Bishop. MoVE; TwAmPo
Invitation to the Bee. Charlotte Smith. OxBChV
Invitation to the Dance. Sidonius Apollinaris, *tr. fr. Latin by* Howard Mumford Jones. AWP
Invitation to the Dance. *Unknown, tr. fr. Latin by* John Addington Symonds. UnTE
Invitation (To the Night and All Other Things Dark). Ronda Davis. JB
Invitation to the Voyage. Baudelaire, *tr. fr. French by* Richard Wilbur. NAWM-2
Invitation to the Zoological Gardens, An. *Unknown.* BoAnP
Invitation to Youth. *Unknown, tr. fr. Latin by* John Addington Symonds. UnTE
Invite to Eternity, An. John Clare. *See* Invitation to Eternity.
Invited guests in silent order sat, Th'. Animal Magnetism; the Pseudo-Philosopher Baffled. Laurence Hynes Halloran. NOEC
Invites His Nymph to His Cottage. Philip Ayres. EnLoPo
Inviting a Friend to Supper. Ben Jonson, *after the Latin of Martial.* AnAnS-2; AWP; BiP; EnRePo; JCP; LiTB; LoBV; NIP; NOBE; NoP; OAEL-1; OAEP; OBS; OxBoli; PAI; PoEL-2; PPP; SeCP; SeCV-1
Invocatio ad Mariam. Chaucer, *mod. vers. by* Frank Ernest Hill. *Fr.* The Canterbury Tales: The Prologue to the Second Nun's Tale. ISi
Invocation: "American muse, whose strong and diverse heart." Stephen Vincent Benét. *Fr.* John Brown's Body. AmFN; CrMA
(American Muse.) PAL
Invocation: "Appear, O Mother, was the perpetual cry." Wilfred Watson. MoCV
Invocation: "As pools beneath stone arches take." John Drinkwater. HBMV; PoA
Invocation: "Bob Southey! You're a poet—Poet-Laureate." Byron. *See* Dedication: "Bob Southey! . . ."
Invocation: "Come down from heaven to meet me when my breath." Siegfried Sassoon. MoBrPo
Invocation: "Come from thy palace, beauteous Queen of Greece." Thomas Randolph. MOON
Invocation: "Come, lovely Muse, desert for me." Samuel Hoffenstein. BXAP
Invocation: "Dolphin plunge, fountain play." Louis MacNeice. SO
Invocation: "Earth, ocean, air, beloved brotherhood !" Shelley. *Fr.* Alastor. WHA
Invocation: "Empty my heart, Lord, of daily vices." Theodore Spencer. TrPWD
Invocation: "Eternal God omnipotent! The One." Caelius Sedulius, *tr. fr. Latin by* George Sigerson. *Fr.* Carmen Paschale. OnYI
Invocation: "Good morning to you, Lord of the world!" Levi Isaac of Berditshev, *tr. fr. Hebrew by* Olga Marx. EaLo
Invocation: "Great-hearted Christ, importunate and mild." Chad Walsh. *Fr.* The Psalm of Christ. TrCP
Invocation, An: "Hear, sweet Spirit, hear the Spell." Samuel Taylor Coleridge. *See* Voice Sings, A.

Invocation, An: "I never prayed for Dryads, to haunt the woods again." William Johnson Cory. HBV-2; OBVV
Invocation: "Land earth-root." Nakasuk, *tr. fr. Eskimo.* WTO
Invocation: "Let me be buried in the rain." Helene Johnson. AmNP; BANP; PoNe
Invocation: "Maidens young and virgins tender." Horace, *tr. fr. Latin by* Louis Untermeyer. Odes, I, 21. AWP
Invocation: "Mother of God, mother of man reborn." Arthur J. Little. *Fr.* Christ Unconquered. ISi
Invocation: "O mother-maid! O maiden mother free! Chaucer, *mod. vers. by* Frank Ernest Hill. *Fr.* The Canterbury Tales: The Prologue of the Prioress's Tale. ISi
(Two Invocations of the Virgin, II.) ACP
Invocation: "O Thou whose equal purpose runs." Wendell Phillips Stafford. TrPWD
Invocation: "Of mans first disobedience, and the fruit." Milton. *See* Invocation to the Heavenly Muse.
Invocation: "Phoebus, arise!" William Drummond of Hawthornden. *See* Phoebus Arise.
Invocation: "Rarely, rarely, comest thou." Shelley. See Song: "Rarely, rarely comest thou."
Invocation: "Senator Smoot (Republican, Ut.)." Ogden Nash. OBAL
Invocation: "Silent, about-to-be-parted-from house." Denise Levertov. PoA
Invocation: "Ten bloody years with this quill lying." Valentin Iremonger. BIrV
Invocation: "There is no balm on earth." Gilbert Thomas. TrPWD
Invocation: "Thou,whose endearing hand once laid in sooth." Edmund Clarence Stedman. AA
Invocation, An: "To God, the everlasting, who abides." John Addington Symonds. WGRP
"O God, unknown, invisible, secure," *sel.* TrPWD; TRV
Invocation: "Truth, be more precious to me than the eyes." Max Eastman. WGRP
Invocation: "Unwinding the spool of the morning." Vassar Miller. NCSH
Invocation and Prelude. Stefan George, *tr. fr. German by* Ludwig Lewisohn. AWP
Invocation before the Rice Harvest. *Malay Oral Tradition, tr. by* R. O. Winstedt. WTO
Invocation for a Storm. *Tr. fr. Hawaiian.* WTO
Invocation for the New Year. Margaret D. Armstrong. STF
Invocation from a Lawn Chair. Mary Jane Irion. AMV-80
Invocation of Comus, The. Milton. *See* Star That Bids the Shepherd Fold, The.
Invocation of Death. Kathleen Raine. *See* Two Invocations of Death.
Invocation to Fancy. Jospeh Warton. *Fr.* Ode to Fancy. OBEC
Invocation to Ireland. *At. to* Amergin, *tr. fr. Old Irish by* R. A. S. Macalister *and* Eoin MacNeill. OnYI
(Aimirgin's Invocation.) AnIV
Invocation to Rain in Summer. William C. Bennett. GN
(Summer Invocation.) HBV-1
Invocation to Sappho. Elsa Gidlow. IHMS
Invocation to Sleep. John Fletcher. *See* Care-charming Sleep.
Invocation to the Faerie Queene. Spenser. *See* Legend of the Knight of the Red Crosse, or of Holinesse, The.
Invocation to the Genius of Greece. Mark Akenside. *Fr.* The Pleasures of Imagination, I. OBEC
Invocation to the Goddess, An. David Wright. NMP; NoAM
Invocation to the Heavenly Muse. Milton. *Fr.* Paradise Lost, I. TreFS
(Invocation: "Of Man's first disobedience, and the fruit.") FaBoEn; POEL-3
(Of Man's First Disobedience.) FiP
("Of Man's first disobedience, and the fruit.") EBEV; FaBoRV; NIP; NoP; OAEL-1; OAEP; SCV; TEP
Invocation to the Muse. Richard Hughes. MoBrPo
Invocation to the Social Muse. Archibald MacLeish. LiTM
Invocation to Urania. Milton. *Fr.* Paradise Lost, VII. FiP; OBS
("Descend from heav'n Urania, by that name.") EBEV
Invocation to Youth. Laurence Binyon. OBEV; OBVV
Invoice, The. Robert Creeley. VGW
Inward Conversation. Baudelaire, *tr. fr. French by* Robert Bly. InPK
Inward Light, The. Henry Septimus Sutton. WGRP
Inward Morning, The. Henry David Thoreau. AmPP; AP
Io. James Shirley. *See* Piping Peace.
Io dwelt within the breathing-space of immensity. Chant to Io. Tiwai Paraone, *tr. by* A. Alpers. WTO
Io! Paean! Io! sing. Triumph of the Whale. Charles Lamb. EtS; ImOP; OBRV
Io Victis. William Wetmore Story. AA; HBV-2; WGRP
Iöas' Epitaph. William Drummond of Hawthornden. PoEL-2
Iolanthe, *sels.* W. S. Gilbert.
Contemplative Sentry, The. FiBHP
House of Peers, The. InMe
(House of Lords, The.) TrGrPo
Nightmare. NOBL; OxBoLi; PoRA
(Chancellor's Nightmare, The.) FaBoNo
(Lord Chancellor's Song.) NBM
("When you're lying awake with a dismal headache.") NoP
Iona. Arthur Cleveland Coxe. AA
Iona. Frederick Tennyson. GoBC
Iona; the Graves of the Kings. Robinson Jeffers. PrIm
Iowa. Michael Dennis Browne. NYBP
Iowa, June. Michael Dennis Browne. AmPA
Iowa Land. Marvin Bell. SaC
Ipecacuanha. George Canning. ChTr; FaBoNo
Iphigeneia and Agamemnon ("Iphigeneia, when she heard her doom"). Walter Savage Landor. *Fr.* The Hellenics. BeLS; EnRP
Iphigenia [*or* Iphigeneia] in Aulis, *sels.* Euripides, *tr. fr. Greek.*
Aftermath, The, *tr. by* Richmond Lattimore. WaaP
Chorus: "And Pergamos,/ City of the Phrygians," *tr. by* Hilda Doolittle ("H. D"). AWP; OBVE
Iphione. Thomas Caulfield Irwin. EnLoPo
Ipomadon, *sel. Unknown.*
Ipomadon Plays the Fool at Court. OxBM
Ipsa Quae. Nicholas Breton. *See* Pastoral, A: "On a hill there grows a flower."
Ipsey Wipsey spider. *Unknown.* OxNR
IpsofactopaperAnswerallquesti. Headrock. Brian Coffey. CIP
Ipswich Bar. Esther Willard Bates *and* Brainard L. Bates. HBMV
Iram indeed is gone with all his rose. Omar Khayyám, *tr. by* Edward Fitzgerald. *Fr.* The Rubáiyát. OBVE
Irapuato. Earle Birney. NIP; PeCV
Ireland. Stephen Lucius Gwynn. HBV-2
Ireland. John Hewitt. CIP; FaBoPP
Ireland. Lionel Johnson. HBV-2
Ireland. Walter Savage Landor. *See* Ireland Never Was Contented.
Ireland. John James Piatt. AA
Ireland. Richard Ryan. CIP
Ireland. Dora Sigerson Shorter. OBEV; OBVV; OxBI
Ireland. Francis Stuart. NeIP
Ireland, Ireland. Sir Henry Newbolt. FaPoR
Ireland Lake. Robert Hershon. NeAC
Ireland Never Was Contented. Walter Savage Landor. FaBoCo; FaBoEE; OxBoLi
(Ireland.) GTBS-P
Ireland, O Ireland, center of my longings. Ireland. Stephen Lucius Gwynn. HBV-2
Ireland was never contented. Ireland. Walter Savage Landor. GTBS-P
Ireland Weeping. William Livingston, *tr. fr. Gaelic.* GoTS
Ireland with Emily. John Betjeman. GTBS-P; OxBTC
Irene, do you yet remember. The Chess-Board. "Owen Meredith." OBVV
Iridescent vibrations of midsummer light, The. John Gould Fletcher. Irradiations, II. TwAmPo
Iris, The. Gasetsu, *tr. fr. Japanese.* TiPo
Iris. David St. John. LCAP
Iris. William Carlos Williams. InPS; LCAP; WeW
Iris-flower with topaz leaves, An. At Delos. Duncan Campbell Scott. PeCV
Iris, lilac, lily, milk. Lalique. Hal Porter. PoAu-2
Irises. Padraic Colum. BoNaP
Irish. Paul Celan, *tr. fr. German by* Michael Hamburger. OBVE
Irish. Edward J. O'Brien. SiSoSe
Irish Airman Foresees His Death, An. W. B. Yeats. CABA; CoBMV; FaBoCh; FaBoMo; GoJo; GTBS-P; HeIP; HoPM; LiTM; MMA; MoAB; MoBrPo; NoAM; NOBE; NoP; OBMV; OBWP; PoPl; PPP; SCV; TrGrPo; WaaP; WaP; WeW
Irish-American Dignitary. Austin Clarke. BIrV
Irish Antiquities. Thomas Moore. FaBoEE
Irish Astronomy. Charles Graham Halpine. HBV-2
Irish Blessing, An. Joan Murray. LTB
Irish Cliffs of Moher, The. Wallace Stevens. DiL; LCAP; NOBA; VGW
Irish Council Bill, 1907, The [*parody on the Shan Van Vocht*], *sel.* Susan Mitchell.
"Is it this you call Home Rule?" OnYI
Irish Dancer, The. *Unknown.* AnIL; FaBoCh; NOBE; OBEV; OxBM; SeCePo
(I Am from Ireland.) HAP; MeEL
(I Am of Ireland.) GBP; OnYI
(Ich Am of Irlonde.) PoEL-1
(Icham of Irlaunde.) HAP
Irish faults are not so very new, The. Written on the Sense of Isolation in Contemporary Ireland. Robert Greacen. NeIP
Irish Girl's Lament, The, *with music. Unknown.* ShS
Irish Grandmother. Katherine Edelman. AmFN; SiSoSe

Irish Harper and His Dog, The. Thomas Campbell. *See* Harper, The.
Irish have the thickest ankles in the world, The. John Berryman. *Fr.* Dream Songs. TAP
Irish Hotel. David Wevill. NYBP
Irish Hurrah, The. Thomas Osborne Davis. OnYI
Irish Lady, The. *Unknown.* *See* Rich Irish Lady, A.
Irish lady can say, that to-day is every day, The. Cézanne. Gertrude Stein. TAP
Irish Lake, An. W. R. Rodgers. BIrV
Irish Lamentation, An. Goethe, *tr. fr. German by* James Clarence Mangan. AWP
Irish Language, The. James Clarence Mangan, *after the Irish of* Philip Fitzgibbon. VLP
Irish Lords. Charles H. Souter. PoAu-1
Irish Love-Song, An. Robert Underwood Johnson. HBV-1
Irish Lullaby, An. Alfred Perceval Graves. HBV-1
Irish Marriage Night, An. Brian Merriman, *tr. fr. Modern Irish by* Frank O'Connor. *Fr.* The Midnight Court. BIrV
Irish Molly O. *Unknown.* HBV-1
Irish Mother in the Penal Days, The. John Banim. AnIV
Irish Music. Larry Levis. MAYP
Irish Peasant Girl, The. Charles Joseph Kickham. AnIV
Irish Peasant to His Mistress, The. Thomas Moore. ACP
Irish Poetry. Michael Longley. CIP
Irish Rapparees, The. Charles Gavan Duffy. AnIV
Irish Satire, An. *Unknown.* *See* Satire on the People of Kildare, A.
Irish Schoolmaster, The. Thomas Hood. BXAP
Irish Schoolmaster, The. James A. Sidney. FiBHP
Irish Wife, The. Thomas D'Arcy McGee. HBV-1
Irish Wild-Flower, An. Sarah Morgan Bryan Piatt. AA
Irish Wind, An. Zelma S. Dennis. AMV-80
Irish Wish, An. *Unknown.* TreFT
Irish Wolf-Hound, The. Denis Florence MacCarthy. GDP
Irishman and the Lady, The. William Maginn. HBV-2
Irishman in Coventry, An. John Hewitt. BIrV; CIP
Irishman's Christening, An. *Unknown.* OnYI
Iron. Walter de la Mare. NOBL
Iron-Door-Woman. Judith Mountain Leaf Volborth. TWSS
Iron flower of the prophet's angry message, The. The Word. Gustave Kahn, *tr. by* Edouard Roditi. VWA
Iron Gate, The, *sel.* Oliver Wendell Holmes.
"As on the gauzy wings of fancy flying." AA
Iron Heaven. Betti Alver, *tr. fr. Estonian by* Willis Barnstone *and* Felix Oinas. BoWoP
Iron horse draweth nigh, with its smoke nostrils high, The. The Utah Iron Horse. *Unknown.* AmFP
Iron Industry in Birmingham, The. Richard Jago. *Fr.* Edge-Hill; or, The Rural Prospect Delineated and Moralised. NOEC
Iron, left in the rain. Rust. Mary Carolyn Davies. HBMV
Iron Lung, The. Stanley Plumly. AmPA; GeTw; LCAP
Iron Music, The. Ford Madox Ford. HBMV
Iron plates, barbells. The Field's Retention. José Y. Terán, Jr. LFAC
Iron queen of uncreations. The Gardens of Proserpine. Turner Cassity. PoA
Iron scallops border the path, barely. Earliest Spring. Denise Levertov. LCAP
Iron, sulphur, steam: the wastes. Saratoga Ending. Weldon Kees. NaP
Iron thing coming from Pompi, from the round-house. The Train. *Unknown, tr. by* D. F. van der Merwe. TTY
Ironic: LL.D. William Stanley Braithwaite. BANP
Ironical Encomium, An. *Unknown.* APAS
Irony. Louis Untermeyer. TrJP
Irony of God. Eva Warner. TrCP
Irradiations, *sels.* John Gould Fletcher.
"Balancing of gaudy broad pavilions, The," IV. TwAmPo
"Brown bed of earth, still fresh and warm with love," VIII. TwAmPo
"Flickering of incessant rain," II *or* V [VII]. MoAmPo; NePA; TwAmPo
"Fountain blows its breathless spray, The," VI. TwAmPo
"Iridescent vibratons of midsummer light, The," II. TwAmPo
"Morning is clean and blue and the wind blows up the clouds, The," V [XXII]. MoAmPo; NePA
"O seeded grass, you army of little men," IV *or* IX [XV]. MoAmPo; NePA; TwAmPo
"Over the roof-tops race the shadows of clouds," I *or* III [V]. MoAmBo; NePA; TwAmPo
"Spattering of the rain upon pale terraces, The," I. TwAmPo
"To-day you shall have but little song from me," X. TwAmPo
"Trees, like great jade elephants, The," III *or* VII [X]. MoAmBo; NePA; TwAmPo
Irreconcilables. Arthur Gregor. NYBP
Irresistible bacilli are at work, The. With the Most Susceptible Element, the Mind, Already Turned under the Toxic Action. Walter Benton. WaP
Irresponsive silence of the land, The. Aloof. Christina Rossetti. *Fr.* The Thread of Life. FaBoEn; NOBE; OBEV; OBNC; OBVV; TrGrPo
Irrevocable. Mary Wright Plummer. WGRP
Irrigation. Susan Tichy. MAYP
Irritable Song. Russell Atkins. AmNP
Irving. James Russell Lowell. *Fr.* A Fable for Critics. TAP
Is. Patrick Kavanagh. FaBoTw
Is/ red beans. Energy. Victor Hernandez Cruz. PoBA
Is a caterpillar ticklish? Only My Opinion. Monica Shannon. FaPON; SoPo; TiPo
I's a little Alabama Coon. Little Alabama Coon. Hattie Starr. AA
Is a monstrance. The Moon Is the Number 18. Charles Olson. CMoP; NMP
Is a son born into this world of woe? Charles Churchill. *Fr.* The Times. OBSV
Is all that fire put out, that passion spent. The Employee. Rudi Holzapfel. DBV
Is an enchanted thing. The Mind Is an Enchanting Thing. Marianne Moore. AP; CMoP; CoBMV; CrMA; HeIP; MOAB; MoAmPo; MoPo; OxBA; PPP; TwAmPo; WPOW
"Is anybody there?" said the Traveller. *See* "Is there anybody there?". . .
Is anything central? The One Thing That Can Save America. John Ashbery. NOBA
I's born in Louisiana. Nothing in Rambling. *Unknown.* BluL
Is by admitting. The Way Things Work. Jorie Graham. NPGG
Is chasing its tail again. Bobbie's Cat. Gerald Locklin. GP
Is drunken,/ Drunken, drunken. A Drunkard. *Unknown.* OxBM
Is God invisible? This very room. Sonnet XI. Adele Greeff. GoYe
I's gonna shine. *Unknown.* WTO
Is it a dream. For My Husband. Ellen Bryant Voigt. NoP
Is it a dream, or not? During my fever. The Blue Gift. David Perkins. NCSH
Is it a happiness? On a Birth. Geoffrey Grigson. NAs
Is It a Month. J. M. Synge. BIrV
"Is it a sail?" she asked. From the Harbor Hill. Gustav Kobbé. HBV-1
Is It a Sin to Love Thee? *Unknown.* BLPA
Is it a sudden thing. Pause. Dorothy Livesay. AMV-81
Is it any better in Heaven, my friend Ford. To Ford Madox Ford in Heaven. William Carlos Williams. AmPP; NoAM; NOBA
Is it bad to have come here. Gallant Château. Wallace Stevens. MoAB; MoAmPo
Is It Because I Am Black? Joseph Seamon Cotter, Jr. BANP
Is It Because of Some Dear Grace. Louis Golding. TrJP
Is it because that lad is dead. Vision. Frank Sidgwick. MMA
Is it birthday weather for you, dear soul? Birthday Poem for Thomas Hardy. C. Day Lewis. CoBMV
Is it cold hard cash? the kind. Three Thousand Dollar Death Song. Wendy Rose. TWSS
Is it dirty. Song. Frank O'Hara. CAD
Is it enough? I'm Here. Theodore Roethke. *Fr.* Meditations of an Old Woman. CoAP; NYBP
Is it enough to think to-day. Memorial Day. Annette Wynne. OHIP
Is it for fear to wet a widow's eye. Sonnets, IX. Shakespeare. MasP
Is it for you/ The Larks sing loud. To the Wind at Morn. W. H. Davies. ELU
Is it her nature or is it her will. Amoretti, XLI. Spenser. OAEP
Is it illusion? or does there a spirit from perfecter ages. A Spirit from Perfecter Ages. Arthur Hugh Clough. *Fr.* Amours de Voyage. EBEV; OBNC
Is it just like picking a lock. The Bomb Disposal. Ciaran Carson. CIP
Is it naught? Is it naught. Cuba. Edmund Clarence Stedman. PAH
Is it no dream that I am he. Walter Savage Landor. GBL
Is it not fine to fling against loaded dice. Hughie at the Inn. Elinor Wylie. NYBP; WPE
Is it not strange that men can die. Reflection. W. J. Turner. OBMV
Is it not sure a deadly pain. *Unknown.* EnLoPo
"Is It Nothing to You?" May Probyn. GoBC; OBEV; OBVV
Is It Possible ? Sir Thomas Wyatt. ELP; EnRePo; GBL; LoBV; NoP
("Is it possible that so high debate.") SiPS
(Varium et Mutabile.) OBSC; QFR
("Ys yt possyble.") AAS; POEL-1
"Is it really very far/ To Zanzibar?" Little Miss Pitt. William Wise. TiPo
Is It Really Worth the While? *Unknown.* BLPA
Is it serious, or funny. B. Larry Eigner. NeAP
Is it so far from thee. The Chamber over the Gate. Longfellow. AP
Is it so small a thing. Matthew Arnold. *Fr.* Empedocles on Etna. OBEV; OBVV
Is it the beauty of the rose. The Reversible Metaphor. "Troubadour." InMe
Is it the fecundating life you see around. Stranger, Why Do You Wonder So? K. B. Jones-Quartey. PBA
Is It the Morning? Is It the Little Morning? Delmore Schwartz. ELU

Is it the petals falling from the rose? The Dance of the Daughters of Herodias. Arthur Symons. BrPo
Is it the tinkling of mandolins which disturbs you? Little Ivory Figures Pulled with String. Amy Lowell. TwAmPo; ViBoPo
Is it the wind of the dawn that I hear. Duet. Tennyson. *Fr.* Becket. GBL
Is it the wind, the many-tongued, the weird. The Draft Riot. Charles de Kay. PAH
Is it this you call Home Rule? Susan Mitchell. *Fr.* The Irish Council Bill, 1907 [*parody on the Shan Van Vocht*]. OnYI
Is it thy wil, thy Image should keepe open. Sonnets, LXI. Shakespeare. PoEL-2
Is it time now to go away? Death of a Vermont Farm Woman. Barbara Howes. MoAmPo
Is it too much to ask that I should be. Toleration. John Barford. PeHV
Is It True? Sarah Williams. BLPA
Is it true that black birds infinitely dispersed. To Krishna Haunting the Hills. Andal, *tr. by* Willis Barnstone. BoWoP
Is it true that you live where there is sorrow, O giver of life? *Unknown, tr. fr. Nahuatl.* ILwL
Is it true, then my girl, that you mean it. Yes? H. C. Bunner. HBV-1
Is it true, ye gods, who treat us. Arthur Hugh Clough. VLP
Is it Ulysses that approaches from the east. The World as Meditation. Wallace Stevens. AP; CABA; HeIP; LCAP; MoAB; PPP
Is it you? Are you there. Poem Wondering If I'm Pregnant. Kathleen Fraser. IHMS; NMM
Is it you, that preach'd in the chapel there. Despair. Tennyson. VLP
Is John Smith within? Mother Goose. OxNR
Is Juno of the ribbons in gelatin. The Medusa. Guy Davenport. GP
Is less like that of a bean. The Manner of a Poet's Germination. José Garcia Villa. PP
Is Life itself but many ways of thought. Substitution. Anne Spencer. BlSi; CDC
Is Life Worth Living? Alfred Austin. FaPoR
"Is life worth living? Yes, so long," *sel.* TreFS
Is Love a Boy? *Unknown.* EnRePo
Is Love, Then, So Simple? Irene Rutherford McLeod. HBMV; WHA
Is man's destructive lust insatiable? Kyrie. David Gascoyne. *Fr.* Miserere. NeBP
Is Mary in the dairy? Where's Mary? Ivy O. Eastwick. TiPo
Is my favorite vegetable. Broccoli. Tom Schmidt. GP
Is My Lover On the Sea? "Barry Cornwall." EtS
Is My Team Ploughing [*or* Plowing]? A. E. Housman. A Shropshire Lad, XXVII. CMoP; CoBMV; EBVV; LiSp; LiTM; MoAB; MoBrPo; NoAM; NoP; OAEP; OBEV; PAI; SeCeV; TrGrPo; VLP; WHA
Is no one awake yet this cold cold winter morn? Who Can Tell When He Is Awake. James Tate. MAYP
Is not man's greatest heart's desire. Omnia Vanitas. Dugald Buchanan. GoTS
Is not something other. Everything That Is. Daniel Berrigan. TwAmPo
Is not the picture strangely like? On Seeing a Pigeon Make Love. Leigh Hunt. FM
Is not this hearth, where goats now feed? The Hearth of Urien. Llywarch the Aged, *tr. by* William Barnes. ChTr
I's reckon Cap'n Fallet. Cap'n & Me. Leon Baker. LFAC
Is seacoast fog, is starfish caught. New England Is New England Is New England. Brenda Heloise Green. GoYe
Is she/ Thoughtless of life. Nun Snow. Alfred Kreymborg. TwAmPo
"Is she fitting for your wife, Billy boy, Billy Boy." Billy Boy. *Unknown.* OBET
Is she not beautiful? reposing there. N. T. Carrington. *Fr.* On Seeing a Fine Frigate at Anchor in a Bay off Mount Edgecumbe. FaBoPP
Is shut/ 22 hours a day and all day Sunday. The Pitt-Rivers Museum, Oxford. James Fenton. FaBoMo
"Is Sin, then, fair?" The Sting of Death. Frederick George Scott. OBCV; PeCV
Is something like the rest. The Politics of Rich Painters. Amiri Baraka. CoPo; VGW
Is tell you my mind, Annes Tayliur: Dame. At the Tavern. *Unknown.* OxBM
Is that dance slowing in the mind of man. Four for Sir John Davies [*or* The Dance]. Theodore Roethke. AP; CoBMV; CrMA; MoAmPo; NePoAm; NoAM; NOBA
Is that enchanted moan only the swell. Tennyson. *Fr.* Maud. SyP
"Is that the Three-and-Twentieth, Strabo mine." The Legion. Robert Graves. BrPo
Is the ability to be. Youth. Richard Shelton. DFF
Is the ball very stupid, *ma mignonne*? At the Ball! Charles H. Webb. OBAL
Is the clock wound up, is it wound? The Insect Kitchen. Nicki Jackowska. BrRo
Is the eternal voice, Coltrane is. Orishas. Larry Neal. NBP
Is the fish ready? You're a tedious while. Dialogue between a Squeamish Cotting Mechanic and His Sluttish Wife, in the Kitchen. Edward Ward. *Fr.* Nuptial Dialogues. NOEC
Is the kitchen tap still dripping? Guest. D. J. Enright. OxBC
Is the Moon Tired? Christina Rossetti. MOON
Is the noise of grief in the palace over the river. A Mother in Egypt. Majorie Pickthall. CaP; HBV-2
Is the struggle and strife. Let the Rest of the World Go By. J. Keirn Brennan. UnPo
Is the total black, being spoken. Coal. Audre Lorde. CNA
Is the unexpected ring of the Cancer. Love. Gerald Jonas. PV
Is the way o'ercast with shadows? Jesus Understands. *Unknown.* BLRP
Is then no nook of English ground secure. Sonnet on the Projected Kendal and Windermere Railway. Wordsworth. VLP
Is there a cause why we should wake the dead? The Yew-Tree. Vernon Watkins. EaLo; LiTB
Is There a Great Green Commonwealth of Thought. John Masefield. *Fr.* Sonnets ("Long, long ago"). LiTM
(Sonnet: "Is there a great green commonwealth of thought.") MoBrPo
Is there a madness underneath the sun. The Starred Mother. Robert Whitaker. PGD
Is There a Voice. Philip Appleman. BXAP
Is there any good man here. A Call for a Song. *Unknown.* OxBM
"Is there anybody [*or* Is anybody] there?" said the Traveller. The Listeners. Walter de la Mare. AWP; BLPL; BrPo; CMoP; CoBMV; FaFP; FaPON; HAP; HBV-2; HBVY; HeIP; HoPM; InPK; InvP; LiTB; LiTM; MoAB; MoBrPo; MoPo; MoVE; NCSH; NoAM; NOBE; NoP; OAEP; OBEV; OBMV; OBVV; OnMSP; PoPl; PoPle; PoRA; SeCeV; SoSe; TreF; TrGrPo; ViBoPo; WeW; WHA; WSC
Is there anything as I can do ashore for you. A Valediction (Liverpool Docks). John Masefield. OBMV
Is there anything else that is better worth. Nothing Better. *Unknown.* STF
Is there anything I can do. The Key to Everything. May Swenson. IHMS; NePoEA
Is there anything left on the floor? Leavetaking. Lisa Reape. AMV-81
Is There for Honest Poverty. Burns. *See* For A' That and A' That.
Is There Life across the Street? Robert Watson. GP
Is there never a man in all Scotland. Johnie Armstrong. *Unknown.* ESPB
Is There No Balm in Christian Lands? *with music.* *Unknown.* AH
Is there no secret place on the face of the earth. The Moneyless Men. Henry T. Stanton. BLPA
Is there no vision in a lovely place? William Montgomerie. *Fr.* Kinfauns Castle. OxBS
Is there no voice in the world to come crying. New Dreams for Old. Cale Young Rice. HBV-2
Is there nothing to be said about the cockroach which is kind? Cockroach. Mary Ann Hoberman. *Fr.* Bugs. OBCA
Is there one desires to hear. Killarney. William Larminie. AnIV
Is there some problem in your life to solve. God's Key. *Unknown.* STF
Is there still any shadow there, on the rainwet window of the coffee pot. Memo. Kenneth Fearing. CMoP
Is this a dagger which I see before me. Macbeth's Words before Murdering. Shakespeare. *Fr.* Macbeth, II, i. TreFS
Is this a fast, to keep. To Keep a True Lent [*or* A True Lent]. Robert Herrick. AnAnS-2; HBV-2; OFD; OHIP; TrCP; TRV
Is this a holy thing to see. Holy Thursday. Blake. *Fr.* Songs of Experience. EnRP; FF; InPS; LAuP; NOEC; NoP; OAEL-2; OAEP; TEP
Is this a time to be cloudy and sad. The Gladness of Nature. Bryant. HBV-1; HBVY
Is this a time to plant and build. Eleventh Sunday after Trinity. John Keble. *Fr.* The Christian Year. VLP
Is This Africa. Roland Tombekai Dempster. PBA
Is this dancing sunlight. Symphony. Frank Horne. AmNP
Is this God's joke? my father screamed. Health. Stewart Parker. CIP
Is This Land Your Land? *Unknown.* FSW
Is this man turning angel as he stares. The Messengers. Thom Gunn. PoA
Is this Sir Philip Sidney, this loud clown. The Knight in Disguise. Vachel Lindsay. HBV-2
Is this the front—this level sweep of life. At the Front. John Erskine. HBMV
Is this the gym?. . .Then this must be the wall. Humiliation Revisited. Nova Trimble Ashley. AMV-80
Is this the Lake, the cradle of the storms. Written on the Banks of Wastwater during a Calm. "Christopher North." OBRV
Is this the object. Sestina. Judith Kroll. AmPA
Is this the price of beauty! Fairest, thou. Charleston. Richard Watson Gilder. PAH
Is this the region, this the soil, the clime. Satan as Rebel-Liberator [*or* Satan Ponders His Fallen State *or* The Fall of the Angels]. Milton. *Fr.* Paradise Lost, I. FF; FiP; TEP; TreFS

"Is this the road that climbs above and bends." The Chalk-Pit. Edward Thomas. BrPo
Is this the Seine? An Ode to Spring in the Metropolis. Sir Owen Seaman. FiBHP; WhC
Is this the self I thought I knew, within. Reflections. Vivian Smith. CBAP
Is this the street? Never a sign of life. Stormy Night. W. R. Rodgers. OxBI
Is this the sum of her, or was she human? Daguerreotype of a Grandmother. Celeste Turner Wright. Str
Is This the Time to Sound Retreat? *Unknown.* BLRP
Is this the ultimate exile no man born. Ultimate Exile IV. Ralph Nixon Currey. PeSA
Is thy face like thy mother's, my fair child! Childe Harold's Pilgrimage, III. Byron. ChER, 15 *sts.*; EnRP; OAEL-2, *abr*; OAEP.
Is to love, this—to nurse a name. Poem. Rhoda Coghill. NeIP
Is true Freedom but to break. Stanzas on Freedom. James Russell Lowell. GN
"Is water nigh?" The Gift of Water. Hamlin Garland. AA; BPAW
Is without world. The Howling of Wolves. Ted Hughes. OxBTC
Is Wolly's wife now dead and gone? A Jacobite Scot in Satire on England's Unparalleled Loss. *Unknown.* APAS
Is yo eye so empty. Signals. Jewel C. Latimore. PoBA
Is your place a small place? Your Place. John Oxenham. BLRP; TRV
Isaac. Stanley Burnshaw. VWA
Isaac. Amir Gilboa, *tr. fr. Hebrew by* Howard Schwartz. VWA
Isaac. Haim Guri, *tr. fr. Hebrew by* Naomi Tauber *and* Howard Schwartz. VWA
Isaac. Barry Holtz. VWA
Isaac. A. C. Jacobs. VWA
Isaac a ransom while he lay. Didn't Old Pharaoh Get Los'? *Unknown.* BoAN-1
Isaac and Archibald. E. A. Robinson. OxBA
Isaac and Esau. Rose Drachler. VWA
Isaac Babel is riding with bloodthirsty Bolshevik soldiers. Babel. Gary Pacernik. AMV-81
Isaac Leybush Peretz. Moishe Leib Halpern, *tr. fr. Yiddish by* Kathryn Hellerstein. VWA
Isabel. Sydney Dobell. OBVV
Isabel. *Unknown, tr. fr. French by* George Lanigan. WHW
Isabel met an enormous bear. Adventures of Isabel. Ogden Nash. CenHV; MoAmPo; MoShBr; NTCP; OBAL; OBCA; OnMSP; OnUR; PDV; RHPC; ShM; TiPo
Isabel of the lily-white hand. Isabel. *Unknown, tr. by* George Lanigan. WHW
Isabella; or, The Morning, *sels.* Sir Charles Hanbury Williams.
  "Monkey, lap-dog, parrot, and her Grace, The." NOEC
  Old General, The. OBEC
Isabella; or, The Pot of Basil. Keats. EnRP
  "Fair Isabel, poor simple Isabel!" *sel.* ViBoPo
Isabella Condemns Tyranny. Shakespeare. *Fr.* Measure for Measure, II, ii. TreFt
  (But Man, Proud Man.) WHA
Isabella spits at Spain. Bourbons. Walter Savage Landor. OBSV
Isabelle. James Hogg. BXAP; Par
Isadora, your body charts a course. Love Poem. Linda Wagner. FAZ
Isaiah, *sels.* Bible, *O. T.*
  All Flesh Is Grass, XL: 6-8. TrJP
  "And there shall come forth a rod out of the stemme of Jesse," XI:1-11. OBVE; TrJP
  "Behold, my servant shall deal prudently," LII:13-LIII. NAWM-1
  "Comfort ye, comfort ye my people," XL: 1-11. EaLo; OBVE (1-8); TreFS (1-11); TrJP (1-5)
  Downfall of the Tyrant, XIV: 4-19. TrGrPo
  For Ye Shall Go Out with Joy, LV: 6-12. TreFT
  For Zion's Sake, LXII: 1-5. TrJP
  God's Rule XI: 6-9. FM
  God's Vengeance XXXIV: 8-15. FM
  Hear the Word of the Lord, I: 10-23. TrJP
  How Beautiful upon the Mountains, LII: 7-10. TrJP
  I Waste Away, XXIV: 16-20. TrJP
  In the End of Days, II: 2-4. TrJP
  Israel, My Servant, XLI: 8-16. TrJP
  Let Me Sing of My Well-Beloved, V. TrJP
  Messiah, The, VII: 14-25. AWP
  My Thoughts Are Not Your Thoughts, LV: 8-13. TrJP
  Peaceable Kingdom, The, XI: 6. FaPON
  Perfect Peace, XXVI: 3. TRV
  Power from God, XL: 28-31. TreFT
  Rod of Jesse, The, XI: 1-10. AWP
  Song of the Harlot, XXIII: 16. TrJP
  "Therefore the Lord Himself/ shall give you a sign," VII: 14-15, *Douay vers.* ISi
  They That Wait upon the Lord, XL: 28-31. TRV
  Vision of the Day of Judgment, LXIII, *Moulton, Modern Reader's Bible.* WGRP
  Watchman, What of the Night? XXI: 11-15. AWP
  Whom Shall One Teach, XXVIII: 9-13. TrJP
  "Wildernesse and the solitarie place shall be glad for them, The," XXX. OBVE
  "Wolf also shall dwell with the lamb, The," XI, 6-9. PDV
Iscah. Howard Schwartz. VWA
I'se got a gal in the Sourwood Mountain. Sourwood Mountain. *Unknown.* AmFP
I'se got a little baby, but she's out of sight. Hello! Ma Baby. Joseph E. Howard *and* Ida Emerson. FSN
I'se the b'y that builds the boat. I'se the B'y. *Unknown.* FSW
I'se wild Nigger Bill. Wild Negro Bill. *Unknown.* BPo
Ishmael. Gabriel Levin. VWA
Ishmael. Herbert Edward Palmer. OBEV
Isidor. Louis Simpson. GP; NNaP
Isis Wanderer. Kathleen Raine. OxBS
Island, The, *sel.* Byron.
  "Highlands' swelling blue, The." OBRV
Island, The. Seán Jennett. NeIP; SeCePo
Island, The. Edwin Muir. OAEL-2
Island, An. Shawn Wong. BrSi
Island, The. George Woodcock. NeBP
Island, The, *sel.* Francis Brett Young.
  Atlantic Charter: 1942. PAL
  (Atlantic Charter, A.D. 1620-1942.) AmFN
Island and the Cattle, The. Nicholas Moore. EAS
Island Cemetery, The. W. H. Auden. NePoAm-2
Island Dogs ("The island crawls with dogs"). Charles G. Bell. NePoAm-2
Island dreams under the dawn, The. The Indian to His Love. W. B. Yeats. VLP
Island in the Evening, The. Fairfield Porter. PoA
Island in the Moon, An, *sels.* Blake.
  Good Hospitality. CoMu
  (Mayors, The.) CH
  In Obtuse Angle's Study. FaBoNo
  Quid the Cynic's Song. FaBoNo
  Sipsop's Song. FaBoNo
  Suction's Anthem. FaBoNo
Island Moment. Ian Hamilton Finlay. NMP
Island of Geological Time, The. Laura Fargas. SUW
Island of Giglio. Harold Norse. GP
Island of Mull. *Unknown, fr. the Gaelic of* Douglas Macphail. PoSH
Island of Night. Galway Kinnell. NePoAm
Island of Rhum, The. Roy Ferguson. PoSH
Island of Shadow. Nostalgie d'Automne. Leslie Daiken. NeIP
Island of the Blest, The. Pindar, *tr. fr. Greek by* Gilbert West. *Fr.* Olympian Ode II. OBEC
Island of the Scots, The, *abr.* William Edmondstoune Aytoun. VLP
Island of Yorrick, The. N. M. Bodecker. WSC
Island Quarry. Hart Crane. CrMA; PPP
Island steams under the opening sky, The. Accident at Three Mile Island. Jim Barnes. AMV-81; FAZ
Island that had flowered to the sun, The. The Coming of Dusk upon a Village in Haiti. Henry Rago. HoPM
Island was a word he woke upon, The. Settler. Stewart Lindh. PoA
Islanders, Inlanders. Michael Mott. PoA
Islands, The. Hilda Doolittle ("H. D."). MoAmPo
Islands, The. Randall Jarrell. EAS
Islands. Ralph Pomeroy. CoPo
Islands. Muriel Rukeyser. GP
Islands and peninsulas, continents and capes. Geography. Eleanor Farjeon. FaPON
Islands and the mountains in the day, The. Shelley. *Fr.* The Revolt of Islam, Canto III. ChER
Islands are islands though in the steady sea. Islands. Ralph Pomeroy. CoPo
Islands move inward. The Name of Our Country. Dennis Schmitz. AmPA
Islands of the Ever Living, The. *Unknown, tr. fr. Irish by* Padraic Colum. AnIV
Islands of the Sea, The. George Edward Woodberry. PAH
Island's Prince, of frame more than celestial, The. The All-seeing Intellect. Phineas Fletcher. *Fr.* The Purple Island, VI. JCP
Islands which whisper to the ambitious, The. At Epidaurus. Lawrence Durrell. LiTB; MoPo
Isle, The. Shelley. SyP
Isle of a summer sea. Cuba. Harvey Rice. PAH
Isle of Arran. Alastair Reid. BSV
Isle of Long Ago, The. Benjamin Franklin Taylor. *See* Isle of the Long Ago, The.

Isle of Man, The. *Unknown.* GBP
Isle of Man Shore, The. *Unknown.* AmFP
Isle of Portland, The. A. E. Housman. A Shropshire Lad, LIX. MoBrPo
Isle of the Long Ago, The. Benjamin Franklin Taylor. FaFP; HBV-1; WBLP
(Isle of Long Ago, The.) TreFS
(Long Ago, The.) BLPA
Isled in the midnight air. The Moth. Walter de la Mare. BrPo; FaBoEn; MoVE
Isles of Greece, The. Byron. *Fr.* Don Juan, III. AWP; ChTr; FaBoEn; FaPoR; FiP; HBV-2; LiTB; NOBE; OBEV; OBRV; RoGo; SeCeV; TreFS; ViBoPo; WHA
Isles of Greece, The. Demetrios Capetanakis. GTBS-P
Islet the Dachs. George Meredith. FM
Isn't it strange. A Bag of Tools. R. L. Sharpe. BLPA; TreFT; YaD
Isn't it strange some people make. Some People. Rachel Field. FaPON; NTCP; PDV; RHPC
Isn't she soft and still? Captive. Marion Strobel. ErPo
"Isn't the violet a dear little flower? And the daisy, too." The Lay Preacher Ponders. Idris Davies. OxBTC
Isn't this grinding the valves a little closer to your ears. Wheat Metropolis. Alfred Starr Hamilton. FAZ
"Isn't this Joseph's son?"—ay, it is He. Jesus the Carpenter. Catharine C. Liddell. HBV-2
Isolation ("We were apart; yet, day by day"). Matthew Arnold. *See* Isolation: To Marguerite.
Isolation ("Yes! in the sea of life enisled"). Matthew Arnold. *See* To Marguerite.
Isolation. Arthur Hugh Clough. *Fr.* Dipsychus. OBVV
Isolation Cell Poem. J. Charles Green. LFAC
Isolation of Genius, The. Byron. WBLP
Isolation: To Marguerite. Matthew Arnold. Switzerland, IV. EBVV; OAEP; TEP; VLP
(Isolation.) TreFT; VLP
Isolation Ward. Robert L. Koenig. AMV-81
Isolda was an Irish queen who always spoke in German. Tristan and Isolda. Newman Levy. InMe
Israel. Israel Zangwill. TrJP
Israel Freyer's Bid for Gold. Edmund Clarence Stedman. PAH
Israel in ancient days. Old-Testament Gospel. William Cowper. TrCP
Israel, My Servant. Bible, *O.T.* Isaiah, XLI: 8-16. TrJP
Israeli Navy, The. Marvin Bell. VWA
Israeli Soldier's Nightmare, An. Alison B. Carb. AMV-80
Israel's Duration. Judah Halevi, *tr. fr. Hebrew by* Nina Davis Salaman. TrJP
Israfel. Poe. AA; AmPP; AP; AWP; BLPL; HBV-2; LiTA; NePA; NOBA; OxBA; PoEL-4; TAP; TreFS; WHA
Issue of great Jove, draw near you Muses nine, The. The Garden. Nicholas Grimald. OAEL-1
"Issues from the hand of God, the simple soul." Animula. T. S. Eliot. LiTB; MoVE; NAs; TwAmPo
Istanbul. 21 March. I woke today. The Thousand and Second Night. James Merrill. NYBP
It. Richmond Lattimore. PP
It. Gary Snyder. LCAP
It ain't gonna rain, it ain't gonna snow. Ain't Gonna Rain. *Unknown.* AS
It Ain't Neccessarily So. Ira Gershwin. OBAL
It ain't no use to grumble and complain. Rain. James Whitcomb Riley. BoNaP
It ain't such a terrible long time ago. Barriers Burned. Charles K. Field. BPAW
It ain't the failures he may meet. The Quitter. *Unknown.* BLPA; WBLP
It ain't the guns nor armament. Co-operation. J. Mason Knox. BLPA; YaD
It all began. Loss. Alex Kuo. BrSi
It all began so easy. Christina. Louis MacNeice. BoLoP; OxBI
It all happened so fast. Fenya was in the straight chair. Pastoral. Norman Dubie. AmPA
It all seems like today: he returns. A Veteran of the Great War. John Bensko. MAYP
It almost doesn't matter who it is. The Hostage and His Takers. Sharon Olds. SOTS
It Always Happens. Horace, *tr. fr. Latin by* Thomas Charles Baring. Odes, I, 33. UnTE
It Always Seems. A. M. Sayers. BXAP
It appeared inside our classroom. The Creature in the Classroom. Jack Prelutsky. RHPC
It appears to be the pampas. The Man in the Dream Is Death. Lynne Butler. IHMS
It Autumne was, and on our hemispheare. Song. William Drummond of Hawthornden. OBS
It baffles the foreigner like an idiom. Drug Store. Karl Shapiro. CMoP; MoVE; MP; OxBA; TwCP
It beats me. The way. Old People. Myra Cohn Livingston. CTBA
It befell at Martynmas. Captain Car; or, Edom o Gordon. *Unknown.* ESPB; OAEP; ViBoFo
It began as a joke: she did not like to leave the house. Another Poem about the Madness of Women. Tom Wayman. NOBC
It began in her pram. The Renaming. Valerie Sinason. BrRo
It Begins Softly ("It begins inside first"). Bernadine. LTB
It begins with my dog, now dead, who all his long life. The Retrieval System. Maxine W. Kumin. WeW
It bends far over Yell'ham Plain. The Comet at Yell'ham. Thomas Hardy. CMoP; GBL; VLP
It billows in a gust of wind. The Homes. Anne Pitkin. AMV-80
It brims in the white cistern; flows. A Meditation upon the Toothache. Laurence Lerner. NePoEA-2
It burns in the void. The World. Kathleen Raine. OxBTC
It came/ Out of the blackness of the spaces between galaxies. The Second Coming. Carl Clark. JB
It came sniffing and nibbling about on the rock terrace. Of a Mouse and Men. A. J. Hovde. AMV-81
It came today to visit. The Visitor. Jack Prelutsky. AmMo
It Came upon the Midnight Clear. Edmund Hamilton Sears. AH, *with music*; FaPON; TreFT
(Angels' Song, The.) AA; FaPO
(Christmas Carols.) HBV-1; HBVY
(Peace on Earth.) FaFP
It can be beautiful this sitting by oneself all alone except for the world. Moon Watching by Lake Chapala. Al Young. NPGG
It can be so tedious, a bore. Moods of Rain. Vernon Scannell. BoNaP
It Cannot Be ("It cannot be that He who made"). David Banks Sickels. HBV-2
(Reincarnation.) AA
It cannot be/ reasoned with. Julius Lester. *Fr.* In the Time of Revolution. PoBA
It cannot be that men who are the seed. Our First Century. George Edward Woodberry. PAH
It cannot come. Balboa, the Entertainer. Amiri Baraka. NoAM
It can't be the passing of time that casts. Rip. James Wright. NaP
It can't happen to me. Age? H. R. Hays. POL
It chanced his lips did meet her forehead cool. George Meredith. Modern Love, VI. ViBoPo
It chanced of late a shepherd swain. Cupid's Pastime. Francis Davison. UnTE
It chanced one day they met. Each in surprise. Seven Sad Sonnets, VII. Mary Aldis. HBMV
It chanced to be our washing day. Oliver Wendell Holmes. *Fr.* The September Gale. FiBHP
It comes about that the drifting of these curtains. The Curtains in the House of the Metaphysician. Wallace Stevens. PoA
It comes back. Deceased. Cid Corman. PCP; VGW
It Comes during Sleep. Philip Dow. NPGG
It comes to me more and more. The Love of the Father. *Unknown.* BLRP
It comes to this. Revelations. David Meltzer. NeAP
It consisted of 8 to 10 pages of short essays. Her Application to Elysium. Kathleen Norris. IHMS
It could be a clip, it could be a comb. Obsessive. Marvin Bell. LCAP
It could be a jaw-bone. Viking Dublin; Trial Pieces. Seamus Heaney. IPY
It could be Louisiana, attracting rain. Pine Barrens: Letter Home. Cleopatra Mathis. TAT
It could only be seen/ when he closed his eyes. Hebrew Script. Tali Loewenthal. VWA
It Couldn't Be Done. Edgar A. Guest. BLPA; FaBoBe; FaFP; FPL; STF; TreFS; WBLP; YaD
It crawled away from 'neath my feet. That Hill. Blanche Taylor Dickinson. CDC
It curls in the closet. The Divorce Dress. Jeanne Finley. AMV-80
It curved below the house. Route 29. Catharine Savage Brosman. AMV-81
It dances. The Newborn Colt. Mary Kennedy. PH
It Did Not Last. J. C. Squire. InPK
("It did not last: the Devil howling Ho.") FaBoCo; FaBoEE; QQQ
It didn't make a grand entrance and I nearly. Snowfall. Hone Tuwhare. OCNZ
It digs the air with green blades. Tulip. Robert Wallace. PPJ
It does, it does, I have seen it. America Bleeds. Angelo Lewis. PoBA
It does not happen. That love, removes. Audubon, Drafted. Amiri Baraka. PPP; TTY
It does not make sense in terms of historical fact. Sans Souci. Lisel Mueller. NePoAm-2
It does not matter. Moonshot. Robert Kelly. MOON

It does not matter who we love or what we think. Inconsistencies. Michelle Roberts. LFAC
It does not worry me that this verse has three stresses. The Eumenides at Home. James Agate. BXAP
It doesn't always do to let a mug know everything. Charlie Piecan. F. Murray *and* F. Leigh. OxBoLi
It doesn't breathe. My Nose. Dorothy Aldis. RHPC
It doesn't look like a finger it looks like a feather of broken glass. Poem. Hugh Sykes Davies. EAS
It don't seem hardly right, John. Jonathan to John. James Russell Lowell. *Fr.* The Biglow Papers. PAH
It don't take sech a lot o' laws. Code of the Cow Country. S. Omar Barker. PoOW
It dropped so low—in my regard. Emily Dickinson. CABA; CMoP; HAP; InPK; OxBA; PoPl
It embarrasses. Personal Poem. Ingrid Wendt. NMM
It ended, and the morrow brought the task. George Meredith. Modern Love, II. HBV-1; OAEP
It faces west, and round the back and sides. Domicilium. Thomas Hardy. FaBoPP
It feels good as it is without the giant. Wallace Stevens. Notes toward a Supreme Fiction, VII. MoPo; NePA; NOBA
It feels so good. One Morning. Ellen Levine. AMV-81
It fell about a Martinmas time. Barbara Allen. *Unknown.* ViBoFo
It fell about the Lambmass tide. Bonny Lizie Baillie. *Unknown.* BaBo; ESPB
It fell about [*or* and about *or* upon] the Lammas tide [*or* time]. The Battle of Otterburn [*or* Otterbourne]. *Unknown.* BSV; ESPB; FaBoCh; GoTS; HBV-2; OnMSP; OxBB
It fell about the Lammas time. Lord Livingston. *Unknown.* ESPB; OxBB
It fell about the Martinmas[s] time. Edom o' Gordon [*or* Captain Car]. *Unknown.* BSV; ESPB; FaBoBa; HBV-2; OxBB; ViBoFo
It fell about the Martinmas time. Get Up and Bar the Door. *Unknown.* BaBo; BiP; BSV; ESPB; FaBoBa; GoTS; HeIP; NoP; OnMSP; OxBS; PDV; TrGrPo; ViBoPo
It fell about the Martinmas tyde. Jamie Telfer of [*or* in] the Fair Dodhead. *Unknown.* BSV; ESPB; OxBB
It fell and about the Lammas time. *See* It fell about the Lammas time.
It fell in the ancient periods. Uriel. Emerson. AP; LiTA; NePA; NOBA; OxBA
It fell on a day, and a bonnie simmer [*or* bonny summer] day. The Bonnie House o' Airlie. *Unknown.* ESPB; OBEV; OxBS
It Fell on a Summer's Day. Thomas Campion. ErPo; HAP; UnTE; WeW
It fell upon a bonny simmer day. The Bonnie House o' Airlie. *Unknown.* OxBB
It fell upon a holy [*or* holly] eve. Perigot and Willye [*or* A Roundelay]. Spenser. *Fr.* The Shepheardes Calender. EIL; InvP; LoBV
It fell upon a Wodensday [*or* Wednesday]. Brown Robyn's [*or* Robin's] Confession [*or* Brown Robyn]. *Unknown.* ACP; CH; ESPB; GBP
It fell upon the Lammas tide. *See* It fell about the Lammas tide.
It fell upon the Lammas time. Young Ronald. *Unknown.* ESPB
It fell upon us like a crushing woe. Colonel Ellsworth. Richard Henry Stoddard. PAH
It fell when I was sleeping. In my dream. The Land-Mine. George MacBeth. OBWP
It felt like the zero in brook ice. The Funeral. Norman Dubie. MAYP
It flows through old hushed Egypt and its sands. The Nile [*or* A Thought of the Nile]. Leigh Hunt. EnRP; EBEV; NBM; NOBE; OBNC; OBRV; ViBoPo
It follows me. Lac Courte Orielles; 1936. Phyllis Wolf. STE
It follows up the hill and down. Market Day. Abigail Cresson. HBMV
It Fortifies My Soul to Know. Arthur Hugh Clough. *See* "With Whom Is No Variableness . . ."
It fortuned (as faire it then befell). Spenser. *Fr.* The Faerie Queene, I, 11. OAEL-1
It gets awful lonely. Lonely. Bloke Modisane. PBA
It gets dark and I get scared. Feeling That Way Too. Arthur Vogelsang. MAYP
It gets run over by a van. Your Dog Dies. Raymond Carver. GeTw
It gleamed above our Old Brigade. The Battle-Flag. Mary Evelyn Moore Davis. BPAW
It goes fwunkety. The Washing Machine. Jeffrey Davies. PCP
It had an autumn smell. Autumn. Allen Tate. *Fr.* Seasons of the Soul. MoVE
It had to be. She from his weariness. Seven Sad Sonnets, I. Mary Aldis. HBMV
It hangs from heaven to earth. Tapestry. Charles Simic. LCAP
It happened/ in a second. Where Is Justice? Eliezer Steinbarg, *tr. by* Seth L. Wolitz. VWA
It happened in Jacksboro in the year of 'seventy-three. The Buffalo Skinners. *Unknown.* AmFP
It happened, it happened all on a Saturday night. Johnny Dyers. *Unknown.* AmFP
It happened not far away. Clonfeacle. Paul Muldoon. CIP
It happened on a certain day. The Ship *Rambolee.* *Unknown.* ShS
It happened on a Sunday. Camp. Patrick Anderson. OBCV
It happened once, before the duller. Green Slates. Thomas Hardy. FaBoPP
It happened once upon a time. James Hatley. *Unknown.* BaBo
It happened so fast. Death Comes to the Salesman. Louis Daniel Brodsky. AMV-81
It happens/ even in my own house. After Your Death. David James. AMV-80
It happens lonely—no one. The Moment. William Stafford. NNaP
It Happens, Often. Edwin Meade Robinson. HBMV
It happens through the blond window, the trees. Ascension. Denis Devlin. BIrV
It has a head like a cat, feet like a cat. Riddle. *Unknown.* NTCP
It has all/ come back today. From Gloucester Out. Edward Dorn. CoPo; NoAM; NOBA; PoM
It has already been said. Winter's Edge. P. R. Roberts. SOTS
It has been a long time now. Marriage and Midsummer's Night. Linda Gregg. NPGG
It has been a month since I gave up shaving. House Plants. David McFadden. NOBC
It has been hours in these rooms. E. W. Mandel. *Fr.* Minotaur Poems. OBCV
It has been many years. Biographical Note. Gabriel Preil, *tr. by* Howard Schwartz. VWA
It has been well said that quietness. A Dog's Best Friend Is His Illiteracy. Ogden Nash. BoAnP
It has certainty, like the fall of a stone. On the Death of Parents. Alfred Barson. AMV-80
It has dawned on me. Flash. Stephen Todd Booker. LFAC
It has happened suddenly. Je Suis une Table. Donald Hall. EAS; NePoEA
It has no wings. Loneliness and July Ninth. Claribel Alegria, *tr. by* Aliki *and* Willis Barnstone. BoWoP
It has not been given me to have a friend. Friend Who Never Came. William Stafford. FAZ
It has snowed. Love Letter. Linda Pastan. DFF
It has to be the end of the day. Surf-casting. W. S. Merwin. NOBA
It has turned to snow in the night. The Horses. Maxine W. Kumin. DuDa
It hath been said of old that plays are feasts. To the Reader of Master William Davenant's Play, The Wits. Thomas Carew. CaPo
It is/ a fuse. Poem Technology. Miroslav Holub, *tr. by* Stuart Friebert *and* Dana Hábová. SUW
It Is a Beauteous Evening [Calm and Free]. Wordsworth. AWP; BLPL; CABA; ChTr, 8 *ll.*; EnRP; FaBoPP; FaBoRV; FiP; HeIP; HBV-1; HBVY; LiTB; NiP; NoP; OAEL-2; OAEP; PAI; POEL-4; PoLF; PPP; SeCePo; SeCeV; TEP; TreFS; WHA
(By the Sea.) EtS; GTBS; GTBS-P; TRV
(Evening on Calais Beach.) OBEV
(On the Beach at Calais.) TrGrPo
(Sonnet: "It is a beauteous evening, calm and free.") ChER; LoBV; ViBoPo
It is a beauteous morning, calm and free. Country Club Sunday. Phyllis McGinley. CrMA
It is a clearing deep in a forest: overhanging boughs. Johnson's Cabinet Watched by Ants. Robert Bly. NoAM; NOBA
It is a clever pushbutton you have, Juan Trippe. What Bright Pushbutton? Samuel Allen. PoNe
It is a cold and snowy night. The main street is deserted. Driving to Town Late to Mail a Letter. Robert Bly. BoNaP; ELU; HeIP; InPK; NaP; VGW
It is a cramped little state with no foreign policy. Shame. Richard Wilbur. ConAP; FaBoMo; OxBC
It is a crude thing as it shapes up here. New Construction: Bath Iron Works. G. Stanley Koehler. NePoAm-2
It is a funny thing, but true. Folks and Me. Lucile Crites. WBLP
It is a God-damned lie to say that these. Another Epitaph on an Army of Mercenaries. "Hugh MacDiarmid." DBV; NoAM; OBWP
It is a good plan, and began with childhood. Monologue of a Deaf Man. David Wright. MP; NoAM
It is a hollow child, delicate, frail. For an Egyptian Boy, Died c.700 B.C. Mary Baron. HoAn
It is a kind of shadow. The Umbrella. Ann Stanford. NYBP
It is a lie—their priests, their pope. The Confessional. Robert Browning. ViBoPo
It is a little pond. Twice. Ian Hamilton Finlay. BSV
It is a lost road into the air. An Airstrip in Essex, 1960. Donald Hall. InPS; LiTM; LCAP; PoCH

It is a milky morning in San Francisco. Another Given: The Last Day of the Year. William Dickey. AMV-80
"It is a month, and isna mair." The White Fisher. *Unknown.* ESPB
It is a new America. Brown River, Smile. Jean Toomer. *Fr.* The Blue Meridian. AmNP; PoBA; PoNe
It is a pilgrim coming from the East. The Pilgrim from the East. Gustave Kahn, *tr. by* Jethro Bithell. TrJP
It is a place where poets crowned may feel the heart's decaying. Cowper's Grave. Elizabeth Barrett Browning. HBV-2; OBVV
It is a small freedom. Minimum Security. James Lewisohn. LFAC
It is a solemn evening, golden-clear. The After-Glow. Mathilde Blind. OBNC
It is a squad car idling. Lust. William Matthews. PCP
It is a steadfast soldier. Heart. Joan LaBombard. PPJ
It is a strange, miraculous thing. Enigma for Christmas Shoppers [*or* Enigma in Altman's]. Phyllis McGinley. PoPl; WhC
It is a sultry day; the sun has drunk. Summer Wind. Bryant. AP; PoEL-4
It is a summer evening. Lullaby. Anne Sexton. NoAM
It is a summer gloaming, balmy-sweet. A Summer Twilight. Charles Tennyson Turner. OBRV
It is a tide pool, shallow. Looking into a Tide Pool. Robert Bly. MAT
It is a time of hunger. Personal Song. Arnatkoak, *tr. fr. Eskimo.* WTO
It is a time to be awake. The clock. Nightpiece. Lewis Turco. SOTS
It is a very curious fact. Lines for a Worthy Person Who Has Drifted by Accident into a Chelsea Revel. A. P. Herbert. NOBL
It is a warm grey afternoon in August. Out of Control; the Quarry. Christopher Dewdney. NOBC
It is a water hand, this right one. Look to the Back of the Hand. Judith Minty. PoA
It is a whisper among the hazel bushes. The Twilight People. "Seumas O'Sullivan." OnYI
It is a willow when summer is over. Willow Poem. William Carlos Williams. NCSH
It is a winter night. Fever and chill. A Winter's Tale. Robert Patrick Dana. NYBP
It is a winter's tale. A Winter's Tale. Dylan Thomas. CMoP; LiTB; SeCeV
It is a wonder foam is so beautiful. Spray. D. H. Lawrence. BoNaP
It is a year of good harvest. Harvesting Wheat for the Public Share. Li Chü, *tr. by* Kenneth Rexroth *and* Ling Chung. BoWoP; PBWP
It is all a rhythm. The Rhythm. Robert Creeley. CoPo; LiTM
It is all falling away, the days fall faster now. Descending. Robert Pack. NePoEA-2
It is all one in Venus' wanton school. Song. John Lyly. SeCePo
It is all right. All they do. To the Muse. James Wright. NNaP; NoP
It is almost dark. Crossing the Colorado River into Yuma. Simon J. Ortiz. TAT
It is almost too simple. Hut. G. J. F. Dutton. PoSH
It is always a temptation to an armed and agile nation. Dane-Geld. Kipling. OxBTC
It is always night here. Star & Garter Theater. Dennis Schmitz. LCAP; NPGG
It is always so: the declining. Returning from Harvest. Vernon Watkins. NYBP
It is always someone else. Destiny of the Poet. Claude Vigée, *tr. by* Anthony Rudolf. VWA
It is an ancestral castle. Life in the Castle. Anne Hébert, *tr. by* Aliki *and* Willis Barnstone. BoWoP
It is an ancient custom. An Ancient Custom. Anatoly Steiger, *tr. by* John Glad. VWA
It is an ancient Mariner. The Rime of the Ancient Mariner. Samuel Taylor Coleridge. BeLS; CABA; CH; ChER; EBEV; EnRP; FaBoBe; FaBoCh; FaBV; FaFP; FiP; HAP; HBV-2; HoPM; InPS; LiTB; MasP; MOS; NOBE; NoP; OAEL-2; OAEP; OBEV; OBNC; OBNV; OBRV; PoEL-4; PrIm; RoGo; SeCeV; TEP; TreF; TrGrPo; ViBoPo; WHA
It is an ancient Mariner. The Ancient Mariner: The Wedding Guest's Version of the Affair from His Point of View. *Unknown.* FaBoPa
It is an auncient waggonere. The Rime of the Auncient Waggonere. William Maginn. BXAP
It is an honorable [*or* honourable] thought. Emily Dickinson. AP; NOCV (Immortality.) TwAmPo
It is an illusion that we were ever alive. The Rock. Wallace Stevens. AP
It is an old stove. Stove. Ken Belford. NeAC
It is as true as strange, else trial feigns. Sonnet. John Davies of Hereford. ElL
It Is at Moments after I Have Dreamed. E. E. Cummings. OxBA
It is at morning, twilight they expire. After Midnight. Charles Vildrac, *tr. by* Jethro Bithell. AWP
It is because the sea is blue. The Great Wave: *Hokusai.* Donald Finkel. PoPl
It is because you were my friend. Mortal Combat. Mary Elizabeth Coleridge. OBVV
It Is Becoming Now to Declare My Allegiance. C. Day Lewis. LiTM
It is best to turn on the set. Violence on Television. Louis Jenkins. NU
"It Is Better. . ." Bible, *O.T.* *Fr.* Ecclesiastes. *See* Better Path, The.
It is better this year. If the Birds Knew. John Ashbery. PoA
It Is Better to Be Together. Ruth Miller. PeSA
It is bleak December noon. December. William Caulfield Irwin. NBM
It is blue-butterfly day here in spring. Blue-Butterfly Day. Robert Frost. RFM
It is borne in upon me that pain. The Human Being Is a Lonely Creature. Richard Eberhart. NePoAm
It is buried and done with. Farewell. John Addington Symonds. OBVV
It is but little that remaineth. Notes of an Interview. William Johnson Cory. NBM
It is Christmas Day in the workhouse, and the cold, bare walls are bright. Christmas Day in the Workhouse [*or* In the Workhouse: Christmas Day]. George R. Sims. BeLS; BLPA; OBCP; PaPo; TreF
It is Christmas in the mansion. Christmas in the Heart. *Unknown.* OHIP; SiSoSe
It is cold here. The Moths. W. S. Merwin. HeIP
"It is cold outside, you will need a coat." The Arabian Shawl. Katherine Mansfield. Two Nocturnes, I. HBMV
It is cold without flesh, without bones. Dead in Wars and in Revolutions. Mary Devenport O'Neill. NeIP
It is colder now. Epistle to Be Left in the Earth. Archibald MacLeish. CMoP; ImOP; MoAB; MoAmPo; NOBA; TrGrPo
It is common knowledge to every schoolboy and even every Bachelor of Arts. Portrait of the Artist as a Prematurely Old Man. Ogden Nash. BLPL; CrMA; FaFP; LiTA; LiTM; NePA
It is consummation, a mad rape. Pitch Seven. Hamish Brown. PoSH
It is creation's morning. Now. Harriet Monroe. HBV-2
It is dangerous for a woman to defy the gods. Letter to My Sister. Anne Spencer. AmNP; BlSi; PoBA; PoNe
It Is Dangerous to Read Newspapers. Margaret Atwood. HeIP; OBWP
It is dangerous to stand in early fall. Having Read Books. Heather McHugh. GeTw
It is dangerous to visit you in your woods in May. Reunion. Heather Cadsby. AMV-81
It is dark. The Last Bus. Mark Strand. TwCP
It is dark and lonesome here. The Lover. Richard Henry Stoddard. AA
It is dark, now, and grave. Melting Pot. Michael Echeruo. TTY
It is December in Wicklow. Exposure. Seamus Heaney. CIP; IPY
It is deep summer. Far out. There. Robert Mezey. NaP
It Is Difficult Now to Speak of Poetry. George Oppen. *Fr.* Of Being Numerous. NNaP
It is difficult to imagine how vulnerable they are. The Birds. David Posner. NYBP
It is disastrous to be a wounded deer. Hello. Gregory Corso. PoM
It is done! Laus Deo! Whittier. AmPP; AP; PAH
It is dusk/ On the bridle path. Memory. Joseph Stroud. NPGG
It is dusk on the Lost Lagoon. The Lost Lagoon. Pauline Johnson. BPAW
It is early dawn. The city forty miles away draws airplanes. Written Forty Miles South of a Spreading City. Robert Bly. NNaP
It is early morning within this room; without. Laurence Binyon. *Fr.* Winter Sunrise. ChMP
It is early, yet. The Grand Canyon. James Merrill. TAP
It is easier to forgive an enemy than to forgive a friend. Blake. *Fr.* Jerusalem. OAEL-2
It is easy enough to be pleasant. Worth While. Ella Wheeler Wilcox. BLPA; FPL; TreF
It is easy enough to love flowers but these. Giant Decorative Dahlias. Molly Holden. OxBTC
It is easy to be young. How to Be Old. May Swenson. MAT; UnPo
It is easy to disturb. As Sun, as Sea. James Sullivan. AMV-81
It is easy to mould the yielding clay. Clay Hills. Jean Starr Untermeyer. HBMV
It Is Enough. Philip Appleman. BXAP
It is enough for me. Old Man Told Me. Lance Henson. VoR
It is enough; time presses, we are thrifty. It Is Enough. Philip Appleman. BXAP
It is equal to living in a tragic land. Dry Loaf. Wallace Stevens. CrMA; NOBA; OxBA; PoRA
It is essential I remember. Man White, Brown Girl and All That Jazz. Gloria C. Oden. PoBA
It is evening. One bat dances. A Soul. Randall Jarrell. CMoP
It is far to Assisi. The Mental Hospital Garden. William Carlos Williams. FYAP
It Is Finished. Barney Bush. STE
It is finished. The enormous dust-cloud over Europe. Armistice. Paul Dehn. OxBTC
"It is finished." The last nail. Tenebrae. David Gascoyne. *Fr.* Miserere. NeBP

It is fitting that you be here. On Seeing Two Brown Boys in a Catholic Church. Frank Horne. BANP; CDC; PoBA; PoNe; TTY
It is folly for any man in the world. The Praises of God. *Unknown, tr. by* Kenneth Jackson. AnIL
It is foolish for Rubens to show her. Susanna and the Elders. Jack Gilbert. NPGG
It is for us/ to praise the Lord of all. The Kingdom of God. Rab. TrJP
It is Friday. We have come. Forgiving My Father. Lucille Clifton. GeTw
It is from the ideas of you that you emerge. Correspondences. Robert Duncan. PoM
It is fun to ride the horse. Horse. Kenneth Rexroth. *Fr.* A Bestiary. NNaP
It is good sometimes to grasp our helplessness. The Flood. Charles G. Bell. GrPl
It is good to be out on the road, and going one knows not where. Tewkesbury Road. John Masefield. TreFT
It is good to see the sunshine ebb on distant hills. The Spirit of the Cairngorms. Axel Firsoff. PoSH
It is good to strive against wind and rain. A Mood. Amélie Rives. AA
It Is Great for Our Country to Die. James Gates Percival. *See* Elegiac.
It is hard. Being a Giant. Robert Mezey. GrPl
It is hard, alone in this room at night to remember. The Eagle. Richard Blessing. AMV–80
It is hard going to the door. The Door. Robert Creeley. NaP; NeAP; NoAM; PoM; VGW
It is hard, inland. In Winter. Robert Wallace. BoNaP
It is hard to beat a good meal. Thomas Kinsella. *Fr.* A Technical Supplement. CIP
It Is Hard to Catch Trout. Piuvkaq, *tr. fr. Eskimo.* WTO
It Is Her Cousin's Death. Gail Fox. NOBC
It is here the bones. The Wing Factory. Dona Stein. AMV–80
It is hot today, dry enough for cutting grain. August from My Desk. Roland Flint. AmFN
It is I, America, calling! A Call to Arms. Mary Raymond Shipman Andrews. PAH
"It Is I, Be Not Afraid." A. B. Simpson. STF
It is I that am under sorrow at this time. Another Song. William Ross. GoTS
It is impossible to find anything good. Flood. Mary Grant Charles. GoYe
It is in captivity. The Bull. William Carlos Williams. LiTM; MoVE; MP; NoP; TwCP
It is in many ways made plain to us. James Branch Cabell. Retractions, V. HBMV
"It is in the fake picture that we first perceive." Plato Instructs a Midwest Farmer. David Palmer. SUW
It is in the rock, but not in the stone. Riddle. *Unknown.* ChTr
It Is in Winter That We Dream of Spring. Robert Burns Wilson. AA
It is Isis the mystery. Don Juan. D. H. Lawrence. PoA
It is January 12. Chronicle. Edward Dorn. TAT
It Is July. Susan Hartley Swett. YeAr
(July.) GN
It is June, it is June. Andraitx—Pomegranate Flowers. D. H. Lawrence. NoAM; NoP
It is late afternoon at the beach; I lie on the swaying dock. "And All the While the Sky is Falling. . ." Lora Dunetz. NePoAm
It is late afternoon. Out of my study window. Out of My Study Window. Reed Whittemore. PoPl
It is late and the others have turned. Late. Daniel Halpern. AMV–81
It is late at night and still I am losing. In Dives' Dive. Robert Frost. VGW
It is late in the year. Night in the House by the River. Tu Fu, *tr. by* Kenneth Rexroth. NaP
It is late last night the dog was speaking of you. The Grief of a Girl's Heart. *Unknown, tr. by* Lady Gregory. ChTr; OLR
It is Leviathan, mountain and world. History. Robert Fitzgerald. FYAP; MoVE
It is like riding Death and not dying. Sometimes Heaven Is a Mean Machine. William Pitt Root. MAYP
It is like the plot of an ol/ novel. Instructions to a Princess. Ishmael Reed. CNA; PoBA
It is likely enough that lions and scorpions. Ante Mortem. Robinson Jeffers. MoAmPo; MoVE
It is little I repair to the matches of the Southron folk. At Lord's. Francis Thompson. EBVV; LiSp
It is made to be rolled down. A Poem like a Grenade. John Haines. EAS
It Is March ("It is March and black dust falls out of the books"). W. S. Merwin. NaP
It is midnight. Poem at Thirty. Sonia Sanchez. BlSi; BPo; CNA; NMM; PoBA
It is midnite. The room is blue. Death Songs. L. V. Mack. PoBA
It Is Mine, This Country Wide. *Unknown.* GOA
It is Monday morning. The Goldfish Wife. Sandra Hochman. NYBP; UnPo
It is moonlight. Alone in the silence. Evening Song of Senlin. Conrad Aiken. *Fr.* Senlin; a Biography. HBMV
It is morning darling look the sun. Aubade: N.Y.C. Robert Wallace. HoPM
It is morning, Senlin says, and in the morning. Morning Song [of Senlin]. Conrad Aiken. *Fr.* Senlin; a Biography. CMoP; HBMV; LiTA; LiTM; MoAB; MoAmPo; NoAM; OxBA; TrGrPo
It is most true that eyes are formed to serve. Astrophel and Stella, V. Sir Philip Sidney. OAEL–1; OBSC; SiPS
It is much like ocean the way it opens. Open Country. Richard Hugo. LCAP; NPAW
It is my joy in life to find. A Prayer. Frank Dempster Sherman. TreFS
It is my own door that is shut. Dialogue. John Erskine. HBMV
It is my sorrow that this day's troubles. Slievenamon. *Unknown, tr. by* Frank O'Connor. KiLC
It is my white horse, just like the dawn. Mi Caballo Blanco (My White Horse). *Tr. fr. Spanish.* FSW
It is myself. To a Dog Injured in the Street. William Carlos Williams. LCAP; LiTM; MoAB; NePoAm; PP; SeCeV
It is necessary to wait until the boss's eyes are on you. Notes from a Slave Ship. Edward Field. PP
It is never enough to know what you want. "The Wish to Be Believed." Mona Van Duyn. PoA
It is New Year's Day. Best Loved of Africa. Margaret Danner. PoBA; PoNe
It is night. At Arm's Length. Shirley Bossert. FAZ
It is night again. Tzu Yeh, *tr. fr. Chinese by* Kenneth Rexroth *and* Ling Chung. WPOW
It is night like a red rag. A Moment of War. Laurie Lee. OBWP
It is no idle fabulous tale, nor is it fayned newes. Newes from Virginia. Richard Rich. PAH
It is no longer necessary to sleep. A Man Walking and Singing. Wendell Berry. AP
It is no madness to say. Hilda Doolittle ("H. D."). *Fr.* The Flowering of the Rod. FaBoMo
It is noble country where we dwell. Our Country. Henry David Thoreau. GOA
It is not. Another Letter to Joseph Bruchac. Jack L. Anderson. LFAC
It is not bad. Let them play. The Bloody Sire. Robinson Jeffers. CMoP; LiTM; NePA; PoA
It Is Not Beauty I Demand. George Darley. HBV–1; OAEL–2
(Loveliness of Love, The.) GTBS; GTBS–P; OBRV
(Song, A: "It is not beauty I demand.") OBNC; OBVV
It is not, Celia, in our power. To a Lady Asking Him How Long He Would Love Her. Sir George Etherege. HBV–1; LoBV; OBEV; ViBoPo
It Is Not Death. Thomas Hood. *See* Sonnet: "It is not death . . ."
It is not easy to be less than lovers. For M. Bruce Williamson. NeIP
It Is Not Enough. David Henderson. PPON
It is not enough. The Prophet's Warning or Shoot to Kill. Ebon Dooley. PoBA
It is not fair to visit all. Eve. Oliver Herford. HBMV; YaD
It is not far to my place. Visit. A. R. Ammons. CoAP; GrPl; TwCP
It is not four years ago. Proffered Love Rejected [*or* The Rejected Offer]. Sir John Suckling. CavP; ErPo; NCEP; UnTE
It is not given to every man to take a bath of multitude. Crowds. Baudelaire, *tr. by* Arthur Symons. SyP
It Is Not Growing like a Tree. Ben Jonson. *See* Noble Nature, The.
It is not hard to tell of a rose. Inscription. Ann Hamilton. HBMV
It is not—I swear it by every fiery omen to be seen these nights. Readings, Forecasts, Personal Guidance. Kenneth Fearing. MoAmPo
It is not in the books. The Three Movements. Donald Hall. NePoEA–2
It is not interesting to see. Thoughts on the Christian Doctrine of Eternal Hell. Stevie Smith. PPON
It is not life upon Thy gifts to live. Life. Jones Very. AP
It Is Not Likely Now. Frances Bellerby. ChMP
It is not my voice, it is not my voice that is tearing. Serenade of Angels. Rina Lasnier, *tr. by* Jan Pallister. AMV–81
It is not raining rain for [*or* to] me. *See* It isn't raining rain for me.
It is not right for you to know, so do not ask, Leuconoë. Ad Leuconoen. Horace, *tr. by* Franklin P. Adams. Odes, I, 13. AWP
It is not so much the image of the man. Photograph of Haymaker, 1890. Molly Holden. OxBTC
It Is Not So with Me. Blake. *Fr.* Vala; or, The Four Zoas. SeCePo
It is not sweet content, be sure. Arthur Hugh Clough. VLP
It is not that I love thee, fairest. Love and Respect. Pathericke Jenkyn. CavP
It is not that I love you less. The Selfe Banished. Edmund Waller. CavP; FaBoEn; MePo; OBS
It is not the earth that I worship. Earth Song. Thomas Peacock. VoR

It is not the fear of death. André's Request to Washington. *Unknown.* PAH
It is not the foreignness *per se* of heroes. Why the British Girls Give In So Easily. Nicholas Moore. WaP
It is not the moon, I tell you. Mock Orange. Louise Glück. MAYP
It is not the still weight. The Jungle. William Carlos Williams. CABA
It is not the weight of the jewel or plate. The Perfect Gift. Edmund Vance Cooke. PChr
It is not the words we work with, words we examine. The Collector. Robert F. Whisler. AMV-81
It is not the young whom we find feeding the pigeons. The Pigeon-Feeders in Battery Park. Julia Cooley Altrocchi. GoYe
It Is Not to Be Thought Of [That the Flood]. Wordsworth. EnRP; FiP; OBRV
(England, 1802, IV.) HBV-2; NOBE; OBEV
(Faith and Freedom, 4 *ll.*) GN
(Sonnet: "It is not to be thought of that the Flood.") LoBV
(We Must Be Free or Die.) FaPoR
It Is Not Too Late. Lucia Trent. PGD
It is not vertue, wisdom, valour, wit. Woman. Milton. *Fr.* Samson Agonistes. OBS
It is not you that move, but the running sand. The Eye. Eithne Wilkins. NeBP
It is nothing I understand any better. Homing. P. C. Bowman. AMV-81
It is now the tenth hour of this October night. October. John Bayliss. NeBP
It is of a fearless highwayman a story I will tell. Quantrell. *Unknown.* CoSo
It is of a fearless Irishman a story I will tell. Brennan on the Moor. *Unknown.* AmFP
It is on the sea and under the waves of the sea. Cycle. Seán Jennett. WaP
It is only death. Journey. Raymond Thompson. LFAC
It is only that this warmth and movement are like. The Woman in Sunshine. Wallace Stevens. BiP; MoVE
It is ordained,—or so Politian said. Arthur Davison Ficke. Epitaph for the Poet V., I. HBMV
It is our hand. Patience of a People. F. J. Bryant, Jr. CNA
It is out in the flimsy suburbs. Sunday in Glastonbury. Robert Bly. ConAP
It is past midnight in a thick fog when sirens. Street Fire. Daniel Halpern. AmPA; NYP
It is people at the edge who say. Sayings from the Northern Ice. William Stafford. NU
It is plain now what you are. Your head has dropped. Carrion. Harold Monro. *Fr.* Youth in Arms. MMA
It is portentous, and a thing of state. Abraham Lincoln Walks at Midnight. Vachel Lindsay. AmFN; AmPP; CMoP; FaBV; FaFP; FaPON; GOA; HBV-2; LiTA; MoAmPo; MoVE; NoAM; NOBA; OFD; OHFP; OHIP; OxBA; PAH; PAI; PAL; PoPl; PPON; TAP; TreF; VGW
It is queer to think that many people. The Man with the Rake. Christopher Morley. *Fr.* Translations from the Chinese. EvOK
It is quite unfair to be. Elephant. Alan Brownjohn. OnUR
It Is Raining. Lucy Sprague Mitchell. SoPo; TiPo
It is reported. Sharks in Shallow Water. Fred Levinson. AmPA
It is rough. Poem about a Seashell. Ranice Henderson Crosby. NMM
It is said that many a king in troubled Europe. Rulers: Philadelphia [*or* Rulers]. Fenton Johnson. AmFN; PoNe
It is said there are those who can never be sane. Bill. Peter Kocan. CBAP
It is sayde full ryfe. *Unknown. Fr.* Shepherd's Play (Townley cycle). FaBoUs
It is she alone that matters. Bouquet of Belle Scavoir. Wallace Stevens. MoAB; MoAmPo
It is, sir, a confest intrusion here. To My Honoured Friend Mr. George Sandys. Henry King. AnAnS-2
It is snowing heavily again. Between Us. Stephen Berg. NaP
It Is So Long Since My Heart Has Been with Yours. E. E. Cummings. NoAM
It is so much easier to forget than to have been Mr. Whittier. Mr. Whittier. Winfield Townley Scott. CrMA; VGW
It is so peaceful on the ceiling! Sleeping on the Ceiling. Elizabeth Bishop. MiAP
It is so pure, so complete. Aesthetics of the Moon. Jack Anderson. MOON
It is so quiet. It is 1957. Sharks, Caloosahatchee River. Greg Pape. MAYP
It is so still in the house. The Mother's Song. *Unknown, tr. by* Peter Freuchen. OBCP; WTO
It is so white. Summer. Bill Manhire. OCNZ
It is some school, brick, green, a sleepy hill. An Officer's Prison Camp Seen from a Troop Train. Randall Jarrell. WaP
It is sometime since I have been. The Hill. Robert Creeley. ConAP; NoAM
It is spring in the mountains. Written on the Wall at Chang's Hermitage. Tu Fu, *tr. by* Kenneth Rexroth. HoPM; NaP
It is springtime and the ants come into the house. Ants. Lewis Hyde. AMV-80; FAZ
It is still the tallest building in the world. Looking at the Empire State Building. Ralph Pomeroy. GP
It is strange to think of the Annas, the Vronskys, the Pierres, all the Tolstoyan lot wiped out. Fate and the Younger Generation. D. H. Lawrence. OxBoLi; WhC
It is strange we trust each other. Why Doubt God's Word? A. B. Simpson. BLRP
"It is such a beautiful day I had to write you a letter." Thoughts of a Young Girl. John Ashbery. ConAP; TAP; VGW
It is summer, city summer. Chicago, Summer Past. Richard Snyder. Psk
It is Sunday afternoon on the Grand Canal. Seurat. Ira Sadoff. PoDr
It is talked the warld all over. Sheath and Knife. *Unknown.* ESPB; ViBoFo
It is ten years, now, since we rowed to Children's Island. The Babysitters. Sylvia Plath. NoP
It is that pale, delaying hour. John Vance Cheney. Evening Songs, II. AA
It is the association after all. A Way of Looking. Elizabeth Jennings. NePoEA; PP
It is the best, erely and late. Be True to Your Condition in Life. John Audelay. MeEL
It is the best thing. Pregnancy. Sandra McPherson. BoWoP; NMM
It is the bittern's solemn cry. Solitude. Frederick Peterson. AA
It is the calm and solemn night! Alfred Domett. *Fr.* A Christmas Hymn. PGD
It Is the Cause, It Is the Cause, My Soul. Shakespeare. *Fr.* Othello, V, ii. BiP; EBEV; PAI
(Othello and Desdemona.) FiP
It is the celestial ennui of apartments. Wallace Stevens. Notes toward a Supreme Fiction, II. MoPo; NePA
It is the counterpoise that minds. Noble Love. Richard Flecknoe. ACP
It is the day of all the year. Mothering Sunday. *Unknown.* OxNR
It is the day when he was born. In Memoriam A. H. H., CVII. Tennyson. EBVV; SBVL
It is the East we dream of: there. The Rider. Leah Bodine Drake. NePoAm-2
It is the endless dance of the dead. Dirge. Quincy Troupe. PoBA
It is the evening hour. To Mary: It Is the Evening Hour [*or* Mary]. John Clare. BoLoP; ChTr; EnLoPo; FaBoEn; GBL
It is the fall, the eternal fall of water. The Fall. Kathleen Raine. MoPo
It is the first mild day of March. To My Sister. Wordsworth. EnRP; OAEL-2; OBRV
It is the football season once more. Autumn. Vernon Scannell. OxBTC
It is the gentle poet's art. Iron. Walter de la Mare. NOBL
It is the Gulf Stream wind's illusion. Indian Summer Here, You in Honolulu. Donald Johnson. AMV-80
It is the Harvest Moon! On gilded vanes. The Harvest Moon. Longfellow. AP; GN
It is the hottest of days. Man on Move Despite Failures. Jeffrey Alan Triggs. AMV-80
It Is the Hush of Night. Byron. *Fr.* Childe Harold's Pilgrimage, III. LiTB
(Night.) LoBV
It is the lake within the lake that drowns. My Lady the Lake. Peter Davidson. WeW
It is the last of the ninth, two down, bases loaded. The Lady Pitcher. Cynthia Macdonald. Psk
It is the light. Aging. Diane Wakoski. AMV-81
It is the littleness I would keep. To a Photograph. Parker Tyler. NePA
It is the man, himself. Aleph. Stuart Z. Perkoff. VWA
It is the memory of the peacock and the muses. Letter to R. Willard Maas. WaP
It is the midnight hour;—the beauteous sea. Calm as the Cloudless Heaven. "Christopher North." EtS
It is the miller's daughter. Song. Tennyson. *Fr.* The Miller's Daughter. HBV-1; OBEV; OBVV; TrGoPo; UnTE
It is the moment of twilight. Sowing Season. Evening. Victor Hugo, *tr. by* Mary Ann Caws. NAWM-2
It is the month of falling stars. The Month of Falling Stars. Ella Higginson. YeAr
It is the morning after. The Blood-letting. Joy Harjo. TWSS
It is the morning of our love. An Aspect of Love, Alive in the Ice and Fire. Gwendolyn Brooks. BPo; CAPP; PAI; TAP
It is the nature of man that puzzles me. The Nature of Man. C.H. Sisson. FaBoTw
It is the Negro's tragedy I feel. The Negro's Tragedy. Claude McKay. BPo
It is the Old Man through the sleeping town. The Fall Again. Howard Nemerov. ConAP

It is the pain, it is the pain, endures. Villanelle. William Empson. ChMP; CMoP; EnLoPo; NoAM; OAEL-2
It is the picnic with Ruth in the spring. The Picnic. John Logan. ConAP; CTBA; NCSH; NePoEA-2
It is the quality that most resembles. Yielding. Shellie Keir Robbins. AMV-80
It Is the Reed. Sister Maris Stella. GoBC
It is the route you took through winter light. Tracking the Sled, Christmas 1951. Jeanne Murray Walker. AMV-81
It is the same infrequent star. The Star of Calvary. Nathaniel Hawthorne. AA
It is the sea: dead calm—and the spring tide. Paris at Night. Tristan Corbière, *tr. by* Kenneth Koch *and* Georges Guy. SyP
It is the sea's edge lubbers love. Sailing, Sailing. Gary Burr. CoPo; NYBP
It Is the Season. Josephine Jacobsen. TAP
It is the season of the sweet wild rose. Modern Love, XLV. George Meredith. GBL; NBM; PoEL-5
It is the silver seeking salvation. The Plight. James W. Thompson. BPo
It is the sinking of things. Rain. James Wright. NaP
It is the sinners' dust-tongued bell claps me to churches. Dylan Thomas. OxBTC
It is the snow-gum silently. The Snow-Gum. Douglas Stewart. PoAu-2
It is the spot I came to seek. An Indian at the Burial-Place of His Fathers. Bryant. HeIP
It Is the Stars That Govern Us. Michael Magee. PoA
It is the thirty-first of March. Peter Bell [*or* Peter Bell; a Lyrical Ballad]. John Hamilton Reynolds. OBNC; OBRV; Par
It is the time of rain and snow. Izumi Shikibu, *tr. fr. Japanese by* Kenneth Rexroth. WPOW
It is the way of a pleasant path. Green Frog at Roadstead, Wisconsin. James Schevill. TAP
It is the whales that drive. Fish. William Carlos Williams. NoAM
It is the white plum tree. 'Tis the White Plum Tree. Shaw Neilson. PoAu-1
It is the word *pejorative* that hurts. Sailing after Lunch. Wallace Stevens. MoPo
It is their way to find the surface. Poem by the Charles River. Robin Blaser. NeAP
It is there, above him, beyond, behind. The Being. James Dickey. NMP
It is this deep blankness is the real thing strange. Let It Go. William Empson. FaBoMo; OxBTC
It is this rainy afternoon that reaches me. This Afternoon. Juan Sáez Burgos, *tr. by* Julio Marzán. InW
It is 3:42 a.m. on a troop train. The Kid in Upper 4. Nelson C. Metcalf. TreFS
It is three o'clock in the morning. Trials of a Tourist. Anne Tibble. FaBoCo
It Is Time. Ted Joans. NNP
It is time for the others to come. The Magus. James Dickey. NAs
It is time for the United States to spend money on education so. It Is Time. Ted Joans. NNP
It is time I wrote my will. W. B. Yeats. The Tower, III. MoVE
It is time to be old. Terminus. Emerson. AA; AmPP; AP; AWP; FPL; HBV-1; NOBA; OxBA; PoEL-4; PoLF; TAP
It is tiresome always to talk about weather, or think about it. The Self and the Weather. Reed Whittemore. NMP
It is to a goodly child well fitting. A Goodly Child. *Unknown.* OxBChV
It is to be my last good memory of you. The Seventies. Tony Beyer. OCNZ
It is to my own as if the man made them a gift. Eadwacer. *Unknown, tr. by* Kemp Malone. PBWP
It is told by seafarers. Told by Seafarers. Galway Kinnell. NePoAm-2
It is told, in Buddhi-theosophic schools. Transcendentalism. *Unknown.* NA
It is tomorrow now. Morning Star. Thomas Hornsby Ferril. VGW
It Is Too Late ("It is too late! Ah, nothing is too late"). Longfellow. *Fr.* Morituri Salutamas. BLPL; PoLF
(Too Late?) WBLP
It is too late for the word. Too Late. Rachel Korn, *tr. by* Seymour Mayne *and* Rivka Augenfeld. VWA
It Is True. Federico García Lorca, *tr. fr. Spanish by* Harriet de Onís. OLR
It is true—/ I've always loved. Alice Walker. *Fr.* Once. NMM; PoBA
It is true, modern life is complicated. For the Market. Jane Mayhall. TAP
It is true, that even in the best-run state. The Murder of William Remington. Howard Nemerov. CMoP; CoAP
It is true that I hold Thero fair. Epigram. Meleager, *tr. by* Peter Whigham. PeHV
It is true that, older than man and ages to oulast him. Gray Weather. Robinson Jeffers. CMoP; NoAM
It is 12:20 in New York a Friday. The Day Lady Died. Frank O'Hara. CAPP; HoAn; NeAP; NoAM; NOBA; NoP; NYP; PAI; PoM; SOTW
It is Ulysses that approaches from the east. The World as Meditation. Wallace Stevens. NIP
It is very aggravating. The Truth about Horace. Eugene Field. InMe
It is what he does not know. On a Squirrel Crossing the Road in Autumn, in New England. Richard Eberhart. HeIP; LiTM; NePA; PoCh; Psk
It is what we both knew in the sunlight of a restaurant's garden. The Circus Ringmaster's Apology to God. Norman Dubie. MAYP
It is whatever day, whatever time it is. Sunday Morning. Wayne Moreland. PoBA
It is when I hear Mozart. Deafness. Richard Ryan. BIrV
It is when I work on the old Volvo. Thoreau. Rodney Jones. MAYP
It Is When the Tribe Is Gone. Duff Bigger. FAZ
It is when they come with questions. Poem for the Atomic Age. Emanuel Litvinov. NeBP
It is winter and the new year. The New Year. Mark Strand. *Fr.* Elegy for My Father. UnPo
It Is Winter, I Know. Merrill Moore. MoAmPo
It is written in the skyline of the city. Pact. Kenneth Fearing. CMoP
It is written that a hurricane holds the power. An Antipastoral Memory of One Summer. Dave Smith. MAYP
It is your last day and hour and you are alone. Who. Edwin Honig. TAP
It is yourself you seek. Man Alone. Louise Bogan. NYBP
It isn't any worse than what. Anxiety about Dying. Alicia Ostriker. AMV-80
It Isn't Far to Bethlehem. Arthur R. Macdougall, Jr. PGD
It isn't freedom, that. That Brings Us to the Woodstove in the Wilds, at Night. Walter Hall. AMV-81
It isn't proper, I guess you know. Read This with Gestures. John Ciardi. RHPC
It isn't [*or* is not] raining rain for [*or* to] me. April Rain [*or* Rain Song]. Robert Loveman. HBV-1; HBVY; SUS; TreFT; TrJP; WBLP
It isn't that I fear. Turning Thirty. W. D. Ehrhart. AMV-81
It isn't that the threat of the bomb is great. Cocoon. Ishigaki Rin, *tr. by* Ayusawa Takako. WPOW
It Isn't the Church—It's You. *Unknown.* BLPA; WBLP
It Isn't the Cough. *Unknown.* FaFP; ShM
It isn't the thing you do, dear. The Sin of Omission. Margaret E. Sangster. BLPA; HBV-2; TreFS; TRV
It Isn't the Town, It's You. R. W. Glover. BLPA
It keeps eternal whisperings around. On the Sea [*or* Sonnet on the Sea]. Keats. CABA; EnRP; EtS; FF; HBV-1; LiTB; MOS; NoP; OAEL-2; SeCePo; SeCeV; TEP; TrGrPo; ViBoPo
It later befell in the years that followed. The Fire-Dragon and the Treasure. *Unknown, tr. by* Charles W. Kennedy. *Fr.* Beowulf. AnOE
It lay, dark in the corner of the field. Suicide Pond. Kathy McLaughlin. PoA
It lies around us like a cloud. The Other World. Harriet Beecher Stowe. AA; HBV-2; WGRP
It Lies Not in Our Power to Love or Hate. Christopher Marlowe. *Fr.* Hero and Leander, First Sestiad. TrGrPo; WHA
(Love at First Sight.) FaBoEn; TreFT
(Who Ever Loved, That Loved Not at First Sight?) BLPL; FaFP; LiTB
It lies not on the sunlit hill. The White Peace. "Fiona Macleod." FaBoBe; HBV-2
It lifts the poor man from his cell. The Powers of Love. George Moses Horton. BALP
It little profits that an idle king. Ulysses. Tennyson. AWP; CABA; EBEV; FaPoR; FF; FiP; FPL; HAP; HBV-2; HeIP; HoPM; InPK; InPS; LiTB; LoBV; MOS; NIP; NOBE; NoP; OAEL-2; OAEP; PAI; PoPle; PoRA; PPoe; PPP; PrIm; SCV; SeCePo; SeCeV; SoSe; TEP; TreF; TrGrPo; UnPo; ViBoPo; VLP; WeW; WHA
It looked extremely rocky for the Mudville nine that day. Casey at the Bat. Ernest Lawrence Thayer. BeLS; BLPA; FaBoBe; FaFP; FPL; InMe; PoRA; TreF; YaD
It looks a piece of golden, broken glass. Onion Skin in Barn. Kenneth Slade Alling. NePoAm
It looks like any building. The Library. Barbara A. Huff. FaPON; RHPC
It makes a man feel happy. Three Sweethearts. Heine, *tr. by* Louis Untermeyer. UnTE
It makes no difference abroad. Emily Dickinson. AP
It May Be. Max Jacob, *tr. fr. French by* Wallace Fowlie. PoPl
It may be a little different. Blood to Blood. Alvin Aubert. GP
It May Be Good. Sir Thomas Wyatt. EnRePo
("It may be good, like it who list.") AAS; SiPS
It may be so,—perhaps thou hast. To the Portrait of "A Gentlemen." Oliver Wendell Holmes. InMe
It may be that a strange dream. It May Be. Max Jacob, *tr. by* Wallace Fowlie. PoPl
It may be these things never did occur. Kinnereth. Rachel, *tr. by* A. M. Klein. TrJP
It may be 'tis observ'd, I want relations. George Wither. *Fr.* The Tired Petitioner. SeCV-1

It may happen again—this much. The Flight. John Haines. EAS
It may indeed be phantasy, when I. To Nature. Samuel Taylor Coleridge. OAEL-2
It May Not Always Be So [and I Say]. E. E. Cummings. *Fr.* Sonnets—Unrealities. BoLoP; FaBV
It Might Be a Lump of Amber. Walter de la Mare. FaBoNo
It might have been in the heart of a deep forest. The False Summer. Marya Zaturenska. CrMA
It mounts at sea, a concave wall. From the Wave. Thom Gunn. NoP
It must be magic. Red White & Another Ism. Harold LaMont Otey. LFAC
It must be so—Plato, thou reason'st well. Cato's Soliloquy. Joseph Addison. *Fr.* Cato, V, i. TreFS; WBLP
It must be spring, the way the light. Another Mother and Child. Joe-Anne McLaughlin. FAZ
It Must Be Summer. Sandor Csoori, *tr. fr. Hungarian by* Nicholas Kolumban. AMV-81
It must have been a Friday. I could hear. Katherine's Dream. Robert Lowell. *Fr.* Between the Porch and the Altar. ConAP
It must have been a year. Fire, Hair, Meat and Bone. Fred Johnson. PoBA
It must have been for one of us, my own. Not Thou but I. Philip Bourke Marston. BLPA; BLPL
It must have been one o'clock at night. To Remain. C. P. Cavafy, *tr. by* John Mavrogordato. ErPo
It must have been one or one-thirty. To Remain. C. P. Cavafy, *tr. by* Nikos Stangos *and* Stephen Spender. BoLoP
It nearly cancels my fear of death, my dearest said. Cremation. Robinson Jeffers. ELU
It neither was the words nor yet the tune. Two Girls Singing. Iain Crichton Smith. BSV
It never occurred to me, never. The Meeting. Howard Moss. HoAn; NYBP
It nods. The Bald Spot. Wesley McNair. AMV-81
It occurred to Marshall. Marshall. George MacBeth. NoAM
It ofttimes has been told, that the British seamen bold. The *Constitution* and the *Guerriére*. *Unknown.* AmFP; AmSS; FSW; ViBoFo
It once might have been, once only. Youth and Art. Robert Browning. CTC; HBV-1; ViBoPo
It ought to be impossible to be mistaken. An Incorrigible Music. Allen Curnow. OCNZ
It ought to come in April. Wearing of the Green. Aileen Fisher. RHPC; YeAr
"It Out-Herods Herod. Pray You, Avoid It." Anthony Hecht. CoAP; NCSH; NiP; NoAM; NOBA; OxBC
It Pays. Arnold Bennett. *See* There Was a Young Man of Montrose.
It Pays to Advertise. *Unknown. See* Advertisement.
It Pleases. Gary Snyder. TAT
It quickned next a toyfull ape, and so. John Donne. *Fr.* The Progresse of the Soule. PoEL-2
It rained in my sleep. September. Linda Pastan. Psk
It rained, it poured, it rained so hard. Sir Hugh. *Unknown.* ViBoFo
It rained quite a lot, that spring. You woke in the morning. Metropolitan Nightmare. Stephen Vincent Benét. ImOP; NYBP
It rained toward day. The morning came sad and white. Colder Fire. Robert Penn Warren. *Fr.* To a Little Girl, One Year Old, in a Ruined Fortress. LiTM; MoVE
It Rains ("It rains, and nothing stirs within the fence"). Edward Thomas. MoVE; OxBTC
It rains in Santiago. Madrigal to the City of Santiago. Federico García Lorca, *tr. by* Norman Di Giovanni. CAD
It rains, it rains in merry Lincoln. Little Sir Hugh. *Unknown.* OBET
It really must. E. E. Cummings. YaD
"It relaxes me," he said. Six Reasons for Drinking. Vernon Scannell. OxBC
It rely is ridikkelus. *See* Itt rely is ridikkelus.
"It rests me to be among beautiful women." Tame Cat. Ezra Pound. ELU; OBAL
It rises over the lake, the farms. The Kite. Mark Strand. NYBP
It Rolls On. Morris Bishop. ImOP
It rose dark as a stack of peat. Suilven. Andrew Young. OxBS
It said welcome. The Second Coming. John William Corrington. HoPM
It sat between my husband and my children. Seele im Raum. Randall Jarrell. CoBMV; LCAP
It say in de Bible. Ku Kluck Klan. Lawrence Gellert. TrAS
It Says. Jon Silkin. VWA
It says much for your life. Grandfather. Mary Joan Coleman. AMV-80
It seconds the crickets of the province. The Rocking Chair. A. M. Klein. CaP; HeIP; NoP; PeCV
It seemed at first like a piece of luck. Camouflage. Amy Clampitt. SUW
It seemed corrival of the world's great prime. A Fallen Yew. Francis Thompson. BrPo; MoAB; MoBrPo
It seemed that out of [the] battle I escaped. Strange Meeting. Wilfred Owen. BrPo; ChMP; CMoP; CoBMV; DTC; FaBoEn; FaBoMo; FaBoRV; GTBS-P; HeIP; HoPM; LiTB; LoBV; MMA; MoAB; MoBrPo; MoPo; MoVE; NoAM; NOBE; NoP; OAEL-2; OAEP; OBWP; SCV; SeCeV; TreFT; TrGrPo; WaaP; WaP
It seemed to be but chance, yet who shall say. May 30, 1893. John Kendrick Bangs. AA
It seemed to me when I saw her. The Torn Nightgown. Joel Oppenheimer. CoPo
It seems a certain time ago: a-maybe. One Time. Douglas Livingstone. PeSA
It seems a day. Nutting. Wordsworth. EnRP; NU; OAEL-2
"It seems a shame." The Last Flower. John Travers Moore. PoSC
It seems I have no tears left. They should have fallen. Tears. Edward Thomas. GTBS-P; LiTB; PoPle
It seems I was always just a guest. Motels, Hotels, Other People's Houses. H. L. Van Brunt. FAZ
It seems like a dream—that sweet wooing of old. Bachelor Hall. Eugene Field. BLPA; FPL
It seems like the same thing all over again. Coming Home from Camp. Lonny Kaneko. BrSi
It seems no work of man's creative hand. Pedra. John William Burgon. BLPA
It seems now far off and foolish, a memory. Lot Later. Howard Nemerov. HoPM; NMP
It seems so simple now, that life of thine. Washington. Geraldine Meyrich. OHIP
It seems so strange that I once loved you so. Twenty Years After. Evan V. Shute. CaP
It Seems That God Bestowed Somehow, *with music.* Amanda Benjamin Hall. AH
It seems that I hear that beauty who. Lament of the Lovely Helmet-Dealer. Villon, *tr. by* Hubert Creekmore. ErPo
It seems the horse they furnished me. Enlightenment. Robert V. Carr. BPAW
It seems they never complete these things. The Classical Style. Michael Palmer. NPGG
It seems to me I'd like to go. Far from the Madding Crowd [*or* Vacation]. Nixon Waterman. BLPA; FaBoBe; WBLP
"It seems to me," said Booker T. Booker T. and W. E. B. Dudley Randall. NoAM
It seems to me the kindliness of old men. Old Men. Alicia Ostriker. AMV-81
It seems too enormous just for a man to be. The Highway. W. S. Merwin. PoA
It seems vainglorious and proud. The Conquerors. Phyllis McGinley. DBV
It seems wrong that out of this bird. A Blackbird Singing. R. S. Thomas. BoAnP
It semes white and is red. The Sacrament of the Altar. *Unknown.* MeEL
It settles softly on your things. The Dust. Gertrude Hall. AA
It shall be said [*or* sayd] I died [*or* dy'de] for Coelia! Sonnet. William Percy. *Fr.* Coelia. AAS; EIL
It shies from the Appalachians through seven states. Route 95 North: New Jersey. P. C. Bowman. AMV-80
It shifts and glides from form to form. The Name. Don Marquis. HBV-2
It shines in the garden. The Garden. Mark Strand. GeTw
It should be brief; if lengthy, it will steep. A Model Sermon. *Unknown.* FaBoUs
It Should Be Easy. Mark Van Doren. CrMA
It sifts from leaden sieves. Emily Dickinson. PoPl; SoSe
It singeth low in every heart. The Abiding Love [*or* Auld Lang Syne]. John White Chadwick. BLPA; FaBoBe; WGRP
It sings to me in sunshine. Segovia and Madrid. Rose Terry Cooke. AA
It sleeps among the thousand hills. The Unnamed Lake. Frederick George Scott. CaP; NOBC
It sleeps by day! Lucky Lion! *Zulu Oral Tradition, tr. by* H. Tracey. WTO
It snowed in New York, I walked on Fifth. Snow in New York. May Swenson. NYP
It snows on this place. Wednesday at North Hatley. Ralph Gustafson. NOBC
It so happens I am sick of being a man. Walking Around. Pablo Neruda, *tr. by* Robert Bly. EAS
It softens now. April snow. The Turning. Philip Booth. NePoAm-2
It sometimes happens. Curse of the Cat Woman. Edward Field. CABA; WeW
It soothes the savage doubts. Apocalypse. D. J. Enright. NMP; OBSV
It sounded as if the streets were running. Emily Dickinson. NePA; PBWP
It sounds unconvincing to say "When I was young." In the Winter of My Thirty-eighth Year. W. S. Merwin. NOBA
It speaks in voices varying with the wind. Africa. Adèle Naudé. PeSA

It spreads, the campaign—carried on. Glory [*or* Carnegie Hall: Rescued]. Marianne Moore. NYBP; NYP
It stands alone. The Sheiling. Edward Thomas. PoSH
It Started. Jimmy Santiago Baca. LFAC
It started into raining. Me an' My Doney-Gal. *Unknown.* CoSo
It started with an alto horn. Jazz. Frank London Brown. PoNe
It started with her shape on the map. Highland Region. Victor Price. PoSH
It starts: a white girl in a dark house. Alternatives. Kingsley Amis. OxBC
It starts out. The Light Year. John Ridland. OFD
It starts, somehow, in the hot damp. Barn Fire. Thomas Lux. LCAP
It stepped into my room. Elegy and Flame. Horace Gregory. FYAP
It stood embosom'd in a happy valley. Norman Abbey. Byron. *Fr.* Don Juan, XIII. OBRV
It stood on a bleak country corner. The Old Brown Schoolhouse. *Unknown.* TreF
It stops the town we come through. Troop Train. Karl Shapiro. OxBA; WaaP; WaP
It struck me every day. Emily Dickinson. PPP
It sushes. Cynthia in the Snow. Gwendolyn Brooks. TiPo
It swings upon the leafless tree. The Snow-filled Nest. Rose Terry Cooke. OBCA
It takes a fast car. Lost Parents. Lawrence Ferlinghetti. GP; PoM
It takes a heap o' children to make a home that's true. Edgar A. Guest Considers "The Good Old Woman Who Lived in a Shoe" and the Good Old Truths Simultaneously [*or* Verities at the Same Time]. Louis Untermeyer. *Fr.* Mother Goose Up-to-Date. FiBHP; MoAmPo; NIP; OBAL; PoPl; WhC
It takes a heap o' livin' in a house t' make it home. Home. Edgar A. Guest. BLPA; BLPL; FaBoBe; NIP; OBAL; OHFP; TreF; YaD
It takes a little courage. The Only Way to Win. *Unknown.* WBLP
It takes a long time to hear what the sands. The Bones. W. S. Merwin. ConAP; LiTM; NePoEA-2
It takes a worried man to sing a worried song. Worried Man Blues. *Unknown.* FSW
It takes more than wind and sleet to. Behind the Stove. James Hearst. TAT
It takes much art. La Carte. Justin Richardson. ELU; FiBHP
It takes time, and there are setbacks. A Difficult Adjustment. Lauris Edmond. OCNZ
It takes time to make. Time to Myself. Paulette Jiles. NOBC
It took generations to mature. Liberace. Jonathan Holden. MAYP
It took the sea a thousand years. Erosion. E. J. Pratt. CaP
It took 27 years to write this poem. Ruth. Colleen J. McElroy. BlSi
It trembled off the keys,—a parting kiss. Her Music. Martha Dickinson Bianchi. AA
It tried to get from out the cage. The Cage. James Stephens. OxBTC
It troubled me as once I was. Emily Dickinson. ImOP
It turns out/ You can kill them. Redwings. James Wright. NNaP
It wants to be somewhere else. Looking at Henry Moore's Elephant Skull Etchings in Jerusalem during the War. Shirley Kaufman. LCAP
It warms my bones. The Uses of Light. Gary Snyder. PAI
It was a bad sign I was born under. The Judas Goat. Susan Musgrave. NOBC
It Was a Beauty That I Saw. Ben Jonson. *Fr.* The New Inn. AnAnS-2; OBS
(Lovel's Song.) TrGrPo
It was a big boxy wreck of a house. The Fall of the House of Usher. Reed Whittemore. GP; InPK
It was a blue fly with wings of pomegranate gold. Blue Fly. Joaquim Maria Machado de Assis, *tr. by* Frances Ellen Buckland. TTY
It was a Borgia-pot, he told me. The Curiosity-Shop. Peter Redgrove. OxBC
It was a bowl of roses. A Bowl of Roses. W. E. Henley. MoBrPo
It was a bright and cheerful afternoon. Summer and Winter. Shelley. BoNaP
It was a bright day and all the trees were still. Silence. W. J. Turner. MoBrPo
It was a chill November eve and on the busy town. Saved. *Unknown.* FaBoUs
It was a chilly winter's night. A Winter Night. William Barnes. ChTr; FaBoRV; NOBE; OBNC
It was a close, warm, breezeless summer night. Conclusion. Wordsworth. *Fr.* The Prelude, XIV. PoEL-4
It was a comely young lady fair. Dark-eyed Canaller. *Unknown.* OuSiCo
It was a cough that carried him [*or* her] off. *Unknown.* FaBoNo; WhC
It was a dance. There Was a Dance, Sweetheart. Joy Harjo. TWSS
It was a dare that made us break. Cruelty. T. R. Hummer. MAYP
It was a dark and stormy night. The Sailor Boy. *Unknown.* ShS
It was a dark, dank, dreadful night. The Malfeasance. Alan Bold. AmMo
It was a day for routine maintenance. The Couch. Fred W. Wright, Jr. AMV-80
It was a day of turning when you came. The Turning. Philip Murray. NePoAm
It was a den where no insulting light. The Den of the Titans. Keats. *Fr.* Hyperion. WHA
It was a dim October day. Thomas Caulfield Irwin. *Fr.* Swift. BIrV
It was a dismal, and a fearful night. On the Death of Mr. William Hervey. Abraham Cowley. AnAnS-2; EBEV; FaBoRV; NOBE; OBEV; OBS; SeCP; SeCV-1; ViBoPo
It was a draper eminent. The Seraph and the Snob. May Kendall. CenHV
It was a dreary day in Padua. Countess Laura. George Henry Boker. BeLS
It was a dreary morning when the chaise. Residence at Cambridge. Wordsworth. *Fr.* The Prelude, III. FaBoPP
It was a famous story, proclaim it far and wide. The Famous Light Brigade. *Unknown.* ShS
It Was A' for Our Rightfu' King. Burns. *See* Farewell, The: "It was a' for our rightfu' king."
It was a foreign ship that sailed. Newcomers. Abraham Reisen, *tr. by* Keith Bosley. VWA
It was a friar of orders free. Song. Thomas Love Peacock. *Fr.* Maid Marian. ViBoPo
It was a friar of orders gray [*or* grey]. The Friar of Orders Gray. *Unknown.* ACP; GoBC; HBV-2; NOEC; OBEC
It was a Funky Deal. Etheridge Knight. BOLo; BPo; PoBA
It was a gallant highwayman. The Gallant Highwayman. James De Mille. WHW
It was a gallant sailor man. The Two Anchors. Richard Henry Stoddard. BeLS
It Was a Goodly Co. E. E. Cummings. CrMA; LiTA; LiTM; MoVE; WaP
It was a great pleasure. Spitting on Ira Rosenblatt. Robert Hershon. NeAC
It was a grey day. Tom Thomson. Arthur S. Bourinot. CaP
It was a hand. God looked at it. The Hand. R. S. Thomas. NOCV; OxBC
It was a hard thing to undo this knot. At a Welsh Waterfall. Gerard Manley Hopkins. FaBoPP
It was a heat to melt the mountains in. Loch Ossian. Syd Scroggie. PoSH
It was a heavenly time of life. The Quest. Ellen Mackay Hutchinson Cortissoz. HBV-1
It was a jolly bed in sooth. Us Idle Wenches. *Unknown.* PoPle
It was a kind and northern face. Praise for an Urn. Hart Crane. AP; AWP; CMoP; CoBMV; HAP; LiTM; MoAB; MoAmPo; MoVE; NoAM; NOBA; OxBA; PPP; WeW
It was a Knight in Scotland borne. The Fair Flower of Northumberland. *Unknown.* ESPB; OxBB
It was a lady of the north she lov'd a gentleman. Room for a Jovial Tinker: Old Brass to Mend [*or* The Jovial Tinker]. *Unknown.* CoMu; OxBB; UnTE
It was a little captive cat. The Singing Cat. Stevie Smith. OxBTC; PCat
It was a long time ago. As I Grew Older. Langston Hughes. AmPP; BANP
It Was a Lording's Daughter. *Unknown, at. to* Shakespeare. *Fr.* The Passionate Pilgrim. ElL
(Contentions.) HBV-1
It Was a Lover, and His Lass. Shakespeare. *Fr.* As You Like It, V, iii. AWP; BiP; CH; ElL; ELP; FSW; GBL; GTBS; GTBS-P; HBV-1; HeIP; InPK; InPS; LiTB; LoBV; NOBE; NoP; OBEV; OLR; PPoe; UnTE; ViBoPo
(Country Song.) TrGrPo
(Pages' Song, The.) OBSC; SeCePo
(Song: "It was a lover and his lass.") CTC; FiP
It was a maid of brenten arse. A Maid of Brenten Arse. *Unknown.* GBP
It was a Maine lobster town. Water. Robert Lowell. CMoP; HeIP; LCAP; NOBA; NoP
It was a merry time. The Courtship, Merry Marriage and Picnic Dinner of Cock Robin and Jenny Wren. *Unknown.* HBV-1
It was a mighty monarch's child. Mir träumte von einem Königskind. Heine, *tr. by* Richard Garnett. AWP
It was a mile of greenest grass. The Occasional Yarrow. Stevie Smith. FaBoNo
It was a miniature country once. Japan. Anthony Hecht. CrMA; InPK; LiTM
It was a mischievous wind that pushed him; a murderous gust that jarred young Jan from the scaffold. Monument. A. M. Sullivan. GoYe
It was a Moorish maiden was sitting by a well. The Broken Pitcher. William E. Aytoun. InMe
It was a mother and a maid. The Milk White Doe. *Unknown, tr. by* Andrew Lang. AWP
It was a night in winter. Clive Sansom. *Fr.* The Witnesses. PChr
It was a night of early spring. Wisdom. Sara Teasdale. MoAmPo
It was a noble Roman. On Fort Sumter. *Unknown.* PAH

It was a perfect day. Sowing. Edward Thomas. HBMV
It was a place of force. The Rabbit Catcher. Sylvia Plath. SBG
It was a puritanical lad [*or* puritanicall ladd]. Two Puritans [*or* Off a Puritane]. *Unknown.* CoMu; UnTE
It was a railway passenger. Striking. Charles Stuart Calverley. CenHV
It was a rainbow impossibly. Prisms. Philip Dacey. Psk
It was a refractory gnu. The Refractory Gnu. *Unknown.* TDH
It was a rich merchant nan. The Merchant and the Fidler's Wife. *Unknown.* CoMu; OxBB
It was a robber's daughter, and her name was Alice Brown. Gentle Alice Brown. W. S. Gilbert. FaBoCo; FiBHP; InMe; NA
It was a room where everything was strained. The Poolhall. Dan Burt. AMV–80
It was a sergeant old and gray. Picciola. Robert Henry Newell. AA
It Was a Special Treat. Luci Tapahonso. STE
It was a still autumnal day. We Walked among the Whispering Pines. John Henry Boner. AA
It was a summer [*or* summer's] evening. The Battle of Blenheim [*or* After Blenheim]. Robert Southey. BeLS; EnRP; FaBV; FaPoR; FPL; GN; GTBS; GTBS–P; HBV–2; HBVY; InMe; OBNC; OBRV; OBWP; PaPo; PoLF; TreF; TrGrPo; TRV; WBLP
It was a summer's night, a close warm night. Conclusion. Wordsworth. *Fr.* The Prelude, XIV. FaBoEn; OBNC
It was a tall young oysterman lived by the river-side [*or* harbor-side]. The Ballad of the Oysterman. Oliver Wendell Holmes. AP; EtS; FaFP; HBV–2; HBVY; MOS; MoShBr; TreFS
It was a time of trouble—executions. Chesspieces. Joseph Campbell. OxBI
It was a time when they were afraid of him. Ancestor. Jimmy Santiago Baca. LFAC
It was a tortoise aspiring to fly. Improvisations on Aesop. Anthony Hecht. OBAL
It was a violent time. Wheels, racks, and fires. A Mirror for Poets. Thom Gunn. LiTM; NePoEA
It was a waning crescent. July Dawn. Louise Bogan. NePoAm–2
It was a wasp, or an imprudent bee. The Wasp. Daryl Hine. NYBP
It was a wild black nicht. In the Hedgeback. "Hugh MacDiarmid." BSV; NeBP
It was a worthy Lord of Lorn. *See* It was the worthy Lord of Lorn.
It was about the deep of night. A Ballad of Christmas. Walter de la Mare. OBCP
It was about the Martinmas time. Barbara Allan. *Unknown.* EnSB
It was after hearing the parish priest. Virgins. Francis Carlin. HBMV
It was afternoon, and my brother split. A Burial, Green. Marcia Southwick. MAYP
It was all the clods at once become. Earth Dweller. William Stafford. LCAP
It Was All Very Tidy. Robert Graves. OxBTC
It was always. Hose and Iron. Greg Kuzma. MAT
It was amusing on that antique grass. Recorders in Italy. Adrienne Rich. TwAmPo
It was an accident, and accidents. The Ring Poem: A Husband Loses His Wedding Band as He Gestures from a Bridge. Phillip Dacey. FAZ
It Was an April Morning. Wordsworth. FaBoPP
It was an English ladye bright. Song of Albert Graeme. Sir Walter Scott. *Fr.* The Lay of the Last Minstrel, VI. EnRP; OBRV
It was an evening in November. The Pig. *Unknown.* FaBoEE
It was an hill placed in an open plain. The Dance of the Graces [*or* The Dance]. Spenser. *Fr.* The Faerie Queene, VI, 10. OBSC; TrGrPo
It was an international rage. Royston Ellis. The Cherry Boy, 6. PeHV
It was an old, old, old, old lady. One, Two, Three. H. C. Bunner. FaPON; HBV–1; PoLF
It was as if the devil of evil had got. García Lorca. Louis Dudek. MoCV; NOBC
It was as if thunder took form upon. Woman Looking at a Vase of Flowers. Wallace Stevens. CrMA
It was at a pow wow. Future Generation. Nila NorthSun. STE
It was at dinner as they sat. The Laird of Wariston. *Unknown.* ESPB
It was at the very date to which we have come. An Anniversary. Thomas Hardy. OxBTC
It was awful. The Day the T.V. Broke. Gerald Jonas. QQQ
It was awful long ago. The Anxious Farmer. Burges Johnson. BoNaP
It was better when we were. For My Mother. Louise Glück. GeTw; UnPo
It was between the night and day. Evening by the Sea. Swinburne. FaBoPP; SyP
It was but now their sounding clamours sung. On the Crucifixion. Giles Fletcher. *Fr.* Christ's Victory and Triumph: Christ's Triumph over Death. EBCP; OxBoCh
It was but the lightest word of the King. The King. Mary Elizabeth Coleridge. OBVV
It was but yesterday, my love, thy little heart beat high. Lament of Anastasius. William Bourne Oliver Peabody. AA
It was by these men's valor that wide-lawned Tegea. Epigram for the Dead at Tegea. *Unknown, tr. by* Richmond Lattimore. WaaP
It was by yonder thorn I saw the fairy host. The Fairy Lover. Moireen Fox. AnIV
It was Captain Pierce of the *Lion* who strode the streets of London. The First Thanksgiving. Clinton Scollard. PAH
It was cause for laughter of a special brand. The Fish. Ralph Gustafson. OBCV
It was Christmas Eve in the year fourteen. Under the Snow. Robert Collyer. AA
It was cold, and all they gave him to wear. Back in the States. Louis Simpson. AMV–81
It was cold then in the cautious hours. Curtain. Lance Henson. VoR
It was dark and frosty, pain congealed into ice. Deportation. "M. B.," *tr. by* A. Glanz-Leyeless. TrJP
It was daybreak a little while ago. Tuesday, 5 March (Morning) 1963. Pier Paolo Pasolini, *tr. by* Nigel Thompson. AMV–81
It was December. Even There. Lyn Lifshin. IHMS
It was down by the Sally Gardens. Down by the Sally Gardens. W. B. Yeats. FSW
It was down in a lone green valley. The Jealous Lover. *Unknown.* ShS
It was down in old Joe's barroom. St. James Infirmary [*or* Gambler's Blues *or* Those Gambler's Blues]. *Unknown.* AS; FSW; TrAS; TreFT
It was down in our far-off village that we heard of the war begun. Sending to War. William Morris. *Fr.* The Pilgrims of Hope. VLP
It was down to Red River I came. The Skew-Ball Black. *Unknown.* CoSo
It was Earl Haldan's daughter. Ballad. Charles Kingsley. GN
It was early/ fall or late summer. Fog 9/76. Richard Morris Dey. AMV–80
It was early, early in the spring. The Croppy Boy. *Unknown.* AmFP; AnIV; FaBoBa; FSW; OxBoLi
It was early, early one mornin'. Stagolee. *Unknown.* TTY
It was early in the season, the fall [*or* in the spring] of 'sixty-three. Michigan-I-O. *Unknown.* AmFP; OuSiCo
It was early last December. The Drunkard and the Pig. *Unknown.* OBAL
It was early Monday morning Willie Leonard arose. Willie Leonard; or, The Lake of Cold Finn. *Unknown.* AmFP; BaBo
It was early morning. Isaac. Amir Gilboa, *tr. by* Howard Schwartz. VWA
It was early one mornin' as I passed St. James Hospital. The Cowboy's Lament. *Unknown.* CoSo
It was early springtime that the strike was on. The Ludlow Massacre. Woody Guthrie. FSW
It was early Sunday morning, in the year of sixty-four. *Kearsarge* and *Alabama. Unknown.* PAH
It was early Sunday mornin. Stagolee. *Unknown.* MAT
It was Easter as I walked in the public gardens. 1929. W. H. Auden. SOTW
It was easy. How I Escaped from the Labyrinth. Philip Dacey. POL; PPJ
It was easy enough. Circe. Hilda Doolittle ("H. D."). PoRA
It was easy to see. Spassky at Reykjavik. David Fisher. AMV–81
It was eight bells in the forenoon and hammocks running sleek. The Little Commodore [*or* How They Do It]. J. C. Squire. HBMV; InMe
It was eight bells ringing. The Fighting Téméraire. Sir Henry Newbolt. HBV–2
It was evening when we came to the river. Crossing. J. Robert Oppenheimer. SUW
It was far in the night and the bairnies grat. Gerry Hamill. BXAP
It was far in the sameness of the wood. The Demiurge's Laugh. Robert Frost. OxBA
It was fifty years ago. The Fiftieth Birthday of Agassiz. Longfellow. ImOP
It Was for Me. Eva Gray. STF
It was for you that the mountains shook at Sinai. Epitaph. *Unknown.* TrJP
It was frosty winter season. Philomela's Second Ode. Robert Greene. *Fr.* Philomela. OBSC
It Was Gentle. Hedva Harkavi, *tr. fr. Hebrew by* Tova Weizman. VWA
It was good for the virgin mary. Poem for Unwed Mothers. Nikki Giovanni. OBAL
It was hurry and scurry at Monmouth town. Molly Pitcher. Kate Brownlee Sherwood. PAL
It was impossible for one to read. Holy Was Demeter Walking th' Corn Furrow. Edward Sanders. PoM
It was in a pleasant deepô, sequestered from the rain. The Ballad of Charity. Charles Godfrey Leland. InMe
It was in and about the Martinmas time. Barbara Allan [*or* Allen] [*or* Bonny Barbara Allan *or* Sir John Graeme and Barbara Allan]. *Unknown.* AWP; BiP; BoLoP; CABA; CH; ESPB; HeIP; InPK; LiTB; NoP; OxBB; OxBoLi; PAI; ViBoFo
It was in autumn that I met. A Picture. Dora Greenwell. EBVV

It was in nineteen-hundred and twenty-nine. Run Come See. Blind Blake. FSW
It was in October, a favorite season. Elegy for a Nature Poet. Howard Nemerov. BoNaP; HoPM; PP
It was in October the woe began. The Fire of Frendraught. *Unknown.* ESPB
It was in the city of Expert. The Oxford Girl; or, Expert Town. *Unknown.* AmFP
It was in the fields. The trees grew still. Jeanne d'Arc. Louise Glück. GeTw
It was in the lovely month of May. The Troubled Soldier. *Unknown.* AS
It was in the merry, merry month of May. Sweet William. *Unknown.* OuSiCo
It was in the merry month of May. The Trail to Mexico. *Unknown.* AS; BPAW
It was in the month of January the hills. Month of January. Frankie Armstrong. BrRo
It was in the Moon when the Cherries Turn Black. What Black Elk Said. R. T. Smith. LTB
It was in the schooner *Ambition.* The Spring Trip of the Schooner *Ambition.* *Unknown.* ShS
It was in the town of Waterford. The Wexford Girl. *Unknown.* ShS (*vers.* II); ViBoFo
It was in the town of Wexford. The Wexford Girl, *vers.* I. *Unknown.* ShS
It was in the year eighteen hundred and forty-nine. Sacramento, *vers.* I. *Unknown.* ShS
It was in the year of forty-four. The Whale. *Unknown.* AmSS
It was in the Yellow Dog Saloon one sultry summer night. Pizen Pete's Mistake. *At. to* Merrill Honey. BPAW
It Was in Vegas. J. V. Cunningham. UnTE
It was intill a pleasant time. Earl Mar's Daughter [*or* The Earl of Mar's Daughter]. *Unknown.* BaBo; CH; ESPB; GN; HBV-2
It was just before the last fierce charge, two soldiers drew a-rein. The Last Fierce Charge. *Unknown.* AmFP
It was justice to see her nude haunches. The Return. Stanley Moss. POL
It was last Monday morning as I have heard them say. Lancashire Lads. *Unknown.* CoMu
It was late afternoon, october. Fort Wayne, Indiana 1964. Steven Lewis. TAT
It was late in the night when the Squire came home. The Gipsy Laddie. *Unknown.* FaBoCh; OxBoLi
It was late last night when my lord come home. The Gypsy Davy. *Unknown.* AmFP
It was late last night when the boss come home. Gypsy Davey. *Ad. by* Woody Guthrie. FSW
It was late last Saturday evening. Blow the Candle Out. *Unknown.* FaBoBa
It was late, we. Man and Wife. Mitchell Goodman. VGW
It was laughing time, and the tall giraffe. Laughing Time. William Jay Smith. FaPON; SoPo
It was less than two thousand we numbered. With Corse at Allatoona. Samuel H. M. Byers. PAH
It was like something done in fever, when nothing fits. Entry August 29. Walter Benton. *Fr.* This Is My Beloved. UnTE
It was like this once: sprinklers mixed. Memo to the 21st Century. Philip Appleman. SOTS; TAT
It was Little Joe, the wrangler, he'll wrangle never more. Little Joe the Wrangler. N. Howard Thorp. FSW
It was lonely in the zero dark, Admetus. Alcestis. Isabel Williams Verry. GoYe
It was love that built the mountains. The Work of Love. Margaret Sangster. BLRP
It was Mabbie without the grammar school gates. The Ballad of Chocolate Mabbie. Gwendolyn Brooks. CAPP
It was Mama who was partial. Emma. Yvonne. CNA
It was many and many a year ago. Samuel Brown. Phoebe Cary. OBAL
It was many and many a year ago. The Cannibal Flea. Tom Hood. SpRo
It was many and many a year ago. A Poe-'em of Passion [*or* Cannibalee; a Po'em of Passion]. Charles Fletcher Lummis. BXAP; ShM; SpRo
It was many and many a year ago. Andrew M'Crie. Robert Fuller Murray. CenHV; FaBoCo
It was many and many a year ago. Annabel Lee. Poe. AA; AmPP; AP; AWP; BeLS; BLPA; CH; DL; EtS; FaFP; FaPON; FPL; HBV-1; HBVY; HeIP; LiTA; NePA; NOBA; NoP; OBCA; OBVV; OnMSP; OxBA; PoPl; PrIm; RoGo; SeCeV; SpRo; TAP; TreF; TrGrPo; ViBoPo; WBLP
It was meetin' night in Rawhide Town. The Raven Visits Rawhide. *Unknown.* BPAW
It was much later in his life he rose. Muriel Rukeyser. *Fr.* Gibbs. ImOP
It was my bridal night I remember. I Remember. Stevie Smith. BoLoP; BoWoP; InPK; OxBC
It Was My Choice. Sir Thomas Wyatt. EnRePo; QFR ("It was my choice, it was no chance.") SiPS
It was my father forced him into the desert. Isaac. A. C. Jacobs. VWA
It was my first/ time in Kula. Kula . . . a Homecoming. Diane Mei Lin Mark. BrSi
It was my thirtieth year to heaven. Poem in October. Dylan Thomas. BiP; CoBMV; LiTB; MoVE; NAs; NeBP; OAEP; PoA; PoPl; PoRA; PrIm; SeCePo; SoSe
It was near evening, the room was cold. The Oath. Allen Tate. FaBoMo; LiTM; NoAM; OxBA; VGW
It was nearly morning when the giant. The Reason for Skylarks. Kenneth Patchen. NaP
It was neither his hunger nor mine. Not Being Wise. Virginia Elson. AMV-80
It was night-time! God, the Father Good. What the Devil Said. James Stephens. CMoP
It was 1945, and it was May. When I Was Conceived. Michael Ryan. MAYP
It was no costume jewellery I sent. With a Gift of Rings. Robert Graves. GBL
It was not by vile loitering in ease. The Praise of Industry. James Thomson. *Fr.* The Castle of Indolence. OBEC
It was not Death, for I stood up. Emily Dickinson. BiP; InPK; MasP; MoPo; NePA; NOBA; NoP; TwAmPo
It was not death to me. The Kiss of God. G. A. Studdert-Kennedy. BLRP
It was not dying: everybody died. Losses. Randall Jarrell. CoBMV; LCAP; LiTM; MoVE; OxBA; PoA; TAP; UnPo; WaP
It Was Not Fate. William H. A. Moore. BANP
It Was Not in the Winter. Thomas Hood. *See* Time of Roses.
It was not like your great and gracious ways! Departure. Coventry Patmore. The Unknown Eros, I, viii. ACP; HBV-1; LO; NOBE; OBEV; OBNC; OBVV; SeCePo; TreFT; VLP
It was not long e're he perceiv'd the skies. Michael Drayton. *Fr.* The Moone-Calfe. PoEL-2
It was not meant for human eyes. The Combat. Edwin Muir. ChMP; CMoP; LiTB; MoBrPo; NOBE
It was not night, not even when the darkness came. The Annunciation. W. S. Merwin. AP
It Was Not Strange. Esther Lloyd Hagg. PGD
It was not that you said I thought you knew. Colloquial. Rupert Brooke. BrPo
It Was Not You. André Spire, *tr. fr. French by* Jethro Bithell. TrJP
It was nothing but a rose I gave her. A Sigh. Harriet Prescott Spofford. AA; HBV-1
It was of a comely young lady fair. The Dark-eyed Sailor. *Unknown.* FSW
It was of a sea captain that followed the sea. The Sea Captain. *Unknown.* ViBoFo
It was on a cold winter's night. When Poor Mary Came Wandering Home. *Unknown.* AS
It was on a May, on a midsummer's day. Sir Hugh; or, The Jew's Daughter. *Unknown.* AmFP; ESPB
It was on a Wednesday night, the moon was shining bright. Jesse James. *Unknown.* AS; BeLS; FaBoBe; UnPo; WiR; YaD
It was on an evning sae saft and sae clear. The Broom of Cowdenknows. *Unknown.* ESPB
It was on one Monday morning,/ All in the month of May. Lisbon. *Unknown.* AmFP
It was on one Monday morning just about one o'clock. The *Titanic.* *Unknown.* AmFP; ViBoPo
It was on one summer's evening,/ Just about the hour of three. Sailor on the Deep Blue Sea. *Unknown.* FSW
It was on Saturday eve, in the gorgeous bright October. The Engagement. Arthur Hugh Clough. NBM
It was on the seventeenth, by break of day. The Battle of Bunker Hill. *Unknown.* PAH
It was on the twenty-first day of December. Ella Speed. *Unknown.* AmFP
It was one afternoon when I was young. The Tale the Hermit Told. Alastair Reid. NePoEA-2
It was one of those kind of days. I was walking down the St. Same Tits. James Tate. FAZ
It was one summer's morning on the fourteenth day of May. The Mower. *Unknown.* CoMu
It was one Sunday morning of June the eighth day. Henry K. Sawyer. *Unknown.* AmFP
It was only a few short years ago. The Cowboy. *Unknown.* CoSo
It was only a kindly smile he gave. Little Things. *Unknown.* STF
It was only a small place and they had cheered us too much. St. Aubin d'Aubigné. Paul Dehn. OBWP
It was only important. The Moss of His Skin. Anne Sexton. CABA; CoAP; IHMS; PAI

It was only my own voice that I had heard. This One Heart-shaken. Sister Maris Stella. GoBC
It was only the clinging touch. The Child. George Edward Woodberry. Wild Eden, XXX. AA
It was only two fields away from the house. In Memoriam I, Elizabeth at Twenty. Richard Weber. ErPo
It was out on the Western frontier. The Clown's Baby. "Margaret Vandegrift." PaPo
It was Pablo who saw him most clearly. Write, Do Write. Marilyn Chin. BrSi
It was plain to see the sense of being a woman. The Inflammable Woman. James K. Baxter. OxBC
It was pleasant and delightful on one midsummer's morn. Pleasant and Delightful. *Unknown.* OBET
It was pneumonia. Lament of the Virtues and Verses on Account of the Death of Don Guido. Antonio Machado, *tr. by* Charles Tomlinson *and* Henry Gifford. OBVE
It was poor little Jesus, yes, yes. Poor Little Jesus. *Unknown.* FSW
It was Private Blair, of the regulars, before dread El Caney. Private Blair of the Regulars. Clinton Scollard. PAH
It was proper for them, awaking in ordered houses. Apology. Anthony Cronin. CIP
It was quite a day at Melrose. All the folks had come to town there. Coronation Day at Melrose. Peter Bladen. PoAu-2
It was roses, roses, all the way. The Patriot. Robert Browning. TrGrPo
It was round, orb being most nearly perfect. The Gift. Ann Stanford. GP
It was running down to the great Atlantic. The Stream. Lula Lowe Weeden. CDC
It was said at the/ flirting creekwater's birth. To an Imaginary Father. Wendy Rose. CDW
It was seven years then. Rachel's Lament. Linda Zisquit. VWA
It was shattered. The Battle of Maldon. *Unknown, tr. by* Kevin Crossley-Holland. OBWP
It was simply a dark. The Color. John Haines. GP
It was six foot four of my father. The Brigg. Robin Skelton. NMP
It was six men of Indostan. The Blind Men and the Elephant. John Godfrey Saxe. BLPA; FaBoBe; FPL; HBV-1; HBVY; OBCA; OnMSP; OnUR; TreF; WBLP
It was so prety a fole. John Skelton. *Fr.* Phyllyp Sparrowe. PB
It was so quiet you could hear. Walls Breathe. Paul Mariah. LFAC
It was something to see that their white was different. Holiday in Reality. Wallace Stevens. NePA; OxBA
It was something you did not know. An Air by Sammartini. Louis Dudek. OBCV
It was sometime in the P.M. of the fall of '92. Doing Railroads for *The Rocky Mountain News.* Cy Warman. PoOW
It was storming and there was someone at the door. The Visitor. George Bogin. FAZ
It was strange, O strange. A Green and Pleasant Land. John Peale Bishop. PoPl
It was strange that morning. Fishin' Blues. Valentino Ramirez. AMV-81
It was strange when I fell to the bottom of Column A. Column A. Michael Silverton. PV
It was such a bright morning. Beautiful Sunday. "Jake Falstaff." BoNaP
It was sudden. The Sea Fog. Josephine Jacobsen. NYBP
It was Sunday morning, I had the *New York Times.* First Love. Sharon Olds. FYAP
It was taken a long time ago. The Verdict. Norman Cameron. SeCePo
It was taken some time ago. This Is a Photograph of Me. Margaret Atwood. NoP
It was that fierce contested field when Chickamauga lay. Thomas at Chickamauga. Kate Brownlee Sherwood. PAH
It was that red moon rising. Looting. Jascha Kessler. HoAn
It was the anniversary of bread. Bread. Constance Urdang. GP
It was the arrival of the kings. The Adoration of the Magi. Christopher Pilling. OBCP
It was the autumn of her madness. Dark Room. Fredrick Zydek. AMV-80
It was the autumn of the year. Left Behind. Elizabeth Akers Allen. HBV-1
It was the beginning of me. Look at My Face, a Collage. Carolyn M. Rodgers. JB
It was. The breech smelling of oil. First Blood. Jon Stallworthy. BoAnP; LiSp
It was the busy hour of 4. Spring Arithmetic. *Unknown.* FiBHP
It was the calm and silent night! A Christmas Hymn [1837]. Alfred Domett. GN; HBV-1; OBVV; WGRP
It was the charming month of May. Chloe. Burns. GN; HBV-1
It was the cooling hour, just when the rounded. Haidée [*or* Haidée and Don Juan]. Byron. *Fr.* Don Juan, II. OBNC; OBRV; ViBoPo
It was the country I loved. The Invaders. John Haines. TAT
It was the departure, the sun was risen. Farewell Voyaging World! Conrad Aiken. NYBP
It was the dingiest bird. Robin Redbreast. Stanley Kunitz. Prf
It was the frog in the well. The Marriage of the Frog and the Mouse. *Unknown.* EBEV
It was the fruit on high. Soul's Kiss. Samuel Greenberg. LiTA
It was the garden of the golden apples. The Long Garden. Patrick Kavanagh. IPY
It was the hour of night, when thus the Son. Milton. *Fr.* Paradise Regained, II. EBEV
It Was the Last of the Parades. Louis Simpson. NYBP
It Was the Lovely Moon. John Freeman. BoNaP
It was the man from Ironbark who struck the Sydney town. The Man from Ironbark. A. B. Paterson. PoAu-1
It was the morning of that blessed day. Petrarch, *tr. by* Joseph Auslander. Sonnets to Laura: To Laura in Life, III. NAWM-1
"It was the morning of the first of May." Popular Songs of Tuscany. *Unknown, tr. by* John Addington Symonds. AWP
It was the night of hardly anyone. The No-Night. Irving Feldman. NoAM
It was the rainbow gave thee birth. The Kingfisher. W. H. Davies. MoVE; NOBE; OBEV
It was the schooner *Hesperus.* The Wreck of the *Hesperus.* Longfellow. BeLS; BLPA; EtS; FaBoBe; FaFP; FaPON; FaPoR; FPL; GN; HBV-2; HBVY; MOS; OBCA; OBNV; PAH; PaPo; TreF; WBLP
It was the season, when through all the land. The Birds of Killingworth. Longfellow. *Fr.* Tales of a Wayside Inn. OnMSP; OxBA
It was the *Stately Southerner*, that carried the Stripes and Stars. The *Stately Southerner. Unknown.* AmFP
It Was the Time of Roses. Thomas Hood. *See* Time of Roses.
It was the time when lilies blow. Lady Clare. Tennyson. BeLS; FaPON; HBV-2; OnMSP
It was the time, when rest, soft sliding downe. Joachim du Bellay, *tr. by* Spenser. *Fr.* Visions. AWP
It was the very noon of night: the stars above the fold. The Story of the Shepherd. *Unknown, tr. fr. Spanish.* OHIP
It was the virgin Zennora, who dwelt. John Heath-Stubbs. *Fr.* Artorius. EBEV
It was the west wind caught her up, as. The Ring Of. Charles Olson. NOBA; VGW
It was the wild midnight. The Death of Leonidas. George Croly. BeLS
It was the wind. Autumn Evening. George Anthony. EAS
It was the winter wild[e]. Hymn on the Morning of Christ's Nativity [*or* On the Morning of Christ's Nativity *or* The Hymn]. Milton. *Fr.* On the Morning of Christ's Nativity. FiP; NOBE; OBEV: WHA
It Was the Worm. James Broughton. GP
It was the [*or* a] worthy Lord of Lorn [*or* Learne]. The Lord of Lorn and the False [*or* Fals] Steward. *Unknown.* ESPB; OxBB
It was the year the Icondic. Ballad of the Icondic. John Ciardi. OBAL
It was then night: the sound[e] and quiet sleep [*or* slepe]. Virgil, *tr. by* the Earl of Surrey. *Fr.* The Aeneid, IV. OAEL-1; PoEL-1
It was then she struck—from behind. The Wanderer: Broadway. William Carlos Williams. TwAmPo
It was there, but I said it couldn't be true in daylight. Nightmare of Mouse. Robert Penn Warren. SO
It was there on the hillside, no tall traveller's story. Pegasus. C. Day Lewis. PoPle
It was this way. Rumoresque Senum Severiorum. Marcus Argentarius, *tr. by* Dudley Fitts. ErPo
It was Thomas Macdonough, as gallant a sailor. The Battle of Plattsburg Bay. Clinton Scollard. PAH
It was three slim does and a ten-tined buck in the bracken lay. The Revenge of Hamish. Sidney Lanier. AP; PoEL-5
It was through a mucous membrane, a kind of mouth. Lion, Leopard, Lady. Douglas Le Pan. OBCV
It was Tiny's habit. Sketches of Harlem. David Henderson. CABA; NNP; PoNe
It was too dark in the chimney corner to see. Cinderella. Cynthia Pickard. DFT; PoPl
It was too lonely for her there. The Impulse. Robert Frost. *Fr.* The Hill Wife. HoPM; NePA; NoAM
It was touching when I started. Aunt Nerissa's Muffin. Wallace Irwin. FiBHP
It was upon a Cristemesse night. The Dancers of Colbek. Robert Mannyng. *Fr.* Handlyng Synne. OxBM
It was upon a Lammas night. The Rigs o' Barley [*or* Corn Rigs Are Bonnie *or* Song]. Burns. BoLoP; BSV; ErPo; LiTB; LoBV; OxBS; UnTE; ViBoPo
It was upon a Shere Thorsday that oure Loverd aras. Judas. *Unknown.* OxBM
It was upon the twilight of that day. Samuel Daniel. *Fr.* The Civil Wars, VIII. OBWP

It was very early in the spring. The Croppy Boy. *Unknown.* AnIL
It was very late at an empty table. Ballad of an Empty Table. Tom Kryss. NeAC
It was very pleasant. A Certain Peace. Nikki Giovanni. CNA
It was water I was trying to think of all the time. Appoggiatura. Donald Jeffrey Hayes. AmNP; PoBA; PoNe
It was way up north in Boothbay Harbor. The Boothbay Whale. *Unknown.* FSW
It was wet & white & swift and where I am. Snow Line. John Berryman. Dream Songs, XXVIII. NaP; PoA
It was when I said. On the Road Home. Wallace Stevens. NU
It was when my songs became quiet. How I Came to Be a Graduate Student. Wendy Rose. STE
It was, when scarce had rang the morning bells. An Almanack for the Year of Our Lord, 1657. Samuel Bradstreet. SCAP
It was when weather was Arabian I went. Allegory of the Adolescent and the Adult. George Barker. LiTB; MasP
It was wild. Assassination. Don L. Lee. AmNP; BOLo; FF; NeAC; OFD; PoBA
It was wintertime. Star of the Nativity. Boris Pasternak, *tr. by* Eugene M. Kayden. PoPl
It was with resolution that she gave up the. The Ice Eagle. Diane Wakoski. InPS
"It Was Wrong to Do This," Said the Angel. Stephen Crane. The Black Riders, LIV. LiTA: NePA; PAI
It was yesterday she roller-skated down. Eighteen. Sister Mary Honora. NePoAm-2
It was you:/ I could have crawled. Watching Salmon Jump. Simon J. Ortiz. CDW
It was you, Atthis, who said. Sappho, *tr. fr. Greek by* Mary Barnard. PeHV
It was your mother wanted you. The Son. R. S. Thomas. NAs
It wasn't Ernest; it wasn't Scott. Song for the Squeeze-Box. Theodore Roethke. NePoAm
It wasn't our battalion, but we lay alongside it. Sergeant-Major Money. Robert Graves. MMA; OBWP
It wasn't ringworm he. New York. Thom Gunn. NYP
It wasn't the daffodils so much. Daffodils. Michael Heffernan. AMV-80
It went many years. The Lockless Door. Robert Frost. NOBA; WSC
It were my soul's desire. The Soul's Desire. *Unknown, tr. by* Eleanor Hull. OxBI
It wes in November an' aw nivor will forget. The Oakey Street Evictions. Tommy Armstrong. OBET
It wes upon a Scere Thorsday that oure Lord aros. Judas Sells His Lord. *Unknown.* MeEL
It will always be like this. Departure Platform. Kenneth Allott. NeBP
It will be all the same in a hundred years. In a Hundred Years. *At. to* Elizabeth Doten. BLPA
It will be easy to love you when I am dead. Muna Lee. Sonnets, XI. HBMV
It will be in the form of an old man. I Want to Write a Jewish Poem. Gary Pacernick. VWA
It will be look'd for, book[e], when some but see. To My Book[e]. Ben Jonson. AnAnS-2; OAEP; SeCV-1
It will be strange. When the Vacation Is Over for Good. Mark Strand. NYBP
It will happen in the summer. Terminal Vision. Diana O Hehir. NPGG
It will not always be like this. A Day in Autumn. R. S. Thomas. BoNaP
It will not hurt me when I am old. Moonlight. Sara Teasdale. VGW
It will not resemble the sea. The New Poem. Charles Wright. GeTw
It will not stay! The robe so pearly white. The April Snow. Jones Very. AP
It will rain tonight. New Life. Joseph E. Kariuki. TTY
It winds o'er prairie and o'er crest. The Santa Fe Trail. Arthur Chapman. BPAW
"It would be/ a mercy if." Phone Call to Rutherford. Paul Blackburn. CTBA; PoM
It would be at the end. The End of the Street. John Haines. LCAP
It would be easier. Vision of 400 Sunrises. Ruth Lisa Schechter. SOTS
It would be nice to simply melt away. Leavings. Gerard Benson. BXAP
It would be painful to interfere. Memo. Charles Ballard. VoR
It would be snowing back there. Pilgrimage to Hennessey's. Steven Sher. AMV-81
It would be wrong for us. It is not right. Sappho, *tr. fr. Greek by* Willis Barnstone. BoWoP
It would have starved a gnat. Emily Dickinson. MoVE; SBG
It would never be morning, always evening. Memory of Brother Michael. Patrick Kavanagh. MoAB; OnYI; OxBI
It wouldn't be so bad if he. In Extremis. Margaret Fishback. FiBHP
It wouldn't do to go crazy. Therapy. Ken Poyner. AMV-81
It wound through strange scarred hills, down cañons lone. The Old Santa Fé Trail. Richard Burton. BPAW; PAH
It wuz one day, I believe in May, when old Si Hubbard to me did say. Si Hubbard. *Unknown.* AS
Italia, Io Ti Saluto. Christina Rossetti. OBVV; WPE
Italia! Oh Italia! thou who hast. Italy. Vincenzo Filicaja, *tr. by* Byron. AWP
Italian. Osbert Lancaster. *Fr.* Afternoons with Baedeker. FaBoCo
Italian Chest, An. Marjorie Allen Seiffert. HBMV
Italian Extravaganza. Gregory Corso. CoPo
Italian in England, The. Robert Browning. OAEP; OBNV
Italian Lullaby. *Unknown.* FaPON
Italian Opera. James Miller. OBEC
Italian Poppies. Joel Elias Spingarn. HBMV
Italian Rhapsody. Robert Underwood Johnson. HBV-2
Italian soldier shook my hand, The. George Orwell. OBWP
Italian Woman. Diane Wakoski. GrPl
Italy. Byron. *Fr.* Beppo. OBRV; SeCePo
(Italy versus England.) NOBE
Italy. Vincenzo Filicaja, *tr. fr. Italian by* Byron. AWP
Italy, *sels.* Samuel Rogers.
Bologna, and Byron. OBRV
Byron Recollected at Bologna. OBNC
Interview near Florence, An. OBNC
Italy and Britain. Joseph Addison. *Fr.* A Letter from Italy. OBEC
Italy of the South. Robert Browning. *Fr.* De Gustibus. FaBoPP
Italy versus England. Byron. *See* Italy.
Itch to Etch, The. Harold A. Larrabee. WhC
Itchin, when I behold thy banks again. To the River Itchin, near Winton. William Lisle Bowles. OAEL-2
Ité. Ezra Pound. HAP; MoAB; MoAmPo; PP; TwAmPo
Item. E. E. Cummings. MoAB; MoAmPo
Iter Boreale. Robert Wild. APAS
Iter Supremum. Arthur Sherburne Hardy. AA
Ithaca last night, Syracuse at noon, Cedar Rapids tonight. Seeing Auden Off. Philip Booth. PoA
'Ithin the woodlands, flow'ry gleaded. My Orcha'd in Linden Lea. William Barnes. EBVV
Ithocles, *sel.* John Addington Symonds.
"That night, when storms were spent and tranquil heavens." PeHV
Itiskit, Itaskit, *with music.* *Unknown.* TrAS
It's/ snowing defective. Self-Pity Is a Kind of Lying, Too. James Schuyler. PoM
It's a box of furniture in a right angle. Where He Hangs His Hat. Deborah Lee. BrSi
It's a brisk young butcher, as I have heard 'em say. Leicester Chambermaid. *Unknown.* CoMu
It's a dark and dreary season. Triolet on a Dark Day. Margaret Fishback. PoSC
It's a debatable land. The winds are variable. Helen Bevington. *Fr.* Report from the Carolinas. AmFN
It's a Different Story When You're Going into the Wind. David McFadden. NeAC
It's a dull poem. Poem. Steve Jonas. PeHV
It's a Far, Far Cry. Patrick Macgill. HBMV
It's a fine kind thought! And yet—I know. Remembrance Day in the Dales. Dorothy Una Ratcliffe. SUMH
It's a Gay Old World. *Unknown.* FaFP
It's a Good Thing to Join a Union. *Unknown.* FSW
It's a great deal better to lose than win. After Reading Certain Books. Mary Elizabeth Coleridge. EaLo
It's a hell/ creeping back into. Back into the Garden. Sarah Webster Fabio. BlSi
It's a kitchen. Its curtains fill. A Room in the Past. Ted Kooser. Str
It's a large town. Wellington. Bill Manhire. OCNZ
It's a late starting dawn that breathes my vision. Late Starting Dawn. Richard Brautigan. PCP
It's a little Walden. You All Know the Story of the Other Woman. Anne Sexton. InPK
It's a lonely road through bogland to the lake at Carrowmore. Carrowmore [*or* The Gates of Dreamland]. "Æ." HBMV; HBV-2
It's a long and dusty road. I Can't Help but Wonder Where I'm Bound. Tom Paxton. FSW
It's a long hot walk up Fathead Mountain you know. Hiking Up Hieizan with Alam Lau/Buddha's Birthday 1974. Garret Kaoru Hongo. BrSi
It's a long walk in the dark. John's Song. Joan Aiken. DuDa
It's a long way out of the past and a long way forward. Written in a Time of Crisis. Stephen Vincent Benét. PAL
It's a low it's a low low. Eagles on a Half. *Unknown.* BluL
It's a madman, I said. Dream. Nana Issaia, *tr. by* Helle Tzalopoulou Barnstone. BoWoP
It's a mighty hard row that my poor hands has hoed. Pastures of Plenty. Woody Guthrie. WTO

It's a mournful tune the rain is making. Spinster Song. Virginia Lyne Tunstall. HBMV
It's a Queer Time. Robert Graves. MoAB; MoBrPo
It's a question of bright stars. Dogwood Blossoms. Peter Blue Cloud. STE
It's a real rock. Wobbly Rock. Lew Welch. PoM
It's a rum. "And Now." J. B. Boothroyd. FiBHP
It's a sitting-pretty, windy-city kind of a place. Tonight in Chicago. *Unknown.* AmFN
It's a south wind that drives you back. Hardon ("Get One Today"). Ian Wedde. OCNZ
It's a strange courage. El Hombre. William Carlos Williams. CABA; CMoP; LiTA
It's a strange courage. Nuances of a Theme by Williams. Wallace Stevens. LiTA
It's a sunny pleasant anchorage, is Kingdom Come. Port of Many Ships. John Masefield. MOS; OBMV
It's a Terrible Thing! Everett Hoagland. BPo
It's a very odd thing. Miss T. Walter de la Mare. CenHV; FaBoBe; GoJo; GrPl; MoShBr; NTCP; OnUR; PDV; SoPo; SUS; TiPo
It's a warm wind, the west wind, full of birds' cries. The West Wind. John Masefield. FaFP; FPL; LiTB; LiTM; MoAB; MoBrPo; PoPl; TreF
It's a white nest! A Small Bird's Nest Made of White Reed Fiber. Robert Bly. NNaP
"It's a Whole World, the Body. A Whole World!"—Swami Satchidandanda. David Young. FF
Its Ain Drap o' Dew. James Ballantine. HBV-2
It's all a trick, quite easy when you know it. Villanelle. W. W. Skeat. FaBoCo; FiBHP
It's all aboard for outer space. Space Travel. Jane W. Krows. SoPo
It's all familiar. A Dream. Bella Akhmadulina, *tr. by* Jean Valentine *and* Olga Carlisle. BoWoP
It's all in/ the sound. A song. The Poem. William Carlos Williams. PCP
It's all out on the old railroad. Jubilee. *Unknown.* FSW
It's All the Same. Thadious M. Davis. BlSi
It's all too swift; it's over all too soon. A Plea for Postponement. Petronius, *tr. by* Louis Untermeyer. UnTE
It's all very well for preachin'. The Pledge at Spunky Point. John Hay. OBAL
It's all very well to dream of a dove that saves. Birdwatchers of America. Anthony Hecht. CoPo; HoPM; NoAM; NOBA; PPP
It's all very well to write reviews. Lasca. Frank Desprez. HBV-2
It's Almost Day. Leadbelly (Huddie Ledbetter). FSW
It's Almost Done (On a Monday). *Unknown.* FSW
It's Already Autumn. Elio Pagliarani. PCP
It's always afternoon somewhere. Night Poem. Wayne Dodd. AMV-80
It's always there, like the drone. Exchange. Dabney Stuart. HoPM
It's an approach. Say what you like. Astrology. Tom Marshall. PeCV
It's an old box camera. Camera. Ted Kooser. Psk
It's another April, and a day. Landscape with Lapwings. James Aitchison. BSV
It's autumn in the country I remember. Mnemosyne. Trumbull Stickney. CrMA; LiTA; NCEP; NOBA; OxBA; TwAmPo; ViBoPo
It's awf'lly bad luck on Diana. Hunter Trials. John Betjeman. FiBHP; PH
It's bad luck with a coughing baby. John Tranter. *Fr.* Crying in Early Infancy. CBAP
It's been a long time since I wrote poems which dance. Dance-Song. Jaroslav Seifert, *tr. by* Paul Jagasich *and* Tom O'Grady. AMV-81
It's been going on a long time. A Way of Life. Howard Nemerov. NIP
It's been like fixing a clock, jamming the wheels. Making Up for a Soul. David Wagoner. VGW
It's best to be best. Best? Siv Widerberg, *tr. by* Verne Moberg. NTCP
Its black fur is suddenly still. In the Surgery. J. M. Ditta. AMV-80
It's Christmas Day. I did not get. Otto. Gwendolyn Brooks. PChr; PDV
It's clear, Trojan cried out to Greek. Why They Waged War. John Peale Bishop. NYBP
Its cloven hoofprint on the sand. How to Catch Unicorns. William Rose Benét. HBMV
It's cold and raw the north winds blow. The Maid That Sold Her Barley. *Unknown.* OnYI
It's Cold in China Blues. *Unknown.* BluL
"It's cold," said the cricket. Halloween Concert. Aileen Fisher. SiSoSe
It's come to this. David Martinson. *Fr.* Nineteen Sections from a Twenty Acre Poem. TAT
It's Comforting. Judy Dothard Simmons. CNA
It's coming, boys. In Trust. Mary Mapes Dodge. SiSoSe
Its Curtains. Ted Joans. PoBA
It's dark on purpose. Visiting the Oracle. Lawrence Raab. AmPA
It's dark out, Jack. All the Roary Night. Kenneth Patchen. LiTM
Its disguise resides in the commonplace. Stinging Nettle. Gwen Head. GP
It's doing your job the best you can. Success! Berton Braley. WBLP
It's easy to fight when everything's right. Carry On! Robert W. Service. HBV-2
It's easy to talk of the patience of Job. Humph! Job hed nothin' to try him! The Inventor's Wife. E. R. Corbett. PoLF
Its echoes. Haunted House. Valerie Worth. WSC
Its edges foamed with amethyst and rose. The Great Breath. "Æ." MoBrPo; OBEV; OBMV; OxBI; WGRP; WHA
It's far I must be going. Via Longa. Patrick McDonough. HBMV
It's fare thee well, my own true love. Mary Ann. FSW
It's fifty miles to Sittingen's Rocks. Prince Robert. *Unknown.* ESPB
It's fifty-one springtimes since she was a bride. Dancing at Whitsun. Austin John Marshall. OBET
It's Fine Today. Douglas Malloch. *See* Ain't It Fine Today!
Its flat, insect-blackened radiator grill. Buffalo. Louis Daniel Brodsky. AMV-80
It's Food. Cid Corman. GP
It's foolish to bring money. Spring Market. Louise Driscoll. HBMV; HBVY
Its former green is blue and thin. The Garden Seat. Thomas Hardy. GoJo; HAP
It's forty in the shade to-day the spouting eaves declare. Pan in Vermont. Kipling. WhC
It's four long years since I reached this land. Lousy Miner. *Unknown.* AmFP
It's full of the moon. Full of the Moon. Karla Kuskin. PDV
It's fun to clean house. I Like Housecleaning. Dorothy Brown Thompson. FaPON
It's fun to go out and buy new shoes to wear. Mary Ann Hoberman. TiPo
It's funny. My Puppy. Aileen Fisher. OnUR
It's funny how a little thing. Reminder. *Unknown.* STF
It's funny that smells and sounds return. Scrapbooks. Nikki Giovanni. CNA
It's funny when understanding. A Truth. Noah Mitchell. LFAC
It's G-L-O-R-Y to Know I'm S-A-V-E-D. *Unknown.* FSW
It's going to be a thick night tonight. Officers' Mess. Gavin Ewart. OxBTC
It's going to come out all right—do you know? Caboose Thoughts. Carl Sandburg. CMoP
It's going to rain. The Watchers. Paul Blackburn. NMP; NYBP
Its got a good shape. Watermelon. Ted Joans. GP
It's growing evening in my soul. In Summer. Trumbull Stickney. NCEP
It's hair and dress, framing old portrait faces. Eternal Contour. Florida Watts Smyth. GoYe
It's Halloween. Jack Prelutsky. NTCP
It's Hard on We Po' Farmers, *with music. Unknown.* OuSiCo
It's hard to breathe in a tenement hall. Song of a Factory Girl. Marya Zaturenska. HBMV
It's hard to know if you're alive or dead. It's a Queer Time. Robert Graves. MoAB; MoBrPo
It's hard to see. Louie. Paul D. Shiplett. LFAC
It's hard to see but think of a sea. Louis Zukofsky. VGW
It's hard to tell what bird it is. After Frost. Brian Patten. EBEV
It's hard to think. To a Human Skeleton. Richard Armour. WhC
It's hard when folks can't find th'work. The Dalesman's Litany. *Unknown.* OBET
It's Here in The. Russell Atkins. AmNP; PoBA
It's his eyes. The Owl. Sue Owen. AMV-81
It's holiday night. Riding Westward. Harvey Shapiro. GP; NYP; VWA
It's in the Egg. Joe Rosenblatt. NOBC
It's in the Name. Kitty Tsui. BrSi
It's in Your Face. *Unknown.* PoLF
It's I've got a ship in the north country. The Golden Vanity. *Unknown.* ELP
It's Jim Farrow and John Farrow and little Simon, too. Jim Farrow. *Unknown.* CoSo
It's just no use. Execution. James A. Randall, Jr. BPo
It's Just the Same to Me. Hermann Hesse, *tr. fr. German.* ILwL
It's kind of you to let me have my hat. Hattage. A. P. Herbert. FiBHP
It's Lamkin was a mason good. Lamkin. *Unknown.* ESPB; FaBoBa; OxBB; ViBoFo
It's like a story. Alive or Not. Al Purdy. NOBC
It's like the riddle Tolstoy. Slow Dance. David St. John. AmPA; LCAP
It's like the sea the way she. One Year After. Gary Allan Kizer. LFAC
It's Little for Glory I Care. Charles James Lever. OnYI
It's little I care what path I take. Departure. Edna St. Vincent Millay. MoAmPo
It's Little Joe, the wrangler. Little Joe, the Wrangler. *Unknown.* CoSo
It's lonely in the world. Party Going. Bill Manhire. OCNZ
Its Lunch. John Hollander. *Fr.* Something about It. GP
It's me/ bathed and ashy. Me, in Kulu Se and Karma. Carolyn M. Rodgers. PoBA
It's Me, O[h], Lord. *Unknown.* BoAN-1, *with music*; FSW

It's midnight in a drizzling fog. North of Santa Monica. Carter Revard. VoR
It's my lunch hour, so I go. A Step Away from Them. Frank O'Hara. ConAP; HoAn; NYP; VGW
Its Name Is Known. Daniel Lawrence Kelleher. NeIP
"It's narrow, narrow, make [*or* mak] your bed. Fair Annie. *Unknown.* BSV; ESPB; FaBoBa; ViBoFo
It's Nation Time. Amiri Baraka. NoP
It's natural the Boys should whoop it up for. Moon Landing. W. H. Auden. MOON; SUW
Its nature is to look back. Poetry. Carol Rakosi. GP
It's nice that though you are casual about me. Sulpicia, *tr. fr. Latin by* Aliki *and* Willis Barnstone. BoWoP
It's 1962 March 28th. Things I Didn't Know I Loved. Nazim Hikmet, *tr. fr. Turkish by* Randy Blasing *and* Mutlu Konuk. LLLT
It's no go the merry-go-round, it's no go the rickshaw. Bagpipe Music. Louis MacNeice. CMoP; GTBS-P; LiTB; LiTM; NoAM; NOBE; NOBL; NoP; OAEL-2; OAEP; OBSV; OnYI; OxBTC; SeCePo; SeCeV; ViBoPo
It's No Good! D. H. Lawrence. InPS; PV
It's no good/ being an actor. Ian Young. NeAC
It's no joke at all, I'm not that sort of poet. The Confession. Wen Yi-tuo. ChTr
It's no secret I've failed. Tending. Paula Rankin. AMV-81
It's no use having good taste in Chicago. Disclaimer of Prejudice. Eli Siegel. PV
It's No Use Raising a Shout. W. H. Auden. OBMV
It's no use, the Christian thinks of himself first. One Thing to Take, Another to Keep. Crescenzo del Monte, *tr. by* Barbara Garvin. VWA
It's none too sociable herdin' sheep. Sheep Ranching. Owen Wister. BPAW
It's not adultery, the lawyers say. Stop, Science—Stop! A. P. Herbert. FiBHP
It's Not Bad Once the Water Goes Down. Thomas Reiter. WOLT
It's not because it is. Those Old Zen Blues. James Broughton. GP
It's not celestial music it's the girl in the bathroom singing. Ode on Celestial Music. Brian Patten. OxBTC
It's not exciting to have a bar of soap. Living with Chris. Ted Berrigan. NoAM
It's not from Argos or Messene that I hail. The Spartan Wrestler. Damagetus, *tr. by* Tom Dodge. LiSp
"It's not I," said the cat. Who Is Tapping at My Window. A. G. Deming. SoPo
It's not so much the things without. Happiness. Walter Isenhour. STF
It's not the age,/ Disease, or accident. Apologia. David Gascoyne. ChMP
It's Not the Heat So Much as the Humidity. James Tate. NoAM
It's not the sun. Psalm. Patricia Hooper. HoAn
It's not the thickened midriff that I mind. So This Is Middle Age! Francis Whiting Hatch. WhC
It's not true that death is a lump like this, or a blow. Death; She Was Always Here. Yona Wallach, *tr. by* Leonore Gordon. VWA
It's not very far to the edge of town. Adventure. Harry Behn. TiPo
It's not you, this dead long moan from the past. Museum of Cruel Days. Richard Hugo. NPAW
It's November. The Song of This House. Stephen Vincent. NeAC
It's O! but aw ken well. A, U, Hinny Burd. *Unknown.* GBP
It's of a blind beggar, and he lost his sight. The Blind Beggar of Bednall (Bethnal) Green. *Unknown.* BaBo
It's of a brisk young butcher, as I have heard them say. The Leicester Chambermaid. *Unknown.* OBET
It's of a crafty miller and he. The Miller and His Sons. *Unknown.* OBET
It's of a fair young creature that dwelt by the sea side. Mary on the Silvery Tide. *Unknown.* ShS
It's of a famous [*or* fearless] highwayman a story I will [*or* now I'll] tell. Brennan on the Moor. *Unknown.* FaBoBa; GBP; OnYI; ViBoFo
It's of a little shepherdess who was keeping of her sheep. The Shepherdess and the Sailor. *Unknown.* OBET
It's of a merchant's daughter. The Constant Farmer's Son. *Unknown.* OBET
It's of a rich squire in Bristol doth dwell [*or* I'll tell]. Squire and Milkmaid; or, Blackberry Fold. *Unknown.* CoMu; InPK; OBET; OxBB
It's of a tradesman and his wife. How Five and Twenty Shillings Were Expended in a Week. *Unknown.* OBET
It's of a young lord o' the Hielands. Lizie Lindsay [*or* Donald of the Isles]. *Unknown.* ESPB; OxBB
It's of flash packet, a packet of fame. The *Dom Pedro.* *Unknown.* AmFP
It's of those Texas cowboys a story I'll tell. The Texas Cowboys. *Unknown.* CoSo
It's of three rioters I have to tell. The Pardoner's Tale. Chaucer, *mod. vers. by* Nevill Coghill. *Fr.* The Canterbury Tales. SCV
It's on this railroad bank I stand. Careless Love. *Unknown.* UnPo
It's once I courted as pretty a lass. *Unknown.* OxNR
It's one thing/ to sing the beloved. Duino Elegies, III. Rainer Maria Rilke, *tr. by* David Young. NAWM-2
It's only we, Grimalkin, both fond and fancy free. The Ride to Cherokee. Amelia Walstien Carpenter. AA
It's Over a (See Just). E. E. Cummings. OxBA; VGW
Its petals do not open of their own accord. That is our part. An Artichoke for Montesquieu. Jorie Graham. NPGG
Its presence is not impeded by visible form. The Human Mind. Ai Shih-te, *tr. by* William C. White. TrJP
Its quick soft silver bell beating, beating. Auto Wreck. Karl Shapiro. BiP; CMoP; FF; LiTM; MiAP; MoVE; NePA; NIP; PoPl; VGW
It's quiet for me, now that I have buried the child. Ritual Three. David Ignatow. ConAP
It's quiet in Hell just now, it's very tame. Lament of an Idle Demon. R. P. Lister. DBV; FiBHP; NOBL
It's Raining. Guillaume Apollinaire, *tr. fr. French.* SOTW
It's raining again in the Southwest. Rain in the Southwest. Reeve Spencer Kelley. AmFN
It's raining, it's pouring. *Unknown.* OxNR; TrAS, *diff. vers., with music*
It's raining, it's raining. *Unknown.* OxNR
It's raining today, a dark rain. Birthday. P. J. Kavanagh. NAs
It's rare to see the morning breeze. The Ingle-Side. Hew Ainslee. HBV-2
It's right to call you son. That cursing alcoholic. Letter to an Absent Son. Madeline DeFrees. GP; NMM
Its roof among the stars projected. Phantasus. Arno Holz, *tr. by* Ludwig Lewisohn. AWP
It's Saturday afternoon at the edge of the world. Laguna Blues. Charles Wright. GeTw
It's seldom wise to generalize. Homage to Texas. Robert Graves. LiTB
It's simple enough. You begin. Middle of the Day. Jack Driscoll. WOLT
It's so cold in China birds can't hardly sing. It's Cold in China Blues. *Unknown.* BluL
It's so hard to coordinate. Late Again. Gabriel Zaid, *tr. by* Eliot Weinberger. AMV-81
It's Spring Returning, It's Spring and Love. *Unknown.* HAP
It's spring; the City, wrapped. To His Chi Mistress. George Starbuck. NYBP
It's step her to your weev'ly wheat. Weevily Wheat. *Unknown.* AS
It's still a good idea. To Friends Who Have Also Considered Suicide. Phyllis Webb. NOBC
It's still inside me. My Mother's Death. Judith Hemschemeyer. Str
"It's strange," my mother said, "to think." My Mother's House. Eunice Tietjens. HBMV
It's strangely like a man. A Film. Albert Goldbarth. MAYP
It's such a/ Bore. Ennui. Langston Hughes. OBAL; OBCA
It's such a static reference; looking. Epistrophe. Amiri Baraka. CAD; NNP; PoNe
It's taken many years to find. The One Song. C. G. Hanzlicek. AMV-80
It's ten. Evening. The room is in half light. My Sister. Alfonsina Storni, *tr. by* Aliki *and* Willis Barnstone. BoWoP
It's the anarchy of poverty. The Poor. William Carlos Williams. MoAB; MoAmPo; NoP; PPP
It's the Buckaroo Sandman. Buckaroo Sandman. *Unknown.* BPAW
It's the first of May. The Anniversary. Roberta Spear. MAYP
It's the first storm of the winter. Subway Psalm. Alden Nowlan. Str
It's the long road to Guinea. Guinea. Jacques Roumain, *tr. by* Langston Hughes. TTY
It's the might, it's the fight. A Football Game. Alice Van Eck. RHPC
It's the old tricks is best tricks. April Fool. Sam Hunt. OCNZ
It's the Same at Four A.M. Joy Harjo. TWSS
It's the Same the Whole World Over. *Unknown.* *See* She Was Poor but She Was Honest.
It's the Spring. Pastoral. W. E. Henley. In Hospital, XXII. BrPo
It's the Syme the Whole World Over. *Unknown.* AS, *with music*; FSW; TrAS, *with music*; TreFS
(It's the Syme the Wide World Over.) BeLS
It's the way she moves. The Accomplice. Ron Slate. AMV-80
It's the way you perceive the world I love. The First Love Poem. Myra Glazer Schotz. VWA
It's there/ in the hole of the sea. The Hole in the Sea. Marvin Bell. NYBP
It's there you'll see confectioners with sugar sticks and dainties. Galway Races. *Unknown.* OxBoLi
It's Three No Trumps. Guy Innes. FiBHP
It's Time. Ian Wedde. Earthly: Sonnets for Carlos, 2. OCNZ
It's time for bloody Watusis to romp through the streets. Time Poem. Quentin Hill. NBP
It's time I told you why. The Hindoo: He Doesn't Hurt a Fly or a Spider Either. A. K. Ramanujan. OxBC
It's time to make love. Douse the glim. Limberick [*or* Limerick]. Conrad Aiken. FaBoNo; FiBHP

It's to you that I speak, men of the Southern hemisphere. By the Waters of Babylon. Benjamin Fondane, *tr. by* Edouard Roditi. VWA
It's too dark to see black. A Mother Speaks: The Algiers Motel Incident, Detroit. Michael S. Harper. AmPA; BPo
It's too late, too late. T.B. Blues. Leadbelly (Huddie Ledbetter). BluL
It's True I'm No Miss America. Stephanie Slowinsky. AMV-80
It's true Mattie Lee. Unidentified Flying Object. Robert Hayden. NCSH
Its trunk as of dead silver cast. The Felled Plane Tree. Anna Hajnal, *tr. by* William Jay Smith. BoWoP
It's 12:21 in New York a Thursday. In Blue. D. C. Berry. BXAP
It's twenty to four. Linen Town. Seamus Heaney. CIP
It's up Glenbarchan's braes I gaed. Sir Walter Scott. PBBP
It's Venice, late August, outside after lunch, and Hart. Portrait of the Artist with Hart Crane. Charles Wright. GeTw
It's Very Unwise to Kill the Goose. Philip H. Rhinelander. WhC
It's we two, it's we two, it's we two for aye. Like a Laverock in the Lift. Jean Ingelow. HBV-1
Its wednesday night baby. Master Charge Blues. Nikki Giovanni. OBAL
Its wingéd lion stands up straight to hide. Venice. Howard Moss. MoAB
It's winter in Paris and women in high heels are strutting. Paris. Jane Garnett. AMV-80
It's Wonderful. Walter E. Isenhour. STF
It's wonderful dogs they're breeding now. Tim, an Irish Terrier. Winifrid M. Letts. GDP
It's wonderful how I jog. Animals Are Passing from Our Lives. Philip Levine. CoAP; NoAM; NOBA; TAP; TW
It's wonderful, so wonderful. It's Wonderful. Walter E. Isenhour. STF
It's worse than death, that hush. Miners. John C. Frohlicher. BPAW
It's You. L. A. McDonald. STF
Itt [*or* It] rely is ridikkelus. Bobby's First Poem. Norman Gale. FiBHP; MoShBr; PV
'Ittle Touzle Head. Ray Garfield Dandridge. BANP
Itum Paradisum all clothed in green. *Unknown.* GBP
Itylus. Swinburne. ChTr; HBV-1; WHA
Iulus. Eleanor Glenn Wallis. NePoAm-2
Ivanhoe, *sels.* Sir Walter Scott.
"Anna-Marie, love, up is the sun," *fr. ch.* 40. ViBoPo
Rebecca's Hymn, *fr. ch.* 39. EnRP
("When Israel, of the Lord beloved.") ViBoPo
I've a letter from thy sire. Baby Mine. Charles Mackey. BLSo
I've a pal called Billy Peg-leg, with one leg a wood leg. Peg-Leg's Fiddle. Bill Adams. EtS
I've a secret in my heart, sweet Marie. Sweet Marie. Cy Warman. TreFS
I've always thought Polonius a dry. Lines to His Son on Reaching Adolescence. John Logan. CAPP; NePoEA-2
I've always wanted brook trout. Looking for Work. Raymond Carver. GeTw
I've always wanted one. Wanting a Mummy. Sandra McPherson. AmPA; LCAP
I've always wanted to say something of you. To Teresa. Iván Silén, *tr. by* Julio Marzán. InW
I've an ingle, shady ingle, near a dusky bosky dingle. Midsummer Jingle. Newman Levy. BoNaP; WhC
I've aye been keen on the heich hills. Ane to Anither. Duncan Glen. PoSH
I've beat my way wherever any winds have blown. Once You Git the Habit. *Unknown.* CoSo
I've been a moonshiner for seventeen [long] years. Kentucky Moonshiner [*or* Moonshiner]. *Unknown.* AS; FSW; OBAL; TrAS
I've been a wandering early and late. Wandering. *Unknown.* FSW
I've been a wild rover for a number of years. Wild Rover. *Unknown.* FSW
I've been after the exotic. The Ethnic Life. Daniel Halpern. AmPA
I've been all around this whole wide world. Don't Let Your Deal Go Down. *Unknown.* FSW
I've been around a long time. Curtain Speech. Michael Braude. AMV-81
I've been called sway. It's in the Name. Kitty Tsui. BrSi
I've been doing some hard traveling. Hard Traveling. Woody Guthrie. FSW
I've been driving for hours. Looking for a Rest Area. Stephen Dunn. AmPA
I've been given this triangular face to wear. Self-Portrait. Nina Cassian, *tr. by* Herbert Kuhner. VWA
I've been going around everywhere without any skin. Josephine Miles. IHMS
I've been in jail from slander. The Rocky Mountains. *Unknown.* AmFP
I've been in love for long. In Love for Long. Edwin Muir. BoLoP; BSV; LiTM; MoBrPo
I've been plannning to tell you. Hesitating Ode. Miklos Radnoti, *tr. by* Steven Polgar, Stephen Berg, *and* S. J. Marks. LLLT
I've been sitting around for weeks reading. Room Service. John W. Moser. FAZ
I've been thinking today. Round Up in Glory. *Unknown.* CoSo
I've been to Haarlem, I've been to Dover. Turn the Glasses Over. *Unknown.* FSW
I've been to Palestine. John Brown. Vachel Lindsay. MoAmPo
I've been to Red Hoss Mountain, where Field once dwelt and wrote. Old Red Hoss Mountain. Cy Warman. PoOW
I've been travlin' all de day. Ride On, Moses. *Unknown.* BoAN-1
I've been trying to fashion a wifely ideal. A Plea for Trigamy. Sir Owen Seaman. NOBL
I've been upon the prairie. Bronc Peeler's Song. *Unknown.* CoSo
I've Been Workin' [*or* Working] on the Railroad. *Unknown.* BLSo, *with music*; FaFP; FSW; SaC; TreF
I've borne full many a sorrow, I've suffered many a loss. The Heaviest Cross of All. Katherine Eleanor Conway. AA
I've changed my ways a little; I cannot now. The House Dog's Grave. Robinson Jeffers. GDP
I've cleaned house. Saturday Afternoon, When Chores Are Done. Harryette Mullen. AMV-81
I've come back many times today. Gift from Kenya. May Miller. BlSi
I've come by the May-tree all times o' the year. The May Tree. William Barnes. LiTB; LoBV
I've come down here to live on a bed of weeds. The Old Lady under the Freeway. Diana O Hehir. NPGG
I've come this far to freedom and I won't turn back. Midway. Naomi Long Madgett. BlSi; BPo; NNP; PoNe
I've come to close your door, my handsome, my darling. Bereft Child's First Night. Frances Bellerby. POL
I've come to give you fruit from out my orchard. The Crossed Apple. Louise Bogan. BiP; HeIP
I've come to see Miss Jennian Jones. Miss Jennian Jones. *Unknown.* AmFP
I've come to town to see you all. Long Tail Blue. *Unknown.* BLSo
I've discovered a way to stay friends forever. Friendship. Shel Silverstein. NTCP
I've dispatch'd, my dear madam, this scrap of a letter. Sent to a Patient, with the Present of a Couple of Ducks. Edward Jenner. FaBoUs
I've done what I could. My boys run wild now. Complaint. Ian Hamilton. NoAM
I've ever lost were. For Both of Us at Fisk. Sharon Scott. JB
I've finished with the listlessness. The Man Who Knew Too Much. David Wojahn. MAYP
I've forgotten what day, but late in December. The Basilisk. Philip Child. CaP
I've found a small dragon in the woodshed. A Small Dragon. Brian Patten. AmMo
I've found my bonny babe a nest. An Irish Lullaby. Alfred Perceval Graves. HBV-1
I've Gone and Stained with the Color of Love. Milton Acorn. NeAC
I've got a bellyful of whisky. Long-Line Skinner. *Unknown.* FSW
I've Got a Dog. *Unknown.* RHPC
("I've got a dog as thin as a rail.") GDP
I've got a gal who loves me so. L'il Liza Jane. *Unknown.* FSW
I've Got a Home in That Rock. Raymond R. Patterson. FF; PoBA; PoNe
I've got a home in-a that Rock, don't you see? Home in That Rock. *Unknown.* FSW
I've got a letter, parson, from my son away out West. Billy, He's in Trouble. James Barton Adams. YaD
I've got a little baby, but she's out of sight. Hello, Ma Baby. Joseph E. Howard *and* Ida Emerson. BLSo; FSW
I've got a mule [and] her name is Sal. The Erie Canal. William S. Allen. AmFN; AS; BLSo; FSW; TrAS
I've Got a New Book from My Grandfather Hyde. Leroy F. Jackson. FaPON; SiSoSe
I've got a pal. My Old Dutch; a Cockney Song. Albert Chevalier. VLP
I've Got a Rocket. *Unknown.* SiSoSe; TiPo
(Rocket in My Pocket, A.) RHPC
I've got a silk-worm. Theobald James. J. B. Morton. *Fr.* When We Were Very Silly. FaBoPa
I've got a sister nine feet tall. 'Way Down in Cuba. *Unknown.* AmSS
I've got a wife and five little children. Rock About My Saro Jane. *Unknown.* FSW
I've got nasty habits. Live with Me. Mick Jagger *and* Keith Richard. InPK
I've Got No Use for the Women. *Unknown.* AmFP
I've got the children to tend. Woman Work. Maya Angelou. SaC
I've Got the Giggles Today. A. P. Herbert. FiBHP
I've got the wiggly-wiggles today. Wiggly Giggles. Stacy Jo Crossen *and* Natalie Anne Covell. RHPC
I've Got the World on a String, *with music.* Ted Koehler. BLSo
I've got to keep moving. Hellhound on My Trail. *Unknown.* BluL
I've Got to Know. Woody Guthrie. FSW

I've had my share of mountain days in snow and rain and sun. Mountain Days. Barclay Fraser. PoSH
I've had tangled feelings lately. Breakthrough. Carolyn M. Rodgers. BPo
I've heard all about musicians. Saxophonetyx. Cyn Zarco. BrSi
I've heard it said that Sir Barnabas Beer. Endurance Test. Dacre Balsdon. DBV; FiBHP
I've heard the lilting at our yowe-milking. *See* I've heard them lilting at our yowe-milking.
I've heard the sea upon the troubled rocks. The Man Whom the Sea Kept Awake. Robert Bly. NePoEA
I've Heard Them Lilting at Loom and Belting. C. Day Lewis. *Fr.* Two Songs. HAP; NoAM; OBMV
I've heard them [*or* the] lilting at our yowe-milking [*or* the ewe-milking]. The Flowers of the Forest [*or* A Lament for Flodden]. Jane Elliot. BSV; CH; FaBoCh; FaBoRV; GoTS; GTBS; GTBS-P; HBV-2; OBEC; OBEV; OxBS; PoPle; ViBoPo; WPE
I've jumped from myself to dawn. The Tree of Diana. Alejandra Pizarnik, *tr. by* Yishai Tobin. VWA
"I've just come from a place." The Little Duck. Joso, *tr. by* Harold G. Henderson. SoPo
I've just got here, through Paris, from the sunny southern shore. The Man Who Broke the Bank at Monte Carlo. Fred Gilbert. FSN; FSW; TreF
I've just had an astounding dream as I lay in the straw. Minstrel's Song. Ted Hughes. OBCP
I've kept a haughty heart thro' grief and mirth. To My Mother. Heine, *tr. by* Matilda Dickson. AWP
I've kissed thee, sweetheart, in a dream at least. Sleep. Theophile de Viau, *tr. by* Sir Edmund Gosse. AWP
I've known ere now an interfering branch. The Axe-Helve. Robert Frost. OxBA
I've known rivers. The Negro Speaks of Rivers. Langston Hughes. AmFN; AmNP; BANP; BPo; CABA; CDC; HAP; HeIP; IDB; NIP; NoAM; NOBA; NoP; OBCA; PAI; PoBA; PoNe; TAP; TTY; WeW
I've known you since the time/ you were amphibian. Songs to a Lady Moonwalker. Abraham Sutskever, *tr. by* Ruth Whitman. VWA
I've labored long and hard for bread. "Black Bart." DBV; PV
I've left my own old home of homes. John Clare. *Fr.* The Flitting. OBRV
I've left the thin autumnal air. Cats and Egypt. Andrew Hudgins. AMV-81
I've listened, when to school I've gone. The Landrail. John Clare. PBBP
I've lived beneath huge portals where marine. Former Life. Baudelaire, *tr. by* Roy Campbell. NAWM-2
I've lived by the world's rules. Lines from an Orchard Once Surveyed by Thoreau. Philip Booth. GP
I've Lost My ———. Harry Cholmondeley Pennell. CenHV
I've made it. Double-Header. John Stone. TAT
I've moved here to the Immortal's place. Staying in the Mountains in Summer. Yü Hsüan-chi, *tr. by* Geoffrey Waters. BoWoP
I've never felt it true. A Delicate Balance. Laura Schreiber. AMV-80
I've never known a dog to wag. The Dog. *Unknown.* WBLP
I've never learned an adequate goodbye. False Cadence. Bruce Berger. AMV-80
I've never traveled for mor'n a day. On the Quay. John Joy Bell. HBV-1
I've no tooth to sing you the song. Pat Cloherty's Version of *The Maisie.* Richard Murphy. IPY
I've oft been asked by prosing souls. A Reason Fair to Fill My Glass. Charles Morris. HBV-2
I've oft been told by learned friars. An Argument [to Any Phillis or Cloë]. Thomas Moore. BoLoP; EnLoPo; NIP
I've often heard my mother say. The Unknown Color. Countee Cullen. FaPON; OBCA
I've reached the land of desert sweet. *See* We've reached the land of desert sweet.
I've paid for your sickest fancies; I've humoured your crackedest whim. The *Mary Gloster.* Kipling. BeLS
I've plucked the berry from the bush, the brown nut from the tree. Sing On, Blithe Bird! William Motherwell. GN; HBV-1; HBVY
I've poached a pickle paitricks. Poaching *in Excelsis.* G. K. Menzies. FaBoCo
I've rambled and gambled all my money away. Rabble Soldier. *Unknown.* AS
I've Rambled This Country Both Earlye and Late, *with music.* *Unknown.* OuSiCo
I've reached the end of my names. In the Season of Wolves and Names. Mariève Rugo. AMV-80
I've Reached the Land of Corn and Wine, *with music.* Edgar P. Stites. AH (Beulah Land.) FSW
I've read that Luther said (it's come to me). The Author to the Reader. Randall Jarrell. OxBC
I've rode the Southern, I've rode the L. & N. I Rode Southern, I Rode L & N. *Unknown.* AmFP
I've said goodbye to the three black kittens. First Departure. Frances Frost. SiSoSe
I've sailed among the Yankees, the Spaniards and Chinees. The Sailor's Way. *Unknown.* ShS
I've saved the milk crystal stone. Palinode. Maura Stanton. MAYP
I've seen a deal of gaiety through out my noisy life. Champagne Charlie. *At. to* George Leybourne. PSoN
I've seen a dying eye. Emily Dickinson. AmPP; BoWoP; FPL; NePA; NOBA; PoEL-5; PoLF; TwAmPo
Ive seen all the sunrises since u left me. Sex Play in Four Acts. Doug Fetherling. NeAC
I've seen it drive straw straight through a fence post. Mid-Plains Tornado. Linda Bierds. AMV-80
I've seen one flying saucer. Only when. Go Fly a Saucer. David McCord. FaPON; ImOP
I've seen strangers. Parole Board. Derek Butler. LFAC
I've seen the grey-haired lyrists come down from the hills. Grand Finale. Irving Layton. NOBC
I've seen the smiling of Fortune beguiling. The Flowers of the Forest. Alison Rutherford Cockburn. BSV; OBEC
I've seen the Thousand Islands. Tadoussac. Charles Bancroft. BLPA
I've served my country nine and twenty years. Edward Thompson. *Fr.* An Humble Wish; off Porto-Sancto, March 29, 1779. NOEC
I've shore at Burrabogie, and I've shore at Toganmain. Flash Jack from Gundagai. *Unknown.* PoAu-1
I've sixpence in my pocket and I've worked hard for it. The Beggar. *Unknown.* OBET
I've slept in five houses, but wakened. This Year. Joseph Hutchison. AMV-81
I've sold the old ranch, stock and all. Last Drift. Arthur Chapman. BPAW
I've stayed in the front yard all my life. A Song in the Front Yard. Gwendolyn Brooks. IDB; NoAM; NOBA; PoBA
I've stitched my dress with continents. Knowledge. Nina Cassian, *tr. by* Michael Impey *and* Brian Swann. BoWoP
I've taken my fun where I've found it. The Ladies. Kipling. MoBrPo; TreFT
I've taken the police squad outline from where you fell. The Immigration Act of 1924. Laureen Mar. BrSi
I've Tasted My Blood. Milton Acorn. MoCV; NOBC
I've taught me other tongues—and in strange eyes. To England. Byron. *Fr.* Childe Harold's Pilgrimage. WHA
I've taught thee Love's sweet lesson o'er. Song. George Darley. *Fr.* Sylvia; or, The May Queen. OBRV
I've Thirty Months. J. M. Synge. OBMV
I've thought of names. Labour of the Brain, Ballad of the Body. Nicole Forman. NMM
I've told you many a tale, my child, of the old heroic days. Madeleine Verchères. William Henry Drummond. CaP
I've tossed an apple at you; if you can love me. The Apple. *At. to* Plato. WeW
I've traveled all over this country. Acres of Clams. *Unknown.* FSW
I've traveled 'round this country. Banks of Marble. Les Rice. FSW
I've tried in vain, day after day. The Promise. Mary B. Fowler. STF
I've tried pitying you. Some Scribbles for a Lumpfish. Thomas Johnson. AMV-80
I've tried the new moon tilted in the air. The Freedom of the Moon. Robert Frost. MOON
I've tried to seal it in. The Knot. Stanley Kunitz. HAP
I've walked along with Jesus. His Presence. Dale Schulz. STF
I've wandered east, I've wandered west. Jeanie Morrison. William Motherwell. HBV-1
I've wandered [*or* wander'd] to the village, Tom, I've sat beneath the tree. Forty [*or* Twenty] Years Ago. *Unknown, at. to* A. J. Gault *and also to* Dill Armor Smith. BLPA; HBV-1
I've watched the clouds by day and night. Watching Clouds. John Farrar. SoPo
I've watched you now a full half-hour. To a Butterfly. Wordsworth. FM; HBV-1; SeCeV
I've weeded their beds, put down manure and bark dust. Elegy while Pruning Roses. David Wagoner. AMV-80
I've wined and dined on Mulligan stew. The Lady Is a Tramp. Lorenz Hart. OBAL
I've wisdom from the East and from the West. The Philosophic Pill. W. S. Gilbert. GLGT
I've Worked for a Silver Shilling. Charles W. Kennedy. HBMV
I've worked on the Nine-Mile, likewise on the River. The Broken-down Digger. *Unknown.* PoAu-1
I've written you a song. Blah, Blah, Blah. Ira Gershwin. OBAL
Ivory Bed, The. Winfield Townley Scott. ErPo
Ivory, Coral, Gold, The. William Drummond of Hawthornden. ELP (Madrigal: "Ivory, coral, gold, The.) ElL

Ivory Dog for My Sister, The. Mary TallMountain. TWSS
Ivory Gate, The, *sel.* Thomas Lovell Beddoes.
Mighty Thoughts of an Old World, The. GoJo
(Song of Thanatos.) NBM
(Stanzas: "Mighty thought of an old world, The.") TrGoPo
(Stanzas from "The Ivory Gate.") EnRP
Ivory in her black, and all intent. Jesu, Joy of Man's Desiring. Robert Fitzgerald. NYBP
Ivory Masks in Orbit. Keorapetse Kgositsile. PoBA
Ivory Paper Weight. Adrien Stoutenburg. GP
Ivory Tower, The. Robert Hillyer. NYBP
Ivry. Macaulay. FaBV; GN; HBV-2; HBVY; OBRV
(Battle of Ivry, The.) WBLP
Ivy and Holly. E. H. W. Meyerstein. ELU
Ivy, Chief of Trees. *Unknown.* OxBM
(In Praise of Ivy.) MeEL
Ivy Crest, The. *Unknown, tr. fr. Old Irish by* Robin Flower. AnIL
Ivy Crown, The. William Carlos Williams. NoP; PrIm
Ivy Green, The. Charles Dickens. *Fr.* The Pickwick Papers, *ch.* 6. BoNaP; HBV-1; HBVY
Ivy o'er the mouldering wall, The. The Sun-Dial. Thomas Love Peacock. *Fr.* Melincourt. OBNC; OBRV
Ivy-Wife, The. Thomas Hardy. VLP
Iwa flies heavy to nest in the brush, The. Love by the Water-Reeds. *Tr. fr. Hawaiian by* M. W. Beckwith. WTO
Iwori wotura. Oracle. *Yoruba Oral Tradition, tr. by* Ulli Beier. WTO
Izaac Walton, Cotton, and William Oldways. Walter Savage Landor. NBM; PoEL-4

J

J. A. G. Julia Ward Howe. PAH
J. Alfred Prufrock to. Said. George Starbuck. OBAL
J. B. H. C. Bunner. AA
J. B., *sel.* Archibald MacLeish.
Curse God and Die, You Said to Me. EaLo
J. J. Walter de la Mare. FaBoNo
J. M. W. Turner on Switzerland. Consolations of Art. Roy Fuller. OxBC
J. Milton Miles. Edgar Lee Masters. *Fr.* Spoon River Anthology. CrMA
J. S. Mill. E. C. Bentley. *See* John Stuart Mill.
J. V. Cunningham Gets Hung Up on a Dirty, of All Things, Joke. Henry Taylor. BXAP
Ja, Ja, Ja! *with music.* *Unknown.* ShS
Ja-Nez—burro with the long ears. Burro with the Long Ears. *Unknown, tr. by* Hilda Faunce Wetherill. FaPON
Jabber-Whacky. Isabelle Di Caprio. QQQ
Jabberwocky. "Lewis Carroll." *Fr.* Through the Looking-Glass, *ch.* 1. AmMo; BiP; CABA; EBEV; EBVV; FaBoBe; FaBoCo; FaBoNo; FaBV; FaFP; FaPON; FF; FiBHP; FPL; GoJo; HBV-2; HeIP; HoPM; InPK; InPS; LiTB; NA; NBM; NIP; NOBE; NOBL; NTCP; OAEL-2; OxBChV; PoPl; PoRA, PPoe; PPP; RHPC; SeCeV; SpRo; TEP; TiPo; TreF; TrGrPo; VLP; WhC
Jabberwocky; as the Author of "The Faerie Queene" Might Have Written It. Junius Cooper. InMe
Jacaranda. Roo Borson. NOBC
J'Accuse. Peter Klappert. AMV-81
Jack. Louis Golding. TrJP
Jack. Charles Henry Ross. OxBChV; RHPC
Jack and Dinah Want Freedom. *Unknown.* BPo
Jack and Gill went up the hill. *See* Jack and Jill went up the hill.
Jack and Gye. *Unknown.* OxNR
Jack and His Pony, Tom. Hilaire Belloc. BoAnP; PH
Jack and Jill. Anthony C. Deane. *See* Here Is the Tale.
Jack and Jill. Charles Battell Loomis. BXAP
Jack and Jill. Harriet S. Morgridge. *Fr.* Mother Goose Sonnets. AA
Jack and Jill. Charles Powell. BXAP
Jack and Jill—as Kipling Might Have Written It. Anthony C. Deane. *See* Here Is the Tale.
Jack and Jill [*or* Gill] went up the hill. Mother Goose. FaBoBe; FaFP; HBV-1; HBVY; OxBoLi; OxNR; SoPo; TiPo
Jack and Jill went up the hill/ To fetch some heavy water. Paul Dehn. *Fr.* Rhymes for a Modern Nursery. DBV; FiBHP; PV
Jack and Joan. Thomas Campion. FaBoCh; FaPoR; HBV-1
("Jack and Joan [*or* Jacke and Jone] they think no ill.") AAS; OAEP; OBSC
Jack and Roger. *At. to* Benjamin Franklin. ChTr
(Impromptu.) NOBL
(Quatrain: "Jack, eating rotten cheese, did say.") WhC
(Sampson Imitated.) FaBoEE
Jack Barrett went to Quetta. The Story of Uriah. Kipling. BrPo; SCV
Jack be nimble. Mother Goose. OxNR; SoPo; TiPo
Jack Creamer. James Jeffrey Roche. PAH
Jack Denver died on Talbragar when Christmas Eve began. Talbragar. Henry Lawson. PoAu-1
Jack Donahoe. *Unknown.* CoSo
Jack, eating rotten cheese, did say. Jack and Roger [*or* Quatrain]. *At. to* Benjamin Franklin. ChTr; FaBoEE; NOBL; WhC
Jack Ellyat Heard the Guns. Stephen Vincent Benét. *Fr.* John Brown's Body. PoLF
"Jack fell as he'd have wished," the Mother said. The Hero. Siegfried Sassoon. OBWP
Jack Frenchman's Defeat. Congreve. APAS
(Jack Frenchman's Lamentation.) CoMu
Jack Frost. "Gabriel Setoun." HBV-1; HBVY
Jack Frost. Helen Bayley Davis. SoPo
Jack Frost. Celia Thaxter. OBCA
Jack Giantkiller took and struck. Driving Cross-Country. X. J. Kennedy. TwCP
Jack had a little pony—Tom. Jack and His Pony, Tom. Hilaire Belloc. BoAnP; PH
Jack Haggerty. *Unknown, at. to* Dan McGinnis. AmFP; ShS, *with music;* ViBoFo
(Flat River Girl, The, *with music.*) AS
Jack Hall. *Unknown.* OBET
Jack his own merit sees: this gives him pride. On a Proud Fellow. *Unknown.* PV
Jack-in-the-Box. Elder Olson. NePA
Jack-in-the-Pulpit. Ivy O. Eastwick. YeAr
Jack in the pulpit, out and in. *Unknown.* OxNR
Jack Is Every Inch a Sailor. *Unknown.* FSW
Jack Monroe. *Unknown.* AmFP
Jack o' Diamonds, *with music.* *Unknown.* OuSiCo
Jack o' Diamonds; or, The Rabble Soldier, *with music.* *Unknown.* CoSo
(Jack of Diamonds, *shorter vers.*) AmFP
Jack o'Lantern. Anna Chandler Ayre. SoPo
Jack Rabbit. *See* Jackrabbit.
Jack Rabbit. Adrien Stoutenburg. BoAnP
Jack Robinson. *Unknown.* OBET
Jack Rose. Maxwell Bodenheim. HBMV
Jack Sprat/ Had a cat. *Unknown.* OxNR
Jack Sprat could eat no fat. Mother Goose. FaBoBe; FaFP; HBV-1; HBVY; OxNR
Jack Tar, *with music.* *Unknown.* ShS
Jack, that nurse at the Veteran's. Uncle Jack. David Kherdian. FAZ
Jack the Giant Queller; an Antique History, *sels.* Henry Brooke.
Air: "Arise, arise, arise!" NOEC
Air: "For often my mammy has told." NOEC
Jack the Guinea Pig. *Unknown.* AmSS
Jack the Jolly Tar. *Unknown.* AmFP
Jack the Piper. *Unknown.* ChTr; GBP
("As I was going up the hill.") OxNR
Jack the Ripper. Allan M. Laing. FiBHP
Jack Was Every Inch a Sailor. *Unknown.* FSW; WHW
Jackals prowl, the serpents hiss, The. Elegy. Arthur Guiterman. InMe
Jackdaw, The. Vincent Bourne, *tr. fr. Latin by* William Cowper. HBV-1; HBVY; PB; PBBP
Jackdaw. Tom Earley. BoAnP
Jackdaw of Rheims, The. "Thomas Ingoldsby." *Fr.* The Ingoldsby Legends. FaBoCo; HBV-2; OBNV; OnMSP; PaPo; VLP
Jacket it winsomely in primrose yellow! Ultimate Anthology. Martin Bell. POL
Jackey Jackey gallops on a horse like a swallow. A Bushranger. Kenneth Slessor. CBAP
Jackfruit, The. Ho Xuan Huong, *tr. fr. Vietnamese by* Nguyen Ngoc Bich. PBWP
Jackie. King D. Kuka. VoR
Jackie Faa. *Unknown.* ChTr
Jackie's gone a-sailing with trouble on his mind. Jack Monroe. *Unknown.* AmFP
Jackknife swandive gainer twist. Elegy for a Diver. Peter Meinke. Psk
Jacklight. Louise Erdrich. TWSS
Jackrabbits. S. Omar Barker. BPAW
Jack's Fidelity. Charles Dibdin. EtS
Jackson. *Unknown.* AS, *with music;* FSW
Jackson at New Orleans. Wallace Rice. PAH
Jackson is on sea, Jackson is on shore. Jackson. *Unknown.* AS; FSW
Jackson, Mississippi. Margaret Walker. FB
Jackson Pollock had a quaint. Squeeze Play. Phyllis McGinley. *Fr.* Spectator's Guide to Contemporary Art. DBV; FaBoEE; OBSV
Jackson State Prison. Leon Baker. LFAC
Jacksonville Blues. *Unknown.* BluL

Jacky, come give me thy fiddle. Mother Goose. OxNR
Jacob. Phoebe Cary. InMe; OBAL
Jacob. Else Lasker-Schüler, *tr. fr. German.* BoWoP, *tr. by* Rosemarie Waldrop; VWA, *tr. by* Joachim Neugroschel
Jacob. Charles Reznikoff. VWA
Jacob. Delmore Schwartz. VWA
Jacob: a bull among his herd. Jacob. Else Lasker-Schüler, *tr. by* Rosemarie Waldrop. BoWoP
Jacob and Esau. Else Lasker-Schüler, *tr. fr. German by* Rosemarie Waldrop. BoWoP
Jacob and the Angel. Stephen Mitchell. VWA
Jacob can have his ladder. Tree Man. Rennie McQuilkin. AMV-81
Jacob Epstein. *Unknown.* FaBoCo
Jacob Godbey. Edgar Lee Masters. *Fr.* Spoon River Anthology. LiTA
Jacob, hear! Jacob's Destiny. Richard Beer-Hofmann, *tr. by* Ida Bension Wynn. *Fr.* Jacob's Dream. TrJP
Jacob Tonson, His Publisher. Dryden. ChTr
Jacob was the buffalo of his herd. Jacob. Else Lasker-Schüler, *tr. by* Joachim Neugroschel. VWA
Jacobean. Clifton Fadiman. FiBHP
Jacobite Scot in Satire on England's Unparalleled Loss, A. *Unknown.* APAS
Jacobite Toast, A. John Byrom. FaBoCo
(Epigram.) HBV-1
(Extempore Verses Intended to Allay the Violence of Party-Spirit.) NOBL; OBEC
("God bless the king—I mean the faith's defender.") FaBoEE
(Toast, A.) ViBoPo
Jacobite's Epitaph, A. Macaulay. FaPoR; NOBE; OBEV; OBNC; OBVV
(Epitaph on a Jacobite.) EBEV; ViBoPo
Jacobite's Exile, A. Swinburne. OBVV
Jacob's Dream, *sel.* Richard Beer-Hofmann, *tr. fr. German by* Ida Bension Wynn.
Jacob's Destiny. TrJP
Jacob's Ladder. *Unknown. See* We Am Clim' in' Jacob's Ladder.
Jacob's Ladder, The. Denise Levertov. AmPP; CoPo; PoM; PPP
Jacob's Well. *Unknown.* OBET
Jacob's Winning. Richard Sherwin. VWA
Jacopone da Todi. Matthew Arnold. *See* Austerity of Poetry.
Jacqueline Gray. Kenneth Pitchford. *Fr.* Good for Nothing Man. CoPo
Jacques Cartier. Thomas D'Arcy McGee. CaP
Jade Flower Palace. Tu Fu, *tr. fr. Chinese by* Kenneth Rexroth. NaP
Jadis. Ernest Dowson. VLP
Jaffar. Leigh Hunt. BeLS; HBV-2
Jagg'd mountain peaks and skies ice-green. Breughel's Winter. Walter de la Mare. SeCePo
Jaguar, The. Ted Hughes. LiTM; PoPl
Jahr der Seele, Das, *sel.* Stefan George, *tr. fr. German by* Daisy Broicher.
"No way too long, no path too steep." AWP
Jailbird. Vernon Scannell. OxBC
Jailhouse Blues ("Thirty days in jail. . ."). *Unknown.* BluL
Jailhouse Blues, The ("When I was lying in jail. . ."). *Unknown.* BluL
Jailhouse Lawyers. Robert B. Smith. LFAC
Jailhouse murder. Wire Monkey. Paul D. Shiplett. LFAC
Jake and Roany was a-chousin' along. The Bosky Steer. Henry Herbert Knibbs. BPAW
Jake Balokowsky, my biographer. Posterity. Philip Larkin. OxBC
Jake Hates All the Girls. E. E. Cummings. CTBA
Jake's store past Pindaric mountain. Purchase of a Blue, Green, or Orange Ode. Josephine Miles. NoP
Jake's Wharf. Philip Booth. NYBP
Jalan Thamrin in Denpasar. Walking down Jalan Thamrin R. F. Brissenden. CBAP
Jam Fa Jamaica. Charles Lynch. LTB
Jam Fish, The. Edward Abbott Parry. AmMo; OxBChV
Jam on Gerry's Rock [*or* Rocks], The. *Unknown.* AmFP; AS, *with music*; BaBo; FaBoBa; FSW; ShS, *vers.* I, *with music*; ViBoFo, *with music*
(Jam on Jerry's Rock, The, *vers.* II, *with music.* ShS
(Young Monroe at Gerry's Rock, *with music.*) AmSS
Jam-Pot, The. Kipling. HBV-1
Jam Trap, The. Charles Tomlinson. MoBrPo
Jamaica Market. Agnes Maxwell-Hall. TTY
Jamaican Bus Ride. A. S. J. Tessimond. OxBTC
James Alan Park/ Came naked stark. Thomas, Lord Erskine. FaBoEE
James Alley. *Unknown.* BluL
James Bird. *Unknown.* AmFP
James Fenimore Cooper. James Russell Lowell. *Fr.* A Fable for Critics. DBV
James Gerard. Paul D. Shiplett. LFAC
James Grant. *Unknown.* ESPB
James Harris. *Unknown. See* Demon Lover, The.
James Hatley. *Unknown.* BaBo; ESPB
James Honeyman. W. H. Auden. MoBS
James James. Disobedience. A. A. Milne. NTCP
James Lee's Wife, *sel.* Robert Browning.
In the Doorway. NCEP
James McCosh. Robert Bridges. AA
James Powell on Imagination. Larry Neal. BPo
James Rigg. James Hogg. BXAP; Par
James Watt. W. H. Auden. InPK
James Wetherell. E. A. Robinson. MoAmPo
James Whaland, *with music. Unknown.* AS
Jamestown. Randall Jarrell. GOA
Jamie Douglas. *Unknown. See* Waly, Waly.
Jamie Telfer in [*or* of] the Fair Dodhead. *Unknown.* BSV; ESPB; OxBB
Jamila. Nazik al-Mala'ika, *tr. fr. Arabic by* Kamal Boullata. WPOW
Jammy. Elizabeth Ripley. TDH
Jan., Jan., is a jeweler-man. January Snow. Aileen Fisher. YeAr
Jan van Hogspeuw staggers to the door. The Card-Players. Philip Larkin. OxBC
Jane and Eliza. Ann Taylor. HBV-1; HBVY
Jane, Jane. *Unknown.* FSW
Jane, Jane,/ Tall as a crane. Aubade. Edith Sitwell. CMoP; MoAB; MoBrPo; NoAM; PoRA
Jane looks down at her organdy skirt. In Bertram's Garden. Donald Justice. BoLoP; ErPo; InPK; NePoEA; VGW
Jane, she could not. Man's Way. L. A. G. Strong. HBMV
Jane Smith. Kipling. HBV-1; SpRo
Jane Williams had a lover true. Shocking Rape and Murder of Two Lovers. *Unknown.* CoMu
Jane won't touch a caterpillar. Why Run? Norah Smaridge. RHPC
Janet Waking. John Crowe Ransom. CABA; CMoP; InPK; MoAB; MoAmPo; NCSH; NoAM; NoP; TAP
Janette's Hair. Charles Graham Halpine. HBV-1
Jangle of the jeering crows, The. Black Humor. Archibald MacLeish. NCSH
Janie Swecker and Me and Gone with the Wind. David Huddle. GrPl
Janis Joplin and the Folding Company. Bayla Winters. AMV-80
Janitor, The; Kindergarten, Corinth. Charles Wright. *Fr.* Tattoos. GP
Janitor Working on Threshold. Margaret Avison. PeCV
Janitor's Boy, The. Nathalia Crane. PoLF
Jankin [the Clerical Seducer]. *Unknown. See* Jolly Jankin.
Janna. King D. Kuka. VoR
Jansenist Journey. Denis Devlin. IPY
Januar: by this fire I warme my handes. *See* January by This Fire.
Januaries, Nature greets our eyes. Brazil, January 1, 1502. Elizabeth Bishop. NoAM
January. Elizabeth J. Coatsworth. PoSC
January. Geoffrey Dutton. PoAu-2
January. Douglas Gibson. OBCP
January. Deborah Godin. AMV-80
January. Robert Hass. NPGG
January. Richard A. Hawley. AMV-80
January. H. R. Hays. EAS
January. John Heath-Stubbs. OBCP
January. Weldon Kees. CoAP
January. Sylvia S. Lambdin. YeAr
January. Daniel James O'Sullivan. NeIP
January. James Reaney. *Fr.* A Suit of Nettles. OBCV
January. Frank Dempster Sherman. YeAr
January. R. S. Thomas. ELU
January. John Updike. PDV; RHPC
January. Ellen Bryant Voigt. NoP
January. William Carlos Williams. MoAB; MoAmPo
January, bleak and drear. January. Frank Dempster Sherman. YeAr
January brings the snow. The Garden Year [*or* The Months]. Sara Coleridge. FaBoBe; HBV-1; HBVY; OxBChV; RHPC; TiPo; TreFT
January by This Fire. *Unknown.* NCEP
("Januar: by this fire I warme my handes.") EBEV
(Labours of the Months.) GBP; SaC
(Months, The.) ChTr; OxBM
January cold and desolate. The Months. Christina Rossetti. FaPON
January: Cover Shooting. Wilfrid Scawen Blunt. *Fr.* An Idler's Calender. VLP
January Eclogue. Spenser. *Fr.* The Shepheardes Calender. FiP
January 15 as a National Holiday. Carter Revard. VoR
January 1. Marnie Pomeroy. PoSC
January first isn't New Year's. Happy New Year, Anyway. Joanna Cole. NTCP
January ice drifts downriver. In the Hellgate Wind. Madeline DeFrees. NYP
January Is Here. Edgar Fawcett. YeAr
January Man. Dave Goulder. OBET
January Morning. William Carlos Williams. InPS; SOTW

January Morning, A. Archibald Lampman. OBCV
January night, A. Moonlight. Significant Fevers. Alison Fell. BrRo
January 1940. Roy Fuller. LiTM; SeCePo; WaP
(War Poet.) HoPM; PP
January 1939. Dylan Thomas. EAS
January sky is deep and calm, The. Reason for Not Writing Orthodox Nature Poetry. John Wain. MP; PP
January Snow. Aileen Fisher. YeAr
January sparkles. January. Sylvia S. Lambdin. YeAr
January 3, 1970. Mae Jackson. PoBA
January wraps up the wound of his arm. Charles Henri Ford. EAS
Janus. Madeline Mason. GoYe
Japan. Anthony Hecht. CrMA; InPK; LiTM
Japan That Sank under the Sea. Satoru Sato. PoPl
Japanese, The. Ogden Nash. DBV; InMe; WhC
Japanese Beetles. X. J. Kennedy. HoAn; OBAL
Japanese Birthday Wish, A. Thomas Burnett Swann. GoYe
Japanese Fan. James Kirkup. GrPl
Japanese Fan. Margaret Veley. NBM
Japanese Girl with Red Table. Stephen Dobyns. MAYP
Japanese Hokku. Lewis Alexander. CDC
Japanese Love-Song, A. Alfred Noyes. OBVV
Japanese Lovers, The. *Unknown.* BeLS; BLPA
Japanese next to me at the bar, The. In a Bar near Shibuya Station, Tokyo. Paul Engle. AmFN; CAD
Japanese Print. Austin Clarke. IPY
Japanesque. Oliver Herford. FiBHP
Jaquerie, The, *sels.* Sidney Lanier.
Betrayal. AA
Hound, The. AA; GDP
Jar, The. Richard Henry Stoddard. AA
(Day and Night My Thoughts Incline.) HBV-2
Jar of cider and my pipe, A. The Sluggard. W. H. Davies. OBMV
Jar of Nations, The. A. E. Housman. LiTB
Jarama Valley. *Unknown.* FSW
Jardin de la Chapelle Expiatoire. Robert Finch. PeCV
Jardin des Fleurs. Charles David Webb. NePoAm-2
Jardin du Palais Royal. David Gascoyne. MoPo
Jarring the air with rumour cool. Small Fountains. Lascelles Abercrombie. *Fr.* Emblems of Love, Epilogue. CH
Jars. Paul Raboff. VWA
Jason. Anthony Hecht. CoPo; DiL
Jason and Medea. John Gower. *Fr.* Confessio Amantis. ACP
Jaunty crop-haired graying, The. Poem about People. Robert Pinsky. NPGG
Javanese Dancers. Arthur Symons. VLP
Javier. José Y. Terán, Jr. LFAC
Jawbone is a platter for the face, The. Dog. D. C. Berry. BXAP
Jay Gould's Daughter. *Unknown.* AS, *with music*; FSW
Jazz. Frank London Brown. PoNe
Jazz. Carolyn M. Rodgers. JB
Jazz Band in a Parisian Cabaret. Langston Hughes. BANP; MoAmPo
Jazz band struck up Dixie, The. . .I could see. Victory in the Cabarets. Louis Untermeyer. HBMV
Jazz Fantasia. Carl Sandburg. MoAB; MoAmPo; PoNe; TwAmPo
Jazz of This Hotel, The. Vachel Lindsay. PoPl
Jazzonia. Langston Hughes. AmNP; BANP; NIP
Je caresserai la belle par amitié, *with music. Unknown, tr. fr. French.* OuSiCo
"Je Ne Sais [*or* Sçay] Quoi," The. William Whitehead. OBEC; SoSe
Je ne veux de personne aupres de ma tristesse. Henri de Regnier, *tr. fr. French by* "Seumas O'Sullivan." AWP
Je suis le frère. Triolets Ollendorfiens. James Kenneth Stephen. WhC
Je Suis une Table. Donald Hall. EAS; NePoEA
Je T'Adore. Thomas Kinsella. NoAM
Jealosie. John Donne. *See* Jealousy.
Jealous Adam. Itzig Manger, *tr. fr. Yiddish by* Jacob Sonntag. TrJP
Jealous Brothers, The. *Unknown.* AmFP
Jealous girls these sometimes were. How Marigolds Came Yellow. Robert Herrick. ChTr
Jealous, I own it, I was once. On Thomas Hood. Walter Savage Landor. PV
Jealous Lover, The. *Unknown. See* Florella; or, The Jealous Lover.
Jealous Lovers, The. Donald Hall. NYBP
Jealous Man, A. Robert Graves. CMoP
Jealous Man, A. *Unknown, tr. fr. Irish by* Frank O'Connor. KiLC
Jealous Wife, The. Vernon Scannell. ErPo
Jealousie Is the Rage of a Man. Countess of Winchilsea. FM
Jealousy. Mary Elizabeth Coleridge. EnLoPo; NBM; OBNC; WPE
Jealousy. Rachel de Vries. AMV-81
Jealousy. John Donne. Elegies, I. FF
(Jealosie.) AnAnS-1
Jealousy. Stephen Vincent. NeAC
Jealousy. *Malay Oral Tradition, tr. by* R. J. Wilkinson *and* R. O. Winstedt. WTO
Jealousy's an awful thing and foreign to my nature. I Can't Think What He Sees in Her. A. P. Herbert. FiBHP
Jealousy. *Unknown, tr. fr. Irish by* Frank O'Connor. KiLC
Jeames of Buckley Square. Thackeray. VLP
Jean. Burns. *See* Of A' the Airts.
Jean. Paul Potts. NeBP
Jean ax'd what ribbon she should wear. Jenny's Ribbons. William Barnes. VLP
Jean, death comes close to us all. The Child Bearers. Anne Sexton. BoWoP
Jean, Jean, Jean. Cat at the Cream. *Unknown.* GBP; POL
Jean Maillard lies buried here. Epitaph for Jean Maillard. *Unknown.* PeHV
Jean Richepin's Song. Herbert Trench. OBMV; OxBI
Jeane. William Barnes. LO
Jeane Dixon's America. Gerald Costanzo. MAYP
Jeanie Morrison. William Motherwell. HBV-1
Jeanie with the Light Brown Hair. Stephen Collins Foster. BLSo, *with music*; FaFP; FSW; TrAS, *with music*; TreF
Jeanne d'Arc. Louise Glück. GeTw
Jeannette. Otto Julius Bierbaum, *tr. fr. German by* Jethro Bithell. AWP
Jeannette and Jeannot. Charles Jeffries. BLPA
Jeannie Marsh. George Pope Morris. AA
Jeannot's Answer. Charles Jeffries. BLPA
Jeans. J. V. Brummels. GP
Jeat Ring Sent, A. John Donne. PoEL-2
Jeep. Charles Stetler. GP
Jeff Buckner. Frank Beddo. WTO
Jefferson and Liberty. *Unknown.* FSW; TrAS, *with music*
Jefferson D. H. S. Cornwell. PAH
Jefferson Davis. Walker Meriwether Bell. PAH
Jefferson, Texas. Naomi Shihab. TAT
Jefferson Valley. John Hollander. PPP
Jehovah. Israel Zangwill. WGRP
Jehovah Buried, Satan Dead. E. E. Cummings. NePA
Jehovah, God, Who Dwelt of Old, *with music.* Lewis R. Amis. AH
Jehovah, Lord and Majesty, *with music.* Conrad Weiser, *tr. fr. German by* Sheema Z. Buehne. AH
Jehovah Our Righteousness. William Cowper. NOCV
Jehovah's Immovable Throne. Bible, *O.T.* Psalms, XCII. WGRP
Jehu. Louis MacNeice. LiTM; MoAB; WaP
Jellicle Cats are black and white. The Song of the Jellicles T. S. Eliot. FaBoCh; FaBoNo; OxBChV; PCat; PoPle
Jellon Grame. *Unknown.* EBEV; ESPB (A *and* B *vers.*); OxBB
Jelly roll/ Jelly roll/ Jelly roll is so hard to find. Hambone Blues. *Unknown.* BluL
Jellyfish, A. Marianne Moore. PCP
Jellyfish, The. Ogden Nash. FaPON
Jellyfish, The. William Pitt Root. BoAnP
Jem writes his verses with more speed. A Rhymester. Samuel Taylor Coleridge. PV
Jemima. *Unknown. See* There Was a Little Girl.
Jemima is my name. Mima. Walter de la Mare. BrPo
Jennie Jenkins. *Unknown. See* Jenny Jenkins.
Jennifer Gentle and Rosemary. *Unknown. See* Riddles Wisely Expounded.
Jenny. Dante Gabriel Rossetti. PoEL-5
"Here nothing warns," *sel.* NBM
Jenny and Me were engaged, you see. Pink Dominoes. Kipling. CenHV
Jenny come tie my. Mother Goose. OxNR
Jenny Jenkins. *Unknown.* FSW
(Jennie Jenkins, *with music.*) OuSiCo
(Jinnie Jinkins.) AmFP
Jenny Kiss'd [*or* Kissed] Me. Leigh Hunt. BLPA; FaBoBe; FaFP; FPL; HBV-1; InMe; NTCP; OBEV; OBVV; PoPl; PoRA; SpRo; TreF
(Rondeau, A: "Jenny kissed me when we met.") BLPA; EnRP; FaBV; FF; HoPM; InPK; NOBE; TEP; ViBoPo
Jenny kiss'd me in a dream. "Such Stuff as Dreams." Franklin P. Adams. FiBHP; SpRo
Jenny kiss'd me when we met. Paul Dehn. *Fr.* A Leaden Treasury of English Verse. FiBHP; SpRo
Jenny White and Johnny Black. Eleanor Farjeon. FaPON
Jenny wi' the Airn Teeth. Alexander Anderson. HBV-1
Jenny Wren. W. H. Davies. MoBrPo
Jenny Wren fell sick. Mother Goose. EvOK; OxNR
Jenny, your mind commands. Reading the Brothers Grimm to Jenny. Lisel Mueller. NYBP
Jenny's Ribbons. William Barnes. VLP
Jephthah's Daughter, *sel.* Charles Heavysege.
"Oh! think how hard it is to die when young!" CaP
Jephthah's Daughter. "Yehoash," *tr. fr. Yiddish by* Alter Brody. TrJP

Jerboa, The. Marianne Moore. FYAP; MoPo
 "Roman had an, A/ artist, a freedman," *sel.* CMoP
Jeremiad. Oscar Williams. LiTA
Jeremiah, *sels.* Bible, *O.T.*
 As Fowlers Lie in Wait, V: 26-31. TrJP
 But Fear Thou Not, O Jacob, XLVI: 27-28. TrJP
 Cry of the Daughter of My People, The, VIII: 18-23. TrJP
 Cursed Be the Day, XX: 14-18. TrJP
 End of the World, The, IV: 19-26. PPON
 "For thus saith the Lord to the men of Judah and Jerusalem," IV: 3-31. OBVE
 O Lord, Thou Hast Enticed Me, XX: 7-10. TrJP
 Oh That I Were in the Wilderness, IX: 1-10. TrJP
Jeremiah. Witter Bynner. CrMA
Jeremiah, *sels.* Stefan Zweig, *tr. fr. German by* Eden *and* Cedar Paul.
 Chosen of God. TrJP
 Flowering without End. TrJP
Jeremiah, blow the fire. *Unknown.* OxNR
Jericho. Willard Wattles. HBMV
Jericho is on the inside. The Walls of Jericho. Blanche Taylor Dickinson. CDC
Jericho, Jericho/ Round and round the walls I go. Jericho. Willard Wattles. HBMV
Jericho's Blind Beggar. Longfellow. WBLP
Jerked Heartstrings in Town. Emily B. C. Jones. HBMV
Jerome. Randall Jarrell. PPP
Jerome was a dizzy giraffe. The Dizzy Giraffe. *Unknown.* TDH
Jeronimo's House. Elizabeth Bishop. MiAP; NoP
Jerry an' Me. Hiram Rich. HBV-1
Jerry, Go an' Ile That Car, *with music.* *Unknown.* AS
Jerry Hall,/ He is so small. Mother Goose. OxNR
Jerry Jones. *Unknown.* ShM
Jersey Bait Shack. Peter Balakian. MAYP
Jersey Belle Blues. *Unknown.* BluL
Jersey Cattle. R. N. Currey. OxBTC
Jersey Marsh, The. David Galler. NYBP
Jerusalem. Rose Ausländer, *tr. fr. German by* Ewald Osers. VWA
Jerusalem. Bernard of Cluny, *tr. fr. Latin by* John Mason Neale. *Fr.* De Contemptu Mundi. HBV-2; OBVV
 (Celestial Country, The, *longer sel.*) GoBC
 (Jerusalem the Golden.) VLP; WGRP, *shorter sel.*
Jerusalem, *sels.* Blake.
 "Ah! weak and wide astray! Ah! shut in narrow doleful form," *fr.* II. OBRV
 "But still the thunder of Los peals loud and thus the thunder's cry." OAEL-2
 "England! awake! awake! awake!" *fr.* IV, Prologue. EnRP; NoP; OBRV
 (Prelude: "England! awake! awake! awake!") OBNC
 "Fearing that Albion should turn his back against the Divine Vision." OAEL-2
 "Fields from Islington to Marybone, The," *fr.* II, Prologue. ChTr, 4 *sts.*; OBNV; OBRV
 (Prelude: "Fields from Islington to Marybone, The.") OBNC
 "I give you the end of a golden string," *fr.* IV, Prologue. OBRV
 (Epigraph: "I give you the end of a golden string.") OBNC
 (To the Christians.) EnRP
 "I saw a Monk of Charlemaine," *fr.* III, Prologue. EnRP; OBRV
 (Monk, The.) LoBV
 In Deadly Fear. SeCePo
 "It is easier to forgive an enemy than to forgive a friend." OAEL-2
 Male & Female Loves in Beulah, *fr. ch.* III. OBNC
 "Rhine was red with human blood, The," *fr.* II, Prologue. ViBoPo
 "Shuddring the Spectre howls. his howlings terrify the night." OAEL-2
 "What are those golden builders doing?" *fr.* I. OBRV
Jerusalem. Blake. *Fr.* Milton. *See* And Did Those Feet in Ancient Time.
Jerusalem, *sel.* Uri Zvi Greenberg, *tr. fr. Hebrew by* Charles A. Cowen.
 Jerusalem the Dismembered. TrJP
Jerusalem. Ruben Kanalenstein, *tr. fr. Spanish by* Yishai Tobin. VWA
Jerusalem. Kadia Molodovski, *tr. fr. Yiddish by* S. F. Chyet. AMV-81
Jerusalem. Jon Silkin. VWA
Jerusalem. Antoni Slonimski, *tr. fr. Polish by* Isaac Komem. VWA
Jerusalem. *Unknown.* *See* New Jerusalem, The.
Jerusalem. Shlomo Vinner, *tr. fr. Hebrew by* Laya Firestone *and* Howard Schwartz. VWA
Jerusalem Delivered. Tasso. *See* Godfrey of Bulloigne.
Jerusalem in the Snow. Anath Bental, *tr. fr. Hebrew by* Howard Schwartz. VWA
Jerusalem is a limestone cracked. Guide to Jerusalem. Dennis Silk. VWA
Jerusalem is Sodom's sister city. Sodom's Sister City. Yehuda Amichai, *tr. by* Shirley Kaufman. VWA
Jerusalem, My Happy Home. *Unknown.* *See* New Jerusalem, The.
Jerusalem Notebook, A. Harvey Shapiro. AMV-81
Jerusalem, Port City. Yehuda Amichai, *tr. fr. Hebrew by* Shirley Kaufman. VWA
Jerusalem Sonnets, *sels.* James K. Baxter.
 "Brother Ass, Brother Ass, you are full of fancies," 36. OCNZ
 "Colin, you can tell my words are crippled now," 37. OCNZ
 "Small grey cloudly louse that nests in my beard," 1. NoP; OCNZ
 "Trap I am setting to catch a tribe, The," 35. OCNZ
 "Yesterday I planted garlic," 18. OCNZ
Jerusalem Street and Paradise Square. Closing Time. James Michie. NePoEA-2
Jerusalem the Dismembered. Uri Zvi Greenberg, *tr. fr. Hebrew by* Charles A. Cowen. *Fr.* Jerusalem. TrJP
Jerusalem the Golden. Bernard of Cluny. *See* Jerusalem.
Jerusalem's autumn has prepared a text. Autumn Music. Gabriel Preil, *tr. by* Howard Schwartz. VWA
Jes' beyan a clump o' pines. The Corn Song. John Wesley Holloway. BANP
Jesous Ahatonhia. Jesse Edgar Middleton. CaP
 (Huron Carol, The.) OBCP
Jess, a wild cowboy, loves whiskey and beer. Jess's Dilemma. *Unknown.* CoSo
Jesse James. William Rose Benét. BPAW; FYAP; MoAmPo; TrGrPo
Jesse James (*diff. versions*). *Unknown.* AmFN; AmFP; BaBo (A, B, *and* C *vers.*); BeLS; CoSo (A *vers., with music*); FaBoBe; FSW; TrAS, *with music;* TreFS; UnPo; ViBoFo (A *and* B *vers.*); WiR; YaD
Jesse James was a boy that downed many a man. Jesse James (D *vers.*). *Unknown.* CoSo
Jesse James was a lad who [*or* that] killed many a man. Jesse James. *Unknown.* AmFP; BaBo (C *vers.*); CoSo (A *vers.*); TrAS; TreFS; ViBoFo
Jesse James was a man, and he had a robber band. Jesse James. *Unknown.* AmFN
Jesse James was a man who traveled through the land. Jesse James (B *vers.*). *Unknown.* CoSo
Jesse James was a two-gun man. Jesse James. William Rose Benét. BPAW; FYAP; MoAmPo; TrGrPo
Jesse James was one of his names, another it was Howard. Jesse James (B *vers.*). *Unknown.* BaBo; ViBoFo
Jessica Jane ("Jessica Jane is the kind of cook"). May Justus. RHPC
Jessie. Thomas Edward Brown. HBV-1
Jessie. Eugene Field. InMe
Jessie ("Jessie is both young and fair"). Bret Harte. GN
Jessie Mitchell's Mother. Gwendolyn Brooks. BoWoP; NAs; NMM
Jessie, my cousin, remembers there were gypsies. Gypsies. Alden Nowlan. NeAC
Jessie, the Flower o' Dunblane. Robert Tannahill. HBV-1
Jess's Dilemma. *Unknown.* CoSo
Jessy. Nora Dauenhauer. TWSS
Jest, The. Austin Clarke. BIrV
Jest a worthless blanket Injun. The Blanket Injun. Arthur Chapman. BPAW
Jest a-wearyin' fer you. Wearyin' fer You. Frank L. Stanton. HBV-1
Jest bronze—you wouldn't ever know. For Valour. May Herschel-Clarke. SUMH
Jest 'fore Christmas. Eugene Field. FaBV; FaFP; FaPON; FPL; HBV-1; HBVY; OHFP; PoLF; TreF
Jester in the Trench, The. Leon Gellert. PoAu-1
Jester shook his hood and bells, and leap'd upon a chair, The. The Jester's Sermon. George Walter Thornbury. BeLS; TreFS
Jester walked in the garden, The. The Cap and Bells. W. B. Yeats. BrPo; ChTr; NoAM; NoP; OBVV; OnMSP; WSC
Jester's Plea, The. Frederick Locker-Lampson. CenHV
Jester's Sermon, The. George Walter Thornbury. BeLS; TreFS
Jesu. George Herbert. EBCP; MeLP
 (Iesu.) OBS
Jesu,/ if Thou wilt make. A Page's Road Song. William Alexander Percy. TrPWD; YeAr
Jesu! by that shuddering dread which fell on Thee. Angel of the Agony. Cardinal Newman. *Fr.* The Dream of Gerontius. OxBoCh
Jesu Christ, My Leman Swete. *Unknown.* OxBM
 (Jesus, My Sweet Lover.) MeEL
Jesu, Come on Board, *with music.* Johann C. Pyrlaeus, *tr. fr. German by* Sheema Z. Buehne. AH
Jesu! for thy mercy endelesse [*or* for thy wondes fife]. Jesu! Send Us Peace. *Unknown.* MeEL
Jesu is in my heart, his sacred name. Jesu. George Herbert. EBCP; MeLP
Jesu, Joy of Man's Desiring. Robert Fitzgerald. NYBP
Jesu, Lord, welcom thou be. A Prayer to the Sacrament of the Altar. *Unknown.* MeEL
Jesu, Lorde, that madest me. A Hymn to Jesus. Richard of Caistre. MeEL
Jesu, Lover of My Soul. Charles Wesley. *See* Jesus, Lover of My Soul.

Jesu, Maria—I am near to death. Cardinal Newman. *Fr.* The Dream of Gerontius. ACP
Jesu, my sweet Son dear. Cradle Song of the Virgin. *Unknown.* ISi. *See also* Jesu, sweete sone dear.
Jesu, no more! it is full tide. On the Bleeding Wounds of Our Crucified Lord [*or* Upon the Bleeding Crucifix]. Richard Crashaw. SeCP; SeCV-1; TrGrPo
Jesu! Send Us Peace. *Unknown.* MeEL
Jesu [*or* Iesu], sweete [*or* swete] sone dear [*or* dere]. The Virgin's Song [*or* Our Lady's Song *or* Cradle Song of the Virgin]. *Unknown.* NOBE; OBEV;OxBM. *See also* Jesu, my sweet Son dear.
Jesu, that hast me dere iboght. A Devout Prayer of the Passion. *Unknown.* MeEL
Jesu, thie love within mee is soe maine. William Alabaster. AnAnS-1
Jesu, to Thee My Heart I Bow, *with music.* Nicolaus L. Zinzendorf, *tr. fr. German by* John Wesley. AH
Jesukin. *At. to* St. Ita, *tr. fr. Old Irish by* George Sigerson. OnYI
(Vision of Ita, The, *tr. by* Whitley Stokes.) AnIL
Jesus. Francis Lauderdale Adams. OxBS
Jesus. James McAuley. CBAP
Jesus. Theodore Parker. AA
Jesus a Child His Course Begun, *with music.* Margaret Fuller. AH
Jesus, almighty King of Blis. The Nativity. *Unknown.* MeEL
Jesus and His Mother. Thom Gunn. EaLo; OxBC
Jesus and I. Dan Crawford. BLRP; TRV
Jesus and the Children. Bible, *N.T.* St. Mark, X: 13-16. TreFT
Jesus and the Woman at the Well. Bible, *N.T.* St. John, IV: 5-26. TreFT
Jesus Answers the Pharisees. Bible, *N.T.* St. John, VIII: 12-32. TreFS
Jesus Bids Man Remember. *Unknown.* MeEL
Jesus Borned in Bethlea. *Unknown.* AmFP
Jesus Christ ("Jesus Christ was a man that travelled through the land"). Woody Guthrie. WTO
Jesus Comforts His Mother. *Unknown. See* Dear Son, Leave Thy Weeping.
Jesus Contrasts Man and Himself. *Unknown.* MeEL
Jesus Drum. Pearl Cleage Lomax. CNA
Jesus Eats with Sinners. Bible, *N.T.* St. Mark, II: 15-17. TreFT
Jesus, Enthroned and Glorified, *with music.* Zachary Eddy. AH
Jesús, Estrella, Esperanza, Mercy. Middle Passage. Robert Hayden. AmNP; BPo; IDB; NoAM; PoBA
Jesus, grant us all a blessing. Shouting Song. *Unknown.* AmFP
Jesus Himself. Henry Burton. BLRP
Jesus His Mother meets. Fourth Station. Padraic Colum. ISi
Jesus, I Come to Thee, *with music.* Nathan S. S. Beman. AH
Jesus, I Live to Thee, *with music.* Henry Harbaugh. AH
Jesus, in Sickness and in Pain, *with music.* Thomas H. Gallaudet. AH
Jesus is born. Peace, such high words forbear. Sonnet. William Alabaster. SBVL
Jesus Is Coming Soon. *Unknown.* BluL
Jesus, Keep Me Near the Cross, *with music.* Fanny J. Crosby. AH
Jesus Lives! C. F. Gellert. PGD
Jesus [*or* Jesu], Lover of My Soul. Charles Wesley. HBV-2; OxBoCh; TreF; WGRP
(Christ, the Refuge of the Soul.) ILwL
(Divine Lover, The, *sl. abr.*) BLRP
(In Temptation.) NOEC; PoEL-3
Jesus Loves Me, This I Know, *with music.* Anna B. Warner. AH
Jesus Make Up My Dying Bed. *Unknown.* BluL
Jesus, Master, O Discover, *with music. Unknown.* AH
Jesus, Merciful and Mild! *with music.* Thomas Hastings. AH
Jesus' mother never had no man. Conception. Waring Cuney. BANP
Jesus, my Lord, when I look upon Thee. Thy Nail-pierced Hands. Kathryn Bowsher. STF
Jesus! my Shepherd, Husband, Friend. John Newton. *Fr.* The Name of Jesus. TrPWD
Jesus, My Sweet Lover. *Unknown. See* Jesu Christ, My Leman Swete.
Jesus Never Fails. Walter E. Isenhour. STF
Jesus never turned on me. The Boys Brushed By. Catherine Gonick. AMV-80
Jesus never will forget me. He Never Will Forget. "M. G. H." STF
Jesus, our brother, kind [*or* strong] and good. The Friendly Beasts. *Unknown.* FaPON; OnMSP; PChr; PoSC; SiSoSe; SoPo
Jesus' Parable of the Sower. Bible, *N.T.* St. Luke, VIII: 5-15. TreFT
Jesus Reassures His Mother. *Unknown. See* As I Lay upon a Night.
Jesus Reproaches His People. *Unknown.* MeEL
Jesus Return. Henry van Dyke. TRV
Jesus Saviour, Pilot Me. Edward Hopper. AH; BLRP
Jesus Shall Reign Where'er the Sun. Isaac Watts. WGRP
(King Triumphant.) BLRP
Jesus, Shepherd of Thy Sheep, *with music.* George Washington Bethune. AH
Jesus Spreads His Banner o'er Us, *with music.* Roswell Park. AH
Jesus, teach me how to be. The Housewife. Catherine Cate Coblentz. BLRP; TrPWD; TRV
Jesus Tender Shepherd. Mary L. Duncan. BLRP
Jesus the Carpenter. Catharine C. Liddell. HBV-2
Jesus, the friend of lonely, beaten folk. Mary's Son. Lucia Trent. PGD
Jesus, there is no dearer name than thine. Jesus. Theodore Parker. AA
Jesus, These Eyes Have Never Seen, *with music.* Ray Palmer. AH
Jesus, thou art the sinner's friend. 'Tis Sweet to Rest in Lively Hope. *Unknown.* AmFP
Jesus, Thou Divine Companion. Henry van Dyke. *See* Hymn of Labor.
Jesus, Thou Joy of Loving Hearts. St. Bernard of Clairvaux, *tr. fr. Latin.* WGRP
Jesus! thy Crucifix. Emily Dickinson. MoVE
Jesus, Thy life is mine! A Prayer. *Unknown.* STF
Jesus to Those Who Pass By. *Unknown.* MeEL
Jesus Understands. *Unknown.* BLRP
Jesus Was Crucified or: It Must Be Deep. Carolyn M. Rodgers. BlSi; PoBA
Jesus was sitting in Moses' chair. Blake. *Fr.* The Everlasting Gospel. OxBoCh
Jesus, Won't You Come B'm-By, *with music. Unknown.* AS
Jesus woundes so wide. The Wells of Jesus Wounds. *Unknown.* MeEL
Jew. Pierre Morhange, *tr. fr. French by* Edouard Roditi. VWA
Jew. James A. Randall, Jr. BPo
Jew, The. Isaac Rosenberg. MoBrPo; VWA
Jew. Karl Shapiro. VWA
Jew at Christmas Eve, The. Karl Shapiro. VGW
Jew, in the painting by Chagall, The. Painting. A. C. Jacobs. VWA
Jew of Malta, The, *sels.* Christopher Marlowe.
Mine Argosy from Alexandria, *fr.* I, i. ChTr
Song of Ithamore, The, *fr.* IV, iv. WHA
Jew to Jesus, The. Florence Kiper Frank. HBMV; TRV; WGRP
Jew Walks in Westminster Abbey, A. Aubrey Hodes. TrJP
Jew was always treated, The. Dubrovnik Poem (Emilio Tolentino). Anthony Rudolf. VWA
Jew Wrecked in the German Cell, The. W. H. Auden. WaP
(Diaspora, The.) LiTA
Jewboy. Julian Tuwim, *tr. fr. Polish by* Isaac Komem. VWA
Jewel, The. James Wright. CAPP; CoAP
Jewel of the secret treasury, The. Hafiz, *tr. by* Gertrude Lowthian Bell. Odes, VI. AWP
Jewel Stairs' Grievance, The ("The jewelled steps are already quite white with dew"). Li Po, *tr. fr. Chinese by* Ezra Pound. InPK; NOBA; OBVE
Jewelled mine of the pomegranate, whose hexagons of honey, The. The Pomegranate. Louis Dudek. OBCV; PeCV
Jewels, The. Baudelaire, *tr. fr. French.* BoLoP, *tr. by* Roy Campbell; ErPo, *tr. by* Paul Blackburn; NAWM-2, *tr. by* David Paul
Jewels, The. Austin Clarke. MoAB
Jewish Arabic Liturgies. *Unknown, tr. fr. Arabic by* Hartwig Hirschfeld. TrJP
Jewish Cemetery, The. Cesar Tiempo, *tr. fr. Spanish by* Angela McEvan-Alvarado. VWA
Jewish Cemetery at Newport, The. Longfellow. AmPP; AP; HAP; HeIP; HoPM; NOBA; NoP; OxBA; PPON; TAP
Jewish Cemetery near Leningrad, A. Joseph Brodsky, *tr. fr. Russian by* Dimitry Pospielovsky *and* Keith Bosley. VWA
Jewish Child Prays to Jesus, A. Ilse Blumenthal-Weiss, *tr. fr. German by* Erna Baber Rosenfeld. VWA
Jewish Conscript, The. Florence Kiper Frank. TrJP
Jewish extremities—cold. In Bed. Myra Sklarew. AMV-81
Jewish king now walks at large and sound, The. Zaph Describes the Haunts of Malzah. Charles Heavysege. *Fr.* Saul. OBCV
Jewish Main Street. Irving Layton. CaP; VWA
Jewish May, The. Morris Rosenfeld, *tr. fr. Yiddish by* Rose Pastor Stokes *and* Helena Frank. TrJP
Jewish Poet Counsels a King, A. Santob de Carrion, *tr. fr. Spanish. Fr.* Consejos y Documentos al Rey Dom Pedro. TrJP
Jewish Woman, The. Gertrud Kolmar, *tr. fr. German by* Henry A. Smith. VWA
Jews, The. George Herbert. JCP
Jews, The. Mieczyslaw Jastrun, *tr. fr. Polish by* Isaac Komem. VWA
Jews, The. Henry Vaughan. OBS
Jews at Haifa. Randall Jarrell. MoAmPo
Jew's Home, The. Robert Eyres Landor. *Fr.* The Impious Feast. OBRV
Jews in Hell, The. Isaac Goldemberg, *tr. fr. Spanish by* David Unger. VWA
Jezebel. Scudder Middleton. HBMV
Jezebel: Her Progress, *sel.* Gillian E. Hanscombe.
"Mrs. Snatcher Thatcher." BrRo
Jezreel. Thomas Hardy. NoP
Jig. C. Day Lewis. OxBI
Jig, A. Robert Greene. *See* Doron's Jigge.
Jig for Sackbuts. D. B. Wyndham Lewis. ErPo

Jig Tune: Not for Love. Thomas McGrath. VGW
Jigsaw Puzzle. Russell Hoban. NTCP
Jill. R. D. Laing. WeW
Jill Came from the Fair. Eleanor Farjeon. TiPo
Jillian of Berry. Beaumont *and* Fletcher. *See* Another Song ("For Jillian of Berry, she dwells on a hill").
Jilted Funeral, The. Gelett Burgess. ShM
Jilted Nymph, The. Thomas Campbell. EnLoPo
Jim. Hilaire Belloc. *See* Jim, Who Ran Away from His Nurse, and Was Eaten by a Lion.
Jim. Bret Harte. AA; WhC
Jim. Barbara Howes. GP
Jim and I as children played together. Oh Lucky Jim! *Unknown.* ChTr; GBP
Jim at the Corner. Eleanor Farjeon. SoPo; SUS
Jim Bludso [of the Prairie Belle]. John Hay. AA; BeLS; FaBoBe; FaFP; HBV-2; PaPo; TreFS; YaD
Jim Bowker, he said, ef he'd had a fair show. Then Ag'in. Sam Walter Foss. HBV-1
Jim Crack Corn. *Unknown. See* Blue-Tail Fly, The.
Jim Crow. Thomas D. Rice. VLP
Jim Desterland. Hyam Plutzik. VGW
Jim Dumps was a most unfriendly man. Force. *Unknown.* FaBoUs
Jim Farrow. *Unknown.* CoSo
Jim Fisk. *Unknown.* AS, *with music;* ViBoFo
Jim Jay. Walter de la Mare. BrPo; CenHV; HBMV; SiSoSe; SO
Jim Jones. *Unknown.* CBAP; PoAu-1
(Jim Jones at Botany Bay.) GBP
Jim the Splitter. Henry Kendall. PoAu-1
Jim was a sailor. Jim at the Corner. Eleanor Farjeon. SoPo; SUS
Jim, Who Ran Away from His Nurse, and Was Eaten by a Lion. Hilaire Belloc. EvOK; OxBChV; ShM
(Jim.) CenHV; ChTr; HBMV
Jiminy Whillikers/ Admiral Samuel. Monarch of the Sea. George Starbuck. OBAL; PV
Jimmie Randall was a-hunting, a-hunting in the dark. Molly Bawn. *Unknown.* ViBoFo
Jimmy Bruder on Quincey Street. Carol Artman Montgomery. AMV-81
Jimmy Jet and His TV Set. Shel Silverstein. CTBA; OBCA; RHPC
Jimmy Judge. *Unknown.* AmFP
Jimmy the Mowdy. *Unknown.* OxNR
Jimmy's Enlisted; or, The Recruited Collier. *Unknown.* CoMu; EBEV
(Recruited Collier, The.) OBET
Jimson lives in a new. A Call to the Wild. Lord Dunsany. OnYI
Jimson weed. Magnetized. Arthur Sze. BrSi
Jingle Bells. James S. Pierpont. BLSo, *with music;* FaFP; FSW; TreF; YaD
(One Horse Open Sleigh, The, *with music.*) PSoN
Jingle bells! jingle, bells! *Unknown.* OxNR
Jingo-Woman, The. Helen Hamilton. SUMH
Jinnie Jinkins. *Unknown. See* Jenny Jenkins.
Jinny Git Around, *with music. Unknown.* OuSiCo
Jinny the Just. Matthew Prior. NOBE; NOEC; OBEC; OBEV; PoEL-3
Jinx Blues, The. *Unknown.* BluL
Jippy and Jimmy. Laura E. Richards. SoPo; TiPo
Jis' Knowin'. Thomas G. Nickens. LFAC
Jitterbug/ is out. Bring the Soul Blocks. Victor Hernandez Cruz. CAD
Jitterbugging in the Streets. Calvin C. Hernton. PoBA
Jittery Jim. William Jay Smith. RHPC
Jo Jo, My Child. *Unknown, tr. fr. Hebrew by* Immanuel Olsvanger. TrJP
Joan/ did you never hear. To Joan. Lucille Clifton. GeTw
Joan Brown, about Her Painting. Kathleen Fraser. NPGG
Joan Miró ("After that war, when death had gone away"). Ruthven Todd. EAS
Joan Miró ("Once there were peasant pots and a dry brown hare"). Ruthven Todd. EAS
Joan of Arc. Hugh McCrae. PoAu-1
Joan of Arc to the Tribunal. Anthony Frisch. CaP
Joan to Her Lady. *Unknown.* UnTE
Job, *abr.* Bible, *O.T.* NAWM-1
Sels.
"Behold, God is great, and we know him not," XXXVI: 26-30, 32. ImOP
"Canst thou draw out Leviathan with an hook[e]?" MOS (XLI: 1-10); OBVE (XLI)
(Leviathan, XLI: 1-21.) TrGrPo
Job's Comforters, XI: 7-8, *Moulton, Modern Reader's Bible.* WGRP
Let the Day Perish [Wherein I Was Born]. NAs (III); OBVE (III: 3-26); TrJP (III)
(Job Complains, III: 3-26.) TrGrPo
(Job's Curse, III: 3-26.) AWP
Lord Gave, The, I: 20-21. TreF
"Man, that is borne of a woman is of a few dayes, and full of trouble," XIV. OBVE
(Job Cries Out.) TrGrPo
(Job's Entreaty.) AWP
"For there is hope for a tree," XIV: 7-17. DL
Immortality, XIV: 1-12, *Moulton, Modern Reader's Bible.* WGRP
Man That Is Born of a Woman, XIV: 1-2. ChTr
Out of the Whirlwind, XL: 7-XLI. AWP
"Moreover the Lord answered Job, and said," XL. OBVE
My Soul Is Weary of My Life, X: 1-22. EaLo
Not Flesh of Brass, VI: 1-13. TrJP
Price of Wisdom, The, XXVIII. TrGrPo
" 'Surely there is a mine for silver,' " XXVIII: 1-11. SaC
Where Shall Wisdom Be Found? XXVIII: 12-20, 28. TreFT
Then the Lord Answered, XXXVIII: 2-XXXIX. AWP
God Replies, XXXVIII: 2-41. TrGrPo
Hast Thou Given the Horse Strength, XXXIX: 19-25. ChTr
(Horse, The.) FaPON, *abr.*; TrGrPo
(War Horse, The.) PH
"Knowest thou the time when the wild goates of the rocke bring forth?" XXXIX. OBVE
"Then the Lord answered Job out of the whirlewind, and sayd," XXXVIII. OBVE
"Where wast thou when I laid the foundations of the earth?" XXXVIII: 4-38. ImOP, *abr.*
"Wilt thou hunt the prey for the lion?" XXXVIII: 38-XXXIX. FM
"Therefore I will not refrain my mouth," VII: 11-21. PAI
(Let Me Alone.) PPON
Job. Eli Mandel. PeCV
Job. Elizabeth Sewell. EaLo
Job, *with music. Unknown.* OuSiCo
Job Complains. Bible, *O.T.* Job, III: 3-26. TrGrPo
Job Cries Out. Bible, *O.T.* Job, XIV. TrGrPo
Job Davies, eighty-five. Lore. R. S. Thomas. OxBC
Job Hunting. Tom Hennen. GP
Job That's Crying to Be Done, The. Kipling. TRV
Job's Ancient Lament. Owen Dodson. FB
Job's Comforters. Bible, *O.T.* (*Moulton, Modern Readers' Bible*). Job, XI: 7-8. WGRP
Job's Curse. Bible, *O.T.* Job, III: 3-26. AWP
Job's Entreaty. Bible, *O.T.* Job, XIV. AWP
Jock o' Hazeldean. Sir Walter Scott. *See* Jock of Hazeldean.
Jock o' the Side ("Now Liddesdale has ridden a raid"). *Unknown.* ESPB; OxBB, *with music*
Jock o' the Side ("Peeter a Whi[t]field he hath slaine"). *Unknown.* ESPB; ViBoFo
Jock of Hazeldean. Sir Walter Scott. BeLS; EnRP; GN; HBV-1; OAEP; OBRV; OxBS; TEP
(Jock o' Hazeldean.) GTBS; GTBS-P
Jock the Leg and the Merry Merchant. *Unknown.* ESPB
Jockie, Thine Hornpipe's Dull. *Unknown.* NCEP
Jocky said to Jeany, Jeany [*or* Jenny, Jenny] wilt thou do't. A Dainty Sang. Allan Ramsay. *Fr.* The Gentle Shepherd. BSV; OBEC
Joculator Domini. Sister Mary John Frederick. GoBC
Jodrell Bank. Patric Dickinson. SUW
Joe. David McCord. TiPo
Joe Beauchamp ees conceited man. De Baby Show. Wilson MacDonald. WhC
Joe Bowers. *Unknown.* AmFP; BaBo; CoSo, *with music;* FSW; TrAS, *with music;* TreFS; ViBoFo
Joe Green Joe Green O how are you doing today? An Old Inmate. Kenneth MacKenzie. PoAu-2
Joe Hill. Alfred Hayes. UnPo
Joe Tinker. Amanda Benjamin Hall. HBMV
Joe Turner, *with music. Unknown.* AS
(Joe Turner Blues, *with music.*) TrAS
Joe, you prefatory mortal. Apostrophe to a Pram Rider. E. B. White. InMe
Jog On, Jog On [the Foot-Path Way]. Shakespeare. *Fr.* The Winter's Tale, IV, ii. FaBoCh; GN; HBV-2; HBVY; ViBoPo
(Autolycus's Song.) OBSC; SpRo; WhC
(Merry Heart, A.) EIL; TrGrPo
Jog On, Jog On, *longer version. Unknown.* ChTr; GBP
Jog-Trot Pair, A, *sel.* Thomas Hardy. "Trite usages in tamest style." PeD
Jogger, The: Denver to Kansas City. David Ray. FAZ
Jogging. Gary Stein. AMV-81
Jogging at Dusk. Andrew Grossbardt. AMV-80
Johann Gaertner (1793-1887). Gary Gildner. FAZ
Johann Joachim Quantz's Five Lessons. W. S. Graham. FaBoMo
Johannes Agricola in Meditation. Robert Browning. OAEL-2; OBVV
Johannes Kepler (1571-1630). Siv Cedering. *Fr.* Letters from the Astronomers. SUW
Johannes Milton, Senex. Robert Bridges. CMoP; LiTB; PoEL-5; PoPl
John. Bible, *N.T. See* St. John.

John. N. M. Bodecker. RHPC
John Adams. Rosemary *and* Stephen Vincent Benét. PAL
John Adams lies here, of the parish of Southwell. On John Adams, of Southwell. Byron. PV
John Adkins' Farewell. *Unknown.* AmFP
John and Karl. *Unknown. Fr.* On Visiting the Graves of Keats and Marx in Hampstead Churchyard. PeD
John and Peter and Robert and Paul. The Chemistry of Character. Elizabeth Dorney. BLPA
"John Anderson, My Jo." Charles G. Blanden. HBV-2
John Anderson My Jo ("John Anderson my jo, John,/ I wonder what you mean"). *At. to* Burns. CoMu; ErPo; FSW; LAuP; OxBS; UnTE
John Anderson, My Jo ("John Anderson, my Jo, John,/ When Nature first began"). *After* Burns. FSW
John Anderson, My Jo ("John Anderson my jo, John,/ When we were first acquent"). Burns. AWP; BoLoP; CABA; EnRP; FaBV; FF; HBV-1; HeIP; InPK; LAUP; NOBE; NOEC; NoP; OAEP; OBEC; OBEV; PAI; PrIm; TreFT; TrGrPo; ViBoPo; WHA
(John Anderson.) GTBS; GTBS-P; HBV-1, LiTB; WBLP
John B. Sails, The. *Unknown.* AS, *with music*; FSW
John Barleycorn. Burns. FaBoCh; HBV-2; SeCeV
John Barleycorn. *Unknown.* OBET
John Barley-Corn, My Foe. Charles Follen Adams. OBAL
John Baynham's Epitaph. Thomas Dermody. OnYI
John Betjeman's Brighton. Gavin Ewart. FaBoPa
John Bird, a laborer, lies here. Epitaph. Sylvia Townsend Warner. MoBrPo
John Bright. Francis Barton Gummere. AA
John Brown. Harry Lyman Koopman. AA
John Brown. Vachel Lindsay. *Fr.* Booker Washington Trilogy. MoAmPo
John Brown. Edna Dean Proctor. PAH
John Brown; a Paradox. Louise Imogen Guiney. PAH
John Brown and Jeanne at Fontainebleau. Students. Florence Wilkinson Evans. HBV-1
John Brown died on the scaffold for the slave. John Brown. Edna Dean Proctor. PAH
John Brown in Kansas settled, like a steadfast Yankee farmer. How Old Brown Took Harper's Ferry. Edmund Clarence Stedman. HBV-2; OnMSP; PAH; PoNe
John Brown of Ossawatomie spake on his dying day. Brown of Ossawatomie. Whittier. HBV-2; PAH
John Brown's Body, *sels.* Stephen Vincent Benét.
  Battle of Gettysburg. BeLS
  Invocation: "American muse, whose strong and diverse heart." AmFN; CrMA
  (American Muse.) PAL
  Jack Ellyat Heard the Guns. PoLF
  John Brown's Prayer. PoNe
  Love Came By from the Riversmoke. MoAmPo
  Out of John Brown's Strong Sinews. WHA
  Robert E. Lee. AmFN
  Song of the Riders. MoAmPo
  Thirteen Sisters, The. TreF
  "This is the hidden place that hiders know." ViBoPo
  Three Elements. EaLo
John Brown's Prayer (*diff. versions*). *Unknown, at. to* Charles Sprague Hall *and to* Thomas Brigham Bishop. BLSo, *with music;* FaFP; ShS; TrAS
(Glory Hallelujah! or, John Brown's Body.) PAH
John Bull, Esquire, my jo John. A New Song to an Old Tune. *Unknown.* PAH
John Bull for pastime took a prance. Nongtongpaw. Charles Dibdin. HBV-1
John Bun. *Unknown.* FaBoCo; PoPle; ShM; WhC
John Burns of Gettysburg. Bret Harte. HBV-2; OHIP; PAH; PAL
John Butler Yeats. Jeanne Robert Foster. GoYe
John Button Birthday. Frank O'Hara. NAs
John Cabot, out of Wilma, once a Wycliffe. Riot. Gwendolyn Brooks. BPo; CAPP; PoBA; TAP
John Calvin whose peculiar fad. Ballade of the Heresiarchs. Hilaire Belloc. MoVE
John Carey's Second Song. Thomas McGrath. FAZ
John Chapman. Richard Wilbur. OxBC
John Charles Frémont. Charles F. Lummis. PAH
John Cherokee. *Unknown.* GBP
John Clare. Jon Anderson. AmPA
John Clare. John Clare. *See* I Feel I Am.
John Coil. *Unknown.* ShM
John Coltrane—an Impartial Review. Alfred B. Spellman. CNA; NNP; PoBA
John Cook had a little grey mare. Mother Goose. OxNR
John could take his clothes off. John. N. M. Bodecker. RHPC
John courts Perrette, but all in vain. To Promise Is One Thing, to Perform Is Another. La Fontaine. UnTE
John Damerlay, *with music. Unknown.* ShS
John Darrow. Donald Davidson. HBMV
John Deere, Allis Chalmers, Farm-All, Oliver. On the Land. Ray Lindquist. TAT
John Delaney of the Rifles has been shot. Casualty. Winifred M. Letts. SUMH
John Done Saw That Number, *with music. Unknown.* OuSiCo
John Donne. James Simmons. CIP
John Donne's Statue. John Peale Bishop. EyDe
John Dory. *Unknown.* ESPB
John Elmer Pettibone Cajee. Sheriff. Ambrose Bierce. DBV
John Endicott, *sels.* Longfellow. PAH
  Proclamation, The.
  Prologue, The: "Tonight we strive to read."
John Evereldown. E. A. Robinson. CMoP; NePA; OxBA
John Fane Dingle. Glaucopis. Richard Hughes. OBMV
John Filson. William Henry Venable. PAH
John Fitzgerald Kennedy. John Masefield. PAL
John Garfield. Nicholas Christopher. MAYP; NYP
John Garner's Trail Herd. *Unknown.* CoSo
John Gilpin. William Cowper. *See* Diverting History of John Gilpin, The.
John Gorham. E. A. Robinson. MoAB; MoAmPo; NoAM
John Graydon. Wilson MacDonald. CaP
John Grumlie. Allan Cunningham. GBP; HBV-2; PoLF; SaC
John had. Happiness. A. A. Milne. TiPo
John Hardy. *Unknown.* AmFP; BaBo (A *and* B *vers.*); FaBoBa; FSW; TrAS, *with music*; ViBoFo (A *and* B *vers.*)
John Harralson, John Harralson, you are a wretched creature. Two Appeals to John Harralson, Agent. *Unknown.* OBAL
John Henry. *Unknown, ad. by* John Jacob Niles. AmFN
John Henry (*diff. versions*). *Unknown.* AmFP; AS, *with music*; BaBo (A *and* B *vers.*); BeLS; BPo; FaBoBa; FaBoBe; FaFP; FSW; NOBA; OuSiCo, *with music*; OxBoLi; TiPo; TrAS, *with music*; TreFT; TrGrPo; ViBoFo (A, B, C, D, E, *and* F *vers.*)
John Henry said to his captain. John Henry. *Unknown.* TreFT
John Henry tol' his cap'n. John Henry. *Unknown.* AS; BeLS
John Henry was a lil [*or* little] baby. John Henry. *Unknown.* FaFP; OxBoLi; TrGrPo
John Henry was a railroad man. John Henry (B *vers.*). *Unknown.* BaBo
John Henry was a very small boy. John Henry (A *vers.*). *Unknown.* ViBoFo
John Henry, who was a baby. John Henry (C *vers.*). *Unknown.* ViBoFo
John Henry's mother had a little baby. John Henry. *Unknown.* OuSiCo
John Hielandman. *Unknown.* GBP
John Horace Burleson. Edgar Lee Masters. *Fr.* Spoon River Anthology. CrMA
John J. Curtis. Joseph Gallagher. AmFP
John Jacob Jingleheimer Schmidt. *Unknown.* FSW
John-John. Thomas MacDonagh. AnIV; AWP; HBMV; OnYI; OxBI
John Jones. Swinburne. *Fr.* The Heptalogia. NA; OAEP
(At the Piano.) FaBoNo
John Keats. Byron. *See* Who Kill'd John Keats?
John Kinsella's Lament for Mrs. Mary Moore. W. B. Yeats. CMoP; DTC; LiTM; MoAB; NoP; OAEL-2; OAEP
John Knox. Iain Crichton Smith. OxBS
John L. Sullivan Enters Heaven. Robert Frost. BXAP
John Landless Leads the Caravan. Iwan Goll, *tr. fr. French by* William Carlos Williams. TrJP
John Marr, *sel.* Herman Melville.
  "Since as in night's deck-watch ye show." ViBoPo
John Masefield Relates the Story of Tom, Tom, the Piper's Son. Louis Untermeyer. *Fr.* Mother Goose Up-to-Date. MoAmPo
John Maynard. Horatio Alger, Jr. BeLS; BLPA; FaBoBe
John McCormack, you are riding again the air. Upon Hearing His High Sweet Tenor Again. Joseph Langland. AMV-81
John Milton said the world in a starry rain. A Willing Suspension. John Holmes. PoCh
John Mouldy. Walter de la Mare. NCSH; OxBChV; PoPle
John Muir on Mt. Ritter. Gary Snyder. Myths and Texts: Burning, VIII. NOBA
John Nobody. Dom Moraes. NoAM
John o' Dreams. Theodosia Garrison. HBMV
John O'Dwyer of the Glen. *Unknown, tr. fr. Irish by* Thomas Furlong. AnIV
John of Gaunt's [Dying] Speech [*or* John of Gaunt Speaks]. Shakespeare. *See* This England.
John of Hazelgreen [*or* Haselgreen]. *Unknown.* BaBo (A, B, *and* C *vers.*); ESPB (A *and* E *vers.*); ViBoFo
John of Tours. *Unknown, tr. fr. French by* Dante Gabriel Rossetti. AWP
John Otto. W. S. Merwin. AP

John Paul Jones. Walt Whitman. *See* Battle of the *Bonhomme Richard* and the *Serapis.*
John Peel. John Woodcock Graves. CH; FSW; OxBoLi
John Pelham. James Ryder Randall. AA; PAH
John Quincy Adams. Stephen Vincent Benét. OBCA; PoPl
John Rabbit, by Dame Eagle chased. The Eagle and the Beetle. La Fontaine, *tr. by* Elizur Wright. OBVE
John Richard William Alexander Dwyer. Horace Smith *and* James Smith. OBRV
John Riley. *Unknown.* FSW; OuSiCo, *with music*
John Rogers' Exhortation to His Children. *Unknown. Fr.* The New England Primer. OBCA
John Saw the Holy Number, *with music. Unknown.* BoAN-1
John Skelton. Robert Graves. BrPo
John Smith, fellow fine. *Unknown.* OxNR
John Smith is my name. *Unknown.* FaBoUs
John Smith of His Friend Master John Taylor. John Smith. SCAP
John Smith's Approach to Jamestown. James Barron Hope. PAH
John Stuart Mill. E. C. Bentley. *Fr.* Clerihews. FaBoCo; FiBHP
(J. S. Mill.) OxBoLi; WhC
John Sutter. Yvor Winters. MoAmPo; MoVE; NoAM; NOBA; PoPl; QFR
John the Baptist. Louis Simpson. NePoEA
John Thomson and the Turk. *Unknown.* ESPB (A *and* B *vers.*)
John, Tom, and James. Charles Henry Ross. OxBChV; RHPC
John Underhill. Whittier. PAH
John warns me of nostalgia. Not Wholly Lost. Raymond Souster. OBCV
John was a bad boy, and beat a poor cat. John, Tom, and James. Charles Henry Ross. OxBChV; RHPC
John Was a-Writin', *with music. Unknown.* OuSiCo
John Webster. Swinburne. InvP
John Wesley Gaines. *Unknown.* ELU; FiBHP
John Wesley's Grace before Meals. John Wesley. *See* Be Present at Our Table, Lord.
John Wesley's Rule. John Wesley. HBVY; TreFT
(Rule, A.) FaFP
John Winter. Laurence Binyon. MOS
John without Heaven. John Malcolm Brinnin. NoAM
John-a-dreams and Harum-Scarum. Ballad of Low-lie-down. Madison Cawein. HBV-1
Johnie Armstrong. *Unknown.* BiP; ESPB (A, B, *and* C *vers.*); FaBoBa; HoPM, *cond.;* NoP (A *vers.*); OxBB, *with music*; TrGrPo; ViBoFo (A *and* B *vers.*)
Johnie Blunt, *with music. Unknown.* OxBB
Johnie Cam to Our Toun. *Unknown.* GBP
Johnie Cock. *Unknown.* ESPB (A, B, C, D, *and* K *vers.*); FaBoBa; ViBoFo (A *and* B *vers.*)
(Johnie o' Cocklesmuir, *with music.*) OxBB
Johnie Scot. *Unknown.* ESPB
Johnnie Bought a Ham, *with music. Unknown.* OuSiCo
Johnnie Cope. Adam Skirving. OxBS
Johnnie Courteau. William Henry Drummond. CaP
Johnnie Crack and Flossie Snail. Dylan Thomas. *Fr.* Under Milk Wood. FaPON; FiBHP; GoJo; PDV; RHPC
Johnnie Norrie. *Unknown.* OxNR
Johnny. Emma Rounds. ShM
Johnny Appleseed, *with music.* Rosemary Benét. TrAS
Johnny Appleseed. Arthur S. Bourinot. CaP
Johnny Appleseed. Vachel Lindsay. FaPON
Johnny Appleseed. William Henry Venable. PAH
Johnny Armstrong killed a calf. *Unknown.* OxNR
Johnny Boker. *Unknown.* AmSS, *with music*; FSW; ShS, *with music*
Johnny Bull, My Jo, John. *Unknown.* FSW
Johnny Carroll's Camp. *Unknown.* AmFP
Johnny Cock, in a May morning. Johnie Cock. *Unknown.* BaBo (B *vers.*); ESPB (C *vers.*)
Johnny Dow. *Unknown.* FaBoCo; WhC
(Johnny Doo.) FaBoEE
("Wha lies here?") FiBHP; PV
Johnny Dyers. *Unknown.* AmFP
Johnny Faa, the Lord of Little Egypt. *Unknown.* EnSB
Johnny Fife and Johnny's Wife. Mildred Plew Meigs. SoPo; TiPo
Johnny Gallagher. *Unknown.* AmFP
Johnny Germany. *Unknown.* AmFP
Johnny Get Your Gun, *with music.* Monroe H. Rosenfeld. PSoN
Johnny he's risen up in the morn. Johnny of Cockley's Well. *Unknown.* EnSB
Johnny, I Hardly Knew Ye. *Unknown.* AnIV; BIrV; ELP; FaBoBa; FSW; GBP; InPK; OnYI; OxBoLi; WaaP
Johnny, I Hardly Knew Ye: In Dublinese, *parody. Unknown.* OnYI
Johnny, I Hardly Knew Ye: In Miltonese, *parody.* Oliver St. John Gogarty. OnYI
Johnny, I Hardly Knew Ye: In Swinburnese, *parody. Unknown.* OnYI
Johnny is a long-haired Blue. Three Cheers for the Black, White and Blue. Ruth Pitter. BoAnP
Johnny made a custard. Some Cook. John Ciardi. PDV
Johnny McCardner, *with music. Unknown.* OuSiCo
Johnny of Cockley's Well. *Unknown.* EnSB
Johnny Raw and Polly Clark. *Unknown.* CoMu
Johnny reading in his comic. Any Day Now. David McCord. QQQ; ShM
Johnny Rich, *sel.* Will Carleton.
"Raise the light a little, Jim." PeD
Johnny Sands. *Unknown.* AmFP; CoMu; OBET; ViBoFo
Johnny shall have a new bonnet. Mother Goose. HBV-1; HBVY; OxNR
Johnny, since today is. Many Happy Returns. W. H. Auden. NAs
Johnny Stiles; or, The Wild Mustard River, *with music. Unknown.* OuSiCo
Johnny Thomson, so they say. Mrs. Vickers' Daughter. *Unknown.* AmFP
Johnny, though clear mine eyes, to speculate. Johnny, I Hardly Knew Ye: In Miltonese, *parody.* Oliver St. John Gogarty. OnYI
Johnny Todd. *Unknown.* FSW
Johnny used to find content. Johnny. Emma Rounds. ShM
Johnny Walk Along to Hilo, *with music. Unknown.* ShS
Johnny, Won't You Ramble, *with music. Unknown.* OuSiCo
Johnny's Hist'ry Lesson. Nixon Waterman. FPL; PoLF
Johnny's in the basement. Subterranean Homesick Blues. Bob Dylan. InPK
Johnny's into England gane. McNaughtan. *Unknown.* OxBB
Johnny's the Lad I Love. *Unknown. See* As I Roved Out.
John's manners at the table. The Visitor. Katherine Pyle. OnUR
John's my name, John Everyone, citizen. John without Heaven. John Malcolm Brinnin. NoAM
John's Song. Joan Aiken. DuDa
John's words were the words. After the Rain. Stanley Crouch. CNA
Johnshaven. *Unknown.* GBP
Johnson. *Unknown.* FSW
(Johnson-Jinkson.) AmFP
Johnson Boys, The. *Unknown.* FSW
Johnson, he was riding along [*or* out], as fast as he could ride. Johnson. *Unknown.* AmFP; FSW
Johnson on Pope. David Ferry. PP
Johnson's Ale. *Unknown.* FSW
Johnson's Cabinet Watched by Ants. Robert Bly. NoAM; NOBA
"Johnsons have her and so must we, The." Piano Lessons. Baron Wormser. MAYP
Johnson's Motor Car. *Unknown.* FSW
Johny Faa, *with music. Unknown.* OxBB
Johny he has risen up i' the morn. Johnie Cock. *Unknown.* ESPB; FaBoBa; ViBoFo
Join hands and circle to the left. Rhymed Dance Calls. *Unknown.* CoSo
Join once again, my Celia, join. Song. Charles Cotton. ViBoPo
Join with the noble-hearted. Distich. Shuraikh. TrJP
Joined the Blues. John Jerome Rooney. AA
Joining, The. Gerda Norvig. VWA
Joining the Colours. Katharine Tynan. SUMH
Jojina, My Love. *Zulu Oral Tradition, tr. by* H. Tracey. WTO
Joke, The. *Unknown.* RHPC
Joke Versified, A. Thomas Moore. *See* Epigram: " 'Come, come,' said Tom's father . . ."
Joke you just told isn't funny one bit, The. The Joke. *Unknown.* RHPC
Jokesmith's Vacation, The. Don Marquis. FiBHP
Jolly Beggar, The. *At. to* James V, King of Scotland. CoMu; OxBB
Jolly Beggars, The. Burns. EnRP, *sl. diff. vers.*; LAuP; OAEP; PoEL-4
Sels.
I Once Was a Maid. OxBoLi; UnTE
"See the smoking bowl before us." BSV; GoTS
(Drinking Song.) TrGrPo
"When lyart leaves bestrow the yird." NOEC
Jolly boating weather. Eton Boating Song. William Cory. ELP
Jolly Cowboy, The, *with music. Unknown.* CoSo
Jolly Driver, The. *Unknown.* CoMu; UnTE
Jolly fat friar loved liquor good store, A. Gluggity Glug. George Colman. *Fr.* The Myrtle and the Vine. HBV-2
Jolly Good Ale and Old. *At. to* William Stevenson *and also to* John Still. *See* Back and Side Go Bove, Go Bare.
Jolly Jack. Thackeray. HBV-1
Jolly Jankin [*or* Jankyn]. *Unknown.* GBP; NoP; OxBM; OxBoLi
(Jankin.) NOBE
(Jankin, the Clerical Seducer.) MeEL
Jolly Juggler, The. *Unknown. See* Juggler and the Baron's Daughter, The.
Jolly Lumbermen, The. *Unknown. See* Colley's Run-I-O.
Jolly old clown, The. The Clown. Mary Catherine Rose. SoPo
Jolly Old Pedagogue, The. George Arnold. HBV-1; TreFS
Jolly old sow once lived in a sty, A. The Three Little Pigs. Sir Alfred Scott Gatty. OxBChV

Jolly Phoebus his car to the coach-house had driven. Homecoming. *Unknown.* AnIV
Jolly Pinder of Wakefield, The. *Unknown.* ESPB (A *and* B *vers.*)
Jolly Plowboy, The. *Unknown.* AmFP
Jolly shepherd, shepherd on a hill. In Praise of His Love. Sir John Wotton. EIL
Jolly Shepherd Wat, The. *Unknown. See* Can I Not Sing.
Jolly Shilling, The. *Unknown.* OBET
Jolly Soldier ("I once was a seaman stout and bold"). *Unknown.* AmFP; OFD
Jolly Soldier, The (" 'Tis of jolly soldier that lately came from war"). *Unknown.* AmFP
Jolly Thresherman, The. *Unknown.* AmFP
Jolly Trades-Men, The. *Unknown.* CoMu
Jolly Waggoner, The. *Unknown.* OBET
(Jolly Wagoner, The, *with music.*) TrAS
Jolly Woodchuck, The. Marion Edey *and* Dorothy Grider. FaPON; PDV; TiPo
Jolly young artist called Bruno, A. Bruno.TDH
Jolly Young Sailor and the Beautiful Queen, The, *with music. Unknown.* ShS
Jolly Young Waterman, The. Charles Dibdin. NOEC; PoPle
Jollymerry/ hollyberry. The Computer's First Christmas Card. Edwin Morgan. FaBoCo; NIP; PChr
Jonah. Bible, *O.T.* NAWM-1
Jonah's Prayer, II: 3-11. TrJP
Jonah. Aldous Huxley. ChTr
Jonah. *Unknown. Fr.* Patience. ACP
Jonah and the Whale. Viola Meynell. EtS
Jonah and the Whale. *Unknown.* BLPA
Jonah Is Cast into the Sea. *Unknown. Fr.* Patience. OxBM
Jonah was an immigrant, so runs the Bible tale. Darky Sunday School. *Unknown.* OxBoLi
Jonah's Prayer. Bible, *O.T.* Jonah, II: 3-11. TrJP
Jonas Kindred's Household. George Crabbe. *Fr.* Tales: The Frank Courtship. FaBoEn; OBNC
Jonathan. Rose Fyleman. TiPo
Jonathan. Rachel, *tr. fr. Hebrew by* L. V. Snowman. TrJP
Jonathan,/ Winesap,/ Sheep-nose. Cider Song. Mildred Weston. BoNaP
Jonathan Bing. Beatrice Curtis Brown. FaPON; OnMSP; PDV; RHPC; SoPo; TiPo
Jonathan Bing Dances for Spring. Beatrice Curtis Brown. SiSoSe
Jonathan Blake. After the Party. William Wise. FaPON
Jonathan Gee. Jonathan. Rose Fyleman. TiPo
Jonathan Houghton. Edgar Lee Masters. *Fr.* Spoon River Anthology. OxBA
Jonathan Moulton lost his wife. The Two Wives. Daniel Henderson. ShM
Jonathan Swift/ Had the gift. Lines on Swift's Ancestors. Pope. FaBoCo
Jonathan Swift Somers. Edgar Lee Masters. *Fr.* Spoon River Anthology. OBAL
Jonathan to John. James Russell Lowell. *Fr.* The Biglow Papers, 2d Series, No. II. PAH
Jone is a wench that's painted. Upon Jone and Jane. Robert Herrick. AnAnS-2
Jone o' Grinfield. *Unknown. See* Poor Cotton Weaver, The.
Jordan ("When first my lines of heav'nly joyes made mention"). George Herbert. AnAnS-1; MePo; OAEL-1; OBS; PP; PPP; SeCP
Jordan ("Who say[e]s that fictions on[e]ly and false hair"). George Herbert. CABA; FaBoEn; HAP; JCP; LiTB; MeLP; MePo; NoP; NOCV; OAEL-1; OBS; PoEL-2; PoPle; PP; PPP; SeCP; TEP; TrCP
Jorkyns was great; he labored in the City. The Tale of Jorkyns and Gertie; or, Vice Rewarded. R. P. Lister. NYBP
Joseph and Mary walked one day. The Cherry-Tree Carol. *Unknown.* AmFP
"Joseph, being seventeen years old, was feeding the flock with his brethren." Bible, *O.T. Fr.* Genesis. NAWM-1
Joseph Ben Tachfin came from the Sahara. Marrakech. Ralph Nixon Currey. PeSA
Joseph, I afraid of stars. Holy Night. Lucille Clifton. GeTw
Joseph, Jesus and Mary. *Unknown.* OHIP
Joseph Mary Plunkett. Wilfrid Meynell. ISi
Joseph Mica. *Unknown.* ViBoFo
Joseph, mild and noble, bent above the straw. Mary's Baby. Shaemas O'Sheel. HBV-1; HBVY
Joseph Rodman Drake. Fitz-Greene Halleck. *See* On the Death of Joseph Rodman Drake.
Joseph was an old man. The Cherry-Tree Carol. *Unknown.* AmFP; ChTr; EBEV; ELP; EnSB; ESPB; FaBoBa; GBP; HeIP; LoBV; OAEL-1; OAEP; OBCP; OBET; OFD; OnMSP; OxBB; OxBoCh; OxBoLi; SBVL; SeCeV; TrGrPo; ViBoFo; ViBoPo
Joseph were a young man, a young man were he. The Cherry-Tree Carol. *Unknown.* AmFP
Josephine. Alexander Resnikoff. RHPC
Joseph's Suspicion. Rainer Maria Rilke, *tr. fr. German. TrCP*
Joses, the Brother of Jesus. Harry Kemp. HBMV
Joshua Fit De [*or* Fought the] Battle of [*or* ob] Jericho. *Unknown.* BoAN-1, *with music*; BPo; FSW; NOBA; TAP; TrAS, *with music*; TrGrPo
Joshua Hight. *Unknown.* ShM
Joshua the son of Nun. *Unknown. Fr.* The Old Testament. FaBoUs
Joshua's Face. Amir Gilboa, *tr. fr. Hebrew by* Shirley Kaufman. VWA
Josie. *Unknown. See* Frankie and Johnny.
Journal. John Ciardi. PoA
Journal, *sel.* Gayl Jones.
3-31-70. BlSi
Journal, *sels.* Edna St. Vincent Millay.
"I read with varying degrees." ImOP
"In the evening I would sit." SaC
Journal Literary Gazette says dozens of irate, The. Women Called Bossy Cowboys. Beth Jankola. AMV-80
Journal of Albion Moolight, The, *sels.* Kenneth Patchen. NaP
"But there is no black jaw which cannot be broken by our word."
"I/ want you/ to listen."
Journal of Society, The. Godfrey Turner. NOBL
Journal of the Storm. Greg Kuzma. AmPA
Journal to Stella. Morton Dauwen Zabel. PoA
Journey. Roy Daniells. MoCV
Journey. Sam Harrison. NeIP
Journey, The. David Ignatow. Psk
Journey, The. Henry Johnson. LFAC
Journey, The. Scudder Middleton. HBMV
Journey, The. Edwin Muir. *See* Mythical Journey, The.
Journey. Raymond Thompson. LFAC
Journey. Diane Wakoski. IHMS
Journey, The. Yvor Winters. MoVE
Journey and Observations of a Countryman, The, *sel.* John Hawthorn.
Deathbed, A. NOEC
Journey Back to Christmas. Gwen Dunn. OBCP
Journey in the Orient. Maria Luisa Spaziani, *tr. fr. Italian by* Ruth Feldman. BoWoP
Journey into France, The. *Unknown.* CoMu; FaBoBa
Journey Nears the Road-End, The. Rabindranath Tagore, *tr. fr. Bengali by* Amiya Chakravarty. DL
Journey of the Magi. T. S. Eliot. CABA; DTC; EaLo; EBCP; FaBoCh; FaBoMo; FaFP; HAP; HeIP; LiTA; LiTM; MoAB; MoAmPo; MP; NePA; NIP; NOCV; NoP; OAEP; OBCP; OBMV; OxBTC; PAI; PChr; PPoe; SBVL; SoSe; TrGrPo; TwCP; TAP
Journey Onwards, The. Thomas Moore. GTBS; GTBS-P; HBV-2; SeCePo
Journey round the World. Ingrid Jonker, *tr. fr. Afrikaans by* Jack Cope *and* William Plomer. PBWP
Journey through the Moonlight, A. Russell Edson. LCAP
Journey through the Night. John Holloway. NePoEA
Journey to a Parallel. Bruce McM. Wright. PoNe
Journey to Hell, A; or, A Visit Paid to the Devil, *sel.* Edward Ward.
Parish Poor-Officers, The. NOEC
Journey to Iceland. W. H. Auden. PoA
Journey to the Insane Asylum, The. Alfred Lichtenstein, *tr. fr. German by* Mary Zilzer. VWA
Journey to the Interior. Theodore Roethke. CABA; LCAP; NYBP; VGW
Journey toward Evening. Phyllis McGinley. GoYe; NYBP
Journey with Hands and Arms, The. Benjamin Saltman. VWA
Journeyman, The. *Unknown, tr. fr. Irish by* Frank O'Connor. KiLC
Journeys. Gary Snyder. NU
Journey's End. Humbert Wolfe. TrJP
Jove descends in sleet and snow. The Storm. Alcaeus, *tr. by* John Hermann Merivale. AWP
Jove for Europaes love, took shape of bull. Parthenophil and Parthenophe, LXIII. Barnabe Barnes. AAS
Jove's Eagle Carries Chaucer into Space. Chaucer. *Fr.* The House of Fame. OxBM
Jovial Marriner, The; or, The Sea-Man's Renown. John Playford. CoMu
Jovial Shepheard's Song, The. Michael Drayton. *See* Trent, The.
Jovial Tinker, The; or, The Willing Couple ("There was a Tinker liv'd of late"). *Unknown.* CoMu
Jovial Tinker, The ("It was a lady of the North"). *Unknown. See* Room for a Jovial Tinker.
Jowl, Jowl and Listen. *Unknown.* OBET
Jowls of his belly crawl and swell like the sea, The. The Glutton. Karl Shapiro. DFF
Joy. Gavin Bantock. OxBTC
Joy. Robert Creeley. PPP
Joy. Clarissa Scott Delany. CDC; PoNe
Joy. Robinson Jeffers. CMoP
Joy—a beginning. Anguish, ardor. Relearning the Alphabet. Denise Levertov. NOBA

Joy and Peace in Believing. William Cowper. NOCV; TRV
Joy and Pleasure. W. H. Davies. OBMV
Joy and the soul are mates, as heart and sorrow. The Cruse. Louise Townsend Nicholl. NYBP
Joy Enough. Barrett Eastman. AA
Joy for the sturdy trees. Tree-planting. Samuel Francis Smith. OHIP
Joy, great joy, was the message. Joy to the World. *Unknown.* STF
Joy, I did lock thee up: but some bad man. The Bunch of Grapes. George Herbert. AnAnS-1
Joy in rebel Plymouth town, in the spring of sixty-four. "Albemarle" Cushing. James Jeffrey Roche. PAH
Joy is a trick in the air. Birth-Dues. Robinson Jeffers. MoAB; MoAmPo
Joy Is the Blossom. Walter Savage Landor. DBV
(Epigram: "Joy is the blossom, sorrow is the fruit.") HBV-1
Joy, joy to mortals! The rejoicing fires. Love's Triumph. Ben Jonson. EnRePo
Joy May Kill. Michelangelo, *tr. fr. Italian by* John Addington Symonds. AWP
Joy-Month. David Atwood Wasson. HBV-1
Joy o' Living. Amanda Benjamin Hall. HBMV
Joy of a Singer, The. Piuvkaq, *tr. fr. Eskimo.* WTO
Joy of Church Fellowship Rightly Attended, The. Edward Taylor. *Fr.* God's Determinations. AmPP; AP; OxBA; SCAP
(In Heaven Soaring.) AH, *with music*
Joy of Cooking, The, *sel.* David Mus.
Conserves. PoA
Joy of Knowledge. Isidor Schneider. TrJP
Joy of Life. Moses ibn Ezra, *tr. fr. Hebrew by* Solomon Solis-Cohen. *Fr.* The Book of Tarshish. TrJP
Joy of Love, The. Allan Dowling. ErPo
Joy of my life, full oft for loving you. Amoretti, LXXXII. Spenser. HeIP
Joy of My Life! While Left Me Here. Henry Vaughan. SeCV-1
(Joy of My Life.) OBS
Joy of the Morning. Edwin Markham. AA; FaPON; HBV-2
Joy, rose-lipped dryad, loves to dwell. Thomas Warton the Elder. *Fr.* Retirement, an Ode. ViBoPo
Joy shakes me like the wind that lifts a sail. Joy. Clarissa Scott Delany. CDC; PoNe
Joy, Shipmate, Joy! Walt Whitman. HBVY; MoAmPo; MOS; OHIP; TAP; TreFT
Joy so short alas, the pain so near, The. Sir Thomas Wyatt. SiPS
Joy Sonnet in a Random Universe. Helen Chasin. HeIP; NIP
Joy to Philip, he this day. Going into Breeches. Charles *and* Mary Lamb. OxBChV
Joy to the bridegroom and the bride. The Milkmaid's Epithalamium. Thomas Randolph. BoLoP
Joy to the World. *Unknown.* STF
Joy to the World. Isaac Watts. FSW
Joyce Kilmer. Amelia Josephine Burr. HBMV
Joyce was afraid of thunder. Volcano. Derek Walcott. OxBC
Joyful. Rose Burgunder. RHPC
Joyful, joyful, we adore Thee. Hymn of Joy. Henry van Dyke. TRV
Joyful [*or* Joyfull] New Ballad, A. Thomas Deloney. CoMu; ViBoPo, *abr.*
Joyful Noise, A. Donald Finkel. CoAP
Joyful Prophecy. Vassar Miller. CoPo
Joyful Sound It Is, A, *with music.* George Strebeck. AH
Joyful Wisdom, The. Coventry Patmore. *Fr.* The Angel in the House. HBV-2
Joyfully, Joyfully Onward I Move, *with music.* William Hunter. AH
Joyless/ what I have [*or* have I] done. Liadan Laments Cuirithir. Liadan, tr. by John Montague. BIrV; PBWP
Joyous birds, hid under greenwood shade, The. Tasso, *tr. by* Edward Fairfax. *Fr.* Godfrey of Bulloigne; or, The Recoverie of Jerusalem, XVI. OBVE
Joyous morning ran and kissed the grass, The. The Wakers. John Freeman. HBMV
Joys of Art, The. Rachel Annand Taylor. OBVV
Joys of Marriage, The. Charles Cotton. InMe
Joys of Mary, The. *Unknown.* AmFP
(Seven Blessings of Mary, The, *diff. version.*) FSW
Joys of the Road, The. Bliss Carman. HBV-1; HBVY; OBVV
Joy's Peak. Robert Farren. ISi
Joy's Treachery. Wilfrid Scawen Blunt. The Love Sonnets of Proteus, XVII. VLP
J's the Jumping Jay-Walker. Phyllis McGinley. *Fr.* All Around the Town. FaPON; RHPC
Juan Belmonte, Torero. Donald Finkel. NePoEA
Juan de Juni the priest said. Aodh Ruadh O'Domhnaill [*or* Red Hugh]. Thomas McGreevy. AnIV; CIP; OBMV; OnYI; OxBI
Juan de Pareja: Painted by Velázquez. Richard A. Long. AmNP
Juan embark'd—the ship got under way. Byron. *Fr.* Don Juan, II. MOS
Juan in England. Byron. *Fr.* Don Juan, XI. FiP
("Don Juan had got out on Shooter's Hill.") OAEP
Juan knew several languages—as well. Byron. *Fr.* Don Juan, XI. OAEL-2
Juan Murray, *with music. Unknown.* CoSo
Juan Quintana. Alice Corbin. BPAW; HBMV
Juan, the moron next door. Report from the Correspondent They Fired. David McElroy. AmPA
Juan who has eaten circles all his life. The Man of O. Marina Rivera. FIA
Juana. Alfred de Musset, *tr. fr. French by* Andrew Lang. AWP
Juanita. Joaquin Miller. AA
Juanita. Caroline Norton. FSW
Juanita, Wife of Manuelito. Simon Ortiz. MAYP
Juan's Song. Louise Bogan. NYBP
Jubalee, *with music. Unknown.* BoAN-2
Jubilant the music through the fields a-ringing. World Music. Frances Louisa Bushnell. AA
Jubilate. George Arnold. EtS
Jubilate Agno, *sels.* Christopher Smart.
"For I am not without authority in my jeopardy." LAuP; NCEP
"For I bless the Prince of Peace and pray that all the guns may be nail'd up." InPS
"For the air is purified by prayer which is made aloud." PrF
"For the doubling of flowers is the improvement of the gard'ner's talent." LauP; NOEC
"For the Greek and Latin are not dead languages." NCEP
"For the spiritual musick is as follows." NOEC
"For thirdly he works it upon stretch with the fore paws extended." NCEP
"Let Elizure rejoice with the partridge." OAEL-1
"Let Ephah rejoice with Buprestis, the Lord endue us with temperance and humanity." NOEC
"Let Shobi rejoice with the Kastrel—blessed be the name Jesus." NOEC
"Let Tobias bless Charity with his dog." NCEP
My Cat Jeoffry. ChTr; FaBoCh; LiTB; SeCePo; WIR
(For I Will Consider My Cat Jeoffry.) CTC; FM; HAP; HeIP; InPK; LAuP; NOEC; NoP; OAEL-1; PAI; PCat; PoEL-3; PPP; PrF; SCV; SeCeV; WeW
(Of Jeoffry, His Cat.) NU; PrIm
"Rejoice in God, O ye tongues; give glory to the Lord, and the Lamb." LAuP
Jubilate Canis. Erica Jong. MAYP
Jubilate Herbis. Norma Farber. PChr
Jubilation T. Cornpone. Johnny Mercer. OBAL
Jubilee. *Unknown.* FSW
Jubilee before Revolution. Andrew Lang. BXAP
Jubilo. Allen Tate. WaP
Judaeus Errans. Louis Golding. TrJP
Judah in Exile Wanders, *with music.* George Sandys. AH
Judaism. Cardinal Newman. ACP
Judas. Vassar Miller. MoAmPo
Judas. *Unknown.* ESPB; OxBM; ViBoFo
Judas Goat, The. Susan Musgrave. NOBC
Judas Iscariot. Robert Williams Buchanan. OBVV; OxBoCh
Judas Iscariot. Countee Cullen. PoLF
Judas Iscariot. Margaret Nickerson Martin. PGD
Judas Iscariot. Stephen Spender. MoAB; MoBrPo; NIP
Judas Iscariot dour and dark. Descent for the Lost. Philip Child. CaP
Judas, Joyous Little Son. Norma Farber. AMV-80
Judas Maccabeus. Bible, Apocrypha. *Fr.* First Maccabeus. TrJP
Judas, Peter. Luci Shaw. AMV-80
Judas Sells His Lord. *Unknown.* MeEL
Judas was I! Ah, the mockery! Judas Iscariot. Margaret Nickerson Martin. PGD
Judean Summer. Fay Lipshitz. VWA
Judeebug's Country. Joe Johnson. PoBA
Judezmo Writer in Turkey Angry, A. Stephen Levy. VWA
Judge, The. Karl Kopp. TAT
Judge, The. Kenneth A. McClane. AMV-81
Judge Bean's court, knowed near and far. Fine! S. Omar Barker. BPAW
Judge enforcing the obsolete law, The. W. H. Auden. TRV
Judge gimme life this morning. Parchman Farm Blues. *Unknown.* BluL
Judge Harsh Blues. *Unknown.* BluL
Judge, judge, tell the judge. *Unknown.* OxBoLi
Judge Kroll. Barbara L. Greenberg. AMV-81
Judge Me, O God, *with music.* Joel Barlow. AH
Judge Not According to the Appearance. Christina Rossetti. TrPWD
Judge Roy Bean of Vinegarroon. The Law West of the Pecos. S. Omar Barker. BPAW
Judge said "Stand up, boy, and dry up your tears," The. Twenty-one Years. *Unknown.* AmFP
Judge Somers. Edgar Lee Masters. *Fr.* Spoon River Anthology. FaBoEE; OBSV

Judge, who lives impeccably upstairs, The. Upstairs Downstairs. Hervey Allen. HBMV; PoA; PoNe
Judge with the Sore Rump, The. St. George Tucker. OBAL
Judged by the Company One Keeps. *Unknown, at. to* Aimor R. Dickson. BLPA; FPL; YaD
(Company One Keeps, The.) TreFT
Judgment, The. Dora Read Goodale. AA
Judgement. George Herbert. AnAnS-1; SeCP
Judgment, The. Kathleen Spivack. BoWoP
Judgement. *Unknown.* TreFT
Judgement and cash and health and faith in God go wrong. But Choose. John Holmes. MiAP
Judgement Day. *Unknown. See* My Lord, What a Mourning.
Judgement of God, The. William Morris. OBVV
Judgement of Tiresias, The. Hildebrand Jacob. NOEC
Judges, Judges. Gene Baro. NePoEA-2
Judges, *sel.* Bible, *O.T.*
Song of Deborah, The, V:1-31. BoWoP; PBWP; WPOW (24-31)
(Song of Deborah and Barak, The, 2-21.) AWP
(Then Sang Deborah and Barak, 1-31.) TrJP
Judging Distances. Henry Reed. Lessons of the War, II. BoLoP; ChMP; GTBS-P; HeIP; LiTB; MoAB; NIP; NOBE; SoSe
Judgment Day. Robert Garioch, *after the Italian of* Giuseppe Belli. OBVE
Judgment Day. William Dean Howells. AA
Judgment Day. John Oxenham. TRV
Judgment in Heaven, A, *sel.* Francis Thompson.
Epilogue: "Heaven, which man's generations draws." MoAB; MoBrPo
Judgment of Paris, The. W. S. Merwin. NNaP
Judgment of Paris, The, *sels.* Ralph Schomberg. TrJP
Ay or Nay?
Courtier's a Riddle, A.
Like Birds of a Feather.
Judgment of the May, The. Richard Watson Dixon. OBNC
Judicious Observation of That Dreadful Comet, A. Ichabod Wiswall. SCAP
Judith, *sel.* Lascelles Abercrombie.
Song: "Balkis was in her marble town." MoBrPo
Judith, *sel.* Bible, Apocrypha.
With Timbrels. TrJP
Judith. William Young. AA
Judith of Bethulia. John Crowe Ransom. CrMA; DTC; FaBoMo; FYAP; LiTA; LiTM; MoPo; NePA; NoAM; NOBA
Judith of Minnewaulken, *sel.* Maxwell Anderson.
Judith Remembers. WHA
Judith Recalls Holofernes. Maura Stanton. AmPA
Judy-One. Don L. Lee. TAP
Judy Sugden! Judy, I made you caper. Barnsley and District. Donald Davie. OxBC
"Jug and a book and a dame, A." The Rubaiyat. Edwin Meade Robinson. Limericised Classics, III. HBMV
Jug Brook. Ellen Bryant Voigt. MAYP
Jug, jug! Fair fall the nightingal. The Nightingale. Richard Brathwaite. *Fr.* Nature's Embassy. EIL; PBBP
Jug of Punch, The. Francis McPeake. FSW
Jug of water in the hand, and on, A. Dawn. Rachel, *tr. by* A. M. Klein. TrJP
Juggle of Myrtle Twigs, A. Edward Codish. VWA
Juggler. Richard Wilbur. CMoP; LiTM; MoAB; NCSH; NePA; NePoEA; NYBP; TAP
Juggler and the Baron's Daughter, The. *Unknown.* OxBM
("Draw me nere, draw me nere.") EBEV
(Jolly Juggler, The.) NoP
(Magician and the Baron's Daughter, The.) MeEL
Jugglers keep six bottles in the air. Hazardous Occupations. Carl Sandburg. SaC
Juggles old bones. Morning Star Man. George Keithley. NPGG
Juggling Jerry. George Meredith. BeLS; HBV-2; OAEP; SeCePo; VLP
Juggy's Christening. *Unknown.* NOEC
Jugs, The. Paul Celan, *tr. fr. German by* Christopher Middleton. OBVE
Jugurtha. Longfellow. AA; AP
Juice glass throbs against his lips, The. A Negro Judge. Frederick Seidel. CoPo
Juice of apples climbs in me, The. The Forbidden. Phyllis Haring. PeSA
JuJu. Askia Muhammad Touré. PoBA
Juju of My Own, A. Lebert Bethune. InPS; PoBA; PoNe
Juke Box Love Song. Langston Hughes. GrPl; IDB; OLR; PoBA
Julia. Wendy Rose. STE; TWSS
Julia and I did lately sit. Cherry-Pit. Robert Herrick. OAEP
Julia, how Irishly you sacrifice. Reproach to Julia. Robert Graves. ELU; FaBoEE
Julia, if I chance to die. His Request to Julia. Robert Herrick. CaPo; OBS
Julia Miller. Edgar Lee Masters. *Fr.* Spoon River Anthology. MoVE
Julia, my dear, how long, I wonder. Lovers and Friends. Henry Luttrell. *Fr.* Advice to Julia. OBRV
Julia, my wife, has grown quite rude. From a Connecticut Newspaper. Levi Rockwell. FaBoUs
Julia was careless, and withal. Upon Julia's Fall. Robert Herrick. UnTE
Julia, when thy Herrick dies. To Julia. Robert Herrick. CaPo
Julian and Maddalo. Shelley. OAEL-2, *much abr.*
Julian Grenfell. Maurice Baring. HBMV
Julian M. and A. G. Rochelle. Emily Brontë. *See* Visionary, The.
Juliana, *sel.* Cynewulf, *tr. fr. Anglo-Saxon by* Charles W. Kennedy.
"I have great need that the Saint grant help." AnOE
Julia's Petticoat. Robert Herrick. AnAnS-2; CaPo
(Upon Julia's Petticoat.) UnTE
Julie-Jane. Thomas Hardy. MoVE
Julie Plante, The. William Henry Drummond. *See* Wreck of the *Julie Plante*, The.
Juliet. Hilaire Belloc. BoLoP; ELU; EnLoPo
Juliet, farewell. I would not be forgiven. Farewell. Wilfrid Scawen Blunt. *Fr.* The Love Sonnets of Proteus. TrGrPo
Juliet's Yearning. Shakespeare. *Fr.* Romeo and Juliet, III, ii. TreFS
Julio. Kell Robertson. TAT
Julius Caesar, *sels.* Shakespeare.
Brutus Explains Why He Murdered Caesar, *fr.* III, ii. TreFT
Cassius Poisons Brutus's Mind, *fr.* I, ii. TreFS
"Cowards die many times before their deaths," *fr.* II, ii. FF
(Death of Cowards, The.) TreFS
(That Men Should Fear.) TrGrPo
"Friends, Romans, countrymen, lend me your ears," *fr.* III, ii. TreF
(Antony's Oration.) PoPL; TrGrPo
(Anthony's Oration over Caesar's Body.) LiTB
(I Come to Bury Caesar.) WHA
Julius Caesar's Preference, *fr.* I, ii. TreFS
Mark Antony Addresses the Mob, *fr.* III, ii. FaPoR
Mark Antony's Lament *fr.* III, i. TreFS
Noblest Roman, The, *fr.* V, v. FaFP; TreFS
(Portrait of Brutus.) TrGrPo
Portrait of Caesar, *fr.* I, ii. TrGrPo
There Is a Tide [in the Affairs of Men], *fr.* IV, iii. PoPl; TRV
(Time to Strike, The.) TreFS
Julius Caesar. *Unknown.* InPK
Julius Caesar and the Honey-Bee. Charles Tennyson Turner. FM; NBM
July. W. Ralph Johnson. AMV-81
July. Susan Hartley Swett. *See* It Is July.
July. *At. to* Whittier. YeAr
July Dawn. Louise Bogan. NePoAm-2
July 1st, French Creek. Kevin Roberts. WOLT
July 1st, 1916. Aimee Byng Scott. SUMH
July 4th. May Swenson. PoA
July 4th, 1981 and all is Hell. Elegy for the Forgotten Oldsmobile. Adrian C. Louis. STE
July ghost, aghast at the strange winter, A. Midsummer Frost. Isaac Rosenberg. MoPo
July in Indiana. Robert Fitzgerald. NYBP
July in the Jardin des Plantes. Claire McAllister. NePA
July in Washington. Robert Lowell. LCAP; NaP; Prf
July is honored with the labor of fields. Labor of Fields. Elizabeth J. Coatsworth. TiPo
July is just in the nick of time! The Mowers. Myron B. Benton. YeAr
July Meadow. Louise Driscoll. YeAr
July 1914. "Anna Akhmatova," *tr. fr. Russian by* Stanley Kunitz. WPOW
July Storm, A: Johnson, Nemaha County, Nebraska. Steve Hahn. AMV-81
July the First. Robert Currie. Psk
July the First, of a morning clear, one thousand six hundred and ninety. The Boyne Water. *Unknown.* AnIV; FaPoR; OnYI
July the redbird (hanh!), redbird, Augus' the fly. Don't Talk About It. *Unknown.* OuSiCo
July: The Succession of the Four Sweet Months. Robert Herrick. *See* Four Sweet Months, The.
July the twenty-second day. The Descent on Middlesex. Peter St. John. PAH
July 31. Norman Jordan. PoBA
July Wakes. Richard Pomfret. OBET
July's dry emperies have fired a snake. Crotalus Rex. Brewster Ghiselin. MoVE
Jumbled in the Common Box. W. H. Auden. PoRA
Jumblies, The. Edward Lear. BLPL; ChTr; EBEV; EvOK; FaBoBe; FaBoNo; FaFP; GoJo; HBV-2; HBVY; LiTB; MOS; NA; OnMSP; OxBChV; OxBoLi; PoRA; SeCeV; SoPo; TEP; TiPo; WiR
Jumbo Jee. Laura E. Richards. SUS
Jump bigness upward. Mwilu/ or Poem for the Living. Don L. Lee. JB
Jump Jim Crow, *with music.* Thomas D. Rice. BLSo

Jump—jump—jump—Jump away. The Little Jumping Girls. Kate Greenaway. FaPON; TiPo
Jump or Jiggle. Evelyn Beyer. TiPo
(Jump or Jingle.) SoPo
Jump over the wall and come to me. Come to Me. *Gond Oral Tradition, tr. by* V. Elwin *and* S. Hivale. WTO
Jump-Rope Rhyme. *Unknown.* NTCP
Jump Shooter, The. Dennis Trudell. LiSp
Jump stone hand leaf shadow sun. The Fire. Robert Duncan. *Fr.* Passages. VGW
Jump-to-Glory Jane. George Meredith. VLP
Jumped his cage. The Gerbil Who Got Away. Judith C. Root. AMV-81
Junction. John Pass. WOLT
Juncture. Rea Lubar Duncan. PoNe
June. Bryant. AA; HBV-2
June. Mary Carolyn Davies. SiSoSe; TiPo
June. Elaine Feinstein. BrRo
June. Aileen Fisher. PDV
June. Nora Hopper. YeAr
June. Francis Ledwidge. BIrV; HBMV; OnYI
June ("Over his keys the musing organist"). James Russell Lowell. *Fr.* The Vision of Sir Launfal. HBV-1; HBVY; OHFP; PoLF
("Over his keys the musing organist.") LiTA
June ("What is so rare as a day in June?"). James Russell Lowell. *Fr.* The Vision of Sir Launfal, Prelude to Pt. 1. FaBV
(Day in June, A.) FaPON
(What Is So Rare as a Day in June.) BLPL; FaBoBe; FaFP
June. Wilson MacDonald. CaP
June. Douglas Malloch. YeAr
June. Harrison Smith Morris. HBV-1
June. Theodore Harding Rand. CaP
June. James Reaney. WHW
June Bracken and Heather. Tennyson. EnLoPo; PPoe
June Day, A. Sara Teasdale. YeAr
June in Wiltshire. Geoffrey Grigson. WaP
June Is Bustin' Out All Over, *with music.* Oscar Hammerstein II. BLSo
June Morning. Hugh McCrae. PoAu-1
June Night. Hazel Hall. HBMV
June, 1915. Charlotte Mew. SUMH
June Rapture. Angela Morgan. HBMV
June Song. Abby Rosenthal. AMV-81
June Song of a Man Who Looks Two Ways. Leslie Daiken. NeIP
June 10. Magdalena de Rodriguez, *tr. fr. Spanish by* Nina Serrano. WPOW
June Thunder. Louis MacNeice. ChMP; CMoP; MoPo
June Twenty-first. Bruce Guernsey. PPJ
June Twilight. John Masefield. GoYe
June Weather. James Russell Lowell. *Fr.* The Vision of Sir Launfal. GN
("For a cap and bells our lives we play.") AA
Junes were free and full, driving through tiny, The. June Thunder. Louis MacNeice. ChMP; CMoP; MoPo
Jungle, The. Diane di Prima. PoM
Jungle, The. Louis Dudek. PeCV
Jungle. Phyllis Haring. PeSA
Jungle, The. Alun Lewis. MoPo
Jungle. Mary Carter Smith. PoNe
Jungle, The. Randolph Stow. *Fr.* Thailand Railway. CBAP
Jungle, The. William Carlos Williams. CABA
Jungle:/ Glaze green and red feathers, jungle. Ezra Pound. *Fr.* Cantos, XX. MoPo
Jungle/ takes over the garden. The Indolent Gardener. Mary Kennedy. BoNaP
Jungle Book, The, *sels.* Kipling.
Road-Song of the Bandar-Log. OAEP
Seal Lullaby. FaPON; SoSe; TiPo
Jungle is the frame for the machine, The. The Bulldozer. Donald A. Stauffer. WaP
Jungle Mammy Song, *with music. Unknown.* AS
Jungle necklaces are hung. Here She Is. Mary Britton Miller. TiPo
Jungle Taste. Edward S. Silvera. CDC
Junglegrave. S. E. Anderson. PoBA
Junior Addict. Langston Hughes. BPo; CNA
Juniper. Eileen Duggan. PChr
Juniper. Robert Francis. VGW
Juniper. Laurie Lee. ChMP; NeBP
Juniper Tree, The. Wilfred Watson. WHW
Junk. Richard Wilbur. HAP; InPK; NoP; SaC; WeW
Junk. William Zaranka. AMV-80
Junk Shop, The. Henri Coulette. NYBP
Junker Schmidt. "Kozma Prutkov," *tr. fr. Russian by* W. D. Snodgrass *and* Tanya Tolstoy. ELU
Junkie with a Flute in the Rain, A. David Fisher. NPGG
Junkyards. Julian Lee Rayford. FAZ; PPJ
Juno, that on her head Loves liverie carried. Caelica, XI. Fulke Greville. NCEP
Jupiter and Ganimede. Thomas Heywood. PeHV
Jupiter and Ten. James Thomas Fields. OBAL
Jurgis Petrakas, the Workers' Angel, Organizes the First Miner's Strike in Exeter, Pennsylvania. Anthony Petrosky. FYAP
Just. Judith Johnson Sherwin. TAP
Just a Closer Walk with Thee. *Unknown.* FSW
Just a few of the roses we gathered from the Isar. Roses on the Breakfast Table. D. H. Lawrence. BrPo
Just a Few Scenes from an Autobiography. John Tagliabue. FAZ
Just a herd of Negroes. Share-Croppers. Langston Hughes. SaC
Just a line to remind my friends that after much trouble. Dear Folks. Patrick Kavanagh. FaBoTw
Just a little rain falling all around. What Have They Done to the Rain. Malvina Reynolds. FSW
Just a picture of somebody's child. Somebody's Child. Louise Chandler Moulton. HBV-1
Just a scuzzy black puddle in the driveway. Our "Civilization." John Morgan. LTB
Just a Smack at Auden. William Empson. FaBoCo; LiTM; MoBrPo; UnPo
Just a solitude. Little Air. Stéphane Mallarmé, *tr. by* Roger Fry. PoPl; SyP
Just a Wearyin' for You. Frank Lebby Stanton. TreF
Just a While. Frantisek Gottlieb, *tr. fr. Czech by* Ewald Osers. VWA
Just a worried old rounder. Lowdown Rounder's Blues. *Unknown.* BluL
Just after Noon with Fierce Shears. Tram Combs. MP; TwCP
Just after supper sheets were passed out. I Am Sure of It. Jimmy Santiago Baca. LFAC
Just after the Board had brought the schools up to date. Modern Ode to the Modern School. John Erskine. YaD
Just an ivy-covered cottage with a brooklet running near. All That Glitters Is Not Gold. *Unknown.* TreFT
Just an Old Man. Mary Goose. STE
Just an Old Sweet Song. Donagh MacDonagh. CIP
Just and fit actions Ptolemy (he saith). Lucan, *tr. by* Ben Jonson. *Fr.* Pharsalia, VII. OBVE
Just and Unjust. Lord Bowen. *See* Rain It Raineth, The.
Just are the ways of God. The Transcendence of God. Milton. *Fr.* Samson Agonistes. OBS
Just as a year might end. Nightsong. Louis Coxe. FYAP
Just as eventide draws near. Song of Longing. *Tr. fr. Maori by* John White. WTO
Just as he is growing a beard. Epigram. Flaccus. PeHV
Just as I Am. Charlotte Elliott. HBV-2
("Just as I am—without one plea.") VLP
Just as I thought I was growing old. The Prime of Life. Walter Learned. HBV-1
Just as my fingers close about the pen. The Spider. Kenneth Mackenzie. BoAnP
Just as my fingers on these keys. Peter Quince at the Clavier. Wallace Stevens. AmPP; AP; CABA; CMoP; CoBMV; HBMV; InPK; InPS; LiTM; MoAB; MoAmPo; MP; NOBA; OxBA; PAI; PPP; TAP; TrGrPo; TwAmPo; TwCP; ViBoPo
Just as soon as summer's done. The Weather Factory. Nancy Byrd Turner. SUS
Just as the day is about to die. Dog in the Fountain. Raymond Souster. GDP
Just as the hour was darkest. The Ballad of New Orleans. George Henry Boker. PAH
Just as the moon was fading amid her misty rings. Kriss Kringle. Thomas Bailey Aldrich. HBVY
Just as the signal tower lights flash. Night at an Airport. David Ignatow. NNaP
Just as the Small Waves Came Where No Waves Were. Pamela Millward. NU
Just as the spring came laughing through the strife. John Pelham. James Ryder Randall. AA; PAH
Just as the Tide Was a-Flowing. *Unknown.* OBET
Just as Thou Art, *with music.* Russell Sturgis Cook. AH
Just at that moment the Wolf. Coup de Grâce. A. D. Hope. DFT; PPP
Just at the blackest bit of my depression. Dirge. Hazel Townson. PV
Just at the self-same beat of Time's wide wings. The Bruised Titans. Keats. *Fr.* Hyperion; a Fragment. OBNC; OBRV
Just back of the beach at Cannes, the afternoon blue as angels swimming. Afternoon. Paul Davis. AMV-81
Just Be Glad. James Whitcomb Riley. WBLP
Just Because. Moishe Leib Halpern, *tr. fr. Yiddish by* Ruth Whitman. VWA
Just because I forget. Letter for Duncan. Larry Eigner. PoM
Just because I smile and smile. Because. B. W. Vilakazi. PeSA
Just before the Battle, Mother. George Frederick Root. FSW; PSoN, *with music;* TreFS

Just behind the Battle, Mother, *parody*. *Unknown.* FiBHP
Just beyond the rainbow's rim a river ripples down. The Sleepytown Express. James J. Montague. HBMV
Just broke from school, pert, impudent, and raw. The Modern Fine Gentleman. Soame Jenyns. OBSV
Just California. John S. McGroarty. BPAW
Just down around the corner of the street where I reside. Sweet Rosie O'Grady. Maude Nugent. FSN
Just Dropped In. William Cole. FiBHP; GoJo; POL; PoPl
Just enough of rain. Haiku. Richard Wright. FAZ
Just ere the darkness is withdrawn. Sleep and His Brother Death. William Hamilton Hayne. AA
Just Exchange. Sir Philip Sidney. *See* My True Love Hath My Heart.
Just Folks. Edgar A. Guest. FaFP; TreFS
Just for a handful of silver he left us. The Lost Leader. Robert Browning. HBV-1; TreFS; TrGrPo; ViBoPo; VLP
Just for a handful of summits he left us. The Lost Leader. Douglas Fraser. PoSh
Just for a space that I met her. Incognita. Austin Dobson. CenHV; EBVV
Just for One Day. Lillian Morrison. RHPC
Just for the Ride. *Unknown.* FaFP
Just for To-Day [*or* Today]. Sybil F. Partridge, *wr. at.* to Samuel Wilberforce. HBV-2; TreF; TRV
Just Forget. Myrtle May Dryden. WBLP
Just Friends. Robert Creeley. NeAP
Just God! and these are they. Clerical Oppressors. Whittier. PAH; PPON
Just hand me my old Martin, for soon I will be startin'. Franklin D. Roosevelt's Back Again. *Unknown.* FSW
Just imagine yourself seated on a shadowy terrace. That Reminds Me. Ogden Nash. FiBHP
Just in the gray of the dawn, as the mists uprose from the meadows. The Expedition to Wessagusset. Longfellow. *Fr.* The Courtship of Miles Standish. PAH
Just Keep On. Clifton Abbott. WBLP
Just Keep On Keepin' On. *Unknown.* STF
(Just Try This.) WBLP
Just like Me. P. W. Sinks. BLRP
Just like that. When he brings the new bike home. The Bicycle Rider. Thomas W. Shapcott. CBAP
Just look at those hands! Soap. Martin Gardner. RHPC
Just look, Manetto, at that wry-mouth'd minx. Sonnet: Of an Ill-favored Lady. Guido Cavalcanti, *tr. by* Dante Gabriel Rossetti. AWP
Just lookee here mama don't treat pigmeat the way you do. Pigmeat. *Unknown.* BluL
Just lost, when I was saved! Emily Dickinson. AmPP; AP; NOBA; NOCV; Prf
(Called Back.) AA; MoAmPo
Just Making It. Richard Thomas. PoNe
Just man followed then his angel guide, The. Lot's Wife. "Anna Akhmatova," *tr. by* Richard Wilbur. BoWoP; PBWP
Just Me. Margaret Hillert. RHPC
Just north of the Yaak River, one man sits bolt up-right. Mount Caribou at Night. Charles Wright. LCAP
Just now/ Out of the strange. The Warning [*or* Cinquain]. Adelaide Crapsey. WeW; WPE; WSC
Just now I visited the monkeys: they. The Petty Officers' Mess. Roy Fuller. ChMP
Just now the lilac is in bloom. The Old Vicarage, Grantchester. Rupert Brooke. BrPo; FaBoPP; FaBV; GoTL; MoBrPo; MoVE; OxBTC; PoRA
Just off the highway to Rochester, Minnesota. A Blessing. James Wright. ConAP; GrPl; HeIP; InPK; LLLT; NaP; NoAM; NOBA; NoP; PPP; TwCP
Just once. That Day. David Kherdian. SaC
Just One Book. *Unknown.* BLRP
Just One Signal. *Unknown.* PAH
Just out of San Francisco one cold December day. The Dying Hobo. *Unknown.* AmFP
Just Passing. *Unknown.* BLRP
Just past the clockhouse is a building of cinder. Letter to My Kinder. Bob Gaskin. AMV-81
Just so it goes—the day, the night. An Ordinary Evening in Cleveland. Lewis Turco. NYBP
Just-so Stories, *sel.* Kipling.
Camel's Hump, The. EvOK
(Hump, The.) OxBChV
Just so that each stark. Crows. Charles Simic. GeTw
Just so you shouldn't have to ask again. What Kind of a Guy Was He? Howard Nemerov. PCP
Just stand aside and watch yourself go by. Watch Yourself Go By [*or* A Cure for Fault-finding]. Strickland Gillilan. BLPA; WBLP
Just Taking Note. Sharon Scott. JB
Just Tell Them That You Saw Me. Paul Dresser. FSN, *with music; TreFS*
"Just the place for a Snark!" the Bellman cried. The Hunting of the Snark. "Lewis Carroll." FaBoNo; FiBHP; MasP; OBNC; OBNV; OnMSP; PoEL-5; WhC
Just the Same To-Day. *Unknown.* BLRP; WBLP
(He's Jus' de Same Today, *diff. vers., with music.*) BoAN-1
Just then, forgetful of the strict command. Homer, *tr. by* William Cowper. *Fr.* The Odyssey, XII. OBVE
Just Think. Paul Celan, *tr. fr. German by* Joachim Neugroschel. VWA
Just This. István Vas, *tr. fr. Hungarian by* Jascha Kessler. VWA
Just this morning I signed the contract. Pearl Harbor Day 1970. Dick Lourie. NeAC
Just three days old. The New Moon. Issa, *tr. by* Harold G. Henderson. MOON
Just to Be Glad. Merlin G. Miller. STF
Just to be tender, just to be true. God's Will for Us [*or* God's Will for You and Me]. *Unknown.* BLRP; SoSe; WBLP
Just Try This. *Unknown. See* Just Keep On Keepin' On.
Just Try to Be the Fellow That Your Mother Thinks You Are. Will S. Adkin. WBLP
Just when each bud was big with bloom. Birth. Grace Raymond. AA
Just when he said the tornado. The Tornado. Norman H. Russell. STE
Just when our drawing-rooms begin to blaze. Winter Evening. William Cowper. *Fr.* The Task. NOEC
Just when you're able to admit. Corps d'Esprit. Heather McHugh. AmPA
Just where the Treasury's marble front. Pan in Wall Street. Edmund Clarence Stedman. AA; HBV-1
Justice. Langston Hughes. BPo
Justice. Petra von Morstein, *tr. fr. German by* Rosemarie Waldrop. BoWoP
Justice Denied in Massachusetts. Edna St. Vincent Millay. GOA; MoAmPo; SBG
Justice Is Reason Enough. Diane Wakoski. AmPA; CoPo
Justice of the Peace, The. Hilaire Belloc. OBSV
Justice to Scotland. *Unknown.* InMe
Justified Mother of Men, The. Walt Whitman. OHIP
Justify all those renowned generations. The Renowned Generations. W. B. Yeats. OxBoLi
Justine, You Love Me Not! John Godfrey Saxe. HBV-1
Justshakeityoucanbreakityoucanhangitonthewall. Hang It on the Wall. *Unknown.* BluL
Justus Quidem Tu Es, Domine. Gerard Manley Hopkins. *See* Thou Art Indeed Just, Lord, If I Contend.
Jutaculla Rock. Robert Morgan. SUW
Jute Mill Song, The. *Unknown.* OBET
Juvenile Court. Sara Henderson Hay. DFT
Juventius, could you not find in this great crowd of men. Catullus, *tr. fr. Latin.* PeHV
Juventius, my honey, while you played. Catullus, *tr. fr. Latin by* James Michie. PeHV
Juxta. Grover Jacoby. GoYe
Juxtaposition. Arthur Hugh Clough. *Fr.* Amours de Voyage. OBNC

K

K. K. K. Disco, The. Noah Mitchell. LFAC
Ka 'Ba. Amiri Baraka. BPo; CAPP; CNA; TAP
Kabbalist, The. Deborah Eibel. VWA
Kabul town's by Kabul river. Ford o' Kabul River. Kipling. FaBoTw
Kacelyevo's slope still felt. The Last Redoubt. Alfred Austin. HBV-2
Kaddish. Allen Ginsberg. VWA
"Strange now to think of you gone without corsets & eyes," *sel.* NeAP; NOBA; PoM
Kaddish. David Ignatow. NU; VWA
Kaddish. Levi Yitzhok, *tr. fr. Yiddish by* Joseph Leftwich. TrJP
Kaddish for Naomi Ginsberg. Allen Ginsberg. *See* Kaddish.
Kadia the Young Mother Speaks. Jessie Sampter. TrJP
Kafka's Other Metamorphosis. Len Gasparini. NeAC
Kafoozalum. *Unknown.* BeLS; BLPA
Kaire. Richard Eberhart. NoAM
Kaiser and Co ("Der Kaiser auf der Vaterland"). Alexander Macgregor Rose. HBV-1
Kaiser Dead. Matthew Arnold. FM
Kakó kakó said grandmother. Red Riding Hood at the Acropolis. Myra Sklarew. DFT
Kalahari. Luis Palés Matos, *tr. fr. Spanish by* Rachel Benson. InW
Kalahari Bushman fires flowing. Firebowl. Sydney Clouts. VWA
Ka-la-kaua, a great name. Praise Song for King Kalakaua. *Tr. fr. Hawaiian by* N. B. Emerson. WTO

Kalaloch. Carolyn Forché. AmPA
Kaleidoscopic memories fall in and out. Memory Movie. Diane Webster. AMV-81
Kallundborg Church. Whittier. BeLS
Kamal is out with twenty men to raise the Border side. The Ballad of East and West. Kipling. FaBoBe
Kamaoktunga . . . I am afraid and I tremble. Manerathiak's Song. *Unknown, tr. by* Raymond De Coccola *and* Paul King. WHW
Kanawâki—"By the Rapid." The Caughnawaga Beadwork Seller. William Douw Lighthall. CaP
Kandinsky: "Improvisation No. 27." Edward Tick. PoDr
Kane. Fitz-James O'Brien. PAH
Kangaroo. D. H. Lawrence. EBEV; InPS; MoVE; OxBTC
Kangaroo, The. Ogden Nash. WhC
Kangaroo, The. *Unknown.* SoPo
Kangaroo by Nightfall ("The kangaroo by the roadside"). Noel Macainsh. PoAu-2
Kangarooster, The. Kenyon Cox. TiPo
Kansas Boy. Ruth Lechlitner. AmFN
Kansas Boys. *Unknown.* AS, *with music;* FSW
Kansas City. Oscar Hammerstein II. OBAL
Kansas City Blues. *Unknown.* FSW
Kansas City West Bottoms. Edward Dahlberg. PoA
Kansas Cowboy, A, *with music. Unknown.* CoSo
Kansas Emigrants, The. Whittier. PAH
Kansas Line, The. *Unknown. See* Cowboy's Life Is a Very Dreary Life, The.
Kanyariri, Village of Toil. The Village. Marina Gashe. PBA
Karamanian Exile, The. James Clarence Mangan. OBVV
Karamazov. Ben Belitt. DiL
Karen can canter, Karen can. Horse-Girl. Henry Petroski. PH
Karl, from your beachhead on that hollow island. V-Letter to Karl Shapiro in Australia. Selden Rodman. WaP
Karl Marx. Al Lee. AmPA
Karl, my friend, caught the crabs. Policy of the House. Charles Stetler. GP
Karma. E. A. Robinson. AmPP; AP; CMoP; CoBMV; HeIP; MoAB; MoAmPo; NoAM; OFD; TrCP
Karolin's Song. Ben Jonson. *Fr.* The Sad Shepherd. LoBV; PoEL-2
(Death and Love.) NOBE
(Song: "Though I am young and cannot tell.") EnRePo; SeCP
(Though I Am Young.) ELP; OAEP
(Though I Am Young and Cannot Tell.) NoP; TEP
Karoo Town. Robert Dederick. PeSA
Karshish and Lazarus. Robert Browning. *See* Epistle Containing the Strange Medical Experience of Karshish, the Arab Physician, An.
Karshish, the Arab Physician ("Karshish, the picker-up of learning's crumbs"). Robert Browning. *See* Epistle Containing the Strange Medical Experience of Karshish, the Arab Physician, An.
Kashmiri Song ("Pale hands I love"). "Laurence Hope." BLPA; BLPL; FaBoBe; FaFP; TreF
Kashrut. Edouard Roditi. VWA
Kasidah, The, *sels.* Sir Richard Francis Burton.
"In these drear wastes of sea-born land, these wilds where none may dwell but He," II. HBV-2
"How then shall man so order life that when his tale of years is told," IX. HBV-2
Kassie Jones. *Unknown.* BluL
"Kat" can play ball, Man, The. Funky Football. Ruby C. Saunders. BlSi
Kate and the Cowhide. *Unknown.* AmFP
Kate Being Pleased. Sir John Davies. POL
(In Katam.) FaBoEE
Kate Dalrymple. *Unknown.* GBP
Kate Kearney. Lady Morgan. BLPA; FaBoBe
Kate meets me at the top of the stairs. At Veronica's. Robert Peterson. NeAC
Kate of Aberdeen. John Cunningham. HBV-1
Kate rose up early as fresh as a lark. Wind's Work. T. Sturge Moore. BrPo; HBMV; HBVY
Kate Temple's Song. Mortimer Collins. HBV-1
Kathaleen Ny-Houlahan. *Unknown, tr. fr. Irish by* James Clarence Mangan. VLP
(Kathleen-Ni-Houlahan.) AnIV
Katharine. Heine, *tr. fr. German by* Louis Untermeyer. UnTE
Katharine Jaffray. *Unknown.* BaBo; ESPB (A, B, *and* C *vers.*); OxBB; ViBoFo (A *and* B *vers.*)
(Katherine Jaffray.) OxBB
Käthe Kollwitz. Muriel Rukeyser. NMM
Katherine is warm. Why? Melba Joyce Boyd. BlSi
Katherine Milton: Died MDCLVIII. Milton. *See* On His Deceased Wife.
Katherine's Dream. Robert Lowell. *Fr.* Between the Porch and the Altar. ConAP
Kathleen Mavourneen. Louisa Macartney Crawford, *sometimes at. to* Julia Crawford. FaBoBe; FSW; HBV-1; TreF
Kathleen-Ni-Houlahan. *Unknown. See* Kathaleen Ny-Houlahan.
Kathleen ni Houlihan. The Celtic Fringe. Stevie Smith. FaBoNo
Katie Lee and Willie Grey. *Unknown, at. to* Josie R. Hunt *and to* J. H. Pixley. BeLS; BLPA
Katie May. *Unknown.* BluL
Katy Cline. *Unknown.* FSW
Katy Cruel. *Unknown.* FSW
Katy Dorey. *Unknown. See* Kitty Morey.
Katydids. Amy Lowell. PBWP
Katzenjammer Kids, The. James Reaney. MoCV; OBCV; PeCV
Kavanagh, The. Richard Hovey. HBV-2
Kayak, The. *Unknown.* FaPON
Kearney Park. Gary Soto. NPGG
Kearny at Seven Pines. Edmund Clarence Stedman. AA; HBV-2; HBVY; PAH
Kearsarge. S. Weir Mitchell. PAH
Kearsarge, The. James Jeffrey Roche. AA; PAH
Kearsarge and *Alabama. Unknown.* PAH
Keats. Longfellow. AP; TAP
Keats. William Wilberforce Lord. *Fr.* Ode to England. AA
Keats. Lizette Woodworth Reese. AA
Keats to Fanny Brawne. Edgar Lee Masters. PoA
Keel Row, The. *Unknown.* PoPle
Keelhauled across the star-wrecked death of God. George Barker. *Fr.* Sonnets of the Triple-headed Manichee. PoA
Keen. Edna St. Vincent Millay. HBMV
Keen blaws the wind o'er the Braes o' Gleniffer. The Braes o' Gleniffer. Robert Tannahill. OBRV
Keen, Fitful Gusts [Are Whispering Here and There]. Keats. CABA; EnRP; OAEP; PoEL-4; TEP
(Sonnet.) PoEL-4
Keen stars were twinkling, The. To Jane. Shelley. NoP
Keen Thyself, Poor Wight. Geoffrey Keating, *tr. fr. Late Middle Irish by* Padraic Pearse. OnYI
Keen winds of cloud and vaporous drift. Nocturne. Richard Garnett. OBVV
Keenan's Charge. George Parsons Lathrop. AA; HBV-2; PAH
Keener tempests come, The: and, fuming dun. Winter. James Thomson. *Fr.* The Seasons. EBEV; EnRP; NoP; ViBoPo
Keening of Mary, The. *Unknown, tr. fr. Gaelic by* Padraic Pearse. ISi
Keep a brave spirit, and never despair. Press Onward. *Unknown.* FaFP
Keep a Good Tongue in Your Head. Martin Parker. CoMu
Keep a Hand on Your Dream. X. J. Kennedy. Psk
Keep a Poem in Your Pocket. Beatrice Schenk de Regniers. PDV; RHPC; SoPo
Keep a Stiff Upper Lip. Phoebe Cary. FaFP
Keep a-Goin'. Frank L. Stanton. FaFP; OHFP; WBLP
Keep a-Inchin' Along, *with music. Unknown.* BoAN-1
Keep away from roads' webs, they always lead. Directions to a Rebel. W. R. Rodgers. LiTM
Keep back the one word more. Reserve. Lizette Woodworth Reese. AA
Keep bees and. Advice to the Young. Miriam Waddington. NOBC
Keep fresh the grass upon his grave. Wordsworth's Grave. Matthew Arnold. *Fr.* Memorial Verses. FaBoPP
Keep Hidden from Me ("Keep from me all that I might comprehend!"). Rachel Korn, *tr. fr. Yiddish by* Carolyn Kizer. PBWP
Keep in God's way; keep pace with evry hour. To Be Engraven on a Dial. Samuel Sewall. SCAP
Keep in the Heart the Journal Nature Keeps. Conrad Aiken. Preludes for Memnon, XLII. CMoP; NePA; OxBA
Keep It Clean. *Unknown.* BluL
Keep It Dark. *Unknown, tr. fr. Zezuru by* Hugh Tracey. PBA
Keep love a-boiling; keep soup in the pot. Recipe. *Unknown, tr. by* Louis Untermeyer. UnTE
Keep Love in Your Life. Thomas Curtis Clark. WBLP
Keep me as your servant, O Girdhar. Mirabai, *tr. fr. Medieval Hindi by* Usha Nilsson. PBWP
Keep me clean. Chamber-Pot Rhyme. *Unknown.* GBP
Keep Me f'om Sinkin' Down, *with music. Unknown.* BoAN-1
Keep me from bitterness. It is so easy. Prayer in Affliction. Violet Alleyn Storey. TrPWD
Keep me from fretting, Lord, today. Prayer. May Carleton Lord. PGD
Keep me, I pray, in wisdom's way. The Bibliomaniac's Prayer. Eugene Field. AA
Keep Me, Jesus, Keep Me. Waverly Turner Carmichael. BANP
Keep Me Still, for I Do Not Want to Dream. Larry Eigner. NeAP
Keep My Skillet Good and Greasy. *Unknown.* FSW
Keep Not Thou Silence. Bible, *O.T.* Psalms, LXXXIII. TrJP
Keep On Praying. Roger H. Lyon. BLRP
Keep On Pushing. David Henderson. PoBA

Keep silence, all created things. God's Dominion and Decrees. Isaac Watts. OBEC
Keep Smiling. *Unknown.* WBLP
Keep Sweet. A. B. Simpson. STF
Keep Talking. Philip Levine. WeW
Keep the commandments, Trapp, and go no further. Abel Evans. FaBoEE
Keep the dream alive and growing always. Song (2). Edwin Rolfe. TrJP
Keep the Glad Flag Flying. *Unknown.* FaFP
Keep the Sea. *Unknown. Fr.* The Libelle of Englyshe Polycye. OxBM
Keep this little light, O Father. A Birthday Prayer. John Finley. TrPWD
Keep Thou My Way, O Lord. Fanny Crosby. TrPWD
Keep thy tunge, thy tunge, thy tunge. Wicked Tongues. *Unknown.* OxBM
Keep to yourself your kisses. Taisigh Agat Fein Do Phog. *Unknown, tr. by* Maire Cruise O'Brien. BIrV
Keep up appearances; there lies the test. Charles Churchill. *Fr.* Night; an Epistle to Robert Lloyd. DBV
Keep Ye Holy Sabbath Rest. *Unknown, tr. fr. Hebrew by* Herbert Loewe. TrJP
Keep you these calm and lovely things. To the Liffey with the Swans. Oliver St. John Gogarty. AnIL; OxBI
Keep your back door locked baby, keep your windows pinned. Keep Your Windows Pinned. *Unknown.* BluL
Keep your copper coin, save your cup of wheat. Never Ask Me Why. Silvia Margolis. GoYe
Keep your distance, Stranger Death, and call. Unwelcome. Irma Dovey. AMV-80
Keep Your Eyes on the Prize. *Unknown. See* All Night Long.
Keep your eyes open when you kiss: do: when. John Berryman. BoLoP
Keep Your Grit. *Unknown.* STF
Keep Your Hands on That Plow, *with music. Unknown.* OuSiCo
Keep Your Lamp Trimmed and Burning. *Unknown.* FSW
Keep your whiskers crisp and clean. The King of Cats Sends a Postcard to His Wife. Nancy Willard. OBCA
Keep Your Windows Pinned. *Unknown.* BluL
Keeper, The. William Carpenter. Psk
Keeper, The. ("The keeper did a hunting go") *Unknown.* FSW
Keeper of the Midnight Gate, The. George Mackay Brown. OxBC
Keeping Christmas. Eleanor Farjeon. OBCP
Keeping Hair. Ramona Wilson. VoR
Keeping On. Arthur Hugh Clough. *See* Say Not the Struggle Nought Availeth.
Keeping Their World Large. Marianne Moore. WaP
Keeping Things Whole. Mark Strand. CoAP; HeIP; LCAP; NoAM; PPP; TAP
Keeping Victory. Walter E. Isenhour. STF
Keeping You Alive. Tess Gallagher. GP
Keepsake Corporation, The. David Fisher. NPGG
Keepsake from Quinault. Dorothy Alyea. GoYe
Kehama's Curse. Robert Southey. *Fr.* The Curse of Kehama. OBNC ("I charm thy life.") LoBV; OBRV
Keith of Ravelston. Sydney Dobell. *Fr.* A Nuptial Eve. CH
Kelly. Robert Hershon. NeAC
Kellyburnbraes, *with music. Unknown.* OxBB
Kelly's kept an unlicensed bull, well away. The Outlaw. Seamus Heaney. NoAM; OxBC
Kelp. Nora Dauenhauer. TWSS
Kelpius's Hymn. Arthur Peterson. AA
Kemp Owyne. *Unknown.* EnSB; ESPB (A *and* B *vers.*); SeCeV; ViBoFo (Kempion, *with music.*) OxBB
Ken when to spend and when to spare. *Unknown.* FaBoUs
Kennedy. Michael Heffernan. AMV-80
Kennedy Airport. Aaron Kramer. AMV-80
Kennedys are dead, The. Wasp. William Welsh. SOTS
Keno. Dara Wier. MAYP
Kensington Garden, *sel.* Thomas Tickell.
Fairies. OBEC
Kensington Gardens. Viviane Verne. SUMH
Kenst doo hoo. The Miller's Wife's Lullaby. *Unknown.* GBP
Kent State Massacre, The. Jack Warshaw *and* Barbara Dane. FSW
Kent State, May 4, 1970. Paul Goodman. MAT
Kentish hamlets gray and old. The Memory of Kent. Edmund Blunden. HBMV
Kentish Sir Byng stood for his King. Marching Along. Robert Browning. Cavalier Tunes, I. HBV-2; OAEP
Kenton and Deborah, Michael and Rose. Ambition. Aline Kilmer. HBMV
Kentucky Babe. Richard Henry Buck. AA; FSN, *with music;* HBV-1
Kentucky Belle. Constance Fenimore Woolson. BeLS; BLPA; FaBoBe; PAH; PH
Kentucky Birthday; February 12, 1815. Frances Frost. SiSoSe; YeAr
Kentucky Blues. *Unknown.* BluL
Kentucky Bootlegger. *Unknown.* FSW
Kentucky Moonshiner. *Unknown.* AS, *with music;* OBAL; TrAS, *with music* (Moonshiner.) FSW
Kentucky Mountain Farm, *sels.* Robert Penn Warren.
Cardinal, The. MoVE
History among the Rocks. GOA; MoAmPo; MoVE
Kentucky Philosophy. Harrison Robertson. HBV-2
Kentucky Thoroughbred, The. James Whitcomb Riley. ELU
Kentucky water, clear springs: a boy fleeing. The Swimmers. Allen Tate. AP; InPS; MoAmPo; MoVE; NOBA
Kepe well x, and flee fro vii. Ten Commandments, Seven Deadly Sins, and Five Wits. *Unknown.* ChTr; FaBoEE
Kéramos, *sel.* Longfellow.
Potter's Song, The. PoEL-5
Keraunograph. Hayden Carruth. NMP
Kerchoo! Margaret Fishback. PoSC
Kerry Dance, The. James Lyman Molloy. OnYI
Kerry Lads, The. Theodosia Garrison. HBMV
Kerry Recruit, The. *Unknown.* FSW
Kettle descants in a cosy drone, The. Satires of Circumstance. Thomas Hardy. BrPo
Kettle sang the boy to a half-sleep, The. Halibut Cove Harvest. Kenneth Leslie. CaP; NOBC
Kevin Barry. Terence Ward. OnYI
Kevin Barry [Died for Ireland, 1st November, 1920]. *Unknown.* AS, *with music;* FaBoBa; FSW
Key to Everything, The. May Swenson. IHMS; NePoEA
Key West. Hart Crane. CMoP
Key-Board, The. Sir William Watson. HBV-2
Keyhole in the Door, The. *Unknown.* CoMu
Keys. Glen Rockwell. AMV-81
Keys of Canterbury, The. *Unknown.* AmFP
Keys of Morning, The. Walter de la Mare. MoVE; NoP
Keys of the Jail, The, *with music. Unknown.* OuSiCo
Keys turning. The Liberator. Emily Holmes Coleman. EAS
Keziah. Gwendolyn Brooks. RHPC
Khamsin. Clinton Scollard. AA
Khristna and His Flute. "Laurence Hope." HBV-1
Khrushchev is coming on the right day! Poem. Frank O'Hara. NeAP; PoM
Kibbutz Sabbath. Levi Ben Amittai, *tr. fr. Hebrew by* Simon Halkin. EaLo
Kick a Little Stone. Dorothy Aldis. SoPo
Kick at the rock, Sam Johnson, break your bones. Epistemology. Richard Wilbur. NePoEA; NoAM; NOBA; SUW
Kicking from Centre Field. David McFadden. NeAC
Kicking his mother until she let go of his soul. Mundus et Infans. W. H. Auden. LiTB; LiTM; MoAB; MoBrPo; NAs
Kicking Mule, The. *Unknown.* AmFP
Kicking the Leaves, *sel.* Donald Hall.
"Kicking the leaves today, as we walk home together." GLGT
Kid, The. Ai. GeTw
Kid, The, *sels.* Conrad Aiken.
Awakening, The. MoVE
Proem. MoAB
Kid. Robert Hayden. CAD; NCSH
Kid Has Gone to the Colors, The. W. M. Herschell. PoLF
Kid in Upper 4, The. Nelson C. Metcalf. TreFS
Kid March had the stuff but his style was hard. The Up-Set. Corey Ford. WhC
Kid Stuff. Frank Horne. AmNP; PChr; PoBA; PoNe
Kidded in April above Glencolumbkille. Care. Richard Murphy. IPY
Kiddy cars of little tikes. Transportation Problem. Richard Armour. WhC
Kidnap Poem. Nikki Giovanni. AmNP; BPo; InPK; NoAM; TAP
Kidnaper. Tess Gallagher. AmPA
Kidnapping of Sims, The. John Pierpont. PAH
Kids are asleep, The. It's a Different Story When You're Going into the Wind. David McFadden. NeAC
Kid's Last Fight, The. *Unknown.* TreF
Kid's packed the last five months, The. Fish. Michael Hogan. GP
Kids want to grow up, The. Last Things. Bill Manhire. OCNZ
Kierkegaard, a/ cripple and a Dane. John Updike. *Fr.* Die Neuen Heiligen. DBV
Kilbarchan now may say alas! The Life and Death of [Habbie Simson] the Piper of Kilbarchan. Robert Sempill. OBS; OxBS
Kilcash. *Unknown, tr. fr. Irish by* Frank O'Connor. BIrV; KiLC; OBMV; OxBI
Kilkenny Boy, The. Eileen Shanahan. NeIP
Kilkenny Cats, The. *Unknown.* FaFP; ShM; TreF (Limerick: "There once were two cats of Kilkenny.") CenHV
Kill a robin or a wren. *Unknown.* PBBP
Kill me not every day. Affliction. George Herbert. TEP
Kill or be killed, the sergeant cried. The Killer Too. Walker Gibson. FF

Kill yourselves with knives and poisoned gas. Strangers Are We All upon the Earth. Franz Werfel, *tr. by* Edith Abercrombie Snow. TrJP
Killarney. Edward Falconer. TreFS
Killarney. Charles Kingsley. WhC
Killarney. William Larminie. AnIV
Killed at the Ford. Longfellow. AP; OHIP
Killed by an omnibus—why not? On a Man Run Over by an Omnibus. Henry Luttrell. FaBoEE
Killed in Action. Terence Tiller. NeBP
Killer, The. *Unknown.* CoSo
Killer Diller. *Unknown.* BluL
Killer Too, The. Walker Gibson. FF
Killers. Carl Sandburg. MoVE
Killers That Run, The. Leonard Cohen. NOBC
Killigrew Wood, The. Norman Dubie. AmPA
Killing. Samuel Greenberg. LiTA
Killing, The. George MacBeth. FaBoMo
Killing, The. Edwin Muir. ChMP; PoPl
Killing a Whale. David Gill. BoAnP
Killing No Murder. Sylvia Townsend Warner. MoBrPo
Killing of the Birds, The. Shirley Williams. BoWoP
Killing Rabbits. Ed Ochester. LTB
Killing the Rooster. Sheryl L. Nelms. Str
Killyburn Brae. *Unknown.* OnYI
Kilmeny. James Hogg. *Fr.* The Queen's Wake. HBV-2; OBEV; OBRV
(Bonny Kilmeny Gaed Up the Glen.) BSV; GoTS
Kilroy. Eugene McCarthy. NIP
Kilroy. Peter Viereck. FF; MoAmPo; NIP
(Kilroy Was Here.) PoRA
Kilroy is gone. Kilroy. Eugene McCarthy. NIP
Kilroy Was Here. Peter Viereck *See* Kilroy.
Kilruddery Hunt, The. Thomas Mozeen. BIrV
Kimono. Jorie Graham. MAYP
Kin. Michael Harper. LCAP
Kin: quiet grasses. Deborah as Scion. James Dickey. SV
Kinchinjunga. Cale Young Rice. HBV-1
Kincora. *Unknown, tr. fr. Middle Irish by* James Clarence Mangan. AnIV; OnYI; OxBI
(Lamentation of Mac Liag for Kincora, The.) AnIL
Kind. A. R. Ammons. NoP; PrIm
Kind Are Her Answers. Thomas Campion. BoLoP; ELP; HBV-1; OBSC; SeCeV; TrGrPo
(Kinde Are Her Answeres.) FaBoEn; PoEL-2
Kind Armadillo, The. Oliver Herford. TDH
Kind country-men listen I pray. All Things Be Dear but Poor Mens Labour; or, The Sad Complaint of Poor People. *Unknown.* CoMu
Kind friends, if you will listen, a story I will tell. Brown-eyed Lee. *Unknown.* CoSo
Kind friends, you must pity my horrible tale [*or* won't you listen to my pitiful tale]. The Dreary Black Hills. *Unknown.* AmFP; CoSo; FSW
Kind gentlemen, will you be patient awhile? Robin Hood's Birth, Breeding, Valor, and Marriage. *Unknown.* ESPB
Kind Hearts. *Unknown.* HBV-1
Kind Heaven, assist the trembling muse. The Wyoming Massacre. Uriah Terry. PAH
Kind Inn, A. George Dillon. GoYe
Kind Keeper, The, *sel.* Dryden.
Song from the Italian, A. SeCV-2
Kind kinderpark. Bears and Waterfalls. May Sarton. GP
Kind Lovers, Love On. John Crowne. InvP
Kind Miss, *with music.* *Unknown.* AS
Kind o'er the kinderbank leans Myfanwy. Myfanwy. John Betjeman. BoLoP
Kind of Act Of, The. Robert Creeley. NeAP
Kind of an Ode to Duty. Ogden Nash. TrGrPo; WhC
Kind of change came in my fate, A. Byron. *Fr.* The Prisoner of Chillon. NOBE
Kind of empty in the way it sees everythng, the earth gets to its feet. For John Clare. John Ashbery. FYAP
Kind of Poetry I Want, The, *sels.* "Hugh MacDiarmid." InPS
"And, constantly, I seek/ A poetry of facts."
"Poetry of one the Russians call 'a broad nature,' The."
Kind of rose she wants called John F. Kennedy, The. Fourth Ode to Persephone. Robert Kelly. The Book of Persephone, 16. PoM
Kind old face, the egg-shapped head, The. On a Portrait of a Deaf Man. John Betjeman. NoAM
Kind pity [*or* Kinde pitty] chokes my spleen[e]; brave scorn forbids. Satire III [*or* Religion *or* Satyre: Of Religion *or* Satyre III *or* Satyre III: On Religion *or* Truth.) John Donne. *Fr.* Satires. AnAnS-1; CABA; EBEV; JCP; MeLP; MePo; NoP; OAEL-1; OBS; PoEL-2; SeCePo; SeCP; SeCV-1
Kind Robin Lo'es Me. *Unknown.* BSV
Kind Sir: These Woods. Anne Sexton. GoYe; TwAmPo
Kind solace in a dying hour! Tamerlane. Poe. AP
Kind Words Can Never Die, *with music.* Abby Hutchinson. AH
Kinde Are Her Answeres. Thomas Campion. *See* Kind Are Her Answers.
Kindergarten. Dennis Schmitz. NPGG
Kindergarten children first come forth, The. The May Day Dancing. Howard Nemerov. NoAM; NYBP
Kindertotenlieder. Michael Longley. CIP
Kindle the Christmas brand and then. The Ceremonies for Candlemas Day. Robert Herrick. OAEP
Kindle the Taper, *with music.* Emma Lazarus. AH
Kindler of glory's embers. In Praise of Aed. *Unknown, tr. by* Robin Flower. AnIL
Kindliest thing God ever made, The. Shade. Theodosia Garrison. OHIP
Kindly I envy thy songs perfection. To Mr. R. W. John Donne. AnAnS-1
Kindly Unhitch That Star, Buddy. Ogden Nash. LiTA; PoPl
Kindly Vision. Otto Julius Bierbaum, *tr. fr. German by* Jethro Bithell. AWP
Kindly watcher by my bed, lift no voice in prayer. Music. George Du Maurier. OBEV; OBVV
Kindness. Catherine Davis. NYBP
Kindness. T. Sturge Moore. OBMV
Kindness. *Unknown.* STF
Kindness during Life. *Unknown.* STF
Kindness to Animals. J. Ashby-Sterry. InMe; NA
Kindness to Animals. Laura E. Richards. NTCP; TiPo
Kindness to Animals. *Unknown.* FaBoUs; HBV-1; HBVY; SoPo
Kinds of Shel-Fish. William Wood. SCAP
Kinds of Trees to Plant. Spenser. *Fr.* The Faerie Queene, I, i. OHIP
Kine of My Father, The. Dora Sigerson Shorter. OnYI; OxBI
Kineo Mountain. Celeste Turner Wright. Psk
Kinfauns Castle, *sel.* William Montgomerie.
"Is there no vision in a lovely place?" OxBS
King, The. Mary Elizabeth Coleridge. OBVV
King, The. Kipling. CABA; VLP
King, The. Douglas Livingstone. BoAnP
King, The. *Unknown.* TDH
King, a pope, and a kaiser, A. The Ship. Charles Mackay. BLPA
King Alexander led the van. Allegro. "McM." InMe
King Alfred Answers the Danes. G. K. Chesterton. *Fr.* Ballad of the White Horse. OxBoCh
King Alfred sensed among his country's words. Anglo-Saxon. E. L. Mayo. MiAP
King and I are more than satisfied, The. The Marriage. Sara Henderson Hay. DFT
King and Queen of Cantelon. Babylon. *Unknown.* ChTr
King and Queen of the Pelicans we. The Pelican Chorus. Edward Lear. FaBoNo; PB
King and the Queen were riding, The. The Naughty Blackbird. Kate Greenaway. HBVY
King Arthur, *sels.* Dryden.
How Happy the Lover. LoBV; ViBoPo
Song: "Your hay it is mow'd, and your corn is reap'd." SeCV-2
(Harvest Home.) PrIm
Song of Venus. LoBV; OxBoLi; PoEL-3; SeCeV
King Arthur, *sel.* Richard Hovey.
Hunting-Song. HBV-1
King Arthur and His Round Table, *sel.* John Hookham Frere.
Bees and Monks. OBRV
King Arthur and King Cornwall. *Unknown.* ESPB
King Arthur, growing very tired indeed. Salad—After Tennyson. Mortimer Collins. CenHV; FaBoCo; Par
King Arthur's Death. *Unknown.* ACP
King Arthur's Waes-hael. Robert Stephen Hawker. ISi; OBEV; OBVV; OxBoCh
King asked, The. The King's Breakfast. A. A. Milne. CenHV; OxBChV
King Berdok. *Unknown.* OxBS
King Billy. Edwin Morgan. BSV
King but an' his nobles a', The. Brown Robin. *Unknown.* ESPB; OxBB
King Cahal Mor of the Wine-red Hand. James Clarence Mangan. AnIV; GoBC
(Vision of Connaught in the Thirteenth Century, A.) AnIL
King can move a single square, The. The Powers of the Pawn. David Solway. AMV-81
King Canute. Stanley J. Sharpless. BXAP
King Charles, and who'll do him right now? Give a Rouse. Robert Browning. Cavalier Tunes, II. HBV-2; OAEP
King Charles he is King James's son. The White Cockade. *Unknown, tr. by* James Joseph Callanan. OnYI
King Charles on [*or* upon] the Scaffold. Andrew Marvell. *Fr.* An Horatian Ode upon Cromwell's Return from Ireland. ChTr; FaBoRV
King Charles II. Earl of Rochester. *See* Epitaph on Charles II.

King Charles the First. *Unknown.* GBP
("As I was going by Charing Cross.") CH; FaBoCh; OxNR
King Charles the First walked and talked. *Unknown.* OxNR
King Charles upon the Scaffold. Andrew Marvell. *See* King Charles on the Scaffold.
King Christian. Johannes Evald, *tr. fr. Danish by* Longfellow. AWP
King Cophetua and the Beggar Maid. Don Marquis. HBMV; InMe
King Croesus carried to Apollo's sibyl. Oracle at Delphi. Robert Bagg. NePoAm-2
King David. Stephen Vincent Benét. HBMV
King David and King Solomon. James Ball Naylor. CenHV
(David and Solomon.) PoPle
King David Dances. John Berryman. OxBC
King Easter has courted her for her gowd. Fause [*or* Fa'se] Foodrage [*or* Footrage]. *Unknown.* ESPB; OxBB
King Edward the Fourth and a Tanner of Tamworth. *Unknown.* BaBo; ESPB
King Edward the Third, *sel.* Blake.
War Song to Englishmen, A. CH; WaaP
(War Song, A.) OHIP
King Enjoys His Own Again, The. Martin Parker. OBS
King Estmere. *Unknown.* ESPB; OBNV; OxBB
King Ethelred the Unready. Bill Greenwell. BXAP
King Fisher courted Lady Bird. The King-Fisher Song. "Lewis Carroll." *Fr.* Sylvie and Bruno Concluded. FaBoNo
King Francis was a hearty king, and loved a royal sport. The Glove and the Lions. Leigh Hunt. BeLS; FaPON; GN; HBV-1; HBVY; TreF; WBLP
King George [*or* The King], observing with judicious eyes. Epigram. Joseph Trapp. FaBoCo; FaBoEE
King Goodheart. W. S. Gilbert. *See* There Lived a King.
King had dropped his crown, A. Out of Whack. Russell Edson. LCAP
King Hancock sat in regal state. A Song about Charleston. *Unknown.* PAH
King Harald's Trance. George Meredith. VLP
King Hart, *sel.* Gavin Douglas.
Hart's Castle. PoEL-1
King has written a braid letter, The. Lord Derwentwater. *Unknown.* ESPB
King he hath been a prisoner, The. Willie o Winsbury. *Unknown.* ESPB
King he sits in Dumferling town, The. *See* King sits in Dunfermline town, The.
King he wrote a love-letter, The. Lord Derwentwater. *Unknown.* AmFP
King Henry. *Unknown.* ESPB; OxBB, *with music*
King Henry IV, Pt. I, *sel.* Shakespeare.
At My Nativity, *fr.* III, i. NAs
King Henry IV, Pt. II, *sels.* Shakespeare.
Cares of Majesty, The, *fr.* III, i. LiTB; TreF
(O Gentle Sleep.) TaBoRV
(Soliloquy on Sleep.) FiP
"My liege, I did deny no prisoners," *fr.* I, iii. WaaP
"O my worshipful lord, an't please your grace," *fr.* II, i. LO
"Wilt thou upon the high and giddy mast," *fr.* III, i. MOS
King Henry V, *sels.* Shakespeare.
Before Agincourt, *fr. Prologue to* IV. ChTr; FaBoRV
("Now entertain conjecture of a time.") EBEV; WaaP
"Boy, bristle thy courage up; for Falstaff he is dead," *fr.* II, iii. LO
(Commonwealth of the Bees, The.) GN
Epilogue: "Thus far, with rough and all-unable pen." CTC
Henry V before Agincourt, *fr.* IV, iii. FaPoR
(St. Crispin's Day.) FF
"I will not change my horse with any that treads," *fr.* III, vi. PH
"Marry, if you would put me to verses or to dance," *fr.* V, ii. LO
"O for a Muse of fire, that would ascend," *fr. Prologue to* I. SCV
(Muse of Fire, A, 2 *ll.*) ChTr
"Once more unto the breach, dear friends, once more," *fr.* III, i. FaBV; PPoe; WaaP
(Blast of War, The.) TrGrPo
(Henry V at Harfleur.) TreF
(Henry Fifth's Address to His Soldiers.) WHA
"Suppose that you have seen," *fr. Prologue to* III. MOS
"Thus with imagin'd wing our swift scene flies," *fr. Prologue to* III. EBEV
Upon the King, *fr.* IV, i. PPON
"We few, we happy few, we band of brothers," *fr.* IV, iii. UnPo
King Henry Fifth's Conquest of France. *Unknown.* ESPB
(Henry V's Conquest of France.) OBET
King Henry VI, Pt. I, *sel.* Shakespeare.
King Is Dead, A, *fr.* I, i. ChTr
King Henry VI, Pt. III, *sels.* Shakespeare.
King Henry VI Yearns for the Simple Life, *fr.* II, v. TreFS
"Now sways it this way, like a mighty sea," *fr.* II, v. MOS
King Henry VIII, *sels.* Shakespeare *and probably* John Fletcher.
Ambition, *fr.* III, ii. TrGrPo
Cranmer's Prophecy of Queen Elizabeth, *fr.* V, v. WGRP
For a Patriot, 3*ll.*, *fr.* III, ii. PGD
Orpheus with His Lute [Made Trees], *fr.* III, i. ChTr; EnRePo; GN; OAEP; OBS; TrGrPo
(Music.) FaBoCh
(Orpheus.) ElL; OBEV; UnS
(Song.) PoEL-2
(Sweet Music's Power.) NOBE
This Royal Infant, *fr.* V, iv. NAs
Wolsey's Farewell to His Greatness, *fr.* III, ii. OHFP
(Cardinal Wolsey's Farewell.) LiTB; TreF
(Farewell to Greatness.) TrGrPo
(Wolsey.) FaBoRV
Wolsey's Regrets, *fr.* III, ii. TreFS
King Henry to Rosamond. Michael Drayton. *Fr.* England's Heroical Epistles. OBSC
(Henry to Rosamond.) AnAnS-2
King I saw who walked a cloth of gold, The. Cloth of Gold. Francis Reginald. MoCV
King I Sit. *Unknown.* OxBM
King in May, The. Michael Dennis Browne. NYBP
King Is Dead, A. Shakespeare. King Henry VI, Pt. I, *fr.* I, i. ChTr
"King is gone, The," the old man said. The Deserted Kingdom. Lord Dunsany. AnIV
King James and Brown. *Unknown.* ESPB
King James II. Dryden. *Fr.* The Hind and the Panther. ACP
King Jamie hath made a vow. Flodden Field. *Unknown.* ESPB
King John, *sels.* Shakespeare.
"Death, death; O amiable lovely death!" *fr.* III, iv. TreFT
To Gild Refinèd Gold, *fr.* IV, ii. LiTB
(Ridiculous Excess, *sl. longer sel.*) TreFT
King John and the Abbot of Canterbury. *Unknown.* GN; HBV-2; TrGrPo
(King John and the Abbot.) EnSB
(King John and the Bishop.) ESPB (A *and* B *vers.*)
King John's Castle. Thomas Kinsella. OxBI
King Lear, *sels.* Shakespeare.
Blow, Winds, *fr.* III, ii. TrGrPo; WHA
(King Lear to the Storm.) TreFT
"Cod-piece that will house, The," *fr.* III, ii. ViBoPo
Death of Lear, *fr.* V, iii. FiP
Dover, the Samphire Cliff, *fr.* IV, vi. FaBoPP
"Get thee glass eyes," *fr.* IV, vi. DBV
"He that has and a little tiny wit," *fr.* III, ii. ViBoPo
"He wakes; speak to him," *fr.* IV, vii. SCV
"How does my royal lord? How fares your Majesty?" *fr.* IV, vii. Prf
King Lear Condemns His Daughter, *fr.* I, iv. TreFT
King Lear Pledges Revenge, *fr.* II, iv. TreFT
Lear and Cordelia, *fr.* V, iii. FiP
Lear's Curse on Goneril, *fr.* I, iv. TW
Lear's Speech to the Storm, *fr.* III, ii. TW
"Please you, draw near.—Louder the music there!" *fr.* IV, vii. EBEV
Poor Naked Wretches, *fr.* III, iii. PPON
Take Physic, Pomp, *fr.* III, iv. TrGrPo
"This is the foul fiend Flibbertigibbet: he begins at," *fr.* III, iii. WSC
"We are not the first," *fr.* V, iii. PoPle
"When priests are more in word than matter," *fr.* III, ii. ViBoPo
King Lives. Jill Witherspoon Boyer. CNA
King Louis on his bridge is he. Le Père Sévère. *Unknown, tr. by* Andrew Lang. AWP
King luikit owre his castle wa', The. Sir Colin. *Unknown.* OxBB
King Midas. Howard Moss. CoAP; TAP
(King's Speech, The.) PoA
King Midas. Ovid, *tr. fr. Latin by* Arthur Golding. *Fr.* Metamorphoses, XI. CTC
King Midas Has Asses' Ears. Donald Finkel. NePoEA-2
King might miss the guiding star, A. Far Trumpets Blowing. Louis F. Benson. TRV
King must rule kingdom. Cities are seen from afar. Maxims (Cotton MS.). *Unknown, tr. by* Charles W. Kennedy. AnOE
King o' Spain's Daughter, The. Jeanne Robert Foster. HBMV
King, observing with judicious eyes, The. *See* King George, observing with judicious eyes.
King of Ai, The. Hyam Plutzik. LiTM; VWA
King of Brentford, The. Thackeray, *after* Béranger. HBV-1
King of Brentford's Testament, The, *abr.* Thackeray, *after* Béranger. OBNV
King of Canoodle-Dum, The. W. S. Gilbert. CenHV
King of Cats Sends a Postcard to His Wife, The. Nancy Willard. OBCA
King of China's Daughter, The. Edith Sitwell. FaBoMo; MoBrPo
(Two Nut Trees, 2.) CH

(Variations on an Old Nursery Rhyme) HBMV
King of comforts! King of life! Praise. Henry Vaughan. AnAnS-1
King of Connacht, The. *Unknown, tr. fr. Irish by* Frank O'Connor. KiLC
King of Cuckooz, The. Kenneth Slessor. *Fr.* The Atlas. PoAu-2
King of Denmark's Ride, The. Caroline Elizabeth Norton. BeLS; GN; HBV-1
King of Dreams, The. Clinton Scollard. HBV-2
King of France, the king of France, The/ with forty thousand men. Mother Goose. OxNR
King of glorie, king of peace,/ With the one make warre to cease. L'Envoy. George Herbert. AnAnS-1
King of glorie, king of peace,/ I will love thee. Praise. George Herbert. AnAnS-1
King of Glory sends his Son, The. Miracles at the Birth of Christ. Isaac Watts. NOCV
King of Harlem, The. Federico García Lorca, *tr. fr. Spanish by* Ben Belitt. NYP
King of Ireland's Cairn, The, *abr.* "Ethna Carbery." WPE
King of Ireland's Son, The. Nora Hopper. AnIL
King of Mercy, King of Love. Begging. Henry Vaughan. AnAnS-1
King of rock 'n roll, The. Painkillers. Thom Gunn. AMV-81
King of stars. The Open Door. *Unknown, tr. by* Frank O'Connor. KiLC
King of Sunshine, The. Michael Silverton. PV
King of the Belgians. Marion Couthouy Smith. PAH
King of the Cradle, The. Joseph Ashby-Sterry. HBV-1
King of the Hobbledygoblins, The. Laura E. Richards. OBCA
King of the perennial holly-groves, the riven sandstone. Geoffrey Hill. Mercian Hymns, I. FaBoMo; HAP
King of Thulé, The. Goethe, *tr. fr. German by* James Clarence Mangan. AWP
King of Ulster, The. *Unknown, tr. fr. Irish by* Frank O'Connor. KiLC
King of waters, the sea shouldering whale, The. William Wood. SCAP
King of Yellow Butterflies, The. Vachel Lindsay. OBCA
King of Yvetot, The. Pierre Jean de Béranger, *tr. fr. French by* William Toynbee. AWP
King Oliver of New Orleans. Satchmo. Melvin B. Tolson. BPo
King, on assuming his reign, A. The King. *Unknown.* TDH
King on the Tower, The. Ludwig Uhland, *tr. fr. German by* Thackeray. OBVV
King Orfeo. *Unknown.* ESPB; OxBB, *with music;* OxBoLi
King Paladin plunged on his moon-coloured mare. Mad Marjory. Hugh McCrae. PoAu-1
King Pellam's Launde. David Jones. In Parenthesis, IV. NoAM; OAEL-2
King Philip had vaunted his claims. A Ballad to Queen Elizabeth [*or* A Ballade of the Armada]. Austin Dobson. FaPoR; OBVV
King Philip's Last Stand. Clinton Scollard. PAH
King Richard hearing of the pranks. The King's Disguise, and Friendship with Robin Hood. *Unknown.* ESPB
King Richard II, *sels.* Shakespeare.
"And nothing can we call our own but death," *fr.* III, ii. DL
Death of Kings, The, *fr.* III, ii. TrGrPo
("For God's sake, let us sit upon the ground.") HoPM
(Let's Talk of Graves.) FaBoRV
("Let's talk of graves, of worms, and epitaphs.") PPoe
(Of the Death of Kings, The.) TrGrPo
(Richard II's Dejection.) TreFS
"I was a poor groom of thy stable, king," *fr.* V, v. PoPle
Perils of Darkness, *fr.* III, ii. TreFT
This England, *fr.* II, i. TreF; TrGrPo
(John of Gaunt Speaks.) FaPoR
(John of Gaunt's Dying Speech.) FiP
(John of Gaunt's Speech.) FaBoPP
(This Blessed Plot . . . This England.) FaBV
Tongues of Dying Men, The, *fr.* II, i. FaBoRV
"Where is the duke my father with his power?" *fr.* III, ii. PoPle
King Richard III, *sels.* Shakespeare.
"As we paced along/ Upon the giddy footing of the hatches," *fr.* I, iv. MOS
Dream of Wrecks, A, *fr.* I, iv. ChTr
(Methought I Saw a Thousand Fearful Wrecks, *shorter sel.*) Ets
Evil Designs, *fr.* I, i. TreF
(Hate the Idle Pleasures.) TrGrPo
King Robert of Sicily. Longfellow. *Fr.* Tales of a Wayside Inn: The Sicilian's Tale, Pt. I. BeLS; OHIP
King Rufus. Y. Y. Segal, *tr. fr. Yiddish by* A. M. Klein. WHW
King Saul. Allan Kolski Horvitz. VWA
King sent for his wise men all, The. W. James Reeves. ChTr; NTCP
King sent his lady on the first Yule day, The. The Yule Days. *Unknown.* ChTr; GBP
King Shall Reign in Righteousness, A, *with music.* Sebastian Streeter. AH
King sits in Dumferline toun, The. The New Ballad of Sir Patrick Spens. Sir Arthur Quiller-Couch. BXAP
King [he] sits in Dunfermline [*or* Dumferling] town [*or* toune], The. Sir Patrick Spens [*or* Spence]. *Unknown.* AmFP; AWP; BiP; BSV; CABA; CH; EBEV; ELP; EnRP; EnSB; ESPB; EtS; FaBoBa; FaBoCh; FaPoR; FF; GN; GoJo; HAP; HBV-2; HoPM: InPK; InPS; InVP; LiTB; LoBV; MOS; NIP; NOBE; NoP; OAEL-1; OAEP; OBEV; OxBB; OxBS; PAI; PoEL-1; PPP; PrIm; RoGo; SeCeV; TreF; TrGrPo; UnPo; ViBoFo; ViBoPo; WeW; WHA
King Solomon stood in the house of the Lord. The Dead Solomon. John Aylmer Dorgan. AA
King still lives. King Lives. Jill Witherspoon Boyer. CNA
King to Oxford sent a troop of horse, The. Epigram [*or* Oxford and Cambridge]. Sir William Browne. FaBoCo; FaBoEE; WhC
King Triumphant. Isaac Watts. *See* Jesus Shall Reign Where'er the Sun.
King walked in his garden green, The. The Three Singing Birds. James Reeves. PDV
King was on his throne, The. The Vision of Belshazzar. Byron. FaPo; GN; HBV-2; OnMSP; RoGo
King was sick, The. His cheek was red. The Enchanted Shirt. John Hay. BLPA; GN; PaPo
King will take the Queen, The. Tom Brown.FSW
King William Was King George's Son. *Unknown.* AmFP; OuSiCo, *with music*
King William's Dispatch to Queen Augusta. Coventry Patmore. FaBoEE
King with all his kingly train, The. Louis XV. John Sterling. BeLS
King Wind. Mark Van Doren. NCSH
Kingcups. Sacheverell Sitwell. MoBrPo
Kingdom. Sir Edward Dyer. LoBV; OBSC
Kingdom, The, *sels.* Louis MacNeice.
"Little dapper man but with shiny elbows, A." ChMP
"Take this old man with the soldierly straight back." LiTM
"Under the surface of flux and of fear there is an underground movement." LiTM
Kingdom, The. Jon Swan. NYBP
Kingdom Coming, *with music.* Henry Clay Work. BLSo; PSoN
(Year of Jubilee, The.) PAH
(Year of Jubilo.) TrAS, *with music*
Kingdom of God, The. Rab, *tr. fr. Hebrew.* TrJP
Kingdom of God, The. Francis Thompson. BrPo; EaLo; FaPoR; GoBC; GTBS-P; ILwL; NOCV; OxBoCh; PoPle; SeCeV; TRV
(In No Strange Land.) EBCP; HAP; HBMV; LiTB; MoAB; MoBrPo; NOBE; OBEV; TrCP; TreFT; TrGrPo; WGRP
Kingdom of God, The. Richard Chenevix Trench. WBLP
Kingdom of Heaven. Léonie Adams. MoAB; MoAmPo
Kingdom of Number is all boundaries, The. W. H. Auden. *Fr.* Numbers and Faces. ImOP
Kingdoms fall in sequence, like the waves on the shore, The. The Sparrow's Skull. Ruth Pitter. EaLo
Kingdoms of the Earth go by, The. In Hoc Signo. Godfrey Fox Bradby. TRV
Kinge Arthur lives in merry Carleile. The Marriage of Sir Gawain. *Unknown.* ESPB
Kingfisher blue along a tangled bank. Poem to the Tune "Riverbank Willows." Yü Hsüan-chi, *tr. by* Geoffrey Waters. BoWoP
Kingfisher Flat. William Everson. PoM
Kingfisher green lines the deserted shore. Composed on the Theme "Willows by the Riverside." Yü Hsüan-chi, *tr. by* Jan W. Walls. WPOW
King-Fisher Song, The. "Lewis Carroll." *Fr.* Sylvie and Bruno Concluded. FaBoNo
Kingfisher, The. W. H. Davies. MoVE; NOBE; OBEV
Kingfisher, The. Blanche Mary Kelly. GoBC
Kingfisher, The. Andrew Marvell. *Fr.* Upon Appleton House. ChTr; FaBoEn; PB
Kingfishers, The. Charles Olson. CMoP; NeAP; NOBA; PoM
Kingis Quair, The, *abr.* James I, King of Scotland. OxBS
Sels.
"Bewailing in my chambers thus alone." BSV
Coming of Love, The. GoTS
He Sees His Beloved. PoEL-1
Nightingale's Song, The. OxBM
("Now was there maid fast by the towris wall.") EBEV
Walking under the Tour. SeCePo
Kingly lyon, and the strong arm'd beare, The. William Wood. SCAP
Kings. *Unknown, tr. fr. Sanskrit by* Arthur W. Ryder. *Fr.* The Panchatantra. AWP
Kings and Queens of England, The. *Unknown.* FaBoUs
Kings and Stars. John Erskine. TrCP
King's Ballad, The. Joyce Kilmer. HBV-1
King's Breakfast, The. A. A. Milne. CenHV; OxBChV
Kings Came Riding. Charles Williams. OBCP
Kings come riding home from the Crusade, The. Crusade. Hilaire Belloc. GoBC

King's Daughter!/ Wouldst thou be all fair. Everymaid. John Oxenham. TrCP
King's Disguise, The, *sel.* John Cleveland.
"And why so coffined in this vile disguise." JCP
King's Disguise, and Friendship with Robin Hood, The. *Unknown.* ESPB
King's Dochter Lady Jean, The. *Unknown.* AmFP; ESPB
Kings don't touch doors. The Delights of the Door. Francis Ponge, *tr. by* Robert Bly. NU
King's Entertainment, The. Thomas Dekker. *See* Entertainment to James
King's Epitaph, The. Earl of Rochester. SeCePo
(Epigram: "Here lies a great and mighty king.") CavP
Kings from the East, The. Heine. *See* Wise Men Ask the Children the Way, The.
Kings go by with jeweled crowns, The. The Choice. John Masefield. MoAB; MoBrPo
King's Highway, The. John Masefield. BLRP; TRV
King's Highway, The. John S. McGroarty. BPAW; HBV-1
King's Highway to the Dare-Not-Know, The. "Dreams Are the Royal Road to the Unconscious." Paul Goodman. PoA
Kings live in palaces, and pigs in sties. Habitations. Hilaire Belloc. PV
King's Men, The. William Heyen. PoA
King's Missive, The. Whittier. PAH
King's most faithful Subjects we, The. England's Triumph. *Unknown.* CoMu
Kings of France. Mary W. Lincoln. BLPA
Kings of the East, The. Katharine Lee Bates. WGRP
Kings of the world are growing old, The. Rainer Maria Rilke, *tr. fr. German by* Robert Bly. NU
King's Own Regulars, The. *Unknown.* PAH
King's poet was his captain of horse in the wars, The. Mount Badon. Charles Williams. FaBoTw
King's Ring, The. Theodore Tilton. *See* Even This Shall Pass Away.
Kings River Canyon. Kenneth Rexroth. NaP
King's Son, The. Thomas Boyd. AnIV; OBMV; OxBI
King's Speech, The. Howard Moss. *Fr.* King Midas. PoA
Kings, The. Louise Imogen Guiney. GoBC; HBV-2
Kings' wares; and dreams; and April dusks. The Portrait of a Florentine Lady. Lizette Woodworth Reese. HBMV
Kings who slept in the caves are awake and out, The. The National Gallery. Louis MacNeice. EyDe
Kings, who would have good subjects, must. Loyalty. W. H. Davies. BrPo
King's young dochter was sitting in her window, The. The King's Dochter Lady Jean. *Unknown.* ESPB
Kingship of the Hills, The. Will H. Ogilvie. PoSH
Kinkaiders, The, *with music.* *Unknown.* AS; CoSo
Kinloch, *sel.* Dorothy Nash.
Road Moves On, The. PoSH
Kinloch Ainort. Sorley MacLean. PoSH
Kinmont Willie. *Unknown.* BSV; ESPB; OxBB
Kinnaird Head. George Bruce. BSV; NeBP
Kinned by hieroglyphic. Kinship. Seamus Heaney. IPY
Kinneret. Judith Herzberg, *tr. fr. Dutch by* Shirley Kaufman. VWA
Kinnereth. Rachel, *tr. fr. Hebrew by* A. M. Klein. TrJP
Kinship. Seamus Heaney. IPY
Kinship. Sir Charles G. D. Roberts. CaP
Kiph. Walter de la Mare. TiPo
Kirk Lonegren's Home Movie Taking Place Just North of Prince George, with Sound. Sharon Thesen. NOBC
Kirk of the Birds, Beasts and Fishes, The. *Unknown.* GBP
Kirk's Alarm, The. Burns. OxBoLi
Kirkyaird by the Sea, The, *sel.* Douglas Young, *after the French of* Paul Valéry.
"Steekit, consecrat, fou o fire but fuel." OBVE
Kirov was shot, Solon will rot in jail. Once More. George Jonas. NeAC
Kiss, A. Austin Dobson. *Fr.* Rose Leaves. HBV-1
Kiss, A. William Drummond of Hawthornden. EIL
Kiss, A. Robert Herrick. CaPo
Kiss, The. Ben Jonson. *See* Song: "O, that joy so soon should waste!"
Kiss, The. Walter Savage Landor. OBVV
Kiss, The. Pierre Louÿs, *tr. fr. French by* Horace M. Brown. *Fr.* The Songs of Bilitis. UnTE
Kiss, The. Thomas Moore. EnLoPo
Kiss, The. Ned O'Gorman. FYAP
Kiss, The. Charles d'Orléans. *See* My Ghostly Father, I Me Confess.
Kiss, The. Robert Pack. AMV-81
Kiss, The. Coventry Patmore. *Fr.* The Angel in the House, II, viii. BoLoP; EnLoPo; FiBHP; OBVV; PoPle
Kiss, The. Dante Gabriel Rossetti. *See* What Smouldering Senses.
Kiss, The. Siegfried Sassoon. MMA
Kiss, The. Anne Sexton. NIP
Kiss, The. Claude Clayton Smith. PoDr
Kiss, The. Sara Teasdale. HBV-1
Kiss, A ("He's my doll!"). *Unknown, tr. fr. Irish by* Frank O'Connor. KiLC
Kiss, The ("Oh, keep your kisses, young provoking girl!"). *Unknown, tr. fr. Late Middle Irish by* the Earl of Longford. OnYI; OxBI
Kiss, The. George Wither. *See* Stolen Kiss, A.
Kiss. Al Young. PoBA
Kiss and the Cup, The. *Unknown, tr. fr. Greek by* Louis Untermeyer. UnTE
Kiss, if you can: Resistance if she make. Ovid, *tr. by* Dryden. *Fr.* Art of Love. ErPo
Kiss in the Morning Early, A. *Unknown.* GBP
Kiss in the Rain, A. Samuel Minturn Peck. OBAL
Kiss in the Ring. *Unknown.* OxBoLi
Kiss, lovely Celia, and be kind. Love's Courtship. Thomas Carew. UnTE
Kiss Me Again. Henry Blossom. BLSo, *with music;* TreFT
(If I Were on the Stage, *longer version.*) FSN
Kiss me again, re-kiss and kiss me whole. Sonnet XVIII. Louise Labé, *tr. by* Raymond Oliver. WPOW
Kiss me again, rekiss me, kiss me more. Sonnet XVIII. Louise Labé, *tr. by* Willis Barnstone. BoWoP
Kiss me and hug me. *Unknown, tr. fr. Spanish by* Willis Barnstone. BoWoP
Kiss Me, Dear. Dryden. *See* Rondelay: "Chloe found Amyntas lying."
Kiss Me Quick and Go, *with music.* Silas S. Steele. BLSo
Kiss me softly and speak to me low. To My Love. John Godfrey Saxe. HBV-1
Kiss [*or* Kisse] me, sweet: the wary [*or* warie] lover. To Celia. Ben Jonson. AnAnS-2; AWP; BiP; EIL; EnRePo; JCP; LoBV; OAEL-1; OBVE; SeCP; SeCV-1; UnTE
Kiss me then, my merry May. Medieval Norman Song. *Unknown, tr. by* John Addington Symonds. AWP
"Kiss me there where pride is glistening." Aria. Delmore Schwartz. ErPo
Kiss me, though you make believe. Make Believe. Alice Cary. HBV-1
Kiss my grey hair, oh, my love. Healing. Abraham Reisen, *tr. by* Joseph Leftwich. TrJP
Kiss of God, The. G. A. Studdert-Kennedy. BLRP
Kiss the one you love. Victor Contoski. *Fr.* Broken Treaties. GP
Kiss'd Yestreen. *Unknown.* ErPo; GBP; POL
Kisse, The. Robert Herrick. CavP
Kisse me, sweet: the warie lover. *See* Kiss me, sweet: the wary lover.
Kissed me from the saddle, and I still can feel it burning. The Smoke-blue Plains. Badger Clark. YaD
Kisses. *At. to* Thomas Campion. EIL; OBSC
(Kisses Make Men Loath to Go. UnTE
(My Love Bound Me.) HBV-1
(Song: "My Love bound me with a kiss.") HBV-1
Kisses. *Malay Oral Tradition, tr. by* R. J. Wilkinson *and* R. O. Winstedt. WTO
Kisses Desired. William Drummond of Hawthornden. EnLoPo
Kisses in the Train. D. H. Lawrence. MoAB; MoBrPo
Kisses Loathesome. Robert Herrick. CaPo
Kisses Make Men Loath to Go. *At. to* Thomas Campion. *See* Kisses.
Kiss-Fest, The. Irwin Edman. InMe
Kissie Lee. Margaret Walker. BlSi; NMM
Kissin'. *Unknown.* FiBHP; TreF
(Kissing's No Sin.) HBV-1; UnTE
Kissing, *sel.* Fred Emerson Brooks.
"Those lustrous eyes but tell met this." PeD
Kissing. Lord Herbert of Cherbury. EnLoPo; ViBoPo
Kissing and Bussing. Robert Herrick. OAEP
Kissing Helena. Plato, *tr. fr. Greek by* Shelley. OBVE
Kissing her hair, I sat against her feet. Rondel. Swinburne. BLPL; FaBoBe; HBV-1; ViBoPo
Kissing Hippomenes, I crave. Epigram. Paulos, *tr. by* Andrew Miller. PeHV
Kissing Natalia. Eldon Grier. NOBC
Kissing of My Dame. *Unknown.* GBP
("Sing jigmijole, the pudding bowl.") OxNR
Kissing the Dancer. Robert Sward. CoPo
Kissing the Toad. Galway Kinnell. DFT
Kissinger has made it, yall. Horatio Alger Uses Scag. Amiri Baraka. GP
Kissing's No Sin. *Unknown.* *See* Kissin'.
Kit Carson's Last Smoke ("Kit Carson came to old Fort Lyons"). Stanley Vestal. PoOW
Kit Carson's Ride. Joaquin Miller. BPAW; TreFS
Kit Hath Lost Her Key. *Unknown.* UnTE
Kit Logan and Lady Helen. Robert Graves. HBMV
Kit, the recording angel wrote. Kitty's "No." Arlo Bates. *Fr.* Conceits. AA
Kitchen Chimney, The. Robert Frost. EyDe
Kitchen Cupboard, The. Allen Curnow. *Fr.* Trees, Effigies, Moving Objects. OCNZ
Kitchen Door Blues. Tennessee Williams. GrPl; OBAL
Kitchen Memory, A. Roy Scheele. Str
Kitchen patio in snowy, The. One A.M. Denise Levertov. CAPP

Kitchen Poem. Francis Scarfe. EAS
Kitchen Prayer, A. M. Peterson. STF
Kitchen Song. Jeannine Dobbs. Str
Kitchen Tables. David Huddle. Str
Kitchen today is so full of appliances, The. Deus ex Machina. Richard Armour. QQQ
Kitchen Window. Ruth N. Ebberts. AMV-80
Kitchen Window. J. E. H. MacDonald. CaP
Kitchenette Building. Gwendolyn Brooks. BALP; BPo; FF; NoP; PoNe; UnPo
Kitchie-Boy, The. *Unknown.* BaBo; ESPB
Kite, The. Harry Behn. FaPON; TiPo
Kite. Laura Jensen. LCAP
Kite. David McCord. PDV
Kite, The. Adelaide O'Keeffe. OxBChV
Kite, The. Mark Strand. NYBP
Kite, A. *Unknown.* SoPo; TiPo
Kite, a sky, and a good firm breeze, A. Kite Days. Mark Sawyer. SiSoSe; TiPo
Kite, completed thus, is borne along, The. Samuel Bowden. *Fr.* The Paper Kite. NOEC
Kite Days. Mark Sawyer. SiSoSe; TiPo
Kite Is a Victim, A. Leonard Cohen. NOBC
Kite Poem. James Merrill. MP; TwCP
Kites, The. Coventry Patmore. *Fr.* The Angel in the House, II, i. VLP
Kithairon sang of cunning Kronos. Korinna, *tr. fr. Greek by* Willis Barnstone. BoWoP
Kitten, A. Eleanor Farjeon. TiPo
Kitten, The. Ogden Nash. DFF; FaPON; MoShBr; WhC
Kitten and [the] Falling Leaves, The, *sels.* Wordsworth.
"But the kitten, how she starts." PCat; HBVY
"See the kitten on the wall." PCat; HBVY
(Kitten at Play, The.) FaPON
"That way look, my infant, Lo!" HBVY
"Where is he, that giddy sprite." PBBP
Kitten can, A. Where Knock Is Open Wide. Theodore Roethke. HAP; VGW
Kittiwakes and cormorants go to sleep, The. Nightfall in Inishtrahull. Daniel James O'Sullivan. NeIP
Kitty. E. Prentiss. MoShBr
"Kitty," The. *Unknown.* TreFT
Kitty Bhan. Edward Walsh. ACP
Kitty-Cat Bird, The. Theodore Roethke. OBAL
Kitty Hawk, *sel.* Robert Frost.
But God's Own Descent. EaLo
Kitty, Kitty Casket, *with music. Unknown.* OuSiCo
Kitty Kline. *Unknown.* AmFP
Kitty Morey. *Unknown.* AmFP
(Katy Dorey, *with music.*) OuSiCo
Kitty Neil. John Francis Waller. HBV-1
Kitty of Coleraine. *Unknown, wr. at. to* Charles Dawson Shanly. HBV-1; OnYI
Kitty: What She Thinks of Herself. William Brightly Rands. *See* Cat of Cats, The.
Kitty's Laugh. Arlo Bates. Conceits, I. AA
Kitty's "No." Arlo Bates. Conceits, II. AA
Kivers. Ann Cobb. AmFN
Klabauterwife's Letter. Christian Morgenstern, *tr. fr. German by* W. D. Snodgrass *and* Lore Segal. WSC
Kleomedes. David Wright. NoAM
Kleptomaniac, The. Leonora Speyer. HBMV
Klondike, The. E. A. Robinson. PAH
Knapweed. A. C. Benson. HBV-1
Knave of darkness, limber in the leaves, The. Death for the Dark Stranger. Thomas McGrath. VGW
Kneading. Barbara Crooker. SOTS
Knedneuch land. In the Pantry. "Hugh MacDiarmid." NoAM
Knee Deep. Ted Joans. GP
Knee-deep in coldness, muzzle buried white. Wisdom. Linda Peavy. PH
Knee-deep in June. James Whitcomb Riley. OHFP
Knee Lunes. Robert Kelly. CoPo
Knee on Its Own, The. Christian Morgenstern, *tr. fr. German by* Geoffrey Grigson. FaBoNo
Kneegrows niggas. Be Cool, Baby. Rob Penny. PoBA
Kneel then with me, fall worm-like on the ground. Night. George Chapman. *Fr.* The Shadow of Night. OBSC
Kneeling Camel, The. Anna Temple Whitney. BLPA
(And So Should You.) STF
(Submission and Rest.) BLRP
Kneeling he spoke the names he loved the most. A Martyr's Mass. Alfred Barrett. GoBC
Kneeling Here, I Feel Good. Marge Piercy. NeAC
Kneeling in the sheepshit. Mountain Oysters. Patrick Lane. NeAC
Knell, The. Muhammad Al-Fītūri, *tr. fr. Arabic by* Samir M. Zoghby. TTY
Knell that dooms the voiceless and obscure, The. Survival. Florence Earle Coates. AA
Knew a poet. W. C. W. David Ray. POL
Knicht had two sons o sma fame, A. Sir Lionel. *Unknown.* ESPB
Knife, The. Juan Gelman, *tr. fr. Spanish by* Yishai Tobin. VWA
Knife, The. Milton Kaplan. TrJP
Knife, The. Richard Tillinghast. MAYP
Knife, The. Jean Valentine. LCAP
Knife and Sap. Kenneth Leslie. POL
Knife-Grinder, The. George Canning *and* John Hookham Frere. *See* Friend of Humanity and the Knife-Grinder, The.
Knife's edge, moon's edge, water's edge. Edge. Robert D. Fitzgerald. CBAP
Knight, The. Rainer Maria Rilke, *tr. fr. German by* John N. Miller. AMV-81
Knight and a lady once met in a grove, A. Sympathy. Reginald Heber. BeLS
Knight and [the] Shepherd's Daughter, The. *Unknown.* AmFP; ESPB (A *and* B *vers.*); ViBoFo
(Shepherd's Dochter, The, *with music.*) OxBB
Knight and the Lady, The. William Cornish. *See* Desire.
Knight, Death, and the Devil, The. Randall Jarrell. CrMA; WeW
Knight Fallen on Evil Days, The. Elinor Wylie. MoAmPo
Knight from the world's end, The. A Dream of Governors. Louis Simpson. NYBP
Knight had ridden down from Wensley Moor, The. Hart-Leap Well. Wordsworth. BeLS
Knight in Disguise, The. Vachel Lindsay. HBV-2
Knight in the Bower, The. *Unknown. See* Heron, The.
Knight in the Wood, The. Lord De Tabley. NCEP; VLP
Knight knock'd at the castle gate, The. Desire [*or* The Knight and the Lady]. William Cornish. NOBD; OBSC; SeCeV
Knight of Curtesy, The, *sel. Unknown, tr. fr. Middle English by* Pearl London.
Eaten Heart, The. TrGrPo
Knight of Ghosts and Shadows, A. Dunstan Thompson. NePA
Knight of Liddesdale, The. *Unknown.* ESPB
Knight of the Burning Pestle, The, *sels.* Beaumont *and* Fletcher.
Another Song, *fr.* IV, i. OBS
Come, You Whose Loves Are Dead; fr. IV, iv. ElL
Jillian of Berry, *fr.* IV, v. ElL
Laugh and Sing, fr. II, viii. TrGrPo
(Mirth.) ElL
Merrythought's Song, *fr.* IV, i. OBS
Month of May, The, *fr.* IV, v. ChTr
"Nose, nose, jolly red nose," *fr.* I, iii. FaBoCh
Knight of the Grail, The. *Unknown. See* Corpus Christi Carol ("Lully, lullay, lully, lullay").
Knight of the Holy Ghost, he goes his way. In Memory of G. K. Chesterton. Walter de la Mare. GoBC
Knight Stained from Battle, The. William Herebert. MeEl
(Who Is This That Cometh from Edom?) OxBM
Knight stands in the stable-door, The. Young Johnstone. *Unknown.* ESPB
Knight ther[e] was, and that a worthy man, A. Chaucer. *See* Knyght ther was . . .
Knight with starry shield, The. Sir Roland; a Fragment. Robert Merry. NOEC
Knight, with Umbrella. Elder Olson. FiBHP
Knight without a Name, The. *Unknown.* WiR
Knightes Tale, The. Chaucer. *See* Knight's Tale, The.
Knightliest of the knightly race, The. The Virginians of the Valley. Francis Orrery Ticknor. AA; HBV-2; PAH
Knight's Ghost, The. *Unknown.* ESPB
Knight's Tale, The. Chaucer. *Fr.* The Canterbury Tales. OBWP, *mod. version by* Dryden
(Knights Tale, The.) GoTL
"Allas the wo! Allas, the peynes stronge," *sel.* LO
Knights to Chrysola, The. Rachel Annand Taylor. OBVV
Knight's Tomb, The. Samuel Taylor Coleridge. EnRP; FaBoCh; GN
Knightsbridge of Libya. Sorley Maclean. NeBP
Knitters, The. Padraic Colum. SaC
Knob and hump upon this tree. A Gnarled Riverina Gum-Tree. Ernest G. Moll. PoAu-2
Knock at the doorie. *Unknown.* OxNR
Knock here's where I live. Message. Gyorgy Raba, *tr. by* Jascha Kessler. VWA
"Knock-me-down sermon, and worthy of Birch, A." An Old Buffer. Frederick Locker-Lampson. CenHV
Knock on Wood. Henry Dumas. CNA; PoBA
Knocking at the Door. John Freeman. HBMV
Knockmany. Richard Ryan. CIP

Knockout, The. Lillian Morrison. RHPC
Knole. C. H. Sisson. NOCV
Knolege, aquayntance, resort, favour with grace. Knowledge, Acquaintance. John Skelton. AAS; NCEP
Knot, The. Tom Clark. HoAn
Knot, The. Stanley Kunitz. HAP
Knot, The. Henry Vaughan. ISi
Knot which first my heart did strain, The. Sir Thomas Wyatt. SiPS
Know, The. Kathleen Fraser. NPGG
Know, Celadon, in vain you use. Song. "Ephelia." CavP
Know Celia, (since thou art so proud). Ingrateful[l] Beauty Threatened. Thomas Carew. AnAnS-2; CaPo; HBV-1; InvP; MeLP; OBEV; OBS; SeCP; SeCV-1
Know him for a white man. Passing into Storm. Patrick Lane. NOBC
Know I not who thou mayst be. At the Hacienda. Bret Harte. AA
Know, that I would accounted be. To Ireland in the Coming Times [*or* Apologia Addressed to Ireland]. W. B. Yeats. BrPo; NoAM; OxBI
Know the world by heart. Theory of Poetry. Archibald MacLeish. AP; DFF
Know then:/ Toward summer when the sun is in Hyades. Ezra Pound, *tr. fr. Chinese*. OBVE
Know then, I was born in a strange country. To My People. Edwin Seaver. TrJP
Know then, my brethren, heaven is clear. Song. *Unknown*. *Fr.* The Song of Anarchus. FaBoCo
Know Then Thyself. Pope. *Fr.* An Essay on Man, Epistle II. BLPL; GoBC; GoTL; LiTB; NOBE; NOEC; NoP; OAEL-1; OBEC; PAI; PoEL-3; PPoe; PrIm; SeCePo; TrGrPo; TRV
(Paragon of Animals, The.) ACP
(Proper Study of Man, The.) TreFS
(Proper Study of Mankind, The.) FiP
(Riddle of the World.) FaFP
Know this. Manifesto of the Soldier Who Went Back to War. Angel Miguel Queremel, *tr. by* Donald Devenish Walsh. WaaP
Know thou, O Virgin, noble-blest. O Noble Virgin. Prudentius, *tr. by* Raymond F. Roseliep. *Fr.* Cathemerinon. ISi
Know Thyself. Kenneth Burke. OBAL
Know Ye Not That Lovely River. Gerald Griffin. OnYI
Know ye not that ye are the temple of God. Ye Are the Temple of God. Bible, *N.T. Fr.* First Corinthians. TreFT
Know ye the land where the cypress and myrtle. The Bride of Abydos. Byron. OAEP
Know ye the willow-tree. The Willow-Tree. Thackeray. CenHV
Know ye the witch's dell? Lincolnshire; from the Wolds to the Fens. Ben Jonson. *Fr.* The Sad Shepherd, II, vii. FaBoPP
Know you faire, on what you looke. On Mr. G. Herberts Booke Intituled the Temple of Sacred Poems, Sent to a Gentlewoman. Richard Crashaw. AnAnS-1; OxBoCh; SeCV-1
Know you her secret none can utter? Alma Mater. Sir Arthur Quiller-Couch. OBVV
Knowest thou the land where bloom the lemon trees. Mignon. Goethe, *tr. by* James Elroy Flecker. AWP
Knowest thou the time when the wild goates of the rocke bring forth? Bible, *O.T. Fr.* Job. OBVE
Knowing. Mary Coghill. BrRo
Knowing her is not knowing her. An Afterword: For Gwen Brooks. Don L. Lee. JB
Knowing I Live in a Dark Age. Milton Acorn. NOBC
Knowing the heart of man is set to be. Samuel Daniel. *Fr.* To the Lady Margaret Countesse of Cumberland. FaBoEn
Knowledge. Louise Bogan. HBMV; PoA
Knowledge. Nina Cassian, *tr. fr. Rumanian by* Michael Impey *and* Brian Swann. BoWoP
Knowledge. Harold M. Grutzmacher. AMV-81
Knowledge, Acquaintance. John Skelton. NCEP
("Knolege, acquayntance, resort, favour with grace.") AAS
Knowledge after Death. Henry Charles Beeching. OBVV
Knowledge and Reason. Sir John Davies. *Fr.* Nosce Teipsum. OBSC
(Much Knowledge, Little Reason.) ChTr
(What Is This Knowledge?) FaBoRV
Knowledge of Age. Margaret Avison. PeCV
Knowledge of Light, The. Henry Rago. PoCh; VGW
Knowledge That Comes through Experience, The. Jane Cooper. NMM
Knowledgeable Child, The. L. A. G. Strong. OBMV
Knowlt Hoheimer. Edgar Lee Masters. *Fr.* Spoon River Anthology. OxBA
Known Soldier, The. Kenneth Patchen. WaaP
Known World, The. Brewster Ghiselin. MoVE
Knows he that never took a pinch. To My Nose. Alfred A. Forrester. BLPA
Know'st thou not at the fall of the leaf. Autumn Song. Dante Gabriel Rossetti. ViBoPo
Know'st thou not. Perils of Darkness. Shakespeare. King Richard II, *fr.* III, ii. TreFT
Know'st thou the land where the fair citron blows. Mignon. Goethe, *tr. by* Edgar A. Bowring. PoPl
Knoxville Girl. *Unknown*. FSW
Knoxville, Tennessee. Nikki Giovanni. AmNP; BlSi; BOLo; BPo; CNA; InPS; PoBA; SO
Knuckles over the flame. Paradigms of Fire. Brian Swann. AmPA
Knyght [*or* Knight] ther[e] was, and that a worthy man, A. Chaucer. *Fr.* The Canterbury Tales: Prologue. BiP; InPS; TrGrPo, *orig. and mod. version by* Louis Untermeyer
Koala. Alan Ross. BoAnP
Kob Antelope. *Yoruba Oral Tradition, tr. by* Ulli Beier. WTO
Kochia. Thomas Hornsby Ferril. NePoAm-2
Kodak, A; Tregantle. Horatio Brown. PeHV
Koheleth. Louis Untermeyer. TrJP
Kohoutek. Richard Ryan. CIP
Koina ta ton Philon. John Addington Symonds. OBVV
Ko-jin goes west from Ko-kaku-ro [*or* Ko-keku-to]. Separation on the River Kiang. Li Po, *tr. by* Ezra Pound. SOTW; UnPo
Kokin Shu, *sels. Tr. fr. Japanese by* Arthur Waley. . AWP
"Although it is not plainly visible to the eye." Fujiwara no Toshiyuki.
"Beloved person must I think, The." Ki no Akimine.
"Did I ever think." Ono no Takamura.
"Hoping all the time." *Unknown*.
"If only, when one heard." *Unknown*.
"My love/ Is like the grasses." Ono no Yoshiki.
"O Cuckoo." *Unknown*.
"Since I heard." Mitsune.
"Thing which fades, A." Ono no Komachi.
"When the dawn comes." *Unknown*.
Koko. Ann Downer. SUW
Ko-Ko's Song ("As some day it may happen that a victim must be found"). W. S. Gilbert. *Fr.* The Mikado. LiTB
(They'll None of 'Em Be Missed.) VLP
Ko-Ko's (Winning) Song ("On a tree by a river"). W. S. Gilbert. *See* Suicides' Grave, The.
Kol Nidra. Joseph Leiser. TrJP
Kona Sea, The. *Tr. fr. Hawaiian by* N. B. Emerson. WTO
Koocoo, The. *Unknown*. GBP
Kookaburra. *Unknown*. FSW
Kopis'taya. Paula Gunn Allen. STE; TWSS
Kore. Robert Creeley. ConAP; CoPo; InPK; InPS; NMP
Kore. Frederic Manning. HBV-1
Korè. Ezra Pound. LoBV
Korea Bound, 1952. William Childress. AmFN
Korean Woman Seated by a Wall, A. William Meredith. NePoEA
Korf's Clock. Christian Morgenstern, *tr. fr. German by* Geoffrey Grigson. FaBoNo
Korf's Enchantment. Christian Morgenstern, *tr. fr. German by* W. D. Snodgrass *and* Lore Segal. WSC
Korf's Joke. Christian Morgenstern, *tr. fr. German by* Max Knight. ELU
Korosta Katzina Song. *Unknown, at. to* Koianimptiwa, *tr. fr. Hopi Indian by* Natalie Curtis. AWP
("Yellow butterflies.") WTO
Koskiusko. Samuel Taylor Coleridge. EnRP
Kraken, The. Tennyson. AmMo; CABA; NoP; OAEL-2; OBNC; OBRV; PoEL-5; SyP; VLP; WiR; WSC
Kral Majales. Allen Ginsberg. GP; PoM
Krankenhaus of Leutkirch, The. Richmond Lattimore. NYBP
Kree. A. C. Gordon. AA
Kreutzer Sonata. Ted Hughes. FaBoMo
Krishna, Krishna,/ Now as I look on. Debate between Arjuna and Sri Krishna. *Unknown, tr. by* Swami Prabhavananda *and* Christopher Isherwood. WaaP
Kriss Kringle. Thomas Bailey Aldrich. HBVY
Kropotkin Poems, The, *sel.* Phyllis Webb.
"Syllables disintegrate ingrate alphabets." NOBC
Ku Kluck Klan, *with music*. Lawrence Gellert. TrAS
Ku Klux. Madison Cawein. AA; PAH
Ku Klux. Langston Hughes. BPo
Kû! Listen! In Alahíyi you repose, O Terrible Woman. Sacred Formula to Attract Affection. *Unknown, tr. by* James Mooney. LiTA
Kubla Khan; or, A Vision in a Dream. Samuel Taylor Coleridge. AWP; BiP; CABA; CH; ChER; ChTr; ELP; EnRP; EyDe; FaBoBe; FaBoCh; FaBoEn; FaBV; FaFP; FF; FiP; FPL; GoJo; GN; HAP; HeIP; HBV-2; HoPM; InPK; InPS; InvP; LiTB; LoBV; MasP; MAT; NIP; NOBE; NoP; OAEL-2; OAEP; OBEV; OBNC; OBRV; PAI; PoEL-4; PoPl; PoRA; PP; PPoe; PrIm; RoGo; SCV; SeCeV; SoSe; SyP; TEP; TreFS; TrGrPo; UnPo; ViBoPo; WeW; WHA; WSC
Kula . . . a Homecoming. Diane Mei Lin Mark. BrSi
Kum Ba Yah (Come By Here). *Unknown*. FSW

Kumulipo, The; a Creation Chant, *sels.* Keaulumoku, *tr. fr. Hawaiian by* M. W. Beckwith. WTO
Birth of Sea and Land Life.
Crawlers, The.
Dawn of Day, The.
Dog Child, The.
Kunai-mai-pa Mo. Ethel Anderson. PoAu-2
Kung walked/ by the dynastic temple. Ezra Pound. Cantos, XIII. CMoP; FaBoMo
Kupris bears trophies away. Sophocles, *tr. by* Ezra Pound. *Fr.* Women of Trachis. CTC
Kutune Shirka (The Ainu Epic), *sel.* Wakarpa, *tr. by* Arthur Waley.
Golden Sea-Otter, The. WTO
Kyng Jamy/ Jamy your Joye is all go. A Ballade of the Scottyshe Kynge. John Skelton. CoMu; FaBoBa
Kyoto: March. Gary Snyder. PPP
Kypros! Andromache's Wedding. Sappho, *tr. by* Willis Barnstone. BoWoP
Kyran's Christening. Alden Nowlan. NeAC
Kyrie. David Gascoyne. *Fr.* Miserere. NeBP
Kyrie Eleison! The Funeral of Philip Sparrow, *abr.* John Skelton. *Fr.* Phyllyp Sparowe. ACP
"Kyrie, so kyrie." Jolly Jankin [*or* Jankin, the Clerical Seducer]. *Unknown.* GBP; MeEL; NOBE; NoP; OxBM; OxBoLi
Kyrielle. John Payne. HBV-2
Kythans. Stewart McGavin. PoSH

L

L (a. E. E. Cummings. NIP; NoP
LMFBR. Gary Snyder. PoM
La Bagarède. Galway Kinnell. NYBP
La Banditaccia, 1979. Rika Lesser. MAYP
La Bella Bona Roba. Richard Lovelace. CaPo; CavP; EBEV; OAEL-1; PoEL-3; SeCP
La Bella Donna Della Mia Mente. Oscar Wilde. UnTE
La Belle Confidente. Thomas Stanley. FaBoEn; JCP; MeLP; MePo; OBS
La Belle Dame sans Merci. Keats. AWP; BeLS; BLPA; CABA; CH; ChTr; DTo; ELP; EnRP; FaBoBe; FaBoCh; FaFP; FiP; FPL; GoJo; GTBS; GTBS-P; HAP; HBV-1; InPK; InPS; InvP; LiTB; LoBV; MasP; NIP; NOBE; NoP; OAEL-2; OAEP; OBEV; OBNC; OBRV; OLR; PAI; PoEL-4; PoPle; PoRA; PPoe; Prf; PrIm; SCV; SeCeV; SoSe; TEP; TreFT; TrGrPo; UnPo; ViBoPo; WeW; WHA; WSC
La Belle Dame sans Merci, *parody.* T. Griffiths. BXAP
La Belle Ennemie. Thomas Stanley. CavP
La Belle Sauvage. John Hunter-Duvar. *Fr.* De Roberval. OBCV
La Bête Humaine. James Kirkup. NeBP
La Carte. Justin Richardson. ELU; FiBHP
La Chute. Charles Olson. InPK; PAI
La Ci Darem la Mano. John Frederick Nims. MiAP
La Condition Botanique. Anthony Hecht. MP; NePoEA; NoAM
La Corona. John Donne. AnAnS-1; OBS
Sels.
Annunciation. SBVL
Nativity. SBVL
La Crosse at Ninety Miles an Hour. Richard Eberhart. AmFN
La Donna E Mobile. "A. K." FiBHP; InMe
La Donna E Perpetuum Mobile. Irwin Edman. FiBHP; NYBP
La Figlia Che Piange. T. S. Eliot. FaBoTw; GBL; HeIP; LiTA; MAT; OxBTC; PoA; UnPo; VGW; ViBoPo
La Fontaine de Vaucluse. Marilyn Hacker. FYAP
La Fuite de la Lune. Oscar Wilde. *Fr.* Impressions. SyP
La Grande Jatte: Sunday Afternoon. Thomas Cole. NePoAm
La Grisette. Oliver Wendell Holmes. AA; HBV-1
La Guerre. E. E. Cummings. MoAB; MoAmPo; SUW
La' laha, il Allah! The Three Khalandeers. James Clarence Mangan. OBVV
La Llorona. Greg Pape. AmPA
La Madonna di Lorenzetti. John Williams Andrews. HBMV
La Máquina a Houston. Edward Dorn. PoM
La Mélinite: Moulin-Rouge. Arthur Symons. SyP
La Mer. Oscar Wilde. *Fr.* Impressions. SyP
La Misère. Philip Appleman. BXAP
La Mort d'Arthur. William Edmonstoune Aytoun. FaBoPa
La Nuit Blanche. Kipling. MoBrPo
La Pesadilla. Gerda Penfold. GP
La Plata chants silver, The/ Where its glittering waters roll. Rivers of the West. "Sunset Joe." PoOW
La Preciosa. Thomas Walsh. ISi
La Préface. Charles Olson. PoM
La Prière de Nostre Dame. Chaucer, *mod. version by* Anselm M. Townsend. ISi
La Reproduction Interdite/Not to Be Reproduced. Kathleen Fraser. NPGG
La Rose des Vents. Richard Wilbur. MiAP
La Rue de la Montagne Sainte-Gèneviève. Dorothy Dudley. HBMV
La Selva. Cid Corman. VGW
La Tricoteuse. George Walter Thornbury. BeLS
La Vie C'est la Vie. Jessie Redmond Fauset. BANP; CDC; PoNe
La Vita Nuova. Weldon Kees. VGW
Labienus, each hair on your bosom that grows. Epigram: To Labienus. Martial. PeHV
Labor. Lucille Day. VWA
Labor. *Unknown.* PGD
Labor and Love. Sir Edmund Gosse. HBV-2
Labor Camp, The. John Pijewski. AMV-81
Labor Day. Gary Pacernick. TAT
Labor Day. Marnie Pomeroy. PoSC
Labor Not in Vain. *Unknown.* STF
Labor of Fields. Elizabeth J. Coatsworth. TiPo
Labor raises honest sweat. The Dignity of Labor. Robert Bersohn. PoPl; WhC
Labor Room: three handed. Oblique Birth Poem. Ann Darr. GP
Labor sweet that I sustained in thee, The. To the Translation of Palingenius. Barnabe Googe. EnRePo
Laboratories explain it away in retrospect as chemistry, The. Sea-Grape Tree and the Miraculous. William Pitt Root. GeTw
Laboratory Midnight, The. Reuel Denney. ImOP; NePA
Laboratory Poem. James Merrill. InPK; MAT; MP; NePoEA-2; TwCP
Laboratory, The; Ancien Régime. Robert Browning. OBEV; OBVV
Laborer, The. Richard Dehmel, *tr. fr. German by* Jethro Bithell. AWP
Laborer, The. José-Maria de Heredia, *tr. fr. French by* Wilfrid Thorley. AWP
Laborer to the lady, The: Yes, there are. Madonna: 1936. John Louis Bonn. ISi
Laborers, domestics, blue. Annunciation. Sister Maura. TAT
Laborers of Christ! Arise, *with music.* Lydia Sigourney. AH
"Laborers Together with God." Lucy Alice Perkins. BLRP
Laboring and Heavy Laden, *with music.* Jeremiah E. Rankin. AH
Laboring men, please all attend. Free Silver. *Unknown.* AmFP
Labors of Hercules, The. Marianne Moore. OxBA
Labors of Thor, The. David Wagoner. GP
Labour. M. Saint-Marthe, *tr. fr. French.* *Fr.* Paedotrophiae; or, The Art of Bringing Up Children. FaBoUs
Labour of the Brain, Ballad of the Body. Nicole Forman. NMM
Labourer in the Vineyard, The. Stephen Spender. NeBP
Labourer's Wife, A. John Davidson. *Fr.* To the Street Piano. EBVV
Labouring man, that tills the fertile soil, The. Pains and Gains. Edward de Vere, Earl of Oxford. ElL
Labouring Man, The. *Unknown.* OBET
Labouring poor, in spite of double pay, The. Daniel Defoe. *Fr.* The True-born Englishman, II. NOBL; SaC
Labours of the Months. *Unknown.* *See* January by This Fire.
Labyrinth, The. W. H. Auden. LiTA; NePA
Labyrinth, The. Edwin Muir. CMoP; MoBrPo; NoAM
Lac Courte Orielles; 1936. Phyllis Wolf. STE
Lace curtain stands effaced, A. Stéphane Mallarmé, *tr. fr. French by* Roger Fry. NAWM-2
Lace grows in her eyes like. Waiting, the Hallways under Her Skin Thick with Dreamchildren. Lyn Lifshin. NeAC
Lace Tell. *Unknown.* OBET
Lacemaker (Vermeer), The. Anne Marx. GoYe
Lachesis. Victor Daley. CBAP
Lachesis. Kathleen Raine. NYBP
Lachin y Gair. Byron. OxBS
Lachlan Gorach's Rhyme. *Unknown.* PoPle
Lachrimae, *sel.* Geoffrey Hill.
Lachrimae Verae. NoP
Lachrimae Amantis. Geoffrey Hill. NOCV
Lachrymae. David Gascoyne. *Fr.* Miserere. NeBP
Lackey Bill. *Unknown.* CoSo
Lacking my Love, I go from place to place. Amoretti, LXXVIII. Spenser. ElL; ViBoPo
Lacking samite and sable. A Christmas Carol. May Probyn. ACP; GoBC; HBMV; ISi; OBVV
Lacking Sense, The. Thomas Hardy. CMoP; PoEL-5
Lacquer Liquor Locker, The. David McCord. FiBHP; InMe
Lacrimae Musarum. Sir William Watson. HBV-2
Lacrimas or There Is a Need to Scream. K. Curtis Lyle. PoBA
Lacy mobile changing lazily, A. Watching a Cloud. Dannie Abse. OxBC; TEP

Lad of Athens, faithful be. Emily Dickinson. FaBoEE
Lad of the Curly Locks. *Unknown, tr. fr. Irish by* Frank O'Connor. KiLC
Lad Philisides, The. A Country Song. Sir Philip Sidney. *Fr.* Arcadia. OBSC; SiPS
Lad That Is Gone, A. Robert Louis Stevenson. *See* Over the Sea to Skye.
Lad when at school, one day stole a pin, A. The Results of Stealing a Pin. *Unknown.* FaBoUs
Ladd I the dance a Midsomer Day. A Night with a Holy-Water Clerk. *Unknown.* MeEL
Ladder, The. Gene Baro. NePoEA-2
Ladder, The. Leonora Speyer. HBMV
Ladder ascends and descends, A. The Drunkenness of Pain. Aliza Shenhar, *tr. by* Linda Zisquit. VWA
Ladder, flag, and amplifier. Corner Meeting. Langston Hughes. CAD
Ladder Has No Steps, The. Jorge Plescoff, *tr. fr. Spanish by* Yishai Tobin. VWA
Ladder of St. Augustine, The, *sel.* Longfellow.
Heights, The. TreF
Laddie, little laddie, come with me over the hills. A Cry from the Canadian Hills. Lillian Leveridge. BLPA
Ladie stude in her bour-door, The. Young Hunting. *Unknown.* ESPB
Ladies, The. Kipling. MoBrPo; TreFT
Ladies' Aid, The. *Unknown.* PoLF
Ladies and gentlemen:/ I have only one question. I Move the Meeting Be Adjourned. Nicanor Parra, *tr. by* Miller Williams. *Fr.* Manifesto. HoPM
Ladies and gentlemen:/ This broadcast comes to you from the city. Voice of the Studio Announcer. Archibald MacLeish. *Fr.* The Fall of the City. HoPM
Ladies and Gentlemen,/ List to my song. Temperance Song. *Unknown.* FaBoUs
Ladies and Gentlemen This Little Girl. E. E. Cummings. CMoP
Ladies and gents, you are here assembled. Gas from a Burner. James Joyce. DBV; TW
Ladies at the Troy Laundry pressed, The. One for the Ladies at the Troy Laundry Who Cooled Themselves for Zimmer. Paul Zimmer. GP
Ladies by Their Windows. Donald Justice. TwAmPo
Ladies' Eyes Serve Cupid Both for Darts and Fire. "A. W." OBSC
Ladies, I do here present you. A Present to a Lady. *Unknown.* ErPo
Ladies in the Dinin' Room, *with music.* *Unknown.* OuSiCo
Ladies men admire, I've heard, The. Interview. Dorothy Parker. *Fr.* Some Beautiful Letters. InMe
Ladies of London, both wealthy and fair. Advice to the Ladies of London in the Choice of Their Husbands. *Unknown.* CoMu
Ladies of St. James's, The. Austin Dobson. HBV-1; PoRA
Ladies of the morning gauze their mouths, The. Canonical Hours. William Dickey. CoAP
Ladies Prayer to Cupid, A. Thomas Carew. *See* Lady's Prayer to Cupid, A.
Ladies rose, The. I held the door. The Dean. Coventry Patmore. *Fr.* The Angel in the House. VLP
Ladies that guild the glittering noon. The General Eclipse. John Cleveland. AnAnS-2
Ladies that have intelligence in love. Dante, *tr. by* Dante Gabriel Rossetti. La Vita Nuova, X. AWP
Ladies, though to your conquering eyes. Song. Sir George Etherege. *Fr.* The Comical Revenge, V, iii. HBV-1; OBS
Ladies, to this advice give heed. A Maxim Revised. *Unknown.* BLPA; FPL; WBLP
Ladies' Voices. Gertrude Stein. SOTW
Ladies, well I deem, delight. My Lady Nature and Her Daughters. Cardinal Newman. GoBC
Ladies, where were your bright eyes glancing. Imogen. Sir Henry Newbolt. HBMV
Ladies, You See Time Flieth. *Unknown.* EnRePo
Lads in Their Hundreds, The. A. E. Housman. A Shropshire Lad, XXIII. CoBMV; MaSP; MoBrPo; OxBTC; VLP
Lad's Love. Esther Lilian Duff. HBMV
Lads of Wamphray, The. *Unknown.* ESPB
Lady, A. Amy Lowell. MoAmPo
Lady, A. W. D. Snodgrass. TW
Lady,/ Baby. *Unknown.* OxNR
Lady,/ how long you been driving a bus? Interview. Laurence Lieberman. AMV-81
Lady,/ You, who are pattering to your carriage door. Genius. Louis Saunders Perkins. PeHV
Lady A. L., My Asylum in a Great Extremity, The. Richard Lovelace. CaPo
Lady Adeline Amundeville. Byron. Don Juan, XIII. PoEL-4
Lady Again Complains, The. Earl of Surrey. SiPS
Lady Alice. *Unknown.* AmFP (4 *versions*); ESPB (A, B, *and* C *vers.*)
Lady Alice, Lady Louise. The Blue Closet. William Morris. NBM; VLP
Lady Alice was sitting in her bower-window. Lady Alice. *Unknown.* ESPB
Lady and Crocodile. Charles Burgess. NePoAm-2
Lady and Queen and Mystery manifold. Ballade to Our Lady of Czestochowa. Hilaire Belloc. ACP; ISi
Lady and the Bear, The. Theodore Roethke. GoJo; SO
Lady Anne Bathing. Anthony Delius. PeSA
Lady Anne Bothwell's Lament. *Unknown.* *See* Balow.
Lady April. Richard Le Gallienne. YeAr
Lady asks me, A. Canzone: Donna Mi Priegha [*or* Donna Me Prega]. Guido Cavalcanti, *tr. by* Ezra Pound. CTC; OBVE
Lady Bates. Randall Jarrell. MiAP
Lady, by yonder blessed moon I swear. Shakespeare. *Fr.* Romeo and Juliet, II, ii. MOON
Lady Byron's Reply to Lord Byron's "Fare Thee Well." *Unknown.* BLPA
Lady came to a bear by a stream, A. The Lady and the Bear. Theodore Roethke. GoJo; SO
Lady Clara Vere de Vere. Tennyson. HBV-1
Lady Clara Vere de Vere! The Wedding. Tom Hood. InMe
Lady Clare. Tennyson. BeLS; FaPON; HBV-2; OnMSP
Lady Comes to an Inn, A. Elizabeth J. Coatsworth. MoAmPo; SO
Lady Complains of Her Lover's Absence, A. Earl of Surrey. *See* Complaint of the Absence of Her Lover . . .
Lady Day. Padraic Fallon. NeIP
Lady Day in Harvest. Sheila Kaye-Smith. ISi
Lady Diamond. *Unknown.* BaBo; ESPB
Lady director is a gentle guide, The. Changsha Shoe Factory. Willis Barnstone. SaC
Lady, do not hold your parasol. By the Beautiful Sea. Thomas Cole. NePoAm-2
Lady Elspat. *Unknown.* ESPB
Lady Erskine sits in her chamber. Child Owlet. *Unknown.* ESPB
Lady, farewell, whom I in silence serve. A Poem Put into My Lady Laiton's Pocket. Sir Walter Ralegh. SiPS
Lady Feeding the Cats, *sel.* Douglas Stewart.
"Shuffling along in her broken shoes from the slums." BoAnP
Lady Fortune, The ("The Lady Fortune is both friend and foe"). *Unknown.* HeIP; NIP
(Fortune.) ACP
Lady Fortune is both friend and foe, The. Fortune. *Unknown.* ACP; HeIP; NIP
Lady Franklin's Lament, *2 vers. with music.* *Unknown.* ShS
Lady Geraldine's Courtship. Elizabeth Barrett Browning. DTo
Lady, giver of Bread. Litany to Our Lady. Caryll Houselander. ISi
Lady Godiva. Edward Shanks. HBMV
Lady Greensleeves. *Unknown.* *See* Greensleeves.
Lady, helpe! Jesu mercy [*or* mercé]! In His Utter Wretchedness [*or* Dread of Death]. John Audelay. MeEL; OxBM
Lady I Know, A. Countee Cullen. *See* For a Lady I Know.
Lady, I loved you all last year. A Song of Impossibilities. Winthrop Mackworth Praed. InMe; NA
Lady, I Thank Thee. *Unknown.* OxBM
(Thanks and a Plea to Mary.) McEL
Lady, I trust it is not to do harm. A Volume of Chopin. James Picot. PoAu-2
Lady in a Distant Face. James Welch. AmPA
Lady in Kicking Horse Reservoir, The. Richard Hugo. CoAP; LCAP; NoP
Lady in the Barbershop, The. Raphael Rudnik. NYBP
Lady in the Pink Mustang, The. Louise Erdrich. TWSS
Lady in the Wood, The. *Unknown.* OxBM
Lady Is a Tramp, The. Lorenz Hart. OBAL
Lady Isabel. *Unknown.* BaBo; ESPB
Lady Isabel and the Elf-Knight ("Fair lady Isabel sits in her bower sewing"). *Unknown.* ESPB; FaBoBa; OAEP
Lady Isabel and the Elf Knight ("O heard ye of a bloody knight"). BaBo
Lady Isabel and the Elf Knight; or, The False-hearted Knight ("I'll tell you of a false-hearted knight"). BaBo
Lady Isabel and the Elf Knight; or, Pretty Polly, *diff. versions.* AmFP; FSW
Lady Isabella's Tragedy, The. *Unknown.* GBP
Lady Jane (Sapphics). Sir Arthur Quiller-Couch. FiBHP; InMe; WhC
Lady Jane, The; a Humorous Novel in Rhyme, *sels.* Nathaniel Parker Willis. OBAL
"If, in well-bred society, ('hear! hear!')."
"Some men, 'tis said, prefer a woman fat."
Lady, Lady. Anne Spencer. BlSi; PoBA
Lady! Lady!/ Upon Heaven-height. In a Boat. Hilaire Belloc. ISi
Lady, lady, lady fair. The Suffolk Miracle. *Unknown.* AmFP
Lady, lady should you meet. Social Note. Dorothy Parker. *Fr.* Some Beautiful Letters. FaBoUs; InMe
Lady Lazarus. Sylvia Plath. CAPP; ConAP; InPK; MAT; NaP; NIP; NoAM; NOBA; NoP; PPoe; PrIm; TAP; VGW
Lady lived in Lancaster, A. Kate and the Cowhide. *Unknown.* AmFP
Lady Lost. John Crowe Ransom. MoAB; MoAmPo; TrGrPo; TwAmPo; UnPo

Lady Love. Paul Eluard, *tr. fr. French by* Samuel Beckett. OBVE
Lady loved a swaggering rover, A. Pirate Treasure. Abbie Farwell Brown. EtS
Lady Luck. Ann Gottlieb. NMM
Lady Maisdry was a lady fair. Lord Ingram and Chiel Wyet (*C vers.*) *Unknown.* ESPB
Lady Maisry. *Unknown.* ESPB (A *and* B *vers.*); OBET; OxBB, *with music;* ViBoFo
Lady Maisry lives intill a bower. Thomas o Yonderdale. *Unknown.* ESPB
Lady Margaret. *Unknown.* FSW
Lady Margaret sat in her bower-door. Prince Heathen. *Unknown.* ESPB
Lady Margaret sat in her bowry all alone. Sweet William's Ghost. *Unknown.* ViBoFo
Lady Margaret sits in her bower door. Hind Etin. *Unknown.* ESPB
Lady Margery May sits in her bower. Prince Heathen. *Unknown.* ESPB
Lady Maria, in you merit and distinction. Bieiris de Romans, *tr. fr. Provençal by* Maud Bogin. PeHV
Lady Mary, blisful Dame. The Mother of God. *Unknown, tr. by* G. R. Woodward. *Fr.* Horologium. ISi
Lady Mary Villiers lies, The. Epitaph on the Lady Mary Villiers. Thomas Carew. AnAnS-2; CaPo; CavP; FaBoEE; NOBE; OAEP; OBEV; SeCV-1; ViBoPo
Lady Moon. Richard Monckton Milnes. MoShBr; OxBChV
Lady Moon. Christina Rossetti. *See* O Lady Moon.
Lady Murasaki says. Murasaki Shikibu, *tr. fr. Japanese by* Kenneth Rexroth *and* Ikuko Atsumi. *Fr.* The Tale of Genji. BoWoP
Lady, my lady, come from out the garden. To a Certain Lady, in Her Garden. Sterling A. Brown. CDC
Lady My Treasure. Sir Philip Sidney. GBL
Lady Named Psyche, A. *Unknown.* *See* Limerick: "Beautiful lady named Psyche, A."
Lady of all the essences, full light. Inanna and the Divine Essences. Enheduanna, *tr. fr. Sumerian.* BoWoP
Lady, of anonymous flesh and face. J. V. Cunningham. HoPM
Lady of Arngosk, The. *Unknown.* ESPB
Lady of Carlisle, The. *Unknown.* AmFP; FSW; OuSiCo, *with music*
Lady of Castlenoire. Thomas Bailey Aldrich. BeLS
Lady of dusk-wood fastnesses. First Praise. William Carlos Williams. VGW
Lady of Heaven and earth, and therewithal. His Mother's Service to Our Lady. Villon, *tr. by* Dante Gabriel Rossetti. AWP; CTC; ISi
Lady of High Degree, A. *Unknown, tr. fr. French by* Andrew Lang. AWP
Lady of Letters. Raymond F. Roseliep. ISi
Lady of Lidice. Fray Angelico Chavez. ISi
Lady of Life, The. Tom Kettle. ACP
Lady of Light, I would admit a dream to you. The Buried Lake. Allen Tate. CrMA
Lady of Miracles. Nina Cassian, *tr. fr. Rumanian by* Laura Schiff. WPOW
Lady of O. James J. Galvin. ISi
Lady of Peace. Fray Angelico Chavez. ISi
Lady of Shalott, The. Tennyson. BeLS; BLPL; FaFP; FiP; GN; HBV-2; NOBE; OAEL-2; OAEP; OBEV; OBNV; OBRV, *diff. vers.*; OBVV; SeCeV; TEP; TreF; VLP; 2 *vers.*; WHA; WiR
Lady of the bright coils and curlings. Eire. David O'Bruadair, *tr. by* Austin Clarke. BIrV
Lady of the Castle, The. John Hollander. GP
Lady of the Ferry Inn. Gwerfyl Mechain, *tr. fr. Welsh by* Willis Barnstone. BoWoP
Lady of the house is on her benders, The. Five Domestic Interiors. Vernon Scannell. OxBC
Lady of the Lake, The, *sels.* Sir Walter Scott.
  Alice Brand, *fr.* IV. BeLS; HBV-2; HBVY; OnMSP
  Boat Song, *fr.* II. OAEP; PoEL-4
    (Hail to the Chief Who in Triumph Advances!) EnRP
    (" 'Proudly our pibroch has thrill'd in Glen Fruin.' ") OAEP
  Chase, The, *fr.* I. EnRP
  Coronach ("He is gone on the mountain"), *fr.* III. BSV; CH; EnRP; GTBS; GTBS-P; HBV-2; OAEP; OHIP; TreFS; TrGrPo; ViBoPo; WHA; WiR
  "Harp of the North, farewell! The hills grow dark," *fr.* VI. OAEP
    (Farewell, Thou Minstrel Harp. OBNC
  "Harp of the North! that mouldering long hast hung," *fr.* I. OAEP; ViBoPo
  Hunter's Song, *fr.* IV. NBM
    (Toils Are Pitched, The.) EnRP
  Hymn to the Virgin, *fr.* IV. EnRP; GoBC
    (Ave Maria.) ISi
  " 'Now yield thee, or by Him who made,' " *fr.* V. OxBS
  Roderick Dhu, *fr.* V. OBRV
  "Rose is fairest when 'tis budding new, The," *fr.* IV. ViBoPo
  Soldier Rest! [Thy Warfare O'er], *fr.* I. AWP; GN; HBV-2; HBVY; MoShBr; NOBE; PoRA; TreFS; TrGrPo
    (Song: "Soldier rest! thy warfare o'er.") OAEP; OBNC; OBRV
  Soldier's Song, *fr.* VI. NBM; ViBoPo
  "Time rolls his careless course. The race of yore," *fr.* III. ViBoPo
    (Gathering, The, *longer sel.*) OBNC
  "Western waves of ebbing day, The," *fr.* I. PoEL-4
Lady of the Lake, The. *Unknown.* ShS
Lady of the Lambs, The. Alice Meynell. *See* Shepherdess, The.
Lady of the legless world I have. Notes after Blacking Out. Gregory Corso. NeAP
Lady of the Manor, The. George Crabbe. *Fr.* The Parish Register: Burials. NOBE; OBNC
Lady of the Manor was dressing for the ball, The. The Highland Tinker. *Unknown.* CoMu
Lady of the Pearls, The, *sel.* Alexandre Dumas, *tr. fr. French by* Gerard Manley Hopkins.
  "We set out yesterday upon a winter drive." TTY
Lady Pitcher, The. Cynthia Macdonald. Psk
Lady Poverty, The. Alice Meynell. HBV-2; OBMV
Lady Poverty, The. Evelyn Underhill. HBV-2
Lady Prayeth the Return of Her Lover Abiding on the Seas, The. *Unknown.* EIL; GBL
    (Seafarer, The.) OBSC
    (To Her Sea-faring Lover.) OBEV
Lady-Probationer. W. E. Henley. In Hospital, IX. BrPo
Lady Queen Anne she sits in the sun. *Unknown.* OxNR
Lady red upon the hill, A. Emily Dickinson. AA; BoNaP; HBV-1; OHIP
Lady Sara Bunbury Sacrificing to the Graces, by Reynolds. Daryl Hine. EyDe
Lady Sings, The. Milton. *See* Song: "Sweet Echo, sweetest Nymph, that liv'st unseen."
Lady stands in her bower door, The. The Twa [*or* Two] Magicians. *Unknown.* ESPB; GBP; OAEL-1; OxBB
Lady Stood, A. Dietmar von Aist, *tr. fr. German by* Jethro Bithell. AWP
Lady, sweet, now do not frown. Joan to Her Lady. *Unknown.* UnTE
Lady Tactics. Anne Waldman. PoM
Lady, take care; for in the diamond eyes. Light and Dark. Barbara Howes. MoVE
Lady that hast my heart within thy hand. Hafiz, *tr. by* Gertrude Lowthian Bell. Odes, VIII. AWP
Lady, the birds right fairly. *Unknown.* PBBP
Lady, the meshes of your coiling hair. He Praises Her Hair. *Unknown, tr. by* the Earl of Longford. AnIL
Lady, the shepherds have all gone. Ya Se Van Los Pastores. Dudley Fitts. FYAP
Lady, the Silly Flea. *Unknown.* NCEP
Lady! the songs of Spring were in the grove. Sonnet: To the Lady Beaumont. Wordsworth. ChER
Lady, there is a hope that all men have. William Ellery Channing. *Fr.* A Poet's Hope. AA
Lady there was of Antigua, A. Limerick. Cosmo Monkhouse. HBV-2
Lady Thinks She Is Thirty, A. Ogden Nash. PoPl
Lady, three white leopards sat under a juniper-tree. T. S. Eliot. *Fr.* Ash Wednesday. LO; LoBV
Lady to a Lover, A. Roden Noel. OBVV
Lady Track Star, A. Roy Blount, Jr. TDH
Lady Venetia Digby, The. Ben Jonson. GoBC
Lady, very fair are you. Ad Chloen, M.A. Mortimer Collins. HBV-1
Lady walked by the ocean strand, The. Strand-Thistle. Gustav Falke, *tr. by* Jethro Bithell. AWP
Lady walked down a roadbed, A. A Gentle Heart: Two. Judith Johnson Sherwin. BoWoP
Lady, Weeping at the Crossroads. W. H. Auden. MoVE
Lady, When I Behold the Roses Sprouting. *Unknown.* InPK
Lady, when we sat together. The Seamy Side of Motley. Sir Owen Seaman. InMe
Lady, when you were alive. The Mortician's Twelve-year-old Son. Ai. GeTw
Lady who intervenes, The. Virgin. Padraic Fallon. OnYI
Lady Who Lived at Bordeaux, A. *Unknown.* TDH
Lady who lived in Uganda, A. The Panda. William Jay Smith. TDH
Lady Who Loved a Swine, The. *Unknown.* OuSiCo, *with music.*
    (Hunc, Said He.) ChTr
    (There Was a Lady Loved a Swine.) GBP
    ("There was a lady loved a swine.") OxNR
Lady Who Offers Her Looking-Glass to Venus, The. Matthew Prior, *after the Greek of* Plato. AWP; FaBoEE; NOEC; OBEV; ViBoPo
    (Farwell, A: "Venus, take my votive glass.") AWP
Lady who signs herself "Vexed," The. Edward Gorey. OBAL
Lady, who with tender word. The Housewife's Prayer. Blanche Mary Kelly. GoBC
Lady, whose ancestor/ Fought for Prince Charlie. The Stirrup Cup. Douglas Ainslie. GoTS

Lady whose name was Miss Hartley, A. Miss Hartley. William Jay Smith. TDH
Lady, whose shrine stands on the promontory. T. S. Eliot. *Fr.* Four Quartets: The Dry Salvages. ISi
Lady, why doth love torment you? Love's Torment. *Unknown.* UnTE
Lady with a Falcon on Her Fist, A. Richard Lovelace. CaPo
Lady with Technique, The. Hughes Mearns. *Fr.* Later Antigonishes. FiBHP; InMe; WhC
Lady with the frilled blouse. Valediction. Seamus Heaney. PPJ
Lady with the Unicorn, The. Vernon Watkins. LiTB; MP; TwCP
Lady without Paragon, A. Chaucer. *See* Balade: "Hide, Absalon, thy gilte tresses clear."
Lady, you are with beauties so enriched. Song. Francis Davison. ElL
Lady, you think too much of speeds. Statistics. Stephen Spender. MoBrPo
Lady, your art or wit could ne'er devise. To a Lady Who Sent Me a Copy of Verses at My Going to Bed. Henry King. PP
Lady, your head is on upside down. After Chagall. Renee Wenger. PoDr
"Lady, you're a poet, do you think about death?" No Signal for a Crossing. Rhoda Donovan. AMV-80
Ladybird. Clive Sansom. GrPl
Ladybird, The. *Unknown.* GBP
Ladybird! Ladybird! Emily Brontë. OnUR
Ladybird, Ladybird fly away home. Mother Goose. FaPON; OxNR; PoPL; SoPo
Ladybirds, The. Edward Lucie-Smith. BoAnP
Ladybug. Joan Walsh Anglund. RHPC
Ladybug. François Dodat, *tr. fr. French by* Bert *and* Odette Meyers. BoAnP
Ladybug. Raymond Souster. MoCV
Ladybug, ladybug, fly away home. Fly, Ladybug. Annette Burr Stowman. AMV-80
Ladybug's Christmas. Norma Farber. PChr
Ladye Marye! today/ Let me say my own say. The Spotless Maid. Vincent McNabb. ISi
Lady's Complaint, The. John Heath-Stubbs. MP; TwCP
Lady's Diary, The. Charles Dibdin. NOEC
Lady's Dressing Room, The. Swift. ErPo; NCEP; NoP; TEP
Lady's Prayer to Cupid, A. Thomas Carew, *after the Italian of* Giovanni Battista Guarini. CaPo
(Ladies Prayer to Cupid, A.) OBVE
Lady's Receipt for a Beau's Dress, The. *Unknown.* CoMu
Lady's Resolve, The. Lady Mary Wortley Montagu. BoWoP
Lady's Song. Milton. *See* Song: "Sweet Echo, sweetest Nymph, that liv'st unseen."
Lady's Song in Leap Year, The. *Unknown.* GBP
Lady's Song, The. Dryden. LoBV; SeCeV
Lady's "Yes," The. Elizabeth Barrett Browning. HBV-1
Lady's Third Song, The. W. B. Yeats. *Fr.* The Three Bushes. FaBoTw
Lady's Trial, The, *sel.* John Ford.
Pleasures, Beauty. ViBoPo
Lady's-Maid's Song, The. John Hollander. ErPo; LiTM; MP; NePoEA; TW; TwCP
La Fayette. Samuel Taylor Coleridge. EnRP
La Fayette. Dolly Madison. PAH; PAL
Lafayette to Washington. Maxwell Anderson. *Fr.* Valley Forge. PAL
Lagoon, The. Ashton Greene. NePoAm
Lagoons, Hanlan's Point. Raymond Souster. NOBC
Laguna Blues. Charles Wright. GeTw
Laguna Perdida. Maynard Dixon. BPAW
Laid in My Quiet Bed [in Study as I Were]. Earl of Surrey. CH; EnRePo; InvP
(How No Age Is Content.) LiTB; LoBV
(How No Age Is Content with His Own Estate, *shorter vers.*) ElL
(Youth and Age.) SiPS
Laid on Thine Altar. *Unknown.* TrPWD
Laid out for dead, let thy last kindness be. To Robin Redbreast. Robert Herrick. OBS; PBBP; TrGrPo
Laid with papyrus to catch fire. Martial, *tr. fr. Latin by* James Michie. FaBoEE
Laieikawai's Lament after Her Husband's Death. *Tr. fr. Hawaiian by* M. W. Beckwith. WTO
L'Aigle A Deux Jambes. Turner Cassity. GP
Laila Boasting. Laila Akhyaliyya, *tr. fr. Arabic by* Willis Barnstone. BoWoP
Laily Worm and the Machrel [of the Sea], The. *Unknown.* ChTr; ESPB; InvP; LoBV; OxBB; PoEL-1
'Laine. Robert Bagg. TwAmPo
Laird, a lord, A. *Unknown.* OxNR; SaC
Laird o' Cockpen, The. Lady Nairne, 2 *added sts. by* Susan Ferrier. BeLS; BSV; HBV-2; OBRV; WPE
Laird o Drum, The. *Unknown.* ESPB
Laird o' Logie, The. *Unknown.* CH; ESPB (A *and* B *vers.*)
Laird o' Ochiltree Wa's, The, *with music.* *Unknown.* OxBB
Laird of Bristoll's daughter was in the woods walking, The. Captain Wedderburn's Courtship. *Unknown.* ESPB
Laird of Leys is on to Edinbrugh [*or* Edinburgh], The. The Baron o [*or* of] Leys. *Unknown.* ESPB; OxBB
Laird of Wariston, The. *Unknown.* ESPB (A *and* B *vers.*)
Lairdless Place, The. Kate Rennie Archer. GoYe
Lairig, The. J. C. Milne. PoSH
Lais. Hilda Doolittle ("H. D."). MoAmPo
Lais Now Old. *Unknown, after the Greek of* Plato. EnRePo
(Lais now old, that erst attempting lass.) FaBoEE
Lais to Aphrodite. E. A. Robinson, *after the Greek of* Plato. FaBoEE
Lak of Stedfastnesse. Chaucer. AWP
Lake, The. Louis O. Coxe. MoVE; NYBP
Lake, The. Ted Hughes. FaBoTw; NYBP
Lake, The. Poe. OBRV
Lake. R. A. Simpson. CBAP
Lake, The. James Stephens. MoBrPo
Lake above Santos, The. Keith Wilson. GP
Lake allows an average father, walking slowly, A. Lakes. W. H. Auden. NePA; NePoAm
Lake and a fairy boat, A. Song. Thomas Hood. HBV-1
Lake Chelan. William Stafford. BiP; NaP
Lake Chemo. James Wilton Rowe. AmFP
Lake, The: Coda. Tom Clark. HoAn
Lake Harriet: Wind. Laurie Taylor. AMV-81
Lake Harvest. Raymond Knister. PeCV
Lake in the Sky, The. John Haines. LCAP
Lake is blue with morning, The; and the sky. Morning on the Shore. Wilfred Campbell. NOBC
Lake is deserted now, The. The Dispossessed. Thomas Kinsella. NOCV
Lake is sharp along the shore, The. Lakeshore. F. R. Scott. MoCV; NOBC; OBCV
Lake Isle, The. Ezra Pound. CABA; CrMA; FaBoCo; FaBoPa; PoA
Lake Isle of Innisfree, The. W. B. Yeats. BrPo; CMoP; CoBMV; FaBoPP; FaBV; FaFP; FaPON; FaPoR; FPL; HBV-1; InPS; LiTM; MoAB; MoBrPo; NoAM; NoBE; NoP; OAEP; OBEV; OBVV; OnYI; OxBTC; PAI; PoPL; PoRA; PrIm; RoGo; TEP; TreF; TrGrPo; VLP; WHA; WeW
Lake lay blue below the hill, The. L'Oiseau Bleu. Mary Elizabeth Coleridge. CH
Lake Leman ("Clear, placid Leman! thy contrasted lake"). Byron. *Fr.* Childe Harold's Pilgrimage, III. OBNC
Lake Leman ("Lake Leman woos me with its crystal face"). Byron. *Fr.* Childe Harold's Pilgrimage, III. PoEL-4
("Lake Leman woos me with its crystal face.") InPS
Lake Leman lies by Chillon's walls. Byron. *Fr.* The Prisoner of Chillon. OBRV
Lake loon paddles, A. Prelude. Rokwaho. STE
Lake Michigan Blues. *Unknown.* BluL
Lake of Gaube, The. Swinburne. OAEL-2; VLP
Lake of the Caogama, The. *Unknown.* WTO
Lake of the Dismal Swamp, The. Thomas Moore. BLPA
Lake Poets, The. Charles Townsend. DBV
(On the Lake Poets.) FaBoEE
Lake Song. Jean Starr Untermeyer. HBMV; TrJP
Lake Success. Robert Conquest. OxBC
Lake sunken among, A. Woman Skating. Margaret Atwood. IHMS
Lake Superior. Samuel Griswold Goodrich. AA
Lake that held a mirror to the sun, The. Northamptonshire Fens. John Clare. *Fr.* Child Harold. FaBoPP
Lake Walk at New Year's. Leigh Perez-Diotima. AMV-81
Lake water lifted a little and fell, The. Crab Orchard Sanctuary, Late October. Thomas Kinsella. IPY
Lakes. W. H. Auden. NePA; NePoAm
Lakes of the Atchafalaya, The. Longfellow. *Fr.* Evangeline. PoEL-5
Lakeshore. F. R. Scott. MoCV; NOBC; OBCV
Lakeside Incident. Robin Skelton. NOBC
La-la-llamas rate as mammals. In Praise of Llamas. Arthur Guiterman. FiBHP
Laleham: Matthew Arnold's Grave. Lionel Johnson. FaBoPP
Lalela Zulu. *Unknown, tr. fr. Zulu.* PeSA
Lalique. Hal Porter. PoAu-2
Lalla Halima! Protect abandoned girls! Like Smoke. Mririda n'Ait Attika, *tr. by* Daniel Halpern *and* Paula Paley. PBWP
Lalla Rookh, *sels.* Thomas Moore.
"Fly to the desert, fly with me," *fr.* The Story of the Sultana Nourmahal. BIrV
Golden Hour, The. OBNC
" 'I never nursed a dear gazelle,' " *fr.* The Fire-Worshippers. SpRo
Light of the Harem, The, *fr.* The Story of the Sultana Nourmahal. EnRP; TEP
Peri's Lament for Hinda, The. OBNC

Lalla Rookh/ Is a naughty book. On Thomas Moore's Poems. *Unknown.* FaBoCo; FiBHP
L'Allegro. Milton. AWP; CABA; FaFP; FiP; GTBS; GTBS-P; HAP; HBV-2; HoPM; JCP; LiTB; LoBV; MasP; NoP; OAEL-1; OBEV; OBS; PPP; SeCePo; SeCeV; TEP; TreFS; TrGrPo; ViBoPo; WHA
Sels.
"And, if I give thee honour due." PoPle
"Haste thee, nymph, and bring with thee." GN
Mirth, with Thee I Mean to Live. FaBV
Lalus a Jolly youthfull Lad. The Second Nimphall. Michael Drayton. *Fr.* The Muses Elizium. AnAnS-2
Laly, Laly. Mark Van Doren. SO
Lama, The. Ogden Nash. FaPON; FiBHP; PV
("One-l lama, The.") FaBoCh
Lamarck Elaborated. Richard Wilbur. AP; NePoEA
Lamb. Michael Dennis Browne. NU
Lamb and Bear; Jet Landing. Laurence Lieberman. DiL
Lamb of God, Thy faithful promise. The Coming and the Appearing. *Unknown.* STF
Lamb, The. Blake. *Fr.* Songs of Innocence. BLPL; CABA; CH; EaLo; EBCP; EnRP; FaBoBe; FaBoCh; FaPON; GoJo; HBV-2; HeIP; InPS; LAuP; LiTB; LoBV; NIP; NOEC; NoP; OAEL-2; OAEP; OBEC; OxBChV; OxBoCh; PAI; PoPl; SBVL; SeCeV; SoSe; SUS; TEP; TrCP; TreF; TrGrPo; TRV; UnPo; WGRP; WHA
Lamb, The. Keith Wilson. Psk
Lamb Was Bleating Softly, The. Juan Ramón Jiménez, *tr. fr. Spanish by* Robert Bly. NU; PChr
Lamb was so skinny I thought it was a baby goat, The. Children among the Hills. Linda Gregg. NPGG
Lamb, whan the hert is laich. Whan the Hert Is Laich. Sidney Goodsir Smith. NeBP
Lambkin. *Unknown. See* Lamkin.
Lambro's Return. Byron. *Fr.* Don Juan, III. OBRV
Lambs Frolicking Home. Fred Lape. BoAnP
Lambs of Grasmere, 1860, The. Christina Rossetti. FM
Lambs on the Green Hills Stood Gazing on Me, The. *Unknown.* AnIV
Lambs that learn to walk in snow. First Sight. Philip Larkin. BoNaP; NCSH; NTCP
Lamda. Melvin B. Tolson. *See* Satchmo.
Lame Angel. Donald Finkel. VWA
Lame Beggar, A. John Donne. FF
Lame, impotent conclusion to youth's dreams. Farewell to Juliet. Wilfrid Scawen Blunt. *Fr.* The Love Sonnets of Proteus. ViBoPo
Lame Soldier, The, *with music. Unknown.* OuSiCo
Lamed-Vov, The. Rose Ausländer, *tr. fr. German by* Ewald Osers. VWA
Lament: "Ban of Time there is no disobeying, The." Gelett Burgess. InMe
Lament: "Because the moon became my mother." Joseph Stroud. NPGG
Lament, A: "O world! O life! O time!" Shelley. ChER; ChTr; EnRP; GTBS; GTBS-P; LoBV; NOBE; OAEP; OBRV; PoRA; TEP; TreFT; TrGrPo; WHA
Lament: "Oh, everything is far." Rainer Maria Rilke, *tr. fr. German by* C. F. MacIntyre. PoPl; TrJP
Lament: "Chaste maids which haunt fair Aganippe's well." William Drummond of Hawthornden. *Fr.* Tears on the Death of Moeliades. LoBV
Lament: "Diameter of the bomb was thirty centimeters, The." Yehuda Amichai, *tr. fr. Hebrew by* Ruth Nevo. VWA
Lament: "Fall now, my cold thoughts, frozen fall." Laurence Binyon. MoVE
Lament: "Farewell Mercy, farewell thy piteous grace." John Lydgate. *Fr.* Court of Sapience. PoEL-1
Lament, A: "Gizzard and some ruby inner parts, A." Margaret Avison. HAP
Lament: "I lie in darkness, as the dead shades gather." Matangi Hauroa, *tr. fr. Maori by* Barry Mitcalfe. WTO
Lament: "Listen, children:/ Your father is dead." Edna St. Vincent Millay. DL; PoPl
Lament: "My man is a bone ringed with weed." Brenda Chamberlain. NeBP; WPE; WPOW
(First Woman's Lament.) NeIP
Lament: "Someone is dead." Anne Sexton. ConAP; WPE
Lament: "We who are left, how shall we look again." W. W. Gibson. MMA; OxBTC
Lament: "What face, in the water." William Carlos Williams. VGW
Lament: "What moved me, was the way your hand." Dorothy Livesay. CaP
Lament: "When I was a windy boy and a bit." Dylan Thomas. ErPo; MasP; PPP
Lament: "When the folk of my household." Edward Walsh. OBVV
Lament: "You did not suck at my mother's breast." Yonathan Ratosh, *tr. fr. Hebrew by* Howard Schwartz. VWA
Lament: "Youth's bright palace." Denis Florence MacCarthy. OBVV
Lament after Her Husband Bishr's Murder. Al-Khirniq, *tr. fr. Arabic by* Willis Barnstone. BoWoP
Lament City. Thomas Lux. AmPA
Lament, A; 1547. Alexander Scott. *See* Lament of the Master of Erskine.
Lament for a Cricket Eleven. Kenneth Allott. OxBTC
Lament for a Dead Lover. Siraad Haad, *tr. fr. Somali by* B. W. Andrzejewski *and* I. M. Lewis. WTO
Lament for a Husband. *Tr. fr. Papuan by* Don Laycock. BoWoP
Lament for a Sailor. Paul Dehn. WaP
Lament for a Warrior. *Unknown, tr. fr. Sotho by* Dan Kunene *and* Jack Cope. PeSA
Lament for Adonis. Bion, *tr. fr. Greek by* John Addington Symonds. AWP
Lament for Apirana Ngata. Arnold Reedy, *tr. fr. Maori by* Barry Mitcalfe. WTO
Lament for Art O'Leary. Eibhlin Dubh O'Connell, *tr. fr. Irish.* AnIL, *tr. by* Frank O'Connor; BIrV, *tr. by* Eilis Dillon *and* John Montague; KiLC, *tr. by* Frank O'Connor
(Dirge on the Death of Art O'Leary, *tr. by* Eleanor Hull.) AnIV
(Lament for Arthur O'Leary, The, *abr., tr. by* Elis Dillon *and* John Montague.) PBWP
Lament for Azazel. Francis Landy. VWA
Lament for Banba. Egan O'Rahilly, *tr. fr. Irish by* James Clarence Mangan. AnIV; AWP
Lament for Barney Flanagan. James K. Baxter. NoP
Lament for Better or Worse. Gene Baro. NePoEA-2
Lament for Bion. Moschus, *tr. fr. Greek by* George Chapman. AWP
Lament for Captain Paton. John Gibson Lockhart. OBRV
Lament for Chaucer. Thomas Hoccleve. OBEV
Lament for Chaucer and Gower. Thomas Hoccleve. *Fr.* De Regimine Principum. OxBM
(Hoccleve's Lament for Chaucer and Gower.) OAEP
("O maister deere and fader reverent!") EBEV
Lament for Corc and Niall of the Nine Hostages. *At. to* Torna, *tr. fr. Old Irish by* Sir Samuel Ferguson. OnYI
Lament for Culloden. Burns. GTBS; GTBS-P; HBV-2; OBEV
(Lovely Lass o'Inverness, The.) GoTS
Lament for Daphnaida. Spenser. FiP
Lament for Flodden, A. Jane Elliot. *See* Flowers of the Forest, The.
Lament for Glasgerion. Elinor Wylie. PoA
Lament for Ignacio Sánchez Mejías. Federico García Lorca, *tr. fr. Spanish by* A. L. Lloyd. OBVE
Lament for Imogen. Shakespeare. *See* Fear No More the Heat o' the Sun.
Lament for Lost Lodgings. Phyllis McGinley. NYBP; SpRo
Lament for Mafukuzela. *Zulu Oral Tradition, tr. by* H. Tracey. WTO
Lament for My Brother on a Hayrake. James Wright. TwAmPo
Lament for O'Sullivan Beare, The. *Unknown, tr. fr. Irish by* Jeremiah Joseph Callanan. AnIV
(Dirge of O'Sullivan Bear.) NBM
Lament for Our Lady's Shrine at Walsingham, A. *Unknown. See* Lament for the Priory of Walsingham, A.
Lament for Pasiphae. Robert Graves. FaBoTw
Lament for Richard Rolston. Sir Osbert Sitwell. ChMP
Lament for Seán. Daniel James O'Sullivan. NeIP
Lament for Sean MacDermott. "Seumas O'Sullivan." AnIV
Lament for Taramoana. Makere, *tr. fr. Maori by* Barry Mitcalfe. WTO
Lament for the Alamo. Arthur Guiterman. AmFN
Lament for the Cuckoo. Alcuin, *tr. fr. Latin by* Helen Waddell. NAWM-1; PeHV
Lament for the Death of Eoghan Ruadh O'Neill. Thomas Osborne Davis. AnIV; OxBI
(Lament for the Death of Owen Roe O'Neill.) OnYI
Lament for the Death of Thomas Davis. Sir Samuel Ferguson. BIrV; NBM; OnYI; OxBI
(Lament for Thomas Davis.) AnIV
Lament for the Dorsets. Al Purdy. NoP
Lament for the European Exile. A. L. Strauss, *tr. fr. Hebrew by* A. C. Jacobs. VWA
Lament for the Graham. Henry the Minstrel. *See* Wallace's Lament for the Graham.
Lament for the Great Music, *sel.* "Hugh MacDiarmid."
"Yet there is no great problem in the world today." OxBTC
Lament for the Makaris [*or* Makars]. William Dunbar. ACP; BSV; ChTr; EBEV; GoTS; NoP; OxBS; PP; ViBoPo, *abr.*
(Fear of Death Confounds Me, The.) MeEL
(I That in Heill Was and Glaidnes.) HAP
(Lament for the Makaris Quhen He Was Seik.) OAEP
(Lament for the Makers.) OAEL-1; OBEV; PoEL-1
(Timor Mortis Conturbat Me.) FaBoRV; NOBE, *abr.*
Lament for the O'Neills. John Montague. CIP
Lament for the Poets: 1916. Francis Ledwidge. AnIV; AWP; OnYI; OxBI
Lament for the Princes of Tyrone and Tyrconnel, A. *Unknown, tr. fr. Irish by* James Clarence Mangan. AnIV

Lament for the Priory of Walsingham, A. *Unknown.* FaBoPP; GBP
(In the Wracks of Walsingham.) NCEP
(Lament for Our Lady's Shrine at Walsingham, A.) ISi; PoEL-2
(Wreck of Walsingham, The.) ACP
"Bitter was it, Oh to view," *sel.* ChTr
Lament for the Two Brothers Slain by Each Other's Hand. Aeschylus, *tr. fr. Greek by* A. E. Housman. *Fr.* The Seven against Thebes. AWP
Lament for the Woodlands. *Unknown, tr. fr. Irish by* Frank O'Connor. KiLC
Lament for Thomas Davis. Sir Samuel Ferguson. *See* Lament for the Death of Thomas Davis.
Lament for Thomas MacDonagh. Francis Ledwidge. AnIV; BIrV
(Thomas MacDonagh.) OnYI; OxBI
Lament for Una, A, *sel.* Tomas Costello, *tr. fr. Gaelic by* Frank O'Connor.
"Young Una, you were a rose in a garden." WTO
Lament for Urien, The. *Unknown, tr. fr. Middle Welsh by* Ernest Rhys. *Fr.* The Red Book of Hergest. OBMV
Lament for Yellow-haired Donough, The. *Unknown, tr. fr. Irish by* Frank O'Connor. KiLC
Lament him, Mauchline husbands a'. On a Wag in Mauchline [*or* Epitaph for James Smith]. Burns. EBEV; ELU; FiBHP
Lament in Autumn. Harold Stewart. PoAu-2
Lament in rhyme, lament in prose. Poor Mailie's Elegy. Burns. FM
Lament, lament, Sir Isaac Heard. Epitaph on Tuft-Hunter. Thomas Moore. FaBoCo; FaBoEE
Lament my losse, my labor, and my payne. Sir Thomas Wyatt. AAS
Lament of a Last Letter. Janet E. Harrison. AMV-80
Lament of a Man for His Son. *Unknown, tr. fr. Paiute Indian by* Mary Austin. AWP; BPAW
(Lament of a Young Man for His Son.) DL
Lament of a Mocking-Bird. Frances Anne Kemble. AA; HBV-1
Lament of an Idle Demon. R. P. Lister. DBV; FiBHP; NOBL
Lament of Anastasius. William Bourne Oliver Peabody. AA
Lament of Barbara Douglas, The. *Unknown.* *See* Waly, Waly ("O waly, waly up the bank").
Lament of Edward Blastock, The. Edith Sitwell. OBMV
Lament of Eve, The. *Unknown.* ACP
Lament of Guiderius and Arviragus. Shakespeare. *See* Fear No More the Heat o' the Sun.
Lament of Hsi-chün. Hsi-chün, *tr. fr. Chinese by* Arthur Waly. BoWoP
Lament of Maev Leith-Dherg, The. *Unknown, tr. fr. Middle Irish by* Thomas W. H. Rolleston. OBWP; OnYI
Lament of the Border Widow, The. *Unknown.* GBP; HBV-1; OxBB, *with music*
(Bonnie Bower, The.) CH
(Border Widow's Lament, The.) BSV
("My love he built me a bonnie bower.") LO
Lament of the Damned in Hell, The. Edward Young. OxBoCh
Lament of the Demobilised, The. Vera Brittain. SUMH
Lament of the Flowers, The. Jones Very. NOBA; OxBA
Lament of the Flutes. Christopher Okigbo. PBA
Lament of the Frontier Guard. Li Po, *tr. fr. Chinese by* Ezra Pound. AP; CoBMV; OBVE; OBWP; TwAmPo; VGW; WaaP
Lament of the Irish Emigrant. Helen Selina Sheridan. HBV-1; OBVV
Lament of the Jewish Women for Tammuz. Charles Reznikoff. VWA
Lament of the Lovely Helmet-Dealer. Villon, *tr. fr. French by* Hubert Creekmore. ErPo
Lament of the Mangaire Sugach. Andrew Magrath, *tr. fr. Modern Irish by* Edward Walsh. OnYI
Lament of the Master of Erskine. Alexander Scott. BSV; GBL
(Lament, A; 1547.) CH, *abr.*
Lament of the Sodomites. George Lestey. *Fr.* Fire and Brimstone; or, The Destruction of Sodom. PeHV
Lament of the Unmarried Girl, The. Brian Merriman, *tr. fr. Modern Irish by* Frank O'Connor. *Fr.* The Midnight Court. OBVE
Lament of the Virtues and Verses on Account of the Death of Don Guido. Antonio Machado, *tr. fr. Spanish by* Charles Tomlinson *and* Henry Gifford. OBVE
Lament of the Voiceless, The. Laura Bell Everett. PGD
Lament the Night before His Execution, A. Chidiock Tichborne. *See* Elegy: "My prime of youth is but a frost of cares."
Lament while Descending a Shaft. *Unknown.* AmFP
Lamentable Ballad of the Bloody Brook, The. Edward Everett Hale. HBV-2; PAH
Lamentable Case, A. Charles Hanbury-Williams. ErPo
Lamentable Case, A. *Unknown.* UnTE
Lamentation. Bible, *O.T.* Ezekiel, XIX: 2-9. TrJP
Lamentation, A. Thomas Campion. CH; OHIP
Lamentation. Nissim Ezekiel. VWA
Lamentation. Harold LaMont Otey. LFAC
Lamentation, A. Carl Rakosi. VWA
Lamentation for Celin, The. *Unknown, tr. fr. Spanish by* John Gibson Lockhart. AWP
Lamentation of Chloris, The. *Unknown.* CoMu
Lamentation of Enion, The. Blake. *Fr.* Vala; or, The Four Zoas. OBNC
Lamentation of Mac Liag for Kincora. *Unknown.* *See* Kincora.
Lamentation of the Old Pensioner, The. W. B. Yeats. HAP; InPK; NoAM; PPON; TW; VLP; WeW
(Old Pensioner, The, *diff. version.*) InPK
Lamentation on My Dear Son Simon, A. John Saffin. SCAP
Lamentation on the Death of the Duke of Wellington. *Unknown.* OBET
Lamentations. Alter Brody. TrJP; VWA
Lamentations. Louise Glück. BoWoP; MAYP
Lamentations. Siegfried Sassoon. OBSV
Lamentations of an Au Pair Girl. Susan Feldman. AmPA
Lamentations of the Fallen Angels. *Unknown, tr. fr. Anglo-Saxon by* Charles W. Kennedy. *Fr.* Christ and Satan. AnOE
Lamentations, *sels.* Bible, *O.T.*
Affliction, III: 1-15. TrJP
Desolation in Zion, I: 12-17. TrJP
How Is the Gold Become Dim, IV: 1-5. ChTr
Misery of Jerusalem, The, I. AWP
Lamenting Maid, The. *Unknown.* OBET
Lamenting Tauba. Laila Akhyaliyya, *tr. fr. Arabic by* Willis Barnstone. BoWoP
Lamia. Keats. EnRP; OAEP
Banquet, The, sel. SeCePo
Lamilia's Song. Robert Greene. *See* Fie, Fie on Blind Fancy!
L'Amitié et l'Amour. John Swanwick Drennan. BIrV
Lamkin (*diff. versions*). *Unknown.* AmFP; ESPB (A, B, *and* K *vers.*); FaBoBa; OxBB, *with music;* ViBoFo
(Lambkin.) OBET
Lamorna Cove. W. H. Davies. BrPo
Lamp, The. Sarah Pratt McLean Greene. AA
Lamp[e], The. Henry Vaughan. AnAnS-1; QFR
Lamp, The. Charles Whitehead. OBEV; OBVV
Lamp burns long in the cottage, The. There's Money in Mother and Father. Morris Bishop. FiBHP
Lamp burns sure, within, The. Emily Dickinson. LiTA
Lamp, don't moan. The Air Vision. Jakov van Hoddis, *tr. by* Charles Guenther. VWA
Lamp in the West, The. Ella Higginson. AA; HBV-2
Lamp must be replenish'd, but even then, The. Manfred. Byron. EnRP
Lamp Now Flickers, The. Alfred Grünewald, *tr. fr. German by* Edouard Roditi. VWA
Lamp of heaven's crystal hall that brings the hours. Sonnet. William Drummond of Hawthornden. JCP
Lamp of Poor Souls, The. Marjorie Pickthall. HBV-2
Lamplight. May Wedderburn Cannan. SUMH
Lamplight lies in a ring. Absence. Peter Meinke. PPJ
Lamplighter, The. "Seumas O'Sullivan. "BIrV; OxBI
Lamplighter, The. Robert Louis Stevenson. EBVV; FaFP; OxBChV; SaC; TreF
Lamprey, glowing with uncommon fires, The. William Diaper, *after the Greek of* Oppian. *Fr.* Halieutica. OBVE
Lamps along the river, The. Estuary. William Montgomerie.
Lamps Are Burning, The. Charles Reznikoff. TrJP
Lamps burn all the night. The Fifth Sense. Patricia Beer. MoBS
Lamps now glitter down the street, The. Armies in the Fire. Robert Louis Stevenson. EBVV
Lan Nguyen; the Uniform of Death, 1971. David Mura. BrSi
L'An Trentiesme de Mon Eage. Archibald MacLeish. LiTM; MoVE; NePA; NoAM; NOBA; TwAmPo
(In My Thirtieth Year.) MoAmPo
Lana Turner has collapsed! Poem. Frank O'Hara. CAPP; VGW
Lancashire Born. *Unknown.* GBP
Lancashire Lads. *Unknown.* CoMu
Lancashire Puritane, The. *Unknown.* CoMu
Lancashire Winter. Tony Connor. OxBTC
Lancaster bore him—such a little town. A Hundred Collars. Robert Frost. YaD
Lancaster County Tragedy. W. Lowrie Kay. ShM
Lancelot. Arna Bontemps. CDC
Lancelot and Elaine, *sel.* Tennyson.
Song of Love and Death, The. OBNC
(Elaine's Song.) FaBoEn
Lancelot and Guinevere. Gerald Gould. HBV-2
Lancelot and the Grail. Tennyson. *Fr.* Idylls of the King. GoBC
Lancer. A. E. Housman. MoBrPo; OBWP
Lancing enhancing. Simfunny of Thee Hold Whorl. Charles Lynch. LTB
Land. Carroll Arnett. VoR
Land, The, *sels.* Struthers Burt.
"Be not afraid, O Dead, be not afraid," III. HBMV

"O Lord of splendid nations let us dream," IV. HBMV
Land, The. Kipling. MoBrPo; OnMSP
Land, The. Dorothy Livesay. *Fr.* The Colour of God's Face. PeCV
Land, The, *sel.* V. Sackville-West.
Spring. PeHV
Land behind the Wind, The. David Wagoner. NPAW
Land Dirge, A. John Webster. *See* Call for the Robin Redbreast and the Wren.
Land earth-root. Invocation. Nakasuk, *tr. fr. Eskimo.* WTO
Land floats by under us, The. Love Making. James Tate. EAS
Land I Came Thro' Last, The. Christopher Brennan. *Fr.* The Wanderer. PoAu-1
Land I plowed last fall, The. Sun and I. Ken Mammone. AMV-81
Land is cold and its men gather earth for no reason, The. A Woman's Song. Colleen J. McElroy. BlSi
Land is lonely now, The: Anathema. Robert Stephen Hawker. *Fr.* The Quest of the Sangraal. EBVV
Land lies in water; it is shadowed green. The Map. Elizabeth Bishop. NOBA
Land-Mine, The. George MacBeth. OBWP
Land not mine, still, A. "Anna Akhmatova," *tr. fr. Russian by* Jane Kenyon. NU
Land o' the Leal, The. Lady Nairne. GTBS; GTBS-P; HBV-2; OBEV; OxBS; WBLP; WGRP
Land of Beginning Again, The. Louisa Fletcher. BLPA
Land of Cockayne, The. *Unknown, at. to* Friar Michael of Kildare. OAEL-1, *paraphrased fr. Middle English by* J. B. Trapp; OxBM
(Cokaygne.) AnIL
(Land of Cockaigne, The, *tr. fr. Middle English by* John Montague.) BIrV
(Land of Cokaygne, The, *mod. vers. by* Russell K. Alspach). OnYI
Land of Counterpane, The. Robert Louis Stevenson. BrPo; EBEV; EvOK; FaBoBe; FaFP; FaPON; HBV-1; HBVY; NTCP; OxBChV; PoPl; SoPo; TreF
Land of Dreams, The. Blake. BeLS; CH; OBRV
Land of Dreams, The. Henry Martyn Hoyt. HBMV
Land of dreams and sleep, Aa poppied land! Nubia. Bayard Taylor. HBV-2
Land of gold!—thy sisters greet thee. California. Lydia Huntley Sigourney. PAH
Land of Heart's Desire, The. Emily Huntington Miller. HBV-1
Land of Heart's Desire, The, *sel.* W. B. Yeats.
"Wind blows out of the gates of the day, The." ViBoPo
(Fairy Song.) MoBrPo; OnYI
Land of Hope and Glory. A. C. Benson. FaPoR
Land of Indolence, The. James Thomson. *Fr.* The Castle of Indolence. OBEC; SeCePo
(Enchanted Ground.) BSV
("In lowly dale, fast by a river's side.") EnRP; NOEC; ViBoPo
Land of leaning ice, A. North Labrador. Hart Crane. CMoP; FaBoMo; POL
Land of Little Sticks, 1945. James Tate. MAYP
Land of my birth! though now, alas! no more. William Charles Wentworth. *Fr.* Australasia. PoAu-1
Land of My Heart. William Dudley Foulke. *Fr.* Ad Patriam. PAL; PGD
Land of Potpourri, The. Jack Prelutsky. RHPC
Land of Story-Books, The. Robert Louis Stevenson. FaBoBe; FaPON; HBV-1; HBVY; TiPo; TreFS
Land of the Evening Mirage, The. *Unknown, tr. fr. Sioux Indian by* A. M. Bede. WGRP
Land of the Free. Arthur Nicholas Hosking. BLPA; PAL
Land of the Free. Sister Mary Honora. NePoAm-2
Land of the Free. Archibald MacLeish. AmFN
"We wonder whether the dream of American liberty," *sel.* MoAB
Land of the Horizontal Yellow. Indian Death. Eda Lou Walton. BPAW
Land of the Wilful Gospel. Sidney Lanier. *Fr.* Psalm of the West. PAH
Land of unconquered Pelayo! land of the Cid Campeador! The Surrender of Spain. John Hay. AA
Land starts *dentelle,* indented, The. Carta Canadensis. Ralph Gustafson. PeCV
Land, that, from the rule of kings, The. The Bartholdi Statue. Whittier. PAH
Land that is lonelier than ruin, A. Swinburne. By the North Sea, I. PoEL-5; VLP
Land wants me to come back, The. Dust Bowl. Langston Hughes. PoA
Land War, The. "Seumas O'Sullivan". OxBI
Land was ours before we were the land's, The. The Gift Outright. Robert Frost. AmFN; AmPP; AP; CMoP; CoBMV; FaBoEn; GOA; LiTM; MoAB; MoAmPo; NoAM; NOBA; NoP; OxBA; PAL; PPP; SeCeV; WaP
Land was overmuch like scenery, The. Beowulf. Richard Wilbur. CrMA
Land was white, The. Riddle. *Unknown.* ChTr, OxNR
Land Where Hate Should Die, The. Denis A. McCarthy. PGD
Land where I was born sits by the seas. Francesca and Paolo. Dante, *tr. by* Byron. *Fr.* Divina Commedia: Inferno. TreFT
Land Where the Columbines Grow. Arthur J. Fynn. PoOW
Land Which No One Knows, The. Ebenezer Elliott. *See* Plaint.
Landcrab. Margaret Atwood. SoSe
Landed: A Valentine. Richard Howard. PoA
Land-Fall. George M. Brady. NeIP
Landfall, The. James Dickey. PoA
Landfall. *Maori Oral Tradition, tr. by* A. S. Thomson. WTO
Landfill. Michael Harper. LCAP
Landing, The. "Lewis Carroll." *Fr.* The Hunting of the Snark. WhC
Landing, The. Daniel Halpern. AmPA
Landing of the Pilgrim Fathers [in New England], The. Felicia Dorothea Hemans. BeLS; BLPA; FaBoBe; FaBV; FaFP; FaPo; FaPON; GN; HBV-2; HBVY; OHIP; PAH; PAL; PaPo; PGD; SBG; TreF; WBLP; WPE
Landing on the Moon. May Swenson. MOON; TAP
Landlady. P. K. Page. CaP; SoSe
Landlord Fill the Flowing Bowl. *Unknown.* FSW
Landlord, landlord. Ballad of the Landlord. Langston Hughes. NOBA
Landlord's coat is tulip red, The. Wild Sports of the West. John Montague. CIP
Landlord's Wife, The. Marilyn Chin. BrSi
Landlubber's Chantey, The. James Stuart. HBMV
Landmarch by camel and shipsail we take. Cargoes of the Radanites. Harry Alan Potamkin. TrJP
Landmark, The. Dante Gabriel Rossetti. The House of Life, LXVII. NBM
Landor. John Albee. AA
Landrail, The. John Clare. PBBP
Land's End. Stanton A. Coblentz. BPAW; EtS
Landscape. David Gascoyne. FaBoMo
Landscape. William Mason. *Fr.* The English Garden, I. OBEC
Landscape. Octavio Paz, *tr. fr. Spanish by* Charles Tomlinson. OBVE
Landscape. Alfred W. Purdy. CaP
Landscape, The. William Shenstone. *See* Song: The Landskip.
Landscape. Abraham Sutskever, *tr. fr. Yiddish by* Ruth Whitman. VWA
Landscape, A/ full of holes. Loose Woman Poem. Sharon Thesen. NOBC
Landscape and Figure. Thomas Kinsella. IPY
Landscape as a Nude. Archibald MacLeish. Frescoes for Mr. Rockefeller's City, I. AmPP; CMoP
Landscape as Metal and Flowers. Winfield Townley Scott. AmFN; GoJo; MiAP
Landscape: Beast/ Yonder, by the eastward sea. Figure for an Apocalypse. Thomas Merton. CrMA
Landscape, Deer Season. Barbara Howes. GoJo; LiSp; POL
Landscape I ("The character of a landscape stands always in a mysterious relation"). Charles Madge. EAS
Landscape Lies within My Head, The. Gervase Stewart. WaaP
Landscape near a Steel Mill. Herschel Horn. PPON
Landscape near an Aerodrome, The. Stephen Spender. CoBMV; LiTM; MoAB; MoBrPo; MoVE; NoAM; OAEP; OxBTC
Landscape, New Mexico. Kell Robertson. TAT
Landscape of Love, The. Thomas Cole. NePoAm
Landscape of Screams. Nelly Sachs, *tr. fr. German by* Michael Roloff. NYBP
Landscape of the Heart, The. Geoffrey Grigson. LiTB; WaP
Landscape of the Vomiting Multitudes. Federico García Lorca, *tr. fr. Spanish by* Ben Belitt. NYP
Landscape of Violence. Ralph Nixon Currey. PeSA
Landscape (the landscape!) again, The: Gloucester. The Librarian. Charles Olson. CoPo
Landscape was, The. Canto 5: Coon Fire. Tom Weatherly. PoBA
Landscape where I lie, The. Song for a Lyre. Louise Bogan. LiTA
Landscape with Figures. Keith Douglas. NePoEA
Landscape with Figures. Theodore Enslin. CoPo
Landscape with Lapwings. James Aitchison. BSV
Landscape with Leaves and Figure. Olga Broumas. BoWoP
Landscape with Little Figures. Donald Justice. LCAP
Landscape with Minute Wildflowers. Hugh Maxton. CIP
Landscape with Next of Kin. Olga Broumas. BoWoP
Landscape with the Fall of Icarus. William Carlos Williams. Pictures from Brueghel, II. LCAP; NIP; PPP
Landscape with the Giant Diana, *sel.* Sacheverell Sitwell.
Orion Seeks the Goddess Diana. MoVE
Landscape with Tractor. Henry Taylor. MAYP
Landscape Workers. Harley Elliott. LTB
Landscapes, *sels.* T. S. Eliot.
Cape Ann, V. BiP; EvOK; GoJo
New Hampshire, I. BiP; FaBoCh; GTBS-P; LoBV; WeW
Rannoch, by Glencoe, IV. BiP; FaBoEn; FaBoPP; PoSH

Usk, III. BiP; FaBoCh; NOCV
Virginia, II. BiP
Landscapes. Richard Hugo. GP
Landscapes. Louis Untermeyer. HBV-2
Landscape's private and all that it contains, The. Artillery Shoot. James Forsyth. WaP
Lane County Bachelor, The. *Unknown. See* Starving to Death on a Government Claim.
Lang Johnny More. *Unknown.* ESPB
Langaig. Richard Hugo. WOLT
Langley Lane. Robert Buchanan. HBV-2
Langston. Mari Evans. BOLo; CNA
Langston Blues. Dudley Randall. CNA; FB
Langston Hughes. Lew Blockcolski. VoR
Langsyne, When Life Was Bonnie. Alexander Anderson. HBV-1
Language, The. Robert Creeley. CAPP; CoPo; TAP
Language has not the power to speak what love indites. Fragment. John Clare. ELU; FaBoEE; NBM; OAEL-2; OBNC; PoEL-4
Language is the first perversion of the senses. Genesis. Brian Higgins. FaBoTw
Language Lesson, 1976. Heather McHugh. MAYP
Language of Ancients. Hayim Lenski, *tr. fr. Hebrew by* Pearl Grodensky. VWA
Language of Erin is brilliant as gold, The. The Irish Language. James Clarence Mangan. VLP
Language of walls, The. Hieroglyph. Paul Auster. VWA
Language on which the sun flows, A. Epos. Harold Rosenberg. PoA
Languages We Are, The. F. J. Bryant. NBP
Langue d'Oc, *sel.* Ezra Pound.
Alba ("When the nightingale to his mate"). OBVE; VGW; WeW
Languid lady next appears in state, The. Characters of Women. Edward Young. *Fr.* Love of Fame. OBEC
Languishing Moon, The. Sir Philip Sidney. *See* Astrophel and Stella: Sonnets, XXXI.
Langwell. Kingsley Amis. *Fr.* The Evans Country. NOBL; OxBC
Lanigan's Ball. *Unknown.* OxBoLi
Lanky hank of a she in the inn over there, The. A Glass of Beer [*or* Righteous Anger]. James Stephens, *after* David O'Bruaidar. AnIV; CMoP; DBV; DTC; FaBoCo; FiBHP; MoAB; MoBrPo; NCSH; NoAM; OBMV; OxBTC; PoPL; SeCePo; TreFT; TW; WhC
L'Annunciazione. Ned O'Gorman. TwAmPo
Lantern. Frank Polite. GP
Lantern. Gary Soto. Str
Lantern light from deeper in the barn, A. The Fear. Robert Frost. BeLS; TwAmPo
Lantern out of Doors, The. Gerard Manley Hopkins. CMoP; LiTB; OxBoCh; TrCP; VLP
Lanternslides grinding out B-flat minor, The. Lunch. Kenneth Koch. SOTW
Lanty Leary. *Unknown.* ChTr
Laocoon. Don Gordon. WaaP
Laocoon. Donald Hall. NePoAm-2
Laodamia. Wordsworth. EnRP; OAEP
Laparotomy revealed a tumor of the insulin-secreting, The. Dr. Dimity Lectures on Unusual Cases. Cynthia Macdonald. SUW
Lapful of Nuts, The. *Unknown, tr. fr. Irish by* Sir Samuel Ferguson. VLP
Lapidary. Bonnie L. Alexander. AMV-80
Lapis. Shawn Wong. BrSi
Lapis Lazuli. W. B. Yeats. ChMP; CMoP; CoBMV; DTC; FaBoMo; FaBoTw; FF; InPK; InPS; LiTB; LiTM; MAT; MoPo; MoVE; NoAM; NOBE; NoP; OAEL-2; OAEP; PP; PPoe; TEP
"L'Apparition" of Gustave Moreau. Gordon Bottomley. BrPo
Lapping of lake water, The. Lake Song. Jean Starr Untermeyer. HBMV; TrJP
Laprairie Hunger Strike. Ronald Everson. MoCV
L'Après Midi d'une Fille aux Cheveux de Lin. Ronald McCuaig. PoAu-2
Lapsus Linguae. Richard Howard. NoAM
Lapsus Linguae. Keith Preston. OBAL; WhC
Lara, *sels.* Byron.
"In him inexplicably mixed appeared." OAEL-2
"There was a vital scorn of all." OBRV
Laramie Trail. Joseph Mills Hanson. BPAW; PoOW
Larch Hill. Leslie Daiken. OnYI
Larch Tree. Laurie Lee. NeBP
Larches. Ivor Gurney. FaBoPP
Large Bad Picture. Elizabeth Bishop. EyDe; MiAP; NoP; NYBP; OxBC
Large, colored dyke from Atlanta, A. Limerick. *Unknown.* PeHV
Large glooms were gathered in the mighty fane. James Thomson. ("B. V."). The City of Dreadful Night, XIV. EBEV; OAEL-2; OAEP
Large porcupine breathes smaller ones, The. There Won't Be Another. Diane Glancy. STE
Large Red Man Reading. Wallace Stevens. HAP; LCAP
Large transparent baby like a skeleton in a red tree, A. The Visible Baby. Peter Redgrove. NAs
Large yellow wings, black-fringed, The. Butterfly on Rock. Irving Layton. NOBC
Larger, gentler slopes of its mouth opening upon the ocean, The. The Dysynni Valley. Theodore Holmes. CoPo
Larger Hope, The. Tennyson. *See* In Memoriam A. H. H.: "Oh yet we trust that somehow good"
Larger Prayer, The. Ednah D. Cheney. BLRP; WGRP
(Prayer—Answer.) STF
Largess, The. Richard Eberhart. LiTA
Largest Life, The. Archibald Lampman. CaP
Largest stock of armaments allows me, The. Civilian. Josephine Miles. WPE
Largo. Sidney Goodsir Smith. NeBP
Largo. Dunstan Thompson. LiTA; MoPo; WaP
Largo e Mesto. W. E. Henley. *See* Out of the Poisonous East.
Lariat snaps, The; the cowboy rolls. The Closing of the Rodeo. William Jay Smith. GOA; MP; NePoEA; SaC; TwCP
Larikie, larikie, lee! *Unknown.* PBBP
Larissa. Thomas Love Peacock. *Fr.* Rhododaphne. OBRV
Lark, The. Bernart de Ventadorn, *tr. fr. Provençal by* Ezra Pound. CTC
Lark, The. Lizette Woodworth Reese. HBMV
Lark, The ("Liverockie, liverockie lee"). *Unknown.* GBP
Lark, The ("Malisons, malisons more than ten"). *Unknown.* GBP
("Malisons, malisons more than ten.") PBBP
Lark, The ("Swift through the yielding air I glide"). *Unknown.* OBS
Lark above our heads doth know, The. A Violinist. Francis William Bourdillon. OBVV
Lark above the Trenches, The. Muriel Elsie Graham. SUMH
Lark as small as a flint arrow, A. The Round Barrow. Andrew Young. SeCePo
Lark Ascending, The. George Meredith. LoBV; OAEP; PBBP; WiR
Lark begins to go up, The. Skylarks. Ted Hughes. HAP
Lark drives invisible pitons in the air. Movements. Norman MacCaig. OxBC
Lark in the mesh of the tangled vine, A. Kyrielle. John Payne. HBV-2
Lark in the Morning, The. *Unknown.* ChTr
Lark is up to meet the sun, The. Morning. Jane Taylor. HBV-1
Lark Now Leaves His Wat'ry [*or* Watery] Nest, The. Sir William Davenant. CH; ChTr; InvP; PoRA; WHA
(Aubade.) NOBE; OBEV
(Lark Now Leaves, The.) ViBoPo
(Morning.) ACP; HBV-1
(Morning Song.) TrGrPo
(Song: "Lark now leaves his wat'ry [*or* watery] nest, The.") AWP; FaBoEn; GBL; GoBC; MeLP; MePo; OBS; PBBP; SeCV-1
Larks. Katharine Tynan. OnYI
Lark's Nest, The. John Clare. PBBP
Lark's Nest, A. Christopher Smart. *See* For Saturday.
Lark's Song, The. Blake. *See* Vision of Beulah, The.
Larks trill in the quiet glen. The Quiet Glen. Douglas Fraser. PoSH
Larkspur and Hollyhock. Names. Dorothy Aldis. SUS
Larrie O'Dee. William W. Fink. HBV-2
Larry M'Hale. Charles James Lever. OnYI
Lars Porsena of Clusium. Horatius at the Bridge. Macaulay. *Fr.* Lays of Ancient Rome. BeLS; FaBoCh; FaFP; FaPoR; HBV-2; HBVY; OBNV; OHFP; PoLF; TreF
L'Art, 1910. Ezra Pound. HeIP; OxBA
Las Trampas U. S. A. Charles Tomlinson. TwCP
Lasagna. X. J. Kennedy. PPJ
Lasca. Frank Desprez. BeLS; BLPA; BPAW; FaBoBe; HBV-2; TreF
Laser. A. R. Ammons. NOBA
Lashes of my eye are clipped away, The. Cataract. Margoret Smith. NYBP
Lass and the Friar, The. Burns. *See* Lovely Lass to a Friar Came, A.
Lass cam' sabbin', A. The Wishin' Well. Helen B. Cruickshank. BSV
Lass from Bally-na-Lee, The. Anthony Raftery, *tr. fr. Irish by* Desmond O'Grady. BIrV
Lass in Wonderland, A. Francis Reginald. MoCV
Lass o' Gowrie, The. Lady Nairne. HBV-1
Lass o' Patie's Mill, The. Allan Ramsay. BSV
Lass of Islington, The. *Unknown.* CoMu
(Fair Lass of Islington, The.) OxBB
Lass of Lochroyan, The. *Unknown.* HBV-2
(Fair Annie of Lochroyan, *with music.*) AS
(Fair Isabell of Rochroyall.) OxBB
(Lass of Roch Royal, The.) AmFP; ESPB (A *and* D *vers.*); FSW; ViBoFo (2 *vers., with music.*)
(True Lover's Farewell, The, *with music.*) AS
(Who Will Shoe Your Pretty Little Foot? *with music.*) AS
(Who's Gonna Shoe Your Pretty Little Foot? *shorter vers.* FSW

Lass of Lynn's New Joy, for Finding a Father for Her Child, The. *Unknown.* CoMu
Lass of Richmond Hill, The. James Upton. HBV-1
Lass of Richmond Hill, The, *with music.* Leonard McNally. BLSo
Lass of Roch Royal, The. *Unknown. See* Lass of Lochroyan, The.
Lass That Died of Love, The. Richard Middleton. HBV-1
Lass That Made the Bed for Me, The. Burns. InvP; UnTE
Lass, when they talk of love, laugh in their face. Love. Francis Jammes, *tr. by* Jethro Bithell. AWP
Lass with a Lump of Land. Allan Ramsay. NOEC
Lasses, like nuts at bottom brown. Epigram. Allan Ramsay. FaBoEE
Lassie, can ye say. For a Wife in Jizzen. Douglas Young. OxBS
Lassie, What Mair Wad You Hae? Heine, *tr. fr. German into Scottish by* Alexander Gray. GoTS; OxBS
Lassie, with the lips sae rosy. Mädchen mit dem rothen Mündchen. Heine, *tr. by* Sir Theodore Martin. AWP
Lassitude. Mathilde Blind. SBG
Lassitude. Paul Verlaine, *tr. fr. French by* Lawrence M. Bensky. ErPo
Last, The. Ezra Zussman, *tr. fr. Hebrew by* D. Shnayorson. VWA
Last Address to My Ghosts, A. Gregory Orr. GeTw
Last Affair: Bessie's Blues Song. Michael S. Harper. GeTw; LCAP
Last All Saints' holy-day, even now gone by. Sonnet: Of Beatrice de' Portinari, on All Saints' Day. Dante, *tr. by* Dante Gabriel Rossetti. AWP; GoBC
Last and greatest herald of Heaven's King, The. For the Baptist [*or* Saint John Baptist]. William Drummond of Hawthornden. BSV; EaLo; GoTS; GTBS; GTBS-P; HBV-2; LoBV; NOBE; OBEV; OBS; OxBoCh; TrCP; TrGrPo
Last Antiphon: To Mary. James J. Donohue. ISi
Last Appendix to "Yankee Doodle," The. *Unknown.* PAH
Last Ascent, The. John Lehmann. ChMP
Last autumn, as we sat, ere fall of night. Cader Idris at Sunset. Charles Tennyson Turner. FaBoPP
Last autumn's chestnuts, rather *passées.* Ingenious Raconteur. Renée Haynes. PV
Last Bison, The, *sel.* Charles Mair.
"Hear me, ye smokeless skies and grass-green earth." NOBC
Last Bite, The. Richard Frost. AMV-80
Last Book of the Ocean to Scinthia, The, *sels.* Sir Walter Ralegh.
"To seeke new worlds, for golde, for prayse, for glory." FaBoEn
"With youth, is deade the hopes of loves returne." FaBoEn
Last Born. Judith Kirkwood. Str
Last Bowstrings, The. Edward Lucas White. AA
Last Breath. Laura Chester. NPGG
Last Buccaneer, The. Charles Kingsley. BeLS; EBVV; EtS; FaBoBe; HBV-1
(Old Buccaneer, The.) EvOK; MoShBr
Last Buccaneer, The. Macaulay. EtS; HBV-1
Last Bus, The. E. V. Knox. BXAP
Last Bus, The. Mark Strand. TwCP
Last Call. Langston Hughes. NePoAm-2
Last Came, and Last Did Go. Milton. *Fr.* Lycidas. TW
Last Campaign, The. Geoffrey Lehmann. PoAu-2
Last Camp-Fire, The. Sharlot M. Hall. HBV-2
Last Cargo. Silence Buck Bellows. EtS
Last chair finally was carried out, The. The House. Paula Nelson. GoYe
Last Chantey, The. Kipling. EtS; FaBoCh; MoBrPo; MOS; OBVV
Last Chapter, The. Walter de la Mare. CMoP; MoBrPo
Last Christmas, Father. Lines for My Father. Patrick Worth Gray. AMV-81
Last Chrysanthemum, The. Thomas Hardy. CMoP; LiTB
Last Coachload, The. Walter de la Mare. SeCePo
Last Communion, The. Leo Ward. GoBC
Last Confession, A. Dante Gabriel Rossetti. NCEP
Last Confession, A. W. B. Yeats. BoLoP; CMoP; ELP; ErPo; HAP; OAEL-2; WeW
Last Conqueror, The. James Shirley. *See* Victorious Men of Earth.
Last Corn Shock, The. Glenn Ward Dresbach. FaPON
Last Cry of the Damp Fly, The. Dennis Lee. NTCP
Last Cup of Canary, The. Helen Gray Cone. AA
Last dark violet, The. Poetry. Abraham Sutskever, *tr. by* Ruth Whitman. VWA
Last Day, The. Lola Derosier. STF
Last Day and the First, The. Theodore Weiss. TwCP; VGW
Last Day of the Trip. Lloyd Davis. WOLT
Last Day of the Year, The (New Year's Eve). Annette von Droste-Hülshoff, *tr. fr. German by* Willis Barnstone. BoWoP
Last Days. Richard Hugo. PoA
Last Days, The. George Sterling. HBMV
Last Days. Elizabeth Stoddard. AA
Last Days of Alice. Allen Tate. NoAM; NOBA; OxBA; TwAmPo; UnPo
Last days of November, and everything so green, The! The Volunteer's Thanksgiving. Lucy Larcom. OBCA
Last Days of Pompeii, The, *sel.* Sir Edward Bulwer-Lytton. Nydia's Song. OBVV
Last decent man alive, The. Across to the Peloponnese. James Welch. CDW
Last Defile, The. Amy Carmichael. TrCP; TRV
Last Democrat, The. D. J. Enright. NMP
Last Dream, The. Ray A. Young Bear. STE
Last Drift. Arthur Chapman. BPAW
Last Drink, A. *Unknown.* OxBM
Last Easter I was married, that night I went to bed. The Lowlands of Holland. *Unknown.* AmFP
Last Easter Jim put on his blue. Easter Zunday. William Barnes. VLP
Last eve I passed [*or* I paused last eve] beside of a blacksmith's door. The Anvil—God's Word [*or* God's Word *or* Hammers and Anvil]. John Clifford. BLPA; BLRP; STF; TRV; WBLP
Last Evening. Rainer Maria Rilke, *tr. fr. German.* OBWP, *tr. by* J. B. Leishman; WaaP, *tr. by* C. F. MacIntyre
Last evening when I went to bed. Our Birthday. Marion Edey. SiSoSe
Last evening you were drinking deep. Hangover Cure. Alexis. FaBoUs
Last Fairy, The. Rosamund Marriott Watson. OBVV
Last Fall of the Alamo. "O. Henry." BPAW
Last Families in the Cabins, The. Millen Brand. GP
Last Farewell to the Hills, *sel.* Duncan Ban MacIntyre, *tr. fr. Gaelic by* Robert Buchanan.
On Ben Dorain. PoSH
Last Farmer in Queens, The. Vickie Karp. NYP
Last Fierce Charge, The. *Unknown.* AmFP; ViBoFo
Last Fight, The. Lewis Frank Tooker. AA; FaBoBe
Last Fire, The. Moishe Steingart, *tr. fr. Yiddish by* Gabriel Preil. VWA
Last Fish, The. Barry Spacks. AMV-80
Last Flight of the Great Wallenda, The. Barbara Helfgott Hyett. AMV-80
Last Flower, The. John Travers Moore. PoSC
Last, for December, houses on the plain. Sonnets of the Months: December. Folgore da San Geminiano, *tr. by* Dante Gabriel Rossetti. AWP
Last Frontier, The. John Thomas. GP
Last Fruit Off an Old Tree, *sels.* Walter Savage Landor.
On His Seventy-fifth Birthday. AWP; BLPL; EBEV; LiTB; OAEL-2; OAEP; SeCeV; TreF; TrGrPo; WHA
(Dying Speech of an Old Philosopher.) FaBoEE; GTBS-P; HeIP; NoP; ViBoPo; VLP
(End, The.) SeCePo
(Envoi.) FaBoEn
(Finis.) GLGT; OBEV; OBVV
(I Strove with None.) ChTr; EnRP; HBV-2
("I strove with none, for none was worth my strife.") FaPoR; NOBE; OBNC
"There falls with every wedding chime." SeCePo
Last full moon of February, The. Hunger Moon. Jane Cooper. CABA
Last Furrow, The. Edwin Markham. AA
Last Galway Hooker, The. Richard Murphy. IPY
Last Generation. Michelle Roberts. LFAC
Last Gloucesterman, The. Gordon Grant. EtS
Last Good-by, The. Louise Chandler Moulton. AA
Last Guest, The. Frances Shaw. HBMV
Last Hour, The. Ethel Clifford. HBV-1
Last hour nears, The. Pshytik. Nahum Bomze, *tr. by* Gabriel Preil. VWA
Last Hunt, The. William Roscoe Thayer. AA; FaBoBe; HBV-2
Last Hymn, The. Marianne Farningham. BLPA
Last Impression of New York. Mason Jordan Mason. PoNe
Last Instructions to a Painter, The. Andrew Marvell. APAS
Sels.
"After two sittings, now our Lady State." OBSV
Charles II. OBS
Dutch in the Medway, The. OBS
"Paint Castlemaine in colours that will hold." OBSV
"Paint last the King, and a dead shade of night." OBSV
Last Invocation, The. Walt Whitman. HBV-2; MoAmPo; OxBA; PoEL-5; TreFT; TrGrPo; TrPWD; TRV
(Imprisoned Soul, The.) WGRP
Last Job I Held in Bridgeport, The. D. W. Donzella. TAT
Last Journey, The. John Davidson. *Fr.* The Testament of John Davidson. BSV; GoTS; PoSH
Last Journey, The. Leonidas of Tarentum, *tr. fr. Greek by* Charles Merivale. AWP
Last Judgment, The. Bible, *N.T.* Revelation, XX: 11-15; XXI: 1-7. TreF
Last Judgment. John Gould Fletcher. AWP
Last Judgment, The. *Unknown, tr. fr. Anglo-Saxon by* Charles W. Kennedy. *Fr.* Christ 3. AnOE
Last Landlord, The. Elizabeth Akers Allen. AA
Last Lap, The. Kipling. OxBTC

Last Lauch. Douglas Young. BSV; FaBoCo; OxBS; SeCePo
Last Leaf, The. Oliver Wendell Holmes. AA; AmPP; AP; FaBoBe; FaPON; HBV-1; OBVV; PoLF; SeCeV; TreF; WBLP
Last Leave. Eileen Newton. SUMH
Last Leave of the Hills. Duncan Ban MacIntyre, *tr. fr. Gaelic.* GoTS
Last Letter to Pablo. Pat Lowther. NOBC
Last Letter to the Western Civilization. D. T. Ogilvie. NBP
Last Light. Robert Kelly. VGW
Last light has gone out of the world, except, The. Liberty. Edward Thomas. MoAB; OAEL-2
Last light muffles itself in cloud and goes, The. Mise en Scène. Robert Fitzgerald. NYBP; VGW
Last Lines. "Thomas Ingoldsby." *See* As I Laye a-Thynkynge.
Last Lines. Emily Brontë. *See* No Coward Soul Is Mine.
Last Lines. Egan O'Rahilly, *tr. fr. Irish by* Frank O'Connor. KiLC
Last Lines. X. J. Kennedy. OBAL
Last Lines, *sel.* "Owen Meredith".
"Lord! if in love, though fainting oft, I have tended thy gracious Vine." TrPWD
Last Longhorn, The. *At. to* R. W. Hall. BPAW; CoSo
Last Longhorn's Farewell, The. John P. Sjolander. BPAW
Last Look at La Plata, Missouri. Jim Barnes. CDW
Last Love. Fyodor Tyutchev, *tr. fr. Russian by* Vladimir Nabokov. BoLoP
Last Man, The, *sel.* Thomas Lovell Beddoes.
"Hard by the lilied Nile I saw." FM
Last Man, The. Thomas Campbell. EnRP; OBRV
Last Man, The. Thomas Hood. OBRV; VLP
Last Mathematician. Hyman Edelestein. CaP
Last May. Carroll Arnett. STE
Last May-day fair I search'd to find a snail. John Gay. *Fr.* The Shepherd's Week. FaBoUs
Last Meeting. Gwen Harwood. PoAu-2
Last Meeting of Pocahontas and the Great Captain, The. Margaret Junkin Preston. PAH
Last Memory, The. Arthur Symons. HBV-1
Last Minstrel, The. Sir Walter Scott. *Fr.* The Lay of the Last Minstrel. TreFS
Last minutes of light, The. My slow Shadow. Jogging at Dusk. Andrew Grossbardt. AMV-80
Last Month. John Ashbery. CAPP; CoAP
Last month in your little Roman house, The. On the Death of Keats. John Logan. Prf
Last Moriori, The. Kendrick Smithyman. OCNZ
Last Night. George Darley. HBV-1; OnYI
Last Night. David Ignatow. VGW
Last night. The Lovers. Joan Murray. LTB
Last night a baby gargled in the throes. A Widow in Wintertime. Carolyn Kizer. NMP
Last night a sword-light in the sky. Stone Trees. John Freeman. BoNaP
Last night, ah, yesternight, betwixt her lips and mine. Non Sum Qualis Eram Bonae sub Regno Cynarae [*or* Cynara]. Ernest Dowson. AWP; BeLS; BLPA; BoLoP; BrPo; CABA; EBVV; EnLoPo; FaBoBe; FaFP; FPL; GBL; GTBS-P; HAP; HBV-1; HeIP; LiTB; MoBrPo; NOBE; NoP; OAEL-2; OBEV; OBMV; OBNC; OBVV; PoPl; PoRA; PrIm; TEP; TreF; TrGrPo; UnPo; UnTE; ViBoPo; VLP
Last night Alicia wore a Tuscan bonnet. Alicia's Bonnet. Elisabeth Cavazza Pullen. AA
Last night along the river banks. The Boats Are Afloat. Chu Hsi, *tr. by* Kenneth Rexroth. NaP
Last night, among his fellow roughs. The Private of the Buffs; or, The British Soldier in China. Sir Francis Hastings Doyle. HBV-2; OBEV; OBVV; PaPo; VLP
Last night as I lay on the prairie. The Cowboy's Dream. *Unknown, at. to* Charles J. Finger. BPAW; CoSo; FSW
Last night, as through the crowd on Market Street. Glimpses. Roy Helton. HBMV
Last night at black midnight I woke with a cry. The Ghosts of the Buffaloes. Vachel Lindsay. BPAW; MoAmPo; NePA
Last night at Bon Odori the drums of Kinnara Taiko. Letter to Tina Koyama from Elliot Bay Park. Jim Mitsui. BrSi
Last night beneath the foreign stars I stood. Sonnet: The Common Grave. Sydney Thompson Dobell. NCEP
Last night, by the Klondike River. By the Klondike River. Alan Coren. OnUr
Last night did Christ the Sun rise from the dark. Easter Sunday. Sedulius Scottus, *tr. by* Helen Waddell. OFD
Last night for the first time since you were dead. To L. H. B. Katherine Mansfield. HBMV
Last night God barr'd the portals of the East. Holiday. Henry Dawson Lowry. OBVV
Last night I did not fight for sleep. In Hospital: Poona, I. Alun Lewis. DTC; NeBP; SeCePo
Last night I dreamed. The Night-Apple. Allen Ginsberg. NoAM
"Last night I dreamed a ghastly dream." Ballad of the Flood. Edwin Muir. MoBS
Last night I dreamed I was the first man to love a woman. Like Wings. Philip Schultz. MAYP
Last night I dreamed of an old lover. Grandmother, Rocking. Eve Merriam. GrPl; PCP
Last night I dreamt I saw. The Lake: Coda. Tom Clark. HoAn
Last night I had a dream. A Dream about an Aged Humorist. Aaron Zeitlin, *tr. by* Ruth Whitman. VWA
Last night I had a dream bad 'cess to my dreaming. The Dream. *Unknown.* WTO
Last night I heard a *rat-tat-too.* Rain Riders. Clinton Scollard. SoPo; TiPo
Last night I heard wolves howling. Wolves. John Haines. BoAnP; LCAP
Last night I lay a-sleeping. The Holy City. Frederic Edward Weatherly. BLRP; WBLP
Last night I lay on the prairie. *See* Last night as I lay on the prairie.
Last night I licked. In Celebration. Ellen Bass. NMM
Last night, I saw a documentary. Losing Track. Cathy Song. BrSi
Last night I saw Merce Cunningham. Merce Cunningham and the Birds. Lisel Mueller. GrPl
Last night I saw the monster near; the big. The White Monster. W. H. Davies. AmMo; LiTB
Last night I saw the savage world. Song for a Birth or a Death. Elizabeth Jennings. EBEV
Last night I saw you in my sleep. Bad Dreams. Robert Browning. OAEP
Last night I saw you in the sky. Starfish. Winifred Welles. FaPON; SiSoSe
Last night I saw your corpse. Joyce Mansour, *tr. fr. French by* Willis Barnstone. BoWoP
Last night I spoke to a dead woman with green face. Last Night. David Ignatow. VGW
Last night I supped on lobster; it nearly drove me mad. The Dream. *Unknown.* OxBoLi
Last night I took a journey. Traveling on My Knees. Sandra Goodwin. STF
Last night I tossed and could not sleep. God Prays. Angela Morgan. WGRP
Last night I watched my brothers play. The Brothers. Edwin Muir. GTBS-P; HeIP; NoP; PrIm
Last night in a land of triangles. Zalinka. Tom MacInnes. PeCV
Last Night in Calcutta. Allen Ginsberg. NoAM
Last Night in Sisseton, S. D. Mary Goose. STE
Last night, in snowy gown and glove. At the Comedy. Arthur Stringer. HBV-1
Last night in the open shippen. Christmas Day. Andrew Young. OBCP
Last night knives flashed. LeChien cried. The Wolves. Galway Kinnell. NePoEA-2
Last night my boy [*or* little boy] confessed to me. The Two Prayers. Andrew Gillies. BLRP; TRV
Last night my friend—he says he is my friend. I Hear It Said. Barbara Young. BLPA
Last night returning from my twilight walk. A Ballad of Past Meridian. George Meredith. OAEL-2; VLP
Last night that she lived, The. Emily Dickinson. BoWoP; CMoP; LiTA; NePA; OxBA; PoEL-5; QFR; SOTW
Last night the cold wind and the rain blew. Sunday at the End of Summer. Howard Nemerov. BoNaP
Last night the first light frost, and now sycamore. Long Walks in the Afternoon. Margaret Gibson. AMV-81; MAYP
Last night the moon poked a long. And the Winner Is. Greg Forker. LFAC
Last night the rainbow. Moon Shadow. George Bowering. MoCV
Last Night There Was a Cricket in Our Closet. Leroy V. Quintana. GP
Last night there was a storm in Tucson. Survivors. Michael Hogan. FAZ
Last night there were four Maries. The Four Maries. *Unknown.* FSW
Last Night They Heard the Woman Upstairs. Leslie Ullman. AMV-80
Last night thin rain, gusty wind. Li Ch'ing-chao, *tr. fr. Chinese by* Willis Barnstone *and* Sun Chu-chin. BoWoP
Last night thou didst invite me home to eat. Upon Showbread: Epigram. Robert Herrick. CaPo
Last night under the stars. Stags. William Montgomerie. PoSH
Last night watching the Pleiades. An Autumn Morning in Shokoku-ji. Gary Snyder. *Fr.* Four Poems for Robin. HAP
Last night we anchored in. Arrival, New York Harbor. Robert Peters. GOA
Last night we sat with the stereopticon. Readings of History. Adrienne Rich. ConAP
Last night we slept in Miami in the house of. September 30. Dick Lourie. NeAC

Last night we started with some dry vermouth. Ballade of Liquid Refreshment. E. C. Bentley. FaBoCo
Last night we talked about God. Furniture. Chana Bloch. GP
Last night when all the stars were still. Three White Birds of Angus. Eleanor Rogers Cox. HBMV
Last night, when my tired eyes were shut with sleep. A Gazelle. Richard Henry Stoddard. AA
Last night when the sun went down. Evensong. Peter Kane Dufault. AMV-80
Last night while we were fast asleep. New Year's Day. Rachel Field. SoPo; TiPo
Last night you stirred in your sleep as the night went through. Before Dawn. Elinor Chipp. HBMV
Last night you would not come. Love Poem. John Logan. CAPP
Last o' the Tinkler, The. Violet Jacob. OxBS
Last of His Tribe, The. Henry Kendall. CBAP; PoAu-1
Last of last words spoken is, Good-bye, The. Good-bye. Walter de la Mare. FaBoEn; NoP
Last of October, The. Fall. Aileen Fisher. YeAr
Last of the Grand Old Masters, The. Tom Patey. PoSH
Last of the Poet's Car. Tony O'Connor. OxBTC
Last of the poets, first of the undead. The Mole. Dennis Schmitz. AmPA
Last of the Princes, The. A. K. Ramanujan. OxBC
Last on legs, last on sax. "Bird Lives": Charles Parker in St. Louis. Michael S. Harper. AmPA
Last One, The. W. S. Merwin. LCAP; NoAM; VGW
Last one, The/ to die here. Nelly Sachs, *tr. fr. German by* Arthur Wensinger. BoWoP
Last Ones, The. Dan Pagis, *tr. fr. Hebrew by* Stephen Mitchell. VWA
Last Picnic, The. Stanley Kunitz. NoAM
Last Plea. Jean Starr Untermeyer. TrPWD
Last Poem. Charles Donnelly. BIrV
(Poem: "Between rebellion as a private study and the public.") CIP
Last Poems. A. E. Housman. *Poems indexed separately by titles and first lines.*
Last pose flickered, failed, The. Rain after a Vaudeville Show. Stephen Vincent Benét. MoAmPo
Last Post, The. Robert Graves. MMA
Last Prayer, A. Helen Hunt Jackson. AA; TrPWD; TRV
Last Prayer. Christina Rossetti. *See* Before the Beginning.
Last Quarter. John Hollander. MOON
Last Quarter Moon of the Dying Year, The. Jonathan Henderson Brooks. CDC
Last Quatrain of the Ballad of Emmet Till, The. Gwendolyn Brooks. CAPP; CNA; PoBA; WPE
Last Redoubt, The. Alfred Austin. HBV-2
Last Refuge, The. Augustus Young. BIrV
Last Republicans, The. Austin Clarke. CIP
Last Reservation, The. Walter Learned. AA; PAH
Last Resort, The. Robert Willson. FAZ
Last Ride Together, The. Robert Browning. BoLoP; FiP; HBV-1; LiTB; OAEP; OBEV; OBVV; PoEL-5; UnPo; VLP; WHA
Last Ride Together, The (from Her Point of View). James Kenneth Stephen. BXAP; CenHV; FaBoCo; Par; UnPo
Last Rite. John V. Hicks. AMV-81
Last Rites. David Citino. AMV-80
Last Rites. Christina Rossetti. OxBChV; RHPC
Last Rose of Summer, The. Thomas Moore. *See* 'Tis the Last Rose of Summer.
Last Round, The. Anna Wickham. MoBrPo
Last Saturday night I called at the house. Johnny McCardner. *Unknown.* OuSiCo
Last sea-thing dredged by sailor Time from Space. Australia. Bernard O'Dowd. PoAu-1
Last settlement scraggled out with a barbed wire fence, The. The Flight in the Desert. William Everson. VGW
Last Sheet. Roy Fuller. TEP
Last Sight, The. Robert Louis Stevenson. BrPo
Last, since a pinch of dust may quench the eyes. Lilith on the Fate of Man. Christopher Brennan. *Fr.* Lilith. PoAu-1
Last Snow. Andrew Young. OxBTC
Last snow is going, The. Spring. Harry Behn. TiPo
Last Song. James Guthrie. PDV; TiPo
Last Song, The. Joy Harjo. TAT; TWSS
Last Songs. Galway Kinnell. PAI
Last Sonnet. Keats. *See* Bright Star! Would I Were Steadfast as Thou Art.
Last specks of sunlight, The. Rural Lines after Breughel. Norbert Krapf. PoDr
Last summer, in the blue heat. La Vita Nuova. Weldon Kees. VGW
Last Summer, The. Vivian Smith. PoAu-2
Last summer was hot and dry, a better time. Delta Farmer in a Wet Summer. James Whitehead. TAT
Last sunbeam, The/ Lightly falls from the finished sabbath. Dirge for Two Veterans [*or* Two Veterans]. Walt Whitman. GN; MoAmPo; PoEL-5
Last Sunday petrified. Wingwalking in Oregon. Robert Peterson. NeAC
Last Supper, The. Stan Rice. NPGG
Last Supper, The. Rainer Maria Rilke, *tr. fr. German by* M. D. Herter Norton. OFD
Last Supper, The. Oscar Williams. FaFP; LiTA; LiTM; NePA; TwAmPo
Last Temptation, The. T. S. Eliot. *Fr.* Murder in the Cathedral. TreFT
Last thin acre of stalks that stood, The. Immortal. Mark Van Doren. MoAmPo
Last thing I put on, The. Vital Message. Robert Phillips. GeTw
Last thing, the very, The. Mountain Creed. Hugh C. Rae. PoSH
Last Things. Bill Manhire. OCNZ
Last Things. William Meredith. NoAM
Last Things. Kathleen Raine. NYBP
Last Things, Black Pines at 4 a.m. Robert Lowell. NOBA
Last Thoughts of a Fighting Man. Frances Angermeyer. *See* Conversion.
Last time around the forest floor. Rainier. Jim Tollerud. VoR
Last time I kissed her, The. Almost Ninety. Ruth Whitman. PCP
Last time I left/ Bill's Twilight Lounge. Sensational Relatives. Alexis Krasilovsky. AMV-80
Last time I left, you pulled your chair. In Search of a Short Poem for My Grandmother. Louise Hardiman. AMV-81
Last time I saw Donald Armstrong, The. The Performance. James Dickey. CoAP; ConAP; LiTM; NePoEA-2; NoAM; NOBA
Last Time I the Well Woke, The. *Unknown.* NCEP
Last time i was home, The. Mothers. Nikki Giovanni. CNA; CTBA; UnPo
Last to leave, The—the first to go. The First Division Marches. Grantland Rice. PAL; YaD
Last Tournament, The, *sels.* Tennyson. *Fr.* Idylls of the King.
Lincolnshire Shores ("As the crest of some slow-arching wave"). FaBoPP
Tristram's Song. FaBoRV
Last Tourney, The. Frederic F. Van de Water. HBMV
Last Trail, The. Stanton A. Coblentz. BPAW
Last Trial, The. Petrarch, *tr. fr. Italian.* *OBSC*
Last truly foolish thing I did was some years ago, The. The Void. Gwendolyn MacEwen. *Fr.* The T. E. Lawrence Poems. NOBC
Last Turn, The. William Carlos Williams. NYP
Last tyme I the wel woke, The. The Last Time I the Well Woke. *Unknown.* NCEP
Last Utterance of the Delphic Oracle, The. *Tr. fr. Greek by* Kenneth Rexroth. OBVE
Last Verses. Thomas Chatterton. TrGrPo
Last Verses. Michael Drayton. *See* Verses Made the Night before He Died.
Last Verses. William Motherwell. HBV-2
Last Verses. Edmund Waller. *See* Old Age.
Last Violet, The. Oliver Herford. OHIP
Last Visit. Robert Finch. NOBC
Last Voyage, The, *sels.* Alfred Noyes. The Torch Bearers, III. GoBC
Messages, *fr.* XIII.
Strong City, The, *fr.* Dedication.
Under the Pyrenees, *fr.* Dedication.
You That Sing in the Blackthorn, *fr.* II.
Last Voyage, The. Katharine Tynan. HBMV
Last Voyage of the Fairies, The. William H. Davenport Adams. HBVY
Last War, The. Kingsley Amis. OBSV; OxBC; SoSe
Last Warmth of Arnold, The. Gregory Corso. CoPo; NoAM
Last week a doctor told me. Beauty I Would Suffer For. Marge Piercy. NIP
Last Week I Took a Wife, *with music.* M. Kelly. BLSo
Last week my old cat fell to the worms. Poem Ending with an Old Cliché. Paul Zimmer. AMV-81
Last Whiskey Cup, The. Paul Engle. YaD
Last Will and Testament, A. John Winstanley. OBSV
Last Will and Testament, A. *Unknown.* MeEL
Last Will and Testament of Anthony, King of Poland, The. *Unknown.* APAS
Last Will of the Drunk. Myra Von Riedemann. OBCV
Last winter a Snowman; and after snow an Iceman. Farmer. Padraic Fallon. OxBI
Last winter we were/ short of firewood. A Letter to Hitler. James Laughlin. LiTA; WaP
Last Wish, The. "Owen Meredith." OBVV
Last Wolf, The. Mary TallMountain. TWSS
Last Word, The. Matthew Arnold. CABA; FaBoEn; FiP; HBV-2; NOBE; OAEL-2; OBNC; OBVV; PoEL-5; TreFT; TrGrPo; VLP; WHA
Last Word, The. Peter Davison. InPK
Last Word, A. Ernest Dowson. MoBrPo; SyP; VLP
Last Word, The. Frederic Lawrence Knowles. HBV-1
Last Word, A. May Sarton. GLGT

Last Word of a Bluebird, The. Robert Frost. FaPON; GoJo; GrPl; SO; TiPo
Last Words. Emily Brontë. WPE
Last Words. John Hollander. OBAL; PV
Last Words, The. Maurice Maeterlinck, *tr. fr. French by* Frederick York Powell. AWP; PoPl
Last Words. James Merrill. TAP
Last Words. Sylvia Plath. FYAP
Last Words before Winter. Louis Untermeyer. MoAmPo
Last Words, 1968. Lance Henson. CDW
Last Words of Don Henriquez, The. Zalman Schneour, *tr. fr. Yiddish by* Joseph Leftwich. TrJP
Last Words of My English Grandmother, The. William Carlos Williams. SOTW
Last words of Shaw, The: "I'm going to die." Alan Bold. POL
Last Words to a Dumb Friend. Thomas Hardy. FM; OAEP; PCat
Last Words to Miriam. D. H. Lawrence. CoBMV
Last World, A. John Ashbery. PoM
Last year at the Feast of Lanterns. Lost. Chu Shu-chen, *tr. by* Kenneth Rexroth. BoWoP
Last year I trod these fields with Di. Mrs. Smith. Frederick Locker-Lampson. HBV-1
Last year, Orlando. The Political Orlando. George MacBeth. NOBL
Last year the fields were all glad and gay. The Fields of Flanders. Edith Nesbit. SUMH
Last year the war was in the northeast. War. Li Po, *tr. by* Rewi Alley. ChTr
Last year when I accompanied you. To a Traveler. Su Tung-p'o, *tr. by* Kenneth Rexroth. HoPM
Last Years, The. W. H. Davies. FM
Last year's decencies. Odysseus. Padraic Fallon. CIP
Last Year's Discussion: The Nobel Russian. Phyllis McGinley. FaBoEE
Lastlie stode warre in glittering armes yclad. *See* Lastly, stood war, in glittering arms yclad.
Lastly came Winter cloathèd all in frize. Winter. Spenser. *Fr.* The Faerie Queene, VII, 7. GN
Lastly, stood war [*or* Lastlie stode warre], in glittering arms yclad. A Vision of War [*or* The Shield of War]. Thomas Sackville. *Fr.* Induction to "A Mirror for Magistrates." FaBoEn; NOBE
Lastness. Galway Kinnell. NNaP
"Black bear sits alone, A," *sel.* DiL; GP
Lat never a man a wooing wend. King Henry. *Unknown.* ESPB; OxBB
Lat no man booste of conning not vertu. Transient as a Rose. John Lydgate. MeEL
Lat Take a Cat. Chaucer. *Fr.* The Canterbury Tales: The Manciples Tale. ChTr
(Mice before Milk.) PCat
Late. Louise Bogan. PBWP; VGW
Late. Daniel Halpern. AMV-81
Late. Helen Salz. GoYe
Late Abed. Archibald MacLeish. NCSH
Late Afternoon on a Good Lake. Dara Wier. MAYP
Late afternoon, summer on the prairie. Bucket in the Well. Connie Wanek. AMV-80
Late Again. Gabriel Zaid, *tr. fr. Spanish by* Eliot Weinberger. AMV-81
Late Air. Elizabeth Bishop. PoPl
Late April and you are three; today. W. D. Snodgrass. Heart's Needle, II. NePoEA
Late April. Taking stock. Generalities. Robert Conquest. OxBC
Late as last summer. Thou Didst Say Me. Miriam Waddington. OBCV; PeCV
Late at een, drinkin' the wine. The Dowie Houms o' Yarrow [*or* The Braes o Yarrow]. *Unknown.* BaBo; BSV; ESPB; GoTS; OBEV; OBS; OxBS
Late at Night. William Stafford. NNaP; POL; RFM
Late at night. The Beads. Jaime Jacinto. BrSi
Late at night our hands stop working. Return to a Place Lit by a Glass of Milk. Charles Simic. GeTw
Late Aubade, A. Richard Wilbur. PAI; SoSe
Late August, given heavy rain and sun. Blackberry-picking. Seamus Heaney. BoNaP
Late Autumn. A. M. Sullivan. GoBC
Late Autumn. Andrew Young. MoVE
Late Autumn Walk. J. D. McClatchy. AMV-80
Late-born and woman-souled I dare not hope. Echoes. Emma Lazarus. SBG
Late Comer. Fanny de Groot Hastings. GoYe
Late Corner. Langston Hughes. NePoAm-2
Late Dandelions. Ben Belitt. NYBP
Late-flowering Lust. John Betjeman. CMoP; ErPo; NMP; TW
Late Game. B. H. Fairchild. AMV-81
Late Gothic. Phyllis Gotlieb. NOBC
Late, I was in the back circle. Auction. William Heyen. MAYP
Late in an evening forth as I went. Archie o Cawfield. *Unknown.* ESPB
Late in Fall. Ramona Wilson. VoR
Late in the afternoon. Spring Burning. Patrick Roland. PeSA
Late in the afternoon the light. Crepuscular. Richard Howard. TwCP
Late in the evening the ale graines and blood. Baits for Various Fish. Thomas Barker. *Fr.* The Art of Angling. FaBoUs
Late, in the louring sky, red, fiery, Streaks. James Thomson. *Fr.* The Seasons: Winter. FaBoEn
Late into the lulling night the pickers toiled. Uneasy Peace. Edmund Blunden. BrPo
Late, just past midnight. Off from Swing Shift. Garrett Kaoru Hongo. MAYP
Late Lark Twitters from the Quiet Skies, A. W. E. Henley. *See* Margaritae Sorori.
Late Last Night. Arthur Gregor. VGW
Late Last Night. Langston Hughes. NoAM
Late Last Night. Harry Graham. *See* Necessity.
Late last night I was a-making my rounds. Bad Man Ballad. *Unknown.* AmFP
Late, Last Rook, The. Ralph Hodgson. MoBrPo
Late Late. George Starbuck. PPON
Late Leaves. Walter Savage Landor. HBV-1
Late lies the wintry sun a-bed. Winter Time. Robert Louis Stevenson. EBVV; MoBrPo; OxBChV
Late Light. Edmund Blunden. EnLoPo
Late Light. Barbara Bellow Watson. NYBP
Late Lights in Minnesota. Ted Kooser. TAT
Late Lunch, San Antonio. Vincent O'Sullivan. OCNZ
Late Manuscript at the Schocken Institute, A. Gabriel Preil, *tr. fr. Hebrew by* Gabriel Levin. VWA
Late May/ and twenty miles east of Fresno. Eclipse. Timothy Sheehan. SUW
Late Miss H. came to us Wednesday at four, The. Swansong. Carol Muske. AmPA
Late Moon. Philip Levine. LCAP
Late Mother, The. Cynthia Macdonald. Psk
Late night, with my bundle of new straws. The Burden of Decision. Peter Everwine. NNaP
Late November in a Field. James Wright. CAPP; NNaP
Late October. Sara King Carleton. GoYe
Late October. Sara Teasdale. PoSC; YeAr
Late October sun, The. White Earth Reservation 1980. Gerald Vizenor. STE
Late of the jungle, wild and dim. Billiards. Walker Gibson. LiSp; NePoAm
Late on a summer night maybe twenty years from now. Midnight, Walking the Wakeful Daughter. Joseph Meredith. AMV-81
Late Passenger, The. C. S. Lewis. EBCP; TrCP
Late Reflections. Babette Deutsch. NYBP
Late, retarding, and unsettled season, The. Autumn; an Ode. Charles Gullans. NePoEA
Late Rising. Jacques Prévert, *tr. fr. French by* Selden Rodman. CAD
Late Saturday afternoons in Emeryville. Butcherboy. Tom Schmidt. NeAC
Late Show, The. William Heyen. GLGT
Late Show, The. Janet Sylvester. MAYP
Late singer of a sunless day. The Linnet in November. Francis Turner Palgrave. EBVV
Late Snow and Lumber Strike of the Summer of Fifty-four, The. Gary Snyder. NaP; NMP
Late Spring. Robert Hass. GeTw; MAYP
Late Spring, A. James Scully. NYBP
Late Spring: A Heaving, a Turning. John Gill. NeAC
Late Spring Day in My Life, A. Robert Bly. NCSH
Late Spring, A: Eastport. Philip Booth. Psk
Late spring I catch them by dozens. Catching Soft Craws. William J. Vernon. WOLT
Late Starting Dawn. Richard Brautigan. PCP
Late summer, and at midnight. The Guttural Muse. Seamus Heaney. NoP
Late that mad Monday evening. Madness One Monday Evening. Julia Fields. NIP; NNP
Late tired with woe, even ready for to pine. Astrophel and Stella, LXII. Sir Philip Sidney. HBV-1; SiPS
Late Tutorial. Vincent Buckley. PoAu-2
Late 'twas in June, the fleece when fully grown. Eclogue. Michael Drayton. *Fr.* The Shepherd's Garland. OBSC
Late Winter. Hazel Hall. HBMV
Late Winter. James McAuley. PoAu-2
Late Wisdom. George Crabbe. HBV-1; OBEV; TrGrPo
("We've trod the maze of error round.") OBRV
Lately, Alas, I Knew a Gentle Boy. Henry David Thoreau. AP; PeHV
Lately his haunch has grown stiff. Father. Jean Lipkin. PeSA

Lately I saw a sight most quaint. "Gross, Coarse, Hideous" (Police Description of My Pictures). D. H. Lawrence. FaBoEE
Lately, I've become accustomed to the way. Preface to a Twenty Volume Suicide Note. Amiri Baraka. AmNP; CABA; CAPP; InPK; InPS; NNP; PoBA; PoM; PoNe; PPP; TTY
Lately I've become religious about atoms. Metamorpho I. Joe Rosenblatt. MoCV
Lately I've felt a grave concern. Countess Beatritz de Die, *tr. fr. Provençal by* Willis Barnstone. BoWoP
Lately Our Poets. Walter Savage Landor. LiTB; NBM; OAEL-2; PoEL-4 ("Lately our poets loitered in green lanes.") CABA; FaBoEE; GTBS-P
Lately the wind burns. Everything. Philip Levine. AMV-80
Later Antigonishes, *sels.* Hughes Mearns.
Alibi. InMe
Crime Note. InMe
Frustrated Male. InMe
Lady with Technique, The. FiBHP; InMe; WhC
Me. InMe
Reveille. InMe
"Later," his mother said; and still those little hands. A Child Accepts. Michael Hamburger. NMP
Later I would say, I have cut myself free from order. Sun Moon Kelp Flower or Goat. Linda Gregg. NPGG
Later that week, when the reddish. Spring Floods Gregory Orr. GeTw
Later, when the scent of early leaves. A Wish for Waving Goodbye. Roberta Hill. AMV-80
Latest Decalogue, The. Arthur Hugh Clough. BiP; CABA; ChTr; DBV; EBEV; EBVV; FaBoCo; FaBoEE; FF; GTBS-P; HAP; HoPM; InMe; LoBV; NBM; NIP; NOBE; OAEL-2; OAEP; OBNC; OBSV; OBVV; PAI; PPP; TreFT; TRV; ViBoPo; VLP; WeW; WGRP
Latest, earliest, of the year. Primroses. Alfred Austin. OBVV
Latest poems, like the most recent, The. Dispatch Number Sixteen. Doug Fetherling. NeAC
Latet Anguis. William Cornish. *See* Desire.
Lather and shave. Barber's Cry. *Unknown.* TrAS
Latimer's Light. *Unknown.* TRV
Latin for Today ("Latin is a dead tongue"). *Unknown.* PoPle (Latin.) ChTr
Latin Tongue, The. James J. Daly. GoBC
Latitude frozen, The. Rout. Philip Booth. FAZ
Latitude, Longitude. George Oppen. CAPP
Latter Day, The. Thomas Hastings. *See* Hail to the Brightness of Zion's Glad Morning.
Latter Day Psalms. Cliff Ashby. NOCV
Latter Purification, A. Haim Guri, *tr. fr. Hebrew by* Mark Elliott Shapiro. VWA
Latter Rain, The. Jones Very. GN; OxBA
Lattice at Sunrise, The. Charles Tennyson Turner. OBVV
Laudanum. *Unknown.* NOEC
Laudate Dominum. Bible, *O.T.* Psalms, CL. ChTr
Laude, honor, praisingis, thankis infinite. The Difficulties of Translation, *abr.* Gavin Douglas. *Fr.* Prologues to the Aeneid. GoTS
Lauded lilies of the field, The. Mrs. Seymour Fentolin. Oliver Herford. HBMV
Lauds. W. H. Auden. *Fr.* Horae Canonicae. TrCP
Lauds. John Berryman. HAP
Laugh and Be Merry. John Masefield. FaFP; MoBrPo; PoPl; TreFT
Laugh and Sing. Beaumont *and* Fletcher. *See* Mirth.
Laugh, and the world laughs with you. Solitude [*or* The Way of the World]. Ella Wheeler Wilcox. FaFP; FPL; HBV-2; OHFP; PaPo; PoLF; TreF; WBLP; YaD
Laugh It Off. Henry Rutherford Elliot. WBLP
Laugh, my friends, and without blame. A Memory-Picture. Matthew Arnold. VLP
Laugh now but by tomorrow you may weep. After Laughter. Grace Buchanan Sherwood. GoYe
Laugh on, laugh on at all the dreams. I Believe. Saul Tchernichowsky, *tr. by* Reginald V. Feldman. TrJP
Laughed at the old deliberate ways. Repression. Timothy Corsellis. WaP
Laughed every goblin. Christina Rossetti. *Fr.* Goblin Market. BrRo
Laughing Child. Carl Sandburg. CTBA; PCP
Laughing eyes followed. Asante Sana, Te Te. Thadious M. Davis. BlSi
Laughing Faces of Pigs, The. Fred Lape. BoAnP
Laughing god born of a startling answer, The. Bacchus. William Empson. NoAM; PoCh
Laughing Hyena, by Hokusai, The. D. J. Enright. MP; TwCP
Laughing knot of village maids, A. The Shaded Pool. Norman Gale. HBV-1; OBVV
Laughing Song. Blake. *Fr.* Songs of Innocence. EnRP; GoJo; LAuP; OxBChV; PoSC; SoPo; SUS; TiPo (When the Green Woods Laugh.) CH
Laughing Time. William Jay Smith. FaPON; SoPo
Laughing Willow, The. Oliver Herford. HBV-2
Laughs not the heart, when giants, big with pride. The Apology Addressed to the Critical Reviewers. Charles Churchill. LAuP
Laughs the happy April morn. Anterotics. W. E. Henley. In Hospital, XXVI. BrPo
Laughter. Isabella Valancy Crawford. CaP
Laughter. Miriam Waddington. WHW
Laughter of children brings. Early Supper. Barbara Howes. DuDa; GoJo; GrPl; NCSH; PoPl
Laughter of the lesser lynx, The. The Lesser Lynx. E. V. Rieu. CenHV; FiBHP; RHPC
Laughter wears a lilied gown. Laughter. Isabella Valancy Crawford. CaP
Launch, The. Alice Meynell. WPE
Launched upon ether float the worlds secure. Authority. William Reed Huntington. AA
Laundress, The. Thomas Kinsella. IPY
Laundromat. David McCord. QQQ
Laundry truck, A. Calamity. F. R. Scott. PeCV
Laura. Thomas Campion. *See* Rose-cheeked Laura, Come.
Laura, *sel.* Robert Tofte.
"Rich damask roses in fair cheeks do bide." ElL
Laura and Lizzie Asleep. Christina Rossetti. *Fr.* Goblin Market. PeHV
Laura Sleeping. Charles Cotton. CavP; ELP; FaBoEn; LoBV; OBS; ViBoPo
Laura Sleeping. Louise Chandler Moulton. AA
Laurana's Song. Richard Hovey. AA
Laura's Song. Oliver Madox Brown. OBVV
Laureate, The. William Edmonstoune Aytoun. BXAP; Par
Laureate, The. Robert Graves. BIrV; FaBoTw; OBSV
Laurel Axe, The. Geoffrey Hill. *Fr.* An Apology for the Revival of Christian Architecture in England. NoP
Laurel-crowned Horatius. Lauriger Horatius. *Unknown, tr. by* John Addington Symonds. HBV-2
Laurel leaf, which you this day do wear, The. Amoretti, XXVIII. Spenser. CABA
Laurel Tree, The. Louis Simpson. NNaP
Laurels and Immortelles. *Unknown.* BLPA
Laurence Bloomfield in Ireland, *sel.* William Allingham.
Eviction, The. BIrV
Laurentian Shield. F. R. Scott. NOBC; OBCV
Lauriger Horatius. *Unknown, tr. fr. Latin by* John Addington Symonds. HBV-2
L'Aurore Grelottante. Peter Levi. NePoEA-2
Laus Deo. Robert Bridges. VLP
Laus Deo! Whittier. AmPP; AP; PAH
Laus Infantium. William Canton. HBV-1
Laus Mortis. Frederic Lawrence Knowles. HBV-2
Laus Veneris. Louise Chandler Moulton. AA; HBV-1
Laus Veneris. Swinburne. VLP
Laus Virginitatis. Arthur Symons. EnLoPo
Lausanne. Thomas Hardy. FaBoRV; FaBoTw
Lavender [*or* Lavender's] Blue. *Unknown.* CH; FSW (Country Lovers, The.) UnTE ("Lavender's blue, diddle diddle.") OxNR
Lavender Cowboy, The. Harold Hersey. BPAW; CoSo, *with music;* FSW
Lavender's for Ladies. Patrick R. Chalmers. HBMV
Lavinia. James Thomson. *Fr.* The Seasons: Autumn. OBEC
Lavish Kindness. Elinor Wylie. CrMA
Law, The. Albert Haynes. NBP
Law, The. Abraham ibn Ezra, *tr. fr. Hebrew by* Alice Lucas. TrJP
Law, The. Grace Schulman. GP
Law, A/ removing from use the monosyllable love. There Is Good News. Josephine Jacobsen. AMV-80
Law against Lovers, The, *sel.* Sir William Davenant.
Wake All the Dead. ELP; FaBoCh; HAP; SeCePo (Song: "Wake all the dead!") LoBV
Law firm commanding, A. Help Wanted. Franklin Waldheim. BLPA
Law in the Country of the Cats. Ted Hughes. TW
Law like Love. W. H. Auden. CMoP; CoBMV; FaBoMo; NoP (Law, Say the Gardeners, Is the Sun.) MoAB; MoBrPo; TrGrPo
Law makes long spokes of the short stakes of men. Legal Fiction. William Empson. CMoP; FaBoMo; InPK; LiTB; LiTM; MoVE; NoAM; NoP; SeCeV
Law of Averages, The. "Troubadour." FiBHP; InMe
Law of Jehovah is perfect, restoring the soul, The. God's Precepts Perfect. Bible, *O.T.* Psalm XIX: 7-9. BLRP
Law of the Jungle, The. Kipling. LiTB; PoEL-5
Law of the Yukon, The. Robert W. Service. CaP; HBV-2; TreFS
Law, Say the Gardeners, Is the Sun. W. H. Auden. *See* Law like Love.
Law there is of ancient fame, A. Tit for Tat; a Tale. John Aikin. OxBChV
Law West of the Pecos, The. S. Omar Barker. BPAW

Lawd, Dese Colored Chillum. Ruby C. Saunders. BlSi
Lawd, if I got my ticket, can I ride? If I Got My Ticket, Can I Ride? *Unknown.* OuSiCo
Lawd, I'm broke and hungry, ragged and dirty, too. Ragged and Dirty. *Unknown.* AmFP
Lawd, tis harder by the day. And "I Know Why the Caged Bird Sings"; a Villanelle. George Mosby, Jr. LFAC
Lawlands o' Holland, The. *Unknown.* *See* Lowlands o' Holland, The.
Lawn as White as Driven Snow. Shakespeare. *Fr.* The Winter's Tale, IV, iii. OAEP; ViBoPo
(Autolycus as Peddler.) OAEL-1
(Autolycus's Song.) LoBV; OBSC
(Come Buy! Come Buy!) EIL
(Pedlar, The.) WiR
(Pedlar's Song, The.) CH
Lawn-Mower. Dorothy Baruch. SoPo; SUS
Lawn Order. William Franklin. LFAC
Lawn Roller, The. Robert Layzer. NePoEA
Lawn-Tennisonian Idyll, A. *Unknown.* FaBoPa
Lawns darken, evening broods in the black, The. Tennyson. Alan Ansen. CoAP
Lawrence here for ever blames. D. H. Lawrence and James Joyce. Humbert Wolfe. FaBoEE
Lawrence—not the bearded one—the one. Any Complaints? Vernon Scannell. OxBTC
Lawrence, of virtuous father virtuous son. To Mr. Lawrence [*or* Sonnet]. Milton. AWP; CABA; GTBS; GTBS-P; OBEV; OBS
Laws-a-massey, what have you done? Negro Reel. *Unknown.* AS
Lawsamassy, for heaven's sake. Lucy Lake! Ogden Nash. ShM
Laws are the secret avengers, The. The Avengers. Edwin Markham. MoAmPo
Laws of God, the Laws of Man, The. A. E. Housman. MoAB; MoBrPo; OAEP; OBSV; PeHV
(Laws of God, The.) OxBoLi; PPP
Lawyer Clark Blues. *Unknown.* BluL
Lawyers, Bob, know too much, The. The Lawyers Know Too Much. Carl Sandburg. BiP; CMoP; HBMV; YaD
Lawyer's Invocation to Spring, The. Henry Howard Brownell. PoLF
Lawyers Know Too Much, The. Carl Sandburg. BiP; CMoP; HBMV; YaD
"Why is there always a secret singing," *sel.* DBV
Lawyers may revere that tree, The. Epigram on a Lawyer's Desiring One of the Tribe to Look with Respect to a Gibbet. Robert Fergusson. OxBS
Lay a Garland on My Hearse. Beaumont *and* Fletcher. *See* Aspatia's Song.
Lay aside phrases; speak as in the night. This Is Not Death. Humbert Wolfe. MoBrPo
Lay down boys, take a little nap. Cumberland Gap. *Unknown.* FSW
Lay down the axe; fling by the spade. Our Country's Call. Bryant. PAH
Lay down these words. Riprap. Gary Snyder. NeAP; NOBA; PoM
Lay his dear ashes where ye will. President Lincoln's Grave. Caroline A. Mason. OHIP
Lay in the house mostly living. Madness. James Dickey. NYBP
Lay me down beneaf de willers in de grass. A Death Song. Paul Laurence Dunbar. BANP; CDC; PoLF; PoNe
Lay me in the woodbox. Last Will of the Drunk. Myra Von Riedemann. OBCV
Lay me in yon place, lad. The Last o' the Tinkler. Violet Jacob. OxBS
Lay me on an anvil, O God. Prayers of Steel. Carl Sandburg. AP; CMoP; FaPON; MoAmPo; PDV; TrCP; TrPWD; YaD
Lay me to rest in some fair spot. Traveller's Hope. Charles Granville. HBV-2; OBVV
Lay me to rest on yon towering height. Simpson's Rest. George S. Simpson. PoOW
Lay me to sleep in [the] sheltering flame. The Mystic's Prayer. "Fiona Macleod." HBV-2; TrPWD; WGRP
Lay not up for yourselves treasures upon earth. Treasures. Bible, *N.T.* St. Matthew, VI: 19-21. TrGrPo
Lay of Ancient Rome. Thomas R. Ybarra. HBV-2; InMe; WhC
Lay of Finn, The. *Unknown, tr. fr. Anglo-Saxon by* Charles W. Kennedy. *Fr.* Beowulf. AnOE
Lay of Ike, The. John Berryman. *Fr.* Dream Songs. LCAP
Lay of Prince Marvan, The. *Unknown, tr. fr. Irish by* Eleanor Hull. AnIV
Lay of St. Gengulphus A, *sel.* "Thomas Ingoldsby." *Fr.* The Ingoldsby Legends.
"But to see now how strangely things sometimes turn out." VLP
Lay of Sigurd, The. *Unknown, tr. fr. Old Norse by* William Morris *and* Eirikr Magnusson. *Fr.* The Elder Elda. AWP
"And now one prayer," *sel.* OBVE
Lay of the Battle of Tombland, The. Dunstan Thompson. LiTA; NePA
Lay of the Captive Count, The. Goethe, *tr. fr. German by* James Clarence Mangan. AWP
Lay of the Deserted Influenzaed. Henry Cholmondeley-Pennell. InMe
Lay of the Ettercap, The. John Leyden. BXAP
Lay of the Famine, A. *Unknown.* OnYI
Lay of the Forlorn. George Darley. OnYI
Lay of the Honeysuckle, The. Marie de France, *tr. fr. French by* Robin Johnson. WPE
Lay of the Labourer, The. Thomas Hood. SaC
Lay of the Last Frontier. Harold Hersey. PoOW
Lay of the Last Minstrel, The, *sels.* Sir Walter Scott.
Breathes There the Man [with Soul So Dead], *fr.* VI. BLPA; EnRP; FPL; OAEP; OBRV; OxBS; TreF
(Innominatus.) OBEV; PAL
(Love of Country.) OHFP; PaPo; WBLP
(My Native Land.) GN
(My Own, My Native Land!) BSV
(Native Land.) TrGrPo
(Patriot, The.) FaPoR; OBNC
(Patriotism.) NOBE; TRV
"O Caledonia!" *sel.* FaBoPP
"Call it not vain; they do not err," *fr.* V. OBRV
(Minstrel Responds to Flattery, The.) OBNC
"Feast was over in Branksome tower, The," *fr.* I. OBRV
"He paused: the listening dames again," *fr.* IV. OBRV
"Humble boon was soon obtain'd, The," *fr. Introd. and* I. OBRV
"In peace, Love tunes the shepherd's reed," *fr.* III. ViBoPo
"It was an English ladye bright," *fr.* VI. OBRV
(Song of Albert Graeme.) EnRP
Last Minstrel, The, *Introd.* TreFS
Love. BSV
Melrose Abbey, *fr.* II. FaBoPP; SeCePo
("If thou wouldst view fair Melrose aright.") OBRV
"Nought of the bridal will I tell," *fr.* VI. OBRV
Dies Irae, *par. fr. Latin of* Thomas of Celano, *sel.* GoBC
Rosabelle, *fr.* VI. BeLS; BSV; GTBS; GTBS-P; HBV-2
(Harold's Song: Rosabelle.) EnRP
Sir William of Deloraine at the Wizard's Tomb, *fr.* II. OBNC
"Sweet Teviot! on thy silver tide," *fr.* IV. OBRV
(Father's Notes of Woe, A.) OBNC
"True Love's the gift which God has given," *fr.* V. OBRV
"Waken, lords and ladies gay." OAEP
(Hunting Song.) EnRP; EvOK; GN; GTBS; GTBS-P; TrGrPo; WiR
Lay of the Levite, The. William Edmondstoune Aytoun. HBV-2
Lay of the Lovelorn, The. William Edmonstoune Aytoun *and* Sir Theodore Martin. FaBoCo
(Cry of the Lovelorn, The.) CenHV
"Comrades, you may pass the rosy," *sel.* VLP
Lay of the Trilobite, The. May Kendall. CenHV
Lay of the Vigilantes, The. *Unknown.* PoOW
Lay out the minutes, row on ordered row. Time Out. Frances Westgate Butterfield. GoYe
Lay Preacher Ponders, The. Idris Davies. OxBTC
Lay this laurel on the one. Emily Dickinson. AP
Lay to Eliza, The. Spenser. *See* Elisa.
Lay up nearer, brother, nearer. The Dying Californian. *Unknown.* BPAW; TrAS
Lay willows under Walsingham. The Holy Land of Walsingham. Benjamin Francis Musser. ISi
Lay Your Arms Aside. Pierce Ferriter, *tr. fr. Irish by* Eilean Ni Chuilleanain. BIrV
Lay Your Head on My Shoulder. Yehuda Amichai, *tr. fr. Hebrew by* Robert Friend. VWA
Lay Your Sleeping Head [My Love]. W. H. Auden. *See* Lullaby: "Lay your sleeping head, my love."
Layer upon layer, with clay and bricks and hard work. A Witch Going Down to Egypt. Raquel Chalfi, *tr. by* Alexandera Meiri *and* Myra Glazer Schotz. VWA
Layers, The. Stanley Kunitz. AMV-80
Laying By. Randall Williams. AMV-80
Laying in the hospital. Little Red Riding Hood. Nila NorthSun. GP
Lays of Ancient Rome, *sels.* Macaulay.
Horatius [at the Bridge]. BeLS; FaBoCh; FaFP; FaPOR; HBV-2; HBVY; OBNV, *abr.;* OBWP; OHFP, *abr.;* PoLF; TreF
"'Horatius,' quoth the Consul." VLP
Lazarus, kindling at the breath of pain. The Second Life of Lazarus. Gwen Harwood. CBAP
Lazily through the clear. The Goldfish. Audrey Alexandra Brown. CaP
Laziness and Silence. Robert Bly. PPP
Lazy and slow, through the snags and trees. In the Bayou. Don Marquis. AmFN
Lazy-bones, lazy-bones, wake up and peep! Nonsense Verses. Charles Lamb. NA
Lazy deuks that sit i' the coal-neuks. *Unknown.* OxNR
Lazy laughing languid Jenny. Jenny. Dante Gabriel Rossetti. PoEL-5

Lazy loop of lozenged gray, A. The Sidewinder. Charles F. Lummis. BPAW
Lazy Man's Song. Po Chü-i, *tr. fr. Chinese by* Arthur Waley. OBVE
Lazy Mary. *Unknown.* AmFP
Lazy People, The. Shel Silverstein. NTCP
Lazy petals of magnolia-bloom float down the sluggish river. Elegy on a Nordic White Protestant. John Gould Fletcher. PoNe
Lazy Pussy, The. Palmer Cox. OBCA
Lazy Roof, The. Gelett Burgess. NA
(Roof, The.) TreFT
Lazy sheep, pray tell me why. The Sheep. Ann *or* Jane Taylor. OxBChV
Lazy Witch. Myra Cohn Livingston. RHPC
Le Chariot. John Wieners. VGW
Le Christianisme. Wilfred Owen. BrPo
Le Hibou et la Poussiquette. Francis Steegmuller. NYBP
Le Jardin ("The lily's withered chalice falls"). Oscar Wilde. *Fr.* Impressions. SeCePo; SyP
(Garden, The.) PoRA
Le Jazz Hot. Anselm Hollo. PoM
Le Jeune Homme Caressant Sa Chimère. John Addington Symonds. OBVV
Le Livre Est sur la Table. John Ashbery. EAS
Le Marais du Cygne. Whittier. PAH
Le Médecin Malgré Lui. William Carlos Williams. PoA; SaC
Le Monocle de Mon Oncle. Wallace Stevens. AP; CoBMV; LiTM; MoAB; NoAM; TwAmPo
Le Musée Imaginaire. Charles Tomlinson. NePoEA-2
Le Repos en Egypte. Agnes Repplier. ISi
Le Rêve. Edgar Bowers. ConAP
Le Roi Est Mort. Agnes Mary Frances Robinson. OBVV
Le Tombeau de Pierre Falcon. James Reaney. MoCV
Lea Rig, The. Burns. *See* My Ain Kind Dearie, O.
Leac A'Chlarsair. Lucy Taylor. PoSH
Lead. Jayne Cortez. PoBA
Lead gently, Lord, and slow. A Hymn [after Reading "Lead, Kindly Light"]. Paul Laurence Dunbar. TrPWD; TRV
Lead, Kindly Light. Cardinal Newman. *See* Pillar of the Cloud, The.
Lead me, O God, and thou my Destiny. God Leads the Way. Cleanthes, *tr. by* C. C. Martindale. EaLo
Lead on, lead on, America. Louise Ayres Garnett. *Fr.* Song of Liberty. PGD
Lead On, O King Eternal, *with music.* Ernest W. Shurtleff. AH
Lead the black bull to slaughter, with the boar. Upon Master Walter Montagu's Return from Travel. Thomas Carew. CaPo
Lead us, Evolution, lead us. Evolutionary Hymn. C. S. Lewis. NOBL
Lead us, heavenly Father, lead us. Prayer to the Trinity. James Edmeston. HBV-2
Lead Us, O Father, in the Paths of Peace, *with music.* William Henry Burleigh. AH
Leadbelly Gives an Autograph. Amiri Baraka. CNA
Leadbelly's Chisholm Trail, *with music. Unknown.* CoSo
Leaden Echo and the Golden Echo, The. Gerard Manley Hopkins. BrPo; CMoP; CoBMV; DTC; FaFP; GTBS-P; LiTB; LiTM; LoBV; MasP; MoAB; MoBrPo; MoVE; OAEP; OBMV; OBNC; SOTW
Leaden-eyed, The. Vachel Lindsay. CMoP; ELU; FaBoEE; LiTA; NePA; PPON
Leaden Treasury of English Verse, A, *sels.* Paul Dehn.
"Flight-Sergeant Foster flattened Gloucester." DBV; PV
"Hark, the herald angels sing/ Glory to the newborn thing." DBV; PV
"Jenny kiss'd me when we met." FiBHP; SpRo
"[O] nuclear wind, when wilt thou blow." DBV; FiBHP; PV; SpRo
"Ring-a-ring o' neutrons." QQQ; SpRo
"We buried him darkly at dead of night." DBV; PV
Leader, A. "Æ." HBMV
Leader, The. Hilaire Belloc. ACP
Leader, The. Dorothy Livesay. MoCV; PeCV
Leaders. *Unknown.* WBLP
Leaders of the Crowd, The. W. B. Yeats. EBEV; MoAB; MoBrPo
Leading a goat to pasture like playing with a toy. Maybe You Cannot Comprehend. Salvador Villanueva, *tr. by* Julio Marźan. InW
Leading liot act to foriage is activity. On Autumn Lake. John Ashbery. LCAP
Leadsman's Song, The. *At. to* J. Pearce *and to* Charles Dibdin. *See* Heaving the Lead.
Leady-Day, an' Ridden House. William Barnes. VLP
Leaf, The. William Carson Fagg. LFAC
Leaf. John Hewitt. NeIP
Leaf, A. Ludwig Uhland, *tr. fr. German by* John S. Dwight. AWP
Leaf, The. John Williams. NePoAm-2
Leaf after Leaf. Walter Savage Landor. TRV; ViBoPo
Leaf bug comes from an egg in June, A. Cockroaches. Kaye Starbird. RHPC
Leaf falls softly at my feet, A. A Leaf. Ludwig Uhland, *tr. by* John S. Dwight. AWP
Leaf floats in endless space, A. Seeking a Mooring. Wang Wei, *tr. by* Kenneth Rexroth *and* Ling Chung. BoWoP; WPOW
Leaf from Freedom's golden chaplet fair, A. To My Father. Henrietta Cordelia Ray. BlSi
Leaf is wilting, The. Summer drains out. Junker Schmidt. "Kozma Prutkov," *tr. by* W. D. Snodgrass *and* Tanya Tolstoy. ELU
Leaf knows sorrow in this time of thorns, The. Anglo-American Chainpoem. *Unknown.* EAS
Leaf-Makers, The. Harold Stewart. PoAu-2
Leaf membranes lid the window. Seamus Heaney. *Fr.* A Northern Hoard. CIP
Leaf of lehua and noni-tint, the Kona Sea. The Kona Sea. *Tr. fr. Hawaiian by* N. B. Emerson. WTO
Leaf-picking, The. Frédéric Mistral, *tr. fr. French by* Harriet Waters Preston. AWP
Leaf-Treader, A. Robert Frost. MoAmPo
Leaf will wrinkle to decay, The. The Crest Jewel. James Stephens. AnIL; MoAB; MoBrPo
Leafless are the trees; their purple branches. The Golden Mile-Stone. Longfellow. PoEL-5
Leafless Trees, Chickahominy Swamp. Dave Smith. MAYP
Leaflets. Adrienne Rich. NoAM
Leaflight. Dorothy Donnelly. NCSH
Leaflight to lamplight, blind with so much sight. The Brahms. Herbert Morris. NePoAm-2
Leafy-with-love banks and the green waters of the canal. Canal Bank Walk. Patrick Kavanagh. CIP; CMoP; FaBoTw; IPY; MoBrPo; NoAM
League of Nations, The. Mary Siegrist. PAH
League of Selves, The. Alvin Toffler. AMV-80
Leagues north, as fly the gull and auk. The *Palatine.* Whittier. EtS; MOS
Leah. Shirley Kaufman. VWA
Leak in the Dike, The. Phoebe Cary. FaFP; FaPON; PaPo; TreF
Lean and tall and stringy are the Navajo. The Navajo. Elizabeth J. Coatsworth. AmFN
Lean back, and get some minutes' peace. Faustine. Swinburne. BeLS; PeHV; UnTE
Lean close and set thine ear against the bark. Heart of Oak. Charles Henry Luders. AA
Lean Day in a Convict's Suit, A. Jean Wahl, *tr. fr. French by* Charles Guenther. VWA
Lean Gaius, who was thinner than a straw. Lucilius, *tr. fr. Greek by* Peter Porter. OBVE
Lean in the greenhood of my fearful years. Fool Song. Cornel Lengyel. GoYe
Lean, lanky son of desert sage. To a Jack Rabbit. S. Omar Barker. BPAW
Lean out of the window. Goldenhair. James Joyce. Chamber Music, V. ChTr; HBMV
Lean out the window: down the street. A Man with a Little Pleated Piano. Winifred Welles. FaPON
Lean Street. G. S. Fraser. NeBP; OxBS
Lean your small head against the Spring. Walking to Dedham. David Wright. NeBP
Leander Stormbound. Sydney Goodsir Smith. OxBS
Leander to the envious light. George Chapman. *Fr.* Hero and Leander, Third Sestiad. OAEL-1
Leane, The. William Barnes. EBVV
Leaning against my books, the sunflowers. Relics. David Wagoner. FAZ
Leaning against the golden undertow. Kenneth Slessor. *Fr.* Out of Time. CBAP
Leaning his chin in his small hard hands. Kentucky Birthday [February 12, 1815]. Frances Frost. SiSoSe; YeAr
Leaning on a Limerick, *sel.* Eve Merriam.
"Let the limerick form be rehoised." TDH
Leap, The. James Dickey. NIP
Leap-Centuries. Paul Celan, *tr. fr. German by* Michael Hamburger. OBVE
Leap for Life, A. Walter Colton. PaPo
Leap in the Dark. Roberta Hill. WPOW
Leap in the Smoke. John Buchan. *Fr.* From the Pentlands. PoSH
Leap out, chill water, over reeds and brakes. The River God. Sacheverell Sitwell. MoBrPo
Leap to the highest height of spring. An Early Bluebird. Maurice Thompson. AA
Leap year is given, when four will divide. Memorial Verses, Adapted to the Gregorian Account, or New Style. *Unknown.* FaBoUs
Leaping Falls. Galway Kinnell. NePoAm-2
Leaping Fire, The. John Montague. IPY
Leaping from oak to oak, tangled-up in the woods. Sacrifice of a Red Squirrel. Joseph Langland. NYBP
Leaping into the Gulf. Patricia Beer. OxBC

Leaping Laughers, The. George Barker. OBMV
Leaps over the Aisle of Syllogism. D. C. Berry. BXAP
Lear. William Carlos Williams. NOBA; PoA
Lear and Cordelia. Shakespeare. *Fr.* King Lear, V, iii. FiP
Lear and Cordelia! 'twas an ancient tale. To England. George Henry Boker. AA; HBV-2
Learn, lads and lasses, of my garden. Francis Daniel Pastorius. SCAP
"Learn to live, and live and learn." The Saturday Review. Dora Greenwell. EBVV
Learn to mak your bed, Annie. Fair Annie. *Unknown.* OxBB
Learn women all from this housewifery. Giovanni Battista Guarini, *tr. by* Sir Richard Fanshawe. *Fr.* Il Pastor Fido. OBVE
Learned and a happy ignorance, A. Eden. Thomas Traherne. AnAnS-1; PoEL-2; SeCV-2; TrGrPo
Learned Man, A. Stephen Crane. The Black Riders, XX. LiTA; MoAmPo; NePA
Learned Men, The. Archibald MacLeish. MoAB
Learned Mistress, A. *Unknown, tr. fr. Irish by* Frank O'Connor. KiLC; OBMV
Learned Song, A. *Unknown.* *Fr.* Mother Goose's Melody. FaBoUs
Learner. J. A. Lindon. PH
Learning. George Chapman. *Fr.* Euthymiae Raptus; or, The Tears of Peace. SeCePo
Learning. Earl Simpson. GrPl
Learning by Doing. Howard Nemerov. HAP; TwCP; WeW
Learning Destiny. Herman Charles Bosman. PeSA
Learning Experience. Marge Piercy. FF
Learning Soul, The. Reed Whittemore. GLGT
Learning the Spells; a Diptych. Anita Endrezze Probst. CDW
Learning to Count. Alberta Turner. LCAP
Learning to Live without You. Susan Wood. AMV-81
Learning to Read. Frances E. W. Harper. BlSi
Learning to Speak. Peter Everwine. NNaP
Learning to Speak. Melvin Wilk. AMV-81
Learning to Type. Diana O Hehir. NPGG
Learning to Understand Darkness. Wendy Rose. TWSS
Lear's Curse on Goneril. Shakespeare. *Fr.* King Lear, I, iv. TW
Lear's Speech to the Storm. Shakespeare. *See* Blow, Winds.
Least little sound sets the coyotes walking, The. Outside. William Stafford. NePoAm-2
Least of Carols, The. Sophie Jewett. OHIP
Leather Bar, The. Ralph Pomeroy. PeHV
Leather belt white shirt black pants. Telegram. Dick Lourie. NeAC
Leather-skinned wrinkled old man, A. Rock Painting. Jack Cope. PeSA
Leatherwing Bat. *Unknown.* FSW
L'Eau Dormante. Thomas Bailey Aldrich. HBV-1
"Leave all and follow—follow!" The Forbidden Lure. Fannie Stearns Davis. HBV-1
Leave Caelia, leave the woods to chase. On His Mistris That Lov'd Hunting. *Unknown.* OBS
Leave go my hands, let me catch breath and see. In the Orchard. Swinburne. BoLoP; UnTE
Leave Helen to her lover. Draw away. The White Isle of Leuce. Sir Herbert Read. FaBoTw
Leave her alone. The Seals. L. A. G. Strong. LO
Leave Her, Bullies, Leave Her, *with music.* *Unknown.* AS
Leave Her, Johnny. *Unknown.* FSW
Leave her now, go out and learn. To Himself. Richard Aldridge. NePoAm
Leave him alone, sweet enemy. The Lonely Traveller. Kwesi Brew. PBA; TTY
Leave him: he's quiet enough: and what matter. Here Lies a Prisoner. Charlotte Mew. MoBrPo
Leave Him Now Quiet. Trumbull Stickney. CrMA; LiTA; NCEP; TwAmPo
Leave in 1917. Lilian M. Anderson. SUMH
Leave It to Me Blues. Joel Oppenheimer. CoPo; VGW
Leave It with Him. *Unknown.* BLRP
Leave Krete and come to this holy temple. Sappho, *tr. fr. Greek by* Willis Barnstone. BoWoP
Leave, leave, converted publican! lay down. Christus Mattaeum et Discipulos Alloquitur. Sir Edward Sherburne. ACP
Leave me a while, for you have been too long. Lover to Lover. David Morton. HBMV
Leave me, all sweet refrains my lip hath made. Sonnet. Luis de Camoes, *tr. by* Richard Garnett. AWP
Leave Me Alone. Felice Holman. RHPC
Leave Me, O Love. Sir Philip Sidney. *Sometimes considered Sonnet CX of* Astrophel and Stella. CABA; ElL; EnRePo; FaBoRV; LiTB; OxBoCh; PoRA; PPP; SeCePo; SeCeV; TrCP; ViBoPo; WHA
(Farewell World.) FaBoEn
("Leave me, O Love, which reachest but to dust.") GBL; NIP; OAEP; TEP; TreFT; TrPWD
(Splendidis Longum Valedico Nugis.) LO; NOBE; NOCV; OBEV; OBSC; SiPS
Leave now the beach, and even that perfect friendship. End of Season. Robert Penn Warren. TwAmPo
Leave off, good Beroe, now. To an Old Gentlewoman, Who Painted Her Face. George Turberville. EnRePo
Leave tarnished sorrow, disappointment, doubt. Thought for a New Year. Gail Brook Burket. PGD
Leave the bars lying in the grass. Fall. Robert Francis. VGW
Leave the flurry/ To the masses. *Unknown.* WhC
Leave the How with Jesus. How? *Unknown.* STF
Leave the lady, Willy, let the racket rip. Willy and the Lady. Gelett Burgess. HBMV
Leave the Miracle to Him. Thomas H. Allan. BLRP
Leave the sluice and "tom" untended. In the Mines. John Swett. BPAW
Leave the Thread with God. *Unknown.* BLRP
Leave the Top Plums. Janet Carncross Chandler. AMV-80
Leave the window open. *Turkish Death Songs, tr. by* Reza Baraheni *and* Zahra-Soltan Shokoohtaezeh. BoWoP
Leave the Word Alone. Edward Marshall. NeAP
Leave these deluding tricks and shows. To a Painted Lady. Alexander Brome. CavP
Leave thine own home, O youth, seek distant shores! Encouragement to Exile. Petronius Arbiter, *tr. by* Howard Mumford Jones. AWP
Leave Train. Alan Ross. ChMP
Leave Us Religion. Blanaid Salkeld. NeIP
Leave we awhile without the turmoil of the town. Our Lady of France. Lionel Johnson. ISi
Leave your home behind, lad. The Recruit. A. E. Housman. FaPoR
Leaves. Frank Asch. NTCP
Leaves. William Barnes. BoNaP; ChTr
(Sonnet: Leaves.) FaBoRV; OBNC
Leaves. W. H. Davies. MoBrPo
Leaves. Ted Hughes. OxBC
Leaves, The. Ron Loewinsohn. GP
Leaves. Sara Teasdale. HBV-2; PoPl
Leaves. Paul Walker. PDV
Leaves/ Murmuring by myriads in the shimmering trees. From My Diary, July 1914. Wilfred Owen. CoBMV; FaBoMo; LiTM; MoAB; MoBrPo
Leaves and branches, flowers and fruits are here. Green. John Gray. SyP
Leaves are fading and falling, The. November. Alice Cary. OBCA
Leaves are falling, The; so am I. Late Leaves. Walter Savage Landor. HBV-1
Leaves are fresh after the rain, The. April Showers. James Stephens. TiPo
Leaves are uncurling, The. Spring. Marchette Chute. TiPo
Leaves at My Window. John James Piatt. AA
Leaves before the Wind. May Sarton. NePoAm
Leaves Come Again, The. Thomas Stanley. FaBoEE
Leaves Compared with Flowers. Robert Frost. NOBA
Leaves Do Not Mind at All, The. Annette Wynne. SoPo
Leaves fall, The. Leaves. Paul Walker. PDV
Leaves fall. The City of Falling Leaves. Amy Lowell. SUS; TiPo; TwAmPo
Leaves fall, fall as if from far away, The. Autumn. Rainer Maria Rilke, *tr. by* C. F. MacIntyre. TrJP
Leaves from eternity are simple things. The Eternity of Nature. John Clare. EBEV
Leaves had a wonderful frolic, The. The Leaves in a Frolic. *Unknown.* OnUR
Leaves have their time to fall. The Hour of Death. Felicia Dorothea Hemans. HBV-2; LoBV; OBNC
Leaves in a Frolic, The. *Unknown.* OnUR
Leaves like Fish. Gladys Cardiff. CDW; TWSS
Leaves looked in at the window, The. The House across the Way. Ralph Hodgson. FaBoTw
Leaves make a slow. Spring Rain. Harry Behn. TiPo
Leaves of autumn drop by two and threes, The. Autumn Change. John Clare. VLP
Leaves of Life, The. *Unknown.* OBET
Leaves of the summer, lovely summer's pride. Sonnet: Leaves. William Barnes. BoNaP; ChTr; FaBoRV; OBNC
Leaves that rustled on this oak-crowned hill, The. Wordsworth. FM; VLP
Leaves, the little birds, and I, The. The Little Shepherd's Song. William Alexander Percy. YeAr
Leaves, though little time they have to live, The. October Maples, Portland. Richard Wilbur. CoPo
Leaves were everywhere in air. In a Maple Wood. Pat Scheider. AMV-81
Leave-Taking, A. Arno Holz, *tr. fr. German by* Jethro Bithell. AWP
Leavetaking. Eve Merriam. PDV
Leave Taking. Milton. *Fr.* Paradise Lost, XII. FaBoEn

Leavetaking. Lisa Reape. AMV-81
Leave-taking, A. Swinburne. CH; FaBoEn; HBV-1; NOBE; OAEP; OBNC; OBVV; PoLF; PoEL-5; ViBoPo; VLP
Leavetaking. Sir William Watson. HBV-1
Leaving. Linda Hogan. WTSS
Leaving. "Michael Lewis," *after the Chinese*. *Fr.* Cherry Blossoms. UnTE
Leaving Barra. Louis MacNeice. EBEV
Leaving beer and apples. For a Friend. Lyn Lifshin. NeAC
Leaving Buffalo. Charles Martin. PoA
Leaving Crete, come visit again our temple. Sappho, *tr. fr. Greek by* John Frederick Nims. WeW
Leaving Here. Stephen Philbrick. AMV-81
Leaving Home. Shirley Cochrane. AMV-80
Leaving Me, and Then Loving Many. Abraham Cowley. AnAnS-2
Leaving Mendota, 1956. Lawrence Locke. GrPl
Leaving Mexico One More Time. Constance Urdang. AMV-80
Leaving of Liverpool, The. *Unknown.* FSW; Shs, *with music*
Leaving One of the State Parks after a Family Outing. Elizabeth Macklin. AMV-81
Leaving Raiford. Mario Petaccia. LFAC
Leaving Seoul; 1953. Walter Lew. BrSi
Leaving Smoke's. Gordon Henry. STE
Leaving Something Behind. David Wagoner. CoAP
Leaving the Atocha Station. John Ashbery. CAPP
Leaving the bar slack-watered, I have left. Two Voyages. Maurice James Craig. NeIP
Leaving the bird house. Responses. Robert Hershon. POL
Leaving the Dance. Alexander Whitaker. NIP
Leaving the island, she believes, to go to the child. Monique Laederach, *tr. by* Charles Guenther. *Fr.* Penelope. BoWoP
Leaving the Motel. W. D. Snodgrass. FF; NIP
Leaving the snows. At the Shelter-Stone. Brenda G. Macrow. PoSH
Leaving the viaduct on the left, and coming over the hill. St. Ursanne. Michael Roberts. LiTM
Leaving the white glow of filling stations. The Strand at Lough Beg. Seamus Heaney. NoP; OBWP
Leaving them, running. 28 VIII 69. Laura Chester. IHMS
Leaving Town Blues. *Unknown.* BluL
Leaving us behind. After the Death of Her Daughter in Child-birth. Izumi Shikibu, *tr. by* Edwin A. Cranston. PBWP
Leavings. Gerard Benson. BXAP
Lebensraum. Thom Gunn. PAI
Lecompton's Black Brigade. Charles Graham Halpine. PAH
Lector Aere Perennior. J. V. Cunningham. QFR
Lecture Hall. Patrick Kavanagh. FaBoTw; NoAM
Lecture Note: Elizabethan Period. Geoffrey Grigson. PV
Lecture upon the Shadow, A. John Donne. AnAnS-1; AWP; CABA; EnRePo; InPK; OBS; SeCP; TEP; UnPo
Lectured by Pa and Ma o'er night. The Lady's Diary. Charles Dibdin. NOEC
Led by the light of an unusual star. W. H. Auden. *Fr.* For the Time Being. PChr
Leda. Hilda Doolittle ("H. D."). HBMV
Leda. Rainer Maria Rilke, *tr. fr. German by* Robert Bly. NU
Leda. Mona Van Duyn. NMM
Leda and Her Swan. Olga Broumas. PeHV
Leda and the Swan. Alice R. Friman. PoDr
Leda and the Swan. Oliver St. John Gogarty. AnIL; HAP; OnYI
Leda and the Swan. W. B. Yeats. AnIL; CABA; ChMP; CMoP; CoBMV; EBEV; ErPo; FaBoEn; FF; FPL; GTBS-P; HAP; HeIP; InPK; LiTM; MoAB; MoBrPo; MoVE; NIP; NoAM; NOBE; NOP; OAEL-2; OAEP; PAI; PBBP; PPoe; PPP; PrIm; SCV; SeCeV; SoSe: TEP; TrGrPo; WeW
Leda in Stratford, Ont. Anne Wilkinson. MoCV
Leda Reconsidered. Mona Van Duyn. NMM
Lede guiterriste was a craftie ladde, The. The Probatioun Officeres Tale. Gerard Benson. BXAP
Lee Handley's dead. Jeep. Charles Stetler. GP
Lee in the Mountains. Donald Davidson. MoVE
Lee Rigg, The. Robert Fergusson. BSV
Lee to the Rear. John Randolph Thompson. PAH
Lee-ers of Hew. James Cunningham. JB
Leering across Pearl Street. Trouble. James Wright. FF; InPK
Lee's Parole. Marion Manville. PAH
Leesome Brand. *Unknown.* ESPB (A *and* B *vers.*)
Leetla Boy, Da. T. A. Daly. HBV-1
Leetla Giorgio Washeenton. T. A. Daly. FaPON; PoSC
Leetle Bateese. William Henry Drummond. CaP
Leezie Lindsay. *Unknown.* FaBoCh
Left/ Forward! He's the leanest in the shower. Soccer. Andrei Voznesensky, *tr. by* Anselm Hollo. LiSp
Left Behind. Elizabeth Akers Allen. HBV-1
Left by his friend to breakfast alone on the white. Edward Lear. W. H. Auden. InvP
Left leg flung out, head cocked to the right. Poet. Karl Shapiro. CMoP; LiTM; MoAB; MoAmPo; NoAM; TwAmPo
Left like an unknown's breath on mirrors. Visitations. Lawrence Durrell. *Fr.* Eight Aspects of Melissa. MoBrPo; NeBP
Left like water in glasses overnight. Love from My Father. Carole Gregory Clemmons. CNA; PoBA
Left right . . . left right. Peter Titheradge. *Fr.* Teatime Variations: After a Thirties Poet. FaBoPa
Left side of her world is gone, The. Strokes. William Stafford. ConAP; PCP
Left to himself, wherever man is found. Americans! Philip Freneau. *Fr.* Reflections. PPON
Left to itself the heart continues, as the tamarind. How Morning Glories Could Bloom at Dusk. Jorie Graham. NPGG
Left to themselves people. Revolutionary Letter # 4. Diane DiPrima. GP
Leg, The. Karl Shapiro. DFF; HAP; MoAB; MoAmPo; TrGrPo; UnPo; WeW
Leg in a Plaster Cast, A. Muriel Rukeyser. MoAmPo
Leg in the Subway, The. Oscar Williams. LiTM; NePA; TwAmPo
Leg over leg. Mother Goose. OxNR
Legacie, The. John Donne. *See* Legacy, The.
Legacies. Nikki Giovanni. CTBA
Legacy. Amiri Baraka. NoAM; NOBA; PoBA
Legacy, The. Bible, *O.T.* Proverbs, IV: 13. TrJP
Legacy [*or* Legacie], The. John Donne. SeCP; TrGrPo
Legacy. Gena Ford. IHMS
Legacy, The. Henry King. AnAnS-2
Legacy, The. Judith Minty. GeTw
Legacy: My South. Dudley Randall. NNP; PoBA; PoNe
Leg-acy of a Blue Capricorn. James Cunningham. JB
Legacy II. Leroy V. Quintana. GP
Legal children of a literary man, The. Relationships. Mona Van Duyn. GP
Legal Fiction. William Empson. CMoP; FaBoMo; InPK; LiTB; LiTM; MoVE; NoAM; NoP; SeCeV
Legem Tuam Dilexi. Coventry Patmore. The Unknown Eros, X. NBM; OxBoCh; PoEL-5
Legend. Hart Crane. CABA; MoVE; NoAM; OxBA; SyP; TwAmPo
Legend. Ralph Gustafson. CaP; PeCV
Legend. Jules Laforgue, *tr. fr. French by* Louis Simpson. Prf
Legend, A. Adelaide Anne Procter. GoBC
Legend. Ridgely Torrence. EtS
Legend, A. *Unknown, at. to* Peter Ilich Tchaikovsky, *tr. fr. Russian by* Nathan Haskell Dole. OHIP
Legend. John Waller. NeBP
Legend. John V. A. Weaver. AmFN; YaD
Legend. Judith Wright. SO
Legend of Boastful Bill, The. Charles Badger Clark, Jr. BPAW
Legend of Camelot, A. George Du Maurier. CenHV
Legend of Cherries, A. Charles Dalmon. HBMV
Legend of Felix is ended, the toiling of Felix is done, The. Envoy. Henry van Dyke. *Fr.* The Toiling of Felix. BLPA
Legend of Ghost Lagoon, The, *sel.* Joseph Schull.
  Pirates' Fight, The. CaP
Legend of Good Women, The: Prologue, *sels.* Chaucer.
  "And as for me, though that I konne [*or* can] but [*or* my wit be] lyte." CH; HeIP; ViBoPo
  Balade: "Hide [*or* Hyd], Absalon [*or* Absalom], thy gilte tresses clear." AWP; ChTr; EBEV; FiP; GBL; LoBV; NOBE; OAEL-1; OBEV; SeCeV ("Hide [*or* Hyd], Absalon, thy gilte tresses clere.") HAP; OxBM (Lady without Paragon, A.) MeEL
  Old Books. OxBM
  This Fresshe Flour. SeCePo
Legend of Grand Lake, The. Joseph L. Westcott. PoOW
Legend of Heinz von Stein, The. Charles Godfrey Leland. HBV-2
Legend of His Lyre. Aaron Schmuller. GoYe
Legend of Montrose, The, *sel.* Sir Walter Scott.
  Annot Lyle's Song: "Birds of omen." EnRP
Legend of Paper Plates, The. John Haines. GP
Legend of Paul Bunyan, A. Arthur S. Bourinot. AmFN
  Paul Bunyan ("He came,/striding"), *sel.* FaPON
Legend of Robert, Duke of Normandy, The, *sel.* Michael Drayton.
  Fame and Fortune. OBSC
Legend of Success, The Salesman's Story, The. Louis Simpson. NYBP
Legend of the Admen, The. Everett W. Lord. BLPA
Legend of the Easter Eggs, The. Fitz-James O'Brien. BeLS
Legend of the First Cam-u-el, The. Arthur Guiterman. CenHV
Legend of the Glaive, The, *sel.* Joseph Sheridan Le Fanu.
  Song of the Spirits, The. OnYI
Legend of the Hive, A. Robert Stephen Hawker. EBVV

Legend of the Knight of the Red Crosse, or of Holinesse, The. Spenser. The Faerie Queene, I, 1-12. OAEP
(Invocation to the Faerie Queen, prologue.) FiP
("Lo! I the man, whose Muse whylome did maske.") OAEL-1
Legend of the Northland, A. Phoebe Cary. HBV-1; HBVY; OBCA; OnMSP
Legend of the Organ-Builder, The. Julia C. R. Dorr. BeLS; BLPA; FaBoBe
Legend of Versailles, A. Melvin B. Tolson. BPo
Legend of Viable Women, A. Richard Eberhart. MiAP; MoVE
Legend of Walbach Tower, The. George Houghton. PAH
Legend of Waukulla, The. Hezekiah Butterworth. PAH
Legend: The god in the sun made two men. J. Michael Yates. *Fr.* The Great Bear Lake Meditations. HoPM
Legends of Evil, The. Kipling. MoShBr
Legerdemain. Kenneth MacKenzie. PoAu-2
Legion, The. Robert Graves. BrPo
Legion Club, The, *sel.* Swift.
"As I strole the city, oft I." BIrV
Legion hall in Atherton contains, The. By-Products. Baron Wormser. MAYP
Legree's big house was white and green. Simon Legree—a Negro Sermon. Vachel Lindsay. The Booker Washington Trilogy, I. HBMV; InMe; LiTA; MoAmPo; MoVE; NePA; TAP
Legs, The. Robert Graves. LiTB; LiTM; NoAM
Legs!/ How we have suffered each other. Poem in Which My Legs Are Accepted. Kathleen Fraser. AmPA; LLLT; NMM
Legs being uneven, The. The Letter. Paul Blackburn. CoPo
Legs of the elk punctured the snow's crust, The. To Christ our Lord. Galway Kinnell. InPK; MP; NIP; PrIm; RFM; TwCP
Legsby, Lincolnshire. *Unknown.* GBP
Lehayyim, my brethren, Lehayyim, I say. Simhat Torah. Judah Leib Gordon, *tr. by* Alice Lucas *and* Helena Frank. TrJP
Lehmann does well with Largactil. Laprairie Hunger Strike. Ronald Everson. MoCV
Leicester Chambermaid, The. *Unknown.* CoMu; OBET
Leichhardt in Theatre, *sel.* Francis Webb.
Room, The. PoAu-2
Leif was a man's name. Hervey Allen. *Fr.* Saga of Leif the Lucky. EtS
Leirioessa Kalyx. Maurice Baring. OBVV
Leisure. W. H. Davies. AWP; BoNaP; CH; FaBoBe; FaFP; FaPON; HBV-2; LiTB; LiTM; MoBrPo; MoShBr; NOBE; OBEV; OBMV; OBVV; PoRA; SeCePo; TiPo; TrGrPo; WHA
Leisure hills, motorway connected. Hills. Robin Munro. PoSH
Leit. Marcos Rodríguez Frese, *tr. fr. Spanish by* Julio Marzán. InW
Leith police dismisseth us, The. *Unknown.* OxNR
Leith Races, *sel.* Robert Fergusson.
My Winsome Dear. SeCePo
Leitrim Woman, A. Lyle Donaghy. OnYI; OxBI
L'Elisir d'Amore. Dallas E. Wiebe. MAT
Lem Catlett had one pretty gal. Hill Hunger. John Foster West. TAT
L'Embarquement pour Cythère. John Manifold. CBAP
Lementable New Ballad upon the Earle of Essex Death, A. *Unknown.* CoMu
Lemme be wid Casey Jones. Odyssey of Big Boy. Sterling A. Brown. BANP; CDC
Lemmings, The. John Masefield. CMoP; NIP; NoAM
Lemmings, The. Donald A. Stauffer. WaP
Lemon. Mario Satz, *tr. fr. Spanish by* Willis Barnstone. VWA
Lemon Pie. Edgar A. Guest. OBAL
Lemon Sherbet. Marvin Solomon. NePoAm
Lemonade. *Unknown.* GBP
(Picnic Rhyme.) FaBoNo
Lemonade Stand. Dorothy Brown Thompson. SiSoSe
Lemons. Ted Walker. NYBP
Lemons, Lemons. Al Young. HeIP
Lemuel's Blessing. W. S. Merwin. CAPP; CoPo; NYBP
Lend a Hand. Edward Everett Hale. *See* Look Up.
Lend me, a little while, the key. The Pedlar. Charlotte Mew. HBMV
Lend me thy fillet, Love! The Lover's Song. Edward Rowland Sill. AA; HBV-1
Lend me your arm. Little Song of the Maimed. Benjamin Péret, *tr. by* David Gascoyne. OBWP
Lend me your song, ye nightingales! oh, pour. James Thomson. *Fr.* The Seasons: Spring. PBBP
L'Enfant Glacé. Harry Graham. FaBoCo
Length o' days ageän do shrink, The. The Fall. William Barnes. NBM; PoEL-4
Length of Moon. Arna Bontemps. CDC; LiTM; PoNe
Lengthy Symphony. Persis Greely Anderson. WhC
Lenin, *sel.* Dorothy Wellesley.
"So I came down the steps to Lenin." OBMV
Leningrad Cemetery, Winter of 1941. Sharon Olds. NIP
Leningrad: 1943. Vera Inber, *tr. fr. Russian by* Dorothea Prall Radin *and* Alexander Kaun. *Fr.* The Pulkovo Meridian. WaaP
Lennox Island. David McFadden. NOBC
Lenora. *Unknown.* TDH
Lenore. Poe. AA; AmPP; AP; LiTA; TreFS; WHA
Lenox Avenue. Sidney Alexander. PoNe
Lenox Avenue/ by daylight. Dive. Langston Hughes. CAD; NYP
Lenox Avenue is a big street. Keep on Pushing. David Henderson. PoBA
Lenox Avenue Mural. Langston Hughes. AmNP; HoPM
Sels.
Harlem ("What happens to a dream deferred"). AmNP; AmPP; BiP; CABA; HeIP; HoPM; InPS; NIP; NoP; PoNe
(Dream Deferred.) FF; InPK; LiTM; PoBA; PPP; SoSe
Same in Blues. InPS
Lenox Christmas Eve 68. Sam Cornish. CNA
Lens. Anne Wilkinson. MoCV; NOBC; OBCV; PeCV
Lens is not an eye, The. It will not leave you. On Being Photographed. William H. Gass. AMV-81
Lens of morning, polished sheer by sleep, The. Celestial Body. Louise Townsend Nicholl. NePoAm
Lent. W. R. Rodgers. AnIL; DTC; NeBP; OxBI
Lent in a Year of War. Thomas Merton. EAS
Lent Lily, The. A. E. Housman. A Shropshire Lad, XXIX. OHIP; PoSC
Lent Tending. J. Barrie Shepherd. AMV-80
Lente, Lente. Ovid, *tr. fr. Latin by* Kirby Flower Smith. Elegies, I, 14. AWP
Lenten Is [*or* Ys] Come [with Love to Toune]. *Unknown.* HAP; MeEL; ViBoPo
(Alysoun.) GoBC
("Lenten is come with love to towne.") EBEV; PBBP
(Spring.) OAEL-1; OxBM
(Spring Has Come to Town with Love.) CABA
(Spring Song.) POEL-1
(Spring-Tide.) OBEV
Lenten stuff is come to the town. Two Old Lenten Rhymes, I. *Unknown.* ACP
Lentinus! thou dost nought but fume, and fret. Martial, *tr. fr. Latin by* Sir Edward Sherburne. OBVE
Lenton has brought us, as I understand. Two Old Lenten Rhymes, II. *Unknown.* ACP
L'Envoi: "Now in a thought, now in a shadowed word." E. A. Robinson. TrCP
L'Envoi: "O love triumphant over guilt and sin." Frederic Lawrence Knowles. TrPWD; TRV
L'Envoi: Return of the Sire de Nesle, The. Herman Melville. *See* Return of the Sire de Nesle, The.
L'Envoi: "There's a whisper down the field where the year has shot her yield." Kipling. *See* Long Trail, The.
L'Envoi: "What is the moral? Who rides may read." Kipling. *See* Winners, The.
L'Envoi: "When Earth's last picture is painted, and the tubes are twisted and dried." Kipling. FaFP; HBV-2; OHFP; PoPl; TRV; WGRP
(When Earth's Last Picture Is Painted.) LiTB; TreFS; VLP
L'Envoi: "Where are the loves that we loved before." Willa Cather. HBV-2
L'Envoi: "Who findeth comfort in the stars and flowers." Thomas Lovell Beddoes. *Fr.* Death's Jest Book. OBNC
L'Envoy: "King of glorie, King of peace." George Herbert. *Fr.* The Church Militant. AnAnS-1
L'Envoy: To His Book. John Skelton. EnRePo
L'Envoy to W. L. H. Ainsworth, Esq. Francis S. Mahony. OnYI
Leo to His Mistress. Henry Dwight Sedgwick. BLPA
Leolin and Edith. Tennyson. *Fr.* Aylmer's Field. GN
Leonardo Da Vinci's. Marianne Moore. NYBP
Leonardo's Secret. Robert Bly. NNaP
Leonidas. George Croly. HBV-2
Leonora. E. A. Robinson. NePA
Leopard. Gretchen Kreps. RHPC
Leopard. *Yoruba Oral Tradition, tr. by* Ulli Beier. WTO
Leopard when told that benzine, A. The Inquisitive Leopard. Oliver Herford. TDH
Leoun, *abr.* Jean Cocteau, *tr. fr. French by* Alan Neame. OBVE
Lepanto. G. K. Chesterton. FaBV; FaPo; FaPoR; GoBC; GoTL; HBMV; HBVY; MoBrPo; MOS; OBMV; OBNV; TreFS; WHA
Leper, The. Ka-'ehu, *tr. fr. Hawaiian by* M. K. Pukui *and* A. L. Korn. WTO
Leper, The. Swinburne. GBL
Leper, The. Nathaniel P. Willis. WGRP
Leper Cleansed, The. John Collop. TrGrPo
Leprahaun, The. Robert Dwyer Joyce. OnYI
Leprechaun, The—the omadhaun!—that lives in County Clare. Of Certain Irish Fairies. Arthur Guiterman. PoLF
Ler to Loven as I Love Thee. *Unknown.* SBVL

Leroy. Amiri Baraka. BPo; PoBA
Les Amours. Charles Cotton. HBV-1
Les Ballons. Oscar Wilde. SyP
Les Belles Roses sans Mercie. Arthur Shearly Cripps. OBVV
Les Chasse-Neige. Ralph A. Lewin. FiBHP
Les Demoiselles de Sauve. John Gray. VLP
Les Etiquettes Jaunes. Frank O'Hara. CAPP
Les Halles d'Ypres. Edmund Blunden. MMA
Les Jours Gigantesques/The Titanic Days. Kathleen Fraser. NPGG
Les Luths. Frank O'Hara. NoAM; NOBA
Les Morts Vont Vite. H. C. Bunner. AA
Les Planches-en-Montagnes. Michael Roberts. OBMV
Les Silhouettes. Oscar Wilde. *Fr.* Impressions. BrPo; EBVV; SyP
Les Sylphides. Louis MacNeice. BoLoP; CoBMV
Les Vaches. Arthur Hugh Clough. OAEP; PeD
Lesbia. Richard Aldington. PoLF
Lesbia. Catullus, *tr. fr. Latin by* Sheridan Baker. PrIm
Lesbia Forever on Me Rails. Catullus, *tr. fr. Latin by* Swift. OBVE
(Lesbia Railing.) AWP
Lesbia loads me night and day with her curses. Catullus, *tr. fr. Latin by* Peter Whigham. BoLoP
Lesbia, my love, let's be gay and enjoy ourselves. The Kiss-Fest. Irwin Edman. InMe
Lesbia on Her Sparrow. William Cartwright. *See* Dead Sparrow, The.
Lesbia Railing. Catullus. *See* Lesbia Forever on Me Rails.
Lesbia Sewing. Harold Vinal. HBMV
Lesbia speaks evil of me with her husband near. Catullus, *tr. fr. Latin by* Horace Gregory. NAWM-1
Lesbian. Paula Jennings. PeHV
Lesbian born under Pisces, A. Limerick. *Unknown.* PeHV
Lesbian girl of Khartoum, A. Limerick. *Unknown.* NOBL
Lesbian Hell, The. Aleister Crowley. PeHV
Lesbian Play on T.V. Caroline Gilfillan. PeHV
Lesbian Poem. Robin Morgan. IHMS
Lesbos. Lawrence Durrell. EBEV
Lèse-Majesté. Herbert S. Gorman. HBMV
Leslie. Marvin Wyche, Jr. AmNP
Lesotho. B. Makalo Khaketla, *tr. fr. Sotho by* Dan Kunene *and* Jack Cope. PeSA
Less and Less Human, O Savage Spirit. Wallace Stevens. VGW
Less Is More. Vern Rutsala. AMV-80
Less Nonsense. A. P. Herbert. OxBTC
Less said about Edward's slut the better, The. Bliss. George Johnston. NOBC
Less said the better. Missing. John Pudney. OxBTC
Less than two hours it took the Iroquois. The Martyrdom of Brébeuf and Lalemant, 16 March 1649. E. J. Pratt. *Fr.* Brébeuf and His Brethren. OBCV
Less the dog begged to die in the sky. Love Poem. George Barker. NeBP
Lesser Lynx, The. E. V. Rieu. CenHV; FiBHP; RHPC
Lesson. Harry Behn. TiPo
Lesson, The. Beth Bentley. GLGT
Lesson, The. Jane W. Krows. SoPo
Lesson, The. Robert Lowell. CMoP; LCAP; NMP
Lesson, The. Edward Lucie-Smith. NCSH; OxBTC; TwCP
Lesson, The. Paul Mariani. MAYP
Lesson, The. Elizabeth Peterson. AMV-80
Lesson, The. Larry Rubin. GoYe
Lesson, A. Wordsworth. GTBS; GTBS-P
(Small Celandine, The.) HBV-1; OBRV
Lesson for Dreamers. Paul B. Janeczko. PCP
Lesson for Mamma, A. Sydney Dayre. OBCA; OxBChV
Lesson for Today, The. Robert Frost. LiTA; LiTM; NePA; WaP
Lesson from a Sun-Dial. *Unknown, ad. fr. German by* Louis Untermeyer. TiPo
Lesson from Van Gogh, A. Howard Moss. MoAB
Lesson in Detachment, A. Vassar Miller. NePoEA-2
Lesson in Hammocks, A. James Schevill. FAZ
Lesson in Handwriting, A. Alastair Reid. NYBP
Lesson in Love, A. Philip Hobsbaum. OxBTC
Lesson in Oblivion, A. Dabney Stuart. GP
Lesson in Translation, A. Gabriel Preil, *tr. fr. Hebrew by* Howard Schwartz. VWA
Lesson of the Water-Mill, The. Sarah Doudney. HBV-2; TreFS
(Water Mill, The.) BLPA; WGRP
Lessoned in a godly school. Mother of Ten. L. A. G. Strong. DBV
Lessons. Helen Weber. PGD
Lessons from the Gorse. Elizabeth Barrett Browning. HBV-1
Lessons in History. Robert Penn Warren. AMV-80
Lessons in Limericks, *sels.* David McCord.
"Bigamist born in Zambezi, A," I. InMe
"British in branding their betters, The," II. InMe
"O limerick, Learest of lyrics," III. InMe
Lessons of Nature, The. William Drummond of Hawthornden. *See* Book of the World, The.
Lessons of the War. Henry Reed. HeIP; LiTB; OBWP
Sels.
Judging Distances, II. BoLoP; ChMP; GTBS-P; MoAB; NIP; NOBE; NoP; SoSe
Naming of Parts, I. DTC; FF; GoJo; HoPM; InPK; InPS; MoAB; MoBrPo; MoVE; MP; NOBE; NoP; OxBTC; PAI; PoPl; PoRA; PrIm; SeCePo; SeCeV; SoSe; UnPo; ViBoPo; WaP
("Today we have naming of parts. Yesterday.") TrGrPo
Lessons of the Year. *Unknown.* BLRP
Lest any doubt that we are glad that they were born today. Emily Dickinson. NAs
Lest it may more quarrels breed. Twelve Articles. Swift. InMe
Lest men suspect your tale to be untrue. The Devil's Advice to Story-Tellers. Robert Graves. LiTM; NoAM
Lest men suspect your tale untrue. The Painter Who Pleased Nobody and Everybody. John Gay. BeLS
Lest the ripple deceive us. Winter Pond. Ben Belitt. NYBP
Lest, tortured by the world's strong sin. Desideravi. Theodore Maynard. HBMV
"Lest we forget!" Let us remember, then. The Tenth Armistice Day. S. Gertrude Ford. SUMH
Lest you should think that verse shall die. The Immortality of Verse. Horace, *tr. by* Pope. Odes, IV, 9. AWP
Lestenyt, lordynges, both elde and yinge. Of a Rose, a Lovely Rose. *Unknown.* OBEV; OxBoCh
Lester Leaps In. Al Young. NPGG
Lester Tells of Wanda and the Big Snow. Paul Zimmer. FAZ
Lester Young. Ted Joans. AmNP
Let a saint cry your praises, O delicate. The Flea Circus at Tivoli. Nancy Willard. HoAn
Let Age no longer toil with feeble strife. The Poor. John Langhorne. *Fr.* The Country Justice. NOEC
Let all chaste matrons, when they chance to see. Upon a Young Mother of Many Children. Robert Herrick. CaPo
Let All Created Things, *with music.* Artis Seagrave. AH
Let all men see the ruins of the shrine. Robert Hillyer. Sonnets, XIV. HBMV
Let all the family gather. Light Another Candle. Miriam Chaikin. NTCP
Let all the little poets be gathered together in classes. To School! Stevie Smith. FaBoEE
Let All Things Pass Away. W. B. Yeats. ChTr
Let all who will. Militant. Langston Hughes. PoBA
Let Allen's eyes be a jukebox of light plugged into the navel of Whitman's verb. Leaps over the Aisle of Syllogism. D. C. Berry. BXAP
Let America Be America Again. Langston Hughes. PoNe
Let azure eyes with coral lips unite. The Value of Dentistry. Solyman Brown. *Fr.* Dentologia; a Poem on the Diseases of the Teeth and Their Proper Remedies. FaBoUs
Let Bacchus's sons be not dismayed. Garryowen. *Unknown.* OnYI
Let Bachus to Venus libations pour forth. "Vive la Compagnie." *Unknown.* PSoN
Let baths and wine-butts be November's due. Sonnets of the Months: November. Folgore da San Geminiano, *tr. by* Dante Gabriel Rossetti. AWP
Let Be. *Unknown.* WBLP
Let Bourbons fight for status quo. Status Quo. Binga Dismond. PoNe
Let but a fellow in a fox-furred gown. Nicholas Breton. *Fr.* An Invective against the Wicked of the World. ViBoPo
Let but a thrush begin. Lyric. John Hewitt. NeIP
Let but the son of earth. The Ages of Man. *At. to* Abraham ibn Ezra, *tr. by* Nina Davis Salaman. TrJP
Let but thy voice engender with the string. Upon Her Voice. Robert Herrick. CaPo
Let by Rain. Edward Taylor. *See* Address to the Soul Occasioned by a Rain, An.
Let certain holdings of stocks and bonds. Codicil. Mabel MacDonald Carver. GoYe
Let Christian Hearts Rejoice Today, *with music.* *Unknown, tr. fr. French by* Francis X. Curley. AH
Let Christmas celebrate greenly. For the fir is king. Jubilate Herbis. Norma Farber. PChr
Let Christmas not become a thing. Christmas Prayer. Madeline Morse. PGD
Let clownish Cymon, in fond rustic strains. St. Anthony and His Pig; a Cantata. Frederick Forrest. NOEC
Let Cynics bark, and the stern Stagirite. The Paradox. *Unknown.* APAS
Let dainty wits cry on the Sisters nine. Astrophel and Stella, III. Sir Philip Sidney. OAEL-1; OBSC; SiPS
Let de peoples know (unnh). Blues for Bessie. Myron O'Higgins. PoNe

Let dirty streets be paved with flow'ry green. *Unknown.* *Fr.* The Comparison. NOEC
Let Dogs Delight to Bark and Bite. Isaac Watts. HBVY; TreFS
(Against Quarrelling and Fighting.) OBEC; OxBChV; SeCePo
(Quarrelling.) BLPA
Let down your hair. Rapunzel. Louis Untermeyer. DFT
Let Dreamers Wake. Lilith Lorraine. PGD
Let due civilities be strictly paid. John Gay. *Fr.* Trivia; or, The Art of Walking the Streets of London, II. OAEL-1
Let dull and ignorant pretenders art condemn. John Oldham. *Fr.* Upon the Works of Ben Jonson. PP
Let each man first seek out his proper totem. A Joyful Noise. Donald Finkel. CoAP
Let Elizur rejoice with the Partridge. Christopher Smart. *Fr.* Jubilate Agno. OAEL-1; PoEL-3
Let 'em censure: what care I? On Critics [*or* In Imitation of Anacreon]. Matthew Prior. FaBoEE; SeCeV
Let Ephah rejoice with Buprestis, the Lord endue us with temperance and humanity. Christopher Smart. *Fr.* Jubilate Agno. NOEC
Let Erin Remember the Days of Old. Thomas Moore. EnRP
Let every good fellow now fill up his glass. Vive la Compagnie (Vive l'Amour). *Unknown.* FSW
Let Fate do her worst; there are relics of joy. Thomas Moore. *Fr.* Farewell! But Whenever. TreFT
Let folly praise that fancy loves, I praise and love that Child. A Child My Choice. Robert Southwell. EBCP; GoBC; HBV-2; OxBoCh
Let fools great Cupid's yoke disdain. Song: The Willing Prisoner to His Mistress. Thomas Carew. CaPo
Let forrain nations of their language boast. The Sonne. George Herbert. SeCP
Let go of the present and death. Once Again. Liz Sohappy Bahe. CDW
Let go of the unicorn's reins. The Beast That Rode the Unicorn. Conny Hannes Meyer, *tr. by* Herbert Kuhner. VWA
Let Go: Once. Gerald Fleming. AMV-81
Let Go the Peak Halyards. *Unknown.* AmSS
Let Go the Reef Tackle, *with music.* *Unknown.* ShS
Let grass grow, and waters flow. Real Old Mountain Dew. *Unknown.* FSW
Let hammer on anvil ring. The Armorer's Song. Harry Bache Smith. AA; OHIP
Let hands be about him white, O his mother's first. The Mother and Child. Vernon Watkins. NeBP
Let happy throats be mute. Threnody. Donald Jeffrey Hayes. AmNP
Let Her Give Her Hand. *Unknown.* ELP
Let her lie naked here, my hand resting. News of the World III. George Barker. FaBoTw; LiTB; LiTM
Let her who walks in Paphos. Lais. Hilda Doolittle ("H. D."). MoAmPo
Let Heroes Account to Love. Alan Dugan. NoAM
Let him answer as he will. The Companion. E. A. Robinson. NoAM
Let him kiss me with the kisses of his mouth. Bible, *O.T.* *Fr.* The Song of Solomon. AWP; TrGrPo; UnTE
Let him that will, ascend the tottering seat. Seneca, *tr. by* Sir Matthew Hale. *Fr.* Thyestes, II. OBVE
Let him who may. To Be Recited to Flossie on Her Birthday. William Carlos Williams. VGW
Let Him with Kisses of His Mouth, *with music.* *Unknown.* AH
Let it be alleys. Let it be a hall. A Lovely Love. Gwendolyn Brooks. BPo
Let It Be Forgotten. Sara Teasdale. HBMV; MoAmPo; TrGrPo
(Song: "Let it be forgotten, as a flower is forgotten.") PoA
Let it be Sabbath, Sabbath! Eternal Sabbath. Isaac Leibush Peretz, *tr. by* Joseph Leftwich. TrJP
Let it disturb no more at first. Fountain. Elizabeth Jennings. PoCh; WPE
Let it end here where the blueprint. Making Chicago. Dennis Schmitz. LCAP; NPGG
Let It Go. William Empson. FaBoMo; OxBTC
Let it no longer be a forlorn hope. On the Baptized Ethiopian. Richard Crashaw. FaBoEE; NoP; PeD; SeCV-1
Let it not be, love, underneath a roof. Golden Bough. Helen Hoyt. HBMV
"Let it not come unto you, all ye that pass by!" Desolation in Zion. Bible, *O.T.* *Fr.* Lamentations. TrJP
Let it not your wonder move. His Excuse for Loving. Ben Jonson. *Fr.* A Celebration of Charis. AnAnS-2; EnRePo; JCP; PoEL-2; QFR; SeCP; SeCV-1
Let kings command, and do the best they may. The Power in the People. Robert Herrick. CaPo
Let love come under your roof. Carol for Advent. John Heath-Stubbs. OxBC
Let man be free! The mighty word. Whittier. *Fr.* The Emancipation Group. PGD
Let man's soul be a sphere, and then in this. Good Friday, 1613. Riding Westward. John Donne. AnAnS-1; EnRePo; JCP; MeLP; MePo; NOCV; NoP; OAEL-1; OBS; OxBoCh; PoEL-2; PPP; SeCP; SeCV-1; TEP
Let Me Alone. Bible, *O.T.* Job, VII: 11-21. PPON
Let me be a little kinder. My Daily Creed [*or* A Creed]. *Unknown.* STF; TRV
Let me be at the place of the castle. Psalm Concerning the Castle. Denise Levertov. TwCP; WPE
Let me be buried as flesh, not burned, I say. Earth Buried. Kenneth Mackenzie. CBAP
Let me be buried in the rain. Invocation. Helene Johnson. AmNP; BANP; PoNe
Let Me Be Held When the Longing Comes. Stephany Fuller. BPO
Let me be marble, marble once again. Galatea Again. Genevieve Taggard. WHA
Let me be my own fool. A Counterpoint. Robert Creeley. NeAP
Let me be the mane that swings. Poem for a Singer. Milton Acorn. NeAC
Let me be to Thee as the circling bird. Gerard Manley Hopkins. VLP
Let me be what I am, as Virgil cold. An Elegie. Ben Jonson. PoEL-2; SeCP
Let me be your salty dog. Salty Dog Blues. *Unknown.* FSW
Let me be your wiggler until your wobbler comes. Jacksonville Blues. *Unknown.* BluL
Let me but do my work from day to day. Work. Henry van Dyke. TRV
Let Me But Live from Year to Year. Henry van Dyke. *Fr.* The Three Best Things. TreFT
(Zest of Life, The.) WBLP
Let me call a ghost. Song of Three Smiles. W. S. Merwin. CoAP; NOBA; VGW
Let me come in where you sit weeping, ay. Bereaved. James Whitcomb Riley. AA
Let me confess that we two must be twain. Sonnets, XXXVI. Shakespeare. OAEP; PeHV
Let me discern by living faith. Discerning the Lord's Body. Carrie Judd Montgomery. STF
Let me do my work each day. A Prayer. Max Ehrmann. BLPA; BLPL; FaBoBe
Let Me Enjoy [(Minor Key)]. Thomas Hardy. AWP; FaBV; HBV-2; NoAM; ViBoPo
Let me fetch sticks. Bliss. Eleanor Farjeon. RHPC
Let Me Flower as I Will. Lew Sarett. TrPWD
Let Me Fly. *Unknown.* FSW
Let Me Go. *Gond Oral Tradition, tr. by* V. Elwin *and* S. Hivale. WTO
Let Me Go Back. Mary E. Albright. BLRP
Let Me Go Down to Dust. Lew Sarett. TrPWD
Let me go forth, and share. Ode in May. Sir William Watson. OBEV; OBVV; WGRP
Let Me Go Warm. Luis de Góngora, *tr. fr. Spanish by* Longfellow. AWP
Let Me Go Where Saints Are Going, *with music.* Lewis Hartsough. AH
Let me go where'er I will. Music. Emerson. FaBV; WGRP
Let Me Grow Lovely. Karle Wilson Baker. BLPA; FaBoBe; HBMV; TrPWD
Let me have a scarlet maple. The Grave-Tree. Bliss Carman. CaP
Let me have men about me that are fat. Julius Caesar's Preference. Shakespeare. *Fr.* Julius Caesar, I, ii. TreFS
Let me just finish off my slender fiddle. My Fiddle. Leib Kwitko, *tr. by* Keith Bosley. VWA
Let me lay it to you gently, Mr. Gone! Ray Bremser. *Fr.* Poem of Holy Madness. NeAP
Let me learn now where Beauty is. Questing. Anne Spencer. CDC
Let me live harmlessly; and near the brink. The Angler's Song. John Dennys. *Fr.* The Secrets of Angling. ElL
Let Me Live Out My Years. John G. Neihardt. HBMV; TreFS; YaD
Let Me Look at Me. Bessie June Martin. STF
Let me look at what I was, before I die. Jamestown. Randall Jarrell. GOA
Let me look back upon thee, O thou wall. Timon Curses Athens and Mankind. Shakespeare. *Fr.* Timon of Athens, IV, i. TW
Let Me Love Bright Things. A. Newberry Choyce. HBMV
Let me not be unfair Lord to New York that sink that sewer. Ode to New York. Reed Whittemore. NYP
Let Me Not Die. Edith Lovejoy Pierce. TrPWD
Let me not die for ever, when I'm gone. A Wish. Fanny Kemble. WPE
Let me not die till death is due to come. Let Me Not Die. Edith Lovejoy Pierce. TrPWD
Let me not go anywhere. Poem Composed in Rogue River Park . . . Tom Wayman. POL
Let me not know how sins and sorrows glide. Prayer. James Elroy Flecker. TrPWD
Let me not live, if I not love. On Himself. Robert Herrick. CaPo
Let me not pass to the house of clay. Forgive, Lord, Have Mercy! *Tr. fr. Sanskrit by* Raimundo Panikkar. *Fr.* Vedic Hymns. ILwL
Let me not to the marriage of true minds. Sonnets, CXVI. Shakespeare.

AWP; CABA; EIL; EnLoPo; EnRePo; FaBoEn; FaBV; FaFP; FPL; GBL; GoBC; GTBS; GTBS-P; HAP; HBV-1; HeIP; InPK; InPS; InvP; LiTB; LoBV; MasP; NIP; NOBE; NoP; OAEL-1; OAEP; OBEV; OBSC; PAI; PeHV; PoEL-2; PoPl; PoRA; PPoe; PPP; PrIm; SCV; SeCePo; SeCeV; SoSe; TEP; TreF; TrGrPo; TRV; UnPo; ViBoPo; WeW; WHA
Let me now set down a picture of New England that will show it to you and explain it. Praise of New England. Thomas Caldecot Chubb. GoYe
Let me obtain forgiveness of thee, Samson. Milton. *Fr.* Samson Agonistes. EBEV
Let Me Play the Fool. Shakespeare. *Fr.* The Merchant of Venice, IV, i. TrGrPo
Let me play to you tunes without measure or end. Bagpipe Music. "Hugh MacDiarmid." OAEL-2
Let me pour [*or* powre] forth. A Valediction: Of Weeping. John Donne. AnAnS-1; CABA; EnRePo; HAP; HeIP; MeLP; MePo; NoP; OAEL-1; OBS; SeCP; WeW
Let me put it this way. George Jonas. NeAC
Let me remember on this day. Others. *Unknown.* STF
Let me say (in anger) that since the day we were married. The Crisis. Robert Creeley. FF; PPP
Let me see if Philip can. The Story of Fidgety Philip. Heinrich Hoffmann, *tr. fr. German.* OxBChV
Let me see you. Mirabai, *tr. fr. Hindi by* Willis Barnstone *and* Usha Nilsson. BoWoP
"Let me show you my love." Webern. Thomas W. Shapcott. *Fr.* Piano Pieces. CBAP
Let Me Sing of My Well-beloved. Bible, *O.T.* *Fr.* Isaiah. TrJP
Let me sit down a minute, stranger. Down in Lehigh Valley. *Unknown.* TreF
Let me sit here by this adobe wall. Summer Comes. Edith Agnew. SiSoSe
Let me speak, sir,/ For Heaven now bids me. Cranmer's Prophecy of Queen Elizabeth. Shakespeare. King Henry VIII, *fr.* V, v. WGRP
Let me strap/ the baby in the seat. If He Let Us Go Now. Shirley Williams. BoWoP
Let me take this other glove off. In Westminster Abbey. John Betjeman. CMoP; DBV; FaBoCo; InPK; NIP; NOBL; OAEL-2; OBSV
Let me tell to you the story. Edith Agnew. PChr
Let me tell you a little story. Miss Gee. W. H. Auden. OxBTC
Let me tell you about our land. The Judge. Karl Kopp. TAT
Let me tell you the story of how I began. Song: Lift Boy. Robert Graves. DTC
Let me tell you what with mirrors. Entoptic Colours (1817). Goethe, *tr. by* Christopher Middleton. SUW
Let me tell you where I have walked. Places I Have Been. Joyce M. Volk. AMV-80
Let me thy properties explain. On An Ill-managed House. Swift. AnIV
Let me work and be glad. A Prayer. Theodosia Garrison. TrPWD
Let me wrap a poem around you. Gift. Judith Hemschemeyer. PCP
Let men take note of her, touching her shyness. The Gift of Song. Anthony Hecht. NYBP
Let Mine Eyes See Thee. St. Theresa of Avila, *tr. fr. Spanish by* Arthur Symons. AWP
Let mine not be the saddest fate of all. Uselessness. Ella Wheeler Wilcox. TrPWD
Let mother Earth now deck herself in flowers. Epithalamium. Sir Philip Sidney. *Fr.* Arcadia. SiPS
Let my sweet song be pleasing unto Thee. A Love Song. Judah Halevi, *tr. by* Nina Davis Salaman. TrJP
Let my voice ring out and over the earth. Song. James Thomson("B. V.") Sunday up the River, XVII. HBV-1; OBVV; TreFT
Let no blasphemer till the sacred earth. Benediction. Mark Turbyfill. PoA
Let No Charitable Hope. Elinor Wylie. HBMV; LiTA; LiTM; MoAB; MoAmPo; NePA; OxBA; PBWP; SBG; TrGrPo; VGW
Let no girl wait on you on that day when you bind your wild. The Alchemy of Day. Anne Hébert, *tr. by* A. Poulin, Jr. BoWoP
Let no man boste of cunning nor vertù. Like a Midsummer Rose. John Lydgate. OxBM
Let no man come [*or* cum] into this hall. Now Is the Time of Christmas [*or* Make We Merry]. *Unknown.* MeEL; OxBM; SBVL
Let no man see my girl. Inconsistent. Mark Van Doren. ELU
Let no one mourn his mount, upholstered bone. Epitaph for a Horseman. Michael Hamburger. NePoEA-2
Let no pirate's sword storm these veins of yours. For Her on the First Day Out. Robert Bagg. NePoAm-2
Let none but guests or clubbers hither come. Ben. Johnsons Sociable Rules for the Apollo. Ben Jonson, *tr. by* Alexander Brome. SeCV-1
Let not Chloris think, because. *Unknown.* OBSC
Let not Death boast his conquering power. On Eleanor Freeman, Who Died 1650, Aged 21. *Unknown.* OBEV
Let not his humble vesture make thee blind. The Poor Scholar. Abraham ibn Chasdai, *tr. by* J. Chotzner. TrJP
Let not old age disgrace my high desire. Old Age. Sir Philip Sidney. *Fr.* Arcadia. SiPS
Let not one sparke of filthy lustfull fyre. Amoretti, LXXXIII. Spenser. TEP
Let not our town be large, remembering. On the Building of Springfield. Vachel Lindsay. OHFP; WHA
Let not the sluggish sleep. Song. *Unknown.* ACP; GoBC; OxBoCh
Let Not Thy Beauty. Aurelian Townshend. AnAnS-2
("Let not thy beauty make thee proud.") JCP
Let not us that youngmen be. Youth. *Unknown.* OBSC
Let not young souls be smothered out before. The Leaden-eyed. Vachel Lindsay. CMoP; ELU; FaBoEE; LiTA; NePA; PPON
Let not your heart be troubled: ye believe in God, believe also in me. The Peace of Christ. Bible, *N.T.* *Fr.* St. John. TreFS
Let nothing disturb thee. Lines Written in Her Breviary [*or* St. Theresa's Book-Mark]. St. Theresa of Avila, *tr. by* Longfellow. AWP; CTC; EaLo; ILwL; PoEL-5; TreFT; TRV; WPOW
Let observation with extensive view. The Vanity of Human Wishes: The Tenth Satire of Juvenal, Imitated. Samuel Johnson. CABA; EBEV; HeIP; LaA; LAuP; LoBV, *abr.;* MasP; NOEC; NoP; OAEL-1; PoEL-3; PrIm; TEP
Let oken club now strike, and poast of might. Seneca, *tr. by* Jasper Heywood. *Fr.* Hercules Furens, IV. OBVE
Let other mount aloft, let other sore. Seneca, *tr. by* John Studley. *Fr.* Hercules Oetaetus, II. OBVE
Let Other People Come as Streams. Charles Reznikoff. VGW
(Dew.) VWA
Let other servants boast a snowy glove. Upon Scarlet and Blush-coloured Ribbands, Given by Two Ladies. James Shirley. GoBC
Let others better mold the running Mass. The Sixth Book of the Aeneis. Virgil, *tr. by* Dryden. *Fr.* The Aeneid. SeCV-2
Let others chaunt a country praise. London Town. Lionel Johnson. FaBoPP
Let others cheer the winning man. A Smile. *Unknown.* BLPA; WBLP
Let others from the town retire. Nonpareil. Matthew Prior. EnLoPo
Let others of the world's decaying tell. Sonnet. Earl of Stirling. *Fr.* Aurora. EIL
Let others pile their yellow ingots high. A Pastoral Elegy. Tibullus, *tr. by* Sir Charles Abraham Elton. AWP
Let others pray for the passenger pigeon. Elegy for the Giant Tortoises. Margaret Atwood. BoWoP
Let Others Share. Edward Anthony. RHPC
Let others sing of knights and pal[l]adin[e]s. Samuel Daniel. *Fr.* To Delia. AAS; EIL; FaBoEn; HBV-1; NOBE; NoP; OAEP; OBEV; OBSC; ViBoPo
Let pious Damon take his seat. Sermon in a Churchyard. Macaulay. OBRV
Let poetry be/ like an air conditioner. Ars Poetica. Arturo Trías, *tr. by* Julio Marzán. InW
Let poets praise the softer winds of spring. J. B. Morton. FaBoEE
Let praise devote thy work, and skill employ. Laus Deo. Robert Bridges. VLP
Let pride grow big my rose, and let the cleare. On a Damaske Rose Sticking upon a Ladies Breast. Thomas Carew. AnAnS-2
Let readers say (description or abuse). The Lemmings. Donald A. Stauffer. WaP
Let sailors watch the waning Pleiades. Cleonicos. Edward Cracroft Lefroy. *Fr.* Echoes from Theocritus. AWP
Let school-masters puzzle their brain. Song [*or* The Three Pigeons]. Goldsmith. *Fr.* She Stoops to Conquer. BIrV; ELP; OAEP; PoRA; ViBoPo
Let Shobi rejoice with the Kastrel—blessed be the name Jesus. Christopher Smart. *Fr.* Jubilate Agno. NOEC
Let shrieking steel and gray stone be set. Psalmodist. Mani Leib, *tr. by* David G. Roskies *and* Hillel Schwartz. VWA
Let sleep take her, let sleep take her, let sleep. Fourth Song the Night Nurse Sang. Robert Duncan. VGW
Let Sol his annual journeys run. Hint from Voiture. William Shenstone. EnLoPo
Let Some Great Joys Pretend to Find. Thomas Shadwell. *Fr.* The Woman-Captain. OAEP
Let Sporus tremble—"What? That thing of silk." Sporus. Pope. *Fr.* Epistle to Dr. Arbuthnot. AWP; ChTr; DBV; NOBE; OBSV; SCV; TW
Let that which is to come be as it may. John Masefield. *Fr.* Sonnets ("Long, long ago"). HBV-2
Let the arched knife. Pruning. John Philips. *Fr.* Cyder. FaBoUs
Let the bells ring, and let the boys sing. John Fletcher. *Fr.* The Spanish Curate, III, ii. OBS
Let the bird of loudest lay. The Phoenix and the Turtle. Shakespeare. EnRePo; FaBoEn; LiTB; LoBV; MasP; NOBE; NoP; OAEL-1; OBEV; OBSC; PoEL-2; SeCePo; SeCeV; TEP
Let the boy try along this bayonet-blade. Arms and the Boy. Wilfred

Owen. BrPo; CABA; CMoP; FaFP; HAP; LiTB; LiTM; MoAB; MoBrPo; OAEL-1; OAEP; WaP; WeW
Let the Catholic Church be now arrayed. Bishop Butler of Kilcash. *Unknown.* OnYI
Let the crows go by hawking their caw and caw. River Roads. Carl Sandburg. VGW
Let the damned ride their earwigs to Hell, but let me not join them. Rock Pilgrim. Herbert Palmer. OxBTC
Let the Day Perish, Wherein I Was Borne. Bible, *O.T.* *Fr.* Job, III. NAs; OBVE; TrJP
(Job Complains.) TrGrPo
(Job's Curse.) AWP
Let the Dead Depart in Peace. *Yoruba Oral Tradition, tr. by* Ulli Beier. WTO
Let the Deep Organ Swell, *with music.* Constantine Pise. AH
Let the door be open wide. Christmas Eve. Liam P. Clancy. ISi
Let the exiles in-gather. Evening of the Rose. Anthony Rudolf. VWA
Let the eye remember the loved face. The Soul Remembers. Richard Burdick Eldridge. GoYe
Let the farmer praise his grounds. The Cruiskeen Lawn. *Unknown.* HBV-2; OnYI
Let the Florid Music Praise. W. H. Auden. MoPo
Let the flowers make a journey. The Fury of Flowers and Worms. Anne Sexton. BoWoP
Let the foul Scene proceed. The Marionettes. Walter de la Mare. MMA
Let the knowing speak. Adjuration. Charles Enoch Wheeler. AmNP; PoNe
Let the Light Enter. Frances E. W. Harper. PoNe
Let the limerick form be rehoised. Leaning on a Limerick. Eve Merriam. TDH
Let the lover his mistress's beauty rehearse. My Bonny Black Bess. *Unknown.* ViBoFo
Let the mountains stand forth! Requiem. Hamilton Warren. GoYe
Let the musicians begin. At a Solemn Musick. Delmore Schwartz. TwAmPo
Let the Nations Be Glad. Bible, *O.T.* Psalms, LXVII. FaPON
Let the night keep. Night. William Rose Benét. MoAmPo
Let the Nile cloak his head in the clouds, and defy. On the Discoveries of Captain Lewis. Joel Barlow. AmPP; PAH
Let the only consistency. "Hugh MacDiarmid." *Fr.* In the Fall. FaBoMo
Let the pines rock in torment of the storm. Horatian Ode. Joseph Warren Beach. PoA
Let the place of the solitaires. The Place of the Solitaires. Wallace Stevens. SyP
Let the rain kiss you. April Rain Song. Langston Hughes. FaPON; NTCP; OBCA; PDV; RHPC; SUS; TiPo
Let the rain plunge radiant. The Way Through. Denise Levertov. NeAP; PoM
Let the Rest of the World Go By. J. Keirn Brennan. UnPo
Let the rich man fill his belly. Spanish Folk Songs. Antonio Machado, *tr. by* Havelock Ellis. AWP
Let the robed kings march in the mind. A Letter from a Friend. John N. Morris. CABA
Let the shark keep to the shelves and closets of coral. From a Litany. Mark Strand. PPP
Let the snake wait under. A Sort of a Song. William Carlos Williams. BiP; FAZ; HoPM; NoP; PP; SeCeV; TAP
Let the still yellow goldenrod, hot with sun, come back. You Are More than I Need. Rebbekka Kaplan. AMV-80
Let the tale's sailor from a Christian voyage. Altarwise by Owl-Light, X. Dylan Thomas. CMoP; FaBoMo; NoAM; OAEL-2
Let the Toast Pass. Sheridan. *Fr.* The School for Scandal, III, iii. HBV-2; OnYI; OxBI
(Famous Toast, A.) TreF
(Here's to the Maiden.) ELP
(Song: "Here's to the maiden [*or* maid] of bashful fifteen.") NOEC; OBEC; OxBoLi; PoRA; ViBoPo
Let the toper regale in his tankard of ale. The Pipe of Tobacco. *At. to* John Usher. HBV-2
Let the waves of slumber billow. To a Lady Troubled by Insomnia. Franklin P. Adams. InMe
Let the wealthy and great. The Rewards of Farming. *Unknown.* PoPle
Let the wick burn low: and suddenly I remember. The Sleepers. Randolph Stow. *Fr.* Thailand Railway. CBAP
Let the Wind Blow High or Low. *Unknown.* OBET
Let the wood be pulled. Surprised by Me. Walter Darring. NYBP
Let the world's sharpness like a clasping knife. Sonnets from the Portuguese, XXIV. Elizabeth Barrett Browning. VLP
Let the youth hardened by a sharp soldier's life. Horace, *tr. by* John Wight. Odes, III, 2. WaaP
Let Them Alone. Robinson Jeffers. AP
Let them bestow on every airth a limb. On Himself, upon Hearing What Was His Sentence [*or* His Metrical Prayer]. James Graham, Marquis of Montrose. CavP; ChTr; FaBoEE; OBS; OxBS; PrIm; SeCePo
Let them bury your big eyes. Elegy. Edna St. Vincent Millay. *Fr.* Memorial to D. C. CMoP; HBMV; MoAB; MoAmPo; NePA; PoRA
Let them call me "froggy," "wart-face," or. Prince Charming. John N. Miller. DFT
Let them come, come never so proudly. God Save Elizabeth! Francis Turner Palgrave. HBV-2
Let them count scalps under the barroom wall. Lying in a Yuma Saloon. Jim Barnes. CDW
Let them go by—the heats, the doubts, the strife. Oasis. Edward Dowden. OxBI
Let them keep it. And Was Not Improved. Lerone Bennett, Jr. CNA; PoBA
Let them lie—their day is over. Refrigerium. Frederick Goddard Tuckerman. AP
Let them say to my lover. Amor Mysticus. Sister Marcela de Carpio de San Felix, *tr. by* John Hay. AWP
Let there be laid, when I am dead. Posthumous Coquetry. Théophile Gautier, *tr. by* Arthur Symons. AWP
Let there be life, said God. And what He wrought. The Power and the Glory. Siegfried Sassoon. OBMV
Let There Be Light, *with music.* William M. Vories. AH
"Let there be light!" said God, and there was light! Byron. *Fr.* Don Juan, VII. OBWP
Let there be many windows to your soul. Progress. Ella Wheeler Wilcox. BLPA; FPL
Let There Be New Flowering. Lucille Clifton. GP; PPJ
Let there be no flowery banks. A Garden of Situations. Jack Anderson. PoA
Let there be ripeness, said the Lord. Their Mouths Full. David Ignatow. GP
Let this day's air praise the Lord. Rinsed with Gold, Endless, Walking the Fields. Robert Siegel. GeTw
Let those who are in favour with their stars. Sonnets, XXV. Shakespeare. OBSC
Let those who from the frozen Arctos reach. The Advantages of Washing. John Armstrong. *Fr.* The Art of Preserving Health. FaBoUs
Let thy gold be cast in the furnace. Cleansing Fires. Adelaide Anne Proctor. WGRP
Let Thy Kingdom, *with music.* *Unknown.* AH
Let thy soul walk slowly in thee. Silence. Samuel Miller Hageman. TRV
Let thy tears, Le Vayer, let them flow. To Monsieur de la Mothe le Vayer. Molière, *tr. by* Austin Dobson. AWP
Let time and chance combine, combine. Adieu. Thomas Carlyle. HBV-1; OBRV
Let Tobias bless Charity with his dog. Christopher Smart. *Fr.* Jubilate Agno. NCEP
Let Tyrants Shake Their Iron Rod, *with music.* William Billings. AH
(Chester, *with music.*) BLSo; TrAS
Let uh revolution come. uh. U Name This One. Carolyn M. Rodgers. BISi; NMM; PoBA
Let us abandon then our gardens and go home. Justice Denied in Massachusetts. Edna St. Vincent Millay. GOA; MoAmPo; SBG
Let Us All be Unhappy on Sunday. Lord Neaves. FaBoCo
Let us arise, and watch by night. Matins—Sunday. Cardinal Newman. VLP
Let us, as by this verdant bank we float. A Water-Party. Robert Bridges. PoPle
Let us ask ourselves some questions; for that man is truly wise. The Higher Catechism. Sam Walter Foss. WGRP
Let us ask you a few questions, without rancor. For Any Member of the Security Police. Josephine Jacobsen. NePoAm
Let us await the great American novel! Critical Observations. Archibald MacLeish. OBAL
Let us be guests in one another's house. Any Wife or Husband. Carol Haynes. BLPA
Let us be like a bird for a moment perched. Wings. Victor Hugo. TRV
Let Us Be Merry before We Go. John Philpot Curran. *See* Deserter's Lamentation, The.
Let us be still. To Usward. Gwendolyn B. Bennett. BlSi
Let us become the overhanging day. Shelley. *Fr.* Epipsychidion. OAEL-2
Let us begin and carry up this corpse. A Grammarian's Funeral. Robert Browning. HBV-2; LoBV; OAEP; VLP; WGRP
Let us begin and portion out these sweets. A Girtonian Funeral. *Unknown.* FaBoCo; Par
Let Us Believe. Hildegarde Flanner. WPE
Let Us Break Bread Together. *Unknown.* AH, *with music*; FSW
(When I Fall on My Knees, *with music.*) BoAN-2
Let us bring out those heavy dice. Birth. Gabriela Melinescu, *tr. by* Willis Barnstone *and* Matei Calinescu. BoWoP

Let Us Cheer the Weary Traveler, *with music*. *Unknown*. AH
(Weary Traveler, *with music*.) BoAN-1
Let us come in to worship Jehovah. Come In. Isaiah Shembe, *tr. by* H. Tracey. WTO
Let Us Consider Where the Great Men Are. Delmore Schwartz. *Fr.* Shenandoah. MoAB; MoAmPo
Let us deal kindly with a heart of old by sorrow torn. Saadabad. James Elroy Flecker. SeCePo
Let Us Declare! *sel.* Angela Morgan.
"Come, workers! Poets, artists, dreamers, more and more." PGD
Let Us Drink. Alcaeus, *tr. fr. Greek by* John Hermann Merivale. AWP
Let Us Drink and Be Merry. Thomas Jordan. PoPle
(Careless Gallant, The.) CoMu; HAP; OxBoLi
(Coronemus Nos Rosis Antequam Marcescant.) HBV-2; OBEV
(Epicure, The, Sung by One in the Habit of a Town Gallant.) NOBE
Let us drink knights of the round table. Chevaliers de la Table Ronde. *Unknown*. FSW
Let us drink old wine, at the sight of which I rejoice. Five Arabic Verses in Praise of Wine, I. *Unknown, tr. by* Hartwig Hirschfeld. TrJP
Let us evoke no phantom throng. Armistice Day. Lucia Trent. PGD
Let Us Forget. Agnes Mary Frances Robinson. WHA
Let us forget tomorrow! For tonight. Last Leave. Eileen Newton. SUMH
Let us forget we loved each other much. Let Us Forget. Agnes Mary Frances Robinson. WHA
Let us forgive Ty Kendricks. Southern Cop. Sterling A. Brown. SoSe
Let Us Gather at the River. Marge Piercy. GeTw
Let us gather hand in hand. A Medieval Poem of the Nativity. *Unknown*. TrCP
Let us gather up the sunbeams. Scatter Seeds of Kindness. May Riley Smith. WBLP
Let us give thanks for the things of the north. The Things of the North. Rennie McOwan. PoSH
Let us give up our trips. Direction. Barbara Guest. WPE
Let Us Go Down, the Long Dead Night Is Done. Christopher Brennan. *Fr.* Towards the Source. PoAu-1
Let us go hence, my songs; she will not hear. A Leave-taking. Swinburne. CH; FaBoEn; HBV-1; NOBE; OAEP; OBNC; OBVV; PoEL-5; PoLF; ViBoPo; VLP
Let us go hence: the night is now at hand. A Last Word. Ernest Dowson. MoBrPo; SyP; VLP
Let Us Go, Then, Exploring. Virginia Woolf. BoNaP
Let us go then, you and I. The Love Song of J. Alfred Prufrock. T. S. Eliot. AmPP; AP; AWP; BiP; CABA; CMoP; CoBMV; EBEV; FF; HAP; HBMV; HeIP; HoPM; InPK; InPS; LiTB; LiTM; MoAB; MoAmPo; MoVE; MP; NePA; NIP; NoAM; NOBA; NOBE; NoP; OAEL-2; OAEP; OxBTC; PAI; PoA; PoRA; PPP; PrIm; SeCeV; SoSe; SOTW; TAP; TreFT; TrGrPo; TwAmPo; TwCP; ViBoPo; WeW
Let us have winter loving that the heart. Winter Love. Elizabeth Jennings. BoLoP; NePoEA; PPJ
Let Us Keep Christmas. Grace Noll Crowell. TRV
Let Us Laugh. Zvi Shargel, *tr. fr. Yiddish by* Gabriel Preil. VWA
Let us lay, and dance, and sing. The Vision of Delight Presented at Court in Chistmas, 1617. Ben Jonson. SeCV-1
Let Us Learn. Melech Ravitch, *tr. fr. Yiddish by* Seymour Mayne *and* Rivka Augenfeld. VWA
Let us leave behind this city. City of Light. Nahum Bomze, *tr. by* Gabriel Preil *and* Howard Schwartz. VWA
Let us leave talking of angelic hosts. Sonnet. Elinor Wylie. *Fr.* One Person. OxBA
Let us live, then, and be glad. Gaudeamus Igitur. *Unknown, tr. by* John Addington Symonds. *Fr.* Carmina Burana. GLGT; HBV-2
Let us make the test. Say God wants you. Gnostics on Trial. Linda Gregg. AMV-80; NPGG
Let us not look upon. Prayer. Witter Bynner. EaLo
Let us not make apologies. Instructions. Anita Skeen. IHMS
"Let us not speak, for the love we bear one another." In a Bath Teashop. John Betjeman. ELV; EnLoPo
Let Us Now Praise Famous Men. Bible, Apocrypha. *Fr.* Ecclesiasticus. ChTr; OBVE
(Our Fathers.) TrJP
"Let Us Now Praise Famous Men." C. Day Lewis. BiP; CMoP
Let us now praise famous men; and the children. Dostoievsky's Daughters. Michael Hamburger. NAs
Let us pause to consider the English. England Expects. Ogden Nash. DBV
Let us play, and dance, and sing. The Vision of Delight. Ben Jonson. PoEL-2
Let us praise our Maker, with true passion extol Him. Anthem. W. H. Auden. NOCV
Let us record/ The evenings when we were innocents of twenty. Winfield Townley Scott. *Fr.* Biography for Traman. ErPo
Let us rejoice on our cots, for His nocturnal miracles. Lauds. John Berryman. HAP
Let us remember Spring will come again. May, 1915. Charlotte Mew. SUMH
Let us remember the yellow. In the Month of Green Fire. Sophie Himmell. GoYe
Let us return from Ilium, and no more. Independence. Guy Mason. CaP
Let Us Rise Up and Live. Francis Sherman. CaP
Let us save the babies. The Babies. Mark Strand. GeTw; NYBP
Let us say good-bye. Bags Packed and We Expected This. Ramona Wilson. VoR
Let us sing of it ever and long. Song of Sukkaartik, the Assistant Spirit. Ajukutooq, *tr. fr. Eskimo*. WTO
Let us sit by the hissing steam radiator a winter's day, grey wind. Horses and Men in the Rain. Carl Sandburg. PoLF
Let Us Smile. Wilbur D. Nesbit. WBLP
Let us stiffen. The Covenant. James Cunningham. JB
Let us suppose the mind. Barbara Moraff. IHMS
Let us suppose, valleys and such ago. John Berryman. *Fr.* Dream Songs. NaP; PPP
Let us synge unto the Lorde, for he is become glorious. Bible, *O.T. Fr.* Exodus. OBVE
Let us take the road. The Highwaymen. John Gay. *Fr.* The Beggar's Opera. WiR
Let us take to our hearts a lesson. The Tapestry Weavers. Anson G. Chester. BLPA; BLRP; WBLP
Let us thank Almighty God. Creatrix. Anna Wickham. MoBrPo
Let us to-day. Song for Memorial Day. Clinton Scollard. OHIP
Let us tunnel. Letters to Walt Whitman, I. Ronald Johnson. VGW
Let us use it while we may. Of Beauty [*or* Beauty]. Giovanni Battista Guarini, *tr. by* Sir Richard Fanshawe. *Fr.* Il Pastor Fido. BoLoP; GBL; InMe
Let us walk in the white snow. Velvet Shoes. Elinor Wylie. CH; FaPON; FPL; GoJo; MoAB; MoAmPo; PAI; PoPl; SiSoSe; SoPo; TreFS; TrGrPo; WHA
Let Us with a Gladsome Mind. Milton. TRV; WGRP
(Praise the Lord.) FaBoCh
Let vain or busy thoughts have there no part. George Herbert. *Fr.* The Church Porch. TRV
Let War's Tempests Cease. Longfellow. OHIP
Let who so lyst with mighty mace to raygne. Seneca, *tr. by* Jasper Heywood. *Fr.* Thyestes, II. OBVE
Let X Equal Half. J. F. Wilson. TDH
Let Y stand for you who says. You. Kenneth Rexroth. *Fr.* A Bestiary. HoPM
Let your eyes look at old people. In Respect of the Elderly. Thomas Peacock. VoR
Let your hands meet. The Death of Meleager. Swinburne. *Fr.* Atalanta in Calydon. OBVV
Let your longing for me, my love. Sulpicia, *tr. fr. Latin by* John Dillon. PBWP
Let Your Pastor Know. *Unknown*. STF
Let your song be delicate. Song Be Delicate. Shaw Neilson. PoAu-1
Let Zeus Record, *sel.* Hilda Doolittle ("H. D.").
"Stars wheel in purple, yours is not so rare." MoAmPo; NOBA; TAP
Let Zulu Be Heard. Isaiah Shembe, *tr. fr. Zulu by* G. C. Oosthuizen. WTO
Lethal Thought, The. Mary Boyd Wagner. GoYe
Lethargy of evil in her eyes, The. A Dying Viper. "Michael Field." FM
Lethe. Hilda Doolittle ("H. D."). CMoP; LiTM; MoAmPo; PoRA; TrGrPo; VGW; ViBoPo; WHA
Lethe. Georgia Douglas Johnson. CDC
Let's away with study. *Unknown, tr. by* Helen Waddell. *Fr.* Carmina Burana. NAWM-1
Let's Be Merry. Christina Rossetti. FaPON
Let's build bridges here and there. Interracial. Georgia Douglas Johnson. PoNe; TTY
Let's contend no more, Love. A Woman's Last Word. Robert Browning. BLPA; BLPL; FaBoBe; FaFP; HBV-1; OAEP; TreFS; TrGrPo; UnTE; ViBoPo
Let's count the bodies over again. Counting Small-boned Bodies. Robert Bly. CAPP; EAS; NaP
Let's Do It. Cole Porter. OBAL
Let's enjoy, while the season invites us. "Giovinette, che fate all'Amore." Lorenzo da Ponte, *tr. by* Natalie MacFarren. *Fr.* Don Giovanni. TrJP
Let's get going. Leylâ Hanim, *tr. fr. Turkish by* Tâlat S. Halman. PBWP
"Let's get hold of one of those deer." Prospero Dreams of Arnaud Daniel Inventing Love in the Twelfth Century. Jack Gilbert. NPGG
Let's go hunting, says Risky Rob. Billy Barlow. *Unknown*. FSW; OuSiCo
Let's go—much as that dog goes. Overland to the Islands. Denise Levertov. ConAP; UnPo
Let's go see Old Abe. Lincoln Monument: Washington. Langston Hughes. OFD

Let's Go to Bed. *Unknown.* ChTr
Let's go to the wood, says this pig. *Unknown.* OxNR
Let's go up to the hillside today. Play Song. Peter Clarke. PBA
Let's go, you and I. Adultery at a Las Vegas Bookstore. Stephen Shu Ning Liu. BrSi
Let's have less nonsense from the friends of Joe. Less Nonsense. A. P. Herbert. OxBTC
Let's hug our grudges, love. The Mill. John Taylor. FAZ
Let's just reject. The Importance of Personal Relationships. Bill Manhire. OCNZ
Let's live, my Lesbia, and love. Lesbia. Catullus, *tr. by* Sheridan Baker. PrIm
Let's not be slow in knowing. On Calvary's Lonely Hill. Herbert Clark Johnson. PoNe
Let's not think of tomorrow. The Trimdon Grange Explosion. Tommy Armstrong. OBET
Let's not use eyes anymore. Dialogue—2 Dollmakers. Gregory Corso. NeAP
Let's paddle, dear, by yonder fort. Invitation. *Malay Oral Tradition, tr. by* R. J. Wilkinson *and* R. O. Winstedt. WTO
Let's say I live here, at any rate. O'Reilly's Reply. Richard Weber. NMP
Let's shake wild music from gray belfry chimes. Resurrection. Margaret Sackville. HBMV
Let's sing a song together once. Song. Louis Simpson. NePoAm
Let's sing the new ministry's praise. The Procession' a New Protestant Ballad. *Unknown.* APAS
Let's skip a few short years of hollow peace. George the Third. Byron. *Fr.* The Vision of Judgment. FiP
Let's smile and be kind—life is so short. Life Is So Short. Margaret S. Hall. STF
Let's step on daddy's head shout. Step on His Head. James Laughlin. VGW
Let's straighten this out, my little man. To a Small Boy Standing on My Shoes While I Am Wearing Them. Ogden Nash. DBV; FiBHP
Let's Talk, Mother. Edith Bruck, *tr. fr. Italian by* Anita Barrows. VWA
Let's Talk of Graves. Shakespeare. *See* Death of Kings, The.
Let's think of eggs. The Poultries. Ogden Nash. CenHV
Let's write a poem about lazy people. The Lazy People. Shel Silverstein. NTCP
Letter, The. W. H. Auden. FaBoTw; NoAM
Letter, The. Patricia Beer. OxBC
Letter. Alexander Bergman. TrJP
Letter, The. Paul Blackburn. CoPo
Letter, The. John Blight. CBAP
Letter. Philip Dow. NPGG
Letter, A. Emerson. OxBA
Letter, A. Anthony Hecht. NYBP; OxBC
Letter, The. John Holmes. NePoAm
Letter, A. Rachel Korn, *tr. fr. Yiddish by* Ruth Whitman. VWA
Letter, A ("That kind o'sogerin' ain't a mite like our October trainin' "). James Russell Lowell. *Fr.* The Biglow Papers, 1st series, No. II. OxBA
Letter, A ("Thrash away, you'll hev to rattle"). James Russell Lowell. *Fr.* The Biglow Papers, 1st series, No. I. OxBA
(Mr. Hosea Biglow Speaks.) PAH
("Thrash away, you'll hev to rattle.") AmPP
Letter. W. S. Merwin. HAP
Letter, The. Beatrice M. Murphy. PoNe
Letter, The. Po Chü-i, *tr. fr. Chinese by* Arthur Waley. LoBV
Letter, A. Matthew Prior. SeCePo
Letter, A. Sir Arthur Quiller-Couch. CenHV
Letter, The. Charles Reznikoff. VWA
Letter. Mark Strand. NoAM
Letter, The. John Tatham. CavP
Letter across Doubt and Distance. M. Carl Holman. AmNP; PoNe
Letter Catches Up with Me, A. Eric Chaet. VWA
Letter Containing a Panegyric on Bath. Christopher Anstey. *Fr.* The New Bath Guide. OBEC
Letter Edged in Black, The. *Unknown.* FSW
Letter VIII ("On the first day of snow, my train)." Randall Swingler. WaP
Letter V ("Lie where you fell and longed"). W. S. Graham. OxBTC
Letter for Allhallows, A. Peter Kane Dufault. NYBP
Letter for Duncan. Larry Eigner. PoM
Letter for Marian, A. Thomas McGrath. VGW
Letter for Melville 1951. Charles Olson. CoPo
Letter IV ("Hatched in a rasping darkness of dry sand"). William Empson. LiTB
Letter from a Black Soldier. Bill Anderson. VGW
Letter from a Coward to a Hero. Robert Penn Warren. MoAmPo
Letter from a Death Bed. John Ciardi. NCSH
Letter from a Friend, A. Carolyn Maisel. IHMS
Letter from a Friend, A. John N. Morris. CABA
Letter from a Girl to Her Own Old Age, A. Alice Meynell. FaBoRV; GoTL; LiTB; MoBrPo; SBG; ViBoPo
Letter from a State Hospital. Frank Mundorf. GoYe
Letter from a Wife. S. Carolyn Reese. PoNe
Letter from a Working Girl. Herbert Scott. GP
Letter from an Institution: III. Michael Ryan. AmPA
Letter from an Island. John Malcolm Brinnin. TAP
Letter from Aragon, A. John Cornford. OBWP
Letter from Artemisa in the Town, to Cloe, in the Country, A. Earl of Rochester. SeCV-2
Letter from Berlin, A. Jon Stallworthy. NoAM; OBWP; OxBC
Letter from Birmingham. Harold Bond. TAT
Letter from Brooklyn, A. Derek Walcott. OxBTC
Letter from Caroline Herschel (1750-1848). Siv Cedering. SUW
Letter from Des Moines. Thomas Swiss. AMV-81
Letter from Ealing Broadway Station, A. Aelfrida Tillyard. SUMH
Letter from Germany. Emily Grosholz. AMV-81
Letter from Home, A. John Paul Minarik. LFAC
Letter from Home, A. Mary Oliver. Str
Letter from Italy [to the Right Honourable Charles Lord Halifax], A. Joseph Addison. NOEC
Italy and Britain, *sel.* OBEC
Letter from Li Po, A, *sel.* Conrad Aiken.
"Winds of doctrine blow both ways at once, The." VGW
"Letter from my love today, A!" A Ballad of Hell [*or* Christmas Eve]. John Davidson. EBVV; HBMV; HoPM; MoBrPo; WHA
Letter from Oregon. William Stafford. NaP
Letter from Rome, A. Arthur Hugh Clough. *Fr.* Amours de Voyage. LoBV
Letter from School, A. Thomas Love Peacock. FaBoUs
Letter from Slough Pond. Isabella Gardner. ELU
Letter from the Caribbean, A. Barbara Howes. CoAP; UnPo
Letter from the Country, A. Howard Baker. TwAmPo
Letter from the Country to a Friend in Town, A. John Oldham. PP
Letter from the Hotel, A. Aliki Barnstone. FAZ
Letter from the Pygmies, A. Theodore Weiss. VGW
Letter from the Street. Thomas Brush. LTB
Letter from the Vieux Carre. Ethel Green Russell. GoYe
Letter from Underground. Ronald Everson. MoCV
Letter from When, A. Bernadine. LTB
Letter in Winter. Raymond R. Patterson. PoBA
Letter Is a Gypsy Elf, A. Annette Wynne. SUS
Letter of a Mother. Robert Penn Warren. MoAmPo
Letter of Advice, A. Winthrop Mackworth Praed. HBV-1; NOBL; OBRV; OxBoLi; WhC
Letter I ("You were amused to find you too could fear"). William Empson. ChMP; LiTB
Letter I ("The midnight streets as I walk back"). Randall Swingler. WaP
Letter Out of the Gray. Gabriel Preil, *tr. fr. Hebrew by* Shirley Kaufman *and* Howard Schwartz. VWA
Letter VI ("A day the wind was hardly"). W. S. Graham. ChMP; FaBoMo
Letter: The Japanese, to Her Husband at War. William Walsh. PoPl
Letter to a Dead Father. Richard Shelton. DFF; GP
Letter to a Friend. Jon Stallworthy. NoAM
Letter to a Friend. John Thompson. PoAu-2
Letter to a Friend. Robert Penn Warren. MoAmPo
Letter to a Friend in an Unknown Place. Anita Barrows. NMM
Letter to a Jealous Friend. James Simmons. CIP
Letter to a Librarian. Irving Layton. MAT; TW
Letter to a Live Poet, A. Rupert Brooke. BrPo
Letter to a Mute. Thomas James. AmPA
Letter to a Substitute Teacher. Gary Gildner. Psk
Letter to a Young Father in Exile. John Logan. CAPP
Letter to a Young Friend. Burns. *See* Epistle to a Young Friend.
Letter to a Young Poet. George Barker. ChMP
Letter to Alex Comfort. Dannie Abse. FaBoTw; MP; TwCP
Letter to an Absent Son. Madeline DeFrees. GP; NMM
Letter to an American Visitor. Alex Comfort. OxBTC
Letter to an Imaginary Friend, Part One, *sels.* Thomas McGrath. NNaP
"And I hear the pad of feet to the union hall," II, 2.
"We go out in the stony midnight," VIII, 4.
Letter to an Imaginary Friend, Part Two, *sels.* Thomas McGrath.
"Begun before Easter. . ./ Sign of the Fish," VI, 4. NNaP
"Evening—another evening—and the lights flare," V, 2. NNaP
"Road outside the window was 'our' road, The," V, 1. GP
"Windless city built on decaying granite, loose ends," II, 2-5. NNaP
Letter to Anne Ridler. G. S. Fraser. OxBS
Letter to Auden, A. Robert Phillips. AMV-81
Letter to Be Disguised as a Gas Bill. Marge Piercy. WPE
Letter to Bell from Missoula. Richard Hugo. NNaP
Letter to Ben Jonson, A. Francis Beaumont. *See* Mr. Francis Beaumont's Letter to Ben Johnson.

Letter to Charles Townsend Copeland, A: Le Baron Russell Briggs, *sel.* Robert Hillyer.
"As dusk comes on, I almost hope to meet." GLGT
Letter to Daphnis [*or* Dafnis], A. Countess of Winchilsea. EnLoPo; SBG
Letter to David Campbell on the Birthday of W. B. Yeats, 1965, A. A. D. Hope. NAs
Letter to E. Franklin Frazier. Amiri Baraka. BPo; PoBA
Letter to Elsa, A. Grace Hazard Conkling. HBMV; HBVY
Letter to Evelyn Baring, A. Edward Lear. FaBoNo
Letter to Garber from Skye. Richard Hugo. AMV-81
Letter to Her Father, A. Inib-sarri, *tr. fr. Akkadian by* Willis Barnstone. BoWoP
Letter to Her Husband, A ("Phoebus, make haste"). Anne Bradstreet. LiTA
Letter to Her Husband, Absent upon Public Employment, A ("As loving hind. . ."). Anne Bradstreet. OxBA; WPE
(Another.) SBG; SCAP
Letter to Her Husband, Absent upon Publick Employment, A ("My head, my heart, mine eyes . . ."). Anne Bradstreet. HAP; HeIP; NoP; SCAP
Letter to Her Mother, A. Eristi-Aya, *tr. fr. Akkadian by* Willis Barnstone. BoWoP
Letter to His Friend Isaac, A. Judah Halevi, *tr. fr. Hebrew by* Emma Lazarus. TrJP
Letter to Hitler, A. James Laughlin. LiTA; WaP
Letter to John Donne, A. C. H. Sisson. NOCV
Letter to John Dryden, A, *sel.* James McAuley.
"Dear John, whoever now takes pen to write." CBAP
Letter to Kafka. Maura Stanton. AmPA
Letter to Karl Shapiro. E. L. Mayo. MiAP
Letter to Lady Margaret Cavendish Holles-Harley, When a Child, A. Matthew Prior. *See* Letter to the Honourable Lady Miss Margaret Cavendish Holles-Harley.
Letter to Levertov from Butte. Richard Hugo. NNaP
Letter to Logan from Milltown. Richard Hugo. NNaP
Letter to Lord Byron, *sels.* W. H. Auden.
"England, my England—you have been my tutrix." OBSV
"I like your muse because she's gay and witty." NOBL
"Ottava Rima would, I know, be proper." NOBL
"Thought of writing came to me today, The." NOBL
"You lived and moved among the best society." OBSV
Letter to Lord Middleton, A. Sir George Etherege. CavP
Letter to "M." *Unknown.* OxBM
Letter to Maria Gisborne, *sels.* Shelley.
To Maria Gisborne in England, from Italy. NOBE
"You are now/ In London, that great sea, whose ebb and flow." ChER; EBEV; OBRV
Letter to My Daughter at the End of Her Second Year. Donald Finkel. CoAP
Letter to My Kinder. Bob Gaskin. AMV-81
Letter to My Mother. Dom Moraes. NoAM
Letter to My Mother. Anita Skeen. IHMS
Letter to My Sister. Anne Spencer. AmNP; BlSi; PoBA; PoNe
Letter to My Wife. Roy Fuller. NeBP
Letter to My Wife. Miklós Radnóti, *tr. fr. Hungarian by* Emery George. VWA
Letter to My Wife. Keidrych Rhys. WaP
Letter to Myself. Christopher Reid. FaBoPa
Letter to N.Y. Elizabeth Bishop. MP; NoP; NYP; TWCP
Letter to P. Robert Friend. NYBP
Letter to Pasternak. Ralph Pomeroy. CoPo
Letter to Paul Celan in Memory, A. Jerome Rothenberg. VWA
Letter to Peter, A. Fay Chiang. BrSi
Letter to R. Willard Maas. WaP
Letter to Reed from Lolo. Richard Hugo. NNaP
Letter to Robert. Mary Fabilli. IHMS
Letter to Robert Fergusson. Alexander Scott. OxBS
Letter to Robert Frost, A. Robert Hillyer. MoAmPo
Letter to Ron Silliman on the Back of a Map of the Solar System, A. Dennis Schmitz. LCAP
Letter to Sara Hutchinson, A. Samuel Taylor Coleridge. *See* Dejection; an Ode.
Letter to Scanlon from Whitehall. Richard Hugo. NNaP
Letter to Sir H. Wotton at His Going Ambassador to Venice. John Donne. *See* To Sir H. W. at His Going . . .
Letter to Statues. John Malcolm Brinnin. EyDe
Letter to the Child Lady Margaret Cavendish Holles-Harley, A. Matthew Prior. *See* Letter to the Honourable Lady Miss Margaret Cavendish Holles-Harley.
Letter to the City Clerk. Frederick A. Wright. FaFP
Letter to the Countess of Denbigh [against Irresolution and Delay in Matters of Religion], A. Richard Crashaw. *See* To the Noblest and Best of Ladies.
Letter to the Front. Muriel Rukeyser. WaP
Sels.
Even during War. TrJP
To Be a Jew in the Twentieth Century. TrJP
Letter to the Honourable Lady Miss Margaret Cavendish Holles-Harley, A. Matthew Prior. LoBV; NOEC; OBEC
(Letter to Lady Margaret Cavendish Holles-Harley, When a Child, A.) NOBE; OBEV
(Letter to the Child Lady Margaret Cavendish Holles-Harley, A.) OxBChV
Letter to the Revolution. Susan Griffin. NPGG
Letter to Three Irish Poets, A. Michael Longley. BIrV
Letter to Tina Koyama from Elliot Bay Park. Jim Mitsui. BrSi
Letter to Viscount Cobham. Congreve. LoBV
Letter to Wagoner from Port Townsend. Richard Hugo. NNaP
Letter to Welch from Browning. Richard Hugo. NNaP
Letter to Wilbur Frohock, A. Daniel Hoffman. CoPo
Letter to William Carlos Williams, A. Kenneth Rexroth. NNaP; PP
Letter 27. Charles Olson. *Fr.* The Maximus Poems. CoPo
(Maximus to Gloucester, Letter 27.) NOBA
Letter II. W. S. Graham. NePoEA
Letter with a Black Border. Sandra McPherson. GeTw
Letter Written on a Ferry Crossing Long Island Sound. Anne Sexton. CoAP; MP; NYBP; TwCP
Letters. Charles Bukowski. GP
Letters. Bernard Spencer. NeBP; WaP
Letters, The. Tennyson. HBV-1
Letters & Other Worlds. Michael Ondaatje. NOBC; NoP
Letters are comforting to get. David McCord. Convalescence, VI. WhC
Letters at School, The. Mary Mapes Dodge. OBCA
Letters for the New England Dead. Mary Baron. HoAn
Letters [*or* Notes] Found near a Suicide. Frank Horne. AmNP; CDC; PoBA; PoNC
Sels.
To "Chick." BPo
To James. BPo
To Mother. BPo
To You. BPo
Letters from a Father. Mona Van Duyn. FYAP
Letters from an Irishman to a Rat. Christopher Logue. BoAnP
Letters from Kazuko (Kyoto, Japan—Summer 1980). Alan Chong Lau. BrSi
Letters from Teignmouth, *sel.* Winthrop Mackworth Praed.
Our Ball. EnRP
Letters from the Astronomers, *sels.* Siv Cedering.
Johannes Kepler (1571-1630). SUW
Nicholas Copernicus (1473-1543). SUW
Letters I, your lone friend, write in sorrow, The. From William Tyndale to John Frith. Edgar Bowers. NePoEA; QFR
Letters, like blood along a weakening body. Letters. Bernard Spencer. NeBP; WaP
Letters of a Name, The. Colette Inez. AMV-81
Letters of Summer, The. Christopher Buckley. AMV-80
Letters of the Book, The. Rose Drachler. VWA
Letters of the Jews as strict as flames, The. The Alphabet. Karl Shapiro. NoAM; PoA; VWA
Letters she left to clutter up the desk. A Gesture by a Lady with an Assumed Name. James Wright. ConAP; LiTM
Letters to a Stranger. Thomas James. AmPA
Letters to Live Poets, *sels.* Bruce Beaver. CBAP
"I shop in the streets of my hometown with/ my family," II.
"I welcome the anonymity of the middle years," XIX.
"Mid-day and a heat haze over all," XXXIV.
"Sou'wester whips the day awake, The," X.
"Three anti-depressants and one diuretic a day," XII.
"Three images of dying stick in my mind like morbid transfers," V.
"Today the self-destroying anger," XXX.
Letters to My Daughters, 11. Judith Minty. AMV-81
Letters to Walt Whitman, *sels.* Ronald Johnson. VGW
"But are these landscapes to be imagined," IX.
"I, too, have plucked a stalk of grass," V.
"Let us tunnel," I.
"Slant sheen/ wrinkled silver," II.
Lettice. Dinah Maria Mulock Craik. HBV-1
Letting Go. Richard Shelton. AMV-81
Letting in Cold. Marvin Bell. DiL
Letting My Feelings Out. Yü Hsüan-chi, *tr. fr. Chinese by* Geoffrey Waters. BoWoP
Letty's Globe. Charles Tennyson Turner. HBV-1; OBEV; OBVV; OnUR
Leukothea. Keith Douglas. NeBP
Levantine, A. William Plomer. OBMV
Levavi Oculos. Marion Campbell. PoSH

Levedy, ich thanke [*or* ic thonke] thee. Lady, I Thank Thee [*or* Thanks and a Plea to Mary]. *Unknown.* MeEL; OxBM
Levee Camp Moan. *Unknown.* BluL
Levee Moan (A *and* B *vers., with music*). *Unknown.* AS
Level and the Square, The. Robert Morris. BLPA
Level ocean lies immeasurably blind, The. The Flying Fish. Jack Cope. PeSA
Level slope of colored sea, The. Metaphysical. Robert Fitzgerald. PoA
Level with duty, days ride a city-express across the calendar page. Coin in the Fist. Florence Kerr Brownell. GoYe
Levelled Churchyard, The. Thomas Hardy. NOBL
Leves Amores. Arthur Symons. UnTE
Levi Yitzhok:/ binding tefillin on. The Morning Prayers of the Hasid, Rabbi Levi Yitzhok. Phyllis Gotlieb. VWA
Leviathan. Bible, *O.T.* Job, XLI, *abr.*
("Canst thou draw out Leviathan with an hook[e].") MOS; OBVE; TrGrPo
Leviathan. Jay Macpherson. MoCV
Leviathan. W. S. Merwin. ConAP; NePoEA; NoAM; NOBA
Leviathan. Milton. *Fr.* Paradise Lost, VII. AmMo
Leviathan, *sel.* Peter Quennell.
"Music met Leviathan returning, A." MoBrPo
Leviathan; a Poem in Four Movements. Kenneth Pitchford. CoPo
Leviathan; or, A Hymn to Poor Brother Ben. *Unknown.* APAS
Levin, on his way to Kitty's love. Secular Games. Richard Howard. PoA
Levitation. Alvin Aubert. GP
Lewd Love Is Loss. Robert Southwell. ACP
Lewesdon Hill, *sel.* William Crowe.
"Up to thy summit, Lewesdon, to the brow." NOEC
Lewis and Clark. Rosemary *and* Stephen Vincent Benét. BPAW
Lewis Carroll. Eleanor Farjeon. OxBChV
Lewis Has a Trumpet. Karla Kuskin. PDV
Lewis, the Lost Lover. Sir Thomas More. OBSC
Lewti. Samuel Taylor Coleridge. EnRP
Lexington. Oliver Wendell Holmes. PAH
Lexington. Sidney Lanier. *Fr.* Psalm of the West. PAH; PAL
Lexington. Whittier. PAH
Lexington, dear heart, you old whore. The Old Athens of the West Is Now a Blue Grass Tour. James Baker Hall. TAT
Lexington Miller, The. *Unknown.* BaBo
Lexington Murder, The. *Unknown.* BaBo; OuSiCo, *with music*
L'Homme Moyen Sensuel, *sels.* Ezra Pound. OBSV
"Alas, eheu, one question that sorely vexes."
"'Tis of my country that I would endite."
Liadan Laments Cuirithir. Liadan, *tr. fr. Irish by* John Montague. BIrV; PBWP
(Liadain, *tr. by* Frank O'Connor). KiLC
(Liadin and Curither, *tr. by* Kuno Meyer.) OnYI
Liady-Day an' Ridden House. William Barnes. OBRV
Liar, The. Amiri Baraka. AmPP; NOBA
Liar, The. *Unknown, tr. fr. Irish by* Frank O'Connor. KiLC
Liar and bragger. Peregrine. Elinor Wylie. BLPL; HBMV
Liar Rumplestiltskin Loves. William Hathaway. *Fr.* Rumplestiltskin Poems. DFT
Liard Hot Springs. Gordon Massman. CTBA
'Lias! 'Lias! Bless de Lawd! In the Morning. Paul Laurence Dunbar. BPo
Libation. Denise Levertov. GP
Libation./ Hey sisters, we the color of our men. Ceremony. Johari M. Kunjufu. BlSi
Libel on Doctor Delaney and a Certain Great Lord, A. Swift. NCEP
Libelle of Englyshe Polycye, The, *sel.* *Unknown.*
Keep the Sea. OxBM
Liber doth vaunt how chastely he hath liv'd. In Librum. Sir John Davies. FaBoEE
Libera nos, Domine—Deliver us, O Lord. Emancipation from British Dependence. Philip Freneau. PAH
Liberace. Jonathan Holden. MAYP
Liberal arts lie eastward of this shore, The. The Seven Sleepers. Mark Van Doren. FYAP
Liberal, blue-eyed, shivering, trying not. The Blue-eyed Precinct Worker. Henri Coulette. MAT
Liberal nature did dispense. Woman's Arms. Anacreon, *tr. by* Abraham Cowley. UnTE
Liberals raised this in their finest hour. Norris Dam. Selden Rodman. PoNe
Liberation. Diane Mei Lin Mark. BrSi
Liberation. Ruth Stone. BoWoP
Liberator, The. Emily Holmes Coleman. EAS
Liberator, The. Lucien Stryk. GP
Liberator of the laboring, The. Talking Union: 1964. L. E. Sissman. TW
Liberia?/ No micro-footnote in a bunioned book. On the Founding of Liberia [*or* Do]. Melvin B. Tolson. *Fr.* Libretto for the Republic of Liberia. PoNe; UnPo
Libertine, The. Louis MacNeice. DTC; NoAM
Liberty. John Hay. AA
Liberty. Archibald MacLeish. GOA
Liberty. Edward Thomas. MoAB; OAEL-2
Liberty, *sel.* James Thomson.
British Commerce, *fr.* IV. OBEC
Liberty, *sel.* Wordsworth.
"Beetle loves his unpretending track, The." FaBoCo; FiBHP; Par
Liberty. Sir Thomas Wyatt. *See* Lover Rejoiceth, The.
Liberty and Independence. *Unknown.* *See* Independence Bell—July 4, 1776.
Liberty and Peace. Phillis Wheatley. SBG
"Lo! Freedom comes. Th' prescient Muse foretold," *sel.* BlSi
Liberty Enlightening the World. Edmund Clarence Stedman. PAH
Liberty for All. William Lloyd Garrison. AA
Liberty Pole, The. *Unknown.* PAH
Liberty Song, The, *with music.* John Dickinson. BLSo; TrAS
Liberty Tree. Thomas Paine. PAH
Librarian, The. Charles Olson. CoPo
Library, The, *sels.* George Crabbe.
Books. OBEC
Crusty Critics. OBEC
Library, The. Barbara A. Huff. FaPON; RHPC
Library. Louis Jenkins. NU
Library, The. John Logan. AMV-80
Library, The. Mary Mills. NePoAm
Library, The. Frank Dempster Sherman. AA
Libretto for the Republic of Liberia, *sel.* Melvin B. Tolson.
On the Founding of Liberia. UnPo
(Do.) PoNe
Lice-Finders, The [*or* The Lice-Hunters *or* The Lice Seekers]. Arthur Rimbaud. *See* Chercheuses de poux, Les.
Licences? Yes. Poetic licence. Ode to Himself. Sir Walter Alexander Raleigh. WhC
Lichen. Mary Fullerton. PoAu-1
Licht begouth to quenschyng out and fail, The. An Evening and Morning in June. Gawin Douglas. *Fr.* Prologues to the Aeneid. BSV
Licia, *sels.* Giles Fletcher the Elder.
"I wish sometimes, although a worthlesse thing," XII. AAS
"In time [*or* tyme] the strong and stately [*or* statelie] turrets fall," XXVIII. AAS; EBEV; NIP
(Time.) OBSC
"Like [*or* Lyke] Memnons rock, touched [*or* rocke toucht] with the rising sun[ne]," XLVII. AAS; FF
(Sonnet.) ElL
Lick your lips, X. darling, it may be the last. The Summer Ending. Glenway Wescott. PoA
Licorice Fields at Pontefract, The. John Betjeman. CMoP; NMP
Liddell and Scott; on the Completion of Their Lexicon. Thomas Hardy. OxBoLi
Liddesdale Crosiers hae ridden a race, The. The Death of Parcy Reed. *Unknown.* ESPB
Lido, The. Edmund Wilson. ErPo
Lie, The. Kipling. NOBL
Lie, The. Al Lee. AmPA
Lie, The. Howard Moss. LiTM; MoAB; NePoAm
Lie, The. Sir Walter Ralegh. AAS; ChTr; CTC; EBEV; EnRePo; HAP; HBV-2; InvP; LiTB; MasP; NOBE; NoP; OAEP; OBSC; PoEL-2; PPoe; PPON; QFR; SCV; SeCeV; SiPS; TEP; TreFT; TrGrPo; ViBoPo
(Soul's Errand, The.) WGRP
Lie back, daughter, let your head. First Lesson. Philip Booth. BiP; LiSp; MP; TwCP
Lie Closed, My Lately Loved. John Woods. ConAP
Lie down on the bright hill. The Dress. Mark Strand. GeTw
Lie Easy in Your Secret Cradle. John Wain. *Fr.* Wildtrack. NAs
Lie heavy on him, earth! for he. For Sir John Vanbrugh, Architect. Abel Evans. WhC
Lie here, without a record of thy worth. Tribute to the Memory of the Same Dog. Wordsworth. FM
Lie on the mats and sweat in summer. Things to Do around Kyoto. Gary Snyder. NaP
Lie on! while my revenge shall be. Revenge. Lord Nugent. PV
"Lie still, my newly married wife." The Griesly Wife. John Manifold. MoBrPo; MoBS
Lie, that we come from water, A. Landcrab. Margaret Atwood. SoSe
Lie up nearer, brother, nearer, for my limbs are growing cold. The Dying Californian. *Unknown.* AmFP
Lie where you fell and longed. Letter V. W. S. Graham. OxBTC
Lied in Crete. Alvaro Mutis. AMV-80
Liefer would I turn and love. Deranged. Padraic Fiacc. NeIP
Lies and Gossip. Raymond Ringo Fernandez. LFAC

Lies on one hip by the fire. The Girl Writing Her English Paper. Robert Wallace. Psk
Lif of this world, The. The Life of This World [*or* This Life]. *Unknown.* FaBoRV; OxBM
Life. Franklin P. Adams. InMe
Life. Sir Francis Bacon. GTBS; GTBS-P
Life. Anna Laetitia Barbauld. BLPA; FaFP; GTBS; GTBS-P; HBV-2; OBEV; OBRV; TreFS; TRV
Life, A. Chana Bloch. MAYP
Life. Alice Brown. AA
Life. Samuel Taylor Coleridge. EnRP
Life. George Crabbe. OBEC
Life. Emily Dickinson. *See* Our share of night to bear.
Life, The. Philip Dow. AmPA
Life. Paul Laurence Dunbar. AmNP; CDC
Life. Artie Gold. NOBC
Life. Amory Hare. HBMV
Life. George Herbert. AnAnS-1; FaBoRV; HBV-2; JCP; LiTB; MeLP; MePo; NoP; OBS; PoPle; SeCeV; SeCP; SeCV-1
Life. Alfred Kreymborg. ELU
Life. Longfellow. *Fr.* Psalm of Life. GN
Life, A. Sylvia Plath. NOBA
Life. Nan Terell Reed. BLPA
Life. Edward Rowland Sill. BLRP; TRV
Life. Grace Treasone. InPK; PeD
Life. Jones Very. AP
Life, A. George Edward Woodberry. EtS
Life, The. James Wright. LCAP; NaP
Life/ anthology of bewilderments. Violins in Repose. Jorge Plescoff, *tr. by* Yishai Tobin. VWA
Life/ is at 2 playing. Childhood. Jewel C. Latimore. JB
Life, a Question. Corinne Roosevelt Robinson. HBV-2
Life Above, the Life on High, The. St. Theresa of Avila, *tr. fr. Spanish by* Edward Caswall. WGRP
Life after Death. Pindar, *tr. fr. Greek by* Walter Headlam. EaLo
Life after Death. Richard W. Thomas. PoBA
Life Again. Keats. *Fr.* Endymion. SeCePo
Life and Death. Edward Benlowes. *Fr.* Theophila. FaBoEn
Life and Death. Sir William Davenant. *Fr.* The Christian's Reply to the Philosopher. OBS
Life and Death. Lilla Cabot Perry. AA
Life and Death. W. J. Turner. FaBoTw
Life and Death of Habbie Simson, the Piper of Kilbarchan, The. Robert Sempill. *See* Life and Death of the Piper of Kilbarchan, The.
Life and Death of Jason, The, *sels.* William Morris.
Garden by the Sea, A, *fr.* IV. NOBE; OAEL-2; OBNC; PoEL-5
(I Know a Little Garden-Close.) CH; ViBoPo
(Nymph's Song to Hylas, The.) HBV-1; OBEV
"O happy seafarers are ye," *fr.* XIV. ViBoPo
Song of the Argonauts, *fr.* IV. EtS
Life and Death of the Piper of Kilbarchan, The. Robert Sempill. OBS
(Life and Death of Habbie Simson, the Piper of Kilbarchan, The.) OxBS
Life and Death of William Longbeard, The, *sels.* Thomas Lodge.
Her Rambling. LoBV; OBSC
My Mistress. TrGrPo
Rose, The. OBSC
(Fancy, A.) ElL
Life and Genuine Character of Dean Swift, The, *sel.* Swift.
"Wise Rochefoucault a maxim writ." NOBL
Life and Love. Whittier. BLRP; TRV
Life and Lucubrations of Crispinus Scriblerus, The, *sels.* James Woodhouse.
Birmingham and Wolverhampton. NOEC
Tribulations of an Uneducated Poet in the 1760's, The. NOEC
Life and Nature. Archibald Lampman. PeCV
Life and the Universe show spontaneity. The Positivists. Mortimer Collins. EBVV
Life and the Weaver. A. W. Dewar. BLRP; WBLP
Life and Thought. Matthew Arnold. *Fr.* Empedocles on Etna. FiP
Life? and worth living? Life, a Question. Corinne Roosevelt Robinson. HBV-2
Life at last I know is terrible. What Is Terrible. Roy Fuller. WaP
Life at War. Denise Levertov. NMM; VGW
Life can be a hassle. Are you free of it, Monsignor. James K. Baxter. Autumn Testament, 32. OCNZ
Life contracts and death is expected. The Death of a Soldier. Wallace Stevens. OBWP; OFD; QFR
Life Cycle of Common Man. Howard Nemerov. NIP
Life Death Does End. Gerard Manley Hopkins. *See* No Worst, There Is None.
Life did not bring me silken gowns. Red Geraniums. Martha Haskell Clark. BLPA
Life-Drama, A, *sel.* Alexander Smith.
"What hope is that?" VLP
Life flows to death as rivers to the sea. Epigram. J. V. Cunningham. POL; VGW
Life, friends, is boring. We must not say so. John Berryman. *Fr.* Dream Songs. CAPP; DBV; HAP; HeIP; InPK; LiTM; NaP; NoAM; NOBA; PAI; PrIm; TAP; TwCP
Life from the Lifeless. Robinson Jeffers. CMoP
Life Half Lived. J. C. F. Hölderlin, *tr. fr. German.* ChTr
Life has conquered, the wind has blown away. Hope. Frank O'Connor, *tr. fr. Irish.* CIP; KiLC
Life has its nauseating ironies. Sonnet Ending with a Film Subtitle. Marilyn Hacker. MAYP
Life has loveliness to sell. Barter. Sara Teasdale. FaBV; FaPON; SoSe; TreFS
Life holds no sweeter thing than this—to teach. No Sweeter Thing. Adelaide Love. PGD
Life-Hook. Juana de Ibarbourou, *tr. fr. Spanish by* Marti Moody. WPOW
Life! I know not what thou art. Life. Anna Laetitia Barbauld. BLPA; FaFP; GTBS; GTBS-P; HBV-2; OBEV; OBRV; TreFS; TRV
Life impaled him high on a cliff. Biography of an Agnostic. Louis Ginsberg. TrJP
Life in a day: he took his girl to the ballet. Les Sylphides. Louis MacNeice. BoLoP; CoBMV
Life in a Half-breed Shack. *Unknown.* CoSo
Life in a Love. Robert Browning. HBV-1; OAEP; OBNC; OBVV; TrGrPo
(Love's Pursuit, 7 *ll.*) TreFT
Life-in-Love. Dante Gabriel Rossetti. The House of Life, XXXVI. HAP; VLP
Life in the Boondocks. A. R. Ammons. HAP
Life in the Castle. Anne Hébert, *tr. fr. French by* Aliki *and* Willis Barnstone. BoWoP
Life in the cellars. In the Cellars. Jiri Gold, *tr. by* Jaroslav Kotan *and* Daniel Weissbort. VWA
Life in the City: In Memoriam Edward Gibbon. Philip Whalen. PoM
Life in the Country. Michael Silverton. ELU
Life is a bitter aspic. We are not. Wallace Stevens. *Fr.* Esthétique du Mal. CMoP
Life Is a Dream. Pedro Calderón de la Barca, *tr. fr. Spanish by* Roy Campbell. NAWM-1
"We live, while we see the sun," *sel., tr. by* Arthur Symons. AWP
Life is a hospital. Anywhere Out of the World. Baudelaire, *tr. by* Arthur Symons. SyP
Life is a jest; and all things show it. My [*or* His] Own Epitaph. John Gay. FaBoEE; FF; HBV-1; NIP; NOEC; SeCePo; SeCEV; TreFT; ViBoPo
Life is a long discovery, isn't it? Discovery. Hilaire Belloc. DBV; ViBoPo
Life is a most extraordinary thing. Tomato Juice. A. P. Herbert. WhC
Life is a pilgrimage, they say. Cockle-Shell and Sandal-Shoon. Herbert T. J. Coleman. CaP
Life Is a Platform, *sel.* Peter Levi.
"Smoke when the sun fell and when it rose." FaBoTw
Life is a poet's fable. *Unknown.* OBSC
Life is a shepherd lad who strides and sings. Life. Amory Hare. HBMV
Life is a sorry mélange of gold and silver and stubble. Nonsense. Robert Haven Schauffler. HBMV
Life is a woven fabric. Life and the Weaver. A. W. Dewar. BLRP; WBLP
Life is butter, life is butter. *Unknown.* FaBoNo
Life is full of horrors and hormones. Kenneth Koch. *Fr.* The Art of Love. GP
Life is inadequate, but there are many real. Independence Day. William Jay Smith. MP; TwCP
Life is like a jagged tooth. Life. Grace Treasone. InPK; PeD
Life Is like a Mountain Railroad. *Unknown.* FSW
Life is long that loathsomely doth last, The. Elegy Wrote in the Tower, 1554, *shorter vers.* John Harington. ElL
Life Is More True. E. E. Cummings. WaP
Life is not dear or gay. The Lass That Died of Love. Richard Middleton. HBV-1
Life is ours like the real. Theme One: The Variations. August Wilson. PoBA
Life is real, life is earnest. A Parody on "A Psalm of Life." *Unknown.* BLPA
Life is seldom if ever dull. Gull. William Jay Smith. TiPo
Life Is So Short. Margaret S. Hall. STF
Life is teeming with evil snares. Where Is Your Boy Tonight? *Unknown.* PaPo
"Life is what you make it," my half-Italian. The Dear Ladies of Cincinnati. Anne Stevenson. HoAn
"Life! length of life!" for this, with earnest cries. Juvenal, *tr. by* William Gifford. *Fr.* Satires, X. OBVE
Life-Lesson, A. James Whitcomb Riley. AA; FPL; HBV-1; PoLF; TreFS

Life may change, but it may fly not. Choruses from "Hellas," 1. Shelley. *Fr.* Hellas. EnRP
Life-Mosaic. Frances Ridley Havergal. TrPWD
Life Must Burn. John Hay. NePoAm
Life Not Given, The. David Habercom. AMV-81
Life of . . ., The. Theodore Weiss. NYBP
Life of a Beau, The. James Miller. OBEC
Life of a Queen. Lisel Mueller. GP
Life of Ages, Richly Poured. Samuel Johnson. *See* Inspiration.
Life of Hard Times, The. Joshua Tan Pai, *tr. fr. Hebrew by* Yishai Tobin. VWA
Life of Hubert, The, *sels.* Thomas Cole.
Memories of a Dorset Childhood in the 1730's. NOEC
"Time allowed for sleep at length elapsed, The." NOEC
Life of itself will be cruel and hard enough. Muna Lee. Sonnets, V. HBMV
Life of Life. Shelley. *Fr.* Prometheus Unbound, II, v. CH; FiP
(Chorus.) LoBV
(Hymn to the Spirit of Nature.) GTBS; GTBS-P
("Life of Life! thy lips enkindle.") LO; NOBE; OBRV; PoEL-4; ViBoPo
Life of Lincoln West, The. Gwendolyn Brooks. FB
Life of Man, The. Francis Bacon. ElL; GTBS; GTBS-P; OBSC; WHA
(World, The.) HBV-1
(World's a Bubble, The.) TreFT
Life of Man, The. Barnabe Barnes. *Fr.* A Divine Century of Spiritual Sonnets. OBSC
("Blast of wind, a momentary breath, A.") EBEV
Life of man, The. The Flight of the Arrow. Richard Henry Stoddard. AA
Life of my learning, fire of all my Art. A Dedication. Mary Elizabeth Coleridge. TrPWD
Life of my life, take not so soon thy flight. To His Dying Brother, Master William Herrick. Robert Herrick. CaPo; OAEP; PoPle; SeCV-1
Life of Particles, The. Michael Benedikt. SUW
Life of Sabbaths here beneath, A! Thomas Traherne. AnAnS-1
Life of Service, The. Donald Davie. NYBP
Life of St. Cellach of Killala, *sels.* *Unknown, tr. fr. Late Middle Irish by* Standish Hayes O'Grady.
Dear Was He. OnYI
Hail, Fair Morning. OnYI
He Who Forsakes the Clerkly Life. OnYI
Life of T. S. Eliot, A. Michael Frayn. FaBoPa
Life of the Blessed, The. Luis de León, *tr. fr. Spanish by* Bryant. AWP
Life of the Letters. Emily Borenstein. VWA
Life of the Mannings. *Unknown.* FaBoBa
Life of the snail is a fight against odds, The. The Snail. A. P. Herbert. BoAnP
Life of the Wolf, The. Gary Gildner. AmPA
Life of This World, The. *Unknown.* OxBM
(This Life.) FaBoRV
Life on Earth, *sel.* Frank O'Hara.
"Shine, 'O world!' don't weary the gulping Pole." UnPo
Life on the Ocean Wave, A. Epes Sargent. AA; EtS; FaBoBe; FSW; GN; HBV-1; TreFS
Life or Death. Glenn Ward Dresbach. *Fr.* In Western Mountains. HBMV
Life pours out images, the accidental. The Rokeby Venus. Robert Conquest. NoAM
Life presents a dismal picture. Family Life. *Unknown.* DBV
Life (priest and poet say) is but a dream. The Dragon-Fly [*or* Lines to a Dragon-Fly]. Walter Savage Landor. FM; OBEV; OBNC; OBRV; OBVV
Life Sculpture. George Washington Doane. BLPA; OHFP; WBLP
Life should be a humane. Lebensraum. Thom Gunn. PAI
Life smitten with a feverish chill. The Wedding. Coventry Patmore. *Fr.* The Angel in the House. VLP
Life Story. J. Kates. AMV-81
Life Story. Tomioka Taeko, *tr. fr. Japanese by* Harry *and* Lynn Guest *and* Kajima Shozo. WPOW
Life Story. Tennessee Williams. PeHV
Life Study. Stephen Orlen. MAYP
Life That Counts, The. "A. W. S." FaFP; WBLP
Life that is free as the bandits' of old, A. Brave Donahue. *At. to* Jack Donahue. PoAu-1
Life the hound. The Hound. Robert Francis. SoSe
Life the very gods in my sight is he. Sappho, *tr. fr. Greek by* Richmond Lattimore. WPOW
Life to the bigot is a whip. Epitaph for a Bigot. Dorothy Vena Johnson. PoNe
Life Upright, The. Thomas Campion. *See* Man of Life Upright, The.
Life was a narrow lobby, dark. For the Bicentenary of Isaac Watts. Norman Nicholson. EaLo
Life will keep hammering the grass blades into the ground. Force. Derek Walcott. OxBC
Life with her weary eyes. Song. Marya Zaturenska. NMP
Life without Passion, The. Shakespeare. *See* Sonnets, XCIV.
Life would be an easy matter. If We Didn't Have to Eat. Nixon Waterman. FiBHP; OBAL
Lifeboat, The. George R. Sims. PaPo
Lifeguard, The. James Dickey. CoPo; LiSp; NoP; NYBP
Lifeguard's whistle organized our swimming, The. The River. Dabney Stuart. NYBP
Lifeless solitude—an angry waste, A. On the Telescopic Moon. John Swanick Drennan. BIrV
Lifelines. Gavin Ewart. EAS
Lifelines. T. R. Hummer. AMV-80
Lifelong. Rachel Boimwall, *tr. fr. Yiddish by* Gabriel Preil *and* Howard Schwartz. VWA
Life-long, Poor Browning. Anne Spencer. CDC; PoNe
Lifers file into the hall, The. In the Cage. Robert Lowell. FF; NOBA; SyP
Life's a Funny Proposition after All. George M. Cohan. PoLF
Life's a Game. *Unknown.* BLPA
Life's Chequer-Board. John Oxenham. TRV
Life's Circumnavigators. W. R. Rodgers. AnIV; GTBS-P; OxBI
Life's Common Duties. Minot J. Savage. WBLP
Life's Common Things. Alice E. Allen. WBLP
Life's Evening. Dudley Foulke. WGRP
Life's Evil. Eugenio Montale, *tr. fr. Italian by* Jan Pallister. AMV-81
Life's Joy. *Unknown.* STF
Life's Last Scene. Samuel Johnson. *Fr.* The Vanity of Human Wishes. OBEC; SeCePo
Life's Lessons. *Unknown.* BLRP; FPL; PoLF; STF
Life's Little Things. *Unknown.* STF
Life's Mirror. "Madeline Bridges." BLPA; FaBoBe; TreF; WBLP
Life's Parallels, A. Christina Rossetti. NBM; PoEL-5
Life's Poor Play. Pope. *Fr.* An Essay on Man. SeCePo
Life's Scars. Ella Wheeler Wilcox. BLPA
Life's Testament, *sels.* William Baylebridge.
"All that I am to Earth Belongs," XI. PoAu-1
"Brain, the blood, the busy thews, The," II. PoAu-1
"Choir of spirits on a cloud, A," XVII. PoAu-1
"God, to get the clay that stayed me," XIII. PoAu-1
"I worshipped, when my veins were fresh," VI. PoAu-1
"This miracle in me I scan," VIII. PoAu-1
Life's Uncertainty. Bible, *O.T.* *Fr.* Ecclesiastes. *See* Cast Thy Bread upon the Waters.
Life's Work. Maxine W. Kumin. GP
Lifesaving. Sandra McPherson. MAYP
Lift, The. Raymond Souster. POL
Lift Every Voice and Sing. James Weldon Johnson. FaBV; FSW; PoNe
Lift her up tenderly. Song of the Ballet. J. B. Morton. DBV; FiBHP
Lift latch, step in, be welcome, Sir. A Luncheon. Max Beerbohm. FaBoCo; NOBL; OBSV; OxBTC
Lift me, O God, above myself. Per Ardua ad Astra. John Oxenham. TrPWD
Lift not the painted veil which those who live. Sonnet. Shelley. EnRP; FaBoEn; OBNC; SyP
Lift, O dark and glorious Wonder. A Hymn to God in Time of Stress. Max Eastman. TrPWD
Lift up thy lips, turn round, look back for love. Hermaphroditus. Swinburne. SyP; TEP; VLP
Lift up, ye poor! your everlasting prayer! The Poor of London. William Forster. CBAP
Lift up your eyes on high. Erige Cor Tuum ad Me in Caelum. Hilda Doolittle ("H. D."). AP; CMoP
"Lift up your hartes [*or* heartes] and be glad." What Cheer [*or* A Cheerful Welcome]. *Unknown.* MeEL; SBVL
Lift up your heads, great gates, and sing. The Ascension. Joseph Beaumont. OxBoCh
Lift Up Your Heads, Rejoice! Thomas T. Lynch. TrCP; VLP; WGRP
Lift up your heads, ye gates of brass! James Montgomery. VLP
Lift Up Your Heads. Bible, *O.T.* *See* Earth Is the Lord's, The.
Lift your arms to the stars. Love and Liberation. John Hall Wheelock. MoAmPo
Lift Your Glad Voices in Triumph on High, *with music.* Henry Ware, Jr. AH
Lifting and Leaning. Ella Wheeler Wilcox. BLPA; WBLP
Lifting, both hands pulling whitely. Grandpa's .45. W. M. Ransom. CDW
Lifting his slowly trickling jaws. Tête-à-Tête. Edwin Honig. NoAM
Lifting Illegal Nets by Flashlight. William Stafford. NNaP
Lifting my eyes from Hesiod's book. Class Dismissed. *Unknown, tr. by* Louis Untermeyer. UnTE
Lifting my fingers. Frozen Hands. Joseph Bruchac. CDW

Lifting the thunder of their acclamation. Shelley. *Fr.* The Revolt of Islam, Canto V. ChER
Lifting their guns easily. Working the Skeet House. Jon Eastman. AMV-80
Liftman, The. H. A. C. Evans. POL
Ligeia, *prose tale, sel.* Poe.
Conqueror Worm, The. AA; AP; AWP; BLPL; HBV-2; LiTA; NOBA
(Emperor Worm, The.) DL
Light. Francis William Bourdillon. *See* Night Has a Thousand Eyes, The.
Light. Carol Coates. CaP
Light, The. John Holloway. NePoEA
Light. Milton. *See* Hail, Holy Light.
Light. Jon Silkin. NoAM
Light, *sels.* Louis Zukofsky. NoAM
"House where every, A."
"These are not my sentiments."
Light/ Lumine. The Women Are Grieving. Linda Hogan. TWSS
Light a Candle. Zelda, *tr. fr. Hebrew by* Marcia Falk. VWA
Light across the courtyard. Saint's Bridge. Lola Ridge. WPE
Light after darkness, gain after loss. Afterwards. Frances Ridley Havergal. BLRP
Light along the hills in the morning, The. Notice What This Poem Is Not Doing. William Stafford. LCAP
Light and Dark. Barbara Howes. MoVE
Light and Glory of the World, The. William Cowper. TRV
(Spirit's Light, The.) BLRP
Light and Love, Hope and Faith. Eva Gray. STF
Light and Rejoicing to Israel. *Unknown, tr. fr. Hebrew by* Israel Abrahams. TrJP
Light Another Candle. Miriam Chaikin. NTCP
Light are the spinning favours, intangible tonight. An English Elegy. Daryl Hine. NoAM
Light as a leaping faun! Doris Ferne. CaP
Light as petals, white as daisies. Butterflies. Clive Sansom. BonAnP
Light at Equinox. Léonie Adams. CrMA
Light at this hour, The. Circles. Elizabeth Knies. AMV-80
Light Baggage. Alice Walker. LTB
Light beats upon me, The. Mid-Day. Hilda Doolittle ("H. D."). ViBoPo
Light became her grace and dwelt among, The. Ballatetta. Ezra Pound. VGW
Light Breaks Where No Sun Shines. Dylan Thomas. CMoP; ErPo; FaBoMo; LiTB; MoAB; MoBrPo; OAEP; OxBTC; SeCePo; ViBoPo
Light Breather, A. Theodore Roethke. NoP
Light breeze rustles the reeds, A. Night Thoughts while Travelling. Tu Fu, *tr. by* Kenneth Rexroth. NaP
Light breezes, drifting through the window. Morning. M. A. George. AMV-80
Light broke in upon my brain, A. Byron. *Fr.* The Prisoner of Chillon. OBRV
Light Casualities. Robert Francis. PPJ
Light diffusing my likeness. Legend of His Lyre. Aaron Schmuller. GoYe
Light do I see within my Lady's eyes. Ballata V. Guido Cavalcanti, *tr. by* Ezra Pound. CTC
Light exists in spring, A. Emily Dickinson. BoWoP; LiTA; NOBA; OxBA
Light falls gently from the dormer-panes, The. On a Spring-Board. Edward Cracroft Lefroy. OBVV
Light fell from the window and the day was done, The. "The Truth Is Blind." David Gascoyne. EAS
Light flower leaves its little core, The. The Changed Woman. Louise Bogan. HBMV
Light flows our war of mocking words, and yet. The Buried Life. Matthew Arnold. OAEL-2; OAEP; SeCeV; VLP
Light foot hears you and the brightness begins, The. A Poem Beginning with a Line by Pindar. Robert Duncan. ConAP; NeAP; NMP; NNaP; PoM
Light forgetting itself light falling loosely. Locations. Kathleen Fraser. NPGG
Light from Within, The. Jones Very. WGRP
Light going out in the forehead, A. Swimming by Night. James Merrill. NYBP; VGW
Light has come again and found. Ark of the Covenant. Louise Townsend Nicholl. ImOP
Light has transformed them. Their utility gone. Apples. Lisel Mueller. NePoAm-2
Light in the Darkness. Aileen Fisher. YeAr
Light in the Darkness. Cardinal Newman. *See* Pillar of the Cloud, The.
Light in the Open Air. Annie Dillard. SUW
Light in the window seemed perpetual, The. The Room above the Square. Stephen Spender. ChMP; NOBE
Light in them stands as clear as water, The. Poppies. Roy Scheele. PPJ
Light into the olive entered. After Greece. James Merrill. ConAP; NOBA; NYBP
Light is a distant world. Touching. Christopher Gilbert. MAYP
Light is a vehicle for shadows. Wonders of the World. Richard Shelton. DFF
Light is around the petals, and behind them. Looking at Some Flowers. Robert Bly. NaP; NOBA
Light is burning late, A. Herbert Street Revisited. John Montague. CIP; IPY
Light is like a spider, The. Tattoo. Wallace Stevens. LiTA
Light is made to shine in darkness. Light and Love, Hope and Faith. Eva Gray. STF
Light is on in my father's study, A. Working Late. Louis Simpson. DiL
Light is on my body also, The. Lilith. Linda Gregg. WPOW
Light Is Sweet, The. Bible, *O.T.* Ecclesiastes, XI: 7. FaPON
Light is the inside, The. Girl Powdering Her Neck. Cathy Song. MAYP
Light lifts from the water. Basil Bunting. *Fr.* Briggflatts, V. OAEL-2
"Light, light, light, my little Scotch-ee." Little Scotch-ee. *Unknown.* AS
Light Listened. Theodore Roethke. BiP; MoAmPo; UnTE
Light little zephyr came flitting, A. Morning Compliments. Sydney Dayre. OxBChV
Light looks from a dazzled leaf. Dazzle. Dorothy Roberts. NOBC
Light Lover. Aline Kilmer. HBMV
Light may be had for nothing. Little Candle. Carl Sandburg. GoYe
Light mist, then dense fog. Li Ch'ing-chao, *tr. fr. Chinese by* Kenneth Rexroth. BoWoP
"Light! more light! the shadows deepen." Let the Light Enter. Frances E. W. Harper. PoNe
Light Morning Snow, We Wait for a Warmer Season. John Garmon. AMV-80
Light Now Shineth, The. *Unknown.* STF
Light of Asia, The, *sels.* Sir Edwin Arnold.
End Which Comes, The, *fr.* III. LoBV
"If we lay bound upon the wheel of change," *fr.* VIII. VLP
"So they rode/ Into a land of wells and gardens, where," *fr.* I. VLP
Light of dim mornings; shield from heat and cold. To Duty. Thomas Wentworth Higginson. AA
Light of dimmed stars goes on, The. The Life of Hard Times. Joshua Tan Pai, *tr. by* Yishai Tobin. VWA
Light of evening, Lissadell, The. In Memory of Eva Gore-Booth and Con Markiewicz. W. B. Yeats. CABA; MoAB; NoAM; OAEL-2; OBMV; OxBI; OxBTC
Light of Faith, The. Edgar Dupree. BLRP
Light of four suns, five moons, The. May I Be Beautiful. *Malay Oral Tradition, tr. by* W. W. Skeat. WTO
Light of Judea. Claude Vigée, *tr. fr. French.* VWA
Light of Life, The. "Hugh MacDiarmid." CMoP
Light of Other Days, The. Alfred Bunn. TreFS
Light of Other Days, The. Thomas Moore. *See* Oft in the Stilly Night.
Light of our cigarettes, The. Pastel. Arthur Symons. SyP
Light of spring, The. Song. Alice Duer Miller. AA
Light of Stars, The. William H. Furness. *See* Evening Hymn.
Light of the Harem [*or* Haram], The. Thomas Moore. *Fr.* Lalla Rookh. EnRP; TEP
Light of the World, The. B. Alquit, *tr. fr. Yiddish by* Howard Schwartz. VWA
Light of the World. John S. B. Monsell. TrPWD
Light on Cape May, The, *with music. Unknown.* ShS
Light on his pins. Roethke Plain. John Malcolm Brinnin. NoAM; TAP
Light Passages, The. Debora Greger. MAYP
Light passes, The. Evening. Hilda Doolittle ("H. D."). CMoP; FaBoMo; LoBV; VGW; WPE
Light pulling away from trees, The. Distance. Peter Everwine. NNaP
Light Rain. Christopher Buckley. AMV-81
Light ripples lace, glitters from the eaves. Still Lives. Emilie Buchwald. PoDr
Light seen suddenly in the storm, snow, A. Melancholia. Robert Bly. NoP
Light Shining out of Darkness. Jane Borthwick. BLRP
Light Shining out of Darkness. William Cowper. EaLo; EBEV; EnRP; FaBoCh; FaFP; FPL; HBV-2; HeIP; LiTB; NoP; NOBE; NOCV; NOEC; OBEC; PoEL-3; SeCePo; SeCeV; TreF; TrGrPo; TRV; WGRP
(God Moves in a Mysterious Way.) ELP; FiP
(Mysterious Way, The.) STF
Light Showers of Light. Kathryn Lindskoog. AMV-80
Light, so low upon earth. Marriage Morning. Tennyson. GBL
Light, stillness and peace lie on the broad sands. The Estuary. Ruth Pitter. MoVE
Light That Came, The. Lucille Clifton. GeTw
Light That Failed, The, *sel.* Kipling. Mother o' Mine. FaFP; TRV; WBLP
Light that fills thy house at morn, The. The Gifts of God. Jones Very. AA

Light that labored to an early fall, The. The Lake. Louis O. Coxe. MoVE; NYBP
Light, that out of the west looked back once more. Night Thoughts in Age. John Hall Wheelock. MoVE; NYBP
Light the candle I will return. Near. Abba Kovner, *tr. by* Shirley Kaufman. VWA
Light the Festive Candles. Aileen Fisher. RHPC
Light the first light of evening, as in a room. Final Soliloquy of the Interior Paramour. Wallace Stevens. HAP; LCAP
Light the first of eight tonight. Light the Festive Candles. Aileen Fisher. RHPC
Light the Lamps Up, Lamplighter! Eleanor Farjeon. CH; SiSoSe; TiPo
Light things falling—I think of rain. Light Casualities. Robert Francis. PPJ
Light under the Door. Marilyn Waniek. MAYP
Light up My world for Me. God to Man. *Fr.* The Talmud. TrJP
Light up thy homes, Columbia. Illumination for Victories in Mexico. Grace Greenwood. PAH
Light wake early in this house. Various Wakings. Vincent Buckley. PoAu-2
Light was burning very dim, The. In the Night. Elizabeth Madox Roberts. WSC
Light will shine again, The; it cannot die. There Will Be Peace. Margaret Miller Pettengill. PGD
Light-winged Smoke, Icarian Bird. Henry David Thoreau. *See* Smoke.
Light Woman, A. Robert Browning. HBV-1; VLP
Light Woman's Song, The. Judith Johnson Sherwin. TAP
Light Year, The. John Ridland. OFD
Light-years in the dark. Kohoutek. Richard Ryan. CIP
Light you down, light you down, love Henry, she said. Young Hunting. *Unknown.* FaBoBa
Light young man lay with a lighter woman, A. On Tom Holland and Nell Cotton. *Unknown.* FaBoEE
Lighten Our Darkness. Lord Alfred Douglas. HBMV
Lighter than dandelion down. Silkweed. Philip Henry Savage. AA
Lighter than thistledown. First Snow. Ivy O. Eastwick. TiPo
Lightest foam, straightest spray. Waters of the Sea. Cecil Goldbeck. EtS
Light-hearted Fairy, The. *Unknown.* FaPON; SUS
Light-hearted I walked into the valley wood. Conversion. T. E. Hulme. FaBoMo; LoBV; ViBoPo
Lighthearted William. William Carlos Williams. SO
Lighthouse, The. John Seller Anson. AMV-80
Lighthouse in the Night. Alfonsina Storni, *tr. fr. Spanish by* Aliki *and* Willis Barnstone. BoWoP
Lighthouse Invites the Storm, The. Malcolm Lowry. NOBC
Lighthouse Keeper's Offspring, The. James Broughton. CrMA
Light-House Keeper's White-Mouse, The. John Ciardi. PDV
Lighthouses. Dorothy Wellesley. WPE
Lighting a spill late in the afternoon. A Winter Talent. Donald Davie. NePoEA-2; OAEL-2
Lighting the Night Sky. Kenneth O. Hanson. FYAP
Light-Keeper, The, *sel.* Robert Louis Stevenson.
"Brilliant kernel of the night, The." EBVV
Lightless, unholy, eldritch thing. The Bat. Ruth Pitter. FM
Lightly forsaking/ the spring mist as it rises. Seeing the Returning Geese. Lady Ise, *tr. by* Etsuko Terasaki *and* Irma Brandeis. BoWoP
Lightly like music running, our blood. Jean Garrigue. MoVE
Lightly stepped a yellow star. Emily Dickinson. AP; MoAmPo; MoShBr; OxBA
Lightness Remembered. Nancy Willard. LCAP
Lightning. D. H. Lawrence. CMoP; MoAB; MoBrPo; UnTE
Lightning Bug. Robert Morgan. GeTw
Lightning Flash, The. *Unknown.* AmFP
Lightning flashes, The! Haiku. Basho, *tr. by* Earl Miner. SoSe
Lightning for Atmosphere. Marya Zaturenska. TwAmPo
Lightning gleam, A. Haiku. Basho, *tr. by* Harold G. Henderson. SoSe
Lightning hits the roof. Woman to Man. Ai. GP
Lightning in the clouds! Basho, *tr. fr. Japanese.* WeW
Lightning is a yellow fork, The. Emily Dickinson. InPK
Lightning! Lightning! Lightning! Without thunder! Flushing Meadows, 1939. Daniel Hoffman. CoPo
Lightning, like an Arab, cross'd, The. The Tree of Rivelin. Ebenezer Elliot. VLP
Lightning of a summer, The. Lady Bates. Randall Jarrell. MiAP
Lightning of the Abyss. Jules Laforgue, *tr. fr. French by* Vernon Watkins. SyP
Lightning rides. P. Wolny. PPJ
Lightning scratched our sugar maple, blood. Injured Maple. Ronald Everson. NOBC
Lightning slices above Texas City. Tornado Watch. Paul Shuttleworth. AMV-80
Lightning-stricken giant gum, The. The Wood-Swallows. "Fiona Macleod." *Fr.* Australian Transcripts. FM
Light'ood Fire, The. John Henry Boner. AA
Lights are burning. Bus Stop. Donald Justice. FYAP; LCAP
Lights from the parlor and kitchen shone out, The. Escape at Bedtime. Robert Louis Stevenson. HBVY; TiPo; TreFS; TrGrPo
Light's Glittering Morn. John Mason Neale. EBCP; OxBoCh
(Hymn for Easter Morn.) TrCP
Lights Go On, The. Mark McCloskey. AMV-80
Lights in the Hallway, The. James Wright. CAPP
Lights in the Quarters Burnin' Mighty Dim, *with music. Unknown.* OuSiCo
Lights in the Sky Are Stars, The, *sel.* Kenneth Rexroth.
Heart of Herakles, The. NU
Lights in the theater fail, The. The long racks. A Dancer's Life. Donald Justice. LCAP
Lights of a hundred cities are fed by its midnight power, The. The River of Stars. Alfred Noyes. OnMSP
Lights of Saturday night beat golden, golden over the pillared street, The. Saturday Night. James Oppenheim. HBV-2
Lights out. How to Meditate. Jack Kerouac. PoM
Lights Out. Edward Thomas. BrPo; MMA; NOBE
Lights out! And a prow turned towards the South. The Race of the *Oregon.* John James Meehan. PAH
Lights out. Shades up. Girl in a Nightgown. Wallace Stevens. OxBA
Like/ treasure hidden in the ground. Mahadevi, *tr. fr. Kannada by* A. K. Ramanujan. WPOW
Like a Beach. Harvey Shapiro. VWA
Like a bird in the butcher's palm you flutter in my hand. Revolt. Rachel, *tr. by* Robert Friend. VWA
Like a bird that trails a broken wing. Prodigal. Ellen Gilbert. GoBC
Like a blind man, with eyes habituated to the darkness. The Diver. Nikos Phocas, *tr. by* Kimon Friar. AMV-81
Like a blind spinner in the sun. Spinning. Helen Hunt Jackson. HBV-2
Like a bread without the spreadin'. Smile. *Unknown.* BLPA; WBLP
Like a bulwark against fate. At Rest in the Blast. Marianne Moore. MoAB; MoAmPo
Like a caught breath. Pause between Clock Ticks. James Hearst. AMV-81
Like a child the wise porpoise. The Zoo. John Logan. LCAP
Like a coy maiden, ease, when courted most. Ease. William Cowper. *Fr.* The Task, I. TEP
Like a crumpled paper cutout. Days Ago. Dianne Hai-Jew. BrSi
Like a deaf man meshed in his endless silence. Poem. John Wain. PoCh
Like a deserted beach. The Man Closing Up. Donald Justice. CoAP
Like a dog before the dog-catcher's sling. Conscience. Melech Ravitch, *tr. by* Keith Bosley. VWA
Like a dragon you have filled the land. Inanna and An. Enheduanna, *tr. fr. Sumerian.* BoWoP
Like a drop of water is my heart. Youth and Maidenhood. Sarah Williams. OBVV
Like a drummer's brush. Rain. Emanuel diPasquale. InPK; POL
Like a dry fish flung inland far from shore. Lost Anchors. E. A. Robinson. CMoP
Like a Field Waiting. Raquel Chalfi, *tr. fr. Hebrew by* Myra Glazer Schotz. VWA
Like a flat sea. Population. George Oppen. PoA
Like a fleet thief, this sparrow has. House and Shutter. Lewis Turco. PoPl
Like a flight of arrows the wind. Stormy Night in Autumn. Chu Shu-chen, *tr. by* Kenneth Rexroth. BoWoP
Like a forsaken theatre art thou. By Cobequid Bay. Alexander Louis Fraser. CaP
Like a fruit wine with earth. Cider and Vesalius. John Peck. AmPA
Like a gaunt, scraggly pine. Lincoln. John Gould Fletcher. HBMV; MoAmPo
Like a genie selling suckers. Boxer Shorts Named Champion. Melvin Douglass Brown. LFAC
Like a glum cricket. Flight. James Tate. InPK
Like a gondola of green scented fruits. Images. Richard Aldington. MoBrPo; PoA
Like a great rock, far out at sea. Lady Sanuki, *tr. by* Curtis Hidden Page. *Fr.* Hyaku-Nin-Isshu. AWP
Like a hidden spring. My Love-Song. Else Lasker-Schüler, *tr. by* Jethro Bithell. TrJP
Like a hot stone your cock weighs on mine, young man. Long Lines: Youth and Age. Paul Goodman. PeHV
Like a hound with nose to the trail. Michaelmas. Norman Nicholson. MoBrPo
Like a hungry fledgeling that watches and hears. Vittoria da Colonna, *tr. fr. Italian by* Lynne Lawner. PBWP
Like a king from a sunrise-land. Days and Nights. T. Sturge Moore. HBMV
Like a Laverock in the Lift. Jean Ingelow. HBV-1

Like a lit-up Christmas Tree. The Lover and the Syringa-Bush. Herman Melville. OBAL
Like a lizard in the sun, though not scuttling. The Laureate. Robert Graves. BlrV; FaBoTw; OBSV
Like a lone Arab, old and blind. Love's Apparition and Evanishment. Samuel Taylor Coleridge. EnRP
Like a loose island on the wide expanse. To a Deaf and Dumb Little Girl. Hartley Coleridge. PoEL-4; VLP
Like a loud-booming bell shaking its tower. The Latin Tongue. James J. Daly. GoBC
Like a madwoman and almost alone. Interior Landscape. Gloria Fuertes, *tr. by* Willis Barnstone. BoWoP
Like a map blanketing a bed. Patches of Sky. Debora Greger. MAYP
Like a Midsummer Rose. John Lydgate. OxBM
Like a mountain whirlwind. Sappho, *tr. fr. Greek by* Willis Barnstone. BoWoP
Like a Mourningless Child. Kenneth Patchen. MoAmPo
Like a pair of companionable porcupines. Baucis and Philemon. Katherine Hoskins. PoA
Like a Pearl. Hayim Naggid, *tr. fr. Hebrew by* Shlomo Vinner *and* Howard Schwartz. VWA
Like a Pearl Dropped. Trumbull Stickney. NCEP
Like a private eye she searches. The Jealous Wife. Vernon Scannell. ErPo
Like a rainstorm, he said, the braided colors. Worsening Situation. John Ashbery. NOBA
Like a ravaged sea/ this bed. Lady Ise, *tr. fr. Japanese by* Etsuko Terasaki *and* Irma Brandeis. BoWoP
Like a river she was. The Memory. Robert Creeley. CAPP; VGW
Like a round loaf, that's how small you were. To the Newborn. Judit Tóth, *tr. by* Laura Schiff. WPOW
Like a scared rabbit running over and. "Graphemics," 1. Jack Spicer. VGW
Like a Shabbos Goy. Elsewhere. Linda Pastan. VWA
Like a she-camel with a large bell. Fortitude. *Somali Oral Tradition, tr. by* B. W. Andrzejewski *and* I. M. Lewis. WTO
Like a shower of rain. Ennius, *tr. by* John Wight. *Fr.* Annales. WaaP
Like a silkworm weaving. Mahādēviyakka, *tr. fr. Kannada by* A. K. Ramanujan. PBWP
Like a skein of loose silk blown against a wall. The Garden. Ezra Pound. AWP; CABA; HeIP; LiTA; MoAB; MoAmPo; MP; NIP; NoP; PPP; SOTW; TwCP
Like a sleeping swine upon the skyline. Muckish Mountain (The Pig's Back). Shane Leslie. AnIV
Like a small gray/ coffee-pot. The Gray Squirrel. Humbert Wolfe. GoJo; MoBrPo
Like a spider that leaves its wind-torn web. To My Wife Asleep. Edward Tick. AMV-80
Like a sweet apple reddening on the high. Sappho, *tr. fr. Greek by* Willis Barnstone. BoWoP
Like a tower above the tortuous. The Pilgrimage to Testour. Ryvel, *tr. by* Edouard Roditi. VWA
Like a Whisper. Ethan Ayer. GoYe
Like a Woman. Uri Zvi Greenberg, *tr. fr. Hebrew by* Robert Mezey *and* Ben Zion Gold. VWA
Like a woman you've longed to make love to, and finally did. Pennsylvania Winter Indian 1974. Harold Littlebird. VoR
Like a Young Levite. Osip Mandelstam, *tr. fr. Russian by* Daniel Weissbort. VWA
Like Abraham and Sarah by the trees of Mamre. Song at the Skirts of Heaven. Uri Zvi Greenberg, *tr. by* Zvi Jagendorf. VWA
Like air on skin, coolness of yachts at mooring. Yachts on the Nile. Bernard Spencer. ChMP
Like an Adventurous Sea-Farer Am I. Michael Drayton. EtS
Like an arrow shot/ To Death from Birth. Wine. Micah Joseph Lebensohn, *tr. by* A. M. Klein. TrJP
Like an elephant. Mahādēviyakka, *tr. fr. Kannada by* A. K. Ramanujan. PBWP
Like an hart, the livelong day. The Relief on Easter Eve. Thomas Pestel. OxBoCh
Like an home-reared animal in a quiet nook. King Pellam's Launde. David Jones. *Fr.* In Parenthesis. OAEL-2
Like an Ideal Tenant. Ruth Daigon. AMV-81
Like an invader, not a guest. Winter's Troops. Charles Cotton. *Fr.* Winter. ChTr
Like an Old Proud King in a Parable. A. J. M. Smith. OBCV
Like an older sister who wasn't quite as pretty. Los Angeles. Eloise Klein Healy. GP
Like any brute, to have a soft heart. Innocence. James Scully. LTB
Like any grey old-timer droving dreams. The Town. David Rowbotham. PoAu-2
Like any merchant in a store. The Ticket Agent. Edmund Leamy. HBMV
Like any of us—you or me. Old Man Pot. Lyon Sharman. CaP
Like Any Other Man. Gregory Orr. FF
Like apple-blossoms, white and red. To Daphne. Walter Besant. HBV-1
Like April morning clouds, that pass. Sir Walter Scott. *Fr.* Marmion, *introd. to* III. OBRV
Like as a flamelet blanketed in smoke. After. W. E. Henley. In Hospital, VI. BrPo
Like [*or* Lyke] as a huntsman after weary chase [*or* chace]. Amoretti, LXVII. Spenser. EnRePo; GBL; HeIP; NoP; OAEP; PoEL-1; SeCePo; TrGrPo
Like [*or* Lyke] as a ship that through the ocean wide [*or* wyde]/ By conduct of some star doth make her way. Amoretti, XXXIV. Spenser. EtS; HBV-1; OBSC
Like as a ship, that through the ocean wyde/Directs her course unto one certaine cost. Spenser. *Fr.* The Faerie Queene, VI, 12. MOS
Like as the armed knight. The Ballad Which Anne Askew Made and Sang When She Was in Newgate. Anne Askew. WPE
Like as the Bay, that bears on branches sweet. In Praise of His Lady. Matthew Grove. *Fr.* Pelops and Hippodamia. ElL
Like as the bird in the cage enclosed. Sir Thomas Wyatt. SiPS
Like as the culver on the bared bough. Amoretti, LXXXIX. Spenser. FF; GBL; PBBP
Like as the damask[e] rose you see. Man's Mortality [*or* Verses of Man's Mortalitie, with an Other of the Hope of His Resurrection]. *Unknown, at. to* Simon Wastell. FaBoCh; HBV-2; LoBV; OBS; WBLP. *See also* Like to the damask rose you see.
Like as the divers-fretchled Butterfly. The Muse Reviving. Sir John Davies. SiPS
Like as the doleful dove delights alone to be. No Pains Comparable to His Attempt. *Unknown.* PBBP
Like as the Dove. Sir Philip Sidney. SiPS
Like as the dumb solsequium, with care ourcome. The Solsequium. Alexander Montgomerie. GoTS; NoP
Like as the fountaine of all light created. Incarnatio Est Maximum Donum Dei [*or* Sonnet]. William Alabaster. MePo; SBVL
Like as the hart, that lifteth up his ears. He Renounceth All the Effects of Love. Thomas, Lord Vaux. EnRePo
Like as the Lark. Thomas William Parsons. AA
Like as the lute delights or else dislikes. To Delia, LIV. Samuel Daniel. OAEP
Like as the rage of rain. The Uncertain State of a Lover. *Unknown.* ElL
Like as the swan towards her death. Sir Thomas Wyatt. SiPS
Like as the tide that comes from th' Ocean main. Spenser. *Fr.* The Faerie Queene, IV. HoPM
Like as the waves make towards the pebbled shore. Sonnets, LX. Shakespeare. ChTr; EBEV; ElL; EnRePo; FaBoEn; FaFP; FPL; GTBS; GTBS-P; HBV-1; LiTB; LoBV; NIP; NOBE; OBSC; PeHV; PoRA; SeCeV; TEP; UnPo; ViBoPo
Like as, to make our appetites more keen. Sonnets, CXVIII. Shakespeare. CABA
Like Attracts Like. Emmett Williams. WeW
Like Barbarossa's beard bright with oil. Boys in October. Irving Layton. OBCV
Like Barley Bending. Sara Teasdale. HBMV
Like battered old millhands, they stand in the orchard. Old Apple Trees. W. D. Snodgrass. FYAP; SV
Like Birds of a Feather. Ralph Schomberg. *Fr.* The Judgment of Paris. TrJP
Like birds when first light breaks. Children Waking: Indian Hill Station. Ralph Nixon Currey. PeSA
Like blood, like good, and like age. *Unknown.* FaBoUs
Like butterflies but lately come. Beautiful Creatures Brief as These. Douglas G. Jones. MoCV
Like chapters of prophecy my days burn, in all the revelations. With My God, the Smith. Uri Zvi Greenberg, *tr. by* Robert Mezey *and* Ben Zion Gold. VWA
Like children in the market-place. Children in the Market-Place. Henry van Dyke. TRV
Like Children of the Summertime Playing at Cards. Julie Herrick White. AMV-80
Like cutting the dry rot out of a potato. Dark Conclusions. Ruth Stone. BoWoP
Like David. Gabriel Preil, *tr. fr. Hebrew by* Laya Firestone. VWA
Like Dolmens Round My Childhood, the Old People. John Montague. EBEV; IPY
Like Etna's dread volcano see the ample forge. The Anchorsmiths. Charles Dibdin. NOEC
Like, everyone wants to look black. Fashions in the 70's. May Swenson. NYP
Like everything else they. For the Man Who Stole a Rose. Harley Elliott. FAZ
Like eyes coming out of the wood. Some Knots. Edwin Honig. NoAM
Like Flowers We Spring. *Unknown.* ElL
Like Ghosts of Eagles. Robert Francis. GOA; LCAP

Like gods who are fêted. They Came to the Wedding. Babette Deutsch. NePoAm
Like gossamer/ On the swift breath of morn, the vessel flew. Ever as We Sailed. Shelley. *Fr.* The Revolt of Islam. SeCePo
Like gript stick. The Sermon. Richard Hughes. OBMV
Like Groping Fingers. Abraham Sutzkever, *tr. fr. Yiddish by* Joseph Leftwich. TrJP
Like Gulliver. Nina Cassian, *tr. fr. Rumanian by* Willis Barnstone *and* Matei Calinescu. BoWoP; VWA
Like Hermit Poor. *At. to* Sir Walter Ralegh. *See* Like to a Hermit Poor. SiPS
Like Jonah in the green belly of the whale. Emily Carr. Wilfred Watson. MoCV; NOBC; OBCV
Like labour-laden moonclouds faint to flee. Through Death to Love. Dante Gabriel Rossetti. The House of Life, XLI. SyP
Like lamp of intricate stained glass which hangs. From Ancient Fangs. Peter Viereck. LiTA; MiAP
Like leaves on trees the race of man is found. Homer, *tr. by* Pope. *Fr.* The Iliad, VI. OBVE
Like liquid gold the wheat-field lies. Color in the Wheat [*or* A Dakota Wheat-Field]. Hamlin Garland. BPAW; OBCA
Like Lise, moreover, my mother was white. The Black Man's Son. Oswald Durand, *tr. by* Edna Worthley Underwood. TTY
Like many a one, when you had gold. The Old Story. Marcus Argentarius, *tr. by* E. A. Robinson. AWP
Like many hard-shelled, luckless creatures. Toward a Theory of Instruction. Danny Rendleman. SUW
Like marble, nude, against the purple sky. The Diver. John Frederic Herbin. CaP
Like [*or* Lyke] Memnon's rock[e], touched [*or* toucht] with the rising sun[ne]. Sonnet. Giles Fletcher the Elder. *Fr.* Licia. AAS; EIL; FF
"Like men riding." Nelly Trim. Sylvia Townsend Warner. ErPo; MoAB; MoBrPo
Like moody beasts they lie along the sands. Condemned Women. Baudelaire, *tr. by* John Gray. SyP
Like most, one way or another, ours. Marriage on a Mountain Ridge. Stewart Conn. PoSH
Like Mother, like Son. Margaret Johnston Grafflin. *See* To My Son.
Like mourners filing into church at a funeral. Trees on the Calais Road. Edmund Blunden. BrPo
Like Musical Instruments. Tom Clark. PPoe
(Poem.) ConAP
Like my father I'm. The Final Cut. Vern Rutsala. AMV-81
Like new waters that form nightly. Blessing of the Firstborn. Howard Schwartz. VWA
Like Noah's Weary Dove, *with music*. William Augustus Mühlenberg. AH
Like Odysseus under the ram. Archilochus, *tr. fr. Latin by* Guy Davenport. OBVE
Like one who'in her third widdowhood doth professe. To Mr. Rowland Woodward. John Donne. AnAnS-1; MePo
Like our father Abraham. With My Grandfather. Zelda, *tr. by* Marcia Falk. VWA
Like Plimsoll lines on British hulls. David McCord. Convalescence, II. WhC
Like plump green floor plans. Rotation. Julian Bond. FF; NIP; NNP
Like right now it's the summertime. The Old O. O. Blues. Al Young. NPGG
Like Ripples on the Water. *Gond Oral Tradition, tr. by* V. Elwin *and* S. Hivale. WTO
Like Rousseau. Amiri Baraka. PoA
Like ruminating cattle on the sands. Women Damned. Baudelaire, *tr. by* Joanna Richardson. PeHV
Like rusted shower-heads at beach resorts. Wintered Sunflowers. Richard Snyder. PPJ
Like shuttles fleet the clouds, and after. Oxford Bells. Gerard Manley Hopkins. FaBoPP
Like Sieur Montaigne's distinction. Golfers. Irving Layton. CABA
Like silver dew are the tears of love. Epitaph. A. E. Coppard. OBMV
Like small curled feathers, white and soft. While Shepherds Watched [Their Flocks by Night]. Margaret Deland. GN; HBVY
Like Smoke. Mririda n'Ait Attik, *tr. fr. French version by* Daniel Halpern *and* Paula Paley. PBWP
Like snails I see the people go. From a Street Corner. Eleanor Hammond. HBMV
Like snakes of golden autumn fire. Nevada. Lawrence Gurney. GoYe
Like snooker balls thrown on the table's faded green. A Poet's Progress. Michael Hamburger. NePoEA; PP
Like so many other young men in those troubled. For Lover Man, and All the Other Young Men Who Failed to Return from World War II. Mance Williams. NNP
Like some kind of ruin, but domed. In a Museum Cabinet. May Swenson. WSC
Like some lone miser, dear, behold me stand. Thysia, XXIII. Morton Luce. HBV-1
Like some school master, kind in being stern. Unanswered Prayers. Ella Wheeler Wilcox. WGRP
Like some weak lords, neighbour'd by mighty kings. Astrophel and Stella, XXIX. Sir Philip Sidney. SiPS
Like South Sea stock, expressions rise and fall. Time's Changes. James Bramston. *Fr.* The Art of Politics. NOEC; OBEC
Like spectral hounds across the sky. Minot's Ledge. Fitz-James O'Brien. OnYI
Like spirits that have wandered too far in a dream. When Both My Fathers Die. Robert Gillespie. FAZ
Like Stephen Vincent Benét, I have fallen in love with American names. Ill Met by Zenith. Ogden Nash. NYBP
Like tall men with a battering-plank—the colt. Letter from Underground. Ronald Everson. MoCV
Like that dying woman in Mexico. If. Patrick Lane. NOBC
Like that oldtimer who has kept by me. Homecoming. Theodore Weiss. TwAmPo
Like the beat, beat, beat of the tom-tom. Night and Day. Cole Porter. BLSo
Like the crash of the thunder. Zionist Marching Song. Naphtali Herz Imber, *tr. by* Israel Zangwill. TrJP
Like the dark germs across the filter clean. Loss. Charles Madge. FaBoMo
Like the ears of wheat in a wheat-field growing. Epilog. Heine, *tr. by* Louis Untermeyer. *Fr.* The North Sea. AWP
Like the Eyes of Wolves. Nachum Yud, *tr. fr. Yiddish by* Joseph Leftwich. TrJP
Like the fey goose-girl in the enchanted wood. Horror. Henry Treece. EAS
Like the ghost of a dear friend dead. Time Long Past. Shelley. HBV-1
Like the honeycomb dropping honey. Hildegard von Bingen, *tr. fr. Latin by* Patrick Diehl. WPOW
Like the Idalian Queen. William Drummond of Hawthornden. *See* Madrigal: "Like the Idalian Queen."
Like the idle fingers of wind caressing the forehead of God. The Falling of the Snow. Raymond Souster. CaP
Like the rusty bronze of a copper kettle. Spring in the Desert. Arthur Truman Merrill. BPAW
Like the shore's alternation of door wave. Crows. Tom Clark. DFF
Like the stalks of wheat in the fields. Epilogue. Heine, *tr. by* Emma Lazarus. *Fr.* The North Sea. TrJP
Like the stench and smudge of the old dump-heap. Dream, Dump-Heap, and Civilization. Robert Penn Warren. NoP
Like the steps of footsore armies. Waiting for Death. Mordecai Gebirtig, *tr. by* Joseph Leftwich. TrJP
Like the sun frozen. Walls of Ice. Janet Campbell Hale. STE
Like the sun on February ice dazzling. Snow, Snow. Marge Piercy. AMV-81
Like the sweet apple which reddens upon the topmost bough. One Girl [*or* Beauty]. Sappho, *tr. by* Dante Gabriel Rossetti. AWP; ViBoPo
Like the Touch of Rain. Edward Thomas. BoLoP; EnLoPo; GBL
Like the tribes of Israel. Sherman's in Savannah. Oliver Wendell Holmes. PAH
Like the universe. Science as Art. Hugh Seidman. AmPA
Like the violet, which alone. Castara [*or* The Description of Castara]. William Habington. *Fr.* Castara, I. AnAnS-2; CavP; HBV-1
Like the white whale, born black, myself grows brighter. Pervigilium Veneris. Suzanne Noguere. PoA
Like the yu'ub wood bell tied to gelded camels that are running away. Poet's Lament on the Death of His Wife. Raage Ugaas, *tr. fr. Somali by* B. W. Andrzejewski *and* I. M. Lewis. WTO
Like thee I once have stemmed the sea of life. An Epitaph Intended for Himself [*or* An Epitaph]. James Beattie. HBV-2; OBEV
Like They Say. Robert Creeley. ELU
Like This Together. Adrienne Rich. CoPo; VGW
Like those boats which are returning. Saigyo Hoshi, *tr. fr. Japanese by* Arthur Waley. AWP
Like thousands, I took just pride and more than just. Reading Myself. Robert Lowell. TAP
Like thunder they run out, like Holstein thunder. The New Cows. Charles Waterman. GP
Like to a baker's oven is the grave. Epitaph in Christ Church, Bristol, on Thomas Turner, Twice Master of the Company of Bakers. Francis Jeffrey. FaBoEE; OxBoLi
Like to a Coin. Arlo Bates. AA
Like to a god he seems to me. Sappho. Catullus, *tr. by* William Ellery Leonard. AWP
Like to a Hermit Poor. *At. to* Sir Walter Ralegh. GBL
(Hermit, The.) OBSC
(Like Hermit Poor) SiPS

(Sonnet: "Like to an hermit poor, in place obscure.") ElL
Like to clear in highest sphere. Rosaline. Thomas Lodge. *Fr.* Rosalynde; or, Euphues' Golden Legacy. GoBC
Like to Diana in her summer weed[e]. Doron's Description of Samela [*or* Samela]. Robert Greene. *Fr.* Menaphon. ElL; GBL; HBV-1; LOBV; NOBE; OBEV; OBSC; PoEL-2; ViBoPo
Like to the Arctic Needle. Francis Quarles. Emblems, V, 4 NOCV; OxBoCh
(I Am My Beloved's, and His Desire Is towards Me.) OBS
("Like to the arctic needle that doth guide.") EBEV; OAEL-1
Like to the clear in highest sphere. Rosaline [*or* Rosalind *or* Rosalynde *or* Rosalind's Description]. Thomas Lodge. *Fr.* Rosalynde; or, Euphues' Golden Legacy. ElL; GoBC; GTBS; GTBS-P; LiTB; OBEV; OBSC; TrGrPo; UnTE
Like to the damaske rose you see. Hos Ego Versiculos. Francis Quarles. *Fr.* Argalus and Parthenia. OBS. *See also* Like as the damask rose you see.
Like to the falling of a star. Sic Vita. Henry King. AnAnS-2; ELP; FF; GoBC; HBV-2; NOBE; OBS; PAI; SeCePo; SeCP; TrGrPo; WHA
Like to the Grass That's Green Today, *with music.* Peter Bulkeley the Younger. AH
Like to the leaf that falls. Epicedium. Horace L. Traubel. AA
Like to the Marigold, I blushing close. Edward Taylor. *Fr.* Preparatory Meditations: Second Series, III. SCAP
Like to the Thundering Tone. Richard Corbet. NA
(Nonsense.) FaBoNo
Like to these unmesurable montayns. Jacopo Sannazaro, *tr. fr. Italian by* Sir Thomas Wyatt. AAS; CABA
Like trains of cars on tracks of plush. The Bee. Emily Dickinson. GN; MoAB; MoAmPo
Like truthles[s] dream[e]s, so are my joys expired. Farewell to the Court. Sir Walter Ralegh. EnRePo; FaBoEn; OBSC; SiPS
Like twilight bleeding on a winter day. Villanelle. John Nist. AMV-81
Like two proud armies marching in the field. Your Beauty and My Reason. *Unknown.* OBSC; TrGrPo
Like two somnambulists we entered the dawn sun. Hunting for Blueberries. Thomas James. AmPA
Like unto Them That Dream. Bible, *O.T.* Psalms, CXXVI. TrJP
Like violets pale i' the Spring o' the year. Song. James Thompson. OBVV
Like Water down a Slope. Zalman Schneour, *tr. fr. Hebrew by* Harry H. Fein. TrJP
Like water pouring from a pitcher, my mouth on your nipples! Sparrow Hills. Robert Lowell. NaP
Like Weary Trees. Jacob Glatstein, *tr. fr. Yiddish by* Ruth Whitman. VWA
Like when/ I drove one of my students. Sparkling Water. Richard Schaaf. TAT
Like when the burning sun doth rise. Epigram. Strato, *tr. by* Sydney Oswald. PeHV
Like Wings. Philip Schultz. MAYP
Like women who are loved very much and are still not sated. Years. Anna Margolin, *tr. by* Ruth Whitman. VWA
Likeness, A. Robert Browning. CTC; InPS; VLP
Likeness, A. Willa Cather. HBMV
Likeness, The. Arthur Gregor. VGW
Likeness, The. Leonard Nathan. GP
Likeness has made them animal and shy. The Twins. Karl Shapiro. MiAP; MoAmPo; TrJP; TwAmPo
Likeness of heaven!/ Agent of power! The Ocean. John Augustus Shea. EtS
Lil' Bro'. Karama Fufuka. RHPC
Lil bro,/ pain done caught me. Haywood. Harold LaMont Otey. LFAC
Li'l Liza Jane. *Unknown.* BLSo, *with music*; FSW
Lilac. F. S. Flint. HBMV
Lilac, The. Humbert Wolfe. FaPON; HBVY
Lilac in my garden comes to bloom, The. My Garden. W. H. Davies. BoNaP
Lilac ribbon is unbound, A. Country of No Lack. Jean Starr Untermeyer. MoAmPo
Lilac Time. Piet Hein. PV
Lilacs. Amy Lowell. BLPL; MoAmPo; MoVE; OxBA; PoRA
Lilacs and the Roses, The. Louis Aragon, *tr. fr. French by* Louis MacNeice. OBWP
Lilacs are flowering, sweet and sublime, The. Lilac Time. Piet Hein. PV
Lilacs blossom just as sweet. Threnody. Dorothy Parker. InMe
Lilacs wither in the Carolinas, The. In the Carolinas. Wallace Stevens. VGW
L'Ile du Levant: The Nudist Colony. Barbara Howes. NePoAm-2; PoCh
Lilian. Tennyson. HBV-1; PeD
Lilian's Song. George Darley. OBNC
Lilies, The. Wendell Berry. GeTw
Lilies. Padraic Colum. NePoAm
Lilies. Shiko, *tr. fr. Japanese by* Olive Beaupré Miller. SUS; TiPo
Lilies Are White. *Unknown.* OxNR; PoPle
Lilies for Neal. James Minor. WOLT
Lilies lie in my lady's bower, The. Oh! Weary Mother. Barry Pain. The Poets at Tea, VIII. NA; Par
Lilies of the Field, The. Compton Mackenzie. OBVV
Lilies of the Valley. Jon Silkin. NoAM
Lilies say on Easter day, The. The Song of the Lilies. Lucy Wheelock. OHIP
Lilies will languish; violets look ill. The Sadness of Things for Sappho's Sickness. Robert Herrick. PoPle
Lilith, *sels.* Christopher Brennan. PoAu-1
Adam to Lilith.
Anguish'd Doubt Broods over Eden, The.
Lilith on the Fate of Man.
Lilith. Ruth Fainlight. VWA
Lilith. Ruth Feldman. VWA
Lilith. Donald Finkel. VWA
Lilith. Yvan Goll. VWA
Lilith. Linda Gregg. WPOW
Lilith. Allen Grossman. VWA
Lilith. X. J. Kennedy. UnTE
Lilith. Primo Levi, *tr. fr. Italian by* Ruth Feldman *and* Brian Swann. VWA
Lilith. Dante Gabriel Rossetti. *See* Body's Beauty.
Lilith, Adam's first companion. Lilith. Ruth Fainlight. VWA
Lilith on the Fate of Man. Christopher Brennan. *Fr.* Lilith. PoAu-1
Lilith our second kinswoman. Lilith. Primo Levi, *tr. by* Ruth Feldman *and* Brian Swann. VWA
Lilith's Child. Edward Francisco. DL
Lilium [*or* Lillium] Regis. Francis Thompson. HBMV; WGRP
Lilli Burlero. Lord Wharton, Thomas. *See* Lilliburlero.
Lillian's Chair ("Lillian had just arisen from her chair"). Olga Cabrall. GP
Lilliburlero. Thomas, Lord Wharton. APAS; ViBoFo; *with music;* (Lilli Burlero.) FSW; OxBoLi
(New Song, A.) CoMu
Lilliput Levee. William Brighty Rands. CenHV
Lilliputian Ode on Their Majesties' Accession, A. Henry Carey. NOEC
Lilliputian's Beer Song. Septimus Winner. OBAL
Lillium Regis. Francis Thompson. *See* Lilium Regis.
Lilly Dale, *with music.* H. S. Thompson. BLSo
Lilly in a Christal, The. Robert Herrick. AnAnS-2; PoEL-3; SeCP
(Lily in a Crystal, The.) NoP; SeCePo
Lilly's Song. Evan Zimroth. AMV-81
Lilt Your Johnnie. *Unknown.* BXAP
Lily. Rosanna Warren. MAYP
Lily Adair. Thomas Holley Chivers. OBAL
Lily and the Rose, The. *Unknown.* *See* Maidens Came, The.
Lily Bed, The. Isabella Valancy Crawford. PeCV
Lily in a Crystal, The. Robert Herrick. *See* Lilly in a Christal, The.
Lily in my garden grew, A. The Maiden and the Lily. John Fraser. HBV-1
Lily, Lois & Flaubert; the Site of Loss. Kathleen Fraser. NPGG
Lily Munro, *with music.* *Unknown.* OuSiCo
Lily of the West, The. *Unknown.* AmFP; FSW
Lily of Yorrow, The. Henry van Dyke. AA
Lily on liquid roses floating. Champagne Rosé[e]. John Kenyon. OBEV; OBRV; OBVV
Lily-white Rose, The. *Unknown.* MeEL
Lilya, *sel.* Eysteinn Asgrímsson, *tr. fr. Icelandic by* Eirik Magnusson.
Author's Entreaty for His Lady. ISi
Lily's withered chalice falls, The. Le Jardin [*or* The Garden]. Oscar Wilde. *Fr.* Impressions. PoRA; SeCePo; SyP
Limb and Mind. John Waller. NeBP
Limb of forests rises up, The. Yvonne Caroutch, *tr. fr. French by* David Cloutier. BoWoP
Limberick. Conrad Aiken. FiBHP
(Limerick: "It's time to make love: douse the glim.") FaBoNo
Limbo. Samuel Taylor Coleridge. OAEL-2
Limbo. Seamus Heaney. CIP; OxBC
Limbo. Marieve Rugo. AMV-81
Limbo. *Unknown.* OBET
Limbs are caught in each other, The. Complicity. Tess Gallagher. GeTw
Limbs that erstwhile charmed your sight, The. Dear, They Have Poached the Eyes You Loved So Well. Rupert Brooke. WhC
Lime condensed on the ceiling, or maybe. Living in the Boneyard. John Oliver Simon. NeAC
Limeraiku. Ted Pauker. NOBL
Limeratomy, The. Anthony Euwer. HBMV
Sels.
As a Beauty I Am Not a Star. InvP
(Face, The.) OBAL; TreF
(Limerick:" As a beauty I'm not a great star.") HBV-2; HBVY
(My Face.) FaFP; NePA; PoLF; WhC

Limerick: "No matter how grouchy you're feeling." WhC
Limericised Classics. Edwin Meade Robinson. HBMV
Limerick: "Aging old queers are no treat." *Unknown.* PeHV
Limerick: "Anal erotic name Herman, An." *Unknown.* PeHV
Limerick: "Angry young husband called Bicket, An." John Galsworthy. CenHV
Limerick: "Animula vagula blandula." Conrad Aiken. FaBoNo; OBAL
Limerick: "Argentine gaucho named Bruno, An." *Unknown.* NOBL
Limerick: "As a beauty I'm not a great star." Anthony Euwer. *See* As a Beauty I Am Not a Star.
Limerick: "At the village emporium in Woodstock." Frederick Winsor. WhC
Limerick: "Beautiful lady named Psyche, A." *Unknown.* WhC
(Lady Named Psychc, A.) TDH
Limerick: "Big bull-dyke, surly and sallow, A." *Unknown.* PeHV
Limerick: "Bottle of perfume that Willie sent, The." *Unknown.* WhC
Limerick: "Breasts of a barmaid of Crale, The." *Unknown.* NOBL
Limerick: "Bright little maid of St. Thomas, A." *Unknown.* *See* St. Thomas.
Limerick: "But he followed the pair to Pawtucket." *Unknown.* TreF
Limerick: "Canner, exceedingly canny, A." Carolyn Wells. HBV-2; HBVY
("Canner, Exceedingly canny, A.") FaPON
(Two Limericks, I.) YaD
Limerick: "Certain young gourmet of Crediton, A." Charles Cuthbert Inge. *See* Certain Young Gourmet, A.
Limerick: "Charlotte Brontë said, 'Wow, sister! *What* a man!'" Victor Gray. NOBL
Limerick: "Charming young woman named Pat, A." *Unknown.* NIP
Limerick: "Cleopatra, who thought they maligned her." Newton Mackintosh. NA
Limerick: "Clergyman in want, A." Ronald Arbuthnott Knox. OxBoLi; WhC
(Limerick: "Evangelical vicar in want.") CenHV
Limerick: "Clergyman out in Dumont, A." Morris Bishop. WhC
Limerick: "Consider the lowering Lynx." Langford Reed. CenHV
Limerick: "Dear Sir, your astonishment's odd." *Unknown.* *See* Reply, A.
Limerick: "Decrepit old gas man named Peter, A." *Unknown.* *See* Decrepit Old Gasman, A.
Limerick: "Eeccentric old person of Slough, An." George Robey. CenHV
Limerick: "Epicure, dining at Crewe, An." *Unknown.* *See* Epicure, Dining at Crewe, An.
Limerick: "Evangelical vicar in want." Ronald Arbuthnott Knox. *See* Limerick: "Clergyman in want, A."
Limerick: "Fire Island pixie called 'Mary,' A." *Unknown.* PeHV
Limerick: "Flea and a fly in a flue, A." *Unknown.* *See* Flea and the Fly, The.
Limerick: "Funny old lady named Borgia, A." *Unknown.* WhC
Limerick: "God's plan had a hopeful beginning." *Unknown.* NIP
Limerick: "H was an indigent Hen." Bruce Porter. NA
Limerick: "Hermaphrodite fairy of Kew, A." *Unknown.* PeHV
Limerick: "I sat next [to] the Duchess at tea." *Unknown.* NIP; SoSe
Limerick: "I wish that my room had a floor." Gelett Burgess. *See* I Wish That My Room Had a Floor.
Limerick: "I'd rather have habits than clothes." Gelett Burgess. NA
Limerick: "In a high-fashion journal for queers." *Unknown.* PeHV
Limerick: "It's time to make love: douse the glim." Conrad Aiken. *See* Limberick.
Limerick: "Lady there was of Antigua, A." Cosmo Monkhouse. HBV-2
Limerick: "Large, colored dyke from Atlanta, A." *Unknown.* PeHV
Limerick: "Lesbian born under Pisces, A." *Unknown.* PeHV
Limerick: "Lesbian girl of Khartoum, A." *Unknown.* NOBL
Limerick: "Man hired by John Smith and Co., A." "Mark Twain." *See* Dirt Dumping.
Limerick: "Miss Minnie McFinney, of Butte." *Unknown.* WhC
Limerick: "My name's Mister Benjamin Bunny." Andrew Lang. CenHV
Limerick: "No matter how grouchy you're feeling." Anthony Euwer. *Fr.* The Limeratomy. WhC
(Smile, The.) HBMV
Limerick: "Old East End worker called Jock, An." Victor Gray. NOBL
Limerick: "On the deck of a ship called the Masm." Conrad Aiken. FaBoNo
Limerick: "One morning old Wilfrid Scawen Blunt." Victor Gray. NOBL
Limerick: "Our ambassador to Venus, Mz Abner." *Unknown.* PeHV
Limerick: "Poor benighted Hindoo, The." Cosmo Monkhouse. HBV-2
Limerick: "Pretty young actress, a stammerer, A." Eille Norwood. CenHV
Limerick: "Reverend Henry Ward Beecher, The." *At. to* Oliver Wendell Holmes. CenHV; HBVY
(Eggstravagance, An.) FaBoNo
(Henry Ward Beecher.) ChTr
Limerick: "S & M bar, oh my dears, The." *Unknown.* PeHV
Limerick: "Said a gabby old queer in Saint-Lô." *Unknown.* PeHV
Limerick: "Said a great Congregational preacher." *Unknown.* WhC
Limerick: "Said old Peeping Tom of Fort Lee." Morris Bishop. WhC
Limerick: "Silly young fellow named Hyde, A." *Unknown.* WhC
("Silly young fellow named Hyde, A.") ShM
Limerick: "Sleeper from the Amazon, A." *Unknown.* WhC
Limerick: "Smooth-bottomed fellow named Fritz, A." *Unknown.* PeHV
Limerick: "Staid schizophrenic named Struther, A." *Unknown.* NIP
Limerick: "Swimmer whose clothing was strewed, A." *Unknown.* NIP
Limerick: "Taxi-cab whore out at Iver, A." Victor Gray. NOBL
Limerick: "That famous old pederast, Wilde." *Unknown.* PeHV
Limerick: "Then the pair followed Pa to Manhasset." *Unknown.* TreF
Limerick: "There is an old he-wolf named Gambart." Dante Gabriel Rossetti. CenHV; FaBoEE
Limerick: "There once was a bonnie Scotch laddie." *Unknown.* WhC
Limerick: "There once was a girl of New York." Cosmo Monkhouse. NA
Limerick: "There once was a girl of Pitlochry." *Unknown.* CenHV
Limerick: "There once was a man from Nantucket." *Unknown.* TreF
Limerick: "There once was a man of Bengal." *Unknown.* CenHV
(Bengal.) OnUR
Limerick: "There once was a man of Calcutta." *Unknown.* WhC
Limerick: "There once was a man [*or* There was a young man] who said, 'Damn!'" Maurice Evan Hare. CenHV; NOBL
(Determinism.) FaBoCo
(Predestination.) PoPle
Limerick: "There once was a man who said 'God.'" Ronald Arbuthnott Knox. *See* Idealism.
Limerick: "There once was a man who said, 'How.'" *Unknown.* NA
Limerick: "There once was a painter named Scott." Dante Gabriel Rossetti. CenHV
Limerick: "There once was a person of Benin." Cosmo Monkhouse. NA
Limerick: "There once was a pious young priest." *Unknown.* NIP
(Pious Young Priest, The.) TDH
Limerick: "There once was a Renaissance man." *Unknown.* PeHV
Limerick: "There once was a spinster of Ealing." *Unknown.* NIP
Limerick: "There once was a warden of Wadham." *Unknown.* PeHV
Limerick: "There once was a wonderful wizard." Conrad Aiken. FaBoNo
Limerick: "There once was an old man of Blackheath." *Unknown.* CenHV
Limerick: "There once was an old man of Lyme." *At. to* Edward Lear, *also at. to* Cosmo Monkhouse. *See* There Was an Old Party of Lyme.
Limerick: "There once were two cats of Kilkenny." *See* Kilkenny Cats, The.
Limerick: "There was a dear lady of Eden." *Unknown.* NA
Limerick: "There was a faith-healer of Deal." *Unknown.* CenHV; WhC
(Faith-Healer.) FaFP
(Mind and Matter.) FaBoCo
Limerick: "There was a fat canon of Durham." *Unknown.* WhC
Limerick: "There was a gay damsel of Lynn." *Unknown.* NA
Limerick: "There was a good Canon of Durham." William Ralph Inge. CenHV
Limerick: "There was a kind Curate of Kew." *Unknown.* CenHV
Limerick: "There was a poor chap called Rossetti." Dante Gabriel Rossetti. CenHV
Limerick: "There was a princess of Bengal." *At. to* Walter Parke. NA
Limerick: "There was a queer fellow named Woodin." "Cuthbert Bede." CenHV
(Queer Fellow Named Woodin, A.) TDH
Limerick: "There was a small boy of Quebec." *At. to* Kipling. *See* Boy of Quebec, The.
Limerick: "There was a young bard of Japan." *Unknown.* CenHV
Limerick: "There was a young critic of King's." Arthur Clement Hilton. CenHV
Limerick: "There was a young curate of Hants." E. V. Knox. CenHV
Limerick: "There was a young fellow called Crouch." Victor Gray. NOBL
Limerick: "There was a young fellow called Green." *Unknown.* CenHV
Limerick: "There was a young fellow named Hall." *Unknown.* WhC
(Fellow Named Hall, A, *at. to* J. F. Wilson.) TDH
Limerick: "There was a young fellow named Nutz." *Unknown.* PeHV
Limerick: "There was a young fellow [*or* person] named Tait [*or* Tate]." *At. to* Carolyn Wells. HBV-2; HBVY; WhC
Limerick: "There was a young Fellow of Caius." *Unknown.* NOBL
Limerick: "There was a young fellow of Ceuta." *Unknown.* CenHV
Limerick: "There was a young Fellow of King's." *Unknown.* NOBL
Limerick: "There was a young fellow of Perth." *Unknown.* WhC
Limerick: "There was a young Fellow of Waldham." *Unknown.* NOBL
Limerick: "There was a young genius of Queens'." Arthur Clement Hilton. CenHV
Limerick: "There was a young girl of Lahore." Cosmo Monkhouse. HBV-2
Limerick: "There was a young gourmand of John's." Arthur Clement Hilton. CenHV
Limerick: "There was a young lady called Starky." *Unknown.* CenHV
Limerick: "There was a young lady in white." Edward Lear. NBM
Limerick: "There was a young lady named Bright." *Unknown, at. to* Arthur Buller. *See* Relativity.
Limerick: "There was a young lady of Corsica." Edward Lear. CenHV; ChTr; FaBoNo

Limerick: "There was a young lady of Ealing." *Unknown.* CenHV
(Young Lady of Ealing, A.) TDH
Limerick: "There was a young lady of Flint." *Unknown.* CenHV
Limerick: "There was a young lady of Hull." Edward Lear. MoShBr
Limerick: "There was a young lady of Kent." *Unknown.* CenHV
Limerick: "There was a young lady of Limerick." Andrew Lang. CenHV
Limerick: "There was a young lady of Lynn." *Unknown.* CenHV; SoSe
(Young Lady of Lynn, A.) ChTr; RHPC
Limerick: "There was a young lady of Milton." *Unknown.* NA
Limerick: "There was a young lady of Niger." *At. to* Cosmo Monkhouse. HBV-2; HBVY; NA; PDV
(Not Just for the Ride.) FaFP
(Satisfied Tiger, The.) TreFT
(There Was a Young Lady of Niger.) FaPON; InvP; ShM; SoPo; TiPo
Limerick: "There was a young lady of Riga." *Unknown.* CenHV; FaBoCo
Limerick: "There was a young lady of Russia." Edward Lear. MoShBr
Limerick: "There was [once] a young lady of Ryde/ Who ate a green apple and died." *Unknown.* CenHV; EvOK; PDV
(There Was a Young Lady of Ryde.) ShM
Limerick: "There was a young lady of Ryde/ Whose shoe-strings were seldom untied." Edward Lear. WhC
("There was a young lady of Ryde.") OxBoLi
Limerick: "There was a young lady of station." "Lewis Carroll." CenHV
(There was a Young Lady of Station.) FaBoNo
Limerick: "There was a young lady of Twickenham." Oliver Herford. WhC
Limerick: "There was a young lady of Wales." *Unknown.* NA
Limerick: "There was a young lady of Wilts." *Unknown.* HBV-2
(Young Lady of Wilts, A.) TDH
Limerick: "There was a young lady of Woosester." *Unknown.* WhC
Limerick: "There was a young lady whose eyes." Edward Lear. GoJo
("There was a young lady whose eyes.") EBEV
Limerick: "There was a young maid who said, 'Why.'" *Unknown.* NA; SoSe
Limerick: "There was a young man of Cohoes." Robert J. Burdette. NA
Limerick: "There was a young man of Devizes." *Unknown, at. to* Archibald Marshall. CenHV; WhC
Limerick: "There was a young man of Madrid." *Unknown.* WhC
Limerick: "There was a young man of Montrose." Arnold Bennett. *See* There Was a Young Man of Montrose.
Limerick: "There was a young man of Sid. Sussex." Arthur C. Hilton. WhC
Limerick: "There was a young man so benighted." *Unknown.* HBV-2
Limerick: "There was a young man who was bitten." *At. to* Walter Parke. NA
Limerick: "There was a young monk of Siberia." *Unknown.* TreFT
Limerick: "There was a young person named Tate." *At. to* Carolyn Wells. *See* Limerick: "There was a young fellow named Tait."
Limerick: "There was a young person of Crete." Edward Lear. FaBoNo
Limerick: "There was a young person of Smyrna." Edward Lear. NBM; TEP
(There Was a Young Person of Smyrna.) OxBoLi
Limerick: "There was a young woman called Starky." *Unknown.* *See* Mendelian Theory.
Limerick: "There was a young woman named Bright." *Unknown.* *See* Relativity.
Limerick: "There was an auld birkie ca'ed Milton." Andrew Lang. CenHV
Limerick: "There was an old fellow of Trinity." *Unknown, at. to* Arthur Clement Hilton. CenHV; WHC
Limerick: "There was an old man in a boat." Edward Lear. EBEV; FaBoNo; HBV-2
(Floating Old Man, The.) WiR
Limerick: "There was an old man in a pew." Edward Lear. MoShBr
Limerick: "There was an old man in a tree." Edward Lear. FaBoNo; HBV-2; OxBChV; TEP
(There Was an Old Man in a Tree.) InvP; NoP; SoPo
Limerick: "There was an old man in a trunk." Ogden Nash. CenHV
(Ultimate Reality.) FaBoCo
Limerick: "There was an old man of Bengal." "F. Anstey." CenHV
Limerick: "There was an old man of Boulogne." *Unknown.* CenHV
(There Was an Old Man of Boulogne.) FaBoCo; OxBoLi
Limerick: "There was an old man of Dumbree." Edward Lear. NBM
(There Was an Old Man of Dumbree.) OxBChV
Limerick: "There was an old man of Dundee." Edward Lear. FaBoNo
Limerick: "There was an old man of El Hums." Edward Lear. FaBoNo
Limerick: "There was an old man of Girgenti." Edward Lear. FaBoNo
Limerick: "There was an old man of Hong Kong." Edward Lear. FaBoCo; NBM
(There Was an Old Man of Hong Kong.) PAI
Limerick: "There was an old man of Kamschatka." Edward Lear. NA; NOBL
Limerick: "There was an old man of Khartoum." *Unknown, at. to* W. R. Inge. NOBL
(There Was an Old Man of Khartoum.) OxBoLi
Limerick: "There was an old man of Leghorn." Edward Lear. NA
Limerick: "There was an old man of Madras." Edward Lear. FaBoNo
Limerick: "There was an old man of Nantucket." *Unknown, at. to* Dayton Voorhees. HBV-2
Limerick: "There was an old man of [*or* from] Peru/ Who dreamt he was eating his shoe." *Unknown.* CenHV; PDV; SoSe; TDH
(Old Man from Peru, An.) FaFP; NTCP
(There Was an Old Man from Peru.) OnUR
Limerick: "There was an old man of Spithead." Edward Lear. FaBoNo
Limerick: "There was an old man of Tarentum." *Unknown.* HBV-2; WhC
Limerick: "There was an old man of the coast." Edward Lear. CenHV; MoShBr
Limerick: "There was an old man of the Dargle." Edward Lear. ChTr
Limerick: "There was an old man of the Dee." Edward Lear. FaBoNo
Limerick: "There was an old man of The Hague." Edward Lear. EvOK
(Old Man of The Hague, The.) TDH
Limerick: "There was an old man of Thermopylae." Edward Lear. EBEV; EvOK; FaBoNo; NA; NBM; NOBL
Limerick: "There was an old man of Three Bridges." Edward Lear. FaBoNo
Limerick: "There was an old man of Vesuvius." Edward Lear. FaBoNo; GLGT
Limerick: "There was an old man of Whitehaven." Edward Lear. EBEV; NBM; VLP
Limerick: "There was an old man on the Border." Edward Lear. CenHV; EBEV
Limerick: "There was an old man who said: 'How.'" Edward Lear. EvOK
(There Was an Old Man Who Said, "How.") OxBCHV
Limerick: "There was an old man who said, 'Do.'" *See* There Was an Old Man Who Said, "Do."
Limerick: "There was an old man who said, 'Hush!'" Edward Lear. FaBoCo; GoJo; HBV-2; NA; NBM; NOBL; OxBChV; OxBoLi; TEP
Limerick: "There was an old man who supposed." Edward Lear. NA; WhC
(There Was an Old Man Who Supposed.) NoP
Limerick: "There was an old man whose despair." Edward Lear. FaBoNo; VLP
Limerick: "There was an old man with a beard." Edward Lear. ChTr; FaBoCo; FaBoNo; HBV-2; NOBL; OxBChV; PDV; TEP
(Old Man with a Beard.) FaPON; NTCP
(There Was an Old Man with a Beard.) NoP; OnUR; RHPC; SoPo; TiPo
Limerick: "There was an old man with a gong." Edward Lear. GoJo
(Old Man with a Gong, The.) TDH
Limerick: "There was an old man with a poker." Edward Lear. HBV-2
Limerick: "There was an old man with a ribbon." Edward Lear. FaBoNo
Limerick: "There was an old person of Anerley." Edward Lear. FaBoCo
Limerick: "There was an old person of Bar." Edward Lear. FaBoNo
Limerick: "There was an old person of Bromley." Edward Lear. NBM
Limerick: "There was an old person of Brussels." Edward Lear. FaBoNo
Limerick: "There was an old person of Crowle." Edward Lear. FaBoNo
Limerick: "There was an old person of Dean." Edward Lear. MoShBr
Limerick: "There was an old person of Diss." Edward Lear. GoJo
Limerick: "There was an old person of Dover." Edward Lear. FaBoNo
Limerick: "There was an old person of Grange." Edward Lear. FaBoNo
Limerick: "There was an Old Person of Gretna." Edward Lear. *See* There Was an Old Person of Gretna.
Limerick: "There was an old person of Harrow." Edward Lear. FaBoNo
Limerick: "There was an old person of Hove." Edward Lear. FaBoNo
Limerick: "There was an old person of Ickley." Edward Lear. EvOK
Limerick: "There was an old person of Lear." Edward Lear. CenHV
Limerick: "There was an old person of Leeds." *Unknown.* WhC
Limerick: "There was an old person of Lyme." *See* There Was an Old Party of Lyme.
Limerick: "There was an old person of Philae." Edward Lear. FaBoNo
Limerick: "There was an old person of Shoreham." Edward Lear. NBM
Limerick: "There was an old person of Skye." Edward Lear. ChTr
Limerick: "There was an old person of Tring." *Unknown.* WhC
(Old Person of Tring, An.) TDH
Limerick: "There was an old person of Twickenham." Edward Lear. FaBoNo
Limerick: "There was an old person of Ware." Edward Lear. NA
(There Was an Old Person of Ware.) PoPl
Limerick: "There was an old person of Wick." Edward Lear. FaBoNo; NA
Limerick: "There was an old person of Woking." Edward Lear. NA
Limerick: "There was an old person whose habits." Edward Lear. FaBoNo
(Hurtful Habits.) TDH
(There Was an Old Person Whose Habits.) FaPON
Limerick: "There was an old stupid who wrote." *At. to* Walter Parke. NA
(Person of Note, A.) TDH
Limerick: "There was an old tailor of Bicester." *Unknown.* CenHV

Limerick: "There was once a maiden of Siam." *Unknown.* TreFT
Limerick: "There was once a man with a beard." Edward Lear. NA
Limerick: "There was once a young lady of Ryde." *Unknown. See* Limerick: "There was a young lady of Ryde/ Who ate a green apple and died."
Limerick: "There were three young women of Birmingham." Cosmo Monkhouse. HBV-2
Limerick: "There's a combative artist named Whistler." Dante Gabriel Rossetti. CenHV
Limerick: "There's a notable family named Stein." *Unknown.* NOBL
("There's a wonderful family called Stein.") DBV
Limerick: "There's a Portuguese person named Howell." *At. to* Dante Gabriel Rossetti *and to* James Abbott McNeill Whistler. CenHV; DBV
Limerick: "There's a vaporish maiden in Harrison." Morris Bishop. *See* Vaporish Woman, A.
Limerick: "There's an Irishman, Arthur O'Shaughnessy." Dante Gabriel Rossetti. CenHV
Limerick: "They say that I was in my youth." *Unknown.* CenHV
Limerick: "Though the music of love is Schubérty." *Unknown.* PeHV
Limerick: "Treatment by old Mr. Mears, The." *Unknown.* PeHV
Limerick: "Trendy young girl from St. Paul, A." *Unknown.* NIP
Limerick: "Tutor who tooted a flute, A." Carolyn Wells. HBV-2; HBVY; SoSe; WhC
(Tutor, The.) MoShBr; RHPC
("Tutor who tooted a flute, A.") TiPo
(Two Limericks, II.) YaD
Limerick: "Two dykes went their separate routes." *Unknown.* PeHV
Limerick: "Vice most obscene and unsavory, A." *Unknown.* NOBL
Limerick: "Well, it's partly the shape of the thing." *Unknown.* SoSe; WhC
Limerick: "Well-bred young girl of Gomorrah, A." *Unknown.* PeHV
Limerick: "Well-buggered boy named Delpasse, A." *Unknown.* PeHV
Limerick: "When Arthur was homeless and broke." *Unknown.* PeHV
Limerick: "When Gauguin was visiting Fiji." Victor Gray. NOBL
Limerick: "When our dean took a pious young spinster." Victor Gray. NOBL
Limerick: "When that Seint George hadde sleyne ye draggon." *Unknown.* NA
Limerick: "When you go to a store in Ascutney." Richard H. Field. WhC
Limerick: "Whenever a fellow called Rex." *Unknown.* NOBL
Limerick: "While Titian was grinding rose madder." *Unknown.* NOBL
Limerick: "While visiting Arundel Castle." Victor Gray. NOBL
Limerick: "Wonderful bird is the pelican, A." Dixon Lanier Merritt. CenHV
Limerick: "Young engine-driver called Hunt, A." Victor Gray. NOBL
Limerick: "Young fairy with habits perverse, A." *Unknown.* PeHV
Limerick: "Young Frederick the Great was a beaut." *Unknown.* PeHV
Limerick: "Young Harvard man, sweet and tender, A." *Unknown.* PeHV
Limerick: "Young lady of fair Mytilene, A." *Unknown.* CenHV
Limerick: "Young things who frequent picture-palaces, The." *Unknown.* NOBL
Limerick of Frankness, A. "X. Y. Z." TDH
Limestone and pine: a dry country. By Rail through Istria. Robert Conquest. NoAM
Limitations. Siegfried Sassoon. MoBrPo
Limited. Carl Sandburg. HAP; MoAB; MoAmPo; OxBA
Limited, The. Robert Penn Warren. PoA
Limits. Emerson. FM; PoEL-4
Limits of Departure, The. Bruce Weigl. AMV-81
Limits of Equitation, The. Barbara Winder. AMV-81
Limits of Submission, The. Faarah Nuur, *tr. fr. Somali by* B. W. Andrzejewski *and* I. M. Lewis. TTY; WTO
Limits of the sphere of dream, The. Goethe, *tr. fr. German by* Shelley. *Fr.* Faust. WSC
Limmerich Towne, *sel.* John Francis O'Donnell.
In the Market-Place. NBM
Limousine up to my brass facade, The. After Mardi Gras. Sister Mary Honora. NePoAm-2
Limp as unwatered flowers, the grey limbs. Homage to the Carracci. Tom Disch. PoA
Limping past the Guthrie theater. Indians at the Guthrie. Gerald Vizenor. VoR
Limpopo and Tugela churned. The Scorpion. William Plomer. NoAM; OBMV
L'Imprévisibilité. Zinaida Hippius, *tr. fr. Russian by* Temira Pachmuss. PBWP
Lim'ricks and Puns. *Unknown.* TDH
Lincoln. George Henry Boker. OHIP
Lincoln. John Vance Cheney. OHIP
Lincoln. Rembrandt William B. Ditmars. HBMV
Lincoln. John Gould Fletcher. HBMV; MoAmPo
"There was a darkness in this man," II. OFD; PAL
Lincoln. Florence Kiper Frank. PGD
Lincoln. Jane L. Hardy. OHIP
Lincoln. Clyde Walton Hill. PGD
Lincoln. Vachel Lindsay. *See* Would I Might Rouse the Lincoln in You All.
Lincoln. James Russell Lowell. *Fr.* Ode Recited at the Harvard Commemoration, VI. HBVY
("Nature, they say, doth date.") PGD
Lincoln. S. Weir Mitchell. PAH
Lincoln. Harriet Monroe. *Fr.* Commemoration Ode. AA
Lincoln. James Whitcomb Riley. OHIP
Lincoln. Corinne Roosevelt Robinson. OHIP
Lincoln. John Townsend Trowbridge. PGD
Lincoln. Nancy Byrd Turner. FaPON; RHPC; TiPo
Lincoln. *Unknown.* OHIP
Lincoln and Liberty. *At. to* F. A. Simpson *and to* Jesse Hutchinson. AS, *with music*; FSW; TrAS, *with music*
Lincoln arose! the masterful great man. The Masterful Man. Henry Tyrrell. PGD
Lincoln at Gettysburg. Bayard Taylor. *Fr.* The Gettysburg Ode. PAH
("After the eyes that looked, the lips that spake.") OHIP
Lincoln-Child, The. James Oppenheim. HBMV
Lincoln, Come Back. Thomas Curtis Clark. PGD
Lincoln Leads. Minna Irving. OHIP
Lincoln Monument: Washington. Langston Hughes. OFD
Lincoln Statue, The. W. F. Collins. OHIP; PGD
Lincoln, the Man of the People. Edwin Markham. GN; HBV-2; MoAmPo; OHFP; OHIP; PAH; PAL; TreFS; TrGrPo
(Lincoln the Great Commoner.) GN
Sels.
"Color of the ground was in him, the red earth, The." PGD
"Up from the log cabin to the capitol." OFD
Lincoln, the man who freed the slave. A Tribute. *Unknown.* PGD
Lincoln! "Thou shouldst be living at this hour!" "Thou Shouldst Be Living at This Hour!" Kenyon West. PGD
Lincoln was a long man. Abraham Lincoln [1809-1965]. Rosemary *and* Stephen Vincent Benét. PoSC; TiPo; YeAr
Lincoln! When men would name a man. Lincoln. *Unknown.* OHIP
Lincoln's Birthday. John Kendrick Bangs. PGD
Lincoln's Grave, *sel.* Maurice Thompson.
Prophecy, A. AA
Lincolnshire; from the Wolds to the Fens. Ben Jonson. *Fr.* The Sad Shepherd, II, vii. FaBoPP
Lincolnshire Poacher, The. *Unknown.* CH; FSW; GBP; OnMSP; OxBoLi
(Poacher, The.) WiR
Lincolnshire Shepherd, A. *Unknown.* OBET
Lincolnshire Shores ("A still salt pool locked in with bars of sand.") Tennyson. *Fr.* The Palace of Art. FaBoPP
Lincolnshire Shores ("As the crest of some slow-arching wave"). Tennyson. *Fr.* Idylls of the King: The Last Tournament. FaBoPP
Lincolnshire Wolds and Lincolnshire Sea. Tennyson. *See* In Memoriam A. H. H.: "Calm is the morn without a sound."
Lincolnshire's Holland Speaks of Her Waterfowl. Michael Drayton. *Fr.* Polyolbion, Song XXV. FaBoPP
Lindamira's Complaint. Mary Sidney Wroth, Countess of Montgomery. *Fr.* Urania. WPE
Lindbergh. *Unknown.* AmFP
Lindeman. Mary Jane White. AMV-81
Linden blossomed, the nightingale sang, The. Farewell. Heine, *tr. by* John Todhunter. AWP
Linden Tree, The. Dietmar von Aist, *tr. by* Edgar Taylor. PoPl
Line in long array where they wind betwixt green islands, A. Cavalry Crossing a Ford. Walt Whitman. AA; AmPP; AP; CABA; ChTr; HeIP; InPK; InPS; NoAM; NoP; OxBA; PAI; PoPl; PPP; TAP; UnPo
Line Like. Nelly Sachs, *tr. fr. German by* Michael Hamburger. BoWoP
Line of an American Poet, The. Reed Whittemore. MoVE; PPON
Line of Beauty, The. Edward Dowden. OnYI
Line of the cut must be clean, The. Lapidary. Bonnie L. Alexander. AMV-80
Line to Heaven by Christ Was Made, The. *Unknown.* BXAP; PeD
Lineage. Reba Terry. AMV-81
Lineage. Margaret Walker. BlSi; BOLo; CNA; NMM; PBWP; PoBA
Linear, encircled youth, The. On Alexander and Aristotle, on a Black-on-Red Greek Plate. Alan Dugan. PPP
Linebacker at Forty, The. Jon Wallace. AMV-81
Lined up single file, they make a point. Concerning the Dead. Mark Halperin. FAZ
Linen Bands. Vance Thompson. AA
Linen Town. Seamus Heaney. CIP
Linen Weaver, The. *Unknown.* NOEC
Liner She's a Lady, The. Kipling. FaBV
Lines, The: "After the centres' naked files, the basic line." Randall Jarrell. CrMA

Lines: "Clear had the day been from the dawn." Michael Drayton. *See* Fine Day, A.
Lines: "Cold earth slept below, The." Shelley. ChER; EnRP; LoBV; NCEP; SyP
Lines: "From fair Jamaica's fertile plains." "Ada." BlSi
Lines: "Here often, when a child, I lay reclined." Tennyson. CABA; FaBoPP; PAI
Lines: "His cock is big and red when I am there." Paul Goodman. PeHV
Lines: "How lovely is the heaven of this night." Thomas Lovell Beddoes. *See* Beautiful Night, A.
Lines: "I followed once a fleet and mighty serpent." Thomas Lovell Beddoes. NBM
Lines ———: "I have been cherish'd and forgiven." Hartley Coleridge. PoEL-4
Lines: I Praise God's Mankind in an Old Woman. Wilfred Watson. NOBC
Lines: Inspired by the Controversy on the Value or Otherwise of Old English Studies. Anthony Burgess. FaBoCo
Lines: "Love within the lover's breast." George Meredith. HBV-1
Lines: "Mine ears have heard your distant moan." J. C. Squire. WhC
Lines: "Other day I was loving a sweet little fruitpie-and-cream, The." Gavin Ewart. EAS
Lines: "Shall earth no more inspire thee." Emily Brontë. *See* Shall Earth No More Inspire Thee.
Lines: "Singularly and in pairs the decade has been ripped by bullets." Herbert Martin. PoBA
Lines: "Slumber did my spirit seal, A." Wordsworth. *See* Slumber Did My Spirit Seal, A.
Lines: "Some are waiting, some can't wait." Heather McHugh. MAYP
Lines: "There can be no power in a square." Brian Swann. AMV-81
Lines: "Though all the Fates should prove unkind." Henry David Thoreau. *See* Though All the Fates Should Prove Unkind.
Lines: To a Movement in Mozart's E-Flat Symphony. Thomas Hardy. ELP
Lines: "When the lamp is shattered." Shelley. *See* When the Lamp Is Shattered.
Lines: "When youthful faith hath fled." John Gibson Lockhart. OBEV; OBVV
Lines Addressed to a Seagull. Gerald Griffin. OnYI
Lines are keen against today's bad sky, The. The Church on Comiaken Hill. Richard Hugo. LCAP; Prf
Lines by a Fond Lover. *Unknown.* NA
Lines by a Medium. *Unknown.* NA
Lines by a Person of Quality. *At. to* Pope, *and to* Swift. InMe; NA
Lines by an Old Fogy. *Unknown. See* Gasbags.
Lines Composed a Few Miles above Tintern Abbey [on Revisiting the Banks of the Wye during a Tour, July 13, 1798]. Wordsworth. BiP; BLPL; CABA; ChER; EnRP; FaBoPP; FF; FiP; GOTL; HBV-2; HeIP; InPS; LiTB; LoBV; MasP; NIP; NoP; OAEL-2; OAEP; OBNC; OBRV; PoEL-4; PPP; PrIm; SeCePo; SeCeV; TEP; TreFS; TrGrPo; WHA
(Lines Written a Few Miles above Tintern Abbey.) HAP
Sels.
"And now, with gleams of half-extinguished thought." ViBoPo
"For I have learned." NU
("I have learned.") TRV
"For thou art with me here upon the banks." Prf
"Sounding cataract, The/ Haunted me like a passion." FaBoEn; WGRP
Lines Composed at Grasmere. Wordsworth. OBRV
Lines Composed in a Wood on a Windy Day. Anne Brontë. EBVV
Lines Concerning the Unknown Soldier, *sel.* Osip Mandelstam, *tr. fr. Russian by* James Greene.
Arteries Juicy with Blood. NAs
Lines Declining a Transatlantic Dinner Invitation. Marilyn Hacker. MAYP
Lines Descriptive of Thomson's Island. Benjamin Lynde. SCAP
Lines for a Bed at Kelmscott Manor. William Morris. *See* Inscription for an Old Bed.
Lines for a Christmas Card. Hilaire Belloc. *See* Season's Greetings.
Lines for a Dead Poet. David Ferry. PP
Lines for a Drawing of Our Lady of the Night. Francis Thompson. ISi
Lines for a Feast of Our Lady. Sister Maris Stella. ISi
Lines for a Friend Who Left. John Logan. DFF
Lines for a Hard Time. Gena Ford. IHMS
Lines for a Sundial. Thomas Herbert Warren. OBVV
Lines for a Wedding Gift. Wesley Trimpi. NePoEA
Lines for a Worthy Person Who Has Drifted by Accident into a Chelsea Revel. A. P. Herbert. NOBL
Lines for a Young Wanderer in Mexico. John Logan. PoA
Lines for an Eminent Poet and Critic. Patric Dickinson. PV
Lines for an Interment. Archibald MacLeish. CMoP; NOBA
Lines for an Old Man. T. S. Eliot. FaBoTw; TW
Lines for Cuscuscaraway and Mirza Murad Ali Beg. T. S. Eliot. FiBHP; OBAL; PoPl; SpRo
Lines for Marking Time. Roberta Hill Whiteman. BoWoP; CDW; TWSS
Lines for Michael in the Picture. John Logan. CAPP
Lines for My Father. Patrick Worth Gray. AMV-81
Lines for the Ancient Scribes. Harvey Shapiro. VWA
Lines for the Hour. Hamilton Fish Armstrong. HBMV
Lines for the Margin of an Old Gospel. Sheila Wingfield. ChMP
Lines for the Planned Parenthood Clinic. Linda Westfall Spurrier. SOTS
Lines for Those to Whom Tragedy Is Denied. Joyce Carol Oates. IHMS
Lines from a Misplaced Person. Jeanne Hill. FAZ
Lines from an Orchard Once Surveyed by Thoreau. Philip Booth. GP
Lines from Catullus. Sir Walter Ralegh. *See* Sun May Set, The.
Lines from Crotchet Castle. Thomas Love Peacock. PV
Lines from Love Letters. *Unknown.* OBEV
"A celuy que plus eyme en mounde," I.
"A soun tres chere et special," II.
Lines grow slack in our hands at full high-water, The. Rock Carving. Douglas Stewart. SeCePo
Lines I Told Myself I Wouldn't Write. Paul Mariani. MAYP
Lines in Order to Be Slandered. Paul Verlaine, *tr. fr. French by* T. Sturge Moore. SyP
Lines in Ridicule of Certain Poems Published in 1777. Samuel Johnson. *See* Lines on Thomas Warton's Poems.
Lines Inscribed upon a Cup Formed from a Skull. Byron. InPK
Lines Left at Mr. Theodore Hook's House in June, 1834. Richard H. Barham. FaBoUs
Lines Occasioned by the Burning of Some Letters. Sarah Dixon. NOEC
Lines of history. Lines of defiance. John Montague. *Fr.* A New Siege; an Historical Meditation. CIP
Lines of this new song are nothing, The. Louis Zukofsky. VGW
Lines on a Bill of Mortality, 1790. William Cowper. OxBoCh
(On a Similar Occasion for the Year 1790.) NOCV
Lines on a Certain Friend's Remarkable Faculty for Swift Generalization. Max Beerbohm. PV
Lines on a Mysterious Occurrence. Alfred Denis Godley. CenHV
Lines on a Purple Cap Received as a Present from My Brother. George Alsop. SCAP
Lines on a Young Lady's Photograph Album. Philip Larkin. EnLoPo; HAP; HeIP; OAEL-2; WeW
Lines on Being Refused a Guggenheim Fellowship. Reed Whittemore. TW
Lines on Bounce. Pope. FM
Lines on Brueghel's *Icarus.* Michael Hamburger. NIP
Lines on Cambridge of 1830. Tennyson. GLGT
Lines on Carmen Sylva. Emma Lazarus. TrJP
Lines on Hearing That Lady Byron Was Ill. Byron. EBEV
Lines on Hearing the Organ. Charles Stuart Calverley. CenHV; FaBoCo; FiBHP; InMe; NBM; NOBL
Lines on His Birthday. John Logan. CAPP
Lines on Leaving a Scene in Bavaria. Thomas Campbell. OBNC
Lines on Milton. Dryden. *See* Lines Printed under the Engraved Portrait of Milton.
Lines on Mountain Villages. "Sunset Joe." PoOW
Lines on Receiving His Mother's Picture. William Cowper. CH; OHIP, *abr.*
Lines on Seeing a Lock of Milton's Hair. Keats. *See* On Seeing a Lock of Milton's Hair.
Lines on Succession of the Kings of England. *Unknown.* FaBoUs
Lines on Swift's Ancestors. Pope. FaBoCo
Lines on the Back of a Confederate Note. Samuel Alroy Jonas. BLPA
Lines on the Celebrated Picture by Leonardo Da Vinci, Called the Virgin of the Rocks. Charles Lamb. ISi
Lines on the Death of Bismarck. John Jay Chapman. PoEL-5
Lines on the Death of Mr. Levett. Samuel Johnson. *See* On the Death of Mr. Levett.
Lines on the Execution of King Charles I. James Graham, Marquess of Montrose. *See* His Metrical Vow.
Lines on the Mermaid Tavern. Keats. AWP; EnRP; HBV-2; InMe; LoBV; OAEP; OBRV; PoRA; PP; SeCeV; TreFS; ViBoPo
(Mermaid Tavern, The.) BLPL; FaBoBe; GTBS; GTBS-P; InvP
Lines on the Sea. Dilys Bennett Laing. NYBP
Lines on the Succession of the Kings of England (Reversed). *Unknown.* FaBoUs
Lines on the Tombs in Westminster. *At. to* Francis Beaumont *and to* William Basse. *See* On the Tombs in Westminster Abbey.
Lines on Thomas Warton's Poems. Samuel Johnson. FaBoEE
(Lines in Ridicule of Certain Poems Published in 1777.) FaBoCo
Lines on the Author's Death. Burns. PV
Lines parallel. The Room. De Leon Harrison. PoBA
Lines Printed under the Engraved Portrait of Milton [in Tonson's Folio of the "Paradise Lost," 1688]. Dryden. HeIP; InPK; SeCeV; SeCV-2
(Epigram on Milton.) TrGrPo
(Lines on Milton.) OAEL-1
(Portrait of Milton, The.) ACP
(Under the Portrait of [John] Milton.) HBV-2; WHA
Lines Scratched in Wet Cement. Ethel Jacobson. ShM

Lines Suggested by the Fourteenth of February. Charles Stuart Calverley. InMe
Lines, Suggested on Reading "An Appeal to Christian Women of the South." "Ada." BlSi
Lines Supposed to Have Been Addressed to Fanny Brawne. Keats. *See* This Living Hand.
Lines to a Blind Girl. Thomas Buchanan Read. AA
Lines to a Don. Hilaire Belloc. DBV, *abr.*; FaBoCo; MoBrPo; OBSV; TW
Lines to a Dragon-Fly. Walter Savage Landor. *See* Dragon-Fly, The.
Lines to a Friend in Trouble. W. S. Di Piero. MAYP
Lines to a Lady-Bird. Lord De Tabley. FM
Lines to a Man Who Thinks That Apple Betty with Hard Sauce Is Food for a Human Being. George S. Kaufman. InMe
Lines to a Nasturtium [a Lover Muses]. Anne Spencer. AmNP; CDC; PoNe
Lines to a Tree. Judah Leib Teller, *tr. fr. Yiddish by* Gabriel Preil *and* Howard Schwartz. VWA
Lines to a World-famous Poet Who Failed to Complete a World-famous Poem; or, Come Clean, Mr. Guest! Ogden Nash. OBAL
Lines to a Young Lady. Edward Lear. *See* How Pleasant to Know Mr. Lear.
Lines to Accompany Flowers for Eve. Carolyn Kizer. BoWoP
Lines to an Indian Air. Shelley. *See* Indian Serenade, The.
Lines to Be Embroidered on a Bib; or, The Child Is Father of the Man, but Not for Quite a While. Ogden Nash. FaBoUs
Lines to Do with Youth. Witter Bynner. PoA
Lines to Dr. Ditmars. Kenneth Allan Robinson. ImOP
Lines to Fanny, *sel.* Keats.
"Where shall I learn to get my peace again?" ChER
Lines to Garcia Lorca. Amiri Baraka. NNP
Lines to His Son on Reaching Adolescence. John Logan. CAPP; NePoEA-2
Lines to Homo Somejerktensis. Earnest A. Hooton. WhC
Lines to Miss Florence Huntingdon. *At. to* James De Mille. NA
(Maiden of Passamaguoddy, The.) WhC
(Sweet Maiden of Passamaguoddy.) WHW
Lines to My Father. Leslie Daiken. NeIP; OxBI
Lines to Our Elders. Countee Cullen. CDC
Lines to Ralph Hodgson, Esqre. T. S. Eliot. OBAL
Lines to Ratclif. Earl of Surrey. SiPS
Lines to the Blessed Sacrament. James Joseph Callanan. OnYI
Lines Where Beauty Lingers. Franklin P. Adams. OBAL
Lines with a Gift of Herbs. Janet Lewis. QFR
Lines Written a Few Miles above Tintern Abbey. Wordsworth. *See* Lines Composed a Few Miles above Tintern Abbey.
Lines Written after a Battle. *Unknown.* InMe
Lines Written after the Discovery by the Author of the Germ of Yellow Fever. Sir Ronald Ross. ImOP
Lines Written among the Euganean Hills. Shelley. EnRP; PoEL-4
(Written in the Euganean Hills, North Italy.) GTBS; GTBS-P
" 'Mid the mountains Euganean," *sel.* PBBP; ViBoPo
Lines Written at Bridgewater, 27 July 1797, *sel.* John Thelwall.
"Day of my double birth, if such the year." NOEC
Lines Written at Cambridge, to W. R., Esquire. Phineas Fletcher. *Fr.* To My Ever-honoured Cousin W. R. Esquire. ElL
Lines Written at the Grave of Alexander [*or* Alexandre] Dumas. Gwendolyn B. Bennett. CDC; PoNe
Lines Written by a Bear of Very Little Brain. A. A. Milne. FaBoNo
Lines Written during a Period of Insanity. William Cowper. EBEV; FiP; HAP; NoP; OAEL-1; PPP; Prf; TW
(Hatred and Vengeance, My Eternal Portion.) FaBoRV; NOEC
(Lines Written under the Influence of Delirium.) PoEl-3
Lines Written Immediately after Parting from a Lady. Sir Samuel Egerton Brydges. NOEC
Lines Written in a Blank Leaf of the Prometheus Unbound. Thomas Lovell Beddoes. OAEL-2
Lines Written in a Country Parson's Orchard. Leslie Daiken. OnYI
Lines Written in a Mausoleum. Lillian Grant. GoYe
Lines Written in a Moment of Vibrant Ill-Health. Morris Bishop. WhC
Lines Written in Dejection. W. B. Yeats. NAs
Lines Written in Early Spring. Wordsworth. EnRP; FPL; HBV-1; OAEL-2; OAEP; OBRV; PAI; PoLF
(Written in Early Spring.) GTBS; GTBS-P; TreFT; TRV
Lines Written in Her Breviary. St. Theresa of Avila, *tr. fr. Spanish by* Longfellow. AWP; EaLo; TRV
(Bookmark.) CTC; WPOW
("Let nothing disturb thee/ Nothing affright thee.") ILwL
(St. Teresa's Book-Mark.) PoEL-5; TreFT
Lines Written in Kensington Gardens. Matthew Arnold. FaBoPP; NIP
Calm Soul of All Things! [Make It Mine], *sel.* TrPWD; TRV; WGRP
Lines Written in Oregon. Vladimir Nabokov. NYBP
Lines Written in the Bay of Lerici. Shelley. OAEL-2
Lines Written in the Dog-Days. William Woty. NOEC
Lines Written in the Front of a Well-read Copy of Burns's *Songs:* To the Reader. *Unknown.* FaBoUs
Lines Written in Windsor Forest. Pope. EBEV
(Hymn Written in Windsor Forest, A.) NOEC
Lines Written near Linton, on Exmoor. Daniel Hoffman. BXAP
Lines Written near Richmond, upon Thames, at Evening. Wordworth. OBEC
Lines Written near San Francisco. Louis Simpson. CABA
Lines Written on a Seat on the Grand Canal, Dublin. Patrick Kavanagh. BIrV; CIP; CMoP; IPY
Lines Written on [*or* upon] a Window Shutter at Weston. William Cowper. LAuP; NOEC
Lines Written on Hearing the News of the Death of Napoleon. Shelley. ChER
Lines Written on November 15, 1933 by a Man Born November 14, 1881 to Another Born November 15, 1881. Clayton Hamilton. InMe
Lines Written on the Antiquity of Microbes. Strickland Gillilan. *See* On the Antiquity of Microbes.
Lines Written under the Influence of Delirium. William Cowper. *See* Lines Written during a Period of Insanity.
Lines Written upon a Window-Shutter at Weston. *See* Lines Written on a Window Shutter at Weston.
Line-up, The. Joan Swift. FiCP
Lingam and the Yoni, The. A. D. Hope. MAT; NoAM
Linger longer, Olga. Molly Fitton. POL
Linger not long. Home is not home without thee. The Wife to Her Husband. *Unknown.* HBV-1
Lingua, *sel.* Thomas Tomkis.
Gordion Knot, The. ElL
Lining Track. *Unknown.* AmFP
Link o' Day, *with music. Unknown.* TrAS
Linked to a clod, harassed, and sad. Circumstance. Thomas Bailey Aldrich. AA
Links. Ricardo Pau-Llosa. AMV-81
Links are chance, the chain is fate, The. Mathematics of Love. Michael Hamburger. NePoEA-2
Links interwoven. Indian Education. Adrian C. Louis. STE
Links of fear. The Sacrifice. Moshe Yungman, *tr. by* Marcia Falk. VWA
Linnet, The. Robert Bridges. *See* I Heard a Linnet Courting.
Linnet, The. Walter de la Mare. HBMV; LiTB; LoBV
Linnet in November, The. Francis Turner Palgrave. EBVV
Linnet in the Rocky Dells, The. Emily Brontë. *See* Song: "Linnet in the rocky dells, The."
Linnet who had lost her way, A. Tenebris Interlucentem. James Elroy Flecker. MoBrPo
Linnets. Larry Levis. LCAP
Linota Rufescens. Lyle Donaghy. OnYI
Linstead Market. *Unknown.* FSW
Lintie in a Cage. Alice V. Stuart. OxBS
Lion, The. Hilaire Belloc. MoBrPo
Lion. Mary Fullerton. PoAu-1
Lion, The. Mary Howitt. FaPON
Lion, The. Vachel Lindsay. HBMV; ShM
Lion, The. Ogden Nash. CenHV; ShM
Lion, The. Jack Prelutsky. RHPC
Lion. Kenneth Rexroth. *Fr.* A Bestiary. HoPM
Lion. William Jay Smith. RHPC
Lion. May Swenson. LiTM; SoSe
Lion, The. W. J. Turner. MoBrPo
Lion. *Unknown, tr. fr. Hottentot.* PeSA
Lion and Albert, The. Marriott Edgar. OBNV
Lion & Honeycomb. Howard Nemerov. PP
Lion and O'Reilly, The. Richard Weber. PPON
Lion and the Cub, The. John Gay. *Fr.* Fables. GN; HBV-1
Lion and the Mouse, The. Jeffreys Taylor. HBV-1; HBVY; OnMSP
Lion and the unicorn, The. Mother Goose. EvOK; HBV-1; OxBoLi; OxNR
Lion and the Wave, The. William Allingham. FM
Lion cub, of sordid mind, A. The Lion and the Cub. John Gay. GN
Lion dishonoured bids death come, The. Reversionary. Stevie Smith. FaBoEE
Lion, even when full of mud, with burrs, The. Birds. Ruth Miller. PeSA
Lion Gate. Vera Rich. PoSH
Lion has a golden mane, The. The Lion. Jack Prelutsky. RHPC
Lion-House, The. John Hall Wheelock. HBMV
Lion-hunger, tiger-leap! The Way of Cape Race. E. J. Pratt. EtS; WHW
Lion Hunts. Patricia Beer. OxBTC
Lion is a beast to fight, The. *See* Lion is the beast to fight, The.
Lion is a kingly beast, The. The Lion. Vachel Lindsay. HBMV; ShM
Lion is called the king, The. Lion. Kenneth Rexroth. *Fr.* A Bestiary. HoPM

Lion is never a lion in a royal hunt, A. Lion Hunts. Patricia Beer. OxBTC
Lion is the [*or* a] beast to fight, The. Sage Counsel. Sir Arthur Quiller-Couch. CenHV; HBV-2; HBVY; NA
Lion, Leopard, Lady. Douglas Le Pan. OBCV
Lion Named Passion, A. John Hollander. NePoEA-2
Lion of my sun, my fiery joy. The Psalm of St. Priapus. James Broughton. ErPo
Lion of St. Mark's upon the glass, The. Her Dead Brother. Robert Lowell. NePoEA
Lion of Winter, The. Shakespeare. *See* Now the Hungry Lion Roars.
Lion over the Tomb of Leonidas, The. *Unknown, tr. fr. Greek by* Walter Leaf. AWP
Lion roars at the enraging desert, The. Wallace Stevens. Notes toward a Supreme Fiction, V. MoPo; NePA
Lion, ruler over all the beasts, The. Lion. William Jay Smith. RHPC
Lion sleeps with open eyes, The. Faces from a Bestiary. X. J. Kennedy. NePoEA-2
Lion tamers wrestle with the lions in a cage, The. Apex. Nate Salsbury. InMe; WhC
Lion, the Lion, he dwells in the waste, The. The Lion. Hilaire Belloc. MoBrPo
Lion with the heat oppressed, A. The Lion and the Mouse. Jeffreys Taylor. HBV-1; HBVY; OnMSP
Lioness whelped, and the sturdy cub, The. The Eagle's Song. Richard Mansfield. HBV-2; HBVY; PAH
Lions and tigers dominate. Jungle. Mary Carter Smith. PoNe
Lion's Bride, The. Gwen Harwood. BoWoP
Lion's Cub, The. Maurice Thompson. AA
Lions in Sweden. Wallace Stevens. BiP
Lions of fire, The. Kenneth Patchen. VGW
Lions of the hill are gone, The. Deirdre's [*or* Deidre's] Lament for the Sons of Usnagh [*or* Usnach]. *Unknown, tr. by* Sir Samuel Ferguson. OnYi; SeCePo
Lions on the mountains I've drove them to their lairs, The. *Unknown.* CoSo
Lion's Skeleton, The. Charles Tennyson Turner. FM; NBM; VLP
Lions who ate the Christians on the sands of the arena, The. Sunt Leones. Stevie Smith. SBG
Lip. J. V. Cunningham. ErPo
("Lip was a man who used his head.") OBAL; PV
Lip and the Heart, The. John Quincy Adams. AA
Lip was a man who used his head. Lip. J. V. Cunningham. ErPo; OBAL; PV
Lip which had once been stolid, now moving, A. Divine Love. Michael Benedikt. AmPA; CoAP; ConAP
Lips and Eyes. Giovanni Battista Marino, *tr. fr. Italian by* Thomas Carew. OBVE
Lips and Eyes. Thomas Middleton. *See* Song: "Love for such a cherry lip."
Lips and Nose. Rodney Hall. *Fr.* The Owner of My Face. CBAP
Lips of the one I love are my perpetual pleasure, The. Hafiz, *tr. fr. Persian by* Peter Avery *and* John Heath-Stubbs. BoLoP
Lips of the Wise, The. Bible, *O.T.* Proverbs, XV: 1-5, 7-8, 15-17. TrGrPo
("Soft answer turneth away wrath, A.") BiP
Lips That Touch Liquor. George W. Young. TreFT
Lips That Touch Liquor Shall Never Touch Mine, The. Harriet A. Glazebrook. PaPo
Lips that touch wine jelly. Wine Jelly. *Unknown.* WhC
Lips Tongueless. Robert Herrick. CaPo
Liquor and Longevity. *Unknown.* FPL; WhC
Liquor don't drown. Blues. Quandra Prettyman. BOLo
Liquor, you turn us into kings. What Matter? *Gond Oral Tradition, tr. by* V. Elwin *and* S. Hivale. WTO
Lisa. Constance Carrier. SoSe
Lisbon. *Unknown.* AmFP
Lise. Rose Terry Cooke. AA
Lis'en to de Lam's, *with music. Unknown.* BoAN-1
Lisnagade. *Unknown.* WTO
Lispy Bails Out. David Barker. GP
Lissen to my story. *See* Listen to my story. . .
List, The. Michael McClure. NU
List no more the ominous din. George Darley. *Fr.* Nepenthe. OBRV
List the harp in window wailing. The Aeolian Harp. Herman Melville. AmPP; AP
List to that bird! His song—what poet pens it? The Mocking-Bird. Edna Proctor Clarke. AA
List while the poet trolls. The Rival Curates. W. S. Gilbert. CenHV; VLP
Listen. E. E. Cummings. WaaP
Listen. Jessica Hagedorn. WPOW
Listen! Lilian Moore. NTCP
Listen. Charles Patterson. NBP
Lis/ -ten/ you know what I mean. Listen. E. E. Cummings. WaaP
Listen:/ There roams, far away, by the waters of Clead. The Giraffe. Nikolai Gumileo, *tr. by* Bowra. *Fr.* The Giraffe. FaPON
Listen!/ Listen to the witch! Listen! Lilian Moore. NTCP
Listen,/ she spent her days. Death. Mildred Jeffrey. AMV-80
Listen . . ./ With faint dry sound. November Night. Adelaide Crapsey. FaPON; PAI
Listen all ye, 'tis the Feast o' St. Stephen. Feast o' St. Stephen. Ruth Sawyer. OHIP
Listen, and when thy hand this paper presses. A Letter from a Girl to Her Own Old Age. Alice Meynell. FaBoRV; GoTL; LiTB; MoBrPo; SBG; ViBoPo
Listen Children. Lucille Clifton. CNA; PoBA
Listen, children:/ Your father is dead. Lament. Edna St. Vincent Millay. DL; PoPl
"Listen, children, listen, won't you come into the night?" Who Calls. Frances Clarke Sayers. SiSoSe
Listen, for example, to the thudding of the winter stream. An Inconclusive Evening. Frances Bellerby. FaBoTw
Listen, gallants, to my words. The Commonwealth of Birds. James Shirley. GoBC
Listen, good people, and you shall hear. The Ballad of Barnaby. W. H. Auden. OBNV
Listen here, Joe. Without Benefit of Declaration. Langston Hughes. AmNP; TTY
Listen! It is the summer's self that ambles. The Good Humor Man. Phyllis McGinley. MoShBr
Listen jealous man. A Jealous Man. *Unknown, tr. by* Frank O'Connor. KiLC
Listen, lass, if you would be. Caution. *Unknown, tr. by* Louis Untermeyer. UnTE
Listen, listen! The small song bird. Song to Imogen [in Basic English.] Richard L. Greene. BXAP; WhC
Listen, lively lordings all. The Rising in the North. *Unknown.* ACP; ESPB
Listen, Lord [a Prayer]. James Weldon Johnson. BANP; BPo
Listen lordings both great and small. The Murder of Saint Thomas of Kent. *Unknown.* ACP
Listen more often. Breaths. Birago Diop, *tr. by* Anne Atik. TTY
Listen, my children, and you shall hear. Paul Revere's Ride [*or* The Midnight Ride of Paul Revere]. Longfellow. *Fr.* Tales of a Wayside Inn, Pt. I: The Landlord's Tale. BeLS; BLPA; FaBoBe; FaBV; FaPo; FaFP; FaPON; FaPoR; FPL; HBV-2; HBVY; OBAL; OBCA; OBNV; OHFP; PAH; PAL; PaPo; TreF; TrGrPo; WBLP; YaD
Listen natives of a dry place. The Old Boast. W. S. Merwin. NOBA
Listen now and ye may lere. The Burgesses of Calais. Laurence Minot. ACP
Listen! Now I have come to step over your soul. Sacred Formula to Destroy Life [*or* A Spell to Destroy Life]. *Unknown, tr. by* James Mooney. LiTA; PAI
"Listen, now, verse should be as natural." Poetry for Supper. R. S. Thomas. OxBC
Listen, Pigeon, Bend an Ear. H. W. Haenigsen. WhC
Listen. Put on Morning. W. S. Graham. FaBoTw; LiTM; MP; NMP
Listen Sally. Phone Call. Tom Crawford. AMV-81
Listen: the ancient voices hail us from the farther shore. Mayflower. Conrad Aiken. MP
Listen! The garbage pouring down the chutes. For David Shapiro. David Lehman. PoA
Listen, the hay-bells tinkle as the cart. The Holy Innocents. Robert Lowell. ConAP; InvP; MoAB; MoAmPo; NePoEA; OBCP; OxBC; SBVL
Listen to Gieseking playing a Berceuse. Berceuse. Amy Clampitt. SUW
Listen to me, as when ye heard our father. Canadian Boat Song. *Unknown, at. to* John Galt *and also to* "Christopher North." BLPA; CaP; FaBoCh; FaPoR; OBEV; OBNC; OBRV
Listen [*or* Lissen] my story, 'tis a story true. John Henry. *Unknown.* TrAS; ViBoFo
Listen to the Bird. Laya Firestone. VWA
Listen to the call of the muezzin. A Denunciation. Mahammed Abdille Hassan, *tr. fr. Somali by* B. W. Andrzejewski. WTO
Listen to the cicada's burning drone. The Cicada. H. M. Green. PoAu-1
Listen to the exhortation of the dawn! The Salutation of the Dawn. *Unknown. PoLF; TreF*
Listen to the Lyre! George Darley. *See* Lyre, The.
Listen to the Mocking Bird. Septimus Winner. BLSo, *with music*; FSW; PSoN, *with music*; TrAS, *with music*; TreFT
Listen to the People: Independence Day, 1941, *sel.* Stephen Vincent Benét. "This is Independence Day." PoSC
Listen to the story of Willie the Weeper. Willie the Weeper. *Unknown.* BeLS; BLPA; OBAL; YaD
Listen to the tale. Slim Greer. Sterling A. Brown.. BALP; BANP
Listen to the water-mill. The Lesson of the Water-Mill [*or* The Water Mill]. Sarah Doudney. BLPA; HBV-2; TreFS; WGRP

Listen to this:/ Yesterday six Vietcong came through my village. Condemnation. Thich Nhat Hanh. PPON
Listen, you drawing men. Snapshots of the Cotton South. Frank Marshall Davis. PoBA
Listen, you who know the pains of love. Epigram. Meleager, *tr. by* Peter Whigham. PeHV
Listen Zulus. Lalela Zulu. *Unknown.* PeSA
Listenen to Big Black at S. F. State. Sonia Sanchez. BPo
Listener's Guide to the Birds, A. E. B. White. NYBP
Listeners, The. Walter de la Mare. AWP; BrPo; BLPL; CMoP; CoBMV; FaPON; FaFP; HAP; HBV-2; HBVY; HeIP; HoPM; InPK; InvP; LiTB; LiTM; MoAB; MoBrPo; MoPo; MoVE; NCSH; NoAM; NOBE; NoP; OAEP; OBEV; OBMV; OBVV; OnMSP; PoPl; PoPle; PoRA; SeCeV; SoSe; TreF; TrGrPo; ViBoPo; WeW; WHA; WSC
Listen—help me! Ears. Sonja Åkesson, *tr. by* Joanna Bankier. WPOW
Listening. Alice Corbin, *after Chippewa Indian.* BPAW
Listening. Douglas Dunn. BSV
Listening. Aileen Fisher. NTCP
Listening. Hanny Michaelis, *tr. fr. Dutch by* Marjolijn de Jager. VWA
Listening. Nancy Passy. AMV-81
Listening. William Stafford. RFM
Listening Dryads hushed the woods, The. The Pewee. John Townsend Trowbridge. HBV-1
Listening for the sound. Nocturne. Pinkie Gordon Lane. BlSi
Listening, listening; it is never still. The Märchen [*or* The Märchen (Grimm's Tales)]. Randall Jarrell. CMoP; DFT
Listening-Post. Martin C. Rosner. AMV-80
Listening to a Broadcast. John Manifold. WaP
Listening to Beethoven on the Oregon Coast. Henry Carlile. Psk
Listening to Confucius. Henryk Grynberg, *tr. fr. Polish by* Isaac Komem. VWA
Listening to Foxhounds. James Dickey. InPS; LiSp
Listening to Grownups Quarreling. Ruth Whitman. NTCP
Listening to hard bop. Zimmer's Last Gig. Paul Zimmer. AMV-80
Listening to Her. Natan Zach, *tr. fr. Hebrew by* Laya Firestone. VWA
Listening to rock 'n roll. Bouzouki. Kenneth O. Hanson. GP
Listening to the man. Poem for Otis Redding. Joyce Carol Thomas. CNA
Listening to the music. Listening. Hanny Michaelis, *tr. by* Marjolijn de Jager. VWA
Listeth, lordes, in good entent. Sir Thopas. [*or* The Tale of Sir Thopas]. Chaucer. *Fr.* The Canterbury Tales. BXAP; Par
Listless beauty of the hour, The. History. D. H. Lawrence. BrPo
Listless he eyes the palisades. In the Prison Pen. Herman Melville. PoEL-5; TAP
Liszt E. C. Bentley. *Fr.* Clerihews. UnS
Litanie, The: "Father of heaven, and him, by whom." John Donne. PoEL-2
Sels.
"Father of heaven, and Him, by whom." NOCV
"From being anxious, or secure." OxBoCh
Litanies of Julia Pastrana (1832-1860), The. Thomas W. Shapcott. CBAP
Litany, A: "Drop, drop, slow tears." Phineas Fletcher. *See* Hymn: "Drop, drop, slow tears."
Litany, The: "Father of heaven, and Him, by whom." John Donne. *See* Litanie, The: "Father of heaven. . ."
Litany, The: "From a ruler that's a curse." Charles Cotton. OBSV
Litany, The: "In the hour of my distress." Robert Herrick. *See* His Litany to the Holy Spirit.
Litany, A: "Ring out your bells, let mourning shows be spread." Sir Philip Sidney. *See* Ring Out Your Bells.
Litany: "When the sun rises on another day." Charles Angoff. TrPWD
Litany at Atlanta, A. W. E. B. Du Bois. *See* Litany of Atlanta.
Litany for Dictatorships. Stephen Vincent Benét. OxBA
Litany for Halloween. *Unknown, tr. fr. Cornish.* SiSoSe; SoPo
("From ghoulies and ghosties.") OFD; ShM; WSC
(Ghoulies and Ghosties.) PoSC
(Things That Go Bump in the Night.) NTCP
Litany for Latter-Day Mystics, A. Cale Young Rice. WGRP
Litany for Old Age, A. Una W. Harsen. TrPWD
Litany for Peace. Leslie Savage Clark. PGD
Litany in Time of Plague, A. Thomas Nashe. *See* Adieu, Farewell Earth's Bliss.
Litany of [*or* at] Atlanta, A. W. E. B. Du Bois. BANP; CDC; PoNe
Litany of Sleep, *sel.* Tristan Corbière, *tr. fr. French by* Christopher Pilling.
"You who snore with your sleeping wife so near." OBVE
Litany of the Dark People, The. Countee Cullen. EaLo; TrPWD
Litany of the Heroes, *sel.* Vachel Lindsay.
Lincoln. OHIP
Litany of the Rooms of the Dead. Franz Werfel, *tr. fr. German by* Edith Abercrombie Snow. TrJP
Litany to Our Lady. Caryll Houselander. ISi
Litany to Satan. Baudelaire, *tr. fr. French by* James Elroy Flecker. AWP; SyP
Litany to the Holy Spirit. Robert Herrick. *See* His Litany to the Holy Spirit.
Litel wot it any mon. An Unfortunate Lover. *Unknown.* OxBM
Literary Criticism. Myles Na Gopaleen. DBV
Literary Dinner, A. Vladimir Nabokov. FiBHP; OBAL
Literary Importation. Philip Freneau. TAP
Literary Landscape with Dove and Poet. Phyllis McGinley. NePoAm-2
Literary Life in the Golden West. Philip Whalen. NAs
Literary Love. Harry Kemp. HBMV
Literary Squabble, A. James Robinson Planché. CenHV
Literary Zodiac. R. A. Piddington. PV
Lithe and listen, gentlemen. Holiday. John Davidson. OBVV
Lithe and long as the serpent train. The Grape-Vine Swing. William Gilmore Simms. HBV-1
Litle black bull kem down de medder, De. *See* Little black bull came down the meadow, The.
Lit'le David Play on Yo' Harp. *Unknown.* *See* Little David.
Littered around Peking, Choukoutien. Peking Man, Raining. Katharine Auchincloss Lorr. SUW
Little. Dorothy Aldis. FaPON; NTCP; SUS; TiPo
Little Ah Sid, *with music.* *Unknown.* AS
Little Air. Stéphane Mallarmé, *tr. fr. French by* Roger Fry. PoPl; SyP
Little Alabama Coon. Hattie Starr. AA
Little Alexander's dead. Obituary. "Max Adeler." DTC
Little and Great. Charles Mackay. HBV-2; HBVY; PoLF
Little anna brown anna. Anna. Joe Johnson. CNA
Little Annie Rooney. Michael Nolan. FSN, *with music*; TreF
Little baby, lay your head. Good-Night. Jane Taylor. HBV-1; HBVY
Little Ball of Yarn. *Unknown.* FSW
Little Beach-Bird, The. Richard Henry Dana. AA; EtS; HBV-1
Little bee returns with evening's gloom, The. A Summer Night in the Beehive. Charles Tennyson Turner. FM
Little Bell. Thomas Westwood. GN; HBV-1
Little Benny sat one evening. Misplaced Sympathy. Charles Follen Adams. OBAL
Little Bessie. *Unknown.* AmFP
Little betrothed has washed her linen, The. Whiteness. Isobel Hume. HBMV
Little Betty Blue. Mother Goose. OxNR
Little Betty Pringle she had a pig. Mother Goose. OxNR
Little Big Horn. Ernest McGaffey. PAH
Little Billee. Thackeray. CenHV; EtS; FaBoCh; FaBoCo; HBV-2; HBVY; MOS; NA; NOBL; PoPle; ShM; TreFS
(Three Sailors, The.) OxBB
Little Billy. *Unknown.* GBP
Little Billy Breek. *Unknown.* OxNR
Little Birches. Effie Lee Newsome. PoNe
Little Bird, The. Walter de la Mare. NAs
Little Bird, A. Aileen Fisher. SoPo
Little Bird, The. *Unknown, tr. by* Rolf Italiaander. PBA
Little bird flew through the dell, A. Autumn Song. Johann Ludwig Tieck, *tr. by* James Clarence Mangan. AWP
Little Bird, Go through My Window, *with music.* *Unknown.* OuSiCo
Little Bird I Am, A. Mme. Guyon, *tr. fr. French by* T. C. Upham. WGRP
Little bird, little bird, go through my window. Little Bird, Go through My Window. *Unknown.* OuSiCo
Little bird of paradise. *Unknown.* OxNR
Little Birdie. *Unknown.* FSW
Little Birds. "Lewis Carroll." *Fr.* Sylvie and Bruno Concluded. FaBoNo; WhC
Little Birds Are Playing, *sel.* OxBoLi
Little Birds. Jacob Sternberg, *tr. fr. Yiddish by* Joseph Leftwich. TrJP
Little Birds, The. *Unknown.* NTCP
Little Birds are dining. Little Birds. "Lewis Carroll." *Fr.* Sylvie and Bruno Concluded. FaBoNo; WhC
Little Birds Are Playing. "Lewis Carroll." *Fr.* Sylvie and Bruno Concluded. OxBoLi
Little birds in a row. Little Birds. Jacob Sternberg, *tr. by* Joseph Leftwich. TrJP
Little birds sit in their nest and beg, The. The Little Birds. *Unknown.* NTCP
Little birds sleep sweetly. Evening Song. Cecil Frances Alexander. OHIP
Little Bits of Soft-boiled Egg. Fay Maschler. RHPC
Little Black Boy, The. Blake. *Fr.* Songs of Innocence. AWP; BiP; CABA; CH; EnRP; HBV-1; HeIP; InPK; LAuP; NOEC; NoP; OAEL-2; OAEP; OBEC; OBEV; OBNC; OxBChV; OxBoCh; PoEL-4; PoNe; SeCeV; TreFS; TrGrPo
Little Black boy. Nigger. Frank Horne. BANP; CDC
Little Black Bug. Margaret Wise Brown. FaPON; NTCP

Little [*or* Litle] black bull came down the meadow, The [*or* kem down de medder, De]. Hoosen Johnny. *Unknown.* AS; FaPON; FSW
Little Black Dog, The. Elizabeth Gardner Reynolds. PoLF
Little black dog ran round the house, The. *Unknown.* OxNR
Little Black Man with a Rose in His Hat. Audrey Wurdemann. YaD
Little Black Rose, The. Aubrey Thomas De Vere. ACP; BIrV; OnYI
Little Black Sheep, The. Paul Laurence Dunbar. WBLP
Little black thing among the snow, A. The Chimney Sweeper. Blake. *Fr.* Songs of Experience. CABA; LAuP; NOEC; OAEL-2; PPoe; PPP; SaC; TEP
Little Black Train, The. *Unknown.* AmFP; OuSiCo, *with music*
Little Black-eyed Rebel, The. Will Carleton. FaPON; PAH
Little blessed Earth that turns, The. O Earth, Turn! George Johnston. MoCV
Little blind girl wandering, A. The Brook. William Wilberforce Lord. AA
Little Blue Ben, who lives in the glen. *Unknown.* OxNR
Little Blue Betty lived in a den. *Unknown.* OxNR
Little Blue Shoes. Kate Greenaway. TiPo
Little boat at anchor, The. Fourth of July Night. Carl Sandburg. OFD
Little Boats of Britain, The. Sara E. Carsley. CaP
Little Bob Robin. Mother Goose. OxNR
Little body I would hold. Unborn. Irene Rutherford McLeod. HBMV
Little Bonny. *Unknown. See* Goodbye, Little Bonnie, Goodbye.
Little Bo-Peep. Frederick Winsor. *Fr.* The Space Child's Mother Goose. QQQ
Little Bo-Peep has lost her sheep. Mother Goose. FaBoBe; HBV-1; HBVY; OxNR; SoPo; SpRo; TiPo
Little bo-peepals. Rhyme for Botanical Baby. Joseph Cook. *Fr.* Boston Nursery Rhymes. InMe; QQQ; SpRo
Little Bow to Books on How To, A. Irwin Edman. WhC
Little Boxes. Malvina Reynolds. FSW
Little boy, The. Junior Addict. Langston Hughes. BPo; CNA
Little Boy and the Old Man, The. Shel Silverstein. RHPC
Little Boy Blue. Eugene Field. AA; BeLs; FaFP; FaPON; FPL; HBV-1; HBVY; OBAL; OBCA; OHFP; PaPo; PoLF; SoSe; TreF
Little Boy Blue. John Crowe Ransom. LiTM; TwAmPo
Little Boy Blue. *Unknown.* BluL
Little Boy Blue, come blow up your horn. Mother Goose. FaBoBe; FaFP; HBV-1; HBVY; OxNR; SoPo; TiPo
Little Boy Found, The. Blake. *Fr.* Songs of Innocence. EnRP; LAuP; NoP
Little Boy in the Morning, A. Francis Ledwidge. OnYI
Little boy is fishing, The. The Fisherman. David McCord. PDV; TiPo
Little boy kneels at the foot of the bed. Vespers. A. A. Milne. OxBChV; SpRo
Little boy, laid sick and low, A. The Dying Child's Request. Hannah F. Gould. OBCA
Little boy, little boy, where wast thou born? Lancashire Born. *Unknown.* GBP
Little Boy Lost, The ("Father, father, where are you going"). Blake. *Fr.* Songs of Innocence. EnRP; LAuP; NoP
Little Boy Lost, A ("Nought loves another as itself"). Blake. *Fr.* Songs of Experience. EnRP; OAEP; PAI; ViBoPo
"Little Boy Lost, A." Jerome Rothenberg. CoPo
Little Boy Lost, The. Stevie Smith. FaBoTw
Little boy lost in the lonely fen, The. The Little Boy Found. Blake. *Fr.* Songs of Innocence. EnRP; LAuP; NoP
Little Boy of heavenly birth, A. Out of Bounds. John Banister Tabb. TRV
Little boy once played so loud, A. Extremes. James Whitcomb Riley. FaPON; HBVY
Little Boy, to show his might and power, The. The Metamorphosis. Sir John Suckling. CaPo; FaBoEE
Little Boy to the Locomotive, The. Benjamin R. C. Low. HBMV
Little Boy was set to keep, A. The Boy and the Wolf. John Hookham Frere. HBV-1; HBVY
Little boy who would not say "Thank you" and "If you please," The. *Unknown.* FaBoUs
Little boys and little maidens. Little Catkins. Alexander Blok, *tr. by* Babette Deutsch. EaLo; OFD
Little Boys of Texas. Robert P. Tristram Coffin. ShM
Little Boy's Vain Regret, A. Edith M. Thomas. AA
Little Brass Wagon. *Unknown.* FSW
Little Breeches. John Hay. AA; BeLS; FaBoBe; HBV-2; PaPo; TreFS
Little Britain. *Unknown.* NOEC
Little Brother, The. James Reeves. DTC; OxBTC
Little Brother of the Rich, A. Edward Sanford Martin. AA; HBV-1
Little Brother Poem, The. Naomi Shihab Nye. Str
Little Brother's Secret. Katherine Mansfield. FaPON; NAs; TiPo
Little Brown Baby. Paul Laurence Dunbar. BANP; NoP; PoNe
Little brown boy. Poem. Helene Johnson. AmNP; BANP; CDC; PoBA
Little brown brother, oh! little brown brother. Baby Seed Song. Edith Nesbit. FaPON; HBV-1; HBVY
Little Brown Bulls, The. *Unknown.* AmFP; BaBo; OuSiCo, *with music*
Little Brown Church in the Vale. William S. Pitts. TreFT
Little Brown Dog. *Unknown.* FSW
Little Brown Jug. *At. to* Joseph E. Winner. BLSo, *with music*; FaFP; FSW; OBAL; PSoN, *with music*; TrAS, *with music*; TreF; YaD
Little brown squirrel hops in the corn, The. The Rejected "National Hymns." "Orpheus C. Kerr." InMe; OBAL
Little bunches of/ grass pretend they are bushes. Stories from Kansas. William Stafford. RFM
Little buoy said, A, "Mother, deer." A Misspelled Tail. Elizabeth T. Corbett. OBCA
Little Busy Bee. Isaac Watts. *See* How Doth the Little Busy Bee.
Little Buttercup. W. S. Gilbert. *Fr.* H. M. S. Pinafore. TreFS
Little Cabin, A. Charles Bertram Johnson. BANP
Little Candle. Carl Sandburg. GoYe
Little Car, The. Guillaume Apollinaire, *tr. fr. French by* Ron Padgett *and others.* SOTW
Little cares that fretted me, The. Out in the Fields with God [*or* A Song from Sylvan]. *At. to* Elizabeth Barrett Browning *and to* Louise Imogen Guiney. BLPA; BLRP; HBV-1; HBVY; TreFS; TRV; WBLP; WGRP
Little Carol of the Virgin, A. Lope de Vega, *tr. fr. Spanish by* Denise Levertov. PChr
Little Cart, The. Ch'en Tzu-lung, *tr. fr. Chinese by* Arthur Waley. LoBV
Little Cat Angel, The. Leontine Stanfield. BLPA
Little caterpillar creeps, The. Cocoon. David McCord. OBCA
Little Catkins. Alexander Blok, *tr. fr. Russian by* Babette Deutsch. EaLo; OFD
Little Charlie Chipmunk. Helen Cowles LeCron. FaPON; SoPo; TiPo
Little Cheat, A. *Malay Oral Tradition, tr. by* R. J. Wilkinson *and* R. O. Winstedt. WTO
Little child, a limber elf, A. Samuel Taylor Coleridge. *Fr.* Christabel, Pt. II. LoBV; ViBoPo
Little Child, The. Albert Bigelow Paine. AA
Little child, A. Puer Aeternus. Kathleen Raine. NYBP
Little child, I counsel you that ye. Customs Change. *Unknown.* OxBChV
Little child is kneeling by his mother's chair, A. Lost after All. Charlie D. Tillman. PeD
Little children here ye may lere. Manners at Table When Away from Home. *Unknown.* OxBChV
Little children, never give. Kindness to Animals. *Unknown.* FaBoUs; HBV-1; HBVY; SoPo
Little Chisel, The. N. P. Van Wyk Louw, *tr. fr. Afrikaans by* Jack Cope *and* Uys Krige. PeSA
Little City. Robert Horan. CrMA; NePA
Little Clan, The. F. R. Higgins. OBMV
Little Clotilda. *Unknown.* RHPC
Little Cock Robin. *Unknown.* PBBP
Little cock sparrow sat on a green tree, A. Mother Goose. OxNR
Little colt, A—broncho, loaned to the farm. The Broncho That Would Not Be Broken. Vachel Lindsay. BPAW; NePA; PH; RoGo
Little Commodore, The. J. C. Squire. HBMV
(How They Do It: Sir Henry Newbolt.) InMe
Little Cosmic Dust Poem. John Haines. SUW
Little cottage stood alone, the pride, The. The Old Cottagers. John Clare. OBRV
Little cousin is dead, by foul subtraction, The. Dead Boy. John Crowe Ransom. CMoP; FaBoMo; LiTA; MP; NoAM; NoP; OxBA; TwCP
Little cousins/ play on your. Victor Hernandez Cruz. *Fr.* Cities #8. BOLo
Little cowboy, what have you heard. The Lepracaun, or Fairy Shoemaker. William Allingham. OnYI
Little Cradle Rocks Tonight in Glory, The. *Unknown.* AmFP
Little Creature, The. Walter de la Mare. EvOK
Little cross, A,/ To tell my loss. Robin's Cross. George Darley. OnYI
Little Dancers, The. Laurence Binyon. CH; MoBrPo; MoVE; OBVV; OxBTC
(Little Dancers, The: A London Vision.) OBVV
Little Dandelion. Helen Barron Bostwick. HBV-1; HBVY
Little Dandelion, The. Lula Lowe Weeden. CDC
Little dapper man but with shiny elbows, A. Louis MacNeice. *Fr.* The Kingdom. ChMP
Little dark Cape girl why is it you roam. Wordspinning. Olga Kirsch, *tr. by* Jack Cope. PeSA
Little Dark Rose, The. *Unknown, tr. fr. Late Middle Irish by* Padraic Pearse. OnYI
Little David. *Unknown.* FSW; TrAS, *with music*
(Lit'le David, Play on Yo' Harp, *with music.*) BoAN-1
Little Derwent's Breakfast, *sel. Unknown.*
Little Gentleman, The. HBV-1; HBVY
Little Dicky Dilver. *Unknown.* OxNR

Little Dirge. Jean Starr Untermeyer. HBMV
Little Dog-Angel, A. Norah M. Holland. PoLF
Little Dog under the Wagon, The. *Unknown.* PoLF
Little Doll, The. Charles Kingsley. *See* Lost Doll, The.
Little Donkey, The. Francis Jammes, *tr. fr. French by* Lloyd Alexander. PChr
Little Donkey Close Your Eyes ("Little donkey on the hill.") Margaret Wise Brown. PDV
Little Dove, The. *Unknown.* AmFP
Little dreams of maidenhood, The. The Wife. Theodosia Garrison. HBV-1
Little drops of water. Little Things. Julia A. Fletcher Carney, *wr. at to* E. C. Brewer *and to* Frances S. Osgood. BLPA; BLPL; FaBoBe; FaFP; FaPON; HBV-1; HBVY; OxBChV; TreF
Little Drummer, The. Richard Henry Stoddard. AmFP; PAH
Little Duck, The. Joso, *tr. fr. Japanese by* Harold G. Henderson. SoPo
Little Dunkeld. *Unknown.* GBP
Little Dutch Garden, A. Harriet Whitney Durbin. AA
Little elbow leans upon your knee, A. Tired Mothers. May Riley Smith. HBV-1
Little Elegy. X. J. Kennedy. CoAP; ConAP; ELU; GoJo; HoPM; NCSH
Little elephant was crying, The. Cradle Song of the Elephants. Adriano del Valle, *tr. by* Alida Malkus. FaPON
Little Elf, The. John Kendrick Bangs. AA; FaBoBe; HBV-1; HBVY; NTCP; OBCA
(Little Elfman, The.) OnUR; PDV; SoPo; TiPo
Little Ellie sits alone. Romance of the Swan's Nest. Elizabeth Barrett Browning. GN
Little Epithalamium. Chester Kallman. CrMA
Little Exercise [at 4. A.M.]. Elizabeth Bishop. CoAP; CrMA; MoAB; MoAmPo; NCSH; NYBP; UnPo
Little face there was, A. In Rama. George Alfred Townsend. AA
Little Factory Girl to a More Fortunate Playmate, The. *Unknown.* SaC
Little fairy comes at night, A. Queen Mab. Thomas Hood. HBV-1; HBVY
Little fairy snowflakes. Santa Claus. *Unknown.* SoPo
Little Falls. Robert Hogg. MoCV
Little Family, The. *Unknown.* BaBo
Little Fan. James Reeves. SO
Little Farm, The; or, The Weary Ploughman. *Unknown.* CoMu
Little Father Poem. Marvin Bell. LCAP
Little Feet. Elizabeth Akers Allen. HBV-1
Little feet too young and soft to walk. The Stranger's Grave. Emily Lawless. OnYI
Little fellow, you're amusing. Song of the Ogres. W. H. Auden. RHPC
Little Fire in the Woods, The. Hayden Carruth. DiL
Little Fish. D. H. Lawrence. OxBTC; SOTW
Little fish swim in the river, big fish swim in the sea. I Don't Let the Girls Worry My Mind. *Unknown.* AmFP
Little fish that in the stream doth fleet, The. To Alexander Neville. Barnabe Googe. EnRePo; NoP
Little Fish That Would Not Do as It Was Bid, The. Jane *and* Ann Taylor. OHIP
Little fishes in a brook. *Unknown.* OxNR
Little flower grew in a lonely vale, A. To Mrs. Ann Flaxman. Blake. OBRV
Little flowers came through the ground, The. At Easter Time. Laura E. Richards. OHIP
Little Fly/ Thy summers play. The Fly. Blake. *Fr.* Songs of Experience. FM; LAuP; TrGrPo
Little fogs were gathered in every hollow. The Country Wedding (A Fiddler's Story). Thomas Hardy. UnPo
Little Fox, The. Marion Edey *and* Dorothy Grider. TiPo
Little French Lawyer, The, *sel.* John Fletcher.
Song in the Wood. EIL
Little Garaine. Sir Gilbert Parker. FaPON
"Little garden little Jowett made, A." *Unknown, sometimes at. to* Richard Porson. WhC
Little gate was reached at last, The. Auf Wiedersehen. James Russell Lowell. AA; HBV-1
Little General Monk. *Unknown.* OxNR
Little General, The. Edwin Muir. BSV
Little Gentleman, The. *Unknown.* *Fr.* Little Derwent's Breakfast. HBV-1; HBVY
Little Ghost, The. Katharine Tynan. HBV-1
Little Ghosts, The. Thomas S. Jones, Jr. HBV-1
Little Gidding. T. S. Eliot. *Fr.* Four Quartets. FaBoEn; FaBoMo; FaBoTw; GTBS-P; NoAM; NOBA; NOBE; OAEL-2; OAEP; OxBTC; PrIm; SeCeV; TAP
"We shall not cease from exploration," *sel.* ImOP
Little Giffen. Francis Orray Ticknor. GOA; HBV-2; PAH; TreFS
Little Girl, A. Charles Angoff. GoYe
Little Girl, The. Nicholas Moore. ErPo; NeBP
Little girl, A/ Had wandered in the night. John W. Lynch. A Woman Wrapped in Silence, V. ISi
Little Girl, Be Careful What You Say. Carl Sandburg. GoYe
Little girl called Silé Javotte. Christmas 1970. Spike Milligan. OBCP
Little Girl Cat. Hy Sibiloff. TwAmPo
Little girl crouches with her little brother, A. The Journey to the Insane Asylum. Alfred Lichtenstein, *tr. by* Mary Zilzer. VWA
Little girl dressed, The. Celebration. Ray A. Young Bear. CDW
Little girl I'd known, The. Flora. Ray Fraser. NeAC
Little girl, little girl,/ Where have you been? Mother Goose. OxNR
Little girl marched around her Christmas tree, A. Ogden Nash. *Fr.* The New Nutcracker Suite. PChr
Little Girl, My Stringbean, My Lovely Woman. Anne Sexton. NYBP
Little Girl on Her Way to School, A. James Wright. GLGT
Little girl running in the street. The Lizards of La Brea. Marc De Baca. AMV-80
Little Girl That Lost a Finger, The. Gabriela Mistral, *tr. fr. Spanish by* Muna Lee. FaPON
Little Girl with Bands on Her Teeth, The. Genevieve Taggard. VGW
Little girl with scarlet enameled fingernails, A. Melodic Trains. John Ashbery. NoP
Little girl won't eat her sandwich, The. Blasting from Heaven. Philip Levine. CoAP
Little girls/ on the sidewalk. Chinatown Games. Wing Tek Lum. BrSi
Little girls—/ You are gay. Day's End. Lesbia Harford. PoAu-1
Little Girl's Dream World, A. Della Burt. BlSi
Little girls' frocks are frilly, The. Ballroom Dancing Class. Phyllis McGinley. MoShBr
Little girls smearing. Schoolyard in April. Kenneth Koch. PoA
Little goat, The. April. Yvor Winters. ELU; RFM
Little gold in law will make, A. Isabella Whitney. *Fr.* A Sweet Nosegay, or Pleasant Posy. WPE
Little Golden Ring, The, *with music.* *Unknown.* ShS
Little granite church upholds, The. Sheepstor. L. A. G. Strong. HBMV
Little gray cat was walking prettily, The. The Little White Cat. *Unknown, tr. by* Mrs. Costello of Tuam. OnYI
Little Gray Pussy. *Unknown.* *See* Catkin.
Little Gray Songs from St. Joseph's, *sels.* Grace Fallow Norton. HBV-2
"My little soul I never saw," XLVII.
"With cassock black, baret and book," XXX.
Little Green Blackbird, The. Kenneth Patchen. PoCh
Little Green Orchard, The. Walter de la Mare. EvOK
Little grey hill-glade, close-turfed, withdrawn, A. Marsyas. Sir Charles G. D. Roberts. PeCV
Little Guinever. Annie Fields. AA
Little Gustava. Celia Thaxter. FaPON; HBV-1; HBVY
"Little Haly! Little Haly!" cheeps the robin in the tree. On the Death of Little Mahala Ashcraft. James Whitcomb Riley. AA
Little hand is knocking at my heart, A. The Return. Arthur Symons. *Fr.* Amor Triumphans. BrPo; HBMV
Little Hands. Laurence Binyon. HBV-1
Little hedgerow birds, The. An Old Man [*or* Old Man Travelling]. Wordsworth. FaBoCh; OBWP
Little Herdboy, sitting there. The Pilgrim and the Herdboy. Robert Buchanan. OBVV
Little Hiawatha, The. Longfellow. *Fr.* The Song of Hiawatha. OnUR
Little hill climbs up to the village and puts its green hands, The. Kenneth Patchen. *Fr.* The Hunted City. NaP
Little hope, a lot of faith, A. Worry. George W. Swarberg. STF
Little Horned Toad. *Unknown, tr. fr. Navajo by* Hilda Faunce Wetherill. FaPON
Little House, The. Pierre Louÿs, *tr. fr. French by* Horace M. Brown. *Fr.* The Songs of Bilitis. UnTE
Little house, a quiet wife, A. The Wish. Rowland Watkyns. CavP
Little House in Lithuania, The. Samuel Marshak, *tr. fr. Russian by* Daniel Weissbort. VWA
Little house there stood within a glen, A. A Deathbed. John Hawthorn. *Fr.* The Journey and Observations of a Countryman. NOEC
Little Hunchback, The. James Whitcomb Riley. PeD
Little Hunger. Richard Murphy. BIrV
Little Hymn to Mary, A. *Unknown.* MeEL
Little I ask; my wants are few. Contentment. Oliver Wendell Holmes. *Fr.* The Autocrat of the Breakfast Table, *ch.* 11. AmPP; AP; HBV-1; InMe; OxBA; TreF
Little, I ween, did Mary guess. His Mother's Joy. John White Chadwick. AA
Little Indian, Sioux or Crow. Foreign Children. Robert Louis Stevenson. GoJo
Little inmate, full of mirth. The Cricket. Vincent Bourne, *tr. by* William Cowper. HBV-1; HBVY; PoLF
Little Ivory Figures Pulled with String. Amy Lowell. TwAmPo; ViBoPo

Little Jack Dandy-prat. *Unknown.* OxNR
Little Jack Frost. *Unknown.* SoPo
Little Jack Horner sat in the corner. Mother Goose. FaBoBe; FaFP; HBV-1; HBVY; OxNR (*orig. and parody*); SoPo; SoSe
Little Jack of Christ, The. St. Stephen's Word. Rayner Heppenstall. ChMP
Little Jack Sprat/ Once had a pig. *Unknown.* OxNR
Little Jenny Wren. *Unknown.* PoPle
Little Jesus. Francis Thompson. *See* Ex Ore Infantium.
Little Jesus came to town, The. A Christmas Folk-Song. Lizette Woodworth Reese. FaPON; HBMV; HBVY; OBCA; OHIP; OnMSP; SUS; TrCP
Little Jesus, wast Thou shy. Ex Ore Infantium [*or* A Child's Prayer *or* Little Jesus]. Francis Thompson. FaBV; HBV-1; HBVY; OBVV; OHIP; OxBChV; PeD; SUS; TreFS; TRV
Little Jew lived in a little straw hut, A. Biography. A. M. Klein. TrJP
Little Jim. Edward Farmer. PaPo
Little joe gould has lost his teeth and doesn't know where. E. E. Cummings. NoAM
Little Joe, the Wrangler, *sl. diff. vers.* *Unknown, at. to* N. Howard Thorp. BPAW; CoSo, *with music*; FSW
Little John a Begging. *Unknown.* ESPB (A *and* B *vers.*)
Little John Bottlejohn. Laura E. Richards. PDV
Little John Jiggy Jag. *Unknown.* OxNR
Little John Nobody. *Unknown.* OxBoLi
Little Johnny Mine, The. Daisy L. Detrick. PoOW
Little Johnny Morgan. *See* Little Shon a Morgan. . .
Little Johnny-jump-up said. Wise Johnny. Edwina Fallis. SiSoSe; SUS; TiPo
Little Johnny's Confession. Brian Patten. CAD
Little Jumping Girls, The. Kate Greenaway. FaPON
("Jump—jump—jump.") TiPo
Little Katy. *Unknown.* ShM
Little King Pippin. Mother Goose. OxNR
Little Kingdom I Possess, A. Louisa May Alcott. AH, *with music*
Little Kings and Queens of May. For Good Luck. Juliana Horatia Ewing. FaPON
Little Kittens, The. Eliza Lee Follen. *See* Where Are You Going.
Little Knight in Green, The. Katharine Lee Bates. AA
Little lad, little lad. *Unknown.* OxNR
Little Lady, The. Russell Edson. GP
Little lady lairdie, The. *Unknown.* OxNR
Little lady of my heart! Ad Domnulam Suam. Ernest Dowson. HBV-1
Little Lady Wren. Tom Robinson. FaPON; TiPo
Little lamb, who made thee? The Lamb. Blake. *Fr.* Songs of Innocence. BLPL; CABA; CH; EaLo; EBCP; EnRP; FaBoBe; FaBoCh; FaPON; GoJo; HBV-1; HeIP; LAuP; LiTB; LoBV; NIP; NOEC; NoP; OAEL-2; OAEP; OBEC; OxBChV; OxBoCh; PoPl; SBVL; SeCeV; SoSe; SUS; TEP; TrCP; TreF; TrGrPo; TRV; UnPo; WGRP; WHA. *See also* Dost thou know who made thee?
Little lame tailor, The. The Starling. Robert Buchanan. FM
Little lamps of the dusk. Fireflies. Carolyn Hall. FaPON; HBMV; HBVY
Little Land, The. Robert Louis Stevenson. SoPo
Little Learning, A. Pope. *Fr.* An Essay on Criticism, Pt. II. ChTr; LiTB; NOBE; OBEC; SeCePo
(Alps on Alps.) FaFP
("Little learning is a dangerous thing, A.") FPL; HAP; HoPM; PoLF; TreF; TrGrPo
Little less returned for him each spring, A. Anglais Mort a Florence. Wallace Stevens. AP
Little Libbie. Julia A. Moore. OBAL; PeD
Little light is going by, A. Firefly. Elizabeth Madox Roberts. GoJo; NTCP; PDV; SUS; TiPo
Little Litany to St. Francis, A. Philip Murray. NePoAm
Little lonely child am I, A. The Moon-Child. "Fiona Macleod." CH; EtS
Little lonely girl, A. Xmas Time. Walta Karsner. ELU
Little Lost Child, The. Edward B. Marks. TreFS
Little Lost Pup. Arthur Guiterman. TreFS
Little Lough, The. John Hewitt. NeIP
Little Love-God, The. Meleager, *tr. fr. Greek by* Walter Headlam. AWP
Little Lover. Leonora Speyer. HBMV
Little Lucy Lavender,/ Aged just three. Lucy Lavender. Ivy O. Eastwick. SiSoSe
Little Lullaby. Irving Feldman. NYBP
Little lute, when I am gone. Richard Corbet. FaBoEE
Little Lyric (of Great Importance). Langston Hughes. OBAL
Little madness in the spring, A. Emily Dickinson. AP; TAP
Little Maggie. *Unknown.* FSW
Little Maid, The. Anna Maria Wells. OBCA
Little maid of Astrakan, A. The Divan. Richard Henry Stoddard. AA
Little maid, pretty maid,/ Whither goest thou? Mother Goose. OxNR
Little maiden climbed [on] an old man's knee, A. After the Ball [Is Over]. Charles Kassell Harris. BLSo; FSN; FSW; TreF
Little maiden, dost thou pine. Valentine to a Little Girl. Cardinal Newman. GoBC
Little man in coal pit. Putting On Nightgown. *Unknown.* OxNR
Little Man That Had a Little Gun, The. "Lewis Carroll." *See* Manlet, The.
Little Man Who Wasn't There, The. Hughes Mearns. FaFP; FaPON; SoPo
(Antigonish.) BLPL; InMe; PoLF; WhC
(Case, A.) FaBoCo
(I Met a Man.) OnUR
(Little Man, The.) RHPC
Little Marble Boy. James Wright. EyDe
Little Marg'et sitting in her high hall door. Fair Margaret and Sweet William. *Unknown.* AmFP
Little marsh-plant, yellow green, A. The Sundew. Swinburne. ELP; NoP; OBNC; VLP
Little Mary Bell had a fairy in a nut. Long John Brown and Little Mary Bell. Blake. InPK
Little Mary Cassidy. Francis A. Fahy. HBV-1
Little masters, hat in hand. Clover. John Banister Tabb. AA
Little Milliner, The. Robert Buchanan. BeLS
Little Miss and Her Parrot. John Marchant. OxBChV
Little Miss Muffet, *parody.* *Unknown.* BXAP; FaBoPa
Little Miss Muffet/ Crouched on a tuffet. Paul Dehn. *Fr.* Rhymes for a Modern Nursery. FiBHP; ShM
Little Miss Muffet/ Sat on a tuffet. Mother Goose. FaBoBe; FaFP; HBV-1; HBVY; OxNR; SoPo; TiPo
Little Miss Muffet discovered a tuffet. The Embarrassing Episode of Little Miss Muffet. Guy Wetmore Carryl. FaPON; OBCA; OnMSP
Little Miss Pitt. William Wise. TiPo
Little Mohee [*or* Mohea], The. *Unknown.* AmFP; AmSS, *with music*; BaBo; FSW
Little More about the Brothers and Sisters, A. Sharon Scott. JB
Little more tired at the close of the Day, A. Growing Old [*or* Growing Older]. Rollin J. Wells. BLPA; TreFT; WBLP
Little more toward the light, A. Growing Gray. Austin Dobson. HBV-1
Little Morning Music, A. Delmore Schwartz. BoNaP; NYBP
Little Moses. *Unknown.* FSW
Little moths are creeping, The. Interior. Padraic Colum. MoBrPo
Little mountain spring I found, A. The Spring. Rose Fyleman. FaPON
Little mouse:/ Are you. Race Prejudice. Alfred Kreymborg. ELU
Little Mouse in gray velvet. Mouse. Hilda Conkling. SoPo; TiPo
Little Musgrave and Lady Barnard, *diff. versions.* *Unknown.* AmFP; ErPo; ESPB (A *and* B *vers.*); FaBoBa; InvP; OBET; ViBoFo
(Little Mousgrove and the Lady Barnet.) OxBB
Little mushroom table spread, A. Robert Herrick. *Fr.* Oberon's Feast. OAEP; ViBoPo
Little Nancy [*or* Nanny] Etticoat. Mother Goose. ChTr; HBV-1; HBVY; NTCP; OxNR; SoPo; TiPo
Little nearer, this time, A. After the Second Operation. Patricia Goedicke. TAP
Little Nellie Cassidy has got a place in town. In Service. Winifred M. Letts. HBMV
Little new neighbor, have you come to be. Welcome. Rose Waldo. SoPo
Little newt, The. The Newt. David McCord. TiPo
Little Ode. Paul Goodman. PoA
Little Ode for X. Maura Stanton. MAYP
Little Old Lady in Lavender Silk, The. Dorothy Parker. InMe; YaD
Little old man of Derby, A. *Unknown.* OxNR
Little old man of the sea, A. The Ingenious Little Old Man. John Bennett. FaPON
Little old shack. Home. Robert V. Carr. BPAW
Little Old Sod Shanty. *Unknown.* AmFP; AS, *with music;* CoSo, *with music*
(Little Old Sod Shanty on My Claim, The.) FSW
(Little Old Sod Shanty on the Claim, The.) BPAW
Little old woman, A. Behind the Waterfall. Winifred Welles. TiPo
Little old-fashioned girl, The. At Grandfather's. Clara Doty Bates. OBCA
Little one, come to my knee! A Story for a Child [*or* A Night with a Wolf]. Bayard Taylor. GN; HBV-1; HBVY
Little one sleeps in its cradle, The. Song of Myself, VIII. Walt Whitman. TrGrPo
Little onion lay by the fireplace, A. Song. Nicholas Moore. EAS
Little onward lend thy guiding hand, A. Samson Agonistes. Milton. OAEL-1; PoEL-3; ViBoPo
Little Orphant Annie. James Whitcomb Riley. AA; FaFON; FaFP; HBV-1; HBVY; MoShBr; OBAL; OBCA; OxBChV; PaPo; TiPo; TreF
Little Pagan Rain Song. Frances Shaw. HBMV
Little Papoose. Arthur Chapman. BPAW
Little Papoose. Hilda Conkling. FaPON
Little Parable, A. Anne Reeve Aldrich. AA; HBV-2
Little park that I pass through. Ellis Park. Helen Hoyt. HBMV

"Little, passionately, not at all, A?" Villanelle of Marguerites. Ernest Dowson. MoBrPo
Little Peach, The. Eugene Field. OBAL; ShM
Little People. Isaac Leibush Peretz, *tr. fr. Yiddish by* Joseph Leftwich. TrJP
Little Person, A. Brian Hooker. HBMV
Little Phoebe. *Unknown.* FSW
Little Pig, The. Zishe Landau, *tr. fr. Yiddish by* Ruth Whitman. VWA
Little Pig. *Unknown.* OxNR
Little Piggy. Thomas Hood. SoPo
Little plant that never sang before, The. Lydia H. Sigourney. *Fr.* On the Death of Mrs. Felicia Hemans. PeD
Little Poem of Life, The. John Oxenham. TRV
Little Political Poem. Edward Hirsch. AMV-81
Little Poll Parrot. *Unknown.* OxNR
Little Polly Flinders. Mother Goose. HBV-1; HBVY; OxNR
Little Ponds. Arthur Guiterman. HBMV
Little poppies, little hell flames. Poppies in July. Sylvia Plath. LCAP; NaP
Little Prayer, A. Paul Goodman. LiTA
Little Pretty Bonny Lass, A. *Unknown.* ElL
("Little prety bony lass was walking, A.") NCEP
Little pretty Nancy girl. *Unknown.* OxNR
Little pretty nightingale, The. *See* Lytyll Prety Nyghtyngale, The.
Little priest of Felton, The. *Unknown.* OxNR
Little Prince Tatters has lost his cap! Prince Tatters. Laura E. Richards. HBV-1; HBVY
Little Pudding. Mary M. Roberts. BXAP
Little Puppy. *Unknown, tr. fr. Navajo by* Hilda Faunce Wetherill. FaPON; TiPo
Little ragged girl, our ball-boy, A. A Game at Salzburg. Randall Jarrell. MiAP; NoAM
Little Rain. Elizabeth Madox Roberts. SoPo; SUS
Little Rain, The. Tu Fu, *tr. fr. Chinese by* L. Cranmer-Byng. FaPON
Little Raindrops. Jane Euphemia Browne. OxBChV
Little Raindrops. *At. to* Ann Hawkshaw. HBV-1; HBVY
Little Red Lark, The. Alfred Perceval Graves. HBV-1
Little Red Ribbon, The. James Whitcomb Riley. HBV-1
Little Red Riding Hood. Olga Broumas. DFT
Little Red Riding Hood. Guy Wetmore Carryl. *See* Red Riding Hood.
Little Red Riding Hood. Nila NorthSun. GP
Little Red-Riding Hood. Anne Sexton. DFT
Little Red Riding Hood and the Wolf. Roald Dahl. DFT
Little Red Sled, The. Jocelyn Bush. SoPo; TiPo
Little Rhyme and a Little Reason, A. Henry Anstadt. BLRP
Little rich girl, glittering with bells. Lost Cinderella. Edith Weaver. DFT
Little river twittering in the twilight, The. Bei Hennef. D. H. Lawrence. BrPo
Little Roach Poem. C. W. Truesdale. PoDr
Little Road says, Go, The. The House and the Road. Josephine Preston Peabody. TreFT
Little Road, The. Nancy Byrd Turner. TiPo
Little robber girl, you sleep. The Story of Good. Phyllis Janik. IHMS
Little Robin Redbreast/ Came to visit me. *Unknown.* OxNR
Little Robin red breast/ I hear you sing your song. Robin Red Breast. Lula Lowe Weeden. CDC
Little Robin Redbreast/ Sat upon a rail [*or* Sitting on a pole]. Mother Goose. OxNR; PBBP
Little Robin Redbreast sat upon a tree. Mother Goose. HBV-1; HBVY; OxNR
Little room, depressing, old, A. The Tailor. "S. Ansky," *tr. by* Joseph Leftwich. TrJP
Little Rose, be not sad for all that hath. The Little Dark Rose. *Unknown, tr. by* Padraic Pearse. OnYI
Little Rose Is Dust, My Dear, The. Grace Hazard Conkling. HBV-1
Little Rose Tree, The. Rachel Field. FaPON; SUS; TiPo
Little Rosewood Casket. *Unknown.* FSW
Little saint best fits a little shrine, A. A Ternarie of Littles, upon a Pipkin of Jellie [*or* Jelly] Sent to a Lady. Robert Herrick. FaBoCh; FaBoUs; GoJo; HBV-1; HBVY; PoEL-3; WhC
Little Saling. Olaf Baker. HBMV
Little Sally Racket. *Unknown.* FSW
Little Sally Waters, *sl. diff. vers.* Mother Goose. AmFP (2 *vers.); TiPo*
(Little Sally Sand, *with music.*) TrAS
(Little Sally Walker.) FSW
Little Satellite. Jane W. Krows. SoPo
Little Scotch-ee, *with music.* *Unknown.* AS
Little Scraping, A. Robinson Jeffers. NoAM
Little Searcher, The. Donna Bowen. AMV-80
Little seed, A. Maytime Magic. Mabel Watts. RHPC
Little Sequence, A, *sels.* Francis Burdett Money-Coutts. OBVV
"No wonder you so oft have wept."
"Forgive!/ And tell me that sweet tale."
Little sharp vexations, The. Our Burden Bearer [*or* The Unfailing One]. Phillips Brooks. BLRP; TRV
Little Shepherd's Song, The. William Alexander Percy. YeAr
Little ships of whitest pearl. A Mother's Song. Francis Ledwidge. EtS
Little Shon a [*or* Johnny] Morgan, shentleman [*or* gentleman] of Wales. Shon a Morgan. *Unknown.* GBP; OxNR
Little shrivelled and humpbacked creature, The! Tim, the Fairy. Florence Randal Livesay. CaP
Little Shroud, The. Letitia E. Landon. PaPo
Little Shrub Growing By, A. Ben Jonson. *See* Ask Not to Know This Man.
Little Sir Hugh. *Unknown.* OBET
Little siren of the stage. To Signora Cuzzoni. Ambrose Philips. LoBV; OBEC
Little Sis. David Kherdian. AMV-80
Little Sister of the Prophet, The. Marjorie Pickthall. HBV-2
Little Sister Rose-Marie. Rose-Marie of the Angels. Adelaide Crapsey. HBV-1
Little Sleep's-Head Sprouting Hair in the Moonlight. Galway Kinnell. LCAP
Little slender lad, toad-headed. The Ambrosia of Dionysus and Semele. Robert Graves. NYBP
Little Snail. Hilda Conkling. FaPON; TiPo
Little snail,/ Dreaming you go. Snail. Langston Hughes. FaPON; TiPo
Little snatch of an ancient song. Of [*or* On] an Old Song. William E. H. Lecky. HBV-2; WGRP
Little Something for William Whipple, A. Dave Oliphant. FAZ
Little Son. Georgia Douglas Johnson. CDC
Little Song, A. Robert Grosseteste, *tr. fr. Latin by* William de Shoreham, *mod. vers. by* F. M. Capes. ISi
Little Song of Life, A. Lizette Woodworth Reese. FaPON; HBMV; OBCA; TiPo; TreFT
Little Song of Spring, A. Mary Austin. YeAr
Little Song of the Maimed. Benjamin Péret, *tr. fr. French by* David Gascoyne. OBWP
Little Song of Work, A. Sarah Elizabeth Sprouse. BLRP
Little Songs. Majorie Pickthall. CaP
Little songs of summer are all gone today, The. End-of-Summer Poem. Rowena Bennett. FaPON; SiSoSe
Little soul, like a cloud, like a feather. To His Soul. Hadrian, *tr. by* Elinor Wylie. PoPl
Little soul so sleek and smiling. The Emperor Hadrian to His Soul. Hadrian, *tr. by* Stevie Smith. OBVE
Little sound, A. Many a Mickle. Walter de la Mare. FaBV
Little Sparrow. *Unknown.* AmFP
(Come All Ye Fair and Tender Maidens.) TreFT
(Come All You Fair and Tender Ladies.) FSW
Little sparrow, A. First Surf. Emanuel Di Pasquale. Str
Little sparrows, The. Pastoral. William Carlos Williams. MP; TwCP
Little Squirrel, A. *Unknown.* TiPo
Little Star, The. *Unknown.* InMe; SpRo
Little state-funded barrack, A. It Started. Jimmy Santiago Baca. LFAC
Little Steamboat. Oscar Williams. PoPl
Little Sticks. Eric Rolls. PoAu-2
Little stones chuckle among the fields, The. At Toledo. Arthur Symons. BrPo
Little sun, a little rain, A. The Earth and Man. Stopford Augustus Brooke. HBV-2; OnYI
Little sycamore, The. Love Song. *Unknown, tr. by* J. E. Manchip White. TTY
Little Talk. Aileen Fisher. FaPON
Little Talk wid Jesus Makes It Right, A, *with music.* *Unknown.* BoAN-2
Little taper set tonight. The Christmas Candle. Kate Louise Brown. SoPo
Little Te Deum of the Commonplace, A, *sels.* John Oxenham.
"For all Thy ministries." TRV
(We Thank Thee.) PGD
(We Thank Thee, Lord.) WBLP
"For maiden sweetness, and for strength of men." TRV
"With hearts responsive." TrPWD
Little Tee-Wee. *Unknown.* OxNR
Little Things. Julia A. Fletcher Carney, *wr. at. to* E. C. Brewer *and to* Frances S. Osgood. BLPA; BLPL; FaBoBe; FaFP; FaPON, 2 *sts.*; HBV-1; HBVY; OxBChV; TreF, 2 *sts.*
Little Things. James Stephens. EaLo; FaPON; GoJo; HBMV; MoBrPo; PDV; PoRA; RHPC; SiSoSe; TiPo
Little Things. Marion Strobel. HBMV
Little Things ("God has no end of material"). *Unknown.* STF
Little Things ("It was only a kindly smile he gave"). *Unknown.* STF
Little things I'll give to you. Little Things. Marion Strobel. HBMV
Little things that crawl and creep. Green Stems. Margaret Wise Brown. RHPC
Little things, that run, and quail. Little Things. James Stephens. EaLo; FaPON; GoJo; HBMV; MoBrPo; PDV; PoRA; RHPC; SiSoSe; TiPo

Little thinks, in the field, yon red-cloaked clown. Each and All. Emerson. AA; AmPP; AP; AWP; BLPL; HBV-2; NePA; NOBA; OHFP; OxBA; TAP; WGRP
Little think'st thou, poor[e] flower. The Blossom[e]. John Donne. AnAnS-1; AWP; LiTB; MeLP; OBS; SeCP; UnPo
Little tigers are at rest, The. Tom Hood, Jr. CenHV
Little time for laughter, A. After. Philip Bourke Marston. HBV-1
Little tiny puppy dog. Spike Milligan. GDP
Little Tippler, The. Emily Dickinson. *See* I taste a liquor never brewed.
Little toe, big toe, three toes between. Close Quarters. John Banister Tabb. OBAL
Little toe is attractive, The. "The Time of Man." Phyllis Webb. MoCV
Little Tom Dogget. Colly, My Cow. *Unknown.* EvOK
Little Tom Tittlemouse/ Lived in a bell-house. *Unknown.* OxNR
Little Tommy Tacket. *Unknown.* OxNR
Little Tommy Tittlemouse/ Lived in a little house. Mother Goose. OxNR
Little Tommy Tucker. Mother Goose. HBVY; OxNR
Little Tommy Yesterday. Alex Glasgow. OBET
Little too abstract, a little too wise, A. Return. Robinson Jeffers. GoYe
Little toy dog is covered with dust, The. Little Boy Blue. Eugene Field. AA; BeLS; FaFON; FaFP; FPL; HBV-1; HBVY; OBAL; OBCA; OHFP; PaPo; PoLF; SoSe; TreF
Little train called 29, A. Number 29. *Unknown.* BluL
Little tree. E. E. Cummings. Chansons Innocentes, II. NTCP; OBCP; PChr; PDV; PoSC; RoGo
Little Trotty Wagtail. John Clare. FaPON; OnUR; PB; UnPo
Little Tumescence, A. Jonathan Williams. ErPo; NeAP; PoM
Little Turtle, The. Vachel Lindsay. FaPON; GoJo; NTCP; OBAL; OBCA; PDV; SoPo; SUS; TiPo
Little Vagabond, The. Blake. *Fr.* Songs of Experience. OBSV; SeCeV
Little Viennese Waltz. Federico García Lorca, *tr. fr. Spanish by* William B. Logan. SOTW
Little Waves of Breffny, The. Eva Gore-Booth. AnIV; HBV-2; HBVY; OnYi
Little Way, A. Frank Lebby Stanton. AA
Little way below her chin, A. On Some Buttercups. Frank Dempster Sherman. AA
Little way to walk with you, my own, A. A Little Way. Frank Lebby Stanton. AA
Little While, A. Horatius Bonar. *See* Beyond the Smiling and the Weeping.
Little While, A. Emily Brontë. *See* Little While, A Little While, A.
Little While, A. Don Marquis. HBV-2
Little While, A. Dante Gabriel Rossetti. ViBoPo; VLP
Little While, a Little While, A. Emily Brontë. OAEP; OBNC; OxBI; ViBoPo
(Holyday.) NBM
(Little While, A.) TreFS
Little While I Fain Would Linger Yet, A. Paul Hamilton Hayne. AA; HBV-1
Little while my love and I, A. A May Song. "Violet Fane." OBVV
Little while the tears and laughter, A. A Little While. Don Marquis. HBV-2
Little Whistler, The. Frances Frost. PDV; SoPo; TiPo
Little White Cat, The. *Unknown, tr. fr. Modern Irish by* Mrs. Costello of Tuam. OnYI
Little white clouds are racing over the sky, The. Magdalen Walks. Oscar Wilde. EBVV; MoBrPo
Little white horses are out on the sea. White Horses. Winifred Howard. SoPo; SUS
Little White Lily. George Macdonald. *Fr.* Within and Without. HBV-1; HBVY
Little white mermaidens live in the sea, The. The Mermaidens. Laura E. Richards. OBCA
Little White Schoolhouse Blues. Florence Becker Lennon. PoNe
Little Wild Baby. "Margaret Vandegrift." AA; HBV-1
Little wild bird sometimes at my ear, A. Ballata: Of True and False Singing. *Unknown, tr. by* Dante Gabriel Rossetti. AWP
Little wild birds have come flying, The. Love-Song. *Unknown, tr. by* W. R. S. Ralston. AWP
Little Willie. Gerald Massey. PaPo
Little Willie ("Little Willie from his mirror"). *Unknown.* MoShBr; PoPle; ShM; WhC
Little Willie ("Little Willie hung his sister"). *Unknown.* NA; TreFS
Little Willie ("Little Willie, mad as hell"). *Unknown.* ShM
Little Willie ("Little Willie, once in ire"). *Unknown.* ShM
Little Willie ("Willie saw some dynamite"). *Unknown.* FaPON
Little Willie;/ Pair of skates. Golden Gates. *Unknown.* ShM
Little Willie, in the best of sashes. Tender-heartedness. Harry Graham. DBV; NA. *See also* Billy, in one of his nice new sashes.
Little Willie's My Darlin', *with music. Unknown.* OuSiCo
Little Wind. Kate Greenaway. GoJo; SUS
(Little wind, blow on the hill-top.) TiPo
Little winter cottontails. The Outdoor Christmas Tree. Aileen Fisher. SiSoSe
Little Word, A. *Unknown.* STF
Little Work, A. George Du Maurier. *Fr.* Trilby, Pt. VIII. FaBoBe; HBV-2; PoLF
(Little Work, a Little Play, A.) TreFS
Little Wren of tender mind, The. The Wren. *Unknown.* OxBChV
Little wrists. So That Even a Lover. Louis Zukofsky. CoPo
Little Yellow Leaf. James Tate. NoAM
Little-League Baseball Fan. W. R. Moses. LiSp; NCSH
Littlest door, the inner door, The. The Door. Mary Carolyn Davies. HBMV
Littoral. Hjalmar Flax, *tr. fr. Spanish by* Julio Marzán. InW
Liu Ch'e. Ezra Pound. AP; OBVE; VGW
Live all thy sweet life thro'. A Summer Wish. Christina Rossetti. OBNC
Live Blindly. Trumbull Stickney. LiTA; NePA; TwAmPo
(Live Blindly and upon the Hour.) TrGrPo
Live Christ. John Oxenham. BLRP
Live ever here, Lorenzo?—shocking thought! Edward Young. *Fr.* Night Thoughts: Night the Third. EnRP
Live fowl squatting on the grapefruit and bananas, The. Jamaican Bus Ride. A. S. J. Tessimond. OxBTC
Live here, great heart; and love and dy and kill. Richard Crashaw. *Fr.* The Flaming Heart. OBS
Live Joyfully. Bible, *O.T.* Ecclesiastes, IX: 7-11. TreFS
Live, live with me, and thou shalt see. To Phillis [*or* Phyllis], to Love and Live with Him. Robert Herrick. CaPo; CavP; OAEP
Live lizard; dead lizard. Witches' Menu. Sonja Nikolay. RHPC
Live Not, Poor Bloom, but Perish. *Unknown.* NCEP
Live so that you. Certain Maxims of Archy. Don Marquis. InMe; OBAL
Live thy Life,/ Young and old. The Oak. Tennyson. FaPON; PoPl
Live, trifling incidents, and grace my song. Robert Bloomfield. *Fr.* The Farmer's Boy. OBRV
Live unlamenting though obscure remaining. To J. S. Collis. Ruth Pitter. OxBoCh
Live While You Live. Philip Doddridge. OxBoCh
(Dum Vivimus, Vivamus). OBEC
Live with Me. Mick Jagger *and* Keith Richard. InPK
Live you by love confined. C. Day Lewis. *Fr.* The Magnetic Mountain. PoPle
Live-a/ humble, humble, Lord. Humble Yo'self de Bell Done Ring. *Unknown.* BoAN-2
Lived on one's back. Vigil. W. E. Henley. In Hospital, VII. BrPo, LoBV
Liveliest effigy of the human race. Ralph Chubb. *Fr.* The Book of God's Madness. PeHV
Lively young turtle lived down by the banks, A. The Turtle and the Flamingo [*or* Song of the Turtle and Flamingo]. James Thomas Fields. GN; HBV-2
Liverockie, liverockie lee. The Lark. *Unknown.* GBP
Liverpool. *Unknown.* AmFP
Lives. Cyril Dabydeen. BrSi
Lives. Gerald Dawe. AMV-81
Lives. Henry Reed. BoNaP; LiTB
Lives and times of Oedipus and Elektra, The. This One's on Me. Phyllis Gotlieb. MoCV; NOBC
Lives in winter. Mother Goose. HBV-1; NTCP; SoPo; TiPo
Lives of Famous Men, The. Jack Gilbert. NPGG
Lives of Great Men. *Unknown.* FaFP; TreFT
(After Emerson.) NOBL
Lives of great men all remind us. Life. Longfellow. *Fr.* Psalm of Life. GN
Lives of great men all remind us/ As their pages o'er we turn. Lives of Great Men [*or* After Emerson]. *Unknown.* FaFP; NOBL; TreFT
Lives of Gulls and Children, The. Howard Nemerov. NePoEA
Lives of the Poet. Ron Miles. AMV-81
Lives of the Saints. Jon Anderson. FiCP
Livid sky on London, A. The Old Song. G. K. Chesterton. FaBoTw
"Living, A." W. S. Di Piero. AMV-80
Living, A. D. H. Lawrence. RFM
Living. Denise Levertov. VGW; WPE
Living. Harold Monro. LiTB; SeCePo
Living. D. S. Savage. NeBP
Living. *Unknown.* BLPA; FaBoBe; TreFS
Living, A. Making a living. "A Living." W. S. Di Piero. AMV-80
Living alone is like floating on blue. So, When I Swim to the Shore. Molly Peacock. MAYP
Living among the Dead. William Matthews. GeTw
Living and Dying. "Michael Lewis," *after the Chinese. Fr.* Cherry Blossoms. UnTE
Living and Dying Prayer for the Holiest Believer in the World, A. Augustus Montagu Toplady. *See* Rock of Ages.

Living being, the Temple was killed, A. The Temple. Gustave Kahn, *tr. by* Edouard Roditi. VWA
Living Book, The. Charlotte Fiske Bates. AA
Living by the Red River. James Wright. NNaP
Living Chalice, The. Susan Mitchell. HBMV
"Living Dog, The," and "The Dead Lion." Thomas Moore. OBRV
Living God, The. Daniel ben Judah, *tr. fr. Hebrew by* Israel Zangwill. TrJP
Living God, The. Charlotte Perkins Gilman. WGRP
Living God, The. Abraham ibn Ezra, *tr. fr. Hebrew by* Alice Lucas. TrJP
Living God O magnify and bless, The. The Living God. Daniel ben Judah, *tr. by* Israel Zangwill. TrJP
Living in a wide landscape are the flowers. Desert Flowers. Keith Douglas. FaBoTw
Living in Sin. Austin Clarke. ELU
Living in Sin. Adrienne Rich. FF; IHMS; NePoEA; NoP; NYBP; SoSe; TAP; UnPo
Living in the Boneyard. John Oliver Simon. NeAC
Living in the earth-deposits of our history. Power. Adrienne Rich. TAP
Living in the Moment. Marilyn Hacker. NYP
Living in the Present. Clarinda Harriss Lott. AMV-81
Living in the World. Alan Chong Lau. BrSi
Living Juliet, The. Shakespeare. *See* He Jests at Scars.
Living man is blind and drinks his drop, A. W. B. Yeats. *Fr.* A Dialogue of Self and Soul. DTC
Living Marble. Arthur O'Shaughnessy. VLP
Living Memory, A. William Augustus Croffut. AA
Living on the river I am able to dip my feet in darkness. One Foot in the River. Gerald Stern. NYP
Living? Our Supervisors Will Do That for Us! David Holbrook. NePoEA-2
Living Pearl, A. Kenneth Rexroth. LiTM
Living Poetry. Hugh Margenat, *tr. fr. Spanish by* Julio Marzán. InW
Living Room, The. Gjertrud Schnackenberg. FYAP
Living someplace else is wrong. The Spring Offensive of the Snail. Marge Piercy. TAP
Living Statue, The. *Unknown, tr. fr. Greek by* Louis Untermeyer. UnTE
Living swim through their photographs, The. Profile. Bronwen Wallace. AMV-81
Living Temple, The. Oliver Wendell Holmes. *Fr.* The Autocrat of the Breakfast Table. AA; AP
Living Tenderly. May Swenson. BoAnP; OBCA
Living Together. Tomioka Taeko, *tr. fr. Japanese by* Sato Hiroaki. WPOW
Living Truth, The. Sterling Plumpp. PoBA
Living Waters. Caroline Spencer. HBV-2
Living with Chris. Ted Berrigan. NoAM
Living with Others. Al Zolynas. LTB
Living with You. Angela Langfield. FF
Liza in the Summer Time (She Died on the Train), *with music. Unknown.* AS
Liza Jane, *with music. Unknown.* AS
(Mountain Top, *diff. vers., with music.*) AS
Lizard, The. John Gardner. RHPC
Lizard. D. H. Lawrence. BoAnP
Lizard, The. Ruth Lechlitner. AMV-81
Lizard. Alan McLean. BoAnP
Lizard, The. Edwin Markham. BPAW
Lizard, The. Rona Murray. NOBC
Lizard, The. Theodore Roethke. GrPl; RHPC
Lizard fidgets in the sun, A. Under Creag Mhor. Stewart Conn. PoSH
Lizard is a timid thing, The. The Lizard. John Gardner. RHPC
Lizard ran out on a rock and looked up, listening, A. Lizard. D. H. Lawrence. BoAnP
Lizard sat on my finger, The. Grey Him. Paul Mariah. LFAC
Lizards and Snakes. Anthony Hecht. CoPo; FaBoMo; NCSH; TwCP
Lizards of La Brea, The. Marc De Baca. AMV-80
Lizie Lindsay. *Unknown.* ESPB (A *and* B *vers.*)
(Donald of the Isles, *with music.*) OxBB
Lizie Wan. *Unknown.* AmFP; ESPB; ViBoFo
Lizzie Borden. *Unknown.* DBV; ShM; TreFS
(Crimes of Lizzie Borden, The.) FaBoCo; FaFP
("Lizzie Borden took an axe.") CenHV
Llama, The. Hilaire Belloc. EvOK; FaBoCh; FaBoNo; FiBHP
Llama seems a sensitive creature, The. A Snap Judgement on the Llama. Peggy Bennett. ELU
Llanberis Summer. Marianne Loyd. AMV-81
Llangollen Vale, *sel.* Anna Seward.
"Now with a vestal lustre glows the Vale." PeHV
Llano Estacado, The. *Unknown, at. to* Joaquin Miller. *See* Tantalus—Texas.
Llewellyn and the Tree. E. A. Robinson. BeLS; HBMV
Lloyd George. *Unknown.* FaBoCo
Lloyd George and Woodrow Wilson and Clemenceau. A Legend of Versailles. Melvin B. Tolson. BPo
Lo! above the mournful chanting. Kol Nidra. Joseph Leiser. TrJP
Lo, alas, I look and seek. The Ageing Hunter. Avane, *tr. fr. Eskimo.* WTO
Lo! all in silence, all in order stand. Books. George Crabbe. *Fr.* The Library. OBEC
Lo, as a careful housewife runs to catch. Sonnets, CXLIII. Shakespeare. BiP; InPK; OAEP
Lo, as a dove when up she springs. In Memoriam A. H. H., XII. Tennyson. LoBV
Lo as I pause in the alien vale of the airport. Twenty-third Flight. Earle Birney. HeIP; OxBC; SoSe
Lo as some venturer, from his stars receiving. Saint Paul, *abr.* F. W. H. Myers. PGD
Lo! As the Potter Mouldeth. *Unknown, tr. fr. Hebrew by* Elsie Davis. TrJP
Lo, as the sun from his ocean bed rising. There She Blows! *Unknown.* EtS
Lo! Beauty flashed forth sweetly; from his eyes. Epigram. Meleager, *tr. fr. Greek by* Sydney Oswald. PeHV
Lo! Death has reared himself a throne. The City in the Sea [*or* The Doomed City]. Poe. AA; AmPP; AP; FaBoEn; HBV-2; LiTA; MAT; MOS; NePA; NOBA; NoP; OBRV; OxBA; PoEL-4; SCV; TAP; TrGrPo; ViBoPo; WHA
Lo, fainter now lie spread the shades of night. Morning Hymn. St. Gregory the Great, *tr. by* Edward Caswell. WGRP
Lo, for I to myself am unknown. Jalal ed-Din Rumi, *tr. fr. Persian. ILwL*
Lo! Freedom comes. Th' prescient Muse foretold. Liberty and Peace. Phillis Wheatley. BlSi; SBG
Lo from our loitering ship a new land at last to be seen. Iceland First Seen. William Morris. VLP
Lo! from the livid East, or piercing North. James Thomson. *Fr.* Winter. FaBoEn
Lo, he comes! Capability Brown. William Cowper. SaC
Lo[e], here a little volume, but great book[e]! Prayer [*or* An Ode Which Was Prefixed to a Prayer Booke Given to a Young Gentlewoman]. Richard Crashaw. AnAnS-1; HBV-2
Lo here I sit at holy head. Holyhead, Sept. 25th, 1727. Swift. BIrV
Lo! Here the Gentle Lark. Shakespeare. *Fr.* Venus and Adonis. ChTr
(Death of Adonis, The.) WHA
Lo, here the state of every mortal wight. Respice Finem. Thomas Proctor. OBSC
Lo! here we come a-reaping, a-reaping. Song. George Peele. *Fr.* The Old Wife's Tale. OBSC
Lo, how I seek and sue to have. Sir Thomas Wyatt. SiPS
Lo! how the lark soars upward and is gone. The Death of Leander. Thomas Hood. *Fr.* Hero and Leander. EnRP
"Lo, I am black but I am comely too." The Dark Brother. Lewis Alexander. CDC
Lo! I am come to autumn. Gold Leaves. G. K. Chesterton. OxBTC
Lo, I Am Stricken Dumb. *Unknown, tr. fr. Hebrew by* Theodor H. Gaster. *Fr.* The Dead Sea Scrolls. TrJP
Lo, I have given thee wings wherewith to fly. To Kuvos. Theognis, *tr. by* G. Lowes Dickinson. PeHV
Lo! I have learned of the loveliest of lands. *Unknown, tr. by* Charles W. Kennedy. *Fr.* The Phoenix. AnOE; OAEL-1
Lo, I have opened unto you the wide gates of my being. Psalm to My Beloved. Eunice Tietjens. ErPo
Lo I the man, whose Muse whilome [*or* whylome] did maske. The Legend of the Knight of the Red Crosse, or of Holinesse [*or* Invocation to the Faerie Queene]. Spenser. *Fr.* The Faerie Queene, I. FiP; OAEL-1; OAEP
Lo! I will tell the dearest of dreams. A Dream of the Rood. *Unknown, at. to* Cynewulf, *tr. by* Charles W. Kennedy. AnOE; OAEL-1
Lo, if some pen should write upon your rafter. The Inner Light. Frederic William Henry Myers. HBV-2; WGRP
Lo! in the mute, mid wilderness. The Unicorn. George Darley. *Fr.* Nepenthe. ChTr; FaBoEn; NBM; OBNC; OBRV; PoEL-4
Lo! in the West, fast fades the ling'ring light. Henry Kirke White. *Fr.* Clifton Grove. OBNC
Lo, it is I, be not afraid! James Russell Lowell. *Fr.* The Vision of Sir Launfal, Pt. II. TreF
Lo, it was the last supper, I leader from gutter. The Drunken Preacher's Sermon. James Reaney. *Fr.* A Suit of Nettles. PeCV
Lo, Joseph dreams his dream again. The League of Nations. Mary Siegrist. PAH
Lo! lemman swete, now may thou see. Christ's Plea to Mankind. *Unknown.* OxBM
Lo, Lord, Thou ridest! The Hurricane. Hart Crane. AP; CMoP; CoBMV; MoAB; MoAmPo; OxBA; TrCP
Lo, Love's obey'd by all. 'Tis right. The Impossibility. Coventry Patmore. *Fr.* The Angel in the House, I. VLP
Lo now he shineth yonder. Epitaph on Prince Henry. Hugh Holland. FaBoEE

Lo! now with red rent cloak and bonnet black. George Crabbe. *Fr.* Phoebe Dawson. EBEV
Lo Que Digo, *with music. Unknown, tr. fr. Spanish.* AS
Lo, quhat it is to love. *See* Lo! what it is to lufe.
Lo, she cometh to us from afar. Assumpta Est Maria. Liam Brophy. ISi
Lo! sun and moon, these minister for aye. Israel's Duration. Judah Halevi, *tr. by* Nina Davis Salaman. TrJP
Lo! the foolish fell. Killing. Samuel Greenberg. LiTA
Lo, the lilies of the field. Providence. Reginald Heber. GN; HBV-2; OHIP
Lo, the moon's self! Phases of the Moon. Robert Browning. *Fr.* One Word More. ChTr; MOON
Lo, the Poor Indian! Pope. *Fr.* An Essay on Man. TreFS
("Lo, the poor Indian! whose untutor'd mind.") NU
Lo! the Sun, among the daughters. Sunset in the Sea. Tom Hood. FaBoNo
Lo, the Winter Is Past. Bible, *O.T. See* For, Lo, the Winter Is Past.
Lo, thou, my Love, art fair. Christ to His Spouse [*or* The Beloved to the Spouse]. William Baldwin. EIL; NOCV; OBSC; OxBoCh
Lo! through a shadowy valley. The Funeral of Time. Henry Beck Hirst. AA
Lo, thus, as prostrate, "In the dust I write." The City of Dreadful Night. James Thomson ("B. V."). GoTS; NOBE; OAEP; OBNC; OxBS; ViBoPo; VLP
Lo, 'tis a gala night. The Conqueror Worm [*or* The Emperor Worm]. Poe. *Fr.* Ligeia, *prose tale.* AA; AP; AWP; BLPL; DL; HBV-2; LiTA; NOBA
Lo, upon the carpet, where. Tamerlane. Victor J. Daley. PoAu-1
Lo! we have listened to many a lay. Beowulf. *Unknown, tr. by* Charles W. Kennedy. OAEL-1
Lo, What Enraptured Songs of Praise, *with music.* Sebastian Streeter. AH
Lo! what [*or* quhat] it is to love [*or* lufe]. A Rondel of Luve [*or* Love]. Alexander Scott. BoLoP; BSV; OBEV; OxBS
Lo, what wonders the day hath brought. Snow. Elizabeth Akers Allen. HBV-1
Lo, when the Lord made North and South. The Rose of the World. Coventry Patmore. The Angel in the House, III. HBV-1
Lo, where envy and where lies. Written on the Walls of His Dungeon. Fray Luís De León, *tr. by* Thomas Walsh. TrJP
Lo, where left 'mid the sheaves, cut down by the iron-/ fanged reaper. On a Forsaken Lark's Nest. Mathilde Blind. FM
Lo! where the four mimosas blend their shade. For an Epitaph at Fiesole. Walter Savage Landor. FaBoEE; OBNC; OBRV; OBVV
Lo! where the rosy-bosomed Hours. Ode on the Spring. Thomas Gray. GTBS; GTBS-P; HBV-1; LAuP; NOEC
Lo! where the stripling, wrapt in wonder, roves. The Youth of a Poet. James Beattie. *Fr.* The Minstrel; or, The Progress of Genius, I. NOEC
Lo, Who Could Stand. *Unknown, tr. fr. Hebrew by* Israel Zangwill. TrJP
Lo worms enjoy the seat of bliss. Burns. FaBoEE
Lo! yon phantom army marching across Heaven. Indian Night Tableau. Hyman Edelestein. CaP
Load. John Hewitt. OnYI
Load of brushes and baskets and cradles and chairs, A. No Buyers; a Street Scene. Thomas Hardy. LiTB; NoP
"Loaded with benefits daily." Mercies and Blessings. *Unknown.* STF
Loaded with gallant soldiers. Ready. Phoebe Cary. PAH
Loads of trash and we light the match. Landfill. Michael Harper. LCAP
Loan of a Stall, The. James L. Duff. ISi
Loan that buildt the barn, The. Tom Ball's Barn. Ted Kooser. GP
Loaves, The. Ronald Everson. WHW
Lob. Edward Thomas. MoVE
Lobbed ball plops, then dribbles to the cup, The. Ford Madox Ford. Robert Lowell. MP; PoCh; TwCP
Lobo. Charles Lillard. NOBC
Lobotomy. Kenneth Pitchford. PoA
Lobster Cove Shindig. Lillian Morrison. BoNaP
Lobster Pot, The. John Arden. ELU
Lobster Quadrille, The. "Lewis Carroll." *Fr.* Alice's Adventures in Wonderland, *ch.* 10. FaPON; MoShBr; OxBChV; Par; PoPle
(Mock Turtle's Song, The.) ChTr; FaBoNo; VLP, 2 *versions*
(Whiting and the Snail, The.) HBV-1; HBVY
Lobster, The. "Lewis Carroll." *See* Alice's Recitation.
Lobsters and the Fiddler Crab, The ("The lobsters came ashore one night"). Frederick J. Forster. RHPC
Lobsters in the Window. W. D. Snodgrass. BiP; BoAnP; HeIP; NCSH; NYBP; TAP
Local groceries are all out of broccoli, The. Against Broccoli [*or* Song against Broccoli]. Roy Blount, Jr. OBAL; PPJ
Local I'll bright my tale on, how. The Children of Greenock. W. S. Graham. FaBoTw
Local Man Remembers Betty Fuller, A. James Whitehead. GP
Local Places. Howard Moss. NePoEA-2
Local Politics. Robert Pinsky. MAYP
Local Storm, A. Donald Justice. NCSH
Locale. Penelope Shuttle. BrRo
Localities. Carl Sandburg. AmFN
Locate I/ love you. The Language. Robert Creeley. CAPP; CoPo; TAP
Location. Knute Skinner. MAT
Location of Things, The. Barbara Guest. NYP
Locations. Kathleen Fraser. NPGG
Locations. Jim Harrison. AmPA
"Loch Achray" was a clipper tall, The. The Yarn of the *Loch Achray.* John Masefield. SeCeV
Loch Coruisk (Skye). "Fiona Macleod." SyP
Loch Leven. Sydney Goodsir Smith. BSV
Loch Lomond. *Unknown, at. to* Lady John Scott. FSW; TreFS
Loch Luichart. Andrew Young. PoSH
Loch Ossian. Syd Scroggie. PoSH
Lochaber No More. Allan Ramsay. HBV-1
Lochan. Roger Smith. PoSH
Lochiel's Warning ("Lochiel, Lochiel! beware of the day"). Thomas Campbell. EnRP
Lochinvar. Sir Walter Scott. *Fr.* Marmion, V. BeLS; BSV; EnRP; EvOK; FaBoBe; FaBV; FaFP; FaPON; FPL; GN; GoTS; HBV-1; NOBE; OAEP; OBNC; OBRV; OxBS; PaPo; PoRA; RoGo; TreF; WHA
(Young Lochinvar.) HBVY; OBNV
Lochmaben Harper, The. *Unknown.* ESPB; OxBB, *with music.*
Lochnagar cam frae the west. Katharine Jaffray (B *vers.*). *Unknown.* ViBoFo
Lock, The. Pope. *Fr.* The Rape of the Lock, V. MOON
Lock the dairy door. *Unknown.* OxNR; PBBP
Lock the Door, Lariston. James Hogg. BSV; GoTS; OxBS
Lock the Place in Your Heart. Zindzi Mandela. LLLT
Lock up, fair lids, the treasure of my heart. Sleep [*or* Sonnet]. Sir Philip Sidney. *Fr.* Arcadia. EIL; OBSC; SiPS
Lock your bedroom doors with terror. Admonition. John Peale Bishop. TwAmPo
Locke sank into a swoon. Fragment. W. B. Yeats. NoAM; PrIm
Locked arm in arm they cross the way. Tableau. Countee Cullen. AmFN; BANP; PoBA
Locked in a glassy iceland lake. Green World Two. Miriam Waddington. PeCV
Lockless Door, The. Robert Frost. NOBA; WSC
Locks. Kenneth Koch. CoAP
Locks and Bolts ("I dreamed last night of my true love"). *Unknown.* FSW; TrAS, *with music*
Locks and Bolts ("Twas over hills and over dales"). *Unknown.* OBET
Locks between her chamber and his will, The. Midnight. Shakespeare. *Fr.* The Rape of Lucrece. OBSC
Locksley Hall. Tennyson. BLPL; EBEV; FaBoBe; FaFP; HBV-2; OAEL-2; OAEP; VLP; WHA
Sels.
For I Dipped into the Future. PoLF
("For I dipped into the future, far as human eye could see.") PGD; PoLF; TRV
(Prophecy.) TreF; WBLP
In the Spring. BoNaP
"Make me feel the wild pulsation that I felt before the strife." SaC
Locksley Hall, Sixty Years After. Tennyson.
"Authors—essayist, atheist, novelist, realist, rimester," *sel.* PeD
Locomotive, The. Emily Dickinson. *See* I like to see it lap the miles.
Locomotive to the Little Boy, The. Benjamin R. C. Low. HBMV
Locrine, *sel. At. to* Charles Tilney.
Cobbler's Song, The. OBSC
Locus, The. Cid Corman. VGW
Locus. Robert Hayden. FYAP
Locust Hunt, The. Philip Murray. NePoAm-2
Locust, The. *Unknown, tr. fr. Zuni Indian by* Frank Cushing. FaPON; SUS
(Coyote and the Locust, The.) AWP
Locust Tree in Flower, The. William Carlos Williams. SOTW
Locusts of Silence. Seymour Mayne. VWA
Locusts, or Appolyonists, The, *sels.* Phineas Fletcher.
"Of Men, nay Beasts: worse, Monsters: worst of all," *fr.* I. SeCV-1
Sin, Despair, and Lucifer, *fr.* I. OBS
Lodestoned salmon, hurtling, The. Weir Bridge. Padraic Fallon. CIP
Lodge Room over Simpkins' Store, The. Lawrence N. Greenleaf. PoOW
Lodgepole/ cone/seed waits for fire. Gary Snyder. Myths and Texts: Logging, XV. NaP
Lodgers. Julian Tuwim, *tr. fr. Polish by* Isaac Komem. VWA
Lodging, The. George Mackay Brown. BSV
Lodging for the Night, A. Elinor Wylie. ErPo
Lodging with the Old Man of the Stream. Po Chü-i, *tr. fr. Chinese by* Arthur Waley. AWP

Loe! formest of a rout that followd him. Virgil, *tr. by* Earl of Surrey. *Fr.* The Aeneid, II. OBVE
Loe here a little volume but great booke. *See* Lo, here a little volume, but great book.
Loe here the precious dust is laid. Epitaph on Maria Wentworth. Thomas Carew. PoEL-3
Loërd, thou clepedest me. Prayer for Forbearance. *Unknown.* LoBV
Loft. Michael Dransfield. CBAP
Lofty against our Western dawn uprises Achilles. Song, Youth, and Sorrow. William Cranston Lawton. AA
Lofty elm-trees darkly dream, The. The Rookery at Sunrise. "Fiona Macleod." *Fr.* Transcripts from Nature. FM
Lofty Lane. Edwin Gerard. PoAu-1
Lofty ship from Salcombe came, A. The Salcombe Seaman's Flaunt to the Proud Pirate [*or* The Pirate of High Barbary]. *Unknown.* ChTr; EtS
Lofty young squire from Portsmouth he came, A. The Golden Glove. *Unknown.* AmFP
Lofty-brow-flourishers. On Philosophers. *Unknown.* TW
Log Jam, The. William Henry Drummond. NOBC
Logan at Peach Tree Creek. Hamlin Garland. PAH
Logan Braes ("By Logan's streams that rin sae deep"). John Mayne. OxBS
Logarithm, The. The fraction. The bead of dew. America the Beautiful. Stan Rice. NPGG
Logging, *sels.* Snyder. *Fr.* Myths and Texts.
"Again the ancient, meaningless," V. CAPP; NaP
"Each dawn is clear," VIII. NaP; NMP
"Groves are down, The," XIV. NaP
"Lodgepole/ cone/seed waits for fire," XV. NaP
"Stood straight/ holding the choker high," III. NaP; NMP; NOBA
Logic. Calvin Murry. LFAC
Logic. *Unknown.* FaBoUs
Logic does well at school. Scholars. Walter de la Mare. NoAM
Logic is my eye. Seeing. John Lyle Donaghy. NeIP
Logical Song, A. *Unknown.* ErPo
Logical Vegetarian, The. G. K. Chesterton. CenHV
Lohengrin. William Morton Payne. AA
Lois in Concert. Charles Moorman. AMV-81
L'Oiseau Bleu. Gordon Bottomley. BrPo
L'Oiseau Bleu. Mary Elizabeth Coleridge. CH
Lollay, Lollay, Little Child! *Unknown.* OxBM
(Adult Lullaby, An.) MeEL
Lollingdon Downs, *sels.* John Masefield. LiTB (I-XV)
Choice, The, VIII. MoAB; MoBrPo
"I could not sleep for thinking of the sky," V. ChMP; LiTM
"Night is on the downland, on the lonely moorland," XVIII. GoYe; LiTM
(Night on the Downland.) MoBrPo; MoPo
Sonnet: "Here in the self is all that men can know." AWP
Lollocks. Robert Graves. ChTr; DTC; EvOK
Lolly-Too-Dum. *Unknown.* *See* Rolly Trudum.
Lollypops, The. Cordia Thomas. SoPo
Lolo died yesterday. Cyn. Zarco. BrSi
Lolotte, who attires my hair. Noblesse Oblige. Jessie Fauset. CDC
London ("I wander through each chartered [*or* dirty] street"). Blake. *Fr.* Songs of Experience. AWP; CABA; ChER; EnRP; FaBoEn; FaBoPP; FF; HAP; HeIP; InPK; InPS; LAuP; LiTB; MAT; NIP; NOBE; NOEC; NoP; OAEL-2; OBNC; PAI; PoEL-4; PPON; PrIm; SCV; SeCePo; SeCeV; TEP; UnPo; ViBoPo; WeW
(London ["I wander thro' each dirty street"], *sl diff.*) ChTr
London ("There souls of men are bought and sold"). Blake. *Fr.* The Human Image. ChTr
London. John Davidson. NOBE; OBNC
London. Daniel Defoe. *Fr.* Reformation of Manners. NOEC
London. Dryden. *Fr.* Annus Mirabilis. SeCePo
London. J. R. Rowland. CBAP
London. T. P. Cameron Wilson. HBMV
London; a Poem in Imitation of the Third Satire of Juvenal. Samuel Johnson. GoTL; LAuP; PoEL-3; TEP
Sels.
"By numbers here from shame or censure free." NOEC; OBSV; ViBoPo
(Poverty in London.) ChTr; OBEC
"Here malice, rapine, accident, conspire." DBV
"Prepare for death, if here at night you roam." OAEL-1
"London: John Lane, The Bodley Head." On the Imprint of the First English Edition of "The Works of Max Beerbohm." Max Beerbohm. InPK; PV
London Adulterations. *Unknown.* OBET
London after the Great Fire, 1666. Dryden. *Fr.* Annus Mirabilis. NOBE
London at Night. John Gay. *Fr.* Trivia; or, The Art of Walking the Streets of London. FaBoPP
London Bells. *Unknown.* *See* Bells of London, The.
London Bridge Is a-Burning Down. *Unknown.* AmFP
London Bridge is broken down. CH; ChTr; EyDe; GBP; OxBoLi; OxNR
("London Bridge is falling down, falling down, falling down.") EyDe
London Bridge is falling down, Rome's burnt, and Babylon. Spring MCMXL. David Gascoyne. MoVE
London Bridge was built. Stranger than the Worst. Babette Deutsch. WPE
London City, *with music.* *Unknown.* AS
London Despair. Frances Cornford. OBMV
London, 1802 ("Milton! thou shouldst be living at this hour"). Wordsworth. AWP; BiP; CABA; EnRP; FaBV; FF; HAP; HeIP; InvP; LiTB; NIP; NoP; OAEP; OBNC; OBRV; PAI; PoEL-4; PoRA; SeCeV; TEP; TreF
(England, 1802, II.) HBV-2; OBEV
(Milton.) FaPoR
(Milton! Thou Shouldst Be Living at This Hour.) WHA
(Sonnet: "Milton! Thou shouldst be living at this hour.") LoBV
(Same, The.) GTBS; GTBS-P
(To Milton.) TrGrPo
London, MDCCCII ("O friend! I know not which way I must look"). Wordsworth. *See* Written in London, September, 1802.
London Evening Post, *sel.* *Unknown.*
"Ye beauties, beaux, ye pleaders at the bar." FaBoUs
London Fête, A. Coventry Patmore. EBVV; HAP; NBM
London, from Hampstead Heath. Wordsworth. *Fr.* Extempore upon the Death of James Hogg. FaBoPP
London, hast thou [*or* thow] accused me. A Satire on London. Earl of Surrey. AAS; OAEP; SiPs
London in War. Helen Dircks. SUMH
London in 1646. Henry Vaughan. FaBoPP
London Interior. Harold Monro. BrPo
London Is a Fine Town. *Unknown.* CoMu
London is full of chickens, on electric spits. Peter Porter. *Fr.* Annotations of Auschwitz. OxBTC
London is painted round them: burly railings. Street Performers, 1851. Terence Tiller. GTBS-P
London Lickpenny. *Unknown wr. at. to* John Lydgate, *tr. fr. Middle English.* CoMu; FaBoPP; GoTL; OxBM; OBSV
(London Lackpenny.) ChTr
London Night. Kathleen Raine. NeBP
London Nightfall. John Gould Fletcher. MoAmPo
London Pavement Artist. James Schevill. TAP
London Plane-Tree, A. Amy Levy. OBVV
London Poets. Amy Levy. OBVV
London Prentice, The. *Unknown.* CoMu; UnTE
London Rain. Louis MacNeice. HeIP; NoP
London Sad London. *Unknown.* OBS
London Snow. Robert Bridges. BoNaP; BrPo; CH; ChTr; CMoP; CoBMV; EBEV; EBVV; FaBoPP; GTBS-P; LiTB; LiTM; LoBV; MoAB; MoBrPo; NBM; NoAM; NOBE; OAEL-2; OBNC; OxBTC; PoEL-5; SeCePo; SeCeV; TrGrPo; VLP; WiR
London Sparrow's If, A. J. A. Lindon. BoAnP
London Spring. Antoni Slonimski, *tr. fr. Polish by* Frances Notley. TrJP
London Suburbs. William Cowper. *Fr.* Retirement. FaBoPP
London, thou art of townes *A per se.* To the City of London [*or* In Honour of the City of London]. William Dunbar. ChTr; EBEV; FaBoPP; OBEV
London, to thee I do present the merry month of May. The Month of May. Beaumont *and* Fletcher. *Fr.* The Knight of the Burning Pestle. ChTr
London Tom-Cat. Michael Hamburger. BoAnP
London Town. Lionel Johnson. FaBoPP
London versus Epping Forest. John Clare. *Fr.* Child Harold. FaBoPP
London Voluntaries, *sels.* W. E. Henley.
Largo e mesto, IV. BrPo
("Out of the poisonous East.") SyP; VLP
Scherzando, III. BrPo
Londoners Gent to the King do present, The. On the Lord Mayor and Court of Aldermen, Presenting the Late King and Duke of York Each with a Copy of Their Freedoms. Andrew Marvell. APAS; CoMu; FaBoBa
Lone and forgotten/ Through a long sleeping. The Lonely. "Æ." AWP; OnYI
Lone Biker, The. R. Wayne Hardy. LFAC
Lone crow caws from the tall dead gum, The. Sheaf-Tosser. Eric Rolls. PoAu-2
Lone Dog. Irene R. McLeod. FaPON; GDP; PDV; RHPC; TiPo
Lone drake, upended, The. The Solitary. Mary Barnard. FAZ
Lone Driftin' Riders. *Unknown.* CoSo
Lone figure is waving, A. A Postcard from North Antrim. Seamus Heaney. IPY
Lone Founts. Herman Melville. LiTA; ViBoPo
Lone Gentleman. Pablo Neruda, *tr. fr. Spanish by* Clayton Eshleman. ErPo
Lone heart, learning. Vigils. Siegfried Sassoon. CMoP
Lone Huntsman. Christie Jeffries. GoYe

Lone kingfisher skims the river's crest, A. The Kingfisher. Blanche Mary Kelly. GoBC
Lone knee wanders through the world, A. The Knee on Its Own. Christian Morgenstern, *tr. by* Geoffrey Grigson. FaBoNo
Lone, lone, and lone I stand. The Myall in Prison. Mary Gilmore. CBAP; PoAu-1
Lone midnight-soothing melancholy bird. The Nightingale. Edward Moxon. OBRV
Lone o'er the moors I stray'd. The Hand. Ebenezer Jones. OBVV
Lone, phallic, Alet's get. Tour de Force. Peter Kane Dufault. ErPo
Lone Prairie, The. *Unknown. See* Bury Me Not on the Lone Prairie.
Lone seas are ominous. Lone Huntsman. Christie Jeffries. GoYe
Lone Star Trail, The, *with music. Unknown.* AS; CoSo
Lone Striker, A. Robert Frost. SaC
Lone watch of the moon over mountains old, The. Mortality. James Devaney. PoAu-1
Lone Wild Fowl, The, *with music.* H. R. MacFayden. AH
Loneliness. Hayden Carruth. FiCP
Loneliness. Edwin Essex. TrPWD
Loneliness. Robert Frost. *Fr.* The Hill Wife. FaBoEn
Loneliness. Hashin, *tr. fr. Japanese by* Harold G. Henderson. PoPl
(No Sky at All.) SoPo
Loneliness. Brooks Jenkins. CTBA
Loneliness. Sandra McPherson. AMV-80
Loneliness. Franz Werfel, *tr. fr. German by* Edith Abercrombie Snow. TrJP
Loneliness. Al Young. PoBA
Loneliness and July Ninth. Clairibel Alegria, *tr. fr. Spanish by* Aliki *and* Willis Barnstone. BoWoP
Loneliness leapt in the mirrors, but all week. Departure's Girl-Friend. W. S. Merwin. ConAP; LCAP
Loneliness of the Long Distance Runner, The. Alden Nowlan. PV; TW
Lonely, The. "Æ." AWP; OnYI
Lonely. Bloke Modisane. PBA
Lonely. André Spire, *tr. fr. French by* Jethro Bithell. AWP; TrJP
Lonely and big. First Pregnancy. Alta. NMM
Lonely and cold and fierce I keep my way. Gulf Stream. "Susan Coolidge." AA; EtS
Lonely and wild it rose. The Mysterious Music of Ocean. *Unknown.* EtS
Lonely Are the Fields of Sleep. Mary Newton Baldwin. GoYe
Lonely Beauty. Samuel Daniel. *Fr.* The Complaint of Rosamond. CTC; OBSC
Lonely-Bird, The. Harrison Smith Morris. AA
Lonely Bugle Grieves, The. Grenville Mellen. AA
Lonely caravan a-rollin' through the night. Star of the Western Skies. *Unknown.* BPAW
Lonely Cloud of Care, The. Coventry Patmore. *Fr.* The Victories of Love, II, vii. FaBoRV
Lonely House, The. Emily Dickinson. *See* I know some lonely houses off the road.
Lonely Isle, The. Claudian, *tr. fr. Latin by* Howard Mumford Jones. AWP
Lonely lake, a lonely shore, A. The Loon. Lew Sarett. HBMV
Lonely Land, The. A. J. M. Smith. CaP; NOBC
Lonely, lonely lay the hill. As Rivers of Water in a Dry Place. Anna Bunston de Bary. HBMV
Lonely Love. Edmund Blunden. OxBTC
Lonely Man, The. Randall Jarrell. OxBC
Lonely Month, The. Ruthven Todd. NeBP
Lonely Mother, The. Fenton Johnson. PoNe
Lonely pond in age-old stillness sleeps, A. Basho, *tr. fr. Japanese by* Curtis Hidden Page. AWP
Lonely Road. Peter Abrahams. PBA
Lonely Road, The. Kenneth Rand. HBV-1
Lonely, save for a few faint stars, the sky. The Little Dancers [a London Vision]. Laurence Binyon. CH; MoBrPo; MoVE; OBVV; OxBTC
Lonely Scarecrow, The. James Kirkup. GrPl; PDV
Lonely season in lonely lands, when fled, The. November. Robert Bridges. NBM; OBNC; PBBP; PoEL-5
Lonely Settler, The. Oliver Goldsmith, the Younger. *Fr.* The Rising Village. NOBC
("What noble courage must their hearts have fired.") OBEC; PeCV
Lonely Shell, The. Martha Eugenie Perry. CaP
Lonely Street, The. William Carlos Williams. MP; PoA; TwCP
Lonely student in a silent room, A. International Brigade Dead. Thomas O'Brien. NeIP
Lonely Traveller, The. Kwesi Brew. PBA; TTY
Lonely wanderer, wounded with iron, A. Shield. *Unknown, tr. by* Charles W. Kennedy. *Fr.* Riddles (Exeter Book). AnOE
Lonesome Dove ("Down in some lonesome piney grove"), 3 *versions. Unknown.* AmFP
Lonesome Dove, The ("Ye weary, heavy laden souls"). *Unknown.* AmFP
Lonesome Dream, The. Lisel Mueller. CoAP
Lonesome Grove, The, *with music. Unknown.* TrAS
Lonesome in the Country. Al Young. MAT; NPGG
Lonesome Road. *Unknown. See* Long Lonesome Road.
Lonesome scenes of winter incline to frost and snow, The. The Rejected Lover. *Unknown.* AmFP
Lonesome Valley, The. *Unknown.* FSW
Lonesome Water. Roy Helton. AmFN; MoAmPo
Long after dark. Scroll. Stanley Moss. VWA
Long after he'd wearied of the work. The Swimming Pool. Jonathan Holden. MAYP
Long after his great carapace was wrenched. Sea Turtle. Liston Pope. AMV-80
Long after you have swung back. Losing Track. Denise Levertov. HeIP; NaP; NoAM; NOBA; PoM
Long afterward, Oedipus, old and blinded. Myth. Muriel Rukeyser. IHMS; NNaP
Long afterwards/ the intelligent could deduce. The Judgment of Paris. W. S. Merwin. NNaP
Long Ago. Syd Scroggie. PoSH
Long Ago, The. Benjamin F. Taylor. *See* Isle of the Long Ago, The.
Long ago how fine was everything! Disillusion. *Tr. fr. Tewa Indian by* H. J. Spinden. WTO
Long ago I learned how to sleep. Wind Song. Carl Sandburg. MoAB; MoAmPo; MoShBr; TwAmPo
Long ago in the north. Songs in the Turtle Dance at Santa Clara. *Tr. fr. Tewa Indian by* H. J. Spinden. WTO
Long ago powerful snake when men also. The Deluge. *Unknown, tr. by* C. S. Rafinesque. *Fr.* The Wallum Olum. LiTA
Long ago when I shouted in red letters. Aubade. Ruth Lechlitner. AMV-80
Long and gray and gaunt he lies. At the Dog Show. Christopher Morley. MoShBr
Long and Lazy. Robert Herrick. FaBoEE
Long and Lonely Winter, The. Dave Goulder. OBET
Long anxiety and time of school, The. Childhood. Rainer Maria Rilke, *tr. by* M. D. Herter Norton. SOTW
Long are the years since he fell asleep. Washington. B. Y. Williams. PGD
Long as I can call to mind. A Childish Game. Reinmar von Hagenau, *tr. by* Jethro Bithell. AWP
Long as the Darkening Cloud Abode, *with music.* George Richards. AH
Long as thine art shall love true love. Dear Land of All My Love. Sidney Lanier. *Fr.* The Centennial Meditation of Columbia. GH; HBVY; PGD
Long Autumn rain. Autumn Song. Edward Dowden. OnYI
Long awaited day at last arrived, The. Walter Savage Landor. *Fr.* Gebir, VII. OBRV
Long Barren. Christina Rossetti. PBWP; TrCP; VLP
Long beardes heartles. The English. *Unknown.* GBP
Long before a woman knows she's pregnant. Progression of the Species. Brian W. Aldiss. FF
Long before he reached our age. Lines Written on November 15, 1933 by a Man Born November 14, 1881 to Another Born November 15, 1881. Clayton Hamilton. InMe
Long before I first left home, my father. Breakings. Henry Taylor. GrPl
Long before I hear it, Naples bright. Napoli Again. Richard Hugo. LCAP
Long before morning they waked me to say. The Lunar Probe. Maxine W. Kumin. MOON
Long before the sun cast a shadow. Gathering the Sparks. Howard Schwartz. VWA
Long Betwixt Love and Fear. Dryden. *Fr.* The Assignation. ViBoPo
Long-billed Gannets. Frances D. Emery. GoYe
Long by the willow-trees. A [*or* The] Willow-Tree. Thackeray. HBV-1; InMe
Long canoe, The/ Toward the shadowy shore. Lullaby. Robert Hillyer. DuDa; FaPON
Long-closed door, oh open it again, The. Love Song. Judah al-Harizi, *tr. by* Emma Lazarus. TrJP
Long desired, the dead return. They Return. Jay MacPherson. *Fr.* The Way Down. NOBC; PoA
Long-Distance. Carol Burns. AMV-81
Long Distance. Dana Naone. CDW
Long Distance. William Stafford. ELU; SO; WSC
Long distance is expensive. For Avi Killed in Lebanon. Mark Osaki. BrSi
Long Distance Moan. *Unknown.* BluL
Long Division; a Tribal History. Wendy Rose. TWSS
Long, Dodington, in debt, I long have sought. Edward Young. *Fr.* Love of Fame, the Universal Passion: Satire III. LAuP
Long-expected one and twenty. A Short Song of Congratulation [*or* One-and-Twenty *or* To a Young Heir]. Samuel Johnson. CABA; EBEV; ELP; HAP; InPK; InPS; InVP; LAuP; LoBV; NOBE; NOEC; NoP; OBEC; OBEV; OBSV; PoEL-3; TEP; UnPo
Long Feud. Louis Untermeyer. MoAmPo
Long flight over, The. MACV Advisor. Patrick Worth Gray. SOTS

Long from the lists of love I stood aloof. Omnia Vincit. Alfred Cochrane. HBV-1
Long Garden, The. Patrick Kavanagh. IPY
Long Gone. Sterling A. Brown. BALP; BANP; BPo; CDC
Long Gone. Jack Prelutsky. RHPC
Long grass searches the wind, The. Shearing Grass. Peter Redgrove. NePoEA-2
Long, gray moss that softly swings, The. In Louisiana. Albert Bigelow Paine. AA; AmFN
Long green shutters are drawn, The. Elsewheres. Donald Justice. LCAP
Long, green swell, A. Chill of the Eve. James Stephens. OnYI
Long had passed the hour of midnight. Dawn. *Malay Oral Tradition, tr. by* R. J. Wilkinson. WTO
Long had this nation been amused in vain. The Spanish Descent. Daniel Defoe. APAS
Long Hair. Gary Snyder. NOBA
Long hair, endless curls trained by the devoted. Epigram. Strato, *tr. by* Teddy Hogge. PeHV
Long-haired preachers come out every night. The Preacher and the Slave. *Unknown, at. to* Joe Hill. AS; FSW; GBP; PPON; TrAS; WTO
Long-haired Yak has long black hair, The. Yak. William Jay Smith. TiPo
Long has the summer sunlight shone. Incognita of Raphael. William Allen Butler. AA
Long hast thou, friend! been absent from thy soil. Mr. Pope's Welcome from Greece. John Gay. EBEV; OBEC; OxBoLi, *abr.*; PoEL-3
Long hath she slept, forgetful of delight. Vita Nuova. Sir William Watson. OBVV
Long have I beat with timid hands upon life's leaden door. The Suppliant. Georgia Douglas Johnson. BALP; CDC; PoBA; PoNe
Long have I dreamed of love's adventure. The Spell. Medora C. Addison. HBMV
Long have I framed weak phantasies of Thee. Agnosto Theo (To an Unknown God). Thomas Hardy. MoPo; WGRP
Long have I looked for my lost child. The Lost Child. James Reaney. NOBC
Long have I loved the terrible clouds that loom. Prayer for Dreadful Morning. E. Merrill Root. TrPWD
Long have I sigh'd for a calm: God grant I may find it at last! Tennyson. *Fr.* Maud. SyP
Long have I yearned and sought for beauty. I Sit and Wait for Beauty. Mae V. Cowdery. BlSi
Long heron feather, The. The Gray Plume. Francis Carlin. HBMV
Long Hill, The. Sara Teasdale. HBMV; LiTA; MoAmPo; PoPl
Long history. Olga Broumas. *Fr.* Backgammon. SUW
Long Hunter, The. Wendell Berry. *Fr.* Inland Passages. GP
Long I followed [*or* follow'd] happy guides. Forerunners. Emerson. AA; OBEV; OBVV; OxBA
Long I Have Loved to Stroll. T'ao Ch'ien, *tr. fr. Chinese by* William Acker. ChTr
Long I Thought That Knowledge Alone Would Suffice. Walt Whitman. NOBA
Long in thy shackles [*or* shackels], liberty. To Lucasta, from Prison. Richard Lovelace. AnAnS-1; CaPo
Long is the day without Usnagh's Children. Deirdre's Lament. *Unknown, tr. by* Whitley Stokes *and* Kuno Meyer. OnYI
Long is the night. Curriculum Vitae. Ingeborg Bachmann, *tr. by* Jerome Rothenberg. BoWoP
Long Island Springs. Howard Moss. GP; HoAn; UnPo
Long John. *Unknown.* FSW
Long John. Padraic Fallon. NeIP
Long John Brown and Little Mary Bell. Blake. InPK
Long Joke, The. R. T. Smith. STE
Long lay the ocean-paths from man conceal'd. The Inspiration. James Montgomery. *Fr.* The West Indies. PAH
Long-legged Fly. W. B. Yeats. CMoP; FaBoEn; FaBoMo; FaBoTw; InPK; InPS; LiTM; NoAM; NOBE; NoP; PAI; PPoe; TEP
Long legs, crooked thighs. Mother Goose. GBP; HBV-1; HBVY; OxNR
Long life to old Whalan of Waitin' a While. Whalan of Waitin' a While. J. W. Gordon. PoAu-1
Long lilies in a blue jug. Crockery. Julia Budenz. AMV-80
Long-Line Skinner. *Unknown.* FSW
Long Lines. Paul Goodman. NMP; VGW
(Long Lines: Youth and Age.) PeHV
Long lines of cliff breaking have left a chasm. Enoch Arden. Tennyson. BeLS
Long live our dear and noble Queen. Edward Edwin Foot. *Fr.* On the Inauguration of the Memorial Statue. FaBoCo
Long Live the Weeds. Theodore Roethke. NoAM; NOBA; PoA
Long Lonely Lover of the Highway. Frederic Will. AMV-81
Long Lonesome Road, *with music.* *Unknown.* OuSiCo
(Lonesome Road, *diff. vers., with music.*) AS
(Look Down That Long Lonesome Road, *diff. vers., with music.*) BLSo; OuSiCo
Long, Long Ago. Thomas Haynes Bayly. BLSo, *with music*; FSW; PSoN, *with music*; TreF
Long, Long Ago. *Unknown.* FaPON; OHIP; PChr; PDV; PoSC
Long, long ago, beyond the misty space. The Celts. Thomas D'Arcy McGee. OnYI; OxBI
Long long ago on Calvary. Victory. *Unknown.* STF
Long, long ago, when all the glittering earth. John Masefield. *Fr.* Sonnets. HBV-2
Long long ago when the world was a wild place. Bedtime Story. George MacBeth. NePoEA-2; NoAM; SoSe
Long, Long Be My Heart with Such Memories Filled. Thomas Moore. *See* Farewell! But Whenever.
Long, long before the Babe could speak. At Bethlehem. John Banister Tabb. *Fr.* The Child. AA
Long, long legs, The. From the Country to the City. Elizabeth Bishop. CrMA; NYP
Long, long sleep, a famous sleep, A. Emily Dickinson. NCEP
Long, long time, and a long time ago, A. A Long Time Ago. *Unknown.* AmSS
Long[e] love, that in my thought doth harbour, The. The Lover for Shamefastnesse Hideth His Desire within His Faithfull Hart. Petrarch, *tr. by* Sir Thomas Wyatt. Sonnets to Laura: To Laura in Life, CIX. AAS; CABA; NoP; OAEL-1; OBVE
Long May. Rosalía de Castro, *tr. fr. Galician by* Benjamin M. Woodbridge, Jr. PBWP
"Long may the lonely one wait for comfort." The Wanderer. *Unknown, tr. by* Mark Caldwell. TEP
Long months He lay within the womb. Signum Cui Contradicetur. Sister Mary Angelita. GoBC
Long Nature travailed, till at last she bore. Nature's Travail. *Unknown, tr. by* Goldwin Smith. AWP
Long Neglect Has Worn Away. Emily Brontë. NoP
Long Night Home, The. Charles F. Gordon. NBP
Long Night Moon, The: December. Frances Frost. YeAr
Long night succeeds thy little day. Margaret Love Peacock [for Her Tombstone, 1826]. Thomas Love Peacock. OBNC; OBRV
Long over, what's on the tree. To Her Body, against Time. Robert Kelly. CoPo
Long Overdue Thankyou Note to the Girl Who Taught Me Loving, A. Tom Schmidt. NeAC
Long Parenthesis, The. Roberta Hill Whiteman. TWSS
Long past midnight I sit here. Forsaken. Zalman Schneour, *tr. by* Joseph Leftwich. TrJP
Long Person. Gladys Cardiff. CDW; STE; TWSS
Long Picnic, The. Russell Edson. LCAP
Long placid evening. Tune: The Butterfly Woos the Blossoms. Li Ching-chao, *tr. by* C. H. Kwock *and* Vincent McHugh. PBWP
Long poles support the branches of the orchards in New Hampshire. Apples in New Hampshire. Marie Gilchrist. BoNaP
Long Prologue to a Short Play, A. Sir Henry Sheers. APAS
Long Pursuit. *Unknown, tr. fr. Greek by* Louis Untermeyer. UnTE
Long Race, The. E. A. Robinson. CrMA
Long, rich breadth of Holland lace, A. Old Flemish Lace. Amelia Walstien Carpenter. AA
Long River, The. Donald Hall. ConAP; LCAP; NePoEA-2
Long Road, The, *sel.* John Gray.
Gazelles and Unicorn. ChTr
Long road and a village, A. Holy Family. Muriel Rukeyser. MoAmPo
Long Road West, The. Henry Herbert Knibbs. BPAW
Long rolling, The. The Main-Deep. James Stephens. MoBrPo; MOS; OBMV; UnPo
Long Season, The. James Haug. AMV-81
Long shines the line of wet lamps dark in gleaming. Rainy Midnight. Ivor Gurney. FaBoPP
Long since I'd ceased to care. The Parrot. W. W. Gibson. OBMV
Long Since Last. Ruth Miller. PeSA
Long Small Room, The. Edward Thomas. BrPo
Long steel grass. Trio for Two Cats and a Trombone. Edith Sitwell. PBWP
Long straggling lines. Wild Geese. William Hart-Smith. BoAnP
Long-Suffering of God. Christopher Smart. Hymns for the Amusement of Children, Hymn 29. LAuP; NOCV
Long Summer. Laurie Lee. BoNaP
Long Summer, *sel.* Robert Lowell.
"Everyone now is crowding everyone." CAPP
Long Summer Day, *with music.* *Unknown.* OuSiCo
Long Tail Blue, *with music.* *Unknown.* BLSo
Long-tailed pig, A. Mother Goose. OxNR
Long-tailed ponies go nosing the pine-lands. Parochial Theme. Wallace Stevens. LiTA

Long Term Suffering. Richard Eberhart. GLGT; GP
Long the proud Spaniard. The Winning of Cales. Thomas Deloney. CoMu
Long the tyrant of our coast. On the Capture of the *Guerrière.* Philip Freneau. PAH
Long, their fixed eyes to Heaven bent. Lord Herbert of Cherbury. *Fr.* An Ode upon a Question Moved, Whether Love Should Continue for Ever? LO
Long they pine in weary woe, the nobles of our land. Kathaleen Ny-Houlahan [*or* Kathleen-Ni-Houlahan]. *Unknown, tr. by* James Clarence Mangan. AnIV; VLP
Long tides shudder over hidden rock, The. By Winter Seas. George Brandon Saul. AMV-80
Long Time a Child. Hartley Coleridge. EnRP; HBV-1; NCEP; OBRV
("Long time a child, and still a child, when years.") PoEL-4
(Sonnet.) OBNC
Long Time Ago, A, *diff. vers.* *Unknown.* AmFP; AmSS, *with music*; ShS, 6 *vers., with music*
Long time ago, A. T'ao Ch'ien, *tr. fr. Chinese by* Arthur Waley. FaBoCh
Long time ago in the big city, A. Small Quiet Song. Robert Paul Smith. CAD
Long time he lay upon the sunny hill. Childhood. Edwin Muir. CMoP; HeIP; NoP; SeCePo
Long time in some forgotten churchyard earth of Warwickshire. Who Were before Me. John Drinkwater. OBMV
Long time, many years, we've had these wars, A. On a Certain Engagement South of Seoul. Hayden Carruth. AmFN; NMP
Long time Plain Dealing in the haughty town. Plain Dealing's Downfall. *Unknown.* OBSV
Long time since it seems to-day, A. W. H. Auden. *Fr.* A New Year Letter. GOA
Long time those gay and spotted hides. Your Chase Had a Beast in View. John Peale Bishop. LiTA
Long Tom. W. W. Gibson. OxBTC
Long, Too Long America. Walt Whitman. GOA; NoAM
Long Trail, The. Kipling. FaBV; HBV-1; MOS; ViBoPo
(L'Envoi: "There's a whisper down the field where the year has shot her yield.") OBEV; OBVV
Long Trip. Langston Hughes. MOS
Long tyme hathe Christ (long tyme I must confesse). On the Reed of Our Lord's Passion. William Alabaster. PoEL-2
Long Voyage, The. Malcolm Cowley. NePA; TwAmPo
Long Walk before the Snows Began, A. Robert Bly. LCAP
Long Walks in the Afternoon. Margaret Gibson. AMV-81; MAYP
Long War, The. Li Po, *tr. fr. Chinese by* Cheng Yu Sun. WaaP
Long war had ended, The. The Next War. Sir Osbert Sitwell. MMA
Long was the great Figg by the prize fighting swains. Extempore Verses upon a Trial of Skill between the Two Great Masters of the Noble Science of Defence, Messrs. Figg and Sutton. John Byrom. OBEC
Long Waters, The. Theodore Roethke. NYBP
Long Way outside Yellowstone, A. Thomas McGrath. VGW
Long ways, A. A Remembrance of a Color inside a Forest. Ray A. Young Bear. CDW
Long whip lingers, the. Horses. Louis MacNeice. PH
Long white barn, A. Riddle. *Unknown.* ChTr; GBP
Long White Seam, The. Jean Ingelow. GN; HBV-1
Long Will in London. William Langland. *Fr.* The Vision of Piers Plowman. OxBM
Long Word, The. Deirdre Ballantyne. AMV-80
Long years ago I blazed a trail. The Pioneer. Arthur Guiterman. TiPo
Long years ago I wandered here. On Recrossing the Rocky Mountains after Many Years. John Charles Frémont. BPAW; PoOW
Long years ago there came to me in sleep. The Beautiful. F. S. Woodley. PeHV
Long years beheld me Patton's mansion grace. A Favourite Cat's Dying Soliloquy. Anna Seward. FM
Longe love that in my thought doth harbour, The. *See* Long love. . .
Longer to muse. Sir Thomas Wyatt. SiPS
Longest and much the dearest. Book Review. Russell Davies. FaBoEE
Longest day in the year had come, The. Midsummer Night. Marion Edey. YeAr
Longest day will drive a crack, The—til Jubilate windows in. Go Round. Laura Chester. NPGG
Longest Tyranny that ever sway'd, The. To My Friend, Dr. Charleton, on His Learned and Useful Works; and More Particularly This of Stone-Heng, by Him Restored to the True Founders. Dryden. SeCV-2
Longface Mahoney Discusses Heaven. Horace Gregory. VGW
Longfellow. James Whitcomb Riley. AA
Longfellow's Visit to Venice. John Betjeman. NOBL
Longford Legend, A. *Unknown.* OnYI
Longing. "Michael Lewis," *after the Chinese.* *Fr.* Cherry Blossoms. UnTE
Longing. Matthew Arnold. FPL; HBV-1; OAEP; PoLF
Longing. *Gond Oral Tradition, tr. by* V. Elwin *and* S. Hivale. WTO
Longing, The. William Goodreau. AMV-80
Longing. Judah Halevi, *tr. fr. Hebrew by* Nina Davis Salaman. TrJP
Longing. George Herbert. AnAnS-1; SeCV-1
Longing. Rachel Korn, *tr. fr. Yiddish by* Ruth Whitman. VWA
Longing at twilight the lovesick Adam saw. The Begetting of Cain. Hyam Plutzik. VWA
Longing for Heaven. Anne Bradstreet. *See* As Weary Pilgrims, Now at Rest.
Longing for Home. Jean Ingelow. *Fr.* Songs of Seven. WGRP
Longing for Jerusalem. Judah Halevi, *tr. fr. Hebrew by* Emma Lazarus. TrJP
Longing for that true comrade of my need. To Liebig. August, Graf von Platen, *tr. by* Reginald Bancroft Cooke. PeHV
Longing for the Emperor. Empress Iwa no Hime, *tr. fr. Japanese by* Geoffrey Bownas *and* Anthony Thwaite. BoWoP
Longing for the Persimmon Tree. Millen Brand. TAT
Longing, I have seen you in the water. Talking Myself to Sleep in the Mountain. Gibbons Ruark. MAYP
Longing that moves me in a second, heavier body, The. The Apartment Hunter. Philip Schultz. NYP
Longing to, The/ make love is a. Privation. Hayden Carruth. FAZ
Longjaunes His Periplus, *sel.* Howard McCord.
"My father gave me the freedom of love." GP
Longshore Intellectual. Sean Lucy. CIP
Lonnie Kramer. Geary Hobson. STE
Lonnie said before this, "I'm." Commanding Elephants. Philip Levine. NaP
Lon's away,/ Cill Garad is sad today. St. Columcille, *tr. by* Robin Flower. *Fr.* On a Dead Scholar. AnIL
Looby Loo. *Unknown.* *See* Here We Go Looby Loo.
Look, The. Elizabeth Barrett Browning. TrCP; TRV
Look, The. Elizabeth Daryush. PoA
Look. William Stafford. FAZ
Look, The. Sara Teasdale. HBV-1
Look and remember. Look upon this sky. Travelogue for Exiles. Karl Shapiro. MoAmPo; TrJP; TwAmPo
Look at a stone and it's nothing. Stone. E. L. Mayo. FAZ
Look at All Those Monkeys. Spike Milligan. OnUr
Look at her, calm and benign. A Bronze Statuette of Kwan-yin. Charles Wharton Stork. GoYe
Look at him, over there. Disillusion. Maureen Burge. BrRo
Look at him there in his stovepipe hat. American Primitive. William Jay Smith. DiL; FF; InPK; MoAmPo; MP; NePoAm; NePoEA; PAI; PoPl; PPON; TwCP
Look at it well. This was the good town once. The Good Town. Edwin Muir. CMoP
Look at itsy-bitsy Mitzi! The Pizza. Ogden Nash. RHPC
Look at Jonah embarking from Joppa, deterred by. Tom Fool at Jamaica. Marianne Moore. AP; NYBP
Look at me 8th. Poem. Sonia Sanchez. PoBA
Look at me: my mouth unlearned complaining early. Mother of Fishermen. Henriëtte Roland-Holst, *tr. by* Ria Leigh-Loohuizen. PBWP
Look at me with thy large brown eyes. Philip, My King. Dinah Maria Mulock Craik. HBV-1
Look at my continent containing. Human Geography. Gloria Fuertes, *tr. by* Willis Barnstone. BoWoP
Look at My Face, a Collage. Carolyn M. Rodgers. JB
Look at my knees. I Wonder What It Feels Like to Be Drowned? Robert Graves. BrPo; MoBrPo
Look at Six Eggs. Carl Sandburg. *Fr.* Prairie. FaPON
Look at That Gal. Julian Bond. PoNe; TTY
Look at the eyes look from my tail! Peacock and Nightingale. Robert Finch. OBCV
Look at the gentle savage, monstrous gentleman. London Tom-Cat. Michael Hamburger. BoAnP
Look at the mare of Farmer Giles! The Mare. Herbert Asquith. PH
Look at the stars! Look, look up at the skies! The Starlight Night. Gerard Manley Hopkins. ACP; BrPo; GoBC; GTBS-P; InPS; LiTM; MoAB; MoBrPo; MoVE; OBVV; OxBoCh; PoPle; PPP; SeCePo; ViBoPo; VLP; WSC
Look at this red pear. The Indigestion of the Vampire. W. S. Merwin. NaP
Look at this skin—at fourscore years. Robert Barnabas Brough. *Fr.* The Marquis of Carabas. FiBHP
Look at this village boy, his head is stuffed. Farm Child. R. S. Thomas. BoNaP; ChMP
"Look at us now, destroyed." The Dead Cities Speak to the Living Cities. Edmond Fleg, *tr. by* Anthony Rudolf. VWA
Look at wealth through warm, misty rain. Looking at Wealth in Newport. James Schevill. TAT
Look at your corn in May. *Unknown.* FaBoUs

Look Away/Look Away. Stephen Todd Booker. LFAC
Look away now from the high lonesome hills. Admonition for Spring. L. A. MacKay. CaP; OBCV; PeCV
Look Back. Carroll Annett. STE
Look back with longing eyes and know that I will follow. The Flight. Sara Teasdale. HBMV
Look, Barker, when you wrote me I lay cringing. Mailed to G. B. Gene Derwood. NePA
Look between the bow and the bowstring, beneath. Backgrounds to Italian Paintings: Fifteenth Century. Anne Ridler. WPE
Look Closely. Morton Marcus. FF
Look, Delia, how we esteem [*or* 'steem] the half-blown rose. The Half-blown Rose [*or* Sonnet]. Samuel Daniel. *Fr.* To Delia. EIL; HBV-1; HeIP; NoP; OBSC; SeCePo; WHA
Look down; be still. Wonga Vine. Judith Wright. PoAu-2
Look Down Fair Moon. Walt Whitman. MOON
Look Down That Lonesome Road. *Unknown. See* Long Lonesome Road.
Look down. The dead have life. Gravestones. Vernon Watkins. ChMP; TEP
Look, Edwin! Edna St. Vincent Millay. GoJo
Look, everyone, look! Easter Joy. Nancy Byrd Turner. YeAr
Look: Florentines and Umbrians have made whole. For a Nativity. Lisel Mueller. NePoAm-2
Look for a place in my skin that may not have been. That Which You Call "Love Me." Luis Rosales, *tr. by* Lynn C. Jacox. AMV-81
Look for Me on England. H. B. Mallalieu. WaP
Look forth and tell me what they do. Hammer and Anvil. Samuel Valentine Cole. PoLF
Look forward, truant, to your second childhood. The Death Room. Robert Graves. NYBP
Look! From my window there's a view. There Is. Louis Simpson. ConAP
Look from the sphere of endless day. Other Sheep I Have, Which Are Not of This Fold. Bryant. TrPWD
Look, God, I have never spoken to You. Conversion [*or* Last Thoughts of a Fighting Man]. Frances Angermayer. PGD; PoLF; TreFS
Look, he is superfluous—for of what use was it to be born? Ovid, *tr. by* L. R. Lind. Tristia, XIII. NAs
Look: Here our bodies lie in a long, long line. But We Shall Bloom. Haim Guri, *tr. by* David Kuselewitz. TrJP
Look[e] Home. Robert Southwell. AnAnS-1; NOCV
Look how evening comes and around us the barbed-wire-hemmed, wild. Seventh Eclogue. Miklós Radnóti, *tr. by* Emery George. VWA
Look, how he shakes for cold! Hymn: Crucifixus pro Nobis. Patrick Carey. OxBoCh
Look how her close defences laddered now. Apollo and Daphne. W. R. Rodgers. ErPo; LiTB
Look! how the clouds are flying south! The Snow-Man. "Marian Douglas." OBCA
Look how the flower which lingeringly [*or* ling'ringly] doth fade. Thy Sun Posts Westward [*or* No Trust in Time]. William Drummond of Hawthornden. LoBV; SeCePo
Look how the golden children. New Leaves. Juan Ramón Jiménez, *tr. by* H. R. Hays. PoPl
Look how the industrious bee in fragrant May. The Bee. Charles Fitzgeffry. *Fr.* Sir Francis Drake. EIL
Look how the lark soars upward and is gone. False Poets and True. Thomas Hood. HBV-2; PP
Look[e] how the pale Queen[e] of the silent night. A Sonnet of the Moon [*or* Of the Moon *or* The Moon *or* Looke How the Pale Queen]. Charles Best. CH; EIL; EtS; HBV-1; MOON; OBSC
Look, I Have Thrown All Right. L. A. MacKay. PeCV
Look in mine eyes, Belovèd! Is it true. Consummation. Elsa Barker. *Fr.* The Spirit and the Bride. HBMV
Look in my face; my name is Might-have-been. A Superscription [*or* Sonnet: A Superscription]. Dante Gabriel Rossetti. The House of Life, XCVII. EBVV; FaBoEn; GTBS-P; HBV-1; NOBE; NoP; OAEL-2; OBNC; PoEL-5; SeCePo; VLP; WHA
Look, in the attic, the unentered room. Before the Carnival. Thom Gunn. NePoEA
Look, in the Labyrinth of Memory. Delmore Schwartz. TrJP
Look in this crystal pool, and you will see. To ———, with an Ivory Hand-Glass. Lord Alfred Douglas. FaBoUs
Look in this mirror, tell me what you see. Glass Dialectic. Howard Nemerov. WaP
Look in thy glass, and tell the face thou viewest. Sonnets, III. Shakespeare. CABA; EnRePo; LiTB; MasP; OBSC
Look into the Gulf, A. Edwin Markham. AA
Look! it is as though the sun. Fern House at Kew. Paul Dehn. ChMP
"Look, it's a fox!"—their two hearts spoke. The Fox. C. Day Lewis. BoAnP
Look, it's morning, and a little water gurgles in the tap. Morning Song. Alan Dugan. CAD; ELU
Look, Loig, behind. The Only Jealousy of Emer. *Unknown, tr. by* John Montague. BIrV
Look! Look at me! Tree Birthdays. Mary Carolyn Davies. OHIP
Look, look! rejoice and wonder! The Return of Astraea. Ben Jonson. NOBE
Look! Look! the spring is come. First Spring Morning. Robert Bridges. BoNaP; YeAr
Look, my love, on the wall, and here, at this Eastern picture. Morning. Henry Reed. MoVE; NeBP
Look Not in My Eyes, for Fear. A. E. Housman. A Shropshire Lad, XV. PeHV; PoEL-5
Look not thou on beauty's charming. Lucy Ashton's Song. Sir Walter Scott. *Fr.* The Bride of Lammermoor, *ch.* 3. BSV; EnRP; GoTS; NoBE; OBEV; OxBS
Look Not to Me for Wisdom. Charles Divine. HBMV
Look now, at this February street in April. A Street in April. Louis Dudek. OBCV
Look now, bride of God. In Praise of Virginity. Hroswitha, *tr. by* John Dillon. PBWP
Look now, directed by yon candle's blaze. Fiction. Charles Sprague. *Fr.* Curiosity. AA
Look off, dear Love, across the sallow sands. Evening Song. Sidney Lanier. AP; TreFT; UnPo; WHA
Look on Him Whom They Pierced, and Mourn. Isaac Watts. NOCV
Look on this cast, and know the hand. The Hand of Lincoln. Edmund Clarence Stedman. AA; OHIP
Look on this maid of honour, now. Philip Massinger. *Fr.* The Maid of Honour. ACP; GoBC
Look once more ere we leave this specular mount. Athens. Milton. *Fr.* Paradise Regained, IV. OBS; ViBoPo
Look one way and the sun is going down. The Mockingbird. Randall Jarrell. DuDa; NYBP; RFM
Look or You Leap. Jasper Heywood. EIL
(Lookers-on, The.) ACP
Look our ransomed shores around. Additional Verses to Hail Columbia. Oliver Wendell Holmes. PAH
Look Out Below! Charles R. Thatcher. PoAu-1
Look out, boys, better wash your hands. The Marrowbone Itch. *Unknown.* OuSiCo
Look out how you use proud words. Primer Lesson. Carl Sandburg. FaPON; MoAmPo; MoShBr; PoPl
Look out! Look out, boys! Clear the track! The Broomstick Train. Oliver Wendell Holmes. *Fr.* The Broomstick Train. FaPON
Look out! Look out! You've spilt the ink. April Fools' Day. Marnie Pomeroy. PoSC
Look out upon the stars, my love. A Serenade. Edward Coote Pinkney. AA; HBV-1
Look over Yonder, *with music.* Lawrence Gellert. TrAS
Look round: You see a little supper room. De Coenatione Micae. Martial, *tr. by* Robert Louis Stevenson. FaBoCh
Look, son, what a skyscraper. My Son Doesn't See a Thing. Tomás Rivera, *tr. by* Toni Empringham. FIA
Look, Stranger, on This Island Now. W.H. Auden. *See* On This Island.
Look, sunset's all undone! Emblems of Evening. Robert Horan. CrMA
Look, the eucalyptus, the atlas pine. Any Night. Philip Levine. AMV-80
Look there at the star! Shepherd's Song at Christmas. Langston Hughes. PChr
Look there! *The Lovers in the Flowers.* Epithalamion. Grace Schulman. FAZ
Look thy last on all things shitty. Shitty. Kingsley Amis. OxBC; TW
Look to the Back of the Hand. Judith Minty. PoA
Look to the Leaf. *Unknown, tr. fr. German by* Louis Untermeyer. UnTE
Look Up. Edward Everett Hale. FaBoBe; FaFP
(Lend a Hand.) TreFS; TRV
Look up. . ./ From bleakening hills. Snow. Adelaide Crapsey. QFR
Look up and not down. Look Up [*or* Lend a Hand]. Edward Everett Hale. FaBoBe; FaFP; TreFS; TRV
Look up into the dome. Altitudes. Richard Wilbur. CMoP
Look up into the light of the lantern. Night Song. Louise Glück. MAYP; SV
"Look up," she said; and all the heavens blazed. Starlight. John White Chadwick. AA
Look up this river in the book of rivers. Border River. Alfred Goldsworthy Bailey. CaP
Look Up to Pentland's Tow'ring Tap. Allan Ramsay. BSV
Look up, you men. Men there at the fire. Rainer Maria Rilke. *Fr.* Annunciation over the Shepherds. PChr
Look upon my face. Once the Striped Quagga. Mary TallMountain. TWSS
Look, we don't give a hoot if Zippo-Fasteners have gone to war. Memorial to the Great Big Beautiful Self-sacrificing Advertisers. Frederick Ebright. WaP

Look what immortal floods the sunset pours. The Sea—in Calm. "Barry Cornwall." EtS
Look where the mist. The Mist over Pukehina. *Maori Oral Tradition, tr. by* E. Shortland. WTO
Look, wild and wide. The Sea. *Unknown, tr. by* Frank O'Connor. KiLC
Look you, my simple friend, 'tis one of those. Arthur Hugh Clough. VLP
"Look!" you said. "Look!" Two Egrets. John Ciardi. PoPl
Look-a How Dey Done My Lord, *with music. Unknown.* BoAN-2
"Lookatitthisway: I have seen some." Where Have All the Indians Gone? Janet Campbell Hale. STE
Looke Home. Robert Southwell. *See* Look Home.
Looke How the Pale Queene. Charles Best. *See* Sonnet to the Moon, A.
Looke how the woods, where enterlaced trees. Bible, *O.T., paraphrased by* Countess of Pembroke. *Fr.* Psalms. OBVE
Looke well about, ye that lovers be. Against Women. *Unknown.* MeEL
Looked stitched together and. Reuben's Cabin. Robert Morgan. TAT
Lookers-on, The. Jasper Heywood. *See* Look or You Leap.
Lookin' for the Bully of the Town. *Unknown.* BaBo
Looking as I've looked before, straight down the heart. The Stranger. Adrienne Rich. NNaP
Looking at a Dead Wren in My Hand. Robert Bly. GP; NNaP
Looking at a Dry Canadian Thistle Brought In from the Snow. Robert Bly. NNaP
Looking at a Picture on an Anniversary. Thomas Hardy. EyDe
Looking at Each Other. Muriel Rukeyser. NNaP
Looking at Henry Moore's Elephant Skull Etchings in Jerusalem during the War. Shirley Kaufman. LCAP
Looking at New-fallen Snow from a Train. Robert Bly. NaP
Looking at Pictures to Be Put Away. Gary Snyder. FF; InPS; NNaP
Looking at Power. Warren Woessner. AMV-80
Looking at Quilts. Marge Piercy. SaC
Looking at Some Flowers. Robert Bly. NaP; NOBA
Looking at the Empire State Building. Ralph Pomeroy. GP
Looking at Wealth in Newport. James Schevill. TAT
Looking at Your Face. Galway Kinnell. PPJ
Looking away from my sin and my shame. That's Faith. S. N. Leitner. STF
Looking Back, *sel.* John Dyer.
Grongar Hill. ChTr; EnRP; FaBoPP; GoTL; LAuP; LoBV; NOEC; NoP; OBEC; PoEL-3
Looking back in my mind I can see. The Elementary Scene. Randall Jarrell. CMoP; LCAP
Looking Both Ways before Crossing. John Woods. ConAP
Looking by chance in at the open window. The Foreboding. Robert Graves. ChMP; ELP; GBL; PoA
Looking Down a Hill. A. R. Thompson. PoSH
Looking down into my father's/ dead face. "Good Night, Willie Lee, I'll See You in the Morning." Alice Walker. WeW
Looking Down on Nether Stowey. Samuel Taylor Coleridge. *Fr.* Fears in Solitude. FaBoPP
Looking Down on West Virginia. John Dickson. AMV-81
Looking eastward from Tablerock. Tablerock. Darryl Wally. AMV-81
Looking for a Country under Its Original Name. Colleen J. McElroy. BlSi
Looking for a Home. Bert Stern. FAZ
Looking for a Rest Area. Stephen Dunn. AmPA
Looking for Buddha. Jaime Jacinto. BrSi
Looking for love, she read cookbooks. The Woman Who Loved to Cook. Erica Jong. TAP
Looking for Maimonides: Tiberias. Shirley Kaufman. VWA
Looking for Mountain Beavers. David Wagoner. VGW
Looking for Mushrooms at Sunrise. W. S. Merwin. NaP; NOBA
Looking for My Old Indian Grandmother in the Summer Heat of 1980. Diane Glancy. STE
Looking for the Buckhead Boys. James Dickey. LiSp
Looking for Work. Raymond Carver. GeTw
Looking Forward. Robert Louis Stevenson. BrPo; OxBChV
("When I am grown to man's estate.") CenHV
Looking-Glass, A. Thomas Carew. CaPo
Looking Glass, The. Kipling. EvOK; FaBoTw; OBMV
Looking-Glass for Smokers, A, *sel.* Lawrence Spooner.
On Giving Up Smoking. NOEC
Looking into a Face. Robert Bly. NOBA
Looking into a Tide Pool. Robert Bly. MAT
Looking into History. Richard Wilbur. VGW
Looking into my daughter's eyes I read. For My Daughter. Weldon Kees. CoAP
Looking into the windows that doom has broken. Sonnet. George Woodcock. NeBP
Looking On. Anthony Thwaite. NePoEA-2
Looking Out. Helen Chasin. NMM
Looking over the water shows nothing but trees. Windowed Habitations. Charles G. Bell. NePoAm-2
Looking to the sea, it is a line. The Innocence. Robert Creeley. NeAP; NoAM
Looking up/ I find myself written. The Paisley Ceiling. Lila Arnold. IHMS
Looking Up at Down. *Unknown.* BluL
Looking Up at Leaves. Barbara Howes. BoNaP
Looking up at the stars, I know quite well. The More Loving One. W. H. Auden. HoPM
Looking West. William Stafford. NYBP
Look—on the topmost branches of the world. Sunday Evening in the Common. John Hall Wheelock. HBV-2; MoAmPo
Lookout, The. William Collins. EtS
Lookout watch must climb and climb, The. Crow's Nest. Richard F. Armknecht. GoYe
Looks of a Lover Enamoured, The. George Gascoigne. ElL; SeCePo
Loom of Dreams, The. Arthur Symons. VLP
Loom of Time, The. *Unknown.* BLPA
Looms are sept an' brass is drawn. July Wakes. Richard Pomfret. OBET
Loon, The. Theodore Harding Rand. CaP
Loon, The. Lew Sarett. HBMV
Loon, The. Alfred Billings Street. AA
Loon, A? No. Chippewa Love Song. *Tr. by* Frances Densmore, *ad. by* Willis Barnstone. BoWoP
See also Loon I Thought It Was, A.
"Loon Call, A." Richard Eberhart. AMV-80
Loon I Thought It Was, A. *Tr. fr. Chippewa Indian by* Frances Densmore. OBVE
See also Chippewa Love Song.
Loon's Egg, The. Peter Dale Scott. MoCV
Loon's long night call, A. Three Seasons. Francis Sparshott. NOBC
Loony, *sels.* William Kloefkorn. GP
During the War.
Good Folks at the Camp Meeting, The.
Loop of rusty cable incises, The. "Luckies." Reginald Gibbons. MAYP
Loose earth falls in the grave like a peaceful regular breathing, The. A Dog's Death. J. C. Squire. FM
Loose eyes of an old man, The. Negroes. Maxwell Bodenheim. PoNe
Loose fold of steam idling, A. Shetland Pony. Maurice Lindsay. BSV
Loose knot of geese crossed the road, vain and squabbling, A. Driving, Driven. David McAleavey. AMV-80
Loose Saraband, A. Richard Lovelace. CaPo; CavP; PoEL-3
Loose Woman. X. J. Kennedy. WeW
Loose Woman Poem. Sharon Thesen. NOBC
Loosed from its bonds my spirit fled away. A Dream, or the Type of the Rising Sun. Jean Adams. NOEC
Loot. Thom Gunn. ErPo; NePoEA-2
Looting. Jascha Kessler. HoAn
Loo-wit. Wendy Rose. STE
Loping along on the day's patrol. The Sheepherder. Lew Sarett. AmFN; FaPON
Loping and sloped with heat, face thatched and red. Drinker. Patrick Anderson. PeCV
Loppèd tree in time [*or* tyme] may grow again [*or* againe *or* agayne], The. Times Go by Turns [or Tymes Goe by Turnes]. Robert Southwell. ACP; ElL; FaBoEn; GoBC; HBV-2; LiTB; OBSC; OxBoCh; PoEL-2
Lopsided with God. On the Road to Vicenza. Ralph Gustafson. CaP
Lord/ forgive me/ if I twist the sunset. The Hungry Black Child. Adam David Miller. PoBA
Lord,/ I am the cat. The Prayer of the Cat. Carmen Bernos de Gasztold. PDV
Lord,/ we have been watching over him. Act of Faith. Arturo Trías, *tr. by* Julio Marzán. InW
Lord,/ What a menagerie! Noah's Prayer. Carmen Bernos de Gasztold, *tr. by* Rumer Godden. TrCP
Lord a big fat woman with the meat shakin' on her bones. Big Fat Woman. *Unknown.* OuSiCo
Lord Abbott. Hilaire Belloc. FaBoNo
Lord above gave man an arm of iron, The. With a Little Bit of Luck. Alan Jay Lerner. FaFP
Lord above, in tender love, The. Thanksgiving Hymn. *Unknown.* PAH
Lord Alcohol. Thomas Lovell Beddoes. WiR
(Song: "Who tames the lion now?") ViBoPo
Lord Apollo, who has never died, The. Many Are Called. E. A. Robinson. MoVE; OxBA
Lord, art thou at the table head above. The Reflexion [*or* Reflection]. Edward Taylor. *Fr.* Preparatory Meditations, First Series. AmPP; AP; NePA; OxBA
Lord, art Thou wrapped in cloud. The Evening Star. Amy Carmichael. TRV
Lord, as thou wilt, bestow. Prayer. Eduard Mörike, *tr. by* John Drinkwater. TrPWD
Lord, at This Closing Hour, *with music.* Eleazar Thompson Fitch. AH

Lord Barrenstock. Stevie Smith. FaBoNo; OBSV
Lord Bateman. *Unknown. See* Young Beichan.
Lord, behold our family here assembled. A Prayer for the Household. Robert Louis Stevenson. TRV
Lord Beichan and Susie Pye. *Unknown. See* Young Beichan.
Lord bless you and keep you, The. Benediction [*or* Blessing of the Priests]. Bible, *O.T. Fr.* Numbers. TrGrPo; TrJP
("Lorde blesse the and kepe the, The," *tr. by* William Tyndale.) OBVE
Lord, by whose breath all souls and seeds are living. Hymn. Andrew Young. EaLo
"Lord Byron" was an Englishman. Sketch of Lord Byron's Life. Julia A. Moore. FiBHP; OBAL
Lord, can a crumb of earth the earth outweigh. Prologue. Edward Taylor. AP
Lord Chancellor's Song. Gilbert. *See* Nightmare.
Lord Chancellours Villanies Discovered; or, His Rise and Fall in the Four Last Years, The. *Unknown.* CoMu
Lord Christ, beneath thy starry dome. Hymn for a Household. Daniel Henderson. HBMV
Lord Clive. E. C. Bentley. *Fr.* Clerihews. DBV; MoShBr; OxBoLi; PoPle; WhC
("What I like about Clive.") CenHV; NOBL
Lord Cockroach, Old Sir Empty Belly. A Curse against the Owner. Barton Sutter. TW
Lord, confound this surly sister. The Curse. J. M. Synge. ChTr; DBV; FaBoCo; FaBoEE; PV; TreFT; TW
Lord Coningsby's Epitaph. Pope. FaBoEE
Lord Cozens Hardy. John Betjeman. OxBTC
Lord Cray. Edward Gorey. RHPC
Lord, Dear God! to Thy Attending, *with music.* Heinrich Otto, *tr. fr. German by* Sheema Z. Buehne. AH
Lord Delamere. *Unknown.* ESPB
Lord, Deliver, Thou Canst Save, *with music.* Eliza Lee Follen. AH
Lord Derwentwater. *Unknown.* AmFP; BaBo; ESPB (A *and* D *vers.*)
Lord Descended from Above, The, *with music.* Thomas Sternhold. AH
(Majesty of God, The.) WGRP
Lord Douglas. *Unknown. See* Waly, Waly.
Lord Epsom. Hilaire Belloc. PH
Lord Erlinton had ae daughter. Erlinton. *Unknown.* ESPB
Lord Erskine, at women presuming to rail. A Wife. Matthew Gregory Lewis. DBV; PV
Lord Finchley. Hilaire Belloc. DTC; ELU; FaBoCo; FaBoEE; FiBHP; NOBL; OxBoLi
Lord Fluting Dreams of America on the Eve of His Departure from Liverpool. Paul Zimmer. VGW
Lord, for the erring thought. A Thanksgiving [*or* A Prayer]. William Dean Howells. HBV-2; TrPWD; WGRP
Lord, for to-morrow and its needs. Just for Today. Sybil F. Partridge, *wr. at.* to Samuel Wilberforce. HBV-2; TreF; TRV
Lord frowned down from every wall, The. Childhood. Donagh MacDonagh. NeIP
Lord Gabriel, wilt thou not rejoice. Cradle Song. Josephine Preston Peabody. HBV-1
Lord Galloway. Burns. DBV; OxBoLi
Lord Gave, The. Bible, *O.T.* Job, I: 20-21. TreF
Lord, God, forgive white Europe. Prayer for Peace: II. Léopold Sédar Senghor, *tr. by* John Reed *and* Clive Wake. TTY
Lord God, how full our cup of happiness! The Cup of Happiness. Gilbert Thomas. TrPWD
Lord God in Paradise. Grace for Gardens. Louise Driscoll. TrPWD
Lord, God of all in Life and Death. Hymn for the Slain in Battle. William Stanley Braithwaite. BALP
Lord God of Hosts, *with music.* Shepherd Knapp. AH
Lord, God of love, the wedded hearts'. The Sanctum. Thomas Augustus Daly. TrPWD
Lord God of the oak and the elm. Prayer. George Villiers. TrPWD
Lord God of trajectory and blast. Man unto His Fellow Man. Norman Corwin. *Fr.* On a Note of Triumph. TrJP
Lord God Planted a Garden, The. Dorothy Frances Gurney. BLPA; FaBoBe; FPL; HBMV; WGRP
Lord God smiled, The. The Preachers. Norman Nicholson. NeBP
Lord God! This was a stone. The Stone. Thomas Vaughan. OBS
Lord Gorbals. Harry Graham. FaBoCo
Lord, Grant Us Calm. Christina Rossetti. OxBoCh
Lord had a job for me, The. Get Somebody Else [*or* Too Busy]. Paul Laurence Dunbar. BLRP; TRV; WBLP
Lord Has a Child, The, *with music.* Langston Hughes. AH
Lord, hast Thou set me here. The Priest's Lament. Robert Hugh Benson. ACP
Lord hath builded for Himself, The. The Unknown God. Henry Francis Lyte. TRV
Lord, Have Mercy On Us. Thomas Nashe. *See* Adieu, Farewell Earth's Bliss.
Lord Hay's Mask, *sel.* Thomas Campion.
Roses. OBSC
Lord, he thought he'd make a man. Dese Bones Gwine to Rise Again. *Unknown.* AS; OxBoLi
Lord, Hear My Prayer. John Clare. NOCV; NoP; TrCP
Lord, heavy hip mama she done moved to piney wood. Piney Wood Money Mama. *Unknown.* BluL
Lord, help me live from day to day. Others. Charles D. Meigs. WBLP
Lord here my prayre and let my crye passe. Bible, *O.T.* Psalms, CII. OBVE
Lord Heygate. Hilaire Belloc. OxBoLi
Lord High-Bo. Hilaire Belloc. FiBHP
Lord, how can man preach thy eternal[l] word? The Windows [*or* The Church Windows]. George Herbert. AnAnS-1; CABA; MeLP; NOCV; NoP; OAEP; OBS; SeCP; SeCV-1; TrCP
Lord, how delightful 'tis to see. For the Lord's Day Evening. Isaac Watts. OxBChV
Lord how many are my foes. Bible, *O.T., paraphrased by* Milton. Psalms, III. OBVE
Lord, how sholde I roule me. How Should I Rule Me? *Unknown.* OxBM
Lord, I am humbled by the great. Scatheless. Marguerite Wilkinson. HBMV
Lord, I am like to [*or* the] mistletoe. To God. Robert Herrick. TrPWD; TRV; WGRP
Lord, I am lonely. A Stranger in This Land. Cliff Ashby. NOCV
Lord I am not entirely selfish. Prayer. Gavin Ewart. OxBC
Lord, I am not one of the just. Seder, 1944. Friedrich Torberg, *tr. by* Erna Baber Rosenfeld. VWA
Lord, I am poor; but it becomes. I Have a Roof. Ada Jackson. TrPWD
Lord, I Am Thine, *with music.* Samuel Davies. AH
Lord I can't see how these hungry women please. Don't Want No Hungry Woman. *Unknown.* BluL
Lord, I confess my sin is great. Repentance. George Herbert. OAEP
Lord, I give thanks! Thanksgiving. Susie M. Best. TrPWD
Lord I hate to hear that Frisco whistle blow. Frisco Whistle Blues. *Unknown.* BluL
Lord, I have fasted, I have prayed. Weakness of Nature. Richard Hurrell Froude. OBRV
Lord, I have knelt and tried to pray to-night. Communion. Edward Dowden. TrPWD
Lord, I have not time to pray. Helene Magaret. *Fr.* Impiety. TrPWD
Lord, I have sinn'd, and the black number swells. The Penitent. Jeremy Taylor. OBS; OxBoCh
Lord, I Know Thy Grace Is nigh Me, *with music.* Hervey Doddridge Ganse. AH
Lord, I my vows to Thee renew. Direct This Day. Thomas Ken. TRV
"Lord, I Owe Thee a Death." Alice Meynell. SUMH
Lord, I remember, and am sore amazed. Hymn of Weeping. Amittai ben Shefatiah, *tr. by* Nina Davis Salaman. TrJP
Lord, I say nothing: I profess. Christ, the Man. W. H. Davies. WGRP
Lord, I Want to Be a Christian in-a My Heart, *with music. Unknown.* BoAN-2
(Lord, I Want to Be a Christian, *with music.*) AH, *sl. diff. version*
Lord! if in love, though fainting oft, I have tended thy gracious Vine. "Owen Meredith." *Fr.* Last Lines. TrPWD
Lord, If Thou Art Not Present. John Gray. TrPWD
Lord, I'm done for: now Margot. Rondeau. William Jay Smith. FiBHP
Lord in His wisdom made the fly, The. The Fly. Ogden Nash. FaPON
Lord, in my silence how do I despise. Frailty. George Herbert. NOCV; OxBoCh
Lord in the Wind, The. James Picot. PoAu-2
Lord, in this day of battle. Prayer during Battle. Hermann Hagedorn. TrPWD
Lord, in this dust Thy sovereign voice. A Thanksgiving. John Henry Newman. TrPWD
Lord, in Thy Presence Here, *with music.* Jesse L. Holman. AH
Lord Ingram and Chiel Wyet. *Unknown.* ESPB (A, B, *and* C *vers.*)
(Lady Maisry.) OBET; OxBB, *with music;* ViBoFo
Lord into His Garden Comes, The, *with music. Unknown.* AH
Lord Is a Man of War, The. Bible, *O.T. Fr.* Exodus. WaaP
Lord Is Good to All, The. Bible, *O.T.* Psalms, CXLV: 9 TRV
Lord Is King, The. *Unknown, tr. fr. Hebrew by* Solomon Solis-Cohen. TrJP
Lord is my light and my salvation, The. The Deliverance of Jehovah. Bible, *O.T.* (*Moulton, Modern Readers' Bible*). Psalms, XXVII. TreFT; WGRP
Lord is my shepherd, I shall not, The. Neo-Thomist Poem. Ernest Hemingway. OBAL
Lord Is My Shepherd, The: [I Shall Not Want]. Bible, *O.T.* Psalms, XXIII. AWP; BiP; BLPL; FaBoBe; FaPON; FPL; NAWM-1; NIP; OHIP; PoPl; SUS; TreF; TrGrPo; TrJP; TRV

("Lord[e] is my shepherd[e], The: therefore can I lack nothing," *tr. by* Miles Coverdale.) ILwL; OBVE
(Lord's My Shepherd, I'll Not Want, The, *Scottish Psalter, ad. by* Francis Rous.) AH, *with music;* TRV; WBLP
(Protection of Jehovah, The, *Moulton, Modern Readers' Bible.*) WGRP
Lord[e] is my shepherd[e]; The: therefore can I lack nothing. Bible, *O.T., tr. by* Miles Coverdale. Psalm, XXIII. ILwL; OBVE
Lord Is Risen, The. William Dunbar. *See* Done Is a Battle.
Lord is the portion of mine inheritance, The. I Have a Goodly Heritage. Bible, *O.T. Fr.* Psalm XVI. TreFT
Lord, It Belongs Not to My Care. Richard Baxter. EBCP; OxBoCh
Lord it is my chief complaint. William Cowper. *Fr.* Lovest Thou Me? TrPWD
Lord! It Is Not Life to Live. Augustus Montague Toplady. *Fr.* Happiness Found. OxBoCh; TrPWD
Lord, it is time. The summer was too long. Autumn Day. Rainer Maria Rilke, *tr. by* C. F. MacIntyre. TrJP
Lord, It's All, Almost Done, *with music.* *Unknown.* OuSiCo
Lord Jesus Christ, We Humbly Pray, *with music.* Henry Eyster Jacobs. AH
Lord Jesus, make Thyself to me. My Prayer. *Unknown.* BLRP
Lord Jesus, Thou hast known. A Mother's Birthday. Henry Van Dyke. OHIP
Lord Jesus! with what sweetness and delights. Ascension-Day. Henry Vaughan. AnAnS-1; OxBoCh
Lord, knights, and squires, the num'rous band. To a Child of Quality [of Five Years Old, the Author Supposed Forty]. Matthew Prior. NOEC; SeCeV
Lord Lavel he stands at his stable-door. Lord Lovel. *Unknown.* ESPB
Lord, lay the taste of prayer upon my tongue. The Taste of Prayer. Ralph W. Seager. TrPWD
Lord, lay your fingers on. Closing Prayer. Johnstone G. Patrick. TrPWD
Lord! Lead the Way the Saviour Went, *with music.* William Crosswell. AH
Lord, let me be the torch that springs to light. The Torch. Theodosia Garrison. BLPA
Lord, let me live like a Regular Man. A Prayer. Berton Braley. BLPA
Lord, let the angels praise thy name. Miserie. George Herbert. PoEL-2
Lord, let war's tempests cease. Let War's Tempests Cease. Longfellow. OHIP
Lord, Listen. Else Lasker-Schüler, *tr. fr. German by* Edouard Roditi. VWA
Lord Livingston. *Unknown.* ESPB; OxBB
Lord, Lord—these miracles, the streets, all say. Stone Too Can Pray. Conrad Aiken. EaLo
Lord, Lord to Thee. A Sailor's Prayer. George Hornell Morris. TrPWD
Lord Lovel. *Unknown.* AmFP; AS, *with music;* BLPA; ESPB (A, B, *and* D *vers.*); FaPON; FSW; TreFS; ViBoFo (A *and* B *vers.*)
(Tale of Lord Lovell, The.) NOBL
Lord Lundy. Hilaire Belloc. FaBoCo; OxBoLi; OBSV
Lord, Make a Regular Man out of Me. Edgar A. Guest. BLPA; BLPL
Lord, Make Me an Instrument of Your Peace. St. Francis of Assisi, *tr. fr. Latin.* TreFS
(Prayer of St. Francis of Assisi [for Peace].) FPL; PoLF; PoPl
(St. Francis' Prayer.) TRV
Lord, make me coy and tender to offend. Unkindness. George Herbert. HBV-2
Lord, make me sensitive to the sight. Prayer. Barbara Marr. TrPWD
"Lord make me the co-ordinator of Thy implementation." The Educational Administration Professor's Prayer. Gerald Bobango. AMV-80
Lord, Make Me to Know Mine End. Bible, *O.T.* Psalms, XXXIX. TrJP
Lord, make my childish soul stand straight. A Prayer. William Laird. HBMV
"Lord, make my loving a guard for them." Mother-Prayer. Margaret Widdemer. HBMV
Lord, make my soul. The Mirror. Blanche Mary Kelly. GoBC; TrPWD
Lord, Many Times. Richard Chenevix Trench. OBRV
Lord, Many Times Thou Pleased Art, *with music.* George Wither. AH
Lord Maxwell's Last Goodnight. *Unknown.* ESPB (A *and* B *vers.*); OxBB, *with music*
Lord, mine eye offended. Matthew V. 29-30. Derek Mahon. CIP
Lord, my first fruits present themselves to thee. The Dedication. George Herbert. AnAnS-1; OAEP
Lord my pasture shall prepare, The. Pastoral Hymn. Joseph Addison. OBEC
Lord my shepherd, me His sheep, The. Psalm XXIII. George Sandys. *Fr.* A Paraphrase upon the Psalms of David. JCP
Lord, My Weak Thought in Vain Would Climb, *with music.* Ray Palmer. AH
Lord North's Recantation. *Unknown.* PAH
Lord, not for light in darkness do we pray. A Prayer. John Drinkwater. HBV-2; OBVV; TrPWD; WGRP
Lord, now lettest Thou Thy servant depart in peace. Nunc Dimittis. Bible, *N.T. Fr.* St. Luke. WGRP
Lord of all being! throned afar. A Sun-Day Hymn. Oliver Wendell Holmes. *Fr.* The Professor at the Breakfast Table. AH, *with music;* TrPWD; TRV; WGRP
Lord of all, himself through all diffused, The. William Cowper. *Fr.* The Task, VI. OAEL-1
Lord of All Pots and Pans and Things. *Unknown, at. to* Cecily Halleck. TRV *See also* Divine Office of the Kitchen, The.
(Home Prayer, A.) STF
Lord of all, who reigned supreme, The. Adon 'Olam. *Unknown, tr. by* F. De Sola Mendes. EaLo
Lord of comfort, hope, and love. Give My Heart a Song. Anna M. Gilleland. STF
Lord of Each Soul, *with music.* Paul Engle. AH
Lord of Life, All Praise Excelling, *with music.* Clement Clarke Moore. AH
Lord of Lorn and the False Steward, The. *Unknown.* ESPB
(Lord of Lorn and the Fals Steward, *with music.*) OxBB
Lord of My Heart's Elation. Bliss Carman. AH, *with music;* HBV-2; NOBC; OBCV; TrPWD
Lord of my years, can life be bare. Common Blessings. Thomas Curtis Clark. TrPWD
Lord of Rosslyn's daughter gaed through the wud her lane, The. Captain Wedderburn's Courtship. *Unknown.* ESPB; ViBoFo
Lord of Sea and Earth and Air. Prayer for a [*or* the] Pilot. Cecil Roberts. FaPON; TrPWD
Lord of the Dance. Sydney Carter. OBET
Lord of the Far Horizons. Bliss Carman. TrPWD
Lord of the grass and hill. Overlord [*or* Veni Creator]. Bliss Carman. CaP; WGRP
Lord of the Isle, The. Stefan George, *tr. fr. German by* Ludwig Lewisohn. AWP
Lord of the Isles, The, *sel.* Sir Walter Scott.
Bannockburn. BSV
Lord of the lands, beneath Thy bending skies. A Hymn for Canada. Albert Durrant Watson. CaP
Lord of the Mountain. Prayer to the Mountain Spirit. *Unknown.* BPAW, *ad. by* Mary Austin; WGRP, *tr. by* G. W. Cronyn
Lord of the pots and pipkins, since I have not time to be. The Divine Office of the Kitchen. Cecily Hallack. BLRP; PoLF; TreFT
Lord of the Winds. Mary Elizabeth Coleridge. OxBoCh; TrPWD
Lord of the World, The. G. A. Studdert-Kennedy. PGD
Lord of the World. *Unknown, tr. fr. Hebrew by* D. A. de Sola. TrJP
Lord of the Worlds Below! *with music.* James Freeman. AH
Lord of Thyself and me, through the sore grief. George Macdonald. *Fr.* Within and Without. TRV
Lord Our God Alone Is Strong, The, *with music.* Caleb T. Winchester. AH
Lord over all! whose power the sceptre swayed. Lord of the World. *Unknown, tr. by* D. A. de Sola. TrJP
Lord over life and all the ways of breath. Ernest Dowson. *Fr.* De Amore. TrPWD
Lord Pam in the church (cou'd you think it) kneel'd down. Epigram. Swift. NCEP
Lord possessed me in the beginning of his way, The. The Voice of Wisdom. Bible, *O.T. Fr.* Proverbs. ISi (*Douay vers.*); TreFT
Lord, purge our eyes to see. Judge Not According to the Appearance. Christina Rossetti. TrPWD
Lord Rameses of Egypt sighed. Birthright. John Drinkwater. CH; HBV-2; OxBTC; WHA
Lord Randal. *Unknown.* AmFP; AWP; BSV; CABA; EBEV; EnRP; ESPB (A, B, *and* J *vers.*); FaBoBA; FF; HAP; HBV-2; HeIP; HoPM; LiTB; LoBV; NIP; NoP (A *vers.*); OAEL-1, *with music;* OxBB, *with music;* OxBS; PAI; SeCeV; TreF; TrGrPo; ViBoFo (A, B, *and* C *vers.*); WeW
(Lord Randall.) FPL; FSW; NIP
(Lord Rendal.) EnSB
Lord reigneth, The; he is apparelled with majesty. Jehovah's Immovable Throne. Bible, *O.T.* Psalms, XCII. WGRP
Lord said, The. Pronouns. Karle Wilson Baker. TreFT
Lord Saltoun and Auchanachie. *Unknown.* BaBo; ESPB
Lord, Save Us, We Perish. Christina Rossetti. TrPWD
(O Lord, Seek Us.) EBCP
Lord, serene on your symbol. Accepting. Vassar Miller. FiCP
Lord Shaftesbury. Dryden. *See* Achitophel: The Earl of Shaftesbury.
Lord, shall I find it in Thy Holy Church. Truth. Claude McKay. BPo
Lord, she won't pick cotton girl won't pull no corn. No More Women Blues. *Unknown.* BluL
Lord she's gone done left me done packed/ up and split. Feeling Fucked Up. Etheridge Knight. GP; NNaP
Lord, since the strongest human hands I know. In the Dark. Sophie Jewett. TrPWD
Lord Sits with Me Out in Front, The. Jack Gilbert. NPGG
Lord, speak to me, that I may speak. For Every Day [*or* A Teacher's Prayer]. Frances Ridley Havergal. BLRP (*both versions*); TRV
Lord Tennyson and Lord Melchett. D. H. Lawrence. FaBoEE
Lord, the newness of this day. Prayer. Henry van Dyke. TRV

Lord, the Roman hyacinths are blooming in bowls. A Song for Simeon. T. S. Eliot. EaLo; EBCP; LiTB; NAs; NOCV; OxBoCh
Lord, the snowful sky. Sailor's Carol. Charles Causley. OBCP
Lord they accused me of murder. Levee Camp Moan. *Unknown.* BluL
Lord, Thine humble servants hear. Hymn for Atonement Day. Judah Halevi, *tr. by* Solomon Solis-Cohen. TrJP
Lord—Thine the Day. Dag Hammarskjöld, *tr. by* Leif Sjöberg *and* W. H. Auden. EaLo
Lord, this humble house we'd keep. Edgar A. Guest. *Fr.* Prayer for the Home. TRV
Lord, this woman who fell into many sins. Mary Magdalene Kassia, *tr. by* Aliki *and* Willis Barnstone *and* Elene Kolb. BoWoP
Lord Thomas and Fair Annet. *Unknown.* AmFP; ESPB (A, D, *and* I *vers.*); FaBoBa; OxBB, *with music*; ViBoFo
(Brown, Girl, The, C *vers.*) BaBo
(Brown Girl or Fair Eleanor, The, *with music.*) AS
(Lord Thomas and Fair Ellender.) AmFP
(Lord Thomas and Fair Ellinor.) OBET
Lord Thomas and Lady Margaret. *Unknown.* BaBo; ESPB
Lord Thomas he was a bold [*or* gay] forrester. Lord Thomas and Fair Annet [*or* Ellinor]. *Unknown.* ESPB; OBET
Lord Thomas is to the hunting gone. Lord Thomas and Lady Margaret. *Unknown.* BaBo; ESPB
Lord Thomas Stuart. *Unknown.* BaBo; ESPB
Lord, Thou art mine, and I am Thine. Clasping of Hands. George Herbert. ILwL; PoEL-2
Lord, Thou Hast Been Our Dwelling Place. Bible, *O.T.* Psalms, XC. AWP; EaLo
("Lord, Thou hast been our dwelling place in all generations.") DL
Lord, Thou hast given me a cell. A Thanksgiving to God for His House. Robert Herrick. AnAnS-2; BLPL; ChTr; FaBoBe; HAP; HBV-2; OBS; OFD; OHIP; PGD; PoRA; SeCeV; SeCP; SeCV-1; TrCP; TreFT; TrPWD; ViBoPo; WGRP
Lord, Thou hast made this world below the shadow of a dream. McAndrew's [*or* M'Andrew's] Hymn. Kipling. OxBTC; PoEL-5; VLP
Lord, Thou Hast Promised, *with music.* Samuel K. Cox. AH
Lord, Thou Hast Suffered. Amy Carmichael. TRV
Lord, thus I sin, repent, and sin again. A Sinner's Lament. Lord Herbert of Cherbury. SeCP
Lord 'tis midnight. Three Phases of Africa. Francis Ernest Kobina Parkes. PBA
Lord to me a shepherd is, The. Psalm 23. *Unknown. Fr.* The Bay Psalm Book. OBCA
Lord Ullin's Daughter. Thomas Campbell. BeLS; EnRP; FaPoN; FaPOR; GN; GTBS; GTBS-P; HBV-2; HBVY; OBRV; RoGo; TreF; WBLP
Lord, very fair my lot and beautiful my story. Very Fair My Lot. Jacob David Kamzon, *tr. by* Sholom J. Kahn. TrJP
Lord Vyet. A. C. Benson. OBVV
Lord Walter's Wife. Elizabeth Barrett Browning. BeLS; HAP
Lord Waterford. *Unknown.* ChTr; GBP
Lord, we look to once for all, The. The Heretic's Tragedy. Robert Browning. OAEL-2
Lord, we thank Thee for affliction. Thank Thee, Lord. Georgia B. Adams. STF
Lord! what a busy [*or* busie], restles[s] thing. The Pursuit[e]. Henry Vaughan. OAEP; SeCP; TrCP; TrPWD
Lord, what a change within us one short hour. Prayer [*or* Prevailing Prayer *or* Sonnet]. Richard Chenevix Trench. BLRP; TrPWD; TRV; WBLP; WGRP
Lord! what a goodly thing is want of shirts. John Cleveland. *Fr.* The Rebel Scot. OBSV
Lord, what a thoughtless wretch was I. *Unknown.* AmFP
Lord, what am I, that, with unceasing care. To-Morrow. Lope de Vega, *tr. by* Longfellow. AWP; TrPWD
Lord, what are the sins. In a U-Haul North of Damascus. David Bottoms. FYAP; MAYP
Lord, what is man? Meditation. Carl Rakosi. AMV-80
Lord what is man, that he should find. Christopher Smart. *Fr.* Psalm VIII. TrPWD
Lord, what is man? why should he cost thee [*or* you]. Charitas Nimia; or, The Dear[e] Bargain. Richard Crashaw. AnAnS-1; JCP; MePo; NOCV; OxBoCh
Lord, what these weders ar cold [*or* Lord! what these weathers are cold]. The Second Shepherds' Play [*or* The Wakefield Second Shepherds Play]. *Unknown.* OAEL-1, *mod. vers.*; PoEL-1
Lord, what unvalued pleasures crown'd. The Invitation. *Unknown.* OxBoCh
Lord, when I find at last Thy Paradise. She Asks for New Earth. Katherine Tynan. HBMV
Lord, when I look at lovely things which pass. In the Fields. Charlotte Mew. BoNaP; MoAB; MoBrPo
Lord, when on my bed I lie. Whirring Wheels. John Oxenham. TRV
Lord, when the sense of Thy sweet grace. A Song [*or* A Song of Divine Love]. Richard Crashaw. GoBC; SeCeV; TrPWD; ViBoPo
Lord, When the Wise Men Came from Far. Sidney Godolphin. *See* Hymn: "Lord, when the wise men came from far."
Lord! when thou didst thy self undress. The Incarnation and Passion. Henry Vaughan. TrCP
Lord, when Thou seest that my work is done. After Work. John Oxenham. TRV
Lord! when Thou wentest from this place. The Lament of Eve. *Unknown.* ACP
Lord, Where Shall I Find Thee? Judah Halevi, *tr. fr. Hebrew by* Nina Davis Salaman. TrJP
Lord, While for All Mankind. John R. Wreford. TrPWD
Lord, who am I to teach the way. The Teacher. Leslie Pinckney Hill. BANP; PoNe; TrPWD
Lord! Who Art Merciful as Well as Just. Robert Southey. TrPWD
(Imitated from the Persian.) EnRP
Lord, who createdst man in wealth and store. Easter Wings. George Herbert. AnAnS-1; CABA; HAP; HeIP; InPK; InPS; LiTB; MeLP; MePo; NIP; NoP; OAEL-1; OAEP; OBS; PAI; PoEL-2; PP; PPP; SeCP; TEP; TrCP; WeW
Lord who ordainst for mankind. The Mother's Hymn. Bryant. OHIP
Lord, Who's the Happy Man, *with music.* Nahum Tate *and* Nicholas Brady. AH
Lord Will Happiness Divine, The. William Cowper. *See* Contrite Heart, The.
Lord William; or, Lord Lundy. *Unknown.* BaBo; ESPB
Lord Willoughby. *Unknown.* CoMu
(Brave Lord Willoughby.) FaPoR
Lord, with glowing heart I'd praise thee. Hymn. Francis Scott Key. TrPWD
Lord, with what care hast thou begirt us round! Sin. George Herbert. NoP; ViBoPo
Lord, with what glorie wast thou serv'd of old. Sion. George Herbert. AnAnS-1
Lord, You may not recognize me. The Gift. Louise Glück. GP
Lord, you visited Paris on the day of your birth. Paris in the Snow. Léopold Sédar-Senghor, *tr. by* Ulli Beier. PBA
Lord, you've sent both. The Cancer Match. James Dickey. GP
Lorde is my shepherde, The: therefore can I lack nothing. *See* Lord Is My Shepherd, The; I Shall Not Want.
Lorde, thou hast bene oure refuge. Bible, *O.T., tr. by* Miles Coverdale. Psalms, XC. OBVE
Lordinges, I wol you singen of a grotë. Sing a Song of Sixpence, *parody.* Frank Sidgwick. WhC
Lordinges, listen, and hold you still. Durham Field. *Unknown.* ESPB
"Lordinges," guod he, "in chirches whan I preche." *See* "Lordings," quod he.
Lordings, Listen to Our Lay. *Unknown.* OHIP
"Lordings [*or* Lordinges]," quod he, "in chirches whan I preche." The Pardoner's Prologue. Chaucer. *Fr.* The Canterbury Tales. NoP; OAEL-1; OAEP
Lordly and Isolate Satyrs, The. Charles Olson. CoAP; NeAP; PoM
Lordly Hudson, The. Paul Goodman. CoAP; NMP; NYP; VGW
Lord's Chameleons, The. Peter Klappert. AmPA
Lords have been made whose hired robes have hidden. On the Relinquishment of a Title. Geoffrey Grigson. FaBoEE
Lords, knights, and squires, the numerous band. To a Child of Quality [Five Years Old, the Author Supposed Forty]. Matthew Prior. GN; HBV-1; LiTB; NIP; NOBE; OBEC; OBEV; PoEL-3
Lord's lost Him His mockingbird. Mourning Poem for the Queen of Sunday. Robert Hayden. HoAn; NoP; PoBA
Lord's Mask[e], The, *sel.* Thomas Campion.
Song: to the Masquers Representing Stars. LoBV
(Stars Dance, The.) OBSC
Lord's My Shepherd, The. Bible, *O.T.* *See* Lord Is My Shepherd, The.
Lord's name be praised, The. The Litanies of Julia Pastrana (1832–1860). Thomas W. Shapcott. CBAP
Lords of Creation, The. *Unknown.* PoLF
Lords of life, the lords of life, The. Experience. Emerson. FPL; LiTA; PoEL-4; TAP
Lords of the Main, The. Joseph Stansbury. PAH
Lords of the Wilderness. John Leyden. OBRV
Lord's Prayer in Verse, The. Aaron Hill. FaBoUs
Lord's Prayer, The. Bible, *N.T.* St. Matthew, VI: 9–13. EaLo; PoLF; TrGrPo; TRV
(Our Father Which in Heaven Art, *with music.*) AH
Lore. R. S. Thomas. OxBC
Lorelei. Heine, *tr. fr. German by* Emma Lazarus. TrJP
(Loreley, The.) NAWM-2, *tr. by* Ernst Feise; WSC, *tr. by* Aaron Kramer
Lorena. H. D. L. Webster. BLPA; FSW; PSoN, *with music*

Lorenzo dwelt at Heighington. Fragment of a Song. "Lewis Carroll." FaBoNo
Lorenzo! such the glories of the world! The Consolation. Edward Young. *Fr.* The Complaint; or, Night Thoughts on Life, Death and Immortality, IX. NOEC
Los Angeles. Eloise Klein Healy. GP
Los is by mortals nam'd Time; Enitharmon is nam'd Space. Blake. *Fr.* Milton, I. OBRV
Los Mineros. Edward Dorn. PoM
Lose This Day Loitering. Goethe, *tr. fr. German by* John Anster. *Fr.* Faust. PoLF
("Lose this day loitering, 'twill be the same story.") TRV
Losers. Jonathan Holden. MAYP
Losers. Carl Sandburg. CMoP; HBMV; MoAB; MoAmPo; MoVE; NoAM; TrGrPo
Losers, The. William Young. *Fr.* Wishmaker's Town. HBMV
(Pawns, The.) AA
Losing a Slave-Girl. Po Chü-i, *tr. fr. Chinese by* Arthur Waley. AWP
Losing the Straight Way. Ian Wedde. OCNZ
Losing Track. Denise Levertov. HeIP; NaP; NoAM; NOBA; PoM
Losing Track. Cathy Song. BrSi
Loss. Richard Aldington. BrPo
Loss. A. R. Ammons. ConAP
Loss. Julia Johnson Davis. HBMV
Loss. Alex Kuo. BrSi
Loss. Charles Madge. FaBoMo
Loss falls from the air as the tables turn. Complaint. Joseph Bennett. LiTA
Loss in Delay. Robert Southwell. OBSC
Loss, my molester, at last patient be. Pamphilia's Sonnet. Mary Sidney Wroth, Countess of Montgomery. *Fr.* Urania. WPE
Loss of an Oil Tanker. Charles Causley. OxBC
Loss of control, parquet, paraqueets, The. Spring Poem. Bin Ramke. AMV-81
Loss of Strength, The. Austin Clarke. IPY
Loss of the *Birkenhead,* The. Francis Hastings Doyle. HBV-2
Loss of the *Cedar Grove*, The, *with music. Unknown.* ShS
Loss of the *Druid,* The, *with music. Unknown.* ShS
Loss of the *Due Dispatch*, The. *Unknown.* AmFP
Loss of the *New Columbia*, The. *Unknown.* AmFP
Loss of the *Ramillies. Unknown. See* Ship *Rambolee,* The.
Loss of the *Royal George.* William Cowper. *See* On the Loss of the Royal George.
Loss of weight. Near Drowning. Ralph Pomeroy. DFF
Losses. Randall Jarrell. CoBMV; LCAP; LiTM; MoVE; OxBA; PoA; TAP; UnPo; WaP
Lost. A. Alvarez. NMP
Lost. Millen Brand. NYBP
Lost. Chu Shu-chen, *tr. fr. Chinese by* Kenneth Rexroth. BoWoP
Lost. Charles d'Orléans. OxBM
Lost. David Fisher. NPGG
Lost, The. *Malay Oral Tradition, tr. by* R. J. Wilkinson *and* R. O. Winstedt. WTO
Lost. Carl Sandburg. AmPP; CMoP; PDV; PoPl; WHA
Lost, The. Jones Very. NOBA; QFR
Lost. David Wagoner. GP; PoA
Lost Acres. Robert Graves. NoAM
Lost after All. Charlie D. Tillman. PeD
Lost among secrets in a tangle. First Days. Tuvia Ruebner, *tr. by* A. C. Jacobs. VWA
Lost Anchors. E. A. Robinson. CMoP
Lost and bewildered in the thickening mist. On the Great Fog in London, December 1762. James Eyre Weeks. NOEC
Lost and Found. George Macdonald. TRV; WGRP
Lost and Given Over. E. J. Brady. PoAu-1
Lost Angel, The. Philip Levine. NOBA
Lost Army, The. Margery Lawrence. SUMH
Lost Baby, The. *Unknown.* AmFP
Lost Baby Poem, The. Lucille Clifton. BlSi; InPK; WPE
Lost Ball, The. Lucy Sprague Mitchell. TiPo
Lost but Found. Horatius Bonar. HBV-2
Lost Child, The. James Reaney. NOBC
Lost Children, The. Richard Eberhart. NePoAm-2
Lost Children, The. Randall Jarrell. CoAP; PrIm; TAP
Lost Children, The. Gregory Orr. GeTw
Lost Chord, A. Adelaide Anne Procter. FaFP; HBV-2; PaPo; TreF; VLP; WBLP; WGRP
Lost Cinderella. Edith Weaver. DFT
Lost City. Ingrid Jonker, *tr. fr. Afrikaans by* Jack Cope *and* Ruth Miller. PeSA
Lost Colors, The. Elizabeth Stuart Phelps Ward. AA; HBV-2; HBVY
Lost Companions. Helen Bryant. AMV-80
Lost Contact. William Cole. POL
Lost Contact. Sylvia Wheeler. FAZ
Lost Continent, The. Jenny Joseph. BrRo
Lost Copper, *sel.* Wendy Rose.
Epilog: "Drop a kernel of corn on a rock." TWSS
Lost Dancer, The. Jean Toomer. BALP; PoBA
Lost, Dancing, The. Edward Field. GP
Lost Days. Dante Gabriel Rossetti. The House of Life, LXXXVI. GoBC; NCEP; OAEP; WHA
Lost Desire. Meleager, *tr. fr. Greek by* William M. Hardinge. AWP
Lost Dog. Frances Rodman. GDP
Lost Doll, The. Charles Kingsley. *Fr.* The Water Babies. FaPON; MoShBr; SoPo
("I once had a sweet little doll, dears.") TiPo
(Little Doll, The.) OxBChV
(Song: "I once had a sweet little doll, dears.") PaPo
Lost Explorer. Edmund Pennant. GoYe
Lost for a Rose's Sake. *Unknown, tr. fr. French by* Andrew Lang. AWP
Lost Garden. "Katherine Hale." CaP
Lost Genius, The. John James Piatt. AA
Lost Girl, The. *Unknown.* TDH
Lost God, A, *sel.* Francis W. Bourdillon.
"Ah, happy who have seen Him, whom the world." WGRP
Lost Heifer, The. Austin Clarke. BIrV; OxBI
Lost Illusion, A. George Du Maurier. CenHV
Lost in a Blizzard. Arthur W. Monroe. PoOW
Lost in a Norther. Hamlin Garland. BPAW
Lost in Heaven. Robert Frost. MoAmPo
Lost in the vastness of the void Pacific. Homecoming. Karl Shapiro. MiAP
Lost in the white world. Winter Climb. Beinn Eunaich. PoSH
Lost in the words. Davening. Rochelle Ratner. VWA
Lost in Translation. James Merrill. FYAP
Lost in Yucatan. Tom McKeown. HoAn
Lost Ingredient, The. Anne Sexton. CoPo
Lost Jewel, A [*or* The]. Robert Graves. EnLoPo; NYBP
Lost Jimmie Whalen. *Unknown.* AmFP; BaBo
Lost Johnny. *Unknown.* AmFP
Lost Lagoon, The. Pauline Johnson. BPAW
Lost Lane. Dorothy Wellesley. WPE
Lost Leader, The. Robert Browning. HBV-1; TreFS; TrGrPo; ViBoPo; VLP
Lost Leader, The. Douglas Fraser. PoSh
Lost Letter to James Wright, with Thanks for a Map of Fano. Gibbons Ruark. MAYP
Lost Light. Elizabeth Akers Allen. HBV-1
Lost Lines from Chaucer's Prologue to "The Canterbury Tales." *Unknown.* PeHV
Lost Little Sister, The. William Barnes. PoEL-4
Lost! lost! lost! Advertisement of a Lost Day. Lydia Huntley Sigourney. WBLP
Lost Love. Robert Graves. AWP; CH; ChMP; FaBoCh; MoAB; MoBrPo; NoP
Lost Love. Andrew Lang. BSV; HBV-1
Lost Love. Tennyson. *See* In Memoriam A. H. H. "I envy not in any moods."
Lost Love. *Tr. fr. Tewa Indian by* H. J. Spinden. WTO
Lost Love, The. Wordsworth. *See* She Dwelt among the Untrodden Ways.
Lost Lover Blues. *Unknown.* BluL
Lost manor where I walk continually. The Pier-Glass. Robert Graves. CMoP; CoBMV; MoAB; NoAM
Lost Mistress, The. Robert Browning. BoLoP; FaBoEn; FiP; HBV-1; NOBE; OBEV; OBNC; OBVV; PoPle
Lost Mohican Visits Hell's Kitchen, A. A. K. Redwing. VoR
Lost Moment. Hoyt W. Fuller. PoBA
Lost Mr. Blake. W. S. Gilbert. InMe
Lost music returns, The: a few bring it. Of the New Prosody. Brewster Ghiselin. MoVE
Lost my partner what'll I do. Skip to My Lou. *Unknown.* FSW
Lost Objects. Diana O Hehir. AMV-80
Lost Occasion, The. Whittier. BLPL; NOBA
Lost on a fogbound spit of sand. W. H. Auden. FaBoEE
Lost on Both Sides. Dante Gabriel Rossetti. The House of Life, XCI. NoP; SeCePo; VLP
Lost on September Trail, 1967. Alberto Ríos. FYAP
Lost Orchard, The. Edgar Lee Masters. CMoP; MoPo
Lost Parasol, The, *sel.* Sándor Weöres, *tr. fr. Hungarian by* Edwin Morgan.
"Where metalled road invades light thinning air." OBVE
Lost Parents. Lawrence Ferlinghetti. GP; PoM
Lost Picture. Ray Fraser. NeAC
Lost Pictures, The. Hollis Summers. HoPM
Lost Pilot, The. James Tate. CoAP; DiL; NoP; OBWP; TwCP; UnPo

Lost Playmate, The. Abbie Farwell Brown. HBVY
Lost Pleiad, The. William Gilmore Simms. AA
Lost Range, The. Henry Herbert Knibbs. BPAW
Lost Sheep, The. Bible, *N.T.* *Fr.* St. Luke, XV. TreF
Lost Sheep, The. Elizabeth Cecilia Clephane. *See* Ninety and Nine, The.
Lost Shipmate, The. Theodore Goodridge Roberts. CaP
Lost Ships. Thomas Hornsby Ferril. EtS
Lost Silvertip. J. D. Reed. NYBP
Lost Son, The. Theodore Roethke. AP; CoBMV; DiL; HAP; LiTM; MiAP; MoPo; NePA; TwAmPo; VGW
Flight, The, *sel.* TrGrPo
Lost Soul, A. Jay Macpherson. NOBC
Lost: The Original, Its Reason and Its Rhyme. Translation. Rika Lesser. PoA
Lost Tribe, The. Robert Finch. CaP
Lost Tribe, The. Ruth Pitter. WPOW
Lost Valley, The. Gordon J. Gadsby. PoSH
Lost War-Sloop, The. Edna Dean Proctor. PAH
Lost Word. Jean Burden. AMV-80
Lost Word of Jesus, A. Henry van Dyke. TrCP; WGRP
Lost World, A. Robert Graves. NYBP
Lost Years. Eugene Lee-Hamilton. OBVV
Lot Later. Howard Nemerov. HoPM; NMP
Lot of boulders lying around, A. Clear Night, Small Fire, No Wind. Reg Saner. NPAW
Lot of love is chosen, The. I learnt that much. Chosen. W. B. Yeats. BoLoP; CMoP
Lot of Night Music, A. Anthony Hecht. NIP; OxBC
Lot of the old folks here, A—all that's left. Reflections in a Slum. "Hugh MacDiarmid." FaBoTw; NMP
Lot would be no loss, the slender stand, The. Wild Cherry. Louise Townsend Nicholl. NePoAm
Loth to depart, but yet at last, each one. The Parting Verse, the Feast There Ended. Robert Herrick. SeCV-1
Lotos-Eaters, The. Tennyson. CABA; FiP; GoTL; HBV-2; LiTB; NoP; OAEL-2; OAEP; OBRV; OnMSP; PoEL-5; SeCeV; TEP; VLP
Sels.
Choric Song: "There is sweet music here that softer falls." HeIP; OBNC
(Choric Song of the Lotus-Eaters.) FaFP; ViBoPo
" 'Courage!' he said, and pointed toward the land." ChTr; TreFT
(Song of the Lotus-Eaters.) NOBE; OBEV; WHA
(There Is Sweet Music Here.) FaBV
Lots of truisms don't have to be repeated. The Anatomy of Happiness. Ogden Nash. LiTA; TAP
Lot's Wife. "Anna Akhmatova," *tr. fr. Russian by* Richard Wilbur. BoWoP; PBWP
Lotus Eaters, The. Tennyson. *See* Lotos-Eaters, The.
Lotus-flower doth languish, The. Die Lotusblume ängstigt. Heine, *tr. by* James Thomson. AWP
Lotus Flowers, The. Ellen Bryant Voigt. MAYP
Lotusblume ängstigt, Die. Heine, *tr. fr. German by* James Thomson. AWP
Loud brayed an ass. Quoth Kate, "My dear." Repartee. *Unknown.* TreFT
Loud deep calls me home even now to feed it, The. Shelley. *Fr.* Prometheus Unbound, III, ii. ChER
Loud drums are rolling, the mad trumpets blow, The! Battle Cry. William Henry Venable. PAH
Loud he sang the psalm of David! The Slave Singing at Midnight. Longfellow. GOA
Loud is the Summer's busy song. John Clare. *Fr.* The Shepherd's Calendar: July. OBRV
Loud is the Vale! Lines Composed at Grasmere. Wordsworth. OBRV
Loud mechanical voices of the sirens, The. Letter To My Wife. Roy Fuller. NeBP
Loud mockers in the roaring street. The Second Crucifixion. Richard Le Gallienne. HBV-2; OBVV; WGRP
Loud pianist summons from the dark, The. Melodie Grotesque. Persis Greely Anderson. WhC
Loud report through Lybian cities goes, The. Virgil, *tr. by* Dryden. *Fr.* The Aeneid, IV. OBVE
Loud roared the winds, dark grew the night. The Old Oak Tree, *with music.* *Unknown.* ShS
Loud through the still November air. The Church of the Revolution. Hezekiah Butterworth. PAH
Loud tumultuous and troubled world, The. Holy Night. Nathaniel A. Benson. CaP
Loud were they, loud, as they rode o'er the hill. Charms for a Sudden Stitch. *Unknown, tr. by* Charles W. Kennedy. AnOE
Loudens the sea-wind, downward plunge the bows. To D'Annunzio: Lines from the Sea. Robert Nichols. OBMV
Loudest thing [*or* sound] in our car, The. Vacation Trip. William Stafford. CTBA; PV
Loudon Hill; or, Drumclog. *Unknown.* ESPB
Loudoun's Bonnie Woods and Braes. Robert Tannahill. HBV-1
Loudspeaker screamed, The. The Akedah. Aliza Shenhar, *tr. by* Linda Zisquit. VWA
Lough Derg. Denis Devlin. BIrV; CIP; IPY
Loughareema! Loughareema. The Fairy Lough. "Moira O'Neill." OBVV
Louie. José Montoya, *tr. fr. Spanish by* Toni Empringham. FIA
Louie. Paul D. Shiplett. LFAC
Louie was buried today. Louie. José Montoya, *tr. by* Toni Empringham. FIA
Louis XV. John Sterling. BeLS
Louis XVI. Blake. *Fr.* The French Revolution. ChER
Louisa. Wordsworth. EnRP; GBL
Louisa May Alcott. Louise Chandler Moulton. AA
Louisa, when I offered. The Clamdigger. Dionis Coffin Riggs. TAT
Louisburg. *Unknown.* PAH
Louise. Stevie Smith. SBG
Louise, have you forgotten yet. Old Loves. Henri Murger, *tr. by* Andrew Lang. AWP
Louise on the Door-Step. Charles Mackay. EBVV
Louisiana Weekly #4, The. David Henderson. PoBA
Lounge in the shade of the luxuriant laurel's. Anyte, *tr. fr. Greek by* Willis Barnstone. BoWoP
Lourenço Marques. Charles Eglington. PeSA
Louse crept out of my lady's shift, A. Gordon Bottomley. ChTr
Louse Hunting. Isaac Rosenberg. EBEV; NoP; OxBTC
Lousy Miner. *Unknown.* AmFP
Lout, The. John Clare. NBM
Lovable Child, The. Emilie Poulsson. HBV-1; HBVY
Love. Henry Baker. NOEC
Love. Joseph Beaumont. OBS
Love. Bible, *N.T.* First Corinthians, XIII. *See* Though I Speak with the Tongues of Men and Angels.
Love. Robert Browning. EnLoPo
Love, *sel.* Samuel Butler.
"Lovers, like wrestlers, when they do not lay." ErPo
Love. Charles Stuart Calverley. FiBHP
Love. John Clare. *See* Song: "Love lives beyond the tomb."
Love. Samuel Taylor Coleridge. BeLS; ChER; EnRP; GTBS; GTBS-P; HBV-1; LoBV; OAEP; OBEV; TreFT
Love ("I'll sing of heroes, and of kings"). Abraham Cowley, *after the Greek of* Anacreon. AWP; OBVE
Love ("I love you,/ Not only for what you are"). *At. to* Roy Croft. BLPA; FaBoBe; TreFT; TRV
Love. Samuel Daniel. *See* Love Is a Sickness.
Love. Tom Dent. NNP
Love. Dryden. *Fr.* The Conquest of Granada, Pt. II, Act III, sc. iii. FiP
Love. Walker Gibson. NePoAm-2
Love. Jorie Graham. NPGG
Love. George Granville. BoLoP
Love ("Immortal love, autho[u]r of this great frame"). George Herbert. HoPM; SeCV-1
Love ("Love bade me welcome; yet my soul drew back"). George Herbert. AnAnS-1; AWP; CABA; CH; ChTr; EBCP; EBEV; FaBoEn; FaBV; HBV-2; HeIP; ILwL; InPK; JCP; LiTB; LO; MAT; MeLP; MePo; NOBE; NOCV; NoP; OAEL-1; OBEV; OBS; OxBoCh; PoEL-2; PoLF; PoPle; PPP; Prf; SCV; SeCePo; SeCeV; SeCP; SeCV-1; TEP; TrCP; TreFT; TrGrPo; TRV; ViBoPo; WeW; WHA
Love. Immanuel di Roma, *tr. fr. Italian by* J. Chotzner. TrJP
Love. Izumi Shikibu, *tr. fr. Japanese by* Hiroaki Sato. *Fr.* Fifty-one Tanka. LLLT
Love. Francis Jammes, *tr. fr. French by* Jethro Bithell. AWP
Love. Gerald Jonas. PV
Love. Ben Jonson. UnTE
Love. Toyohiko Kagawa. TRV
Love. Patrick Lane. NeAC
Love. Gordon LeClaire. CaP
Love. Pierre Louys, *tr. fr. French.* *Fr.* Chansons de Bilitis. PeHV
Love. "Hugh MacDiarmid." CMoP
Love. Nicholas Moore. ErPo
Love. Anthony Munday. *Fr.* Zelanto, the Fountain of Fame. OBSC
Love. Anthony Ostroff. FAZ
Love. John Oxenham. BLRP
Love. George Peele. *See* What Thing Is Love?
Love. Samuele Romanelli, *tr. fr. Hebrew by* A. B. Rhine. TrJP
Love. Sappho, *tr. fr. Greek by* William Ellery Leonard. AWP
Love. Sir Walter Scott. *Fr.* The Lay of the Last Minstrel. BSV
Love. Shakespeare. *See* Tell Me Where Is Fancy Bred.
Love. Shelley. *See* To ———: "One word is too often profaned."
Love. William Jay Smith. RHPC
Love. Spenser. *Fr.* The Faerie Queene, IV. OBSC
("Rugged forehead that with grave foresight, The.") OAEL-1
Love. Anne Stevenson. NCSH

Love. Tasso, *tr. fr. Italian by* John Hermann Merivale. AWP
Love. Henry David Thoreau. OBVV
Love. Thomas Traherne. SeCV-2
Love. Katrina Trask. AA
Love. Darwin T. Turner. BALP
Love ("I am a fool, I can no good"). *Unknown.* OxBM
Love ("Love is a funny thing"). *Unknown.* TTY
Love ("Love was before the light began"). *Unknown, tr. fr. Arabic by* E. Powys Mather. *Fr.* The Thousand and One Nights. AWP
Love ("My love is no short year's sentence"). *Unknown, tr. fr. Irish by* John Montague. BIrV
Love ("There's the wonderful love of a beautiful maid"). *Unknown.* SoSe
Love. Louis Untermeyer. HBMV
Love. Jones Very. AP
Love, *sel.* Alice Walker.
"Old man in White, An." NMM
Love. Sir William Watson. *Fr.* Two Epigrams. TrGrPo
Love a woman? You're an ass! Song [*or* Love a Woman]. Earl of Rochester. CavP; GBL; NOBL; PeHV; TEP; TW
Love Affair, A. Arnold Bennett. OxBTC
Love all the senses doth beguile. Of Love. James Sandford. ElL
Love among the Manichees. William Dickey. PoCh
Love among the Ruins. Robert Browning. FaBV; HAP; HBV-1; NOBE; OAEL-2; OAEP; OBEV; OBVV; PoEL-5; PrIm; VLP
Love and a Question. Robert Graves. MoBS
Love and Age. Walter Savage Landor. GBL
Love and Age. Thomas Love Peacock. *Fr.* Gryll Grange. HBV-1; OBEV; OBNC; PoPle
Love and Death. Byron. EBEV; NOBE
Love and Death. Catullus, *tr. fr. Latin by* H. W. Garrod. AWP
Love and Death. Margaret Deland. AA; HBV-2
Love and Death. Rosa Mulholland. HBV-1
Love and Death. John Frederick Nims. HoPM
Love and Death. *Unknown.* WeW
Love and Debt Alike Troublesome. *At. to* Sir John Suckling. AnAnS-2; CavP
Love and Discipline. Henry Vaughan. TrPWD
Love and Folly. La Fontaine, *tr. fr. French by* Bryant. AWP
Love and forgetting might have carried them. Two Look at Two. Robert Frost. AP; CoBMV; CrMA; MoAB; MoAmPo; NU
Love and Fortune. Fulke Greville. *Fr.* Caelica. OBSC
("Faction, that ever dwells.") EnRePo
Love and Friendship. Emily Brontë. EBVV; VLP
(Love Is like the Wild Rose-Briar.) ELP
Love and Friendship. Keats. *Fr.* Endymion, I. OBRV
Love and harmony combine. Song. Blake. EnRP
Love and Hate. *Unknown, tr. fr. Irish by* Frank O'Connor. KiLC; TW
Love and Honour. Fulke Greville. *Fr.* Caelica. OBSC
Love and Jealousy. Robert Greene. ElL
Love and Jealousy. Sir Philip Sidney. *Fr.* Arcadia. SiPS
Love and Jealousy. William Walsh. BoLoP
Love and Liberation. John Hall Wheelock. MoAmPo
Love and Liberty; a Cantata. Burns. *See* Jolly Beggars, The.
Love and Life. Julie Mathilde Lippmann. AA; HBV-1
Love and Life. Earl of Rochester. BoLoP; ELP; EnLoPo; GBL; HAP; HBV-1; MePo; NIP; NOBE; OBEV; TrGrPo; ViBoPo
("All my past life is mine no more.") FF
(Love and Life; a Song.) CavP; FaBoEn; LoBV; OBS; PoEL-3; SeCV-2
Love and Lust. Isaac Rosenberg. ChMP; TrJP
Love and Marriage. Ray Mathew. PoAu-2
Love and Music. *Gond Oral Tradition, tr. by* V. Elwin *and* S. Hivale. WTO
Love and Philosophy. George Chapman. *See* Sonnet: "Muses that sing Love's sensual empery."
Love and Poetry. Louis Simpson. PPoe
Love and Poverty. Elisabeth Cavazza Pullen. AA
Love and Reason. Matthew Prior. *Fr.* Solomon. OBEC
Love and Reason. Sir Philip Sidney. *Fr.* Arcadia. SiPS
Love and Respect. Patthericke Jenkyn. CavP
Love and Sleep. Swinburne. BoLoP; UnTE; VLP
Love and the gentle heart are one same thing. Dante, *tr. by* Dante Gabriel Rossetti. La Vita Nuova, XI. AWP
Love and the Lady Lagia, Guido and I. Sonnet: On the Detection of a False Friend. Guido Cavalcanti, *tr. by* Dante Gabriel Rossetti. AWP
Love and Time. Sir Walter Ralegh. *See* Nature, That Washed Her Hands in Milk.
Love and Wine. Thomas Shadwell. UnTE
Love Arm'd. Aphra Behn. *See* Song: "Love in fantastic triumph sate."
Love at First Sight ("It lies not in our power"). Christopher Marlowe. *See* It Lies Not in Our Power.
Love at First Sight ("On this feast day"). Christopher Marlowe. *Fr.* Hero and Leander, First Sestiad. NOBE
("On this feast day, O cursed day and hour.") ViBoPo
"Love at first sight," some say, misnaming. At First Sight. Robert Graves. FaBoEE
Love at Large. Coventry Patmore. *Fr.* The Angel in the House. EBVV
Love at Roblin Lake. Al Purdy. NoP
Love at Sea. Swinburne, *after the French of* Théophile Gautier. AWP; HBV-1
Love at the closing of our days. Last Love. Fyodor Tyutchev, *tr. by* Vladimir Nabokov. BoLoP
Love at the Door. Meleager, *tr. fr. Greek by* J. A. Symonds. AWP
Love at the lips was touch. To Earthward. Robert Frost. AP; BiP; BLPL; CABA; CoBMV; HBMV; LiTA; MoAB; MoAmPo; MoPo; MoVE; NePA; NoAM; NOBA; NoP; OxBA; PPoe; TAP; TwAmPo
Love bade me welcome; yet my soul drew back. Love. George Herbert. AnAnS-1; AWP; CABA; CH; ChTr; EBCP; EBEV; FaBoEn; FaBV; HBV-2; HeIP; ILwL; InPK; JCP; LiTB; LO; MAT; MeLP; MePo; NOBE; NOCV; NoP; OAEL-1; OBEV; OBS; OxBoCh; PoEL-2; PoLF; PoPle; PPP; Prf; SCV; SeCePo; SeCeV; SeCP; SeCV-1; TEP; TrCP; TreFT; TrGrPo; TRV; ViBoPo; WeW; WHA
Love being what it is, full of betrayals. Poem. Ruth Herschberger. HoAn
Love between Brothers and Sisters. Isaac Watts. FaBoUs
Love Bit, The. Joel Oppenheimer. CoPo; PoM
Love—bittersweet, irrepressible. Sappho, *tr. fr. Greek by* Willis Barnstone. BoWoP
Love, born in Greece, of late fled from his native place. Astrophel and Stella, VIII. Sir Philip Sidney. SiPS
Love born of knowledge, love that gains. George Meredith. *Fr.* The Thrush in February. FaBoEn
Love, brave vertue's [*or* virtue's] younger brother. Love's Horoscope. Richard Crashaw. HBV-1; MeLP; OBS
Love Breathing Thanks and Praise, *sel.* Richard Baxter.
"I preached as never sure to preach again." TRV
Love brought by night a vision to my bed. Lost Desire. Meleager, *tr. by* William M. Hardinge. AWP
Love brought me quietly in the dreaming night. Epigram. Meleager, *tr. by* Sydney Oswald. PeHV
Love brought me to a silent grove. Upon Love. Robert Herrick. TrGrPo
Love built a stately house; where Fortune came. The World. George Herbert. OBS; SeCV-1
Love, by sure proof I may call thee unkind. Astrophel and Stella, LXV. Sir Philip Sidney. SiPS
Love, by that loosened hair. Song. Bliss Carman. HBV-1
Love by the Water-Reeds. *Tr. fr. Hawaiian by* M. W. Beckwith. WTO
Love Calls Us to the Things of This World. Richard Wilbur. AmPP; CAPP; CMoP; HAP; HeIP; InPS; MoAmPo; NePA; NePoEA; NIP; NoAM; PoRA; PPP; SeCeV; TAP; TrGrPo; TwAmPo; UnPo; VGW
Love Came Back at Fall o' Dew. Lizette Woodworth Reese. HBV-1
Love Came By from the Riversmoke. Stephen Vincent Benét. *Fr.* John Brown's Body. MoAmPo
Love can do all but raise the dead. Emily Dickinson. LiTA; NePA
Love Cannot Live. *Unknown.* ElL
Love Charm. *Malay Oral Tradition, tr. by* R. O. Winstedt. WTO
Love-Charms. Thomas Campion. *See* Thrice Toss These Oaken Ashes in the Air.
Love Child—a Black Aesthetic. Everett Hoagland. BPo
Love comes back to his vacant dwelling. The Wanderer. Austin Dobson. HBV-1
Love comes laughing up the valleys. The Call. Reginald Wright Kauffman. HBV-1
Love Comes Quietly. Robert Creeley. LLLT
Love Concealed. Shakespeare. *Fr.* Twelfth Night, II, iv. TreFS
(Patience on a Monument.) TrGrPo
Love Constraining to Obedience. William Cowper. NOCV
Love Dies. George Meredith. *See* Modern Love: "In our old shipwrecked days. . ."
Love Dirge. *Tr. fr. Maori by* John White. WTO
Love Dirge to the Whitehouse, A. Bob Fletcher. NBP
Love Dislikes Nothing. Robert Herrick. AnAnS-2; CavP
Love Divine, All Loves Excelling. Charles Wesley. NOCV
(Divine Love.) WGRP
Love doth again. Sir Thomas Wyatt. SiPS
Love drooped when Beauty fled the bower. On the Death of a Recluse. George Darley. OxBI
Love, drunk the other day, knocked at my breast. The Dual. Richard Lovelace. CaPo
Love Enthroned. Richard Lovelace. CaPo
Love Enthroned. Dante Gabriel Rossetti. *Fr.* The House of Life. OBNC
Love Equals Swift and Slow. Henry David Thoreau. NoP
Love ere he bleeds, an eagle in high skies. Modern Love, XXVI. George Meredith. HBV-1
Love essential unto youth. Ninety. "E." CBAP
Love ever gives. Love's Prerogative. John Oxenham. BLRP

Love Ever Green. Henry VIII, King of England. *See* As the Holly Groweth Green.
Love-Faith. Harry Kemp. HBMV
Love Fallen to Earth. Paul Verlaine, *tr. fr. French by* Arthur Symons. SyP
Love Feast, The. W. H. Auden. ErPo
Love feeds, like Intellect, his lamp with truth. William Baylebridge. *Fr.* Love Redeemed, XXXII. PoAu-1
Love flies with bow unstrung when Time appears. Love and Age. Walter Savage Landor. GBL
Love Flows from God. Mechthild von Magdeburg, *tr. fr. German by* Lucy Menzies. WPOW
Love for a Beautiful Lady. *Unknown.* *See* Blow, Northern Wind.
Love for a Hand. Karl Shapiro. CoAP; NYBP
Love for a Hare. Melvin Walker La Follette. NePoEA-2
Love for Instance. Dan Gerber. FAZ
Love for Love, *sel.* Congreve.
Souldier and a Sailor, A. OAEP
(Buxom Joan.) InMe
(Soldier and a Sailor, A.) CoMu
Love for Patsy, A. John Thompson, Jr. LiTA; NePA; WaP
Love for such a cherry lip. Song [*or* Lips and Eyes]. Thomas Middleton. *Fr.* Blurt, Master Constable. ElL; HBV-1; ViBoPo
Love forged for me a golden chain. Wildness. Blanche Shoemaker Wagstaff. HBMV
Love, forget me when I'm gone! Love's Last Suit. Thomas Davidson. BSV
Love from My Father. Carole Gregory Clemmons. CNA; PoBA
Love, give me leave to serve thee, and be wise. An Elegie. Thomas Randolph. MePo
Love gives its best. Love. John Oxenham. BLRP
Love God—/ my mother said. The Will's Love. Besmilr Brigham. IHMS
Love-grip, first excited by the eye, The. In Panelled Rooms. Ruth Herschberger. LiTA
Love Guards the Roses of Thy Lips. Thomas Lodge. *Fr.* Phyllis. ElL
(Fidelity.) OBSC
(Phillis 2.) OBEV
(To Phyllis.) ViBoPo
Love has been sung a thousand ways. Songs Ascending. Witter Bynner. HBV-1
Love Has Eyes. William Forster. CBAP
Love has gone and left me, and the days are all alike. Ashes of Life. Edna St. Vincent Millay. BLPL; FaBoBe; HBV-1
Love has its morn, its noon, its eve, and night. Too Late. Philip Bourke Marston. OBNC
Love has its secrets, joy has its revealings. The Love Secret. *Unknown, tr. by* Wilfrid Scawen Blunt. AWP
Love has never read the Ave Maria. Love. Immanuel di Roma, *tr. by* J. Chotzner. TrJP
Love has seven names. Hadewijch, *tr. fr. Dutch by* Willis Barnstone *and* Elene Kolb. BoWoP
Love Hath a Language. Helen Selina Sheridan. To My Son. HBV-1
Love hath his poppy-wreath. Love in Dreams. John Addington Symonds. HBV-1
Love hath me brought in evil thought. A Rhyme-Beginning Fragment. *Unknown.* AnIL
Love hath so long possessed me for his own. Dante, *tr. by* Dante Gabriel Rossetti. La Vita Nuova, XVIII. AWP
Love he tomorrow, who loved never. The Vigil of Venus. *Unknown, tr. by* Thomas Stanley. UnTE
Love heeds no more the sighing of the wind. The Garden of Shadow. Ernest Dowson. FaBoEn; HBV-1; OBNC
Love her he doesn't but the thought he puts. John Berryman. *Fr.* Dream Songs. FaBoMo
Love, how ignobly has thou met thy doom! He Has Fallen from the Height of His Love. Wilfrid Scawen Blunt. *Fr.* The Love Sonnets of Proteus. ViBoPo
Love, how thou'rt tired out with rhyme! Margaret Cavendish, Duchess of Newcastle. EnLoPo
Love, I adore the contours of thy shape. To a Sicilian Boy. Theodore Wratislaw. PeHV
Love, I am guilty of listening to hot rods. Confession. Ralph Pomeroy. CoPo
Love, I am sick for thee, sick with an absolute grief. The Grief of Love. *Unknown, tr. by* Wilfrid Scawen Blunt. AWP
Love, I have lain awake by night. J. V. Cunningham Gets Hung Up on a Dirty, of All Things, Joke. Henry Taylor. BXAP
Love, I have warmed the car. News from the House. Michael Dennis Browne. NYBP
Love, I love beyond. Edmond Rostand, *tr. by* Brian Hooker. *Fr.* Cyrano de Bergerac, Act III. OLR
Love I love whose lips I love, A. The Accomplices. Conrad Aiken. NOBA
Love, I Marvel What You Are. Trumbull Stickney. HBV-1
Love, I should be content. Duality. Katherine Thayer Hobson. GoYe
Love? I'd rather be condemned to Grand Opera. Do You Love Me? Robert Watson. POL
Love, if a God thou art. To Cupid. Francis Davison. OBSC
Love! if Thy destined sacrifice am I. The Acquiescence of Pure Love. William Cowper, *after* Mme Guyon. ILwL
Love in a Cottage. J. A. R. McKellar. *Fr.* Fourth Napoleon. PoAu-2
Love in a Cottage. Nathaniel Parker Willis. HBV-1
Love in a cottage: candles in the dark. Love in a Cottage. J. A. R. McKellar. *Fr.* Fourth Napoleon. PoAu-2
Love in a Life. Robert Browning. HBV-1; InvP; NOBE; OAEP; OBNC; OBVV
Love in a Valley, *sel.* George Meredith.
White Owl, The. ChTr
Love in a Village, *sels.* Isaac Bickerstaffe.
Song: "How happy were my days, till now." OBEC
Song: "There was a jolly miller once." OBEC; OnYI
(There Was a Jolly Miller.) HBV-1; ViBoPo
("There was a jolly miller once," *st.* 1.) OxNR
Love in a Warm Room in Winter. James Wright. OBAL
Love in a Wood, *sel.* William Wycherley.
Spouse I Do Hate, A. OAEP
Love in Age. Charles G. Bell. NePoAm-2
Love in America. Marianne Moore. GOA
Love in Brooklyn. John Wakeman. AMV-81; SoSe
Love in Dreams. John Addington Symonds. HBV-1
Love in Exile, *sels.* Mathilde Blind.
"Dost thou remember ever, for my sake." OBNC
"I charge you, O winds of the West, O." TrJP
Love in fantastic [*or* fantastique] triumph sate [*or* sat]. Song [*or* Love Arm'd]. Aphra Behn. *Fr.* Abdelazer. CavP; HBV-1; NOBE; OAEP; OBEV; OBS; PAI; SBG; TrGrPo; ViBoPo; WeW; WPE
Love in Her Eyes [Sits Playing]. John Gay. *Fr.* Acis and Galatea. ELP; ViBoPo
(Song: "Love in her eyes sits playing.") FaBoEn; OBEC
Love in her sunny eyes does basking play. The Change. Abraham Cowley. *Fr.* The Mistress. AnAnS-2; FaBoEn; MeLP; MePo; SeCP; SeCV-1; OBS
Love-in-Idleness. Thomas Lovell Beddoes. ViBoPo
Love-in-Idleness. Shakespeare. *Fr.* A Midsummer Night's Dream, II, i. TrGrPo
Love in Labrador. Carl Sandburg. VGW
Love in Magnolia Cemetery. Paula Rankin. AMV-80
Love in May. Jean Passerat, *tr. fr. French by* Andrew Lang. AWP
Love in my bosom like a bee. Rosalind's [*or* Rosalynd's] Madrigal[l]. Thomas Lodge. *Fr.* Rosalynde; or, Euphues' Golden Legacy. ElL; EnRePo; FaBoEn; GoBC; HBV-1; InvP; LoBV; NOBE; NoP; OBEV; OBSC; PoEL-2; SeCePo; TrGrPo; UnTE; ViBoPo
Love in Particular. John Malcolm Brinnin. NYP
Love in the First Age: To Chloris. Sir John Denham. AnAnS-2
Love in the Museum. Adrienne Rich. NePoEA; NYBP
Love in the peaceful u.s.a. Love u.s.a. Kathleen Spivack. BoWoP
Love in the Valley. George Meredith. AWP; EBVV; HBV-1; LiTB, *abr.*; NOBE; OAEL-2; OBEV, *abr.*; OBVV; TreFT; ViBoPo; VLP, 2 *versions*
"Under yonder beech-tree single on the greensward," *sel.* ErPo; TrGrPo; UnTE; WHA
Love in the Winds. Richard Hovey. AA; HBV-1
Love in Thy Youth [Fair Maid]. *Unknown.* HBV-1; ViBoPo
Love in Vain. Robert Johnson. UnPo
Love Indestructible. Robert Southey. *Fr.* The Curse of Kehama. OBNC
("They sin who tell us love can die.") OBRV
Love Is. Ann Darr. GrPl
Love is a circle that doth restless[e] move. Love What It Is. Robert Herrick. AnAnS-2; FaBoEE; GBL
Love is a funny thing. Love. *Unknown.* TTY
Love Is a Hunter Boy. Thomas Moore. OnYI
Love Is a Keeper of Swans. Humbert Wolfe. MoBrPo
Love Is a Law. *Unknown, at. to* John Webster *and* William Rowley. *Fr.* The Thracian Wonder. ElL
("Love is a law, a discord of such force.") GBL
Love is a light burden that gladdeneth young and old. Richard Rolle of Hampole. *Fr.* Love Is Life. GoBC
Love is a little golden fish. The Golden Fish. George Arnold. HBV-1
Love is a place. E. E. Cummings. FaBoEE; OLR
Love is a queer little elfin sprite. Because You're You. Henry Blossom. BLSo
Love Is a Shark. *Tr. fr. Hawaiian by* N. B. Emerson. WTO
Love Is a Sickness[e]. Samuel Daniel. *Fr.* Hymen's Triumph. ELP; LoBV; NOBE; OBEV; PoEL-2; TreFS; ViBoPo
(Love.) ElL; OBSC
(Love Is a Sickness Full of Woes.) OAEP
(Song: "Love is a sickness full of woes.") HBV-1

Love Is a Terrible Thing. Grace Fallow Norton. HBV-1
Love is a torment, there's no question. Love's Torment. *Unknown, tr. by* Louis Untermeyer. UnTE
Love is a universal migraine. Symptoms of Love. Robert Graves. BoLoP
Love is a well that never runs dry. No Fear. Mary Doyle Curran. AMV-80
"Love is all/ Unsatisfied." Crazy Jane on the Day of Judgment. W. B. Yeats. CMoP; SOTW
Love is and was my lord and king. My Lord and King. Tennyson. In Memoriam A. H. H., CXXVI. ChTr; HBV-2; NOBE; NOCV; OBEV; OBNC; SeCeV
Love is begot by fancy, bred. Love. George Granville. BoLoP
Love Is Bitter. *Unknown, tr. fr. Zulu.* PeSA
Love is cruel, Love is sweet. Song. Thomas MacDonagh. ACP
Love Is Enough, *sels.* William Morris.
"Love is enough: ho ye who seek saving." OBVV
"Love is enough: though the World be a-waning." FaBV; OBEV; OBVV; PoEL-5; ViBoPo; VLP
Love Is Life, *orig. and mod. English prose.* Richard Rolle of Hampole. OxBM
(Song of the Love of Jesus.) PoEL-1
Sels.
"For now, love thou, I rede, Christ, as I thee tell." ACP
"Love is a light burden that gladdeneth young and old," 3 *sts., mod. vers. by* Alfred Noyes. GoBC
Love Is like a Dizziness. James Hogg. HBV-1; InMe
Love is like butter, Evans mused, and stuck. Pendydd. Kingsley Amis. *Fr.* The Evans Country. NOBL
Love is like the wild rose-briar. Love and Friendship. Emily Brontë. EBVV; ELP; VLP
Love Is Loathing & Why. Dan Ford. AMV-81
Love Is Love. Sir Edward Dyer. *See* Silent Love, A.
Love is not all; it is not meat nor drink. Sonnet. Edna St. Vincent Millay. CMoP; FPL; HAP; MasP; NoAM; OxBA; PrIm; TAP
Love is not blind. I see with single eye. Edna St. Vincent Millay. SBG
Love is not mocked whatever use. "Graphemics," 10. Jack Spicer. VGW
Love Is Not Solace. Sister Maris Stella. GoBC
Love is not worth so much. Coda. James Tate. AmPA; NYBP
Love Is of God. Horatius Bonar. TRV
Love is sharper than stones or sticks. Ballade of Unfortunate Mammals. Dorothy Parker. InMe
Love is soft, love is swete, love is good sware. Love Is Weal, Love Is Wo. *Unknown.* OxBM
Love Is Strong. Richard Burton. AA; HBV-1
Love Is Stronger than Death. Christina Rossetti. LO
Love Is Teasing. *Unknown.* OBET
Love is that later thing than death. Emily Dickinson. LiTA; NePA
Love is that madness which all lovers have. Love. Dryden. *Fr.* The Conquest of Granada, Pt. II. FiP
Love is the blossom where there blows. Wooing Song. Giles Fletcher. *Fr.* Christ's Victory and Triumph. ElL; HBV-1; LO; OBEV; ViBoPo
Love is the cause of war and death in battle. Affidavit in Platitudes. E. B. White. InMe
Love is the peace, whereto all thoughts do[e] strive. Sonnet. Fulke Greville. *Fr.* Caelica. AAS; JCP
Love is the plant of peace and most precious of virtues. Et Incarnatus Est. William Langland. *Fr.* The Vision of Piers Plowman. NOBE
Love is too young to know what conscience is. Sonnets, CLI. Shakespeare. BiP; EBEV; HeIP; PoEL-2
Love Is Weal, Love Is Wo. *Unknown.* OxBM
Love is where the glory falls. Hafiz, *tr. fr. Persian.* ILwL
Love It Is Pleasing. *Unknown.* OBET
Love-Joy. George Herbert. OAEL-1
Love-Knot, The. Nora Perry. AA; HBV-1
Love Knot. *Unknown.* NIP
Love laid his sleepless head. Song. Swinburne. TrGrPo
Love Laughs at Winter. *Unknown, tr. fr. Latin by* George F. Whicher. UnTE
Love-Lesson, A. Clement Marot, *tr. fr. French by* Leigh Hunt. AWP
Love Letter. Carole C. Gregory. BlSi
Love Letter. Linda Pastan. DFF
Love Letter. Sylvia Plath. NOBA
Love Letter. David Ray. TW
Love Letter. Karl Shapiro. *See* V-Letter.
Love Letter, A. *Unknown.* MeEL
Love Letter from an Impossible Land. William Meredith. WaP
Love-Letter One ("To C——/ her lover"). *Unknown, tr. fr. Latin.* PeHV
Love Letter Postmarked Van Beethoven. Diane Wakoski. BiP
Love Letter to Elizabeth Thatcher, A. Thomas Thatcher. SCAP
Love-Letter Two ("To G, her one and only rose"). *Unknown, tr. fr. Latin.* PeHV
Love Letters, Unmailed. Eve Merriam. DFF
Love Lies Sleeping. Elizabeth Bishop. NYP
Love Lifted Me. Paris Leary. CoPo
Love, light for me/ Thy ruddiest blazing torch. Deliciae Sapientiae de Amore. Coventry Patmore. The Unknown Eros, XXVIII. OxBoCh
Love, like a bird, hath perched upon a spray. Love. Sir William Watson. *Fr.* Two Epigrams. TrGrPo
Love, like a mountain-wind upon an oak. Love. Sappho, *tr. by* William Ellery Leonard. AWP
Love like heat and cold. Jealousy. *Unknown, tr. by* Frank O'Connor. KiLC
Love, like Ulysses. Counsel. Roselle Mercier Montgomery. HBMV
Love Lives Beyond the Tomb. John Clare. *See* Song: "Love lives beyond the tomb."
Love long dormant showing itself. Palais des Arts. Louise Glück. MAYP
Love-lorn microbe met by chance, A. The Microbe's Serenade. George Ade. OBAL
Love, love, a lily's my care. Words for the Wind. Theodore Roethke. AP; CoAP; NoAM; NOBA; PoCh
Love, Love today, my dear. Song. Charlotte Mew. MoBrPo
Love, love! What nonsense it is. Natalya Gorbanevskaya, *tr. fr. Russian by* Daniel Weissbort. WPOW
Love, love, what wilt thou with this heart of mine? Rondel. Jean Froissart, *tr. by* Longfellow. AWP
Love Made in the First Age: To Chloris. Richard Lovelace. CaPo; CavP; JCP; OAEL-1; SeCP
Love made me such that I live in fire. Gaspara Stampa, *tr. fr. Italian by* Lynne Lawner. PBWP
Love Making. James Tate. EAS
Love-making, The: His and Hers. Eve Merriam. UnTE
Love Me. Maria Wine, *tr. fr. Swedish by* Nadia Christensen. PBWP
Love Me Again. *Unknown.* ElL
Love me and leave me; what love bids retrieve me? John Jones [*or* At the Piano]. Swinburne. *Fr.* The Heptalogia. FaBoNo; NA; OAEP
Love Me and Never Leave Me. Ronald McCuaig. POL
Love Me, and the World Is Mine. David Reed, Jr. TreFT
Love Me at Last. Alice Corbin. HBMV
Love me broughte. Christ's Love-Song. *Unknown.* OxBM
Love Me Little, Love Me Long. Robert Herrick. BLPA; CaPo; ElL; FaBoBe; FaFP; NoP; TreF
Love Me, Love My Dog. Isabella Valancy Crawford. WHW
Love Me Not for Comely Grace. *Unknown.* *See* Love Not Me.
Love me, not with smiles, or with flutes, or with the plaited flowers. The Despairing Embrace. Pierre Louÿs, *tr. by* Horace M. Brown. *Fr.* The Songs of Bilitis. UnTE
Love Me, O Love. Sir Philip Sidney. *Sometimes considered Sonnet CX of* Astrophel and Stella. HeIP
Love Me or Not. Thomas Campion. ElL; HBV-1; ViBoPo
Love me with the left hand. The Light Woman's Song. Judith Johnson Sherwin. TAP
Love Medicine. Eda Lou Walton. BPAW
Love Medley: Patrice Cuchulain. Michael S. Harper. GeTw
Love, Meet Me in the Green Glen. John Clare. ELP
Love me—I love you. Lullaby. Christina Rossetti. PoPle
Love mocks us all. Then cast aside. Albi, Ne Doreas. Horace, *tr. by* Austin Dobson. Odes I, 33. AWP
"Love my heart for an hour, but my bone for a day." Street Song. Edith Sitwell. CMoP; CoBMV; MoPo; MoVE
Love Necessitates. Eugene Redmond. CNA
Love, 1916. May Wedderburn Cannan. SUMH
Love Not. Caroline Elizabeth Sarah Norton. HBV-1; OBVV
Love not a loveliness too much. Ownership. Lizette Woodworth Reese. MoAmPo
Love not, love not, ye hapless sons of clay! Love Not. Caroline Elizabeth Sarah Norton. HBV-1; OBVV
Love Not Me [for Comely Grace]. *Unknown.* BLPL; CH; ElL; ELP; FaFP; HBV-1; LiTB; PoLF; TreFT; ViBoPo
(Love Me Not for Comely Grace.) GTBS; GTBS-P; OBEV
(Love's Unreason.) TrGrPo
Love not too much. But how. The Affliction of Richard. Robert Bridges. QFR
Love now no fire hath left him. Madrigal. Giovanni Battista Marino, *tr. by* Richard Crashaw. OBVE
Love, O love, O careless love. Careless Love. *Unknown.* *See* Love, oh love, oh careless love.
Love of a woman, The. Air. Robert Creeley. VGW
Love of Country. Sir Walter Scott. *See* Breathes There the Man.
Love of England. William Cowper. *See* England.
Love of Fame, the Universal Passion, *sels.* Edward Young.
"Britannia's daughters, much more fair than nice," *fr.* Satire V. OBSV
Characters of Women, *fr.* Satire V. OBEC
"Long, Dodington, in debt, I long have sought," Satire III. LAuP
"Love of praise, howe'er concealed by art, The," *fr.* Satire I. OBSV

"See commons, peers, and ministers of state," *fr.* Satire III. OBSV
"These all their care expend on outward show," *fr.* Satire II. OBSV
"With what, O Codrus! is thy fancy smit?" *fr.* Satire II. OBSV
Love of field and coppice, The. My Country. Dorothea MacKellar. PoAu-1
Love of God, The. John Audelay. OxBM
Love of God, The. Bernard Rascas, *tr. fr. Provençal by* Bryant. WGRP
Love of Hell, The. Abraham Burstein. TrJP
Love of King David and Fair Bethsabe, The. George Peele. *See* David and Bethsabe.
Love of man and woman is as fire, The. My Comrade. James Jeffrey Roche. AA
Love of men for each other, The—so tender, heroic, constant. Edward Carpenter. *Fr.* A Mightier than Mammon. PeHV
Love of Nature. Mark Akenside. *See* Nature's Influence on Man.
Love of Nature. James Thomson. *Fr.* The Seasons: Autumn. OBEC
Love of Older Men, The. James Kirkup. PeHV
Love of praise, howe'er concealed by art, The. Edward Young. *Fr.* Love of Fame, the Universal Passion. OBSV
Love of the Father, The. *Unknown.* BLRP
Love, of this clearest, frailest Glass. In a Glass-Window for Inconstancy. Lord Herbert of Cherbury. AnAnS-2; SeCP
Love, oh love, oh careless love. Careless Love. *Unknown.* AS; BLSo; BluL; FSW; TrAS; UnTE
Love on a day (wise poets tell). How Violets Came Blue. Robert Herrick. CaPo
Love on the Farm. D. H. Lawrence. CMoP; ErPo; FaBV; FF; MoAB; MoBrPo; TrGrPo
Love on the Mountain. Thomas Boyd. AnIV; HBV-1; OxBI
Love Once Was like an April Dawn. Robert Underwood Johnson. HBV-1
Love One Another. Bible, *N.T.* St. John, XIII: 33-35. TreFT
Love Perfumes All Parts. Robert Herrick. UnTE
Love Pictures You as Black and Long-faced. Lance Jeffers. FB
Love Play. William Cavendish, Duke of Newcastle. ErPo
Love Poem: "Black biplane crashes into [*or* through] the window, The." Gregory Orr. GeTw; MAT
Love Poem: Dispossessed, The. T. R. Hummer. MAYP
Love Poem: "Everything will happen. Your friend." Lauris Edmond. OCNZ
Love Poem: "First line." Maurice James Craig. NeIP
Love Poem: "I like/ the feel of your pulsating fibers." Yuri Kageyama. BrSi
Love Poem: "I want/ to make a myth of you." Rosemary Aubert. AMV-80
Love Poem: "Instinctively, unwittingly." Janet Lewis. QFR
Love Poem: "Isadora, your body charts a course." Linda Wagner. FAZ
Love Poem: "Last night you would not come." John Logan. CAPP
Love Poem: "Less the dog begged to die in the sky." George Barker. NeBP
Love Poem: "My clumsiest dear, whose hands shipwreck vases." John Frederick Nims. FF; HoPM; InPK; MiAP; SoSe
Love Poem: "My joy, my jockey, my Gabriel." George Barker. *See* My Joy, My Jockey, My Gabriel.
Love Poem: "O tender under her right breast." George Barker. *See* O Tender under Her Right Breast.
Love Poem: "Oh your thighs." Judson Crews. UnTe
Love Poem: "Rain smell comes with the wind." Leslie Silko. UnPo; VoR
Love Poem: "Six o'clock and/ the sun rises. . ." Miller Williams. MAT
Love Poem: "There is a white mare that my love keeps." Alex Comfort. *Fr.* The Postures of Love. ErPo
("There is a white mare that my love keeps.") NeBP
Love Poem: "Warned, warned for years." Susan Irene Rea. AMV-80
Love Poem: "When we are in love, we love the grass." Robert Bly. BiP; InPS; PCP
Love Poem: "Written under Capricorn, a land." Chris Wallace-Crabbe. PoAu-2
Love Poem: "Yours is the face that the earth turns to me." Kathleen Raine. LiTB; MoAB; MoBrPo; MoPo; NeBP
Love Poem Investigation for A. T. Frank Frate. AMV-80
Love Poem—1940. Miriam Hershenson. GoYe
Love Poem on Theme by Whitman. Allen Ginsberg. CAPP; NaP
Love poems they read. Uses of Poetry. Winfield Townley Scott. DFF; PoA
Love Pursued. *Unknown.* *See* Art Thou Gone in Haste?
Love, Reason, Hate, did once bespeak. A Barley-Break [*or* Love, Reason, Hate]. Sir John Suckling. CaPo; NCEP; SeCV-1
Love Redeemed, *sels.* William Baylebridge.
"As fire, unfound ere pole approaches pole," LXXXVIII. PoAu-1
"Love feeds, like Intellect, his lamp with truth," XXXII. PoAu-1
"Quiet moon, immaculate of face, The," CVII. CBAP
"Who questions if the punctual sun unbars," LXXXII. PoAu-1
Love Rejected. Lucille Clifton. BPo
Love scorch'd my finger, but did spare. Upon Love. Robert Herrick. SeCV-1
Love Secret, The. *Unknown, tr. fr. Arabic by* Wilfrid Scawen Blunt. AWP
"Love seeketh not itself to please." The Clod and the Pebble. Blake. *Fr.* Songs of Experience. CABA; EBCP; EnLoPo; EnRP; FaBoEn; FaBV; InPS; LAuP; LoBV; NOBE; NoP; OAEP; OBEC; OBNC; PAI; PrIm; SCV; TEP; TrGrPo; ViBoPo
Love Serviceable. Coventry Patmore. *Fr.* The Angel in the House. EnLoPo
Love set you going like a fat gold watch. Morning Song. Sylvia Plath. BoWoP; HeIP; IHMS; InPK; InPS; LCAP; NAs; NOBA; PrIm; SBG
Love Sets Order in the Elements. Thomas Nabbes. *Fr.* Microcosmus. UnS
Love Should Grow Up like a Wild Iris in the Fields. Susan Griffin. NPGG
Love should intend realities: good-bye! Exit Line. John Ciardi. WeW
Love Sight. Dante Gabriel Rossetti. *See* Lovesight.
Love signed the contract blithe and leal. Epigram. John Swanwick Drennan. BIrV
Love Sleeping. Plato, *tr. fr. Greek by* Thomas Stanley. AWP; FaBoEE
Love Somebody, Yes I Do. *Unknown.* AS, *with music;* FSW
Love-Song, A, *sel.* Thomas of Hales.
Where is Paris and Heleyne? ChTr
Love-song, A. W. J. Turner. OBMV
Love Song: "Arrow rides upon the sky, An." Samuel Allen. NNP
Love Song: "Beautiful is she, this woman." *Unknown, tr. fr. Haida Indian by* Constance Lindsay Skinner. AWP
Love Song, A: "By the fierce flames of love I'm in a sad taking." Royall Tyler. TAP
Love Song, A: "Come to me in the night—we shall sleep closely together." Else Lasker-Schüler, *tr. fr. German by* Michael Gillespie. BoWoP; TrJP
Love Song, A: "Do I love you?" Raymond Richard Patterson. BOLo
Love Song: "Do not love me, my friend." Flavien Ranaivo, *tr. fr. French by* Miriam Koshland. PBA
Love Song: "Early I rose." *Unknown, tr. fr. Papago Indian by* Mary Austin. AWP; LiTA
Love Song: "For love one must risk." Bob Zmuda. AMV-81
Love Song: "Had I concealed my love." Elinor Wylie. BLPL
Love Song, A: "He is a heart." *Unknown, tr. fr. Old Irish by* Myles Dillon. AnIL
Lovesong: "How shall I whithhold my soul so that." Rainer Maria Rilke, *tr. fr. German by* M. D. Herter Norton. OLR
Love Song: I and Thou. Alan Dugan. AP; CAPP; FF; HoPM; InPK; NoAM; SoSe
Love Song: "I know not how to speak to thee, girl (damselle?)." Reed Whittemore. AmFN
Love Song: "I painted my eyes with black antimony." *Tr. fr. Bagirmi by* H. Gaden. BoWoP
Love Song: "I passed by the house of the young man who loves me." *Unknown, tr. fr. Egyptian by* J. E. Manchip White. TTY
Love Song: "I was/ the girl of the chain letter." Anne Sexton. NCSH
Love Song: "In the light of the moon." Hayim Be'er, *tr. fr. Hebrew by* Stephen Mitchell. VWA
Love Song A: "Let my sweet song be pleasing unto Thee." Judah Halevi, *tr. fr. Hebrew by* Nina Davis Salaman. TrJP
Love Song: "Little sycamore, The." *Unknown, tr. fr. Egyptian by* J. E. Manchip White. TTY
Love-Song: "Little wild birds have come flying, The." *Unknown, tr. fr. Russian by* W. R. S. Ralston. AWP
Love Song: "Long closed door, oh open it again, The." Judah Al-Harizi, *tr. fr. Hebrew by* Emma Lazarus. TrJP
Love Song: "My boat sails downstream." *Unknown, tr. fr. Egyptian by* J. E. Manchip White. TTY
Love Song: "My love is a lotus blossom." *Unknown, tr. fr. Egyptian by* J. E. Manchip White. TTY
Love Song: "My loved one is unique, without a peer." *Unknown, tr. fr. Egyptian by* J. E. Manchip White. TTY
Love Song: "My own dear love, he is strong and bold." Dorothy Parker. InMe
Love Song: "Now the lusty Spring is seen." John Fletcher. *See* Love Emblems.
Love Song: "O lovely pussy, O pussy, my love." Edward Lear. *Fr.* The Owl and the Pussy-Cat. PCat
Love Song: "One with eyes the fairest." Euripides, *tr. fr. Greek by* Shelley. *Fr.* Cyclops. AWP
Love-Song: "Out of one golden breath." Else Lasker-Schüler, *tr. fr. German by* Jethro Bithell. TrJP
Love Song, The: "Out of the blackthorn hedges." Ivor Gurney. EnLoPo
Love Song: "See'st thou o'er my shoulders falling." Judah Halevi, *tr. fr. Hebrew by* Emma Lazarus. TrJP
Love Song: "Soft as the wind your hair." Adam Drinan. NeBP
Love Song: "Sweep the house clean." William Carlos Williams. MoAB; MoAmPo
Love Song: "Take, Oh take those lips away." Shakespeare. *See* Take, O Take Those Lips Away.

Love Song: "That haughty tyranny of thine." Fray Luís de León, *tr. fr. Spanish by* Thomas Walsh. TrJP
Love Song: "Though to think/ Rejoiceth me." Margot Ruddock. OBMV
Love Song: "Tiny children." Yityangu Ejong, *tr. fr. Yindjibarndi by* Frank Wordick. CBAP
Love Song: "Wherever your voice moves." Kosrof Chantikian. AMV–81
Love Song, A: "Yes, I will love thee when the sun." W. F. Hawley. OBCV
Love Song: "You've got nice knees." Gavin Ewart. OxBTC
Love-Song by a Lunatic, A. *Unknown.* NA
Love Song for a Tyrant. Marion Brimm Rewey. AMV–81
Love Song for the Future. Vassar Miller. NCSH
Love Song from New England. Winifred Welles. HBMV
Love Song of J. Alfred Prufrock, The. T. S. Eliot. AmPP; AP; AWP; BiP; CABA; CMoP; CoBMV; EBEV; FF; HAP; HBMV; HeIP; HoPM; InPK; InPS; LiTB; LiTM; MoAB; MoAmPo; MoVE; MP; NePA; NIP; NoAM; NOBA; NOBE; NoP; OAEL–2; OAEP; OxBTC; PAI; PoA; PoRA; PPP; PrIm; SeCeV; SoSe; SOTW; TAP; TreFT; TrGrPo; TwAmPo; TwCP; ViBoPo; WeW
Love Song of J. Alfred Prufrock, The, *parody.* J. Walker. BXAP
Love-Song of the Water Carriers. *Unknown, tr. fr. Zulu.* PeSA
Love Song out of Nothing. Vassar Miller. NePoEA
Love Song to Eohippus. Peter Viereck. MoAmPo
Love Song to King Shu-Suen. Kubatum, *tr. fr. Sumerian by* Thorkild Jacobsen. WPOW
Love Song to Lucy. Helen Ehrlich. SUW
Love Songs. Mina Loy. VGW; WPE, *abr.*
Love Songs (Dadaria). *Gond Oral Tradition, tr. by* V. Elwin *and* S. Hivale. WTO
Love-Songs, at Once Tender and Informative. Samuel Hoffenstein. OBAL
Love Songs in Age. Philip Larkin. PPP
Love Sonnet, A. George Wither. *See* I Loved a Lass.
Love Sonnets, *sels.* Zora Cross.
"In me there is a vast and lonely place," XLIX. CBAP
"What have you more than I, who crave you so?" LIV. CBAP
Love Sonnets of Proteus, The, *sels.* Wilfrid Scawen Blunt.
"And then fate strikes us. First our joys decay," LXXV. VLP
Depreciating Her Beauty, VI. OBMV
Farewell to Juliet, *sels.*
Farewell: "Juliet, farewell. I would not be forgiven," XXXIX. TrGrPo
Farewell to Juliet ("I see you, Juliet, still, with your straw hat"), XLVII. BoLoP; EnLoPo; OxBTC; ViBoPo
(Farewell to Juliet ("Lame, impotent conclusion"), LII. ViBoPo
Fear Has Cast Out Love, XXXVI. VLP
He Has Fallen from the Height of His Love, XIV. ViBoPo
In Answer to a Question, XXVIII. ViBoPo
Joy's Treachery, XVII. VLP
Mockery of Life, The, LXXIV. VLP
On the Nature of Love, XXII. ViBoPo
St. Valentine's Day, LV. EnLoPo; NBM; OBVV; ViBoPo
To Manon, as to His Choice of Her, VIII. HBV–1
(As to His Choice of Her.) ViBoPo
To Manon, Comparing Her to a Falcon, II. OBVV
(Falcon, The.) ACP
To Manon, on Her Lightheartedness, XI. NBM
To One on Her Waste of Time, LVIII. ViBoPo
To One Who Would Make a Confession, LXII. HBV–1; ViBoPo
Love Sonnets, VIII. Charles Harpur. PoAu–1
Love Speaks at Last. Lord Herbert of Cherbury. AnAnS–2
Love steered my course, while yet the sun rode high. Of Fiammetta Singing. Boccaccio, *tr. by* Dante Gabriel Rossetti. *Fr.* Sonnets. AWP; GoBC
Love still a boy, and oft a wanton is. Astrophel and Stella, LXXIII. Sir Philip Sidney. HBV–1; OAEP; SiPS
Love still has something of the sea. Song. Sir Charles Sedley. CavP; EtS; FaBoEn; GBL; HBV–1; LoBV; NOBE; OBS; SeCV–2; ViBoPo
Love Story, A. Robert Graves. CMoP; FaBoTw; LiTB; MoVE
Love, strong as Death, is dead. An End. Christina Rossetti. FaBoRV; GBL
Love struck into his life. The Dove-Breeder. Ted Hughes. PAI
Love Suicides at Sonezaki, The, *sel.* Chikamatsu Monzaemon, *tr. fr. Japanese.*
"Farewell to the world, and to the night farewell." DL
Love, Sweet Love. Felix McGlennon. PaPo
Love-Sweetness. Dante Gabriel Rossetti. *Fr.* The House of Life. OAEP
Love Symphony, A. Arthur O'Shaughnessy. HBV–1
Love-Talker, The. "Ethna Carbery." AnIV; CH; OnYI; OxBI; WPE
Love That Doth Reign and Live within My Thought. Petrarch, *tr. fr. Italian by* the Earl of Surrey. Sonnets to Laura: To Laura in Life, CIX. HeIP; NoP; OAEL–1
(Complaint of a Lover Rebuked.) AWP; CABA; TrGrPo
("Love that doth raine and live within my thought.") AAS; OBVE
("Love that liveth and reigneth in my thought.") SiPS
Love, that drained her, drained him she'd loved, though each. The Turtle Dove. Geoffrey Hill. FaBoTw; NePoEA
"Love that I hae chosen, The." The Lawlands o' Holland. *Unknown.* AmSS; CH
Love that is not pardoned, A. Doors. Tom Clark. ConAP
Love, that liveth and reigneth in my thought. *See* Love That Doth Reign and Live within My Thought.
Love That's Pure, Itself Disdaining, *with music.* Johann A. Gruber, *tr. fr. German by* Sheema Z. Buehne. AH
Love the Beautiful. Moses Mendelssohn, *tr. fr. German.* TreFT
Love, the delight of all well-thinking minds. Caelica, I. Fulke Greville. GBL; OBSC
Love, the great master of true eloquence. Love. Tasso, *tr. by* John Hermann Merivale. AWP
Love, the Light-Giver. Michelangelo, *tr. fr. Italian by* John Addington Symonds. AWP
(To Tommaso de' Cavalieri: "With your fair eyes a charming light I see.") PeHV
Love the Ruins. Malka Heifetz Tussman, *tr. fr. Yiddish by* Marcia Falk. VWA
Love the unholy, that frost which quickens summer. Didactic Sonnet. Melvin Walker La Follette. NePoEA; PoA
Love the Wild Swan. Robinson Jeffers. HeIP; InPS; MoAB; MoAmPo; TW; TwAmPo
Love, thou art absolute, sole Lord. A Hymn to the Name and Honour of the Admirable Saint[e] Teresa [*or* Hymn to Saint Teresa *or* In Memory of the Vertuous and Learned Lady Madre de Teresa]. Richard Crashaw. ACP; AnAnS–1; EBEV; FaBoEn; HAP; JCP; LoBV; MeLP; MePo; NOBE; NoP; OAEP; OBEV; OBS; OxBoCh; PoEL–2; SeCV–1, *abr.*; WGRP
Love thy country, wish it well. Ode. George Bubb Dodington. OBEC
Love thy God and love Him only. Reality. Sir Aubrey De Vere. WGRP
Love Tight. Ted Joans. CNA
Love, Time and Death. Frederick Locker-Lampson. HBV–2
Love to faults is always blind. Blake. *Fr.* Poems from MSS. ViBoPo
Love to his singer held a glistening leaf. Love's Last Gift. Dante Gabriel Rossetti. The House of Life, LIX. VLP
Love to the Church. Timothy Dwight. *See* I Love Thy Kingdom, Lord.
Love took my life and thrill'd [*or* thrilled] it. Song [*or* The Surface and the Depths]. Sir Lewis Morris. HBV–1; OBVV
Love Triumphant, *sel.* Dryden.
Prologue to "Love Triumphant." OxBoLi
Love Triumphant. Frederic Lawrence Knowles. HBV–1; TreFT
Love, 20¢ the First Quarter Mile. Kenneth Fearing. HAP; WeW
Love twists. The Pressures. Amiri Baraka. BPo
Love Unchangeable. Rufus Dawes. AA
Love Undeclared. *Unknown.* OxBM
Love Unfeigned. Chaucer. *Fr.* Troilus and Criseyde. LO; NOBE; OBEV
(O Yonge Freshe Folkes.) OxBM
("O yonge fresshe folkes, he or she.") LO
Love Unfeigned, The. Chaucer. OBEV
Love Unknown. George Herbert. JCP; Prf
Love unlike Love. *Unknown.* *See* Divine Love.
Love, unrequited, robs me of my rest. When You're Lying Awake with a Dismal Headache. W. S. Gilbert. *Fr.* Iolanthe. NoP
Love unreturn'd, how ere the flame. Constancye. Sidney Godolphin. MePo
Love Unsought. Emma Catharine Embury. AA
Love u.s.a. Kathleen Spivack. BoWoP
Love was before the light began. Love. *Unknown, tr. by* E. Powys Mathers. *Fr.* The Thousand and One Nights. AWP
Love Was Once Light as Air. C. Day Lewis. *Fr.* Two Songs [Written to Irish Airs]. OAEP
Love was true to me. Song. John Boyle O'Reilly. ACP
Love, we curve downwards, we are set to night. After Midsummer. E. J. Scovell. OxBTC
Love we define for ourselves, The. Prothalamion. Michael Ryan. AmPA
Love wears roses' elegance. Sister Bertke. LLLT
Love What It Is. Robert Herrick. AnAnS–2; FaBoEE; GBL
Love, when all the years are silent, vanished quite and laid to rest. Hereafter. Harriet Prescott Spofford. HBV–1
Love Which Frees. Gloria Fuertes, *tr. fr. Spanish by* Philip Levine. WPOW
Love which is here a care. William Drummond of Hawthornden. OxBoCh
Love which is the most difficult mystery. Psyche with the Candle. Archibald MacLeish. PCP
Love Who Will, for I'll Love None. William Browne. CavP; HBV–1
Love, Whose Month Was Ever May. Ulrich von Liechtenstein, *tr. fr. German by* Jethro Bithell. AWP
Love, why have you led me here. The Young Cordwainer. Robert Graves. MoBS
Love Will Find Out the Way. *Unknown.* FaBoCh; GBL; GN; HBV–1; OBEV; TreFS; WiR

(Great Adventurer, The.) FaFP; GTBS; GTBS-P
Love will not have me cry. Canzonetta: He Will Neither Boast nor Lament to His Lady. Jacopo da Lentino, *tr. by* Dante Gabriel Rossetti. AWP
Love Winged My Hopes. *Unknown.* EIL; TrGrPo
(Icarus.) OBEV
("Love winged my hopes and taught me how to fly.") OBSC
Love within the lover's breast. Lines. George Meredith. HBV-1
Love without Hope. Robert Graves. BoLoP; ChTr; ELU; FaBoEE; GBL; GTBS-P; OAEL-2; OxBI
Love without Longing. *Unknown. See* I Have a Young Sister.
Love without Love. Luis Lloréns Torres, *tr. fr. Spanish by* Julio Marzán. InW
Love you alone have been with us. Rumi, *tr. fr. Persian by* W. S. Merwin *and* Talat Sait Halman. LLLT
Love, You have struck me straight, my Lord! Resolution. Charles L. O'Donnell. GoBC; TrPWD
"Love you?" said I, then I sighed, and then I gazed upon her sweetly. Ferdinando and Elvira, or the Gentle Pieman. W. S. Gilbert. NA
Love Your Enemy. Yusef Iman. BPo; TTY
"Love your neighbor as yourself." Thoughts on the Commandments. George Augustus Baker. AA; HBV-1
Love your toys, my darling. Toys. Abraham Sutskever, *tr. by* Seymour Levitan. VWA
Love, You've Been a Villain. James Planché. NOBL
Lovebirds. William Jay Smith. ErPo
Loved I am, and yet complain[e] of Love. Complaint of Love. Sir Philip Sidney. *Fr.* Arcadia. PoEL-1; SiPS
Loved of My Soul. Israel Najara, *tr. fr. Hebrew by* Nina Davis Salaman. TrJP
Loved One, The. Joseph Hansen. NYBP
Loved stream, that meanders along. Memories of Childhood. John Carr. *Fr.* Derwent; an Ode. NOEC
Loveliest dawn of gold and rose. The Least of Carols. Sophie Jewett. OHIP
Loveliest of Counties, Shropshire Now. Ian Sainsbury. BXAP
Loveliest of Pies. Peter De Vries. OBAL
Loveliest of Trees [the Cherry Now]. A. E. Housman. A Shropshire Lad, II. AWP; BiP; BLPL; BoNaP; ChTr; CMoP; CoBMV; ELP; FaBoBe; FaBV; FaFP; FF; HAP; HeIP; InPK; LiTB; LiTM; MasP; MoAB; MoBrPo; NAs; NoAM; NoP; OAEL-2; OAEP; OHIP; OxBTC; PAI; PoLF; PrIm; SoSe; TEP; TreFT; TrGrPo; ViBoPo; VLP; WeW
Loveliest of trees, the cherry now. In a Town Garden. Donald Mattam. ELU; FiBHP
Loveliest of what I leave. Adonis, Dying. Praxilla of Sicyon. PBWP, *tr. by* John Dillon; WPOW, *tr. by* Richmond Lattimore
Lovelight. Georgia Douglas Johnson. AmNP
Loveliness. Hilda Conkling. TiPo
Loveliness. Christopher Smart. Hymns for the Amusement of Children, 14. NOCV
Loveliness of Love, The. George Darley. *See* It Is Not Beauty I Demand.
Loveliness that dies when I forget. Loveliness. Hilda Conkling. TiPo
Lovelocks. Walter de la Mare. MoVE
Lovel's Song. Ben Jonson. *See* It Was a Beauty That I Saw.
Lovely! all the essential parts. These Purists. William Carlos Williams. OBAL
Lovely are curves of the white owl sweeping. The White Owl. George Meredith. *Fr.* Love in a Valley. ChTr
Lovely body of the dead, The. Lament for Glasgerion. Elinor Wylie. PoA
Lovely boy, thou art not dead. Epitaph. Francis Davison. OBSC
Lovely cherries on the tree. Adjectives. Moishe Nadir, *tr. by* Joseph Leftwich. TrJP
"Lovely courier of the sky." Anacreon's Dove. Samuel Johnson. AWP
Lovely days of spring have clothed the plains, The. The Round-up. Sarah Elizabeth Howard. PoOW
Lovely Fia was the summer queen. A Mare. Kate Barnes. NYBP; PH
Lovely form there sate beside my bed, A. Phantom or Fact. Samuel Taylor Coleridge. EnRP
Lovely girl, you look at me through the window. Praxilla, *tr. fr. Greek by* John Dillon. PBWP
Lovely Girls with Flounder on a Starry Night. Anselm Parlatore. SUW
Lovely grapes and apples. A Tabernacle Thought. Israel Zangwill. TrJP
Lovely hill-torrents are. Song. W. J. Turner. GoJo; MoBrPo
Lovely in the winter sunshine lies the Haslemere Hotel. John Betjeman's Brighton. Gavin Ewart. FaBoPa
Lovely kind, and kindly loving. An Odd Conceit. Nicholas Breton. EIL; OBSC
Lovely lady dressed in blue. To Our Lady. Mary Dixon Thayer. TreFS
Lovely lady, rein thy will. Death's Warning to Beauty. *Unknown, tr. by* Robin Flower. AnIL
Lovely lady sat and sange, A. Mary and Her Child. *Unknown.* OxBoCh
Lovely Lass o' Inverness, The. Burns. *See* Lament for Cullodeen.
Lovely Lass to a Friar Came, A. *At. to* Burns, *also at. to* the Earl of Rochester. CoMu
(Lass and the Friar, The.) UnTE
Lovely, lasting peace of mind! A Hymn to Contentment. Thomas Parnell. NOEC; OBEC
Lovely Love, A. Gwendolyn Brooks. BPo
Lovely Lucinda, blame not me. The Innocent Gazer. John, Lord Cutts. CavP
Lovely maid, with rapture swelling. Lines by a Fond Lover. *Unknown.* NA
Lovely Mary Donnelly. William Allingham. AnIV; HBV-1
Lovely morn, so still, so very still, A. May, 1840. Hartley Coleridge. OBVV
Lovely of hair and breast and face. The Question. Norman Gale. ELU; FiBHP
Lovely Pamela, who found. Epitaph on a Party Girl. Richard Usborne. FaBoEE
Lovely Rivers and Lakes of Maine, The. George B. Wallis. BLPA
Lovely Rose Is Sprung, A. *Unknown, tr. fr. German by* Margarete Münsterberg. AWP
Lovely Semiramis. The Fan. Edith Sitwell. HBMV
Lovely Shall Be Choosers, The. Robert Frost. CoBMV; MoAB; MoAmPo; NOBA; OxBA
Lovely Tear of Lovely Eye ("Lovely ter of lovely eye [*or* eiye]"). *Unknown.* OxBM
(Christ's Tear Breaks My Heart.) MeEL
Lovely Village Fair, The; or, I Dont Mean to Tell You Her Name. *Unknown.* CoMu
Lovely was the death. Samuel Taylor Coleridge. *Fr.* Religious Musings. EnRP
Lovely whore though. Cathleen. *Unknown, tr. by* Thomas MacIntyre. BIrV
Lovely years went lightly by, The. A Child's Song to Her Mother. Winifred Welles. HBMV
Lovely young lady I mourn in my rhymes, A. An Epitaph. George John Cayley. ELU; FiBHP; HBV-1
Lovely young Lavinia once had friends, The. Lavinia. James Thomson. *Fr.* The Seasons: Autumn. OBEC
Lovely Young Moor, A. *Unknown, tr. fr. Spanish by* Willis Barnstone. BoWoP
Lovelye William, 2 *versions. Unknown.* AmFP
Lovemaker, The. Robert Mezey. NePoEA-2
Lovemusic. Carolyn Kizer. ErPo
Lover, The. Robert Duncan. PeHV
Lover, The. Richard Henry Stoddard. AA
Lover, The; a Ballad. Lady Mary Wortley Montagu. NoP; OBEC
Lover Abused Renounceth Love, The, *sel.* George Turberville.
"Was never day came on my head." EIL
Lover and Birds, The. William Allingham. *See* Spring: The Lover and the Birds.
Lover and Echo. Carrol O'Daly, *tr. fr. Irish by* George Sigerson. OnYI
Lover and Philosopher. Sir William Davenant. *See* Philosopher and the Lover, The: To a Mistress Dying.
Lover and the Nightingale, The. *Unknown, tr. fr. Latin by* John Addington Symonds. UnTE
Lover and the Syringa-Bush, The. Herman Melville. OBAL
Lover Beseecheth His Mistress Not to Forget His Steadfast Faith and True Intent, The. Sir Thomas Wyatt. *See* Forget Not Yet.
Lover Compareth Himself to the Painful Falconer, The. *Unknown.* PBBP
Lover Compareth His State to a Ship in Perilous Storm Tossed on the Sea, The. Petrarch, *tr. fr. Italian by* Sir Thomas Wyatt. Sonnets to Laura: To Laura in Life, CLVI. EIL; GBL; HeIP; PoEL-1
(Galley, The.) OBSC
(Lover Like to a Ship Tossed on the Sea.) EtS
(My Galley.) LiTB; MOS
(My Galley Charged with Forgetfulness.) BiP; CABA; HAP; NoP; OAEL-1; PPP; TEP; WeW
("My galy charged with forgetfulnes.") AAS; OBVE
(Sonnet.) SiPS
Lover Complaineth [*or* Complayneth] the Unkindness of His Love, The. Sir Thomas Wyatt. EIL; FaBoEn; GBL; OAEP; PoEL-1; ViBoPo
(Lover Complaineth, The.) TrGrPo
("My lute, awake! perform the last.") AAS; CABA; EBEV; HAP; OAEL-1
(To His Lute.) BoLoP; NOBE; OBEV; OBSC; QFR
Lover Consults with Reason, The. Thomas Carew. *See* Lover, upon an Accident Necessitating His Departure, Consults with Reason.
Lover Deceived Writes to His Lady, The, *sels.* Thomas Howell.
Who Would Have Thought. EIL
("Who would have thought that face of thine.") POL
Lover Exhorteth His Lady to Be Constant, The. *Unknown.* OBSC

Lover Exhorteth His Lady to Take Time, While Time Is, The. George Turberville. EnRePo
Lover for Shamefastnesse Hideth His Desire within His Faithfull Hart, The. Petrarch, *tr. fr. Italian by* Sir Thomas Wyatt. Sonnets to Laura: To Laura in Life, CIX. AAS, 2 *versions*
(Long Love That in My Thought Doth Harbour, The.) NoP
("Long[e] love that in my thought doth harbour, The.") CABA; OAEL-1; OBVE
Lover Forsaken, The. Sir Thomas Wyatt. *See* Lover Showeth How He Is Forsaken of Such as He Sometime Enjoyed, The.
Lover Having Dreamed Enjoying of [*or* Enjoying of] His Love, Complaineth That the Dream Is Not either Longer or Truer, The. Sir Thomas Wyatt. AAS, 2 *versions;* WHA
(Unstable Dream, According to the Place.) OAEP
Lover in Liberty Smileth at Them in Thraldom, That Sometime Scorned His Bondage, The. *Unknown.* EIL
Lover in Winter Plaineth for the Spring, The. *Unknown. See* Western Wind.
Lover Left Alone, A. *Unknown.* MeEL
Lover Like to a Ship Tossed on the Sea, The. Sir Thomas Wyatt. EtS
Lover Mourns for the Loss of Love, The. W. B. Yeats. WeW
Lover of child Marjory, The. A Sea Child. Bliss Carman. HBV-1
Lover of her body said, The. The Two Lovers. Richard Harvey. HBV-1
Lover of mine, if upland you journey. Ave atque Vale. *Malay Oral Tradition, tr. by* R. J. Wilkinson *and* R. O. Winstedt. WTO
Lover of swamps. To the Snipe. John Clare. NCEP; OBNC
Lover of the Lord. *Unknown.* AmFP
Lover of the moorland bare, A. To K[atharine] de M[attos]. Robert Louis Stevenson. OBNC
Lover Proved False, The. *Unknown.* AmFP
Lover Rejoiceth, The. Sir Thomas Wyatt. AAS; SiPS; TrGrPo
(Liberty.) OBSC
("Tangled I was in love's snare.") SiPS
("Tanglid I was yn love's snare.") AAS
Lover Rejoiceth the Enjoying of His Love, The. Sir Thomas Wyatt. FaBoEn
("Once as methought Fortune me kissed.") BoLoP; SiPS
("Ons as me thought fortune me kyst.") AAS
(Promise, A.) OBSC
Lover Renounceth Love, The. Sir Thomas Wyatt. *See* Renouncing of Love, A.
Lover Showeth [*or* Showeth] How He Is Forsaken of Such as He Sometime Enjoyed, The. Sir Thomas Wyatt. AAS, 2 *versions;* EIL; ELP; FaBoEn; HoPM; InPS; OAEP; PoEL-1; PoRA; TrGrPo; ViBoPo
(How Like You This?) SeCePo
(Lover Forsaken, The.) UnTE
(Remembrance.) BoLoP; NOBE; OBSC; PoPle; QFR
(They Flee from Me.) BLPL; EnRePo; HeIP; LiTB; LoBV; MasP; NIP; NoP; PrIm; SCV; SeCeV; WeW
(They Flee from Me That Sometime Did Me Seek [*or* Seke].) BiP; CABA; EnLoPo; FF; HAP; InPK; OAEL-1; OxBC; PPP; SiPS; TEP
(Vixi Peullis Nuper Idoneus.) OBEV
Lover Tells of the Rose in His Heart, The. W. B. Yeats. CMoP; ViBoPo
(Aedh Tells of the Rose in His Heart.) BrPo; MoBrPo; VLP
Lover That I Hope You Are. Milton Acorn. NeAC
Lover, the lover will always remember, The. Act of Love. Nicholas Moore. NeBP
Lover Thinks of His Lady in the North, The. Shaemas O'Sheel. HBV-1
Lover to Himself, The. David Phillips. NeAC
Lover to His Lady, The. George Turberville. CTC; OBSC
Lover to His Lady, The. *At. to* Plato, *tr. fr. Greek by* George Turberville. CTC; FaBoEE; FF; OBSC
Lover to Lover. David Morton. HBMV
Lover to the Thames of London, to Favour [*or* Favor] His Lady Passing Thereon, The. George Turberville. ChTr; EIL; NoP; OBSC
Lover under burthen of his love, The. A Gulling Sonnet. Sir John Davies. Gulling Sonnets, I. EIL
Lover, upon an Accident Necessitating His Departure, Consults with Reason, A. Thomas Carew. CaPo
(Lover Consults with Reason, The.) TrGrPo
Loverd, thou clepedest me. Wait a Little! *Unknown.* NOCV; OxBM
Lovers, The. Conrad Aiken. AP; NYBP
Lovers, The. Phoebe Cary. HBV-2
Lovers, The. Alex Comfort. NeBP; PoA
Lovers. Mary Fullerton. PoAu-1
Lovers, The. Joan Murray. LTB
Lovers, The. W. R. Rodgers. BIrV
Lovers, The. William Jay Smith. MoAmPo
Lovers, The. Marya Zaturenska. MoAmPo
Lovers, and a Reflection. Charles Stuart Calverley. FaBoCo; FaBoPo; NA; SpRo; VLP; WhC
Lovers and Friends. Henry Luttrell. *Fr.* Advice to Julia. OBRV
Lovers and madmen have such seething brains. The Lunatic, the Lover, and the Poet [*or* Imagination *or* The Tricks of Imagination]. Shakespeare. *Fr.* A Midsummer Night's Dream, V, i. FiP; LiTB; MaSP; PP
Lover's Anger, A. Matthew Prior. ErPo; UnTE
Lover's Appeal, The. Sir Thomas Wyatt. *See* And Wilt Thou Leave Me Thus?
Lover's Arithmetic, The. *Unknown.* OxBoLi
Lover's Choice, The. Thomas Bedingfield. HBV-1
Lover's Complaint, A. *Unknown, sometimes at. to* Sir Walter Ralegh. *See* As You Came from the Holy Land.
Lover's Complaint, A. Shakespeare. NCEP
Lovers conceits are like a flattring glasse. *Unknown.* OBS
Lover's Confession, A. Charles d'Orléans. *See* My Ghostly Father, I Me Confess.
Lovers' Death, The. Baudelaire, *tr. fr. French by* "Michael Field." SyP
Lovers' Debouchment. William Zaranka. BXAP
Lovers' Dialogue. Sir Philip Sidney. *See* Astrophel and Stella, Eleventh Song.
Lover's Envy, A. Henry van Dyke. HBV-1
Lovers everywhere are bringing babies into the world. Make Love Not War. Howard Nemerov. NoAM; NAs
Lover's eyes will gaze an eagle blind, A. Shakespeare. *Fr.* Love's Labour's Lost, IV, iii. GBL
Lovers, fast in their longing, The. March. William Everson. ErPo
Lovers Go Fly a Kite, The. W. D. Snodgrass. NYBP
Lovers How They Come and Part. Robert Herrick. GBL; OxBoLi; PoEL-3
Lovers in ladies' magazines. Song. Thomas McGrath. VGW
Lovers in the act dispense. The Thieves. Robert Graves. BoLoP; CMoP; GTBS-P; LiTM; OAEL-2; OxBI
Lovers in Winter. Robert Graves. FaBoEE; NYBP
Lovers Infiniteness[e]. John Donne. AnAnS-1; EIL; FaBoEn; LiTB; MeLP; OAEL-1; OBS; PoEL-2; SeCP; SeCV-1
Lover's Invitation, The. John Clare. VLP
Lover's Lament, A [*or* The]. *Unknown.* AmFP (3 *vers.*); AS (A *and* B *vers.*)
Lover's Lament, A ("My little breath"). *Unknown, tr. fr. Tewa Indian by* H. J. Spinden. AWP
Lover's Lament for Her Sailor, The. *Unknown.* AmFP
Lover's Lane. Paul Laurence Dunbar. BANP
Lover's Leap, The; a Tale. Andrew Macdonald. NOEC
Lovers, like wrestlers, when they do not lay. Samuel Butler. *Fr.* Love. ErPo
Lovers loitered on the deck talking, The. The Feast. Robert Hass. GeTw
Lover's Lullaby, A. George Gascoigne. *See* Lullaby of a Lover, The.
Lover's Lute Cannot Be Blamed, The. Sir Thomas Wyatt. *See* Blame Not My Lute for He Must Sownde.
Lovers may find similitudes. The Cascade. Edgell Rickword. ChMP; FaBoTw
Lover's Meeting. Ray Mathew. CBAP
Lover's Melancholy, The, *sels.* John Ford.
Fly Hence, Shadows, *fr.* V, i. ViBoPo
(Dawn.) OBEV
(Song: "Fly hence, shadows, that do keep.") LoBV
"If thou canst wake with me, forget to eate," *fr.* IV, ii. PoEL-2
"Minutes are are numbered by the fall of sands," *fr.* IV, iii. PoEL-2
Lover's New Year's Gift, A. John Lydgate. PoEL-1
Lovers of Marchaid, The. Marjorie Pickthall. HBV-1
Lovers of pleasure more than God. Lover of the Lord. *Unknown.* AmFP
Lovers of the Poor, The. Gwendolyn Brooks. BiP; CAPP; NoAM; NOBA
Lover's Plea, A. Thomas Campion. *See* Shall I Come, Sweet Love, to Thee?
Lover's Posy, The. Rufinus, *tr. fr. Greek by* W. H. D. Rouse. AWP
Lover's Prayer, The. *Malay Oral Tradition, tr. by* R. J. Wilkinson *and* R. O. Winstedt. WTO
Lover's Progress, The, *sel.* John Fletcher.
Dead Host's Welcome, The, *fr.* III, i. TrGrPo
('Tis Late and Cold.) ViBoPo
Lover's Protestation, A. Thomas Lodge. *See* Fancy, A.
Lovers Rejoyce [*or* Rejoice]. Beaumont *and* Fletcher. *Fr.* Cupid's Revenge. EIL; FaBoEn
Lovers Relentlessly. Stanley Kunitz. TwAmPo; UnTE
Lover's Reply to Good Advice. Richard Hughes. MoBrPo
Lover's Resolution, A. George Wither. *Fr.* Fair Virtue. *See* Shall I, Wasting in Despair.
Lover's Song, The. Alfred Austin. OBVV
Lover's Song, The. Edward Rowland Sill. AA; HBV-1
Lover's Stratagem, A. *Unknown.* *Fr.* Floris and Blauncheflour. OxBM
Lovers' Walk, The. Dante Gabriel Rossetti. *Fr.* The House of Life. OAEP
Lovers who/ came to me. Ghost Poem Five. Mary Norbert Körte. IHMS
Lovers who are young indeed, and wish to know the sort of life. Love, You've Been a Villain. James Planché. NOBL
Lovers whose lifted hands are candles in winter. For a Child Expected. Anne Ridler. LiTM; MoVE; NeBP; SeCePo
Lover's Words, A. Vernon Watkins. DTC

Love's a Jest, *sel.* Peter Anthony Motteux.
Slaves to London. OAEP
Love's Alchemy [*or* Alchymie]. John Donne. AnAnS-1; CABA; MePo; NoP; OAEL-1; OAEP; SeCP; SUW; ViBoPo
Love's an headstrong wild desire. Love. Henry Baker. NOEC
Loves and sorrows of those who lose an orchard. The Lost Orchard. Edgar Lee Masters. CMoP; MoPo
Love's Apparition and Evanishment. Samuel Taylor Coleridge. EnRP
Love's Arithmetic. Sir Edward Sherburne. CavP
Love's Calendar. William Bell Scott. HBV-1
Love's Caution. W. H. Davies. ChMP
Love's Change. Anne Reeve Aldrich. AA
Love's Clock. Sir John Suckling. CaPo
("That none beguiled be by time's quick flowing.") PoEL-3
Love's Coming. Shaw Neilson. PoAu-1
Love's Consolation, *sel.* Richard Watson Dixon.
"All who have loved, be sure of this from me." OBNC
Love's Cosmopolitan. Annie Matheson. OBVV
Love's Courtship. Thomas Carew. UnTE
Love's Cure, *sel.* Beaumont *and* Fletcher.
Song: "Turn, turn thy beauteous face away." PoEL-2
Love's Deity [*or* Deitie]. John Donne. AnAnS-1; AWP; ElL; EnRePo; GBL; LiTB; MePo; OAEP; SeCePo; SeCP; SeCV-1; WHA
Love's Despair. Dryden. *See* Farewell, Ungrateful Traitor.
Love's Despair. Shakespeare. *See* Come Away, Come Away, Death.
Love's Despair. Richard Lynch. *Fr.* Diella. ElL
Love's Despair. Diarmad O'Curnain, *tr. fr. Irish by* George Sigerson. OnYI; OxBI
Love's Diet. John Donne. OAEP
Love's domain, supernal Zion. Brynbwrla. Kingsley Amis. *Fr.* The Evans Country. NOBL
Love's Emblem. John Clare. NIP
Love's Emblems. John Fletcher. *Fr.* The Tragedy of Valentinian, II, iv. BoLoP; ElL; HBV-1; NIP; NOBE; OBEV; UnTE
(Love Song: "Now the lusty Spring is seen.") FaBoEn
(Now the Lusty Spring.) ELP; ErPo; FF; ViBoPo
Loves End. Lord Herbert of Cherbury. AnAnS-2; SeCP
(Sonnet: "Thus ends my love, but this death grieve me most.") ViBoPo
Love's Ending. *Unknown.* OBSC
Love's Entreaty. Michelangelo, *tr. fr. Italian by* John Addington Symonds. AWP
("Thou knowest, love, I know that thou dost know.") PeHV
Love's equinoctial gales are past. Winter. Maurice Craig. OnYI
Love's Fancy. Dryden. *See* After the Pangs of a Desperate Lover.
Love's Farewell. Michael Drayton. *See* Idea: "Since there's no help. . ."
Love's Fidelity. Petrarch. *See* Vow to Love Faithfully.
Love's Flight. Else Lasker-Schüler, *tr. fr. German by* Jethro Bithell. TrJP
Love's Fool. John Rosenthal. AMV-81
Love's Force. Thomas Carew. CaPo
Love's Franciscan. Henry Constable. ACP; GoBC
Love's Glory. Fulke Greville. *Fr.* Caelica. OBSC
("Fie, foolish, Earth, think you the heaven wants glory.") EnRePo
("Fye foolish Earth, Thinke you the heaven wants glory.") PoEL-1
Love's god is a boy. Cupid. *Unknown.* ElL
Love's Grave. George Meredith. *See* Modern Love: "Mark where the pressing wind. . ."
Love's Grave. Thomas Watson. *See* Here Lieth Love.
Love's Growth. John Donne. AnAnS-1; JCP; MePo; NoP; SeCV-1
Loves Heretick. Thomas Stanley. CavP
Love's Horoscope. Richard Crashaw. HBV-1; MeLP; OBS
Love's Immaturity. E. J. Scovell. GBL; LiTB
Love's Immortality. Elsa Barker. *Fr.* The Spirit and the Bride. HBMV
Love's Inconsistency. Petrarch. *See* Description of the Contrarious Passions . . .
Love's Justification. Michelangelo. *See* To the Marchesana of Pescara.
Love's Labour Lost. Robert Tofte. *Fr.* Alba. ElL
Love's Labour's Lost, *sels.* Shakespeare.
"But love, first learned in a lady's eyes," *fr.* IV, iii. PP
Did Not the Heavenly Rhetoric of Thine Eye, *fr.* IV, iii. LiTB
(Sonnet: "Did not the heavenly rhetoric of thine eye.") ViBoPo
"If she be made of white and red," *fr.* I, ii. CTC
"Lover's eyes will gaze an eagle blind, A," *fr.* IV, iii. GBL
On a Day—Alack the Day, *fr.* IV, iii. ElL; ViBoPo
(Blossom, The.) OBEV
(Dumain's Rhymes.) OBSC
(Love's Perjuries.) GTBS; GTBS-P; HBV-1
So Sweet a Kiss, *fr.* IV, iii. ElL; InvP
When Daisies Pied and Violets Blue, *fr.* V, ii. BiP; EnRePo; FF; InPK; NOBE; NoP; PoRA; PrIm; SeCeV
(Cuckoo Sing, The.) PoPle
(Song: "When daisies pied and violets blue.") FiP; HBV-2; PBBP; PoEL-2
(Song: Spring and Winter.) LoBV
(Spring.) ElL; HAP; HeIP; NIP; OAEL-1; OBEV; PAI; PoEL-2; SeCePo; TEP; TrGrPo; UnPo; ViBoPo
(Spring Song.) TreFT
When Icicles Hang by the Wall, *fr.* V, ii. AWP; BiP; EnRePo; FaPON; FF; GN; GoJo; InPK; InPS; LiTB; NOBE; PoRA; PoSC; PrIm; RoGo; SeCeV
(Hiems.) FaBoCh
(Merry Note, A.) WiR
(Song: "When icicles hang by the wall.") FiP; HBV-2; PBBP; PoEL-2
(Tu-Whit To-Who.) CH
(Ver and Hiems.) OBSC
(Winter.) BoNaP; ChTr; ElL; GTBS; GTBS-P; HAP; HeIP; NIP; OAEL-1; OBEV; PAI; SeCePo; TEP; TreFS; TrGrPo; UnPo; ViBoPo; WeW; WHA
(Winter Song.) FaBoEn
Love's Land. Isabella Valancy Crawford. CaP
Love's Language. Donagh MacDonagh. NeIP
Love's Last Gift. Dante Gabriel Rossetti. The House of Life, LIX. VLP
Love's Last Resource. Sadi, *tr. fr. Persian by* L. Cranmer-Byng. *Fr.* The Gulistan. AWP
Love's Likeness. George Darley. OBVV
Love's Limit. *Unknown.* TrGrPo
Love's Longing. *Unknown, tr. fr. Latin by* John Addington Symonds. UnTE
Love's Lord. Edward Dowden. HBV-2
Love's Martyr, *sels.* Sir Robert Chester.
Ditty: "O holy Love, religious saint!" ElL
Her Hair. ElL
Love's Martyrs. John Ford. *See* Song: "Oh no more, no more, too late."
Love's Matrimony. William Cavendish. SeCePo
Love's Mortality. Richard Middleton. WHA
Love's multitudinous boneyard. Chorus. Jack Kerouac. *Fr.* Mexico City Blues. NeAP
Love's night and a lamp. Meleager, *tr. fr. Greek by* Peter Whigham. BoLoP
Love's Nightingale. Richard Crashaw. LoBV
Love's Nobility. Emerson. *Fr.* Celestial Love. TreF
Love's Not Time's Fool. Shakespeare. *See* Sonnets, CXVI.
Loves of the Birds, The. *Malay Oral Tradition, tr. by* R. J. Wilkinson *and* R. O. Winstedt. WTO
Loves of the Plants, The. Erasmus Darwin. *See* Botanic Garden, The.
Loves of the Puppets. Richard Wilbur. CoPo; OxBC
Loves of the Triangles, The, *sel.* John Hookham Frere.
"Stay your rude steps, or e'er your feet invade." FaBoNo
Love's Offence. Sir John Suckling. CaPo
Love's Old Sweet Song. G. Clifton Bingham. BLSo, *with music*; FaBoBe; FSN, *with music*; TreF
Love's Omnipresence. *At. to* Joshua Sylvester. *See* Were I as Base as Is the Lowly Plain.
Love's on the highroad. Song. Dana Burnet. HBV-1
Love's own form. R. G. Vliet. POL
Love's pallor and the semblance of deep ruth. Dante, *tr. by* Dante Gabriel Rossetti. La Vita Nuova, XXIV. AWP
Love's perfect blossom only blows. Courtesy. Coventry Patmore. OBVV
Love's Perjuries. Shakespeare. *See* On a Day—Alack the Day.
Love's Philosophy. Shelley. BLPA; BLPL; BoLoP; EnRP; FaBoBe; FaBV; GTBS; GTBS-P; HBV-1; HoPM; OAEP; OBRV; OLR; TreFT; TrGrPo; UnTE; ViBoPo
Love's Pilgrims. Thomas Campion. *See* What Faire Pompe.
Love's Prayer. James Whitcomb Riley. AA
(Dear Lord! Kind Lord!) TreFT
Love's Prerogative. John Oxenham. BLRP
Love's Prisoner. Mariana Griswold Van Rensselaer. HBV-1
Love's Progress. John Donne. Elegies, XVIII. LiTB; OAEL-1; ViBoPo
Love's Protestation. Thomas Lodge. *See* Fancy, A.
Love's Pursuit. Robert Browning. *See* Life in a Love.
Love's Reality. Coventry Patmore. *Fr.* The Angel in the House, I, i. VLP
Love's Rebel. Earl of Surrey. OBSC
("When sommer take in hand the winter to assail.") AAS
("When summer took in hand the winter to assail.") SiPS
Love's Remorse. Edwin Muir. OxBTC
Love's Résumé. Heine. *See* Rose, die Lilie, die Taube, die Sonne, Die.
Love's Resurrection Day. Louise Chandler Moulton. AA; HBV-1
Love's Rosary. Alfred Noyes. HBV-1
Love's Rosary. George Edward Woodberry. AA
Love's Secret. Blake. *See* Never Seek to Tell Thy Love.
Love's Servile Lot. Robert Southwell. ACP
Loves She Like Me? Samuel Woodworth. AA
Love's Siege. Sir John Suckling. *See* 'Tis Now, Since I Sat Down Before.
Love's Spite. Aubrey Thomas De Vere. HBV-1
Love's Stratagems. Donald Justice. NYBP
Love's Torment. *Unknown, tr. fr. German by* Louis Untermeyer. UnTE
Love's Tribute. Lorena W. Sturgeon. PGD

Love's Trinity. Alfred Austin. OBVV
Love's Triumph. Ben Jonson. EnRePo
Love's Unreason. *Unknown. See* Love Not Me.
Love's Victories. James Shirley. *Fr.* Cupid and Death. GoBC
Loves Victory. Aurelian Townshend. *See* To the Countesse of Salisbury.
Love's Vision. Edward Carpenter. WGRP
Loves who many years held all my mind, The. Walter Savage Landor. GBL
Love's Wisdom. Margaret Deland. AA
Love's Witchery. Thomas Lodge. ElL
Love's without Reason. Alexander Brome. OBS
Love's Witness. Aphra Behn. BoWoP
Loves World. Sir John Suckling. SeCV-1
Love's worshipers alone can know. Love and Folly. La Fontaine, *tr. by* Bryant. AWP
Love's Young Dream. Thomas Moore. HBV-1; WBLP
Lovesick. *Unknown, tr. fr. Greek by* Louis Untermeyer. UnTE
Lovesick Cowboy, The. *Unknown.* CoSo
Love-sick Lass, The. "Hugh MacDiarmid." BSV
Lovesight. Dante Gabriel Rossetti. The House of Life, IV. EBVV; FaBoEn; GTBS-P; HBV-1; OAEP; OBNC; OBVV; TrGrPo; ViBoPo; VLP; WHA
Lovesleep, The. Gavin Ewart. OxBC
Lovest Thou Me? William Cowper. HBV-2; OBEC
"Lord it is my chief complaint," *sel.* TrPWD
Lovewell's Fight. *Unknown.* BaBo; HBV-2; PAH
Loving. Shirley Kaufman. VWA
Loving. Jane Stembridge. NMM
Loving/ the pottery goodness. The Parts of a Poet. Wendy Rose. TWSS
Loving and Beloved. Sir John Suckling. CaPo; FaBoEn; OBS
Loving and Liking. Dorothy Wordsworth. OxBChV
Loving Ballad of Lord Bateman, The. *Unknown. See* Young Beichan.
Loving care! Leave Me Alone. Felice Holman. RHPC
Loving in truth, and fain in verse my love to show. Astrophel and Stella, I. Sir Philip Sidney. AAS; AWP; BLPL; CABA; EBEV; FaBoEn; GBL; HAP; HBV-1; LiTB; MasP; NoP; OAEL-1; OAEP-1; OBSC; PP; SeCePo; SeCeV; SiPS; TEP; TreFT; TrGrPo; ViBoPo
Loving looks the large-eyed cow. A Christmas Prayer. George Macdonald. PChr; SUS
Loving Mad Tom. *Unknown. See* Tom o' Bedlam's Song.
Loving she is, and tractable, though wild. Characteristics of a Child Three Years Old. Wordsworth. OBRV
Loving She Stood Apart. Patrick Lane. NeAC
Loving the rituals that keep men close. Palladas, *tr. fr. Greek by* Tony Harrison. OBVE
Lovingly I turn me down. After Mass. "Michael Field." WPE
Low-anchored Cloud. Henry David Thoreau. *See* Mist.
Low-backed Car, The. Samuel Lover. HBV-1
Low Barometer. Robert Bridges. CMoP; CoBMV; LiTB; LoBV; NoAM; NOCV; QFR
Low beating of the tom-toms, The. African Dance. Langston Hughes. FaPON
Low Doun in the Broom. *Unknown.* BSV; GoTS
Low Down. *See also* Lowdown.
Low Down Chariot, *with music. Unknown.* OuSiCo
Low Fields and Light. W. S. Merwin. ConAP; LCAP
Low in the eastern sky. To the Maiden in the East. Henry David Thoreau. OxBA
Low in thy grave with thee. David's Lament for Jonathan. Peter Abelard, *tr. by* Helen Waddell. NAWM-1; PeHV
Low lies the land upon the sea. The Lookout. William Collins. EtS
Low, like another's, lies the laureled head. Lacrimae Musarum. Sir William Watson. HBV-2
Low prayer, a high prayer, I send through space, A. *Tr. from Gaelic by* Douglas Hyde. WTO
Low Road, The. Marge Piercy. LTB
Low-set island this September, A. Tresco. Goeffrey Grigson. FaBoPP
Low spake the knight to the peasant maid. The Rose and the Gauntlet. John Wilson. BeLS
Low sun whitens on the flying squalls, The. Rounding the Cape. Roy Campbell. PeSA
Low Tide. Lynette Roberts. NeBP
Low Tide. Warren Woessner. WOLT
Low Tide on Grand Pré. Bliss Carman. CaP; NOBC; OBCV; PeCV
Low Trick, A. Gelett Burgess. OBCA
Low was our pretty cot: our tallest rose. Reflections on Having Left a Place of Retirement. Samuel Taylor Coleridge. EnRP; OBEC
Lowdown. *See also* Low Down.
Lowdown Dirty Blues. *Unknown.* AmFP
Low-down, Lonesome Low, The. *Unknown. See* Golden Vanity, The.
Lowdown Rounder's Blues. *Unknown.* BluL
Lowell. James Russell Lowell. *Fr.* A Fable for Critics. AmPP; AP; NOBA; OxBA; TAP
(On Himself.) AA
Lower Court. Carolyn Baxter. LFAC
Lower Criticism, The. John Hollander. DBV; PV
Lower Forms of Life. Mary Winter. GoYe
Lower him gently, gently, now, into the quiet deep. Sea Burial. Robina Monkman. EtS
Lower the flags. Special Bulletin. Langston Hughes. PoBA
Lower the Standard: That's My Motto. Karl Shapiro. NoAM
Lowering night, with muggy sultry air, A. The Stampede. Earl Alonzo Brininstool. PoOW
Lowery Cot. L. A. G. Strong. MoBrPo
Lowest Place, The. Christina Rossetti. TrPWD
Lowest Trees Have Tops, The. Sir Edward Dyer. *See* Silent Love, A.
Lowland hills and rivers. The War Year. Ts'Ao Sung, *tr. by* C. H. Kwock *and* Vincent McHugh. PPON
Lowlands ("I dreamt [*or* dreamed] a dream the other night"). *Unknown.* ChTr; FSW; OxBoL
Lowlands Away ("Lowlands, Lowlands away, my John"), *diff. versions. Unknown.* AmSS, 2 *vers., with music*; GBP; ShS, 3 *vers., with music*; TrAS, *with music*
Lowlands o' [*or* of] Holland, The. *Unknown.* AmFP, *diff. version*; BSV; OxBB, *with music*
(Lawlands o' Holland, The.) AmSS, *with music;* CH
Lowly Bethlehem, *with music.* Count Zinzendorf, *tr. fr. German.* TrAS
Lowly Peasant, The. *Unknown, tr. fr. Ladino by* Rina Benmayor. PBWP
Lowpin owre a burn. O Aa the Manly Sports. J. K. Annand. PoSH
Lowriders #2 ("Lowriders/ cruising the barrio"). Reyes Cárdenas, *tr. fr. Spanish by* Toni Empringham. FIA
Lowshot Light. William Barnes. VLP
Lowveld, The. Charles Eglington. PeSA
Low-voiced girls that go, The. The Invisible Bride. Edwin Markham. HBV-1
Loyal. William Matthews. MAYP
Loyal Effusion. Horace Smith *and* James Smith. OBRV
Loyal General, The, *sel.* Nahum Tate.
Prologue: "If yet there be a few that take delight" (*by* Dryden). SeCV-2
"Loyal Hearts of London City, come I pray, and sing my ditty." The Dutchess of Monmouth's Lamentation for the Loss of Her Duke. *Unknown.* CoMu; FaBoBa
Loyal Scot, The, *sel.* Andrew Marvell.
"But who considers well will find indeed." ViBoPo
Loyal Sins. Jacob Glatstein, *tr. fr. Yiddish by* Ruth Whitman. VWA
Loyal subject, thou, to that bright Queen, A. To W. L. G. On Reading His "Chosen Queen." Charlotte Forten. BlSi
Loyalty. Berton Braley. BLPA
Loyalty. Allan Cunningham. *See* Hame, Hame, Hame.
Loyalty. W. H. Davies. BrPo
Loyalty Confin'd. Sir Roger L'Estrange. OBS
Lo-yang. Emperor Ch'ien Wen-ti, *tr. fr. Chinese by* Arthur Waley. AWP
Luath. Burns. GDP
Lubber Breeze. T. Sturge Moore. CH
Lubly Fan, *with music.* Cool White. TrAS
Lucasia, Rosania and Orinda Parting at a Fountain, July 1663. Katherine Philips. PeHV
Lucasta, frown and let me die. To Lucasta: Her Reserved Looks. Richard Lovelace. CaPo; SeCV-1
Lucasta Laughing. Richard Lovelace. PoEL-3
"Lucasta," said Terence O'Connor. "To Lucasta, on Going to the Wars." Edwin Meade Robinson. *Fr.* Limericised Classics, IV. HBMV
Lucasta Weeping ("Lucasta wept, and still the bright"). Sir John Denham. AnAnS-2
Lucasta's Fan, with a Looking-Glass in It. Richard Lovelace. CaPo
Lucasta's World. Richard Lovelace. CaPo; SeCP
Lüchow's and After. L. E. Sissman. NYP
Lucifer. D. H. Lawrence. OAEP
Lucifer in Starlight. George Meredith. AWP; CABA; CH; EBVV; FF; HAP; HBV-2; InPK; LiTB; LoBV; NOBE; NoP; OAEL-2; OAEP; OBEV; OBNC; OBVV; PoEL-5; PPoe; SeCeV; TreFT; TrGrPo; UnPo; ViBoPo; VLP; WeW
Lucifer in the Train. Adrienne Rich. EaLo; NePoEA-2; TwAmPo
Lucifer, The. Guy Glover. CaP
Lucile, *sel.* "Owen Meredith."
What We May Live Without. TreF
Lucilia, wedded to Lucretius, found. Lucretius. Tennyson. OAEL-2; VLP
Lucilla, saved from shipwreck on the seas. A Dedication. Claire McAllister. TwAmPo
Lucina Schynning in Silence of the Night. Eilean Ni Chuilleanain. CIP
Lucinda Matlock. Edgar Lee Masters. *Fr.* Spoon River Anthology. CMoP; FaBV; FF; HAP; LiTA; LiTM; MoAmPo; MoVE; NoAM; NOBA; OxBA
Luck. Elaine Epstein. AMV-81
Luck. W. W. Gibson. EtS; MoShBr; OBMV

Luck. Evan V. Shute. CaP
Luck has no songs, luck has no thoughts, luck has nothing. Pain. Edith Södergran. PBWP
Luck? I am upset. My dog is ill. A Rune for C. Barbara Howes. NYBP
Luck is not smiling upon us. Smile at Me. Musa Moris Farhi. VWA
Luck of Edenhall, The. Ludwig Uhland, *tr. fr. German by* Longfellow. AWP
Luckes, my faire falcon, and your fellowes all. Sir Thomas Wyatt. *See* Lux, My Fair Falcon.
"Luckies." Reginald Gibbons. MAYP
Luckless man/ Avoids the miserable bodkin's point. Man's Anxious, but Ineffectual Guard against Death. Thomas Lovell Beddoes. ChER
Lucky. Cathy Song. BrSi
Lucky Chance, The, *sel.* Aphra Behn.
Song: "Oh! Love, that stronger art than wine." WPE; WPOW
Lucky Coin, The. Austin Clarke. NeIP
Lucky like Cook to travel and return. "Heureux Qui comme Ulysse." John Manifold. WaaP; WaP
Lucky Lion! *Zulu Oral Tradition, tr. by* H. Tracey. WTO
Lucky Marriage, The. Thomas Blackburn. GTBS-P
Lucky the husband. Mabel Kelly. Turlough O'Carolan, *tr. by* Austin Clarke. BIrV; CIP
Lucky the living child, born in a land. American Child. Paul Engle. AmFN
Lucrative offices are seldom lost. Absence of Occupation. William Cowper. *Fr.* Retirement. OBEC
Lucretius. Tennyson. OAEL-2; VLP
Lucretius could not credit centaurs. Invitation to Juno. William Empson. CMoP; FaBoMo
Lucretius felt the change of the world in his time. Prescription of Painful Ends. Robinson Jeffers. LiTA; MoAB; MoAmPo; OxBA
Lucretius versus the Lake Poets. Robert Frost. GLGT
Lucy. Walter de la Mare. CMoP
Lucy, *complete, in 5 parts.* Wordsworth. EnRP; FiP; HBV-1; NOBE; OAEL-2; OBEV; OBNC; TrGrPo
Sels.
I Traveled [*or* travell'd] among Unknown Men. FaBV; GTBS; GTBS-P; OAEP; OBNC; OBRV
She Dwelt among the Untrodden Ways. AWP; BLPA; BoLoP; CABA; ELP; EnLoPo; FaBoEn; FaBV; FF; FPL; HAP; HBVY; HeIP; LiTB; LoBV; NIP; NoP; OAEP; OBRV; PAI; PPP; PrIm; SpRo; TEP; TreF; UnPo; ViBoPo; WeW; WHA
(Lost Love, The.) GTBS; GTBS-P
Slumber Did My Spirit Seal, A. BiP; BLPL; CABA; HAP; HeIP; InPK; InPS; InvP; NIP; PoEL-4; TreFS
Strange Fits of Passion Have I Known. EBEV; GBL; LO
Three Years She Grew in Sun and Shower. GN; HAP; HBVY; LoBV; NoP; OAEP; OBRV; PoEL-4; SeCeV; TreFS
(Education of Nature, The.) GTBS; GTBS-P
Lucy/ blessed among women. Hominization. Miroslav Holub, *tr. by* David Young *and* Dana Háová. SUW
Lucy Answers. Helen Ehrlich. SUW
Lucy Ashton's Song. Sir Walter Scott. *Fr.* The Bride of Lammermoor, *ch.* 3. BSV; EnRP; GoTS; NOBE; OBEV; OxBS
(Look Not Thou.) OBRV
Lucy goes down the celestial escalator in light. Lucy Taking Birth. Diana Scott. BrRo
Lucy Gray; or, Solitude. Wordsworth. BeLS; CH; EnRP; FiP; HBV-1; OAEL-2; OAEP; OBRV; OxBChV; SeCeV; TEP; TreFS
Lucy Lake. Newton Mackintosh. BXAP; HBV-1; SpRo
Lucy Lake. Ogden Nash. ShM
Lucy Lavender. Ivy O. Eastwick. SiSoSe
Lucky Lock lost her pocket. Mother Goose. OxNR; OxBoLi; TiPo
Lucy Taking Birth. Diana Scott. BrRo
Lucy, you brightnesse of our spheare, who are. To Lucy, Countesse of Bedford, with Mr. Donnes Satyres. Ben Jonson. AnAnS-2; OBS; SeCV-1
Lud! what a group the motley scene discloses! Goldsmith. *Fr.* Epilogue to "The Sister." OBSV
Ludlow Massacre, The. Woody Guthrie. FSW
Ludmilla; an Ode on the Occasion of Her Departure from These Shores ("Ludmilla, the Soviet lassie"). Ernest W. Thiele. WhC
Ludwig's Death Mask. Ted Hughes. NoAM
Luer, faulkners! give warning to the feild! *Unknown. See* Lure, falconers, lure!. . .
Luf es lif that lastes ay, thar it in Criste es feste. *See* Love Is Life.
Lugubrious Whing-Whang, The. James Whitcomb Riley. NA; YaD
Luini in porcelain! Medallion. Ezra Pound. *Fr.* Hugh Selwyn Mauberley. SeCeV
Luis de Camões. Roy Campbell. FaBoTw; PeSA
Luke. Bible, *N.T. See* St. Luke.
Luke and John. Handwriting on the Wall. *Unknown.* AmFP
Luke Havergal. Robert Bridges. QFR
Luke Havergal. E. A. Robinson. AA; AmPP; AP; AWP; CoBMV; CrMA; GBL; LiTA; LiTM; MoAB; MoAmPo; MoPo; MOVE; NePA; NoAM; NOBA; PoEL-5; TreFT; UnPo
Luke tells us how the boy Jesus. The Temple. Clifford Dyment. ChMP
Luke XI: Blessed Be the Paps Which Thou Hast Sucked. Richard Crashaw. BXAP; CABA; JCP
(Blessed Be the Paps Which Thou Hast Sucked.) PeD
Lula Vires. *Unknown.* AmFP
Lulee, lullay. A Lullaby. Janet Lewis. NOCV
Lull, The. Molly Peacock. MAYP
Lulla La, Lulla Lulla Lullaby. William Byrd. SBVL
Lullabie of a Lover, The. George Gascoigne. *See* Lullaby of a Lover, The.
Lullaby: "Baloo, loo, lammy, now baloo, my dear." Carolina Nairne. HBV-1
Lullaby: "Beloved, may your sleep be sound." W. B. Yeats. BoLoP; FaBoTw; OBMV
Lullaby: "Come sleep, and with the sweet deceiving." Beaumont *and* Fletcher. *See* Come Sleep.
Lullaby: "Din of work is subdued, The." W. H. Auden. FaBoMo
Lullaby, A: "For wars his life and half a world away." Randall Jarrell. OxBC
Lullaby: "Golden slumbers kiss your eyes." Thomas Dekker. *See* Golden Slumbers.
Lullaby: "Gray goose and gander." *Unknown. See* Grey Goose and Gander.
Lullaby: "Hush dove the summer." Miriam Waddington. CaP
Lullaby: "Hush, lullay." Léonie Adams. MoAB; MoAmPo
Lullaby: "Husheen, the herons are crying." "Seumas O'Sullivan." OnYI
Lullaby: "I wish to God my child was born." *Unknown.* AmFP
Lullaby: "It is a summer evening." Anne Sexton. NoAM
Lullaby: "Lay your sleeping head, my love." W. H. Auden. CMoP; HAP; LLLT; NoAM; NOBE; OAEL-2; OxBTC; PPP; UnPo; WeW
(Lay Your Sleeping Head, My Love.) BoLoP; ChMP; CoBMV; FaBoEn; LiTB; MoAB; MoBrPo; MoPo; MoVE; SeCePo; TEP
(Song XI.) EnLoPo
Lullaby: "Long canoe, The." Robert Hillyer. DuDa; FaPON
Lullaby: "Love me—I love you." Christina Rossetti. PoPle
Lullaby, A: "Lulee, lullay." Janet Lewis. NOCV
Lullaby: "Lullaby baby, lullaby baby." John Phillip. ELI
Lullaby: "O! hush thee, my darling, sleep soundly my son." *Unknown, tr. fr. Yiddish by* Alice Lucas. TrJP
Lullaby: "O men from the fields." Padraic Colum. *See* Cradle Song, A: "O men from the fields."
Lullaby: "O my son, born on a winter's morn." Nohomaiterangi, *tr. fr. Maori by* Barry Mitcalfe. WTO
Lullaby: "Puva . . . puva . . . puva." *Unknown, tr. by* Natalie Curtis. SUS
Lullaby: "Rockaby, lullaby, bees in the clover!" Josiah Gilbert Holland. *Fr.* The Mistress of the Manse. AA; HBV-1
Lullaby: "Rook's nest do rock on the tree-top, The." William Barnes. VLP
Lullaby: "Sleep, little baby, sleep and rest." Elinor Chipp. HBMV
Lullaby: "Sleep, love, sleep." Quandra Prettyman. BOLo
Lullaby: "Sleep, mouseling, sleep." Elizabeth J. Coatsworth. SiSoSe
Lullaby: "Sleep, my little baby, sleep." Samuel Hoffenstein. TrJP
Lullaby: "Sleep now." Shlomo Vinner, *tr. fr. Hebrew by* Laya Firestone. VWA
Lullaby: "Slumber, Jesu, lightly dreaming." *Unknown, tr. fr. Latin by* Raymond R. Roseliep. ISi
Lullaby: "Softly now the burn is rushing." Seumas MacManus. AnIV
Lullaby, A: "Speak roughly to your little boy." "Lewis Carroll." *See* Speak Roughly to Your Little Boy.
Lullaby: "Sweet and low, sweet and low." Tennyson. *Fr.* The Princess. *See* Sweet and Low.
Lullaby, A: "Sweet baby, sleep! what ails my dear." George Wither. *See* Hymn L: Rocking Hymn, A.
Lullaby: "This is where/ the light sleeps." Sue Owen. AMV-80
Lullaby: "Though the world has slipped and gone." Edith Sitwell. ChMP; CMoP; LiTM; SBVL; WaP
Lullaby: "Upon my lap my sovereign sits." Richard Verstegan. CH; EIL; HBV-1; LoBV; OBEV
(Our Lady's Lullaby.) ACP; GoBC; IS
(Upon My Lap My Sovereign Sits.) ViBoPo
Lullaby: "What if, every time you walked, things." Frederick Eckman. FAZ
Lullaby: "Wide as this night, old as this night is old and young as it is young." Kenneth Fearing. CMoP
Lullaby: "With lights for eyes, our city turns." Dom Moraes. NePoEA-2
Lullaby baby, lullaby baby. Lullaby. John Phillip. EIL
Lullaby for an Emigrant. Benjamin Fondane, *tr. fr. French by* Keith Bosley. VWA
Lullaby for Ann-Lucian. Calvin Forbes. PoBA

Lullaby for Miriam. Richard Beer-Hofmann, *tr. fr. German by* Jonathan Griffin. VWA
Lullaby for My Dead Child. Denise Jallais, *tr. fr. French by* Maxine Kumin *and* Judith Kumin. BoWoP
Lullaby for Titania. Shakespeare. *See* You Spotted Snakes.
Lullaby in Auschwitz. Pierre Morhange, *tr. fr. French by* Edouard Roditi. VWA
Lullaby in Bethlehem. Henry Howarth Bashford. HBV-1; HBVY
Lullaby, my little one. Cradle Song. Carl Michael Bellman. FaPON
Lullaby, O Lullaby. William Cox Bennett. HBV-1
Lullaby [*or* Lullabie] of a Lover, The. George Gascoigne. AAS; EBEV; ElL; EnRePo; HAP; OAEP; QFR
(Gascoigne's Lullaby [*or* Lullabie].) NoP; PoEL-1; TrFrPo
(Lover's Lullaby, A.) HBV-1; OBEV
(Sing Lullaby, as Women Do.) InvP
Lullaby of an Infant Chief. Sir Walter Scott. EnRP; FaPON; HBV-1; OxBChV
Lullaby of the Catfish and the Crab. William Rose Benét. WhC
Lullaby of the Nativity, A. *Unknown.* MeEL
(Lullay Mine [*or* My] Liking.) ELP; SBVL
Lullaby of the Woman of the Mountain. Padraic Pearse, *tr. fr. Modern Irish by* Thomas MacDonagh. OnYI
Lullaby Town. John Irving Diller. BLPA
Lullabye! "Snow is lying on my roof." Kathryn Stripling. AMV-80
Lullay, By-by, Lullay. *Unknown. See* This Endris Night.
Lullay, Lullay. John Skelton. *See* My Darling Dear, My Daisy Flower.
Lullay, Lullay. *Unknown.* OxBoCh
Lullay, lullay, la, lullay. Jesus Reassures His Mother. *Unknown.* MeEL
Lullay, lullay, litel child. Lullay, Lullay. *Unknown.* OxBoCh
Lullay Mine Liking. *Unknown. See* Lullaby of the Nativity.
Lullay, My Child. *Unknown.* OxBM
Lullay, My Liking. *Unknown. See* Lullaby of the Nativity, A.
Lulled, at silence, the spent attack. Baggot Street Deserta. Thomas Kinsella. CIP; CMoP; IPY; NMP
Lulled by La Belle Dame sans Merci he lies. The Enchanted Knight. Edwin Muir. MoVE
Lulls swears he is all heart, but you'll suppose. Upon Lulls. Robert Herrick. CaPo
Lully, lulla, thou little tiny child. Coventry Carol. *Unknown.* EBCP; ELP; MeEL; OFD; PChr
Lully, lullay [*or* lulley], lully, lullay [*or* lulley]. Corpus Christi Carol [*or* The Bereaved Maid *or* The Falcon *or* The Knight of the Grail *or* Over Yonder's a Park.] *Unknown.* ACP; BaBo; CH; ChTr; EBEV; FaBoBa; GBP; HAP; LiTB; LoBV; MeEL; NOBE; NoP; NU; OAEL-1; OAEP; OBEV; OxBM; OxBoCh; SCV; SeCeV; TrGrPo; ViBoPo; WeW
Lulu, *with music. Unknown.* CoSo
Lumber Camp Song, The. *Unknown.* ShS
Lumber of a London-going dray, The. An Incident in the Early Life of Ebenezer Jones, Poet, 1828. John Betjeman. CMoP; NoAM
Lumber of Spring. Anne Ridler. NYBP
Lumbering haunches, pussyfoot tread, a pride of. Circus Lion. C. Day Lewis. BoAnP; PoPle
Lumbering tractor rolls its panting round, The. The Agricultural Show, Flemington, Victoria. "Furnley Maurice." CBAP
Lumberman's Alphabet, The. *Unknown.* AmFP; ShS, *with music*
Lumberyard, The. Ruth Herschberger. LiTA; WPE
Lumen de Lumine. Shelley. *Fr.* Adonais. GoBC
("One remains, the many change and pass, The.") SCV
Lumière. H. L. Van Brunt. AMV-81; LTB
Luminous, The. Barbara Guest. PoM
Luminous almonds have. Anne Sexton. Hans Juergensen. AMV-81
Luminous blaze! An Ode on Gas. *Unknown.* OBAL
Lump. Robert Phillips. AMV-80
Lump says that Caliban's of gutter breed. On Two Ministers of State. Hilaire Belloc. PV
Lumps. Judith Thurman. RHPC
Lumumba's Grave. Langston Hughes. CNA
Lunar Baedeker. Mina Loy. VGW
Lunar Eclipse. Diane Glancy. STE
Lunar Eclipse. Jessica Scarbrough. LFAC
Lunar Games, The. Eeva-Liisa Manner, *tr. fr. Finnish by* Jaakko A. Ahokas. WPOW
Lunar Paraphrase. Wallace Stevens. MOON
Lunar Probe, The. Maxine W. Kumin. MOON
Lunar Stanzas. Henry Coggswell Knight. FaBoNo; NA
Lunar Tides, The. Marya Zaturenska. MOON
Lunatic, the Lover, and the Poet, The. Shakespeare. *Fr.* A Midsummer Night's Dream, V, i. FiP; MasP
(Imagination.) LiTB
("Lovers and madmen have such seething brains.") PP
(Tricks of Imagination, The.) TreFS
Lunch. Kenneth Koch. SOTW
Lunch at the Coq d'Or. Peter Davison. TwCP
Lunch with Girl Scouts. Sharon Bryan. MAYP
Luncheon, A. Max Beerbohm. FaBoCo; NOBL; OBSV; OxBTC;
Lunching with you at a restaurant on Commonwealth Ave. Letters to My Daughters. Judith Minty. AMV-81
Lunchroom Bus Boy Who Looked like Orson Welles, The. Horace Gregory. *Fr.* The Passion of M'Phail. NYP; TwAmPo
(They Were All Like Geniuses.) NYBP
Lune Concrete. Raymond Federman. MOON
Lungs draw in the air and rattle it out again, The. Remorse. John Betjeman. MoBrPo
Lupercalia. Ted Hughes. CMoP; NMP
Lupine Dew. Jarold Ramsey. NIP
Lupracaun, or Fairy Shoemaker, The. William Allingham. OnYI
Lupus in Fabula. Malcolm Lowry. OBCV; PeCV
(Xochitepec.) MoCV; NOBC
Lurching from gloomy limousines we slip. My Father's Funeral. Karl Shapiro. DiL
Lure, The. John Boyle O'Reilly. HBV-1
Lure, falconers, lure! [*or* Luer, faulkners!] give warning to the field! For the Hern [*or* Hearne] and Duck. *Unknown.* NCEP; PBBP
Lure me with lovers. Monogamania. Eve Merriam. UnTE
"Lured," little one? Nay, you've but heard. Nested. Habberton Lulham. HBV-1
Luriana, Lurilee. Charles Elton. PoPle
Luscious and Sorrowful. Christina Rossetti. PoEL-5; SeCePo
Luscious lobster, with the crabfish raw, The. Kinds of Shel-fish. William Wood. SCAP
Lusiads, The, *sels.* Luis de Camoes, *tr. fr. Portuguese by* Sir Richard Fanshawe.
"Now through the ocean in great haste they flunder." OBVE
"Shores are crown'd with people, The." OBVE
Luss! be for ever sunk beneath. Mercury; on Losing My Pocket Milton at Luss near Ben Lomond, and Other Mountains. Robert Andrews. NOEC
Luss Village. Iain Crichton Smith. BSV
Lust. William Matthews. PCP
Lust for Murder, The. Gerda Penfold. GP
Lust in Song. Robert Graves. *See* Bards, The.
Lust is the oldest lion of them all. An Italian Chest. Marjorie Allen Seiffert. HBMV
Lust of Gold, The. James Montgomery. *Fr.* The West Indies. PAH
Lustra, *sels.* Ezra Pound.
Further Instructions. MP; TwCP
("Come, my songs, let us express our baser passions.") PoA
Rest, The. AmPP; MoAB; MoAmPo; NoAM; NOBA; OxBA; PP
("O helpless few in my country.") PoA
Lusty Fryer of Flanders, The. *Unknown.* CoMu
Lusty Juventus. Charles Madge. FaBoMo
Lusty Juventus, *sel.* Robert Wever.
In Youth Is Pleasure. ChTr; NOBE; OBEV
("In a herber green, asleep whereas I lay.") GBL
(In an Arbour Green.) ELP
(Of Youth He Singeth.) ElL
(Youth.) OBSC
Lusty May. *Unknown.* OBEV
(Four May Poems.) OxBS
Lute and the pear are your half sisters, The. A Flock of Guinea Hens Seen from a Car. Eudora Welty. GrPl; NYBP; PrIm
Lute, companion of my calamity. Sonnet XII. Louise Labé, *tr. by* Aliki *and* Willis Barnstone. BoWoP
Lute Music. Kenneth Rexroth. TAP
Lute Obeys, The. Sir Thomas Wyatt. *See* Blame Not My Lute for He Must Sound.
Lutea Allison. Sir John Suckling. ErPo
Luther. W. H. Auden. PAI
Luther B—— stepped from his air-conditioned house. I Hear America Griping. Morris Bishop. AmFN; QQQ
Luther, they say, was unwise. A Letter from Rome. Arthur Hugh Clough. *Fr.* Amours de Voyage. LoBV
Lutra, the Fisher. James McMichael. AmPA
Luvin' wumman is a licht, A. Love. "Hugh MacDiarmid." CMoP
Lux in Tenebris. Katherine Tynan. OxBI; TrPWD
Lux in Tenebris. *Unknown.* GoBC
Lux, My Fair Falcon. Sir Thomas Wyatt. NoP
(Epigram: "Lux my fair falcon, and your fellows all.") SiPS
("Luckes, my faire falcon, and your fellowes all.") AAS
Luxurious house had a huge mirror, The. The Mirror in the Front Hall. C. P. Cavafy, *tr. by* Edmund Keeley *and* Philip Sherrard. PeHV
Luxurious man, to bring his vice in use. The Mower against Gardens. Andrew Marvell. AnAnS-1; EBEV; LiTB; NoP; OAEL-1; OAEP; PoEL-2; PP; PPP; SeCV-1

Luxury. Donald Justice. HeIP
Luxury, then, is a way of. Political Poem. Amiri Baraka. CoAP; NoAM
Luzzato. Charles Reznikoff. VWA
Lyarde Is an Old Horse. *Unknown.* OxBM
Lyce. William Walsh. BoLoP
Lychee, The. Wang I, *tr. fr. Chinese by* Arthur Waley. FaBoCh
Lycias. Earl of Rochester. ErPo
Lycidas. Milton. AWP; BiP; CABA; ChTr; EBEV; FaBoEn; FiP; GTBS; GTBS-P; HAP; HBV-2; InPK; InPS; JCP; LiTB; LoBV; MasP; NIP; NOBE; NoP; OAEL-1; OAEP; OBEV; OBS; PAI; PoEL-3; PPoe; PPP; PrIm; SeCeV; TrGrPo; UnPo; ViBoPo; WeW; WGRP; WHA, *abr.*
Sels.
"Ayme! Whilst thee the shores and sounding seas." Prf
Last Came, and Last Did Go. TW
"Weep no more, woful shepherds weep no more." FaBoRV
Lycidas and Moeris. Virgil, *tr. fr. Latin by* Dryden. Eclogues, IX. AWP
Lycon begin—begin the mournful tale. Eclogue. William Diaper. *Fr.* Nereides; or, Sea-Eclogues. SeCePo
Lycoris darling, once I burned for you. Martial, *tr. fr. Latin by* Peter Porter. BoLoP
Lydford Journey. William Browne. CavP
Lydia. Lizette Woodworth Reese. AA
Lydia, in Heavens Name. Horace, *tr. by* Sir Richard Fanshawe. Odes, I, 8. OBVE
Lydia Is Gone This Many a Year. Lizette Woodworth Reese. CH; GoJo; HBV-1
Lydia Pinkham, *with music. Unknown.* AS
Lydia Sherman, *sel. Unknown.*
"Lydia Sherman is plagued with rats." ShM
Lyell's Hypothesis Again. Kenneth Rexroth. MoVE; NoAM
Lyf so short, the craft so long to lerne, The. Proem to the Parlement of Foules. Chaucer. *Fr.* The Parlement of Foules. FiP; ViBoPo
Lying. Thomas Moore. FiBHP
Lying. Richard Wilbur. SV
Lying along the wide branch. Tiger People. Geary Hobson. STE
Lying apart now, each in a separate bed. One Flesh. Elizabeth Jennings. OxBTC; PBWP
Lying asleep between the strokes of night. Love and Sleep. Swinburne. BoLoP; UnTE; VLP
Lying at night poised between sleep and waking. East Coast—Canada. Elizabeth Brewster. CaP
Lying Awake. Thomas Hardy. FaBoRV
Lying Awake. W. D. Snodgrass. HoPM; MoAmPo; NYBP
Lying awake. White. Marguerite Bouvard. AMV-81
Lying Down with Men and Women. John Woods. GP
Lying here alone. Izumi Shikibu, *tr. fr. Japanese.* WeW
Lying here, everything in me. Margaret Atwood. NeAC
Lying here quietly beside you. Quietly. Kenneth Rexroth. ErPo
Lying in a Hammock at William Duffy's Farm. James Wright. CAPP; ConAP; HAP; HoPM; InPS; NaP; NOBA
Lying in a Yuma Saloon. Jim Barnes. CDW
Lying in State. Adrian Mitchell. ELU
Lying in the dark music. The Enigma Variations. Paul Petrie. NYBP
Lying in the Grass. Sir Edmund Gosse. EBVV; OBVV
Lying in the sunshine among the buttercups and dandelions. Tribute to Grass. John James Ingalls. WBLP
Lying is an occupation. Song. Laetitia Pilkington. WPE
Lying Muslims, The. *Yoruba Oral Tradition, tr. by* Ulli Beier. WTO
Lying south of sweet Northumber. Rhymed Mnemonic of the Forty Counties of England. Donald Monat. FaBoUs
Lying under the stars. The Heart of Herakles. Kenneth Rexroth. *Fr.* The Lights in the Sky are Stars. NU
Lying with unstable pego 'twixt a brace of vigorous boys. Epigram: To Phoebus. Martial. PeHV
Lyk as the dum. The Solsequium. Alexander Montgomerie. OxBS
Lyke as a huntsman, after weary chace. *See* Like as a huntsman after weary chase.
Lyke as a ship, that through the ocean wyde. *See* Like as a ship, that through the ocean wide.
Lyke Memnons rocke toucht, with the rising sunne. *See* Like Memnon's rock. . .
Lyke-Wake Dirge, A [*or* The]. *Unknown.* CH; ChTr; EaLo; EvOK; FaBoCh; FaBoRV; GBP; GoBC; HAP; HBV-2; HoPM; LoBV; NOBE; NoP; OBEV; OxBoCh; PoEL-1; SeCeV; WeW
(Cleveland Lyke Wake Dirge, The.) EnSB
(Final Dirge.) ACP
Lyke-Wake Song, A. Swinburne. PAI
Lynchburg Town, *with music. Unknown.* OuSiCo
Lynched. Stephen Todd Booker. LFAC
Lynched Negro. Maxwell Bodenheim. PoNe
Lynching, The. Claude McKay. BALP; BANP; IDB; PoBA
Lynching and Burning. Primus St. John. PoBA
Lynton Verses, *sel.* Thomas Edward Brown.
"Milk! milk! milk!" PeD
Lynx. R. A. D. Ford. CaP
Lynx. Ben Howard. GrPl
Lyon. Herman Melville. PeD
Lyre, The. George Darley. OBVV
(Listen to the Lyre, *sl. abr.*) LO
Lyre. Patrick White. AMV-80
Lyre Player, The. Stefan George, *tr. by* Carol North Valhope *and* Ernst Morowitz. PeHV
Lyre! though such power do in thy magic live. Wordsworth. VLP
Lyre-Bird, The. Roland Robinson. PoAu-2
Lyrebirds. Judith Wright. BoAnP; GoJo
Lyric: "Embodiment of what, The." Arthur Gregor. TAP
Lyric: "From now on kill America out of your mind." James Agee. *See* Millions Are Learning How.
Lyric: "I touched a shining mote of sand." Philip Child. CaP
Lyric: "Let but a thrush begin." John Hewitt. NeIP
Lyric, A: "There's nae lark loves the lift, my dear." Swinburne. HBV-1
Lyric: "You would have understood me, had you waited." Paul Verlaine. *See* You Would Have Understood Me.
Lyric Barber. Liboria E. Romano. GoYe
Lyric by Nine. *Unknown.* EAS
Lyric for Legacies. Robert Herrick. JCP
Lyric from a Play, A. *Unknown.* MeEL
Lyric Love. Robert Browning. *See* O Lyric Love.
Lyric night of the lingering Indian Summer. September Midnight. Sara Teasdale. PoA
Lyric to Mirth, A. Robert Herrick. CaPo
Lyric to Spring. Joseph W. Stilwell. DBV; OBAL
Lyricism of the Weak, The. Peter Viereck. *See* To Helen (of Troy, N.Y.).
Lyrick for Legacies. Robert Herrick. FaBoRV; OBS
Lyrics, *sels.* James Agee.
"I loitered weeping with my bride for gladness." MoAmPo; PoPl
"No doubt left. Enough deceiving." MoAmPo; PoPl
"Not met and marred with the year's whole turn of grief." MoAmPo; PoPl
Lysidike dedicates. Kenneth Rexroth, *after the Greek of* Asklepiades. NNaP
Lysistrata. Aristophanes, *tr. fr. Greek by* Charles T. Murphy. NAWM-1
How the Women Will Stop War, *sel.* WaaP
Lyth and listen, gentlemen. Robin Hood and the Beggar, II. *Unknown.* ESPB
Lythe and listin, gentilmen. A Gest of Robyn Hode. *Unknown.* ESPB; OxBB
Lyttel Boy, The. Eugene Field. AA
Lytyll Prety Nyghtyngale, The. *Unknown.* OAEP
(Nightingale, The.) TrGrPo
Lyve thowe gladly, yff so thowe may. Sir Thomas Wyatt. AAS

M

M. Edward Lear. WhC
MACV Advisor. Patrick Worth Gray. SOTS
M. A. P. Calvin Forbes. MAYP
M and A, R and I. *Unknown.* OxBM
M & O Blues. *Unknown.* BluL
M. Crashaw's Answer for Hope. Richard Crashaw. *See* For Hope.
M Sgt. Robert G. Levi 1915-1943. Uncle Robert. Robert Morgan. GeTw
M., Singing. Louise Bogan. CrMA; GoJo; LiTA; NePA
M was once a little mouse. M. Edward Lear. WhC
Ma Canny Hinny. *Unknown.* FaBoPP; GBP
Ma Jesus. Troubled Jesus. Waring Cuney. BANP
Ma lass by munelicht fesht me frae the fail. The Deean Tractorman, Deleerit. Edith Anne Robertson. OxBS
Ma'am dear, did ye never hear of pretty Molly Brannigan. Molly Brannigan. *Unknown.* FSW
Mab the Mistress-Fairy. Ben Jonson. *Fr.* The Satyr. EIL
(Mab.) WiR
(Queen Mab.) HBV-1
Mabel, in New Hampshire. James Thomas Fields. HBV-1
Mabel Kelly. Turlough O'Carolan, *tr. fr. Irish by* Austin Clarke. BIrV
(Mable Kelly.) CIP
Mabel, little Mabel. The Face against the Pane. Thomas Bailey Aldrich. TreFS
Mabel—when is the bomb set to. An Anarchist's Letter. Harald Wyndham. POL

Mac. Mark Vinz. Str
Mac had a place to drink and talk downtown. McSorley's Bar. Reuel Denney. TwAmPo
Macadam, gun-grey as the tunny's belt. Van Winkle. Hart Crane. *Fr.* The Bridge. AmPP; CrMA; FaBV; MoAB; MoAmPo
Macaffie's Confession. *Unknown.* BeLS; CoSo, *with music*
(McAfee's Confession, *diff. vers.*) AmFP
McAndrew's Hymn. Kipling. OxBTC; VLP
(M'Andrew's Hymn.) PoEL-5
Macaulay at Tea. Barry Pain. *Fr.* The Poets at Tea. CenHV
Macavity: The Mystery Cat. T. S. Eliot. BiP; CenHV; FaBoCo; InPS; NOBL; OBCA; OnUR; OxBChV; PoRA; TiPo
Macaw preens upon a branch outspread, A. Decoration. Louise Bogan. MoAB; MoAmPo
Macbeth. Andrew of Wyntoun. OxBS
Macbeth's Dream, *sel.* BSV
Macbeth, *sels.* Shakespeare.
"Hang out our banners on the outward walls," *fr.* V, v. EBEV
"I have lived long enough," *fr.* V, iii. TrGrPo
"If it were done when 'tis done, then 'twere well," *fr.* I, vii. UnPo
Macbeth Does Murder Sleep, *fr.* II, ii. FiP
("I have done the deed—Didst thou not hear a noise?") EBEV
(Murderers, The.) WHA
(Sleep.) TreFS
Macbeth's Words before Murdering, *fr.* II, i. TreFS
Mind Diseased, A, *fr.* V, iii. TreFT
("Canst thou not minister to a mind diseas'd.") TRV
Murder Pact, The, *fr.* I, vii. WHA
(Vaulting Ambition.) FiP
O! Full of Scorpions, *fr.* III, ii. FiP
"She should have died hereafter," *fr.* V, v. DL; FiP; SoSe
Tomorrow, and Tomorrow, and Tomorrow, *fr.* V, v. FaBoRV; FaFP; FF; LiTB; MasP; PoPl; TrGrPo; TRV; WHA
(Macbeth Learns of His Wife's Death.) TreF
(Out, Out, Brief Candle!) ChTr
Witches' Brew, The, *fr.* IV, i. TreFT
(Charm, The.) ElL
(Song of the Witches.) RHPC
("Thrice the brinded cat hath mew'd.") InvP; OFD; WSC
Macbeth. Horace *and* James Smith. BXAP
McCaffery. *Unknown.* OBET
McCord and Liddy and all those bums. Watergate. Ruth Herschberger. FAZ
McCullam Camp. Larry Gorman. *See* Winter of '73, The.
Mac Diarmod's Daughter. Francis Carlin. HBMV
Macdonald's Raid. Paul Hamilton Hayne. PAH
McDonogh Day in New Orleans. Marcus B. Christian. AmNP; PoNe
MacDuff. Charles Tomlinson. NAs; OxBC
Maceo. Luis Lloréns Torres, *tr. fr. Spanish by* Julio Marzán. InW
M'Fingal, *sels.* John Trumbull.
"At once with resolution held." AmPP
"Rise then, ere ruin swift surprize." GOA
MacFlecknoe; or, A Satire [*or* Satyr] upon the True-Blue [*or*-Blew] Protestant Poet T. S. Dryden. CABA; HAP, *abr.*; NoP; OAEL-1; OAEP; OBSV; OxBoLi; PP; QFR; SeCV-2; TEP
"All human[e] things are subject to decay," *sel.* SCV; TrGrPo; ViBoPo
(Crown Prince of Dullness, The.) NOBE
(Poet Shadwell, The.) FiP
(Primacy of Dullness, The.) OBS
MacGregor's Gathering. Sir Walter Scott. OxBS
Machberoth, *sels.* Immanuel di Roma, *tr. fr. Hebrew by* J. Chotzner.
Oh, Let Thy Teachings. TrJP
Virtue. TrJP
Macheath and Polly. John Gay. *See* Song: "Were I laid on Greenland's coast."
Machine Hand, A. Thomas Ashe. OBVV
Machine Out of the God. Thomas E. Sanders. AMV-81
Machine stitched rivets on a tree. The Pilot in the Jungle. John Ciardi. MiAP
Machinery is enough for a Scientist. James Oppenheim. *Fr.* Night. TRV
Machupuchare. What the Mountain Said. Shaking the Dead Bones, Christmas Eve, 1974. Joseph Stroud. NPGG
McIlrath of Malate. John Jerome Rooney. PAH
Macinnes's Mountain Patrol. Tom Patey. PoSH
McIntosh Apple. Steven Kroll. RHPC
MacKenna's Dream. *Unknown.* OnYI
Mackerel-man drives down the street, The. A Pretty Ambition. Mary E. Wilkins Freeman. OBCA
Mackerel sky. *Unknown.* FaBoUs; OxNR
McKinley. *Unknown.* PAH
McKinley Brook, *with music.* George Calhoun. ShS
McKinley called for volunteers. Battleship of Maine. *Unknown.* FSW
McKinley hollered, McKinley squalled. White House Blues. *Unknown.* FSW
McLean's Welcome. James Hogg. OxBS
MacLugach! says Finn. *Unknown, tr. by* Standish Hayes O'Grady *and* Kuno Meyer. *Fr.* The Colloquy of the Ancients. OnYI
McLuhan put his telescope to his ear. The Taste of Space. A. J. M. Smith. PV
McNaughtan, *with music. Unknown.* OxBB
MacPhairson Clonglocketty Angus M'Clan. Ellen M'Jones Aberdeen. W. S. Gilbert. HBV-2; InMe
Macpherson's Farewell. Burns. BSV; FSW, *diff. vers.*
Macquarie Place. Robert D. Fitzgerald. PoAu-2
Macramé. Michael D. Riley. AMV-81
Macrinus against Trees. "Michael Field." WPE
Macrobius Mingling with Nature. Rochelle Owens. CoPo
Macrocosm. Philip Child. CaP
McSorley's Bar. Reuel Denney. TwAmPo
Macy's Poem, The. James Reiss. POL
Mad Answer of a Madman, A. Robert Hayman. FF
Mad are predators, The. Too often lately they harbor. Geoffrey Hill. Mercian Hymns, VIII. NoP
Mad as the Mist and Snow. W. B. Yeats. ChTr
Mad Berkeley believed, with his gay cavaliers. The Burning of Jamestown. Thomas Dunn English. PAH
Mad Blake. William Rose Benét. HBMV
Mad Day in March. Philip Levine. NYBP
Mad Dogs and Englishmen. Noel Coward. CenHV; FiBHP; NOBL; WhC
Mad Farmer Stands Up in Kentucky for What He Thinks Is Right, The. James Baker Hall. TAT
Mad Fight Song for William S. Carpenter, 1966, A. James Wright. LiSp
Mad Gardener's Song, The. "Lewis Carroll." *Fr.* Sylvie and Bruno. BLPL; FaBoCo; FaBoNo; FiBHP, 6 *sts.*; NBM; OnUR, 4 *sts.*; OxBChV; TreFS; WiR
(Gardener's Song, The.) EvOK; HBV-2
(He Thought He Saw, 6 *sts.*) HBVY
("He thought he saw a banker's clerk," 5 *sts.*) NA
Mad girl with the staring eyes and long white fingers, The. Cassandra. Robinson Jeffers. HeIP; LiTA; LiTM; NePA; WaP
Mad Hatter's Song. "Lewis Carroll." *Fr.* Alice's Adventures in Wonderland, *ch.* 7. FaBoNo; SpRo
("Twinkle, twinkle, little bat!") NOBL; Par; WhC
Mad Lover, The, *sels.* John Fletcher.
Arm, Arm, Arm, Arm! *fr.* V, iv. ElL
"O divine star of heaven," *fr.* IV, i. GBL
"Orpheus I am, come from the deeps below," *fr.* IV, i. GBL
Mad Maid's Song, The. Robert Herrick. AWP; CaPo; CH; EnLoPo; LoBV; OAEL-1; OBEV; SeCV-1; TrGrPo; ViBoPo; WiR
Mad male-hearted woman in a prouder age, A. Desmond O'Grady. NoAM
Mad Marjory. Hugh McCrae. PoAu-1
Mad Negro Soldier Confined at Munich, A. Robert Lowell. FaBoMo; NMP; OxBC
Mad Patsy said, he said to me. In the Poppy Field. James Stephens. PoRA
Mad Queen Aeronautical Corporation . . Cyclone . 3030. Telephone Directory. Harry Crosby. EAS
Mad Rapist of Calaveras County, The. Pete Winslow. PV
Mad Scene, The. James Merrill. CoAP; NoAM; NOBA; PoA; TAP
Mad Song. Blake. EnRP; NOEC; OAEL-2; PrIm; TEP; TrGrPo
Mad Song. Denise Levertov. TAP
Mad Song. Hester Sigerson. AnIV
Mad Sonnet 1. Michael McClure. PoM
Mad Sweeney. *Unknown. See* Sweeney the Mad.
Mad Woman of Punnet's Town, The. L. A. G. Strong. MoBrPo
Mad World, My Masters, A, *sel.* Thomas Middleton.
O for a Bowl of Fat Canary. *Also in* Alexander and Campaspe (*by* John Lyly). ViBoPo
Mad Yak, The. Gregory Corso. CoPo; NoAM
Madaket Beach. Isabel Harriss Barr. GoYe
Madam,/ If you're deceived, it is not by my cheat. A Very Heroical Epistle in Answer to Ephelia. Earl of Rochester. APAS
Madam,/ Were you but only great, there are some men. To the Excellent Pattern of Beauty and Virtue, Lady Elizabeth, Countess of Ormond. James Shirley. GoBC
Madam and Her Madam. Langston Hughes. BALP
Madam and the Minister. Langston Hughes. NOBA
Madam Eglantine. Chaucer. *See* Prioress, The.
Madam Gabrina, or the Ill-favourd Choice. Henry King. CavP
Madam, he thinks you've become his lover. Ode to the Muse on Behalf of a Young Poet. David Wagoner. AMV-80
Madam Hickory. Wilbur Larremore. AA
Madam Life's a Piece in Bloom. W. E. Henley. CABA; EBVV; InPK; NBM

(Madam Life.) MoBrPo; TrGrPo
(To W. R.) VLP
Madam Mouse Trots. Edith Sitwell. SyP
(Madame Mouse Trots.) FaBoCh
Madam, no more! The time has come to eat. The Elegy. A. D. Hope. ErPo; NoP
Madam, 'tis true, your beauties move. Sonnet. Sidney Godolphin. JCP
Madam, twice through the Muses Grove I walkt. Upon Mrs. Anne Bradstreet Her Poems. John Rogers. SCAP
Madam, withouten Many Words. Sir Thomas Wyatt. *See* Madame, withouten Many Wordes.
Madam, you are right, the fight was a great pity. To the Woman in Bond Street Station. Edward Weismiller. LiTA; NePA; WaP
Madame d'Albert's Laugh. Clement Marot, *tr. fr. French by* Leigh Hunt. AWP
Madame Dill. *Unknown.* FiBHP
Madame, for your[e] newefangelnesse. Against Women Unconstant [*or* A Ballade against Woman Inconstant]. Chaucer. CABA
Madame, had all antiquitie been lost. To Mary Lady Wroth. Ben Jonson. OBS
Madame, his grace will not be absent long. Cyril Tourneur. *Fr.* The Revenger's Tragedy, III, v. PoEL-2
Madame, I Have Come a-Courting. *Unknown.* AmFP
Madame Louise sleeps well o' nights. Aux Carmélites. Katharine Tynan. OnYI
Madame Maynard of the hard pebble. Stranded in My Ontario. Ronald Everson. NOBC
Madame Mouse Trots. Edith Sitwell. *See* Madam Mouse Trots.
Madame, withouten Many Wordes. Sir Thomas Wyatt. AAS; CABA; OBVE
(Madam, withouten Many Words.) EnLoPo; EnRePo; NoP; SiPS
(To a Lady to Answer Directly with Yea or Nay.) EIL
(To His Lady.) OBSC; SeCePo
Madame, ye been [*or* ben] of alle [*or* all *or* al] beautee [*or* beaute] shrine [*or* shryne] To Rosemond [*or* Rosemounde *or* Ballade to Rosamund]. Chaucer. CABA; MeEL; NoP; OAEL-1
Madam's Past History. Langston Hughes. NoAM
Madboy's Song. Muriel Rukeyser. MoAmPo; TrJP
Mädchen mit dem rothen Mündchen. Heine, *tr. fr. German by* Sir Theodore Martin. AWP
Made in Heaven. Peter Porter. PPON
Made in his maker's image? Tree of Knowledge. Edward Lowbury. VWA
Made in the Hot Weather. W. E. Henley. *See* Ballade Made in the Hot Weather.
Made Lake, The. Louise Townsend Nicholl. NePoAm-2
Made Shine. Josephine Miles. NoAM
Made to See. John Nist. AMV-80
Madeleine in Church. Charlotte Mew. SBG
"How old was Mary out of whom you cast," *sel.* LO; MoAB; MoBrPo
Madeleine Verchères. William Henry Drummond. CaP
Madeline at Jefferson Market Night Court. Margaret McGovern. WhC
Mademoiselle from Armentières. *Unknown.* BLSo, *with music*; FSW; OBAL
(Hinky Dinky, [Parlee-Voo].) AS, *with music*; TrAS, *with music*
Mademoiselle Richarde. Edith Sitwell. MoVE
Madge Wildfire's [Death] Song [*or* Madge Wildfire Sings]. Sir Walter Scott. *See* Proud Maisie.
Madhouse. Calvin C. Hernton. IDB; NNP; PoNe
(Patient, The: Rockland County Sanitarium.) PoBA
Madison Square. A. Glanz-Leyeles, *tr. fr. Yiddish by* Keith Bosley. VWA
Madman, The. S. J. Pretorius, *tr. fr. Afrikaans by* Uys Krige *and* Jack Cope. PeSA
Madman, The. Constance Urdang. PoPl
Madman's Song, The. John Webster. *Fr.* The Duchess of Malfi, IV, ii. EIL
(Song: "O, let us howl some heavy note.") InvP
Madman's Song. Elinor Wylie. MoAB; MoAmPo; MOON; PoRA
Madman's Wife, The. Stephen Orlen. MAYP
Madness. John Armstrong. *Fr.* The Art of Preserving Health. NOEC
Madness. James Dickey. NYBP
Madness. Sachiko Yoshihara, *tr. fr. Japanese by* James Kirkup *and* Shozo Tekunaga. BoWoP
Madness One Monday Evening. Julia Fields. NIP; NNP
Madone! my lady, I will build for thee. To a Madonna. John Gray. SyP
Madonna di Campagna. Alfred Kreymborg. HBMV
Madonna, Madonna [*or* Madonnina]/ Sat by the grey road-side. Cradle-Song. Adelaide Crapsey. HBMV; ISi
Madonna Mia. Swinburne. HBV-1
Madonna Natura. "Fiona Macleod." WGRP
Madonna: 1936. John Louis Bonn. ISi
Madonna of the Dons. Arthur MacGillivray. ISi
Madonna of the Empty Arms. Maurice Francis Egan. ISi
Madonna of the Evening Flowers. Amy Lowell. PeHV; TreFT
Madonna of the Exiles. James Edward Tobin. ISi
Madonna of the Hills. Paula Gunn Allen. TWSS
Madonna's Lullaby. St. Alphonsus Liguori, *tr. fr. Italian by* James J. Galvin. ISi
Madras,/ 1965, and rain. Some Indian Uses of History on a Rainy Day. A. K. Ramanujan. OxBC
Madrid. "Pai Wei," *tr. fr. Chinese by* Kenneth Rexroth *and* Ling Chung. PBWP
Madrid, Iowa. Ron Ikan. PPJ
Madrigal: "Ay me, alas, heigh ho, heigh ho!" Thomas Weelkes. OxBoLi
Madrigal: "Beauty [*or* Beautie], and the life, The." William Drummond of Hawthornden. EIL; PoEL-2
(Her Passing.) OBEN
Madrigal: "Beside the rivers of the midnight town." John Frederick Nims. MiAP
Madrigal, A: "Crabbed Age and Youth." Shakespeare. *See* Crabbed Age and Youth.
Madrigal: "Dear, when I did from you remove." Lord Herbert of Cherbury. EIL
Madrigal: "Ha ha! ha ha! This world doth pass." *Unknown. See* Fara Diddle Dyno.
Madrigal: "How should I love my best?" Lord Herbert of Cherbury. AnAnS-2; PoEL-2; SeCP; ViBoPo
Madrigal: "I always loved to call my lady Rose." *Unknown.* EIL
Madrigal: "Ivory, coral, gold, The." William Drummond of Hawthornden. *See* Ivory, Coral, Gold, The.
Madrigal: "Like the Idalian Queen[e]." William Drummond of Hawthornden. EIL; ELP; FaBoEn; GBL; InvP; NOBE; OAEL-1; OBEV; OBS; PoEL-2; ViBoPo
(Like the Idalian Queen.) BSV; GoTS; SeCePo
Madrigal: "Love now no fire hath left him." Giovanni Battista Marino, *tr. fr. Italian by* Richard Crashaw. OBVE
Madrigal: Love Vagabonding. William Drummond of Hawthornden. LoBV
Madrigal: "My love in her attire doth show her wit." *Unknown. See* My Love in Her Attire.
Madrigal: "My mistress frowns when she should play." *At. to* John Hilton. OxBoLi
(Fa La La.) CH
Madrigal: "My mistress is as fair as fine." Thomas Ravenscroft. OxBoLi
Madrigal: "My thoughts hold mortal[l] strife." William Drummond of Hawthornden. EIL; GTBS; GTBS-P; LoBV; OBS
(Inexorable.) NOBE; OBEV
Madrigal: "O I do love, then kiss me." Robert Jones. OxBoLi
(O I Do Love, Then Kisse Me.) NCEP
Madrigal: "Poor turtle, thou bemoans." William Drummond of Hawthornden. PBBP
Madrigal: "Since Bonny-boots was dead, that so divinely." *Unknown. See* Since Bonny-Boots Was Dead.
Madrigal: "Some there are as fair to see to." Francis Davison. *See* Her Commendation.
Madrigal: "Sound of thy sweet name, my dearest treasure, The." Francis Davison. EIL
Madrigal, A: "Swans, whose pens as white as ivory, The," *sel.* Robert Greene. ViBoPo
Madrigal: "Take, O take those lips away." Shakespeare. *See* Take, O Take Those Lips Away.
Madrigal: "Tell me where is Fancy bred." Shakespeare. *See* Tell Me Where Is Fancy Bred.
Madrigal: "This life, which seem[e]s so fair[e]." William Drummond of Hawthornden. EIL; OAEL-1; OBS; SeCePo
(This Life.) CH; TrGrPo
("This Life which seems so fair.") GTBS; GTBS-P
Madrigal: "To be a whore, despite of grace." Charles Cotton. FaBoEE
Madrigal: To His Lady Selvaggia Vergiolesi; Likening His Love to a Search for Gold. Cino da Pistoia, *tr. fr. Italian by* Dante Gabriel Rossetti. AWP
Madrigal: "Unhappie Light." William Drummond of Hawthornden. OBS
Madrigal: "When in her face mine eyes I fix." Earl of Stirling. *Fr.* Aurora. EIL
Madrigal: "Why dost thou haste away?" Sir Philip Sidney. *Fr.* Arcadia. OBSC; SiPS
Madrigal: "Your love is dead, lady, your love is dead." R. S. Thomas. BoLoP; ELU; EnLoPo
Madrigal de Verano. Federico García Lorca, *tr. fr. Spanish by* Paul Blackburn. ErPo
Madrigal Macabre. Samuel Hoffenstein. ShM
Madrigal to the City of Santiago. Federico García Lorca, *tr. fr. Spanish by* Norman Di Giovanni. CAD
Madroño. Bret Harte. AA
Madwoman at Rodmell. Michele Roberts. BrRo
Madwomen of the Plaza de Mayo, The. Eli Mandel. NOBC
Mae West. Edward Field. FYAP

Maerchen. Walter de la Mare. CoBMV
Mae's Rent Party. Ernest J. Wilson, Jr. PoNe
Maesia's Song. Robert Greene. *Fr.* Farewell to Folly. CTC; HBV-2; OBSC; UnPo
(Mind Content, A.) ElL; ViBoPo
(Poor Estate, The.) TrGrPo
(Song: "Sweet are the thoughts that savour of content.") PoEL-2
Maestro's Barber Shop, The. Ricardo Vásquez, *tr. fr. Spanish by* Toni Empringham. FIA
Mafukuzela, rain-giving clouds. Lament for Mafukuzela. *Zulu Oral Tradition, tr. by* H. Tracey. WTO
Magalu. Helene Johnson. BlSi; CDC; PoBA; PoNe
Magazine Fort, Phoenix Park, Dublin, The. William Wilkins. SeCePo
Magdalen. Henry Kingsley. HBV-2; OBVV
(At Glastonbury.) PoRA
Magdalen, The. Sir Edward Sherburne. *See* And She Washed His Feet with Her Tears.
Magdalen Walks. Oscar Wilde. EBVV; MoBrPo
Maggie. *Unknown.* OnUR
(Shaggy Dog, A.) TDH
Maggie and Milly and Molly and May. E. E. Cummings. NePoAm-2; NOBA; RHPC
(Poem.) PoSC
Maggie Campbell Blues. *Unknown.* BluL
Maggie Lauder. *Unknown, at. to* Francis Sempill. OBS; OxBS
Maggie Mac. Unknown. AmFP
Maggie's Star. Charles Tennyson Turner. FM
Magi, The. Louise Glück. PoA
Magi, The. Milton. *Fr.* On the Morning of Christ's Nativity. ChTr
Magi, The. W. B. Yeats. BiP; BrPo; CABA; CMoP; CoBMV; ELU; FaBoRV; HAP; InPK; InPS; NoAM; OAEL-2; OFD; PChr; PoA; PPoe; SBVL; TrCP
Magic. Lionel Johnson. VLP
Magic. Shakespeare, *after the Latin of* Ovid. *Fr.* The Tempest, V, i. AWP
("Ye elves of hills, brooks, standing lakes, and groves.") EBEV; SCV
Magic. Thomas Wolfe. PoPl
Magic/ my man. Black Magic. Sonia Sanchez. BPo
Magic Apple Tree, The. Elaine Feinstein. BrRo
Magic Car Moved On, The. Shelley. *Fr.* Queen Mab. GN
Magic Casements. Keats. *Fr.* Ode to a Nightingale. FaBV
Magic Flute, The. W. D. Snodgrass. NYBP
Magic Fox. James Welch. CDW
Magic Lantern. William Stafford. FAZ
Magic Mirror, The. Henry Mills Alden. HBV-2
Magic of the day is the morning, The. Ballad of the Morning Streets. Amiri Baraka. CNA; SOTW
Magic Piper, The. E. L. Marsh. SiSoSe
Magic Wood, The. Henry Treece. DuDa; EAS
Magic Word. Edgar Jackson. LFAC
Magic Words, The. Ronald Koertge. AMV-81
Magic Words. *Unknown, tr. fr. Eskimo.* NU
Magical Eraser. Shel Silverstein. WSC
Magical Mouse, The. Kenneth Patchen. SO
Magical Nature. Robert Browning. VLP
Magical prognosticator. Halloween Witches. Felice Holman. WSC
Magically awakened to a strange, brown night. Fog. Laurence Binyon. SyP
Magician, The. Joan Colby. PoDr
Magician, The. Bin Ramke. MAYP
Magician and the Baron's Daughter, The. *Unknown. See* Juggler and the Baron's Daughter, The.
Magician Suspends the Children, The. Carole Oles. SoSe
Magistrate's Escape, The. Alice Fulton. PoDr
Magma. G. J. F. Dutton. PoSH
Magna Est Veritas. Coventry Patmore. *Fr.* The Unknown Eros. GoBC; GTBS-P; HAP; NOBE; OBEV; OBNC; OBVV; TreFT
(Here, in This Little Bay.) BoNaP
(Truth.) TrGrPo
Magna Est Veritas. Stevie Smith. OxBC
Magnanimous, The. Ellen de Young Kay. NePoEA
Magnet, The. Thomas Stanley. MePo; NOBE
Magnet, The. Ruth Stone. MoAmPo; NePA
Magnet hung in a hardware shop, A. The Fable of the Magnet and the Churn. W. S. Gilbert. *Fr.* Patience. FaPON; OnMSP
Magnetic Mountain, The, *sels.* C. Day Lewis.
"Live you by love confined." PoPle
Nearing Again the Legendary Isle, VI. CoBMV; FaBoTw; LiTB; MoAB; MoBrPo
"Tempt me no more; for I," XXIV. PoA; PoPl
(Tempt Me No More.) MoAB; MoBrPo; OAEP; OBMV
Third Enemy Speaks, XXI. EaLo
Magnetism. Emma Lazarus. SBG
Magnetized. Arthur Sze. BrSi
Magnets. Laurence Binyon. HBMV
Magnets. Countee Cullen. BALP
Magnificat, The. Bible, *N.T.* St. Luke, I: 46-55. BoWoP; ILwL; WGRP
("And Marie said, My soule doth magnifie the Lord.") OBVE
Magnificat. Michele Roberts. BrRo
Magnificat. Arthur Symons. UnTE
Magnificat in Transit from the Toledo Airport. George Starbuck. SUW
Magnolia trees, The. Genealogy. Frank Lamont Phillips. AmNP
Magnolia's Shadow, The. Robert Lowell, *ad. fr. the Italian of* Eugenio Montale. NaP
Magpie. Peter Davison. GrPl
Magpie, magpie, flutter and flee. *Unknown.* OxNR
Magpie Rhyme, Northumberland, A. *Unknown.* GBP
Magpie Song. *Tr. fr. Navajo Indian by* Washington Matthews. OBVE
Magpies in Picardy. T. P. Cameron Wilson. HBV-2; MMA
Mag's Song, *with music. Unknown.* AS
Maguire is not afraid of death, the Church will light him a candle. Patrick Kavanagh. *Fr.* The Great Hunger. CIP
Magus, A. John Ciardi. MAT
Magus, The. James Dickey. NAs
Mah mule is white, mah chahcoal is black. Charcoal Man. *Unknown.* TrAS
Mahabalipuram. Louis MacNeice. NoAM
Mahabharata, The, *sel. Unknown, tr. fr. Sanskrit by* Franklin Edgerton.
"So, pure and dutiful, she sought that place." DL
Mahalia. Michael S. Harper. FAZ
Maharani of midnight tresses, The. In the Seraglio. David R. Slavitt. ErPo; PeHV
Mahler, *sel.* Jonathan Williams.
Symphony No. 3, in D Minor. VGW
Mahogany Tree, The. Thackeray. HBV-2
Mahoney. Seán Jennett. NeIP
Mahony's Mountain. Douglas Stewart. PoAu-2; SeCePo
Maia was one, all gold, fire, and sapphire. A Legend of Viable Women. Richard Eberhart. MiAP; MoVE
Maid, The. Katherine Brégy. GoBC
Maid, The. Theodore Goodridge Roberts. HBV-2; MoShBr
Maid and the Palmer, The. *Unknown.* ACP; ESPB (A *and* B *vers.*)
Maid Freed from the Gallows, The. *Unknown.* AmFP, 2 *vers.*; AS, *with music*; AWP; ESPB (A *and* I *vers.*); ViBoFo (A, B, C, *and* D *vers.*)
(Gallows Pole, The.) FSW
(Hangman, *with music.*) AS
(Hangsaman, *with music.*) TrAS
Maid going to Comber, her markets to larn, A. The Next Market Day. *Unknown.* FSW
Maid, I dare not tell her name, A. The Nameless Maiden. *Unknown.* ErPo
Maid I Left Behind, The, *with music. Unknown.* ShS
Maid I love ne'er thought of me, The. The Kiss. Walter Savage Landor. OBVV
Maid in the Mill, The, *sel.* John Fletcher *and* William Rowley.
"Now having leisure, and a happy wind," *fr.* V, i. GBL
Maid Marian, *sels.* Thomas Love Peacock.
For the Slender Beech and the Sapling Oak. EnRP
(Song: "For the tender beech and the sapling oak.") OHIP
Song: "It was a friar of orders free." ViBoPo
Maid Marjory sits at the castle gate. Medieval Norman Song. *Unknown, tr. by* John Addington Symonds. AWP
Maid Mars Me, A. *Unknown.* OxBM
Maid o' the West, The. John Clare. OAEL-2
Maid of Amsterdam. *Unknown. See* Fair Maid of Amsterdam, The.
Maid of Arc, The. Gordon Bottomley. GoTL
Maid of Athens [Ere We Part]. Byron. EBEV; EnRP; FaBV; FaFP; HBV-1; OAEP; PrIm; TreF
Maid of Brenten Arse, A. *Unknown.* GBP
Maid of Honour, The, *sel.* Philip Massinger.
"Look on this maid of honour, now," *fr.* V, ii. ACP; GoBC
Maid of Kent, A. *Unknown.* OxBoLi
(There Was a Maid.) ElL
Maid of Monterey, The. *Unknown.* AmFP
Maid of Neidpath, The. Thomas Campbell. GoTS; GTBS; GTBS-P
(Song: "Earl March looked on his dying child.") HBV-1
Maid of Neidpath, The. Sir Walter Scott. BeLS; EnRP; GTBS; GTBS-P
Maid of Orleans, The. Schiller, *tr. fr. German by* James Clarence Mangan. AWP
Maid of the Moor, The. *Unknown. See* Maiden in the Moor, A.
Maid of the Moor, The; or, The Water-Fiends, *sel.* George Colman the Younger.
"Cold blows the blast—the night's obscure." NOEC
Maid of the Sweet Brown Knowe, The. *Unknown.* AnIV; OnYI
Maid of Tottenham, The. *Unknown.* CoMu

Maid, Out of Thine Unquarried Mountain-Land. *Unknown, tr. fr. Greek by* G. R. Woodward. ISi
Maid she[e] went to the well to wash[e], The. The Maid and the Palmer. *Unknown.* ACP; ESPB
Maid That Sold Her Barley, The. *Unknown.* OnYI
Maid, where's my lawrel? Oh my rageing soul! The Enchantment. Theocritus, *tr. by* Thomas Creech. *Fr.* Idylls, II. CTC; OBVE
Maid who binds her warrior's sash, The. The Brave at Home. Thomas Buchanan Read. *Fr.* The Wagoner of the Alleghanies. HBV-2
Maid who, on the first [day] of May, The. Old Superstitions. *Unknown.* HBVY; TreF
Maiden, The. Peter Hille, *tr. fr. German by* Jethro Bithell. AWP
Maiden, The. Rochelle Ratner. PCP
Maiden and Her Hair, A. W. H. Davies. BrPo
Maiden, and mistress of the months and stars. Swinburne. *Fr.* Atalanta in Calydon. PoEL-5
Maiden and the Lily, The. John Fraser. HBV-1
Maiden caught me in the wild, The. The Crystal Cabinet. Blake. CH; FaBoCh; NCEP; OAEL-2; OBNC; OBRV; PAI; PoEL-4
Maiden caught stealing a dahlia, A. Caught Stealing a Dahlia. *Unknown.* TDH
Maiden City, The. Charlotte Elizabeth Tonna. HBV-2
Maiden Eyes. Gerald Griffin. HBV-1
Maiden from the Bosphorus, A. How the Helpmate of Blue-Beard Made Free with a Door. Guy Wetmore Carryl. InMe
Maiden in the Moor [*or* Mor], A. *Unknown.* LoBV; PoEL-1
(Maid of the Moor, The.) NOBE; OAEL-1; OxBM
(Maiden in the Moor Lay.) NCEP
(Maiden Lay in the Wilds, The.) MeEL
Maiden Lane. Al Lee. NYP
Maiden Lay in the Wilds, The. *Unknown. See* Maiden in the Moor, A.
Maiden Lies in Her Chamber, A. Heine, *tr. fr. German by* Louis Untermeyer. AWP
Maiden Makeles, The. *Unknown. See* I Sing of a Maiden.
Maiden Name. Philip Larkin. GTBS-P
Maiden of Passamaquoddy, The. James De Mille. *See* Lines to Miss Florence Huntingdon.
Maiden of the Smile, The. Alfred Austin. TEP
Maiden Queen, The, *sel.* Dryden.
"I feed a flame within, which so torments me." PoPle
Maiden ran away to fetch the clothes, The. Deluge. John Clare. BoNaP
Maiden Ring-Adorned, A. Cynewulf, *tr. fr. Anglo-Saxon by* Mother Margaret Williams. *Fr.* The Christ. ISi
Maiden sat in an apple-tree, A. The Apple-Tree. Brian Vrepont. PoAu-2
Maiden That Is Makeless, A. *Unknown. See* I Sing of a Maiden.
Maiden There Lived, A. *Unknown.* NOBL
Maiden! with the meek, brown eyes. Maidenhood. Longfellow. HBV-1
Maidenhead. "Ephelia." WPE
Maidenhood. Longfellow. HBV-1
Maiden's Best Adorning, The. *Unknown.* OxBChV
Maidens Came, The. *Unknown.* GBL; PoEL-1; ViBoPo
(Bailey Beareth the Bell Away, The.) LiTB; SeCePo; SeCeV
(Bridal Morn, The.) NOBE
(Bridal Morning.) OBEV
(Lily and the Rose, The.) DTC; OxBoLi
(Young Girl's Song.) TrGrPo
Maiden's Complaint, The. *Unknown.* OLR
Maiden's Denial, A. *Unknown.* ErPo
(Reluctant Lady, The.) UnTE
Maidens, gather not the yew. Prologue to a Saga. Dorothy Parker. InMe
Maiden's Ideal of a Husband, A. Henry Carey. The Contrivances. HBV-1
Maidens, kilt your skirts and go. Celia's Home-coming. Agnes Mary Frances Robinson. OBEV; OBVV
Maiden's Plight, The. Brian Merriman, *tr. fr. Modern Irish by* Frank O'Connor. *Fr.* The Midnight Court. BIrV
Maidens shall weep at merry morn. The Summer Malison. Gerard Manley Hopkins. CMoP; NoAM; PoEL-5
Maidens who this bursting [*or* burning] May. A Young Man's Song. William Bell. FaBoTw; NePoEA
Maidens, why spare ye? To Cupid. Michael Drayton. ElL
Maidens young and virgins tender. Invocation. Horace, *tr. by* Louis Untermeyer. Odes, I, 21. AWP
Maid's Complaint, A. Thomas Campion. UnTE
Maid's Complaint for Want of a Dil Doul, The. *Unknown.* CoMu
Maids Conjuring Book, The. *Unknown.* CoMu
Maid's Lament, The. Walter Savage Landor. *Fr.* The Citation and Examination of William Shakespeare. HBV-1; OBEV; OBNC; OBRV; OBVV
Maids, not to you my mind doth change. "Michael Field." *Fr.* Variations on Sappho. PeHV
Maids of Elfin-Mere, The. William Allingham. OnYI
Maids of Honour, The. *Unknown.* CoMu
Maids of Simcoe, The, *with music. Unknown.* ShS
Maid's Thought, The. Robinson Jeffers. ErPo
Maids to bed and cover coal. The Bellman's Song. *Unknown.* EBEV; ElL; SeCePo
Maid's Tragedy, The, *sels.* Beaumont *and* Fletcher.
Aspatia's Song, *fr.* II, i. AWP; HAP; HBV-1; NOBE; OBEV; OBS; PoPle; TrGrPo
(I Died True.) CH
("Lay a garland on my hearse.") ElL; GBL; OAEP; ViBoPo; WHA
Bridal Song ("Cynthia, to thy power"), *fr.* I, ii. OBEV
Bridal Song ("Hold back thy hours"), *fr.* I, ii. ElL; ErPo; TrGrPo
(Hold Back Thy Hours.) UnTE; ViBoPo
To Bed, to Bed, *fr.* I, ii. UnTE
Maids When You're Young, Never Wed an Old Man. *Unknown.* FSW
Mail Call. John Bensko. MAYP
Mail has come from home, The. To My Friend, Grown Famous. Eunice Tietjens. HBMV
Mailed to G. B. Gene Derwood. NePA
Mailman, The. Victor Contoski. GP
Maimed and enormous in the air. The Feast. David Wagoner. NePoEA-2
Maimed [*or* Maim'd] Debauchee, The. Earl of Rochester. *See* Disabled Debauchee, The.
Main artery of fighting. War. Guillaume Apollinaire, *tr. by* Jessie Degen *and* Richard Eberhart. WaaP
Main-Deep, The. James Stephens. MoBrPo; MOS; OBMV; UnPo
Main Man Blues. Eugene B. Redmond. GP
Main-Sheet Song, The. Thomas Fleming Day. EtS
Main-Truck, The; or, A Leap for Life. George Pope Morris. BLPL; PoLF
Maine. Philip Booth. AmFN
Maine Sea Gulls. Russell Hoban. BoAnP
Maine Trail, A. Gertrude Huntington McGiffert. HBV-1
Mainline. John Ditsky. AMV-80
Mainsail Haul, *2 vers., with music. Unknown.* ShS
Mainspring, The. Martha Eugenie Perry. CaP
Maire My Girl. John Keegan Casey. AnIV; OnYI
Majestic tomes, you are the tomb. Epitaph on the Proofreader of the Encyclopedia Britannica. Christopher Morley. ShM
Majesty and Mercy of God, The. Sir Robert Grant. OHIP; WGRP
Majesty of God, The. Thomas Sternhold. WGRP
Major abstraction is the idea of man, The. Wallace Stevens. *Fr.* Notes toward a Supreme Fiction. NOBA
Major André. *Unknown.* AmFP
Major-General Scott. On to Richmond. John R. Thompson. PAH
Major-General's Song. W. S. Gilbert. *See* Modern Major-General, The.
Major Macroo. Stevie Smith. SBG
Major, with wonderful force, A. An Atrocious Pun. *Unknown.* RHPC; TDH
Majuba Hill. Roy Macnab. PeSA
Makar, The. William Soutar. OxBS
Make a joyful noise unto the Lord, all ye lands. A Psalm of Praise [*or* Be Thankful unto Him]. Psalm C, Bible, *O.T.* FaPON; OFD; OHIP; SiSoSe; SUS; TRV
Make Believe. Alice Cary. HBV-1
Make every bargain clear and plain. *Unknown.* FaBoUs
Make Friends. Ali Ben Abu Taleb. TRV
"Make it sweet and delicate to eat." The Eaten Heart. *Unknown, tr. by* Pearl London. *Fr.* The Knight of Curtesy. TrGrPo
Make Love Not War. Howard Nemerov. NAs; NoAM
Make me a bowl, a mighty bowl. The Cup. John Oldham. AWP
Make me a captive, Lord. Christ's Bondservant [*or* Christian Freedom]. George Matheson. STF; TrPWD; TRV
Make Me a Garment, *with music. Unknown.* OuSiCo
Make me a grave where'er you will. Bury Me in a Free Land. Frances E. W. Harper. BPo
Make me a handle as straight as the mast of a ship. To the Blacksmith with a Spade. Owen O'Sullivan, *tr. by* Frank O'Connor. KiLC
Make me a heaven, and make me there. The Eye. Robert Herrick. CaPo
Make Me a Pallet on Your Floor. *Unknown.* BluL
Make me an intercessor. An Intercessor. *Unknown.* STF
Make me content, O Lord, with daily bread. Prayer for Contentment. Edwin McNeill Poteat. TrPWD
Make me, dear Lord, polite and kind. A Child's Prayer. John Banister Tabb. FaPON; TreF; YaD
Make me feel the wild pulsation that I felt before the strife. Tennyson. *Fr.* Locksley Hall. SaC
Make Me Hear You. Reginald Gibbons. MAYP
Make me no vows of constancy, dear friend. Until Death. Elizabeth Akers Allen. HBV-1
Make me, O Lord, thy spinning [*or* spining] wheel[e] complete [*or* compleat *or* compleate] [*or* of use for thee]. Huswifery [*or* Housewifery.] Edward Taylor. AP; EaLo; EBCP; FaBV; LiTA; NePA; NIP; NOBE; NoP; OxBA; SaC; SCAP; TAP

Make me one, my Only One, in such true God-is-One. The Ecstasy. Al-Hallaj. ILwL
Make me over, Mother April. Spring Song. Bliss Carman. HBV-1; HBVY, *abr.*
Make me too brave to lie or be unkind. A Prayer for Every Day. Mary Carolyn Davies. BLPA; FaBoBe
Make miniatures of the once-monstrous theme. A Short History of British India. Geoffrey Hill. OxBC
Make Music with Your Life. Bob O'Meally. CNA
Make my mortal dreams come true. Whittier. *Fr.* Andrew Rykman's Prayer. TrPWD
Make new friends, but keep the old. New Friends and Old Friends. Joseph Parry. BLPA; BLPL; TreFT
Make no mistake: if He rose at all. Seven Stanzas at Easter. John Updike. EaLo; EBCP; TrCP
Make room, all ye kingdoms, in history renown'd. American Independence. Francis Hopkinson. PAH
Make room on our banner bright. Song of Texas. William Henry Cuyler Hosmer. PAH
Make the most of it, mood. Separation. John L. Sweeney. TwAmPo
Make this night loveable. Song. W. H. Auden. TW
Make this thing plain to us, O Lord! Clean Hands. Austin Dobson. TrPWD
Make three-fourths of a cross, and a circle complete. *Unknown.* HBV-1; HBVY; OxNR
Make thyself known, Sibyl, or let despair. Mona Lisa. Edward Dowden. OnYI
Make us Thy mountaineers. The Last Defile. Amy Carmichael. TrCP; TRV
Make Way! Florence Crocker Comfort. PGD
Make Way! Ada Negri, *tr. fr. Italian by* Lynne Lawner. PBWP
Make Way for Liberty. James Montgomery. TreFS
(Arnold von Winkelried.) BeLS
(Patriot's Pass-Word.) HBV-2
Make way for the beast with chrome teeth. The Beast with Chrome Teeth. Thurmond Snyder. NNP
Make way, make way. The Stream's Song. Lascelles Abercrombie. OBMV
Make We Merry. *Unknown. See* Now Is the Time of Christmas.
Make we mirth. Sing We Yule. *Unknown.* MeEL
Make Ye a Joyful Sounding Noise, *with music. Unknown.* AH
Make your cotton and make your corn. *Unknown.* OuSiCo
Maker, The. R. S. Thomas. ELU
Maker of Heaven and Earth. Cecil Frances Alexander. *See* All Things Bright and Beautiful.
Maker-of-Sevens in the scheme of things. The Wife-Woman. Anne Spencer. BANP; NoAM
Maker of Songs. Hazel Hall. HBMV
Makers, The. David Galler. NYBP
Makers, The. Richard Kell. CIP
Makers, The. Howard Nemerov. FYAP
Makes the Little Ones Dizzy. Samuel Hoffenstein. BXAP
Makhno's Philosophers. John Manifold. CBAP
Making. Phyllis Webb. PoCh
Making a Door. Dennis Schmitz. LCAP
Making a Fist. Naomi Shihab Nye. MAYP
Making a Man. Nixon Waterman. BLPA
Making a meaning out of everything that has happened. Ramble on What in the World Why. Ralph Gustafson. AMV-81
Making an Impression. William (Haywood) Jackson. AMV-80
Making Chicago. Dennis Schmitz. LCAP; NPGG
Making Contact. John Manifold. CBAP
Making Feet and Hands. Benjamin Péret, *tr. fr. French by* David Gascoyne. EAS
Making his advances. Tortoise Gallantry. D. H. Lawrence. CMoP; NoAM
Making It Simple December 8, 1969. David McElroy. AmPA
Making Land. Thomas Fleming Day. EtS
Making Love, Killing Time. Anne Ridler. NMP
Making Miso. Lawson Fusao Inada. GP
Making Music. Judith Minty. GeTw
Making of Birds, The. Katharine Tynan. HBMV; OxBI
Making of Color, The. Hugh Seidman. AmPA
Making of Man, The. John White Chadwick. AA
Making of the Cross, The. William Everson. VGW
Making Port. J. T. McKay. EtS
Making toast at the fireside. Misfortunes Never Come Singly. Harry Graham. FaFP; TreFT
Making Up for a Soul. David Wagoner. VGW
Malacoda. Samuel Beckett. CIP
Malady of Love Is Nerves, The. Petronius Arbiter, *tr. fr. Latin by* Howard Mumford Jones. AWP
Malaga. Pearse Hutchinson. BIrV
Malbecco and Hellenore. Spenser. The Faerie Queene, III, 9 *and* 10. NoP
Malcolm. Lucille Clifton. CNA
Malcolm. Kattie M. Cumbo. BOLo
Malcolm. Welton Smith. BPo
Malcolm, a Thousandth Poem. Conrad Kent Rivers. CNA
Malcolm X. Gwendolyn Brooks. BALP; CNA; OFD; PoBA; TTY
Malcolm X—An Autobiography. Larry Neal. AmNP; BPo
Malcolm X spoke to me. My Ace of Spades. Ted Joans. BOLo
Malcolm's Katie, *sels.* Isabella Valancy Crawford.
"Bite deep and wide, O Axe, the tree." OBCV
"South Wind laid his moccasins aside, The." OBCV
Malcom, Iowa. Charles Itzin. FAZ
Malcontent, The, *sel.* John Marston.
"I cannot sleepe, my eyes ill neighbouring lids." PoEL-2
Malcontents, The. Dryden. *Fr.* Absalom and Achitophel, I. OBS
Maldive Shark, The. Herman Melville. AmPP; AP; MOS; NePA; NOBA; NoP; OxBA; PAI; PoEL-5; TAP; TW
Male and Female. W. Craddle. WhC
Male & Female Loves in Beulah. Blake. *Fr.* Jerusalem, III. OBNC
Male mite Adactylidium, The. Teaching about Arthropods. Miroslav Holub, *tr. by* Stuart Friebert *and* Dana Hábová. SUW
Male Rage Poem. Pier Giorgio Di Cicco. NOBC
Male Rain. Laura Tohe. STE
Male Torso. Christopher Middleton. NePoEA-2
Malediction. Phyllis McGinley. DBV
Malediction. Barry Spacks. InPK; TW
Malefic Return, The. Ramón López Velarde, *tr. fr. Spanish by* Samuel Beckett. OBVE
Malefic Surgeon, The. Gerrit Lansing. CoPo
Malemute Dog, A. Pat O'Cotter. BLPA
Malest Cornifici Tuo Catullo. Allen Ginsberg. NeAP
Malfeasance, The. Alan Bold. AmMo
Malice Domestic. Ogden Nash. DBV
Malice of Innocence, The. Denise Levertov. NNaP
Malicious Envy rode. Envy. Spenser. *Fr.* The Faerie Queene, I, 4. TW
Malignant planets! do ye still combine. The Sow of Feeling. Robert Fergusson. NOEC
Malison of the Stone-chat. *Unknown.* GBP
Malisons, malisons more than ten. The Lark. *Unknown.* GBP; PBBP
Mallee in October. Flexmore Hudson. PoAu-2
Mallow evenings on the shallow lake. The Heron. Philip Murray. BoAnP
Maltese Dog, A. Tymnes *tr. fr. Greek by* Edmund Blunden. FaBoCh; TiPo
(Dog from Malta, The.) GDP
("He came from Malta, and Eumelus says.") FaBoEE
Maltworm's Madrigal, The. Austin Dobson. HBV-2
Malum Opus. James Appleton Morgan. FaBoCo; NA
Malvern Hill. Herman Melville. AmPP; AP; FPL; PAH; TAP
Malvern Hills, *sel.* Joseph Cottle.
Industrial Evils. NOEC
Malvern Waters. *Unknown.* FaBoEE
Malvolio. Walter Savage Landor. Par
Malzah's Song. Charles Heavysege. *Fr.* Saul. OBCV
Mama/ eats death/ tastes like fish. Monogram 4. Martina Werner, *tr. by* Rosemarie Waldrop. BoWoP
Mama,/ papa,/ and us. An Inconvenience. John Raven. BPo
Mama and Daughter. Langston Hughes. UnPo
Mama Don't 'Low. *Unknown.* FSW
Mama Have You Heard the News, *with music. Unknown.* AS
Mama Knows. Sharon Scott. JB
Mama, please brush off my coat. Mama and Daughter. Langston Hughes. UnPo
Mama sent me to the spring. *See* Mamma sent me to the spring, she told me not to stay.
Mama, they're gonna give me. The Keys of the Jail. *Unknown.* OuSiCo
Mama writes. Under Your Voice, among Legends. Phyllis Beauvais. NMM
Mama, you turn from the sink, shaking water. To My Mother. L. M. Rosenberg. AMV-81
Mama's Advice. Kurt M. Stein. InMe
Mama's God. Carolyn Rodgers. GP
Mama's Gone to the Mail Boat, *with music. Unknown.* OuSiCo
Mamba the Bright-eyed, *sel.* George Gordon McCrae.
"Day had fled, the moon arose, The." PoAu-1
Mamma! Frank Horne. BPo
Mamma and Papa, Wo-ho, Lawdy. Godamighty Drag. *Unknown.* OuSiCo
Mamma, Mamma, *with music. Unknown.* OuSiCo
Mamma, Mamma, make me a garment. Make Me a Garment. *Unknown.* OuSiCo
Mamma [*or* Mama] sent me to the spring, she told me not to stay. Chewing [Chawing] Gum. *Unknown.* AmFP; FSW
Mamma Sings. Samuel Hoffenstein. DBV
Mamma, there's Rachel making hay. The Mistake. *Unknown.* PaPo

Mammals are a varied lot. Dogs and Cats and Bears and Bats. Jack Prelutsky. RHPC
Mammon emovéd was with inward wrath. Spenser. *Fr.* The Faerie Queene, II, 7. ViBoPo
Mammon Marriage. George Macdonald. BoLoP; EBVV; NBM; OBVV
Mammoth morning moved grey flanks and groaned, A. Walking Wounded. Vernon Scannell. OBWP
Mammy Hums. Carl Sandburg. PoNe
Mamua, when our laughter ends. Tiare Tahiti. Rupert Brooke. BrPo; SeCeV
Man, The. Michael Dennis Browne. GP
Man, The. Robert Creeley. OBAL
Man. Sir John Davies. *Fr.* Nosce Teipsum. ElL; OBEV, 2 *sts.*
(I Know Myself a Man.) ChTr
(Which Is a Proud, and Yet a Wretched Thing.) WHA
Man. Samuel Greenberg. CrMA
Man. George Herbert. AnAnS-1; CABA; MePo; NoP; OAEP; PoEL-2; SeCP; SeCV-1; TrGrPo; TrPWD
Man, A! Clinton Scollard. OHIP
Man ("What a piece of work is a man!"). Shakespeare. *Fr.* Hamlet, II, ii. TreF
Man. Swinburne. *See* Before the Beginning of Years.
Man. Henry Vaughan. AnAnS-1; FaBoEn; HBV-1; MeLP; MePo; NOBE; NOCV; OBEV; OBS; PoEL-2; SeCV-1
Man. Humbert Wolfe. MoBrPo
Man, A (a Tom, a Dick, or some such epithet). The Bayonet and the Needle. Eliezer Steinbarg, *tr. by* Curt Leviant. VWA
Man about the Kitchen, A. Rodney Hobson. QQQ
Man Adrift on a Slim Spar, A. Stephen Crane. CrMA; MOS
Man against the Sky, The. E. A. Robinson. AmPP; AP; CMoP; CoBMV; LiTA; MoVE; OxBA; TwAmPo
Man All Grown Up Is Supposed To, A. Terry Stokes. AmPA
Man Alone. Louise Bogan. NYBP
Man and a woman walk out into the summer night, A. Such Comfort as the Night Can Bring to Us. Peter Cooley. MAYP
Man and Bat. D. H. Lawrence. BoAnP
Man and Beast. Clifford Dyment. BoAnP
Man and Cows. Andrew Young. EBEV
Man and Dog. Edward Thomas. FM
Man and His Image, The. La Fontaine, *tr. fr. French by* Elizur Wright. OBVE
Man and Machine. Robert Morgan. Str
Man and Nature. Robert Kelley Weeks. AA
Man and the Ascidian. Andrew Lang. HBV-1
Man and the maid go side by side, The. Sunday Afternoon in Italy. D. H. Lawrence. BrPo
Man and the Weasel, The. Phaedrus, *tr. fr. Latin by* Christopher Smart. AWP
Man and Wife. Mitchell Goodman. VGW
Man and Wife. Robert Lowell. AmPP; BoLoP; ConAP
Man and Wife. Anne Sexton. CAPP
Man and Wife Is One Flesh. Ann Deagon. NIP
Man and Woman. Robert Conquest. OxBTC
Man and Woman. Don L. Lee. NeAC
Man and woman, A. The Woman's Dream. Frances Horovitz. BrRo
Man and woman lie on a white bed, A. Happiness. Louise Glück. MAYP
Man and woman walking, A. The Feather. Lilian Bowes Lyon. ChMP
Man-apes. Between the Karim Shahir. Rochelle Owens. CoPo
Man Arrested in Hacking Death Tells Police He Mistook Mother-in-Law for Raccoon. Susan Ludvigson. MAYP
Man as He Shall Be. Rochelle Owens. CoPo
Man Asleep in the Desert. Thomas Lux. LCAP
Man at the end. Hamewith. Sydney Goodsir Smith. BSV
Man at the moment of departure, turning, A. Ritual of Departure. Thomas Kinsella. CIP; CMoP
Man at Work. John Holmes. WhC
Man Awakened by a Song above His Roof, The. Tomas Tranströmer, *tr. fr. Swedish by* Robert Bly. EAS
Man, be merry, I thee rede. Three Christmas Carols, II. *Unknown.* ACP
Man, be ware and wise in dede. Assay a Friend. *Unknown.* OxBM
Man before me stands, black muscles, The. Base Chapel, Lejeune 4/79. Archie Hobson. AMV-81
Man behind the book may not be man, The. The Intellectual. Karl Shapiro. CMoP
Man bent over his guitar, The. The Man with the Blue Guitar. Wallace Stevens. CMoP; LiTA; NoAM
Man, born to toil, in his labour rejoiceth. A Hymn of Nature. Robert Bridges. YeAr
Man bows out of the employment office, A. The Long Season. James Haug. AMV-81
Man-brained and man-handed ground-ape, physically, The. Original Sin. Robinson Jeffers. MoAB; MoAmPo; MoVE
Man by the Name of Bolus, A. James Whitcomb Riley. AA
Man by the wall snores, The. *Unknown, tr. by* J. G. O'Keefe. *Fr.* Mad Sweeney. AnIL
Man Called Dante, I Have Heard, A. Georgiana Goddard King. HBV-2
Man came slowly from the setting sun, A. The Death of Cuchulain [*or* Cuchulain's Fight with the Sea]. W. B. Yeats. AnIL; ChTr; GoTL
Man Cannot Name Himself. Luci Shaw. TrCP
Man carries a skull of red yarn, A. In an Empty Field at Night. Gregory Orr. PAI
Man Carrying Bale. Harold Monro. BrPo; MoBrPo
Man Carrying Thing. Wallace Stevens. SyP
Man Christ, The. Therese Lindsey. TRV
Man Closing Up, The. Donald Justice. CoAP
Man comes in the door, A. The Man. Michael Dennis Browne. GP
Man Coming toward You, The. Oscar Williams. LiTA; TwAmPo
"Man coming toward you is falling forward on all fronts, The," I *and* II. NePA
Man could love the city he detested, The. Ovid. Richard Pevear. AMV-81
Man cut his throat and left his head there, The. The Creation of the Moon. *Unknown, tr. by* W. S. Merwin. MOON
Man divided into animal, A. Sun of the Center. Robert Kelly. CoPo
Man, dream[e] no more of curious mysteries. Fulke Greville. Caelica, LXXXVIII. EnRePo; JCP; MePo; OBS; QRF
Man Exalted. *Unknown.* MeEL
(Out of Your Sleep Arise and Wake.) NoP
Man fell out of grace, A. A Funny Joke. Leon Stokesbury. MAYP
Man Flammonde, from God knows where, The. Flammonde. E. A. Robinson. AmPP; CMoP; LiTA; LiTM; NoAM; SeCeV
Man! Foolish Man! On Exodus 3: 14: "I am that I am." Matthew Prior. NOCV
Man fools about with self-analysis. The Collective Portrait. Robert Finch. MoCV
Man for Galway, The. Charles James Lever. OnYI
Man Frail, and God Eternal. Isaac Watts. *See* O God, Our Help in Ages Past.
Man from Ironbark, The. Andrew Barton Paterson. PoAu-1
Man from Porlock, The. Helen Bevington. EvOK
Man from Snowy River, The. Andrew Barton Paterson. CBAP; PH; PoAu-1
Man from the Crowd, The. Sam Walter Foss. PoLF
Man from the Top of the Mind, The. David Wagoner. NePoEA-2
Man from the Woods, The. John Ciardi. SO
Man from Washington, The. James Welch. CDW; GP
Man Goin' Roun'. *Unknown.* *See* There's a Man Goin' 'Round Takin' Names.
Man growing old is going, A. Shalom. Denise Levertov. NoAM
Man had died on the cross, The. The Sepulcher. Annie Johnson Flint. STF
Man had just married an automobile, A. The Automobile. Russell Edson. LCAP
Man had nothing to write about, The. Success Story. Bruce Bennett. LTB
Man had something in the look of him, The. Karshish and Lazarus. Robert Browning. *Fr.* An Epistle Containing the Strange Medical Experience of Karshish, the Arab Physician. GoBC
Man has a soul of vast defines. Putney Hymn. *Unknown.* TrAS
Man has been standing, A. The Tunnel. Mark Strand. HeIP; TwCP; WeW
Man Has No Smokestack. *Unknown.* STF
Man has separated lust and sorrow. All Is God's. Jakov de Haan, *tr. by* David Soetendorp. VWA
Man He Killed, The. Thomas Hardy. BrPo; CMoP; CoBMV; DL; FaFP; FF; HAP; HeIP; InPS; LiTB; LiTM; MoAB; MoBrPo; NIP; OBWP; PAI; PoPl; TreF; WaaP; WeW; WHA
Man, hef in mind and mend thy mis. Remember the Last Things. *Unknown.* MeEL
Man Hidden behind the Drapes, The. Pattiann Rogers. MAYP
Man hired by John Smith and Co., A. Dirt Dumping [*or* Limerick]. "Mark Twain." FaBoNo; TDH
Man Holding Boy. Melvin Dixon. LTB
Man, husband existence: ne'er launch on the sea. Epitaph of Cleonicus. Theocritus, *tr. by* Charles Stuart Calverley. FaBoEE
Man, I Felt Like Running All Night. Salomón R. Baldenegro, Jr., *tr. fr. Spanish by* Toni Empringham. FIA
Man I had a love for, The. An Old Woman's Lamentations. Villon, *tr. by* J. M. Synge. MoBrPo; OBMV
Man I know wrote a book about a man he knew, A. Dichtung und Wahrheit. Allen Curnow. OCNZ
Man I married twice, The. Reject Jell-o. Lucille Day. AMV-81
Man I saw in the forest, The. Dream 2: Brian the Still-Hunter. Margaret Atwood. BoWoP

Man I Thought You Was Talking Another Language That Day. Victor Hernandez Cruz. BOLo
Man, if I said once, "I know." The Islands. Randall Jarrell. EAS
Man, if you gonna love your woman. You Got to Love Her with a Feeling. *Unknown.* BluL
Man in Black, The. Mark Strand. EAS
Man in Harmony with Nature. Jones Very. AP
Man in his secret shrine. Hymn in Columbus Circle. Stephen Vincent Benét. OBAL
Man in Nature. William Roscoe Thayer. AA
Man in Our Village, A. Leslie Norris. GDP
Man in righteousness arrayed, The. To Sally. John Quincy Adams, *after* Horace. AA; AWP; OBAL
Man in terror of impotence, A. The Ninth Symphony of Beethoven Understood at Last as a Sexual Message. Adrienne Rich. NoP; TAP
Man in That Airplane, The. Oscar Williams. WaP
Man in the Dream Is Death, The. Lynne Butler. IHMS
Man in the Dress Suit, The. Robert L. Wolf. HBMV
Man in the feed store called them mountain beavers, The. Looking for Mountain Beavers. David Wagoner. VGW
Man in the Mirror, The. Mark Strand. NYBP
Man in the Moon, The. "Hugh MacDiarmid." NeBP
Man in the Moon, The. James Whitcomb Riley. HBV-1; HBVY; InMe; NA
Man in the Moon, The ("Man in the moone stand [*or* mone stond] and strit"). *Unknown.* MeEL; OxBM
Man in the moon, The/ As he sails in the sky. Mother Goose. SoPo
Man in the moon, The/ Came down too soon [*or* Came tumbling down]. *Unknown.* MOON; OxBoLi; OxNR
Man in the Moon Drinks Claret, The ("Bacchus, the father of drunken Nowls"). *Unknown.* CoMu
Man in the moon drinks claret, The/ But he is a dull jack-a-dandy. *Unknown.* OxNR
Man in the moon looked down on the field, The. Jack o'Lantern. Anna Chandler Ayre. SoPo
Man in the moon was caught in a trap, The. *Unknown.* MOON; OxNR
Man in the mune, The/ is making shune. *Unknown.* OxNR
Man in the Ocelot Suit, The. Christopher Brookhouse. CAD
Man in the Onion Bed, The. John Ciardi. SO
Man in the red scarf comes—from five split places, The. The Raspberry in the Pudding. Philip O'Connor. EAS
Man in the Street. Robert Penn Warren. OBAL
Man in the street is fed, The. Carl Sandburg. OxBA
Man in the Tree, The. Mark Strand. EAS
Man in the Trilby hat has furtively shifted it, The. The Cenotaph. Ursula Roberts. SUMH
Man in the wilderness asked [of] me [*or* said to me], The [*or* A]. Mother Goose. FaBoCh; FaBoCo; FaBoNo; GBP; NA; OxNR
Man into a Churchyard. Bernard Gutteridge. EAS
Man, introverted man, having crossed. Science. Robinson Jeffers. NU; OxBA
Man Is a Fool. Joseph Capp. FaFP
(Generalization.) TreFT, *diff. vers.*
Man is a fool and a bag of wind! Hakluyt Unpurchased. Franklin McDuffee. EtS
Man is a lumpe, where all beasts kneaded bee. To Sir Edward Herbert at Julyers. John Donne. SeCV-1
Man is a sacred city built of marvelous earth. John Masefield. *Fr.* The Tragedy of Pompey the Great. WGRP
Man Is a Spirit. Stevie Smith. OxBC
Man is a torch borne in the wind; a dream. The Pilot. George Chapman. *Fr.* Bussy d'Ambois, I, i. EtS
Man Is a Weaver. Moses ibn Ezra, *tr. fr. Hebrew by* Emma Lazarus. TrJP
Man is born, a man dies, A. Tir-Nan-Og. J. F. Hendry. NeBP
Man Is but a Castaway. Clarence Day. ImOP
Man is clothed, The. And When the Green Man Comes. John Haines. ConAP; NCSH
Man Is for Woman Made. Peter Anthony Motteux. UnTE
Man Is God's Nature. Richard Eberhart. EaLo
Man Is in Pain. Philip Lamantia. NeAP
Man is in the fields, let us look with his eyes, A. Enigma. R. S. Thomas. ChMP
Man is mind. Progress. Peter Meinke. POL
Man is most anxious not to stir. That Corner. Blanaid Salkeld. OnYI; OxBI
Man Is Nothing But. Shaul Tchernichovsky, *tr. fr. Hebrew by* Robert Friend. VWA
Man is permitted much. The Elements [*or* Chorus of the Elements]. Cardinal Newman. GoBC; OBRV; OBVV
Man knocked strongly at the door, The. The Man from Porlock. Helen Bevington. EvOK
Man knows not love—such love as woman feels. Woman's Love. *Unknown.* WBLP
Man knows where first he ships himself, but he. Man's Dying-Place Uncertain. Robert Herrick. CaPo
Man looking into the sea. A Grave. Marianne Moore. CABA; CMoP; CrMA; FaBoEn; HAP; HeIP; InPK; LiTA; MoPo; MOS; MoVE; NoAM; NOBA; PPoe; SeCeV; TAP; UnPo; WeW; WPE
Man Lying on a Wall. Michael Longley. CIP
Man-made bay, its fat weeds, The. Mission Bay. John Koethe. PoA
Man-made stars. In the Planetarium. Siv Cedering Fox. LTB
Man-Making. Edwin Markham. PGD
Man, Man, Man. *Unknown.* ErPo; FaFP
(Man, Man, Man Is for the Woman Made). Prf
Man, matron, maiden. Robert Baden-Powell. CenHV
Man may be martyred in bondage. The Mainspring. Martha Eugenie Perry. CaP
Man May Live Thrice Nestor's Life, A. Thomas Norton. *See* Against Women either Good or Bad.
Man may work from sun to sun. *Unknown.* SaC
Man Meeting Himself. Howard Sergeant. EAS
Man more kindly, in his careless way, A. A Portrait. Caroline Duer. AA
Man-Moth, The. Elizabeth Bishop. LiTA; LiTM; MAT; MiAP; MoAB; MoAmPo; NoAM; NOBA; NYP; PoCH; PPP
Man moves toward himself as old, A. In Random Fields of Impulse and Repose. Jeanine Hathaway. AMV-81
Man-muckle was I or I saw. What Finer Hills? J. K. Annand. PoSH
Man, my friend, whose conscious heart, The. To Aristius Fuscus. Horace, *tr. by* Samuel Johnson. Odes, I, 22. OBVE
Man Named Hods, A. *Unknown.* CoSo
Man New Made. Shakespeare. *Fr.* Measure for Measure, II, ii. GoBC
Man next to me with the gray hair, The. In the Bar. Robert Vander Molen. TAT
Man, Not His Arms. Selden Rodman. WaP
Man o' War Bird. Derek Walcott. TTY
Man of bone confirms his throne, The. The New Ancient of Days. Herman Melville. OBAL
Man of Calvary, The. "Sin-Killer" Griffin. OuSiCo
"Roman soldiers come riding in full speed,"*sel.* AmFP
Man of Constant Sorrow. *Unknown.* FSW
Man of Experience, A. Laoiseach Mac an Bhaird, *tr. fr. Irish by* Frank O'Connor. KiLC
Man of independent means, A. No Occupation. George Rostrevor Hamilton. FaBoEE
Man of Kerioth, The, *sel.* Robert Norwood.
"But, this I found," *fr.* V. CaP
Man of Letters. Warren Knox. QQQ
Man of Life Upright, The. Thomas Campion. AAS; ElL; EnRePo; OAEP; OBSC; PoRA; ViBoPo
(Integer Vitæ.) HBV-2; NOBE; OBEV
(Life Upright, The.) HBVY
Man of marble holds the throne, A. The Roman Stage. Lionel Johnson. BrPo
Man of massive meditation, A. Analogue of Unity in Multeity. Richard Eberhart. NoAM
Man of Men, A. Leonard Charles Van Noppen. PGD
Man of My Time. Salvatore Quasimodo, *tr. fr. Italian by* Allen Mandelbaum. PoPl
Man of O, The. Marina Rivera. FIA
Man of Peace, The, *abr.* Bliss Carman. OHIP
Man of Prayer, The. Christopher Smart. *Fr.* The Song of David. LiTB
Man of Sense, A. Richard Eberhart. MiAP
Man of Sorrows, The. *Unknown.* PGD
Man of Taste, The, *sels.* James Bramston.
"Huge commentators grace my learned shelves." FaBoCo
"Whoe'er he be that to a Taste aspires." NOEC
Man of the North Countrie, The. Thomas D'Arcy McGee. OnYI
Man of the Open West, The. Arthur W. Monroe. PoOW
Man of the World. Michael Hamburger. NePoEA-2
Man of Thessaly, The. *Unknown.* FaBoCo
("There was a man of Thessaly.") FaBoNo; OxNR
Man of Valour to His Fair Lady, The. William Dunbar. MeEL
Man of Words, A. John Ashbery. PoA
Man of Words, A. *Unknown.* FaFP; FF; TreFS
("Man of words, and not of deeds.") FaBoBe; FaBoCh; OxBoLi
(Proverb.) HBV-1
Man on Move Despite Failures. Jeffery Alan Triggs. AMV-80
Man on the Bed, The. Debora Greger. MAYP
Man on the dubious waves of error toss'd. William Cowper. *Fr.* Truth. NOCV
Man on the Dump, The. Wallace Stevens. HAP
Man on the Flying Trapeze, The. *Unknown, at. to* George Leybourne.

BeLS; BLPA; BLSo, *with music*; FaBoBe; FaFP, *diff. vers.*; FSW; OxBoLi, *diff. vers.*; YaD
(Flying Trapeze, The.) PSoN, *with music*; TreF
Man on Wheels. Karl Shapiro. PCP
Man or woman walking today, A. To Xanadu, Which Is Beth Shaul. Arye Sivan, *tr. by* Anthony Rudolf *and* Natan Zach. VWA
Man pays that debt with new munificence. "Lord, I Owe Thee a Death." Alice Meynell. SUMH
Man picked up a stick, which felt, A. The Stick. Bruce Bennett. LTB
Man plays harmonica at midnight, The. Ruston, Louisiana: 1952. Cleopatra Mathis. AMV-80
Man possessed a cat on which he doted, A. Cat into Lady. La Fontaine, *tr. by* Edmund Marsh. PCat
Man Proposes. Thomas à Kempis. *Fr.* Imitation of Christ, I, 19. TreF
Man proposes, God in His time disposes. On a Dead Child. Richard Middleton. OBVV; SoSe
Man rejects imprisonment. Fall To. Howard Jones. NBP
Man said, The. An Historic Moment. William J. Harris. BOLo
Man said to the universe, A. War Is Kind, XXI. Stephen Crane. AmPP; CrMA; FaBoEE; FF; ImOP; LiTM; NCEP; OBAL; OBSV; PrIm; TAP; TreFT; WeW; YaD
Man said unto his Angel, A. The Kings. Louise Imogen Guiney. GoBC; HBV-2
Man Sails the Deep a While. Robert Louis Stevenson. MOS
Man sat in the felon's tank, alone, A. In the Tank. Thom Gunn. NoAM
Man sat in the gallery, The. Words without Music. *Unknown.* WhC
Man Saw a Ball of Gold in the Sky, A. Stephen Crane. The Black Riders, XXXV. EvOK; LiTA; NePA; PoPl
Man say I had something look like new, A. Stew Meat Blues. *Unknown.* BluL
Man says lilacs against white houses, two sparrows, one streaked, A. Spring Drawing II. Robert Hass. MAYP
Man seasick with drink. Brendan Gone. Padraic Fiacc. CIP
Man Sentenced to Death, The, *sel.* Jean Genet, *tr. fr. French by* Steven Finch.
"Murderers of the wall wrap themselves in sunrise, The." PeHV
Man shall come into this land, A. Bard's Chant. James Shirley. *Fr.* Saint Patrick for Ireland. ACP
Man She Called Honey, and Married, The. Alberto Ríos. MAYP
Man she had was kind and clean, The. Tombstones in the Starlight: The Fisherwoman. Dorothy Parker. NIP
Man should live in a garret aloof, A. The Flight of the Goddess. Thomas Bailey Aldrich. HBV-2
Man should never earn his living, A. A Living. D. H. Lawrence. RFM
Man sits in a timelessness, The. The Rescue. Robert Creeley. CAPP
Man so sick that the sexual soup, A. Sexual Soup. Erica Jong. GP
Man, standing in the shadows of a, A. For H. W. Fuller. Carolyn M. Rodgers. BPo
Man steps in out of the blizzard with his Klootch, The. The Sweet. Ai. GP
Man stood in the laurel tree, A. Things. Louis Simpson. OxBC
Man stoops low on the overcast plain, A. He is earthing. Landscape and Figure. Thomas Kinsella. IPY
Man that had six mortal wounds, a man, A. Cuchulain Comforted. W. B. Yeats. CMoP; LiTM; OAEL-2
Man that hails you Tom or Jack, The. William Cowper. *Fr.* On Friendship. POL; TreFT
Man that hath great griefs I pity not, The. Thomas Edward Brown. *Fr.* Pain. PeD
Man That Is Born of a Woman. Bible, *O.T.* Job, XIV: 1-2. ChTr
("For there is hope for a tree," XIV: 7-17.) DL
(Immortality, XIV: 1-12, *Moulton, Modern Reader's Bible.*) WGRP
(Job Cries Out, XIV.) TrGrPo
(Job's Entreaty, XIV.) AWP
("Man that is borne of woman, is of a few dayes, and full of trouble," XIV.) OBVE
Man that joins in life's career, The. The Parting Glass. Philip Freneau. AA
Man That Lives, The. *Unknown.* OBET
Man that mates wi' Poverty, The. Comfort in Puirtith. Helen B. Cruickshank. OxBS
Man that never will declare his thought, The. On the Deception of Appearances. Sadi, *tr. by* L. Cranmer-Byng. *Fr.* The Gulistan. AWP
Man that sees by chance his picture made, A. The Growth of Love, XXXIX. Robert Bridges. NoAM
Man that was old came a-courtin' one day, A. Old Shoes and Leggin's. *Unknown.* OuSiCo
Man That Waters the Workers' Beer, The. Paddy Ryan. FSW
Man, that with me trod, The. Tennyson. *Fr.* In Memoriam A. H. H, Epilogue. TRV
Man, the egregious egoist. Cold-blooded Creatures. Elinor Wylie. ImOP; SBG
Man the Enemy of Man. Sir Walter Scott. *Fr.* Rokeby. WBLP
Man, them revolutionary niggers is all. Just Taking Note. Sharon Scott. JB
Man there is of fire and straw, A. William Wilson. Malcolm Cowley. MoVE
Man Thinking about Woman. Don L. Lee. CNA; NoAM; PAI
Man to Man. John McClure. HBMV
Man to the Angel, The. "Æ." OBVV
Man under the Bed, The. Erica Jong. AmPA
Man unto His Fellow Man. Norman Corwin. *Fr.* On a Note of Triumph. TrJP
Man upon mold, whatsoever thou be. Money Is What Matters. *Unknown.* MeEL
Man Upright, The. Thomas MacDonagh. BIrV
Man Walking and Singing, A. Wendell Berry. AP
Man walks into a room, A. There is a corpse on the floor. Gorg, a Detective Story. B. P. Nichol. NOBC
Man walks through a district, A. Animation and Ego. Jody Swilky. AMV-80
"Man wants but little here below." The Wants of Man. John Quincy Adams. OBAL; PoLF
Man was all shot through that came to-day, The. Connolly. Liam MacGowan. OnYI
Man was called Methuselah I remember, The. Methuselah. Rosemary Dobson. *Fr.* The Devil and the Angel. PoAu-2
"Man was in such deep distress, The." Advice. Ambrose Bierce. DBV
Man was sitting underneath a tree, A. Seumas Beg. James Stephens. EvOK; FaPON; GrPl; OxBTC; RoGo
Man Watching, The. Rainer Maria Rilke, *tr. fr. German by* Robert Bly. NU
Man waxy, The—he jogs along the fields. Napoleon after Sedan. Arthur Rimbaud, *tr. by* Robert Lowell. *Fr.* Eighteen-Seventy. OBWP
Man went forth one day at eve, A. Tragedy. "Æ." MoBrPo
Man went forth with gifts, A. Martin Luther King, Jr. Gwendolyn Brooks. BOLo; CNA; PoBA
Man went walking up and down, A. One Fish Ball. *Unknown.* FSW
Man White, Brown Girl and All That Jazz. Gloria C. Oden. PoBA
Man Who Broke the Bank at Monte Carlo, The. Fred Gilbert. FSN, *with music*; FSW; TreF
Man Who Buys Hides, The. Dennis Schmitz. LCAP
Man who cloaked his bitterness within, The. Thomas Hood. E. A. Robinson. HBMV
Man Who Dreamed of Faeryland, The. W. B. Yeats. CMoP; NoAM; NoP; OAEP; PoPle
Man Who Dreamt He Was Turquoise, The. Wendy Rose. TWSS
Man who drew his strength from all, A. The Lincoln Statue. W. F. Collins. OHIP; PGD
Man who feels not, more or less, somewhat, The. Sonnet: Of Love in Men and Devils. Cecco Angiolieri da Siena, *tr. by* Dante Gabriel Rossetti. AWP
Man Who Finds That His Son Has Become a Thief, The. Raymond Souster. NOBC; OBCV
Man who follow English ways. Civil Irish and Wild Irish. Laoiseach Mac an Bhaird, *tr. by* Kenneth Jackson. AnIL
Man who for his race might supersede, The. Richard Henry Horne. *Fr.* Orion. VLP
Man who found the aardvark, The. A Bestiary. Kenneth Rexroth. OBAL
Man Who Frets at Worldly Strife, The. Fitz-Greene Halleck *and* Joseph Rodman Drake. *Fr.* The Croaker Papers. AA
Man who goes for Christian resignation, The. Epigram. J. V. Cunningham. NePoAm; PV
Man Who Had Fallen among Thieves, A. E. E. Cummings. AP; CoBMV; HAP; LiTM; MoVE; NoAM; NOBA; OxBA; TAP
Man, who had no rivals in the love, A. The Man and His Image. La Fontaine, *tr. by* Elizur Wright. OBVE
Man who, having collapsed, rises, takes steps, is insane, The. Forced March. Miklós Radnóti, *tr. by* Emery George. VWA
Man Who Hid His Own Front Door, The. Elizabeth MacKinstry. FaPON; TiPo
Man who in his life trusts in this world, A. Epitaph. *Unknown.* TrJP
Man Who Invented Las Vegas, The. Gerald Costanzo. TAT
Man Who Knew Too Much, The. David Wojahn. MAYP
Man who loves hiking, A. Hiking. Joseph Bruchac. CDW
Man Who Married Magdalene, The. Louis Simpson. NePoEA; NoAM; TAP
Man Who Married Magdalene, The: Variation on a Theme by Louis Simpson. Anthony Hecht. CoPo
Man who met a phalanx with their spears, The. The Good Hour. Louise Driscoll. HBMV
Man Who Named Children, The. Alberto Ríos. LTB
Man Who Rode to Conemaugh, The. John Eliot Bowen. PAH
Man Who Sang the Sillies, The. John Ciardi. OBCA

Man who saw the light hanging on the tall end, The. The Borrower of Salt. Oscar Williams. *Fr.* Variations on a Theme. LiTA; NePA
Man who seeks one thing in life, and but one, The. One Thing. "Owen Meredith." WBLP
Man who sold his lawn to standard oil, The. The War against the Trees. Stanley Kunitz. HAP; NoAM; PAI; PPON
Man Who Thinks He Can, The. Walter D. Wintle. *See* Thinking.
Man Who Thought He Was a Horse, The. Thomas Hornsby Ferril. NePoAm-2
Man who told the hawk, The. Much of Me. Chuck Eggerth. AMV-80
Man who with undaunted toils, The. The Elephant and the Bookseller. John Gay. LoBV
Man who would woo a fair maid, A. W. S. Gilbert. *Fr.* The Yeomen of the Guard. FaBoUs
Man whom many held for wise, A. Memo. Hans Sahl, *tr. by* Edouard Roditi. VWA
Man Whom Men Deplore, A. Alfred Kreymborg. HBMV
Man Whom the Sea Kept Awake, The. Robert Bly. NePoEA
Man whose height his fear improved he, The. Medgar Evers. Gwendolyn Brooks. NoP; PoBA
Man whose name was Johnny Sands, A. Johnny Sands. *Unknown.* CoMu; OBET; ViBoFo
Man with a leaf in his head, A. The Mulch. Stanley Kunitz. GP
Man with a Little Pleated Piano, A. Winifred Welles. FaPON
Man with a marvelous mug, A. A Ballad in "G." Eugene Fitch Ware. PoLF
Man with a scythe: the torrent of his swing. Gardens No Emblems. Donald Davie. LiTM; NePoEA-2; OAEL-2
Man with a thousand hearts, The. Image-Nation 13 (the Telephone). Robin Blaser. PoM
Man with his burning soul. Truth. John Masefield. WGRP
Man with his lion under the shed of wars, The. The Song of the Borderguard. Robert Duncan. NeAP; PoM
Man with One Small Hand. P. K. Page. MoCV; OBCV
Man with the blood in his sight, The. To Strike for Night. Lebert Bethune. NBP
Man with the Blue Guitar, The. Wallace Stevens. LiTA
Sels.
"I cannot bring a world quite round," II. CMoP
"Man bent over his guitar, The," I. CMoP; NoAM
"Tom-tom, c'est moi. The blue guitar," XII. CMoP
"Tune beyond us as we are, A," VI. CMoP
Man with the camera comes, The. Reservation Special. Lew Blockcolski. VoR
Man with the Hoe, The. Edwin Markham. AA; BLPA; BLPL; EaLo; FaFP; HBV-2; LiTA; MoAmPo; OHFP; PPON; PrIm; SaC; TreF; TrGrPo; TRV; WBLP; WGRP
Man with the Hoe, The: A Reply. John Vance Cheney. AA; HBV-2
Man with the Hollow Breast, The. Tania van Zyl. PeSA
Man with the Rake, The. Christopher Morley. *Fr.* Translations from the Chinese. EvOK
Man with the red hat, The. Glazunoviana. John Ashbery. LCAP
Man with Three Friends, The. Dora Greenwell. OBVV
Man Within, The. Annemarie Ewing. NePoAm-2
Man without Sense of Direction. John Crowe Ransom. LiTM; OxBA
Man, you are at the first door. The Seven Houses. George Mackay Brown. NAs
Man you know, assured and kind, The. Almost Human. C. Day Lewis. NoAM
"Man, you too, aren't you, one of these rough followers of the criminal?" In the Servants' Quarters. Thomas Hardy. MoAB; MoBrPo
Mana Aboda. T. E. Hulme. FaBoMo
Manahatta. . ./ A lovely name, he thought, and a lovely island. Early Dutch. Jennie M. Palen. GoYe
Manassas. Catherine M. Warfield. PAH
Manatee, The. Carey Blyton. AmMo
Manchester by Night. Mathilde Blind. SBG
Manchester Ship Canal, The ("I sing a theme deserving praise"). *Unknown.* OBET
Manchester Ship Canal, The ("Oh the SS *Irwell* left this port the stormy sea to cross"). *Unknown.* OBET
Manchouli. William Empson. CoBMV
Manciple's Tale, The, *sels.* Chaucer. *Fr.* The Canterbury Tales.
Controlling the Tongue. OxBChV
Lat Take a Cat. ChTr
(Mice before Milk.) PCat
Mandalay. Kipling. BrPo; FaBV; FPL; HBV-2; LiTB; MoBrPo; NOBE; TreF; TrGrPo
Mandarin/ in a silent film. The Yellow Bird. James W. Thompson. PoBA
Mandelstam. Richard Burns. VWA
Mandelstam. David Young. AmPA
Mandoline. Paul Verlaine, *tr. fr. French by* Arthur Symons. AWP; OBMV
Mandrake Hert, The. Sydney Goodsir Smith. OxBS
Mandrakes for Supper. James K. Baxter. OxBC
Mandrake's Song. Thomas Lovell Beddoes. *Fr.* Death's Jest Book. NBM
Mandrill, The. Conrad Aiken. RHPC
Manerathiak's Song. *Unknown, tr. fr. Eskimo by* Raymond De Coccola *and* Paul King. WHW
Manerly Margery Mylk and Ale. John Skelton. AAS
(Mannerly Margery Milk and Ale.) FaBoNo; NoP
Manfred: A Dramatic Poem. Byron. EnRP
Sels.
"By thy cold breast and serpent smile," *fr.* I, i. DBV
Incantation, An, *fr.* I, i. OBRV
"Stars are forth, the moon above the tops, The," *fr.* III, iv. OAEL-2
Mango on the Mango Tree, The. Robert Penn Warren. Mexico Is a Foreign Country: Four Studies in Naturalism, IV. NoAM
Mango Tree, The. Eric Chock. BrSi
Mangoes grow in clusters, The. So Close Should Be Our Love. *Gond Oral Tradition, tr. by* V. Elwin *and* S. Hivale. WTO
Manhattan. Morris Abel Beer. AmFN
Manhattan. Lorenz Hart. OBAL
Manhattan. H. R. Hays. EAS
Manhattan. Osbert Lancaster. *Fr.* Afternoons with Baedeker. NOBL
Manhattan is no island, it. Under. George Bowering. NeAC
Manhattan Lullaby. Rachel Field. AmFN
Manhattan Menagerie. Joseph Cherwinski. GoYe
Manhole Covers. Karl Shapiro. AmFN; GoJo; GP; NCSH
Manhood. Oliver Wendell Holmes. *Fr.* Wind-Clouds and Star-Drifts. AP
Manhood. Sir Thomas More. EnRePo
Manhood End. Anthony Thwaite. NMP
Maniac, The. Thomas Russell. OBEC
MANICdepressant. Kim Dammers. POL
Manichaeans, The. Gary Snyder. VGW
Manicheans did no idols make, The. Caelica, LXXXIX. Fulke Greville. NOCV
Manifest Destiny. Anita Endrezze Probst. CDW
Manifesto. Paris Leary. CoPo
Manifesto, *sel.* Nicanor Parra, *tr. fr. Spanish by* Miller Williams.
I Move the Meeting Be Adjourned. HoPM
Manifesto of the Soldier Who Went Back to War. Angel Miguel Queremel, *tr. fr. Spanish by* Donald Devenish Walsh. WaaP
Manila. Eugene Fitch Ware. FiBHP; InMe; PV; YaD
Manila Bay. Arthur Hale. PAH
Manitou. Ron Ikan. PPJ
Mankend I cale. Christ Calls Man Home. *Unknown.* MeEL
Mankind Is Sick. Thomas Traherne. *Fr.* Christian Ethics. OxBoCh
Manless Society, The. Pierre Unik, *tr. fr. French by* David Gascoyne. EAS
Manlet, The. "Lewis Carroll." BXAP; Par
(Little Man That Had a Little Gun, The.) FaBoNo
Manly Diversion. Karl Kopp. GP
Manly Heart, The. George Wither. *See* Shall I, Wasting in Despair.
Manly Man, The. *Unknown.* BLPA; WBLP
Mannahatta. Walt Whitman. AA; EyDe; GOA; HBV-2; MoAmPo; NYP
Mannequins. Daniel Mark Epstein. MAYP
Manner of a Poet's Germination, The. José Garcia Villa. PP
Manner of her death was thus, The. *Unknown.* WhC
Mannerly Margery Milk and Ale. John Skelton. *See* Manerly Margery Mylk and Ale.
Manners [for a Child of 1918]. Elizabeth Bishop. CTBA; NCSH; OxBC
Manners. Edith Marcombe Shiffert. WPE
Manners. Mariana Griswold Van Rensselaer. FaPON; HBMV; HBVY; RHPC
Manners at Table When Away from Home. *Unknown.* OxBChV
Manners in the dining-room. *Unknown.* OxNR
Manoeuvre, The. William Carlos Williams. PCP
Manomin. Phyllis Wolf. STE
Manong Benny. Virginia Cerenio. BrSi
Manong Federico Delos Reyes and his Golden Banjo. Al Robles. BrSi
Manong Jacinto Santo Tomas. Al Robles. BrSi
Manor Farm, The. Edward Thomas. SeCeV
Manor Garden, The. Sylvia Plath. LCAP
Manor Lord, The. George Houghton. AA
Manor Water. *Unknown.* GBP
Manos Karastefanís. James Merrill. TAP
Man's a Man for A' That, A. Burns. *See* For A' That and A' That.
"Man's a man, A," says Robert Burns. For A' That and A' That. *Unknown.* BXAP
Man's Amazement. *Unknown.* CoMu
Man's and woman's bodies lay without souls. A Childish Prank. Ted Hughes. OAEL-2; OxBC
Man's Anxious, but Ineffectual Guard against Death. Thomas Lovell Beddoes. ChER

Man's been pitying himself all Sunday long, The. The Apron. Stuart Friebert. FiCP
Man's Bread, A. Josephine Preston Peabody. YeAr
Man's Days. Eden Phillpotts. HBV-2; OBEV; OBVV; OxBTC
Man's dead, The. The Edward Hopper Retrospective. Edward Quagliano. PoDr
Man's Dying-Place Uncertain. Robert Herrick. CaPo
Mans Fall, and Recovery. Henry Vaughan. AnAnS-1
Man's Going Hence. Samuel Rogers. *Fr.* Human Life. OBNC
Man's ingress into the world is naked and bare. A Brief Sermon. *Unknown.* TreFS
Man's Inhumanity to Man. Burns. BLPA; FaFP
Man's inhumanity to man is hard. Inverse Ratio. *Unknown.* WhC
Man's Life. William Hammond. OBS
Man's life is death. Yet Christ endured to live. Wednesday in Holy Week. Christina Rossetti. PGD; TrCP
Man's life is laid in the loom of time. The Loom of Time. *Unknown.* BLPA
Man's life is like a rose, that in the spring. Meditation 9. Philip Pain. NOBA
Man's life is well compared to a feast. A Comparison of the Life of Man. Richard Barnfield. OBSC
Man's life was once a span; now one of those. Man's Life. William Hammond. OBS
Man's life's a tragedy: his mother's womb. De Morte. Sir Henry Wotton. OBS
Man's Littleness in Presence of the Stars. Henry Kirke White. WBLP
Man's love is of man's life a thing apart. Byron. *Fr.* Don Juan, I. TreF
Man's Medley. George Herbert. ViBoPo
Man's Mortality. *At. to* Simon Wastello. *Fr.* Microbiblion. FaBoCh; HBV-2; WBLP. *See also* Has Ego Versiculos, *sl. diff. vers. by* Francis Quarles, *fr.* Argalus and Parthenia.
(Verses of Man's Mortalitie.) OBS
Man's Need, A. *Gond Oral Tradition, tr. by* V. Elwin *and* S. Hivale. WTO
Man's no bigger than the way he treats his fellow man, The. Measuring a Man. *Unknown.* STF
Man's parts tell us such a lot, A! Parts. Zishe Landau, *tr. by* Ruth Whitman. VWA
Man's Pillow. Irving Browne. AA
Man's Prayer, The. T. A Daly. TrPWD
Mans restlesse soule hath restlesse eyes and ears. Roger Williams. SCAP
Man's Sliding Mood, A. "E." CBAP
Man's Way. L. A. G. Strong. HBMV
Man's Woman, A. Mary Carolyn Davies. PoLF
Man's World Dissolving. Derek Butler. LFAC
Manservants on the last trains. North to Milwaukee. Gerald Vizenor. VoR
Mansion stood apart in its own ground, The. James Thomson ("B. V."). The City of Dreadful Night, X. BSV
Mantelpiece of Shells, A. Ruthven Todd. NYBP
Mantis. David McCord. OBAL
"Mantis." Louis Zukofsky. PoA
Mantis Friend, The. Vincent McHugh. NePoAm-2
Mantis with translucent grin, The. Confrontation. John Hart. POL
Mantle. William Heyen. MAYP
Mantle of Mary, The. Patrick O'Connor. ISi
Mantle So Green, The. *Unknown.* AmFP
Mantova. James Wright. LCAP; NNaP
Manual, The. Larry Rubin. GP
Manuelzinho. Elizabeth Bishop. NYBP
Manufactured Gods. Carl Sandburg. WGRP
Manuscripts of God, The. Longfellow. TRV
Many a curious mortal have I seen. The Aquarium, San Francisco. V. Sackville-West. SBG
Many a fairer face than yours. To a Lady. Franklin P. Adams. FiBHP
Many a flower have I seen blossom. Gibberish. Mary Elizabeth Coleridge. MoVE
Many a green isle needs must be. Lines Written among the Euganean Hills. Shelley. EnRP; GTBS; GTBS-P; PoEL-4
Many a hearth upon our dark globe sighs after many a vanish'd face. Vastness. Tennyson. VLP
Many a lip is gaping for drink. Eliza Cook. *Fr.* Song of the Seaweed. FiBHP
Many a long, long year ago. The Alarmed Skipper [*or* The Nantucket Skipper]. James T. Fields. AmSS; EtS; HBV-2; YaD
Many a Long Year. *Unknown.* PoPle
Many a Mickle. Walter de la Mare. FaBV
Many a summer is dead and buried, A. Spirits Everywhere. Ludwig Uhland, *tr. by* James Clarence Mangan. AWP
Many a time your arms 'round me would cling. The Teasing Lovers. Horace, *tr. by* Louis Untermeyer. Odes, III, 9. UnTE
Many and sharp the numerous ills. Man's Inhumanity to Man. Burns. BLPA; FaFP
Many Are Called. E. A. Robinson. MoVE; OxBA
Many are praised, and some are fair. In Spain: Drinking Song. Emily Lawless. AnIV
Many are the deceivers. Little Red-Riding Hood. Anne Sexton. DFT
Many are the doors of the spirit that lead. Doors of the Temple. Aldous Huxley. HBMV
Many are the joys. Intimations of Sublimity. Wordsworth. *Fr.* The Prelude, II. OBNC
Many are the sayings of the wise. The Ways of God to Men. Milton. *Fr.* Samson Agonistes. OBS; SeCeV
Many are the wand-bearers. Evoe! Edith M. Thomas. HBV-2
Many are the ways and many the recipes. Recipe: Hare. Archestratus. FaBoUs
Many as noticed by the one, The. De Imagine Mundi. John Ashbery. FaBoMo
Many Birds. Anne Welsh. PeSA
Many days of sorrow, many nights of woe. Chain Gang Blues. *Unknown.* WTO
Many desire, but few or none deserve. The Advice. Sir Walter Ralegh. AAS; NCEP; SiPS
Many Die Here. Gayl Jones. BlSi
Many Happy Returns. W. H. Auden. NAs
Many hundred years ago. Noah's Carpenters. *Unknown.* STF
Many in aftertimes will say of you. Christina Rossetti. Monna Innominata, XI. OBNC; ViBoPo
Many Indeed Must Perish in the Keel. Hugo von Hofmannsthal, *tr. fr. German by* Jethro Bithell. AWP; TrJP
Many ingenious lovely things are gone. Nineteen Hundred and Nineteen. W. B. Yeats. BIrV; LiTB; MasP; MoAB; MoPo
Many liberals don't just. Respectabilities. Jon Silkin. NePoEA-2; NoAM
Many little cuss words, bother, dash and blow. *Unknown.* FaBoUs
Many love music but for music's sake. On Music. Walter Savage Landor. GoJo; HBV-2
Many-maned scud-thumper, tub. Winter Ocean. John Updike. ELU; InPK; MOS; PAI; SoSe
Many men of many minds. *Unknown.* WhC
Many paths lead. Paths to God. Musa Moris Farhi. VWA
Many people have been frighted & died in cemeteries. My Gang. Jack Kerouac. PoM
Many people have gathered together. Foot Race Song. *Unknown, tr. by* Frank Russell. NU; OBVE
Many people seem to think. Nonsense Quatrains [*or* Parisian Nectar]. Gelett Burgess. CenHV; FaBoNo
Many poems may be composed upon the same theme. Praising the Poets of That Country. Howard Nemerov. PP; TwAmPo
Many red devils ran from my heart. The Black Riders, XLVI. Stephen Crane. TAP
Many shapes of wings. Environs. Larry Eigner. NeAP
Many things I might have said today. Aprons of Silence. Carl Sandburg. NoAM; NOBA
Many Things Thou Hast Given Me, Dear Heart. Alice Wellington Rollins. AA
Many Thousand Gone. *Unknown.* *See* No More Auction Block.
Many times a last time I will look. Harmless Streets. Tess Gallagher. LTB
Many times the size of man. The Horse. Francis Ponge, *tr. by* Beth Archer. NU
Many trees can stand unshaded. Trees and Cattle. James Dickey. NePoEA-2
Many weary weeks divide me. The Ship's Cook, a Captive Sings. Hugo von Hofmannsthal, *tr. by* Charles Wharton Stork. TrJP
Many were happy. Fresh News from the Past. Marvin Bell. LCAP
Many Wings. Isabel Fiske Conant. HBMV
Many without Elegy. W. S. Graham. OxBS
Many women call on me to sleep with them. A Mourning-Song for Rangiaho. Te Heuheu Herea, *tr. by* Barry Mitcalfe. WTO
Many Workmen. Stephen Crane. The Black Riders, XXXI. LiTA; NePA; TAP
Many years ago my mother and I skated. My Grandmother and the Voice of Tolstoy. Steve Orlen. AMV-81
Many years back was an evening. Then and Now. Anne B. Murray. PoSH
Manyo Shu, *sels.* *Var. authors, tr. fr. Japanese by* Arthur Waley. AWP
"Because he is young." Okura.
"By way of pretext." Yakamochi.
"Dress that my brother has put on is thin, The." Lady Otomo of Sakanoe.
"For my sister's sake." Hitomaro.
"How will you manage." Princess Daihaku.
"I wish I could lend a coat." Akahito.
"May the men who are born." Hitomaro.

"Men of valor, The." Akahito.
"My heart, thinking." Lady Otomo of Sakanoe.
"O boy cutting grass." Hitomaro.
"O pine-tree standing." Hakutsu.
"On the moor of Kasuga." Hitomaro.
"On the shore of Nawa." Hioki no Ko-okima.
"Plum-blossom, The." Akahito.
River of Heaven, The. *Unknown, tr. by* Lafcadio Hearn.
"Shall we make love." *Unknown.*
"Unknown love." Lady Otomo Sakanoe. AWP; PBWP
("Unknown love/ is bitter," *tr. by* Willis Barnstone.) BoWoP; LLLT
"What am I to do with my sister?" Prince Yuhara.
"When evening comes." Yakamochi.
Manzanita, The. Yvor Winters. VGW
Manzini; Escape Artist. Gwendolyn MacEwen. NOBC
Maori Girl's Song, A. Alfred Domett. OBVV
Map, The. Elizabeth Bishop. NOBA
Map, The. Gloria C. Oden. AmNP; NNP; PoNe
Map, The. Gary Soto. MAYP
Map, The. Mark Strand. NYBP
Map, The/ takes me back. Passover. Rose Ausländer, *tr. by* Ewald Osers. VWA
Map of Mock-Begger Hall, The. *Unknown.* CoMu
Map of Montana in Italy, A. Richard Hugo. LCAP
Map of My Country. John Holmes. AmFN; MiAP
Map of Places, The. Laura Riding. LiTA; NoAM
Map of the Western Part of the County of Essex in England, A. Denise Levertov. ConAP; CoAP
Map of Verona, A. Henry Reed. ChMP
Map Reading. David Citino. AMV-81
Map Reference T994724. John Pudney. WaP
Map shows me where it is you are, The. A Private Letter to Brazil. Gloria C. Oden. AmNP; NNP; PoNe
Maple and Sumach. C. Day Lewis. CoBMV; FaBoMo
Maple buds are red, are red, The. A Song of Waking. Katharine Lee Bates. OHIP
Maple buds were blossoming reddish tufts, The. The Grotto. Ray Fraser. NeAC
Maple Feast. Frances Frost. RHPC; SiSoSe
Maple is a dainty maid, The. Autumn Fancies. *Unknown.* FaPON
Maple Leaf Rag, *with music.* Sydney Brown. BLSo
Maple Leaves. Thomas Bailey Aldrich. GN
(October.) RHPC
Maple Leaves. Shiko, *tr. fr. Japanese by* Harold G. Henderson. SoPo
Maple owned that she was tired, The. Autumn Fashions. Edith M. Thomas. YeAr
Maples. Philip Appleman. BXAP
Maples flare among the spruces, The. Harvest Home. Arthur Guiterman. RHPC; YeAr
Maples have turned, The. Fire snaps on my tongue. On a Recent Protest against Social Conditions. David Posner. NYBP
Mapmaker on His Art, The. Howard Nemerov. NYBP
Mappemounde. Earle Birney. OBCV; PeCV
Maps. Robert Hass. NPGG
Maps. Dorothy Brown Thompson. RHPC; TiPo
Maps for a Son Are Drawn as You Go. Samuel Hazo. AMV-81
Maps to Nowhere. David Rosenberg. VWA
Maquillage. Arthur Symons. VLP
Maratea Porto: Saying Goodbye to the Vitolos. Richard Hugo. MAT
Marathon Runner, The. Fenton Johnson. CDC
Marban, a Hermit Speaks. *Unknown, tr. fr. Irish by* Michael Hartnett. BIrV; CIP
Marble mausoleum solemnly holds the rich, A. Quatrains. Salah Jahin, *tr. by* Samir M. Zoghby. TTY
Marble Statuette Harpist. Sara Van Alstyne Allen. GoYe
Marble-streeted Town, The. Thomas Hardy. FaBoPP
Marble-Top. E. B. White. FiBHP; OBAL; WhC
Marble, weepe, for thou dost cover. On Margaret Ratcliffe. Ben Jonson. SeCP
Marceline, to Her Husband. Elizabeth Libbey. AmPA
Marcellus. Virgil, *tr. fr. Latin by* Dryden. *Fr.* The Aeneid, VI. OBS
March. Bryant. GN
March. Elizabeth J. Coatsworth. PDV; RHPC; YeAr
March. Hart Crane. BoNaP
March. Emily Dickinson. *See* Dear March, come in!
March. William Everson. ErPo
March. Arthur Guiterman. YeAr
March. Nora Hopper. HBV-1
March. A. E. Housman. FaBoCh
March ("He ended; and midst those who heard were some"). William Morris. *Fr.* The Earthly Paradise. VLP
March ("Slayer of winter, art thou here again?"). William Morris. HBV-1
March, The. J. C. Squire. HBMV; OHIP; PoSC
March. *Unknown.* GBP
March. Charles Henry Webb. AA
March. William Carlos Williams. NCSH
March Bee, The. Edmund Blunden. PoPle
March Calf, A. Ted Hughes. NoP
March Evening. L. A. G. Strong. MoBrPo
March 1st. Kathleen Spivack. NYBP
March 4th Anno 1698/9; a Charracteristicall Satyre. John Saffin. *See* Satyretericall Charracter of a Proud Upstart, A.
March Hares. Walter de la Mare. FaBoNo
March Hares. Andrew Young. MoVE
March has come in roaring. Spring and All. Grace Bauer. PPJ
March has come to the bridge head. Poem by the Bridge at Ten-shin. Li Po, *tr. by* Ezra Pound. OBVE
March in the Ranks Hard-Prest, and the Road Unknown, A. Walt Whitman. AmPP; OxBA; PAI
March into Virginia, The. Herman Melville. AP; BLPL; HAP; LiTA; NoP; TAP; TrGrPo; ViBoPo; WaaP
March Light. Ralph J. Mills, Jr. AMV-81
March, March, Ettrick and Teviotdale. Sir Walter Scott. *See* Border Ballad.
March, march, head erect. Mother Goose. OxNR
March! March! March! from sunrise till it's dark. The Marching Song of Stark's Men. Edward Everett Hale. PAH
March, May, July, October; these are they. The Roman Calendar. Benjamin Hall Kennedy. FaBoUs
March, 1941. Paul Goodman. LiTA
March of Humanity, The. J. Corson Miller. HBMV
March of the Three Kings. *Unknown, tr. fr.* French. OHIP
March of the Women, The. Cicely Hamilton. BrRo
March 1, The. Robert Lowell. NoP
March said to Averil. The Borrowing Days. *Unknown.* GBP
March Snow. Don McKay. NOBC
March. . .someone has walked across the snow. Vacancy in the Park. Wallace Stevens. LCAP
March Sound. Harry Thurston. AMV-81
March 10th and the snow flees like eloping brides. May You Always Be the Darling of Fortune. Jane Miller. AMV-80
March the 3rd. Edward Thomas. NAs
March Thoughts from England. Margaret L. Woods. OBVV
March to Moscow, The. Robert Southey. FaBoCo
March 23, 1982; Tuesday Night. Thomas Waltner. LFAC
March Twilight. Louise Bogan. NePoAm-2
March 2, The. Robert Lowell. NoP
March, Upstate. William Bronk. NYBP
March Weather. Jon Swan. NYBP
March went out like a lion. June Is Bustin' Out All Over. Oscar Hammerstein II. BLSo
March Wind, The. *Unknown.* RHPC
March Wind. Maud E. Uschold. YeAr
March Winds, The. George Washington Wright Houghton. YeAr
March Winds. Cecil Francis Lloyd. CaP
March winds and April showers. Weather Wisdom. *Unknown.* FaBoBe; HBV-1; HBVY; OxNR; SoPo; TreF
March with All Drums Muffled, A. Reuel Denney. NYP
March with his wind hath struck a cedar tall. On Queen Anne's Death. *Unknown.* ElL
March yeans the lammie. March. *Unknown.* GBP
Marchant was ther with a forked berd, A. Chaucer. *Fr.* The Canterbury Tales: Prologue. CTC, *abr.*; ViBoPo
Märchen, The (Grimm's Tales). Randall Jarrell. CMoP; DFT, *abr.*
Märchenbilder. John Ashbery. LCAP; NOBA
Marches Now the War Is Over. Walt Whitman. *See* By Blue Ontario's Shore.
Marches of Glynn, The. Sidney Lanier. PrIm
Marching. Isaac Rosenberg. BrPo
Marching Along. Robert Browning. Cavalier Tunes, I. HBV-2; OAEP
Marching 'round the Levee. *Unknown.* AmFP
Marching Song. Dana Burnet. PAH
Marching Song. Robert Louis Stevenson. FaPON; TiPo
Marching Song of Stark's Men, The. Edward Everett Hale. PAH
Marching through Georgia. Henry Clay Work. FaPoR; FSW; PAH; PSoN, *with music*
Marching to Pretoria. *Unknown.* FSW
Marching to Quebec. *Unknown.* AmFP
Marching to Utah. *Unknown.* AmFP
Marcia and I went over the curve. Millions of Strawberries. Genevieve Taggard. FaPON; MoShBr; TiPo
Marcia Thompane was light and compact. Dancing School. Jonathan Holden. Psk
Marco Bozzaris. Fitz-Greene Halleck. AA; BeLS; GN; HBV-2; TreF; WBLP

"At midnight, in his guarded tent," *sel.* HoPM
Marcus Antoninus Cui Cognomen Erat Aurelius. Burns Singer. OxBS
Marcus Argentarius. Kenneth Rexroth. CrMA
Marcus Aurelius. C. H. Sisson. OxBC
Marcus Curtius. Oliver St. John Gogarty. OBMV
Mardi Gras. Miller Williams. TAT
Mardi Gras / Grandmothers—Portrait in Red and Black Crayon. James Nolan. Str
Mare, The. Herbert Asquith. PH
Mare, A. Kate Barnes. NYBP; PH
Mare. Judith Thurman. PH
Mare Liberum. Henry van Dyke. PAH
Mare Nostrum. Joel Oppenheimer. NeAP
Mare roamed soft about the slope, The. Orchard. Ruth Stone. PH; TwAmPo
Mares of Night. Virginia Long. AMV-81
Mares of the Camargue, The. Frédéric Mistral, *tr. fr. Provençal by* George Meredith. *Fr.* Mirèio. AWP; PoPl
Marezle toats. *Unknown.* FaBoNo
Margaret. Charles Cotton. *See* Resolution in Four Sonnets . . . Concerning Four Rural Sisters.
Margaret and Dora. Thomas Campbell. HBV-1
Margaret Are You Drug. George Starbuck. MAT
Margaret, are you grieving. Spring and Fall [To a Young Child]. Gerard Manley Hopkins. BiP; BrPo; ChTr; CMoP; EBEV; ELP; FaBoUs; FF; GoJo; GTBS-P; HAP; HeIP; HoPM; InPK; InPS; LiTB; LiTM; MAT; MoAB; MoPo; MoVE; NIP; NOBE; NoP; OAEP; PAI; PoEL-5; PoPl; PoPle; PPoe; PPON; PPP; SCV; SeCeV; SOTW; TEP; VLP; WeW
Margaret Fuller. Amos Bronson Alcott. AA
Margaret Grady—I fear she will burn. The Witch. Katharine Tynan. OnYI
Margaret Love Peacock [for Her Tombstone, 1826]. Thomas Love Peacock. OBNC; OBRV
Margaret mentioned Indians. Indians. John Fandel. AmFN; NYBP
Margaret my sweetest, Margaret I must go. The Souldiers Farewel to His Love. *Unknown.* CoMu
Margaret of humbler stature by the head. Margaret. Charles Cotton. TrGrPo; UnTE
Margaret, Seen through a Picture Window. Judy Grahn. *Fr.* The Common Woman, VI. GP
Margaret to Dolcino. Charles Kingsley. HBV-1
Margaret's beauteous—Grecian arts. Margaret and Dora. Thomas Campbell. HBV-1
Margarita first possest [*or* possessed]. The Chronicle; a Ballad. Abraham Cowley. GoTL; SeCV-1; ViBoPo
Margaritae Sorori [I. M.]. W. E. Henley. Echoes, XXXV. MoBrPo;NOBE; OBEV; OBNC; OBVV; TrGrPo; WGRP; WHAT
(In Memoriam: Margaritae Sorori.) TreFT
(Late Lark, A.) PORA
(Late Lark Twitters from the Quiet Skies, A.) HBV-2
(So Be My Passing.) HBVY
(Some Late Lark Singing.) TRV
Margarite of America, A, *sel.* Thomas Lodge.
Sonnet: "O shady vales, O fair enriched meads." EIL; OBSC
Margery Mutton-pie. Mother Goose. OxNR
Marginal Field, The. Stephen Spender. PoA
Marginal Music. R. K. Meiners. AMV-81
Marginalia, *sel.* W. H. Auden.
"Dead man, A/ who never caused others to die." OAEL-2
Marginalia. Richard Wilbur. CMoP; NMP; PoA
Mari Magno, *sel.* Arthur Hugh Clough.
Currente Calamo. LoBV
Maria Bright. Walther von der Vogelweide, *tr. fr. Medieval German by* Ian G. Colvin. ISi
Maria intended a letter to write. How to Write a Letter. Elizabeth Turner. MoShBr; OxBChV
Maria Wentworth [Thomæ Comitis Cleveland, Filia Præmortuæ Prima Virgineam Animam Exhalauit]. Thomas Carew. AnAnS-2; CaPo; JCP; MeLP; MePo; SeCV-1
(Inscription on the Tombe of the Lady Mary Wentworth, The.) OBS
Mariam, *sels.* Lady Elizabeth Carey.
"Fairest action of our human life, The," *fr.* IV. WPE
" 'Tis not enough for one that is a wife," *fr.* III. WPE
Marian. George Meredith. HBV-1
Marian at the Pentecostal Meeting. Alden A. Knowlan. ELU
Marian Drury. Bliss Carman. HBV-1
Marian I cannot begrudge. Marian at the Pentecostal Meeting. Alden A. Knowlan. ELU
Mariana. Tennyson. AWP; BiP; CH; ChER; HBV-1; InPS; NOBE; NoP; OAEL-2; OAEP; OBEV; OBNC; OBRV; OBVV; PoEL-5; PoPle; TEP; TrGrPo; UnPo; ViBoPo; VLP; WiR
Mariana in the South. Tennyson. VLP
Marianne, Madeline, Alys. Three Little Girls. Richard Aldington. BrPo
Marianne Moore (1887-1972). Raymond Roseliep. SOTS
Marie Curie Contemplating the Role of Women Scientists in the Glow of a Beaker. Robert Frazier. SUW
Marie Hamilton. *Unknown. See* Mary Hamilton.
Marie Magdalene. George Herbert. AnAnS-1
Marie Magdalens Complaint at Christs Death. Robert Southwell. AnAnS-1; MePo
Marigold, The. William Forrest. ACP
Marigold. Richard Garnett. PCat
Marigold. John Haines. POL; PPJ
Marigold, The. George Wither. OBS
Marigolds. Robert Graves. BrPo
Marin. Philip Booth. NYBP
Marin-An. Gary Snyder. TAT
Marina. T. S. Eliot. ChMP; CMoP; FaBoMo; GTBS-P; HeIP; LiTA; MOS; NOBE; NOCV; TwAmPo
Marina's gone, and now sit I. Celadyne's Song [*or* Memory *or* So Shuts the Marigold Her Leaves]. William Browne. *Fr.* Britannia's Pastorals, III, Song 1. ChTr; HBV-1; OBS
Marine Aquarium, The. Louis Dudek. *Fr.* Atlantis. MoCV
Mariner, The. Allan Cunningham. EtS
Mariner, in the green spire. Land-Fall. George M. Brady. NeIP
Mariner sat on the shrouds one night, A. The Drowned Mariner. Longfellow. AA
Mariner that on smooth waves doth glide, The. Anne Bradstreet. *Fr.* Contemplations. WPOW
Mariner, what of the deep? Deep Sea Soundings. Sarah Williams. EtS; WGRP
Mariners. David Morton. EtS
Mariners, The. Margaret L. Woods. OBVV
Mariners' Carol. W. S. Merwin. EaLo
Mariner's Dream, The. William Dimond. BeLS; HBV-1
Mariners sleep by the sea, The. The Mariners. Margaret L. Woods. OBVV
Mariners' Song. Thomas Lovell Beddoes. *See* To Sea, to Sea!
Mariner's Song, The. Sir John Davies. OBSC
Mariner's Wife, The. William Julius Mickle. *See* Sailor's Wife, The.
Marines' Hymn, The. *Unknown, wr. at. to* L. Z. Phillips. BLSo, *with music*; TreF; YaD
(Marines' Song.) PAL
Marionettes, The. Walter de la Mare. MMA
Mariposa Lily, The. Ina Coolbrith. AA; BPAW
Maritae Suae. William Philpot. OBEV; OBVV
Marital Tragedy. Keith Preston. WhC
Maritimes. Penelope Shuttle. BrRo
Marjorie's Almanac. Thomas Bailey Aldrich. FaPON
Mark. Bible, *N.T. See* St. Mark.
Mark, The. Louise Bogan. MoPo; MoVE
Mark. Ernest McGaffey. AA
Mark Anderson. W. W. Gibson. MMA
Mark Anthony [*or* Antony]. John Cleveland. AnAnS-2; InvP; OAEL-1; SeCP; ViBoPo
(Whenas the Nightingale.) UnTE
Mark Anthony would now rouse fears. Transplantitis. Lester A. Sobel. QQQ
Mark Antony Addresses the Mob. Shakespeare. *See* Antony's Oration.
Mark Antony's Lament. Shakespeare. *Fr.* Julis Caesar, III, i. TreFS
Mark [*or* Marke] but this flea, and mark[e] in this. The Flea. John Donne. AnAnS-1; BiP; BLPL; BoLoP; CABA; EBEV; FF; FM; HoPM; JCP; LiTB; MAT; MePo; NIP; OAEL-1; PAI; PoPle; PPoe; SCV; SeCP; SeCV-1; SoSe; TEP; TrGrPo
Mark [*or* Marke] how the bashful[l] morn[e] in vain[e]. Boldness[e] in Love. Thomas Carew. AnAnS-1; CaPo; ErPo; MePo; SeCV-1; UnTE
Mark how the feathered tenants of the flood. Water Fowl. Wordsworth. FM
Mark how the lanterns cloud mine eyes! A Non Sequitor. Richard Corbet. FaBoNo
Mark how the lark and linnet sing. Dryden. *Fr.* An Ode on the Death of Mr. Henry Purcell. PBBP
Mark [*or* Marke] how yon[d] eddy steal[e]s away. To My Mistress [*or* Mistris] Sitting by a River's Side: An Eddy. Thomas Carew. AnAnS-2; CaPo
Mark me how still I am!—The sound of feet. The Statue of Lorenzo de' Medici. James Ernest Nesmith. AA
Mark the dark rook, on pendent branches hung. George Canning. *Fr.* The Progress of Man. FaBoNo
Mark Van Doren. James Worley. AMV-81
Mark well my heavy doleful tale. A Carol for Twelfth Day. *Unknown.* OHIP
Mark when she smiles with amiable cheer. Amoretti, XL. Spenser. OBSC
Mark where the pressing wind shoots javelin-like. Modern Love, XLIII.

George Meredith. EnLoPo; FaBoEn; GBL; HBV-1; NBM; NOBE; OAEP; OBEV; OBNC; PoEL-5; SeCeV; TEP
Mark yon round parson, fat and sleek. Robert Lloyd. *Fr.* A Familiar Epistle to J. B. Esq. OBSV
Mark you how the peacock's eye. Fragment. Gerard Manley Hopkins. FM
Mark you the floor [*or* floore]? that square and speckled stone. The Church-Floor [*or* Floore]. George Herbert. AnAnS-1; EBEV; MeLP; OAEL-1; OBS; SeCePo; SeCeV
Marke but this flea, and marke in this. *See* Mark but this flea. . .
Marke how the bashfull morne, in vaine. *See* Mark how the bashful . . .
Marke how yond eddy steales away. *See* Mark how yon eddy . . .
Marke, when the Evenings cooler wings. To Amoret. Henry Vaughan. SeCP
Marker slants, flowerless, day's almost done, The. John Berryman. *Fr.* Dream Songs. CAPP; DiL
Market, The. Gary Snyder. *Fr.* Mountians and Rivers. CoPo
"Seventy-five feet hoed rows equals," *sel.* NaP
Market Day. Abigail Cresson. HBMV
Market Day. Mary Webb. CH
Market Economy, The. Marge Piercy. GeTw
Market Square. A. A. Milne. TiPo
Market square's admiring throngs, The. Goethe, *tr. by* John Weiss. *Fr.* West-Easterly Divan, *Bk.* 9. PeHV
Market Town, The. Francis Carlin. HBMV
Market Women's Cries. Swift. *See* Verses for Fruitwomen.
Markings. Frank Steele. Psk
Marks. Linda Pastan. NIP
Mark's Fingers. Mary O'Neill. RHPC
Marl white road, the Dorée rushing cool, The. Tales of the Islands. Derek Walcott. OxBTC
Marlborough, *sel.* Charles Hamilton Sorley.
"So, there, when sunset made the downs look new." WGRP
Marlburyes Fate. Benjamin Tompson. SCAP
Marlow and Nancy. Sandra McPherson. AmPA
Marlowe. Arthur Bayldon. PoAu-1
Marm Grayson's Guests. Mary E. Wilkins Freeman. OBCA
Marmion, *sels.* Sir Walter Scott.
Abbess, The, *fr.* II. GoBC
Battle, The ("But as they left the dark'ning heath"), *fr.* VI. ELP
Battle, The ("By this, though deep the evening fell"), *fr.* VI. PoEL-4
(Flodden.) BSV
Christmas in the Olden Time, *fr. Introd. to* VI. GoBC
(Christmas in England, *abr.*) GN
(Heap on More Wood!) OBCP
("Heap on more wood!—the wind is chill.") TiPo
(Old Christmastide.) SiSoSe
Edinburgh from the Pentland Hills, *fr.* IV. FaBoPP
"Like April morning clouds, that pass," *fr. Introd. to* III. OBRV
Lochinvar, *fr.* V. BeLS; BSV; EnRP; EvOK; FaBoBe; FaBV; FaFP; FaPON; FPL; GN; GoTS; HBV-1; NOBE; OAEP; OBNC; OBRV; OxBS; PaPo; PoRA; RoGo; TreF; WHA
(Young Lochinvar.) HBVY; OBNV
Marmion and Douglas ("Not far advanc'd was morning day"), *fr.* VI. WHA
(Battle, The.) EnRP
Marmion and Douglas ("Train from out the castle drew, The"), *fr.* VI. OHFP
Nelson, Pitt, Fox, *fr. Introd. to* I. OBEV.
"November's sky is chill and drear," *Introd. to* I. OBRV
(Ettrick Forest in November, *abr.*) FaBoPP
(November in Ettrick Forest, *abr.*) BSV
O, Woman! *fr.* I. TreFS
Song: "Where shall the lover rest," *fr.* III. NBM; OBRV; PoEL-4; ViBoPo
(Where Shall the Lover Rest.) CH, *abr.;* EnRP
"Thus while I ape the measure wild," *fr. Introd.* to III. OBRV
"When dark December glooms the day," *fr. Introd.* to V. OBRV
Marquis of Carabas, The. Robert Barnabas Brough. HBV-1
"Look at this skin—at fourscore years," *sel.* FiBHP
Marrakech. Ralph Nixon Currey. PeSA
Marrakech. Richard Eberhart. LiTM
Marrakesh Women. Lyn Lifshin. LTB
Marriage, A. Anthony Barnett. VWA
Marriage. Blake. *See* When a Man Has Married a Wife.
Marriage. Raymond Carver. GeTw
Marriage. Austin Clarke. BlrV; GTBS-P; OxBI
Marriage. Mary Elizabeth Coleridge. PeHV
Marriage. Gregory Corso. CABA; CoAP; InPS; LiTM; NeAP; NoAM; NoP; OBAL; PPP; PrIm; TAP
Marriage. Nathaniel Cotton. *See* Early Thoughts of Marriage.
Marriage, A. Robert Creeley. LiTM; NeAP
Marriage. W. W. Gibson. HBV-1
Marriage. Marea Gordett. AMV-81
Marriage. Donald Hall. NePoEA
Marriage, The. Sara Henderson Hay. DFT
Marriage, *sels.* Robert Lowell.
Ninth Month, *st.* 11. NAs
Overhanging Cloud, *st.* 14. NAs
Robert Sheridan Lowell, *st.* 13. NAs
Marriage. Marianne Moore. NOBA
Marriage. Mary Ellen Solt. BoWoP
Marriage, The. Mark Strand. EAS; NoAM
Marriage ("Here we go around this ring"). *Unknown.* AmFP
Marriage ("Put your hand in the creel"). *Unknown.* GBP
Marriage. William Carlos Williams. PoA
Marriage, The. Yvor Winters. MoVE; QFR
Marriage à la Mode, *sels.* Dryden.
Whil'st Alexis Lay Prest [*or* Press'd], *fr.* IV, ii. ErPo; FF; PrIm; UnTE
(Song: "Whilst Alexis lay pressed.") BoLoP; CavP
Why Should a Foolish Marriage Vow, *fr.* I, i. HeIP; NIP; OAEP; ViBoPo
(Song: "Why should a foolish marriage vow.") AWP; SeCV-2
Marriage and Midsummer's Night. Linda Gregg. NPGG
Marriage and Money. Sir Charles Sedley. *Fr.* The Happy Pair. OBSV
Marriage and the Care o't. Robert Lochore. HBV-1
Marriage betwixt Scrape, Monarch of the Maunders, and Blobberlips, Queen of the Gypsies, A, *sel.* Alexander Pennecuik.
"Below fair Peebles, on the river's side." NOEC
Marriage Charm, A. Nora Hopper. HBV-1
Marriage Contract. Vern Rutsala. DFF
Marriage Couplet. William Cole. OBAL
Marriage Dance, The. Eda Lou Walton, *after Blackfoot Indian.* BPAW
Marriage-Hater Match'd, The, *sel.* Thomas D'Urfey.
Brother Solon's Hunting Song, *fr.* II, i. CavP
Marriage is a lovely thing. Christine de Pisan, *tr. fr. French by* Joanna Bankier. WPOW
Marriage is not/ a house or even a tent. Habitation. Margaret Atwood. BoWoP
Marriage Morning. Tennyson. GBL
Marriage of a Virgin, The. Dylan Thomas. ErPo
Marriage of Earth and Heaven, The. Jay Macpherson. OBCV
Marriage of Heaven and Earth, The. Howard Nemerov. NYBP
Marriage of Heaven and Hell, The. Blake. EnRP; LAuP; OAEL-2
Sels.
"In seed time learn, in harvest teach, in winter enjoy." FF
Memorable Fancy, A ("An angel came to me and said"). NU
Memorable Fancy, A ("As I was walking . . ."). NU
"Pride of the peacock is the glory of God, The." FF
"Rintrah roars and shakes his fires in the burden'd air." LoBV
Voice of the Devil, The. NU
Marriage of Hector and Andromache, The. Sappho, *tr. fr. Greek by* Guy Davenport. OBVE
Marriage of Pocahontas, The. M. M. Webster. PAH
Marriage of Sir Gawain, The. *Unknown.* ESPB
Marriage of the Frog and the Mouse, The. *Unknown.* EBEV
Marriage of Two. C. Day Lewis. ChMP
Marriage on a Mountain Ridge. Stewart Conn. PoSH
Marriage Ring, A. George Crabbe. BoLoP; LO; OBEV
(His Late Wife's Wedding-Ring.) NOBE
(His Mother's Wedding Ring.) OBNC
(His Wife's Wedding Ring.) OBRV
Marriage Song. Judah Halevi, *tr. fr. Hebrew by* Alice Lucas. TrJP
Marriage, which might have been a mateship sweet. Elizabeth Wolstenholme-Elmy. *Fr.* Woman Free. BrRo
Marriage Wig, The. Ruth Whitman. IHMS
Marriages. George Crabbe. *Fr.* The Parish Register, II. FaBoUs
Marrie dear. When in Rome. Mari Evans. AmNP; SoSe
Married and Single Life. *Unknown.* AmFP
Married for one year. Making It Simple December 8, 1969. David McElroy. AmPA
Married in white, you have chosen all right. Wedding Signs. *Unknown.* TreFT
Married Lover, The. Coventry Patmore. *Fr.* The Angel in the House, II, xii. GoBC; HBV-1; OBEV; TreFT; TrGrPo; VLP
Married Man, The. Robert Phillips. GeTw
Married Man Blues. *Unknown.* BluL
Married man comes nearest to the dead, A. Samuel Butler. FaBoEE
Married Man Gonna Keep Your Secret, *with music. Unknown.* OuSiCo
Married Me a Wife, *with music. Unknown.* OuSiCo
Married to rural goldmines. The Dark Way Home: Survivors. Michael S. Harper. CNA
Married twice now, I've had two. Mothers-in-Law. Robert Sward. CoPo
Marrog, The. R. C. Scriven. AmMo; RHPC
Marrow, The. Theodore Roethke. NYBP

Marrow of My Bone. Mari Evans. BPo
Marrowbone Itch, The, *with music.* *Unknown.* OuSiCo
Marry in Lent. *Unknown.* FaBoUs
Marry in May. *Unknown.* FaBoUs
Marry Monday, marry for wealth. *Unknown.* HBV-1; HBVY; TreF
Marry the Lass? Andrew Greig. PoSH
Marrying left your maiden name disused. Maiden Name. Philip Larkin. GTBS-P
Marrying the Hangman. Margaret Atwood. NOBC
Mars and Venus. Robert Greene. *Fr.* Tullie's Love. OBSC
(Sonnet or Dittie: "Mars in a fury 'gainst love's brightest queen.") LoBV
Mars is braw in crammasy. The Bonnie Broukit Bairn. "Hugh MacDiarmid." FaBoCh; HAP; InPS
Mars, most-strong, gold-helm'd, making chariots crack. To Mars. *Unknown, tr. by* George Chapman. LoBV
Marseillaise, The [*or* La]. Claude Joseph Rouget de Lisle, *tr. fr. French.* FSW, *tr. by* Albert Morehead; HBV-2, TreFS *and* WBLP; *tr. by* Charles H. Kerr
Marsh, The. W. D. Snodgrass. BoNaP; NePoEA
Marsh, The. Marcia Southwick. MAYP
Marsh bank, lotus rank. Confucius, *tr. by* Ezra Pound. *Fr.* Songs of Ch'en. CTC
Marsh Leaf. David Wagoner. PoA
Marsh, New Year's Day, The. Peter Everwine. NNaP
Marsh Song—At Sunset. Sidney Lanier. NOBA
Marshall. George MacBeth. NoAM
Marshall, the thinges for to attayne. *See* Martial, the things for to attain.
Marshes, The. Jane Mayhall. TAP
Marshes of Glynn, The. Sidney Lanier. AA; AmPP; AP; HBV-1; LiTA; NePA; NOBA; OxBA; WGRP; WHA
Sels.
"Glooms of the live-oaks, beautiful-braided and woven." TreFT
"Oh, what is abroad in the marsh and the terminal sea?" EtS
"Ye marshes, how candid and simple and nothing-withholding and free." TRV
Marshlands. Pauline E. Johnson. NOBC
Marsiliun at Saragossa, Charles at the siege. Charles at the Siege. George Hetherington. AnIV
Marston. Stephen Spender. FaBoTw
Marsyas. Sir Charles G. D. Roberts. PeCV
Marten flew to the finch's nest, The. Feathers and Moss. Jean Ingelow. SpRo
Martha. Walter de la Mare. MoBrPo; TreFS
Martha/ Mary passed this morning. Mary Passed This Morning. Owen Dodson. PoBA
Martha Blake at Fifty-one. Austin Clarke. CIP; IPY
Martha Graham. Lyn Lifshin. LTB
Marthy Had a Baby, *with music.* *Unknown.* OuSiCo
Marthy Virginia's Hand. George Parsons Lathrop. PAH
Martial. Thomas Heyrick. CavP
Martial Cadenza. Wallace Stevens. NePA; NIP; OxBA; VGW
Martial in London. Mortimer Collins. InMe
Martial [*or* Marshall *or* My Friend], the thing[e]s that do [*or* for to] attain [*or* attayne]. The Happy Life [*or* The Means to Attain Happy Life *or* Martial's Quiet Life *or* The Things That Cause a Quiet Life]. Martial, *tr. by* Earl of Surrey. CABA; EIL; EnRePo; FaBoEE; HBV-2; NOBE; NoP; OBEV; OBSC; OBVE; SiPS; TrGrPo; ViBoPo
Martial, thou gav'st farre nobler epigrammes. To the Ghost of Martial. Ben Jonson. OAEP
Martial's Quiet Life. Martial. *See* Happy Life, The.
Martian named Harrison Harris, A. Interplanetary Limericks. Al Graham. QQQ
Martian Sends a Postcard Home, A. Craig Raine. NoP
Martin Buber in the Pub. Max Harris. PoAu-2
Martin cat long shaged of courage good, The. John Clare. FM
"Martin, I wonder who makes all the songs." Child and Boatman. Jean Ingelow. *Fr.* Songs on the Voices of Birds. FM
Martin Luther at Potsdam. Barry Pain. NA
Martin Luther King. Myra Cohn Livingston. RHPC
Martin Luther King, Jr. Gwendolyn Brooks. BOLo; CNA; PoBA
Martin sat young upon his bed. St. Martin and the Beggar. Thom Gunn. MoBS
Martin to His Man. *Unknown.* NA
("Martin said to his man.") FaBoNo
Martin's Blues. Michael S. Harper. CNA; PoBA
Martins skim the pond. When the Cows Come Down to Drink. Allen Hoey. WOLT
Martyr. "E." CBAP
Martyr, The. Natalie Flohr. PGD
Martyr, The. Herman Melville. PoEL-5; TAP; TrGrPo
Martyr and the Army, The. Jock Henderson. AMV-81
Martyr poets, The—did not tell. Emily Dickinson. EyDe
Martyr worthiest of the bleeding name, The. The True Martyr. Thomas Wade. OBVV
Martyrdom. Rufus Learsi. TrJP
Martyrdom. Richard W. Thomas. PoBA
Martyrdom of Brébeuf and Lalemant, 16 March 1649, The. E. J. Pratt. *Fr.* Brébeuf and His Brethren. NOBC; OBCV
Martyrdom of Father Campion, The. Henry Walpole. ACP; GoBC
Martyrdom of Mary, Queen of Scots, The. Robert Southwell. ACP
Martyrdom of St. Teresa, The. A. D. Hope. CBAP
Martyrdom of Two Pagans. Philip Whalen. NeAP
Martyred Democrat, The. C. J. Dennis. CBAP
Martyred Earth, The. Ewart Milne. BIrV
Martyred Saint, he lies upon his bier, A. Lincoln. Corinne Roosevelt Robinson. OHIP
Martyrs, The. Jay Macpherson. MoCV
Martyr's Death, A. Menahem ben Jacob, *tr. fr. Hebrew.* TrJP
Martyr's Mass, A. Alfred Barrett. GoBC
Martyr's Memorial. Louise Imogen Guiney. AA
Martyrs of the *Maine,* The. Rupert Hughes. PAH
Marvel, A. Carolyn Wells. OBCA
Marvel [*or* Marvaill] no more although [*or* all tho]. Fortune. Sir Thomas Wyatt. AAS; OBSC; SiPS
Marvel of Marvels. Christina Rossetti. NOBE; OBVV; OxBoCh; WGRP
Marvell! I think you'd neither seen nor smelt. Hibernia. Stuart Howard-Jones. DBV; NOBL
Marvell, still your fragrant rhyme. The Poet of Gardens. Daniel Henderson. HBMV
Marvellous Martin. Charles Harpur. CBAP
Marvell's Garden. Phyllis Webb. OBCV
Marvell's Ghost. John Ayloffe. APAS
Marvelous. Allan Kaplan. POL
Marvels. *Unknown.* OxBM
Marx the Sign Painter. Edgar Lee Masters. *Fr.* The New Spoon River. NoAM; TAP
Mary. Fray Angelico Chavez. ISi
Mary. John Clare. *See* To Mary: It Is the Evening Hour.
Mary. Robert Farren. ISi
Mary Ackerman, 1938. Diane Glancy. STE
Mary Ames. *Unknown.* NA
Mary an' Martha Jes' Gone 'Long, *with music.* *Unknown.* BoAN-2
Mary and Gabriel. Rupert Brooke. ISi
Mary and Her Child. *Unknown.* OxBoCh
Mary and Her Dead Canary. Alexander Kerr. InPK
Mary and Her Lamb. Sarah Josepha Hale. *See* Mary's Lamb.
Mary and Her Son Alone. *Unknown, at. to* James Ryman. OxBM
Mary and Martha. Annie Johnson Flint. STF
Mary and the Baby, Sweet Lamb. *Unknown.* AmFP
Mary and the Bramble. Lascelles Abercrombie. OBMV
Mary and the Lamb. Frank Dempster Sherman. InMe
Mary Ann. Joseph Tabrar. PV
Mary Ann ("It's fare thee well, my own true love"). *Unknown.* FSW
Mary Ann ("Mary Ann has gone to rest"). *Unknown.* FaBoCo
Mary Anne Lowder. *Unknown.* WhC
Mary Arnold the Female Monster. *Unknown.* GBP; OBET
Mary at the Cross. Clyde McGee. PGD
Mary Beaton's Song. Swinburne. *Fr.* Chastelard. HBV-1
Mary Booth. Thomas William Parsons. AA
Mary Complains to Other Mothers. *Unknown.* MeEl
Mary, for the love of thee. Carol: The Five Joys of the Virgin. *Unknown.* ACP; ISi
Mary Gloster, The. Kipling. BeLS
Mary Gulliver to Captain Lemuel Gulliver, *abr.* John Gay *and* Alexander Pope. OAEL-1
Mary Had a Baby. *Unknown.* FSW
(Mary Had a Baby, Yes, Lord, *with music, sl. diff. vers.*) BoAN-2
Mary had a baby. Crooked Carol. Norma Farber. POL
Mary had a little bird. The Canary. Elizabeth Turner. OxBChV
Mary had a little lamb. Mary's Lamb [*or* Mary and Her Lamb]. Sarah Josepha Hale. FaBoBe; FaFP; FaPON; HBV-1; HBVY; OBCA; OxBChV; OxNR; SoPo; TiPo; TreFS
Mary had a little lamb. The True Story of Mary and Her Little Lamb. *Unknown.* DBV
Mary Had a William Goat, *with music.* *Unknown.* AS
Mary [*or* Marie] Hamilton. *Unknown.* AmFP; BSV; ESPB (A *and* B *vers.*); FaBoBa; NoP (A *vers.*); NOBE; OAEP; OxBB, *with music*; ViBoFo, *with music*
(Queen's Marie, The.) OBEV; PoPle
Mary Hamilton's Last Goodnight. *Unknown.* ViBoFo
Mary hath born alone. Mary and Her Son Alone. *At. to* James Ryman. OxBM
Mary, Helper of Heartbreak. Margaret Widdemer. HBMV

Mary Hynes. Padraic Fallon, *after the Irish of* Anthony Raftery. AnIV; OxBI
Mary Hynes. Frank O'Connor, *after the Irish of* Anthony Raftery. KiLC
Mary! I want a lyre with other strings. To Mary Unwin [*or* Sonnet to Mrs. Unwin]. William Cowper. GTBS; GTBS-P; HBV-1; OAEP; OBEC; OBEV; TrGrPo
Mary, in a dream of love. Dialogue between Mary and Gabriel. W. H. Auden. *Fr.* For the Time Being; a Christmas Oratorio. ISi
Mary in the Silvery Tide. *Unknown.* OBET
Mary is a gentle name. Gentle Name. Selma Robinson. MoShBr
Mary is a lady bright. Nunc Gaudet Maria. *Unknown.* ISi
Mary Is with Child. *Unknown.* MeEL
Mary Jane. *Unknown.* NA
Mary laid her Child among. Carol. Norman Nicholson. NeBP; OBCP
Mary Le More. George Nugent Reynolds. OnYI
Mary Lifted from the Dead, *with music.* William Alfred. AH
Mary, long by Boss's kisses bored. Don't Look Now but Mary Is Everybody. Peter Viereck. LiTA
Mary Magdalene. Kassia, *tr. fr. Byzantine Greek by* Aliki *and* Willis Barnstone *and* Elene Kolb. BoWoP
Mary Magdalene. Leonora Speyer. HBMV
Mary Magdalene at the Door of Simon the Pharisee. Dante Gabriel Rossetti. GoBC
Mary Magdalene, that easy woman. Lent. W. R. Rodgers. AnIL; DTC; NeBP; OxBI
Mary, maiden, mild and free. A Little Song. Robert Grosseteste, *tr. by* William de Shoreham, *mod. vers. by* F. M. Capes. ISi
Mary, Mary. Anthony C. Deane. FaBoPa
Mary, Mary [*or* Mistress Mary], quite contrary. Mother Goose. FaBoBe; FaFP; HBV-1; HBVY; OxNR; SoPo; TiPo
Mary McGuire's our cook, you know. This and That. Florence Boyce Davis. FaPON
Mary Middling. Rose Fyleman. SUS
Mary Modyr, cum and see. *Unknown.* OxBoCh
Mary Morison. Burns. EnRP; GTBS; GTBS-P; HBV-1; OAEP; OBEC; OBEV; OxBS; TreFT; TrGrPo; WHA
(Song: Mary Morison.) AWP
Mary, most serenely fair. To the Sistine Madonna. Cornelia Otis Skinner. ISi
Mary, Mother of Christ. Countee Cullen. PChr
Mary, Mother of our Maker. The Annunciation. Nerses, *tr. by* W. H. Kent. ISi
Mary of Bethlehem. Mary King. ISi
Mary of Nazareth, *sel.* Abby Maria Hemenway.
Annunciation Night. ISi
Mary of the Wild Moor. *Unknown.* BaBo
Mary on Her Way to the Temple. Ruth Schaumann, *tr. fr. German by* Edwin Buers. ISi
Mary on the Silvery Tide. *Unknown.* ShS
Mary Passed This Morning. Owen Dodson. PoBA
Mary Passes. *Unknown, tr. fr. German.* ISi
Mary, Queen of Heaven. *Unknown.* MeEL
Mary, Queen of Scots. Henry Glassford Bell. BeLS; BLPA; FaBoBe
Mary Queen of Scots. Charles Tennyson Turner. HBV-2
Mary sat in the corner dreaming. In the Carpenter's Shop. Sara Teasdale. HBMV
Mary sat musing on the lamp-flame at the table. The Death of the Hired Man. Robert Frost. AmPP; CMoP; HoPM; MoAB; MoAmPo; NoP; OxBA; SeCeV; SoSe; TrGrPo
Mary Shepherdess. Marjorie Pickthall. ISi
Mary Star of the sea! Lionel Johnson. Cadgwith, III. ISi
Mary Suffers with Her Son. *Unknown.* MeEL
Mary, the Blessed Virgins name. Profit and Loss: An Elegy upon the Decease of Mrs. Mary Gerrish. John Danforth. SCAP
Mary, the Christ long slain, passed silently. Motherhood. Agnes Lee. BLPA; HBMV
Mary the Cook-Maid's Letter to Dr. Sheridan. Swift. LoBV; OnYI; OxBoLi
Mary, the maiden, walked out in the country. After the Annunciation. Eileen Duggan. ISi
Mary the Mother/ Sang to her son. A Carol. Lizette Woodworth Reese. HBMV
Mary the Mother of Jesus. The Spinner. Charles L. O'Donnell. GoBC; ISi
Mary, the mother, sits on the hill. Carol. Langdon E. Mitchell. OHIP
Mary Tired. Marjorie Pickthall. PeCV
Mary walked in the daisies. Gabriel. Willard Wattles. HBMV
Mary Was a Red Bird, *with music. Unknown.* OuSiCo
Mary was busy and hurried. Mary and Martha. Annie Johnson Flint. STF
Mary Was Watching. *Unknown, tr. fr. Czech by* Mary Cochrane Vojâcek. ISi
Mary, we hail thee, Mother and Queen compassionate. Salve Regina. *At. to* Hermanus Contractus, *tr. by* Winfred Douglas. ISi
Mary Weeps for Her Child. *Unknown.* OxBoLi
Mary went through the thorn-wood wild. Mary Passes. *Unknown.* ISi
Mary,—what melodies mingle. Mary and the Lamb. Frank Dempster Sherman. InMe
Mary, will you ever grow? Water, blessed by bishops. Song for Healing. Roberta Hill. CDW
Mary Winslow. Robert Lowell. MiAP; MoVE; PPP
Mary wore her red dress. Mary Was a Red Bird. *Unknown.* OuSiCo
Mary Wore Three Links of Chain. *Unknown. See* Hold On.
Mary Wyatt and Henry Green. *Unknown. See* Henry Green.
Marye, maide milde and fre[e]. Hymn to the Virgin [*or* A Song to Mary]. *At. to* William of Shoreham. MeEL; OxBM
Maryland Battalion, The. John Williamson Palmer. AA; HBV-2; PAH
Maryland, My Maryland! James Ryder Randall. *See* My Maryland.
Maryland Resolves. *Unknown.* PAH
Maryland Virginia Caroline. Emblems. Allen Tate. AWP; VGW
Maryland Yellow-Throat, The. Henry van Dyke. HBV-1
Mary's a Grand Old Name. George M. Cohan. BLSo, *with music*; FSN, *with music*; TreFT
Mary's Assumption. Alfred J. Barret. ISi
Mary's Baby. Shaemas O'Sheel. HBV-1; HBVY
Mary's Ghost. Thomas Hood. FiBHP
Mary's Girlhood. Dante Gabriel Rossetti. GoBC; ISi; WGRP
Mary's gone a-milking. Milking Pails. *Unknown.* CH
Mary's Lamb. Sarah Josepha Hale. FaBoBe; FaFP; FaPON; HBV-1; HBVY; OBCA; OxBChV; OxNR; SoPo; TiPo
(Mary and Her Lamb.) TreFS
Mary's Son. Lucia Trent. PGD
Mary's Song. Marion Angus. BSV
Mary's Song. Charles Causley. OBCP
Mary's Song. Sylvia Plath. CAPP; FaBoMo
Mary's Vision. *Unknown, tr. fr. Gaelic by* Eleanor Hull. ISi
Maryuma. Frank Lamont Phillips. AmNP
Masa bin an' sol' yeh O! Link o' Day. *Unknown.* TrAS
Masada. Isaac Elchanan Mozeson. AMV-81
Masai warrior is not, The. Outbreak. Bill Anderson. VGW
Masar. Walter Savage Landor. *Fr.* Gebir, V. LoBV
("Once a fair city, courted then by kings.") LOBV
Mashkin Hill. Louis Simpson. SaC
Mask, The. Elizabeth Barrett Browning. OBNC; OBVV
Mask. Elizabeth Cox. GoYe
Mask, The. Clarissa Scott Delany. CDC; PoNe
Mask, The. Patty L. Harjo. VoR
Mask, The. Irma McClaurin. BlSi
Mask, A. Milton. *See* Star That Bids the Shepherd Fold, The.
Mask. Stephen Spender. MoAB; MoBrPo
Mask and the Poem, The. Alejandra Pizarnik, *tr. fr. Spanish by* Alina Rivero. VWA
Mask-Maker. Michael Jackson. OCNZ
Mask [*or* Masque] of Anarchy, The. Shelley. EnRP
Sels.
"As I lay asleep in Italy." OBSV; SCV
"Stand ye calm and resolute." LOBV
Mask of Cupid, The. Spenser. *See* Masque of Cupid, The.
Mask of Love. Thomas Kinsella. CMoP; NMP
Mask of Mutability, The. Spenser. *Fr.* The Faerie Queene, VII, 7. OBSC
(Seasons, The.) GN
Mask of Stone. Henry Johnson. LFAC
Mask the Wearer of the Mask Wears, The. William Bronk. GP
Maske for Lydia, A. Thomas Randolph. AnAnS-2
Masked Shrew, The. Isabella Gardner. ImOP
Masks. Thomas Bailey Aldrich. AA
Masks. Elizabeth Fenton. NMM
Masks. Brian Swann. AMV-81
Masochist, The. Maxine W. Kumin. IHMS; PoA
Masochistic Tendencies. Carolyn Baxter. LFAC
Mason, The. Robert Farren. OnYI; OxBI
Mason Jar. David Steinberg. AMV-81
Masque of Anarchy, The. Shelley. *See* Mask of Anarchy, The.
Masque of Augurs, The, *sel.* Ben Jonson.
Apollo's Song. LoBV
Masque of Balliol, The. *Var. authors. See* Balliol Rhymes.
Masque of Beauty, The, *sel.* Ben Jonson.
Song: "When love at first did move." GoBC
Masque of Christmas, The. Ben Jonson. OxBoLi
Masque of Cupid, The. Spenser. *Fr.* The Faerie Queene, III, 12. NOBE; PoEL-1
(Mask of Cupid, The.) OBSC
Masque of Queens, The, *sels.* Ben Jonson.
"What our Dame bids us do." OFD; WSC

Witches' Charm, The. FaBoCh; LoBV; NOBE
(Charme.) FM
("Owl is abroad, the bat and the toad, The.") PoPle
Witches' Sabbath, The. WSC
Masque of the Gypsies, The Ben Jonson.
See Gypsies Metamorphosed, The.
Masque of the Inner Temple and Gray's Inne, The, *sels.* Francis Beaumont.
"More pleasing were these sweet delights," III. OBS
"On blessed youths, for Jove doth pause," II. OBS
"Peace and silence be the guide," V. OBS
(Three Songs, 3.) GoBC
Shake Off Your Heavy Trance, I. ELU; OBS; TrGrPo; ViBoPo
(Fit Only for Apollo.) ChTr
(Song for a Dance.) ElL; FaBoCh
(Three Songs, 1.) GoBC
"Ye [*or* We] should stay longer if we durst," IV. OBS; TrGrPo; ViBoPo
(Three Songs, 2.) GoBC
Masque of the Middle Temple and Lincoln's Inn, The, *sel.* George Chapman.
Bridal Song. ElL
Descend, Fair Sun! ElL
Masque of the Twelve Months, The, *sels.* *At. to* George Chapman.
Shine Out, Fair Sun, with All Your Heat. ChTr
(Song: "Shine out, fair sun, with all your heat.") ElL
Masque of the Virtues against Love. Mary Monck, *after the Italian of* Guarini. NOEC
Masquerade. Carolyn M. Rodgers. BlSi
Masquerader, The. Aline Kilmer. HBMV
Mass at Dawn. Roy Campbell. PeSA
Mass hysteria, wave after breaking wave. Willowware Cup. James Merrill. NoP
Mass of Love. *Unknown, tr. fr. Spanish by* Anna Pursche. PoPl
Mass was sung, and prayers were said, The. Dies Irae. Thomas of Celano, *paraphrased by* Sir Walter Scott. *Fr.* The Lay of the Last Minstrel. GoBC
Massa ob de sheepfol', De. De Dheepfol'. Sarah Prat McLean Greene. AA; HBV-2
Massachusetts Song of Liberty. *At. to* Mrs. Mercy Warren. PAH
Massacre of the Innocents, The, *sel.* Giovanni Battista Marino, *tr. fr. Italian by* Richard Crashaw.
"Yet on the other side, faine would he start." OBVE
Massacre of the Innocents, The. William Jay Smith. EaLo
Massacre of the Macpherson, The. William Edmondstoune Aytoun. BXAP; CenHV; ChTr; FaBoCo
Massada, *sel.* Yitzhak Lamdan, *tr. fr. Hebrew by* A. C. Jacobs.
"On an autumn night, lying restless, far from her broken homeland." VWA
Massa's in de Cold Cold Ground. Stephen Collins Foster. AA; TreF
Massasauga. Hamlin Garland. AA; BPAW
Massenet/ Never wrote a Mass in A. Antony Butts. FiBHP
Massive engines lift beautifully from the deck. The Teeth Mother Naked at Last. Robert Bly. NNaP
Massive gates of circumstance, The. Trifles. *Unknown.* HBV-2
Master, The. "C. G. L." ImOP
Master, The. W. S. Merwin. NePoEA
Master, The. E. A. Robinson. HBV-2; LiTA; LiTM; MoAB; MoAmPo; OHIP
Master and Boatswain. W. H. Auden. *See* Song of the Master and Boatswain.
Master and Man. Sir Henry Newbolt. OxBTC; WhC
Master and the slave go hand in hand, The. Sonnet. E. A. Robinson. PP
Master Brunetto, this my little maid. Sonnet: To Brunetto Latini. Dante, *tr. by* Dante Gabriel Rossetti. AWP
Master Charge Blues. Nikki Giovanni. OBAL
Master City, The. Rose J. Orente. GoYe
Master Francesco, I have come to thee. Petrarch. Giosuè Carducci, *tr. by* William Dudley Foulke. AWP
"Master has come over Jordan, The." Christ and the Little Ones. Julia Gill. BLPA
Master Hugues of Saxe-Gotha. Robert Browning. OAEL-2
Master I have, and I am his man. Master and Man. Mother Goose. NA; OxNR; TiPo
Master Mariner, The. George Sterling. HBV-1
Master McGrath. *Unknown.* *See* Ballad of Master McGrath, A.
Master, No Offering, *with music.* Edwin Pond Parker. AH
Master of Arts. Cosmo Monkhouse. TDH
Master of beauty, craftsman of the snowflake. Eleven Addresses to the Lord, I. John Berryman. OxBC; PAI; UnPo
Master of blood I am yours. Nocturnal Heart. Anne-Marie Kegels, *tr. by* W. S. Merwin. BoWoP
Master of discords John. The Harper. *Unknown, tr. by* Frank O'Connor. AnIL; KiLC
Master of human destinies am I! Opportunity. John James Ingalls. AA; FaFP; HBV-2; HBVY; OHFP; PoLF; TreF; WBLP; YaD
Master of Laborers, The. George Edward Day. PGD
Master of metaphor, at three. David. Walker Gibson. CrMA; NePoAm
Master of spirits! hear me: King of souls! The Darkness. Lionel Johnson. BrPo
Master-Player, The. Paul Laurence Dunbar. TRV
Master said, The: "The Fang bird does not come." A Chinese Mural. Carlos Baker. *Fr.* A Visit to the Art Gallery. EyDe
Master Singers, The. Rhys Carpenter. WGRP
Master Sky-Lark, *sels.* John Bennett.
Sky-Lark's Song, The. AA
Song of the Hunt, The. AA
Master-songs are ended, and the man, The. Walt Whitman. E. A. Robinson. NePA; OxBA
Master Spirit, The. George Chapman. *Fr.* The Conspiracy of Charles Duke of Byron, III, i. EtS
("Give me a spirit that on life's rough sea.") ViBoPo
Master stood in His garden, The. For the Master's Use [*or* The Watered Lilies]. *Unknown.* BLPA; BLRP
Master, the swabber, the boatswain and I, The. Song [*or* Stephano's Song]. Shakespeare. *Fr.* The Tempest, II, ii. DBV; FF; MOS; NOBL; PoPle; ViBoPo; WhC
Master, they say that when I seem. Prayer. C. S. Lewis. TrCP
Master, this very hour. This Very Hour. Lizette Woodworth Reese. HBMV
Master, to do great work for Thee my hand. Life-Mosaic. Frances Ridley Havergal. TrPWD
Master Weaver, The. *Unknown.* STF
Master, whose fire kindled our glad surprise. The Master. "C. G. L." ImOP
Masterful Man, The. Henry Tyrrell. PGD
Masterly lens-polisher, A. The Spectacle of Truth. John Hewitt. CIP
Masterpiece, The. Walter Malone. PGD
Masterpiece of the taxidermist's art, A. Phar Lap in the Melbourne Museum. Peter Porter. PoAu-2
Masters. Kingsley Amis. NePoEA; PoPl
Masters, The. "Laurence Hope." HBV-2
Masters, The. Margaret Widdemer. HBMV
Masters, be kind to the old house that must fall. Rockland. Julia Randall. WPE
Master's Call, The. Oswald J. Smith. STF
Master's in the Garden Again. John Crowe Ransom. AP; NoAM
Masters, in This Hall. William Morris. ChTr; FSW
Master's Invitation, The. Anson Davies Fitz Randolph. AA
Master's Touch, The. Horatius Bonar. HBV-2; TrPWD
Mastery. Sara Teasdale. HBV-2; WGRP
Mastrim; a Meditation, *sel.* Hugh Maxton.
"Halt in the desert where I have in mind, A." CIP
Matadors, The. Josephine Jacobsen. TAP
Match, The. Andrew Marvell. EBEV
Match, A. Swinburne. ELP; HBV-1; OBVV
Match, The. Henry Vaughan. AnAnS-1
Match-bark of the younger dog sets fire to, The. Table-Birds. Kenneth MacKenzie. PoAu-2
Match with the Moon, A. Dante Gabriel Rossetti. NCEP; VLP
"Mater á Dios, preserve us." With Cortez in Mexico. W. W. Campbell. PAH
Mater Amabilis. Aubrey Thomas De Vere. ISi
Mater Amabilis. Emma Lazarus. OHIP
Mater Dei. Padraic Fallon. NOCV
Mater Dei. Katharine Tynan. ISi
Mater Desiderata. Winthrop Mackworth Praed. OBVV
Mater Dolorosa. William Barnes. CH; HBV-1; OBEV
Mater Incognita. Sister Mary Benvenuta. ISi
Materia Nupcial. Pablo Neruda, *tr. fr. Spanish by* Clayton Eshleman. ErPo
Materialism. C. E. M. Joad. FaBoCo
Materialized into an Owl. Louis (LittleCoon) Oliver. STE
Maternal Despotism; or, The Rights of Infants. Richard Graves. NOEC
Maternal Earth stirs redly from beneath. Roy Campbell. The Flaming Terrapin, I. MoBrPo
Maternal Lady with the Virgin Grace. Mary Lamb. ISi
Maternity. Jean Ingelow. *Fr.* Songs of Seven. OHIP
Maternity Gown. David Holbrook. OxBTC
Math. It's deliberately solutionless. "Titus, Son of Rembrandt: 1665." Richard J. Lyons. AMV-81
Mathematical Problem, A. Samuel Taylor Coleridge. FaBoUs
Mathematician named Bath, A. Let X Equal Half. J. F. Wilson. TDH
Mathematician named Rose, A. IBM Hired Her. W. J. J. Gordon. QQQ
Mathematics. Joel Oppenheimer. CoPo
Mathematics of Encounter. Isabella Gardner. ErPo
Mathematics of Love. Michael Hamburger. NePoEA-2

Mathematics or the Gift of Tongues. Anna Hempstead Branch. ImOP
Mathmid, The. Hayyim Nahman Bialik, *tr. fr. Hebrew by* Maurice Samuel. AWP
Matilda. Hilaire Belloc. CenHV; FaBoCh; NOBE; OnMSP; OxBChV
Matilda Jane, you never look. Doll Song. "Lewis Carroll." SoPo
Matilda Maud Mackenzie frankly hadn't any chin. How a Girl Was Too Reckless of Grammar [by Far]. Guy Wetmore Carryl. FiBHP; OBAL
Matilda told such dreadful lies. Matilda. Hilaire Belloc. CenHV; FaBoCh; NOBE; OnMSP; OxBChV
Matin Pandemoniums, The. Richard Eberhart. NYBP
Matin Song. Nathaniel Field. *See* Rise, Lady Mistress, Rise.
Matin Song. Thomas Heywood. *See* Pack, Clouds, Away.
Matinal. Cilla McQueen. OCNZ
Matinees. James Merrill. NOBA; Prf
Mating Answer. Ronald Bottrall. PoA
Mating the Goats. Aliki Barnstone. AMV-81; BoWoP
Matins. Denise Levertov. AmPP; CoPo; IHMS; NoAM; NOBA
Matins—Friday. Cardinal Newman. VLP
Matins, or Morning Prayer. Robert Herrick. CaPo
Matins—Sunday. Cardinal Newman. VLP
Matisse. Edward Hirsch. PoDr
Matisse Tits. David Barker. GP
Matlock Bath. John Betjeman. NYBP
Matmiya. Mary TallMountain. TWSS
Matrimony. John Williams. NOEC
Matrix, *sel.* Dorothy Wellesley.
"Spiritual, the carnal, are one, The." OBMV
Matrix III. Ed Lipman. LFAC
Matron of Jedborough and Her Husband, The, *sel.* Wordsworth.
"More I looked, I wondered more, The." PeD
Matron well known in Montclair, A. Uncertain What to Wear. William Jay Smith. TDH
Matronita. Dennis Silk. VWA
Matt Casey formed a social club that beat the town for style. The Band Played On. John F. Palmer. BLSo; FSN; FSW; OBAL; TreF
Mattens. George Herbert. AnAnS-1; TrPWD
Matter,/ with this look. The Vow. Carl Rakosi. FAZ
Matter is palsy: the land heaving, water. From Heraclitus. Alan Dugan. PoA
Matter of Life and Death, A. Richard Aldridge. NePoAm
Matter of Life and Death, A. Anne Ridler. MP
Matter of Taste. *Unknown, tr. fr. Greek by* Louis Untermeyer. UnTE
Matter whose movement moves us all. Entropy. Theodore Spencer. ImOP
Matthew. Bible, *N.T.* *See* St. Matthew.
Matthew and Mark, and Luke and John. The New Testament. Thomas Russell. TreFS
Matthew V. 29-30. Derek Mahon. CIP
Matthew left his place of toil. Discipleship. C. O. Bales. STF
Matthew, Mark, Luke, and John/ Bless the bed that I lie on.
Before Sleeping [*or* Bed Charm *or* Prayer *or* White Paternoster]. *Unknown.* CH; FaBoCh; GBP; HBVY; OxBoLi; OxNR; TreF
Matthew, Mark, Luke, and John,/ Hold my horse till I leap on. *Unknown.* OxNR
Matthew, Mark, Luke, and John./ The Book of Acts then think upon. The New Testament. *Unknown.* FaBoUs
Matthew X. 28. Roger Wolcott. SCAP
Matthias, *sels.* Matthew Arnold.
"Cruel, but composed and bland." POL
"Rover, with the good brown head." PCat
Matty Groves. *Unknown.* FSW
Maturity. J. Elgar Owen. WaP
Mauberley. Ezra Pound. *See* Hugh Selwyn Mauberley.
Maud Tennyson. OAEP; VLP
Sels.
"But the broad light glares and beats," *fr.* Pt. II, iv. SyP
"Cold and clear-cut face, why come you so cruelly meek," Pt. I, iii. SyP
Come into the Garden, Maud, Pt. I, xxii. EBVV; FaBV; FiP; HBV-1; NOBE; OAEL-2; OBVV; PaPo; TreF
(Maud.) OBEV
(Song: "Come into the garden, Maud.") AWP
"Dead, long dead," Pt. II, v. OAEL-2; SyP
"Go not, happy day," Pt. I, xvii. EBVV; OBVV
"I have led her home, my love, my only friend," Pt. I, xviii. ChER; EBVV; ELP; FiP; PoEL-5
"I was walking a mile," Pt. I, ix. EBVV
"Is that enchanted moan only the swell," *fr.* Pt. I, xviii. SyP
"Long have I sigh'd for a calm: God grant I may find it at last!" Pt. I, ii. SyP
"Million emeralds break from the ruby-budded lime, A," Pt. I, iv. SyP
"My life has crept so long on a broken wing," Pt. III. OAEL-2; OBWP; SyP
"Oh! that 'twere possible," Pt. II, iv. BoLoP; HBV-1; NOBE; OAEL-2; OBVV
"See what a lovely shell," Pt. II, ii. BoNaP; GoJo; PoEL-5
(Shell, The.) GN
"She came to the village church," Pt. I, viii. EBVV
Sleeping House, The, *fr.* Pt. I, xiv. FaBoEn; OBNC
"There is none like her, none," *fr.* Pt. I, xviii. FaBoEn
(There Is None Like Her.) OBNC
"What is she now? My dreams are bad. She may bring me a curse," *fr.* Pt. I, i. SyP
Maud Muller. Whittier. AA; BeLS; BLPL; FaBoBe; HBV-1; OHFP; PoLF; TAP; TreF; WBLP
Maud Muller all that summer day. Mrs. Judge Jenkins (Being the Only Genuine Sequel to "Maud Muller"), *parody.* Bret Harte. BxAP; CABA; FiBHP; HBV-1; WhC
Maud Muller Mutatur. Franklin P. Adams. HBMV
Maud went to college. Sadie and Maud. Gwendolyn Brooks. NoAM; NOBA; TAP
Maude Clare. Christina Rossetti. BeLS; EBVV
Maudle-in Ballad, A. *Unknown.* BXAP; FaBoPa
Maumee Ruth. Sterling A. Brown. CDC
Maunder's Praise of His Strowling Mort, The. *Unknown.* OxBoLi
Maunding Soldier, The; or, The Fruits of Warre Is Beggery. Martin Parker. CoMu; WaaP
Maureen. John Todhunter. HBV-1; OBVV
Maurice de Guérin. Maurice Francis Egan. AA
Maurice, I dreamed of you last night. You wore. Spring 1974. C. K. Stead. Twenty-one Sonnets, 1. OCNZ
Maurice was in an exhibition hall. Austin Clarke. Mnemosyne Lay in Dust, V. IPY
Mavrone. Arthur Guiterman. BXAP; FiBHP; InMe; SpRo
Maw Bonnie Lad. *Unknown.* GBP
Max Schling, Max Schling, Lend Me Your Green Thumb. Ogden Nash. PV
Max Schmitt in a Single Scull. Richmond Lattimore. EyDe; NePoAm-2
Maxim Revised, A. *Unknown.* BLPA; FPL; WBLP
Maximian Elegy V. Kenneth Rexroth. CrMA
Maxims (Cotton MS). *Unknown, tr. fr. Anglo-Saxon by* Charles W. Kennedy. AnOE
Maxims (Exeter Book). *Unknown, tr. fr. Anglo-Saxon by* Charles W. Kennedy. AnOE
Maxims of a Park Vagrant. Nicholas Swift. AMV-80
Maximus Poems, The, *sels.* Charles Olson.
Celestial Evening, October 1967. PoM
Cole's Island. PoM
I, Maximus of Gloucester, to You ("By ear, she sd"). NeAP
I, Maximus of Gloucester, to You ("Off-shore, by islands hidden in the blood"). LiTM; NoAM; NOBA; PoM
Maximus, from Dogtown, I. CoPo
Maximus, to Gloucester, Letter 19. CMoP; NMP
Maximus, to Gloucester, Letter 27. NOBA
(Letter 27.) CoPo
Maximus, to Gloucester, Letter 2. NoAM
Maximus, to Himself. CMOP; NeAP; NMP; NOBA; PoM; VGW
River Map, The, and We're Done. CoPo
Songs of Maximus, The. NeAP
Sels.
"All/wrong," II. NoAM
"Colored pictures," I. NoAM
"I have seen faces of want," V. PAI
"I know a house made of mud & wattles," IV. PAI
"This morning of the small snow," III. PAI; PPP
"You sing, you," VI. PAI
Maxixe. Sir Osbert Sitwell. PoA
Maxwel[l]ton[’s] braes are bonnie. Annie Laurie. William Douglas, *revised by* Lady Jane Scott. FaBoBe; FaBV; FaFP; FSW; GN; HBV-1; PoPle; TreF; WBLP
May. William Barnes. PoSC
"Mother o' blossoms, and ov all," *sel.* ChTr
May. Stephen Moylan Bird. HBMV
May. Henry Sylvester Cornwell. HBV-1
May. Thomas Dekker. *See* O, the Month of May.
May. Richard Edwards. OBSC
May. Edward Hovell-Thurlow. HBV-1; OBEV; OBRV
May ("O love, this morn when the sweet nightingale"). William Morris. *Fr.* The Earthly Paradise. VLP
May. Shaw Neilson. PoAu-1
May. Christina Rossetti. GBL
May. Spenser. *Fr.* The Fairie Queene, VII. GN
May. *Unknown, tr. fr. Old Irish by* Frank O'Connor. AnIl; KiLC
May. John Updike. *Fr.* A Child's Calendar. OBCA
May. John Stevens Wade. AMV-80

May afternoon with birds in every bush. Poem in May. John Hewitt. NeIP
May All Earth Be Clothed in Light. George Hitchcock. VGW
May all my enemies go to hell. Season's Greetings [*or* Lines for a Christmas Card]. Hilaire Belloc. DBV; TW
May all that dread the cruel feind of night. Warning to Travailers Seeking Accomodations at Mr. Devills Inn. Sarah Kemble Knight. SCAP
"May an unforeseen disaster." The Horse and the Whip. Eliezer Steinbarg, *tr. by* Curt Leviant. VWA
May and Death. Robert Browning. FaBoRV; NOBE
May, and the air is light. The Road's End. John Montague. A Severed Head, I. IPY
May, and the wall was warm again. For miles. Winter's Cold. W. R. Rodgers. EnLoPo
May! be thou never graced with birds that sing. [Epitaph] In Obitum M.S., X° Maij [*or* Maii], 1614. William Browne. ElL; FaBoEE; JCP; NOBE; OBEV; OBS; SeCeV
May Burden, A. Francis Thompson. HBV-1
May Carol. *Unknown.* OBET
May Carols, *sels.* Aubrey Thomas De Vere.
  Divine Presence, The, I, 3. GoBC
  Implicit Faith, II, 64. GoBC
May Collin. Lady Isabel and the Elf-Knight. *Unknown.* ESPB
May Colvin [*or* Colven]. *Unknown.* OxBB, *with music;* TrGrPo
May come up with bird-din. Nuts in May. Louis MacNeice. MoAB; MoBrPo
May-Day, *sel.* Emerson.
  April and May. GN; OHIP
May-Day. Aaron Hill. NOEC
Mayday. Ed Roberson. PoBA
May Day. Sara Teasdale. BoNaP; PoSC
May day. *Unknown.* OxNR
May Day, A. Sir Henry Wotton. *See* On a Bank as I Sate a-Fishing.
May-Day at Sea. John F. Finerty. EtS
May Day Carol, A. *Unknown.* PoSC
  ("Moon shines bright, The.") GBL
May Day Dancing, The. Howard Nemerov. NoAM; NYBP
May-day! delightful day!/ Bright colours play the vale along. In Praise of May. *At. to* Fionn MacCunhaill, *tr. by* T. W. Rolleston. AnIV
May-day, delightful time! How beautiful the color! The Song of Finn. *Unknown, tr. by* John O'Donovan. OnYI
May Day Garland, The. Edmund Blunden. HBMV
May-Day on Magdalen Tower. Thomas Herbert Warren. OBVV
May Day Rounds: Renfrew County, *sel.* Joan Finnigan.
  "Stoop on the log-house is brown with sweet rain-rot, The." WPE
May de Lord—He will be glad of me. Bright Sparkles in de Churchyard. *Unknown.* AA
May, 1840. Hartley Coleridge. OBVV
May Evening. Eileen Brennan. NeIP
May 1506 (Christopher Columbus Speaking). Winfield Townley Scott. GOA
May 15th. Raymond Souster. MoCV
May Garden. John Drinkwater. HBMV
May God above. A Curse on Mine-Owners. *Unknown.* TW
May God be praised for woman. On Woman. W. B. Yeats. BiP; CMoP
May God Give Strength. Peter Van Wynen. BLRP
May has come out from the showers. The Jewish May. Morris Rosenfeld, *tr. by* Rose Pastor Stokes *and* Helena Frank. TrJP
May have killed the cat; more likely. Curiosity. Alastair Reid. SoSe
May he fall in with beasts that scatter fire. Ballad against the Enemies of France. Villon, *tr. by* Swinburne. AWP
May he have new life like the fall. John Coltrane: An Impartial Review. Alfred B. Spellman. CNA; NNP; PoBA
May he lose his way on the cold sea. Archilochus, *tr. fr. Latin by* Guy Davenport. OBVE
May His Body make me safer. Thanksgiving after Communion. *Tr. fr. Gaelic by* Douglas Hyde. WTO
May his lines lose their lures. Curse of a Fisherman's Wife. Lila Chalpin. AMV-80
May I Be Beautiful. *Malay Oral Tradition, tr. by* W. W. Skeat. WTO
May I borrow your handpainted cravat? Neckwear. Michael Silverton. PV
May I Feel Said He. E. E. Cummings. BoLoP; ErPo; FF; HeIP; LiTA; NOBE; UnTE
May I find a woman fair. True Beauty. Francis Beaumont. ElL; HBV-1
May I for my own self song's truth reckon. The Seafarer. *Unknown, tr. by* Ezra Pound. AP; CTC; FaBoTw; HeIP; LiTA; NoP; OxBA; SeCeV
May I forever a Muse-/ um. Vow. John Updike. NYBP
May I put my head on your shoulder, Mr. Mac Adams, Sr.? Nuts and Bolts Poem for Mr. Mac Adams, Sr. Kathleen Fraser. NPGG
May in the Green-Wood. *Unknown.* *See* Robin Hood and the Monk.
May Is Building Her House. Richard Le Gallienne. HBVY; OHIP; YeAr
May is Mary's month, and I. The May Magnificat. Gerard Manley Hopkins. ISi; VLP
May is the moneth maist amene. Of May. Alexander Scott. OxBS
May is the month when "the white throat builds." The Merry Month. "Miss X *and* Miss Y." InMe
May It Be. Boris Pasternak, *tr. fr. Russian by* C. M. Bowra. TrJP
May Janet. Swinburne. VLP
May-June, 1940. Robinson Jeffers. LiTA; MoAB; MoAmPo; NePA; WaP (Battle.) LiTM
May Magnificat, The. Gerard Manley Hopkins. ISi; VLP
May Margaret. Théophile Marzials. HBV-1
May Margret stood in her bouer door. Hind Etin. *Unknown.* ESPB
May moon rises bright and clear, The. Tom Pringle. Louis Simpson. NePoAm-2
May Morn. Michael McClure. EAS
May Morning, *mod. vers.* Chaucer. *Fr.* The Book of the Duchesse. WHA
May Morning. Milton. *See* Song on May Morning.
May Morning. Celia Thaxter. AA
May Mornings. Ivy O. Eastwick. SiSoSe
May-Music. Rachel Annand Taylor. HBV-1
May my Irish grandfather from Tyrells Pass. The Buzz Plane. Robert Francis. TW
May, 1915. Charlotte Mew. SUMH
May, 1945. Peter Porter. OxBC
May No Man Sleep in Your Hall [*or* Halle]. *Unknown.* GBP; NCEP
May nothing evil cross this door. Prayer for This [*or* a New] House. Louis Untermeyer. BLPL; FaPON; PoLF; TrPWD
May one kind grave unite each hapless name. Eloisa's Prayer for Abelard. Pope. *Fr.* Eloisa to Abelard. GoBC
May others fear, fly, and traduce thy name. To the Learned Critic. Ben Jonson. PP
May poverty, without offence, approach. Nicholas James. *Fr.* The Complaints of Poverty. NOEC
May! queen of blossoms. May. Edward Hovell-Thurlow. HBV-1; OBEV; OBRV
May seven tears in every week. A Wish. J. M. Synge. FaBoEE
May Song. Wendell Berry. AP
May Song, A. "Violet Fane." OBVV
May Song. *Unknown.* OBET
May Sun Sheds an Amber Light, The. Bryant. AA
May 10th. Maxine W. Kumin. BoNaP; NYBP; RFM
May the Ambitious Ever Find. Charles Sackville. UnTE
May the Babylonish curse. A Farewell to Tobacco. Charles Lamb. NBM; OxBoLi; OBRV
May the blessing of light be on you. An Old Irish Blessing. *Unknown.* TRV
May the castle lie in slumber. And When the Prince Came. Robert Hillyer. DFT
May the dread Three in One, who sways. Matins—Friday. Cardinal Newman. VLP
May the foemen's wives, the foemen's children. Europa. William Johnson Cory. NBM
May the grace of Christ our Saviour. In Sweet Communion. John Newton. TRV
May the harpoon rust, may the cold steel be gone. Blood on the Sails. Phil *and* June Colclough. OBET
May the man who gained my trust yet did not come. Ryojin Hisho, *tr. fr. Japanese by* Geoffrey Bownas *and* Anthony Thwaite. BoWoP
May the men who are born. Hitomaro. *Fr.* Manyo Shu. AWP
May the Milky Way enter my Father's fading eyes. To My Father. Ralph Pomeroy. DFF
May the road rise to meet you. An Irish Wish. *Unknown.* TreFT
May the strong curse of crushed affections light. Shelley. *Fr.* To the Lord Chancellor. DBV
May the will come from Thee. Annul Wars. Rabbi Nahman of Bratzlav, *tr. by* Jacob Sloan. TrJP
May the wrath of the heart of my god be pacified! Penitential Psalm to the Goddess Anunit. *Unknown.* WGRP
May they come, may they come. Song of the Highest Tower. Arthur Rimbaud, *tr. by* Edgell Rickword. AWP
May they stumble [*or* wander], stage by stage. The Travel[l]er's Curse after Misdirection. Robert Graves. BrPo; CMoP; DBV; DTC; FiBHP; HoPM; LiTM; MoAB; MoBrPo; NCSH; TW
May Thirtieth. *Unknown.* PoSC
May 30, 1893. John Kendrick Bangs. AA
May Time. Sir Thomas Wyatt. *See* Sonnet: "You that in love find luck and abundaunce."
May Tree, The. William Barnes. LiTB; LoBV
May Trees in a Storm. Geoffrey Grigson. GBL
May 20: Very Early Morning. Luci Shaw. EBCP
May we and all who bear thy name. By Gentle Love. *Unknown.* TRV

May we have leave to ask, illustrious Mother. Purification of the Blessed Virgin. Joseph Beaumont. ISi
May with its light behaving. W. H. Auden. EBEV
May You Always Be the Darling of Fortune. Jane Miller. AMV-80
May you drinke beare, or that adult'rate wine. To a Friend, Inviting Him to a Meeting upon Promise. William Habington. AnAnS-2
May you live long and be well. Vigndig a Fremd Kind (Babysitter's Song). *Unknown.* FSW
May your sleep be calm as snow in the pleats of clouds. For You, Falling Asleep after a Quarrel. Diane Middlebrook. AMV-81
Mayakovsky was right. Kiss. Al Young. PoBA
Maybe all I saw was the mirror. Vision. Delmira Augustini, *tr. by* Marti Moody. WPOW
Maybe Alone on My Bike. William Stafford. NYBP
Maybe he dreamed of/ new snow. Retired Farmer. David Allan Evans. Psk
Maybe I should go back to the white leather. Desnos Reading the Palms of Men on Their Way to the Gas Chambers. Stephen Berg. VWA
Maybe it is her birth. The Blanket around Her. Joy Harjo. TWSS
Maybe it is true we have to return. Obsessions. Denise Levertov. LiTM; NePoEA-2
Maybe it was the way. Finding You. Virginia Gilbert. IHMS
Maybe Love. Allen Ginsberg. PeHV
Maybe morning lightens over. For My Grandmother, Bridget [*or* Bridgid] Halpin. Michael Hartnett. BIrV; CIP
Maybe nothing can save us tonight. Vivaldi on the Far Side of the Bars. Michael Knoll. LFAC
Maybe this is what ghost is. Recovery. Patricia Y. Ikeda. BrSi
Maybe You Cannot Comprehend. Salvador Villanueva, *tr. fr. Spanish by* Julio Marzán. InW
Maybe you ranted in the grove. Ezry. Archibald MacLeish. MoVE; NOBA
Maybrick trial is over now, there's been a lot of jaw, The. Penal Servitude for Mrs. Maybrick. *Unknown.* OxBoLi
Mayday. *See* May Day.
Mayde ther was, y-clept Joan Hunter Dunn, A. The Summonee's Tale. Stanley J. Sharpless. BXAP; FaBoPa
Mayde's Metamorphosis, The, *sels.* *Unknown, at. to* John Lyly *and to* Thomas Ravenscroft.
  By the Moon. CH
  (Fairy Dances, 1.) ElL
  Elves' Dance, The. CH; FaPON
Mayers' Song, The. *Unknown.* *See* Song of the Mayers.
Mayflower. Conrad Aiken. MP
Mayflower, The. Erastus Wolcott Ellsworth. AA; FaBoBe; HBV-2; PAH
Mayflower. John Boyle O'Reilly. AA; PAH
Maymie's Story of Red Riding-Hood. James Whitcomb Riley. DFT
Mayor of Lagos. *Yoruba Oral Tradition, tr. by* Ulli Beier. WTO
Mayor of Scuttleton, The. Mary Mapes Dodge. NA
Mayors, The. Blake. *See* Good English Hospitality.
Maypole, A. Swift. NCEP
May's the merriest time of all. May. *Unknown, tr. by* Frank O'Connor. AnIL; KiLC
Mayst thou die desp'rate in some dirty pool. An Adieu to My Landlady. George Farewell. NOEC
Maytime. Thomas Dekker. *See* O, the Month of May.
Maytime. *Unknown, tr. fr. Chinese by* L. Cranmer-Byng. *Fr.* Shi King. AWP
Maytime Magic. Mabel Watts. RHPC
Mazeppa. Byron. EnRP
  "Up rose the sun; the mists were curl'd," *sel.* OBRV
Mazilla and Mazura. *Unknown.* ChTr
Mbuyazi of the Bay! Praises of Henry Francis Fynn. *Zulu Oral Tradition, tr. by* T. Cope. WTO
Me. Walter de la Mare. FaPON; RHPC; TiPo
Me. Karla Kuskin. RHPC
Me. Hughes Mearns. *Fr.* Later Antigonishes. InMe
Me Alone. Lula Lowe Weeden. CDC
Me an' My Doney-Gal. *Unknown.* CoSo
Me and my brother. My Brother, Beautiful Shinault, That Goat. David Huddle. GrPl
Me and My Chauffeur Blues. *Unknown.* BluL
Me and My Dog. *Unknown.* PoAu-1
Me and Prunes. Rupe Sherwood. PoOW
Me and Samantha. Pyke Johnson, Jr. GDP
Me and the Devil Blues. *Unknown.* BluL
Me and the Mule. Langston Hughes. IDB
Me clairvoyant. Variations on an Air: After Walt Whitman. G. K. Chesterton. BXAP; FaBoPa; NOBL; Par
Me, Colored. Peter Abrahams. *Fr.* Tell Freedom. PBA
Me Cupid made a happy slave. Song. Sir Richard Steele. OBEC
Me! dutiful son going back to South Wales, this time afraid. Down the M4. Dannie Abse. OxBC
Me father was the keeper of the Eddystone light. Eddystone Light. *Unknown.* FSW
Me first/ you all. Mardi Gras. Miller Williams. TAT
Me from myself—to banish. Emily Dickinson. NoAM; SBG
Me, go to Florida! This Is Pioneer Weather. William Carlos Williams. NePoAm-2
Me happy, night, night full of brightness. Elegy VII. Ezra Pound. *Fr.* Homage to Sextus Propertius. ErPo; InvP; VGW
Me I Am! Jack Prelutsky. RHPC
Me I will throw away. The Self-slaved. Patrick Kavanagh. MoBrPo
Me, I'm the man that dug the Murray for Sturt to sail down. They'll Tell You about Me. Ian Mudie. PoAu-2
Me Imperturbe. Walt Whitman. NOBA
Me, in Kulu Se and Karma. Carolyn M. Rodgers. PoBA
Me Johnny Mitchell Man, *with music.* *Unknown.* TrAS
Me liketh ever the lengere the bet. In Praise of Winchester. *Unknown.* OxBM
Me list no more to sing. Sir Thomas Wyatt. AAS; SiPS
Me Lord? can'st Thou mispend. Phineas Fletcher. *Fr.* The Divine Wooer. TrPWD
"Me loving subjects," sez she. Percy French. *Fr.* The Queen's Afterdinner Speech. OxBI
Me mother kept a boarding house. Hullabaloo Belay. *Unknown.* FSW
Me nappy hair dream child. Image in the Mirror. Peggy Susberry Kenner. JB
Me needeth not to boast; I am Eternity. Eternity. Sir Thomas More. EnRePo
Me Polytimus vexes and provokes. Epigram. Martial. PeHV
Me Rueth, Mary. *Unknown.* *See* Now Goeth Sonne under Wode.
Me so oft my fancy drew. The Choice. George Wither. OBEV
Me that 'ave been what I've been. Chant-Pagan. Kipling. OAEP; VLP
Me thinkes this draught such vertue does infuse. The Office of Poetry. Nathaniel Whiting. *Fr.* Il Insonio Insonado. OBS
Me thinks I see our mighty monarch stand. *Unknown.* *Fr.* The Royal Angler. OBSV
Me thinks [*or* Methinks], I see, with what a busie [*or* busy] hast[e]. On Zacheus [*or* Zacchaeus]. Francis Quarles. HAP; LoBV; MePo; OBS
Me thought I was in wildernesse walking al one. A Dream. *Unknown.* *Fr.* Mum and the Sothsegger. OxBM
Me thoughte thus: that [h]it was May. The Dream. Chaucer. *Fr.* The Book of the Duchesse. FiP; PBBP
Me to You. Alastair Reid. NYBP
Me Up at Does. E. E. Cummings. NYBP; WeW
Me, whom no muse of heav'nly birth inspires. On Himself. Charles Churchill. *Fr.* The Prophecy of Famine. OBEC
Mea Culpa. Ethna Carbery. TrPWD
Meadow, The. John Wieners. CoPo
Meadow and the mountain with desire, The. Attraction. Ella Wheeler Wilcox. PeD
Meadow-Field, The. Charles Sangster. *Fr.* Pleasant Memories. OBCV
Meadow Grass. Michael Mott. AMV-80
Meadow Lark, The. Hamlin Garland. AA
Meadow Mouse, The. Theodore Roethke. HeIP; InPK; NaP; PAI; PPoe; SeCeV
Meadowland. *Unknown, tr. fr. Russian.* FSW
Meadows are empty, The. There are two villages. The Hours. Norman Dubie. GeTw
Meadows in Spring, The. Edward Fitzgerald. *See* Old Song.
Meadows with yellow cowslips all aglow. The Wood-Dove's Note. Emily Huntington Miller. HBV-1
Meadowsweet. William Allingham. OBNC
Mean Drunk Poem. Sharon Thesen. NOBC
Mean Mistreater Mama. *Unknown.* BluL
Mean Old Twister. *Unknown.* BluL
Mean Trick, A. *Unknown.* TDH
Mean while. *See* Meanwhile.
Meandering abroad in the Lincolnshire meadows day. George Barker. *Fr.* Calamiterror, VI. EAS
Meandering Wye. Robert Bloomfield. *Fr.* The Banks of Wye. OBNC
Meanest trick I ever knew, The. A Low Trick. Gelett Burgess. OBCA
Meaning, The. Ralph Gustafson. OBCV
Meaning of Africa, The. Abioseh Nicol. PBA
Meaning of Love, The. *Malay Oral Tradition, tr. by* R. O. Winstedt. WTO
Meaning of the Look, The. Elizabeth Barrett Browning. TrCP; TRV
Meaning of Violence, The. John Williams. NePoAm-2
Means of Propulsion for Steam-Ships. Thomas Baker. *Fr.* The Steam Engine; or, The Power of Flame. FaBoUs
Means to Attain Happy Life, The. Martial. *See* Happy Life, The.
Meantime. Heather McHugh. GeTw

Meanwhile Achilles, plung'd. Homer, *tr. by* Edward, Earl of Derby. *Fr.* The Iliad. PoPl
Meanwhile surely there must be something to say. The Constructed Space. W. S. Graham. PoA
Meanwhile [*or* Mean while] the adversary of God and man. Sin and Death. Milton. *Fr.* Paradise Lost, II. DL; EBEV; OBNV
Meanwhile the choleric Captain strode wrathful away to the council. The War-Token. Longfellow. *Fr.* The Courtship of Miles Standish. PAH
Meanwhile the Queen with many piteous drops. Titania. Thomas Hood. *Fr.* The Plea of the Midsummer Fairies. OBRV
Meanwhile the tepid caves and fens and shores. The Creation of Birds. Milton. *Fr.* Paradise Lost, VII. PB; PBBP
Meanwhile the troops beneath Patroclus' care. Homer, *tr. by* Pope. *Fr.* The Iliad, XVI. OBVE
Meanwhile the woman, from her strawberry lips. Metamorphoses of the Vampire. Baudelaire, *tr. by* Jackson Mathews. ErPo
Meare's milk and deer's milk. A Witch's Spell [*or* Witch's Milking Charm]. *Unknown.* ChTr; GBP
Measles. Kaye Starbird. RHPC
Measles in the Ark. "Susan Coolidge." OxBChV
Measure. Robert Hass. GeTw
Measure, The. Patrick Lane. NOBC
Measure for Measure, *sels.* Shakespeare.
Be Absolute for Death, *fr.* III, i. FaBoRV
But Man, Proud Man, *fr.* II, ii. WHA
Fear of Death, The, *fr.* III, i. TreFT
(On Death.) FiP
Man New Made, *fr.* II, ii. GoBC
"O, it is excellent," *fr.* II, ii. TreFT
Take, O Take Those Lips Away, *fr.* IV, i (*also given, with add. st., in* The Bloody Brother, *by* John Fletcher, *and others*). AWP; BiP; EBEV; ElL; ELP; EnLoPo; EnRePo; FaBV; GBL; HBV-1; HeIP; InPS; LiTB; NoP; OAEL-1; OAEP; OBEV; SeCeV; ViBoPo; WHA
(At the Moated Grange.) NOBE
(Love Song: "Take, O take those lips away.") FaBoEn
(Madrigal: "Take, O take those lips away.") GTBS; GTBS-P
(Seals of Love.) TrGrPo
(Song: "Take, O take those lips away.") FiP; PoEL-2
(Song at the Moated Grange, A.) OBSC
Measure Me, Sky. Leonora Speyer. FaPON; HBMV
Measure of a Man, The. *Unknown.* BLPL; PoLF; STF
Measure of Success. *Unknown.* STF
Measured blood beats out the year's delay, The. Simple Autumnal. Louise Bogan. MoAB; MoAmPo; QFR
Measurement. A. M. Sullivan. RHPC
Measuring, The. Jared Carter. AMV-80
Measuring a Man. *Unknown.* STF
Measuring worm with a hump on his back, A. Pedagogical Principles. Harry Amoss. CaP
Meat Epitaph, The. Michael Benedikt. FiCP
Mechanic, The. Robert Creeley. NaP
Mechanic, The. Diane Wakoski. AmPA
Mechanical/ Oracles dot the sky. Gods in Vietnam. Eugene Redmond. NBP; PoBA
Mechanical digger wrecks the drill, A. At a Potato Digging. Seamus Heaney. IPY
Mechanism. A. R. Ammons. HAP
Mechanophilus, *sel.* Tennyson.
"Dash back that ocean with a pier." FaBoCo
Mecklenburg Declaration, The. William C. Elam. PAH
Medal of John Bays, The; a Satire against Folly and Knavery. Thomas Shadwell. APAS
Medal Reversed, The. Elkanah Settle. APAS
Medal [*or* Medall], The, *sel.* Dryden.
Vox Populi. NOBE; OBS
Medallion. Sylvia Plath. HeIP; NoP
Medallion. Ezra Pound. *Fr.* Hugh Selwyn Mauberley. SeCeV
Meddlesome Matty. Ann Taylor. HBV-1; HBVY; OnMSP; OxBChV
Meddow Verse, The; or, Aniversary to Mistris Bridget Lowman. Robert Herrick. SeCV-1
Medea, *sel.* Lord De Tabley.
Chorus: "Sweet are the ways of death to weary feet." NBM; OBEV; OBVV
Medea. Euripides, *tr. fr. Greek by* Rex Warner. NAWM-1
Medea, *sels.* Seneca, *tr. fr. Latin by* John Studley.
"Her chaunging lookes no colour longe can holde," *fr.* IV. OBVE
"That Orpheus Calliops sonne who stayde the running brooke," *fr.* III. OBVE
Medea Casts a Spell to Make Aeson Young Again. Ovid, *tr. fr. Latin by* Arthur Golding. *Fr.* Metamorphoses, VII. MOON
Medea in Athens, *sel.* Augusta Webster.
"Oh smooth adder/ who with fanged kisses changedst my natural blood." BrRo
Medea's Magic. John Gower. *Fr.* Confessio Amantis. OxBM
Medgar Evers. Gwendolyn Brooks. NoP; PoBA
Mediator, The. Elizabeth Barrett Browning. TrPWD
Mediatrix of Grace, The. Francis Burke. ISi
Medical Aid. Walter Hard. BXAP; WhC
Medicine. Alice Walker. NMM; PAI
Medicine plants blooming beneath. Another Old Song. Barney Bush. STE
Medicine song. For Mabel: Pomo Basketmaker and Doctor. Wendy Rose. TWSS
Medieval Christ Speaks on a Spanish Sculpture of Himself. Rochelle Owens. CoPo
Medieval Mirth. *Unknown.* *Fr.* The Squire of Low Degree. ACP
Medieval Norman Songs. *Unknown, tr. fr. French by* John Addington Symonds. AWP
Medieval Poem of the Nativity, A. *Unknown.* TrCP
Medieval town, with frieze, The. What Is Poetry. John Ashbery. LCAP
Mediocrity [*or* Mediocritie] in Love Rejected. Thomas Carew. AnAnS-2; HBV-1; MeLP; MePo; NoP; PAI; SeCV-1; TEP
(Give Me More Love.) UnTE
(More Love or More Disdain.) TrGrPo
(Song: "Give me more love or more disdain.") ViBoPo
(Song: Mediocrity in Love Rejected.) CaPo; GBL
Meditatio. Ezra Pound. FaBoCh; OBAL
Meditation. Baudelaire, *tr. fr. French by* Robert Lowell. InPK; NAWM-2
Meditation, A. Richard Eberhart. LiTA
Meditation. Toyohiko Kagawa. TRV
Meditation, A. Herman Melville. GOA
Meditation ("How long will you remain a boy?"). Carl Rakosi. VWA
Meditation ("Lord, what is a man?"). Carl Rakosi. AMV-80
Meditation ("Men are children of this world"). Carl Rakosi. VWA
Meditation ("Three things remind me of you"). Carl Rakosi. VWA
Meditation. Blanaid Salkeld. OnYI
Meditation. Beyle Schaechter-Gottesman, *tr. fr. Yiddish by* Gabriel Preil. VWA
Meditation at Kew. Anna Wickham. FaBoTw; MoBrPo
Meditation at Lagunitas. Robert Hass. MAYP; NoP; NPGG
Meditation at Oyster River. Theodore Roethke. CMoP; NYBP
Meditation by Mascoma Lake. Donald C. Babcock. NePoAm-2
Meditation 8 ("Scarce do I pass a day but that I hear"). Philip Pain. NOBA; QFR
Meditation for a Pickle Suite. R. H. W. Dillard. HoPM
Meditation for Christmas, A. Selwyn Image. OBEV
Meditation for His Mistress[e], A. Robert Herrick. CaPo; JCP; NOBE; OBEV; OBS; SeCP
Meditation in Winter. William Dunbar. BSV; NCEP
(Meditatioun in Wynter.) OxBS; SeCePo
Meditation 9 ("Man's life is like a rose, that in the spring"). Philip Pain. NOBA
Meditation of a Mariner. Dorothy Auchterlonie. CBAP
Meditation on a Bone. A. D. Hope. TW
Meditation on a Memoir. J. V. Cunningham. QFR
Meditation on Communion with God. Judah Halevi, *tr. fr. Hebrew by* Solomon Solis-Cohen. TrJP
Meditation on John Constable, A. Charles Tomlinson. NePoEA-2
Meditation on Statistical Method. J. V. Cunningham. CoAP; QFR; VGW
Meditation on the BMT. Paul Blackburn. CoPo
Meditation on the Nativity. Elizabeth Jennings. NAs
Meditation on the Rhode Island Coal, A. Bryant. TAP
Meditation 62 ("How is it that I am so careless here"). Philip Pain. NOBA
Meditation 10 ("Alas, what is the world? A sea of glass"). Philip Pain. NOBA
Meditation 29 ("How mutable is every thing that here"). Philip Pain. NOBA
Meditation under Stars. George Meredith. OAEP
Meditation upon the Toothache, A. Laurence Lerner. NePoEA-2
Meditations. Solomon ibn Gabirol, *tr. fr. Hebrew by* Emma Lazarus. TrJP
Meditations. Edward Taylor. *See* Preparatory Meditations.
Meditations at Oyster River. Theodore Roethke. MoAmPo
Meditations for a Savage Child. Adrienne Rich. LCAP
Meditations for August 1, 1666. Philip Pain. SCAP
Meditations for July 19, 1666. Philip Pain. SCAP
Meditations for July 25, 1666. Philip Pain. SCAP
Meditations for July 26, 1666. Philip Pain. SCAP
Meditation 29 ("How mutable is every thing that here"), *sel.* NOBA
Meditations in an Emergency. Frank O'Hara. TAP
Meditations in Time of Civil War, *sels.* W. B. Yeats.
Ancestral Houses, I. ChMP; LiTB; MoVE; OAEL-2
I See Phantoms of Hatred and of the Heart's Fullness and of the Coming Emptiness, VII. LiTB

My Descendants, IV. LiTB
My House, II. LiTB
My Table, III. LiTB
Road at My Door, The, V. BIrV; LiTB; NOBE
Stare's Nest by My Windows, The, VI. BIrV; GTBS-P; LiTB; NOBE
Meditations of a Hindu Prince. Sir Alfred Comyns Lyall. WGRP
Meditations of a Tortoise Dozing under a Rosetree near a Beehive at Noon While a Dog Scampers about and a Cuckoo Calls from a Distant Wood. E. V. Rieu. FiBHP
Meditations of an Old Woman. Theodore Roethke. NaP
Sels.
First Meditation. AP; LCAP; NOBA
I'm Here. CoAP; NYBP
Meditations on the Sepulchre in the Garden. Philip Doddridge. NOCV; NOEC
Meditatioun in Wyntir. William Dunbar. *See* Meditation in Winter.
Mediterranean. Israel Pincas, *tr. fr. Hebrew by* A. C. Jacobs. VWA
Mediterranean, The. Allen Tate. AP; FaBoMo; GOA; HAP; LiTA; LiTM; MoAB; MoAmPo; MOS; MoVE; NePA; PoCh; SeCeV; TwAmPo; VGW; WeW
Mediterranean. Ruth Whitman. VWA
Medium, The. Elaine Feinstein. BrRo
Medium IV, The: Sights. Carl Rakosi. InPS
Medlars and Sorb-Apples. D. H. Lawrence. OAEL-2
Medoro's Inscription for a Cave. John Stewart of Baldynnis. *Fr.* Roland Furious. BSV
Medusa. Louise Bogan. AWP; BoWoP; HoPM; MoAB; MoAmPo; MoPo; MoVE; NoP; PAI; WPE
Medusa, The. Guy Davenport. GP
Medusa. Vincent O'Sullivan. PAI
Medusa. Sylvia Plath. CAPP
Medusa. Robert Kelley Weeks. AA
Medusa's Hair Was Snakes. Was Thought, Split Inward. Kathleen Fraser. NPGG
Meek and the Proud, The. Abraham ibn Chasdai, *tr. fr. Hebrew by* J. Chotzner. TrJP
Meek dew shone, the grass lay prostrate, The. The Tree. Ilya Ehrenburg, *tr. by* Babette Deutsch. TrJP
Meek Francis lies here, friend, without stop or stay. Epitaph. Matthew Prior. FaBoEE
Meek-ey'd morn appears, mother of dews, The. Summer Morning. James Thomson. *Fr.* The Seasons: Summer. OBEC
Meet Me in St. Louis, Louis. Andrew B. Sterling. FSN, *with music*; FSW; OBAL; TreFT
Meet me my love, meet me my love. The Juniper Tree. Wilfred Watson. WHW
Meet me tonight. Jackie. King D. Kuka. VoR
Meet me tonight as usual at nine. Love Poem—1940. Miriam Hershenson. GoYe
Meet me to-night, lover, meet me. Moonlight. *Unknown.* AS
Meet Rabbi Shatz in his correct black homburg. Tales of Shatz. Dannie Abse. OxBC; VWA
Meet was at "The Cock and Pye," The. John Masefield. *Fr.* Reynard the Fox. OxBTC
Meet We No Angels, Pansie? Thomas Ashe. HBV-1; OBVV
Meet women with tender bearing. The Voice of Experience. Goethe, *tr. by* Walter Kaufman. ErPo; PV
Meet your Saviour in the morning. Keeping Victory. Walter E. Isenhour. STF
Meeting. Matthew Arnold. Switzerland, I. ELP; OAEP; VLP
Meeting, The. Louise Bogan. NePoAm-2; NYBP
Meeting, The. Gerald Costanzo. MAYP
Meeting. George Crabbe. HBV-1; OBEV
"My Damon was the first to wake." LO
Meeting, A. C. Day Lewis. NYBP
Meeting, The. Tess Gallagher. GeTw
Meeting. Sam Harrison. NeIP
Meeting, A. Daniel Hoffman. CoPo
Meeting, The. Jocelyn Hollis. AMV-80
Meeting, The. Nicki Jackowska. BrRo
Meeting, The. Pierre Louys, *tr. fr. French. Fr.* Chansons de Bilitis. PeHV
Meeting, The. Howard Moss. HoAn; NYBP
Meeting ("If we shall live, we live"). Christina Rossetti. GBL
Meeting ("They made the chamber sweet with flowers and leaves"). Christina Rossetti. *Fr.* Monna Innominata. HBV-1
Meeting, The. Muriel Rukeyser. MoAmPo; TrJP
Meeting, The. Kathleen Spivack. NMM
Meeting, The. Ramona Wilson. VoR
Meeting a Bear. David Wagoner. HAP
Meeting after Long Absence, *sels.* Lilla Cabot Perry.
As It Was, II. AA
As She Feared It Would Be, I. AA
Meeting after Separation. Marula, *tr. fr. Sanskrit by* Tambimuttu *and* G. V. Vaidya. BoWoP
Meeting Anais Nin's Elena. Gene Frumkin. AMV-81
Meeting and Passing. Robert Frost. OxBA
Meeting at Night. Robert Browning. AWP; BoLoP; ELP; FaBoEn; FaBV; FF; FiP; GBL; HBV-1; HeIP; InPS; InvP; MOS; NOBE; OAEP; OBEV; OBNC; OLR; PAI; PoPl; PoPle; PoRA; SCV; SeCePo; SoSe; TreFT; TrGrPo; UnPo; ViBoPo; VLP; WeW
Meeting at the Building. *Unknown.* FSW
Meeting at the Local. Tom Parson. SOTS
Meeting by the Gjulika Meadow. Geoffrey Grigson. WaP
Meeting Halfway. R. Wayne Hardy. LFAC
Meeting his mother makes him lose ten years. Between the Porch and the Altar. Robert Lowell. MiAP; NePoEA
Meeting-House Hill. Amy Lowell. MoAmPo; OxBA; PoRA; SBG
Meeting-house is not what it used to be, The. Elegy in a Presbyterian Burying-Ground. R. N. D. Wilson. BIrV
Meeting Mick Jagger. Robert Peters. BXAP
Meeting Myself. Edward Lucie-Smith. NePoEA-2
Meeting of Cultures, A. Donald Davie. OxBC
Meeting of the Ships, The. Thomas Moore. EtS
Meeting of the Waters, The. Thomas Moore. AnIL; NBM; OxBoLi; PoEL-4
Meeting Point. Louis MacNeice. ChMP
Meeting the Easter Bunny. Rowena Bastin Bennett. SiSoSe; SoPo; SUS; TiPo
Meeting the first time for many years. A Meeting. C. Day Lewis. NYBP
Meeting the Mountains. Gary Snyder. NoAM; TAP
Meeting the Reincarnation Analyst. Gary Gildner. AmPA
Meeting Together of Poles & Latitudes: In Prospect. Margaret Avison. NOBC; OBCV
Meeting when all the world was in the bud. Loves of the Puppets. Richard Wilbur. CoPo; OxBC
Meeting with Time, "Slack thing!" said I. Time. George Herbert. TEP
Meetings and Absences. Roy Fuller. OnUR
Meeting's in order, The. What's coming? What's to come? Town Meeting. John Hay. NePoAm
Meetings meetings meetings. Yuh Lookin Good. Carolyn M. Rodgers. BPo
Meg/ Likes/ A regular egg. Meg's Egg. Mary Ann Hoberman. RHPC
Meg Merrilies [*or* Merrilees]. Keats. FaBoCh; FaPON; FiP; OxBChV; PoPle; TEP; TiPo
Megaceph, chosen to serve the State. Ambrose Bierce. *Fr.* The Devil's Dictionary. OBAL
Meg's Egg. Mary Ann Hoberman. RHPC
Mehitabel Sings a Song. Don Marquis. *Fr.* Archy and Mehitabel. InMe
Mein Herz, mein Herz ist traurig. Heine. *See* My Heart, My Heart Is Mournful.
Mein Kind, Wir Waren Kinder. Heine, *tr. fr. German by* Elizabeth Barrett Browning. AWP; TrJP
("My child, we were two children.") OBVE
Mein Liebchen, wir sassen zusammen. Heine, *tr. fr. German by* James Thomson. AWP
Melampus. George Meredith. OBVV; PoEL-5; VLP
Melampus, when will love be void of fears? Song of Coridon and Melampus. George Peele. *Fr.* The Hunting of Cupid. OBSC
Melancholetta, *sel.* "Lewis Carroll."
"My dismal sister! Couldst thou know." FiBHP
Melancholia. Robert Bly. NoP
Melancholia. Robert Bridges. CMoP
Melancholia. *Unknown.* NA
Melancholy. John Fletcher. *Fr.* The Nice Valor. GTBS; GTBS-P; HBV-2; OBEV; PoPle
(Hence, All You Vain Delights.) OAEP; ViBoPo
(O Sweetest Melancholy.) TrGrPo
(Passionate Man's Song, The.) OBS
(Song.) PoEL-2
Melancholy. William Habington. *Fr.* Castara, II. LoBV
Melancholy. Thomas Lodge. *See* Earth Late Choked with Showers.
Melancholy. Edward Thomas. MoVE; NoP
Melancholy Cowboy, The. *Unknown.* CoSo
Melancholy days are come, the saddest of the year, The. The Death of the Flowers. Bryant. AA; BLPL; BoNaP; GN; HBV-1; OBCA; PoLF; TreF; WBLP
Melancholy days have come, The. Autumn Leaves. Charles H. Webb. OBAL
Melancholy desire of ancient things, A. On an Air of Rameau. Arthur Symons. OBNC
Melancholy face Charles Carville had, A. Charles Carville's Eyes. E. A. Robinson. CMoP; NePA; OxBA; TAP
Melancholy Knight, The, *sels.* Samuel Rowlands.
Poetaster, The. EIL

Sir Eglamour. ElL; FaBoCh; FaBoNo; InvP
Melancholy Lay, A. Marjory Fleming. FaBoCh; FiBHP
(Six-Year-Old Marjory Fleming Pens a Poem.) TreFT
Melancholy lieth dolorously ill. Arabs. Alfred Kreymborg. TwAmPo
Melancholy little man was seated on the ground, A. Home. *Unknown.* HBV-2
Melancholy Pig, The. "Lewis Carroll." *See* Pig-Tale, A.
Melancholy slackening that ensued, The. Cambridge and the Alps. Wordsworth. *Fr.* The Prelude, VI. PoEL-4
Melancholy Year, The. Trumbull Stickney. NCEP
Melancthon. Marianne Moore. CrMA
(Black Earth.) FaBoMo
Melchior, Gaspar, Balthazar. The Ballad of the Cross. Theodosia Garrison. HBMV; HBVY
Melchior Vulpius. Marianne Moore. AP
Meleager. Ovid, *tr. fr. Latin by* Arthur Golding. *Fr.* Metamorphoses, VIII. CTC
Melfort Dalton, I knew you well. To an Old Tenor. Oliver St. John Gogarty. WhC
Melhill Feast. William Barnes. OBNC
Melincourt, *sels.* Thomas Love Peacock.
Glee—The Ghosts. ViBoPo
Sun-Dial, The. OBNC; OBRV
Melinda, who had never been. The Coquette. Aphra Behn. TrGrPo; ViBoPo
Melissa. Don Marquis. *Fr.* Savage Portraits. HBMV
Melissa. Carolyn D. Redl-Hlus. AMV-80
Melissa. *Unknown, tr. fr. Greek by* Louis Untermeyer. UnTE
Melita, Rhodópis, and young Rhodocleia. Embarrassed Judge. *Unknown, tr. by* Louis Untermeyer. UnTE
Melkon. David Kherdian. FAZ
Mellifluous as bees, these brittle men. On First Looking in on Blodgett's *Keats's "Chapman's Homer."* George Starbuck. NIP; OBAL; PP
Mellisandra. Harriet Rose. BrRo
Méllonta taûta. Samuel Butler. GLGT
Mellow Groove Grave Elegy. Michael C. Ford. SOTS
Mellow the moonlight to shine is beginning. The Spinning-Wheel. John Francis Waller. AnIV; ChTr
Mellow year is hasting to its close, The. November. Hartley Coleridge. Sonnets to the Seasons, XII. LoBV; OBNC; OBRV
Mellowness and Flight. George Barlow. CNA
Melodic Trains. John Ashbery. NoP
Melodie Grotesque. Persis Greely Anderson. WhC
Melodies of Time, The. Thomas Hood. *Fr.* The Plea of the Midsummer Fairies. OBNC
Melody. Shmuel Moreh, *tr. fr. Arabic by* Yoffee Berkovitz. VWA
Melon-Slaughterer; or, A Sick Man's Praise for a Well Woman. Robert Peters. BXAP
Melons. Mary Mapes Dodge. TiPo
Melons. Moshe Yungman, *tr. fr. Yiddish by* Gabriel Preil *and* Howard Schwartz. VWA
Melpomene (at whose mischeifous tove). Carmen Elegiacum. Thomas Morton. SCAP
Melpomene, the Muse of tragic songs. Oenone's Complaint. George Peele. *Fr.* The Arraignment of Paris. ElL; OBSC
Melrose Abbey. Sir Walter Scott. *Fr.* The Lay of the Last Minstrel, II. FaBoPP; SeCePo
("If thou wouldst view fair Melrose aright.") OBRV
(Sir William of Deloraine at the Wizard's Tomb.) OBNC
Melting in thin mist and heavy clouds. Li Ch'ing-chao, *tr. fr. Chinese by* J. P. Seaton. BoWoP
Melting Pot. Michael Echeruo. TTY
Melting Pot, The. Dudley Randall. BALP; BPo
Melton Mowbray Pork Pie, A. Richard Le Gallienne. BXAP; Par
Member of the modern great, A. Epigram. John Cunningham. FaBoEE
Members, Don't Git Weary, *with music. Unknown.* BoAN-2
Membrane, The. Mei-mei Berssenbrugge. LTB
Memento for Mortality [*or* Mortalitie], A. *At. to* William Basse *and to* Francis Beaumont. *See* On the Tombs in Westminster Abbey.
Memento Homo Quod Cinis Es et in Cinerem Reverteris. *Unknown. See* Earth upon Earth.
Memento Mori. Moishe Leib Halpern, *tr. fr. Yiddish by* Ruth Whitman. VWA
Memento Vivendi. Eva Brudne. VWA
Mementos, *sel.* Charlotte Brontë.
"And heaven did curse—they found him laid." PeD
Mementos, 1 ("Sorting out letters and piles of my old"). W. D. Snodgrass. CABA; FF; HeIP; MoAmPo; NePoEA-2; PPP; UnPo
Mementos, II ("I found them there today"). W. D. Snodgrass. NePoEA-2
Memnon. Clinton Scollard. AA
Memo. Charles G. Ballard. VoR
Memo. Kenneth Fearing. CMoP
Memo. Hildegarde Flanner. NYBP
Memo. Charles Lynch. PoBA
Memo. Hans Sahl, *tr. fr. German by* Edouard Roditi. VWA
Memo from the Desk of X. Donald Justice. TwCP
Memo to the 21st Century. Philip Appleman. SOTS; TAT
Memoir. R. G. Howarth. PV
Memoir. Roger Weingarten. AMV-80
Memoirs, The. Carl Rakosi. PoA
Memoirs of a Spinach-Picker. Sylvia Plath. GrPl
Memoirs of a Turcoman Diplomat. Denis Devlin. IPY
Memorabilia. Robert Browning. CABA; FaBoEn; FiP; HBV-2; LoBV; NoP; OAEL-2; OAEP; OBNC; PP; SeCePo; TreFT; WHA
Memorable Fancy, A ("An Angel came to me and said"). Blake. *Fr.* The Marriage of Heaven and Hell. NU
Memorable Fancy, A ("As I was walking among the fires of hell"). Blake. *Fr.* The Marriage of Heaven and Hell. NU
Memorandum. Rudy Bee Graham. PoNe
Memorandum. William Stafford. NYBP
Memorandum for Minos. Richard Kell. ELU
Memorandum/ The Accountant's Notebook. Kathleen Norris. OBAL
Memoria Technica for the Books of the Bible. *Unknown.* FaBoUs
Memoria Technica for the Plays of Shakespeare. *Unknown.* FaBoUs
Memorial. Mae Winkler Goodman. PGD
Memorial. Sonia Sanchez. BlSi
Memorial Couplets for the Dying Ego. George Barker. EBEV
Memorial Day. William E. Brooks. PAL; PGD
Memorial Day. Laureen Ching. AMV-80
Memorial Day. Theodosia Garrison. OHIP; PoSC
Memorial Day. Richard Watson Gilder. OHIP
Memorial Day. Emma A. Lent. WBLP
Memorial Day. Josephine Miles. NoP
Memorial Day. Annette Wynne. OHIP
Memorial Day; a Collaboration, *sel.* Anne Waldman *and* Ted Berrigan.
"And now the book is closed." EAS
Memorial Lines on the Gender of Latin Substantives. Benjamin Hall Kennedy. FaBoUs
Memorial Ode. Chief John Buck. GOA
Memorial: On the Slain at Chickamauga. Herman Melville. AA
Memorial Pillar, The. Felicia Dorothea Hemans. SBG
Memorial Poem. Jacob Glatstein, *tr. fr. Yiddish by* Ruth Whitman. VWA
Memorial Rain. Archibald MacLeish. AmPP; CMoP; LiTA; MoAB; MoAmPo; NoAM; OBWP; TwAmPo
Memorial Service. Ursula Vaughan Williams. POL
Memorial Service for the Invasion Beach Where the Vacation in the Flesh Is Over. Alan Dugan. MP; NMP; TwCP
Memorial to D. C., *sel.* Edna St. Vincent Millay.
Elegy: "Let them bury your big eyes," V. CMoP; HBMV; MoAB; MoAmPo; NePA; PoRA
("O, loveliest throat of all sweet throats.") OxBA
Memorial to the Great Big Beautiful Self-sacrificing Advertisers. Frederick Ebright. WaP
Memorial Verses. Matthew Arnold. CABA; FiP; HBV-2; OAEL-2; OAEP; PP; VLP
Wordsworth's Grave, *sel.* FaBoPP
Memorial Verses, Adapted to the Gregorian Account, or New Style. *Unknown.* FaBoUs
Memorial Verses for Travellers. Sir Anthony Fitzherbert. *Fr.* Husbandry. FaBoUs
Memorial Wreath. Dudley Randall. CNA; IDB; NNP; PoBA; PoNe
Memories. Thomas Bailey Aldrich. AA
Memories. George Gascoigne. *See* Gascoigne's Memories.
Memories. George Denison Prentice. AA
Memories. Arthur Stringer. HBV-1
Memories. Walt Whitman. PCP
Memories. Whittier. AP; OBVV
Memories are hidden. The Book. William Carson Fagg. LFAC
Memories of a Dorset Childhood in the 1730's. Thomas Cole. *Fr.* The Life of Hubert. NOEC
Memories of a good life are not enough. A Good Life. Robert Watson. AMV-81
Memories of a Lost War. Louis Simpson. NePoAm; OBWP; VGW
Memories of Aunt Maria-Martha. William Zaranka. BXAP
Memories of Childhood. John Carr. *Fr.* Derwent; an Ode. NOEC
Memories of President Lincoln. Walt Whitman.. *See* When Lilacs Last in the Dooryard Bloomed *and* O Captain, My Captain!
Memories of West Street and Lepke. Robert Lowell. AmPP; CAPP; CMoP; ConAP; InPS; NaP; NOBA
Memory. Thomas Bailey Aldrich. AA; BoNaP; PoLF; TreFS
Memory, A. William Allingham. *See* Four Ducks on a Pond.
Memory, A. Marvin Bell. GP
Memory. Anne Brontë. EBVV
Memory, A. Rupert Brooke. BrPo

Memory ("Marina's gone, and now sit I"). William Browne. *See* Celadyne's Song.
Memory ("So shuts the marigold her leaves"). William Browne. *Fr.* Britannia's Pastorals, III, Song 1. OBEV
("So shuts the marigold her leaves.") ViBoPo
Memory, The. Robert Creeley. CAPP; VGW
Memory. Babette Deutsch. PoA
Memory, The. Lord Dunsany. OxBI
Memory. Goldsmith. *Fr.* The Captivity. OBEC; OBEV
(Song: "O memory, thou fond deceiver.") ViBoPo
Memory. Michael Hamburger. OxBTC
Memory. Helen Hoyt. PoLF
Memory, A. Frederic Lawrence Knowles. HBV-1
Memory. Walter Savage Landor. EBEV; OAEL-2
Memory. Abraham Lincoln. BLPA; FaBoBe; FPL; WBLP
Memory ("I have a room whereinto no one enters"). Christina Rossetti. OBNC
Memory ("I nursed it in my bosom while it lived"). Christina Rossetti. OBNC
Memory, A. Margaret Sackville. SUMH
Memory. Erik Johann Stagnelius, *tr. fr. Swedish by* Sir Edmund Gosse. AWP
Memory, A. L. A. G. Strong. FaBoCo; NOBL; PoPl; WhC
Memory. Joseph Stroud. NPGG
Memory, A. Katharine Tynan. OxBI
Memory. W. B. Yeats. BIrV
Memory, a Small Brown Bird. Rich Ives. AMV-81
Memory Air. Charles Dobzynski, *tr. fr. French by* Anita Barrows. VWA
Memory as Memorial in the Last. Edward Marshall. CoPo
Memory cannot linger long. So Wags the World. Ellen Mackay Hutchinson Cortissoz. AA
Memory carries my fancy back. The Little Golden Ring, *with music.* *Unknown.* ShS
Memory comes, like the shadow of fog. Deja Vu. J. B. Mulligan. AMV-80
Memory: farfields of morning. Persephone. Robert Duncan. NoAM; NOBA
Memory feeds us on a prison diet. Mandrakes for Supper. James K. Baxter. OxBC
Memory Gardens. Allen Ginsberg. NNaP
Memory, hither come. Song. Blake. PoEL-4
Memory: I can take my head and strike it on a wall on Cumberland Island. The Shark's Parlor. James Dickey. NYBP
Memory is a full pocket. Fishing, at Coot Shallows. Don Welch. WOLT
Memory is a watery flower, when watered. In the Garden. Richard Eberhart. NePoAm-2
Memory Movie. Diane Webster. AMV-81
Memory of a Porch. Donald Justice. NCSH
Memory of a Scholar. Richmond Lattimore. GLGT
Memory of Another Climate. Gabriel Preil, *tr. fr. Hebrew by* Jeremy Garber. VWA
Memory of Boxer Benny (Kid) Paret, The. Frank Lima. PoNe
Memory of Brother Michael. Patrick Kavanagh. MoAB; OnYI; OxBI
Memory of Earth, A. "Æ." OBVV
Memory of Elena, The. Carolyn Forché. MAYP
Memory of Hills, *sel.* Rex Ingamells.
"There are rock-rooted ranges to dominate." CBAP
Memory of Kent, The. Edmund Blunden. HBMV
Memory of summer is winter's consciousness. Early Winter. Weldon Kees. NaP
Memory of the Dead, The. John Kells Ingram. AnIV; HBV-2; OnYI; OxBI
Memory of the face, A. After the War. Hayim Naggid, *tr. by* Shlomo Vinner *and* Howard Schwartz. VWA
Memory of the Night of the Fourth. Victor Hugo, *tr. fr. French by* Mary Ann Caws. NAWM-2
Memory of the Players in a Mirror at Midnight, A. James Joyce. InvP; NoAM; ViBoPo
Memory of you may be. Night Song for an Old Lover. Susan Glickman. AMV-81
Memory, out of the mist, in a long slow ripple. Seagulls on the Serpentine. Alfred Noyes. EtS
Memory pales in the face of the moon. On Leaving Baltimore. Duane Niatum. CDW
Memory parachutes in. Birthday: Tara Regina. George Mosby, Jr. AMV-81
Memory-Picture, A. Matthew Arnold. VLP
Memphis Blues. Sterling A. Brown. BANP
Memphis Minnie-Jitis Blues. *Unknown.* BluL
Men. Archibald MacLeish. AmFN; MoAB; YaD
Men. Dorothy Parker. DBV
Men against the Sky. John Haines. LCAP
Men and women round thee, what are they, The? Companionship. Mary Elizabeth Coleridge. NBM
Men Are Children of This World. Moses ibn Ezra, *tr. fr. Hebrew by* Solomon Solis-Cohen. TrJP
Men are children of this world. Meditation. Carl Rakosi. VWA
Men Are Coming Back, The. Barry Cole. OxBTC
Men are running across a field. Letter. Mark Strand. NoAm
Men Are the Devil. Mary Carolyn Davies. HBMV; YaD
Men are what they are, and what they do. Intimate Parnassus. Patrick Kavanagh. MoBrPo
Men are what they do, women are what they are. In Nature There Is neither Right nor Left nor Wrong. Randall Jarrell. OxBC
Men at Forty. Donald Justice. DiL; GP; LCAP; Prf; PPP
Men behind the Guns, The. John Jerome Rooney. AA; BLPA; EtS; FaBoBe; HBV-2; PAH; YaD
Men, brother men, that after us yet live. The Epitaph in Form of a Ballad. Villon, *tr. by* Swinburne. CTC
Men call you fair [*or* fayre], and you do credit it. Amoretti, LXXIX. Spenser. AWP; BLPL; FaBoBe; HBV-1; NoP
Men chase the boy into the hog shed, The. Rape. Thomas Rabbitt. MAYP
Men do not long endure the light. Fleur de Lys. Rayner Heppenstall. WaP
Men don't believe in a devil now. The Devil. *Unknown.* STF
Men dying make their wills—but wives. Woman's Will [*or* Wills]. John Godfrey Saxe. FaFP; HBV-1; ShM; TreFT
Men en masse. Observation. Richard Weber. POL
Men Fade like Rocks. W. J. Turner. OBMV
Men grew sae cauld, maids sae unkind. The Blind Boy's Pranks. William Thom. OBEV
Men halt in the littered spot before the bank. Saturday in the County Seat. Elijah L. Jacobs. AmFN
Men have left God not for other gods, they say, but for no god. T. S. Eliot. *Fr.* The Rock. TRV
Men have made them gods of love. Pain. "Æ." MoBrPo
Men heard this roar of parleying starlings, saw. February Afternoon. Edward Thomas. NoAM
Men if you love us, play no more. In the Person of Woman Kind. Ben Jonson. NIP; SeCP; SeCV-1
Men in Green. David Campbell. PoAu-2
Men in her department envied her, The. Sayre. Lynn Strongin. IHMS
Men in the City. Alfonsina Storni, *tr. fr. Spanish by* Rachel Benson. PBWP
Men late at night cook coffee in rusty cans. The County Jail. Jimmy Santiago Baca. LFAC
Men lean toward the wood. Lynching and Burning. Primus St. John. PoBA
Men Loved Wholly beyond Wisdom. Louise Bogan. HBMV; LiTA; LiTM; NePA; PBWP; VGW
Men Made Out of Words. Wallace Stevens. MoAB; NOBA; TAP; VGW
Men may leve all games. Pilgrims to St. James. *Unknown.* OxBM
Men May Talk of Country-Christmasses. Philip Massinger. OBCP
Men meet and part. Words Made of Water. Burns Singer. NePoEA-2
Men moving in a trench, in the clear noon. These Men. Leon Gellert. PoAu-1
Men never know. The Radical. Waring Cuney. CDC
Men never speak a good word. The Women Speak Out in Defense of Themselves. Aristophanes, *tr. by* B. B. Rogers. *Fr.* The Thesmophoriazusae. TreFT
Men of careful turns, haters of forks in the road. Gwendolyn Brooks. *Fr.* The Womanhood. BALP
Men of England, wherefore plough. Song to the Men of England. Shelley. EnRP; FiP; InPS; PAI; SaC; SeCeV; TrGrPo; ViBoPo
Men of Gotham, The. Thomas Love Peacock. *See* Three Men of Gotham.
Men of Old, The. Richard Monckton Milnes. OBEV; OBVV
Men of sin prevail, The! The Convenanter's Lament for Bothwell Brigg. Winthrop Mackworth Praed. OBRV
Men of Sudbury, The. Carlos Baker. GOA
Men of the Alamo, The. James Jeffrey Roche. BPAW; PAH
Men of the earth said, The: "We must war." Why. Robert Freeman. PGD
Men of the East, The. Feathers of Snow. *Unknown.* GBP
Men of the *Maine,* The. Clinton Scollard. PAH
Men of the *Merrimac,* The. Clinton Scollard. PAH
Men of the North. John Neal. AA
Men of the North and West. Richard Henry Stoddard. PAH
Men of the Rocks, *sels.* Joseph Gordon Macleod ("Adam Drinan").
"Below the dancing larches freckled." OxBS
"Fire the heather." OxBS
"Our pastures are bitten and bare." OxBS
Men of valor, The. Akahito. *Fr.* Manyo Shu. AWP
Men on Ice, *sel.* Andrew Greig.
On Falling. PoSH
Men Only Pretend. *Unknown.* MeEL

Men openly call you the enemy, call you the swine. Take Down the Fiddle, Karl! Shaw Neilson. CBAP
Men proffer presents here to my people. Wulf and Eadwacer. *Unknown.* TrGrPo
Men rent me on rode. Jesus Bids Man Remember. *Unknown.* MeEL
Men said at vespers: "All is well!" Chicago. Whittier. PAH
Men saw no portents on that night. Young Lincoln. Edwin Markham. OHIP
Men say, Columbia, we shall hear thy guns. Sydney Dobell. *Fr.* America. OBVV
Men say the sullen instrument. In the Twilight. James Russell Lowell. AA; HBV-1
Men Say They Know Many Things. Henry David Thoreau. ImOP; PoPl
Men seem as alike as the leaves on the trees. The Man from the Crowd. Sam Walter Foss. PoLF
Men seldom make passes. News Item. Dorothy Parker. *Fr.* Some Beautiful Letters. FaBoUs; InMe; OBAL; TreF; YaD
Men share perceptions. The Switch Blade; or, John's Other Wife. Jonathan Williams. NeAP
Men smile like they know everything. Oil. Linda Hogan. TWSS
Men, some to bus'ness, some to pleasure take. Pope. *Fr.* Moral Essays, Epistle II. OBSV
Men Tell and Talk. Nia Francisco. STE
Men that are safe, and sure, in all they doe. An Epistle Answering to One That Asked to be Sealed of the Tribe of Ben. Ben Jonson. AnAnS-2; OAEP; SeCV-1
Men, that delight to multiply desire. Caelica, XCIV. Fulk Greville. OBS
Men That Don't Fit In, The. Robert W. Service. BLPA; BLPL
Men that worked for England, The. Elegy in a Country Churchyard. G. K. Chesterton. DBV; EvOK; FaPoR; HBMV; MMA; MoBrPo; OBWP; TreFT; TrGrPo; ViBoPo; WhC
Men they may have many faults. Faults, Male and Female. *Unknown.* DBV
Men Told Me, Lord! David Starr Jordan. WGRP
Men tortured children. Children of Auschwitz. Naum Korzhavin, *tr. by* Daniel Weissbort. VWA
Men Walked To and Fro. Blanaid Salkeld. NeIP
Men went to Gododdin, laughter-loving. Aneirin, *tr. by* Joseph P. Clancy. *Fr.* The Gododdin. OBWP
Men went up on these sands along the sea. Children's Song. Arye Sivan, *tr. by* David Shevin. VWA
Men were connected with animals. The Shock. Larry Eigner. CoPo
Men were looking up. Austin Clarke. Mnemosyne Lay in Dust, III. IPY
Men who have loved the ships they took to sea. Mariners. David Morton. EtS
Men Who March Away ("We be the King's men"). Thomas Hardy. *Fr.* The Dynasts, Pt. I. CH
Men Who March Away ("What of the faith and fire within us"). Thomas Hardy. MMA; OBWP
Men! whose boast it is that ye. Stanzas on Freedom. James Russell Lowell. OHIP; PGD; PoNe
Men with crew-cuts. Crew-cuts. Donald Hall. MAT
Men with ventilators of black straw, The. Confab. Kenneth Rosen. AmPA
Men worked, men loafed, men sired. Ulster. Hans Adler. AMV-81
Men Working. Edna St. Vincent Millay. SaC
Men would never have come to need an attic. Up There. W. H. Auden. OxBTC
Menacing machine turns on and off, The. Terror Conduction. Philip Lamantia. NeAP
Menagerie, The. William Vaughn Moody. AP; YaD
Menaion, *sel.* Saint Cosmas, *tr. fr. Greek.*
  Purification, The. ISi
Menaphon, *sels.* Robert Greene.
  Doron's Jigge. PoEL-2
  (Jig, A.) ElL
  Menaphon's Ditty. OBSC
  Menaphon's Song. OBSC
  ("Some say Love.") LoBV
  Of His Mistress. ElL
  Samela. ElL; GBL; HBV-1; NOBE; OBEV; OBSC; ViBoPo
  (Doron's Description of Samela.) LoBV; PoEL-2
  Sephestia's Song to Her Child. ELP; EnRePo; LoBV; OBSC; PoEL-2; TrGrPo
  (Sephestia's Lullaby.) HBV-1; NOBE; OBEV
  (Weep Not My Wanton.) ElL; SeCePo; ViBoPo
Mend my broken mood. Prayer for Song. Fay Lewis Noble. TrPWD
Mendacious Mole, The. Oliver Herford. TDH
Mendacity. A. E. Coppard. OBMV
Mendax. *Unknown, tr. fr. German by* Gotthold Lessing. PV
Mendelian Theory. *Unknown.* FaBoCo
  (Limerick: "There was a young woman called Starkey.") NOBL
Mendel's Law. Peter Meinke. SUW
Mendicants, The. Bliss Carman. HBV-1
Mending Crab Pots. Dave Smith. GeTw
Mending Sump. Kenneth Koch. BXAP; HeIP; InPK; NeAP; NoAM; PV
Mending the Adobe. Hayden Carruth. EyDe; Psk
Mending Wall. Robert Frost. AmFN; AmPP; AP; CMoP; CoBMV; FaBV; FaFP; FPL; HAP; HBV-2; HeIP; HoPM; InPS; LiTA; LiTM; MoAB; MoAmPo; MoVE; NePA; NoAM; NOBA; NoP; OHFP; OxBA; PAI; PrIm; SCV; SeCeV; SoSe; TAP; VGW; ViBoPo; WeW; WHA
Mendings. Muriel Rukeyser. SaC
"Mene, Mene, Tekel, Upharsin." Madison Cawein. PAH
Menelaus and Helen. Rupert Brooke. SeCePo
Meningitis killing me, The. Memphis Minnie-Jitis Blues. *Unknown.* BluL
Menodotis. Leonidas of Alexandria, *tr. fr. Greek by* Richard Garnett. AWP
Men's hearts love gold and jade. Lodging with the Old Man of the Stream. Po Chü-i, *tr. by* Arthur Waley. AWP
Men's Impotence. *Unknown, tr. fr. Eskimo.* WTO
Men's Room in the College Chapel, The. W. D. Snodgrass. GP; MoAmPo; PPP; TW
Men's Voices. Inger Christensen, *tr. fr. Danish by* Nadia Christensen. BoWoP
Menstruation at Forty. Anne Sexton. CAPP
Mental Cases. Wilfred Owen. BiP; BrPo; CMoP; FaBoMo; MMA; NoAM; WaP
Mental Health. Elliot Fried. GP
Mental Hospital Garden, The. William Carlos Williams. FYAP
Mental Traveller, The. Blake. EnRP; LAuP; MasP; OAEL-2; PoEL-4
Mentis Trist. Robert Hillyer. HBMV
"Mentrechè il Vento, Come Fa, Si Tace." Delmore Schwartz. TwAmPo
Menu, The. Thomas Bailey Aldrich. HBV-2
Menu. Edward Lear. FaBoNo
Menzi son of Ndaba! Senzangakhona. *Zulu Oral Tradition, tr. by* T. Cope. WTO
Mephistopheles enters. Choosing the Devil. Linda Gregg. NPGG
Mercado. Greg Pape. AmPA
Merce Cunningham and the Birds. Lisel Mueller. GrPl
Merce of Egypt. Charles Olson. NoP
Merced. Adrienne Rich. NOBA
Mercedes. Elizabeth Stoddard. AA
Mercedes, Her Aloneness. Colette Inez. IHMS
Merchandise. Seán Jennett. NeIP
Merchant addressing a debtor, A. Persuasive Go-Gebtor. "R. C." TDH
Merchant and the Fidler's Wife, The. *Unknown.* CoMu; OxBB, *with music*
Merchant, as crafty a man is he, The. Do You Plan to Speak Bantu? Ogden Nash. FiBHP
Merchant Marine. Josephine Miles. TAP; VGW
Merchant of Venice, The, *sels.* Shakespeare.
  All That Glisters Is Not Gold, *fr.* II, vii. CTC
  Birdsong, *fr.* V, i. PB
  Fire Seven Times Tried This, The, *fr.* II, ix. CTC
  "How sweet the moonlight sleeps upon this bank," *fr.* V, i. FaBoRV; TreFS; TrGrPo
  (Moonlight.) OHFP
  In Such a Night, *fr.* V, i. ChTr; FiP; WHA
  (Divine Harmony, The.) GoBC
  ("Moon shines bright, The. In such a night as this.") GBL; PoPle
  Let Me Play the Fool, *fr.* I, i. TrGrPo
  Power of Music, The, *fr.* V, i. GN
  Quality of Mercy [Is Not Strain'd], The, *fr.* IV, i. FaFP; LiTB; TRV
  (Mercy.) OHFP; TrGrPo; WBLP
  (Portia's Plea for Mercy.) TreF
  Shylock's Defense, *fr.* III, i. TreFS
  "Tell me where is fancy bred," *fr.* III, ii. CH; ElL; ELP; EnRePo; LiTB; OAEL-1; OAEP; SeCeV; ViBoPo; WHA
  (Casket Song, A.) OBSC
  (Fancy.) FaPON; TreFS; TrGrPo
  (Love.) OBEV
  (Madrigal.) GTBS; GTBS-P
  (Song.) CTC; PoEL-2
Merchant, to secure his treasure, The. An Ode [*or* Song]. Matthew Prior. AWP; CABA; EnLoPo; GTBS; GTBS-P; HBV-1; NOEC; NoP; OBEV; PoPle; PoRA; TrGrPo; ViBoPo
Merchantmen, The. John Davidson. OBVV
Merchants from Cathay. William Rose Benét. HBMV; MoAmPo
Merchants have multiplied more than the stars of heaven. The Executive's Death. Robert Bly. CoAP; NaP
Merchant's Tale, The, *abr.* Chaucer, *mod. vers. by* Frank Ernest Hill. *Fr.* The Canterbury Tales. UnTE
Mercian Hymns, *sels.* Geoffrey Hill.
  "And it seemed, while we waited, he began to walk," XXX. NoP
  "At Pavia, a visitation of some sorrow. Boethius' dungeon," XVIII. FaBoMo

"Brooding on the eightieth letter of *Fors Clavigera,*" XXV. HAP
"Coins handsome as Nero's; of good substance and weight," XI. FaBoMo; HAP
"Clash of salutation. As keels thrust into shingle," XVI. NoP
"Dismissing reports and men, he put pressure on the wax," XIV. HAP
"Gasholders, russet among fields," VII. HAP; NoP
"He adored the desk, its brown-oak inlaid with ebony," X. HAP; NoP
"King of the perennial holly-groves, the riven sandstone," I. FaBoMo; HAP
"Mad are predators, The. Too often lately they harbor," VIII. NoP
" 'Not strangeness, but strange likeness,' " XXIX. FaBoMo; HAP
"On the morning of the crowning we chorused our remission from school," III. HAP
"Princes of Mercia were badger and raven, The," VI. HAP; NoP
"Processes of generation; deeds of settlement," XXVIII. NoP
"Trim the lamp; polish the lens; draw, one by one, rare coins," XIII. FaBoMo
"We ran across the meadow scabbed with the cow-dung," XXII. HAP
Mercies and Blessings. *Unknown.* STF
Mercies of the Year, The. John Danforth. SCAP
Merciles[s] Beaute [*or* Beautée *or* Beauty]. Chaucer. CTC; EBEV; EnLoPo; HAP; NoP; OxBM
(Three Roundels of Love Unreturned.) MeEL
Merciless Beauty, I, *mod. vers., sel.* ACP
(Rondel of Merciles Beaute, A.) TrGrPo
(Rondel of Merciless Beauty, A, *mod. vers.* by Louis Untermeyer.) TrGrPo
("Your eyen two will slay me suddenly," *mod. vers.*) BoLoP
Merciless love, whom nature hath denied. John Fletcher. *Fr.* The Chances. GBL
Mercury; on Losing My Pocket Milton at Luss near Ben Lomond, and Other Mountains. Robert Andrews. NOEC
Mercury shew'd Apollo, Bartas Book. Nathaniel Ward. SCAP
Mercury's Song to Phædra. Dryden. *See* Song: "Fair Iris I love, and hourly I die."
Mercutio's Queen Mab Speech. Shakespeare. *Fr.* Romeo and Juliet, I, iv. LiTB; TreF
(Mercutio Describes Queen Mab.) TrGrPo
("Oh, then I see Queen Mab hath been with you.") WSC
(Queen Mab.) FaPON; FiP
Mercy ("Mercy is hendest where sinne is mest"). *Unknown.* OxBM
Mercy ("The quality of mercy is not strained"). Shakespeare. *See* Quality of Mercy, The.
Mercy and Love. Robert Herrick. SeCV-1
Mercy is whiter than laundry. Angels in Winter. Nancy Willard. FiCP; LCAP
Mercy Killing. Kenneth Burke. TwAmPo
Mercy Pleads for Mankind. Giles Fletcher. *Fr.* Christ's Victory and Triumph. JCP
Mercy to Animals: A Ballad of Humanity. Martin Farquhar Tupper. PeD
Meredith Phyfe. Edgar Lee Masters. *Fr.* The New Spoon River. GOA
Merely the landscape of a vanished whim. Versailles. Adrienne Rich. NePoEA
'Mergency Man, The. J. M. Synge. PoPle
Merideth. *Unknown.* WhC
Meridian. Brewster Ghiselin. AMV-80
Meridians are a net. Objects. Richard Wilbur. FF; NoP
Merit of True Passion, The. Sir Walter Ralegh. *See* Wrong Not, Sweet Empress of My Heart.
Merits of Laughter and Lust. Eli Mandel. PeCV
Merlin. Emerson. AmPP; AP; NOBA
Sels.
Merlin, I. AA; OxBA
Merlin, II. PoEL-4
Merlin. Geoffrey Hill. POL
Merlin. Edwin Muir. FaBoTw; OxBS
Merlin and the Gleam. Tennyson. OAEL-2; OAEP; VLP
Follow the Gleam, IX. TreFT
Merlin and the Snake's Egg. Leslie Norris. WSC
Merlin and Vivien. Tennyson. *See* Idylls of the King.
Merlin Enthralled. Richard Wilbur. CMoP; NePoEA; NYBP
Merlin in the Cave: He Speculates without a Book. Thom Gunn. NePoEA
Merlin, they say, an English prophet borne. Caelica, XXIII. Fulke Greville. NCEP
Merlin's Apple-Trees. Thomas Love Peacock. *Fr.* The Misfortunes of Elphin. OBRV
Merlin's Riddling. Tennyson. *Fr.* Idylls of the King: The Coming of Arthur. FaBoRV
Mermaid Tavern, The. Keats. *See* Lines on the Mermaid Tavern.
Mermaid, The. Ben King. OBAL
Mermaid, The. Tennyson. FaPON; GN; WSC
Mermaid, The ("One [*or* 'Twas a] Friday morn"). *Unknown.* AmFP, *sl. diff. vers.* (A *and* B *vers.*); BaBo, *sl. diff. vers.*; ESPB (A *and* B *vers.*); FSW; OuSiCo, *sl. diff. vers., with music;* TreF; ViBoFo (A *vers.;* B *vers., with music*)
(One Friday Morn.) CH; OnMSP
Mermaid, The ("To yon fausse stream"). *Unknown.* CH
Mermaiden, A. Thomas Hennell. FaBoTw
Mermaidens, The. Laura E. Richards. OBCA
Mermaidens' Vesper-Hymn, The. George Darley. Syren Songs, VI. FaBoEn; GBL; LoBV; OBNC; OBRV; PoEL-4
(Chorus of Sirens.) NBM
(Siren Chorus.) BIrV; FaBoRV; OxBI; ViBoPo; WSC
(Song of the Mermaids.) ChTr
Mermaids, The. Walter de la Mare. BrPo
Mermaids. Kenneth Slessor. *Fr.* The Atlas. PoAu-2
Mermaids, The. Spenser. *Fr.* The Faerie Queene, II, 12. ChTr
Mermaids and Mermen. Sir Walter Scott. *Fr.* The Pirate, *ch.* 16. EtS
(Song of the Mermaids and Mermen.) WSC
Mermaid's not a human thing, A. Lost and Given Over. E. J. Brady. PoAu-1
Merman, The. Tennyson. FaPON; GN; WSC
Mer-Man, and Marstig's Daughter, The. *Unknown, tr. fr. Danish by* Robert Jamieson. AWP
Merops. Emerson. FaBoEn; OxBA
Merrie world did on a day, The. *See* Merry world did on a day, The.
Merrily swim we, the moon shines bright. Song of the White Lady of Avenel. Sir Walter Scott. *Fr.* The Monastery. NBM
Merrily swinging on brier and weed. Robert of Lincoln. Bryant. FaBoBe; FaPON; HBV-1; HBVY; OBCA; WBLP, *abr.*
Merritt Parkway. Denise Levertov. AmPP; NeAP; PoM
Merry Are the Bells. *Unknown.* HBV-1; HBVY; MoShBr; TiPo
Merry Bagpipes, The. *Unknown.* CoMu
Merry Bee, A. Joseph Skipsey. OBVV
Merry car, A. Three Car Poems. Richard Jones. FAZ
Merry Christmas. Aileen Fisher. RHPC
Merry Christmas! Elder Olson. FAZ
Merry Country Lad, The. Nicholas Breton. *See* Shepherd and Shepherdess.
Merry Crocodile, The. Gertrude E. Heath. TDH
Merry Cuckold, The. *Unknown.* CoMu
Merry cuckoo, messenger of spring, The. Amoretti, XIX. Spenser. OBSC
Merry-go-round. Dorothy Baruch. SoPo; SUS; TiPo
Merry-go-round. Langston Hughes. CTBA; PAI; PoNe
Merry-go-round. Oliver Jenkins. GoYe
Merry-go-round. James McAuley. CBAP
Merry-go-round, The. Rainer Maria Rilke, *tr. fr. German by* C. F. MacIntyre. CAD; WeW
Merry-go-round. Mark Van Doren. SO
Merry-go-round, The/ Plays a bouncy tune! June. Mary Carolyn Davies. SiSoSe; TiPo
Merry Guide, The. A. E. Housman. A Shropshire Lad, XLII. OAEP
Merry Hay-Makers, The; or, Pleasant Pastime between the Young-Men and Maids, in the Pleasant Meadows. *Unknown.* CoMu; ErPo
Merry Heart, A. Shakespeare. *See* Jog On, Jog On.
Merry Hoastess, The. *Unknown.* CoMu
Merry It Is, *modern vers.* *Unknown.* HAP, (How Long This Night Is, *medieval vers.*) MeEL
(Mirie It Is while Sumer Ilast, *medieval vers.*) HAP
(Now Comes the Blast of Winter, *medieval vers.*) SeCePo
(Winterfall, *medieval vers.*) OxBM
Merry [*or* Mery] it is in May morning. By a Chapel as I Came. *Unknown.* ChTr; GBP; OxBM
Merry it is in the good greenwood. Alice Brand. Sir Walter Scott. *Fr.* The Lady of the Lake. BeLS; HBV-2; HBVY; OnMSP
Merry Jovial Beggar, The. Peter Casey, *tr. fr. Gaelic by* Douglas Hyde. WTO
Merry Little Maid and Wicked Little Monk, The. *Unknown.* ErPo
Merry-ma-Tanzie, The. *Unknown.* GBP
("Here we go dancing jingo-ring," 1st.) OxNR
Merry Man of Paris, The. Stella Mead. SUS
Merry [*or* Mirry] Margaret,/ As midsummer flower. To Mistress Margaret Hussy. John Skelton. *Fr.* The Garlande of Laurell. AAS; ACP; EBEV; EnLoPo; ErPo; FaBoCh; GN; GoBC; GoJo; HBV-1; HeIP; HoPM; LoBV; NOBE; NoP; OAEL-1; OAEP; OBEV; OBSC; PoEL-1; PoRA; PPoe; PPP, SCV; SeCeV; TreFT; ViBoPo
Merry May the Keel Row. *Unknown.* GBP
Merry may the maid be. The Miller. Sir John Clerk. ChTr
Merry, merry, merry, cheery, cheery, cheery! Harvest. Thomas Nashe. *Fr.* Summer's Last Will and Testament. OBSC
Merry, merry sparrow! The Blossom. Blake. *Fr.* Songs of Innocence. GoJo; PB; PBBP
Merry Minuet, The. Sheldon Harnick. DBV
Merry Month, The. "Miss X *and* Miss Y." InMe

Merry Month of March, The. Wordsworth. *See* Written in March.
Merry month of May, sunny skies of blue. I've Got the World on a String. Ted Koehler. BLSo
Merry Note, A. Shakespeare. *See* When Icicles Hang by the Wall.
Merry Old Souls. Morris Bishop. WhC
"Old Savonarola was a merry old soul," *sel.* DBV
Merry sang the monks who in Ely fare. The Monks of Ely. *Unknown.* ACP
Merry the green, the green hill shall be merry. Another Song [*or* Tune for a Lonesome Fife]. Donald Justice. ConAP; NePoEA-2; NYBP; VGW
Merry voices chatterin'. Two-an'-Six. Claude McKay. BANP
Merry Window, The. Francis Scarfe. EAS
Merry Wives of Windsor, The, *sel.* Shakespeare.
"Fie on sinful fantasy!" *Fr.* V, v. ViBoPo
Merry [*or* Merrie] World did on a day, The. The Quip. George Herbert. JCP; LiTB; OAEP; OBS; OxBoCh; SeCP; SeCV-1
Merrythought's Song. Beaumont *and* Fletcher. *Fr.* The Knight of the Burning Pestle, IV, i. OBS
Merthe of all this land, The. God Speed the Plough! *Unknown.* OxBM
Merthymawr. George Woodcock. NeBP
Meru. W. B. Yeats. InPS; NoAM; OAEL-2; PoA
Mery Gest How a Sergeaunt Wolde Lerne to Be a Frere, A. Sir Thomas More. AAS
Mery it is in May morning. *See* Merry it is in May morning.
Mery it was in grene forest. Adam Bel [*or* Bell], Clym [*or* Clim] of the Cloughe, and Wyllyam [*or* William] of Cloudesle [*or* Cloudesly]. *Unknown.* ESPB; OxBB
Mery [*or* Mirie] it is while sumer y-last [*or* ilast]. Winterfall. *Unknown.* HAP; OxBM
Mesdames, never dare to deem those lovers yours. The Man Within. Annemarie Ewing. NePoAm-2
Meseem'd that Love, with swifter feet than fire. An Utter Passion Uttered Utterly. John Todhunter. BXAP
Meseemeth I heard cry and groan. The Complaint of the Fair Armoress [*or* Armouress]. Villon, *tr. by* Swinburne. AWP; CTC; OBVE; UnTE; VLP
Mesh cast for mackerel. Fishermen. Basil Bunting. PoA
Meshed in a glow of nickel, glass. Ballad of the Drinker in His Pub. N. F. Van Wyk Louw, *tr. by* Uys Krige, Jack Cope, *and* Ruth Miller. PeSA
Mesnevi. Sadi, *tr. fr. Persian by* L. Cranmer-Byng. *Fr.* The Gulistan. AWP
Mesón Brujo. E. A. Lacey. PeHV
Mesopotamia. Kipling. MMA
Mess Deck Casualty. Alan Ross. WaP
Mess is all asleep, my candle burns, The. A Wry Smile. Roy Fuller. WaaP; WaP
Mess of Love, The. D. H. Lawrence. OAEL-2
Mess-tent is full, and the glasses are set, The. The Battle Eve of the [Irish] Brigade. Thomas Osborne Davis. AnIV; OnYI
Message, The. John Donne. EIL; HBV-1; MeLP; OBS; ViBoPo; WHA
Message. Allen Ginsberg. ConAP; NeAP; VGW
Message, The. Heine, *tr. fr. German by* Kate Freiligrath Kroeker. AWP
Message, The. *At. to* Thomas Heywood. *See* Ye Little Birds That Sit and Sing.
Message, A. George Ives. PeHV
Message. Renata Pallottini, *tr. fr. Portuguese by* Monique *and* Carlos Altschul. WPOW
Message, A. Elizabeth Stuart Phelps. PAH
Message, The. Jacques Prévert, *tr. fr. French by* John Frederick Nims. WeW
Message. Gyorgy Raba, *tr. fr. Hungarian by* Jascha Kessler. VWA
Message. Dorothy M. Richardson. PoA
Message at Sunset for Bishop Berkeley. Heather McHugh. GeTw
Message-Bringer Woman. Prologue. Carol Lee Sanchez. TWSS
Message Clear. Edwin Morgan. NIP
Message for Peace, A. Longfellow. WBLP
Message from a Mouse, Ascending in a Rocket. Patricia Hubbell. RHPC
Message from Home. Kathleen Raine. ImOP; WPE
Message from Ohanapecosh Glacier. W. M. Ransom. CDW
Message from Reverend Fat Back Made Possible by the International Society of Social Suckers, A. Melvin Douglass Brown. LFAC
Message from Space, A. William Stafford. SUW
Message of Peace, The. Julia Ward Howe. PGD
Message of Peace, A. John Boyle O'Reilly. OnYI
Message of the Bells, The. Thomas Curtis Clark. PGD
Message of the March Wind, The. William Morris. OBNC; OBVV; WiR
Message of the Rain, The. Norman H. Russell. STE
Message to General Montgomery. H. F. Ellis. WhC
Message to Siberia. Pushkin, *tr. fr. Russian by* Max Eastman. AWP; TTY
Message to the Bard. William Livingston, *tr. fr. Gaelic.* GoTS
Message to the Photographer Whose Prints I Purchased, A. Beryle Williams. PoDr
Messages, The. W. W. Gibson. OHIP
Messages. Alfred Noyes. *Fr.* The Last Voyage, XIII. GoBC
Messages. Francis Thompson. CH
Messages—from the dead? Messages. Alfred Noyes. *Fr.* The Last Voyage, XIII. GoBC
Messe of Nonsense, A. *Unknown.* OBS
Messed Damozel, The. Charles Hanson Towne. SpRo
Messenger, The. Thom Gunn. PoA
Messenger, The. Frances Horovitz. BrRo
Messenger, The. Alfred Noyes. GoBC
Messenger, The. Jean Valentine. LCAP
Messenger dispatch'd, again she view'd, The. Ave atque Vale. Dryden. *Fr.* Sigismonda and Guiscardo. OBS
Messenger Song, The. *At. to* John Calhoun. ShS
Messiah, The. Bible, *O.T.* Isaiah, VII: 14–25. AWP
Messiah, The. Milton. *Fr.* Paradise Regained, I. OBS
Messiah. Pope. OxBoCh
Rise, Crowned with Light [Imperial Salem Rise], *sel.* GoBC; WGRP
Messiah, The. Virgil, *tr. fr. Latin by* Dryden. Eclogues, IV. AWP
Messiah, The. Moshe Yungman, *tr. fr. Yiddish by* David G. Roskies *and* Hillel Schwartz. VWA
Messiah-Blower, The. Paul Goodman. FAZ
Messiah will not come. The Field of Night. Miriam Waddington. VWA
Messmates. Sir Henry Newbolt. CH; EBVV; HBV-1
Metagnomy. N. H. Pritchard. NBP
Metal Fatigue. Adam Le Fevre. AMV-81
Metallic apparition whirring. Hummingbird. Marge Piercy. GeTw
Metamorpho I. Joe Rosenblatt. MoCV
Metamorphosed Gipsies, The. Ben Jonson. *See* Gypsies Metamorphosed, The.
Metamorphoses. Roy Fuller. OxBTC
Metamorphoses. Howard Nemerov. EyDe
Metamorphoses, *sels.* Ovid, *tr. fr.* Latin.
Acteon, *fr.* III, *tr. by* Arthur Golding. CTC
"And from the citie Tegea there came the Paragone," *fr.* X, *tr. by* Arthur Golding. OBVE
Daphne and Apollo, *fr.* I, *tr. by* Matthew Prior. NOEC
Death of Eurydice and Orpheus' Journey to Hell, The, *tr. by* George Sandys. JCP
"Floods, by nature enemies to land, The," *fr.* I, *tr. by* Dryden. OBVE
(Flood, The, *shorter sel., tr. by* Dryden.) ChTr
Golden Age, The, *fr.* I, *tr. by* Arthur Golding. OAEL-1
"I pray thee Nymph Penaeis stay, I chase not as a fo," *fr.* I, *tr. by* Arthur Golding. OBVE
"In the Shire of Phestos hard by Cnossus dwelt of yore," *fr.* IX, *tr. by* Arthur Golding. PeHV
King Midas, *fr.* XI, *tr. by* Arthur Golding. CTC
Magic, *tr. by* Shakespeare. AWP
Meleager, *fr.* VIII, *tr. by* Arthur Golding. CTC
"More whyght thou art than primrose leaf my Lady Galatee," *fr.* VIII, *tr. by* Arthur Golding. OBVE
(Cyclops, *tr. by* Arthur Golding.) CTC
"Near the Cymmerians, in his dark abode," *fr.* XI, *tr. by* Dryden. OBVE
"Neare Enna walles there standes a Lake Pergusa is the name," *fr.* V, *tr. by* Arthur Golding. OBVE
"Northern breath, that freezes floods, he binds, The," *fr.* I, *tr. by* Dryden. OBVE
"Not Pallas, not ev'n Spleen it self could blame," *fr.* VI, *tr. by* John Gay. OBVE
"Now have I brought a woork to end which neither Joves fierce wrath," *fr.* XV, *tr. by* Arthur Golding. OBVE
(Conclusion.) CTC
"Now in this while gan Daedalus a wearinesse to take," *fr.* VIII, *tr. by* Arthur Golding. OBVE
(Daedalus.) CTC
"Now whyle Hippomenes/ Debates theis things," *fr.* X, *tr. by* Arthur Golding. OBVE
(Atalanta, *longer sel., tr. by* Rolfe Humphries.) LiSp
Of the Pythagorean Philosophy, *fr.* XV, *tr. by* Dryden. FM; OBVE
"Pallas an old-wife. Haughtie thoughts o're-throw," *fr.* VI, *tr. by* George Sandys. AnAnS-2
Phoenix Self-born, The, *fr.* XV, *tr. by* Dryden. ChTr
"Pygmalion seeing these to spend their times," *fr.* X, *tr. by* George Sandys. OAEL-1
Pygmalion's Statue Comes to Life, *fr.* X, *tr. by* Arthur Golding. OAEL-1
"Seeing as the father saw the rosy morn," *fr.* II, *tr. by* Joseph Addison. OBVE
"Stones (a Miracle to Mortal View), The," *fr.* I, *tr. by* Dryden. OBVE
"Then Lelex rose, an old experienc'd man," *fr.* VIII, *tr. by* Dryden. OBVE
(Baucis and Philemon.) AWP; OAEL-1
(Philemon and Baucis, *tr. by* Arthur Golding.) CTC; OBSC
"To thee obeyeth all the East as far as Ganges goes," *fr.* IV, *tr. by* Arthur Golding. OBVE

"Ye ayres and windes, ye elves of hilles," *fr.* VII, *tr. by* Arthur Golding. OBVE
(Medea Casts a Spell to Make Aeson Young Again, *longer sel., tr. by* Arthur Golding.) MOON
Metamorphoses of M. John Peale Bishop. ErPo
Metamorphoses of the Vampire. Baudelaire, *tr. fr. French by* Jackson Mathews. ErPo
Metamorphosis. Sylvia Plath. PoA
Metamorphosis. Peter Porter. OxBTC
Metamorphosis. Wallace Stevens. InPK; VGW
Metamorphosis, The. Sir John Suckling. CaPo; FaBoEE
Metamorphosis of Aunt Jemima, The. William Childress. MAT
Metamorphosis of Pygmalion's Image, The, *sel.* John Marston.
"O gracious gods, take compassion." OAEL-1
Metaphor as Degeneration. Wallace Stevens. LCAP
Metaphor for My Son. John Holmes. MiAP
Metaphors. Sally McNall. FAZ
Metaphors. Sylvia Plath. HeIP; InPK; SoSe
Metaphors. Miklós Radnóti, *tr. fr. Hungarian* by Steven Polgar *and* Stephen Berg *and* S. J. Marks. VWA
Metaphors of a Magnifico. Wallace Stevens. SOTW
Metaphysic of Snow. Donald Finkel. PoA
Metaphysical. Robert Fitzgerald. PoA
Metaphysical Amorist, The. J. V. Cunningham. TwAmPo; VGW
Metaphysical Paintings, The. John Perreault. EAS
Metaphysical Sectarian, The ("He was in logick a great critic"). Samuel Butler. *Fr.* Hudibras. MeLP
(Hudibras, the Presbyterian Knight, *abr.*) OxBoLi
(Portrait of Hudibras.) PoEL-3
(Presbyterian Knight and Independent Squire, *abr.*) OBS
(Sir Hudibras, His Passing Worth.) FaBoCo
Metaphysical Shock while Watching a TV Cartoon. Stan Rice. NPGG
Metaphysician. Robert Fitzgerald. PoA
Metaphysics. Oliver Herford. NA
Metempsychosis. Kenneth Slessor. ViBoPo
Meteorologists, like old lovers, know. Spring. Frederick Feirstein. AMV-81
Meteor's arc of quiet, The; a voiceless rain. Faint Music. Walter de la Mare. FaBoCh
Methinks all things have travelled since you shined. On the Sun Coming Out in the Afternoon. Henry David Thoreau. PoEL-4
Methinks already, from this chymick flame. The New London [*or* London]. Dryden. *Fr.* Annus Mirabilis. FaBoCh; NOBE; OBS; SeCePo
Methinks, dear Tom, I see thee stand demure. To the Revd. Mr. ——— on His Drinking Sea-Water. John Winstanley. NOEC
Methinks Death like one laughing lyes. Epitaph. Caecil. Boulstr. Lord Herbert of Cherbury. AnAnS-2; SeCP
Methinks heroick poesie till now. To Sir William Davenant, Upon His Two First Books of Gondibert. Abraham Cowley. AnAnS-2; SeCV-1
Methinks I am a prophet new inspir'd. John of Gaunt's Dying Speech. Shakespeare. King Richard II, *fr.* II, i. FiP
Methinks I draw but sickly breath. The Farewell. *Unknown.* OxBoCh
Methinks I see great Diocletian walk. Great Diocletian. Abraham Cowley. *Fr.* The Garden. ChTr
Methinks I see some crooked mimic jeer. Sonnet—To the Critic. Michael Drayton. Idea, XXXI. LoBV
Methinks I see, with what a busy haste. *See* Me thinks . . .
Methinks I spy Almighty holding in. Edward Taylor. *Fr.* Preparatory Meditations, Second Series, LXVIII. AP; HAP
Methinks the poor town has been troubled too long. Song. Charles Sackville. CavP; SeCV-2
Methinks thou writhest as in rage. To a Worm Which the Author Accidentally Trode Upon. William Hawkins. FM
Methinks 'Tis Pretty Sport [to Hear a Child]. Thomas Bastard. EIL; InvP
Method must be purest meat, The. On Burroughs' Work. Allen Ginsberg. NoAM; NOBA
Method of Preserving Hay from Being Mow-Burnt, or Taking Fire, A. Robert Dodsley. *Fr.* Agriculture. FaBoUs
Methodist, The, *sels.* Evan Lloyd.
Religion and the Lower Classes. NOEC
"Sons of War sometimes are known, The." OBSV
Methods of Cooking Trout. Thomas Barker. *Fr.* The Art of Angling. FaBoUs
Methought I heard a butterfly. The Butterfly and the Bee. William Lisle Bowles. HBV-1; HBVY
Methought I heard a voice cry "Sleep no more!" Sleep. Shakespeare. *Fr.* Macbeth, II, ii. TreFS
Methought I met a lady yester even. William Alexander. *Fr.* A Vision of Oxford. OBVV
Methought I Saw. Milton. *See* On His Deceased Wife.
Methought I saw/ Life swiftly treading over endless space. The Sea of Death. Thomas Hood. FaBoEn; LiTB; LoBV; OBNC; PoEL-4
Methought I Saw a Thousand Fearful Wrecks. Shakespeare. *See* Dream of Wrecks, A.
Methought I saw (as I did dream in bed). The Vision [*or* The Second Vision]. Robert Herrick. CaPo; UnTE
Methought I saw my late espoused saint. On His Deceased [*or* Dead *or* Late] Wife. Milton. BLPL; BoLoP; CABA; EBEV; EnLoPo; FaBoEn; FaFP; GBL; HAP; LiTB; LoBV; NOBE; NoP; OAEL-1; OBEV; OBS; PoEL-3; PoPle; PPP; SCV; SeCeV; TEP; TreFS; WeW
Methought I Saw the Footsteps of a Throne. Wordsworth. SyP
Methought I saw the grave, where Laura lay. A Vision upon This Conceit of the Faerie Queene [*or* Of Spenser's Faery Queen, *or* The Faery Queen]. Sir Walter Ralegh. OBSC; SiPS; ViBoPo
Methought I stood where trees of every clime. A Dream. Keats. *Fr.* The Fall of Hyperion, I. OBNC; OBRV
Methuselah. Rosemary Dobson. *Fr.* The Devil and the Angel. PoAu-2
Methuselah ("Methuselah ate what he found on his plate"). *Unknown.* BLPA; BLPL; FaBoBe; QQQ; TreFS
Meticulous, past midnight in clear rime. Hart Crane. Voyages, V. MoPo; MoVE
Metonymy as an Approach to a Real World. William Bronk. VGW
Metre Columbian, The. *Unknown.* BXAP; Par; SpRo
Metric Figure. William Carlos Williams. MoAB; MoAmPo
Metrical Feet. Samuel Taylor Coleridge. HBV-2; NIP; OxBChV; SoSe
(Metrical Feet: Lesson for a Boy.) FaBoUS
Metrical Index to the Bible, A, *sel.* Josiah Chorley.
"All things created, Moses writes." FaBoUs
Metrical Version of the Bible, Said to Have Been Composed by a Negro Christian in the State of Massachusetts, and Published in Louisville, Kentucky, in 1858, A, *sel.* *Unknown.*
"Adam was de first man and Eve was de udder." FaBoUs
Metroliner. Jack DuVall. AMV-80
Metropolitan Night. Jorge Guillén, *tr. fr. Spanish by* Barbara Howes. NYP
Metropolitan Nightmare. Stephen Vincent Benét. ImOP; NYBP
Metropolitan Railway, The. John Betjeman. EBEV; OxBTC
Metrum Parhemiacum Tragicum. Eugenius Vulgarius, *tr. fr. Latin by* Helen Waddell. WaaP
Metrum V. Boethius, *tr. by* Henry Vaughan. *See* Happy That First White Age When We.
Meuse and Marne have little waves, The. A Girl's Song. Katharine Tynan. OnYI; SUMH
Mewlips, The. J. R. R. Tolkien. AmMo; SO; WSC
Mews Flat Mona. William Plomer. FaBoTw
Mexican dwarfs can dance for miles, The. Maxixe. Sir Osbert Sitwell. PoA
Mexican Jo and Mexican Jane. Raking Walnuts in the Rain. Monica Shannon. SiSoSe
Mexican Market Woman. Langston Hughes. SaC
Mexican Quarter. John Gould Fletcher. Arizona Poems, II. BPAW
Mexican Scrapbook, A. Dave Oliphant. FAZ
Mexican Serenade. Arthur Guiterman. FiBHP
Mexico, *sel.* Robert Lowell.
"No artist perhaps, you go beyond their phrases." BiP
México:/ When I'm that far south, the old words. Visions of Mexico While at a Writing Symposium in Port Townsend, Washington. Lorna Dee Cervantes. FIA
Mexico City Blues, *sels.* Jack Kerouac.
Chorus: "Big Engines, The," 146. NeAP
Chorus: "Essence of Existence, The," 182. NeAP
Chorus: "Glenn Miller and I were heroes," 179. NeAP
Chorus: "Got up and dressed up," 113. NeAP
Chorus: "In the ocean there's a very sad turtle," 229. PoM
Chorus: "Love's multitudinous boneyard," 230. NeAP
Chorus: "Nobody knows the other," 127. NeAP
Chorus: "Old Man Mose," 221. NeAP
Chorus: "Only awake to Universal Mind," 183. NeAP
Chorus: "Praised be man, he is existing in milk," 228. NeAP
Chorus: "Saints, I give myself up to thee," 219. NeAP
Chorus: "Void that's highly embraceable, The," 225. NeAP
Chorus: "Wheel of the quivering Meat, The," 211. NeAP; PoM
Mexico City Hand Game. Rayna Green. TWSS
Mexico City, 150 Pesos to the Dollar. Jim Mitsui. BrSi
Mexico Is a Foreign Country: Four Studies in Naturalism, *sel.* Robert Penn Warren.
Mango on the Mango Tree, The, IV. NoAM
Meyer and I, we drove. Herman Nibbelink. AMV-80
Mezzo Cammin. Longfellow. FPL; NoP; TAP
Mi Abuelo. Alberto Ríos. MAYP
Mi Caballo Blanco (My White Horse.). *Tr. fr. Spanish.* FSW
Mi Corazón. Gordon W. Norris. BPAW
Mi Y'Malel (Who Can Retell?). *Tr. fr. Hebrew.* FSW
Mia Carlotta. T. A. Daly. InMe; TreFS; WhC
Miami. Daniel Mark Epstein. MAYP

Mica shines on the beach. Extract. Paul Bowles. PoA
Micah, *sels.* Bible, *O.T.*
And They Shall Beat Their Swords into Plowshares, IV: 1-5. TreF
(Neither Shall They Learn War Anymore, IV: 1-4.) TRV
Wherewith Shall I Come before the Lord? VI: 6-8. TRV
Woe Is Me! VII: 1-6. TrJP
Mice. Rose Fyleman. EvOK; FaPON; NTCP; PDV; RHPC; SoPo; SUS; TiPo
Mice at the Door, The. Vincent McHugh. NePoAm-2
Mice before Milk. Chaucer. *See* Lat Take a Cat.
Mice in the garbage. For Rosa Yen, Who Lived Here. Greg Pape. AmPA
Mice in the Hay. Leslie Norris. OBCP; PChr
Mice masticate from crumb to tooth. Repast. Gertrude Tiemer-Wille. GoYe
Michael. Sandra McPherson. LCAP
Michael. Wordsworth. EnRP; GoTL; OAEP; WHA
(Michael: A Pastoral Poem.) OAEL-2
Michael Finnigan. *Unknown.* FSW
("There was an old man named Michael Finnegan.") TiPo
Michael Hayd'n and Patrick Buggy one night got very druggy. The Scow on Cowden Shore, *vers.* III. Larry Gorman. ShS
Michael Robartes and the Dancer. W. B. Yeats. OAEL-2
Michael Robartes Bids His Beloved Be at Peace. W. B. Yeats. BrPo; NoAM
(Shadowy Horses, The.) SyP
Michael Robartes Remembers Forgotten Beauty. W. B. Yeats. *See* He Remembers Forgotten Beauty.
Michael, Row the Boat Ashore. *Unknown.* BLSo, *with music;* FSW
Michael Walked in the Wood. Robert Greacen. NeIP
Michaelmas. Norman Nicholson. MoBrPo
Michael's Room. Reginald Gibbons. AMV-81
Michelangelo: "The Creation of Adam." Gregory Djanikian. AMV-81
Michigan-I-O. *Unknown.* AmFP
("It was early in the season in the spring of '63.") OuSiCo
Mick. James Reeves. GDP
Microbe's Serenade, The. George Ade. OBAL
Microbiblion, *sel. At. to* Simon Wastell.
Man's Mortality. FaBoCh; HBV-2; WBLP. *See also* Hos Ego Versiculos, *sl. diff. vers. by* Francis Quarles, *Fr.* Argalus and Parthenia.
(Verses of Man's Mortalitie.) OBS
Microcosm. Bertram Dobell. OBVV
Microcosmos, *abr.* Nigel Heseltine. NeBP
Microcosmos. Susan Miles. OxBTC
Microcosmus, *sel.* Thomas Nabbes.
Love Sets Order in the Elements. UnS
Micromutations. James Wright. NYBP
Microscope, The. Maxine W. Kumin. QQQ
Microscopic Trout and the Machiavellian Fisherman, The. Guy Wetmore Carryl. WhC
'Mid all the ceaseless rush of life. Refuge. Mabel E. McCartney. BLRP
'Mid pleasures and palaces though we may roam. H. C. Bunner. *Fr.* Home, Sweet Home with Variations. InMe; OBAL
Mid pleasures and palaces though we [*or* I] may roam. Home, Sweet Home. John Howard Payne. *Fr.* Clari, the Maid of Milan. AA; BLPA; BLSo; FaBoBe; FaFP; FSW; HBV-2; PaPo; PSoN; TreF; WBLP
'Mid roaring brooks and dark moss-vales. On the Death of a Recluse. George Darley. OBVV
'Mid sunshine, cloud or stormy days. In Every Thing Give Thanks. *Unknown.* STF
'Mid the flower-wreathed tombs I stand. Decoration. Thomas Wentworth Higginson. AA; OHIP
'Mid the mountains Euganean. Shelley. *Fr.* Lines Written among the Euganean Hills. PBBP; ViBoPo
Mid the squander'd colour. Cheddar Pinks. Robert Bridges. ChMP; MoVE; SeCePo
Mid the white spouses of the Sacred Heart. To St. Mary Magdalen. Benjamin Dionysius Hill. AA
Mid-afternoons. Daysleep. Virginia E. Smith. AMV-81
Midas, *sels.* John Lyly.
Daphne. ElL
(Apollo's Song.) HBV-1
(Song of Daphne to the Lute, A.) OBSC
Pan's Song. OBSC
(Pan's Syrinx.) ELP
(Pan's Syrinx Was a Girl.) ViBoPo
(Syrinx.) ElL; LoBV; SeCePo; WHA
Song to Apollo. OBSC
Midas, they say, possessed the art of old. Epigram. "Peter Pindar." DBV; ELU; NIP
Midas watched the golden crust. The Ungrateful Garden. Carolyn Kizer. NePoEA-2
Midas, we are in story told. The Fable of Midas. Swift. APAS
Mid-August. Louise Driscoll. YeAr
Mid-August at Sourdough Mountain Lookout. Gary Snyder. HAP; MAT; NaP; NCSH; NoP; TAP
Mid-Century. Mary Elizabeth Osborn. NePoAm
Midcentury Love Letter. Phyllis McGinley. ViBoPo
Mid-Country Blow. Theodore Roethke. BoNaP
Mid-Day. Hilda Doolittle ("H. D."). ViBoPo
Mid-day and a heat haze over all. Bruce Beaver. Letters to Live Poets, XXXIV. CBAP
Midday half-moon slopes in heaven, A. Gold. Glyn Jones. NeBP
Midday, midsummer, the field is watercolor green. Five Horses. May Swenson. PH
Midden of rotting bodies of men, A. Corpses in the Wood. Ernst Toller, *tr. by* E. Ellis Roberts. TrJP
Middle-Age. Emily B. C. Jones. HBMV
Middle Age. Rudolph Chambers Lehmann. HBV-1
Middle Age. Robert Lowell. PAI
Middle Age. Paula Rankin. MAYP
Middle-aged, The. Adrienne Rich. NePoEA-2
Middle aged. 40——Love. Roger McGough. LiSp; NoAM
Middle-aged Conversation. A. S. J. Tessimond. POL
Middle-aged king, The. King Saul. Allan Kolski Horvitz. VWA
Middle-aged life is merry, and I love to lead it. Peekaboo, I Almost See You. Ogden Nash. PoLF
Middle-aged Man, The. Louis Simpson. NNaP
Middle Ages, The. John Haines. LCAP
Middle Ages. Siegfried Sassoon. SO
Middle Ages, The: Two Views. Leah Bodine Drake. NePoAm-2
Middle of a War, The. Roy Fuller. OBWP
Middle of the Day. Jack Driscoll. WOLT
Middle of the Night, The. Karla Kuskin. RHPC
Middle of the Way. Galway Kinnell. NU
Middle of the World. D. H. Lawrence. HAP
Middle of the World, The. Kathleen Norris. GP
Middle Passage. Robert Hayden. AmNP; BPo; IDB; NoAM; PoBA
Middle-Time, The. Lona M. Fowler. TRV
Middleness of the Road, The. Robert Frost. CrMA; LiTA; NOBA
Middlesex. John Betjeman. OxBTC
Midewiwan. Phyllis Wolf. STE
Midges Dance aboon the Burn, The. Robert Tannahill. BoNaP; HBV-1
Midget, The. Philip Levine. NaP; NoAM
Midnight. Dryden. ACP
Midnight. Weldon Kees. NoAM
Midnight. Archibald Lampman. OBCV; PeCV
Midnight. John Masefield. BrPo
Midnight. Thomas Middleton. *Fr.* Blurt, Master Constable. ElL; SeCePo
Midnight. Gabriela Mistral, *tr. fr. Spanish by* David Garrison. BoWoP
Midnight. Michael Roberts. OBMV
Midnight. Thomas Sackville. *Fr.* The Mirror for Magistrates. CH
Midnight. Margaret E. Sangster. TRV
Midnight. Shakespeare. *Fr.* The Rape of Lucrece. OBSC
Midnight. James Stephens. DTC
Midnight. Tennyson. VLP
Midnight. Henry Vaughan. AnAnS-1; OAEP
Midnight and Ten Minutes. Shlomo Vinner, *tr. fr. Hebrew by* Laya Firestone *and* Howard Schwartz. VWA
Midnight, and three women. Auguries for Three Women. Jacquelyne Crews. AMV-81
Midnight at Baiae; a Dream Fragment of Imperial Rome. John Addington Symonds. PeHV
Midnight at midwinter: the dead land laid. Turning Point. W. L. Holshouser. AMV-81
Midnight black with clouds is in the sky, A. Earth. Bryant. AP
Midnight Court, The. Brian Merriman, *tr. fr. Modern Irish by* Frank O'Connor. AnIL; KiLC; OnYI, *tr. by* Arland Ussher
Sels.
Country's Crisis, The, *tr. by* David Marcus. BIrV
Husband's Lament, The, *tr. by* Frank O'Connor. OBVE
Irish Marriage Night, An, *tr. by* Frank O'Connor. BIrV
Lament of the Unmarried Girl, The, *tr. by* Frank O'Connor. OBVE
Maiden's Plight, The, *tr. by* Frank O'Connor. BIrV
Now God Stand Up for Bastards, *tr. by* Arland Ussher. BIrV
Old Man's Tale, The, *tr. by* David Marcus. BIrV
Solution, The, *tr. by* Arland Ussher. BIrV
Walk, *tr. by* Brendan Behan. BIrV
Midnight cry appalls the gloom, A. Johnny Appleseed. William Henry Venable. PAH
Midnight Dancer. Langston Hughes. FF
Midnight, December Thirty-first. Song for December Thirty-first. Frances Frost. YeAr
Midnight has come, and the great Christ Church Bell. All Souls' Night. W. B. Yeats. *Fr.* A Vision. MoVE

Midnight in Bonnie's Stall. Siddie Joe Johnson. PChr
Midnight is no time for. No Time for Poetry. Julia Fields. AmNP
Midnight Lamentation. Harold Monro. BrPo; ChMP; LO; OxBTC; ViBoPo
"When you and I go down," *sel.* OBMV
Midnight March, The. Fred Gilbert. VLP
Midnight Mass for the Dying Year. Longfellow. GoBC
Midnight on Front Street. Roberta Hill Whiteman. CDW; TWSS
Midnight on the Great Western. Thomas Hardy. CH; CoBMV; NOBE
Midnight past! Not a sound of aught. The Portrait. "Owen Meredith." HBV-1
Midnight plane with its riding lights, The. Night Plane. Frances Frost. FaPON; PDV; TiPo
Midnight Prayer. Hayyim Nahman Bialik, *tr. fr. Hebrew by* Helena Frank. TrJP
Midnight Ramble, The. Charles Woodward. NOEC
Midnight Ride of Paul Revere, The. Longfellow. *See* Paul Revere's Ride.
Midnight—September 19, 1881. John Boyle O'Reilly. PAH
Midnight Show. Karl Shapiro. OxBA
Midnight Skaters, The. Edmund Blunden. FaBoTw; GoJo; GTBS-P; MoBrPo; NOBE
Midnight Special. Leadbelly (Huddie Ledbetter). FSW
Midnight Special. Kenneth Patchen. VGW
Midnight Special ("If you evah go to Houston"). *Unknown.* AS
Midnight Special ("Yonder come Roberta!"), *with music. Unknown.* AS
Midnight streets as I walk back, The. Letter I. Randall Swingler. WaP
Midnight Tennis Match, The. Thomas Lux. AmPA
Midnight the years last day the last. New Year's Eve, 1938. John Frederick Nims. MiAP
Midnight Train, The, *with music. Unknown.* AS
Midnight, Walking the Wakeful Daughter. Joseph Meredith. AMV-81
Midnight was come, when every vital thing. Midnight. Thomas Sackville. *Fr.* The Mirror for Magistrates. CH
Midnight's bell goes ting, ting, ting, ting, ting. Midnight. Thomas Middleton. *Fr.* Blurt, Master Constable. EIL; SeCePo
Mid-Noon in January. "Fiona Macleod." *Fr.* Australian Transcripts. FM
Mid-Ocean in War-time. Joyce Kilmer. MOS
Midocean like a pale blue morning-glory. Calm Morning at Sea. Sara Teasdale. EtS; MOS
Mid-Plains Tornado. Linda Bierds. AMV-80
Midpoint. Charles Simic. GeTw
Mid-Rapture. Dante Gabriel Rossetti. *See* The House of Life, XXVI.
Midrash, *sel.* David Meltzer.
"Rabbi is before me, The." GP
Midrash on Hamlet. Francis Landy. VWA
Midshipman, The. William Falconer. MOS
Midst the fair range of buildings which, new-reared. George Keate. *Fr.* A Burlesque Ode, on the Author's Clearing a New House of Some Workmen. NOEC
Midstream. D. J. Enright. OxBC
Midstream. Mao Tse-tung, *tr. fr.* Chinese *by* Earle Birney. MoCV
Midstream they met. Challenger and champion. The Swans. Clifford Dyment. BoAnP; MoVE
Midsummer. Robert Fitzgerald. PoA
Midsummer. Thomas Kinsella. IPY
Midsummer. Sydney King Russell. BLPA; FaBoBe
Midsummer. James Scully. MP; NYBP; TwCP
Midsummer. John Townsend Trowbridge. AA; HBV-1; HBVY
Midsummer. Ella Wheeler Wilcox. HBV-1
Midsummer Courtship. James Thompson. OBVV
Midsummer Day in France. Alexander Hume. *See* Summer Day, A.
Midsummer Eve, a year ago, my mother she commanded. Midsummer Magic. Ivy O. Eastwick. TiPo
Midsummer Fantasy. Newman Levy. PoSC
Midsummer Frost. Isaac Rosenberg. MoPo
Midsummer Holiday, A, *sel.* Swinburne.
Cliffside Path, The, VI. VLP
Midsummer Jingle. Newman Levy. BoNaP; WhC
Midsummer Magic. Ivy O. Eastwick. TiPo
Midsummer Melancholy. Margaret Fishback. PV
Midsummer Night. Marion Edey. YeAr
Midsummer Night's Dream, A, *sels.* Shakespeare.
Asleep, My Love? *fr.* V, i. CTC
Bottom's Song, *fr.* III, i. CTC
("Ousel [*or* Woosel] cock so black of hue, The.") PB; PBBP; ViBoPo
Course of True Love, The, *fr.* I, i. TreFS; WHA
Epilogue: "If we shadows have offended," *fr.* V, ii. OBSC
Flower of This Purple Dye, *fr.* III, ii. CTC
Helena and Hermia, *fr.* III, ii. GN
Love-in-Idleness, *fr.* II, i. TrGrPo
Lunatic, the Lover, and the Poet, The, *fr.* V, i. FiP; MasP
(Imagination.) LiTB
("Lovers and madmen have such seething brains," *sl. longer sel.*) PP
(Tricks of Imagination, The.) TreFS
"My hounds are bred out of the Spartan kind," *fr.* IV, i. GDP; PoPle
Now the Hungry Lion Roars, *fr.* V, ii. CH, ChTr; CTC; EIL; EnRePo; LiTB; SeCeV; ViBoPo; WSC
(Epilogue: "Now the hungry lion roars.") LoBV, *longer sel.*; OBSC
(Fairy Blessing, The.) OxBoLi
(Fairy Songs: "Now the hungry lion roars.") TrGrPo
(Lion of Winter, The.) WiR
(Puck's Song.) MoShBr
"Now until the break of day," *fr.* V, ii. GN
(Fairy Songs: "Now, until the break of day.") TrGrPo
(Through the House.) CTC
Oberon and Titania to the Fairy Train, *fr.* V, ii. GN
Over Hill, over Dale, *fr.* II, i. EIL; ViBoPo
(Fairy Land, 1.) OBEV
(Fairy Song: "Over hill, over dale.") HBV-1; HBVY; NOBE; OBSC; PoPle; TrGrPo
(Fairy's Wander-Song.) FaPON
(Puck and the Fairy.) GN
(Song.) InvP
Sunrise on the Sea, *fr.* III, ii. ChTr
Through the Forest Have I Gone, *fr.* II, ii. CTC
Up and Down, *fr.* III, ii. CTC
Violet Bank, A, *fr.* II, i. FaPON
("I know a place whereon the wild thyme blows.") BoNaP; PoPle
(Where the Wild Thyme Blows.) TrGrPo
Yet but Three? *fr.* III, ii. CTC
You Spotted Snakes [with Double Tongue], *fr.* II, ii. InvP; LiTB; NOBE; PoRA; ViBoPo; WSC
(Fairies' Lullaby, The.) EIL; WHA
(Fairies' Song, The.) LoBV
(Fairy Land, 2.) OBEV
(Fairy Lullaby.) FaPON
(Fairy Songs: "You spotted snakes with double tongue.") HBV-1; OBSC; TrGrPo
(Lullaby for Titania.) GN
(Song: "You spotted snakes with double tongue.") FiP
Midsummer Night's Dream. Byron Vazakas. NePA
Midsummer Noon in the Australian Forest, A. Charles Harpur. PoAu-1
Midsummer Pause. Fred Lape. PoSC
Midsummer Song, A. Richard Watson Gilder. BoNaP; HBV-1
Mid-Term Break. Seamus Heaney. NCSH; NoP
Midway. John D. Engle, Jr. AMV-81
Midway. Naomi Long Madgett. BlSi; BPo; NNP; PoNe
Midway along the journey of our life. Inferno. Dante, *tr. by* Mark Musa. *Fr.* Divina Commedia. NAWM-1
Midway between Mecca and Medina. To a Hero Dead at al-Safra. Hind bint Uthatha, *tr. by* Bridget Connelly *and* Deirdre Lashgari. WPOW
Midway, he paces the cheap hotel room. The Jogger: Denver to Kansas City. David Ray. FAZ
Midway in the Night: Blackman. Eugene B. Redmond. GP
Midway the hill of science, after steep. To Mr. S. T. Coleridge. Anna Laetitia Barbauld. NOEC
Midways of a walled garden. Golden Wings [*or* An Ancient Castle]. William Morris. ChTr; OBNC; SeCePo; WHA
Midweek. Josephine Miles. NoP
Midwest. John Frederick Nims. MoVE; PoPl
Midwest Town. Ruth Delong Peterson. AmFN
Midwestern Man. Paul Giandi. AMV-81
Midwife. Earl Gene Box. LFAC
Midwife laid her hand on his thick skull, The. Thomas Shadwell the Poet. John Dryden *and* Nahum Tate. *Fr.* Absalom and Achitophel: Part II. ChTr
Midwife's Story, A; Two. Anne Szumigalski. NOBC
Midwinter. John Townsend Trowbridge. AA; GN; HBV-1
Midwinter spring is its own season. Little Gidding. T. S. Eliot. *Fr.* Four Quartets. FaBoEn; FaBoMo; GTBS-P; NoAM; NOBA; NOBE; OAEL-2; OAEP; OxBTC; PrIm; SeCeV; TAP
Midwinter Stars. Roberta Hill Whiteman. STE
Midwinter Thaw. Lenore Pratt. CaP
Mid-Winter Waking. Robert Graves. MoAB
Might and Right. Clarence Day. InMe
Might as well bury her. Maumee Ruth. Sterling A. Brown. CDC
Might have been. This Place Rumord to Have Been Sodom. Robert Duncan. NeAP; NOBA; PoM; PPP
Might I, if you can find it, be given. Saint Nicholas. Marianne Moore. NYBP; WPE
"Might Is Right." Israel Zangwill. TrJP
Might these be thrushes climbing through almost. E. E. Cummings. CrMA
Mightier than Mammon, A, *sel.* Edward Carpenter.
"Love of men for each other, The—so tender, heroic, constant." PeHV

Mighty bell is six o'clock, A. Six to Six. *Unknown, tr. by* A. C. Jordan. PBA
Mighty Brahma, Lord Almighty. The Pariah's Prayer. Goethe. ILwL
Mighty change it is, and ominous, A. The Winter Shore. Thomas Wade. NBM; OAEL-2
Mighty creature is the germ, A. The Germ. Ogden Nash. CenHV; MoShBr
Mighty Day. *Unknown.* FSW
Mighty Fortress, A. Bible, *O.T.* Psalms, XCI. TrGrPo
(Everlasting Arms, The, *Moulton, Modern Reader's Bible.*) WGRP
("He that dwelleth in the secret place of the most High.") AWP
Mighty Fortress Is Our God, A. Martin Luther, *tr. fr. German by* Frederick Henry Hedge. AWP; EaLo; HBV-2; TreFS
(Feste Burg Ist Unser Gott, Ein, *tr. by* M. Woolsey Stryker.) CTC
(Hymn: "Mighty fortress is our God, A.") WGRP
(Paraphrase of Luther's Hymn.) AA
Mighty hand, from an exhaustless urn, A. The Flood of Years. Bryant. AA
Mighty Heart, The. Emerson. *Fr.* Woodnotes, II. AA
Mighty Hunter, The. J. B. Worley. PoLF
Mighty Lak' a Rose, *with music.* Frank L. Stanton. BLSo; FSN
Mighty Love. John Fletcher. *See* Hear, Ye Ladies.
Mighty Mother, and her son who brings, The. Pope. *Fr.* The Dunciad, I. OBSV
Mighty One, before Whose Face, *with music.* Bryant. AH
Mighty, praised beyond compare. Rock of My Salvation. Mordecai, *tr. by* Solomon Solis-Cohen. TrJP
Mighty river flowing dark and deep, The. James Thomson. The City of Dreadful Night, XIX. EBVV
Mighty Runner, A (Variation of a Greek Theme.) E. A. Robinson. LiSp; OBAL
Mighty Sea! Cameleon-like Thou Changest. Thomas Campbell. EtS
Mighty soul that is ambition's mate, The. Disenchantment. Charles Leonard Moore. AA
Mighty spirit, and its power, which stains, The. Inebriety. George Crabbe. BXAP
Mighty Thoughts of an Old World, The. Thomas Lovell Beddoes. *Fr.* The Ivory Gate. GoJo
(Song of Thanatos.) NBM
(Stanzas: "Mighty thought of an old world, The.") TrGrPo
(Stanzas from "The Ivory Gate.") EnRP
Mighty waste of moaning waters lay, The. The Deep Dark Night. Tennyson. *Fr.* The Devil and the Lady. SeCePo
Mighty wave rush'd o'er him as he spoke, A. Homer, *tr. by* Pope. *Fr.* The Odyssey, V. OBVE
Mignon. Goethe, *tr. fr. German.* *Fr.* Wilhelm Meister's Apprenticeship, Bk. I, *ch.* 1. AWP, *tr. by* James Elroy Flecker; NU, *tr. by* Robert Bly; PoPl, *tr. by* Edgar A. Bowring
Migod, a picture window. The One-Night Stand: An Approach to the Bridge. Paul Blackburn. ErPo
Migrant, The. Donald G. Babcock. NePoAm
Migration. Joseph Bruchac. AMV-81
Migration. Carole Gregory Clemmons. *See* Ghetto Lovesong—Migration.
Migration. Pinkie Gordon Lane. BlSi
Migration as a Passage in Time. Judy Bolz. SUW
Migration of the Grey Squirrels, The. William Howitt. OxBChV
Migrations of People, The. Dorothy Leiser. AMV-80
Migratory Rats, The. Heine, *tr. fr. German by* Ernst Feise. NAWM-2
Mihailovich. Roy McFadden. NeIP
Mikado, The, *sels.* W. S. Gilbert.
Flowers That Bloom in the Spring, The, *with music.* BLSo
Ko-Ko's Song ("As some day it may happen"). LiTB
(They'll None of 'Em Be Missed.) VLP
Mikado's Song, The. LiTB
(My Object All Sublime.) TreFT
Suicide's Grave, The. TreF; VLP; WhC
(Ko-Ko's Song ["On a tree by a river a little tom-tit"].) FaFP
(Ko-Ko's Winning Song.) LiTB
(Titwillow.) NoP
Three Little Maids from School. TreFT
To Sit in Solemn Silence. WhC
Wand'ring Minstrel, A. TreFS
Mike O'Day. *Unknown.* TreFT; WhC
(On Mike O'Day.) FaBoEE
Mike 65. Lennox Raphael. PoBA
Miklos Radnoti. Willis Barnstone. VWA
Mikveh, The. Blu Greenberg. AMV-80
Mild and slow and young. Girl Help. Janet Lewis. HeIP; QFR
Mild day of sorts, today, A. St. Valentine. Pancho Aguila. LFAC
Mild Is the Parting Year. Walter Savage Landor. *Fr.* Ianthe. OBRV
(Autumn.) TrGrPo
("Mild is the parting year, and sweet.") EnLoPo; TEP
Mild, melancholy, and sedate, he stands. The Hottentot. Thomas Pringle. OBRV
Mild offspring of a dark and sullen sire! To an Early Primrose. Henry Kirke White. HBV-1; OBNC; OBRV
Mild yoke of Christ, most harsh to me not bearing. Paradox. Vassar Miller. NePoEA
Mile an' a Bittock, A. Robert Louis Stevenson. OxBS; SeCePo
Mile and mile and mile; but no one would gather. The Sea. Francis Webb. CBAP; PoAu-2
Mile behind is Gloucester town [*or* Moors], A. Gloucester Moors. William Vaughn Moody. AP; HBV-2; NOBA; OxBA; TreFT; WHA
Mile below Blue Canyon on the lonely Pinon Trail, A. Curly Joe. *Unknown.* BPAW
Mile down the road from us, A. Children Not Kept at Home. Joyce Carol Oates. DFF
Mile from Eden, A. Anne Ridler. MoPo
Mile Hill. Dennis Schmitz. LCAP
Mile out in the marshes, under a sky, A. The Town Dump. Howard Nemerov. BiP; CMoP; MAT; NIP
Mile with Me, A. Henry van Dyke. BLPA; FPL
Miles, and miles, and miles of desolation! Suffolk. Swinburne. *Fr.* By the North Sea, III. FaBoPP
Miles and miles of giraffes galloping. Serengeti Sunset. Andrew Oerke. POL
Miles away, the dome. Looking at Power. Warren Woessner. AMV-80
Miles' Delight. Ted Joans. PoNe
Miles Keogh's Horse. John Hay. PAH; PoOW
Miles of pram in the wind and Pam in the gorse track. Potpourri from a Surrey Garden. John Betjeman. CenHV; DTC; FiBHP; NOBL; PoCh
Militant. Langston Hughes. PoBA
Military Harpist, The. Ruth Pitter. FaBoTw; MoVE
Militia, The. Dryden. *Fr.* Cymon and Iphigenia. OBSV
Milk at the Bottom of the Sea. Oscar Williams. LiTA; MoPo
Milk-cart Pony, The. Eleanor Farjeon. SUS
Milkcow Blues. *Unknown.* BluL
Milkcow's Calf Blues. *Unknown.* BluL
Milk for the Cat. Harold Monro. FaBoBe; FaFP; HBVY; MoBrPo; OBMV; PCat
Milk-glass bowl hanging by three chains, A. The Corpse-Plant. Adrienne Rich. CoPo
Milk Jug, The. Oliver Herford. HBMV; HBVY
Milk! milk! milk! Thomas Edward Brown. *Fr.* Lynton Verses. PeD
Milk White Doe, The. *Unknown, tr. fr. French by* Andrew Lang. AWP
Milk-white Dove, The. *Unknown.* *See* Song of the Murdered Child.
Milk white Hind, immortal and unchang'd, A. Dryden. The Churches of Rome and of England. *Fr.* The Hind and the Panther, Pt. I. ACP; SeCV-2
Milk-white Moon, Put the Cows to Sleep. Carl Sandburg. FaPON
Milk-white mouse immortal and unchang'd, A. The Town Mouse and the Country Mouse. Matthew Prior. BXAP
Milke before wine, I would 'twere mine. *Unknown.* FaBoUs
Milking-Maid, The. Christina Rossetti. BeLS
Milking Pails. *Unknown.* CH
Milking Shed, The. John Clare. VLP
Milking Time. Elizabeth Madox Roberts. FaPON; GoJo; OBCA; SUS
Milkmaid, The. Austin Dobson. HBV-1
Milkmaid. Laurie Lee. BoLoP; ChMP; FaBoTw
Milkmaid, The. *Unknown.* AmFP
Milkmaid singing leaves her bed, The. John Clare. *Fr.* The Shepheard's Calendar: February. OBRV
Milkmaid's Epithalamium, The. Thomas Randolph. BoLoP
Milkman, The. Isabella Gardner. NePA
Milkman, The. Jane W. Krows. SoPo
Milkman, The. "Seumas O'Sullivan." SUS
Milkman's Horse, The. *Unknown.* SoPo
Milkweed. Philip Levine. LCAP
Milkweed. James Wright. LCAP; NaP; NOBA; NU
"Milkweed, and a buttercup, and cowslip, A," said sweet Mary. Her Dairy. Peter Newell. NA
Milk weed pods. Open. Joseph Bruchac. FAZ
Milk-Wort and Bog-Cotton. "Hugh MacDiarmid." BSV; NeBP
Milky Way, The. Jon Anderson. MAYP
Milky Way above, The. Fire Island. May Swenson. PoA; TAP
Mill, A. William Allingham. FaBoEE; NBM; POL; SeCePo
Mill, The. William Heyen. EyDe
Mill, The. E. A. Robinson. CMoP; DL; HAP; MoVE; NePA; NoAM; NoP; PAI; PrIm; SoSe; WeW
(Miller's Wife, The.) TAP
Mill, The. John Taylor. FAZ
Mill, The. Richard Wilbur. Psk; SoSe
Mill at Romesdal. Richard Hugo. AMV-80

Mill at Trumpington, The. Chaucer. *Fr.* The Canterbury Tales: The Reeve's Tale. OxBM
("At Trumpyngtoun nat fer from Cantebrigge.") ViBoPo
Mill goes toiling slowly around, The. Nightfall in Dordrecht. Eugene Field. AA
Mill Valley. Myra Cohn Livingston. RFM
"Millennium," yes; "pandemonium"! Hometown Piece for Messrs. Alston and Reese. Marianne Moore. OBAL
Miller, The. Sir John Clerk. ChTr
Miller, The. John Cunningham. OBEC
Miller, The. *Unknown.* FSW
Miller and His Sons, The. *Unknown.* OBET
Miller of [the] Dee, The ("There dwelt a miller hale and bold"). *Unknown at. to* Charles Mackay. GBP; HBV-2
Miller, stout and sturdy as the stones, The. Chaucer, *mod. vers. by* Louis Untermeyer. *Fr.* The Canterbury Tales: Prologue. TrGrPo
Miller[e] was a stout carl, for the nones, The. Chaucer. *Fr.* The Canterbury Tales: Prologue. TrGrPo; ViBoPo
Milleres Tale, The. Chaucer. *See* Miller's Tale, The.
Miller's daughter, The. Spinning Song. Edith Sitwell. MoAB; MoBrPo
Miller's Daughter, The. Tennyson. OBEV; OBVV; TrGrPo; UnTE; VLP
Song: "It is the miller's daughter," *sel.* HBV-1
Miller's mill-dog lay at the mill-door, The. Bingo. *Unknown.* CH
Miller's Prologue, The. Chaucer. *Fr.* The Canterbury Tales. OAEL-1
Miller's Tale, The. Chaucer. *Fr.* The Canterbury Tales. OAEL-1; TEP, *mod. vers. by* Nevill Coghill
(Milleres Tale, The.) OxBoLi
"Fair was this yonge wyf, and therwithal," *sel.* EBEV
Miller's wife had waited long, The. The Mill [*or* The Miller's Wife]. E. A. Robinson. CMoP; DL; HAP; MoVE; NePA; NoAM; NoP; PAI; PrIm; SoSe; TAP; WeW
Miller's Wife's Lullaby, The. *Unknown.* GBP
Millery, millery, dustipole. *Unknown.* OxNR
Millicent can play the flute. Broom Balancing. Kathleen Fraser. RHPC
Million, The. Peter Redgrove. OxBC
Million butterflies rose up from South America, A. Annual Legend. Winfield Townley Scott. CoAP; LiTA; LiTM; WaP
Million emeralds break from the ruby-budded lime, A. Tennyson. *Fr.* Maud. SyP
Million Little Diamonds, A. Mary Frances Betts. AA
Million years of death some star, A. Micromutations. James Wright. NYBP
Millions Are Learning How. James Agee. PoPl
(Lyric: "From now on kill America out of your mind.") GOA
Millions of Strawberries. Genevieve Taggard. FaPON; MoShBr; TiPo
Millions who pass you see. To a Blue Hippopotamus. Ellen de Young Kay. NePoEA
Millman Song, The, *with music.* *Unknown.* ShS
Millom Old Quarry. Norman Nicholson. ChMP
Mills of the Gods, The. *Unknown.* BLPA; FPL
Mill-stream, now that noises cease, The. A. E. Housman. GBL
Milne's Bar. Norman MacCaig. FaBoTw
Milord, how beautifully you write! To Li Po from Tu Fu. Carolyn Kizer. GP
Milo's from home; and, Milo being gone. Epigram. Martial, *tr. by* Elijah Fenton. OBVE
Milton, *sels.* Blake.
And Did Those Feet in Ancient Time, *fr.* Preface. AWP; CABA; EnRP; FaBoCh; FaBV; HAP; HeIP; InPS; LoBV; MAT; NoP; OAEL-2; OAEP; OBRV; PAI; PoEL-4; PoRA; PrIm; SeCeV; ViBoPo; WGRP
(Jerusalem.) EaLo; EvOK; FaPoR; NOBE; NOCV; OBEV; WaaP
(New Jerusalem, The.) FaBoEn; FSW; LiTB; TrGrPo
(Preface: "And did those feet in ancient time.") PPoe
(Prelude: "And did those feet in ancient time.") OBNC
"Los is by mortals nam'd Time," *fr.* I. OBRV
Nightingale and Flowers, *fr.* II. LoBV
(Birds, The, *shorter sel.*) PB
(Birdsong, *shorter sel.*) FaBoEn
(Choir of Day, The.) EnRP
(Lark's Song, The, *shorter sel.*) WiR
("Thou hearest the nightingale begin the song of spring.") OBRV; PBBP
(Vision of Beulah, The.) NOBE; OAEL-2
(Vision of the Lamentation of Beulah, A.) OBNC
Reason and Imagination, *fr.* II. EnRP
"Then Milton rose up from the heaven of Albion ardorous!" *fr.* I. OAEL-2
Wild Thyme, The, *fr.* II. WiR
Wine-Press of Los, The, *fr.* I. EnRP
("This Wine-press is call'd War on Earth," *shorter sel.*) EBEV
Milton. Longfellow. AA; AmPP; AP; AWP; NePA; NoP; TAP; TrGrPo
Milton. Lloyd Mifflin. AA
Milton. Henrietta Cordelia Ray. BlSi
Milton. Tennyson. OAEP; VLP
Milton! Wordsworth. *See* London, 1802 ("Milton! thou shouldst be living. . .").
Milton by Firelight. Gary Snyder. CAPP; CoAP; ConAP; InPK; InPS; PPP
Milton! I think thy spirit hath passed away. To Milton. Oscar Wilde. BrPo
Milton, thou shouldest be living at this hour. The Poet and the Butcher. Catherine Durning Whetham. SUMH
Milton! Thou Shouldst Be Living at This Hour. Wordsworth. *See* London, 1802.
Miltonic Sonnet for Mr. Johnson on His Refusal of Peter Hurd's Official Portrait, A. Richard Wilbur. CAPP; TW
Milton's Prayer for [*or* of] Patience. Elizabeth Lloyd Howell. AA; TRV; WGRP
Milton's the prince of poets—so we say. Byron. *Fr.* Don Juan, III. NOBL; OAEL-2
Milton's Wife on Her Twenty-third Birthday. Jane Conant-Bissell. AMV-80
Milwaukee Fire, The. *Unknown.* AmFP
Mima. Walter de la Mare. BrPo
Mime. Dick Allen. AMV-81
Mimi, do you remember. Biftek aux Champignons. Henry Augustin Beers. AA; HBV-1
Mimma Bella, *sels.* Eugene Lee-Hamilton. HBV-1
"Have dark Egyptians stolen Thee away," I.
"Oh, bless the law that veils the Future's face," VI.
"Oh, rosy as the lining of a shell," IV.
"One day, I mind me, now that she is dead," VIII.
"Two springs she saw—two radiant Tuscan springs," II.
"What essences from Idumean palm," XX.
Mimnermus in Church. William Johnson Cory. HBV-1; LO; NOBE; OBEV; TreFT; VLP
Mimnermus Incert. Walter Savage Landor. PoEL-4
Mimosa. Cleopatra Mathis. MAYP
Minarets wave on the plains of Stamboul, The. Eastern Serenade. William E. Aytoun *and* Sir Theodore Martin. InMe
Mince-Python, The. Carolyn Wells. *Fr.* A Baker's Dozen of Wild Beasts. OBCA
Mind. Richard Wilbur. CMoP; HoPM; NCSH; NePA; NePoEA; PPP; TwAmPo
Mind a clutter: sick with love for another. Night Trip across the Chesapeake and After. Sydney Lea. MAYP
Mind and Matter. *Unknown.* *See* Limerick: "There was a faith-healer of Deal."
Mind Content, A. Robert Greene. *See* Maesia's Song.
Mind Diseased, A. Shakespeare. *Fr.* Macbeth, V, iii. TreFT
Mind drowned in the sun may dream of birds, The. A Balcony with Birds. Howard Moss. NePoEA
Mind Flying Afar. Edgar Lee Masters. PoA
Mind from nature, divorced by love, The. Around the Fish: After Paul Klee. Howard Moss. MoPo
Mind has shown itself at times, The. For the Marriage of Faustus and Helen. Hart Crane. AP; InPS; NePA; NoAM; NOBA
Mind in its [*or* the] purest play is like some bat. Mind. Richard Wilbur. CMoP; HoPM; NCSH; NePA; NePoEA; PPP; TwAmPo
Mind, Intractable Thing, The. Marianne Moore. LiTM; NYBP
Mind Is an Ancient and Famous Capital, The. Delmore Schwartz. NoAM; TAP
Mind is an Enchanting Thing, The. Marianne Moore. AP; CMoP; CoBMV; CrMA; HeIP; InvP; MoAB; MoAmPo; MoPo; OxBA; PPP; TwAmPo; WPOW
Mind is not, The. The Perishing Bird. Douglas G. Jones. MoCV
Mind Is Still, The. Ursula K. Le Guin. AMV-80
Mind of Man is fram'd even like the breath, The. In Patterdale. Wordsworth. *Fr.* The Prelude, I. FaBoRV
Mind of the people is like mud, The. Talking with Soldiers. W. J. Turner. ChMP; MoBrPo
Mind Reader Blues. *Unknown.* BluL
Mind, with its own eyes and ears, The. The Mind's Liberty. W. H. Davies. MoBrPo
Mindful of the/ shambles of the day. Nightwalker. Thomas Kinsella. IPY
Minds awake in bodies that were asleep. Pandora and the Moon. Merrill Moore. MoAmPo
Mind's eye aches from Henry James, The. Satie, at the End of Term. Simon Curtis. NOBL
Mind's eye sees as the heart mirrors, The. To Sleep. Robert Graves. MoVE
Mind's Liberty, The. W. H. Davies. MoBrPo
Mine. Andrew Hudgins. AMV-80
Mine. Frank Polite. NYBP

Mine are the night and morning. Song of Nature. Emerson. HBV-1
Mine Argosy from Alexandria. Christopher Marlowe. *Fr.* The Jew of Malta, I, i. ChTr
Mine be a cot beside the hill. A Wish. Samuel Rogers. FaPoR; GTBS; GTBS-P; HBV-1; NOBE; OBEC; OBEV; OBVV; TreFS
Mine—by the right of the white election. Emily Dickinson. NoP
Mine ears have heard your distant moan. Lines. J. C. Squire. WhC
Mine enemy is growing old. Emily Dickinson. TW
Mine eye and heart are at a mortal war. Shakespeare. Sonnets, XLVI. EyDe
Mine eye bewrays. Love Cannot Live. *Unknown.* ElL
Mine eye hath play'd the painter, and hath steel'd. Shakespeare. Sonnets, XXIV. EyDe
Mine eyes beheld the blessed pity spring. Sonnet. Dante, *tr. by* Dante Gabriel Rossetti. La Vita Nuova, XXIII. AWP; PoPl
Mine eyes have seen the glory of the coming of the Lord. The Battle Hymn of the [American] Republic. Julia Ward Howe. AA; AH; BLPA; BLSo; CH; EaLo; FaBoBe; FaFP; FaPo; FaPON; FaPoR; FSW; GN; HBV-2; HBVY; NePA; NOBA; NOCV; OBVV; OBWP; OHIP; PAH; PAL; PSoN; SCV; TAP; TrAS; TreF; TRV; WBLP; WGRP; WPE; YaD
Mine eyes have seen the guru. *Unknown.* POL
Mine Host of "The Golden Apple." Thomas Westwood. GN; OHIP
Mine is a dark and twisting place. Coal Miner's Grace. Jay Divine. AMV-80
Mine is the freedom of the tranquil hills. Freedom of the Hills. Douglas Fraser. PoSH
Mine old dear enemy, my froward master. Translation from Petrarch. Petrarch, *tr. by* Sir Thomas Wyatt. SiPS
Mine own [*or* Myne owne] John Poins [*or* Poyntz *or* Poynz], since ye delight to know. Of the Courtier's Life. Sir Thomas Wyatt. Satires, I. AAS; GoTL; NoP; OBSC; OBSV; OBVE; PoEL-1; SiPS
Mine owne good Bat, before thou hoyse up saile. Councell Given to Master Bartholmew Withipoll. George Gascoigne. AAS
Mine to the core of the heart, my beauty! Plighted. Dinah Maria Mulock Craik. HBV-1
Mine was a Midwest home—you can keep your world. One Home. William Stafford. AmFN; CoAP; NePA; VGW
Mine will last though others fall to dust. The Enigma. Richard Eberhart. NYBP
Miner, The. Alfred Castner King. PoOW
Miner Boy, The. *Unknown.* AmFP
Miner Coming Home One Night, A. *Unknown.* GBP
Mineral Point. Robert Dana. FAZ
Minerals of Cornwall, Stones of Cornwall. Peter Redgrove. FaBoMo
Miners. John C. Frohlicher. BPAW
Miners. Wilfred Owen. BrPo; MoAB; MoBrPo; NOBE
Miners. James Wright. ConAP; CTBA
Miner's Doom, The. *Unknown.* AmFP
Miner's Helmet, The. George MacBeth. OxBTC
Miner's Lament, The ("High on a rough and dismal crag"). *At. to* "Mark Twain." BPAW
Miner's Lament, The ("When the gold fever raged I was doing very well"). *Unknown.* AmFP
Miner's Life, A. *Unknown.* OBET
Miner's Lifeguard ("Miner's life is like a sailor's"). *Unknown.* FSW
Miner's Progress, The. *At. to* Alanzo Delano. BPAW
Miners' Wives. Joe Corrie. OxBS
Ming the Merciless. Jessica Hagedorn. BrSi
Mingled aye with fragrant yearnings. Blue Moonshine. Francis G. Stokes. NA
Mingled the moonlight with daylight. Thomas Hardy. Walter de la Mare. NoAM
Mingled Yarns. X. J. Kennedy. OBCA
Mingling my prayer. Saigyo Hoshi, *tr. fr. Japanese by* Arthur Waley. AWP
Mingus. Bob Kaufman. PoBA
Miniatures IV. Lynn Strongin. IHMS
Minimal, The. Theodore Roethke. BiP; NoAM; NOBA
Minimum Security. James Lewisohn. LFAC
Minion Wife, A. Nicholas Udall. *Fr.* Ralph Roister Doister. ElL
Miniskirtminiskirt. A Concrete Poem. Anthony Mundy. PV
Minister of birds, islands, and pools. Cortege for Colette. Jean Garrigue. NYBP
Minister said it wad [*or* wald] dee, The. Last Lauch. Douglas Young. BSV; FaBoCo; OxBS; SeCePo
Minister, why do you direct your artillery against. A Fisher's Apology. *Unknown, tr. by* Arthur Johnstone. GoTS
Ministers who've sold the King. Are You Glad? *Mongol Oral Tradition, tr. by* C. R. Bawden. WTO
Miniver Cheevy. E. A. Robinson. AmPP; AP; AWP; CABA; ChTr; CMoP; CoBMV; FaBoCh; FaBV; FaFP; FaPo; FF; FPL; HBV-1; HeIP; InMe; LiTA; LiTM; MoAB; MoAmPo; NePA; NIP; NoAM; NOBA; NoP; OBSV; OxBA; PAI; PoEL-5; PoLF; PoPl; PoRA; SCV; SeCeV; SpRo; TAP; TreF; TrGrPo; WHA; WhC; YaD
Miniver Cheevy, Jr., *parody.* David Fisher Parry. BXAP; InMe; SpRo; WhC
Minneapolis Poem, The. James Wright. FYAP; NoAM; UnPo
Minnesota Camp Grounds. Gerald Vizenor. STE
Minnesota Thanksgiving. John Berryman. GOA
Minnie and Her Dove. Charles Tennyson Turner. FM
Minnie and Mattie. Christina Rossetti. *Fr.* Sing-Song. GoJo; InvP; SUS; TiPo
Minnie and Mrs. Hoyne. Kenneth Fearing. PoRA
Minnie and Winnie. Tennyson. HBV-1; HBVY; NA; OxBChV
Minnie, I canna caa my wheel. Douglas Young, *after the Greek of* Sappho. OBVE
Minnie Morse. Kaye Starbird. PH
Minnows. Keats. FaPON; GN
Minoan Snake Goddess is flanked by a Chardin still-life, The. The Postcards; a Triptych. Denise Levertov. PoDr
Minor Bird, A. Robert Frost. CMoP; PB
Minor Elegy. Henriqueta Lisboa, *tr. fr. Portuguese by* Willis Barnstone *and* Nelson Cerqueira. BoWoP
Minor Key. Judah Leib Teller, *tr. fr. Yiddish by* Gabriel Preil *and* Howard Schwartz. VWA
Minor Prophet, A, *sel.* "George Eliot."
  Tide of Faith, The. TRV; WGRP
Minor Victorian Painter, A. John Hewitt. CIP
Minority Report. John Updike. GOA
Minority, The: 1917. May O'Rourke. SUMH
Minotaur. Robert Fisher. AmMo
Minotaur, The. Robert Gibb. FAZ
Minotaur Poems, *sels.* E. W. Mandel.
  "It has been hours in these rooms," I. OBCV
  "My father was always out in the garage," II. MoCV; OBCV
  Orpheus, VI. OBCV
Minot's Ledge. Fitz-James O'Brien. OnYI
Minott, Lee, Willard, Hosmer, Meriam, Flint. Hamatreya. Emerson. FaBoEn *See also* Bulkeley, Hunt, Willard . . .
Minstrel, The, *sels.* James Beattie.
  But Who the Melodies of Morn Can Tell, 2 *sts., fr.* I. ViBoPo
    (Nature and the Poets.) OBEC, 5 *sts.*; SeCePo, 3 *sts.*
  Nature's Charms, 4 *sts., fr.* I. OBEC
    (Youth of a Poet, The.) NOEC, 7 *sts.*
Minstrel, The. Goethe, *tr. fr. German by* James Clarence Mangan. AWP
Minstrel and Genius, to whose songs or sighs. Autumnal Ode. Aubrey Thomas De Vere. OBNC
Minstrel Boy, The. Thomas Moore. ACP; AnIL; FaBoBe; FaFP; FSW; GN; GoBC; HBV-2; OAEP; OnYI; PrIm; RoGo; TreF
Minstrel Responds to Flattery, The. Sir Walter Scott. *Fr.* The Lay of the Last Minstrel. OBNC
  ("Call it not vain; they do not err.") OBRV
Minstrels and Maids. William Morris. *See* Outlanders, The.
Minstrel's Last Lay, The. John Barth. OBAL
Minstrel's Song. Thomas Chatterton. *Fr.* Aella. HAP; HBV-1; LoBV; TrGrPo, *sl. abr.*; WHA
  (My Love Is Dead.) WiR
  (Mynstrelles Songe.) EnLoPo; EnRP; NOEC; OBEC
  (O, Sing unto My Roundelay.) CH, *abr.*; LiTB
  ("O! Synge untoe mie roundelaie.") NOBE
  (Song: "O sing unto my roundelay.") LO, *abr.*; OBEV
Minstrel's Song. Ted Hughes. OBCP
Mint Julep, The. Charles Fenno Hoffman. AA
Minuet, The. Mary Mapes Dodge. OHFP
Minuet on Reaching the Age of Fifty, A. George Santayana. BLPL; FaFP; HBMV; NePA
Minus One. John Ciardi. HoAn
Minute, The. Karl Shapiro. MiAP; MoVE
Minute before Meeting, The. Thomas Hardy. VLP
Minute flowers harden. Depend. Lilies of the Valley. Jon Silkin. NoAM
Minute-Men of Northboro', The. Wallace Rice. PAH
Minutes. Denis Johnson. MAYP
Minutes are numbered by the fall of sands. John Ford. *Fr.* The Lover's Melancholy, IV, iii. PoEL-2
Minyan, The. Jack Myers. VWA
Mir träumte von einem Königskind. Heine, *tr. fr. German by* Richard Garnett. AWP
Mir träumte wieder der alte Traum. Heine, *tr. fr. German by* James Thomson. AWP
Mira is dancing with bells tied on her ankles. Mirabai, *tr. fr. Hindi by* Willis Barnstone *and* Usha Nilsson. BoWoP
Mirabeau Bridge, The. Guillaume Apollinaire, *tr. fr. French.* BoLoP, *tr. by* Quentin Stevenson; OBVE, *tr. by* W. S. Merwin
Miracle. Liberty Hyde Bailey. OHIP; YeAr

Miracle, The. Walter de la Mare. LiTB; UnPo
Miracle, The. Allan Dowling. ErPo
Miracle, The. Emerson. FM
Miracle, The. Chaim Grade, *tr. fr. Yiddish by* Ruth Whitman. VWA
Miracle, The. Sir John Suckling. CaPo
Miracle for Breakfast, A. Elizabeth Bishop. LiTA; MiAP
Miracle Indeed, A. Purohit. OBMV
Miracle of the children the brilliant. Exodus. George Oppen. GP
Miracle of the Dawn, The. Madison Cawein. HBV-1
Miracle of the world, I never will deny. Henry Constable. *Fr.* Diana. NIP; OBSC
Miracles. Conrad Aiken. HBMV; MoAmPo
Miracles. Arna Bontemps. PoNe
Miracles. Walt Whitman. HBVY
Miracles at the Birth of Christ. Isaac Watts. NOCV
Miracles offend because they lack proportion. Why I Am Offended by Miracles. David Bergman. AMV-80
Mirage. R. P. Blackmur. *Fr.* Sea Island Miscellany. MoVE
Mirage. Christina Rossetti. BoLoP; LLLT; PoRA
Mirage, A. Ruth Setterberg. AMV-80
Mirage, The. Oscar Williams. CrMA; LiTM; NePA
Miramar Beach. J. V. Cunningham. To What Strangers, What Welcome, VIII. PoA
Miramichi Fire, The. *Unknown.* AmFP
Miramichi Lightning. Alfred Goldsworthy Bailey. OBCV
Mira's Will. Mary Leapor. NOEC
Mirèio, *sels.* Frédéric Mistral, *tr. fr.* Provençal.
  Cocooning, The, *tr. by* Harriet Waters Preston. AWP; PoPl
  Mares of the Camargue, The, *tr. by* George Meredith. AWP; PoPl
Miriam, *sel.* Whittier.
  Bible, The. TreFT
    (Book Our Mothers Read.) BLRP; TRV
Miriam, Mary, Maria, Marie. Mary. Fray Angelico Chavez. ISi
Miriam Tazewell. John Crowe Ransom. TW
Miriamne—Miriamne—yes, and Mio. In All These Turning Lights I Find No Clue. Maxwell Anderson. *Fr.* Winterset. TreFT
Mirie It Is while Sumer Ilast. *Unknown. See* Merry It Is.
Mirror, The. Edgar Bowers. QFR
Mirror. Tada Chimako, *tr. fr. Japanese by* Kenneth Rexroth *and* Ikuko Atsumi. BoWoP
Mirror. Peter De Vries. PoA
Mirror, The. Louise Glück. GeTw; GP; MAYP
Mirror, The. Judah Halevi, *tr. fr. Hebrew by* Emma Lazarus. TrJP
Mirror. Donald Hall. DFT
Mirror, The. Blanche Mary Kelly. GoBC; TrPWD
Mirror. James Merrill. CoAP; NePoEA-2; TwAmPo
Mirror, The. John N. Morris. PoA
Mirror. Sylvia Plath. HAP; NYBP; PAI
Mirror, The. Dante Gabriel Rossetti. SyP
Mirror cared less and less at the last, The. At the Grave of My Brother. William Stafford. Str
Mirror for Magistrates, A. Thomas Sackville. *See* Induction to "A Mirror for Magistrates."
Mirror for Poets, A. Thom Gunn. LiTM; NePoEA
Mirror for the Barnyard. Jack Myers. AmPA
Mirror Images. Laurel Speer. AMV-80
Mirror in February. Thomas Kinsella. CIP; GTBS-P; NoAM
Mirror in the Front Hall, The. C. P. Cavafy, *tr. fr. Greek by* Edmund Keeley *and* Philip Sherrard. PeHV
Mirror in Which Two Are Seen as One, The. Adrienne Rich. NNaP
Mirror, let us through the glass. The Flight into Egypt. W. H. Auden. *Fr.* For the Time Being. OAEP; OxBA
Mirror, Mirror. Robert Graves. HBMV
"Mirror, mirror, on the wall/ Who is Donald Andrew Hall?" Mirror. Donald Hall. DFT
Mirror, mirror, tell me. Mirror, Mirror. Robert Graves. HBMV
Mirror of Knighthood, The, *sels.* Robert Parry. EIL
  Except I Love.
  Song: "Fond affection, hence, and leave me."
Mirror of men's eyes delights me less, The. Laus Virginitatis. Arthur Symons. EnLoPo
Mirror of poets, mirror of our age. Upon Ben Johnson. Edmund Waller. SeCV-1
Mirror Perilous, The. Alan Dugan. LiTM; MP; TwCP
Mirrorment. A. R. Ammons. PCP
Mirrors, The. Sophia de Mello Breyner Andresen, *tr. fr. Portuguese by* Allan Francovich. PBWP
Mirrors. Elizabeth Jennings. NePoEA
Mirrors, no one yet has really described. Rainer Maria Rilke, *tr. by* Christopher Hawthorne. *Fr.* Sonnets to Orpheus. SOTW
Mirrors of Jerusalem, The. Barbara F. Lefcowitz. AMV-80; VWA
Mirry Margaret,/ As mydsomer flowre. *See* Merry Margaret . . .
Mirth. Beaumont *and* Fletcher. *Fr.* The Knight of the Burning Pestle. EIL
  (Laugh and Sing.) TrGrPo
Mirth. Robert Herrick. LiTB
Mirth. Christopher Smart. *Fr.* Hymns for the Amusement of Children. LAuP; OxBChV
Mirth and Melancholy. Margaret Cavendish, Duchess of Newcastle. WPE
Mirth, with Thee I Mean to Live. Milton. *Fr.* L'Allegro. FaBV
  ("Haste thee, nymph, and bring with thee.") GN
Mirthful Lunacy. Thomas Stoddart. *Fr.* The Death-Wake or Lunacy. OBNC
Mis Flora McFlimsey of Madison Square. *See* Miss Flora McFlimsey of Madison Square.
Mis' Smith. Albert Bigelow Paine. PoLF
Misadventures at Margate. "Thomas Ingoldsby." *Fr.* The Ingoldsby Legends. HBV-2
Misanthropos, *sel.* Thom Gunn.
  "Serving man, A. Curled my hair." OxBC
Misapprehended Goose, The. Oliver Herford. TDH
Misapprehension. Paul Laurence Dunbar. BPo
Miscarriage. Michael Longley. POL
Miscegenous Zebra, The. Roland Young. BoAnP
Miscellaneous screaming that comes from nowhere, A. The Geese. Hyam Plutzik. BiP
Mischievous, they say, as a monkey. Jackdaw. Tom Earley. BoAnP
Misconception, A. James Russell Lowell. OBAL
Misconceptions. Robert Browning. OBEV; OBVV
Misdeeming eye! that stoopest to the lure. Lewd Love Is Loss. Robert Southwell. ACP
Misdemeanor. Eve Triem. GP
Mise en Scène. Robert Fitzgerald. NYBP; VGW
Miser. Gordon LeClaire. CaP
Miserable Catullus, stop being foolish. Catullus, *tr. fr. Latin by* Louis Zukofsky. NoAM
Miserable change now at my end, The. Shakespeare. *Fr.* Antony and Cleopatra, IV, xiii. EBEV; PoPle
Miserable day, his dog had leapt, A. Riven Doggeries. James Tate. MAYP
Miserable shower those Corrs. The Corrs. Tom MacIntyre, *tr. fr. Irish.* CIP
Miserere. David Gascoyne. NeBP
  Sels.
  Ecce Homo. ChMP; LiTM; OBWP
  Ex Nihilo. GTBS-P
Miserere, My Maker. *Unknown.* NOCV
Misericordia. Margaret Mead. PoA
Miserie. George Herbert. PoEL-2
Miserly Patron, A. *Unknown, tr. fr. Old Irish by* Myles Dillon. AnIL
Miser's mind thou hast, A. Of a Rich Miser. George Turberville. EnRePo
Misery. John Holmes. NYBP
"Misery," he said, "to have no chin." Aldous Huxley. *Fr.* Soles Occidere et Redire Possunt. ViBoPo
Misery is a good thing if misery is spread. Misery. John Holmes. NYBP
Misery of Jerusalem, The. Bible, *O.T.* Lamentations, I. AWP
Misery of Mechanics, The. Philip Booth. MAT
Misfortune is as huge/ and heavy as this cold. Snow-Girl. Yunna Moritz, *tr. by* Elaine Feinstein. VWA
Misfortune to have lived not knowing thee. Emerson. Amos Bronson Alcott. AA
Misfortunes Never Come Singly. Harry Graham. FaFP; TreFT
Misfortunes of Elphin, The, *sels.* Thomas Love Peacock.
  Merlin's Apple-Trees. OBRV
  "Not drunk is he, who from the floor." ViBoPo
  Song of Gwythno. OBRV
  Song of the Four Winds, The. OBRV; WiR
  War Song of Dinas Vawr, The. AWP; CABA; EnRP; EvOK; FaPoR; HAP; InvP; LoBV; NOBE; OAEL-2; OBRV; OnMSP; PoPle; PrIm; ViBoPo; WaaP; WeW; WhC
Misgivings. Herman Melville. AP; NePA; NOBA; OxBA
Mishka. John Gray. SyP; VLP
Mishnah says I blind you with my hair, The. The Marriage Wig. Ruth Whitman. IHMS
Mismatch. Carl Lindner. AMV-80
Misnomer. Eve Merriam. RHPC
Misnomer really, A. With a few exceptions. Squares. Michael Hamburger. FF
Misogynist. Richard Conniff. DBV
Misogynist, The. Jean Morgan. FF
Misplaced Sympathy. Charles Follen Adams. OBAL
Misplacing—Mistaking. On Sir Nathaniel Wraxall the Historian. George Colman the Younger. FaBoEE
Miss Ada. Christopher Fahy. TAT
Miss Alderman. Robert Winner. GP

Miss Bailey's Ghost. George Colman the Younger. *See* Unfortunate Miss Bailey.
Miss Betty's Singing-Bird. John Winstanley. NOEC
Miss Biddy Fudge to Miss Dorothy. Thomas Moore. NBM
Miss Bitter. N. M. Bodecker. NTCP
Miss Brown, before these walls unquote. Notation in Haste. Elias Lieberman. GoYe
Miss Buss and Miss Beale. *Unknown.* CenHV; FaBoEE; PoPle
Miss Cho Composes in the Cafeteria. James Tate. WeW
Miss Creighton. Henry Taylor. GrPl
Miss Crustacean. Robert Phillips. GeTw
Miss Danae, when Fair and Young. An English Padlock. Matthew Prior. FaBoEn; OBEC
Miss Dickinson is gone. A New England Sampler. John Malcolm Brinnin. GOA
Miss Ellen Gee of Kew. *Unknown.* FaBoNo
Miss Emily Brittle Sails for India. Sir George Dallas. *Fr.* The India Guide; or, Journal of a Voyage to the East Indies in 1780. NOEC
Miss Euphemia. John Crowe Ransom. CMoP
Miss [*or* Mis] Flora McFlimsey, of Madison Square. Nothing to Wear. William Allen Butler. HBV-2; OBAL; PoLF
Miss Foggerty's Cake. *Unknown.* BLPA
Miss Gee. W. H. Auden. OxBTC
Miss Hartley. William Jay Smith. TDH
Miss Helen Slingsby was my maiden aunt. Aunt Helen. T. S. Eliot. OBAL; PoA
Miss her, Catullus? don't be so inept to rail. Catullus, *tr. fr. Latin by* Celia *and* Louis Zukofsky. OBVE
Miss Hocket. *Unknown.* TDH
Miss Israel Nineteen-Sixty-Eight is new. Ballade of Beauties. Alexander Scott. BSV
Miss J. Hunter Dunn, Miss J. Hunter Dunn. A Subaltern's Love-Song. John Betjeman. BoLoP; ChMP; EvOK; HAP; LiSp; MP; NOBL; OxBTC; TwCP
Miss James. A. A. Milne. MoShBr
("Diana Fitzpatrick Maulverer James.") TiPo
Miss Jennian Jones. *Unknown.* AmFP
Miss Kilmansegg and Her Precious Leg, *sels.* Thomas Hood.
"Born in wealth and wealthily nursed." EBVV
Her Fancy Ball, *abr.* VLP
Miss Kilmansegg's Birth. OxBoLi
(What Different Dooms Our Birthdays Bring!, *shorter sel.*) NAs
Miss Lavender. Jon Stallworthy. OxBC
Miss Loo. Walter de la Mare. CMoP; OxBTC
(Miss Lou.) HBV-1
Miss Lucy she is slender, Miss Lucy she is stout. I Am Fur from My Sweetheart. *Unknown.* CoSo
Miss Marnell. Austin Clarke. IPY
Miss Melerlee. John Wesley Holloway. BANP; PoNe
Miss Minnie McFinney, of Butte. Limerick. *Unknown.* WhC
Miss M.'s a nightingale. 'Tis well. On a Poetess. Gerard Manley Hopkins. PP
Miss Nancy Ellicott. Cousin Nancy. T. S. Eliot. OBAL
Miss Norma Jean Pugh. Mary O'Neill. RHPC
Miss One, Two, and Three. *Unknown.* OxNR
Miss Packard and Miss Giles. Owen Dodson. GLGT
Miss Pheasant. Walter de la Mare. FaBoNo
Miss Rafferty wore taffeta. The Private Dining Room. Ogden Nash. NYBP; PoCh
Miss Ravenel's Conversion, *sel.* John William DeForest.
National Hymn, A. PAL
Miss Rosie. Lucille Clifton. AmPA; BlSi; CAPP; CNA; NMM; PoBA; TwCP
Miss Snooks, Poetess. Stevie Smith. PV
Miss T. Walter de la Mare. CenHV; FaBoBe; GoJo; GrPl; MoShBr; NTCP; OnUR; PDV; SoPo; SUS; TiPo
Miss Tillie McLush. Joseph S. Newman. TDH
Miss Twye. Gavin Ewart. ErPo; FiBHP; NeBP; NOBL; PV
"Miss Ulalume, there are questions that linger here." Abbreviated Interviews with a Few Disgruntled Literary Celebrities. Reed Whittemore. FiBHP
Miss Wagnalls, when I brought you here. The Girl I Took to the Cocktail Party. Trevor Williams. FiBHP
Miss You. David Cory. BLPA; FaBoBe; TreFS
Missel-Thrush's Nest, The. John Clare. VLP
Misshapen, black, unlovely to the sight. A Bulb. Richard Kendall Munkittrick. AA; POL
"Mis-shapen Time, copesmate of ugly Night." Shakespeare. *Fr.* The Rape of Lucrece. OAEL-1
Missing. W. H. Auden. OxBTC
Missing. A. A. Milne. MoShBr; PDV
Missing. John Pudney. OxBTC
Missing. John Banister Tabb. TrPWD
Missing. *Unknown.* WGRP
Missing all, prevented me, The. Emily Dickinson. AP
Missing Beat. Carolyn M. Rodgers. JB
Missing Dates. William Empson. ChMP; CMoP; CoBMV; FaBoEn; HAP; LiTB; LiTM; MoAB; MoBrPo; MoPo; NoAM; NOBE; NoP; OAEL-2; UnPo; ViBoPo
Missing from the map, the abandoned roads. Old Roads. Eilean Ni Chuilleanain. CIP
Missing Link, The. Oliver Herford. CenHV
Missing My Daughter. Stephen Spender. GTBS-P; Str
Missing Person, The. Donald Justice. NYBP
Missing the Children. Paul Zimmer. Str
Mission. *Unknown.* AmFP
Mission Bay. John Koethe. PoA
Mission Bells of Monterey, The. Bret Harte. PeD
Mission of the Flowers, The. Frances E. W. Harper. BlSi
Mission Tire Factory, 1969. Gary Soto. NPAW; NPGG
Missionaries in the Jungle. Linda Piper. BlSi
Missionary from the Mau Mau told me, A. A Magus. John Ciardi. MAT
Missionary Visits Our Church in Scranton, The. Jay Parini. MAYP
Missions. *Unknown.* STF
Mississippi Blues. *Unknown.* AmFP
Mississippi Born. Pearl Cleage Lomax. CNA
Mississippi Sawyer. *Unknown.* AmFP
Missive, The. Sir Edmund Gosse. HBV-1
Missouri Maiden's Farewell to Alabama, A. "Mark Twain." InMe
Missouri Sequence, *sel.* Brian Coffey.
"Our children have eaten supper." CIP
Missouri Town. John Palen. AMV-80
Missouri Traveller Writes Home, A: 1830. Robert Bly. NePoEA
Misspelled Tail, A. Elizabeth T. Corbett. OBCA
Misspelt scrawl, upon the wall, The. In an Album. James Russell Lowell. OBAL
"Missy Sick." *Unknown.* CoMu
Mist. Gill Man. PoSH
Mist. Henry David Thoreau. *Fr.* A Week on the Concord and Merrimack Rivers. AA; AmPP; AWP; OxBA
(Low-anchored Cloud.) ImOP; NoP; ViBoPo
Mist. Andrew Young. PoSH
Mist and All, The. Dixie Willson. FaPON; SoPo; YeAr
Mist and cold descend from the hills of Wales. Evening in Camp. Patricia Ledward. WaP
Mist condenses, The. A Warm Winter Day. Julian Cooper. BoNaP
Mist drenched, moonlit, the sculpture. Kenneth Rexroth. *Fr.* On Flower Wreath Hill. GP
Mist-foot man who forms within my cellars, The. Nightfall. Elder Olson. DFF
Mist Forms. Carl Sandburg. CMoP; HBMV
Mist lay still on Heartbreak Hill, The. Ipswich Bar. Esther Willard Bates *and* Brainard L. Bates. HBMV
Mist-moist, past the rainbow, we make a small row. Niagara. Richard Emil Braun. NoAM
Mist—no sky. Mist. Gill Man. PoSH
Mist over Pukehina, The. *Maori Oral Tradition, tr. by* E. Shortland. WTO
Mist that from the moor arose, A. Tregardock. John Betjeman. FaBoPP
Mist was driving down the British Channel, A. The Warden of the Cinque Ports. Longfellow. AA; HBV-2; WHA
Mistah Berrybones, you daid? Ode. William Zaranka. BXAP
Mistakable Identity. Elaine V. Emans. AMV-80
Mistake, The. Theodore Roethke. NePoAm-2; UnTE
(Epigram: The Mistake.) NIP
Mistake, The. *Unknown.* PaPo
Mistaken fair, lay Sherlock by. Verses Written in a Lady's Sherlock "Upon Death" [*or* To a Lady on Reading Sherlock "Upon Death"]. Earl of Chesterfield. EBEV; NOEC; OBEC
Mistaken Resolve, The. Martial. *See* To Julius.
Mistakes. George W. Swarberg. STF
Mistakes are dredged up again. Unalterables. Arthur Gregor. NYBP
Mr. A. E. Housman on the Olympic Games. E. V. Knox. WhC
Mr. and Mrs. Discobbolos. Edward Lear. BLPL
Mr. and Mrs. Spikky Sparrow. Edward Lear. OxBChV
Mr. and Mrs. Vite's Journey. *Unknown.* NOBL
Mr. Apollinax. T. S. Eliot. PoA
Mr. Attila. Carl Sandburg. ImOP
Mister Backlash, Mister Backlash. The Backlash Blues. Langston Hughes. BPo
Mister Beers. Hugh Lofting. FaPON
Mr. Bernard Shaw. E. C. Bentley. *Fr.* Clerihews. CenHV
Mr. Bidery's Spidery Garden. David McCord. RHPC
Mr. Blake was a regular out-and-out hardened sinner. Lost Mr. Blake. W. S. Gilbert. InMe
Mr. Bleaney. Philip Larkin. HoPM; InPS; NePoEA-2; OxBC; PPoe

Mr. Brodsky. Charles Tomlinson. NoAM; OxBC
Mr. Brunt. Robert Siegel. GeTw
Mister Charlie. *Unknown.* BluL
Mr. Cherry. Paul Baker Newman. AMV-81
Mr. Coggs. E. V. Lucas. HBV-1; HBVY
(Mr. Coggs, Watchmaker.) FaPON
"Mr. Colwell"/ says Sharon the nurse. The Cry of an Aged One. Ray Fraser. NeAC
Mr. Cooper. Anthony Thwaite. OxBTC
Mr. Cromek. Blake. ChTr
("Pretty sneaking knave I knew, A.") FaBoEE
Mr. Cromek to Mr. Stothard. Blake. FaBoEE
Mr. Davis's Experience. *Unknown.* AmFP
Mr. Edwards and the Spider. Robert Lowell. AP; CABA; CAPP; CMoP; CoAP; FaBoMo; HeIP; InPS; LiTM; MoAB; MoPo; MoVE; MP; NePoEA; NOBA; NoP; SeCeV; SoSe; TwCP
Mr. Eliot Pastor of the Church of Christ at Roxbury. Edward Johnson. SCAP
Mr. Eliot's Day. Robert Francis. NYBP
Mr. Finney's Turnip. *Unknown.* HBV-2; HBVY; NA
Mr. Flood's Party. E. A. Robinson. AmPP; AP; AWP; BiP; BLPL; CABA; CMoP; CoBMV; CrMA; EvOK; FaFP; FF; HAP; HeIP; HoPM; InPK; LiTA; LiTM; MAT; MoAB; MoAmPo; NePA; NIP; NoAM; NOBA; NoP; OxBA; PoPl; PoRA; PPoe; PPP; PrIm; SeCeV; SoSe; TAP; TreFT; TrGrPo; UnPo; ViBoPo; WeW
Mr. Francis Beaumont's Letter to Ben Johnson. Francis Beaumont. OBS
(Francis Beaumont's Letter from the Country to Jonson.) SeCP
(Letter to Ben Jonson, A.) LoBV
"Sun, which doth the greatest comfort bring, The," *sel.* ViBoPo
Mister Frog Went a-Courting. *Unknown. See* Frog Went a-Courting.
Mr. Frost Goes South to Boston. Firman Houghton. Par
Mr. 'Gator. N. M. Bodecker. NTCP; OnUR
Mr. Giraffe. Geoffrey LaPage. OnUR
Mr. Gunman. Vin Garbutt. OBET
Mr. Heath-Stubbs as you must understand. Epitaph. John Heath-Stubbs. NePoEA; OxBTC
Mr. Hilaire Belloc. E. C. Bentley. *Fr.* Clerihews. CenHV
Mr. Hosea Biglow to the Editor of the Atlantic Monthly. James Russell Lowell. *Fr.* The Biglow Papers, 2nd Series, X. AA; PoEL-5
Mr. Housman's Message. Ezra Pound. FaBoEE; FaBoPa
Mr. Hughes. David Campbell. CBAP
Mr. Ibister, and Betsy his sister. *Unknown.* OxNR
Mister Johnson. Ben Harney. OBAL
"Mr. Johnson's Policy of Reconstruction." Charles Graham Halpine. PAH
Mr. Jones. Harry Graham. FaBoCo; FaFP
(Common Sense.) FiBHP
(Some Ruthless Rhymes.) CenHV
Mr. Kartoffel ("Mr. Kartoffel's a whimsical man"). James Reeves. RHPC
Mr. Klein says, "Milagres, hold Angelo's hand." The Retarded Class at F. A. O. Schwarz's Celebrates Christmas. David Fisher. NPGG
Mr. Kurtz. Robert McGovern. SOTS
Mr. Leach made a speech. Forensic Jocularities [*or* A Chancery Suit]. Sir George Rose. FaBoCo; OxBoLi
Mr. Lear, I'm the Akond of Swat. A Reply from the Akond of Swat. Ethel Talbot Scheffauer. FiBHP
Mr. Macklin's Jack O'Lantern ("Mr. Macklin takes his knife"). David McCord. FaPON
Mr. Mandragon, the Millionaire, he wouldn't have wine or wife. The Good Rich Man. G. K. Chesterton. DTC
Mr. Meant-to. *Unknown.* WBLP
Mr. Merry's Lament for "Long Tom." John Gardiner Calkins Brainard. AA
Mr. Minnitt. Rose Fyleman. HBVY
Mr. Molony's Account of the Ball. Thackeray. HBV-2
Mr. Moon. Bliss Carman. FaPON; SUS
Mr. Murple's got a dog that's long. Noctambule. George Johnston. MoCV
Mr. Muscle-on. Faye Kicknosway. GeTw
Mr. Nixon. Ezra Pound. *Fr.* Hugh Selwyn Mauberley. MoAmPo
Mr. Nobody. *Unknown.* FaPON; HBVY
"Mr. Nowlan, are you asleep?" Semi-Private Room. Alden Nowlan. NeAC
Mr. Ody met a body. Edith Nesbit. CenHV; FaBoNo
Mr. Over. Stevie Smith. NoP
Mr. P.—I have heard it rumored. Letter to a Librarian. Irving Layton. MAT; TW
Mr. Pope. Allen Tate. AP; CABA; MoAB; MP; NoAM; NOBA; TwCP; VGW
Mr. Pope's Welcome from Greece. John Gay. EBEV; OBEC; OxBoLi, *abr.*; PoEL-3
Mr. Pratt ("Mr. Pratt has never left"). Myra Cohn Livingston. RHPC
Mr. Pratt, your sheep are very fat. The Norfolk Rebellion. *Unknown.* GBP
Mr. Pyme. Harry Behn. PDV; TiPo
Mr. Rand and Mr. McNally. I Wonder What Became of Rand, McNally. Newman Levy. InMe; WhC
Mr. Rhind is very kind. The Schoolmaster. *Unknown.* GBP; GLGT
Mr. Rockefeller's Hat. Helen Bevington. OBAL
Mr. Roosevelt Regrets. Pauli Murray. PoBA
Mr. Secretary. Karl Patten. SOTS
Mr. Slimmer's Funeral Verses for the *Morning Argus.* "Max Adeler." OBAL
(Out of the Hurly-Burly.) CenHV
Mr. Smiling teeth. Nuclear Racial Lockdowns. Pancho Aguila. LFAC
Mr. Smith/ (With Nods to Mr. Lear and Mr. Eliot.) William Jay Smith. SpRo
(Mr. Smith.) FiBHP
Mister Socrates Snooks, a lord of creation. Socrates Snooks. Fitz Hugh Ludlow. BLPA
Mr. Speeds will clean his auto. Some Who Do Not Go to Church. *Unknown.* WBLP
Mr. Strugnell. Wendy Cope. FaBoPa
Mr. Symons at Richmond, Mr. Pope at Twickenham. Julian Symons. WaP
Mr. T./ bareheaded. The Artist. William Carlos Williams. InPS; LCAP; NYBP; PAI
Mr. T. S. Eliot Cooking Pasta. József Tornai, *tr. fr. Hungarian by* Richard Wilbur. GrPl
Mister Tambourine Man. Bob Dylan. NIP
Mister Thomas Jones. Bringing Him Up. Lord Dunsany. PV
Mr. Thomas Shepheard. Edward Johnson. SCAP
Mr. Tom Narrow. James Reeves. SO
Mr. U Will Not Be Missed. E. E. Cummings. FaBoEE; VGW
Mr. Vachel Lindsay Discovers Radio. Samuel Hoffenstein. BXAP
Mr. Vanessa took the phone. Parallax. Maxwell Anderson. NYBP
Mr. Walter de la Mare Makes the Little Ones Dizzy. Samuel Hoffenstein. Par
"Speckled with glints of star and moonshine," *sel.* SpRo
Mr. Ward of Anagrams Thus. Nathaniel Ward. SCAP
Mr. Wells. Elizabeth Madox Roberts. FaPON; HBMV; HBVY
Mr. Whittier. Winfield Townley Scott. CrMA; VGW
Mister Williams/ lets youn me move. Uncle Iv Surveys His Domain from His Rocker. Jonathan Williams. OBAL
Mr. Wright went out to fish. The Right Way to Fish. *Unknown.* WhC
Mr. Z. M. Carl Holman. SoSe
Mistletoe. Walter de la Mare. SO
Mistletoe Bough, The. Thomas Haynes Bayly. BLPA; HBV-2; PaPo; TreFS; VLP
Mistral. Barbara Howes. NYBP
Mistral blows, the plane leaves, The. On the Eve of the Plebiscite. Kenneth Rexroth. NNaP
Mistress, The. Joan Barton. OxBTC
Mistress, The, *sels.* Abraham Cowley.
Against Hope. LiTB; MeLP; OBS; SeCV-1
(On Hope.) MePo; NOBE
Change, The. AnAnS-2; FaBoEn; MeLP; MePo; OBS; SeCP; SeCV-1
Clad All in White. SeCV-1
Platonic[k] Love. NoP; SeCV-1
Spring, The. HAP; JCP; MeLP; OBS
Thief, The. JCP; OAEP; WHA
Thraldome, The. SeCV-1
Welcome, The. BoLoP; SeCV-1
Wish, The. CavP; HBV-1; LiTB; NOBE; NoP; OAEP; OBS; SeCV-1; TrGrPo; ViBoPo; WHA
Written in Juice of Lem[m]on. AnAnS-2; CABA; SeCP; SeCV-1
Mistress, The. Sir William Davenant. JCP
Mistress, The; a Song. Earl of Rochester. CavP; EBEV; MePo; NOBE; OBS
"Age in her embraces past, An," *sel.* ViBoPo
Mistress Addresses the Wife, The. Naomi Replansky. GP
Mrs. Albion You've Got a Lovely Daughter. Adrian Henri. OxBTC
Mrs. Alfred Uruguay. Wallace Stevens. AP; InPS; MoPo; MP; NePA; TwCP
Mistress allows an average lover, A. To His Coy Mistress. John Flood. BXAP; FaBoPa
Mrs. Ambrose watched the iridescence. Water-Images. Mary Elizabeth Osborn. NePoAm-2
Mrs. Applebaum's Sunday Dance Class. Philip Schultz. AMV-81; MAYP
Mrs. Asquith Tries to Save the Jacarandas. Harold Witt. AMV-81
Mrs. Brown. Rose Fyleman. OxBChV; TiPo
Mrs. Bubb was gay and free, fair, fat and forty-three. The One Horse Chay. *Unknown.* OxBoLi
Mrs. Busk. Sir Osbert Sitwell. OxBTC

Mrs. Chub was rich and portly. Jupiter and Ten. James Thomas Fields. OBAL
Mrs. Coley's three-flat brick. The Vacant Lot. Gwendolyn Brooks. NoAM; NOBA
Mrs. Frances Harris's Petition. Jonathan Swift. *See* To Their Excellencies the Lords Justices of Ireland, the Humble Petition of Frances Harris [Who Must Starve, and Die a Maid if It Miscarries].
Mrs. Golightly. Gertrude Hall. AA
Mrs. Green. David Huddle. PPJ
Mistress Hale of Beverly. Lucy Larcom. PAH
Mrs. Hamer. Jane Stembridge. NMM
Mrs. Hobart-Constantine awakens. Two Ladies Bidding Us "Good Morning." James P. Vaughn. NNP
Mrs. Hopley, on Seeing Her Children Say Goodnight to Their Father. Gerard Manley Hopkins. FaBoEE
Mrs. Huff is up a miff tree. Let Your Pastor Know. *Unknown.* STF
Mrs. Jaypher. Edward Lear. FaBoNo
Mrs. Jaypher on Lemons. Edward Lear. FaBoNo
Mrs. Johnson Objects. Clara Ann Thompson. BlSi
Mrs. Judge Jenkins [Being the Only Genuine Sequel to "Maud Muller"], *parody.* Bret Harte. BXAP; CABA; FiBHP; HBV-1; WhC
Saddest Words, The, *sel.* NePA
Mrs. Kriss Kringle. Edith M. Thomas. OBCA
Mrs. Loewinsohn &c. Ron Loewinsohn. NeAP
Mrs. Lombardi's month-old son is dead. Italian Extravaganza. Gregory Corso. CoPo
Mrs. McGrath. *Unknown.* FaBoBa; FSW; OnYI
Mrs. Macintosh. Rodney Hall. CBAP
Mrs. Malone. Eleanor Farjeon. OxBChV
Mistress Margaret Hussey. John Skelton. *See* To Mistress Margaret Hussey.
Mrs. Marmaduke Moore, at the age of ten. The Seven Spiritual Ages of Mrs. Marmaduke Moore. Ogden Nash. MoAmPo
Mistress Mary, quite contrary. Mother Goose. *See* Mary, Mary, quite contrary.
Mrs. Mary Blaize. Goldsmith. *See* Elegy on That Glory of Her Sex. . .
Mrs. Mason bought a basin. *Unknown.* OxNR
Mistress Murphy gave a party just about a week ago. Who Threw the Overalls in Mistress Murphy's Chowder? George L. Geifer. FSN
Mrs. Noah in the Ark. The Ballad of Mrs. Noah. Robert Duncan. NoAM; NOBA
Mistress of the Manse, The, *sel.* Josiah Gilbert Holland.
Lullaby: "Rockaby, lullaby, bees in the clover!" AA; HBV-1
Mistress of the Matchless Mine. Clyde Robertson. PoOW
Mistress of the Roses, The. Unguarded. Ada Foster Murray. HBV-1
Mistress of Vision, The. Francis Thompson. BrPo; CH, *abr.*; OBVV
Mrs. Peck-Pigeon. Eleanor Farjeon. NTCP; OnUR; PDV; SoPo; SUS; TiPo
Mistress Penelope Penwick, she. The Ballad of Sweet P. Virginia Woodward Cloud. PAH
Mrs. Sadie Grindstaff, Weaver and Factotum. Jonathan Williams. OBAL
Mrs. Santa Claus' Christmas Present. Alice S. Morris. PoSC
Mrs. Saunder's Experience. *Unknown.* AmFP
Mrs. Severin. Winfield Townley Scott. NePoAm
Mrs. Seymour Fentolin. Oliver Herford. HBMV
Mrs. Shepherd of Danbury, Conn., A. Malice Domestic. Ogden Nash. DBV
Mistress, Since You So Much Desire. Thomas Campion. OAEL-1
Mrs. Smith. Frederick Locker-Lampson. HBV-1
Mrs Snatcher Thatcher. Gillian E. Hanscombe. *Fr.* Jezebel: Her Progress. BrRo
Mrs. Snipkin and Mrs. Wobblechin. Laura E. Richards. OxBChV; SoPo; TiPo
Mrs. Someone's been to Asia. An Importer. Robert Frost. FaBoCo
Mrs. Southern's Enemy. Sir Osbert Sitwell. ViBoPo
Mrs. Spider. Myra Cohn Livingston. PDV
Mrs. Throckmorton's bull-finch sang a song. Homage to William Cowper. Donald Davie. NePoEA
Mistress Towl. *Unknown.* FaBoNo
("There was an old woman named Towl.") OxBChV
Mrs. Trollope in America. Helen Bevington. OBAL
Mrs. Velez of the Tenants' Association. Ordinary Women II. Marilyn Hacker. LTB
Mrs. Vickers' Daughter. *Unknown.* AmFP
Mrs. Walpurga. Muriel Rukeyser. NMM
Mistress without Compare, A. *At. to* Charles d'Orléans. MeEL
Mistresses. *Unknown, tr. fr. Irish by* Frank O'Connor. KiLC
Mistrustful minds be moved. Sir Thomas Wyatt. SiPS
Mists and Rain. Baudelaire, *tr. fr. French by* Arthur Symons. SyP
Mists Are Rising Now, The. Hasye Cooperman. GoYe
Mists rise over, The. Yamabe no Akahito, *tr. fr. Japanese by* Kenneth Rexroth. HoPM
Misty and dim, a bush in the wilds of Kapa's. Song. Kaiama, *tr. fr. Hawaiian by* N. B. Emerson. WTO
Misty Island. *Unknown.* PoSH
Misty-Moisty Was the Morn. *Unknown.* GBP
(How Do You Do?) ChTr
Misunderstanding. Irving Layton. PV
Mites go up, The. Stalagmites and Stalactites. *Unknown.* FaBoUs
Mitherless Bairn, The. William Thom. HBV-1
Mither's Lament, The. Sydney Goodsir Smith. OxBS
Mithraic Emblems, *sel.* Roy Campbell.
To the Sun. EaLo
Mithridates. Emerson. AP; NOBA
Mitten Song, The. Marie Louise Allen. NTCP; SoPo; SUS; TiPo
Mix a Pancake. Christina Rossetti. *Fr.* Sing-Song. NTCP; SoPo; SUS
(Pancake, The.) HBVY
Mixed Feelings. John Ashbery. GP; HAP
Mixed Media. James Schevill. AMV-81
Mixed Sketches. Don L. Lee. BPo; TAP
Mixer, The. Louis MacNeice. FaBoTw
Mixture of chloroform and oil of cloves. The Place of Pain in the Universe. Anthony Hecht. CrMA
Mixtures of this garden, The. In the Garden: Villa Cleobolus. Lawrence Durrell. ChMP
Mizpah. Julia A. Baker. BLPA; FaBoBe
MJQ, The. Joyce Carol Thomas. CNA
Mmmmmmmm lordy lordy lord. Savannah Mama. *Unknown.* BluL
Mnemosyne. Trumbull Stickney. CrMA; LiTA; NCEP; NOBA; OxBA; TwAmPo; ViBoPo
Mnemosyne Lay in Dust, *sels.* Austin Clarke.
"Maurice was in an Exhibition Hall," V. IPY
"Men were looking up," III. IPY
"One night he heard heart-breaking sound." VI. CIP; CMoP; IPY
"Past the house where he was got," I. CMoP; IPY
"Rememorised, Maurice Devane," XVIII. CMoP (1970 ed.); IPY
"Straight-jacketing sprang to every lock," II. CMoP; IPY
"Summer was sauntering by," XVII. IPY
"Tall, handsome, tweeded Dr. Leeper," IV. IPY
Moan in the Form of a Ballade. Maurice Baring. WhC
Moan, Moan, Ye Dying Gales. Henry Neele. HBV-2
Moaning. They lay in bed. Last Night They Heard the Woman Upstairs. Leslie Ullman. AMV-80
Moanish Lady, *with music.* *Unknown.* AS
Mobile, immaculate and austere. A Pastoral. Geoffrey Hill. NePoEA-2
Moby Dick, *sel.* Herman Melville.
Father Mapple's Hymn, *fr. ch.* 9. EtS
(Ribs and Terrors, The.) EaLo; ViBoPo
(Whale, The.) PoPl; TrGrPo
Mock Charon, A. Richard Lovelace. CaPo
Mock Invocation to Genius, A, *sel.* William Woty.
"I now solicit not the Muses nine." NOEC
Mock Medicine. *Unknown.* *See* For Sore Eyes.
Mock Miracle, A. Oliver Herford. TDH
Mock On, Mock On, Voltaire, Rousseau. Blake. BiP; CABA; EnRP; HAP; LAuP; NoP; OAEL-2; OAEP; OBNC; OBRV; OxBoCh; PoEL-4; PPoe; PPP; PrIm
(Mockery.) TrGrPo
(Scoffers, The.) LiTB; SeCeV; UnPo
Mock Orange. Louise Glück. MAYP
Mock Song, A. Richard Lovelace. CaPo
Mock Turtle's Song, The. "Lewis Carroll." *See* Lobster Quadrille, The.
Mockado, Fustian, and Motley. John Taylor. *Fr.* Odcomb's Complaint. FaBoNo
(Sonnet: "Sweet semi-circled Cynthia played at maw.") ElL
Mockery. Blake. *See* Mock On, Mock On, Voltaire, Rousseau.
Mockery murders love, they say, and this. Foolish Proverb. *Unknown, tr. fr. Greek by* Louis Untermeyer. UnTE
Mockery of Life, The. Wilfrid Scawen Blunt. The Love Sonnets of Proteus, LXXIV. VLP
Mocking Fairy, The. Walter de la Mare. MoBrPo; MoShBr
Mocking Song against Qaqortingneq. Piuvkaq, *tr. fr. Eskimo.* WTO
Mocking the water with their wings. To One Older. Marion M. Boyd. HBMV
Mocking your slow sepulchral horns. Song for a Proud Relation. Patrick MacDonogh. OnYI
Mocking-Bird, The. Edna Proctor Clarke. AA
Mockingbird, The. Randall Jarrell. DuDa; NYBP; RFM
Mocking Bird, The. Sidney Lanier. AA
Mocking-Bird, The. Frank Lebby Stanton. AA
Mocking-Bird, The. Henry Jerome Stockard. AA
Mocking Bird, The. *Unknown.* *See* Hush Little Baby.
Mocking-Bird, The. Walt Whitman. *Fr.* Out of the Cradle Endlessly Rocking. PB

Mockingbird, Copy This. Jack Myers. AMV-81
Mockingbird in Winter. Ernest Kroll. AMV-80
Mockingbird, I've been working hard. Mockingbird, Copy This. Jack Myers. AMV-81
Mockingbird shrieks and dives again and again at the squirrel, A. Can-Opener. David McAleavey. AMV-81
Mode of the person becomes the mode of the world, The. Conversation with Three Women of New England. Wallace Stevens. NePA
Model. A. R. Ammons. FAZ
Model for the Laureate, A. W. B. Yeats. CMoP
Model Sermon, A. *Unknown.* FaBoUs
Model T. Adrien Stoutenburg. CTBA
Moderation. Robert Herrick. FaBoEE
Moderation. Christopher Smart. Hymns for the Amusement of Children, Hymn 9. NOCV
Modern American Nursing. Lucy Hricz. AMV-80
Modern Architecture. Norman Nathan. AMV-81
Modern Baby, The. William Croswell Doane. BLPA; YaD
Modern Beauty. Arthur Symons. HBV-1
Modern Chinese History Professor Plays Pool Every Tuesday and Thursday, The. James Baker Hall. TAT
Modern Critics. Samuel Taylor Coleridge. FaBoEE
Modern Dragon, A. Rowena Bastin Bennet. PDV; SoPo; TiPo
Modern Fine Gentleman, The, *sel.* Soame Jenyns.
"Just broke from school, pert, impudent, and raw." OBSV
Modern Fine Lady, The. Soame Jenyns. NOEC
"For love no time has she, or inclination," *sel.* OBSV
Modern Grimm. Dorothy Lee Richardson. DFT
Modern Hiawatha, The, *parody*. George A. Strong. *Fr.* The Song of Milkanwatha. FaBoCo; FaBoPa; FaFP; FaPON; FiBHP; HBV-1; InMe; MoShBr; NA; Par; RHPC; SpRo; TreFS; WhC; YaD
(Hiawatha Revisited.) BXAP
Modern house, with great glass eye, The. Anecdote of the Sparrow. Robert Pack. NePA
Modern Jonas, The. *Unknown.* PAH
Modern Kabbalist. Marcia Falk. VWA
Modern Language Association, The. A Salute to the Modern Language Association, Convening in the Hotel Pennsylvania, December 28th-30th. Morris Bishop. WhC
Modern Love. J. V. Cunningham. POL
Modern Love. Keats. OBNC
Modern Love. George Meredith. VLP
Sels.
"All other joys of life he strove to warm," IV. OAEP
"Am I falling? For no longer can I cast," XXIX. CABA; GBL; OAEP
"At dinner, she is hostess, I am host," XVII. HeIP; NoP; OAEP
"At last parley: we so strangely dumb," XLVII. OAEP
"But where began the change; and what's my crime?" X. NBM; PoEL-5
"By this he knew she wept with waking eyes," I. EnLoPo; HBV-1; HeIP; NBM; NoP; OAEL-2; OAEP; PoEL-5
(End of Love, The.) HoPM
"He found her by the ocean's moaning verge," XLIX. HBV-1; NoP; OAEL-2; OAEP
"Here Jack and Tom are paired with Moll and Meg," XVIII. InvP; NBM; PoEL-5
"How many a thing which we cast to the ground," XLI. HBV-1
"I am to follow her. There is much grace," XLII. ViBoPo
" 'I play for seasons, not eternities!' " XIII. FaBoEn; OBNC
"In our old shipwrecked days there was an hour," XVI. BoLoP; HBV-1; WHA
(Love Dies.) SeCePo
"It chanced his lips did meet her forehead cool," VI. ViBoPo
"It ended, and the morrow brought the task," II. HBV-1; OAEP
"It is the season of the sweet wild rose," XLV. GBL; NBM; PoEL-5
"Love ere he bleeds, an eagle in high skies," XXVI. HBV-1
"Mark where the pressing wind shoots javelin-like," XLIII. EnLoPo; FaBoEn; GBL; HBV-1; NBM; NOBE, OAEP; OBNC; PoEL-5; SeCeV; TEP
(Love's Grave.) OBEV
"Not solely that the future she destroys," XII. GBL; TEP; ViBoPo
"Out in the yellow meadows, where the bee," XI. GBL
"Their sense is with their senses all mixed in," XLVIII. NoP; OAEL-2; OAEP
"This was the woman; what now of the man?" III. HBV-1
"Thus piteously Love closed what he begat," L. EBEV; EnLoPo; FaBoEn; GTBS-P; HAP; HBV-1; LoBV; NBM; NOBE; NoP; OAEL-2; OAEP; OBNC; PoEL-5; SeCeV; TreFT; TrGrPo; ViBoPo; WHA
(Dusty Answer, A.) SeCePo
"We saw the swallows gathering in the sky," XLVII. EnLoPo; FaBoEn; GTBS-P; NOBE; OAEL-2; OBNC; SeCeV; ViBoPo; WHA
(We Saw the Swallows.) ELP
"We three are on the cedar-shadowed lawn," XXI. OAEP
"What are we first? First, animals; and next," XXX. GBL; HAP; NBM; NoP; OAEP; PoEL-5; ViBoPo
"What soul would bargain for a cure that brings," XIV. HBV-1
"Yet it was plain she struggled, and that salt," VIII. OAEP
Modern Love. Gerald Stern. AMV-80
Modern Love Poems. *Somali Oral Tradition.* TTY, *tr. by* B. W. Andrzejewski *and* I. M. Lewis; WTO, *tr. by* B. W. Andrzejewski *and* M. Laurence
Modern Major-General, The. W. S. Gilbert. *Fr.* The Pirates of Penzance. FaPo; InMe; NOBL
(I Am the Very Model of a Modern Major-General.) NoP
(Major-General's Song, The.) NBM
Modern malady of love is nerves, The. Nerves. Arthur Symons. BrPo; FaBoTw; SyP
Modern Ode to the Modern School. John Erskine. YaD
Modern Poetry. Anita Skeen. IHMS
Modern Romance, A. Paul Engle. PoPl
Modern Romance. William J. Harris. GP
Modern Romans, The. Charles Frederick Johnson. AA
Modern Woman to Her Lover, The. Margaret Widdemer. HBMV
Modern World, The. Colin Ellis. FaBoEE
Modernist married a fundamentalist wife, A. Marital Tragedy. Keith Preston. WhC
Modernists, The. Tom MacInnes. CaP
Modes of Pleasure. Thom Gunn. PeHV; PPP
Modes of the Court, The. John Gay. *Fr.* The Beggar's Opera, III, iv. HeIP
Modes of Vallejo Street, San Diego, Los Angeles, The, *sels.* Hugh Seidman.
"He imagines her," 3. UnPo
"He knows he must explain this," 9. UnPo
Modest and needy is my destiny in thy world, O God! Kibbutz Sabbath. Levi Ben Amittai, *tr. by* Simon Halkin. EaLo
Modest front of this small floore, The. An Epitaph upon Mr. Ashton, a Conformable Citizen. Richard Crashaw. OBS
Modest Love, A. Sir Edward Dyer. *See* Silent Love, A.
Modest Wit, A. Selleck Osborn. BLPA; HBV-1
Modo and Alciphron. Sylvia Townsend Warner. MoBrPo
Moenkopi. Arthur Sze. BrSi
Mog the Brunette. *Unknown.* CoMu
Moggy and Me. James Hogg. HBV-1
Mohammed and Seid. Harrison Smith Morris. AA
Mohammed Ibrahim Speaks. Martha Beidler. FF
Mohini Chatterjee. W. B. Yeats. NoAM
Moiré. Michael McClure. EAS
Moishe Leib stood up. Just Because. Moishe Leib Halpern, *tr. by* Ruth Whitman. VWA
Moist Moon People. Carl Sandburg. MoAmPo
Moistened osier of the hoary willow, The. The Coracle. Lucan, *tr. by* Sir Walter Ralegh. ChTr
Mojo Hiding Woman. *Unknown.* BluL
Molasses River. Richard Kendall Munkittrick. OBCA
Molded to the owl is what the owl spits out. Natural Architecture. John Hay. NePoAm
Mole, The. John Clare. SeCeV
Mole, The. Roy Daniells. WHW
Mole, The. John Haines. NCSH
Mole, The. Dennis Schmitz. AmPA
Mole and the Eagle, The. Sarah Josepha Hale. OBCA
Mole Catcher. Edmund Blunden. OBMV
Molecatcher. Albert D. Mackie. GoTS
Mole in the Ground *Unknown.* FSW
Mole is blind, and under ground, The. The Mole and the Eagle. Sarah Josepha Hale. OBCA
Mole, The (it may have been vole: I can't distinguish). The Mole. Roy Daniells. WHW
Mole Talk. Leo Kennedy. PeCV
Mole who knows. Back to Base. Jenny Joseph. BrRo
Moles. William Stafford. NYBP; RFM
Moll-in-the-wad and I fell out. *Unknown.* OxNR
Mollesse. Josephine Jacobsen. NePoAm-2
Mollis Abuti. Jonathan Swift. ChTr
Molly Bawn. *Unknown.* *See* Young Molly Ban.
Molly Bawn and Brian Oge. *Unknown.* OnYI
Molly Brannigan, *Unknown.* FSW
Molly Malone. *Unknown.* *See* Cockles and Mussels.
Molly Means. Margaret Walker. AmNP; BlSi; NMM; PoNe
Molly Mog; or, The Fair Maid of the Inn. John Gay. CoMu
Molly Moor. George Farewell. NOEC
Molly of the North Country. *Unknown.* OBET
Molly Pitcher. Laura E. Richards. PAH; YAD
Molly Pitcher. Kate Brownlee Sherwood. PAH; PAL
Moly. Thom Gunn. HAP; NoAM; PrIm

Moly. Edith M. Thomas. HBV-1
Mom said I was old enough to decide. Sunday Crappies. Jim Thomas. WOLT
Moment, The. Theodore Roethke. NYBP
Moment, The. William Stafford. NNaP
Moment before Conception, The. Eve Merriam. UnTE
Moment by Moment. Daniel W. Whittle. BLRP
Moment Eternal, The. Robert Browning. *See* Now.
Moment I glanced at the mirk-windowed mansion, The. The Spectre. Walter de La Mare. WhC
Moment in Summer, A. Charlotte Zolotow. RHPC
Moment in the morning, ere the cares of day begin, A. To Begin the Day. *Unknown.* BLRP
Moment is what moves us, after all, The. A Discussion of the Vicissitudes of History under a Pine Tree. Katha Pollitt. MAYP
Moment Musical in Assynt. Norman MacCaig. PoSH
Moment Musicale. Bliss Carman. HBMV
Moment of desire, The! the moment of desire! the virgin. Blake. *Fr.* Visions. ErPo
Moment of silence first, then there it is, A. The Dial Tone. Howard Nemerov. NYBP
Moment of the Rose, The. Dunstan Thompson. LiTA
Moment of War, A. Laurie Lee. OBWP
Moment Please, A. Samuel Allen. AmNP; IDB; PAI; PoBA
Moment the wild swallows like a flight, A. A Thunderstorm. Archibald Lampman. CaP; NOBC
Moment to/ moment the/ body seems. Time. Robert Creeley. LCAP
Momento for Mortality, A. William Basse. EIL
Moments. Hervey Allen. HBMV
Moments. Marcel Schwob, *tr. fr. French by* William Brown Meloney. TrJP
Moments He Remembers, The. Mark Van Doren. NYBP
Moments of Vision. Thomas Hardy. OAEL-2
Moments there are when heart and brain ring clear. Moments. Hervey Allen. HBMV
Momist. Amy Groesbeck. GoYe
Momma Momma Momma. Getting Down to Get Over. June Jordan. TAP
Momma's Not Gods Image. Noah Mitchell. LFAC
"Mommy, take me home, I'm a changed boy." Ontogeny. Jarold Ramsey. NIP
Momotara. Rose Fyleman. TiPo
Momus. E. A. Robinson. ViBoPo
Mon in the mone stond and strit. The Man in the Moon. *Unknown.* MeEL
Mon that wist for raine, The. Amedie Eva List. BXAP
Mona Lisa. Edward Dowden. OnYI
Mona Lisa, A. Angelina Weld Grimké. BlSi; CDC
Mona Lisa. Walter Pater. OBMV
Monadnock, The. John Gould Fletcher. PoA
Monaghan. Shane Leslie. OnYI
Monangamba. Antonio Jacinto, *tr. fr. Portuguese by* Alan Ryder. TTY
Monarch, The. William Cowper. *See* Verses Supposed to be Written by Alexander Selkirk . . .
Monarch oak, the patriarch of the trees, The. The Oak. Dryden. OHIP
Monarch of gods and daemons, and all spirits. Prometheus Unbound. Shelley. EnRP; FiP, *abr.*; OAEL-2
Monarch of the Sea. George Starbuck. OBAL
("Jiminy Whillikers.") PV
Monarch sat on his judgment-seat, The. The Fay's Sentence. Joseph Rodman Drake. *Fr.* The Culprit Fay. AA
Monarche, The, *sel.* Sir David Lindsay.
After the Flood. OxBS
Monasteries. Charles David Webb. NePoAm-2
Monasteries Lift Gold Domes, The. Yocheved Bat-Miriam, *tr. fr. Hebrew by* Robert Friend. VWA
Monastery, The, *sels.* Sir Walter Scott.
Book of Books, The ("Within this ample volume lies"), *fr. ch.* 12. TreFT
(Bible, The.) BLRP; TRV
(Sir Walter Scott's Tribute.) WBLP
Border Ballad, *fr. ch.* 25. GN; HBV-2
(Blue Bonnets over the Border.) OxBS
(Border March.) EnRP
("March, march, Ettrick and Teviotdale.") BSV; ViBoPo
"Indifferent, but indifferent pshaw! he doth it not," *fr. ch.* 21. NBM
Song of the White Lady of Avenel, *fr. ch.* 5. NBM
Monastery on Athos. Richmond Lattimore. EyDe
Mond ist aufgegangen, Der. Heine, *tr. fr. German by* James Thomson. AWP
Monday. William Stafford. NYBP
Monday for wealth. Propitious Days for Weddings [*or* Days of the Week]. *Unknown.* FaBoUs; TreFT
Monday I found a boot. Beachcomber. George Mackay Brown. OxBC
Monday I was 'rested, Tuesday I was fined. Lookin' for the Bully of the Town. *Unknown.* BaBo
Monday morning back to school. David McCord. TiPo
Monday's child is fair of face. Mother Goose. BLPA; BLPL; FaBoBe; FaBoCh; HBV-1; HBVY; MoShBr; OxNR; SoPo; TreF
Monet: "Les Nymphéas." W. D. Snodgrass. CoAP; ConAP
Monet Refuses the Operation. Lisel Mueller. FYAP
Money. Richard Armour. FaFP; PoPl; TreFS; WhC
Money. Victor Contoski. GP
Money. W. H. Davies. OBEV; OBMV; OBVV
Money. Howard Nemerov. OxBC; WeW
Money. C. H. Sisson. POL
Money, *with music.* *Unknown.* AS
Money and a Friend. *Unknown.* BLPA
Money Cry, The. Peter Davison. FYAP
Money Gets the Mastery. Robert Herrick. CaPo
Money in the Bank. W. D. Ehrhart. FAZ
Money Is King. *Unknown.* FSW
Money Is What Matters. *Unknown.* MeEL
Money Isn't Everything! Oscar Hammerstein II. OBAL
Money Makes the Marriage. *Unknown.* TDH
Money Makes the Mirth. Robert Herrick. CaPo
Money men collect in high rise, The. Thumbing Old Magazines. Gerald Vizenor. VoR
Money! Money! *Yoruba Oral Tradition, tr. by* O. Ogunba. WTO
Money, thou bane of bliss and source of woe. Avarice. George Herbert. FaBoRV; LiTB
Money thou ow'st me; prithee fix a day. Upon Bunce: Epigram. Robert Herrick. CaPo
Money was once well known, like a townhall or the sky. Behaviour of Money. Bernard Spencer. LiTB
Moneyless Men, The. Henry T. Stanton. BLPA
Mongan Laments the Change That Has Come upon Him and His Beloved. W. B. Yeats. VLP
Mongol Quine. Alastair Mackie. BSV
Mongoloid boy is astounded, The. In the Dome Car of the "Canadian." Sid Marty. NOBC
Mon-goos, The. Oliver Herford. *Fr.* Child's Natural History. AA; HBV-2
'Mongst all the hard names that denote reproach. Burnet's Character. *Unknown.* APAS
Mongst all the Palaces in Hells command. Sospetto d'Herode. Giambattista Marini, *tr. by* Richard Crashaw. *Fr.* La Strage degli Innocenti. SeCV-1
'Mongst illustrious men in the Bible there be. An Aristocratic Trio. Judson France. PV
Monk, The. Blake. *Fr.* Jerusalem. LoBV
("I saw a Monk of Charlemaine.") EnRP; OBRV
Monk, The, *sel.* Matthew Gregory Lewis.
Alonzo the Brave and Fair Imogine. OBEC
Monk and His Pet Cat, The. *Unknown, tr. fr. Old Irish.* CH, *tr. by* Kuno Meyer; OnYI, *tr. by* Whitley Stokes, John Strachan, *and* Kuno Meyer, *arr. by* Kathleen Hoagland
(Pangur Ban, *tr. by* Robin Flower.) AnIL; FaBoCh; OnYI; OxBI
(Scholar and the Cat, The, *tr. by* Frank O'Connor.) KiLC
Monk Arnulphus uncorked his ink, The. The Court Historian. Walter Thornbury. HBV-1; OBVV
Monk can do his work on bended knees, A. Mendel's Law. Peter Meinke. SUW
Monk in the Kitchen, The. Anna Hempstead Branch. MoAmPo
Monk of Casal-Maggiore, The. Longfellow. *Fr.* Tales of a Wayside Inn: The Sicilian's Tale, Pt. III. AmPP; OxBA
(Sicilian's Tale, The.) AP
Monk of Great Renown, The. *Unknown.* CoMu
Monk sat in his den, The. The Weak Monk. Stevie Smith. BoWoP; FaBoTw
Monk ther was, a fair for the maistrye [*or* maistrie], A. Chaucer. *Fr.* The Canterbury Tales: Prologue. CTC, *abr.*; TrGrPo
Monk there was, a monk of mastery, A. Chaucer, *mod. vers. by* Louis Untermeyer. *Fr.* The Canterbury Tales: Prologue. TrGrPo
Monk was preaching, The: strong his earnest word. A Legend. Adelaide Anne Procter. GoBC
Monk, when his rites sacerdotal were o'er, A. The Philosopher's Scales. Jane Taylor. HBV-1
Monkey, The. Mary Howitt. GN
Monkey. Josephine Miles. LiTM
Monkey. William Jay Smith. TiPo
Monkey Difference. Barbara Howes. GP
Monkey-flower, or mimulus, The. Floral Tribute. Sir Charles Jeffries. PoPle
Monkey, lap-dog, parrot, and her Grace, The. Sir Charles Hanbury Williams. *Fr.* Isabella; or, The Morning. NOEC
Monkey, little merry fellow. The Monkey. Mary Howitt. GN

Monkey married the Baboon's sister, The. The Monkey's Wedding. *Unknown.* AS; BLPA; NA
Monkey Monkey Moo! So Many Monkeys. Marion Edey *and* Dorothy Grider. SoPo; TiPo
Monkeys. Padraic Colum. OxBTC
Monkeys, The. Marianne Moore. CMoP; LiTA; NoAM; NOBA; OxBA; SeCeV; TwAmPo
Monkeys, The. Edith Osborne Thompson. TiPo
Monkeys and the Crocodile, The. Laura E. Richards. FaPON; ShM; SoPo; SUS; TiPo
Monkey's Glue, The. Goldwin Goldsmith. NA
Monkeys in a forest. Where. Walter de la Mare. NYBP
Monkeys on Mt. Hiei. Edith Marcombe Shiffert. WPE
Monkey's Raincoat, The. Basho, *tr. fr. Japanese by* Harold G. Hendeson. SoPo
Monkey's Wedding, The. *Unknown.* AS, *with music*; BLPA; NA
Monkeys winked too much and were afraid of snakes, The. The Monkeys. Marianne Moore. LiTA; OxBA
Monkish Mind of the Speculative Physicist, The. Bin Ramke. SUW
Monks. Cardinal Newman. GoBC
Monks at Ards, The. Patrick Maybin. NeIP
Monks of Ely, The. *Unknown.* ACP
Monna Innominata. Christina Rossetti. VLP
Sels.
First Day, The. BLPL; BoLoP; FaBoBe; HBV-1; OLR
("I wish I could remember that first day.") GBL
"Many in aftertimes will say of you." OBNC; ViBoPo
Meeting: "They made the chamber sweet with flowers and leaves." HBV-1
Remember ("Remember me when I am gone away"). HBV-1
Rest ("O Earth lie heavy upon her eyes"). HBV-1
"Youth gone, and beauty gone if ever there." GBL; OBNC; ViBoPo
Monody. Herman Melville. AP; LiTA; NCEP; PoEL-5
Monody on a Century. Earle Birney. CaP
Monody to the Sound of Zithers. Kay Boyle. PoA
Monogamania. Eve Merriam. UnTE
Monogamy, *sel.* Gerald Gould.
"You were young—but that was scarcely to your credit." OxBTC
Monogram 4. Martina Werner, *tr. fr. German by* Rosemarie Waldrop. BoWoP
Monogram 29. Martina Werner, *tr. fr. German by* Rosemarie Waldrop. BoWoP
Monogram 23. Martina Werner, *tr. fr. German by* Rosemarie Waldrop. BoWoP
Monologue of a Deaf Man. David Wright. MP; NoAM
Monologue of the Rating Morgan in Rutherford County. C. F. MacIntyre. PH
Monologue of Two Moons, Nudes with Crests. 1938. Norman Dubie. FiCP
Monologue through Bars. Nelson Hubbell. AMV-81
Monotonous evil clock, The. A Round Number. Keith Douglas. NeBP
Monseigneur Plays. Theodosia Garrison. HBMV
Monserrat. William Edwin Collin. CaP
Monsieur Etienne de Silhouette. Some Frenchmen. John Updike. FaBoCo
Monsieur Ezra Pound croit que. Another Canto. J. B. Morton. FaBoPa
Monsieur Gaston. A. M. Klein. MoCV
Monsieur Pussy-Cat, Blackmailer. Stevie Smith. PCat
Monsieur Qui Passe. Charlotte Mew. SBG
Monsieur the Curé down the street. The Curé's Progress. Austin Dobson. HBV-1
Monsignore,/ Right Reverend Bishop Valentinus. A Blue Valentine. Joyce Kilmer. ISi
Monsoon. Kenneth Slade Alling. NePoAm
Monsoon. David Wevill. NYBP
Monster, The. Greg Kuzma. AmPA
Monster, The. Edward Lowbury. AmMo
Monster, The. Henry Rago. PoA
Monster Alphabet. Robert Fisher. AmMo
Monster has escaped from the dungeon, The. Frankenstein. Edward Field. FF
Monster rests upon my roof, A. The Chimera. Alfred Mombert, *tr. by* Erna Baber Rosenfeld. VWA
Monster taught, A/ To come to hand. Song of a Train. John Davidson. BrPo
Monster who lives in Loch Ness, A. The Monster. Edward Lowbury. AmMo
Monstrous Marriage, The. William Carlos Williams. MoPo
Monstrous, uncouth, their vast leaves amply spread. Palm House, Botanic Gardens. George Hetherington. NeIP
Mont Blanc. Shelley. EnRP; NIP; NoP; OAEL-2; PP; TEP
Montalbert, *sel.* Charlotte Smith.
"Swift fleet the billowy clouds along the sky." BoWoP; WPE
Montana Eclogue. William Stafford. NYBP
Montana Fifty Years Ago. J. V. Cunningham. Prf
Montana Pastoral. J. V. Cunningham. MAT; MoAmPO; PrIm; VGW
Montana Remembered from Albuquerque; 1982. Ron Rogers. STE
Montana Wives. Gwendolen Haste. AmFN
Montanus' Sonnet. Thomas Lodge. *Fr.* Rosalynde. PoEL-2
Montauk/ Shagwong to Great Eastern Rock to Pollock Rip. 12 Oct. Allen Planz. WOLT
Montcalm and Wolfe. *Unknown.* AmFP
Monte Albán. Joseph Stroud. NPGG
Montefiore. Ambrose Bierce. AA
Monterey. Charles Fenno Hoffman. AA; FaBoBe; HBV-2; PAH
Montgomery. Sam Cornish. CNA; PoBA; Psk
Montgomery. H. A. C. Evans. GDP
Montgomery. J. C. Hall. ChMP
Montgomery at Quebec. Clinton Scollard. PAH
Month after month the gathered rains descend. To the Nile. Shelley. OBRV
Month can never forget the year, The. Carol. John McClure. HBMV
Month is amber, The. October. John Updike. PDV
Month of Falling Stars, The. Ella Higginson. YeAr
Month of gold, A: gold flowers, gold sun. The Golden Month. Marion Doyle. YeAr
Month of January. Frankie Armstrong. BrRo
Month of May, The. Beaumont *and* Fletcher. *Fr.* The Knight of the Burning Pestle. ChTr
Month of the drowned dog, The. After long rain the land. November. Ted Hughes. CMoP; GTBS-P; NePoEA-2; NMP; NoP
Month of the Thunder Moon, The. Marion Doyle. YeAr
Months, The. Sara Coleridge. *See* Garden Year, The.
Months, The. Christina Rossetti. FaPON
Months, The. *Unknown.* *See* January by This Fire.
Months after the Muse. The Illustration—a Footnote. Denise Levertov. PoA
Months of the Year, The. Richard Grafton. FaBoUs
Months of the Year, The. *Unknown.* FaBoUs
Months of waiting: then everyone. At Summer's End. Saul Hillel Benjamin. AMV-81
Monticello. May Sarton. GOA
Montreal. A. M. Klein. CaP; MoCV; OBCV
Montrose to His Mistress. James Graham, Marquess of Montrose. LoBV, *abr.*; ViBoPo
"My dear and only Love, I pray," *sel.* OxBS
Monument. Milton Acorn. NeAC
Monument, The. Elizabeth Bishop. LiTA; MoPo; NoAM; NOBA; PP; PPoe
Monument, A. Charles Madge. FaBoMo
Monument. A. M. Sullivan. GoYe
Monument and the Shrine, The. John Logan. LCAP
Monument Mountain. Bryant. BeLS
Monument of Cleita, The. Edward Cracroft Lefroy, *after the Greek of* Theocritus. *Fr.* Echoes from Theocritus. AWP
Monument to a Boxer. Lucilius, *tr. fr. Greek by* Tom Dodge. LiSp
Monument to Pushkin. Joseph Brodsky, *tr. fr. Russian by* Dimitry Pospielovsky *and* Keith Bosley. VWA
Monument which thou beholdest here, The. Epitaph for Himself. Lord Herbert of Cherbury. AnAnS-2
Monumental Memorial of Marine Mercy, A. Richard Steere. SCAP
Monumentum Aere, Etc. Ezra Pound. NOBA
Mony ane talks [*or* speaks] o the grass, the grass. Willie and Earl Richard's Daughter (B *and* C *vers.*). *Unknown.* ESPB
Moo! Robert Hillyer. OBAL; WhC
Moo-Cow-Moo, The. Edmund Vance Cooke. FaFP; MoShBr
Moochie ("Moochie likes to keep on playing"). Eloise Greenfield. NTCP
Mood, A. Winifred Howells. AA
Mood, The. Quandra Prettyman. PoBA
Mood, A. Amélie Rives. AA
Moods, The. Fannie Stearns Davis. HBV-2
Moods. Leib Kwitko, *tr. fr. Yiddish by* Joseph Leftwich. TrJP
Moods, The. W. B. Yeats. CTC; VLP
Moods have laid their hands across my hair, The. The Moods. Fannie Stearns Davis. HBV-2
Moods of Rain. Vernon Scannell. BoNaP
"Mooly cow, mooly cow, home from the wood." The Cow-Boy's Song. Anna Maria Wells. OBCA
Moom moom. Troll Chanting. Anselm Hollo. *Fr.* Out of the "Kalevala." WSC
Moon, The. Charles Best. *See* Sonnet of the Moon, A.
Moon, The. Robert Creeley. VGW
Moon, The. W. H. Davies. BrPo; MoBrPo; MoVE
Moon, The. Eliza Lee Follen. HBV-1; HBVY
Moon, The. Louise Ayres Garnett. SiSoSe
Moon, The. Donald Hall. NCSH

Moon. Frances Horovitz. BrRo
Moon. Henry Rowe. OBEV
Moon, The. Ryuho, *tr. fr. Japanese.* SoPo
Moon, The. Shelley. *See* Waning Moon, The.
Moon, The. Sir Philip Sidney. *See* Astrophel and Stella, XXXI.
Moon. William Jay Smith. PDV
Moon. Derek Walcott. NoAM
Moon, The/ is a white/ bull. Images. Alastair Campbell. MOON
Moon/ you lift your white skirts. Talking to the Moon #002. Joy Harjo. TWSS
Moon, a sweeping scimitar, dipped in the stormy straits, The. Winged Man. Stephen Vincent Benét. MoAmPo
Moon above the milky field, The. Night-Piece. Léonie Adams. MoAB; MoAmPo
Moon and I a-tiptoe peer within, The. The Old Casa. Torrey Connor. BPAW
Moon and seven Pleiades have set, The. Alone. Sappho, *tr. by* William Ellery Leonard. AWP
Moon and the Night and the Men, The. John Berryman. CoAP; VGW; WaP
Moon and the Nightingale, The. Milton. *See* Evening in Paradise.
Moon and the Salt Flats, The. Mary Di Michele. NOBC
Moon and the Yew Tree, The. Sylvia Plath. CoAP; FaBoMo; MOON; NaP; NYBP; PPP; VGW; WPE; WPOW
Moon as Medusa. Vinnie-Marie D'Ambrosio. IHMS
Moon at the Fortified Pass, The. Li Po, *tr. fr. Chinese by* Witter Bynner *and* Kiang Kang-hu. WaaP
Moon at the full. Europe has burst its banks. The Inundation. Howard Sergeant. EAS
Moon at Three A.M. Lance Henson. CDW
Moon behind High Tranquil Leaves, The. Robert Nichols. OBMV
Moon behind the Hill, The. *Unknown.* WTO
Moon Bird, The. V. C. Vickers. AmMo
Moon Blast. Michelle Roberts. LFAC
Moon bloats full and white, The. Omalos. Rosanna Warren. AMV-80
Moon-Bone Song [*or* Cycle], The. *Unknown, tr. fr. Wonguri by* Ronald M. Berndt. CBAP
Sels.
Birds, The. WTO
Evening Star, The. WTO
New Moon. WTO
Moon came to the forge, The. Ballad of Luna, Luna. Federico García Lorca, *tr. by* William B. Logan. SOTW
Moon-Child, The. "Fiona Macleod." CH; EtS
Moon-Come-Out. Eleanor Farjeon. TiPo
Moon comes every night to peep, The. The White Window. James Stephens. SUS; TiPo
Moon Compasses. Robert Frost. MOON; MoVE
Moon-cradle's rocking and rocking, The. The Ballad of Downal Baun. Padraic Colum. SUS
Moon cuts through, The. Somewhere near Phu Bai. Yusef Komunyakaa. MAYP
Moon Deer, how near. By the Waters of Minnetonka. J. M. Cavanass. BLSo
Moon Eclipse Exorcism. *Unknown, tr. fr. American Indian by* Armand Schwerner. MOON
Moon-faced baby with cocaine arms. Blues for Sister Sally. Lenore Kandel. NMM
Moon Festival. Tu Fu, *tr. fr. Chinese by* Kenneth Rexroth. NaP
Moon fills up its hollow bowl of milk, The. Alex Comfort. *Fr.* The Postures of Love. NeBP
Moon Fishing. Lisel Mueller. CoAP
Moon, Flowers, Man. Su Tung-p'o, *tr. fr. Chinese by* Kenneth Rexroth. NaP
Moon goes over the water, The. Half Moon. Federico García Lorca, *tr. by* W. S. Merwin. RFM
Moon Going Down. *Unknown.* BluL
Moon going orange, The. The Point. Gary Soto. MAYP
Moon Ground, The. James Dickey. MOON
Moon had climbed the highest hill, The. The Banks of Dee. *Unknown.* AmFP
Moon had risen on the eastern hill, The. The Sailor and His Bride. *Unknown.* AmFP
Moon has gone to her rest, The. A Nocturne. Wilfrid Scawen Blunt. OBMV
Moon has left the sky, The. A Night in Lesbos. George Horton. AA
Moon Has Set, The. Sappho, *tr. fr. Greek.* ChTr
Moon his mare, all silver-bright, The. The Chase. W. H. Davies. BrPo
Moon in heaven's garden, among the clouds that wander. Spinning in April. Josephine Preston Peabody. HBV-1
Moon, in her pride, once glanced aside, The. The Moon Sings. *Unknown.* MOON; OxBoLi
Moon in the bureau mirror, The. Insomnia. Elizabeth Bishop. LLLT
Moon in the Water, The. Ryota, *tr. fr. Japanese.* SoPo
Moon in your eyes is best, The. Tracking Rabbits: Night. Jim Barnes. CDW
Moon in Your Hands, The. Hilda Doolittle ("H. D."). BoWoP; NYBP
Moon Is a Diamond, The. Arthur Sze. AMV-81
Moon is a dusty place, The. Moon-Witches. Ted Hughes. WSC
Moon is a poor woman, The. Sidney Keyes. *Fr.* The Foreign Gate. OBWP
Moon is a sow, The. Song for Ishtar. Denise Levertov. NaP; NMM; NoAM; PoM
Moon is able to command the valley tonight, The. Moist Moon People. Carl Sandburg. MoAmPo
Moon is an ivory tusk in the Utah sky, The. The Moon and the Salt Flats. Mary Di Michele. NOBC
Moon is an usurer, whose gain. Upon Moon. Robert Herrick. MOON
Moon is at her full, and, riding high, The. The Tides. Bryant. TAP
Moon is down, The. Night Up There. G. D. Valentine. PoSh
Moon is eaten and renewed, The. The Lunar Games. Eeva-Liisa Manner, *tr. by* Jaakko A. Ahokas. WPOW
Moon is fully risen, The. Der Mond ist aufgegangen. Heine, *tr. by* James Thomson. AWP
Moon is not green cheese, The. Night Light. Nancy Willard. LCAP
Moon is round as a jack-o'-lantern, The. Hallowe'en. Frances Frost. TiPo
Moon is setting in the west, The. Song of the Hesitations. Paul Blackburn. NMP
Moon Is Teaching Bible, The. Zelda, *tr. fr. Hebrew by* Marcia Falk. VWA
Moon is the mother of pathos and pity, The. Lunar Paraphrase. Wallace Stevens. MOON
Moon Is the Number 18, The. Charles Olson. CMoP; NMP
Moon Is to Blood. Richard Duerden. NeAP
Moon Is Up, The. *Unknown.* NA
Moon is up, The. Old Mole. James Reeves. WSC
Moon, The? It is a griffin's egg. Yet Gentle Will the Griffin Be. Vachel Lindsay. Poems about the Moon, II. MOON; PDV; TwAmPo
Moon labours through black cloud, The. Lionel Johnson. Sancta Silvarum, II-IV. VLP
Moon Landing. W. H. Auden. MOON; SUW
Moon like a flower, The. Blake. *Fr.* Songs of Innocence: Night. MOON
Moon-Madness. Victor Starbuck. HBMV
Moon-Man. Dorothy Hewett. CBAP
Moon Man. Jean Valentine. MOON
Moon Mattress. Diane DiPrima. NMM
Moon mentions, The. Grunion. Myra Cohn Livingston. RFM
Moon, moon/ Mak' me a pair o'shoon. *Unknown.* OxNR
Moon moon moon moon this. This May Be Your Captain Speaking. C. K. Stead. OCNZ
Moon more indolently dreams tonight, The. The Sadness of the Moon. Baudelaire, *tr. by* F. P. Trurm. MOON
Moon, my mother opened up. Talking to the Moon. Joy Harjo. TWSS
Moon Now Rises [to Her Absolute Rule], The. Henry David Thoreau. FaBoEn; PoEL-4
Moon of Huckleberries. Phillip William George. VoR
Moon of Id came, The. Empress Nur Jahan, *tr. fr. Persian by* Willis Barnstone. BoWoP
Moon of Mobile, The. Thomas Holley Chivers. OBAL
Moon of the Earth. *Gond Oral Tradition, tr. by* V. Elwin *and* S. Hivale. WTO
Moon on the one hand, the dawn on the other, The. The Early Morning. Hilaire Belloc. BoNaP; HBMV; HBVY
Moon Poem. Saundra Sharp. QQQ
Moon Poems. John Wieners. VGW
Moon Rises, The. Federico García Lorca, *tr. fr. Spanish by* William B. Logan. SOTW
Moon rises, The, a vengeance on anguish. Sleepwalkers. Bella Akhmadulina, *tr. by* Barbara Einzig. BoWoP
Moon rises, The. The red cubs rolling. The Breath of Night. Randall Jarrell. CrMA
Moon Rock. E. Louise Mally. POL
Moon Shadow. George Bowering. MoCV
Moon shall be a darkness, The. Valentine Promise. *Unknown.* PoSC
Moon, The: she shakes off her cloaks. Promontory Moon. Galway Kinnell. MOON; TwAmPo
Moon shines bright, The. *Unknown.* OBET; OxNR
Moon shines bright, The: in such a night as this. In Such a Night [*or* The Divine Harmony]. Shakespeare. *Fr.* The Merchant of Venice, V, i. ChTr; FiP; GBL; GoBC; PoPle; WHA
Moon shines bright, The; [and] the stars give a light. A May Day Carol. *Unknown.* GBP; OBET; PoSC
Moon shines on the Isle of Inishtrahull, The. Dawn in Inishtrahull. D. J. O'Sullivan. OnYI

Moon shining in silence of the night. Lucina Schynning in Silence of the Night. Eilean Ni Chuilleanain. CIP
Moon silvers the bay, she waxes, she wanes, The. The Eternal Kinship. Maurice E. Peloubet. GoYe
Moon Sings, The. *Unknown.* MOON; OxBoLi
Moon, So Round and Yellow. Matthias Barr. HBV-1; HBVY
Moon, Son of Heaven. Miyazawa Kenji, *tr. fr. Japanese by* Gary Snyder. MOON
Moon Song. Hilda Conkling. TiPo
Moon Song. Hildegarde Flanner. AMV-81
Moon Song. Chuba Nweke. PBA
Moon Song, Woman Song. Anne Sexton. MOON; PPP
Moon, Sun, Sleep, Birds, Live. Kenneth Patchen. WeW
Moon that is a cow, being horned like her. Because the Three Moirai Have Become the Three Maries. Constance Urdang. MOON
Moon that now and then last night, The. Snow Harvest. Andrew Young. BoNaP
Moon, they say, called Mantis, The. How Death Came. *Unknown, tr. by* W. H. I. Bleek. PeSA; TTY
Moon Tiger. Denise Levertov. MOON
Moon upon her fluent route, The. Emily Dickinson. QFR
Moon was but a chin of gold, The. Emily Dickinson. MOON
Moon was like a full cup tonight, The. The Cows at Night. Hayden Carruth. SV
Moon was round, The. The Whisperer. James Stephens. WGRP
Moon was shining brightly upon the battle plain, The. The Maid of Monterey. *Unknown.* AmFP
Moon was up, the lake was shining clear, The. Wordsworth. *Fr.* The Prelude. FaBoEn
Moon Watching by Lake Chapala. Al Young. NPGG
Moon-Witches. Ted Hughes. WSC
Moon, with the pace of a wolf, The. Harvest Poem. David Fisher. NPGG
Moon, worn thin to the width of a quill. Moon's Ending. Sara Teasdale. MOON
Moon beams and yams. Rapping Along with Ronda Davis. James Cunningham. JB
Moonbeams kelter i the lift, The. The Man in the Moon. "Hugh MacDiarmid." NeBP
Moonbeams over Arno's vale in silver flood were pouring, The. The Veery. Henry van Dyke. AA
Moone-Calfe, The, *sel.* Michael Drayton.
  "It was not long e're he perceiv'd the skies." PoEL-2
Mooni. Henry Clarence Kendall. OBEV; OBVV
Moonless Darkness Stands Between. Gerard Manley Hopkins. OBCP
Moonless night—a friendly one, A. Running the Batteries. Herman Melville. PAH
Moonlight. Guillaume Apollinaire, *tr. fr. French by* William Meredith. MOON
Moonlight. Walter de la Mare. EnLoPo
Moonlight. Joy Harjo. TWSS
Moonlight. Longfellow. MOON
Moon Light. Freya Manfred. PH
Moonlight. Edward Moxon. OBRV
Moonlight. Berta Hart Nance. AmFN
Moonlight. Shakespeare. *See* How Sweet the Moonlight Sleeps.
Moonlight. Jacques Tahureau, *tr. fr. French by* Andrew Lang. AWP
Moonlight. Sara Teasdale. VGW
Moonlight, *with music. Unknown.* AS
Moonlight. Paul Verlaine, *tr. fr. French by* John Gray. SyP
Moonlight among the Pines. "Hugh MacDiarmid." OAEL-2
Moonlight and death were on the Narrow Seas. Leave in 1917. Lilian M. Anderson. SUMH
Moonlight breaks upon the city's domes, The. A Song of the Moon. Claude McKay. PoNe
Moonlight drifts like snow across the sheets, The. Those Guyana Nights. Richard Foerster. SOTS
Moonlight filled them both with sundry glamors, The. Et Sa Pauvre Chair. Alec Brock Stevenson. HBMV
Moonlight—fluorescently shining. Materialized into an Owl. Louis (LittleCoon) Oliver. STE
Moonlight has touched them all, The. Ryder. John Haines. LCAP
Moonlight in Autumn. James Thomson. *Fr.* The Seasons: Autumn. OBEC
Moonlight, The: Juice flowing from an overripe pomegranate. Enchantment. Lewis Alexander. PoBA
Moonlight Night: Carmel. Langston Hughes. MOS
Moonlight Night on the Port. Sidney Keyes. DTC
Moonlight on Lake Sydenham. Wilson MacDonald. CaP
Moonlight . . . Scattered Clouds. Robert Bloomfield. *Fr.* The Farmer's Boy. OBNC
Moonlight silvers the shaken tops of trees. Nocturne of Remembered Spring. Conrad Aiken. HBMV
Moonlight Song of the Mocking-Bird. William Hamilton Hayne. AA
Moonlight through my gauze curtains. The Skein. Carolyn Kizer. PrIm; VGW
Moonlight touched the sombre waters white, The. The Abandoned. Arthur Symons. SyP
Moonlight washes the west side of the house. Winter Verse for His [*or* My] Sister. William Meredith. NYBP; TAP
Moon-like Is All Other Love. *Unknown, tr. fr. Middle English by* Donald Davie. NOCV
Moonlit Apples. John Drinkwater. BoNaP; OBMV; OxBTC; PoRA
Moonlit Night in Kansas. Victor Contoski. TAT
Moonmoth and grasshopper that flee our page. A Name for All. Hart Crane. PP; VGW
Moonpoison, mullock of sacrifice. Joseph Gordon Macleod. *Fr.* The Ecliptic: Cancer, or, The Crab. NeBP
Moonrise. Hilda Doolittle ("H. D."). PoA
Moonrise. Gerard Manley Hopkins. FaBoPP; MoAB; MoBrPo; MOON; SeCePo
Moonrise. D. H. Lawrence. LiTM; MOON; PoA
Moonrise. Frank Dempster Sherman. AA
Moonrise in the Rockies. Ella Higginson. AA
Moon's a devil jester, The. The Traveler. Vachel Lindsay. MoAmPo
Moon's a little arch, The. A Classic Case. Gilbert Sorrentino. NeAP
Moon's a steaming chalice, The. What Semiramis Said. Vachel Lindsay. Poems about the Moon, IV. MOON; TwAmPo
Moon's Ending. Sara Teasdale. MOON
Moon's glow by seven fold multiplied, turned red. After Reading St. John the Divine. Gene Derwood. LiTM; NePA; WPE
Moon's greygolden meshes make, The. Alone. James Joyce. InvP
Moon's little skullcap, The. Front Street. Howard Moss. NYBP
Moon's my constant mistress, The. Tom o' Bedlam. *Unknown.* CH; FaBoCh; PoPle; PoRA
Moon's on the lake, and the mist's on the brae, The. MacGregor's Gathering. Sir Walter Scott. OxBS
Moon's the North Wind's Cooky, The. Vachel Lindsay. EvOK; FaFP; FaPON; OBCA; PDV; RHPC; SoPo; SUS
Moon's up-riding makes a line, The. Night Scenes. Robert Duncan. VGW
Moonset. Sir Henry Newbolt. EBVV
Moonsheep, The. Christian Morgenstern, *tr. fr. German.* FaBoNo, *tr. by* Geoffrey Grigson; MOON, *tr. by* E. M. Valk
Moonshine. Walter de la Mare. FiBHP; TDH
Moonshine. *Unknown.* BluL
Moonshiner. *Unknown. See* Kentucky Moonshiner.
Moonshot. Robert Kelly. MOON
Moonshot Sonnet. Mary Ellen Solt. BoWoP
Moonsweet the summer evening locks. Sheepbells. Edmund Blunden. BrPo
Moontan. Mark Strand. NYBP
Moonwalk. John Engels. MAT
Moor, The. Ralph Hodgson. MoBrPo
Moor:/ point my horse. Haiku. Basho, *tr. by* Lucien Stryk *and* Takashi Ikemoto. FAZ
Moorburn in Spring. *Unknown.* PoSH
Moored wes i Cornwale and somnede cnihtes feole. The Death of Arthur. Layamon. *Fr.* The Brut. OxBM
Moorhen Pond, The. Tom Earley. BoAnP
Moorings. Norman MacCaig. OxBTC
Moorland Night. Charlotte Mew. ChMP; ViBoPo
Moorland sheep is frightened and amazed, The. Philosophy Is Born. Christian Morgenstern, *tr. by* Geoffrey Grigson. FaBoNo
Moorlands of the Not. *Unknown.* NA
Moose. Robert Wiljer. AMV-81
Moose Lake State Hospital. Dennis Shady. LFAC
Moosehead Lake, *with music. Unknown.* OuSiCo
Mopoke. Louis Lavater. PoAu-1
Moral, The. Theodore Weiss. Prf
Moral Alphabet, A, *sels.* Hilaire Belloc.
  B Stands for Bear. ShM
  "Dreadful Dinotherium he, The." NOBL
Moral Essays, *sels.* Pope.
  As the Twig Is Bent, 2 *ll., fr.* Epistle I. TreF
  Duke of Buckingham, The, *fr.* Epistle III. NOBE; OBEC
  (Death of Buckingham, The.) FiP
  Gem and the Flower, The, *fr.* Epistle I. OBEC
  "Search then the Ruling Passion: there, alone," *fr.* Epistle I. ViBoPo
  Epistle to a Lady: Of the Characters of Women, Epistle II. FaBoEn, *abr.*; NOEC; OAEL-1, OxBoLi, *shorter sel.*
    Characters of Women: Flavia, Atossa, and Cloe. OBEC
    Heaven's Last Best Work. OBEC
    "Men, some to bus'ness, some to pleasure take." OBSV
    Women's Ruling Passions. OBEC
    "Yet Chloe [*or* Cloe] sure was formed without a spot." ErPo; OBSV

(Chloe.) AWP; NOBE
To Richard Boyle, Earl of Burlington: Of the Uses of Riches, Epistle IV. OAEL-1, PoEL-3; PPP
"At Timon's villa let us pass a day." NOEC; OBSV
(Timon's Villa.) OBEC
Moral in Sevres, A. Mildred Howells. HBV-1
Moral Ode. David Rosenmann-Taub, *tr. fr. Spanish by* Charles Guenther. VWA
Moral Poem, A. J. V. Cunningham. VGW
Moral Story II. David Wright. ChMP; PeSA
Moral Taxi Ride, The. Erich Kästner, *tr. fr. German by* Jerome Rothenberg. ErPo
Moral Tetrastich, A. Sir William Jones. *See* Epigram: "On parents knees, a naked new-born child."
Moral Warfare, The. Whittier. PAL; TreFT
Morality. Matthew Arnold. HBV-2
(We Cannot Kindle.) TRV
Morality. Jean Garrigue. ELU
Morality of Poetry, The. James Wright. PP
Morality, thou deadly bane. Burns. *Fr.* A Dedication to G**** H******* Esq. OBSV
Morals. James Thurber. *Fr.* Further Fables for Our Time. FaBV
More. Philip Appleman. BXAP
More. Gertrude Stein. *Fr.* Tender Buttons. PBWP
More Ancient Mariner, A. Bliss Carman. OBAL
More Animals, *sel.* Oliver Herford.
Cow, The. NA
More Ballads! here's a spick and span new Supplication. A Free Parliament Litany. *Unknown.* OxBoLi
More beautiful and soft than any moth. The Landscape near an Aerodrome. Stephen Spender. CoBMV; LiTM; MoAB; MoBrPo; MoVE; NoAM; OAEP; OxBTC
More beautiful than any gift you gave. The Token. F. T. Prince. FaBoTw; OxBTC
More beautiful than the remarkable moon and her noble light. To the Sun. Ingeborg Bachmann, *tr. by* Michael Hamburger. BoNaP
More brightly must my spirit shine. The Spirit's Grace. Janie Screven Heyward. HBMV
More Clues. Muriel Rukeyser. IHMS
More discontents I never had. Discontents in Devon. Robert Herrick. AnAnS-2; CaPo; OAEP; POL; SeCV-1
More distant than the dead sea. Nadia Tuéni, *tr. fr. French by* Carol Cosman. PBWP
More Foreign Cities. Charles Tomlinson. NePoEA-2
More gaily, dance. Quick-Step. Robert Creeley. VGW
More Good Whiskey Blues. *Unknown.* BluL
More grotesque than a row of laundromats. The Novelty Shop. Duane Niatum. CDW
More haughty than the rest, the wolfish race. The Presbyterians. Dryden. *Fr.* The Hind and the Panther, I. OBS
More humane Mikado never, A. My Object All Sublime. W. S. Gilbert. *Fr.* The Mikado. LiTB; TreFT
More I chew this stuff, The. O'Connor the Bad Traveler. Peter Klappert. FiCP
More I looked, I wondered more, The. Wordsworth. *Fr.* The Matron of Jedborough and Her Husband. PeD
More ill at ease was never man than Walbach, that Lord's day. The Legend of Walbach Tower. George Houghton. PAH
More It Snows, The. A. A. Milne. NTCP; RHPC
More kicks than pence. To Hell with Commonsense. Patrick Kavanagh. CIP; FaBoTw
More Letters Found near a Suicide. Frank Horne. BANP
"More Light! More Light!" Anthony Hecht. CoAP; ConAP; HAP; NePoEA-2; NoAM; NOBA; NoP; OBWP; SoSe; TwCP; UnPo; VGW; VWA
More Love or More Disdain. Thomas Carew. *See* Mediocrity in Love Rejected.
More love or more disdain I crave. Against Indifference. Charles Webbe. HBV-1; OBEV
More Love to Thee, O Christ, *with music.* Elizabeth Payson Prentiss. AH
More Love, *with music. Unknown.* AH
More Lovely Grows the Earth. Helena Coleman. CaP
More Loving One, The. W. H. Auden. HoPM
More Luck to Honest Poverty. Shirley Brooks. *See* For A' That and A' That.
More Nudes for Florence. Harold Witt. ErPo
More of a Corpse than a Woman. Muriel Rukeyser. NMM
More of Thee. Horatius Bonar. BLRP
More oft than once Death whispered in mine ear. Sonnet: Death's Last Will. William Drummond of Hawthornden. JCP
More paper blackened with more signatures. The Night There Was Dancing in the Streets. Elder Olson. NePA
More pleasing were these sweet delights. Francis Beaumont. *Fr.* The Masque of the Inner Temple and Gray's Inne. OBS
More Power to Cromwell ("More power to thee, O Cromwell"). Egan O'Rahilly, *tr. fr. Modern Irish by* P. S. Dinneen *and* T. O'Donoghue. OnYI
(More Power, *tr. by* John Montague.) BIrV
More Prayer. *Unknown.* STF
More Reformation, *sel.* Daniel Defoe.
"To sin's a vice in nature, and we find." OBSV
More secure is no one ever. Security. Lina Sandell. STF
"More ships!" some cry; "more guns!" More Prayer. *Unknown.* STF
More shower than shine. Valentines to My Mother, 1880. Christina Rossetti. OFD
More shy than the shy violet. Quaker Ladies. Ellen Mackay Hutchinson Cortissoz. AA
More Songs from Vagabondia, *sel.* Richard Hovey.
Envoy: "Whose furthest footstep never strayed." AA; HBV-2
More Sonnets at Christmas. Allen Tate. LiTA; LiTM; NePA; WaP
Sels.
"Day's end and there's nowhere to go, The," II. SBVL
"Give me this day a faith not personal," III. SBVL
More Strong than Time. Victor Hugo, *tr. fr. French by* Andrew Lang. AWP
More Than. Susan Fitzpatrick. AMV-80
More than Fifty. Jack Gilbert. NPGG
More than Flowers We Have Brought. Nancy Byrd Turner. SiSoSe
More than half beaten, but fearless. Battle Cry. John G. Neihardt. HBMV
More than he mourned for walking he grieved. The Amputation. Helen Sorrells. DFF
More than leaves, more than flakes. More. Philip Appleman. BXAP
More than moon-measure. Between the Tides. Emily Sargent Councilman. AMV-80
More than Morgan, I desire to eat people. Morgan. John Blight. CBAP
More than Most Fair. Fulke Greville. *Fr.* Caelica. ElL
(To His Lady.) OBSC
More than most fair, full of the living fire. Amoretti, VIII. Spenser. CABA; HBV-1; OAEP; NoP; TEP; TrGrPo
More Than Most People. Eldon Grier. MoCV
More than People. Robin Fulton. *Fr.* A Cleared Land. PoSH
More than the ash stays you from nothingness! The Phoenix. J. V. Cunningham. NoAM; QFR
More than the gems/ locked away and treasured. Sent from the Capital to Her Elder Daughter. Lady Otomo of Sakanone, *tr. by* Geoffrey Bownas *and* Anthony Thwaite. BoWoP; WPOW
More than the shortest distance. A Barbed Wire Fence Meditates upon the Goldfinch. Don McKay. NOBC
More than those. Rosa Nascosa. Maurice Hewlett. OBVV
More than We Ask. Faith Wells. BLRP
More things are wrought by prayer. Prayer. Tennyson. *Fr.* Idylls of the King *and* Morte d'Arthur. BLRP; TreF
More to It than Riding. J. A. Lindon. PH
More Truth and Light. John Robinson. TRV
More we live, more brief appear, The. The River of Life [*or* A Thought Suggested by the New Year]. Thomas Campbell. BSV; FaFP; GTBS; GTBS-P; HBV-1; LiTB; OBNC
More White than Whitest Lilies. Robert Herrick. UnTE
More whyght thou art then Primrose leaf my Lady Galatee. Cyclops. Ovid, *tr. by* Arthur Golding. *Fr.* Metamorphoses, XIII. CTC; OBVE
More years ago than I can state. My Last Illusion. John Kendall. FiBHP; WhC
Morea's Sonnet. Mary Sidney Wroth, Countess of Montgomery. *Fr.* Urania. WPE
Morels. William Jay Smith. BoNaP; MAT; NYBP; RFM
Moreover the Lord answered Job, and said. Bible, *O.T.* Job, XL. OBVE
Moreton Bay. *Unknown.* CBAP
Morgan. John Blight. CBAP
Morgan. Edward Harrington. PoAu-1
Morgan. Edmund Clarence Stedman. AA; HBV-2
Morgan Stanwood. Hiram Rich. PAH
Morgans in October. Suzanne Brabant. PH
Morgante Maggiore, Il, *sel.* Luigi Pulci, *tr. fr. Italian.*
Prophecy. PAH
Morituri Salutamus, *sel.* Longfellow.
It Is Too Late! BLPL; PoLF
(Too Late?) WBLP
Moriturus. "Marie Madelaine," *tr. fr. French by* Ferdinand E. Kappey. PeHV
Moriturus. Edna St. Vincent Millay. LiTA
Morley's light went out. Power Failure. Michael Dennis Browne. AmPA
Mormon Bishop's Lament, The. *Unknown.* CoSo
Mormon Immigrant Song, A. *At. to* George A. Hicks. CoSo

Mormons, led by Colonel Cooke, The. On the Road to California; or, The Buffalo Bullfight. *Unknown.* AmFP
Morn. Helen Hunt Jackson. AA
Morn of life is past, The. Old Dog Tray. Stephen Collins Foster. FSW; GDP
Morn of the year, of day and May the prime! May-Day on Magdalen Tower. Thomas Herbert Warren. OBVV
Morn was cloudy and dark and gray, The. The Battle of Morris' Island. *Unknown.* PAH
Morn when first it thunders in March, The. Old Pictures in Florence. Robert Browning. VLP
Morning. Blake. FaBoCh; LoBV; OAEL-2; OBRV
Morning. Keats. *See* Imitation of Spenser.
Morning. Charles Stuart Calverley. FiBHP; NBM
Morning. Chu Shu-chen, *tr. fr. Chinese by* Kenneth Rexroth. BoWoP
Morning. John Cunningham. *See* Day; a Pastoral.
Morning. Sir William Davenant. *See* Lark Now Leaves His Wat'ry Nest, The.
Morning. Emily Dickinson. *See* Will there really be a morning?
Morning. Tove Ditlevsen, *tr. fr. Danish by* Nadia Christensen. PBWP
Morning. Harry Fainlight. POL
Morning. Dorothy Hamilton Gallagher. SiSoSe
Morning. M. A. George. AMV-80
Morning. Patrick Kavanagh. GLGT
Morning. John Keble. OBRV
Morning. Henry Reed. MoVE; NeBP
Morning. Alberto Ríos. MAYP
Morning. Marjorie Saiser. AMV-80
Morning. Philip Henry Savage. AA
Morning, A. Mark Strand. GeTw
Morning. Jane Taylor. HBV-1
Morning. *Unknown.* NOEC
Morning. Samuel Waddington. OBVV
Morning./ and she awoke to. Five Sense. Marvin Wyche, Jr. AmNP
Morning After, The. Walter Clark. NCSH
Morning After, The. Heine, *tr. fr. German by* Louis Untermeyer. ErPo; UnTE
Morning After. Langston Hughes. NoAM
Morning After. Mark Vinz. PPJ
Morning After, The. Dorothy Wellesley. OBMV
Morning after Death, The. Emily Dickinson. *See* Bustle in a house, The.
Morning after . . . Love, The. Kattie M. Cumbo. BlSi
Morning after your departure. Marianne Moore. Raymond Roseliep. SOTS
Morning again, nothing has to be done. Second Poem. Peter Orlovsky. NeAP
Morning and Evening. Antoni Slonimski, *tr. fr. Polish by* Watson Kirkconnell. TrJP
Morning and evening. Goblin Market. Christina Rossetti. DTo; EBEV; GoTL; OAEP; OBNV; SBG; VLP
Morning and evening a heron flies. Neighbor. Charles Waterman. GP
Morning and evening, drunk and singing. For Kuo Hsiang. Yu Hsuah-chi, *tr. by* Geoffrey Waters. BoWoP
Morning and evening, sleep she drove away. The Spinning Woman. Leonidas of Tarentum, *tr. by* Andrew Lang. AWP
Morning and Evening Star. Plato. *See* To Stella.
Morning and Myself. Nia Francisco. STE
Morning, and streaks of heavenly blue. London Spring. Antoni Slonimski, *tr. by* Frances Notley. TrJP
Morning. And the alleys give up. Letter from the Street. Thomas Brush. LTB
Morning, and the poet up again and out and about. The Poet's Day. Richard Weber. CIP
Morning and the snow might fall forever. Going to Remake This World. James Welch. CDW
Morning at Arnheim. William Jay Smith. NePoEA
Morning at nine, seven ultra-masculine men. In Your Bad Dream. Richard Hugo. LCAP
Morning at the Window. T. S. Eliot. AWP; CABA; CAD; NePA; PoA
Morning: blue, cold, and still. January. Weldon Kees. CoAP
Morning breaks like a pomegranate, The. Wedding Morn. D. H. Lawrence. MoAB; MoBrPo
Morning Bright, with Rosy Light, The, *with music.* Thomas O. Summers. AH
Morning Bus. John Coulter. CaP
Morning comes, and thickening clouds prevail, The. The Clouded Morning. Jones Very. AP; NOBA
Morning comes, The; not slow, with reddening gold. Frederick Goddard Tuckerman. Sonnets, I, xxii. AP
Morning comes, the night decays, the watchmen leave their stations, The. Empire Is No More. Blake. *Fr.* America: A Prophecy. EnRP
Morning comes, The. The old woman, a spot. Grief. Wendell Berry. GeTw
Morning comes to consciousness, The. Preludes, II. T. S. Eliot. HeIP; NoP; OBMV; WeW
Morning Compliments. Sydney Dayre. OxBChV
Morning Dialogue. Conrad Aiken. NoAM
Morning Duke Ellington Praised the Lord, The. Owen Dodson. FB
Morning Fog. Quinton Duval. AMV-81
Morning from My Office Window. John A. Wood. AMV-81
Morning-Glory, The. Florence Earle Coates. HBV-1
Morning-Glory, The. Maria White Lowell. AA; HBV-1
Morning Glory. Siegfried Sassoon. TrCP
Morning Glory, The. *Unknown, tr. fr. Chinese by* Helen Waddell. *Fr.* Shi King. AWP
Morning-glory, climbing the morning long, A. Indiana. Hart Crane. *Fr.* The Bridge. TwAmPo
Morning Glory Pool. Sandra McPherson. LCAP
Morning Has No House. Rosemarie Waldrop. MAT
Morning he had gone. My Face Is My Own, I Thought. Tom Raworth. EAS
Morning Hours, The. *Unknown, tr. fr. Arabic by* Mohammed Marmaduke Pickthall. PoPl
Morning Hymn. Joseph Beaumont. OxBoCh; TrPWD
Morning Hymn. St. Gregory the Great, *tr. fr. Latin by* Edward Caswell. WGRP
Morning Hymn. John Keble. NOCV
(Hymn: "New every morning is the love.") NBM
(New Every Morning.) FaPoR
Morning Hymn. Thomas Ken. FaFP; OBS; TreFS
(Awake, My Soul.) OxBoCh
Morning Hymn, A. Christopher Smart. OxBChV
Morning Hymn, A. Charles Wesley. NOEC; OBEC; PoEL-3; TrPWD
(Christ, Whose Glory Fills the Skies.) ELP; OxBoCh
Morning Hymn of Adam [and Eve]. Milton. *See* Adam's Morning Hymn.
Morning, if this late withered light can claim. The Zonnebeke Road. Edmund Blunden. MMA; OBWP
Morning in Spring. Louis Ginsberg. GoYe
Morning in the Hills. Bliss Carman. NOBC
Morning in the North-west. Arthur Stringer. CaP
Morning in the Park. John Ciardi. MiAP
Morning is bright and sunlit, and the west wind running smoothly, The. Message to the Bard. William Livingston. GoTS
Morning is cheery, my boys, arouse, The! Reveille. Michael O'Connor. AA; HBV-2
Morning is clean and blue and the wind blows up the clouds, The. John Gould Fletcher. Irradiations, XXII. MoAmPo; NePA
Morning is hot and windy, The. Lonnie Kramer. Geary Hobson. STE
Morning is lost in a maze. We're OK. Gloria Fuertes, *tr. by* Philip Levine. WPOW
Morning is the gate of day, The. The Sentinel. *Unknown.* BLRP
Morning Kiss, A. Andrew McCord Jones. LFAC
Morning Letter, A. Robert Duncan. PoA
Morning Light. Louis Dudek. AMV-80
Morning Light [the Dew Drier]. Mary Effie Lee Newsome. AmNP; CDC; PoBA; PoNe
Morning Light Is Breaking, The. Samuel F. Smith. AH, *with music*; WGRP
(Daybreak.) BLRP
Morning Light Song. Philip Lamantia. NeAP
Morning Light, The. Louis Simpson. NNaP; NoAM
Morning like others, and a father, A. Why I Am Afraid to Have Children. Bin Ramke. MAYP
Morning man came in to report, The. People Who Went By in Winter. William Stafford. GP
Morning, May rain. The Man Awakened by a Song above His Roof. Tomas Tranströmer, *tr. by* Robert Bly. EAS
Morning mists still haunt the stony street, The. Enter Patient. W. E. Henley. In Hospital, I. BrPo
'Morning, Morning. Ray Mathew. PoAu-2
Morning, Noon, And. Hawley Truax. NYBP
Morning of a cold month, The. The International Brigade Arrives at Madrid. Pablo Neruda, *tr. by* Angel Flores. WaaP
Morning of our rest has come, The. The Poor Man's Sunday Walk. Charles Mackay. EBVV
Morning of the Red-tailed Hawk, The. Bettie M. Sellers. AMV-80
Morning of the winter's, The. Leaping Falls. Galway Kinnell. NePoAm-2
Morning, on a beach. A man & woman sitting by fire. Moon Is to Blood. Richard Duerden. NeAP
Morning on the misty highlands. Sandpipers. Helen Merrill Egerton. CaP
Morning on the St. John's. Jane Cooper. NYBP
Morning on the Shore. Wilfred Campbell. NOBC
Morning Once More. Joy Harjo. TWSS
Morning opened/ Like a rose. Song. Donald Justice. DFF; NCSH

Morning ought not. Pas de Deux for Lovers. Michael Dransfield. CBAP
Morning-Piece, A; or, An Hymn for the Hay-Makers. Christopher Smart. NOEC
Morning Poem. Jennivien-Diana Beenen. AMV-81
Morning Porches, The. Donald Hall. NePoAm-2
Morning Prayer. Aua, *tr. fr. Eskimo.* WTO
Morning Prayer. Ogden Nash. GrPl; OxBChV
Morning Prayer, A. Betty Perpetuo. STF
Morning Prayers of the Hasid, Rabbi Levi Yitzhok, The. Phyllis Gotlieb. VWA
Morning Serenade. Madison Cawein. HBV-1
Morning service! parson preaches. The House of God. A. D. Hope. OxBC
Morning sits outside afraid, The. Night and Morning. Dorothy Aldis. PoSC; YeAr
Morning sky glitters, The. De Civitate Hominum. Thomas MacGreevy. CIP
Morning Song. Conrad Aiken. *See* Morning Song of Senlin.
Morning Song. Karle Wilson Baker. HBMV
Morning Song. Henry Blakely. CNA
Morning Song. Sir William Davenant. *See* Lark Now Leaves His Wat'ry Nest, The.
Morning Song. Charlotte DeClue. STE; TWSS
Morning Song. Alan Dugan. CAD; ELU
Morning Song. Afanasi Afanasievich Fet, *tr. fr. Russian by* Max Eastman. AWP
Morning Song. Solomon ibn Gabirol, *tr. fr. Hebrew by* Nina Davis Salaman. TrJP
Morning Song. Gregory Orr. MAYP
Morning Song. Sylvia Plath. BoWoP; HeIP; IHMS; InPK; InPS; LCAP; NAs; NOBA; PrIm; SBG
Morning Song, A ("Hark! hark! the lark"). Shakespeare. *See* Hark, Hark the Lark.
Morning Song. Kurt M. Stein. FiBHP
Morning Song. Leon Stokesbury. AMV-80
Morning Song. Sara Teasdale. MOON
Morning Song of [*or* from] Senlin. Conrad Aiken. *Fr.* Senlin; a Biography, II, ii. HBMV; LiTA; MoAmPo; OxBA
("It is morning, Senlin says, and in the morning.") LiTM; NoAM
(Morning Song.) CMoP; MoAB; TrGrPo
Morning spreads over. May All Earth Be Clothed in Light. George Hitchcock. VGW
Morning Star, The. Emily Brontë. ChTr
Morning Star. Thomas Hornsby Ferril. VGW
Morning Star. James J. Galvin. ISi
Morning Star, The. Primus St. John. PoBA
Morning Star Man. George Keithley. NPGG
Morning Star, O Cheering Sight! *with music. Unknown.* AH
Morning Sun. Louis MacNeice. MoAB; MoBrPo; MP; TwCP
Morning sun, The. Poem for Myself and Mei: Abortion. Leslie Silko. VoR
Morning sun shines from the east, The. Ode on Science. Jezaniah Sumner. TrAS
Morning Swim. Maxine W. Kumin. LiSp; WPE
Morning: the soft release. Meditation for a Pickle Suite. R. H. W. Dillard. HoPM
Morning They Shot Tony Lopez, Barber and Pusher Who Went Too Far, 1958, The. Gary Soto. MAYP
Morning to Remember, A; or, E Pluribus Unum. Edward Dorn. NoAM
Morning Track, The. Edward Parone. NYBP
Morning trickles over the bruised vegetables. The Manless Society. Pierre Unik, *tr. by* David Gascoyne. EAS
Morning uptown, quiet on the street. Song Form. Amiri Baraka. CTBA; SOTW
Morning Vigil. Phillip William George. VoR
Morning wakens on time. Get Up. Philip Levine. NYP
Morning was never here, nor more dark ever. Blue Cockerel. W. S. Merwin. TwAmPo
Morning-watch, The. Henry Vaughan. AnAnS-1; LiTB; LoBV; MePo; OBS; OxBoCh; SeCePo; ViBoPo
Morning Work. D. H. Lawrence. MoAB; MoBrPo
Morning Workout. Babette Deutsch. LiSp; NePoAm-2
Morning Worship. Mark Van Doren. NePoAm-2; TwAmPo
Mornings/ before the sun's liquid. Lagoons, Hanlan's Point. Raymond Souster. NOBC
Mornings/ I got up early. The Way It Was. Lucille Clifton. WPE
Mornings everything is grey. Morning Has No House. Rosemarie Waldrop. MAT
Mornings, from my upstairs window, I can see a gray. Permission to Speak. Stephen Orlen. MAYP
Mornin's Mornin', The. Gerald Brennan. BLPA
Morns are meeker than they were, The. Emily Dickinson. AA; BoNaP; FaPON; HBV-1; OBCA; PoPl; TiPo; TreFT; YeAr
Moron, The. *Unknown.* TreFT; YaD
("See the happy moron.") CenHV
Morpheus, the lively son of deadly Sleep. Astrophel and Stella, XXXII. Sir Philip Sidney. SiPS
Morphine. Heine, *tr. fr. German by* Ernst Feise. NAWM-2
Morrigan, The. *Unknown, tr. fr. Irish by* Thomas Kinsella. BIrV
Morrissey and the Russian Sailor, *with music. Unknown.* AS
Mors Benefica. Edmund Clarence Stedman. AA
Mors et Vita. Richard Henry Stoddard. AA
Mors et Vita. Samuel Waddington. HBV-2
Mors Iabrochii. *Unknown.* NA
Mors, Morituri Te Salutamus. Francis Burdett Money-Coutts. OBVV
Mort/ alentity in. Syl La Ble Speaks En Erg y/ Sound, The. Carol Lee Sanchez. TWSS
Mort aux Chats. Peter Porter. OxBC
Mortal Combat. Alice Fay di Castagnola. GoYe
Mortal Combat. Mary Elizabeth Coleridge. OBVV
Mortal mixed of middle clay. Guy. Emerson. NOBA
Mortal my mate, bearing my rock-a-heart. To His Watch. Gerard Manley Hopkins. MoAB; MoBrPo
Mortal Prudence, handmaid of divine Providence. The Testament of Perpetual Change. William Carlos Williams. GOA
Mortal, Sneer Not at the Devil. Heine, *tr. by* Emma Lazarus. *Fr.* Homeward Bound. TrJP
Mortality. James Devaney. PoAu-1
Mortality. Naomi Long Madgett. NNP; PoBA; PoNe
Mortality [*or* Mortalitie], behold and fear[e]! Lines on the Tombs in Westminster [*or* A Momento for Mortality]. *At. to* Francis Beaumont *and to* William Basse. ACP; CH; ElL; FaBoCh; FaPoR; GoBC; GTBS; GTBS-P; HAP; HBV-2; LoBV; NOBE; OBEV; OBS; PoPle; TrGrPo; ViBoPo
Mortally. James Kirkup. NeBP
"Mortals, that behold a Woman." Assumpta Maria. Francis Thompson. ISi
Mortars are/ the devil coughing. Remembrance of Things Past. Horace Coleman. FAZ
Morte Arthur, *sel. Unknown.*
Sir Gawain Encounters Sir Priamus. PoEL-1
Morte d'Arthur. Tennyson. *Incorporated in* Idylls of the King, *with changes, as* The Passing of Arthur. DL; DTo; FaBoBe; FiP; HBV-2; NIP; OAEL-2; OAEP; OBNV; PoEL-5, SeCeV; VLP; WHA
Sels.
"And answer made King Arthur, breathing hard." EBEV
"And slowly answered Arthur from the barge." FaBoEn
Arthur's Disillusionment. TreFS
" 'But now farewell. I am going a long way.' " FaBoRV
"Old order changeth, yielding place to new, The." TRV
(Prayer for the Dead.) GoBC
Prayer ("[Pray for my soul.] More things are wrought by prayer"). BLRP; TreF; WGRP
"So all day long the noise of battle rolled." FaBoRV
Mortem, Quae Violat Suavia, Pellit Amor. William Johnson Cory. NBM
Mortician's Twelve-year-old Son, The. Ai. GeTw
Mortification. George Herbert. AnAnS-1; MePo; OAEP; SeCP; ViBoPo
Mortified Genius, The. James Graeme. NOEC
Mortifying Mistake, A. Anna Maria Pratt. AA; HBV-1; HBVY
Mortmain. Robert Penn Warren. PoCh
"In Time's concatenation and/ Carnal conventicle," I. NOBA; Prf
(After Night Flight.) DiL
Morvin. John Fuller. NePoEA-2
Morwennæ Statio. Robert Stephen Hawker. GoBC
Mos' Done Toilin' Here, *with music. Unknown.* BoAN-2
Mosaic Worker, The. Arthur Wallace Peach. BLRP
Mosby at Hamilton. Madison Cawein. PAH
Moschatel. Daniel James O'Sullivan. NeIP
Moschus Moschiferus. A. D. Hope. CBAP; GrPl
Moscow Nights. M. Matusovskii *and* V. Solovyov-Sedoi, *tr. fr. Russian.* FSW
Moses. Amir Gilboa, *tr. fr. Hebrew by* Stephen Mitchell. VWA
Moses. Sydney Tremayne. OxBS
Moses. *Unknown.* OxNR; RHPC
Moses' Account. Milan Fuest, *tr. fr. Hungarian by* Andrè Ungar. VWA
Moses and Jesus. Israel Zangwill. TrJP
Moses and Joshua. Else Lasker-Schüler, *tr. fr. German by* Joachim Neugroschel. VWA
Moses, from whose loins I sprung. The Jew. Isaac Rosenberg. MoBrPo; VWA
Moses on Mount Nebo. Abraham Regelson, *tr. fr. Hebrew by* Richard Flantz. VWA
Moses supposes his toeses are roses. Moses. *Unknown.* OxNR; RHPC

Mosquito, The. Rodney Jones. MAYP
Mosquito, The. D. H. Lawrence. BoAnP; PoPle
(Mosquito Knows, The.) FaBoEE; OxBTC
Mosquito. John Updike. BoAnP
Moss. Nancy Willard. HoAn
Moss-gathering Theodore Roethke. CoBMV; RFM; VGW
Moss of His Skin, The. Anne Sexton. CABA; CoAP; IHMS; PAI
Moss-Rose, The. Sir Henry Newbolt. HBV-2
Moss Supplicateth for the Poet, The. Richard Henry Dana. AA
Mossbawn: Two Poems in Dedication. Seamus Heaney. CIP
Mossbawn Sunlight, I. BlrV
(Sunlight.) NoP
Most Acceptable Gift, The. Matthias Claudius, *tr. fr. German by* J. M. Campbell. BLRP
Most animals have no houses, only holes. Housing Starts. Peter Davison. EyDe
Most are dead already. Cleaning Fish. Richard Behm. WOLT
Most are innocent, shy, will not undress. Angels. Dannie Abse. PoA
Most Beautiful Girl in the World, The. Lorenz Hart. OBAL
Most beautiful of things I leave is sunlight. Praxilla, *tr. fr. Greek by* Willis Barnstone. BoWoP
Most beautiful! the red flowering eucalyptus. The Torso: Passages 18. Robert Duncan. GP
Most Beautiful Woman at My Highschool Reunion, The. Ellen Marie Bissert. PeHV
Most Blessed Lady, Comfort to such as call. Dedication of the Chronicles of England and France. Robert Fabyan. ISi
Most chivalrous fish of the ocean. The Rhyme of the Chivalrous Shark [*or* The Chivalrous Shark]. Wallace Irwin. FSW; ShM
Most don't teach. Teacher. Sonya Dorman. GLGT
Most Expensive Picture in the World, The. Howard Nemerov. EyDe
Most folks believe in doctors, but there's my old girl she don't. Household Remedies. *Unknown.* OBET
Most glorious Lord of life [*or* lyfe], that on this day. Amoretti, LXVIII. Spenser. CABA; EBCP; ElL; EnRePo; HAP; HBV-1; LiTB; NOBE; NOCV; NoP; OBEV; OHIP; OxBoCh; SeCeV; TRV
Most glorious of all the Undying, many-named, girt round with awe! Hymn to Zeus. Cleanthes, *tr. by* Edward Hayes Plumptre. WGRP
Most Gracious Queen, we thee implore. On Queen Caroline. *Unknown.* FaBoEE
Most high Lord. Cantico del Sole. Saint Francis of Assisi, *tr. by* Ezra Pound. CTC
Most high, omnipotent, good Lord. The Canticle of the Sun. St. Francis of Assisi, *tr. by* P. Robinson. PAI
Most Holy Night, that still dost keep. The Night. Hilaire Belloc. HBV-2; OBEV; OBVV
Most holy Satyr. Holy Satyr. Hilda Doolittle ("H. D."). MoAmPo
Most inexplicable the wiles of boys I deem. Epigram. Rhianus, *tr. by* Sydney Oswald. PeHV
Most Ingenious Paradox, A. W. S. Gilbert. *Fr.* The Pirates of Penzance. NAs
Most is your name the name of this dark stone. Rainy Mountain Cemetery. N. Scott Momaday. CDW
Most Like an Arch This Marriage. John Ciardi. PoPl; WeW
Most like some agèd king it seemed to me. Recollections of Burgos. Richard Chenevix Trench. OBRV
Most Lovely Shade ("Most lovely dark, my Æthiopia born"). Edith Sitwell. FaBoTw; GTBS-P
Most Men Know Love But as a Part of Life. Henry Timrod. AA
(Sonnet.) HBV-2
Most men use/ their eyes. The Mechanic. Diane Wakoski. AmPA
Most near, most dear, most loved and most far. Sonnet to My Mother [*or* To My Mother]. George Barker. DTC; FaBoMo; FaFP; FF; LiTB; LiTM; MoAB; MP; NCSH; OxBTC; SeCePo; TwCP; ViBoPo; WaP
Most needy [*or* Ac that most neeeden] aren oure neighebores, The. Our Needy Neighbours [*or* The Poor]. William Langland. *Fr.* The Vision of Piers Plowman. OxBM; PoEL-1
Most of It, The. Robert Frost. BiP; CABA; CrMA; HAP; MoPo; NePA; NoP; NU; PPoe; WeW
Most of my days are passed away, yet my heart is still impure. The Worthless Heart. Immanuel di Roma. TrJP
Most people simply ignore it, they have to. The Death Balloon. Patricia Goedicke. FAZ
Most people think. Initials. Michael S. Glaser. AMV-81
Most poets to a muse that is stone-deaf cry. On the Oxford Book of Victorian Verse. "Hugh MacDiarmid." MoBrPo
Most present of all the watchers where we camped, The. When We Looked Back. William Stafford. NYBP
Most Quietly at Times. Cäsar Flaischlen, *tr. fr. German by* Jethro Bithell. AWP
Most reverend Father, I have borne all wrong. Two Souls. Marjorie Pickthall. NOBC
Most reverend lords, the church's joy and wonder. On Calamy's Imprisonment and Wild's Poetry. *Unknown.* APAS
Most-Sacred Mountain, The. Eunice Tietjens. HBMV
Most Souls, 'Tis True, but Peep Out Once an Age. Pope. *Fr.* Elegy to the Memory of an Unfortunate Lady. CH, *longer sel.*; ELU; PAI
(Dull, Sullen Prisoners.) FaBoRV
Most Sovereign Lady. *Unknown.* MeEL
Most stupendous show they ever gave, The. In Memory of the Circus Ship *Euzkera.* Walker Gibson. FiBHP; NCSH; NePoAm
Most Sweet It Is with Unuplifted Eyes. Wordsworth. *See* Inner Vision, The.
Most that can be said, The. Parade's End. Barbara Guest. PoM
Most that I know but one. Care. Josephine Miles. NYBP
Most Unloving One, The. Samuel Daniel. *Fr.* To Delia. SeCePo
Most Vital Thing in Life, The. Grenville Kleiser. SoSe
Most weeds, whilst young. Francis Daniel Pastorius. SCAP
Most worthy of praise were the virtuous ways. [Little] Red Riding Hood. Guy Wetmore Carryl. DFT; FiBHP; HBV-2
Most worthye she is in towne, The. In Praise of Ivy. *Unknown.* MeEL
Most wounds can Time repair. At Ease. Walter de la Mare. ChMP; GTBS-P
Most wretched heart, most miserable. Sir Thomas Wyatt. SiPS
Mostly Are We Mostless. José Garcia Villa. TwAmPo
Mot eran dous miei cossir. Arnaut Daniel, *tr. fr. French by* Harriet Waters Preston. AWP
Motels, Hotels, Other People's Houses. H. L. Van Brunt. FAZ
Motet: "I am a young girl." *Unknown, tr. fr. Old French by* Carol Cosman. PBWP
("I am a young girl, gay.") BoWoP
Motet: "My love, how could your heart consider." *Unknown, tr. fr. Old French by* Carol Cosman. PBWP
Moth, The. Walter de la Mare. BrPo; FaBoEn; MoVE
Moth. Lance Henson. VoR
Moth, The. Vernon Scannell. OxBC
Moth and the Flame, The. George Taggert. FSN, *with music*; TreF
Moth ate a word, A. To me it seemed. Book Moth. *Unknown, tr. by* Charles W. Kennedy. *Fr.* Riddles (Exeter Book). AnOE
Moth flew a bee-line, The. Mothy Monologue. Ralph Gustafson. NOBC
"Moth has got into it, The." The Moth. Vernon Scannell. OxBC
Moth is a shadow without a source, The. Getting Older Here. Barbara Hauk. AMV-80
Moth-Song. Ellen Mackay Hutchinson Cortissoz. AA
Moth-Terror. Benjamin De Casseres. TrJP
Mother, The. Gwendolyn Brooks. BlSi; BPo; CAPP; GP; NMM
Mother. Aldo Camerino, *tr. fr. Italian by* Anita Barrows. VWA
Mother. Thomas Curtis Clark. PGD
Mother, The. Sara Coleridge. OBVV
Mother. Barry Dempster. AMV-80
Mother. Philip Dow. NPGG
Mother. Rose Fyleman. SiSoSe
Mother, The. S. S. Gardons. NePoEA-2
Mother. Seamus Heaney. NAs
Mother. Theresa Helburn. FaPON; HBV-1; OHIP
Mother. Daniel Lawrence Kelleher. NeIP
Mother. Nagase Kiyoko, *tr. fr. Japanese by* Kenneth Rexroth *and* Ikuko Atsumi. BoWoP
Mother. Sharon Mayer Libera. IHMS
Mother, The. Catulle Mendès, *tr. fr. French by* W. J. Robertson. TrJP
Mother. José Montoya, *tr. fr. Spanish by* Toni Empringham. FIA
Mother, The. Nettie Palmer. PoAu-1
Mother, The. Padraic Pearse. OnYI
Mother. Anwar Shaul, *tr. fr. Arabic by* Yoffee Berkovitz. VWA
Mother. Emily Taylor. PGD
Mother. Julian Tuwim, *tr. fr. Polish by* Isaac Komem. VWA
Mother ("Each day to her a miracle"). *Unknown.* PGD
Mother, The ("From out the south the genial breezes sigh"). *Unknown, tr. fr. Chinese by* George Barrow. OHIP
Mother. Stephen Vincent. NeAC
Mother. Whittier. *Fr.* Snow-bound. AA; OHIP
Mother. Margaret Widdemer. *See* Watcher, The.
Mother/Deer/Lady. Harold Littlebird. VoR
Mother,/ If I am where I am. From an Asylum; Kathy Chattle to Her Mother, Ruth Arbeiter. Anne Stevenson. BrRo
Mother,/ You did not leave me an inheritance of necklaces for a wedding. Mother's Inheritance. Fawziyya Abu Khalid, *tr. by* Kamal Boullata. WPOW
Mother—a Portrait. Ethel Romig Fuller. PGD
Mother, among the Dustbins. Stevie Smith. PBWP
Mother and Child. Ivy O. Eastwick. SiSoSe
Mother and Child, The. Vernon Watkins. NeBP
Mother and child! whose blending tears. The Memorial Pillar. Felicia Dorothea Hemans. SBG

Mother and daughter German refugees. Schwiegermutterlieder. Tony Harrison. InPS
Mother and Her Son on the Cross, The. *Unknown.* MeEL
Mother and listener she is, but she does not listen. The Question. Muriel Rukeyser. IHMS; WPOW
Mother and maid and soldier, bearing best. A Portrait. Brian Hooker. HBV-1
Mother and Poet. Elizabeth Barrett Browning. HBV-2; SBG
Mother and Sister of the Artist. Olga Cabral. PoDr
Mother and Son. William Heyen. GeTw
Mother and Son. Allen Tate. LiTA; MoAB; MoAmPo; MoVE
Mother, because you never spoke to me. More Clues. Muriel Rukeyser. IHMS
Mother before a Soldier's Monument, A. Winnie Lynch Rockett. PGD
Mother Bombie, *sel.* John Lyly.
O Cupid! Monarch over Kings. ElL
(Fools in Love's College.) TrGrPo
(Song of Accius and Silena.) OBSC
Mother Carey's Chicken. Theodore Watts-Dunton. OBVV
Mother Country, The. Benjamin Franklin. PAH
Mother Country. Christina Rossetti. OxBoCh
Mother Crab and Her Family, The. L. T. Manyase, *tr. fr. Xhosa by* Jack Cope *and* C. M. Mcanyangwa. PeSA
Mother Dark. Francesca Yetunde Pereira. PBA
Mother darling, I cannot work the loom. Sappho, *tr. fr. Greek by* Willis Barnstone. BoWoP
Mother Dear, I am being careful. Letter from a Working Girl. Herbert Scott. GP
"Mother dear, may I go downtown." Ballad of Birmingham. Dudley Randall. BPo; HeIP; InPK; NIP; NoAM
Mother Dear, O! Pray for Me, *with music. Unknown.* AH
Mother Doesn't Want a Dog. Judith Viorst. RHPC
Mother, don't read. Preface. Carol Shauger. AMV-80
Mother Earth. Anna Margolin, *tr. fr. Yiddish by* Keith Bosley. VWA
Mother Earth; Her Whales. Gary Snyder. LCAP; WeW
Mother England. Edith M. Thomas. AA; HBV-2
Mother fragrant in her dust and grace, The. Celestine. Robert Fitzgerald. MoVE
Mother Goose. *Unknown.* SoPo
Mother Goose (circa 2054). Irene Sekula. QQQ; ShM
Mother Goose Rhyme. Kenneth Rexroth. ErPo
Mother Goose Sonnets, *sel.* Harriet S. Morgridge.
Jack and Jill. AA
Mother Goose Up-to-Date, *parodies.* Louis Untermeyer. MoAmPo
Edgar A. Guest Considers "The Good Old Woman Who Lived in a Shoe" and the Good Old Truths Simultaneously, *sel.* NIP; PoPl
(Edgar A. Guest Considers "The Old Woman Who Lived in a Shoe" and the Good Old Verities at the Same Time.) FiBHP; OBAL; WhC
Mother Goose's Garland. Archibald MacLeish. OBAL
Mother Goose's Melody, *sel. Unknown.*
Learned Song, A. FaBoUs
Mother-heart doth yearn at eventide, The. When Even Cometh On. Lucy Evangeline Tilley. AA
Mother, here there are shadowy salmon. Letter from Oregon. William Stafford. NaP
Mother, Home, Heaven. William Goldsmith Brown. FaBoBe; HBV-2
Mother, I Am. Lucille Clifton. GeTw
Mother!, I am sick. For an Obligate Parasite. Alan Dugan. TW
Mother, I am something more. Looking Out. Helen Chasin. NMM
Mother, I Cannot Mind My Wheel. Walter Savage Landor, *first st. par. fr. the Greek of* Sappho. AWP, *st.* 1; BoLoP; CABA; EnRP; GBL; HBV-1; InPK; NOBE; OAEP; OBEV; OBRV; OBVE; TEP; TrGrPo
Mother, I long[s] to get married. Whistle, Daughter, Whistle. *Unknown.* AmFP; ErPo
Mother, I may do violence to you. Mother. Sharon Mayer Libera. IHMS
Mother, I want to go. *Unknown, tr. fr. Spanish by* Willis Barnstone. BoWoP
Mother, I went to China this morning. Who Can Say. Alastair Reid. NePoEA
Mother, I would marry, yes I would be a bride. Whistle, Daughter, Whistle. *Unknown.* FSW
Mother in Egypt, A. Majorie Pickthall. CaP; HBV-2
Mother in her office holds the key, The. Queen of the World. *Unknown.* PGD
Mother, in my unwanted suffering, I turn to you. Threnody. David Ignatow. FAZ
Mother in old Alabama, A. Beulah Louise. William Jay Smith. TDH
Mother, in the 45¢ Bottle. Paul Blackburn. NYP
Mother in the House, The. Hermann Hagedorn. HBMV; OHIP
Mother in the Snow-Storm, The. Seba Smith. PaPo
Mother Is a Sun, A. Peggy Bennett. PoSC
Mother is drinking to forget a man. Frying Trout While Drunk. Lynn Emanuel. MAYP
Mother is gone. Bird songs wouldn't let her breathe. Requiem. William Stafford. NaP
Mother, is this the darkness of the end. For "Our Lady of the Rocks." Dante Gabriel Rossetti. EBEV; OxBoCh; VLP
Mother Land/ Long lain asleep. Mother Dark. Francesca Yetunde Pereira. PBA
Mother, let me congratulate you on/ the birthday of your son. Birthday. Yevgeny Yevtushenko, *tr. by* Peter Levi *and* Robin Milner-Gulland. NAs
Mother likes the frocks and hats. Shop Windows. Rose Fyleman. SoPo; TiPo
Mother Love. Janie Alford. PGD
Mother Marie Therese. Robert Lowell. CoPo
Mother Maudlin the Witch. Ben Jonson. *Fr.* The Sad Shepherd. ChTr
Mother, May I Go Out to Swim? *Unknown.* FaPON; OxNR
"Mother, may I stay up tonight?" Conversation. David McCord. GrPl; SO
Mother mine, Mother mine, what do you see? Ballad. Annemarie Ewing. NePoAm
Mother, mother,/ Why is it not you? The One Who Struggles. Ernst Toller, *tr. by* E. Ellis Roberts. TrJP
Mother, Mother, Make My Bed. *Unknown.* ELP
Mother Mother shave me. Song. *Tr. fr. Nyasa by* Ulli Beier. BoWoP
Mother, mother, what illbred aunt. The Disquieting Muses. Sylvia Plath. NMM; SBG
Mother, my eyes wait on you, unfulfilled. Mother. Anwar Shaul, *tr. by* Yoffee Berkovitz. VWA
Mother my good girl. Life's Work. Maxine W. Kumin. GP
Mother, my Mary Gray. The Division of Parts. Anne Sexton. NePoEA-2
Mother needs Thee, Lord, A. A Mother's Prayer. Jeanette Saxton Coon. STF
Mother o' blossoms, and ov all. May. William Barnes. *Fr.* May. ChTr
Mother o' Mine. Kipling. FaFP; TRV; WBLP
Mother of Christ the Priest and of His, The/ royal and priestly people. The Mediatrix of Grace. Francis Burke. ISi
Mother of Fisherman. Henriëtte Roland-Holst, *tr. fr. Dutch by* Ria Leigh-Loohuizen. PBWP
Mother of God, The. *Unknown, tr. fr. Greek by* G. R. Woodward. *Fr.* Horologium. ISi
Mother of God, The. W. B. Yeats. SBVL
Mother of God, mother of man reborn. Invocation. Arthur J. Little. *Fr.* Christ Unconquered. ISi
Mother of God! no lady thou. Our Lady. Mary Elizabeth Coleridge. OBEV; OBMV; OBVV; WPE
Mother of God! Our Lady! For Eleanor and Bill Monahan. William Carlos Williams. VGW
Mother of God that's Lady of the Heavens. Prayer of the Old Woman, Villon's Mother. Villon, *tr. by* J. M. Synge. *Fr.* Two Translations from Villon. MoBrPo
Mother of God, whose burly love. On the Eve of the Feast of the Immaculate Conception: 1942. Robert Lowell. WaaP
"Mother of heaven, regina of the clouds." Le Monocle de Mon Oncle. Wallace Stevens. AP; CoBMV; LiTM; MoAB; NoAM; TwAmPo
Mother of Hermes! and still youthful Maia! Fragment of an Ode to Maia [Written on May Day, 1818]. Keats. EnRP; OAEL-2; OAEP; OBEV; OBRV; PoEL-4
Mother of life indulges all our wandering, The. Return to Ritual. Mark Van Doren. MoVE
Mother of light! how fairly dost thou go. Ode to the Moon. Thomas Hood. OBVV
Mother of Man. Vesna Parun, *tr. fr. Croatian by* Mary Coote. PBWP
Mother of memories! O mistress-queen! Le Balcon. Baudelaire, *tr. by* Lord Alfred Douglas. AWP
Mother of Men. Brian Hooker. HBMV
Mother of Men. Stephen Southwold. HBMV
Mother of Men, grown strong in giving. Mother of Men. Brian Hooker. HBMV
Mother of musings, contemplation sage. The Pleasures of Melancholy. Thomas Warton, the Younger. EnRP; LAuP
Mother of my birth, for how long were we together. Kaddish. David Ignatow. NU; VWA
Mother of nations, of them eldest we. America to England. George Edward Woodberry. AA
Mother of revolutions, stern and sweet. To France. Ralph Chaplin. HBMV
Mother of Ten. L. A. G. Strong. DBV
Mother of the Fair Delight. Ave. Dante Gabriel Rossetti. GoBC; ISi; OxBoCh
Mother of the Groom. Seamus Heaney. PAI
Mother of the House, The. Bible, *O.T.* Proverbs, XXXI: 25-29 (*American Standard Version*). PGD
("Strength and honour are her clothing.") PoSC

Mother of the Muses, we are taught, The. Memory. Walter Savage Landor. EBEV; OAEL-2
Mother of Us All, The, *sel.* Gertrude Stein.
"We cannot retrace our steps." CrMA
Mother Pin a Rose on Me, *with music.* David Lewis, Paul Schindler, *and* Bob Adams. FSN
Mother plays a march. Away We Go. Aileen Fisher. TiPo
Mother Poem. Joel Oppenheimer. PoM
Mother-Prayer. Margaret Widdemer. HBMV
Mother rock is black basalt, The. Human Geography. Ruth Whitman. AMV-80
Mother said if I wore this hat. My Hat. Stevie Smith. BrRo
Mother said to call her if the H bomb exploded. Belief. Josephine Miles. NoAM; TAP
Mother Sarah's Lullaby ("Mother Sarah rocks the cradle"). Itzig Manger, *tr. fr. Yiddish by* Jacob Sonntag. TrJP
Mother says. Counting Sheep. Aileen Fisher. SoPo
Mother sent me on the holy quest, The. The Living Chalice. Susan Mitchell. HBMV
Mother shake the cherry-tree. Let's Be Merry. Christina Rossetti. *Fr.* Sing-Song. FaPON; TiPo
Mother Shipton's Prophecies. *At. to* Charles Hindley. BLPA
Mother-Song. Alfred Austin. *Fr.* Prince Lucifer. HBV-1
Mother Speaks, A: The Algiers Motel Incident, Detroit. Michael S. Harper. AmPA; BPo
Mother Superior. George MacBeth. NMP
Mother Tabbyskins. Elizabeth Anna Hart. CenHV; OxBChV
Mother the Wardrobe Is Full of Infantrymen. Roger McGough. MAT
Mother to Her Waking Infant, A. Joanna Baillie. NOEC
Mother to Son. Langston Hughes. AmNP; CABA; CDC; CTBA; NTCP; OBCA; PoNe; SO; TTY
Mother told me the directions. Memorial Day. Laureen Ching. AMV-80
Mother Was a Lady; or, If Jack Were Only Here. Edward B. Marks. *See* My Mother Was a Lady . . .
Mother was a wolf; snarled her long. Recollection. Donald D. Govan. NBP
Mother Wept. Joseph Skipsey. EBVV; HBV-1; OBVV; VLP
Mother wept, A: where were You, God. Calvary. Libby Stopple. GoYe
Mother Who Died Too, The. Edith M. Thomas. AA
Mother, who knew/ what hardship shakes. Our Lady of the Refugees. Sister Mary Maura. ISi
Mother who owns Christ as Lord, The. God's Ideal Mother. Cora M. Pinkham. STF
Mother! Whose virgin bosom was uncrossed. The Virgin [*or* Sonnet to the Virgin]. Wordsworth. GoBC; ISi
Motherhood. Josephine Daskam Bacon. HBV-1
Motherhood. Charles Stuart Calverley. FM
Motherhood. Karl M. Chworowsky. PGD
Motherhood. Agnes Lee. BLPA; HBMV
Motherhood. Susan Ludvigson. AMV-81
Motherhood. William L. Stidger. PGD
Motherhood. May Swenson. CoAP
Motherless Child Blues. *Unknown.* BluL
Motherless Children. *Unknown.* BluL; FSW
Mothers. Nikki Giovanni. CNA; CTBA; UnPo
Mothers. Anne Sexton. Str
Mothers. Tristan Tzara, *tr. fr. French by* Willis Barnstone *and* Matei Calinescu. VWA
Mothers. *Unknown.* PGD
Mothers/ cranking the machine. The Greater Friendship Baptist Church. Carole C. Gregory. BlSi
Mothers,/ That hope of yours, your joyful burden. To the Mothers. Ernst Toller, *tr. by* E. Ellis Roberts. TrJP
Mother's Advice. *Unknown.* AmFP
Mothers and Children. Orrick Johns. HBMV
Mothers and Daughters. David Campbell. POL
Mothers and fathers of sons, what will you be saying. It Is Not Too Late. Lucia Trent. PGD
Mothers—and Others. Amos R. Wells. WBLP
Mothers are hardest to forgive. The Adversary. Phyllis McGinley. OBCA
Mother's Birthday, A. Henry van Dyke. OHIP
Mother's Choice, The. *Unknown.* OxBoLi
Mothers, Daughters. Shirley Kaufman. BoWoP; GP; NMM
Mother's Dream, The. William Barnes. NOBE
Mother's Habits. Nikki Giovanni. BlSi
Mother's hardest to forgive, A. The Adversary. Phyllis McGinley. DBV; FaBoEE
Mother's home early, out of bed. After Illness. Vi Gale. GP
Mother's Hymn, The. Bryant. OHIP
Mother's Idol Broken, The, *sel.* Gerald Massey.
Our Wee White Rose. HBV-1
Mother's Inheritance. Fawziyya Abu Khalid, *tr. fr. Arabic by* Kamal Boullata. WPOW
Mothers' Lament at the Slaughter of the Innocents, The. *Unknown, tr. fr. Middle Irish by* Kuno Meyer. OnYI
Mother's Lament for the Death of Her Son, A. Burns. HoPM
Mother's Love. Ross B. Clapp. WBLP
Mother's Love ("A mother's love—how sweet the name!"). F. Montgomery. PGD
Mother's Lullaby, The. John Clare. NAs
Mother's Malison, The; or, Clyde's Water. *Unknown. See* Clyde's Water.
Mother's Name, A. *Unknown.* PGD
Mother's Nerves. X. J. Kennedy. GrPl; RHPC
Mothers of America. Ave Maria. Frank O'Hara. NNaP; NoP; PoM
Mothers of Men, The. Joaquin Miller. *See* Bravest Battle, The.
Mothers of our forest-land, The! The Mothers of the West. William D. Gallagher. PAH
Mothers of sailors, I hope you will draw nigh. Johnny Gallagher. *Unknown.* AmFP
Mothers of Sons. Lesley Saunders. BrRo
Mothers of the West, The. William D. Gallagher. PAH
Mother's Picture, A. Edmund Clarence Stedman. OHIP
Mother's Prayer, A. Jeanette Saxton Coon. STF
Mother's Prayer, A. Margaret E. Sangster. *See* Father Speaks, A.
Mother's Prayer, The. Dora Sigerson Shorter. HBV-1
Mother's Sacrifice, The. Lydia Huntley Sigourney. PaPo
Mother's Song, The. Virginia Woodward Cloud. AA
Mother's Song, A. Francis Ledwidge. EtS
Mother's Song ("If snow falls on the far field"). *Unknown, tr. fr. Japanese by* Willis Barnstone. BoWoP
Mother's Song, The ("It is so still in the house"). *Unknown, tr. fr. Eskimo by* Peter Freuchen. OBCP; WTO
Mother's Song ("My heart is like a fountain true"). *Unknown.* GN; HBV-1
Mothers who have seen him die—your first child, your only one. Fourth Station. Paul Claudel, *tr. by* Sister Mary David. ISi
Mothers who raise. Double Duty. W. E. Farbstein. PoPl; WhC
Mothers-in-Law. Robert Sward. CoPo
Moths. Julia Fields. *Fr.* Poems: Birmingham 1962-1964. PoBA; PoNe
Moths, The. W. S. Merwin. HeIP
Moth's Kiss, First, The! Robert Browning. *Fr.* In a Gondola. BoLoP; GBL; OBEV; OBVV, UnTE
(Song: "Moth's kiss, first, The!") HBV-1; TrGrPo
Mothy Monologue. Ralph Gustafson. NOBC
Motif for Mary's Dolors. Sister Mary Madeleva. ISi
Motion, The. Theodore Roethke. SeCeV
Motion of gathering loops of water, The. The Glass Bubbles. Samuel Greenberg. LiTA; NePA
Motion of the Earth, The. Norman Nicholson. ImOP
Motionless—His sons. Death Bed. Thomas Kinsella. CIP
Motions and means, on land and sea at war. Steamboats, Viaducts, and Railways. Wordsworth. VLP
Motion's the dead giveaway. Viable. A. R. Ammons. TAP
Motive. Cecilia Meireles, *tr. fr. Portuguese by* Don Wilson. AMV-81
Motive. Muriel Rukeyser. *See* Motive of All of It, The.
Motive for Mercy. Ken Milburn. PoSH
Motive for Metaphor, The. Wallace Stevens. AP; MoAB; MoAmPo
Motive of All of It, The. Muriel Rukeyser. MiAP
(Motive.) PoA
Motives of Rhythm, The. Robert Conquest. PP
Motley. Walter de la Mare. HoPM; MMA
Motley's the Only Wear. Shakespeare. *Fr.* As You Like It, II, vii. TrGrPo
(Worthy Fool, A.) TreFT
Motor Bus. Alfred Denis Godley. FaBoCo; NOBL
(On the Motor Bus.) FaBoNo
Motor Cars. Rowena Bastin Bennett. FaPON; SoPo; TiPo
Motorcycle. Benjamin Sturgis Pray. GoYe
Motorcycle Irene. Skip Spence. MAT
Motorcyclists, The. James Tate. MAYP
Motown/Smokey Robinson. Jessica Hagedorn. BrSi
Motto, The. Abraham Cowley. AnAnS-2; SeCP
Motto. Langston Hughes. PoBA; PoNe
Motto. *Unknown, ad. fr. German by* Louis Untermeyer. TiPo
Motto for a Dog House. Arthur Guiterman. GDP
Motto for a Sun Dial. J. V. Cunningham. InPK
(Epigram: "I who by day am function of the light.") VGW
Motto for a Sundial. *Unknown.* FaBoEE
Mould of Castile. Jack Clemo. NOCV
Mouldering Vine, The. *Unknown.* AmFP
Mound, The. Thomas Hardy. OxBTC
Mounds of humped rust-colored hills. Safed. Dovid Knut, *tr. by* Daniel Weissbort. VWA
Mount, The. Léonie Adams. MoAB; MoAmPo; MoVE
Mount Badon. Charles Williams. FaBoTw

Mount Caribou at Night. Charles Wright. LCAP
Mount Gilboa. Malka Heifetz Tussman, *tr. fr. Yiddish by* Marcia Falk. PBWP
Mount Lykaion. Trumbull Stickney. *Fr.* Sonnets from Greece. MoVE; NePA; OxBA; TrGrPo
Mount, mount for the chase! let your lassos be strong. The White Steed of the Prairies. J. Barber. BPAW; CoSo
Mount of Olives. Henry Vaughan. AnAnS–1
Mount of the Muses, The. Robert Herrick. CaPo
Mount Saint Helens/ Loowit; an Indian Woman's Song. Wendy Rose. TWSS
Mount Vernon. *Unknown.* AmFP; OFD
Mount Vernon, the Home of Washington. William Day. OHIP
Mount Zion. *Unknown.* AmFP
Mountain, The. Robert Finch. CaP
Mountain, The. Robert Frost. FaBV
Mountain, The. Mikhail Yuryevich Lermontov, *tr. fr. Russian by* Max Eastman. AWP
Mountain, The. W. S. Merwin. VGW
Mountain/ rises out of paper. Pastoral. Robin Magonan. PoDr
Mountain Afterglow, The. James Laughlin. VGW
Mountain and the Squirrel, The. Emerson. *See* Fable: "Mountain and the squirrel, The."
Mountain Born. Marcia Inzer Bost. AMV–80
Mountain Bride. Robert Morgan. GeTw; GP; MAYP
Mountain Brook. Elizabeth J. Coatsworth. RHPC
Mountain Cemetery, The. Edgar Bowers. ConAP; NePoEA
Mountain Convent. Laura Benét. GoYe
Mountain Corral. Helen Sorrells. WPE
Mountain Creed. Medora Addison Nutter. GoYe
Mountain Creed. Hugh C. Rae. PoSH
Mountain Days. Barclay Fraser. PoSH
Mountain Dew. *Unknown.* FSW
Mountain Evenings. Jamie Sexton Holme. PoOW
Mountain, Fire, Thornbush. Harvey Shapiro. VGW
Mountain gorses, ever-golden. Lessons from the Gorse. Elizabeth Barrett Browning. HBV–1
Mountain Greenery. Lorenz Hart. OBAL
Mountain Heart's-Ease, The. Bret Harte. HBV–1
Mountain held the town as in a shadow, The. The Mountain. Robert Frost. FaBV
Mountain Heritage, A. Joan Wyrick Ellison. AMV–80
Mountain in Labor, The. Aesop, *tr. fr. Greek by* William Ellery Leonard. AWP
Mountain is a sort of music, A: theme. Moment Musical in Assynt. Norman MacCaig. PoSH
Mountain is wild with men, The. Matronita. Dennis Silk. VWA
Mountain Liars. Ann Woodbury Hafen. PoOW
Mountain Lion. D. H. Lawrence. BoAnP; OxBTC; RFM
Mountain Meadows. Martha Keller. BoNaP
Mountain Medicine. Elizabeth-Ellen Long. AmFN
Mountain Oysters. Patrick Lane. NeAC
Mountain peaks put on their hoods, The. Twilight Song. John Hunter-Duvar. *Fr.* De Roberval. WHW
Mountain pine is a man at arms, The. The Elm. Odell Shepard. HBMV
Mountain road ends here, The. Lyell's Hypothesis Again. Kenneth Rexroth. MoVE; NoAM
Mountain road is steep, the stone steps are dangerous, The. Spring Thoughts Sent to Tzu-an. Yü Hsüan-chi, *tr. by* Geoffrey Waters. BoWoP
Mountain sat upon the plain, The. Emily Dickinson. FaBV
Mountain Sculpture. James Will. PoSH
Mountain sheep are sweeter, The. The War Song of Dinas Vawr. Thomas Love Peacock. *Fr.* The Misfortunes of Elphin. AWP; CABA; EnRP; EvOK; FaBoCh; FaPoR; HAP; InvP; LoBV; NBM; NOBE; OAEL–2; OBRV; OnMSP; PoPle; PrIm; ViBoPo; WaaP; WeW; WhC; WiR
Mountain Song. Harriet Monroe. HBV–2
Mountain Study. Peter van Toorn. NOBC
Mountain summits sleep, The: glens, cliffs, and caves. Sleep Upon the World [*or* Fragment]. Alcman, *tr. by* Thomas Campbell. AWP; ChTr
Mountain teeth, tips of anemious rippled stone. On the Subject of Waves. Eldon Grier. MoCV; PeCV
Mountain That Got Little, The. William Stafford. FAZ
Mountain tips are white and dead, The. The River. Leo Vroman. VWA
Mountain-Toilet Thief, A. Al Robles. BrSi
Mountain Top. *Unknown.* *See* Liza Jane.
Mountain Town—Mexico. Eldon Grier. NOBC
Mountain Tree, The. Hugh Connell. NeIP
Mountain Vigil. Douglas Fraser. PoSH
Mountain was in great distress and loud, A. The Mountain in Labor. Aesop, *tr. by* William Ellery Leonard. AWP
Mountain where I danced on moonlit stones, The. Cairngorm, November 1971. Martyn Berry. PoSH
Mountain Whippoorwill, The. Stephen Vincent Benét. TrGrPo; YaD
Mountain Wind, A. "Æ." AWP
Mountain Wind. Barbara Kunz Loots. RHPC
Mountaineer, The. Robert Nathan. TrJP
Mountaineer is working with his Bible, The. Quatrina. Joseph Bennett. LiTA
Mountaineering Bus. Rennis McOwan. PoSH
Mountaineers, The. Dannie Abse. PP
Mountains, The. Walter de la Mare. BrPo
Mountains, The. Louis Dudek. CaP
Mountains. Lucy Larcom. WBLP
Mountains and cold places on the earth. The Cloud Factory. John Haines. EAS
Mountains and Other Outdoor Things. Ruth Good. PoDr
Mountains and Rivers, *sels.* Gary Snyder.
  Market, The. CoPo
  "Seventy-five feet hoed rows equals." NaP
Mountains, and the lonely death at last, The. To a Traveler. Lionel Johnson. MoBrPo; NBM
Mountains Are a Lonely Folk, The. Hamlin Garland. TreFT
Mountains are dragons, The. Nightmare on Rhum. James Macmillan. PoSH
Mountains are moving, rivers. The Redwoods. Louis Simpson. AmFN; CoAP; PP
Mountains are steadfast but the mountain streams. Hwang Chin-i, *tr. fr. Korean by* Peter H. Lee. PBWP
Mountains blue now, The. The Mountains in the Desert. Robert Creeley. CoPo
Mountain's giddy height I sought, A. The Lay of the Trilobite. May Kendall. CenHV
Mountains grow unnoticed, The. Emily Dickinson. MoAB; MoAmPo; TrGrPo
Mountains have gathered in the distance. Sleep on the Fraser. Patrick Lane. NeAC
Mountains in the Desert, The. Robert Creeley. CoPo
Mountains loom upon the path we take. Song to the Mountains. *Unknown, tr. by* Alice C. Fletcher. AWP
Mountains stand, and stare around, The. The Paps of Dana. James Stephens. NoAM
Mountains taught us speechlessness, The. Alps. Rosanna Warren. MAYP
Mountains they are silent folk, The. The Mountains Are a Lonely Folk. Hamlin Garland. TreFT
Mountainy Childer, The. Elizabeth Shane. HBMV
Mountebanks, The. Charles Henry Luders. AA
Mountebank's Mask, The, *sel.* Thomas Campion.
  Hours of Sleepy Night, The. EIL
    (Dismissal.) OBSC
Mounting lark, day's herald, got on wing, The. William Browne. *Fr.* Britannia's Pastorals, I, Song 3. PBBP
Mounting the Tehachapis. Entering the Desert; Big Circles Running. Wendy Rose. TWSS
Mountown! Thou Sweet Retreat. William King. *Fr.* Mully of Mountown. FaBoPP
Mourn for Yourself. Geoffrey Keating, *tr. fr. Irish by* Sean Lucy. BIrV
Mourn, hapless Caledonia, mourn. The Tears of Scotland. Tobias Smollett. NOEC; OBEC
Mourn No More. John Fletcher. *See* Weep No More.
Mourn Not for Adonais. Shelley. *See* Elegy on the Death of John Keats, An.
Mourn Not the Dead. Ralph Chaplin. HBMV; ViBoPo
Mourn, ye wee songsters o' the wood. Burns. *Fr.* Elegy on Captain Matthew Henderson. PBBP
Mourners, The. Bevil Higgons. APAS
Mourners Came at Break of Day, The. Sarah Flower Adams. HBV–2
Mourners drive away, The. The Mowing Crew. Baron Wormser. MAYP
Mournful Dove, The. *Unknown.* AmFP
Mournful Numbers. Morris Bishop. WhC
Mourning. Andrew Marvell. CABA; SeCP
Mourning. Josephine Van Fossan. STF
Mourning and Melancholia. A. Alvarez. VWA
Mourning Bride, The, *sels.* William Congreve.
  "Heaven hath no rage like love to hatred turned," *fr.* III, viii, 2 *ll.* TreF
  "Music has charms to soothe a savage breast," *fr.* I, i. ViBoPo
Mourning Conquest , The. *Unknown.* CoMu
Mourning Garment, The. Robert Greene. *See* Greene's Mourning Garment.
Mourning Letter from Paris, A. Conrad Kent Rivers. BPo
Mourning Letter, March 29 1963. Edward Dorn. ConAP
Mourning Pablo Neruda. Robert Bly. LCAP
Mourning Picture. Adrienne Rich. CoAP
Mourning Poem for the Queen of Sunday. Robert Hayden. HoAn; NoP; PoBA

Mourningsong for Anne. David Posner. FAZ
Mourning-Song for Rangiaho, A. Te Heuheu Herea, *tr. fr. Maori by* Barry Mitcalfe. WTO
Mourning Women. Mathilde Blind. SBG
Mouse, The. Elizabeth J. Coatsworth. FaPON; MoShBr; OBCA; SoPo; SUS; TiPo
Mouse. Hilda Conkling. SoPo; TiPo
Mouse, The. Jean Garrigue. MP; TwCP
Mouse, The. Hugh McCrae. PoAu-1
Mouse, The. Laura E. Richards. OBCA
Mouse and the Cake, The. Eliza Cook. OxBChV
Mouse Dinners, The. Russell Edson. SoSe
Mouse in the Wainscot, The. Ian Serraillier. PDV
Mouse Night: One of Our Games. William Stafford. NCSH
Mouse the trap had slapped on, but not caught, A. Ballad of the Mouse. Robert Wallace. NYBP
Mousemeal. Howard Nemerov. MP; NCSH; TwCP
Mouse's Lullaby, The. Palmer Cox. OBCA
Mouse's Nest. John Clare. ChTr; InPK; LiTB; LoBV; PAI; SeCeV; VLP
Mouse's Petition, The. Anna Laetitia Barbauld. FM; OxBChV
Mouse's Tale, The. "Lewis Carroll." *See* Fury Said to a Mouse.
Mouth. Clarisse Nicoïdski, *tr. fr. Judezmo by* Stephen Levy. VWA
Mouth and the Ears, The. Shem-Tob ben Joseph Palquera, *tr. fr. Hebrew by* J. Chotzner. TrJP
Mouth. Can blow or breathe, A. Cardinal Ideograms. May Swenson. OBCA
Mouth down in the timothy. Grass. John Holmes. MiAP
Mouth like old silk soft with use, A. A Levantine. William Plomer. OBMV
Mouth of a girl who had been lying, The. Beautiful Youth. Gottfried Benn, *tr. by* Joachim Neugroschel. POL
Mouth of the Amazon. R. P. Gira. AMV-80
Mouth of the Hudson, The. Robert Lowell. AmFN; CAD; CoPo; NaP; NYP
Mouth to mouth joined we lie, her naked breasts. Tantalos. Paulus Silentiarius, *tr. by* Dudley Fitts. ErPo
Mouths. Louis Dudek. PeCV
Mouth's disfurnished eyes. Three. John N. Morris. GP
Move Continuing, The. Al Young. PoBA
Move him into the sun. Futility. Wilfred Owen. ChMP; CMoP; CoBMV; FaBoMo; GTBS-P; MMA; MoAB; MoBrPo; NoAM; NoP; OAEP; OBWP; PAI; SeCePo; TrGrPo
Move into/ the past tense. Grammar Lesson. Linda Pastan. Psk
Move on with a will, nor dream thou back. At Dawn of the Year. George Klingle. PGD
Move On, Yiddish Poet. Jacob Glatstein, *tr. fr. Yiddish by* Ruth Whitman. VWA
Move over, Ali Baba! Now there comes. Autosonic Door. Dorothy Brown Thompson. GoYe
Move over, ham. Hiding Place. Richard Armour. NIP
Move to California, The, *sel.* William Stafford.
Written on the Stub of the First Paycheck. InPK
Moved by Her Music. Richard Gillman. NePoAm-2
Moved by the miracles of saints. The Raising of the Dead. Rosemary Dobson. PoAu-2
Moved towards a Future. Laura Chester. NPGG
Movement. Denise Levertov. LLLT
Movement,/ Feet hit pavement. Running under Street Lights. Christy White. AMV-80
Movement of Fish, The. James Dickey. NYBP; VGW
Movement, she explained, would bring poetry to the rich, The. Ralph Hodgson. *Fr.* Flying Scrolls. FaBoTw
Movement Song. Audre Lorde. CNA
Movements. Norman MacCaig. OxBC
Moves in me now the tongues, the gongs. To the Ladies. Arnold Kenseth. PPON
Movie Actors Scribbling Letters Very Fast in Crucial Scenes. Jean Garrigue. TAP
Movie-Going. John Hollander. CoAP; NYP; PPP
Movie Queen. James P. Vaughn. NNP
Movies, The. Jack Gilbert. NPGG
Movies are badder. Saturday Afternoon at the Movies. John Logan. NNaP
Movies for the Home. Howard Moss. NePoEA-2; NYBP
Movies, Left to Right. Robert Sward. NYBP
Moving. Barbara Crooker. AMV-80
Moving. Randall Jarrell. DFF
Moving. William Matthews. POL
Moving. Janet Reed McFatter. GrPl
Moving. Eunice Tietjens. TiPo
Moving Again. William Matthews. NPAW
Moving Ahead. Rainer Maria Rilke, *tr. fr. German by* Robert Bly. NU
Moving between Beloit and Monroe. Bink Noll. GrPl
Moving Day. Lewis B. Horne. HoAn
Moving form or rigid mass, A. Song of the Screw. *Unknown.* NA
Moving from Cheer to Joy, from Joy to All. Next Day. Randall Jarrell. HAP; NoAM; NoP; NYBP; WeW
Moving from left to left, the light. View of the Capitol from the Library of Congress. Elizabeth Bishop. AmFN
Moving In. Paul Engle. PoA
Moving In. Josephine Miles. NoP
Moving In. Karl Shapiro. NAs
Moving in Winter. Adrienne Rich. DFF
Moving: New York—New Haven Line. Alfred Corn. MAYP
Moving Out. Joyce Carol Oates. AMV-81
Moving out. Thing Poem. Petra von Morstein, *tr. by* Rosemarie Waldrop. BoWoP
Moving over the hills, crossing the irrigation. Some San Francisco Poems. George Oppen. NNaP
Moving sun-shapes on the spray, The. Going and Staying. Thomas Hardy. CMoP; NoAM
Moving through the Silent Crowd. Stephen Spender. NOBE
Mower, The. *Unknown.* CoMu; OBET
Mower against Gardens, The. Andrew Marvell. AnAnS-1; EBEV; LiTB; NoP; OAEL-1; OAEP; PoEL-2; PP; PPP; SeCV-1
Mower in Ohio, The. John James Piatt. AA
Mower to the Glow-Worms [*or* Glowworms], The. Andrew Marvell. AWP; ELP; InvP; NOBE; NoP; OAEL-1; OxBoLi; PoPle; PPP; TrGrPo
(Mower to the Glo-Worms, The.) AnAnS-1; EnLoPo; MePo; OBS; PoEL-2; SeCP
Mowers, The. Myron B. Benton. YeAr
Mowers, The: An Anticipation of the Cholera, 1848. Charles Mackay. EBVV
Mowers begin, The. Watchers. W. S. Merwin. NaP
Mower's Song, The. Andrew Marvell. AnAnS-1; CavP; LoBV; PoEL-2; PPP; SeCP; SeCV-1
Mowers, weary and brown, and blithe. Scythe Song. Andrew Lang. GN; HBV-1
Mowing. Robert Frost. BLPL; CMoP; HBMV; HoPM; LiTA; NOBA; OxBA; PPP; TwAmPo; VGW
Mowing, The. Sir Charles G. D. Roberts. NOBC; OBCV
Mowing Crew, The. Baron Wormser. MAYP
Mowing the Lawn. John Bensko. MAYP
Moxford Book of English Verse, The, *sels.* Archibald Stodart-Walker. CenHV
Counsel to Girls.
Early Bacon.
Inflictis.
Moyst with one drop of thy blood, my dry soule. Resurrection. John Donne. AnAnS-1; OBS
Moytura, *sel.* William Larminie.
Sword of Tethra, The. OnYI
Mozart. Jacob Glatstein, *tr. fr. Yiddish by* Ruth Whitman. VWA
Mozart. John Heath-Stubbs. EBEV
Mozart, Goethe, and the Duke of Wellington. The Augsburg Adoration. Randall Jarrell. NYBP
Mozart's Grave. Paul Scott Mowrer. GoYe
Mririda. Mririda n'Ait Attik, *tr. fr. Berber into French by* René Euloge; *English vers. by* Daniel Halpern *and* Paula Paley. WPOW
Ms. Minnie McFinney. *Unknown.* TDH
Ms. Whatchamacallit Thingamajig. Miriam Chaikin. RHPC
Mu'allaqat, The, *sels. Tr. fr. Arabic.*
Abla. Antar, *tr. by* E. Powys Mathers. AWP
"Have the poets left a single spot for a patch to be sewn?" Antar, *tr. by* A. J. Arberry. TTY
Ode: "Weep, ah weep love's losing." Imr el Kais, *tr. by* Lady Anne Blunt *and* Wilfrid Scawen Blunt. AWP
Pour Us Wine. Ibn Kolthum, *tr. by* E. Powys Mathers. AWP
Much Ado about Nothing, *sels.* Shakespeare.
Beauty Is a Witch, *fr.* II, i. TrGrPo
Epitaph: "Done to death by slanderous tongues," *fr.* V, iii. CTC
(Claudio's Lament: "Done to death by slanderous tongues.") OBSC
"Pardon, goddess of the night," *fr.* V, iii. ViBoPo
(Claudio's Lament: "Pardon, goddess of the night.") OBSC
(Song: "Pardon, goddess of the night.") CTC
Sigh No More, Ladies [Sigh No More], *fr.* II, iii. AWP; CTC; ElL; ELP; FF; HBV-1; InMe; LiTB; OAEP; PAI; SeCeV; TreFS; TrGrPo; ViBoPo
(Balthasar's Song.) OBSC
(Song: "Sigh no more, ladies, sigh no more.") FiP; PoEL-2
Much Ado about Nothing in the City. *Unknown.* FaBoPa
Much as he left it when he went from us. Why He Was There. E. A. Robinson. CMoP; NOBA
Much cry and little wool. Back. Weldon Kees. NaP; PrIm; TwAmPo

Much did I rage when young. Youth and Age. W. B. Yeats. ELU; FaBoEE
Much-discerning public hold, A. La Nuit Blanche. Kipling. MoBrPo
Much Distressed. *Unknown.* CBAP
Much had passed/ Since last we parted. Byron Recollected at Bologna. Samuel Rogers. *Fr.* Italy. OBNC
Much Has Been Said . . . *Unknown.* CoMu
Much have I labored, much read o'er. Alas for Youth. Firdausi, *tr. by* R. A. Nicholson. AWP
Much have I roved by Sandy River. By Sandy Waters. Jesse Stuart. AmFN
Much have I spoken of the faded leaf. November. Elizabeth Stoddard. AA
Much have I travail'd in the realms of gold. On First Looking into the Dark Future. Roger Lancelyn Green. CenHV
Much have I travell'd [*or* travelled *or* traveled] in the realms of gold. On First Looking into Chapman's Homer. Keats. BiP; BLPA; CABA; CH; ChER; ChTr; EnRP; FaBoBe; FaBoCh; FaBoEn; FaBV; FaFP; FaPo; FF; FiP; FPL; GN; GTBS; GTBS-P; HAP; HBV-2; HBVY; HeIP; HoPM; InPK; LiTB; LoBV; NIP; NOBE; NoP; OAEL-2; OAEP; OBEV; OBNC; OBRV; PAI; PoEL-4; PPoe; PPP; PrIm; RoGo; SeCeV; SoSe; TEP; TreF; TrGrPo; ViBoPo; WHA
Much have I travelled in East Lothian and Dundee. On First Looking into Chapman's Homer. W. S. Brownlie. BXAP
Much have we heard the peevish world complain. On Friendship. William Whitehead. OBEC
Much here is historical. In the Hamptons. John N. Morris. NYP
Much-hugged rag-doll is oozing cotton from her ruined figure, The. September. Robert Lowell. NaP
Much I remember of the death of men. The Tomb of Michael Collins. Denis Devlin. OxBI
Much Knowledge, Little Reason. Sir John Davies. *See* Knowledge and Reason.
Much madness is divinest sense. Emily Dickinson. AmPP; AP; BoWoP; CMoP; ELU; HeIP; LiTM; MAT; NoAM; NOBA; NoP; OxBA; WPE
(Much Madness.) LiTA
Much of Me. Chuck Eggerth. AMV-80
Much of the transfiguration that we hear. The Interlude. Karl Shapiro. MoVE
Much of what is seen is best avoided. Running Back. Dave Smith. LiSp
Much suspected by me. Written with a Diamond on Her Window at Woodstock. Elizabeth I, Queen of England. PBWP; WPE
Much tobacco is burnt. Rolling Thunder. Phyllis Wolf. STE
Muckers. Carl Sandburg. CTBA; SaC
Muckers drive muckers' cars. Heroes of the Strip. Sheila Cudahy. TAT
Muckish Mountain (The Pig's Back). Shane Leslie. AnIV
Muckle-Mouth Meg. Robert Browning. HBV-1
Mud ("Mud is very nice to feel"). Polly Chase Boyden. FaBV; NTCP; RHPC; SoPo; TiPo
Mud put. The House. Robert Creeley. CoPo
Mud through my toes I'm from this land. Testimony to an Inquisitor. William Stafford. NePoAm-2
Mud turkle settin' on de end of a log. The Turtle's Song. *Unknown.* BPo
Mud Turtle, The. Howard Nemerov. NYBP
Muddled Metaphors. Tom Hood. NA
(Few Muddled Metaphors by a Moore-ose Melodist, A.) FaBoNo
Muddling up the wooden stairs one night, in my socks. Spiders. David Wevill. MoCV
Muddy meek river, oh, it was splendid sport. Big Dam. W. R. Moses. AmFN
Muddy Puddle, The. Dennis Lee. RHPC
Mudtower, The. Anne Stevenson. HoAn
Mufaddaliyat, The, *sels.* *Tr. fr. Arabic by* Sir Charles Lyall. AWP
Gone Is Youth. Salamah, Son of Jandal.
His Camel. Alqamah.
Old Age. Al-Aswad, Son of Ya'fur.
Muffle the wind. Orders. A. M. Klein. WHW
Muffled drum's sad roll has beat, The. The Bivouac of the Dead. Theodore O'Hara. AA; BLPA; HBV-2; PAH; PAL; TreF
Mugford's Victory. John White Chadwick. PAH
Mugger, The. Robert Pack. GP
Muhammedan Call to Prayer. Bilal, *tr. fr. Arabic by* Raoul Abdul. TTY
Muirland Meg. Burns. ErPo
(She'll Do It.) UnTE
Mulberry Garden, The, *sel.* Sir Charles Sedley.
Child and Maiden, *fr.* III, ii. GTBS; GTBS-P
("Ah Cloris! That I could now sit.") CavP; OAEP; OBS
(Song: "Ah Cloris! That I could now sit.") SeCV-2; ViBoPo
(To Chloris.) HBV-1; OBEV
Mulberry Mountain. *Unknown.* AmFP
Mulberry Street. Ruth Herschberger. HoAn
Mulch, The. Stanley Kunitz. GP
Mule, The. Coleman Barks. POL
Mule In the Mines, The. *Unknown.* *See* My Sweetie's the Mule in the Mine.
Mule Skinner Blues. *Unknown.* FSW
Mule-Skinners, The. *At. to* John Caldwell. BPAW
Mule Skinner's Song, *with music.* *Unknown.* AS
Mule-Train. John L. Sellers. LFAC
Mules. C. Fox-Smith. BoAnP
Mules. Paul Muldoon. CIP
Mules. Ted Walker. NYBP
Mules, I think, will not be here this hour, The. Empedocles on Etna. Matthew Arnold. VLP
Mulford. Whittier. AA
Mulier Amicta Sole. Fray Angelico Chavez. ISi
Mullabinda. David Rowbotham. CBAP; PoAu-2
Mullet Snatching. Malcolm Glass. WOLT
Mulligan Guard, The, *with music.* Ned Harrigan. BLSo
Mully of Mountown, *sels.* William King.
"How fleet is air! how many things have breath." FM
Mountown! Thou Sweet Retreat. FaBoPP
Multipara: Gravida 5. Marie Ponsot. VGW
Multiplication is vexation. Arithmetic. *Unknown.* TreFS
Multiplicity. Eleanor Berry. AMV-80
Multitude of masts in the harbour, A. The Victim of Aulis. Dannie Abse. NoAM
Multitude of the skies, gold riddle of millions of stars. Sorley Maclean. Dain do Eimhir, XVII. NeBP
Multitudes Turn in Darkness. Conrad Aiken. PoA
Multitudinous Stars, *sel.* "Ping Hsin," *tr. fr. Chinese by* Kenneth Rexroth *and* Ling Chung.
"Void only." PBWP
"Multum Dilexit." Hartley Coleridge. EnRP; HBV-2
Mum and the Sothsegger, *sel.* *Unknown.*
Dream, A. OxBM
Mumford. Ina M. Porter. PAH
Mummia. Rupert Brooke. BrPo
Mummies, The. Maxine W. Kumin. Psk
Mummy, The. Vernon Watkins. MoPo; NeBP
Mummy of a Lady Named Jemutesonekh XXI Dynasty. Thomas James. AmPA
Mummy Slept Late and Daddy Fixed Breakfast. John Ciardi. PDV; RHPC
Mumps. Elizabeth Madox Roberts. FaPON; SoPo
Munch lime sip sky juice slurp kiskimo pine. Jam Fa Jamaica. Charles Lynch. LTB
Munch made. The Kiss. Claude Clayton Smith. PoDr
Munching a plum on/ the street. To a Poor Old Woman. William Carlos Williams. OBAL; SOTW; TAP
Munch's Scream. Donald Hall. NePoEA
Mundus et Infans. W. H. Auden. LiTB; LiTM; MoAB; MoBrPo; NAs
Mundus Morosus. Frederick William Faber. ACP; NBM
(World Morose, The.) OBVV
Mundus Qualis. Joshua Sylvester. FaBoEE
Munestruck. "Hugh MacDiarmid." NeBP
Munich Elegy No. 1. George Barker. SeCePo; WaP
Munich Mannequins, The. Sylvia Plath. NaP
Municipal. Kipling. BrPo; BXAP; WhC
Municipal Gallery Revisited, The. W. B. Yeats. GTBS-P; LiTB; OxBTC
Munition Wages. Madeline Ida Bedford. SUMH
Muppim and Huppim! Strike blows on your drums! The Dance of Despair. Hayyim Nahman Bialik, *tr. by* A. M. Klein. TrJP
Mural, *sel.* Vicente Rodríguez Nietzche, *tr. fr. Spanish by* Julio Marzán.
"We must burn up." InW
Muramoto knew all this as a child. Making Miso. Lawson Fusao Inada. GP
Murder, The. Gwendolyn Brooks. DBV
Murder in the Cathedral, *sels.* T. S. Eliot.
Chorus: "We do not wish anything to happen." OxBTC
Chorus: "We have not been happy, my Lord, we have not been too happy." OxBTC
Forgive Us, O Lord. EaLo
Last Temptation, The. TreFT
Murder Mystery. Timothy Steele. AMV-81
Murder Mystery. David Wagoner. TwAmPo
Murder of a Community. Daniel Weissbort. VWA
Murder of Goins, The. *Unknown.* AmFP
Murder of Maria Marten, The. W. Corder. CoMu; OBET
Murder of Moses, The. Karl Shapiro. EaLo
Murder of Saint Thomas of Kent, The. *Unknown.* ACP
Murder of William Remington, The. Howard Nemerov. CMoP; CoAP
Murder Pact, The. Shakespeare. *See* Vaulting Ambition.
Murder self slowly. And die like ants shuffling up under. Reckoning A.M. Thursday. Doris Turner. JB
Murder Trial, The. Perseus Adams. PeSA

Murdered Girl Is Found on a Bridge, The. Jane Hayman. NYBP
Murdered, I went, risen. The Life. James Wright. LCAP; NaP
Murdered Little Bird. *Unknown.* FiBHP
Murderer, The. Paul Petrie. NYBP
Murderer, The. Stevie Smith. TEP
Murderers/ of Emmett Till. Salute. Oliver Pitcher. PoBA
Murderers, The. Shakespeare. *Fr.* Macbeth, II, ii. WHA
Murderers of the wall wrap themselves in sunrise, The. Jean Genet, *tr. by* Steven Finch. *Fr.* The Man Sentenced to Death. PeHV
Murdering Beauty. Thomas Carew. *See* Song: Murdring Beautie.
Murderous owls off Malo bay, The. Owls. John Fuller. POL
Murgatroyd. Celeste Turner Wright. Str
Murie Sing. A. Y. Campbell. FaBoPa
Murmur of a bee, The. Emily Dickinson. MoAmPo; TRV
Murmur of the mourning ghost, The. The Ballad of Keith of Ravelston. Sydney Dobell. *Fr.* A Nuptial Eve. CH; HBV-2; OBEV; OBVV
Murmurers, The. Josephine Jacobsen. GrPl
Murmuring in empty shells, A. The Relic. Robert Hillyer. GoYe; UnS
Murphy in Manchester. John Montague. NMP
Murrough Defeats the Danes, 994. *Unknown. See* On the Defeat of Ragnall by Murrough King of Leinster A.D. 994.
Mus Ridiculus Non. Marie De L. Welch. BoAnP
Musa, Musae,/ The Gods were at tea. The Muses. *Unknown.* FaBoNo
Muscae Volitantes. Lewis B. Horne. HoAn
Muscles flex, contract, The. Spring Poem. Julian Symons. NeBP
Muscovy Drake, The. E. A. S. Lesoro, *tr. fr. Sotho by* Dan Kunene *and* Jack Cope. PeSA
Muse, The. W. H. Davies. BrPo
Muse, The. Barry Spacks. MAT; POL
Muse. David Wagoner. PoA
Muse, The,/ in her dark habit. The Well. Denise Levertov. AP
Muse and Poet. Robert Bridges. OBMV
Muse, bid the morne awake. To His Valentine. Michael Drayton. PoEL-2
Muse, disgusted at an age and clime, The. On the Prospect of Planting Arts and Learning in America [*or* Verses on . . .]. George Berkeley. FaFP; HBV-2; NIP; NOEC; OBEC; OnYI; PP; SeCePo; SeCeV; TreF; TrGrPo; ViBoPo
Muse, first of Arden tell, whose footsteps yet are found. The Dwindling Forest of Arden. Michael Drayton. *Fr.* Polyolbion, Thirteenth Song. FaBoPP
Muse-haunted. Hugh McCrae. PoAu-1
Muse in Late November. Jonathan Henderson Brooks. PoNe
Muse in the New World, The. Walt Whitman. *Fr.* Song of the Exposition. MoAmPo
("Come, Muse, migrate from Greece and Ionia.") PP
Muse, June, Related, *sel.* Brian Coffey.
"Blooms such as wither at finger-touch." BIrV
Muse of Amergin, The. *Unknown, tr. fr. Irish by* John Montague. BIrV
Muse of Fire, A. Shakespeare. *Fr.* King Henry V, Prologue to Act I. ChTr
("O for a Muse of fire, that would ascend.") SCV
Muse of my native land! loftiest Muse! Keats. Endymion, IV. EnRP
Muse of the many-twinkling feet! whose charms. Byron. *Fr.* The Waltz. OBSV
Muse of Water, A. Carolyn Kizer. NMM
Muse Poem. Kathryn Van Spanckeren. FF
Muse Reviving, The. Sir John Davies. SiPS
Muse should be sprightly, The. A Skeltoniad. Michael Drayton. PoEL-2; PP
Muse, sing the stir that happy Whitbread made. George III Visits Whitbread's Brewery. "Peter Pindar." *Fr.* Instructions to a Celebrated Laureat. NOEC
Muse that stirs my blood, The. Bird and the Muse. Marya Zaturenska. PoA
Muse to an Unknown Poet, The. Paul Potts. FaBoTw
Muse with the hero's brave deeds being fired, The. Captain Death. *Unknown.* CoMu
Musée des Beaux Arts. W. H. Auden. BiP; CABA; ChMP; CMoP; CoBMV; FaFP; FF; GTBS-P; HAP; HeIP; InPK; InPS; LiTB; LiTM; MoAB; MoPo; MP; NePA; NIP; NoAM; NOBE; NoP; OAEP; PAI; PoRA; PPP; PrIM; SCV; SeCePo; SeCeV; SoSe; TEP; TrCP; TreFT; TrGrPo; TwCP; WeW
Muses, The. Edith M. Thomas. HBV-2
Muses, The. *Unknown.* FaBoNo
Muses' Elysium [*or* Elizium], *sels.* Michael Drayton.
Cloris and Mertilla. LoBV
Description of Elizium, The. AnAnS-2; OAEL-1
(Poet's Paradise, The.) WiR, *much abr.*
Second Nimphall, The. AnAnS-2
"I have two sparrows white as snow," *sel.* PBBP
Seventh Nimphall, The. AnAnS-2
Sixt Nimphall, The. OBS
(Fine Day, A.) GN
(Lines: "Clear had the day been from the dawn.") LoBV
Tenth Nimphall [*or* Nymphal], The. AnAnS-2; JCP
Muses' friend, The, (grey-eyed Aurora) yet. William Browne. *Fr.* Britannia's Pastoral, II, Song 2. JCP
Muses' garden, with pedantic weeds, The. On the Death of Donne. Thomas Carew. *Fr.* Elegy upon the Death of the Dean of Paul's, Dr. John Donne. NOBE
Muses, I oft invoked your holy aid. Astrophel and Stella, LV. Sir Philip Sidney. SiPS
Muses of Sicily, loftier be our song! The Sibylline Prophecy. Virgil, *tr. by* Thomas Walsh. *Fr.* Eclogues, IV. ISi
Muses that sing Love's sensual empery [*or* emperie]. Sonnet [*or* Love and Philosophy]. George Chapman. A Coronet for His Mistress Philosophy, I. ElL; LoBV; OBSC; SeCePo
Muses wrapped in mysteries of light, The. The Whirlwind Road. Edwin Markham. AA
Museum, The. William Abrahams. WaP
Museum. Robert Hass. NPGG
Museum is gone from my bones now, The. Calling Home the Scientists. Wendy Rose. AMV-81
Museum of Cruel Days. Richard Hugo. NPAW
Museum of Man. Earle Birney. OxBC
Museum of Modern Art on West Fifty-third Street, The. Tulips and Addresses. Edward Field. NYBP; Psk
Museum of the Second Creation, The. Sandra McPherson. LCAP
Museum-Piece. Audrey Alexandra Brown. CaP
Museum Piece. Lawrence P. Spingarn. GoYe
Museum Piece. Richard Wilbur. CMoP; ConAP; FaBoMo; MiAP; NePA; NIP; NoP; PoPl; TAP
Museum Piece No. 16228. Elaine Watson. AMV-81
Museum with Chinese Landscapes. Walter Cybulski. AMV-81
Museums. Louis MacNeice. MoBrPo
Museums and stockmarkets protect me, The. Four Stanzas Written in Anxiety. George Jonas. MoCV
Museums offer us, running from among the buses. Museums. Louis MacNeice. MoBrPo
Musgrove. *Unknown.* AmFP
Mushroom Gatherers, The. Donald Davie. NePoEA-2
Mushroom Hunting in Late August, Peterborough, N.H. Michael Blumenthal. MAYP
Mushroom is the elf of plants, The. Emily Dickinson. NePA
Mushroom, Soft Ear, Old Memory. Bring the North. William Stafford. LCAP
Mushrooms. Sylvia Plath. BoNaP; NePoEA-2; WeW; WPOW
Mushrooms grew near the tree. Peter Rabbit. Sandra McPherson. LCAP
Music. Conrad Aiken. *See* Calyx of the Oboe Breaks, The.
Music, The. Baudelaire, *tr. fr. French by* Arthur Symons. SyP
Music, A. Wendell Berry. VGW
Music. Bible, Apocrypha. Ecclesiasticus, XXXII: 5-6. TrJP
Music. George Du Maurier, *after the French of* Sully-Prudhomme. OBEV; OBVV
Music. Alice Dunbar-Nelson. BlSi
Music. Emerson. FaBV; WGRP
Music. Eleanor Farjeon. TiPo
Music. *At. to* John Fletcher. *See* Orpheus with His Lute.
Music. W. E. Henley. In Hospital, XXIII. BrPo
Music. Robert Herrick. CaPo
Music, The. Everett Hoagland. CNA
Music. Amy Lowell. YaD
Music. *Malay Oral Tradition, tr. by* R. O. Winstedt. WTO
Music. Naomi Shihab Nye. Str
Music. Frank O'Hara. NoP; NYP
Music. Shakespeare. *See* Food of Love, The.
Music. Shelley. *See* Music, When Soft Voices Die.
Music. Edith M. Thomas. HBV-2
Music Alone Shall Live. *Unknown.* FSW
Music and its harmony, The. The Design. Clarence Major. PoBA
Music and Memory. John Albee. AA
Music at Twilight. George Sterling. HBV-2
Music by the Waters. John Hay. AMV-81
Music Crept by Us, The. Leonard Cohen. FF
Music first and foremost of all! Art Poétique [*or* The Art of Poetry]. Paul Verlaine, *tr. by* Arthur Symons. AWP; SyP
"Music for a while." Song at Night. Norman Nicholson. FaBoTw
Music God. Mark Van Doren. UnS
Music Grinders, The. Oliver Wendell Holmes. WhC
Music has charms to soothe a savage breast. Congreve. *Fr.* The Mourning Bride. ViBoPo
Music I Heard [with You]. Conrad Aiken. Discordants, I. AWP; BLPL; CMoP; FaFP; HBV-1; LiTA; LiTM; NOBA; OxBA; PoRA; TreFT

(Bread and Music.) MoAB; MoAmPo
Music in an Empty House. Hugh Sykes Davies. EAS
Music in Camp. John R. Thompson. AA; BLPA; HBV-2
Music in the Air. George Johnston. PeCV
Music in the Air. Ronald McCuaig. ErPo
Music in the Night. Harriet Prescott Spofford. AA
Music in the Rec Hut. Hubert Creekmore. WaP
Music in Venice. Louis Simpson. NYBP
Music Is Unevennesses. Geoffrey Lehmann. *Fr.* Ross's Poems. CBAP
Music lifting and falling. Aria. Rolfe Humphries. NYBP
Music! Lilting, soft and languorous. Music. Alice Dunbar-Nelson. BlSi
Music Makers, The. Arthur O'Shaughnessy. *See* Ode: "We are the music-makers."
Music met Leviathan returning, A. Peter Quennell. *Fr.* Leviathan. MoBrPo
Music of a Tree, The. W. J. Turner. MoBrPo
Music of Colours: The Blossom Scattered. Vernon Watkins. LiTB
Music of Colours—White Blossom. Vernon Watkins. LiTM; WaP
Music of Forefended Spheres, The. Coventry Patmore. *Fr.* The Victories of Love, I, ii. FaBoRV
(Fragment: "He that but once too nearly hears.") NBM
Music of His Steps, The, *with music.* Samuel Wakefield. AH
Music of Hungary. Anne Reeve Aldrich. AA
Music of the autumn winds sings low, The. Autumn. Edwin Curran. HBMV
Music of the Dawn. Virginia Bioren Harrison. HBV-1
Music of the dignity of souls, The. Crass Times Redeemed by Dignity of Souls. Peter Viereck. MiAP
Music of the Future, The. Oliver Herford. CenHV
Music of the Night. John Neal. AA
Music of the Spheres, The. Marvin Bell. PoA
Music on the Water. George Johnston. MoCV
Music stirs me, for you. Ricarda Huch, *tr. fr. German by* Susan C. Strong. PBWP
Music [*or* Musick], thou queen of heaven, care-charming spell. To Music: A Song. Robert Herrick. CaPo; UnS
Music, thou soul of heaven, care-charming spell. Music. Robert Herrick. CaPo
Music [*or* Musick] to hear, why hear'st thou music sadly? Sonnets, VIII. Shakespeare. ViBoPo
Music touches me with your hands, The. Leit. Marcos Rodríguez Frese, *tr. by* Julio Marzán. InW
Music was going on, The. At the Fillmore. Philip Levine. NNaP
Music, When Soft Voices Die. Shelley. FaBV; GTBS; GTBS-P; LiTB; NOBE; OBEV; OBRV; PAI; PCP; TreFT; TrGrPo; WHA
(Music.) CH
(To ———.) AWP; EnRP; FiP; HeIP; LoBV; NoP; OAEP; OBNC; PoEL-4; SeCePo; ViBoPo
Musica No. 3. Richard Duerden. NeAP
Musical Critic Anticipates Eternity, A. Siegfried Sassoon. UnS
Musical Instrument, A. Elizabeth Barrett Browning. EBVV; FaBoBe; FaPON; HBV-2; HBVY; NoP; OAEL-2; OAEP; OBEV; OBVV; OnMSP; WPE
(Great God Pan, The.) WiR
Musical Lion, The. Oliver Herford. OBCA; TDH
Musical Maiden, The. *Unknown.* TDH
Musical Orchard, The. Douglas Dunn. FaBoMo
Musical Shuttle. Harvey Shapiro. VWA
Musician. Louise Bogan. GoJo; NYBP
Musician at His Work, The. Robert Currie. Str
Musician Returning from a Cafe Audition, A. Michael D. Minard. AMV-80
Musicians wrestle everywhere. Emily Dickinson. UnS
Musick, thou Queen of Heaven, Care-charming-spel. *See* Music, thou queen of heaven . . .
Musick to heare, why hear'st thou musick sadly. *See* Music to hear . . .
Music's Duel. Richard Crashaw. GoTL; OAEL-1; PBBP
(Musick's Duell.) OBS; SeCP; SeCV-1
Music's Silver Sound. Shakespeare. *Fr.* Romeo and Juliet, IV, V. GN
Musing on [*or* of] roses and revolution[s]. Roses and Revolutions. Dudley Randall. BPo; CNA; ConAP; NIP; NoAM; PoBA; TAP
Musing upon the restles bisinesse [*or* restless bisynesse]. Prologue [*or* Anxious Thought]. Thomas Hoccleve. *Fr.* De Regimine Principum. OxBM; PoEL-1
Musings. William Barnes. HAP; NOBE; OBNC
Musk-ox smells, The. The Long River. Donald Hall. ConAP; LCAP; NePoEA-2
Musk Oxen. Igjugarjuk, *tr. fr. Eskimo.* WTO
Musketaquid. Emerson. AP
Muskogee's hokpi, The. The Sharpbreasted Snake. Louis (LittleCoon) Oliver. STE
Muskrat. *Unknown.* FSW
Muslims are still lying, The. The Lying Muslims. *Yoruba Oral Tradition, tr. by* Ulli Beier. WTO
Musophilus; or, Defence of All Learning, *sels.* Samuel Daniel.
English Poetry. OBSC
(Heavenly Eloquence.) NOBE
"How many thousands never heard the name." PP
O Blessed Letters. FaBoRV
Poet and Critic. OBSC
Muss I Denn (Must I Then). *Tr. fr. German.* FSW
Mussel Hunter at Rock Harbor. Sylvia Plath. NYBP
Musselburgh Field. *Unknown.* ESPB
Mussels. Mary Oliver. NU
Mussoorie and Chakrata Hill. The Hills. Julian Grenfell. HBV-1
Must/ All this aching. Alun Lewis. ELU
Must all successful rebels grow. 1912–1952, Full Cycle. Peter Viereck. OBAL
Must Be the Season of the Witch. Alurista, *tr. fr. Spanish by* Toni Empringham. FIA
Must delicate women die in vain. The Pill. Austin Clarke. TW
Must hapless man, in ignorance sedate. Celestial Wisdom. Juvenal, *tr. by* Samuel Johnson. AWP
Must I go bound and you go free. *Unknown.* WTO
Must I shoot the. Watts. Conrad Kent Rivers. BOLo; PoBA
Must I tell again. The Daemon. Louise Bogan. NYBP
Must I then, must I then leave the village today. Muss I Denn (Must I Then). *Tr. fr. German.* FSW
Must I then see, alas! eternal night. Elegy over a Tomb. Lord Herbert of Cherbury. AnAnS-2; EIL; FaBoEn; MeLP; MePo; NOBE; OBEV; OBS; PoEL-2; QFR; ViBoPo
Must noble Hastings immaturely die. Upon the Death of the Lord Hastings. Dryden. SeCV-2
Must then my crimes become thy scandal too? To Antenor. Katherine Philips. SBG
Must we part, Von Hügel, though much alike. W. B. Yeats. *Fr.* Vacillation. OBMV
Mustacheless Bard, A. J. Gordon Coogler. OBAL
Mustang Gray, *with music.* *Unknown.* CoSo
Mustapha, *sels.* Fulke Greville.
Chorus Primus: Wise Counsellors. OBS
Chorus Quintus: Tartarorum. OBS
Chorus Sacerdotum. FaBoEn; InvP; JCP; MePo; NOBE; OAEL-1; OBS; PoEL-1; PPP; SeCePo
(Chorus: "O wearisome condition of humanity.") ViBoPo
(O Wearisome Condition of Humanity.) HAP; LiTB; SeCeV
Chorus Tertius: Of Time; Eternitie. OBS
Eternity's Speech against Time, *sel.* JCP
Muster Out the Rangers. *Unknown.* CoSo
Mutability. Rupert Brooke. BrPo
Mutability. Shelley. EnRP; FaBoEn; HBV-2; NoP; OBNC; TEP; ViBoPo
Mutability ("For, all that from her springs, and is ybredde"). Spenser. *Fr.* The Faerie Queene. FaBoEn
Mutability ("When these were past, thus gan the Titanesse"). Spenser. *Fr.* The Faerie Queene. PoEL-1
"When I bethink me on that speech whilere," *sel.* OAEL-1; OxBoCH
Mutability. Wordsworth. Ecclesiastical Sonnets, Pt. III, Sonnet XXXIV. CABA; EBEV; EnRP; HeIP; InPK; LiTB; NOBE; NoP; OAEL-2; OBEV; OBRV; PoEL-4; PrIM; SeCeV
Mutations of the Phoenix, *sel.* Sir Herbert Read.
"Phoenix, bird of terrible pride." FaBoTw
Mute/ the hand moves from the heart. Miniatures IV. Lynn Strongin. IHMS
Mute bird sidles through soft valleys of air, A. Afternoon in Anglo-Ireland. Bruce Williamson. NeIP
Mute City, The. Lazer Eichenrand, *tr. fr. Yiddish by* Gabriel Preil *and* Howard Schwartz. VWA
Mute figures with bowed heads. The Refugees. Sir Herbert Read. BrPo
Mute he sat in the saddle—mute 'midst our full acclaim. A Christopher of the Shenandoah. Edith M. Thomas. PAH
Mute Is Thy Wild Harp, Now, O Bard Sublime! Charlotte Smith. SBG
Mute Opinion. Thomas Hardy. CMoP
Mute, sightless visitant. Helen Keller. Edmund Clarence Stedman. AA
Muted Screen of Graham Greene, The. Phyllis McGinley. FaBoEE
Mutes, The. Denise Levertov. IHMS; NaP; NOBA
Mutilated choir boys, The. Heine, *tr. by* Ezra Pound. *Fr.* Die Heimkehr. AWP
Mutilated Soldier, The. David Fisher. NPGG
Mutter sagt, Die, "Nau Lieschen listen here." Mama's Advice. Kurt M. Stein. InMe
Muttering at the crowd, indifferent. The Death of an Old Man. Michael Hamburger. NePoEA
Mutterings over the Crib of a Deaf Child. James Wright. LCAP; PoPl
Mutton. *Unknown.* BXAP

Mutton and Leather. *Unknown.* CoMu
Mutual Congratulations of the Poets Anna Seward and Hayley, The. Richard Porson. FaBoEE; OBSV
Mutual Forgiveness of each Vice. For the Sexes; the Gates of Paradise. Blake. LiTB; PoEL-4
Mutual Love. William Hammond. JCP
Mutual Problem. William Cole. OBAL; POL
Mutual Subjection. Christopher Smart. Hymns for the Amusement of Children, Hymn 26. NOCV
(Consideration for Others.) OxBChV
Muvver was barfin' 'er biby one night, A. "Biby's" Epitaph. *Unknown.* FiBHP
Muzzle and jowl and beastly brow. Fearfull Symmetry. Basil Bunting. PoA
Muzzy with drink, I let my humor recline. The Ghost of an Education. James Michie. NYBP
Mwilu/ or Poem for the Living. Don L. Lee. JB
My/ father/ dreams. The Eyes of Flesh. Sandra Hochman. NMM
My/ soul is a witness for my Lord. Who'll Be a Witness for My Lord? *Unknown.* BoAN-1
My absent daughter—gentle, gentle maid. A Living Memory. William Augustus Croffut. AA
My accountant father. Sum. James Nolan. Str
My Ace of Spades. Ted Joans. BOLo
My adored statue. The Arid Husband. E. L. T. Mesens. EAS
My Africa. Michael Dei-Anang. PBA
My age fallen away like white swaddling. Age. Philip Larkin. CMoP
My age is three hundred and seventy-two. The Sleepy Giant. Charles Edward Carryl. OnUR
My aged friend, Miss Wilkinson. The Bards. Walter de la Mare. DTC; FaBoNo; NOBL; PV
My Aim. George Linnaeus Banks. *See* What I Live For.
My Ain Countree. Mary Lee Demarest. HBV-2; TRV; WGRP
My Ain Fireside. Elizabeth Hamilton. FaBoBe; HBV-2
My Ain Kind Dearie, O. Burns. GoTS
(Lea Rig, The.) BSV
My Ain Wife. Alexander Laing. HBV-1
My Airedale Dog. W. L. Mason. SoPo
My Alba. Allen Ginsberg. NoAM; NOBA
My ambition as I remember and. Love at Roblin Lake. Al Purdy. NoP
My America. Oliver La Grone. NNP
My American host in Madras in his moist air-conditioned apartment. Americans Are Afraid of Lizards. Karl Shapiro. AmFN
My ancestor was called on to go out. Wind at Your Door, The. Robert D. FitzGerald. PoAu-2
My ancestors were fine, long men. Square-toed Princes. Robert P. Tristram Coffin. AmFN
My Angel. Jonathan Henderson Brooks. PoNe
My Angel. Philip Levine. AMV-81
My Angeline. Harry B. Smith. InMe
My anguish, my anguish! I writhe in pain! The End of the World. Bible, *O.T. Fr.* Jeremiah. PPON
My Anna! though thine earthly steps are done. Frederick Goddard Tuckerman. Sonnets, II, xxxiv. AP
My Anna! When for her my head was bowed. Frederick Goddard Tuckerman. Sonnets, II, xxxi. AP
My annals have it so. Emus. Mary Fullerton. BoAnP; PoAu-1
My answer would have to be music. The Medium. Elaine Feinstein. BrRo
My April Lady. Henry van Dyke. HBV-1
My ardors for emprize nigh lost. On an Invitation to the United States. Thomas Hardy. AWP
My Arkansas. Maya Angelou. BlSi
My arm sweeps down. Gesture. Donald Finkel. InPK
My arms are [a]round you, and I lean. To the Oaks of Glencree. J. M. Synge. ELU; MoBrPo; OxBI
My arms smell good. Think. Please Forward. James Welch. CDW
My arms were always quiet. Gesture. Winifred Welles. HBMV
My aspens dear, whose airy cages quelled. Binsey Poplars [Felled 1879]. Gerard Manley Hopkins. BoNaP; BrPo; CoBMV; EBVV; ELP; FaBoPP; InPS; MoVE; NoAM; NoP; PAI; VLP
My Atlas Poet. George Bowering. NeAC
My attention is a wild/ animal. Pet Panther. A. R. Ammons. NoP
My Atthis, although our dear Anaktoria. Sappho, *tr. fr. Greek by* Willis Barnstone. BoWoP
My attire is noiseless when I tread the earth. Wild Swan. *Unknown, tr. by* Charles W. Kennedy. *Fr.* Riddles (Exeter Book). AnOE
My Auld Wife. *Unknown.* GBP
My Aunt. Oliver Wendell Holmes. AmPP; HBV-1; TAP; TreFS
My Aunt. Ted Hughes. WSC
My Aunt. Peggy Wood. POL
My Aunt Bebe. The Aga Khan. Steve Orlen. Psk
My aunt Beulah said to me. Aunt Beulah's Wisdom. Earl Gene Box. LFAC
My aunt! my dear unmarried aunt! My Aunt. Oliver Wendell Holmes. AmPP; HBV-1; TAP; TreFS
My aunt she died a month ago. Death of My Aunt. *Unknown.* OxBoLi
My aunt was an herb doctor. To-ta Ti-om. Peter Blue Cloud. STE
My aunts washed dishes while the uncles. Paper Matches. Paulette Jiles. NOBC
"My author and disposer, what thou biddest." Thus Eve to Adam. Milton. *Fr.* Paradise Lost, IV. FaBV
My Autumn Walk. Bryant. AA
My Babe My Babe. *Unknown.* BluL
My Babes in the Wood. Sarah Morgan Bryan Piatt. AA
My baby ain't good looking and she don't dress fine. Robbing and Stealing Blues. *Unknown.* BluL
My baby done quit me. Squabbling Blues. *Unknown.* BluL
My Baby Has No Name Yet. Kim Nam-jo, *tr. fr. Korean by* Ko Won. PBWP
My bands of silk and miniver. Full Moon. Elinor Wylie. CrMA; MoAmPo; SBG; VGW
My banks they are furnished with bees. The Shepherd's Home. William Shenstone. *Fr.* Pastoral Ballad. BoNaP; GN
My Baptismal Birthday. Samuel Taylor Coleridge. NOCV
My Barbaric Yawp. Walt Whitman. *Fr.* Song of Myself. NePA
("Spotted hawk swoops by and accuses me, The.") BiP; NOP; PP
My barefoot steps lie broad and big. Spring. Moishe Kulbak, *tr. by* Ruth Whitman. VWA
My Baselard. *Unknown.* OxBM
My beak is bent downward, I burrow below. Plow. *Unknown, tr. by* Charles W. Kennedy. *Fr.* Riddles (Exeter Book). AnOE
My Beautiful Lady. Thomas Woolner. OBVV
My beautiful! my beautiful! that standest meekly by. The Arab to His Favorite Steed [*or* The Arab's Farewell to His Horse]. Caroline Norton. BeLS; BLPA; PaPo; TreFS
My beautiful picture of pirates and treasure. Jigsaw Puzzle. Russell Hoban. NTCP
My beauty is not wine to me. The Song of the Narcissus. *Unknown, tr. by* E. Powys Mathers. *Fr.* The Thousand and One Nights. AWP
My Beauty, My Love, You Have Bound Me. Heine, *tr. fr. German by* Meno Spann. NAWM-2
My Bed. Lucy Sprague Mitchell. SoPo
My Bed Is a Boat ("My bed is like a little boat"). Robert Louis Stevenson. HBV-1; HBVY; TreFS
My bed rocks me gently. Aubade. Dilys Laing. NMP
My bed will fold up where I fold. David McCord. Convalescence, III. WhC
My belly joined the Belly Potential Movement. Psychology Today. Judson Jerome. AMV-81
My Beloved Is Mine, and I Am His; He Feedeth among the Lillies. Francis Quarles. *Fr.* Emblems. MePo; NOBE; OBS; TrGrPo, *abr.*
(Canticle.) FaBoEn
(Divine Rapture.) HBV-2; LO; OBEV
(E'en like Two Little Bank-dividing Brooks.) MeLP
My beloved land. Minority Report. John Updike. GOA
My beloved spake, and said unto me. For, Lo, the Winter Is Past. Bible, *O.T. Fr.* Song of Solomon. TreF
My best belovit brother of the band. To R. Hudson. Alexander Montgomerie. OxBS
My best Christmases. The Day before Christmas. Raymond Souster. PeCV
My Best Clothes. Eli Netser, *tr. fr. Hebrew by* Bernhard Frank. AMV-81
My best friend's name is Billy. Puzzle. Arnold Spilka. RHPC
My Betsey-Jane, it would not do. To Betsey-Jane, on Her Desiring to Go Incontinently to Heaven. Helen Parry Eden. HBMV
My better half, why turn a peevish scold. Epigram. Martial. PeHV
My Bible and I. *Unknown.* STF
My bibliography has grown. Epilogue. Dallas Wiebe. TW
My Bird. "Fanny Forester." AA
My Bird-wrung Youth. Patrick Anderson. PeCV
My Birth. Minot Judson Savage. AA; WGRP
My Birth-Day. Thomas Moore. HBV-1
My birthdays take so long to start. Between Birthdays. Ogden Nash. OnUR
"My birth-day"—what a different sound. My Birth-Day. Thomas Moore. HBV-1
My Bishop's Eyes. *Unknown.* WhC
My Black Gal Blues. *Unknown.* BluL
My black hills have never seen the sun rising. Shancoduff. Patrick Kavanagh. BIrV; CIP; FaBoTw; IPY; NoP; OxBI
My Black Mama. *Unknown.* BluL
My black mothers I hear them singing. Black Star Line. Henry Dumas. CNA

My black-eyed lover broke my back. The Masochist. Maxine W. Kumin. IHMS; PoA
My Blackness is the Beauty of this Land. Lance Jeffers. NBP; PoBA
My Blessed Lord, how doth thy Beautious Spouse. Edward Taylor. *Fr.* Preparatory Meditations: Second Series, CL. SCAP
My blessed mother dozing in her chair. A Valentine to My Mother. Christina Rossetti. OHIP
My Blessing Be on Waterford. Winifred M. Letts. HBMV
My blessing on the patient cows. A Blessing on the Cows. "Seumas O'Sullivan." BoAnP
My blood so red. The Call. *Unknown.* OBEV
My bloodstream chokes on gall and spleen. Quatrain. Barend Toerien. PeSA
My boat goes west, yours east. Farewell. Chao Li-hua, *tr. by* J. P. Seaton. BoWoP
My boat is on the shore. To Thomas Moore. Byron. EnRP; OAEP; TreFT
My boat sails downstream. Love Song. *Unknown, tr. by* J. E. Manchip White. TTY
My Body. Rachel Korn, *tr. fr. Yiddish by* Ruth Whitman. VWA
My body a rounded stone. Living Tenderly. May Swenson. BoAnP; OBCA
My body answers you, my blood. Music of Hungary. Anne Reeve Aldrich. AA
My body being dead, my limbs unknown. The Preparative. Thomas Traherne. AnAnS-1; OxBoCh; PoEL-2
My body, eh? Friend Death, how now? Habeas Corpus. Helen Hunt Jackson. AA; WGRP
My body holds its shape. The genius is intact. Mummy of a Lady Named Jemutesonekh XXI Dynasty. Thomas James. AmPA
My Body in the Walls Captived. Sir Walter Ralegh. SeCePo; SiPS
My body is like/ a field wasted by winter. On Seeing the Field Being Singed. Lady Ise, *tr. by* Etsuko Terasaki *and* Irma Brandeis. BoWoP
My body is made of waves and foam. Sea-Games. Aliza Shenhar, *tr. by* Linda Zisquit. VWA
My body is weary to death of my mischievous brain. Nebuchadnezzar. Elinor Wylie. MoAmPo; SBG
My body knows it will never bear children. Waiting. Jane Cooper. TAP
My body's like a tree trunk in the wood. My Body. Rachel Korn, *tr. by* Ruth Whitman. VWA
My body's passion-hide. Two Times Two Is Four. H. Leivick, *tr. by* Ruth Whitman. VWA
My Bonie Mary. Burns. *See* Silver Tassie, The.
My Bonnie Highland Laddie. Burns. *See* As I Came O'er Cairney Mount.
My Bonnie Lies over the Ocean. *Unknown.* FSW
My Bonnie Mary. Burns. *See* Silver Tassie, The.
My Bonny Black Bess ("Dick Turpin bold! Dick, hie away"). *Unknown. See* Dick Turpin's Ride.
My Bonny Black Bess ("Let the lover his mistress's beauty rehearse"). *Unknown.* ViBoFo
My bonny keel laddie, my canny keel laddie. The Bonny Keel Laddie. *Unknown.* GBP
My bonny lass, thine eye. Love's Witchery. Thomas Lodge. ElL
My bonny moorhen, my bonny moorhen. The Bonny Moorhen. *Unknown.* GBP
My Book of Life. Frances Humphrey. STF
My Books. Longfellow. AA
My Books I'd Fain Cast Off, I Cannot Read. Henry David Thoreau. AP
My Boots. Henry David Thoreau. PeD
My boy Kree? Kree. A. C. Gordon. AA
My Boy Tammy. Hector MacNeill. CH
My boy was scarcely ten years auld. Leesome Brand. *Unknown.* ESPB
My boyhood went: it went where went the trace. Lost Years. Eugene Lee-Hamilton. OBVV
My brain is like the ravaged shores—the sand. At Night. Frances Cornford. MoBrPo
My Breath. Orpingalik, *tr. fr. Eskimo by* K. Rasmussen. WTO
My brethren all attend. The Zealous Puritan. *Unknown.* OBS
"My brethren. . ." And a bland, elastic smile. The Evangelist. Donald Davie. NePoEA
"My bride is not coming, alas!" says the groom. At the Altar-Rail. Thomas Hardy. *Fr.* Satires of Circumstance. MoAB; MoBrPo
My Brigantine. James Fenimore Cooper. *Fr.* The Water Witch, *ch.* 15. AA; EtS; MOS
My Brother. Dorothy Aldis. SoPo; TiPo
My Brother. Marci Ridlon. RHPC
My Brother, Beautiful Shinault, That Goat. David Huddle. GrPl
My Brother Ben's face, thought Eugene. Ben. Thomas Wolfe. NCSH
My Brother Bert. Ted Hughes. RHPC
My brother Cain, the wounded, liked to sit. Abel. Demetrios Capetanakis. GTBS-P; WaaP
My brother came back from the field. My Brother Was Silent. Amir Gilboa, *tr. by* Shirley Kaufman. VWA
My brother came home from a Princeton club. Eastward to Eden. Edgar Bogardus. POL
My brother has on/ a thin robe. Lady Otomo of Sakanone, *tr. fr. Japanese by* Willis Barnstone. BoWoP
My brother is inside the sheet. My Brother. Dorothy Aldis. SoPo; TiPo
My brother is skull and skeleton now. Epitaph. William Montgomerie. OxBS; POL
My brother Jack was nine in May. The Baby's Debut. Horace Smith *and* James Smith. OBRV; Par
My brother knows the man. An Example of How a Daily Temporary Madness Can Help a Man Get the Job Done. John Stone. TAT
My brother was not a camel driver. On Her Brother. Al-Khansa, *tr. by* Willis Barnstone. BoWoP
My Brother Was Silent. Amir Gilboa, *tr. fr. Hebrew by* A. C. Jacobs. VWA
My Brothers. Anna Walters. VoR
My brother's worth about two cents. My Brother. Marci Ridlon. RHPC
My brow with pain is often coryougated. Take Nothing for Granite. Nate Salsbury. InMe
My brudder sittin' on de tree of life. Roll, Jordan, Roll. *Unknown.* AA
My bully boys of Liverpool. The Banks of Newfoundland. *Unknown.* GBP
My Burial Place. Robinson Jeffers. AP
My Buried Friends. *Unknown.* AmFP
My business is words. Words are like labels. Said the Poet to the Analyst. Anne Sexton. TwAmPo
My button gloves are very white. Easter Parade. Marchette Chute. SiSoSe
My Cabinets Are Oyster-Shells. Margaret Cavendish, Duchess of Newcastle. *Fr.* The Convent of Pleasure. ELP
(Song: "My cabinets are oyster-shells.") WPE
My calm and herculean dad. Gaiety of Descendants. Douglas Newton. NeBP
My camel kneels at Ibn Marwan's door. Camel. Laila Akhyaliyya, *tr. by* Willis Barnstone. BoWoP
My Camping Ground. Morris Rosenfeld, *tr. fr. Yiddish by* Aaron Kramer. TrJP
My Candidate. Norman H. Crowell. YaD
My candle burns at both ends. First Fig. Edna St. Vincent Millay. *Fr.* Figs from Thistles. FaBV; FaFP; FF; FPL; NoAM; NoP; PoA; PoLF; TAP
My canoe slowly drifting downriver. Moose. Robert Wiljer. AMV-81
My Captain. Dorothea Day. BLPA
My cares draw on mine everlasting night. To Delia, XXX. Samuel Daniel. OBSC
My cartridge belt is empty. The Huntsman. John Wheelwright. CrMA
My cat/Is quiet. Cat. Dorothy W. Baruch. SoPo; SUS; TiPo
My Cat and I. Roger McGough. OxBTC; POL
My cat can look at a king. No-Kings and the Calling of Spirits. Nancy Willard. LCAP
My Cat Jeoffry [*or* Jeoffrey]. Christopher Smart. *See* For I Will Consider My Cat Jeoffry.
My cat jumps to the window sill. Waiting for It. May Swenson. BoAnP
My cat was a southerner and a lady. A Farewell. Hildegarde Flanner. AMV-81
My cat, washing her tail's tip, is a whorl. Cat on Couch. Barbara Howes. DFF; NCSH
My Catbird. William Henry Venable. AA; HBV-1
My Cats. Stevie Smith. FaBoNo
My cellpartner quick. Freedom. J. Charles Green. LFAC
My chant must enclose hell. The Tusks of Blood. Samuel Greenberg. MoPo
My cheap toy lamp. Child's Song. Robert Lowell. NMP
My cherrystones! I prize them. Precious Stones. Charles Stuart Calverley. InMe
My Child. Susan Griffin. NPGG
My Child. John Pierpont. AA; HBV-1
My child and I hold hands on the way to school. September, the First Day of School. Howard Nemerov. GLGT; OxBC
My child came to me with the equinox. The Storm-Child. May Byron. HBV-1
My child deep in the/ snow of illusion. My Child. Susan Griffin. NPGG
My child, my sister, dream. Invitation to the Voyage. Baudelaire, *tr. by* Richard Wilbur. NAWM-2
My child, the Duck-billed Plat-y-pus. The Platypus. Oliver Herford. FiBHP; NA
My child, we were two children. Mein Kind, wir waren Kinder. Heine, *tr. by* Elizabeth Barrett Browning. AWP; OBVE; TrJP
My childhood all a myth. The Myth. Edwin Muir. CMoP
My childhood is a sphere. Childhood. Thomas Traherne. TrGrPo
My childhood was like a dark passage. Intimations. Alma Johanna Koenig, *tr. by* Edouard Roditi. VWA

My Childhood's Bedroom. Charles Tisdale. AMV-80
My childhood's home I see again. Memory. Abraham Lincoln. BLPA; FaBoBe; FPL; WBLP
My children, my little dears. The Mother Crab and Her Family. L. T. Manyase, *tr. by* Jack Cope *and* C. M. Mcanyangwa. PeSA
My children! speak not ill of one another. To Poets. Walter Savage Landor. ViBoPo
My Children's Book. John N. Morris. AMV-80
My Chinese uncle, gouty, deaf, half-blinded. Grotesques. Robert Graves. CMoP
My Christmas gifts were few: to one. To a Lady. Thomas William Parsons. AA
My Christmas; Mum's Christmas. Sarah Forsyth. OBCP
My Church ("My church has but one temple"). "E. O. G." BLPA; SoSe
My City. James Weldon Johnson. BANP; CDC; PoNe
My city, my beloved, my white! Ah slender. N.Y. Ezra Pound. NYP
My city slept. The Beginning of a Long Poem on Why I Burned the City. Lawrence Benford. NBP; TTY
My clear-cut heart, my tender soul. Jules Laforgue, *tr. by* William Jay Smith. *Fr.* Asides from the Clowns. PoPl
My Cleo's blush is tender, slow. Tender, Slow. *Unknown, tr. by* Wallace Rice. ErPo
My closest and dearest! Dirge on the Death of Art O'Leary. "Dark Eileen," *tr. by* Eleanor Hull. AnIV
My clothes are silent when I walk on the earth. Riddle: Mute Swan. *Unknown.* PBBP
My clothing was once of the linsey woolsey fine. Poor Old Horse. *Unknown.* CH
My clumsiest dear, whose hands shipwreck vases. Love Poem. John Frederick Nims. FF; HoPM; InPK; MiAP; SoSe
My coachman, in the moonlight there. Without and Within. James Russell Lowell. HBV-1
My Cobra Girl. *Gond Oral Tradition, tr. by* V. Elwin *and* S. Hivale. WTO
My cock? Chicken. Dennis Kelly. PeHV
My Coffin Is a Deckchair. Rodney Hall. *Fr.* Black Bagatelles. CBAP
My comforts drop and melt away like snow. The Answer. George Herbert. FaBoRV; TEP
My Companion. Charles Wesley. STF
My Company. Sir Herbert Read. BrPo; MMA
My Comrade. Edwin Markham. AA
My Comrade. James Jeffrey Roche. AA
My conscience has given me several twitches. To My Cousin Mary, for Mending My Tobacco Pouch. Francis Scott Key. OBAL
My couch lay in a ruined Hall. A Dream. Emily Bronte. NBM
My counterpane is soft as silk. A Child's Song of Christmas. Marjorie Pickthall. HBV-1; HBVY; YeAr
My Country. Dorothea MacKellar. PoAu-1
My Country, *sels.* George Edward Woodberry.
"O destined Land, unto thy citadel." AA
O Land Beloved. PAH
My country is not a country. Envoi. Eli Mandel. NOBC
My Country Is the World. Robert Whitaker. PGD
My country need not change her gown. Emily Dickinson. AmFN; GOA
My Country, Right! Thomas Curtis Clark. PGD
"My country, 'tis of thee." Assembly: Harlem School. Eugene T. Maleska. GoYe
My country 'tis of thee. America. Samuel Francis Smith. AA; BLSo; FaBoBe; FaFP; FaPON; HBV-2; HBVY; PAL; PoLF; PSoN; TreF; WBLP; YaD
My country, 'tis of thee./ Land where things used to be. New National Anthem. *Unknown.* CoSo
My country 'tis of thee./ Sweet land of felony. Ambrose Bierce. YaD
My Country, to Thy Shore, *with music.* Theodore Chickering Williams. AH
My countryman, the poet, wears a Stetson. David Wright. *Fr.* Seven South African Poems. PeSA
My countrymen have now become too base. April 1962. Paul Goodman. NMP; VGW
My coursers are fed with the lightning. Shelley. *Fr.* Prometheus Unbound. OBRV
My Cousin Agueda. Ramón López Velarde, *tr. fr. Spanish by* Samuel Beckett. OBVE
My Cousin German came from France. *Unknown.* FaBoCh
My cousins, lean hunters. Love Lifted Me. Paris Leary. CoPo
My Cow. Howard McCord. GP
My Creed. Alice Cary. WGRP
My Creed. Jeanette Gilder. WGRP
My Creed. Howard Arnold Walter. FaFP; PoLF; WBLP
(I Would Be True.) TRV
My Crime. *Unknown.* BluL
My Cross. Zitella Cocke. HBV-2
My crown desired, my true love and joy. A Love Letter to Elizabeth Thatcher. Thomas Thatcher. SCAP
My curse be on the day when first I saw. Sonnet: To the Lady Pietra degli Scrovigni. Dante, *tr. by* Dante Gabriel Rossetti. AWP
My cuticles are a mess. Oh honey, by the way. The Motorcyclists. James Tate. MAYP
My Dad and Mam They Did Agree. *Unknown.* POL
My dad gave me one dollar bill. Smart. Shel Silverstein. RHPC
My dad was a soldier and fought in the wars. The Hero. Leroy F. Jackson. SiSoSe
My daddie is a cankert carle. Low Doun in the Broom. *Unknown.* BSV; GoTS
My daddy come home this morning drunk as he could be. Don't Fish in My Sea. *Unknown.* BluL
My daddy don't know. For Sapphires. Carolyn M. Rodgers. CNA
My Daddy has paid the rent. Good Times. Lucille Clifton. AmNP; AmPA; BPo; CNA; FF; GrPl; InPS; NCSH; PAI; PoBA; TAP; TwCP
My daddy is an engineer. Wanderin'. *Unknown.* AS
My Daddy smells like tobacco and books. Smells (Junior). Christopher Morley. TiPo
My Dad's Dinner Pail. Edward Harrigan. BLPA
My Daily Creed. *Unknown.* TRV
(Creed, A.) STF
My Daily Prayer. Eva Gray. STF
My Daily Prayer. Grenville Kleiser. BLRP
My dame hath a lame tame crane. *Unknown.* OxNR
My Damon was the first to wake. Meeting. George Crabbe. HBV-1; LO; OBEV
My Dancing Day. *Unknown.* OxBoLi
("Tomorrow shall be my dancing day.") PoEL-1
My dancing is, in my opinion, good. Of Dancing. Alan Brownjohn. FaBoMo
My Daphne's hair is twisted gold. A Song of Daphne to the Lute [*or* Apollo's Song, *or* Daphne]. John Lyly. *Fr.* Midas. EIL; HBV-1; OBSC
My Dark Fathers. Brendan Kennelly. BIrV; CIP
My dark-headed Käthchen, my spit-kitten darling. Song. John Manifold. DTC
My darkling child the stars have obeyed. George Barker. *Fr.* To My Son. MP; TwCP
My Darling Dear, My Daisy Flower. John Skelton. EnRePo; HAP; NoP
(Lullay, Lullay.) PoEL-1
(Sleeper Hood-winked, The.) MeEL
(With Lullay, Lullay, like a Child.) InvP; NCEP
("With, Lullay, lullay, lyke a chylde.") AAS
My darling little fishing rods. A Song of Satisfaction on Completing an Overhauling of Fishing Tackle. Leslie P. Thompson. WhC
My darling, we sat together. Mein Liebchen, wir sassen zusammen. Heine, *tr. by* James Thomson. AWP
My Darling's on the Deep Blue Sea. *Unknown.* AmFP
My daughter, at eleven. Little Girl, My Stringbean, My Lovely Woman. Anne Sexton. NYBP
My daughter, Blake, is in kindergarten. Poop. Gerald Locklin. Str
My daughter cries, and I. Child Crying. Anthony Thwaite. NePoEA-2
My daughter cries when we have to talk about money. The Money Cry. Peter Davison. FYAP
My daughter denies she is like me. Breaking Tradition. Janice Mirikitani. BrSi
My daughter has given me a grandchild. Celebration. Elizabeth Newton Sachs. AMV-81
My daughter is drawing a picture. Art Work. Ronald Wallace. PPJ
My Daughter Louise. Homer Greene. HBV-1
My daughter plays on the floor. Spelling. Margaret Atwood. NoP
My daughter pleads with me. Chile. Susan Griffin. NPGG
My daughter's heavier. Light leaves are flying. John Berryman. *Fr.* Dream Songs. CAPP
My day and night are in my lady's hand. Rondeau Redoublé. John Payne. HBV-1
My day was filled with many things. Crowded Out. Florence White Willett. STF
My Days among the Dead Are Passed [*or* Past]. Robert Southey. EnRP; HBV-2; OBRV; TEP; TreFT
(His Books.) OBEV
(Scholar, The.) GTBS; GTBS-P
My Days are Gliding Swiftly By, *with music.* David Nelson. AH
My days are in the yellow leaf. Byron. *Fr.* On This Day I Complete My Thirty-sixth Year. TRV
My days' delights, my springtime joys fordone. A Poem Entreating of Sorrow. Sir Walter Ralegh. SiPS
My Days Have Been So Wondrous Free, *with music.* *Unknown.* TrAS
My Days of Love are Over. Byron. *Fr.* Don Juan. FaBoEn; OBNC
My Dead. Frederick Lucian Hosmer. WGRP
My Dead. Rachel, *tr. fr. Hebrew by* Robert Mezey. VWA

My dead Love came to me, and said. The Apparition. Stephen Phillips. OBEV; OBVV
My dear ———:/ I do thank you. Letter for Melville 1951. Charles Olson. CoPo
My dear,/ Today a letter from Berlin. A Letter from Berlin. Jon Stallworthy. NoAM; OBWP; OxBC
My Dear and Only Love. James Graham, Marquess of Montrose. BSV; CavP; JCP; LO; OBS
(I'll Never Love Thee More.) GBL; HBV-1; NOBE; OBEV; PoPle
(Montrose to His Mistress.) LoBV; OxBS, 2 *sts.;* ViBoPo
My dear brother Ned. The *South Carolina.* *Unknown.* PAH
My dear child, first thyself enable. The Boy Serving at Table. John Lydgate. OxBChV
My dear companion, and my faithful friend! An Address to His Elbow-Chair, New Cloath'd. William Somervile. OBEC
My dear Daddie bought a mansion. The Little Bird. Walter de la Mare. NAs
My dear, darkened in sleep turned from the moon. To Judith Asleep. John Ciardi. LiTM; MiAP
My dear deaf father, how I loved him then. John Betjeman. *Fr.* Summoned by Bells. OxBTC
My dear, do you know. The Babes in the Wood. *Unknown.* OxBChV; PBBP
My dear, do you remember that country. Remember That Country. Jean Garrigue. VGW
My dear, dumb friend, low lying there. To My Dog "Blanco." Josiah Gilbert Holland. PoLF
"My dear fellow!" said the great poet. Fiction: A Message. Gavin Ewart. OxBC
My dear, I wonder if before the end. To D——, Dead by Her Own Hand. Howard Nemerov. PoA
My Dear Lady. *Unknown.* ElL
My dear little crane. A Pet Crane. *Unknown, tr. by* Myles Dillon. AnIL
My dear Mr. Murray. Epistle to Mr. Murray. Byron. FaBoUs
My dear Mistress has a heart. A Song. Earl of Rochester. HBV-1; LoBV; SeCV-2
My dear, my dear, I know. To a Young Girl. W. B. Yeats. EBEV; OLR
My dear, naïve, ingenuous child. Don't Say You Like Tchaikowsky. Paul Rosner. FiBHP
My dear, observe the rose! though she desire it. Elegy IX. William Bell. NePoEA
My Dear Son John's deceas'd ah! gone from hence. A Brief Elegie on My Dear Son John. John Saffin. SCAP
My dear Telemachus,/ The Trojan War. Odysseus to Telemachus. Joseph Brodsky, *tr. by* George L. Kline. PAI
My dear, the time has come to say. A Song of Parting. Compton Mackenzie. HBV-1; OBVV
My dear, when I was very young. To a Lady on Her Marriage. William Bell. NePoEA
My dearely loved friend how oft have we. *See* My dearly loved friend . . .
My dearest Betty, my more lovéd heart. Phineas Fletcher. *Fr.* Elisa, or an Elegy upon the Unripe Decease of Sir Antony Irby. ViBoPo
My dearest dear, the time draws near. The Lover's Lament. *Unknown.* AS
My dearest dust, could not thy hasty day. Epitaph on the Monument of Sir William Dyer at Colmworth, 1641. Lady Catherine Dyer. *Fr.* Sir William Dyer, Knight. BoLoP; EnLoPo; NIP
My dearest love! when thou and I must part. The Legacy. Henry King. AnAnS-2
My Dearest Mistress. *Unknown.* EnRePo
My dearest Rival, least our Love. Sir John Suckling. MeLP
My Dearling. Elizabeth Akers Allen. AA
My dearly [*or* dearely] loved friend, how oft have we. To My Most Dearly-loved Friend, Henry Reynolds, Esquire, of Poets and Poesy. Michael Drayton. AnAnS-2; OAEP; OBS
First Steps Up Parnassus, *sel.* NOBE
My dears, 'tis said in days of old. The Bee, the Ant, and the Sparrow. Nathaniel Cotton. OxBChV
My Death. A. J. M. Smith. OBCV
My Death. Carl Zuckmayer, *tr. fr. German by* E. B. Ashton. TrJP
My death was arranged by special plans in Heaven. A New England Bachelor. Richard Eberhart. MoAmPo; NoAM
My debt to you, Belovèd. Debts. Jessie B. Rittenhouse. HBMV
My Definition of Poetry. Douglas Blazek. LTB
My Delight. Gamaliel Bradford. HBMV
My Delight and Thy Delight. Robert Bridges. CMoP; HBV-1; NBM; NOBE; OAEP; OBEV; PoEL-5
My Descendants. W. B. Yeats. *Fr.* Meditations in Time of Civil War, IV. LiTB
My desire for revenge, the bitterness. Till Death Do Us Part. Leila Miccolis, *tr. by* Willis Barnstone *and* Nelson Cerqueira. BoWoP
My desk's at the back of the class. The Marrog. R. C. Scriven. AmMo; RHPC
"My deth I love, my lif ich hate." A Cleric Courts His Lady [*or* De Clerico et Puella]. *Unknown.* MeEL; OxBM
My Didyma is dark, but I aspire. Didyma. *Unknown, tr. by* Louis Untermeyer. UnTE
My Dim-wit Cousin. Theodore Roethke. DFF
My dishes went unwashed today. Labor Not in Vain. *Unknown.* STF
My dismal sister! Couldst thou know. "Lewis Carroll." *Fr.* Melancholetta. FiBHP
My Dog. John Kendrick Bangs. BLPA; BLPL; FaBoBe
My Dog. Marchette Chute. FaPON; PDV; SoPo; TiPo
My Dog. Tom Robinson. SoPo
My Dog Dash. John Ruskin. FM
My Dog I was ever well pleased to see. My Dog Tray. John Bryon. SeCePo
My Dog Jock. Hayden Carruth. FAZ
My dog lay dead five days without a grave. The Pardon. Richard Wilbur. NePoEA; NIP; NoAM; NOBA; NoP; PAI
My dog listens when I talk. My Dog. Tom Robinson. SoPo
My Dog Ponto. Edgar Lee Masters. FM
My Dog Tray. John Bryon. SeCePo
My dog's so furry I've not seen. The Hairy Dog. Herbert Asquith. FaPON; PDV; RHPC; SoPo; SUS; TiPo
My dolour is ane cup. Ressaif My Saul. R. Crombie Saunders. OxBS
My Dolphin, you only guide me by surprise. Dolphin. Robert Lowell. NOBA
My Donkey. Rose Fyleman. TiPo
My Doves. Elizabeth Barrett Browning. VLP
My Dream. Lew Blockcolski. VoR
My Dream. Christina Rossetti. BrRo; VLP
My Dream. *Unknown.* NA
My dream a drink with Lonnie Johnson. Sonnet. Ted Berrigan. NoAM
My dreams are so full of longing. Longing. Rachel Korn, *tr. by* Ruth Whitman. VWA
My Dreams by Henry James. Michael Ryan. SV
My Dreams, My Works, Must Wait Till after Hell. Gwendolyn Brooks. NoP
My dreams wear thinner as the years go by. The Years. John Hall Wheelock. CrMA
My Drinking Song. Richard Dehmel, *tr. fr. German by* Ludwig Lewisohn. AWP
My drooping eyelids veil waking. To Sleep. Barbara Fialkowski. AMV-81
My drum, hollowed out thru the thin slit. La Chute. Charles Olson. InPK; PAI
My duchess was the werst she laffed she bitte. Sonnet. Ernest Walsh. ErPo
My dugout canoe goes. Paddling Song. *Unknown, tr. by* Max Exner. PBA
My ear, still keyed to summer, failed to label. Partial Draft. Robert B. Shaw. AMV-81
My Early Home. John Clare. HBV-2; PoLF
My Education. James Kenneth Stephen. WhC
My Elbow Ancestry. Larry Mollin. NeAC
My embarrassment at his nakedness. The Pool. Robert Creeley. CoAP
My Enemy. Alice Williams Brotherton. AA
My enemy came nigh. Hate. James Stephens. MoAB; MoBrPo; OBVV
My enemy had bidden me as guest. The Compassionate Fool. Norman Cameron. GTBS-P; OxBTC
My enemy is dead. The news arrived. Enemy, Enemy. Cecil J. Mullins. AMV-80
My Epitaph. H. J. Daniel. FaBoEE
My Epitaph. David Gray. EBVV; OBVV
My Erotic Double. John Ashbery. LCAP
My Estate. John Drinkwater. HBMV
My Evening Prayer. Charles H. Gabriel. BLPA; FaBoBe
My eye cried and woke me. The Night. Al-Khansa, *tr. by* Willis Barnstone. BoWoP
My eye descending from the hill surveys. The Thames from Cooper's Hill. Sir John Denham. *Fr.* Cooper's Hill. OAEL-1; OBS; SeCePo; ViBoPo
My eye is not on Calvary, nor on Bethlehem the Blessed. Sorley Maclean. *Fr.* Dain Eile. NeBP
My eyelids red and heavy are. A Poor Scholar of the 'Forties. Padraic Colum. AnIL; GLGT; OxBI
My eyes are filmed, my beard is grey. The Time of the Barmecides. James Clarence Mangan. EnRP; RoGo
My eyes are thirsty. Mirabai, *tr. fr. Hindi by* Willis Barnstone *and* Usha Nilsson. BoWoP
My eyes are white stones. River God's Song. Anne Ridler. NYBP
My eyes catch ruddy necks. Marching. Isaac Rosenberg. BrPo
My eyes went away from me. The Fickle One. Pablo Neruda, *tr. by* Donald D. Walsh. FF; OLR
My eyes were all too wary. The Kerry Lads. Theodosia Garrison. HBMV
My Face. Anthony Euwer. *See* As a Beauty I Am Not a Star.

My face is [*or* is wet] against the grass—the moorland grass is wet. Moorland Night. Charlotte Mew. ChMP; ViBoPo
My face is black. See the moon? My eyes. Crystal. Faye Kicknosway. IHMS
My Face Is My Own, I Thought. Tom Raworth. EAS
My face is wet with rain. Walking at Night. Amiry Hare. PoLF
My faint spirit was sitting in the light. From the Arabic [an Imitation]. Shelley. HBV-1; OBEV
My Fair Lady. *Unknown.* UnTE
(Under the Leaves Green.) OxBoLi
("Who shall have my fair[e] lady?") EnLoPo; PoEL-1
My fair, look from those turrets of thine eyes. Michael Drayton. Idea's Mirrour, XXXIV. OBSC
My fair says, she no spouse but me. On the Inconstancy of Women. Catullus. PV
My fairest child, I have no song to give you. A Farewell. Charles Kingsley. BLPA; EBVV; GN; HBV-1; HBVY; OxBChV; TreF
My Fairy. "Lewis Carroll." FaBoNo
My Faith. Ananda Acharya. WGRP
My faith is all a doubtful thing. Symbol. David Morton. HBMV
My Faith Looks Up to Thee. Ray Palmer. AH, *with music;* BLSo, *with music;* WGRP
(Faith.) AA; HBV-2
My faithful friend, if you can see. Impossibilities to His Friend. Robert Herrick. OLR
My Familiar. John Godfrey Saxe. HBV-2; TreFS
My Family's under Contract to Cancer. Greg Simison. AMV-80
My Fancy. "Lewis Carroll." *See* Disillusioned.
My Father. Abraham Chalfi, *tr. fr. Hebrew by* Shlomo Vinner *and* Howard Schwartz. VWA
My Father. Rae Dalven. GoYe
My father/ lets his hair down now. Father Takes to the Road and Lets His Hair Down. Alan Chong Lau. BrSi
My Father above, beholding the meekest [*or* meekness]. The Child Jesus to Mary the Rose. John Lydgate. GoBC; ISi
My Father after Work. Gary Gildner. AMV-80; Psk
My father and mother were Irish. The Ninepenny Fidil. Joseph Campbell. HBMV
My father and mother were Irish. Irish. Edward J. O'Brien. SiSoSe
My father and mother (what ails 'em?). The Rural Lass. Catherine Jemmat. NOEC
My father and my mother died and left me young and poor. The Orphan. *Unknown, tr. by* Frank O'Connor. KiLC
My father and my mother never quarrelled. Because. James McAuley. CBAP
My Father and the Fig Tree. Naomi Shihab Nye. GP
My father asks me how I stand it all. Parents. Vincent Buckley. CBAP
My father bequeathed me no wide estates. Heirloom. A. M. Klein. NIP; NOBC; OBCV; PeCV; TrJP
My father bound me to a trade in Waterford's fair town. The *Flying Cloud. Unknown.* AmSS
My father brought that dog home. Bony. Simon J. Ortiz. CDW
My father brought the emigrant bundle. Europe and America. David Ignatow. AmFN; NNaP; UnPo
My father by some strange conjunction had mice for sons. In All the Days of My Childhood. Russell Edson. AmPA
My father came in the darkness. Hyena. *Unknown, tr. by* George Economou. TTY
My father carries a pearl-handled knife. A Wonderful Man. Aileen Fisher. SiSoSe
My father casts a stone whose ripples ride. L. E. Sissman. *Fr.* Going Home, 1945. DiL
My Father Christmas passed away. The Skeptic. Robert Service. PV
My father comes to see me on Friday night. Bar Mitzvah. Isaac Goldemberg, *tr. by* David Unger. VWA
My father coming home. One Summer. Robert Mezey. DiL
My father could go down a mountain faster than I. That Dark Other Mountain. Robert Francis. LiSp; NCSH
My father could hear a little animal step. Listening. William Stafford. RFM
My father dear, so far from here. My Father Gave Me a Lump of Gold. *Unknown.* OuSiCo
My father didn't really belong in history. Parentage. William Stafford. BiP
My father died a month ago. *Unknown.* OxNR; PoPle
My Father Died This Spring. Joanne Kyger. PoM
My Father Dragged by Horses. T. Alan Broughton. AMV-80
My Father Dreams of Baseball. Laurence Lieberman. LiSp
My father entered the kingdom of roots. 1933. Philip Levine. VWA
My father, folding toward the earth again, plays. Waving Good-bye to My Father. Michael Blumenthal. DiL
My father found it after the war. The House on Buder Street. Gary Gildner. TAP
My father, fresh out of dental school. Old Photo, 1942. George Uba. BrSi
My father, gasping, in his white calked shoes. The Course. Robert Huff. CoAP
My Father Gave Me a Lump of Gold, *with music. Unknown.* OuSiCo
My father gave me the freedom of love. Howard McCord. *Fr.* Longjaunes His Periplus. GP
My father got me strong and straight and slim. The End. Marguerite Wilkinson. HBMV
My father had a glass eye. My Father's Eye. Eléni Vakaló, *tr. by* Kimon Friar. BoWoP
My father had terrible words for you. For My Brother Jesus. Irving Layton. NoP
My father has a pair of shoes. Shoes. Tom Robinson. SoPo; TiPo
My father hated moonlight. Moonlight. Berta Hart Nance. AmFN
My father he died, but I can't tell you how. Mother Goose. OxNR
My father, he gave me a bantam man. The Bantam Husband. *Unknown.* OuSiCo
My father, he was a mountaineer. The Ballad of William Sycamore. Stephen Vincent Benét. HBMV; MoAmPo; PoRA; TreFT
My father, his mouth full of nails. Nails. Gary Gildner. TAP
My father in his. Beryl Lyn Lifshin. NeAC
My Father in the Night Commanding No. Louis Simpson. CoAP; ConAP; DiL; HeIP; LCAP; MP; NePoEA-2; NoAM; NOBA; NYBP; PAI; TAP; TwCP; VGW
My father is a fugitive/ from the villages of Chagall. Two Refugees. Mordecai Marcus. VWA
My father is a hard man. The Armorer's Daughter. Debora Greger. MAYP
"My father is a knight and a man of high renown." The Bold Dragoon. *Unknown.* OBET
My father is a quiet man. Fruit of the Flower. Countee Cullen. PoLF
My father is dead. Song of the Bush-Shrike. *Unknown.* PeSA
My father is dead and there is nothing left. Not Saying Much. Linda Gregg. NPGG
My father is happy or we should be poor. From the Day-Book of a Forgotten Prince. Jean Starr Untermeyer. HBMV
My Father Kept a Horse. *Unknown.* GBP
My Father Kept His Cats Well Fed. Kenneth Sherman. HeIP
My Father Knows. Wilbur Fisk Tillet. BLRP
My father left me a book of Hemingway's stories. The Hemingway House in Key West. Philip Schultz. MAYP
My father left me three acres of land. Three Acres of Land. *Unknown.* NA; OxNR
My father lies black and hushed. The Worker. Richard W. Thomas. PoBA; PoNe
My father listening to opera, that's me. A Requiem. David Ignatow. DiL
My father made a synagogue of a boat. Two Fishermen. Stanley Moss. CoAP; DiL; VWA
My Father Moved through Dooms of Love. E. E. Cummings. AP; CMoP; CoBMU; CrMA; DiL; FYAP; HAP; LiTA; MoAB; MoPo; MoVE; NoAM; NOBA; NoP; OxBA; PoCh; TAP; TwAmPo; UnPo
My father moves through the South hunting duck. Treetops. Marvin Bell. AmPA; DiL
My Father, My Son. John Malcolm Brinnin. DiL; NYBP
My Father; October 1942. William Stafford. DiL; NaP
My father once broke a man's hand. Winter Stars. Larry Levis. DiL; MAYP
My father owns the butcher shop. *Unknown.* FaFP; RHPC
My Father Paints the Summer. Richard Wilbur. DiL; NCSH; NOBA
My father played the melodion. Patrick Kavanagh. *Fr.* A Christmas Childhood. DTC; PChr
My father preached full, powerful. Hudson Hornet. William W. Cook. AMV-80
My father returned. The Return. Shmuel Moreh, *tr. by* Yoffee Berkovitz. VWA
My father sang the songs. Yiddish. Judith Herzberg, *tr. by* Shirley Kaufman. VWA
My father sleeps in the sun porch. When at Night. Mark Perlberg. AMV-80
My father smiled this morning when. Keep Smiling. *Unknown.* WBLP
My father talked too much. How My Father Died. Nissim Ezekiel. VWA
My father talked with ghosts. Story from Another World. Paul Petrie. AMV-81
My father taught. Whose Voice. Barney Bush. STE
My father, the least happy. The Cage. John Montague. CIP
My father thought that fact was dull. Garland for a Storyteller. Jessie Farnham. GoYe
My father tore out his native roots. My Father. Rae Dalven. GoYe
My father used to say. Silence. Marianne Moore. CMoP; FaBoEn; FaBoMo; LiTA; NOBA; PAI; SBG; ViBoPo

My father used to say. The Seed of Reality. Max von Hartmann. AMV-80
My father used to show off by putting his forefinger. Fire. 10/78. Bart Plantenga. AMV-80
My Father Used to Tell of An. A. R. Ammons. DiL
My father was a farmer gay. One-and-Twenty. *Unknown.* AmFP
My father was a Frenchman. *Unknown.* OxNR
My father was a gambler, he learnt me how to play. The Gambler. *Unknown.* ViBoFo
My father was a sailor. Spanish Folk Songs. Antonio Machado, *tr. by* Havelock Ellis. AWP
My Father was a scholar and knew Greek. Development. Robert Browning. GLGT, *shorter vers.*; VLP
My father was a working man. Red-Herring. D. H. Lawrence. NoAM
My father was always out in the garage. Minotaur Poem II. Eli Mandel. MoCV; OBCV
My father was born with a spade in his hand and traded it. Elegy. John Ciardi. DiL
My father was hung for sheep-stealing. My God, How the Money Rolls In. *Unknown.* DBV
My father was hung from a star. Song of the Last Jewish Child. Edmond Jabès, *tr. by* Anthony Rudolf. VWA
My father was not inarticulate. False Prophet. Emanuela O'Malley. AMV-81
My father was the keeper of the Asteroid Light. The Asteroid Light. *Unknown.* FSW
My father when the sulphur boats were in. Song about My Father. Elizabeth Smither. OCNZ
My father, who works with stone. A Story of How a Wall Stands. Simon Ortiz. MAYP
My Father, Who's Still Alive. José Kozer, *tr. fr. Spanish by* Jorge Guitart. VWA
My father wore it working coal at Shotts. The Miner's Helmet. George MacBeth. OxBTC
My father worked with a horse-plough. Follower. Seamus Heaney. IPY
My father would have saved us, had the occasion of fire arisen. Netting. Jorie Graham. NPGG
My father would walk about for hours with a lit cigarette. The Stranger. Juan Gelman, *tr. by* Yishai Tobin. VWA
My father, wreathed in smoke. Crossing Raquette Lake at Night. Greg Kuzma. WOLT
My Fatherland. William Cranston Lawton. AA
My Father's a Still Day. Geoffrey Lehmann. *Fr.* Ross's Poems. CBAP
My father's body was a globe of fear. Letters & Other Worlds. Michael Ondaatje. NOBC; NoP;
My Fathers Came from Kentucky. Vachel Lindsay. AmFN; HBMV
My Father's Child. "Stuart Sterne." AA
My Father's Close. *Unknown, tr. fr. French by* Dante Gabriel Rossetti. AWP
My father's cluttered workbench stands, heaped up. Cleaning Up, Clearing Out. Daniel Ross Bronson. AMV-80
My fathers come to me in an old film. The Worm. Willis Barnstone. FAZ; VWA
My Father's Cot, *sel.* J. C. Squire.
"I left thee with a courage high." BXAP
My Father's Eye. Eléni Vakaló, *tr. fr. Modern Greek by* Kimon Friar. BoWoP
My Father's Face. Hayden Carruth. DiL
My father's face is brown with sun. Father. Frances Frost. FaPON; SiSoSe; TiPo
My father's father gave. The Gold Nest. Robert Wallace. PPJ
My father's friend came once to tea. A Recollection. Frances Cornford. ELU
My Father's Funeral. Karl Shapiro. DiL
My Father's Ghost. David Wagoner. Str
My Father's Heart. Stuart Friebert. Str
My Father's Leaving. Ira Sadoff. AmPA; DiL
My Father's Martial Art. Stephen Shu Ning Liu. BrSi
My father's memory book. Coat of Arms. Alan Dugan. DiL
My father's name is Frankenstein. Father and Mother. X. J. Kennedy. GrPl; RHPC
My Fathers sit on benches. Song for the Old Ones. Maya Angelou. SaC
My Father's Song. Simon J. Ortiz. MAYP; STE
My Father's Voice in Prayer. May Hastings Nottage. BLRP
My Father's Watch. John Ciardi. ImOP
My Father's way may twist and turn. He Maketh No Mistake. A. M. Overton. STF
My Father's Wedding. Robert Bly. DiL
My father's white uncle became. Todd. Stewart Conn. BSV
My Father's World. Maltbie D. Babcock. BLRP
My fathers wrote their names in sweat. Signatures. Candace Thurber Stevenson. AmFN
My favorite dress. Her Favorites. Mattie Lee Hausgen. PoPl
My favorite student lately is the one who wrote about feeling clumbsy. The Spell against Spelling. George Starbuck. FYAP
My Feet. Gelett Burgess. NA
(Nonsense Verses.) HBV-2
My Feet. Louis Jenkins. GP
My feet and limbs, young friend, are no longer. Nestor. Homer, *tr. by* Ennis Rees. *Fr.* The Iliad, XXIII. LiSp
My feet are elms, roots in the earth. They Tell Me I Am Lost. Maurice Kenny. STE
My feet fall in step with absent whores. Amelia Street. Frank Ormsby. CIP
My feet have felt the sands. Determination. John Henrik Clarke. CNA; PoBA
My feet strike an apex of the apices of the stairs. Infinity. Walt Whitman. *Fr.* Song of Myself, XLIV-XLV. AA
My feet taste funny. Why I Didn't Go to Delphi. James Welch. CDW
My feet, they haul me round the house. My Feet [*or* Nonsense Verses]. Gelett Burgess. HBV-2; NA
My feet took a walk in heavenly grass. Heavenly Grass. Tennessee Williams. PoPl
My feets is so sore can't hardly wear my shoes. Big Night Blues. *Unknown.* BluL
My, Fellowship, with, God. José Garcia Villa. EaLo
My female friends, whose tender hearts. Swift. *Fr.* Verses on the Death of Doctor Swift. NOBL; SeCePo; ViBoPo
My Fiddle. Leib Kwitko, *tr. fr. Yiddish by* Keith Bosley. VWA
My fifthe housbonde, god his soule blesse! Chaucer. *Fr.* The Canterbury Tales: The Wife of Bath's Prologue. FiP
My 50th year having arrived. On the Birth of Dan Goldman. Daniel Berrigan. NAs
My fingers/ find it. The Raquette River, Potsdam, New York; Lying on a Rock Drinking Scotch while My Friends Fish Upstream. Anthony Piccione. WOLT
My fingers are but stragglers at the rear. Stragglers. Pietro Aretino, *tr. by* Samuel Putnam. ErPo
My fingers feed in the fields of wood. Picture Framing. Bert Meyers. ELU
My First Love. Harry Graham. FiBHP
My first love sighed for brooches. Prices. Louis Ginsberg. TrJP
My first thought was, he lied in every word. "Childe Roland to the Dark Tower Came." Robert Browning. DTo; NoP; OAEL-2; OAEP; OBNV; PPP; SeCeV; VLP
My flattering fortune, look thou never so fair. To Fortune. Sir Thomas More. ACP
My flesh is racked by plague. The New Ahasuerus. Jozsef Kiss, *tr. by* André Ungar. VWA
My flock feeds [*or* flocks feed] not, my ewes breed[s] not. The Unknown Shepherd's Complaint [*or* A Shepherd's Complaint]. Richard Barnfield. EIL; OBSC
My flowery and green age was passing away. He Understands the Great Cruelty of Death. Petrarch, *tr. by* J. M. Synge. Sonnets to Laura: To Laura in Death, XLVII. BIrV; OBMV
My Flying Machine. Louis Daniel Brodsky. AMV-80
My foe was dark, and stern, and grim. My Enemy. Alice Williams Brotherton. AA
My folk, now answere me. Jesus Reproaches His People. *Unknown.* MeEL
My Folk, What Have I Done Thee? William Herebert. OxBM
My food was pallid till I heard it ring. King Midas. Howard Moss. CoAP; TAP
My foot in the stirrup, my pony won't stan'. Good-by, Old Paint. *Unknown.* BPAW; CoSo
My foot-steps press where, centuries ago. The Red Men. Charles Sangster. CaP
My Former Hopes Are Fled. William Cowper. OxBoCh
My fortitude is all awry. She Sees Another Door Opening. Firman Houghton. Par
My forty-year-old father learned to fly. The Hang-Glider's Daughter. Marilyn Hacker. MAYP
My foster-brother and foster-sister. The Golden Sea-Otter. Wakarpa, *tr. by* Arthur Waley. *Fr.* Kutune Shirka (The Ainu Epic.) WTO
My foster-children were not slack. Lament for Corc and Niall of the Nine Hostages. *At. to* Torna, *tr. by* Sir Samuel Ferguson. OnYI
My frame of nature is a ruffled sea. The Hurry of the Spirits, in a Fever and Nervous Disorders. Isaac Watts. NOEC
My freshmen/ settle in. Achilles. Freshmen. Barry Spacks. NYBP
My Friend. Samuel Allen. FB
My Friend. Philip Appleman. BXAP
My Friend. Marjorie Lorene Buster. STF
My friend and I have decided to write for money. Writing for Money. Edward Field. PPJ

My friend cannot speak any more. Waiting for a Second Time. Tauhindauli. STE
My friend conceived the soul hereafter dwells. Aspiration. Edward William Thomson. OBVV
My friend from Asia has powers and magic. Credo. Robinson Jeffers. MoAB; MoAmPo; PoPl
My friend, have you heard of the town of Nogood. The Town of Nogood. W. E. Penny. BLPA
My friend is lodging high in the Eastern Range. To Tan Ch'iu. Li Po, *tr. by* Arthur Waley. AWP
My friend must be a bird. Emily Dickinson. TAP
My friend says I was not a good son. Yesterday. W. S. Merwin. DiL; FYAP
My friend, speak always once, but listen twice. The Mouth and the Ears. Shem-Tob ben Joseph Palquera, *tr. by* J. Chotzner. TrJP
My friend, the things that do attain. *See* Martial, the things that do attain.
My Friend the Wind. King D. Kuka. VoR
My friend, this body is made of bone. The Origin of the Praise of God. Robert Bly. NU
My friend thy beauty seemeth good. The Penurious Quaker; or, The High Priz'd Harlot. *Unknown.* CoMu
My friend who married the girl I. Watts. Shirley Kaufman. NMM
My friend, who was a heroin addict. Certain Choices. Richard Shelton. Psk
My friend, you don't understand. My Friend. Philip Appleman. BXAP
My friend, your face. Who Is My Brother? Pinkie Gordon Lane. BlSi
My friends,/ I am amazed. Acceptance Speech. Marvin Bell. AmPA
My friends are borne to one another. Martin Buber in the Pub. Max Harris. PoAu-2
My friends are on vacation. Mothers. Tristan Tzara, *tr. by* Willis Barnstone *and* Matei Calinescu. VWA
My friends have left. Far away, my darling is asleep. A Small Elegy. Jiri Orten, *tr. by* Lyn Coffin. AMV-81
My friends, my sweet barbarians. A Breakfast for Barbarians. Gwendolyn MacEwen. NOBC
My funeral-shaft, and marble shapes that dwell. Baucis. Erinna, *tr. by* Richard Garnett. AWP
My gal don' wear button-up shoes. Georgia Land. *Unknown.* OuSiCo
My Gal Sal. Paul Dresser. BLSo, *with music;* FSW, *with music;* TreFT
My galleon of adventure. San Francisco. Walter Adolphe Roberts. PoNe
My Galley Charged with Forgetfulness. Petrarch. *See* Lover Compareth His State to a Ship . . .
My Gang. Jack Kerouac. PoM
My Garden. Thomas Edward Brown. BLPL; EBCP; FaBV; HBV-1; HBVY; InPK; OBEV; OBVV; PeD; PoLF; TreF; TRV; WBLP; WGRP
My Garden. W. H. Davies. BoNaP
My Garden, *parody.* J. A. Lindon. DBV; InPK; POL
My Garden. Janice Appleby Succorsa. HoPM
My garden blazes brightly with the rose-bush and the peach. In Springtime. Kipling. BrPo
My garden is a pleasant place. Louise Driscoll. BLPA; FaBoBe
My Garden, My Daylight. Jorie Graham. MAYP
My gentle child, behold this horse. The Racing-Man. A. P. Herbert. BoAnP; FiBHP; PH; WhC
My gentle father. Feliks Skrzynecki. Peter Skrzynecki. CBAP
My ghost pets are like shadows on the wall. Ghost Pet. Horatio Colony. GoYe
My Ghostly Father, I Me Confess. Charles d'Orléans. BoLoP
(Confession.) ChTr
(Confession of a Stolen Kiss.) MeEL
(Kiss, The.) ACP
(Lover's Confession, A.) NOBE; OxBM
("My ghostly fadir I me confess.") GBL
(My Gostly Fader, I Me Confesse.) EnLoPo
My Gift. Christina Rossetti. *Fr.* A Christmas Carol: "In the bleak of mid-winter." FaPON; SiSoSe
("What can I give Him.") PChr
My girl hath violet eyes and yellow hair. The Little Milliner. Robert Buchanan. BeLS
My girl I say be on your guard. Death and the Maiden. *Unknown, tr. by* Frank O'Connor. KiLC
My girl is thin, yet that is why. True Love. *Unknown, tr. by* Louis Untermeyer. UnTE
My girl the voluptuous creature. Love and Poetry. Louis Simpson. PPoe
My girl, thou gazest much. The Lover to His Lady. *At. to* Plato, *tr. by* George Turberville. CTC; FaBoEE; FF; OBSC
My girlfriend, at my urging. Domestic Duties. Richard Emil Braun. NoAM
My girl's tall with hard long eyes. E. E. Cummings. *Fr.* Sonnets—Realities. UnTE
My glad feet shod with the glittering steel. The Skater. Sir Charles G. D. Roberts. NOBC
My Glass Is Half Unspent. Francis Quarles. OxBoCh
My glass shall not persuade me I am old. Sonnets, XXII. Shakespeare. OBSC
My glittering sky, high, clear, profound. The Lovers. Marya Zaturenska. MoAmPo
My glory, honor, all depend. The Gentleman. Menahem ben Judah Lonzano, *tr. by* A. B. Rhine. TrJP
My Glumdalclitch, come here and sit with me. A Tryst in Brobdingnag. Adrienne Rich. NYBP
My goats leave deep tracks in the mud. Tracks. Joseph Torain. FAZ
My God. Solomon ibn Gabirol, *tr. fr. Hebrew by* Alice Lucas. *Fr.* The Royal Crown. TrJP
My God, a verse is not a crown. The Quidditie. George Herbert. PoEL-2
My God, how gracious art thou! I had slipt. The Relapse. Henry Vaughan. AnAnS-1; TrCP
My God, how perfect are thy ways! Jehovah Our Righteousness. William Cowper. NOCV
My God, How the Money Rolls In. *Unknown.* DBV; FSW
My God, How Wonderful Thou Art. Frederick W. Faber. *Fr.* Our Heavenly Father. GoBC; TrPWD
My God, I heard this day. Man. George Herbert. AnAnS-1; CABA; MePo; NoP; OAEP; PoEL-2; SeCP; SeCV-1; TrGrPo; TrPWD, *abr.*
My God, I know that those who plead. My God. Solomon ibn Gabirol, *tr. by* Alice Lucas. *Fr.* The Royal Crown. TrJP
My God, I love thee, not because. Hymn. St. Francis Xavier. WGRP
My God, I Thank Thee, *with music.* Andrews Norton. AH
My God, I thank Thee who hast made. Thankfulness. Adelaide Anne Procter. TrPWD
My God, if writings may. Obedience. George Herbert. AnAnS-1
My God, is any hour so sweet. The Hour of Prayer. Charlotte Elliott. STF
My God is just, yes he is. *Unknown, tr. fr. Pashto by* Saduddin Shpoon. PBWP
My God is Love. Love. Toyohiko Kagawa. TRV
My God is not a chiselled stone. True Knowledge. Panatattu. WGRP
My God! looke on me with thine eye. His Ejaculation to God. Robert Herrick. SeCV-1
My God most glad to look, most prone to hear. Bible, *O.T., paraphrased by* Countess of Pembroke. Psalms, LV. OBVE; WPE
My God, my God, have mercy on my sin. Ash Wednesday. Christina Rossetti. TrCP; VLP
My God, my God, let me for once look on thee. Robert Browning. *Fr.* Pauline. TrPWD
My God, My God, Look upon Me. Chad Walsh. *Fr.* The Psalm of Christ. TrCP
My God, my god, what queer corner am I in? In the Deep Museum. Anne Sexton. MoAmPo; Prf
My God, my God, why hast thou forsaken me? A Cry in Distress. Bible, *O.T.* Psalm XXII. TrGrPo
My God (oh, let me call Thee mine). A Prayer. Anne Brontë. TrPWD
My God said: "Love me, son! Dost thou not see." Mystical Dialogue. Paul Verlaine, *tr. by* Alan Conder. LO
My God, the bitter-tasting mouth was me. Homage. R. J. Schoeck. GoYe
My God, thou that didst dye for me. The Dedication. Henry Vaughan. AnAnS-1
My God, when I walk in those groves. Religion. Henry Vaughan. AnAnS-1; NOCV; OAEL-1; OBS; OxBoCh
My God, where is that ancient heat towards thee. To His Mother [*or* Sonnet]. George Herbert. AnAnS-1; OAEL-1
My God, you have wounded me with love. Paul Verlaine, *tr. fr. French. Fr.* Sagesse. ILwL
My god you shall not thus forsake me, you. Prayer of a Little Hope. Jean Wahl, *tr. by* Charles Guenther. VWA
My godmother invited my cousin. My Cousin Agueda. Ramón López Velarde, *tr. by* Samuel Beckett. OBVE
My good blade carves the casques of men. Sir Galahad [*or* The Purple Heart]. Tennyson. HBV-2; OBVV; TreF
My goodness, my goodness,/ It's Christmas again. Christmas. Marchette Chute. SiSoSe
My Gostly Fader, I Me Confesse. Charles d'Orléans. *See* My Ghostly Father . . .
"My Grace Is Sufficient for Thee." *Unknown.* BLRP
My Gracious Lord, I would thee glory doe. Edward Taylor. *Fr.* Preparatory Meditations: Second Series, IV. SCAP
My Grandaddy Mostly with His Knife. David Huddle. GrPl
My granddad, viewing earth's worn cogs. Going to the Dogs. *Unknown.* TreFS
My Grandfather Always Promised Us. Liam Rector. AMV-80
My Grandfather Burning Cornfields. Roger Sauls. Str
My Grandfather Dying. Ted Kooser. Str
My grandfather leads me through snow. Blessing. Melvin Wilk. VWA
My grandfather placed wood. Mythology. Earle Thompson. STE

My grandfather prayed. Bury Me in America. Arno Karlen. FAZ
My grandfather said to me. Manners [for a Child of 1918]. Elizabeth Bishop. CTBA; NCSH; OxBC
My grandfather told me I had a choice. Grandfather's Heaven. Naomi Shihab Nye. Str
My grandfather used to pray. The Wicked Neighbor. Zelda, *tr. by* Hannah Hoffman. WPOW
My Grandfather Was a Quantum Physicist. Duane Big Eagle. STE
My grandfather was an elegant gentleman. David Wright. *Fr.* Seven South African Poems. PeSA
My grandfather worked when he was very young. An Old Man's Advice. *Unknown.* OBET
My grandfather's beard/ Was blacker than God's. On the Photograph of a Man I Never Saw. Hyam Plutzik. VWA
My grandfather's clock was too large for the shelf. Grandfather's Clock. Henry Clay Work. BLPA; BLSo; FaFP; FSW; PSoN; TreF
My Grandfather's Days. *Unknown.* OBET
My Grandfather's Funeral. James Applewhite. TAT
My grandfather's hands were wise and hard. Rivets. N. S. Olds. EtS
My grandfather's mind was a covered ark. The Law. Grace Schulman. GP
My Grandmama/ dont believe they walked in space. It's All the Same. Thadious M. Davis. BlSi
My Grandmother. Perseus Adams. PeSA
My Grandmother. Karl Shapiro. VGW
My grandmother. The Dust Will Settle. Luci Tapahonso. STE
My Grandmother and the Voice of Tolstoy. Steve Orlen. AMV-81
My Grandmother Green. *Unknown.* AmFP
(Grandma's Advice, *sl. diff. vers.*) OBET
My Grandmother Had Bones. Judith Hemschemeyer. DFF
My grandmother had braids. Keeping Hair. Ramona Wilson. VoR
My grandmother is old, not old. Grandmother Poems. Marilyn Chin. BrSi
My grandmother lived in yonder little lane. Grandma's Advice. *Unknown.* OBET
My grandmother lived on yonder green. My Grandmother Green. *Unknown.* AmFP
My grandmother (Lord, love her jackdaw soul!). Touchstone. James Worley. AMV-80
My grandmother moves to my mind in context of sorrow. My Grandmother. Karl Shapiro. VGW
My grandmother sent me a new-fashioned three-cornered cambric country-cut handkerchief. *Unknown.* OxNR
My grandmother, she, at the age of eighty-three. Grandmother's Old Armchair. *Unknown.* BLPA
My grandmother was a wrinkled little girl. Genealogy. Eléni Vakaló, *tr. by* Paul Merchant. PBWP
My Grandmother was buried here. Epitaph in a Churchyard at Thetford, in Norfolk. *Unknown.* FaBoUs
My grandmother's/brother here. At a Chinaman's Grave. Wing Tek Lum. BrSi
My Grandmother's Funeral. Thomas Lux. WeW
My Grandmother's Love Letters. Hart Crane. BLPL; CMoP; FaBoBe; MoAB; NoAM; NOBA; NoP;
My grandmothers were strong. Lineage. Margaret Walker. BlSi; BOLo; CNA; NMM; PBWP; PoBA;
My Grandpa lives in a wonderful house. The Painted Ceiling. Amy Lowell. OBAL
My grandparents lived to a great age in the cold. Cold. Dorothy Roberts. NOBC
My Grandser was a fearsome man! Grandser. Abbie Farwell Brown. HBMV
My grandsire sailed three years from home. The Master Mariner. George Sterling. HBV-1
My grasp of what he wrote or meant. Literary Criticism. Myles na Gopaleen. DBV
My Grave. Thomas Osborne Davis. OnYI
My great brother. A Psalm Praising the Hair of Man's Body. Denise Levertov. CAPP
My Great Great etc. Uncle Patrick Henry. James Tate. GP; OBAL
My Great-Grandfather's Slaves. Wendell Berry. GeTw
"My green leaves are more beautiful." Leaves. Frank Asch. NTCP
My grey-barked trees wave me in. I Stroll. Peter Redgrove. NePoEA-2
My grey-eyed father kept pigs on his farm. The Pigs. Geoffrey Lehmann. CBAP
My grief, my grief, maid without sin. The Body's Speech. Donal MacCarthy, First Earl Clancarty, *tr. by* Frank O'Connor. KiLC
My Grief on Fál's Proud Plain, *sel.* Geoffrey Keating, *tr. fr. Late Middle Irish by* Padraic Pearse.
"From my grief on Fál's proud plain I sleep." OnYI
My Grief on the Sea. *Unknown, at. to* Biddy Cussrooee, *tr. fr. Modern Irish by* Douglas Hyde. AnIL; OBEV; OBVV; OnYI; OxBI; WTO
My grief, quoth I, is called Ignorance. Rachel Speght. *Fr.* A Dream. WPE
My grief! that they have laid you in the town. Synge's Grave. Winifred Letts. AnIV
My Guardian Angel Stein. Philip Schultz. MAYP
My gudame wes a gay wif, bot scho wes ryght gend. The Ballad of Kynd Kittok. William Dunbar. BSV; GoTS; OxBoLi
My guest! I have not led you thro'. Interlude. Walter Savage Landor. GTBS-P
My hair has dried. Self Dirge. Wendy Rose. CDW
My hair is gray, but not with years. The Prisoner of Chillon. Byron. DTo; EnRP; PoLF
My hair is springy like the forest grasses. Black Woman. Naomi Long Madgett. BlSi; FB; OLR; PoBA
My hair's falling fast. Afternoon. Lucien Stryk. *Fr.* Zen Poems, after Shinkichi Takahashi. FAZ
My Hairt Is Heich Aboif. *Unknown.* OxBS
My hand cannot smooth your sigh. Microcosmos, III. Nigel Heseltine. NeBP
My hand has a pain from writing. *See* My hand is weary with writing.
My hand is lonely for your clasping, dear. You and I. Henry Alford. BLPA; FaBoBe
My hand is weary with [*or* has a pain from] writing. St. Columcille the Scribe. *At. to* St. Columcille. AnIL, *tr. by* Kuno Meyer; BlrV, *tr. by* Flann O'Brien; OnYI, *tr. by* Kuno Meyer
My hand on your breasts the kitchen. The Knife. Juan Gelman, *tr. by* Yishai Tobin. VWA
My hand plunged into the waters of night. Memory of Another Climate. Gabriel Preil, *tr. by* Jeremy Garber. VWA
My hand waving from the window. Platform Goodbye. H. B. Mallalieu. WaP
My hands/ Open the curtains of your being. Touch. Octavio Paz, *tr. by* Charles Tomlinson. BoLoP
My hands are tender feathers. Calypso's Song to Ulyssess. Adrian Mitchell. GBL
My hands did numb to beauty. I Held a Shelley Manuscript. Gregory Corso. VGW
My hands have developed eyes! Conversion. Geof Hewitt. NeAC
My hands have not touched water since your hands. Carrier Letter. Hart Crane. BoLoP
My hands in pockets worn out at the seams. The Strolling Player. Arthur Rimbaud, *tr. by* William Jay Smith. GrPl
My hands, my fists, my small bells. Oh Yes. William Matthews. AmPA
My hands of silk and miniver. Full Moon. Elinor Wylie. MoAB
My hands shook as I bargained for passage. Oedipus. David Ignatow. PAI
My Handsome Gilderoy. *Unknown. See* Gilderoy.
My Happiness. Greg Pape. MAYP
My happiness depends on an electric appliance. The Telephone. Edward Field. CAD; PPJ
My Happy Life. Mildmay Fane, Earl of Westmorland. CavP
My Harry was a gallant gay. Highland Harry Back Again. *At. to* Burns. EBEV
My Hat. Stevie Smith. BrRo
My hated birthday is here, and I must go. Sulpicia, *tr. fr. Latin by* Aliki *and* Willis Barnstone. BoWoP
My hazard wouldn't be yours, not ever. Advice. Ruth Stone. NMM
My head aches. Going through Changes. Jean Tepperman. NMM
My head and shoulders, and my book. The Signature of All Things. Kenneth Rexroth. NNaP; NU
My head is bald, my breath is bad. Late-flowering Lust. John Betjeman. CMoP; ErPo; NMP; TW
My head is drawing closer to the bar again. Indian Guys at the Bar. Simon J. Ortiz. STE
My head is like lead, and my temples they bulge. Hangover. Philip H. Rhinelander. WhC
My head, my heart, mine eyes, my life, nay more. A Letter to Her Husband, Absent upon Publick Employment. Anne Bradstreet. HAP; HeIP; NoP; SCAP
My head on moss reclining. A Song. *Unknown.* NOEC
My Head on My Shoulders. Jeremy Ingalls. GoYe
My heart aches and a drowsy numbness pains. Ode to a Nightingale [*or* To a Nightingale]. Keats. AWP; BiP; BLRP; CABA; ChER; ChTR; EBEV; EnRP; FaBoBe; FaBoEn; FaFP; FiP; GTBS; GTBS-P; HAP; HBV-1; HBVY; HeIP; InPK; InPS; LiTB; LoBV; MasP; NIP; NOBE; NoP; OAEL-2; OAEP; OBEV; OBNC; OBRV; PAI; PB; PBBP; PoEL-4; PoRA; PPoe; PPP; PrIm; SeCeV; SoSe; SpRo; TEP; TreF; TrGrPo; UnPo; ViBoPo; WeW; WHA
My Heart and I. Elizabeth Barrett Browning. HBV-1
My heart beating, my blood running. Time's Dedication. Delmore Schwartz. VGW
My heart beats to the feet of the first faithful. An Interlude. Robert Duncan. CMoP

My Heart Belongs to Daddy. Cole Porter. OBAL
My Heart Burns for Him. *Gond Oral Tradition, tr. by* V. Elwin *and* S. Hivale. WTO
My heart, complaining like a bird. Burning Bush. Karle Wilson Baker. HBMV
My heart cried like a beaten child. Song Making. Sara Teasdale. WGRP
My heart dissolved to see Thee bleed. At the Cross. *Unknown.* STF
My heart doth in the Lord rejoice, that living Lord of might. The Song of Hannah. Bible, *O.T., ad. by* Michael Drayton. *Fr.* First Samuel. TrCP
My heart felt need to die. The Scourge. Stanley Kunitz. CrMA
My heart grows sick before the wide-spread death. The Grave-Yard. Jones Very. NOBA
My heart has an opening that discharges blood. The Heart. David Ignatow. VWA
My heart has become capable of every form. Ibn al-Arabi, *tr. fr. Arabic.* ILwL
My heart has fed to-day. Completion. Eunice Tietjens. HBMV
My heart has grown rich with the passing of years. The Solitary. Sara Teasdale. MoAmPo; WHA
My heart has thank'd thee, Bowles! for those soft strains. To the Reverend W. L. Bowles. Samuel Taylor Coleridge. EnRP
My Heart, How Very Hard It's Grown, *with music.* Cotton Mather. AH
My heart, I cannot still it. Auspex. James Russell Lowell. AP; HBV-1; NePA; OBVV; PoEL-5; TAP
My heart, imprisoned in a hopeless isle. Michael Drayton. Idea's Mirrour, XXII. OBSC
My Heart Is a Lute. Anne Barnard. HBV-1
My heart is a-breaking, dear tittie. Tam Glen. Burns. AWP; BSV; OAEP; OBEC; OxBS
My heart is an oil lamp. A Rapier of Treason. *Tr. fr. Arabic by* Willis Barnstone. BoWoP
My heart is chilled and my pulse is slow. Lost Light. Elizabeth Akers Allen. HBV-1
My heart is empty. All the fountains that should run. The Naked Seed. C. S. Lewis. TrCP
My Heart Is High Above. *At. to* Alexander Scott. OBEV
(My Heart Is Heich Above.) BSV; GoTS
(My Heart Is Heich Abufe.) ErPo
My Heart Is in the East. Judah Halevi, *tr. fr. Hebrew.* TrJP
My heart is in woe. The Downfall of the Gael. Fearflatha O'Gnive, *tr. by* Sir Samuel Ferguson. AnIV; AWP; OnYI
My heart is lighter than the poll. The New-slain Knight. *Unknown.* ESPB
My heart is like a fountain true. Mother's Song. *Unknown.* GN; HBV-1
My heart is like a singing bird. A Birthday. Christina Rossetti. AWP; BLPL; CH; FaFP; InvP; LiTB; LoBV; NAs; NOBE; OAEL-2; OAEP; OBEV; OBVV; OLR; TreFS; TrGrPo; ViBoPo; VLP; WHA; WiR; WPE
My heart is like one asked to dine. An Unexpected Pleasure. *Unknown.* FaBoCo
My heart is on my fist. The Tomb of the Kings. Anne Hébert, *tr. by* Aliki *and* Willis Barnstone. BoWoP
My heart is sair—I dare na tell. Somebody. Burns. BSV
My Heart Is Set upon a Lusty Pin. Queen Elizabeth of York. WPE
My Heart Is Woe. *Unknown.* OxBM
My heart is young—the breath of blowing trees. Certainties. Helen Frazee-Bower. Two Married, IV. HBMV
My Heart Leaps Up [When I Behold]. Wordsworth. BiP; CABA; EnRP; FaBoEn; FaBV; FaFP; GTBS; GTBS-P; InPK; LoBV; NOBE; NoP; OAEL-2; OAEP; OBNC; OBRV; PAI; PoPl; SoPo; TEP; TiPo; TreF; TrGrPo; TRV; ViBoPo
(Rainbow, The.) BLPA; FPL; HBV-1; HBVY; LiTB; OBEV; RoGo
My heart leaps up when I behold. Song to be Sung by the Father of Infant Female Children. Ogden Nash. MoAmPo
My heart lies light in my own breast. The Wind Bloweth Where It Listeth. Susan L. Mitchell. AnIV
My heart moves as heavy as the horse that climbs the hill. *Unknown, tr. fr. Welsh by* Menna Gallie. ELU
My Heart, My Heart Is Mournful. Heine, *tr. fr. German by* James Thomson. PoPl
(Mein Herz, mein Herz ist traurig.) AWP
My heart of gold as true as steel. A Nonsense Carol. *Unknown.* OxBoLi
My heart rebels against my generation. Ode. George Santayana. ViBoPo
My heart rejoiceth in the Lord. Hannah's Song of Thanksgiving. Bible, *O.T. Fr.* First Samuel. AWP
My Heart Shall Be Thy Garden. Alice Meynell. HBV-1
My heart still hovering round about you. Epigram. Robert, Earl Nugent. NOEC
My heart stirs quietly now to think. A Hermit's Song. *Unknown, tr. by* James Simmons. BIrV
My Heart Stood Still, *with music.* Lorenz Hart. BLSo
My heart that was so passionless. Rencontre. Jessie Fauset. CDC
My heart the anvil where my thoughts do beat. Idea, XL. Michael Drayton. HBV-1
My heart, thinking/ "How beautiful he is." Lady Otomo of Sakanoe, *tr. fr. Japanese by* Arthur Waley. AWP; PBWP
My heart was fired, as from his sight it turned. The Dream of Dakiki. Firdausi, *tr. by* A. V. Williams Jackson. WGRP
My heart was heavy, for its trust had been. Forgiveness. Whittier. TrCP
My Heart Was Wandering in the Sands. Christopher Brennan. *Fr.* The Twilight of Disquietude. PoAu-1
My Heart's Desire. *Unknown.* STF
My heart's despair. Isabel. Sydney Dobell. OBVV
My heart's friend, will you tell me who this mischievous youngster is? Dancing-Girl's Song. Kshetrayya, *tr. fr. Teluga.* BoWoP
My Heart's in the Highlands. Burns. AWP, *sl. var.*; EnRP, *sl. var.*; FaBoBe; FaBoPP; FaFP, *sl. var.*; FaPON. *sl. var.*; GN; HBV-1; PoPl; PoPle; TreFT
My heart's so heavy with a hundred things. Sonnet: In Absence from Becchina. Cecco Angiolieri da Siena, *tr. by* Dante Gabriel Rossetti. AWP
My help, my hope, my strength shall be. The Law. Abraham ibn Ezra, *tr. by* Alice Lucas. TrJP
My Hereafter. Juanita de Long. WGRP
My Hero. Benjamin Brawley. BANP; PoNe
My hero is na decked wi' gowd. The Hero. Robert Nicoll. HBV-2
My Hiding Place. Kathryn T. Bowsher. STF
My highway is unfeatured air. Hymn of the Earth. William Ellery Channing. AA
My history crucified, buried under the muddy flood of time. The Rusted Chain. Yosef Damana ben Yeshaq, *tr. by* Ephraim Isaac. VWA
My history extends/ Where moved my tourist hands. Abroad Thoughts from Home. Donald Hall. NePoEA
My hoary locks I dye with care. Self-Defense. Santob de Carrion, *tr. by* George Ticknor. TrJP
My Home ("My home is on the rolling deep"). *Unknown.* NA
My home is the mountain. Akhtar Amiri, *tr. by* Fereshte Mahamadi. *Fr.* I Am a Woman. WPOW
My Home's across the Smoky Mountains. *Unknown.* AmFP; FSW
My home's in Montana, I wear a bandanna. The Cowboy's Lament. *Unknown.* CoSo
My homestead's with lightning aflame. The Meaning of Love. *Malay Oral Tradition, tr. by* R. O. Winstedt. WTO
My homeward barque is stocked with treasure. Homecoming. Stefan George, *tr. by* Peter Viereck. AMV-81
My Honey, My Love. Joel Chandler Harris. *Fr.* Uncle Remus and His Friends. AA; FaBoBe
My Honeyed Languor. Edward Bagritzky, *tr. fr. Russian by* Babette Deutsch. TrJP
My hope, alas, hath me abused. Sir Thomas Wyatt. SiPS
My Hope, My Love. *Unknown, tr. fr. Irish by* Edward Walsh. BIrV
My hopes retire; my wishes as before. Walter Savage Landor. *Fr.* Ianthe. GBL; OBNC
My horny feet are cutting through the fog. Satyr. Charles Gullans. PoA
My Horses. Jean Jaszi. SoPo
My Horses Ain't Hungry. *Unknown.* FSW
My horse's feet beside the lake. A Farewell. Matthew Arnold. Switzerland, III. OAEP; VLP
My hounds are bred out of the Spartan kind. Shakespeare. *Fr.* A Midsummer Night's Dream, IV, i. GDP; PoPle
My hour switched on the cameras take. The Voice of America, 1961. James Liddy. CIP
My House. Robert Adamson. CBAP
My House. George Bruce. OxBS
My House. Jane W. Krows. SoPo
My House. Claude McKay. CDC
My House. W. B. Yeats. *Fr.* Meditations in Time of Civil War, II. LiTB
My house also has/ an oversized room. Possible Love Poem to the Usurer. Octavio Armand, *tr. by* Carol Maier. AMV-81
My house, I say. But hark to the sunny doves. Robert Louis Stevenson. FM
My house is not quiet, I am not loud. Fish in River. *Unknown, tr. by* Charles W. Kennedy. *Fr.* Riddles (Exeter Book). AnOE
My house, my fairy/ palace. Jeronimo's House. Elizabeth Bishop. MiAP; NoP
My humanoid friend, myself, a limited animal. The Week-End Naturalist. Tom Buchan. BSV
My humble Muse sad, and in lonely state. To His Excellency Joseph Dudley. John Saffin. SCAP
My humid hand against your/ breast. An Island. Shawn Wong. BrSi
My Husband. *Unknown.* CoMu
My husband gives me an A. Marks. Linda Pastan. NIP
My husband is the same [man] who took my maidenhead [*or* who first pierced

me]. Silabhattarika, *tr. fr. Sanskrit. Fr.* The Wanton. BoWoP, *tr. by* Willis Barnstone; PBWP, *tr. by* Daniel H. H. Ingalls
My husband smiles in sleep beside me. Charlotte Nicholls. Jack Clemo. NAs
My husband's a jockey, a jockey, a jockey. My Husband. *Unknown.* CoMu
My Indian Girl. Ali Sedat Hilmi Törel. PeD
My Influence. *Unknown.* STF
My Infundibuliform Hat. Charles Follen Adams. OBAL
My Inmost Hope. Sarah Copia Sullam, *tr. fr. Italian.* TrJP
My inquisitive little brown children. Song for My Little Friends. Leonard Adame, *tr. by* Toni Empringham. FIA
My Inside-Self. Rachel Field. FaPON
My Invention. Shel Silverstein. PV; QQQ
My Jack Spratt parents, full of spite and bile. Family History. Wendy Bishop. AMV-81
My Jacket Old. Herman Melville. SaC
My Jesus, as Thou wilt! Consecration. Benjamin Schmolck. BLRP
My Johnny. *Unknown.* OBET
My Joy, My Jockey, My Gabriel. George Barker. First Cycle of Love Poems, V. ErPo; MoAB; MoBrPo
(Love Poem.) NeBP
My Joy, my Life, my Crown! A True Hymn. George Herbert. InvP; NOCV; OxBoCh
My Kate. Elizabeth Barrett Browning. OBVV; OHFP; WBLP
My ketch must lead into the fray. Parting at Dawn. *Malay Oral Tradition, tr. by* R. J. Wilkinson *and* R. O. Winstedt. WTO
My Kin Talk. Anna Margolin, *tr. fr. Yiddish by* Keith Bosley. VWA
My kite is three feet broad, and six feet long. The Kite. Adelaide O'Keeffe. OxBChV
My kitten walks on velvet feet. Night. Lois Weakley McKay. SiSoSe
My kitty has a little song. Song for a Child. Helen B. Davis. SoPo
My knee against the ground. The Ladder Has No Steps. Jorge Plescoff, *tr. by* Yishai Tobin. VWA
My Laddie. Amélie Rives. HBV-1
My Laddie's Hounds. Marguerite Elizabeth Easter. AA
My ladies haire is threeds of beaten gold. Bartholomew Griffin. *Fr.* Fidessa, More Chaste than Kind. AAS
My Lady. Philip James Bailey. OBVV
My lady/ fair with. A Token. Robert Creeley. VGW
My Lady Carenza of the lovely body. *Unknown, tr. fr. Provençal by* Willis Barnstone. BoWoP
My lady carries love within her eyes. Dante, *tr. by* Dante Gabriel Rossetti. La Vita Nuova, XII. AWP
My Lady Esther, beautiful. Esther. Fray Angelico Chavez. GoBC
My Lady Has the Grace of Death. Joseph Plunkett. OxBI
My Lady Is a Pretty One. *Unknown.* OxBoLi
My lady looks so gentle and so pure. Dante, *tr. by* Dante Gabriel Rossetti. La Vita Nuova, XVI. AWP
My Lady mine, I send. Canzonetta: Of His Lady, and of His Making Her Likeness. Jacopo da Lentino, *tr. by* Dante Gabriel Rossetti. AWP
My Lady Nature and Her Daughters. Cardinal Newman. GoBC
My lady seems of ivory. Praise of My Lady. William Morris. HBV-1
My Lady Takes the Sunlight for Her Gown. Thomas Cole. NePoAm
My Lady the Lake. Peter Davidson. WeW
My lady walks her morning round. The Henchman. Whittier. HBV-1; OBEV; OBVV
My lady was found mutilated. Ballad. Leonard Cohen. OBCV
My lady went to Canterbury. Carol. *Unknown.* FaBoCo; FaBoNo
My Lady Wind. *Unknown.* HBV-1; HBVY
My lady woke upon a morning fair. On His Lady's Waking. Pierre de Ronsard, *tr. by* Andrew Lang. AWP
My Lady's birthday crowns the growing year. In February. Henry Simpson. HBV-1
My Lady's face it is they worship there. Sonetto XXXV: To Guido Orlando. Guido Cavalcanti, *tr. by* Ezra Pound. CTC
My Lady's Grave. Emily Brontë. *See* Song: "Linnet in the rocky dells, The."
My Lady's Presence Makes the Roses Red. Henry Constable. *Fr.* Diana. HBV-1; NIP; OBSC
(Sonnet: "My lady's presence makes the roses red.") EIL
My Lady's Tears. *Unknown. See* I Saw My Lady Weep.
My lamp, full charged with its sweet oil, still burns. Hero Entombed I. Peter Quennell. LiTB
My Land. Thomas Osborne Davis. HBV-2; PAL
My land is fair for any eyes to see. Jesse Stuart. FaPON; TiPo
My landlady has been to Hawaii. I look at her diamante. Vincent O'Sullivan. Brother Jonathan, Brother Kafka, 33. OCNZ
My lank limp lily, my long lithe lily. A Maudle-in Ballad. *Unknown.* BXAP; FaBoPa
My Last Afternoon with Uncle Devereux Winslow. Robert Lowell. NoP; VGW
My Last Duchess. Robert Browning. AWP; BeLS; BiP; CABA; EBVV; FaBoEn; FaFP; FF; FiP; FPL; GTBS-P; HAP; HBV-1; HeIP; HoPM; InPS; LiTB; MasP; MAT; NIP; NOBE; NoP; OAEL-2; OAEP; OBNC; PAI; PoEL-5; PoLF; PoPle; PPP; PrIm; SCV; SeCeV; SoSe; TEP; TreFS; TrGrPo; VLP; WeW; WHA
My Last Illusion. John Kendall. FiBHP; WhC
My Last Terrier. John Halsham. HBV-1
My Latest Sun Is Sinking Fast, *with music.* Jefferson Haskell. AH
My least height flowers late with buds. Where Unimaginably Bright. Oliver Hale. GoYe
My lefe is faren in a lond. The One I Love Is Gone Away [*or* Separated Lovers]. *Unknown.* MeEL; OAEL-1; OxBM
My left eye is blind and jogs like. Sketch for a Job Application Blank. Jim Harrison. AmPA; NoAM
My left upper/ lip and half. After the Dentist. May Swenson. DFF; GP
My Legacy. Helen Hunt Jackson. HBV-2
My Lesbia, I will not deny. Upon Lesbia—Arguing. Alfred Cochrane. HBV-1
My Lesbia, let us live and love. Courtship. Alexander Brome. CavP
My Lesbia let us love and live. Catullus, *tr. fr. Latin by* Wordsworth. OBVE
My Lessons in the Jail. Miriam Waddington. MoCV
My Letter. Grace Denio Litchfield. AA
My letters! all dead paper, mute and white! Elizabeth Barrett Browning. Sonnets from the Portuguese, XXVIII. HAP; HBV-1; ViBoPo
My liege, I did deny no prisoners. Shakespeare. *Fr.* King Henry IV, Pt. I. WaaP
My life/ is/ a/ bald headed match. Black Taffy. Peggy Susberry Kenner. JB
My Life by Somebody Else. Mark Strand. GP
My life closed twice before its close. Emily Dickinson. AmPP; AP; BoLoP; BoWoP; FaBoEn; GBL; HBVY; HeIP; MoAmPo; MoVE; NePA; NIP; NoAM; NOBA; OLR; OxBA; PoPl; PPP; SBG; SCV; SoSe; TreFT; TrGrPo; ViBoPo; WHA
(My Life Closed Twice.) MoAB
(Parting.) AA; LiTA; OBEV; OBVV; TwAmPo
My life flows on in endless song. How Can I Keep from Singing? *Unknown.* FSW
My life had stood—a loaded gun. Emily Dickinson. AmPP; AP; HAP; NoP; SBG; WeW; WPOW
My life had taken the shape of the small square. The Small Square. Sophia de Mello Breyner Andresen, *tr. by* Alexis Levitin. WPOW
My life has crept so long on a broken wing. Tennyson. *Fr.* Maud. OAEL-2; OBWP; SyP
My Life Is a Bowl. May Riley Smith. BLPA
My life is a wearisome journey. The End of the Way. Harriet Cole. BLRP
My life is cast. Sifting. Victor E. Beck. GoYe
"My life is done, yet all remains." Robert the Bruce. Edwin Muir. OxBS
My life is engraved on my poems. Of Myself. Leah Goldberg, *tr. by* Ramah Commanday. BoWoP
My life is legends of the yellow haired. Nor Mars His Sword. Dunstan Thompson. NePA
My life is like a dream. From Disciple to Master. Monk Gibbon. AnIV
My life is like a music-hall. Prologue to "London Nights." Arthur Symons. BrPo; VLP
My life is like a stroll upon the beach. The Fisher's Boy. Henry David Thoreau. AA; ChTr; MOS
My Life Is like the Summer Rose. Richard Henry Wilde. HBV-2; TreFT
(Stanzas.) AA
My Life is measur'd by this glasse, this glasse. On an Houre-glasse. John Hall. MeLP; MePo
My Life like Any Other. Philip Levine. AMV-81
My life more civil is and free. Independence. Henry David Thoreau. TreFS
My life must touch a million lives in some way ere I go. My Prayer. *Unknown.* BLRP
My life, my love, you say our love will last forever. Catullus, *tr. fr. Latin by* Horace Gregory. NAWM-1
My life shall touch a dozen lives. My Influence. *Unknown.* STF
My Life, the Quality of Which. Etheridge Knight. NNaP
My life—to Discontent a prey. Rhymes (?). Henry S. Leigh. NOBL
My life was never so precious. Inscription for the Tank. James Wright. TwCP
My life, your light green eyes. Last Words. James Merrill. TAP
My Life's Delight. Thomas Campion. TrGrPo
("Come, O! come, my life's delight.") EIL; InvP; OBSC
My light will tip tankards of fire in the sky. A Constant Labor. James W. Thompson. BPo
My limbs are wasted with a flame. La Bella Donna della Mia Mente. Oscar Wilde. UnTE
My lines falter. Arriving. Gabriel Preil, *tr. by* Robert Friend. VWA

My lips from this day forgot how to smile. Auguste Lacaussade. *Fr.* Les Salaziennes. TTY
My lips lack prophecy. Lamentation. Nissim Ezekiel. VWA
My lips murmur. The Vigil. Shlomo Reich, *tr. by* Mira Reich. VWA
My little bed is wide enough. The White Dream. May Doney. HBMV
My little Ben, whilst thou art young. To His Son Bennet. John Hoskyns. FaBoEE
My Little Bird. Bunyan. OBS
(Of the Child with the Bird on the Bush.) OxBChV
My Little Birds. *Unknown, tr. fr. Arabic by* Henrietta Siksek-Su'ad. FaPON
My little boy, with pale, round cheeks. The Shadows. George Macdonald. TRV
My little breath, under the willows by the water-side we used to sit. A Lover's Lament [*or* The Willows by the Water Side]. *Unknown, tr. by* H. J. Spinden. AWP; WTO
My Little Buckaroo. *Unknown.* BPAW
My little cousin, if you'll be. To My Youngest Kinsman, R. L. Abraham Chear. OxBChV
My little dears, who learn to read, pray early learn to shun. Cautionary Verses to Youth of Both Sexes [*or* Address to Children]. Theodore Hook. FaBoUs; HBV-2; OxBChV
My little doves have left a nest. My Doves. Elizabeth Barrett Browning. VLP
My Little Dreams. Georgia Douglas Johnson. BANP; BlSi; CDC; PoNe
My little finger's stuck in a/ Coca-Cola bottle. Constant Defender. James Tate. MAYP
My Little Girl. Samuel Minturn Peck. AA
My little lady I may not leave behind. To My Lady Mirriel Howard. John Skelton. *Fr.* The Garlande of Laurell. LoBV
My Little Lodge. *Unknown, tr. fr. Old Irish by* F. N. Robinson. OnYI
My little lord, methinks 'tis strange. A Prognostication on Will Laud, Late Archbishop of Canterbury. *Unknown.* OxBoLi
My Little Love. Charles B. Hawley. HBV-1
My little love, do you remember. The Chess-Board. "Owen Meredith." HBV-1
My Little Love Lies on the Ground. Larin Paraske, *tr. fr. Finnish by* Jaakko A. Ahokas. PBWP
My little Mädchen found one day. A Chrysalis. Mary Emily Bradley. AA; HBV-1
My little milliner has slipp'd. A Machine Hand. Thomas Ashe. OBVV
My Little Neighbor. Mary August Mason. AA
My little old man and I fell out. Mother Goose. OxNR
My little one begins his feet to try. The First Step. Andrew Bice Saxton. AA
My Little Pretty Mopsy. *Unknown.* OxBM
My little scholar, to thy book inclined. A Schoolmaster's Precepts. John Penkethman. OxBChV
My Little Sister. William Wise. RHPC
My little son, I have cast you out. Choosing a Name. Anne Ridler. NOBE
My little son, who looked from thoughtful eyes. The Toys. Coventry Patmore. The Unknown Eros, I, x. ACP; BeLS; EBEV; EBVV; FaFP; GoBC; HBV-1; OBEV; OBVV; SoSe; TreFS; TrGrPo; TrPWD; TRV; ViBoPo
My little soul I never saw. Grace Fallow Norton. Little Gray Songs from St. Joseph's, XLVII. HBV-2
My little soul, my vagrant charmer. Emperor Hadrian, *tr. fr. Latin by* J. V. Cunningham. OBVE. *See also* Hadrian's Address to His Soul When Dying.
My little stone. Letters [*or* Notes] Found near a Suicide. Frank Horne. AmNP; CDC; PoBA; PoNe
My lizard just beyond the lamp's shine. The Small Lizard. Linda Gregg. MAYP
My lizard, my lively writher. Wish for a Young Wife. Theodore Roethke. NoAM; NoP; TAP
My locker, green steel. Game Resumed. Richmond Lattimore. LiSp; NYBP
My lodging it is on the cold ground. Sir William Davenant. *Fr.* The Rivals. JCP
My long two-pointed ladder's sticking through a tree. After Apple-Picking. Robert Frost. AmPP; AP; CMoP; CoBMV; FPL; LiTA; MoAB; MoAmPo; MoPo; MoVE; NoAM; NOBA; NU; OxBA; PAI; PPP; PrIM; RoGo; TAP; UnPo; ViBoPo
My Lord/ if I worship Thee from fear of Hell. Rabi'a al-Adawiyya, *tr. fr. Arabic by* Margaret Smith, *ad. by* Deirdre Lashgari. WPOW
My Lord and King. Tennyson. *See* In Memoriam A. H. H.: "Love is and was my lord and king."
My Lord, fallen, sin-stained. Sticheron for Matins, Wednesday of Holy Week. Kassia, *tr. by* Patrick Diehl. WPOW
My Lord has departed. Longing for the Emperor. Empress Iwa no Hime, *tr. by* Geoffrey Bownas *and* Anthony Thwaite. BoWoP
My lord, I was accustomed to swill about the sky. The Dove Apologizes to His God for Being Caught by a Cat. Anthony Eaton. PeSA
My Lord, my Life, can Envy ever bee. Edward Taylor. *Fr.* Sacramental Meditations. PoEL-3
My lord said to my lady. Lamkin. *Unknown.* ESPB
My Lord Says He's Gwineter Rain Down Fire, *with music.* *Unknown.* BoAN-2
My Lord Tomnoddy. Robert Barnabas Brough. FiBHP; VLP
My Lord Tomnoddy got up one day. Hon. Mr. Sucklethumbkin's Story. "Thomas Ingoldsby." *Fr.* The Ingoldsby Legends. OBRV
My Lord Tomnoddy's the son of an Earl. My Lord Tomnoddy. Robert Barnabas Brough. FiBHP; VLP
My Lord, What a Morning. Waring Cuney. TTY
My Lord, What a Mourning [*or* Mornin']. *Unknown.* BoAN-1, *with music;* FSW
(Judgement Day.) WTO
My Lord would make a cross for me. My Cross. Zitella Cocke. HBV-2
My Lord's a-Writin' All de Time, *with music.* *Unknown.* BoAN-1
My Lords, my Lord of Warwick. Joan of Arc to the Tribunal. Anthony Frisch. CaP
My lords, with your leave. A New War Song by Sir Peter Parker. *Unknown.* PAH
My Lost Youth. Longfellow. AA; AmPP; AP; AWP; EtS; FaBoBe; FaBV; FaFP; FaPoR; FPL; GoJo; HBV-1; LiTA; NePA; NOBA; OBEV; OxBA; PoEL-5; PoLF; PoRA; RoGo; SeCeV; TAP; TreF; ViBoPo
(Sea Memories.) FaPON
My loud machine for making hay. An Old Field Mowed. William Meredith. NYBP
My lov'd, my honour'd, much respected friend! The Cotter's Saturday Night. Burns. EnRP; LAuP; OAEP
My Love. E. E. Cummings. ErPo; LiTM; VGW
My Love. Bartholomew Griffin. *See* Sonnet: "Fair is my love that feeds among the lilies."
My Love. James Russell Lowell. BLPL; FaBoBe; HBV-1
My love/ Is like the grasses. Ono no Yoshiki, *tr. by* Arthur Waley. *Fr.* Kokin Shu. AWP
My love and I for kisses play'd. William Strode. FaBoEE
My love and I, the other day. The Snake. Thomas Moore. HBV-1
My love and my delight. The Lament for Art O'Leary. Eileen O'Leary, *tr. by* Frank O'Connor. AnIL; KiLC
My Love behind Walls. Heather Spears. OBCV
My Love bound me with a kiss. Kisses Make Men Loath to Go [*or* Kisses *or* Song]. *At. to* Thomas Campion. ElL; HBV-1; OBSC; UnTE
My love came back to me. All Souls' Night. Frances Cornford. EnLoPo; OxBTC
My love came up from Barnegat. The Puritan's Ballad. Elinor Wylie. HBMV; PoRA
My love comes down from the mountain. Love on the Mountain. Thomas Boyd. AnIV; HBV-1; OxBI
My love dwelt in a northern land. Romance. Andrew Lang. HBV-1
My Love Eats an Apple. Ralph Gustafson. MoCV
My Love for All Things Warm and Breathing. William Kloefkorn. AMV-81
My love for him shall be. Medieval Norman Song. *Unknown, tr. by* John Addington Symonds. AWP
My Love for Thee. Richard Watson Gilder. HBV-1
"My love for you has faded"—thus the Bad. Versions of Love. Roy Fuller. LiTM
My love forever! The Lament for Art [*or* Arthur] O'Leary. Eibhlin Dubh O'Connell, *tr. by* Eilis Dillon *and* John Montague. BIrV; PBWP
My love gave me a king's robe. Wardrobe. Sister Mary Madeleva. GoBC
My love gave me a passion-flower. The Passion-Flower. Margaret Fuller. HBV-1
"My love has built a bonny ship, and set her on the sea." The Lowlands o' Holland. *Unknown.* BSV
My love has gone down to his garden. Bible, *O.T., ad. by* Willis Barnstone. *Fr.* The Song of Solomon. BoWoP
My love has left me has gone from me. Souvenirs. Dudley Randall. BPo
My love hath vowed he will forsake me. A Maid's Complaint. Thomas Campion. UnTE
My love he built me a bonnie bower. The Lament of the Border Widow [*or* The Border Widow's Lament *or* The Bonnie Bower]. *Unknown.* BSV; CH; GBP; HBV-1; LO; OxBB, *with music*
My love he is fairer than a summer day. The Drynaun Dhun. *Unknown.* GBP
My love, how could your heart consider. Motet. *Unknown, tr. by* Carol Cosman. PBWP
My Love, I Cannot Thy Rare Beauties Place. William Smith. *Fr.* Chloris. InvP
(Sonnet: "My Love, I cannot thy rare beauties place.") ElL
My Love I Gave for Hate. *Unknown, tr. fr. Irish by* George Hay. BIrV

My love I give to you a threefold thing. Branwell's Sestina. James Reaney. *Fr.* A Suit of Nettles. MoCV
My Love in Her Attire. *Unknown.* BLPL; FF; GTBS; GTBS-P; HeIP; LiTB; NiP; ViBoPo
(Beauty's Self.) TrGrPo; UnTE
(Madrigal: "My love in her attire doth show her wit.") BoLoP; EIL; HBV-1; NOBE; OBEV; OBSC
My love is a lotus blossom. Love Song. *Unknown, tr. by* J. E. Manchip White. TTY
My love is a rider, [wild] broncos he breaks. *See* My lover's a cowboy, wild broncos he breaks.
My love is as a fever, longing still. Sonnets, CXLVII. Shakespeare. EBEV; HoPM; PoEL-2; TEP
My love is but a shepherd lad. The Shepherd and the Shepherdess. *Unknown.* OBET
My Love Is Dead. Thomas Chatterton. *See* Minstrel's Song.
My love is in my house. Mirabai, *tr. fr. Hindi by* Willis Barnstone *and* Usha Nilsson. BoWoP
My love is lessened and must soon be past. The Beginning of the End. Gerard Manley Hopkins. VLP
My Love is Like a Myrtle. Moses ibn Ezra, *tr. fr. Hebrew by* Solomon Solis-Cohen. TrJP
My Love Is like a Red, Red Rose. Burns. *See* Red, Red Rose, A.
My Love Is like the Sun. *Unknown.* AnIV
My Love Is like to Ice. Spenser. Amoretti, XXX. ErPo; FF; FPL; LiTB; PAI; TrGrPo
My love is living. South of the Great Sea. *Unknown, tr. by* Arthur Waley. OLR
My love is male and proper-man. The Contemplative Quarry. Anna Wickham. HBMV
My Love Is neither Young nor Old. *Unknown.* EnRePo; OBSC
My love is no short year's sentence. Love. *Unknown, tr. by* John Montague. BIrV
My love is o' comely height, an' straight. White an' Blue. William Barnes. GBL; GTBS-P
My love is of a birth as rare. The Definition of Love. Andrew Marvell. AnAnS-1; BLPL; BoLoP; EBEV; FaBoEn; GBL; HoPM; InPK; InPS; JCP; LiTB; LoBV; MeLP; MePo; NOBE; NoP; OAEL-1; OAEP; OBEV; OBS; PoEL-2; SeCePo; SeCeV; SeCP; SeCV-1; TEP; TreFT; TrGrPo; UnPo; WHA
My Love is Past. Thomas Watson. PBBP
My love is playing on a fiddle. *Gond Oral Tradition, tr. by* V. Elwin *and* S. Hivale. WTO
My Love Is Sleeping. Kenneth Leslie. OBCV
My love is strengthen'd, though more weak in seeming. Sonnets, CII. Shakespeare. AWP; EIL; OAEP; OBEV; OBSC; ViBoPo
My love is tasting the fragrance. *Unknown, tr. fr. Pashto by* Saduddin Shpoon. PBWP
My love is the flaming Sword. Song. James Thompson. OBVV
My love is the maid ov all maidens. In the Spring. William Barnes. GBL
My love is the red sky before a rain. Signals. Keith Waldrop. AMV-81
My Love is the voice of a song. David McKee Wright. *Fr.* Dark Rosaleen. PoAu-1
My love is white and ruddy. Bible, *O.T., ad. by* Willis Barnstone. *Fr.* The Song of Solomon. BoWoP
My Love Is Young. Earle Birney. NOBC
My love leads the white bulls to sacrifice. Processionals. Alice Archer James. AA
My love lies in the gates of foam. The Churchyard on the Sands. Lord De Tabley. CH, *abr.;* FaBoPP; GBL; HBV-1; LoBV; OBNC
My love lies underground. Hymn to Priapus. D. H. Lawrence. CMoP; CoBMV; MoAB; OBMV
My love, like the vast majority. Erotic Suite. José Luis Vega, *tr. by* Julio Marzán. InW
My love looks like a girl tonight. The Bride. D. H. Lawrence. NoAM; OxBTC
My Love, Oh, She Is My Love. *Unknown, tr. fr. Irish by* Douglas Hyde. AnIV
My love on Wednesday letting fall her body. In Crisis. Lawrence Durrell. LiTM
My love sent me a chicken without e'er a bone. *Unknown.* OxNR
My love she is a gentlewoman. Auld Matrons. *Unknown.* BaBo; ESPB
My Love, She Passed Me By. *Unknown.* AmFP
My love she was born in the north country wide. Molly of the North Country. *Unknown.* OBET
My Love, She's But a Lassie Yet. Burns. ViBoPo
My Love She's But a Lassie Yet. James Hogg. HBV-1
My Love-Song. Else Lasker-Schüler, *tr. fr. German by* Jethro Bithell. TrJP
My love takes an apple to bed. Evesong. Maureen Duffy. PeHV
My love, this is the bitterest, that thou. Any Wife to Any Husband. Robert Browning. FaBoEn; OBNC; VLP
My love tonight is far away. Harry Edward Mills. *Fr.* On a Rainy Night. PeD
My love too stately is to be but fair. Electra. Francis Howard Williams. AA
My love took scorn my service to retain. Sonnet. Sir Thomas Wyatt. SiPS
My Love Wants to Park. Eloise Klein Healy. GP
My Love Was Light. Tennessee Williams. PoA
My Love When This Is Past. Stephany Fuller. BPo
My love will come. Waiting. Yevgeny Yevtushenko, *tr. by* Robin Milner-Gulland *and* Peter Levi. LLLT
My love, you are timely come, let me lie by your heart. The Door and the Window. Henry Reed. NeBP
My loved, my honored, much-respected friend! The Cotter's Saturday Night. Burns. BeLS; FaBoBe; HBV-2; PoLF
My loved one is unique, without a peer. Love Song. *Unknown, tr. by* J. E. Manchip White. TTY
My lovely child all clothed in blue. Lullaby in Auschwitz. Pierre Morhange, *tr. by* Edouard Roditi. VWA
My lover capable of terrible lies. Kaccipettu Nannakaiyar, *tr. fr. Tamil by* A. K. Ramanujan. BoWoP; PBWP; WPOW
My lover he is a cowboy. The Jolly Cowboy. *Unknown.* CoSo
My lover is ridiculous. Nocturnal Visitor. Carolyn Miller. AMV-80
My lovers/ (Simple chaps). Ode: To My Lovers. Paul Verlaine, *tr. by* J. Murat *and* W. Gunn. PeHV
My lover's [*or* love is] a cowboy [*or* rider], wild [*or* and] broncos he breaks. Bucking Bronco. *Unknown.* AmFP; BPAW; CoSo; FSW
My lovers do not belong to the two rich classes. Thousands and Three. Paul Verlaine, *tr. by* François Pirou. PeHV
My Loves. John Stuart Blackie. OBVV
My love's eyes are red as the sargasso. The Talking Fish. Ruth Stone. BoWoP
My Love's Guardian Angel. William Barnes. GBL; NBM; PoEL-4
My love's manners in bed. The Way. Robert Creeley. AP; BoLoP; LiTM; NeAP; PPP
My loyal sins. Loyal Sins. Jacob Glatstein, *tr. by* Ruth Whitman. VWA
My Lucy was charming and fair. The Shepherd's Despair. Thomas Dermody. OnYI
My Lulu, *with music.* *Unknown.* AS
My Lute and I. Sir Thomas Wyatt. MeEL
("At most mischief.") SiPS
My lute, awake! perform at last. The Lover Complaineth the Unkindness of His Love [*or* To His Lute]. Sir Thomas Wyatt. AAS; BoLoP; CABA; EBEV; EIL; ELP; EnRePo; FaBoEn; GBL; HAP; NOBE; NoP; OAEL-1; OAEP; OBEV; OBSC; PoEL-1; QFR; SiPS; TrGrPo; ViBoPo
My lute, be as thou wast [*or* wert] when thou didst grow. Sonnet [*or* To His Lute]. William Drummond of Hawthornden. EIL; GTBS; GTBS-P; LoBV; OBS; ViBoPo
My Luve Is like a Red, Red Rose. Burns. *See* Red, Red Rose, A.
"My luve she lives in Lincolnshire." Alison and Willie. *Unknown.* BaBo; ESPB
My Luve's in Germany. *Unknown.* CH
My Luve's like a Red, Red Rose. Burns. *See* Red, Red Rose, A.
My madman bathes in the golden tank. The Right True End. *Gond Oral Tradition, tr. by* V. Elwin *and* S. Hivale. WTO
My madness is dear to me. Mad Song. Denise Levertov. TAP
My Madonna. Robert W. Service. BLPA
"My magic is dead," said the witch. "I'm astounded." The Witch's Cat. Ian Serraillier. SO; WSC
My maid Mary,/ She minds the dairy. Mother Goose. OxNR
My Maisters all attend you. Turners Dish of Lentten Stuffe or A Galymaufery. William Turner. CoMu
My Maker shunneth me. Spiritual Isolation. Isaac Rosenberg. TrJP
My Mall, I mark that when you mean to prove me. The Author to His Wife, of a Woman's Eloquence. Sir John Harington. BoLoP; ErPo
My Mama Moved among the Days. Lucille Clifton. *Fr.* Good Times. BlSi; PoBA
My mamma is dead and she's buried. My Darling's on the Deep Blue Sea. *Unknown.* AmFP
My mammy she told me to open the door. Old Gray Beard a-Shaking. *Unknown.* AmFP
My Mammy Was a Wall-eyed Goat. *Unknown.* ChTr; FaBoNo
My mammy's in the cold, cold ground. Po' Boy. *Unknown.* AS
My man is a bone ringèd with weed. [First Woman's] Lament. Brenda Chamberlain. NeBP; NeIP; WPE; WPOW
My Man John. *Unknown.* OBET
My man loved me so much. So Long. Jayne Cortez. BoWoP
My Many-Coated Man. Laurie Lee. NYBP
My Marriage with Mrs. Johnson. Jack Gilbert. NPGG
My Mary. William Cowper. *See* To Mary.
My Maryland. James Ryder Randall. AA; FaBoBe; FaFP; HBV-2; PAH; TreF
(Maryland, My Maryland!) FaPo; PSoN, *with music*

My Master and I. *Unknown.* CoMu; OBET
My Master Hath a Garden. *Unknown.* CH
My Master Was So Very Poor. Harry Lee. TRV
My masters twain made me a bed. Said the Canoe [*or* The Canoe]. Isabella Valancy Crawford. NOBC; OBCV; OnYI
My Mate Bill. G. H. Gibson. PoAu-1
My meaning passes like wild nightbirds. Credo. Brewster Ghiselin. PoA
My Midnight Meditation. Henry King. MePo; OBS
'My milk-white doo,' said the young man. The Young Man and the Young Nun. A. D. Mackie. OxBS
My mill grinds pepper and spice. *Unknown.* OxNR
My mind has thunderstorms. Thunderstorms. W. H. Davies. HBV-2
My mind i th' mines of rich Philosophy. On My Lord Bacon. John Danforth. SCAP
My mind is sad and weary thinking how. Odell. James Stephens. MoAB; MoBrPo
My mind is so evil and unjust. Human Relations. C. H. Sisson. POL; TW
My mind is stuffed with tablecloths. Poland/ 1931 "The Wedding." Jerome Rothenberg. PoM; Prf
My Mind Keeps Out the Host of Sin. Edmund Elys. NCEP
My mind lets go a thousand things. Memory. Thomas Bailey Aldrich. AA; BoNaP; PoLF; TreFS
My mind shrugs off his threadbare winter poems. Time Out. Donald Finkel. HoPM
My Mind [*or* Minde *or* Mynde] to Me a Kingdom [*or* Kyngdome] Is. Sir Edward Dyer. BLPL; ElL; EnRePo; FaBoBe; HBV-2; LiTB; NIP; NOBE; PoEL-1; TreFS; TrGrPo; ViBoPo; WGRP
(Kingdom.) LoBV; OBSC
My mind was once the true survey. The Mower's Song. Andrew Marvell. AnAnS-1; CavP; LoBV; PoEL-2; PPP; SeCP; SeCV-1
My mirror is always a little taller than I am. Mirror. Tada Chimako, *tr. by* Kenneth Rexroth *and* Ikuko Atsumi. BoWoP
My Mistress. Thomas Lodge. *Fr.* The Life and Death of William Longbeard. TrGrPo
My Mistress. William Warner. ElL
My mistress' eyes are nothing like the sun. Sonnets, CXXX. Shakespeare. AWP; BiP; BoLoP; CABA; EBEV; FF; HAP; HBV-1; HoPM; InPK; InPS; InvP; LiTB; NIP; NoP; OAEL-1; OAEP; PAI; PoPle; PP; PPP; PrIm; SeCeV; SoSe; TEP; WeW
My mistress frowns when she should play. Madrigal [*or* Fa La La]. John Hilton. CH; OxBoLi
My mistress' innermost heart. Beauty, Sleeping. Arthur Freeman. DFT
My Mistress is a paragon. My Mistress. William Warner. ElL
My mistress is as fair as fine. Madrigal. Thomas Ravenscroft. CH; OxBoLi
My Mistress Makes Music ("My mistress is in music passing skillful"). *Unknown.* UnTE
My mistress sayes she'll marry none but me. Catullus, *tr. fr. Latin by* Richard Lovelace. OBVE
My mistress when she goes. Her Rambling [*or* My Mistress]. Thomas Lodge. *Fr.* The Life and Death of William Longbeard. LoBV; OBSC; TrGrPo
My Mistress's Boots. Frederick Locker-Lampson. HBV-1
My misunderstandings: for years I thought "muso bello" meant. Taking a Walk with You. Kenneth Koch. CABA; CAPP
My mither sent me to the well. Whistle o'er the Lave o't. *Unknown.* GBP
My mom says I'm her sugarplum. Some Things Don't Make Any Sense at All. Judith Viorst. RHPC
My money! O, my money! Mavimbela, *tr. fr. Zulu by* H. Tracey. WTO
My Morning Song. George Macdonald. TRV
My mortal love's a rabbit skin. Apology. Vassar Miller. NePoEA
My most distinguished guest and learnèd friend. Edna St. Vincent Millay. VGW
My most pious songs I have written. God's Gifts. Jakov de Haan, *tr. by* David Soetendorp. VWA
My Mother. Amelia Josephine Burr. HBMV
My Mother. Josephine Rice Creelman. OHIP
My Mother. Francis Ledwidge. HBMV; OHIP
My Mother. Robert Mezey. NaP
My Mother. Hayim Naggid, *tr. fr. Hebrew by* Rose Drachler. VWA
My Mother. Bertha Nolan. PGD
My Mother. Ann *or* Jane Taylor. BLPA; BLPL; OHIP; OxBChV; PaPo; TreF, *sl. abr.*
My Mother. *Unknown.* STF
My mother/sits. My Mother Takes a Bath. Yuri Kageyama. BrSi
My mother, a great believer in presences. Keeping You Alive. Tess Gallagher. GP
My mother always said. Sappho, *tr. fr. Greek by* Willis Barnstone. BoWoP
My Mother and My Sisters. Simon J. Ortiz. GP
My mother and your mother. *Unknown.* OxNR
My Mother Bids Me Bind My Hair. Anne Hunter. HBV-1; OBEC
My mother bore me. Foolish Child. *Unknown, tr. by* J. B. Danquah. PBA
My mother bore me in an island town. Sea Born. Harold Vinal. HBMV
My mother bore me in the heat of summer. On Approaching My Birthday. Vassar Miller. IHMS; NMM
My mother bore me in the southern wild. The Little Black Boy. Blake. *Fr.* Songs of Innocence. AWP; BiP; CABA; CH; EnRP; HBV-1; HeIP; InPK; LAuP; NOEC; NoP; OAEL-2; OAEP; OBEC; OBEV; OBNC; OxBChV; OxBoCh; PoEL-4; PoNe; SeCeV; TreFS; TrGrPo
My mother called me to her deathbed side, these words she said to me. Coon Can (Poor Boy). *Unknown.* AS
My mother called my father "Mr Hunt." Stabat Mater. Sam Hunt. OCNZ
My mother calls it. The City. Linda Pastan. NYP
My mother came/ From a village of grasses. Beginnings. Erez Biton, *tr. by* Judith Katz. VWA
My mother gathered balls of dust. The Housecleaner. Gail White. AMV-80
My mother groaned! my father wept. Infant Sorrow. Blake. *Fr.* Songs of Experience. FaBoEn; InPS; LAuP; NAs; OBNC; PAI; PoEL-4; PoPle
My mother had two faces and a frying pot. From the House of Yemanjá. Audre Lorde. NoP
My mother has the prettiest tricks. A Song for My Mother Her Words. Anna Hampstead Branch. *Fr.* Song for My Mother. FaPON; OHIP; SiSoSe; TiPo; YeAR
My mother is beautiful as a flapper. Among His Effects We Found a Photograph. Ed Ochester. Str
My mother is peeling an apple over the sink. A Kitchen Memory. Roy Scheele. Str
My mother lives in a house. My House. Robert Adamson. CBAP
My mother makes beer in the bathtub. My God, How the Money Rolls In. *Unknown.* FSW
My mother never forgave my father. The Portrait. Stanley Kunitz. CTBA; DiL; GP; Psk
My mother of the blue/ Anglo-Saxon eyes. The Eyes, the Blood. David Meltzer. PoM; VWA
My Mother on an Evening in Late Summer. Mark Strand. FYAP; GeTw
My Mother Once Told Me. Yehuda Amichai, *tr. fr. Hebrew by* Assia Gutmann. NYBP
My mother once was a doe. My Nightingale. Rose Ausländer, *tr. by* Ewald Osers. VWA
My Mother Pieced Quilts. Teresa Palma Acosta. FIA; WPOW
My mother, poor woman, lies tonight. Goodbye. Galway Kinnell. Str
My mother said I must not have a collier. I'll Have a Collier for My Sweetheart. William Oliver. WTO
My mother said, "If just once more." Mother's Nerves. X. J. Kennedy. GrPl; RHPC
My mother said that I never should. Gypsies in the Wood. *Unknown.* DTC; OxBoLi; OxNR; PoPle
My mother sate me at her glass. The Comb. Walter de la Mare. FaBoRV
My mother saw the green tree toad. Lorine Niedecker. VGW
My mother says I must not pass. The Witch in the Glass. Sarah Morgan Bryan Piatt. AA
My Mother sends our neighbors things. Neighborly. Violet Alleyn Storey. TiPo
My mother sent us to the school. The Shoemakker. *Unknown.* OBET
My mother she's so good to me. A Boy's Mother. James Whitcomb Riley. HBVY; OHIP
My mother sliced the south for us. Lullaby for Ann-Lucian. Calvin Forbes. PoBA
My Mother Takes a Bath. Yuri Kageyama. Brsi
My mother taught me to be good. Poem for Mother's Day. Margaret Fishback. InMe
My mother thinks. Living in the World. Alan Chong Lau. BrSi
My mother told me just before she died. Motherless Child Blues. *Unknown.* BluL
My mother took us, when we went walking. The Dell. Gavin Ewart. OxBC
My mother twice in her life on worn feet. Frederick Douglass. Sam Cornish. PoBA
My Mother Was a Lady; or, If Jack Were Only Here. Edward B. Marks. TreF; YaD
(Mother Was a Lady; or, If Jack Were Only Here, *with music.*) FSN
My mother was a romantic girl. Papa Love Baby. Stevie Smith. DBV; SBG
My mother was an ill woman. The Death of Lord Warriston. *Unknown.* OxBB
My mother was old. Piccante. Mary Di Michele. AMV-81
My mother was taken up to heaven in a pink cloud. Ordinary People in the Last Days. Jay Macpherson. PAI
My mother wept loudly. Austin Clarke. *Fr.* Tiresias. CIP
My mother, when young, scrubbed laundry in a tub. In an Iridescent Time. Ruth Stone. MoAmPo; PoPl; TwAmPo

My mother whispers to my father. At Wonder Donut. Laureen Mar. BrSi
My mother whistled softly. The Little Whistler. Frances Frost. PDV; SoPo; TiPo
My Mother, Who Came from China, Where She Never Saw Snow. Laureen Mar. WPOW
My mother, who has a hide. The Hide of My Mother. Edward Dorn. NeAP
My mother who loses a piece. Now It Is Broccoli. Jeff Tagami. BrSi
My Mother Would Be a Falconress. Robert Duncan. PAI; PoM
My mother writes from Trenton. My Mother. Robert Mezey. NaP
My mother—preferring the strange to the tame. The Intruder. Carolyn Kizer. BoWoP; GP; NePoEA-2
My Mother's Bible. George Pope Morris. AA; BLRP; PaPo; WBLP
My Mother's Birthday, *sel.* Kathleen Raine.
I Used to Watch You, Sleeping. NAs
My mother's brother hauled me to the big-boys' club. Fall In. Lincoln Kirstein. NoAM
My Mother's Childhood. Barry Spacks. GP
My mother's cigarette flares and fades. June Twenty-first. Bruce Guernsey. PPJ
My mother's Council house is occupied. Ornaments. Frank Ormsby. CIP
My Mother's Death. Judith Hemschemeyer. Str
My Mother's Feet. Stanley Plumly. GeTw
My mother's form was spare and keen. Generations. Robert Clark. PoAu-2
My Mother's Garden. Alice E. Allen. BLPA; BLPL; FaBoBe
My Mother's Hands. *Unknown. See* Beautiful Hands.
My mother's hands are cool and fair. A Song for My Mother: Her Hands. Anna Hampstead Branch. OHIP
My Mother's House, *sel.* Leah Goldberg, *tr. fr. Hebrew.*
"My mother's mother died," *tr. by* Robert Alter. PBWP
(From My Mother's Home, *tr. by* Robert Friend.) VWA
My Mother's House. Eunice Tietjens. HBMV
My mother's lamp once out. Scenes of Childhood. James Merrill. CoAP; DiL
My Mother's Life. William Meredith. AMV-81
My Mother's Love. *Unknown.* STF
My mother's maids [*or* maydes], when they did sew and spin [*or* sowe and spynne]. Sir Thomas Wyatt. Satires, II. AAS; SiPS
My mother's mother died. Leah Goldberg. *Fr.* My Mother's House. PBWP; VWA
My mother's mother's underpants. Grandma Shorba and the Pure in Heart. Freya Manfred. FAZ
My mother's name was Mary. Mary's a Grand Old Name. George M. Cohan. BLSo; FSN; TreFT
My Mother's Prayer. T. C. O'Kane. BLPA; FaBoBe
My Mother's Shoes. Rayzel Zychlinska, *tr. fr. Yiddish by* Marc Kaminsky. VWA
My Mother's Sister. C. Day Lewis. OxBTC
My Mother's Table. Hy Sobiloff. NePA; TwAmPo
My mountains, God has company in heaven. In High Places. Harriet Monroe. PoA
My mouse, my girl in gray, I speak to her. Afternoon. Donald Hall. Str
My Mouth. Arnold Adoff. RHPC
My mouth blooms like a cut. The Kiss. Anne Sexton. NIP
My mouth doth water, and my breast doth swell. Astrophel and Stella, XXXVII. Sir Philip Sidney. SiPS
My mouth is often joined against his mouth. Arthur Rimbaud, *tr. fr. French by* François Pirou. PeHV
My Mouth Is Very Quiet. José Garcia Villa. TwAmPo
My mouth to utter a cry. A Time of Night. David Ignatow. FAZ
My Muse and I, Ere Youth and Spirits Fled. George Colman the Younger. ELU
My muse in meads has spent her many hours. To Mistress Katherine Bradshaw, the Lovely, That Crowned Him with Laurel. Robert Herrick. CaPo
My Muse may well grudge at my heavenly joy. Astrophel and Stella, LXX. Sir Philip Sidney. SiPS
My Muse, though airy, glides softly along. The Song of the Pen. Judah al-Harizi, *tr. by* J. Chotzner. TrJP
My muse, what ails this ardour? Sappho, *tr. fr. Greek by* Sir Philip Sidney. OBVE
My Muse will now by chymistry draw forth. To the Learned and Reverend Mr. Cotton Mather, on His Excellent Magnalia. Grindall Rawson. SCAP
My Mynde to Me a Kyngdome Is. Sir Edward Dyer. *See* My Mind To Me a Kingdom Is.
My Naked Aunt. Archibald MacLeish. NePA
My naked simple life was I. My Spirit. Thomas Traherne. SeCV-2
My Name and I. Robert Graves. NoAM; NYBP
My name engraved herein. A Valediction: Of My Name in the Window. John Donne. EnRePo; QFR
My Name Is. Pauline Clarke. RHPC
My Name Is Afrika. Keorapetse Kgositsile. PoBA
My name is Captain Hall. Captain Hall. *Unknown.* GBP
My name is Colin Clout. The Prelates. John Skelton. *Fr.* Colin Clout. TrGrPo
My name is Edgar Poe and I was born. On the Edge. Philip Levine. CoAP; TAP
My name is Edward Hollander [*or* Holland *or* Hallahan *or* Hollahan], as you may [*or* shall] understand. The *Flying Cloud. Unknown.* AmFP; BaBo; OBET; ShS; ViBoFo
My name is Frank Taylor [*or* Frank Bolar *or* Tom Hight], a [*or* 'nole *or* an old] bachelor I am. Starving to Death on a Government Claim [*or* The Lane County Bachelor]. *Unknown.* AmFP; AS; FSW; OBAL
My name is George Nathaniel Curzon. John William Mackail *and* Cecil Arthur Spring-Rice. *Fr.* Balliol Rhymes. FaBoCo; FaBoEE; NOBL
My name is "I am living." I Have Bowed before the Sun. Anna Lee Walters. WPOW
My name is Jew. The Permanent Delegate. Yuri Suhl, *tr. by* Max Rosenfeld *and* Walter Lowenfels. PAI; PPON
My name is Joe Bowers. *See* My name it is Joe Bowers.
My name is John J. Curtis. John J. Curtis. Joseph Gallagher. AmFP
My name is Johnson. Madam's Past History. Langston Hughes. NoAm
My name is Juan Murray, and sad for my fate. Juan Murray. *Unknown.* CoSo
My name is Larry Gorman, to you I mean no harm. The Scow on Cowden Shore, *vers.* I. Larry Gorman. ShS
My name is not my own. The Meeting. Tess Gallagher. GeTw
My name is O'Kelly, I've heard the Revelly. Shillin' a Day. Kipling. OAEP; ViBoPo
My name is old Jack Palmer. The Old Keg of Rum. *Unknown.* PoAu-1
My name is Old Mortality—mine is the hand. Surviving a Poetry Circuit. William Stafford. FAZ
My name is Parrot, a bird [or byrd] of paradise. Parrot's Soliloquy [*or* The Parrot *or* Speke, Parrot]. John Skelton. *Fr.* Speak, Parrot. ACP; OxBoLi, *abr.*; PoEL-1
My name is Peter Emberley [*or* Embley *or* Emily]. Peter Emberley [*or* Amberley]. John Calhoun. AmFP; ShS, *diff. vers.*
My name is Phyllis Janik. In the Field. Phyllis Janik. IHMS
My name is Sam, an' I don't give a damn. A Cowboy Dance Song. *Unknown.* CoSo
My name is Samuel Hall, Samuel Hall. Sam Hall. *Unknown.* AmFP
My name is Sanford Barney [*or* Stamford *or* Stanford Barnes], and I came from Little Rock [*or* Nobleville] town. Sanford Barney [*or* The State of Arkansas]. *Unknown.* AmFP; CoSo; FSW; TrAS
My name is Sluggery-wuggery. My Name Is. Pauline Clarke. RHPC
My name is Solomon Levi. An Old Cracked Tune. Stanley Kunitz. GP
My name is Stanford Barnes. *See* My name is Sanford Barney. . .
My name is sweet Jenny, my age is sixteen. A Song. *Unknown.* POL
My name is Tom Hight, an old bach'lor I am. *See* My name is Frank Taylor, a bachelor I am.
My name is William Edwards, I live down Cove Creek way. The T.V.A.. *Unknown.* TrAS
My name it is Bill Stafford; I was born in Buffalo town. The Arkansaw Traveler. *Unknown.* ViBoFo
My name it is Jack Hall, chimney sweep, chimney sweep. Jack Hall. *Unknown.* OBET
My name it is [*or* is] Joe Bowers, I have [*or* I've got] a brother Ike. Joe Bowers. *Unknown.* AmFP; BaBo; CoSo; FSW; TrAS; TreFS; ViBoFo
My name it is Nell, quite [*or* right] candid I tell. Nell Flaherty's Drake. *Unknown.* AnIV; OnYI; TW
My name, my country, what are they to thee? No Matter [*or* An Epitaph]. Paulus Silentiarius, *tr. by* William Cowper. AWP; FaBoEE; OBVE
My name was Amaryllis. On Amaryllis, a Tortoyse. Marjorie Pickthall. PeCV
My Name Was Legion. Hildegarde Hoyt Swift. AmFN
My name was William Kidd, when I sailed, when I sailed. The Ballad of Captain Kidd. *Unknown.* AmSS
My name's Mister Benjamin Bunny. Limerick. Andrew Lang. CenHV
My name's Polly Parker I come o'er. The Collier Lass. Frankie Armstrong. BrRo
My namesake, Little Boots, Caligula. Caligula. Robert Lowell. CoPo
My Nannie's Awa'. Burns. GN; HBV-1
My native clay. Growing in Grace. Jack Clemo. NOCV
My Native Land. Sir Walter Scott. *See* Breathes There the Man.
My Native Land, thy Puritanic stock. The Rejected "National Hymns." "Orpheus C. Kerr." InMe; OBAL
My Need. *Unknown.* STF
My neighbor, a scientist and art-collector, telephones me. The Burning of Paper instead of Children. Adrienne Rich. LCAP
My neighbor brings me bottom fish. My Garden, My Daylight. Jorie Graham. MAYP

My neighbor Hunks's house and mine. Near Neighbors. Martial, *tr. by* Swift. AWP
My neighbor lives on the hill. Differences. Paul Laurence Dunbar. TreFS
My neighbor's boy has lifted his father's shotgun and stolen. Snowy Egret. Bruce Weigl. MAYP
My Neighbor's Roses. Abraham L. Gruber. BLPA
My neighbor's willow sways its frail. The Willow. Tu Fu, *tr. by* Kenneth Rexroth. NaP
My New Garden Field. *Unknown.* AmFP
My new province is a land of bamboo-groves. Eating Bamboo-Shoots. Po Chü-i, *tr. by* Arthur Waley. OBVE
My New World. Irving Browne. AA
My New Year Prayer. *Unknown.* STF
My new-cut ashlar takes the light. A Dedication. Kipling. HBV-2; OBVV; PoEL-5
My Nightingale. Rose Ausländer, *tr. fr. German by* Ewald Osers. VWA
My nights is so lonely days is so doggone long. Jersey Belle Blues. *Unknown.* BluL
My Nkosi you loved me. I Am the Beginning. Isaiah Shembe, *tr. by* G. C. Oosthuizen. WTO
My noble, lovely, little Peggy. A Letter [to the Honourable Lady Miss Margaret Cavendish-Holles-Harley] Matthew Prior. LoBV; NoAM; NOBE; NOEC; NoP; OBEC; OBEV; OxBC; OxBChV; SeCePo
My normal dwelling is the lungs of swine. Autobiography of a Lungworm. Roy Fuller. NoAM; NoP; OxBC
My Nose. Dorothy Aldis. RHPC
"My nose is blue." Me. Karla Kuskin. RHPC
My November Guest. Robert Frost. BLPL; HBMV; MoVE; OxBA; PoLF; TwAmPo; ViBoPo
My Object All Sublime. W. S. Gilbert. *Fr.* The Mikado. TreFT
My occupation is river man, as you may well know. Jack Haggerty. Dan McGinnis. ShS
My Old Bible. *Unknown.* BLRP; STF
My Old Black Billy. Edward Harrington. PoAu-1
My Old Cat. Hal Summers. OxBTC; PCat
My old companion! and my friend! To My Worthy Friend, Mr. James Bayley. Nicholas Noyes. SCAP
My Old Counselor. Gertrude Hall. AA
My Old Dutch; a Cockney Song. Albert Chevalier. VLP
My old flame, my wife! The Old Flame. Robert Lowell. BoLoP; NoAM; NOBA; PAI
My old friend, Lord O., owned a parcel of land. False Dawn. Walter de la Mare. FaBoNo
My Old Hammah, *with music.* *Unknown.* AS
My Old Kentucky Home. Stephen Collins Foster. AA; BLSo, *with music*; FaBoBe; FaBV; FaFP; FSW; HBV-2; PoLF; PSoN, *with music*; TrAS, *with music;* TreF; TrGrPo
My old lady died. Kitchen Door Blues. Tennessee Williams. GrPl; OBAL
My old man's a white old man. Cross. Langston Hughes. AmNP; BANP; IDB; LiTM; PoBA; PoLF; SoSe; TAP
My old massa he's got the dropser. Down in Alabam'; or, Aint I Glad I Got Out de Wilderness. *At. to* J. Warner. PSoN
My old master promised me. Raise a Ruckus Tonight. *Unknown.* FSW
My old Mistiss promise me. Promises of Freedom. *Unknown.* BPo
My old mule. Me and the Mule. Langston Hughes. IDB
My Old Straw Hat. Eliza Cook. BrRo
My Old True Love, *with music.* *Unknown.* OuSiCo
My Old Wife's a Good Old Cratur. *Unknown.* OBET
My oldest friend, mine from the hour. Guardian Angel. Cardinal Newman. GoBC
My oldest sister wears thick glasses. My Mother and My Sisters. Simon J. Ortiz. GP
My ole massa promised me. Shine On. Luke Schoolcraft. TrAS
My Olson Elegy. Irving Feldman. Prf
My once dear love; hapless that I no more. The Surrender. Henry King. AnAnS-2; BoLoP; EBEV; JCP; MePo; TrGrPo
My only desire was to make myself over. The Outwit Song. Daniel Hoffman. SaC
My only son, more God's than mine. Jesus and His Mother. Thom Gunn. EaLo; OxBC
My Only Star. Francis Davison. ElL
My Orcha'd in Linden Lea. William Barnes. EBVV
My ornaments are arms. The Wandering Knight's Song. John Gibson Lockhart. ChTr; HBV-1
My Other Chinee Cook. Brunton Stephens. PoAu-1
My Other Me. Grace Denio Litchfield. AA; HBV-1
My Owen. Ellen Mary Patrick Downing. HBV-1
My Own Brand. Art Cuelho. TAT
My Own Cáilin Donn. George Sigerson. FaBoBe; HBV-1
My own dear love, he is strong and bold. Love Song. Dorothy Parker. InMe
My own dim life should teach me this. In Memoriam A. H. H., XXXIV. Tennyson. SeCePo
My Own Epitaph. John Gay. FaBoEE; FF; NIP; NOEC; SeCePo; SeCeV; TreFT
(Epigram.) HBV-1
(His Own Epitaph.) ViBoPo
My own family. Immigrants. Stanley Nelson. AMV-81
My Own Hallelujahs. Zack Gilbert. PoBA
My own head. Seen in mirrors. Cleanly axed. Edward Lucie-Smith. Caravaggio Dying, Porto Ercole, July 1610, Aged 36, II. PeHV
My own heart let me more have pity on. Gerard Manley Hopkins. BrPo; CoBMV; FaBoMo; InPS; LiTM; MoAB; MoBrPo; NoP; VLP
My Own Hereafter. Eugene Lee-Hamilton. WGRP
My Own House. David Ignatow. AMV-80
My own in a foreign land. The Jewish Conscript. Florence Kiper Frank. TrJP
My Own, My Native Land! Sir Walter Scott. *See* Breathes There the Man.
My Ox Duke. John Dyer. NOEC
My pa held me up to the moo-cow-moo. The Moo-Cow-Moo. Edmund Vance Cooke. FaFP; MoShBr
My Packard Bell was set up in the vacant lot near the stump. The Campaign. Josephine Miles. WPE
My Papa's Waltz. Theodore Roethke. CMoP; CrMA; CTBA; DiL; FF; HAP; HeIP; HoPM; InPK; InPS; LCAP; LiTM; MiAP; MoAB; NCSH; NIP; NoAM; NOBA; NoP; PAI; PPoe; PPP; PrIm; TAP; VGW; WeW
My parents are making the journey. Spirit-like before Light. Arthur Gregor. VWA
My parents couldn't know, in 1950. Corner Lot. Sharon Bryan. MAYP
My parents felt those rumblings. The Hongo Store 29 Miles Volcano Hilo, Hawaii. Garrett Kaoru Hongo. MAYP
My parents have come to town for my wedding. The Form and Function of the Novel. Albert Goldbarth. GeTw
My Parents Kept Me from Children Who Were Rough. Stephen Spender. OAEP
(Rough.) NoAM
My parents raised me tenderly. The Girl [*or* Maid] I Left behind Me. *Unknown.* AmFP; ShS
My Paris is a land where twilight days. Paris. Arthur Symons. SyP
My passion is as mustard strong. A New Song [of New Similies]. John Gay. FaBoCo; InMe; NOBL
My passion is like turbulence at the head of waters. *Tr. fr. Arabic by* Willis Barnstone. BoWoP
My "Patch of Blue." Mary Newland Carson. BLPA
My patent pardouns, ye may see. The Pardoner's Sermon. Sir David Lindsay. *Fr.* Ane Satyre of the Thrie Estaitis. BSV; OBSV
My pathway lies through worse than death. Conquest. Georgia Douglas Johnson. AmNP
My Peace I Give unto You. G. A. Studdert-Kennedy. EBCP
"My peace," the peace of the Lord Most High. Peace. Margaret E. Sangster. TRV
My Peggy [Is a Young Thing]. Allan Ramsay. *Fr.* The Gentle Shepherd. BSV; GN; HBV-1; OxBS
(Peggy.) OBEV; ViBoPo
(Sang: "My Peggy is a young thing.") LoBV; OBEC
My Pen, Take Pain a Little Space. Sir Thomas Wyatt. PP; SiPS
(To His Pen.) OBSC
My Penis. Ed Ochester. GP
My pensive Sara! thy soft cheek reclined. The Eolian [*or* Aeolian] Harp. Samuel Taylor Coleridge. EnRP; NoP; OAEL-2
My People. Margery Himel. IHMS
My People. Else Lasker-Schüler. *See* Rock Crumbles, The.
My people have married me. Lament of Hsi-chün. Hsi-chün, *tr. by* Arthur Waley. BoWoP
My people? Who are they? Who Are My People? Rosa Zagnoni Marinoni. BLPA
My period had come for prayer. Emily Dickinson. EaLo
My Phillis [*or* Phyllis] hath the morning sun. Phillis [*or* Phyllis *or* To Phyllis, the Fair Shepherdess]. Thomas Lodge. *Fr.* Phyllis. ACP; ElL; LoBV; OBEV; OBSC; ViBoPo
My photograph already looks historic. The Middle of a War. Roy Fuller. OBWP
My Phyllis hath the morning sun. *See* My Phillis hath . . .
My Physics Teacher. David Wagoner. SUW
My Picture. Adelaide Anne Proctor. PeD
My Picture Left in Scotland. Ben Jonson. AnAnS-2; EnRePo; MePo; PoEL-2; QFR; SeCP; SeCV-1
My pictures blacken in their frames. Death of the Day. Walter Savage Landor. NoP
My Pilgrimage. Sir Walter Ralegh. *See* Passionate Man's Pilgrimage, The.
My plaid awa, my plaid awa. Lady Isabel and the Elf-Knight [*or* The Elfin Knight]. *Unknown.* CH; FaBoBa; GBP; ViBoFo (A *vers.*)
My Plan. Marchette Chute. FaPON

My plan is to fish wets down. Bad Day on the Boulder. Lloyd Davis. WOLT
My plan was to generate light. The Project. Gregory Orr. GeTw
My Playmate. Whittier. AP; HBV-1; NOBA; OBVV
My pocket book was empty. Danville Girl. *Unknown.* FSW
My Poem. Nikki Giovanni. AmNP; BOLo; BPo; PoBA
My poem would eat nothing. The Poem You Asked For. Larry Levis. AmPA
My poet, thou canst touch on all the notes. Elizabeth Barrett Browning. Sonnets from the Portuguese, XVII. BrRo; HBV-1; VLP; WHA
My Poker Girl. Tom Masson. OBAL
My Policeman. Rose Fyleman. SoPo; TiPo
My Polish Grandma. Edward Field. Prf
My Political Faith. George Frederick Cameron. PeCV
My poor body is alas unworthy. Ch'in Chia's Wife's Reply. *Tr. fr. Chinese by* Arthur Waley. BoWoP
My poor old bones—I've only two. The Lonely Scarecrow. James Kirkup. GrPl; PDV
My poor Pegasus must go on foot. In Life's Stable. Kadya Molodovsky, *tr. by* Ruth Whitman. VWA
My poplars are like ladies trim. The Poplars. Theodosia Garrison. HBMV; OHIP
My portion is defeat—today. Emily Dickinson. OBWP
My Portrait. Moishe-Leib Halpern, *tr. fr. Yiddish by* Joseph Leftwich. TrJP
My Prairies. Hamlin Garland. FaPON
My Prayer. Horatius Bonar. BLRP
My Prayer. Henry David Thoreau. HBV-2; HBVY; PoPl
(Great God, I Ask Thee for No Meaner Pelf.) AP; NOBA; TrPWD
My Prayer ("I asked the Lord that I might grow"). *Unknown.* STF
My Prayer ("Lord Jesus, make Thyself to me"). *Unknown.* BLRP
My Prayer ("My life must touch a million lives in some way ere I go"). *Unknown.* BLRP
My precious life I spent considering. Take the Crust. Sadi, *tr. by* L. Cranmer-Byng. *Fr.* The Gulistan. AWP
My pretty Marten, my winter friend. The Dead Marten. Walter Savage Landor. FM
My Pretty [Little] Pink. *Unknown.* AmFP; AS, *with music*
My Pretty Rose Tree. Blake. *Fr.* Songs of Experience. BoLoP; LAuP
My prime of youth is but a frost of cares. [Tichborne's] Elegy [*or* A Lament the Night before His Execution *or* On the Eve of His Execution *or* Retrospect *or* Written on the Eve of Execution]. Chidiock Tichborne. ACP; ChTr; DL; EBEV; ElL; FaBoRV; FF; GoBC; HAP; HBV-1; HelP; InPK; InPS; LiTB; LoBV; NOBE; NoP; OAEL-1; OBSC; PAI; PPoe; SCV; TreFT; TrGrPo; ViBoPo; WeW
My prow is tending toward the west. My New World. Irving Browne. AA
My Puppy. Aileen Fisher. OnUR
(Puppy.) SoPo
My Puritan Grandmother!—I see her now. Sea Lavender. Louise Morey Bowman. CaP
My purpose is to tell my own true tale. The Seafarer. *Unknown, tr. by* John Wain. EBEV
My Purse. *Unknown.* OxBM
("Singe we alle and say we thus.") EBEV
My Queen. William Winter. AA
(Queen, The.) HBV-1
My Queen. *Unknown.* HBV-1
My quiet kin, must I affront you. Preliminary to Classroom Lecture. Josephine Miles. NoAM
My quietness has a man in it, he is transparent. In Memory of My Feelings. Frank O'Hara. NeAP; PoM
My quill is charged with fire. Song of Hate. Jacob ben David Frances, *tr. by* A. B. Rhine. TrJP
My Ramblin' Boy. Tom Paxton. FSW
My Ratclif [*or* Ratcliffe], when thy retchlesse [*or* rechless] youth offendes. Exhortation to Learn by Others' Trouble [*or* Lines to Ratclif]. Earl of Surrey. AAS; FaBoEE; SiPS
My ravist spreit in that desart terribill. Nightmare. Gavin Douglas. *Fr.* The Palace of Honor. PoEL-1
My Recollectest Thoughts. Charles Edward Carryl. *Fr.* Davy and the Goblin, *ch* 7. HBV-2; HBVY; NA
My Record ends: But hark! e'en now I hear. George Crabbe. *Fr.* The Parish Register. OBRV
My red horse has his stable. My Horses. Jean Jaszi. SoPo
My Relatives for the Most Part. Frederick B. Hudson. AMV-80
My Return to Czechoslovakia. Murray Edmond. OCNZ
My Rival. Kipling. OxBTC
My Road. Oliver Opdyke. HBV-1
My room as usual a disorder of books. Crises. G. S. Fraser. NeBP
My room in Florence was the color of air. Above the Arno. May Swenson. NYBP
My room is so small. Leah Goldberg, *tr. by* Ramah Commanday. *Fr.* Nameless Journey. BoWoP
My room's a square and candle-lighted boat. The Country Bedroom. Frances Cornford. MoBrPo
My room's bigger than a coffin. On Saint-Urbain Street. Milton Acorn. NeAC; NOBC
My rug is red. My couch, whereon I deal. The Map. G. C. Oden. AmNP; NNP; PoNe
My Sabine Farm. Eugene Field. InMe
My Sad Captains. Thom Gunn. CMoP; FaBoMo; InPS; LiTM; NePoEA-2; PoCH
My Sad Self. Allen Ginsberg. NoAM; UnPo
My Sadness Sits around Me. June Jordan. BPo
My Saigon daughter I saw only once. A Black Soldier Remembers. Horace Coleman. FAZ
My Samsons. Haim Guri, *tr. fr. Hebrew by* Mark Elliott Shapiro. VWA
My sange es in sihting. A Song of Love for Jesus. Richard Rolle. MeEL
My saull and lyfe [*or* saul and life], stand up and see. Ane Sang of the Birth of Christ, with the Tune of Baw Lula Low. Martin Luther, *tr. by* John Wedderburn. BSV, *abr.*; ChTr
My Saxon shrine! the only ground. Morwennæ Statio. Robert Stephen Hawker. GoBC
My secret way of waking. Waking. Lilian Moore. RHPC
My secrets cry aloud. Open House. Theodore Roethke. AP; CoBMV; NoAM; NOBA; NoP
My Sense of Sight. Oliver Herford. HBMV; HBVY
My serious son! I see thee look. Before a Saint's Picture. Walter Savage Landor. OxBChV
My seven sons came back from Indonesia. Homecoming. Peter Viereck. CoAP
My 71st Year. Walt Whitman. NAs
My sexual feats. Fred Apollus at Fava's. Nicholas Moore. ErPo; NeBP
My Shadow. Robert Louis Stevenson. FaBoBe; FaBV; FaPON; HBV-1; HBVY; OnUR; OxBChV; PDV; SoPo; TEP; TiPo; TreF
My shadow/ I woke to a wind swirling the curtains light and dark. Absence. Edwin Morgan. BSV
My shag-hair Cyclops, come, lets ply. The Song in Making of the Arrows [*or* Vulcan's Song]. John Lyly. *Fr.* Sapho and Phao. EBEV; ElL; LoBV; OBSC
My Share of the World. Alice Furlong. HBV-1; OBVV
My shattred Phancy stole away from mee. Edward Taylor. *Fr.* Preparatory Meditations: First Series, XXIX. AP; SCAP
My Sheep Are Thoughts. Sir Philip Sidney. *Fr.* Arcadia. SiPS
My sheep I neglected, I broke my sheep-crook. Amynta. Gilbert Elliot. HBV-1
My Shepherd Is the Living Lord, *with music.* Thomas Sternhold. AH
My Shepherd's unkind; alas, what shall I do? The Lamentation of Chloris. *Unknown.* CoMu
My Ship and I. Robert Louis Stevenson. SUS
My Ship Is on de Ocean, *with music. Unknown.* BoAN-2
My ship passes over-slowly through the foreign lands. First Prelude. Dream in Ohio; the Father. John Logan. *Fr.* Poem in Progress. LCAP
My Ships. Ella Wheeler Wilcox. PoLF
My Shoes. Charles Simic. CoAP
My shoes./ I have just taken them off. 17. IV. 71. Paul Blackburn. PoM
My shoes are almost dead. Caesar. W. S. Merwin. LCAP; NaP
My short and happy day is done. The Stirrup-Cup. John Hay. AA; HBV-2
My shoulders ache beneath the pack. Prayer of a Soldier in France. Joyce Kilmer. GoBC
My shoulders once were yours for riding. Now That Your Shoulders Reach My Shoulders. Robert Francis. Str
My signs are a rain-proof coat, good shoes, and a staff cut from the woods. Walt Whitman. *Fr.* Song of Myself, XLVI. Prf
My Silks and Fine Array. Blake. *See* Song: "My silks and fine array."
My simple heart, bred in provincial tenderness. Sonnet. G. S. Fraser. NeBP
My sin! my sin, my God, these cursed dregs. Edward Taylor. Preparatory Meditations: First Series, XXXIX. SCAP
My Singing Aunt. James Reeves. ShM
My sinnes are like the haires upon my head. The Authour's Dreame. Francis Quarles. *Fr.* Argalus and Parthenia. OBS
My Sister. Alfonsina Storni, *tr. fr. Spanish by* Aliki *and* Willis Barnstone. BoWoP
My sister and I. Plans. Helen Morgan Brooks. NNP; PoNe
My sister and I when we were close together. Sisters. Dorothy Roberts. CaP
My sister in her well-tailored silk blouse hands me. The Photos. Diane Wakoski. NIP
My Sister Jane. Ted Hughes. OnUR; SO
My Sister Laura. Spike Milligan. NTCP
My sister! my sweet sister! if a name. Epistle to Augusta. Byron. EnRP
My sister rubs the doll's face in mud. The Kid. Ai. GeTw

My sister says. Rhinos Purple, Hippos Green. Michael Patrick Hearn. RHPC
My Sister She Works in a Laundry. *Unknown. See* How the Money Rolls In.
My sister was quicker at everything than I. The Paper Lantern. Tennessee Williams. *Fr.* Recuerdo. CTBA
My sister writes, "Come out, I need you." Seal Rock. Sue Baugh. AMV-81
My sister, you are a stranger to this place. God Hasn't Made Room. Mririda n'Ait Attik, *tr. by* Daniel Halpern *and* Paula Paley. PBWP
My sisters played beyond the doorway. Detail from an Annunciation by Crivelli. Rosemary Dobson. PoAu-2
My Sister's Sleep. Dante Gabriel Rossetti. LoBV; OAEP; SeCeV; VLP
My Six Toothbrushes. Phyllis McGinley. GoYe
My skin is black, my arms are long. Four Women. Nina Simone. MAT
My skin is so thin. And Yet. Kadya Molodovsky, *tr. by* Seymour Levitan. VWA
My slain! Oh silver-hoof! Oh clover breath! Laura Lourene LeGear. GoYe
My sleep falters and the good dreams. Lost. A. Alvarez. NMP
My softness heaves its spiral canopy. Snail. Elisabeth Eybers. PeSA
My Son. James D. Hughes. BLPA
My Son. Ruth Stone. WPE
My son/ I promised you a world and see. Why I Never Went into Politics. Richard Shelton. Str
My Son and I. Philip Levine. DiL; FAZ; GP; NYP
(New Season.) NNaP
My Son and I. Rosemary Norman. BrRo
My son & I, between *Fu-Sang* and/ Cathay. Philip Dow. *Fr.* Sussyissfriin. NPGG
My son Augustus, in the street, one day. Quiet Fun. Harry Graham. DBV; ShM
My son, despise not the chastening of the Lord. Happy Is the Man That Findeth Wisdom. Bible, *O.T. Fr.* Proverbs. TreF
My Son Doesn't See a Thing. Tomás Rivera, *tr. fr. Spanish by* Toni Empringham. FIA
My Son, Forsake Your Art. Mahon O'Heffernan, *tr. fr. Irish by* Maire Cruise O'Brien. BIrV
(A Mhic, ná Meabhraigh Éigse.) OxBI, *tr. by* Máire MacEntee
My son has birds in his head. Daedalus. Alastair Reid. NCSH; NYBP
My son invites me to witness with him. Mousemeal. Howard Nemerov. MP; NCSH; TwCP
My son, keep well thy tongue, and keep thy friend. Controlling the Tongue. Chaucer. *Fr.* The Canterbury Tales: The Manciple's Tale. OxBChV
My son leaps across my back. Still Wrestling. Phil Boiarski. AMV-81
My Son, My Executioner. Donald Hall. DiL; InPK; NePoEA
My Son, My Son. Seymour Cain. AMV-81
My son tells his aunt. A San Diego Poem. Simon J. Ortiz. CDW
My son, thou wast my heart's delight. On the Death of My Son Charles. Daniel Webster. AA
My son was killed while laughing at some jest. A Son. Kipling. *Fr.* Epitaphs of the War. ChMP; FaBoEE
My son wears a nappy. My Son and I. Rosemary Norman. BrRo
"My son!" What simple, beautiful words! To My Unborn Son. Cyril Morton Thorne. BLPA
My son who is stranger. A Variation. Robert Creeley. DiL
My Song. Hayim Nachman Bialik, *tr. fr. Hebrew by* Ruth Nevo. VWA
My Song. Hazel Hall. HBMV
My Song. King D. Kuka. VoR
My Song. Rabindranath Tagore. OHIP
My song, I fear that thou wilt find but few. Epipsychidion. Shelley. EnRP
My Song Is Love Unknown. Samuel Crossman. OxBChV
My song that was a sword is still. My Song. Hazel Hall. HBMV
My Song to the Jewish People. Leib Olitski, *tr. fr. Yiddish by* Jacob Sonntag. TrJP
My song today is the storm-cock's song. The Storm-Cock's Song. "Hugh MacDiarmid." OxBTC
My Songs Are Poisoned ("My songs, they say, are poisoned"). Heine, *tr. fr. German by* Louis Untermeyer. AWP
My songs to sell, good sir! Vendor's Song. Adelaide Crapsey. HBV-2
My Sons. Ron Loewinsohn. DFF; NeAP
My sons/ sometimes I can. Efficiency Apartment. Gerald W. Barrax. PoBA
My Sore Thumb. Burges Johnson. HBVY
My Sorrow. "Seumas O'Sullivan." *See* Starling Lake, The.
My sorrow is so wide. Kings River Canyon. Kenneth Rexroth. NaP
My sorrow that I am not by the little dún. The Starling Lake [*or* My Sorrow]. "Seumas O'Sullivan." AnIV; AWP; HBV-2
My sorrow, when she's here with me. My November Guest. Robert Frost. BLPL; HBMV; MoVE; OxBA; PoLF; TwAmPo; ViBoPo
My Sort o' Man. Paul Laurence Dunbar. AmNP
My soul, be not disturbed. Address to My Soul. Elinor Wylie. AWP; LiTM; OxBA
My Soul before Thee Prostrate Lies, *with music.* C. F. Richter, *tr. fr. German by* John Wesley. AH
My soul, calm sister, towards thy brow, whereon scarce grieves. Sigh. Stéphane Mallarmé, *tr. by* Arthur Symons. AWP; SyP
My soul doth magnify [*or* magnifies] the Lord. [The] Magnificat. Bible, *N.T.* St. Luke I: 46-56. BoWoP; ILwL; WGRP
My Soul Doth Pant towards Thee. Jeremy Taylor. TrPWD
My soul goes clad in gorgeous things. Souls. Fannie Stearns Gifford. HBMV
My soul has solitudes. Loneliness. Edwin Essex. TrPWD
My Soul Hovers over Me. Joshua Tan Pai, *tr. fr. Hebrew by* Yishai Tobin. VWA
My Soul in the Bundle of Life. *Unknown, tr. fr. French by* E. Margaret Rowley. *Fr.* The Dead Sea Scrolls. TrJP
My soul is an enchanted boat. Shelley. *Fr.* Prometheus Unbound. ViBoPo
My soul is awakened, my spirit is soaring. Lines Composed in a Wood on a Windy Day. Anne Brontë. EBVV
My soul is like a well of dead, deep water. The Well. Luis Palés Matos, *tr. by* Donald Walsh. InW
My soul is like the oar that momently. Struggle. Sidney Lanier. LiTA; OxBA
My Soul Is Robbed. Isaac Rosenberg. MoPo
My Soul Is Weary of My Life. Bible, *O.T.* Job, X: 1-22. EaLo
My soul looked down from a vague height with Death. The Show. Wilfred Owen. LiTB; LiTM; MoAB; MoBrPo; NoAM; OxBTC; WaaP; WaP
My soul magnifies the Lord. *See* My soul doth magnify the Lord.
My soul, my pleasant soul and witty. Animula Vagula, Blandula. Emperor Hadrian, *tr. by* Henry Vaughan. FaBoRV
My Soul, Sit Thou a Patient Looker-on. Francis Quarles. *See* Epigram: "My soul, sit thou a patient looker-on."
My soul stands at the window of my room. Nostalgia. Karl Shapiro. AP; CMoP; CoAP; CoBMV; MP; NePA; TrJP; TwAmPo; TwCP; WaaP
My soul surcharged with grief now loud complains. Sonnet. Rachel Morpurgo, *tr. by* Nina Davis Salaman. TrJP
My Soul, there is a country [*or* countrie]. Peace. Henry Vaughan. AnAnS-1; AWP; ChTr; EaLo; EBEV; ELP; FaBoCh; GN; HAP; HBV-2; MePo; NOBE; NOCV; OAEP; OBEV; OBS; SeCV-1; TEP; TrCP; WeW; WGRP; WHA
My Soul Thirsteth for God. Bible, *O.T.* Psalms, XLII. *See* As the Hart Panteth.
My Soul Thirsts for God. William Cowper. TrCP
My soul, thy love is dear: 'twas thought a good. Epigram. Francis Quarles. *Fr.* Emblems, V, 4. OAEL-1
My soul thy sacrifice! I choose thee out. Poems of the Arabic. *Unknown, tr. by* Sir Richard Burton. *Fr.* The Thousand and One Nights. ErPo
My soul to-day. Drifting. Thomas Buchanan Read. AA; GN; HBV-1
My soul was an old horse. Pegasus [*or* A Glut on the Market]. Patrick Kavanagh. MoAB; OnYI; OxBI
My Soul, Weigh Not Thy Life, *with music.* Leonard Swain. AH
My soul, what's lighter than a feather? Wind. Francis Quarles. FaBoEE
My Soul Would Fain Indulge a Hope, *with music.* Joseph Steward. AH
My soule a world is by Contraccion. William Alabaster. AnAnS-1
My soule is like a bird; my flesh, the cage. Francis Quarles. *Fr.* Emblems, V, 10. AnAnS-1
My Soul's Been Anchored in de Lord, *with music. Unknown.* BoAN-2
My South. Don West. PoNe
My specialty is living said. E. E. Cummings. MoVE; NOBA
My Spectre around Me Night and Day. Blake. NCEP; OAEL-2; OxBoCh
My Spirit. Thomas Traherne. SeCV-2
My spirit is a pestilential city. Desolate. Claude McKay. CDC
My spirit is too weak—mortality. On Seeing the Elgin Marbles. Keats. BLPL; CABA; EnRP; EyDe; LiTB; NIP; PrIm; SeCeV; TrGrPo; WHA
My spirit leans in joyousness tow'rd thine. Lines. "Ada." BlSi
My spirit like a shepherd boy. Song. V. Sackville-West. HBMV
My Spirit Longeth for Thee. John Byrom. BLPL; EBCP; NOBE; OxBoCh
(Desponding Soul's Wish, The.) OBEC; TrPWD
My Spirit Will Not Haunt the Mound. Thomas Hardy. MoBrPo; OBNC; QFR
My spotless love hovers with purest wings. The Most Unloving One. Samuel Daniel. To Delia, XII. HBV-1; OBEV; OBSC; SeCePo
My spouse, Chunaychunay. *Tr. fr. Quechua (Peru) by* W. S. Merwin. BoWoP
My Spring Thing. Everett Hoagland. BPo
My Springs. Sidney Lanier. UnPo
My Star. Robert Browning. EvOK; FaPON; HBV-1; OAEP; SoSe; TrGrPo
My star, star-gazing?—if only I could be. Aster. Plato, *tr. by* Peter Jay. PeHV
My stare like God's in space. The Well-aimed Stare. Hugo Margenat, *tr. by* Julio Marzán. InW
My Stars. Abraham Ibn Ezra, *tr. fr. Spanish by* Robert Mezey. OFD

My stepfather was a hobo because he didn't know any better. Open Roads. David Donnell. Str
My steps are wet from the cold death. Old Jewish Cemetery in Worms. Alfred Kittner, *tr. by* Herbert Kuhner. VWA
My stick fingers click with a snicker. Player Piano. John Updike. WeW
My stock lies dead, and no increase. Grace. George Herbert. JCP; SeCV-1
My stocking's where. David McCord. *Fr.* A Christmas Package. PChr; RHPC
My stomach is of many minds. Stomach. Kathleen Norris. OBAL
My Strawlike Hair. Asya, *tr. fr. Yiddish by* Gabriel Preil *and* Howard Schwartz. VWA
My straying thoughts, reduced stay. Song. Anne Collins. WPE
My Street Baby's Lament. William Franklin. LFAC
My study's ornament, thou shell of death. Cyril Tourneur. *Fr.* The Revenger's Tragedy. ViBoPo
My stutter, my cough, my unfinished sentences. The Second-fated. Robert Graves. NoAM
My Style. Charles Bukowski. AMV-81
My Subtle and Proclamant Song. Seán Jennett. NeIP
My suffering public, take it not amiss. The Problem of the Poles. John Kendall. WhC
My suite is just, just lord to my suite hark. Bible, *O.T.* Psalms, XVII, *paraphrased by* Sir Philip Sidney. OBVE
My Sun,/ You smile at the granite of Milton. The Street of Named Houses. Robert David Cohen. NYBP
My Sun-killed Tree. Marguerite Harris. GoYe
My sunlight came pre-packaged. Nomen. Naomi Long Madgett. BlSi
My sweet did sweetly sleep. Stolen Pleasure. William Drummond of Hawthornden. EnLoPo
My sweet-faced, tattle-tale brother was born blind. The Twins. Mona Van Duyn. GP
My Sweet Gazelle! Immanuel di Roma, *tr. fr. Italian.* TrJP
My Sweet Old Etcetera. E. E. Cummings. AmPP; CABA; CMoP; FF; HeIP; NePA; InPS; OBAL; OBWP; OxBa; PAI; PoPl; PPP; SOTW; WaaP; WaP
My Sweet Sweeting. *Unknown.* CH
My Sweetest Lesbia [Let Us Live and Love]. Thomas Campion, *after the Latin of* Catullus. AAS; AWP; BiP; CABA; ElL; EnRePo; FF; GBL; HAP; HeIP; LoBV; NIP; NoP; OAEL-1; OBSC; OBVE; PoRA; PrIm; TEP; TrGrPo; UnTE; WeW
(To Lesbia.) HBV-1
(Vivamus, Mea Lesbia, atque Amemus.) EBEV; SeCeV
My sweetheart in the rippling hills of sand. *Tr. fr. Hawaiian by* S. H. Elbert *and* N. Mahoe. WTO
My Sweetheart's a Mule in the Mines. *Unknown. See* My Sweetie's a Mule in the Mine.
My Sweetheart's Dainty Lips. Judah Halevi, *tr. fr. Hebrew by* Emma Lazarus. TrJP
My Sweetie's a Mule in the Mine. *Unknown.* AmFP; BPAW
(Driving the Mule.) GBP
(My Sweetheart's the [*or* a] Mule in the Mines.) CoSo; FSW
(Mule in the Mines, The.) ChTr
My swirling wants. Your frozen lips. A Valediction Forbidding Mourning. Adrienne Rich. NoAM; NoP
My sword I shook. The Sword. Abu Bakr, *tr. by* A. J. Arberry. TTY
My Table. W. B. Yeats. Meditations in Time of Civil War, III. LiTB
My tail is not impresssive. Ode to the Pig: His Tail. Walter R. Brooks. RHPC
My tailor is against parting. Against Parting. Natan Zach, *tr. by* Jon Silkin. VWA
My tall sunflowers love the sun. Sunflowers. Clinton Scollard. HBMV
My tap is run; then Baxter, tell me why. The Last Will and Testament of Anthony, King of Poland. *Unknown.* APAS
My tea is nearly ready and the sun has left the sky. The Lamplighter. Robert Louis Stevenson. EBVV; FaFP; OxBChV; SaC; TreF
My tears are true, though others be divine. Henry Constable. *Fr.* Diana. OBSC
My tears were Orion's splendor with sextuple suns. Tears. Edith Sitwell. CMoP; MoPo
My Teeth. Ed Ochester. DFF; GP
My teeth dare not trust you. Bridgework. Annette Lynch. FF
My Temper. *Unknown.* STF
My temples throb, my pulses boil. To Minerva. Thomas Hood. ChTr; FaBoCo; FaBoNo; FiBHP; HBV-2; InMe; NOBL; OxBoLi; WhC
My tender parents brought me up [*or* who brought me here], providing me full well. The Lexington Murder [*or* The Wexford Girl]. *Unknown.* AmFP; BaBo; OuSiCo
My tent stands in a garden. An Autumn Garden. Bliss Carman. HBV-1
My thanks, friends of the County Scientific Association. Perry Zoll. Edgar Lee Masters. *Fr.* Spoon River Anthology. CrMA
My Thing Is My Own. *Unknown.* CoMu
My thirsty soul desires her drought. A Prisoner's Song of Jerusalem. *Unknown.* ACP
My Thirty Years. Juan Fransico Manzano, *tr. fr. Spanish by* Oliver Cobarn *and* Ursula Lehrburger. TTY
My Thompson, least attractive character. Elegy. Howard Nemerov. PPJ
My thought awaked me with Thy Name. Meditation on Communion with God. Judah Halevi, *tr. by* Solomon Solis-Cohen. TrJP
My thought is caught in the eyes of love. Entanglement. Francis Sparshott. MoCV
My thought shall never be that you are dead. Reported Missing. Anna Gordon Keown. SUMH
My Thought Was on a Maid So Bright. *Unknown.* ISi
My thought was thus—that it was May. May Morning, *mod. vers.* Chaucer. *Fr.* The Book of the Duchesse. WHA
My thoughts are all in yonder town. The Friend's Burial. Whittier. OBVV
My thoughts are as a garden-plot, that knows. Thy Garden. Mu'tamid, King of Seville, *tr. by* Dulcie L. Smith. AWP
My thoughts are fixed in contemplation. John Marston. *Fr.* Antonio and Mellida. ViBoPo
My Thoughts Are Not Your Thoughts. Bible, *O.T.* Isaiah, LV: 8-13. TrJP
My Thoughts Are Winged with Hopes. *At. to* George Clifford *and to* Sir Walter Ralegh. ElL; GBL
(To Cynthia.) OBSC
My thoughts by night are often filled. Castles in the Air. Thomas Love Peacock. HBV-1
My Thoughts Do Harbour. Shakespeare. *Fr.* The Two Gentlemen of Verona, III, i. CTC
My thoughts hold mortal strife. Madrigal [*or* Inexorable]. William Drummond of Hawthornden. ElL; GTBS; GTBS-P; LoBV; NOBE; OBEV; OBS
My thoughts impelled me to the resting-place. Elegy. Moses ibn Ezra, *tr. by* Emma Lazarus. TrJP
My thoughts, like sailors becalmed in Cape Town harbor. Sailor's Harbor. Henry Reed. MoAB; MoBrPo; MOS
My thoughts, my grief! are without strength. A Poem Written in Time of Trouble by an Irish Priest Who Had Taken Orders in France. *Unknown, tr. by* Lady Gregory. OBMV
My Thread. David Hofstein, *tr. fr. Yiddish by* Joseph Leftwich. TrJP
My three sisters are sitting. Women. Adrienne Rich. NMM
My Three Wives. *Unknown, after the Latin of* Etienne Pasquier. FaBoEE
My Thrush. Mortimer Collins. HBV-1
My tidings for you: the stag bells. Summer Is Gone. *Unknown, tr. by* Kuno Meyer. FaBoCh; OnYI
My time, O ye muses, was happily spent. A Pastoral. John Byrom. OBEC
My Tocher's the Jewel. Burns. BSV
My Tommy's gone, what shall I do. Tommy's Gone to Hilo. *Unknown.* ShS
"My towers at last!" Herman Melville. Conrad Aiken. NoAM; NOBA; TAP
My towers at last! These rovings end. L'Envoi: The Return of the Sire de Nesle. Herman Melville. NOBA; ViBoPo
My townspeople, beyond in the great world. Gulls. William Carlos Williams. FaBoEn; NoP; OxBA; TwAmPo
My trade takes me frequently into decaying houses. From a Museum Man's Album. John Hewitt. OxBTC
My traveling provisions are short, and won't see me through. Sufi Quatrain. Rabi'a bint Isma'il of Syria, *tr. by* Deirdre Lashgari. WPOW
My trewest tresowre sa trayturly was taken. A Song of the Passion. Richard Rolle of Hampole. OxBoCh
My Triumph. Whittier. NOBA
My triumph lasted till the drums. Emily Dickinson. OBWP; WaaP
My True Love. Ivy O. Eastwick. SiSoSe
My true love breathed her latest breath. The Murderer. Stevie Smith. TEP
"My True Love Hath My Heart and I Have His." Mary Elizabeth Coleridge. BoLoP
My True Love Hath My Heart [and I Have His.] Sir Philip Sidney. *Fr.* Arcadia. BoLoP; CH; FaBoBe; GBL; HBV-1; OAEP; PoEL-1; PoPle; SeCeV; TrGrPo; ViBoPo; WHA
(Arcadian Duologue.) SiPS
(Bargain, The.) NOBE; OBEV; TreFS
(Ditty, A.) AWP; GTBS; GTBS-P
(Heart Exchange.) LiTB; LoBV
(Just Exchange.) FaBoEn
(Sonnet: "My true love hath my heart.") ElL
(True Love.) ChTr; OBSC
My true love makes me happy. Beatrice de Die, *tr. fr. Provençal by* Doris Earnshaw. WPOW
My True Memory. Asya, *tr. fr. Yiddish by* Gabriel Preil *and* Howard Schwartz. VWA
My Trundle Bed. J. G. Baker. BLPA; FaBoBe

My Trust, *sel.* Whittier.
"Picture memory brings to me, A," *first 3 sts.* OHIP; PGD
My Twelve Oxen. *Unknown.* OxBM
My twenty-six-year-old ensign. To a Portrait of Lermontov. Margarita Aliger, *tr. by* Elaine Feinstein. VWA
My two white rabbits. Rabbits. Dorothy W. Baruch. SoPo; SUS; TiPo
My uncle, a craftsman of hammers and wood. Willy Lyons. James Wright. NNaP
My uncle believed he had. Parity. Kenneth Rexroth. GP
My Uncle Ben, who's been. Kiph. Walter de la Mare. TiPo
My uncle is a small man. Hills Brothers Coffee. Luci Tapahonso. STE
My Uncle Jasper in Siam. Ponjoo. Walter de la Mare. ShM
My Uncle Jehoshaphat. Laura E. Richards. OxBChV
My Uncle Joe. Robert B. Smith. LFAC
My Uncle Paul of Pimlico. Mervyn Peake. OnUR
My uncle sleeps in the image of death. Lawrence Durrell. *Fr.* The Death of General Uncebunke; a Biography in Little. FaBoMo
My uncle was Sabbath crazed. Ichthycide. Joe Rosenblatt. NOBC
My Uninvited Guest. May Riley Smith. AA; WGRP
My urine smells of smoke. Desert in the Sea. Brian Swann. AmPA
My Valentine. Kitty Parsons. SoPo
My Valentine. Robert Louis Stevenson. *See* Romance.
My various fleets for fowl, O who is he can tell. Michael Drayton. *Fr.* Polyolbion: The Twenty-fifth Song. PBBP
My Voice. Oscar Wilde. BrPo; EBVV
My voice has been imprisoned. Voice. Stanley Moss. AMV-80
My voice rings down through thousands of years. Sappho's Reply. Rita Mae Brown. PeHV
My Wage. Jessie B. Rittenhouse. BLPA
My walls outside must have some flowers. Truly Great. W. H. Davies. HBV-1; OBMV; OBVV
My walls tonight are lined with ancestors. Ancestors. Harold Schimmel. VWA
My wand strikes me no joy till loosened weeping. Third Madrigal. Gene Derwood. NePA
My wavering mind resembles. In the Balance. *Unknown, tr. by* George Whicher. *Fr.* Carmina Burana. OLR
My Way Is Not Thy Way. D. H. Lawrence. CMoP
My Way's Cloudy, *with music. Unknown.* BoAN-1
My wearied bark, O let it now be crowned! To Crown It. Robert Herrick. CaPo
My well-beloved was stripped. Knowing my whim. The Jewels. Baudelaire, *tr. by* Roy Campbell. BoLoP
My whining lover, what needs all. Against Absence. Sir John Suckling. CaPo
My whiskey is/ a tough way of life. Drink. William Carlos Williams. OxBA
My White Book of Poems. Rachel, *tr. fr. Hebrew by* N. N.. VWA
My white canoe, like the silvery air. The Camp of Souls. Isabella Valancy Crawford. NOBC
My white tiger bounding in the west! Welcome My World. Denis Devlin. AnIV
My whole eye was sunset red. Eye and Tooth. Robert Lowell. CAPP
My whole life. At the Well. Malka Heifetz Tussman, *tr. by* Marcia Falk. VWA
My whole life has been a chronology of—changes. For Malcolm: After Mecca. Gerald W. Barrax. OFD
My Wicked Uncle. Derek Mahon. OxBC
My Wife. Robert Louis Stevenson. DL
(To My Wife.) TRV
(Trusty, Dusky, Vivid and True.) HBV-1
My wife already there to comfort. The Berries. William Heyen. GeTw; MAYP
My wife and I lived all alone. Ballad of the Despairing Husband. Robert Creeley. NeAP; NoP; OBAL
My wife and I lived [*or* live] all alone. Little Brown Jug. *At. to* Joseph E. Winner. BLSo; FaFP; FSW; OBAL; PSoN; TrAS; TreF; YaD
My wife broke a dollar tube of perfume. The Problem. Paul Blackburn. NeAP
My wife bursts into the room. The Loneliness of the Long Distance Runner. Alden Nowlan. PV; TW
My wife comes home. Refusing What Would Bind You to Me Irrevocably. Ronald Koertge. GP
My wife had an ulcer. Pain Paint. Peter Minck. FaBoUs
My wife is left-handed. For Hettie. Amiri Baraka. NeAP; NoAM; NOBA
My Wife Is My Shirt. Stephen Tropp. InPK; PeD
My wife saw it first. Blackbird. Christopher Leach. BoAnP
My wife sits reading in a garden chair. October. Barry Spacks. PoA
My wife with the hair of a wood fire. Freedom of Love. André Breton. EAS
My Wife's a Wanton Wee Thing. *Unknown.* CoMu
My Wife's a Winsome Wee Thing. Burns. HBV-1
My Wild Irish Rose. Chauncey Olcott. FSN, *with music*; BLSo, *with music*; FSW; TreFT
My will lies there, my hope, and all my life. Thomas Lovell Beddoes. *Fr.* Death's Jest Book. LO
My Wind Is Turned to Bitter North. Arthur Hugh Clough. OAEP; VLP
My window is the open sky. Immortality. Arthur Sherburne Hardy. AA
My window opens out into the trees. Solace. Clarissa Scott Delany. AmNP; CDC; PoBA; PoNe
My window shows the travelling clouds. The Alchemist in the City. Gerard Manley Hopkins. NoP
My windows open to the autumn night. Cadgwith. Lionel Johnson. OBVV
My Winsome Dear. Robert Fergusson. *Fr.* Leith Races. SeCePo
My Winter Past. Eldon Grier. NOBC
My wish for you/ that God should make your love. Rabi'a of Balkh, *tr. fr. Farsi by* Deirdre Lashgari. WPOW
My Wishes. Patrick Healy, *tr. fr. Modern Irish by* John D'Alton. OnYI
My wives do not write. Memory. Michael Hamburger. OxBTC
My Woe Must Ever Last. Sir Walter Ralegh. ElL
My Woman. Catullus, *tr. fr. Latin by* Gilbert Highet. PoPl
My Woman. A.D. Winans. AMV-80
My woman says she wants no other lover. My Woman. Catullus, *tr. by* Gilbert Highet. PoPl
My woman says that she would rather wear the wedding-veil for me. Catullus, *tr. fr. Latin by* Horace Gregory. NAWM-1
My Woodcock. Patrick Reginald Chalmers. CenHV
My woorthy Lord, I pray you wonder not. *See* My worthy Lord . . .
My words and thoughts do both express this notion. Our Life Is Hid with Christ in God. George Herbert. OAEL-1
My words for you. The Words of Finn. *Unknown.* ChTr
My words I know do well set forth my mind. Astrophel and Stella, LXIV. Sir Philip Sidney. SiPS
My work is done. Angel. Cardinal Newman. *Fr.* The Dream of Gerontius. GoBC
My world is a painted fresco, where coloured shapes. Dreams Old and Nascent. D. H. Lawrence. WGRP
My worthy [*or* woorthy] Lord, I pray you wonder not. Gascoigne's Woodmanship. George Gascoigne. AAS; EnRePo; PoEl-1; QFR
My Yoke Is Easy. Bible, *N.T.* St. Matthew, XI: 28-30. TreFS
My young love said to me, "My brothers won't mind." She Moved through the Fair. Padraic Colum. BIrV; InvP
My young Mary do's mind the Dairy. The Happy Husbandman; or, Country Innocence. *Unknown.* CoMu
My Young Mother. Jane Cooper. NMM
My Zipper Suit. Marie Louise Allen. SUS; TiPo
Myall in Prison, The. Mary Gilmore. CBAP; PoAu-1
Mycenae. David Fisher. NPGG
Mycilla dyes her locks, 'tis said. On an Old Woman. Lucillius, *tr. by* William Cowper. AWP
Mye love toke skorne my servise to retaine. Sir Thomas Wyatt. AAS
Myfanwy. John Betjeman. BoLoP
Myne owne John Poynz, sins ye delight to know. *See* Mine own John Poins . . .
Mynstrelles Songe: "Angelles bee wrogte to bee of neidher kynde." Thomas Chatterton. *Fr.* Aella. EnLoPo
Mynstrelles Songe: "Boddynge flourettes bloshes atte the lyghte, The." Thomas Chatterton. *See* Song of the Three Minstrels.
Mynstrelles Songe ("O! synge untoe mie roundelaie"). Thomas Chatterton. *See* Minstrel's Song.
Myra. Fulke Greville. *Fr.* Caelica. ElL; LoBV; NOBE; OBEV; OBSC; PoPle
("I, with whose colors [*or* colours] Myra dressed [*or* dress'd] her head.") EnRePo; GBL; HAP; InVP; QFR
(To Myra.) LiTB; ViBoPo
Myra Song, The ("Myra, Myra, sing-song"). John Ciardi. RHPC
Myriads of motley molecules through space. Soul and Sense. Hannah Parker Kimball. AA
Myriads of wasps now also clustering hang. How to Catch Wasps. John Philips. *Fr.* Cyder. FaBoUs
Myrtilla, early on the lawn. Sweet Slug-a-Bed. *Unknown.* FaBoCo
Myrtilla, to-night. A Corsage Bouquet. Charles Henry Lüders. HBV-1
Myrtis, *sel.* Walter Savage Landor. *Fr.* Pericles and Aspasia.
"Friends, whom she lookt at blandly from her couch." OBRV
Myrtle, and eglantine. The Flower-Seller. William Young. *Fr.* Wishmaker's Town. AA
Myrtle and the Vine, The, *sel.* George Colman.
Gluggity Glug. HBV-2
Myrtle bush grew shady, The. Jealousy. Mary Elizabeth Coleridge. CH; EnLoPo; NBM; OBNC; WPE
"Myrtle loves Harry"—It is sometimes hard to remember a thing like that. Aphrodite Metropolis. Kenneth Fearing. CAD
Myself. Edgar A. Guest. BLPA; BLPL

Myself. Walt Whitman. Song of Myself, I. BLPL; FaBoBe
(I Celebrate Myself.) NePA
Myself grown old do fearfully frequent. Case History. Arthur W. Bell. WhC
Myself, I rather like the bat. The Bat. Ogden Nash. PV
Myself unto myself will give. The Holy Office. James Joyce. FaBoTw; NoAM; OxBTC
Myself When I Am Real. Al Young. CNA; PoBA
Myself When Young. Tom Donnelly. BXAP
Myself When Young Did Eagerly Frequent. Omar Khayyám, *tr. fr. Persian by* Edward Fitzgerald. *Fr.* The Rubáiyát of Omar Khayyám. EaLo; ILwL; WGRP
Myselves/ the grievers. Ceremony after a Fire Raid. Dylan Thomas. CMoP; CoBMV; MoPo; WaP
Mysteries. Emily Dickinson. *See* Murmur of a bee, The.
Mysteries: if a nymph naked and golden. Microcosmos, XX. Nigel Heseltine. NeBP
Mysteries Remain, The. Hilda Doolittle ("H. D."). NOBA; TAP; VGW; WPOW
Mysteries Revealed after Death. John Reynolds. *Fr.* Death's Vision. NOEC
Mysterious Biography. Carl Sandburg. OFD; SiSoSe
Mysterious Britain. Amy Clampitt. AMV-81
Mysterious Cat, The. Vachel Lindsay. ChTr; FaPON; GoJo; OBCA; SoPo; TiPo
Mysterious East. William Cole. OBAL
Mysterious Music of Ocean, The. *Unknown.* EtS
Mysterious night! Spread wide thy silvery plume! Night. John Addington Symonds. HBV-1
Mysterious Night! when our first parent knew. To Night. Joseph Blanco White. AnIV; EBEV; GoBC; HBV-1; OBEV; OBRV; RoGo; TreFS; ViBoPo; WGRP
Mysterious Presence! Source of All, *with music.* Seth Curtis Beach. AH
Mysterious Way, The. William Cowper. *See* Light Shining Out of Darkness.
Mystery, The. *At. to* Amergin, *tr. fr. Old Irish by* Douglas Hyde. OnYI
Mystery. Elizabeth Barrett Browning. OBVV
Mystery, The. Ralph Hodgson. CH; HBV-2; MoAB; MoBrPo; WGRP
Mystery. Claire McAllister. TwAmPo
Mystery, The. Sara Teasdale. HBMV
Mystery, The. *Unknown, tr. fr. Irish by* Douglas Hyde. OxBI
Mystery, The. Lilian Whiting. AA
Mystery. "Yehoash", *tr. fr. Yiddish by* Marie Syrkin. TrJP
" 'Mystery Boy' Looks for Kin in Nashville." Robert Hayden. LCAP; NoAM
Mystery of a kind, A. Planting a Magnolia. W. D. Snodgrass. NoAM
Mystery of Cro-a-tàn, The. Margaret Junkin Preston. PAH
Mystery of Dawn, ere yet the glory streams. Laurence Binyon. *Fr.* The Sirens. GoTL
Mystery of Emily Dickinson, The. Marvin Bell. LCAP
Mystery of Life, The. John Gambold. NOEC
Mystery of the Caves, The. Michael Waters. GeTw; MAYP
Mystic, The. Witter Bynner. HBV-1
Mystic. D. H. Lawrence. PAI
Mystic. Sylvia Plath. NYBP
Mystic, The. Cale Young Rice. WGRP
Mystic, The. Tennyson. OAEP; VLP
Mystic and Cavalier. Lionel Johnson. MoBrPo; SeCePo; VLP
Mystic as Soldier, A. Siegfried Sassoon. WGRP
Mystic Borderland, The. Helen Field Fischer. WBLP
Mystic Drum, The. Gabriel Okara. TTY
Mystic finishes in Time, The. The Insomniacs. Adrienne Rich. NYBP
Mystic in the morning, half asleep, A. Bachelor. William Meredith. NoAM
Mystic Magi, The. Robert Stephen Hawker. ChTr; OBCP
(Southern Cross, The.) OxBoCh
Mystic River. John Ciardi. NYBP
Mystic Song, A. *Unknown, tr. fr. French by* Percy Allen. WGRP
Mystical Dialogue. Paul Verlaine, *tr. fr. French by* Alan Conder. LO
Mystical strains unheard. A Clymène. Paul Verlaine, *tr. by* Arthur Symons. AWP
Mysticism, but let us have no words. Conrad Aiken. *Fr.* Time in the Rock, XI. VGW
"Mysticism Has Not the Patience to Wait for God's Revelation." Richard Eberhart. MoPo; NoAM
Mystic's Prayer, The. "Fiona Macleod." HBV-2; TrPWD; WGRP
Myth, A. Charles Kingsley. GN
Myth, The. Edwin Muir. CMoP
Myth. Ned O'Gorman. TwAmPo
Myth. Muriel Rukeyser. IHMS; NNaP
Myth lilies. A smog-edge sky blurs his eyes. Crow's Way. Duane Niatum. CDW
Myth of Arthur, The. G. K. Chesterton. HBMV
Myth on Mediterranean Beach: Aphrodite as Logos. Robert Penn Warren. HAP; WeW
Mythical Journey, The. Edwin Muir. NoAM; OxBS
(Journey, The.) MoVE
Mythics. Helen Chasin. DFT; IHMS
Myth-maker drags his myth, The. Alone by the Road's Edge. Diana O Hehir. NPGG
Mythmaking. Kathleen Spivack. NMM
Mythological Sonnets, *sels.* Roy Fuller.
"How startling to find the portraits of the gods," XVI. ErPo
"Suns in a skein, the uncut stones of night," VIII. GTBS-P
Mythology. Lawrence Durrell. DTC; OxBTC
Mythology. Earle Thompson. STE
Mythology. Michael Waters. MAYP
Mythos of Samuel Huntsman, The. Hyam Plutzik. LiTM
Myths. Guy Butler. PeSA
Myths. D. L. Klauck. LTB
Myths and Texts, *sels.* Gary Snyder.
Burning *abr.* NeAP; PoM
"He's out stuck in a bird's craw," IV. NaP
" 'If, after attaining Buddhahood, anyone in my land,' " X. NaP
"John Muir on Mt. Ritter," VIII. NOBA
"Night here, a covert," IX. NaP
Second Shaman Song, I. NOBA
"Sourdough mountain called a fire in," XVII. NaP; NoP
"Spikes of new smell driven up nostrils," XIII. NaP
"Stone-flake and salmon," XV. NaP
Hunting. CoPo
"All beaded with dew," VII. NaP
"Birds in a whirl, drift to the rooftops," III. NaP
First Shaman Song, I. NOBA
"How rare to be born a human being!" XVI. CAPP; NaP
"Out the Greywolf valley," XII. NaP
"Swallow-shell that eases birth, The," IV. NaP
This Poem Is for Bear, VI. NOBA; NU
("Bear down under the cliff, A.") NaP
This Poem Is for Deer, VIII. CAPP; NOBA
(" 'I dance on all the mountains.' ") NaP
Logging.
"Again the ancient, meaningless," V. CAPP; NaP
"Each dawn is clear," VIII. NaP; NMP
"Groves are down, The," XIV. NaP
"Lodgepole/ cone/seed waits for fire," XV. NaP
"Stood straight/ holding the choker high," III. NaP; NMP; NOBA
Myxomatosis. Philip Larkin. CMoP; ELU; NMP; NoAM; NoP

N

N. Hugh Seidman. PoA
N. B., Symmetrians. Gene Derwood. LiTA; NePA
NFL/ Going backward. In the Pocket. James Dickey. LiSp
NHR. Jack Hirschman. VWA
N is for Naughty Young Nat. Naughty Young Nat. Isabel Frances Bellows. TDH
NN 616410. Bill Tulloch. PoSH
NW5 and N6. John Betjeman. SCV
N.Y. Ezra Pound. NYP
N.Y. to L.A. by Jet Plane. Sonya Dorman. GOA
Nabara, The. C. Day Lewis. OBNV
Naboth's Vineyard. John Caryll. APAS
Nae man wha loves the lawland tongue. The Makar. William Soutar. OxBS
Nae shoon to hide her tiny taes. The Babie. Jeremiah Eames Rankin. AA; HBV-1
Nahant. Emerson. AmPP
(Waves.) AA
Naiad, hid beneath the bank. Anteros [*or* A Dirge]. William Johnson Cory. OBNC; OBVV
Nailed to a cross, your beauty still aglow. Crucifixion. "Marie Madelaine," *tr. by* Ferdinand E. Kappey. PeHV
Nails. Gary Gildner. TAP
Naked/ I have lain in beastly days. Dawn. Alejandra Pizarnik, *tr. by* Alina Rivero. VWA
Naked all night the field. Sports Field. Judith Wright. LiSp
Naked and breast to breast we lie. Tormenting Virgin. *Unknown, tr. by* Louis Untermeyer. UnTE
Naked and grey the Cotswolds stand. Edgehill Fight. Kipling. PoPle

Naked and knowing my heart my love had left on. The Jewels. Baudelaire, *tr. by* Paul Blackburn. ErPo
Naked and the Nude, The. Robert Graves. NYBP; SoSe
Naked as from the earth we came. Submission to Afflictive Providences. Isaac Watts. NOCV
Naked before the glass she said. Young Woman. Howard Nemerov. ErPo
Naked earth is warm with Spring, The. Into Battle. Julian Grenfell. FaPoR; HBV-2; LoBV; MMA; OBEV; OBMV; OBWP; OxBTC; WaaP
Naked Eve shared the last bite. Like Weary Trees. Jacob Glatstein, *tr. by* Ruth Whitman. VWA
Naked house, a naked moor, A. The House Beautiful. Robert Louis Stevenson. NOBE
Naked I came, naked I leave the scene. Epitaph for Someone or Other. J. V. Cunningham. NIP; OBAL; VGW
Naked I reached the world at birth. Palladas, *tr. fr. Greek by* A. J. Butler. NIP
Naked I saw thee. Ideal. Padraic Pearse, *tr. by* Thomas MacDonagh. AnIV; AWP; OnYI
Naked in Borneo. May Swenson. NYBP
Naked is the earth. Poems. Antonio Machado, *tr. by* John Dos Passos. AWP
Naked Land, The. Kenneth Patchen. EAS
Naked love did to thine eye. Ice and Fire. Sir Edward Sherburne. CavP
Naked out of the dark we came. Kenneth Rexroth, *after the Persian.* FaBoEE
Naked Seed, The. C. S. Lewis. TrCP
Naked she lay, clasped in my longing arms. The Imperfect Enjoyment. Earl of Rochester. BoLoP; ErPo; UnTE
Naked to earth was I brought—naked to earth I descend. Vanity of Vanities. Palladas, *tr. by* William M. Hardinge. AWP; TRV
Naked War. Michael Heffernan. BXAP
Naked woman, black woman. Black Woman. Léopold Sédar Senghor, *tr. by* Anne Atik. TTY
Naked World, The. Sully-Prudhomme, *tr. fr. French by* William Dock. ImOP
Nakedness of women, The. Blake. POL
Nam. Mike Lowery. Psk; SOTS
Namby-Pamby; or, A Panegyric on the New Versification. Henry Carey. FaBoNo; FaBoPa; NOEC, *abr.;* OBSV; Par
Name, The. Robert Creeley. CoPo
Name, The. Eileen Duggan. ISi
Name, The. Sara Henderson Hay. DFT
Name, The. Don Marquis. HBV-2
Name, The. Jalal ed-Din Rumi, *ad. fr. Persian by* Robert Bly. NU
Name, The/ never left his lips. Scribe. Paul Auster. VWA
Name for All, A. Hart Crane. PP; VGW
Name Giveaway. Phillip William George. VoR
Name in a footnote. Faceless name. Crispus Attucks. Robert Hayden. CNA
Name in block letters. *None that signified.* A Form of Epitaph. Laurence Whistler. GTBS-P
Name in the Sand, A. Hannah Flagg Gould. AA
Name is hard, The. On the 25th Anniversary of the Liberation of Auschwitz. Eli Mandel. NOBC
Name is immortal but only the name, for the rest, The. Jew. Karl Shapiro. VWA
Name—of it—is "Autumn," The. Emily Dickinson. InPS
Name of Jesus, The. John Newton. NOEC; OBEC; STF
(How Sweet the Name of Jesus Sounds.) NOCV; OxBoCh
"Jesus! my Shepherd, Husband, Friend," *sel.* TrPWD
Name of Mother, The. George Griffith Fetter. PGD
Name of my heroine, simply "Rose." The Tale of a Pony. Bret Harte. OBNV
Name of Old Glory, The. James Whitcomb Riley. GN
Name of Our Country, The. Dennis Schmitz. AmPA
Name of the beast is, The. Small Comment. Sonia Sanchez. NBP
Name of the game is beat the lame, The. The Hustler. *Unknown.* TW
Name of the product I tested is "Life," The. A Consumer's Report. Peter Porter. FaBoCo; NOBL
Name of this poem is, The. Cameo No. II. June Jordan. BPo
Name of Washington, The. Arthur Gordon Field. PAL; PGD
Name the leaves on all the trees. My Loves. John Stuart Blackie. OBVV
Name they gave me is lost, The. Privilege. Alejandra Pizarnik, *tr. by* Yishai Tobin. VWA
Name thou wearest does thee grievous wrong, The. The Mocking-Bird. Henry Jerome Stockard. AA
Named them. Orpheus. Donald Davie. TEP
Nameless/ white poppy. White Summer Flower. W. S. Merwin. DFF
Nameless Doon [or Dun], The. William Larminie. AnIL; BIrV; NBM; OxBI
(Nameless Ruin, The.) OnYI
Nameless Epitaph, A. Matthew Arnold. FaBoEE; VLP
Nameless, he crept from the hutch of creation. Love for a Hare. Melvin Walker La Follette. NePoEA-2
Nameless Journey, *sel.* Leah Goldberg, *tr. fr. Hebrew by* Ramah Commanday.
"My room is so small." BoWoP
Nameless Maiden, The. *Unknown.* ErPo
Nameless One, A. Margaret Avison. HeIP; NOBC
Nameless One, The. James Clarence Mangan. ACP; BIrV; EnRP; GoBC; HBV-2; NBM; OBEV; OBVV; OnYI; OxBI
Nameless Ones, The. Conrad Aiken. NePA; OxBA
Nameless presence on the paling green, A. The Child. Frank Ormsby. AMV-81
Nameless Recognition, A. Arthur Gregor. GP
Nameless Ruin, The. William Larminie. *See* Nameless Doon, The.
Nameless Saints, The. Edward Everett Hale. WGRP
Nameless, the village. The People: Village. Dorothy Livesay. *Fr.* The Colour of God's Face. PeCV
Names. Dorothy Aldis. SUS
Names, The. Lauris Edmond. OCNZ
Names. D. J. Enright. FaBoCo
Names and Order of the Books of the Old Testament. Thomas Russell. *See* Old Testament, The.
Names for everything I touch. The Hollow Thesaurus. Roger McDonald. CBAP
Names from the War. Bruce Catton. AmFN
Names in Monterchi: To Rachel. James Wright. NNaP
Names of Georgian Women, The. Bella Akhmadulina, *tr. fr. Russian by* Stanley Noyes *and* Olga Carlisle. BoWoP
Names of Horses. Donald Hall. HAP; LCAP; LLLT; PH
Names of the Humble, The. Les A. Murray. CBAP
Names of things, The—sparks! Resigning from a Job in a Defense Industry. Sandra McPherson. LCAP
Names of those who fought and died, The. Sitting in Bib Overalls, Workshirt. Louis Daniel Brodsky. AMV-81
Names, the people, the times, The. Come unto Us Who Are. . .Laden. Harry Roskolenko. FAZ
Naming, The. Terry Hummer. AMV-81
Naming. Joseph Stroud. NPGG
Naming of Parts. Henry Reed. Lessons of the War, I. DTC; FF; GoJo; HeIP; HoPM; InPK; InPS; LiTB; LiTM; MoAB; MoBrPo; MoVE; MP; NOBE; OxBTC; PAI; PoRA; PrIm; SeCePo; SeCeV; SoSe; UnPo; ViBoPo; WaP
Naming of Private Parts. John Lloyd Williams. BXAP; FaBoPa
Naming of the Beasts, The. Francis Sparshott. NOBC
Naming Power. Wendy Rose. TWSS
Naming the Rain. Annette Arkeketa West. TWSS
Namkwin Pul. Bernard Gutteridge. WaP
Nana Kru. *Unknown, tr. fr. Kru by* R. Van Richards. PBA
Nanak and the Sikhs, *sel. Unknown, tr. fr. Hindustani.*
"How shall I address Thee, O God? how shall I praise Thee?" WGRP
Nancy Cock. *Unknown.* OxNR
Nancy Dawson. Herbert P. Horne. HBV-1
Nancy Hanks. Rosemary *and* Stephen Vincent Benét. FaBV; FaPON; NTCP; PoPl; SiSoSe; TiPo
Nancy Hanks. Harriet Monroe. OHIP
Nancy Hanks, Mother of Abraham Lincoln. Vachel Lindsay. CMoP
Nancy Lee, *with music. Unknown.* AmSS
Nancy, the hogs don't know us. Mirror for the Barnyard. Jack Myers. AmPA
Nancy, You Dance. Michael L. Johnson. AMV-81
Nani. A. A. Rios. GP
Nanny. Francis Davis. HBV-1
Nano's Song. Ben Jonson. *See* Fools, They Are the Only Nation.
Nansen. Gary Snyder. InPS
Nanta was nominated for a W(hore). Aenigma on the Six Cases. *Unknown.* FaBoUs
Nantucket. William Carlos Williams. HAP; OxBA; SOTW; TAP; WeW
Nantucket/Mussels/October. Stephen Lewandowski. WOLT
Nantucket Skipper, The. James T. Fields. *See* Alarmed Skipper, The.
Nantucket Whalers. Daniel Henderson. EtS
Nantucket's Widows. Richard Foerster. AMV-81
Nanye'hi (Nancy Ward), the Last Beloved Woman of the Cherokees, 1738–1822. Rayna Green. TWSS
Naomi and Ruth. Bible, *O.T.* Ruth, I:8–17. TrJP
Naomi (Omie) Wise. *Unknown.* AmFP; BaBo (A *and* B *vers.*); ViBoFo, *with music*
(Omie Wise.) FSW
Nap. Mark Van Doren. TwAmPo
Napa, California. Ana Castillo. WPOW
Napery in heaven's wind, The. The Feast of All Saints. Elizabeth Smither. OCNZ
Napkin and Stone. Vernon Watkins. NYBP

Naples Again. Arthur Freeman. NYBP
Napoleon. Byron. *Fr.* Childe Harold's Pilgrimage, III. OBRV
Napoleon. Walter de la Mare. FaBoCh; FaBoTw; MoVE; NOBE
Napoleon after Sedan. Arthur Rimbaud, *tr. fr. French by* Robert Lowell. *Fr.* Eighteen-seventy. OBWP
Napoleon and the British Sailor. Thomas Campbell. BeLS
Napoleon hoped that all the world would fall beneath his sway. *Unknown.* FaBoCo
Napoleon is standing with his pants upon the floor. The Poor Old Prurient Interest Blues. John Hartford. MAT
Napoli Again. Richard Hugo. LCAP
Nappy Edges (A Cross Country Sojourn). Ntozake Shange. BlSi
Nappy Head Blues. *Unknown.* BluL
Narcissa. Gwendolyn Brooks. GrPl; NTCP
Narcissist's eye is blue, fringed with white and covered, The. The Eye. Michael Benedikt. ConAP
Narcissus. Charles Gullans. NePoEA
Narcissus. Donald Petersen. NePoEA-2
Narcissus. John Press. UnTE
Narcissus. Paul Valéry, *tr. fr. French by* Joseph T. Shipley. AWP
Narcissus and Some Tadpoles. Victor J. Daley. PoAu-1
Narcissus, Come Kiss Us! *Unknown.* ErPo
Narcissus in a Cocktail Glass. Frances Minturn Howard. GoYe
Narcissus in Camden. Helen Gray Cone. BXAP
Narcissus: To Himself. David Galler. PoA
Narcotic plash of water from the kitchen sink. The Girl Who Learned to Sing in Crow. Paul Mariani. GeTw
Narrative. Russell Atkins. PoBA
Narrative. Louis Dudek. CaP
Narrative. Elisabeth Eybers, *tr. fr. Afrikaans by author.* PeSA
Narrative, A. Theodore Spencer. WhC
Narrative Hooper and L.D.O. Sestina with a Long Last Line, The. James Whitehead. HoPM; TAT
Narrator's Trance, The, *sels.* James Cunningham. JB
"And birds came crying."
"Song thumbed down a cruiser for a ride, A."
"There were blood spots on the skirt."
"Woods are overhead over everywhere, The."
Narrow Door, The. Charlotte Mew. SBG
Narrow Doors, The. Fannie Stearns Gifford. HBMV
Narrow fellow in the grass, A. Emily Dickinson. AmPP; AP; BoWoP; CABA; CMoP; FaFP; FM; FPL; GoJo; HAP; HoPM; LiTM; NIP; NOBA; NoP; OBCA; OxBA; PAI; PoEL-5; PoLF; PPoe; PPP; SeCeV; SoSe; TAP; WeW
(Snake, The.) LiTA; MoAB; TwAmPo
Narrow glade unfolded, such as Spring, A. An Interview near Florence. Samuel Rogers. *Fr.* Italy. OBNC
Narrow Sea, The. Robert Graves. FaBoEE; FaBoMo; MOS
Narrow, thorny path he trod, The. The Ascetic. Victor J. Daley. PoAu-1
Narrow water, channel water. Channel Water. Virginia Scott Miner. AMV-80
Narrowing of knowledge to one window to a door, A. Elegy for William Soutar. William Montgomerie. NeBP; OxBS
Narrowing sea embraces it forever, The. The Urumbula Song. *Unknown, tr. by* T. G. H. Strehlow. CBAP
Narrows, The. Joseph Bruchac. FAZ
Narrows of Birth, The. William Everson. PoM
Nasal whine of power whips a new universe, The. Power. Hart Crane. *Fr.* The Bridge: Cape Hatteras. MoAB; MoAmPo
Nashville Stonewall Blues. *Unknown.* BluL
Naso, you are many men's man; and yet. To Naso. Catullus, *tr. by* Jack Lindsay. ErPo
Naso, you're all men's man, yet few. Catullus, *tr. fr. Latin by* James Michie. DBV
Nasturtiums with. Rainbow Writing. Eve Merriam. GrPl
Nat Turner. Samuel Allen. CNA; FB
Natalya Nikolayevna Goncharov. Don Coles. NOBC
Nathan Hale. Francis Miles Finch. PAH; PAL
Nathan Hale. William Ordway Partridge. PAL
Nathan Hale. *Unknown.* PAH
Nathan, no thought today. The Bratzlav Rabbi to His Scribe. Jacob Glatstein, *tr. by* Jacob Sloan. TrJP
Nathaniel Lee to Sir Roger L'Estrange. Nathaniel Lee. FaBoEE
Nation. Charlie Cobb. PoBA
Nation. Mendel Naigreshel, *tr. fr. Yiddish by* Joachim Neugroschel. VWA
Nation of hayricks spotting the green solace, A. The Airman Who Flew over Shakespeare's England. Hyam Plutzik. PoPl
Nation of trees, drab green and desolate gray, A. Australia. A. D. Hope. NoP
Nation Wrapped in Stone, A. Roberta Hill. BoWoP; CDW
National Cold Storage Company. Harvey Shapiro. MAT; NYP; VGW
National Gallery, The. Louis MacNeice. EyDe
National Hymn, A. John William DeForest. *Fr.* Miss Ravenel's Conversion. PAL
National Hymn. Daniel C. Roberts. *See* God of Our Fathes, Whose Almighty Hand.
National Miner, The. *Unknown.* AmFP
National Ode, July 4, 1876, The. Bayard Taylor. PAH
America, *sel., fr.* III. AA; PAL
National Paintings, The. Fitz-Greene Halleck *and* Joseph Rodman Drake. *Fr.* The Croaker Papers. AA
National Presage. John Kells Ingram. OnYI
National Security. Archibald MacLeish. GOA
National Song. William Henry Venable. PAH
National Winter Garden. Hart Crane. *Fr.* The Bridge: Three Songs. ErPo; InPS; LiTM; OxBA
Nationalism. Harry Roskolenko. AMV-80
Nationality. Mary Gilmore. CBAP; PoAu-1
Nation's Strength, A. *Unknown, wr. at. to* Emerson. PAL; PGD; TRV
"Not gold, but only man can make," *sel.* AmFN; FaPON
Nations That Long in Darkness Walked, *with music.* John Barnard. AH
Nation's Wealth, A. John Dyer. *Fr.* The Fleece, III. OBEC
Native, The. W. S. Merwin. NePoEA-2; PoRA
Native African Revolutionaries. Paul Jones. AMV-80
Native Born. Eve Langley. PoAu-2; WPE
Native Irishman, The. *Unknown.* OnYI
Native Land. Sir Walter Scott. *See* Breathes There the Man.
Native Moments. Walt Whitman. NePA; OxBA
Native Origin. Beth Brant. STE
Native Working on the Aerodrome. Roy Fuller. NeBP
Natives, The. David Mura. BrSi
Natives here have given up their backyards, The. Champagne. Rita Dove. MAYP
Natives of America, The. Ann Plato. BlSi
Nativitie [*or* Nativity]. John Donne. *Fr.* La Corona. AnAnS-1; OBS; SBVL
Nativitie, The. William Drummond of Hawthornden. *See* Angels, The.
Nativity, The. Richard Crashaw. *See* In the Holy Nativity of Our Lord God.
Nativity. John Donne. *See* Nativitie.
Nativity. Gladys May Casely Hayford (Aquah Laluah). CDC; PBA; TTY
Nativity. Linda Hogan. TWSS
Nativity, A. Kipling. NAs
Nativity, The. C. S. Lewis. EBCP; TrCP
Nativity. James Montgomery. *See* Angels, from the Realms of Glory.
Nativity. W. R. Rodgers. NeBP
Nativity. May Sarton. NePoAm-2
Nativity, The. *Unknown.* MeEL
Nativity, The. Henry Vaughan. SBVL
Nativity, The. Charles Wesley. *See* Hark! the Herald Angels Sing.
Nativity Chant, The. Sir Walter Scott. *Fr.* Guy Mannering. ChTr; FaBoCh; NAs
Nativity of Christ, The. Robert Southwell. EBCP
Nativity of Our Lord and Saviour Jesus Christ, The. Christopher Smart. *Fr.* Hymns and Spiritual Songs. EBEV; HAP; LAuP; LoBV; NOBE; NOCV; PoEL-3; SBVL
(Christmas Day, *sts.* 6-9.) ChTr; OBCP
(Hymn: Nativity of Our Lord and Saviour Jesus Christ, The.) NAs; NOEC
Nativity Song. Jacopone da Todi, *ad. fr. Latin by* Sophie Jewett. OHIP
Natura Naturans. Arthur Hugh Clough. HAP; VLP
Natura Naturans. Kathleen Raine. NYBP
Natura Naturata. Sir John Denham. NCEP
Natural alexandrites are very rare. The Causes of Color. Ann Rae Jonas. SUW
Natural Architecture. John Hay. NePoAm
Natural History. Laura Fargas. SUW
Natural History. Richard Howard. TAP
Natural History, *sel.* Harold Monro.
"Vixen woman, The." OBMV
Natural History. Robert Penn Warren. FF
Natural History of Dragons and Unicorns My Daughter and I Have Known, A. William Pitt Root. AMV-81
Natural History of Pliny, The. Vincent McHugh. NePoAm-2
Natural Magic. Robert Browning. VLP
Natural Mother, The. Jay MacPherson. CABA
Natural Order of Things, The. Harley Elliott. NeAC
Natural pussy. Bitter Herbs. Alta. NMM
Natural silence of a tree, The. Fortune. Charles Madge. FaBoMo
Natural Tears. Thomas Hood. *See* Epigram: "After such years of dissension and strife."
Natural world is a spiritual house, The. Intimate Associations. Baudelaire, *tr. by* Robert Bly. NU
Naturalist's Summer Evening Walk, The. Gilbert White. NOEC; PBBP

Naturally. Audre Lorde. BlSi; CNA
Naturally it is night. Air. W. S. Merwin. CAPP; CoPo; NaP
Naturally it was the naked moon. Moon Song. Hildegarde Flanner. AMV-81
Nature. Mark Akenside. *Fr.* The Pleasures of Imagination, IV. LoBV
Nature. Emerson. AWP
Nature. George Herbert. OAEP
Nature. Longfellow. AA; AP; BoNaP; FaBoBe; FPL; HBV-1; PoLF; TAP; TreFT; TrGrPo; TRV; WHA
Nature. Walter Stone. NYBP
Nature. Henry David Thoreau. BLPL; FaBoBe; HBV-1
Nature. Jones Very. AP; HBV-1
Nature. Alfred de Vigny, *tr. fr. French by* Margaret Jourdain. AWP
Nature and Art. Oliver Herford. TDH
Nature and Art. Pope. *Fr.* Essay on Criticism, I. TreFT
("First follow Nature, and your judgment frame.") HAP; PP
Nature and Nature's laws lay hid in Night. Epitaph Intended for [*or* Epitaph on] Sir Isaac Newton. Pope. FaBoCo; FaBoEE; FaBoEn; FiP; ImOP; InPK; OAEP; QQQ; SeCeV; TreFT; ViBoPo; WeW
Nature and the Child. John Lancaster Spalding. *Fr.* God and the Soul. AA
Nature and the Poet. Wordsworth. *See* Elegiac Stanzas . . .
Nature and the Poets. James Beattie. *Fr.* The Minstrel. OBEC; SeCePo
("But who the melodies of morn can tell?") ViBoPo
Nature Be Damned. Anne Wilkinson. NOBC; OBCV
"I took my watch beside the rose," *sel.* PeCV
Nature, creations law, is judg'd by sense. Upon Love Fondly Refus'd for Conscience['s] Sake. Thomas Randolph. AnAnS-2; OAEL-1
Nature Green Shit. Gary Snyder. LCAP
Nature had long a treasure made. The Match. Andrew Marvell. EBEV
Nature had made them hide in crevices. New Hampshire, February. Richard Eberhart. LiTM; MP; TwCP
Nature herself doth Scotchmen beasts confess. John Cleveland. *Fr.* The Rebel Scot. OBSV
Nature in Couplets. Charlton Ogburn. GrPl
Nature in her wisdom has formed the human head. Four Heads & How to Do Them. John Forbes. CBAP
Nature in Her Working. Richard Stanyhurst. NCEP
Nature, in thy largess, grant. To Mother Nature. Frederic Lawrence Knowles. HBV-1
Nature in War-Time. S. Gertrude Ford. SUMH
Nature Is. Jack Prelutsky. RHPC
Nature is a temple where living pillars. Correspondences. Baudelaire, *tr. by* Anthony Hartley. NAWM-2
Nature is a temple where we live ironically. Correspondences. Baudelaire, *tr. by* Arthur Symons. SyP
"Nature is blind." Overheard in a Barbershop. Irving Layton. NMP
Nature is rising from the dead. Epigram on the First of April. John Winstanley. NOEC
Nature is the endless sky. Nature Is. Jack Prelutsky. RHPC
Nature might chicken out, but "I love you." X. J. Kennedy. PeD
Nature Morte. Louis MacNeice. NoAM
Nature most calm is often a crisis. Chesapeake. Gerta Kennedy. NYBP
Nature Note. Arthur Guiterman. SUS
Nature nothing shows more rare. Shells. T. Sturge Moore. SeCePo
Nature of an Action, The. Thom Gunn. NePoEA
Nature of Jungles, The. W. R. Moses. NCSH
Nature of Love, The. James Kirkup. EaLo
Nature of Love, The. Lucretius, *tr. fr. Latin by* Dryden. *Fr.* De Rerum Natura. UnTE
Nature of Man, The. C. H. Sisson. FaBoTw
Nature of the Eagle, The. *Unknown, tr. fr. Middle English. Fr.* The Bestiary. PBBP
Nature of the Turtle Dove, The. *Unknown, tr. fr. Middle English. Fr.* The Bestiary. PBBP
Nature one hour appears a thing unsexed. Francis Thompson. *Fr.* Contemplation. OBNC
Nature reads not our labels, "great" and "small." The Man with the Hoe; a Reply. John Vance Cheney. AA; HBV-2
Nature selects the longest way. A Northern Suburb. John Davidson. NBM; OBNC
Nature Study, after Dufy. Helen Bevington. NYBP
Nature that day a woman was in weakness. A Storm in Summer. Wilfrid Scawen Blunt. FaBoTw
Nature That Framed Us of Four Elements. Christopher Marlowe. *Fr.* Tamburlaine the Great, Pt. I, Act II, sc. vii. PoEL-2; TrGrPo
(Perfect Bliss and Sole Felicity.) SeCePo
Nature, That Washed [*or* Washt] Her Hands in Milk[e]. Sir Walter Ralegh. CABA; EnRePo; NoP
(Love and Time.) SiPS
(Poem of Sir Walter Raleighs, A.) AAS
Nature: The Artist. Frederic Lawrence Knowles. AA
Nature, they say, doth dote. Lincoln. James Russell Lowell. *Fr.* Ode Recited at the Harvard Commemoration. HBVY; PGD
Nature! thou may'st fume and fret. To Miss Arundell. Walter Savage Landor. OBVV
Nature, which is the vast creation's soul. To Mr. Henry Lawes. Katherine Philips. SBG; WPE
Nature, with endless being rife. A Demonstration. Coventry Patmore. *Fr.* The Angel in the House. VLP
Nature withheld Cassandra in the skies. Fragment of a Sonnet. Pierre de Ronsard, *tr. by* Keats. AWP; OBVE
Nature's Charms. James Beattie. *Fr.* The Minstrel. OBEC
Nature's confectioner the bee. Fuscara; or, The Bee Errant. John Cleveland. AnAnS-2
Nature's Cook, *sel.* Margaret Cavendish, Duchess of Newcastle.
"Death is the cook of nature, and we find." PBWP
Nature's Creed. *Unknown.* OHIP
(Handiwork of God, The.) TRV
Nature's decorations glisten. Christmas Day. Christopher Smart. *Fr.* Hymns and Spiritual Songs, XXXII. ChTr; OBCP
Nature's Easter Music. Lucy Larcom. OHIP
Nature's Embassy, *sel.* Richard Brathwaite.
Nightingale, The. EIL
("Jug, jug! Fair fall the nightingal.") PBBP
Nature's first green is gold. Nothing Gold Can Stay. Robert Frost. AmPP; GrPl; MoAB; MoAmPo; NCSH; NOBA; PAI; PPP; SoSe; TAP; VGW; WHA
Nature's Hymn to the Deity. John Clare. EBCP; VLP
Nature's Influence on Man. Mark Akenside. *Fr.* The Pleasure of Imagination, III. OBEC
(Created Universe, The.) LoBV
(Love of Nature.) NOEC
Nature's lay idiot [*or* ideot], I taught thee to love. Elegy. John Donne. Elegies, VII. NoP; SeCP
Nature's Lineaments. Robert Graves. FaBoTw
Natures Naked Jem. George Chapman. *See* Corinna Bathes.
Nature's Questioning. Thomas Hardy. CoBMV; MoPo; TEP; VLP
Nature's Reply to Mutability. Spenser. *Fr.* The Faerie Queene, VII, 7. NOBE
Nature's Travail. *Unknown, tr. fr. Greek by* Goldwin Smith. AWP
Naughty Blackbird, The. Kate Greenaway. HBVY
Naughty Boy. Robert Creeley. NoAM; NOBA
Naughty Lord and the Gay Young Lady, The. *Unknown.* CoMu
Naughty Paughty Jack-a-Dandy. Namby-Pamby; or, A Panegyric on the New Versification. Henry Carey. FaBoNo; FaBoPa; NOEC; OBSV; Par
Naughty Preposition, The. Morris Bishop. FiBHP; NYBP; PV
Naughty Young Nat. Isabel Frances Bellows. TDH
Nausea. Catherine Davis. NePoEA
Nausea. E. L. Mayo. MiAP
Nausicaa. Homer, *tr. fr. Greek by* George Chapman. *Fr.* The Odyssey, VI. OBS
Nausicäa. Irving Layton. ErPo
Nausicaa with Some Attendants. Tom Lowenstein. VWA
Nautical Ballad, A. Charles Edward Carryl. *See Walloping Window-Blind, The.*
Nautilus Island's hermit. Skunk Hour. Robert Lowell. AmPP; AP; BiP; CAPP; CMoP; CoAP; ConAP; FaBoMo; HAP; HeIP; InPK; LCAP; MoAmPo; NIP; NMP; NoAM; NOBA; NoP; OxBC; PAI; PPP: PrIm; SCV; TAP; WeW
Nauty Pauty Jack-a-Dandy. *Unknown.* OxNR
Nauvoo. Bayard Taylor. OBAL
Navajo, The. Elizabeth J. Coatsworth. AmFN
Navajo. William Haskel Simpson. BPAW
Navajo Song. Maynard Dixon. BPAW
Navigators, The. W. J. Turner. OBMV
Nay, be you pardoner or cheat. Villon's Ballade. Andrew Lang. HBV-1
Nay but you, who do not love her. Song. Robert Browning. HBV-1; TrGrPo; ViBoPo
Nay, come and visit me, sweet friend. Invitation to a Mistress. *Unknown, tr. by* George F. Whicher. UnTE
Nay, gather not that filbert, Nicholas. The Filbert. Robert Southey. FM
Nay, I have loved thee. Theseus and Ariadne. Lloyd Mifflin. AA
Nay, Ivy, Nay. *Unknown. See* Holly and Ivy ("Holly standeth in the hall").
Nay, lady, one frown is enough. To Helen in a Huff. Nathaniel Parker Willis. OBAL
Nay, Lord, not thus! white lilies in the spring. Sonnet on Hearing the *Dies Irae* Sung in the Sistine Chapel. Oscar Wilde. TrPWD
Nay, nay, Ivy! Holly Beareth Berries [*or* Holly against Ivy]. *Unknown.* MeEL; PBBP
Nay, nay, my boy—'tis not for me. Fie on Eastern Luxury! Horace, *tr. by* Hartley Coleridge. Odes, I, 38. InPK

Nay, painter, if thou dar'st design that fight. The Second Advice to a Painter. Andrew Marvell. APAS
Nay, pish; nay, phew! nay, faith and will you? fie! A Maiden's Denial [*or* The Reluctant Lady]. *Unknown.* ErPo; UnTE
Nay, prethee [*or* prithee] dear, draw nigher. A Loose Saraband. Richard Lovelace. CaPo; CavP; PoEL-3
Nay, prithee do, be coy and slight me. The Contrary. Alexander Brome. CavP
Nay, prithee tell me, Love, when I behold. The Transfiguration of Beauty. Michelangelo, *tr. by* John Addington Symonds. AWP
Nay, tell me now in what strange air. Ballade of Dead Ladies. Villon, *tr. by* Andrew Lang. HBV-1
Nay, tempt me not, my Corydon; I tell you once again. Football and Rowing—an Eclogue. Alfred Denis Godley. CenHV
Nay, tempt me not to love again. Thomas Moore. *Fr.* Odes to Nea. OBNC
Nay, *that*, furini, never I at least. With Francis Furini. Robert Browning. *Fr.* Parleyings with Certain People of Importance in Their Day. VLP
Nay then, farewell, if this be so. To Avisa. Henry Willoby. *Fr.* Willobie His Avisa. EIL
"Nay then," quoth Adon, "you will fall again." Venus Abandoned. Shakespeare. *Fr.* Venus and Adonis. OBSC
Nay, thou art my eternal attribute. Whym Chow. "Michael Field." FM
Nay, why should I fear Death. Laus Mortis. Frederic Lawrence Knowles. HBV-2
Nay, Xanthias, feel unashamed. Ad Xanthiam Phoceum. Horace, *tr. by* Franklin P. Adams. Odes, II, 4. AWP
Nay, you wrong her, my friend, she's not fickle; her love she has simply outgrown. Outgrown. Julia C. R. Dorr. HBV-1
Nazi in a Zeppelin, A. Anxiety Pastorale. Ted Schaefer. FAZ
Ndaaya's Kàsàlà, *sel.* Citèkù Ndaaya, *tr. after French-Luba texts by* Judith Gleason
"Ndaaya, I, am so poor." PBWP
Ne Plus Ultra. Samuel Taylor Coleridge. OAEL-2
Neaera when I'm there is adamant. J. V. Cunningham, *after the Latin of* George Buchanan. OBVE
Neaera's Kisses. Johannes Secundus, *tr. fr. Latin by* John Nott. *Fr.* Basia. UnTE
Neanderthal. Michael Jackson. OCNZ
Neap-tide and the ebbing days slide. A Song of Sickness. Hine Tangikuku, *tr. by* Barry Mitcalfe. WTO
Near. Abba Kovner, *tr. fr. Hebrew by* Shirley Kaufman. VWA
Near. William Stafford. ConAP
Near a shady wall a rose once grew. The Rose Still Grows beyond the Wall. A. L. Frink. BLPA
Near a Waterfall at Ryumon. Lady Ise, *tr. fr. Japanese by* Etsuko Terasaki *and* Irma Brandeis. BoWoP
Near an Old Prison. Frances Cornford. OBMV
Near Avalon. William Morris. OAEL-2
Near Barbizon. Galway Kinnell. NePoAm-2
Near dark/ snow falling like flakes of light. The First Hunt. Gordon Anderson. PPJ
Near Dover, September 1802. Wordsworth. EnRP
(September 1802; near Dover.) OAEP
(Sonnet: September, 1802.) ChER
Near Drowning. Ralph Pomeroy. DFF
Near Dusk. Joseph Auslander. FaPON
Near Hampton Court there lies a common. Hounslow Heath. *Unknown.* APAS
Near Helikon. Trumbull Stickney. LiTA; NCEP; TwAmPo
Near Lanivet, 1872. Thomas Hardy. AWP; CMoP; LoBV; NoAM
Near me a black and shaggy pony is eating grass. Black Pony Eating Grass. Robert Bly. FAZ
Near Neighbors. Martial, *tr. fr. Latin by* Swift. AWP
Near Perigord. Ezra Pound. FaBoMo; LiTA; LiTM
Near strange, weird temples, where the Ganges' tide. The Bayadere. Francis Saltus Saltus. AA
Near the Base Line. Samuel L. Albert. NePoAm-2
Near the Border of Insanities. Dannie Abse. PoA
Near the celebrated Lido where the breeze is fresh and free. Longfellow's Visit to Venice. John Betjeman. NOBL
Near the Cymmerians, in his dark abode. Ovid, *tr. by* Dryden. *Fr.* Metamorphoses, XI. OBVE
Near the Death of Ovid. Robert Conquest. NoAM
Near the dry river's water-mark we found. A Note Left in Jimmy Leonard's Shack. James Wright. NoP
Near the edge, as on a shelf. Cat on the Porch at Dusk. Dorothy Harriman. GoYe
Near the headwaters of the longest river. The Banished Gods. Derek Mahon. OxBC
Near the Lake. George Pope Morris. AA
Near the Ocean. Robert Lowell. NOBA
Near the river with white waves, we probed. Apology of the Young Scientists. Celia Dimmette. GoYe
Near the road brim. Pittsburgh. Hy Sobiloff. NePA
Near the School for Handicapped Children. Thomas W. Shapcott. CBAP
Near the top a bad turn some dare. Whether There Is Sorrow in the Demons. John Berryman. LiTM
Near the Vipsanian columns where the aqueduct. Martial, *tr. fr. Latin by* Peter Porter. OBVE
Near this spot. Epitaph to a Dog [*or* An Epitaph: Inscription on a Monument at Newstead Abbey *or* Epitaph to a Newfoundland Dog]. Byron. BLPA; BoAnP; GDP; TreFS
Near to me as my flesh, my flesh and blood. Allen Tate. *Fr.* Sonnets of the Blood. PoA
Near to the Rose where punks in numbers flock. The Play-House. Joseph Addison. APAS
Near [*or* Neare] to the silver Trent. The Trent [*or* The Jovial Shepheard's Song *or* Sirena]. Michael Drayton. *Fr.* The Shepherd's Sirena. FaBoPP; OBEV; PoEL-2
Near where I live there is a lake. Fringed Gentians. Amy Lowell. FaPON
Near where yonder evening star. Cockayne Country. Agnes Mary Frances Robinson. OBVV
Near Wilton sweet hugh heaps of stone are found. Stonehenge. Sir Philip Sidney. *Fr.* The Seven Wonders of England. FaBoPP
Near yonder copse, where once the garden smiled. The Village Parson. Goldsmith. *Fr.* The Deserted Village. OBEC; TRV; WGRP
Neare Enna walles there standes a Lake Pergusa is the name. Ovid, *tr. by* Arthur Golding. *Fr.* Metamorphoses, V. OBVE
Nearer. Judith Herzberg, *tr. fr. Dutch by* Shirley Kaufman. BoWoP; VWA
Nearer Home. Phoebe Cary. AA; BLRP; FaFP; HBV-2; TreF; WBLP; WGRP
(One Sweetly Solemn Thought, *with music.*) AH
Nearer, My God, to Thee. Sarah Flower Adams. BLRP; FaBoBe; FaFP; FSW; TreF; VLP; WBLP; WGRP
(Nearer to Thee.) HBV-2; PoLF
Nearer the pulse than other themes. A True Picture Restored. Vernon Watkins. NoAM
Nearest Friend, The. Frederic W. Faber. TreFS
Nearest the Dearest. Coventry Patmore. *Fr.* The Angel in the House, II, i. HBV-1
Nearing Again the Legendary Isle. C. Day Lewis. The Magnetic Mountain, VI. CoBMV; FaBoTw; LiTB; MoAB; MoBrPo
Nearing La Guaira. Derek Walcott. TTY
Nearing Winter. Ernest Sandeen. NYBP
Nearly dark; warm stones of the wall in the woods. The Owl. Thorkild Bjornvig, *tr. by* Robert Bly. NU
Nearly Everybody Loves Harvey Martin. William D. Barney. LiSp
Nearly right, The. To the Tune of the Coventry Carol. Stevie Smith. FaBoTw
Nearly seven. The New Mothers. Carol Shields. Str
Nearly winter. All day the sky gray. Earth heavy. A Long Walk before the Snows Began. Robert Bly. LCAP
Nearsighted child has taken off her glasses, The. Country Stars. William Meredith. GrPl
Neat little packet from Hobart set sail, A. The Waterwitch. *Unknown.* PoAu-1
Neat young lady at work in the garden, A. A Sweetheart in the Army. *Unknown.* BaBo
'Neath blue-bell or streamer. Song from "Al Aaraaf." Poe. *Fr.* Al Aaraff. AmPP; NePA; OxBA
'Neath northern skies thou hid'st thy punctual nest. The Loon. Theodore Harding Rand. CaP
Neatness, madam, has. The Truth Is Quite Messy. William J. Harris. BOLo
Nebraska. Jon Swan. RFM
Nebuchadnezzar. Irwin Russell. HBV-2
Nebuchadnezzar. Elinor Wylie. MoAmPo; SBG
Nebuchadnezzar, von Hoffman the Great, then. Lines I Told Myself I Wouldn't Write. Paul Mariani. MAYP
Necessary Miracle, A. Eda Lou Walton. NYBP
Necessitarian's Epitaph, A. Thomas Hardy. FaBoEE
Necessities of Life. Adrienne Rich. NIP; NoAM; NOBA
(33.) CuPo
Necessity. Harry Graham. FaBoCo
(Late Last Night.) ShM
Necessity. Langston Hughes. NOBA
Necessity of Rejection, The. James Schevill. FAZ
Nechama. Shirley Kaufman. LCAP
Neckwear. Michael Silverton. PV
Necromancers, The. John Frederick Nims. PoCh
Necropolis. Karl Shapiro. MoAB; PoA
Nectar, puff of sails, lily. To a Young Girl. David Rosenmann-Taub, *tr. by* Charles Guenther. VWA

Ned Braddock. John Williamson Palmer. PAH
Ned Bratts. Robert Browning. VLP
Ned Christie. Robert J. Conley. STE
Ned knew I was short of tobacco one day. Ned's Delicate Way. Henry Lawson. CBAP
Ned Vaughan. Walter de la Mare. FaBoEE
Neddy Nibble'm and Biddy Finn. *Unknown.* GBP
Ned's Delicate Way. Henry Lawson. CBAP
Need. Babette Deutsch. PCP
Need, The. Siegfried Sassoon. TrPWD
Need from excess—excess from folly growing. Epigram. Samuel Bishop. NOEC
Need Is Our Name. Luci Shaw. TrCP
Need of an Angel. Raymond Souster. CaP
Need of Being Versed in Country Things, The. Robert Frost. FaBoEn; NoAM; NOBA; OxBA; UnPo
Need of Loving. Strickland Gillilan. *See* Folks Need a Lot of Loving.
Need of the Hour, The. Edwin Markham. PAL
Need to explore, The. Explorers as Seen by the Natives. Doug Fetherling. NOBC
Need to Love, The. Shlomo Vinner, *tr. fr. Hebrew by* Laya Firestone *and* Howard Schwartz. VWA
Needle, The. Grace Cornell Tall. GoYe
Needle, The. Samuel Woodworth. GN; HBV-2
Needle and Thread. Pan Chao, *tr. fr. Chinese by* Richard Mather *and* Rob Swigart. WPOW
Needle quivering from its pole, The. To a Lady, with a Compass. George Napier. FaBoUs
Needle Travel. Margaret French Patton. HBMV
Needles and Pins. Mark Van Doren. SO
Needles and pins, needles and pins. Proverb. *Unknown.* FaBoBe; HBV-1
Needles are starved, brown, The. Acceleration near the Point of Impact. Joyce Carol Oates. GeTw
Needle's Eye, The. *Unknown.* AmFP
Needles' Lighthouse from Keyhaven, Hampshire, The. Charles Tennyson Turner. FaBoPP
Needless Alarm, The. John Ruskin. FM
Needless to catalogue heroes. No Man Knows War. Edwin Rolfe. TrJP; WaP
Needless Worry. Emerson. TreFT
Needs. A. R. Ammons. NIP; OBAL
Needs. Elizabeth Rendall. HBMV
Needs Must I Leave, and Yet Needs Must I Love. Henry Constable. *Fr.* Diana. InvP; OBSC
Needs no introduction. My Woman. A. D. Winans. AMV-80
"Needy knife-grinder! whither are you going?" The Friend of Humanity and the Knife Grinder [*or* The Knife-Grinder *or* Sapphics]. George Canning *and* John Hookham Frere. BXAP; FaBoCo; HBV-1; InMe; NOEC; OBEC; Par
Needy were lined up by order of famine, The. The Offended. Anne Hébert, *tr. by* Willis Barnstone. BoWoP
Negation is the spectre, the reasoning power in man, The. Reason and Imagination. Blake. *Fr.* Milton. EnRP
Negative Passage. Michael Newman. PoA
Negative tree, you are belief. Bound. Theodore Roethke. PoA
Negatives, The. Philip Levine. NePoEA-2
Negatives. Charles Wright. PoA
Neglected long had been my useless lyre. On the Defeat at Ticonderoga or Carilong. *Unknown.* PAH
Neglectful Edward. Robert Graves. BrPo; MoBrPo
Negritude. James A. Emanuel. BPo; CNA
Negro, The. James A. Emanuel. HoPM
Negro, The/ With the trumpet at his lips. Trumpet Player. Langston Hughes. TTY
Negro Dreams. Doughtry Long. PoBA
Negro Hero. Gwendolyn Brooks. CAPP
Negro holds firmly the reins of his four horses, The. The Drayman. Walt Whitman. *Fr.* Song of Myself. PoNe
Negro Judge, A. Frederick Seidel. CoPo
Negro Love Song, A. Paul Laurence Dunbar. BANP; PoNe
Negro Peddler's Song, A. Fenton Johnson. AmNP
Negro Poets. Charles Bertram Johnson. BANP
Negro Reel, *with music. Unknown.* AS
Negro Serenade. James Edwin Campbell. BANP
Negro Sermon, A: Simon Legree. Vachel Lindsay. *See* Simon Legree—a Negro Sermon.
Negro Servant. Langston Hughes. VGW
Negro Singer, The. James David Corrothers. BANP
Negro Soldiers, The. Roscoe Conkling Jamison. BANP
Negro Soldier's Civil War Chant. *Unknown.* BPo
(Black Soldier's Civil War Chant.) TAP
Negro Soldier's Viet Nam Diary, A. Herbert Martin. PoBA
Negro Speaks of Rivers, The. Langston Hughes. AmFN; AmNP; BANP; BPo; CABA; CDC; HAP; HeIP; IDB; NIP; NoAM; NOBA; NoP; OBCA; PAI; PoBA; PoNe; TAP; TTY; WeW
Negro Spiritual. Perient Trott. PoNe
Negro Spirituals. Rosemary *and* Stephen Vincent Benét. AmFN; FaPON
Negro sprouts from the pavement like an asparagus, A. Stumpfoot on 42nd Street. Louis Simpson. NNaP; NYP; UnPo; VGW
Negro Woman. Lewis Alexander. CDC; PoBA
Negroes. Maxwell Bodenheim. PoNe
Negroes/ Sweet and docile. Warning. Langston Hughes. BPo
Negroes, labouring, The. Guadalupe, W.I. Nicolás Guillén, *tr. by* Anselm Hollo. TTY
Negroes turned black overnight. The Sixties. Thomas Listmann. AMV-80
Negro's Tragedy, The. Claude McKay. BPo
Nehi Blues. *Unknown.* BluL
Neighbor. Charles Waterman. GP
Neighbor, The. Miller Williams. GP
Neighbor, A/ rejects chemotherapy and the hospital. The Cloud Chamber. Arthur Sze. BrSi
Neighbor sits in his window and plays the flute, The. Music. Amy Lowell. YaD
Neighbor thought that they, A. The Planetary Arc-Light. August Derleth. GoYe
Neighborly. Violet Alleyn Storey. TiPo
Neighbors. David Allan Evans. Psk
Neighbors. Marilyn Francis. GoYe
Neighbors, The. Theodosia Garrison. HBMV
Neighbors. "Lennox." DBV; InMe
Neighbors. Charles Malam. AMV-80
Neighbors. Anne Spencer. CDC
Neighbors of Bethlehem, The. *Unknown, tr. fr. French.* OHIP
Neighbour mine not long ago there was, A. A Tale for Husbands. Sir Philip Sidney. *Fr.* Arcadia. SiPS
Neighing North, The. Annie Charlotte Dalton. CaP
Neïla. Yvan Goll, *tr. fr. French by* Anthony Rudolf. VWA
Neither blemish this book, nor the leaves double down. *Unknown.* FaBoUs
Neither Here nor There. W. R. Rodgers. LiTB; LiTM; MoAB; MoBrPo; NeBP; ViBoPo
Neither Hook nor Line. Bunyan. LiSp
Neither in idleness consume thy days. Walter Savage Landor. FaBoEE
Neither love, the subtlety of refinement. The Presence. William Everson. ErPo
Neither malt nor Milton can. In Humbleness. Daniel G. Hoffman. NePA
Neither of them was better than the other. From Plane to Plane. Robert Frost. MoAmPo
Neither on horseback nor seated. Walt Whitman at Bear Mountain. Louis Simpson. ConAP; LiTM; NePoEA-2; PoCh; PP
Neither our vices nor our virtues. Poetry, a Natural Thing. Robert Duncan. NoAM; NOBA
Neither Out Far nor In Deep. Robert Frost. AmPP; AP; CABA; ChTr; CoBMV; CrMA; HAP; LiTA; MoAB; MOS; NoAM; NOBA; NoP; TAP; WeW
Neither Poverty nor Riches. Bible, O.T. Proverbs, XXX: 7-9. TrJP
Neither Shadow of Turning. Jack Clemo. NOCV
Neither Shall They Learn War Anymore. Bible, *O.T. Fr.* Micah. *See* And They Shall Beat Their Swords into Plowshares.
Neither snow, nor rain. On Their Appointed Rounds. *Unknown.* FaPON
Neither Spirit nor Bird. *Unknown, tr. fr. Shoshone Indian by* Mary Austin. AWP; BPAW
Neither This nor That. Luis Palés Matos, *tr. fr. Spanish by* Julio Marzán. InW
Neither tribal nor trivial he shouts. Newsboy. Irving Layton. CaP
Neither war, nor cyclones, nor earthquakes. Antipater of Thessalonica. Kenneth Rexroth. CrMA
Neither will I put myself forward as others may do. Eternal Masculine. William Rose Benét. AWP; MoAmPo
Nell. Raymond Knister. *Fr.* A Row of Stalls. NOBC; OBCV
Nell Flaherty's Drake. *Unknown.* AnIV; OnYI; TW
Nell Gwynne's Looking-Glass. Laman Blanchard. HBV-1
Nellie Rakerfield. Nell. Raymond Knister. *Fr.* A Row of Stalls. NOBC; OBCV
Nelly Bly. Stephen Collins Foster. FSW
Nelly Kelly loved baseball games. Take Me Out to the Ball Game. Jack Norworth. OBAL
Nelly, methinks, 'twixt thee and me. To a Cat. Hartley Coleridge. FM
Nelly Trim. Sylvia Townsend Warner. ErPo; MoAB; MoBrPo
Nelson, Pitt, Fox. Sir Walter Scott. *Fr.* Marmion, *Introd. to* I. OBEV
Nelson Street. "Seumas O'Sullivan." OxBI
Nelson's Death. *Unknown.* OBET
Nemea. Lawrence Durrell. ChMP; FaBoTw; GTBS-P
Nemesis. Emerson. NOBA
Nemo Canem Impune Lacessit. Robert Garioch. BSV

Neo-classical Poem. William Jay Smith. WaP
Neon glitter of night. Beale Street, Memphis. Thurmond Snyder. NNP
Neon glow escapes from, The. West End Blues. John Hollander. NYP
Neoplatonic Soliloquy. Donald G. Babcock. NePoAm
Neo-Thomist Poem. Ernest Hemingway. OBAL
Nepenthe, *sels.* George Darley.
"As from the moist and gelid sleep." OnYI
Hundred-gated Thebes. NOBE
Hurry Me Nymphs. NBM
In Dreamy Swoon. OBNC
("Over a bloomy land, untrod.") OBRV
"List no more the ominous din." OBRV
O Blest Unfabled Incense Tree. BIrV; ChER; FaBoCh; FaBoRV; OBRV; PBBP
(Hundred-sunned Phenix.) OBNC
(Nepenthe.) AnIV
(Phoenix, The.) ChTr; LoBV; NOBE; OAEL-2; OBVV; WiR
"O fast her amber blood doth flow." OBRV
(Phoenix, The.) OBEV
Onward to Far Ida. OBNC
"Solitary wayfarer!" OBRV; PBBP
(Hoopoe.) OBNC
"Thou whose thrilling hand in mine." OBRV
Unicorn, The. ChTr; FaBoEn; NBM; OBNC; PoEL-4
("Lo! in the mute mid wilderness.") OBRV
Nephelidia. Swinburne. *Fr.* The Heptalogia. BXAP; FaBoCo; FaBoNo; FaBoPa; HBV-1; HoPM; InMe; NA; OAEP; Par; SpRo
Nephews and Nieces, love your leaden statues. Paul and Virginia. John Wheelwright. CrMA
Neptune. Thomas Campion. *See* In Praise of Neptune.
Neptune and Mars in council sate. Louisburg. *Unknown.* PAH
Neptune—Polka. Edith Sitwell. NOBE
Neptune, the mighty Marine God, I sing. Homeric Hymn to Neptune. George Chapman. EtS
Neptune's Triumph, *sel.* Ben Jonson.
Chorus: "Spring all the Graces of the age." OBS
Nereid, Grand Turk, Good Intent. Waterfront. Oliver Jenkins. EtS
Nereides; or, Sea-Eclogues, *sels.* William Diaper.
"Believe not, Fair, that I can prove untrue," *fr.* Eclogue I. PeD
Eclogue: "Lycon begin—begin the mournful tale." SeCePo
Sea Eclogue: "Otys, begin." LoBV
Nereids, The. Charles Kingsley. *Fr.* Andromeda. NBM
Nerves. "Sagittarius." OxBTC
Nerves. Arthur Symons. BrPo; FaBoTw; SyP
Nervous hose is dribbling on the tar, A. The Roof Garden. Howard Moss. MAT; NYP
Nervous Prostration. Anna Wickham. TW
Nervy with neons, the main drag. At Barstow. Charles Tomlinson. NoAM; TwCP
Nescit Vox Missa Reverti. J. V. Cunningham. ELU
Nessie. Ted Hughes. AmMo
Nest Eggs. Robert Louis Stevenson. FM
Nested. Habberton Lulham. HBV-1
Nesting. Dennis Saleh. NeAC
Nesting Ground, The. David Wagoner. PoCh
Nesting Time. Douglas Stewart. BoAnP; PoAu-2
Nestor. Homer, *tr. fr. Greek by* Ennis Rees. *Fr.* The Iliad, XXIII. LiSp
Nests are in the hedgerows, The. To a Child of Fancy. Lewis Morris. HBV-1
Nestus Gurley. Randall Jarrell. MP; TwCP
Net, The. W. R. Rodgers. AnIL; BoLoP; CIP; ErPo; NMP; OxBI
Net and the Sword, The. Douglas LePan. NOBC
Net Menders, The. Brian Vrepont. PoAu-2
Net of Law, The. James Jeffrey Roche. HBV-1; PV
Net rests on the water's surface, The. Elena Clementelli, *tr. by* Ruth Feldman *and* Brian Swann. *Fr.* Etruscan Notebook. PBWP
Net to Snare the Moonlight, A. Vachel Lindsay. PoLF
Netley Abbey; Midnight. William Sotheby. NOEC
Nets are real, The—heroin (sniffed) clears them. For Artaud. Michael McClure. NeAP
Nets on the Andrea Doria, The. Karen G. Tepfer. AMV-81
Nets to Catch the Wind. John Webster. *See* All the Flowers of the Spring.
Netting. Jorie Graham. NPGG
Nettles. Neil Munro. PoSH
Network, The. Robert Finch. CaP
Neural Folds. Lucille Day. SUW
Neuteronomy. Eve Merriam. QQQ
Neutral British Gentlemen, The. "Orpheus C. Kerr." OBAL
Neutral island facing the Atlantic, The. Neutrality. Louis MacNeice. CoBMV
Neutral Tones. Thomas Hardy. BrPo; CABA; CMoP; CoBMV; EBVV; HAP; HeIP; InPK; MoBrPo; NoAM; OAEL-2; PPP; SyP; TEP; UnPo; VLP
Neutrality. Sidney Keyes. MoAB; MoBrPo
Neutrality. Louis MacNeice. CoBMV
Neutrality Loathsome. Robert Herrick. LiTB; NoP
Nevada. Lawrence Gurney. GoYe
Nevada. Stanley Noyes. PH
Nevadaville upon a hill/ The home of Cousin Jack and Jill. The Fight at Nevadaville. *Unknown.* PoOW
Never. George Reavey. BIrV
Never a beak has my white bird. Thistle-Down. Clara Doty Bates. AA
Never a careworn wife but shows. Wives in the Sere. Thomas Hardy. BrPo; NOBE; VLP
Never a trial that He is not there. Moment by Moment. Daniel W. Whittle. BLRP
Never Admit the Pain. Mary Gilmore. PoAu-1
Never Again, The. Charles Dobzynski, *tr. fr. French by* Anita Barrows. VWA
Never again, Orpheus. Antipater of Sidon, *tr. fr. Greek by* Kenneth Rexroth. OBVE
Never again shall we beat out to sea. Fiddler's Green. Theodore Goodridge Roberts. CaP
Never Again Would Birds' Song Be the Same. Robert Frost. CrMA; FYAP; HAP; InPK; NIP; NoAM; NoP; VGW
Never and never, my girl riding far and near. In Country Sleep. Dylan Thomas. LiTB
Never Ask Me Why. Silvia Margolis. GoYe
Never ask of money spent. The Hardship of Accounting. Robert Frost. FaBoCh; FaBoCo; FaFP; OBAL; WhC
Never, being damned, see paradise. Those Not Elect. Léonie Adams. MoVE
Never believe all you hear. Wolf. Kenneth Rexroth. *Fr.* A Bestiary. NNaP
Never, believe me/ Appear the Immortals. The Visit of the Gods. Schiller, *tr. by* Samuel Taylor Coleridge. OBVE
Never believe me, if I love. The Careless Lover. Sir John Suckling. CavP
"Never burn witchwood," my old Granny said. Witchwood. May Justus. SiSoSe
Never could I think/ Our love a worldly commonplace. Izumi Shikibu, *tr. fr. Japanese by* Edwin A. Cranston. PBWP
Never, even in a dream. Abroad. William Carlos Williams. TwAmPo
Never fear the phantom bird. Mentis Trist. Robert Hillyer. HBMV
Never forget this when the talk is clever. The Sacred Order. May Sarton. ImOP
Never forget who brings the rain. Turn of the Moon. Robert Graves. TEP
Never Get a Lickin' Till I Go Down to Bimini, *with music.* *Unknown.* OuSiCo
Never Give All the Heart. W. B. Yeats. BoLoP; CMoP; HBV-1
Never going off, always here, I. Away. Josephine Miles. GP
Never had child a more adventurous life. Iulus. Eleanor Glenn Wallis. NePoAm-2
Never have I seen the sky more clear. Depressed by the Death of the Horse That He Bought from Robert Bly. Henry Taylor. BXAP
Never Let Your Left Hand Know. *Unknown.* BluL
Never Love [Unless You Can]. Thomas Campion. AAS; ElL; LoBV; TrGrPo; ViBoPo
(Advice to a Girl.) HBV-1
Never love with all your heart. Song in Spite of Myself. Countee Cullen. BALP
Never May the Fruit Be Plucked. Edna St. Vincent Millay. CrMA; SBG
Never mind avarice; the hills. Thinking of Hölderlin. Christopher Middleton. NePoEA-2
Never mind how the pedagogue proses. To Fanny. Thomas Moore. HBV-1
Never mind the clouds which gather. I Have Always Found It So. Birdie Bell. BLRP
Never mind the day we left, or the way the women clung to us. The Klondike. E. A. Robinson. PAH
Never More. *See* Nevermore.
Never, Never Can Nothingness Come. Norma Keating. GoYe
Never, never let your gun. A Rule for Shooting. *Unknown.* FaBoUs
Never, never may the fruit be plucked from the bough. Never May the Fruit Be Plucked. Edna St. Vincent Millay. CrMA
Never on this side of the grave again. A Life's Parallels. Christina Rossetti. NBM; PoEL-5
Never once—since the world began. God's Sunshine. John Oxenham. WBLP
Never pain to tell thy love. Blake. OAEL-2
Never pass a nun. How to Walk in a Crowd. Robert Hershon. FF
Never presume that in this marble stable. The Brass Horse. Drummond Allison. FaBoTw

Never said/a word. Adam's Apple. Coleman Barks. PPJ
Never Said a Mumbalin' Word. *Unknown.* GBP; TrAS; *with music*
Never saw him. The Negro. James A. Emanuel. HoPM
Never say that there is only death for you. Zog Nit Keynmol (Tell Us No More). *Unknown, tr. fr. Yiddish.* FSW
Never Seek to Tell Thy Love. Blake. ChER; ELP; EnLoPo; EnRP; FaBV; InPS; LO; NOBE; OAEP; OBEC; OBNC; PoEL-4; PoPle; TreFT; ViBoPo
(Love's Secret.) FaFP; OBEV; OLR; PPoe; TrGrPo
(Song: "Never seek to tell thy love.") LoBV
"Never shall a young man." For Anne Gregory. W. B. Yeats. BiP; CMoP; DTC; FaFP; InPK; LiTM; LoBV; SeCeV; SOTW
Never sings a city-robin on the gray-stone window-ledges. Returning. Ruth Guthrie Harding. HBV-2
Never stoops the soaring vulture. The Ghosts. Longfellow. *Fr.* The Song of Hiawatha. LoBV
Never Such Love. Robert Graves. BoLoP; FaBoEn
Never talk down to a glowworm. Glowworm. David McCord. NTCP
Never the nightingale. Dirge. Adelaide Crapsey. HBV-1
Never the Spirit Was Born. *Unknown, tr. fr. Sanskrit by* Sir Edwin Arnold. *Fr.* Bhagavad-Gita. TreFT
Never the Time and the Place. Robert Browning. EnLoPo; HBV-1
Never the tramp of foot or horse. Farewell to Anactoria. Sappho, *tr. by* Allen Tate. AWP
Never think she loves him wholly. Appraisal. Sara Teasdale. MoAmPo
Never think you fortune can bear the sway. On Fortune. Elizabeth I, Queen of England. PBWP; WPE
Never this scratched world, its human. To Mark Rothko. Anne Cherner. PoDr
Never to be lonely like that. Face to Face. Adrienne Rich. LiTM; NoP
Never to remember. Accident. Sydney Lea. NYP
Never to see a nation born. The Great Virginian. James Russell Lowell. *Fr.* Under the Old Elm. GOA; PGD
Never to see ghosts? Then to be. Ghosts. Alastair Reid. NYBP
Never Too Late, *sels.* Robert Greene.
Infida's Song. OBSC
Palmer's Ode, The. CTC; EnRePo; OBSC
Never twice that river. By the River Eden. Kathleen Raine. NYBP
Never until the mankind making. A Refusal to Mourn the Death, by Fire, of a Child in London. Dylan Thomas. BLPL; CABA; ChMP; CMoP; CoBMV; EBEV; FaBoEn; FaBoMo; FaFP; FF; GTBS-P; HeIP; HoPM; LiTB; LiTM; MasP; MoAB; MoBrPo; MoPo; MoVE; MP; NeBP; NoAM; NOBE; NoP; OAEL-2; OAEP; OxBTC; PAI; PoPl; SeCePo; TEP; TwCP; UnPo; WaaP
Never was there a man much uglier. Vain Gratuities. E. A. Robinson. NePA
Never was there path our childhood used to roam. New Horizons. Sidney Royse Lysaght. HBMV
Never we needed Thee so sore. In Time of Need. Katharine Tynan. TrPWD
Never Weather-beaten Sail[e]. Thomas Campion. ChTr; ElL; GoBC; OAEL-1, OBSC; OxBoCh; PoEL-2
(O Come Quickly!) NOBE; OBEV; TreFT
Never Will You Hold Me. Charles Divine. HBMV
Never yet was a springtime. Awakening. Margaret E. Sangster. AA
Nevermore/ Shall the shepherds of Arcady follow. The God-Maker, Man. Don Marquis. HBV-2; WGRP
Never More, Sailor. Walter de la Mare. EtS; MOS
Never more will I protest. The Indifferent. Francis Beaumont. ElL; HBV-1
Never More Will the Wind. Hilda Doolittle ("H. D."). *Fr.* Hymen. CTC; TrGrPo; ViBoPo
Nevertheless. Gustav Davidson. GoYe
Nevertheless. Marianne Moore. CMoP; MoAB; OxBA; SeCeV; SoSe
Nevertheless I prefer . . .1968. . . Petra von Morstein, *tr. by* Rosemarie Waldrop. BoWoP
Nevertheless you've seen a strawberry. Nevertheless. Marianne Moore. OxBA
New Ahasuerus, The. Jozsef Kiss, *tr. fr. Hungarian by* André Ungar. VWA
New air has come around us. Dakota: October, 1822; Hunkpapa Warrior. Rod Taylor. WeW
New Ancient of Days, The. Herman Melville. OBAL
New and Old Gospel. Nate Mackey. CNA
New Approach Needed. Kingsley Amis. OxBTC; PPON
New Arrival, The. George Washington Cable. AA; HBV-1
New Baby Calf, The. Edith Newlin Chase. SoPo; TiPo
New Ballad, A. Arthur Mainwaring. APAS
New Ballad, A ("Rouse, Britons! at length"). *Unknown.* PAH
New Ballad, A (" 'Twere folly if ever"). *Unknown.* APAS
New Ballad of Sir Patrick Spens, The. Sir Arthur Quiller-Couch. BXAP
New Ballad, to an Old Tune, Called, I Am the Duke of Norfolk, etc., A. *Unknown.* APAS
New Ballade of the Marigolde, A. William Forrest. CoMu
New Balow, The. *Unknown.* CoMu
New Bath Guide, The, *sels.* Christopher Anstey.
"Hearken, Lady Betty, hearken." NOEC
Letter Containing a Panegyric on Bath. OBEC
New Birth, The. Jones Very. AP; NOBA
New Brooms. Robert Wilson. *Fr.* The Three Ladies of London. ElL
(Conscience's Song.) OBSC
New Bundling Song, A. *Unknown.* ErPo
New Bury Loom, The. *Unknown.* OBET
New Calf, The. James Hearst. TAT
New Calf, The. Frances Downing Vaughan. AMV-80
New Canaans Genius; Epilogus. Thomas Morton. SCAP
New Castalia, The. William Hayes Ward. AA
New Catch in Praise of the Reverend Bishops, A. *Unknown.* APAS
New Cecilia, The. Thomas Lovell Beddoes. OAEL-2
New Chitons for Old Gods, *sel.* David McCord.
Euterpe; a Symmetric. UnS
New-Chum's First Trip, The. *Unknown.* FaBoBa
New Church Organ, The. Will Carleton. PoLF
New Coasts and Poseidon's Son. Homer, *tr. fr. Greek by* Robert Fitzgerald. The Odyssey, IX. WTO
New Colossus, The. Emma Lazarus. AmFN; FaBV; FaFP; FaPo; FaPON; FPL; PAL; PGD; PoLF; PoPl; PrIm; SBG; TreFS; TRV; WPE
New Construction: Bath Iron Works. G. Stanley Koehler. NePoAm-2
New Courtly Sonnet of the Lady Greensleeves, A. *Unknown. See* Greensleeves.
New Cows, The. Charles Waterman. GP
New Dance, A. S. E. Anderson. NBP
New-dated from the terms that reappear. To Oxford. Gerard Manley Hopkins. BrPo; FaBoPP
New Day, The, *sels.* Richard Watson Gilder.
Prelude: "Night was dark, though sometimes a faint star, The." HBV-1; PoLF
Song: "Not from the whole wide world I chose thee." AA
Song: "Years have flown since I knew thee first." AA
New Day, The. Fenton Johnson. BANP
New Day. Naomi Long Madgett. BlSi
New Dial, The. *Unknown.* OBET
New Doctor, The. "Parmenas Mix." DBV
New doth the sun appear. Change Should Breed Change. William Drummond of Hawthornden. OBEV; OxBoCh
New Dreams for Old. Cale Young Rice. HBV-2
New Dress, A. Rachel Korn, *tr. fr. Yiddish by* Ruth Whitman. VWA
New Duckling, The. Alfred Noyes. FaPON
New Emigration, The. Kay Boyle. WPE
New England. James Gates Percival. AA
New England. George Denison Prentice. AA
New England. E. A. Robinson. CABA; FaBoEn; GOA; HeIP; MoAB; MoAmPo; MoVE; NOBA; NoP; OxBA; TAP; WhC
New England Bachelor, A. Richard Eberhart. MoAmPo; NoAM
New-England Boy's Song about Thanksgiving Day, The. Lydia Maria Child. *See* Thanksgiving Day.
New England Church, A. Wilson Agnew Barrett. WGRP
New England Greenhouse. Rennie McQuilkin. AMV-80
New England Is New England Is New England. Brenda Heloise Green. GoYe
New England Primer, The, *sels. Unknown.*
"In Adam's Fall/ We sinned all." OBCA
(ABC, An.) GBP
John Rogers' Exhortation to His Children. OBCA
New England Sampler, A. John Malcolm Brinnin. GOA
New England Suite. Charles Philbrick. TwAmPo
New England Verses, *sel.* Wallace Stevens.
Statue against a Clear Sky. EyDe
New England's Annoyances. *Unknown.* PAH
(Old Song, Wrote by One of Our First New-England Planters, An.) SCAP
New England's Chevy Chase, April 19, 1775. Edward Everett Hale. HBVY; PAH; PAL; YaD
New-Englands Crisis. Benjamin Tompson. SCAP
New England's Dead! Isaac McLellan, Jr. AA
New England's Growth. William Bradford. PAH
New English Canaan; Prologue. Thomas Morton. SCAP
New Every Morning. "Susan Coolidge." STF
New Every Morning. John Keble. *See* Morning Hymn.
New every morning now the clerk docks off. Summer Holidays. W. R. Rodgers. LiTB
New Ezekiel, The. Emma Lazarus. AA
New Faces, The. W. B. Yeats. GTBS-P; MoVE
New Farm Tractor. Carl Sandburg. FaPON
New-fashioned Farmer, The. *Unknown.* OBET

New Fashions. George Moses Horton. OBAL
New follies spring; and now we must be taught. Picturesque; a Fragment. John Aikin. NOEC
New Formalists, The. Marvin Bell. AMV-81
New Forms. Peter Redgrove. NMP
New Freedom, The. Olive Tilford Dargan. HBMV
New Friends and Old Friends. Joseph Parry. BLPA; BLPL; TreFT
New Garden Fields. *Unknown.* OBET
New Genesis, A. Avraham Shlonsky, *tr. fr. Hebrew by* Francis Landy. VWA
New Ghost, The. Fredegond Shove. ChMP; HBMV; MoVE; OxBoCh
New God, The. Witter Bynner. *Fr.* The New World. WGRP
New God, The. James Oppenheim. WGRP
New Graveyard: Jerusalem. Shirley Kaufman. VWA
New Guinea. James McAuley. NOCV; PoAu-2
New Hampshire. T. S. Eliot. Landscapes, I. BiP; FaBoCh; GTBS-P; LoBV; WeW
New Hampshire. Donald Hall. LCAP; NePoEA-2
New Hampshire Boy, A. Morris Bishop. HBMV
New Hampshire Farm Woman. Rachel Graham. GoYe
New Hampshire, February. Richard Eberhart. LiTM; MP; TwCP
New Hampshire, *sel.* Robert Frost.
"I met a Californian who would." DBV
New Heart, The. *Unknown, tr. fr. Chinese.* WGRP
New Heaven and Earth. D. H. Lawrence. CMoP
New Heaven, New War[re]. Robert Southwell. AnAnS-1; LoBV; MePo; NOBE; NoP; OBSC; SBVL
("Come to your heaven, you heavenly choirs!") OxBoCh
New Hellas, The. Irwin Edman. InMe
New Holland is a barren place, in it there grows no grain. The Lowlands of Holland. *Unknown.* OxBB
New Horizons. Sidney Royse Lysaght. HBMV
New House, The. Joseph Easton McDougall. CaP
New House, The. Edward Thomas. EBEV; HBMV; MoAB; MoBrPo; NOBE; OBEV
New Household, A. Longfellow. *Fr.* The Hanging of the Crane. GN
New Hunting Song, A. *Unknown.* CoMu; OBET
New Hymns for Solitude, *sel.* Edward Dowden.
"I found Thee in my heart, O Lord." TrPWD
New Improved Sonnet XVIII. Peter Titheradge. FaBoPa
New Inn, The, *sel.* Ben Jonson.
It Was a Beauty That I Saw. AnAnS-2; OBS
(Lovel's Song.) TrGrPo
New Integrationist, The. Don L. Lee. BOLo
New Jail. *Unknown.* AmFP
New Jersey city where I did dwell. The Butcher Boy. *Unknown.* BaBo
New Jersey White-tailed Deer. Joyce Carol Oates. GeTw
New Jerusalem, The. Bible, *N.T.* Revelation, XXI: 1-6, 10-12, 21, 23-25. TrGrPo
New Jerusalem, A. Blake. *See* And Did Those Feet in Ancient Time.
New Jerusalem, The. *Unknown, at. to* "F. B. P.," *after the Latin* Urbs Beata Hierusalem. HBV-2; OBEV; OxBoCh; ViBoPo, *longer vers.*
(Heavenly City, The.) GoBC
(Hierusalem.) CTC; NOCV; OBSC
(Hierusalem, My Happy [*or* Happie] Home.) FaPoR; NOBE; PoEL-2
(Jerusalem.) FaBoCh
(Jerusalem, My Happy Home.) ElL; TrCP
(O Mother Dear, Jerusalem.) WGRP
(Song Made by F. B. P., A.) CoMu
New Jewish Hospital at Hamburg, The. Heine, *tr. fr. German by* Charles Godfrey Leland. TrJP
"New King Arrives in His Capital by Air. . ."—Daily Newspaper. John Betjeman. OxBoLi; WhC
(Death of King George V.) NOBE
New Leaf, A [*or* The]. Kathleen Wheeler. BLRP; PGD; STF; WBLP
New Leaves. Juan Ramón Jiménez, *tr. fr. Spanish by* H. R. Hays. PoPl
New Life. Amelia Josephine Burr. HBV-1
New Light, A. William Hawkins. MoCV
New light gives new directions, fortunes new. George Chapman. *Fr.* Hero and Leander, Third Sestiad. OAEL-1
New Lines for Cuscuscaraway and Mirza Murad Ali Beg. Louis Simpson. OBAL
New Litany, The. Rita Mae Brown. PeHV
New Litany in the Year 1684, A. *Unknown.* APAS
New London, The. Dryden. *Fr.* Annus Mirabilis. FaBoCh; OBS
New Love, New Life. Amy Levy. OBVV
New Man, The. Jones Very. AP; NOBA
New man flies in from Manchester, A. A New Poet Arrives. Gavin Ewart. OxBTC
New Manong, The. Luis Syquia. BrSi
New Married Couple, The; or, A Friendly Debate between the Country Farmer and His Buxome Wife. *Unknown.* CoMu
New Mars, The. Florence Earle Coates. PGD
New Maths. Tom Lehrer. FaBoUs
New mercies, new blessings, new light on the way. A New Year Wish. Frances Ridley Havergal. BLRP
New Mexican Desert. Witter Bynner. BPAW
New Mexican Mountain. Robinson Jeffers. GOA; InPS; NoAM
New Mexico. Polly Chase Boyden. TiPo
New Mexico and Arizona. George Canterbury. PoOW
New Minglewood Blues. *Unknown.* BluL
New Mistress, The. A. E. Housman. A Shropshire Lad, XXXIV. MoBrPo
New Moon. *Aborigine Oral Tradition, tr. by* R. M. Berndt. *Fr.* The Moon-Bone Cycle. WTO
New Moon, The. Edmund Blunden. BrPo
New Moon, The. Issa, *tr. fr. Japanese by* Harold G. Henderson. MOON
New Moon. D. H. Lawrence. BoNaP
New Moon, The. Sara Teasdale. MOON
New moon hangs like an ivory bugle, The. The Penny Whistle. Edward Thomas. MoAB; MoBrPo
New moon hung in the sky, The. Prescience. Thomas Bailey Aldrich. AA OBVV
New moon, new moon, I hail thee! *Unknown.* FaBoUs
New moon, of no importance, The. New Moon. D. H. Lawrence. BoNaP
New Morality, *sel.* George Canning *and* John Hookham Frere.
"From mental mists to purge a nation's eyes." NOEC
New Mothers, The. Carol Shields. Str
New-mown hay smell and wind of the plain. Population Drifts. Carl Sandburg. OxBA
New Music. Gwen Harwood. CBAP
New National Anthem. *Unknown.* CoSo
New National Hymn. Francis Marion Crawford. PAH
New Navigation, The. John Freeth. OBET
New Negro, The. James Edward McCall. CDC
New Neighbor, The. Rose Fyleman. SoPo; TiPo
New Night Thoughts on Death; a Parody. William Whitehead. NOEC
New Notebook, The. Maria Banus, *tr. fr. Rumanian by* Laura Schiff *and* Dana Beldiman. PBWP
New Nutcracker Suite, The, *sel.* Ogden Nash.
"Little girl marched around her Christmas tree, A." PChr
New occasions teach new duties. James Russell Lowell. *Fr.* The Present Crisis. TreFT
New Order, The. Phyllis McGinley. AmFN
New Order of Chivalry, A. Thomas Love Peacock. CenHV
New Orleans. Hayden Carruth. AmFN
New Orleans. Joy Harjo. STE; TWSS
New Pastoral, The, *sel.* Thomas Buchanan Read.
Blennerhassett's Island. PAH
New Patriotism, A. Chauncey R. Piety. PGD
New Physician, The. Stephen Chalmers. HBMV
New Pietà, The: For the Mothers and Children of Detroit. Clarence Major. PoBA
New Poem, A. Robert Duncan. NNaP; PoM
New Poem, The. Charles Wright. GeTw
New Poet, A. William Canton. HBV-1
New Poet Arrives, A. Gavin Ewart. OxBTC
New Potatoes. Ken Belford. NeAC
New Prince, New Pomp[e]. Robert Southwell. AnAnS-1; ELP; GN; NOBE; NOCV; OBSC; OHIP; SBVL; TrCP
New professional group, A. Stacking Up. Rita Rosenfeld. AMV-81
New Proverb. Shirley Brooks. FaBoNo
New River Head, a Fragment, The. E. Dower. NOEC
New River Train. *Unknown.* FSW
New road runs into, The. Directions. William Matthews. AmPA
New Romance. Nellie Wong. BrSi
New Roof, The. Francis Hopkinson. PAH
New Saddhus, The. Robert Pinsky. MAYP
New Season. Philip Levine. NNaP
New season brought sure the visible good. Restoration. Woodridge Spears. GoYe
New servant maid named Maria, A. Fire! *Unknown.* TDH
New Shakespeare, A. Andrew Lang. CenHV
"New Shirt, A!" Why? Paul Grano. PoAu-2
New Shoes. Marjorie S. Watts. SoPo
New Shoes. Alice Wilkins. SUS; TiPo
New shoes, new shoes. Choosing Shoes. ffrida Wolfe. SoPo; SUS; TiPo
New Siege, A; an Historical Meditation, *sel.* John Montague.
"Lines of history. Lines of defiance." CIP
New-silver-crescented the moon forth came. The New Moon. Edmund Blunden. BrPo
New Simile in the Manner of Swift, A. Goldsmith. LAuP
New Skills. Naomi Shihab Nye. PH
New-slain Knight, The. *Unknown.* ESPB
New Snow. Catharine Bryant Rowles. YeAr

New Song, The. Arthur Gordon Field. PGD
New Song, A. John Gay. *See* New Song of New Similes, A.
New Song, A. Seamus Heaney. FaBoTw
New Song, A. Joseph Stansbury. PAH
New Song, A ("As near beauteous Boston lying"). *Unknown.* PAH
New Song Called the Curling of the Hair, A. *Unknown.* CoMu
New Song Called the Gaspee, A. *Unknown.* PAH
New Song Composed on the Death of Lord Nelson, A. *Unknown.* *See* Death of Nelson, The.
New Song Entitled the Warming Pan, A. *Unknown.* CoMu
New Song of an Orange, A. *Unknown.* CoMu
New Song of Mary, A. *Unknown.* MeEL
New Song of New Similies, A. John Gay. FaBoCo; NOBL
(New Song, A.) InMe
New Song of Wood's Halfpence, A. *At. to* Swift. OxBoLi
New Song on the Birth of the Prince of Wales, A. *Unknown.* CoMu; FaBoBa; VLP
New Song on the Taxes, A. *Unknown.* WTO
New Song, A; or, Lilliburlero. Thomas, Lord Wharton. *See* Lilliburlero.
New Song to an Old Tune, A. *Unknown.* PAH
New Song to Sing about Jonathan Bing, A. Beatrice Curtis Brown. SoPo
New Spoon River, The, *sels.* Edgar Lee Masters.
Benjamin Franklin Hazard. GOA
Catherine Ogg. GLGT
Howard Lamson. ViBoPo
Marx the Sign Painter. NoAM; TAP
Meredith Phyfe. GOA
Rhoda Pitkin. NoAM
Unknown Soldiers. NoAM; TAP
Willis Beggs. SaC
New Spring. Juan Ramón Jiménez, *tr. fr. Spanish by* H. R. Hays. OLR
New Spring, A. A. D. Mackie. OxBS
New Storefront. Russell Atkins. FB
New Story, A. Simon J. Ortiz. STE
New Strain. George Starbuck. MP; TwCP
New Students. Marvin Bell. GLGT
New Style, The. David O'Bruadair, *tr. fr. Irish by* John Montague. BIrV
New Sun, The. John Wain. NePoEA-2
New Tenants, The. E. A. Robinson. NoAM
New Territory. Eavan Boland. CIP
New Testament, The. Thomas Russell. TreFS
New Testament, The. *Unknown.* FaBoUs
New Testament; Revised Edition. Sister Mary Catherine. ISi
New Things and Old. Sister Mary Madeleva. GoBC
New ties, fifteen each, ten. Ties. Raymond Souster. MoCV; OBCV
New Time. *Unknown.* BLRP
New Trinity, The. Edwin Markham. PGD
New Vestments, The. Edward Lear. RHPC
New Vicar of Bray, The. Colin Ellis. NOBL
New Victory, The. Margaret Widdemer. WGRP
New View, The. John Holmes. MiAP
New Vintage, The. Douglas Le Pan. OBCV
New War Song by Sir Peter Parker, A. *Unknown.* PAH
New Warden, The. Jimmy Santiago Baca. LFAC
New Wife, The. *Gond Oral Tradition, tr. by* V. Elwin *and* S. Hivale. WTO
New Wind a-Blowin', A, *with music.* Langston Hughes. TrAS
New Wings for Icarus, *sel.* Henry Beissel.
"In the one-two domestic goose one-two one-two step." MoCV
New Words for an Old Song. Babette Deutsch. NePoAm
New Words to the Tune of "O'Donnel Abu." Jim Connell. OnYI
New World, The. Amiri Baraka. NoAM; NoP
New World, The, *sel.* Louis James Block.
Final Struggle, The. PAH
New World, The, *sel.* Witter Bynner.
New God, The. WGRP
New World, The. Paul Engle. AmFN
New World. Brewster Ghiselin. MoVE
New World, The, *sel.* Edgar Lee Masters.
"This America is an ancient land." AmFN
New World, A. Shelley. *See* Chorus: "World's great age begins anew, The."
New World, The. Jones Very. AA; AP
New World. Derek Walcott. OxBC
New Worlds. Milton. *Fr.* Paradise Lost, III. OBS
New Year, The. Charles Cotton. GoTL; OBS
New Year, The. Dinah Maria Mulock Craik. YeAr
New Year, A. Mary Carolyn Davies. YeAr
New Year. Gail N. Harada. BrSi
New Year, The. Homera Homer-Dixon. BLRP
New Year, A. Dora Sigerson Shorter. YeAr
New Year. Stephen Spender. AWP
New Year, The. Mark Strand. *Fr.* Elegy for My Father. UnPo
New Year, The. J. D. Templeton. PGD
New Year, The ("God gives to you another year"). *Unknown.* STF
New Year Carol, A ("Here we bring new water"). *Unknown.* CH; OxBoLi; PoSC
(New Year, The.) OBCP
(New Year's Water.) GBP; OFD; POL
New Year for Trees, The. Howard Schwartz. VWA
New Year Idyl, A, *sel.* Eugene Field.
"Upon this happy New Year night." PoSC
New Year Letter, *sels.* W. H. Auden.
"Long time since it seems to-day, A." GOA
"O Unicorn among the cedars." FaBoEn; NoAM
"Our news is seldom good: the heart." FaBoRV
New Year, 1916. Ada M. Harrison. SUMH
New Year Prayer, A. Theodore Parker. *See* Higher Good, The.
New Year Song. Ted Hughes. *See* New Year's Song.
New Year Wish, A. Frances Ridley Havergal. BLRP
New Year Wish, A. *Unknown.* BLRP
New yeares, expect new gifts: Sister, your Harpe. Ben Jonson. SeCP
New-Yeares-Gift Sung to King Charles, 1635, A. Ben Jonson. SeCP
New Year's. Charles Reznikoff. VGW
"This is the autumn and our harvest," *sel.* OFD
New Years and Old. Maud Frazer Jackson. PGD
New Year's Carol. *Unknown.* OBET
New Year's Day. Richard Crashaw. JCP
New Year's Day. Rachel Field. SoPo; TiPo
New Year's Day. Robert Lowell. AmPP; CABA; ConAP; LiTM; NePoEA; PPoe
New Year's Eve. John Berryman. LiTM; NMP
New Year's Eve, *sel.* John Davidson.
Imagination. MoBrPo
New Year's Eve. Thomas Hardy. MoBrPo; NoAM
New Year's Eve. A. E. Housman. VLP
New Year's Eve. D. H. Lawrence. BoLoP; ErPo
New Year's Eve. H. B. Mallalieu. WaP
New Year's Eve in Solitude. Robert Mezey. NaP; VWA
New Year's Eve in Troy. Adrienne Rich. NePoEA-2
New Year's Eve, 1938. John Frederick Nims. MiAP
New-Year's Gift Sent to Sir Simeon Steward, A. Robert Herrick. CaPo
New-Years-Gift to Brian Lord Bishop of Sarum, A. William Cartwright. MePo
New Year's morning. After the Gentle Poet Kobayashi Issa. Robert Hass. GeTw
New Year's, 1978. Howard Nemerov. SOTS
New Year's Poem. Margaret Avison. LiTM; NOBC; OBCV
New Year's Promise, A. *Unknown.* BLRP
New Year's Sacrifice, A: To Lucinda. Thomas Carew. CaPo
New Year's Song. Ted Hughes. OFD
(New Year Song.) OBCP
New Year's Water. *Unknown.* *See* New Year Carol, A.
New Year's Wish, A. "J. H. S." BLRP
New Year's Wishes. Frances Ridley Havergal. BLRP; STF
New-Yeeres Gift, The; or, Circumcisions Song, Sung to the King in the Presence at White Hall. Robert Herrick. SeCV-1
New York. "Æ." OBMV
New York. Edward Field. NYP
New York. Federico García Lorca, *tr. fr. Spanish by* Robert Bly. NU; NYP
New York. Thom Gunn. NYP
New York. Marianne Moore. NYP
New York. Léopold Sédar Senghor, *tr. fr. French.* NYP, *tr. by* Ellen Conroy Kennedy
(To New York.) PBA, *tr. by* Ulli Beier
New York. John Hall Wheelock. NYP
New York—Albany. Lawrence Ferlinghetti. PoCh
New York! At first I was confused by your beauty, by those great golden long-legged girls. To New York. Léopold Sédar-Senghor, *tr. by* Ulli Beier. PBA
New York! At first I was confused by your beauty, those tall long-legged golden girls. New York. Léopold Sédar Senghor, *tr. by* Ellen Conroy Kennedy. NYP
New York Bird. Andrei Voznesensky, *tr. fr. Russian by* William Jay Smith. NYP
New York City. George Abbe. GoYe
New York City. Maxwell Bodenheim. HBMV
New York City—1935. Gregory Corso. Psk
New York—December, 1931. Babette Deutsch. ImOP
New York deserted—without a person! Deep Night. Juan Ramón Jiménéz, *tr. by* Robert Bly. NYP
New York in August. Donald Davie. NMP
New York in the Spring. David Budbill. CAD
New York, it would be easy to revile. New York City. Maxwell Bodenheim. HBMV
New York 1962: Fragment. Robert Lowell. *See* Picture, The.

New York, Summer. Jack Gilbert. NPGG
New York Woman, The. L. E. Sissman. MAT
New York's lovely weather. Bean Spasms. Ted Berrigan. EAS
New Zealand. James K. Baxter. NoP
Newark Abbey. Thomas Love Peacock. NOBE; OBNC
Newark, for Now (68). Carolyn M. Rodgers. PoBA
Newberry. *Unknown.* AmFP
Newborn Baby. Miroslav Holub, *tr. fr. Czech by* Stuart Friebert *and* Dana Hábová. SUW
Newborn Colt, The. Mary Kennedy. PH
Newborn, on the naked sand. Song for the Newborn. *Unknown, tr. by* Mary Austin. OFD; WPE
New-come Chief, The. *Unknown. Fr.* Under the Old Elm. PAH
Newcomers. Abraham Reisen, *tr. fr. Yiddish by* Keith Bosley. VWA
Newcomer's Wife, The. Thomas Hardy. BoLoP; OxBTC
Newes from Virginia. Richard Rich. PAH
Newest Banana Plant Leaf, The. Ingrid Wendt. NMM
Newgate's Garland. John Gay. FaBoBa
Newly Born, The. *Unknown. Fr.* The Pricke of Conscience. OxBM
Newly Discovered "Homeric" Hymn, A. Charles Olson. NeAP; NoAM; PoM
Newly Pressed Suit, The. Roger McGough. NoAM
Newly-wedded, The. Winthrop Mackworth Praed. HBV-1
Newlyweds, The. Cloyd Mann Criswell. PoLF
Newlyweds, The. John Updike. PV
Newmarket Song, The. *Unknown.* APAS
Newport Railway, The. William McGonagall. PeD
Newport Street, E. Douglas Goldring. HBMV
News. Louis Dudek. *Fr.* Provincetown. MoCV
News. Marnie Pomeroy. POL
News. Dennis Schmitz. NPGG
News, The. "Sec." TRV
News, The. Charles Sprague. *Fr.* Curiosity. AA
News. Thomas Traherne. *Fr.* The Third Century. MePo; NOBE; OBEV; PoPle; SeCV-2
(On News.) AnAnS-1; FaBoEn; QFR
News & the Weather, The. Rika Lesser. MAYP
News for the Delphic Oracle. W. B. Yeats. CMoP; CoBMV; FaBoMo; LiTB; LiTM; MoPo; NoAM; OAEP
News from a foreign [*or* forein *or* forrein] country came. News [*or* On News]. Thomas Traherne. *Fr.* The Third Century. AnAnS-1; FaBoEn; MePo; NOBE; OBEV; PoPle; QFR; SeCV-2
News from a Pacified Area. James K. Baxter. OxBC
News from abroad does a secret reveal, The. An Excellent New Song Called "Mat's Peace." Arthur Mainwaring. APAS
News from Detroit. Judith Minty. SOTS
News from Mount Amiata. Robert Lowell, *ad. fr. the Italian of* Eugenio Montale. NaP
News from Norwood. Christopher Middleton. FaBoMo; NePoEA-2
News from the Cabin. May Swenson. NMP; NYBP
News from the Court. David Wagoner. NePoAm-2; NePoEA-2
News from the heavens! All wars are at an end. Rare News. Nicholas Breton. NIP
News from the House. Michael Dennis Browne. NYBP
News from Yorktown. Lewis Worthington Smith. PAH
News Item. Dorothy Parker. FaBoUs; OBAL; TreF; YaD
(Some Beautiful Letters: News Item.) InMe
News lapped at us out of all, The. The Sirens. Donald Finkel. NePoEA
News! News! Eleanor Farjeon. SiSoSe
News of the dead is heard through words of the living. The Speech of the Dead. Anne Ridler. ChMP
News of the palace. Lady Ise, *tr. fr. Japanese by* Etsuko Terasaki *and* Irma Brandeis. BoWoP
News of the Phoenix. A. J. M. Smith. ELU; MoCV; PeCV
News of the World. Philip Levine. AMV-81
News of the World I ("Cold shuttered loveless star, skulker in clouds"). George Barker. LiTB
News of the World II ("In the first year of the last disgrace"). George Barker. DTC; FaBoTw; LiTB
News of the World III ("Let her lie naked here, my hand resting"). George Barker. FaBoTw; LiTB; LiTM
News, The! our morning, noon, and evening cry. The News. Charles Sprague. *Fr.* Curiosity. AA
News Reel. *See* Newsreel.
News Report. David Ignatow. ErPo; TwCP
News Stand, The. Daniel Berrigan. CAD
News That Stays News. Paul Mariani. GeTw
Newsboy. Irving Layton. CaP
Newsletter from My Mother. Michael S. Harper. PoBA
Newspaper, The, *sel.* George Crabbe.
"I sing of news, and all those vapid sheets." PPON
Newspaper. Aileen Fisher. SoPo
Newspaper Hats. Jim Howard. AMV-81; FAZ
Newspaper Is a Collection of Half-Injustices, A. Stephen Crane. War Is Kind, XII. AmPP; DBV; NCEP
(Newspaper Is, A.) ViBoPo
Newspapers rise high in the air over Maryland. At a March against the Vietnam War. Robert Bly. EAS
Newsreel. C. Day Lewis. MoAB; MoBrPo
News Reel. David Ross. GoYe
Newstead Abbey. Byron. ChER
Newsvendor with his hut and crutch, The. The Imprisoned. Robert Fitzgerald. MP; TwCP
Newt, The. David McCord. TiPo
Newton. Wordsworth. *Fr.* The Prelude, III. ImOP
Newton to Einstein. Jeannette Chappell. GoYe
Newton's Statue. Wordsworth. *Fr.* The Prelude, III. FaBoRV
("Evangelist St. John my patron was, The.") HAP
Newton's Third. Jake T. W. Hubbard. AMV-80
Next. Tina Koyama. BrSi
Next after comes coyote, Stretched-out-in-Dew. Scalp Dance Song. *Tr. fr. Tewa Indian by* H. J. Spinden WTO
Next at our altar stood a luckless pair. George Crabbe. *Fr.* The Parish Register, II. OBRV
Next bidding all draw near on bended knees. Pope. *Fr.* The Dunciad, IV. OBSV
Next bring some lawyers to thy bar. Daniel Defoe. *Fr.* A Hymn to the Pillory. DBV
Next came one/ Who mourn'd in earnest. Milton. *Fr.* Paradise Lost, I. EBEV
Next comes that [*or* the] dull disciple of thy school. That Idiot, Wordsworth. Byron. *Fr.* English Bards and Scotch Reviewers. DBV; OBRV; PP
Next Day. Rachel Field. *Fr.* A Circus Garland. SoPo
(Epilogue: "Nothing now to mark the spot.") OBCA
Next Day. Randall Jarrell. HAP; NoAM; NoP; NYBP; WeW
Next day they rambled round the town, and swore. James Bisset. *Fr.* Ramble of the Gods through Birmingham. NOEC
Next died the Lady, who yon Hall possess'd. The Lady of the Manor. George Crabbe. *Fr.* The Parish Register, III. NOBE; OBNC
Next door they've finally brought home the new baby. For Every Last Batch When the Next One Comes Along. William Dickey. GP
Next Door to Monica's Dance Studio. Barbara Smith. AMV-81
Next, for October, to some sheltered coign. Sonnets of the Months: October. Folgore da San Geminiano, *tr. by* Dante Gabriel Rossetti. AWP
Next grand adjunct to our hero's cause, The. The Electric Telegraph. Thomas Baker. *Fr.* The Steam Engine; or, The Power of Flame. FaBoUs
Next Heaven, my vows to thee, O sacred Muse! Upon the Saying That My Verses Were Made by Another. Anne Killigrew. WPE
Next him Jack Squire through his own tear-drops sploshes. Roy Campbell. *Fr.* The Georgiad. OxBTC
Next his chamber, beside his study. The Bishop's Harp. Robert Mannyng. ACP
Next is your lot, fair, to be numbered one. To His Kinswoman, Mistress Penelope Wheeler. Robert Herrick. CaPo
Next Market Day, The. *Unknown.* FSW
Next Marlowe, bathed in the Thespian springs. Christopher Marlowe. Michael Drayton. *Fr.* To Henry Reynolds, of Poets and Poesy. ChTr
Next of Kin. H. B. Mallalieu. WaP
Next of Kin. Christina Rossetti. HBV-2
Next painting, she said to me, should be white, The. Trying to Stay. Diana Chang. PoDr
Next, Please. Philip Larkin. HeIP; MoBrPo; NePoEA
Next Table, The. C. P. Cavafy, *tr. fr. Greek by* John Mavrogordato. PeHV
Next these, a troop of busy [*or* buisy] spirits press. Dryden. *Fr.* Absalom and Achitophel, Pt. II. PPP; SeCV-2
Next Time. Laura Simmons. PGD
Next Time You Were There, The. Samuel Hazo. FAZ
Next, to a Lady I must bid adieu. The Dean's Lady. George Crabbe. LoBV
Next to my counsels an attention pay. Hesiod, *tr. by* Thomas Cooke. *Fr.* Works and Days. FaBoUs
Next to of Course God America I. E. E. Cummings. AmFN; AmPP; AP; BiP; CABA; InPK; LiTM; NCSH; NePA; NoP; OBWP; OFD; OxBA; PAI; TAP; VGW; WaaP
Next to the Apostolic Church of God. The Maestro's Barber Shop. Ricardo Vásquez, *tr. by* Toni Empringham. FIA
Next to will/ I value reason. Swimming Pool. Maria Teresa Horta, *tr. by* Suzette Macedo. PBWP
Next unto him was Neptune pictured. Spenser. *Fr.* The Faerie Queene, III, 11. EtS
Next War, The. Robert Graves. BrPo
Next War, The. Wilfred Owen. WaP
Next War, The. Sir Osbert Sitwell. MMA

Next week they're goin' to lay me off because I'm gettin' old. The Old Quartermaster. Gordon Grant. EtS
Next week will be publish'd (as "Lives" are the rage). "The Living Dog" and "The Dead Lion." Thomas Moore. OBRV
Next whose fortune 't was a tale to tell, The. Fitz Adam's Story. James Russell Lowell. AmPP
Next year, I'm forty years old. Lantern. Frank Polite. GP
Next Year, in Jerusalem. Shirley Kaufman. VWA
Next year the grave grass will cover us. Street Corner College. Kenneth Patchen. MoAmPo
Next year we are to bring the soldiers home. Homage to a Government. Philip Larkin. EBEV
Ngaa . . . now then. Paddy Biran's Song. Paddy Biran, *tr. by* R. M. W. Dixon. CBAP
Ngoni Burial Song. *Unknown, tr. fr. Zulu.* PeSA
Niagara. Richard Emil Braun. NoAM
Niagara. Adelaide Crapsey. PAI
Niagara Falls. Alan Dugan. PoA
Niagara Falls. Philip Parisi. FAZ
Niagara Falls Nocturne. Len Gasparini. NeAC
"Nibble, nibble, little mouse." Modern Grimm. Dorothy Lee Richardson. DFT
Nibble, nibble, little sheep. Sheep. Samuel Hoffenstein. TrJP
Nicander, ooh, your leg's got hairs! Epigrams. Alkaios, *tr. by* Tony Harrison. PeHV
Nice Correspondent, A. Frederick Locker-Lampson. HBV-1
Nice Day for a Lynching. Kenneth Patchen. PoNe
Nice Mrs. Eberle early had been told. La Donna È Perpetuum Mobile. Irwin Edman. NYBP
Nice Part of Town, A. Alfred Hayes. NYBP
Nice Valour, The, *sel.* John Fletcher.
Melancholy, *fr.* III, iii. GTBS; GTBS-P; HBV-2; OBEV; PoPle
(Hence All You Vain Delights.) OAEP; ViBoPo
(O Sweetest Melancholy.) TrGrPo
(Passionate Man's Song, The.) OBS
(Song: "Hence all you vaine delights.") PoEL-2
Nice young man about the town, A. I've Got the Giggles Today. A. P. Herbert. FiBHP
Nice young mawawan, A. The Rattlesnake. *Unknown.* CoSo
"Nicest Phantasies Are Shared, The." Brian Coffey. CIP
Nicholas Copernicus (1473-1543). Siv Cedering. *Fr.* Letters from the Astronomers. SUW
Nicholas Ned. *Unknown.* NTCP
Nicholas Nye. Walter de la Mare. HBMV; HBVY
Nichols Fountain. Virginia Scott Miner. FAZ
Nicht Is Neir Gane, The. Alexander Montgomerie. *See* Night Is Near Gone, The.
Nick and the Candlestick. Sylvia Plath. CAPP; CoAP; LCAP; PBWP
Nick could hardly wait. The Graduate. Charles Stetler. GP
Nickle Bet, A. Etheridge Knight. CAD
Nickleplate moon, The. Kansas City West Bottoms. Edward Dahlberg. PoA
Nicky, the word has come to the West Coast. Smoke. Charles Wright. NYBP
Nicodemus, the slave, was of African birth. Wake Nicodemus. Henry Clay Work. FSW
Nicolas Gatineau. Arthur S. Bourinot. CaP
Nid-nod through shuttered streets at dead of night. The Last Bus. E. V. Knox. BXAP
Nievie nievie nick nack. *Unknown.* OxNR
Nigerian Unity/ or Little Niggers Killing Little Niggers. Don L. Lee. NeAC
Nigga Section, The. Welton Smith. BPo
Nigger. Frank Horne. BANP; CDC
Nigger. Sonia Sanchez. BPo
Nigger. Karl Shapiro. OxBA
Nigger/ Can you kill. The True Import of Present Dialogue, Black vs. Negro. Nikki Giovanni. BPo; PoBA
Nigger: as if it were not. Internal Injuries. Robert Penn Warren. NYP
Nigger mighty happy w'en he layin' by co'n. The Plough-Hands' Song. Joel Chandler Harris. *Fr.* Uncle Remus, His Songs and His Sayings. AA
Nigger Song; an Odyssey. Rita Dove. AmPA
Nigguhs with naturrals. So This Is Our Revolution. Sonia Sanchez. GP
Nigh seated where the river flows. Bible, *O.T., paraphrased by* the Countess of Pembroke. Psalms, CXXXVII. OAEL-1
Nigh to a grave that was newly made. The Old Sexton. Park Benjamin. AA; HBV-2
Night, The. Al-Khansa, *tr. fr. Arabic by* Willis Barnstone. BoWoP
Night, The. Hilaire Belloc. HBV-2; OBEV; OBVV
Night. William Rose Benét. MoAmPo
Night. Hayyim Nahman Bialik, *tr. fr. Hebrew by* Maurice Samuel. AWP
Night. Blake. *Fr.* Songs of Innocence. BLPL; BoNaP; CH; EnRP; FaBoBe; FaPON; HBV-1; HBVY; OBEC; OBEV; OxBChV; OxBoCh; PoLF; TreFT; WiR
Night. Robert Bly. NaP
Night. Louise Bogan. UnPo
Night. John Brown. *See* Rhapody, Written at the Lakes in Westmorland, A.
Night. Byron. *See* It Is the Hush of Night.
Night. Aldo Camerino, *tr. fr. Italian by* Anita Barrows. VWA
Night. George Chapman. *Fr.* The Shadow of Night. OBSC
Night. Hartley Coleridge. NCEP
Night, *sel.* Victor J. Daley.
"Suns, planets, stars, in glorious array." PoAu-1
Night, The. Lawrence Durrell. *Fr.* Eight Aspects of Melissa. NeBP
Night. Peter Everwine. NNaP
Night. Solomon ibn Gabirol, *tr. fr. Hebrew by* Emma Lazarus. TrJP
Night. Donald Jeffrey Hayes. CDC
Night. Charles Heavysege. OBCV
Night. Hermann Hesse, *tr. fr. German by* Ludwig Lewisohn. AWP
Night. Mary Ann Hoberman. RHPC
Night. Patricia Hubbell. PDV
Night. Robinson Jeffers. AP; AWP; CoBMV; LiTA; MoAmPo; MoPo; NOBA; OxBA; WHA
Night. Glyn Jones. NeBP
Night, The. Myra Cohn Livingston. PDV
Night. Richard Lovelace. CaPo
Night. Lois Weakley McKay. SiSoSe
Night. James Montgomery. HBV-1
Night. Joyce Carol Oates. GeTw
Night, *sel.* James Oppenheim.
"Machinery is enough for a Scientist." TRV
Night. Anne Radcliffe. WPE
Night. Henri de Regnier, *tr. fr. French by* "Seumas O'Sullivan." AWP
Night. Thomas William Rolleston. HBV-2
Night. Shelley. *See* To Night.
Night. Sir Philip Sidney. *Fr.* Arcadia. SiPS
Night. Robert Southey. GN
Night. Earl of Surrey. *See* Complaint by Night of the Lover Not Beloved, A.
Night. S. D. R. Sutu, *tr. fr. Sotho by* Dan Kunene *and* Jack Cope. PeSA; TTY, *abr.*
Night. John Addington Symonds. HBV-1
Night. Sara Teasdale. FaPON; SoPo; SUS; TiPo
Night, The. Henry Vaughan. AnAnS-1; EBEV; LiTB; MeLP; MePo; NOBE; NoP; OAEL-1; NOCV; OBEV; OBS; OxBoCh; PoEL-2; SeCeV; SeCV-1
"Dear night! this world's defeat," *sel.* TrGrPo
Night. Joseph Blanco White. AnIV
Night. Edward Young. *Fr.* Night Thoughts. OBEC; SeCePo
Night/ And death rides fast on foul breath. Night Slivers. Darwin T. Turner. NBP
Night/ and in the warm blackness. Upon Your Leaving. Etheridge Knight. NeAC; NNaP
Night:/ And the taut. Night Music. Chester Kallman. PoPl
Night,/ And the yellow pleasure of candlelight. Song of the Rain. Hugh McCrae. CBAP; PoAu-1
Night, The/ creeps in. The Night. Myra Cohn Livingston. PDV
Night, a grey sky, a ghostly sea. On the Beach. Arthur Symons. At Dieppe, II. SyP; VLP
Night a Sailor Came to Me in a Dream, The. Diane Wakoski. TAP; VGW
Night after Night. "Stuart Sterne." AA
Night after night I dream about my losses. Lost Objects. Diana O Hehir. AMV-80
Night Airs. Walter Savage Landor. BoNaP
(Night Airs and Moonshine.) ChTr
(On Grey Cliffs.) VLP
Night Alert. Alison Boodson. NeBP
Night along the Mackinac Bridge. Roberta Hill. CDW; STE
Night; an Epistle to Robert Lloyd. Charles Churchill. NCEP
Sels.
"Keep up appearances; there lies the test." DBV
Nut, a World, a Squirrel, and a King, A. FaBoRV
"Spectators only on this bustling stage." OBSV
What Is't to Us? SeCePo
Night and a Distant Church. Russell Atkins. PoBA
Night and Day. Michael Drayton. *See* Idea: "Dear, why should you . . ."
Night and Day. Sidney Lanier. AA
Night and Day, *with music.* Cole Porter. BLSo
Night and day arrive, and day after day goes by. For My Son, Noah, Ten Years Old. Robert Bly. DiL
Night and day under the rind of me. Parodies of Cole Porter's "Night and Day." Ring Lardner. OBAL

Night and Love. Sir Edward Bulwer-Lytton. *Fr.* Ernest Maltravers. HBV-1
Night and Morning. Dorothy Aldis. PoSC; YeAr
Night and Morning. Austin Clarke. AnIL; CIP; IPY; MoAB; NeIP; NoAM
Night, and on all sides only the folding quiet. Night. S. D. R. Sutu, *tr. by* Dan Kunene *and* Jack Cope. PeSA; TTY
Night, and one single ridge of narrow path. Water and Air. Robert Browning. *Fr.* Pauline. OBRV; VLP
Night and Sleep. Coventry Patmore. EBVV
(Shadow of Night, The, *sl. abr.*) CH
Night and the Child. Judith Wright. SeCePo
Night and the distant rumbling; for the train. The Last Evening. Rainer Maria Rilke, *tr. by* C. F. MacIntyre. WaaP
Night, and the down by the sea. Rain on the Down. Arthur Symons. At Dieppe, III. BrPo; OBNC; OBVV; SyP
Night, and the heavens beam serene with peace. Night. Solomon ibn Gabirol, *tr. by* Emma Lazarus. TrJP
Night, and the hill to me! From Russian Hill. Ina Coolbrith. BPAW
Night and the hood. Prelude. Conrad Kent Rivers. PoBA
Night and the Pines. Duncan Campbell Scott. OBCV
Night and we heard heavy and cadenced hoofbeats. The Return. John Peale Bishop. LiTA; MoPo; MoVE; OxBA; TwAmPo; WaP
Night and Wind. Arthur Symons. BrPo
Night-Apple, The. Allen Ginsberg. NoAM
Night approaches. Glenpool. Annette Arkeketa West. TWSS
Night arches England, and the winds are still. Peace. Walter de la Mare. MoAB; MoBrPo
Night at an Airport. David Ignatow. NNaP
Night at Gettysburg. Don C. Seitz. OHIP
Night at the Napi in Browning, A. Richard Hugo. TAT
Night attendant, a B. U. sophomore, The. Waking in the Blue. Robert Lowell. CoAP; MoAmPo; PPP; UnPo
Night before Christmas, The. Clement Clarke Moore. *See* Visit from St. Nicholas, A.
Night before Larry Was Stretched, The. *Unknown.* AnIV; BIrV; FaBoBa; GBP; NOBL; OnYI; OxBoLi
Night before my uncle Carter got shot, The. Support Your Local Police Dog. Carter Revard. VoR
Night before the Battle of Waterloo, The. Byron. *See* Waterloo.
Night before Waterloo, The Byron. *See* Waterloo.
Night before you left, as you lay, The. Lawrence Russ. *Fr.* The Wedding Poem. AMV-80
Night Blessing. *Unknown.* HBVY
Night-blooming Cactus, The. John Bensko. MAYP
Night-blooming Cereus, The. Robert Hayden. FB; HoAn; NoP; NU
Night Blooming Flowers. Katha Pollitt. MAYP
Night Boat. Audrey Alexandra Brown. CaP
Night breathes in the window. Death Comes for the Old Cowboy. Kevin Clark. AMV-81
Night breaths, short ones. In the Hospital. Laura Jensen. AmPA
Night by nightfall more benighted. Garcia Lorca Murdered in Granada. John Manifold. CBAP
Night by the Sea, A. Heine, *tr. fr. German by* Howard Mumford Jones. *Fr.* The North Sea. AWP
Night came, but without darkness or repose. The Fire of London. Dryden. *Fr.* Annus Mirabilis. FaBoEn
Night Catch. Heather McHugh. AmPA
Night Character. Dino Campana, *tr. fr. Italian by* Frank Stewart. AMV-81
Night Clouds. Amy Lowell. MoAmPo; PoPl; WHA
Night Clouds. Tom McKeown. HoAn
Night Club. F. R. Scott. NOBC
Night Comes. Beatrice Schenk de Regniers. RHPC
Night comes, an angel stands. Nocturne. Kathleen Raine. ChMP
Night Comes Apace. Evan V. Shute. CaP
Night comes. Day runs for its life into my eyes. Gil Orlovitz. *Fr.* Art of the Sonnet. PoA
Night comes to the man who can pray. New Year's Eve in Solitude. Robert Mezey. NaP; VWA
Night Court, The. Ruth Comfort Mitchell. HBV-2
Night Crackles. Elizabeth Woody. STE
Night Cries, Wakari Hospital. Charles Brasch. OCNZ
Night Crow. Theodore Roethke. DFF; ELU; HoPM; InPK; MoVE; NCSH; VGW
Night Dances, The. Sylvia Plath. LCAP
Night, Death, Mississippi. Robert Hayden. FF; LCAP; VGW
Night Dive. Don Johnson. MAYP
Night Don Juan came to pay his fees, The. Don Juan in Hell. Baudelaire, *tr. by* James Elroy Flecker. AWP; SyP
Night draws itself as tight. Lord, Listen. Else Lasker-Schüler, *tr. by* Edouard Roditi. VWA
Night Driving. Sharyn November. AMV-80
Night Duty. Eva Dobell. SUMH
Night Encampment outside Troy. Homer, *tr. fr. Greek by* Tennyson. *Fr.* The Iliad, VIII. RoGo
("So Hector spake; the Trojans roared applause.") OBVE
Night Enchantment. Eleanor Muth. SiSoSe
Night Expedition from Ben Alder Cottage. Roger A. Redfern. PoSH
Night, expositor of love. Musical Shuttle. Harvey Shapiro. VWA
Night Express, The. Cosmo Monkhouse. OBVV
Night Falls on China. W. H. Auden. CoBMV
Night Falls on Eden. Milton. *See* Evening in Paradise.
Night Feeding. Muriel Rukeyser. MiAP; NMM; WPE
Night Fishing. Greg Kuzma. WOLT
Night Fishing. Stephen Lewandowski. WOLT
Night Fishing. Michael Waters. WOLT
Night Fishing for Blues. Dave Smith. GeTw; LiSp; WOLT
Night Flight. Ruth Daigon. AMV-81
Night Flight. Don Johnson. AMV-81
Night Flight. George Whalley. CaP
Night flutters. Hasidim Dance. Nelly Sachs, *tr. by* Keith Bosley. VWA
"Night. Fog. Tall through the murky gloom." A Letter from Ealing Broadway Station. Aelfrida Tillyard. SUMH
Night for Adventures. Victor Starbuck. HBV-1
Night Funeral in Harlem. Langston Hughes. InPS
Night ghosts are dancing. A Morning Kiss. Andrew McCord Jones. LFAC
Night grows no flower children. Ascendancy. Herbert A. Simmons. NBP
Night Harvest. Susan Pence. AMV-80
Night Has a Thousand Eyes, The. Francis William Bourdillon. BoLoP; FaFP; HBV-1; OBEV; OBVV; OHFP; TreF; WBLP
(Light.) BLPA; BLPL; FaBoBe
Night has come on like a woman sleeping, The. Moon Poems. John Wieners. VGW
Night has drawn its knees up. Learning to Understand Darkness. Wendy Rose. TWSS
Night has secreted us. Amen. Richard W. Thomas. PoBA
Night Has Twenty-four Hours, The. Pedro Juan Pietri. InW
Night he died, earth's images all came, The. Poet [*or* The Planted Skull]. Peter Viereck. HoPM; MiAP; MoAmPo; PP
Night held me as I scrawled and scrambled near. The Turkish Trench Dog. Geoffrey Dearmer. GDP
Night her blackest sables wore, The. A Song. Thomas D'Urfey. CavP
Night Herder, The. Charles Badger Clark, Jr. BPAW
Night-herding Song. Harry Stephens. BPAW; CoSo, *with music;* TrAS, *with music*
(Cowboy Songs: "Oh, slow up, dogies, quit your roving round.") OuSiCo
Night here, a covert. Gary Snyder. Myths and Texts: Burning, IX. NaP
Night Heron. Frances Frost. RHPC
Night hides our thefts; all faults then pardoned be. In the Dark None Dainty. Robert Herrick. CaPo; ELU; PoPle
Night hides outside. City. Timothy P. Mocarski. AMV-81
Night huddled our town. In Dear Detail, by Ideal Light. William Stafford. NaP
Night Hunt, The. Thomas MacDonagh. GDP; OxBI; RoGo
Night Hymns on Lake Nipigon. Duncan Campbell Scott. OBCV
Night I brought the cows home, The. The Herd Boy. Haniel Long. HBMV
Night, I know you are powerful and artistic. For Bill Hawkins, a Black Militant. William J. Harris. PoBA
Night in a Village, A. Ivan Savvich Nikitin, *tr. fr. Russian by* P. E. Matheson. AWP
Night in June, A. Duncan Campbell Scott. OBCV
Night in June, a lovely moon, A. Coax Me. Andrew Sterling. FSN
Night in Lesbos, A. George Horton. AA
Night in Martindale. Kathleen Raine. NeBP
Night in Odessa, A. Louis Simpson. NNaP
Night in the bloodstained snow: the wind is chill. Hialmar Speaks to the Raven. Leconte de Lisle, *tr. by* James Elroy Flecker AWP
Night in the Forest. Galway Kinnell. TAP
Night in the House by the River. Tu Fu, *tr. fr. Chinese by* Kenneth Rexroth. NaP
Night in the Royal Ontario Museum, A. Margaret Atwood. PBWP
Night, in the sweetness of his murky dominion. Nocturnal Thoughts. Avraham Huss, *tr. by* Mark Elliott Shapiro. VWA
Night Interpreted. Everett Hoagland. NBP
Night Is a Big Black Cat, The. G. Orr Clark. RHPC
Night is a furrow, a queasy, insistent wound, The. Nightletter. Charles Wright. PoA
Night is a purple pumpkin. Night. Patricia Hubbell. PDV
Night is beautiful, The. Poem. Langston Hughes. CDC
Night is black swan wholly adrift. Hotel in Paris. Dennis Trudell. PoA

Night is calm, the cygnet's down, The. On a Calm Summer's Night. John Nicholson. EnLoPo
Night is cloudy, The. The Middle of the World. Kathleen Norris. GP
Night is come. Finis. Sir Henry Newbolt. TiPo
Night is come, like to the day, The. A Colloquy with God [*or* Evening Hymn]. Sir Thomas Browne. *Fr.* Religio Medici. OBS; OxBoCh
Night is coming softly, slowly, The. Night. Mary Ann Hoberman. RHPC
Night is covered with signs, The. Akiba. Muriel Rukeyser. VWA
Night is dark, The. And Yet. Errol B. Sloan. BLRP
Night is dark, the wind has dashed, The. Midnight Prayer. Hayyim Nahman Bialik, *tr. by* Helena Frank. TrJP
Night Is Darkening round Me. Emily Brontë. OBNC; PoEL-5
(Song.) NBM
(Spellbound.) NOBE
Night Is Freezing Fast, The. A. E. Housman. CMoP; LiTM; LoBV; MoPo; PoPle; PrIm
Night is full of stars, full of magnificence, The. Bagley Wood. Lionel Johnson. VLP
Night is late, the house is still, The. For Charlie's Sake. John Williamson Palmer. HBV-1
Night is light and chill, The. Night and Wind. Arthur Symons. BrPo
Night is long, The. Grandpa Bear's Lullaby. Jane Yolen. RHPC
Night is my sister, and how deep in love. Edna St. Vincent Millay. HAP
Night Is Near [*or* Neir] Gone, The. Alexander Montgomerie. GoTS; OBEV; OxBS
(Hey! Now the Day Dawns.) CH
(Nicht Is Neir Gane, The.) BSV
Night is o'er England, and the winds are still. Peace. Walter de la Mare. MMA
Night Is on the Downland, on the Lonely Moorland. John Masefield. Lollingdon Downs, XVIII. GoYe; LiTM
(Night on the Downland.) MoBrPo; MoPo
Night is soft with summer, The; yon faint arch. John Plummer Derwent Llwyd. *Fr.* The Vestal Virgin. CaP
Night is still silky, The. Curtains are drawn. Observation at Dawn. Abba Kovner, *tr. by* Shirley Kaufman. VWA
Night is still, The. The unfailing surf. Miramar Beach. J. V. Cunningham. To What Strangers, What Welcome, VIII. PoA
Night is the time for rest. Night. James Montgomery. HBV-1
Night is the true democracy. Night's Mardi Gras. Edward J. Wheeler. HBV-1
Night is very dark, The. Assassination Poems. John Ridland. MAT; OFD
Night is warm and hot, my arms, The. Death Is a Second Cousin Dining with Us Tonight. Geraldine Kudaka. BrSi
Night is white, The. Birch Trees. John Richard Moreland. HBMV; HBVY; OHIP; RHPC
Night it was a holy night, The. Godly Girzie. Burns. CoMu; ErPo; UnTE
Night it was horribly dark, The. Measles in the Ark. "Susan Coolidge." OxBChV
Night John Henry is born an ax, The. The Birth of John Henry. Melvin B. Tolson. *Fr.* Harlem Gallery. BPo; TTY
Night Journey, The. Rupert Brooke. BrPo
Night Journey. Theodore Roethke. AmFN; GOA; InPS; NYBP
Night: Landing at Newark. Jonathan Holden. PPJ
Night Landscape. Joan Aiken. DuDa
Night Las Vegas caught fire, The. The Case. H. R. Hays. EAS
Night last night was strange and shaken, The. At a Month's End. Swinburne. VLP
Night Letter. Marge Piercy. NMM
Night letter. Charles Wright. PoA
Night lies blue and white, The. Minor Key. Judah Leib Teller, *tr. by* Gabriel Preil *and* Howard Schwartz. VWA
Night-life. Letters, journals, bourbon. Origins and History of Consciousness. Adrienne Rich. NIP
Night Light. Nancy Willard. LCAP
Night like a silver peacock in the sky. Poetry and Science. W. J. Turner. SeCePo
Night like purple flakes of snow. Night. Donald Jeffrey Hayes. CDC
Night! loathèd jailor of the locked-up sun. Night. Richard Lovelace. CaPo
Night Loves Us, The. Louis Adeane. NeBP
Night Mail, The. W. H. Auden. ChTr; GrPl; OxBTC
Night Mail North, The. Henry Cholmondeley Pennell. EBVV
Night makes no difference 'twixt the priest and clerk. No Difference in the Dark. Robert Herrick. CaPo
Night-March, The. Herman Melville. LiTA
Night Mare. *See* Nightmare.
Night miles force us to a self-serve. Filling Station. Edward Morin. SOTS
Night Mirror, The. John Hollander. NYBP; Prf
Night Mists. William Hamilton Hayne. AA
Night Moths, The. Edwin Markham. HBMV
Night moves in fast. Across the Charles. Nocturne: Homage to Whistler. Ruth Feldman. AMV-81
Night Music. Chester Kallman. PoPl
Night-Music. Philip Larkin. InPS
Night music slanted. Cell Song. Etheridge Knight. NNaP; PoBA
Night Musick for Thérèse. Dachine Rainer. NePoAm-2
Night, A: mysterious, tender, quiet, deep. A Common Inference. Charlotte Perkins Gilman. AA; WGRP
Night Nurse Goes Her Round, The. John Gray. LoBV; OBNC
Night of Battle. Yvor Winters. PoA
Night of Frost in May. George Meredith. VLP
Night of Gods, The. George Sterling. *Fr.* Three Sonnets on Oblivion. HBV-2; WHA
Night of iron wheels and rain, A. The Red Flag. Michael Jackson. OCNZ
Night of night's drew to its tardy close, The. Love's Mortality. Richard Middleton. WHA
Night of Rain. Bernice Lesbia Kenyon. HBMV
Night of Sine. Léopold Sédar-Senghor, *tr. fr. French by* Ulli Beier. PBA
Night of Souls. Ann Stanford. WPE
Night of Spring. Thomas Westwood. OBVV; SoSe
Night of the Dance, The. Thomas Hardy. BrPo
Night of Trafalgar, The. Thomas Hardy. *Fr.* The Dynasts, Pt. I, Act V, sc. vii. ChTr; FaBoCh; MoBrPo; MOS; OBMV
(Trafalgar.) CH
Night of utter silences, A. Shadows. "Yehoash," *tr. by* Elias Lieberman. TrJP
Night of Wind. Frances Frost. FaPON; TiPo
Night on Clinton. Robert Mezey. AmPA; NaP
Night on earth and sky. A Terrible Thought. Eliezer Steinberg, *tr. by* Joseph Leftwich. TrJP
Night on the bloodstained snow: the wind is chill. Hialmar Speaks to the Raven. Leconte de Lisle, *tr. by* James Elroy Flecker. SyP
Night on the Downland. John Masefield. *See* Night Is on the Downland, on the Lonely Moorland.
Night on the Prairie. Rufus B. Sage. PoOW
Night on the Prairies, *sel.* Walt Whitman.
"Night on the prairies." RFM
Night on the Shore. Marie Carmichael Stopes. SUMH
Night opens like an almond. Yvonne Caroutch, *tr. fr. French by* Elene Kolb. BoWoP
Night, our black summer, simplifies her smells. Nights in the Gardens of Port of Spain. Derek Walcott. OxBC
Night Out. R. A. Simpson. PoAu-2
Night Out, Tom Cat. Charles deGravelles. AMV-81
Night-owl shrieked, The: a gibbous moon peered pallid o'er the yew. The Conscience-Curst! "F. Anstey." CenHV
Night passd and Enitharmon eer the dawn returnd in bliss. Blake. *Fr.* Vala; or, The Four Zoas. OAEL-2
Night-Piece. Léonie Adams. MoAB; MoAmPo
Night-Piece. Robert Herrick. *See* Night-Piece, to Julia.
Nightpiece. James Joyce. NoAM; PoA; SyP
Night Piece. John Manifold. LiTM; MoBrPo; WaP
Night-Piece. Raymond Richard Patterson. CAD; PoBA, WSC
Night Piece, A. Edward Shanks. HBMV
Night Piece. Mark Strand. NYP
Nightpiece. Lewis Turco. SOTS
Night-Piece, A. *Unknown. See* O Jealous Night.
Night-Piece, A. Wordsworth. EnRP; MOON
Night Piece on Death. Thomas Parnell. NOEC; OBEC; SeCePo
"Death speaks:/ When men my scythe and darts supply," *sel.* OnYI
Night-Piece, A; or, Modern Philosophy. Christopher Smart. NOEC
Night-Piece, to Julia, The. Robert Herrick. AnAnS-2; CaPo; CH; ELP; HBV-1; InvP; JCP; LiTB; LoBV; NoP; OAEL-1; OAEP; OBEV; OBS; PoEL-3; PoPle; PoRA; SeCeV; SeCP; SeCV-1; TreFT; UnTE; WHA
("Her eyes the glow-warm lend thee.") TEP
Night-piercing, whitely illuminant. Keraunograph. Hayden Carruth. NMP
Night Plane. Frances Frost. FaPON; PDV; TiPo
Night pockets the house. The Gone Years. Alice Fulton. Str
Night Poem. Wayne Dodd. AMV-80
Night Poem in an Abandoned Music Room. William Pillen. VWA
Night Quarters. Henry Howard Brownell. GN
Night sank upon the dusky beach, and on the purple sea. Macaulay. *Fr.* The Armada. OBNC
Night saw the crew like pedlars with their packs. Lunar Stanzas. Henry Coggswell Knight. FaBoNo; NA
Night, say all, was made for rest, The. Upon Visiting His Lady by Moonlight. "A. W." CTC; MOON; OBSC
Night Scenes. Robert Duncan. VGW
Night sea quickens, The. On the shoal or rock. Lighthouses. Dorothy Wellesley. WPE
Night Serene, The. Luís de León, *tr. fr. Spanish by* Thomas Walsh. TrJP
Night Shift. Naomi Shihab. GP

Night Shore. Barry O. Higgs. PeSA
Night should be fuller than this. Now and Again. Roo Borson. AMV-81
Night sleeps, but the chill, The. The Harp of David. Jacob Cohen, *tr. by* Sholom J. Kahn. TrJP
Night Slivers. Darwin T. Turner. NBP
Night Song. Frances Cornford. FM; GDP
Nightsong. Louis Coxe. FYAP
Night Song. Louise Glück. MAYP; SV
Night Song. Lisel Mueller. AMV-80
Night Song at Amalfi. Sara Teasdale. MoAmPo
Night Song for a Child. Charles Williams. OBEV
Night Song for a Woman. Al Purdy. NOBC
Night Song for an Old Lover. Susan Glickman. AMV-81
Night Song for Two Mystics. Paul Blackburn. NeAP
Night Song from Backbone Mountain. Daniel Mark Epstein. TAT
Night Sowing. David Campbell. CBAP; PoAu-2
Night stilled the field, and every golden stook. Cornfield. Leo Cox. CaP
Night stirs but wakens not, her breathings climb. Animula Vagula. A. Y. Campbell. HBMV
Night stirs the trees. By Achmelvich Bridge. Norman MacCaig. OxBS
Night Storm. William Gilmore Simms. EtS; MOS
Night, street, a lamp, a chemist's window. Alexander Blok, *tr. by* Jon Stallworthy *and* Peter France. *Fr.* Dances of Death. OBVE
Night Sweat. Robert Lowell. TAP; VGW
Night Teeth. Peter Brett. AMV-80
Night that ends so soon. The Short Night. Buson, *tr. by* Harold G. Henderson. MOON
Night that has no star lit up by God, The. The New World. Jones Very. AA; AP
Night that lives protectively, The. Stone. Juliet Chayat. AMV-80
Night, that old woman, jabs the sun. 29 (A Dream in Two Parts). Ai. MAYP
Night that Paddy Murphy died, The. Paddy Murphy. *Unknown.* PV
Night the green moth came for me, The. Green Moth. Winifred Welles. FaPON; TiPo
Night the Ninth Being the Last Judgment. Blake. *Fr.* Vala; or, The Four Zoas. OAEL-1
Night, the rain, who could forget, The? In the Street. Shaw Neilson. CBAP
Night, the starlesse night of passion, The. William Alabaster. AnAnS-1
Night There Was Dancing in the Streets, The. Elder Olson. NePA
Night Thought. Gerald Jonas. NYBP
Night Thought of a Tortoise Suffering from Insomnia on a Lawn. E. V. Rieu. FiBHP
Night Thoughts. Henri Coulettte. FYAP
Night-Thoughts. Solomon ibn Gabirol, *tr. fr. Hebrew by* Emma Lazarus. TrJP
Night Thoughts, *sels.* Edward Young.
  Consolation, The, *fr.* Night IX. NOEC
  Happiness an Art, *fr.* Night VIII. OBEC
  (Art of Happiness, The.) POL
  "How poor, how rich, how abject, how august," *fr.* Night I. OAEL-1
  Infidel Reclaimed, The, *fr.* Night NOEC
  "Live ever here, Lorenzo?—shocking thought!" *fr.* Night III. EnRP
  Night I ("Tir'd nature's sweet restorer, balmy Sleep!"). EnRP, *abr.;* LAuP; NOEC, *abr.*
  (Night.) OBEC, *much abr.;* SeCePo, *much abr.*
  Procrastination ("Be wise today; 'tis madness to defer"), *fr.* Night I. OBEC
  "Where, thy true treasure? Gold says, 'Not in me,' " *fr.* Night VI. OAEL-1
Night Thoughts: Baby & Demon. Gwen Harwood. CBAP
Night Thoughts in Age. John Hall Wheelock. MoVE; NYBP
Night Thoughts over a Sick Child. Philip Levine. NePoEA-2
Night Thoughts while Travelling. Tu Fu, *tr. fr. Chinese by* Kenneth Rexroth. NaP
Night throbs on, The; O, let me pray, dear lad! Motherhood. Josephine Daskam Bacon. HBV-1
Night tinkles like ice in glasses, The. November Night, Edinburgh. Norman MacCaig. BSV; NMP
Night, too long illumined, comes a stranger, The. In the Proscenium [*or* War's Clown in the Proscenium]. Gene Derwood. LiTA; NePA
Night Train. Mary C. Fineran. AMV-81
Night Train. Robert Francis. DuDa
Night Train. Adrien Stoutenburg. PDV
Night Trip across the Chesapeake and After. Sydney Lea. MAYP
Night up There. G. D. Valentine. PoSH
Night Visitors. Kadya Molodovsky, *tr. fr. Yiddish by* Ruth Whitman. VWA
Night Walk. Sylvia Plath. *See* Hardcastle Crags.
Night walked down the sky, The. A Memory. Frederic Lawrence Knowles. HBV-1
Night-Walker, The. Horace Gregory. MOON
Nightwalker. Thomas Kinsella. IPY
  "I must lie down with them all soon and sleep," *sel.* BIrV
Night was as sweet, The. Airwaves. Warren Woessner. TAT
Night was coming very fast, The. The Hens. Elizabeth Madox Roberts. FaPON; GoJo; HBMV; OBCA; PDV; SoPo; SUS; TiPo
Night was creeping on the ground, The! Check. James Stephens. AnIL; HBMV; OnUR; RHPC; SiSoSe; SuS; TiPo
Night was dark and fearful, The. The Watcher. Sara Josepha Hale. AA
Night was dark, though sometimes a faint star, The. Prelude. Richard Watson Gilder. *Fr.* The New Day. HBV-1; PoLF
Night was faint and sheer, The. A Nocturne for October 31st. Yvor Winters. PoA
Night was growing old, The. In the Night. *Unknown.* FaBoNo; NA
Night was made for cooling shade, The. At Sea. John T. Trowbridge. EtS
Night was made for rest and sleep, The. Interim. Clarissa Scott Delany. CDC; PoNe
Night Was Smooth, The. James Bertolino. POL
Night was stormy and dark, The. The Speculators. Thackeray. OBSV
Night was thick and hazy, The. Robinson Crusoe [*or* Robinson Crusoe's Story]. Charles Edward Carryl. *Fr.* Davy and the Goblin. AA; BeLS; FiBHP; HBV-2; HBVY; InMe; PoRA; TreFT
Night was wet, spun luminous, The. The Fisherman. Susan Fawcett. WOLT
Night was winter in his roughest mood, The. The Winter Walk at Noon [*or* Winter Scene]. William Cowper. *Fr.* The Task, VI. EnRP; OBEC; TEP
Night Watch. Margo Magid. NMM
Night Watch, A. *Unknown.* *Fr.* The Passionate Pilgrim, XIV. OBSC
Night Watch, The. William Winter. AA
Night-watchmen think of dawn and things auroral. Blindman's Buff. Peter Viereck. LiTM; MiAP; MoAmPo
Night we heard the news from space, The. Doorman. Martin Galvin. SUW
Night we went to see the Brisbane River, The. Profiles of My Father. Rhyll McMaster. CBAP
Night when last I saw my lad, The. Forgettin'. "Moira O'Neill." HBV-1
Night Will Never Stay, The. Eleanor Farjeon. CH; FaPON; HBMV; NTCP; OxBChV; SiSoSe; SoPo
Night Wind, The. Emily Brontë. ChER; ChTr; NCEP; OAEP; RoGo; TEP; VLP
  ("In summer's mellow midnight.") EBVV
Night Wind, The. Eugene Field. FaPON
Night Wind in Fall. W. R. Moses. NCSH
Nightwind sings and rustles through the reeds, The. Nocturne in G Minor. Karl Gustave Vollmoeller, *tr. by* Ludwig Lewisohn. AWP
Night Winds. Adelaide Crapsey. QFR
Night with a Holy-Water Clerk, A. *Unknown.* MeEL
Night with a Wolf, A. Bayard Taylor. *See* Story for a Child, A.
Nightbreak. Adrienne Rich. IHMS
Nightcrawlers. I waken my son. The First Lesson. Thomas Reiter. WOLT
Nightdream. Charles Wright. LCAP
Nightfall. Elder Olson. DFF
Nightfall in Dordrecht. Eugene Field. AA
Nightfall in Inishtrahull. Daniel James O'Sullivan. NeIP
Nightfall on Sedgemoor. Andrew Young. FaBoPP
Nightfall, that saw the morning-glories float. On the Skeleton of a Hound. James Wright. LiTM; NePoEA; TwAmPo
Nightfishing, The, *sel.* W. S. Graham. BSV
  "We are at the hauling then hoping for it." BSV
Nightgown, Wife's Gown. Robert Sward. ELU
Nighthawks circle/ through the midwestern elms. For a Winnebago Brave. Joseph Bruchac. CDW
Nightingale, The. Mark Akenside. HBV-1; OBEV
Nightingale, The. Richard Barnfield. *See* As It Fell upon a Day.
Nightingale, The. Richard Brathwaite. *Fr.* Nature's Embassy. EIL
  ("Jug, jug! Fair fall the nightingal.") PBBP
Nightingale, The. John Clare. EBVV
Nightingale, The. Samuel Taylor Coleridge. EnRP; FM
  Sels.
  Nightingales. ChTr
  "No cloud, no relique of the sunken day." PBBP
  " 'Tis the merry Nightingale." OBRV
Nightingale, The. Marie de France, *tr. fr. French by* Patricia Terry. BoWoP
Nightingale, The. Edward Moxon. OBRV
Nightingale, The. Petrarch, *tr. fr. Italian by* Thomas LeMesurier. Sonnets to Laura: To Laura: To Laura in Death, XLIII. PoPl
Nightingale, The. Sir Philip Sidney. EBEV; EIL; LiTB; LoBV; NoP; OBSC; SiPS; WHA
  (Nightingale, as Soon as April Bringeth, The.) EnRP; PBBP
  (Philomela.) HBV-1; NOBE; OBEV
Nightingale, The. William Strode, *after the Latin of* Famianus Strada. OBVE

Nightingale, The ("Both old and young, I pray lend an ear"), *with music.* *Unknown* ShS
Nightingale, The ("The little pretty nightingale, "). *Unknown.* TrGrPo
Nightingale, The ("One morning, one morning, one morning in May"). *Unknown.* *See* One Morning in May.
Nightingale and Flowers. Blake. *See* Vision of Beulah, The.
Nightingale and the Glowworm, The. William Cowper. HBV-1; OnMSP; PBBP
Nightingale, as Soon as April Bringeth, The. Sir Philip Sidney. *See* Nightingale, The.
Nightingale has a lyre of gold, The. The Blackbird [*or* To A. D.]. W. E. Henley. Echoes, XVIII. HBV-1; HoPM; MoBrPo; TrGrPo; ViBoPo
Nightingale I never heard. My Catbird. William Henry Venable. HBV-1
Nightingale, in dead of night, The. The Happy Nightingale. *Unknown.* OxBChV
Nightingale made a mistake, A. The Singing-Lesson. Jean Ingelow. HBV-1
Nightingale near the House, The. Harold Monro. HBMV; MoBrPo
Nightingale, that all day long, A. The Nightingale and the Glowworm. William Cowper. HBV-1; OnMSP; PBBP
Nightingale, the organ of delight, The. *Unknown.* PBBP
Nightingale, whose happy noble hart, The. The Steele Glas. George Gascoigne. AAS
Nightingales. Robert Bridges. BrPo; CMoP; CoBMV; FaBoEn; HBMV; LiTB; LiTM; MoAB; MoBrPo; MoPo; NOBE; OAEL-2; OBEV; OBMV; OBNC; OBVV; PBBP; PoPl; SeCeV; TrGrPo; UnPo; VLP
Nightingales. Samuel Taylor Coleridge. *Fr.* The Nightingale. ChTr
Nightingales. Grace Hazard Conkling. HBMV
Nightingales Are Not Singing. Moshe Dor, *tr. fr. Hebrew by* Dennis Johnson. VWA
Nightingales of Spring, The. *Unknown.* AmFP
Nightingale's Song, The. James I, King of Scotland. *Fr.* The Kingis Quair. OxBM
("Now was there maid fast by the towris wall.") EBEV
Nightingales warble about it. The Secret. George Edward Woodberry. Wild Eden, VI. AA; HBV-1
Nightingales warbled without. In the Garden at Swainston [*or* Valedictory, II]. Tennyson. GoBC; OBEV; OBNC; OBVV; VLP
Nightletter. *See* Night Letter.
Nightlong you lie and mock the idle moon. Moon Rock. E. Louise Mally. POL
Nightly Deed, A. Charles Madge. NeBP
Nightly I mark and praise, or great or small. James Branch Cabell. Retractions, XV. HBMV
Nightly off Route 50. Stars Shine So Faithfully. Jane Flanders. AMV-80
Nightly tormented by returning doubt. The Struggle. Sully-Prudhomme, *tr. by* Arthur O'Shaughnessy. AWP; PoPl
Nightmare. Erasmus Darwin. *Fr.* The Botanic Garden. NOEC
Nightmare. Gavin Douglas. *Fr.* The Palace of Honor. PoEL-1
Night Mare. Anita Endrezze-Danielson. STE
Nightmare. James A. Emanuel. BPo
Nightmare. Edward Field. Str
Nightmare. Isabella Gardner. CoAP
Nightmare. W. S. Gilbert. *Fr.* Iolanthe. NOBL; OxBoli; PoRA
(Chancellor's Nightmare, The.) FaBoNo
(Lord Chancellor's Song.) NBM
("When you're lying awake with a dismal headache.") NoP
Nightmare, The. Sorley Maclean. NeBP
Nightmare Abbey, *sels.* Thomas Love Peacock.
Song by Mr. Cypress *fr. ch.* 11. OAEL-2; OBNC; OBRV; Par
Wise Men of Gotham, The, *fr. ch.* 11. BXAP; FaBoNo; LoBV
(Catch; A.) ViBoPo
(Men of Gotham, The.) CH
(Seamen Three.) OBRV; WiR
(Three Men of Gotham.) FaBoCh; OBEV
Nightmare at Noon. Stephen Vincent Benét. OxBA
Nightmare Begins Responsibility. Michael S. Harper. DiL; GeTw; LCAP; TAP
Nightmare Inspection Tour for American Generals. Gibbons Ruark. TW
Nightmare leaves fatigue. Louis MacNeice. *Fr.* Autumn Journal. AnIL; BIrV
Nightmare Number Three. Stephen Vincent Benét. MoAmPo; SaC
Nightmare of a Cook. Chester Kallman. CrMA
Nightmare of beasthood, snorting, how to wake. Moly. Thom Gunn. HAP; NoAM; PrIm
Nightmare of Mouse. Robert Penn Warren. SO
Nightmare on Rhum. James Macmillan. PoSH
Nightmare, with Angels. Stephen Vincent Benét. MAT
Nightmares. Siv Cedering Fox. WSC
Nightmares: Part Three. Lynn Moskowitz. AMV-81
Nightpiece. *See* Night Piece.
Night's Ancient Cloud. Thomas Keohler. AnIV
Nights and days we stumble over each other. Stumbling. Dick Lourie. NeAC
Nights bring you the fever. Prometheus. Jenny Mastoraki, *tr. by* Nikos Germanakos. BoWoP
Night's diadem around thy head. Fairest of Freedom's Daughters. Jeremiah Eames Rankin. PAH
Night's drifts, The. A Winter Daybreak above Vence. James Wright. LCAP
Night's Fall. W. S. Graham. NeBP
Night's first sweet silence fell, and on my bed. The Malady of Love Is Nerves. Petronius Arbiter, *tr. by* Howard Mumford Jones. AWP
Nights hang heavy on the winter air, The. Winter Nights. Lora Dunetz. AMV-80
Nights here are usually clear and the shadows, The. Addio a la Mamma. Noe Jitrik, *tr. by* Yishai Tobin. VWA
Nights in Hackett's Cove. Mark Strand. GeTw
Nights in the Gardens of Port of Spain. Derek Walcott. OxBC
Night's Mardi Gras. Edward J. Wheeler. HBV-1
Nights on the Indian Ocean. Cale Young Rice. EtS
Nights Passed on Ward's Island, Toronto Harbour. Doug Fetherling. NeAC
Nights Primarily III. Ed Lipman. LFAC
Nights Remember, The. Harold Vinal. HBMV
Nights, the railway-arches, the bad sky, The. Rimbaud. W. H. Auden. SyP
Nights you wake to sudden stars. Wolf Hunting near Nashoba. Jim Barnes. STE
Nightsea and violet wave. A Storm of Love. Hilary Corke. NYBP
Nightsong. *See* Night Song.
Nightswim. William Pitt Root. MAYP
Nighttime. The faithful prison guard. Bedtime Story. Lou Lipsitz. VGW
Nightwalker. *See* Night Walker.
Nightwood. William Jay Smith. PoA
Nihil Humani Alienum. Titus Munson Coan. AA
Nijinsky. Doris Ferne. CaP
Nijinsky. Parker Tyler. PoA
Nike. Adam Wazyk, *tr. fr. Polish by* Isaac Komem. VWA
Nike of Samothrace, The. Hilda Morley. FAZ
Nikki-Rosa. Nikki Giovanni. AmNP; BlSi; HeIP; IHMS; NoAM; NYP; PAI; PoBA; TAP
(Nikki-Roasa.) CAD; NBP
Nikolina. Celia Thaxter. GN; HBV-1
Nikos Painting. Kenneth O. Hanson. FAZ
Nil Admirari. Congreve. OBEC
Nile, The. Leigh Hunt. EBEV; EnRP; NOBE; OBNC; OBRV; ViBoPo
(Thought of the Nile, A.) NBM
Nilotic Elegy. G. S. Fraser. WaP
Nima, The. Jorge Isaacs, *tr. fr. Spanish by* Alice Jane McVan. TrJP
Nimble as dolphins to. Gimboling. Isabella Gardner. ErPo
Nimble cat and lazy maid, A. On Maids and Cats. Henricus Selyns. SCAP
Nimble sigh, on thy warm wings. To Amoret. Henry Vaughan. EnLoPo
Nimble Stag, The. E. V. Knox. HBMV
Nimbus. Douglas Le Pan. MoCV; OBCV; PeCV
Niminy piminy/ Gilbert and Sullivan. Geeandess. William Cole. PV
Nimium Fortunatus. Robert Bridges. *See* Fortunatus Nimium.
Nimmo. E. A. Robinson. HBMV
Nimphidia. Michael Drayton. *See* Nymmphidia
Nimphs Reply to the Sheepheard, The. Sir Walter Ralegh. *See* Nymph's Reply to the Shepherd, The.
Nina loved compromising. Three Women. Alan Dienstag. ErPo
Nina Simone. Lance Jeffers. CNA
Nina's cross: her alphabet. Cubes. Mary Fullerton. PoAu-1
Nine, The. John Sheffield, Duke of Buckingham and Normanby. APAS
Nine adulteries, 12 liaisons, 64 fornications and something approaching a rape. The Temperaments. Ezra Pound. BoLoP; ErPo; NoAM; NOBA; PAI
Nine Bean-Rows on the Moon. A. W. Purdy. MOON
Nine Birds. E. E. Cummings. UnPo
Nine Charms against the Hunter. David Wagoner. TW
Nine drops of water bead the jessamine. A Wet August. Thomas Hardy. PPP
Nine grenadiers, with bayonets in their guns. The Dream of a Boy Who Lived at Nine Elms. William Brighty Rands. OxBChV
900 Miles. *Unknown.* FSW
Nine Inch Will Please a Lady. Burns. ErPo
Nine Little Goblins, The. James Whitcomb Riley. OBCA
Nine Men out of a Minyan. Haim Guri, *tr. fr. Hebrew by* Mark Elliott Shapiro. VWA
Nine months I waited in the dark beneath. Pro Sua Vita. Robert Penn Warren. MoAmPo
Nine Nectarines and Other Porcelain. Marianne Moore. OxBA

9:00. Patricia Hooper. AMV-81; HoAn
Nine o'Clock. Katherine Pyle. *Fr.* The Wonder Clock. OBCA
Nine-o'clock Bell! School-Bell. Eleanor Farjeon. FaPON; SiSoSe
Nine o'Clock Thoughts on the 73 Bus. Peter Porter. POL
Nine Pound Hammer. *Unknown.* FSW
Nine Times a Night. *Unknown.* OBET
9 Verses of the Same Song, *sel.* Wendell Berry.
"And my love has come to me." LLLT
Nine white chickens come. A Black November Turkey. Richard Wilbur. BoAnP; LCAP; MoAB; NCSH
Nine Years after Viet Nam. Leroy V. Quintana. AMV-80
Nine years ago I was diggin' up the land. The True Paddy's Song. *Unknown.* OuSiCo
Ninepenny Fidil, The. Joseph Campbell. HBMV
1918–1941. Robert D. Fitzgerald. CBAP
1915: A Pre Raphaelite Ending, London. Richard Howard. NoAM
1955. Bruce Weigl. MAYP
1956. Daniel G. Hoffman. PoCh
1905. David Ignatow. VWA
1945. Sheila Cussons, *tr. fr. Afrikaans by* Jack Cope *and* Uys Krige. PeSA
1945. Sir Herbert Read. OxBTC
1944—On the Invasion Coast. Jack Beeching. WaP
1914, *sels.* Rupert Brooke.
Dead, The ("Blow out, you bugles, over the rich dead!"), III. HBV-2; TreF; WGRP
Dead, The ("These hearts were woven"), IV. BrPo; CH; HBV-2; LiTB; MMA; PoA; SeCeV
Peace, I. HBV-2; MMA; OBWP; PoA; TreFT, WGRP
Safety, II. BrPo; EnLoPo; HBV-2
Soldier, The, V. BrPo; FaBoEn; FaBV; FaFP; FaPoR; FF; FPL; HBV-2; HeIP; LiTB; LiTM; MoBrPo; MOVE; NIP; NOBE; OBEV; OBWP; OxBTC; PoA; PoLF; PoPl; PoRA; TEP; TreF; TrGrPo; ViBoPo; WaP; WHA
MCMXIV. Philip Larkin. EBEV; OBWP
Nineteen Hundred and Nineteen. W. B. Yeats. BlrV; LiTB; MasP; MoAB; MoPo
Nineteen long lines hanging over my door. Lace Tell. *Unknown.* OBET
Nineteen! of years a pleasant number. Aetate XIX. Herman Charles Merivale. OBVV
Nineteen Pieces for Love, *sel.* Susan Griffin.
Trying to Say, #15. LLLT
Nineteen Sections from a Twenty Acre Poem, *sels.* David Martinson. TAT
"All morning I watched," 12.
"How the kerosene outlasted," 1.
"It's come to this," 8.
"Sharpening grandpa's scythe," 19.
"Where pollen crusts the pine bough," 4.
1917–1919. Henry Martyn Hoyt. HBMV
1976. Harvey Shapiro. FAZ
1916 Seen from 1921. Edmund Blunden. MMA
. . . 1968 . . . Petra von Morstein, *tr. fr. German by* Rosemarie Walkdrop BoWoP
1967. Thomas Hardy. NoAM
1913 Massacre, The. Woody Guthrie. FSW
1930's. Robert Lowell. NoP
1930. Kathleen Fraser. NPGG
1935. Stephen Vincent Benét. MoAmPo
1934. Richard Eberhart. TwAmPo
1934. Donald Hall. PoPl
1937 Ford Convertible. Tom McKeown. PPJ
1933. Philip Levine. VWA
1912–1952, Full Cycle. Peter Viereck. OBAL
1929. W. H. Auden. SOTW
1926. Weldon Kees. CoAP; NaP
Nineteenth Century and After, The. W. B. Yeats. FaBoEE
Nineteenth of April, The. Lucy Larcom. PAH
Ninetieth Psalm, The. Isaac Watts. *See* O God, Our Help in Ages Past.
90th Year, The. Denise Levertov. FiCP
Ninety. "E." CBAP
Ninety and Nine, The. Elizabeth Cecilia Clephane. FSW; TreF
("There were ninety and nine that safely lay.") VLP; WGRP
Ninety-fifth. Isaac Watts. AmFP
(Saint's Delight, The, *with music.*) TrAS
90 North. Randall Jarrell. AP; CoAP; CoBMV; FYAP; MoAB; MoPo; MoVE; NoAM; NOBA; TAP
Ninety percent of the mass of the Universe. Certainty before Lunch. John Berryman. LCAP; OxBC
96 Vandam. Gerald Bickford. NYP
Nineveh. Robert Eyres Landor. *Fr.* The Impious Feast. OBRV
Nineveh, Tyre. Memphis Blues. Sterling A. Brown. BANP
Niño Leading an Old Man to Market. Leonard Nathan. CTBA; NCSH
Nino, the Wonder Dog. Roy Fuller. FF
Ninth Eclogue, The. Michael Drayton. *See* Gorbo and Batte.
Ninth Month. Robert Lowell. *Fr.* Marriage. NAs
Ninth of July, The. John Hollander. CoAP
Ninth Philosopher's Song. Aldous Huxley. ViBoPo
Ninth Symphony of Beethoven Understood at Last as a Sexual Message, The. Adrienne Rich. NoP; TAP
Niobe on Phrygian sands. The Wish. Thomas Stanley. AWP
Niplets. *Unknown, tr. fr. Greek by* Wallace Rice. ErPo
Nirvana. Ali S. Hilmi Törel. PeD
Nirvana. John Hall Wheelock. HBMV; MoAmPo
Nisei Picnic, A. David Mura. BrSi
'Nita, Juanita. Elegy for Helen Trent. Paris Leary. CoPo
Nixons at Calvary. Howard Nemerov. SOTS
No! Thomas Hood. ChTr; FiBHP; HBV-2
(November.) GN
No. Natan Sach, *tr. fr. Hebrew by* Laya Firestone. VWA
No. E. M. Schorb. AMV-80
No!!/ Anywhere my father goes. War. William Alfred McLean, Jr. BOLo
No,/ I cannot/ turn from love. To Turn from Love. Sarah Webster Fabio. BlSi
No,/ I never could talk with my father. Love Song for a Tyrant. Marion Brimm Rewey. AMV-81
No/ No/ No/ I am not doing. Our Lives. Sharon Scott. JB
No,/ people are feared to fall off. On Falling. Andrew Greig. *Fr.* Men on Ice. PoSH
No Accident. Norman MacCaig. PoSH
No and Yes. Thomas Ashe. HBV-1
No Answer. Laurence Whistler. MoVE
No answer, yet I called her name. The Trick. W. H. Davies. ChMP
No argument, no anger, no remorse. Hedges Freaked with Snow. Robert Graves. OxBTC
No Armistice in Love's War. Ralph Cheyney. PGD
No artist perhaps, you go beyond their phrases. Robert Lowell. *Fr.* Mexico. BiP
No Baby in the House. Clara Dolliver. HBV-1
No Bargains Today. Peggy Susberry Kenner. JB
No bars are set too close, no mesh too fine. The Sparrow in the Zoo [*or* Epigram: Political Reflection]. Howard Nemerov. ELU; NIP; NoAM
No beggar she in the mighty hall where her bay-crowned sisters wait. Arizona. Sharlot M. Hall. PAH
No bells rang in her house. The silver plate. Miss Marnell. Austin Clarke. IPY
No berserk thirst of blood had they. Lexington. Whittier. PAH
No bird, no fabled fowl it is. A Little Cheat. *Malay Oral Tradition, tr. by* R. J. Wilkinson *and* R. O. Winstedt. WTO
No bitterness: our ancestors did it. Ave Caesar. Robinson Jeffers. MoVE; NoAM; NOBA; OxBA
No black and swirling cloak, no faceless grin. Waiting for the Post. Dorothy Auchterlonie. CBAP
No blacker than others in winter, but. Burning Mountain. W. S. Merwin. NYBP
No bottom,/ Mark four. *Unknown.* AmFP
No boy chooses war. Sailors on Leave. Owen Dodson. AmNP
No branch nor the last grass. Fossil. E. D. Blodgett. NOBC
No breath of wind. Snow. Walter de la Mare. OnUR
No, Bro, I ain't gotta'. "Gotta' Smoke?" William Franklin. LFAC
No butler, no second maid, no blood upon the stair. Crime Club. Weldon Kees. NaP
No Buyers; a Street Scene. Thomas Hardy. LiTB; NoP
No camellia. Yosano Akiko, *tr. fr. Japanese by* Geoffrey Bownas *and* Anthony Thwaite. PBWP
No Categories! Stevie Smith. NoP
No ceaseless vigil with hard toil we keep. Compensation. Thomas Stephens Collier. AA
No Change in Me. *Unknown.* AmFP
No Change of Place. W. H. Auden. OxBTC
No changes of support—only. Last Month. John Ashbery. CAPP; CoAP
No charm can stay, no medicine can assuage. Walter Savage Landor. FaBoEE
No Cherub's heart or hand for us might ache. Good Friday Evening. Christina Rossetti. PGD
No Child. Padraic Colum. OBMV
No, children, my trips are over. The Engineer's Story. *Unknown.* BeLS
"No Christian upbringing, no old wive's tales." My Street Baby's Lament. William Franklin. LFAC
No city in the spacious universe. London. Daniel Defoe. *Fr.* Reformation of Manners. NOEC
No city primness train'd my feet. Rustic Childhood. William Barnes. OBNC
No closer the glove clings to the sweaty hand. Little-League Baseball Fan. W. R. Moses. LiSp; NCSH

No cloud can hide the glow of living faith. The Light of Faith. Edgar Dupree. BLRP
No cloud, no relique of the sunken day. The Nightingale. Samuel Taylor Coleridge. EnRP; FM; PBBP
No clouds are in the morning sky. Going a-Nutting. Edmund Clarence Stedman. GN
No Cold Approach. *At. to* Burns. EBEV
No Coming to God without Christ. Robert Herrick. EBCP; OxBoCh; TRV
No considerable picture. All Too Little on Pictures. Charles Black. AMV-80
No Country You Remember. Robert Mezey. FF
No Coward Soul [Is Mine]. Emily Brontë. BrRo; EaLo; EBVV; FaBoEn; FaFP; HeIP; LiTB; NoP; OAEP; OBNC; OxBI; PoEL-5; TrCP; TreFS; TrPWD; ViBoPo; VLP
(Last Lines.) BLPA; ChER; EBCP; FaBoBe; FPL; GoBC; HBV-2; NOBE: OAEL-2; OBEV; OBVV; PoPle; TrGrPo; WGRP; WHA
"Though earth and man were gone," *sel.* TRV
No Credit. Kenneth Fearing. CMoP
No crooked leg, no bleared eye. Written in Her French Psalter. Elizabeth I, Queen of England. PBWP; WPE
No, Daisy! lift not up thy ear. To a Spaniel. Walter Savage Landor. FM
No David could send a stone as high. Central Park West. Stanley Moss. PCP
No Dawns. Julianne Perry. PoBA
No day was sad as the day Sakhr. On Her Brother Sakhr. Al-Khansa, *tr. by* Willis Barnstone. BoWoP
No Difference. Beverly Lawn. AMV-81
No Difference in the Dark. Robert Herrick. CaPo
No dignity without a chromium. Ballad of Faith. William Carlos Williams. OBAL
No dip and dart of swallows wakes the black. The Canal. Aldous Huxley. HBMV
No distant Lord have I. Companionship. Maltbie D. Babcock. STF
No Doubt. Helen Baker Adams. STF
No doubt in the mind of Brébeuf that this was the last. The Martyrdom of Brébeuf and Lalemant, 16 March 1649. E. J. Pratt. *Fr.* Brébeuf and His Brethren. NOBC
No doubt left. Enough deceiving. James Agee. *Fr.* Lyrics. MoAmPo; PoPl
No doubt this way is best. No Use. W. D. Snodgrass. BoLoP
No doubt to-morrow I will hide. At Mass. Vachel Lindsay. VGW
No dream of mortal joy. Love and Lust. Isaac Rosenberg. ChMP; TrJP
No dust have I to cover me. An Inscription by the Sea. E. A. Robinson, *after* Glaucus. AWP; ChTr; ELU; FaBoEE
No early buds of laughing spring. Valentine. "C. W. T." YeAr
No earthquake. Chapped, a lifting in this field. Dead Center. Chester Kallman. PoA
No East or West. John Oxenham. TRV
(All One in Christ.) BLRP
(In Christ.) STF
No, editors don't care a button. Thoughts on Editors. Thomas Moore. WhC
No Escape. Harriet L. Delafield. GoYe
No "fan is in his hand" for these. The Threshing Machine. Alice Meynell. SeCePo; WPE
No Fault in Women. Robert Herrick. HBV-1
No Fear. Mary Doyle Curran. AMV-80
No fence will keep a growing boy outside. Father of the Man. Elizabeth Mabel Bryan. GoYe
No Fig. Stephen Todd Booker. LFAC
No first-class war can now be fought. Civil Defense. Kenneth Burke. OBAL
No flowers now to wear at/ Sunset. The Waning of the Harvest Moon. John Wieners. CoPo
No, for I'll save it! Seven years since. Apparent Failure. Robert Browning. NOBE
No for you, my queyn, will I prepare. The Real Muse. Tom Scott. PoA
No form of human framing. One in Christ. Henry van Dyke. TRV
No Foundation. John Hollander. OBAL
No freeman, saith the wise, thinks much on death. The End. Wallace Rice. AA
No Funeral Gloom. Ellen Terry. BLPA
No Furlough. Stephen Stepanchev. WaP
No further, fathering logos, withering son. The Worm in the Whirling Cross. John Malcolm Brinnin. MoPo
No Ghost Is True. Leslie A. Fiedler. PoA
No Girls Allowed. Jack Prelutsky. RHPC
No Goddess is thy parent, nor th'art of Dardanus offspring. Dido to Aeneas. Virgil, *tr. by* Richard Stanyhurst. *Fr.* The Aeneid, IV. AnIV
No Great Matter. David Lawson. VGW
No Greater Love. *Unknown.* STF
No hand has been allowed to touch. Inscription on a Chemise. *Unknown, tr. by* E. Powys Mathers. *Fr.* The Thousand and One Nights. ErPo
No haste but good, where wisdome makes the waye. George Gascoigne. AAS
No hawk hangs over in this air. The Snow Storm. Edna St. Vincent Millay. PoA
No hay nada nuevo en nueva york. There Is Nothing New in New York. Miguel Piñero. NYP
No, He is too quick. We never. Getting Inside the Miracle. Luci Shaw. TrCP
No heavier lies the everlasting snow. Truth. Cecil Francis Lloyd. CaP
No heralding daffodils. Row of Houses. John Robert Quinn. AMV-80
No hesitation. Mourning Letter, March 29 1963. Edward Dorn. ConAP
No Hiding Place ("There's no hiding place down there"). *Unknown. See* Dere's No Hidin' Place Down Dere.
No Hiding Place Down There ("A sinner man sat on the gates of hell"). *Unknown.* GBP
No Hint of Stain. William Vaughan Moody. *Fr.* An Ode in Time of Hesitation. AA
No hint upon the hill top shows. Inspiration. John Banister Tabb. WGRP
No Holes Marred. Suzanne Douglass. QQQ; RHPC
"No home, no home," cried an orphan girl. The Orphan Girl. *Unknown.* AmFP; AS
No, Honoria, I am greatly flattered. Time's Revenges. Sir Owen Seaman. FaBoUs
No hope have I to live a deathless name. Poietes Apoietes. Hartley Coleridge. OBNC
No house of stone. The Elements. W. H. Davies. MoBrPo; OBVV
No hungr[y] hawke poore patridge to devoure. Mr. Thomas Shepeard. Edward Johnson. SCAP
No, I Am Not as Others Are. Villon, *tr. fr. French by* Arthur Symons. AWP
No, I am not death wishes of sacred rapists. I, Too, Know What I Am Not. Bob Kaufman. NBP
No, I am through and you can call in vain. Admonition. Philip Stack. BLPA
No, I don't love you. Anti-Love Poems. Elizabeth Brewster. NOBC
No, I had set no prohibiting sign. Trespass. Robert Frost. FaBV
No, I have never found. Places, Loved Ones. Philip Larkin. CMoP; NePoEA
"No, I have tempered haste." The Mount. Léonie Adams. MoAB; MoAmPo
No! I shan't envy him, who'er he be. The Choice. John Norris. CavP
No Idle Boast. Edward C. Lynskey. WOLT
No—I'll endure ten thousand deaths. Chaste Florimel. Matthew Prior. BoLoP; ErPo
No. I'll have no bawds. Ben Jonson. *Fr.* The Alchemist. ViBoPo
No, I'm not afraid of death. Soliloquy I. Richard Aldington. BrPo
No. I'm not an Englishman with a partisan religion. Tragic Guilt. Keidrych Rhys. WaP
No Images. Waring Cuney. AmNP; BANP; CDC; MAT; TTY
No! Indeed. Sir Thomas Wyatt. *See* Rondeau "What no, perdie! ye may be sure!"
No Irish Need Apply. *Unknown.* FSW; WTO
No, it is not an elephant or any such grasshopper. Nessie. Ted Hughes. AmMo
No, it's a tenement. "It's a Whole World, the Body. A Whole World!"—Swami Satchidandanda. David Young. FF
No. It's an impudent falsehood. Men did not. On a Vulgar Error. C. S. Lewis. OxBTC
No Job Blues. *Unknown.* BluL
No John. *Unknown. See* O, No, John.
No-Kings and the Calling of Spirits. Nancy Willard. LCAP
No Labor-saving Machine. Walt Whitman. PCP
No landscape ever fancies or delights me. In Front of the Seine, Recalling the Rio de la Plata. Silvina Ocampo, *tr. by* Jason Weiss. AMV-80
No Laws. Brian Allwood. WaP
No leaf is left unmoistened by the dew. Prayer by Moonlight. Roberta Teale Swartz. TrPWD
No leaf moves. The weather. The Shirt. Hilda Morley. AMV-81
No Less than Prisoners. Frederick T. Macartney. CBAP
No life in earth, or air, or sky. Crotalus. Bret Harte. AA
No lifeless thing of iron and stone. Brooklyn Bridge. Sir Charles G. D. Roberts. PAH
No light except the stars, but from the cliff. The Sea Birds. Van K. Brock. NYBP
No Loathsom[e]nesse in Love. Robert Herrick. AnAnS-2; GBL
No Lock against Lechery. Robert Herrick. CaPo
No longer a real thing. Still Life. Regina M. Austin. AMV-80
No longer casual hand to lip. Blind, I Speak to the Cigarette. Joanne deLongchamps. GoYe
No longer heed we war and strife. Thus Speak the Slain. Carl Holliday. PGD

No longer homes are flame against. Litany for Peace. Leslie Savage Clark. PGD
No longer mourn for me when I am dead. Sonnets, LXXI. Shakespeare. AWP; EBEV; EIL; EnRePo; FaBoRV; GBL; GTBS; GTBS-P; HAP; HBV-1; LiTB; LO; NoP; OAEP; OBSC; PAI; PoRA; PPoe; SeCeV; TEP; TreFT; TrGrPo; ViBoPo; WHA
No longer now do perfumed swains and merry wanton youths. The Passing of Lydia. Horace, *tr. by* Louis Untermeyer. UnTE
No longer tension, no dimension, only the words without letters. To Morris Louis. Anne Cherner. PoDr
No longer the drifting. To Some Few Hopi Ancestors. Wendy Rose. TWSS
No longer the wife of the hero. The Vamp Passes. James J. Montague. HBMV
No longer throne of a goddess to whom we pray. Full Moon. Robert Hayden. BPo
No longer to lie reading Strauss's *Life.* Memories of Aunt Maria-Martha. William Zaranka. BXAP
No longer to lie reading *Tess of the d'Urbervilles.* The Lesson. Robert Lowell. CMoP; LCAP; NMP
No Love, to Love of Man and Wife. Richard Eedes. InvP
(Of Man and Wife.) EIL
No lover saith, I love, nor any other. The Paradox. John Donne. OAEP
No luck/ this still afternoon. Fishing Drunk. Bob Mondy. WOLT
No Madam Butterfly. Louise Hajek. AMV-80
No man can bid a fool or sage. The Power of Thought. Süsskind von Trimberg. TrJP
No man can serve two masters. Bible, *N.T.* St. Matthew, VI: 24-29. OBVE
No man e'er found a happy life by chance. The Art of Happiness [*or* Happiness an Art]. Edward Young. *Fr.* Night Thoughts, VIII. OBEC; POL
No Man, if Men Are Gods. E. E. Cummings. InvP; MoPo; NePA; VGW
No man in the West ever won such renown. The Ballad of Billy the Kid. Henry Herbert Knibbs. BPAW
No man is born into the world whose work. Work. James Russell Lowell. PoSC
No Man Knows War. Edwin Rolfe. TrJP; WaP
No man outlives the grief of war. The Permanence of the Young Men. William Soutar. NeBP; OxBS
No man should stand before the moon. A Sense of Humour. Vachel Lindsay. Poems about the Moon, III. TwAmPo
No Man's Land. Eric Bogle. OBET
No man's trust let woman claim. The Roman Earl. *Unknown, tr. by* Douglas Hyde. OBVE
No Marvel Is It. Bernard de Ventadour, *tr. fr. Provençal by* Harriet Waters Preston. AWP
No Matter. Paulus Silentiarius, *tr. fr. Greek by* William Cowper. AWP
No matter how grouchy you're feeling. Limerick [*or* The Smile]. Anthony Euwer. *Fr.* The Limeratomy. HBMV; WhC
No matter how hard I listen, the wind speaks. For Zbigniew Herbert, Summer, 1971, Los Angeles. Larry Levis. FYAP; LCAP
No matter how the chances are. Jerry an' Me. Hiram Rich. HBV-1
No matter how tough the job. Handyman. Homer Phillips. QQQ
No matter what life you lead. Snow White and the Seven Dwarfs. Anne Sexton. DFT
No matter what we are and who. Routine. Arthur Guiterman. RHPC
No. Maybe Indigos. Perdido, Duke? Robert McGovern. SOTS
No McTavish. Genealogical Reflection. Ogden Nash. OBAL
No Mean City. Patrick MacDonogh. BIrV
No memory but this new day, dark wings. City Butterfly. Charles Siebert. NYP
No. Merely to have writ. Peruke of Poets. William Zaranka. BXAP
No Miracle. Daniel Corkery. AnIV
No Mixed Green Salad for Me, Thanks. Georgie Starbuck Galbraith. QQQ
No mo meetings. Listenen to Big Black at S. F. State. Sonia Sanchez. BPo
No monuments or landmarks guide the stranger. A Country without a Mythology. Douglas Le Pan. MoCV; NOBC
No moon. Night water shapes all light. Night Dive. Don Johnson. MAYP
No moon, no chance to meet. Ono no Komachi, *tr. fr. Japanese by* Rob Swigart. WPOW
No moon No road No thunder. Poem on the Suicide of My Teacher. Joseph Stroud. NPGG
No Moon, No Star. Babette Deutsch. NYBP
No More. Carl Clark. JB
No more alone sleeping, no more alone waking. Marriage. Mary Elizabeth Coleridge. PeHV
No more, America, in mournful strain. Phillis Wheatley. *Fr.* To the Right Honourable William, Earl of Dartmouth, His Majesty's Principal Secretary of State for North America, & C. WPOW
No More Auction Block. *Unknown.* BPo
(Many Thousand Gone). FSW
No more be grieved at that which thou hast done. Sonnets, XXXV. Shakespeare. CABA; PeHV; TEP; UnPo
No More beneath the Oppressive Hand, *with music. Unknown.* AH
No More Booze. *Unknown.* OBAL; TrAS, *with music;* TreF
(Fireman Save My Child.) AS, *with music.*
No more chant your old rhymes about bold Robin Hood. General Ludd's Triumph. *Unknown.* OBET
No more dams I'll make for fish. Shakespeare. *Fr.* The Tempest, II, ii. ViBoPo
No More Destructive Flame. Francis X. Connolly. ISi
No more exercises of style for him. A Younger Poet. Peter Schjeldahl. PoA
No more for them shall evening's rose unclose. Epicedium. J. Corson Miller. HBMV; PAH
No more from out the sunset. Sandy Star. William Stanley Braithwaite. Sandy Star and Willie Gee, V. HBMV
No More Good Water. *Unknown.* BluL
No more in any house can I be at peace. A Dream. Charles Williams. OBEV
No More Love Poems #1. Ntozake Shange. BlSi
No more marble let him have. Epitaph Inscribed on a Small Piece of Marble. James Shirley. CavP
No more, my Dear, no more these counsels try. Astrophel and Stella, LXIV. Sir Philip Sidney. HBV-1; OBSC; SiPS
No more, my Stella, to the sighing shades. To Stella. Hester Chapone. OBEC
No more my visionary soul shall dwell. Pantisocracy. Samuel Taylor Coleridge. EnRP
No more, no more. The Riddle. Alexander Brome. OBS
No more—no more in Cashel town. The Roving Worker. *Unknown, tr. by* George Sigerson. OnYI
No more, no more Jewish townships in Poland. Elegy. Antoni Slonimski, *tr. by* Isaac Komem. VWA
No more—no more—Oh! never more on me. My Days of Love Are Over. Byron. *Fr.* Don Juan. FaBoEn; OBNC
No More, O My Spirit. Euripides, *tr. fr. Greek by* Hilda Doolittle ("H. D."). *Fr.* Hippolytus. AWP
No more of talk where God or angel guest. The Subject of Heroic Song. Milton. *Fr.* Paradise Lost, IX. NoP; OBS
No more of your titled acquaintances boast. Burns. FaBoEE
No more phrases, Swenson: I was once. Lions in Sweden. Wallace Stevens. BiP
"No more shall I see." Frithiof's Farewell. Esaias Tegner, *tr. by* Longfellow. *Fr.* Frithiof's Saga. AWP
No more shall I, since I am driven hence. To Lar[r]. Robert Herrick. CaPo; SeCV-1
No more shall I work in the factory. The Factory Girl. *Unknown.* FSW; SaC
No more shall meads be deckt with flowers. The Protestation. Thomas Carew. CavP
No more shall walls, no more shall walls confine. Hosanna. Thomas Traherne. PoEL-2; SeCV-2
No More Soft Talk. Diane Wakoski. FF; IHMS
No More than Five. Fred Levinson. AmPA
No more the battle or the chase. Indian Summer. John Banister Tabb. AA
No more the English girls may go. High Germany. Edward Shanks. OBMV
No More the Slow Stream. Floris Clark McLaren. OBCV
No more the swanboat on the artificial lake. Blind Date. Conrad Aiken. DL; MoVE; ViBoPo
No More the Thunder of Cannon. Julia C. R. Dorr. OHIP
No more waiting. Electrocution Script. P. L. Jacobs. LFAC
No more wine? Then we'll push back chairs and talk. Bishop Blougram's Apology. Robert Browning. OBNC; PoEL-5; VLP
No more with candied words infect mine ears. Tell Me No More. William Drummond of Hawthornden. TrGrPo
No more with overflowing light. For a Dead Lady. E. A. Robinson. AP; CMoP; CoBMV; DL; FaBoEn; FYAP; HeIP; HoPM; InvP; LiTA; LiTM; MoAB; MoAmPo; NoAM; NOBA; OxBA; PoEL-5; PoRA; TreFT; TwAmPo; ViBoPo; WHA
No More Women Blues. *Unknown.* BluL
No More Words. Franklin Lushington. PAH
No more words! To the field, to arms. Veronica Franco, *tr. fr. Italian by* Lynne Lawner. PBWP
"No mortal man beneath the sky." Epitaph for George Moore. Thomas Hardy. FaBoEE
No mortal thing enthralled these longing eyes. Celestial Love. Michelangelo, *tr. by* John Addington Symonds. AWP

No movement on the hill: the old soldiers. Old Soldiers Home at Marshalltown, Iowa. Jim Barnes. AMV-80; FAZ
No myrtle can obliterate a name. Your Glory, Lincoln. Mae Winkler Goodman. PGD
No Names. *Unknown, tr. fr. Irish by* Frank O'Connor. KiLC
No need for confusion if we but recall. Rhyme for Remembering the Date of Easter. Justin Richardson. FaBoUs
No need to cling. Haiku. Joso, *tr. by* Lucien Stryk *and* Takashi Ikemoto. FAZ
No need to dial the doctor. I have. The Legacy. Judith Minty. GeTw
"No need to get home early." Father's Voice. William Stafford. RFM
No need to hush the children for her sake. Out of Hearing. Jane Barlow. HBV-2
No! never such a draught was poured. A Ballad of the Boston Tea-Party. Oliver Wendell Holmes. PAH; PAL
No, Never Think. Pushkin, *tr. fr. Russian by* Babette Deutsch. ErPo
No new delights to our desire. Singers to Come. Alice Meynell. WPE
No new moon in its arms. Last Quarter. John Hollander. MOON
No New Music. Stanley Crouch. PoBA
No New Thing. Vincent Buckley. CBAP
No news of navies burnt at seas. A New-Year's Gift Sent to Sir Simeon Steward. Robert Herrick. CaPo
No-Night, The. Irving Feldman. NoAM
No! No!/ Bird in the darkness singing. The Tsigane's Canzonet. Edward King. AA
No No Blues. *Unknown.* BluL
No, no, don't, please. Crimes of Passion: The Phone Caller. Terry Stokes. AmPA
No, no, fair heretic[k], it needs must be. Song. Sir John Suckling. *Fr.* Aglaura. AnAnS-2; CABA; CaPo; LoBV; OBS; PrIm
"No, no; for my virginity." A True Maid. Matthew Prior. ErPo; FaBoCo; FaBoEE; NIP; NOEC; PV
No, no! Go from me. I have left her lately. A Virginal. Ezra Pound. AP; CMoP; CoBMV; MoAB; MoAmPo; NePA; NIP; NoAM; NOBA; OxBA; TAP; TwAmPo
No, no! go not to Lethe, neither twist. Ode on Melancholy [*or* On Melancholy]. Keats. CABA; EnRP; FaBoEn; FiP; HAP; HBV-2; InPS; LiTB; MAT; NIP; NOBE; NoP; OAEL-1; OAEP; OBEV; OBNC; PoEL-4; PoPle; PoRA; PPP; PrIm; SeCeV; TEP; TreFS; TrGrPo; ViBoPo
No, no I did not bargain for so much. Too Much. Edwin Muir. LiTB
No, no, I well remember—proofs, you said. The Demon-Lover. James Abraham Hillhouse. *Fr.* Hadad. AA
No, no, my friend, we're off! Six months have passed. Phaedra (Phèdre). Racine, *tr. by* Robert Lowell. NAWM-2
No, No, Nigella! *Unknown.* EnRePo
No, no, no, I know I was not important as I moved. Come Dance with Kitty Stobling. Patrick Kavanagh. NoAM
No, no, no, no, I cannot hate my foe. Song. Sir Philip Sidney. SiPS
No, No, Poor Suffering Heart. Dryden. *Fr.* Cleomenes. LiTB; LoBV; QFR; ViBoPo
(One Happy Moment.) OBEV
(Song: "No, no, poor suff'ring heart, no change endeavor.") SeCV-2
No, no, this bitterness is no new thing. Northwind. Gene Baro. NePoEA-2
No noise is here, or none that hinders thought. The Winter Walk at Noon. William Cowper. *Fr.* The Task, VI. BoAnP; PBBP
No, not far beneath some foreign sky then. Requiem. "Anna Akhmatova," *tr. by* Robin Kemble. NAWM-2
No; not for those of women born. From a Hint in the Minor Poets. Samuel Wesley. OBEC
No, not in the halls of the noble and proud. The Quakeress Bride. Elizabeth Clementine Kinney. AA
No, not the last Last Supper, and yet. Extreme Unction in PA. David Ray. AMV-81; FAZ
No, not this leaf haunts me. Some year I might. Not This Leaf Haunts Me. Tony Cosier. AMV-81
No not this old whalehall can whelm us. Mappemounde. Earle Birney. OBCV; PeCV
No, not tonight. In Teesdale. Andrew Young. FaBoPP
No, not under the vault of another sky. Requiem 1935—1940. "Anna Akhmatova," *tr. by* Richard McKane. BoWoP
No, nothing is asleep in this demesne. The Sleeping Beauty. Robert Layzer. NePoEA
No Occupation. George Rostrevor Hamilton. FaBoEE
No Offence. D. J. Enright. OxBTC
No one/ ran up. In-Group. Lionel Kearns. PeCV
No one alive has seen such ice but the five-mile floor. Photographic Plate, Partly Spidered, Hampton Roads, Virginia, with Model T Ford Mid-Channel. Dave Smith. MAYP
Noone and a Star Stand,Am to Am. E. E. Cummings. NePoAm-2
Noone" autumnal this great lady's gaze. E. E. Cummings. CrMA
No one but him. Swimmer in the Rain. Robert Wallace. FiCP; LiSp
No one can come here for the first time. Limbo. Marieve Rugo. AMV-81
No one can communicate to you. Face of Poverty. Lucy Smith. NNP; PoNe
No one can hurt me. They've tried to kill me. Alone. "Anna Akhmatova," *tr. by* Stephen Berg. BoWoP
No one can tell you why. Heart's Needle, IV. W. D. Snodgrass. ConAP; NePoEA
No one cares less than I. Edward Thomas. MoVE
No one could find his grave for relic-plunder. Casanova. Richard Usborne. POL
No one could have a blacker tail. Othello Jones Dresses for Dinner. Ed Roberson. PoBA; PoNe
No one could tell me where my Soul might be. The Search. Ernest Crosby. AA
No one dies cleanly now. Eclogue. Frederic Prokosch. ViBoPo
No one ever walking this our only earth. Muriel Rukeyser. NNaP
No one for spelling at a loss is. What's the Plural? *Unknown.* FaBoUs
No one has sung "Let the world know!" Antiphonal Hymn in Praise of Inanna. Enheduanna, *tr. fr. Sumerian.* BoWoP
No One Is Asleep Even while Dreaming. Michelle Roberts. LFAC
No one is home today doing usual chores. Becoming a Frog. Paul R. Jones. DFT
No one is the homeland. Not even the horseman. Ode Written in 1966. Jorge Luis Borges, *tr. by* Lynn C. Jacox. AMV-81
No one kneads us again of earth and clay. Psalm. Paul Celan, *tr. by* Joachim Neugroschel. VWA
No one knows the way out of his mother. String. Dennis Schmitz. LCAP
No one knows us here. Love in Magnolia Cemetery. Paula Rankin. AMV-80
No one knows what the banging is all about. The Neighbor. Miller Williams. GP
No one moulds us again out of earth and clay. Psalm. Paul Celan, *tr. by* Michael Hamburger. OBVE
No one need feel alone looking up at leaves. Looking Up at Leaves. Barbara Howes. BoNaP
No one remembered when she first discovered God. Grandmother. Henry Carlile. DFF; GP
No One Remembers Abandoning the Village of White Fir. Duane Niatum. CDW
No one sat in the chair. Sundays Visiting. Alberto Rios. Str
No One So Much as You. Edward Thomas. ChMP; GBL
No one spells out the unwritten agreement. Marriage Contract. Vern Rutsala. DFF
No one standing. How the Joy of It Was Used Up Long Ago. Linda Gregg. NPGG
No One Talks about This. Carl Rakosi. GP
No one understands the Windigo, his voice like. Windigo. Paulette Jiles. NOBC
No one wants to hear about the war. Nam. Mike Lowery. Psk; SOTS
No one was with me there. Estranged. Walter de la Mare. FaBoEn
"No one will milk a cow within." Forbidden Drink. Robert Lovett. WhC
No one writes to me. Letter Out of the Gray. Gabriel Preil, *tr. by* Shirley Kaufman *and* Howard Schwartz. VWA
No one's dancing here tonight. The Dance. Daniel Halpern. MAYP
No one's going to read. A Dance for Militant Dilettantes. Al Young. PoBA
No Other Choice. *Unknown. See* Fain Would I Change That Note.
No, our kind cannot live with these. Oreads. Kathleen Raine. PoSH
No Pains Comparable to His Attempt. *Unknown.* PBBP
No painter's brush, nor poet's pen. A Mother's Name. *Unknown.* PGD
No passenger was known to flee. Emily Dickinson. MoVE
No path at all goes somewhere. Woodlore. Kim Kurt. NePoAm-2
No pavement chalks the plain with memories. Beginning the Year at Rosebud, S. D. Roberta Hill. CDW; TWSS
No people are uninteresting. People. Yevgeny Yevtushenko, *tr. by* Robin Milner-Gulland *and* Peter Levi. DL
No photographs exist. This man. Crazy Horse Returns to South Dakota. Harley Elliott. NeAC
No place seemed farther than your death. And I Am Old to Know. Pauline Hanson. TAP
No Place So Grand. *Unknown.* WTO
No Platonic Love. William Cartwright. CABA; ErPo; GBL; InvP; JCP; LiTB; OAEL-1
(No Platonique Love.) PAI; PoEL-2
No Pleasure without Some Pain. Thomas, Lord Vaux. ElL; EnRePo
(Death in Life.) OBSC
No porter guards the passage of your door. To My Honour'd Kinsman, John Driden, of Chesterton. Dryden. EBEV
No Possum, No Sop, No Taters. Wallace Stevens. MoVE; OxBA; TAP; VGW

No price is set on the lavish summer. What Is So Rare as a Day in June? James Russell Lowell. *Fr.* The Vision of Sir Launfal. NePA
No private grudge they need, no personal spite. Modern Critics. Samuel Taylor Coleridge. FaBoEE
No purple mars the chalice; not a bird. The Exquisite Sonnet. J. C. Squire. HBMV
"No Quarrel." A. P. Herbert. DBV
No quarrel ever stirred. Of Quarrels. Arthur Guiterman. TiPo
No quirt—right?—nor spur. To My Mouse-colored Mare. Tristan Corbière, *tr. by* C. F. MacIntyre. ErPo
No rack can torture me. Emily Dickinson. MoAB; MoPo
No Remedy. Drummond Allison. OxBTC
No Return. Vassar Miller. CoPo
No Road. Philip Larkin. EBEV; MoBrPo
No rock along the road but knows. Poet. Donald Jeffrey Hayes. AmNP; PoNe
No rooftops to rest on. Madison Square. A. Glanz-Leyeles, *tr. by* Keith Bosley. VWA
No Room. Dorothy Conant Stroud. STF
No Room at the Inn. *Unknown.* FSW
No room for mourning: he's gone out. William Wordsworth. Sidney Keyes. ChMP; OxBTC; SeCePo
No room in the inn, of course. What the Donkey Saw. U. A. Fanthorpe. OBCP
No rooster wakes them. A donkey brays. In the Madison Zoo. Roberta Hill. CDW
No round-shouldered pitchers here, no stewards. Cana Revisited. Seamus Heaney. FaBoMo
No runner clears the final fence. The Unfinished Race. Norman Cameron. OxBS
"No," said Charles Peace. E. C. Bentley. *Fr.* Clerihews. NOBL
No saint on a disc of snow. Emily Dickinson Postage Stamp. Lynn Strongin. NMM
No season/ brings conclusion. Outlook Uncertain. Alastair Reid. NePoEA-2
No Second Troy. W. B. Yeats. BrPo; CABA; CMoP; EnLoPo; GTBS-P; NoAM; NOBE; OAEL-2; OxBTC; PoEL-5; PPP; SeCePo; WeW
No Sects [or Sect] in Heaven. Elizabeth H. Jocelyn Cleaveland. BLPA; TreFS
No Sense Grieving. Ilya Rubin, *tr. fr. Russian by* Linda Zisquit. VWA
No shepherds now, in smooth alternate verse. George Crabbe. *Fr.* The Village. PP
No ship of all that under sail or steam. Immigrants. Robert Frost. GOA
No Shop Does the Bird Use. Elizabeth J. Coatsworth. OBCA
No show of bolts and bars. Love. Henry David Thoreau. OBVV
No sign is made while empires pass. Continuity. "Æ." MoBrPo; NBM
No Signal for a Crossing. Rhoda Donovan. AMV-80
No single hour can stand for naught. John Clare. OBNC
No Single Thing Abides. Lucretius, *tr. fr. Latin by* W. H. Mallock. *Fr.* De Rerum Natura. AWP; ImOP; *abr.*
No, Sir, No. *Unknown.* AmFP
"No, sir," said General Sherman. E. C. Bentley. *Fr.* Clerihews. NOBL
No Sky at All. Hashin. *See* Loneliness.
No sleep! I rise and burn the night away. The Protagonist. Peter Hopegood. PoAu-2
No sleep in the sky; nobody, nobody. Unsleeping City. Federico García Lorca, *tr. by* Ben Belitt. NYP
No sleep. The sultriness pervades the air. The House-Top. Herman Melville. AP; LiTA; NCEP; NOBA; NYP; Prf
No sleep tonight. Summary. Sonia Sanchez. BPo
No slightest golden rhyme he wrote. A Hint from Herrick. Thomas Bailey Aldrich. HBV-2
No sly usurping dream defeats the will. The Settled Men. George M. Brady. NeIP
No Smiles. Frank Lamont Phillips. AmNP
No song of a soldier riding down. The Ride of Collins Graves. John Boyle O'Reilly. PAH
No sooner come, but gone, and fal'n asleep. On My Dear Grand-Child Simon Bradstreet. Anne Bradstreet. SCAP
No sooner had I left A. Midpoint. Charles Simic. GeTw
No sooner had th' Almighty ceas't, but all. Heaven. Milton. *Fr.* Paradise Lost, III. OBS
No sorrows or plagues popped. Hope. Kenneth L. Anderson. AMV-80
No sound—a spell—on, on out. Father and Son. William Stafford. GP
No sound of any storm that shakes. Hillcrest. E. A. Robinson. AP; CoBMV; FaBoEn; MoAB; OxBA; PPoe
No sound—yet my room fills up with thunder. The Peeper. Peter Davidson. ErPo
No specious splendour of this stone. The Cornelian. Byron. PeHV
No Speech from the Scaffold. Thom Gunn. OxBTC
No spot of earth where men have so fiercely for ages of time. Antrim. Robinson Jeffers. BIrV; NOBA; VGW
No spring, nor summer beauty hath such grace. The Autumnal[l]. John Donne. Elegies, IX. InPS; JCP; OAEP; PoEL-2; SeCV-1; TEP; ViBoPo
No stately column marks the hallowed place. Alamance. Seymour W. Whiting. PAH
No Stewart art thou, Galloway. On Lord Galloway. Burns. FaBoEE
No stir in the air, no stir in the sea. The Inchcape Rock. Robert Southey. BeLS; ChTr; FaBoBe; GN; HBV-1; HBVY; OBNV; OBRV; PaPo; PoPle; TreFS
No storehouse nor barn have we. The Birds of the Air. Hollis Freeman. STF
No stranger pilgrims wear the shepherd's way. To Mary at Christmas. John Gilland Brunini. ISi
No strength of Nature can suffice. Love Constraining to Obedience. William Cowper. NOCV
No such luck under the lush, bumpy orange and leaf sky, the owner. Americans in an Orange Grove. Arthur Vogelsang. MAYP
No Such Thing. Marcia Southwick. AMV-81
No Sufferer for Her Love. *Unknown, tr. fr. Late Middle Irish by* Robin Flower. AnIL
No sun—no moon! No! [or November]. Thomas Hood. ChTr; FiBHP; GN; HBV-2
No sunny ray, no silver night. Threnody. Thomas Lovell Beddoes. EnRP
No Swan So Fine. Marianne Moore. AP; CoBMV; EyDe; NoP; OxBA; PoA; PrIm; UnPo
No Sweeter Thing. Adelaide Love. PGD
No Talking Shop. Minnie Leona Upton. TDH
No teacher I of boys or smaller fry. Allen Beville Ramsay. CenHV; PV
No telling his age. The Piano Tuner. W. Atmar Smith II. AMV-80
"No, Thank You, John." Christina Rossetti. TEP
No, the serpent did not. Theology. Ted Hughes. FaBoMo; NoAM; PAI
No, the serpent was not. Reveille. Ted Hughes. PPP
No Theory. David Ignatow. NNaP
No; there he moves, the thoughtful engineer. Ebenezer Elliott. *Fr.* Steam. VLP
No, they are come; their horn is lifted up. Gerard Manley Hopkins. *Fr.* Six Epigrams. SeCePo
No thing/ no-thing. Cathexis. F. J. Bryant, Jr. PoBA
No! those days are gone away. Robin Hood. Keats. AWP; EnRP
No, thou hast never griev'd but I griev'd too. Walter Savage Landor. GBL
No thyng is to man so dere. Praise of Women. Robert Mannyng. OBEV
No Time. Terence Tiller. NeBP
No Time for God. Norman L. Trott. BLRP; STF
No Time for Lamentation Now. Milton. *See* Death of Samson.
No Time for Poetry. Julia Fields. AmNP
No time, no time. The Suburb. Anne Stevenson. NMM
No, Time, thou shalt not boast that I do change. Sonnets, CXXIII. Shakespeare. OAEP; OBSC; TrGrPo
No Time to Hate. Emily Dickinson. *See* I had no time to hate, because.
No time to read, no time to pray. Stop a Minute! *Unknown.* STF
No, 'tis in vain to seek for bliss. Felicity. Isaac Watts. OxBoCh
No tranquil ordered day of ours. In Memoriam. Ada Jackson. PGD
No Truer Word. Walter Savage Landor. *See* Epigram: "No truer word, save God's . . ."
No Trust in Time. William Drummond of Hawthornden. *See* Thy Sun Posts Westward.
No trust to metals nor to marbles, when. Epitaph on the Tomb of Sir Edward Giles and His Wife [or Epitaph on Sir Edward Giles and His Wife]. Robert Herrick. PoPle; QFR
No two eyes gaze alike. Janus. Madeline Mason. GoYe
No Uneasy Refuge. Blanaid Salkeld. AnIV
No Use. W. D. Snodgrass. BoLoP
No use/ being angry at the dead. Fragment. Bruce Berlind. FAZ
No use, no use, now, begging Recognize! Amnesiac. Sylvia Plath. NYBP
No use to speak, no good to tell you that. Communication. Elizabeth Jennings. NePoEA
No use trying to hurry it. The Wait. Phyllis Janowitz. AMV-80
No use waiting for it to stop. Apples. Shirley Kaufman. NMM
No Voice of Man. Raymond Falconer. PoSH
No walls confine! Can nothing hold my mind? Insatiableness. Thomas Traherne. OxBoCh
No warm, downy pillow His sweet head pressed. The Heavenly Stranger. Ada Blenkhorn. BLRP
No water is still, on top. The Movement of Fish. James Dickey. NYBP; VGW
"No water so still as the/ dead fountains of Versailles." No Swan So Fine. Marianne Moore. AP; CoBMV; EyDe; NoP; OxBA; PoA; PrIm; UnPo
No way too long—no path too steep. Stefan George, *tr. by* Daisy Broicher. *Fr.* Das Jahr der Seele. AWP
No White Bird Sings. John Ciardi. AMV-80
No wind of Life may strike within. Dutch Seacoast. Kenneth Slessor. *Fr.* The Atlas. PoAu-2

No wind-wakeness here. A cricket's creed. Sunday in the Country. May Swenson. NePoAm-2
No Woman Born. Robert Farren. OxBI
No woman has ever lost her man. Nine Bean-Rows on the Moon. A. W. Purdy. MOON
No woman, if she is honest, can say that she's/ been blessed with greater love, my Lesbia. Catullus, *tr. fr. Latin by* Horace Gregory. NAWM-1
No Woman No Nickel. *Unknown.* BluL
No woman's pleasure did I feel. Evidence at the Witch Trials. James K. Baxter. OxBC
No wonder the birds make whittlings of sound, that the hemlock. Sun-up in March. Abbie Huston Evans. NePoAm
No wonder Wendy's coat blew off. Wendy in Winter. Kaye Starbird. RHPC
No wonder you so oft have wept. Francis Burdett Money-Coutts. *Fr.* A Little Sequence. OBVV
No word, no lie, can cross a carven lip. Silence. T. Sturge Moore. QFR; SyP
No word that is not flesh, he said. A Reason for Writing. Theodore Spencer. TwAmPo
No, worldling, no, 'tis not thy gold. The Second Rapture. Thomas Carew. CaPo; UnTE
No Worst, There Is None. Gerard Manley Hopkins. BrPo; CABA; CMoP; EBCP; EBVV; FaBoMo; GTBS-P; HeIP; InPS; LiTB; LiTM; LoBV; MoAB; MoBrPo; MoVE; NoAM; NOBE; NoP; OAEL-2; OAEP; PoEL-5; PPON; PPP; VLP
(Life Death Does End.) SeCePo
(Sonnet: "No worst, there is none.") FaBoEn; OBNC
(Terrible Sonnets, II, The.) MoPo
Noah. Chana Bloch. VWA
Noah. Roy Daniells. PeCV; WHW
Noah an' Jonah an' Cap'n John Smith. Don Marquis. PoLF
Noah and the Waters, *sel.* C. Day Lewis.
Chorus: "Since you have come thus far." OAEP
Noah in New England. Tom Lowenstein. VWA
Noah sailed his ark and skimmed his inner world. Proust on Noah. Eisig Silberschlag. VWA
Noah's Ark. Marguerite Young. MoPo; WPE
Noah's Carpenters. *Unknown.* STF
Noah's daughter. Sibyl of the Waters. Ruth Fainlight. VWA
Noah's Flood, *sels.* Michael Drayton.
"And as our God the beasts had given in charge." PBBP
"Eternall and all-working God, which wast." PoEL-2
Noah's Flood. *Unknown, tr. fr. Anglo-Saxon by* Charles W. Kennedy. *Fr.* Genesis. AnOE
Noah's Prayer. Carmen Bernos de Gasztold, *tr. fr. French by* Rumer Godden. TrCP
Noah's Song. Evan Jones. PoAu-2
Nobility. Alice Cary. OHFP; WBLP
Noble, The. Wordsworth. *Fr.* The Prelude, IX. ChTr
Noble Balm, The. Ben Jonson. OBEV
Noble Duke of York, The. *Unknown.* FSW
(Brave Old Duke of York, The.) OxNR
("O, the grand old Duke of York.") GBP
Noble executors of the munificent testament. Application for a Grant. Anthony Hecht, *ad. fr.* Horace. SaC
Noble Fisherman, The; or, Robin Hood's Preferment. *Unknown.* ESPB
Noble hart, that harbours vertuous [*or* virtuous] thought, The. The Fight of the Red Cross Knight and the Heathen Sansjoy. Spenser. *Fr.* The Faerie Queene, I, 5. FiP; ViBoPo
Noble hedge of ancient yew, A. Open to Visitors. E. V. Milner. ELU
Noble horse with courage in his eye, The. Aristocrats. Keith Douglas. FaBoMo; NePoEA; OBWP
Noble is he who falls in front of battle. How Can Man Die Better. Tyrtaeus, *tr. by* T. F. Higham. WaaP
Noble King of Brentford, The. The King of Brentford's Testament, *abr.* Thackeray, *after the French of* Pierre-Jean de Béranger. OBNV
Noble Love. Richard Flecknoe. ACP
Noble mayde, still standing, all this vewd, The. The Masque of Cupid. Spenser. *Fr.* The Faerie Queene, III, 7. PoEL-1
Noble, nasty course he ran, A. Epitaph on the Late King of the Sandwich Isles. Winthrop Mackworth Praed. DBV; FiBHP
Noble Nature, The. Ben Jonson. *Fr.* To the Immortal Memory and Friendship of That Noble Pair, Sir Lucius Cary, and Sir Henry Morison. GN; GoBC; GTBS; GTBS-P; HBV-2; HBVY; TreFT
(It Is Not Growing like a Tree.) CABA; ChTr; HeIP; LiTB
(Oak and Lily.) TrGrPo
(Part of an Ode, A.) OBEV
(Proportion.) FaBoEn
Noble range it was, of many a rood, A. Places of Nestling Green. Leigh Hunt. *Fr.* The Story of Rimini. EnRP; OBRV
Noble Ritter Hugo, Der. Ballad by Hans Breitmann [*or* Ballad of the Mermaid]. Charles Godfrey Leland. BXAP; CenHV; FiBHP; NOBL; PaPo
Noble Tuck-Man, The. Jean Ingelow. NA
Nobleman and Thresherman, The. *Unknown.* OBET
Nobleman's House, A, *sel.* May Sarton.
"After the palaces." EyDe
Nobleman's Wedding, The. *Unknown.* AnIV
Nobles and heralds, by your leave. Epitaph on Himself [*or* Epigram *or* On Himself *or* Prior's Epitaph]. Matthew Prior. FaBoEE; HBV-1; TreFS; TrGrPo
Noblesse Oblige. Jessie Fauset. CDC
Noblesse Oblige. Celeste Turner Wright. Psk
Noblest Charis, you that are. His Discourse with Cupid. Ben Jonson. *Fr.* A Celebration of Charis. AnAnS-2; SeCP
Noblest Roman, The. Shakespeare. *See* Portrait of Brutus.
Noblest thoughts my soul can claim, The. The Name of Mother. George Griffith Fetter. PGD
Nobly, nobly Cape Saint Vincent to the North-west died away. Home-Thoughts, from the Sea. Robert Browning. AWP; EBVV; FaBoCh; FiP; MOS; NOBE; OAEP; OBEV; OBVV
Nobody believes in Fate any more, nobody listens to the Norns. Waiting and Peeking. V. R. Lang. NePA
Nobody but Lester let Lester leap. Lester Leaps In. Al Young. NPGG
Nobody but me can know the sorrow that wrings me. Complaint of a Young Girl. Wang Chung-ju, *tr. by* Kenneth Rexroth. PCP
Nobody Comes. Thomas Hardy. BiP; MoVE
Nobody comes to the graveyard on the hill. The Hill above the Mine. Malcolm Cowley. PoPl; SaC
Nobody comes up from the sea as late as this. You Will Know When You Get There. Allen Curnow. OCNZ
Nobody ever galloped on this road. The Dead Ride Fast. R. P. Blackmur. MoPo
Nobody heard him, the dead man. Not Waving but Drowning. Stevie Smith. FF; GTBS-P; HAP; HeIP; NoAM; NOBE; NoP; OAEL-2; OxBTC; POL; PPP; PrIm; TEP; WeW
Nobody I know would like to be buried. Thanksgiving for a Habitat. W. H. Auden. NYBP
Nobody in the lane, and nothing, nothing but blackberries. Blackberrying. Sylvia Plath. HAP; NoAM; NOBA; NYBP
Nobody knew when it would start again. Schizophrenic. P. K. Page. HeIP
Nobody knows/ Whither our delirium. The Need. Siegfried Sassoon. TrPWD
Nobody Knows but Mother. Mary Morrison. BLPA
Nobody knows me. Number 5—December. David Henderson. BOLo
Nobody knows the other side. Chorus. Jack Kerouac. *Fr.* Mexico City Blues. NeAP
Nobody Knows the [*or* de] Trouble I've Seen [*or* I See]. *Unknown.* AH, *with music;* BLSo, *with music;* BoAN-1, *with music;* BoAN-2, *with music;* FSW
Nobody knows what I say. Alone. Itzik Manger, *tr. by* Ruth Whitman. VWA
Nobody knows what love is anymore. For a Masseuse and Prostitute. Kenneth Rexroth. NNaP
Nobody knows what's growing in Bridget. The Bulge. George Johnston. MoCV; PV
Nobody Lives on Arthur Godfrey Boulevard. Gerald Costanzo. MAYP
Nobody Loses All the Time. E. E. Cummings. CMoP; DL; FaBoCo; FF; LiTM; MP; NOBA; TwCP
Nobody loves you Chloe, you sly minx. To His Coy Mistress. Edward Bird. BXAP; FaBoPa
Nobody mentioned war. Malcolm. Lucille Clifton. CNA
Nobody noogers the shaff of a sloo. On a Flimmering Floom You Shall Ride. Carl Sandburg. GoYe; OBAL
Nobody painted Mrs. Aherne's store. Dakota: Five Times Six. Joseph Hansen. NYBP
Nobody planted roses, he recalls. "Summertime and the Living." Robert Hayden. BPo; NCSH; PoBA; PPP; TwCP
Nobody Riding the Roads Today. June Jordan. BPo
Nobody said Apples for nearly a minute. Political Intelligence. A. J. M. Smith. EAS
Nobody sees what I can see. Just Me. Margaret Hillert. RHPC
Nobody stays here long. Not in the Guide-Books. Elizabeth Jennings. LiTM; MP; NePoEA
Nobody stuffs the world in at your eyes. Snow. Margaret Avison. NOBC
Nobody wanted this infant born. Burial. Mark Van Doren. MoBS
Nobody will open the door for you. Blanca Varela, *tr. fr. Spanish by* Willis Barnstone. BoWoP
Nobody will quarrel with the woodcock. Quarrel. *Yoruba Oral Tradition, tr. by* Ulli Beier. WTO
Nobody's Child. Phila H. Case. TreF
Nocht o' Mortal Sicht. Bessie J. B. Macarthur. OxBS
Noctambule. George Johnston. MoCV

Nocturn. W. E. Henley. In Hospital, XXVII. BrPo
Nocturn at the Institute. David McElroy. Psk
Nocturn Cabbage. Carl Sandburg. DuDa
Nocturnal. Os Marron. NeBP
Nocturnal Heart. Anne-Marie Kegels, *tr. fr. French by* W. S. Merwin. BoWoP
Nocturnal Landscape. Malcolm Cowley. PoA
Nocturnal Reverie, A. Countess of Winchilsea. EBEV; FaBoEn; GoTL; LoBV; NOEC; NoP; OBEC; PBWP; PoEL-3; SBG; SeCePo; WPE
Nocturnal Sketch, A. Thomas Hood. FaBoCo; FiBHP
Nocturnal Sounds. Kattie M. Cumbo. BlSi
Nocturnal Thoughts. Avraham Huss, *tr. fr. Hebrew by* Mark Elliott Shapiro. VWA
Nocturnal upon St. Lucy's Day [Being the Shortest Day], A. John Donne. EBEV; EnRePo; GBL; JCP; LiTB; NOBE; NoP; OAEL-1; PoPle; PPP; TEP
(Nocturnall upon S. Lucies Day, A.) AnAnS-1; FaBoEn; MeLP; MePo; OBS; PoEL-2; SeCP; SeCV-1
Nocturnal Visitor. Carolyn Miller. AMV-80
Nocturnal water, primaeval silences. Useless Day. Rosario Castellanos, *tr. by* Maureen Ahern. WPOW
Nocturne: "All the earth a hush of white." Amelia Josephine Burr. HBV-1
Nocturne: "Be thou at peace this night." Edward L. Davison. CH
Nocturne: "Blade of a knife, The." Richard Murphy. IPY
Nocturne: Georgia Coast. Daniel Whitehead Hicky. AmFN
Nocturne: Homage to Whistler. Ruth Feldman. AMV-81
Nocturne: "If the deep wood is haunted, it is I." Robert Hillyer. FYAP
Nocturne: "Keen winds of cloud and vaporous drift." Richard Garnett. OBVV
Nocturne: Lake Huron. Conor Kelly. AMV-80
Nocturne: "Listening for the sound." Pinkie Gordon Lane. BlSi
Nocturne, A: "Moon has gone to her rest, The." Wilfrid Scawen Blunt. OBMV
Nocturne: "Night comes, an angel stands." Kathleen Raine. ChMP
Nocturne: "Nothin' or everythin' it's got to be." John V. A. Weaver. HBMV
Nocturne: "Over New England now, the snow." Frances Frost. BoNaP
Nocturne: "Red flame flowers bloom and die, The." Crosbie Garstin. CH
Nocturne: "See how dark the night settles on my face." Naomi Long Madgett. BALP
Nocturne: "See how the dying west puts forth her song." Richard Church. ChMP
Nocturne: "Softly blow lightly." Donald Jeffrey Hayes. CDC
Nocturne: "This cool night is strange." Gwendolyn Bennett. BANP
Nocturne: "Up to her chamber window." Thomas Bailey Aldrich. HBV-1
Nocturne: "Wildness of haggard flights." Roussan Camille, *tr. fr. French by* Seth L. Wolitz. TTY
Nocturne II: "You who have listened to the heart of the night." Ruben Dario, *tr. fr. Spanish by* Jan Pallister. AMV-81
Nocturne at Bethesda. Arna Bontemps. AmNP; BALP; BANP; CDC; PoNe
Nocturne, Central Park South. L. E. Sissman. NYP
Nocturne for October 31st, A. Yvor Winters. PoA
Nocturne for the U.S. Congress. Victor Contoski. GP
Nocturne in a Deserted Brickyard. Carl Sandburg. MoAmPo
Nocturne in G Minor. Karl Gustave Vollmoeller, *tr. fr. German by* Ludwig Lewisohn. AWP
Nocturne in the Women's Prison. Maria Beneyto, *tr. fr. Spanish by* Catherine Rodriguez-Nieto. WPOW
Nocturne of Remembered Spring. Conrad Aiken. HBMV
Nocturne of the Self-evident Presence. Thomas MacGreevy. BIrV; CIP
Nocturne of the Wharves. Arna Bontemps. BANP; BPo; PoNe
Nocturne Varial. Lewis Alexander. PoBA; PoNe
Nod. Walter de la Mare. HBMV; MoAB; MoBrPo; OxBTC
Nodding, its great head rattling like a gourd. Original Sin; a Short Story. Robert Penn Warren. CrMA; HoPM; LiTA; LiTM; MoVE; NOCV; PPP; TAP
Nodding oxeye bends before the wind, The. The Fear of Flowers. John Clare. NBM; OBRV; SeCeV
Noe longer torture mee, in dreams. Anti-Platonicke. George Daniel. CavP
Noe more unto my thoughts appeare. Song [*or* Quatrains]. Sidney Godolphin. MeLP; MePo; OBS
Noël. Hilaire Belloc. HBMV
Noel. Gail Brook Burket. PGD
Noel. Richard Watson Gilder. AA
Noel; Christmas Eve, 1913. Robert Bridges. LiTB; MoVE; NOCV; OBCP; OxBoCh; PoEL-5
Noel! Noel! Laura Simmons. PGD
Noel, noel, noel. Out of Your Sleep Arise and Wake. *Unknown.* NoP
Noel of the marvelous night. To Noel. Gabriela Mistral. PChr
Noël Tragique. Ramon Guthrie. ErPo
Noise Grimaced. Larry Eigner. NeAP
Noise of hammers once I heard. The Hammers. Ralph Hodgson. GoJo; MoBrPo; NOBE; OxBTC
Noise of passing feet, The. Listening. Alice Corbin, *after Chippewa Indian.* BPAW
Noise of the Village, The. *Tr. fr. Chippewa Indian by* Frances Densmore. OBVE
Noise of trampling, the wind of trumpets, The. Louis XVI. Blake. *Fr.* The French Revolution. ChER
Noise of water teased his literal ears, The. Persistent Explorer. John Crowe Ransom. OxBA
Noise of Waters, The. James Joyce. *See* All Day I Hear.
Noise That Time Makes, The. Merrill Moore. MoAmPo; TrGrPo; YaD
Noiseless Patient Spider, A. Walt Whitman. AmPP; AP; AWP; BiP; BLPL; CABA; EvOK; FF; HAP; HeIP; InPK; LiTA; MoAmPo; NePA; NIP; NOBA; NoP; OxBA; PAI; PP; SCV; SoSe; TAP; TrGrPo; TRV; WiR
Noises. Fred Johnson. CNA
Noises coming down the stairs. Rest Hour. George Johnston. WHW
Noises from underground made gibber some. John Berryman. *Fr.* Dream Songs. CAPP
Noises of the harbour die, the smoke is petrified, The. The Statue. Roy Fuller. NOBE
Noises of the street come up subdued, The. An Upper Room. Daniel Lawrence Kelleher. NeIP
Noises round my house, The. On cobbles bounding. Regent's Park Terrace. Bernard Spencer. FaBoPP
Noises that strive to tear. The Inner Silence. Harriet Monroe. HBMV
Noisette on my garden path, A. The Shadow Rose. Robert Cameron Rogers. AA
Noisy politicians confuse the world. Rhyming with a Friend. Yü Hsüan-chi, *tr. by* Geoffrey Waters. BoWoP
Noisy urchins scampered round, The. Much Distressed. *Unknown.* CBAP
Nokes went, he thought, to Styles's wife to bed. A Case to the Civilians. *Unknown.* FaBoEE
Noli Me Tangere. Robert Lowell. *See* Death of the Sheriff, The.
Nomads gather in autumn. Assembly. W. S. Merwin. GP
Nomen. Naomi Long Madgett. BlSi
Nominativo hic gallant asse. The Declining of a Gallant. *Unknown.* FaBoUs
Nomine Domini/ Theotocopoulos. High Renaissance. George Starbuck. OBAL
Non Amo Te. Thomas Brown. *See* Doctor Fell.
Non Dolet. Oliver St. John Gogarty. OBMV; OnYI; OxBI
"Non ego hoc ferrem calida juventâ." At Thirty Years. Byron. *Fr.* Don Juan, I. FiP
Non Nobis. Henry Cust. OBEV; OBVV
Non Nobis Domine. Kipling. EBCP
Non Piangere, Liù. Peter Porter. OxBC
Non Que Je Veuille Ôter la Liberté. Pernette de Guillet, *tr. fr. French by* Raymond Oliver. WPOW
Non Sequitor, A. Richard Corbet. FaBoNo
Non Sum Qualis Eram Bonae sub Regno Cynarae. Ernest Dowson. AWP; BLPA; BoLoP; BrPo; CABA; EBVV; EnLoPo; FaBoBe; FPL; GBL; GTBS-P; HAP; HBV-1; HeIP; MoBrPo; NOBE; NoP; OAEL-2; OBEV; OBMV; OBNC; OBVV; PoPl; PrIm; TEP; TreF; TrGrPo; ViBoPo; VLP
(Cynara.) BeLS; FaFP; LiTB; PoRA; UnPo; UnTE
Non Sum Qualis Eram in Bona Urbe Nordica Illa. John Hollander. ErPo
Non Ti Fidar. Louis Zukofsky. VGW
Nona poured oil on the water and saw the eye. The Evil Eye. John Ciardi. MoBS; NAs
Non-Combatant. Cicely Hamilton. SUMH
None. Josephine Miles. VGW
None but a Muse in love, can tell. On Fruition. Charles Sedley. ErPo
None but a Tuscan hand could fix ye here. On the Picture of the Three Fates in the Palazzo Pitti, at Florence. Arthur Henry Hallam. OBRV
None but the mouse-brown wren. The Young Martins. Andrew Young. FM
None call thee flower! . . . I will not so malign. To the Milkweed. Lloyd Mifflin. AA
"None can usurp this height," return'd that shade. Keats. *Fr.* The Fall of Hyperion, I. OBRV
None could ever say that she. True or False. Catullus, *tr. by* Walter Savage Landor. AWP; OBVE
None ever was in love with me but grief. "My True Love Hath My Heart and I Have His." Mary Elizabeth Coleridge. BoLoP
None Is Happy. Hartmann von Aue, *tr. fr. German by* Jethro Bithell. AWP
None of our warnings sank in. Contentment. Mark Osaki. BrSi
None of Self and All of Thee. Theodore Monod. BLRP
(Christ Alone.) STF
None other fame mine unambitious muse. Samuel Daniel. *Fr.* To Delia. AAS

None Other Lamb [None Other Name]. Christina Rossetti. OxBoCh; TrPWD; TRV
None spake when Wilson stood before. Catherine Kinrade. Thomas Edward Brown. OBVV
None walked behind that shoddy rain-swept hearse. Mozart's Grave. Paul Scott Mowrer. GoYe
Nones. W. H. Auden. *Fr.* Horae Canonicae. CoBMV
Nonetheless Ali Baba had no richer cave. Quebec Liquor Commission Store. A. M. Klein. OBCV
Non-Euclidean Elegy. John Frederick Nims. MoVE
Nongtongpaw. Charles Dibdin. HBV-1
Noni Daylight left the morning. Origins. Joy Harjo. TWSS
Noni Daylight Remembers the Future. Joy Harjo. TWSS
Nonne Preestes Tale, The. Chaucer. *See* Nun's Priest's Tale, The.
Nonny, The. James Reeves. AmMo
Nonpareil. Matthew Prior. EnLoPo
Nonsense. Richard Corbet. *See* Like to the Thundering Tone.
Nonsense. Thomas Moore. FaBoEE; InMe; NA
Nonsense! Jack Prelutsky. RHPC
Nonsense. Robert Haven Schauffler. HBMV
Nonsense ("The cricket and the greshope. . ."). *Unknown.* OxBM
("Cricket and the greshope wenten hem to fight, The.") EBEV
Nonsense ("Oh that my lungs . . ."). *Unknown. See* Odd but True.
Nonsense Alphabet, A. Edward Lear. SoPo; SUS
("A was once an apple-pie.") TiPo
(Alphabet, An.) OxBChV
Nonsense Carol, A. *Unknown.* OxBoLi
Nonsense Quatrains: "Ah, yes! I wrote the 'Purple Cow.'" Gelett Burgess. *See* Ah, Yes, I Wrote "The Purple Cow."
Nonsense Quatrains: "I never saw a purple cow." Gelett Burgess. *See* Purple Cow, The.
Nonsense Quatrains: "I sent my Collie to the wash." Gelett Burgess. CenHV
Nonsense Quatrains: "Many people seem to think." Gelett Burgess. *See* Parisian Nectar.
Nonsense Quatrains: "Proper way to leave a room, The." Gelett Burgess. CenHV
Nonsense Song, A. Stephen Vincent Benét. OBAL
Nonsense? That's what makes no sense. Nonsense! Jack Prelutsky. RHPC
Nonsense Verses: "I wish that my room had a floor." Gelett Burgess. *See* I Wish That My Room Had a Floor.
Nonsense Verses: "I'd rather have fingers than toes." Gelett Burgess. *See* On Digital Extremities.
Nonsense Verses: "My feet they haul me 'round the house." Gelett Burgess. *See* My Feet.
Nonsense Verses: "Remarkable truly, is art!" Gelett Burgess. *See* Remarkable Art.
Nonsense Verses: "Window has four little panes, The." Gelett Burgess. *See* Window Pane, The
Nonsense Verses. Charles Lamb. NA
Noodle-Vendor's Flute, The. D. J. Enright. NoP
Nooked underneath steep, sterile hills that rise. An Old Seaport. *Unknown.* EtS
Nooksack Valley. Gary Snyder. NaP
Noon. John Clare. OBRV; SeCePo
Noon. Robinson Jeffers. MoAmPo
Noon: and the gentle air. A swallow's wing. The Dead. John Williams. NePoAm-2
Noon Glare. Matthew Brennan. AMV-80
Noon heat in the yard, The. Hen Woman. Thomas Kinsella. CIP; IPY
Noon is beautiful, The: the perfect wheel. An Elegy. Yvor Winters. VGW
Noon of the Sunbather. Marge Piercy. NMM
Noon on the mountain! Walt Whitman. Emanuel Carnevali. PoA
Noon Quatrains. Charles Cotton. LoBV
Noon sun beats down the leaf; the noon. Grapes Making. Léonie Adams. FYAP; MoVE; NePA; UnPo
Noon. The luminous tide. Ballydavid Pier. Thomas Kinsella. BIrV
Noon was shady, and soft airs, The. The Dog and the Water-Lily. William Cowper. OAEP
Noonday April Sun, The. George Love. IDB; NNP
Noonday Sun. Kathryn Jackson *and* Byron Jackson. FaPON; TiPo
Noonlight is sudden full of the spirits. The Storm. Robert Wallace. NYBP
Nooses of double meanings swing. Conversation Piece. Arthur Freeman. ErPo
Nor bring, to see me cease to live. A Wish. Matthew Arnold. DBV
Nor do these heads sing. Lightness Remembered. Nancy Willard. LCAP
Nor dread nor hope attend. Death. W. B. Yeats. ChMP
Nor exults he nor complains he; silent bears whate'er befalls him. Ever Watchful. Ta' Abbata Sharra, *tr. by* W. G. Palgrave. AWP
Nor force nor fraud shall sunder us! America, II. Sydney Dobell. HBV-2; OBVV; PAL
Nor Hammond's love nor Shenstone's was sincere. Elegy. John Maclaurin. NOEC
Nor happiness, nor majesty, nor fame. Political Greatness. Shelley. EnRP
Nor House nor Heart. Elinor Lennen. PGD
Nor Is It Written. Laura Riding. Three Sermons to the Dead, III. LiTA
Nor less the spaniel, skillful to betray. John Gay. *Fr.* Rural Sports. PBBP
Nor lingered Paris in the lofty house. Homer, *tr. by* Tennyson. *Fr.* The Iliad, VI. OBVE
Nor long the trench or lofty walls oppose. Homer, *tr. by* Pope. *Fr.* The Iliad, XII. OBVE
Nor Mars His Sword. Dunstan Thompson. NePA
Nor practising virtue nor committing crime. Epitaph. Geoffrey Taylor. FaBoEE
Nor shall you for your fields neglect your stock. Young Stock. V. Sackville-West. OxBTC
Nor skin nor hide nor fleece. Lethe. Hilda Doolittle ("H. D."). CMoP; LiTM; MoAmPo; PoRA; TrGrPo; VGW; ViBoPo; WHA
Nor think, in nature's state they blindly trod. Pope. *Fr.* An Essay on Man, III. OAEL-1
Nor truth nor good did they know. Gloss. Padraic Fiacc. CIP
Nor was this fellowship vouchsaf'd to me. Wordsworth Skates on Esthwaite Water. Wordsworth. *Fr.* The Prelude, I. FaBoPP
Nor when the youthful pair more closely join. Concerning the Nature of Love. Lucretius, *tr. by* Dryden. *Fr.* De Rerum Natura. ErPo
Nor, will anyone dare say to. Sharon Will Be No/Where on Nobody's Best-selling List. Sharon Scott. JB
Nor will the search be hard or long. Epistle to the President of the Scottish Society of Antiquaries: On Being Chosen a Correspondent Member. Alexander Geddes. OxBS
Nor with less waste the whisker'd vermin race. How to Exterminate Rats. James Grainger. *Fr.* The Sugar-Cane. FaBoUs
Nor yet do I, your knowing lover. Portrait. John Lyle Donaghy. BIrV
Nora. Dora Sigerson Shorter. HBMV
Norah. Zoë Akins. HBV-1
Nor'easter. Bianca Bradbury. EtS
Norembega. Whittier. PAH
Norfolk. John Betjeman. ChMP
Norfolk Girls, The, *with music. Unknown.* AmSS
Norfolk Memorials. Coman Leavenworth. LiTA
Norfolk Rebellion, The. *Unknown.* GBP
Norfolk sprang [*or* sprung] thee, Lambeth holds thee dead. Epitaph on Thomas Clere. Earl of Surrey. AAS; NCEP; OBWP; SiPS
Normal as Two Ships in the Night. Walta Borawski. AMV-81
Norman Abbey. Byron. *Fr.* Don Juan, XIII. OBRV
Norman Baron, The, *sel.* Longfellow.
"In his chamber, weak and dying." PeD
Norman conquest all historians fix, The. The English Succession. *Unknown.* OxBChV
Norman Morrison. Adrian Mitchell. FF
Norris Dam. Selden Rodman. PoNe
Norse am I when the first snow falls. The Song of the Ski. Wilson MacDonald. CaP
Norse Lullaby. Eugene Field. SUS
Norse Sailor's Joy. Wilfrid Thorley. EtS
Norsemen, The. Whittier. PAH
North. Philip Booth. NePoEA; PoPl
North. Lance Henson. STE
North, The. Barry McKinnon. NOBC
North, The. Stephen Spender. *See* Polar Exploration.
North American Sequence. Theodore Roethke. NaP
North and South. Claude McKay. AmPP
North and the South, The. Elizabeth Barrett Browning. OBVV
North Atlantic. Carl Sandburg. MOS
North Clark Street. Raymond Thompson. LFAC
North Country, The. D. H. Lawrence. OAEP
North Country. Kenneth Slessor. CBAP
North Country Maid, The. *Unknown. See* Oak and the Ash, The.
North Express. Joyce Mansour, *tr. fr. French by author.* WPOW
North Haven. Elizabeth Bishop. PAI
North Infinity Street. Conrad Aiken. AP
North is weather, Winter, and change. North. Philip Booth. NePoEA; PoPl
North Labrador. Hart Crane. CMoP; FaBoMo; POL
North, near the tip, where the island. Approaching Washington Heights. James Reiss. NYP
North of Berwick. Sydney Tremayne. BSV
North of Chillicothe. Blessing at Kellenberger Road. Maxine Kent Valian. AMV-80
North of here where. Snowgoose. Paula Gunn Allen. TWSS
North of my grandfathers house. North. Lance Henson. STE
North of 96th where the tracks come out from under. From a Diary. Frederick Morgan. NYP

North of Santa Monica. Carter Revard. VoR
North of Wales, The. Herbert Morris. NePoAm-2
North Percy, *sel.* Paul Goodman.
Pagan Rites. DiL
North Philadelphia, Trenton, and New York. Richmond Lattimore. NYBP
North Pickenham. Coman Leavenworth. Norfolk Memorials, I. LiTA
North Pole Story, A. Menella Bute Smedley. OxBChV
North Sea off Carnoustie. Anne Stevenson. HoAn
North Sea, The, *sels.* Heine, *tr. fr. German.*
Epilog: "Like the ears of wheat in a wheat-field growing," *tr. by* Louis Untermeyer. AWP
(Epilogue: "Like the stalks of wheat in the fields," *tr. by* Emma Lazarus.) TrJP
Evening Twilight, *tr. by* John Todhunter. AWP
Night by the Sea, A, *tr. by* Howard Mumford Jones. AWP
North Sea Undertaker's Complaint, The. Robert Lowell. NePoEA
North Shore. Peter Davison. CoPo
North to Milwaukee. Gerald Vizenor. VoR
North Wind Came Up Yesternight, The. Robert Bridges. SeCeV
North wind doth blow, The. Mother Goose. HBV-1; OnUR; OxNR; PBBP; SoPo
North Wind in October. Robert Bridges. VLP
North winds send hail, south winds bring rain. The Winds. Thomas Tusser. WiR
Northamptonshire Fens. John Clare. *Fr.* Child Harold. FaBoPP
Northboun'. Lucy Ariel Williams Holloway. BANP; BlSi; CDC; PoNe
Northeast wind was the wind off the lake, The. Cook County [*or* Weather]. Archibald MacLeish. CrMA; MoAmPo
Northern Boulevard. Edwin Denby. CrMA
Northern breath, that freezes floods, he binds, The. Ovid, *tr. by* Dryden. *Fr.* Metamorphoses, I. OBVE
Northern Cobbler, The. Tennyson. EBEV
Northern Farmer: New Style. Tennyson. BiP; VLP
Northern Farmer: Old Style. Tennyson. OAEP; VLP
Northern Hoard, A, *sel.* Seamus Heaney.
"Leaf membranes lid the window." CIP
Northern Ireland: Two Comments. Seamus Deane. CIP
Northern Legion, A. Sir Herbert Read. SeCePo
Northern pair, we waive the name, A. The Power of Innocence. "C. G. H." NOEC
Northern Seas, The. William Howitt. GN
Northern Spring, A. Gene Baro. NePoEA-2
Northern Star, The. *Unknown.* HBV-1
Northern Suburb, A. John Davidson. NBM; OBNC
Northern Vigil, A. Bliss Carman. OBEV; OBVV; PeCV
Northern Water Thrush. D. G. Jones. PeCV
Northern Wind/ sweeping down from the Sahara. Exile in Nigeria. Ezekiel Mphahlele. PBA
Northumberland Betrayed by Douglas [*or* Dowglas]. *Unknown.* ESPB; OxBB
Northward. Dominick J. Lepore. AMV-80
Northwest Airlines (My Emergency Instructions Were in Chinese). Fred Chappell. HoPM
Northwind. Gene Baro. NePoEA-2
Northwind dies half way to the Gobi Desert, A. I Lie on the Chilled Stones of the Great Wall. Stephen Shu Ning Liu. BrSi
Northwind fallen, in the newstarrèd night, The. The Hesperides. Tennyson. OAEL-2; SyP
Norway. Norman Dubie. GeTw
Nosce Teipsum. Sir John Davies. SiPS
Sels.
Affliction. NOBE; OBSC
Dedication II: "Strongest and the noblest argument, The." SiPS
Dedication I: "To that clear majesty which in the north." SiPS
(To Queen Elizabeth.) OBSC
Knowledge and Reason. OBSC
(Much Knowledge, Little Reason.) ChTr
(What Is This Knowledge?) FaBoRV
Man, 3 *sts.* ElL; OBEV, 2 *sts.*
(I Know Myself a Man.) ChTr
(Which Is a Proud, and Yet a Wretched Thing.) WHA
Soul and the Body, The. CTC; NOBE; OBSC
(In What Manner the Soul[e] Is United to the Body.) LiTB; PoEL-2
Nose becomes a triangular history, The. Terra Cotta. K. Curtis Lyle. CNA
Nose, nose, jolly red nose. Mother Goose (*also appears in* Beaumont *and* Fletcher's "The Knight of the Burning Pestle"). FaBoCh; OxNR
Nosegay. Elizabeth J. Coatsworth. OBCA
("Violets, daffodils.") TiPo
Nosegay, A. John Reynolds. OBEV
Nosegay Always Sweet, for Lovers to Send for Tokens of Love at New Year's Tide, or for Fairings, A. William Hunnis. ElL
Noses are running at our house, The. A Winter Scene. Reed Whittemore. NCSH
Nostalgia. Walter de la Mare. CoBMV; LiTM
Nostalgia. D. H. Lawrence. PoA
Nostalgia. Louis MacNeice. OnYI
Nostalgia. Gertrude Millard. BPAW
Nostalgia. Karl Shapiro. AP; CMoP; CoAP; CoBMV; MP; NePA; TrJP; TwAmPo; TwCP; WaaP
Nostalgia for 70. Jim Wayne Miller. AMV-81
Nostalgia's a rough trip. Mainline. John Ditsky. AMV-80
Nostalgie d'Automne. Leslie Daiken. NeIP
Not a bark was heard, not a warning note. The Lay of the Vigilantes. *Unknown.* PoOW
Not a breath of air. Airey-Force Valley. Wordsworth. VLP
Not a Cloud in the Sky. Richard Armour. WhC
Not a drum was heard, not a funeral note. A Fragment. *Unknown.* FaBoPa
Not a drum was heard, not a funeral note. The Burial of Sir John Moore after [*or* at] Corunna. Charles Wolfe. AnIV; ChTr; EnRP; FaBoRV; FaFP; FaPoR; GN; GTBS; GTBS-P; HBV-2; HBVY; NOBE; OBEV; OBRV; OBWP; OnYI; OxBI; PaPo; PoRA; RoGo; TreF; WaaP; WBLP; WHA
Not a laugh was heard, not a frivolous note. The Burial of the Bachelor. *Unknown.* FaBoPa
Not a line of her writing have I. Thoughts of Phena [at News of Her Death]. Thomas Hardy. EBVV; NoP; OxBTC
Not a sign of life we rouse. Battery Moving Up to a New Position from Rest Camp: Dawn. Robert Nichols. MMA
Not a Sou Had He Got. "Thomas Ingoldsby." *Fr.* The Ingoldsby Legends: The Cynotaph. FaBoCo; HBV-1
Not a sound disturbs the air. A Midsummer Noon in the Australian Forest. Charles Harpur. PoAu-1
Not a sound to pull. There Is Something I Want to Say. Alex Kuo. BrSi
Not a thing on the river McCluskey did fear. The Little Brown Bulls. *Unknown.* AmFP; BaBo; OuSiCo
Not a tree but the tree. There Is Only One of Everything. Margaret Atwood. NOBC
Not a viper with milk beneath its tongue. Who Will Give Cover? Anadad Eldan, *tr. by* Ruth Nevo. VWA
Not All Immaculate. Laura Riding. Three Sermons to the Dead, II. LiTA
Not all of them must suffer. Some. Saints. George Garrett. EaLo
Not all of them were human. The Village of Tudda. Kenneth Patchen. VGW
Not all of us were warm, not all of us. Spring. James Still. GrPl
Not all pale Hecate's direful charms. Lines Occasioned by the Burning of Some Letters. Sarah Dixon. NOEC
Not all the time. People. Orban Veli Kanik, *tr. by* Talat Sait Halman. LLLT
Not All There. Robert Frost. FaBoCo
Not all thy flushing suns are set. An Ode to Master Endymion Porter, upon His Brother's Death. Robert Herrick. CaPo
Not Alone for Mighty Empire. William Pierson Merrill. AH, *with music;* TrPWD
Not alone in Palestine those blessed Feet have trod. "Where the Blessed Feet Have Trod." "Michael Field." OxBoCh
Not alwayes give a melting kiss. Johannes Secundus, *tr. fr. Latin by* Thomas Stanley. *Fr.* Basia, VIII. OBVE
Not always as the whirlwind's rush. The Call of the Christian. Whittier. NOCV
Not always to the swift the race. The Law of Averages. "Troubadour." FiBHP; InMe
Not an editorial-writer, bereaved with bartlett. Portrait of the Poet as Landscape. A. M. Klein. NOBC
Not an epic, being not loosely architectured. King John's Castle. Thomas Kinsella. OxBI
Not another bite, not another cigarette. Search. Raymond Souster. ELU; OBCV
Not any sunny tone. Emily Dickinson. TwAmPo
Not as all other women are. My Love. James Russell Lowell. BLPL; FaBoBe; HBV-1
"Not as Black Douglas, bannered, trumpeted." Two Wise Generals. Ted Hughes. MoBS
Not as height rises into lightness. Breadth. Circle. Desert. Monarch. Month. Wisdom. John Hollander. PoA
Not as the white nations. The Black Madonna. Albert Rice. CDC
Not as These. Dante Gabriel Rossetti. The House of Life, LXXV. VLP
Not as they planned it or will plan again. The Day. Witter Bynner. PGD
Not as when some great captain falls. Abraham Lincoln. Richard Henry Stoddard. AA; FaBoBe; PAH
Not as you had dreamed was the battle's issue. To a Young Leader of the First World War. Stefan George, *tr. by* E. B. Ashton. WaaP

Not at midnight, not at morning, O sweet city. Caryatid. Léonie Adams. LiTM; MoVE
Not at night, no, altogether, tomorrow. No. Natan Zach, *tr. by* Laya Firestone. VWA
Not at the first sight, nor with a dribbed shot. Astrophel and Stella, II. Sir Philip Sidney. OAEL-1; SiPS
Not because of their beauty—though they are slender. The Twins. Judith Wright. PoAu-2
Not because of victories. Te Deum. Charles Reznikoff. TrJP; VWA
Not because of you, not because of me, just that. Natalya Gorbanyevskaya, *tr. fr. Russian by* Daniel Weissbort. BoWoP
Not because you didn't call. The Heart Has Its Reasons. Felice Picano. PeHV
Not being Breedlove, whose immortal skid. To Dorothy on Her Exclusion from the *Guinness Book of World Records.* X. J. Kennedy. Psk
Not Being Oedipus. John Heath-Stubbs. OxBC; TEP
Not-Being was not, Being was not then. Brahma, the World Idea. *Unknown. Fr.* The Rig-Veda. WGRP
Not Being Wise. Virginia Elson. AMV-80
Not believing that igneous dream. Nothing Inside and Nothing Out. Ray Amorosi. FiCP
Not Blindly in the Dark. Robert M. Stanley. AMV-81
Not born to the forest are we. Song of the Camels. Elizabeth J. Coatsworth. FaPON
Not but they die, the teasers and the dreams. The Teasers. William Empson. OxBTC
Not by Bread Alone. *Unknown, tr. fr. Greek by* James Terry White. PoLF; TreFT
Not by chance/ the cock sparrow. Christographia 35. Eugene Warren. AMV-80
Not by hammering the furious word. Harlem Riot, 1943. Pauli Murray. PoBA
Not by lost killers stranded. The Biggest Killing. Edward Dorn. CoPo; VGW
Not by the ball or brand. Vanquished. Francis Fisher Browne. AA; HBV-2
Not by the poets. Discovery of This Time. Archibald MacLeish. LiTA; WaP
Not by wayout hairdos, bulbous Afro blowouts and certainly. Only in This Way. Margaret Goss Burroughs. BlSi
Not Canaan and its cities, the splendor of towers. Moses on Mount Nebo. Abraham Regelson, *tr. by* Richard Flantz. VWA
Not caring to observe the Wind. Of Loving at First Sight. Edmund Waller. SeCP
Not, Celia, that I juster am. To Celia [*or* Song *or* Song to Celia]. Sir Charles Sedley. AWP; CavP; FaBoEn; GTBS; GTBS-P; NOBE; OBEV; OBS; SeCePo; ViBoPo
Not Changed, but Glorified. *Unknown.* STF
Not "common speech." Denise Levertov. *Fr.* A Common Ground. PP
Not Dead. Robert Graves. HBMV
Not drowsihood and dreams and mere idleness. In Sleep. Richard Burton. AA
Not drunk is he, who from the floor. Thomas Love Peacock. *Fr.* The Misfortunes of Elphin. ViBoPo
Not easy to state the change you made. Love Letter. Sylvia Plath. NOBA
Not entirely enviable, however envied. The Master. W. S. Merwin. NePoEA
Not even dried-up leaves. Thesis, Antithesis, and Nostalgia. Alan Dugan. CAD; PCP
Not even for a moment. He knew, for one thing, what he was. Leda. Mona Van Duyn. NMM
Not even in dreams/ Can I meet him anymore. Lady Ise, *tr. fr. Japanese by* Donald Keene. WPOW
Not even my pride will suffer much. Theme and Variations. Edna St. Vincent Millay. SBG
Not even the angels could bring a breath of air. The Old Biograph Girl. Margaret Benbow. AMV-81
Not even when the early birds. The Rabbit. W. H. Davies. BoAnP
Not Every Day Fit for Verse. Robert Herrick. PoRA
Not every man has gentians in his house. Bavarian Gentians. D. H. Lawrence. CMoP; FaBoCh; FaBoMo; GoJo; GTBS-P; HAP; InPK; InPS; LiTB; NoAM; NOBE; NoP; OAEL-2, 2 *versions;* OAEP; PAI; PPoe; SeCeV; SOTW; ViBoPo
Not far/ From the cat dropped. The Street. Gary Soto. NPAW
Not far advanc'd was morning day. The Battle [*or* Marmion and Douglas]. Sir Walter Scott. *Fr.* Marmion, VI. EnRP; WHA
Not far beyond the town wild flowers grow. Sanctuary. Clifford Dyment. PoA
Not far from Cambridge, close to Trumpington. The Reeve's Tale. Chaucer, *mod. version. by* Frank Ernest Hill. *Fr.* The Canterbury Tales. UnTE
Not far from old Kinvara, in the merry month of May. The Ould Plaid Shawl. Francis A. Fahy. HBV-1
Not far from Paris, in fair Fontainebleau. The Angelus. Florence Earle Coates. HBV-2
Not far from these Phoenician Dido stood. Dido among the Shades. Virgil, *tr. by* Dryden. *Fr.* The Aeneid, VI. OBS
Not fifty summers yet have passed thy clime. Oliver Goldsmith, the Younger. *Fr.* The Rising Village. OBCV
Not fighting if for once. Insomnia. Elizabeth Zelvin. AMV-80
Not Flesh of Brass. Bible, *O.T.* Job, VI: 1-13. TrJP
Not for Its Own Sake. Hazel Littlefield. GoYe
Not for me a giantess. Requirements. Niarchus, *tr. by* Wallace Rice. ErPo
Not for one single day. The Day—the Way. John Oxenham. TRV
Not for our lands, our wide-flung prairie wealth. We Thank Thee! Thomas Curtis Clark. PGD
Not for That City. Charlotte Mew. MoBrPo
Not for the broken bodies. Broken Bodies. Louis Golding. HBMV
Not for the fishermen's sake. Backwater Pond: The Canoeists. W. S. Merwin. PoPl
Not for the promise of the laboured field. Ode to the Poppy. Henrietta Oneil. WPE
Not forgetting Ko-jen, that. More Foreign Cities. Charles Tomlinson. NePoEA-2
Not Fortune's worshipper, nor Fashion's fool. Apologia pro Vita Sua. Pope. *Fr.* Epistle to Dr. Arbuthnot. NOBE
Not from my reverent sires hath come. Poet's Prayer. Adelaide Love. TrPWD
Not from successful love alone. Halcyon Days. Walt Whitman. NePA; OxBA
Not from that/ could you get it. The City. Robert Creeley. LCAP
Not from the earth, or skies. Health of Body Dependent on Soul. Jones Very. WGRP
Not from the glory of the cloud's pile and rift. Elegy on the Eve. George Barker. WaaP
Not from the stars do I my judgement pluck. Sonnets, XIV. Shakespeare. MasP
Not from the unmapped valleys of darkness, nor. Hall of Ocean Life. John Hollander. PoA
Not from the whole wide world I chose thee. Song. Richard Watson Gilder. *Fr.* The New Day. AA
Not from This Anger. Dylan Thomas. LiTB
("Not from this anger, anticlimax after.") PoA
Not from Titania's Court do I. Hob Gobbling's Song. James Russell Lowell. OBCA
Not furred nor wet, the pointing words yet make. Beaver Pond. Anne Marriott. NOBC
Not Going with It. Zali Gurevitch, *tr. fr. Hebrew by* Gabriel Levin. VWA
Not gold, but only man can make. *Unknown. Fr.* A Nation's Strength. AmFN; FaPON
Not greatly moved with awe am I. The Two Deserts. Coventry Patmore. BoNaP
Not guns, not thunder, but a flutter of clouded drums. Fireworks. Babette Deutsch. NYBP; OFD
Not he who holds the sceptre high atop the eagle's throne. Why the Resurrection Was Revealed to Women. Catharina Regina von Greiffenberg, *tr. by* Michael Hamburger. PBWP
Not Heat Flames Up and Consumes. Walt Whitman. NePA
Not Heaving from My Ribb'd Breast Only. Walt Whitman. NePA
Not hell but a street, not. 209 Canal. Richard Howard. NYP; TAP
Not Her, She Aint No Gypsy. Al Young. GP
Not Here. Edmund Wilson. PoA
Not Here, O Apollo. Matthew Arnold. *See* Song of Callicles, The.
Not Honey. Hilda Doolittle ("H. D."). MoPo; TwAmPo
(Fragment 113.) LiTA
Not—"How did he die?" But—"How did he live?" The Measure of a Man. *Unknown.* BLPL; PoLF; STF
Not I. Robert Louis Stevenson. NA; NOBL
Not I ("Not I, but Christ"). *Unknown.* BLRP
Not I, but God. Annie Johnson Flint. STF
Not I myself know all my love for thee. The Dark Glass. Dante Gabriel Rossetti. The House of Life, XXXIV. HBV-1
Not I, not I, but the wind that blows through me! Song of a Man Who Has Come Through. D. H. Lawrence. ChMP; CMoP; CoBMV; FaBoMo; GTBS-P; InPS; LiTM; MoPo; NoAM; OxBTC; SeCeV; ViBoPo
Not Ideas about the Thing but the Thing Itself. Wallace Stevens. HAP; LCAP; TAP; ViBoPo
Not if men's tongues and angels' all in one. Shakespeare. Swinburne. TrGrPo
Not, I'll not, carrion comfort, Despair, not feast on thee. Carrion Comfort [*or* Sonnet]. Gerard Manley Hopkins. CABA; CMoP; FaBoEn; HeIP; InPK; LiTB; MoPo; MoVE; NoAM; NoP; OAEL-2; OAEP; OBNC; OxBoCh; PoEL-5; PPP; TEP

Not in a silver casket cool with pearls. Edna St. Vincent Millay. CMoP; VGW
Not in Dumb Resignation. John Hay. WGRP
(Thy Will Be Done.) WBLP
Not in India, where fire rivers are. Jalal al-Din Rumi, *tr. fr. Persian.* ILwL
Not in my saddle, but above it. Indian Summer: Montana, 1956. W. M. Ransom. CDW
Not in our time, O Lord. Hilda Doolittle ("H. D."). *Fr.* Tribute to the Angels. NOBA
Not in rich furniture, or fine array. The H. Communion. George Herbert. AnAnS-1
Not in sleep I saw it, but in daylight. Kindly Vision. Otto Julius Bierbaum, *tr. by* Jethro Bithell. AWP
Not in the ancient abbey. Threnody for a Poet. Bliss Carman. CaP
Not in the cities, nor among fabricated towers. Boulder Dam. May Sarton. SaC
Not in the crises of events. The Spirit's Epochs. Coventry Patmore. *Fr.* The Angel in the House. EBEV; GBL; GoBC
Not in the dire, ensanguined front of war. The Men of the *Maine.* Clinton Scollard. PAH
Not in the Guide-Books. Elizabeth Jennings. LiTM; MP; NePoEA
Not in the rustle of water, the air's noise. Night in Martindale. Kathleen Raine. NeBP
Not in the sepulchre Thou art. Passiontide Communion. Katharine Tynan. TrPWD
Not in the silence only. My Prayer. Horatius Bonar. BLRP
Not in the sky. The Lost Pleiad. William Gilmore Simms. AA
Not in the world of light alone. The Living Temple. Oliver Wendell Holmes. *Fr.* The Autocrat of the Breakfast Table. AA; AP
Not in those climes where I have late been straying. To Ianthe. Byron. *Fr.* Childe Harold's Pilgrimage. FaBoEn; OBNC
Not in thy body is thy life at all. Life-in-Love. Dante Gabriel Rossetti. The House of Life, XXXVI. HAP; VLP
Not in Vain. *Unknown.* BLRP
Not in works or vain endeavors. The God in Whom We Trust. *Unknown.* STF
Not Iris in Her Pride. George Peele. *Fr.* The Arraignment of Paris. ViBoPo
Not Jerusalem—lowly Bethlehem. Lowly Bethlehem. Count Zinzendorf. TrAS
Not just folklore, or. Fast Ball. Jonathan Williams. NeAP
Not Just for the Ride. *At. to* Cosmo Monkhouse. *See* Limerick: "There was a young lady of Niger."
Not just the temples, lifting. Waiting for the Fire. Philip Appleman. SOTS
Not Just Yet. Carter Revard. VoR
Not Knowing, *sel.* Mary Gardiner Brainard.
"I know not what shall befall me: God hangs a mist o'er my eyes." TRV
Not-Knowing. Dawn Hinshaw. AMV-81
Not knowing in what season this again. Parting: 1940. John Frederick Nims. PoA
Not knowing where he was or how he got there. A Bewilderment at the Entrance of the Fat Boy into Eden. Daryl Hine. NOBC; OBCV
Not Late Enough. Hazel Townson. PV
Not least, 'tis ever my delight. Morning. Philip Henry Savage. AA
Not less because in purple I descended. Tea at the Palaz of Hoon. Wallace Stevens. FaBoMo; PoA
Not light of love, lady! The Lover Exhorteth His Lady to Be Constant. *Unknown.* OBSC
Not like a Cypress. Yehuda Amichai, *tr. fr. Hebrew by* Stephen Mitchell. VWA
Not like the brazen giant of Greek Fame. The New Colossus. Emma Lazarus. AmFN; FaBV; FaFP; FaPo; FaPON; FPL; PAL; PGD; PoLF; PoPl; PrIm; SBG; TreFS; TRV; WPE
Not lips of mine have ever said. In Youth. Evaleen Stein. AA
Not long ago from hence I went. The Lusty Fryer of Flanders. *Unknown.* CoMu
Not long ago it was a bird. A Volunteer's Grave. William Alexander Percy. HBMV
Not long this transport held its place. The Third Voice. "Lewis Carroll." *Fr.* The Three Voices. VLP
Not Lost, but Gone Before. Caroline Elizabeth Sarah Norton. BLRP; PaPo; WBLP
Not Lost in the Stars. Bruce Bliven. QQQ
Not lost or won but above all endeavor. Fidelity. Trumbull Stickney. LiTA; TwAmPo
Not Lotte. Katherine Hoskins. ErPo
Not magnitude, not lavishness. Greek Architecture. Herman Melville. NoP
"Not Marble nor the Gilded Monuments." Archibald MacLeish. AP; BoLoP; CMoP; CoBMV; HoPM; MoAB; MP; NIP; PoRA; TwCP; ViBoPo
Not marble, nor the gilded monuments. Sonnets, LV. Shakespeare. AWP; BLPL; CABA; CTC; EnRePo; FaBoEn; FaFP; FF; HeIP; InPK; LiTB; LoBV; MasP; NIP; NOBE; NoP; OAEL-1; OAEP; OBSC; PAI; PeHV; PoEL-2; PoRA; PP; PPoe; SeCeV; TEP; TrGrPo; ViBoPo
Not Marching Away to Be Killed. Jean Overton Fuller. FF
Not marching in the fields of Thrasimene. Doctor Faustus. Christopher Marlowe. OAEL-1
Not Me. Shel Silverstein. *See* Slithergadee, The.
Not merely for our pleasure, but to purge. "Ej Blot til Lyst." William Morton Payne. AA
Not merely in matters material, but in things of the spirit. America First! G. Ashton Oldham. PGD
Not met and marred with the year's whole turn of grief. James Agee. *Fr.* Lyrics. MoAmPo; PoPl
Not midst the lightning of the stormy fight. Stonewall Jackson. Henry Lynden Flash. AA; PAH
Not mine own fears, nor the prophetic soul. Sonnets, CVII. Shakespeare. AWP; CABA; CTC; EBEV; FiP; HAP; LiTB; LoBV; MasP; NoP; OAEL-1; OAEP; OBSC; PPoe; SeCeV
Not mine to draw the cloth-yard shaft. The Satirist. Harry Lyman Koopman. AA
Not my hands but green across you now. The Lady in Kicking Horse Reservoir. Richard Hugo. CoAP; LCAP; NoP
Not now, but in the coming years. Some Time We'll Understand. Maxwell N. Cornelius. BLRP; WBLP
Not now expecting to live forever. Dublin Bay. Ewart Milne. NeIP
Not now the sun yellows the vine. Sparrows in College Ivy. Edgar Wolfe. AMV-81
Not of all my eyes see, wandering on the world. Ashboughs. Gerard Manley Hopkins. VLP
Not, of course, the monster hunched downtown. Dome Poem. Dave Smith. PoA
Not of Itself but Thee. *Unknown, tr. fr. Greek by* Richard Garnett. AWP
Not of ourselves are we free. Heritage. Mary Gilmore. CBAP
Not of School Age. Robert Frost. GLGT
Not of the princes and prelates with periwigged charioteers. A Consecration. John Masefield. HBMV; MoAB; MoBrPo; NoAM; WHA
Not of the sunlight. Follow the Gleam. Tennyson. *Fr.* Merlin and the Gleam, IX. TreFT
Not oft such marvel the years reveal. The People's King. Lyman Whitney Allen. PGD
Not Often. Ray Fraser. NeAC
Not often *con brio*, but *andante, andante*. Stanley Matthews. Alan Ross. LiSp; OxBTC
Not on a prayerless bed, not on a prayerless bed. Exhortation to Prayer. Margaret Mercer. AA
Not on an altar shall mine eyes behold thee. Real Presence. Ivan Adair. WGRP
Not on our golden fortunes builded high. The Forgotten Man. Edwin Markham. BLPL; PoLF
Not on sad Stygian shore, nor in clear sheen. Méllonta taûta. Samuel Butler. GLGT
Not on Sunday Night. *Unknown.* STF
Not on the neck of prince or hound. The Splendid Spur. Sir Arthur Quiller-Couch. HBVY
Not One Is Turned Away from God. Dorothy Conant Stroud. STF
Not one of them has seen it, but the fox. Field Trip. Gary Miranda. AMV-81
Not one poem about an animal, she said. Florida. Dannie Abse. OxBC
Not Only around Our Infancy. James Russell Lowell. *Fr.* The Vision of Sir Launfal. FaFP; NePA
Not only how far away, but the way that you say it. Judging Distances. Henry Reed. Lessons of the War, II. BoLoP; ChMP; GTBS-P; HeIP; LiTB; MoAB; NIP; NOBE; SoSe
Not only once, and long ago. Christ Is Crucified Anew. John Richard Moreland. PGD
Not only that thy puissant arm could bind. Wellington. Benjamin Disraeli. OBVV
Not only the soot from the city air. The Floor Is Dirty. Edward Field. NeAP
Not only we, the latest seed of Time. Godiva. Tennyson. BeLS
Not Only Where God's Free Winds Blow, *with music.* Shepherd Knapp. AH
Not only with no sense of shame. Tennyson. FaBoEE
"Not ours," say some, "the thought of death to dread." The Great Misgiving. Sir William Watson. HBV-2; OBVV
Not Ours the Vows. Bernard Barton. HBV-1
Not out of the East but the West. The Star of Sangamon. Lyman Whitney Allen. PGD
Not overwhelming, this morning's little dream. The Know. Kathleen Fraser. NPGG

Not Palaces [an Era's Crown]. Stephen Spender. CMoP; FaBoMo; LiTB; LiTM; MoAB; MoBrPo; NoAM; NoP; WaP
Not Pallas, not ev'n Spleen it self could blame. Ovid, *tr. by* John Gay. *Fr.* Metamorphoses, VI. OBVE
Not picnics or pageants or the improbable. Terror. Robert Penn Warren. MoPo; NePA; PoA; WaP
Not Poppy, nor Mandragora. Shakespeare. *Fr.* Othello, III, iii. WHA
Not power nor the storied hand of God. Allen Tate. *Fr.* Sonnets of the Blood. PoA
Not Quite Fair. H. S. Leigh. InMe
Not quite organs, they sprout from the ankles. Feet, a Sermon. James Paul. HoAn
Not Quite Spring. Lyn Lifshin. NeAC
Not quite yet. Dining Out with Doug and Frank. James Schuyler. NYP
Not Ragged-and-Tough. *Unknown.* ChTr; FaBoNo
Not realizing. Six Feet Under. Janet Campbell Hale. VoR
Not rose of death. Rose in the Afternoon. Jenny Joseph. BrRo
Not roses, joyn'd with lillies, make. Pure Platonicke. George Daniel. CavP
Not Saying Much. Linda Gregg. NPGG
Not Seeing Is Believing. Paul Petrie. TAP
Not serried ranks with flags unfurled. What Makes a Nation Great? Alexander Blackburn. WBLP
Not she with traitorous kiss her Saviour stung. Woman. Eaton Stannard Barrett. HBV-1; OnYI; OxBI
Not slowly wrought, nor treasured for their form. Snowflakes. Howard Nemerov. PCP
Not so, for living yet are those. A Dead Past. *At. to* C. C. Munson. BLRP; WBLP
Not-so-good Earth, The. Bruce Dawe. CBAP
Not so in haste, my heart. Be Still, My Heart. *Unknown.* STF
Not solely that the future she destroys. George Meredith. Modern Love, XII. GBL; TEP; ViBoPo
Not soon shall I forget. Farewell. Katharine Tynan. CH
"Not strangeness, but strange likeness." Geoffrey Hill. Mercian Hymns, XXIX. FaBoMo; HAP
Not Such Your Burden. Agathias, *tr. fr. Greek by* William M. Hardinge. AWP
Not sure if he heard. Philonous' Paradox. Chris Gilbert. FAZ
Not that broad path chose he, which whoso wills. Unknown Warrior. Elizabeth Daryush. SUMH
Not that by this disdain. The Repulse. Thomas Stanley. AnAnS-2; MeLP; MePo; OBS
Not That Far. May Miller. BlSi
Not that God's dead. Jacob's Winning. Richard Sherwin. VWA
Not that he promised not to windowshop. One Man's Wife. Philip Booth. NIP; VGW
Not that I have cause for celebration. New Year's Eve. H. B. Mallalieu. WaP
Not that I wish to take the liberty. Non Que Je Veuille Ôter la Liberté. Pernette de Guillet, *tr. by* Raymond Oliver. WPOW
Not That, If You Had Known. Trumbull Stickney. NCEP
Not that my hand could make of stubborn stone. Death-Bed Reflections of Michel-Angelo. Hartley Coleridge. EyDe
Not that the earth is changing, O my God! On Refusal of Aid between Nations. Dante Gabriel Rossetti. EBEV; LoBV; VLP
Not that the Pines were darker there. The Long Voyage. Malcolm Cowley. NePA; TwAmPo
Not that thy hand is soft, is sweet, is white. Henry Constable. *Fr.* Diana. OBSC
Not that we are weary. In the Trenches. Richard Aldington. MMA
Not the attendance of stones. Black Maps. Mark Strand. PoA
Not the beautiful youth with features of bloom & brightness. Beauty. Walt Whitman. WeW
Not the branch that taps at the widow. Leaving Mexico One More Time. Constance Urdang. AMV-80
Not the delicate mare who came nosing. White Horse of the Father, White Horse of the Son. William Pitt Root. MAYP
Not the last struggles of the Sun. On the Death of Southey. Walter Savage Landor. OBVV
Not the round natural world, not the deep mind. Frederick Goddard Tuckerman. Sonnets, I, xxvii. NoP
Not There. *Unknown.* STF
Not these appal/ The soul. Faith's Difficulty. Theodore Maynard. TrPWD
Not Thinking of America. Judith Kroll. AmPA
Not This Leaf Haunts Me. Tony Cosier. AMV-81
Not this spring shall return again. Aftermath. Margaret McCulloch. PGD
Not those patient men who knocked and were unheeded. 1918-1941. Robert D. Fitzgerald. CBAP
Not Thou but I. Philip Bourke Marston. BLPA; BLPL
Not Three—but One. Esther Lilian Duff. HBMV
Not to be confused. The Origin of Species. Myra Sklarew. SUW
Not to Be Ministered To. Maltbie D. Babcock. TrPWD
Not to be the mother of solitude will I give myself. A Busy Man Speaks. Robert Bly. ConAP
"Not to be tuneless in old age!" Henry Wadsworth Longfellow. Austin Dobson. HBV-2
Not to dance with her. A Triviality. Waring Cuney. CDC
Not to do but work. The Pessimist. Ben King. TreFT
Not to Forget Miss Dickinson. Marshall Schacht. LiTM
Not to Keep. Robert Frost. CMoP; OxBA
Not to know vice at all, and keepe true state. Epode. Ben Jonson. SeCP; SeCV-1
Not to lose the feel of the mountains. The Double-headed Snake. John Newlove. MoCV
Not to Love. Robert Herrick. CaPo; OAEP
Not to March. Kris Hackleman. AMV-80
Not to say what everyone else was saying. Different. Clere Parsons. FaBoTw
Not to scatter bread and gold. Love's Nobility. Emerson. *Fr.* Celestial Love. TreF
Not to sigh and to be tender. Aphra Behn. BoWoP
Not to the butcher did he pass. The Old Ox. George Rostrevor Hamilton, *after* Addaios of Makedon. FaBoEE
Not to the fury of the storm, though loud. The Pine of Whiting Wood. John P. Sjolander. BPAW
Not to the I-80 where. Where I Walk in Nebraska. Nancy G. Westerfield. AMV-80
Not to the swift, the race. Reliance. Henry van Dyke. FaFP
Not to the weak alone. The Call to the Strong. William Pierson Merrill. BLRP
Not to Us, Not unto Us, Lord, *with music. Unknown.* AH
Not Tonight, Josephine. Colin Curzon. ErPo
Not too chary, not too fast. Requirements. Rufinus, *tr. by* Wallace Rice. ErPo
Not too lean, and not too fat. Requirements. Rufinus, *tr. by* Wallace Rice. ErPo
Not-too-near slip softly by, The. David McCord. Convalescence, I. WhC
Not too old, and not too young. Requirements. Honestus, *tr. by* Wallace Rice. ErPo
Not too pallid, as if bleacht. Requirements. Xenos Palaestes, *tr. by* Wallace Rice. ErPo
Not twice a twelvemonth you appear in print. Epilogue to the Satires. Pope. OAEL-1
Not Ulysses, no, nor any other man. Sonnet I. Louise Labé, *tr. fr. Italian by* Willis Barnstone. BoWoP
Not Understood. Thomas Bracken. BLPA
Not unto the Forest. Margaret Widdemer. HBMV
Not unto us, not unto us. America Prays. Arthur Gordon Field. PGD
Not unto us, O Lord. Non Nobis. Henry Cust. OBEV; OBVV
Not upon earth, as you suppose. "Tu Non Se' in Terra, Si Come Tu Credi." Kathleen Raine. NeBP; WPE
Not us, I say, not us. Psalm CXV. Countess of Pembroke. NOCV
Not walking, in my dreams, my dreams. Infidelity. Olga Berggolts, *tr. by* Daniel Weissbort. BoWoP
Not Wanting Myself. Linda Gregg. NPGG
Not Waving but Drowning. Stevie Smith. FF; GTBS-P; HAP; HeIP; NoAM; NOBE; NoP; OAEL-2; OxBTC; POL; PPP; PrIm; SBG; TEP; WeW
Not weaned yet, without comprehension loving. Love's Immaturity. E. J. Scovell. GBL; LiTB
Not what, but Whom, I do believe. Credo. John Oxenham. BLRP
Not what I am, O Lord, but what Thou art. More of Thee. Horatius Bonar. BLRP
Not what you get, but what you give. Of Giving. Arthur Guiterman. TiPo
Not when, with self dissatisfied. With Self Dissatisfied. Frederick L. Hosmer. TrPWD
Not where the battle red. On the Death of "Jackson." *Unknown.* PAH
Not while, but long after he had told me. Each Bird Walking. Tess Gallagher. MAYP; SV
Not Wholly Lost. Raymond Souster. OBCV
Not with a club the heart is broken. Emily Dickinson. AP; LiTA; WHA
Not with Libations. Edna St. Vincent Millay. *See* Sonnet: "Not with libations, but with shouts and laughter."
Not with more glories, in the ethereal plain. The Voyage on the Thames. Pope. *Fr.* The Rape of the Lock, II. EBEV; FaBoEn; NOBE; NOEC; ViBoPo; WHA
Not with my hands. Benediction. Donald Jeffrey Hayes. AmNP; PoNe
Not with slow, funereal sound. An Ode, on the Unveiling of the Shaw Memorial on Boston Common, May 31st, 1897. Thomas Bailey Aldrich. AA; HBV-2; PAH
Not with vain tears, when we're beyond the sun. Sonnet. Rupert Brooke. BrPo

Not without Beauty. John A. B. McLeish. CaP
Not without heavy grief of heart did he. Epitaphs, VIII. Gabriello Chiabrera, *tr. by* Wordsworth. AWP
Not working, not breathing. Autumn. Bella Akhmadulina, *tr. by* Barbara Einzig. BoWoP
Not writ in water nor in mist. For John Keats, Apostle of Beauty. Countee Cullen. Four Epitaphs, 2. CDC
Not wrongly moved by this dismaying scene. Sonnet. William Empson. LiTM; WaP
"Not ye who have stoned, not ye who have smitten us," cry. Arraignment. Helen Gray Cone. AA
Not yesterday, nor yet a day. The Annunciation. Margaret Devereaux Conway. ISi
Not yet dead, not yet alone. Osip Mandelstam, *tr. fr. Russian by* James Greene OBVE
Not yet, dear love, not yet: the sun is high. The Parting Hour. Olive Custance. HBV-1
Not yet! Do not touch. The Turning of the Leaves. Vernon Watkins. NeBP
Not yet enslaved, not wholly vile. O My Mother Isle! Samuel Taylor Coleridge. *Fr.* Ode on the Departing Year. FaBoPP
Not yet five, and the light. After Hours. Robert Mezey. NaP
Not yet, not yet; it's hardly four. One More Quadrille. Winthrop Mackworth Praed. OBRV
"Not yet, not yet; steady, steady!" Bunker Hill. George Henry Calvert. BeLS; FaBoBe; PAH
Not yet, not yet. The Tree. Joel Sloman. VGW
Not yet will those measureless fields be green again. The Cenotaph. Charlotte Mew. MMA; SUMH; WPE
Not you, lean quarterlies and swarthy periodicals. To the Film Industry in Crisis. Frank O'Hara. NoAM; NOBA; OBAL; SOTW
Nota: man is the intelligence of his soil. The Comedian as the Letter C. Wallace Stevens. NePA; OxBA; TwAmPo
Notably fond of music, I dote on a sweeter tone. The Clink of the Ice. Eugene Field. InMe
Notation in Haste. Elias Lieberman. GoYe
Note. Anthony Euwer. *Fr.* The Limeratomy. HBMV
Note/ O. O. Gabugah writes that he "was born in a taxicab right smack on 125th." "Boogie with O. O. Gabugah." Al Young. NPGG
Note-Book of a European Tramp, The, *sel.* Michael Hamburger.
"Townsman on his yielding bed, The." NePoEA
Note Delivered by a Female Impersonator. Heather McHugh. AmPA
Note from an Exhibition. Albert Goldbarth. AMV-81
Note from an Intimate Diary. Emanuel Litvinov. NeBP
Note from my dying sister stirs up, The. Bordello, Revisited. Eve Triem. GP
Note from the Pipes, A. Leonora Speyer. HBMV
Note how the desert takes form, easily as wax. In Scorching Time. Alex Stevens. AMV-81
Note in a Sanitorium. Ray Amorosi. FAZ
Note in Lieu of a Suicide. Donald Finkel. CoPo
Note Left in Jimmy Leonard's Shack, A. James Wright. NoP
Note of Humility, A. Arna Bontemps. PoNe
Note on Feeding. *Unknown.* FaBoUs
Note on Intellectuals. W. H. Auden. FiBHP; PoPl
Note on Lizard's Feet, A. James Van Rensselaer. BPAW
Note on Local Flora. William Empson. EBEV; FaBoMo; MoVE
Note on Master Crow, A. Jean Garrigue. BoAnP
Note on Modern Journalism during the Last Campaign. E. L. Mayo. FAZ
Note on Propertius 1.5. Fleur Adcock. BoLoP
Note on the Latin Gerunds, A. Richard Porson. FaBoCo
(On the Latin Gerunds.) FaBoUs
("When Dido found Aeneas would not come.") FaBoEE
Note on Wyatt, A. Kingsley Amis. WeW
Note the stump, a peach tree. Places and Ways to Live. Richard Hugo. GP
Note this survivor, bearing the mark of the violator. Swendenborg's Skull. Vernon Watkins. FaBoTw
Note to Olga (1966), A. Denise Levertov. CAPP
Note to Wang Wei. John Berryman. NYBP
Notes after Blacking Out. Gregory Corso. NeAP
Notes for a History of Poetry. David Daiches. PoA
Notes for a Lecture. David Ignatow. NNaP
Notes for a Movie Script. M. Carl Holman. AmNP; PoBA; PoNe
Notes for a Revised Sonnet. Edward Pygge. BXAP
Notes for a Sonnet. Edward Pygge. BXAP
Notes for a Speech. Amiri Baraka. CoPo
Notes for Albuquerque. Roberta Hill Whiteman. STE
Notes for Echo Lake 5. Michael Palmer. NPGG
Notes for My Son. Alex Comfort. LiTM; MoBrPo; NeBP; SeCePo
Notes for the Chart in 306. Ogden Nash. NYBP
Notes Found near a Suicide. Frank Horne. *See* Letters Found near a Suicide.
Notes from a Journey. Sam Hunt. OCNZ
Notes from a Slave Ship. Edward Field. PP
Notes from an Analyst's Couch. Anita Endrezze Probst. CDW
Notes Made in the Piazza San Marco. May Swenson. CoAP
Notes of an Interview. William Johnson Cory. NBM
Notes on a Certain Terribly Critical Piece. Reed Whittemore. PP
Notes on a Child's Coloring Book. Robert Patrick Dana. PoPl
Notes on a Girl. Peter Kane Dufault. ErPo
Notes on a Life to Be Lived. Robert Penn Warren. NYBP
Sels.
Blow, West Wind. NoAM
Small White House. NoAM
Ways of Day. NoAM
Notes on a Long Evening. David Phillips. NeAC
Notes on My Father, *sel.* Katerina Anghelaki-Rooke.
"Old man moved into his night, The." PBWP
Notes on the Post-Industrial Revolution. Edward Morin. FAZ
Notes to the Reader. Robert Bringhurst. NOBC
Notes toward a Supreme Fiction, *sels.* Wallace Stevens.
"And for what, except for you, do I feel love?" NOBA
"Begin, ephebe, by perceiving the idea." NOBA
"Bethou me, said sparrow, to the crackled blade." LiTM; MoPo
(Bethou Me, Said Sparrow.) CrMA; NePA
"First idea was not our own, The. Adam." NOBA
Great Statue of the General Du Puy, The. LiTA
"It feels good as it is without the giant." MoPo; NePA; NOBA
"It is the celestial ennui of apartments." MoPo; NePA
"Lion roars at the enraging desert, The." MoPo
"Major abstraction is the idea of man, The." NOBA
President Ordains the Bee to Be, The. LiTA
Soldier, There Is a War between the Mind. LiTM; NePA
We Reason of These Things. CrMA
Whistle Aloud, Too Weedy Wren. LiTA
Notes towards a Poem That Can Never Be Written. Margaret Atwood. NOBC
"Nothin' or everythin' it's got to be." Nocturne. John V. A. Weaver. HBMV
Nothin very bad happen to me lately. Henry's Confession. John Berryman. Dream Songs, LXXVI. LCAP; NaP; NoAM; TwCP
Nothing. Julia de Burgos, *tr. fr. Spanish by* Aliki *and* Willis Barnstone. BoWoP
Nothing. Walter de la Mare. WSC
Nothing. Charles Simic. NNaP
Nothing. Burns Singer. OxBS
Nothing/ substance utters or time. The Word. Basil Bunting. PoA
Nothing before, nothing behind. Faith. Whittier. TRV
Nothing Better. *Unknown.* STF
Nothing but a man. Nadia Tueni, *tr. fr. French by* Willis Barnstone. BoWoP
Nothing but Death. Pablo Neruda, *tr. fr. Spanish by* Robert Bly. EAS
Nothing but Image. Jody Swilky. AMV-81
Nothing but no and I, and I and no. Michael Drayton. Idea, V. GBL; PoEL-2
Nothing could make me sooner to confesse. Of the Progres[se] of the Soule; the Second Anniversary [*or* Anniversarie]. John Donne. AnAnS-1; SeCP
Nothing doing here. New England Greenhouse. Rennie McQuilkin. AMV-80
Nothing, either great or small. What Must I Do to Be Saved? *Unknown.* STF
Nothing Elegant. Gertrude Stein. *Fr.* Tender Buttons. PBWP
Nothing for a dirty man. All That Is Lovely in Men. Robert Creeley. NaP
Nothing Gold Can Stay. Norma Farber. AMV-81
Nothing Gold Can Stay. Robert Frost. AmPP; GrPl; MoAB; MoAmPo; NCSH; NOBA; PAI; PPP; SoSe; TAP; VGW; WHA
Nothing grows in vain. Use plants to heal. Creed of Mr. Nicholas Culpeper. Patricia Beer. OxBC
Nothing has been quite the same. After Reading the Reviews of "Finnegans Wake." Melville Cane. WhC
Nothing here is bitter. Wisdom. Phyllis Hanson. GoYe
Nothing if not utterly in death. So? James P. Vaughn. AmNP
Nothing in Rambling. *Unknown.* BluL
Nothing in this bright region melts or shifts. From the Highest Camp. Thom Gunn. MP; TwCP
Nothing Inside and Nothing Out. Ray Amorosi. FiCP
Nothing Is. Sun-Ra. PoBA
Nothing is better, I well think. The Leper. Swinburne. GBL
Nothing Is Enough. Laurence Binyon. MoBrPo
Nothing Is Lost. Anne Ridler. WPE

Nothing is new: we walk where others went. Nothing New. Robert Herrick. CaPo
Nothing is pacified. It will be. Written. Mary Ruelfe. AMV-81
Nothing is plumb, level or square. Love Song: I and Thou. Alan Dugan. AP; CAPP; FF; HoPM; InPK; NoAM; SoSe
Nothing is so beautiful as spring. Spring. Gerard Manley Hopkins. BoNaP; BrPo; EBCP; EBVV; FaBoEn; FaBV; HAP; InvP; LiTM; LO; MoAB; MoBrPo; MoVE; NoAM; NOBE; OAEL-2; OAEP; OBMV; OBNC; OxBoCh; SoSe; TrCP; VLP
Nothing is too small for my sarcasm. Immensity. Gerald Stern. AMV-80
Nothing like that road runs from me. A Cabin in Minnesota. Marvin Bell. HoPM
Nothing More than a Sister. *Unknown.* TDH
Nothing More Will Happen. Marge Piercy. NeAC
(Different Persuasions.) InPK
"Nothing moves," you say, and stare across the lawn. The Recruits. Ian Hamilton. NoAM
Nothing New. Robert Herrick. CaPo
Nothing, not the hotel's beige darkness, not. The Chelsea. Derek Walcott. NYP
Nothing now to mark the spot. Next Day [*or* Epilogue]. Rachel Field. *Fr.* A Circus Garland. OBCA; SoPo
Nothing older than stone but the soil and the sea and the sky. The Mason. Robert Farren. OnYI; OxBI
Nothing out of which to create a new, A. None. Josephine Miles. VGW
Nothing remained: Nothing, the wanton name. The Annihilation of Nothing. Thom Gunn. NePoEA-2; NoAM
Nothing Sacred. Roger Woddis. NOBL
Nothing sacred here: no hysterical woman chewing. Verse. Richmond Lattimore. PP
Nothing sings from these orange trees. On Watching the Construction of a Skyscraper. Burton Raffel. PCP
Nothing so difficult as a beginning. Romantic to Burlesque. Byron. *Fr.* Don Juan, IV. EnRP; FiP; OAEL-2
Nothing so sharply reminds a man he is mortal. Departure in the Dark. C. Day Lewis. ChMP; CoBMV; MoPo; MP; TwCP
Nothing so startles us as tumbleweeds in December. Weeds. Ann Stanford. GrPl
Nothing so true as what you once let fall. To a Lady; of the Characters of Women [*or* Epistle to a Lady]. Pope. *Fr.* Moral Essays, II. FaBoEn; NOEC; OAEL-1; OxBoLi
Nothing Strange. Tom Kryss. NeAC
Nothing that is said or done. At First. C. H. Sisson. OxBC
Nothing! thou elder brother ev'n to shade. Upon Nothing. Earl of Rochester. MePo; OBS; OBSV; PoEL-3; TrGrPo; ViBoPo
Nothing to Be Said. Philip Larkin. OxBTC
Nothing to be said about it, and everything. Dying. Robert Pinsky. AMV-81; MAYP
Nothing to do but work. The Pessimist [*or* The Sum of Life]. Ben King. BLPA; CTC; FaBoCo; FaBoNo; FaFP; InMe; NA; OBAL
Nothing to do, Nellie Darling. School Days. Will D. Cobb. TreFT
Nothing to Fear. Kingsley Amis. DBV; ErPo; OxBC
Nothing to Report. May Herschel-Clarke. SUMH
Nothing to Save. D. H. Lawrence. SOTW
Nothing to Say, You Say? Conrad Aiken. Preludes for Memnon, IX. LiTA; TwAmPo
Nothing to Wear. William Allen Butler. HBV-2; OBAL; PoLF
Nothing was left of me. A Dream of Burial. James Wright. NaP
Nothing wild. Inertia. Audrey McGaffin. NePoAm
Nothing will ever change beside this river. Changeless Shore. Sarah Leeds Ash. GoYe
Nothing will fill the salt caves our youth wore. Alone. E. J. Scovell. GBL
Nothing will give delight. Nausea. Catherine Davis. NePoEA
Nothing would sleep in that cellar, dank [*or* dark] as a ditch. Root Cellar. Theodore Roethke. AmPP; BoNaP; HeIP; NoP; PAI; PPP
Nothing you could know, or name, or say. Peppergrass. Stanley Plumly. LCAP
Nothingness. Aharon Amir, *tr. fr. Hebrew.* VWA
Nothing's going to become of anyone. Play. A. R. Ammons. PoA
Nothing's too good for the women. The Best Dance Hall in Iuka, Mississippi. Thomas Johnson. FAZ
Notice. David McCord. SoPo
Notice at the factory gate, The. Hands. Alex Glasgow. OBET
Notice the Convulsed Orange Inch of Moon. E. E. Cummings. VGW
Notice What This Poem Is Not Doing. William Stafford. LCAP
Noticing from what they talk about, and how they stand, or walk. Remembering Lunch. Douglas Dunn. OxBC
Notify someone of authority. If You See This Man. Thomas Lux. AmPA
Noting in slow sequence by waterclock of rain. The Walk in the Garden. Conrad Aiken. PoCh
Notions of freedom are tied up with drink. The Drunkards. Malcolm Lowry. NYBP
Notorious Glutton, The. Ann Taylor. OxBChV
Notre Dame. Osip Mandelstam, *tr. fr. Russian by* James Greene. OBVE
Notre Dame des Champs. J. M. Synge. SyP
Notre Dame des Petits. Louis Mercier, *tr. fr. French by* Liam Brophy. ISi
Notre Dame Perfected by Reflection. Harold Witt. HoAn
Nottamun Town. *Unknown.* FaBoNo; NCEP; OxBoLi
Nottingham Fair. *Unknown.* AmFP
Nottinghamshire Poacher, The. *Unknown.* OBET
Nou Goth Sonne under Wode. *Unknown. See* Now Goeth Sonne under Wode.
Nought have I to bring. November. Christina Rossetti. YeAr
Nought is on earth more sacred or divine. Spenser. *Fr.* The Faerie Queene, V, 7. OAEL-1
Nought loves another as itself. A Little Boy Lost. Blake. *Fr.* Songs of Experience. EnRP; OAEP; PAI; ViBoPo
Nought of the bridal will I tell. Sir Walter Scott. *Fr.* The Lay of the Last Minstrel, VI. OBRV
Nova. Robinson Jeffers. CMoP; HAP
Nova. Charles Levendosky. SOTS
Novel, The. Denise Levertov. AP; NoAM
Novella. Adrienne Rich. PPP
Novelty Shop, The. Duane Niatum. CDW
November. Margaret Atwood. NOBC
November. Laurence Binyon. SyP
November. Robert Bridges. NBM; OBNC; PBBP; PoEL-5
November. Alice Cary. OBCA
November. C. L. Cleaveland. HBV-1
November. Elizabeth J. Coatsworth. YeAr
November. Hartley Coleridge. Sonnets to the Seasons, XII. LoBV; OBNC; OBRV
November. Elizabeth Daryush. QFR
November. Aileen Fisher. SiSoSe; TiPo
November. Mahlon Leonard Fisher. HBV-1
November. F. W. Harvey. OxBTC
November. Thomas Hood. *See* No!
November. Ted Hughes. CMoP; GTBS-P; NePoEA-2; NMP; NoP
November. John Keble. *Fr.* Forest Leaves in Autumn. OBEV; OBVV
(Red o'er the Forest.) OxBoCh
("Red o'er the forest glows the setting sun.") OBNC
November. James Reaney. *Fr.* A Suit of Nettles. OBCV
November. Christina Rossetti. YeAr
November. Spenser. *Fr.* The Shepheardes Calender. PoEL-1
Dido My Dear, Alas, Is Dead, *sel.* ChTr
November. Elizabeth Stoddard. AA
November. Frederick Goddard Tuckerman. NOBA
November. Samuel S. Turner. AMV-80
November Afternoons. Sister Mary Madeleva. GoBC
November air, The. Hotel Sierra. David St. John. MAYP
November Blue. Alice Meynell. MoBrPo
November chill blaws loud wi' angry sugh. The Cotter's Saturday Night. Burns. OBEC
November comes. November. Elizabeth J. Coatsworth. YeAr
November Cotton Flower. Jean Toomer. CDC; NoAM; UnPo
November dawns and dewy-glooming downs. November in the Isle of Wight. Tennyson. *Fr.* Enoch Arden. FaBoPP
November Day at McClure's. Robert Bly. NU
November, 1806 ("Another year! another deadly blow"). Wordsworth. OBRV; OBWP
November Eves ("November evenings! Damp and still"). James Elroy Flecker. MoVE; SyP
November Fugitive. Henry Morton Robinson. GoYe
November Garden. Louise Driscoll. YeAr
November in Ettrick Forest. Sir Walter Scott. *Fr.* Marmion. BSV
(Ettrick Forest in November.) FaBoPP
("November's sky is chill and drear.") OBRV
November in the Isle of Wight. Tennyson. *Fr.* Enoch Arden. FaBoPP
November Morning. Evaleen Stein. YeAr
November Night. Adelaide Crapsey. FaPON; PAI
November Night, Edinburgh. Norman MacCaig. BSV; NMP
November, 1941. Roy Fuller. MoPo
November 1968. Adrienne Rich. NMM
November Poppies. Hilary Corke. NYBP
November Rain. Maud E. Uschold. YeAr
November should be cold and grey. Weather Vanes. Frances Frost. SiSoSe
November Snow. E. J. Carson. AMV-81
November Song. Mark Vinz. Psk
November Sun. Elizabeth Daryush. PBWP
November Sunday Morning. Alvin Feinman. CoAP
November Surf. Robinson Jeffers. CrMA; MoPo; OxBA
November the Fifth. Leonard Clark. OnUR
November through a Giant Copper Beech. Edwin Honig. NoAM; NYBP

November Twenty-sixth Nineteen Hundred and Sixty-three. Wendell Berry. AP; LiTM
November Walk. Susanne Doyle. AMV-81
November Wears a Paisley Shawl. Hilda Morris. YeAr
November woods are bare and still. Down to Sleep. Helen Hunt Jackson. GN
November's sky is chill and drear. November in Ettrick Forest [*or* Ettrick Forest in November]. Sir Walter Scott. *Fr.* Marmion. BSV; FaBoPP; OBRV
Novice, The. Edward Davison. ErPo
Novice when I came beneath thy gaze, A. Stanzas concerning Love. Stefan George, *tr. by* Ludwig Lewisohn. AWP
Novices, The. Denise Levertov. NaP
Now. Robert Browning. VLP
(Moment Eternal, The.) UnTE
Now. Mary Barker Dodge. AA
Now. Christopher Gilbert. MAYP
Now. Thomas Ken. OxBoCh
Now. Harriet Monroe. HBV-2
Now. Richard Murphy. The Battle of Aughrim, I. IPY
Now. William Stafford. NNaP
Now,/ asked sweet mama, let me. Milkcow Blues. *Unknown.* BluL
Now/ Change in the ocean. Everybody Ought to Make a Change. *Unknown.* BluL
Now/ Got offices in town. Lawyer Clark Blues. *Unknown.* BluL
Now/ I know the people. Street Car Blues. *Unknown.* BluL
Now/ with your head thrown back. I Tell of Another Young Death. Cesar Tiempo, *tr. by* Donald Devenish Walsh. TrJP
Now a whole year has waxed and waned and whitened. Anniversary of the Great Retreat. Isabel C. Clarke. SUMH
Now, after a party with the consul and our best friend. Summer, 1970. Daniel Halpern. AmPA
Now after David had lived seventy years. The Death of David. Hayyim Nahman Bialik, *tr. by* Herbert Danby. TrJP
Now again the world is shaken. Foundation. Henry van Dyke. TRV
Now, age came on, and all the dismal traine. Clarinda's Indifference at Parting with Her Beauty. Countess of Winchilsea. SBG
Now Ain't That Love? Carolyn M. Rodgers. BPo
Now al is done; bring home the bride againe. Spenser. *Fr.* Epithalamion. FiP
Now all aloud the wind and rain. The Watercress Seller. Thomas Miller. OxBChV
Now all day long the man who is not dead. Mother and Son. Allen Tate. LiTA; MoAB; MoAmPo; MoVE
Now all of change. Sir Thomas Wyatt. SiPS
Now all that sound of laughter, sound of singing. Rosalia de Castro, *tr. fr. Galician by* John Frederick Nims. BoWoP
Now all the cloudy shapes that float and lie. Such Stuff as Dreams Are Made Of. Thomas Wentworth Higginson. AA
Now all the dogs with folded paws. Suburban Song. Elizabeth Riddell. CBAP
Now all the flowers that ornament the grass. Unreturning. Elizabeth Stoddard. AA
Now all the peacefull regents of the night. George Chapman. *Fr.* Bussy D'Ambois. PoEL-2
Now all the truth is out. To a Friend Whose Work Has Come to Nothing. W. B. Yeats. AWP; BiP; LiTM; MoAB; MoBrPo; OAEL-2; OBMV; PoA
Now all the ways are open. The New Freedom. Olive Tilford Dargan. HBMV
Now along the solemn heights. The Recessional. Sir Charles G. D. Roberts. HBV-2
Now am I a tin whistle. A Fresh Morning. J. C. Squire. WhC
Now and Afterwards. Dinah Maria Mulock Craik. HBV-2; PoLF; WGRP
Now and Again. Roo Borson. AMV-81
Now and, I fear, again. Table Talk. Donald Mattam. FiBHP
Now and it's moon shine. Moonshine. *Unknown.* BluL
Now and Then. Ian Hamilton. NoAM
Now and Then. Margaret E. Sangster. TRV
Now and then there will arise. Song. *Tr. fr. Chippewa Indian by* Frances Densmore. OBVE
Now another day is breaking. Morning Prayer. Ogden Nash. GrPl; OxBChV
Now apprehension, with terrible dragon-eyes. The Annual Solution. Edwin Meade Robinson. InMe
Now are our labours crowned with their reward. Hops along the Medway. Christopher Smart. *Fr.* The Hop Garden. FaBoPP
Now are our prayers divided, now. At the "Ye That Do Truly." Charles Williams. NOCV; OxBoCh
Now are the forests dark and the ways full. Southern Summer. Francis Stuart. NeIP
Now are the winds about us in their glee. Song in March. William Gilmore Simms. AA; HBV-1
Now Arethusa from her snow couches arises. Shelley's "Arethusa" Set to New Measures. Robert Duncan. CMoP
Now, a-roving, a-roving. A-Roving, *vers.* II. *Unknown.* ShS
Now art thou fair, Diodorus. Epigram. Strato, *tr. by* Sydney Oswald. PeHV
Now as at all times I can see in the mind's eye. The Magi. W. B. Yeats. BiP; BrPo; CABA; CMoP; CoBMV; ELU; FaBoRV; HAP; InPK; InPS; NoAM; OAEL-2; OFD; PChr; PoA; PPoe; SBVL; TrCP
Now as even's warning bell. Solitude. John Clare. EnRP
Now as I was young and easy under the apple boughs. Fern Hill. Dylan Thomas. BiP; CABA; ChMP; CMoP; CoBMV; EvOK; FaBoEn; FaBoPP; FaBV; FPL; GoJo; GTBS-P; HAP; HeIP; InPK; InPS; LiTB; LiTM; MasP; MoAB; MoBrPo; MoPo; MoVE; MP; NIP; NoAM; NOBE; NoP; OAEL-2; OAEP; OxBTC; PAI; PoLF; PoPl; PoRA; PPoe; PPP; RoGo; SoSe; TrGrPo; TwCP; ViBoPo; WeW
Now as the train bears west. Night Journey. Theodore Roethke. AmFN; GOA; InPS; NYBP
Now as the year turns toward its darkness. Going Away. Howard Nemerov. DFF
Now as Then. Anne Ridler. WaP
Now as these slaughtered seven hundreds hear. On the *Struma* Massacre. Ralph Gustafson. OBCV
Now as we cross this white page together. The Escape. William Stafford. NNaP
Now at the end I smell the smells of spring. Exit Molloy. Derek Mahon. POL
Now at the road's quick turn. Edwin Muir. *Fr.* Variations on a Time Theme. NoAM
Now, at the time that was before agreed. Spenser. *Fr.* The Faerie Queene, VII, 7. OAEL-1
Now austere lips are laid. The Hard Lovers. George Dillon. PoA
Now Autumn comes, the wise fool of the year. Autumn. Frances Winwar. GoYe
Now Be the Gospel Banner, *with music.* Thomas Hastings. AH
Now be ye lords or commoners. The Tod's Hole. *Unknown.* GBP
Now, before Shaving. Aaron Kramer. AMV-81
Now beginneth Glutton [*or* biginneth Glotoun] for to go to shrift[e]. The Glutton [*or* Glutton in the Tavern]. William Langland. *Fr.* The Vision of Piers Plowman. ACP; OxBM
Now Behold the Saviour Pleading, *with music.* John Leland. AH
Now, being invisible, I walk without mantilla. The Souls of Women at Night. Wallace Stevens. CMoP
Now Bekotsidi, that am I. For them I make. The Song of Bekotsidi. *Tr. fr. Navajo Indian by* Washington Matthews. OBVE
Now bethink thee, gentilman. Adam Driven from Eden. *Unknown.* OxBM
Now blest be the Briton, his beef and his beer. Bacon and Eggs. A. P. Herbert. WhC
Now Blue October. Robert Nathan. FYAP
Now bold Robin Hood to the north would go. Robin Hood and the Scotchman. *Unknown.* ESPB
Now, boys, if you will listen, I will sing to you a song. The Lumber Camp Song. *Unknown.* ShS
Now Brigham Young is a Mormon bold. Brigham Young. *Unknown.* CoSo
Now burst above the city's cold twilight. Six o'Clock. Trumbull Stickney. NCEP; OxBA
"Now, by Columba!" Con exclaimed. Denis Florence MacCarthy. *Fr.* The Foray of Con O'Donnell A.D. 1495. OnYI
Now, by the verdure on thy thousand hills. Adequacy. Elizabeth Barrett Browning. SGB
Now by this lake, this fallen thunderstorm. Four Poems for April, I. Louis Adeane. NeBP
Now call to mind Edom, remember well. The Church of England's Glory. *Unknown.* APAS
Now Came Still Evening On ("Uriel to his charge . . ."). Milton. *Fr.* Paradise Lost, IV. FaBoRV
Now came still evening on, and twilight gray. Evening in Paradise [*or* Night Falls on Eden *or* The Moon and the Nightingale]. Milton. *Fr.* Paradise Lost, IV. ChTr; FaBoEn; GN; LoBV; MOON; NOBE; TreFS
Now can you see the monument? It is of wood. The Monument. Elizabeth Bishop. LiTA; MoPo; NoAM; NOBA; PP; PPoe
Now Charito is sixty. But her hair. Ageless. *Unknown, tr. by* Louis Untermeyer. UnTE
Now, Charles Gustavus Anderson is my right and proper name. Charles Gustavus Anderson, *vers.* I. *Unknown.* ShS
Now children may. May. John Updike. *Fr.* A Child's Calendar. OBCA
Now Christendom bids her cathedrals call. Elegy X. William Bell. NePoEA
Now Christmas Day is drawing near at hand. Christmas Now Is Drawing Near. *Unknown.* OBET

Now Christmas is come. *Unknown.* PChr
Now clear the triple region of the air. Christopher Marlowe. *Fr.* Tamburlaine the Great, Pt. I, Act IV, sc. ii. TrGrPo
Now coil up your nonsense 'bout England's great Navy. Charge the Can Cheerily. *Unknown.* AmSS
Now coldness comes sifting down, layer after layer. Flute Notes from a Reedy Pond. Sylvia Plath. FaBoMo
Now, come all you young sailors and listen to me. As I Went a-Walkin' down Ratcliffe Highway, *vers.* I. *Unknown.* ShS
Now, come all you young sailors and listen to me. Blow the Man Down, *vers.* I. *Unknown.* ShS
Now come the rosy dogwoods. In October. Bliss Carman. YeAr
Now come, ye naiads, to the fountains lead. The Home of the Naiads. John Armstrong. *Fr.* The Art of Preserving Health, II. OBEC
Now come young men and list to me. Macaffie's Confession. *Unknown.* BeLS; CoSo
Now comes my lover tripping like the roe. George Peele. *Fr.* David and Bethsabe. ViBoPo
Now Comes the Blast of Winter. *Unknown. See* Merry It Is.
Now comes the fisherman to terms. Fisherman. Robert Francis. PPJ
Now comes the graybeard of the north. Winter Days. Henry Abbey. AA
Now cometh alle ye that been y-brought. God, the Port of Peace. John Walton. OxBM
Now conscience wakes despair. Satan's Address to the Sun. Milton. *Fr.* Paradise Lost, IV. BiP
Now corn pushes past the foam. Ode to a Dead Dodge. David McElroy. AmPA; DFF
Now cracking grass encrusts the yard. For My Students, Returning to College. John Williams. NePoAm-2
Now crouch, ye kings of greatest Asia. The Bloody Conquests of Mighty Tamburlaine. Christopher Marlowe. *Fr.* Tamburlaine the Great, Pt. II, Act IV, sc. iii. ChTr; TrGrPo
Now Cynthia shone serene, and ev'ry star. The Daventry Wonder. "Agricola." NOEC
Now dandelions in the short, new grass. Dandelions. John Albee. AA
Now death has sealed my warthog's eyes. Epitaph on a Warthog. J. B. Morton. PV
Now dis-band all the bands of kin. Family Poem. John Holloway. NMP
Now do our eyes behold. Lament for the Two Brothers Slain by Each Other's Hand. Aeschylus, *tr. by* A. E. Housman. *Fr.* The Seven against Thebes. AWP
Now do you suppose that bee. The Buzzing Doubt. Donald L. Hill. NCSH
Now Does Our World Descend. E. E. Cummings. AP; NYBP
Now don't you see a little turtle dove. Turtle Dove. *Unknown.* FSW
Now dreams. Oppression. Langston Hughes. CNA
Now Dreary Dawns the Eastern Light. A. E. Housman. CMoP
Now each creature joys the other. Ode. Samuel Daniel. EIL; LoBV; OBSC
Now England lessens on my sight. To England. Charles Leonard Moore. AA
Now entertain conjecture of a time. Before Agincourt. Shakespeare. King Henry V, *prologue to* IV. EBEV; FaBoRV; WaaP
Now especially, each flower moves. Variation on the Gothic Spiral. W. S. Merwin. PoA
Now Europe's balanc'd neither side prevails. The Balance of Europe. Pope. SeCeV
Now Evening Puts Amen to Day, *with music.* Paul Horgan. AH
Now evermore, lest some one hope might ease. The Portents. Lucan, *tr. by* Christopher Marlowe. *Fr.* Pharsalia, I. OBSC
Now Every Child. Eleanor Farjeon. SUS
Now every leaf, though colorless, burns bright. Sonnet to the Moon. Yvor Winters. TwAmPo
Now every man at my request. *Unknown.* OBCP
Now every thing that shadowy thought. In Festubert. Edmund Blunden. OBMV
Now ev'ning fades! her pensive step retires. Night. Anne Radcliffe. WPE
Now Fade the Rose and Lily-Flower. *Unknown, tr. fr. Middle English by* Brian Stone. NOCV
Now fades the last long streak of snow. In Memoriam A. H. H., CXV [*or* Spring]. Tennyson. EBVV; FaBoEn; FaBoRV; GTBS-P; HBV-1; NOBE; OBNC; SeCeV; TreFT; ViBoPo
Now faith is the substance of things hoped for. The Evidence. Bible, *N.T. Fr.* Hebrews. TRV
Now far and near on field and hill. So This Is Autumn. W. W. Watt. PoPl
Now ferkes to the firthe thees fresche men of armes. Sir Gawain Encounters Sir Priamus. *Unknown. Fr.* Morte Arthur. PoEL-1
Now fie upon that everlasting life, I dye! Valiant Love. Richard Lovelace. SeCP
Now fields are striped in green and brown. The Busy Body. Rachel Field. InMe
Now first, as I shut the door. The New House. Edward Thomas. EBEV; HBMV; MoAB; MoBrPo; NOBE; OBEV
Now first of all he means the night. A Song for the Middle of the Night. James Wright. WeW
"Now for a brisk and cheerful fight!" The Fight at [the] San Jacinto. John Williamson Palmer. AA; BPAW; HBV-2; PAH
Now for a little I have fed on loneliness. Fruit of Loneliness. May Sarton. PoA
Now for the crown and throne of Israel. George Peele. *Fr.* David and Bethsabe. ViBoPo
Now for your sixtieth birthday am I to send you. To Wystan Auden. Geoffrey Grigson. NAs
Now friends if you'll listen to a horrible tale. The Dreary Black Hills. *Unknown.* BPAW
Now from each van. War Poetry. John Philips. *Fr.* Blenheim. NOEC
Now from Labor and from Care, *with music.* Thomas Hastings. AH
Now from Leander's place she rose, and found. George Chapman. *Fr.* Hero and Leander, Fourth Sestiad. EBEV
Now from the dark, a deeper dark. Calling in the Cat. Elizabeth J. Coatsworth. BoAnP; PCat
Now from the darkness of myself. Escape and Return. Elizabeth Jennings. NePoEA
Now from the east. Masahongva, *tr. fr. Hopi Indian by* Natalie Curtis. WTO
Now from their slumber waking. Comrades. Henry R. Dorr. PAH
Now front to front the hostile armies stand. Homer, *tr. by* Pope. *Fr.* The Iliad, III. OBVE
Now gentle sleep hath closed up those eyes. A Stolen Kiss [*or* The Kiss]. George Wither. HBV-1; UnTE
Now gently winding up the fair ascent. Homer, *tr. by* Pope. *Fr.* The Odyssey, XXI. OBVE
Now get thee back, retreat, depart, O Serpent. He Overcometh the Serpent of Evil in the Name of Ra. *Unknown, tr. by* Robert Hillyer. *Fr.* Book of the Dead. AWP
Now, Gibbon has told the story of old. Fighting McGuire. William Percy French. CenHV
Now, Gilbert, you know you're our man. To G. K. Chesterton. Joseph Mary Plunkett. OnYI
Now Gilderoy was a bonny boy, and he would not the ribbons wear. Gilderoy. *Unknown.* OBET
Now ginnes this goodly frame of Temperaunce. The Bower of Bliss. Spenser. *Fr.* The Faerie Queene, II, 12. PoEL-1
"Now give us lands where the olives grow." The North and the South. Elizabeth Barrett Browning. OBVV
Now glory to the Lord of Hosts, from whom all glories are! Ivry [*or* The Battle of Ivry]. Macaulay. FaBV; GN; HBV-2; HBVY; OBRV; WBLP
Now, God be thanked Who has matched us with His hour. Peace. Rupert Brooke. 1914, I. HBV-2; MMA; OBWP; PoA; TreFT; WGRP
Now God preserve, as you well do deserve. The Masque of Christmas. Ben Jonson. OxBoLi
Now God Stand Up for Bastards. Brian Merriman, *tr. fr. Modern Irish by* Arland Ussher. *Fr.* The Midnight Court. BIrV
Now Goeth [*or* Goth] Sonne under Wode. *Unknown.* HAP; PAI
(Me Rueth, Mary.) GBP
(Now Goeth Sun under Wood.) NCEP; NoP
(Pity for Mary.) MeEL
(Under the Wood, *mod. English.*) HAP
Now gowans sprout, an' lavrocks sing. Ode to Mr. F—— [*or* Mr. Forbes]. Allan Ramsay, *after* Horace. NOEC; OBVE
Now gracious plenty rules the board. Thanksgiving. Florence Earle Coates. TrPWD
Now grapes are plush upon the vines. Contrary Theses (I). Wallace Stevens. OxBA
Now green, now burning, I make a way for peace. Tenth Elegy: Elegy in Joy. Muriel Rukeyser. MiAP
Now grimy April comes again. For City Spring. Stephen Vincent Benét. BXAP; PoPl
Now had night measured with her shadowy cone. Then When I Am Thy Captive, Talk of Chains. Milton. *Fr.* Paradise Lost, IV. WHA
Now had th' Almighty Father from above. Milton. *Fr.* Paradise Lost, III. NIP
"Now half a hundred years had I been born." His Statement of the Case. James Herbert Morse. AA
Now hand in hand, you little maidens, walk. Spring. André Spire, *tr. by* Jethro Bithell. AWP
Now hands to seedsheet, boys! The Sower's Song. Thomas Carlyle. OBVV
Now handy high and handy low. So Handy, Me Boys, So Handy. *Unknown.* AmFP
Now hardly here and there a[n] hackney-coach. A Description of the Morning. Swift. CABA; EBEV; FaBoEn; FF; HAP; HelP; InPS;

NIP; NOBE; NOEC; NoP; OAEL-1; PAI; PPP; Prf; SeCeV; SoSe; TEP; ViBoPo; WeW
Now has ended the battle of Saul. Saul. Nathan Alterman, *tr. by* Dov Vardi. TrJP
Now haste, my Muse, pursue thy destin'd way. Soame Jenyns. *Fr.* The Art of Dancing. FaBoUs
Now hath Flora robbed her bowers. Roses. Thomas Campion. *Fr.* Lord Hay's Mask. OBSC
Now hath my life across a stormy sea. On the Brink of Death. Michelangelo, *tr. by* John Addington Symonds. AWP
Now hath the summer reached her golden close. September. Archibald Lampman. PeCV
Now haud your tongue, baith wife and carle. Red Harlaw. Sir Walter Scott. *Fr.* The Antiquary, *ch.* 40. OxBB
Now have good day, now have good day! I Am Christmas. *Unknown.* OxBM
Now have I brought a woork too end which neither Joves fierce [*or* feerce] wrath. Conclusion. Ovid, *tr. by* Arthur Golding. *Fr.* Metamorphoses, XV. CTC
Now having leisure, and a happy wind. John Fletcher *and* William Rowley. *Fr.* The Maid in the Mill. GBL
"Now, he belongs to the ages." The Soul of Lincoln. Chauncey R. Piety. PGD
Now he is gone and we had not understood one another. The Year's Ending. St. J. Page Yako, *tr. by* C. M. Mcanyangwa *and* Jack Cope. PeSA
Now he who knows old Christmas. Old Christmas. Mary Howitt. GN
Now Help Us, Lord, *with music.* *Unknown, ad. by* Charles E. Ives. AH
Now here, now there, lightheaded, crazed with grief. A Psalm of the Early Buddhist Sisters. *Unknown.* WGRP
Now high and low, where leaves renew. Autet e bas. Arnaut Daniel, *tr. by* Ezra Pound. CTC
Now his nose's bridge is broken, one eye. On Hurricane Jackson. Alan Dugan. CoAP; LiSp; NCSH; PAI; POL
Now hoisteth sail the pinnace of my wit. Dante, *tr. by* Laurence Binyon. Divina Commedia: Purgatorio, I-II. NAWM-1
Now homing tradesmen scatter through the streets. Place Pigalle. Richard Wilbur. HeIP
Now how I came to get this hat 'tis very strange and funny. Where Did You Get That Hat? Joseph J. Sullivan. FSN; TreF
Now I ain't no butcher. All Around Man. *Unknown.* BluL
Now I Am a Man. Russell Marano. AMV-80
Now I am slow and placid, fond of sun. With Child. Genevieve Taggard. MoAmPo
Now I am sure. Beast Enough. Robert Billings. AMV-81
Now I am thankful this unbroken flesh. Fisherman's Son. Charles Bruce. CaP
Now I am tired of being Japanese. Picture of a Castle. William Meredith. NePoEA
Now I believe tradition, which doth call. Upon the Author; by a Known Friend. Benjamin Woodbridge. SCAP
Now I can be sure of my sleep. On the Hill below the Lighthouse. James Dickey. NePoEA-2
Now I can straighten your wires. Brownsville Blues. *Unknown.* BluL
Now I find [*or* see] thy looks were feigned. Ode [*or* Song]. Thomas Lodge. *Fr.* Phyllis. EIL; EnRePo; LoBV; OBSC
Now I go, do not weep, woman. Parting. Alice Corbin. BPAW
Now I go down here and bring up a moon. Auctioneer. Carl Sandburg. PDV
Now I got a brown skin girl. Brown Skin Girl. *Unknown.* BluL
Now I have come to reason. C. Day Lewis. CMoP
Now I Have Forgotten All. David Vogel, *tr. fr. Hebrew by* A. C. Jacobs. VWA
Now I have found thee I will evermore. Upon the Crucifix. William Alabaster. AnAnS-1; PoEL-2
Now I have lost you, I must scatter. Farewell, Sweet Dust. Elinor Wylie. LiTA
Now I Have Nothing. Stella Benson. OxBTC
Now I have tempered haste. The Mount. Léonie Adams. MoVE
Now I have touched you near the grated bone. Postscript. Mary Mills. NePoAm
Now I knew I lost her. Emily Dickinson. PeHV
Now I know/ why God ordered Abe. On Living with Children for a Prolonged Time. Mark Lowey. AMV-81
"Now I Lay Me Down to Sleep." Eugene Henry Pullen. AA; FaBoBe
Now I Lay Me Down to [Take My] Sleep, *diff. versions.* *Unknown.* BLRP; FaFP; GBP; OxNR; SoPo; TreF
Now I lay me down to sleep. Now I Set Me. Reinhold W. Herman. QQQ
Now I love you/ as the sea loves its water. Pedro Salinas, *tr. by* Linda Gutierrez *and* Lawrence Pitkethly. *Fr.* Razón de Amor. LLLT
Now I must betray myself. Prothalamion. Delmore Schwartz. OxBA
Now I never will forget that floating bridge. Floating Bridge. *Unknown.* BluL
Now I out walking. Away! Robert Frost. NOBA
Now I pray the man who may love this lay. Cynewulf, *tr. by* Charles W. Kennedy. *Fr.* Fates of the Apostles. AnOE
Now I put on the thimble of dream. The Red Bird Tapestry. May Swenson. TwAmPo
Now I see its whiteness. The Dead Butterfly. Denise Levertov. NoP
Now I see the leaves tilting. Variations on a Still Morning. Thomas Cole. NePoAm
Now I see their faces stamped forever. Why I Can't Write a Poem about Lares. Iván Silén, *tr. by* Julio Marzán. InW
Now I see thy looks were feigned. *See* Now I find thy looks were feigned.
Now I see you. Grandfather. Joseph Stroud. NPGG
Now I Set Me. Reinhold W. Herman. QQQ
Now I shall reach over. With Lilacs in My Eye. Lucile Coleman. GoYe
Now I tell you mama now I'm sure gonna leave this town. Leaving Town Blues. *Unknown.* BluL
Now I wake and see the light. Eugene Henry Pullen. BLRP
Now I was born on the Rio Grande. Rio Grande, *vers.* II. *Unknown.* ShS
Now I will do nothing but listen. Walt Whitman. Song of Myself, XXVI. HoPM
Now I will fashion the tale of a fish. The Whale. *Unknown, tr. by* Charles W. Kennedy. *Fr.* Physiologus. AnOE; MOS
Now I woke up this morning, mama. You Can't Keep No Brown. *Unknown.* BluL
Now I would remind you, brethren. Bible, *N.T.* First Corinthians, XV: 1-8. DL
Now ich see blostme springe. Of Jesu Christ I Sing. *Unknown.* OxBM
Now if a man has money today. Money Is King. *Unknown.* FSW
Now if ever it is time to cleanse Helicon. Ezra Pound. *Fr.* Homage to Sextus Propertius. CrMA; VGW
Now, if ever, let poets sing. Let Dreamers Wake. Lilith Lorraine. PGD
"Now, if the fish will only bite, we'll have some royal fun." Timid Hortense. Peter Newell. NA
Now if thou hast one dram of grace. Nahum Tate, *after the Latin of* Catullus. OBVE
Now if you want an onion, just consider. Recipe: Onions. Philemon. FaBoUs
Now if you will listen I'll tell you a story. The New-Chum's First Trip. *Unknown.* FaBoBa
Now, if You Will Look in My Brain. José Garcia Villa. TwAmPo
Now I'm Easy. Eric Bogle. OBET
Now, I'm leaving old England, the land that I love. The First of the Emigrants. *Unknown.* ShS
Now in a thought, now in a shadowed word. L'Envoi. E. A. Robinson. TrCP
Now in golden glory goes. Songs. Lionel Johnson. VLP
Now in her green mantle blythe [*or* blithe] nature arrays. My Nannie's Awa'. Burns. GN; HBV-1
Now in middle age, my blood like a thief who. Irish Music. Larry Levis. MAYP
Now in midsummer come and all fools slaughtered. Credences of Summer. Wallace Stevens. AP; CoBMV
Now in my/ heart I/ see clearly. Sappho, *tr. fr. Greek by* Willis Barnstone. BoWoP
Now in my Samarkand of blue enamels. Journey in the Orient. Maria Luisa Spaziani, *tr. by* Ruth Feldman. BoWoP
Now in old age, quiet in his tent. Isaac. Barry Holtz. VWA
Now in the after play. Blackheads. Knute Skinner. GP
Now in the Bloom. Florence Kiper Frank. GoYe
Now in the circulating torrent of the stars. In Conjunction. Charles Madge. NeBP
Now in the dawn before it dies, the eagle swings low. The Story of a Well-made Shield. N. Scott Momaday. CDW; GrPl
Now, in the evenings, when the light. The Generations. George M. Brady. OnYI
Now in the Palace Gardens. Trumbull Stickney. Eride, V. LiTA; NCEP; TwAmPo
Now in the patron's mansion see the wight. Richard Savage. *Fr.* The Progress of a Divine. OBSV
Now in the suburbs and the falling light. Father and Son. Stanley Kunitz. DiL; MP; NoAM; TwCP
Now in the summer of life, sweetheart. Will You Love Me in December as You Do in May? James J. Walker. FSN; TreFT
Now in the third voice. W. S. Graham. The Dark Dialogues, III. OxBS
Now in the Time of This Mortal Life. Norman Nicholson. NeBP
Now in this mirthfull tyme of May. Four May Poems, II. *Unknown.* OxBS
Now in this while gan Daedalus a wearinesse to take. Daedalus. Ovid, *tr. by* Arthur Golding. *Fr.* Metamorphoses, VIII. CTC; OBVE
Now in thy dazzling half-oped eye. A Mother to Her Waking Infant. Joanna Baillie. NOEC

Now, innocent, within the deep. M., Singing. Louise Bogan. CrMA; GoJo; LiTA; NePA
Now into the saddle, and over the grass. The Pony Express. Dorothy Brown Thompson. AmFN
Now is a bursting in me. Argent Solipsism. Howard Blake. PoA
Now is a great and shining company. Resurgam. Struthers Burt. HBMV
Now is come Midsummer Night. Song for Midsummer Night. Elizabeth J. Coatsworth. YeAr
Now Is Farewell. Blanaid Salkeld. NeIP
Now is Ingland all in fight. On the Times. *Unknown.* OxBM
Now is it most like as if on ocean. The Voyage of Life. Cynewulf, *tr. by* Charles W. Kennedy. *Fr.* Christ 2. AnOE; MOS
Now is it pleasant in the summer-eve. George Crabbe. *Fr.* The Borough, Letter IX. FM; OBRV
Now is Light, sweet mother down the west. John Vance Cheney. Evening Songs, III. AA
Now is mon hol and soint. When Death Comes. *Unknown.* MeEL
Now is my Chloris fresh as May. *Unknown.* OBSC
Now is my father. Poem for My Father's Ghost. Mary Oliver. Str
Now is my misery full, and namelessly. Pieta. Rainer Maria Rilke, *tr. by* M. D. Herter Norton. OFD
Now is my way clear, now is the meaning plain. The Last Temptation. T. S. Eliot. *Fr.* Murder in the Cathedral. TreFT
Now is the autumn of the Tree of Life. Progress of Unbelief. Cardinal Newman. GoBC
Now is the globe shrunk tight. Snowdrop. Ted Hughes. FaBoMo
Now Is the High-Tide of the Year. James Russell Lowell. *Fr.* The Vision of Sir Launfal: Prelude to Part First. TreFS
Now is the hour when, swinging in the breeze. Harmonie du Soir. Baudelaire, *tr. by* Lord Alfred Douglas. AWP
Now is the month of maying. *Unknown.* EBEV; OBSC
Now is the night, foreshadowed of our fears. Edwin Booth. Alice Brown. HBV-2
Now is the ox-eyed daisy out. June. James Reaney. WHW
Now is the pause between asleep and awake. The Spring Equinox. Anne Ridler. NeBP
Now is the time for all good men. Testing, Testing. Dan Dillon. PV
Now is the time for mirth. To Live Merrily, and to Trust to Good Verses. Robert Herrick. AnAnS-2; AWP; CaPo; InvP; LoBV; OBS; PP; SeCP; SeCV-1
Now is the time for the burning of the leaves. The Burning of the Leaves. Laurence Binyon. ChMP; DTC; GTBS-P; MoVE; NOBE; OxBTC
Now Is the Time of Christmas. *Unknown.* MeEL; OxBM
(Make We Merry.) SBVL
Now is the time that hills put on. Spring Signs. Rachel Field. InMe
Now is the time, when all the lights wax dim. To Anthea. Robert Herrick. OAEP; OBS; PoEL-3
Now is the time when cheery crickets. Autumn! Nancy Byrd Turner. YeAr
Now is the winter of our discontent. Evil Designs [*or* Hate the Idle Pleasures]. Shakespeare. King Richard III, *fr.* I, i. TreF; TrGrPo
Now is the world withdrawn all. Carol. Howard Nemerov. TrCP
Now Is Yule Come. *Unknown. See* Hay, Ay, Hay, Ay.
Now Israel May Say, and That Truly, *with music.* William Whittingham. AH
Now it begins. Now the subaqueous evening. A Is for Alpha: Alpha Is for A. Conrad Aiken. NePA
Now It Can Be Told. Philip Levine. VWA
Now it grows dark. Hymn to Night. Melville Cane. MoAmPo
Now it is autumn and the falling fruit. The Ship of Death. D. H. Lawrence. CMoP; FaBoRV; FaBoTw; GTBS-P; LiTB; LoBV; MasP; MOS; NoAM; NoP; OAEL-2; OAEP; PrIm
Now It Is Broccoli. Jeff Tagami. BrSi
Now it is fifteen years you have lain in the meadow. Lines for an Interment. Archibald MacLeish. CMoP; NOBA
Now it is only hours before you wake. Letter to My Daughter at the End of Her Second Year. Donald Finkel. CoAP
Now it is time to be cut out. Hansel and Gretel Return. David Ray. DFT
Now it is winter and the fallen snow. Los Mineros. Edward Dorn. PoM
Now, it takes all 'ands to man the capstan. Rolling Home, *vers.* II. *Unknown.* ShS
Now it was Spring. Grant at Appomattox. Gertrude Claytor. GoYe
Now it was that the Morrigan settled in bird shape. The Morrigan. *Unknown, tr. by* Thomas Kinsella. BIrV
Now, it's blow, you winds, 'ow I long to hear you. Blow, Boys, Blow, *vers.* III. *Unknown.* ShS
Now, it's one cold and dreary morning in December. Mainsail Haul, *vers.* I. *Unknown.* ShS
Now it's stingy mama. Mojo Hiding Woman. *Unknown.* BluL
Now it's Uncle Sam sitting on top of the world. Carl Sandburg. *Fr.* Good Morning America. OFD
Now, I've got no use for the women. Bury Me Out on the Prairie. *Unknown.* BPAW; CoSo
Now Jentil Belly Down. *Unknown.* GBP
Now Jesus knew that they were desirous to ask him. Be of Good Cheer; I Have Overcome the World. Bible, *N.T. Fr.* St. John. TreFS
Now John come home all in a wonder. Everyday Dirt. *Unknown.* FSW
Now Johnson would go up to join the great simulacra of men. Up Rising. Robert Duncan. *Fr.* Passages. NNaP
Now, jolly Swains! the harvest of your cares. How to Shear Sheep. John Dyer. *Fr.* The Fleece, II. FaBoUs
Now Jones had left his new-wed bride. A Code of Morals. Kipling. FaBoCo
Now joy be to the Trinity. Wassail, Wassail, Wassail, Sing We. *Unknown.* SBVL
Now, Joy is born of parents poor. Joy and Pleasure. W. H. Davies. OBMV
Now keep that long revolver at your side. Sonnet. George Hetherington. NeIP
Now Kindness. Peter Viereck. LiTA
Now kisse me, lovely Ganimed, for see. Jupiter and Ganimede. Thomas Heywood. PeHV
Now, ladies, if you'll listen, a story I'll relate. Pearl Bryan. *Unknown.* BaBo
Now, landsmen, list! There is no sight more fair. Norse Sailor's Joy. Wilfrid Thorley. EtS
Now leave the check-reins slack. To the Man after the Harrow. Patrick Kavanagh. CIP; GTBS-P
Now let me alone, though I know you won't. Barney O'Hea. Samuel Lover. OnYI
Now let no charitable hope. Let No Charitable Hope. Elinor Wylie. HBMV; LiTA; LiTM; MoAB; MoAmPo; NePA; OxBA; PBWP; SBG; TrGrPo; VGW
Now Let Our Hearts Their Glory Wake, *with music.* Elizabeth Scott. AH
Now let the cycle sweep us here and there. Sigil. Hilda Doolittle ("H. D."). VGW
Now let the drums roll muffled; let the bells'. Charles Heavysege. *Fr.* Count Filippo. PeCV
Now let the golden prison ope its gates. Cardinal Newman. *Fr.* The Dream of Gerontius. VLP
Now let the legless boy show the great lady. In the Children's Hospital. "Hugh MacDiarmid." NoP; PAI
Now let us praise heaven's Emperor. Caedmon's Hymn. *Unknown, tr. by* Walter Kendrick. TEP
Now Liddesdale [*or* Liddisdale] has ridden a raid. Jock o' the Side. *Unknown.* ESPB; OxBB
Now Liddisdale has lain long in. Dick o' the Cow. *Unknown.* ESPB; OxBB
"Now life alone is left me, to maintain." Near the Death of Ovid. Robert Conquest. NoAM
Now Lift Me Close. Walt Whitman. DFF
Now light the candles; one; two; there's a moth. Repression of War Experience. Siegfried Sassoon. BrPo; CMoP; MMA; NoAM
Now lighted windows climb the dark. Manhattan Lullaby. Rachel Field. AmFN
Now, like a magpie, he collects the bright. "Trade" Rat. Eleanor Glenn Wallis. NePoAm
Now list and lithe, you gentlemen. Northumberland Betray[e]d by Douglas [*or* Dowglas]. *Unknown.* ESPB; OxBB
Now list you, lithe you, gentlemen. Robin Hood and Queen Katherine. *Unknown.* ESPB
Now listen to boasting which leaves the heart dazed. Al-Samau'al ibn Adiya, *tr. by* Hartwig Hirschfeld. *Fr.* Are We Not the People. TrJP
Now, listen, Ye who established the Great League. Memorial Ode. Chief John Buck. GOA
Now Little Billy is gone to the kirk. Little Billy. *Unknown.* GBP
Now Look What Happened. Molly Peacock. MAYP
Now look, you see, it's this way like. The Road to Hogan's Gap. Andrew Barton Paterson. CBAP
Now, Lord, or never they'll believe on Thee. On the Miracle of Loaves. Richard Crashaw. ACP
Now lufferis cummis with larges lowd. The Petition of the Gray Horse, Auld Dunbar. William Dunbar. OxBS
Now manhood and garbroyls I chaunt. Virgil, *tr. by* Richard Stanyhurst. *Fr.* The Aeneid, I. BIrV; OBVE
Now many are the stately ships that northward steam away. The Lover Thinks of His Lady in the North. Shaemas O'Sheel. HBV-1
Now may we turn aside and dry our tears. Inis Fal. Egan O'Rahilly, *tr. by* James Stephens. BIrV; OBMV
Now me and my baby we talked last night. Welfare Store. *Unknown.* BluL
Now milkmaids' pails are deckt with flowers. Stool Ball. *Unknown.* CH

Now, miners, if you'll listen, I'll tell you quite a tale. Coming around the Horn. John A. Stone. AmFP
Now mirk December's dowie face. The Daft Days. Robert Fergusson. BSV; NOEC
Now Mr. Boomer Johnson was a gettin' old in spots. Boomer Johnson. Henry Herbert Knibbs. BPAW
Now Mrs. Eberle early had been told. La Donna È Perpetuum Mobile. Irwin Edman. FiBHP
Now more and more on my concern with the lifted waves of genius gaining. On the Ocean Floor. "Hugh MacDiarmid." FaBoMo; HAP
Now Morning from her orient chamber came. Imitation of Spenser [*or* Morning]. Keats. EnRP; GN
Now Muse assist me, aptly to describe. A. D. Hope. *Fr.* Dunciad Minor, V. BXAP
Now must all satisfaction. Certain Mercies. Robert Graves. CoBMV; GTBS-P
Now must I learn to live [*or* lerne to lyve] at rest. Sir Thomas Wyatt. AAS; SiPS
Now must I these three praise. Friends. W. B. Yeats. NoAM
Now must I wait. The Blank Book Letter. Samuel Greenberg. LiTA
Now must we hymn heaven's Guardian. Caedmon's Hymn. Caedmon. EBCP
Now must we praise of heaven's kingdom the keeper. Caedmon's Hymn. Caedmon. OAEL-1
Now my charms are all o'erthrown. Epilogue. Shakespeare. *Fr.* The Tempest, V, i. CTC
Now, my co-mates and brothers in exile. The Uses of Adversity. Shakespeare. *Fr.* As You Like It, II, i. LiTB; TreFS; TrGrPo
Now, my dear, we're getting down. A Delicate Impasse. Kenneth John Atchity. AMV-80
Now, my fair'st friend. Some Flowers o' the Spring. Shakespeare. *Fr.* The Winter's Tale, IV, iii. ChTr
Now my father carries his old heart. Christmas Eve. Ted Kooser. GP
Now my heart turns to and fro. Hatshepsut, *tr. fr. Egyptian by* Miriam Lichtheim. *Fr.* Obelisk Inscriptions. WPOW
Now my legs begin to walk. Thaw in the City. Lou Lipsitz. MAT; NCSH
Now, my name is Samuel Hall, Sam Hall. Sam Hall. *Unknown.* ViBoFo
Now, my son, is life for you. Wishes for My Son. Thomas MacDonagh. AnIV; GoBC; HBMV
Now my thick years bend your back. The Turn of the Road. Fannie Stearns Gifford. HBMV
Now, My Usefulness Over. Edwin Honig. NoAM
Now 'neath the silver moon. Santa Lucia. Teodoro Cottrau. FSW
Now new-vamped silks the mercer's window shows. A Description of Spring in London. *Unknown.* NOEC
Now, night; and once again. Avalon. Audrey McGaffin. NePoAm
Now, not a tear begun. A Woman Mourned by Daughters. Adrienne Rich. IHMS; NCSH
Now, now's the time so oft by Truth. An Epithalamy to Sir Thomas Southwell and His Lady. Robert Herrick. CaPo
Now, O Lord, please lend me thine/ ear. The Cowman's Prayer. *Unknown.* CoSo
Now o'er the rugged peasants' cot. Ye Simple Men. John Stuart Blackie. PoSH
Now o'er the topmost pine. Morning. Samuel Waddington. OBVV
Now of all the trees by the king's highway. Aunt Mary. Robert Stephen Hawker. OHIP
Now of that vision I, bereaven. Francis Thompson. *Fr.* Grace of the Way. MoAB; MoBrPo
Now old Dan Tucker's a fine old man. Old Dan Tucker. Daniel Decatur Emmett. FSW
Now, on a sudden, I know it, the secret, the secret of life. Revealed. Harry Lyman Koopman. AA
Now on the verge of spring the icy silver leaf. Return to Spring. Florence Ripley Mastin. GoYe
Now once again the gloomy scene explore. The Pauper's Funeral. George Crabbe. *Fr.* The Village. FaBoEn; OBNC
Now once upon a time the King of Astrakhan, at that. The Lacquer Liquor Locker. David McCord. FiBHP; InMe
Now one and all, you roses. A Wood Song. Ralph Hodgson. GoJo; HBV-1
Now or Never. Astra. BrRo
Now orange blossoms filigree. Ain't Nature Commonplace! Arthur Guiterman. FiBHP; InMe
Now ore the sea from her old love comes she. Ovid, *tr. by* Christopher Marlowe. Amores, I, 13. OBVE
Now over there across the sea they've got another war. That Crazy War. *Unknown.* FSW
Now Phillipa Is Gone. Anne Ridler. FaBoTw
Now Phoebus did the world with frowns survey. Abigail's Lamentation for the Loss of Mr. Harley. William Walsh. APAS
Now Poem. For Us. Sonia Sanchez. CNA; PoBA
Now ponder well, you parents dear. The Babes [*or* Children] in the Wood. *Unknown.* EnSB; HBV-1; HBVY; OBNV
Now, poor Rufus he has come to town. Rufus's Mare. George Calhoun. ShS
Now poor Tom Dunstan's cold. Tom Dunstan; or, The Politician. Robert Buchanan. HBV-2
Now put aside the flute; sing no sweet air. Consummation. *Unknown, tr. by* Louis Untermeyer. UnTE
Now quenched each midnight window is. Now unimpeded. The Single Woman. Frances Cornford. ELU
"Now rede me, dear mither, a sonsy rede." The Mer-Man, and Marstig's Daughter. *Unknown, tr. by* Robert Jamieson. AWP
Now rest for evermore, my weary heart! A Sè Stesso. Giacomo Leopardi, *tr. by* Lorna De' Lucchi. AWP
Now Robin Hood, Will Scadlock and Little John. Robin Hood and the Prince of Aragon. *Unknown.* ESPB
Now rock the boat to a fare-thee-well. Rite of Passage. Audre Lorde. CNA; PoBA
Now St. Joseph's cottage stood. A Legend of Cherries. Charles Dalmon. HBMV
Now science is a dandy thing—explaining, as it can. Folks, I Give You Science! Al Graham. WhC
Now secretness dies of the open. For the Nightly Ascent of the Hunter Orion over a Forest Clearing. James Dickey. TwCP
Now seven days from land the gulls still wheel. Transport. William Meredith. WaP
Now shal y tellen to ye, y wis. The Lay of the Ettercap. John Leyden. BXAP
Now shall I walk. The Best Friend. W. H. Davies. OBMV
Now shall the body. The Cloud of Unknowing. Philip Murray. NePoAm-2
Now shall we see, that nature hath no end. George Chapman. *Fr.* Bussy D'Ambois. PoEL-2
Now she burnes as well as I. Song: To Her Againe, She Burning in a Feaver. Thomas Carew. AnAnS-2; SeCP
Now She Is like the White Tree-Rose. C. Day Lewis. *Fr.* From Feathers to Iron. CMoP; FaBoTw; MoBrPo
Now she will lean away to fold. A Girl in a Window. James Wright. ErPo
Now shout into my dream. These trumpets snored. Farewell in a Dream. Stephen Spender. MoAB; MoBrPo
Now show thy joy, frolic in Angels' sight. Leviathan. Jay Macpherson. MoCV
Now Shrinketh Rose and Lily-Flower. *Unknown.* OxBM
(Penitent Hopes in Mary, The.) MeEL
Now side by side, with like unweary'd care. Homer, *tr. by* Pope. *Fr.* The Iliad, XIII. OBVE
"Now since mine even is come at last." The Ridè to the Lady. Helen Gray Cone. AA
Now since the members of the world we view. Lucretius, *tr. by* Thomas Creech. *Fr.* De Rerum Natura, V. OBVE
Now sinks another day to rest. The Bull. V. Sackville-West. WPE
Now skrinketh rose and lilye-flour. *See* Now Shrinketh Rose and Lily-Flower.
Now, Sleep, bind fast the flood of air. Bridal Song. George Chapman. *Fr.* The Masque of the Middle Temple and Lincoln's Inn. ElL
Now Sleep My Little Child So Dear, *with music.* Casper Kriebel, *tr. fr. German by* Sheema Z. Buehne. AH
Now Sleeps the Crimson Petal. Tennyson. *Fr.* The Princess. BoLoP; CABA; ChER; ChTr; EBEV; EBVV; ELP; FiP; GBL; GTBS-P; LLLT; NIP; NOBE; NoP; OBNC; OBVV; PoEL-5; PPoe; PPP; SCV; TreFT; TrGrPo; UnTE; ViBoPo
(Song: "Now sleeps the crimson petal, now the white.") BLPL; FaBoBe; LoBV; OAEP; SeCeV
(Summer Night.) OBEV; SeCePo
Now Snow Descends. Jean Garrigue. WPE
Now, solitary, and in pensive Guise. James Thomson. *Fr.* The Seasons: Winter. FaBoEn
Now some may drink old vintage wine. Early Morning Meadow Song. Charles Dalmon. CH; HBMV
Now some people thinks it's jolly for to lead a single life. Wedding Song. *Unknown.* OBET
Now south and south and south the mallard heads. The North Sea Undertaker's Complaint. Robert Lowell. NePoEA
Now spears lift them by their ribs. Dog Sacrifice at Lake Ronkonkoma. William Heyen. AmPA
Now Spring brings back the tepid breeze. Spring. Catullus, *tr. by* L. R. Lind. PoPl
Now Spring returns: but not to me returns. Michael Bruce. *Fr.* Elegy: In Spring. BSV
Now Springs the Spray. *Unknown.* OxBM; OAEL-1
(Now Sprinkes the Spray.) PoEL-1

(Singing Maid, The.) MeEL
Now stands our love on that still verge of day. James Agee. Sonnets, XX. MoAmPo
Now stood Eliza on the wood-crown'd height. Eliza. Erasmus Darwin. PaPo
Now stoops the sun, and dies day's cheerful light. The Gauls Sacrifice. C. M. Doughty. *Fr.* The Dawn in Britain. FaBoTw
Now stop your noses, readers, all and some. Og and Doeg. Dryden. *Fr.* Absalom and Achitophel, Pt. II. FiP; TW
Now strike your sailes, ye[e] jolly mariners. Spenser. *Fr.* The Faerie Queene, I, 12. EtS; MOS
Now, suddenly, the table rocks, a bell. Séance. William Abrahams. NYBP
Now Summer finds her perfect prime. Heaven, O Lord, I Cannot Lose. Edna Dean Proctor. AA
Now sunk the sun, now twilight sunk, and night. A Rhapsody, Written at the Lakes in Westmorland [*or* Night]. John Brown. NOEC; OBEC
Now swarthy Summer, by rude health embrowned. Summer Images. John Clare. OBNC
Now sways it this way, like a mighty sea. Shakespeare. King Henry VI, Pt. III, *fr.* II, v. MOS
Now take your fill of love and glee. A Double Ballad of Good Counsel. Villon, *tr. by* Swinburne. AWP
Now tell me again about Miss Terrer's dog. A Colloquy with Gregory on the Balcony. Howard Moss. FAZ
Now tell me where my easy rider gone. Easy Rider Blues. *Unknown.* BluL
Now Thank We All Our God. Martin Rinkart, *tr. fr. German by* Catherine Winkworth. TreFS
Now that black ground and bushes. Winter Sketches. Charles Reznikoff. PoA
Now That Can Never Be Done. Sister Maris Stella. GoBC
Now that compelling silver throat. Haydn; the Horn. Daniel Barrigan. TwAmPo
Now that day doth end. At Day's End. *Unknown.* TreFT
Now that Fate is dead and gone. Song. Edith Sitwell. MoAB; MoBrPo
Now that guy was a real fruit. A peach. A Musician Returning from a Cafe Audition. Michael D. Minard. AMV-80
"Now that he is in grave condition." Pushkin, *tr. by* Walter Arndt. *Fr.* Eugene Onegin. NAWM-2
Now that he's left the room. Univac to Univac. Louis B. Salomon. FF; QQQ
Now that high, oft-affronted bosom heaves. To the Lady Portrayed by Margaret Dumont. John Hollander. OBAL; PoA
Now that I am dressed I'll go. Paedar Og Goes Courting. James Stephens. WhC
Now that I am fifty-six. Rondel. Muriel Rukeyser. FF
Now That I Am Forever with Child. Audre Lorde. PoBA
Now that I am Oxford Professor of Poetry. Unsolicited Letters to Five Artists. Clive James. FaBoPa
Now that I have your face by heart, I look. Song for the Last Act. Louise Bogan. NePoAm; NoP; NYBP; UnPo; WPE
Now that I have your hand, let me persuade you. One Last Word. John Glassco. NOBC
Now that I know. Knowledge. Louise Bogan. HBMV; PoA
Now that I live no longer among mountains. Among Friends. Greg Kuzma. AMV-80
Now that I, tying thy glass mask tightly. The Laboratory; Ancien Régime. Robert Browning. OBEV; OBVV
Now that I've nearly done my days. The Things That Matter. Edith Nesbit. OxBTC
Now that I've taken a wife. The Groom's Lament. Robert Peterson. NeAC
Now that I've wasted. My Alba. Allen Ginsberg. NoAM; NOBA
Now That My Father Lies Down beside Me. Stanley Plumly. DiL; GeTw
Now that my seagoing self-possession wavers. Autobiography. Charles Causley. LiTM
Now that night is creeping. Evensong. C. S. Lewis. TrCP
Now that of absence the most irksome night. Astrophel and Stella, LXXXIX. Sir Philip Sidney. SiPS
Now that our love has drifted. Finis. Waring Cuney. AmNP; BANP
Now that the April of your youth adorns. A Ditty in Imitation of the Spanish. Lord Herbert of Cherbury. AnAnS-2; ElL; OBS
Now that the barbarians have got as far as Picra. Translation. Roy Fuller. ChMP; NOBE; OxBTC
Now that the cameras zero in from space. The Weather of the World. Howard Nemerov. SUW
Now that the causeway spans the channel. Causeway. Allan Block. TAT
Now that the day is done. Centaur Song. Hilda Doolittle ("H. D."). VGW
Now that the days are growing light and long. Cuckoo. R. P. Lister. BoAnP
Now That the Flowers. Cullen Jones. GoYe
Now that the harth [*or* hearth] is crown'd with smiling fire. Ode to Sir William Sydney, on His Birth-Day [*or* Another Birthday]. Ben Jonson. NAs; WiR
Now that the midd day heate doth scorch my shame. William Alabaster. AnAnS-1
Now that the others are gone, all of them, forever. Tomorrow. Kenneth Fearing. CMoP
Now that the red glare of thy fall is blown. Francis Thompson. *Fr.* Ode to the Setting Sun. OBNC
Now that the Spring hath filled our veins. A Round. William Browne. ViBoPo
Now that the time has come wherein. Advice from Poor Robin's Almanack. *Unknown.* OBCP
Now That the Truth Is Tried. Thomas Whythorne. ElL
Now that the Village-Reverence doth lye hid. A New-Years-Gift to Brian Lord Bishop of Sarum. William Cartwright. MePo
Now That the Winter's Gone. Thomas Carew. *See* Spring, The.
Now that the world is all in a maze. The Unconcerned. Thomas Flatman. FaBoCh
Now that the young buds are tipped with a falling sun. Early Spring. Sidney Keyes. MoBrPo
Now that these wings to speed my wish ascend. The Philosophic Flight. Giordano Bruno, *tr. by* John Addington Symonds. AWP
Now that they've got it settled whose I be. The Pauper Witch of Grafton. Robert Frost. CrMA
Now that we're almost settled in our house. In Memory of Major Robert Gregory. W. B. Yeats. AnIL; EBEV; OAEL-2; OAEP
Now that we're alone we can talk prince man to man. Elegy of Fortinbras. Zbigniew Herbert, *tr. by* Czeslaw Milosz. OBVE
Now that we've done our best and worst, and parted. The Busy Heart. Rupert Brooke. HBV-1; MoBrPo
Now that you have freely given me leave to love. To a Lady that Desired I Would Love Her. Thomas Carew. CavP
Now that you lie. Before Sleep. Anne Ridler. NeBP
Now That You Too. Eleanor Farjeon. SUMH
Now that you would leave me. Love-Faith. Harry Kemp. HBMV
Now That Your Shoulders Reach My Shoulders. Robert Francis. Str
Now the bat circles on the breeze of eve. Sonnet. Anne Radcliffe. WPE
Now, the boys and the girls went out huckleberry hunting. Huckleberry Hunting. *Unknown.* ShS
Now the bright crocus flames, and now. In the Spring. Meleager, *tr. by* Andrew Lang. AWP
Now the bright morning star, day's [*or* dayes] harbinger. Song on [*or* of] May Morning. Milton. BoNaP; CH; GN; HBV-1; HBVY; PoPl; TrGrPo; YeAr
Now the *Chesapeake* so bold. The *Shannon* and the *Chesapeake*. *Unknown.* AmSS
Now the cup of grasses and down is cool. In This Life. Robert Mezey. SUW
Now the Day Is Over. Sabine Baring-Gould. OxBChV
(Child's Evening Hymn.) WGRP
(For Evening.) TreFT
(Hymn.) NBM
Now the declining fulgent orb of day. J. C. Squire. *Fr.* Doris and Philemon. BXAP
Now the declining sun 'gan downwards bend. The Nightingale. William Strode, *after* Famianus Strada. OBVE
Now the descending triumph stops its flight. The Day of Judgement. Edward Young. OxBoCh
Now the dreary winter's over. Spring Song. Nahum, *tr. by* Emma Lazarus. TrJP
Now the drowsy sunshine. Evening. Harry Behn. TiPo
Now the ears, so I always had thunk. The Ears. Anthony Euwer. *Fr.* The Limeratomy. HBMV
Now the Earth, the Skies, the Air. *Unknown.* ElL
Now the Earth turns, and tilts me from the sun. Evensong. Judith Moffett. LTB
Now the first silly bastard he got in an aeroplane. Ops in a Wimpey. *Unknown.* CoMu
Now the frog, all lean and weak. The Sweet o' the Year. George Meredith. BoNaP
Now the frontiers are all closed. Ultimatum. Peggy Pond Church. TRV
Now the frosty stars are gone. Ariel in the Cloven Pine. Bayard Taylor. AA
Now the full-throated daffodils. C. Day Lewis. *Fr.* From Feathers to Iron. ViBoPo
Now the golden morn aloft. Ode on the Pleasure Arising from Vicissitude. Thomas Gray. GTBS; GTBS-P; LAuP; NOEC; OBEC
Now the good man's away from home. Sally Sweetbread. Henry Carey. CoMu
Now the hard margin bears us on, while steam. Dante, *tr. by* Dorothy L. Sayers. *Fr.* Divina Commedia: Inferno. PeHV

Now the heart sings with all its thousand voices. The Gateway. A. D. Hope. BoLoP; ErPo; UnTE
Now the Holy Lamp of Love. Patrick MacDonogh. BIrV
Now the Hungry Lion Roars. Shakespeare. *Fr.* A Midsummer Night's Dream, V, ii. CH; ChTr; CTC; EIL; EnRePo; LiTB; SeCeV; ViBoPo; WSC
(Epilogue.) LoBV; OBSC
(Fairy Blessing, The.) OxBoLi
(Fairy Songs.) TrGrPo
(Lion of Winter, The.) WiR
(Puck's Song.) MoShBr
Now the ice lays its smooth claws on the sill. Scotland's Winter. Edwin Muir. OxBS; OxBTC
Now the joys of the road are chiefly these. The Joys of the Road. Bliss Carman. HBV-1; HBVY; OBVV
Now the Laborer's Task Is O'er. John Lodge Ellerton. BLPA; HBV-2; TreFS; WGRP
Now the last day of many days. To Jane: The Recollection [*or* The Recollection]. Shelley. ChER; GTBS; GTBS-P; OBNC; OBRV
Now the last drop, both sweet and fierce. Middle-Age. Emily B. C. Jones. HBMV
Now the last step! Behold. M. Krishnamurti. *Fr.* The Cloth of Gold. PeD
Now the late fruits are in. For a Wine Festival. Vernon Watkins. OxBTC
Now the Leaves Are Falling Fast. W. H. Auden. CMoP; CoBMV
Now the light o' the west is a-turn'd to gloom. Evenen in the Village. William Barnes. EBVV
Now the little rivers go. Winter Streams. Bliss Carman. YeAr
Now the long blade of the sun, lying. Thebes of the Seven Gates. Sophocles, *tr. by* Dudley Fitts *and* Robert Fitzgerald. *Fr.* Antigone. WaaP
Now, the Lord made the bee and the bee did make the honey. Swansea Town. *Unknown.* ShS
Now the lotuses in the imperial lake. Wang Ch'ing-hui, *tr. fr. Chinese by* Kenneth Rexroth *and* Ling Chung. BoWoP
Now the Lusty Spring. John Fletcher. *See* Love's Emblems.
Now the midwinter grind. Middle Age. Robert Lowell. PAI
Now the Most High Is Born. James Ryman. MeEL
Now the narrowing track. The Look. Elizabeth Daryush. PoA
Now the New Moon is hanging, having cast away his bone. New Moon. *Aborigine Oral Tradition, tr. by* R. M. Berndt. *Fr.* The Moon-Bone Cycle. WTO
Now the Noisy Winds Are Still. Mary Mapes Dodge. YeAr
Now, the people are getting their art. Ballet under the Stars. Robert Stewart. FAZ
Now the People Have the Light. Charles G. Ballard. VoR
Now the pines lift. Burning the Tomato Worms. Carolyn Forché. AmPA
Now the plains come to adore the mountain wall. Colorado. Robert Fitzgerald. MoPo
Now the rich cherry, whose sleek wood. Country Summer. Léonie Adams. GoJo; LiTM; MoAB; MoAmPo; MoPo; MoVE; TrGrPo; TwAmPo; ViBoPo
Now the rite is duly done. The Newly-wedded. Winthrop Mackworth Praed. HBV-1
Now the river is rich, but her voice is low. The River in March. Ted Hughes. OxBC
Now the shiades o' the elems da stratch muore an muore. Evening, and Maidens. William Barnes. OBEV; OBVV
Now, the showground is quiet. The Horse Show at Midnight. Henry Taylor. PH
Now the small birds come to feast. Winter Feast. Frances Frost. YeAr
Now the sneeze is a joy-vent, I s'pose. The Sneeze. Anthony Euwer. *Fr.* The Limeratomy. HBMV
Now the snow/ lies on the ground. Winter. William Carlos Williams. NCSH
Now the snow is vanished clean. Québec May. Earle Birney. WHW
Now the sprinkled blackthorn snow. Spring in War-Time. Edith Nesbit. SUMH
Now the stone house on the lake front is finished and the workmen are beginning the fence. A Fence. Carl Sandburg. WeW
Now the storm begins to lower. The Fatal Sisters. Thomas Gray. EnRP; LAuP; OAEP
Now the Summer's Come. *Unknown.* *See* Cuckoo Song.
Now the sun again, like a bloody convict. The Rising Sun. Lawrence Durrell. *Fr.* Eight Aspects of Melissa. NeBP
Now the sun's gane out o' sight. Up in the Air. Allan Ramsay. BSV; NOEC
Now, the times are hard and the wages low. Time for Us to Leave Her. *Unknown.* ShS
Now the trouble with SETting down a: written calypso. Calypsomania. Anthony Brode. FiBHP
Now the wheat is in the ear, and the rose is on the brere. The Lover's Invitation. John Clare. VLP
Now the white roses, wilted and yellowing fast. Lament of the Jewish Women for Tammuz. Charles Reznikoff. VWA
Now the white-buskined lamb. At Bungendore. James McAuley. PoAu-2
Now the Widow McGee. Larrie O'Dee. William W. Fink. HBV-2
Now the wild bees that hive in the rocks. The Brown Bear. Mary Austin. FaPON; PoSC
Now the winds are all composure. St. Philip and St. James [*or* Hymn: St. Philip and St. James *or* Spring]. Christopher Smart. Hymns and Spiritual Songs, Hymn 13. LoBV; NOCV; NOEC; OBEC
Now the winter is gone and the summer is come. As I Walked through the Meadows. *Unknown.* OBET
Now the word of the Lord came unto Jonah. Jonah. Bible, *O.T.* NAWM-1
Now, the wry Rosenbloom is dead. Cortège for Rosenbloom. Wallace Stevens. TwAmPo
Now Thebes stood in good estate, now Cadmus might thou say. Acteon. Ovid, *tr. by* Arthur Golding. *Fr.* Metamorphoses, III. CTC
Now then, for love of Crist and of His joye. Keep the Sea. *Unknown.* *Fr.* The Libelle of Englyshe Polycye. OxBM
Now then, shipmates, come gather and join in my ditty. The *Cumberland's* Crew. ShS
Now then, take your seats! for Glasgow and the North. The Night Mail North. Henry Cholmondeley Pennell. EBVV
"Now then, what are you up to, Dai?" Langwell. Kingsley Amis. *Fr.* The Evans Country. NOBL; OxBC
Now there are gold reflections on the water. In Time of Gold. Hilda Doolittle ("H. D."). PoA
Now there are no bonds except the flesh; listen. Manzini; Escape Artist. Gwendolyn MacEwen. NOBC
Now there are no walls. Passover Dachau. B. Z. Niditch. AMV-81
Now there comes/ The Christmas rose. New Year's [*or* Year] Song. Ted Hughes. OBCP; OFD
Now there is a love of which Dante does not speak unkindly. Sonnet I. Robert Duncan. GP
Now there is frost upon the hill. Where It Is Winter. George O'Neil. HBMV
Now There Is Nothing Left. L. A. MacKay. CaP; PeCV
Now there's many fool things a woman will do. Gold Tooth Blues. Tennessee Williams. OBAL
Now they are resting. Fine Work with Pitch and Copper. William Carlos Williams. OxBA
Now they call me Hanging Johnny. Hanging Johnny. *Unknown.* ShS
Now they have come, those afternoons in November. November Afternoons. Sister Mary Madeleva. GoBC
Now they have two cars to clean. Do It Yrself. Larry Eigner. NeAP; PoM
Now they're pillaging the last coast. The Vandals. Jenny Mastoraki, *tr. by* Nikos Germanakos. BoWoP
Now thin mists temper the slow-ripening beams. The Garden in September. Robert Bridges. PoPle
Now think on't, Nell the glover fair. Ballade of the Fair Helm-Maker. Villon, *tr. by* John Payne. UnTE
Now this dark cloud is rising. Mean Old Twister. *Unknown.* BluL
Now this is my first counsel. Part of the Lay of Sigrdrifa [*or* Counsels of Sigrdrifa]. *Unknown, tr. by* William Morris *and* Eirikr Magnusson. *Fr.* The Elder Edda. AWP; OBVE
Now this is new: that I (habitué). First Day of Teaching. Bonaro W. Overstreet. TrPWD
Now this is the Law of the Jungle—as old and as true as the sky. The Law of the Jungle. Kipling. LiTB; PoEL-5
Now those that are low spirited I hope won't think it wrong. A New Hunting Song. *Unknown.* CoMu
Now thou art dead, no eye shall ever see. Upon His Spaniell Tracie. Robert Herrick. FM
Now thou hast lov'd me one whole day. Woman's Constancy. John Donne. AnAnS-1; NoP; SeCV-1
Now thought seeks shelter, lest the heart melt. Recovery. F. R. Scott. CaP
Now Thrice Welcome Christmas. *Unknown.* OHIP
Now through Night's Caressing Grip. W. H. Auden. PoRA
Now through the ocean in great haste they flunder. Luis de Camoes, *tr. by* Sir Richard Fanshawe. *Fr.* The Lusiads. OBVE
Now Time's Andromeda on this rock rude. Andromeda. Gerard Manley Hopkins. EBEV; FaBoMo; LiTB; VLP
Now to attune my dull soul, if I can. Bleue Maison. Edmund Blunden. BrPo
Now to be clean he must abandon himself. The Swan Bathing. Ruth Pitter. BoAnP; MoBrPo
Now to dispose the dead, the care remains. Homer, *tr. by* Pope. *Fr.* The Odyssey, XXII. OBVE
Now to Great Britain we must make our way. Of England, and of Its Marvels. Fazio degli Uberti, *tr. by* Dante Gabriel Rossetti. AWP

Now to pick wild plums. Leave the Top Plums. Janet Carncross Chandler. AMV-80
Now to th'ascent of that steep savage hill. Satan Journeys to the Garden of Eden. Milton. *Fr.* Paradise Lost, IV. ChTr
Now toils the heroe; trees on trees o'erthrown. Homer, *tr. by* Pope. *Fr.* The Odyssey, V. OBVE
Now Tomlinson gave up the ghost in his house in Berkeley Square. Tomlinson. Kipling. BeLS
Now touch the air softly. A Pavane for the Nursery. William Jay Smith. DuDa; GoJo; MoAmPo; NePoAm-2; PoSC
Now tow'rd the Hunter's gloomy sides we came. The Hospital Prison Ship. Philip Freneau. The British Prison Ship, III. AmPP
Now trees are weedy mazes, upright, still. Larch Hill. Leslie Daiken. OnYI
Now, 'twas twenty-five or thirty years since Jack first saw the light. Jack Was Every Inch a Sailor. *Unknown.* FSW; WHW
Now, Until the Break of Day. Shakespeare. *Fr.* A Midsummer Night's Dream, V, ii. NAs
(Fairy Songs.) TrGrPo
Now upon sale, a bankrupt island. Four Epigrams on the Naturalization Bill. John Byrom. NOBL
Now upon this piteous year. The Stranger. Jean Garrigue. LiTA; LiTM; MP; NOBA; TwCP
Now van to van the foremost squadrons meet. Dryden. *Fr.* Annus Mirabilis. OBWP
Now Venus is an evening star. Waiting. Hilary Corke. ErPo
Now vows connubial chain the plighted pair. Reproduction of Life. Erasmus Darwin. *Fr.* The Temple of Nature; or, The Origin of Society, II. PBBP
Now—wagon full of thunder. Wagon Full of Thunder. Louis (LittleCoon) Oliver. STE
Now War Is All the World About; or, An Ode, upon Occasion of His Majesties Proclamation in the Year 1630. Sir Richard Fanshawe. *Fr.* Il Pastor Fido. LoBV
(Ode on His Majesty's Proclamation, Commanding the Gentry to Reside on Their Estates.) NOBE
(Ode, An, upon Occasion of His Majesties Proclamation in the Year[e] 1630.] MePo; OBS
Now was there maid fast by the towris wall. The Nightingale's Song. James I, King of Scotland. *Fr.* The Kingis Quair. EBEV; OxBM
Now watch this autumn that arrives. Song at the Beginning of Autumn. Elizabeth Jennings. OxBTC
Now we are civilized, the old men die. Old Men's Ward. Elma Dean. GoYe
Now we are left out. Funeral Song. *Unknown, tr. by* Dan Kunene *and* Jack Cope. PeSA
Now We Are Sick. J. B. Morton. *Fr.* When We Were Very Silly. FaBoPa; PV; SpRo
Now we are thirty-five we no longer enjoy red neon. Literary Life in the Golden West. Philip Whalen. NAs
Now we begin another day together. Prayer at Dawn. Edwin McNeill Poteat. TrPWD
Now we enter a strange world, where the Hessian Christmas. After the Industrial Revolution, All Things Happen at Once. Robert Bly. CoAP; ConAP
Now we have always with us these men—these men! Memo. Hildegarde Flanner. NYBP
Now we have in our group a lot. Should We Legalize Abortion? Frank O'Hara. NoAM
Now we must get up quickly. Two Lines from the Brothers Grimm. Gregory Orr. AmPA
Now we must praise heaven-kingdom's Guardian. Hymn. Caedmon. TrCP
Now we remember all: the wild pear-tree. Pictures by Vuillard. Adrienne Rich. TwAmPo
Now we shall learn to live in the dark. Dusk of the Revolutionaries. John Haines. NPAW
Now we should praise Heaven-kingdom's guard. Hymn. Caedmon, *tr. by* D. K. Fry. PAI
Now weave the winds to music of June's lyre. June. Theodore Harding Rand. CaP
Now Welcom[e], Somer [*or* Summer]. Chaucer. *Fr.* The Parliament of Fowls. HAP; OxBM; SeCePo
(Birds' Rondel, The, *mod. vers. by* Louis Untermeyer.) TrGrPo
(Foules Rondel.) TrGrPo
(Qui Bien Aime a Tard Oublie.) EnLoPo
(Roundel: "Now welcom[e], somer, with thy sunne [*or* sonne] softe.") CTC; OAEL-1
(Welcome, Summer.) MeEL
Now welcome, welcome, baby-boy, unto a mother's fears. The Irish Mother in the Penal Days. John Banim. AnIV
Now wend we to the Palmalle. Domine, Quo Vadis? *Unknown.* ACP
Now we're afloat upon the tropic sea. Tropical Weather. Epes Sargent. EtS
Now we're met, my brethren Benchers. The Humours of the King's Bench Prison, a Ballad. Leonard Howard. NOEC
Now we're stuck there. Heaving the Lead Line. *Unknown.* AmFP
Now westward Sol had spent the richest beam[e]s. Music[k]'s Duel[l]. Richard Crashaw. GoTL; OAEL-1; OBS; PBBP; SeCP; SeCV-1
Now we've made a child. And What About the Children. Audre Lorde. PoBA
Now We've Met. *Unknown.* OBET
Now, what did you do with the gun in your hand. Take a Drink on Me. *Unknown.* FSW
Now what do you think. *Unknown.* OxNR
Now what in the world shall we dioux. The Sioux. Eugene Field. FiBHP; GoJo
Now What Is Love. Sir Walter Ralegh. *See* Description of Love, A.
Now, what news on the Rialto? Shylock's Defense. Shakespeare. *Fr.* The Merchant of Venice, III, i. TreFS
Now what you all know about this? Stagolee. *Unknown.* ViBoFo
Now when drowning imagination clutches. Word over All. C. Day Lewis. OAEP
Now when I drove to the sand pit, the horizon. Red Wing Hawk. James Applewhite. AMV-81
Now when I have thrust my body. To Forget Me. Theodore Weiss. CoAP
Now when I sleep the thrush breaks through my dreams. A Dream in Early Spring. Fredegond Shove. MoVE
Now when I walk around at lunchtime. Personal Poem. Frank O'Hara. CAPP; NYP
Now, when the cheerless empire of the sky. Winter. James Thomson. *Fr.* The Seasons. BSV; OxBS
Now when the solemn rites of pray'r were past. Homer, *tr. by* Dryden. *Fr.* The Iliad, I. OBVE
Now when those Seven of the First Heaven stood still. Dante, *tr. by* Laurence Binyon. Divina Commedia: Purgatorio, XXX-XXXI. NAWM-1
Now, when thou hast decreed to seize their stores. The Care of Bees. Virgil, *tr. by* Dryden. *Fr.* Georgics, IV. FaBoUs
Now, when twelve days complete had run their race. Homer, *tr. by* Dryden. *Fr.* The Iliad, I. OBVE
Now when we leave the windows of hay. To a Horse. Jill Hoffman. PH
Now, when you cut me dead and say that I'm. On a Female Snob, Surprised. Patric Dickinson. DBV
"Now where are ye goin'," ses I, "wid the shawl." The Road. Patrick R. Chalmers. HBV-1
Now whether folks are Methodists. The Radio Religion. William Ludlum. WBLP
Now, whether it were by peculiar grace. Wordsworth. *Fr.* Resolution and Independence. Par
Now which is wrong or right? Too glib we talk. Falkland at Newbury, 1643. Hugh Conway. EBVV
Now, while our money is piping hot. The Merchantmen. John Davidson. OBVV
Now while Rogero learns the arms and name. Angelica and the Ork. Ariosto, *tr. by* Sir John Harington. *Fr.* Orlando Furioso, X. OBSC
Now, while the birds thus sing a joyous song. Wordsworth. *Fr.* Ode: Intimations of Immortality from Recollections of Early Childhood. Prf
Now while the solemn evening shadows sail. Swans. Wordsworth. *Fr.* An Evening Walk. OBEC
Now while the sunset offers. Santa Barbara Beach. Ridgely Torrence. HBMV
Now, while thou hast the wondrous power of word. The Gift of Speech. Sadi, *tr. by* L. Cranmer-Byng. *Fr.* The Gulistan. AWP
Now Whitehall's in the grave. A Mock Song. Richard Lovelace. CaPo
Now who is he on earth that lives. Medieval Norman Song. *Unknown, tr. by* John Addington Symonds. AWP
Now whyle Hippomenes/ Debates theis things. Ovid, *tr. by* Arthur Golding. *Fr.* Metamorphoses, X. OBVE
Now will I a lover be. The Combat. Thomas Stanley. AWP
Now will you stand for me, in this cool light. Love in the Museum. Adrienne Rich. NePoEA; NYBP
Now wilt me take for Jesus' sake. A Prayer. Katharine Tynan. OBVV
Now winds of winter glue. Upon New Year's Eve. Sir Arthur Quiller-Couch. OBVV
Now winter downs the dying of the year. Year's End [*or* At Year's End]. Richard Wilbur. CAPP; CoAP; HeIP; LiTM; MiAP; NePoEA; NePA; NYBP
Now Winter Nights Enlarge. Thomas Campion. AAS; EBEV; ElL; ELP; EnRePo; HeIP; LoBV; NoP; OBSC; QFR; SeCePo; TEP; ViBoPo
(Winter Nights.) NOBE; OBEV
Now Winter's winds are banished from the sky. Spring. Meleager, *tr. by* William M. Hardinge. AWP

Now wintry blasts have come again. Love Laughs at Winter. *Unknown, tr. by* George F. Whicher. UnTE
Now with a general peace the world was blest. Dryden. *Fr.* Astraea Redux. OBS
Now with a vestal lustre glows the Vale. Anna Seward. *Fr.* Llangollen Vale. PeHV
Now with earth riven and a bloodied sun. We Shall Say. Miriam Allen deFord. GoYe
Now with gray hair begins defeat. Farewell to Town. Laurence Housman. HBMV
Now with the coming in of the spring the days will stretch a bit. The County Mayo. Anthony Raftery, *tr. by* James Stephens. AnIL
Now with the springtime the days will grow longer. County Mayo. Anthony Raftery, *tr. by* Frank O'Connor. KiLC
Now, with your palms on the blades of my shoulders. Dead Still. Andrei Voznesensky, *tr. by* Richard Wilbur. BoLoP
Now wolde I fayne sum merthis [*or* faine some merthes] mak[e]. Song for My Lady [*or* An Absent Lover *or* A Song in His Lady's Absence]. A. Godwin. CH; MeEL; OxBM; OxBoLi
Now would I weave her portrait out of all dim. Portrait. Ezra Pound. OBVV
Now would to God swift ships had ne'er been made! Sopolis. Callimachus, *tr. by* William M. Hardinge. AWP
"Now, yield thee, or by Him who made." Sir Walter Scott. *Fr.* The Lady of the Lake, V. OxBS
Now you/ tell me mama, do you. Saturday Blues. *Unknown.* BluL
Now you are going, what can I do but wish you. The Poet's Farewell to His Teeth. William Dickey. DFF; GP; PoA
Now you are holding my skull in your hand. A Meditation. Richard Eberhart. LiTA
Now you are one with us, you know our tears. To America, on Her First Sons Fallen in the Great War. E. M. Walker. PAH
Now you are standing face to face with the clear light. Prayer for the Little Daughter between Death and Burial. Diana Scott. BrRo
Now you clown with your grocery man. Go Back to the Country. *Unknown.* BluL
Now you come again. Happiness of 6 A.M. Harvey Shapiro. NYBP
Now you depart, and though your way may lead. To a Friend Going on a Journey. Mahammed Abdille Hassan, *tr. fr. Somali by* M. Laurence. WTO
Now you done spent all my 1940 rent. Working Man Blues. *Unknown.* BluL
Now You Have Burned. John Thompson. NOBC
Now you have freely given me leave to love. To a Lady That Desired I Would Love Her. Thomas Carew. AnAnS-2; CaPo; LoBV; MeLP; MePo; OBS; SeCV-1
Now you have stabbed her good. Kreutzer Sonata. Ted Hughes. FaBoMo
Now you have to promise. Cousin Ella Goes to Town. George Ella Lyon. Str
Now "you," if you are still yourself. Witness. Jon Anderson. MAYP
Now you may have Him, Mary, they are done. Thirteenth Station. William A. Donaghy. ISi
"Now you must die," the young one said. The Rite. Dudley Randall. HoPM
Now you take ol Rufus. He beat drums. For Freckle-faced Gerald. Etheridge Knight. BPo; LFAC; NeAC
Now your cheeks are as old and bald. For Allen Ginsberg, Who Cut Off His Beard. Sanford Pinsker. AMV-80
Now You're Content. André Spire, *tr. fr. French by* Stanley Burnshaw. TrJP
Now you've been an Abbess for years. Abelard at Cluny. Grover Rees III. AMV-80
Nowadays the mess is everywhere. The Survivors. Daryl Hine. TwCP
Nowe welcome, Somor, with sonne softe. *See* Now Welcome, Somer.
Nowel! nowel! nowel! Man Exalted. *Unknown.* MeEL
Nowel! nowel! nowel! Mary Is with Child. *Unknown.* MeEL
Nowell Sing We. *Unknown.* ChTr
Nowhere are we safe. Hymn Written after Jeremiah Preached to Me in a Dream. Owen Dodson. AmNP
Nowhere can flesh feel more limp. Voting Machine. Norman Nathan. AMV-80
Nowhere, not among the warriors at their festival. Atimantiyar, *tr. fr. Tamil by* A. K. Ramanujan. WPOW
Nowhere, on the way to the meaning. Sayer. George P. Elliott. FAZ
Now's the time for mirth and play. For Saturday [*or* A Lark's Nest]. Christopher Smart. *Fr.* Hymns for the Amusement of Children. FaBoCh; LAuP; NOEC; OxBChV
Nox Est Perpetua. Marion Lochhead. LO
Nox Nocti Indicat Scientiam. William Habington. *Fr.* Castara, III. ACP; AnAnS-2; GoBC; HBV-2; JCP; LoBV; MeLP; MePo; NOBE; OBEV; OBS; OxBoCh
Nox was lit by lux of Luna, The. Carmen Possum. *Unknown.* BLPA
Nuances of a Theme by Williams. Wallace Stevens. CMoP; LiTA
Nubia. Bayard Taylor. HBV-2
Nubs Lilly liked to use his fists. The Fighter. Dave Etter. TAT
Nuclear Family, The. Melvin Douglass Brown. LFAC
Nuclear Land. Ellen Tifft. AMV-81
Nuclear Racial Lockdowns. Pancho Aguila. LFAC
Nuclear wind, when wilt thou blow. *See* O Nuclear wind, when wilt thou blow.
Nude. Daniel Halpern. MAYP
Nude. Harold Witt. ErPo
Nude Beneath the Willows, leaves hanging down. Art Gallery. John Dickson. AMV-81
Nude Descending a Staircase. X. J. Kennedy. CoAP; ConAP; HeIP; HoAn; HoPM; NePoEA-2; NIP; PoA; POL
Nude in a Fountain. Norman MacCaig. OxBS
Nude Kneeling in Sand. John Logan. ErPo
Nude on the Bathroom Wall, The. Gena Ford. IHMS
Nude Swim, The. Anne Sexton. WPE
Nude with Green Chair. Antony Oldknow. AMV-81
Nudes—stark and glistening. Louse Hunting. Isaac Rosenberg. EBEV; NoP; OxBTC
Nudging and thrusting to the light. Gideon at the Well. Geoffrey Hill. NePoEA
Nudities. André Spire, *tr. fr. French.* AWP; *tr. by* Jethro Bithell; ErPo; *tr. by* Jethro Bithell; TrJP, *tr. by* Stanley Burnshaw; VWA, *tr. by* Stanley Burnshaw
Nuflo de Olano (Who Sailed with Balboa). Antar S. K. Mberi. LTB
Nuisance at Home, A. *Unknown.* TDH
Nuit Blanche. Katherine Hoskins. NMP
Nuit Blanche: North End. Conrad Aiken. OxBA
Numb, stiff, broken by no sleep. Night Thoughts over a Sick Child. Philip Levine. NePoEA-2
Number 5—December. David Henderson. BOLo
Number Four. Doughtry Long. CNA; PoBA; SO
Number is dialed, a window opened, A. Telephone Ghosts. Robert Frazier. SUW
Number Nine, Penwiper Mews. Edward Gorey. RHPC
(From Number Nine, Penwiper Mews.) TDH
Number One/ I slouch in bed. Two Hangovers. James Wright. LCAP
Number one is a good clean number, The. The Million. Peter Redgrove. OxBC
Number Twelve Train. *Unknown.* FSW
Number 29. *Unknown.* BluL
Numbers, *sels.* Bible, *O.T.*
Balaam's Blessing, XXIV: 5-9. TrGrPo
("How goodly are the tentes of Jacob and thine habitacions Israel," *tr. by* William Tyndale.) OBVE
Benediction, VI: 24-26. TrGrPo
(Blessing of the Priests.) TrJP
("Lorde blesse the and kepe the, The," VI: 24-27, *tr. by* William Tyndale.) OBVE
Song of the Well, XXI: 17-18. TrJP
Numbers. Harley Elliott. LTB
Numbers, The. Joel Oppenheimer. CoPo
Numbers and Faces, *sel.* W. H. Auden.
"Kingdom of Number is all boundaries, The." ImOP
Numbers, Letters. Amiri Baraka. BPo; NOBA
Numerella Shore, The. "Cockatoo Jack." PoAu-1
Numerous Celts. J. C. Squire. BXAP; SpRo
Numerous host of dreaming saints succeed, A. Zimri: The Duke of Buckingham. Dryden. *Fr.* Absalom and Achitophel, Pt. I. FaBoEn; NOBE; OBSV
Nummum et secalis sacculum cantate! Four and Twenty Merulae. J. Moyr Smith. FaBoNo
Nun, The. Leigh Hunt. HBV-1; InMe; OBRV; OBVV
Nun, The. Arthur Symons. BrPo
Nun Snow. Alfred Kreymborg. TwAmPo
Nun Speaks to Mary, A. Sister Mary Madeleva. ISi
Nun to Mary, Virgin, A. Sister Mary St. Virginia. ISi
Nun walked on her prayer, The. The Friar and the Nun. *Unknown.* GBP
*Nunaptigne. . .*In our land—*ahe, ahe, ee, ee, iee.* The Wind Has Wings. *Unknown, tr. by* Raymond de Coccola *and* Paul King. GrPl; WHW
Nunc Dimittis. Bible, *N.T.* St. Luke, II: 29-32. WGRP
Nunc Gaudet Maria. *Unknown.* ISi
Nunc Scio, Quid Sit Amor. L. A. Mackay. OBCV
Nunc Viridant Segetes. Sedulius Scottus, *tr. fr. Medieval Latin by* Helen Waddell. BIrV
(He Complains to Bishop Hartgar of Thirst.) NAWM-1
Nuns at Eve. John Malcolm Brinnin. MoAB; MP; TwCP
Nuns Fret Not at Their Convent's Narrow Room. Wordsworth. CABA; EBEV; EnRP; NIP; NoP; OAEP; PP
(Prefatory Sonnet.) OBRV

(Sonnet: "Nuns fret not at their convent's narrow room.") OBEV; ViBoPo
Nuns, his nieces, bring the priest in the next. A Far Cry after a Close Call. Richard Howard. NYBP; UnPo
Nuns in the Wind. Muriel Rukeyser. NNaP
Nun's Priest's Prologue, The. Chaucer. *Fr.* The Canterbury Tales. OAEL-1
Nun's Priest's Tale, The. Chaucer. *Fr.* The Canterbury Tales. NoP; OAEL-1; OAEP; OBVE, *mod. version by* Dryden; PoEL-1; SeCeV; TrGrPo, *orig. and mod. version by* Frank Ernest Hill.
(Cock and the Hen, The.) OBNV
(Nonne Preestes Tale, The.) FiP
Sels.
Chauntecleer. PB
"His comb was redder than the fine coral." PBBP
"This Chauntecleer stood hye up-on his toos." FiP
Nu-numma-kwiten formerly sang. The Song of Nu-Numma-Kwiten. *Unknown.* PeSA
Nuptial Dialogues, *sel.* Edward Ward.
Dialogue between a Squeamish Cotting Mechanic and His Sluttish Wife, in the Kitchen. NOEC
Nuptial Eve, A. Sydney Dobell. OBNC
Ballad of Keith of Ravelston, The, *sel.* HBV-2; OBEV; OBVV
(Keith of Ravelston.) CH
Nuptial Hymn. Henry Peacham. *Fr.* The Period of Mourning. ElL
Nuptial Sleep. Dante Gabriel Rossetti. The House of Life, VI. LoBV; VLP
(Sonnet: Nuptial Sleep.) EBVV
Nuptial Song. Lord De Tabley. GTBS-P; OBVV
Nuptial Song. Henricus Selyns. *See* O Christmas Night.
Nuptial[l] Song, or Epithalamie [*or* Epithalamy], on Sir Clipseby Crew and His Lady, A. Robert Herrick. CaPo; JCP; PoEL-3; SeCP; SeCV-1
Nuremberg. Longfellow. AmPP; HBV-2
Nurse carried him up the stair, The. At Thomas Hardy's Birthplace, 1953. James Wright. ConAP
Nurse-life wheat, within his green[e] husk[e] growing, The. Youth and Maturity [*or* Sonnet]. Fulke Greville. *Fr.* Caelica. AAS; EnRePo; JCP; NCEP; OBSC
Nurse looks round my clinic screen, The. David McCord. Convalescence, IV. WhC
Nurse No Long Grief. Mary Gilmore. PoAu-1
Nurse Sharks. William Matthews. FiCP
Nurse, who is neither young nor pretty, The. Rivalry. Alden Nowlan. POL
Nursery boast, The. On Seeing My Birthplace from a Jet Aircraft. John Pudney. NYBP
Nursery Rhyme. Kenneth Burke. OBAL
Nursery Rhyme of Innocence and Experience. Charles Causley. GoJo
Nursery Rhymes for the Tender-hearted, *sels.* Christopher Morley.
"I knew a black beetle, who lived down a drain," IV. HBMV
"Scuttle, scuttle little roach," I. FaFP; HBMV; YaD
Nursery Song, A. Laura E. Richards. HBV-1; HBVY
Nursery Song in Pidgin English. *Unknown.* SpRo; WhC
(Song: "Singee songee sick a pence.") BXAP
Nurse's Dole in the Medea, The. Byron. OBVE
Nurse's Song ("When the voices of children are heard on the green/ And laughing is heard on the hill"). Blake. *Fr.* Songs of Innocence. AWP; BLPL; CH; EnRP; FaBoBe; HBV-1; HBVY; LAuP; OBEC; OxBChV;
(Play Time.) FaPON
Nurse's Song ("When the voices of children are heard on the green/ And whisprings are in the dale"). Blake. *Fr.* Songs of Experience. CABA; EnRP; FF; LAuP
Nursing the Hide. Carol Dunne. AMV-81
Nursing your nerves. The Afterwake. Adrienne Rich. NOBA; Prf
Nut, a World, a Squirrel, and a King, A. Charles Churchill. *Fr.* Night; an Epistle to Robert Lloyd. FaBoRV
Nut-brown Ale, The. John Marston. ElL
Nut-brown Maid, The. *Unknown.* OBEV; OBSC
Nut Tree, The. *Unknown.* MoShBr; SoPo
Nutcrackers and the Sugar-Tongs, The. Edward Lear. BLPL; PoLF; PoPle
Nut-gathering Lass, The. Burns. UnTE
Nuts an' May. *Unknown.* EvOK
Nuts and Bolts Poem for Mr. Mac Adams, Sr. Kathleen Fraser. NPGG
Nut's Birthday, The. Jessie Pope. SUMH
Nuts in May. Louis MacNeice. MoAB; MoBrPo
Nutting. Wordsworth. EnRP; NU; OAEL-2
Nyanu was appointed. Early Losses; a Requiem. Alice Walker. BlSi
Nycht he thocht in his dreming, A. Macbeth's Dream. Andrew of Wyntoun. BSV
Nydia's Song. Sir Edward Bulwer-Lytton. *Fr.* The Last Days of Pompeii. OBVV
Nymph and a Swain, A. Congreve. UnTE
Nymph Complaining for the Death of Her Faun, The. Andrew Marvell. AnAnS-1; CH; FM; GoTL; HBV-1; HeIP; LoBV; MePo; OAEL-1; OBS, *abr.;* PoEL-2; SeCP; SeCV-1
Nymph and Her Fawn, The, *sel.* FaBoCh
Nymph Fanaret, the gentlest maid. The Penance. Nahum Tate. CavP
Nymph I come once more awooing. Ay or Nay? Ralph Schomberg. *Fr.* The Judgment of Paris. TrJP
Nymph, nymph, what are your beads? Overheard on a Saltmarsh. Harold Monro. CH; FaPON; GoJo; MoShBr; SO; TiPo; WSC
Nymph of the garden where all beauties be. Astrophel and Stella, LXXXII. Sir Philip Sidney. InvP; SiPS
Nymph that undoes me is fair and unkind, The. Silvia. Sir George Etherege. CavP
Nymph turnd home, The. He fell to felling downe. Homer, *tr. by* George Chapman. *Fr.* The Odyssey, V. OBVE
Nymphidia, the Court of Fairy. Michael Drayton. OAEP
Sels.
Arming of Pigwiggen, The. GN
(Pigwiggin Arms Himself.) MoShBr
"Pigwiggen was this fairy knight." ViBoPo
Queen's Chariot, The. OBS
Nymphing through Car Windows (East Gallatin). Greg Keeler. WOLT
Nympholept, A. Swinburne. VLP
Nymphs, The, *sel.* James Leigh Hunt.
"There are the fair-limbed Nymphs o' the woods, (Look ye.)" OBNC; OBRV
Nymphs and Satyrs. Gavin Ewart. PV
Nymphs and shepherds dance no more. Song. Milton. *Fr.* Arcades. ELP; FiP; ViBoPo
Nymph's Disdain of Love, A. *Unknown.* ElL
Nymphs of sea and land, away. Nuptial Hymn. Henry Peacham. *Fr.* The Period of Mourning. ElL
Nymph's Reply to the Shepherd, The. Sir Walter Ralegh. BiP; CABA; CTC; ElL; FF; HAP; HeIP; HoPM; LiTB; LoBV; NIP; NOBE; NoP; OAEP; OLR; PAI; PPP; SeCePo; SeCeV; SiPS; TreFS; TrGrPo; WeW; WHA
(Answer to Marlowe.) OAEL-1; OBSC
(Her Reply.) BoLoP; OBEV
(Nimphs Reply to the Sheepheard, The.) AAS
(Nymph's Reply to the Passionate Sherpherd.) FaBoPa; HBV-1
(Reply to Marlowe's "The Passionate Shepherd to His Love.") ViBoPo
Nymph's Secret, A. Ben Jonson. OBEV
Nymph's Song to Hylas, The. William Morris. *See* Garden by the Sea, The.
"Nymphs! your fine hands ethereal floods amass." The Action of Electricity. Erasmus Darwin. *Fr.* The Economy of Vegetation. FaBoUs
Nystagmus. Joseph Matuzak. SUW
Nyum-Nyum, The. *Unknown.* NA

O

Ö. Rita Dove. MAYP
O. Richard Wilbur. LiTA; MoPo
O. *See also* Oh.
O/ out of a bed of love. Holy Spring. Dylan Thomas. WaP
O a dainty plant is the Ivy green. *See* Oh a dainty plant is the Ivy green.
O a gallant set were they. A Huguenot. Mary Elizabeth Coleridge. OBVV
O a' the isles of this braid sea. Skye. John Gawsworth. PoSH
O, a wonderful steam is the river Time. *See* Oh, a wonderful stream is the river Time.
O a year from tomorrow I left my own people. Clonmel Jail. *Unknown, tr. by* Valentin Iremonger. BIrV
O Aa the Manly Sports. J. K. Annand. PoSH
"O, Aaron Burr, what have you done?" Aaron Burr. Stephen Vincent Benét. InMe
O Abishag, my little serving-maid. Abishag. André Spire, *tr. by* Emanuel Eisenberg. TrJP
O absent presence! Stella is not here. Astrophel and Stella, CVI. Sir Philip Sidney. SiPS
O African mother, so full of fear. To Whom Shall They Go? *Unknown.* STF
O ah drove three mules foh Gawge McVane. Mule Skinner's Song. *Unknown.* AS
O Alison Gross, that lives in yon tower [*or* tow'r]. Alison [or Allison] Gross. *Unknown.* CH; ESPB; FaBoCh; OxBB; WSC
O All Down within the Pretty Meadow. Kenneth Patchen. HAP; WeW
O all the problems other people face. Alcoholic. John Berryman. NOCV
O all ye fair ladies with your colours and your graces. The Revenant. Walter de la Mare. GBL
O all you little blackety-tops. *Unknown.* OxNR; PBBP

O all your ages at the mercy of my loves. John Berryman. *Fr.* Homage to Mistress Bradstreet. NOBA
O Allison Gross, that lives in yon towr. *See* O Alison Gross. . .
O Amber Day, amid the Autumn Gloom. William Talbot Allison. CaP
O amiable prospect! New Lines for Cuscuscaraway and Mirza Murad Ali Beg. Louis Simpson. OBAL
O an old King in a story. After W. B. Yeats. G. K. Chesterton. NOBL
O, answer me a question, Love, I pray. *See* Oh, answer me a question, Love, I pray.
O Apple Betty fiend, attend. Lines to a Man Who Thinks That Apple Betty with Hard Sauce Is Food for a Human Being. George S. Kaufman. InMe
O apple blossoms. Japanese Hokku. Lewis Alexander. CDC
O! Are Ye Sleepin [*or* Sleeping], Maggie? Robert Tannahill. OBRV; OxBS
O Artemis and your virgin girls. Telesilla, *tr. fr. Greek by* Willis Barnstone. BoWoP
O Atthis. Ezra Pound. PoA
O Autumn, laden with fruit, and stained. To Autumn. Blake. BoNaP; WiR
O, aye! they had woone child bezide. The Child an' the Mowers. William Barnes. VLP
O baby, where you been so long? Lord, Lord, Lord, Lord. Levee Moan. *Unknown.* AS
O-Bar Cowboy. *Unknown.* CoSo
O barn reality! I saw you swimming. Iowa Land. Marvin Bell. SaC
O, Be Not Too Hasty, My Dearest. "Orpheus C. Kerr." OBAL
O be swift. The Helmsman. Hilda Doolittle ("H. D."). CMoP; OxBA
O beams of steel are slim and black. Song of the Builders. Jessie Wilmore Murton. AmFN
O beautiful bones. The Tough Ones. Errol Miller. AMV-80
O beautiful calm. Tu-kehu *and* Wetea, *tr. fr. Maori by* J. C. Andersen. WTO
O beautiful for spacious skies. America the Beautiful. Katharine Lee Bates. BLPA; EaLo; FaBoBe; FaBV; FaFP; FaPON; FSW; GOA; HBMV; HBVY; PAL; TAP; TreF; WBLP; WGRP; YaD
O Beautiful Forever! I Saw Eternity. Louise Bogan. LiTA
O Beautiful, My Country. Frederick L. Hosmer. AH, *with music;* PGD
O, Beautiful They Move. William Pillen. VWA
O beauty (beams, nay, flame). A Description of Beauty. Samuel Daniel. OBSC
O beech, unbind your yellow leaf, for deep. Ghostly Tree. Léonie Adams. MoAB; MoAmPo
O bells that rang, O bells that sang. The Mission Bells of Monterey. Bret Harte. PeD
O Bessie Bell and Mary Gray. Bessy [*or* Bessie] Bell and Mary Gray. *Unknown.* BSV; ESPB; LO; OxBB; ViBoFo
O Billie, billie, bonny billie. The Battle of Bothwell Bridge [*or* Bothwell Bridge]. *Unknown.* ESPB; OxBB,
O Billows Bounding Far. A. E. Housman. BoNaP
(Profoundly True Reflections on the Sea.) FaBoNo
O Bird at night, who, hearing, could forget. Bird at Night. Marion Ethel Hamilton. GoYe
O Bird, So Lovely. Louis Golding. TrJP
O Bird, thou dartest to the sun. Song. Maria White Lowell. AA
O bitter moon, O cold and bitter moon. Clement Wood. Eagle Sonnets, IX. HBMV
O bitter sea, tumultuous sea. Song of the Argonauts. William Morris. *Fr.* The Life and Death of Jason, IV. EtS
O bitter wind toward the sunset blowing. The Only Son. Sir Henry Newbolt. HBV-2
O Black and Unknown Bards. James Weldon Johnson. AmNP; BANP; BPo; HeIP; PoBA; PoNe; TTY; UnPo
O blackbird! sing me something well. The Blackbird. Tennyson. FM; PB; PBBP
O black-maned, horse-haired, unworthy one. To the Noble Woman of Llanarth Hall. Evan Thomas, *tr. by* Anthony Conran. PV
O blazing Sun, how happy you are there. Sonnet XXII. Louise Labé, *tr. by* Willis Barnstone. BoWoP
O blessed bodie! Whither art thou thrown. Sepulchre. George Herbert. AnAnS-1
O Blessèd House, That Cheerfully Receiveth. Karl Johann Philipp Spitta, *tr. fr. German by* Charles William Schaeffer. TrPWD
O Blessed Letters. Samuel Daniel. *Fr.* Musophilus. FaBoRV
O blessed man, that in th' advice. Bible, *O.T.* Psalms, I. SCAP
O Blest Estate, Blest from Above, *with music.* George Sandys. AH
O Blest Unfabled Incense Tree. George Darley. *Fr.* Nepenthe. BIrV; ChER; FaBoCh; FaBoRV; OBRV; PBBP
(Hundred-sunned Phenix.) OBNC
(Nepenthe.) AnIV
(Phoenix, The.) ChTr; LoBV; NOBE; OAEL-2; OBVV; Wir
O blisful light, of which the bemes clere. The Wooing of Criseide. Chaucer. *Fr.* Troilus and Criseide, III. PoEL-1
O blithe new-comer! I have heard. To the Cuckoo. Wordsworth. ELP; EnRP; FaFP; FiP; GTBS; GTBS-P; HBV-1; LoBV; OBRV; PB; PBBP; PoLF; TreFT; TrGrPo
O blithely shines the bonnie sun. *See* Oh blythely shines the bonnie sun.
O blush not so! O blush not so! Sharing Eve's Apple. Keats. ChER; ErPo
O Bonny Baby Livingston. Bonny Baby Livingston. *Unknown.* BaBo; ESPB
O bonny, bonny sang the bird. The Unquiet Grave. *Unknown.* EnSB
O Boston, though thou now art grown. Of Boston in New England. William Bradford. SCAP
O Boston wives and maids, draw near and see. To the Boston Women. *Unknown.* PAH
O boy cutting grass. Hitomaro. *Fr.* Manyo Shu. AWP
O Boy God, Muse of Poets. Ode to Fidel Castro. Edward Field. CoPo; CABA
O boys and men of British mould. Mercy to Animals: A Ballad of Humanity. Martin Farquhar Tupper. PeD
O Boys! O Boys! Oliver St. John Gogarty. DTC; OBMV
O boys, we're goin' for to fight. Way Down in Mexico. *Unknown.* CoSo
O Brazil, the Isle of the Blest. Gerald Griffin. ACP
(Hy-Brasail—the Isle of the Blest.) BLPA
O bretheren, my way. My Way's Cloudy. *Unknown.* BoAN-1
O [*or* Oh], Brignal[l] banks are wild and fair. Brignall Banks [*or* Edmund's Song *or* The Outlaw *or* Song]. Sir Walter Scott. *Fr.* Rokeby, III. EnRP; GTBS; GTBS-P; HBV-2; OAEP; OBEV; OBRV; PoRA
O broad-breasted queen among nations! Boston. John Boyle O'Reilly. PAH
O brother, as you've given me so much. The Bride's Farewell: Two Songs. *Gond Oral Tradition, tr. by* V. Elwin *and* S. Hivale. WTO
O brother in the restless rest of God! Zora Cross. *Fr.* Elegy on an Australian Schoolboy. PoAu-1
O brother, lift a cry, a long world cry. Peace. Edwin Markham. PGD
O Brother Man. Whittier. TRV
O Brother Tree. Max Michelson. TrJP
O brother, what is there to say to you. Ernest Dowson. John Hall Wheelock. HBMV
O brothers mine, take care! Take care! The White Witch. James Weldon Johnson. BANP; CDC
O brothers mine, today we stand. Fifty Years. James Weldon Johnson. BANP
O brothers, why do you talk. Mahadevi, *tr. fr. Kannada by* A. K. Ramanujan. WPOW
O, brothers, you oughta been there. Roll, Jordan, Roll. *Unknown.* FSW
O Bruadair. *See* O'Bruadair.
O Bury Me Beneath the Willow, *with music.* *Unknown.* AS
"O [*or* Oh], bury me not in the deep, deep sea." The Ocean Burial. Edwin H. Chapin. PSoN; ShS; ViBoFo
"O [*or* Oh] bury me not on the lone prairie." Bury Me Not on the Lone Prairie [*or* The Dying Cowboy *or* The Lone Prairie]. *Unknown.* AS; BPAW; CoSo; FaBoBe; FaBV; FaFP; FSW; TrAS; TreF; ViBoFo
O, but how white is white, white from shadows come. Music of Colours: The Blossom Scattered. Vernon Watkins. LiTB
O, but I saw a solemn sight. The Wicked Hawthorn Tree. W. B. Yeats. WSC
O, but life went gaily, gaily. In the House of Idiedaily. Bliss Carman. OBVV
O, but they say the tongues of dying men. The Tongues of Dying Men. Shakespeare. King Richard II, *fr.* II, i. FaBoRV
O but we talked at large before. Sixteen Dead Men. W. B. Yeats. OBWP
O, by an' by, by an' by. By an' By. *Unknown.* BoAN-1
O By the By. E. E. Cummings. OxBA
O Caledonia! Sir Walter Scott. *Fr.* The Lay of the Last Minstrel, VI. FaBoPP
O California. Alejandro Murguía, *tr. fr. Spanish by* Toni Empringham. FIA
O' cam' ye here to hear a lilt. The Battle of Glentilt (1847). Sir Douglas Maclagan. PoSH
O cam ye in by the House o Rodes. John Thomson and the Turk. *Unknown.* ESPB
O Cambridge, attend. Satire upon the Heads. Thomas Gray. FaBoCo
O camel in the zoo. Camel. Mary Britton Miller. TiPo
O camp of flowers, with poplars girdled round. Memory. Erik Johann Stagnelius, *tr. by* Sir Edmund Gosse. AWP
O Canada! Adolphe Routhier, *tr. fr. French by* Robert Stanley Weir. FSW
O Captain! My Captain! Walt Whitman. *Fr.* Memories of President Lincoln. AA; AP; FaBoBe; FaBoCh; FaBV; FaFP; FaPo; FaPON; FaPoR; FPL; GN; GOA; HBV-2; HBVY; InPK; LiTA; MoAmPo; MOS; NePA; OBCA; OBEV; OHFP; OHIP; PAH; PAI; PAL; PoLF; PoPl; RoGo; TAP; TreF; TrGrPo
O captain of the wars, whence won Ye so great scars? The Veteran of Heaven. Francis Thompson. HBV-2
O Carib Isle! Hart Crane. AP; MoPo; NePA; NoAM; PoA; VGW

O cat of churlish [*or* carlish] kind. A Curse on the Cat. John Skelton. *Fr.* Phyllyp Sparowe. ChTr; EvOK

O Cedar-tree, Cedar, my Mother. Song of Basket-weaving. Constance Lindsay Skinner. BPAW

O chansons foregoing. Epilogue. Ezra Pound. OxBA

O Charnwood, be thou called the choicest of thy kind. Charnwood Forest. Michael Drayton. *Fr.* Polyolbion, the Sixth and Twentieth Song. FaBoPP

O child, had I thy lease of time! such unimagined things. A Child of To-Day. James Buckham. AA

O Child of Beauty Rare. Goethe, *tr. fr. German by William Edmonstoune Aytoun ISi*

O Child of Lowly Manger Birth, *with music.* Ferdinand Q. Blanchard. AH

O Child of Nations, giant-limbed. Canada. Sir Charles G. D. Roberts. PeCV

O child of sunrise. Sister Bernardo. Heather Wilde. FAZ

O children of men, O sons and daughters of sorrow. Song for Tomorrow. Lucia Trent. PGD

O Children, Would You Cherish? *with music.* Christopher Dock, *tr. fr. German by* Samuel W. Pennypacker. AH

O child's tremble. Forming Child Poems. Simon J. Ortiz. CDW

O chillen, run, Cunjah man. De Cunjah Man. James Edwin Campbell. BANP

O Christ of Bethlehem, *with music.* H. Glenn Lanier. AH

O Christ of God! whose life and death. Vesta. Whittier. TrPWD; WHA

O Christ of Olivet, you hushed the wars. Edwin Markham. *Fr.* The Christ of the Andes. TrPWD

O Christ, the glorious Crown. Hymn. Philip Howard. ACP

O Christ, Thou Art within Me Like a Sea. Edith Lovejoy Pierce. TrPWD

O Christ, Who Died. John Calvin Slemp. TrPWD

O Christ who holds the open gate. John Masefield. *Fr.* The Everlasting Mercy. ILwL; TreFS; TRV

O Christmas Night. Henricus Selyns, *tr. fr. Dutch by* Howard Murphy. AH, *sts.* 1, 2, 4, 6, *with music*
(Nuptial Song.) SCAP

O city metropole, isle riverain! Montreal. A. M. Klein. CaP; MoCV; OBCV

O city of the world, with sacred splendor blest. Longing for Jerusalem. Judah Halevi, *tr. by* Emma Lazarus. TrJP

O Clipper Ships! where are, where are ye now? Clipper Ships. John Anderson. EtS

O cloud that wants to be the sky's arrow. Rosario Castellanos, *tr. fr. Spanish by* Willis Barnstone. BoWoP

O Columbia, the gem of the ocean. Columbia, the Gem of the Ocean [*or* The Red, White and Blue]. David T. Shaw. FaBoBe; FSW; PAL; WBLP

O come, all my young lovers. The Unconstant Lover. *Unknown.* TrAS

O Come, All Ye Faithful. *Unknown, at. to* John Francis Wade, *tr. fr. Latin by* Frederick Oakeley. FaFP; FSW; TreFS
(Adeste Fideles.) PSoN; WGRP

"O come and be my mate!" said the Eagle to the Hen. Wedded Bliss. Charlotte Perkins Stetson Gilman. HBV-1

O come and take thou me/ Beneath thy wing. Beneath Thy Wing. Hayyim Nahman Bialik, *tr. by* Helena Frank. TrJP

O [*or* Oh] come let us sing unto the Lord [*or* Jehovah]. Bible, *O.T.* Psalms, XCV. AWP; BLRP; OHIP

O, come, list awhile, and you soon shall hear. The Female Smuggler. *Unknown.* AmSS

O come, my body is alone. Come Laugh with Me. *Gond Oral Tradition, tr. by* V. Elwin *and* S. Hivale. WTO

O come, our Lord and Saviour. *Unknown.* BLRP

O Come Quickly! Thomas Campion. *See* Never Weather-beaten Sail.

O! Come, soft rest of cares, come Night. Bridal Song [*or* Song]. George Chapman. *Fr.* Hero and Leander, Fifth Sestiad. NOBE; OBEV; ViBoPo

O come sweet death, sang Bach. Horn. James Hayford. NePoAm-2

O come to me, my brother Green, for I am shot and bleeding. Brother Green. *Unknown.* AmFP

O! Come to the Greenwood Shade. Alexander McLachlan. PeCV

O come you pious youth! adore. Jupiter Hammon. *Fr.* An Address to Miss Phillis Wheatley. AmPP

O commemorate me where there is water. Lines Written on a Seat on the Grand Canal, Dublin. Patrick Kavanagh. BIrV; CIP; CMoP; IPY

O comrades, come gather and join in my ditty. The *Cumberland*'s Crew. *Unknown.* AmFP

O cool in the summer is salad. Salad: After Swinburne. Mortimer Collins. *Fr.* Salad. Par

"O Cormac, grandson of Conn," said Carbery. *Unknown, tr. by* Kuno Meyer. *Fr.* The Instructions of King Cormac. BIrV

O Could I Find from Day to Day, *with music.* Benjamin Cleavland. AH

O courteous Christkind guest, most gracious host. To a Crucifix. Anna Wickham. MoBrPo

O cricket, from your cheery cry. Basho, *tr. fr. Japanese by* Curtis Hidden Page. AWP

"O crikey, Bill!" she ses to me, she ses. Culture in the Slums. W. E. Henley. CenHV; HBV-1; InMe

O crimson blood. Hildegard von Bingen, *tr. fr. Latin by* Patrick Diehl. WPOW

O cruel cloudless space. Nativity. May Sarton. NePoAm-2

"O cruel Death, give three things back." Three Things. W. B. Yeats. DTC; FaBoEn; OBMV

O cruel Death! thou hast cut down. Epitaph—on the Wife of Dr. Greenwood. Dr. ——— Greenwood. FaBoUs

O cruel Love! on thee I lay. Sapho's Song. John Lyly. *Fr.* Sapho and Phao. OBSC

O cruel!—could thy infant bosom find. To a Little Boy, Who Had Destroyed a Nest of Young Birds. *Unknown.* FaBoUs

O Cuckoo. *Unknown, tr. by* Arthur Waley. *Fr.* Kokin Shu. AWP

O Cuckoo! shall I call thee Bird. To the Cuckoo. F. H. Townsend. ChTr; FaBoNo

O cuckoo that sang to us and art fled. Lament for the Cuckoo. Alcuin, *tr. by* Helen Waddell. NAWM-1; PeHV

O Cupid! Monarch over Kings. John Lyly. *Fr.* Mother Bombie. EIL
(Fools in Love's College.) TrGrPo
(Song of Accius and Silena.) OBSC

O curfew of the setting sun! O Bells of Lynn! The Bells of Lynn. Longfellow. AA

"O.D." Zack Gilbert. CNA

O Daedalus, Fly Away Home. Robert Hayden. BiP; HAP; IDB; NCSH; PoBA; PoNE; WeW

O dainty gland, whose lobulated grace. To the Parotid Gland. ——— Schlesinger. WhC

O dappled throat of white! Shy, hidden bird! The Lonely-Bird. Harrison Smith Morris. AA

O Dark, Dark, Dark. Milton. *Fr.* Samson Agonistes. WHA

O dark-haired girl, let us now. From an Irish-Latin Macaronic. Geoffrey Taylor. NeIP

O David, highest in the list. Christopher Smart. *Fr.* A Song to David. NOEC, 38 *sts.;* OxBoCh

O David, if I had. That Harp You Play So Well. Marianne Moore. HBMV; MoAB; MoAmPo; PoA

O dawn upon me slowly, Paradise. Come Slowly, Paradise. James Benjamin Kenyon. AA

O Day most calm, most bright. Sunday. George Herbert. OBS; SeCV-1; TrCP

O Day of God, Draw Nigh, *with music.* Robert B. Y. Scott. AH

O Day of Light and Gladness, *with music.* Frederick Lucian Hosmer. AH

O Day of Rest and Gladness. Christopher Wordsworth. WGRP

O days and hours, your work is this. In Memoriam A. H. H., CXVII. Tennyson. HBV-2

O, de birds ar' sweetly singin'. 'Weh Down Souf. Daniel Webster Davis. BANP

O de Glory Road! O de Glory Road! De Glory Road. Clement Wood. HBMV; YaD

O, de light-bugs glimmer down de lane. Negro Serenade. James Edwin Campbell. BANP

O' de wurl' ain't flat. Northboun'. Lucy Ariel Williams. BANP; BISi; CDC; PoNe

O dear and loving God. Prayer for Living and Dying. Christopher La Farge. TrPWD

O dear! I cannot choose but write. Eve. Oliver Herford. OBAL

O Dear Life, When Shall It Be. Sir Philip Sidney. Astrophel and Stella, Tenth Song. EnRePo; SiPS

O Dear O. *Unknown.* ErPo

O dear, what can the matter be? *See* Oh, Dear! What Can the Matter Be?

O dearest, canst thou tell me why. Warum sind denn die Rosen so blass. Heine, *tr. by* Richard Garnett. AWP

O Dearest Dread, most glorious King. A Prayer unto Christ the Judge of the World. Michael Wigglesworth. SCAP

O dearly-bought revenge, yet glorious! Heroic Vengeance. Milton. *Fr.* Samson Agonistes. OBS

O Death. Bible, Apocrypha. Ecclesiasticus, XLI: 1–4. TrJP

O Death. *Unknown.* TrAS, *with music*
(Oh! Death.) AmFP

O Death, Rock Me Asleep. *At. to* George Boleyn, *also at. to* Anne Boleyn. EiL; FaBoRV; FF; TrGrPo; WPE
(Death.) OBSC
(O Death, Rock Me on Sleep) ChTr

O death, thy certainty is such. Henry Luttrell. FaBoEE

O death, when thou shalt come to me. Strong as Death. H. C. Bunner. HBV-1

O deep and clear as is the sky. To Silence. T. Sturge Moore. BrPo

O deep-blue sea, O god Uli! Prayer of the Fishing Net. *Tr. fr. Hawaiian by* N. B. Emerson. WTO

O deep, creating Light. Eagle Song. Gordon Bottomley. *Fr.* Suilven and the Eagle. MoBrPo
O depth of wealth, wisdom, and knowledge in God! To Him Be Glory. Bible, *N.T.* *Fr.* Romans. TRV
O depth sufficient to desire. Adam's Song to Heaven. Edgar Bowers. ConAP; QFR
O Desolate Eves. Christopher Brennan. *Fr.* The Wanderer. PoAu-1
O destined Land, unto thy citadel. George Edward Woodberry. *Fr.* My Country. AA
O Deus, Ego Amo Te. Gerard Manley Hopkins. TrPWD
O Did you ever hear of the brave Earl Brand. Earl Brand. *Unknown.* OxBB
O did you see a troop go by. The Camp within the West. Roderic Quinn. PoAu-1
O differing human heart. Personality. Archibald Lampman. PeCV
O, Dinna ask me gin I lo'e ye. Dinna Ask Me. John Dunlop. HBV-1
O Diodorus, in a storm of spring. Epigram. *Unknown, tr. by* Sydney Oswald. PeHV
O Dirty Bird Yr Gizzard's Too Big & Full of Sand. James Koller. PoM
O distant Christ, the crowded, darkening years. Doubt. Margaret Deland. TrPWD
O divine star of heaven. John Fletcher. *Fr.* The Mad Lover, IV, i. GBL
O do not grieve, Dear Heart, nor shed a tear. Margaret Cavendish, Duchess of Newcastle. EnLoPo
O do not use me/ After my sinnes! Sighs and Grones. George Herbert. PoEL-2
O, do not wanton with those eyes. *See* Oh, do not wanton with those eyes.
O Doctor Dear My Love. Anne Halley. NMM
O Domine Deus! Speravi in te. Prayer before Execution. Mary Queen of Scots, *tr. by* John Fawcett. WGRP
O Donal[l] Oge, if you go across the sea. Donal[l] Oge: Grief of a Girl's Heart. *Unknown, tr. by* Lady Gregory. GBL; OnYI; OxBI; PBWP
O don't be sorrowful, darling. Don't Be Sorrowful, Darling. Rembrandt Peale. HBV-1
O don't, don't ever ask me for alms. Death and the Plowman. Sidney Keyes. OxBTC
O dream from the blackness. Sappho, *tr. fr. Greek by* Willis Barnstone. BoWoP
O Dreams, O Destinations. C. Day Lewis. MoPo
"To travel like a bird, lightly to view," *sel.* GTBS-P
(Sonnet: "To travel like a bird, lightly to view.") ChMP
"O Dreary life," we cry, "O dreary life!" Patience Taught by Nature. Elizabeth Barrett Browning. EBCP; OxBoCh
O dull, cold northern sky. Robert Louis Stevenson. EBVV
O Duty,/ Why hast thou not the visage of a sweetie or a cutie? Kind of an Ode to Duty. Ogden Nash. TrGrPo; WhC
"O Earl Rothes, an thou wert mine." Earl Rothes. *Unknown.* BaBo; ESPB
O early one morning I walked out like Agag. The Streets of Laredo. Louis MacNeice. ChTr; MoBS; OBWP
O Earnest Be, *with music. Unknown.* AH
O earth,/ I count the praises thou art worth. Praise of Earth. Elizabeth Barrett Browning. OBVV
O Earth-and-Autumn of the Setting Sun. Indian Summer. William Ellery Leonard. *Fr.* Two Lives. HBMV
O Earth! Art Thou Not Weary? Julia Caroline Ripley Dorr. AA
O Earth, I will have none of thee. The Heart's Low Door. Susan Mitchell. HBMV
O earth, lie heavily upon her eyes. Rest. Christina Rossetti. HBV-1; NOBE; OAEL-2; OBEV; OBNC; OBVV; TrGrPo
O Earth, O dewy mother, breathe on us. A Prayer. Archibald Lampman. TrPWD
O Earth, Sufficing All Our Needs. Sir Charles G. D. Roberts. CaP
O Earth, thou hast not any wind that blows. The Word. Richard Realf. AA; TRV; WGRP
O Earth, throughout thy borders. Easter Carol. George Newell Lovejoy. OHIP; PGD
O Earth, Turn! George Johnston. MoCV
O Ease My Spirit. "Hugh MacDiarmid." BSV
O, Eleazar Wheelock was a very pious man. *See* Oh, Eleazar Wheelock was a very pious man.
O elephant, possessor of a savings-basket full of money. Salute to the Elephant. Odeniyi Apolebieji, *tr. by* S. A. Babalola. WTO
O embittered joy. Fiend's Weather. Louise Bogan. MoVe
O Empress high, celestial Queen most rare. Ballad of Our Lady. William Dunbar, *mod. version by* E. M. Clerke. ISi
O Englishwoman on the Pincian. Thomas Edward Brown. *Fr.* Roman Women. OBNC
O eternal grass. On the Meadow. "Katri Vala," *tr. by* Jaakko A. Ahokas. PBWP
O Eternal, in thy majesty ride. Jewish Arabic Liturgies. *Unknown, tr. by* Hartwig Hirschfeld. TrJP
O ever beauteous, ever friendly, tell. Elegy to the Memory of an Unfortunate Lady. Pope. ACP
O everie living warldly wight. Of Gods Omnipotencie. Alexander Hume. NOCV
O everlasting Kingdom of the Scepter. He Maketh Himself One with the Only God, Whose Limbs Are the Many Gods. *Unknown, tr. by* Robert Hillyer. *Fr.* Book of the Dead. AWP
O eye, weep for a rider. Rain to the Tribe. Al-Khansa, *tr. by* Willis Barnstone *and* Tony Nawfal. BoWoP
O eyes clear with beauty, O tender gaze. Sonnet XI. Louise Labé, *tr. by* Willis Barnstone. BoWoP
O eyes which do the spheres of beauty move. Astrophel and Stella, XLII. Sir Philip Sidney. SiPS
O, fain would I, before I die. *Unknown.* LO
O faint, delicious, spring-time violet! The Violet. William Wetmore Story. HBV-1
O fair! O Sweet! when I do look on thee. Song. Sir Philip Sidney. SiPS
O faire sweet face, O eyes celestiall bright. *See* Oh fair sweet face, oh eyes celestial bright.
O Fairest of the Rural Maids. Bryant. *See* Oh Fairest of the Rural Maids!
O faithless thorn. *Gond Oral Tradition, tr. by* V. Elwin *and* S. Hivale. WTO
O faithless world, and thy more faithless part. A Poem Written by Sir Henry Wotton, in His Youth. Sir Henry Wotton. AnAnS-2
O Fall of the leaf, I am tired. Leaf. John Hewitt. NeIP
O, Falmouth is a fine town with ships in the bay. Home [*or* Falmouth]. W. E. Henley. GN; HBV-2; MoBrPo; MOS; PoLF
O false and treacherous Probability. Caelica; CIII[CIV]. Fulke Greville. *Fr.* AAS; OBS; OxBoCh
O fan of white silk. Fan-Piece, for Her Imperial Lord. Ezra Pound. MoAB
O far, fantastic line of notch and spire. A'Chuilionn. A. G. Hutchison. PoSh
O far-off darling in the South. Coeur de Lion to Berengaria. Theodore Tilton. AA
O far withdrawn into the lonely West. To K. H. Thomas Edward Brown. OBNC
O fare ye weel, my auld wife! My Auld Wife. *Unknown.* GBP
"O fare you well, my darling." Ten Thousand Miles. *Unknown.* AmFP
O fast her amber blood doth flow. The Phoenix. George Darley. *Fr.* Nepenthe. OBEV; OBRV
O, fastidious mind, gorging on absolutes, remember. Promises. Ruth Forbes Sherry. GoYe
O fate, O fault, O curse, child of my bliss! Astrophel and Stella, XCIII. Sir Philip Sidney. SiPS
O father, answer me. *See* Oh father, answer me.
O Father, give the spirit power to climb. Boethius, *tr. by* Helen Waddell. *Fr.* The Consolation of Philosophy. NAWM-1
O Father, keep me through this day. My Daily Prayer. Eva Gray. STF
O Father, O Supreme of heav'nly Thrones. Milton. *Fr.* Paradise Lost, VI. ILwL
O Father, we approach Thy throne. Adam's Hymn in Paradise. Joost van den Vondel, *tr. by* Sir John Bowring. WGRP
O, father's gone to market town, he was up before the day. A Midsummer Song. Richard Watson Gilder. BoNaP; HBV-1
O Faustus. Faustus Faces His Doom. Christopher Marlowe. *Fr.* Doctor Faustus. TreFT
"O favourable spirit, propitious guest." Adam Unfallen. Milton. *Fr.* Paradise Lost, V. NOCV
O Fearfull, Frowning Nemesis. Samuel Daniel. *Fr.* Cleopatra. PoEL-2
"O Felix Culpa!" *Unknown. See* Adam Lay Ibounden.
O first created and creating source. Ode to the Sea. Howard Baker. OxBA
O Flame of Living Love. St. John of the Cross, *tr. fr. Spanish by* Arthur Symons. AWP; ILwL
(O Living Flame of Love, *tr. by* Willis Barnstone.) PAI
O fleece, that down the neck waves to the nape! Her Hair. Baudelaire. NAWM-2
O flower of all that springs from gentle blood. Epitaphs, VII. Gabriello Chiabrera, *tr. by* Wordsworth. AWP
O flower of all wind-flowers and sea-flowers. Sark. Swinburne. *Fr.* The Garden of Cymodoce. FaBoPP
O Flower of flowers, our Lady of the May! Our Lady of the May. Lionel Johnson. ISi
O flowers of Mekhmekh, give us peace! Ezra Pound *and* Noel Stock, *fr. Egyptian hieroglyphics BoWoP*
O Fly My Soul. James Shirley. *Fr.* The Imposture, II, ii. OBS; OxBoCh
(Hymn, A: "O fly my soul! What hangs upon.") GoBC
(Song of Nuns, A.) ACP
O fly not, Pleasure, pleasant-hearted Pleasure. *See* Oh fly not, Pleasure . . .
O fond, but fickle and untrue. Walter Savage Landor. GBL
O fondest, and O frailest fair. Ode to Popularity. Winthrop Mackworth Praed. VLP

O foolish builders! Danger. Theodora L. Paine. PGD
O foolishnes of men! that lend their ears. Comus's Praise of Nature. Milton. *Fr.* Comus. PoEL-3
O for a Booke. *Unknown.* CH; PoSC; SiSoSe
O for a Bowl of Fat Canary. John Lyly. *See* Serving Men's Song, A.
O [*or* Oh] for a Closer Walk with God. William Cowper. *See* Walking with God.
O for a faith that will not shrink. Unshrinking Faith. W. H. Balhurst. BLRP
O for a ferryman to steer my yearning. Home-Sickness. Hedwig Lachmann, *tr. by* Jethro Bithell. TrJP
O for a heart of calm repose. Peace. *Unknown.* STF
O for a muse of fire, a sack of dough. Sonnet with a Different Letter at the End of Every Line. George Starbuck. OBAL
O for a Muse of fire, that would ascend. A Muse of Fire. Shakespeare. *Fr.* King Henry V, Prologue to Act I. ChTr; SCV
O for a sculptor's hand. Balaam. John Keble. OBNC; OBVV
O for a toe, such as the funeral pyre. Sir Thomas Browne. FaBoEE
O, for Ane-and-twenty. Burns. BSV
O for Doors to Be Open and an Invite with Gilded Edges. W. H. Auden. OAEP; ViBoPo
(O for Doors to Be Open.) CoBMV
O for God's sake. Islands. Muriel Rukeyser. GP
O for one minute hark what we are saying! A Prayer. Frederic W. H. Myers. TrPWD
O for our upland meads. Shepherd and Shepherdess. Thomas Hennell. FaBoTw
O! for some honest lover's ghost. *See* Oh! for some honest lovers ghost.
O for ten years, that I may overwhelm. Keats. *Fr.* Sleep and Poetry. OAEL-2
O for that warning voice, which he who saw. The Prospect of Eden. Milton. *Fr.* Paradise Lost, IV. PoEL-3; TEP
O for the Happy Hour, *with music.* George Washington Bethune. AH
O for the perfumes that arise. Non Sum Qualis Eram in Bona Urbe Nordica Illa. John Hollander. ErPo
O for the times which were. Tempora Acta. "Owen Meredith." OBVV
O for the Wings of a Dove. Euripides, *tr. fr. Greek by* Gilbert Murray. *Fr.* Hippolytus. AWP
O fortunate, O happy day. A New Household. Longfellow. *Fr.* The Hanging of the Crane. GN
O fountain of Bandusia! To the Fountain of Bandusia. Horace, *tr. by* Eugene Field. Odes, III, 13. AA; AWP
O Frail Adam. Epitaph for Mr. Moses Levy. *Unknown.* TrJP
O France, with what a shamed and sorry smile. An American to France. Alice Duer Miller. HBMV
O Friend! I know not which way I must look. Written in London, September, 1802 [*or* England, 1802, I *or* In London, September 1802 *or* London, MDCCCII *or*, Sonnet: Written in London, September, 1802]. Wordsworth. ChER; EnRP; GTBS; GTBS-P; HBV-2; OBEV; PPON; TrGrPo
O friends! who have accompanied thus far. Walter Savage Landor. GBL
O friends! with whom my feet have trod. The Eternal Goodness. Whittier. AA; OHFP; WGRP
O Friendship! Friendship! the shell of Aphrodite. Walter Savage Landor. GBL
O, Frisco was a strumpet. Nostalgia. Gertrude Millard. BPAW
O! Full of Scorpions. Shakespeare. *Fr.* Macbeth, III, ii. FiP
O furrowed plaintive face. The Hurrier. Harold Monro. MoBrPo
O Future bards. A Prophecy. Allen Ginsberg. TAP
O gaily sings the bird! and the wattle-boughs are stirr'd. Whisperings in Wattle-Boughs. Adam Lindsay Gordon. OBVV
O gallant brothers of the generous South. Henry Peterson. *Fr.* Ode for Decoration Day. AA; FaBoBe
O Galuppi, Baldassare, this is very sad to find! *See* Oh Galuppi, Baldassaro, this is very sad to find.
O, Gambler, Git Up Off o' Yo' Knees, *with music.* *Unknown.* BoAN-1
O Gather Me the Rose. W. E. Henley. Echoes, III. MoBrPo
(Collige Rosas.) OBVV
O generation of the thoroughly smug and thoroughly uncomfortable. Salutation. Ezra Pound. HeIP; MoAB; MoAmPo; NOBA; OxBA; TAP; VGW
O Genevieve, I'd give this world. *See* Oh Genevieve, I'd give the world.
O gentle, gentle land. Night Sowing. David Campbell. CBAP; PoAu-2
O gentle, gentle summer rain. Invocation to Rain in Summer [*or* Summer Invocation]. William C. Bennett. GN; HBV-1
O Gentle Love. George Peele. *Fr.* The Arraignment of Paris. ElL
(Colin's Passion of Love.) OBSC
O gentle Love, do not forsake the guide. Upon Some Alterations in My Mistress, after My Departure into France. Thomas Carew. CaPo
O gentle queen of the afternoon. Poem. W. S. Graham. NeBP
O gentle, restless earth. Night Harvest. Susan Pence. AMV-80
O Gentle Ships. Meleager, *tr. fr. Greek by* Andrew Lang. AWP
O Gentle Sleep. Shakespeare. *See* Cares of Majesty, The.
O gie the lass her fairin' lad. Gie the Lass Her Fairin'. Burns. CoMu; ErPo
O Gin My Love Were Yon Red Rose. *Unknown.* GBP
O girl, you torment me, you are so deceiving. *Gond Oral Tradition, tr. by* V. Elwin *and* S. Hivale. WTO
O give me back my rigorous English Sunday. The Fresh Start. Anna Wickham. ViBoPo
"O give thanks unto the Lord, for He is good." O Give Thanks. Bible, *O.T.* Psalms, CXVIII. TrJP
O give thanks unto the Lord for he is good [*or* gracious]. Bible, *O.T.* Psalms, CXXXVI. AWP; OHIP
O Give yee thanks unto the Lord. Bible, *O.T.* Psalms, CVII. SCAP
O Glorious Childbearer. Joseph Campbell. OnYI
O Glorious Christ of God; I live. Cotton Mather. SCAP
O Glory of Virgins. Fortunatus, *tr. fr. Latin by* Sister Maura. ISi
"O go again," said the King. King Arthur's Death. *Unknown.* ACP
O God,/ forever I turn in this hard crystal. The Prayer of the Goldfish. Carmen Bernos de Gasztold. PDV
O god above, relent. Here Followeth the Songe of the Death of Mr. Thewlis. *Unknown.* CoMu
O God, above the Drifting Years, *with music.* John Wright Buckham. AH
O God, Accept the Sacred Hour, *with music.* Samuel Gilman. AH
O God, beneath thy guiding hand. *See* oh, God, beneath thy guiding hand.
O God, grant us the serenity to accept. Prayer for Serenity. Reinhold Niebuhr. TreFT
O God, Great Father, Lord, and King, *with music.* E. Embree Hoss. AH
O God! Have Mercy, in This Dreadful Hour. Robert Southey. MOS; TrPWD
O God, How Many Years Ago. Frederick W. H. Myers. HBMV
O God, I Cried, No Dark Disguise, *with music.* Edna St. Vincent Millay. AH
O God, I love thee, I love thee. O Deus, Ego Amo Te. Gerard Manley Hopkins. TrPWD
O God! if this indeed be all. If This Be All. Anne Brontë. TrPWD
O God, in Restless Living. Harry Emerson Fosdick. TrPWD
O God, in the dream the terrible horse began. The Dream. Louise Bogan. LiTA; LiTM; MAT; MoAB; MoAmPo; SBG
O God, in whom my deepest being dwells. A Psalm. Edmund Blunden. TrPWD
O God, in Whom the Flow of Days, *with music.* Donald C. Babcock. AH
O God, in Whose Great Purpose, *with music.* James G. Gilkey. AH
O God, keep not Thou silence. Keep Not Thou Silence. Bible, *O.T.* Psalms LXXXIII. TrJP
O God, make this age great that we may be. To Poesy. Tennyson. VLP
O God! methinks it were a happy life. King Henry VI Yearns for the Simple Life. Shakespeare. King Henry VI, Pt. III, *fr.* II, v. TreFS
O God most glorious, called by many a name. Hymn to Zeus. Cleanthes, *tr. by* James Adam. ILwL
O God! My God! have mercy now. Supposed Confessions of a Second-rate Sensitive Mind. Tennyson. VLP
O God, my master God, look down and see. The Artisan. Alice Brown. TrPWD
O God! O Montreal! Samuel Butler. DTC; FaBoCo; NBM; OxBoLi
(Psalm of Montreal.) OBSV
O God, O Venus, O Mercury, patron of thieves. The Lake Isle. Ezra Pound. CABA; CrMA; FaBoCo; FaBoPa; PoA
O God of battles, who art still. On the Eve of War. Danske Dandridge. PAH
O God of Bethel. Philip Doddridge *and* John Logan WTO
O God of Calvary and Bethlehem. The Hem of His Garment. Anna Elizabeth Hamilton. TrPWD
O God of earth and altar. A Hymn [*or* Prayer]. G. K. Chesterton. HBMV; TreFT; TrPWD; WGRP
O God of Goodness, Forwardness, and Fulness. Prayer. Doris Hedges. GoYe
O God of love unbounded! Lord supreme! Prayer to God. "Placido," *tr. by* Raoul Abdul. TTY
O God of Mercy. God of Mercy. Kadia Molodowsky, *tr. by* Irving Howe. WPOW
O God of My Salvation, Hear, *with music.* Joel Barlow. AH
O God of Stars and Distant Space, *with music.* John Franzen. AH
O God of Youth, *with music.* Bates G. Burt. AH
O God, our Father, if we had but truth! A Prayer. Edward Rowland Sill. AA
O God, Our Help in Ages Past. Isaac Watts. EaLo; FaPoR; HBV-2; OxBoCh; WGRP
(Man Frail, and God Eternal.) NOCV; NOEC; OBEC; PoEL-3
(Ninetieth Psalm, The.) BLRP
(Our God, Our Help in Ages Past.) NoP; OBVE
(Recessional.) TreF; WBLP

O God, our loving Father, help us. A Christmas Prayer. Robert Louis Stevenson. TrCP
O God, Send Men, *with music.* Elizabeth Burrowes. AH
O God, the cleanest offering. Father Damien. John Banister Tabb. ACP
O God, the heathen are come into Thine inheritance. The Heathen Are Come into Thine Inheritance. Bible, *O.T.* Psalms, LXXIX. TrJP
O God, the Rock of Ages. Edward H. Bickersteth. BLPA; FPL
O God, though Countless Worlds of Light, *with music.* James D. Knowles. AH
O God, thy moon is on the hills. Kelpius's Hymn. Arthur Peterson. AA
O God, unknown, invisible, secure. John Addington Symonds. *Fr.* An Invocation. TrPWD; TRV
O God, we thank Thee for everything. The One Thousandth Psalm. Edward Everett Hale. TRV
O God, when You send for me, let it be. Prayer to Go to Paradise with the Asses. Francis Jammes, *tr. by* Jethro Bithell. AWP
O God, where do they tend—these struggling aims? Robert Browning. *Fr.* Pauline. WGRP
O God, who made me. The Prayer of the Donkey. Carmen Bernos de Gasztold. PChr
O God, whose daylight leadeth down. George Macdonald. *Fr.* Evening Hymn. TrPWD
O God Whose Presence Glows in All, *with music.* Nathaniel L. Frothingham. AH
O God! whose thunder shakes the sky. Resignation. Thomas Chatterton. TrCP
O God, why hast thou thus. Psalm LXXIV: "O God, why hast thou cast us off for ever?" Countess of Pembroke. NOCV
O goddess! give me back the ready laughter. To the Frivolous Muse. George Meason Whicher. InMe
O Goddess! hear these tuneless numbers, wrung. Ode to Psyche [*or* To Psyche]. Keats. CABA; ChER; EnRP; HBV-2; InPS; LiTB; LoBV; NOBE; NoP; OAEL-2; OAEP; OBEV; OBNC; OBRV; PoEL-4; PP; PPP; ViBoPo; WHA
O goddess Laka! Altar Prayers. *Tr. fr. Hawaiian by* N. B. Emerson. WTO
O gold Hyperion, love-lorn Porphyro. Keats. William Wilberforce Lord. *Fr.* Ode to England. AA
O Golden Fleece. George Barker. Secular Elegies, V. MoAB; MoBrPo ("O Golden Fleece she is where she lies tonight.") ErPo; LiTM; NeBP
O golden tongued Romance, with serene lute! On Sitting Down to Read *King Lear* Once Again. Keats. EBEV; EnRP; NoP
O Gongyla, my darling rose. Sappho, *tr. fr. Greek by* Willis Barnstone. BoWoP
O good gigantic smile o' the brown old earth. The Ancient Doctrine. Robert Browning. OBVV
"O good Lord Judge, and sweet Lord Judge." The Maid Freed from the Gallows. *Unknown.* AWP; ESPB; ViBoFo
O good painter, tell me true. An Order for a Picture. Alice Cary. BLPA
O good Sun,/ Look thou down upon us. Song for Fine Weather. *Unknown, tr. by* Constance Lindsay Skinner. AWP
O Goodly Hand. Sir Thomas Wyatt. InvP; SiPS (His Lady's Hand.) OBSC
O Goody, it's coming, the circus parade. The Circus Parade. Olive Beaupré Miller. TiPo
O Gracious Father of Mankind, *with music.* Henry Hallam Tweedy. AH
O Gracious God, O Saviour sweet. O That I Had Wings like a Dove. *Unknown.* OxBoCh
O gracious gods, take compassion. John Marston. *Fr.* The Metamorphosis of Pygmalion's Image. OAEL-1
O Gracious Jesus, Blessed Lord! *with music.* Andrew Fowler. AH
O Gracious Shepherd. Henry Constable. OxBoCh
O grammar-rules, O now your virtues show. Astrophel and Stella, LXIII. Sir Philip Sidney. FaBoUs; SiPS
O grandest of the Angels, and most wise. Litany to Satan. Baudelaire, *tr. by* James Elroy Flecker. AWP; SyP
O grasses wet with dew, yellow fallen leaves. A Glimpse. Frances Cornford. OBMV
O great humming nymphet and mother and moth and. 25 Spontaneous Lines Greeting the World. Jim Tyack. AMV-80
O Great Mary. The Gaelic Litany to Our Lady. *Unknown, tr. by* Eugene O'Curry. ISi
O Great Spirit! A Voyager's Prayer. *Unknown, tr. by* Tanner. TRV; WGRP
O Grief! *Unknown.* EIL
O guide my judgement and my taste. Taste. Christopher Smart. Hymns for the Amusement of Children, Hymn 15. NOCV
O guns, fall silent till the dead men hear. The Anxious Dead. John McCrae. OHIP
O had truth power, the guiltless could not fall. His Petition to Queen Anne of Denmark (1618). Sir Walter Ralegh. SiPS
O [*or* Ah] had you seen the Coolun. The Coolun. Maurice O'Dugan, *tr. by* Sir Samuel Ferguson. AnIV; OnYI; OxBI
O handsome chestnut eyes, evasive gaze. Sonnet II. Louise Labé, *tr. by* Willis Barnstone. BoWoP
O happiest village! how I turned to you. Old Homes. Edmund Blunden. MoVE
O happy [*or* happie] dames, that may embrace. Complaint of the Absence of Her Lover Being upon the Sea [*or* A Lady Complains of Her Lover's Absence *or* The Seafarer]. Earl of Surrey. AAS; EBEV; EIL; ELP; GBL; NOBE; OBEV; OBSC; SiPS
O happy, golden age! *See* Oh happy golden age.
O happy hour. *Unknown, tr. by* Helen Waddell. *Fr.* Carmina Burana. NAWM
O happy life, whose love is found! Queen and Slave. Mortimer Collins. OBVV
O happy seafarers are ye. William Morris. *Fr.* The Life and Death of Jason. ViBoPo
O happy Sleep! thou bear'st upon thy breast. Sleep. Ada Louise Martin. HBV-2
O happy souls, that mingle with your kind. "Social Science." Thomas Edward Brown. PeD
O happy Thames that didst my Stella bear. Astrophel and Stella, CIII. Sir Philip Sidney. HBV-1; SiPS
O happy Tithon! if thou know'st thy hap. Aurora. Earl of Stirling. OBEV
O hard endeavor, to blend in with these. Elegy in Six Sonnets. Frederick Goddard Tuckerman. *Fr.* Sonnets. QFR
"O hark, the drums do beat, my love, I can no longer stay." The Banks of the Nile. *Unknown.* OBET
O hark! 'tis the note of the Schmaltztenor! Schmaltztenor! M. W. Branch. FiBHP
O Hark to the Herald. Eleazar ben Kalir, *tr. fr. Hebrew by* Israel Zangwill. TrJP
O harmless feast. Song. Barten Holyday. *Fr.* Technogamia. EIL
O Harry Heine, curses be. Translator to Translated. Ezra Pound. FaBoEE
O hate me not for my grey hair. A Song: In the Name of a Lover, to His Mistress; Who Said, She Hated Him for His Grey Hairs, Which He Had at Thirty. William Wycherley. SeCV-2
O hateful harm! condicion of poverte! Prologue to the Man of Law's Tale. Chaucer. *Fr.* The Canterbury Tales. FiP
O, have ye been in love, me boys. I Met Her in the Garden Where the Praties Grow. *Unknown.* AS
O have ye na heard o' the fause Sakelde? Kinmont Willie. *Unknown.* BSV; ESPB; OxBB
O, have you been in Gudbrand's dale, where Laagen's mighty flood. Thoralf and Synnöv. Hjalmar Hjorth Boyesen. AA
O Have You Caught the Tiger? A. E. Housman. BXAP; FaBoNo; SpRo
O have you seen my fairy steed? "She Wandered after Strange Gods." Laura Benét. HBMV
O, have you seen the leper healed. The Healing of the Leper. Vernon Watkins. FaBoTw
O have you seen the Stratton flood. Stratton Water. Dante Gabriel Rossetti. OxBB
O hear a pensive prisoner's prayer. The Mouse's Petition. Anna Laetitia Barbauld. FM; OxBChV
O Hear My Prayer, Lord, *with music.* John Craig. AH
O hear ye that foul and fiendish laughter. War! J. Gilchrist Lawson. WBLP
O heard ye never of Wat o' the Cleuch? Walsinghame's Song. James Hogg. BXAP
O heard ye of a silly Harper. The Lochmaben Harper. *Unknown.* OxBB
O heard ye of Sir James the Rose. Sir James the Rose. *Unknown.* ESPB
O hearken, all ye little weeds. Candlemas. Alice Brown. AA
O hearken and hear, and I will you tell. The Friar in the Well (B *vers.*). *Unknown.* ESPB
O hearken and hear the while I will tell. The Friar and the Fair Maid. *Unknown.* UnTE
O heart of hearts, the chalice of love's fire. Cor Cordium. Swinburne. VLP
O heart of mine, we shouldn't worry so! Just Be Glad. James Whitcomb Riley. WBLP
O heart, small urn. Hilda Doolittle ("H. D."). *Fr.* The Walls Do Not Fall. LLLT
O heart submissive in this martyrdom. The Assumption. John Gilland Brunini. ISi
O Heart! the equal poise of love's both parts. Richard Crashaw. *Fr.* The Flaming Heart. TrGrPo
O heart, why dost thou sigh, and wilt not break? When He Thought Himself Contemned. Thomas Howell. EIL
O Heaven Indulge, *with music.* Stephen Tilden. AH
O heavenly color, London town. November Blue. Alice Meynell. MoBrPo
O Heavy Step of Slow Monotony. Ernst Toller, *tr. fr. German by* Ashley Dukes. TrJP
O Hector, thou wert rooted in my heart. Helen's Lamentation. Homer, *tr. by* Congreve. *Fr.* The Iliad, XXIV. OBVE

O Heitsi-Eibib. Hunter's Prayer. *Unknown.* PeSA
O Hell! what do mine eyes with grief behold! Satan Beholds Adam and Eve in Eden. Milton. *Fr.* Paradise Lost, IV. TW
O helpless few in my country. The Rest. Ezra Pound. *Fr.* Lustra. AmPP; MoAB; MoAmPo; NoAM; NOBA; OxBA; PoA; PP
O herbis green, and pretty plants formois. Medoro's Inscription for a Cave. John Stewart of Baldynnis. *Fr.* Roland Furious. BSV
O hermitage well found. The Young Pilgrim Finds Refuge with the Goatherds. Luis de Góngora, *tr. by* Edward Meryon Wilson. *Fr.* The First Solitude. OBVE
O Hesperus! thou bringest all good things. Evening [*or* Hesperus the Bringer]. Byron. *Fr.* Don Juan, III. AWP; TrGrPo
O hideous little bat, the size of snot. The Fly. Karl Shapiro. LiTM; MiAP; MoVE; NePA; NIP; NoAM; TW; TwAmPo
O hill-hung city of my West. San Francisco Arising. Edwin Markham. BPAW
O Holy Aether, and swift-wingèd Wings. The Wail of Prometheus Bound. Aeschylus, *tr. by* Elizabeth Barrett Browning. *Fr.* Prometheus Bound. WGRP
O Holy City Seen of John, *with music.* Walter Russell Bowie. AH
O Holy, Holy, Holy, Lord, *with music.* James Wallis Eastburn. AH
O holy Jerusalem, Vision of peace. Advent Lyrics, III. *Unknown, tr. by* Charles W. Kennedy. *Fr.* Christ 1. AnOE
O holy Love, religious saint! Ditty. Sir Robert Chester. *Fr.* Love's Martyr. ElL
O Holy Mother, thou who still dost send. At the Tomb of Rachel. "Yehoash," *tr. by* Isidore Goldstick. TrJP
O holy virgin! clad in purest white. To Morning. Blake. EnRP
O Holy Water. Margot Ruddock. OBMV
"O hone a rie'! O hone a rie'!" Glenfinlas; or, Lord Ronald's Coronach. Sir Walter Scott. GoTL
O! Honour! Honour! Honour! Oh! the Gain! God's Selecting Love in the Decree. Edward Taylor. *Fr.* God's Determinations. PoEL-3
O how came I that loved stars, moon, and flame. The Image of Delight. William Ellery Leonard. HBMV
O how canst thou renounce the boundless store. Nature's Charms. James Beattie. *Fr.* The Minstrel. OBEC
O, how comely it is, and how reviving. *See* Oh, how comely it is, and how reviving.
O' How deep is thy love says. Sept. 1957. Edward Marshall. CoPo
O How I Love Thy Law. Isaac Watts. STF
O, how I remember the pain of it. Blood. Nina Cassian, *tr. by* Herbert Kuhner. VWA
O [*or* Oh], how much more doth [*or* doeth] beauty beauteous seem. Sonnets, LIV. Shakespeare. AWP; ElL; OBEV; OBSC; ViBoPo
O how my mind. Confusion. Christopher Hervey. BXAP; Par
O! How my thoughts do beat me. *Unknown.* OBSC
O! how shall I picture, in delicate strain. Miss Emily Brittle Sails for India. Sir George Dallas. *Fr.* The India Guide; or, Journal of a Voyage to the East Indies in 1780. NOEC
O How Sweet Are Thy Words! Anne Steele. BLRP
O how the nights are short. Midsummer Courtship. James Thompson. OBVV
O how the pleasant airs of true love be. Astrophel and Stella, LXXVIII. Sir Philip Sidney. SiPS
O, how this spring of love resembleth. This Spring of Love. Shakespeare. *Fr.* Two Gentlemen of Verona, I, iii. ChTr
O how this sullen, careless world. The Idiot. John Ashbery. *Fr.* Two Sonnets. VGW
O human hearts,/ Beating through fear, through jealousy. Prepare. Witter Bynner. PGD
O hurry where by water among the trees. The Ragged Wood. W. B. Yeats. GBL
O, hush thee, my babie [*or* baby], thy sire was a knight. Lullaby of an Infant Chief. Sir Walter Scott. EnRP; FaPON; HBV-1; OxBChV
O! hush thee, my darling, sleep soundly my son. Lullaby. *Unknown, tr. by* Alice Lucas. TrJP
O hushed October morning mild. October. Robert Frost. GoJo
O Hymen! O Hymenee! Walt Whitman. ErPo
O I am sick for the sagebrush. Sagebrush. Charles Erskine Scott Wood. BPAW
O I C. *Unknown.* WhC
O I Do Love, Then Kisse Me. Robert Jones. *See* Madrigal: "O I do love, then kiss me."
O I feel like the kinks in the paws of the Sphinx! Hotel Continental. William Jay Smith. WaP
"O I forbid you, maidens a' [*or* all]." Tam Lin [*or* Tamlane]. *Unknown.* BSV; ESPB; FaBoBa; NOBE; OBEV; OBNV; OxBB; OxBS; ViBoFo; WSC
O I gaed furth and far awa to see what I cou'd see. Dolomites. J. C. Milne. PoSH
O I had a future. I Had a Future. Patrick Kavanagh. BIrV; NoAM
O I had been to sunny Spain. On First Looking into Chapman's Homer I. T. Griffiths. BXAP
O I hae come from far away. The Witch's [*or* Witches'] Ballad. William Bell Scott. CH; EvOK; NBM; OBEV; OBVV; VLP
O, I love to hear the frogs. The Early Frogs. Harry Edward Mills. PeD
O, I shall run mad! John Webster. *Fr.* The Devil's Law Case. LO
O, I tell you. Lament of a Last Letter. Janet E. Harrison. AMV-80
O, I wad like to ken—to the beggar-wife says I. The Spaewife. Robert Louis Stevenson. BrPo; OxBS
O I went into the stable. Our Goodman. *Unknown.* ESPB
O I will sing to you a sang. The Clerk's Twa Sons O Owsenford. *Unknown.* ESPB
O! I wish the sun was bright in the sky. The Terrible Robber Men. Padraic Colum. HBMV
O if all the young maidens was blackbirds and thrushes. Blackbirds and Thrushes. *Unknown.* GBP
O if love were had for asking. The Sailor's Sweetheart. Duncan Campbell Scott. PeCV
O, if the world I make. The Dream. Arthur Symons. SyP
O if thou knew'st how thou thyself dost harm. *See* Oh, if thou knew'st how thou thyself dost harm.
O ignorant poor man! what dost thou bear. An Acclamation. Sir John Davies. OxBoCh
O, Inexpressible as Sweet. George Edward Woodberry. Wild Eden, VII. AA; HBV-1
(Song.) InMe
O interminable desires, O futile hope. Sonnet III. Louise Labé, *tr. by* Willis Barnstone. BoWoP
O Isis, Mother of God, to thee I pray! Prayer to Isis. Christina Walsh. BrRo
O it fell out upon a day. The Laird o Drum. *Unknown.* ESPB
O, it is excellent. Isabella Condemns Tyranny [*or* But Man, Proud Man]. Shakespeare. *Fr.* Measure for Measure, II, ii. TreFT; WHA
O, it is great for our country to die, where ranks are contending! Elegiac. James Gates Percival. AA; HBV-2
O, it was out by Donnycarney. Song. James Joyce. Chamber Music, XXXI. MoBrPo; OBVV
O Italy, I see the lonely towers. To Italy. Giacomo Leopardi, *tr. by* Romilda Rendel. AWP
O it's hippity hop to bed! Hippity Hop to Bed. Leroy F. Jackson. TiPo
O it's I that am the captain of a tidy little ship. My Ship and I. Robert Louis Stevenson. SUS
O it's up in the Highlands, and along the sweet Tay. Bonnie James Campbell. *Unknown.* BaBo; ESPB
O Jealous Night. *Unknown.* UnTE
(Night Piece, A.) OBSC
(To Night.) ElL; MOON
O Jean Baptiste, pourquoi. Pourquoi You Greased [*or* Pourquoi?]. *Unknown.* ChTr; GDP
O Jean, my Jean, when the bell ca's the congregation. Tam i' the Kirk. Violet Jacob. BSV; GBL; GoTS; HBMV
O Jellon Grame sat in Silver Wood. Jellon Grame. *Unknown.* EBEV; ESPB; OxBB
O Jenny, don't sobby! vor I shall be true. A Zong. William Barnes. BoLoP
O Jesu Parvule ("His mither sings to the bairnie Christ"). "Hugh MacDiarmid." BSV
O Jesu Parvule ("I saw a sweet and silly sight"). *Unknown.* ISi
O Jesus Christ, True Light of God, *with music.* John F. Ernst. AH
O Jesus, I have promised. To the End. John E. Bode. BLRP
O Jesus, My Savior, I Know Thou Art Mine, *with music.* Caleb J. Taylor. AH
O Job, Job (uh-huh). Job. *Unknown.* OuSiCo
O John "Doctor" Donne, O John "Doctor" Donne. Death Again. T. Hope. BXAP
O Johney was as brave a knight. Johnie Scot. *Unknown.* ESPB
O, Johnny Bull, my jo, John, I wonder what you mean. Johnny Bull, My Jo, John. *Unknown.* FSW
O Jojina my love, I always miss you. Jojina, My Love. *Zulu Oral Tradition, tr. by* H. Tracey. WTO
O Jonathan Bing, O Bingathon Jon. A New Song to Sing about Jonathan Bing. Beatrice Curtis Brown. SoPo
O joy of creation. What the Bullet Sang. Bret Harte. AA; OBEV; OBVV; PeD
O joy! that in our embers. Wordsworth. *Fr.* Ode: Intimations of Immortality. PoPle
O joy too high for my low style to show! Astrophel and Stella, LXIX. Sir Philip Sidney. SiPS; TrGrPo
O joys [*or* joyes]! Infinite sweetness! with what flowers [*or* flowres]. The Morning Watch. Henry Vaughan. AnAnS-1; LiTB; LoBV; MePo; OBS; OxBoCh; SeCePo; ViBoPo
O Joys of love and joys of fame. The Last Hour. Ethel Clifford. HBV-1

O June, O June, that we desired so. William Morris. *Fr.* The Earthly Paradise. ViBoPo
O Kane, O Ku-ka-Pao. Old Creation Chant. *Tr. fr. Hawaiian.* WTO
O Kane, O Lono of the blue sea. *Tr. fr. Hawaiian by* N. B. Emerson. WTO
O kangaroo, O kangaroo. The Kangaroo. Ogden Nash. WhC
O Keeper of the Sacred Key. Forceythe Willson. *Fr.* In State. AA
O Kentucky! my parents were driving. A Poem of the Forty-eight States. Kenneth Koch. NNaP; OBAL
O kindly house, where time my soul endows. The Old House. George Edward Woodberry. HBMV
O King Amasis, hail! Amasis. Laurence Binyon. OBVV
O King, I know you gave me poison. Mirabai, *tr. fr. Medieval Hindi by* Usha Nilsson. PBWP; WPOW
O King of Saints, We Give Thee Praise and Glory, *with music.* Mary A. Thomson. AH
O king of terrors! whose unbounded sway. To Death. Countess of Winchilsea. HBV-2
O King of the Friday. *Unknown, tr. fr. Irish by* Douglas Hyde. BIrV
O King of the starry sky. Starry Sky. *Unknown, tr. by* Sean O'Faolain. AnIL
O King of the World. *Tr. fr. Gaelic by* Douglas Hyde. WTO
O kiss, which dost those ruddy gems impart. Astrophel and Stella, LXXXI. Sir Philip Sidney. SiPS
O knit me, that am crumbled dust! the heape. Distraction. Henry Vaughan. NCEP; SeCP
O Lady amorous,/ Merciless lady. Canzonetta: A Bitter Song to His Lady. Pier Moronelli da Fiorenza, *tr. by* Dante Gabriel Rossetti. AWP; OBVE
O lady leal and lovesomest. To Our Lady. Robert Henryson. ACP
O Lady Moon. Christina Rossetti. MOON
(Lady Moon.) OxBChV
O lady of all truths bright light going forth. Enheduanna, *tr. by* Anne Draffkorn Kilmer, *based on text by* W. W. Hallo *and* J. J. A. van Dijk. *Fr.* Inanna Exalted. WPOW
O Lady of the Passion, dost thou weep? Our Lady of the Passion. John Mauropus, *tr. by* Elizabeth Barrett Browning. ISi
O Lady, rock never your young son young. Young Hunting. *Unknown.* BaBo (A *vers.*); ESPB; OxBB; ViBoFo
O Lady, together with the Child you take. Cry from the Battlefield. Robert Menth. ISi
O lady, when the tipped cup of the moon blessed you. Song. Ted Hughes. LLLT
O Lamb Give Me My Salt. *Unknown, tr. fr. Ibo by* Dennis C. Osadebay. PBA
O Land Beloved. George Edward Woodberry. *Fr.* My Country. PAH
O land of Empire, art and love! Resignation—to Faustus. Arthur Hugh Clough. VLP
O Land, of every land the best. Peace. Phoebe Cary. PAH
O, land of mud and mist, where man is wet and shivers. Such Is Holland! Petrus Augustus de Genestet, *tr. by* Adriaan Barnouw. POL
O Lapwing! Blake. ChTr
("O lapwing, thou fliest around the heath.") FaBoEE; PBBP
O last and best of Scots! who didst maintain. *See* Oh last and best of Scots! who did'st maintain.
O Lawd I Went Up on the Mountain, *with music.* *Unknown.* OuSiCo
O, Lay Thy Hand in Mine, Dear! Gerald Massey. EBVV; HBV-1
"O leaders and counselors." Odysseus and the Phaeacian Games. Homer, *tr. by* Ennis Rees. *Fr.* The Odyssey, VIII. LiSp
O leafy yellowness you create for me. October. Patrick Kavanagh. CIP; GTBS-P
O learned man who never learned to learn. The Myth of Arthur. G. K. Chesterton. HBMV
O leave them, Muse! O leave them to their woes. Keats. *Fr.* Hyperion. ViBoPo
O leave this barren spot to me! The Beech Tree's Petition. Thomas Campbell. HBV-1
O leeze me on my spinning-wheel. Bess and Her Spinning-Wheel. Burns. BSV
O lend to me, sweet nightingale. The Daughter of Mendoza. Mirabeau Bonaparte Lamar. AA; BPAW; HBV-1
O, lest your true love may seem false in this. Shakespeare. Sonnets, LXXII. LO
O let me be in loving nice. Punctilio. Mary Elizabeth Coleridge. OBEV; OBVV
O, Let Me Kiss. Karl Gjellerup, *tr. fr. Danish by* Charles Wharton Stork. PoPl
O let me leave the plains behind. Shakespeare. Sir William Watson. HBV-2
O let me love my love unto myself alone. Arthur Hugh Clough. *Fr.* Dipsychus, Pt. II, sc. ii. OAEP
O, let me reverently kiss thine eye. O, Let Me Kiss. Karl Gjellerup, *tr. by* Charles Wharton Stork. PoPl
O, let the solid ground. Song. Tennyson. *Fr.* Maud. HBV-1
O let your strong imagination turn. J. C. Squire. *Fr.* The Birds. PBBP
O life is a game of poker. Cash In. Sharlot M. Hall. BPAW
O Life That Maketh All Things New, *with music.* Samuel Longfellow. AH
O, Lift One Thought. Samuel Taylor Coleridge. *See* Epitaph: "Stop, Christian passer-by!—Stop, child of God."
O Light Invisible, we praise Thee! T. S. Eliot. *Fr.* The Rock, X. ILwL; OxBoCh; TrPWD
O Ligurinus. Horace. Odes, IV, 10. PeHV
O, like a queen's her happy tread. Song. Sir William Watson. HBV-1
O lily of the King! low lies the silver wing. Lillium Regis. Francis Thompson. HBMV; WGRP
O, limerick, Learest of lyrics. Lessons in Limericks, III. David McCord. InMe
O Lionel has the itch to etch. The Itch to Etch. Harold A. Larrabee. WhC
O, listen for a moment, lads, and hear me tell my tale. Jim Jones [*or* Jim Jones at Botany Bay]. *Unknown.* CBAP; GBP; PoAu-1
O listen, gude peopell, to my tale. The Laird o Logie. *Unknown.* ESPB
O [*or* Oh] listen, listen, ladies gay! Rosabelle [*or* Harold's Song: Rosabelle]. Sir Walter Scott. *Fr.* The Lay of the Last Minstrel. BeLS; BSV; EnRP; GTBS; GTBS-P; HBV-2
O little bird, you sing. The Secret. Arthur Wallace Peach. HBMV
O little buds, break not so fast! Budding-Time Too Brief. Evaleen Stein. AA
O little fleet! that on thy quest divine. Columbus and the Mayflower. Richard Monckton Milnes. PAH
O little friend, your nose is ready; you sniff. Dog. Harold Monro. MoBrPo
O little head of gold! O candle of my house! Lullaby of the Woman of the Mountain. Padraic Pearse, *tr. by* Thomas MacDonagh. OnYI
O little hearts, beat home, beat home. Swallow Song. Majorie Pickthall. CaP
O little Land of lapping seas. The Promised Land. Jessie E. Sampter. TrJP
O little mouse, so frightened of each sound. O Pity Our Small Size. Benjamin Rosenbaum. TrJP
O little self, within whose smallness lies. John Masefield. *Fr.* Sonnets ("Long long ago"). HBV-2; WGRP
O little soldier with the golden helmet. Dandelion. Hilda Conkling. FaPON; PDV; RHPC; TiPo
O Little Town of Bethlehem. Phillips Brooks. AA; AH, *with music;* BLRP; FaFP; FaPON; FSW; GN; HBV-1; OHIP; TreF; WBLP; WGRP
O little well, you give no water. *Gond Oral Tradition, tr. by* V. Elwin *and* S. Hivale. WTO
O Living Always, Always Dying. Walt Whitman. NOBA
O Living Flame of Love. St. John of the Cross. *See* O Flame of Living Love.
O living image of eternal youth! Trilby. Alice Brown. AA
O living pine, be still! Sleep. Yvor Winters. POL
O living will that shalt endure. In Memoriam A. H. H., CXXXI [*or* The Prayer]. Tennyson. EBVV; FaBoBe; HBV-2; WGRP
O London is a dainty place. London Is a Fine Town. *Unknown.* CoMu
O lonely bay of Trinity. The Cable Hymn. Whittier. PAH
O lonely workman, standing there. In the Moonlight. Thomas Hardy. NoAM
O lonesome sea-gull, floating far. Sea-Birds. Elizabeth Akers Allen. AA; FaBoBe; HBV-1
O, look at the moon! The Moon. Eliza Lee Follen. HBV-1; HBVY
O look how the loops and balloons of bloom. Stormy Day. W. R. Rodgers. LiTB
O, Lord/ If in life eternal. "Ping Hsin," *tr. by* Kai-yu Hsu. *Fr.* The Spring Waters. WPOW
O Lord,/ Thou hast given me a body. Thanksgiving for the Body. Thomas Traherne. ImOP
O Lord, Almighty God, *with music.* *Unknown.* AH
O Lord, at Joseph's humble bench. The Carpenter. George Macdonald. TrPWD; TRV
O Lord, Bow Down Thine Ear, *with music.* Thomas Prince. AH
O Lord, How Excellent Is Thy Name. Bible, *O.T.* Psalms, VIII. *See* What Is Man?
O Lord, How Lovely Is the Place, *with music.* *Ad. by* Francis Hopkinson. AH
O Lord, how wonderful in depth and height. Cardinal Newman. *Fr.* The Dream of Gerontius. VLP
O Lord, I been a-working. Trifling Women. *Unknown.* AmFP
O Lord, I Come Pleading. James Gilchrist Lawson. BLRP
O lord, I dred, and that I did not dred. Bible, *O.T.* Psalms, VI. OBVE
O Lord, I pray/ That for this day. Not to Be Ministered To. Maltbie D. Babcock. TrPWD
O Lord, I pray: that for each happiness. Petition. John Drinkwater. TrPWD

O Lord, I wonder at thy lov. Thomas Traherne. *Fr.* The Approach. TrPWD
O Lord, in me there lieth nought. Psalm CXXXIX. Countess of Pembroke. NOCV; OBSC; OxBoCh; WPE
O Lord, it is not hard to love. Prayer for Neighborhood Evangelism. Annette Jansen. STF
O Lord, it was all night. Sun. James Dickey. CAPP
O Lord! methought, what pain it was to drown. A Dream of Wrecks. Shakespeare. King Richard III, *fr.* I, iv. ChTr
"O Lord, My Best Desire Fulfill." William Cowper. OxBoCh
O Lord my sinne doth over-charge thy brest. Sinnes Heavie Loade. Robert Southwell. AnAnS-1
O Lord of all compassionate control. The Portrait. Dante Gabriel Rossetti. The House of Life, X. VLP
O Lord of Life, *with music.* Washington Gladden. AH
O Lord of life, Thy quickening voice awakes my morning song! My Morning Song. George Macdonald. TRV
O Lord of splendid nations let us dream. Struthers Burt. The Land, IV. HBMV
O Lord, our God, Thy mighty hand. Peace Hymn of the Republic. Henry van Dyke. AH; TRV
O Lord, our Lord, how excellent is thy name. Bible, *O.T.* Psalms, VIII. AWP; NAWM-1; TreFS; TrGrPo; TrJP
O Lord, our Lord! how wondrously (quoth she). The Prioress' Tale. Chaucer, *mod. by* Wordsworth. *Fr.* The Canterbury Tales. GoBC (*incl.* prologue)
O lord our lord, thy name how merveillous. The Prioress's Tale. Chaucer. *Fr.* The Canterbury Tales. OxBoCh (*incl.* prologue)
O Lord, Save We Beseech Thee. *Unknown.* TrJP
O Lord, Seek Us. Christina Rossetti. *See* Lord, Save Us, We Perish.
O Lord, since we have feasted thus. Grace after Dinner. Burns. FaBoEE
O Lord, So Sweet. *Unknown.* NCEP
O Lord, support us all the day long. Until the Shadows Lengthen. Cardinal Newman. TRV
O Lord, That Art My God and King, *with music.* John Craig. AH
O Lord, that rul'st the human heart. Bible, *O.T., paraphrased by* Christopher Smart. Psalms, VIII. OBVE
O Lord, the hard-won miles. A Prayer. Paul Laurence Dunbar. TrPWD
O Lord, the whistling sword is beauty. Headsong. Joseph Bennett. NePA
O Lord, Thou Hast Been to the Land, *with music. Unknown.* AH
O Lord, Thou Hast Enticed Me. Bible, *O.T.* Jeremiah, XX: 7-10. TrJP
O Lord, Turn Not Away Thy Face, *with music. At. to* John Marckant. AH
O Lord, we come this morning. Listen, Lord [—a Prayer]. James Weldon Johnson. BANP; BPo
O Lord! who seest from yon starry height. The Image of God. Francesco de Aldana, *tr. by* Longfellow. WGRP
O Lord whose mercy never fails. Pro Libra Mea. Joseph I. C. Clarke. TrPWD
O Lord, why must thy poets peak and pine. Priest or Poet. Shane Leslie. WGRP
O Lord, wilt thou not look upon our sore afflictions. Blake. *Fr.* Vala; or, The Four Zoas. ViBoPo
O Lord, you know my inmost hope and thought. My Inmost Hope. Sarah Copia Sullam. TrJP
O Lorde oure governoure, howe excellent is thy name. Bible, *O.T.* Psalms, VIII. OBVE
O lords! O rulers of the nation! The People's Petition. Wathen Mark Wilks Call. OBVV
O Lordy, jes' give me a long white robe! Choose You a Seat 'n' Set Down. *Unknown.* OuSiCo
O Loss of sight, of thee I most complain. The Blindness of Samson. Milton. *Fr.* Samson Agonistes. LiTB
O Love, Answer. Anne Ridler. SeCePo
O love, be fed with apples while you may. Sick Love [*or* O Love in Me]. Robert Graves. BoLoP; CMoP; EBEV; FaBoMo; GTBS-P; HAP; NoAM; NOBE; OAEL-2
O Love, bringer of fire. Aut Neutrum . . . Vel Duos. Rufinus Domesticus, *tr. by* Dudley Fitts. OLR
O Love Divine, That Stooped to Share. Oliver Wendell Holmes. *See* Hymn of Trust.
O Love, give me a passionate heart. A Prayer. Irene Rutherford McLeod. TrPWD
O Love, how strangely sweet. Song. John Marston. ElL
O love, I never, never thought. Cancion. Juan II of Castile, *tr. by* George Tichnor. AWP
O Love, if you were here. If You Were Here. Philip Bourke Marston.
O Love in Me. Robert Graves. *See* Sick Love.
O, love, in your sweet name enough. Anne Finch. *Fr.* Essay on Marriage. FaBoTw
O, Love Is Not a Summer Mood. Richard Watson Gilder. HBV-1
O Love, Love, Love! O withering might! Fatima. Tennyson. GBL; SeCePo; UnPo; UnTE
O Love, my love, and perfect bliss! Medieval Norman Song. *Unknown, tr. by* John Addington Symonds. AWP
O Love, O thou that, for my fealty. Sonnet: To Love, In Great Bitterness. Cino da Pistoia, *tr. by* Dante Gabriel Rossetti. AWP
O love of God, God's love, love that alone. For All Sorts and Conditions. Norman Nicholson. EaLo
O Love of God incarnate. Incarnate Love. Wilbur Fisk Tillett. BLRP
O love, so sweet at first. Disarmed. Laura Redden Searing. AA
O Love, That Dost with Goodness Crown. John W. Chadwick. TrPWD
O Love That Lights the Eastern Sky, *with music.* Louis F. Benson. AH
O Love That Wilt Not Let Me Go. George Matheson. TreFS; TrPWD; TRV; WGRP
O love, the interest itself in thoughtless Heaven. Perhaps [*or* Prologue]. W. H. Auden. EBEV; FaBoMo; MoPo; NePA; OAEP
O love, this morn when the sweet nightingale. May. William Morris. *Fr.* The Earthly Paradise. VLP
O love triumphant over guilt and sin. L'Envoi. Frederic Lawrence Knowles. TrPWD; TRV
O love, turn from the unchanging sea, and gaze. October. William Morris. *Fr.* The Earthly Paradise. FaBoEn; OBNC
O love, what hours were thine and mine. The Daisy. Tennyson. EnLoPo; OBNC; OBVV; PoEL-5
O Love! what shall be said of thee. Fragoletta. Swinburne. UnTE
O Love, when in my day of doom. The Gardener. Laurence Housman. TrPWD
O Love, who all this while hast urged me on. Canzone: To Love and to His Lady. Guido delle Colonne, *tr. by* Dante Gabriel Rossetti. AWP
O Love, whose patient pilgrim feet. The Golden Wedding. David Gray. FaBoBe; HBV-1
O, loveliest throat of all sweet throats. Edna St. Vincent Millay. Memorial to D.C., V. OxBA
O lovely age of gold! The Golden Age. Tasso, *tr. by* Leigh Hunt. *Fr.* Aminta. AWP; OBVE
O lovely April, rich and bright. Song. Gustave Kahn, *tr. by* Ludwig Lewisohn. TrJP
O lovely maiden, thou hast drawn my heart. The Unhappy Lover. Judah al-Harizi, *tr. by* J. Chotzner. TrJP
O lovely O most charming pug. A Sonnet on a Monkey [*or* A Sonnet]. Marjory Fleming. FaBoCo; FaFP; FiBHP
O lovely pussy! O pussy my love. Love Song. Edward Lear. *Fr.* The Owl and the Pussy-Cat. PCat
O [*or* Oh], lovers' eyes are sharp to see. The Maid of Neidpath. Sir Walter Scott. BeLS; EnRP; GTBS; GTBS-P
O loyal to the royal in thyself. To the Queen. Tennyson. *Fr.* Idylls of the King. VLP
O ludicrous and pensive trinity. Romeo and Juliet. H. Phelps Putnam. ErPo
O luely, luely, cam she in. The Tryst [*or* Trysting Place]. William Soutar. BoLoP; BSV; EBEV; ErPo; GoTS; NeBP; OxBS
O Lusty May, with Flora queen! Lusty May [*or* Four May Poems]. *Unknown.* OBEV; OxBS
O luxury! Thou curst by Heaven's decree. Goldsmith. *Fr.* The Deserted Village. BIrV
O Lyric Love. Robert Browning. *Fr.* The Ring and the Book, I. FiP (Lyric Love.) OBVV
("O lyric Love, half-angel and half-bird.") OAEP
O Lyric Love. Winfield Townley Scott. VGW
"O madam, I will give to thee a new silk gown." My Man John. *Unknown.* OBET
O madam, I will give to you the keys of Canterbury. The Keys of Canterbury. *Unknown.* AmFP
O magic sleep! O comfortable bird. Life Again. Keats. *Fr.* Endymion. SeCePo
O maister deer[e] and fader reverent! Lament for Chaucer and Gower [*or* Hoccleve's Lament]. Thomas Hoccleve. *Fr.* De Regimine Principum. EBEV; OAEP; OxBM
O Maistres Myn. *Unknown. See* O Mistress Mine.
O make me a mask and a well to shut from your spies. Dylan Thomas. PoA
O Maker of the infinite starry spaces. Petition. Harold McCurdy. AMV-81
O Maker of the Mighty Deep. Voyagers. Henry van Dyke. TRV
O Maker of the starry world. Boethius, *tr. by* Helen Waddell. *Fr.* The Consolation of Philosophy. NAWM-1
O Mally's Meek, Mally's Sweet. Burns. GN; HBV-1
"O man of little wit." The Pine to the Mariner, *abr.* George Turberville. EtS
O Man of mine own people, I alone. The Jew to Jesus. Florence Kiper Frank. HBMV; TRV; WGRP
O man that for Fergus of the feasts dost kindle fir. Song of the Forest Trees. *Unknown, tr. by* Standish Hayes O'Grady. OnYI
O Man Unkind. *Unknown.* OxBM

O! Mankinde. See! Here, My Heart. *Unknown.* MeEL
O many a day have I made good ale in the glen. *See* Oh, many a day have I made good ale in the glen.
O Marduk, lord of countries, terrible one. *Unknown.* *Fr.* Hymn to Marduk. WGRP
O Mariners! Archibald Rutledge. EtS
O mark yon rose-tree! When the west. Love's Likeness. George Darley. OBVV
O Martyred Spirit. George Santayana. TrPWD
O [*or* Oh] Mary, at the window be. Mary Morison [*or* Song: Mary Morison]. Burns. AWP; EnRP; GTBS; GTBS-P; HBV-1; OAEP; OBEC; OBEV; OxBS; TreFT; TrGrPo; WHA
O Mary, Don't You Weep, Don't You Mourn. *Unknown.* *See* Pharoah's Army Got Drownded.
"O [*or* Oh] Mary, go and call the cattle home." The Sands of Dee. Charles Kingsley. *Fr.* Alton Lockes, *ch.* 26. BeLS; CH; EBVV; FaBoPP; FaPON; FaPoR; GN; HBV-1; PoPle; TreF; VLP; WBLP
O Mary Hamilton [*or* Marie Hamilton's] to the kirk [is] gane. Mary Hamilton [*or* Marie Hamilton *or* The Queen's Marie]. *Unknown.* BSV; NOBE; OBEV; OxBB; PoPle
O Mary Mary lying on the wheel. Visitor's Parking. Anne Szumigalski. NOBC
O Mary Pierced with Sorrow. Kipling. *Fr.* Song before Action. ISi
O Mary's lovelier than anything that grows. Prisoner's Song. Horace Gregory. OLR
O Master, Let Me Walk with Thee. Washington Gladden. AH, *with music;* WGRP
(Service.) BLRP; TRV
O Master Masons. Ernst Toller, *tr. fr. German by* Ashley Dukes. TrJP
O Master of the common weal. The Master of Laborers. George Edward Day. PGD
O Master-Workman of the Race. Jay T. Stocking. AH, *with music;* TRV
O [*or* Oh] may I join the choir invisible. The Choir Invisible. "George Eliot." EBVV; HBV-2; OBNC; OBVV; OHFP; TreFS; TRV; WBLP; WGRP
O may I with myself agree. John Dyer. Grongar Hill. TrGrPo
O May she comes, and May she goes. The Bonny Hind [*or* Heyn]. *Unknown.* ESPB; OxBB; ViBoFo
O me, oh my, oh you. Does the Spearmint Lose Its Flavor on the Bedpost Overnight? Billy Rose. OBAL
O me! what eyes hath love put in my head. Sonnets, CXLVIII. Shakespeare. GTBS; GTBS-P
O meikle thinks my luve o' my beauty. My Tocher's the Jewel. Burns. BSV
O melancholy bird, a winter's day. The Heron. Edward Hovell-Thurlow. HBV-1
"O 'Melia, my dear, this does everything crown!" The Ruined Maid. Thomas Hardy. BoLoP; BrPo; CABA; CMoP; ErPo; FiBHP; HeIP; InPK; LiTB; NIP; NOBL; NOP; OxBTC; PAI; PPoe; SCV; SeCeV; TEP; WeW
O Memory, could I but loose thee now. Lindamira's Complaint. Mary Sidney Wroth, Countess of Montgomery. *Fr.* Urania. WPE
O memory, thou fond deceiver. Memory [*or* Song]. Goldsmith. *Fr.* The Captivity. OBEC; OBEV; ViBoPo
O, men from the fields! A Cradle Song [*or* Lullaby]. Padraic Colum. GoBC; ISi; OnYI; OxBI; WTO
O men, the beautiful world is going to be spoiled. The Suez Crisis. *Somali Oral Tradition, tr. by* B. W. Andrzejewski. WTO
O men, walk on the hills. Poem. Maxwell Bodenheim. TrJP
O merciful Father, my hope is in thee! Prayer before [Her] Execution. Mary Queen of Scots, *tr. by* John Fawcett. TRV; WGRP
O merciful God, hear this our request. A Prayer to Be Said When Thou Goest to Bed. Francis Seager. OxBChV
O Merlin in your crystal cave. Merlin. Edwin Muir. FaBoTw; OxBS
O Merry Hae I Been Teethin' a Heckle. Burns. BSV
O Merry May the Maid Be. John Clerk. HBV-1
O! mestress, why. Distant as the Duchess of Savoy. *Unknown.* MeEL
O Michael, you are at once the enemy. Garden-Lion. Evelyn Hayes. ChTr
O mickle yeuks the keckle doup. Justice to Scotland. *Unknown.* InMe
O might those sigh[e]s and tear[e]s return again[e]. Holy Sonnets, III. John Donne. AnAnS-1; BiP; MasP; OBS
O mighty Caesar! dost thou lie so low? Mark Antony's Lament. Shakespeare. *Fr.* Julius Caesar, III, i. TreFS
O mighty God, Which for us men. A Prayer. Humphrey Gifford. OxBoCh
O Mighty, Melancholy Wind. John Todhunter. *See* Song: "Bring from the craggy haunts of birch and pine."
O mighty-mouth'd inventor of harmonies. Milton. Tennyson. OAEP; VLP
O Mighty Nothing! unto thee. And He Answered Them Nothing. Richard Crashaw. MePo
O Mighty, powerful, strong one of Ashur. *Unknown.* *Fr.* Hymn to Marduk. WGRP
O mighty river! strong, eternal Will. The Great River. Henry van Dyke. TrPWD
O Mind of God, Broad as the Sky. Oliver Huckel. TrPWD
O mine own sweet heart. Simon and Susan. *Unknown.* OxBoLi
O miserable sorrow, withouten cure. Sir Thomas Wyatt. SiPS
O Mister Giraffe, you make me laugh. Mr. Giraffe. Geoffrey LaPage. OnUR
O Mistress Mine ("O mistress mine, till you I me commend"). *Unknown.* GoTS; MeEL
(O Maistres Myn.) OxBS
O Mistress Mine, Where Are You Roaming? Shakespeare. *Fr.* Twelfth Night, II, iii. AWP; BiP; ElL; ELP; EnRePo; GBL; HAP; InPS; LoBV; NOBE; OAEL-1; OAEP; OLR; ViBoPo; WHA
(Carpe Diem.) GTBS; GTBS-P
(Clown's Song.) FaBoEn
(Feste's Song.) BoLoP; OBSC
(O [*or* Oh] Mistress Mine.) CTC; FaBV; FaFP; HeIP; InMe; LiTB; NoP; PoRA; SeCeV; TreFT; TrGrPo
(Song.) FiP; HBV-1
(Sweet-and-Twenty.) OBEV
O mitsch mein inkum stinkum buckeroom. Ja, Ja, Ja! *Unknown.* ShS
O Mollie, O Mollie, 'tis for your sake alone. Jack o' Diamonds; or, The Rabble Soldier. *Unknown.* CoSo
O money is the meat in the cocoanut. Money. *Unknown.* AS
O mongrel land! My America. Oliver La Grone. NNP
O months of blossoming, months of transfigurations. The Lilacs and the Roses. Louis Aragon, *tr. by* Louis MacNeice. OBWP
O Moon, Mr. Moon. Mr. Moon. Bliss Carman. FaPON; SUS
O moon, O hide thy golden light. O World, Be Not So Fair. Maria Jäger, *tr. by* Grace Fallow Norton. HBV-2
O Moon! the oldest shades 'mong oldest trees. Keats. *Fr.* Endymion, III. EnRP
O Moon, When I Gaze on Thy Beautiful Face. *Unknown.* *See* Poetic Thought.
O Morning-Maker, deign that ray. Plea for Hope. Francis Carlin. TrPWD
O Mors! Quam Amara Est Memoria Tua Homini Pacem Habenti in Substantiis Suis. Ernest Dowson. BrPo; OBMV
O mortal[l] folk[e]! you may behold and se[e]. The Epitaph of [la] Grande Amoure [*or* An Epitaph *or* His Epitaph]. Stephen Hawes. *Fr.* The Pastime of Pleasure. ACP; ChTr; EBEV; FaBoEE; FaBoRV; GoBC; OBEV; OBSC; SeCeV; TrGrPo; ViBoPo
O mortal man, that lives by bread. *At. to* Julius Caesar Ibbetson. FaBoEE
O mortal man, that lives by bread. Sally Birkett's Ale. *Unknown.* ChTr
O mortal Man, who livest here by toil. The Castle of Indolence, Canto I. James Thomson. LAuP
O [*or* Oh] most high, almighty, good Lord God. Canticle of the Sun [*or* The Song of the Creatures]. St. Francis of Assisi. GoBC, *tr. by* Matthew Arnold; TreFS, *tr. by* Matthew Arnold; WGRP, *tr. by* Maurice Francis Egan
O most unconscious daisy! To a School-Girl. Shaw Neilson. PoAu-1
O Mother Dear, Jerusalem. *Unknown.* *See* New Jerusalem, The.
O Mother Eve, I do believe that after all you're glad you ate. Ode to Eve. Edwin Meade Robinson. InMe
"O mother, I longs to get married." Whistle, Daughter, Whistle. *Unknown.* OBET
O mother, lay your hand on my brow! The Sick Child. Robert Louis Stevenson. CH; PoSC
O mother-maid! O maiden-mother free! Invocation. Chaucer [*or* Two Invocations of the Virgin, II]. *Fr.* The Canterbury Tales: The Prologue of the Prioress's Tale. ACP, *mod.*; ISi, *mod. version by* Frank Ernest Hill
O Mother Mary, Flower of all womankind. Ballade to Our Lady. Alexander Barclay. *Fr.* The Ship of Fools. ISi
O Mother of Fair Love, it was not alone. Cause of Our Joy. Sister Maris Stella. ISi
O Mother Race! to thee I bring. Ode to Ethiopia. Paul Laurence Dunbar. BALP
O Mothers of the Human Race. Robert Whitaker. PGD
O move in me, my darling. Woman's Song. Judith Wright. PAI
O Muse! by thee conducted down, I dare. The Court of Neptune. John Hughes. EtS
O Muse! relate (for you can tell alone). The Triumph of Dulness. Pope. *Fr.* The Dunciad, IV. OBEC
O [*or* Oh] my aged uncle Arly! Incidents in the Life of My Uncle Arly. Edward Lear. FaBoNo; FPL; MoShBr; NA; NBM; OAEL-2; OxBoLi; TrGrPo; WhC
O My Belly. *Unknown.* GBP; POL
O my black[e] Soul[e]! now thou art summoned. *See* Oh my black[e] soul[e]! now thou art summoned.
O my body! I dare not desert the likes of you in other men and women, nor

the likes of the parts of you. Walt Whitman. *Fr.* I Sing the Body Electric. ErPo
O My Bonny, Bonny May. *Unknown.* GBP
O my brother I heard u. Before/ and After. Jewel C. Latimore. JB
O my chief good! The Passion. Henry Vaughan. AnAnS-1
O my comrade, it is cold. Cold and Heat. *Tr. fr. Hawaiian by* M. W. Beckwith. WTO
O my cousin, my beloved. Girl's Song. *Unknown, tr. by* Willard Trask. LLLT
O my coy darling, still. Ode to a Dressmaker's Dummy. Donald Justice. DFF
O [*or* Oh] my dark Rosaleen. Dark Rosaleen. *Unknown, at. to* Owen Roe MacWard *and to* Hugh O'Donnell, *tr. by* James Clarence Mangan. ACP; AnIL; AnIV; AWP; BIrV; CH; EnRP; HBV-2; OBEV; OBVV; OnYI; OxBi; ViBoPo
O my deerest I shall grieve thee. The Complement. Thomas Carew. CavP
O my deir hert, young Jesus sweit. Balulalow [*or* Cradle Song]. James, John, *and* Robert Wedderburn. EaLo; LoBV; OBEV; OxBoCh
O my earliest love, who, ere I number'd. First Love. Charles Stuart Calverley. FiBHP; InMe
O my God, thou hast wounded me with love. A Confession. Paul Verlaine, *tr. by* Arthur Symons. WGRP
O my heart is the unlucky heir of the ages. Personal History; for My Son. Ruthven Todd. NeBP
O my Heart, my Mother, my Heart, my Mother. He Approacheth the Hall of Judgment. *Unknown, tr. by* Robert Hillyer. *Fr.* Book of the Dead. AWP
O My Honey, Take Me Back, *with music. Unknown.* AS
O my hornbill husband, you have a bad smell. Lament for a Husband. *Tr. fr. Papuan by* Don Laycock. BoWoP
O my lady, the Anunna, the great gods. Inanna and the Anunna. Enheduanna, *tr. fr. Sumerian.* BoWoP
O my land! O my love! Lament for Banba. *Unknown, at. to* Egan O'Rahilly, *tr. by* James Clarence Mangan. AnIV; AWP
O my life is so simple and the world. The Fiddlehead. David McFadden. NeAC
O my Lord, if I worship you from fear of Hell. Rabi'a the Mystic, *tr. fr. Arabic by* Willis Barnstone. BoWoP
O my Lord, the stars glitter and eyes of men are closed. Rabi'a the Mystic, *tr. fr. Arabic by* Willis Barnstone. BoWoP
O my lost husband! let me ever mourn. Andromache's Lament. Homer, *tr. by* Congreve. *Fr.* The Iliad, XXIV. OBVE
O my love/ The pretty towns. Kenneth Patchen. VGW
O my love! my wife! Everlasting Rest. Shakespeare. *Fr.* Romeo and Juliet, V, iii. WHA
O my lover, blind me. The Tired Woman. Anna Wickham. MoBrPo
O my Lucasia, let us speak our love. To My Lucasia, in Defence of Declared Friendship. Katherine Phillips. MeLP
O [*or* Oh], My Luve [*or* Love] Is like a Red, Red Rose. Burns. *See* Red, Red Rose, A.
O My Mother Isle! ("Not yet enslaved, not wholly vile.") Samuel Taylor Coleridge. *Fr.* Ode on the Departing Year. FaBoPP
O My Mother Isle! ("O native Britain! O my Mother Isle!") Samuel Taylor Coleridge. *Fr.* Fears in Solitude. FaBoPP
O, my name is Samuel Hall. *See* Oh, my name is Sam Hall.
O My Poor Darling. Wilfred Watson. EnLoPo
O my sinner, let us spend this night together. Tonight, at Least, My Sinner. *Gond Oral Tradition, tr. by* V. Elwin *and* S. Hivale. WTO
O my son,/ Only your name remains. Lament for Taramoana. Makere, *tr. fr. Maori by* Barry Mitcalfe. WTO
O my son, born on a winter's morn. Lullaby. Nohomaiterangi, *tr. fr. Maori by* Barry Mitcalfe. WTO
O my songs. Coda. Ezra Pound. NOBA
O my soul be patient, she is very beautiful. She Is Not for Me. *Gond Oral Tradition, tr. by* V. Elwin *and* S. Hivale. WTO
O my soul, keep the rest unknown! He Resolves to Say No More. Thomas Hardy. TEP
O My Swallows! Ernst Toller, *tr. fr. German by* Ashley Dukes. TrJP
O my thoughts' sweet food, my only owner. Lady My Treasure. Sir Philip Sidney. GBL
O my trade it is the rarest one. The Stranger's Song. Thomas Hardy. BrPo
O my true love's a smuggler and sails upon the sea. The Smuggler. *Unknown.* WhC
O Nancy! Wilt Thou Go with Me. Thomas Percy. HBV-1
O native Britain! O my Mother Isle! O My Mother Isle! Samuel Taylor Coleridge. *Fr.* Fears in Solitude. FaBoPP
O nature! I do not aspire. Nature. Henry David Thoreau. BLPL; FaBoBe; HBV-1
O Nectar! O Delicious Stream! Love. Thomas Traherne. SeCV-2
O [*or* Oh], never say that I was false of heart. Sonnets, CIX. Shakespeare. EIL; GTBS; GTBS-P; HBV-1; NOBE; OBEV; OBSC
O Never Star Was Lost. Robert Browning. TreFT
O New England, thou canst not boast. A Word to New England. William Bradford. SCAP
O Night! dark Night! wrapped round with Stygian gloom! New Night Thoughts on Death; a Parody. William Whitehead. NOEC
O Night, O jealous Night, repugnant to my pleasures [*or* measures] O Jealous Night [*or* A Night Piece *or* To Night]. *Unknown.* EIL; MOON; OBSC; UnTE
O Night O Trembling Night. Stephen Spender. ErPo; NeBP
O Night of the Crying Children. Nelly Sachs, *tr. fr. German by* Keith Bosley. VWA
O night, the ease of care, the pledge of pleasure. Night. Sir Philip Sidney. *Fr.* Arcadia. SiPS
O Nightingale. Milton. *See* To the Nightingale.
O nightingale of woodland gay. Medieval Norman Song. *Unknown, tr. by* John Addington Symonds. AWP
O Nightingale, That on Yon Bloomy Spray. Milton. *See* To the Nightingale.
O nightingale, the poet's bird. A Song about Singing. Anne Reeve Aldrich. AA
O Nightingale! Thou Surely Art. Wordsworth. HBV-1; PBBP
O no, beloved, I am most sure. Lord Herbert of Cherbury. *Fr.* An Ode upon a Question Moved, Whether Love Should Continue for Ever? ViBoPo
O [*or* Oh], No, John. *Unknown.* ErPo; OBET; UnTE
(No John.) FSW
(One Answer, The.) PDV
O, no more, no more, too late. *See* Oh, no more, no more, too late.
O noble brow, so wise in thought! Washington [*or* When Shall We See Thy Like Again?]. Mary Wingate. OHIP; PGD
O noble England. A Joyfull New Ballad. Thomas Deloney. CoMu; ViBoPo
O noble, gracious English tongue. A Grub Street Recessional. Christopher Morley. InMe
O noble Oisin, son of the king. Oisin in the Land of Youth. Michael Comyn, *tr. by* Tomás O'Flannghaile. AnIL
O Noble Virgin. Prudentius, *tr. fr. Latin by* Raymond F. Roseliep. *Fr.* Cathemerinon. ISi
O! Nothing earthly save the ray. Al Aaraaf. Poe. AP
O nothing, in this corporal earth of man. All's Vast [*or* Correlated Greatness]. Francis Thompson. *Fr.* The Heart. GTBS-P; MoAB; MoBrPo; OBMV
O, now for ever/ Farewell the tranquil mind! Othello's Farewell to His Career [*or* Farewell Content]. Shakespeare. *Fr.* Othello, III, iii. TreFT; TrGrPo
O now I know: a smile. Rest O Sun I Cannot. Joseph Tusiani. GoYe
O Now the Drenched Land Wakes. Kenneth Patchen. PoA
O now you come in rut. To Frighten a Storm. Gladys Cardiff. CDW; STE
O nuclear [*or* Nuclear] wind, when wilt thou blow. *Fr.* A Leaden Treasury of English Verses. Paul Dehn. FiBHP; DBV; PV; SpRo
O nymph, compar'd with whose young bloom. To Lady Anne Fitzpatrick, When about Five Years Old, with a Present of Shells, 1772. Horace Walpole. NOEC; OBEC
O often have I prayed, and thought. Oblique. Archibald Rutledge. TRV
O [*or* Oh] ole Zip Coon he is a larned skoler. Zip Coon [*or* Old Zip Coon]. *Unknown.* PSoN; TrAS; YaD
O [*or* Oh] once I was happy but now I'm forlorn. The Man on the Flying Trapeze [*or* The Flying Trapeze]. George Lebourne. BLSo; FSW; TreF
O only Source of all our light and life. Qui Laborat, Orat. Arthur Hugh Clough. TrPWD; VLP
O, open the door, some pity to show. *See* Oh, open the door, some pity to shew.
O, Opportunity, thy guilt is great. Opportunity [*or* An Outcry upon Opportunity]. Shakespeare. *Fr.* The Rape of Lucrece. LiTB; NOBE; OBSC; PoEL-2
O [*or* Oh] Paddy, dear, and [*or* an'] did you hear the news that's going [*or* goin'] 'round? The Wearing of [*or* Wearin' o'] the Green. *Unknown.* AnIL; AnIV; AWP; FaFP; FaPoR; FSW; GBP; HBV-2; OnYi; OxBoLi; PoSC; TreF; WTO
O pale! O vivid! dear! Conquered. Zoë Akins. HBMV
"O Paleys [*or* palace], whylom [*or* whilom] croune [*or* crown] of houses all[e]." The Complaint of Troilus. Chaucer. *Fr.* Troilus and Criseyde. NOBE; OBEV
O pansy-eye, O polished face. Debutantrum. William Rose Benét. InMe
O Paradise! O Paradise! Frederick William Faber. *See* Paradise.
O Parcy Reed has Crozer ta'en. Parcy Reed. *Unknown.* OxBB
"O Passenger, pray list and catch." The Levelled Churchyard. Thomas Hardy. NOBL
O pastoral heart of England! like a psalm. Upon Eckington Bridge, River Avon. Sir Arthur Quiller-Couch. OBVV
O patron saints of all my friends! Friends. Lionel Johnson. GoBC

O peony, O pink inverted bell. A Peony for Apollo. Charles Edward Eaton. GoYe
O people who live in the world. Andal, *tr. fr. Tamil by* Willis Barnstone. BoWoP
O people-chosen! are ye not. To the Thirty-ninth Congress. Whittier. PAH
O perfect Light, which [*or* whilk *or* quhilk] shaid [*or* shed *or* schaid] away. A Summer Day [*or* Of the Day Estivall]. Alexander Hume. BSV; LoBV; NOCV; OxBS
"O Peter, O Apostle, hast thou seen my bright love?" The Keening of Mary. *Unknown, tr. by* Padraic Pearse. ISi
O Phoebus embattling the high wall of Ilium. Chorus: The Kings of Troy. Euripides, *tr. by* George Allen. *Fr.* Andromache. WaaP
O piano I heard at evening. Piano at Evening. Palea, *tr. fr. Hawaiian by* M. K. Pukui *and* A. L. Korn. WTO
O pine-tree standing. Hakutsu. *Fr.* Manyo Shu. AWP
O, Pioneers! John Peale Bishop. VGW
O piteous race! Judaism. Cardinal Newman. ACP
O Pity Our Small Size. Benjamin Rosenbaum. TrJP
O pitying angel, pause, and say. In Paradise. Arlo Bates. AA
O [*or* Oh] pleasant exercise of hope and joy! Residence in France (Continued) [*or* The French Revolution as It Appeared to Enthusiasts at Its Commencement]. Wordsworth. *Fr.* The Prelude, XI. FiP; HAP; OBRV; PoEL-4
O plump head-waiter at The Cock. Will Waterproof's Lyrical Monologue. Tennyson. VLP
O, po' sinner, O, now is yo' time. What Yo' Gwine to Do When Yo' Lamp Burn Down? *Unknown.* BoAN-1; BPo
O, poet gifted with the sight divine! Milton. Henrietta Cordelia Ray. BlSi
O poet of the future! I. The Future. George Frederick Cameron. OBCV
O poet rare and old! Astræa. Whittier. AA
O poet strutting from the sandbagged portal. As One Non-Combatant to Another. George Orwell. OxBTC
O poet, what do you do? I praise. Praise. Rainer Maria Rilke. ChTr
O Polly dear, O Polly, the rout has now begun. *See* Oh Polly love, Oh Polly, the rout has now begun.
"O Polly, you might have toy'd and kist." John Gay. *Fr.* The Beggar's Opera. EnLoPo
"O poppy Death!—sweet poisoner of sleep!" Scylla's Lament. Thomas Hood. *Fr.* Hero and Leander. EnRP
O Possible and Probable. Adventure. Grace Fallow Norton. HBMV
O potent Earth, and Heaven god-built. Earth and Sky. Euripides, *tr. by* C. M. Bowra. EaLo
O pour upon my soul again. Rosalie. Washington Allston. AA
O power of Love, O wondrous mystery! Love. Katrina Trask. AA
O Powers Celestial, with what sophistry. Barnabe Barnes. *Fr.* Parthenophil and Parthenophe. EnLoPo
O, praise an' tanks! De Lord he come. Song of the Negro Boatman. Whittier. *Fr.* At Port Royal. GN
O praise God in his holiness: praise him in the firmament of his power. Laudate Dominum. Bible, *O.T.* Psalms, CL. ChTr; ILwL
O praying one, who long has prayed. Ask, and Ye Shall Receive. Mrs. Havens. BLRP
O precious codex, volume, tome. To a Thesaurus. Franklin P. Adams. BLPL; PoPl; WhC
O Prince of Life, Thy Life hath tuned. The Prince of Life. John Oxenham. TrPWD
O Proserpina!/ For the flowers now that frighted thou let'st fall. Perdita's Garden. Shakespeare. *Fr.* The Winter's Tale, IV, iii. WHA
O pumpkins! O periwinkles! Wet Weather at Cannes. Edward Lear. FaBoNo
O Queen, awake to thy renown. Honor and Desert. Coventry Patmore. The Angel in the House, II. HBV-1
O Queen of heaven, be joyful, alleluia. Regina Coeli. *Unknown, tr. by* Winfred Douglas. ISi
O quick quick quick, quick here the song-sparrow. Cape Ann. T. S. Eliot. Landscapes, V. BiP; EvOK; GoJo
O Quondam Pre-and-Post-Bellum. The Bitch-Kitty. Jonathan Williams. PoM
O, Rachel, your very gait. A Vilna Puzzle. Sasha Chorny, *tr. by* Daniel Weissbort. VWA
O radiant luminary of light interminable. A Prayer to the Father of Heaven. John Skelton. HoPM; TrPWD
O raging seas, and mighty Neptune's reign! Coming Homeward out of Spain. Barnabe Googe. ElL; EnRePo
O rain, depart with blessings. Song of the Dew. *Unknown, tr. by* Solomon Solis-Cohen. TrJP
O! raise the woefull Pillalu. An Irish Lamentation. Goethe, *tr. by* James Clarence Mangan. AWP
O rare circle. Americana XV: Simplicity. Carl Rakosi. GP; InPS
O [*or* Oh] rare Harry Parry. Harry Parry. *Unknown.* GBP; OxNR
O Reader! hast thou ever stood to see. The Holly Tree. Robert Southey. EnRP; HBV-1
O Realm Bejewelled. Forugh Farrokhzad, *tr. fr. Farsi by* Jascha Kessler *and* Amin Banani. WPOW
O reapers and gleaners. Harvest Song. Joseph Campbell. OFD
O reverend Chaucere, rose of rethoris all. William Dunbar. *Fr.* The Goldyn Targe. PP
O, rich young lord, thou ridest by. Compensation. James Edwin Campbell. BANP
O Ride On, Jesus, *with music. Unknown.* AH
"O, rise up, Willie Riley, and come along with me." *See* Oh, rise up Willy Reilly, and come along with me.
O Risen Lord upon the Throne, *with music.* Louis F. Benson. AH
O river, green and still. Boy in Ice. Laurie Lee. NYBP
O, Rocks Don't Fall on Me, *with music. Unknown.* BoAN-1
O Romeo, Romeo! wherefore art thou Romeo? Shakespeare. *Fr.* Romeo and Juliet, II, ii. WHA
O Rose, O Rainbow. Nicholas Moore. NeBP
O Rose the Red and White Lil[l]y. Rose the Red and White Lil[l]y. *Unknown.* ESPB; OxBB
O Rose, thou art sick! The Sick Rose. Blake. *Fr.* Songs of Experience. AWP; BoLoP; CABA; ChER; ChTr; ELP; EnLoPo; FaBoEn; HAP; HeIP; InPK; InPS; LAuP; LoBV; NIP; NOBE; NOEC; NoP; OAEL-2; OAEP; OBNC; PAI; PoEL-4; PPP; PrIm; SeCeV; SoSe; TrGrPo; ViBoPo; WeW
O Ross, thou wale of hearty cocks. To Mr. Alexander Ross. James Beattie. OxBS
O roving muse, recall that wondrous [*or* wond'rous] year. The Great Frost. John Gay. *Fr.* Trivia, or, the Art of Walking the Streets of London. OBEC; SeCePo
O rowan tree, O rowan tree! thou'lt aye be dear to me! The Rowan Tree. Lady Nairne. HBV-2
O Ruddier than the Cherry. John Gay. *Fr.* Acis and Galatea. ELP; ViBoPo
(Air: "O ruddier than the cherry.") NOEC
(Song: "O ruddier than the cherry.") HBV-1; NOBE; OBEC
O ruddy Lover. The Clover. Margaret Deland. AA
O ruined father dead, long sweetly rotten. For the Word Is Flesh. Stanley Kunitz. DiL; VGW
O sacred poesie, thou spirit of artes. Ben Jonson. *Fr.* The Poetaster, I, ii. PoEL-2
O sad for me Glen Aora. Nettles. Neil Munro. PoSH
O sailor, come ashore. Christina Rossetti. *Fr.* Sing-Song. FM
O sailor sailor tell me why. Scarabs for the Living. R. P. Blackmur. TwAmPo
"O sailor, tell me, tell me true." Elihu. Alice Cary. PaPo
O sairly may I rue the day. The Women Folk. James Hogg. HBV-1
"O Sally my dear, shall I come up to see you?" Hares on the Mountain. *Unknown.* OBET
O Saviour of a World Undone, *with music.* Leonard Withington. AH
O, Saw Ye Bonny Lesley. Burns. *See* Bonnie Lesley.
"O saw ye my father? or saw ye my mother?" The Grey Cock [*or* Saw You My Father?]. *Unknown.* BaBo; ESPB
O saw ye not fair Ines? Fair Ines. Thomas Hood. EnRP; HBV-1; OBEV; OBRV; OBVV
O, Saw Ye the Lass. Richard Ryan. FaBoBe; HBV-1
O, say, can you see, by the dawn's early light. *See* Oh, say, can you see, by the dawn's early light.
O Say, My Brown Drimin. *Unknown, tr. fr. Modern Irish by* James Joseph Callanan. OnYI
O say, my flattering heart. Loves She Like Me? Samuel Woodworth. AA
O say what is that thing call'd Light. The Blind Boy. Colley Cibber. GTBS; GTBS-P; HBV-1; NOEC; OBEC; OxBChV; RoGo; TreFS
O sea born and obscene. An Invocation to the Goddess. David Wright. NMP; NoAM
O season of repetition and return. Spring 1940. W. H. Auden. OAEP
O see how narrow are our days. Prayer of the Maidens to Mary. Rainer Maria Rilke, *tr. by* Jethro Bithell. AWP
O seeded grass, you army of little men. John Gould Fletcher. Irradiations, IV *or* IX [XV]. MoAmPo; NePA; TwAmPo
O, Seeger, the night you tied the cabbie. Quarry/Rock. Paul Mariah. PeHV
O seeker of Greater Light. The Circle. Carol Coates. CaP
O! sely anker, that in thy celle. Go, Sad Complaint. Charles d' Orléans. MeEL
O servant of God's holiest charge. Christopher Smart. *Fr.* Song to David. ViBoPo
O Shadow. Shadow Dance. Ivy O. Eastwick. SoPo; TiPo
O shady vales, O fair enriched meads. Sonnet. Thomas Lodge. *Fr.* A Margarite of America. ElL; OBSC
O! shairly ye hae seen my love. Ballad. William Soutar. NeBP
O Shannadore, I love your daughter. The Wide Mizzoura. *Unknown.* AS

O she looked out of the window. The Two Magicians. *Unknown.* ChTr; OxBoLi
O, she walked unaware of her own increasing beauty. She Walked Unaware. Patrick MacDonogh. NeIP; OnYI; OxBI
O ship incoming from the sea. Off Rivière du Loup. Duncan Campbell Scott. EtS; HBV-1; OBCV
O Ship of State. Longfellow. *See* Ship of State.
O shut your bright eyes that mine must endanger. At the Manger [Mary Sings]. W. H. Auden. *Fr.* For the Time Being; a Christmas Oratorio. EBCP; ILwL; SBVL
O Sicily, O Tuscany, where I. Easter Sunday, 1945. G. A. Borgese. NePoAm
O sight of pity, shame and dole! The Singer in the Prison. Walt Whitman. BeLS
O Silent God, Thou whose voice afar in mist and mystery. A Litany of Atlanta. W. E. B. Du Bois. BANP; CDC; PoNe
O [*or* Oh] silver-throated swan. The Dying Swan. T. Sturge Moore. OBMV; SeCePo; SyP
O Simplicitas. Madeleine L'Engle. *Fr.* Three Songs of Mary. EBCP; OBCP; PChr
O sing the glories of our Lord. A Psalm for Sunday Night. Thomas Pestel. OxBoCh
O Sing to Me of Heaven, *with music.* Mary Stanley Bunce Dana. AH
O sing unto my roundelay. *See* Oh sing unto my roundelay.
O [*or* Oh] sing unto the Lord [*or* Jehovah] a new song. The Floods Clap Their Hands [*or* Sing unto Jehovah.] Bible, *O.T.* Psalms, XCVIII. BLRP; EaLo; TrGrPo; TrJP
O singer of Persephone! Theocritus. Oscar Wilde. HBV-2; NOBE; OxBI
O singer of the field and fold. For a Copy of Theocritus. Austin Dobson. HBV-2
O singing wind. The Fir-Tree. Edith M. Thomas. OHIP
O, sinner, sinner, you better pray. Death's Gwinter Lay His Cold Icy Hands on Me, *rare version. Unknown.* BoAN-2
O Sion, Haste, Thy Mission High Fulfilling, *with music.* Mary A. Thomson. AH
O! sisters too. The Coventry Carol. *Unknown.* MeEL
O sixteen hundred and ninety one. The Two Witches. Robert Graves. SO
O Sleep. Grace Fallow Norton. HBV-2
O sleep, my babe, hear not the rippling wave. Sara Coleridge. *Fr.* Phantasmion. OBNC; OBRV
O Sleep, O tranquil son of noiseless Night. To Sleep. Giovanni della Casa, *tr. by* John Addington Symonds. AWP
O sleeper rise, if thou would'st see. Sleeper Rise. *Gond Oral Tradition, tr. by* V. Elwin *and* S. Hivale. WTO
O sleepy city of reeling wheelchairs. The Wheelchair Butterfly. James Tate. NoAM
O, slow to smite and swift to spare. *See* Oh, slow to smite and swift to spare.
O smitten mouth! O forehead crowned with thorn! For Our Sakes. Oscar Wilde. PGD
O smooth flatterers, go over sea. Reflection and Advice. Ezra Pound. OBSV
O [*or* Oh] snatch'd away in beauty's bloom! Elegy. Byron. EnRP; FiP; GTBS; GTBS-P; HBV-1; LoBV; OBRV
O soft embalmer of the still midnight. To Sleep [*or* Sonnet to Sleep]. Keats. ChTr; EnRP; FaBoRV; LoBV; NIP; OAEP; OBEV; OBRV; PoEL-4; PrIm; TEP; ViBoPo; WHA
O Softly Singing Lute. Francis Pilkington. OAEP
"O soldier, O soldier, won't you marry me now." Soldier, Won't You Marry Me? *Unknown.* AmFP; OLR
O Solitary of the Austere Sky. Sir Charles G. D. Roberts. CaP
O Solitude! if I must with thee dwell. Solitude. Keats. EnRP
O solitude, romantic maid! James Grainger. *Fr.* Solitude [*or* Ode to Solitude]. OBEC; ViBoPo
O sometimes in the street, or in the Paris Metro. Remembrance. Antoni Slonimski, *tr. by* Frances Notley. TrJP
O Son of God, Afflicted. *Unknown, tr. fr. Greek by* John Brownlees. STF
O Son of Man, Thou Madest Known. Milton S. Littlefield. AH, *with music;* TrPWD
O son of man, when thou findest wine. Five Arabic Verses in Praise of Wine. *Unknown, tr. by* Hartwig Hirschfeld. TrJP
O son of mine, when dusk shall find thee bending. From Generation to Generation. Sir Henry Newbolt. FaBoTw
O song as yet unsung! A Song as Yet Unsung. "Yehoash," *tr. by* Isidore Goldstick. TrJP
O sons of earth! Pope. *Fr.* An Essay on Man, IV. TreFT
O sons of men,/ Lean death perches upon your shoulder. Inscriptions at the City of Brass. *Unknown, tr. by* E. Powys Mathers. *Fr.* The Thousand and One Nights. AWP
O sons of men,/ Why do you put your hands before your eyes. Inscriptions at the City of Brass. *Unknown, tr. by* E. Powys Mathers. *Fr.* The Thousand and One Nights. AWP
O sons of men,/ You add the future to the future. Inscriptions at the City of Brass. *Unknown, tr. by* E. Powys Mathers. *Fr.* The Thousand and One Nights. AWP
O sons of men,/ You see a stranger upon the road. Inscriptions at the City of Brass. *Unknown, tr. by* E. Powys Mathers. *Fr.* The Thousand and One Nights. AWP
O sons of men, that toil, and love with tears! The Fair Maid and the Sun. Arthur O'Shaughnessy. BeLS
O! sop of sorrow, sonkin into cair. Cresseid's Complaint against Fortune. Robert Henryson. *Fr.* The Testament of Cresseid. MeEL
O Sorrow! Keats. *See* Song of the Indian Maid.
O sorrow, cruel fellowship! Tennyson. In Memoriam A. H. H., III. HAP
O sorrow! He is one who jumps. Springbok. *Unknown.* PeSA
O sorrowful and ancient days. Metrum Parhemiacum Tragicum. Eugenius Vulgarius, *tr. by* Helen Waddell. WaaP
O soul, canst thou not understand. Aridity. "Michael Field." OBMV; OxBoCh; TRV
O soul, 'tis thine in season meet. Ode on Theoxenos. Pindar, *tr. by* John Addington Symonds. PeHV
O Soul, with Storms Beset. Solomon ibn Gabirol, *tr. fr. Hebrew by* Alice Lucas. TrJP
O sovereign power of love! O grief! O balm! Keats. *Fr.* Endymion, II. EnRP; OBNC; ViBoPo
O spare a tear for poor Tom Hood. Elegy on Thomas Hood [*or* Elegy]. Martin Fagg. BXAP; FaBoPa; NOBL
O sperm, testes, paradidymus! o scrotum, septum, and rectum! Gay Epiphany. James Mitchell. PeHV
O spirit of Venus whom I adore. *Unknown, tr. fr. Latin.* PeHV
O spiteful bitter thought. Assurance. George Herbert. OxBoCh
O spread agen your leaves an' flow'rs. The Woodlands. William Barnes. BoNaP; OBVV
O Spring, I know thee! Seek for sweet surprise. In Early Spring. Alice Meynell. HBV-1
O spring, O spring. Ode to Spring. Walter R. Brooks. RHPC
O Spring, thou youthful beauty of the year. Spring. Giovanni Battista Guarini, *tr. by* Leigh Hunt. AWP
O spring's a pleasant time. Aye Waukin' O! *Unknown.* BSV; GoTS
O stagnant east-wind, palsied mare. A Room on a Garden. Wallace Stevens. NoP
O Star of Galilee. Girolamo Savonarola, *tr. fr. Latin by* R. R. Madden. ISi
O star of morning and of liberty! Longfellow. *Fr.* Divina Commedia, VI. GoBC; NePA
O Star (the fairest one in sight). Choose Something like a Star. Robert Frost. MoAB; MoAmPo; PoCh
O starry temple of unvalted space. William Alabaster. AnAnS-1
O! Start a Revolution. D. H. Lawrence. FaBoEE
O statue, stand still. Hans Christian Andersen in Central Park. Hy Sobiloff. PoPl
O Stay, Sweet Love. *Unknown.* TrGrPo
O stay that covetous hand! First turn all eye. Upon the Curtain of Lucasta's Picture It Was Thus Wrought. Richard Lovelace. CaPo
O steadfast trees that know. Man and Nature. Robert Kelley Weeks. AA
O stealthily-creeping *Merrimac.* The Victory-Wreck. Will Carleton. PAH
O stiffly shapen houses that change not. Suburbs on a Hazy Day. D. H. Lawrence. OBMV
O still, white face of perfect peace. Ripe Grain. Dora Reed Goodale. HBV-2
O stony grey soil of Monaghan. Stony Grey Soil. Patrick Kavanagh. CIP
O stoodent A has gone and spent. Ballad with an Ancient Refrain. *Unknown.* NA
O strange devices that alone divide. Eyes. Walter de la Mare. BrPo
O Strassburg. *Unknown, tr. fr. German by* C. F. MacIntyre. WaaP
O Strong to Bless. Elizabeth Daryush. QFR
O strong was the wood in the ashen oar. Lament for Seán. Daniel James O'Sullivan. NeIP
O, Struck beneath the Laurel. George Edward Woodberry. Wild Eden, XXXIII. AA
O Suen, the usurper Lugalanne means nothing to me! Appeal to the Moongod Nanna-Suen to Throw Out Lugalanne. Enheduanna, *tr. fr. Sumerian.* BoWoP
O suitably-attired-in-leather-boots. Fragment of a Greek Tragedy. A. E. Housman. CenHV; FaBoNo; NOBL; Par; SpRo
O sun, and moonlight shining in the woods. Carmen Saeculare. Charles H. Sisson, *after the Latin of* Horace. OBVE
O suns [*or* sun] and skies and clouds of June. October's Bright Blue Weather. Helen Hunt Jackson. BLPA; BLPL; FaBoBe; GN; HBVY; PoSC; TreFT
O Sun, when I stand in my green leaves. To the Sun from a Flower. Guido Gezelle, *tr. by* Jethro Bithell. FaPON
O sunstruck spray, where change and changeless meet. Some Refrains at the Charles River. Peter Viereck. PoCh
O surely surely life is fair. Fiorentina. Ernest Myers. OBVV

O! Susanna. Stephen Collins Foster. *See* Oh! Susanna!
O Swallow, Swallow, Flying South. Tennyson. *Fr.* The Princess, Pt. IV. HBV-1
O swan, come slowly from the sky. Song of Poverty. *Gond Oral Tradition, tr. by* V. Elwin *and* S. Hivale. WTO
O swan of slenderness. The Little Red Lark. Alfred Perceval Graves. HBV-1
O Sweet Anne Page. William Shenstone. SeCePo
O sweet are tropic lands for waking dreams. North and South. Claude McKay. AmPP
O sweet delight, O more than human bliss. Song. Thomas Campion. HBV-1
O sweet everlasting voices be still. The Everlasting Voices. W. B. Yeats. AWP
O, sweet is the vale where the Mohawk gently glides. Bonny Eloise. C. W. Elliott *and* J. R. Thomas FSW
O sweet September! thy first breezes bring. Sweet September. George Arnold. GN
O Sweet Spontaneous. E. E. Cummings. AP; NoP; PAI; PrIm
(La Guerre.) SUW
(O Sweet Spontaneous Earth.) NoAM; OxBa; TrGrPo
O sweet the time, when neither folly might. Truth's Complaint over England. Thomas Lodge. ACP
O sweet wild April came over the hills. Sweet Wild April. William Force Stead. HBV-1; HBVY
O [*or* Oh] sweet woods, the delight of solitariness. Solitariness [*or* The Delight of Solitariness *or* Dorus's Song]. Sir Philip Sidney. *Fr.* Arcadia. FaBoRV; LiTB; LoBV; OBSC; PoEL-1; SiPS
O sweete and bitter monuments of paine. Upon the Ensignes of Christes Crucifyinge. William Alabaster. AnAnS-1; MePo
O Sweetest Melancholy. John Fletcher. *Fr.* The Nice Valor. TrGrPo
O Sweetheart, Hear You [*or* Thou]. James Joyce. Chamber Music, XVIII. FaBoRV; GBL; HBMV; MoBrPo
O swift forerunners, rosy with the race! Sunrise on Mansfield Mountain. Alice Brown. HBV-1
O swinging sword of Carroll hail! Carroll's Sword. Dallan MacMore, *tr. by* Frank O'Connor. KiLC
O Sylvan prophet, whose eternal fame. Hymn for St. John's Eve. *Unknown, tr. by* Dryden. AWP
O! synge untoe mie roundelaie. *See* Oh! sing unto my roundelay.
O take me to the sullen flats. From the Righteous Man Even the Wild Beasts Run Away. David Bromwich. PoA
O talk not to me of a name great in story. *See* Oh talk not to me of a name great in story.
O Tan-faced Prairie-Boy. Walt Whitman. FaPON; OxBA; PeHV
O Taste and See. Denise Levertov. NoP; PBWP; PPP; TAP
O tears! no tears, but rain from Beauty's skies. Astrophel and Stella, C. Sir Philip Sidney. SiPS
O Tell Me How to Woo Thee. Robert Graham. *See* If Doughty Deeds.
O tell me, little children, have you seen her. Nikolina. Celia Thaxter. GN; HBV-1
O tell me whence that joy doth spring. The Queer. Henry Vaughan. PoEL-2
O tender dove, sweet circling in the blue. Vale! Roden Noel. OBVV
O Tender under Her Right Breast. George Barker. Second Cycle of Love Poems, II. MoAB; MoBrPo
(Love Poem.) NeBP
O tender-heartedness right bitter grown. Fragmenti. Ezra Pound. PoA
O tenderly the haughty day. Ode. Emerson. AA; GN; PAL
O terrible is the highest thing. Kenneth Patchen. VGW
O Terry why is sex so quick. Ruth Herschberger. POL
O Thalassa! Thalassa! Where, where. The Singers. George Bruce. OxBS
O, That I Had Some Secret Place. *Unknown.* AmFP
O That I Had Wings like a Dove. *Unknown.* OxBoCh
O that I were lying under the olives. March Thoughts from England. Margaret L. Woods. OBVV
O that joy so soon should waste! Song [*or* The Kiss]. Ben Jonson. *Fr.* Cynthia's Revels, IV, iii. HBV-1; UnTE; ViBoPo
"O That My Love Were in My Arms." *Malay Oral Tradition, tr. by* R. J. Wilkinson *and* R. O. Winstedt. WTO
O that our dreamings all, of sleep or wake. Keats. *Fr.* Epistle to John Hamilton Reynolds. OAEL-2
O that the chemist's magic art. On a Tear. Samuel Rogers. HBV-2
O that the pines which crown yon steep. Evening Melody. Aubrey Thomas De Vere. GoBC; HBV-1
"O that this too [too] solid flesh would melt." On a Young Lady's Going into a Shower Bath. Francis Scott Key. UnTE; YaD
O, that this too too solid flesh would melt. Frailty, Thy Name Is Woman [*or* Hamlet Broods over the Death of His Father]. Shakespeare. *Fr.* Hamlet, I, i. SCV; TreFS; TrGrPo
O that those lips had language! Life has passed. *See* Oh that those lips had language! Life has passed.
O [*or* Oh] that 'twere possible. Tennyson. *Fr.* Maud, Pt. II, iv. BoLoP; HBV-1; NOBE; OAEL-2; OBEV; OBVV
O [*or* Oh]! that you were yourself; but, love, you are. Sonnets, XIII. Shakespeare. OAEP; TEP
O the aching pain of that long, long night. Sundered. John Barford. PeHV
O, the captain went below. The Captain Went Below. *Unknown.* AmSS
O the Chimneys. Nelly Sachs, *tr. fr. German by* Keith Bosley. VWA
O the crossbones of Galway. Galway. Louis MacNeice. OxBI
O the cuckoo she's a pretty bird. The Cuckoo. *Unknown.* GBP. *See also* Cuckoo is a bonny bird, The.
O the days gone by! O the days gone by! *See* Oh the days gone by! Oh the days gone by!
O, the days of the Kerry dancing, O, the ring of the piper's tune! The Kerry Dance. James Lyman Molloy. OnYI
O the days of the Messiah are at hand, are at hand! Ballad of the Days of the Messiah. A. M. Klein. TrJP
O the evening's for the fair, bonny lassie O! Bonny Lassie O! John Clare. CH
O the French are on the sea. *See* Oh! the French are on the sea.
O, the fun, the fun and frolic. Interlude. W. E. Henley. In Hospital, XVII. BrPo
O the gallant fisher's life. The Angler. John Chalkhill. HBV-1
O the goose and the gander walk'd over the green. The Goose and the Gander. *Unknown.* GBP
O, the grand old Duke of York. *See* Oh, the noble Duke of York.
O the green glimmer of apples in the orchard. Ballad of Another Ophelia. D. H. Lawrence. ChTr; CoBMV; MoVE
O the green things growing, the green things growing. Green Things Growing. Dinah Maria Mulock Craik. FaFP; HBV-1; HBVY; OHIP
O the hog-eye men are all the go. The Hog-Eye Man. *Unknown.* AS
O the hurt, the hurt, and the hurt of love! The Hurt of Love. George Macdonald. TrCP
O the instrument draws close. The Wasp. Joyce Carol Oates. GeTw
O the little rusty dusty miller. *Unknown.* OxNR
O, the lovely rivers and lakes of Maine! The Lovely Rivers and Lakes of Maine. George B. Wallis. BLPA
O, the Marriage! Thomas Osborne Davis. OBVV
O [*or* Oh], the Month of May. Thomas Dekker. *Fr.* The Shoemaker's Holiday, III, v. ElL; ViBoPo
(May.) OBSC
(Maytime.) TrGrPo
(Song: "O the month of May, the merry month of May.") PBBP
O the opal and the sapphire of that wandering western sea. Beeny Cliff. Thomas Hardy. OBNC
O the Ploughboy was a-ploughing. The Simple Ploughboy. *Unknown.* FaBoCh
O the pride of Portsmouth water. The Lost War-Sloop. Edna Dean Proctor. PAH
O the Raggedy Man! He works fer Pa. The Raggedy Man. James Whitcomb Riley. FaPON; HBV-1; HBVY; OBCA; OxBChV; TiPo; TreFS
O, the rain, the weary, dreary rain. Twenty Golden Years Ago. James Clarence Mangan. NBM; OnYI
O the sad day! The Sad Day. Thomas Flatman. OBEV
O the Spring will come. The Spring Will Come. H. D. Lowry. BoNaP
O the vexation. Lost Contact. William Cole. POL
O the vines were golden, the birds were loud. Fable. Frederic Prokosch. WaP
O the wonder man rides his space ship. African Things. Victor Hernández Cruz. InW
O [*or* Oh], then, I see Queen Mab hath been with you. Mercutio's Queen Mab Speech [*or* Queen Mab]. Shakespeare. *Fr.* Romeo and Juliet, I, iv. FaPON; FiP; LiTB; TreF; WSC
O, there are times/ When all this fret. Daily Trials. Oliver Wendell Holmes. PoEL-5
O there is a little artist. The Fairy Artist. Nellie M. Garabrant. PoPl
O there is blessing in this gentle breeze. *See* Oh there is blessing in this gentle breeze.
O [*or* Oh] there was a woman, and she was a widow. Flowers in the Valley. *Unknown.* OLR; OnMSP; OxBoLi
O [*or* Oh] there was an old soldier and he had a wooden leg. There Was an Old Soldier. *Unknown.* AS; TrAS, *with* Old Zip Coon
O Thirsty Wind. *Tr. fr. Hawaiian by* N. B. Emerson. WTO
O this fair volume which we World do name. On the Margin Wrought. William Drummond of Hawthornden. SeCePo
O, this is a sin-tryin' world. This Is a Sin-trying' World. *Unknown.* TrAS
O thorn-crowned brow. Behold the Man! *Unknown.* STF
O thorn-crowned Sorrow, pitiless and stern. Sorrow. Katrina Trask. AA
O Thou/ God of all long desirous roaming. Rupert Brooke. *Fr.* The Song of the Pilgrims. TrPWD

O thou afflicted, drunken not with wine! Dirge for the Ninth of Ab. *Unknown, tr. by* Nina Davis Salaman. TrJP
O thou all-eloquent, whose mighty mind. Man's Going Hence. Samuel Rogers. *Fr.* Human Life. OBNC
O Thou almighty will. Strength, Love, Light. Robert II, King of France. WGRP
O thou bright jewel in my aim I strive. On Virtue. Phillis Wheatley. TAP
O thou by Nature taught. Ode to Simplicity. William Collins. EnRP; LAuP; NOBE; OBEC; OBEV; TEP
O, Thou Eternal One! Gavril Romanovich Derzhavin, *tr. fr. Russian by* Sir John Bowring. WGRP
O Thou Eternal Source of Life. Rolland W. Schloerb. TrPWD
O Thou Eternal Victim Slain. Charles Wesley. NOCV
O thou fair silver Thames, O clearest crystal flood! Song to Beta. Michael Drayton. *Fr.* The Shepherd's Garland, Eclogue III (1593 ed.). OBSC
O Thou Great Being! what Thou art. Prayer under the Pressure of Violent Anguish. Burns. TrPWD
O Thou great Friend to all the sons of men. The Way, the Truth, and the Life. Theodore Parker. HBV-2; TrPWD; TRV; WGRP
O thou great movement of the universe. Bryant. *Fr.* An Evening Revery. AA
O Thou great mystery. Indian Prayer. Chief Joseph Strongwolf. TRV
O thou great wrong, that, through the slow-paced years. The Death of Slavery. Bryant. AA
O Thou Immortal Deity. Shelley. TrPWD
O thou in heaven and earth the only peace. The Plan of Salvation. Milton. *Fr.* Paradise Lost, III. WGRP
O thou Moor of Morería. Abenamar, Abenamar. *Unknown, tr. by* Robert Southey. AWP
O Thou Most High Who Rulest All, *with music.* Anne Bradstreet. AH
O Thou my monster, Thou my guide. Prayer in Mid-Passage. Louis MacNeice. EaLo
O Thou my soule, Jehovah blesse. Bible, *O.T.* Psalms, CIII. SCAP
O thou newcomer who seek'st Rome in Rome. Rome. Joachim du Bellay, *tr. by* Ezra Pound. AWP
O Thou not made with hands. The City of God. Francis Turner Palgrave. WGRP
O thou of little faith. Hitherto Hath the Lord Helped. *Unknown.* BLRP
O thou that achest, pulse o' the unwed vast. Adam to Lilith. Christopher Brennan. *Fr.* Lilith. PoAu-1
O Thou, that dost cover the heavens. Song of the Wind and the Rain. Solomon ibn Gabirol, *tr. by* Solomon Solis-Cohen. TrJP
O thou that from the green vales of the West. To Spring: On the Banks of the Cam. William Stanley Roscoe. OBVV
O thou that from thy mansion. For My Funeral. A. E. Housman. CMoP; TrPWD; ViBoPo
O thou that held'st the blessed Veda dry. Hymn to Vishnu. Jayadeva, *tr. by* Sir Edwin Arnold. *Fr.* The Gita Govinda. AWP
O Thou, that [*or* wha] in the heavens does [*or* dost] dwell. Holy Willie's Prayer. Burns. BSV; EBEV; EnRP; GoTS; InPS; LAuP; NOEC; NoP; OAEL-1; OBSV; OxBoLi; OxBS; PoEL-4; PPP; TW; ViBoPo
O thou that lovest a pure, and whitend soul. Dressing. Henry Vaughan. AnAnS-1
O thou that often hast within thine eyes. Sonnet: He Speaks of a Third Love of His. Guido Cavalcanti, *tr. by* Dante Gabriel Rossetti. AWP
O thou, that sendest out the man. England and America in 1782. Tennyson. PAH; PAL
O thou, that sit'st upon a throne. A Song to David. Christopher Smart. ChTr; EBEV; GoTL; LaA; LAuP; LoBV; MasP; NOBE; OAEL-1; OBEC; PoEL-3; TrGrPo
O Thou That Sleep'st like Pig in Straw. Sir William Davenant. InvP
O [*or* Oh] thou that swing'st upon the waving hair [*or* haire *or* ear *or* eare]. The Grasshopper. Richard Lovelace. AnAnS-2; CaPo; EBEV; FaBoEn; JCP; LoBV; MeLP; MePo; NOBE; NoP; OAEL-1; OBEV; OBS; PPP; SeCePo; SeCV-1
O thou that to the moonlight vale. Ode: To the Nightingale. Joseph Warton. PBBP
O thou that with surpassing glory crowned [*or* crownd]. Satan's Soliloquy. Milton. *Fr.* Paradise Lost, IV. LiTB; OBS
O Thou! the first fruits of the dead. Buriall. Henry Vaughan. SeCV-1
O thou, the friend of man assign'd. Ode to Pity. William Collins. LAuP
O thou undaunted daughter of desires! Upon the Book and Picture of the Seraphical Saint Teresa. Richard Crashaw. *Fr.* The Flaming Heart. HAP; NOBE; OBEV; WHA
O Thou unknown, Almighty Cause. A Prayer in the Prospect of Death. Burns. HBV-2; TrPWD; WGRP
O thou, wha in the heavens does dwell. *See* O thou that in the heavens does dwell!
O thou! whatever title suit thee. Address to the Deil. Burns. EnRP; GoTS; LAuP; NOEC; OAEL-1; OAEP; OxBS; PoEL-4
O Thou who all-things has of nothing made. Deo Opt. Max. George Sandys. *Fr.* Paraphrase on the Psalms of David. OBS
O thou who art of all that is. Through Unknown Paths. Frederick L. Hosmer. TrPWD
O Thou Who Art Our Author and Our End. Sir John Beaumont. TreFT
O Thou Who Bidst the Torrent Flow. Whittier. *Fr.* Hymn from the French of Lamartine. TrPWD
O Thou Who Camest from Above. Charles Wesley. TrPWD
(Hymn: "O thou who camest from above.") OBEC; SeCePo
(Inextinguishable Blaze.) NOEC
O thou who didst furnish. Hymn to Moloch. Ralph Hodgson. HBMV; OxBTC
O Thou, Who Didst Ordain the Word, *with music.* Edwin Hubbell Chapin. AH
O thou, who lately closed my eyes. A Morning Hymn. Christopher Smart. OxBChV
O Thou who lovest not alone. The Aim. Sir Charles G. D. Roberts. PeCV
O Thou, Who Man of Baser Earth Didst Make. *See* Oh Thou, Who Man of Baser Earth Didst Make.
O thou who movest onward with a mind. Epitaphs, III. Gabriello Chiabrera, *tr. by* Wordsworth. AWP
O thou, who passest through our valleys [*or* thro' our vallies] in. To Summer. Blake. LAuP; WiR
O thou, who plumed with strong desire. The Two Spirits [an Allegory]. Shelley. CH; OAEL-2; Prf; WiR
O thou, who sit'st a smiling bride. Ode to Mercy. William Collins. LAuP
O Thou who speedest Time's advancing wing. He Asketh Absolution of God. *Unknown, tr. by* Robert Hillyer. *Fr.* Book of the Dead. AWP
O thou whom Poetry [*or* Poesy] abhors. On Elphinston's Translation of Martial [*or* Epigram on Elphinstone's Translation of Martial's Epigrams]. Burns. FaBoCo; FaBoEE; TW
O Thou whose equal purpose runs. Invocation. Wendell Phillips Stafford. TrPWD
O thou, whose eyes were closed in death's pale night. Epitaph on a Child Killed by Procured Abortion. *Unknown.* NOEC
O thou whose face hath felt the Winter's wind. What the Thrush Said. Keats. EBEV; NIP
O thou! whose fancies from afar are brought. To H. C. Wordsworth. ChER; EnRP; HBV-1; OBRV; PoEL-4
O Thou Whose Feet Have Climbed Life's Hill, *with music.* Louis F. Benson. AH
O Thou, whose glorious orbs on high. Hymn of [*or* to] the West. Edmund Clarence Stedman. HBV-2; PAH; TrPWD
O Thou Whose Gracious Presence Blest. Louis F. Benson. TrPWD
O Thou Whose Gracious Presence Shone, *with music.* Marion Franklin Ham. AH
O Thou Whose Image. Arthur Hugh Clough. TrPWD
O thou, whose mighty palace roof doth hang. Hymn to Pan. Keats. *Fr.* Endymion, I. ChER; OBRV; PoEL-4
O thou whose name shatters the universe. Eli the Thatcher. Max Beerbohm *and* William Rothenstein. FaBoNo
O Thou Whose Own Vast Temple Stands, *with music.* Bryant. AH
O Thou Whose Power. Boethius, *tr. fr. Latin by* Samuel Johnson. The Consolation of Philosophy, III, 9. TrPWD
("O thou whose pow'r o'er moving worlds presides.") OBVE
O Thou! Whose Presence Went Before, *with music.* Whittier. AH
O Thou with dewy locks, who lookest down. To Spring. Blake. BLPL; BoNaP; EnRP; HBV-1; LAuP; NOEC; OAEL-2; OBEC; OBEV; PoEL-4; PoLF; PPP; WiR
O Thought! Süsskind von Trimberg, *tr. fr. Middle High German.* TrJP
O [*or* Oh] thy bright eyes must answer now. Plead for Me [*or* God of Visions *or* To Imagination]. Emily Brontë. BrPo; NBM; PoEL-5; TrGrPo
O tide-enwreathed and time-tormented Man. The Gatineaus. James Wreford Watson. CaP
O Time the fatal wrack of mortal things. Anne Bradstreet. *Fr.* Contemplations. PBWP; WPOW
"O Time, whence comes the Mother's moody look amid her labours." The Lacking Sense. Thomas Hardy. CMoP; PoEL-5
O Time! who know'st a lenient hand to lay. Time and Grief [*or* Influence of Time on Grief *or* Sonnet July 18th 1787]. William Lisle Bowles. EnRP; FaBoEn; HBV-2; LO; OBEC; OBEV
O times most bad. Upon the Troublesome Time. Robert Herrick. CaPo
O to Be a Dragon. Marianne Moore. CTC; GoYe; PoPl
O to be blind! The Blind Man at the Fair. Joseph Campbell. AnIV; AWP
O, to be in England. *See* Oh, to be in England.
O to Be Up and Doing. Robert Louis Stevenson. TreFT; TRV
O to break loose, like the chinook. Waking Early Sunday Morning. Robert Lowell. FaBoMo; NOBA; OxBC
O [*or* Oh], to have a little house! An Old Woman of the Roads. Padraic Colum. CH; FaBoBe; FaPON; FYAP; GoBC; HBMV; MoBrPo; OBEV; PoRA; TreFS; WHA
O to lie in long grasses! In the Grass. Hamlin Garland. AA
O to scuttle from the battle and to settle on an atoll far from brutal mortal

neath a wattle portal! What'll Be the Title? Justin Richardson. FiBHP
O, to vex me, contraries meet in one. *See* Oh, to vex me . . .
O touch me not, unless thy soul. Unless. Ella Dietz Glynes. AA
"O Trade! O Trade! would thou wert dead!" The Symphony. Sidney Lanier. AmPP; AP; LiTA
O tragic hours when lovers leave each other! Partings. Charles Guérin, *tr. by* Jethro Bithell. AWP
O trees, to whom the darkness is a child. Advice to a Forest. Maxwell Bodenheim. TrJP
O tremble, all ye earthly princes. The Revolutionaries. R. P. Lister. NOBL
O tremble! O tremble, O tremble. Six Sunday. Hart Leroi Bibbs. NBP
"O Troy Muir, my lily-flower." The Queen of Scotland. *Unknown.* ESPB
O. T.'s Blues. Waring Cuney. MAT
O, Tuomy! you boast yourself handy. Andrew Magrath's Reply to John O'Tuomy. Andrew Magrath, *tr. by* John O'Daly. OnYI
O [*or* Oh] turn away those cruel eyes. The Relapse. Thomas Stanley. AnAnS-2; OBEV
O Turn Ye, O Turn Ye, *with music.* Josiah Hopkins. AH
O 'twas on a bright mornin' in summer. Who's the Pretty Girl Milkin' the Cow? *Unknown.* AS
O Twilight, Twilight! evermore to hear. Music at Twilight. George Sterling. HBV-2
O Ubi? Nusquam. R. W. Dixon. LO
O unicorn among the cedars. W. H. Auden. *Fr.* New Year Letter. FaBoEn; NoAm
O universal Mother, who dost keep. Hymn to Earth the Mother of All. *Unknown, tr. by* Shelley. *Fr.* Homeric Hymns. AWP
O Urizen! Creator of men! mistaken Demon of heaven! Take Thy Bliss, O Man. Blake. *Fr.* Visions of the Daughters of Albion. EnRP
O valiant Hearts, who to your glory came. The Supreme Sacrifice. John S. Arkwright. WGRP
O, very gloomy is the House of Woe. The Haunted House. Thomas Hood. SeCePo
O vile ingratefull me. Biothanatos. Joseph Beaumont. OBS
O Virgin. *Tr. fr. Gaelic by* Douglas Hyde. WTO
O virgin mother, daughter of thy Son. Saint Bernard's Prayer to Our Lady. Dante, *tr. by* Louis How. *Fr.* Divina Commedia: Paradiso. ISi
O Virtuous Light. Elinor Wylie. MoAB; MoAmPo; MoPo; NePA
O Visionary who adjust your lens. The Higher Empiricism. Francis C. Golffing. PoA
O wad this braw hie-heapit toun. The Prows o' Reekie. Lewis Spence. OxBS
O Wahkonda (Master of Life) pity me! A Dance Chant. *Unknown, tr. by* D. G. Brinton. WGRP
O wall-flower! or ever thy bright leaves fade. The Wall-Flower. Henrik Arnold Thaulov Wergeland, *tr. by* Sir Edmund Gosse. AWP
"O waly, waly, my gay goss-hawk." The Gay Goshawk. *Unknown.* ESPB
O waly, waly, up the [*or* yon] bank. Waly, Waly [*or* The Forsaken Bride *or* Jamie Douglas *or* Lord Douglas]. *Unknown.* BSV; ELP; EnLoPo; EnSB; FaBoBa; GBP; GoTS; GTBS; GTBS-P; HAP; HBV-1; OBEV; OBS; OxBB; OxBS; PoPle; PrIm; ViBoFo; ViBoPo
O waly waly waly waly. The Holloe Menn. Harrison Everard. BXAP
O warm, enthusiastic maid. Joseph Warton. *Fr.* Ode to Fancy. NOEC
O was an ossified oyster. An Ossified Oyster. Carolyn Wells. TDH
O, Wasn't Dat a Wide River? *with music.* *Unknown.* BoAN-1
O wastfull riot, never well content. Lucan, *tr. by* Sir Walter Ralegh. *Fr.* Pharsalia, IV. OBVE
O water-girl! with tinkling anklets. Water-Girl. *Gond Oral Tradition, tr. by* V. Elwin *and* S. Hivale. WTO
O we can wait no longer. Walt Whitman. *Fr.* Passage to India. ILwL
O, we loved long and happily, God knows! The Custom of the World. Louis Simpson. BoLoP
"O we were sisters seven, Maisry." Fair Mary of Wallington [*or* The Bonny Earl of Livingston]. *Unknown.* ESPB; OxBB
O we were sisters, sisters seven. Earl Crawford. *Unknown.* BaBo; ESPB
O wearisome condition of humanity. *See* Oh wearisome condition of humanity.
O Weary Pilgrims. Robert Bridges. The Growth of Love, XXIII. MoAB; MoBrPo
O well I love the Spring. A Wife's Song. William Cox Bennett. HBV-1
"O well is [*or* well's] me, [o] my gay goshawk." The Gay Goshawk. *Unknown.* ESPB; GN; HBV-2; OxBB; WPE
O Were My Love Yon Lilac Fair. Burns. ChTr; GBL; HBV-1; OBEV
O, were you on the mountain, or saw you my love? Were You on the Mountain. *Unknown, tr. by* Douglas Hyde. PV
O [*or* Oh], Wert Thou in the Cauld Blast. Burns. EBEV; ELP; EnRP; HAP; HeIP; NOBE; NoP; OAEP; OBEC; OxBS; TrGrPo; WHA
O Western Wind. *Unknown.* *See* Western Wind.
O wha my babie-clouts will buy? The Rantin' Dog, the Daddie o't. Burns. OxBoLi; PPP
"O wha will bake my bridal bread." Fair Annie. *Unknown.* ESPB
"O wha will lace my shoes sae small?" The Lass of Roch Royal (A *vers.*). *Unknown.* ViBoFo
"O wha will shoe my bonny foot?" The Lass of Lochroyan. *Unknown.* HBV-2
"O wha will shoe my fair foot?" The Lass of Roch Royal. *Unknown.* ESPB
O wha would [*or* wou'd] wish the win to blaw. Brown Adam. *Unknown.* ESPB; OxBB
"O whare are ye gaun?" [*or* "O where are you going?"] The False Knight [*or* Fause Knicht] upon the Road [*or* The False Knight and the Wee Boy]. *Unknown.* CH; EnSB; ESPB; FaBoCh; GBP; OxBoLi; OxBS
"O whare hae ye been a' day, Lord Donald, my son?" Lord Randal (B *vers.*). *Unknown.* ESPB
"O [*or* Oh] whare hae ye been a' day, my bonnie wee croodlin dow?" Lord Randal. *Unknown.* ESPB (J *vers.*); ViBoFo (C *vers.*)
"O whare hae ye been, my dearest dear." *See* "O where have you been, my dear, dear, love?"
O whare hae ye been, my dearest dear. The Carpenter's Wife. *Unknown.* OAEL-1; OxBB
"O whare hae ye been, Peggy?" Young Peggy. *Unknown.* BaBo; ESPB
O Wha's the Bride? "Hugh MacDiarmid." BoLoP; BSV; CMoP; ErPo; GTBS-P; LiTM; NoAM; OxBS
(O Wha's Been Here afore Me, Lass, *shorter version.*) FaBoTw; NeBP; OBMV
O [*or* Oh] what a cunning guest. Confession. George Herbert. AnAnS-1; JCP
O what a happy soul am I! Blind but Happy. Fanny Crosby. TRV
O what a loud and fearful shriek was there. Koskiusko. Samuel Taylor Coleridge. EnRP
O what a physical effect it has on me. In Love with You. Kenneth Koch. CAPP
O! what a plague is love! *See* Oh! what a plague is love!
O, what a rogue and peasant slave am I. Shakespeare. *Fr.* Hamlet, II, ii. TreFT
O what a tangled web we weave. A Word of Encouragement. J. R. Pope. ELU; FiBHP; FPL; NOBL; PV
O, what a war of looks was then between them! Shakespeare. *Fr.* Venus and Adonis. UnTE
O what an endlesse worke have I in hand. Spenser. *Fr.* The Faerie Queene, IV, 12. MOS
O what are you waiting for here, young man? The Bridge. James Thompson. OBVV
O what avails the sceptred race. *See* Ah, what avails the sceptred race.
O [*or* Oh *or* Ah] what can ail thee, knight-at-arms [*or* wretched wight]. La Belle Dame sans Merci. Keats. AWP; BeLS; BLPA; CABA; CH; ChTr; DTo; ELP; EnRP; FaBoBe; FaBoCh; FaFP; FiP; FPL; GoJo; GTBS; GTBS-P; HAP; HBV-1; InPK; InPS; InvP; LiTB; LoBV; MasP; NIP; NOBE; NoP; OAEL-2; OAEP; OBEV; OBNC; OBRV; OLR; PAI; PoEL-4; PoPle; PoRA; PPoE; Prf; PrIm; SCV; SeCeV; SoSe; TEP; TreFT; TrGrPo; UnPo; ViBoPo; WeW; WHA; WSC
O, what can be the matter with thee, Knight-at-arms. La Belle Dame sans Merci. T. Griffiths. BXAP
O what can you give me? Idris Davies. *Fr.* Gwalia Deserta. DTC
O what could be more nice. Light Listened. Theodore Roethke. BiP; MoAmPo; UnTE
O what harper could worthily harp it. The Schoolmaster Abroad with His Son. Charles Stuart Calverley. NOBL
O What If the Fowler. Charles Dalmon. CH
O What Is That Sound [Which So Thrills the Ear]. W. H. Auden. BiP; LiTB; SoSe
(Ballad: "O what is that sound . . .") MoAB; MoBrPo; ViBoPo; WaP
(Quarry, The.) CMoP
O What Pleasure 'Tis to Find. Aphra Behn. UnTE
O what their joy and their glory must be. Hymn for the Close of the Week. Peter Abelard. TrCP
O what transparent waves, what a tranquil sea. Vittoria Colonna, *tr. fr. Italian by* Lynne Lawner. PBWP
O what's the blood that's [*or* 'at's] on your sword. Son David. *Unknown.* OxBB; OxBS
O What's the Rhyme to Porringer. *Unknown.* GBP
O what's the weather in a beard? Dinky. Theodore Roethke. OBAL; OBCA; RHPC
O, when I hear at sea. Wind and Wave. Charles Warren Stoddard. AA
O when in San Francisco do. Scenic. John Updike. CAD
O, when our clergie [*or* clergy], at the dreadful[l] day. On Those That Deserve It. Francis Quarles. MePo; NOCV; OBS
O [*or* Oh] when the saints go marchin' [*or* marching] in. When the Saints Go Marchin' [*or* Marching] In. *Unknown.* EaLo; FSW
O when, through ev'ry province, shall be raised. The Happy Workhouse and the Good Effects of Industry. John Dyer. *Fr.* The Fleece, Bk. III. NOEC

O Where Are You Going? W. H. Auden. *Fr.* The Orators. CMoP; LiTB; MoVE; NOBE; SoSe
(Epilogue: " 'O where are you going?' said reader to rider.") FaBoCh
(Five Songs.) LiTM
(Song: " 'O where are you going?' said reader to rider.") OAEL-2
O, where are you going, "Goodspeed" and "Discovery"? Southern Ships and Settlers. Rosemary *and* Stephen Vincent Benét. AmFN
"O where are you going?" said reader to rider. O Where Are You Going? [*or* Epilogue *or* Song]. W. H. Auden. *Fr.* The Orators. CMoP; FaBoCh; LiTB; LiTM; MoVE; NOBE; OAEL-2; SoSe
O [*or* Oh] where are you going? says [*or* said] Milder to Malder. The Cutty Wren. *Unknown.* FSW; GBP; NCEP; OxBoLi; WiR
"O where are you going?" *See* "O whare are ye gaun?"
"O where hae ye been, my long, long love." *See* "O where have you been, my dear, dear love."
"O [*or* Oh] where have [*or* ha *or* hae] you [*or* ye] been, Lord Randal my son?" Lord Randal. *Unknown.* AmFP; AWP; BSV; CABA; EBEV; EnRP; ESPB; FaBoBa; FF; FPL; FSW; HAP; HBV-2; HeIP; HoPM; LiTB; LoBV; NIP; NoP; OAEL-1; OxBB; OxBS; PAI; SeCeV; TreF; TrGrPo; ViBoFo (A *and* B *vers.*); WeW
"O where have you been, Lord Rendal my son." Lord Rendal. *Unknown.* EnSB
"O where [*or* whare] have you [*or* hae ye] been, my dear, dear [*or* dearest dear *or* long, long] love." The Demon [*or* Daemon] Lover [*or* James Harris]. *Unknown.* BaBo; CABA; EnSB; ESPB; FaBoBa; HAP; HoPM; LiTB; MAT; MOS; NU; UnPo; ViBoFo; WeW
O where is tiny Hewe? The Goblin's Song. James Telfer. ChTr
"O where were ye, my milk-white steed." The Broomfield Hill. *Unknown.* CH
O, where, where are the winter grounds of angels. The Angels. Marguerite Young. WPE
O wherefore was my birth from heaven foretold. O Dark, Dark, Dark. Milton. *Fr.* Samson Agonistes. WHA
O while within a Jewish breast. Hatikvah—a Song of Hope. Naphtali Herz Imber, *tr. by* Henry Snowman. TrJP
O whisper, O my soul! The afternoon. The Tired Worker. Claude McKay. BANP; BPo
O Whistle, and I'll Come to You, My Lad. Burns. *See* Whistle and I'll Come to Ye, My Lad.
O white and midnight sky! O starry bath! The Celestial Passion. Richard Watson Gilder. AA
O white clay, O fine clay of the earth cold. Fine Clay. Winifred Shaw. PoAu-1
O White Mistress. Don Johnson. NNP
O white priest of eternity, around. Kinchinjunga. Cale Young Rice. HBV-1
O white, white, light moon, that sailest in the sky. Donald. Henry Abbey. AA
O whither goest thou, pale student. Ye Laye of Ye Woodpeckore. Henry A. Beers. NA
O, whither sail you, Sir John Franklin? A Ballad of Sir John Franklin. George Henry Boker. AA; HBV-2; OnMSP
O Whither Shall I Fly? Francis Quarles. OxBoCh
O who are thou with that queenly brow. Roisin Dubh. Aubrey Thomas De Vere. AnIV
O who can ever praise enough. Poem. W. H. Auden. PoA
O who rides by night thro' the woodland so wild? The Erl-King. Goethe, *tr. by* Sir Walter Scott. AWP; OBVE; WSC
O [*or* Oh] who shall, from this dungeon, raise. A Dialogue between the Soul and [the] Body. Andrew Marvell. AnAnS-1; HAP; JCP; MeLP; MePo; NoP; OAEL-1; OBS; OxBoCh; PoEL-2; PPP; SeCP; SeCV-1; TEP; WeW
O, who will drive the chariot when she comes? She'll Be Comin' Round the Mountain. *Unknown.* AS
"O who will shoe my fair foot." Fair Annie of Lochyran. *Unknown.* AS
"O who will shoe my little feet." The Lass of Roch Royal. *Unknown.* AmFP
O who will shoe your pretty little foot. Who Will Shoe Your Pretty Little Foot? *Unknown.* AS
O who will show me those delights on high? Heaven. George Herbert. AnAnS-1; SeCP; TrCP; TrGrPo
"O, who will speak from a womb or cloud," and cloud. To George Barker. Gene Derwood. NePA
O who will walk a mile with me. A Mile with Me. Henry van Dyke. BLPA; FPL
"O who'll get me a healthy child." A Practical Woman. Thomas Hardy. NAs
O Whose Are These Children. Richard Snyder. SOTS
O why do you walk through the fields in gloves. To a Fat Lady Seen from the Train. Frances Cornford. BLPA; ELU; GoJo; MoBrPo; OBMV; SpRo; WeW
O Why Should the Spirit of Mortal Be Proud? William Knox. *See* Oh! Why Should the Spirit of Mortal Be Proud?
O why was I born with a different face? Blake. POL
O wild West Wind, thou breath of Autumn's being. Ode to the West Wind. Shelley. AWP; BiP; BoNaP; CABA; CH; EBEV; EnRP; FaBoBe; FaBoEn; FaBV; FaFP; FiP; FPL; GTBS; GTBS-P; HAP; HBV-1; HeIP; InPS; LiTB; LoBV; MOS; NOBE; NoP; NIP; OAEL-2; OAEP; OBEV; OBNC; OBRV; OHFP; PAI; PoEL-4; PoLF; PoRA; PPoe; PPP; PrIm; SeCeV; TEP; TreFS; TrGrPo; ViBoPo; WeW; WHA
O will ye choose to hear the news? Mr. Molony's Account of the Ball. Thackeray. HBV-2
O Willie brew'd a peck o' maut. Willie Brew'd [*or* Brewed] a Peck o' Maut. Burns. AWP; EnRP; OAEP; OxBS; ViBoPo
O Willie's large o' limb and lith. The Birth of Robin Hood [*or* Willie and Earl Richard's Daughter]. *Unknown.* ESPB; OAEL-1; OxBB
O Willy was as brave a lord. Willie o Douglas Dale. *Unknown.* ESPB
O, wilt thou have my hand, Dear, to lie along in thine? *See* Oh, wilt thou have a hand, Dear, to lie along in thine?
O wind, rend open the heat. Heat. Hilda Doolittle ("H. D."). *Fr.* The Garden. AP; CMoP; HeIP; InPK; MoAmPo; NoAM; OxBA; PrIm; TAP; UnPo; WHA
O wind, why do you never rest. Christina Rossetti. *Fr.* Sing-Song. TiPo
O winds that blow across the sea. The Wind's Song. "Gabriel Setoun." HBV-1; HBVY
O Winter! bar thine adamantine doors. To Winter. Blake. WiR
O Winter, ruler of th' inverted year. Winter. William Cowper. *Fr.* The Task, IV. OBEC
O winter wind, lat grievin be. Villanelle. Margaret Winefride Simpson. OxBS
O, winter, your gesture. Winter. Bella Akhmadulina, *tr. by* Barbara Einzig. BoWoP
O with what key. Skeleton Key. John Hollander. InPK; NoP
O woe, woe,/ People are born and die. Mr. Housman's Message. Ezra Pound. FaBoEE; FaBoPa
O, Woman! ("O woman, in our hours of ease"). Sir Walter Scott. *Fr.* Marmion. TreFS
O Woman Full of Wile. *At. to* Geoffrey Keating, *tr. fr. Late Middle Irish by* Padraic Pearse. OnYI
O woman, let thy heart not cleave. Forepledged. John Lancaster Spalding. AA
O woman of the piercing wail. A Lament for the Princes of Tyrone and Tyrconnel. *Unknown, tr. by* James Clarence Mangan. AnIV
O Woman of Three Cows, agra [*or* agragh]! The Woman of Three Cows. *Unknown, tr. by* James Clarence Mangan. AnIL; EnRP; OnYI; OxBI
O Woman, Shapely as the Swan. *Unknown.* *See* I Shall Not Die for Thee.
O wonder!/ How many goodly creatures are there here! Brave New World. Shakespeare. *Fr.* The Tempest, V, i. TrGrPo
O wonderful nonsense of lotions of Lucky Tiger. Haircut. Karl Shapiro. MoPo; MoVE; MP; TwCP
O wondrous scene is Meeker. Lines on Mountain Villages. "Sunset Joe." PoOW
O Word of God Incarnate. William Walsham How. TRV
"O words are lightly spoken." The Rose Tree. W. B. Yeats. CMoP; ELP; OBMV
O words, which fall like summer dew on me! Rural Poesy. Sir Philip Sidney. *Fr.* Arcadia. EIL
O World. George Santayana. Sonnets, III. FPL; HBV-2; PoLF; TRV
(Faith.) WGRP
(O World, Thou Choosest Not the Better Part.) TreFS
(Sonnets, III.) TrGrPo
O World, Be Nobler. Laurence Binyon. HBV-1; MoBrPo; OBEV
O World, Be Not So Fair. Maria Jäger, *tr. fr. German by* Grace Fallow Norton. HBV-2
"O World-God, give me Wealth?" the Egyptian cried. *See* "Oh, World-God, give me Wealth!" the Egyptian cried.
O world, I cannot hold thee close enough! God's World. Edna St. Vincent Millay. BLPL; CMoP; FaBoBe; FaBV; HBV-1; MoAmPo; PoPl; PoSC; TrCP
O world, in very truth thou art too young. Written at Florence. Wilfrid Scawen Blunt. OBVV
O world invisible, we view thee. The Kingdom of God [*or* In No Strange Land]. Francis Thompson. BrPo; EaLo; EBCP; FaPoR; GoBC; GTBS-P; HAP; HBMV; ILwL; LiTB; MoAB; MoBrPo; NOBE; NOCV; OBEV; OxBoCh; PoPle; SeCeV; TrCP; TreFT; TRV; TrGrPo; WGRP
O world! O life! O time! A Lament. Shelley. ChER; ChTr; EnRP; GTBS; GTBS-P; LoBV; NOBE; OAEP; OBRV; PoRA; TEP; TreFT; TrGrPo; WHA
O world that turneth as a vane that veers! Heliodore. J. D. Logan. CaP
O World, Thou Choosest Not the Better Part! George Santayana. *See* O World.
O worthy of belief I hold it was. Pan and Luna. Robert Browning. VLP
O would I were where I would be! Suspiria. *Unknown.* OBEV

O Wretch, Beware. William Dunbar. BSV
O wretch! hath madness cured thy dire despair? On Seeing an Officer's Widow Distracted. Mary Barber. NOEC
O wretched offspring! O unhappy state. Death the Consequence of the Fall. Dryden. *Fr.* The State of Innocence. NOCV
O write it up above your hearth. A Dublin Ballad: 1916. "Dermot O'Byrne." AnIV; OxBI
O, write my name. De Angels in Heab'n Gwineter Write My Name. *Unknown.* BoAN-2
O ye dales. Nature. Mark Akenside. *Fr.* The Pleasures of Imagination, IV. LoBV
O ye Northumbrian shades, which overlook. Early Influences. Mark Akenside. *Fr.* The Pleasures of Imagination, IV. OBEC
O Ye Sweet Heavens! Thomas William Parsons. AA
O ye that look on Ecstasy. Ecstasy. Rachel Annand Taylor. GoTS
O ye that put your trust and confidence. A Rueful Lamentation on the Death of Queen Elizabeth. Sir Thomas More. AAS; FaBoRV; LiTB; OBSC
O Ye That Would Swallow the Needy. Bible, *O.T.* Amos, VIII: 4–10. TrJP
O [*or* A *or* Oh] ye wha are sae guid yoursel. Address to the Unco Guid, or the Rigidly Righteous. Burns. EnRP; HBV-1; LoBV; NOBE; NOCV; NoP; OAEP; OBEC; OxBS; SeCeV; TreFS; TrGrPo; ViBoPo
O ye who see with other eyes than ours. Life and Death. Lilla Cabot Perry. AA
O ye wretched Scots. John Skelton. *Fr.* How the Doughty Duke of Albany like a Coward Knight Ran Away Shamefully. OBSV
O years, and age, farewell! Eternity. Robert Herrick. WHA
O Years Unborn. John Richard Moreland. PGD
O yee, whome lorde of lande and waters wyde. Seneca, *tr. by* Jasper Heywood. *Fr.* Thyestes, III. OBVE
O yes, I love you, book of my confessions. Water under the Earth. Robert Bly. NNaP
O yes, O yes! if any maid. Cupid's Indictment [*or* A Song of Diana's Nymphs]. John Lyly. *Fr.* Galathea. EIL; OBSC
O yes O yes. Archilochos. John Tagliabue. FAZ
O yet we trust that somehow good. *See* Oh yet we trust that somehow good.
O yonge fresshe folkes, he or she. *See* O younge freshe folkes, he or she.
O you,/ Who came upon me once. Carrefour. Amy Lowell. BoWoP
O You among Women. F. R. Higgins. BIrV
O you are a rajah in your rage. Courage for the Pusillanimous. Paul Roche. GoYe
O you chorus of indolent reviewers. Hendecasyllabics. Tennyson. EBEV; FaBoCo; NOBL; PV; VLP
O you clouds. Callypso Speaks. Hilda Doolittle ("H. D."). SBG
O you dear trees, you have learned so much of beauty. This Way Only. Lesbia Harford. PoAu-1
O you hollow-cheeked offspring. Baboon. *Zulu Oral Tradition, tr. by* C. *and* W. Leslav. WTO
O you liar tell me this. The Liar. *Unknown, tr. by* Frank O'Connor. KiLC
O you not only worshipful but dear. Credo. Zona Gale. TrPWD
O, you plant the pain in my heart with your wistful eyes. Maureen. John Todhunter. HBV-1; OBVV
O you so long dead. To My Brother. Louise Bogan. NYBP
O you that from some southern land. Ode to the Nightingale. John Kendall. InMe
O You That Hear This Voice. Sir Philip Sidney. Astrophel and Stella, Sixth Song. OBSC; SiPS
O you who come to me—alas! Laieikawai's Lament after Her Husband's Death. *Tr. fr. Hawaiian by* M. W. Beckwith. WTO
O you would clothe me in silken frocks. The Wild Goat. Claude McKay. CDC
O young and brave, it is not sweet to die. Dulce et Decorum. T. P. Cameron Wilson. HBMV
O Young and Fearless Prophet. S. Ralph Harlow. AH, *with music;* TrPWD; TRV
O, young Lochinvar is come out of the west. *See* Oh, young Lochinvar is come out of the west.
O young Mariner. Merlin and the Gleam. Tennyson. OAEL-2; OAEP; VLP
O younge [*or* yonge] fres[s]he folkes, he or she. Love Unfeigned. Chaucer. *Fr.* Troilus and Criseyde. LO; NOBE; OBEV; OxBM
O, you're braw wi' your pearls and your diamonds. Lassie, What Mair Wad You Hae? Heine, *tr. by* Alexander Gray. GoTS; OxBS
O Youth with Blossoms Laden. Arthur Wallace Peach. HBMV
O zummer clote! when the brook's a-gliden [*or* a-sliden]. The Clote (Water-Lily). William Barnes. ELP; PoEL-4
O' zummer night, as day did gleam. The Lost Little Sister. William Barnes. PoEL-4
Oa! hoy! awe! ba! mey! Canedolia. Edwin Morgan. FaBoCo; PoSH
Oak. Philip Child. CaP
Oak, The. Dryden. OHIP
Oak, The. Tennyson. FaPON; PoPl
Oak and Lily. Ben Jonson. *See* Noble Nature, The.
Oak and Olive. James Elroy Flecker. HBMV
Oak and the Ash, The. *Unknown.* FaBoCh; FSW
(North County Maid, The.) OBET
Oak and the Brere, The. Spenser. *Fr.* The Shepheardes Calender: February. OBSC
Oak and the Olive, The. George Barker. FaBoMo
Oak and the Reed, The. La Fontaine, *tr. fr. French by* Marianne Moore. NAWM-2
Oak, fern, ivy and pine. Little Epithalamium. Chester Kallman. CrMA
Oak is called the king of trees, The. Trees. Sara Coleridge. OHIP; OxBChV; RHPC
Oak leaves are big as the mouse's ear. Every One to His Own Way. John Vance Cheney. AA
Oak-Tree, The. William Barnes. *See* Girt Woak Tree That's in the Dell, The.
Oakeley, whenas the bass you beat. To E. M. O. Thomas Edward Brown. WhC
Oaken, broken elbow-chair, An. A True and Faithful Inventory of the Goods Belonging to Dr. Swift, Vicar of Laracor; upon Lending His House to the Bishop of Meath, Till His Palace Was Rebuilt. Swift. FaBoUs
Oakey Street Evictions, The. Tommy Armstrong. OBET
Oaks are old at birth and ornery. At the Woodpile. Raymond Henri. SaC
Oaks, how subtle and marine, The. Bearded Oaks. Robert Penn Warren. LiTM; MoAmPo; MoVE; MP; NoAM; NOBA; PAI; PoA; TAP; TwCP
Oars fell from our hands, The. The Island. George Woodcock. MoCV; NeBP
Oasis. Edward Dowden. OxBI
Oath, The. Allen Tate. FaBoMo; LiTM; NoAM; OxBA; VGW
Oatmeal Deluxe. Stephen Dobyns. AMV-81
Oatmeal was in their blood and in their names. The Gathering. Edwin John Pratt. *Fr.* Towards the Last Spike. MoCV; OBCV
Obatala, the Creator. *Yoruba Oral Tradition, tr. by* Ulli Beier. WTO
Obedience. George Herbert. AnAnS-1
Obedience. George Macdonald. BLRP; TreFT; TRV; WGRP
(What Christ Said.) HBV-2
Obelisk Inscriptions, *sel.* Hatshepsut, *tr. fr. Egyptian.*
"Now my heart turns to and fro," *tr. by* Miriam Lichtheim. WPOW
Oberammergau. Leonora Speyer. HBMV
Obermann Once More. Matthew Arnold. PoEL-5
Oberon and Titania to the Fairy Train. Shakespeare. *Fr.* A Midsummer Night's Dream, V, ii. GN
(Through the House.) CTC
Oberon, the Fairy Prince, *sel.* Ben Jonson.
Buz, Quoth the Blue Fly. NA; TEP
("Buzz, quoth the blue fly," *sl. diff.*) OxNR
(Catch, A.) EIL
(Satyrs' Catch, The.) FaBoNo; FM
(Song of the Satyrs.) PoPle
Oberon's Feast. Robert Herrick. CaPo; OAEP; SeCV-1; TrGrPo
"Little mushroom table spread, A," *sel.* ViBoPo
Oberon's Palace. Robert Herrick. CaPo
Obit on Parnassus. F. Scott Fitzgerald. InMe; NYBP; PrIm; WhC
Obituary. "Max Adeler." DTC
Obituary. Anthony Brode. FiBHP
Obituary. Kenneth Fearing. VGW
Obituary. Weldon Kees. BoAnP
Obituary. Thomas William Parsons. AA; HBV-1; HBVY
Obituary in Bitcherel. Conrad Aiken. OBAL
Object among dreams, you sit here with your shoes off, An. A Girl in a Library. Randall Jarrell. NoAM; NOBA; NoP
Objects. W. H. Auden. NePoAm-2
Objects. Richard Wilbur. FF; NoP
Objects are disposed, The: the sky is suitable. November, 1941. Roy Fuller. MoPo
Objects of the Summer Scene, The. William Caulfield Irwin. NBM
Objets d'Art. Cynthia Macdonald. NMM
Oblation. A. Newberry Choyce. HBMV
Oblation, The. Swinburne. HBV-1; VLP
Obligations. Jane Cooper. NePoEA-2
Obligatory Love Poem. P. L. Jacobs. LFAC
Oblique. Archibald Rutledge. TRV
Oblique Birth Poem. Ann Darr. GP
Obliterate/ mythology as you unwind. The Cavern. Charles Tomlinson. CMoP; NMP
Oblivion. Jessie Redmond Fauset, *fr. the French of* Massillon Coicou. BANP; PoNe
Oblivion. Ellis Ayitey Komey. PBA
Oblivion. George Sterling. *Fr.* Three Sonnets on Oblivion. HBV-2
Oblivion! Skin. Nelly Sachs, *tr. fr. German by* Michael Roloff. PBWP

Oboes on the terrace held a chord, The. Professor Drinking Wine. Alasdair Clayre. PV
Obon by the Hudson. Richard Oyama. BrSi
O'Bruadair. David O'Bruadair, *tr. fr. Irish by* James Stephens. BIrV
(O Bruadair.) OxBI
Obscene Caller, The. Philip Dacey. AmPA
Obscene Caller, The. Cheri Fein. TW
Obscene Phone Call #2. Joy Harjo. TWSS
Obscure Night of the Soul, The. St. John of the Cross. *See* Dark Night, The.
Obscure Pleasure of the Indistinct, The. Bin Ramke. MAYP
Obscured Prince, The; or, The Black Box Boxed. *Unknown.* APAS
Obscurely yet most surely called to praise. Praise in Summer. Richard Wilbur. CAPP; NoP; PP
Obscurest night involved [*or* involv'd] the sky. The Castaway. William Cowper. CABA; ELP; EnRP; FaBoEn; FiP; HelP; LAuP; MOS; NOBE; NOEC; NoP; OAEL-1; OAEP; OBEC; PoEl-3; PPoe; PPP
Obsequies of Stuart. John Randolph Thompson. PAH
Obsequies to the Lady Anne Hay. Thomas Carew. AnAnS-2
Observant of the way she told. Tact. E. A. Robinson. NoAM
Observation. Robert Herrick. FaBoUs
Observation. Dorothy Parker. *Fr.* Some Beautiful Letters. FiBHP; InMe
Observation. Richard Weber. POL
Observation. Derk Wynand. AMV-80
Observation at Dawn. Abba Kovner, *tr. fr. Hebrew by* Shirley Kaufman. VWA
Observation Car. A. D. Hope. NoAM
Observation Car and Cigar. William Stafford. LCAP
Observation of a Bee. Leah Goldberg, *tr. fr. Hebrew by* Stephen Mitchell. WPOW
Observation of Facts. Charles Tomlinson. NePoEA-2
Observations in a Cornish Teashop. Kenneth Rexroth. OBAL
Observatory Ode, The. John Frederick Nims. SUW
Observe God in His works: here fountains flow. Henry Vaughan. *Fr.* Rules and Lessons. TRV
Observe how he negotiates his way. Swimmer. Robert Francis. CrMA; DFF; LiSp; NePoAm; WeW
Observe how it will be at last. Summing Up in Italy. Elizabeth Barrett Browning. VLP
Observe. I myself will proceed/ To put him in his place. Cyrano de Bergerac Discusses His Nose. Edmond Rostand, *tr. by* Brian Hooker. *Fr.* Cyrano de Bergerac. TreFS
Observe! I turn the key in this new door. After the Blitz, 1941. J. R. Ackerley. PeHV
Observe. Ridged, raised, tactile, the horror. Munch's Scream. Donald Hall. NePoEA
Observe the Cat upon this page. The Cat. Oliver Herford. FaBV
Observe the daily circle of the sun. Virgil, *tr. by* Dryden. *Fr.* The Georgics, I. FaBoUs
Observe the Roman Forum; turn away. Morality. Jean Garrigue. ELU
Observe the weary birds e're night be done. Orinda to Lucasia. Katherine Philips. LO; PeHV
Observe the Whole of It. Thomas Wolfe. TreFT
Observe these pirates bold and gay. On the Dangers Attending Altruism on the High Seas. G. K. Chesterton. FaBoNo
Observe this man, he is an engineer. Revelation. Nancy Keesing. PoAu-2
Observer, The. David C. Yates. AMV-81
Observing a Vulgar Name on the Plinth of an Ancient Statue. Walter Savage Landor. EyDe
Observing point by point mere instances. On a Baltimore Bus. Charles G. Bell. NePoAm
Obsession, The. Rosy Liggett. AMV-80
Obsessions. Denise Levertov. LiTM; NePoEA-2
Obsessions governing an art, The. Aids to Composition. Robert Conquest. PP
Obsessive. Marvin Bell. LCAP
Obtuse Angle, Scopprell, Aradobo, and Tilly Lally. In Obtuse Angle's Study. Blake. *Fr.* An Island in the Moon. FaBoNo
Occam's Razor Starts in Massachusetts. Edward Pygge. BXAP
Occasional mornings when an early fog. Housewife. Josephine Miles. PCP
Occasional Poem. A. E. Housman. *See* When Adam Day by Day.
Occasional Yarrow, The. Stevie Smith. FaBoNo
Occasioned by General Washington's Arrival in Philadelphia, on His Way to His Residence in Virginia. Philip Freneau. PAH
Occultist and the New York Times coffee man, The. The Planets Line Up for a Demonstration. Josie Kearns. SUW
Occupation: Housewife. Phyllis McGinley. *Fr.* I Know a Village. DBV; WPE
Occupational Hazards. David Young. FiCP
Ocean, The. Bible, *O.T.* Psalms, CVII: 23-33:. WGRP
Ocean, The ("Oh! that the desert were my dwelling-place"). Byron. *Fr.* Childe Harold's Pilgrimage, IV. PoEL-4
(By the Deep Sea.) OBNC
Ocean ("Roll on, thou deep and dark blue ocean—roll!"). Byron. *Fr.* Childe Harold's Pilgrimage. *See* To the Ocean.
Ocean, The ("There is a pleasure in the pathless woods"). Byron. *See* Sea, The.
Ocean, The. Louis Dudek. *Fr.* Provincetown. MoCV
Ocean. Robinson Jeffers. AP; CoBMV
Ocean, The. Moschus, *tr. fr. Greek by* Shelley. AWP
(From the Greek of Moschus.) MOS
("When winds that move not its calm surface sweep.") OBVE
Ocean. Robert Pollok. EtS
Ocean, The. George D. Prentice. EtS
Ocean, The. John Augustus Shea. EtS
Ocean, The/ holds the bass. Rope's End. Peter F. Neumeyer. WOLT
Ocean Burial, The. Edwin H. Chapin. PSoN, *with music;* ShS; ViBoFo, *with music*
Ocean-Fight, The. *Unknown.* PAH
Ocean has not been so quiet for a long while, The. Evening Ebb. Robinson Jeffers. NoAM
Ocean is a strange, The. Laura St. Martin. FF
Ocean Is like a Wreath, The. Kuapakaa, *tr. fr. Hawaiian.* WTO
Ocean Lullaby, An. Charles Keeler. EtS
Ocean of Life, The. Longfellow. *See* Ships That Pass in the Night.
Ocean said to me once, The. Stephen Crane. The Black Riders, XXXVIII. MOS
Ocean Springs Missippy. Al Young. The Song Turning Back into Itself, 3. CNA; NPGG
Ocean stood like crystal, The. The soft air. The Birth of Venus. *Unknown.* EtS
Ocean thunders in the caverned sky, The. Homecoming in Storm. Bernice L. Kenyon. EtS
Ocean to Cynthia, The. Sir Walter Ralegh. *See* 11th and Last Book of the Ocean to Cynthia.
Ocean too has winter-views serene, The. Winter Views Serene. George Crabbe. *Fr.* The Borough. OBNC
Ocean Wanderer, The. *Unknown.* NA
Oceana and Britannia. John Ayloffe. APAS
Oceans. Juan Ramón Jiménez, *tr. fr. Spanish by* Robert Bly. NU
Ocean's Love to Cynthia, The. Sir Walter Ralegh. *See* 11th and Last Book of the Ocean to Cynthia.
Oceans separated us. Hunger Striker. William Franklin. LFAC
Och hey! for the splendour of tartans! The Return. Pittendrigh Macgillivray. GoTS; OxBS
Och hon for somebody! Somebody. *Unknown.* OxBS
Och! what will [*or* shall] we do for linen? What Will We Do for Linen? *Unknown.* GBP; WTO
Och, when we lived in ould Glenann. A Song of Glenann. "Moira O'Neill." HBV-2
Ochil Hills, The. *Unknown, after* "Hugh Haliburton." PoSH
Ock Gurney and old Pete were there. John Masefield. *Fr.* Reynard the Fox. CMoP
O'Connor the Bad Traveler. Peter Klappert. FiCP
Ocotillo in Bloom, The. Marilla Merrimar Guild. PBAW
October. Thomas Bailey Aldrich. *See* Maple Leaves.
October. John Bayliss. NeBP
October. Robert Frost. GoJo
October. Rose Fyleman. SiSoSe; TiPo
October. Judith Goren. AMV-81
October. Steve Hahn. PPJ
October. Rodney Hall. *Fr.* Black Bagatelles. CBAP
October. Patrick Kavanagh. CIP; GTBS-P
October. Frederic Koeppel. AMV-80
October, *sels.* William Morris. *Fr.* The Earthly Paradise.
"Ah, these, with life so done with now, might deem." VLP
"O, love, turn from the unchanging sea, and gaze." FaBoEn; OBNC
October. Greg Pape. AmPA
October. Maurice Sendak. RHPC
October. Barry Spacks. PoA
October. Spenser. *Fr.* The Shepheardes Calender. OAEL-1
(Contempt of Poetry, The.) OBSC
(October Eclogue.) PP
October. Dylan Thomas. *Fr.* Poem in October. YeAr
October. Edward Thomas. ChMP; MoVE; NoAM
October. John Updike. PDV
October and November. Robert Lowell. MAT
October: and the fires go out along the coast. October. Rodney Hall. *Fr.* Black Bagatelles. CBAP
October at last has come! The thicket has shaken. Autumn. Pushkin, *tr. by* Max Eastman. AWP

October! Can I stand it one more year? The Game. Walker Gibson. NePoAm-2
October Dusk. C. Stephen Finley. AMV-80
October Eclogue. Spenser. *See* October.
October 1803. Wordsworth. EnRP
October Elegy. Margaret Gibson. FYAP
October 1. Karl Shapiro. MoAB; MoAmPo; PoA
October 14, 1644. Lord Herbert of Cherbury. AnAnS-2
October gave a party. October's Party. George Cooper. HBV-1; HBVY; PoLF; SiSoSe
October. Here in this dank, unfamiliar kitchen. Photograph of My Father in His Twenty-second Year. Raymond Carver. WOLT
October Hill. R. Wayne Hardy. LFAC
October in New England. Home Thoughts. Odell Shepard. HBMV
October in Tennessee. Walter Malone. AA
October Journey. Margaret Walker. AmNP; IDB; PoBA; PoNe
October Magic. Myra Cohn Livingston. PDV
October Maples, Portland. Richard Wilbur. CoPo
October Morning. John James Piatt. YeAr
October Night. Agnes Louise Dean. YeAr
October nights, wild geese string. The Impulse of October. W. R. Moses. NCSH
October 1942. Roy Fuller. WaP
October Redbreast, The. Alice Meynell. MoBrPo
October 16: The Raid. Langston Hughes. BOLo; PoBA
October turned my maple's leaves to gold. Maple Leaves [*or* October]. Thomas Bailey Aldrich. GN; RHPC
October XXIX, 1795. William Stanley Braithwaite. CDC
October Winds. Virginia D. Randall. YeAr
October's Bright Blue Weather. Helen Hunt Jackson. BLPA; BLPL; FaBoBe; GN; HBVY; PoSC; TreFT
October's end. A day of sunny still. Indian Summer. Gray Burr. AMV-80
October's Party. George Cooper. HBV-1; HBVY; PoLF; SiSoSe
October's Song. Eleanor Farjeon. PoSC
Octopus. A. C. Hilton. BXAP; CenHV; FaBoCo; FaBoPa; Par
Octopus, The. "Hugh MacDiarmid." TW
Octopus, The. James Merrill. CoAP; GP; TwAmPo
Octopus, The. Ogden Nash. MOS; NePA; SoPo; TiPo
Octopussycat, The. Kenyon Cox. FaPON; SoPo; TiPo
"Oculist prescribes me spectacles, The." On Oculists. Sir J. C. Squire. WhC
Odalisque. Brian Coffey. CIP
Odcomb's Complaint, *sel.* John Taylor.
  Sonnet: "Sweet semi-circled Cynthia played at maw." ElL
    (Mockado, Fustian, and Motley.) FaBoNo
Odd but True. *Unknown.* FaBoCo
    (Nonsense.) FaBoNo; NA
    (Oh That My Lungs.) NOBL
Odd Conceit, An. Nicholas Breton. ElL; OBSC
Odd, friendless boy raised by four aunts, The. Thumb. Philip Dacey. POL; PPJ
Odd Old Man in Hackensack, An. *Unknown.* TDH
Odd silence, An/ Falls as we enter. Dreams of Water. Donald Justice. LCAP; NYBP
Odd to a Krokis. *Unknown.* NA
Odd way you comb your hair, The. Lady in a Distant Face. James Welch. AmPA
Odd Woman, The. Madeline DeFrees. GP
Oddities composed the sum of the news. For the Lost Generation. Galway Kinnell. NePoAm; PAI; PPON
Oddity Land, *sel.* Edward Anthony.
  "I know seven mice." TiPo
Ode: "Absence, hear thou my protestation." John Hoskins. *See* Absence.
Ode: Acme and Septimius. Catullus, *tr. fr. Latin by* Abraham Cowley. *See* Acme and Septimius.
Ode, An: "As it fell upon a day." Richard Barnfield. *See* As It Fell upon a Day.
Ode: "At her fair hands how have I grace entreated." Walter Davison. *See* At Her Fair Hands.
Ode: Autumn. Thomas Hood. *See* Autumn.
Ode, An: "Awake, faire Muse; for I intend." William Browne. OBS
Ode: "Bards of passion and of mirth." Keats. *See* Bards of Passion and of Mirth.
Ode: "Come, let us drink away the time." *At. to* Charles Cotton. *See* Song of Sack, A.
Ode: First of April, The, *sel.* Thomas Warton, the Younger.
  "Swallow, for a moment seen, The." PBBP
Ode: "God save the Rights of Man!" Philip Freneau. AP; GOA
Ode: "Good night, my love, may gentle rest." Charles Cotton. ViBoPo
Ode: "How are thy servants blest, O Lord!" Joseph Addison. *See* How Are Thy Servants Blest.
Ode: "How sleep the brave, who sink to rest." William Collins. *See* How Sleep the Brave.
Ode: "I am the spirit of the morning sea." Richard Watson Gilder. AA
Ode: "I hate that drum's discordant sound." John Scott of Amwell. *See* I Hate That Drum's Discordant Sound.
Ode, An: "I sing a song of sixpence, and of rye." Anthony C. Deane. NOBL
Ode: "Idea of justice may be precious, An." Frank O'Hara. NeAP
Ode, An: "I'm going to write a novel, hey." John Updike. FiBHP
Ode: Inscribed to W. H. Channing. Emerson. *See* Ode Inscribed to W. H. Channing.
Ode: Intimations of Immortality from Recollections of Early Childhood. Wordsworth. AWP; BiP; BLPL; CABA; ChER; EnRP; FaBoRV; FiP; HAP; HeIP; InvP; LiTB; LoBV; MasP; NAs; NOBE; NoP; OAEL-2; OAEP; OBEV; OBNC; OBRV; PAI; PoEL-4; PPoE; PPP; PrIm; SeCeV; TEP; TrGrPo; ViBoPo
    (Ode on Intimations of [*or* on] Immortality [from Recollections of Early Childhood].) FaFP; GTBS; GTBS-P; HBV-1; OHFP; TreF, *abr.*; WHA
  Sels.
  "Now, while the birds thus sing a joyous song." Prf
  "O joy! that in our embers." PoPle; Prf
  "Our birth is but a sleep and a forgetting." EaLo; FaBoEn; ILwL; TRV; WGRP
    (Intimations of Immortality.) ChTr
    (Our Birth Is But a Sleep.) FaBV
Ode: "Love thy country, wish it well." George Bubb Dodington. OBEC
Ode, An: "Merchant, to secure his treasure, The." Matthew Prior. AWP; CABA; EnLoPo; NOEC; NoP; PoRA; ViBoPo
    ("Merchant, to secure his treasure, The.") GTBS; GTBS-P
    (Song: "Merchant, to secure his treasure, The.") HBV-1; OBEV; PoPle; TrGrPo
Ode: "Mistah Berrybones, you daid?" William Zaranka. BXAP
Ode: "My heart rebels against my generation." George Santayana. ViBoPo
Ode: "Now each creature joys the other." Samuel Daniel. ElL; LoBV; OBSC
Ode: "Now I find thy looks were feigned." Thomas Lodge. *Fr.* Phyllis. ElL; EnRePo; OBSC
Ode: "O tenderly the haughty day." Emerson. AA; GN; PAL
Ode: Of Wit. Abraham Cowley. AnAnS-2; MeLP; MePo; OAEL-1; OAEP; SeCP; SeCV-1
    (Of Wit.) OBS
Ode: On the Death of William Butler Yeats. A. J. M. Smith. OBCV; PeCV
Ode: On the Morning of Christ's Nativity. Milton. *See* On the Morning of Christ's Nativity.
Ode: "Once more the country calls." Allen Tate. WaP
Ode: "People in the middle ages didn't think they were living." David Lehman. AMV-81
Ode: "Poor bird, I do not envy thee." George Daniel. *See* Robin, The.
Ode: Salute to the French Negro Poets. Frank O'Hara. NeAP; NNaP; PoM; PoNe
Ode: Secundum Artem, An. William Cowper. PP
Ode: "Sire of the rising day." Lord De Tabley. OBVV
Ode: "Sleep sweetly in your humble graves." Henry Timrod. GOA; HBV-2; NOBA; OxBA; TAP
    (At Magnolia Cemetery.) AA
    (Ode Sung on the Occasion of Decorating the Graves of the Confederate Dead.) AP
    (Ode to the Confederate Dead.) TreFT
    (Ode to the Confederate Dead in Magnolia Cemetery.) PAL
    (Sleep Sweetly.) AH, *with music*
Ode: "Spacious firmament on high, The." Joseph Addison. *See* Spacious Firmament on High, The.
Ode: Spirit Wooed, The. Richard Watson Dixon. OBNC
Ode: "Tell me, thou soul of her I love." James Thomson. OBEC
Ode: "That I have often been in love, deep love." "Peter Pindar." NOEC
Ode: "They journeyed,/ When the darkness of night." Ibn al-Arabi, *tr. fr. Arabic by* R. A. Nicholson. AWP
Ode: To Himself[e] ("Come leave the loathed stage"). Ben Jonson. *See* Ode to Himself ("Come leave the loathed stage").
Ode: To Himself[e] ("Where dost thou careless lie"). Ben Jonson. *See* Ode to Himself, An ("Where do'st thou careless lie").
Ode: To My Lovers. Paul Verlaine, *tr. fr. French by* J. Murat *and* W. Gunn. PeHV
Ode: To My Pupils. W. H. Auden. MoBrPo
    (Which Side Am I Supposed to Be On?) CoBMV
Ode: To the Cuckoo. Michael Bruce. *See* To the Cuckoo.
Ode: To the Evening Star. Mark Akenside. PBBP
Ode: To the Nightingale. Joseph Warton. PBBP
Ode: "Until thine hands clasp girdlewise the waist of the Belov'd." Sadi, *tr. fr. Persian by* R. A. Nicholson. AWP
Ode: "Was ever man of Nature's framing." Charles Cotton. CavP

Ode: "We are the music-makers." Arthur O'Shaughnessy. FaPoR; HBV-2; OBEV; OBVV; OnYI; OxBi; *abr.*; TreF, *abr.*; TrGrPo; ViBoPo, *abr.*; VLP; WHA
(Music Makers, The.) FaBV
Ode: "Weep, ah weep love's losing." Imr el Kais, *tr. fr. Arabic by* Lady Anne Blunt *and* Wilfrid Scawen Blunt. *Fr.* The Mu'allaqât. AWP
Ode: "Who can support the anguish of love?" Ibn al-Arabi, *tr. fr. Arabic by* R. A. Nicholson. AWP
Ode: "Why doth heaven bear a sun." Barnabe Barnes. *Fr.* Parthenophil and Parthenophe. ElL; OBSC
Ode: "Why will they never sleep." John Peale Bishop. LiTA; LiTM; MoPo; MoVE; NePA; TwAmPo
Ode: "Without the evening dew and showers." Charles Cotton. ViBoPo
Ode against St. Cecilia's Day. George Barker. PoA
Ode for a Master Mariner Ashore. Louise Imogen Guiney. AA; GoBC
Ode for a Social Meeting. Oliver Wendell Holmes. OBAL
Ode for Ben Jonson, An. Robert Herrick. AWP; InvP; LoBV; SeCP; TrGrPo
(Ode for Him, An.) AnAnS-2; CaPo; NoP; OAEP; OBS; SeCV-1
Ode for Decoration Day. Henry Peterson. OHIP
"O gallant brothers of the generous South," *sel.* AA; FaBoBe
Ode for Him, An. Robert Herrick. *See* Ode for Ben Jonson, An.
Ode for Music on St. Cecilia's Day, *sel.* Pope.
Descend, Ye Nine. GN
Ode for Soft Voice. Michael McClure. NeAP
Ode for the American Dead in Korea. Thomas McGrath. NePoEA; PoPl; VGW
Ode for the Burial of a Citizen. John Ciardi. LiTM; MiAP
Ode for the New Year, An. *At. to* John Gay. OxBoLi
Ode in Honour. Francis Scarfe. EAS
Ode in Honor of St. Cecilia's Day, The. Dryden. *See* Alexander's Feast.
Ode in Imitation of Alcæus, An. Sir William Jones. *See* What Constitutes a State?
Ode in May. Sir William Watson. OBEV; OBVV; WGRP
Ode in Memory of the American Volunteers Fallen for France. Alan Seeger. PAH
Ode in the Praise of Sack, An. *Unknown.* OBS
Ode in Time of Hesitation, An. William Vaughn Moody. AP; HBV-2; OxBA; PAH
Sels.
No Hint of Stain. AA
Robert Gould Shaw. AA
Ode Inscribed to the Earl of Sunderland at Windsor, An. Thomas Tickell. OBEC
Ode Inscribed to W. H. Channing. Emerson. AmPP; AP; HAP; NOBA; NoP; OxBA; PPON; TAP
"God who made New Hampshire, The," *sel.* ViBoPo
Ode Occasioned [*or* Occasion'd] by the Death of Mr. Thomson. William Collins. LAuP; NOEC
(Ode on the Death of Thomson.) OBEC; SeCePo
Ode of Lament. Randolph Jeck. WhC
Ode of Odium on Aquariums. Arthur Guiterman. BoAnP
Ode of the Birth of Our Saviour, An, *sel.* Robert Herrick.
Instead of Neat Inclosures. ChTr
Ode on a Decision to Settle for Less. William Pillen. VWA
Ode on a Distant Prospect of Clapham Academy. Thomas Hood. BXAP
Ode on a Distant Prospect of Eton College. Thomas Gray. BLPL; CABA; GTBS; GTBS-P; HeIP; LAuP; LiTB; NOBE; NOEC; NoP; OAEL-1; OAEP; OBEC; PoEL-3; PrIm; SeCeV; ViBoPo
Ode on a Grecian Urn. Keats. AWP; BiP; CABA; ChER; EBEV; EnRP; FaBoBe; FaBoEn; FaFP; FF; FiP; FPL; HAP; HBV-2; HBVY; HeIP; HoPM; InPK; InPS; LiTB; LoBV; MasP; NIP; NOBE; NoP; OAEL-2; OAEP; OBEV; OBNC; OBRV; OHFP; PAI; PoEL-4; PPoe; PPP; PrIm; SeCeV; SoSe; TEP; TreF; TrGrPo; UnPo; WHA
(On a Grecian Urn.) ViBoPo
Ode on a Grecian Urn, *parody.* E. O. Parrott. BXAP
Ode on a Grecian Urn Summarized. Desmond Skirrow. NIP; NOBL
Ode on [*or* to] a Jar of Pickles. Bayard Taylor. BXAP; FaBoPa; SpRo
Ode on a Plastic Stapes. Chad Walsh. HoAn
Ode on Advancing Age. Richard Watson Dixon. NBM
Ode on Celestial Music. Brian Patten. OxBTC
Ode on Contemplating Clapham Junction. Christopher Middleton. *Fr.* Herman Moon's Hourbook. NePoEA-2
Ode on Gas, An. *Unknown.* OBAL
Ode on His Majesty's Proclamation, Commanding the Gentry to Reside on Their Estates. Sir Richard Fanshawe. *See* Now War Is All the World About.
Ode on Indolence. Keats. EnRP; LiTB; OBNC
Ode on Intimations of Immortality from Recollections of Early Childhood. Wordsworth. *See* Ode: Intimations of Immortality . . .
Ode on Leaving the Great Town. Thomas Randolph. *See* Ode to Mr. Anthony Stafford to Hasten Him into the Country, An.
Ode on Lord Macartney's Embassy to China. William Shepherd. NOEC
Ode on [*or* to] Melancholy. Keats. CABA; EnRP; FaBoEn; FiP; HAP; InPS; LiTB; MAT; NIP; NOBE: NoP; OAEL-2; OAEP; OBEV; OBNC; PoEL-4; PoPle; PoRA; PPP; PrIm; SeCeV; TEP; TreFS; TrGrPo
(On Melancholy.) HBV-2; ViBoPo
Ode on Miss Harriet Hanbury at Six Years Old, An. Sir Charles Hanbury Williams. OBEC
Ode on Science, *with music.* Jezaniah Sumner. TrAS
Ode on [*or* to] Solitude. Pope. AWP; FiP; GoBC; HBV-1; HBVY; HeIP; InvP; NIP; OAEP; OBEC; PAI; PoPl; PoPle; PoRA; PPoe; Prf; SeCeV; TEP; TreFS; ViBoPo
(Contented Man, The.) InMe
(Quiet Life, The.) GTBS; GTBS-P
(Solitude.) FaFP; TrGrPo
Ode on the Birth of Our Saviour, An. Robert Herrick. GN; SBVL
Ode on the Celebration of the Battle of Bunker Hill, June 17, 1825, *sel.* Grenville Mellen.
Lonely Bugle Grieves, The. AA
Ode on the Death of a Favourite [*or* Favorite] Cat, Drowned in a Tub [*or* Bowl] of Gold Fishes. Thomas Gray. EBEV; FaBoBe; FM; HoPM; LAuP; NOBE; NOBL; NOEC; NoP; OAEL-1; OAEP; OBEC; PCat; PoEL-3; PPP; TEP
(Cat and the Fish, The.) WiR
(On a Favorite Cat Drowned in a Tub of Goldfishes.) BeLS; FaBoCo; GN; GTBS-P; InvP; LiTB; OBEV; PoPle
(On the Death of a Favourite Cat, Drowned in a Tub of Gold Fishes.) FPL; HBV-1; InMe; PoLF; PoRA; SeCeV
Ode on the Death of Mr. Henry Purcell, An, *sel.* Dryden.
"Mark how the lark and linnet sing." PBBP
Ode on the Death of the Duke of Wellington. Tennyson. HBV-2; OBVV; VLP
Ode on the Death of Thomson. William Collins. *See* Ode Occasioned by the Death of Mr. Thomson.
Ode on the Departing Year, *sel.* Samuel Taylor Coleridge.
O My Mother Isle! ("Not yet enslaved, not wholly vile"). FaBoPP
Ode on the Intimations of Immortality from Recollections of Early Childhood. Wordsworth. *See* Ode: Intimations of Immortality from Recollections of Early Childhood.
Ode on the Morning of Christ's Nativity. Milton. *See* On the Morning of Christ's Nativity.
Ode on the Pleasure Arising from Vicissitude. Thomas Gray. GTBS; GTBS-P; LAuP; OBEC
"Now the golden Morn aloft," *sel.* NOEC
Ode on the Poetical Character. William Collins. EnRP; LAuP; NOEC; OAEL-1; OAEP; PoEL-3; TEP
Ode on the Poets. Keats. *See* Bards of Passion and of Mirth.
Ode on the Popular Superstitions of the Highlands of Scotland, An [Considered as the Subject of Poetry]. William Collins. EnRP; LAuP; NOEC; OAEL-1; OAEP; OBEC
Sels.
St. Kilda. FaBoEn
Stormy Hebrides, The. NOBE
Ode on the Spring. Thomas Gray. GTBS; GTBS-P; HBV-1; LAuP; NOEC
Ode, on the Unveiling of the Shaw Memorial on Boston Common [May 31st, 1897], An. Thomas Bailey Aldrich. AA; HBV-2; PAH
Ode on Theoxenos. Pindar, *tr. fr. Greek by* John Addington Symonds. PeHV
Ode on Zero. Phoebe Pettingell. PoA
Ode Recited at the Harvard Commemoration, *sel.* James Russell Lowell. AA; AP; HBV-2; NOBA; OBWP; PAH
Sels.
"I with uncovered head," *fr.* VIII *and* XII. OHIP
Lincoln, *fr.* VI. HBVY
("Nature, they say, doth dote.") PGD
Ode Sung at the Opening of the International Exhibition. Tennyson. VLP
Ode Sung on the Occasion of Decorating the Graves of the Confederate Dead. Henry Timrod. *See* Ode: "Sleep sweetly in your humble graves."
Ode to a Beautiful Woman. Carl Clark. JB
Ode to a Butterfly. Thomas Wentworth Higginson. AA; FaBoBe; HBV-1
Ode to a Country Hoyden. "Peter Pindar." NOEC
Ode to a Dead Dodge. David McElroy. AmPA; DFF
Ode to a Dental Hygienist. Earnest A. Hooten. FiBHP; WhC
Ode to a Ditch. *Unknown.* PeD
Ode to a Dressmaker's Dummy. Donald Justice. DFF
Ode to a Fat Cat. Annabel Farjeon. PCat
Ode to a Friend. William Mason. OBEC
Ode to a Homemade Coffee Cup. Marine Robert Warden. AMV-81
Ode to a Jar of Pickles. Bayard Taylor. *See* Ode on a Jar of Pickles.
Ode to a Lebanese Crock of Olives. Diane Wakoski. GP

Ode to a Model. Vladimir Nabokov. OBAL; PoPl
Ode to a Nightingale. Keats. AWP; BiP; BLPL; CABA; ChER; EBEV; EnRP; FaBoBe; FaBoEn; FaFP; FiP; GTBS; GTBS-P; HAP; HBV-1; HBVY; HeIP; InPK; InPS; LiTB; LoBV; MasP; NIP; NOBE; NoP; OAEL-2; OAEP; OBEV; OBNC; OBRV; PAI; PB; PBBP; PoEL-4; PPoe; PPP; PoRA; PrIm; SeCeV; SoSe; SpRo; TEP; TreF; TrGrPo; UnPo; WeW
(Ode to the Nightingale.) WHA
(To a Nightingale.) ChTr; ViBoPo
Magic Casements, *sel.* FaBV
Ode to a Nightingale, *parody.* Roy Kelly. BXAP
Ode to a Pig while His Nose Was Being Bored. Robert Southey. NOBL
Ode to a Skylark. Shelley. *See* To a Skylark.
Ode to a Vanished Operator in an Automatized Elevator. Loyd Rosenfield. QQQ
Ode to Anactoria. Sappho, *tr. fr. Greek by* William Ellery Leonard. AWP
("Peer of the gods is that man, who, " *tr. by* William Carlos Williams.) OBVE
Ode to Aphrodite. Sappho, *tr. fr. Greek by* William Ellery Leonard. AWP
Ode to Arnold Schoenberg. Charles Tomlinson. NePoEA-2
Ode to Autumn. Thomas Hood. *See* Autumn.
Ode to Autumn. Keats. *See* To Autumn.
Ode to Beauty. Emerson. AmPP; AP; PoEL-4
Ode to Chloris. Charles Cotton. CavP
Ode to Cupid. Charles Cotton. CavP
Ode to Duty. Wordsworth. AWP; BiP; EnRP; FPL; GTBS; GTBS-P; HBV-2; NoP; OAEL-2; OBEV; OBRV; TreFS; TRV; WGRP
Stern Daughter of the Voice of God, *sel.* HBVY
Ode to England, *sels.* William Wilberforce Lord.
Keats. AA
Wordsworth. AA
Ode to Ethiopia. Paul Laurence Dunbar. BALP
Ode to Eve. Edwin Meade Robinson. Inme
Ode to Evening. William Collins. AWP; CABA; EBEV; EnRP; FaBoBe; FaBoEn; HAP; HBV-1; LAuP; LiTB; LoBV; MasP; NOBE; NOEC; NoP; OAEL-1; OAEP; OBEC; OBEV; PoEL-3; PPP; SeCePo; SeCeV; TreFT; TrGrPo; ViBoPo; WHA
(To Evening.) GTBS; GTBS-P
Ode to Fancy, *sels.* Joseph Warton.
Invocation to Fancy. OBEC
"O warm, enthusiastic maid." NOEC
Ode to Fanny, *sel.* Keats.
"Ah! dearest love, sweet home of all my fears." ChER
Ode to Fear. William Collins. LAuP; NOEC; OAEP; TrGrPo, *abr.*
Ode to Fidel Castro. Edward Field. CABA; CoPo
Ode to Fortune. Fitz-Greene Halleck *and* Joseph Rodman Drake. *Fr.* The Croaker Papers. AA
Ode to Freedom. Aaron Zeitlin, *tr. fr. Yiddish by* Keith Bosley. VWA
Ode to Himself[e] ("Come leave the loathèd stage"). Ben Jonson. AnAnS-2; OAEL-1; OBS; SeCP
Ode to Himself[e], An ("Where do'st thou careless lie"). Ben Jonson. AnAnS-2; EnRePo; FaBoEn; HAP; JCP; LiTB; NOBE; NoP; OAEP; OBS; PoEL-2; PrIm; QFR; SeCePo; SeCeV; SeCV-1
Ode to Himself. Sir Walter Ralegh. WhC
Ode to Jamestown. James Kirke Paulding. PAH
Ode to Joy. Daniel Hoffman. AMV-81
Ode to Joy. Michael McClure. GP
Ode to Joy. Frank O'Hara. NeAP; PPP
Ode to Leven-Water. Tobias Smollett. BSV; OBEC
Ode to Liberty. Thomas Chatterton. *Fr.* Goddwyn. TrGrPo
Ode to Master Anthony Stafford to Hasten Him into the Country, An. Thomas Randolph. *See* Ode to Mr. Anthony Stafford . . .
Ode to Master Endymion Porter, upon His Brother's Death, An. Robert Herrick. CaPo
Ode to Me. Kingsley Amis. NAs
Ode to Melancholy. Keats. *See* Ode on Melancholy.
Ode to Memory. Tennyson. VLP
Ode to Mercy. William Collins. LAuP
Ode to Michael Goldberg's Birth and Other Births. Frank O'Hara. NeAP
I Don't Remember Anything of Then, *sel.* NAs
Ode to Miss Hoyland. Thomas Chatterton. BXAP
Ode to Mr. [*or* Master] Anthony Stafford to Hasten Him into the Country, An. Thomas Randolph. AnAnS-2; FaBoEn; HBV-1; NOBE; OBEV; OBS; ViBoPo
(Ode on Leaving the Great Town.) GoTL
Ode to Mr. F—— [*or* Forbes]. Allan Ramsay, *after* Horace. NOEC; OBVE
Ode to Moderation, *sel.* Annabella Plumptre.
"To thee, whose cautious step and specious air." NOEC
Ode to Myself, An. Thomas Dermody. OnYI
Ode to Naples, *sel.* Shelley.
At Pompeii. FaBoPP
Ode to Napoleon Buonaparte, *sel.* Byron.
Washington. OHIP; PAH; PAL
Ode to New York. Reed Whittemore. NYP
Ode to Peace. *Unknown.* PAH
Ode to Pity. William Collins. LAuP
Ode to Popularity. Winthrop Mackworth Praed. VLP
Ode to Pornography. Jack Anderson. PoA
Ode to Psyche. Keats. CABA; ChER; EnRP; HBV-2; InPS; LiTB; LoBV; NOBE; NoP; OAEL-2; OAEP; OBEV; OBNC; OBRV; PoEL-4; PP; PPP; WHA
(To Psyche.) ViBoPo
Ode to Quinbus Flestrin. Pope. OAEP
Ode to Salt. Pablo Neruda, *tr. fr. Spanish by* Robert Bly. NU
Ode to Simplicity. William Collins. EnRP; LAuP; NOBE; OBEC; OBEV; TEP
Ode to Sir Lucius Cary and Sir H. Morison, An, *sel.* Ben Jonson.
Noble Nature, The. HBV-2
Ode to Sir William Sydney, on His Birth-Day. Ben Jonson. NAs
(Another Birthday.) WiR
Ode to Solitude, *sel.* James Grainger. *See* Solitude.
Ode to Solitude. Pope. *See* Ode on Solitude.
Ode to Spring. Walter R. Brooks. RHPC
Ode to Spring in the Metropolis, An. Sir Owen Seaman. FiBHP; WhC
Ode to Stephen Dowling Bots, Dec'd. "Mark Twain." *See* Emmeline Grangerford's "Ode to Stephen Dowling Bots, Dec'd."
Ode to Terminus. W. H. Auden. HAP
Ode to the Alien. Diane Ackerman. SUW
Ode to the Cameleopard. Thomas Hood. FaBoNo
Ode to the Chinese Paper Snake. Richard Eberhardt. CrMA
Ode to the Confederate Dead. Allen Tate. AP; CABA; FaBoMo; HeIP; LiTA; LiTM; MoAB; MoAmPo; MoPo; MoVE; NoAM; NOBA; NoP; OBWP; OxBA; PrIm; SeCeV; TAP; TwAmPo; UnPo; ViBoPo
Ode to the Confederate Dead [in Magnolia Cemetery]. Henry Timrod. *See* Ode: "Sleep sweetly in your humble graves."
Ode to the Country Gentlemen of England, An, *sel.* Mark Akenside.
England, Unprepared for War. OBEC
Ode to the Departing Year. Samuel Taylor Coleridge. EnRP
Ode to the Evening Star. Mark Akenside. OBEC
Ode to the Finnish Dead. Chad Walsh. HoAn
Ode to the Fourth of July, *with music.* Daniel George. TrAS
Ode to the Framers of the Frame Bill, An. Byron. CoMu; SaC
Ode to the German Drama. *Unknown.* NOEC
Ode to the Hayden Planetarium. Arthur Guiterman. ImOP
Ode to the Human Heart. Laman Blanchard. InMe; NA; NOBL
Ode to the Inhabitants of Pennsylvania. Longfellow. PAH
Ode to the Maguire. *See* O'Hussey's Ode to the Maguire.
Ode to the Medieval Poets. W. H. Auden. PoA
Ode to the Mediterranean. George Santayana. *Fr.* Odes. EtS
Ode to the Moon. Thomas Hood. OBVV
Ode to the Muse on Behalf of a Young Poet. David Wagoner. AMV-80
Ode to the Nightingale. Keats. *See* Ode to a Nightingale.
Ode to the Nightingale. John Kendall. InMe
Ode to the North-east Wind. Charles Kingsley. FaPoR; GN
Ode to the Norther. William Lawrence Chittenden. BPAW
Ode to the Pig: His Tail. Walter R. Brooks. RHPC
Ode to the Pious Memory of the Accomplished Young Lady, Mrs. Anne Killigrew. Dryden. *See* To the Pious Memory of the Accomplished Young Lady, Mrs. Anne Killigrew.
Ode to the Poppy. Henrietta Oneil. WPE
Ode to the Sea. Howard Baker. OxBA
Ode to the Setting Sun. Francis Thompson. GoBC
Sels.
"Now that the red glare of thy fall is blown." OBNC
Sun, The. MoAB; MoBrPo
Ode to the Spirit of Earth in Autumn. George Meredith. TEP; VLP
Ode to the Virgin. Petrarch, *tr. fr. Italian by* Helen Lee Peabody. *Fr.* Sonnets to Laura: Songs. ISi
Ode to the Watermelon. Pablo Neruda, *tr. fr. Spanish by* Robert Bly. EAS; NU
Ode to the West Wind. Shelley. AWP; BiP; BoNaP; CABA; CH; EBEV; EnRP; FaBoBe; FaBoEn; FaBV; FaFP; FiP; FPL; GTBS; GTBS-P; HAP; HBV-1; HeIP; InPS; LiTB; LoBV; MOS; NIP; NOBE; NoP; OAEL-2; OAEP; OBEV; OBNC; OBRV; OHFP; PAI; PoEL-4; PoLF; PoRA; PPoe; PPP; PrIm; SeCeV; TEP; TreFS; TrGrPo; ViBoPo; WeW; WHA
Ode to Tobacco. Charles Stuart Calverley. FaBoCo; FiBHP; HBV-2; InMe; WhC
Ode to Walt Whitman. Federico García Lorca, *tr. fr. Spanish.* PeHV
Ode to Winter. Thomas Campbell. GTBS; GTBS-P
Ode to Wisdom. Elizabeth Carter. OBEC
Ode to Work in Springtime. Thomas R. Ybarra. HBMV
Ode to Zion. Judah Halevi, *tr. fr. Hebrew by* Nina Davis Salaman. TrJP
Ode upon a Question Moved, Whether Love Should Continue for Ever, An?

Lord Herbert of Cherbury. AnAnS-2; JCP; MeLP; MePo; NOBE; OBS; SeCP
Sels.
"Long, their fixed eyes to Heaven bent." LO
"O no, beloved, I am most sure." ViBoPo
Ode upon Doctor Harvey. Abraham Cowley. PoEL-2
"Coy Nature (which remain'd, though aged grown)," *sel.* Par
Ode, upon Occasion of His Majesties Proclamation in the Year[e] 1630, An. Sir Richard Fanshawe. *See* Now War Is All the World About.
Ode Which Was Prefixed to a Prayer Booke Given to a Young Gentlewoman, An. Richard Crashaw. *See* Prayer: "Lo, here a little volume, but great book!"
Ode Written during the War with America, 1814, *sel.* Robert Southey. Bower of Peace, The. PAH
Ode Written in the Beginning of the Year 1746. William Collins. *See* How Sleep the Brave.
Ode Written in the Peak[e], An. Michael Drayton. FaBoPP; OBS
Ode Written in 1746. William Collins. *See* How Sleep the Brave.
Ode Written in 1966. Jorge Luis Borges, *tr. fr. Spanish by* Lynn C. Jacox. AMV-81
Odell. James Stephens. MoAB; MoBrPo
Odes, *sels.* Hafiz, *tr. fr. Persian.* AWP
"Comrades, the morning breaks, the sun is up," II, *tr. by* Richard Le Gallienne.
"Days of spring are here, The! the eglantine," X, *tr. by* Gertrude Lowthian Bell.
"Grievous folly shames my sixtieth year, A," IV, *tr. by* Richard Le Gallienne.
"I cease not from desire till my desire," IX, *tr. by* Gertrude Lowthian Bell.
"I have borne the anguish of love, which ask me not to describe," XI, *tr. by* John Hindley.
"I said to heaven that glowed above," XII, *tr. by* Emerson.
"Jewel of the secret treasury, The," VI, *tr. by* Gertrude Lowthian Bell.
"Lady that hast my heart within thy hand," VIII, *tr. by* Gertrude Lowthian Bell.
"Oft have I said, I say it once more," XIII, *tr. by* Emerson.
"Rose is not the rose unless thou see, The," III, *tr. by* Richard Le Gallienne.
"Saki, for God's love, come and fill my glass," I, *tr. by* Richard Le Gallienne.
"Where is my ruined life, and where the fame," V, *tr. by* Gertrude Lowthian Bell.
"Wind from the east, oh Lapwing of the day," VII, *tr. by* Gertrude Lowthian Bell.
Odes, *sels.* Horace, *tr. fr. Latin.*
I, 3. To the Ship on Which Virgil Sailed to Athens ("Sic te diva potens Cyri"), *tr. by* Dryden. AWP
I, 5. "What slender youth bedewed with liquid odours" ("Quis multa gracilis"), *tr. by* Milton. OBVE
(Another to the Same, *tr. by* William Browne.) WiR
(Fifth Ode of Horace, The, *tr. by* Milton.) EBEV; EnLoPo; PoEL-3
("Pyrrha, what slender well-shap'd beau," *tr. by* Anthony Horneck.) OBVE
("Say what slim youth, with moist perfumes," *tr. by* Christopher Smart.) OBVE
("Tell me, Pyrrha, what fine youth," *tr. by* William Browne.) OAEL-1
(To a Girl, *tr. by* Milton.) WiR
(To Pyrrha, *tr. by* Milton.) AWP
("To whom now, Pyrrha, art thou kind?" *tr. by* Abraham Cowley.) OBVE
("What stripling now thee discomposes," *tr. by* Sir Richard Fanshawe.) OBVE
I, 8. "Lydia, in Heavens Name" ("Lydia, dic, per omnes"), *tr. by* Sir Richard Fanshawe. OBVE
I, 9. To Thaliarchus ("Vides ut alta"). AWP, *tr. by* Dryden; OBVE, *tr. by* Sir Richard Fanshawe
("Behold yon' mountains hoary hieght," *tr. by* Dryden.) CaVP; OBVE
I, 11. To Leuconöe ("Tu ne quaesieris"). AA, *tr. by* Eugene Field; LoBV, *tr. by* Charles Stuart Calverley
(Ad Leuconoen, *par. by* Franklin P. Adams.) AWP
(Ask Not Ungainly, *tr. by* Ezra Pound.) CTC
I, 14. Ship of State, The ("O navis, referent"), *tr. by* William Ewart Gladstone. AWP
I, 21. To Apollo and Diana ("Dianam tenerae dicite virgines"), *tr. by* Branwell Brontë. OBVE
(Invocation: "Maidens young and virgins tender," *tr. by* Louis Untermeyer.) AWP
I, 22. "Virtue, dear friend, needs no 'defence' " ("Integer vitae"), *tr. by* Earl of Roscommon. OBVE
(To Aristius Fuscus, *tr. by* Samuel Johnson.) OBVE
(To Sally, *tr. by* John Quincy Adams.) AWP
I, 23. To Chloe ("Vitas hinnuleo"). AWP, *tr. by* Austin Dobson; OBVE, *tr. by* Branwell Brontë
I, 25. Ribald Romeos Less and Less Berattle ("Parcius iunctas quatiunt fenestras"), *tr. by* John Frederick Nims. MAT
("Bloods and bucks of this lewd town, The," *tr. by* the Young Gentlemen of Mr. Rule's Academy at Islington.) OBVE
(To Lydia, *tr. by* Philip Francis.) OBVE
("Young bloods come round less often now, The," *tr. by* James Michie.) BoLoP
I, 31. By the Flat Cup ("Quid dedicatum"), *tr. by* Ezra Pound. CTC
I, 33. Albi, Ne Doreas, *tr. by* Austin Dobson. AWP
(It Always Happens, *tr. by* Thomas Charles Baring.) UnTE
I, 38. Fie on Eastern Luxury! ("Persicos odi"), *tr. by* Hartley Coleridge. InPK
("Ah child, no Persian—perfect art!" *tr. by* Gerard Manley Hopkins.) InPK; OBVE
("Dear Lucy, you know what my wish is," *tr. by* Thackeray.) OBVE
(Persian Fopperies, *tr. by* William Cowper.) AWP
("Persian pomps, boy, ever I renounce them," *tr. by* Christopher Smart.) OBVE
(Persicos Odi.) HBMV, *par. by* Franklin P. Adams; OBEV, *tr. by* Thackeray
(Preference Declared, The, *tr. by* Eugene Field.) InPK
(Simplicity, *tr. by* William Cowper.) InPK
("Boy, I hate their empty shows," *tr. by* William Cowper.) OBVE
II, 4. Ad Xanthiam Phoceum ("Ne sit ancillae"), *tr. by* Franklin P. Adams. AWP
II, 7. "Pompeius, best of all my comrades, you and I" ("O saepe mecum"), *tr. by* John Wight. WaaP
("Pompeius, chief of all my friends, with whom," *tr. by* James Michie.) OBWP
II, 8. Barine, the Incorrigible ("Ulla si iuris"), *tr. by* Louis Untermeyer. UnTE
II, 10. "Receive, dear friend, the truths I teach" ("Rectius vives"), *tr. by* William Cowper. OBVE
("Of thy lyfe, Thomas, this compass well mark," *tr. by* Earl of Surrey.) OBVE
(To Licinius, *tr. by* William Cowper.) AWP
("You better sure shall live, not evermore," *tr. by* Sir Philip Sidney.) OBVE
II, 11. To an Ambitious Friend ("Quid bellicosus"), *tr. by* Matthew Arnold. AWP
II, 18. "Gold or iv'ry's not intended" ("Non ebur neque aureum"), *tr. by* Christopher Smart. OBVE
III, 1. "Tread back—and back, the lewd and lay!" ("Odi profanum vulgus"), *tr. by* Gerard Manley Hopkins. OBVE
("Hence ye prophane; I hate ye all," *tr. by* Abraham Cowley.) OBVE, 2 *sts.*
(Profane, The, *tr. by* Abraham Cowley.) AWP
III, 2. "Let the youth hardened by a sharp soldier's life" ("Angustam amice"), *tr. by* Gardner Taplin *and* Richard Eberhart. WaaP
("Disciplined in the school of hard campaigning," *tr. by* James Michie.) OBWP
III, 7. "Dear Molly, why so oft in tears?" ("Quid sles, asterie"), *tr. by* George Stepney. OBVE
III, 9. A Dialogue between Horace and Lydia ("Donec gratus eram"), *tr. by* Robert Herrick. OBVE
(Teasing Lovers, The, *tr. by* Louis Untermeyer.) UnTE
III, 10. Extremum Tanain, *tr. by* Austin Dobson. AWP
III, 13. To the Fountain[s] of Bandusia ("O fons Bandusiae"), *tr. by* Eugene Field. AA; AWP
III, 22. Pine Tree for Diana, The ("Montium custos memorumque"), *tr. by* Louis Untermeyer. AWP
III, 23. To Phidyle ("Caelo supinas si tuleris"), *tr. by* Austin Dobson. AWP
III, 28. Holiday ("Festo quid potius die"), *tr. by* Louis Untermeyer. AWP
III, 29. "Descended of an ancient line" ("Tyrrhena regum progenies"), *paraphrased by* Dryden. OBVE
(Happy the Man, *st.* 8 *only.*) FaPoR
(Horat. Ode 29. Book 3.) SeCV-2
(To Maecenas, *tr. by* Dryden.) AWP
III, 30. This Monument Will Outlast ("Exegi momumentum aere perennius," *tr. by* Ezra Pound.) CTC
IV, 1. To Venus ("Intermissa, Venus"), *tr. by* Ben Jonson. AWP; OBVE
("Again? New tumults in my breast?" *tr. by* Pope.) PeHV
IV, 2. The Praise of Pindar ("Pindarum quisquis studet aemulari"), *tr. by* Abraham Cowley. OAEL-1
IV, 7. "The snow dissolv'd no more is seen" ("Diffugere nives"), *tr. by* Samuel Johnson. LAuP; OBVE
(Diffugere Nives, *tr. by* A. E. Housman.) OBVE
IV, 9. Immortality of Verse, The, *tr. by* Pope. AWP

IV, 10. "O Ligurinus" ("O crudelis adhuc"). PeHV
(To Ligurinus, *tr. by* Sir Edward Sherburne.) CavP
IV, 13. Revenge ("Audivere, Lyce"), *tr. by* Louis Untermeyer. AWP
Odes, *sel.* Pindar, *tr. fr. Greek.*
Island of the Blest, The, *fr.* Olympian Ode II, *tr. by* Gilbert West. OBEC
Odes, *sel.* George Santayana.
Ode to the Mediterranean. EtS
Odes, *sels.* Tibullus, *tr. fr. Latin by* John Dart. PeHV
"And you, whate'er your Fav'rite does, approve," *fr.* I, 4.
"Far from the tender tribe of boys remove," *fr.* I, 4.
Odes of Anacreon, *sel.* Thomas Moore.
"Women tell me every day, The," VII. LoBV
Odes to Nea, *sels.* Thomas Moore.
"I pray you, let us roam no more." OBNC
(I Pray You.) OBRV
"Nay, tempt me not to love again." OBNC
Odi et Amo. Catullus, *tr. fr. Latin by* Ezra Pound. CTC
("I hate and love. Why? You may ask but," *tr. by* Ezra Pound.) OBVE
("I love and hate. Ah! never ask why so!" *tr. by* Walter Savage Landor.) OBVE
(To Lesbia, *tr. by* Abraham Cowley.) PoPl
Odiham. John Gray. FaBoCo
O'Donnell Aboo. Michael Joseph McCann. FSW; OnYI
Odor of Blood, The. Thomas McGrath. NePoEA
Odorous shade lingers the fair day's ghost, An. Night. Henri de Regnier, *tr. by* "Seumas O'Sullivan." AWP
Odour, The. George Herbert. AnAnS-1; OBS
O'Driscoll drove with a song. The Host of the Air. W. B. Yeats. BrPo; CH; OnYI; SeCeV
O'Duffy's Ironsides. "Tom Moore, Jr." OnYI
Odysseus. Padraic Fallon. CIP
Odysseus. W. S. Merwin. NOBA; NoP
Odysseus and the Phaeacian Games. Homer, *tr. fr. Greek by* Ennis Rees. *Fr.* The Odyssey, VIII. LiSp
Odysseus Dying. Sheila Wingfield. OxBI
Odysseus heard the sirens; they were singing. The Sirens. John Manifold. LiTB; LiTM; MoBrPo; WaP
Odysseus' Song to Calypso. Peter Kane Dufault. ErPo
Odysseus to Telemachus. Joseph Brodsky, *tr. fr. Russian by* George L. Kline. PAI
Odysseus, twenty years gone, was recognized. Advice to a Prizefighter. Lucilius, *tr. fr. Greek by* Tom Dodge. LiSp
Odyssey, The, *sels.* Homer, *tr. fr. Greek.*
"And now Eurynome had bath'd the king," *fr.* XXIII, *tr. by* George Chapman. OBVE
"And now his well-known bow the master bore," *fr.* XXI, *tr. by* Pope. OBVE
"And now man-slaughtering Pallas took in hand," *fr.* XXII, *tr. by* George Chapman. OBVE
"And now the Queene of women had intent," *fr.* XXI, *tr. by* George Chapman. OBVE
"Cave we found, but vacant all within, The," *fr.* IX, *tr. by* Pope. OBVE
"Close to the gates a spacious garden lies," *fr.* VII, *tr. by* Pope. OBVE
"Downe to the king's most bright-kept baths they went," *fr.* IV, *tr. by* George Chapman. CTC
End of the Suitors, The, *fr.* XXII, *tr. by* George Chapman. OBS
"Far gone in weariness, in oblivion," *fr.* VI, *tr. by* Robert Fitzgerald. NAWM-1
"For my part, I'le not meddle with the cause," *fr.* XIV, *tr. by* George Chapman. CTC
"From her bed's high and odoriferous roome," *fr.* IV, *tr. by* George Chapman. CTC
Gardens of Alcinous, The ("Close to the gates a spacious garden lies"), *fr.* VII, *tr. by* Pope. OAEL-1
Gardens of Alcinous, The ("Without the hall, and close upon the gate"), *fr.* VII, *tr. by* George Chapman. OAEL-1
"God who mounts the winged winds, The," *fr.* V, *tr. by* Pope. OBVE
"He ended, nor the Argicide refus'd," *fr.* V, *tr. by* William Cowper. OBVE
"Just then, forgetful of the strict command," *fr.* XII, *tr. by* William Cowper. OBVE
"Mighty wave rush'd o'er him as he spoke, A," *fr.* V, *tr. by* Pope. OBVE
Nausicaa, *fr.* VI, *tr. by* George Chapman. OBS
New Coasts and Poseidon's Son, IX, *tr. by* Robert Fitzgerald. WTO
"Now gently winding up the fair ascent, " *fr.* XXI, *tr. by* Pope. OBVE
"Now to dispose of the dead, the care remains," *fr.* XXII, *tr. by* Pope. OBVE
"Now toils the Heroe; trees on trees o'erthrown," *fr.* V, *tr. by* Pope. OBVE
"Nymph turnd home, The. He fell to felling downe," *fr.* V, *tr. by* George Chapman. OBVE
Odysseus and the Phaeacian Games, *fr.* VIII, *tr. by* Ennis Rees. LiSp
Sacrifice, The, *fr.* III, *tr. by* George Chapman. OBS
Scylla and Charybdis, *fr.* XII, *tr. by* George Chapman. OBS
" 'She thus; when I had great desire to prove,' " *fr.* XI, *tr. by* George Chapman. OBVE
"Then tooke they seate, and forth our passage strooke," *fr.* XII, *tr. by* George Chapman. MOS
"There grew two olives, closest of the grove," *fr.* V, *tr. by* Pope. OBVE
"This spoke, a huge wave tooke him by the head," *fr.* V, *tr. by* George Chapman. MOS; OBVE
"Thus charg'd he; nor Argicides denied," *fr.* V, *tr. by* George Chapman. OBVE
"Trembling the spectres glide, and plaintive vent," *fr.* XXIV, *tr. by* Pope. OBVE
"Twelve herds of oxen, no less flockes of sheepe," *fr.* XIV, *tr. by* George Chapman. CTC
Ulysses and His Dog, *fr.* XVII, *tr. by* Pope. FiP; OBEC
Ulysses Hears the Prophecies of Tiresias, *fr.* XI, *tr. by* George Chapman. LoBV
Ulysses Leaves the Nymph Calypso, *fr.* V, *tr. by* George Chapman. JCP
Ulysses in the Waves, *fr.* V, *tr. by* George Chapman. OBS
"Under the opening fingers of the dawn," *fr.* VIII-XI, *tr. by* Robert Fitzgerald. NAWM-1
"Where neither king nor shepheard want comes neare," *fr.* IV, *tr. by* George Chapman. CTC
"While thus he thought, a monst'rous wave up-bore," *fr.* V, *tr. by* Pope. OBVE
"Without the hall, and close upon the gate," *fr.* VII, *tr. by* George Chapman. OBVE
"Youth there was, Elpenor was he nam'd, A," *fr.* X, *tr. by* Pope. OBVE
Odyssey, The. Andrew Lang. HBV-2; LoBV; OBEV; OBNC; OBVV; PoLF; PoRA; ViBoPo; WHA
Odyssey of Big Boy. Sterling A. Brown. BANP; CDC
Oeconomy of Love, The; a Poetical Essay, *sel.* John Armstrong.
Advice to Lovers. NOEC
Oedipus. Thomas Blackburn. FaBoTw
Oedipus, *sel.* Dryden.
Incantation to Oedipus, *fr.* III, i. OFD; WSC
(Spell, A.) WiR
Oedipus. David Ignatow. PAI
Oedipus. Josephine Miles. WPE
Oedipus. Edwin Muir. CMoP
Oedipus at Colonus, *sels.* Sophocles, *tr. fr. Greek.*
Chorus: "What man is he that yearneth," *tr. by* A. E. Housman. AWP
("Endure what life God gives and ask no longer span," *tr. by* W. B. Yeats). DTC; OBMV
Colonus' Praise, *tr. by* W. B. Yeats. OBVE
Oedipus at San Francisco. Donald Finkel. CoPo
Oedipus, Pentheus. David Bromwich. AMV-81
Oedipus Rex [*or* Oedipus Tyrannus]. Sophocles, *tr. fr. Greek by* Luci Berowitz *and* Theodore F. Brunner. NAWM-1 Chorus: "Oh, may my constant feet not fail," *tr. by* Robert Whitelaw, *sel.* WGRP
Oedipus to the Oracle. Wesley Trimpi. NePoEA
Oedipus Tyrannus. Sophocles. *See* Oedipus Rex.
Oenone. Tennyson. OAEP; OBRV; ViBoPo; VLP
Oenone and Paris. George Peele. *See* Fair and Fair.
Oenone's Complaint. George Peele. *Fr.* The Arraignment of Paris. ElL; OBSC
O'er a low couch the setting sun had thrown its latest ray. The Baron's Last Banquet. Albert Gorton Greene. AA; BeLS
O'er a small suburban borough. The Domineering Eagle and the Inventive Bratling. Guy Wetmore Carryl. OBAL
O'er all my song the image of a face. The Negro Singer. James David Corrothers. BANP
O'er [*or* Over] all the hill-tops. Wanderer's Night-Songs, II [*or* The Second Poem the Night-Walker Wrote]. Goethe. AWP, *tr. by* Longfellow; NU, *tr, by* Robert Bly; PoPl, *tr. by* Longfellow
O'er books the mind inactive lies. Conversation. Hannah More. *Fr.* Bas Bleu. OBEC
O'er Cambridge set the yeoman's mark. Lexington. Sidney Lanier. *Fr.* Psalm of the West. PAH; PAL
O'er Continent and Ocean, *with music.* John Haynes Holmes. AH
O'er desert plains, and rushy meers. Song. William Shenstone. FaBoEn
O'er faded heath-flowers spun or thorny furze. The Gossamer. Charlotte Smith. ViBoPo
O'er golden sands my waters flow. The Enchanted Spring. George Darley. BoNaP; NBM
O'er Huron's wave the sun was low. The Battle of Bridgewater. *Unknown.* PAH
O'er sunbaked plains he winds his way. The Rattlesnake. Robert V. Carr. PoOW
O'er the glad waters of the dark-blue sea. Song of the Corsairs. Byron. EtS
O'er the high and o'er the lowly. Our National Banner. Dexter Smith. PAH

O'er the level plains, where mountains greet me as I go. Time's Song. Winthrop Mackworth Praed. EnRP; NBM
O'er the men of Ethiopia she would pour her cornucopia. Husband and Heathen. Sam Walter Foss. OBAL
O'er the rough main, with flowing sheet. The *Bonhomme Richard* and *Serapis.* Philip Freneau. PAH
O'er the rugged mountain's brow. Some Ruthless Rhymes, VI. Harry Graham. CenHV
O'er [*or* O're] the smooth enamel[l]ed green. Song. Milton. *Fr.* Arcades. LoBV; OBEV; TrGrPo; ViBoPo
O'er the snow, through the air, to the mountain. Alpine Spirit's Song. Thomas Lovell Beddoes. OBNC
O'er the warrior gauntlet grim. Parricide. Julia Ward Howe. PAH
O'er the waste of waters cruising. Song. Philip Freneau. PAH
O'er the Water to Charlie. Burns. FaBoCh
O'er the wet sands an insect crept. An Autograph. James Russell Lowell. AA
O'er the wide-spreading plains rolled the emigrant trains. The Dust of the Overland Trail. James Barton Adams. PoOW
O'er the Wild Gannet's Bath. George Darley. *Fr.* Ethelstan. ChTr; PoEL-4
(Runilda's Chant.) OnYi
O'er the yellow crocus on the lawn. A Russian Fantasy. Nathan Haskell Dole. AA
O'er this huge town, rife with intestine wars. Manchester by Night. Mathilde Blind. SBG
O'er town and cottage, vale and height. Valley Forge. Thomas Buchanan Read. *Fr.* The Wagoner of the Alleghanies. PAH
O'er Waiting Harp-Strings of the Mind, *with music.* Mary Baker Eddy. AH
Of a brazier's daughter who lived near. The Betrayed Maiden. *Unknown.* OBET
Of a Certain Green-eyed Monster. Esther Lilian Duff. HBMV
Of a Contented Mind. Thomas, Lord Vaux. ElL; EnRePo; GoBC
(Content.) OBSC; QFR
(On a Contented Mind.) HBV-2
Of a Daw. John Heywood. PBBP
Of a Fair Lady Playing with a Snake. Edmund Waller. *See* To a Fair Lady Playing . . .
Of a Fair Shrew. Sir John Harington. *See* Fair, Rich, and Young.
Of a fallen sparrow, the prairie dog first softens. Gnawing the Breast. Sandra McPherson. LCAP
Of a great heroine I mean to tell. Earl of Rochester. *Fr.* A Panegyric on Nelly. UnTE
Of a Lady That Refused to Dance with Him. Earl of Surrey. SiPS
Of a little take a little. *Unknown.* OxNR
Of a Mistress. Sir Aston Cokayne. CavP
Of a pendulum's mildness, with her feet up. A Timepiece. James Merrill. HoPM; NePoEA-2; NoAM
Of a Poet Patriot. Thomas MacDonagh. HBMV; OnYI; OxBI
(On a Poet Patriot.) AnIV
Of a Rich Miser. George Turberville. EnRePo
Of a Rose, a Lovely Rose. *Unknown.* OBEV; OxBM; OxBoCh
Of a Spider. Wilfred Thornley. FaPON; PDV
Of a steady winking beat between. Paraphrase. Hart Crane. MoVE; TwAmPo
Of a tall stature and of sable hue. Charles II [*or* An Historical Poem]. *Unknown.* APAS; FaBoEE
Of A' the Airts [the Wind Can Blaw]. Burns. AWP; EnRP; GoTS; LoBV; NoP; OAEP; OBEC; OxBS; ViBoPo
(I Love My Jean.) BiP; GN; HBV-1, *with 2 add. sts. by* John Hamilton; LAuP
(Jean.) GTBS; GTBS-P; OBEV; TreFS; TrGrPo
Of a' the festivals we hear. Hallowe'en. John Mayne. HBV-2
Of a' the maids o' fair Scotland. Young Benjie. *Unknown.* OxBB
Of a Woman, Dead Young. Dorothy Parker. SBG
Of a Zealous Lady. Sir John Harington, *after the Latin of* Martial. FaBoEE
Of Adam's first wife, Lilith, it is told. Body's Beauty [*or* Lilith]. Dante Gabriel Rossetti. The House of Life, LXXVIII. HBV-1; OAEL-2; PoEL-5; TrGrPo; VLP
Of all chaste birds the phoenix doth excel. Of Rosalind. Thomas Lodge. GoBC
Of all creatures women be best. What Women Are Not. *Unknown.* MeEl
Of all great Nature's tones that sweep. Implicit Faith. Aubrey Thomas De Vere. May Carols, Pt. II, lxiv. GoBC
Of all mad creatures, if the learn'd are right. Why Did I Write? Pope. *Fr.* Epistle to Dr. Arbuthnot. OBEC
Of all our bath-house thieves the cleverest one. Catullus, *tr. fr. Latin by* James Michie. DBV; PeHV
Of All Plants, the Tree. Mary Jane White. AMV-80
Of all sad words of tongue or pen. The Saddest Words. Whittier. *Fr.* Maud Muller. NePA
Of all that Orient lands can vaunt. The Haschish. Whittier. OBAL
Of all the animals on earth. Christmas Song. Elizabeth-Ellen Long. SiSoSe
Of all the beasts which we for our veneriall name. Michael Drayton. *Fr.* Polyolbion, Thirteenth Song. OBS
Of All the Birds. George Gasciogne. *See* Praise of Philip Sparrow, The.
Of all the birds from East to West. Chanticleer. Katharine Tynan. HBV-1; HBVY; TiPo
Of all the birds I know. The Toucan. Pyke Johnson, Jr. NTCP
Of All the Birds That I Do Know. George Gascoigne. *See* Praise of Philip Sparrow, The.
Of all the brave captains that ever were seen. Sir Dilberry Diddle, Captain of Militia. *Unknown.* NOEC
Of all the causes which conspire to blind. Pride, the Never-Failing Vice of Fools. Pope. *Fr.* Essay on Criticism, Pt. II. FaBoEn; NOEC; NoP; OAEP; PPoe; TreFT
Of all the creatures, in the world, that be. John Oldham, *after the French of* Boileau. *Fr.* Satires, VIII. OBVE
Of all the flowers rising now. Maritae Suae. William Philpot. OBEV; OBVV
Of all the fonts from which man's heart has drawn. The Guerdon of the Sun. George Sterling. HBMV
Of all the gay birds that e'er I did see. *Unknown.* PBBP
Of all the gay places the world can afford. Letter Containing a Panegyric on Bath. Christopher Anstey. *Fr.* The New Bath Guide. OBEC
Of all the gentle tenants of the place. Sons of Indolence. James Thomson. *Fr.* The Castle of Indolence. OBEC
Of all the girls that are so smart. Sally in Our Alley [*or* The Ballad of Sally in our Alley]. Henry Carey. AWP; BLPL; BLSO, *with music;* BoLoP; CoMu; FaBoBe; FaFP; FSW; GTBS; GTBS-P; HBV-1; InMe; NOBE; NOEC; OBEC; OBEV; PoPle; PoSC, *abr.;* TreF; ViBoPo
Of all the girls that e'er were seen. Ballad. John Gay. CoMu; ErPo
Of all the grain our nation yields. A Panegyric upon Oates. Richard Duke. APAS
Of all the kings that ever here did reign. Astrophel and Stella, LXXV. Sir Philip Sidney. SiPS
Of all the Lombards, by their trophies knowne. Sir William Davenant. *Fr.* Gondibert, I, i. SeCV-1
Of All the Men. Thomas Moore. FiBHP
Of all the old times. The China Policy. Carl Rakosi. FAZ
Of all the pleasant ways. Driving in the Park. *Unknown.* OxBoLi
Of all the problems no one's solved. Minnie Morse. Kaye Starbird. PH
Of all the rides since the birth of time. Skipper Ireson's Ride. Whittier. AA; AP; BeLS; HBV-2; InMe; NOBA; OBAL; OBCA; OxBA; PAH; PoLF; TreFS; YaD
Of all the sayings in this world. *Unknown.* OxNR
Of all the seas that's coming. *Unknown.* EBEV
Of all the shafts to Cupid's bow. The Three Arrows. Edward Fitzgerald. OBVV
Of all the ships upon the blue. Captain Reece. W. S. Gilbert. CenHV; EvOK; FiBHP; GN; HBV-2
Of all the souls that stand create. Emily Dickinson. AmPP; AP; NePA; TrGrPo
(Choice.) AA
Of all the sounds despatched abroad. The Wind. Emily Dickinson. TwAmPo
Of all the stars that bathe the heavens in glory. La Donna È Mobile. "A. K." FiBHP; InMe
Of all the tales of human struggle, hear this one from Tennessee. Bryan's Last Battle. *Unknown.* AmFP
Of all the tales was ever told. Mary Arnold the Female Monster. *Unknown.* GBP; OBET
Of all the thoughts of God that are. The Sleep. Elizabeth Barrett Browning. HBV-2; TRV; WGRP
Of all the torments, all the cares. Rivals [*or* The Rival *or* Song]. *At. to* Sir George Etherege *and to* William Walsh CavP; HBV-1; OBEC; OBEV; ViBoPo
Of all the trees in England. Trees. Walter de la Mare. OHIP
Of all the various lots around the ball. The Poet: A Rhapsody. Mark Akenside. PP
Of all the ways of traveling in earth and air and sea. Flight Plan. Jane Merchant. RHPC
Of all the weathers wind is king. King Wind. Mark Van Doren. NCSH
Of all the wild deeds upon murder's black list. Verses on Daniel Good. *Unknown.* CoMu; OxBB
Of all the wimming doubly blest. A Grain of Salt. Wallace Irwin. HBV-2; WhC
Of all the wives as e'er you know. Nancy Lee. *Unknown.* AmSS
Of all thes kene conquerours to carpe it were kynde. The Tournament of Tottenham. *Unknown.* OxBoLi
Of All Things for You to Go Away Mad. Joanne Kyger. PoM
Of all things human which are strange and wild. James Thomson. *Fr.* The City of Dreadful Night. LoBV; ViBoPo

Of all trades agoing, begging it is my delight. The Happy Beggarman. *Unknown.* OnYI
Of all wemen that ever were borne. Mary Complains to Other Mothers. *Unknown.* MeEl
Of all who died in silence far away. Iris Tree. SUMH
Of Ameinias nothing more is known for sure. Ameinias. John Simon. ELU
Of an Ancient Spaniel in Her Fifteenth Year. Christopher Morley. GDP
Of an Heroical Answer of a Great Roman Lady to Her Husband. Sir John Harington. BoLoP; ErPo
Of an Old Con. George Mosby, Jr. LFAC
Of an old King in a story. Variations on an Air: After W. B. Yeats. G. K. Chesterton. BXAP; FaBoPa; NOBL; Par
Of an Old Song. William E. H. Lecky. WGRP
(On an Old Song.) HBV-2
Of an old souldier of the Queens. An Old Souldier of the Queens. *Unknown.* OBS
Of an Orchard. Katharine Tynan. GoBC; HBV-1; OBVV; WGRP
Of Angels. E. L. Mayo. FAZ
Of asphodel, that greeny flower. William Carlos Williams. *Fr.* Asphodel, That Greeny Flower. CMoP; PP
Of Astraea. Sir John Davies. *Fr.* Hymns to Astraea. TrGrPo
Of Autumn. Veronica Porumbacu, *tr. fr. Rumanian by* Willis Barnstone *and* Matei Calinescu. BoWoP; VWA
Of Baiting the Lion. Sir Owen Seaman. NA
Of beasts am I, of men was he most brave. The Lion over the Tomb of Leonidas. *Unknown, tr. by* Walter Leaf. AWP
Of Beauty. Giovanni Battista Guarini, *tr. fr. Italian by* Sir Richard Fanshawe. BoLoP; InMe
(Beauty.) GBL
Of Being Numerous, *sels.* George Oppen.
"In this nation." GOA
It Is Difficult Now to Speak of Poetry. NNaP
Of Birds and Birders. John Heywood. PBBP
Of Books. John Florio. ElL
Of Boston in New England. William Bradford. SCAP
Of bricks . . . Who built it? Like some crazy balloon. Our Youth. John Ashbery. CAPP; ConAP; SOTW; VGW
Of bright cities/ and citrus. Florida. Carl Rakosi. TAP
Of bronze and blaze. Emily Dickinson. AP; MoPo
(Aurora.) TwAmPo
Of caterpillars Fabre tells how day after day. Caterpillars. John Freeman. ChMP
Of Caution. Francesco da Barberino, *tr. fr. Italian by* Dante Gabriel Rossetti. AWP
Of Certain Irish Fairies. Arthur Guiterman. PoLF
Of Clementina. Walter Savage Landor. HBV-1; OBEV; OBRV
(In Clementina's Artless Mien.) ViBoPo
Of college I am tired; I wish to be at home. Home-Sickness. Charlotte Brontë. GLGT
Of comfort no man speak! Let's Talk of Graves. Shakespeare. King Richard II, *fr.* III, ii. FaBoRV
Of Commerce and Society. Geoffrey Hill. NePoEA-2; PPoe
Of composts shall the Muse descend to sing. Compost [*or* How to Fertilize Soil]. James Grainger. *Fr.* The Sugar Cane. FaBoUs; NOEC
Of cool sweet dew and radiance mild. Simples. James Joyce. HBMV; PoPl
Of Corinna's Singing. Thomas Campion. *See* When to Her Lute Corinna Sings.
Of Course I Know. Zishe Landau, *tr. fr. Yiddish by* Ruth Whitman. VWA
Of course I prayed. Emily Dickinson. AP; BoWoP; MoAmPo
Of course I tried to tell him. Poets Hitchhiking on the Highway. Gregory Corso. NeAP; NoAM; PoM
Of course it is snowing. Dear Old Stockholm. Al Young. NPGG
Of course, the entire effort is to put myself. Thoughts during an Air Raid. Stephen Spender. MoBrPo; ViBoPo
Of course the heart is nothing. City. Joseph Stroud. NPGG
Of course when someone leaves you forever. Back. Angela McCabe. AmPA
Of course you have read of the wicked ways. The Ballad of Chicken Bill. F. E. Vaughn. PoOW
Of Courtesy. Arthur Guiterman. TiPo
Of Courtesy, it is much less. Courtesy. Hilaire Belloc. ACP; HBMV
Of Cupid. Henry Chettle. *Fr.* Piers Plainness' Seven Years' Prenticeship. ElL
(Aeliana's Ditty.) OBSC
Of Curious Questions. Martin Farquhar Tupper. VLP
Of Cynthia. *Unknown.* OBSC
Of Dancing. Alan Brownjohn. FaBoMo
Of Dandelions & Tourists. Joe Rosenblatt. NOBC
Of De Witt Williams on His Way to Lincoln Cemetery. Gwendolyn Brooks. CAPP; NoAM; NOBA
Of Death. Countess of Pembroke. *Fr.* Antonius. ElL
Of Death. James Shirley. *See* Glories of Our Blood and State, The.
Of deepest blue of summer skies. Alice. Herbert Bashford. HBV-1
Of Disdainful Daphne. M. H. Nowell. ElL
Of diverse monsters I have sometimes read. Strange Monsters. Rowland Watkyns. FaBoEE
Of Drunkenness. George Turberville. NoP
Of Dying Beauty. Louis Zukofsky. PoA
Of Eden lost, in ancient days. Rondeau Humbly Inscribed to the Right Hon. William Eden, Minister Plenipotentiary of Commercial Affairs at the Court of Versailles. *At. to* George Ellis. OBEC
Of Edenhall the youthful lord. The Luck of Edenhall. Ludwig Uhland, *tr. by* Longfellow. AWP
Of England, and of Its Marvels. Fazio degli Uberti, *tr. fr. Italian by* Dante Gabriel Rossetti. AWP
Of English Verse. Edmund Waller. AnAnS-2; CavP; OAEL-1; OBS; PP; SeCP
Of every kinne [*or* everykune] tree, of every kinne tree. The Hawthorn. *Unknown.* ChTr; GBP; OxBM
Of every vice pursued by those. Gambling. Royall Tyler. TAP
Of everykunė tre. *See* Of every kinne tree . . .
Of Februar the fifteen nicht. *See* Off Februar the fyiftene nycht.
Of few words, Sir, you seem to be. *Unknown.* SiPS
Of Fiammetta Singing. Boccaccio, *tr. fr. Italian by* Dante Gabriel Rossetti. *Fr.* Sonnets. AWP
(Fiammetta.) GoBC
Of Flowers. Alan Loney. OCNZ
Of Fortune, *abr.* Thomas Kyd. *Fr.* Cornelia. ElL
Of fret, of dark, of thorn, of chill. Opposition. Sidney Lanier. LiTA
Of Giving. Arthur Guiterman. TiPo
Of God we ask one favor. Emily Dickinson. EaLo
Of Gods Omnipotencie. Alexander Hume. NOCV
Of green and hexagonal glass. The Bottle. Walter de la Mare. MoPo
Of Heaven Considered as a Tomb. Wallace Stevens. PoA; QFR
Of Heaven or Hell I have no power to sing. An Apology [*or* Prologue *or* The Singer's Prelude]. William Morris. *Fr.* The Earthly Paradise. AWP; EBVV; FaBoEn; HBV-2; LiTB; LoBV; NoP; OAEL-2; OAEP; OBNC; ViBoPo; VLP
Of heavenly stature, but most human smile. Written in the Visitors' Book at the Birthplace of Robert Burns. George Washington Cable. AA
Of her friends at the textile mill. The Labor Camp. John Pijewski. AMV-81
Of heroes and statesmen I'll just mention. Paul Jones—a New Song. *Unknown.* PAH
Of high Honour should be her hood. The Garment of Good Ladies. Robert Henryson. ACP
Of Himself. Meleager, *tr. fr. Greek by* Richard Garnett. AWP
Of His Cynthia. Fulke Greville. Caelica, LII. ElL; ELP; NoP
("Away with these self-loving lads.") EnRePo
(Cynthia.) OBSC
(Song to His Cynthia.) ViBoPo
Of His Dear Son, Gervase. Sir John Beaumont. *Fr.* Of My Dear Son, Gervase Beaumont. OBEV
("Dear Lord, receive my son, whose winning love.") GoBC
Of His Death. Meleager, *tr. fr. Greek by* Andrew Lang. AWP
Of His Divine Poems. Edmund Waller. *See* Of the Last Verses in the Book.
Of His Lady. *Unknown.* ElL
Of His Lady's Old Age. Pierre de Ronsard, *tr. fr. French by* Andrew Lang. AWP; CTC
Of His Last Sight of Fiammetta. Boccaccio, *tr. fr. Italian by* Dante Gabriel Rossetti. *Fr.* Sonnets. AWP
(Fiammetta.)
Of His Majesties Receiving the News of the Duke of Buckingham's Death. Edmund Waller. SeCV-1
Of His Mistress. Robert Greene. *Fr.* Menaphon. ElL
Of His Returne from Spaine. Sir Thomas Wyatt. *See* Tagus, Farewell.
Of History More Like Myth. Jean Garrigue. NYBP
Of How Scientists Are Often Ahead of Others in Thinking, While the Average Man Lags Behind; and How the Economist (Who Can Only Follow in the Footsteps of the Average Man Looking for Clues to the Future), Remains Thoroughly Out of It. Michael Benedikt. SUW
Of how your poems. A Letter to Paul Celan in Memory. Jerome Rothenberg. VWA
Of Human Bondage. Miller Williams. NYP
Of Human Learning, *sel.* Fulke Greville.
"Chiefe use then in man of that he knowes, The." OBS
Of Human Life. Henry King. *See* Sic Vita.
Of Invention, *sel.* Martin Farquhar Tupper.
"Behold the barren reef, which an earthquake hath just left dry." VLP
Of inviting to dine, in Epirus. A Difficult Guest. Carroll Watson Rankin. TDH
Of Iron Am I. *Malay Oral Tradition, tr. by* W. W. Skeat. WTO

Of Jeoffry, His Cat. Christopher Smart. *See* For I Will Consider My Cat Jeoffry.
Of Jesu Christ I Sing. *Unknown.* OxBM
Of Joan's Youth. Louise Imogen Guiney. AA; HBV-1
Of John Bunyans Life. John James. SCAP
Of John Cabanis' wrath and of the strife. The Spooniad. Edgar Lee Masters. OBAL
Of Jolly Good Ale and Old. William Stevenson. *See* Back and Side Go Bare, Go Bare
Of Jonathan Chapman two things are known. Johnny Appleseed. Rosemary Benét. TrAS
Of Kate's Baldness. John Davies of Hereford. FaBoEE
Of Kings and Things. Lillian Morrison. CAD; NCSH
Of Late. George Starbuck. VGW
Of late/ Since I parted from Liadin. Liadin and Curither. *Unknown, tr. by* Kuno Meyer. OnYI
Of late a noble steamer, the *Cedar Grove* by name. The Loss of the *Cedar Grove. Unknown.* ShS
Of lead and emerald. A Note to Olga (1966). Denise Levertov. CAPP
Of Leinster, fam'd for maidens fair. Colin and Lucy. Thomas Tickell. OBEC
Of Liddisdale [*or* Liddesdale] the common thievis [*or* thieves]. Aganis the Thievis of Liddisdale [*or* Against the Thieves of Liddesdale]. Sir Richard Maitland. BSV; GoTS
Of Life and Death, *sel.* Henry Vaughan.
Winged Heart, A. FaBoRV
Of life the darkest part is solitude. From Mistra: A Prospect. Ted Higgs. AMV-80
Of Little Faith. Harold T. Pulsifer. EtS
Of little use the man you may suppose. The Poet's Use. Pope. *Fr.* The First Epistle of the Second Book of Horace. EBEV; OBEC
Of living creatures most I prize. Butterfly. William Jay Smith. GoJo; TiPo
Of London Bridge, and the Stupendous Sight, and Structure Thereof. James Howell. ChTr; FaBoPP
Of Love. Kahlil Gibran. *Fr.* The Prophet. PoLF
Of Love. James Sandford. ElL
Of love he sang, full hearted one. A Forced Music. Robert Graves. MoBrPo
Of Love of Silence and of Solitude. Thomas à Kempis. *Fr.* Imitation of Christ. TreF
Of loves perfection perfectly to speake. Spenser. *Fr.* Colin Clouts Come Home Againe. OAEL-1
Of Loving at First Sight. Edmund Waller. SeCP
Of M, A, R, I,/ Sing I will a new song. M and A, R and I. *Unknown.* OxBM
Of Maids' Inconstancy. Richard Brathwaite. *Fr.* A Strappado for the Devil. ElL
Of Man and Nature. Horace Mungin. BOLo
Of Man and Wife. Richard Eedes. *See* No Love, to Love of Man and Wife.
Of Manners gentle, of affections mild. On Mr. Gay; In Westminster Abbey, 173). PoPe; Fip
Of Man's first disobedience, and the fruit. Invocation to the Heavenly Muse. Milton. *Fr.* Paradise Lost, I. EBEV; FaBoEn; FaBoRV; FiP; NIP; NoP; OAEL-1; OAEP; PoEL-3; SCV; TEP; TreFS
Of many marvels in my time. A Description of a Strange (and Miraculous) Fish. Martin Parker. CoMu
Of many things adulterate. Epitaph. Tristan Corbière, *tr. by* Joseph T. Shipley. AWP
Of Mary. A New Song of Mary. *Unknown.* MeEL
Of May. Alexander Scott. OxBS
Of men, nay beasts: worse, monsters: worst of all. Phineas Fletcher. *Fr.* The Locusts, or Apollyonists. SeCV-1
Of Misery. Thomas Howell. ElL; FF
Of Mistress D. S. Barnabe Googe. EnRePo
Of Modern Poetry. Wallace Stevens. CABA; InvP; NePA; NIP; NoAM: OxBA; PP; PrIm; TAP
Of Money. Barnabe Googe. ElL; EnRePo; FF; NoP
Of Mouse and Men. A. J. Hovde. AMV-81
Of My Dear Son, Gervase Beaumont. Sir John Beaumont. JCP; NOBE, OBS; ViBoPo, *abr.*
"Dear Lord, receive my son, whose winning love, *sel*". GoBC
(Of His Dear Son, Gervase.) OBEV
Of My Lady Isabella Playing on the Lute. Edmund Waller. HAP; MePo
(On My Lady Isabella Playing on the Lute.) SeCP
Of my lady, wel me rejoise I may. Hoccleve's Humorous Praise of His Lady [*or* A Description of His Ugly Lady]. Thomas Hoccleve. MeEL; OAEP
Of my ould loves, of their ould ways. Memories. Arthur Stringer. HBV-1
Of Myself. Abraham Cowley. *See* This Only Grant Me.
Of Myself. Leah Goldberg, *tr. fr. Hebrew by* Ramah Commanday. BoWoP
Of myself, my dear joy, if you wish to be told. An Irishman's Christening. *Unknown.* OnYI
Of Nelson and the North. Battle of the Baltic. Thomas Campbell. EnRP; FaPoR; GN; GTBS; GTBS-P; HBV-2; NBM; OBEV; RoGo
Of Neptune's empire let us sing. A Hymn[e] in Praise [*or* Prayse] of Neptune. Thomas Campion. BoNaP; EtS; MOS; NOBE; OBEV; OBSC; WiR
Of Nicolette. E. E. Cummings. HBMV
Of Objects Considered as Fortresses in a Baleful Place. Hyam Plutzik. VGW
Of old, a man who died. Immortal Flowers. Wallace Rice. AA
Of old, all invitations ended. Thoughts on Being Invited to Dinner. Christopher Morley. HBMV
Of old our fathers' God was real. Exit God. Gamaliel Bradford. HBMV; InMe
Of Old Sat Freedom on the Heights. Tennyson. *Fr.* On a Mourner. HBV-2; OAEP
Of old the Muses sat on high. The Muses. Edith M. Thomas. HBV-2
Of old when folk lay sick and sorely tried. On Hygiene. Hilaire Belloc. DBV; MoBrPo
Of old when Nature, in her verve defiant. The Giantess. Baudelaire, *tr. by* Roy Campbell. OBVE
Of old, when Scarron his companions invited. Retaliation. Goldsmith. LaA; OAEP; OxBoLi
Of One Dead. Tennyson. *See* In Memoriam A. H. H.: "If one should bring me this report."
Of One Self-slain. Charles Hanson Towne. WGRP
Of One That Had a Great Nose. George Turberville, *after the Greek of* Trajan. FaBoEE
Of One [*or* On] That Is So Fair [or Fayr] and Bright. *Unknown. See* Hymn to the Virgin, A.
Of one who grew up at Gallipoli. War Story. Jon Stallworthy. DFF; ELU; OxBC
Of One Who neither Sees nor Hears. Richard Watson Glider. AA
Of One Who Seemed to Have Failed. S. Weir Mitchell. AA
Of Only a Single Poem. G. J. F. Dutton. PoSH
Of Order in Our Lord Christ. St. Francis of Assisi, *tr. by* Dante Gabriel Rossetti. *See* Cantica: Our Lord Christ: of Order.
Of Oystermen, Workboats. Dave Smith. MAYP
Of Pardons, Presidents, and Whiskey Labels. Richard Snyder. SOTS
Of people running down the street. A Picture. Howard Nemerov. OxBC
Of Perfect Friendship. Henry Cheke. ElL
Of Phyllis. William Drummond of Hawthornden. ElL; HBV-1
(Phyllis.) GN
Of priests we can offer a charmin' variety. Father O'Flynn. Alfred Perceval Graves. HBV-2; OnYI
Of Quarrels. Arthur Guiterman. TiPo
Of Rama. Herman Melville. LiTA
Of Robert Frost. Gwendolyn Brooks. NoAM; NOBA
Of Rome. Herman Melville. *Fr.* Clarel. OxBA
Of Rosalind. Thomas Lodge. GoBC
Of Scolding Wives and the Third Day Ague. Henricus Selyns. SCAP
Of seven sparrows on a country wire. Minus One. John Ciardi. HoAn
Of Sir Philip Sidney. Sir John Beaumont. GoBC
Of Snow. Norman Brick. WaP
Of Solitude. Abraham Cowley. OBS
(Essay on Solitude, *abr.*) ViBoPo
Solitude and Reason, in the Village, *sel.* FaBoPP
Of speckled eggs the birdie sings. Singing. Robert Louis Stevenson. SUS
Of Spencer's Faery Queen. Sir Walter Ralegh.
See Vision upon this Conceit of the Faerie Queene, A.
Of Suicide. John Berryman. NoAM
Of Tact. Arthur Guiterman. *See* How Are You?
Of Taste; an Essay, *sel.* James Cawthorn.
"Time was, an Englishman would join." NOEC
Of that Medusa strange. The Statue of Medusa. William Drummond of Hawthornden. EyDe
Of that time in a Southern jail. Galway Kinnell. *Fr.* The Call across the Valley of Not Knowing. GP
Of that wherein thou art a questioner. To Dante Alighieri: He Interprets Dante Alighieri's Dream. Dante da Maiano, *tr. by* Dante Gabriel Rossetti. AWP
Of that world, having returned from it, I may say. Voyage to the Moon. William Dickey. MOON
Of the beast. . .an angel. The Everlasting Contenders. Kenneth Patchen. CrMA; NaP
Of the beauty of kindness I speak. Kindness. T. Sturge Moore. OBMV
Of the Beloved Caravan. Conny Hannes Mayer, *tr. fr. German by* Herbert Kuhner. VWA
Of the birds that fly in the farthest sea. John Gray. The Flying Fish, II. ChTr; LoBV; OBNC

Of the Birth and Bringing Up of Desire. Edward de Vere, Earl of Oxford, *after the Latin of* George Buchanan. FaBoEE; OBSC
Of the Blessed Sacrament of the Altar. Robert Southwell. GoBC; OBEV
Of the Boy and Butterfly. Bunyan. NIP; OxBChV
Of the Characters of Women. Pope. *See* Moral Essays: Epistle to a Lady.
Of the Child with the Bird on the Bush. Bunyan. *See* My Little Bird.
Of the Clock and the Cock. George Turberville. EnRePo
Of the Courtier's Life. Sir Thomas Wyatt. GoTL; OBSC
(Mine Own John Poins.) NoP
(Satire I: "Mine own John Poynz.") AAS; OBSV; OBVE; PoEL-1; SiPS
Of the Cuckoo. Bunyan. PBBP
Of the dark past. Ecce Puer. James Joyce. BIrV; EBEV; NAs; NoAM; PoPl; TrCP
Of the Day Estivall. Alexander Hume. *See* A Summer Day.
Of the Death of Kings. Shakespeare. King Richard II, *fr.* III, ii. ChTr
("For God's sake, let us sit upon the ground.") HoPM
Of the Death of Sir T[homas]. W[yatt]. Earl of Surrey. FaBoEn
Of the Elmira Wood. Her Apron through the Trees. Roger Weingarten. AmPA
Of the fifth and order of the world. A Series 5.8. John Wieners. CoPo
Of the first Paradice there's nothing found. On St. James's Park, as Lately Improved by His Majesty. Edmund Waller. AnAnS-2
Of the Four Ages of Man, *sel.* Anne Bradstreet.
Four Ages of Man: Childhood. SBG
Of the French Kings Nativity. Benjamin Harris. SCAP
Of the Gentle Heart. Guido Guinicelli, *tr. fr. Italian by* Dante Gabriel Rossetti. GoBC
Of the goddess there is only the marble shoulder and one. The Interrupted. Josephine Jacobsen. GP
Of the Going Down of the Sun. Bunyan. CH
Of the Great and Famous Ever to Be Honoured Knight, Sir Francis Drake [and of My Little-Little Selfe]. Robert Hayman. CH; FaBoCh; NoP
Of the Holy Eucharist. *Unknown.* ACP
Of the Incomparable Treasure of the Scriptures. *Unknown.* TRV
Of the Last Verses in the Book. Edmund Waller. AnAnS-2; EBEV; FaBoEn; FaBoRV; HAP; HBV-1; MePo; NoP; OAEP; OBS; SeCP; SeCV-1; ViBoPo
(Of His Divine Poems.) LoBV
Sels.
Old Age. BLPL; NOBE; OBEV; TreFT
(Last Verses.) OxBoCh
("Seas are quiet when the winds give o'er, The.") NoCV
Soul's Dark Cottage, The. ChTr
Of the Loss of Time. John Hoskyns. FaBoEE
Of the manner in which he moves. A Walk in Early March. Paul Mariani. DiL
Of the Manner of Addressing Clouds. Wallace Stevens. PoA
(On the Manner of Addressing Clouds.) QFR
Of the many ills afflicting Greece. The Greek Athlete. Euripides, *tr. fr. Greek by* Tom Dodge. LiSp
Of the Mathematician. Alice Clear Matthews. GoYe
Of the million or two, more or less. Instans Tyrannus. Robert Browning. EBEV
Of the Moon. Charles Best. *See* Sonnet of the Moon, A.
Of the Nativity of the Lady Rich's Daughter. Henry Constable. OBSC
Of the New Prosody. Brewster Ghiselin. MoVE
Of the old house, only a few crumbled. The House That Was. Laurence Binyon. MoBrPo
Of the onset, fear-inspiring, and the firing and the pillage. The Sack of Deerfield. Thomas Dunn English. PAH
Of the Progress[e] of the Soule; the Second Anniversarie [*or* Anniversary]. John Donne. AnAnS-1; SeCP
Sels.
"Forget this rotten world; and unto thee." FaBoEn
Our Companie in the Next World. OBS
"Poor soul, in this thy flesh what dost thou know?" OAEL-1
(Soules Ignorance in This Life and Knowledge in the Next, The.) OBS
"Think then, my soul, that death is but a groom." OxBoCh
(Contemplation of Our State in Our Deathbed.) OBS
Of the Pythagorean Philosophy. Ovid, *tr. fr. Latin by* Dryden. *Fr.* Metamorphoses, XV. FM; OBVE
Of the Realme of Scotland. Sir David Lindsay. *Fr.* The Dreme. OxBS
Of the Resurrection of Christ. William Dunbar. *See* Done Is a Battle.
Of the Sad Lot of the Humanists in Paris. George Buchanan, *tr. fr. Latin.* GoTS
Of the Stalking of the Stag. Sir Owen Seaman. CenHV
Of the Surface of Things. Wallace Stevens. ELU
Of the Terrible Doubt of Appearances. Walt Whitman. NePA
Of the three Wise Men. Carol of the Brown King. Langston Hughes. PChr; SBVL
Of the unended in the speed of. Anne-Marie Albiach, *tr. by* Paul Auster. *Fr.* État. PBWP
Of the Use of Riches. Pope. Moral Essays, Epistle IV. PoEL-3
Of thee (kind boy) I ask no red and white. Sonnet [*or* Song]. Sir John Suckling. AnAnS-2; CaPo; LoBV; MeLP; MePo; NoP; OBS; OxBoLi; SeCP; SeCV-1
Of thee the Northman by his beachèd galley. Ode to the Mediterranean. George Santayana. *Fr.* Odes. EtS
Of them all—those laboring men who knew my first name. At the Sign-Painter's. Jared Carter. FYAP
Of thes four letters purpose I. A New Song of Mary. *Unknown.* MeEL
Of thes Frer Minours me thenkes moch wonder. Friars' Enormities. *Unknown.* MeEL
Of these the false Achitophel was first. Achitophel [*or* The False Achitophel *or* Shaftesbury]. Dryden. *Fr.* Absalom and Achitophel, Pt. I. AWP; FiP; HAP; InPS; OBS; PoEL-3; SeCePo; ViBoPo; WHA
Of these two spitefull rocks, the one doth shove. Scylla and Charybdis. Homer, *tr. by* George Chapman. *Fr.* The Odyssey, XII. OBS
Of this bad world the loveliest and the best. On a Dead Hostess. Hilaire Belloc. MoBrPo; MoVE
Of this fair[e] volume which we[e] World do[e] name. The Book of the World [*or* The Book *or* The World *or* The Lessons of Nature]. William Drummond of Hawthornden. CH; GTBS; GTBS-P; HBV-1; OBS
Of this house I know the backwindow. Eyeglasses. Tom Clark. ConAP
Of this world's theater in which we stay. Amoretti, LIV. Spenser. NIP; NoP; OAEL-1
Of Thomas Traherne and the Pebble Outside. Sydney Clouts. VWA
Of those around thee there is none who heeds. To Bülow. August, Graf von Platen, *tr. by* Reginald Bancroft Cooke. PeHV
Of those rebellions that we start in jest. Fear Test: Integrity of Heroes. James Simmons. CIP
Of Those Who Walk Alone. Richard Burton. HBV-1
Of those whom I have known, the few and fatal friends. Largo. Dunstan Thompson. LiTA; MoPo; WaP
Of Three Damsels in a Meadow. John Payne. OBVV
Of three eyes, I would still give two for one. The Third Eye. Jay Macpherson. MoCV
Of Three Girls and of Their Talk. Boccaccio, *tr. fr. Italian by* Dante Gabriel Rossetti. *Fr.* Sonnets. AWP
Of Three or Four in a Room. Yehuda Amichai, *tr. fr. Hebrew by* Stephen Mitchell. VWA
Of thy life [*or* lyfe], Thomas, this compass[e] well mark. The Golden Mean. Earl of Surrey, *after* Horace. OBVE; SiPS
Of Treason. Sir John Harington. FaBoEE; FF; InPK; OxBoLi
(Epigram: Of Treason.) NIP
(Epigram: "Treason doth never prosper; what's the reason?") HBV-1
(On Treason.) ELU; FiBHP
(Treason.) FaBoCo
(Treason Never Prospers.) InvP
Of True Liberty. Sir John Beaumont. OBS
Of two fair virgins, modest, though admired. On a Nun. Jacopo Vittorelli, *tr. by* Byron. AWP
Of Tyndarus, That Frumped a Gentlewoman. *Unknown, tr. fr. Latin by* Richard Stanyhurst. BIrV
Of us/ not much is known. Degli Sposi. Rika Lesser. FYAP
Of Use. John Heywood. FaBoEE; PBBP
Of virtures I most warmly bless. Gerard Manley Hopkins. FaBoEE
Of virtuous amusements, i.e. good conditions, are numbered. The Discriminations; Virtuous Amusements and Wicked Demons. Jim Bogan. PoDr
Of W. W. (Americanus). James Kenneth Stephen. *See* Sincere Flattery of W. W. (Americanus).
Of wealthy lustre was the banquet-room. The Banquet. Keats. *Fr.* Lamia. SeCePo
Of what a quality is courage made. Donagh MacDonagh. *Fr.* Charles Donnelly. CIP
"Of what are you afraid, my child?" inquired the kindly teacher. Wild Flowers. Peter Newell. NA; RHPC
Of what good can Paradise be. Paradise. Immanuel di Roma, *tr. by* J. Chotzner. TrJP
Of what mould did Nature frame me? The Tinder. Thomas Carew. CaPo
Of white and tawny, black as ink. Variation on a Sentence. Louise Bogan. FM; ImOP
Of Wit. Abraham Cowley. *See* Ode: Of Wit.
Of woman and wine, of woods and spring. Inexhaustible. Israel Zangwill. TrJP
Of Women. Richard Edwards. EIL
Of Women. *Unknown, tr. fr. Arabic by* E. Powys Mathers. *Fr.* The Thousand and One Nights. ErPo; PV
Of Women No More Evil. *Unknown, tr. fr. Late Middle Irish by* Robin Flower. AnIL

Of woods, of plains, of hills and dales. Upon a Rich Country Gentleman. *Unknown.* FaBoEE
Of worthy Captain Lovewell I purpose now to sing. Lovewell's Fight. *Unknown.* BaBo; HBV-2; PAH
Of Wounds. Sister Mary Madeleva. ISi
Of Wounds and Sore Defeat. William Vaughn Moody. *Fr.* The Fire-Bringer. HBV-2
Of you, if anyone, it can be said. Catullus, *tr. fr. Latin by* James Michie. DBV
Of Your Father's Indiscretions and the Train to California. Lynn Emanuel. MAYP
Of your trouble, Ben, to ease me. Her Man Described by Her Owne Dictamen. Ben Jonson. *Fr.* A Celebration of Charis. AnAnS-2; SeCP.
Of Youth He Singeth. Robert Wever. *See* In Youth Is Pleasure.
Off a Puritane. *Unknown. See* Two Puritans.
Off all the lords in faire Scottland. The Heir of Linne. *Unknown.* ESPB
Off an ancient story Ile tell you anon. King John and the Bishop. *Unknown.* ESPB
Off Brighton Pier. Alan Ross. OBWP
Off Broadway, where they sell those photographs. Manhattan Menagerie. Joseph Cherwinski. GoYe
Off Crane's Neck the sun. The Spirit of Wrath. William Heyen. AmPA; WOLT
Off [*or* Of] Februar the fyiftene nycht [*or* fifteen nicht]. The Dance of the Sevin Deidly Synnis [*or* Seven Deadly Sins]. William Dunbar. BSV; GoTS; OxBS
Off from Boston. *Unknown.* PAH
Off from Swing Shift. Garrett Kaoru Hongo. MAYP
Off from the shore at last he took his way. The Discoverer. Arthur Gordon Field. PGD
Off Guard. *Unknown.* CoSo
Off Highway 106. Cherrylog Road. James Dickey. BiP; CABA; CoAP; HAP; InPK; InPS; NIP; NYBP; PrIm; TwCP; WeW
Off in the twilight hung the low full moon. Full Moon. Sappho, *tr. by* William Ellery Leonard. AWP
"Off Manilly." Edmund Vance Cooke. PAH
Off Mindanao warm salt wind. Postcard from Zamboanga. Barbara J. Esbensen. PoDr
Off Molokai. Norman Hindley. WOLT
Off Portland: wind east, visibility eight. Hydrographic Report. Frances Frost. EtS
Off Rivière du Loup. Duncan Campbell Scott. EtS; HBV-1; OBCV
Off that landspit of stony mouth-plugs. Medusa. Sylvia Plath. CAPP
Off the coast of Hispaniola. Columbus and the Mermaids. Elizabeth J. Coatsworth. GOA
Off the track/ I blew. Phoenix. Carolyn M. Rodgers. JB
Off to Patagonia. Theodore Weiss. TAP
Off to Sea Once More, *2 vers., with music. Unknown.* ShS
Off to the Fishing Ground. L. M. Montgomery. CaP
Off Viareggio. Kenneth Pitchford. CoPo
Off with sleep, love, up from bed. Love in May. Jean Passerat, *tr. by* Andrew Lang. AWP
Off with your hat! along the street. The Marquis of Carabas. Robert Brough. HBV-1
Off with your hat as the flag goes by! The Old Flag. H. C. Bunner. PAL; PGD
Off Womanheid Ane Flour Delice. *Unknown.* OxBS
Offended, The. Anne Hébert, *tr. fr. French by* Willis Barnstone. BoWoP
Offender, The. Denise Levertov. NePoEA-2
Offensive, The. Keith Douglas. NeBP
Offer, An. Arthur Guiterman. DBV; TrJP
Offered a sexless heaven I'd say "No thank you." Ovid, *tr. by* Guy Lee. Amores, II, 9b. NAWM-1
Offering of the Heart Tapestry from Arras, XV Century, The. Rolfe Humphries. FYAP
Offering. *Unknown, tr. fr. Zuni Indian by* Ruth Bunzel, *ad. by* Robert Bly. NU
Offering, The: Part One. Mary Lee, Lady Chudleigh. WPE
Office building treads the marble dark, The. The Minute. Karl Shapiro. MiAP; MoVE
Office feels like a sealed glass case today, The. What Grandma Knew. Edward Field. CoPo; Psk
Office of Poetry, The. Nathaniel Whiting. *Fr.* Il Insonio Insonado. OBS
Office Party. Phyllis McGinley. OBSV
Officer Brady. Robert W. Chambers. InMe
Officers get all the steak[s], The. World War[s]. *Unknown.* FaFP; TreFT
Officers' Mess. Gavin Ewart. OxBTC
Officers' Mess (1916). Harold Monro. BrPo
Officers' Prison Camp Seen from a Troop Train, An. Randall Jarrell. WaP
Official document blows through a forest, An. The Long Picnic. Russell Edson. LCAP
Off'rings of the Eastern[e] kings of old, The. Royal[l] Presents. Nathaniel Wanley. OBS; OxBoCh
Offshore Breeze. Milton Acorn. NeAC
Off-shore, by islands hidden in the blood. I, Maximus of Gloucester, to You. Charles Olson. *Fr.* The Maximus Poems. LiTM; NoAM; NOBA; PoM
Offspring. Naomi Long Madgett. FB
Offspring of modern poetry, attend. Morning. *Unknown.* NOEC
Oft am I by the women told. Age. Abraham Cowley. AWP; CavP
Oft, as we run the weary way. Courage. Stopford Brooke. WGRP
Oft did I hear our eyes the passage were. Sir John Davies. *Fr.* Sonnets to Philomel. SiPS
Oft do I return/ To my little song. The Song of the Trout Fisher. Ikinilik, *tr. fr. Eskimo.* WTO
Oft has it been my lot to mark. The Chameleon. James Merrick. HBV-1
Oft has our Poet wisht, this happy Seat. Epilogue Spoken by Mrs. Boutell [*or* To the University of Oxford, 1674: Epilogue]. Dryden. FaBoEn; SeCV-2
Oft has this planet rolled around the sun. Sir Samuel Garth. *Fr.* The Dispensary. OBSV
Oft have I brooded on defeat and pain. Success. Emma Lazarus. SBG
Oft have I heard my lief[e] Corydon [*or* Coridon] report on a love-day. Hexametra Alexis in Laudem Rosamundi. Robert Greene. *Fr.* Greene's Mourning Garment. EIL; GBL; PoEL-2
Oft have I heard thee mourn the wretched lot. Charles Churchill. *Fr.* The Prophecy of Famine. OBSV
Oft Have I Mused. Sir Philip Sidney. *See* Farewell, A: "Oft have I mused, but now at length I find."
Oft have I mused the cause to find. Ladies' Eyes Serve Cupid Both for Darts and Fire. "A. W." OBSC
Oft have I played at cards and dice. The Rantin Laddie. *Unknown.* AmFP
Oft have I said, I say it once more. Hafiz, *tr. by* Emerson. Odes, XIII. AWP
Oft Have I Seen At Some Cathedral Door. Longfellow. Divina Commedia, I. GoBC; HBV-2; NePA; TreF
(Dante.) OBEV
(Divina Commedia, I [*or* I-IV].) AmPP; AP; HAP; OxBa; TAP; ViBoPo
(Three Sonnets on the Divina Commedia.) SeCeV
Oft have I seen, ere Time had ploughed my cheek. Decay of Piety. Wordsworth. TrCP
Oft have I seen, when that renewing breath. Resurrection and Immortality. Henry Vaughan. AnAnS-1
Oft have I sigh'd for him that heares me not. Thomas Campion. FaBoEn
Oft have I wakened ere the spring of day. Will It Be So? Edith M. Thomas. *Fr.* The Inverted Torch. AA
Oft have I walked these woodland paths. Under the Leaves. Albert Laighton. HBV-1; OHIP
Oft have we heard of impious sons before. The Female Parricide. *Unknown.* APAS
Oft have you seen a swan superbly frowning. To Charles Cowden Clarke. Keats. EnRP; PBBP, *abr.*
Oft I had heard of Lucy Gray. Lucy Gray; or, Solitude. Wordsworth. BeLS; CH; EnRP; FiP; HBV-1; OAEL-2; OAEP; OBRV; OxBChV; SeCeV; TEP; TreFS
Oft I have known thee, Hogarth, weak and vain. Hogarth. Charles Churchill. DBV
Oft I must strive with wind and wave. Anchor. *Unknown, tr. by* Charles W. Kennedy. *Fr.* Riddles (Exeter Book). AnOE
Oft in danger yet alive. To Mrs. Thrale [on Her Thirty-fifth Birthday]. Samuel Johnson. FaBoEE; NaS
Oft in My Thought. Charles d'Orléans. NoP
Oft in the after days, when thou and I. Ad Matrem. Julian Fane. HBV-1
"Oft in the hall I have heard my people." *Unknown, tr. by* Charles W. Kennedy. *Fr.* Beowulf. HeIP
Oft, in the silence of the night. Our Little Ghost. Louisa May Alcott. OBCA
Oft in the Silent Night. Otto Julius Bierbaum, *tr. fr. German by* Ludwig Lewisohn. AWP
Oft, in the Stilly Night. Thomas Moore. BLBL; EnRP; FaBoBe; GoBC; LiTB; LoBV; OAEP; OBNC; OBRV; OxBI; PoEL-4; Prf; WHA
(Light of Other Days, The.) FaFP; GTBS; GTBS-P; HBV-1; OBEV; TreF; NOBE
Oft it befalls by the grace of God. Fates of Men (Exeter Book). *Unknown, tr. by* Charles W. Kennedy. AnOE
Oft I've implor'd [*or* implored] the Gods in vain. A Prayer for Indifference. Frances Greville. LoBV; NOEC; OBEC
Oft o'er my brain does that strange fancy roll. Sonnet: Oft o'er My Brain. Samuel Taylor Coleridge. ChER
Oft on a dusky night of March, I've watched. Moorburn in Spring. *Unknown.* PoSH

Oft shall the soldier think of thee. Ben Milam. William H. Wharton. PAH
Oft since thine earthly eyes have closed on mine. Sarah Helen Whitman. Sonnet from the Series Relating to Edgar Allan Poe, III. AA
Oft Thou Hast with Greedy Ear. *Unknown.* EnRePo
Oft times I get to thinkin' of the changes times has wrought. A Veteran Cowboy's Ruminations. John M. Kuykendall. PoOW
Oft to the Wanderer, weary of exile. The Wanderer. *Unknown, tr. by* Charles W. Kennedy. AnOE; OAEL-1
Oft when I'm sitting without anything to read. Lines to a World-famous Poet Who Failed to Complete a World-famous Poem; or, Come Clean, Mr. Guest! Ogden Nash. OBAL
Oft when my spirit doth spre[a]d her bolder wing[e]s. Amoretti, LXXII. Spenser. OAEP; OBSC
Oft with true sighs, oft with uncalled tears. Astrophel and Stella, LXI. Sir Philip Sidney. SiPS
Often/ he wears my son's face. Child. Tom MacIntyre. CIP
Often'/ Stepping so delicately through the shrubbery of learning. Salt. Monk Gibbon. OxBI
Often beneath the wave, wide from this ledge. At Melville's Tomb. Hart Crane. AP; CoBMV; HAP; MoAmPo; MOS; NePA; NoAM; NoP; PoA; SeCeV; TAP; UnPo; VGW
Often, for pastime, mariners will ensnare. The Albatross. Baudelaire, *tr. by* Richard Wilbur. SyP
Often had I found her fair. Chorale. A. D. Hope. ErPo; UnTE
Often, half-way to sleep. In Procession. Robert Graves. MP; TwCP
Often I Am Permitted to Return to a Meadow. Robert Duncan. CMoP; HeIP; NMP; NOBA; NU
Often I compare my lord to heaven. Gaspara Stampa, *tr. fr. Italian by* Lynne Lawner. PBWP. *See also* Often when alone I liken my lord/to the cosmos.
Often I have heard it said. Song. Walter Savage Landor. HBV-1
Often I have stumbled on life's evil. Life's Evil. Eugenio Montale, *tr. by* Jan Pallister. AMV-81
Often I saw, as on my balcony. Christ Church Meadows, Oxford. Donald Hall. NYBP
Often I sit in the sun and brooding over the city, always. Dennis Lee. *Fr.* Civil Elegies. NOBC
Often I talk to men, on this or that. Talk. Philip A. Stalker. FiBHP
Often I think of my Jewish friends. The Pripet Marshes. Irving Feldman. NoAM; VWA
Often I think of the beautiful town. My Lost Youth [*or* Sea Memories]. Longfellow. AA; AmPP; AP; AWP; EtS; FaBoBe; FaBV; FaFP; FaPON; FaPoR; FPL; GoJo; HBV-1; LiTA; NePA; NOBA; OBEV; OxBA; PoEL-5; PoLF; PoRA; RoGo; SeCeV; TAP; TreF; ViBoPo
Often in summer, on a tarred bridge plank standing. Wild Bees. James K. Baxter. NoP
Often in the morning the fog is thick over Jersey. A View of Jersey. Edward Field. NeAP
Often, in these blue meadows. Pursuit from Under. James Dickey. HAP; PPP
Often in this life. Poem to Han-shan. Joseph Stroud. NPGG
Often I've wished that I'd been born a woman. A Wish. Laurence Lerner. FF; OxBTC
Often rebuked, yet always back returning. Stanzas [*or* Stanza]. *At. to* Emily Brontë, *also at. to* Charlotte Brontë ChER; FaBoEn; HBV-2; LiTB; LoBV; OAEL-2; OAEP; OBEV; OBNC; OBVV; PBWP
Often the western wind has sung to me. A Prayer. Alfred Bruce Douglas. TrPWD
Often the woodman scares them as he comes. Wood-Pigeons. John Masefield. ChMP
Often this thought wakens me unawares. Night. Hermann Hesse, *tr. by* Ludwig Lewisohn. AWP
Often waking/ before the sun decreed. The Author of *Christine.* Richard Howard. CoAP
Often when alone I liken my lord/ to the cosmos. Gaspara Stampa, *tr. fr. Italian by* J. Vitiello. BoWoP. *See also* Often I compare my lord to heaven.
Often, when o'er tree and turret. Hic Vir, Hic Est. Charles Stuart Calverley. NBM; OxBoLi
Often you seem them sitting, solitary, on a dune. The Beach Homos. Forrest Anderson. PeHV
Often you walked at night, houselights made. In Sepia. Jon Anderson. PoA
Oftener seen, the more I lust, The. Out of Sight, Out of Mind. Barnabe Googe. ElL; EnRePo; InPS; InvP
Ofttimes I get to thinking of the changes time has wrought. The Old-Time Cowboy. *Unknown.* CoSo
Og and Doeg. Dryden. *Fr.* Absalom and Achitophel, Pt. II. AWP; FiP, *shorter sel.*
(Og, *shorter sel.*) TW
Ogier the Dane. William Morris. *See* Song from "Ogier the Dane."
O'Grady's Goat. Will S. Hays. PoLF
Ogres and Pygmies. Robert Graves. CABA; CMoP; FaBoMo; LiTB; LiTM; NoAM; SeCePo; SeCeV
oh. *See also* O.
Oh, a capital ship for an ocean trip. The *Walloping Window Blind.* Charles Edward Carryl. MoShBr. *See also* Capital ship for an ocean trip, A.
Oh [*or* O], a dainty plant is the Ivy green. The Ivy Green. Charles Dickens. *Fr.* The Pickwick Papers, *ch.* 6. BoNaP; HBV-1; HBVY
Oh a high holiday, on a high holiday. Little Musgrave and Lady Barnard. *Unknown.* AmFP
Oh, a long, long time and a very long time. A Long Time Ago, *vers.* IV. *Unknown.* ShS
Oh, a lush green English meadow—it's there that I would lie. The Poplars. Bernard Freeman Trotter. CaP
Oh, a man there lives on the Western plains. The Cowboy. *Unknown.* BPAW; CoSo
Oh! a private buffoon is a light-hearted loon. The Family Fool. W. S. Gilbert. *Fr.* Yeoman of the Guard. InMe
Oh, a sailor's life is the life for me. The Warrior's Lament. Sir Owen Seaman. FiBHP
Oh a shantyman's life is a wearisome [*or* drearisome] life. A Shantyman's Life. *Unknown.* AS; ShS (*vers.* I); TrAS
Oh, a ship she was rigged and ready for sea. The Fishes. *Unknown.* GBP
Oh [*or* O], a wonderful stream is the River Time. The Isle of the Long Ago [*or* The Long Ago]. Benjamin Franklin Taylor. BLPA; FaFP; HBV-1; TreFS; WBLP
Oh, a Yankee ship came down the river. Blow, Boys, Blow, *vers.* II. *Unknown.* ShS
Oh Achilles of the moleskins. To "Chick." Frank Horne. *Fr.* Letters Found near a Suicide. BPo
"Oh, Albert," she said. How Einstein Started It Up Again. R. H. W. Dillard. SUW
Oh all ye, who passe by, whose eyes and minde. The Sacrifice. George Herbert. PoEL-2
Oh Ambulance Man. *Unknown.* BluL
Oh, ancient sin, oh, bathtub gin. Bathtub Gin. Philip H. Rhinelander. WhC
Oh [*or* O], answer me a question, love, I pray. The Sweetest Story Ever Told. R. M. Stults. BLSo; FSN; TreFS
Oh, as I walked down the Landing Stage. We're All Bound to Go. *Unknown.* AmSS
Oh, as I went a-walkin' down Ratcliffe 'Ighway. As I Went a-Walkin' down Ratcliffe Highway, *vers.* II. *Unknown.* ShS
Oh, as I went a-walkin' down Ratcliffe 'Ighway. Paddy West. *Unknown.* ShS
Oh, as I went down to Derby Town. The Derby Ram. *Unknown.* AmFP
Oh, away down South where I was born. Roll the Cotton Down. *Unknown.* AmFP
Oh, Babe, It Ain't No Lie. Elizabeth Cotton. FSW
Oh baby/ You can't have armies charging in here. Obscene Phone Call #2. Joy Harjo. TWSS
Oh, back in the fall of nineteen-two. "Haec Olim Meminisse Iuvabit." Deems Taylor. InMe
Oh, bad the march, the weary march. Fontenoy, 1745. Emily Lawless. AnIV
Oh, band in the pine-wood, cease! The Band in the Pines. John Esten Cooke. AA
Oh, be not ether-borne, poet of earth. Poet of Earth. Stephen Henry Thayer. AA
Oh be thou blest with all that Heav'n can send. To Mrs. M[artha]. B[lount] on Her Birthday. Pope. EnLoPo; FaBoEn; OBEC
Oh Beach Love Blossom. Judson Crews. UnTE
Oh Beverly, do you remember. September 7. Ellen Bass. NMM
Oh, bid my tongue be still. Song. Richard Watson Dixon. VLP
Oh Blame Not the Bard. Thomas Moore. OnYI
Oh, bless the law that veils the future's face. Eugene Lee-Hamilton. Mimma Bella, VI. HBV-1
Oh! blest [*or* bless'd] of heav'n [*or* Heaven], whom not the languid songs. Nature's Influence on Man [*or* Love of Nature *or* The Created Universe]. Mark Akenside. *Fr.* The Pleasures of Imagination, III. LoBV; NOEC; OBEC
Oh! blest with temper, whose unclouded ray. Heaven's Last Best Work. Pope. *Fr.* Moral Essays, Epistle II. OBEC
Oh, blithe and bonny is fair Scotland, where the bluebells gently grow. The Paisley Officer, *vers.* I. *Unknown.* ShS
Oh blithely shines the bonny sun. *See* Oh blythely shines the bonnie sun.
Oh, blow away, I long to hear you. Blow, Boys, Blow, *vers.* I. *Unknown.* ShS
Oh, blow the man down, boys [*or* bullies], blow the man down. Blow the Man Down. *Unknown.* AmSS; FSW; TrAS
Oh, blow the man down, Johnny, blow him right down. Blow the Man Down, *vers.* III. *Unknown.* ShS

Oh blythely [*or* O blithely] shines the bonnie [*or* bonny] sun. We'll Go to Sea No More [*or* Fisherman's Song]. *Unknown.* ChTr; EtS; GBP; PoPle
Oh, Boney was a warrior. Boney, *vers.* II. *Unknown.* ShS
Oh Boney's on the sea. The Shan Van Vocht. *Unknown.* OxBoLi
Oh, Bonnie is the little cow. Midnight in Bonnie's Stall. Siddie Joe Johnson. PChr
Oh Book! infinite sweetnesse! let my heart. The H. Scriptures. George Herbert. AnAnS-1
Oh, Boston, Boston, thou hast nought to boast on. Boston, Lincolnshire. *Unknown.* FaBoPP; GBP
Oh, Boston's a fine town with ships in the bay. Home, Boys [*or* Dearie], Home. *Unknown.* AmSS; FSW
Oh, both my shoes are shiny new. Autobiography. Dorothy Parker. WhC
Oh, bow your head, Tom Dooley. Tom Dooley. *Unknown.* AmFP; ViBoFo
Oh, Brandy leave me alone. Brandy Leave Me Alone. *Unknown.* FSW
Oh, Breathe Not His Name! Thomas Moore. AnIL; EnRP; HBV-2; TreFS
Oh! breathe upon this hapless world. Ode to Peace. *Unknown.* PAH
Oh Bright Oh Black Singbeast Lovebeast Catkin Sleek. Michael McClure. CoPo
Oh Brignall banks are wild and fair. *See* O Brignal banks are wild and fair.
Oh! bring me one sweet orange bough. The Orange Bough. Felicia Dorothea Hemans. VLP
Oh Britannia's got a baby, a baby, a baby. Britannia's Baby. D. H. Lawrence. NAs
"Oh, brother, oh, brother, can you play ball." The Two Brothers. *Unknown.* AmFP
Oh, bury me beside my knife and six-shooter. *Unknown.* CoSo
"Oh, bury me not in the deep, deep sea." *See* "O, bury me not in the deep, deep sea."
Oh, Bury Me Not on the Lone Prairie, *with music. Unknown. See* Bury Me Not on the Lone Prairie.
Oh, but it is dirty! Filling Station. Elizabeth Bishop. FaBoMo; HAP; NoP; NYBP; WeW
Oh but It Was Good. Harold Littlebird. VoR
Oh but, says one, tradition set aside. Tradition. Dryden. *Fr.* Religio Laici. OBS
Oh, call my brother back to me. The [Child's] First Grief. Felicia Dorothea Hemans. BLPA; CH
Oh, Cape Cod girls are very fine girls. Cape Cod Girls. *Unknown.* TrAS
Oh, cease, my wandering soul. Fulfillment. William A. Muhlenberg. WGRP
Oh, Charlie, he's my darling. Charlie Is My Darling. *Unknown.* FSW
Oh, Charlie's sweet and Charlie's neat. Weevily Wheat. *Unknown.* AmFP
Oh Christmas, that your Gift of Gifts might be. Noel! Noel! Laura Simmons. PGD
Oh Christmas Tree. *Unknown. See* Oh Tannenbaum.
Oh, come all ye true bold raftsmen and friends both far and near. Whalen's Fate. *Unknown.* ShS
Oh come and listen to my song. The Oxford and Hampton Railway. *Unknown.* OBET
Oh come and live with me, my love. Invitation au Festin. Aelfrida Tillyard. SUMH
Oh, come, cowboys, and listen to my song! The U-S-U Range. *Unknown.* CoSo
Oh come, let us sing unto Jehovah. *See* O come, let us sing unto the Lord.
Oh, come let us welcome sweet Sabbath the Queen! Welcome, Queen Sabbath. Zalman Schneour, *tr. by* Harry H. Fein. TrJP
Oh Come, Little Children. Phyllis McGinley. FaBV
Oh, come my joy, my soldier boy. Ballad. Henry Treece. WaP
Oh, Come to Me When Daylight Sets. Thomas Moore. EnRP
Oh, come with me in my little canoe. Ossian's Serenade [*or* The Burman Lover]. Calder Campbell. BLPA; TrAS
Oh, concerning of some gentlemen who lived down below. Hog Rogues on the Harricane. *Unknown.* OuSiCo
Oh! could I acquire my fullest desire. My Wishes. Patrick Healy, *tr. by* John D'Alton. OnYI
Oh, could we keep the Christmas thrill. The Whole Year Christmas. Angela Morgan. TRV
Oh, could we weep. Nurse No Long Grief. Mary Gilmore. PoAu-1
Oh Cruel Was the Press-Gang. *Unknown.* GBP
Oh, cut me reeds to blow upon. Tampico. Grace Hazard Conkling. HBMV
Oh Danaan brethren. At My Whisper. Lyle Donaghy. AnIV
Oh Danny boy, the pipes, the pipes are calling. Danny Boy. *Unknown.* FSW
Oh, Day of Days, *with music.* LeRoy V. Brant. AH
Oh, days of beauty standing veiled apart. Prevision. Ada Foster Murray. HBV-1
Oh, de boll weevil am a little black bug. *See* Oh, the boll weevil is a little black bug.
Oh, de good ole chariot swing so low. Swing Low, Sweet Chariot. *Unknown.* AA
Oh, de hearse keep a-rollin'. I Feel Like My Time Ain't Long. *Unknown.* OuSiCo
Oh, de ole sheep, dey know de road. De Ole Sheep Dey Know de Road. *Unknown.* BPo
Oh, de white gal ride in a automobile. De Black Girl. *Unknown.* GBP
Oh! Dear! *Unknown. See* Oh! Dear! What Can the Matter Be?
Oh dear me, the mill's ga'in' fast. The Jute Mill Song. *Unknown.* OBET
Oh [*or* O], Dear! What Can the Matter Be? *Unknown.* FSW; OxNR; PoPle (Oh! Dear!) CH
Oh, dear, what can the matter be?/ Two old women got up in an apple-tree. *Unknown.* FaBoNo
Oh! dearer by far than the land of our birth. Richard Henry Wilde. GOA
Oh dearest Bess. Queen Elizabeth. *Unknown.* DBV
"Oh, dearest grandpa, come and see." The Dead Sister. Caroline Gilman. OBCA
Oh! Death. *Unknown.* AmFP
Oh! Death Will Find Me. Rupert Brooke. *See* Sonnet: "Oh! Death will find me, long before I tire."
Oh, Dem Golden Slippers! James A. Bland. PSoN, *with music* (Golden Slippers.) FSW
Oh, dewy was the morning, upon the first of May. Manila. Eugene Fitch Ware. FiBHP; InMe; PV; YaD
Oh, dey whupped him up de hill, up de hill, up de hill. Never Said a Mumbalin' Word. *Unknown.* GBP; TrAS
Oh, did you go to see the show. The Orange Lily. *Unknown.* GBP
Oh Did You Hear? Shelley Silverstein. PoSC
Oh! Did you ne'er hear of Kate Kearney? Kate Kearney. Lady Morgan. BLPA; FaBoBe
Oh, did you see him riding down. Riding Down. Nora Perry. AA; HBV-1
Oh, dis is de day we pick on de banjo. Gimme de Banjo. *Unknown.* ShS
Oh, ditch of all ditches. Ode to a Ditch. *Unknown.* PeD
Oh, do buzz off, you bumptious Sun. Busy Old Fool. Ian Kelso. BXAP
Oh, do, my Johnny Boker. Johnny Boker. *Unknown.* AmSS
Oh do not die, for I shall hate. A Fever. John Donne. OAEL-1
Oh, do not tease the Bluffalo. The Bluffalo. Jane Yolen. RHPC
Oh [*or* O], do[e] not wanton with those eyes. A Song. Ben Jonson. AnAnS-2; HBV-1; OBS; SeCP; TEP
Oh, do [*or* don't] you remember sweet Bets[e]y from Pike. Sweet Betsy from Pike. *Unknown.* AmFP; AS; BaBo; BLSo; BPAW; FSW; OBAL; OxBoLi; TrAS; TreFT; ViBoFo
Oh doe not wanton with those eyes. *See* Oh do not wanton with those eyes.
Oh! don't you remember black Alice, Sam Holt. A Ballad of Queensland (Sam Holt). G. H. Gibson. PoAu-1
Oh! don't you remember sweet Alice, Ben Bolt. Ben Bolt; or, Ah! Don't You Remember. Thomas Dunn English. FSW; PSoN
Oh, don't you remember sweet Betsey from Pike. *See* Oh, do you remember sweet Betsy from Pike.
"Oh! don't you see the turtle-dove." The Turtle-Dove. *Unknown.* OxBoLi
Oh! Dublin sure there is no doubtin'. No Place So Grand. *Unknown.* WTO
Oh, Dunderbeck, oh Dunderbeck. Dunderbeck. *Unknown.* FSW
Oh, Earlier Shall the Rosebuds Blow. William Johnson Cory. HBV-2
Oh, early in the evenin', just after dark. The Blackleg Miners. *Unknown.* GBP; OBET; VLP
Oh Ease Oh Body-Strain Oh Love Oh Ease Me Not! Wound-Bore. Michael McClure. CoPo
Oh East is East, and West is West, and never the twain shall meet. The Ballad of East and West. Kipling. BeLS; BLPL; BrPo; FaBoBe; FaBV; FaPoR; HBV-2; OBNV; TRV, *abr.*
Oh effervescent palisades of ferns in drippage. From Rome, for More Public Fountains in New York City. Alan Dugan. NYP; Prf
Oh [*or* O], Eleazar Wheelock was a very pious man. Eleazar Wheelock. Richard Hovey. OBAL; WhC
Oh, England./ Sick in head and sick in heart. England. *Unknown.* ELU; FaBoEE
Oh, England is a pleasant place for them that's rich and high. The Last [*or* Old] Buccaneer. Charles Kingsley. BeLS; EBVV; EtS; EvOK; FaBoBe; HBV-1; MoShBr
"Oh, Eve, where is [*or* where's] Adam?" Adam in the Garden Pinnin' Leaves. *Unknown.* FSW; OuSiCo
Oh, ever skill'd to wear the form we love! To Hope. Helen Maria Williams. OBEC
Oh, ever thus from childhood's hour, I've seen my fondest hopes recede. Muddled Metaphors [*or* A Few Muddled Metaphors by a Moore-ose Melodist]. Tom Hood. FaBoNo; NA
Oh, every fall the chestnut men. Chestnut Stands. Rachel Field. SiSoSe
Oh, everything is far. Lament. Rainer Maria Rilke, *tr. by* C. F. MacIntyre PoPl; TrJP

Oh [*or* O] fair[e] sweet face, oh [*or* O] eyes celestial[l] bright. Song. John Fletcher. *Fr.* Women Pleased, III, iv. OBS; PoEL-2
Oh, Fair to See. Christina Rossetti. *Fr.* Sing-Song. FaPON; OHIP; TiPo
(Cherry Tree.) YeAr
Oh Fairest of the Rural Maids! Bryant. AP; TAP; ViBoPo
(Forest Maid, The.) OBVV
(O Fairest of the Rural Maids.) AA
Oh, fare you well, I wish you well! Good-bye, Fare You Well. *Unknown.* AmSS
Oh, fare you well, my darling. Fare You Well, My Darling. *Unknown.* AmFP
Oh farmer have you a daughter fair, parlay-voo. Hinky Dinky. *Unknown.* TrAS
Oh Father. Wendy Rose. CDW
Oh [*or* O] father, answer me. Dialogue. Howard Nemerov. NYBP; PoPl
Oh Father—if Thou wouldst indeed. Father. Arthur Davison Ficke. TrPWD
Oh, father, oh, father, come riddle to me. Fair Ellender. *Unknown.* FSW
Oh, fields of wonder. Birth. Langston Hughes. NAs
Oh flame falling, as shaken, as the stories. The Fire. Robert Creeley. NOBA
Oh [*or* O] fly not, Pleasure, pleasant-hearted Pleasure. Song. Wilfrid Scawen Blunt. OBVV; ViBoPo
Oh, For a Bowl of Fat Canary. John Lyly. *See* Serving Men's Song, A.
Oh! [*or* O!] for a Closer Walk with God. William Cowper. *See* Walking with God.
Oh, for a heart that weeps o'er souls. A Heart That Weeps. Oswald J. Smith. STF
Oh for a lodge in some vast wilderness. Against Slavery. William Cowper. *Fr.* The Task, II: The Timepiece. EnRP; NOEC; OAEP
Oh, for a man to take me out. Wanted: One Cave Man with Club. Margaret Fishback. WhC
Oh, for a Pentecost! ("Oh, for a passionate passion for souls!") *Unknown.* BLRP
Oh for a Poet-for a Beacon Bright. E. A. Robinson. NePA; OxBA
(Sonnet.) PP
Oh, for an hour when the day is breaking. Nanny. Francis Davis. HBV-1
Oh, for 'is heart is like the sea. They All Love Jack. *Unknown.* ShS
Oh for one hour of youthful joy! The Old Man Dreams. Oliver Wendell Holmes. BLPL; HBV-1; PoLF
Oh [*or* O] for some honest lovers ghost. Sonnet [*or* Actuality *or* A Doubt of Martyrdom]. Sir John Suckling. AnAnS-2; BoLoP; BXAP; CaPo; FaBoEn; HBV-1; JCP; LoBV; MeLP; MePo; NOBE; OBEV; OBS; Par; PoEL-3; PoPle; SeCP; SeCV-1
Oh for the face and footstep!—Woods and shores! Frederick Goddard Tuckerman. Sonnets, II, xxxii. AP
Oh for the good old times! When all was new. The Della Cruscans. William Gifford. *Fr.* The Baviad. OBEC
Oh for the Swedish law enacted here! John Oldham. *Fr.* Satires upon the Jesuits. DBV
Oh fortune, thy wresting wavering state. Written on a Wall at Woodstock. Elizabeth I, Queen of England. PBWP; WPE
Oh, frame some little word for me. The Clue. Charlotte Fiske Bates. AA
Oh Freedom. *Unknown.* FSW
Oh friend, we arrived too late. Friedrich Hölderlin, *tr. by* Robert Bly. *Fr.* Bread and Wine. NU
Oh, Frog Prince, Frog Prince. The Princess Addresses the Frog Prince. Elizabeth Brewster. DFT
Oh frog [*or* Froggie] went a-courtin' and he did ride, u-huh uh-huh. Frog [*or* Froggie] Went a-Courtin'. *Unknown.* BLSo; TrAS
Oh! fye upon care. The Ranting Wanton's Resolution; 1672. *Unknown.* CoMu
Oh gallant was our galley from her carven steering-wheel. The Galley-Slave. Kipling. BrPo
Oh, [*or* O] Galuppi, Baldassaro, this is very sad to find! A Toccata of Galuppi's. Robert Browning. EBVV; GTBS-P; HAP; HBV-2; LiTB; LoBV; NCEP; NOBE; NoP; OAEL-2; OAEP; TEP; WHA
Oh gather the thoughts of your early years. Early Thoughts. William Edward Hartpole Lecky. OnYI
Oh [*or* O] Genevieve, I'd give the [*or* this] world. Sweet Genevieve. George Cooper. BLSo; FSW; PSoN; TreFS
"Oh, Georgie Wedlock is my name." Georgie Wedlock. *Unknown.* AmFP
"Oh, get you forth, my son Willy." Marm Grayson's Guests. Mary E. Wilkins Freeman. OBCA
Oh gin I were a doo. Gin I Were a Doo. *Unknown.* GBP
Oh, Gingilee, my aching heart. Gingilee. Moishe-Leib Halpern, *tr. by* Joseph Leftwich. TrJP
Oh, git around, Jinny, git around. Jinny Git Around. *Unknown.* OuSiCo
Oh give attention, you maidens dear. Constance Kent. *Unknown.* OBET
Oh, Give Me a Home Where the Buffalo Roam. *Unknown.* *See* Home on the Range, A.
Oh give me a pup. Poetic Tale. Grace Maddock Miller. GDP
Oh, give me, Lord, Thy love for souls. The Soul Winner's Prayer. Eugene M. Harrison. STF
Oh, Give Me the Hills. *Unknown.* AmFP
Oh, Give Us Back the Days of Old'. John Mason Neale. NOCV
Oh, Give Us Pleasure in the Flowers Today. Robert Frost. *See* Prayer in Spring, A.
Oh glorious spirits, who after all your bands. To All Angels and Saints. George Herbert. SeCV-1
Oh, go to old Ireland and then you will know. Go to Old Ireland. *Unknown.* AmFP
Oh [*or* O], God, beneath thy guiding hand. The Pilgrim Fathers. Leonard Bacon. AH; WGRP
Oh God, I offer Thee my heart. Consecration. *Unknown.* TRV
Oh, God, let me be beautiful in death. Last Plea. Jean Starr Untermeyer. TrPWD
Oh God, let me forget the things he said. Rapunzel. Sara Henderson Hay. DFT
Oh God made a trance on Sunday. God Made a Trance. *Unknown.* OBET
Oh, God of dust and rainbows, help us see. Two Somewhat Different Epigrams. Langston Hughes. NePoAm-2
Oh God, she said. Song My. Susan Griffin. NMM; WPOW
Oh! Golden Rose! Oh! Glittering Lilly White. Edward Taylor. Preparatory Meditations: Second Series, II. SCAP
Oh! Good, good, good, my Lord. What more love yet. Edward Taylor. Preparatory Meditations: Second Series, CXII. NOBA
Oh, green grow the lilacs and so does the rue. Green Grow the Lilacs. *Unknown.* TreFT
Oh, greenly and fair in the lands of the sun. The Pumpkin. Whittier. OHIP
Oh, grieve not, ladies, if at night. Grieve Not, Ladies. Anna Hempstead Branch. FaFP; HBV-1
"Oh, hangman, hangman, slacken your rope." The Sycamore Tree. *Unknown.* AmFP
Oh, hapless sire, distraught with cares. The Yoke. Kalonymos ben Kalonymos, *tr. by* J. Chotzner. *Fr.* The Touchstone. TrJP
Oh [*or* O] happy golden age. A Pastoral[l]. Tasso, *tr. by* Samuel Daniel. *Fr.* Aminta. OAEL-1; OBSC; PoEL-2
Oh, happy, happy maid. A Nuptial Eve. Sydney Dobell. OBNC
Oh happy shades! to me unblest. The Shrubbery. William Cowper. FaBoEn; FaBoRV; NCEP; NOBE; OBEC
Oh happy trees that we plant today. Tree Planting. *Unknown.* OHIP
Oh, hard is the fortune of all womankind. Hard Is the Fortune of All Womankind. *Unknown.* FSW
Oh, hark the dogs are barking, love. The Banks of the Condamine. *Unknown.* FaBoBa; GBP; PoAu-1
Oh, hark the pulses of the night. The Reason. James Oppenheim. HBV-1
Oh, hark to the brown thrush! hear how he sings! Joy-Month. David Atwood Wasson. HBV-1
Oh, haul away the bowline, the packet ship's a-rollin'! Haul Away, Joe, *vers.* II. *Unknown.* ShS
Oh, have you heard de lates'. De Ballit of de Boll Weevil. *Unknown.* NOBA
Oh have you heard the story 'bout Aimee McPherson? Aimee McPherson. *Unknown.* FSW
Oh, have you seen the *Tattlesnake.* The Journal of Society. Godfrey Turner. NOBL
Oh, he was a handsome trotter, and he couldn't be completer. How We Drove the Trotter. W. T. Goodge. PH
Oh, Hear Me Prayin', *with music.* *Unknown.* BoAN-2
"Oh, hear you a horn, mother, behind the hill?" The Horn. James Reeves. SO
Oh, heard ye yon pibroch sound sad in the gale. Glenara. Thomas Campbell. HBV-2
Oh heart rejoice! For I Have Done a Good and Kindly Deed. Franz Werfel, *tr. by* Edith Abercrombie Snow. TrJP
Oh, heavens! the weakness of my unkind father! The Obscured Prince; or, The Black Box Boxed. *Unknown.* APAS
Oh Heav'ns! I'm choack'd with smoak, I'm burn'd with fire. Lament of the Sodomites. George Lestey. *Fr.* Fire and Brimstone; or, The Destruction of Sodom. PeHV
"Oh hell, what do mine eyes." Milton by Firelight. Gary Snyder. CAPP; CoAP; ConAP; InPK; InPS; PPP
Oh, here you see old Tom Moore. The Days of Forty-nine. *Unknown.* FSW
Oh, here's a jolly lark. The Old Marquis and His Blooming Wife. *Unknown.* CoMu
Oh he's God. God Don't Never Change. *Unknown.* BluL
Oh hinny, Geordie, canny man. California. Joseph Philip Robson. VLP
"Oh, hold your hand, butcher!" this fair one she cried. The Silk Merchant's Daughter, *vers.* I. *Unknown.* ShS
Oh, Hollow! Hollow! Hollow! W. S. Gilbert. FaBoNo

Oh, holy cause/ That points the grass. Sung on a Sunny Morning. Jean Starr Untermeyer. TrPWD
Oh [*or* O], how comely it is, and how reviving. The Deliverer. Milton. *Fr.* Samson Agonistes. NOBE; NOCV; OBEV; OBS; SeCeV
Oh, how far away things are. The Grief. Rainer Maria Rilke, *tr. by* Steven Lautermilch. AMV-81
Oh, How He Lied. *Unknown.* FSW
Oh, how I love Humanity. The World State. G. K. Chesterton. DBV
Oh, how I love to skip alone. Skipping Along Alone. Winifred Welles. SoPo; TiPo
Oh how I wish that an embargo. The Nurse's Dole in the Medea. Byron. OBVE
Oh, How Lovely Is the Evening. *Unknown.* FSW
Oh, how much more doeth beauty beauteous seem. *See* O, how much more doth beauty beauteous seem.
Oh, how my love/ With a whirling power. Tu-kehu *and* Wetea, *tr. fr. Maori by* J. C. Andersen. WTO
Oh, how my pulse pipes to go riding, go riding. Riding. Harry Amoss. CaP
Oh how oft I wake and find. To My God. George Macdonald. TrPWD; TRV
Oh, how with brightness hath Love filled my way. George Edward Woodberry. Ideal Passion, XXX. HBMV
Oh, Huntsman, when will the hunting stop. To Charlotte Corday. Sir Osbert Sitwell. ChMP
Oh, hush, my heart, and take thine ease. April Weather. Lizette Woodworth Reese. HBMV
Oh hush thee, little Dear-my-soul. Christmas Eve. Eugene Field. OHIP
Oh! hush thee, my baby, the night is behind us. Seal Lullaby. Kipling. *Fr.* The Jungle Book. FaPON; SoSe; TiPo
Oh I am a cat that likes to/ Gallop. The Galloping Cat. Stevie Smith. BrRo
Oh, I am a poor girl, my fortune is sad. The Wagoner's Lad. *Unknown.* FSW
Oh, I am a rusty cowboy. The Drifter. *Unknown.* CoSo
Oh, I am a Texas cowboy, far away from home. The Texas Cowboy. *Unknown.* CoSo
Oh, I am a Texas cowboy, just off the Texas plains. The Texas Cowboy. *Unknown.* AmFP
Oh, I be vun of the useful troibe. A Rustic Song. Anthony C. Deane. FiBHP; InMe
Oh, I can hear you, God, above the cry. Wind in the Pine. Lew Sarett. TrPWD; TRV
Oh, I can smile for you, and tilt my head. A Certain Lady. Dorothy Parker. NIP
Oh, I come from the world below. Rise Me Up from Down Below. *Unknown.* ShS
Oh, I couldn't hear nobody pray. I Couldn't Hear Nobody Pray. *Unknown.* FSW
Oh, I don't want to be a gambler. I Don't Want to Be a Gambler. *Unknown.* AS
Oh I got up and went to work. On a Seven-Day Diary. Alan Dugan. OBAL
Oh, I had a bird and the bird pleased me. The Barnyard. *Unknown.* AmFP
Oh, I had a horse and his name was Bill. The Horse Named Bill. *Unknown.* AS
Oh, I have slipped the surly bonds of earth. High Flight. John Gillespie Magee, Jr. FaFP; FaPON; PGD; TreFS; TRV
Oh! I know why the alder trees. I Know. Elsa Barker. HBMV
Oh, I laugh to hear what grown folk. Mrs. Kriss Kringle. Edith M. Thomas. OBCA
Oh! I love to travel far and near throughout my native land. Wizard Oil. *Unknown.* AS
Oh, I never had but one true love. The Unquiet Grave. *Unknown.* AmFP
Oh, I should like to ride the seas. Song of Perfect Propriety. Dorothy Parker. DBV; InMe
Oh, I should love to be like one of those. The Youth Dreams. Rainer Maria Rilke, *tr. by* Ludwig Lewisohn. AWP; TrJP
Oh I suppose I should. Le Médecin Malgré Lui. William Carlos Williams. PoA; SaC
Oh, I used to sing a song. The Endless Song. Ruth McEnery Stuart. OBAL
Oh! I vu'st know'd o' my true love. Heedless o' My Love. William Barnes. GBL
Oh I want to/ tell you. Perversity. Susan Griffin. LLLT
Oh I was born in Boston, a city you all know well. *See* I was born in Boston.
"Oh, I was good, man." The Boxer Turned Bartender. Gary Allan Kizer. LFAC
Oh, I went down South for to see my Sal. Polly Wolly Doodle. *Unknown.* FSW; TreF; YaD
Oh, I went down to Framingham. Spooks. Nathalia Crane. ShM
Oh, I went to California in the spring of seventy-six. Root, Hog, or Die. *Unknown.* FSW
"Oh, I will put my ship in order." The Drowsy Sleeper. *Unknown.* BaBo
Oh, I Wish I Were Single Again. *Unknown.* *See* I Wish I Were Single Again.
Oh, I wonder where my lost Johnny's gone. Lost Johnny. *Unknown.* AmFP
Oh, I woud I wee a cose, cose fiend. Sim Ines. Jane Stubbs. FiBHP
Oh, I would be a cowboy. *Unknown.* CoSo
Oh, if but a single hour. Permanence in Change. Goethe, *tr. by* Mark Doyle. HoPM
Oh! if by any unfortunate chance I should happen to die. The Soldier. J. Y. Watson. BXAP
Oh, if ever I get married, it will be in June. The Banks of the Roses. *Unknown.* ShS
Oh, if I could only make you see. Her Mother. Alice Cary. OHIP
Oh, if the world were mine, Love. If. James Jeffrey Roche. HBV-1
Oh, If They Only Knew! Edith L. Mapes. BLRP; WBLP
Oh [*or* O], if thou knew'st how thou thyself dost harm. To Aurora [*or* Sonnet]. Earl of Stirling. Aurora, XXXIII. EIL; FaFP; GTBS; GTBS-P
Oh, if you love her. Advice to a Lover. S. Charles Jellicoe. HBV-1
Oh, I'm a good old Rebel. The Rebel [*or* The Good Old Rebel]. Innes Randolph. FSW; OBAL; OxBoLi; TW
Oh I'm Dirty Dan, the world's dirtiest man. The Dirtiest Man in the World. Shel Silverstein. OBCA
Oh, I'm goin' round the world, baby mine. Baby Mine. *Unknown.* FSW
Oh, I'm gonna get me a religion. Preachin' the Blues. *Unknown.* BluL
Oh I'm in love with the janitor's boy. The Janitor's Boy. Nathalia Crane. PoLF
Oh, I'm mad for Don Juan. How to Tell Juan Don from Another. Gardner E. Lewis. FiBHP
Oh, in Byrontown of high renown. Byrontown. Larry Gorman. ShS
Oh in eighteen hundred and forty-one. Paddy [*or* Poor Paddy] Works on the Railway. *Unknown.* AmSS; AS
Oh, in South Australia where I was born. South Australia. *Unknown.* ShS
Oh, in the merry month of May. Bonny Barbara Allan. *Unknown.* AmFP
Oh in whose grove have we wakened, the bees. Two Horses. W. S. Merwin. NePA; TwAmPo
"Oh is it the jar of nations." The Jar of Nations. A. E. Housman. LiTB
Oh, is it, then, Utopian. De Profundis. Dorothy Parker. ErPo
Oh, is not this a holy spot? On Laying the Corner-Stone of the Bunker Hill Monument. John Pierpont. PAH
"Oh! isn't it a pity, such a pretty girl as I." Harriet H. Robinson. SaC
Oh it happen'd in Vienna not so very long ago. Doctor Freud. David Lazar. FSW
Oh, it was not a pheasant cock. The Drowned Lady. *Unknown.* ChTr
Oh, it will be fine. Valentine for Earth. Frances Frost. QQQ
Oh, it's a southerly wind and a cloudy sky. Southerly Wind. *Unknown.* ShS
Oh it's all under the leaves and the leaves of life. The Leaves of Life. *Unknown.* OBET
Oh, it's beer, beer, that makes you feel so queer. The Quartermaster Store. *Unknown.* FSW
Oh, it's fiddle-de-dum and fiddle-de-dee. The Dancing Bear. Albert Bigelow Paine. OBCA
Oh, it's H-A-P-P-Y I am, and it's F-R-double-E. The Bells. *Unknown.* FiBHP
"Oh, it's Hynde Horn fair, and it's Hynde Horn free." Hynde Horn. *Unknown.* GN
Oh, it's move along, you dogies, don't be driftin' by th' way. Cowboy's Salvation Song. Robert V. Carr. PoOW
Oh, It's Nine Years Ago I Was Digging in the Land. *Unknown.* AmFP
Oh, it's treat the cook with a pleasant look. *Unknown.* CoSo
Oh, it's twenty gallant gentlemen. The Last Hunt. William Roscoe Thayer. AA; FaBoBe; HBV-2
"Oh! I've got a plum-cake, and a fine feast I'll make." The Plum-Cake. Ann Taylor. HBVY
Oh, I've got no use for the women. I've Got No Use for the Women. *Unknown.* AmFP
"Oh, I've had ten men before you." Ballad of Mistress Death. Denis Devlin. NMP
Oh, I've ridden plenty of horses. Noonday Sun. Kathryn *and* Byron Jackson. FaPON; TiPo
Oh, Jack's come home from sea today. Our Jack's Come Home Today. *Unknown.* ShS
Oh, Jesse was the man, he traveled through the land. Jesse James. *Unknown.* CoSo
Oh, Johnny Fife and Johnny's wife. Johnny Fife and Johnny's Wife. Mildred Plew Meigs. SoPo; TiPo

Oh, keep your kisses, young provoking girl! The Kiss. *Unknown, tr. by* Earl of Longford. OnYI; OxBI
Oh, kind folks, listen to my song. Abraham's Daughter. Septimus Winner. TrAS
Oh, kind friend you may ask me what makes me sad and still. Utah Carroll. *Unknown*FSW
Oh King of grief! (a title strange, yet true). The Thanksgiving. George Herbert. AnAnS-1
Oh King of Saints, how great's thy work, say we. Edward Johnson. SCAP
Oh King of stars! Hospitality in Ancient Ireland. *Unknown, tr. by* Kuno Meyer. OnYI
Oh, King of the fiddle, Wilhelmj. Wilhelmj. Robert J. Burdette. TDH
Oh! King who hast the key. Exspecto Resurrectionem. Charlotte Mew. LO
Oh! Ladies and gentlemen, please to draw near. Down, Down Derry Down. *Unknown.* AS
Oh, lady, wake! the azure moon. Ballad of Bedlam. *Unknown.* NA
Oh, land of Castile, you do raise me up. Castile. Miguel de Unamuno, *tr. by* Eleanor L. Turnbull. PoPl
Oh, larch tree with scarlet berries. Larch Tree. Laurie Lee. NeBP
Oh! Larry M'Hale he had little to fear. Larry M'Hale. Charles James Lever. OnYI
Oh [*or* O] last and best of Scots! who did'st maintain. Upon the Death of the Viscount [*or* Earl] of Dundee. Dryden. ACP; OBS
Oh last Thursday morning while playing at ball. Willie. *Unknown.* AmFP
Oh Lawd have mussy now upon us. Blessing without Company. *Unknown.* BPo; POL
Oh, lead me to a quiet cell. Portrait of the Artist. Dorothy Parker. WhC
Oh leaden heeld. Lord, give, forgive I pray. Edward Taylor. Preparatory Meditations: Second Series, I. SCAP
Oh leave his body broken on the rocks. On a Dying Boy. William Bell. NePoEA
Oh, leave me! It's time for the horizon to. Reverie. Victor Hugo, *tr. by* Mary Ann Caws. NAWM-2
Oh! leave the past to bury its own dead. To One Who Would Make [a] Confession. Wilfrid Scawen Blunt. The Love Sonnets of Proteus, LXII. HBV-1; ViBoPo
Oh, let a father's curse be on thy soul. Shelley. *Fr.* To the Lord Chancellor. ViBoPo
Oh, let me run and hide. Spring Ecstasy. Lizette Woodworth Reese. MoAmPo
Oh, Let Thy Teachings. Immanuel di Roma, *tr. fr. Hebrew by* J. Chotzner. *Fr.* Machberoth. TrJP
Oh, let us howl some heavy note. The Madman's Song [*or* Song]. John Webster. *Fr.* The Duchess of Malfi, IV, ii. ElL; InvP
Oh let your shining orb grow dim. To the Sun. Roy Campbell. *Fr.* Mithraic Emblems. EaLo
Oh, let-n me ride, oh, let-n me ride. Low Down Chariot. *Unknown.* OuSiCo
Oh, let's fix us a julep and kick us a houn'. Boogie-woogie Ballads. St. Clair McKelway. PoNe
Oh, let's go up the hill and scare ourselves. The Bonfire. Robert Frost. InvP
Oh, life is a glorious cycle of song. Comment. Dorothy Parker. *Fr.* Some Beautiful Letters. InMe; NIP; OBAL
Oh Light Was My Head. C. Day Lewis. *Fr.* Two Songs [Written to Irish Airs]. OAEP
O-o-o-oh, lil' man. Chahcoal Man. *Unknown.* AS
Oh, limpid stream of Tyrus, now I hear. A Classic Ode. Charles Battell Loomis. NA
Oh! list to the lay of a poor Irish harper. Bold Phelim Brady, the Bard of Armagh. *Unknown.* FSW; OnYI
Oh listen, listen, ladies gay! *See* O listen, listen, ladies gay.
Oh! Listen, man! Immortality. Richard Henry Dana. WGRP
Oh, little body, do not die. A Child Ill. John Betjeman. DTC
Oh, little cat beside my stool. Cinderella's Song. Elizabeth Madox Roberts. DFT
Oh, little Christ, why do you sigh. Christmas Eve in France. Jessie Redmund Fauset. BANP
Oh! little loveliest lady mine. A Valentine. Laura E. Richards. AA; YeAr
Oh! lives there, Heaven! beneath thy dread expanse. The Pilgrim of a Day. Thomas Campbell. OBRV
Oh loathsome place! where I. Earl of Surrey. SiPS
Oh! London town, you are grim and gray. London. T. P. Cameron Wilson. HBMV
Oh! lonely is our old green fort. Old Fort Meigs. *Unknown.* PAH
Oh, long before the bere was steeped for malt. Last Journey. John Davidson. *Fr.* The Testament of John Davidson. PoSH
Oh, long, long/ The snow has possessed the mountains. The Grass on the Mountain. *Unknown, tr. by* Mary Austin. AmFN; AWP; FaPON; GOA
Oh, look up and down that long, lonesome road. Long Lonesome Road. *Unknown.* OuSiCo
Oh, loosen the snood that you wear, Janette. Janette's Hair. Charles Graham Halpine. HBV-1
Oh Lord Cozens Hardy. Lord Cozens Hardy. John Betjeman. OxBTC
Oh Lord, give me a plane. Queen of Horizons. Joseph Dever. ISi
Oh Lord, I have been staring into a mirror. Psalm. Eugene Heimler, *tr. by* Anthony Rudolf. VWA
Oh, Lord, Oh, my Lord! Keep Me f'om Sinkin' Down. *Unknown.* BoAN-1
Oh Lord! thou hast known me, and searched me out. An Hymn on the Omnipresence. John Byrom. TrPWD
Oh Lord, when all our bones are thrust. Supplication. Edgar Lee Masters. TrCP; TrPWD
Oh lordy, lord, oh lordy, lord. Worried Life Blues. *Unknown.* AmFP
Oh, Lordy, pick a bale of cotton. Pick a Bale of Cotton. *Unknown.* FSW
Oh! lose the winter from thine heart, the darkness from thine eyes. May-Music. Rachel Annand Taylor. HBV-1
Oh, love builds on the azure sea. Love's Land. Isabella Valancy Crawford. CaP
"Oh love is fair, and love is rare;" my dear one she said. There's Wisdom in Women. Rupert Brooke. HBV-1
Oh love! no habitant of earth thou art. The Fatal Spell. Byron. *Fr.* Childe Harold's Pilgrimage, IV. OAEL-2; OBNC; ViBoPo
Oh! Love, that stronger art than wine. Song. Aphra Behn. *Fr.* The Lucky Chance. WPE; WPOW
"Oh! Love," they said, "is King of Kings." Song. Rupert Brooke. HBV-1
Oh, Lovely Appearance of Death, *with music.* George Whitefield. OuSiCo
Oh Lovely Fishermaiden. Heine, *tr. fr. German by* Louis Untermeyer. AWP
Oh, lovely Mary Donnelly, my joy, my only best [*or* it's you I love best]. Lovely Mary Donnelly. William Allingham. AnIV; HBV-1
Oh, Lovely Rock. Robinson Jeffers. NoAM; NU
Oh! lovely voices of the sky. Hymn for Christmas. Felicia Dorothea Hemans. GN
Oh, lovers' eyes are sharp to see. *See* O, lovers' eyes are sharp to see.
Oh Lucky Jim! *Unknown.* ChTr; GBP
Oh Lydia, when I hear you rave. To the Polyandrous Lydia. Franklin P. Adams. HBMV
Oh, make me, sphere-descended Queen. A Wykehamist's Address to Learning. P. N. Shuttleworth. FaBoCo
Oh, make my bed in the warm air. To Carry on Living. Yehuda Amichai, *tr. by the author.* LLLT
"Oh, Mammy, Mammy, now I'm married." Will the Weaver. *Unknown.* AmFP
Oh, man's capacity/ For spiritual sorrow. The Crucifixion. Alice Meynell. OxBoCh
Oh [*or* O], many a day have I made good ale in the glen. The Outlaw of Loch Lene. *Unknown, tr. by* Jeremiah Joseph Callanan. AnIV; BIrV; CH; GBL; OBEV; OBRV; OnYI; OxBI
Oh, Mary and the Baby, sweet Lamb. Mary and the Baby, Sweet Lamb. *Unknown.* AmFP
Oh, Mary, at thy window be. *See* O Mary, at thy window be.
Oh, Mary, Don't You Weep, Don't You Mourn. *See* Pharoah's Army Got Drownded.
"Oh, Mary, go and call the cattle home." *See* "O, Mary, go and call the cattle home."
Oh, Mary had a little lamb, regarding whose cuticular. The Original Lamb. *Unknown.* InMe
Oh, Masters, you who rule the world. The Masters. "Laurence Hope." HBV-2
Oh May, bonnie May is to the Yowe buchts gane. The Laird o' Ochiltree Wa's. *Unknown.* OxBB
Oh, may I join the choir invisible. *See* O, may I join the choir invisible.
Oh, may my constant feet not fail. Chorus. Sophocles, *tr. by* Robert Whitelaw. *Fr.* Oedipus Rex. WGRP
Oh, meet me tonight in the moonlight. New Jail. *Unknown.* AmFP
Oh Menelaus. On Hearing the First Cuckoo. Richard Church. OBMV
Oh, Mexico, my Mexico. Santy Anna, *vers.* II. *Unknown.* ShS
Oh, mighty America, hast thou come to this? Fare Thee Well. Eli Siegel. GOA
Ohhhhhhh Mister Charlie your rolling mill is burning down. Mister Charlie. *Unknown.* BluL
Oh, Mr. Cross! Address to Mr. Cross, of Exeter 'Change, on the Death of the Elephant. Thomas Hood. FM
Oh Mr. Froude, how wise and good. Killarney. Charles Kingsley. WhC
"Oh, Mrs. McGrath," the sergeant said. Mrs. McGrath. *Unknown.* FaBoBa; FSW; OnYI
Oh Mistress Mine. Shakespeare. *See* O Mistress Mine, Where Are You Roaming?
Oh, Molly, oh, Molly, I've told you before. Red Whiskey. *Unknown.* AmFP
Oh Monday night's the night for me! Y.M.C.A. "C. A. L. T. " SUMH

Oh Moon, discreetly worshipped by our sires. The Injured Moon. Baudelaire, *tr. by* Robert Lowell. MOON
Oh moon, oh moon! *Tr. fr. Papuan by* Mari Marase. BoWoP
Oh [*or* O] Moon! when I look [*or* gaze] on thy beautiful face. Poetic Thought. *Unknown.* FiBHP; InPK
Oh, Most High, Almighty, Good Lord God, to Thee belong praise, glory, honor and all blessing. *See* O most high, almighty good Lord God.
Oh, most natural grandson I was. Apology for E. H. William Hathaway. FAZ
Oh mother,/ here in your lap. Mothers. Anne Sexton. Str
Oh, mother, I shall be married to Mr. Punchinello. To Mr. Punchinello. *Unknown.* OxNR
Oh Mother of a Mighty Race. Bryant. AP; FaBoBe; HBV-2; HBVY; PAH; PAL
(America.) AA
Oh, mountains loom the grandest in Montana. In Montana. Washington Jay McCormick. WhC
Oh! mourn not for Anacreon dead. On Tom Moore's Translation of Anacreon. Thomas, Lord Erskine. FaBoEE
Oh, Musgrove, he persuaded me. Musgrove. *Unknown.* AmFP
Oh! my aged Uncle Arly. *See* O my aged Uncle Arly.
Oh, my belovèd, have you thought of this. Sonnet. Edna St. Vincent Millay. HBMV
Oh, my beloved, shall you and I. Afterwards. Margaret Postgate Cole. SUMH
Oh [*or* O] my black[e] soul[e]! now thou art summoned. John Donne. Holy Sonnets, IV. AnAnS-1; EBEV; JCP; MasP; MePo; OAEL-1; OBS; TEP
Oh my boy: Jesus. The Confession Stone. Owen Dodson. TTY
Oh! my dark Rosaleen. *See* O, my dark Rosaleen.
Oh, My Darling Clementine. *Unknown, at. to* Percy Montross. FaBoBe; FaFP; PSoN, *with music*; TreF
(Clementine.) AmFP; BLSo, *with music*; FSW; OBAL
Oh, my fair Pastheen is my heart's delight. Páistín Fionn. *Unknown, tr. by* Sir Samuel Ferguson. OxBI
Oh my fine, my honey-colored Duke of Marmalade! Elegy for the Duke of Marmalade. Luis Palés Matos, *tr. by* Julio Marzán. InW
Oh, My Geraldine. F. C. Burnand. NA
Oh my God, screamed Mommy, you went and ate the baby. The Snack. L. L. Zeiger. BXAP
Oh, my golden slippers am [*or* are] laid away. Oh, Dem Golden Slippers. James A. Bland. FSW; PSoN
Oh, My Good Lord, Show Me de Way, *with music.* *Unknown.* BoAN-2
Oh, my laddie, my laddie. My Laddie. Amélie Rives. HBV-1
Oh, My Liver and My Lungs, *with music.* *Unknown.* OuSiCo
Oh, my Lord. My Lord, What a Morning. Waring Cuney. TTY
Oh My Love's [*or* Luve Is] like a Red, Red Rose. Burns. *See* Red, Red Rose, A.
Oh, my mother's moaning by the river. The Lonely Mother. Fenton Johnson. PoNe
Oh, my name is Bob the Swagman, before you all I stand. The Old Bark Hut. *Unknown.* PoAu-1
Oh, my name is Captain Kidd. *See* Oh, my name was Robert Kidd, as I sailed and sailed.
Oh! my name is John Wellington Wells. W. S. Gilbert. *Fr.* The Sorcerer, Mr. Wells. WSC
Oh, my name is Larry Gorman, to you I mean no har-rm. The Scow on Cowden Shore, *vers.* II. Larry Gorman. ShS
Oh, my name is Peter Emberley. Peter Emberley, *vers.* I. John Calhoun. ShS
Oh [*or* O], my name it is Sam [*or* Samuel] Hall, it is Sam [*or* Samuel] Hall. Sam [*or* Samuel] Hall. *Unknown.* ChTr; CoSo; DBV; FSW; TW; UnPo; VLP
Oh, my name was Robert [*or* is Captain] Kidd, as I sailed, as I sailed. Captain Kidd. *Unknown.* FSW; MoShBr; TrAS; ViBoFo
Oh My People I Remember. Wendy Rose. CDW
Oh, my sweet mother, 'tis in vain. On My Sweet Mother. Sappho, *tr. by* Thomas Moore. PoPl
Oh, my wandering melody. Melody. Shmuel Moreh, *tr. by* Yoffee Berkovitz. VWA
Oh! Mystery of Man. Wordsworth. *Fr.* The Prelude, XII. FiP
Oh, Nancy Dawson, hio! Cheer'ly, Man. *Unknown.* AmSS
"Oh, Nancy, my heart." To Milk in the Valley Below. *Unknown.* OBET
Oh, neighbors! I'll have such a quest shortly. Cops and Robbers. Bill Middleton. AMV-80
Oh Neïla/ borne away by evening. Neïla. Yvan Goll, *tr. by* Anthony Rudolf. VWA
Oh never in this hard world was such an absurd. Nesting Time. Douglas Stewart. BoAnP; PoAu-2
Oh never marry Ishmael! Song for Unbound Hair. Genevieve Taggard. PoRA
Oh, never, never more will I go to Cashel. The Journeyman. *Unknown, tr. by* Frank O'Connor. KiLC
Oh, never say that I was false of heart. *See* O, never say that I was false of heart.
Oh, never say that you have reached the very end. We Survive! Hirsch Glick, *tr. by* Ruth Rubin. TrJP
Oh nimber, nimber Will-o! Chuck Will's Widow Song. *Unknown.* BPo
Oh! ninna and anninia! Sleep, Baby Boy. *Unknown.* FaPON
Oh No. Robert Creeley. HeIP; InPK; NaP
Oh No John. *Unknown.* *See* O, No, John.
Oh [*or* O], no more, no more, too late. Song [*or* Love's Martyrs]. John Ford. ELP; GBL; LO; LoBV; NOBE; OBS; PoEL-2; SeCePo; ViBoPo
Oh, no one can deny. Self's the Man. Philip Larkin. NOBL
Oh, No! We Never Mention Her. Thomas Haynes Bayly. PaPo
Oh, Northern men—true hearts and bold. Cast Down, but Not Destroyed. *Unknown.* PAH
Oh, not to be in England. Abroad Thoughts. Edward Blishen. NOBL
"Oh, now I've come back to you, Mother." The Cripple for Life; or, The Poor Volunteer. *Unknown.* AmFP
Oh, now that it's vacation time. Vacation Time. Rowena Bennett. SiSoSe
Oh, now we're leaving home, me boys; to Ottawa we're goin'. The Lake of the Caogama. *Unknown.* WTO
Oh Oh Blues. *Unknown.* BluL
Oh—oh: death is awful. Death Is Awful. *Unknown.* BluL
Oh, oh, you will be sorry for that word! Edna St. Vincent Millay. BoWoP
Oh - ohh/ Smokestack lightnin'. Smokestack Lightnin'. *Unknown.* BluL
Oh, ole Zip Coon he is a larned skolar. *See* O, ole Zip Coon he is a larned skolar.
Oh, on an early morning I think I shall live forever! Poem in Three Parts. Robert Bly. CAPP; ConAP; NaP; NOBA; PAI
Oh, once I lived in Cottonwood and owned a little farm. Once I Lived in Cottonwood. *Unknown.* AmFP
Oh once I was a shepherd boy. Once I Was a Shepherd Boy. *Unknown.* OBET
Oh, once I was happy but now I'm forlorn. *See* O once I was happy but now I'm forlorn.
Oh, once upon a time in Arkansas. The Arkansas Traveler. *Unknown.* FSW
Oh, open the door, my hinnie, my heart. The Padda Song. *Unknown.* GBP
Oh [*or* O], open the door, some pity to shew [*or* show]. Open the Door to Me, Oh! Burns. FaBoCh; PoEL-4
Oh our Mother the Earth oh our Father the Sky. Song of the Sky Loom. *Unknown, tr. by* Herbert J. Spinden. WTO
Oh Paddy dear, and did you hear the news that's going [*or* goin'] round? *See* O Paddy dear, and did you hear the news that's going round?
Oh, pass around your bottle, we'll all take a drink. Pass Around Your Bottle. *Unknown.* OuSiCo
Oh, Passage town is of great renown. The Town of Passage. *Unknown.* OxBoLi
Oh, passer-by, should you inquire. Epitaph on Pegasus, a Limping Gay. Panormitanus. PeHV
Oh, Peterkin Pout and Gregory Grout. A Nursery Song. Laura E. Richards. HBV-1; HBVY
Oh, Pillykin Willykin Winky Wee! Punkydoodle and Jollapin. Laura E. Richards. OBCA
Oh, pity Reuben Ranzo! Reuben Ranzo, *vers.* III. *Unknown.* FSW
Oh pleasant eventide! Twilight Calm. Christina Rossetti. BoNaP; OBNC
Oh! pleasant exercise of hope and joy! *See* O pleasant exercise of hope and joy!
Oh, Please Don't Get Up! Ogden Nash. NePA
Oh-h-h-h, po' roustabout don't have no home. Roustabout Holler. *Unknown.* OuSiCo
"Oh [*or* O] Polly love [*or* dear], Oh Polly [*or* my dear Polly], the rout [*or* war] has now begun." High Germany. *Unknown.* FSW; OBET; WaaP
Oh, poor old Reuben [*or* pore old Roving] Ranzo *Unknown.* AmSS; ShS, *vers.* I *and* II
Oh! poverty is a weary thing, 'tis full of grief and pain. The Sale of the Pet Lamb. Mary Howitt. CH
"Oh, pray come in." Rather Too Good, Little Peggy! Adelaide O'Keeffe. FaBoUs
Oh Promise Me. Clement Scott. BLSo, *with music;* FaFP; FSN, *with music*; TreF
Oh, Prue she has a patient man. She Is Overheard Singing. Edna St. Vincent Millay. InMe
Oh, quiet peoples sleeping bed by bed. A Solis Ortus Cardine. Ford Madox Ford. ViBoPo
Oh, rare Harry Parry. *See* O rare Harry Parry.
"Oh [*or* O], rise up, Willy Reilly [*or* Willie Riley], and come along with me." Willy Reilly [*or* Willie Riley]. *Unknown.* BaBo; HBV-2; OnYi; OuSiCo.
Oh Roberta honey where you been so long. Roberta. *Unknown.* BluL

Oh, rock-a my soul in the bosom of Abraham. Rock-a My Soul. *Unknown.* FSW
Oh, rock-a-by, baby mouse, rock-a-by, so! The Mouse's Lullaby. Palmer Cox. OBCA
Oh, Roll On, Babe, *with music.* *Unknown.* OuSiCo
Oh, roll the cotton, roll me, boys. Roll the Cotton Down, *vers.* I. *Unknown.* ShS
Oh Roses for the Flush of Youth. Christina Rossetti. *See* Song: "Oh roses for the flush of youth."
Oh, rosy as the lining of a shell. Eugene Lee-Hamilton. Mimma Bella, IV. HBV-1
Oh, rouse you, rouse you, men at arms. The Great Swamp Fight. Caroline Hazard. PAH
Oh, row me cross the river. Rock 'n' Row Me Over. *Unknown.* FSW
Oh! St. Patrick was a gentleman. St. Patrick Was a Gentleman. Henry Bennett. SiSoSe
Oh, Sally Brown, of New York City. Sally Brown. *Unknown.* AmSS
Oh, Sally, my dear, I wish I could wed you. Sally My Dear. *Unknown.* FSW
Oh, Santa Anna fought for fame. Santa Anna; or, The Plains of Mexico. *Unknown.* AmSS
Oh [*or* O], say, can you see, by the dawn's early light. The Star-spangled Banner. Francis Scott Key. AA; BLPA; BLSo; FaBoBe; FaFP; FaPo; FaPON; FaPoR; FSW; HBV-2; HBVY; NePA; PAH; PAL; TAP; TreF; WBLP; YaD
Oh! say not woman's love is bought. Song. Isaac Pocock. *Fr.* The Heir of Vironi. HBV-1
Oh, say, were you ever in Rio Grande? Rio Grande. *Unknown.* FSW; TrAS
Oh, say, what is this fearful, wild. The Hippopotamus. Oliver Herford. NA
Oh, say you can hear/ On the Watergate tapes. Final Curtain. Roger Woddis. FaBoPa
Oh! say you so, bold sailor. The Herald Crane. Hamlin Garland. HBV-1
Oh, says the linnet, if I sing. Birds' Lament. John Clare. PoEL-4
Oh, See How Thick the Goldcup Flowers. A. E. Housman. A Shropshire Lad, V. FaBV; MoBrPo
Oh, see my little boat. The Boat. Caroline Gilman. OBCA
Oh, seek me not within a tomb. Envoi. John G. Neihardt. HBV-2; WGRP
Oh send to me an apple that hasn't any kernel. *Unknown, tr. fr. Welsh by* Gwyn Williams. FaBoCh
Oh, setting sun, had you no aureole? February 12, 1809. Gail Brook Burket. PGD
Oh shall I never never be home again? Brumana. James Elroy Flecker. BrPo
Oh she called to her little page boy. Lady Maisry. *Unknown.* OBET
Oh! she is good, the little rain! and well she knows our need. The Little Rain. Tu Fu, *tr. by* L. Cranmer-Byng. FaPON
Oh, she walked unaware of her own increasing beauty. She Walked Unaware. Patrick MacDonogh. BoLoP; ErPo; FaBoTw
Oh, Shenandoah, I long to hear [*or* see] you. Shenandoah. *Unknown.* AmFN; BLSo; FSW; TrAS; TreFT
Oh, Shenandoah, I love your daughter. Shenandoah. *Unknown.* AmSS
Oh Ship! new billows sweep thee out. The Ship of State. Horace, *tr. by* William Ewart Gladstone. Odes, I, 14. AWP
"Oh, sick I am to see you, will you never let me be?" The New Mistress. A. E. Housman. A Shropshire Lad, XXXIV. MoBrPo
Oh silver-throated Swan. *See* O silver-throated swan.
Oh, silver tree! Jazzonia. Langston Hughes. AmNP; BANP; NIP
Oh, sing a song of phosphates. Rhyme for a Chemical Baby. Joseph Cook. *Fr.* Boston Nursery Rhymes. InMe; QQQ; SpRo
Oh, sing me the song of the factory girl! Song of the Factory Girls. *Unknown.* SaC
Oh, Sing to God, *with music.* Jacob Steendam, *tr. fr. Dutch.* AH
Oh sing unto Jehovah a new song. *See* O sing unto the Lord a new song.
Oh! sing unto my roundelay [*or* O! Synge untoe mie roundelaie]. The Minstrel's Song [*or* My Love Is Dead *or* Mynstrelles Songe]. Thomas Chatterton. *Fr.* Aella. CH; EnLoPo; EnRP; HAP; HBV-1; LiTB; LO; LoBV; NOBE; NOEC; OBEC; OBEV; TrGrPo; WHA; WiR
Oh, sinner man, where you gonna run to? Sinner Man. *Unknown.* FSW
Oh sister/ how those Nulato sled dogs howl. The Ivory Dog for My Sister. Mary TallMountain. TWSS
Oh, sister Phoebe, how merry were we. Tom Jones's Plum Tree. *Unknown.* AmFP
Oh Sky, you look so drear! Earth and Sky. Eleanor Farjeon. PoSC; SUS
Oh, Sleep, Fond Fancy. *Unknown.* EIL
Oh, Sleep Forever in the Latmian Cave. Edna St. Vincent Millay. CMoP; LiTM; MoAmPo; MoVE; NoAM; NoP; SeCeV; ViBoPo
Oh! sleep in peace where poppies grow. Reply to "In Flanders Fields." John Mitchell. BLPA; PAL
Oh sleep, thou holy baby. Duérmete, Niño Lindo. *Tr. fr. Spanish.* FSW
Oh [*or* O], slow to smite and swift to spare. The Death of Lincoln [*or* Abraham Lincoln *or* To the Memory of Abraham Lincoln]. Bryant. AP; OHIP; PAH; TAP
Oh, slow up, dogies, quit your roving round. Night-herding Song. Harry Stephens. BPAW; CoSo; OuSiCo; TrAS
Oh smooth adder/ who with fanged kisses changedst my natural blood. Augusta Webster. *Fr.* Medea in Athens. BrRo
Oh! snatch'd away in beauty's bloom. *See* O snatch'd away beauty's bloom.
Oh soft flowing rivers. My South. Don West. PoNe
Oh some are fond of red wine, and some are fond of white. Captain Stratton's Fancy. John Masefield. MoBrPo; OBEV
Oh! some folks boast of quail on toast. The Abalone Song. George Sterling. BPAW
Oh some have killed in angry love. A Rope for Harry Fat. James K. Baxter. MoBS
Oh, somewhere there are people who. Midsummer Melancholy. Margaret Fishback. PV
Oh! spring was in his shining eyes. True and False. Isabella Valancy Crawford. PeCV
Oh, Stop Being Thankful All over the Place. Ogden Nash. NePA
Oh stormy, stormy world. Happiness Makes Up in Height for What It Lacks in Length. Robert Frost. MoAB; MoAmPo; MoPo
Oh, Stormy's gone, that good old man. Stormalong. *Unknown.* AmSS
Oh, strong and faithful and enduring. The Return. Martha Ostenso. CaP
Oh strong ridged and deeply hollowed. Smell. William Carlos Williams. MoAB; MoAmPo; TAP
Oh, Susan Blue. Kate Greenaway. TiPo
Oh! [*or* O] Susanna. Stephen Collins Foster. BLSo, *with music;* FaFP; FSW; OBAL; PSoN, *with music;* TrAS, *with music;* TreF
Oh swearing and telling. Cockcrow. Eithne Wilkins. NeBP
Oh, Sweet Content. W. H. Davies. CH
Oh sweet woods, the delight of solitariness! *See* O sweet woods, the delight of solitariness.
Oh, take my hand and stroll with me. The Land of Potpourri. Jack Prelutsky. RHPC
Oh [*or* O], talk not to me of a name great in story. Stanzas Written on the Road between Florence and Pisa [*or* All for Love]. Byron. EnRP; GTBS; GTBS-P; HBV-1; OBRV; TreFT
Oh Tannenbaum (Oh Christmas Tree). *Unknown, tr. fr. German.* FSW
Oh, Teddy wants a nine-dollar shawl. I Wish I Was a Mole in the Ground. *Unknown.* AmFP
Oh! tell me have you ever seen a red, long-leg'd Flamingo? The Flamingo. Lewis Gaylord Clark. NA
"Oh, tell me, sailor, tell me true." The Gray Swan. Alice Cary. BeLS; GN
"Oh, tell me what was on yer road, ye roarin' norlan' wind." The Wild Geese. Violet Jacob. BSV
Oh thank you cowboy with four-wheel drive. For Drum Hadley. Harold Littlebird. VoR
Oh thank you for giving me the chance. Thank You. Kenneth Koch. NeAP; PoM
Oh thanks for all since the days long past. Synnöve's Song. Björnstjerne Björnson, *tr. by* Charles Wharton Stork. PoPl
Oh that bright impossible beast of the mind. Virgin and Unicorn. John Heath-Stubbs. NeBP
Oh, that day there was a great demand for sailors. Mainsail Haul, *vers.* II. *Unknown.* ShS
Oh that horse I see so high. A Gift of Great Value. Robert Creeley. LCAP; NaP
Oh! that I always breath'd in such an air. The Experience. Edward Taylor. Preparatory Meditations: First Series, III. AmPP
Oh that I had wings like a dove! Wings. Bible, *O.T.* Psalms, LV. FaPON
Oh that I was the Bird of Paradise! Edward Taylor. *Fr.* Preparatory Meditations. NOCV
Oh that I were/ Where I would be. *Unknown.* OxNR
Oh, that I were a lovely flower. The Flower. Samuel Speed. OxBoCh
Oh! that I were a poet now in grain! An Elegie upon that Reverend. . .Mr. Thomas Shepard. Urian Oakes. SCAP
Oh That I Were in the Wilderness. Bible, *O.T.* Jeremiah, IX: 1-10. TrJP
Oh, that last day in Lucknow fort! The Relief of Lucknow. Robert Traill Spence Lowell. HBV-2
Oh! that mine eye might closed be. Prayer. Thomas Ellwood. WGRP
Oh that moon is going down, baby. Moon Going Down. *Unknown.* BluL
Oh that my lungs could bleat like butter'd pease. Odd but True [*or* Nonsense]. *Unknown.* FaBoCo; FaBoNo; NA; NOBL
Oh that my soul a marrow-bone might seize! Sonnet Found in a Deserted Madhouse. *Unknown.* FaBoCo; FaBoNo; InvP; NA
Oh! That my young life were a lasting dream. Dreams. Poe. AmPP; OxBA; TAP
Oh! that the desert [*or* desart] were my dwelling-place. The Ocean [*or* By the

Deep Sea]. Byron. *Fr.* Childe Harold's Pilgrimage, IV. OBNC; PoEL-4
Oh [*or* O] that those lips had language! Life has passed [*or* pass'd]. On the Receipt of [*or* Lines on Receiving] My Mother's Picture out of Norfolk. William Cowper. CH; EnRP; FiP; HBV-2; NOEC; OAEP; OBEC; OHIP
Oh! that 'twere possible. *See* O that 'twere possible.
Oh! that we two were Maying. Song. Charles Kingsley. *Fr.* The Saint's Tragedy. HBV-1
Oh that you were yourself! But, love, you are. *See* O that you were yourself! But, love, you are.
Oh, the anchor's aweigh, the anchor's aweigh. The Anchor's Aweigh. *Unknown.* ShS
Oh, the anguish of Mary! Not There. *Unknown.* STF
Oh, the auld house, the auld house. The Auld House. Lady Nairne. HBV-2
Oh, the beautiful maiden has gone away. A Garland of Recital Programs. Franklin P. Adams. InMe
Oh, the big ice axe, it hangs on the wall. The Scottish Mountaineering Club Song. John G. Stott. PoSH
Oh, the bitter shame and sorrow. None of Self and All of Thee [*or* Christ Alone]. Theodore Monod. BLRP; STF
Oh, the blue blue bloom. Pansy. Mary Effie Lee Newsome. CDC
Oh, the [*or* de] boll weevil is [*or* am] a little black bug. The Boll Weevil Song [*or* Ballad of the Boll Weevil]. *Unknown.* AS; BLSo; FSW; TrAS
Oh, the bosses' tricks of '76. Two-Cent Coal. *Unknown.* AmFP
Oh, the brave old Duke of York. *See* Oh, the noble old Duke of York.
Oh the broom, the yellow broom. The Broom Flower. Mary Howitt. HBV-1
Oh, the Camptown ladies sing this song. Camptown Races. Stephen Collins Foster. FSW
Oh, the candidate's a dodger. The Dodger Song. *Unknown.* FSW
Oh the charming month of May! Song. Joseph Addison. NOEC
Oh, the comfort—the inexpressible comfort of feeling safe with a person. Friendship. Dinah Maria Mulock Craik. BLPA
Oh the corrugated-iron town. Douglas Stewart. *Fr.* The Birdsville Track. CBAP
Oh the dance of our Sister! The Dance of the Rain. Eugène Marais, *tr. by* Jack Cope *and* Uys Krige. PeSA
Oh! the days are gone, when beauty bright. Love's Young Dream. Thomas Moore. HBV-1; WBLP
Oh [*or* O], the days gone by! Oh [*or* O], the days gone by! The Days Gone By. James Whitcomb Riley. OBCA; TreF
Oh, the deacon went down. Ain't Gonna Grieve My Lord No More. *Unknown.* FSW
Oh, the Devil in hell they say he was chained. Hell in Texas. *Unknown.* CoSo
Oh! the eastern winds are blowing. The Cornish Emigrant's Song. Robert Stephen Hawker. EBVV
Oh the falling snow! For Snow. Eleanor Farjeon. CH
Oh [*or* O]! the French are on the sea [*or* say]. The Shan Van Vocht. *Unknown.* AnIL; AnIV; FSW; GBP; OnYI
Oh, the Funniest Thing. *Unknown.* EvOK
Oh, the gen'ral raised the devil with the kernel, so 'tis said. Bugs. Will Stokes. MoShBr
Oh, the girl that I loved she was handsome. The Man on the Flying Trapeze. *Unknown.* FaFP; OxBoLi
Oh, the gold hills of Ireland. They Who Wait. Charles Buxton Going. HBMV
Oh, the hearts of men, they are rovers, all! Ulysses Returns, IV. Roselle Mercier Montgomery. HBMV
Oh the Inconstant. N. P. Van Wyk Louw, *tr. fr. Afrikaans by* Uys Krige *and* Jack Cope. PeSA
Oh the January man he walks abroad in woollen coat and boots of leather. January Man. Dave Goulder. OBET
Oh, the joy of looking forward. He Is Coming. Gladys M. Gearhart. STF
Oh! the king's gane gyte. Cophetua. "Hugh MacDiarmid." OxBS; POL
Oh, the little birds sang east, and the little birds sang west. Round Our Restlessness. Elizabeth Barrett Browning. TRV
Oh, the littles that remain! After. Lizette Woodworth Reese. HBV-1
Oh, the lives of men, lives of men. Bindlestiff. Edwin Ford Piper. HBMV
Oh the many joys of a harlot's wedding. Hail Wedded Love! Jay Macpherson. MoCV
Oh, the men who laughed the American laughter. American Laughter. Kenneth Allan Robinson. AmFN; TreFS
Oh the Miller, the dusty, musty Miller. A Ballad of All the Trades. *Unknown.* CoMu; ErPo; UnTE
Oh, the minstrels sing of an English king of many long years ago. The Bastard King of England. *Unknown.* FSW
Oh, the Month of May! Thomas Dekker. *See* O, the Month of May.
Oh! the night that I struck New York. The Bowery. Charles Hale Hoyt. FSN; TreF; YaD
Oh [*or* O], the noble [*or* brave *or* grand old] duke of York. The Noble [*or* Brave Old] Duke of York. *Unknown.* FSW; GBP; OxNR
Oh the north countree is a hard countree. The Ballad of Yukon Jake. Edward E. Paramore, Jr. BeLS; BLPA
Oh, the old gray mare, she ain't what she used to be. Old Gray Mare. *Unknown.* AS; GBP
Oh! the old swimmin'-hole! whare the crick so still and deep. The Old Swimmin'-Hole. James Whitcomb Riley. BeLS; FaFP; HBV-1
Oh, the Pilliwinks lived by the portals of Loo. The Cooky-Nut Trees. Albert Bigelow Paine. OBCA
Oh, the Polliwog is woggling. The Polliwog. Arthur Guiterman. RHPC
Oh, the praire dogs are screaming. A Cow Camp on the Range. *Unknown.* CoSo
Oh, the praties they grow small. The Praties. *Unknown.* FSW; WTO
Oh, the rain is slanting sharply, and the Norther's blowing cold. Ballad of the Hyde Street Grip. Gelett Burgess. BPAW
Oh, the revenue men is riding. Revenue Man Blues. *Unknown.* BluL
Oh, the Rifles have stolen my dear jewel away. The Rifles. *Unknown.* OBET
Oh, the Roman was a rogue. Lay of Ancient Rome. Thomas R. Ybarra. HBV-2; InMe; WhC
Oh, the sea is deep. Song for a Suicide. Langston Hughes. PoNe
Oh, the sexual life of the camel. The Sexual Life of the Camel. *Unknown.* DBV
Oh, the shambling sea is a sexton old. The Gravedigger. Bliss Carman. BoNaP
Oh! the shearing is all over. The Old Bullock Dray. *Unknown.* PoAu-1
Oh, the sheer joy of it! Sheer Joy. Ralph Spaulding Cushman. TRV
Oh, the slimy, squirmy, slithery eel! Song of Hate for Eels. Arthur Guiterman. OBAL
Oh! the snow, the beautiful snow. The Beautiful Snow. John Whittaker Watson. BLPA; TreF; WBLP
Oh the SS *Irwell* left this port the stormy sea to cross. The Manchester Ship Canal. *Unknown.* OBET
Oh the streams of lovely Nancy are divided into three parts. The Streams of Lovely Nancy. *Unknown.* FaBoBa; OBET
Oh, the summer time is coming. Will You Go, Lassie, Go? *Unknown.* FSW
Oh, the sun sets red, the moon shines white. The *Armstrong* at Fayal. Wallace Rice. PAH
Oh, the sweet contentment. Coridon's Song. John Chalkhill. HBV-1; ViBoPo
Oh, the tidal waves of our suffering. The Law. Albert Haynes. NBP
Oh! the time that is past. *Unknown.* BoLoP
Oh, the times are hard and the wages low. Across the Western Ocean. *Unknown.* AmSS; AS; FSW
Oh the times are hard and the wages low. Leave Her, Bullies, Leave Her. *Unknown.* AS
Oh the Toe-Test! Norma Farber. RHPC
Oh, the train's off the track. The Train Is off the Track. *Unknown.* AmFP
Oh the white seagull, the wild seagull. The Seagull. Mary Howitt. OxBChV
Oh, the Wild Joy[s] of Living. Robert Browning. *Fr.* Saul. FaBV; TreFT
Oh, the wind blow east. The Wind Blow East. *Unknown.* OuSiCo
Oh, the wind from the desert blew in!—Khamsin. Khamsin. Clinton Scollard. AA
Oh the wine's fine. Song for New Orleans, A. George Keithley. NPGG
Oh the wold, the wold. Wind. Sydney Dobell. PeD
Oh, the work was hard and the wages low. Time to Leave Her. *Unknown.* AmSS
Oh, them days on Red Hoss Mountain, when the skies was fair 'nd blue. Casey's Table d'Hote. Eugene Field. PoOW
Oh, then, I see Queen Mab hath been with you. *See* O, then, I see Queen Mab hath been with you.
"Oh, then tell me, Shawn [*or* Sean] O'Ferrall [*or* O'Farrall]." The Rising of the Moon. John Keegan Casey. AnIV; FSW; OnYI
Oh, there are those, a sordid clan. The Child's Heritage. John G. Neihardt. HBV-1
Oh [*or* O] there is blessing in this gentle breeze. Wordsworth. *Fr.* The Prelude, I. EnRP; OAEL-2; TreFT
Oh, there once was a merry crocodile. The Merry Crocodile. Gertrude E. Heath. TDH
Oh, there once was a Puffin. There Once Was a Puffin. Florence Page Jaques. NTCP; SoPo; TiPo
Oh! there once was a swagman camped in a Billabong. Waltzing Matilda. A. B. Paterson. WhC
Oh! there was a moanish lady. Moanish Lady. *Unknown.* AS
Oh there was a woman and she was a widow. *See* O there was a woman and she was a widow.
Oh, there was a youth and a noble youth. The Bailiff's Daughter of Islington. *Unknown.* AmFP

Oh! There was an old soldier. *See* O there was an old soldier and he had a wooden leg.
Oh, there was once a tree. The Green Grass Grew All Around. *Unknown.* FSW
Oh, there were fifteen men in green. Men in Green. David Campbell. PoAu-2
Oh they built the ship *Titanic* to sail the ocean blue. The *Titanic.* *Unknown.* FSW
Oh, they call me Hanging Johnny. Hanging Johnny. *Unknown.* FSW
Oh! think how hard it is to die when young! Charles Heavysege. *Fr.* Jephthah's Daughter. CaP
Oh, Think Not I Am Faithful to a Vow! Edna St. Vincent Millay. FaBV (Sonnet.) MasP
Oh, this is the place where fishermen gather. The Squid-jiggin' Ground. *Unknown.* FSW
Oh, this is the tale of John Cherokee. John Cherokee. *Unknown.* GBP
Oh this man. Magnificat. Michele Roberts. BrRo
Oh those were happy days, heaped up with wineskins. Silenus in Proteus. Thomas Lovell Beddoes. EnRP
Oh thou great Power, in whom I move. A Hymn to My God in a Night of My Late Sicknesse. Sir Henry Wotton. AnAnS-2; MeLP; MePo; OBS
Oh, thou immortal bard! Byron. J. Gordon Coogler. OBAL
Oh thou, that dear and happy isle. Andrew Marvell. *Fr.* Upon Appleton House. OxBoLi
Oh thou that swing'st upon the waving ear [*or* eare *or* haire]. *See* O thou that swing'st upon the waving hair.
Oh, Thou! Who Dry'st the Mourner's Tear. Thomas Moore. TrPWD
Oh [*or* O] Thou, Who Man of Baser Earth Didst Make. Omar Khayyám, *tr. fr. Persian by* Edward Fitzgerald. *Fr.* The Rubáiyát of Omar Khayyám. EaLo; SeCeV
Oh, thy bright eyes must answer now. *See* O thy bright eyes must answer now.
Oh, 'tis little Mary Cassidy's the cause of all my misery. Little Mary Cassidy. Francis A. Fahy. HBV-1
Oh! 'tis of a bold major a tale I'll relate. A Longford Legend. *Unknown.* OnYI
Oh! 'tis of a rich merchant, in London did dwell. *See* 'Tis of a rich merchant who in London did dwell.
Oh! 'tis pretty to be in Ballinderry. Ballinderry. *Unknown.* WTO
"Oh, 'tis time I should talk to your mother." Ask and Have. Samuel Lover. HBV-1; TreFS
Oh to be a bride. The Bride. Bella Akhmadulina, *tr. by* Stephen Stepanchev. BoWoP; PBWP
Oh to be at Crowdieknowe. Crowdieknowe. "Hugh MacDiarmid." InPS; NoAM; NoP; OxBS
Oh [*or* O], to be in England. Home-Thoughts, from Abroad. Robert Browning. AWP; BoNaP; EBVV; FaBoBe; FaBoEn; FaBV; FaFP; FaPON; FaPoR; FiP; FPL; GN; HBV-1; HBVY; HeIP; LiTB; NOBE; NoP; OAEP; OBEV; OBNC; OBVV; PoLF; PoRA; PrIm; SeCeV; TEP; TreF; TrGrPo; WHA
"Oh! to be in England." Home Thoughts from Abroad, *parody.* *Unknown.* Par
Oh to be in England now that Winston's out. Ezra Pound. *Fr.* Cantos, LXXX. PoA
Oh, to be in Oleanna! Oleanna. Pete Seeger. FSW
Oh to be moving as we once were. After Sex. Greg Kuzma. GP
Oh, to be there to-night! Ada Cambridge. *Fr.* On Australian Hills. PoAu-1
Oh! to be wafted away. Quatrain. *Unknown.* NA
Oh, to come home once more, when the dusk is falling. A Song of Twilight. *Unknown.* HBV-1
Oh, to feel the fresh breeze blowing. The Song of the Forest Ranger. Herbert Bashford. HBV-1; OHIP
Oh, to have a little house! *See* O, to have a little house.
Oh, to those who know no better. That Little Lump of Coal. *Unknown.* AmFP
Oh [*or* O], to vex me, contraryes [*or* contraries] meet in one. Devout Fits. John Donne. Holy Sonnets, XIX. AnAnS-1; MasP; OAEL-1; PoEL-2; SeCePo
Oh, Tommy's gone, what shall I do? Tommy's Gone to Hilo. *Unknown.* AmSS; FSW
Oh! trouble not Menèdemos by guile. Epigram. Strato, *tr. by* Sydney Oswald. PeHV
Oh! true was his heart while he breathed. The King of Thulé. Goethe, *tr. by* James Clarence Mangan. AWP
Oh turn away those cruel eyes. *See* O turn away those cruel eyes.
Oh, 'twas bitter cold/ As our steamboat rolled. The Red-Breast of Aquitania. Francis S. Mahony. OnYI
Oh! 'twas Dermot O'Nowlan McFigg. The Humours of Donnybrook Fair. Charles O'Flaherty. OnYI
Oh very early all in the spring. Early, Early in the Spring. *Unknown.* OBET
Oh virgin queen of mountain-side and woodland. The Pine Tree for Diana. Horace, *tr. by* Louis Untermeyer. Odes, III, 22. AWP
Oh, wake her, oh, shake her. Johnny Walk Along to Hilo. *Unknown.* ShS
Oh wanderer in the southern weather. An Indian Song. W. B. Yeats. VLP
Oh! water for me! Bright water for me! The Water-Drinker. Edward Jonson. BXAP; PeD
Oh, we come on the sloop *John B.* The *John B.* Sails. *Unknown.* AS
Oh, we don't get no justice here in Atlanta. We Don't Get No Justice Here in Atlanta. *Unknown.* OuSiCo
Oh, we had an old hen and she had a wooden leg. Another Little Drink. *Unknown.* TrAS, *with* Old Zip Coon
Oh, we started down from Roto when the sheds had all cut out. On the Road to Gundagai. *Unknown.* PoAu-1
Oh [*or* O] wearisome condition of humanity. Chorus Sacerdotum. Fulke Greville. *Fr.* Mustapha. FaBoEn; HAP; InVP; JCP; LiTB; MePo; NOBE; OAEL-1; OBS; PoEL-1; PPP; SeCePo; SeCeV; ViBoPo
Oh! Weary Mother. Barry Pain. The Poets at Tea, VIII. NA ("Lilies lie in my lady's bower, The.") Par
Oh, weep for Mr. and Mrs. Bryan! The Lion. Ogden Nash. CenHV; ShM
Oh well done Lord E[ldo]n! and better done R[yde]r! An Ode to the Framers of the Frame Bill. Byron. CoMu; SaC
Oh well it's our Father who art in Heaven. You Shall. *Unknown.* BluL
Oh, we'll rally 'round the flag, boys, we'll rally once again. The Battle Cry of Freedom. George Frederick Root. FSW
Oh, Wellington! (or "Villainton") for Fame. Wellington [*or* On Wellington]. Byron. *Fr.* Don Juan, IX. FiP; OBRV; OBSV; OxBoLi
Oh were I at the moss house, where the birds do increase. The Streams of Bunclody. *Unknown.* BIrV
Oh, we're up in the morning ere breaking of day. The Railroad Corral. *Unknown.* CoSo; FSW
Oh Wert Thou in the Cauld Blast. Burns. *See* O Wert Thou in the Cauld Blast.
Oh wha are sae happy as me an' my Moggy? Moggy and Me. James Hogg. HBV-1
Oh, whar shill we go w'en de great day comes. Revival Hymn. Joel Chandler Harris. *Fr.* Uncle Remus. HBV-2
"Oh whare hae ye been a' day, my bonnie wee croodlin dow?" *See* "O whare haeye been a'day. . ."
Oh, what a beautiful city. Twelve Gates to the City. *Unknown.* FSW
Oh what a cunning guest. *See* O what a cunning guest.
Oh, what a drear dark close to my poor day! Robert Browning. *Fr.* Pippa Passes, sc. iv. PeD
Oh, what a dreary place this was when first the Mormons found it. St. George. Charlie Walker. AmFP
Oh what a host of questions in me rose. Back Again for the Holidays. John Betjeman. *Fr.* Summoned by Bells. FaBoPP
Oh, what a lark to fish for shark. The Shark. J. J. Bell. RHPC
Oh, what a night for a soul to go! Iter Supremum. Arthur Sherburne Hardy. AA
Oh [*or* O]! what a plague is Love! Phillida Flouts Me [*or* The Disdainful Shepherdess]. *Unknown.* CoMu; ElL; HBV-1; InVP; OBEV; OBSC; TrGrPo; ViBoPo
Oh, what a set of Vagabundos. Morgan. Edmund Clarence Stedman. AA; HBV-2
Oh! What a thing is man? Lord, who am I? Edward Taylor. Preparatory Meditations: First Series, XXXVIII. AP; NOBA; OxBA
Oh, what a you say, seekers. Die in de Fiel'. *Unknown.* BoAN-1
Oh, what amiss may I forgive in Thee. Sidney Lanier. *Fr.* The Crystal. TRV
Oh, what an effort it is. It Is True. Federico García Lorca, *tr. by* Harriet de Onís. OLR
Oh, what are you waiting for here, young man? James Thomson. Sunday up the River, II. OBVV
Oh, what can ail thee, knight-at-arms. *See* O, what can ail thee, knight-at-arms.
Oh, what can be more pleasant. Chorus of Scyrian Maidens. Philip Bainbrigge. *Fr.* Achilles in Scyros. PeHV
Oh, what can you do with a Christmas pup. Gift with the Wrappings Off. Mary Elizabeth Counselman. RHPC
Oh, what have you got for dinner, Mrs. Bond? *Unknown.* OxNR
Oh, what is abroad in the marsh and the terminal sea? Sidney Lanier. *Fr.* The Marshes of Glynn. EtS
Oh, what is Jeanie weeping for. All on a Summer's Day. *Unknown.* PoPle
"Oh! what is that comes gliding in." Sally Simpkin's Lament. Thomas Hood. EnRP; MOS; ShM
Oh what is that country. Mother Country. Christina Rossetti. OxBoCh
Oh, what is that I see yonder coming. Union Train. Lee Hays, Millard Lampell, *and* Pete Seeger. FSW
Oh, what know they of harbors. Plymouth Harbor. Mrs. Ernest Radford. HBV-1
Oh, what precious peace I find. The Hour of Prayer. Georgia B. Adams. STF

Oh, what shall we do with a drunken sailor. The Drunken Sailor; or, Early in the Morning. *Unknown.* ShS
Oh, what was your name in the States? What Was Your Name in the States? *Unknown.* AS
"Oh, what's that stain on your shirt sleeve?" Edward. *Unknown.* AmFP
Oh! what's the matter? what's the matter? Wordsworth. *Fr.* Goody Blake and Harry Gill. Par
Oh, what's the matter wi' [*or* with] you, my lass. Jimmy's Enlisted; or, The Recruited Collier. *Unknown.* CoMu; EBEV; OBET
Oh, what's the way to Arcady. The Way to Arcady. H. C. Bunner. AA; InMe
Oh, when I come to die. Give Me Jesus. *Unknown.* BoAN-1; BPo
Oh, when I go down to Bimini. Never Get a Lickin' Till I Go Down to Bimini. *Unknown.* OuSiCo
Oh when I think of my long-suffering race. Enslaved. Claude McKay. BALP; BPo
Oh, When I Was in Love with You. A. E. Housman. A Shropshire Lad, XVIII. BoLoP; FaBV; LiTB; MoBrPo; NBM; OAEP; OLR
Oh, when I was single, oh then, oh then! I Wish I Were Single Again. *Unknown.* AmFP
Oh, when I'm in trouble. Do, Lord, Remember Me. *Unknown.* AmFP
Oh! when my friend and I. Friendship. Robert Blair. *Fr.* The Grave. OBEC
Oh, When Shall I See Jesus? *with music.* *Unknown.* AH
(Ecstasy, 1 *st., at. to* John Leland.) AmFP
Oh when the early morning at the seaside. East Anglian Bathe. John Betjeman. NoP
Oh, when the saints go marching in. *See* O when the saints go marchin' in.
Oh, when this earthly tenement. "Ada." BlSi
"Oh, when we going to marry, to marry, to marry." Buffalo Boy. *Unknown.* AmFP
"Oh whence do you come, my dear friend, to me." The Poor Ghost. Christina Rossetti. GBL
Oh, whenever I went away, the story I'd like to tell. The Campañero. *Unknown.* ShS
Oh where! and oh where is your Highland laddie gone? The Blue Bells of Scotland. *Unknown.* HBV-2; TreFS. *See also* Oh where, please tell me where.
Oh, where are you going, my good old man? Where Are You Going, My Good Old Man? *Unknown.* FSW
"Oh, where are you going, my kind old husband." The Best Old Fellow in the World. *Unknown.* AmFP
"Oh, where are you going, my little maiden fair." The Milkmaid. *Unknown.* AmFP
Oh, where are you going, says Milder to Malder. *See* O where are you going, says Milder to Malder.
Oh where are you going to, all you Big Steamers. Big Steamers. Kipling. Par
Oh, where are you going to, my pretty little dear. Dabbling in the Dew. *Unknown.* CH
"Oh, where are you going with your lovelocks flowing." Amor Mundi. Christina Rossetti. NBM; NoP; PoEL-5
Oh! Where Do Fairies Hide Their Heads? Thomas Haynes Bayly. HBV-1; HBVY
Oh, where do you come from. Little Raindrops. *At. to* Ann Hawkshaw, *also to* Jane Euphemia Browne. HBV-1; HBVY; OxBChV
"Oh, where have you been, Billy boy, Billy boy?" Billy Boy. *Unknown.* AmFP; BLPA; HoPM
"Oh, where have you been, Lord Randal, my son?" *See* O where have you been, Lord Randal, my son?
Oh, where, Kincora! is Brian the Great? Kincora [*or* Lamentation of Mac Liag for Kincora]. *Unknown, tr. by* James Clarence Mangan. AnIL; OnYI; OxBI
Oh where, oh where has my little dog gone? Mother Goose. OxNR
Oh where, Oh where ish mine little dog gone. Der Deitcher's Dog. Septimus Winner. PSoN
Oh where, please tell me where. The Blue Bells of Scotland. *Unknown, ad. by* Annie McVicar *and* Dorothy Jordan. FSW. *See also* Oh where! and oh where is your Highland laddie gone?
Oh! where shall I bury my poor dog Tray. The Cynotaph. "Thomas Ingoldsby." *Fr.* The Ingoldsby Legends. FM
Oh, where the white quince blossom swings. Japanesque. Oliver Herford. FiBHP
Oh, where will be the birds that sing. A Hundred Years to Come. Hiram Ladd Spencer, *wr. at. to* William Goldsmith Brown. HBV-2
Oh! wherefore come ye forth, in triumph from the North. The Battle of Naseby. Macaulay. HBV-2; OBRV
Oh, where's that girl that will go with me. *Unknown.* CoSo
Oh, whiffaree an' a-whiffo-rye. Honey, Take a Whiff on Me. *Unknown.* OxBoLi
Oh, whiskey is the life of man. Whiskey, Johnny [*or* Whiskey for My Johnny]. *Unknown.* AmSS; ShS (*vers.* II)
Oh, whisky here, and whisky there. Whisky, Johnny, *vers.* I. *Unknown.* AmFP
Oh whither, oh why, and oh wherefore. Goosey Goosey Gander—By Various Authors (Swineburne's Version). William Percy French. CenHV
Oh, who can sleep/ On a summer night. Night Enchantment. Eleanor Muth. SiSoSe
Oh who can speak, what numbers can reveal. Pompey and Cornelia. Lucan, *tr. by* Nicholas Rowe. *Fr.* Pharsalia, V. OBEC
Oh, who has not heard of the Northmen of yore. America. Arthur Cleveland Coxe. PAH
Oh, who is so merry, so merry, heigh ho! The Light-hearted Fairy. *Unknown.* FaPON; SUS
Oh! who is that poor foreigner that lately came to town. Irish Molly O. *Unknown.* HBV-1
Oh Who Is That Young Sinner [with the Handcuffs on His Wrists?] A. E. Housman. ChMP; FaBoTw; PeHV; SoSe
Oh! who is there of us that has not felt. November. Frederick Goddard Tuckerman. NOBA
Oh! who on the mountain, the plain, or the wave. The Song of the Micmac. Joseph Howe. CaP
Oh, Who Regards. *Unknown.* EIL
Oh, who shall from this dungeon raise. *See* O who shall from this dungeon raise.
Oh, who will follow old Ben Milam into San Antonio? The Valor of Ben Milam. Clinton Scollard. HBV-2; PAH
"Oh, who will shoe your feet, my love." The Mournful Dove. *Unknown.* AmFP
"Oh, who will shoe your foot, my dear?" The Lass of Roch Royal. *Unknown.* ViBoFo
Oh, who would stay indoor, indoor. Hunting-Song. Richard Hovey. *Fr.* King Arthur. HBV-1
Oh who'll replace this old miner. The Old Miner. *Unknown.* OBET
"Oh, why did God,/ Creator wise." Adam Speaks. Milton. *Fr.* Paradise Lost, X. NU
Oh, why does New York go to France for its fun? Come to Britain; a Humble Contribution to the Movement. A. P. Herbert. WhC
Oh, why does the white man follow my path. The Indian Hunter. Eliza Cook. BLPA
Oh, why don't you [*or* I] work like other men do? Hallelujah, I'm a Bum [*or* Hallelujah, Bum Again. *Unknown.* AS, *with music;* FSW; GBP; SaC, *abr.;* TrAS, *with music*
Oh, why left I my hame? The Exile's Song. Robert Gilfillan. HBV-2
Oh [*or* O]! Why Should the Spirit of Mortal Be Proud? William Knox. BLPA; FaFP; HBV-2; TreF; WBLP; WGRP
Oh, will you wear red? I'll Wear Me a Cotton Dress. *Unknown.* BPo
Oh, will you wear white, oh my dear, oh my dear? Jenny Jenkins *Unknown.* FSW
Oh, Willie was a plowboy. The Banks of Dundee. *Unknown.* BaBo
Oh [*or* O], wilt thou have my hand, Dear, to lie along in thine? Inclusions. Elizabeth Barrett Browning. HBV-1; OBVV; UnTE
Oh, women dear, and did ye hear the news that's going round. The Purple, White and Green. L. E. Morgan-Browne. BrRo
Oh wond'rous power of words, how sweet they are. The Young Wordsworth's London. Wordsworth. *Fr.* The Prelude, VII. FaBoPP
"Oh [*or* O], World-God, give me Wealth!" the Egyptian cried. Gifts. Emma Lazarus. TrJP; WGRP
Oh, worship the King all glorious above. The Majesty and Mercy of God. Sir Robert Grant. OHIP; WGRP
Oh would I could subdue the flesh. Senex. John Betjeman. DTC
Oh, Would That I Knew. Al-Samau'al ibn Adiya, *tr. fr. Arabic.* TrJP
Oh, would that working I might shun. Ode to Work in Springtime. Thomas R. Ybarra. HBMV
Oh would you know why Henry sleeps. Inhuman Henry. A. E. Housman. FiBHP
Oh, Ye Censurers. Al-Samau'al ibn Adiya, *tr. fr. Arabic by* Hartwig Hirschfeld. TrJP
Oh ye wha are sae guid yoursel'. *See* O ye wha are sae guid yoursel'.
Oh ye! who teach the ingenuous youth of nations. Byron. *Fr.* Don Juan, II. EnRP
Oh ye who tread the Narrow Way. The Buddha at Kamakura. Kipling. LoBV
Oh—-Yeah! Sharon Scott. JB
Oh Yes. William Matthews. AmPA
Oh yes/ We got Mr. President Roosevelt. President Roosevelt. *Unknown.* BluL
Oh, yes, I'm gwine up, gwine up. Gwine Up. *Unknown.* BoAN-1
Oh, yes, my lads, we'll roll alee. Come Down, You Bunch of Roses, Come Down. *Unknown.* ShS
Oh, Yes! Oh, Yes! Wait 'til I Git on My Robe, *with music.* *Unknown.* BoAN-2

Oh yes, we are so thankful. The Black Army. S. E. K. Mqhayi, *tr. by* C. M. Mcanyangwa *and* Jack Cope. PeSA
Oh yesterday the cutting edge drank thirstily and deep. Tomorrow. John Masefield. MoBrPo; TrGrPo
Oh! yet a few short years of useful life. Wordsworth. *Fr.* The Prelude, XIII. OBRV
Oh [*or* O] yet we trust that somehow good. In Memoriam A. H. H., LIV. Tennyson. BiP; EaLo; EBVV; HBV-2; LiTB; LoBV; NoP; OBNC; SeCeV; TreFS; TrGrPo; TRV; WGRP
Oh Yield, Fair Lids. Sheridan. OnYI
Oh, you are a kilt which a young dandy set out to choose. A Woman Sings of Her Love. *Somali Oral Tradition, tr. by* B. W. Andrzejwski *and* I. M. Lewis. WTO
Oh you canna spend a dollar when you're dead. Ding Dong Dollar. Hamish Henderson. FSW
Oh, you come along, boys, you listen to my tale. The Old Chisholm Trail. *Unknown.* AmFP
Oh, you foulbreathed destroyer of children and villages. Warming Up for the Real Thing. Lee Rudolph. TW
Oh, you know Joe Silovatesky. Me Johnny Mitchell Man. *Unknown.* TrAS
"Oh, you must answer my questions nine." The Devil's Nine Questions. *Unknown.* AmFP; WSC
Oh, you tall traveler. A Friend's Passing. Barclay Sheaks. AMV-80
Oh you used to told me you could drive me like a cow. From Now On. *Unknown.* BluL
Oh, You Wholly Rectangular. E. R. Cole. GoYe
Oh! young Lochinvar has [*or* is] come out of the West. Young Lochinvar, *parody. Unknown.* FiBHP; InMe
Oh [*or* O], young Lochinvar is come out of the west. Lochinvar [*or* Young Lochinvar]. Sir Walter Scott. *Fr.* Marmion. BeLS; BSV; EnRP; EvOK; FaBoBe; FaBV; FaFP; FaPON; FPL; GN; GoTS; HBV-1; HBVY; NOBE; OAEP; OBNC; OBNV; OBRV; OxBS; PaPo; PoRA; RoGo; TreF; WHA
Oh, your sweetness, softness, smoothness! Lassitude. Paul Verlaine, *tr. by* Lawrence M. Bensky. ErPo
Oh, your thighs. Love Poem. Judson Crews. UnTE
"Oh, you're welcome home again," said the young man to his love. The Grey Cock. *Unknown.* BaBo
Oh youth, beware! that laurel-rose. Larissa. Thomas Love Peacock. *Fr.* Rhododaphne. OBRV
Oh Zlotchev, my home, my town. Zlotchev, My Home. Moishe Leib Halpern, *tr. by* Richard J. Fein. VWA
Ohio. John Updike. AMV-80
Ohio Valley Swains. James Wright. NNaP
Ohioan Pastoral. James Wright. LCAP
Ohms. Irving Layton. NeAC
Oho for the woods where I used to grow. The Song of the Christmas Tree. Blanche Elizabeth Wade. OHIP
O'Hussey's Ode to the Maguire. Eochadh O'Hussey, *tr. fr. Middle Irish by* James Clarence Mangan. AnIV; SeCePo
(Ode to the Maguire.) BIrV; OnYI; OxBI
Oil. Linda Hogan. TWSS
Oil. Hansjörg Mayer. WeW
Oil. Gary Snyder. LCAP
Oil and Blood. Gary Allan Kizer. LFAC
Oil, came, The. NHR. Jack Hirschman. VWA
Oil Lamp, The. William Jay Smith. TDH
Oileus by his brother's side stood close. Homer, *tr. by* George Chapman. *Fr.* The Iliad, XIII. OBVE
Oiseaurie. Margaret Widdemer. BXAP
Oisin. *Unknown, tr. fr. Irish by* Frank O'Connor. KiLC
Oisin in the Land of Youth. Michael Comyn, *tr. fr. Modern Irish by* Tomás O'Flannghaile. AnIL
Oisin, tell me the famous story. The Wanderings of Oisin. W. B. Yeats. BrPo
Oithona; a Poem. James Macpherson. LAuP
Ojibwa War Songs. *Unknown, tr. fr. Ojibwa Indian by* H. H. Schoolcraft. AWP
Ojisan after the Stroke; Three Notes to Himself. Tina Koyama. BrSi
Ojistoh. Pauline E. Johnson. NOBC
OK, it's imperishable or a world as Will. The Same Old Jazz. Philip Whalen. NeAP
Okay. Sharon Scott. JB
Okay a nightingale. An Appearance. Robin Blaser. *Fr.* The Faerie Queene. CoPo
Okay "Negroes." June Jordan. BPo
Okeechobee. John Allison. GrPl
Okefenokee Swamp. Daniel Whitehead Hicky. AmFN
Okinawa Kanashii Monogatari. Geraldine Kudaka. BrSi
Oklahoma Ligno and Lithograph Co., The. Corporate Entity. Archibald MacLeish. OBAL
Ol' Ark's a-Moverin' an' I'm Goin' Home, De, *with music. Unknown.* BoAN-2
Ol' Bunk's Band. William Carlos Williams. NOBA
Ol' Doc' Hyar. James Edwin Campbell. BANP
Ol' Dynamite. Phil Le Noir. BPAW
Ol' Hag, You See Mammy? *with music. Unknown.* OuSiCo
Ol' Hannah. *Unknown.* BluL
Ol' Jinny Mine, The. Daisy L. Detrich. PoOW
Ol' Man River, *with music.* Oscar Hammerstein II. BLSo
Ol' Sheep Done Know de Road, De, *with music. Unknown.* BoAN-2
Old. Ralph Hoyt. AA
Old, The. George Mosby, Jr. LFAC
Old, The. Roden Noel. OBVV
Old, The/ Old winds that blew. Night Winds. Adelaide Crapsey. QFR
Old Abe Lincoln Came Out of the Wilderness. *Unknown.* AS, *with music;* FSW
(Old Abe Lincoln, *with music.*) TrAS
Old Abram Brown is dead and gone. *Unknown.* OxNR
Old Adam. Thomas Lovell Beddoes. *See* Song: "Old Adam, the carrion crew."
Old Adam, The. William Rose Benét. YaD
Old Adam, The. Denise Levertov. NaP; UnPo
Old Adam, *with music. Unknown.* AS
Old Adam, the Carrion Crow. Thomas Lovell Beddoes. *See* Song: "Old Adam, the carrion crew."
Old Age. Al-Aswad, Son of Ya'fur, *tr. fr. Arabic by* Sir Charles Lyall. *Fr.* The Mufaddaliyat. AWP
Old Age. *Gond Oral Tradition, tr. by* V. Elwin *and* S. Hivale. WTO
Old Age. Sir Philip Sidney. *Fr.* Arcadia. SiPS
Old Age. Edmund Waller. *Fr.* Of the Last Verses in the Book. BLPL; NOBE; OBEV; TreFT
(Last Verses.) OxBoCh
("Seas are quiet when the winds give o'er, The.") NOCV
Old Age. *Zulu Oral Tradition, tr. by* H. Tracey. WTO
Old Age am I, with lockës thin and hoar. Age. Sir Thomas More. EnRePo
Old Age Compensation. James Wright. NNaP
Old age has come, my head is shaking. Once I Played and Danced in My Parents' Kingdom. *Gond Oral Tradition, tr. by* V. Elwin *and* S. Hivale. WTO
Old Age Home, The. Daniel Hoffman. CoPo
Old Age in His Ailing. Herman Melville. TAP
Old age is. To Waken an Old Lady. William Carlos Williams. HAP; InPK; NoP; PAI; QFR; WeW
Old Age of Michelangelo, The. F. Templeton Prince. PeSA
Old Age, on tiptoe, lays her jewelled hand. A Minuet on Reaching the Age of Fifty. George Santayana. BLPL; FaFP; HBMV; NePA
Old Age Pensioner, The. Joseph Campbell. AnIL
Old Age Sticks. E. E. Cummings. InPS
Old Air, An. F. R. Higgins. AnIL
Old already?—Provable still. New Students. Marvin Bell. GLGT
Old am I in years and wisdom and. Old I Am. Herman Charles Bosman. PeSA
Old Amusement Park. Marianne Moore. NYBP
Old, and abandon'd by each venal friend. On Lord Holland's Seat near Margate, Kent [*or* Impromptu]. Thomas Gray. CABA; LAuP; NCEP; NOEC; OAEL-1; SeCePo; SeCeV; TW
Old and alone sit we. The Old Men. Walter de la Mare. MoAB; MoBrPo
Old and New ("Farewell, Old Year!"). *Unknown.* BLRP
Old and New ("She went up the mountain to pluck wild herbs"). *Unknown, tr. fr. Chinese by* Arthur Waley. AWP
Old and New Year Ditties, *sel.* Christina Rossetti.
"Passing away, saith the world, passing away," III. NoP; OBNC
(Passing Away.) GoBC; OAEL-2; OBVV; WPE
Old and quiet house set down, An. Possessions. Lizette Woodworth Reese. HBMV
Old and sick, you turn away from mirrors, whether. Late Reflections. Babette Deutsch. NYBP
Old and the New, The. "Q. B. M." SoPo
Old and the New Courtier, The. *Unknown. See* Old and Young Courtier, The.
Old and the New Masters, The. Randall Jarrell. InPK
Old and Young Courtier, The. *Unknown.* ViBoPo
(Old and the New Courtier, The.) CoMu
Old Angler, The. Walter de la Mare. GoTL; OAEP
Old Anguish, The. Chu Shu-chen, *tr. fr. Chinese by* Kenneth Rexroth. BoWoP
Old Apple Trees. W. D. Snodgrass. FYAP; SV
Old Argonaut. Sara Saper Gauldin. AMV-81
Old Ark's a-Moverin', The. *Unknown.* FSW
Old Arm-Chair, The. Eliza Cook. BrRo; InPK; PaPo; WBLP
Old as I am, for ladies' love unfit. Cymon and Iphigenia. Dryden. OBNV

Old astronomer there was, An. A Marvel. Carolyn Wells. OBCA
Old Astronomer to His Pupil, The. Sarah Williams. BLPA
"Though my soul may set in darkness, it will rise in perfect light," 2 *ll.* TRV
Old Atheist Pauses by the Sea, An. Thomas Kinsella. ELU; PAI
Old Athens of the West Is Now a Blue Grass Tour, The. James Baker Hall. TAT
Old Bachelor, The, *sel.* Congreve.
"Thus grief still treads upon the heels of pleasure," 2 *ll. fr.* V, iii. TreF
Old Balaam. *Unknown.* PoOW
Old Bangham [*or* Bangum], *sl. diff. vers.* *Unknown.* FSW; OuSiCo, *with music*
Old Barbarossa. Sleeping Heroes. Edward Shanks. OBMV
Old Bark Hut, The. *Unknown.* PoAu-1
Old Battalion,The. *Unknown.* OBET
Old battle field, fresh with Spring flowers again. All That Is Left. Basho, *tr. by* Curtis Hidden Page. AWP; WaaP
Old Beauty, The. Phyllis McGinley. FaBoEE
Old Beebe had three full grown sons, Buster, Bill and Bee. Didn't He Ramble. Will Handy. FSW
Old Ben Franklin was a merry old soul. Merry Old Souls. Morris Bishop. WhC
Old Ben Golliday. Mark Van Doren. SO
Old Bibles. Marilyn Waniek. MAYP
Old Bill the Whaler said to me. Bill the Whaler. Will Lawson. PoAu-1
Old Bill's Memory Book. William Rose Benét. InMe
Old Bing, The. Stanley Roger Green. BSV
Old Biograph Girl, The. Margaret Benbow. AMV-81
Old Birch, who taught the village school. The Retort. George Pope Morris. HBV-2
Old bitch labrador swims, The. The End of Summer. Judith Minty. FiCP; GeTw
Old black dog comes in one evening, The. First Snow. Ted Kooser. GrPl
Old Black Joe. Stephen Collins Foster. FaFP; PSoN, *with music;* TreFS
Old Black ladies. Weeksville Women. Elouise Loftin. PoBA
Old Black Men. Georgia Douglas Johnson. CDC; PoBA; PoNe
Old Black Men Say. James A. Emanuel. PoBa
Old Blue. *Unknown.* FSW; GDP; OuSiCo
(Old Dog Blue.) BluL
Old Boards. Robert Bly. CAPP; NaP
Old Boast, The. W. S. Merwin. NOBA
Old Boat, The. Lenore Pratt. CaP
Old Boniface he loved good cheer. *Unknown.* OxNR
Old Books. Chaucer. *Fr.* The Legend of Good Women: Prologue. OxBM
Old Books, The. Vernon Scannell. OxBC
Old Books Are Best. Beverly Chew. HBV-1
Old Botany Bay. Mary Gilmore. PoAu-1
Old boys, the cracked boards spread before. Bread. James Dickey. LCAP
Old Brass Wagon, *with music.* *Unknown.* AS
Old Bridge at Florence, The. Longfellow. EyDe
Old brown hen and the old blue sky, The. Continual Conversation with a Silent Man. Wallace Stevens. LiTM; NePA; NoP
Old Brown Schoolhouse, The. *Unknown.* TreF
Old brown thorn-trees break in two high over Cummen Strand, The. Red Hanrahan's Song about Ireland. W. B. Yeats. CMoP; FaBoCh; OnYI; OxBI
Old Brown's Daughter. *Unknown.* OBET
Old Buccaneer, The. Charles Kingsley *See* Last Buccaneer, The.
Old Buck's Ghost. Frank Benton. PoOW
Old Buffer, An. Frederick Locker-Lampson. CenHV
Old Bullock Dray, The. *Unknown.* PoAu-1
Old Burying-Ground, The. Whittier. AP
Old Cabin, The. Paul Laurence Dunbar. PoLF
Old canoe in, The. Sunrise. Jim Tollerud. VoR
Old Casa, The. Torrey Connor. BPAW
Old castles on the cliff arise. John Dyer. *Fr.* Grongar Hill. ViBoPo
Old Cat Care. Richard Hughes. OBMV
Old Cat's Confessions, An. Christopher Pearse Cranch. OBCA
Old Cat's Dying Soliloquy, An. Anna Seward. NOEC
Old Charcoal Seller, An. Po Chü-i, *tr. fr. Chinese by* Eugene Eoyang. SaC
Old Charley Garber delivered ice. Desert Holy Man. John Beecher. TAT
Old Chartist, The. George Meredith. NBM
Old Chaucer doth of Thopas tell. Nymphidia, the Court of Fairy. Michael Drayton. OAEP
Old Chaucer, like the morning Star. On Mr. Abraham Cowley, His Death and Burial amongst the Ancient Poets. Sir John Denham. AnAnS-2; OBS, *abr.;* SeCV-1
Old Chisholm Trail, The, *sl. diff. vers.* *Unknown.* AmFP; BeLS; BPAW; CoSo, *add. st., with music;* FaBoBe; FSW; TreFT
(Chisholm Trail, The.) TrAS, *with music*
Old Christmas. Mary Howitt. GN
Old Christmas. *Unknown.* OHIP
Old Christmas Greeting, An. *Unknown.* FaPON; TiPo
(Christmas Greeting.) SiSoSe
("Sing hey! Sing hey!/ For Christmas Day.") PChr
Old Christmas Morning. Roy Helton. MoAmPo
Old Christmas Returned. *Unknown.* GN; OHIP
Old Christmastide. Sir Walter Scott. *See* Christmas in the Olden Time.
Old Churchyard of Bonchurch, The. Philip Bourke Marston. EBVV; HBV-2; NBM; OBNC; OBVV
Old City, The. Ruth Manning-Sanders. CH
Old Cloak, The. *Unknown.* OBEV; OBSC; TrGrPo
(This Winter's Weather It Waxeth Cold.) InvP
Old Clock on the Stairs, The. Longfellow. HBV-2; WBLP
Old cloud passes mourning her daughter. Sunset after Rain. W. S. Merwin. PoA
Old College Song with Variant Lines to Suit. *Unknown.* TreFT
Old Colony Times, *with music.* *Unknown.* BLSo
Old Conservative, The. L. Frank Tooker. EtS
Old Cornish Litany, An. *Unknown.* *See* Litany for Halloween.
Old Cottagers, The. John Clare. OBRV
Old Counsel. Herman Melville. FaBoRV
Old Countryside. Louise Bogan. HAP; LiTA; NePA; TwAmPo; WPE
Old Couple, The. F. Pratt Green. OxBTC
Old couple living in Gloucester, An. The Lost Girl. *Unknown.* TDH
Old Cove, The. Henry Howard Brownell. PAH
Old Cow Died, The. *Unknown.* FSW
Old Cowboy, The. *Unknown.* CoSo
Old Cowboy's Lament, The. Robert V. Carr. BPAW; PoOW
Old Cowman, The/ cross-legged, sat before the fire. Eighteen-Ninety. E. Richard Shipp. PoOW
Old Crabbed Men. James Reeves. ChMP; ErPo
Old Cracked Tune, An. Stanley Kunitz. GP
Old cradle of an infant world. Ode to Jamestown. James Kirke Paulding. PAH
Old Creation Chant. *Tr. fr. Hawaiian.* WTO
Old Cumberland Beggar, The. Wordsworth. EnRP; LaA
Old Damon's Pastoral. Thomas Lodge. OBSC
Old Dan Tucker. Daniel Decatur Emmett. BLSo, *with music;* FSW; PSoN, *with music;* TrAS, *with music*
Old Dan'l. L. A. G. Strong. ELU; MoBrPo; PoSC; WhC
Old Davis owned a solid mica mountain. A Fountain, a Bottle, a Donkey's Ears and Some Books. Robert Frost. VGW
Old dears gardening in fur coats. The House Next Door. Douglas Dunn. OxBC
Old decrepit city like London, An. Roaches. Edward Field. NYP
Old Devil. *Unknown.* BluL
Old Diamond Joe was a rich old jay. Diamond Joe. *Unknown.* CoSo; OuSiCo
Old Dick Johnson, gentleman, adventurer. The Dick Johnson Reel. "Jake Falstaff." EvOK; WhC
Old Doc. Mark Vinz. Psk
Old Doctor Foster. *Unknown.* OxNR
Old Dog. Raymond Souster. GDP
Old Dog. William Stafford. BoAnP; GDP
Old dog barks backward without getting up, The. The Span of Life. Robert Frost. GDP; HoPM; LiTM; SoSe
Old Dog Blue. *Unknown.* *See* Old Blue.
Old Dog in the Ruins of the Graves at Arles, The. James Wright. NNaP
Old Dog lay in the summer sun. Sunning. James S. Tippett. GDP; RHPC; SiSoSe; SUS; TiPo
Old Dog, New Dog. Sydney Lea. MAYP
Old Dog Tray. Stephen Collins Foster. FSW; GDP
Old Dominion. Robert Hass. MAYP
Old dream comes again to me, The. Mir träumte wieder der alte Traum. Heine, *tr. by* James Thomson. AWP
Old Dubuque. Dave Etter. AmFN
Old earth, how she sulks. Jacaranda. Roo Borson. NOBC
Old East End worker called Jock, An. Limerick. Victor Gray. NOBL
Old Eben Flood, climbing alone one night. Mr. Flood's Party. E. A. Robinson. AmPP; AP; AWP; BiP; BLPL; CABA; CMoP; CoBMV; CrMA; EvOK; FaFP; FF; HAP; HeIP; HoPM; InPK; LiTA; LiTM; MAT; MoAB; MoAmPo; NePA; NIP; NoAM; NoBA; NoP; OxBA; PoPl; PoRA; PPoe; PPP; PrIm; SeCeV; SoSe; TAP; TreFT; TrGrPo; UnPo; ViBoPo; WeW
Old Ego Song ("Old ego climbing out of the trap door on the top of my head"). John Minczeski. AMV-80
Old Egyptians hid their wit, The. On Mr. Nash's Picture at Full Length. Jane Brereton. WPE
Old Ellen Sullivan. Winifred Welles. FaPON; TiPo
Old elm trees flock round the tiled farmstead, The. Childhood. Sir Herbert Read. BrPo
Old Emily. Hyacinthe Hill. GoYe
Old enemies. Safed and I. Molly Myerowitz Levine. VWA

Old England. Nahum Tate. APAS
Old England Forever and Do It No More. *Unknown.* GBP
Old England is eaten by knaves. Song. Alexander McLachlan. *Fr.* The Emigrant. NOBC; OBCV
Old England's long-expected heavy news from our fleet. Nelson's Death. *Unknown.* OBET
Old England's sons are English yet. Ready, Ay, Ready. Herman Charles Merivale. HBV-2
Old English Prayer. *Unknown.* TreFT
Old Ernie Anderson eating peanuts. Peanuts. Ken Belford. NeAC
Old Essex Door. Agnes MacCarthy Hickey. GoYe
Old Euclid drew a circle. Euclid. Vachel Lindsay. Poems about the Moon, I. ImOP; TwAmPo; YaD
Old Familiar Faces, The. Charles Lamb. AWP; BLPA; EnRP; FaBoBe; FaBoRV; FaFP; FaPoR; FPL; GTBS; GTBS-P; HBV-1; NBM; NOBE; OBEV; OBRV; PoPl; TreF; ViBoPo
Old Farmer and His Young Wife, The. *Unknown.* GBP
Old Farmer Giles. *Unknown.* OxNR
Old farmer, nearing death, asked, The. Field Day. W. R. Rodgers. BIrV
Old Farmer Oats and his son Ned. Song. John Jay Chapman. PoEL-5
Old Fashioned Fun. Thackeray. InMe
Old-fashioned Garden, The. John Russell Hayes. AA
Old-fashioned Pitcher, The. George E. Phair. SoSe
Old-fashioned Poet, An. Ada Foster Murray. HBV-2
Old Father Annum. Leroy F. Jackson. SiSoSe
Old Father Greybeard. *Unknown.* OxNR
Old Father Ocean calls my Tyde. A Song of the River Thames. Dryden. *Fr.* Albion & Albanius. FaBoEn
Old father tongue sticking out. Rehearsal. Cyril Dabydeen. BrSi
Old Fellow. Ernest Walsh. ErPo
Old Fence Post. Leigh Hanes. GoYe
Old Field Mowed, An. William Meredith. NYBP
Old Figurehead Carver, The. H. A. Cody. EtS
Old, Filthy Beer Pail, The. Katie V. Hall. InPK; PeD
Old fish fiddle with their fins and glide, The. Aquarium. George T. Wright. NYBP
Old Fisherman, The. George Campbell Hay. BSV
Old Fisherman with Guitar. George Mackay Brown. BSV; OxBC
Old Fitz, who from your suburb grange. To Edward Fitzgerald. Tennyson. LoBV; PoEL-5
Old Flag, The. H. C. Bunner. PAL; PGD
Old Flagman, The. Carl Sandburg. YaD
Old Flame, The. Robert Lowell. BoLoP; NoAM; NOBA; PAI
Old Flemish Lace. Amelia Walstien Carpenter. AA
Old Flood Ireson! all too long. A Plea for Flood Ireson. Charles Timothy Brooks. PAH
Old Florist. Theodore Roethke. CTBA; NCSH; PCP; SaC
Old Folk, The. Tove Ditlevsen, *tr. fr. Danish by* Nadia Christensen. PBWP
Old Folks at Home. Stephen Collins Foster. AA; BLSO, *with music;* FaBoBe; FaFP; FSW; HBV-2; PSoN, *with music;* TreF; WBLP
Old Folks Home, An. Paul Lake. AMV-81
Old forms are like birdhouses that, The. Poetry. Greg Kuzma. PoA
Old Fort Meigs. *Unknown.* PAH
Old Fortunatus, *sels.* Thomas Dekker.
"Behold you not this globe, this golden bowl." ViBoPo
Fortune. OBSC
(Fortune and Virtue.) GoTL
Song: "Virtue's branches wither, virtue pines." ElL; WHA
(Priest's Song, A.) OBSC
Old Forty-five Per Cent. *Unknown.* FaBoEE
Old Friedrich Barbarossa. Barbarossa. Friederich Rückert, *tr. by* John W. Thomas. WSC
Old friend, I greet you! you are still the same. To One Who Denies the Possibility of a Permanent Peace. Margaret Sackville. HBMV
Old friend, kind friend! lightly down. To My Old Schoolmaster. Whittier. NOBA
Old friend, your place is empty now. No more. To Scott. Winifred Letts. PoLF
Old Fritz, on this rotating bed. A Flat One. W. D. Snodgrass. AP; CAPP; LiTM; NePoEA-2; PoCh
Old Furniture. Thomas Hardy. MoVE; OxBTC
Old Gardens. Arthur Upson. HBV-1
Old General, The. Sir Charles Hanbury Williams. *Fr.* Isabella. OBEC
Old Ghost, The. Thomas Lovell Beddoes. WiR
Old gilt vane and spire receive, The. The Late, Last Rook. Ralph Hodgson. MoBrPo
Old Glory! say, who. The Name of Old Glory. James Whitcomb Riley. GN
Old Gods, The. Edwin Muir. BSV; EaLo
Old gods, avaunt! The rosy East is waking. Courage, All. Edwin Markham. HBMV
Old Gospel Ship, The. *Unknown.* FSW
Old Grahame he is to Carlisle gone. Bewick and Graham. *Unknown.* BaBo; ESPB
Old Gramophone Records. James Kirkup. NYBP
Old grand piano, The. Fantasia. Leonard Nathan. PPJ
Old Grandpaw Yet. *Unknown.* AmFP
Old Graves fell asleep. George Keithley. *Fr.* The Donner Party. NPGG
Old Gray Beard a-Shaking. *Unknown.* AmFP
Old Gray [*or* Grey] Goose, The. *Unknown.* ChTr, *sl. diff. vers.;* GBP
(Aunt Rhody.) FSW
("Go tell Aunt Rhody.") AmFP
Old gray hen is dying, The. Hen Dying. Alasdair Maclean. BoAnP
Old Gray Mare. *Unknown.* AS, *with music;* FSW; GBP
Old Green River knife had to be scraped, An. Canst Thou Draw Out Leviathan with an Hook. Allen Curnow. OCNZ
Old Grey. Fred Lape. BoAnP
Old Grey Goose, The. *Unknown.* *See* Old Gray Goose, The.
Old grey hearse goes rolling by, The. The Hearse Song. *Unknown.* AS; DTC; OxBoLi
Old grey shade of the mountain, The. In the Selkirks. Duncan Campbell Scott. CaP
Old Grey Wall, The. Bliss Carman. CaP
Old Grimes. Albert Gorton Greene. BeLS; HBV-2; HBVY; InMe; TreFS
Old guy put down his beer, The. Do the Dead Know What Time It Is? Kenneth Patchen. HoPM; MoAmPo
Old Habitant, An. Frank Oliver Call. CaP
Old Hannah. *Unknown.* FSW
Old Haven. Jean Garrigue. WPE
Old he was but not yet wax. My Father's Face. Hayden Carruth. DiL
Old Hokum Buncombe, The. Robert E. Sherwood. InMe
Old Home, The. Madison Cawein. HBV-2
Old Homes. Edmund Blunden. MoVE
Old homes and human lives—both. Reflections. David R. Pichaske. AMV-80
Old Horn to All Atlantic said. Frankie's Trade. Kipling. EtS
Old horse dies slow, The. When Structure Fails Rhyme Attempts to Come to the Rescue. William Carlos Williams. PP
Old horse, old horse, what brought you here. Blow the Man Down, *vers.* V. *Unknown.* ShS
Old horse, old horse, what brought you here. The Sailor's Grace. *Unknown.* ShS
Old House, The. William Barnes. OBVV
Old House, The. George Edward Woodberry. HBMV
Old house felt unfriendly, The. The Empty House. Max Williams. CBAP
Old House Place. Velma Sanders. AMV-80
Old house with trees and twisting river, An. A Visit to Bridge House. Richard Weber. BIrV
Old Houses of Flanders, The. Ford Madox Ford. CTC
Old houses were scaffolding once. Images. T. E. Hulme. InPK; OxBTC
Old Humpy. *Unknown.* AmFP
Old Hundredth. William Kethe. BLSo, *with music;* FaPoR
(Old Hundred.) FSW
(Psalm C.) NOCV
(Scotch Te Deum.) WGRP
Old Hymns, The. Frank L. Stanton. BLRP
Old I Am. Herman Charles Bosman. PeSA
Old I Am. Thomas Stanley, *after the Greek of* Anacreon. AWP
Old Indian Trick. Rayna Green. TWSS
Old Inmate, An. Kenneth MacKenzie. PoAu-2
Old Inn on the Eastern Shore. William H. Matchett. NePoEA
Old Irish Blessing, An. *Unknown.* TRV
Old Ironsides. Oliver Wendell Holmes. AA; AP; BLPA; EtS; FaBoBe; FaFP; FaPo; FaPON; FPL; GN; GOA; HBV-2; HBVY; MOS; PAH; PAL; PoPl; TAP; TreF; YaD
Old Ironsides at anchor lay. The Main-Truck; or, A Leap for Life. George Pope Morris, *also at. to* Walter Colton. BLPL; PaPo; PoLF
Old January. Spenser. *Fr.* The Faerie Queene, VII, 7. YeAr
Old Jew, The. Paradise. Willis Barnstone. VWA
Old Jew asked me by the Jaffa Gate, An. Conversation with a Countryman. Antoni Slonimski, *tr. by* Isaac Komem. VWA
Old Jewish Cemetery in Worms. Alfred Kittner, *tr. fr. German by* Herbert Kuhner. VWA
Old Jockey, The. F. R. Higgins. AnIV; OBMV; OxBI; OxBTC
Old Joe. *Unknown.* OxBoLi
Old Joe Clark[e]. *Unknown.* FSW; TrAS, *with music*
Old Joe Yazzie died after working. The Death of Old Joe Yazzie. Ron Rogers. STE
Old John Bax. Charles H. Souter. PoAu-1
Old Joyce. Seán Jennett. NeIP
Old Jumpety-Bumpety-Hop-and-Go-One. The Kangaroo. *Unknown.* SoPo
Old Keg of Rum, The. *Unknown.* PoAu-1
Old Kimball. *Unknown.* AmFP
Old King, The. John Heath-Stubbs. NePoEA

Old King Cabbage. Richard Kendall Munkittrick. OBCA
Old King Cole ("Me clairvoyant"). G. K. Chesterton. *Fr.* Variations on an Air. BXAP
Old King Cole ("Of an old king in a story"). G. K. Chesterton. *Fr.* Variations on an Air. BXAP
Old King Cole ("Who smoke-snorts toasts o' My Lady Nicotine"). G. K. Chesterton. *Fr.* Variations on an Air. BXAP
Old King Cole was a merry old soul. Mother Goose. FaBoBe; FaFP; FSW; HBV-1; HBVY; OuSiCo, *with music*; OxNR; SoPo
Old King Cole. E. A. Robinson. HBV-1
Old King of Dorchester, The. The Ceremonial Band. James Reeves. OnUR
Old Knight, The. George Peele. *See* His Golden Locks.
Old Ladies. Will Allen Dromgoole. WeW
Old Ladies, The. Colin Ellis. OxBTC
Old Lady from Dover, The. Carolyn Wells. TDH
Old lady, I now celebrate. The Leaping Fire. John Montague. IPY
Old Lady of Harrow, An. *Unknown.* TDH
Old Lady of London, The. *Unknown.* AmFP
Old Lady Sitting in the Dining Room. *Unknown.* AmFP
Old Lady under the Freeway, The. Diana O Hehir. NPGG
Old Lady Watching TV, An. Knute Skinner. SOTS
Old lady, when last year I sipped your tea. To an Old Lady Dead. Siegfried Sassoon. PoPle
Old Lady Who Swallowed a Fly, The. *Unknown.* ShM
Old lady writes me in a spidery style, An. A Letter from Brooklyn. Derek Walcott. OxBTC
Old Lady's Lament for Her Youth, The. Villon. *See* Complaint of the Fair Armouress, The.
Old Lambro pass'd unseen a private gate. Byron. *Fr.* Don Juan, III. EnRP
Old lane, an old gate, an old house by a tree, An. The Old Home. Madison Cawein. HBV-2
Old Leadville was booming in eighty-eight. The Little Johnny Mine. Daisy L. Detrick. PoOW
Old Lecher, The. Louis O. Coxe. TwAmPo
Old Lem. Sterling A. Brown. BPo; FB; IDB; PoBA; PoNe; TTY
Old Lesson. *Unknown.* TreFT
Old Liberals, The. John Betjeman. ChMP
Old light & owl-light. 2nd Light Poem: For Diane Wakoski. Jackson MacLow. PoM
Old Lizette on Sleep. Agnes Lee. HBMV
Old Log House. James S. Tippett. FaPON
Old-long Syne. *Unknown.* OBS
Old looking glass grows darker, it is true. Color Alone Can Speak. Louise Townsend Nicholl. NePoAm
Old Looney, An. *Unknown.* TDH
Old Love. William Morris. PeD; VLP
Old Love, The. Katharine Tynan. HBMV
Old Loves. Henri Murger, *tr. fr. French by* Andrew Lang. AWP
Old MacDonald Had a Farm. *Unknown.* FSW
Old, mad, blind, despised, and dying king, An. England in 1819 [*or* Sonnet: England in 1819]. Shelley. CABA; EnRP; FF; FiP; MAT; NiP; NOBE; NoP; OAEL-2; OAEP; OBRV; PPP; SeCePo; SeCeV; TrGrPo; TW; UnPo
Old Maggie's sweat would drip and sizzle. John Beecher. *Fr.* To Live and Die in Dixie. GP
Old Maid. John U. Nicolson. HBMV
Old maid, an old maid, An. *Unknown.* OxNR
Old Maid Factory, The. Constance Urdang. GP
Old Maids. *Unknown.* AmFP
Old Maid's Song. *Unknown.* AmFP; FSW
Old Malediction, An. Anthony Hecht, *after* Horace. TW
Old Man. Philip Booth. AMV-80
Old Man. Alan J. Carr. AMV-80
Old Man, The. David Fisher. NPGG
Old Man. Elizabeth Jennings. NePoEA-2
Old Man. David E. Stern. AMV-81
Old Man. Edward Thomas. ChMP; LiTM; MoVE; SCV; SeCeV
Old Man, An. Wordsworth. FaBoCh
(Old Man Travelling.) OBWP
Old man, The/ He is gone now. The Old Man Who Is Gone Now. Margarita Baldenegro Reyes. FIA
Old man/ man black man. Tony Get the Boys. D. L. Graham. PoBA
Old man, An/ on st catherine street. For Your Inferiority Complex. David O'Rourke. AMV-81
Old man alone in the dark, muttering, An. Girls' Voices. Brendan Gill. POL
Old Man and His Wife, An. *Unknown.* OxBM
Old Man and Jim, The. James Whitcomb Riley. AA
Old Man and Young Wife, The. *Unknown.* CoMu
Old Man at the Crossing, The. L. A. G. Strong. OBMV
Old man bending I come among new faces, An. The Wound-Dresser. Walt Whitman. AmPP; AP; NOBA; OBWP; PrIm; TAP; ViBoPo
Old man Brown. The Cheerful Chilterns. Frank Sidgwick. BXAP
Old Man by Salt Lake, An. William Jay Smith. TDH
Old man came a-courting me, An. Maids When You're Young, Never Wed an Old Man. *Unknown.* FSW
Old Man Con. Earl Gene Box. LFAC
Old man dozed, The. The hospital quietened. Burns Singer. Sonnets for a Dying Man, XV. NePoEA-2
Old Man Dreams, The. Oliver Wendell Holmes. BLPL; HBV-1; PoLF
Old Man from Darjeeling. *Unknown.* NTCP
Old Man from Peru, An. *Unknown.* *See* Limerick: "There was an old man of Peru/ Who dreamt he was eating his shoe."
Old man from the North, immaculate liar. Borges. Willis Barnstone. AMV-80
Old man gets up turns, An. Zeimbekiko. Robin Magowan. EAS
Old man, going [*or* traveling] a lone highway, An. The Bridge Builder [*or* Building the Bridge for Him]. Will Allen Dromgoole. BLPA; STF; TreFS; TRV; WeW
Old man had been listless, but he perked, The. End of Steel. Thomas Saunders. CaP
Old man had his box and wheel, The. The Scissors-Grinder. Vachel Lindsay. Poems about the Moon, V. TwAmPo
Old Man Hall. P. L. Jacobs. LFAC
Old man in a lodge within a park, An. Chaucer. Longfellow. AA; AP; AWP; HeIP; InvP; NePA; NOBA; NoP; OBEV; OBVV; OxBA; PoRA; PP; PrIm; TAP; TrGrPo
Old man in the crystal morning after snow. Poem. Delmore Schwartz. PoA
Old Man in the Park. Mary Elizabeth Osborn. NePoAm-2
Old Man in the Wood. *Unknown.* *See* Father Grumble.
Old man in white, An. Alice Walker. *Fr.* Love. NMM
Old man is seated, The. The Old Man. David Fisher. NPGG
Old Man Know-All. *Unknown.* BPo
Old Man Larsen fishes for bass. Charlie Johnson in Kettletown. Claude Clayton Smith. WOLT
Old man leaning on a gate, An. From My Window. Mary Elizabeth Coleridge. OBNC
Old man, listening to the careful, The. The First Snow of the Year. Mark Van Doren. NCSH
Old Man Mose. Chorus. Jack Kerouac. *Fr.* Mexico City Blues. NeAP
Old Man Mountain. Alfred Noyes. GoBC
Old man moved into his night, The. Katerina Anghelaki-Rooke. *Fr.* Notes on My Father. PBWP
Old man never had much to say. The Old Man and Jim. James Whitcomb Riley. AA
Old man of eighty. Hasidic Jew from Sadagora. Rose Ausländer, *tr. by* Ewald Osers. VWA
Old Man of Hawaii, An. *Unknown.* TDH
Old Man of Tennessee. John Hay. NePoAm-2
Old Man of the Hague, The. Edward Lear. *See* Limerick: "There was an old man of the Hague."
Old Man of the Nile, An. Edward Lear. TDH
("There was an old man of the Nile.") VLP
Old man of the sea, briny bell. Now Is Farewell. Blanaid Salkeld. NeIP
Old Man of Toulon, An. William Jay Smith. TDH
Old Man of Verona, The. Claudian, *tr. fr. Latin by* Abraham Cowley. AWP; OBVE
Old man, old father, old argonaut. Old Argonaut. Sara Saper Gauldin. AMV-81
Old Man, or Lad's-Love,—in the name there's nothing. Old Man. Edward Thomas. ChMP; LiTM; MoVE; SCV; SeCeV
Old Man Platypus. A. B. Paterson. BoAnP
Old Man Pondered. John Crowe Ransom. MoAmPo
Old Man Pot. Lyon Sharman. CaP
Old Man Rain. Madison Cawein. PoSC
Old man raises his bones, The. Levitation. Alvin Aubert. GP
Old Man Said, The. Carroll Arnett. STE
Old Man Said, An. Padraic Colum. OxBI
Old man Sargent, sittin' at the desk. Winnsboro Cotton Mill Blues. *Unknown.* FSW
Old man sits in wrinkled reverie, An. An Evasion. Douglas Livingstone. PeSA
Old Man, the Sweat Lodge. Phil George. GrPl
Old Man to His Scythe, The. Denis Wrafter. NeIP
Old Man Told Me. Lance Henson. VoR
Old man, traveling a lone highway, An. *See* Old man, going a lone highway, An.
Old Man Travelling. Wordsworth. *See* Old Man, An.
Old man walks to me, The. Lawrence McGaugh. *Fr.* Glimpses, xii. BOLo
Old man was already well ahead, The. The Last Dream. Ray A. Young Bear. STE

Old man was cold, The. Translating. Ruth Whitman. VWA
Old man went to meetin', for the day was bright and fair, The. The Preacher's Vacation. *Unknown.* BLPA; BLPL
Old man who had dug the small pit, The. Burial. May Sarton. GP
Old Man Who Is Gone Now, The. Margarita Baldenegro Reyes. FIA
Old Man Who Lived in a Wood [*or* the Woods], The. *Unknown. See* Father Grumble.
Old man who seined. Lorine Niedecker. VGW
Old man whose black face, An. The Rainwalkers. Denise Levertov. CAD; CTBA; NePoEA-2; PPP
Old Man with a Beard. Edward Lear. FaPON; NTCP
Old Man with a Gong, The. Edward Lear. *See* Limerick: "There was an old man with a gang."
Old Man with a Mowing Machine. May Carleton Lord. GoYe
Old man, you surface seldom. Full Fathom Five. Sylvia Plath. MOS
Old Mandarin, The/ Always perplexes his friend the Adjuster. Unearned Increment. Christopher Morley. WhC
Old Mandarin was always pleased, The. Psychoanalysts. Christopher Morley. WhC
Old Man's Advice, An. *Unknown.* OBET
Old Man's Carousal, The. James Kirke Paulding. AA
Old Man's Comforts [and How He Gained Them], The. Robert Southey. HBV-1; HoPM; OxBChV; PaPo; Par; SpRo; UnPo
Old man's fair-haired consort, whose dewy axle-tree, The. Lente, Lente. Ovid, *tr. by* Kirby Flower Smith. Elegies, I, 14. AWP
Old Man's Idyl, An. Richard Realf. AA; HBV-1
Old Man's Son, An. Russell Edson. LCAP
Old man's son was killed far away, An. The Colors of Night. N. Scott Momaday. STE
Old Man's Song, An. Richard Le Gallienne. HBV-1
Old Man's Song, The. *Tr. fr. Eskimo.* WTO
Old Man's Tale, The. Brian Merriman, *tr. fr. Modern Irish by* David Marcus. *Fr.* The Midnight Court. BIrV
Old Man's Thought of School, An. Walt Whitman. GLGT
Old Man's Winter Night, An. Robert Frost. AWP; HAP; HBMV; MoAB; MoAmPo; MoVE; NoAM; OxBA; VGW
Old Man's Wish, The. Walter Pope. CoMu; OBS
Old Mansion. John Crowe Ransom. HeIP; NOBA; OxBA
Old Maps and New. Norman MacCaig. OxBC
Old Mare, The. Elizabeth J. Coatsworth. MoAmPo
Old Marlborough Road, The. Henry David Thoreau. PoEL-4
Old Marquis and his Blooming Wife, The. *Unknown.* CoMu
Old-Marrieds, The. Gwendolyn Brooks. AmNP; PoBA
Old Marse John. *Unknown.* TTY
Old master yourself now, Auden, An. As You Like It. Theodore Weiss. TAP
Old May Song. *Unknown.* CH
Old mayor climbed the belfry tower, The. The High Tide on the Coast of Lincolnshire (1571). Jean Ingelow. BeLS; EBVV; FaBoPP; GN; HBV-2; NBM; OBVV; OnMSP; PaPo
Old Meg she was a gipsy [*or* gypsy]. Meg Merrilies [*or* Merrilees]. Keats. ELP; FaBoCh; FaPON; FiP; OxBChV; PoPle; TEP; TiPo
Old Men, The. Cid Corman. PCP
Old Men, The. Walter de la Mare. MoAB; MoBrPo
Old Men, The. Irving Feldman. MP; TwCP
Old Men, The. Alexander Javitz. TrJP
Old Men, The. Kipling. OBSV
Old Men. Ogden Nash. DFF; EvOK
Old Men. Alicia Ostriker. AVM-81
Old Men, The. Charles Reznikoff. DFF
Old Men Admiring Themselves in the Water, The. W. B. Yeats. CMoP; FaBoCh; GoJo; PCP
Old Men and Old Women Going Home on the Street Car. Merrill Moore. MoAmPo
Old men beneath the mountain. With a Sliver of Marble from Carrara. James Wright. EyDe
Old men in blue: and heavily encumbered. Pihsien Road. Robin Hyde. WPE
Old Men on the Blue. Thomas Hornsby Ferril. PoOW
Old Men Pitching Horseshoes. X. J. Kennedy. AMV-81
Old men sit by the chimney-piece and drink the good red wine, The. The Green Estaminet. A. P. Herbert. HBMV
Old men sit on park benches. Perspective. Robert L. Vorpahl. AMV-80
Old men sleeping. The List. Michael McClure. NU
Old men stand. Bulldozers. Frederick Dec. PCP
Old men, white-haired, beside the ancestral graves. Basho, *tr. fr. Japanese by* Curtis Hidden Page. AWP
Old Men Working Concrete. Phillip Hey. FiCP
Old Menalcas on a day. The Palmer's Ode. Robert Greene. *Fr.* Never Too Late. CTC; EnRePo; OBSC
Old Men's Ward. Elma Dean. GoYe
Old Michael. George M. Brady. NeIP
Old Mill, The. Thomas Dunn English. AA
Old Miner, The. *Unknown.* OBET
Old Miner's Refrain, The. *Unknown.* AmFP
Old Miniatures. Leo Vroman. VWA
Old Miser Named Quince, An. John Ciardi. TDH
Old Mr. Hardy, upright in his chair. At Max Gate. Siegfried Sassoon. NoAM
Old Mister Johnson had troubles of his own. The Cat Came Back. Harry S. Miller. FSW
Old Moke. Harold Littlebird. VoR
Old Mole. James Reeves. WSC
Old Molly Means was a hag and a witch. Molly Means. Margaret Walker. AmNP; BlS; NMM; PoNe
Old moon is tarnished, The. Sea Lullaby. Elinor Wylie. BoNaP; MOS
Old moon my eyes are new moon with human footprint. Poem Rocket. Allen Ginsberg. CoPo; VGW
Old Mortality, *sels.* Sir Walter Scott.
  And What though Winter Will Pinch Severe, *fr. ch.* 19. EnRP
  Sound, Sound the Clarion, *fr. ch.* 34. Thomas O. Mordaunt, *formerly at. to* Scott. FaBoEE; FaPoR; NOBE
  (Call, The.) OBEV
  (One Crowded Hour.) TrGrPo
  ("Sound, sound the clarion, fill the fife!") OAEP
  (Sound the Clarion.) TreFS
Old Mother Earth woke up from her sleep. A Spring Song. *Unknown.* PoLF
Old Mother Goose/ When she wanted to wander. Mother Goose.. OxNR; PBBP; SoPo
Old Mother Hubbard. Sarah Catherine Martin. FaBoBe; HBV-1; HBVY; OnMSP; OxNR; SoPo; TiPo
  (Comic Adventures of Old Mother Hubbard and Her Dog.) OxBChV
Old Mother Niddity Nod. *Unknown.* OxNR
Old Mother Shuttle. *Unknown.* EvOK; OxNR
Old Mother Twitchett had [*or* has] but one eye. Mother Goose. HBV-1; HBVY; NTCP; OxNR; SoPo; TiPo
Old Mountain Road. Charles Simic. FYAP
Old Mountaineer, The. W. K. Holmes. PoSH
Old Movies. John Cotton. FF
Old Munro Bagger, The. *Unknown.* PoSH
Old Navy, The. Frederick Marryat. *See* Captain Stood on the Carronade, The.
Old Nick in Sorel. Standish O'Grady. *Fr.* The Emigrant. OBCV
Old Noah he built himself an ark. One More River to Cross. *Unknown.* FSW
Old Noah he had an ostrich farm and fowls on the largest scale. Wine and Water. G. K. Chesterton. *Fr.* The Flying Inn. ACP; CenHV; FaBoCo; FiBHP; GoBC; HBMV; InMe; MoBrPo; ViBoPo
Old Noah once he built the Ark. One More River. *Unknown.* TreFS
Old Nudists, The. Joan Colby. AMV-80
Old O. O. Blues, The. Al Young. NPGG
Old oak, old timber, sunk and rooted. G. M. B. Donald Davie. OxBC
Old Oak Tree, The, *with music.* *Unknown.* ShS
Old Oaken Bucket, The, *parody.* *Unknown.* BLPA; FaFP; WBLP
Old Oaken Bucket, The. Samuel Woodworth. BLPA; BLSo, *with music;* FaBoBe; FaFP; FPL; FSW; PaPo; PSoN, *with music;* TreF; WBLP
  (Bucket, The.) AA; HBV-1
  Old Oaken Bucket, The ("How dear to this heart are the scenes of my childhood"), *sel.* FaPON
Old ocean was/ Infinity of ages ere we breathed. The Beatific Sea. Thomas Campbell. EtS
Old October. Thomas Constable. HBV-1
Old One and the Wind, The. Clarice Short. IHMS
Old One, lie down. Up the Hill, Down the Hill. Eleanor Farjeon. PoSC
Old ones go to each other's funerals, The. Burials Geoffrey Grigson. PoA
Old ones to the side. Psalm. Charles Simic. AmPA; LCAP
Old ones whose ancestors hunted, The. Raven. Duane Niatum. STE
Old [*or* Ould] Orange Flute, The. *Unknown.* FaBoBa; FSW; GBP; OxBoLi; WTO, *at. to* Nugent Bohen
"Old order changeth, yielding place to new." Prayer for the Dead. Tennyson. *Fr.* Morte d'Arthur. GoBC; TRV
Old Ox, The. George Rostrevor Hamilton, *after the Greek of* Addaios of Makedon. FaBoEE
Old Pack, The. *Unknown.* APAS
Old Paint. *Unknown.* BPAW
  (Good-bye [*or* Good-by], Old Paint.) CoSo; FSW; TrAS, *with music*
Old Paintings on Italian Walls. Kathleen Raine. NYBP
Old Parish Church, Whitby, The. Hardwick Drummond Rawnsley. OBVV
Old Parson Beanes hunts six dayes of the week. Upon Parson Beanes. Robert Herrick. AnAnS-2
Old Peasant Woman at the Monastery of Zagorsk, The. James Schevill. NMP
Old Penobscot Indian, The. Flux. Richard Eberhart. Psk; VGW

Old Pensioner, The. W. B. Yeats. *See* Lamentation of the Old Pensioner, The.
Old People. Myra Cohn Livingston. CTBA
Old people are like birds. City Pigeons. Helen Chasin. WeW
Old People Speak of Death, The. Quincy Troupe. CNA
Old People Working (Garden, Car). Gwendolyn Brooks. SaC
Old Person of Cromer, An. Edward Lear. TDH
Old Person of Tring, An. *Unknown.* *See* Limerick: "There was an old person of Tring."
Old Peter Grimes made fishing his employ. Peter Grimes. George Crabbe. The Borough, Letter XXII. EnRP; NoP; OBNV; PoEL-4; TEP
Old Peter Prairie-Dog. Prairie-Dog Town. Mary Austin. BPAW; FaPON; TiPo
Old Photo, 1942. George Uba. BrSi
Old Photographs. David Harsent. POL
Old Pictures in Florence. Robert Browning. VLP
Old Pilot, The. Donald Hall. LCAP
Old Pines, The. Cid Corman. GP
Old Pluvius, month of rains, in peevish mood. Spleen LXXV. Baudelaire, *tr. by* Kenneth O. Hanson. NAWM-2
Old Poem. *Unknown, tr. fr. Chinese by* Arthur Waley. AWP
("Cold, cold the year draws to its end.") BoWoP
Old Poet, Poetry's final subject glimmers months ahead. Don't Grow Old. Allen Ginsberg. DiL
Old poets fostered under friendlier skies. Poets and Their Bibliographies. Tennyson. PP
Old Polish Lesson, An. Deanna Louise Pickard. AMV-81
Old Pond, The. Basho, *tr. fr. Japanese.* SoPo
Old Poulter's Mare. *Unknown.* PeD
Old priest Peter Gilligan, The. The Ballad of Father Gilligan. W. B. Yeats. AnIV; EaLo; EBVV; HBV-2; MoBrPo; OnYI; PoRA
Old Prison, The. Judith Wright. PoAu-2
Old professor of zoology, The. The Parrot. James Elroy Flecker. FaBoTw
Old Pro's Lament, The. Paul Petrie. LiSp; TAP
Old Python Nose with the wind-rolling ears. To a Dead Elephant. Douglas Livingstone. PeSA
Old Quartermaster, The. Gordon Grant. EtS
Old Quin Queeribus. Nancy Byrd Turner. EvOK; RHPC; SoPo; TiPo
Old Rattler. *Unknown.* FSW
Old Red Hoss Mountain. Cy Warman. PoOW
Old Reilly (In Dem Long Hot Summer Days). Leadbelly (Huddie Ledbetter). FSW
Old Repair Man, The. Fenton Johnson. AmNP
Old restlessness is gone, The. In Praise of Blur. G. Sharat Chandra. FAZ
Old ridiculous partner is back again, The. The She Wolf. Muriel Spark. NYBP
Old river, once blue-mercurial. We Are a Young Nation, Uncle. Marilyn Chin. BrSi
Old River Road. Blanche Whiting Keysner. GoYe
Old Road, The. Jones Very. AA
Old Road to Paradise, The. Margaret Widdemer. HBMV
Old Roads. Eilean Ni Chilleanain. CIP
Old Roadside Resorts. Molly Peacock. MAYP
Old Robin of Portingale. *Unknown.* ESPB
Old Roger. *Unknown.* OxBoLi
Old Room, The. W. S. Merwin. NYBP
Old Rosin the Beau. *Unknown.* BLSo, *with music*; CoSo; FSW; PSoN, *with music*
Old Ross, Cockburn, and Cochrane too. The Battle of Baltimore. *Unknown.* PAH
Old rude church, with bare, bald tower, is here, The. Wordsworth's Grave. Sir William Watson. GoTL; HBV-2; OBNC; VLP
Old Rugged Cross, The, *with music.* George Bennard. AH
Old Ruralities. Charles Tennyson Turner. EBVV
Old rusty-belly thing will soon be gone. The Sappa Creek. Gary Snyder. NCSH
Old rutted roads have been turned to macadams, The. John Adams. Rosemary Benét *and* Stephen Vincent Benét. PAL
Old Sailor, The. Glenn Ward Dresbach. EtS
Old Sailor, The. A. A. Milne. CenHV
Old Saint, The. Muriel Stuart. HBMV
Old Sam Smith. The Shepherd. Mary Gilmore. PoAu-1
Old Sam's Wife. *Unknown.* ChTr
(On the Wife of a Parish Clerk.) ShM
Old sandpiper contemplates his age, The. Summer's Early End at Hudson Bay. Hayden Carruth. NYBP
Old Santa Fe Trail, The. Richard Burton. BPAW; PAH
Old Savonarola was a merry old soul. Morris Bishop. *Fr.* Merry Old Souls. DBV
Old Saxony Clock, The. Stéphane Mallarmé, *tr. fr. French by* George Moore. SyP
Old Scent of the Plum Tree. Fujiwara Ietaka, *tr. fr. Japanese by* E. Powys Mathers. AWP
Old School List, The. James Kenneth Stephen. CenHV
Old School Tie-up, The. Laurence McKinney. WhC
Old Scottish Cavalier, The. William Edmondstoune Aytoun. GN; HBV-2
Old Scout's Lament, The. William F. Drannan. CoSo; PoOW
Old scythe in the hedge. The Old Man to His Scythe. Denis Wrafter. NeIP
Old sea captains, when their work, The. Between Brielle and Manasquan. Oliver St. John Gogarty. OnYI
Old sea-dog on a sailor's log, An. The Powerful Eyes o' Jeremy Tait. Wallace Irwin. FiBHP
Old Seaport, An. *Unknown.* EtS
Old Seawoman. Gordon LeClaire. CaP
Old Section Boss, The. *Unknown.* BPo
Old Sergeant, The. Forceythe Willson. AA; BeLS
Old Settler's Song, The. Francis Henry. BPAW
Old Sexton, The. Park Benjamin. AA; HBV-2
Old Shadow Woman, old thing. Dusk Chant. Judith Mountain Leaf Volborth. TWSS
Old Shellover. Walter de la Mare. OxBChV; PoPle
Old Shepherd's Prayer. Charlotte Mew. EaLo; MoAB; MoBrPo; OxBTC; WPE
Old Ship of Zion. *Unknown.* FSW
(What Ship Is This? *with music.*) AH
Old Ship Riggers. H. A. Cody. EtS
Old Ships, The. James Elroy Flecker. BrPo; CH; EtS; EvOK; FaBoRV; MoBrPo; MOS; MoVE; OBMV; PoPle; PoRA; RoGo; WHA
Old Ships. Louis Ginsberg. HBMV
Old Ships. David Morton. EtS
Old shoe, an old pot, an old skin, An. Autumn Sequence. Adrienne Rich. VGW
Old Shoes and Leggin's, *with music.* *Unknown.* OuSiCo
Old silver church in a forest, An. Poet to His Love. Maxwell Bodenheim. PoPl
Old Sir Simon the king. *Unknown.* OxNR
Old sisters at our Maris Stella House. Mother Marie Therese. Robert Lowell. CoPo
Old Skinflint. W. W. Gibson. OBMV
Old Smoky. *Unknown.* *See* On Top of Old Smoky.
Old snake, old hole in the corner man. A Dead Weasel. David Helwig. NOBC
Old Snapshot. Ronald Everson. MoCV
Old snow gets up and moves taking its, The. December among the Vanished. W. S. Merwin. NaP
Old Socrates, whose wisdom did excel. To Master Edward Cobham. Barnabe Googe. EnRePo
Old Soldier. Padraic Colum. OBMV
Old Soldiers Home at Marshalltown, Iowa. Jim Barnes. AMV-80; FAZ
Old Soldiers Never Die. *Unknown.* FSW
Old soldiers true, ah, them all men can trust. A Prophecy. Maurice Thompson. *Fr.* Lincoln's Grave. AA
Old Song, The. G. K. Chesterton. FaBoTw
Old Song. Edward Fitzgerald. GN; OBEV; OBVV
(Meadows in Spring, The.) HBV-1
Old Song, The. Charles Kingsley. OBVV
Old Song. F. R. Scott. PeCV
Old Song, An. "Yehoash," *tr. fr. Yiddish by* Marie Syrkin. AWP
Old Song Ended, An. Dante Gabriel Rossetti. BoLoP; EBVV
(Frier of Orders Gray, The.) GoBC
Old song made by an agéd old [*or* old aged] pate, An. The Old and Young [*or* the New] Courtier. *Unknown.* CoMu; ViBoPo
Old Song Resung, An. Charles Larcom Graves. CenHV
Old Song Re-sung, An. John Masefield. EvOK; LiTB
Old Song Resung, An. W. B. Yeats. *See* Down by the Salley Gardens.
Old Song Reversed, An. Richard Henry Stoddard. AA
Old Song Written during Washington's Life. *Unknown.* OHIP
Old Song, Wrote by One of Our First New-England Planters, An. *Unknown.* *See* New England's Annoyances.
Old Songs, The. Sir Owen Seaman. InMe
Old Sorrow I shall meet again. Childhood. John Banister Tabb. HBV-1
Old Souldier of the Queens, An. *Unknown.* OBS
Old South Boston Aquarium stands, The. For the Union Dead. Robert Lowell. AmPP; CABA; CoAP; FYAP; HAP; HeIP; InPS; LCAP; LiTM; MP; NaP; NMP; NoAM; NOBA; NoP; OBWP; PPoe: PPP; SCV; SeCeV; TwCP; UnPo; WeW
Old spoon, An. The Spoon. Charles Simic. NNaP
Old squaw, The. Indian Sky. Alfred Kreymborg. BPAW
Old Squire, The. Wilfrid Scawen Blunt. FaPoR; HBV-1; OBEV; OBVV
Old Stephen. Charles Tennyson Turner. EBVV
Old Stoic, The. Emily Brontë. FaPoR; FPL; NOBE; OAEP; OBEV; OBNC; OBVV; OxBI; PoLF; PoPl; TreFT; TrGrPo; ViBoPo

Old Stories, The. Gene Frumkin. AMV-80
Old stories of a Tyler sing. Tom Tiler; or, The Nurse. *Unknown.* APAS
Old Storm. David Phillips. NeAC
Old Stormalong was a gay old man. Stormalong. *Unknown.* ShS
Old Story, The. Marcus Argentarius, *tr. fr. Greek by* E. A. Robinson. AWP
Old Story. Lance Henson. VoR
Old Story, An. Rena Lee. VWA
Old Story, The. Louis MacNeice. GBL
Old Story, An. E. A. Robinson. HBMV; MoAmPo; TreFS
Old Story Over Again, The. James Kenney. OnYI
Old Street, An. Virginia Woodward Cloud. AA
Old Stuff. Bert Leston Taylor. HBMV
Old Summerhouse, The. Walter de la Mare. CMoP; FaBoPP; FaBoRV; GTBS-P; MoPo
Old Susan. Walter de la Mare. CMoP; MoBrPo; TreFS
Old Sussex Road, The. Ian Serraillier. NTCP
Old Sweetheart of Mine, An. James Whitcomb Riley. BeLS; BLPA; FPL
"As one who cons at evening o'er an album all alone," *sel.* TreFS
Old Swimmer, The. Christopher Morley. LiSp
Old Swimmin'-Hole, The. James Whitcomb Riley. BeLS; FaFP; HBV-1
Old tales were told of Sigemund's daring. The Tale of Sigemund. *Unknown, tr. by* Charles W. Kennedy. *Fr.* Beowulf. AnOE
Old Tawny's mane is moth. The King. Douglas Livingstone. BoAnP
Old Tennis Player. Gwendolyn Brooks. LiSp
Old Testament, The. Thomas Russell. TreFS
(Names and Order of the Books of the Old Testament.) BLPA
Old Testament, The, *sel.* *Unknown.*
"Joshua the son of Nun." FaBoUs
Old Testament, a bygone age, The. The Flood. Lev Mak, *tr. by* Neil Muhlberger *and* Marvin Misemer. VWA
Old Testament Contents. *Unknown.* BLPA
Old-Testament Gospel. William Cowper. TrCP
Old Thad Stevens. Kenneth Porter. NePoAm-2
Old, the mad, the blind have fairest daughters, The. The Beauty of Job's Daughters. Jay MacPherson. MoCV; NOBC; PoCh
Old thorn tree in a stony place, An. Ode: On the Death of William Butler Yeats. A. J. M. Smith. OBCV; PeCV
Old Thought, An. Charles Henry Luders. AA
Old Tillie Turveycombe. Tillie. Walter de la Mare. TiPo
Old Timbrook Blues. *Unknown.* BluL
Old-Time Cowboy, The. *Unknown.* CoSo
Old Time is lame and halt. Wie langsam kriechet sie dahin. Heine, *tr. by* Richard Monckton Milnes. AWP
Old-Time Sea-Fight, An. Walt Whitman. *See* Battle of the *Bonhomme Richard* and the *Serapis.*
Old-Time Service. Thomas Churchyard. *Fr.* A Fayned Fancy between the Spider and the Gowte. OBSC
Old Timers. Carl Sandburg. NoAM; YaD
Old Times Were the Best, The. James Whitcomb Riley. FaFP
Old Tippecanoe. *Unknown.* PAH
Old tips come out as good as new. John William Mackail. *Fr.* The Masque of Balliol. CenHV
Old Tityrus to Eugenia, *sel.* Charles Cotton.
"Eugenia, young and fair and sweet." ViBoPo
Old town lies afar, An. There Is an Old City. Karl Bulcke, *tr. by* Ludwig Lewisohn. AWP
Old Trail Town, Cody Wyoming. John Garmon. TAT
Old Tree, The. Andrew Young. GoJo
Old Trouper, The. Don Marquis. *Fr.* Archy and Mehitabel. FaBoCo
Old Tubal Cain was a man of might. Tubal Cain. Charles Mackay. WBLP
Old Tune, An. Gérard de Nerval, *tr. fr. French by* Andrew Lang AWP; HBV-1
Old Uncle Jim was as blind as a mole. Echoes of Childhood. Alice Corbin. PoNe
Old Vicarage, Grantchester, The. Rupert Brooke. BrPo; FaBoPP; FaBV; GoTL; MoBrPo; MoVE; OxBTC; PoRA
"Cambridge people rarely smile," *sel.* DBV
Old Violin, The. Maurice Francis Egan. AA
Old Virginny. James A. Bland. *See* Carry Me Back to Old Virginny.
Old Voyager. Walter Blackstock. GoYe
Old Walking Song, The. J. R. R. Tolkien. RFM
Old Walt. Langston Hughes. HeIP
Old warder of these buried bones. In Memoriam A. H. H., XXXIX. Tennyson. PoEL-5
Old watch, The: their/ thick eyes. Vapor Trail Reflected in the Frog Pond. Galway Kinnell. NoP; OBWP; VGW
Old Waterford Woman, An. Mary Devenport O'Neill. NeIP
Old West, the old time, The. Spanish Johnny. Willa Cather. BPAW; FaPON; HBMV
Old Wharves, The. Rachel Field. SoPo
Old Whim Horse, The. Edward Dyson. CBAP
Old Wife, The. Rolly Kent. FF
Old Wife and the Ghost, The. James Reeves. PDV; ShM
Old Wife in High Spirits. "Hugh MacDiarmid." CMoP; NMP; OxBTC
Old Wife's Tale, The. George Peele. *See* Old Wives' Tale, The.
Old wind stirs the hawthorn tree, The. The Road of Remembrance. Lizette Woodworth Reese. HBV-1
Old wine filled him, and he saw, with eyes, The. Maurice de Guérin. Maurice Francis Egan. AA
Old wine to drink! A Winter Wish [*or* Give Me the Old]. Robert Hinckley Messinger. AA; HBV-2; ViBoPo
Old Winter. Thomas Noel. GN; HBV-1; PoSC
Old Witherington. Dudley Randall. ConAP; NoAM; TW
Old Wives Prayer, The. Robert Herrick. SeCV-1
Old Wives' [*or* Wife's] Tale, The, *sels.* George Peele.
Harvester's Song. TrGrPo
Song: "Lo! here we come a-reaping, a-reaping," 4 *ll.* OBSC
Song: "When as [*or* Whenas] the rye [*or* rie] reach to the chin." ElL; FaBoEn; LoBV; OBSC; OxBoLi; PoEL-2
(Summer Song, A.) NOBE; OBEV
(When as [*or* Whenas] the Rye [Reach to the Chin].) ELP; NoP; SeCePo; ViBoPo
("When as [*or* Whenas] the rye reach to the chin.") EnLoPo; FaBoCh; GBL
Spell, A. ChTr
Voice from the Well [of Life Speaks to the Maiden], The. ChTr; FaBoEn; NOBE
(Celanta at the Well of Life.) LoBV
(Fair Maiden.) PoEL-2
(Gently Dip.) ELP
("Gently dip, but not too deep.") InPS
(Song at the Well.) SeCeV
(Voice Speaks from the Well, A.) FaBoCh; OBSC; OxBoLi
Old Woman, The. Joseph Campbell. AWP; GoBC; HBMV; MoBrPo; OnYI; OxBI; OxBTC; TreFT; ViBoPo
Old Woman. Linda Pastan. FiCP
Old Woman, The. Beatrix Potter. GoJo; NTCP; PDV
Old Woman, An. Charles Henry Ross. OxBChV
Old Woman, An. Edith Sitwell. CoBMV; MoPo
Old Woman. Iain Crichton Smith. BSV; FaBoTw; NePoEA-2; OxBTC
Old Woman. *Unknown.* AmFP
Old woman across the way, The. The Whipping. Robert Hayden. GP; GrPl; IDB; NCSH; PAI; PoBA; TW
Old Woman All Skin and Bone, *with music.* *Unknown.* TrAS
Old Woman Awaiting the Greyhound Bus. Duane Niatum. CDW
Old woman has forgotten her face, The. Evasion. Blanaid Salkeld. NeIP
Old woman in me walks patiently to the hospital, An. Revelation. Carole C. Gregory. BlSi
Old Woman Laments in Spring-Time, An. Edith Sitwell. ViBoPo
Old woman must stand, The. *Unknown.* OxNR
Old Woman of Beare [Regrets Lost Youth], The. *Unknown.* *See* Hag of Beare, The.
Old Woman of Berkeley, The. Robert Southey. OBRV
(Witch, The.) WiR
Old Woman of Harrow. *Unknown.* FaBoNo
Old Woman of the Roads, An. Padraic Colum. CH; FaBoBe; FaPON; FYAP; GoBC; HBMV; MoBrPo; OBEV; PoRA; TreFS; WHA
Old woman, old and bent and worn. Morning Bus. John Coulter. CaP
Old woman, old woman,/ Shall we go a-shearing? Mother Goose. OxNR
"Old woman, old woman, are you fond of carding?" Old Woman. *Unknown.* AmFP
Old Woman, outside the Abbey Theater, An. L. A. G. Strong. DBV; FiBHP; MoBrPo
Old Woman Remembers, An. Sterling A. Brown. CNA; PoBA
Old Woman Remembers, The. Lady Gregory. OnYI
Old woman sits, The. Leasa Davis. CTBA
Old woman sits on a bench before the door and quarrels, The. Fawn's Foster-Mother. Robinson Jeffers. NoAM; NOBA
Old Woman Speaks of the Moon, An. Ruth Pitter. WPE
Old woman went to market and bought a pig, An. *Unknown.* OxNR
Old Woman Who Lived in a Shoe, The. *Unknown.* OxBoLi
For Mother Goose *vers., see* There was an old woman who lived in a shoe.
Old Woman's Lamentations, An. Villon, *tr. fr. French by* J. M. Synge. MoBrPo; OBMV
Old Woman's Song, An. Akjartoq, *tr. fr. Eskimo into Danish by* Knud Rasmussen; *tr. into English by* Tom Lowenstein. WPOW
Old Woman's Song. Thomas Cole. NePoAm-2
Old Woman's Three Cows, The. *Unknown.* OxNR
Old Women, The. George Mackay Brown. NePoEA-2; OxBS
Old Women. Babette Deutsch. HBMV
Old women/ fire clay ovens. Nativity. Linda Hogan. TWSS
Old women all their lives, they're a mixture of whitelime and brine. Women

at the Market. Angela Figueroa Aymerich, *tr. by* Hardie St. Martin. PBWP
Old women are gathered in the Longhouse, The. Native Origin. Beth Brant. STE
Old Women beside a Church. Keith Wilson. Psk
Old women in this town never sleep. Cold Front. Peter Sharpe. AMV-80
Old Women of Toronto. Miriam Waddington. NOBC
Old women say that children asleep are saints, The. The Sleeping Saint. Melvin Walker La Follette. CoPo
Old women say that men don't know. Becoming a Dad. Edgar A. Guest. BLPL; PoLF
Old women sit at Willowsleigh and spin, The. Spinners at Willowsleigh. Marya Zaturenska. HBMV
Old women sit, stiffly, mosaics of pain. Old Women. Babette Deutsch. HBMV
Old Women Still Sing, The. Charles H. Rowell. CNA
Old World, New World. Harry Roskolenko. AMV-81
Old world staggers, but a young, triumphant world is born, The. Toward a True Peace. Lucia Trent *and* Ralph Cheyney. PGD
Old-World Thicket, An. Christina Rossetti. SBG
Old, worn harp that had been played, An. The Master-Player. Paul Laurence Dunbar. TRV
Old wound in my ass, The. Fabrication of Ancestors. Alan Dugan. NoAM
Old Year, The. John Clare. OBCP
Old Year, The. Clarence Urmy. PGD
Old Year and the New, The. Annie Johnson Flint. BLRP
Old Year, going, take with you. Farewell and Hail! Thomas Curtis Clark. PGD
Old Year is a diary where is set, The. Ethel Romig Fuller. *Fr.* Diary. PGD
Old Year's gone away, The. The Old Year. John Clare. OBCP
Old Year's Prayer, The. Minna Irving. PGD
Old yellow stucco, The. Winter Nightfall. J. C. Squire. OxBTC
Old yew, which graspest at the stones. In Memoriam, A. H. H., II. Tennyson. EBVV; ELP; FaBoEn; GTBS-P; NOBE; NoP; OBNC; PAI; PoEL-5; SeCeV; UnPo
Old Zip Coon. *Unknown, at. to* Bob Farrell. *See* Zip Coon.
Olden Days, The. Richard Barnfield. *Fr.* Virgidemiarum. OBSC
Olden Love-making. Nicholas Breton. OBSC
Older I grow, The. Triolet on a Downhill Road. Margaret Fishback. WhC
Older Now. Dave Gingell. PoSH
Older than the ancient Greeks. Pigeons. Marianne Moore. PoA
Oldest of friends, the trees! Trees. Thomas Curtis Clark. PGD
Oldest Soldier, The. Robert Graves. DTC
Ole Abe (God bless 'is ole soul!). Negro [*or* Black] Soldier's Civil War Chant. *Unknown.* BPo; TAP
Ole Aunt Dinah, she's jes lak me. Jack and Dinah Want Freedom. *Unknown.* BPo
Ole Sheep Dey Know de Road, De. *Unknown.* BPo
Oleander on the wall, The. By the Arno. Oscar Wilde. EBVV
Oleanna. Pete Seeger, *after the Norwegian.* FSW
Olga Poems. Denise Levertov. LCAP; NNaP
Olger the Dane and Desiderio. Charlemagne. Longfellow. FaFP
O'Lincon Family, The. Wilson Flagg. HBV-1; HBVY
Oliphaunt. J. R. R. Tolkien. AmMo; RHPC
Olive, The. A. E. Housman. NoAM
Olive Grove. James Merrill. NePoAm
Olive journeys. Journey round the World. Ingrid Jonker, *tr. by* Jack Cope *and* William Plomer. PBWP
Olive Tree, The. Sabine Baring-Gould. GN
Olive Trees. Padraic Colum. NePoAm
Oliver Wiggins. "Stanley Vestal." BPAW
Olives and Mountains. Elizabeth Barrett Browning. *Fr.* Aurora Leigh, VII. FaBoPP
Olivia. Edward Pollock. AA
Olivia. Tennyson. *Fr.* The Talking Oak. GN
Olivier Metra's Waltz of Roses. La Mélinite: Moulin-Rouge. Arthur Symons. SyP
Ollie, Answer Me. Stephen Berg. NaP
Olympian sunlight is the Poet's sphere. The Crystal. Titus Munson Coan. AA
Om. *Malay Oral Tradition, tr. by* R. O. Winstedt. WTO
Omalos. Rosanna Warren. AMV-80
Omar for Ladies, An. Josephine Daskam Bacon. HBV-1
Ombre and basset laid aside. A Song on the South Sea. Countess of Winchilsea. NOEC
Ombre at Hampton Court. Pope. *Fr.* The Rape of the Lock, III. OBEC
("Close by those meads, for ever crowned with flowers.") FaBoPP, *shorter sel.;* FIP; OBSV, *shorter sel.,* OxBoLi
Omelet of A. MacLeish, The. Edmund Wilson. NYBP; Par
Omen of Victory Mina Loy. InPK
Omens. James H. Cousins. OnYI
Omens. Michael Hamburger. NMP
Omens, The. Ann Stanford. WSC
Omie Wise. *Unknown. See* Naomi Wise.
Ominous length uncoiling and thin, An. The Rattlesnake. Alfred Purdy. WHW
Omit, omit, my simple friend. To an Ambitious Friend. Horace, *tr. by* Matthew Arnold. Odes, II, 11. AWP
Omnes gentes plaudite. A Last Drink. *Unknown.* OxBM
Omnia Exeunt in Mysterium. George Sterling. WGRP
Omnia Somnia. Joshua Sylvester. FaBoEE; OBS
(Go, Silly Worm.) ElL
Omnia Somnia. Rosamund Marriott Watson. HBV-1
Omnia Vanitas. Dugald Buchanan, *tr. fr. Gaelic.* GoTS
Omnia Vincit. Alfred Cochrane. HBV-1
Omnia Vincit. *Unknown. See* Fain Would I Change That Note.
Omnibus across the bridge, An. Symphony in Yellow. Oscar Wilde. EBVV; FaBoPP; MoBrPo; SyP
Omnipotent and steadfast God. John Brown's Prayer. Stephen Vincent Benét. *Fr.* John Brown's Body. PoNe
Omnipotent confederate of all good. Prayer. Amos N. Wilder. TrPWD
Omnipresence. Edward Everett Hale. TRV; WGRP
Omnipresence of the Deity, The, *sel.* Robert Montgomery.
"Stupendous God! how shrinks our bounded sense." VLP
Omniscience. Blanche Mary Kelly. TrPWD
Omnivorous Bookworm, The. Oliver Herford. TDH
Omphalos: The Well. Seán Jennett. NeIP
On a Bad Singer. Samuel Taylor Coleridge. FaBoEE; RHPC; TreF
(Desired Swan-Song, The.) WhC
(Epigram: "Swans sing before they die.") HBV-1
(Swans Sing [before They Die].) EvOK; FaBaCo
On a Baltimore Bus. Charles G. Bell. NePoAm
On a Bank [*or* Banck] as I Sat [*or* Sate] a-Fishing; a Description of the Spring. Sir Henry Wotton. AnAnS-2; LoBV; OBS; SeCP
(May Day, A.) CH
On a bank of flowers, in a summer-day. Blooming Nelly. Burns. UnTE
On a Bas-Relief. Wesley Trimpi. NePoEA
On a battle-trumpet's blast. Shelley. *Fr.* Prometheus Unbound, I. OBRV
On a Beautiful Youth Struck Blind with Lightning. Goldsmith, *after the Spanish.* OAEP
On a Bed of Guernsey Lilies. Christopher Smart. NOEC; OBEC
On a Birth. Geoffrey Grigson. NAs
On a Birthday. J. M. Synge. ChTr; GBL; OBMV
On a Blind Girl. Baha Ad-din Zuhayr, *tr. fr. Arabic by* E. H. Palmer. AWP
On a Bookseller. Goldsmith. PV
On a Bougainvillæa Vine at the Summer Palace. Barbara Howes. MoAmPo; NYBP
On a Boxer. X. J. Kennedy. PPJ
On a Boy's First Reading of "King Henry V." S. Weir Mitchell. AA
On a Bright and Summer's Morning. *Unknown.* AmFP
On a Bust of Dante. Thomas William Parsons. AA; HBV-2
On a Bust of Lincoln. Clinton Scollard. OHIP
On a Calm Summer's Night. John Nicholson. EnLoPo
On a Cast from an Antique. George Pellew. AA
On a Cat, Ageing. Sir Alexander Gray. BSV
On a Catholic Childhood. Janet Campbell Hall. VoR
On a Celtic Mask by Henry Moore. Horace Gregory. PoA
On a Certain Alderman. John Cunningham, *after the Greek of* Simonides. FaBoEE
On a Certain Effeminate Peer. John Winstanley. FaBoEE
On a Certain Engagement South of Seoul. Hayden Carruth. AmFN; NMP
On a Certain Lady at Court. Pope. HBV-1; NOBE; NOEC; OAEP; OBEC; OBEV; PoPle; TrGrPo
On a Certain Lord Giving Some Thousand Pounds for a House. David Garrick. PV
("So many thousands for a house!") FaBoEE
On a Certain Scholar. W. Craddle. WhC
On a Child. Walter Savage Landor. OBVV
On a Child Who Lived One Minute. X. J. Kennedy. DFF; HoAn; HoPM; NYBP
On a Child with a Wooden Leg. Bertram Warr. OBCV
On a Clear Day I Can See Forever. Alex Kuo. BrSi
On a Clergyman's Horse Biting Him. *Unknown.* FaBoCo; FaBoEE; OxBoLi; TreFT; WhC
On a clothesline hangs the moon. Room Poems. Eli Bachar, *tr. by* Jeremy Garber. VWA
On a Cock at Rochester. Sir Charles Sedley. FaBoEE; POL; TW
On a Cock Which Was Stolen from a Good Priest. Egan O'Rahilly, *tr. fr. Modern Irish by* P. S. Dinneen *and* T. O'Donoghue. OnYI
On a cold night I came through the cold rain. J. V. Cunningham. HAP; QFR

On a Contented Mind. Thomas, Lord Vaux. *See* Of a Contented Mind.
On a Contentious Companion. John Hoskyns. FaBoEE
On a Country Road. Harley Elliott. NeAC
On a Damaske Rose Sticking upon a Ladies Breast. Thomas Carew. AnAnS-2
On a dark and stormy night. The Wreck of the Royal Palm. *Unknown.* AmFP
On a dark and stormy night, as the train rattled on, all the passengers had gone to bed. In the Baggage Coach Ahead. Gussie L. Davis. FSN; TreFS
On a dark stormy mornin' when the snow was a-fallin'. The Wreck on the Somerset Road. *Unknown.* OuSiCo
On a dark winter morning, I couldn't see. Unseen Horses. Joan Byers Grayston. PH
On a Day—Alack the Day! Shakespeare. *Fr.* Love's Labour's Lost, IV, iii. ElL; ViBoPo
(Blossom, The.) OBEV
(Dumain's Rhymes.) OBSC
(Love's Perjuries.) GTBS; GTBS-P; HBV-1
On a day, alack the day! Love's Wooing Song. Giles Fletcher. *Fr.* Christ's Victory. HBV-1
On a day long and wet we fall upon. Arriving. Daniel Halpern. HoPM
On a day of grief. Misdemeanor. Eve Triem. GP
On a day sweet with April showers. In Canterbury Cathedral. E. W. Oldenburg. EBCP
On a day when smoke lies down in alleys. Looking Both Ways before Crossing. John Woods. ConAP
On a day when the breath of roses. The Unwanted. C. Day Lewis. PoPl
On a Day's Stint. Sir Walter Scott. NBM
On a Dead Child. Robert Bridges. BrPo; CMoP; EBEV; LiTB; LiTM; NoAM; NOBE; OAEP; OBMV; OBNC; ViBoPo
On a Dead Child. Richard Middleton. OBVV; SoSe
On a Dead Hostess. Hilaire Belloc. MoBrPo; MoVE
On a Dead Poet. Frances Sargent Osgood. AA
On a Dead Scholar, *sel.* St. Columcille, *tr. fr. Old Irish by* Robin Flower.
"Lon's away,/ Cill Garad is sad today." AnIL
On a Discovery Made Too Late. Samuel Taylor Coleridge. EnRP
On a Distant Prospect of an Absconding Bookmaker. G. Rostrevor Hamilton. FaBoCo
On a Distant Prospect of Eton College. Thomas Gray. HBV-2
Where Ignorance Is Bliss, *sel.* TreFs
On a Distinguished Politician. J. E. Thorold Rogers. FaBoEE
On a Doctor of Divinity. Richard Porson. FaBoCo
("Here lies a Doctor of Divinity.") FaBoEE
On a Drawing by Flavio. Philip Levine. VWA
On a Dream. Keats. EnRP
On a Drop of Dew. Andrew Marvell. AnAnS-1; GoBC; HAP; JCP; LiTB; MeLP; MePo; NIP; OBS; OxBoCh; SeCP; SeCV-1; TEP
On a Dying Boy. William Bell. NePoEA
On a Fair Beggar. Philip Ayres. EnLoPo; OBS
On a Fair Morning. *Unknown.* ViBoPo
On a fair summer's morning of soft recreation. The Blackbird. *Unknown.* OnYI
On a Fair Woman. Francis Burdett Money-Coutts. OBVV
On a Fan That Belonged to the Marquise de Pompadour. Austin Dobson. HBV-1; OBVV; ViBoPo
On a Favorite Cat Drowned in a Tub of Goldfishes. Thomas Gray. *See* Ode on the Death of a Favourite Cat . . .
On a Female Rope-Dancer. *Unknown.* NOEC
On a Female Snob, Surprised. Patric Dickinson. DBV
On a Ferry Boat. Richard Burton. AA
On a Field at Fredericksburg. Dave Smith. GeTw
On a Fifteenth-Century Flemish Angel. David Ray. NePoEA-2
On a Fine Morning. Thomas Hardy. VLP
On a flat road runs the well-train'd runner. The Runner. Walt Whitman. InPS; LiSp
On a Flimmering Floom You Shall Ride. Carl Sandburg. GoYe; OBAL
On a Fly Drinking Out of [*or* from] His Cup. William Oldys. FaFP; OBEV; TrGrPo; ViBoPo
(Anacreontick, An.) OBEC
On a Fly-Leaf of Burns's Songs. Frederic Lawrence Knowles. HBV-2
On a Forsaken Lark's Nest. Mathilde Blind. FM
On a Fortification at Boston Begun by Women. Benjamin Thompson. GOA; PAH; SCAP
On a Fowler. Isidorus, *tr. fr. Greek by* William Cowper. AWP
On a Friend's Suicide. Michael Yots. AMV-81
On a Frightful Dream. John Codrington Bampfylde. NOEC
On a General Election. Hilaire Belloc. FaBoCo; FaBoEE; MoVE; NOBE; NOBL; OBSV; OxBTC
(On a Great Election.) OxBoLi; WhC
On a Gentleman Marrying His Cook. Colin Ellis. FaBoEE
On a Gentlewoman Walking in the Snowe. William Strode. *See* On Chloris Walking in the Snow.
On a German Tour. Richard Porson. *See* Epigram on an Academic Visit to the Continent.
On a Girdle. Edmund Waller. AnAnS-2; AWP; BLPL; CABA; CavP; FF; GTBS; GTBS-P; HBV-1; HeIP; InMe; InPK; LiTB; LoBV; NoP; OAEP; OBEV; OBS; PoRA; SeCePo; SeCV-1; TreFS; TrGrPo; UnTE; ViBoPo; WHA
On a Gloomy Easter. Alice Freeman Palmer. OHIP
On a granite boulder. The Narrows. Joseph Bruchac. FAZ
On a grassy pillow. Happy Myrtillo. Henry Carey. SeCePo
On a Grave in Christchurch, Hants. Oscar Fay Adams. AA
On a Great Election. Hilaire Belloc. *See* On a General Election.
On a Great Man Whose Mind Is Clouding. Edmund Clarence Stedman. AA
On a Grecian Urn. Keats. *See* Ode on a Grecian Urn.
On a Greek Vase. Frank Dempster Sherman. AA
On a green island in the Main Street traffic. Pro Patria. Constance Carrier. NePoAm; NYBP; WPE
On a Grey-haired Old Lady Knitting at an Orchestral Concert. "Furnley Maurice." CBAP
On a Hand. Hilaire Belloc. ELU
On a hill there blooms a palm. Hayyim Nahman Bialik, *tr. by* Maurice Samuel. Songs of the People, II. AWP
On a hill there grows a flower. A Pastoral [*or* Ipsa Quae *or* Phyllida and Corydon.] Nicholas Breton. ElL; OBSC; TrGrPo
On a hillside in Italy. On an Italian Hillside. Richard Weber. NMP
On a holy day when sails were blowing southward. The Straying Student. Austin Clarke. AnIL; BIrV; CIP; IPY; MoAB; NeIP; OxBI
On a Honey Bee. Philip Freneau. AP; TAP
(To a Honey Bee.) AA; YaD
On a Horse and a Goat. R. P. Lister. PV
On a Horse Carved in Wood. Donald Hall. EyDe
On a hot summer Sunday. The Cemetery at Academy, California. Philip Levine. NaP
On a ladder, in an old checkered shirt. Washing Windows. Barry Spacks. NCSH
On a Lady Who Beat Her Husband. *Unknown.* FiBHP
On a Landscape of Sestos. Carlos Baker. *Fr.* A Visit to the Art Gallery. EyDe
On a Ledge. William Bell. PoSH
On a Line in Sandburg. R. S. Thomas. NAs
On a Little Bird. Martin Armstrong. CH
On a Little Boy's Endeavouring to Catch a Snake. Thomas Foxton. OxBChV
On a little green knoll. Old Log House. James S. Tippett. FaPON
On a little piece of wood. Mr. and Mrs. Spikky Sparrow. Edward Lear. OxBChV
On a Lonely Spray. James Stephens. OnYI
On a Lord. Samuel Taylor Coleridge. FaBoCo; FiBHP; PV
On a lorry the centre of a gaping crowd. W. H. Auden. *Fr.* A Happy New Year. OBSV
On a Lover of Books. Geoffrey Grigson. FaBoEE
On a Magazine Sonnet. Russell Hillard Loines. OBAL
On a Maid[e] of Honour Seen[e] by a Schol[l]ar in Som[m]erset Garden. Thomas Randolph. JCP; MePo
On a Man Run Over by an Omnibus. Henry Luttrell. FaBoEE
On a Memory of Beauty. G. S. Fraser. NeBP
On a mid-December day. Since. W. H. Auden. InPS
On a midsummer night, on a night that was eerie with stars. August Night. Sara Teasdale. MoAmPo
On a Miniature. Henry Augustin Beers. AA
On a Monday I was arrested. It's Almost Done (On a Monday). *Unknown.* FSW
On a Monday mornin' it began to rain. Jay Gould's Daughter. *Unknown.* AS
On a Monday Morning. Cyril Tawney. OBET
On a Monday morning early as my wandering steps did lead me. The Boys of Mullabaun [*or* Mullaghbawn]. *Unknown.* BIrV; GBP
On a Monday morning it began to rain. On the Charlie So Long. *Unknown.* AS
On a Monument in France Which Marks the Last Resting Place of an Army Mule. *Unknown.* ShM
On a Monument to Martí. Walter Adolphe Roberts. TTY
On a Morning Full of Sun. Philip Appleman. SOTS
On a morning such as this. Veteran. Lola Ridge. WPE
On a mountain of sugar-candy. Arno Holz. *Fr.* Phantasus. PChr
On a Mourner, *sel.* Tennyson.
Of Old Sat Freedom on the Heights. HBV-2; OAEP
On a New Duke. *Unknown.* FaBoEE
On a Newcastle Architect. *Unknown.* WhC
On a night of mist and rain. Phyllis. Sydney King Russell. ErPo

On a Night of Snow. Elizabeth J. Coatsworth. MoAmPo; MoShBr; OBCA
On a Nightingale in April. "Fiona Macleod." HBV-1; OBVV
On a Noisy Polemic. Burns. FaBoEE
On a Nomination to the Legion of Honour. *Unknown.* FaBoEE
On a Note of Triumph, *sel.* Norman Corwin.
Man unto His Fellow Man. TrJP
On a Nun. Jacopo Vittorelli, *tr. fr. Italian by* Byron. AWP
On a Painted Woman. Shelley. FaBoCo
On a Painting by Patient B of the Independence State Hospital for the Insane. Donald Justice. CoAP; ConAP; NePoEA-2
On a Pair of Garters. Sir John Davies. SiPS
On a Pair of Shoes Presented to Him, *sel.* Egan O'Rahilly, *tr. fr. Modern Irish by* P. S. Dinneen *and* T. O'Donoghue.
"I have received jewels of conspicuous beauty." OnYI
On a Parisian Boulevard. James Kenneth Stephen. DBV; NOBL
(England and America, II.) InMe.
On a patrician evening in Ireland. The Woman of the House. Richard Murphy. IPY
On a Peacock. Thomas Heyrick. PB
On a Photo of a Baby Killed in the War. Mark DeFoe. SOTS
On a Photo of Sgt. Ciardi a Year Later. John Ciardi. MiAP
On a Picture by J. M. Wright, Esq. Robert Southey. FM
On a Picture by Michele da Verona, of Arion as a Boy Riding upon a Dolphin. Anne Ridler. PoA
On a Picture by Pippin, Called "The Den." Selden Rodman. PoNe
On a Picture by Poussin Representing Shepherds in Arcadia. John Addington Symonds. FaBoBe; HBV-1
On a Picture of a Black Centaur by Edmund Dulac. W. B. Yeats. SyP
On a Picture of Lincoln. John Vance Cheney. PGD
On a Picture of Your House. D. G. Jones. NOBC
On a Piece of Unwrought Pipeclay. John Frederick Bryant. NOEC
On a Poet. Henry Parrot. FaBoEE
On a Poet Patriot. Thomas MacDonagh. *See* Of a Poet Patriot.
On a Poetess. Gerard Manley Hopkins. PP
On a Poet's Lips I Slept. Shelley. *Fr.* Prometheus Unbound, I. ChER; ELP; FiP; ViBoPo
(Poet's Dream, The.) GTBS; GTBS-P
On a Political Prisoner. W. B. Yeats. OAEL-2; OBMV
On a Politician. Hilaire Belloc. *See* Epitaph on the Politician Himself.
On a Portrait by Copley. Arthur Freeman. DBV
On a Portrait of a Deaf Man. John Betjeman. NoAM
On a Portrait of Columbus. George Edward Woodberry. AA
On a Portrait of Mme. Rimsky-Korsakov. Kingsley Amis. NePoEA-2
On a Portrait of Wordsworth by B. R. Haydon. Elizabeth Barrett Browning. HeIP
On a Prayer Book Sent to Mrs. M.R., *sel.* Richard Crashaw.
"Dear soul be strong!" ErPo
On a Prize Crucifix by a Student Sculptor. Robert Logan. CAPP
On a Professional Couple in a Side-Show. Alan Dugan. GP
On a Prohibitionist Poem. G. K. Chesterton. ViBoPo
On a Proud Fellow. *Unknown.* PV
On a Puritan. Hilaire Belloc. FaBoEE
On a Puritanicall Lock-Smith. William Camden. ShM; WhC
("Zealous locksmith died of late, A.") FaBoEE
On a Quaker's Tankard. Walter Savage Landor. FaBoEE
On a Quiet Conscience. Charles I, King of England. CH; PoPle
On a Rainy Night, *sel.* Harry Edward Mills.
"My love tonight is far away." PeD
On a Recent Protest against Social Conditions. David Posner. NYBP
On a Replica of the Parthenon. Donald Davidson. MoVE
On a Return from Egypt. Keith Douglas. NeBP; NePoEA
On a Rhine Steamer. James Kenneth Stephen. NBM; NOBL; TW
(England and America, I.) InMe
On a rock, whose haughty brow. A Pindaric Ode. Thomas Gray. *Fr.* The Bard. SeCePo
On a Romantic Lady. Mary Monck. NOEC
On a Rope Maker Hanged. William Browne. CavP
On a Rose in December. Ebenezer Elliott. FaBoEE
On a Row of Nuns in a Cemetery. R. G. Howarth. ELU
On a Royal Demise. Thomas Hood. FiBHP; PV
On a Ruined House in a Romantic Country. Samuel Taylor Coleridge. FaBoPa; Par
On a Saturday afternoon in the football season. Laziness and Silence. Robert Bly. PPP
On a School-Teacher. *Unknown, tr. fr. Greek by* Dudley Fitts. GLGT
On a Scooter. D. A. Greig. PeSA
On a Sculptured Head of the Christ. Mahlon Leonard Fisher. HBV-2
On a Sea-Grape Leaf. Katherine Garrison Chapin. GrPl
On a Seal. Plato, *tr. fr. Greek by* Thomas Stanley. AWP; FaBoEE
On a Sea-Storm nigh the Coast. Richard Steere. SCAP
On a Seven-Day Diary. Alan Dugan. OBAL
On a shining silver morning long ago. David McKee Wright. *Fr.* Dark Rosaleen. PoAu-1
On a Similar Occasion for the Year 1790. William Cowper. *See* Lines on a Bill of Mortality, 1790.
On a Similar Occasion for the Year 1792. William Cowper. NOCV
On a Skeleton of a Hound. James Wright. TwAmPo
On a small six-acre farm dwelt John Grist the miller. Under the Drooping Willow Tree. *Unknown.* OxBoLi
On a Snowy Day. Dorothy Aldis. *See* Snow.
On a snug evening I shall watch her fingers. Piano after War. Gwendolyn Brooks. AmNP
On a Soldier Fallen in the Philippines. William Vaughn Moody. AP; HBV-2; NOBA; PAH
On a Spaniel Called Beau Killing a Young Bird. William Cowper. FaBoCh
On a Spring-Board. Edward Cracroft Lefroy. OBVV
On a squeaking cart, they push the usual stuff. A Removal from Terry Street. Douglas Dunn. FaBoMo; OxBC; POL
On a Squinting Poetess. Thomas Moore. FaBoCo
On a Squirrel Crossing the Road in Autumn, in New England. Richard Eberhart. HeIP; LiTM; NePA; PoCH; Psk
On a starred [*or* starr'd] night Prince Lucifer uprose. Lucifer in Starlight. George Meredith. AWP; CABA; CH; EBVV; FF; HAP; HBV-2; InPK; LiTB; LoBV; NOBE; NoP; OAEL-2; OAEP; OBEV; OBNC; OBVV; PoEL-5; PPoe; SeCeV; TreFT; TrGrPo; UnPo; ViBoPo; VLP; WeW
On a Statue of Sir Arthur Sullivan. G. Rostrevor Hamilton. FaBoCo
On a Steamer. Dorothy W. Baruch. FaPON
On a Stingy Beau. John Winstanley. FaBoEE
On a straw-colored day. Dream. Solomon Edwards. NNP; PoNe
On a street in Knoxville. Street Scene—1946. Kenneth Porter. PoNe
On a Stupendous Leg of Granite, Discovered Standing by Itself in the Deserts of Egypt, with the Inscription Inserted Below. Horatio H. Smith. PrIm
On a Subway Express. Chester Firkins. YaD
On a summer day in the month of May. The Big Rock Candy Mountains. *Unknown.* NOBA
On a Summer Day, 1972. Calvin Murry. LFAC
On a summer's day when the sea [*or* wave] was rippled. The Ship That Never Returned. Henry Clay Work. BLPA; FSW
On a summer's day while the waves were rippling, with a quiet and gentle breeze. The Ship That Never Returned. *Unknown.* AS
On a Sunbeam. Thomas Heyrick. MePo
On a Sunday. Charles Reznikoff. DFF
On a Sunday Afternoon, *with music.* Andrew B. Sterling. FSN
On a Sunday morn, sat a maid forlorn. Wait till the Sun Shines, Nellie. Andrew B. Sterling. BLSo; FSN; FSW; TreFS
On a Sunday mornin' it begins to rain. Casey Jones. *Unknown.* ViBoFo
On a Sundial ("I am a sundial, and I make a botch"). Hilaire Belloc. FaBoEE; PV; QQQ
On a Sundial ("Save on the rare occasion when the sun"). Hilaire Belloc. POL
On a Sundial ("Stealthy the silent hours advance, and still"). Hilaire Belloc. MoVE
On a sunny brae alone I lay. A Day Dream. Emily Brontë. VLP
On a Tear. Samuel Rogers. HBV-2
On a throne of new gold the Son of the Sky. The Emperor. Tu Fu, *tr. by* E. Powys Mathers. AWP
On a Thrush Singing in Autumn. Sir Lewis Morris. OBVV
On a Time the Amorous Silvy. *Unknown.* GBL; ViBoPo
(Amorous Silvy, The.) UnTE
(Awakening, The.) NOBE
(Wakening, The.) OBEV
On a Tired Housewife. *Unknown.* *See* Epitaph: "Here lies a poor woman who always was tired."
On a train in Texas German prisoners eat. Defeat. Witter Bynner. PoNe
On a Travelling Speculator. Philip Freneau. AA
On a tree by a river, a little tom-tit. The Suicide's Grave [*or* Ko-Ko's Song *or* Titwillow]. W. S. Gilbert. *Fr.* The Mikado, II. FaFP; LiTB; NoP; TreF; VLP; WhC
On a Very Young, Very Dead Soldier. Richard Gillman. NePoAm
On a View of Pasadena from the Hills. Yvor Winters. QFR
On a Violet in Her Breast. Thomas Stanley. OBS
On a Virtuous Young Gentlewoman That Died Suddenly. William Cartwright. HAP; OBEV
On a Visit to Ch'ung Chen Taoist Temple. Yü Hsüan-chi, *tr. fr. Chinese by* Kenneth Rexroth *and* Ling Chung. PBWP
On a Vulgar Error. C. S. Lewis. OxBTC
On a Wag in Mauchline. Burns. ELU; FiBHP
(Epitaph for James Smith.) EBEV
On a Waiter. David McCord. *See* Epitaph on a Waiter.
On a Watchman Asleep at Midnight. James Thomas Fields. CenHV
On a Wednesday. Jody Aliesan. AMV-80
On a Wet Day. Franco Sacchetti. *See* Catch: On a Wet Day.

On a wet night, laden with books for luggage. The Poet on the Island. Richard Murphy. CIP; NMP
On a Wet Summer. John Codrington Bampfylde. NOEC
On a white field. The Sower. R. Olivares Figueroa, *tr. by* Dudley Fitts. FaPON
On a Whore. John Hoskyns. FaBoEE
On a wide-open, windless Autumn morning. The Plough-Horse. Rhoda Coghill. OnYI
On a Wife. Francis Burdett Money-Coutts. OBVV
On a winter night/ when the moon is low. Christmas Eve. Marion Edey. YeAr
On a winter's night long time ago. Noël. Hilaire Belloc. HBMV
On a withered branch. Basho, *tr. fr. Japanese.* WeW
On a Woman's Inconstancy. Sir Robert Ayton. *See* I Loved Thee Once.
On a World War Battlefield. Thomas Curtis Clark. PGD
On a Young Lady's Going into a Shower Bath. Francis Scott Key. UnTE; YaD
On Aesthetics, More or Less. Peter Kane Dufault. NYBP
On Alexander and Aristotle, on a Black-on-Red Greek Plate. Alan Dugan. PPP
On Alexis. Plato, *tr. fr. Greek by* Thomas Stanley. AWP
On alien ground, breathing an alien air. Where a Roman Villa Stood, above Freiburg. Mary Elizabeth Coleridge. OBNC
On alien ground I dwelt and also. The Dwelling. Moshe Dor, *tr. by* Dennis Johnson. VWA
On all the whole nacyon. Anathema of Cats. John Skelton. *Fr.* Phyllyp Sparowe. PCat
On Amaryllis, a Tortoyse. Marjorie Pickthall. PeCV
On an Aberdeen Favourite. *Unknown.* FaBoEE; FaBoPP
(Epitaph from Aberdeen.) DBV
On an Air of Rameau. Arthur Symons. OBNC
On an Anniversary. J. M. Synge. FaBoEE; OBMV; POL
On an apple-ripe September morning. Patrick Kavanagh. *Fr.* Tarry Flynn. IPY
On an autumn night, lying restless, far from her broken homeland. Yitzhak Lamdan, *tr. by* A. C. Jacobs. *Fr.* Massada. VWA
On an early Sunday in April, a feeble day. An Extract from Addresses to the Academy of Fine Ideas. Wallace Stevens. LiTA; LiTM
On an East Wind from the Wars. Alan Dugan. AP
On an Engraving by Casserius. A. D. Hope. CBAP
On an Houre-glasse. John Hall. MeLP; MePo
On an Ill-managed House. Swift. AnIV
On an Imaginary Journey to the Continent. Richard Porson. *See* Epigram on an Academic Visit to the Continent.
On an Indian Tomineois, the Least of Birds. Thomas Heyrick. FM
On an Infant Dying as Soon as Born. Charles Lamb. GTBS; GTBS-P; OBEV; OBRV
On an Infant Eight Months Old. *Unknown.* WhC
On an Insignificant Fellow. Lord Curzon. PV
On an Intaglio Head of Minerva. Thomas Bailey Aldrich. HBV-1; InMe
On an Invitation to the United States. Thomas Hardy. AWP
On an Island, *abr.* "Ethna Carbery." WPE
On an Island. J. M. Synge. BIrV; MoBrPo; OBVV
On an island the soft hue of memory. Hugging the Jukebox. Naomi Shihab Nye. MAYP
On an Italian Hillside. Richard Weber. NMP
On an oak in autumn. Survivor. Archibald MacLeish. NCSH; PrIm
On an Old Horn. Wallace Stevens. LiTA
On an Old Muff. Frederick Locker-Lampson. CenHV
On an Old Song. William E. H. Lecky. *See* Of an Old Song.
On an Old Sun Dial. *Unknown.* TreFT
On an Old Toper Buried in Durham Churchyard, England. *Unknown.* ShM
On an Old Woman. Lucillius, *tr. fr. Greek by* William Cowper. AWP
On an Old Woman Who Sold Pots. *Unknown.* PAI
On an olive-crested steep. Virgil's Tomb. Robert Cameron Rogers. AA
On an Upright Judge. Swift. DBV
On and on,/ O white brother! The Sea Bird to the Wave. Padraic Colum. EtS; SUS
On Andrew Turner. Burns. DBV; PV
On Angels. W. W. Eustace Ross. MoCV
On Another's Sorrow. Blake. *Fr.* Songs of Innocence. AWP; EBCP; EnRP; FaBV; PoEL-4; ViBoPo
On Apples. David Ross. NYBP
On Approaching My Birthday. Vassar Miller. IHMS; NMM
On Archaeanassa. Plato, *tr. fr. Greek by* Thomas Stanley. AWP
On Arrival. Richard Howard. TAP
On Arthur Hugh Clough. Swinburne. FaBoEE
On August nights. Driving By. Robert Wallace. LiSp
On Australian Hills, *sel.* Ada Cambridge.
"Oh, to be there to-night!" PoAu-1
On Authors and Booksellers. Pope. FaBoEE
On Autumn Lake. John Ashbery. LCAP
On Barclay's Apology for the Quakers. Matthew Green. NOEC
On beaches washed by seas. What She Said to Her Girl-Friend. Venmanipputi, *tr. by* A. K. Ramanujan. PBWP
On Becoming Man. R. P. Lister. PV
On Behalf of Some Irishmen Not Followers of Tradition. "Æ." AnIL
On Being a Woman. Dorothy Parker. FPL; PoLF
On Being Asked for a Peace Poem. Howard Nemerov. OxBC
On Being Asked for a War Poem. W. B. Yeats. MoVE; NIP; OBWP; PP
On Being Brought from Africa to America. Phillis Wheatley. BALP; FF; GOA; HeIP; NOBA; NOEC; SBG; TAP; TTY; WPE
On Being Head of the English Department. Pinkie Gordon Lane. BlSi
On Being Invited to a Testimonial Dinner. William Stafford. NePoAm-2
On Being Photographed. William H. Gass. AMV-81
On Being Sixty. Po Chü-i, *tr. fr. Chinese by* Arthur Waley. AWP
On Being Told That One's Ideas Are Victorian. Sara Henderson Hay. InMe
On Bell-Ringers. Voltaire, *tr. fr. French.* ShM
On Ben Dorain. Duncan Ban MacIntyre, *tr. fr. Gaelic by Robert Buchanan. Fr.* Last Farewell to the Hills. PoSH
On Ben Jonson. Robert Herrick. FaBoEE
On Bertrand Russell's "Portraits from Memory." Donald Davie. FaBoTw
On black bare trees a stale cream moon. Eau-Forte. F. S. Flint. OxBTC
On Blenheim House. Abel Evans. OBEC
On blessed youths, for Jove doth pause. Francis Beaumont. *Fr.* The Masque of the Inner Temple and Gray's Inne. OBS
On blood, smoke, rain and the dead. Who Knows Where. Detlev von Liliencron, *tr. by* Ludwig Lewisohn. AWP
On blue summer evenings I'll go down the pathways. Sensation. Arthur Rimbaud, *tr by* Kenneth Koch. SOTW
On bluish inlets bristling. The Painter. Robert Fitzgerald. MoVE
On Board the *Cumberland.* George Henry Boker. PAH
On Board the '76. James Russell Lowell. MOS
On Botching. John Heywood. FaBoCo; FaBoEE
On Broad Cairn, I remember still. Long Ago. Syd Scroggie. PoSH
On broad plains of bright sound. The White Peacock. Mary Mills. NePoAm
On Burning a Dull Poem. Swift. TW
On Burroughs' Work. Allen Ginsberg. NoAM; NOBA
On Butler who can think without just rage. John Oldham. *Fr.* A Satire. OBSV
On Button the Grave-Maker. *Unknown.* FaBoEE
On Buying a Dog. Edgar Klauber. GDP; NTCP
On Buying a Horse. *Unknown.* PH
On Calamy's Imprisonment and Wild's Poetry. *Unknown.* APAS
On Calvary's Lonely Hill. Herbert Clark Johnson. PoNe
On Calvert's plains new faction reigns. Maryland Resolves. *Unknown.* PAH
On Cardinal Wolsey. *Unknown.* FaBoCo
(Cacophonous Couplet on Cardinal Wolsey.) DBV
On Catching a Dog-Daisy in the Mower. Peter Redgrove. NePoEA-2
On Catullus. Walter Savage Landor. OBEV; ViBoPo
On Certain Days of the Year. Nancy Simpson. AMV-81
On Certain Ladies. Pope. FaBoCo
(Epigram.) PoEL-3
("When other ladies to the groves go down.") FaBoEE
On Certain Wits. Howard Nemerov. OxBC
On charts they fall like lace. Delos. Lawrence Durrell. NeBP
On Children. Kahlil Gibran. *Fr.* The Prophet. PoPl
On China Blue. Sir Stephen Gaselee. WhC
On Chloris Walking in the Snow. William Strode. ELP; HBV-1; JCP; OAEL-1
(Chloris in the Snow.) NOBE; OBEV
(On a Gentlewoman Walking in the Snowe.) OBS
On Christmas Day. Clement Paman. OxBoCh
(On Christmas Day to My Heart.) OBS
On Christmas Day. Thomas Traherne. OBS; PoEL-2
"Shake off thy sloth, my drowsy soul, awake," *sel.* OxBoCh
On Christmas Day ("On Christmas Day it happened so"). *Unknown.* OBET
On Christmas Day I weep. Christmas Mourning. Vassar Miller. CoPo; MoAmPo
On Christmas-day in seventy-six. The Battle of Trenton. *Unknown.* PAH
On Christmas Day to My Heart. Clement Paman. *See* On Christmas Day.
On Christmas Eve. W. S. Di Piero. AMV-81
On Christmas Eve I lay abed. Christmas Eve. John Drinkwater. HBMV
On Christmas Eve I turned the spit. *Unknown.* OxNR
On Christmas eve they filled the house, some fifty guests all told. Christmas at Babbitt's. Henry Hallam Tweedy. TRV
On Christmas Morn. *Unknown.* *See* Words from an Old Spanish Carol.
On Christmas morn awake did I. He Sports by Himself. Susan Miles. BXAP

On Christopher Wordsworth, Master of Trinity. Benjamin Hall Kennedy. FaBoCo; FaBoEE
(On "Who Wrote Icon Basilike" by Dr. Christopher Wordsworth, Master of Trinity. PV
On Clarastella Singing. Robert Heath. OBS
On Clarastella Walking in Her Garden. Robert Heath. CavP; OBS
On Clark Street in Chicago. George Keithley. NPGG
On clear May evenings the old sheep. Lambs Frolicking Home. Fred Lape. BoAnP
On Clergymen Preaching Politics. John Byrom. SeCePo
On cold days. Becoming a Nun. Erica Jong. MAYP
On coming to this sprawled and lazy city. How Night Falls in the Courtyard. Christine Rimmer. AMV-80
On Common Ground. R. P. Blackmur. Scarabs for the Living, III. CrMA
On Commonwealth, on Marlborough. Technologies. George Starbuck. NYBP
On Communists. Ebenezer Elliott. NOBL
On Corwen Road. Jay Ames. AMV-80
On Court-Worme. Ben Jonson. SeCP
On Critics. Matthew Prior. SeCeV
(In Imitation of Anacreon.) FaBoEE
On Cromek. Blake. *See* Cromek.
On crystal rims, they wheel in space. Snowflakes. Alice Behrend. GoYe
On Cupid's bow how are my heart-strings bent. Astrophel and Stella, XIX. Sir Philip Sidney. SiPS
On dark days the clouds. Sarentino-South Tyrol. Philip Brantingham. AMV-80
On Dean Inge. Humbert Wolfe. *See* Dean Inge.
On Death. John Donne. *See* Death, Be Not Proud.
On Death. Keats. SyP
On Death. Anne Killigrew. BoWoP
On Death. Walter Savage Landor. *See* Death Stands above Me.
On Death. Shakespeare. *Fr.* Measure for Measure, III, i. FiP
On Death and Love. Janet Campbell Hale. VoR
On Death, thy murd'rer, this revenge I take. An Epitaph upon My Dear Brother, Francis Beaumont. Sir John Beaumont. JCP
On Death's domain intent I fix my eyes. To a Gentleman and Lady on the Death of the Lady's Brother and Sister, and a Child of the Name Avis, Aged One Year. Phillis Wheatley. BlSi
On December, the sixth. Trenton and Princeton. *Unknown.* PAH
On Dennis. Pope. FaBoEE
On Devenish Island. Frank Ormsby. CIP
On Digital Extremities. Gelett Burgess. FaPON; HBVY
(Nonsense Verses.) HBV-2
On Disbanding the Army. David Humphreys. PAH
On Discovering a Butterfly. Vladimir Nabokov. NYBP
On Diverse Deviations. Maya Angelou. BlSi
On Dives. Richard Crashaw. ACP
On Dr. Evans Cutting Down a Row of Trees. *Unknown.* FaBoEE
On Dr. Isaac Letsome. *Unknown.* FaBoCo
(Candid Physician, The.) TreFT
(On Dr. Lettsom.) FaBoEE
(On Dr. Lettsom, by Himself, *at. to* John Coakley Lettsom.) PV
(Self-Composed Epitaph on a Doctor by the Name of I. Letsome.) WhC
On Dr. Keene, Bishop of Chester. Thomas Gray. FaBoEE
On Dr. Lettsom [by Himself]. *Unknown.* *See* On Dr. Isaac Letsome.
On Dr. Samuel Ogden. R. P. Arden. FaBoCo
On Don Juan del Norte, Not Don Juan Tenorio del Sur. Alan Dugan. ErPo
On Don Surly. Ben Jonson. FaBoEE
On Donne's Poem "To a Flea." Samuel Taylor Coleridge. FM
On Donne's Poetry. Samuel Taylor Coleridge. CABA; InvP; NoP; OAEL-2; OAEP; PAI; PP; SeCePo
On Douglas Bridge I met a man. Ballad of Douglas Bridge. Francis Carlin. AnIV; HBMV; OxBI
On Drawing-Room Amenities. Gelett Burgess. FaBoNo
On Dreams. Swift. BlrV
On Dressing to Go Hunting. *Unknown.* PH
On Drinking and a New Moon through the Window. Keith Wilson. GP
On dry days, I remember. First Rainfall. Alan P. Lightman. SUW
On Dulcina. *At. to* Sir Walter Ralegh. CoMu
(Come to Me Soon.) UnTE
On dull mornings. Mrs. Busk. Sir Osbert Sitwell. OxBTC
On dusty benches in the park. Reflections in a Little Park. Babette Deutsch. ELU; NePoAm
On Dwelling. Robert Graves. CMoP; FaBoMo; MoVE
On ear and ear two noises too old to end. The Sea and the Skylark. Gerard Manley Hopkins. FM; LiTB; OBMV
On Earth. Forugh Farrokhzad, *tr. fr. Persian by* Girdhard Tikku. BoWoP
On Earth There Is a Lamb So Small, *with music.* Nicolaus L. Zinsendorf, *tr. fr. German by* Sheema Z. Buehne. AH
On Easter Day. Celia Thaxter. FaPON; YeAr
On Easter morn,/ on Easter morn. Easter. Elizabeth J. Coatsworth. YeAr
On Easter morn at early dawn. Meeting the Easter Bunny. Rowena Bastin Bennett. SiSoSe; SoPo; SUS; TiPo
On Easter Morning. Eben E. Rexford. BLRP
On Eastnor Knoll. John Masefield. CH
On Editing Scott Fitzgerald's Papers. Edmund Wilson. CrMA; NYBP
On Edward Seymour, Duke of Somerset. *Unknown.* OBSC
On either side the river lie. The Lady of Shalott. Tennyson. BeLS; BLPL; FaFP; FiP; GN; HBV-2; NOBE; OAEL-2; OAEP; OBEV; OBNV; OBRV, *diff. vers.;* OBVV; SeCeV; TEP; TreF; VLP; WHA; WiR
On Eleanor Freeman, Who Died 1650, Aged 21. *Unknown.* OBEV
On Elizabeth Ireland. *Unknown.* FaBoEE
(Outside the Chancel Door.) ShM
On Ellson Fell. William Landles. PoSH
On Elm & Main a dreamy cur has recollected. Madrid, Iowa. Ron Ikan. PPJ
On Elphinston's Translation of Martial. Burns. FaBoCo
(Epigram on Elphinstone's Translation of Martial's Epigrams.) TW
("O thou, whom Poesy abhors.") FaBoEE
On Enclosures. *Unknown.* *See* On Inclosures.
On English Monsieur. Ben Jonson. NoP
On Entering a Forest. Elinor Lennen. PGD
On Even Keel. Matthew Green. *Fr.* The Spleen. OBEC
On every branch sat birdes three. *Unknown.* *Fr.* The Squire of Low Degree. PBBP
On every schoolhouse, ship, and staff. Half-Mast. Lloyd Mifflin. PAH
On eves of cold, when slow coal fires. Town Owl. Laurie Lee. PB
On Evolution. John Ciardi. OBAL
On Exodus 3: 14: "I am that I am." Matthew Prior. NOCV
On fair Augusta's towers and trees. A Tale of Drury Lane. Horace Smith. FaBoCo
On Falling. Andrew Greig. *Fr.* Men on Ice. PoSH
On Falling Asleep by Firelight. William Meredith. NoAM; NYBP
On Falling Asleep to Birdsong. William Meredith. PoCh
On Fame ("Fame, like a wayward girl, will still be coy"). Keats. *See* Two Sonnets on Fame.
On Fame ("How fever'd is that man"). Keats. *See* Two Sonnets on Fame.
On Fanny Godwin. Shelley. ChER; FaBoEn; OBNC
On Fell. Gotthold Lessing, *tr. fr. German.* ShM
On File. John Kendrick Bangs. WBLP
On Finding a Small Fly Crushed in a Book. Charles Tennyson Turner. FM
On Finding the Truth. Jones Very. TrCP
On First Entering Westminster Abbey. Louise Imogen Guiney. AA
On First Knowing God. Reed Whittemore. *Fr.* The Seven Days. GP
On First Looking in on Blodgett's Keats's "Chapman's Homer." George Starbuck. NIP; OBAL; PP
On First Looking into Chapman's Homer. Keats. BiP; BLPA; CABA; CH; ChTr; EnRP; FaBoBe; FaBoCh; FaBoEn; FaBV; FaFP; FaPo; FF; FiP; FPL; GN; GTBS; GTBS-P; HAP; HBV-2; HBVY; HelP; HoPM; InPK; LiTB; LoBV;NIP; NOBE; NoP; OAEL-2; OAEP; OBAL; OBEV; OBNC; OBRV; PAI; PoEL-4; PPoe; PPP; PrIm; RoGo; SeCeV; SoSe; TEP; TrGrPo; ViBoPo; WHA
(Sonnet: On First Looking into Chapman's Homer.) ChER
On First Looking into Chapman's Homer, *parody.* W. S. Brownlie. BXAP
On First Looking into Chapman's Homer I, *parody.* T. Griffiths. BXAP
On First Looking into Chapman's Homer II, *parody.* Peter Peterson. BXAP
On First Looking into Loeb's Horace. Lawrence Durrell. FaBoMo; LiTM
On First Looking into the Dark Future. Roger Lancelyn Green. CenHV
On Fleas. Augustus De Morgan. *See* Great Fleas.
On Fleas. Swift. TreFS
On Flower Wreath Hill, *sels.* Kenneth Rexroth.
"Aging pilgrim on a, An," GP
"Clustered in the forest around." GP
"Mist drenched, moonlit, the sculpture." GP
On Foinaven. Donald G. Saunders. PoSH
On Forelands High in Heaven. A. E. Housman. InPS
On Fort Sumter. *Unknown.* PAH
On Fortune. Elizabeth I, Queen of England. PBWP; WPE
On Freedom. James Russell Lowell. *See* Slaves.
On Friendship, *sel.* William Cowper.
"Man that hails you Tom or Jack, The." POL; TreFT
On Friendship. William Whitehead. OBEC
On Frosty Days. David Campbell. CBAP
On Fruition. Charles Sedley. ErPo
On Galveston Beach. Barbara Howes. MoAmPo
On Garland Sunday, the weaver told me. Garland Sunday. Padraic Colum. GoYe
On gay Anacreon's joy-inspiring line. On the Translation of Anacreon. Horace Walpole. FaBoEE
On Gay Wallpaper. William Carlos Williams. MoAB; MoAmPo; TAP
On getting a card. Poem. William Carlos Williams. VGW
On Getting a Natural. Dudley Randall. FB; PoBA

On Giles and Joan. Ben Jonson. NOBL
("Who says that Giles and Joan at discord be?") TEP
On Giving. Kahlil Gibran. *Fr.* The Prophet. PoPl
On Giving Up Smoking. Lawrence Spooner. *Fr.* A Looking-Glass for Smokers. NOEC
On Glaister's Hill, *sel.* William Jeffrey.
Carlyle on Burns. OxBS
On glossy wires artistically bent. Waspish. Robert Frost. BoAnP
On Going Home. Marjorie L. Agnew. GoYe
On Going to the Wars. Earle Birney. WaP
On golden seas of drink, so the Greek poet said. Alcohol. Louis MacNeice. LiTM
On gossamer nights when the moon is low. The Fairy Thrall. May Byron. HBV-1; HBVY
On Grey Cliffs. Walter Savage Landor. *See* Night Airs.
On Growing Old. John Masefield. CMoP; FaFP; FPL; HBMV; LiTB; LiTM; MoAB; MoBrPo; PoLF; PoRA; TreFS; ViBoPo; WHA
On Growing Old in San Francisco. Jack Gilbert. NPGG
On Gustavus Adolphus, King of Sweden. Sir Thomas Roe. FaBoEE
On Gut. Ben Jonson. AnAnS-2; JCP; NoP
On gypsum slabs of preternatural whiteness. Animal, Vegetable and Mineral. Louise Bogan. FM; SBG
On Hallow-Mass Efe, ere you boune ye to rest. St. Swithin's Chair. Sir Walter Scott. WSC
On Halloween. Shelley Silverstein. PoSC
On Hampstead Heath. W. W. Gibson. HBV-1
On hand is 27. Macrobius Mingling with Nature. Rochelle Owens. CoPo
On Hardscrabble Mountain. Galway Kinnell. RFM
On Harting Down. T. Sturge Moore. OxBTC
On Having Piles. Sir Walter Scott. FaBoEE
On he goes, the little one. Tortoise Family Connections. D. H. Lawrence. BrPo; ChMP
On Hearing a Beautiful Young Woman Describe Her Class in Physical Anthropology. A. J. Hovde. AMV-81
On Hearing a Broadcast of Ceremonies in Connection with Conferring of Cardinals' Hats. Denis Wrafter. NeIP
On Hearing a Lady Praise a Certain Rev. Doctor's Eyes. George Outram. DBV; EBVV; TreFT
On Hearing a Symphony of Beethoven. Edna St. Vincent Millay. LiTA; LiTM; MasP; MoAB; MoAmPo; NePA; TrGrPo; TwAmPo
On Hearing Mrs. Woodhouse Play the Harpsichord. W. H. Davies. BrPo
On Hearing Prokofieff's Grotesque for Two Bassoons, Concertina and Snare-Drums. Louis Untermeyer. BXAP
On Hearing That the Students of Our New University Have Joined the Agitation against Immoral Literature. W. B. Yeats. NoAM
On Hearing the Airlines Will Use a Psychological Profile to Catch Potential Skyjackers. Stephen Dunn. AmPA
On Hearing the First Cuckoo. Richard Church. OBMV
On Hearing the Marsh Bird's Water Cry. Duane Niatum. CDW
On Heaven. Ford Madox Ford. CTC
"And my dear one sat in the shadows," *sel.* ViBoPo
On Hellespont, guilty [*or* guiltie] of true love's blood. Hero and Leander. Christopher Marlowe. AAS; CABA; LoBV; NoP; OAEL-1; OAEP; OBSC; PoEL-2; SeCePo; TEP
On her beautiful face there are smiles of grace. A Pretty Girl. J. Gordon Coogler. OBAL
On Her Brother. Al-Khansa, *tr. fr. Arabic by* Willis Barnstone. BoWoP
On Her Brother Sakhr. Al-Khansa, *tr. fr. Arabic by* Willis Barnstone. BoWoP
On Her Coming to London. Edmund Waller. HBV-1
On Her Dancing. James Shirley. PoPle
On Her Loving Two Equally. Aphra Behn. SBG
On her side, reclining on her elbow. So-and-So Reclining on Her Couch. Wallace Stevens. AmPP; LiTM; NOBA
On her white breast a sparkling cross she wore. Pope. *Fr.* The Rape of the Lock. ACP
On him the unpetitioned heavens descend. A Counsel of Moderation. Francis Thompson. MoBrPo
On Himself. Charles Churchill. *Fr.* The Prophecy of Famine. OBEC
On Himself[e] ("Born[e] I was to meet with age"). Robert Herrick. ChTr; FaBoEE; SeCV-1
On Himself ("Here down my wearied limbs I'll lay"). Robert Herrick. CaPo
On Himself ("I fear no earthly powers"). Robert Herrick. CaPo
On Himself ("I will no longer kiss"). Robert Herrick. CaPo
On Himself ("I'll write no more of love, but now repent"). Robert Herrick. CaPo
On Himself ("Let me not live, if I not love"). Robert Herrick. CaPo
On Himself[e] ("The work[e] is done. Young men and maidens, set"). Robert Herrick. CaPo; SeCP
On Himself ("Weep for the dead, for they have lost this light"). Robert Herrick. FaBoEE
On Himself ("Young I was who now am old"). Robert Herrick. UnTE
On Himself. Walter Savage Landor. *See* On His Seventy-fifth Birthday.
On Himself. James Russell Lowell. *See* Lowell.
On Himself. William Oldys. FaBoEE
On Himself. Matthew Prior. *See* Epitaph on Himself.
On Himself. Dante Gabriel Rossetti. FaBoEE
On Himself. Swift. AnIV
On Himself, upon Hearing What Was His Sentence. James Graham, Marquis of Montrose. CavP; OBS; SeCePo
(His Metrical Prayer.) OxBS; PrIm
(Verses Composed on the Eve of His Execution.) ChTr; FaBoEE
On his airy perch among the branches. The Fox and the Crow. La Fontaine, *tr. by* Marianne Moore. NAWM-2; OBVE; PPP
On his arms he wears. Tattooed. William Plomer. ChMP
On His Blindness. Milton. AWP; ChTr; EBCP; FaBoEn; FaBV; FaFP; FaPoR; FiP; FPL; GN; GTBS; GTBS-P; HAP; HBV-2; HBVY; HeIP; InPS; LiTB; NOBE; OBEV; OxBoCh; PoEL-3; PoLF; PoPl; PoRA; PPoe; PrIm; SoSe; TEP; TreF; TrGrPo; TRV; WeW; WHA
(Sonnet: On His Blindness.) FaBoBe; NOCV; OHFP; WGRP
(Sonnet: "When I consider how my light is spent.") EBEV; JCP; LoBV; OAEL-1; OBS
(When I Consider How My Light Is Spent.) BiP; CABA; FF; InPK; MAT; NIP; NoP; OAEP; PAI; PPP; SeCeV; TrCP; ViBoPo
On His Books. Hilaire Belloc. ACP; FaBoCo; FaBoEE; MoBrPo; OxBoLi; PoPl; TreFT; WeW; WhC
On His Dead Wife. Milton. *See* On His Deceased Wife.
On his deathbed my grandfather. Gooseberries. Peter Wild. DFF; GP
On his death-bed poor Lubin lies. A Reasonable Affliction. Matthew Prior. HBV-1; NOEC; NoP; ShM; TreFT; TrGrPo; WhC
On His Deceased Wife. Milton. BLPL; FaFP; LiTB; OBEV; PoPle; SCV; SeCeV; TEP; TreFS
(Katherine Milton: Died MDCLVIII.) FaBoEn
(Methought I Saw.) NoP
("Methought I saw my late espoused saint.") BoLoP; CABA; EnLoPo; PPP
(On His Dead Wife.) GBL; HAP; NOBE; WeW
(On His Late Wife.) PoEL-3
(Sonnet: "Methought I saw my late espoused saint.") EBEV; OAEL-1; OBS
(Sonnet on His Deceased Wife.) LoBV
On His First Sonne. Ben Jonson. *See* On My First Son.
On His Friend, Joseph Rodman Drake. Fitz-Greene Halleck. *See* On the Death of Joseph Rodman Drake.
On His Garden Book. Francis Daniel Pastorius. SCAP
On His Having Arrived at the Age of Twenty-Three. Milton. *See* How Soon Hath Time.
On His Lady's Waking. Pierre de Ronsard, *tr. fr. French by* Andrew Lang. AWP
On his last swing around. Field Work. Doug Cockrell. Psk
On His Late Espoused Saint. Sir Kenelm Digby. ACP
On His Late Wife. Milton. *See* On His Deceased Wife.
On His Mistress Drown'd. Thomas Spratt. EnLoPo
On His Mistress Going from Home. *Unknown.* OBS
On His Mistress Looking in a Glass. Thomas Carew. CaPo
On His Mistress [*or* Mistris]. John Donne. Elegies, XVI. AnAnS-1; BoLoP; EBEV; LiTB; PoEL-2; SeCeV; SeCP; ViBoPo
(Elegy [*or* Elegie] on His Mistress.) GBL; LoBV; MeLP; MePo; SeCV-1
(To His Mistress Desiring to Travel with Him as His Page.) NOBE
On His Mistress. *Unknown.* *See* Beauty Extolled.
On His Mistress [*or* Mistris], the Queen of Bohemia. Sir Henry Wotton. AnAnS-2; EIL; EnLoPo; GBL; HAP; JCP; LoBV; MeLP; MePo; NoP; OBS; SeCP; TrGrPo; ViBoPo
(Elizabeth of Bohemia.) BoLoP; FaBoCh; GTBS; GTBS-P; HBV-1; NOBE; OBEV; PoPle
On His Mistresse Going to Sea. Thomas Cary. OBS
On His Mistris. John Donne. *See* On His Mistress.
On His Mistris That Lov'd Hunting. *Unknown.* OBS
On His Mistris, the Queen of Bohemia. Sir Henry Wotton. *See* On His Mistress, the Queen of Bohemia.
On his morning rounds the Master. Incident Characteristic of a Favourite Dog. Wordsworth. FM
On His Ninth Decade. Walter Savage Landor. *See* To My Ninth Decade.
On His Own Agamemnon and Iphigeneia. Walter Savage Landor. OBRV
On His Own Deafness Swift. BIrV; FaBoEE
On His Own Death. Walter Savage Landor. *See* Death Stands above Me.
On His Own Poetry. Charles Churchill. *Fr.* The Prophecy of Famine. NOEC
On His Portrait. William Cowper. EyDe
On His Queerness. Christopher Isherwood. OxBTC; PeHV
On His Seventy-fifth Birthday. Walter Savage Landor. *Fr.* The Last Fruit

off an Old Tree. AWP; BLPL; EBEV; LiTB; OAEL-2; OAEP; SeCeV; TreF; TrGrPo; WHA
(Dying Speech of an Old Philosopher.) FaBoEE; GTBS-P; HeIP; NoP; ViBoPo; VLP
(End, The.) SeCePo
(Envoi.) FaBoEn
(Finis.) GLGT; OBEV; OBVV
(I Strove with None.) ChTr; EnRP; HBV-2
("I strove with none, for none was worth my strife.") FaPoR; NOBE; OBNC
(On Himself.) FaBoEE
On His Twenty-third [*or* 24th] Birthday. Milton. *See* How Soon Hath Time.
On His Writing Verses. John Hawthorn. NOEC
On hoary Conway's battlemented height. With a Rose from Conway Castle. Julia Caroline Ripley Dorr. AA
On Honour. Bernard Mandeville. NOEC
On Hope by Way of Question and Answer between Abraham Cowley and Richard Crashaw. Abraham Cowley *and* Richard Crashaw. *See* Against Hope (Cowley) *and* For Hope (Crashaw).
On Hot Days. James Reiss. AmPA
On hot September nights, when sleep is scarce. My Father Dreams of Baseball. Laurence Lieberman. LiSp
On How the Cobler. *Unknown.* SCAP
On Hubbard Street, among factory signs. On the Upside. G. E. Murray. MAYP
On humming rubber along this white concrete. Driving in Oklahoma. Carter Revard. VoR
On Hurricane Jackson. Alan Dugan. CoAP; LiSp; NCSH; PAI; POL
On Hygiene. Hilaire Belloc. DBV; MoBrPo
On Imagination. Phillis Wheatley. AmPP; BlSi; PoNe
On Inclosures. *Unknown.* FaBoCo
(Epigram: On Inclosures.) OxBoLi
(On Enclosures.) FaBoEE
On Independence. Jonathan Mitchell Sewall. PAH
On Inhabiting an Orange. Josephine Miles. NoAM; PoA
On Installing an American Kitchen in Lower Austria. W. H. Auden. NYBP
On Its Way. May Swenson. WPE
On itself. His red hair was standing up. "I just began to weep." The Woman Who Could Read the Minds of Dogs. Leslie Scalapino. NPGG
On J. M. S. Gent. Pope. FaBoEE
On J. W. Ward. Samuel Rogers. DBV
On Jacob Tonson, His Publisher. Dryden. FaBoEE; OBSV
On James Grieve, Laird of Boghead, Tarbolton. Burns. DBV
(Epitaph on James Grieve, Laird of Boghead.) TW
On Jocky Bell. *Unknown.* FaBoEE
On John Adams, of Southwell. Byron. PV
On John Donne's Book of Poems. John Marriot. CH
On John Grubb. *Unknown.* WhC
On John So. *Unknown.* FaBoEE
On Jordan's Bank. Byron. ChER
On Jordan's stormy banks I stand. The Promised Land. Samuel Stennett. AmFP; TrAS
On July 5 the Associated Press gave the news to the world. Harangue on the Death of Hayyim Nahman Bialik. César Tiempo, *tr. by* Donald Devenish Walsh. TrJP
On Keats. Shelley. FaBoEE
On King Richard the Third, Who Lies Buried under Leicester Bridge. Sir John Suckling. CaPo
On Kingston Bridge. Ellen Mackay Hutchinson Cortissoz. AA
On Knighthood. Folgore da San Geminiano, *tr. fr. Italian by* John Addington Symonds. AWP
On Knowing Nothing. A. J. M. Smith. PeCV
On Ladies' Accomplishments. *Unknown.* FaBoUs
On Lady Anne Hamilton. Sheridan. FaBoEE
On Lady Poltagrue, a Public Peril. Hilaire Belloc. FaBoCo; MoBrPo; POL; PV; TreFT; WhC
On Lake Pend Oreille. Richard Shelton. NYBP
On Late-acquired Wealth. *Unknown, tr. fr. Greek by* William Cowper. OBVE
(Riches.) AWP
On Lavater's Song of a Christian to Christ. Goethe, *tr. fr. German by* Walter Kaufmann. ELU
On Laying the Corner-Stone of the Bunker Hill Monument. John Pierpont. PAH
On Laying Up Treasure. Lois Smith Hiers. GoYe
On Leander's Swimming over the Hellespont to Hero. Thomas Warton the Younger, *after the Latin of* Martial. FaBoEE
On Leaping over the Moon. Thomas Traherne. LiTB; LoBV; MOON; SeCV-2
On Learning That Certain Peat Bogs Contain Perfectly Preserved Bodies. Susan Ludvigson. MAYP
On Learning to Adjust to Things. John Ciardi. OBCA
On Learning to Play the Guitar. Ray Fraser. NeAC
On Leaving. Gertrudis Gomez de Avellaneda, *tr. fr. Spanish by* Frederick Sweet. PBWP
On Leaving Baltimore. Duane Niatum. CDW
On Leaving Cuba, Her Native Land. Gertrudis Gomez de Avellaneda, *tr. fr. Spanish by* Catherine Rodriguez-Nieto. WPOW
On Leaving Mrs. Brown's Lodgings. Sir Walter Scott. NBM
(To-Day I Leave Mrs. Brown's Lodgings.) FaBoEE
On Leaving Prison. Luis de Leon, *tr. fr. Spanish.* ILwL
On Leaving Ullswater. Kathleen Raine. NeBP
On Lebanon. David Gray. AA
On Lending a Punch-Bowl. Oliver Wendell Holmes. AA
On Leven's banks, while free to rove. Ode to Leven Water. Tobias Smollett. BSV; OBEC
On Liberty and Slavery. George Moses Horton. PoNe
On Lieutenant Shift. Ben Jonson. OBSV
On Linden Street. Shelley Ehrlich. AMV-80
On Linden, when the sun was low. Hohenlinden [*or* The Battle of Hohenlinden]. Thomas Campbell. BeLS; Ch; ChTr; EnRP; FaBoCh; FaBoRV; FaPoR; GN; GTBS; GTBS-P; HBV-2; NOBE; OBNC; OBRV; OBWP; OnMSP; PaPo; RoGo; TreF; WaaP; WBLP; WHA
On Listening to the Spirituals. Lance Jeffers. PoBA
On Living with Children for a Prolonged Time. Mark Lowey. AMV-81
On London fell a clearer light. Summer in England, 1914. Alice Meynell. BrRo; SBG; SUMH; WPE
On Long Island, they moved my clapboard house. Whitman. Larry Levis. MAYP
On long, serene midsummer days. Wild Roses. Edgar Fawcett. HBV-1
On longer evenings. Coming. Philip Larkin. MoBrPo; OxBTC
On Looking at a Copy of Alice Meynell's Poems. Amy Lowell. SBG
On Looking at an Old Climbing Photograph. Douglas Fraser. PoSH
On Looking at Stubb's Anatomy of the Horse. Edward Lucie-Smith. NePoEA-2
On Looking into Henry Moore. Dorothy Livesay. OBCV
On Looking Up by Chance at the Constellations. Robert Frost. CMoP; NePA
On Lord Chesterfield and His Son. *Unknown.* FaBoCo
On Lord Galloway. Burns. FaBoEE
On Lord Holland's Seat near Margate, Kent. Thomas Gray. CABA; LAuP; NOEC; OAEL-1; SeCeV; TW
(Impromptu.) NCEP; SeCePo
On Love. Kyōgoku Tamekane, *tr. fr. Japanese by* Burton Watson. *Fr.* Twenty-three Tanka. LLLT
On love's worst ugly day. First Meditation. Theodore Roethke. *Fr.* Meditations of an Old Woman. AP; LCAP; NaP; NOBA
On Lucretia Borgia's Hair. Walter Savage Landor. *See* On Seeing a Hair of Lucretia Borgia.
On Lucy Countess[e] of Bedford. Ben Jonson. AnAnS-2; EnRePo; OAEP; OBS; SeCP; SeCV-1
On Lydia Distracted. Philip Ayres. EnLoPo
On Maids and Cats. Henricus Selyns. SCAP
On Malverne Hilles, the Place of Piers Plowman's Vision. William Langland. *Fr.* The Vision of Piers Plowman. FaBoPP
On Mammon. Herman Melville. *Fr.* Clarel. OxBA
On Man. Walter Savage Landor. NBM; OBNC; OBRV
On man, on nature, and on human life. Prospectus [*incl. in* The Excursion]. Wordsworth. *Fr.* The Recluse. EnRP; NoP; OAEL-2; OBRV
On many a lazy river, in many a sparkling bay. The Little Boats of Britain. Sara E. Carsley. CaP
On Margaret Ratcliffe. Ben Jonson. SeCP
On Marriage. Richard Crashaw. FaBoEE
On Marriage. Thomas Flatman. ELU; FaBoUs; FiBHP; NOBL; WhC
(Bachelor's Song, The.) EnLoPo
On Mary Magdalene. William Drummond of Hawthornden. OAEL-1
On Meall nan Con, the Peak of the Dogs. Envoy. Alasdair MacLean. PoSH
On Meesh-e-gan, *with music.* *Unknown.* TrAS
On Meeting a Gentlewoman in the Dark. *Unknown.* FaBoEE
On Meeting a Stranger in a Bookshop. Oscar Williams. NePA
On Meeting the Clergy of the Holy Catholic Church in Osaka. Joy Kogawa. BrSi
On Melancholy. Keats. *See* Ode on Melancholy.
On Mercenary and Unjust Bailiffs. Henricus Selyns. SCAP
On Middleton Edge. Andrew Young. ELU
On Midsummer night the witches shriek. Owl. Sylvia Read. RHPC
On Mike O'Day. *Unknown.* *See* Mike O'Day.
On Minding One's Own Business. James Wright. PoPl
On miserable Nearchos' bones lie lightly, earth. Last Lines. X. J. Kennedy. OBAL
On Miss Eleanor Ambrose, a Celebrated Beauty in Dublin. Earl of Chesterfield. FaBoEE

On Mr. Abraham Cowley [His Death and Burial amongst the Ancient Poets]. Sir John Denham. AnAnS-2; OBS, *abr.;* SeCV-1
On Mr. Edward Howard, upon His British Princes. Charles Sackville. OBSV
On Mr. Francis Beaumont (Then Newly Dead). Richard Corbet. OBS
On Mr. G[eorge] Herbert's Book[e] [Intituled the Temple of Sacred Poems, Sent to a Gentlewoman]. Richard Crashaw. AnAnS-1; OxBoCh; SeCV-1
On Mr. Gay; in Westminster Abbey, 1732. Pope. FiP
On Mr. Hobbs, and His Writings. John Sheffield, Duke of Buckingham and Normanby. PoEL-3
On Mr. Milton's Paradise Lost. Andrew Marvell. JCP; OAEP
"Well mighst thou scorn thy readers to allure," *sel.* PP
On Mr. Nash's Picture at Full Length. Jane Brereton. WPE
On Mr. Nash's Present of His Own Picture at Full Length. Earl of Chesterfield. NOEC
On Mr. Partridge. *Unknown.* WhC
On Mr. Pitt's Hair-Powder Tax. Burns. FaBoEE
On Mr. Pricke. *Unknown.* FaBoEE
On Mr. Wm. Shakespeare. William Basse. *See* Elegy on Shakespeare.
On Mistress Nicely, a Pattern for Housekeepers. Thomas Hood. OBRV
On Mrs. Reynolds's Cat. Keats. *See* To a Cat.
On Mrs. W——. Nicolas Bentley. DBV; FiBHP
On Mites; to a Lady. Stephen Duck. FM
On Monday man gave God. Adam and God. Anne Wilkinson. MoCV
On Monday, Monday. My True Love. Ivy O. Eastwick. SiSoSe
On Monday morning as we set sail. Bold General Wolfe. *Unknown.* OBET
On Monday, when the sun is hot. Lines Written by a Bear of Very Little Brain. A. A. Milne. FaBoNo
On Monsieur Coué. Charles Inge. FaFP
On Monsieur's Departure. Elizabeth I, Queen of England. WPE
On moonlight bushes. Nightingales. Samuel Taylor Coleridge. *Fr.* The Nightingale. ChTr
On moonlit heath and lonesome bank. A. E. Housman. A Shropshire Lad, IX. BrPo; CMoP; OAEP; SoSe
On moony nights the dogs bark shrill. Night Song. Frances Cornford. FM; GDP
On Mother's Day. Aileen Fisher. NTCP; RHPC
On Mundane Acquaintances. Hilaire Belloc. ELU; FaBoEE; FiBHP; MoVE; OxBTC
On Music. Walter Savage Landor. GoJo; HBV-2
On My Bed I Sought Him. Bible, *O.T.* The Song of Solomon, III: 1-15. TrJP
On My Birthday, July 21. Matthew Prior. OBEV
On My Dear Grand-Child Simon Bradstreet. Anne Bradstreet. SCAP
On My First Daughter. Ben Jonson. AnAnS-2; EBEV; EnRePo; FaBoEE; HoPM; JCP; LoBV; NOBE; NoP; OBS; SeCP; SeCV-1; TEP
On My First Son [*or* Sonne]. Ben Jonson. AnAnS-2; AWP; CABA; EBEV; EIL; EnRePo; FaBoEE; FaBoEn; FF; HAP; HeIP; HoPM; JCP; LiTB; LoBV; NIP; NoP; OAEL-1; OAEP; OBS; PoEL-2; PPoe; QFR; SeCP; SeCV-1; TEP; WeW
(On His First Sonne.) OBS
(On My Son.) NOBE
On My Fortieth Birthday. John Tripp. NAs
On My Joyful Departure [from the City of Cologne]. Samuel Taylor Coleridge. FaBoCo; InvP; TW
(On My Joyful Departure from the Same [City].) WhC
On my knees. In the Garden. Tom Schmidt. NeAC
On My Lady Isabella Playing on the Lute. Edmund Waller. *See* Of My Lady Isabella . . .
On My Late Dear Wife. Jonathan Richardson. NOEC
On my little guitar. On My Old Ramkiekie. C. Louis Leipoldt, *tr. by* Anthony Delius. PeSA
On My Lord Bacon. John Danforth. SCAP
On My Old Ramkiekie. C. Louis Leipoldt, *tr. fr. Afrikaans by* Anthony Delius. PeSA
On My Own. Philip Levine. FYAP
On my perambulator. Perambulator Poems, I. David McCord. WhC
On My Pretty Marten. Charles Cotton. FM
On My Son. Ben Jonson. *See* On My First Son.
On My Sorrowful Life. Moses ibn Ezra, *tr. fr. Hebrew by* Solomon Solis-Cohen. TrJP
On My Stand. Sharon Scott. JB
On My Sweet Mother. Sappho, *tr. fr. Greek by* Thomas Moore. PoPl
On My Thirty-third Birthday. Byron. FaBoEE; NAs; OBRV
On My Wandering Flute. Abraham Sutskever, *tr. fr. Yiddish by* Ruth Whitman. VWA
On my way home from school. The Testing-Tree. Stanley Kunitz. FYAP; MAT; UnPo
On my way to Mass. The Lass from Bally-na-Lee. Anthony Raftery, *tr. by* Desmond O'Grady. BIrV
On My Wife's Birth-Day. Christopher Smart. NAs
On my windowsill. New York Bird. Andrei Voznesensky, *tr. by* William Jay Smith. NYP
On Myself. Edith Bone. FaBoEE
On Myself[e]. Countess of Winchilsea. SBG; TrGrPo
On Neal's Ashes. Allen Ginsberg. PoM
On New-Year's Day 1640, to the King. Sir John Suckling. SeCV-1
On New Year's Eve. Ts'uei T'u, *tr. fr. Chinese by* Witter Bynner. OFD
On News. Thomas Traherne. *See* News.
On nights when hail/ falls noisily. Izumi Shikibu, *tr. fr. Japanese by* Willis Barnstone. BoWoP
On No Work of Words. Dylan Thomas. LiTB
On Noman, a Guest. Hilaire Belloc. DBV; FaBoEE; PV
On Not Hearing the Birds Sing in Ireland. Padraic Colum. NePoAm
On Not Saying Everything. C. Day Lewis. NoP
On November 2nd 1965. Norman Morrison. Adrian Mitchell. FF
On ochre walls in ice-formed caves shaggy Neanderthals. To My Son Parker, Asleep in the Next Room. Bob Kaufman. PoBA; TwCP; VGW
On Oculists. Sir J. C. Squire. WhC
On old Cold Crendon's windy tops. The Fox Awakes. John Masefield. *Fr.* Reynard the Fox. MoVE
On Old Olympia's Towering Top. The Cranial Nerves. *Unknown.* FaBoUs
On old slashed spruce boughs. On Hardscrabble Mountain. Galway Kinnell. RFM
On Oliver Goldsmith. David Garrick. FaBoEE
On, on, on. The Dirigible. Chris Wallace-Crabbe. CBAP
On, on the vessel steals. Charles Stuart Calverley. *Fr.* Dover to Munich. NOBL
On One Condition. Charles Madge. EAS
On one fix'd point all nature moves. On the Uniformity and Perfection of Nature. Philip Freneau. AmPP
On one occasion. Visit to the Hermitage. Jack L. Anderson. LFAC
On one of those days with the Legion. A Day with the Foreign Legion. Reed Whittemore. CoAP; ConAP; LiTM; NePoEA
On one Saturday evenin'. Harvey Logan. *Unknown.* OuSiCo
On one summer [*or* summer's] day, sun was shining fine. Bill Bailey, Won't You Please Come Home. Hughie Cannon. BLSo; FSN; OBAL
On One That Lived Ingloriously. John Hoskyns, *after the Greek of* Simonides. FaBoEE
On One Who Died Discovering Her Kindness. John Sheffield, Duke of Buckingham and Normanby. LO; OBEV
On One Who Died in May. Clarence Chatham Cook. AA
On Opening a New Book. Abbie Farwell Brown. YeAr
On other cloudy afternoons. The Double. Irving Feldman. NYBP
On Our Crucified Lord, Naked and Bloody. Richard Crashaw. CABA; HoPM; OAEL-1; PAI; SeCV-1; TrCP
(Upon the Body of Our Blessed Lord Naked and Bloody.) ACP; InvP; OAEP; OBS; SeCP
On Our Lady of Blachernae. *Unknown, tr. fr. Greek by* Shane Leslie. ISi
On our lone pathway bloomed no earthly hopes. Sarah Helen Whitman. Sonnets, from the Series Relating to Edgar Allan Poe, V. AA
On our Pharsalian Plaines, comprizing space. Seaconk Plain Engagement. Benjamin Tompson. SCAP
On Our Thirty-ninth Wedding Day. Jonathan Odell. CaP
On Oxford. Keats. Par
On Pali Lookout. Stephen Shu Ning Liu. BrSi
On Parent Knees. Sir William Jones. *See* Epigram: "On parent knees, a naked new-born child."
On Parting with Moses ibn Ezra. Judah Halevi, *tr. fr. Hebrew by* Solomon Solis-Cohen. TrJP
On Passing the New Menin Gate. Siegfried Sassoon. OBMV
On Passing Two Negroes on a Dark Country Road Somewhere in Georgia. Conrad Kent Rivers. IDB; NNP
On Paunch, a Parasite. Hilaire Belloc. POL
On, Pegasus! Why, whither turn ye? A Survey of the Amphitheatre. Moses Browne. NOEC
On Peter Robinson. Francis Jeffrey. DBV; FaBoCo; FaBoEE; WhC
(Epitaph on Peter Robinson.) OxBoLi
On Philiphaugh a fray began. The Battle of Philiphaugh. *Unknown.* ESPB
On Philosophers. *Unknown.* TW
On Philosophy. Jonas Goldstein. AMV-81
On pianos and organs she lbs. The Musical Maiden. *Unknown.* TDH
On Playwright. Ben Jonson. NoP
On Poet Ninny. Earl of Rochester. APAS
On Poetry; a Rhapsody. Swift. OBSV
Sels.
"All human race would fain be wits." HAP; PoEL-3
"Hobbes clearly proves that every creature." HAP; PP; SCV
(Critics.) OBEC; SeCePo
On poetry and geometric truth. Wordsworth. *Fr.* The Prelude, V. SyP
On Poets. Pope. FaBoEE

On Portents. Robert Graves. FaBoMo
On Presenting to a Lady a White Rose and a Red on the Tenth of June. William Somervile. OBEC
On primal rocks she wrote her name. Our Country. Julia Ward Howe. PAH; PAL
On Prince Frederick. *Unknown.* FaBoCo; FaBoEE; NOBL; TreFS; WhC
(Epitaph on Frederick, Prince of Wales.) DBV
(Epitaph on Prince Frederick.) OxBoLi
On Professor Drennan's Verse. Roy Campbell. GTBS-P; WhC
On quarry walls the spleenwort spreads. Rockferns. Norman Nicholson. MoBrPo
On Queen Anne's Death. *Unknown.* ElL
On Queen Caroline. *Unknown.* FaBoEE
On Queen Caroline's Deathbed. Pope. TW
On Rachmaninoff's Birthday. Frank O'Hara. CAPP; PoM
On rainy days alone I dine. On Himself. Swift. AnIV
On Rape Unattempted. Alan Dugan. NoAM
On Reading. Thomas Bailey Aldrich. AA
On Reading a Poet's First Book. H. C. Bunner. AA
On Reading Aloud My Early Poems. John Williams. WeW
On Reading: Four Limericks. Myra Cohn Livingston. TDH
On Reading Gene Derwood's "The Innocent." Willard Maas. NePA
On Reading Mr. Ytche Bashes' Stories in Yiddish. Lester Ehrilichman. AMV-80
On Reading Poems to a Senior Class at South High. D. C. Berry. SoSe
On Reading the *Metamorphoses.* George Garrett. NePoAm-2
On Rears. Mary Hedin. PH
On Receiving a Copy of Mr. Austin Dobson's "Old World Idylls." James Russell Lowell. AP
On Receiving News of the War. Isaac Rosenberg. MMA; MoBrPo; OBWP
On Recrossing the Rocky Mountains after Many Years. John Charles Frémont. BPAW; PoOW
On Refusal of Aid between Nations. Dante Gabriel Rossetti. EBEV; LoBV; VLP
On Revisiting Cintra after the Death of Catarina. Luis de Camoes, *tr. fr. Spanish by* Richard Garnett. AWP
On Richard Hind. *Unknown. See* Epitaph: "Here lies the body of Richard Hind."
On Richmond Hill there lives a lass. The Lass of Richmond Hill. *At. to* Leonard McNally *and to* James Upton. BLSo; HBV-1
On Riding to See Dean Swift in the Mist of the Morning. Alexander Pope *and* Thomas Parnell. FaBoEE
On Riots. Cy Leslie. NBP
On Robert Buchanan, Who Attacked Him under the Pseudonym of "Thomas Maitland." Dante Gabriel Rossetti. FaBoEE
On Roman Feet my stumbling Muse declines. An Elegiack Verse on. . .Mr. Elijah Corlet. Nehemiah Walter. SCAP
On Roofs of Terry Street. Douglas Dunn. OxBTC
"On royal crowns and purples, I." Long John. Padraic Fallon. NeIP
On Rÿneveld, an Unpopular Dutch Judge. *Unknown.* FaBoEE
On St. James's Park, as Lately Improved by His Majesty. Edmund Waller. AnAnS-2
On St. Martin's evening green. Nuns at Eve. John Malcolm Brinnin. MoAB; MP; TwCP
On Saint-Urbain Street. Milton Acorn. NeAC; NOBC
On St. Winefred. Gerard Manley Hopkins. SaC
On Samuel Pease. *Unknown.* ShM
(Epitaph, An: "Under this sod and beneath these trees.") MoShBr
On Saturday mornings. Lines for the Planned Parenthood Clinic. Linda Westfall Spurrier. SOTS
On Saturday night shall be my care. Mother Goose. OxNR
On Saturday sailed from Bremen. Gerard Manley Hopkins. *Fr.* The Wreck of the *Deutschland.* SeCePo
On Saturday with joy Bill dubs his half. The Linen Weaver. *Unknown.* NOEC
On Scafell Pike. Ted Walker. NYBP
On Scaring Some Waterfowl in Loch Turit, a Wild Scene among the Hills of Oughtertyre. Burns. PBBP
On scent of game from town to town he flew. On a Travelling Speculator. Philip Freneau. AA
On Scotland. John Cleveland. DBV; PV
On Scott's [Poem] "The Field of Waterloo." Thomas, Lord Erskine. DBV; FaBoCo; FiBHP; WhC
On Seein an Aik-Tree Sprent Wi Galls. Robert Garioch. OxBS
On Seeing a Fine Frigate at Anchor in a Bay off Mount Edgecumbe, *sel.* N. T. Carrington.
"Is she not beautiful? reposing there." FaBoPP
On Seeing a Hair of Lucretia Borgia. Walter Savage Landor. CABA; HAP; InPK; OAEP; WeW
(On Lucretia Borgia's Hair.) EnRP
On Seeing a Lady's Garter. *Unknown.* ErPo
On Seeing a Lock of Milton's Hair. Keats. PP
(Lines on Seeing a Lock of Milton's Hair.) PeD
On Seeing a Pigeon Make Love. Leigh Hunt. FM
On Seeing a Poet of the First World War on the Station at Abbeville. Charles Causley. ChMP; LiTM; NMP
On Seeing a Pompous Funeral for a Bad Husband. *Unknown.* ShM
On Seeing a Torn Out Coin Telephone. Martin Robbins. MAT
On Seeing an Officer's Widow Distracted. Mary Barber. NOEC
On Seeing Francis Jeffrey Riding on a Donkey. *At. to* Sydney Smith. FaBoEE
On Seeing My Birthplace from a Jet Aircraft. John Pudney. NYBP
On Seeing Swift in Laracor. Brinsley MacNamara. AnIV; OxBI
On Seeing the Elgin Marbles [for the First Time]. Keats. BLPL; CABA; EnRP; EyDe; LiTB; NIP; PrIm; SeCeV; TrGrPo; WHA
On Seeing the Field Being Singed. Lady Ise, *tr. fr. Japanese by* Etsuko Terasaki *and* Irma Brandeis. BoWoP
On Seeing the Royal Palace at Stirling in Ruins. Burns. DBV
On Seeing Two Brown Boys in a Catholic Church. Frank Horne. BANP; CDC; PoBA; PoNe; TTY
On Seeming to Presume. Lawrence Durrell. LiTM
On Shakespeare. Milton. InvP; LoBV; MeLP; MePo; NoP; OAEP; PoRA; SeCePo; TrGrPo; WHA
(Epitaph on the Admirable Dramatic Poet, W. Shakespeare, An.) FaBoEE; HBV-2; ViBoPo
On Shakespeare and Voltaire. Thomas Holcroft. NOEC
On Shakespeare Critics. A. D. Hope. *Fr.* Dunciad Minor, V. OxBC
On shallow straw, in shadeless glass. Take One Home for the Kiddies. Philip Larkin. ELU; OxBTC
On Shiloh's dark and bloody ground. The Drummer Boy of Shiloh. *Unknown.* AmFP
On Shooting a Swallow in Early Youth. Charles Tennyson Turner. FM
On Shooting Particles beyond the World. Richard Eberhart. LiTA; LiTM; TW
On Sight of a Gentlewoman's Face in the Water. Thomas Carew. CaPo; SeCV-1
On Sir Henry Clinton's Recall. *Unknown.* PAH
On Sir Henry Ferrett, M.P. J. B. Morton. PV
On Sir John Calf. *Unknown.* FaBoEE
On Sir John Fenwick. Henry Hall. APAS
On Sir John Hill, M.D., Playwright. David Garrick. FaBoCo; FaBoEE
(David Garrick, the Actor, to Sir John Hill.) TreFT
On Sir John Vanbrugh [Architect]. Abel Evans. FaBoCo; FaBoEE; FiBHP; OBEC; PV
(Epitaph on Sir John Vanbrugh [Architect].) TreFT; ViBoPo
(For Sir John Vanbrugh, Architect, 2 *ll.*) WhC
On Sir Nathaniel Wraxall the Historian. George Colman, the Younger. FaBoEE
On Sir Philip Sidney. Henry Constable. *See* On the Death of Sir Philip Sidney.
On Sir Philip Sidney. Matthew Royden. *Fr.* An Elegy, or Friend's Passion for His Astrophil. ElL
On Sitting Down to Read "King Lear" Once Again. Keats. EBEV; EnRP; NoP
On Sitting Up Late, Watching Kittens. Eric W. Paff. AMV-81
On Sivori's Violin. Frances Sargent Osgood. AA
On sloping, shattered granite, the snake man. Snake Hunt. David Wagoner. GP
On small donkeys they bring in suns. Melons. Moshe Yungman, *tr. by* Gabriel Preil *and* Howard Schwartz. VWA
On Snow-Flakes Melting on His Lady's Breast. William Martin Johnson. AA
On soft puff of satin he now lies. Cat of Many Years. Gertrude May Lutz. AMV-80
On softest pillows my dim eyes unclose. Vita Benefica. Alice Wellington Rollins. AA
On Solomon Pavy, a Child of Queen Elizabeth's Chapel. Ben Jonson. *See* Epitaph on S.P., a Child of . . .
On Some Buttercups. Frank Dempster Sherman. AA
On Some Humming-Birds in a Glass Cage. Charles Tennyson Turner. FM
On some island I long to be. St. Columcille, *tr. fr. Irish by* John Montague. BIrV
On some mad magnificent mornings. Tidying Up. Nancy Weber. AMV-80
On Some Shells Found Inland. Trumbull Stickney. LiTA; NCEP; NePA; TwAmPo
On Some South African Novelists. Roy Campbell. ChMP; FaBoCo; FaBoEE; GTBS-P; InPK; MoBrPo; NOBL; OxBTC; PoPl; WhC
On Some Trees Needlessly Slain. Stanton A. Coblentz. TRV
On some Vermont road. Mating the Goats. Aliki Barnstone. AMV-81; BoWoP
On Something, That Walks [*or* Walkes] Somewhere. Ben Jonson. PAI; SeCP; SeCV-1

On Spies. Ben Jonson. NoP
On Springfield Mountain there did dwell. Springfield Mountain. *Unknown.* AmFP; BaBo; BLSo; FSW; TrAS; ViBoFo (A, B, C, *and* D *vers.*)
On Squire Neale's Projects. *Unknown.* APAS
On starry heights. The Conflict of Convictions. Herman Melville. AP; NOBA
On Startling Some Pigeons. Charles Tennyson Turner. PB
On Stella's Birthday, 1719. Swift. *See* Stella's Birthday, 1718-19.
On stifling summer days/ While a listless peacock strays. Old Inn on the Eastern Shore. William H. Matchett. NePoEA
On still black waters where the stars lie sleeping. Ophelia. Arthur Rimbaud, *tr. by* Brian Hill. ChTr
On still days when country telephone. Trouble-shooting. William Stafford. AMV-80
On stormy days. Brooms. Dorothy Aldis. SoPo
On stormy seas we six years sailed. Seven Years at Sea. *Unknown.* OuSiCo
On Stripping Bark from Myself. Alice Walker. LTB
On Sturminster Foot-Bridge. Thomas Hardy. FaBoPP; OAEP
On Such a Day. Mary Elizabeth Coleridge. LO; MoVE
On such a day as this I think. An April Day. Joseph S. Cotter, Jr. CDC
On such a morning as this. In Memory of Basil, Marquess of Dufferin and Ava. John Betjeman. OBWP
On Such a Windy Afternoon. Theodore Enslin. AMV-80
On summer afternoons I sit. La Vie C'est la Vie. Jessie Redmond Fauset. BANP; CDC; PoNe
On summer evenings blue, pricked by the wheat. Sensation. Arthur Rimbaud, *tr. by* Jethro Bithell. AWP
On summer evenings blue, where ears of wheat. Sensation. Arthur Rimbaud, *tr. by* T. Sturge Moore. SyP
On summer mornings when it's hot. The Milkman's Horse. *Unknown.* SoPo
On summer nights they swarm. Termites. Eric Chock. BrSi
On summer Saturday nights in Persia, Iowa, I saw. Watching the Out-Door Movie Show. Ann Struthers. FAZ
On Sunday Afternoons. Sunday Afternoons. Anthony Thwaite. OxBTC
On Sunday in the Sunlight. William Rose Benét. HBMV
On Sunday morning, then he comes. Mr. Wells. Elizabeth Madox Roberts. FaPON; HBMV; HBVY
"On Sunday morning well I knew." Popular Songs of Tuscany. *Unknown, tr. by* John Addington Symonds. AWP
On Sunday, when she visits him, she must come prepared. Erev Shabbos. Marc Kaminsky. VWA
On Sweet Killen Hill. Tom MacIntyre. CIP; NCSH
On Sympathisers with the American Revolution. Charles Wesley. NOCV
On T. Moore's Poems. *Unknown. See* On Thomas Moore's Poems.
On Taking a Wife. Thomas Moore. *See* Epigram: " 'Come, come,' said Tom's father . . ."
On Taking Up One's Cross. Bible, *N.T.* St. Luke, IX: 23-26. TreFT
On taut airbells; lifted, adoring eyes. Immolation. Robert Farren. OnYI
On Teaching David to Shoot. Walter McDonald. AMV-80
On Teaching the Young. Yvor Winters. NoAM; NOBA
On Ternissa's Death. Walter Savage Landor. *See* Ternissa! You Are Fled.
On that big estate there is no rain. Monangamba. Antonio Jacinto, *tr. by* Alan Ryder. TTY
On that last night before we went. In Memoriam A. H. H., CIII. Tennyson. PoEL-5
On that slope. An Autumn Day. Sorley MacLean. AMV-81
On that wild verge in the light he stood. Conrad Aiken. *Fr.* Time in the Rock. TwAmPo
On the/ dashboard. September Butterfly. Mollie Boring. AMV-80
On the American Rivers. James Smith. FaBoUs
On the Annunciation. *Unknown, tr. fr. Greek by* Shane Leslie. ISi
On the Antiquity of Microbes. Strickland Gillilan. WhC
(Lines Written on the Antiquity of Microbes.) TreFT
On the Apparition of Oneself. William Burford. PoA
On the Appeal from the Race of Sheba: II. Léopold Sédar Senghor, *tr. fr. French by* John Reed *and* Clive Wake. TTY
On the Aristocracy of Harvard. John Collins Bossidy. *See* Boston Toast, A.
On the Army of Spartans, Who Died at Thermopylae. Simonides. *See* On the Spartan Dead at Thermopylae.
On the Assumption. Richard Crashaw. *see* In the Glorious Assumption of Our Blessed Lady.
On the Astrologer and Almanac Maker, John Partridge. Swift. FaBoEE
On the Asylum Road. Charlotte Mew. MoBrPo
On the Atchafalaya. Longfellow. *Fr.* Evangeline. AA
On the Athenian Dead at Ecbatana. Plato, *tr. fr. Greek by* Ralph Gladstone. PoPl
On the athletic field. A Day of Notes. J. Charles Green. LFAC
On the Author of the *Treatise of Human Nature.* James Hay Beattie. FaBoCo
On the avenue the faces change each day. Hope. F. D. Reeve. PoA
On the Balcony D. H. Lawrence. BrPo; GBL
(Illicit.) PoA
On the banks of Allan Water. Allan Water. Matthew Gregory Lewis. HBV-1
On the Banks of Salee. *Unknown.* AmFP
On the Banks of the Little Eau Pleine. *Unknown.* AmFP
On the banks of the Potomac there's an army so grand. The Red, White and Red. *Unknown.* AmFP
On the Banks of the Wabash, Far Away, *with music.* Paul Dresser. BLSo; FSN
On the Baptized Ethiopian. Richard Crashaw. NoP; PeD
(On the Baptized Aethiopian.) FaBoEE; SeCV-1
On the bare mountain. Distant View. Uys Krige, *tr. by* Uys Krige *and* Jack Cope. PeSA
On the bare veld where nothing ever grows. A Veld Eclogue: The Pioneers. Roy Campbell. OBSV
On the Beach. Charles Stuart Calverley. FiBHP
On the Beach. Frances Cornford. BoAnP
On the Beach. Arthur Symons. *Fr.* At Dieppe. SyP; VLP
On the beach/ a big dog lies. Pati Hill. FAZ
On the Beach at Calais. Wordsworth. *See* It Is a Beauteous Evening.
On the Beach at Fontana. James Joyce. MoBrPo; OBMV; PoA; SoSe
On the Beach at Night. Walt Whitman. AmPP; AWP; ChTr; InPS; MoAmPo; NePA; NOBA; NoP; OBVV; OxBA
On the Beach at Night Alone. Walt Whitman. NePA; TAP
On the beach where we had been idly. Gracious Goodness. Marge Piercy. BoAnP; HoAn; Psk
On the Benefactions in the Late Frost. Pope. NOEC
On the beryl-rimmed rebecs of Ruby. Lily Adair. Thomas Holley Chivers. OBAL
On the Big Horn. Whittier. PAH
On the Birth of a Black/Baby/Boy. Etheridge Knight. DiL
On the Birth of a Posthumous Child, Born in Peculiar Circumstances of Family Distress. Burns. NAs
On the Birth of Dan Goldman. Daniel Berrigan. NAs
On the Birth of His Son. Su Tung-p'o, *tr fr. Chinese by* Arthur Waley. AWP; OBVE; OFD; TRV
("Families, when a child is born.") PV
On the Birth of My Son, Malcolm Coltrane. Julius Lester. PoBA
On the black tarmac playground dark. Deaf-and-Dumb School. Anthony Delius. PeSA
On the Bleeding Wounds of Our Crucified Lord. Richard Crashaw. SeCV-1
(Upon the Bleeding Crucifix, *later vers.*) SeCP
"Jesu, no more! It is full tide," *sel.* TrGrPo
On the Blessed Virgin's Bashfulness. Richard Crashaw. HAP; ISi; OAEP
On the bloody field of Monmouth. Captain Molly. William Collins. PAL
On the blue corner's top rope. Ripper Collins' Legacy. Don Johnson. LiSp
On the bluff of the Little Big Horn. Miles Keogh's Horse. John Hay. PAH; PoOW
On the bog road the blackthorn flowers, the turf-stacks. Anthony Cronin. *Fr.* R.M.S. *Titanic.* BIrV
On the boulder a lizard. Recognition. Georgette Perry. AMV-80
On the Breaking-up of a School. Tadhg O'g O'Huiginn, *tr. fr. Late Middle Irish by* Osborn Bergin. AnIL
On the Bridge. Kate Greenaway. RHPC
On the bridge at Avignon. Sur le Pont d'Avignon (On the Bridge at Avignon). *Tr. fr. French.* FSW
On the Bridge of Athlone; a Prophecy. Donagh MacDonagh. OxBI
On the Bridge of Sighs. Byron. *See* Venice.
On the Bright Side. Carter Revard. VoR
On the Brink of Death. Michelangelo, *tr. fr. Italian by* John Addington Symonds. AWP
On the British Invasion. Philip Freneau. PAH
On the British King's Speech. Philip Freneau. PAH
On the Building of a New Church. *Unknown. See* Building of a New Church, The.
On the Building of Springfield. Vachel Lindsay. OHFP; WHA
On the Burial of His Brother. Catullus, *tr. fr. Latin by* Aubrey Beardsley. AWP
On the Bus. Mitsuye Yamada. *Fr.* Camp Notes. WPOW
On the Bust of Helen by Canova. Byron. EyDe
On the Calculus. J. V. Cunningham. QFR
On the Campagna. Elizabeth Stoddard. AA
On the Candidates for the Laurel. Pope. FaBoEE
On the Capture and Imprisonment of Crazy Snake, January, 1900. Alexander L. Posey. BPAW
On the Capture of the *Guerrière.* Philip Freneau. PAH
On the Cards and Dice. Sir Walter Ralegh. EnRePo
(Prognostication upon Cards and Dice, A.) SiPS
On the Castle of Chillon. Byron. *See* Sonnet on Chillon.

On the chalk cliff edge struggles the final field. The Marginal Field. Stephen Spender. PoA
On the Charlie So Long, *with music. Unknown.* AS
On the Circuit. W. H. Auden. NOBL; OxBTC
On the Clerk of a Country Parish. William Shenstone. FaBoEE
On the Cliff. Hal Summers. ChMP
On the Cliffs. Swinburne. VLP
On the Closing of Millom Ironworks. Norman Nicholson. FaBoTw
On the Coast near Sausalito. Robert Hass. WOLT
On the Coast of Coromandel. Sir Osbert Sitwell. MoBrPo; SeCePo
On the Coast of Coromandel. The Courtship of the Yonghy-Bonghy-Bo. Edward Lear. EnLoPo; EvOK; FaBoNo; HBV-2; NA; OAEL-2; OnMSP; WiR
On the Collar of Mrs. Dingley's Lap-Dog. Swift. FaBoEE; FM
On the College Archery Range. Robert Wallace. LiSp
On the Columbia River near Vantage. Bobber. Raymond Carver. GeTw
On the Coming of Age of a Rich Extravagant Young Man, *sel.* Samuel Johnson.
"Wealth, my lad, was made to wander." ViBoPo
On the Completion of the Pacific Telegraph. Jones Very. AP; TAP
On the cool porch of "Wannamasset." Vignette: 1922. Lawrence P. Spingarn. AMV-81
On the corner—116th and Lenox. Harlem Freeze Frame. Lebert Bethune. PoBA
On the corner where s. klien's used to be. 14th St/New York. Patricia Jones. NYP
On the Couch. Oscar Williams. WaP
On the Countess Dowager of Pembroke. William Browne. AWP; CABA; CavP; HAP; InvP; JCP; NoP; PoEL-2; PoRA; SeCeV; TreFS; WeW
(Epitaph on the Countess Dowager of Pembroke.) FaBoEE; HBV-2; LoBV; NOBE; OBEV; OBS
(On the Death of Marie, Countess of Pembroke.) NIP; OAEL-1; WHA
(On the Dowager Countess of Pembroke.) ViBoPo
(Underneath This Sable Hearse.) PoPle
On the Countess of Dorchester ("Dorinda's sparkling wit, and eyes"). Charles Sackville. *See* Song: "Dorinda's sparkling wit, and eyes."
On the Countess of Dorchester (Tell me, Dorinda, why so gay"). Charles Sackville. APAS; CavP
On the cover of the book of 19th-century. The Cyclists. Lawrence Kearney. AMV-80
On the craggy mountain-top the mist. Majuba Hill. Roy Macnab. PeSA
On the Creation and Ontogony. *Unknown, tr. fr. Lenape Indian by* C. S. Rafinesque. *Fr.* The Wallum Olum. LiTA
On the Crocodile. Thomas Heyrick. FM
On the crooked arm of Columbus, on his cloak. Pigeons. Alastair Reid. MP; NePoEA; NYBP; NYP; TwCP
On the Croun o Bidean. J. K. Annand. PoSH
On the Crucifixion. Giles Fletcher. *Fr.* Christ's Triumph over Death. EBCP; OxBoCh
On the Cuckoo. Francis Quarles. PBBP
On the Curve-Edge. Abbie Huston Evans. NYBP
On the Danger of War. George Meredith. PPON
On the Dangers Attending Altruism on the High Seas. G. K. Chesterton. FaBoNo
On the Danube. Robert Conquest. NMP
On the Dark, Still, Dry, Warm Weather Occasionally Happening in the Winter Months. Gilbert White. NOEC
On the Dates of Poets. Michael L. Johnson. AMV-80
On the day I was born. My Stars. Abraham Ibn Ezra, *tr. by* Robert Mezey. OFD
On the day my father died a flame-tree. Vincent O'Sullivan. Brother Jonathan, Brother Kafka, 8. OCNZ
On the Day of Atonement. Yehuda Amichai, *tr. fr. Hebrew by* Shirley Kaufman. VWA
On the Day of Atonement we fasted. Day of Atonement. Jack Myers. VWA
On the day of the explosion. The Explosion. Philip Larkin. EBEV; FaBoMo; HAP; OxBC; SCV; WeW
On the Dead. Walter Savage Landor. NBM
On the Death of a Cat. Christina Rossetti. PCat
On the Death of a Child. Edward Silvera. PoNe
On the Death of a Favorite Cat, Drowned in a Tub of Gold Fishes. Thomas Gray. *See* Ode on the Death . . .
On the Death of a Favourite Old Spaniel. Robert Southey. FM
On the Death of a Female Officer of the Salvation Army. A. E. Housman. *See* Hallelujah!
On the Death of a Lady's Dog. Earl of Roscommon. CavP
On the Death of a Lady's Owl. Moses Mendes. TrJP
On the Death of a Metaphysician. George Santayana. ViBoPo
On the Death of a Monkey. Thomas Heyrick. FM; MePo
On the Death of a New Born Child. Mei Yao Ch'en, *tr. fr. Chinese by* Kenneth Rexroth. NaP
On the Death of a Nightingale. Thomas Randolph. AnAnS-2; PBBP
On the Death of a Particular Friend. James Thomson. *See* Finis.
On the Death of a Pious Lady. Olof Wexionius, *tr. fr. Swedish by* Sir Edmund Gosse. AWP
On the Death of a Prince; a Meditation. Thomas Philipott. JCP
On the Death of a Recluse. George Darley. OBVV; OxBI
On the Death of a Young and Favorite Slave. Martial, *tr. fr. Latin by* Goldwin Smith. AWP
On the Death of an Acquaintance. Oscar Williams. *Fr.* Variations on a Theme. LiTA; NePA
On the Death of an Emperor Penguin in Regent's Park, London. David Wright. NYBP
On the Death of Anne Brontë. Charlotte Brontë. ViBoPo; WPE
On the Death of Benjamin Franklin. Philip Freneau. PAH
On the Death of Captain Nicholas Biddle. Philip Freneau. PAH
On the Death of Catarina de Attayda. Luis de Camoes, *tr. fr. Spanish by* R. F. Burton. AWP
On the Death of Commodore Oliver H. Perry. John G. C. Brainard. PAH
On the Death of Crashaw. Abraham Cowley. GoBC
On the Death of Dermody, the Poet. Henry Kirke White. PeD
On the Death of Dr. Robert Levet. Samuel Johnson. *See* On the Death of Mr. Robert Levet.
On the Death of Doctor Swift. Swift. *See* Verses on the Death of Doctor Swift.
On the Death of Donne. Thomas Carew. *Fr.* Elegy upon the Death of the Dean of Paul's, Dr. John Donne. NOBE
On the Death of Echo. Hartley Coleridge. BoAnP; GDP
On the Death of Edward III. *Unknown.* OxBM
On the Death of Elizabeth, Queen of Henry VII, and Mother of Henry VIII. *Unknown.* FaBoRV
On the Death of Emperor Tenji. *Unknown, tr. fr. Japanese by* Geoffrey Bownas *and* Anthony Thwaite. BoWoP
On the Death of Francis Thompson. Alfred Noyes. OBVV
On the Death of Friends in Childhood. Donald Justice. ConAP; LCAP; NCSH
On the Death of His Son. Lewis Glyn Cothi, *tr. fr. Welsh by* Gwyn Williams. PoPl
On the Death of His Son. Charles Wesley. NOCV
On the Death of His Wife. Muireadach O'Dalaigh, *tr. fr. Irish by* Frank O'Connor. BIrV; CIP
On the Death of Ho Chi Minh. Eli Mandel. NIP
On the Death of "Jackson." *Unknown.* PAH
On the Death of Joseph Rodman Drake. Fitz-Greene Halleck. AA; HBV-2; PAH; PoEL-4; TreFS
(Joseph Rodman Drake.) BLPA
(On His Friend, Joseph Rodman Drake.) OBVV
On the Death of Karl Barth. Jack Clemo. NOCV
On the Death of Keats. John Logan. Prf
On the Death of Lisa Lyman. Della Burt. BlSi
On the Death of Little Mahala Ashcraft. James Whitcomb Riley. AA
On the Death of M. D'Ossoli and His Wife, Margaret Fuller. Walter Savage Landor. PAH
On the Death of Marie, Countess of Pembroke. William Browne. *See* On the Countess Dowager of Pembroke.
On the Death of Mary. Rainer Maria Rilke, *tr. fr. German by* M. D. Herter Norton. ISi
On the Death of Mr. Crashaw. Abraham Cowley. AnAnS-2; MeLP; MePo; OBS; SeCP; SeCV-1; ViBoPo
On the Death of Mr. Pope. *Unknown.* NOEC
On the Death of Mr. Richard West. Thomas Gray. *See* Sonnet on the Death of Richard West.
On the Death of Mr. [*or* Dr.] Robert Levet, a Practiser in Physic. Samuel Johnson. EBEV; HBV-2; HeIP; InPS; LAuP; NOBE; NOEC; NoP; OAEL-1; OBEC; OBEV; PoEL-3; PPP; SCV; TEP
(Lines on the Death of Mr. Levett.) FaBoEn
"In misery's darkest cavern known," *sel.* ViBoPo
On the Death of Mr. William Aikman the Painter, *sel.* James Thomson. Finis. BSV
(On the Death of a Particular Friend.) OBEV
(Verses Occasioned by the Death of Dr. Aikman.) OBEC
On the Death of Mr. William Hervey [*or* Harvey]. Abraham Cowley. AnAnS-2; EBEV; FaBoRV; OBEV; OBS; SeCP; SeCV-1
"It was a dismal and a fearful night," *sel.* NOBE; ViBoPo
On the Death of Mrs. Bowes. Lady Mary Wortley Montagu. BoWoP
On the Death of Mrs. Felicia Hemans, *sel.* Lydia H. Sigourney.
"Little plant that never sang before, The." PeD
On the Death of Mistress Mary Prideaux. William Strode. JCP
On the Death of Mrs. Throckmorton's Bullfinch. William Cowper. HBV-1; NOEC; PBBP; PPP
(On the Lamented Death of Mrs. Throckmorton's Bullfinch.) LAuP
On the Death of My Son Charles. Daniel Webster. AA
On the Death of Neruda. Olga Cabral. SOTS

On the Death of Neruda. H. L. Van Brunt. LTB
On the Death of Old Bennet the News-Crier. *Unknown.* NOEC
On the Death of Parents. Alfred Barson. AMV-80
On the Death of Phillips. *Unknown.* OBSC
On the Death of President Garfield. Oliver Wendell Holmes. PAH
On the Death of Richard West. Thomas Gray. *See* Sonnet on the Death of Richard West.
On the Death of Sir Albert Morton's Wife. Sir Henry Wotton. *See* Upon the Death of Sir Albert Morton's Wife.
On the Death of Sir Philip Sidney. Henry Constable. GoBC; OBEV
(On Sir Philip Sidney.) OBSC
(To Sir Philip Sidney's Soul.) ElL; SeCePo
On the Death of Sir Thomas Wyatt. Earl of Surrey. *See* Wyatt Resteth Here.
On the Death of Southey. Walter Savage Landor. OBVV
On the Death of Sylvia Plath. Judith Herzberg, *tr. fr. Dutch.* VWA, *tr. by* Shirley Kaufman; WPOW, *tr. by* Manfred Wolf
On the Death of the Evansville University Basketball Team in a Plane Crash, December 13, 1977. Robert W. Hamblin. AMV-80
On the Death of the Giraffe. Thomas Hood. FaBoEE
On the Death of the Great Chef Alexis Soyer. *Unknown.* FaBoEE
On the Death of the Lord Treasurer. *Unknown.* FaBoEE
On the Death of William Edward Burghardt Du Bois [by African Moonlight and Forgotten Shores]. Conrad Kent Rivers. NBP; PoBA
On the Deaths of Thomas Carlyle and George Eliot. Swinburne. HBV-2
On the Debt My Mother Owed to Sears Roebuck. Edward Dorn. ConAP
On the Decease of the Religious and Honourable Jno Haynes Esqr. John James. SCAP
On the Deception of Appearances. Sadi, *tr. fr. Persian by* L. Cranmer-Byng. *Fr.* The Gulistan. AWP
On the deck of a ship called the Masm. Limerick. Conrad Aiken. FaBoNo
On the deck of Patrick Lynch's boat I sat in woeful plight. The County of Mayo. *At. to* Thomas Flavell [*or* Lavelle], *tr. by* George Fox. AnIV; BIrV; OBEV; OnYI; OxBI
On the Defeat at Ticonderoga or Carilong. *Unknown.* PAH
On the Defeat of Henry Clay. William Wilberforce Lord. PAH
(On the Defeat of a Great Man.) AA
On the Defeat of Ragnall by Murrough King of Leinster A.D. 994. *Unknown, tr. fr. Middle Irish by* Kuno Meyer. OnYI
(Murrough Defeats the Danes, 994, *tr. by* Frank O'Connor.) KiLC
On the Democracy of Yale. Frederick Scheetz Jones. HBV-1; WhC; YaD
(To New Haven.) TreFS
On the Departure of Sir Walter Scott from Abbotsford, for Naples. Wordsworth. EBEV; EnRP
On the Departure of the British from Charleston. Philip Freneau. PAH
On the Departure Platform. Thomas Hardy. NOBE; OBNC; OxBTC
On the Deputy of Ireland's Child. Sir John Davies. FaBoEE
On the Desert. Stephen Crane. War Is Kind, XI. LiTM
On the Detraction Which Followed upon My Writing Certain Treatises. Milton. SeCeV
On the Disadvantages of Central Heating. Amy Clampitt. AMV-80
On the Discoveries of Captain Lewis. Joel Barlow. AmPP; PAH
On the distant prairie, where the heather wild. Rosalie, the Prairie Flower. George Frederick Root. BLSo
On the Doorstep. Thomas Hardy. MoVE
On the Dowager Countess of Pembroke. William Browne. *See* On the Countess Dowager of Pembroke.
On the Duke of Buckingham. James Shirley. *See* Epitaph on the Duke of Buckingham.
On the Duke of Buckingham, Slain by Felton, the 23rd August, 1628. Owen Felltham. JCP
On the dusty earth-drum. Rain Music. Joseph S. Cotter, Jr. BANP; CDC
On the Earl of Kildare. *Unknown.* FaBoEE
On the Earl of Leicester. *Unknown.* FaBoEE
On the Earl of Strafford's Trial and Death. John Denham. LoBV
On the Eclipse of the Moon of October 1865. Charles Tennyson Turner. OBNC
On the Edge. Frank Dwyer. AMV-81
On the Edge. Philip Levine. CoAP; TAP
On the Edge at Santorini. Michael C. Blumenthal. AMV-80
On the Edge of a Safe Sleep. Teresa D. Cader. AMV-81
On the Edge of the Copper Pit. Pauline Henson. GoYe
On the Edition of Mr. Pope's Works with a Commentary and Notes. Thomas Edwards. TW
On the 18th of April in '28. Happy Lifetime to You. Franklin P. Adams. InMe
On the eighteenth of August, at the eighth month of the year. New Garden Fields. *Unknown.* OBET
On the eighteenth of September in eighteen seventy three. The Winter of '73. Larry Gorman. ShS
On the eighth day God died: his bearded mouth. The Worms of History. Robert Graves. MoPo
On the eighth day of March it was, some people say. The Birth of Saint Patrick. Samuel Lover. HBV-2; PoSC
On the eighth day, the rain stopped before dusk. The Loon's Egg. Peter Dale Scott. MoCV
On the Emigration to America. Philip Freneau. PAH; TAP
(Stanzas on the Emigration to America, and Peopling the Western Country.) GOA
On the Erection of Shakespeare's Statue in Westminster Abbey. Pope. FaBoEE
On the Erie Canal, it was. The Aged Pilot Man. "Mark Twain." OBAL
On the Esplanade des Invalides. David Fisher. NPGG
On the Eve of a Birthday. Geoffrey Grigson. NAs
On the Eve of His Execution. Chidiock Tichborne. *See* Elegy: "My prime of youth is but a frost of cares."
On the Eve of Our Anniversary. Gary Margolis. Str
On the Eve of the Feast of the Immaculate Conception: 1942. Robert Lowell. WaaP
On the Eve of the Plebiscite. Kenneth Rexroth. NNaP
On the Eve of War. Danske Dandridge. PAH
On the Extinction of the Venetian Republic. Wordsworth. EnRP; FaBoRV; FaPo; GTBS; GTBS-P; HBV-2; LoBV; NOBE; NoP; OAEP; OBEV; OBNC; OBRV; TrGrPo; ViBoPo
On the fair green hills of Rio. The Burglar of Babylon. Elizabeth Bishop. NYBP
On the far edge of a plain. The Watcher. John Peck. AmPA
On the far reef the breakers. The Tide Will Win. Priscilla Leonard. TRV
On the far rock. Lives. Gerald Dawe. AMV-81
On the far side. A Late Spring: Eastport. Philip Booth. Psk
On the Farm. R. S. Thomas. OxBTC
On the Farm. Barbara Winder. PH
On the farm it never mattered. The Assistance. Paul Blackburn. NeAP; PoM
On the Farther Wall, Marc Chagall. Phyllis McGinley. *Fr.* Spectator's Guide to Contemporary Art. OBSV
On the Fifth Anniversary of Bluma Sach's Death. Vinnie-Marie D'Ambrosio. IHMS
On the Fine Arts Garden, Cleveland. Russell Atkins. PoBA
On the fine wire of his whine he walked. Mosquito. John Updike. BoAnP
On the first day/ malcolm. The Easter Bunny Blues or All I Want for Xmas Is the Loop. Ebon Dooley. PoBA
On the first day good enough father and son. Target Practice. Donald Finkel. NePoEA-2
On the first day of Christmas. The Twelve Days of Christmas. *Unknown.* FSW
On the first day of school the teacher asked me. How a Girl Got Her Chinese Name. Nellie Wong. WPOW
On the first day of snow, my train. Letter VIII. Randall Swingler. WaP
On the first day of the week cometh Mary Magdalene. Bible, *N.T.* *Fr.* St. John LO
On the first day, the lifted siege at last. A Death in Hospital. John Lehmann. ChMP
On the first hour of my first day. The Beginner. Kipling. *Fr.* Epitaphs of the War. FaBoTw
On the first morning of the moon, in land. The Good Beasts. Willis Barnstone. VWA
On the first of March. The Rooks. *Unknown.* GBP; OxNR
On the first of May. Mountain Greenery. Lorenz Hart. OBAL
On the first of the Feast of Feasts. Epilogue. Robert Browning. *Fr.* Dramatis Personae. VLP
On the first page of my dreambook. Empire of Dreams. Charles Simic. LCAP
On the first summer day I lay in the valley. On the Third Day. Stephen Spender. NeBP
On the Flightiness of Thought. *Unknown, tr. fr. Middle Irish by* Kuno Meyer. OnYI
On the floodis of Babiloyne there we saten. Bible, *O.T.* (Second Wycliffite Version). Psalms, CXXXVII. OAEL-1
On the Fly-Leaf of a Book of Old Plays. Walter Learned. HBV-1
On the Fly-Leaf of Manon Lescaut. Walter Learned. AA
On the Fly-Leaf of Pound's Cantos. Basil Bunting. FaBoTw; NoAM; OxBTC
On the Following Work and Its Author. Jonathan Mitchell. SCAP
On the forgotten si-/ ding. Tank Town. John Atherton. NYBP
On the Founding of Liberia. Melvin B. Tolson. *Fr.* Libretto for the Republic of Liberia. UnPo
(Do.) PoNe
On the Four Georges. Walter Savage Landor. *See* Georges, The.
On the fourteenth of April we sailed from the strand. The Bold *Princess Royal, vers.* I. *Unknown.* ShS
On the Frequent Review of the Troops. "M." NOEC

On the Friendship betwixt Two Ladies. Edmund Waller. PeHV
On the Frozen Lake. Wordsworth. *Fr.* The Prelude. FaBoCh
(Skaters, The.) LiSp
(Skating.) GN
On the Glorious Assumption of Our Blessed Lady. Richard Crashaw. *See* In the Glorious Assumption of Our Blessed Lady.
On the Gold Mines. B. W. Vilakazi. *See* In the Gold Mines.
On the Grand Canal. David Gascoyne. SeCePo
On the Grasshopper and [the] Cricket. Keats. BiP; EnRP; FaBoBe; GN; HBV-1; LiTB; NIP; OAEL-2; SeCeV; TrGrPo
(Poetry of Earth, The) WiR
On the Grave of a Young Cavalry Officer Killed in the Valley of Virginia. Herman Melville. AP
On the gray days, when the sky. Gray Days. Joanne Lawlor. AMV-80
On the Great Fog in London, December 1762. James Eyre Weeks. NOEC
On the Great Plateau. Edith Wyatt. HBMV
On the green banks of Shannon, when Sheelah was nigh. The Harper [*or* The Irish Harper and His Dog]. Thomas Campbell. CH; NCEP
On the green lawn of a city park. The Will to Live. Mekeel McBride. MAYP
On the green sheep-track, up the heathy hill. Samuel Taylor Coleridge. *Fr.* Fears in Solitude. OBNC
On the grey sand beside the shallow stream. Ego Dominus Tuus. W. B. Yeats. CMoP
On the ground are my sketches of the contours. The Painter in the Lion Cage. Betti Alver, *tr. by* Willis Barnstone *and* Felix Oinas. BoWoP
On the ground there was a tree. The Tree in the Wood. *Unknown.* AmFP
On the Hall at Stowey. Charles Tomlinson. CMoP; NoAM
On the Happy Corydon and Phyllis. *At. to* Sir Charles Sedley. BoLoP
(Young Coridon and Phillis.) CoMu; ErPo
On the Hazards of Smoking. Leah Goldberg, *tr. fr. Hebrew by* Bernhard Frank. AMV-81
On the headland's grassed and sheltered side. Storm. Judith Wright. PoAu-2; WPE
On the hearth a little fire burns. Oyfn Pripetshuk (On the Hearth). Mark Warshawsky. FSW
On the Heart's Beginning to Cloud the Mind. Robert Frost. CMoP
On the Height. Eunice Tietjens. HBMV
On the Heights. Lucius Harwood Foote. AA
On the Heights. W. K. Holmes. PoSH
On the Heights. Walter Savage Landor. FaBoEE
On the heights of great endeavor. Attainment. Madison Cawein. WGRP
On the Hellenics. Walter Savage Landor. *Fr.* The Hellenics. EnRP
(Proem to Hellenics.) ViBoPo
On the High Cost of Dairy Products. James McIntyre. FiBHP
On the highway. Está Muy Caliente. George Bowering. MoCV
On the Hill. William Soutar. PoSH
On the hill above the pond. October Dusk. C. Stephen Finley. AMV-80
On the Hill below the Lighthouse. James Dickey. NePoEA-2
On the hill of weeping. The Two Mothers. Shane Leslie. ISi
On the hill's top we stood. Distances. Jeremy Kingston. NYBP
On the hillside's upper garden a dressmaker's dummy. The Dressmaker's Dummy as Scarecrow. Barbara Howes. DFF
On the Historians Freeman and Stubbs. J. E. Thorold Rogers. FaBoEE
On the holiest day we fast till sundown. The Converts. Chana Bloch. AMV-81
On the holy day of your going out to war. Mohodahi, *tr. fr. Sanskrit by* Willis Barnstone. BoWoP
On the hottest day of the year I rode the mail. The Insult. Robert Layzer. NePoEA
On the House of a Friend. John Logan. DFF
On the Hurry of This Time. Austin Dobson. HBV-1
On the Ice Islands Seen Floating in the German Ocean. William Cowper. OAEL-1; PrIm
On the idle hill of summer. A. E. Housman. A Shropshire Lad, XXXV. MoBrPo; NOBE; OAEL-2; OAEP; OBNC; OBWP; SoSe
On the Ile de Gorée, M. Diop elegant. Double Take at Relais de L'Espadon. Thadious M. Davis. BlSi
On the Imprint of the First English Edition of "The Works of Max Beerbohm." Max Beerbohm. InPK; PV
On the Inconstancy of Women. Catullus, *tr. from Latin.* PV
On the Ineffable Inspiration of the Holy Spirit. Catharina Regina von Greiffenberg, *tr. fr. German by* Michael Hamburger. PBWP
On the Infancy of Our Saviour. Francis Quarles. OBS; OxBoCh; SeCePo
On the Instability of Youth. Thomas, Lord Vaux. EnRePo
On the Irish Club. Swift. OBSV
On the Island. L. E. Sissman. NYBP
On the Island, finding you naked and pearled. That Summer's Shore. John Ciardi. ErPo
On the island of Hokkaido. Hokkaido. Jim Trifilio. FAZ
On the island of Skip-scoop-anellie. Skip-Scoop-Anellie. Tom Prideaux. FiBHP
On the Isle of Man shore, I carelessly wandered. The Isle of Man Shore. *Unknown.* AmFP
On the isle of Penang there is 'stablished a city. Regret. *Malay Oral Tradition, tr. by* R. J. Wilkinson. WTO
On the itching back. Teemothy Hatch. Wilson MacDonald. WhC
On the jetty, our fingers shading. In the Beginning. Daniel G. Hoffman. PP
On the Jewish Day of Judgment in the Year 1942 (5703). Jozef Wittlin, *tr. fr. Polish by* Issaac Komem. VWA
On the Jubilee of Queen Victoria, *abr.* Tennyson. UnPo
On the kitchen wall a flash. The World Outside. Denise Levertov. ConAP
On the Lacedaemonian Dead at Plataea. Simonides, *tr. fr. Greek by* Richard Eberhart. WaaP
On the Lady Mary Villiers. Thomas Carew. *See* Epitaph on the Lady Mary Villiers.
On the Lake. V. Sackville-West. ChMP; MoVE; OBMV; SBG
On the Lake Poets. Charles Townsend. *See* Lake Poets, The.
On the Lakes of Ponchartrain. *Unknown.* AmFP
On the Lamented Death of Mrs. Throckmorton's Bullfinch. William Cowper. *See* On the Death of Mrs. Throckmorton's Bullfinch.
On the Land. Ray Lindquist. TAT
On the large highway of the awful air that flows. The Fish-Hawk. John Hall Wheelock. EtS; HBMV
On the Last Page of the Last Yellow Pad in Rome before Taking Off for Dacca on Air Bangladesh. Miller Williams. AMV-80
On the last year's trip I enjoyed this place. On the Road through Chang-te. Sun Yün-feng, *tr. by* Kenneth Rexroth *and* Ling Chung. BoWoP; WPOW
On the Late Massacre in Piedmont [*or* Piemont]. Milton. AWP; BiP; CABA; FaPo; GTBS; GTBS-P; HAP; HBV-2; HeIP; InPK; LiTB; LoBV; NIP; NOBE; NoP; OAEP; OBWP; PAI; PPoe; PPP; SeCeV; UnPo; ViBoPo; WaaP; WeW
(On the Late Massacher in Piemont.) PoEL-3
(On the Massacre in Piedmont.) WHA
(Sonnet: "Avenge, O Lord, thy slaughtered saints, whose bones.") OAEL-1; TW
(Sonnet: On the Late Massacre in Piedmont.) JCP; NOCV; OBS
On the Late Metamorphosis of an Old Picture of Oliver Cromwell's. *Unknown.* APAS
On the Late S. T. Coleridge. Washington Allston. AA
On the Late Successful Expedition against Louisbourg. Francis Hopkinson. PAH
On the Latest Crisis of Confidence. Haywood Jackson. SOTS
On the Latin Gerunds. Richard Porson. *See* Note on the Latin Gerunds, A.
On the Lawn at Ira's. Gregory Orr. GeTw
On the Lawn at the Villa. Louis Simpson. CoAP; GOA; LCAP; OBAL; OxBC; PPP
On the ledges of Newbury Street. The Beasts of Boston. Betty Lowry. AMV-80
On the levee the Saarinen Arch. Riverfront, St. Louis. John Knoepfle. TAT
On the Life-Mask of Abraham Lincoln. Richard Watson Gilder. AA; HBV-2
On the Life of Man. Sir Walter Ralegh. *See* What Is Our Life? A Play of Passion.
On the Life of Man. Henry King, *wr. at. to* Francis Beaumont. *See* Sic Vita.
On the lips a taste of tolling we are blind. (Poem) (Chicago) (The Were-Age). William Knott. EAS
On the long shore, lit by the moon. The Goose Fish. Howard Nemerov. CMoP; HeIP; InPK; LiTM; NePoEA; NIP; NMP; NoAM; NoP
On the Lord Gen. Fairfax at the Siege of Colchester. Milton. OBS
On the Lord Mayor and Court of Aldermen, Presenting the Late King and Duke of York Each with a Copy of Their Freedoms. Andrew Marvell. CoMu; FaBoBa
(Upon His Majesty's Being Made Free of the City.) APAS
On the Loss of the *Royal George.* William Cowper. EBEV; EtS; FiP; GN; HBV-2; NOBE; OAEP; OBEC; RoGo; TrGrPo
(Loss of the *Royal George.*) GTBS; GTBS-P; WHA
(*Royal George,* The.) FaPoR
On the Loss of U.S. Submarine S4, *sel.* H. C. Canfield.
"Entrapped inside a submarine." FaBoCo; FiBHP
On the low table by the bed. Mark Anderson. W. W. Gibson. MMA
On the Manner of Addressing Clouds. Wallace Stevens. *See* Of the Manner of Addressing Clouds.
On the March. Richard Aldington. BrPo
On the marches of Pamplonaout to sun and wind and star. La Preciosa Thomas Walsh. ISi
On the Margin, *sel.* David Wright.
Anniversary Approaches, An; of the Birth of God. NAs
On the Margin Wrought. William Drummond of Hawthornden. SeCePo
On the Marginal Way. Richard Wilbur. CAPP; CoAP; NOBA

On the Margins of a Poem. Jiri Mordecai Langer, *tr. fr. Hebrew by* Gabriel Preil *and* Howard Schwartz. VWA
On the Marriage of a Beauteous Young Gentlewoman with an Ancient Man. Francis Beaumont. ViBoPo
On the Marriage of a Virgin. Dylan Thomas. EnLoPo
On the Marriage of T. K. and C. C., the Morning Stormy. Thomas Carew. BoLoP
On the Masquerades. Christopher Pitt. NOEC
On the Massacre in Piedmont. Milton. *See* On the Late Massacre in Piedmont.
On the Meadow. "Katri Vala," *tr. fr. Finnish by* Jaakko A. Ahokas. PBWP
On the Meetings of the Scotch Covenanters. *Unknown.* FaBoEE
On the Memorial building's. Under Cancer. John Hollander. CoAP
On the Memory of Mr. Edward King, Drowned in the Irish Seas. John Cleveland. AnAnS-2; OAEL-1; OBS; SeCP
(Upon the Death of Mr. King Drowned in the Irish Seas.) HAP
On the Miracle of Loaves. Richard Crashaw. ACP
On the Moon's rim. Three Songs to Mark the Night. Judith Mountain Leaf Volborth. TWSS
On the Moor. Cale Young Rice. HBV-1
On the moor of Kasuga. Hitomaro. *Fr.* Manyo Shu. AWP
On the Morning of Christ's Nativity. Milton. GoTL; HBV-1; MasP; MeLP; NAs; NOCV; NoP; OBS; OxBoCh; PoEL-3; SeCeV; WGRP
(Ode on the Morning of Christ's Nativity.) GTBS; GTBS-P; LiTB; SBVL
Sels.
"But peaceful was the night." FaBoCh
Hymn on the Morning of Christ's Nativity. NOBE; OBEV
(Hymn, The: "It was the winter wild.") WHA, *abr.*
(On the Morning of Christ's Nativity.) FiP
Magi, The. ChTr, 2 *ll.*
On the morning of noise. Poem at Thirty. John Woods. CoPo
On the morning of the crowning we chorused our remission from school. Geoffrey Hill. Mercian Hymns, III. HAP
On the morning of the Käthe Kollwitz exhibit, a young man and woman. Museum. Robert Hass. NPGG
On the Morning of the Third Night above Nisqually. W. M. Ransom. CDW; NU
On the most westerly Blasket. The Given Note. Seamus Heaney. NCSH
On the Motor Bus. Alfred Denis Godley. *See* Motor Bus, The.
On the Mountain. Neidhart von Reuental, *tr. fr. German by* Jethro Bithell. AWP
On the Mountain. Ruth Stone. BoWoP
On the mountain peak, called "Going-to-the-Sun." The Apple-Barrel of Johnny Appleseed. Vachel Lindsay. AmFN; OxBA
On the mountains of Judea. The Expectation. Frederick William Faber. *Fr.* Our Lady's Expectation. ACP
On the Move. Thom Gunn. CMoP; HAP; LiTM; MP; NePoEA-2; NIP; NMP; NOP; OAEL-2; OxBTC; PPP; TwCP
On the Murder of Sir Edmund Berry Godfrey. *Unknown.* APAS
On the Name of Jesus. Richard Crashaw. *See* To the Name above Every Name, the Name of Jesus.
On the Naming Day. Jewel C. Latimore. CNA
On the narrow road. The Poppy. Cid Corman. HoAn
On the Nativity of Christ. William Dunbar. *See* Rorate Coeli Desuper.
On the Nativity of Christ Our Lord. Joseph Bennett. NePA
On the Nativity of Our Saviour. Thomas Philipott. JCP
On the Nature of Love. Wilfrid Scawen Blunt. *Fr.* The Love Sonnets of Proteus. ViBoPo
On the Nature of Things. Lucretius. *See* De Rerum Natura.
On the navel of the Boer's domain. Lesotho. B. Makalo Khaketla, *tr. by* Dan Kunene *and* Jack Cope. PeSA
On the Needle of a Sundial. Francis Quarles. OBS; TrGrPo
On the New Forcers of Conscience under the Long Parliament. Milton. CABA
On the New Laureate. *Unknown.* FaBoCo
On the New Road. Lyn Lifshin. NeAC
On the news today they spoke. Oil and Blood. Gary Allan Kizer. LFAC
On the Night Express to Madrid. Lora Dunetz. AMV-81
On the Night in Question. Patricia Goedicke. TAP
On the night of the Belgian surrender the moon rose. The Moon and the Night and the Men. John Berryman. CoAP; VGW; WaP
On the night of the execution. The Execution. Alden Nowlan. PeCV
On the Night Train from Oxford. E. L. Mayo. FAZ
On the Ning Nang Nong. Spike Milligan. RHPC
On the North Shore a reptile lay asleep. The Precambrian Shield. E. J. Pratt. *Fr.* Towards the Last Spike. MoCV; NoBC; OBCV
On the Ocean Floor. "Hugh MacDiarmid." FaBoMo; HAP
On the ocean that hollows the rocks where ye dwell. O Brazil [*or* Hy-Brasail], the Isle of the Blest. Gerald Griffin. ACP; BLPA
On the Origin of Evil. John Byrom. NOEC
On the other side. Ohioan Pastoral. James Wright. LCAP
On the other side/ of my world. To the Man I Live With. Ann Menebroker. IHMS
On the outer Barcoo where the churches are few. A Bush Christening. A. B. Paterson. PoAu-1
On the outermost far-flung ridge of ice and snow. Inspiration. W. W. Gibson. WGRP
On the outside grows the furside. The Sleeping-bag. Herbert George Ponting. CenHV
On the Oxford Book of Victorian Verse. "Hugh MacDiarmid." MoBrPo
On the Oxford Carrier. Milton. NA
On the Painter Val Prinsep. Dante Gabriel Rossetti. FaBoEE
On the Park Bench. Kenneth Slade Alling. NePoAm
On the Passion. *Unknown.* OxBM
On the Path. A. L. Strauss, *tr. fr. Hebrew by* Robert Friend. VWA
On the path. Under the Maud Moon. Galway Kinnell. NNaP
On the path winding. The Path among the Stones. Galway Kinnell. NNaP; NOBA; Prf
On the pathway mica glints. Water and Worship: An Open-Air Service on the Gatineau River. Margaret Avison. HAP
On the Pavement. David A. Sam. AMV-80
On the Persistence of Humanity. G. S. Fraser. BSV
On the phonograph, the voice. Reunion. Carolyn Forché. MAYP
On the Photograph of a Man I Never Saw. Hyam Plutzik. VWA
On the Phrase, "To Kill Time." Voltaire. PV
On the Picture of a "Child Tired of Play." Nathaniel Parker Willis. HBV-1
On the Picture of the Three Fates in the Palazzo Pitti, at Florence. Arthur Henry Hallam. OBRV
On the Pilgrim's Way in Kent, as It Leads to the Coldrum Stones. Asphodel. BrRo
On the Pilots Who Destroyed Germany in the Spring of 1945. Stephen Spender. NeBP
On the Plains, crows speak in raucous caws. Crow Voices. Gail Tremblay. AMV-81
On the Planet of Flies. Christian Morgenstern, *tr. fr. German by* Geoffrey Grigson. FaBoNo
On the Plough-Man. Francis Quarles. OBS
On the Poet O'Shaughnessy. Dante Gabriel Rossetti. ChTr
On the Poet's Leer. David Ray. NePoEA-2
On the Pole. Uri Zvi Greenberg, *tr. fr. Hebrew by* Robert Mezey *and* Ben Zion Gold. VWA
On the poplars and oaks. The Bard's Song. Sir Robert Stapylton. SeCePo
On the Porch. Harriet Monroe. SUMH
On the Porch at the Frost Place, Franconia, NH. William Matthews. MAYP
On the porch like night peelings. A Fish to Feed All Hunger. Sandra Alcosser. WOLT
On the Porch of the Antique Dealer. Paul Ramsey. FAZ
On the Portrait of a Woman about to Be Hanged. Thomas Hardy. CMoP
On the Portrait of Shakespeare Prefixed to the First Folio Edition, 1623. Ben Jonson. *See* To The Reader. (This figure, that thou here seest put").
On the Power of Sound. Wordsworth. VLP
On the Princess Mary. John Heywood. *See* Praise of His Lady, A.
On the Projected Kendal and Windermere Railway. Wordsworth. VLP
On the Proposal to Erect a Monument in England to Lord Byron. Emma Lazarus. AA
On the Prorogation. *Unknown.* APAS
On the Prospect of Planting Arts and Learning in America. George Berkeley. FaFP; HBV-2; NIP; NOEC; OnYI; PP; SeCeV; TreF; TrGrPo
(Verses on the Prospect of Planting Arts and Learning in America.) OBEC; SeCePo; ViBoPo
On the proud banks of great Euphrates' flood. Bible, *O.T., paraphrased by* Richard Crashaw. Psalms, CXXXVII. OAEL-1
On the prow. The Landing. Daniel Halpern. AmPA
On the Quay. John Joy Bell. HBV-1
On the Queen's Return from the Low Countries. William Cartwright. MePo; OBEV
On the Queen's Visit to London, the Night of the Seventeenth of March, 1789, *sel.* William Cowper.
"When, long sequester'd from his throne." PeD
On the Receipt of My Mother's Picture out of Norfolk [the Gift of My Cousin Ann Bodham]. William Cowper. EnRP; HBV-2; NOEC; OAEP; OBEC
Sels.
"Could Time, his flight reversed, restore the hours." WHA
"Oh that those lips had language! Life has pass'd." FiP
On the Receipt of My Mother's Picture Out of Norfolk, the Gift of My Cousin Ann Bodham. William Cowper. NOEC
On the Reed of Our Lord's Passion. William Alabaster. PoEL-2
On the Relative Merit of Friend and Foe, Being Dead. Donald Thompson. WaP
On the Religion of Nature. Philip Freneau. AmPP
On the Relinquishment of a Title. Geoffrey Grigson. FaBoEE

On the Resurrection of Christ. William Dunbar. *See* Done Is a Battle.
On the Reverend Jonathan Doe. *Unknown.* ChTr; FaBoEE
On the Ridgeway. Andrew Young. FaBoPP
On the Road. Tudor Jenks. NA
On the road. Driving to the Beach. Joanna Cole. RHPC
On the Road at Night There Stands the Man. Dahlia Ravikovitch, *tr. fr. Hebrew by* Chana Bloch. WPOW
On the Road Home. Wallace Stevens. NU
On the road over head. An Old Waterford Woman. Mary Devenport O'Neill. NeIP
On the road, the lonely road. The Stab. Will Wallace Harney. AA
On the Road There Stands a Tree. Itzik Manger, *tr. fr. Yiddish by* Stephen Griffin. VWA
On the Road through Chang-te. Sun Yün-feng, *tr. fr. Chinese by* Kenneth Rexroth *and* Ling Chung. BoWoP; WPOW
On the road through the hills I thought I heard it. Half-heard. Christopher Koch. PoAu-2
On the Road to Anster Fair. William Tennant. *Fr.* Anster Fair. OBRV
On the Road to California; or, The Buffalo Bullfight. *Unknown.* AmFP
On the Road to Chorrera. Arlo Bates. AA
On the Road to Emmaus. Bible, *N.T.* St. Luke, XXIV: 13-36. TreFS
On the Road to Gundagai. *Unknown.* PoAu-1
On the Road to Paradise. Garrett Hongo. HoAn
On the Road to the Sea. Charlotte Mew. BrRo; PeHV
On the Road to Vicenza. Ralph Gustafson. CaP
On the roads at night I saw the glitter of eyes. Eyes of Night-Time. Muriel Rukeyser. BoWoP; MiAP; NePA
On the rock overlapping the huddled rock-gorge. The Detail. Cid Corman. PCP
On the roof cloudy sky fading sun rays. Allen Ginsberg. *Fr.* Waking in New York. NYP
On the Rouge. Raymond Souster. NOBC
On the rough diamond. Sign for My Father, Who Stressed the Bunt. David Bottoms. MAYP
On the Ruins of a Country Inn. Philip Freneau. *See* Stanzas Occasioned by the Ruins of a Country Inn . . .
On the run is the Otoe County corn rootworm. Otoe County in Nebraska. William Kloefkorn. GP
On the Sabbath-day. Barbara. Alexander Smith. BSV; GoTS; HBV-1; OBVV
On the Safe Side. Lord Dunsany. OxBI
On the salt water streets. Venice Recalled. Bruce Boyd. NeAP
On the Same. Milton. *See* I Did But Prompt the Age.
On the Same [Some South African Novelists]. Roy Campbell. OxBTC
On the school platform, draping the folding seats. Political Meeting. A. M. Klein. MoCV; OBCV
On the Sea. Keats. CABA; EnRP; FF; HBV-1; LiTB; NoP; OAEL-2; SeCeV; TEP; TrGrPo
(Sonnet: On the Sea.) MOS
(Sonnet on the Sea.) EtS; SeCePo; ViBoPo
On the sea and at the Hogue, sixteen hundred ninety-two. Hervé Riel. Robert Browning. BeLS; FaBoBe; GN; HBV-2; HBVY; MOS; OnMSP
On the sea or in the air. God Is with Me. Oswald J. Smith. STF
On the Sea Wall. C. Day Lewis. SeCePo
On the second of October, a Monday at noon. Walter Lesly. *Unknown.* BaBo; ESPB
On the secret map the assassins. Rivers and Mountains. John Ashbery. CoAP; NoAM; NOBA
On the Sentence Passed by the House of Lords on Dr. Sacheverell. *Unknown.* APAS
On the Setting Up [of] Mr. Butler's Monument in Westminister Abbey. Samuel Wesley. InvP; NOEC; OBEC; PPON; WhC
On the Seventh Anniversary of the Death of My Father. Robert Pack. NePoEA
On the seventh day the storm lay dead. The Dyke-Builder. Henry Treece. LiTB; WaP
On the sheep-cropped summit, under hot sun. Cat and Mouse. Ted Hughes. EaLo
On the shining china white and gold. Its Lunch. John Hollander. *Fr.* Something about It. GP
On the shore of Nawa. Hioki no Ko-okima. *Fr.* Manyo Shu. AWP
On the sicilian strand a hare well wrought. Decimus Magnus Ausonius, *tr. fr. Latin by* Richard Lovelace. OBVE
On the side of the road. Song. Edmond Jabès, *tr. by* Anthony Rudolf. VWA
On the "Sievering" Tram. Bernard Spencer. NAs
On the sightless seas of ether. Mikhail Yuryevich Lermontov, *tr. by* Babette Deutsch *and* Avrahm Yarmolinsky. *Fr.* The Daemon. AWP
On the Site of a Mulberry-Tree. Dante Gabriel Rossetti. NCEP; TW
On the sixteenth day of September, nineteen twenty-eight. The West Palm Beach Storm. *Unknown.* AmFP
On the Skeleton of a Hound. James Wright. LiTM; NePoEA
On the skim of the wharf where the planks split. Bucket of Sea-Serpents. Howard Ant. GoYe
On the Slope of the Desolate River. Rabindranath Tagore. *Fr.* Gitanjali. OBMV
On the smooth brow and clustering hair. Walter Savage Landor. GBL
On the Snake. *Unknown.* PAH
On the Snuff of a Candle. Sir Walter Ralegh. FaBoEE; SiPS
On the Solitary Fells around Hawkshead. Wordsworth. *Fr.* The Prelude, I. FaBoPP
("Fair seed-time had my soul and I grew.") HAP
(Introduction—Childhood and School-Time.) PoEL-4
On the Sonnet. Keats. CABA; NIP; NoP; OAEL-2
(If by Dull Rhymes Our English Must Be Chained.) PP
On the South Downs. Sara Teasdale. MoAmPo
On the southwest side of Capri. The Nude Swim. Anne Sexton. WPE
On the southwest up-escalator. The Macy's Poem. James Reiss. POL
On the Spartan Dead at Thermopylae. Simonides, *tr. fr. Greek.* WeW
(At Thermopylae, *tr. unknown.*) WaaP
(Inscription to the Spartans Dead at Thermopylae, *tr. by* William Lisle Bowles.) TreF
(On the Army of Spartans, Who Died at Thermopylae, *tr. unknown.*) ChTr
("Stranger, when you come to/ Lakedaimon," *tr. by* Kenneth Rexroth.) OBVE
("Tell them in Lakedaimon, passer-by.") FaBoEE
(Thermopylae, *tr. by* William Lisle Bowles.) AWP; OBVE; OBWP
On the stage I stumbled. Indian Blood. Mary TallMountain. STE; TWSS
On the stage, mirrored many times. The Stripper. Anita Endrezze Probst. CDW
On the Staircase. Eleanor Farjeon. SiSoSe
On the stairway fragrance assails the bosom. A Spring Song of Tzu-yeh. Hsiao Yen, *tr. by* Jan W. Walls. LLLT
On the steep road. Dreamscape. Philip Booth. FiCP
On the steps of the bright madhouse. In the Fleeting Hand of Time. Gregory Corso. NAs
On the steps of the Pentagon I tucked my skull. Revised Notes for a Sonnet. Edward Pygge. BXAP
On the stiff twig up there. Black Rook in Rainy Weather. Sylvia Plath. LiTM; MP; NePoEA-2; NIP; PP
On the stone terrace, underneath the shade. The Summer Landscape; or, The Dragon's Teeth. Rolfe Humphries. NYBP
On the Street. C. P. Cavafy, *tr. fr. Greek by* Rae Dalven. BoLoP
On the street/ Slung on his shoulder. The Shovel Man. Carl Sandburg. HAP
On the street at dusk. Visitations. Jennifer Crewe. AMV-80
On the street-corner. What It Means, Living in the City. William Dickey. POL
On the street we two pass. Commitment in a City. Margaret Tsuda. CTBA
On the *Struma* Massacre. Ralph Gustafson. OBCV
On the Subject of Poetry. W. S. Merwin. PAI; PP
On the Subject of Waves. Eldon Grier. MoCV; PeCV
On the suburban street, guarded by patient trees. I Did Not Know the Truth of Growing Trees. Delmore Schwartz. LiTM
On the Suicide of a Friend. Reed Whittemore. ConAP; NMP
On the summer road that ran by our front porch. Lizards and Snakes. Anthony Hecht. CoPo; FaBoMo; NCSH; TwCP
On the Sun Coming Out in the Afternoon. Henry David Thoreau. PoEL-4
On the Sunday morning, just at the hour of ten. The Bigler. *Unknown.* AmSS
On the Supposed Author of a Late Poem "In Defense of Satire." Earl of Rochester. APAS
On the tallest day in time, the dead came back. V-J Day. John Ciardi. MiAP; PoPl
On the taut shore, the bald skull. Resurrection. Robert Pack. NePoEA-2
On the Telescopic Moon. John Swanwick Drennan. BIrV
On the temple bell. Spring Scene. Taniguchi Buson, *tr. by* Harold G. Henderson. PoPl
On the tenth day of December. Musselburgh Field. *Unknown.* ESPB
On the Tercentenary of Milton's Death. Gavin Ewart. OxBC
On the Third Day. Stephen Spender. NeBP
On the third day from this (Saint Brendan said). The Burial of Saint Brendan. Padraic Colum. OxBI
On the third day of May. The Boy and the Mantle. *Unknown.* UnTE
On the third day rose Arp. Resurrection of Arp. A. J. M. Smith. MoCV; NOBC
On the third finger of my left hand. Ceremony. William Stafford. LCAP
On the third planet too, life is found. Excerpt from a Report to the Galactic Council. Robert Conquest. OxBC
On the Thirteenth Day of Christmas. Charles Causley. OBCP
On the Threshold. Karl Kraus, *tr. fr. German by* Albert Bloch. TrJP
On the Threshold. *Unknown.* BLPA

On the threshold of heaven, the figures in the street. To an Old Philosopher in Rome. Wallace Stevens. AP; NoAM; NOBA
On the threshold of the stable smelling. The Stable. Jill Hoffman. PH
On the tidal mud, just before sunset. Daybreak. Galway Kinnell. LCAP
On the Times. *Unknown.* OxBM
On the Tombs in Westminster Abbey. *At. to* Francis Beaumont *and to* William Basse ACP; CH; GTBS; GTBS-P; LOBV; NOBE; OBEV; PoPle; TrGrPo; ViBoPo
(In Westminster Abbey, *shorter version.*) FaPoR
(Lines on the Tombs in Westminster.) GoBC
(Memento for Mortality, A.) FaBoCh; HAP; OBS
(On the Tombs in Westminster.) HBV-2
On the tongue of smoke. How Came She to Such Poppy-Breath? Judith Mountain Leaf Volborth. TWSS
On the top of old Smoky all covered in snow. Old Smoky. *Unknown.* BaBo
On the top of the Crumpetty Tree. The Quangle Wangle's Hat. Edward Lear. AmMo; EBEV; OnUR
On the top step with soft kitchen light. Coloring Margarine. William Hathaway. AMV-81
On the Tower. Annette von Droste-Hülshoff, *tr. fr. German by* James Edward Tobin. PBWP; WPOW
On the tower of Little Saling. Little Saling. Olaf Baker. HBMV
On the Trail to Idaho. *Unknown.* CoSo
On the Train. Rachel McAlpine. OCNZ
On the train/ old ladies playing football. Going Uptown to Visit Miriam. Victor Hernandez Cruz. FF; MAT; NYP
On the Translation of Anacreon. Horace Walpole. FaBoEE
On the Triumph of Rationalism. Alfred Ainger. FaBoCo
On the twelfth day of July. Orange Lilies. James Reaney. WHW
On the 25th Anniversary of the Liberation of Auschwitz. Eli Mandel. NOBC
On the Twenty-fifth of July. David Cornel DeJong. NYBP
On the twenty-second of June. *At. to* Ben Jonson. WhC
On the twenty-sixth of August, our fatal moss gave way. The Donibristle Moss Moran Disaster. *Unknown.* WTO
On the 26th of October, in the evening. Winter Journey Stanislaw Wygodski, *tr. by* Isaac Komen. VWA
On the Twenty-third Psalm. *Unknown, at. to* H. H. Barry. TRV
(He Leadeth Me.) BLRP
On the unbreathing sides of hills. Squatter's Children. Elizabeth Bishop. NePoAm-2; NoP
On the Uniformity and Perfection of Nature. Philip Freneau. AmPP
On the Universality and Other Attributes of the God of Nature. Philip Freneau. AP
On the University Carrier (Who Sickn'd in the Time of His Vacancy). Milton. EBEV; FaBoCh; FaBoEE; MePo; PoPle; PrIm; SaC
On the University of Cambridge's Burning the Duke of Monmouth's Picture. George Stepney. APAS
On the Unusual Cold and Rainie Weather in the Summer, 1648. Robert Heath. OBS
On the up-platform at Morpeth station. The Complaint of the Morpethshire Farmer. Basil Bunting. CTC
On the Upside. G. E. Murray. MAYP
On the Use of Jayshus. Oliver St. John Gogarty. FaBoEE
On the Vanity of Earthly Greatness. Arthur Guiterman. BXAP; HeIP; HoPM; InPK; NIP; OBCA; PAI; PoPl; PV; TrJP; WhC
On the Vanity of Man's Life. *Unknown.* OBSC
On the Verge. William Winter. AA
On the verge of the infinite. Jerusalem. Kadia Molodovski, *tr. by* S. F. Chyet. AMV-81
On the "Vita Nuova" of Dante. Dante Gabriel Rossetti. VLP
On the volcanic hill. Precarious Ground. Leah Bodine Drake. GoYe
On the Vowels—a Riddle. Swift. FaBoUs
(Riddle, A: "We are little airy creatures.") GN
(Riddle, A; the Vowels.) OnYI
On the Wall. Immanuel di Roma, *tr. fr. Hebrew by* Solomon Solis-Cohen. TrJP
On the Wall. *Unknown.* BluL
On the Wallowy. Laura Chester. NPGG
On the wan sea-strand. Evening Twilight. Heine, *tr. by* John Todhunter. *Fr.* The North Sea. AWP
On the water the first wind. Spring. W. S. Merwin. NaP
On the Way. Mordechai Husid, *tr. fr. Yiddish by* Seymour Mayne *and* Rivka Augenfeld. VWA
On the way back, more than halfway. Junction. John Pass. WOLT
On the way down. The Way Down. Philip Levine. NOBA
On the Way to Kew. W. E. Henley. Echoes, XXXVIII. EBVV; OBNC; OBVV; ViBoPo
On the Way to Language. Michael Palmer. NPGG
On the way to my daily occupation. Life. Franklin P. Adams. InMe
On the Way to the Island. David Ferry. NePoAm-2
On the Way to the Mission. Duncan Campbell Scott. CaP; NOBC
On the way up from Sheet I met some children. To Edward Thomas. Alun Lewis. WaP
On the Welsh Marches. Walter Stone. NYBP
On the wet sand the queen emerged from forest. Theseus: A Trilogy. Yvor Winters. NOBA
On the white throat of the useless passion. Ad Finem. Ella Wheeler Wilcox. BLPA; FPL
On the Wide Heath. Edna St. Vincent Millay. CMoP; WPE
On the wide level of a mountain's head. Time, Real and Imaginary. Samuel Taylor Coleridge. EnRP; NOBE; OBEV; OBRV
On the Wide Stairs. Yehuda Amichai, *tr. fr. Hebrew by* Laya Firestone *and* Howard Schwartz. VWA
On the Wife of a Parish Clerk. *Unknown. See* Old Sam's Wife.
On the wind, a drifting echo. Christmas Night. Lawrence Sail. OBCP
On the wind of January. The Wind of January. Christina Rossetti. YeAr
On the Wing. Christina Rossetti. SBG
On the Wings of a Dove. Jim Wayne Miller. AMV-80
On the World. Francis Quarles. HAP
On the World. Swift. *See* Day of Judgement, The.
On the Wrong Side. A. W. Webster. TDH
On the Young Statesmen. Charles Sackville. APAS
On Their Appointed Rounds. *Unknown.* FaPON
On these ancient discs, smooth-backed, severe. Old Gramophone Records. James Kirkup. NYBP
On these occasions, the feelings surprise. Father and Son. Delmore Schwartz. DiL; LiTA
On these sunny steps. View from the Planetarium. David Barker. GP
On these white cliffs, that calm above the flood. At Dover Cliffs [*or* Dover Cliffs *or* Sonnet]. William Lisle Bowles. EnRP; HBV-2; OBEC; ViBoPo
On things asleep, no balm. North American Sequence. Theodore Roethke. NaP
On Third Street there's a naked spot. The Ballad of Mary Baldwin. Stephen Sandy. MAT
On this black night of rain. The Son, Condemned. Larry Rubin. GP
On This Day. M. B Goffstein. NTCP
On This Day I Complete My Fortieth Year. Peter Porter. NAs
On This Day I Complete My Thirty-sixth Year. Byron. CABA; EnRP; FiP; HBV-1; NAs; NoP; OAEL-2; OAEP; OBWP; TreFT; ViBoPo
"My days are in the yellow leaf," *sel.* TRV
On this day man's disgust is known. On Shooting Particles beyond the World. Richard Eberhart. LiTA; LiTM; TW
On this day of longed-for peace. Armistice. Elizabeth Daryush. AMV-81
On this feast day, oh, cursed day and hour! Love at First Sight. Christopher Marlowe. *Fr.* Hero and Leander, First Sestiad. NOBE; ViBoPo
On this floor. Floor: O. Stephen Vincent. *Fr.* Elevator Landscapes. NeAC
On this hill crossed. The Poem. Galway Kinnell. NaP
On this hotel, their rumpled royalties. The West Forties: Morning, Noon, and Night. L. E. Sissman. CoAP; NYBP; NYP
On This Island. W. H. Auden. CMoP; InPS
(Look, Stranger.) MoAB; MoBrPo; TrGrPo
(Look, Stranger, on This Island Now.) CoBMV; InVP; OAEP
(Seascape.) GTBS-P
On this island, species subdivide so fast. The Island of Geological Time. Laura Fargas. SUW
On this lone Isle, whose rugged rocks affright. Sonnet: Suppos'd to Be Written at Lemnos [*or* Philoctetes]. Thomas Russell. FaBoEn; LoBV; NOEC; OBEC
On this map white. A state thick as a fist. A Map of Montana in Italy. Richard Hugo. LCAP
On This My Sick-Bed Beats the World. Jiří Wolker, *tr. fr. Czech by* Karl W. Deutsch. WaaP
On this piece of earth I seize a knife. Conversation. Gyorgy Raba, *tr. by* Jascha Kessler. VWA
On This Sea-Floor. Ralph Gustafson. PeCV
On this side of the tapestry. The Tapestry. Howard Nemerov. Prf
On this sweet bank your head thrice sweet and dear. Youth's Spring-Tribute. Dante Gabriel Rossetti. The House of Life, XIV. VLP
On this tree thrown up. Spindrift. Galway Kinnell. NaP; NYBP
On this winter night. Izumi Shikibu, *tr. fr. Japanese by* Willis Barnstone. BoWoP
On this wondrous sea. Eternity. Emily Dickinson. AA
On Thomas Hood. Walter Savage Landor. PV
On Thomas Moore's Poems. *Unknown.* FiBHP
(On T. Moore's Poems.) FaBoCo
On Thomas, Second Earl of Onslow. *Unknown.* FaBoCo
(On Tom Onslow, Earl of Onslow.) FaBoEE
On Thomas Woodcock. *Unknown.* WhC
On Those That Deserve It. Francis Quarles. MePo; NOCV; OBS

On thrones from China to Peru. A Model for the Laureate. W. B. Yeats. CMoP
On, through the lovely Archipelago. Charles Sangster. *Fr.* The St. Lawrence and the Saguenay. PeCV
On thy stupendous summit, rock sublime! Charlotte Smith. *Fr.* Beachy Head. SBG
On thy wild and windy upland, Tornamona. Shane O'Neill. Seumas MacManus. OnYI
On Time. Richard Hughes. MoBrPo
On Time. Milton. BLPL; CABA; LiTB; LoBV; MePo; OBEV; OBS; OxBoCh; SeCeV; TRV
On Time with God. C. D. Nutter. STF
On Tintock-Tap there is a mist. Tintock. *Unknown.* GBP
On tip-toe comes the gentle dark. Good Night. Dorothy Mason Pierce. SiSoSe
On to Richmond. John R. Thompson. PAH
On to the beach the quiet waters crept. The Quiet Tide near Ardossan. Charles Tennyson Turner. FaBoPP
On to the Morgue, *with music. Unknown.* AS
On Tobacco. Charles Cotton. OBSV
On Tobacco. Thomas Pestel. ElL
On Tom Holland and Nell Cotton. *Unknown.* FaBoEE
On Tom Moore's Translation of Anacreon. Thomas, Lord Erskine. FaBoEE
On Tom Onslow, Earl of Onslow. *Unknown. See* On Thomas, Second Earl of Onslow.
On Tomato Ketchup. *Unknown.* FaBoUs
On Tom-o-Combe. *Unknown.* FaBoEE
On top of: my main man (dummy) fails to burn the tapes. On the Latest Crisis of Confidence. Haywood Jackson. SOTS
On Top of Old Smoky, *sl. diff. vers. Unknown.* BLSo, *with music;* FaFP; FSW; InPK; TreFT
(Old Smoky.) AmFP; BaBo (B *vers. of* The Wagoner's Lad)
(Way Up on Old Smoky, *with music.*) TrAS
On top of that if you know me I pronounce you an ignu. Ignu. Allen Ginsberg. NaP
On Treason. Sir John Harington. *See* Of Treason.
On tree-topped hill, on tufted green. Tree-topped Hill. *Unknown.* NOEC
On Trinity Sunday, *sel.* John Byrom.
"One Divinity of Father, Son, The." PeD
On Troy. Oliver St. John Gogarty. WhC
On Trust in the Heart. Seng-ts'an, *tr. fr. Chinese.* ILwL
On Tuesday morn at half-past six o'clock. James Rigg. James Hogg. BXAP; Par
On Two Brothers. Simonides, *tr. fr. Greek by* W. H. D. Rouse. AWP
On Two Ministers of State. Hilaire Belloc. PV
On Two Monopolists. John Byrom. FaBoCo
("Bone and Skin.") FaBoEE
On Ullswater. Wordsworth. *Fr.* The Prelude, I. FaBoPP
("One evening (surely I was led by her)"). OBRV
On Venus, time passes slowly because. Here. Marvin Bell. AmPA
On Viewing a Florist's Whimsy at Fifty-ninth and Madison. Margaret Fishback. WhC
On village green, whose smooth and well-worn sod. A Disappointment. Joanna Baillie. NOEC
On Virtue. Phillis Wheatley. TAP
On Visiting Central Park Zoo. Alan Dugan. NYP
On Visiting My Son, Port Angeles, Washington. Duane Niatum. CDW
On Visiting the Graves of Hawthorne and Thoreau. Jones Very. AP; TAP
On Visiting the Graves of Keats and Marx in Hampstead Churchyard, *sel. Unknown.*
"John and Karl." PeD
On Vital Statistics. Hilaire Belloc. POL
On Waking. Joseph Campbell. AnIV
On Waking. Alida Carey Gulick. GoYe
On Waking from a Dreamless Sleep. Annie Fields. AA
On Walking Back to the Bus. Alan Gardner. PoSH
On wan dark night on Lac St. Pierre. The Wreck of the *Julie Plante* [*or* The *Julie Plante*]. William Henry Drummond. BeLS; BLPA; CaP; FaBoBe; FaPON; HBV-2; InMe; NA; OBCV; PeCV; TreFS; WhC
On warm days in September the high school band. The High School Band. Reed Whittemore. GLGT; NCSH
On warm summer evenings. Poem for the Conguero in D-Yard. Raymond Ringo Fernandez. LFAC
On Watching Politicians Perform at Martin Luther King's Funeral. Etheridge Knight. NNaP
On Watching the Construction of a Skyscraper. Burton Raffel. PCP
On Waterloo's ensanguined plain. On Scott's Poem "The Field of Waterloo." Thomas, Lord Erskine. DBV; FaBoCo; FiBHP; WhC
On Wearing Ears. William J. Harris. BOLo
On Wednesday night. Wednesday Night Prayer Meeting. Jay Wright. PoBA
On Wellington. Byron. *See* Wellington.
On Wenlock Edge [the Wood's in Trouble]. A. E. Housman. A Shropshire Lad, XXXI. BrPo; CABA; CoBMV; GTBS-P; HBV-1; LiTB; MasP; MoAB; MoBrPo; NBM; NOBE; NoP; OAEP; OBNC; OxBTC; PoEL-5; PoRA; PrIm; VLP
(Wenlock Edge.) OBEV
On Westwall Downes. William Strode. FaBoEn; FaBoPP; JCP; PoEL-2
On what a brave and curious whim. Clocks. Louis Ginsberg. TrJP
On what foundation stands the warrior's pride. Charles XII [of Sweden]. Samuel Johnson. *Fr.* The Vanity of Human Wishes. NOBE; OBEC; OBWP; ViBoPo
On what long tides. Fires of Driftwood. Isabel Ecclestone MacKay. CaP
On what pure mission do the seagulls fly. On the Beach. Frances Cornford. BoAnP
On When McCarthy Was a Wolf amoung a Nation of Queer-Queers. Alan Dugan. GP
On "Who Wrote Icon Basilike" by Dr. Christopher Wordsworth, Master of Trinity. Benjamin Hall Kennedy. *See* On Christopher Wordsworth, Master of Trinity.
On Why I Would Betray You. Jorie Graham. AMV-81
On Will Smith. *Unknown.* FaBoCo
On William Graham, Esq., of Mossknowe. Burns. DBV
On William Prynne. Samuel Butler. FaBoEE
On William Wilson, Tailor. *Unknown.* FaBoEE
On Willy's birthday, as you see. A Party. Laura E. Richards. SiSoSe; SoPo
On Windermere; Bowness Bay and Belle Isle. Wordsworth. *Fr.* The Prelude, I. FaBoPP
On windy days the mill. The Unfortunate Miller. A. E. Coppard. FaBoTw
On winter days, about the gloamin hour. Auld Sanct-Aundirans—Brand the Builder. Tom Scott. BSV
On winter nights. The Car Cemetery. Ciaran Carson. CIP
On with the Message. Wesley Duewel. STF
On Wodin's day, sixth of December, thirty-nine. *In re* Solomon Warshawer. A. M. Klein. MoCV
On Woman. W. B. Yeats. BiP; CMoP
On woodlands ruddy with autumn. My Autumn Walk. Bryant. AA
On wool-soft feet he peeps and creeps. Santa Claus. Walter de la Mare. PChr
On Wordsworth. Hartley Coleridge. *See* He Lived admidst th' Untrodden Ways.
On Writing Asian-American Poetry. Geraldine Kudaka. BrSi
On Writing for the Stage. John Sheffield, Duke of Buckingham and Normanby. *Fr.* Essay on Poetry. FaBoUs
On Yes Tor. Sir Edmund Gosse. CH
On yon hill's top which this sweet plain commands. Invites His Nymph to His Cottage. Philip Ayres. EnLoPo
On yonder hill there is a red deer. Riddle. *Unknown.* ChTr; GBP
On yonder hill there stands a creature. O, No, John [*or* No John *or* The One Answer] *Unknown.* ErPo; FSW; OBET; PDV; UnTE
On your bare rocks, O barren moors. The Barren Moors. William Ellery Channing. AA
On your dazzling throne, Aphrodite. Sappho, *tr. fr. Greek by* Willis Barnstone. BoWoP
On your hospital bed of terminal illness. On the Death of Neruda. Olga Cabral. SOTS
On your slender body. For the Courtesan Ch'ing Lin. Wu Tsao, *tr. by* Kenneth Rexroth *and* Ling Chung. BoWoP; WPOW
On your way home you stopped to shop. A Nameless Recognition. Arthur Gregor. GP
On Youth, the Warden & Solitary! Leon Baker. LFAC
On Zacheus [*or* Zacchaeus]. Francis Quarles. HAP; LoBV; MePo; OBS
On Zion and on Lebanon, *with music.* Henry Ustic Onderonk. AH
Onan. Paris Leary. CoPo
Once. Eric N. Batterham. CH
Once. George Ives. PeHV
Once. *Unknown.* CH
("Once I was a monarch's daughter.") PBBP
Once. Alice Walker. BlSi
Sels.
"Green lawn/ a picket fence." PoBA
"I/ never liked/ white folks." PoBA
"It is true—/ I've always loved." NMM; PoBA
Once. Siv Widerberg, *tr. fr. Swedish by* Verne Moberg. NTCP
Once/ I went for an ocean trip. On a Steamer. Dorothy W. Baruch. FaPON
Once a Big Molicepan. *Unknown.* FaPON
Once a boy beheld a bright. The Rose. Goethe, *tr. by* James Clarence Mangan. AWP
Once a Child. Emily Dickinson. *See* It troubled me as once I was.

Once a dream did weave a shade. A Dream. Blake. *Fr.* Songs of Innocence. CH; EnRP; LAuP; PoPle
Once a fair city, courted then by kings. Masar. Walter Savage Landor. *Fr.* Gebir, V. LoBV; OBRV
Once a Frenchman. *Unknown.* TDH
Once a gay wit, subsequently a wretched instructor. The Father. Richmond Lattimore. EyDe; NePoAm-2
Once a girl. Hieroglyphic. Myra Sklarew. SUW
Once a grasshopper (food being scant). The Humorous Ant. Oliver Herford. TDH
Once a jolly swagman camped by a billabong. Waltzing Matilda. Andrew Barton Paterson. CBAP; ChTr; FSW; GBP; PoAu-1; WhC
Once a Kansas zephyr strayed. Zephyr. Eugene Fitch Ware. PoLF
Once a little baby lay. The First Christmas. Emilie Poulsson. OHIP
Once a little satellite. Little Satellite. Jane W. Krows. SoPo
Once a man is born he has to die. All Intents. Larry Eigner. VGW
Once a pallid vestal. The Vestal. Nathalia Crane. TrJP
Once a pound-keeper chanced to impound. The Ounce of Detention. Oliver Herford. TDH
Once a raven from Pluto's dark shore. The True Facts of the Case. Anthony Euwer. OBAL
Once a rover of the sea, captain of a barkentine. The Captain of St. Kitts. Beulah May. EtS
Once a snowflake fell. Winter Poem. Nikki Giovanni. PAI
Once a wife in Bethlehem. A Prayer for a Sleeping Child. Mary Carolyn Davies. OHIP
Once a winter bayou child knew the green music. Troubador. J. Edgar Simmons. TAT
Once a young "Canadien." Un Canadien Errant (An Exiled Canadien). *Unknown, tr. fr. French.* FSW
Once after he'd come back from Ohio. On the Wings of a Dove. Jim Wayne Miller. AMV-80
Once Again. Liz Sohappy Bahe. CDW
Once again I'm integrated with machinery. My Flying Machine. Louis Daniel Brodsky. AMV-80
Once again our glad thanksgivings. Thanksgiving. A. B. Simpson. STF
Once again, tell me, what was it like? Summer. Gary Soto. WeW
Once again the scurry of feet—those myriads. The Face of the Waters. Robert D. Fitzgerald. CBAP; PoAu-2
Once again they've quarreled on a tram. Two. Margarita Aliger, *tr. by* Elaine Feinstein. VWA
Once Alien Here. John Hewitt. CIP; NeIP
Once, and but once found in thy company. The Perfume. John Donne. Elegies, IV. AnAnS-1; SeCP
Once and Future. Diana Chang. BrSi
Once and Upon. Madeline Gleason. NeAP
Once around a daisy counting. Counting on Flowers. John Ciardi. PP
Once, as a child, I ate raspberries. And forgot. Raspberries. Laurence Lerner. EBEV
Once as a child I loved to hop. Adam's Footprint. Vassar Miller. NePoEA; NIP
Once as Congress sat in session. The Reagan, *parody*. Richard Quick. FaBoPa
Once as I travelled through a quiet evening. Egrets. Judith Wright. GoJo; NCSH
Once as I went by rail to Epping Street. The Wasp. John Davidson. FM
Once [*or* Ons] as methought [*or* me thought], fortune me kissed [*or* kist *or* kyst]. The Lover Rejoiceth the Enjoying of His Love [*or* A Promise]. Sir Thomas Wyatt. AAS; BoLoP; FaBoEn; OBSC; SiPS
Once, as old Lord Gorbals motored. Lord Gorbals. Harry Graham. FaBoCo
Once as we were sitting by. Spring 1942. Roy Fuller. LiTM; NeBP; OxBTC; WaaP
Once at Swanage. Thomas Hardy. FaBoPP
Once before, this self-same air. Mary Mapes Dodge. AA
Once between us the Atlantic. Sundered. Israel Zangwill. TrJP
Once—but no matter when. A Chronicle. *Unknown.* BLPL; NA
Once by the Pacific. Robert Frost. BPAW; CMoP; CoBMV; HAP; HeIP; LiTA; LiTM; MoAB; MoAmPo; MOS; NePA; NOBA; PrIm; VGW; WeW
Once came an exile, longing to be free. Blennerhassett's Island. Thomas Buchanan Read. *Fr.* The New Pastoral. PAH
Once did I love, and yet I live. *Unknown.* OBSC
Once did my Philomel reflect on me. Sir John Davies. *Fr.* Sonnets to Philomel. SiPS
Once Did My Thoughts. *Unknown.* ELP
("Once did my thoughts both ebb and flow.") EBEV
Once did she hold the gorgeous east in fee. On the Extinction of the Venetian Republic. Wordsworth. EnRP; FaBoRV; FaPo; GTBS; GTBS-P; HBV-2; LoBV; NOBE; NoP; OAEP; OBEV; OBNC; OBRV; TrGrPo; ViBoPo
Once, dreaming of eternal fire. On a Horse and a Goat. R. P. Lister. PV
Once, ere God was crucified. The Abdication of Fergus Mac Roy. Sir Samuel Ferguson. AnIL
Once every so often the risible makes me think of my friends. The Friendship Game. Pier Giorgio Di Cicco. AMV-81
Once for candy cook had stolen. W. H. Auden. PV
Once for our consolation it seemed, O Lord. No More Destructive Flame. Francis X. Connolly. ISi
Once from a big, big building. A Visit to the Asylum. Edna St. Vincent Millay. SO
Once git a smell o' musk into a draw. Sunthin' in the Pastoral Line. James Russell Lowell. *Fr.* The Biglow Papers. AP
Once, grave Laodicean profiteer. Lourenço Marques. Charles Eglington. PeSA
Once he puts out the light. The Hermit Has a Visitor. Maxine W. Kumin. BoWoP
Once he will miss, twice he will miss. Death. *Unknown, tr. by* E. Powys Mathers. *Fr.* The Thousand and One Nights. AWP
Once her brother's child, for fun. The Careless Niece. Carolyn Wells. ShM
Once hid in a fiery twist. The Scratch. James Dickey. AP
Once hoary winter chancedalas! Why Ye Blossome Cometh Before Ye Leafe. Oliver Herford. AA
Once hooked ever after lives in lack, The. Nescit Vox Missa Reverti. J. V. Cunningham. ELU
Once I am sure there's nothing going on. Church Going. Philip Larkin. CMoP; GTBS-P; InPK; LiTM; MoBrPo; MP; NePoEA; NIP; NoAM; NoP; OAEL-2; PAI; PPP; PrIm; SCV; TwCP; UnPo
Once I courted a fair beauty bride. The Fair Beauty Bride. *Unknown.* AmFP
Once I cried for new songs to sing. I Sing No New Songs. Frank Marshall Davis. PoBA; PoNe
Once I did have a dear companion. Dear Companion. *Unknown.* FSW
Once—I didn't mean to. Accidentally. Maxine W. Kumin. RHPC
Once I fought a shadow. The Duel. Harold Trowbridge Pulsifer. HBMV
Once I hauled a catfish home from the river. The Catfish. Michael Waters. WOLT
Once I heard a hobo, singing by the tie-trail. The Long Road West. Henry Herbert Knibbs. BPAW
Once I heard an old bachelor say. The Bachelor's Complaint. *Unknown.* AmFP
Once I knew a fine song. 'Scaped. Stephen Crane. The Black Riders, LXV. AA
Once I knew a little girl, and I loved her as my life. Do Come Back Again. *Unknown.* OuSiCo
Once I knowed old lady. The Rich Old Lady. *Unknown.* OuSiCo
Once I learnt in wilful hour. On a Wife. Francis Burdett Money-Coutts. OBVV
Once I liked pablum. Once. Siv Widerberg, *tr. by* Verne Moberg. NTCP
Once I Lived in Cottonwood. *Unknown.* AmFP
Once I lived with my brothers, images. The Centaur Overheard. Edgar Bowers. ConAP
Once I lost my temper. My Temper. *Unknown.* STF
Once I loved a spider. The Spider and the Ghost of the Fly. Vachel Lindsay. VGW
Once I Pass'd through a Populous City. Walt Whitman. AmPP; NePA; OxBA
Once I Played and Danced in My Parents' Kingdom. *Gond Oral Tradition, tr. by* V. Elwin *and* S. Hivale. WTO
Once, I remember well the day. The Enthusaist; an Ode. William Whitehead. OBEC
Once I saw a little bird. Mother Goose. OxNR
Once I saw a wolf tread a circle in his cage. Traverse City Zoo. Jim Harrison. BoAnP
Once I saw large waves. At Sea. Jean Toomer. BALP
Once I seen a human ruin. Ambrose Bierce. *Fr.* The Devil's Dictionary. OBAL
Once I stood in a green bough. Portrait of the Father. Lindy Hough. IHMS
Once I Thought to Die for Love. *Unknown.* ElL
Once I was a boy and I sat in a meadow with flowers in it. Time Passes. R. P. Lister. NYBP
Once I was a lady's [*or* serving] maid way down [*or* who worked] in Drury Lane. Bell-bottomed Trousers. *Unknown.* FSW; UnTE
Once I was a little boy. The Foggy Dew. *Unknown.* OBET (B *vers.*)
Once I was a monarch's daughter. Once. *Unknown.* CH; PBBP
Once I was a serving maid who worked in Drury Lane. *See* Once I was a lady's maid way down in Drury Lane.
Once I Was a Shepherd Boy. *Unknown.* OBET
Once I was a tiny tad. Innocence. George S. Chappell. YaD
Once I was a young horse all in my youthful prime. Poor Old Horse. *Unknown.* OBET

Once I was at a nobleman's wedding. The Nobleman's Wedding. *Unknown.* AnIV
Once I was common wood, a shapeless log. John Oldham. *Fr.* Satires upon the Jesuits. DBV
Once I was good like the Virgin Mary and the Minister's wife. The Scarlet Woman. Fenton Johnson. BANP; PoBA; PoNe
Once I was happy, but now I'm forlorn. The Man on the Flying Trapeze [*or* The Flying Trapeze]. *Unknown, at. to* George Leybourne. BeLS; BLPA; FaBoBe; PSoN; YaD
Once I was jealous of lovers. Now I am. The Valley. Stanley Moss. NYBP; PCP
Once I went through the lanes, over the sharp. Spring. V. Sackville-West. *Fr.* The Land. PeHV
Once in a dream (for once I dreamed of you). On the Wing. Christina Rossetti. SBG
Once in a dream I saw the flowers. Paradise. Christina Rossetti. HBV-2; OxBoCh; WGRP
Once, in a finesse of fiddles found I ecstasy. *See* Once, in finesse . . .
Once in a golden hour. The Flower. Tennyson. HBV-2
Once, in a great while. Icon. Mark Osaki. BrSi
Once in a hundred years the lemmings come. The Lemmings. John Masefield. CMoP; NIP; NoAM
Once in a Lifetime, Snow. Les A. Murray. CBAP
Once in a lifetime, we may see the veil. Midnight—September 19, 1881. John Boyle O'Reilly. PAH
Once, in a roostery. The Hen and the Carp. Ian Serraillier. OnUR
Once in a Saintly Passion. James Thomson ("B. V."). FF; TreFS (Vanity.) DBV; PV
Once in a while/ we'd find a patch. The Children. William Carlos Williams. NePoAm-2
Once in a while a curious weed unknown to me. William Jones. Edgar Lee Masters. *Fr.* Spoon River Anthology. ImOP
Once in a wood at winter's end. Winter's End. Howard Moss. NePoEA
Once in an Ancient Book. Marya Zaturenska. GP
Once in Canandaigua, hitchhiking from Ann Arbor. Faces. John Ciardi. BiP; WeW
Once, in [a] finesse of fiddles found I ecstasy. The Embankment [*or* Fantasia of a Fallen Gentleman]. T. E. Hulme. EBEV; ELU; FaBoMo; GTBS-P; OxBTC; SeCePo
Once in Love with Amy, *with music.* Frank Loesser. BLSo
Once, in my darkest hour, in some dim place. Lux in Tenebris. *Unknown.* GoBC
Once in our lives,/ Let us drink to our wives. *Unknown.* FaBoEE
Once in Persia reigned a King. Even This Shall Pass Away [*or* The King's Ring]. Theodore Tilton. BLPA; HBV-2; TreFS; WGRP
Once in Royal David's City. Cecil Frances Alexander. OxBChV (Christmas Hymn, A: "Once in royal David's City.") OHIP
Once, in the burning age. Apprentices. Robin Munro. PoSH
Once in the dark of night. The Dark Night. St. John of the Cross, *tr. by* John Frederick Nims. WeW
Once in the dear dead days beyond recall. Love's Old Sweet Song. G. Clifton Bingham. BLSo; FaBoBe; FSN; TreF
Once in the Jurassic, about 150 million years ago. Smokey the Bear Sutra. *Unknown.* MAT
Once in the wind of morning. The Merry Guide. A. E. Housman. A Shropshire Lad, XLII. OAEP
Once in the winter. The Forsaken. Duncan Campbell Scott. CaP; NOBC; WHW
Once, in this Tuscan garden, noon's huge ball. A Snail's Derby. Eugene Lee-Hamilton. FM
Once in winter shone the ground and full sped. On the Nativity of Christ Our Lord. Joseph Bennett. NePA
Once, it happened I'd been dining, on my couch I slept reclining. The Goblin Goose. *Unknown.* FaBoPa
Once it smiled a silent dell. The Valley of Unrest. Poe. AmPP; AP; PoEL-4; ViBoPo
Once it was enough simply. Reaching the Horizon. Robert Mezey. NaP
Once, Lily and I fell from a ladder. Monologue of Two Moons, Nudes with Crests. 1938. Norman Dubie. FiCP
Once, long ago, set close beside a wood. The Nun's Priest's Tale. Chaucer, *mod. vers. by* Frank Ernest Hill. *Fr.* The Canterbury Tales. TrGrPo
Once looked Gudrun. The First Lay of Gudrun: Gudrun Laments over Sigurd. *Unknown, tr. by* William Morris *and* Eirikr Magnusson. *Fr.* The Elder Edda: The First Lay of Gudrun. OBVE
Once man entirely free, alone and wild. The Swiss Peasant. Wordsworth. OBEC
Once mermaids mocked your ships. Mermaids. Kenneth Slessor. *Fr.* The Atlas. PoAu-2
Once More. Forugh Farrokhzad, *tr. fr. Persian by* Jascha Kessler *and* Amin Banani. BoWoP
Once More. George Jonas. NeAC
Once More a-Lumbering Go. *Unknown.* AmFP
Once more around should do it, the man confided. Flight of the Roller Coaster. Raymond Souster. NOBC; PeCV; SO; WHW
Once more, before I move on. To the Unknown God. Friedrich Nietzsche. ILwL
Once more beneath my thumb the globe turns. Childhood. Donald Justice. LCAP
Once more by the brook the alder leaves. Hayden Carruth. NNaP
Once more, Cesario. Shakespeare. *Fr.* Twelfth Night. SCV
Once more evening on the earth. The Lake in the Sky. John Haines. LCAP
Once More Fields and Gardens. T'ao Ch'ien, *tr. fr. Chinese by* Amy Lowell *and* Florence Ayscough. AWP
Once more I came to Sarum Close. The Cathedral Close [*or* Salisbury; the Cathedral Close]. Coventry Patmore. *Fr.* The Angel in the House. EBVV; FaBoPP
Once more I move among you, dear familiar places. Amagansett Beach Revisited. John Hall Wheelock. NYBP
Once more I saw him. In the lofty room. The Last Sight. Robert Louis Stevenson. BrPo
Once more in misted April. An April Morning. Bliss Carman. HBMV; HBVY
Once more into the breach, dear friends, once more. Shakespeare. *See* Once More unto the Breach.
Once more it seems. Zohara. Jack Hirschman. VWA
Once more, listening to the wind and rain. The Return. Arna Bontemps. CDC; PoBA; PoNe
Once more my deeper life goes on with more strength. Moving Ahead. Rainer Maria Rilke, *tr. by* Robert Bly. NU
Once More, O Lord, *with music.* George Washington Doane. AH
Once more, once more, my Mary dear. Memories. George Denison Prentice. AA
Once more Orion and the sister Seven. A Welcome to Dr. Benjamin Apthorp Gould. Oliver Wendell Holmes. ImOP
Once More, Our God, Vouchsafe to Shine! *with music.* Samuel Sewall. AH (Wednesday, January 1, 1701.) SCAP
Once more the Ancient Wonder. Easter, 1923. John G. Neihardt. HBMV; OHIP
Once more the changed year's turning wheel returns. Barren Spring. Dante Gabriel Rossetti. The House of Life, LXXXIII. EBVV; FaBoEn; NoP; OAEL-2; OBNC; PoEL-5; VLP
Once more the country calls. Ode. Allen Tate. WaP
Once more the cuckoo's call I hear. Spring. Aubrey Thomas De Vere. *Fr.* The Year of Sorrow. OBNC
Once more the flower of Essex is marching to the wars. Essex Regiment March. George Edward Woodberry. PAH
Once more the Heavenly Power/ Makes all things new. Early Spring. Tennyson. HBV-1; HBVY
Once more the liberal year laughs out. Harvest Hymn. Whittier. *Fr.* For an Autumn Festival. OHIP; PGD
Once more the miracle, still unexplained. On the Heights. W. K. Holmes. PoSH
Once more the storm is howling, and half hid. A Prayer for My Daughter. W. B. Yeats. BLPL; CABA; CMoP; CoBMV; HAP; LiTB; LiTM; LoBV; MasP; MoAB; NAs; NoAM; NoP; OxBTC; PoA; PoLF; PoRA; PrIm; TEP
Once more this autumn-earth is ripe. The Australian. Arthur H. Adams. PoAu-1
Once More unto the Breach. Shakespeare. King Henry V, *fr.* III, i. FaBV
(Blast of War.) TrGrPo
(Henry V at Harfleur.) TreF
(Henry Fifth's Address to His Soldiers.) WHA
(King Henry the Fifth before Harfleur.) PPoe
("Once more into the breach, dear friends, once more.") Waap
Once Musing as I Sat. Barnabe Googe. *See* Fly, The.
Once my feet trod Nineveh. The Babe. Monk Gibbon. OxBI
Once my heart was a summer rose. Song. Edith Sitwell. ChMP
Once my parents were older. Chiyo, *tr. fr. Japanese by* David Ray. BoWoP
Once neighbor to the dinosaur. The Star-nosed Mole. Robert Wallace. BoAnP
Once, new, you rolled easy and maroon. Packard. David Barker. DFF; GP
Once on a silver and green day, rich to remember. Brindabella. Douglas Stewart. PoAu-2
Once on a Time. Kendall Banning. HBV-1
Once on a Time. Margaret Benson. HBV-1
Once on a time a knight of high degree. The Merchant's Tale, *abr.* Chaucer, *mod. vers. by* Frank Ernest Hill. *Fr.* The Canterbury Tales. UnTE
Once on a time, a monarch, tired [*or* tir'd] with whooping. The Apple Dumplings and a King. "Peter Pindar." OBEC; OBSV
Once on a time a young giraffe. Oliver Herford. *Fr.* The Untutored Giraffe. ShM

Once on a time, as old stories rehearse. A Ballad to the Tune of "The Cut-Purse." Swift. PP
Once on a time did Eucritus and I. Harvest-Home. Theocritus, *tr. by* Charles Stuart Calverley. *Fr.* Idylls. AWP
Once on a time I used to be. Harlot's Catch. Robert Nichols. ErPo; FaBoTw
Once on a time I used to dream. Once on a Time. Margaret Benson. HBV-1
Once on a time, it came to pass. The Fable of the Piece of Glass and the Piece of Ice. John Hookham Frere. OxBChV
Once on a time, some centuries ago. The Monk of Casal-Maggiore [*or* The Sicilian's Tale]. Longfellow. *Fr.* Tales of a Wayside Inn. AmPP; AP; OxBA
Once on a time there lived a man. Peter Gray. *Unknown.* BLSo; FSW; OuSiCo
Once on a time there was a pool. Rev. Homer Wilbur's "Festina Lente." James Russell Lowell. *Fr.* The Biglow Papers. OBAL
Once, on that highway where a traveler works hard. Pornography, Nebraska. Sandra McPherson. MAYP
Once, once, in Washington. Patriotic Tour and Postulate of Joy. Robert Penn Warren. NYBP
"Once . . . once upon a time." Martha. Walter de la Mare. MoBrPo; TreFS
Once Only. Gary Snyder. SUW
Once-over, The. Paul Blackburn. ErPo; NeAP; PoM
Once over summer streams the ice-crusts harden. No Return. Vassar Miller. CoPo
Once, Paumanok. The Mocking-Bird. Walt Whitman. *Fr.* Out of the Cradle Endlessly Rocking. PB
Once riding in Old Baltimore. Incident. Countee Cullen. BiP; BPo; CABA; CDC; CTBA; FF; IDB; NoAM; NTCP; OBCA; PoBA; PoNe; SoSe; VGW
Once (says an author, where I need not say). Verbatim from Boileau. Pope. DBV
Once, so long ago. For Paddy Mac. Padraic Fallon. CIP
Once some people were visiting Chekhov. Chocolates. Louis Simpson. LCAP; OxBC
Once the family meeting place. Fish Story. B. Jo Kinnick. AMV-81
Once the head is gray. A Catch. Richard Henry Stoddard. AA
Once the land had no great names and no history. Names from the War. Bruce Catton. AmFN
Once the orioles sang in chorus. Ballade of Big Plans. Dorothy Parker. InMe
Once the Striped Quagga. Mary TallMountain. TWSS
Once the Wind. Mark Van Doren. TwAmPo
Once There Came a Man. Stephen Crane. PAI
(Four Poems, II.) CrMA
Once there lived side by side two little maids. I Don't Want to Play in Your Yard. Philip Wingate. FSN; TreFT
Once there was a fence here. Former Barn Lot. Mark Van Doren. FaBV; MoAmPo; PDV; PoPl
Once there was a little boy whose name was Robert Reese. An Overworked Elocutionist. Carolyn Wells. BLPA; BLPL
Once there was a little kitty. Kitty. Elizabeth Prentiss. MoShBr
Once there was an elephant. Eletelephony. Laura E. Richards. FaPON; GoJo; NTCP; OBCA; OnUR; OxBChV; PDV; RHPC; SoPo; TiPo; YaD
Once there were peasant pots and a dry brown hare. Joan Miró. Ruthven Todd. EAS
Once There Were Three Fishermen. *Unknown.* FSW
Once there were 3 little Indian girls. Charité Espérance et Foi. Earle Birney. OxBC
Once they minted Our Lady in multiple golden medallions. Ox-Bone Madonna. James J. Galvin. ISi
Once this soft turf, this rivulet's sands. The Battle-Field. Bryant. AA; FPL; PAL; PoLF
Once to Every Man and Nation. James Russell Lowell. *Fr.* The Present Crisis. FaPoR, *sl. diff. sel.;* PAL
("Once to every man and nation comes the moment to decide.") TRV
Once to life I said, yes! To Life I Said Yes. Chaim Grade, *tr. by* Joseph Leftwich. TrJP
Once, Twice, Thrice. *Unknown.* DBV; ErPo; PV
Once, twice, thrice/ I give thee warning. *Unknown.* OxNR
Once up u hurl a stone. Mike 65. Lennox Raphael. PoBA
Once upon a colony. Can. Hist. Earle Birney. OxBC
Once upon a Great Holiday. Anne Wilkinson. WHW
Once upon a midnight dreary, eerie, scary. Ravin's of Piute Poet Poe. C. L. Edson. BXAP
Once upon a midnight dreary, while I pondered [*or* ponder'd], weak and weary. The Raven. Poe. AA; AmPP; AP; BeLS; BLPA; CH; FaBoBe; FaBoCh; FaBV; FaFP; FPL; GN; GoJo; HBV-2; LiTA; NePA; NOBA; OBCA; OBNV; OHFP; OxBA; PaPo; PoRA; RoGo; TAP; TreF; ViBoPo; WBLP; WHA
Once upon a Nag. Michael Beirne McMahon. PH
Once upon a time. Issa, *tr. fr. Japanese by* Harry Behn. WSC
Once upon a Time. Gabriel Okara. PBA
Once upon a time/ I caught a little rhyme. Catch a Little Rhyme. Eve Merriam. OBCA; PDV
Once upon a time/ I composed a witty rhyme. The Minstrel's Last Lay. John Barth. OBAL
Once upon a time,/ In the realm of Dewajing. Zong Belegt Baatar. *Mongol Oral Tradition, tr. by* C. R. Bawden. WTO
Once upon a time/ Old Mr. Pyme. Mr. Pyme. Harry Behn. PDV; TiPo
Once upon a time/ there was a lonely wolf. Fable. Janos Pilinszky, *tr. by* Ted Hughes *and* János Csokits. OBVE
Once upon a time I spent a summer. Remembering Kevan MacKenzie. Henry Taylor. InPK
Once upon a time I was. To the Tune "The Fall of a Little Wild Goose." Huang O, *tr. by* Kenneth Rexroth *and* Ling Chung. WPOW
Once upon a time, in a little wee house. The Funny Old Man and His Wife. D'Arcy W. Thompson. OnUR; SoPo; SUS
Once upon a time in California. A Friend of the Family. Louis Simpson. NNaP
Once upon a time there was an Italian. Columbus. Ogden Nash. NoP; OFD
Once upon a time there were three little foxes. The Three Foxes. A. A. Milne. GoJo; GrPl; MoShBr; OxBChV
Once upon the earth at the midnight hour. The Wooing Lady. William Jay Smith. NePoEA
Once, walking home, I passed beneath a tree. The Music of a Tree. W. J. Turner. MoBrPo
Once, walking in the woods. Getting at the Root of the Matter. Henry Taylor. BXAP
Once was every woman the witch. Witches. Ted Hughes. GoYe
Once we dreamed of eagles. Reading Indian Poetry. Ramona Wilson. VoR
Once we felt at home with Nature if we knew the nomenclature. Progress. Felicia Lamport. QQQ
Once we shared the view. The Cyclone. Stewart Brisby. LFAC
Once we were small and real. On the Night Train from Oxford. E. L. Mayo. FAZ
Once we were strong. Charles Mair. *Fr.* Tecumseh. PeCV
Once we were wayfarers, then seafarers, then airfarers. Post Early for Space. Peter J. Henniker-Heaton. AmFN
Once we'd packed up your clothes. Partial Eclipse. W. D. Snodgrass. MOON
Once when I walked into a room. Between Ourselves. Audre Lorde. WPOW
Once, when I was little, as the summer night was falling. The Wastrel. Reginald Wright Kauffman. HBV-1
Once when I was looking at some decoys. Carved by Obadiah Verity. Don Welch. PoDr
Once when I was very scared. A Riddle. Charlotte Zolotow. NTCP
Once when my heart was passion free. Communion. John Banister Tabb. WGRP
Once when the snow of the year was beginning to fall. The Runaway. Robert Frost. AWP; CH; FaBoCh; FaPON; GoJo; MoAB; MoAmPo; MP; PDV; PH; TiPo; TwCP; VGW
Once when the wind was on the roof. Beyond. Hannah Parker Kimball. AA
Once, when their hearts were wild with joy. On Harting Down. T. Sturge Moore. OxBTC
Once When You Were Walking. Annette Wynne. SUS
Once, with a whirl of thought oppressed. The Day of Judgment. Swift. InPK; TW. *See also* With a whirl of thought oppressed.
Once You Git the Habit. *Unknown.* CoSo
Once you said joking slyly, "If I'm killed." The Faithful. Jane Cooper. NePoEA-2
Oncet in the museum. Two Ways. John V. A. Weaver. HBMV
Ondt and the Gracehoper, The. James Joyce. *Fr.* Finnegans Wake. BIrV
One! E. E. Cummings. CAD
One, The. Patrick Kavanagh. MoBrPo
One, The Other, And. Wendy Wieber. NMM
One. Carolyn M. Rodgers. BPo
One, The. *Tr. fr. Sanskrit by* Raimundo Panikkar. *Fr.* Bhagavadgita. ILwL
One afternoon as I was wandering around. A Lesson in Oblivion. Dabney Stuart. GP
One afternoon, finding nothing to do. Getting On. Stephen Sandy. CAD
One afternoon in my room. A True Story. Marvin Bell. SV
One Almost Might. A. S. J. Tessimond. ChMP
One alone is God; there cannot be a second. *Tr. fr. Sanskrit by* Raimundo Panikkar. *Fr.* Upanishads. ILwL

One A.M. X. J. Kennedy. ELU
One A.M. Denise Levertov. CAPP
One and One. C. Day Lewis. OAEP
One and One. Mary Mapes Dodge. HBV-1; HBVY
One and one only/ Is the splendid lover. The Splendid Lover. John Richard Moreland. PGD
One-and-Twenty. Samuel Johnson. *See* Short Song of Congratulation, A.
One-and-Twenty. *Unknown.* AmFP
One Answer, The. *Unknown. See* O, No, John.
One arch of the sky. Love in Labrador. Carl Sandburg. VGW
One arm hooked around the frayed strap. Yellow Light. Garrett Kaoru Hongo. HoAn; MAYP
One Art. Elizabeth Bishop. HAP; SoSe
One ask'd me where the roses grew! The Rosarie. Robert Herrick. InMe
One asked a madman if a wife he had. A Mad Answer of a Madman. Robert Hayman. FF
One asked a sign from God; and day by day. The Seekers. Victor Starbuck. WGRP
One bails out into space. Flight. Barbara Howes. NYBP
One before the Last, The. Rupert Brooke. OBVV
One biting winter morning. The Spider. Hannah F. Gould. OBCA
One bland elipse in cornflower blue. Rigor Viris. Margaret Avison. CaP
One blessing had I, than the rest. Emily Dickinson. LiTA
One bliss for which. Taboo to Boot. Ogden Nash. FiBHP
One block away from my house is an office building. Tie Your Tongue, Sir? Robert Paul Smith. CAD
One born to hardship in his place and station. Vidya, *tr. by* Daniel H. H. Ingalls. *Fr.* Substantiations. PBWP
One boy alone in all the world for me. Epigram. Meleager, *tr. by* Sydney Oswald. PeHV
One Bright Morning. *Unknown.* EvOK
One brought me the news of your death, O Herakleitos my friend. Elegy on Herakleitos. Callimachus, *tr. by* Dudley Fitts. InPK
One by One. Adelaide Anne Procter. GN; HBV-2
One by one, as harvesters, all heavy laden. Sacheverell Sitwell. *Fr.* Agamemnon's Tomb. MoBrPo
One by one, like leaves from a tree. Leaves. Sara Teasdale. HBV-2; PoPl
One by one, the ancient. Next Year, in Jerusalem. Shirley Kaufman. VWA
One by one the pale stars die before the day now. Sailing at Dawn. Sir Henry Newbolt. EtS
One by one the sands are flowing. One by One. Adelaide Anne Procter. GN; HBV-2
One by one they appear in. My Sad Captains. Thom Gunn. CMoP; FaBoMo; InPS; LiTM; NePoEA-2; PoCH
One calm and cloudless winter night. Medusa. Robert Kelley Weeks. AA
One can do one begins to one can only. Reincarnation (II). James Dickey. CAPP
One candidate has been nominated. The Election. Robert Pack. CoPo
One cannot have enough. Soliloquy of a Tortoise on Revisiting the Lettuce Beds after an Interval of One Hour While Supposed to Be Sleeping in a Clump of Blue Hollyhocks. E. V. Rieu. FiBHP; RHPC
One cannot possess. Heritage. Augustus Young. CIP
One Centred System. Joel Barlow. *Fr.* The Columbiad. AP
("Eager he look'd. Another train of years.") AmPP
One Certainty, The. Christina Rossetti. OBNC
One chain-smoked cigarettes. Grandfathers. Michael Castro. VWA
One Chip of Human Bone. Ray A. Young Bear. STE
One chop uncovered. Chops. Alan Dixon. BoAnP
One Chord. Nelly Sachs, *tr. fr. German by* Keith Bosley. VWA
One Christmastime Fats Waller in a fur coat. History of My Heart. Robert Pinsky. NPGG
"One ciarog knows another ciarog." The Tinkers. Joseph Campbell. OnYI
One comes to language from afar, the ear. A Vulnerary. Jonathan Williams. PoM
One Country. Frank Lebby Stanton. AA; PAL
One Crowded Hour. Sir Walter Scott. *See* Sound, Sound the Clarion.
One cup for my self-hood. The Poets at Tea, X. Barry Pain. Par
One dark world is all I am. Born Again. Forugh Farrokhzad, *tr. by* Jascha Kessler *and* Amin Banani. PBWP
One day/ as I was lying on the lawn. The Gift. Ed Ochester. DFF; GP; Psk
One day/ Marilyn marched. Chic Freedom's Reflection. Alice Walker. NMM
One day/ two people decide to build a bed. The Bed. Dennis Saleh. NeAC
One day/ You gonna walk in this house. Seduction. Nikki Giovanni. NMM
One day, a fine day, a high-flying-sky day. The Cat Heard the Cat-Bird. John Ciardi. SO
One day a wag—what would the wretch be at? Art. Ambrose Bierce. InPK
One day a week I stay home. When You Are Gone. Nance Van Winckel. AMV-81
One day across the lake where echoes come now. The Animal That Drank Up Sound. William Stafford. VGW
One day after school. Tanya. Jay Parini. AMV-80
One day as I rambled, down by the seashore. I Never Will Marry. *Unknown.* FSW
One day as I sat and suffered. The Heretic. Bliss Carman. WGRP
One day as I strolled down the Royal Albion. The Sailor Cut Down in His Prime. *Unknown.* OBET
One day as I unwarily did gaze. Amoretti, XVI. Spenser. OAEL-1
One day as I was a-rambling around. Will Bill Jones. *Unknown.* AmFP
One day as I was sitting still. The Battle of Sole Bay. *Unknown.* GBP
One day between the Lip and the Heart. The Lip and the Heart. John Quincy Adams. AA
One day, by appointment, Maria I met. Maria. G. A. Stevens. UnTE
One day I complained about the periphery. Periphery. A. R. Ammons. NOBA
One day I could not read or play. Clouds. Norman Ault. HBVY
One day I found a lost dog in the street. Dead Dog. Vernon Scannell. OxBC
One day I looked at myself. Reflection. *Unknown.* STF
One day, I mind me, now that she is dead. Mimma Bella, VIII. Eugene Lee-Hamilton. HBV-1
One day I observed a grey hair in my head. The Grey Hair. Judah Halevi, *tr. by* J. Chotzner. TrJP
One day I saw a downy duck. Good Morning. Muriel Sipe. SoPo; SUS; TiPo
One day I saw a ship upon the sands. Sea Irony. John Langdon Heaton. AA
One day I thought I'd have some fun. The Horse Wrangler. *Unknown, at. to* D. J. O'Malley. CoSo
One day I thought I'd have some fun. The Tenderfoot. *Unknown.* AS
One day I was walking, I heard a complaining. The Housewife's Lament. *Unknown.* FSW; MAT
One day I was walking out on the mountain. The Cowboy's Lament. *Unknown.* ViBoFo
One day I went down in the golden harvest field. *Unknown.* GBP
One day I wrote her name upon the strand. Amoretti, LXXV. Spenser. AWP; BLPL; BoLoP; CABA; EBEV; ElL; FiP; GBL; HAP; HBV-1; HeJP; LiTB; NoP; OAEL-1; OAEP; PAI; SeCePo; SeCeV; ViBoPo; WeW
One day in a dream as I lay at the edge of a cliff. Dream. William Jay Smith. MoVE
One day in a lonesome grove. The Lonesome Grove. *Unknown.* TrAS
One day in April. Softly Softly. Richard Shelton. NPAW
One day in the Library. Further Advantages of Learning. Kenneth Rexroth. TAP
One day, it thundered and lightened. Adam, Lilith, and Eve. Robert Browning. HBV-1
One day Mamma said "Conrad dear." The Story of Little Suck-a-Thumb. Heinrich Hoffmann, *tr. fr. German.* EvOK; HBV-1; HBVY; SpRo
One Day More, *with music. Unknown.* AmSS
One day more/ These muttering shoalbrains leave the helm to me. James Russell Lowell. *Fr.* Columbus. PGD
One day my life will end; and lest. Biography. Jan Struther. InMe
One day, not here, you will find a hand. Again. Charlotte Mew. MoAB; MoBrPo
One day on our village in the month of July. Death of an Aircraft. Charles Causley. MoBS
One day, one day, (one day, one day). Long John. *Unknown.* FSW
One day people will touch and talk perhaps easily. Daydream. A. S. J. Tessimond. SeCePo
One day ringing men will be a race gone. The Ringers. John Peck. AmPA
One day soon he'll tell her it's time to start packing. Drifters. Bruce Dawe. CBAP
One day Sun found a new canyon. People of the South Wind. William Stafford. NNaP
One day that we mustered on Sliabh Truim. *Unknown. Fr.* The Hunt of Sliabh Truim. OnYI
One day the amorous Lysander. The Disappointment. *At. to* Aphra Behn *and to* Earl of Rochester. SBG; UnTE
One day the Chinese Bird of Royalty, Fum. Fum and Hum, the Two Birds of Royalty. Thomas Moore. OBSV
One day the Earth will be. Prophecy. Jules Supervielle, *tr. by* Jan Pallister. AMV-81
One day the god of fond desire. Song. James Thomson. EnLoPo
One day the letters went to school. The Letters at School. Mary Mapes Dodge. OBCA

One day the nouns were clustered in the street. Permanently. Kenneth Koch. CAPP; CoAP; NoP; PoA; PoM; PPP
One day the sun was rising high. The Peddler and His Wife. *Unknown.* AmFP
One day the tired sea will open to the sun. Like a Pearl. Hayim Naggid, *tr. by* Shlomo Vinner *and* Howard Schwartz. VWA
One day, the vine. The Rebellious Vine. Harold Monro. BrPo
One day the water merchants came. Fable of the Water Merchants. Stephen Dixon. LTB
One day there came with glowing soul. The Story of Macha. *Unknown, tr. by* Sir Samuel Ferguson. *Fr.* Dinnshenchas. OnYI
One day there entered at my chamber door. My Uninvited Guest. May Riley Smith. AA; WGRP
One day there reached me from the street. The Goatherd. Grace Hazard Conkling. TiPo
One day they just started rolling up. Beached Whales off Margate. Stephen Dunn. LTB
One day thou didst desert me—then I learned. To Imagination. Edith M. Thomas. AA
One day, through the primeval wood. The Calf-Path. Sam Walter Foss. HBV-1; HBVY; PoLF
One day we took our lunches. The Circus Parade. Katherine Pyle. OBCA
One day, when childhood tumbled the spongy tufts. Crane. Joseph Langland. NYBP
One day when I was a child, long ago. Grace Paley. NMM
One day when I was studying with Stan Musial. Baseball. Tom Clark. LiSp
One day when I went visiting. I Held a Lamb. Kim Worthington. SoPo; TiPo
One Day When We Went Walking. Valine Hobbs. RHPC; SoPo
One day, while in a lonesome grove. Newberry. *Unknown.* AmFP
One day while walking down Thirty Fifth Street. He's a Fool. *Unknown.* FSW
One day you look at the mirror and it's open. Glass. W. S. Merwin. EAS
One day you were there, the next day gone. Flight. Judith Hemschemeyer. PPJ
One day you'll have to go to the City of the Dead. Elephants May Parade before Your House. *Gond Oral Tradition, tr. by* V. Elwin *and* S. Hivale. WTO
One dignity delays for all. Emily Dickinson. SoSe
One Divinity of Father, Son, The. John Byrom. *Fr.* On Trinity Sunday. PeD
One doctor, singly like the sculler plies. Samuel Garth. *Fr.* The Dispensary. DBV
One does such work as one will not. In the Matter of Two Men. James David Corrothers. BANP
One dollar down. $. Abelardo. FIA
One dolphin./ Strongly curved, watertight. Dolphin Seen Alone. Richmond Lattimore. BoAnP
One dot/ Grainily shifting. The Bee. James Dickey. LiSp; SoSe
One dove has its head turned. Girl with Doves. Stephen Gray. PeSA
One Down. Richard Armour. WhC
One dream of passion and of beauty more! Properzia Rossi. Felicia Dorothea Hemans. SBG
One duck stood on my toes. Feeding Ducks. Norman MacCaig. OxBS
One eats/ the moon in a tortilla. Food. Victor M. Valle, *tr. by* Toni Empringham. FIA
One effort more, my altar this bleak sand. Walt Whitman. *Fr.* The Prayer of Columbus. PGD
One elf, I trow, is diving now. Song of the Elfin Steersman. George Hill. AA
One-erum, two-erum. *Unknown.* OxNR
One-ery, two-ery, [*or* ore-ery], ickery, Ann. *Unknown.* FaPON; OxNR
One-ery, two-ery, tickery, seven. *Unknown.* OxNR
One evenin' in de month of May. Johnny Get Your Gun. Monroe H. Rosenfeld. PSoN
One evening a goose, for a treat. The Misapprehended Goose. Oliver Herford. TDH
One evening a young lady fair, her estate rode out to see. On the Banks of Salee. *Unknown.* AmFP
One evening as a maid did walk. The Trooper and Maid. *Unknown.* BaBo
One evening as I chanced to stray along the banks of Clyde. The *Lady of the Lake*. *Unknown.* ShS
One evening as the sun went down [*or* when the sun was low]. The Big Rock Candy Mountains. *Unknown.* AmFP; ChTr; FSW; GBP; OBAL; TreFT
One evening bright stars they were shining. The Brooklyn Theater Fire. *Unknown.* AmFP
One evening fair when Venus bright her radiant beams displayed. The Irish Girl's Lament. *Unknown.* ShS
One evening in November I happened for to stray. Johnny Carroll's Camp. *Unknown.* AmFP
One evening last June as I rambled. On the Banks of the Little Eau Pleine. *Unknown.* AmFP
One evening late I chanced to stray. MacKenna's Dream. *Unknown.* OnYI
One evening (surely I was led by her). On Ullswater. Wordsworth. *Fr.* The Prelude, I. FaBoPP; OBRV
One evening, when the sun was just gone down. On the Death of Old Bennet the News-Crier. *Unknown.* NOEC
One evening when the sun was low. *See* One evening as the sun went down.
One evening when we were lounging in his apartment in a relaxed mood. Rain. Anselm Hollo. PoM
One evening, while the cooler shade she sought. Dryden. *Fr.* The Hind and the Panther, I. PoEL-3
One eye without a head to wear it. On the Farther Wall, Marc Chagall. Phyllis McGinley. *Fr.* Spectator's Guide to Contemporary Art. OBSV
One Eyed Black Man in Nebraska. Sam Cornish. PoBA
One-eyed Bridegroom, The. Constance Urdang. MOON
One face looks out from all his canvases. In an Artist's Studio. Christina Rossetti. NoP; OAEP; PAI
One fall not far from Ozark, Arkansas. The Narrative Hooper and L.D.O. Sestina with a Long Last Line. James Whitehead. HoPM; TAT
One fantee wave. Edith Sitwell. *Fr.* Gold Coast Customs. OBMV
One feather is a bird. The Voice. Theodore Roethke. VGW
One fine day in the middle of the night. *Unknown.* CenHV
One fine morning, in the country of a very gentle people. Royalty. Arthur Rimbaud, *tr. by* Enid Rhodes Peschal. *Fr.* Illuminations. SOTW
One Fish Ball. *Unknown.* FSW
One Flesh. Elizabeth Jennings. OxBTC; PBWP
One flower at a time, please. Bouquets. Robert Francis. DFF; GP
One flutter of memory, then all becomes. Burning the Letters. Gwendolyn Grew. HoPM
One Foot in Eden. Edwin Muir. BSV; CMoP; GTBS-P; NoAM; NOBE
One foot in front of the other, heel to toe. Highway Patrol Stops Me, Going Too Slow. Robert Peterson. NeAC
One Foot in the Door. Anne Elder. CBAP
One Foot in the River. Gerald Stern. NYP
One for her club and her own latch-key fights. An Omar for Ladies. Josephine Daskam Bacon. HBV-1
One for money. *Unknown.* OxNR
One for sorrow, two for joy. *Unknown.* OxNR
One for sorrow, two for mirth. *Unknown.* PBBP
One for the Ladies at the Troy Laundry Who Cooled Themselves for Zimmer. Paul Zimmer. GP
One Friday morn when we set sail. The Mermaid. *Unknown.* CH; ESPB; OnMSP; ViBoFo (A *vers.*)
One Furrow, The. R. S. Thomas. HoPM; OxBC
One Gift I Ask. Virginia Bioren Harrison. HBV-2
One Girl. Sappho, *tr. fr. Greek by* Dante Gabriel Rossetti. AWP (Beauty.) ViBoPo
One Girl at the Boys Party, The. Sharon Olds. MAYP
One girl in a red dress leaves the shopping center. Suburban Dusk. Bert Meyers. EAS
One-gloved beasts in cleats, they come clattering. Golfers. John Updike. LiSp
One Goes with Me along the Shore. Manfred Winkler, *tr. fr. Hebrew by* Mary Zilzer. VWA
One Good Turn Deserves Another. *Unknown.* ShM
One granite ridge. Piute Creek. Gary Snyder. CAPP; CoAP; ConAP; NaP; NOBA
One great vision unites us. World Youth Song. *Unknown.* FSW
One grey and foaming day. R. P. Blackmur. *Fr.* Sea Island Miscellany. MoVE
One had a lovely face. Memory. W. B. Yeats. BIrV
One had grown almost affluent: one had. Elegy for an Estrangement. John Holloway. NePoEA
One half of me was up and dressed. The Gentle Check. Joseph Beaumont. PBBP
One hand is smaller than the other. It. Man with One Small Hand. P. K. Page. MoCV; OBCV
One hand, two hands. Nothing more. Sphinxes Inclined to Be. Olga Orozco, *tr. by* Leslie Keffer. WPOW
One Happy Moment. Dryden. *See* No, No, Poor Suffering Heart.
One has a feeling it is all coming to an end. The Feeling. William Bronk. VGW
One hay-wire sawmill, nice new location. For Sale. *Unknown.* BPAW
One hears Light harnessing the strong back of the sky-ox. There Are Three Bones in the Human Ear. Anita Endrezze-Danielson. STE
One heifer and one fleecy sheep. Aristeides. Antipater, *tr. by* Charles Whibley. AWP
One hero dies, a thousand new ones rise. Nathan Hale. William Ordway Partridge. PAL
One high, one high, one high holiday. Matty Groves *Unknown.* FSW

One Hogmany, at Glesca Fair. Rothesay, O *Unknown.* FSW
One holy church of God appears. The Church Universal. Samuel Longfellow. WGRP
One Home. William Stafford. AmFN; CoAP; NePA; VGW
One honest John Tomkins, a hedger and ditcher. Contented John. Jane Taylor. HBV-1; HBVY
One Hope, The. Dante Gabriel Rossetti. The House of Life, CI. HBV-2; OAEL-2; VLP
One-horned Ewe, The. *Unknown.* GBP
One Horse Chay, The. *Unknown.* OxBoLi
One Horse Open Sleigh, The. James S. Pierpont. *See* Jingle Bells.
One-Hoss Shay, The. Oliver Wendell Holmes. *See* Deacon's Masterpiece, The.
One hot Bengali night returning home. Grand Hotel, Calcutta. Layle Silbert. AMV-81
One house in my walk holds a corner. The Corner. Rita Johnson. AMV-80
One hue of our flag is taken. The Rejected "National Hymns." "Orpheus C. Kerr." InMe; OBAL
108 Tales of a Po'Buckra, *sel.* Will Inman.
"Dark brother touches me, The." GP
One hundred feet from off the ground. Long-Suffering of God. Christopher Smart. Hymns for the Amusement of Children, Hymn 29. LAuP; NOCV
151st Psalm, The. Karl Shapiro. EaLo; VWA
104 Boulevard Saint-Germain. Kenneth Pitchford. NYBP
110 Year Old House. Ed Ochester. Psk
112 at Pesidio. Virginia Long. AMV-80
100 Year Old Woman at Christmas Dinner. Colin Style. AMV-80
One I love. *Unknown.* OxNR
One I Love Is Gone Away, The. *Unknown.* MeEL
(Separated Lovers.) OAEL-1; OxBM
One if by land. Early Warning. Shirley Marks. QQQ
One imagines the lives of the Prince. Winter in Étienburgh. Stephen Parker. NYBP
One in Christ. Henry van Dyke. TRV
One in herself, not rent by schism, but sound. The Catholic Church. Dryden. *Fr.* The Hind and the Panther, II. OBS
One in the boat cried out. The Door. L. A. G. Strong. MoBrPo
One in thy thousand statues we salute thee. The Black Virgin. G. K. Chesterton. ISi
One Inch Tall. Shel Silverstein. OBCA
One infant grows up and becomes a jockey. Confessions of a Born Spectator. Ogden Nash. LiSp
One is a sign of mischief. *Unknown.* PBBP
One is an ex-professor of biology. Dykes in the Garden. Sharon Barba. PeHV
One is enough, she cried. Technicalities for Jack Spicer. Philip Whalen. PoM
One is not hale until one inhales. On Apples. David Ross. NYBP
"One is reminded of a certain person." Kite Poem. James Merrill. MP; TwCP
One is sorrow, two mirth. *Unknown.* PBBP
One keeps a secret for me. The Secret. Mary Morison Webster. PeSA
One kick/ of Cossack's boots. Golda. Adrienne Wolfert. AMV-80
One kind of teacher is the bhikku, the Buddhist monk. The Teacher. Helen Bevington. GLGT
One Kingfisher and One Yellow Rose. Eileen Brennan. NeIP
One king's daughter said to anither. Sheath and Knife. *Unknown.* CH; ESPB
One-l lama, the. The Lama. Ogden Nash. FaBoCh; FaPON; FiBHP; PV
One last look at your hills, Lysander. Learning Destiny. Herman Charles Bosman. PeSA
One Last Word. John Glassco. NOBC
One late afternoon I hitched from Galway down to Kinvara. Kennedy. Michael Heffernan. AMV-80
One-legged Colonel, The. *Unknown.* TDH
One-legged Man, The. Siegfried Sassoon. CMoP
One lesson, Nature, let me learn of [*or* from] thee. Quiet Work. Matthew Arnold. FaBoBe; HBV-1; OAEP; TrGrPo
One little Indian boy making a canoe. Ten Little Indian Boys. M. M. Hutchinson. SoPo
One little minute more, Maud. Darling, Tell Me Yes. John Godfrey Saxe. HBV-1
One little noise of life remained—I heard. On the Eclipse of the Moon of October 1865. Charles Tennyson Turner. OBNC
One lives by commerce, said the guide. Guide to the Ruins. Howard Nemerov. EyDe
One look at this mill and the adjacent croft. Mill at Romesdal. Richard Hugo. AMV-80
One looks from the train. The Orient Express. Randall Jarrell. AP; CMoP; CoAP; CoBMV; NOBA
One Lost, The. Isaac Rosenberg. MoBrPo
"One lump or two? It's comforting to think." Conversation. Berenice C. Dewey. InMe
One Man Down. Ai. GeTw
One man in a house. To Landrum Guy, Beginning to Write at Sixty. James Dickey. PP
One Man's Goose; or, Poetry Redefined. George Starbuck. PP
One Man's Wife. Philip Booth. NIP; VGW
One midnight, deep in starlight still. Bankrupt. Cortlandt W. Sayres. PoLF
One minute we was laughin', me an' Ted. Nothing to Report. May Herschel-Clarke. SUMH
One Mr. B,/ A joker he. Repartée. Charles Follen Adams. OBAL
One misty, moisty morning. Mother Goose. FaBoBe; HBV-1; HBVY; OxNR; RHPC; TiPo. *See also* Misty-Moisty Was the Morn.
One Modern Poet. Carl Sandburg. OBAL
One month after my tenth birthday. August 12, 1952. Charles Fishman. AMV-81
One More Day's Work for Jesus, *with music.* Anna B. Warner. AH
One more little spirit to Heaven has flown. Little Libbie. Julia A. Moore. OBAL; PeD
One More New Botched Beginning. Stephen Spender. CMoP; NoAM; NYBP
One More Quadrille. Winthrop Mackworth Praed. OBRV
One more rendezvous. John Neihardt. *Fr.* The Song of Jed Smith. FYAP
One More River [to Cross], *sl. diff. vers.* *Unknown.* FSW; TreFS
One More Time. Alvin Aubert. GP
One More Time. Patricia Goedicke. AMV-80
One More Time. Richard Shelton. GP
One more unfortunate. The Bridge of Sighs. Thomas Hood. BeLS; EBEV; EnRP; FaPoR; FPL; GTBS; GTBS-P; HBV-2; OBEV; OBVV; PeD; TreF; WBLP; WHA
One morn as through Hyde Park we walk'd. Epilogue to Lessing's Laocoön. Matthew Arnold. VLP
One morn before me were three figures seen. Ode on Indolence. Keats. EnRP; LiTB; OBNC
One morn I watch'd the rain subside. Devonshire Scenes. Coventry Patmore. *Fr.* Tamerton Church-Tower or First Love. FaBoPP
One Morning. Ellen Levine. AMV-81
One Morning. Vassar Miller. AMV-80
One morning a weasel came swimming. The Weasel. *Unknown.* ChTr
One morning as I rambled. The Miner Boy. *Unknown.* AmFP
One morning, as we travelled in the fields. The Riders Held Back. Louis Simpson. ConAP
One morning before Titan thought of stirring his feet. The Reverie [*or* Reverie at Dawn]. Egan O'Rahilly, *tr. by* Frank O'Connor. AnIL; KiLC
One morning I got up. The Little Bird. *Unknown, tr. by* Rolf Italiaander. PBA
One Morning in May. *Unknown.* AS, *with music*; BaBo; FSW
(Nightingale, The.) AmFP; UnTE
One Morning in May; or, The Young Girl Cut Down in Her Prime. *Unknown.* AmFP
One morning in spring. Fife Tune. John Manifold. CBAP; FaFP; GoJo; LiTB; LiTM; WaaP; WaP
One morning in St. Thomas, when I tried. The Eye. Richard Wilbur. FiCP
One morning in the month of June. The Royal Fisherman. *Unknown.* ChTr
One morning in the month of May. Just as the Tide Was a-Flowing. *Unknown.* OBET
One Morning, Oh, So Early! Jean Ingelow. HBV-1; OxBChV
One morning old Wilfrid Scawen Blunt. Limerick. Victor Gray. NOBL
One morning, one morning, one morning in May. One Morning in May [*or* The Nightingale]. *Unknown.* AmFP; AS; BaBo; FSW; UnTE
One morning, one morning, one morning in May. The Rebel Soldier. *Unknown.* OxBoLi
One morning, one morning, one morning in Spring. I'll Be Fourteen Next Sunday. *Unknown.* AmFP; OLR
One morning, one morning, the weather being fine. I Must and I Will Get Married. *Unknown.* TrAS
One Morning the World Woke Up. Oscar Williams. FaFP; WaaP; WaP
One Morning We Brought Them Order. Al Lee. FF
One morning when I went downtown. Morning in Spring. Louis Ginsberg. GoYe
One Morning When the Rain-Birds Call. Lloyd Roberts. CaP
One morning with a 12-gauge my brother shot what he said was a linnet. Linnets. Larry Levis. LCAP
One most like himself is not this mirror's, The. Himself. Daniel Hoffman. AMV-80
One mouse adds up to many mice. Singular Indeed. David McCord. OBCA

One Music. Edwin Markham. *See* There Is a High Place.
One must have a mind of winter. The Snow Man. Wallace Stevens. AP; CABA; CMoP; CoBMV; CrMA; GoJo; HAP; HeIP; InPK; MAT; NoP; NU; PAI; PrIm; QFR; SoSe; WeW
One nears with Harvard-men expression. Crossing Boston Common. Louise Dyer Harris. WhC
One need not be a chamber—to be haunted. Emily Dickinson. SyP
One needs a lyric poet in these. Julius Lester. In the Time of Revolution, IV. PoBA
One Night. Millicent Sutherland. SUMH
One night a bird came to me. Night Visitors. Kadya Molodovsky, *tr. by* Ruth Whitman. VWA
"One night," a doctor said, "last fall." Ambrose Bierce. *Fr.* The Devil's Dictionary. OBAL
One night all tired with the weary day. The Gnat. Joseph Beaumont. FM; LoBV; OBS
One night as Dick lay fast asleep. Full Moon. Walter de la Mare. BoNaP; TiPo
One night, as dreaming on my bed I lay. "There Was No Place Found." Mary Elizabeth Coleridge. OxBoCh
One night as Polly Oliver was lying in her bed. Polly Oliver's Rambles. *Unknown.* OBET
One Night Away from Day. John Digby. EAS
One night, being pressed by his old friend Chubb. The Undertakers' Club. *Unknown.* GBP
One night came on a hurricane. The Sailor's Consolation. William Pitt, *wr. at. to* Charles Dibdin. BeLS; EtS; FaBoCo; HBV-2; PoPle; TreFS
One night came Winter noiselessly and leaned. The Frosted Pane. Sir Charles G. D. Roberts. HBV-1
One-Night Expensive Hotel. Ronald Everson. NOBC
One night from the stern I thought, as I watched. Braemar. Galway Kinnell. PoA
One night he dreamed he was a. The Young Man Who Loved the Girl Who Took Care of Her Aged Father. Greg Kuzma. AmPA
One night he heard heart-breaking sound. Austin Clarke. Mnemosyne Lay in Dust, VI. CIP; CMoP; IPY
One night I dreamed I was locked in my Father's watch. My Father's Watch. John Ciardi. ImOP
One night I held all Europe in my arms. The Enemy. John Waller. NeBP
One night I lay asleep in Africa. Bookra. Charles Dudley Warner. AA; HBV-2
One night I met when stepping out. Frustrated Male. Hughes Mearns. *Fr.* Later Antigonishes. InMe
One night I reached a cave: I slept, my head. Incident on a Journey. Thom Gunn. NePoEA
One night i' th' yeare [*or* in the year], my dearest Beauties, come. To His Lovely Mistresses. Robert Herrick. CaPo; CTC; OAEP; SeCP
One night in late October. Judged by the Company One Keeps [*or* The Company One Keeps]. *Unknown, at. to* Aimor R. Dickson. BLPA; FPL; TreFT; YaD
One night in the year, my dearest beauties, come. *See* One night i' th' yeare . . .
One night of the two bad years. The Nightmare. Sorley Maclean. NeBP
One night on the fall beef round-up. The Cowboy's Fate. Wallace D. Coburn. PoOW.
One night Polly Oliver lay musing in bed. Polly Oliver's Rambles. *Unknown.* ViBoFo
One night poor Jim had not a sou. Facts. W. H. Davies. BrPo
One night quite bang up to the mark, ri tol de lol. Johnny Raw and Polly Clark. *Unknown.* CoMu
One Night Stand. Amiri Baraka. NeAP
One-Night Stand, The: An Approach to the Bridge. Paul Blackburn. ErPo
One night the Brownies reached a mound. The Brownies' Celebration. Palmer Cox. OBCA
One night the wind it blew cold. Mary of the Wild Moor. *Unknown.* BaBo
One night when I got frisky. I'll Never Get Drunk Any More. *Unknown.* OnYI
One night when I was in the House of Death. Birth. Harold Monro. *Fr.* Strange Meetings. PoA
One night when I was walking. Let the Wind Blow High or Low. *Unknown.* OBET
One night when I went down. The Heap of Rags. W. H. Davies. BrPo
One night, your mother is listening to the walls. How You Get Born. Erica Jong. UnPo
One noonday, at my window in the town. Ball's Bluff. Herman Melville. OBWP
One nostril means latin. Queer Things. Emanuel Carnevali. EAS
One No. 7. John Frederick Frank. GoYe
One o'Clock. Katherine Pyle. *Fr.* The Wonder Clock. OBCA
One o'clock in the letter-box. The Meeting. Muriel Rukeyser. MoAmPo; TrJP
One of Many. Stevie Smith. OxBC
One of my father; he stands. Photographs. Charles Wright. HoPM
One of my names, and I have many others. The Name. Sara Henderson Hay. DFT
One of our gulls. On a Morning Full of Sun. Philip Appleman. SOTS
One of the Boys. Philip Dacey. Str
One of the clock, and silence deep. One o'Clock. Katherine Pyle. *Fr.* The Wonder Clock. OBCA
One of the difficulties is in being. Russian Asylum. Marilyn Bowering. NOBC
One of the Jews. C.P. Cavafy, *tr. fr. Greek.* TrJP
One of the Many Days. Norman MacCaig. PoSH
One of the more intelligent members. For the Fly-Leaf of a School-Book. Norman Cameron. OxBS
One of the other things. Toad Suck Ferry. H. R. Stoneback. TAT
One of the Pharisees desired [Jesus] that he would eat with him. Bible, *N.T. Fr. St.* Luke. LO
One of the Regiment. Douglas Le Pan. CaP
One of the Seven Has Somewhat to Say. Sara Henderson Hay. DFT
One of the two according to your choice. Haidee. Byron. *Fr.* Don Juan, IV, xxv. SeCePo
"One of the wits of the school" your chum would say. Your Birthday in Wisconsin You Are 140. John Berryman. NAs
One of their horses was Nancy Hanks. Going to Town. Fred Lape. PH
One of them seems to offer her breasts. Two Women with Mangoes. Steven Cramer. AMV-80
One of these/ mornings. Cell-Rap #27. Raymond Ringo Fernandez. LFAC
One of these days under the white. The Boarding. Denis Johnson. AMV-80; MAYP
One of these last summer nights. Finding a Friend Home. Timothy Hamm. AMV-80
One of these mornings bright and fair. Great Day. *Unknown.* FSW
One of these nights about twelve o'clock. The Heavenly Aeroplane. *Unknown.* NOCV
One of those golden oldies from the fifties. Golden Oldie. Paul Mariani. GeTw
One of those queer, artistic dives. The Women of the Better Class. Oliver Herford. HBMV
One of us/ will/ be. Devils. Norman Mailer. OBAL
One of Wally's Yarns. John Masefield. BrPo
One of you is a major made of cord and catskin. Lent in a Year of War. Thomas Merton. EAS
"One old Chinese man told me," he said. The Mango Tree. Eric Chock. BrSi
One Old Ox. *Unknown.* ChTr; FaBoNo
One old woman, Lord, in this town. Oh, Babe, It Ain't No Lie. Elizabeth Cotton. FSW
One, one, one, one. The Universe Is Closed and Has REMs. George Starbuck. SUW
One other bitter drop to drink. The Rubicon. William Winter. HBV-2
One ought not to have to care. The Hill Wife. Robert Frost. CMoP; FaBoEn; HAP; LiTM; NoP; VGW
One ounce of truth benefits. Nikki Giovanni. CNA
One Paddy Doyle lived near Killarney. Doran's Ass. *Unknown.* OnYI
One pale November day. Affaire d'Amour. Margaret Deland. HBV-1
One Perfect Rose. Dorothy Parker. FiBHP; NIP; NoP; OBAL; OLR
One person present steps on his pedal of speech. The Talker. Mona Van Duyn. POL
One Person, *sels.* Elinor Wylie.
  Sonnet: "I hereby swear that to uphold your house." LiTA; MoAB; OXBA
  (I Hereby Swear That to Uphold Your House.) NePA
  (Sonnet from "One Person.") MoAmPo
  Sonnet: "Let us leave talking of angelic hosts." OxBA
One petal of a blood-red tulip pressed. Hallucination, I. Arthur Symons. SyP
One Piecee Thing. *Unknown, quoted by* "Lewis Carroll" *in* A Tangled Tale, VI. WhC
One pleasant summer morning it came a storm of snow. The Crooked Gun. *Unknown.* OuSiCo
One Poet Visits Another. W. H. Davies. DTC; TW
One potato, two potato. Counting-out Rhymes. *Unknown.* FaPON
One Presenting a Rare Book to Madame Hull. John Saffin. SCAP
One remains, the many change and pass, The. Lumen de Lumine. Shelley. *Fr.* Adonais. GoBC; SCV
One said to me, "Seek Love, he is Joy." Love, 1916. May Wedderburn Cannan. SUMH
One sat within a hung and lighted room. Love and Poverty. Elisabeth Cavazza Pullen. AA
One Saturday. "Marian Douglas." AA
One Saturday night as we set sail. The Mermaid. *Unknown.* AmFP

One scene as I bow to pour her coffee. Vacation. William Stafford. AmFN; POL; Psk
One seem'd all dark and red—a tract of sand. Tennyson. *Fr.* The Palace of Art. UnPo
1 September 1939. John Berryman. NIP
One set on the highway to sing. Li Po, *tr. fr. Chinese by* Ezra Pound. OxBA
One shadow glides from the dumb shore. Gloucester Harbor. Elizabeth Stuart Phelps Ward. AA
One ship drives east and another drives west. The Winds of Fate. Ella Wheeler Wilcox. BLPA; FPL; TRV; WBLP
One shoulder up, the other down. The Scarecrow. H. L. Doak. OnYI
One side of his world is always missing. Riding a One-eyed Horse. Henry Taylor. HeIP; PH
One side of the coin has a vicious monarch's face. Render unto Cæsar. Rolfe Humphries. CrMA
One side of the potato-pits was white with frost. A Christmas Childhood. Patrick Kavanagh. AnIL; IPY; OxBI
One Sided Shoot-out. Don L. Lee. BPo; PoBA
One silent night of late. The Cheat of Cupid; or, The Ungentle Guest. Robert Herrick, *after* Anacreon. AWP; OBVE; SeCeV
One simple and effective rhyme. Woodpigeons at Raheny. Donald Davie. PP
One sister for sale! For Sale. Shel Silverstein. CTBA
One Snowy Night in December. John N. Morris. NYP
One solitary bird melodiously. Evening. Charles Sangster. CaP
One son was a jewel to me. On the Death of His Son. Lewis Glyn Cothi, *tr. by* Gwyn Williams. PoPl
One Song, The. C. G. Hanzlicek. AMV-80
One sound. Then the hiss and whir. The Garden. Louise Glück. AmPA; FiCP
One standing on the empty beach. Ballykinlar: May 1940. Patrick Maybin. NeIP
One Star Fell and Another. Conrad Aiken. Preludes for Memnon, LVII. MoAmPo
One star is Minnesota. The Flag. Shelley Silverstein. PoSC
One steed I have of common clay. Comrades. Henry Ames Blood. AA
One Step at a Time. *Unknown.* WBLP
One step twix't me and death, (twas Davids speech). Roger Williams. SCAP
One still dark night, I sat alone and wrote. Frederick Goddard Tuckerman. Sonnets, II, xxxiii. AP
One stone sufficeth (lo what death can do). On a Whore. John Hoskyns. FaBoEE
One stood still, looking stupid. The other. The Willets. May Swenson. WPE
One stormy day in winter. The Splinter. James Kenneth Stephen. CenHV
One stormy morn I chanced to meet. A Kiss in the Rain. Samuel Minturn Peck. OBAL
One Summer. Robert Mezey. DiL
One Summer Evening. Wordsworth. *Fr.* The Prelude, I. FiP
("One summer evening (led by her) I found.") NU; ViBoPo
One summer he stole the jade buttons. Of Your Father's Indiscretions and the Train to California. Lynn Emanuel. MAYP
One summer, high in Wyoming. Before the Storm. Kenneth O. Hanson. CoAP
One summer morning a daring band. The Ballad of Ishmael Day. *Unknown.* PAH
One summer morning the sun fell gold. Waking Up. Edward Lense. AMV-80
One sun has set. On my wall. Another Sunset. John Minczeski. PoDr
One Sunday morning as I went walking, by Brisbane waters I chanced to stray. Moreton Bay. *Unknown.* CBAP
One Sunday morning, into Youghall walking. Youghall Harbor. *Unknown, tr. by* Sir Samuel Ferguson. OnYI
One Sunday morning soft and fine. Brigadier. Arthur James Marshall Smith. MoCV; NMP
One sweet of hands, one starred for grace. A Woman of Words. Amanda Benjamin Hall. HBMV
One Sweetly Solemn Thought. Phoebe Cary. *See* Nearer Home.
One tawny paw is all it takes to squash. Some Lines in Three Parts. Peter Viereck. MiAP
One that I cherished. Falstaff's Lament over Prince Hal Become Henry V. Herman Melville. ViBoPo
One that is ever kind said yesterday. The Folly of Being Comforted. W. B. Yeats. AnIL; AnIV; BrPo; GBL; HeIP; VLP
One they hunt by night, The. I Am Ham Melanite. William Millett. GoYe
One Thing. "Owen Meredith." WBLP
One thing at a time. *Unknown.* OxNR
One thing has a shelving bank. A Drumlin Woodchuck. Robert Frost. GoYe; NoAM; NOBA
One Thing I of the Lord Desire. *Unknown.* STF
One thing in all things have I seen. The Secret. "Æ." MoBrPo
One thing is sure. The Pulse. Mark Van Doren. MoAmPo; PoPl
One Thing Needful, The. Vassar Miller. PoCh
One Thing Needful, The. Max Isaac Reich. BLRP
One Thing That Can Save America, The. John Ashbery. NOBA
One thing that literature would be greatly the better for. Very like a Whale. Ogden Nash. BLPL; DTC; HAP; InPK; PoLF; TrGrPo; WeW
One Thing to Take, Another to Keep. Crescenzo del Monte, *tr. fr. Judeo-Romanesque by* Barbara Garvin. VWA
One thing work gives. Wendell Berry. *Fr.* Reverdure. SaC
One thing you left with us, Jack Johnson. Strange Legacies. Sterling A. Brown. CNA; PoBA; TTY
One thing you taught me I'm grateful for. The Lesson. Elizabeth Peterson. AMV-80
One Thought for My Lady ("One thought into one word.") Bloke Modisane. PBA
One thought the recurring "image" in the poet's song. Handbook of Versification. Gilbert Sorrentino. PoA
One thousand eight hundred and twenty-four. The Greenland Whale Fishery. *Unknown.* AmFP
One Thousand Fearful Words for Fidel Castro. Lawrence Ferlinghetti. CoPo; VGW
One Thousand Feet of Shadow. David Craig. PoSH
One thousand saxophones infiltrate the city. Battle Report. Bob Kaufman. AmNP; CAD; TTY
One Thousand Seven Hundred and Thirty Eight. Pope. *See* Epilogue to the Satires.
One Thousandth Psalm, The. Edward Everett Hale. TRV
One Time. Douglas Livingstone. PeSA
One Time Henry Dreamed the Number. Doughtry Long. BPo; CNA; PoBA
One time in Alexandria, in wicked Alexandria. Thaïs. Newman Levy. FiBHP; InMe
One Times One, *sel.* E. E. Cummings.
"Plato told/ him:he couldn't," XIII. CTC
One tiny golden upward-pointing flame. Candle and Book. Nina Willis Walter. TRV
One to destroy is murder by the law. The Criminality of War. Edward Young. FF; PGD
One to make ready. *Unknown.* OxNR
One to Nothing. Carolyn Kizer. OBAL
One Token. W. H. Davies. BrPo
One, two,/ Buckle my shoe. Mother Goose. HBV-1; HBVY; OxNR; SoPo; TiPo
One, two, Buckle my shoe. The Late Mother. Cynthia Macdonald. Psk
One, Two, Three. Samuel L. Albert. NePoAm-2
One, Two, Three. H. C. Bunner. FaPON; HBV-1; PoLF
One—Two—Three. Hannah Senesh, *tr. fr. Hungarian by* Peter Hay. WPOW
One, two, three,/ I love coffee. *Unknown.* OxNR
One! Two! Three!/ Outside the school. Sing-Song Rhyme. *Unknown.* SiSoSe
One, two, three, four,/ Mary at the cottage door. Mother Goose. OxNR
1, 2, 3, 4, 5!/I caught a hare alive. Mother Goose.. TiPo
One, two, three, four, five/Once I caught a fish alive. Mother Goose. OxNR
One, Two, Three—Gough! Eve Merriam. NTCP
1-2-3 was the number he played but today the number came 3-2-1. Dirge. Kenneth Fearing. FF; HeIP; HoPM; InPK; NIP; PoRA; TrJP
One, two, whatever you do. *Unknown.* OxNR
One ugly trick has often spoiled. Meddlesome Matty. Ann Taylor. HBV-1; HBVY; OnMSP; OxBChV
One-Upmanship. Miriam Chaikin. NTCP
One wading a Fall meadow finds on all sides. The Beautiful Changes. Richard Wilbur. CMoP; CoAP; InPS; NIP; SeCeV
One wants a Teller in a time like this. Gwendolyn Brooks. *Fr.* The Womanhood. WPE
One was fifteen years old, the other sixteen, The. Pensionnaires. Paul Verlaine, *tr. by* François Pirou. PeHV
One was fire and fickleness, a child, The. Voltaire and Gibbon. Byron. *Fr.* Childe Harold's Pilgrimage, III. OBRV
One was kicked in the stomach. Gangrene. Philip Levine. VGW
One Way Down. David Craig. PoSH
One Way Gal. *Unknown.* BluL
One Way of Love. Robert Browning. HBV-1
One-Way Song, *sels.* Wyndham Lewis.
"I would set all things whatsoever front to back." CTC
"In any medium except that of verse." PP
One We Knew. Thomas Hardy. VLP
One weapon I would keep. Preparedness. Jean Grigsby Paxton. PGD
One Wept Whose Only Child Was Dead. Alice Meynell. TreFT
One West Coast. Al Young. NPGG

One white foot, run him for your life. How to Choose a Horse. *Unknown.* FaBoUs
One white foot, try him. On Buying a Horse. *Unknown.* PH
One White Hair, The. Walter Savage Landor. HBV-1
One who does not love me, The. Song of Abuse. *Yoruba Oral Tradition, tr. by* Ulli Beier *and* B. Gbadamosi. WTO
One Who Grew to Be a Wolf, The. Patricia Monaghan. PoDr
One Who Is Missing, The. Abraham Chalfi, *tr. fr. Hebrew by* Shlomo Vinner *and* Howard Schwartz. VWA
One, who is not, we see: but one, whom we see not, is. The Higher Pantheism in a Nutshell. Swinburne. *Fr.* The Heptalogia. BXAP; FaBoNo; HBV-1; NA; Par; SpRo
One Who Is Within, The. Nia Francisco. STE
One Who Runs Away, The. Callimachus, *tr. fr. Greek by* Tom Dodge. LiSp
One Who Struggles, The. Ernst Toller, *tr. fr. German by* E. Ellis Roberts. TrJP
One Who Watches. Siegfried Sassoon. TrJP
One whom I knew, a student and a poet. Epitaph [*or* Poem]. Alex Comfort. MoBrPo; MOS; SeCePo
One Whose Reproach I Cannot Evade, The. George Hitchcock. EAS
One Wife for One Man. Frank Aig-Imoukhuede. PBA
One winter afternoon. E. E. Cummings. NCSH
One Winter Night in August. X. J. Kennedy. OBCA
One with eyes the fairest. Love Song. Euripides, *tr. by* Shelley. *Fr.* Cyclops. AWP
One without looks in to-night. The Fallow Deer at the Lonely House. Thomas Hardy. AWP; BoAnP; CH; CMoP; MoVE
One woman may robe herself in a tunic of white wool. Bilitis. Pierre Louÿs, *tr. by* Horace M. Brown. *Fr.* The Songs of Bilitis. UnTE
One word beyond all rules. Love. Gordon LeClaire. CaP
One word in your letter &, again, that quail trots from the vineyard, spurts. Letter. Philip Dow. NPGG
One word is too often profaned. To ——— [*or* Love]. Shelley. BLPL; BoLoP; ELP; EnRP; FaBoEn; FaBV; FIP; GTBS; GTBS-P; HBV-1; LiTB; LoBV; NOBE; OAEP; OBEV; OBNC; OBRV; PoLF; PPP; TreFT; TrGrPo; ViBoPo; WHA
One Word More. Robert Browning. FiP; HBV-1; OAEP; PoEL-5; VLP
Sels.
Phases of the Moon. ChTR; MOON
"There they are, my fifty men and women." ViBoPo
One would be in less danger. Family Court. Ogden Nash. FiBHP
One would never assume, from the toy bulldogs taking the air. A Nice Part of Town. Alfred Hayes. NYBP
One would not hope to meet. Thoughts at the Museum. Eileen Brennan. OnYI
One writes, that "other friends remain." In Memoriam A. H. H., VI. Tennyson. PoEL-5
One writes when. Two Poems. Edward Marshall. CoPo
One Writing against His Prick. *Unknown.* TW
One X. E. E. Cummings. FaBoMo
One Year After. Gary Allan Kizer. LFAC
One Year Later. Eric Torgerson. POL
One year there were too many/ frogs. Calendar. Cecil Bodker, *tr. by* Nadia Christensen *and* Alexander Taylor. BoWoP
One Year to Life on the Grand Central Shuttle. Audre Lorde. CNA
O'Neill's War Song. Michael Hogan. OnYI
Onely a little more. *See* Only a little more.
Onely the Reverend Grave and Godly Mr. Buckly Remaines. Edward Johnson. SCAP
Oneness of the Philosopher with Nature, The. G. K. Chesterton. FaBoNo
One's grand flights, one's Sunday baths. The Sense of the Sleight-of-Hand Man. Wallace Stevens. AP; CABA; CoBMV; HAP; LiTM; MoAB; MoAmPo; MoPo; MP; NOBA; PoA; TwCP; WeW
One's none. Little Hundred. *Unknown.* OxNR
One's-Self I Sing. Walt Whitman. NOBA; OxBA
Ones of the old days, The. As in the Old Days, Passages 8. Robert Duncan. PoM
Ones who hammer the air with fists, The. Cripples. J. D. Reed. NeAC
Onion, The. John Thompson. NOBC
Onion Bucket. Lorenzo Thomas. PoBA
Onion, Memory, The. Craig Raine. NoP
Onion Skin, The. Kenneth Pitchford. *Fr.* Good for Nothing Man. CoPo
Onion Skin in Barn. Kenneth Slade Alling. NePoAm
Onions. Swift. *Fr.* Verses for Fruitwomen. AnIV; OnYI
(Onyons.) BIrV; FaBoUs
Only. Harriet Prescott Spofford. HBV-1
Only/ a little/ yellow/ school bus. Snow Country. Dave Etter. AmFN
Only/ the gray wind. Something for Supper. Carroll Arnett. VoR
Only a baby, fair, and small. George Washington. *Unknown.* OHIP
Only a Baby Small. Matthias Barr. HBV-1; HBVY; PaPo
Only a bit of color. Our Flag. Frances Crosby Hamlet. PGD
Only a Cowboy. *Unknown.* CoSo
Only a dish of blueberries could pull me. It's Not the Heat So Much as the Humidity. James Tate. NoAM
Only a few could understand his ways and his outfit queer. The Lost Range. Henry Herbert Knibbs. BPAW
Only a few will really understand. One Sided Shoot-out. Don L. Lee. BPo; PoBA
Only a hundred yards, says Bob. Space and Time. Syd Scroggie. PoSH
Only a Little Litter. Myra Cohn Livingston. QQQ
Only [*or* Onely] a little more. His Poetry [*or* Poetrie] His Pillar. Robert Herrick. AnAnS-2; CaPo; FaBoEn; JCP; LoBV; OBS; QFR; SeCP
Only a little while since first we met. Song. Brian Hooker. HBMV
Only a man harrowing clods. In Time of "The Breaking of Nations." Thomas Hardy. BoLoP; CMoP; CoBMV; EBEV; HAP; LiTB; LiTM; LoBV; MMA; MoAB; MoBrPo; NoAM; NOBE; NoP; OAEL-2; OAEP; OBEV; OBWP; POL; PPP; QFR; SeCeV; TreF; WeW
Only a Miner. *Unknown.* AmFP
Only a Smile ("Only a smile that was given me.") *Unknown.* STF
Only a tender little thing. A Snowdrop, *abr.* Harriet Prescott Spofford. GN
Only a touch, and nothing more. Kate Temple's Song. Mortimer Collins. HBV-1
Only after, wading waist deep. The Ring. Paul Mariani. GeTw
Only awake to Universal Mind. Chorus. Jack Kerouac. *Fr.* Mexico City Blues. NeAP
Only Bar in Dixon, The. James Welch. AmPA; FF
Only Be Willing to Search for Poetry. Yuan Mei, *tr. fr. Chinese.* PDV
Only blossoms of the plains are black, The. The Plains. Roy Fuller. MoPo
Only brooms. Brooms. Charles Simic. AmPA; LCAP; NNaP
Only Daughter, The. *Unknown.* OBET
Only difference, I said, The. Poetry Workshop in a Reform School. Betty Adcock. AMV-80
Only for Me. Mark Van Doren. NCSH
Only for Morning Glories. Basho, *tr. fr. Japanese by* Nobuyuki Yuasa. PAI
Only for these I pray. Two Prayers. Charlotte Perkins Gilman. WGRP
Only from chaos /Is creation. Song for These Days. Patrick F. Kirby. GoBC
Only from day to day. To-Day. John Boyle O'Reilly. OnYI
Only ghost I ever saw, The. Emily Dickinson. NePA; WSC
Only head in the sky, The. Giraffe. Stanley Plumly. AmPA
Only in my deep heart I love you, sweetest heart. A Farewell. "Æ." OBVV
Only in This Way. Margaret Goss Burroughs. BlSi
Only Jealousy of Emer, The. *Unknown, tr. fr. Irish by* John Montague. BIrV
Only Jealousy of Emer, The, *sel.* W. B. Yeats.
Song: "Woman's beauty is like a white, A." MoAB
Only joy, now here you are. Astrophel and Stella: Fourth Song. Sir Philip Sidney. EIL; EnRePo; GBL; HAP; InVP; NoP; OBSC; SiPS; UnTE
Only kid, An! an only kid. Had Gadyaa Kid, a Kid. *Unknown.* TrJP
Only last week, walking the hushed fields. Father and Son. F. R. Higgins. BIrV; OBMV; OxBI
Only leaf upon its tree of blood, The. The Red Heart. James Reaney. CaP
Only light at this hour, The. My Grandfather Burning Cornfields. Roger Sauls. Str
Only man that e'er I knew, The. Blake. PV
Only moment held, The. Night Train. Mary C. Fineran. AMV-81
Only monument, The. On the Pavement. David A. Sam. AMV-80
Only mother he could afford was a skinny old man, The. Because They Were Very Poor That Winter. Kenneth Patchen. NaP
Only My Opinion. Monica Shannon. FaPON; SoPo; TiPo
Only news I know, The. Emily Dickinson. NOCV
Only, O Lord, in Thy dear love. Help Us to Live. John Keble. TRV
Only of Thee and Me. Louis Untermeyer. HBV-1
Only on the rarest occasions, when the blue air. The Mountain. W. S. Merwin. VGW
Only once more and not again—the larches. In Ampezzo. Trumbull Stickney. CrMA; NCEP; TwAmPo
Only One. Ralph Burns. PoDr
Only One. George Cooper. *See* Only One Mother.
Only One King. John Richard Moreland. PGD
Only One Life. Gladys M. Bowman. STF
Only one more day, my Johnny. One Day More. *Unknown.* AmSS
Only One Mother. George Cooper. FaPON; SiSoSe
(Only One.) AA
(Our Mother.) OHIP
Only our love hath no decay. John Donne. *Fr.* The Anniversary. LO
Only quiet death. Threnody. Waring Cuney. AmNP; BANP
Only real airship, The. The Dirigible. Ralph Bergengren. FaPON; SoPo
Only response, The. Poem. William Knott. InPK
Only Seven. Henry S. Leigh. BXAP; HBV-1; SpRo
Only Silence. Arthur S. Bourinot. CaP

Only snake writes, a coil sprung in my fingers. Yetzer ha Ra. Edward Codish. VWA
Only Son, The. Sir Henry Newbolt. HBV-2
Only, sweet Love, afford me but thy heart. For Her Heart Only. *Unknown.* EIL
Only teaching on Tuesdays, book-worming. Memories of West Street and Lepke. Robert Lowell. AmPP; CAPP; CMoP; ConAP; InPS; NaP; NOBA
Only Teasing. *Unknown.* TDH
Only tell her that I love. Song. John Cutts. HBV-1
Only the air-spirits know. Solitary Song. *Tr. fr. Eskimo.* WTO
Only the Beards Are Different. Bruce Dawe. PoAu-2
Only the Dead. Reed Whittemore. NYBP
Only the deep well. I Break the Sky. Owen Dodson. PoBA
Only the diamond and the diamond's dust. Edna St. Vincent Millay. Epitaph for the Race of Man, II. MoPo
Only the flawlessly beautiful. Night Cries, Wakari Hospital. Charles Brasch. OCNZ
Only the hands are living; to the wheel attracted. Casino. W. H. Auden. MoPo
Only the Heart. Marjorie Freeman Campbell. CaP
Only the illegitimate are beautiful. Thesis. Edward Dorn. NOBA
Only the lion and the cock. After Galen. Oliver St. John Gogarty. FaBoEE; OBMV; PoRA
Only the Polished Skeleton. Countee Cullen. PrIm; VGW
Only the sand, only the sand. El Alamein Revisited. Roy Macnab. PeSA
Only the short, broad, splayed feet. Young Shepherd Bathing His Feet. Peter Clarke. PBA
Only the wanderer. Song. Ivor Gurney. FaBoPP
Only the wholesomest foods you eat. Samuel Hoffenstein. Poems in Praise of Practically Nothing, II. InMe; TrJP
Only thing I have of Jane MacNaughton, The. The Leap. James Dickey. NIP
Only thing that can be relied on, The. The Snow on Saddle Mountain. Kenji Miyazawa, *tr. by* Gary Snyder. NoAM; NOBA; PAI
Only thing we know is the thing, The. Red Light. Amiri Baraka. SOTW
Only think, dearest Louisa, what fearful scenes we have witnessed! Arthur Hugh Clough. *Fr.* Amours de Voyage, Canto II, viii. EBVV
Only this evening I saw again low in the sky. Martial Cadenza. Wallace Stevens. NePA; NIP; OxBA; VGW
Only those coral insects live. The Builders. Judith Wright. SeCePo
Only Thy Dust. Don Marquis. PoLF
Only to find Forever, blest. Heaven. Martha Dickinson Bianchi. AA; HBV-1
Only to have a grief. Peeling Onions. Adrienne Rich. BoWoP; TAP
Only today and just for this minute. The Withdrawal. Robert Lowell. NoP
Only totems protrude. An Inhabited Emptiness. Jiri Gold, *tr. by* Jaroslav Kotan *and* Daniel Weissbort. VWA
Only Tourist in Havana Turns His Thoughts Homeward, The. Leonard Cohen. CABA; MoCV; NoAM
Only two beds. The Family of Eight. Abraham Reisen, *tr. by* Marcia Falk. VWA
Only two patient eyes to stare. Faded Pictures. William Vaughn Moody. AP
Only Waiting. Frances Laughton Mace. BLPA
Only Way to Win, The. *Unknown.* WBLP
Only what I bring to this room will exist here. At the Jewish Museum. Olga Cabral. PoDr
Only what is heroic and courageious moves our blood. The Flowers of Politics, II. Michael McClure. NeAP
Only Years. Kenneth Rexroth. TAP
Onne Ruddeborne bank twa pynynge maydens sate. Elinoure and Juga. Thomas Chatterton. LAuP
Onondaga Madonna, The. Duncan Campbell Scott. PeCV
Ons as me thought fortune me kyst. Sir Thomas Wyatt. *See* Once as methought Fortune me kissed.
Ons in your grace I knowe I was. What Once I Was. Sir Thomas Wyatt. MeEL
Onset, The. Robert Frost. AP; CMoP; CoBMV; MoAB; MoAmPo; OxBA; PPP
Onto the hallowit steid bryng in, thai cry. Virgil, *tr. by* Gavin Douglas. *Fr.* The Aeneid, II. OBVE
Ontogeny. Jarold Ramsey. NIP
Onward, Christian Soldiers. Sabine Baring-Gould. FaBoBe; FaPoR; FSW; HBV-2; TreF; VLP; WGRP
"Onward Christian Soldiers!" Frank Marshall Davis. FB
Onward, Christian soldiers! Duty's way is plain. Christians at War. John F. Kendrick. TW
Onward led the road again. Hell Gate. A. E. Housman. NoAM; UnPo
Onward, Onward, Men of Heaven, *with music.* Lydia H. Sigourney. AH
Onward they came in their joy. The Nereids. Charles Kingsley. *Fr.* Andromeda. NBM
Onward to Far Ida. George Darley. *Fr.* Nepenthe. OBNC
Onwardness. Doris Hedges. CaP
Onyons. Swift *See* Onions.
Oocuck, The. Justin Richardson. BoAnP; FiBHP
Oodles of Noodles. Lucia *and* James L. Hymes, Jr. RHPC
Oor best-lo'ed makar has but late grown cauld. Carlyle on Burns. William Jeffrey. *Fr.* On Glaister's Hill. OxBS
Opal heart of afternoon, The. The Bracelet of Grass. William Vaughn Moody. AP
Opal ring and a holly tree, An. Sailor's Woman. Annette Patton Cornell. GoYe
Ope your doors and take me in. The House of the Trees. Ethelwyn Wetherald. CaP
Open. Joseph Bruchac. FAZ
Open. Larry Eigner. NeAP
Open Air Performance of "As You Like It," An. E. J. Scovell. ChMP
Open and Closed Space. Tomas Tranströmer, *tr. fr. Swedish by* Robert Bly. EAS
Open-backed dumpy junktruck. In Passing. Gerald Jonas. GrPl
Open Casket. Sandra McPherson. GeTw
Open Country. Richard Hugo. LCAP; NPAW
Open Door, The. Elizabeth J. Coatsworth. DuDa
Open Door, The. Grace Coolidge. TRV
Open Door, The. *Unknown, tr. fr. Irish by* Frank O'Connor. KiLC
Open Dream Sequence. Carol Lee Sanchez. TWSS
Open Earth. Clarisse Nicoïdski, *tr. by* Stephen Levy. VWA
Open Heart. Michael Salcman. AMV-80
Open House. Theodore Roethke. AP; CoBMV; NoAM; NOBA; NoP
Open Hydrant. Marci Ridlon. RHPC
Open Letter. Owen Dodson. BALP
Open Letter for John Doe. Edward Doro. TwAmPo
Open Letter from a Constant Reader. Mona Van Duyn. GP; PoA
Open Letter-Poem-Note to Vincent van G, An. Bernadine. LTB
Open, love. Unclench Yourself. Marge Piercy. NeAC
Open me like a meadow lily. The Seduction. Suzanne Berger Rioff. NMM
Open My Eyes. Betty Scott Stam. STF
Open Poetry Reading. Jesús Papoleto Meléndez. AMV-81
Open Range. Kathryn Jackson *and* Byron Jackson. FaPON; TiPo
Open Range. Thomas Mitchell. AMV-81
Open Roads. David Donnell. Str
Open Sea, The. William Meredith. CoAP; GrPl; MOS; NePoEA; TAP; UnPo
Open Secret, An. Caroline Atherton Mason. AA
Open the Door. Marion Edey. SiSoSe; TiPo
Open the Door. *Malay Oral Tradition, tr. by* R. J. Wilkinson *and* R. O. Winstedt. WTO
Open the Door. *Unknown.* EIL
("Open the door, who's there within?") GBL
Open the door and who'll come in? Open the Door. Marion Edey. SiSoSe; TiPo
Open the Door to Me, Oh! Burns. PoEL-4
(O, Open the Door to Me, O!) FaBoCh
Open the door, who's there within? Open the Door. *Unknown.* EIL; GBL
Open the Gates. *Unknown, tr. fr. Hebrew by* Israel Zangwill. TrJP
"Open the gates." The Bonny Earl of Murray. *Unknown.* ESPB
Open the old cigar-box, get me a Cuba stout. The Betrothed. Kipling. HBV-1
Open the window on the high. Earth Tremor in Lugano. James Kirkup. NYBP
Open Thy Doors, O Lebanon. Bible, *O.T.* Zechariah, XI: 1-14. AWP
Open to Me! He Commandeth a Fair Wind. *Unknown, tr. by* Robert Hillyer. *Fr.* Book of the Dead. AWP
Open to Visitors. E. V. Milner. ELU
Open wound which has been healed anew, An. Sonnet. Richard Chenevix Trench. TrPWD
"Open, ye everlasting gates!" they sung. The Great Creator from His Work Returned. Milton. *Fr.* Paradise Lost, VII. TreFT
Open your gates for him. Harold at Two Years Old. Frederick W. H. Myers. HBMV
Open Your Hand. Dorothy R. Fulton. AMV-81
Opened, clear as a child's geography. The Summer Countries. Henry Rago. VGW
Opening of Eyes. Laura Riding. NoAM
Opening of the Tomb of Charlemagne, The. Sir Aubrey De Vere. HBV-2
Opening the Seams. Stephen Lewandowski. WOLT
Opening Year, The. *Unknown, tr. fr. Latin by* F. Pott. BLRP
Openly, yes,/ with the naturalness. Melancthon [*or* Black Earth]. Marianne Moore. CrMA; FaBoMo
Opera in English? Benjamin M. Steigman. WhC
Opera singer softly sang, The. Essence. Samuel Greenberg. MoPo; NePA

Operatic Olivia. Isabel Frances Bellows. TDH
Operation. A. Alvarez. NMP
Operation, The. Robert Creeley. NaP
Operation. W. E. Henley. In Hospital, V. BrPo
Operation, The. W. D. Snodgrass. InPK; TAP
Operation—Souls. *Unknown.* STF
Operative No. 174 Resigns. Kenneth Fearing. NYBP
Ophelia. Arthur Rimbaud, *tr. fr. French by* Brian Hill. ChTr
Ophelia. Vernon Watkins. MoVE
Ophelia's Death. Shakespeare. *Fr.* Hamlet, V, i. ChTr
Ophelia's Song. Marya Zaturenska. OLR
Ophelia's Songs. Shakespeare. *Fr.* Hamlet, IV, v.
And Will He [*or* A'] Not Come Again. PoEL-2; ViBoPo
("He is dead and gone, Lady," 1 *st.*) LO
(Ophelia's Songs, 2.) TrGrPo
How Should I Your True Love Know. EBEV; EnLoPo; LiTB; PoRA; QFR; ViBoPo
(Friar of Orders Grey, The, *diff. sel.*) GoBC
(Ophelia's Song.) ChTr; GBL; OBSC
(Ophelia's Songs, 1.) TrGrPo
(Song.) CH
Tomorrow Is Saint Valentine's Day. EnLoPo; OFD; PV; ViBoPo
(Ophelia's Song.) UnTE
(Saint Valentine's Day.) LiTB
(Song.) FaPON; NTCP
(Song: "Good morrow, 'tis . . .") SiSoSe
Ophra. Judah Halevi, *tr. fr. Hebrew by* Nina Davis Salaman. TrJP
Opifex. Thomas Edward Brown. OBVV
Opinion is not worth a rush. Michael Robartes and the Dancer. W. B. Yeats. OAEL-2
Opinions of the New Student. Regino Pedroso, *tr. fr. Spanish by* Langston Hughes. TTY
Opium Clippers. Daniel Henderson. EtS
Opium-Den, The. *Malay Oral Tradition, tr. by* R. J. Wilkinson *and* R. O. Winstedt. WTO
Opossum. William Jay Smith. TiPo
Opponent Charm Sustained, The. Samuel Greenberg. MoPo
Opportunity. Berton Braley. WBLP
Opportunity. Madison Cawein. AA
Opportunity. Harry Graham. DTC; FaBoCo
Opportunity. John James Ingalls. AA; FaFP; HBV-2; HBVY; OHFP; PoLF; TreF; WBLP; YaD
Opportunity. Machiavelli, *tr. fr. Italian by* James Elroy Flecker. AWP
Opportunity. Walter Malone. BLPA; BLPL; FaBoBe; HBV-2; WBLP; YaD
Opportunity. Shakespeare. *Fr.* The Rape of Lucrece. LiTB; OBSC
("O opportunity thy guilt is great.") PoEL-2
(Outcry upon Opportunity, An.) NOBE
Opportunity. Edward Rowland Sill. BLPA; GN; HBV-2; HBVY; OHFP; TreFS; WGRP; YaD
Opportunity's Knock. Morris Bishop. TDH
Opposite House, The. Robert Lowell. CMoP; NYP
Opposite of Two, The. Richard Wilbur. RHPC
Opposition. Sidney Lanier. LiTA
Oppressed and few, but freemen yet. The Mecklenburg Declaration. William C. Elam. PAH
Oppression. Langston Hughes. CNA
Ops in a Wimpey. *Unknown.* CoMu
Optimism. Blanaid Salkeld. NeIP
Optimism. Ella Wheeler Wilcox. BLPA; BLPL; FaBoBe
Optimist, The ("The optimist fell ten stories"). *Unknown.* BLPA; TreFT; YaD
Optimist, The ("When the world is all against you"). *Unknown.* PV
Optimist and Pessimist. *At. to* McLandburgh Wilson. TreFT
Options. "O. Henry." FiBHP
Opulent oracle—it's a terrible thing! It's a Terrible Thing! Everett Hoagland. BPo
Opus rises to fortissimo, The. Lengthy Symphony. Persis Greely Anderson. WhC
Opusculum paedagogum. Study of Two Pears. Wallace Stevens. AP; InPK; InPS; NU; OxBA
Or a ship's mast. Speak like Rain. Jerred Metz. VWA
Or: all dolls come. Five Poems for Dolls, V. Margaret Atwood. NIP
Or did we make them. Five Poems for Dolls, IV. Margaret Atwood. NIP
Or else, in an afternoon of minor reflection. Conrad Aiken. *Fr.* Time in the Rock. MoVE
Or ever a lick of Art was done. Bygones. Bert Leston Taylor. HBMV
Or Ever God Created Adam. *Malay Oral Tradition, tr. by* R. J. Wilkinson. WTO
Or Ever the Earth Was. Charles Leonard Moore. AA
Or Ever the Knightly Years Were Gone. W. E. Henley. Echoes, XXXVII. HBV-1
(Echoes: "Or ever the knightly years were gone.") BLPA; BLPL; TreF
(When I Was a King in Babylon.) PaPo
Or I shall live your epitaph to make. Sonnets, LXXXI. Shakespeare. OAEP; OBSC
Or is it all illusion? Do the years. David P. Berenberg. *Fr.* Two Sonnets. HBMV
Or lookt I back unto the times hence flown. To Master Denham, on His Prospective Poem. Robert Herrick. AnAnS-2
Or love me[e] less[e], or love me[e] more. Song. Sidney Godolphin. CavP; JCP; MePo; OBS
Or, Pyrrha, tell me who's the guy. Horace the Wise. Morrie Ryskind. HBMV
Or scorn[e] or pity [*or* pittie] on me take. The Dream[e]. Ben Jonson. NOBE; PoEL-2
Or the black centaurs, statuesquely still. Ambuscade. Hugh McCrae. PoAu-1
Or, trying simple charms and spells. John Clare. *Fr.* The Shepherd's Calendar. FaBoUs
Or what is closer to the truth. When I Buy Pictures. Marianne Moore. EyDe; OxBA
Or wren or linnet. Samuel Taylor Coleridge. PBBP
Or yield or die's the word, what could he mean. Ignotum per Ignotius, or a Furious Hodge-Podge of Nonsense; a Pindaric. *Unknown.* NOEC
Oracle, The. Arthur Davison Ficke. HBV-1
Oracle. E. L. Mayo. MiAP
Oracle ("Iwori wotura"). *Yoruba Oral Tradition, tr. by* Ulli Beier. WTO
Oracle at Delphi. Robert Bagg. NePoAm-2
Oracles, The. A. E. Housman. HAP; OAEP; RoGo
Oracular Portcullis, The. James Reaney. ErPo; PeCV
Oraga Haru, *sels.* Issa, *tr. fr. Japanese by* Nobuyuki Yuasa. OFD
Buddha's Birthday: April 8, 1819.
Buddha's Death Day: February 15, 1815.
"For a fresh start."
Oral Messages, *sel.* Lawrence Ferlinghetti.
I Am Waiting. CAPP
("I am waiting for my case to come up," *shorter sel.*) GOA; PoPl
Orange air grows fetid with smoke, The. The uneasy dark. Mess Deck Casualty. Alan Ross. WaP
(Epilogue: " 'O where are you going?' said reader to rider") (Five Songs.) FaBoCh; LiTM
Orange and purple, shot with white and mauve. Orchids. Theodore Wratislaw. VLP
Orange Bears, The. Kenneth Patchen. NaP
Orange Bough, The. Felicia Dorothea Hemans. VLP
Orange Chiffon. Jayne Cortez. BlSi
Orange County Plague: Scenes. Laurence Lieberman. CoPo
Orange fish are swimming. Watching the Sun Rise over Mount Zion. Ruth Whitman. VWA
Orange in the middle of a table. Against Still Life. Margaret Atwood. MoCV; NMM
Orange is a tiger lily. What Is Orange? Mary O'Neill. RHPC
Orange is the single-hearted color. I remember. Poppies. Sandra McPherson. GeTw
Orange Jews. Ted Berrigan *and* Ron Padgett. EAS
Orange Juice Song. David Phillips. NeAC
Orange leaves are gone. Izumi Shikibu, *tr. fr. Japanese by* Willis Barnstone. BoWoP
Orange Lilies. James Reaney. WHW
Orange Lily, The. *Unknown.* GBP
Orange line splits the sky, An. The Flint Hills. Lew Blockcolski. VoR
Orange on its way. On Its Way. May Swenson. WPE
Orange on the table, An. Alicante. Jacques Prévert, *tr. by* Lawrence Ferlinghetti. BoLoP
Orange Tree, The. Shaw Neilson. CBAP; PoAu-1
Orange Tree, The. Ellen Pearce. IHMS
Oranges, The. Abu Dharr, *tr. fr. Arabic by* A. J. Arberry. TTY
Oranges at Jaffa gate, The. Gates. Sister Mary Madeleva. GoBC
Oranges in a wooden bowl. Still-Life. Ronald Perry. NePoEA-2
Oranges in th bowl, Th. Windfall. David Mitchell. OCNZ
Orara. Henry Kendall. CBAP; PoAu-1
Oration, Entitled "Old, Old, Old, Old Andrew Jackson," An, *abr.* Vachel Lindsay. YaD
Oration on the Toes. Edward Brynes. AMV-81
Orator. Emerson. *Fr.* Quatrains. OxBA
Orator, The. Roy McFadden. OnYI
Orator dismal of Nottinghamshire, An. An Excellent New Song, Being the Intended Speech of a Famous Orator against Peace. Swift. APAS
Orator Prigg. Blake. OBSV
Oratorical Crab, The. Oliver Herford. TDH
Orators, The, *sel.* W. H. Auden.
O Where Are You Going? CMoP; LiTB; MoVE; NOBE; SoSe
(Song: " 'O Where Are You Going?' said reader to rider.") OAEL-2

Orb Weaver, The. Robert Francis. PPON
Orbed Maiden. Shelley. *Fr.* The Cloud. MOON
Orbiter 5 Shows How Earth Looks from the Moon. May Swenson. SUW
Orchard. Hilda Doolittle ("H. D."). CMoP; LiTA; LiTM; MoAmPo; OxBA
Orchard, The. Gretel Ehrlich. MAYP
Orchard, The. Michael Spence. AMV-80
Orchard. Ruth Stone. PH; TwAmPo
Orchard and the Heath, The. George Meredith. OBNC
Orchard at Avignon, An. Agnes Mary Frances Robinson. HBV-1
Orchard by the Shore, The; a Pastoral. Elinor Sweetman. OBVV
Orchard-Pit, The. Dante Gabriel Rossetti. EnLoPo; NBM; NCEP; OAEL-2; PoEL-5; SCV; SyP; VLP
Orchard Snow. J. B. Goodenough. AMV-81
"Orchards," said Johnny Appleseed. Johnny Appleseed. Arthur S. Bourinot. CaP
Orchards, we linger here because. For a Second Marriage [*or* Upon a Second Marriage]. James Merrill. NePoEA; NoP
Orchestra. Reg Saner. AMV-80
Orchestra, The. William Carlos Williams. HAP
Orchestra of the dark tangled field, The. The Transparence of November. Roo Borson. PPJ
Orchestra; or, A Poem[e] of Da[u]ncing. Sir John Davies. OBSC; SiPS
Sels.
Dance of Love, The. EIL; SeCePo
Dancing Sea, The. ChTr
(Sea Danceth, The.) EtS
"Dauncing (bright Lady) then began to bee." FaBoEn; PoEL-2
(Praise of Dancing, The.) NOBE
Dedications, I: To His Very Friend, Master Richard Martin. SiPS
Dedications, II: To the Prince. SiPS
"Or from what spring doth your opinion rise." UnS
"Yet, once again, Antinous did reply." LO
Orchids. Judith Minty. GeTw
Orchids. Theodore Roethke. CMoP; NMP; PPoe
Orchids. Theodore Wratislaw. VLP
Ordained I was a beggar. The File-Hewer's Lamentation. Joseph Mather. NOEC
Ordeal. Nina Cassian, *tr. fr. Rumanian by* Michael Impey *and* Brian Swann. PBWP
Ordeal by Fire, The, *sel.* Edmund Clarence Stedman.
"Thou, who dost feel Life's vessel strand." WGRP
Order and Degree. Shakespeare. *Fr.* Troilus and Cressida, I, iii. NIP
("Heavens themselves, the planets and this center, The.") ImOP; PAI
Order for a Picture, An. Alice Cary. BLPA
Order goes, The; what if we rush ahead. Next Time. Laura Simmons. PGD
Order is a lovely thing. The Monk in the Kitchen. Anna Hempstead Branch. MoAmPo
Ordered to strip prior to execution. Murder of a Community. Daniel Weissbort. VWA
Orders. A. M. Klein. WHW
Ordinance on Winning. Naomi Lazard. GP
Ordinarily I call it "my cock," but. My Penis. Ed Ochester. GP
Ordinary, The, *sel.* William Cartwright.
House Blessing, A, *fr.* III, i. ChTr
(Saint Francis and Saint Benedight.) EaLo
Ordinary Day beyond Kaitaia, An. Kendrick Smithyman. OCNZ
Ordinary Dog, The. Nancy Byrd Turner. TiPo
Ordinary Evening in Cleveland, An. Lewis Turco. NYBP
Ordinary people are peculiar too. Conversation. Louis MacNeice. TEP
Ordinary People in the Last Days. Jay Macpherson. PAI
Ordinary valour only works, The. "F. Anstey." CenHV
Ordinary Women I ("I am the woman you see in Bloomingdale's"). Marilyn Hacker. LTB
Ordinary Women II ("Mrs. Velez of the Tenants' Association"). Marilyn Hacker. LTB
Ordinary Women, The. Wallace Stevens. OxBA
Ordination. Sister Mary Immaculate. GoBC
Ore is waiting in the tubs, the snow's upon the fells, The. Fourpence a Day. *Unknown.* FSW; OBET
O're the smooth enameld green. *See* O'er the smooth enameled green.
Oread. Hilda Doolittle ("H. D."). AP; AWP; CMoP; GoJo; MoAmPo; MoVE; NoAM; NOBA; OxBA; SBG; TAP
Oreads. Kathleen Raine. PoSH
Oregon Message, An. William Stafford. CoAP; MOON
Oregon Trail, The. Arthur Guiterman. BPAW; FaPON
Oregon Trail, The. *Unknown.* BPAW
Oregon Trail: 1851. James Marshall. BPAW
Oregon Winter. Jeanne McGahey. AmFN
O'Reilly's Reply. Richard Weber. NMP
Orestes Pursued. Charles David Webb. NePoAm-2
Organ Cactus, The. Dorothy Scarborough. BPAW
Organ Grinders' Garden, The. Mildred Plew Merryman. SoPo
Organ Solo. Knute Skinner. GP
Organ Transplant. J. D. Reed. POL
Organist, The. George W. Stevens. BLPA
Organist in Heaven, The. Thomas Edward Brown. OBVV
(Wesley in Heaven.) OBNC
Orgasm completely, The. Sonnet. Tom Clark. CoAP
Orgy. Norman MacCaig. OxBC
Orgy (That Is, Vegetable Market, at Sarno). Gina Labriola, *tr. fr. Italian by* Edgar Pauk. WPOW
Orient Express, The. Randall Jarrell. AP; CMoP; CoAP; CoBMV; NOBA
Orient Wheat. Adrienne Rich. NePoEA
Oriental Apologue, An. James Russell Lowell. PoEL-5
Orientale. W. E. Henley. PeD
Oriflamme. Jessie Redmond Fauset. BANP; BlSi; PoBA
Origin, far side of a lake, The. The Alchemist. Robert Kelly. CoPo
Origin of Baseball, The. Kenneth Patchen. LiSp
Origin of Centaurs, The. Anthony Hecht. NePoEA
Origin of Cities, The. Robert Hass. NPGG
Origin of Didactic Poetry, The. James Russell Lowell. PoEL-5
Origin of Dreams. Marvin Bell. LCAP
Origin of Species, The. Myra Sklarew. SUW
Origin of the Praise of God, The. Robert Bly. NU
Original./ Ragged-round. Malcolm X. Gwendolyn Brooks. BALP; CNA; OFD; PoBA; TTY
Original Child Bomb, *sel.* Thomas Merton.
In the Year 1945 an Original Child Was Born. NAs
Original Cuss, An. Keith Preston. WhC
Original Epitaph on a Drunkard. Royall Tyler. OBAL
Original family rock is three parts restored, The. Anniversary. Daniel Weissbort. VWA
Original Lamb, The. *Unknown.* InMe
Original man lies down to be copied, The. Xerox. Ben Belitt. NYP
Original Sin. Robinson Jeffers. MoAB; MoAmPo; MoVE
Original Sin. Alexander Laing. NYBP
Original Sin: A Short Story. Robert Penn Warren. CrMA; HoPM; LiTA; LiTM; MoVE; NOCV; PPP; TAP
Original Strawberry. Nancy Willard. LCAP
Origins. Joy Harjo. TWSS
Origins. Keorapetse Kgositsile. PoBA
Origins and History of Consciousness. Adrienne Rich. NIP
Origins of Escape, The. Charles P. R. Tisdale. AMV-81
Oriki Erinle. *Unknown, tr. fr. Yoruba by* Ulli Beier. PBA; TTY
Orinda to Lucasia. Katherine Philips. PeHV
("Observe the weary birds ere night be done.") LO
Orinda to Lucasia Parting, October, 1661, at London. Katherine Philips. OBS
Oriole with joy was sweetly singing, The. In the Shade of the Old Apple Tree. Harry H. Williams. FSN; TreFT
Orion, *sels.* Richard Henry Horne.
"Man who for his race might supersede, The." VLP
"There was a slumbrous silence in the air." VLP
Orion. Adrienne Rich. NIP; NoAM; NoP; WPE
Orion Seeks the Goddess Diana. Sacheverell Sitwell. *Fr.* Landscape with the Giant Orion. MoVE
Orisha. Jayne Cortez. BlSi
Orishas. Larry Neal. NBP
Orkney Interior. Ian Hamilton Finlay. NMP
Orlando Commercial, The. George MacBeth. NOBL
Orlando Furioso, *sels.* Ariosto, *tr. fr. Italian by* Sir John Harington.
"Alcyna met them at the outer gate," *fr.* VII. OBVE
Angelica and the Ork, *fr.* X. OBSC
"Blessed angell not a word replies, The, " *fr.* XIV. OBVE
"Go soule, go sweetest soule for ever blest," *fr.* XXIX. OBVE
Orlando's Rhymes. Shakespeare. *Fr.* As You Like It, III, ii. OBSC
Orlo's Valediction. Jon Manchip White. NePoEA
Ormerod was deeply troubled. Distractions and the Human Crowd. Stevie Smith. OxBC
Ornamental Water. Louise Townsend Nicholl. NePoAm
Ornaments. Frank Ormsby. CIP
Ornithology in Florida. Arthur Guiterman. BoAnP; InMe
Oro Stage, The. Henry Herbert Knibbs. BPAW
Oro, the islandmen. The Waistcoat. Padraic Fallon. OxBI
Orotava Road, The. Basil Bunting. NoAM
O'Rourke's Feast. Hugh MacGowran, *tr. fr. Irish by* Charles Wilson. BIrV
(Description of an Irish Feast, The, *tr. by* Swift.) OBVE; OnYI
Orphan, The. *Unknown, tr. fr. Chinese by* Arthur Waley. PoA
Orphan, The. *Unknown, tr. fr. Irish by* Frank O'Connor. KiLC
Orphan, The; or, The Unhappy Marriage, *sel.* Thomas Otway.
Come, All Ye Youths. OAEP

Orphan beat of my heart, The. "Ping Hsin," *tr. fr. Chinese by* Kenneth Rexroth *and* Ling Chung. BoWoP
Orphan Born. Robert Jones Burdette. OBAL
Orphan Boy, The. *Unknown.* OBET
Orphan Boy, Fishing. Albert Goldbarth. WOLT
Orphan Boy's Tale, The. Amelia Opie. PaPo
Orphan Girl, The. *Unknown.* AmFP; AS, *with music*
"Orphan Hours, the Year is dead." Dirge for the Year. Shelley. GN; HBV-1; HBVY
Orphan, yes, An. But not. Fragment Reflection I. Doris Turner. JB
Orphaned/ I am your child. Strings/Himo. Yuri Kageyama. BrSi
Orphans. David Ray. FiCP
Orphan's Song, The. Sydney Dobell. CH; ELP; OBNC
Orpheus. Donald Davie. TEP
Orpheus. *At. to* John Fletcher *See* Orpheus with His Lute.
Orpheus. J. F. Hendry. NeBP
Orpheus. Robert Herrick. CaPo
Orpheus. Elizabeth Madox Roberts. MoAmPo
Orpheus. Yvor Winters. MoVE; NOBA; VGW
Orpheus and Eurydice. Robert Browning. CTC
Orpheus and Eurydice. Geoffrey Hill. NePoEA-2
Orpheus and Eurydice. Jean Valentine. LCAP
Orpheus he went (as poets tell). Orpheus. Robert Herrick. CaPo
Orpheus I am, come from the deeps below. John Fletcher. *Fr.* The Mad Lover, IV, i. GBL
Orpheus in Greenwich Village. Jack Gilbert. NPGG; POL; PP
Orpheus in the Underworld. David Gascoyne. FaBoTw
Orpheus to Beasts. Richard Lovelace. CaPo
Orpheus to Eurydice. Frederick Morgan. AMV-80
Orpheus to Woods. Richard Lovelace. CaPo
Orpheus with His Lute [Made Trees]. *At. to* John Fletcher, *also to* Shakespeare. King Henry VIII, *fr.* III, i. ChTr; EnRePo; GN; OAEP; OBS; TrGrPo; ViBoPo
(Music.) FaBoCh
(Orpheus.) EIL; OBEV; UnS
(Song.) PoEL-2
(Sweet Music's Power.) NOBE
Orthodox, Orthodox, wha believe in John Knox. The Kirk's Alarm. Burns. OxBoLi
Orthodoxy's staunch adherent. To Dr. Kipling. Richard Porson. FaBoCo
Ortho's Epitaph. Theocritus, *tr. fr. Greek by* Charles Stuart Calverley. FaBoEE
Ortiz. Hezekiah Butterworth. PAH
Ortus. Ezra Pound. LiTA; NePA
O'Ryan was a man of might. Irish Astronomy. Charles Graham Halpine. HBV-2
O's Operatic Olivia. Operatic Olivia. Isabel Frances Bellows. TDH
Osawatomie. Carl Sandburg. *See* Ossawatomie.
Osculation. Henry Sydnor Harrison. InMe
Oshun, the River Goddess. *Yoruba Oral Tradition, tr. by* Ulli Beier. WTO
Osip Mandelshtam. Irving Layton. NeAC
Osprey sails about the sound, The. The Fisherman's Hymn. Alexander Wilson. AA; EtS
Osprey Suicides, The. Laurence Lieberman. HoAn
Ossawatomie. Carl Sandburg. OxBA
(Osawatomie.) CMoP
Ossian's Serenade. Calder Campbell. BLPA
(Burman Lover, The.) TrAS, *with music*
Ossified Oyster, An. Carolyn Wells. TDH
Ostia Antica. Anthony Hecht. NePA
'Ostler Joe. George R. Sims. BeLS; BLPA; HBV-2; TreF
Ostracized as we are with God. Apology of Genius. Mina Loy. QFR
Ostrich is a silly bird, The. Mary E. Wilkins Freeman. FaPON; OBCA; SoPo; TiPo
Ostrich who lived at the zoo, An. The Bored Ostrich. *Unknown.* TDH
Ostriches and Grandmothers! Amiri Baraka. NeAP
Oterborne. *Unknown. See* Battle of Otterburn, The.
Othello, *sels.* Shakespeare.
"Behold, I have a weapon," *fr.* V, ii. BiP
Death of Othello, *fr.* V, ii. FiP
(Othello's Farewell.) TreFS
Desdemona's Song, *fr.* IV, iii. LoBV
Good Name, A, *fr.* III, iii. FaFP; TreFS
It Is the Cause, It Is the Cause, My Soul, *fr.* V, ii. BiP; EBEV; PAI
(Othello and Desdemona.) FiP
Not Poppy, nor Mandragora, *fr.* III, iii. WHA
Othello's Defense, *fr.* I, iii. TreF
("Her father lov'd me; oft invited me.") EBEV; SCV
Othello's Farewell to His Career, *fr.* III, iii. TreFT
(Farewell Content.) TrGrPo
"Perdition catch my soul," *br. sel. fr.* III, iii. LO
" 'Tis not a year or two shows us a man," *fr.* III, iv. DBV
Othello Jones Dresses for Dinner. Ed Roberson. PoBA; PoNe
Othello's Farewell to His Career. Shakespeare. *Fr.* Othello, III, iii. TreFT
(Farewell Content.) TrGrPo
Other, An ("The purest soule that e're was sent"). Thomas Carew. *See* Another [Epitaph on the Lady Mary Villiers].
Other, An ("This little vault, this narrow roome"). Thomas Carew. Epitaph on the Lady Mary Villiers, An.
Other, The. Peter Cooley. AMV-80; MAYP
Other, The. Ruth Fainlight. BrRo
Other. Lance Henson. VoR
Other bright days of action have seemed great. John Masefield. *Fr.* Biography. OxBTC
Other day a partridge, The. The Talk of the Town. Ed Fisher. FiBHP
Other day I was loving a sweet little fruitpie-and-cream, The. Lines. Gavin Ewart. EAS
Other day, when I looked at a tree, The. Roots. Louis Ginsberg. TrJP
Other Fabrics, Other Mores! Anna Maria Lenngren, *tr. fr. Swedish by* Nadia Christensen *and* Mariann Tiblin. PBWP
Other Fellow's Job, The. Strickland Gillilan. WBLP
Other Journey, The. Katherine Garrison Chapin. MoVE
Other Lives. Patricia Hooper. AMV-81; HoAn
Other loves I have known. Proof. Bessie Calhoun Bird. BlSi
Other men are thorn. Mahadevi, *tr. fr. Kannada by* A. K. Ramanujan. BoWoP
Other night while I was sparking sweet Terlina Spray, The. Kiss Me Quick and Go. Silas S. Steele. BLSo
Other One, The. Harry Thurston Peck. AA
Other Person's Place, The. Donald H. Hover. STF
Other props are gone, The. Je T'Adore. Thomas Kinsella. NoAM
Other Sheep I Have, Which Are Not of This Fold. Bryant. TrPWD
Other Side, The. Roy Fuller. OxBC
Other Side, The. Thomas Reiter. AMV-80
Other Side of a Mirror, The. Mary Elizabeth Coleridge. BoWoP
Other Side of Jordan, The. *Unknown.* FSW
Other Side of This World, The. Calvin Forbes. MAYP
Other states were carved or born. Cattle. Berta Hart Nance. BPAW
Other Women's Children. Mary Nelson Waniek. AMV-80
Other World, The. Harriet Beecher Stowe. AA; HBV-2; WGRP
Other World, The. *Unknown, tr. fr. Egyptian by* Robert Hillyer. *Fr.* Book of the Dead. AWP
Others. Harry Behn. SoPo; TiPo
Others. Charles D. Meigs. WBLP
Others, The. "Seumas O'Sullivan." AnIV; HBMV; OxBI
Others. *Unknown.* STF
Others abide our question. Thou art free. Shakespeare. Matthew Arnold. BiP; CABA; FiP; HBV-2; InvP; NoP; OAEP; OBEV; OBVV; TrGrPo; ViBoPo; WHA
Others are tunneled in sleep, The. Night Flight. Don Johnson. AMV-81
Others because you did not keep. A Deep-sworn Vow. W. B. Yeats. CMoP; ELU; OAEL-2; PCP; UnPo
Others have seen men die. On Knowing Nothing. A. J. M. Smith. PeCV
Others Hunters in the North the Cree, The. Jerome Rothenberg. PoM
Others, I Am Not the First. A. E. Housman. A Shropshire Lad, XXX. CMoP; LiTB; MoBrPo; OxBTC; PPP
Others made danceroom for us, she was so fine. Some Semblance of Order. Charles David Wright. FAZ
Others make verses of grace. Ardor. Gamaliel Bradford. HBMV
Others, many others, must have known. Leaving Buffalo. Charles Martin. PoA
Others May Praise What They Like. Walt Whitman. Par
Others stand in their imported, The. Giving Up Butterflies. Geraldine Kudaka. BrSi
Others taunt me with having knelt at well-curbs. For Once, Then, Something. Robert Frost. AP; NoAM; NOBA
Others weary of the noise. Mothers—and Others. Amos R. Wells. WBLP
Others would think I was walking somewhere. Friday Evening. Julio Marzán. InW
Otherwise. Aileen Fisher. SoPo; SUS
Otoe County in Nebraska. William Kloefkorn. GP
Ottava Rima would, I know, be proper. W. H. Auden. *Fr.* Letter to Lord Byron. NOBL
Otter, The. Seamus Heaney. IPY
Otter, An. Ted Hughes. CMoP; NePoEA-2; NMP; NoAM
Otter is known, The. Lutra, the Fisher. James McMichael. AmPA
Otters. William Hart-Smith. BoAnP
Otto. Gwendolyn Brooks. PChr; PDV
Otto. Theodore Roethke. DiL
O'Tuomy's Drinking Song. John O'Tuomy, *tr. fr. Modern Irish by* John O'Daly, *vers. by* James Clarence Mangan. OnYI
Otys, begin. Sea Eclogue. William Diaper. Nereides; or Sea-Eclogues, X. LoBV
Ou Phrontis. Charles Causley. NePoEA

Ouch! *Unknown.* TDH
"O-U-G-H-"; or, The Cross Farmer. D. S. Martin. TDH
Oui, oui Monsieur, Timagami. Pierre of Timagami in New York. Wilson MacDonald. WhC
Oul' Gray Mare, The. *Unknown.* AnIV
Ould Orange Flute, The. *Unknown. See* Old Orange Flute, The.
Ould Plaid Shawl, The. Francis A. Fahy. HBV-1
Ounce of Detention, The. Oliver Herford. TDH
Ouphe and goblin! imp and sprite! Elfin Song. Joseph Rodman Drake. *Fr.* The Culprit Fay. AA
Our age bereft of nobility. A Poem for Painters. John Wieners. NeAP; PoM
Our ambassador to Venus, Mz Abner. Limerick. *Unknown.* PeHV
Our anchors drag and our cables surge. The Cheer of the *Trenton.* Walter Mitchell. EtS
Our Andy's gone with cattle now. Andy's Gone with Cattle. Henry Lawson. PoAu-1
Our Angels. Howard Schwartz. VWA
Our Annual Return to the Lake. Robert D. Hoeft. AMV-81
Our author by experience finds it true. Prologue. Dryden. *Fr.* Aureng-Zebe. FiP; OBS; OxBoLi; PP; SeCEV; SeCV-2
Our Backs Are to the Cypress. Leah Goldberg, *tr. fr. Hebrew by* Ramah Commanday. BoWoP
Our backyards touched somewhere upon the hill. Neighbors. Marilyn Francis. GoYe
Our Ball. Winthrop Mackworth Praed. *Fr.* Letters from Teignmouth. EnRP
Our balloon man has balloons. The Balloon Man. Dorothy Aldis. TiPo
Our band is few, but true and tried. Song of Marion's Men. Bryant. HBV-2; HBVY; PAH; TreF
Our bark was [out] far, far from [the] land. The Sailor's Grave. *Unknown, at. to* Eliza Cook. BLPA; ShS
Our Barrio. Alurista, *tr. fr. Spanish by* Toni Empringham. FIA
Our beauty is to us that which to men. Giovanni Battista Guarini, *tr. by* Sir Richard Fanshawe. *Fr.* Il Pastor Fido. OBVE
Our Bias. W. H. Auden. NoAM; NoP
Our birth is but a sleep and a forgetting. Wordsworth. *Fr.* Ode: Intimations of Immortality from Recollections of Early Childhood. ChTr; EaLo; FaBoEn; FaBV; ILwL; TRV; WGRP
Our Birthday. Marion Edey. SiSoSe
Our Blackness Did Not Come to Us Whole. Linda Brown Bragg. CNA
Our Blood and State. James Shirley *See* Glories of Our Blood and State, The.
Our Bodies. Denise Levertov. NaP; PPP
Our bodies were sunlit spattered. The Serpent of God. Cerise Farallon. UnTE
Our Bog is Dood. Stevie Smith. FaBoNo; WeW
Our Bondage It Shall End, *with music. At. to* Peter Cartwright. AH
Our Bonny-boots Could Toot It, Yea and Foot It. *Unknown.* NCEP
Our boots and clothes are all in pawn. Blood Red Roses. *Unknown.* FSW
Our brains ache, in the merciless iced east winds that knive us. Exposure. Wilfred Owen. FaBoMo; InPS; MMA; MoVE; NoAM; OBWP; WaP
Our brother Clarence goes to school. Big Brother. Elizabeth Madox Roberts. FaPON
Our brows are wreathed with spindrift and the weed is on our knees. The Coastwise Lights. Kipling. EtS
Our bugles sang truce, for the night-cloud had lowered [*or* lower'd]. The Soldier's Dream. Thomas Campbell. BeLS; EnRP; FaPoR; GTBS; GTBS-P; HBV-2; RoGo; TreFS
Our Burden Bearer. Phillips Brooks. TRV
(Unfailing One, The.) BLRP
Our camp-fires shone bright on the mountains. Sherman's March to the Sea [*or* Song of . . .]. Samuel H. M. Byers. HBV-2; PAH
Our candles, lit, re-lit, have gone down now. Twelfth Night. Peter Scupham. OBCP
Our Canoe Idles in the Idling Current. Kenneth Rexroth. ErPo
Our Captain Cried All Hands. *Unknown.* OBET
Our captain stood upon the deck, a spyglass in his hand. Captain Bunker. *Unknown.* AmFP
Our car was fierce enough. The Trip. William Stafford. PCP
Our caves do not go Boom! and make one nervy. Sterkfontein. Ruth Miller. PeSA
Our chairs drawn to one end of the living/ room. Aunt Gladys's Home Movie No. 31, Albert's Funeral. Jim Wayne Miller. Str
Our cherished dualism gone? Journal to Stella. Morton Dauwen Zabel. PoA
Our Childhood Spilled into Our Hearts. David Vogel, *tr. fr. Hebrew by* A. C. Jacobs. VWA
Our children have eaten supper. Brian Coffey. *Fr.* Missouri Sequence. CIP
Our Children's Children Will Marvel. Ilya Ehrenburg, *tr. fr. Russian by* Jeannette Eyre. WaaP
Our Christ. Harry Webb Farrington *See* I Know Not How That Bethlehem's Babe.
Our church had no theology. Woods Gets Religion. John Woods. GP
Our city's sons and daughters. School Days in New Amsterdam. Arthur Guiterman. FaPON
Our "Civilization." John Morgan. LTB
Our Clock. Florence Eakman. SiSoSe
Our collective wastebin. In the Outhouse. Mitsuye Yamada. *Fr.* Camp Notes. WPOW
Our Companie in the Next World. John Donne. *Fr.* Of the Progresse of the Soul; the Second Anniversarie. OBS
"Our couch shall be roses all spangled with dew." A Sensible Girl's Reply to Moore's. Walter Savage Landor. FaBoEE
Our Country. Julia Ward Howe. PAH; PAL
Our Country. Henry David Thoreau. GOA
Our country hath a gospel of her own. America's Gospel. James Russell Lowell. PGD
Our Country Is Divided. Faarah Nuur, *tr. fr. Somali by* B. W. Andrzejewski *and* I. M. Lewis. WTO
Our Country's Call. Bryant. PAH
Our Country's Emblem. *Unknown.* WBLP
Our darkness stays, the only dark we know. Degrees of Shade. H. A. Pinkerton. NePoAm
Our daughter, Alicia. Hot Line. Louella Dunann. QQQ; RHPC
Our day was composed of resemblances, take. Sail Away. Robert Adamson. CBAP
Our days, alas! our mortal days. The Shortness and Misery of Life. Isaac Watts. NOCV
Our Dead. Robert Nichols. WGRP
Our doctor had called in another, I never had seen him before. In the Children's Hospital. Tennyson. HBV-1
Our dog Fred. The Diners in the Kitchen. James Whitcomb Riley. GDP; OBAL
Our doom is in our being. We began. James Agee. Sonnets, II. MoAmPo
Our earth in 1969. Doggerel by a Senior Citizen. W. H. Auden. NOBL
Our Earth Mother. *Tr. fr. Zuni Indian by* R. Bunzel. WTO
Our earthly homes are simple things. Home. Martha Snell Nicholson. STF
Our English gamesters scorne to stake. Roger Williams. SCAP
Our epoch takes a voluptuous satisfaction. Hypocrite Auteur. Archibald MacLeish. AmPP; MoVE; NePA
Our eyeless bark sails free. The Earth. Emerson. AA
Our eyes are holden that we do not see. Faith and Sight. Anna M. King. BLRP
Our eyes have viewed the burnished vineyards where. Letter to a Friend. Robert Penn Warren. MoAmPo
"Our Fadder, Which are in Heaben!" He Paid Me Seven. *Unknown.* BPo
Our fairest garland, made of Beauty's flowers. Contention between Four Maids Concerning That Which Addeth Most Perfection to That Sex. Sir John Davies. SiPS
Our families in Thine arms enfold. In Thine Arms. Oliver Wendell Holmes. TRV
Our famous Harvey hath made good. The Circulation. Thomas Washbourne. NOCV
Our Father, by Whose Name, *with music.* F. Bland Tucker. AH
Our Father, God, *with music.* Adoniram Judson. AH
Our Father, grant us to lie down in peace. Evening Prayer. *Unknown, tr. by* Solomon Solis-Cohen. TrJP
Our Father in Heaven, *with music.* Sarah Josepha Hale. AH
Our Father Land! and wouldst thou know. Father Land and Mother Tongue. Samuel Lover. HBV-2
Our father our all-wielding is. The "Pater Noster." *Unknown.* ACP
Our Father, Our King. *Unknown.* TrJP
Our Father which [*or* who] art in heaven. The Lord's Prayer. Bible, *N.T. Fr.* St. Matthew. EaLo; PoLF; TrGrPo; TRV
Our Father! While Our Hearts Unlearn, *with music.* Oliver Wendell Holmes. AH
Our Father, who art in heaven. *See* Our Father which . . .
Our Father, whose creative Will. W. H. Auden. *Fr.* For the Time Being. ILwL; TrPWD
Our father works in us. A Father of Women. Alice Meynell. BrRo; SBG; WPE
Our Fathers. Bible, *Apocypha. See* Let Us Now Praise Famous Men.
Our fathers all were poor. The Fathers. Edwin Muir. OxBS
Our fathers came to search for gold. Australia's on the Wallaby. *Unknown.* PoAu-1
Our Fathers Fought for Liberty. James Russell Lowell. PAL
Our Fathers' God, *with music.* Benjamin Copeland. AH
Our fathers' God! from out whose hand. Centennial Hymn. Whittier. AA; PAH; PAL
Our Father's Hand. Annie Johnson Flint. BLRP

Our fathers in their books and speech. Orient Wheat. Adrienne Rich. NePoEA
Our fathers to creed and tradition were tied. Commercial Candour. G. K. Chesterton. WhC
Our fathers to their graves have gone. The Moral Warfare. Whittier. TreFT
Our fathers took oaths as of old they took wives. Thomas Brown. FaBoEE
Our fathers were fellows of substance and weight. Commissary Report. Stoddard King. ShM
Our fathers, who were wondrous wise. *Unknown.* FaBoUs
Our fathers wrung their bread from stocks and stones. Children of Light. Robert Lowell. AP; CMoP; MoAB; OxBA; PoPl
Our feet have wandered from thy path. Wanderers. Thomas Curtis Clark. TrPWD
Our first ancestor (Abram) alone received his religion from Heaven. Therefore We Preserve Life. Shen Ch'üan, *tr. by* William C. White. TrJP
Our First Century. George Edward Woodberry. PAH
Our Flag. Frances Crosby Hamlet. PGD
Our Flag Forever. Frank L. Stanton. PGD
Our Flag Was Still There. Richard Tillinghast. MAYP
Our flesh was a battle-ground. The Litany of the Dark People. Countee Cullen. EaLo; TrPWD
Our forefather once wished a wife. How Our Forefather Got His Wife. Eda Lou Walton. BPAW
Our forty-gun frigate from Baltimore came. Paul Jones. *Unknown.* BaBo
Our friends go with us as we go. Non Dolet. Oliver St. John Gogarty. OBMV; OnYI; OxBI
Our friendship, Robert, firm through twenty years. A Letter to Robert Frost. Robert Hillyer. MoAmPo
Our God and Father surely knows. The Father Knows. "F. L. H." BLRP
Our God and God of our fathers. Prayer for Dew. Eleazar ben Kalir, *tr. by* Israel Zangwill. TrJP
Our God and soldiers we alike adore. Francis Quarles. FaBoEE
Our God, Our Help in Ages Past. Isaac Watts. *See* O God, Our Help in Ages Past.
Our golden age was then, when lamp and rug. Family Prime. Mark Van Doren. VGW
Our good King Charles within his youthful prime. The Royal Love Scene. Voltaire. UnTE
Our Goodman. *Unknown.* AmFP; BaBo; ESPB (A *and* B *vers.*); UnTE; ViBoFo (A *and* B *vers.*)
(Four Nights Drunk, *diff. vers.*) FSW; OBAL
(Three Nights Drunk.) OuSiCo, *with music*
Our Ground Time Here Will Be Brief. Maxine W. Kumin. AMV-81
Our guttural muse. Traditions. Seamus Heaney. FaBoMo
Our Hands in the Garden. Anne Hébert, *tr. fr. French by* A. Poulin, Jr. BoWoP
Our haughty life is crowned with darkness. London, from Hampstead Heath. Wordsworth. *Fr.* Extempore Effusion upon the Death of James Hogg. FaBoPP
Our hearths are gone out, and our hearts are broken. The Raven Days. Sidney Lanier. NePA; OxBA
Our Heavenly Father, *sel.* Frederick William Faber.
"My God! how wonderful Thou art." GoBC; TrPWD
Our Help ("Our help is in the name of the Lord"). Bible, *O.T.* Psalms, CXXIV: 8. TRV
Our Heritage. Joseph Mary Plunkett. *See* This Heritage to the Race of Kings.
Our Heritage. Jesse Stuart. AmFN
Our Heroes. Phoebe Cary. BLPA
Our Hired Girl. James Whitcomb Riley. HBV-1; HBVY
Our Hired Man (and His Daughter, Too). Monica Shannon. FaPON
Our hired man is the kindest man. The Hired Man's Way. John Kendrick Bangs. OBCA
Our History. Catherine Cate Coblentz. FaPON
Our history is grave noble and tragic. Men. Archibald MacLeish. AmFN; MoAB; YaD
Our history sings of centuries. Our History. Catherine Cate Coblentz. FaPON
Our homes are eaten out by time. The Town Betrayed. Edwin Muir. CMoP
Our horse fell down the well around behind the stable. Good-By Liza Jane. *Unknown.* AS
Our Hoste sey wel that the brighte sonne. Introduction to the Man of Law's Prologue. Chaucer. *Fr.* The Canterbury Tales. FiP
Our House. Dorothy Brown Thompson. RHPC
Our house had wings for children, chandeliers. The Exile. Larry Rubin. GoYe
Our house is small. Our House. Dorothy Brown Thompson. RHPC
Our Hunting Fathers. W. H. Auden. FaBoMo; NoAM
Our images withdraw, the rose returns. Beyond Possession. Elizabeth Jennings. NePoEA
Our indolence was despair. We were still at times struck. An Interlude. John Peale Bishop. LiTA
Our Insufficiency to Praise God Suitably for His Mercy. Edward Taylor. LiTA
Our Islet out of Helgoland, dismissed. Islet the Dachs. George Meredith. FM
Our Jack's Come Home Today, *with music. Unknown.* ShS
Our journey had advanced. Emily Dickinson. ILwL; LiTA; LiTM; MoAB; NOCV; PoEL-5; QFR
Our Joyful Feast. George Wither. *See* Christmas Carol, A: "So now is come our joyful'st feast."
Our keels are furred with tropic weed that clogs the crawling tides. The Captive Ships at Manila. Dorothy Paul. PAH
Our Kind. William Stafford. AMV-81
Our Kind Creator, *with music.* Solomon Howe. AH
Our king has wrote a lang letter. Lord Derwentwater. *Unknown.* BaBo; ESPB
Our king he has a secret to tell. The Bonny Lass of Anglesey. *Unknown.* ESPB
Our king he kept a false steward. Sir Aldingar. *Unknown.* ESPB; OxBB
Our king lay at Westminster. Hugh Spencer's Feats in France. *Unknown.* ESPB
Our[e] king[e] went forth to Normandy. *Unknown.* The Agincourt Carol [*or* A Carol of Agincourt]. MeEL; OAEL-1; OBET; OxBM
Our King went up upon a hill high. Henry before Agincourt: October 25, 1415. John Lydgate. CH
Our Lady. Robert Bridges. ISi
Our Lady. Mary Elizabeth Coleridge. OBEV; OBMV; OBVV; WPE
Our Lady, Help of Christians. Paul Claudel, *tr. fr. French by* Sister Mary David. ISi
Our Lady in the Middle Ages. Frederick William Faber. ACP; ISi
Our Lady is my fear. Family Portrait. Leonard Feeney. ISi
Our Lady of France. Lionel Johnson. ISi
Our Lady of Good Voyage. Lucy A. K. Adee. ISi
Our Lady of Mercy. Sister Mary Bertrand. ISi
Our Lady of the Libraries. Sister Mary Ignatius. ISi
Our Lady of the May. Lionel Johnson. ISi
Our Lady of the Passion. John Mauropus, *tr. fr. Greek by* Elizabeth Barrett Browning. ISi
Our Lady of the Refugees. Sister Mary Maura. ISi
"Our Lady of the Rocks." Dante Gabriel Rossetti *See* For "Our Lady of the Rocks" . . .
Our Lady of the Sea. Alfred Noyes. OBVV
Our Lady of the Skies. James M. Hayes. ISi
Our Lady of the Waves. George Mackay Brown. NePoEA-2
Our Lady on Calvary. Sister Michael Marie. ISi
Our Lady Peace. Mark Van Doren. WaP
Our Lady walks the parapets of heaven. Our Lady of Mercy. Sister Mary Bertrand. ISi
Our Lady went forth pondering. The Annunciation. *Unknown.* ISi
Our Lady went into a strange country. Regina Angelorum. G. K. Chesterton. ISi
Our Lady with Two Angels. Wilfred Rowland Childe. ISi
Our Lady's Expectation, *sel.* Frederick William Faber.
Expectation, The. ACP
Our Lady's Labor. John Duffy. ISi
Our Lady's Lullaby. Richard Verstegan *See* Lullaby: "Upon my lap my sovereign sits."
Our Lady's Salutation. Robert Southwell. ISi
Our Lady's Song. *Unknown. See* Virgin's Song, The.
Our last bridge. Marina Tsvetayeva, *tr. by* Paul Schmidt. *Fr.* The Daughter of Jairus. BoWoP
Our last free summer we mooned about at odd hours. Chrysalides. Thomas Kinsella. BIrV; NoAM
Our Last Toast. Bartholomew Dowling. *See* Revel, The.
"Our Left." Francis Orrery Ticknor. PAH
Our life is but a summer's day. *Unknown.* WhC
Our Life Is Hid with Christ in God. George Herbert. OAEL-1
Our life is like a forest, where the sun. Charles Sangster. Sonnets Written in the Orillia Woods, VII. NOBC
Our life is two-fold: Sleep hath its own world. The Dream. Byron. BeLS; ChER; TEP
"Our life together," she says. Widow. Felix Pollak. FAZ
Our Light Afflictions. *Unknown.* BLRP
Our Lips and Ears. *Unknown.* BLPA; TreF; WBLP
Our little bird in his full day of health. The Vacant Cage. Charles Tennyson Turner. FM
Our Little Calf. Dorothy Aldis. TiPo
Our little fleet in July first. The Armada, 1588. John Wilson. OxBChV
Our Little Ghost. Louisa May Alcott. OBCA

Our little kinsmen after rain. Emily Dickinson. FaPON; ImOP
Our little systems have their day. Tennyson. In Memoriam A. H. H., *fr.* Proem. TRV
Our little tantrum, flushed and misery-hollow. Rebeca in a Mirror. Judith Rodriguez. CBAP
Our Lives. Sharon Scott. JB
Our lives are sketched in the simplest lines. Cartoon. Jim Simmerman. AMV-81
Our lives are Swiss. Emily Dickinson. AP; NOBA; POL; TAP
Our lives float on quiet waters. Quiet Waters. Blanche Shoemaker Wagstaff. BLPA
Our Lombard country-girls along the coast. A Last Confession. Dante Gabriel Rossetti. NCEP
Our Lord and Our Lady. Hilaire Belloc. GoBC; HBMV; ISi
Our lords are to the mountains gane. Hughie Graham. *Unknown.* OxBB
Our Love Shall Be the Brightness. James Wreford Watson. CaP
Our love was conceived in silence and must live silently. At the Dark Hour. Paul Dehn. BoLoP; WaP
Our love was like most other loves. Winthrop Mackworth Praed. *Fr.* The Belle of the Ball-Room. ViBoPo
Our love was pure. Song of Snow-white Heads. Cho Wen-chün, *tr. by* Arthur Waley. BoWoP
Our low cabin above the river is lost. Staying up on Jack's Fork near Eminence, Missouri. Albert Salsich. AMV-80
Our Lucy (1956-1960). Paul Goodman. GDP
Our many years are made of clay and cloud. Destiny. Harrison Smith Morris. AA
Our March. Vladimir Mayakovsky, *tr. fr. Russian by* Babette Deutsch *and* Avrahm Yarmolinsky. AWP
Our Martyr-Chief. James Russell Lowell. OHIP
Our Master. Whittier. *See* Immortal Love, Forever Full.
Our masters of satire are vigorous gents. Wasted Ammunition. Stoddard King. InMe
Our millions rose in arms, one fateful day. Armistice Day Vow. Dorothy Gould. PGD
Our Mr. Toad. David McCord. TiPo
Our Modest Doughboys. Charlton Andrews. PAH
Our molting days are in their twilight stage. Far from Africa. Margaret Danner. NNP
Our Mother. George Cooper. *See* Only One Mother.
Our mother knew our worth. Our Kind. William Stafford. AMV-81
Our Mother, loved of all thy sons. Sea and Shore. Harry Lyman Koopman. AA
Our mother makes a pot of tea. Pot of Tea. Susan Griffin. NPGG
Our mother sits by the/ pool. Sitting. Susan Griffin. NPGG
Our mother tells us it is time to clean up. Tissue. Susan Griffin. NPGG
Our mother, the pride of us all. Mugford's Victory. John White Chadwick. PAH
Our Mother Tongue. Richard Monckton Milnes. GN
Our mother was the pussy-cat, our father was the owl. The Children of the Owl and the Pussy-Cat. Edward Lear. FaBoNo
Our mother, while she turned her wheel. Mother. Whittier. *Fr.* Snow-bound. AA; OHIP
Our Mother's Body Is the Earth. Mary McAnally. AMV-80
Our mother's kingdom does not fall. Stark County Holidays. Mary Oliver. Str
Our moulting days are in their twilight stage. Garnishing the Aviary. Margaret Danner. Far from Africa, I. AmNP; BPo; PoBA
Our mound of earth dug up. Epithalamion. Olga Broumas. LTB
Our names burn in the air. Fame. Vern Rutsala. GP
Our Nation Forever. Wallace Bruce. OHIP
Our National Banner. Dexter Smith. PAH
Our Nation's birth gave history your name. Washington. John A. Prentice. OHIP
Our nation's movies, foolish, false, erotic. Essay in Defense of the Movies. Walker Gibson. NePoAm
Our Needy Neighbours. William Langland. *Fr.* The Vision of Piers Plowman. OxBM
(Poor, The.) PoEL-1
Our neighbor's dog ate. The Man in the Ocelot Suit. Christopher Brookhouse. CAD
Our new clothes fool no one. Yom Kippur. Chana Bloch. VWA
Our news is seldom good: the heart. W. H. Auden. *Fr.* New Year Letter. FaBoRV
Our Norman betters. Lines: Inspired by the Controversy on the Value or Otherwise of Old English Studies. Anthony Burgess. FaBoCo
Our nuns come out to shop in the afternoon. Intercessors. Austin Clarke. CMoP; NMP
Our objections to the war. For the Minority. Robert Peterson. NeAC
Our old cat has kittens three. Choosing Their Names. Thomas Hood. PCat
Our old new house climbs a hill. Hush, Hush, New House in Charlotte. E. M. Schorb. AMV-81
Our Orders. Julia Ward Howe. AA
Our Own. Margaret E. Sangster. BLPA
Our passions are most like to floods and streams. The Silent Lover [*or* Sir Walter Ralegh to the Queen *or* To the Queen *or* To His Mistress]. Sir Walter Ralegh. AAS; EIL; OAEP; OBSC; SiPS. *See also* Passions are liken'd best to floods and streams.
Our pastures are bitten and bare. "Adam Drinan." *Fr.* Men of the Rocks. OxBS
Our paths began at distant points in space. Juncture. Rea Lubar Duncan. PoNe
Our People. Teresa Anderson. LTB
Our People. Diane Burns. STE; TWSS
Our perverse old *pisatel'* Vladimir. Something for My Russian Friends. Edmund Wilson. OBAL
Our Photographs. Frederick Locker-Lampson. DBV; NoBL
Our portion of fire. The Manichaeans. Gary Snyder. VGW
Our Prayer. George Herbert. PGD
Our Prayer of Thanks, *sel.* Carl Sandburg.
"For the gladness here where the sun is shining at evening." TRV
Our Presidents. *Unknown.* BLPA
Our private foliage has unscrolled. Early Fall: The Adirondacks. Carolyne Wright. AMV-81
Our quin's seek, an very seek. Queen Eleanor's Confession. *Unknown.* ESPB
Our Revels Now Are Ended. Shakespeare. *Fr.* The Tempest, IV, i. LiTB; WHA
(Prospero Ends the Revels.)TreF
(Stuff of Dreams, The.) FaBV
(Such Stuff as Dreams Are Made On.) TrGrPo
Our roads are ridden. For Sammy Younge. Charlie Cobb. PoBA
Our Rock. Francis Scott Key. STF
Our Rock with loving care. Grace after Meals. *Unknown, tr. by* Alice Lucas. TrJP
Our roofs are adjacent. *Turkish Love Songs, tr. by* Reza Baraheni *and* Zahra-Soltan Shokoohtaezeh. BoWoP
Our rural ancestors, with little blest. The Ideals of Satire. Pope. *Fr.* First Epistle of the Second Book of Horace. FiP
"Our saints are poets, Milton and Blake." Encounter. Denis Devlin. BIrV; OnYI
Our sardine fishermen work at night in the dark of the moon. The Purse-Seine. Robinson Jeffers. CMoP; HAP; NoAM; NOBA; NoP; OxBA; PrIm; WeW
Our Saviour/ (Paterne of true holinesse). Ensamples of Our Savior. Robert Southwell. PoEL-2
Our Saviour's Golden Rule. Isaac Watts. OxBChV
Our Saviour's Love. *Unknown.* OBET
Our School Now Closes Out, *with music.* Edmund Dumas. AH
Our share of night to bear. Emily Dickinson. AA
Our shepherds all. Boots and Saddles. Nicolas Saboly, *tr. fr. Provençal.* OHIP
Our ship is a cradle on ocean's blue billow. An Ocean Lullaby. Charles Keeler. EtS
Our ship lay tumbling in an angry sea. On Board the '76. James Russell Lowell. MOS
Our Ship She Lies in Harbour. *Unknown.* OBET
Our short fat, lord bishop. Bad Bishop Jegon. *Unknown.* GBP
Our Silly Little Sister. Dorothy Aldis. EvOK; FaPON
Our single purpose was to walk through snow. Polar Exploration [*or* The North]. Stephen Spender. ChMP; FaBoMo; MoAB; MoPo; NoAM
Our Sister. Horatio Nelson Powers. HBV-1
Our skin loosely lies. Long Division; a Tribal History. Wendy Rose. TWSS
Our Smoke Has Gone Four Ways. Lance Henson. CDW
Our songs are dead, and dead in vain. The Flower. Lee Wilson Dodd. HBMV
Our soprano is on the wind tonight. Autumn Song on Perry Street. Lloyd Frankenberg. GrPl
Our sorrow sends its shadow round the earth. J. A. G. Julia Ward Howe. PAH
Our Stars Come from Ireland. Wallace Stevens. GOA
Our States, O Lord, *with music.* John Mycall. AH
Our steeds remounted and the summons given. Wordsworth. *Fr.* The Prelude, II. SyP
Our steps are scattered far. In the Wilderness. Edith Lovejoy Pierce. TrPWD
Our storm[e] is past, and that storm's tyrannous rage. The Calm[e]. John Donne. LoBV; MePo; MOS
Our Strange and Lovable Weather. William Matthews. NPAW
Our Sunday morning when dawn-priests were applying. John Berryman. BoLoP

Our tarin' Dan O'Connell sure he was a mighty man. Cushendall. *Unknown.* WTO
Our tears have fallen for this world of stone. My Subtle and Proclamant Song. Seán Jennett. NeIP
Our Tense and Wintry Minds, *with music.* Hayden Carruth. AH
Our Times Are in His Hands. Mary D. Freeze. STF
Our toes touched stone. Sleeping in a Cave. Naomi Shihab Nye. AMV-81
Our top-sails reef'd and filled away. The Norfolk Girls. *Unknown.* AmSS
Our town is not unusual. The University sits on a hill. Home. Hollis Summers. SOTS
Our Traveller. Henry Cholmondeley-Pennell. InMe
Our trivial fights over spading. For My Father: Two Poems. David Kherdian. GP
Our True Beginnings. Wrey Gardiner. NeBP
Our trust is now in thee, Beauregard! Beauregard. Catherine Ann Warfield. PAH
Our twelve months go round and round. January 1. Marnie Pomeroy. PoSC
Our Two Opinions. Eugene Field. AA
Our Two Worthies. John Crowe Ransom. OBAL
Our uncle called us on the phone. Surprise. Harry Behn. TiPo
Our vales are sweet with fern and rose. The Old Burying-Ground. Whittier. AP
Our Vegetable Love Shall Grow. Elaine Feinstein. POL
Our vernal signs the RAM begins. The Signs of the Zodiac. Ebenezer Cobham Brewer. FaBoUs
Our Vicar. *Unknown.* TDH
Our vicar still preaches that Peter and Poule. Soldier's Song. Sir Walter Scott. *Fr.* The Lady of the Lake, VI. NBM; ViBoPo
Our Village—by a Villager. Thomas Hood. InMe; OBSV; PoPle
(Our Village.) PoEL-4
Our Visit to the Zoo. Jessie Pope. PoPle
Our Washing Machine. Patricia Hubbell. RHPC
Our Wee White Rose. Gerald Massey. *Fr.* The Mother's Idol Broken. HBV-1
Our window-panes enthral our summer bees. The Bee-Wisp. Charles Tennyson Turner. FM
Our Youth. John Ashbery. CAPP; ConAP; SOTW; VGW
Our youth began with tears and sighs. Ballade of Middle Age. Andrew Lang. HBV-1
Our youth is like a rustic at the play. The Rustic at the Play. George Santayana. HBV-2; OBVV
Our youth was happy: why repine. Walter Savage Landor. FaBoEE
Our zummer way to church did wind about. Green. William Barnes. VLP
Oure hoste gan to swere as he were wood. The Pardoner's Prologue and Tale. Chaucer. *Fr.* The Canterbury Tales. NoP; OAEL-1
Oure kinge went forth to Normandy. *See* Our king went forth to Normandy.
Ourobouros. Jorge Plescoff, *tr. fr. Spanish by* Yishai Tobin. VWA
Ours, and All Men's. James Russell Lowell. *Fr.* Under the Old Elm. PAL; PGD
(Washington.) GN; OHIP
Ours are the streets where Bess first met her/ cancer. Bess. William Stafford. GP; NNaP; NoP
Ours is a dark Easter-tide. The Old Road to Paradise. Margaret Widdemer. HBMV
Ourselves we do inter with sweet derision. Emily Dickinson. FaBoEE
Ourselves were wed one summer—dear. Emily Dickinson. PeHV
Ousel-cock, so black of hue, The. *See* Woosel cock so black of hue, The.
Out amongst the flowers sweet. Hearts and Flowers. Mary D. Brine. FSN
Out and Fight. Charles Godfrey Leland. PAH
Out back by the garage, the pumpkin tilts. Forecasting the Economy. Edward Morin. SOTS
Out beyond the grasses growing. Drifting. D. Maitland Bushby. BPAW
Out Fishin'. Edgar A. Guest. BLPL; PoLF
Out Fishing. Barbara Howes. LiSp; WPE
Out for a walk, after a week in bed. An Urban Convalescence. James Merrill. CoAP; NOBA; NYP
Out for a walk on the ice. Ice. Jack Driscoll. AMV-80
Out for a walk the other day. A Mystic Song. *Unknown, tr. by* Percy Allen. WGRP
Out frae the wüd the gowk cries still. On the Hill. William Soutar. PoSH
Out from Gloucester. Harlan Trott. EtS
Out from his bed the breaking seas. A Dream Observed. Anne Ridler. NeBP
Out from Lobster Cove. J. D. Reed. NeAC
Out from muted bee-sounds and musketry. Origin of Dreams. Marvin Bell. LCAP
Out from the harbor of Amsterdam. Henry Hudson's Quest. Burton Egbert Stevenson. HBV-2; PAH; PAL
"Out from the horror of infernal deeps." The Complaint of Rosamond. Samuel Daniel. OAEP; OBSC, *sel.*
Out Goes She. *Unknown.* PoPle
(Up in the North.) OxBoLi
Out goes the rat. Counting-out Rhymes. *Unknown.* FaPON
Out here on Cottage Grove it matters. The galloping. Pyrography. John Ashbery. PoM
Out here the dogs of war run loose. From a Trench. Maud Anna Bell. SUMH
Out here there are no hearthstones. Sleep in the Mojave Desert. Sylvia Plath. NoP
Out here where the summer air. Driving through the Pima Indian Reservation. Paul H. Cook. AMV-80
Out I came from the dancing-place. Ashore. "Laurence Hope." HBV-1
Out in a dark, lost kingdom of their own. Nor'easter. Bianca Bradbury. EtS
Out in a world of death, far to the northward lying. The Winter Lakes. Wilfred Campbell. BoNaP; NOBC; OBCV
Out in Arizona where the bad men are. Rag Time Cowboy Joe. Grant Clarke, Lewis F. Muir, *and* Maurice Abrahms. FSW
Out in back. Train Song. Diane Siebert. RHPC
Out in the Cold. George Starbuck. NYBP
Out in the Country, Back Home. Jeff Daniel Marion. PPJ
Out in the Dark. Edward Thomas. BrPo; CH; FaBoEn; GTBS-P; LiTM; MoAB; MoBrPo; MoVE; NOBE; PoPle
Out in the dark beyond my gates. New Year's Eve in Troy. Adrienne Rich. NePoEA-2
Out in the dark it throbs and glows. On the Verge. William Winter. AA
Out in the dark night-long. Countersign. Arthur Ketchum. HBMV
Out in the dark over the snow. Out in the Dark. Edward Thomas. BrPo; CH; FaBoEn; GTBS-P; LiTM; MoAB; MoBrPo; MoBE; NoBE; PoPle
Out in the Fields. *Unknown, at. to* Elizabeth Barrett Browning *and to* Louise Imogen Guiney. *See* Out in the Fields with God.
Out in the fields which were green last May. A Child's Thought of Harvest. "Susan Coolidge." OHIP; PoSC
Out in the Fields with God. *At. to* Elizabeth Barrett Browning *and to* Louise Imogen Guiney. BLRP; HBV-1; HBVY; TreFS; TRV; WBLP; WGRP
(Song from Sylvan, A.) BLPA
Out in the late amber afternoon. In Shadow. Hart Crane. NOBA; TwAmPo
Out in the misty moonlight. Ghosts. Richard Kendall Munkittrick. AA
Out in the night thou art the sun. Star of Ethiopia. Lucian B. Watkins. BANP
Out in the rain a world is growing green. Easter Monday. Christina Rossetti. NOCV
Out in the sky the great dark clouds are massing. Ships That Pass in the Night. Paul Laurence Dunbar. BANP; CDC; MOS
Out in the snow. Snowman. Andrew McCord Jones. LFAC
Out in the south, when the day is done. The Song of the Spanish Main. John Bennett. HBV-2
Out in the yellow meadows, where the bee. George Meredith. *Fr.* Modern Love. GBL
Out in this desert we were testing bombs. Trying to Talk with a Man. Adrienne Rich. NIP
Out-island once, on a south slope. Deer Isle. Philip Booth. BiP; VGW
Out it spake Lizee Linzee. Lizie Lindsay. *Unknown.* ESPB
Out of a cavern on Parnassus' side. The New Castalia. William Hayes Ward. AA
Out of a cell into this darkened space. Frank Drummer. Edgar Lee Masters. *Fr.* Spoon River Anthology. NoAM
Out of a fired ship, which, by no way. A Burnt Ship. John Donne. EBEV; InPK; OBWP; WaaP
Out of a gothic North, the pallid children. Good-bye to the Mezzogiorno. W. H. Auden. OxBTC
Out of a Northern city's bay. The Cruise of the *Monitor.* George Henry Boker. PAH
Out of a vacancy of sky. On the Death of Neruda. H. L. Van Brunt. LTB
Out of a War of Wits. Dylan Thomas. PoA
Out of adult hearing. A Picture of Okinawa. Dennis Schmitz. LCAP; NPGG
Out of all the wild horse bands. The Golden Stallion. Paul Thompson. BPAW
Out of autumn like a blade. Autumn Journey. Denise Levertov. NeBP
Out of blue nowhere came guns. Indian Death. Alice Corbin. BPAW
Out of Body. Janice Townley Moore. AMV-81
Out of Bounds. John Banister Tabb. TRV
Out of brightness, a brightness out of brightness. The Waltz. Hilary Corke. NYBP
Out of burlap sacks, out of bearing butter. They Feed They Lion. Philip Levine. LCAP; MAT; NNaP; NoAM; NOBA; Prf
Out of Catullus. Catullus, *tr. fr. Latin by* Richard Crashaw. CavP
("Come and let us live my deare.") OBVE
Out of chaos. Star. Joanie Whitebird. GP
Out of Chaos Out of Order Out. Michele Roberts. BrRo

Out of Control; the Quarry. Christopher Dewdney. NOBC
Out-of-Doors. Robert Whitaker. TrPWD
Out of every hundred of us. American Commencement. Aram Boyajian. NeAC
Out of French. Sir Charles Sedley. FaBoEE
Out of friendship and a slow retreat of the blood. Ascending Red Cedar Moon. Duane Niatum. CDW
Out of gas south. Autumn. Philip Levine. NNaP
Out of Hearing. Jane Barlow. HBV-2
Out of her house she crept. Miss Euphemia. John Crowe Ransom. CMoP
Out of her own body she pushed. Grandmother. Paula Gunn Allen. STE; TWSS
Out of him that I loved. Our Stars Come from Ireland. Wallace Stevens. GOA
Out of his cottage to the sun. Old Dan'l. L. A. G. Strong. ELU; MoBrPo; PoSC; WhC
Out of hunger/ or out of great love. To My Child. Abraham Sutskever, *tr. by* David G. Roskies *and* Hillell Schwartz. VWA
Out of icy storms the white hare came. Ecclesiastes. Joseph Langland. NePoEA
Out of John Brown's Strong Sinews. Stephen Vincent Benét. *Fr.* John Brown's Body. WHA
Out of Luck. Abraham ibn Ezra, *tr. fr. Hebrew by* Solomon Solis-Cohen. TrJP
Out of me unworthy and unknown. Anne [*or* Anne] Rutledge. Edgar Lee Masters. *Fr.* Spoon River Anthology. AmFN; CMoP; FaFP; FaPo; HAP; LiTA; LiTM; MoAmPo; MoVE; NePA; NoAM; NOBA; OFD; OHFP; OxBA; PAI; PoPl; PoSC; TrGrPo
Out of Mobile I saw a 60 Ford. Plain. Miller Williams. TAT
Out of money, so I'm sitting in the shade. More than Fifty. Jack Gilbert. NPGG
Out of Mourning. Anthony S. Abbott. AMV-81
Out of my birth. Horoscope. J. V. Cunningham. NePoAm
Out of my clothes, I ran past the boathouse. Under the Boathouse. David Bottoms. MAYP
Out of my door I step into. The Old Love. Katharine Tynan. HBMV
Out of my heart, one day, I wrote a song. Misapprehension. Paul Laurence Dunbar. BPo
Out of my longing, dusk-aware. Candle Song. Anna Elizabeth Bennett. GoYe
Out of my own great woe. Proem. Heine, *tr. by* Elizabeth Barrett Browning. AWP
Out of my sorrow/ I'll build a stair. Duet. Leonora Speyer. HBMV
Out of My Soul's Depth. Thomas Campion. OxBoCh
Out of My Study Window. Reed Whittemore. PoPl
Out of my window I could see. Blossoms. Frank Dempster Sherman. OBCA
Out of my window late at night I gape. In the Night. Elizabeth Jennings. MP; NePoEA; NYBP
Out of one golden breath. Love-Song. Else Lasker-Schüler, *tr. by* Jethro Bithell. TrJP
Out of our daylight into death you burn. Paper Anarchist Addresses the Shade of Nancy Ling Perry. George Woodcock. NOBC
Out of Our Shame. Norman Rosten. TrJP
Out of Palestine, out of Babylon. Wandering Jews. Nancy Keesing. VWA
Out of Question & Mind. Noah Mitchell. LFAC
Out of Sight, Out of Mind. Barnabe Googe. ElL; EnRePo; InPS
(Oftener Seen, the More I Lust, The.) InvP
Out of Soundings. Padraic Fallon. NeIP
Out of That Sea. David Ferry. NePoAm-2
Out of the air a time of quiet came. The Clipper Loitered South. John Masefield. *Fr.* Dauber. EtS
Out of the blackthorn edges. The Love Song. Ivor Gurney. EnLoPo
Out-of-the-Body Travel. Stanley Plumly. AmPA; DiL; GeTw
Out of the bosom of the air. Snow-Flakes. Longfellow. AP; ChTr; FaBoRV; FPL; NOBA; NoP; PoEL-5; TAP; UnPo; WiR
Out of the breath of Gehennah. Germination. Arlene Stone. VWA
Out of the church she followed [*or* follow'd] them. Maude Clare. Christina Rossetti. BeLS; EBVV
Out of the cleansing night of stars and tides. Brooklyn Bridge at Dawn. Richard Le Gallienne. HBMV
Out of the clover and blue-eyed grass. Driving Home the Cows. Kate Putnam Osgood. AA; BeLS; HBV-2; PAH; TreFS
Out of the complicated house, come I. The Hills. Frances Cornford. MoBrPo
Out of the corner of my eye. Shadow Life. Robert F. Reid III. AMV-81
Out of the corpse-warm vestibule of heaven steps the sun. Ingeborg Bachmann, *tr. fr. German by* Janice Orion. BoWoP
Out of the Cradle Endlessly Rocking. Walt Whitman. AA; AmPP; AP; AWP; CABA; HAP; HeIP; MoAmPo; NePA; NOBA; NoP; OxBA; PoEL-5; PPoe; PrIm; SeCeV; TAP; TreFS; WeW; WHA
(Brown Bird, The.) OBVV
Sels.
Mocking-Bird, The. PB
"Out of the cradle endlessly rocking." ViBoPo
Out of the damp black night. The End of a Leave. Roy Fuller. NeBP
Out of the dark. The Open Door. Elizabeth J. Coatsworth. DuDa
Out of the dark raw earth. Alabama. Julia Fields. PoBA; PoNe
Out of the dark shadow. Evolution. John Banister Tabb. TreF
Out of the Dark Wood. Peter. AmMo
Out of the Darkness. Frankie Armstrong. BrRo
Out of the Darkness. Gertrud Kolmar, *tr. fr. German by* Michael Hamburger. WPOW
Out of the darkness of time and the stress of an impulse unending. The Wave. John Curtis Underwood. EtS
Out of the debris of dying stars. Little Cosmic Dust Poem. John Haines. SUW
Out of the deep and the dark. The Poet. Yone Noguchi. WGRP
Out of the deep have I called unto thee, O Lord. *See* Out of the depths have I cried. . .
Out of the Deepness. William (Haywood) Jackson. AMV-81
Out of the deeps I cry to thee, O God! A Prayer. Richard Le Gallienne. TrPWD
Out of the Depths. Frederic Lawrence Knowles. TrPWD
Out of the depths [*or* deep] have I cried [*or* called] (unto) Thee, O Lord. De Profundis [*or* A Song of Supplication]. Bible, *O.T.* Psalms, CXXX. Bible, *O.T.* BLRP; ILwL; TreF; TrGrPo; TrJP; WGRP
Out of the dusk a shadow. Evolution. John Banister Tabb. AA; HBV-2; PoPl
Out of the Earth. Mary Carolyn Davies. HBMV
Out of the earth beneath the water. The Mud Turtle. Howard Nemerov. NYBP
Out of the earth, out of the air, out of the water. Rapparees. Richard Murphy. *Fr.* The Battle of Aughrim. BIrV
Out of the earth to rest or range. The Passing Strange. John Masefield. LiTB; MoAB; MoBrPo; MoPo; OBEV
Out of the factory chimney, tall. Smoke Animals. Rowena Bastin Bennet. PDV
Out of the fire. Pool. Carl Sandburg. AP
Out of the focal and foremost fire. Little Giffen. Francis Orrery Ticknor. AA; GOA; HBV-2; PAH; TreFS
Out of the fog. The Fog Dream. Sandra M. Gilbert. PoA
Out of the garden in the gathering gloom. Shrine in Nazareth. Sister Mary St. Virginia. ISi
Out of the ghetto streets where a Jewboy. Autobiographical. Abraham Moses Klein. MoCV
Out of the golden remote wild west where the sea without shore is. Hesperia. Swinburne. OBNC; OBVV
Out of the grey air grew snow and more snow. Snow. W. R. Rodgers. LiTM
Out of the heart there flew a little singing bird. Youth. Virginia Woodward Cloud. AA
Out of the hills of Habersham. Song of the Chattahoochee. Sidney Lanier. AA; AmFN; AP; BoNaP; FaBoBe; FaBV; HBV-1; LiTA; NePA; OHFP; TreF; YaD
Out of the Hitherwhere. James Whitcomb Riley. BLPA; FPL
Out of the Hurly-Burly. "Max Adeler." *See* Mr. Slimmer's Funeral Verses for the *Morning Argus.*
Out of the icy storms the white hare came. Ecclesiastes. Joseph Langland. PoPl
Out of the Italian: A Song. Richard Crashaw. SeCV-1
Out of the "Kalevala," *sel.* Anselm Hollow.
Troll Chanting. WSC
Out of the lamplight. Mice in the Hay. Leslie Norris. OBCP; PChr
Out of the Land of Heaven. Leonard Cohen. MoCV
(Poem for Marc Chagall.) OBCV
Out of the light that dazzles me. My Captain. Dorothea Day. BLPA
Out of the living word. The Book of Kells. Howard Nemerov. EaLo
Out of the marbled underwaters. Music by the Waters. John Hay. AMV-81
Out of the midnight sky a great dawn broke. The Shepherd Speaks. John Erskine. TrCP
Out of the mid-wood's twilight. In the Forest. Oscar Wilde. SyP
Out of the mighty Yule log came. The Yule Log. William Hamilton Hayne. AA
Out of the mud two strangers came. Two Tramps in Mud Time. Robert Frost. AP; BLPL; CMoP; CoBMV; LiTA; LiTM; MasP; MoAB; MoAmPo; NePA; NoAM; PrIm; TrGrPo
Out of the mud which covers me. Inflictis. Archibald Stodart-Walker. *Fr.* The Moxford Book of English Verse. CenHV
Out of the night and the north. The Train Dogs. Pauline Johnson. GDP; WHW
Out of the night of the sea. At Carbis Bay. Arthur Symons. FaBoPP
Out of the night that covers me. Invictus [*or* Echoes *or* I. M.—R. T.

Hamilton Bruce]. W. E. Henley. Echoes, IV. BLPA; FaBoBe; FaBV; FaFP; FaPo; FaPoR; FPL; HBV-2; HBVY; HoPM; LiTB; LoBV; MoBrPo; NOBE; OBEV; OBMV; OBNC; OBVV; OHFP; PoPl; TEP; TreF; TrGrPo; ViBoPo; VLP; WGRP; WHA
Out of the night to my leafy porch they came. The Night Moths. Edwin Markham. HBMV
Out of the north the wild news came. The Rising. Thomas Buchanan Read. *Fr.* The Wagoner of the Alleghanies. PAH; TreFS
Out of the Northeast. The White Horse. Tu Fu, *tr. by* Rewi Alley. ChTr
Out of the Old House, Nancy. Will Carleton. AA
Out of the Past. Robert Wallace. POL
Out of the Poisonous East. W. E. Henley. London Voluntaries, IV. SyP; VLP
(Largo e Mesto.) BrPo
Out of the Rolling Ocean the Crowd. Walt Whitman. ViBoPo
Out of the scabbard of the night. Dawn. Frank Dempster Sherman. TRV
Out of the scraped surface of the land. The End of World War One. Sharon Olds. AMV-81
Out of the Sea, Early. May Swenson. RFM
Out of the shadow, I am come in to you whole a black holy man. Study Peace. Amiri Baraka. PoBA
Out of the sighs and breath of each small citizen. The City: Midnight. Bruce Dawe. PoAu-2
Out of the Strong, Sweetness. Charles Reznikoff. VWA
Out of the table endlessly rocking. Just Friends. Robert Creeley. NeAP
Out of the tense awed darkness, my Frangepani comes. Rainy Season Love Song. Gladys May Casely Hayford (Aquah Laluah). CDC
Out of the terra cotta still a voice. Etruscan Warrior's Head. Helen Rowe Henze. GoYe
Out of the utmost pitch of wilderment. De Profundis. Amos N. Wilder. TrPWD
Out of the Vast. Augustus Wright Bamberger. TRV
Out of the Vastness that is God. A Litany for Latter-Day Mystics. Cale Young Rice. WGRP
Out of the western chaparral. Road Runner. Sharlot M. Hall. BPAW
Out of the Whirlwind. Bible, *O.T.* Job, XL: 7-XLI. AWP
Out of the wild sweet grape, I have trampled a wine. On Laying Up Treasure. Lois Smith Hiers. GoYe
Out of the Wilderness. Ulrich Troubetzkoy. GoYe
Out of the window the trees in the Square. Red May. Agnes Mary Frances Robinson. HBMV
Out of the winds' and the waves' riot. Ebb Tide. Majorie Pickthall. CaP
Out of the wine-pot cry'd [*or* cried] the fly. The Fly. Philip Ayres, *after the Spanish of* Quevedo. CavP; OBVE
Out of the wood of thoughts that grows by night. Cock-Crow. Edward Thomas. GTBS-P; MoAB; MoBrPo
Out of these depths. De Profundis. David Gascoyne. *Fr.* Miserere. NeBP
Out of these thin, thin cups I drink pale tea. Bone China. R. P. Lister. NYBP
Out of this anteroom whose light is broken. The Anteroom. Denise Levertov. NeBP
Out of This Life. *Unknown.* STF
Out of this ugliness may come. Glasgow Street. William Montgomerie. OxBS
Out of this wilderness, this stony time. What Sanguine Beast? LeRoy Smith, Jr. NePoAm
Out of thise blake wawes for to saile. Chaucer. *Fr.* Troilus and Criseide. PP
Out of Time, *sel.* Kenneth Slessor.
"Leaning against the golden undertow." CBAP
Out of Tune. W. E. Henley. MoBrPo
Out of Whack. Russell Edson. LCAP
Out of what calms and pools the cool shell grows. The Atoll in the Mind. Alex Comfort. LiTB; LiTM; SeCePo
Out of You. Rodney Phillips. POL
Out of Your Hands. Theodore Weiss. CoPo
Out of your slepe arise and wake. Man Exalted. *Unknown.* MeEL; NoP
Out of your whole life give but a moment! Now [*or* The Moment Eternal]. Robert Browning. UnTE; VLP
Out on a limb and frantically sawing. Martyrdom of Two Pagans. Philip Whalen. NeAP
Out on a ranch way out West. Son of a Gun. *Unknown.* CoSo
Out on Santa Fe—Blues. *Unknown.* BluL
Out on the bare grey roads, I pass. Touch It. Robert Mezey. NaP
Out on the board the old shearer stands. Click Go the Shears, Boys. *Unknown.* PoAu-1
Out on the breeze. Flag Song. Lydia Avery Coonley Ward. YeAr
Out on the desert. A Note on Lizard's Feet. James Van Rensselaer. BPAW
Out on the furthest tether let it run. The Undiscovered Planet. Norman Nicholson. ChMP
Out on the lawn I lie in bed. A Summer Night. W. H. Auden. FaBoRV
Out on the margin of moonshine land. The Lugubrious Whing-Whang. James Whitcomb Riley. NA; YaD
Out on the ocean, great wide ocean. Great *Titanic. Unknown.* AmFP
Out on the roads of sky the moon stands poised. Elegy. Roy McFadden. NeIP
Out on the tormented, midnight sea. Poem and Message. Dannie Abse. TEP
Out on the wastes of the Never Never. Where the Dead Men Lie. Barcroft Boake. CBAP; PoAu-1
Out on the water was the same display. E. J. Pratt. *Fr.* The *Titanic. PeCV*
Out on the windy hill. The Shepherd's Dog. Leslie Norris. OBCP
"Out, Out." Robert Frost. CABA; DL; FF; HAP; HeIP; OxBA; PAI; PPoe; SoSe; UnPo; VGW; WeW
Out, Out, Brief Candle! Shakespeare. *see* Tomorrow and Tomorrow and Tomorrow.
Out, out, harrow! Into bale am I brought. Satan and Pilate's Wife. *Unknown.* ACP
Out rides the knight in dusky steel. The Knight. Rainer Maria Rilke, *tr. by* John N. Miller. AMV-81
Out rode from his wild, dark castle. The Legend of Heinz von Stein. Charles Godfrey Leland. HBV-2
Out shopping, little Julia spied. The Coconut. "Ande." FiBHP
Out the back window the sky is dead. Rain for Ka-waik. Paula Gunn Allen. TWSS
Out the Greywolf valley. Gary Snyder. Myths and Texts: Hunting, XII. NaP
Out there, beyond the boundary fence, beyond. The Singing Bones. Randolph Stow. CBAP
Out There Somewhere. Henry Herbert Knibbs. BLPA
Out there, we've walked quite friendly up to Death. The Next War. Wilfred Owen. WaP
Out there, with little else to do. Robben Island. Robert Dederick. PeSA
Out they came from Liberty, out across the plains. Oregon Trail: 1851. James Marshall. BPAW
Out through the fields and the woods. Reluctance. Robert Frost. CMoP; MoAB; MoAmPo; NOBA; OxBA
Out to Old Aunt Mary's. James Whitcomb Riley. FaFP; OHFP
Out, traitor Absence, darest thou counsel me. Astrophel and Stella, LXXXVIII. Sir Philip Sidney. SiPS
Out under the sprinkler, naked as toads. They Grow Up Too Fast, She Said. Diana O Hehir. NPGG
Out upon It! I Have Loved. Sir John Suckling. *See* Constant Lover, The.
Out upon the round-up, boys, tell you what you get. *Unknown.* CoSo
Out upon you California. Pennsylvania Places. T. A. Daly. OBAL
Out walking in the frozen swamp one gray [*or* grey] day. The Wood-Pile. Robert Frost. CABA; CoBMV; LiTA; NoAM; NoP; SeCeV; TwAmPo; VGW
Out walking ties left over from a track. Cross Ties. X. J. Kennedy. CoPo; HoPM
Out went the taper as she hurried in. Keats. *Fr.* The Eve of St. Agnes. ViBoPo
Out West. Gary Snyder. NNaP
Out West is windy. New Mexico. Polly Chase Boyden. TiPo
Out West, they say, a man's a man; the legend still persists. Étude Géographique. Stoddard King. AmFN; BPAW; WhC
Out where the handclasp's a little stronger. Out Where the West Begins. Arthur Chapman. BLPA; BPAW; FaBoBe; FaFP; HBV-2; PoOW; TreF
Out where the talk is a little stronger. Out Where the West Begins: A Parody. Ernest Douglas. BPAW
Out Where the West Begins. Arthur Chapman. BLPA; BPAW; FaBoBe; FaFP; HBV-2; PoOW; TreF
Out Where the West Begins: A Parody. Ernest Douglas. BPAW
Out where the white waves whisper. Out from Gloucester. Harlan Trott. EtS
Out with the mountain moon, stinging clear. Mill Valley. Myra Cohn Livingston. RFM
Outbreak. Bill Anderson. VGW
Outburst from a Little Face. John Woods. GP
Outcast, The. "Æ." LO; OxBI
Outcast. Claude McKay. AmNP; BALP; CABA; PoBA
Outcast, The. Frank Elwood Sanford. PeD
Outcast, The. James Stephens. MoBrPo
Outcast bones from a thousand biers. Ballade. Don Marquis. WhC
Outcrop stone is miserly. Still-Life. Ted Hughes. NYBP
Outcry upon Opportunity, An. Shakespeare. *See* Opportunity.
Outdoor Christmas Tree, The. Aileen Fisher. SiSoSe
Outdoor Litany, An. Louise Imogen Guiney. TrPWD
Outer provinces are never secure, The. Peace with Honor. Philip Appleman. SOTS
Outer Space, Inner Space. Gladys Cardiff. TWSS

Outgoing Sabbath. *Unknown, tr. fr. Yiddish by* Joseph Leftwich. TrJP
Outgrown. Julia C. R. Dorr. HBV-1
Outlanders, The. Andrew Glaze. NYBP
Outlanders, The. William Morris. *Fr.* The Earthly Paradise. EBVV
(Minstrels and Maids.) GN
("Outlanders, whence come ye last?") OxBoCh
Outlandish Knight, The. *Unknown.* OBET; ShM
Outlaw, The. Seamus Heaney. NoAM; OxBC
Outlaw, The. Sir Walter Scott. *See* Brignall Banks.
Outlaw Murray, The. *Unknown.* ESPB; OxBB
Outlaw of Loch Lene, The. *Unknown, tr. fr. Modern Irish by* Jeremiah Joseph Callanan. AnIV; BIrV; CH; GBL; OBEV; OBRV; OnYI; OxBI
Outlaw stands with blindfold eyes, The. Ol' Dynamite. Phil Le Noir. BPAW
Outlaw's Song, The. Joanna Baillie. OBEV
(Song of the Outlaws.) OBRV
Outlook Uncertain. Alastair Reid. NePoEA-2
Outlook wasn't brilliant for the Mudville nine that day, The. Casey at the Bat. Ernest Lawrence Thayer. FaPON; HBV-2; LiSp; OBAL; OBCA; PaPo; PoPl
Outlook wasn't brilliant for the Mudvillettes, it seems, The. Casey's Daughter at the Bat. Al Graham. InMe
Outside. Phyllis Beauvais. IHMS
Outside. Audre Lorde. NIP
Outside. William Stafford. NePoAm-2
Outside/ yellow leaves rattle. Voice in the Blood. Barney Bush. STE
Outside, a delicate arch. The Curse. John Hollander. UnPo
Outside, affectionate eyes. Ursula. David Ray. VGW
Outside Bristol Rovers Football Ground. The Ballad of Billy Rose. Leslie Norris. MoBS
Outside Dunsandle. Sacheverell Sitwell. ChMP
Outside Every Window Is a Flowering Thing. Anita Skeen. AMV-81
Outside Fargo, North Dakota. James Wright. LCAP; NNaP
Outside my blind a bird lit in a tree. A Play of Opposites. Gray Burr. CoPo
Outside my cheap candle. To Myself, Late, in a Myrtle Grove. Robert Peterson. NeAC
Outside my window. A Good Start. Larry Moffi. AMV-81
Outside New York, a high place where with one glance. Schubertiana. Tomas Tranströmer, *tr. by* Robert Bly. NU
Outside that bulbous Babylon. English Beach Memory: Mr. Thuddock. Sir Osbert Sitwell. NYBP
Outside the cats are wailing. Leah Goldberg, *tr. by* Robert Alter. *Fr.* The Symposium. PBWP
Outside the Chancel Door. *Unknown. See* On Elizabeth Ireland.
Outside the courtroom. Sharpeville Inquiry. Anne Welsh. PeSA
Outside, the cubist fells are drawn again. Cockley Moor, Dockray, Penrith. Norman Nicholson. NeBP
Outside the Door. Annette Wynne. SoPo; SUS
Outside the door the bare tree stands. Outside the Door. Annette Wynne. SoPo
Outside the Holy City, *with music.* James G. Gilkey. AH
Outside the house an ash-tree hung its terrible whips. Discord in Childhood. D. H. Lawrence. ELU
Outside, the last kids holler. Leaving the Motel. W. D. Snodgrass. FF; NIP
Outside, the rain, pinafore of gray water, dresses the town. Child Beater. Ai. BoWoP
Outside the Supermarket. Roy Fuller. OxBC
Outside the tent on the Little Fork. Horace Kephart. Robert Morgan. MAYP
Outside the window, at the top. Starlings. Laura Jensen. AMV-81
Outside the world crackles like a daily. A lion. A Room I Once Knew. Henry Birnbaum. GoYe
Outside the world was full, plural. The Christmas Tree. Patricia Beer. OBCP
Outside White Earth. Gordon Henry. STE
Outspoken buttocks in pink beads. National Winter Garden. Hart Crane. *Fr.* The Bridge: Three Songs. ErPo; InPS; LiTM; OxBA
Outward. John G. Neihardt. HBV-1
Outward. Louis Simpson. NYBP
Outward Bound. Thomas Bailey Aldrich. AA; EtS
Outward Bound. Edward Sydney Tylee. PAH
Outward from the planets are blown the fumes of thought. The Awakening. Don Marquis. HBMV
Outward Man Accused, The. Edward Taylor. LiTA
Outwardly splendid as of old. The Church Today. Sir William Watson. WGRP
Outweighing all, heavy out of the souvenir bundle. Three American Women and a German Bayonet. Winfield Townley Scott. NMP
Outwit me, Lord, if ever hence. Security. Charles L. O'Donnell. TrPWD
Outwit Song, The. Daniel Hoffman. SaC
Outwitted. Edwin Markham. BLPA; ELU; FPL; MoAmPo; TreFT; TRV
Out-worn heart, in a time out-worn. Into the Twilight. W. B. Yeats. HBV-2
"Ouu/ gee whiz." Moon Poem. Saundra Sharp. QQQ
Ov all the birds upon the wing. The Blackbird. William Barnes. HBV-1
Oven Bird, The. Robert Frost. AmPP; AP; AWP; CoBMV; CrMA; HeIP; NoAM; NOBA; NoP; OxBA; PPP; TAP; TwAmPo
Over. R. S. Thomas. FF
Over a bloomy land, untrod. In Dreamy Swoon. George Darley. *Fr.* Nepenthe. OBNC; OBRV
Over a ground of slate and light gravel. The Sanctuary. Howard Nemerov. NePoEA
Over a mountain-slope with lentisk, and with abounding. Actaeon. Arthur Hugh Clough. VLP
Over a pipe the Angel of Conversation. Inter Sodales. W. E. Henley. HBV-2
Over a slow-dying fire. Lachesis. Victor Daley. CBAP
Over a trail glinting with flakes. Indian Painting, Probably Paiute, in a Cave near Madras, Oregon. Jarold Ramsey. TAT
Over a wild and stormy sea. Mother Shipton's Prophecies. *At. to* Charles Hindley. BLPA
Over against the treasury. His Gift and Mine. *Unknown.* BLRP
Over all the face of earth/ Main ocean flow'd. Milton. *Fr.* Paradise Lost, VII. EtS
Over all the hilltops. *See* O'er all the hill-tops.
Over an ash-fawn beach fronting a sea which keeps. Fiascherino. Charles Tomlinson. NoAM
Over and back. At Ithaca. Hilda Doolittle ("H. D."). VGW
Over and over again he remembers that huge black sound. The Coal Mine Disaster's Last Trapped Man Contemplates Salvation. William Meissner. AMV-80
Over and over again to people. The Limits of Submission. Faarah Nuur, *tr. by* B. W. Andrzjewski *and* I. M. Lewis. TTY; WTO
Over and over, when the wayside dust had grayed us. To Be Said at the Seder. Karl Wolfskehl, *tr. by* Carol North Valhope *and* Ernst Morwitz. TrJP
Over and Under. William Jay Smith. TiPo
Over back where they speak of life as staying. The Investment. Robert Frost. CMoP; OxBA
Over Bright Summer Seas. Robert Hillyer. NYBP
Over by my bedroom wall. The Ugstabuggle. Peter Wesley-Smith. AmMo
Over Case's Door. John Case. FaBoUs
Over deep cushions, drenched with drowsy scents. Damned Women. Baudelaire, *tr. by* Roy Campbell. BoLoP
Over-Heart, The. Whittier. NOCV; WGRP
Over her shoulder, the window framed the stars. Eve in Old Age. Rob Holland. NIP
Over here in England I'm helpin' wi' the hay. Corrymeela. "Moira O'Neill." AnIV; AWP; HBV-2
Over Hill, over Dale. Shakespeare. *Fr.* A Midsummer Night's Dream, II, i. EIL; ViBoPo
(Fairy Land, 1.) OBEV
(Fairy Song.) HBV-1; HBVY; NOBE; OBSC; PoPle; TrGrPo
(Fairy's Wander-Song.) FaPON
(Puck and the Fairy.) GN
(Song.) InvP
Over hill, over dale, we have hit the dusty trail. The Caisson Song [*or* The Caissons Go Rolling Along]. Edmund L. Gruber. BLSo; PAL; TreF
Over hills and high mountains. The Wandering Maiden; or, True Love at Length United. *Unknown.* CoMu
Over his head were the maple buds. Emerson. *Fr.* Excelsior. PeD
Over his keys the musing organist. James Russell Lowell. The Vision of Sir Launfal, Prelude to Part First. HBV-1; HBVY; LiTA; OHFP; OnMSP; PoLF
Over his millions Death has lawful power. On the Death of M. D'Ossoli and His Wife, Margaret Fuller. Walter Savage Landor. PAH
Over in the Meadow. *Unknown.* SoPo
Over in the Meadow. Oliver A. Wadsworth. MoShBr
Over Jordan. *Unknown. See* Poor Wayfaring Stranger.
Over logs jammed between rocks. The Fish Will Swim as Before. Michael Spence. AMV-81
Over Manhattan island when gales subside. City without Smoke. Edwin Denby. NYP
Over mountains, pride. The Praise of Ben Dorain. Duncan Ban MacIntyre, *tr. by* "Hugh MacDiarmid." GoTS
Over my head, I see the bronze butterfly. Lying in a Hammock at William Duffy's Farm. James Wright. CAPP; ConAP; HAP; HoPM; InPS; NaP; NOBA
Over my head the fan moves slowly. In the Turkish Ward. Peter Balakian. MAYP
Over New England now, the snow. Nocturne. Frances Frost. BoNaP
Over now. Attica Is. Stewart Brisby. LFAC; SOTS

Over our heads the branches made. The Mountebanks. Charles Henry Luders. AA
Over our heads the missiles ran. Loss of an Oil Tanker. Charles Causley. OxBC
Over our scattered tents by night. Psalm—People Power at the Die-in. Denise Levertov. FAZ
Over rock and wrinkled ground. Beagles. W. R. Rodgers. FaBoTw; GDP; OnYI
Over Salève. George Herbert Clarke. CaP
Over Sir John's Hill. Dylan Thomas. LiTB; MoAB
Over that breathing waste of friends and foes. Sonnet: The Army Surgeon. Sydney Thompson Dobell. NCEP
Over that morn hung heaviness, until. Seascape. Francis Brett Young. OxBTC
Over the Arafura sea, the China sea. For John Chappell. Gary Snyder. NNaP
Over the black mountain, across the black bay, into the/ black night and beyond. Encounter. Uys Krige. PeSA
Over the bleak and barren snow. Tony O. Colin Francis. CH; FaBoCo; PV
Over the books of bricks. Landscape near a Steel Mill. Herschel Horn. PPON
Over the bridge. Crossing Portsmouth Bridge. Alan Chong Lau. BrSi
Over the briny wave I go. The Kayak. *Unknown.* FaPON
Over the chessboard now. Artificial Intelligence. Adrienne Rich. SUW
Over the climbing meadows. Dandelions. Frances M. Frost. TiPo
Over the cradle the mother hung. Where Shall the Baby's Dimple Be. Josiah G. Holland. BLPA
Over the Dark World Flies the Wind. Tennyson. FaBoRV
Over the deep sea Love came flying. The Two Burdens. Philip Bourke Marston. VLP
Over the dim blue hills. Maire, My Girl. John Keegan Casey. AnIV; OnYI
Over the dim confessional cried. A Priest's Prayer. Martha Dickinson Bianchi. AA
Over the downs there were birds flying. On the South Downs. Sara Teasdale. MoAmPo
Over the eye behind the moon's cloud. Raison d'Etre. Oliver Pitcher. AmNP; NNP
Over the fence. Emily Dickinson. SBG
Over, the four long years! And now there rings. Oxford. Lionel Johnson. FaBoPP; OBNC; OBVV
Over the Great City. Edward Carpenter. WGRP
Over the gulf and soaring of the city. Diretro al Sol. Charles G. Bell. NePoAm
Over the half-finished houses. The Roofwalker. Adrienne Rich. CoAP; PPP
Over the harbor at St. James. The Mill. William Heyen. EyDe
Over the hearth with my minishing eyes I muse. The Cat of the House. Ford Madox Ford. PCat
Over the heather the wet wind blows. Roman Wall Blues. W. H. Auden. DTC
Over the hill and over the dale. Dawlish Fair. Keats. PoPle
Over the hill the farm-boy goes. Evening at [*or* on] the Farm. John Townsend Trowbridge. FaPON; GN; MoShBr
Over the Hill to the Poor-House. Will Carleton. BeLS; BLPA; FaFP; PaPo; TreF
Over the hills/ Where the edge of the light. The Witches' Ride. Karla Kuskin. PDV
Over the Hills and Far Away. John Gay. *See* Song: "Were I laid on Greenland's coast."
Over the Hills and Far Away. W. E. Henley. HBVY; TreF
(Stanzas.) HBV-2
Over the hills I went one day, a lovely maid I spied. The Foggy Dew. *Unknown.* FSW
Over the Hills with Nancy. Gelett Burgess. WhC
Over the hiss of the coffee urns. Next Door to Monica's Dance Studio. Barbara Smith. AMV-81
Over the land freckled with snow half-thawed. Thaw. Edward Thomas. EBEV; ELU; FaBoTw; FM; GTBS-P; MoAB; MoBrPo; OxBTC
Over the lids of thine eye. Images. Richard Schaukal, *tr. by* Ludwig Lewisohn. AWP
Over the lonesome hollows. A Paris Nocturne. "Fiona Macleod." SyP
Over the long-shut house. Greek Excavations. Bernard Spencer. ChMP
Over the low, barnacled, elephant-colored rocks. Meditation at Oyster River. Theodore Roethke. CMoP; MoAmPo; NYBP
Over the mantel in the settlement house in Gary. For Great Grandmother and Her Settlement House. Ann Darr. GP
Over the Mindanao Deep. Gary Snyder. *Fr.* Hitch Haiku. InPK
Over the monstrous shambling sea. Marsh Song—at Sunset. Sidney Lanier. NOBA
Over the mountains/ And over the waves. Love Will Find Out the Way [*or* The Great Adventurer]. *Unknown.* FaBoCh; FaFP; GBL; GN; GTBS; GTBS-P; HBV-1; OBEV; TreFS; WiR
Over the mountains/ Over the plains. Trains. James S. Tippett. FaPON; SoPo; SUS; TiPo
Over the Phone. Mekeel McBride. MAYP
Over the plain two dark. The Triumph of Chastity. Barbara Howes. NePoAm-2
Over the plains where Persian hosts. The Cyclamen. Arlo Bates. AA; HBV-1
Over the quarry the children went rambling. The Fossil Raindrops. Harriet Prescott Spofford. OBCA
Over the rainy day mountain. Wishes. Patty L. Harjo. VoR
Over the right/ triangle formed. The Slogan. Paul Blackburn. PoM
Over the rim of glory. After Reading Twenty Years of Grantland Rice. Don Skene. InMe
Over the rim of the glass. The Ghost in the Martini. Anthony Hecht. OxBC
Over the River. Nancy Woodbury Priest. HBV-2
Over the river. Ferry-Boats. James S. Tippett. SoPo; SUS; TiPo
Over the river and through the wood. Thanksgiving Day [*or* The New-England Boy's Song about Thanksgiving Day]. Lydia Maria Child. FaPON; NTCP; OBCA; OHIP; RHPC; SiSoSe; TreFS
Over the river, on the hill. Two Villages. Rose Terry Cooke. HBV-2
Over the river they beckon to me. Over the River. Nancy Woodbury Priest. HBV-2
Over the roof-tops race the shadows of clouds. John Gould Fletcher. Irradiations, I or III [V]. MoAmBo; NePA; TwAmPo
Over the sea our galleys went. The Wanderers [*or* Song]. Robert Browning. OBEV; OBRV; OBVV
Over the Sea to Skye. Robert Louis Stevenson. EtS; MOS
(Lad That Is Gone, A.) HBV-1
(Sing Me a Song.) NOBE
("Sing me a song of a lad that is gone.") BrPo
Over the seagulls and the gull white roofs the music lies like heat. Tabernacles. Gerrit Lansing. CoPo
Over the sheer rocks over the gorges. An Inscription. Stanislav Vinaver, *tr. by* Vasa D. Mihailovich. VWA
Over the shining pavement of the sea. The Ship. Louise A. Doran. EtS
Over the shoulders and slopes of the dune. The Daisies. Bliss Carman. BoNaP; HBV-1
Over the snow at night. The Winter Lightning for Paul. Howard Nemerov. MoVE
Over the stern, my sad heart, drool. The Tortured Heart. Arthur Rimbaud. PeHV
Over the stones still rattling, up Pall Mall. Byron. *Fr.* Don Juan. NOBL
Over! the sweet summer closes. Prologue. Tennyson. *Fr.* Becket. GBL
Over the Top. Sybil Bristowe. SUMH
Over the turret, shut in his ironclad tower. Craven. Sir Henry Newbolt. HBV-2; HBVY; PAH
Over the utmost hill at length I sped. Shelley. *Fr.* The Revolt of Islam. OBWP
Over the Wall: Berlin, May 1975. C. H. Sisson. OxBC
Over the warts on the bumpy. Sadie's Playhouse. Margaret Danner. PoBA
Over the water an old ghost strode. The Old Ghost. Thomas Lovell Beddoes. WiR
Over the water and over the lea. *Unknown.* OxNR
Over the waters but a single bough. Robert Hillyer. Sonnets, XXIII. HBMV
Over the wave-patterned sea-floor. Greeting. Ella Young. AnIV
Over the west side of the mountain. Lyrebirds. Judith Wright. BoAnP; GoJo
Over the western sea hither from Niphon come. A Broadway Pageant. Walt Whitman. NYP
Over the winter glaciers. Beyond Winter. Emerson. RHPC
Over the wintry. Soseki, *tr. fr. Japanese by* Henry Behn. PDV
Over the wintry fields the snow drifts; falling, falling. Winter Evening. Walter de la Mare. FaBoRV
Over the Wintry Threshold. Bliss Carman. HBV-1
Over the years, they've darkened, like old paintings. In Memory. Katha Pollitt. MAYP
Over their edge of earth. The Little Clan. F. R. Higgins. OBMV
Over Their Graves. Henry Jerome Stockard. AA; OHIP
Over them all, we sit aloft and sing. Shadows of Sails. John Anderson. EtS
Over there in your fields you have. Rains for the Harvest. *Tr. fr. Tewa Indian by* H. J. Spinden. WTO
Over this battered track. Express Train. Karl Kraus, *tr. by* Albert Bloch. TrJP
Over Three Nipple-Stones. Paul Celan, *tr. fr. German by* Joachim Neugroschel. VWA
Over to God. Stephen Harrigan. FAZ

Over two shadowless waters, adrift as a pinnace in peril. Evening on the Broads. Swinburne. TEP
Over 2000 Illustrations and a Complete Concordance. Elizabeth Bishop. LCAP; NoAM
Over Yonder's a Park (Corpus Christi). *Unknown.* *See* Corpus Christi Carol ("Lully, lullay. . .")
Over yonder's a park, which is newly begun. The Corpus Christi Carol. *Unknown.* BaBo (B *vers.*); GBP
Over you falls the sea-light, festive yet pale. Ireland. Francis Stuart. NeIP
Over your body the clouds go. Gulliver. Sylvia Plath. NOBA
Over your dear dead heart I'll lift. I'll Be Your Epitaph. Leonora Speyer. HBMV
Over-all picture is winter, The. The Hunters in the Snow, III. William Carlos Williams. *Fr.* Pictures from Brueghel. LCAP
Overcoats. Larry Kramer. AMV-80
Overcoats are gone from Central Park, The. "Grandfather" in Winter. Frederick Feirstein. NYP
Overdose of beautiful words, An. 12th Raga: For John Wieners. David Meltzer. *Fr.* Ragas. NeAP
Overdue Balance Sheet. Therese Plantier, *tr. fr. French by* Maxine W. Kumin *and* Judith Kumin. BoWoP
Overflow. John Banister Tabb. HBV-1
Overflowing eyes. Meditation. Beyle Schaechter-Gottesman, *tr. by* Gabriel Preil. VWA
Overgrown Back Yard, The. John Holmes. CrMA; NePoAm
Overhanging Cloud. Robert Lowell. *Fr.* Marriage. NAs
Overhead at sunset all heard the choir. The Singers in a Cloud. Ridgely Torrence. HBMV
Overhead on a Saltmarsh. Harold Monro. GoJo
Overheard. Denise Levertov. PoM
Overheard in a Barbershop. Irving Layton. NMP
Overheard in an Orchard. Elizabeth Cheney. BLRP; TRV
Overheard in the Louvre. X. J. Kennedy. ELU
Overheard on a Saltmarsh. Harold Monro. CH; FaPON; MoShBr; SO; TiPo; WSC
Overheard over S.E. Asia. Denise Levertov. BoWoP
Overland to the Islands. Denise Levertov. ConAP; UnPo
Overlander, The. *Unknown.* PoAu-1
Overlooking the River Stour. Thomas Hardy. FaBoPP
Overlord. Bliss Carman. CaP
(Veni Creator.) WGRP
Overnight, a Rose. Caroline Giltinan. HBMV
Overnight Guest. Ramona Wilson. VoR
Overnight in the Apartment by the River. Tu Fu, *tr. fr. Chinese.* ChTr
Overnight my garden is Yoknapatawpha. Starlings. Ted Olson. PV
Overnight the new green grass. Cinderella Grass. Aileen Fisher. DFT
Overnight, very/ whitely, discreetly. Mushrooms. Sylvia Plath. BoNaP; NePoEA-2; WeW; WPOW
Overreacher, The. Christopher Marlowe. *Fr.* Tamburlaine the Great, Part I, I. NIP
Overripe Fruit. Kasmuneh, *tr. fr. Arabic.* TrJP
Overseer of the Poor. James Hayford. NePoAm-2
Overthrow of Lucifer, The. Phineas Fletcher. *Fr.* The Purple Island. OBS
Overtones. William Alexander Percy. HBMV; HBVY
Overture, An. Michael Knoll. LFAC
Overture to Strangers. Phyllis Haring. PeSA
Overtures to Death, *sel.* C. Day Lewis.
"For us, born into a still," VII. CMoP
Overturned Lake, The. Charles Henri Ford. EAS
Overworked Elocutionist, An. Carolyn Wells. BLPA; BLPL
Ovibos, The. Robert Hale. FiBHP
Ovid. Richard Pevear. AMV-81
Ovid in the Third Reich. Geoffrey Hill. FaBoMo; NoAM; POL
Ovid is the surest guide. Written in an Ovid. Matthew Prior. FaBoEE; FaBoUs
Ovid, Meet a Metamorphodite. Jonathan Williams. PoM
Ovid on the Dacian Coast. Dunstan Thompson. NYBP
Ovid's Banquet of Sense, *sel.* George Chapman.
Corinna Bathes. OBSC
(Natures Naked Jem.) FaBoEn
Ovid's Fifth Elegy. Ovid. *See* In Summer's Heat.
Oviparous Tailor, The. Thomas Lovell Beddoes. NBM
(Tailor, The.) WiR
Owed to Dickens, 1956. Jan Burroway. NePoAm-2
Owed to New York. Byron Rufus Newton. BLPA; TreFS
Owen of Carron, *sel.* John Langhorne.
"Does nature bear a tyrant's breast?" FaBoCo
Owen's praise demands my song. The Triumphs of Owen. Thomas Gray. EnRP; PoEL-3
Ower the grey sentinel hills. No Voice of Man. Raymond Falconer. PoSH
Owl, The. Thorkild Bjornvig, *tr. fr. Danish by* Robert Bly. NU
Owl, The. Edward Davison. PoA
Owl, The. Michael Drayton. *See* Owle, The.
Owl. Peter Kane Dufault. NYBP
Owl, The. W. S. Merwin. PPP
Owl, The. Sue Owen. AMV-81
Owl. Sylvia Read. RHPC
Owl. Rokwaho. STE
Owl, The. V. Sackville-West. SBG
Owl, The. William Jay Smith. PDV
Owl, The. Tennyson. FaBoCh; MoShBr; OBRV; PoPle
(Song—the Owl.) FaPON; GoJo; HBV-1; PB; PBBP; SUS
(When Cats Run Home.) CH
Owl, The. Edward Thomas. ChTr; DTC; EBEV; FaBoRV; FaBoTw; FF; GTBS-P; LiTB; NoAM; NOBE; NoP; OAEL-2; PoPle; PPoe; SoSe; UnPo
Owl, The. Robert Penn Warren. MoAmPo
Owl and Rooster. Gladys Cardiff. STE
Owl and the Eel and the Warming-Pan, The. Laura E. Richards. EvOK; HBV-1; HBVY; OBCA
Owl and the Fox, The. *Unknown.* BLPA
Owl and the Nightingale, The, *sel.* *Unknown, at. to* Nicholas de Guildford.
Owl against Nightingale, *orig. and mod. English prose.* OxBM
("When I was in a summer valley," *tr. fr. Middle English by* John William Hey Atkins.) PBBP
Owl and the Pussy-Cat, The. Edward Lear. BeLS; FaBoBe; FaBoCh; FaBoNo; FaFP; FPL; FaPON; GoJo; GTBS-P; HBV-2; HBVY; MoShBr; NA; NOBE; NoP; NTCP; OxBChV; OxBoLi; PDV; PoLF; PoPl; PoRA; RHPC; SoPo; SUS; TiPo; TreFS; TrGrPo; WHC
Love Song, *sel.* PCat
Owl-Critic, The. James Thomas Fields. BLPA; CenHV; EvOK; HBV-1; OBAL; TreFS; WBLP; YaD
Owl expires, The! Death gave the dreadful word. On the Death of a Lady's Owl. Moses Mendes. TrJP
Owl has come, The/ Right into my house. Eyes. W. H. Davies. BrPo; FM
Owl in the Oak, The. *Unknown.* FaBoNo
("There was an owl lived in an oak," *sl. diff. vers.*) OxNR
Owl in the Rabbi's Barn, The. Dan Jaffe. VWA
Owl in the Sarcophagus, The. Wallace Stevens. FaBoMo
Owl[e] is abroad, the bat, and the toad, The. The Witches' Charm [*or* Charme]. Ben Jonson. *Fr.* The Masque of Queens. FaBoCh; FM; LoBV; NOBE; PoPle
Owl Is an Only Bird of Poetry, An. Robert Duncan. NeAP; PoM
Owl is hooting in the grove, An. Winter Night. Roy Fuller. NeBP
Owl King, The. James Dickey. CoPo
(Call, The.) NePoEA-2
Owl swoops, An. The Visit. William J. Rewak. AMV-80
Owl that lives in the old oak tree, The. The Owl. William Jay Smith. PDV
Owl, the Eel, and the Warming-Pan, The. Laura E. Richards. *See* Owl and the Eel and the Warming-Pan, The.
Owl to her mate is calling, The. The Fate of the Oak. "Barry Cornwall." OHIP
Owl winks in the shadows, An. Mother Earth; Her Whales. Gary Snyder. LCAP; WeW
Owl Woman's Death Song. *Tr. fr. Papago Indian by* Ruth Underhill. BoWoP
Owle is abroad, the bat, and the toad. *See* Owl is abroad . . .
Owle, The, *sel.* Michael Drayton.
"And every bird shew'd in his proper kind." FM
Owls. John Fuller. POL
Owls. W. D. Snodgrass. BoAnP; Psk
Owls roost like gray lamps up there, The. Brobdingnag. Adrien Stoutenburg. NYBP
Owl's Song. Ted Hughes. PAI
Owner of My Face, The, *sels.* Rodney Hall.
After a Sultry Morning. CBAP
Lips and Nose. CBAP
Some Magnetism in the Sea. CBAP
Ownership. Lizette Woodworth Reese. MoAmPo
Ownership of the Night, The. Larry Levis. LCAP
Owning. Wilmot B. Lane. CaP
Owning a Dead Man. Marcia Southwick. AMV-80; MAYP
Owre the Hill. William Soutar. PoSH
Owre the Muir amang the Heather. Jean Glover. HBV-1
Owslesbury Lads, The. *Unknown.* OBET
Ox, The. Mary Morison Webster. PeSA
Ox and the Ass, The. Five Carols for Christmastide, V. Louise Imogen Guiney. ISi
Ox-Bone Madonna. John Duffy. ISi
Ox-Bone Madonna. James J. Galvin. ISi
Ox Cart Man. Donald Hall. FYAP; LCAP

Ox-Driver, The. *Unknown.* FSW
(Ox-driving Song, *with music.*) OuSiCo
Ox he openeth wide the Doore, The. Tryste Noël [*or* Five Carols for Christmastide, I]. Louise Imogen Guiney. HBV-1; ISi; OBVV
Oxen, The. Thomas Hardy. BiP; CMoP; CoBMV; EBEV; HAP; HBMV; InPK; LiTM; MoAB; MoBrPo; NoAM; NOBE; OAEL-2; OAEP; OBCP; OxBTC; PChr; PPoe; PPP; SoSe; WeW
Oxen have voices, The. Don Giovanni on His Way to Hell. Jack Gilbert. NPGG
Oxen: Ploughing at Fiesole. Charles Tomlinson. OxBTC
Oxen that rattle the yoke and chain or halt in the leafy shade. Walt Whitman. *Fr.* Song of Myself. FM
Oxford, *sel.* Edward Dorn.
Comforted by Limestone. NOBA
Oxford. Keith Douglas. NePoEA
Oxford. Lionel Johnson. FaBoPP; OBNC; OBVV
Oxford abounds in fern and bird-watcher. Views of the Oxford Colleges. Barbara Howes. GLGT
Oxford and Cambridge. Sir William Browne. *See* Epigram: "King to Oxford sent a troop of horses, The."
Oxford and Hampton Railway, The. *Unknown.* OBET
Oxford Barber's Verses on the Queen's Death. *Unknown.* APAS
Oxford Bells. Gerard Manley Hopkins. FaBoPP
Oxford Bells. Sister Maris Stella. GoBC
Oxford Canal. James Elroy Flecker. OxBTC
Oxford Commination. Paris Leary. AMV-81
Oxford Girl, The; or, Expert Town. *Unknown.* AmFP
Oxford Is a Stage. Edward Nolan. CenHV
Oxford Nights. Lionel Johnson. BrPo
Oxford, since late I left thy peaceful shore. Sonnet: To Oxford. Thomas Russell. OBEC
Oxford to London, 1884. In a Railway Compartment. John Fuller. NePoEA-2
Oxygen. Joan Swift. NYBP
Oya. Audre Lorde. CNA
Oye, oyeye. Battle Songs of the King Tshaka. *Unknown.* PeSA
Oyfn Pripetshuk (On the Hearth). Mark Warshawsky, *tr. fr. Yiddish.* FSW
Oyster, The. Ogden Nash. PV
Oyster, The ("The oyster, about as large as a medium-sized stone"). Francis Ponge, *tr. fr. French by* Robert Bly. NU
Oyster boats are moored. Boom. Julian Lee Rayford. AMV-80
Oyster-Crabs. Carolyn Wells. BXAP
Oyster that went to bed x-million years ago, An. Goodnight. John Ciardi. OBAL
Oystercatchers. Christopher Middleton. FaBoTw
Oystering. Richard Howard. NoAM
Oysters. Swift. ErPo
Oyster's a confusing suitor, The. The Oyster. Ogden Nash. PV
Ozymandias. Shelley. AWP; BiP; CABA; DL; EnRP; FaBoBe; FaBoCh; FaBoEn; FaBoRV; FaFP; FaPo; FaPoR; FF; FiP; FPL; HAP; HeIP; HoPM; InPK; LoBV; NIP; NOBE; NoP; OAEL-2; OAEP; OBNC; PAI; PoLF; PoPle; PoRA; PrIm; RoGo; SCV; SeCeV; SoSe; SpRo; TEP; TrGrPo; WeW; WHA
(Ozymandias of Egypt.) BeLS; CH; GTBS; GTBS-P; HBV-2; HBVY; TreF
(Sonnet: Ozymandia.) SyP
Ozymandias Revisited. Morris Bishop. BXAP; SpRo

P

P. C. Plod Versus the Dale St Dog Strangler. Roger McGough. NoAM
P Is for Paleontology. Milton Bracker. FiBHP; InMe; WhC
Pa. Leo Dangel. AMV-81; Str
Pa lays around 'n' loafs all day. Options. "O. Henry." FiBHP
Pa, Pa, Build Me a Boat. *Unknown.* AmFP
Pacelli and the Ethiop. Turner Cassity. GP
Pachuco Remembered. Tino Villanueva. FIA
Pachuta, Mississippi/ A Memoir. Al Young. TAT
Pacific Door. Earle Birney. PeCV
Pacific Engagement, The. *Unknown.* *Fr.* Bungiana. WhC
Pacific Epitaphs. Dudley Randall. NoAM
Pacific Railway, The. C. R. Ballard. PAH
Pacific Sonnets, *sels.* George Barker.
"And now there is nothing left to celebrate," XII. LiTM; NeBP
"At midday they looked up and saw their death," VII [*or* IX]. LiTM; MasP; MOS; WaP
"From thorax of storms the voices of verbs," VI [*or* VIII]. LiTM; MasP; MOS; WaP
"Seagull, spreadeagled, splayed on the wind, The," V [*or* VII]. LiTM; MasP; MOS; WaP
Pacified. Thomas G. Nickens. LFAC
Pacifist, The. Hilaire Belloc. MoVE
Pacifists. George Woodcock. NOBC
Pacing with bag-pipe in a bosky square. Caledonia. Anthony Powell. NOBL
Pack, Clouds, Away. Thomas Heywood. *Fr.* The Rape of Lucrece. ElL; SoSe; ViBoPo; WHA
(Good Morrow.) CH
(Matin Song.) HBV-1; OBEV
("Pack, clouds, away, and welcome day.") GBL; GTBS; GTBS-P; PBBP
Pack Rat, The. Robert Pack. PPP
Package, The. Aileen Fisher. SoPo
Packard. David Barker. DFF; GP
Packed in my mind lie all the clothes. The Inward Morning. Henry David Thoreau. AmPP; AP; NoP
Packed with woodpeckers, my head knocks. Raking Leaves. Robert Pack. CoPo; NYBP
Packet of Letters. Louise Bogan. GrPl; PCP
Packin' Trunk Blues. *Unknown.* BluL
Packing a Photograph from Firenze. William H. Matchett. NePoEA
Packing In with a Man. Judith McCombs. LTB
Pact. Kenneth Fearing. CMoP
Pact, A. Ezra Pound. AmPP; ELU; LiTA; NePA; NoAM; NOBA; OxBA; PAI; PoPl; TAP
Pact, The. Larry Rubin. AMV-81
Pact that we made was the ordinary pact, The. From a Survivor. Adrienne Rich. GP; PAI
Pad, Pad. Stevie Smith. ELU
Padda Song, The. *Unknown.* GBP
Paddle Your Own Canoe. Sarah K. Bolton. FaFP
Paddling Song. *Unknown, tr. fr. Bantu by* Max Exner. PBA
Paddock's a lonely space to stay inside, The. The Gate's Open. John Blight. CBAP
Paddy Biran's Song. Paddy Biran, *tr. fr. Girramay by* R. M. W. Dixon. CBAP
Paddy Doyle, *with music.* *Unknown.* AmSS; ShS
Paddy, Get Back. *Unknown.* AmFP; AmSS, *with music;* ShS, *with music*
Paddy, I have but stol'n your living. Ebenezer Elliott. FaBoEE
Paddy, in want of a dinner one day. Paddy O'Rafther. Samuel Lover. HBV-2
Paddy McCabe was dying one day. Father Molloy. Samuel Lover. HBV-2
Paddy Murphy. *Unknown.* PV
Paddy O'Rafther. Samuel Lover. HBV-2
Paddy West, *with music.* *Unknown.* ShS
Paddy Works on the Railway, *with music.* *Unknown.* AmSS
(Pat Works on the Railway.) FSW; TrAS, *with music*
(Poor Paddy Works on the Railway, *with music.*) AS
Paddy's Metamorphosis. Thomas Moore. OnYI
Padraic O'Conaire, Gaelic Storyteller. F. R. Higgins. OBMV; OnYI; OxBI
Padstow Night Song, The. *Unknown.* ChTr; GBP
Paean. Jonathan Henderson Brooks. CDC
Paean to Eve's Apple. James Liddy. CIP
Paedar Og Goes Courting. James Stephens. WhC
Paedotrophiae; or, The Art of Bringing Up Children, *sels.* M. Saint-Marthe, *tr. fr. French.* FaBoUs
Choosing a Wet-Nurse.
Cravings during Pregnancy.
Infant Diseases and Their Treatment.
Labour.
Pagan Epitaph. Richard Middleton. OBVV
Pagan Isms, The. Claude McKay. BPo
Pagan Prayer. Alice Brown. WGRP
Pagan Reinvokes the Twenty-third Psalm, A. Robert L. Wolf. HBMV; TrPWD
Pagan Rites. Paul Goodman. *Fr.* North Percy. DiL
Pagan's myths through marble lips are spoken, The. Worship. Whittier. NOCV
Pagans wild confesse the bonds, The. Roger Williams. SCAP
Page. Sandra McPherson. PoA
Page from a Diary. Desmond O'Grady. NoAM
Pageant of Seamen, The. May Byron. HBV-2
Pageant Verses. Sir Thomas More. *See* I Am Called Childhood.
Pages of history open, The. Elegy. Sandra M. Gilbert. PoA
Pages of the album, The. Sonatina in Yellow. Donald Justice. DiL; LCAP
Page's Road Song, A. William Alexander Percy. TrPWD; YeAr
Pages' Song, The. Shakespeare. *See* It Was a Lover and His Lass.
Pagett, M. P. Kipling. BrPo

Pagget, a schoolboy, got a sword, and then. Upon Pagget. Robert Herrick. CaPo; FaBoCh
"Paid by my lord, one portrait, Lady Anne." Child with a Cockatoo. Rosemary Dobson. CBAP
Paid on Both Sides, *sel.* W. H. Auden.
Chorus: "To throw away the key and walk away." MoBrPo
(Walking Tour, The.) CMoP
Pain. "Æ." MoBrPo
Pain, *sel.* Thomas Edward Brown.
"Man that hath great griefs I pity not, The." PeD
Pain. St. John Lucas. HBV-2
Pain. Edith Södergran, *tr. fr. Swedish by* Jaakko A. Ahokas. PBWP; WPOW, *tr. by* Samuel Charters
Pain. Alfonsina Storni, *tr. fr. Spanish by* Merrilee Antrim. WPOW
Pain. Leonora Speyer. HBMV
Pain. Robert Wrigley. AMV-81
Pain and laughter of the day are gone, The. Night Duty. Eva Dobell. SUMH
Pain for a Daughter. Anne Sexton. SoSe; WeW
Pain gnaws at my heart like a rat that gnaws at a beam. The Rat. Arthur Symons. SyP
Pain has an element of blank. Emily Dickinson. AP; LiTA; LiTM; MoAB; MoAmPo; PPP; SBG
Pain is a beckoning hand. Pain. Leonora Speyer. HBMV
Pain is a blacksmith. Blacksmith Pain. Otto Julius Bierbaum, *tr. by* Jethro Bithell. AWP
Pain is my familiar now. To My New Mistress. Beverly Bowie. PoPl
Pain of loving you, The. A Young Wife. D. H. Lawrence. BrPo; ChMP; ELP; MoBrPo
Pain of too poignant beauty fills the heart. The World's Desire. William Rose Benét. TrPWD
Pain Paint. Peter Minck. FaBoUs
Painful and brief the act. Eve on the barren shore. Eve in Reflection. Jay Macpherson. OBCV
Painful Love Song, A. Yehuda Amichai, *tr. fr. Hebrew by the author.* LLLT
Painful Plough, The. *Unknown.* OBET
Painfully writhed the few last weeds. An Infantryman. Edmund Blunden. ViBoPo
Painkillers. Thom Gunn. AMV-81
Painlessly out of Ourselves. William Page. AMV-81
Pains and Gains. Edward de Vere, Earl of Oxford. ElL
Pains of Education, The. Charles Churchill. *Fr.* The Author. FaBoCo
(Against Education) TW
Pains of insecurity surround me. Back Again, Home. Don L. Lee. BALP; BPo
Pains of Sleep, The. Samuel Taylor Coleridge. EnRP; NCEP; OAEP; OBNC; OBRV; SeCePo; SyP; TEP
(Child's Evening Prayer, A.) OxBChV; TrPWD
Pains, reading, study, are their just pretence. Verbal Critics. Pope. *Fr.* Epistle to Dr. Arbuthnot. OBEC; PP
Pains the sharp sentence the heart in whose wrath it was uttered. Pardon. Julia Ward Howe. PAH
Paint Box, The. E. V. Rieu. RHPC; SO
Paint Castlemaine in colours that will hold. Andrew Marvell. *Fr.* The Last Instructions to a Painter. OBSV
Paint last the King, and a dead shade of night. Charles II. Andrew Marvell. *Fr.* The Last Instructions to a Painter. OBS; OBSV
Paint me a cavernous waste shore. Sweeney Erect. T. S. Eliot. OxBTC; VGW
Paint samples. Bruises. Coleman Barks. PPJ
Painted autumn overwhelms, The. Epilogue. John Meade Falkner. FaBoPP
Painted Ceiling, The. Amy Lowell. OBAL
Painted Fan, A. Louise Chandler Moulton. AA
Painted Head. John Crowe Ransom. AP; CoBMV; CrMA; LiTA; LiTM; MoPo; MoVE; NoAM; NOBA; OxBA
(Painting: A Head.) MoAB; MoAmPo
Painted Hills of Arizona, The. Edwin Curran. BPAW; HBMV
Painted Indian rides no more, The. *Unknown.* WhC
Painted Lady, The. Margaret Danner. BPo
Painted Passages. Gail N. Harada. BrSi
Painted stars. Pictures on the Wall. Zvi Shargel, *tr. by* Gabriel Preil *and* Howard Schwartz. VWA
Painted with one fish, a cucumber. Japanese Fan. James Kirkup. GrPl
Painter, The. John Ashbery. NOBA; NoP; SOTW
Painter, The. Robert Fitzgerald. MoVE
Painter and poet, runner and disk-thrower. One of the Jews. C. P. Cavafy. TrJP
Painter, by unmatch'd desert. The Picture. Anacreon, *tr. by* Thomas Stanley. AWP; UnTE
Painter Dreaming in the Scholar's House, The. Howard Nemerov. PoDr
Painter in New England, A. Charles Wharton Stork. HBMV
Painter in the Lion Cage, The. Betti Alver, *tr. fr. Estonian by* Willis Barnstone *and* Felix Oinas. BoWoP
Painter of Dante's awful ferry-ride, The. The Poem. Babette Deutsch. PoA
Painter Who Pleased Nobody and Everybody, The. John Gay. BeLS
Painter, you're come, but may be gone. The Picture of Her Mind. Ben Jonson. *Fr.* Elegy on the Lady Venetia Digby, Wife of Sir Kenelm Digby. GoBC
Painters, The. Judith Hemschemeyer. Psk
Painters. Muriel Rukeyser. EyDe
Painter's eye follows relation out, The. The Painter Dreaming in the Scholar's House. Howard Nemerov. PoDr
Painter's Mistress, The. James Elroy Flecker. BrPo
Paint-flaken, it is paint-flaken. March, Upstate. William Bronk. NYBP
Painting. A. C. Jacobs. VWA
Painting: A Head. John Crowe Ransom. *See* Painted Head.
Painting of a Lobster by Picasso. Hy Sobiloff. NePA; TwAmPo
Painting of a White Gate and Sky. Louise Erdrich. TWSS
Painting the Gate. May Swenson. WeW
Paintings with stiff. Primitives. Dudley Randall. BALP; BPo; CABA
Painture. Richard Lovelace. CaPo
Pair, A. Karl Gjellerup, *tr. fr. Danish by* Charles Wharton Stork. PoPl
Pair, A. May Swenson. RFM
Pair of Fireflies, A. Stephen Shu Ning Liu. BrSi
Pair of funnels stroll by night, A. The Funnels. Christian Morgenstern, *tr. by* Geoffrey Grigson. FaBoNo
Pair of Lovers, A. Jeanne Robert Foster. HBMV
Pair of muscular calves, A. Harold Norse. *Fr.* You Must Have Been a Sensational Baby. GP
Pair of Wings, A. Stephen Hawes. MeEL
Paired Lives. W. R. Rodgers. CIP
Paisley Ceiling, The. Lila Arnold. IHMS
Paisley Officer, The. *Unknown.* ShS, 2 *vers., with music.*
Páistín Fionn. *Unknown, tr. fr. Irish by* Sir Samuel Ferguson. OxBI
Paiute Ponies. Jim Barnes. CDW
Pal, in the Pals of Death Club. This Is a Poem for the Fathers [and for Michael Ryan]. Thomas Lux. AmPA; DiL
Palabras Cariñosas. Thomas Bailey Aldrich. AA; HBV-1
Palabras Grandiosas. Bayard Taylor. OBAL
Palace, The. Charles Stuart Calverley. EBVV
Palace clocks are stiff as coats of mail, The. The King's Speech. Howard Moss. *Fr.* King Midas. PoA
Palace Dancer, Dancing at Last. Rayna Green. TWSS
Palace for Teeth, The. Abigail Luttinger. AMV-80
Palace of Art, The. Tennyson. OAEP; VLP
Sels.
Lincolnshire Shores ("A still salt pool locked in with bars of sand"). FaBoPP
"One seem'd all dark and red—a tract of sand." UnPo
Palace of Honor, The, *sel.* Gavin Douglas.
Nightmare. PoEL-1
Palace of humbug, The. "Lewis Carroll." FaBoNo
Palace of Pleasant Regard, The. Lady of the Assembly. *Fr.* The Assembly of Ladies. WPE
Palace of Pleasure, The. Stephen Hawes. *See* Pastime of Pleasure, The.
Palace of the Gnomes. Maria Gowen Brooks. *Fr.* Zophiël. AA
Palace of Truth, The. William Langland. *Fr.* The Vision of Piers Plowman. ACP
Palace with revolving doors, was mine, The. Atameros. John Beevers. EAS
Palaces are sombre cliffs by night, The. On the Grand Canal. David Gascoyne. SeCePo
Palaces of Gold. Leon Rosselson. OBET
Palais des Arts. Louise Glück. MAYP
Palamon and Arcite, *sel.* Dryden.
Parts of the Whole Are We; but God the Whole. NAs
Palatine, The. Willa Cather. HBMV
Palatine, The. Whittier. EtS; MOS
Pale amber sunlight falls across. Autumnal. Ernest Dowson. EBVV; OBNC
Pale beech and pine so [*or* pine-tree] blue. In a Wood. Thomas Hardy. OAEP; OBNC; PAI; PoPl; VLP
Pale beryl sky, with clouds. A Winter Twilight. Arlo Bates. AA
Pale, beyond porch and portal. Proserpine. Swinburne. *Fr.* The Garden of Proserpine. ChTr; FaBoEn
Pale Blue Casket, The. Oliver Pitcher. NNP; PoBA; TTY
Pale brown Moses went down to Egypt land. Benediction. Bob Kaufman. PoNe
Pale brows, still hands and dim hair. The Lover Mourns for the Loss of Love. W. B. Yeats. WeW
Pale, climbing disk, who dost lone vigil keep. To the Moonflower. Craven Langstroth Betts. AA

Pale darts still quivering, crocuses. Poem at Equinox. Hilary Corke. NYBP
Pale, drooping girl and the swaggering soldier, The. Just an Old Sweet Song. Donagh MacDonagh. CIP
Pale Ebenezer thought it wrong to fight. The Pacifist. Hilaire Belloc. MoVE
Pale-faced rat! To Noël Coward. Noël Coward. FaBoPa
Pale faced, tight laced. Margaret Southgate. POL
Pale from the watery west, with the pallor of winter a-cold. In Winter. Arthur Symons. BrPo
Pale gold of the walls, gold. Gold. Donald Hall. ConAP; InPS
Pale green of the English Hymnal! Yattendon hymns. The Old Liberals. John Betjeman. ChMP
Pale grey, her guns hooded, decks clear of all impediment. H. M. S. *Hero.* Michael Roberts. OxBTC
Pale hands I love beside the Shalimar. Kashmiri Song. "Laurence Hope." BLPA; BLPL; FaBoBe; FaFP; TreF
Pale Heinrich he came sauntering by. The Window-Glance. Heine, *tr. by* John Todhunter. AWP
Pale Italian peasant, A. At the Shrine. Richard Kendall Munkittrick. AA
Pale light tatters the stones beyond the hemlock. Sudden Frost. David Wagoner. PoPl
Pale moon was rising above the green mountain, The. The Rose of Tralee. William Pembroke Mulchinock, *also at. to* C. Mordaunt Spencer. FSW; OnYI; TreFT
Pale morning in June 4 AM, A. Country Roads. Rolf Jacobsen, *tr. by* Robert Bly. NU
Pale Punk drinks liquid naugahyde on porch of Cafe Flor. Round Trip. Stan Rice. NPGG
Pale road winds faintly upward into the dark skies, The. The Glow-Worm. Edward Shanks. WHA
Pale sand edges England's Old/ Dominion. Virginia Britannia. Marianne Moore. MoVE
Pale sky that lies above a world, The. The Future Phenomenon. Stéphane Mallarmé, *tr. by* George Moore. SyP
Palely intent, he urged his keel. At the Cannon's Mouth. Herman Melville. PAH
Palermo, Mother's Day, 1943. William Belvin. PoPl
Palestine. Whittier. WBLP
Palimpsest. Hyman Edelestein. CaP
Palindrome. Lisel Mueller. IHMS; WeW
Palinode, A. Edmund Bolton. ElL; InvP; OBSC; PoEL-2; PrIm
Palinode. Oliver St. John Gogarty. OBMV
Palinode, A. Robert Greene. *Fr.* Greene's Groatsworth of Wit. OBSC
Palinode. James Russell Lowell. AA
Palinode. Maura Stanton. MAYP
Palladium. Matthew Arnold. FaBoEn; GTBS-P; OAEL-2; OAEP; OBNC; PPP; VLP
Pallas an old-wife. Haughtie thoughts o're-throw. Ovid, *tr. by* George Sandys. Metamorphoses, VI. AnAnS-2
Pallid Cuckoo. David Campbell. CBAP; PoAu-2
Pallid cuckoo, The. Late Winter. James McAuley. PoAu-2
Pallid, mis-shapen he stands. The World's grimed thumb. In the Dock. Walter de la Mare. ChMP; LiTM
Pallid Thunderstricken Sigh for Gain, The. Tennyson. TW
Pallid with too much longing. Laus Veneris. Louise Chandler Moulton. AA; HBV-1
Pallidly sleeping, the Ocean's mysterious daughter. Elegy on a Dead Mermaid Washed Ashore at Plymouth Rock. Robert Hillyer. EtS
Palm, The. Roy Campbell. MoBrPo
Palm House, Botanic Gardens. George Hetherington. NeIP
Palm Leaves of Childhood. G. Adali-Mortti. PBA
Palm of the Hand. Rainer Maria Rilke, *tr. fr. German by* Robert Bly. NU
Palm of the hand, The,/ is not aware of dying. Fumi Saito, *tr. fr. Japanese by* Edith Marcombe Shiffert *and* Yuki Sawa. BoWoP
Palm-Sunday Hymn, A. William Herebert. MeEL
Palm Sunday: Naples. Arthur Symons. BrPo
Palm Tree, The. Abd-ar-Rahman I, *tr. fr. Arabic by* J. B. Trend. AWP
Palm-Tree, The. Henry Vaughan. AnAnS-1
Palm-Tree and the Pine, The. Richard Monckton Milnes. HBV-1
Palm tree grows in the far bush, The. Election Songs. *Yoruba Oral Tradition, tr. by* Ulli Beier. WTO
Palm Willow, The. Robert Bridges. VLP
Palmer, The. John Heywood. *Fr.* The Play of the Four P.P. ACP
Palmer, The. William Langland. *Fr.* The Vision of Piers Plowman. ACP
Palmer's Ode, The. Robert Greene. *Fr.* Never Too Late. CTC; EnRePo; OBSC
Palms, The. David Knight. MoCV
Palms and Myrtles. Eleazar ben Kalir, *tr. fr. Hebrew by* Alice Lucas. TrJP
Palo Alto; the Marshes. Robert Hass. NPGG
Palomino Stallion, The. Alden Nowlan. BoAnP; PH; POL
Pamela in Town. Ellen Mackay Hutchinson Cortissoz. AA; HBV-1
Pampered steed, of swiftness proud. The. The Horse and the Mule. John Huddlestone Wynne. OxBChV
Pamphilia to Amphilanthus. Mary Sidney Wroth, Countess of Montgomery. *Fr.* Urania. WPE
Pamphilia's Sonnet. Mary Sidney Wroth, Countess of Montgomery. *Fr.* Urania. WPE
Pan and Luna. Robert Browning. VLP
Pan and Syrinx. W. R. Rodgers. NMP
Pan and the Cherries. Paul Fort, *tr. fr. French by* Jethro Bithell. AWP
Pan, blow your pipes and I will be. A Note from the Pipes. Leonora Speyer. HBMV
Pan came out of the woods one day. Pan with Us. Robert Frost. OxBA
Pan—did you say he was dead, that he'd gone, and for good. Pan-Pipes. Patrick Chalmers. HBMV
Pan, grant that I may never prove. Song by the Wavering Nymph. Aphra Behn. SBG
Pan in Vermont. Kipling. WhC
Pan in Wall Street. Edmund Clarence Stedman. AA; HBV-1
Pan leave piping, the gods have done feasting. The Green-Gown. *Unknown.* CoMu
Pan loved his neighbour Echo—but that child. Moschus, *tr. fr. Greek by* Shelley. OBVE
Pan Piping. Plato, *tr. fr. Greek by* Thomas Stanley. FaBoEE
Pan-thrilled saplings swayed in sportive bliss, The. May. Stephen Moylan Bird. HBMV
Pan with Us. Robert Frost. OxBA
Panama. Amanda T. Jones. PAH
Panama. James Jeffrey Roche. PAH
Panama Limited, The. *Unknown.* BluL
Pan-Asian Holiday Tour. Luis Syquia. BrSi
Pancake, The. Christina Rossetti. *See* Mix a Pancake.
Pancake Collector, The. Jack Prelutsky. OBCA
Panchatantra, The, *sels.* *Unknown, tr. fr. Sanskrit by* Arthur W. Ryder. AWP
  Fool and False.
  Kings.
  Penalty of Virtue, The.
  Poverty.
  True Friendship.
Pancho Villa. Lou Lipsitz. NCSH
Panda, The. Harley Elliott. *Fr.* Animals That Stand in Dreams. NeAC
Panda, The. William Jay Smith. TDH
Pandemonium and Its Architect. Milton. *Fr.* Paradise Lost, I. TreFS
Pandora and the Moon. Merrill Moore. MoAmPo
Pandora Speaks. William Vaughn Moody. *See* I Stood within the Heart of God.
Pandosto, *sel.* Robert Greene.
  Fawnia. HBV-1; OBEV; OBSC
    (Ah Were She Pitiful.) TrGrPo, *abr.*; ViBoPo
    (In Praise of His Loving and Best-beloved Fawnia.) PoEL-2
Panegyric. Harris Lenowitz. VWA
Panegyric, A ("Hail happy William, thou art strangely great"). *Unknown, at. to* Henry Hall *and to* John Grubham Howe. APAS
Panegyric, A ("Of a great heroine I mean to tell"). *Unknown.* APAS
Panegyric on Geese, A. Francis S. Mahony. OnYI
Panegyric on Nelly, A, *sel.* Earl of Rochester.
  "Of a great heroine I mean to tell. UnTE
Panegyric on the Author of "Absalom and Achitophel," A. *Unknown.* APAS
Panegyric [*or* Panegyrick] to My Lord Protector, A. Edmund Waller. OBS
  "While with a strong and yet a gentle hand," *sel.* JCP; SeCV-1
Panegyric to Sir Lewis Pemberton, A. Robert Herrick. CaPo
Panegyric upon Oates, A. Richard Duke. APAS
Panegyrick upon O. Cromwell. Edmund Waller. *See* Panegyric to My Lord Protector, A.
Panes of light cracking. A Wet Night. Richard Ryan. CIP
Panfilo's head was shaped awkwardly. The Man Who Named Children. Alberto Ríos. LTB
Pang of the long century of rains, The. The Lament of Edward Blastock. Edith Sitwell. OBMV
Pangloss' [*or* Pangloss's] Song. Richard Wilbur. NePoAm-2; NoAM; OxBC
  (Pangloss's Song: A Comic-Opera Lyric.) AP
Pangolin, The. Marianne Moore. AP; CoBMV; CrMA; HAP; NoAM; NOBA; PBWP
Pangur Ban. *Unknown.* *See* Monk and His Pet Cat, The.
Panhandle Cob. *Unknown.* CoSo
Panic. Lloyd Davis. WOLT
Panic, *sels.* Archibald MacLeish. MoAmPo
  Final Chorus.
  Panic ("Slowly the thing comes").
Pannyra of the Golden Heel. Albert Samain, *tr. fr. French by* James Elroy Flecker. AWP

Panope. Edith Sitwell. MoAB; MoBrPo
Panorama, The. Milton. *See* New Worlds.
Pan-Pipes. Patrick Chalmers. HBMV
Pan's/ spring rain. Symphony No. 3, in D Minor. Jonathan Williams. *Fr.* Mahler. VGW
Pans Anniversarie. Ben Jonson. OBS
(Pans Anniversarie; or, The Shepherds Holy-Day). AnAnS-2
Pan's Song. John Lyly. *Fr.* Midas, IV, i. OBSC
(Pan's Syrinx). ELP
(Pan's Syrinx Was a Girl.) ViBoPo
(Syrinx.) ElL; LoBV; SeCePo; WHA
Pansies, lilies, kingcups, daisies. To the Small Celandine. Wordsworth. EnRP; HBV-1; OBRV
Pansy, The. Samuel Hoffenstein. DBV
Pansy. Mary Effie Lee Newsome. CDC
Pansy and the Prayer-Book, The. Matilda Betham Edwards. OBVV
Pansy makes such weird grimaces, The. The Pansy. Samuel Hoffenstein. DBV
Panther. Sam Cornish. PoBA
Panther, The. Ogden Nash. FaPON; MoShBr; OBAL; OBCA; SoPo; TiPo
Panther, The. Rainer Maria Rilke, *tr. fr. German.* NU, *tr. by* Robert Bly; PoPl, *tr. by* Paul Engle
Panther, The. *Unknown.* NA
Panther and Peacock. Gwen Harwood. CBAP; PoAu-2
Panther is like a leopard, The. The Panther. Ogden Nash. FaPON; MoShBr; OBAL; OBCA; SoPo; TiPo
Panther, knowing that his spotted hide, The. Amoretti, LIII. Spenser. EnRePo
Panther lies next to Wharncliffe. Appalachian Front. Robert Lewis Weeks. AmFN; NYBP
Panther Man. James A. Emanuel. BPo
Panther sure the noblest, next the Hind, The. The Church of England. Dryden. *Fr.* The Hind and the Panther, I. OBS
Pantisocracy. Samuel Taylor Coleridge. EnRP
Pantomime. Paul Verlaine, *tr. fr. French by* Arthur Symons. AWP; SyP
Pantomime Diseases. Dannie Abse. DFT
Papa above! Emily Dickinson. AmPP; FM
Papa finally left us. Divorce. Siv Widerberg, *tr. by* Verne Moberg. CTBA
Papa John. Jorge de Lima, *tr. fr. Portuguese by* John Nist. TTY
Papa Love Baby. Stevie Smith. DBV; SBG
Papa's Letter. *Unknown.* WeW
Paper Anarchist Addresses the Shade of Nancy Ling Perry. George Woodcock. NOBC
Paper Boats. Rabindranath Tagore. FaPON
Paper come out—done strewed de news. Scottsboro. *Unknown.* InPK
Paper Cutter, The. David Ignatow. CTBA
Paper Dragons. Susan Alton Schmeltz. RHPC
Paper Kite, The, *sel.* Samuel Bowden.
"Kite, completed thus, is borne along, The." NOEC
Paper Lantern, The. Tennessee Williams. *Fr.* Recuerdo. CTBA
Paper Matches. Paulette Jiles. NOBC
"Paper Men to Air Hopes and Fears." Robert Francis. LCAP
Paper Nautilus, The. Marianne Moore. VGW
Paper of Pins. *Unknown.* AmFP; BLSo, *with music*; FSW
Paper tiger throw H-bomb in south pole. Pepsi Generation. Walasse Ting. MAT
Paper tigers roar at noon, The. Tiger. A. D. Hope. OxBC
Paper Words. William Franklin. LFAC
Papermill Graveyard. Ben Belitt. NYBP
Paperweight Escape. Stephen Todd Booker. LFAC
Paphnutius, *sel.* Hroswitha von Gandersheim, *tr. fr. Latin by* Patrick Diehl.
"I bring you a goat." WPOW
Paphos. Lawrence Durrell. NYBP
Papio. Eric Chock. BrSi
Pap's got his patent right, and rich as all creation. Back to Griggsby's Station. James Whitcomb Riley. BLPA; BLPL
Paps of Dana, The. James Stephens. NoAM
Paps of Jura, The. Andrew Young. PoSH
Papuan Shepherd, A. Francis Webb. *Fr.* A Drum for Ben Boyd. PoAu-2
Parable. W. H. Auden. FaBoCo
Parable. Peggy Bennett. ELU
Parable, A. George L. Kress. STF
Parable, A, *sel.* James Russell Lowell.
" 'Have ye founded your thrones and altars, then.' " PGD
Parable. Robert Pack. NePoEA-2
Parable for Poetasters, A. Oliver St. John Gogarty. WhC
Parable: November. Stephen Tapscott. FAZ
Parable of the Old Man and the Young, The. Wilfred Owen. FaBoRV; PAI
Parabola. A. D. Hope. PoA
Paracelsus, *sels.* Robert Browning.
Awakening of Man, The, *fr.* V. WGRP
Faith, *fr.* V. TreFT
Song: "Heap cassia, sandal-buds, and stripes." OBEV; OBRV; WHA
Thus the Mayne Glideth, *fr.* V. OBEV
Wanderers, The, *fr.* IV. OBEV; OBVV
(Song: "Over the sea our galleys went.") OBRV
Parachute. Dwight Okita. Brsi
Parachute Descent. David Bourne. WaP
Parachutes, My Love, Could Carry Us Higher. Barbara Guest. NeAP
Parachuting Thoor Ballylee. William Zaranka. BXAP
Parachutist, The. Jon Anderson. AmPA; LiSp; NYBP
Parade. Rachel Field. *Fr.* A Circus Garland. OBCA; SoPo
Parade, The. Ashton Greene. NePoAm
Parade, A. Mary Catherine Rose. SoPo
Parade's End. Barbara Guest. PoM
Paradice on earth is found, A. *See* Paradise on earth is found, A.
Paradigm. Babette Deutsch. TrJP
Paradigm, The. Allen Tate. NOBA
Paradigms of Fire. Brian Swann. AmPA
Parading near Saint Peter's flood. The Battle of Lake Champlain. Philip Freneau. PAH
Paradise. Willis Barnstone. VWA
Paradise. George Birdseye. DBV
(Paradise; a Hindoo Legend.) HBV-1
Paradise. Chana Bloch. VWA
Paradise. Frederick William Faber. HBV-2
(O Paradise! O Paradise!) WGRP
Paradise. George Herbert. OAEL-1; SeCP; TrGrPo
Paradise. Milton. *Fr.* Paradise Lost, IV. OBS
Paradise. Immanuel di Roma, *tr. fr. Hebrew by* J. Chotzner. TrJP
Paradise. Christina Rossetti. HBV-2; OxBoCh; WGRP
Paradise. E. N. Sargent. NYBP
Paradise; a Hindoo Legend. George Birdseye. *See* Paradise.
Paradise Lost, *sels.* Milton.
Adam and Eve ("So passed they naked on, nor shunned the sight"), *Bk.* IV, *ll.* 319-355. SeCePo
Adam Fallen ("He ended, and they both descended the hill"), *Bk.* XII, *ll.* 606-649. NOCV
Adam Speaks ("Oh, why did God,/ Creator wise"), *Bk.* X, *ll.* 888-908. NU
Adam Unfallen ("Oh favourable spirit, propitious guest"), *Bk.* V, *ll.* 507-543. NOCV
"And God created the great whales, and each," *Bk.* VII, *ll.* 391-416. EtS; MoS
Ark, The ("At length a reverend sire among them came"), *Bk.* XI, *ll.* 719-753. EtS
Atonement, The ("Father, Thy word is past, man shall find grace"), *Bk.* III, *ll.* 227-265. OBS
Banishment, The ("So spake our Mother Eve, and Adam heard"), *Bk.* XII, *ll.* 624-649. NOBE; OBS
(Exit from Eden, The.) FaBoRV
(Their Banishment.) SeCePo
Banishment from Paradise ("Descended Adam to the bower where Eve"), *Bk.* XII, *ll.* 607-649. TreFS
"Beneath him with new wonder now he views," *Bk.* IV, *ll.* 205-268. PPP
Council of Satan, The ("So Satan spake, and him Beëlzebub"), *Bk.* I, *ll.* 271-669. PoEL-3
Creation of the Animals ("And God said, let the waters generate"), *Bk.* VII, *ll.* 387-505. FM
"Descend from Heaven, Urania, by that name," *Bk.* VII, *ll.* 1-39. EBEV; OAEL-1
(Invocation to Urania.) FiP; OBS
"Earth was form'd, but in the womb as yet, The," *Bk.* VII, *ll.* 276-309. MOS
Eden ("Thus was this place"), *Bk.* IV, *ll.* 246-268. FaBoEn
Eve Penitent ("Forsake me not thus, Adam, witness Heav'n"), *Bk.* X, *ll.* 914-946. OBS
Evening in Paradise ("Now came still evening on, and twilight gray"), *Bk.* IV, *ll.* 598-609. FaBoEn; GN; LoBV, *ll.* 598-688; NOBE, *ll.* 598-656
(Moon and the Nightingale, The.) ChTr; MOON
(Night Falls on Eden.) TreFS
Expulsion from Paradise ("The brandish't sword of God before them blazed"), *Bk.* XII, *ll.* 633-649. ChTr
Fall, The ("Thus saying, from her husband's hand her hand"), *Bk.* IX, *ll.* 385-1189. PoEL-3
First Day of Creation, The ("So sang the hierarchies; meanwhile the Son"), *Bk.* VII, *ll.* 192-260. OxBoCh
Gabriel Meets Satan ("Which of those rebell spirits adjudg'd to Hell"), *Bk.* IV, *ll.* 823-1015. LoBV
Great Creator from His Work Returned, The (" 'Open, ye everlasting gates!' they sung"), *Bk.* VII, *ll.* 565-601. TreFT
"Hail holy light, ofspring [*or* offspring] of Heav'n first born," *Bk.* III, *ll.* 1-55. OAEL-1; OAEP; SCV; ViBoPo
(Hail, Holy Light.) FiP; LoBV; WHA

(Holy Light.) NOBE
(Hymn to Light, *ll.* 1-50.) FaBoEn
(Light.) LiTB; OBEV; OBS
"Hail wedded love, mysterious law, true source," *Bk.* IV. BiP, *ll.* 750-755
(Their Wedded Love, *ll.* 750-775.) SeCePo
(Wedded Love, *ll.* 750-775.) OBS
"He ended; and thus Adam last replied," *Bk.* XII, *ll.* 552-649. HeIP
(Retreat from Paradise, The.) PoEL-3
Heaven ("No sooner had th' Almighty ceas't, but all"), *Bk.* III, *ll.* 344-371. OBS
Hell ("At once with him they rose"), *Bk.* II, *ll.* 475-628. OBS
"Her long with ardent look his eye pursu'd," *Bk.* IX, *ll.* 397-470. UnPo
"High on a throne of royal state, which far," *Bk.* II. NIP, *ll.* 1-42; OAEL-1; *ll.* 1-309; OAEP, *complete*
"His pride/ Had cast him out from Heaven, with all his host," *Bk.* I, *ll.* 37-236, *abr.* PPoe
"If thou beest he; but O how fall'n! how chang'd," *Bk.* I, *ll.* 84-124. SCV
Immortal Hate ("There the companions of his fall, o'erwhelmed"), *Bk.* I, *ll.* 76-124. NOBE
"In bower and field he sought, where any tuft," *Bk.* IX, *ll.* 417-792. TEP
(Eve, *ll.* 417-466.) OBS
"Into thir inmost bower," *Bk.* IV, *ll.* 738-757. FF
"Is this the region, this the soil, the clime," *Bk.* I, *ll.* 242-270. TEP
(Fall of the Angels, The, *ll.* 242-363.) FiP
(Satan as Rebel-Liberator, *ll.* 242-255.) FF
(Satan Ponders His Fallen State, *ll.* 242-263.) TreFS
Leave Taking ("Whence thou returnst, and whither wentst, I know"), *Bk.* XII, *ll.* 610-649. FaBoEn
Leviathan ("There leviathan/Hugest of living creatures, on the deep"), *Bk.* VII, *ll.* 412-416. AmMo
"Meanwhile the adversary of God and man," *Bk.* II. DL, *ll.* 629-841; EBEV, *ll.* 629-734
(Sin and Death, *ll.* 629-889.) OBNV
"Meanwhile the tepid caves and fens and shores," *Bk.* VII, *ll.* 417-448. PBBP
(Creation of Birds, The, *ll.* 417-446.) PB
Morning Hymn of Adam ("These are thy glorious works, parent of good"), *Bk.* V, *ll.* 153-165, 195-208. TrPWD
(Adam's Morning Hymn, *ll.* 153-210.) WGRP
(Morning Hymn of Adam and Eve, *ll.* 153-208.) OxBoCh
New Worlds ("As when a Scout/through dark and desart wayes with peril gone"), *Bk.* III, *ll.* 543-571. OBS
"Next came one/ Who mourn'd in earnest," *Bk.* I. *ll.* 457-489. EBEV
"No more of talk where God or angel guest," *Bk.* IX, *complete.* NoP; OAEL-1
(Subject of Heroic Song, The, *ll.* 1-47.) OBS
Now Came Still Evening On ("Uriel to his charge/ Returned on that bright beam"), *Bk.* IV, *ll.* 589-609. FaBoRV
"Now had th' Almighty Father from above," *Bk.* III, *ll.* 54-76. NIP
"Now Morn her rosy steps in the eastern clime," *Bk.* V, *ll.* 1-128. OAEL-1
"O Father, O Supreme of heav'nly Thrones," *Bk.* VI, *ll.* 723-745. ILwL
"O for that warning voice, which he who saw," *Bk.* IV. OAEL-1, *complete;* TEP, *ll.* 1-324
(Prospect of Eden, The, *ll.* 1-775.) PoEL-3
"Of man's first disobedience, and the fruit," *Bk.* I. EBEV, *ll.* 1-270; FaBoRV, *ll.* 1-26; NIP, *ll.* 1-49; NoP, *ll.* 1-26; OAEL-1, *ll.* 1-375; OAEP, *complete;* SCV, *ll.* 1-26; TEP, *ll.* 1-75
(Invocation, *ll.* 1-26.) FaBoEn; PoEL-3
(Invocation to the Heavenly Muse, *ll.* 1-26.) TreFS
(Of Man's First Disobedience, *ll.* 1-26.) FiP
"Over all the face of earth/ Main ocean flow'd," *Bk.* VII, *ll.* 278-308. EtS
Pandemonium and Its Architect ("Anon out of the earth a fabric huge"), *Bk.* I, *ll.* 710-746. TreFS
Panorama, The ("Satan from hence now on the lower stair"), *Bk.* III, *ll.* 540-565. WHA
Paradise ("Another side, umbrageos grots and caves"), *Bk.* IV, *ll.* 257-294. OBS
Place of the Damned, The ("Farr off from these a slow and silent stream"), *Bk.* II, *ll.* 582-603. FaBoEn
Plan of Salvation, The ("O thou in heaven and earth the only place"), *Bk.* III, *ll.* 274-343. WGRP
Satan ("He ceased; and Satan stayed not to reply"), *Bk.* II, *ll.* 1010-1055. SeCePo
(Satan Views the World.) WHA
Satan ("He scarce had ceas't when the superior Fiend"), *Bk.* I, *ll.* 283-313. SeCePo
(Satan and the Fallen Angels.) LiTB; OBS
Satan ("His pride/ Had cast him out from Heaven, with all his host"), *Bk.* I, *ll.* 36-75. TreFT; TrGrPo, *ll.* 36-75, 221-237, 524-543
("His pride/ Had cast him out from Heaven," *ll.* 36-237, *abr.*) PPoe
Satan and His Host ("But he his wonted pride"), *Bk.* I, *ll.* 527-699. OBS
Satan Beholds Adam and Eve in Eden ("O Hell! what do mine eyes with grief behold!"), *Bk.* IV, *ll.* 358-392. TW
Satan Defiant ("Him the Almighty Power"), *Bk.* I, *ll.* 44-109. WHA
(Fallen Angels, The, *ll.* 44-74.) FaBoEn
Satan Journeys to the Garden of Eden ("Now to th' ascent of that steep savage hill"), *Bk.* IV, *ll.* 172-201. ChTr
Satan Looks upon Adam and Eve in Paradise ("Two of far nobler shape, erect and tall"), *Bk.* IV, *ll.* 288-324. TreFS
Satan's Address to the Sun ("Now conscience wakes despair"), *Bk.* IV, *ll.* 23-113. BiP
(Scene in Paradise, A, *ll.* 23-55, *abr.*) GN
Satan's Adjuration ("What though the field be lost?"), *Bk.* I, *ll.* 105-124. FaBoEn
(What Though the Field Be Lost?) EaLo
Satan's Soliloquy ("O thou that with surpassing glory crown'd"), *Bk.* IV, *ll.* 32-113. LiTB; OBS
"She, as a veil down to the slender waist," *Bk.* IV, *ll.* 304-311. ErPo
(Before the Fall, *ll.* 304-355.) NIP
"So spake the Archangel Michaël, then paused," *Bk.* XII, *ll.* 466-649. OAEL-1
"So spake the enemy of mankind, enclosed," *Bk.* IX, *ll.* 494-526. FM
"So stretched out huge in length the Arch-Field lay," *Bk.* I, *ll.* 209-238. TEP
"Southward through Eden went a river large," *Bk.* IV, *ll.* 223-311. ViBoPo
Standing on Earth ("Standing on Earth, not rapt above the Pole"), *Bk.* VII, *ll.* 23-39. ChTr
"Stygian council thus dissolved; and forth, The," *Bk.* II, *ll.* 506-870. OAEL-1
Summons, The ("He stood and call'd/ His legions, angel forms, who lay intranst"), *Bk.* I, *ll.* 300-345, 522-587. WHA
(Satan's Legions and the Beech Leaves of the Casentino, *ll.* 300-304.) FaBoPP
"Thee, Father, first they sung Omnipotent," *Bk.* III, *ll.* 372-415. ILwL
Their Banishment ("For now too nigh"), *Bk.* XII, *ll.* 625-649. SeCePo
Then When I Am Thy Captive, Talk of Chains ("Now had night measured with her shadowy cone"), *Bk.* IV, *ll.* 776-1015. WHA
"There stood a hill not far whose grisly top," *Bk.* I, *ll.* 670-798. OBEL-1
"They ended parle, and both addressed for fight," *Bk.* VI, *ll.* 296-353. OBWP
"This having learnt, thou hast attaind the summe," *Bk.* XII, *ll.* 575-649. SCV
"Thus Adam himself lamented loud," *Bk.* X, *ll.* 845-1104. OAEL-1
Thus Eve to Adam ("My author and disposer, what thou biddest"), *Bk.* IV, *ll.* 635-658. FaBV
"Thus saying, from her side the fatal key," *Bk.* II, *ll.* 871-1055. EBEV
"Thus talking hand in hand alone they pass'd," *Bk.* IV, *ll.* 689-775. EBEV
"Thus they in Heav'n above the starry sphear," *Bk.* III, *ll.* 416-515. EBEV
"To whom thus also th' angel last replied," *Bk.* XII, *ll.* 574-649. FiP
What Words Have Passed ("What words have passed thy lips, Adam severe"), *Bk.* IX, *ll.* 1144-1189. TrCP
"While thus he spake, th'Angelic Squadron bright," *Bk.* IV, *ll.* 977-1004. SCV
"With thee conversing, I forget all time," *Bk.* IV, *ll.* 639-656. WiR
(Eve Speaks to Adam.) ChTr; GBL
(Eve to Adam.) FaBoEn; TreFS; TrGrPo
World Beautiful, The ("Sweet is the breath of morn, her rising sweet"), *Bk.* IV, *ll.* 641-649. GN
Paradise Lost. Stanley J. Sharpless. BXAP
Paradise [*or* Paradice] on earth is found, A. The Description of Elizium [*or* The Poet's Paradise]. Michael Drayton. *Fr.* The Muses' Elizium. AnAnS-2; OAEL-1; WiR
Paradise Regained, *sels.* Milton.
"At thy nativity a glorious quire," *Bk.* I, *ll.* 242-254. PChr
But to His Mother Mary ("But to his mother Mary, when she saw"), *Bk.* II, *ll.* 60-108. ISi
First Temptation, The ("Full forty days he pass'd, whether on a hill"), *Bk.* I, *ll.* 303-502. OxBoCh
"It was the hour of night, when thus the Son," *Bk.* II, *ll.* 260-389. EBEV
"Look once more ere we leave this specular Mount," *Bk.* IV, *ll.* 236-284. ViBoPo
(Athens, *ll.* 236-364.) OBS
Messiah, The ("So they in Heav'n their odes and vigils tun'd"), *Bk.* I, *ll.* 182-293. OBS
Parthians, The ("He looked and saw what numbers numberless"), *Bk.* III, *ll.* 310-343. OBS
Rome ("The City which thou seest no other deem"), *Bk.* IV, *ll.* 44-108. OBS
Satan's Guile ("Whom thus answer'd th' Arch Fiend now undisguis'd"), *Bk.* I, *ll.* 357-405. LiTB; OBS
Table Richly Spread, A ("A table richly spread, in regal mode"), *Bk.* II, *ll.* 340-365. FaBoCh
"Therefore let pass, as they are transitory," *Bk.* IV, *ll.* 209-364. OAEL-1

True and False Glory ("To whom our Saviour calmly thus reply'd"), *Bk.* III, *ll.* 43-107. LiTB; OBS
Paradise Saved. A. D. Hope. OxBC
Paradisi Gloria. Thomas William Parsons. AA
Paradiso. Dante. *See* Divina Commedia.
Paradox. Benjamin K. Bennett. POL
Paradox, The. John Donne. OAEP
Paradox, The. Paul Laurence Dunbar. CABA; PoBA
Paradox. Angelina Weld Grimké. CDC
Paradox. Vassar Miller. NePoEA
Paradox, The. Francesca Yetunde Pereira. PBA
Paradox, A. Aurelian Townshend. AnAnS-2; SeCP
Paradox, The ("Let Cynics bark, and the stern Stagirite"). *Unknown.* APAS
Paradox, A ("Though we boast of modern progress"). *Unknown.* ShM
Paradox of Time, The. Pierre de Ronsard, *tr. fr. French by* Austin Dobson. AWP; HBV-1
Paradox: That Fruition Destroys Love, *sel.* Henry King.
"Since lovers' joys then leave so sick a taste." ErPo
Paradox: The Birds. Karl Shapiro. CrMA
Paradoxes and Oxymorons. John Ashbery. NoP
Paragon of Animals, The. Pope. *Fr.* An Essay on Man. ACP
Paragraph, A. Hayden Carruth. FAZ
Parallax. Maxwell Anderson. NYBP
Parallel Texts. Robert Kelly. CoPo
Paralytic man has dropped in death, The. In Manchester Square. Alice Meynell. SBG
Paranoia. Michael Dennis Browne. AmPA
Paranoia in Crete. Gregory Corso. NeAP
Paraphrase. Hart Crane. MoVE; TwAmPo
Paraphrase from the French, A. Matthew Prior. OxBoLi
Paraphrase of Luther's Hymn. Martin Luther. *See* Mighty Fortress Is Our God, A.
Paraphrase on the Psalms of David, *sels.* George Sandys.
Deo Opt. Max, Psalm CIV. OBS
Psalm XXIII: "Lord my shepherd, me His sheep, The." JCP
Psalme CXXXVII. OBS
Paraphrase on Thomas á Kempis, A. Pope. GoBC; OBEC
"Speak, Gracious Lord, oh speak; thy Servant hears," *sel.* TrPWD
Parasite lichen. Lichen. Mary Fullerton. PoAu-1
Parasitosis. Ronda Davis. JB
Parcae, The, or Three Dainty Destinies: The Armillet. Robert Herrick. CaPo
Parchman Farm Blues. *Unknown.* BluL
Parchment and paper left clean. The Making of Color. Hugh Seidman. AmPA
Parcy Reed, *with music. Unknown.* OxBB
Pardon. Julia Ward Howe. PAH
Pardon, The. Richard Wilbur. NePoEA; NIP; NoAM; NOBA; NoP; PAI
Pardon, goddess of the night. Song [*or* Claudio's Lament]. Shakespeare. *Fr.* Much Ado about Nothing, V, iii. CTC; OBSC; ViBoPo
Pardon, Lord, the lips that dare. Whittier. *Fr.* Andrew Rykman's Prayer. TrPWD
Pardon me, lady, but I wanta ast you. Drug Store. John V. A. Weaver. HBMV; YaD
Pardon mine ears, both I and they do pray. Astrophel and Stella, LI. Sir Philip Sidney. SiPS
Pardon, Old Fathers. W. B. Yeats. *Fr.* Responsibilities. OAEP
("Pardon, old fathers, if you still remain.") PoEL-5
Pardon our visit to this place. The Framework-Knitters Petition. C. Briggs. CoMu
Pardoner's Prologue and Tale, The. Chaucer. *Fr.* The Canterbury Tales. NoP. *See also* Pardoner's Tale, The.
Pardoner's Prologue, The, *sel.* OAEL-1; OAEP
Pardoner's Sermon, The. Sir David Lindsay. *Fr.* Ane Satyre of the Thrie Estaitis. BSV
Pardoner's Tale, The. Chaucer. *Fr.* The Canterbury Tales. BiP, *mod. version by* Nevill Coghill; FiP; HAP, *abr.;* OAEL-1; OAEP; PoEL-1; SCV, *mod. vers. by* Nevill Coghill
(Pardoner's Prologue and Tale, The.) NoP
Sels.
"But, sires o word forgat I in my tale." EBEV
Death and the Three Revellers. OBNV
("These rioters, of whom I make my rime," *mod. version.*) WHA
(Three Revellers Search for Death.) OxBM
Parent of all, omnipotent. The American Patriot's Prayer. *Unknown.* PAH
Parentage. Alice Meynell. SBG
Parentage. William Stafford. BiP
Parental Ode to My Son [Aged Three Years and Five Months], A. Thomas Hood. FiBHP, *abr.;* HBV-1; PoLF
(To My Son, Aged Three Years and Five Months, *abr.*) FaPON
Parental Recollections. Charles Lamb. OBRV
Parenthood. John Farrar. OHIP
Parents. Vincent Buckley. CBAP
Parents. William Meredith. FYAP
Parents are sinful now, for they must whisper. Marriage. Austin Clarke. BlrV; GTBS-P; OxBI
Parents in Winter, *sel.* L. E. Sissman.
"Brick plant like a school, The. The winter set." DiL
Parents of Psychotic Children, The. Marvin Bell. SUW
Parents-Without-Partners Picnic, The. Ted Schaefer. FAZ
Parfum Exotique. Baudelaire, *tr. fr. French by* Arthur Symons. AWP
Pariah's Prayer, The. Goethe, *tr. fr. German.* ILwL
Paring the Apple. Charles Tomlinson. CMoP; NePoEA-2; NMP; OxBTC
Paris. Gregory Corso. VGW
Paris. Jane Garnett. AMV-80
Paris. Gertrud Kolmar, *tr. fr. German by* David Kipp. PBWP
Paris. Arthur Symons. SyP
Paris at Night. Tristan Corbière, *tr. fr. French by* Kenneth Koch *and* Georges Guy. SyP
Paris by Night. Gustave Kahn, *tr. fr. French by* Edouard Roditi. VWA
Paris in the Snow. Léopold Sédar Senghor, *tr. fr. French by* Ulli Beier. PBA
Paris Nocturne, A. "Fiona Macleod." SyP
Paris; the Seine at Night. Charles Divine. HBMV
Paris; This April Sunset Completely Utters. E. E. Cummings. SOTW
Parish. Norman Dubie. MAYP
Parish Poor-House, The. George Crabbe. *Fr.* The Village. OBEC
Parish Poor-Officers, The. Edward Ward. *Fr.* A Journey to Hell; or, A Visit Paid to the Devil. NOEC
Parish priest, The. The Preacher's Mistake. William Croswell Doane. BLPA
Parish-priest was of the pilgrim train, A. The Character of a Good Parson. Dryden. NOCV
Parish Register, The, *sels.* George Crabbe.
Baptisms, Pt. I.
"Behold the cot!" OBRV
Marriages, Pt. II.
"Disposed to wed, e'en while you hasten, stay." FaBoUs
"Next at our altar." OBRV
Burials, Pt. III, *abr.* OAEL-1
Ancient Virgin, An. OBNC
Lady of the Manor, The. NOBE; OBNC
"My record ends." OBRV
Parisian Idyl, A, *sel.* George Moore.
"This is the twilight of the summer dead." SyP
Parisian Nectar. Gelett Burgess. FaBoNo
(Nonsense Quatrains: "Many people seem to think.") CenHV
Parity. Kenneth Rexroth. GP
Park, The. Robin Blaser. CoPo
Park. David Ignatow. Psk
Park, The. James A. Tippett. SUS; TiPo
Park at Evening, The. Leslie Norris. DuDa
Park Avenue. Robert Fitzgerald. NYP
Park in Milan, The. William Jay Smith. CAD; CoAP;
Park is filled with night and fog, The. Spring Night. Sara Teasdale. BLPL; FaBoBe; HBMV; LiTA; MoAmPo
Park Pigeons. Melville Cane. CAD
Park Poem. Paul Blackburn. CoPo
Park, the heart, you see at town's center is soft, The. Last Look at La Plata, Missouri. Jim Barnes. CDW
Parked in the fields. The Forms of Love. George Oppen. NNaP
Parklands, The. Stevie Smith. MoBS
Parks and Ponds. Emerson. PoEL-4
Park's beautiful, The. On the Fine Arts Garden, Cleveland. Russell Atkins. PoBA
Parlement of Foules, The, *sels.* Chaucer.
"Lyf so short, the craft so long to lerne, The." ViBoPo
(Proem to the Parlement of Foules.) FiP
Roundel: "Now welcom [*or* welcome] somer, with thy sonne softe." CTC; OAEL-1
(Foules Rondel, *orig., with mod. vers.* [The Birds' Rondel] *by* Louis Untermeyer.) TrGrPo
(Now Welcom [*or* Welcome] Somer.) HAP; SeCePo
(Now Welcome Summer.) OxBM
(Qui Bien Aime a Tard Oublie.) EnLoPo
(Welcome Summer.) MeEL
Seynt Valentynes Day. PB
"There mighte men the royal eagle find." PBBP
Parlement [*or* Parliament] of the Thre Ages, The, *sels. Unknown.*
Poacher, The, *orig. and mod. English prose.* OxBM
"When the water fowl are found, the falconers hasten." PBBP
Parley of Beasts. "Hugh MacDiarmid." BoAnP; MoBrPo; NoAM; NoP; OBMV
("Auld Noah was at hame wi' them a'.") LO
Parley with His Empty Purse, A. Thomas Randolph. JCP; OBS

Parleyings with Certain People of Importance in Their Day, *sel.* Robert Browning.
With Francis Furini. VLP
Parliament Dissolved at Oxford, The. *Unknown.* APAS
Parliament Hill Fields. John Betjeman. FaBoTw; NOBE
Parliament of Bees, The, *sel.* John Day.
"I will have one built/ Like Pompey's theatre." ViBoPo
Parliament of Cats. D. J. Enright. NMP
Parliament of England, Ye. *Unknown. See* Ye Parliament of England.
Parliament of Fowls, The. Chaucer. *See* Parlement of Foules, The.
Parliament Soldiers, The. *Unknown.* GBP
("High diddle ding, did you hear the bells ring?" *diff. vers.*) OxNR
Parnell. Thomas Kettle. AnIV
(Parnell's Memory.) ACP
Parnell. W. B. Yeats. CMoP
Parochial Theme. Wallace Stevens. LiTA
Parodie, A: "Souls joy, when thou art gone." George Herbert. AnAnS-1; OBS
Parodies of Cole Porter's "Night and Day." Ring Lardner. OBAL
Parody. Martha Paley Francescato, *tr. fr. Spanish by* Willis Barnstone. BoWoP
Parody on "A Psalm of Life," A. *Unknown, at. to* Oliver Wendell Holmes. BLPA
Parody on Thomas Hood's "The Bridge of Sighs." *Unknown.* FiBHP
Parole Board. Derek Butler. LFAC
Parole Denial. J. Charles Green. LFAC
Paros. Robin Magowan. EAS
Parrhasius. Nathaniel Parker Willis. AA
Parricide. Julia Ward Howe. PAH
Parrot, The. Thomas Campbell. FM; PB
Parrot, The. James Elroy Flecker. FaBoTw
Parrot, The. W. W. Gibson. OBMV
Parrot, The. Edward Lucie-Smith. BoAnP; SO
Parrot, The. John Skelton. *See* Parrot's Soliloquy.
Parrot, The/ Is eating a carrot. Who Killed Lawless Lean? Stevie Smith. TEP
Parrot and Dove. Walter Savage Landor. PB
Parrot and the carrot we may easily confound, The. Robert W. Wood. PV
Parrot Cry, The. "Hugh MacDiarmid." OxBS
Parrot Fish, The. James Merrill. NOBA
Parrot, from the Spanish main, A. The Parrot. Thomas Campbell. PB
Parrot, if I had your wings. The Boy and the Parrot. John Hookham Frere. OxBChV
Parrot is a thief, The. The Parrot. Edward Lucie-Smith. BoAnP; SO
Parrots, The. W. W. Gibson. CH; RoGo
Parrots have richly color'd wings. Parrot and Dove. Walter Savage Landor. PB
Parrot's Soliloquy. John Skelton. *Fr.* Speak, Parrot. PoEL-1
(Parrot, The.) ACP
(Speke, Parrot, *abr.*) OxBoLi
Parrot's voice snaps out, The. "Psittachus Eois Imitatrix Ales ab Indis." Sacheverell Sitwell. MoBrPo
Parsifal. Paul Verlaine, *tr. fr. French by* John Gray. *Fr.* Amour. PAI; SyP
Parsnip, The. Ogden Nash. NePA
Parson Allen's Ride. Wallace Bruce. PAH
Parson Gray. Goldsmith. NA
Parson Grocer, The. *Unknown.* CoMu
Parson him answered, The, "Bendicite!" The Shipman. Chaucer. *Fr.* The Canterbury Tales: Prologue to the Shipman's Tale. ACP
Parson of a country town was he, The. The Good Parson. Chaucer, *mod. version by* H. C. Leonard. *Fr.* The Canterbury Tales, Prologue. TRV; WGRP
Parson, these things in thy possessing. The Happy Life of a Country Parson. Pope. BXAP
Parsons, The. Thomas Edward Brown. DBV
Parson's Job, The. Madeline Ida Bedford. SUMH
Parson's Looks, The. Burns. OxBoLi
Parson's Pleasure. Barry O. Higgs. PeSA
Part fenced by man, part by a rugged steep. A Place of Burial in the South of Scotland. Wordsworth. VLP
Part for the Whole. Robert Francis. PoA
Part of a Letter. Richard Wilbur. CMoP
Part of a Novel, Part of a Poem, Part of a Play, *sels.* Marianne Moore.
Hero, The. CMoP; NOBA; OxBA; PoA; TwAmPo
Steeple-Jack, The. AP; BoWoP; CMoP; CoBMV; CrMA; FaBoMo; HAP; MoPo; NoAM; NOBA; NoP; OxBA; PBWP; SBG; TwAmPo; WeW; WPE
Part of an Ode, A. Ben Jonson. *See* Noble Nature, The.
Part of Fortune, The. Ann Sanfedele. AMV-81
Part of Plenty. Bernard Spencer. ErPo; GBL; LiTB; LiTM
Part of the Darkness. Isabella Gardner. BoAnP
Part of the Lay of Sigrdrifa. *Unknown, tr. fr. Old Norse by* William Morris *and* Eirikr Magnusson. *Fr.* The Elder Edda. OBVE
(Counsels of Sigrdrifa.) AWP
Part of the Vigil. James Merrill. NoAM
Part of the work remains; one part is past. The End of His Work. Robert Herrick. CaPo
Part-Sequence for Change, A. Robert Duncan. VGW
Parta Quies. A. E. Housman. NOBE; TEP
(Alta Quies.) SeCeV
Partaking of the miraculous. Apparition of Splendor. Marianne Moore. NePoAm
Parted Souls. Lord Herbert of Cherbury. AnAnS-2; SeCP
Parterre, The. E. Harriet Palmer. FaBoCo; NA; NOBL
Parthenophil and Parthenophe, *sels.* Barnabe Barnes.
"Ah, sweet Content! where is thy mylde abode?" LXVI. AAS
(Content.) OBSC
(Sonnet: "Ah, sweet Content! where is thy mild abode.") ElL
"Jove for Europaes love tooke shape of bull," LXIII. AAS
"O Powers Celestial, with what sophistry." EnLoPo
Ode, An: "Why doth heaven bear a sun." ElL; OBSC
"Soft, lovely, rose-like lips, conjoined with mine." EnLoPo
Parthians, The. Milton. *Fr.* Paradise Regained, III. OBS
Partholan went out one day. The First Lawcase. *Unknown, tr. by* John Montague. BIrV
Partial Comfort. Dorothy Parker. FaBoCo; OBAL
Partial Draft. Robert B. Shaw. AMV-81
Partial Eclipse. W. D. Snodgrass. MOON
Partial Explanation, The. Charles Simic. FiCP; NoP
Partial Resemblance. Denise Levertov. CoAP; NaP
Parting. Matthew Arnold. Switzerland, II. OAEP; VLP
Parting. Alice Corbin. BPAW
Parting. Emily Dickinson. *See* My life closed twice before its close.
Parting, The. Michael Drayton. *See* Idea: "Since there's no help . . ."
Parting. Judah Halevi, *tr. fr. Hebrew by* Nina Salaman. AWP; TrJP
Parting. Lady Heguri, *tr fr. Japanese by* Geoffrey Bownas *and* Anthony Thwaite. OLR
("Thousand years, you said, A.") BoLoP
Parting. Michael Hogan. GP
Parting, The. Elizabeth Jennings. NePoEA-2
Parting ("High towers the grass where once we'd meet and wander"). *Malay Oral Tradition, tr. by* R. J. Wilkinson *and* R. O. Winstedt. WTO
Parting. Gerald Massey. HBV-1
Parting. Thomas Middleton. *Fr.* A Chaste Maid in Cheapside. ElL
Parting. Gabriel Preil, *tr. fr. Hebrew by* Laya Firestone. VWA
Parting. William Caldwell Roscoe. OBVV
(For Ever.) HBV-1
Parting. Shlomo Vinner, *tr. fr. Hebrew by* Laya Firestone *and* Howard Schwartz. VWA
Parting. W. B. Yeats. FaBoTw
Parting; a Game. Lynn Sukenick. NMM
Parting, a thousand cups won't wash away the sorrow. To Tzu-an. Yü Hsüan-chi, *tr. by* Geoffrey Waters. BoWoP
Parting after a Quarrel. Eunice Tietjens. HBMV
Parting as Descent. John Berryman. LiTA; MoAmPo
Parting at Dawn. *Malay Oral Tradition, tr. by* R. J. Wilkinson *and* R. O. Winstedt. WTO
Parting at Morning. Dietmar von Aist, *tr. fr. German by* Frank C. Nicholson. AWP
Parting at Morning. Robert Browning. AWP; FaBoEn; FaBV; FF; FiP; HBV-1; HeIP; MOS; NOBE; OAEP; OBEV; OBNC; OBVV; PAI; SoSe; TreFT; UnPo; VLP; WiR
Parting friends put me the query. Anglo-Eire Vignette. Patric Stevenson. NeIP
Parting from My Son. Evangeline Paterson. AMV-80
Parting Gift. Elinor Wylie. OxBA
Parting Glass, The. Philip Freneau. AA
Parting golden haze, A. L'Oiseau Bleu. Gordon Bottomley. BrPo
Parting Guest, A. James Whitcomb Riley. HBV-2; TreFT
Parting Hour, The. Olive Custance. HBV-1
Parting Hymn, A. Charlotte Forten. BlSi
Parting Hymn We Sing, A, *with music.* Aaron R. Wolfe. AH
Parting in Wartime. Frances Cornford. NIP
Parting injunctions, The. Clarence Day. DBV
Parting Is Hard. *Unknown, tr. fr. Chinese by* Geoffrey Waters. BoWoP
Parting: 1940. John Frederick Nims. PoA
Parting of Hector and Andromache, The. Homer, *tr fr. Greek by* William B. Smith *and* Walter Miller. *Fr.* Iliad. TreFS
Parting of the Red Sea, The. *Unknown, tr. fr. Anglo-Saxon by* Charles W. Kennedy. *Fr.* Exodus. AnOE
Parting of the Ways, The. Joseph B. Gilder. HBV-2; PAH
Parting of Venus and Old Age, The. John Gower. *Fr.* Confessio Amantis, VIII. PoEL-1

Parting Verse, the Feast There Ended, The. Robert Herrick. SeCV-1
Parting with Lucasia; a Song. Katherine Philips. PeHV
Parting, without a Sequel. John Crowe Ransom. DTC; MoAB; MoAmPo; MoVE; OxBA; SoSe
Partings. Charles Guérin, *tr. fr. French by* Jethro Bithell. AWP
Partings. Maria Jane Jewsbury. OxBChV
Partly to My Cat. Ellen Bass. NMM
Partner, The. Theodore Roethke. NePA; NePoAm
Partnership dissolved. Sale. Miller Williams. WeW
Partridge and quail, of course. Occasional woodcock. The Sportsman. David McCord. LiSp
Partridge berry, bittersweet. Counting-out Rhyme for March. Frances Frost. YeAr
Partridges. John Masefield. LiSp; OxBTC
Parts. Zishe Landau, *tr. fr. Yiddish by* Ruth Whitman. VWA
Parts of a Poet. The. Wendy Rose. TWSS
Parts of Speech, The. *Unknown. See* Grammar in a Nutshell.
Parts of the Whole Are We; but God the Whole. Dryden. *Fr.* Palamon and Arcite. NAs
Party, The. Margaret Avison. PoA
Party. Constance Carrier. NePoAm-2
Party, The. Paul Laurence Dunbar. AmNP
Party. Donald Justice. GP
Party, A. Laura E. Richards. SiSoSe; SoPo
Party, The. W. R. Rodgers. BIrV
Party, The. Reed Whittemore. CAD; CoAP; ConAP; NCSH
Party at Bannon Brook. Alden Nowlan. NeAC
Party at Hydra. Irving Layton. HeIP
Party at the Contessa's House, The. Brian Robertson. AMV-80
Party finished early, 'twas on the stroke of nine, The. The Keyhole in the Door. *Unknown.* CoMu
Party Going. Bill Manhire. OCNZ
Party in Winter. Karl Shapiro. PCP
Party is going strong, The. Tribute to Kafka for Someone Taken. Alan Dugan. CAPP; NoAM
Party Knee. John Updike. FiBHP
Party Piece. Brian Patten. BoLoP
Partying by a river near Ellwood City, Pennsylvania. Coming Home in March. Harold Littlebird. STE; VoR
Parzival, *sel.* Eithne Wilkins.
Dreamers and the Sea, The. NeBP
Pas de Deux for Lovers. Michael Dransfield. CBAP
Pasa Thalassa Thalassa. E. A. Robinson. EtS; MOS
Pascal's abyss went with him at his side. The Abyss. Baudelaire, *tr. by* Robert Lowell. SyP
Paschal Lamb. Robert Hass. NPGG
Pasquin to the Queen's Statue at St. Paul's. William Shippen. APAS
Pass, The. John Logan. LCAP
Pass Around Your Bottle, *with music. Unknown.* OuSiCo
Pass forth, my wonted cries. Sir Thomas Wyatt. SiPS
Pass It On. Henry K. Burton. BLRP
Pass It On! *Unknown.* STF
Pass It On Grandson. Ted D. Palmanteer. STE
Pass of Kirkstone, The. Wordsworth. HBV-2
Pass Office Song. *Unknown, tr. fr. Afrikaans by* Peggy Rutherford. PBA; TTY
("Take off your hat," *tr. by* H. Tracey.) WTO
Pass, thou wild light. Leavetaking. Sir William Watson. HBV-1
Pass we the ills, which each man feels or dreads. Power. Matthew Prior. *Fr.* Solomon on the Vanity of the World, Bk. III. LoBV; NOEC; PoEL-3
Passage. Hart Crane. CMoP; MoVE; NoAM; NOBA
Passage. Richard Eberhart. FAZ
Passage of a Year, The. *Unknown. Fr.* Sir Gawain and the Green Knight. PoEL-1
Passage of an August. Eithne Wilkins. NeBP
Passage over Water. Robert Duncan. NoAM; NOBA
Passage Steamer. Louis MacNeice. MOS
Passage to India. Walt Whitman. AmPP; PoEL-5
Sels.
"Ah, more than any priest, O soul, we too believe in God." WGRP
"Bathe me O God in thee, mounting to thee." TrPWD
"O we can wait no longer." ILwL
"Sail forthsteer for the deep waters." TRV
Passages. Larry Eigner. NeAP
Passages. David Walker. AMV-80
Passages, *sels.* Robert Duncan.
At the Loom. VGW
Envoy. VGW
Fire, The. VGW
Tribal Memories. NOBA
Up Rising. NNaP
Passed the end of a day in the provinces. The End of a Day in the Provinces. Jules Laforgue, *tr. by* Margaret Crosland. SyP
Passed through the dark well. The Long Hunter. Wendell Berry. *Fr.* Inland Passages. GP
Passenger Pigeons. Robert Morgan. GeTw; MAYP
Passenger Train. Edith Newlin Chase. SoPo
Passengers, The. David Antin. NYBP
Passengers. Denis Johnson. MAYP
Passenjare, The. Isaac H. Bromley. FiBHP
Passer, The. George Abbe. LiSp
Passer Mortuus Est. Edna St. Vincent Millay. CMoP; MoAmPo; OxBA
Passer-by, A. Robert Bridges. BrPo; CMoP; CoBMV; EtS; HBV-1; LiTB; LiTM; MoAB; MoBrPo; MOS; NBM; OAEL-2; OAEP; OBEV; OBNC; OBVV; OxBTC; PoPle; SeCeV; WiR
Passerby being fair about sacrifice, A. Chickens the Weasel Killed. William Stafford. NaP
Passer-by might just as well be blind, A. Walls. Robert Francis. CrMA
Passes are blocked by snow, The. Persia. V. Sackville-West. WPE
Passetyme, The. Stephen Hawes. *See* Pastime of Pleasure, The.
Passin Ben Dorain. Alastair MacKie. *Fr.* At the Heich Kirk-Yaird. PoSH
Passing a dull red college-block. A Walk in Würzburg. William Plomer. NYBP
"Passing across the billowy sea." Popular Songs of Tuscany. *Unknown, tr. by* John Addington Symonds. AWP
Passing and Glassing. Christina Rossetti. FaBoEn; OBNC
Passing Away, Saith the World, Passing Away. Christina Rossetti. Old and New Year Ditties, III. NoP; OBNC
(Passing Away.) GoBC; OAEL-2; OBVV; WPE
Passing Bell, The. Thomas Heywood. *Fr.* The Rape of Lucrece. FaBoRV
Passing Bell, The. James Shirley. ACP
Passing Bell at Stratford, The. William Winter. AA
Passing between the stumbling generations. The Wandering Jew Comes to the Wall. Edmond Fleg, *tr. by* Humbert Wolfe. *Fr.* The Wall of Weeping. TrJP
Passing By. *Unknown. See* There Is a Lady Sweet and Kind.
Passing Flower, The. Harry Kemp. HBMV
Passing glance, a lightning long the skies, A. Sonnet. William Drummond of Hawthornden. ViBoPo
Passing I saw her as she stood beside. The Gypsy Girl. Henry Alford. HBV-1
Passing into Storm. Patrick Lane. NOBC
Passing It On. Reg Saner. GP
Passing like a Strauss waltz. The Hoofer. A. K. Redwing. VoR
Passing Love. Langston Hughes. BiP
Passing motorist glanced back, A. The Shack. Nellie Burget Miller. PoOW
Passing of Arthur, The. J. C. Squire. BXAP
Passing of Arthur, The. Tennyson. *See* Idylls of the King.
Passing of Lydia, The. Horace, *tr. fr. Latin by* Louis Untermeyer. UnTE
Passing of March, The. Robert Burns Wilson. HBV-1
Passing of the Buffalo, The. Hamlin Garland. BPAW
Passing of the Shee, The. J. M. Synge. BIrV; FaBoEE; OnYI
Passing out of a great city. Initial. Arthur Boyars. NePoEA-2
Passing out of the shadow. Just Passing. *Unknown.* BLRP
Passing policeman found a little child, A. The Little Lost Child. Edward B. Marks. TreFS
Passing Remark. William Stafford. GP
Passing Strange, The. John Masefield. LiTB; MoAB; MoBrPo; MoPo; OBEV
Passing stranger! you do not know how longingly I look upon you. To a Stranger. Walt Whitman. NoAM; NOBA
Passing the American graveyard, for my birthday. Poem for My Twentieth Birthday. Kenneth Koch. PoA
Passing the flower-stalls there did I perceive. Epigram. Strato, *tr. fr. Greek by* Sydney Oswald. PeHV
Passing the Graveyard. Andrew Young. DTC
Passing the great plane tree in the square. The Beginning of the End. Jon Stallworthy. OxBC
Passing the Masonic Home for the Aged. Herbert Scott. PPJ
Passing Through. Annie Johnson Flint. BLRP
(Through the Waters.) STF
Passing through huddled and ugly walls. The Harbor. Carl Sandburg. NCSH; PoPl; TAP
Passing today by a cottage, I shed tears. C. S. Lewis. LO
Passing Visit to Helen. D. H. Lawrence. CMoP
Passion. Galway Kinnell. NePoAm
Passion, The. Ralph Knevet. JCP
Passion, The. Henry Vaughan. AnAnS-1
Passion and Exaltation of Christ, The. Isaac Watts. NOCV
Passion Drinker, The. Anita Endrezze Probst. VoR
Passion-Flower, The. Margaret Fuller. HBV-1

"Passion o' me!" cried Sir Richard Tyrone. The Sally from Coventry. Walter Thornbury. HBV-2
Passion of a Lover, The. George Gascoigne. EnRePo
(Gascoigne's Passion.) NCEP
Passion of Christ, The. Denis Devlin. IPY
Passion of Jesus, The. *Unknown.* MeEL
Passion of M'Phail, The, *sels.* Horace Gregory.
Lunchroom Bus Boy Who Looked like Orson Welles, The. NYP; TwAmPo
(They Were All like Geniuses.) NYBP
This Is the Place to Wait. MoAmPo
Passion of Our Lady, The, *sel.* Charles Péguy, *tr. fr. French by* Julian Green.
"For the past three days she had been wandering, and following." ISi
Passionate are palms that clasp in double fist. In the Wind's Eye. R. P. Blackmur. Scarabs for the Living, II. CrMA
Passionate Encyclopedia Britannica Reader to his Love, The. "Maggie." InMe
Passionate love is temporary. Landscape with Leaves and Figure. Olga Broumas. BoWoP
Passionate Man's Pilgrimage, The. Sir Walter Ralegh. AAS; CABA; ChTr; ElL; EnRePo; LiTB; LoBV; MePo; NOBE; NoP; OAEP; OBSC; OxBoCh; PoEL-2; SeCePo; TrGrPo
(Give Me My Scallop-Shell of Quiet.) PoRA
(His Pilgrimage.) DTC; HBV-2; ILwL; OBEV
(My Pilgrimage.) WGRP
(Pilgrimage, The.) EBCP; SiPS
"Give me my scallop shell of quiet," *sel.* TRV; ViBoPo
(Pilgrimage, The.) TreFS
Passionate Man's Song, The. John Fletcher. *Fr.* The Nice Valour, III. OBS
Passionate Pilgrim, The, *sels.* Shakespeare *and others.*
Beauty ("Beauty is but a vain and doubtful good"), XIII. *Unknown.* OBSC
Crabbed Age and Youth, XII. Shakespeare. HBV-1; InPS; LiTB; NIP; OBEV; TreFS; UnTE; ViBoPo
(Age and Youth.) ElL; FaBoEn
("Crabbed age and youth cannot live together.") GBL
(Madrigal, A: "Crabbed age and youth.") GTBS; GTBS-P
(Youth and Age.) OBSC
Fair Is My Love, VII. *At. to* Shakespeare. ElL
If Music and Sweet Poetry, VIII. Richard Barnefield. ViBoPo
It Was a Lording's Daughter. *Unknown, at. to* Shakespeare. ElL
(Contentions.) HBV-1
Philomel. Richard Barnefield. CH; HBV-1; NOBE; OBEV
("As it fell upon a day.") GBL; PBBP; ViBoPo
(Nightingale, The.) AWP; GTBS; GTBS-P
(Ode, An.) ElL; LoBV; OBSC
Sweet Rose, Fair Flower, X. *At. to* Shakespeare. ElL
Venus, with Young Adonis Sitting by Her, XI. Bartholomew Griffin. ViBoPo
Passionate Reader to His Poet, The. Richard Le Gallienne. HBV-2
Passionate Sheepheard To His Love, The. Christopher Marlowe. *See* Passionate Shepherd to His Love.
Passionate Shepherd, The, *sels.* Nicholas Breton.
Aglaia. OBSC
Merry Country Lad, The. ElL; LoBV
(Happy Countryman, The, *shorter sel.*) CH
(Pastoral: "Who can live in heart so glad.") ELP
(Shepherd and Shepherdess.) OBSC
("Who can live in heart so glad.") ViBoPo
Pretty Twinkling Starry Eyes. ElL
Passionate Shepherd to His Love, The, 6 *sts.* Christopher Marlowe. AAS; AWP; BiP; BoLoP; CABA; CTC; ElL; ELP; FaBoBe; FaFP; FF; FPL; GTBS, 7 *sts.*; GTBS-P, 7 *sts.*; HAP; HBV-1; HeIP; HoPM; InPK; InPS; LiTB; LoBV; NIP; NOBE; NoP; OAEL-1; OAEP; OBEV; OBSC; OLR; PAI; PoLF; PoRA, 7 *sts.*; PPoe, 7 *sts.*; PPP; SCV; SeCePo; SeCeV; TreF; TrGrPo; UnTE; ViBoPo, 7 *sts.*; WeW; WHA
(Passionate Sheepherd to His Love, The. FaBoEn
(Shepherd to His Love, The.) GN, 7 *sts.*
(Shepherd's Plea, The.) SiPS
Passionate Shepherd to His Love, The. Delmore Schwartz. NIP
Passionate Sword, The. Jean Starr Untermeyer. HBMV; TrJP; TrPWD
Passions, The; an Ode for [*or* to] Music. William Collins. GOTL; GTBS; GTBS-P; HBV-2; LAuP; LoBV; OBEC
Passions are liken'd [*or* likened] best to floods and streams. The Silent Lover [*or* Passions]. Sir Walter Ralegh. LiTB; OBEV; PoPle, 1 *st.*; ViBoPo. *See also* Our passions are most like to floods and streams.
Passions That We Fought With, The. Trumbull Stickney. NCEP
Passiontide Communion. Katharine Tynan. TrPWD
Passive I lie, looking up through leaves. Seventh Day. Kathleen Raine. ChMP
Passive Resistance. Joseph Bruchac. SOTS
Passive within the heart. The Meaning of Violence. John Williams. NePoAm-2
Passover. Rose Ausländer, *tr. fr. German by* Ewald Osers. VWA
Passover Dachau. B. Z. Niditch. AMV-81
Passover Eve. Fania Kruger. GoYe
Passover in the Holy Family, The. Dante Gabriel Rossetti. GoBC
Past, The. Bryant. AA
Past, The. Emerson. FaBoCh; FPL; LiTA; PoEL-4; TAP
Past. John Galsworthy. HBV-1
Past. Winifred Howells. AA
Past, The. William Oandasan. STE
Past/ Is but the cinders, The. The Search. Kwesi Brew. PBA
Past, a glacier, gripped the mountain wall, The. Full Moon at Tierz; before the Storming of Huesca. John Cornford. OBWP
Past a swim-by of deep sea fish. At the Natural History Museum. William Meredith. NYP
Past and Present. Thomas Hood. *See* I Remember, I Remember.
Past arenas, sanctuaries. Pilgrims. Joseph Brodsky, *tr. by* Dimitry Pospielovsky *and* Keith Bosley. VWA
Past Burwash and the White River delta. At Slim's River. John Haines. NPAW
Past can be no more, The. Now. Thomas Ken. OxBoCh
Past comes back, The. Ralph Hodgson. POL
Past crag and scarp. History. Robert Penn Warren. NoAM
Past exchanges have left orbits of rain around my face. An Apology. Diane Wakoski. TAP
Past factory workshops, empty. Marina Tsvetayeva, *tr. by* Paul Schmidt. *Fr.* The Daughter of Jairus. BoWoP
Past Is Dark with Sin and Shame, The, *with music.* Thomas Wentworth Higginson. AH
Past is fresh, dust is fresh, The. Ebb. John Lyle Donaghy. NeIP
Past is past, and if one. Salute. James Schuyler. FYAP; NeAP
Past Is the Present, The. Marianne Moore. PP
Past love, past sorrow, lies this darkness. Requiem. Kathleen Raine. NeBP
Past my window runs a tree. The Changing Wind. Julian Orde. NeBP
Past ploughed and fallow, at the top. Glenarm. John Lyle Donaghy. NeIP
Past Ruined [*or* Ruin'd] Ilion Helen Lives. Walter Savage Landor. CTC; ELP; EnRP; GBL; HAP; HeIP; LoBV; NoP; OAEP; OBRV; POL; PoRA; TreFT; TrGrPo; ViBoPo; WeW
(Ianthe.) FaBoEn; LiTB; PoEL-4
(Past Ruin'd Ilion.) AWP
(To Ianthe.) NOBE; VLP
(Verse: "Past ruin'd [*or* ruined] Ilion Helen lives.") HBV-2; OBEV
Past sends images to beach, The. Lines for the Ancient Scribes. Harvey Shapiro. VWA
Past seven o'clock: time to be gone. Moonset. Sir Henry Newbolt. EBVV
Past the barred windows. Escape. Andrew McCord Jones. LFAC
Past the blueing humus. Vigil of the Wounded. Phillip Yellowhawk Minthorn. STE
Past the house where he was got. Austin Clarke. Mnemosyne Lay in Dust, I. CMoP; IPY
Past the old barbershop on Jefferson. Gary Gotow. George Uba. BrSi
Past the school and down. Directions to the Nomad. James Welch. CDW
Past them he strode. The Hinds of Kerry. William S. Wabnitz. GoYe
Past Time. Harvey Shapiro. POL
"Past two o'clock and Cornwallis is taken." News from Yorktown. Lewis Worthington Smith. PAH
Past walks here, noiseless, unasked, alone, The. An Old Street. Virginia Woodward Cloud. AA
Past we glide, and past, and past! Robert Browning. *Fr.* In a Gondola. PeD
Pastel. Francis Saltus Saltus. AA
Pastel. Arthur Symons. SyP
Pastel, A. Paul Verlaine, *tr. fr. French by* Arthur O'Shaughnessy. SyP
Pastel the flowers, the wreaths in the pastel gardens. Moon Mattress. Diane Di Prima. NMM
Pastime. Henry VIII, King of England. CTC; EBEV; OBSC
(Good Company.) TrGrPo
Pastime of Pleasure, The, *sels.* Stephen Hawes.
Dame Music. PoEL-1
Epitaph of Graunde [*or* La Graunde] Amoure, The, *fr. ch.* 42. ChTr; EBEV; FaBoRV; OBSC; SeCeV
(Epitaph, An.) ACP; OBEV; TrGrPo
(Epitaphy of la Graunde Amoure.) FaBoEE
(His Epitaph.) GoBC
("O mortal folk, you may behold and see.") ViBoPo
Seven Deadly Sins, The. PoEL-1
Time and Eternity. PoEL-1
True Knight, The, *fr. ch* 27. ACP; OBEV
(True Knighthood.) TrGrPo

Pastime with good company. Pastime [*or* Good Company]. Henry VIII, King of England. CTC; EBEV; OBSC; TrGrPo
Pastor, The. William C. Summers. STF
Pastor M'Gadi's startling blackness. Halo. Ralph Nixon Currey. PeSA
Pastor sips weak hock and seltzer, The. The Pastor Speaks Out. David Fisher. NPGG
Pastor Speaks Out, The. David Fisher. NPGG
Pastoral: "Afternoon wears on, The." David Wright. NYBP
Pastoral, A: "Along the lane beside the mead." Norman Gale. HBV-1
Pastoral, A: "By the side of a [*or* the] green stagnate pool." G. A. Stevens. CoMu; ErPo
Pastoral: "Crouched in the yard." Ellen Bryant Voigt. MAYP
Pastoral: "Death./ The death of a million." Ron Loewinsohn. NeAP
Pastoral: "Dominic Francis Xavier Brotherton-Chancery." Gavin Ewart. OxBC
Pastoral: "Dove walks with slick feet, The." Kenneth Patchen. NaP
Pastoral: "Enquiring fields, courtesies, The." Allen Tate. AP
Pastoral: "Farmhouse skyline, draped with trees, The." Alan Creighton. CaP
Pastoral, A: "Flower of the medlar." Théophile Marzials. HBV-1
Pastoral, A: "From thence into the open fields he fled." Spenser. *Fr.* The Faerie Queene, VI, 9. OBSC
Pastoral: "I came to a field." Charles Simic. NNaP
Pastoral, A: "In the merry month of May." Nicholas Breton. *See* Phyllida and Corydon ("In the merry month of May").
Pastoral: "In the old days the white gates swung." Clifford Dyment. MoVE
Pastoral: "It all happened so fast. Fenya was in the straight chair." Norman Dubie. AmPA
Pastoral: "It's the Spring." W. E. Henley. In Hospital, XXII. BrPo
Pastoral: "Little sparrows, The." William Carlos Williams. MP; TwCP
Pastoral, A: "Mobile, immaculate and austere." Geoffrey Hill. NePoEA-2
Pastoral: "Mountain/ rises out of paper." Robin Magonan. PoDr
Pastoral, A: "My time, O ye muses, was happily spent." John Byrom. OBEC
Pastoral [*or* Pastorall], A: "Oh [*or* O] happy golden age." Tasso, *tr. fr. Italian by* Samuel Daniel. *Fr.* Aminta. OAEL-1; PoEL-2
(Golden Age, The, *tr. by* Leigh Hunt.) AWP
(Pastoral of Tasso, A, *tr. by* Samuel Daniel.) OBSC
("O lovely age of gold!" *tr. by* Leigh Hunt.) OBVE
Pastoral, A: "On a hill there grows a flower." Nicholas Breton. EIL
(Ipsa Quae.) OBSC
(Phyllida and Corydon.) TrGrPo
Pastoral: "So soft in the hemlock wood." Robert Hillyer. MoAmPo
Pastoral, A: "Sweet birds! that sit and sing amid the shady valleys." Nicholas Breton. *See* Phyllis.
Pastoral, A: "There went out in the dawning light." *Unknown, tr. fr. Latin by* John Addington Symonds. AWP; UnTE
Pastoral: "This is a place of ease." Marion Strobel. PoA
Pastoral: "Today in Peru, this first day of summer." Lawrence Raab. AmPA
Pastoral: "When I was younger." William Carlos Williams. AmPP; OxBA
Pastoral: "Who can live in heart so glad." Nicholas Breton. *See* Shepherd and Shepherdess.
Pastoral, A: "Wise old apple tree in spring, The." Robert Hillyer. BoNaP
Pastoral Ballad. William Shenstone. OBEC
Shepherd's Home, The, *sel.* GN
("My banks they are furnish'd with bees.") BoNaP
Pastoral Ballad by John Bull, A. Thomas Moore. BIrV; OBSV
Pastoral Courtship, A, *sel.* Thomas Randolph.
"Being set, let's sport a while, my fair." ViBoPo
Pastoral Courtship, A. Earl of Rochester. UnTE
Pastoral Dialogue, A. Thomas Carew. *See* Pastorall Dialogue, A ("This mossie bank they prest").
Pastoral Elegy, A. Tibullus, *tr. fr. Latin by* Sir Charles Abraham Elton. AWP
Pastoral Hymn. Joseph Addison. OBEC
Pastoral [*or* Pastorall] Hymn, A. John Hall. MeLP; OBS; OxBoCh; TrPWD
Pastoral, A; in the Modern Style. "Worcester." NOEC
Pastoral Landscape. Ambrose Philips. *Fr.* Pastorals. OBEC
Pastoral of Tasso, A. Tasso. *See* Pastoral: "Oh happy golden age."
Pastoral on the King's Death, The; Written in 1648. Alexander Brome. OBS
Pastoral Poesy. John Clare. OAEL-2
Pastorall, A: "O happy golden age." Tasso. *See* Pastoral, A: "Oh happy golden age."
Pastorall Dialogue, A ("As Celia rested in the shade"). Thomas Carew. AnAnS-2; CavP
Pastorall [*or* Pastoral] Dialogue, A ("This mossie [*or* mossy] bank they prest"). Thomas Carew. AnAnS-2; CaPo; GBL; SeCP
Pastorall Hymne, A. John Hall. *See* Pastoral Hymn, A.
Pastorals, *sel.* Ambrose Philips.
Pastoral Landscape. OBEC
Pastorals, *sel.* Pope.
Sylvan Delights. NOBE
Pastor's Friend, The. *Unknown.* STF
Pastourelle. Donald Jeffery Hayes. AmNP
Pastourelle. *Unknown.* OBSC
("Hey, troly, loly lo, maid, whither go you?") LO
Pasture, The. Robert Frost. BiP; BLPL; CMoP; FaPON; GoJo; MoAB; MoAmPo; MoShBr; NOBA; OxBA; PDV; PoPl; SoPo; SUS; TiPo; ViBoPo
Pasture, A. Frederic Lawrence Knowles. AA
Pasture, stone wall, and steeple. Question in a Field. Louise Bogan. NYBP; SBG
Pastures of Plenty. Woody Guthrie. WTO
Pat-a-cake, pat-a-cake, baker's man. Mother Goose. OxNR
Pat Cloherty's Version of *The Maisie.* Richard Murphy. IPY
Pat Works On the Railway. *Unknown.* *See* Paddy Works on the Railway.
Pat Young. Kenneth MacKenzie. PoAu-2
Pat your foot. Leadbelly Gives an Autograph. Amiri Baraka. CNA
Patapan. Bernard de la Monnoye, *tr. fr. French.* PChr
Patch of Old Snow, A. Robert Frost. CMoP; WeW
Patch-Shaneen. J. M. Synge. LoBV
Patches of it. The Luminous. Barbara Guest. PoM
Patches of Sky. Debora Greger. MAYP
Patching Together, A, *sel.* Murray Edmond.
Cell Lay Inside Her Body, The, 3. NAs
Patchwork Quilt, The. Dora Sigerson Shorter. HBMV
Pater Filio. Robert Bridges. CMoP; OBEV; OBVV; ViBoPo
"Pater Noster," The. *Unknown.* ACP
Paternal. Ernest J. Wilson, Jr. PoNe
Pater's Bathe. Edward Abbott Parry. OxBChV
Paterson, *sels.* William Carlos Williams.
"Beautiful thing/ I saw you." CMoP
Delineaments of the Giants, The. NoAM
Episode 17. OxBA
"Paterson lies in the valley under the Passaic Falls." NoAM; TAP
Preface: "To make a start." AP; CMoP; CoBMV; NoAM; NOBA
Sunday in the Park. CrMA
"There is a woman in our town." CMoP
"Without invention nothing is well spaced." PP
Path, The. Edward Thomas. BrPo; MoVE; NoAM
Path across a meadow fair and sweet, A. Two Paths. Julia Caroline Ripley Dorr. AA
Path among the Stones, The. Galway Kinnell. NNaP; NOBA; Prf
Path by which we twain did go, The. In Memoriam A. H. H., XXII. Tennyson. EBVV; SCV
Path crossed green closes and went down the lane, The. We Passed by Green Closes. John Clare. VLP
Path Flower. Olive Tilford Dargan. HBMV
Path of the Old Spells, The. Donald Sinclair, *tr. fr. Gaelic.* GoTS
Path of the Padres, The. Edith D. Osborne. AmFN
Path of the Stars, The. Thomas S. Jones, Jr. WGRP
Path of Wisdom, The. Bible, Apocrypha. Baruch, II: 9-IV: 4. TrJP
Path That Leads to Nowhere, The. Corinne Roosevelt Robinson. BLPA; HBMV
Path through which that lonely twain, The. Shelley. *Fr.* Prometheus Unbound. ViBoPo
Pathedy of Manners. Ellen Kay. SoSe
Pathfinder—and Path-clincher! John Charles Frémont. Charles F. Lummis. PAH
Path-let . . . leaving home, leading out. Footpath. Stella Ngatho. WPOW
Paths of Prayer, The. Edouard Roditi. VWA
Paths They Kept Barren. John Garmon. AMV-81
Paths to God. Musa Moris Farhi, *tr. fr. Turkish by the author.* VWA
Patience. Bartola Cattafi, *tr. fr. Italian by* Rina Ferrarelli. AMV-81
Patience. Elaine Feinstein. BrRo
Patience, *sels.* W. S. Gilbert.
Bunthorne's Song. FiBHP; LiTB; NBM
(Bunthorne's Song: The Aesthete.) OAEL-2
(Aesthete, The.) EBVV; VLP
Fable of the Magnet and the Churn, The. FaPON; OnMSP
Oh, Hollow! Hollow! Hollow! FaBoNo
Patience. Harry Graham. FiBHP; MoShBr; WhC
Patience. Frank Horne. BPo
Patience. Bobbi Katz. RHPC
Patience. E. E. Nott-Bower. WhC
Patience. G. A. Studdert-Kennedy. TrPWD
Patience. Sir Thomas Wyatt. *See* Patience, Though I Have Not.
Patience, *sel.* *Unknown.*
Jonah. ACP
(Jonah Is Cast into the Sea.) OxBM, *orig. and mod. prose vers.*

Patience! coy singers of the Delphic wood. To Poets. Walter Savage Landor. FaBoEE
Patience, for I have wrong. Sir Thomas Wyatt. SiPS
Patience for my device. Sir Thomas Wyatt. SiPS
Patience, Hard Thing! Gerard Manley Hopkins. *See* Sonnet: "Patience hard thing! the hard thing but to pray."
Patience, Hard Virtue. Daniel Berrigan. LFAC
Patience is a virtue. *Unknown.* OxNR
Patience, my lord! why, 'tis the soul of peace. Thomas Dekker. *Fr.* The Honest Whore. ViBoPo
Patience of a People. F. J. Bryant, Jr. CNA
Patience of all my smart. Sir Thomas Wyatt. SiPS
Patience of Job is a story old, The. Will God's Patience Hold Out for You? Edythe Johnson. STF
Patience on a Monument. Shakespeare. *See* Love Concealed.
Patience . . . patience. Patience. Frank Horne. BPo
Patience Taught by Nature. Elizabeth Barrett Browning. EBCP; OxBoCh
Patience, tedious non Virtue. Patience, Hard Virtue. Daniel Berrigan. LFAC
Patience, Though I Have Not. Sir Thomas Wyatt. NoP; SiPS
(Patience.) OBSC; TrGrPo
Patient, The. Nicholas Moore. EAS
Patient above his tinted tiles he bent. The Mosaic Worker. Arthur Wallace Peach. BLRP
Patient Church, The. Cardinal Newman. GoBC
Patient Griselda. Chaucer, *mod. by* Edward Hodnett. *Fr.* The Canterbury Tales: The Clerk's Tale. PoRA
Patient Grissel [*or* Grissell *or* Grissill]. Thomas Dekker. *See* Pleasant Comedy of Patient Grissell, The.
Patient Is Rallying, The. Weldon Kees. NaP
Patient, The: Rockland County Sanitarium. Calvin C. Hernton. *See* Madhouse.
Patient, we pray and wait and weep and pray. The Sit-in. Darwin T. Turner. BALP
Patmos. David Gascoyne, *after the German of* Friedrich Hölderlin. OBVE
Patmos. Edith M. Thomas. HBV-1
Patriach, The. Burns. CoMu
Patriarch in black takes, The. The Sacrifice. Chana Bloch. VWA
Patricians, The. Douglas Dunn. OxBC
Patrick Ewing Takes a Foul Shot. Diane Ackerman. MAYP
Patrick Sarsfield, Lord Lucan. *Unknown.* *See* Farewell to Patrick Sarsfield.
Patrick you chatter too loud. The Praise of Fionn. *Unknown, tr. by* Frank O'Connor. KiLC
Patrico's Song. Ben Jonson. *See* Faery Beam upon You, The.
Patriot, The. Robert Browning. TrGrPo
Patriot, The. J. C. Milne. PoSH
Patriot, A. Langford Reed. TDH
Patriot Game, The. Dominic Behan. FSW
Patriot, The. Sir Walter Scott. *See* Breathes There the Man.
Patriotic Ode on the Fourteenth Anniversary of the Persecution of Charlie Chaplin. Bob Kaufman. PoBA
Patriotic Poem. Diane Wakoski. OFD; VGW
Patriotic Tour and Postulate of Joy. Robert Penn Warren. NYBP
Patriotism [I] ("Breathes there the man with soul so dead"). Sir Walter Scott. *See* Breathes There the Man.
Patriotism [II] ("To mute and to material things"). Sir Walter Scott. *See* Nelson, Pitt, Fox.
Patriot's Pass-Word, The. James Montgomery. *See* Make Way for Liberty.
Patroclus' Body Saved. Homer, *tr. fr. Greek by* E. R. Dodds. *Fr.* The Iliad, XVII. WaaP
Patrol. Ralph Pomeroy. CoPo
Patrol; Buonamary. Bernard Gutteridge. WaP
Patrol[l]ing Barnegat. Walt Whitman. LoBV; MOS; NePA; NoP
Patron of all those who do good by stealth. December: Prayer to St. Nicholas. John Heath-Stubbs. OBCP
Patron of Flawless Serpent Beauty. Friederike Mayröcker, *tr. fr. German by* Michael Hamburger. WPOW
Patrum Propositum. Robert Fitzgerald. GOA
Pat's Opinion of Flags. Fred Emerson Brooks. InPK
Patter of the Shingle, The. *Unknown.* BLPA
Patter, patter, little feet. To Beatrice Stuart Wortley: Aetat 2. Alfred Austin. PeD
Pattern of Saint Brendan. Francis MacManus. AnIV; OxBI
Pattern Poem with an Elusive Intruder. Reinhold Döhl. WeW
Patterns. Amy Lowell. AWP; BoWoP; DL; FaFP; FPL; HBV-1; LiTA; MoAmPo; NePA; OnMSP; OxBA; TreFS; TrGrPo
Patterns. Ruth Setterberg. AMV-81
Patterns of old green-gold trees. Autumn. D. R. Beeton. PeSA
Pattonio, the Pride of the Plain, *with music. Unknown.* CoSo
Patty-cake, patty-cake/ Marcus Antonius. Tact. Paul Pascal. PV; WeW
Patty Hearst Hoists the Carbine. Sibyl James. SOTS
Patty, 1949-1961. Sharon Mayer Libera. IHMS
Pauca Mea, *sel.* Christopher Brennan.
I Said, This Misery Must End." PoAu-1
Paudeen. W. B. Yeats. HAP; InPS; PoEL-5
Paul. John Oxenham. TRV
Paul. James Wright. NePoEA; PoPl
Paul and Silas, bound in jail. All Night Long [*or* Keep Your Eyes on the Prize]. *Unknown.* AS; FSW
Paul and Virginia. John Wheelwright. CrMA
Paul Bunyan ("He came, /striding"). Arthur S. Bourinot. *Fr.* A Legend of Paul Bunyan. FaPON
Paul Faber, Surgeon, *sel.* George Macdonald.
That Holy Thing. HBV-2; OBEV; OBVV; TrPWD; TRV; WGRP
Paul Jones ("An American [*or* A forty-gun *or* Our forty-gun] frigate from Baltimore came"). *Unknown.* BaBo; PAH; PAL; ViBoFo
Paul Jones ("A song unto Liberty's brave buccaneer"). *Unknown.* PAH
Paul Jones—a New Song. *Unknown.* PAH
Paul Jones's [*or* Jones'] Victory ("An American frigate, a frigate of fame"). *Unknown.* AmFP; TrAS, *with music*
Paul Klee. John Haines. LCAP
Paul Klee. Ruthven Todd. EAS
Paul Laurence Dunbar. James David Corrothers. BANP; PoNe
Paul Laurence Dunbar. Robert Hayden. NoP
Paul on the Road to Damascus. Bible, *N.T.* Acts, IX: 3-6. TreF
Paul Revere's Ride. Longfellow. *Fr.* Tales of a Wayside Inn: The Landlord's Tale, Pt. I. BeLS; BLPA; FaBoBe; FaBV; FaFP; FaPo; FaPON, FaPoR; FPL; HBV-2; HBVY; OBAL; OBCA; OBNV; OHFP; PAH; PAL; TreF; TrGrPo; WBLP; YaD
(Midnight Ride of Paul Revere, The.) PaPo
Paul Robeson. Gwendolyn Brooks. CNA; PoBA
Pauline, *sels.* Robert Browning.
Andromeda. OBRV
"My God, my God, let me for once look on thee." TrPWD
"Night, and one single ridge of narrow path." VLP
(Water and Air.) OBRV
"O God, where do they tend—these struggling aims?" WGRP
"Sun-treader, life and light be thine for ever!" VLP
(Shelley.) OBRV
"Thou wilt remember. Thou art not more dear." OAEL-2
Pauline ("Pauline Pauline, I don' love nobody but you"), *with music. Unknown.* OuSiCo
Paul's clock struck twelve, 'twas time to go to bed. The Midnight Ramble. Charles Woodward. NOEC
Paul's midnight voice prevail'd; his music's thunder. Epigram. Francis Quarles. Emblems, V, 10. LoBV
Paunch talks against good liquor to excess. On Paunch, a Parasite. Hilaire Belloc. POL
Pauper, A. Allen Tate. LiTM
Pauper Witch of Grafton, The. Robert Frost. CrMA
Pauper Woodland. Ronald Everson. NOBC
Pauper's Drive, The. Thomas Noel. PaPo
Pauper's Funeral, The. George Crabbe. *Fr.* The Village. FaBoEn; OBNC
Pause. Ann Hamilton. HBMV
Pause. Dorothy Livesay. AMV-81
Pause a Moment. Asya, *tr. fr. Yiddish by* Gabriel Preil *and* Howard Schwartz. VWA
Pause between Clock Ticks. James Hearst. AMV-81
Pause, courteous spirit!—Balbi supplicates. Epitaphs, IX. Gabriello Chiabrera, *tr. by* Wordsworth. AWP
Pause en Route. Thomas Kinsella. OxBI
Pause for Breath, A. Ted Hughes. NYBP
Pause of Thought, A. Christina Rossetti. FaBoEn; NOBE; OBNC
Pause stranger at the porch: nothing beyond. A Gateway to the Sea—St. Andrews. George Bruce. BSV
Pause, Traveller! whosoe'er thou be. Inscribed upon a Rock. Wordsworth. SyP
Pavane for the Nursery, A. William Jay Smith. DuDa; GoJo; MoAmPo; NePoAm-2; PoSC
Pavane for the Passing of a Child. Laura Chester. FiCP
Pavilion on the Pier, The. Byron Vazakas. NePA
Pavlov. Naomi Long Madgett. BPo
Paw-Paw Patch. *Unknown.* FSW
Pawky auld carle cam[e] ower [*or* owre *or* o'er] the lea [*or* lee], The. The Gaberlunzie Man. *Unknown.* BSV; EnSB; GoTS; OxBB; OxBS
Pawky Duke, The. David Rorie. BSV; GoTS
Pawnbrokers. Marguerite Wilkinson. HBMV
Pawns, The. Frank Betts. HBMV
Pawns, The. William Young. *See* Losers, The.
Pawn-shop man knows hunger, The. Street Window. Carl Sandburg. PCP
Pawnshop Window. R. H. Grenville. GoYe
Pax. D. H. Lawrence. TrCP
Pax Paganica. Louise Imogen Guiney. AA
"Pax vobis," quod the fox. The Fox and the Goose. *Unknown.* OxBM

Pay Day [*or* Payday] at Coal Creek. *Unknown.* AmFP; FSW; OuSiCo, *with music*
Pay Me My Money Down. Lydia A. Parrish. FSW
Payments. Diana O Hehir. NPGG
Pay-off. Kenneth Fearing. CMoP
Paysage Choisi. Francis Sparshott. MoCV
Paysage Moralisé. W. H. Auden. *See* Hearing of Harvests Rotting in the Valleys.
Paysage Moralisé. John Hollander. ErPo; NePoEA
Pcheek pcheek pcheek pcheek pcheek. The Avenue Bearing the Initial of Christ into the New World. Galway Kinnell. CAD (1); CoPo (1-14); LiTM (1-2); NePoEA-2 (1)
Pea-Fields, The. Sir Charles G. D. Roberts. *Fr.* Songs of the Common Day. NOBC; OBCV; PeCV
Peace. Bhartrihari, *tr. fr. Sanskrit by* Paul Elmer More. AWP
Peace. Rupert Brooke. *Fr.* 1914. HBV-2; MMA; OBWP; PoA; TreFT; WGRP
Peace. Charles Stuart Calverley. EBVV; NBM; WhC
Peace. Phoebe Cary. PAH
Peace. Walter de la Mare. MoAB; MoBrPo; MMA
Peace. Irwin Edman. TrJP
Peace. Eleanor Farjeon. SUMH
Peace. Samuel Greenberg. CrMA
Peace. George Herbert. AnAnS-1; AWP; ChTr; ELP; NOCV; OxBoCh; SeCeV; TEP
Peace. Gerard Manley Hopkins. EBCP; ELP; GTBS-P; OAEP; TrCP
Peace. Langston Hughes. BPo
Peace. George Jonas. NeAC
Peace. D. H. Lawrence. FaBoPP
Peace. Michael Longley. CIP
Peace, The. Henry Luttrell. *Fr.* Advice to Julia. OBRV
Peace. Edwin Markham. PGD; WBLP
Peace. Margaret E. Sangster. TRV
Peace. Samuel Speed. OxBoCh
Peace. Henry Vaughan. AnAnS-1; AWP; ChTr; EaLo; EBEV; ELP; FaBoCh; GN; HAP; HBV-2; MePo; NOBE; NOCV; OAEP; OBEV; OBS; SeCV-1; TEP; TrCP; WeW; WGRP; WHA
Peace. Adeline D. T. Whitney. PAH
Peace. *Unknown.* MeEL; STF
Peace and Joy. Shelley Silverstein. PoSC
Peace and Mercy and Jonathan. First Thanksgiving of All. Nancy Byrd Turner. FaPON; PAL; SiSoSe
Peace and silence be the guide. Three Songs, III. Francis Beaumont. *Fr.* The Masque of the Inner Temple and Gray's Inne. GoBC; OBS
Peace? and to all the world? sure, one. The Nativity. Henry Vaughan. SBVL
Peace, Be at Peace, O Thou My Heaviness. Baudelaire, *tr. fr. French by* Lord Alfred Douglas. InPK
(Sois sage o ma douleur.) AWP
Peace be unto you,/ Ye ministering angels. Shalom Aleichem. *Unknown.* TrJP
Peace be unto you, Penglima Lenggang Laut! Invitation to a Spirit. *Malay Oral Tradition, tr. by* W. W. Skeat. WTO
Peace be with you, gentle scrivener. Sholom Aleichem. Elias Lieberman. TrJP
Peace be with you, O Tin-ore. Tin-Ore. *Malay Oral Tradition, tr. by* W. W. Skeat. WTO
Peace Beldam Eve, surcease thy suit. A Young Man to an Old Woman Courting Him. John Cleveland. AnAnS-2
Peace by Night. Sister Mary Madeleva. GoBC
Peace; come away: the song of woe. Tennyson. In Memoriam A. H. H., LVII. EBVV
Peace, deep and rich. Prayer to Peace. Euripides, *tr. by* Moses Hadas. PoPl
Peace Delegate. Douglas Livingstone. PeSA
Peace does not mean the end of all our striving. G. A. Studdert-Kennedy. *Fr.* The Christian Soldier. TRV
Peace Hymn of the Republic. Henry van Dyke. TRV
(O Lord Our God, Thy Mighty Hand.) AH, *with music.*
Peace in the sober house of Jonas dwelt. Jonas Kindred's Household. George Crabbe. *Fr.* Tales: The Frank Courtship. OBNC
Peace in the valley will sing to me like a choir, The. A Clash with Cliches. Vassar Miller. AMV-80; FAZ
Peace in the Welsh Hills. Vernon Watkins. ChMP; GTBS-P; OxBTC
Peace in the World. John Galsworthy. PoLF
Peace in thy hands. The Ghost. Walter de la Mare. OAEP
Peace is declared, and I return. The Return. Kipling. MoBrPo
Peace is made with a warlike man. *Unknown, tr. fr. Irish by* John Montague. BIrV
Peace is the men not marching away to be killed. Not Marching Away to Be Killed. Jean Overton Fuller. FF
Peace Is the Mind's Old Wilderness, *with music.* John Holmes. AH
"Peace Is the Tranquillity of Order." Robert Wilberforce. GoBC
Peace is written on the doorstep. Peace. D. H. Lawrence. FaBoPP
Peace lies profound on these forgotten acres. Meditation by Mascoma Lake. Donald C. Babcock. NePoAm-2
Peace Message, The. Burton Egbert Stevenson. PAH
Peace of a Good Mind, The. Sir Thomas More. *Fr.* The Twelve Weapons of Spiritual Battle. EnRePo; FaBoRV
Peace of Christ, The. Bible, *N.T.* St. John, XIV: 1-27. TreFS
Peace of great doors be for you, The. For You. Carl Sandburg. MoAmPo
Peace of the Roses, The. Thomas Philipps. ACP
Peace of Wild Things, The. Wendell Berry. GeTw; HeIP; NU; PCP; VGW
Peace on Earth. Bacchylides, *tr. fr. Greek by* John Addington Symonds. AWP
Peace on Earth. Longfellow. PGD
Peace on Earth. Edmund H. Sears. *See* It Came upon the Midnight Clear.
Peace on Earth. William Carlos Williams. LiTA; ViBoPo
Peace on New England, on the shingled white houses, on golden. Jehu. Louis MacNeice. LiTM; MoAB; WaP
Peace on the earth,/ Joyfully sang the angels long ago. Through the Ages. Margaret Hope. PGD
Peace! peace! A mighty Power, which is as darkness. Shelley. *Fr.* Prometheus Unbound, IV. OAEP
Peace, peace! he is not dead, he doth not sleep. An Elegy on the Death of John Keats [*or* Mourn Not for Adonais *or* Against Oblivion]. Shelley. *Fr.* Adonais. FaBoEn; LO; NOBE; OBNC; TreFS
Peace, peace, my friend; these subjects fly. George Crabbe. *Fr.* Sir Eustace Grey. PoEL-4
Peace, Peace, my hony, do not cry. Christ's Reply. Edward Taylor. *Fr.* God's Determinations. PoEL-3
Peace, peace on earth! the heart of man forever. Peace on Earth. Longfellow. PGD
Peace, peace, peace, make no noise. A Ditty. John Day. *Fr.* Humour Out of Breath. EIL
Peace, Perfect Peace. Edward H. Bickersteth. BLRP; WGRP
Peace pratler, do not lowre. Conscience. George Herbert. AnAnS-1
Peace, Shepherd, peace! What boots it singing on? Genius Loci. Margaret L. Woods. HBV-2; OBEV; OBVV
Peace, So That. Greg Kuzma. InPK
Peace, the one-time radiant goddess. The Child of Peace. Selma Lagerlof, *tr. by* Charles Wharton Stork. PoPl
Peace! The perfect word is sounding, like a universal hymn. In the Dawn. Odell Shepard. WGRP
Peace, the wild valley streaked with torrents. The Straw. Robert Graves. MoVE; OxBTC
Peace, there is peace in this awaking. Waking. Patrick MacDonogh. NeIP
Peace to all such! but were there one whose fires. Atticus. Pope. *Fr.* Epistle to Dr. Arbuthnot. AWP; NOBE; OBEC; SeCePo; ViBoPo; WHA
Peace to the Slumberers! Thomas Moore. HBV-2; OnYI
Peace to these little broken leaves. Leaves. W. H. Davies. MoBrPo
Peace to-night, heroic spirit! Requiem for a Young Soldier. Florence Earle Coates. OHIP
"Peace upon earth!" was said. We sing it. Christmas: 1924. Thomas Hardy. FaBoEE; OBCP; PV
Peace Walk. William Stafford. Psk
Peace, war, religion. This Tokyo. Gary Snyder. CAPP; NeAP
Peace with Honor. Philip Appleman. SOTS
Peaceable Kingdom, The. Bible, *O.T.* Isaiah, XI: 6-9. FaPON
(God's Rule.) FM
("Wolf also shall dwell with the lamb, The.") PDV
Peaceable Kingdom, The. Marge Piercy. TwCP
Peaceable Race, The. T. A. Daly. HBV-2
Peaceful life, A—just toil and rest. Lincoln. James Whitcomb Riley. OHIP
Peaceful Shepherd, The. Robert Frost. *Fr.* A Sky Pair. MoAB; MoAmPo
Peaceful Song, A. Natan Zach, *tr. fr. Hebrew by* Peter Everwine *and* Shula Starkman. VWA
Peaceful spot is Piper's Flat, A. The folk that live around. How McDougal Topped the Score. Thomas E. Spencer. PoAu-1
Peaceful Western Mind, The. Thomas Campion. EnRePo; LoBV
Peach, The. Abbie Farwell Brown. TDH
Peach Orchard Mama. *Unknown.* BluL
Peach Tree with Fruit. Padraic Colum. BoNaP
Peaches, The. Joel Oppenheimer. CoPo
Peaches in, and pears late. Orchard Snow. J. B. Goodenough. AMV-81
Peaches so sweet this summer. Indulgences. Michael Hogan. AMV-80
Peachstone. Dannie Abse. OxBC
Peachtree, The. Denise Levertov. *Fr.* During the Eichmann Trial. CAPP
Peacock and Nightingale. Robert Finch. OBCV
Peacock "At Home," The. Catherine Ann Dorset. OxBChV
"Peacock colored tears and rotten oranges." Midnight on Front Street. Roberta Hill. CDW; TWSS

Peacock in Leucadia loved a maid, A. From Burton the Anatomist. Maurice James Craig. NeIP
Peacock Room, The. Robert Hayden. FB
Peak, The. W. W. Gibson. PoSH
Peaks, The. Stephen Crane. War Is Kind, XVIII. AA; HBV-1; WGRP
Peanut sat on a railroad track, A. Toot! Toot! *Unknown.* RHPC
Peanuts. Ken Belford. NeAC
Peanuts ("The boy stood on the burning deck"). *Unknown.* FaFP
Pear, The. Ruth Stone. TwAmPo
Pear Tree. Hilda Doolittle ("H. D."). AP; BoWoP; CMoP; HBMV; MoAmPo; NOBA; UnPo
Pear-Tree, The. Mary Gilmore. PoAu-1
Pear-Tree, The. Iwan Goll, *tr. fr. German by* Babette Deutsch *and* Avram Yarmolinsky. TrJP
Pear Tree, The. Edna St. Vincent Millay. MoAmPo
Pear-Tree, The ("I have a new garden, and new is begun"). *Unknown. See* I Have a New Garden.
Pear-Tree, The ("This shade-bestowing pear-tree, thou"). *Unknown, tr. fr. Chinese by* Allen Upward. *Fr.* Shi King. AWP
Pear Tree, the sun has reached the corner. Strawberries. Dorothy Hughes. AMV-81
Pearl, The. George Herbert. AnAnS-1; EBEV; FaBoEn; HAP; JCP; MePo; NOCV; OAEL-1; OxBoCh; PoEL-2; SeCP
(Pearl, The. Matth. 3.) SeCV-1
Pearl, *sels. Unknown.*
"Perle, plesaunte to prynces paye." OxBM, *sts.* 1-15, *orig. and mod. English prose;* EBEV, *sts.* 1-5, *orig. only*
Queen of Courtesy, The, *sts.* 36-8. ACP; ISi; *mod vers. by* Stanley Perkins Chase
Pearl Avenue runs past the high-school lot. Ex-Basketball Player. John Updike. CTBA; LiSp; NYBP
Pearl Bryan. *Unknown.* AmFP; 2 *vers.*; BaBo; ViBoFo
Pearl Harbor Day 1970. Dick Lourie. NeAC
Pearl. Matth. 13, The. George Herbert. *See* Pearl, The.
Pearl of the sea! Star of the West! On Leaving Cuba, Her Native Land. Gertrudis Gómez de Avellaneda, *tr. by* Catherine Rodriguez-Nieto. WPOW
Pearl of the White Breast. *Unknown, tr. fr. Modern Irish by* George Petrie. AnIV; OnYI
Pearl Perch. John Blight. CBAP
Pearly Beads. *Gond Oral Tradition, tr. by* V. Elwin *and* S. Hivale. WTO
Pearly Everlasting, The. Ernest Fewster. CaP
Pears. Linda Pastan. VWA
Peas [and Honey]. *Unknown. See* I Eat My Peas with Honey.
Peasant. W. S. Merwin. NYBP
Peasant, The. Leonard Wolf. NYBP
Peasant and the Sheep, The. Ivan Andreevich Kriloff, *tr. fr. Russian by* C. Fillingham Coxwell. AWP
Peasant Declares His Love, The. Emile Roumer, *tr. fr. French by* John Peale Bishop. ErPo; TTY
Peasant haled a sheep to court, A. The Peasant and the Sheep. Ivan Andreevich Kriloff, *tr. by* C. Fillingham Coxwell. AWP
Peasant Poet, The. John Clare. OAEL-2; OBNC; WGRP
Peasant stood before a king and said, A. Ahab Mohammed. James Matthew Legaré. AA
Peasant sun went crushing grapes, The. Song. Laurence Dakin. *Fr.* Tancred, I, i. CaP
Peasant with the black tooth, The. The Bad Apple. Bruce Bennett. LTB
Peasants, The. Alun Lewis. LiTM; PPP
Peasants my forebears were. Forebears. Monk Gibbon. NeIP
Pease porridge [*or* pudding] hot. Mother Goose. FaFP; HBV-1; HBVY; OxNR (2 *vers.*); SoPo; TiPo
Peat Bog Soldiers. *Unknown.* FSW
Peau de Chagrin of State Street, The. Oliver Wendell Holmes. AP
Pebble, The. Elinor Wylie. MoAmPo
Pebbles. Herman Melville. AP
Peblis to the Play. *Unknown.* GoTS
Peck of Gold, A. Robert Frost. BPAW; PDV; SO
Pecos Puncher, The. *Unknown.* CoSo
Peculiar ghost! great and immortal ghost! Arthur Davison Ficke. Epitaph for the Poet V, XVII. HBMV
Pedagogical Principles. Harry Amoss. CaP
Pedagogue Arraigned. John Wain. GLGT
Pedagogy. Gerald Locklin. GP
Pedant dove, the poet who admires him, The. Literary Landscape with Dove and Poet. Phyllis McGinley. NePoAm-2
Peddler and His Wife, The. *Unknown.* AmFP
Peddler's Caravan, The. William Brighty Rands. HBV-1; HBVY; SoPo
Peddler's Song, A. *Unknown. See* Fine Knacks for Ladies.
Pedestrian's Plaint, The. E. V. Lucas. CenHV
Pedigree. Emily Dickinson. *See* Pedigree of honey, The.
Pedigree, The. Thomas Hardy. CoBMV
Pedigree. Mary Mills. NePoAm
Pedigree of honey, The. Emily Dickinson. BLPL; FaBV; NoAM; NOBA (Pedigree.) YaD
Pedlar. Confucius, *tr. fr. Chinese by* Ezra Pound. *Fr.* Wei Wind. CTC; OBVE
Pedlar, The. Charlotte Mew. HBMV
Pedlar. Sharon Nelson. VWA
Pedlar, The. Shakespeare. *See* Lawn as White as Driven Snow.
Pedlar, A. *Unknown. See* Fine Knacks for Ladies.
Pedlar of Small-Wares, A ("A pedlar I am, that take great care"). Sir John Suckling. CaPo
Pedlar's Caravan, The. William Brighty Rands. OxBChV
Pedlar's Song, The. Shakespeare. *See* Lawn as White as Driven Snow *and also* When Daffodils Begin to Peer.
Pedra. John William Burgon. BLPA
Pedro. Phoebe W. Hoffman. GoYe
Pedro. Luis Omar Salinas. FF
Peek-a-Boo. Robert Lowenstein. AMV-81
Peekaboo, I Almost See You. Ogden Nash. PoLF
Peel off me. Incantation to Get Rid of a Sometime Friend. Emanuel diPasquale. TW
Peeler and the Goat, The. *Unknown.* AnIL
Peeler, hast thou found my treasure. I've Lost My ———. Harry Cholmondeley Pennell. CenHV
Peeler's Lament, The. *Unknown.* CoSo; WTO
Peeling Onions. Adrienne Rich. BoWoP; TAP
Peeper, The. Peter Davidson. ErPo
Peepers in Our Meadow, The. Archibald MacLeish. NCSH
Peepin' through the knothole. Go Get the Axe. *Unknown.* AS; TrAS
Peeping Tom. Francis Hope. ErPo
Peer Gynt. Charles Hamilton Sorley. HBMV
Peer of the gods is that man, who. Sappho, *tr. fr. Greek by* William Carlos Williams. OBVE
Peer of the golden gods is he to Sappho. Ode to Anactoria. Sappho, *tr. by* William Ellery Leonard. AWP
Peerless yet hopeless maid of Q. Miss Ellen Gee of Kew. *Unknown.* FaBoNo
Pees maketh plente. Peace. *Unknown.* MeEL
Peeter a Whi[t]feild he hath slaine. Jock o' the Side. *Unknown.* ESPB; ViBoFo
Peg Leg Snelson. Melvin B. Tolson. FAZ
Peg-Leg's Fiddle. Bill Adams. EtS
Pegasos are steaming, The. Winter Rains: Cataluña. Philip Levine. NaP
Pegasus. C. Day Lewis. PoPle
Pegasus. Patrick Kavanagh. MoAB; OxBI
(Glut on the Market, A.) OnYI
Pegasus Lost. Elinor Wylie. MoAmPo
Peggy. Allan Ramsay. *See* My Peggy.
Peggy. Blanaid Salkeld. OnYI
Peggy Browne. Turlough O'Carolan. BIrV
Peggy-O. *Unknown.* FSW
Peggy Said Good Morning. John Clare. ELP
Peking Man, Raining. Katharine Auchincloss Lorr. SUW
Pelican, The. Greg Kuzma. AmPA
Pelican, The. *Unknown.* TreFS
Pelican Chorus, The. Edward Lear. FaBoNo
"King and Queen of the Pelicans we," *sel.* PB
Pelicanaries ("Pelicanaries are homely birds"). J. Patrick Lewis. PPJ
Pelicans. Robinson Jeffers. FM; MoAmPo
Pelicans My Father Sees, The. Sister Maris Stella. GoBC
Pelleas and Ettarre, *sel.* Tennyson.
"Rose, but one, none other rose had I, A." PoEL-5
Pelops and Hippodamia, *sel.* Matthew Grove.
In Praise of His Lady. EIL
Pelvic Meditation. Bruce Smith. AMV-80
Pen Hy Cane ("Pen Hyrogliphic Cane"). Mason Jordan Mason. PoNe
"Pen is mightier than the sword, The." A Feather's Weight. G. P. Lathrop. FaBoUs
Pen stops in a phrase of a letter home, The. Music in the Rec Hut. Hubert Creekmore. WaP
Penal Law. Austin Clarke. BoLoP; ELU; GTBS-P; IPY; NoAM; PAI
Penal Servitude for Mrs. Maybrick. *Unknown.* OxBoLi
Penalties of Baldness, The. Sir Owen Seaman. FiBHP
Penalty of Virtue, The. *Unknown, tr. fr. Sanskrit by* Arthur W. Ryder. *Fr.* The Panchatantra. AWP
Penance, The. Nahum Tate. CavP
Pencil and Paint. Eleanor Farjeon. PDV
Pendant Watch. Madeline DeFrees. NMM
Pendennis, *sel.* Thackeray.
At the Church Gate. HBV-1
Pendulous mouth, you flap in a wind. Mouths. Louis Dudek. PeCV
Pendulum Rhyme. Selma Robinson. InMe

Pendydd. Kingsley Amis. *Fr.* The Evans Country. NOBL
Penelope, *sels.* Monique Laederach, *tr. fr. French by* Charles Guenther. BoWoP
"And so I speak/ in place of that primordial cry."
"(Leaving the island, she believes, to go to the child.)"
Penelope, for her Ulysses' sake. Amoretti, XXIII. Spenser. NIP
Penelope, That Longed for the Sight. *Unknown.* EnRePo
Penetration and Trust. George Meredith. VLP
P'eng That Was a K'un, The. Chuang Tzu, *at. to* Lao-tse, *tr. fr. Chinese by* Robert Graves. AmMo
Penguin, A. Oliver Herford. FiBHP; PV
Penguin hailed me at the door, A. Penguins in the Home. Helen Bevington. OBAL
Penguin on the Beach. Ruth Miller. PeSA
Pen-guin sits up-on [*or* upon] the shore, The. A Penguin. Oliver Herford. FiBHP; PV
Penguins in the Home. Helen Bevington. OBAL
Penguins must have had it once, The. Teaching Penguins to Fly. Barry Spacks. GP
Pengur Bán. *Unknown, tr. fr. Irish by* Robin Flower. OxBI
Penitent, The. Jeremy Taylor. OBS; OxBoCh
Penitent, The, *satire.* Edna St. Vincent Millay. YaD
Penitent Considers Another Coming of Mary, A. Gwendolyn Brooks. NoAM; PChr
Penitent Hopes in Mary, The. *Unknown. See* Now Shrinketh Rose and Lily-Flower.
Penitent Nun, The. John Lockman. ErPo; UnTE
Penitent Palmer's Ode, The. Robert Greene. *Fr.* Francesco's Fortunes. LoBV; OBSC
Penitential Psalm: "I, thy servant, full of sighs, cry unto thee." *Unknown, tr. fr. Babylonian.* WGRP
Penitential Psalm to the Goddess Anunit: "May the wrath of the heart of my god be pacified!" *Unknown, tr. fr. Babylonian.* WGRP
Pen-knife, quills, ink-horn, books, paper, table-books, caps; take. Verses to Be Repeated by an Attorney Leaving His Lodging to Wait upon Judges Riding the Circuits from One County to Another, Least He Forget Some Necessary Thing. John Willis. FaBoUs
Penn Central Station at Beacon, N.Y., The. Ed Ochester. TAT
Penn Station at three in the morning. One Snowy Night in December. John N. Morris. NYP
Pennines in April. Ted Hughes. PPP
Pennsylvania Academy of Fine Arts. Ernest Kroll. AMV-80
Pennsylvania Dutch mouse. Lancaster County Tragedy. W. Lowrie Kay. ShM
Pennsylvania Places. T. A. Daly. OBAL
Pennsylvania Song. *Unknown.* PAH
Pennsylvania Station. Langston Hughes. AmNP
Pennsylvania Winter Indian 1974. Harold Littlebird. VoR
Penny and penny. *Unknown.* OxNR
Penny for a spool [*or* ball] of thread, A. Pop! Goes the Weasel. *Unknown.* SoPo; TreFT
Penny Is a Hardy Knight. *Unknown.* OxBM
Penny is heavier than the shrew, A. The Masked Shrew. Isabella Gardner. ImOP
Penny lost in the lak, The. *Unknown. Fr.* Colkelbie Sow. OxBS
Penny Trumpet. Raphael Rudnik. MAT; NYBP
Penny Whistle, The. Edward Thomas. MoAB; MoBrPo
Penny Whistle Blues. E. H. L. Island. InMe
Pennycandystore beyond the El, The. Lawrence Ferlinghetti. *Fr.* A Coney Island of the Mind. BiP; CAD; CAPP; CTBA; HeIP; PoM; TAP
Penological Study: Southern Exposure, *sel.* Robert Penn Warren.
Wet Hair: If Now His Mother Should Come. NoAM
Pénsees de Noël. A. D. Godley. DBV; InMe
Penshurst. Ben Jonson. FaBoPP
Pensioners fondle the books in the sidewalk bins. The Band. Carl Dennis. AMV-80
Pensionnaires. Paul Verlaine, *tr. fr. French by* François Pirou. PeHV
Pensy Ant, right trig and clean, A. The Caterpillar and the Ant. Allan Ramsay. SeCePo
Pentachromatic. Julia de Burgos, *tr. fr. Spanish by* Julio Marzán. InW
Pentagonia. G. E. Bates. NYBP; SpRo
Pentecost. Ai. GeTw; LTB
Pentecost. John Bennett. EBCP
Pentecost. Adelbert Sumpter Coats. TrPWD
Pentecost Castle, The, *abr.* Geoffrey Hill. HAP
Pentimento. Lori Fisher. PoDr
Pentland Hills, The. *Unknown.* GBP
Pentucket. Whittier. PAH
Penumbra. Pierre Louys, *tr. fr. French. Fr.* Chansons de Bilitis. PeHV
Penumbra. Dante Gabriel Rossetti. VLP
Penurious Quaker or The High Priz'd Harlot, The. *Unknown.* CoMu
Penus envy, they call it. Alta. NMM
Peony for Apollo, A. Charles Edward Eaton. GoYe
People, The. Tomasso Campanella, *tr. fr. Italian by* John Addington Symonds. AWP; DBV
People, The. Robert Creeley. VGW
People. Orban Veli Kanik, *tr. fr. Turkish by* Talat Sait Halman. LLLT
People. D. H. Lawrence. BrPo
People. Lois Lenski. FaPON; SoPo
People, The. Elizabeth Madox Roberts. GoJo; RHPC; SoPo; TiPo
People, The. W. B. Yeats. CMoP
People. Yevgeny Yevtushenko, *tr. fr. Russian by* Robin Milner-Gulland *and* Peter Levi. DL
People. Charlotte Zolotow. RHPC
People,/ male and female. Mahadevi, *tr. fr. Kannada by* A. K. Ramanujan. BoWoP
People all over at this time of year. Resolutions?—New and Old. Harvey E. Rolfe. STF
People along the sand, The. Neither Out Far nor In Deep. Robert Frost. AmPP; AP; CABA; ChTr; CoBMV; CrMA; HAP; LiTA; MoAB; MOS; NoAM; NOBA; NoP; TAP; WeW
People always say to me. The Question. Karla Kuskin. NTCP; PDV
People—and a lot/ I don't care for. Perambulator Poems, IV. David McCord. WhC
People are making a camp of branches in that country at Arnhem Bay, The. The Moon-Bone Song. *Unknown, tr. by* Ronald M. Berndt. CBAP
People are putting up storm windows now. Storm Windows. Howard Nemerov. ConAP
People are saying that I am your enemy, The. To Julia de Burgos. Julia de Burgos, *tr. by* Grace Schulman. BoWoP; PBWP
People are standing, as if out of the rain. Fifth and 94th. Stanley Plumly. NYP
People arrive to worship in their church. The Church. Jules Romains, *tr. by* Jethro Bithell. WGRP
People at the Party, The. Lisel Mueller. NePoAm-2
People Buy a Lot of Things. Annette Wynne. PDV; SoPo
People buying and selling, consuming pleasures, The. Reference to a Passage in Plutarch's Life of Sulla. Robinson Jeffers. CrMA
People chained to aurora, A. Civilization and Its Discontents. John Ashbery. CAPP; LCAP; TwCP
People die from loneliness. One. Carolyn M. Rodgers. BPo
People do gossip. Sappho, *tr. fr. Greek by* Mary Barnard. PBWP
People expect old men to die. Old Men. Ogden Nash. DFF; EvOK
People going straight up to heaven. Amazing Grace. Anselm Hollo. PoM
People Hide Their Love. Emperor Wu Ti, *tr. fr. Chinese by* Arthur Waley. OLR
People I love the best, The. To Be of Use. Marge Piercy. GeTw; HoAn
People in the middle ages didn't think they were living. Ode. David Lehman. AMV-81
People in the Park, The. Léonie Adams. MoVE
People is a beast of muddy brain, The. The People. Tomasso Campanella, *tr. by* John Addington Symonds. AWP; DBV
People know, The. A Little More about the Brothers and Sisters. Sharon Scott. JB
People like us are meant to share some loving moment. For Chicle & Justina. Diana Bickston. LFAC
People love war, The. War. Anthony Ostroff. FAZ
People made a ring, The. The Hemorrhage. Stanley Kunitz. NYP; WaP
People married by pictures then. Relocation. David Mura. BrSi
People of Blakeney, The. *Unknown.* GBP
People of Ireland—I am an old woman; I am near my end. A Leitrim Woman. John Lyle Donaghy. OnYI; OxBI
People of Spain think Cervantes, The. Cervantes. E. C. Bentley. *Fr.* Clenhews. CenHV; EvOK; FiBHP
People of Tao-chou, The. Po Chü-i, *tr. fr. Chinese by* Arthur Waley. ChTr
People of the Phoenix do not say "the Phoenix," The. Conventicle. Gerrit Lansing. CoPo
People of the South Wind. William Stafford. NNaP
People said, "Indian children are hard to teach." Indian Children Speak. Juanita Bell. PAI
People say they have a hard time. For de Lawd. Lucille Clifton. CNA; PoBA; TAP; TwCP
People south of Gibbon call him, The. Blue Heron. Don Welch. GP
People spoiled by too many masters. Poetics. André Spire, *tr. by* Edouard Roditi. VWA
People, the People, The. George Oppen. GP
People Trying to Love. Stephen Berg. NaP
People upstairs, The. Ogden Nash. RHPC
People vs. the People, The. Kenneth Fearing. MoAmPo
People, The: Village. Dorothy Livesay. *Fr.* The Colour of God's Face. PeCV
People walk upon their heads, The. Topsy-turvy Land. H. E. Wilkinson. SoPo
People watch the young, The. Love. Anthony Ostroff. FAZ

People were bathing and posturing themselves on the beach. The Gods! The Gods! D. H. Lawrence. CMoP
People who came to see the great gorilla. The Gorilla. Baxter Hathaway. HoAn
People who have no children can be hard. The Children of the Poor. Gwendolyn Brooks. *Fr.* The Womanhood. PoA; WPE
People who have what they want are very fond of telling people. The Terrible People. Ogden Nash. NePA; TAP
People Who Must. Carl Sandburg. PDV
People Who Went By in Winter. William Stafford. GP
People Will Live On, The. Carl Sandburg. *Fr.* The People, Yes. MoAB; MoAmPo; MoPo; NePA; NoAM; NOBA; OxBA; TrGrPo
People Will Talk. Samuel Dodge. TreFS, *sl. diff.*; WBLP, *sl. abr.*
People Will Talk. *Unknown.* TreFS
People, Yes, The, *sels.* Carl Sandburg.
"Englishman in the old days, An," Sec. 11. FYAP
"From the four corners of the earth," *fr.* Sec. 1. CMoP
"People will live on, The," Sec. 107. MoAB; MoAmPo; MoPo; NePA; NoAM; NOBA; OxBA; TrGrPo
"They have yarns, Sec. 45." AmFN; LiTA; MoAmPo
"What the people learn out of lifting and hauling," Sec. 32. OBAL
"Who shall speak for the people?" Sec. 24. OxBA
" 'Why did the children,' " Sec. 41. OBAL
"Why repeat? I heard you the first time," Sec. 42. OBAL
People's Attorney, servant of the Right! Wendell Phillips. Amos Bronson Alcott. AA
People's Choice, The: The Dream Poems II. Amiri Baraka. BiP
People's [*or* Worker's] flag is deepest red, The. The Red Flag. Jim Connell. FSW; VLP
People's King, The. Lyman Whitney Allen. PGD
People's Petition, The. Wathen Mark Wilks Call. OBVV
Pep. Grace G. Bostwick. WBLP
Pepita, my paragon, bright star of Arragon. Saragossa. Henry Sambrooke Leigh. FaBoCo
Peppergrass. Stanley Plumly. LCAP
Peppertrees, the peppertrees, The! Scenes from the Life of the Peppertrees. Denise Levertov. LiTM; NeAP; NoP; PoM
Peppery Man, The. Arthur Macy. FaPON
Pepsi Generation. Walasse Ting. MAT
Pepys Bar, West Forty-eighth Street, 8 a.m. L. E. Sissman. NYP
Per Ardua ad Astra. John Oxenham. TrPWD
Per Aspera. Florence Earle Coates. HBMV
Per Iter Tenebricosum. Oliver St. John Gogarty. AnIL; OBMV; OxBI
Per Pacem ad Lucem. Adelaide Anne Procter. TrPWD
Perambulator Poems, I-VII. David McCord. WhC
Perambulator Poem, V. OFD
(When I Was Christened.) OBCA
Perceiving the mediocrity of blackness. The K.K.K. Disco. Noah Mitchell. LFAC
Perception of an object costs. Emily Dickinson. NOBA
Perchance in days to come. Strange Love. Moses ibn Ezra, *tr. by* Solomon Solis-Cohen. TrJP
Perchance she died in age—surviving all. Rome, by Metella's Tomb. Byron. *Fr.* Childe Harold's Pilgrimage, IV. FaBoPP
Perchance some coming after. Epigram. Strato, *tr. by* Sydney Oswald. PeHV
Perchance that I might learn what pity is. A Prayer for Purification. Michelangelo, *tr. by* John Addington Symonds. AWP
Perched in a tower of this ancestral wall. At the Great Wall of China. Edmund Blunden. GTBS-P
Perched on a birch stump. The Hooded Crow. Rennie McOwan. PoSH
Perched on a great fall of air. Landscape with Figures. Keith Douglas. NePoEA
Percival Wilberforce Henderson Crane. The Scandalous Tale of Percival and Genevieve. Newman Levy. WhC
Percivale's Quest. Tennyson. *Fr.* Idylls of the King. OAEL-2
Percolating Highway. Michael Castro. VWA
Percussions. Ron Welburn. CNA
Percussive, furious, this wind. Mistral. Barbara Howes. NYBP
Percy/ 68. Glenn Myles. NBP
Percy out of Northumberland, The [*or* Perse out of Northombarlande, The]. Chevy Chase [*or* The Hunting of the Cheviot *or* The Ancient Ballad of Chevy-Chase]. *Unknown.* BaBo; EnRP; ESPB; OxBB; ViBoPo; WHA
Percy Shelley. John Peale Bishop. ErPo
Perdido, Duke? Robert McGovern. SOTS
Perdie, I said it not. *See* Perdy! I said it not.
Perdita. Florence Earle Coates. AA
Perdita. Louis MacNeice. PoA
Perdita's Garden. Shakespeare. *Fr.* The Winter's Tale, IV, iii. WHA
Perdition catch my soul. Shakespeare. *Fr.* Othello, III, iii. LO
Perdy [*or* Perdie *or* Perdye]! I said[e] it not. Constancy. Sir Thomas Wyatt. EnRePo; OBSC; PoEL-1; SiPS
Père Lalemant. Marjorie Pickthall. CaP; NOBC; OBCV; PeCV
Père Sévère, Le. *Unknown, tr. fr. French by* Andrew Lang. AWP
Peregrine. Elinor Wylie. BLPL; HBMV
Peregrine Prykke's Pilgrimage, *sel.* Clive James.
"Blood has soaked the bone which hides the stone, The." FaBoPa
Peregrine White and Virginia Dare. Rosemary *and* Stephen Vincent Benét. OBCA
Peregrine's Sunday Song. Elinor Wylie. NYBP
Perfect. "Hugh MacDiarmid." NeBP
Perfect Bliss and Sole Felicity. Christopher Marlowe. *See* Nature, That Framed Us of Four Elements.
Perfect Day, A. Carrie Jacobs Bond. BLSo, *with music;* TreF; WBLP
Perfect dear whom no one blames, The. Lady Sara Bunbury Sacrificing to the Graces, by Reynolds. Daryl Hine. EyDe
Perfect Garden, The. Winifred Robertson. PoSH
Perfect Gift, The. Edmund Vance Cooke. PChr
Perfect Husband, The. Ogden Nash. DFF; FaBoUs
Perfect little body, without fault or stain on thee. On a Dead Child. Robert Bridges. BrPo; CMoP; EBEV; LiTB; LiTM; NoAM; NOBE; OAEP; OBMV; OBNC; ViBoPo
Perfect Love ("Perfect love the Father giveth"). *Unknown.* STF
Perfect Mother, The. Susan Griffin. NPGG
Perfect Peace. Bible, *O. T.* Isaiah, XXVI: 3. TRV
Perfect rainbow, A! a wide. The Storm. William Carlos Williams. PCP; PPJ
Perfect Reactionary, The. Hughes Mearns. NTCP; WhC
Perfect Way is only difficult for those who pick and choose, The. On Trust in the Heart. Seng-ts'an, *tr. fr. Chinese.* ILwL
Perfect Woman. Wordsworth. *See* She Was a Phantom of Delight.
Perfection. Francis Carlin. FaFP; HBMV
Perfection, if't hath ever been attayned. In the Due Honor of the Author Master Robert Norton. John Smith. SCAP
Perfection is terrible, it cannot have children. The Munich Mannequins. Sylvia Plath. NaP
Perfection, of a kind, was what he was after. Epitaph on a Tyrant. W. H. Auden. ELU; HeIP
Perfection of Dentistry, The. Marvin Bell. AmPA; CoAP
Perfectionist, The. Bernice Fleisher. PoDr
Perfectly happy now, he looked at his estate. Voltaire at Ferney. W. H. Auden. NePA; PoA
Perfectly rounded yet how slender. Boy at a Certain Age. Robert Francis. DFF
Perfervid Roc, sitting on candle light, The. The Roc. Richard Eberhart. CMoP
Perforated Spirit, The. Morris Bishop. FiBHP; QQQ
Performance, The. James Dickey. CoAP; ConAP; LiTM; NePoEA-2; NoAM; NOBA
Performance at Hog Theater, A. Russell Edson. AmPA
Performances, assortments, résumés. The Tunnel. Hart Crane. *Fr.* The Bridge. AP; CMoP; MAT; MoAB; MoAmPo; MoVE; NePA; NYP; OxBA
Performer numbs toward the moribund, The. The Martyr and the Army. Jock Henderson. AMV-81
Performing Seal, The. Rachel Field. *Fr.* A Circus Garland. OBCA; SoPo; RHPC; TiPo
Perfume, The. John Donne. Elegies, IV. AnAnS-1; SeCP
Perfume, The. Robert Herrick. CaPo
Perfume. *Unknown, tr. fr. Greek by* Louis Untermeyer. UnTE
Perfume of the iris, sweet citron, The. The Words, the Words, the Words. William Carlos Williams. BiP
Perfume of your body dulls my sense, The. Flower of Love. Claude McKay. BALP
Pergamon city of the Phrygians. The Aftermath. Euripides, *tr. by* Richmond Lattimore. *Fr.* Iphigenia in Aulis. WaaP
Perhaps. W. H. Auden. MoPo; NePA; OAEP
(Prologue: "O love, the interest itself in thoughtless heaven.") EBEV; FaBoMo
Perhaps. Vera Brittain. SUMH
Perhaps. Lucille Clifton. GeTw
Perhaps. Rachel, *tr. fr. Hebrew by* A. C. Jacobs. VWA
Perhaps. Stephen Spender. NoAM
Perhaps/ they are trying to tell us. Metaphors. Sally McNall. FAZ
Perhaps/ This is the way. Antigone I. Herbert Martin. PoBA
Perhaps/ You will remember/ John Brown. October 16: The Raid. Langston Hughes. BoLo; PoBA
Perhaps a dream; yet surely truth has beamed. Frederick Goddard Tuckerman. Sonnets, I, xxiv. AP
Perhaps because/ you won everything you lost. Hubert Horatio Humphrey (1911-1978). Martin Galvin. SOTS
Perhaps biography is the flat map. Biography. Maura Stanton. MAYP
Perhaps Eve in the garden knew the sun. The Fortunate Fall. A. Alvarez. VWA

Perhaps he plays with cherubs now. A Phantasy of Heaven. Harry Kemp. HBMV
Perhaps He will come at the dawning. When Will He Come? *Unknown.* STF
"Perhaps I may allow, the Dean." Swift. *Fr.* Verses on the Death of Doctor Swift. FaBoEn; OnYI; NOBE
Perhaps if we could begin some definite way. A Bird Sings to Establish Frontiers. Jack Gilbert. NPGG
Perhaps it is no matter that you died. To Hasekawa. Walter Conrad Arensberg. HBV-2
Perhaps it is to avoid some great sadness. Sleeping on the Wing. Frank O'Hara. SOTW
Perhaps it is well now. We Who Are Left. George Whalley. CaP
Perhaps it was because. Nightswim. William Pitt Root. MAYP
Perhaps it was being inside of something. The History of the World as Pictures. Nancy Sullivan. CoPo
Perhaps it was never so. Perhaps. Rachel, *tr. by* A. C. Jacobs. VWA
Perhaps It's as You Say. Peter Everwine. NNaP
Perhaps It's Only Music. Natan Zach, *tr. fr. Hebrew by* Peter Everwine *and* Shula Starkman. VWA
Perhaps, long hence, when I have pass'd away. She, to Him. Thomas Hardy. OBEV
Perhaps she said, lively at first but once. Farmer Goes Beserk. Anne Elder. CBAP
Perhaps she watches where a silver bay. La Madonna di Lorenzetti. John Williams Andrews. HBMV
Perhaps some day the sun will shine again. Perhaps. Vera Brittain. SUMH
Perhaps some needful service of the state. Epitaphs, II. Gabriello Chiabrera, *tr. by* Wordsworth. AWP
Perhaps the accident of a bird. An Instance. Alastair Reid. PP
Perhaps the Best Time. William Meredith. NePoEA
Perhaps the children of a future day. Unless We Guard Them Well. Jane Merchant. QQQ
Perhaps the Socrates he had never read. Why Hast Thou Forsaken Me? Chad Walsh. *Fr.* The Psalm of Christ. TrCP
Perhaps this valley too leads into the head of long-ago days. Grand Abacus. John Ashbery. EAS; PoA
Perhaps Today ("Perhaps today the clouds will part asunder"). *Unknown.* STF
Perhaps when I am gaunt. To Drift Down. Janet Carncross Chandler. AMV-81
Perhaps you expected a face that was free from tears. Narcissus. Paul Valéry, *tr. by* Joseph T. Shipley. AWP
Perhaps you find the angel most improbable. Poem for a Christmas Broadcast. Anne Ridler. NeBP
Perhaps—well/ It may not matter! Men's Impotence. *Tr. fr. Eskimo.* WTO
Peri Poietikes. Louis Zukofsky. CoPo
Pericles, *sels.* Shakespeare.
  "Terrible childbed hast thou had, my dear, A," *fr.* III, i. EBEV
  Thou God of This Great Vast, Rebuke These Surges, *fr.* III, i. MOS; NAs
Pericles and Aspasia, *sels.* Walter Savage Landor.
  Behold, O Aspasia! I Send You Verses, *fr.* CXC. LoBV; OBNC
    ("Beauty! thou art a wanderer on the earth.") ViBoPo
  Copy of Verses Sent by Cleone to Aspasia, A, *fr* CXXI. LoBV
  Corinna, from Athens, to Tanagra, *fr.* XLIV. OBEV; OBVV
    (Corinna to Tanagra.) OBNC; OBRV; ViBoPo, *abr.*
    (Corinna, to Tanagra, from Athens.) NOBE
  Death of Artemidora, The, *fr.* LXXXV. EnRP; OBNC; SeCeV
    ("'Artemidora! Gods invisible.'") ViBoPo
  Dirce, *fr.* CCXXX. AWP; CTC; EBEV; EnRP; FaBoEE; FaBoEn; GBL; HAP; LiTB; LoBV; NOBE; NoP; OAEL-2; OAEP; OBEV; OBNC; OBRV; PAI; PoEL-4; PoPle; PoRA; SeCeV; TreFT; TrGrPo; ViBoPo; VLP; WeW; WHA; WhC
    (Stand Close Around.) ChTr
  Myrtis, *fr.* LIII. OBRV
Perigoo's Horse. *At. to* George Calhoun *or* John Calhoun. ShS
Perigot and Willye. Spenser. *Fr.* The Shepheardes Calender. LoBV
  (It Fell upon a Holy Eve.) InvP
  (Roundelay, A: "It fell upon a holy eve.") ElL
Perilla! to thy fates resign'd. A Copy of Verses Sent by Cleone to Aspasia. Walter Savage Landor. *Fr.* Pericles and Aspasia. LoBV
Perilous Life, A ("A perilous life, and hard as life may be"). *Unknown.* EtS
Perils and the dangers of the voyage being past, The. Jack Robinson. *Unknown.* OBET
Perils of Darkness. Shakespeare. King Richard II, *fr.* III, ii. TreFT
Perils of Obesity, The. Harry Graham. FiBHP
Perimedes [*or* Perimedes, the Blacksmith], *sels.* Robert Greene.
  Coridon and Phillis. OBSC
    (Phillis and Corydon.) HBV-1
  Fair Is My Love for April's in Her Face. HBV-1
    (Fair Is My Love.) ElL
    (Sonnet: "Fair is my love, for April's in her face.") ViBoPo
Period of Mourning, The, *sel.* Henry Peacham.
  Nuptial Hymn. ElL
Period Piece. Bruce Berlind. FAZ
Periods of Adjustment. Shawn Wong. BrSi
Peripatetic. Robert Lima. AMV-81
Periphery. A. R. Ammons. NOBA
Periphery. Ruth Stone. GP
Periphrastic Insult, Not a Banal, A. J. V. Cunningham. TW
Peri's Lament for Hinda, The. Thomas Moore. *Fr.* Lalla Rookh. OBNC
Perishing Bird, The. Douglas G. Jones. MoCV
Perle, plesaunte to prynces paye. *Unknown.* *Fr.* Pearl. EBEV; OxBM
Permanence. Francis Meynell. HBMV
Permanence in Change. Goethe, *tr. fr. German by* John Frederick Nims; *diff. tr. by* Mark J. Doyle. HoPM
Permanence of the Young Men, The. William Soutar. NeBP; OxBS
Permanent Delegate, The. Yuri Suhl, *tr. fr. Yiddish by* Max Rosenfeld *and* Walter Lowenfels. PAI; PPON
Permanent Tourists, The. P. K. Page. LiTM; NOBC
Permanently. Kenneth Koch. CAPP; CoAP; NoP; PoA; PoM; PPP
Permission to Speak. Stephen Orlen. MAYP
Permit me here a simple brief aside. To Calliope. Robert Graves. CMoP
Permit Me Voyage. James Agee. MoAmPo
Permit Us, Lord, to Consecrate, *with music.* Joseph Green. AH
Permitted to assist you, let me see. St. Valentine. Marianne Moore. NYBP; OFD
Pernicious Weed. William Cowper. InMe; WhC
Perpetual Christmas. Arthur Gordon Field. PGD
Perpetual Motion. David Lehman. SUW
Perpetual night and endless sleep. Nox Est Perpetua. Marion Lochhead. LO
Perpetual rebozo man, The. Mexico City Hand Game. Rayna Green. TWSS
Perpetuum Immobile. Bruce Dawe. CBAP
Perpetuum Mobile. Edith Sitwell. HBMV
Perplex'd with trifles thro' the vale of life. A Nut, a World, a Squirrel, and a King. Charles Churchill. *Fr.* Night; an Epistle to Robert Lloyd. FaBoRV
Perplext in faith, but pure in deeds. Tennyson. *Fr.* In Memoriam A. H. H., XCVI. TRV
Perrette's milk-pot fitted her head-mat just right. The Dairymaid and Her Milk-Pot. La Fontaine, *tr. by* Marianne Moore. NAWM-2
Perry Zoll. Edgar Lee Masters. *Fr.* Spoon River Anthology. CrMA
Perry's Victory. *Unknown.* PAH
Perry's Victory—a Song. *Unknown.* PAH
Perse owt of [*or* off] Northombarlonde, The. *See* Percy out of Northumberland, The.
Persephone. Robert Duncan. NoAM; NOBA
Persephone is the woman buried. Robert Kelly. The Book of Persephone, 11. PoM
Perseus. Louis MacNeice. CoBMV; LiTM
Perseverance. *Unknown.* *See* Always Finish.
Perseverance; or, Half a Coronet, *sel.* A. P. Herbert.
  Finale. InMe
Pershing at the Tomb of Lafayette. Amelia Josephine Burr. PAH
Persia. V. Sackville-West. WPE
Persian Fopperies. Horace. *See* Fie on Eastern Luxury!
Persian galleys plumed with warriors, The. Before Salamis. William Bedell Stanford. NeIP
Persian Miniature. William Jay Smith. CoAP; MoVE
Persian pomps, boy, ever I renounce them. Horace, *tr. by* Christopher Smart. Odes, I, 38. OBVE
Persian Song of Hafiz, A. Hafiz, *tr. fr. Persian by* Sir William Jones. AWP; OBEC
Persian Version, The. Robert Graves. CMoP; FaBoCo; LiTB; LiTM; NoAM; NOBL; OBWP; WeW
Persians, The, *sel.* Aeschylus, *tr. fr. Greek by* G. M. Cookson.
  Salamis. WaaP
Persicos Odi. Horace. *See* Fie on Eastern Luxury!
Persimmon Tree, The. *Unknown.* GBP
Persimmon Trees, She Remembers, Not Far Away. David Baker. AMV-81
Persimmon woman. Donna. Paula Gunn Allen. TWSS
Persimmons and Plums. Elizabeth Hodges. GrPl
Persistence of Memory, the Failure of Poetry, The. Robert Phillips. GeTw
Persistency of Poetry. Matthew Arnold. VLP
Persistent Explorer. John Crowe Ransom. OxBA
Person, a Mexican, A. Lorri Martinez. LFAC
Person after person. Buddha's Birthday: April 8, 1819. Issa, *tr. by* Nobuyuki Yuasa. *Fr.* Oraga Haru. OFD

Person is very self-conscious about his head, A. Thoughts on One's Head. William Meredith. HAP
Person of Note, A. *At. to* Walter Parke. *See* Limerick: "There was an old stupid who wrote."
Person, or A Hymn on and to the Holy Ghost. Margaret Avison. PeCV
Person who can do, The. Poem. Alan Dugan. ErPo; NoAM
Personal. Langston Hughes. AmNP; NOBA; PoNe
Personal. Samuel Yellen. NYBP
Personal Helicon. Seamus Heaney. IPY
Personal History; for My Son. Ruthven Todd. NeBP
Personal Poem. Frank O'Hara. CAPP; NYP
Personal Poem. Ingrid Wendt. NMM
Personal Song. Arnatkoak, *tr. fr. Eskimo.* WTO
Personal Talk. Wordsworth. CABA; EnRP; NOBE
Personality. Archibald Lampman. PeCV
Personality. Carl Sandburg. CrMA
Personality Sketch, A: Bill. Ronda Davis. JB
Personals. Leatrice W. Emeruwa. PCP
Personified Sentimental, The. Bret Harte. NA
Perspective. Margaret Avison. OBCV; PeCV
Perspective. Coventry Patmore. *Fr.* The Angel in the House, II, i. FaBoEE; GBL
Perspective. Robert L. Vorpahl. AMV-80
Perspective and Limits of Snapshots, The. Dave Smith. MAYP
Perspective He Would Mutter Going to Bed. Jack Gilbert. NPGG
Perspective never withers from their eyes. Quaker Hill. Hart Crane. *Fr.* The Bridge. LiTM
Perspective of Co-ordination. Arthur Davison Ficke. PoA
Perspectives. Dudley Randall. AmNP
Perspectives Are Precipices. John Peale Bishop. LiTA; MoVE; NePA
Persuasions [*or* Perswasions] to Enjoy. Thomas Carew. HBV-1; MePo; NOBE; SeCV-1
(Persuasions to Joy; a Song.) OBEV
(Song: Persuasions [*or* Perswasions] to Enjoy.) AnAnS-1; CaPo; SeCP
Persuasions to Love, *sel.* Thomas Carew.
"For that lovely face will fail." ViBoPo
Persuasive Go-Gebtor. "R. C." TDH
Perswasions to Enjoy. Thomas Carew. *See* Persuasions to Enjoy.
Perturbations of Uranus, The. Roy Fuller. ErPo
Perugia. Amelia Josephine Burr. HBV-2
Peruke of Poets. William Zaranka. BXAP
Peruse my leaves thro' ev'ry part. Verses Wrote in a Lady's Ivory Table-Book. Swift. NCEP
Perverse Custom, A ("A perverse custom it is to prefer boys to girls"). *Unknown, tr. fr. Latin by* John Boswell. PeHV
Perverse habit of cat goddesses, A. Cat Goddesses. Robert Graves. MoVE; NYBP
Perversion interests me. Note Delivered by a Female Impersonator. Heather McHugh. AmPA
Perversity. Susan Griffin. LLLT
Pervigilium Veneris. Suzanne Noguere. PoA
Peschiera. Arthur Hugh Clough. HBV-2
Pesci Misti. Leonard Aaronson. FaBoTw
Peshach Has Come to the Ghetto Again. Binem Heller, *tr. fr. Yiddish by* Max Rosenfeld. TrJP
Pessimist, The. Ben King. BLPA; FaBoCo; FaBoNo; FaFP; InMe; NA; OBAL; TreFT
(Sum of Life, The, *abr.*) CTC
Pet Crane, A. *Unknown, tr. fr. Old Irish by* Myles Dillon. AnIL
Pet Deer, The. James Tate. EAS
Pet Lamb, The. Wordsworth. OxBChV
Pet Name, The. Elizabeth Barrett Browning. HBV-1
Pet Panther. A. R. Ammons. NoP
Pet Shop. Louis MacNeice. BoAnP
Pet Shop. Robert Sward. ELU
Pet was never mourned as you. Last Words to a Dumb Friend. Thomas Hardy. FM; OAEP; PCat
Petals fall in the fountain, The. Ts'ai Chi'h. Ezra Pound. NoP
Pete at the Seashore. Don Marquis. GDP
Pete at the Zoo. Gwendolyn Brooks. PDV
Pete Orman. *Unknown.* BPAW
Pete Petersen, before this bit, a professional entertainer. Vaudeville. Lincoln Kirstein. NoAM
Pete Rousecastle the sailor's son. Rousecastle. David Wright. MoBS
Peter. Laura Benét. HBMV
Peter. Michael Dennis Browne. NYBP
Peter. Marianne Moore. CMoP; NoP; OxBA
Peter Amberley. John Calhoun. *See* Peter Emberley.
Peter and John. Elinor Wylie. HBMV; MoAB; MoAmPo; MoBS
Peter at Fourteen. Constance Carrier. NePoAm
Peter at some immortal cloth, it seemed. The Death of Peter Esson. George Mackay Brown. NePoEA-2
Peter Bell [a Lyrical Ballad]. John Hamilton Reynolds. OBNC; OBRV; Par
Peter Bell the Third, *sels.* Shelley.
"Among the guests who often stayed." ChER
"Devil now knew his proper cue, The." OBSV
"Hell is a city much like London." OBSV
Peter Cooper. Joaquin Miller. AA
Peter Emberley, *vers.* I-III, *with music.* John Calhoun. ShS
(Peter Amberley.) AmFP
Peter, Go Ring Dem Bells, *with music. Unknown.* BoAN-1
Peter Gray. *Unknown.* BLSo, *with music;* FSW; OuSiCo, *with music*
Peter Grimes. George Crabbe. The Borough, Letter XXII. EnRP; OBNV; PoEL-4; TEP
(Poor of the Borough, The: Peter Grimes.) NoP
Sels.
"Alas! for Peter not a helping hand." OBRV
(Peter Grimes at Aldeburgh.) FaBoPP
"He built a mud-wall'd hovel, where he kept." SaC
"Thus by himself compell'd to live each day." FaBoEn; OBNC; SeCePo
(Peter Grimes; the Outcast.) NOBE
Peter had experienced the tight, nauseous desire. The Wickedness of Peter Shannon. Alden Nowlan. MoCV
Peter Hath Lost His Purse. *At. to* Henry Parrot. FF
Peter of the brothers three. Peter. Laura Benét. HBMV
Peter-Penny, The. Robert Herrick. CaPo
Peter, Peter, pumpkin eater. Mother Goose. FaBoBe; FaFP; HBV-1; HBVY; OxNR; SoPo; TiPo
Peter Piper picked a peck of pickled peppers. Mother Goose. FaBoBe; FaFP; FaPON; HBV-1; HBVY; OxNR; TiPo; TreFS
Peter Quince at the Clavier. Wallace Stevens. AmPP; AP; CABA; CMoP; CoBMV; HBMV; InPK; InPS; LiTM; MoAB; MoAmPo; MP; NOBA; OxBA; PAI; PPP; TAP; TrGrPo; TwAmPo; TwCP; ViBoPo
Peter Rabbit. Sandra McPherson. LCAP
Peter sleep-walks. Peter. Michael Dennis Browne. NYBP
Peter Stuyvesant's New Year's Call. Edmund Clarence Stedman. PAH
Peter White will ne'er go right. Mother Goose. OxBoLi; OxNR
Peterhead in May. Burns Singer. OxBS
Peterhof. Edmund Wilson. GoJo
Peter's not friendly. He gives me sideways looks. John Berryman. *Fr.* Dream Songs. CAPP
Peter's Tears. Thomas Hood. TreFT
Pete's Error. Arthur Chapman. BPAW
Petit Mari, Le, *with music. Unknown.* OuSiCo
Petit, the Poet. Edgar Lee Masters. *Fr.* Spoon River Anthology. CMoP; InPK; MoAmPo; MoVE; NoAM; NOBA; OxBA; PPoN; TAP
Petition, A. Thomas Bailey Aldrich. AA
Petition. W. H. Auden. CMoP; CoBMV; LiTB; MoPo; OAEP
Petition. John Drinkwater. TrPWD
Petition. Harold McCurdy. AMV-81
Petition. Eleanor Slater. TrPWD
Petition. R. S. Thomas. FaBoMo
Petition for a Miracle. David Morton. *Fr.* Boke of Two Ladies. ISi
Petition for an Absolute Retreat, The. Countess of Winchilsea. OBEC, *abr.*; PoEL-3; SBG; WPE, *abr.*
"Give me, O indulgent fate!" *sel.* TrGrPo
Petition of the Gray Horse, Auld Dunbar, The. William Dunbar. OxBS
Petition of Tom Dermody to the Three Fates in Council Sitting, The. Thomas Dermody. AnIV
Petition to Have Her Leave to Die. "A. W." *See* Give Me Leave.
Petrarch. Giosuè Carducci, *tr. fr. Italian by* William Dudley Foulke. AWP
Petrified Fern, The. Mary Bolles Branch. AA; HBV-2
Petrillo, *parody.* "Gilbertulus." WhC
Petron, the Desert Father. Lawrence Durrell. *Fr.* Eight Aspects of Melissa. NeBP
Petruchio Is Undaunted by Katharina. Shakespeare. *Fr.* The Taming of the Shrew, I, ii. TreFT
Pets, The. Robert Farren. OxBI
Pets are the hobby of my brother Bert. My Brother Bert. Ted Hughes. RHPC
Pettichap's Nest, The. John Clare. PBBP
Pettitoes are little feet, The. *Unknown.* OxNR
Petty Officers' Mess, The. Roy Fuller. ChMP
Petty sneaking knave I knew, A. Cromek [*or* On Cromek]. Blake. FaBoCo; FiBHP; PoPle; PV
Petulance is purple. Spectrum. Mari Evans. BPo
Petunias in mass formation. Giardino Pubblico. Osbert Sitwell. ChMP
Peveril of the Peak, *sel.* Sir Walter Scott.
" 'Speak not of niceness, when there's chance of wreck,' " *fr. ch.* 38. FaBoEE; NBM
Pew, pew,/ My minny me slew. Song of the Murdered Child [*or* The Milk-white Dove]. *Unknown.* ChTr; GBP
Pewee, The. John Townsend Trowbridge. HBV-1
Pewter. Jack Gilbert. NPGG

Peyote Poem. Michael McClure. PoM
"Clear—the senses bright—sitting in the black chair—Rocker," *sel.* NeAP
Peyote Vision. Lew Blockcolski. VoR
Phaedra. Hilda Doolittle ("H. D."). SBG
Phaedra. Osip Mandelstam, *tr. fr. Russian by* James Greene. OBVE
Phaedra (Phèdre). Racine, *tr. fr. French by* Robert Lowell. NAWM-2
Phaeton. Eli Mandel. PeCV
Phallic Root. Shiraishi Kazuko. *See* Phallus.
Phallic Symbol, The. Nicholas Moore. NeBP
Phallus. Shiraishi Kazuko, *tr. fr. Japanese by* Ikuko Atsumi. BoWoP
(Phallic Root, *tr. by* Thomas Fitzsimmons.
Phallus going around a corner, A. Banana. Adrian Mitchell. PV
Phantasia for Elvira Shatayev. Adrienne Rich. LiSp
Phantasmion, *sels.* Sara Coleridge.
He Came Unlook'd For. OBRV
(Song: "He came unlook'd for, undesir'd.") OBVV
I Was a Brook. OBRV
"O sleep, my babe, hear not the rippling wave." OBNC; OBRV
Phantasus. Arno Holz, *tr. fr. German by* Ludwig Lewisohn. AWP
"On a mountain of sugar-candy," *sel.* PChr, *tr. by* Babette Deutsch
Phantasy. *Unknown.* ACP
Phantasy of Heaven, A. Harry Kemp. HBMV
Phantom. Samuel Taylor Coleridge. OAEL-2; PoEL-4
("All look and likeness caught from earth.") LO
Phantom Bark, The. Hart Crane. CMoP
Phantom Horsewoman, The. Thomas Hardy. CMoP; FaBoPP; LO; NOBE; PoEL-5; WSC
Phantom Light of the Baie des Chaleurs, The. Arthur Wentworth Hamilton Eaton. CaP
Phantom or Fact. Samuel Taylor Coleridge. EnRP
Phantom Ship, The. J. W. de Forest. EtS
Phantom Ship, The. Longfellow. EtS
Phantom streams were in the distance—mocking lights of lake and pool. Christmas Creek. Henry Kendall. CBAP
Phantoms All. Harriet Prescott Spofford. AA
Phantoms of the Steppe. Pushkin, *tr. fr. Russian by* Edna Worthley Underwood. WSC
Phantom-Wooer, The. Thomas Lovell Beddoes. EnRP; OBRV; TrGrPo; ViBoPo; WiR
("Ghost, that loved a lady fair, A.") LO
Phar Lap in the Melbourne Museum. Peter Porter. PoAu-2
Pharaoh and Joseph ("Pharaoh rejects his blossoming wives"). Else Lasker-Schüler, *tr. fr. German by* Joachim Neugroschel. VWA
Pharao's Daughter. Michael Moran. BIrV
Pharisee and the Publican, The. Bible, *N. T.* St. Luke, XVIII: 9-14. TreFT
Pharisee murmurs when the woman weeps, conscious of guilt, The. Sequaire. Godeschalk, *tr. by* Ezra Pound. CTC
Pharoah's Army Got Drownded, *with music. Unknown.* AS
(Oh, Mary Don't You Weep.) FSW
Pharsalia, *sels.* Lucan, *tr. fr. Latin.*
Cato's Address to His Troops in Lybia, *fr.* IX, *tr. by* Nicholas Rowe. OBEC
"Just and fit actions Ptolemy (he saith)," *fr.* VII, *tr. by* Ben Jonson. OBVE
"O wastfull riot, never well content," *fr.* IV, *tr. by* Sir Walter Ralegh. OBVE
Pompey and Cornelia, *fr.* V, *tr. by* Nicholas Rowe. OBEC
Portents, The, *fr.* I, *tr. by* Christopher Marlowe. OBSC
"Thee Pompey thy past deeds by turns infest," *fr.* I, *tr. by* Nicholas Rowe. OBVE
Phases of Darkness, The. Paul Petrie. TAP
Phases of the Moon. Robert Browning. *Fr.* One Word More. ChTr; MOON
Pheasant, The ("The pheasant cock sprang into view"). Robert P. Tristram Coffin. TiPo
Pheasant Hunter and the Arrowhead, The. Julian Gitzen. AMV-80
Phèdre. Racine. *See* Phaedra.
Phenomena. Robinson Jeffers. NoAM; NOBA; OxBA
Phenomenal Survivals of Death in Nantucket. Louise Glück. AmPA
Phenomenon, The. Karl Shapiro. CMoP; NMP; NYBP
Phi Beta Kappa Poem, The. Richmond Lattimore. GLGT
Phil. Ted Kooser. AMV-81
Philadelphia ("Philadelphia is a handsome town"). *Unknown.* AmFP
Philadelphia sky. Alfred-Seeable Philadelphia Sky. Eli Siegel. CAD
Philander. Donald Hall. ELU; ErPo
Philander Knox!—I know him by the sound. An Attorney General. Ambrose Bierce. DBV
Philanderer, The. Moses Mendes. *Fr.* The Chaplet. TrJP
Philaret on Willy cals. The Fourth Eglogue. George Wither. *Fr.* The Shepherd's Hunting. SeCV-1
Philarete Praises Poetry. George Wither. *Fr.* The Shepherd's Hunting. OBS
Philarete to His Mistress, *sel.* George Wither.
"Thee entirely I have loved." PeD
Philatelic Lessons: The German Collection. Lawrence P. Spingarn. NYBP
Philatelist Royal. Robert Graves. FaBoCo
Philemon and Baucis. Ovid, *tr. fr. Latin by* Arthur Golding. *Fr.* Metamorphoses, VIII. CTC; OBSC
Philip, foozling with his cleek. Some Ruthless Rhymes, VII. Harry Graham. CenHV
Philip, My King. Dinah Maria Mulock Craik. HBV-1
Philip returned to his books, but returned to his Highlands after. Arthur Hugh Clough. *Fr.* The Bothie of Tober-na-Vuolich. VLP
Philip Sparrow. John Skelton. *See* Phyllyp Sparowe.
Philip van Artevelde, *sel.* Sir Henry Taylor.
Elena's Song, *fr.* II. OBEV; OBRV; OBVV
Philippians, *sel.* Bible, *N.T.*
Think on These Things, IV: 8. TreFT
Philippine Madonna. Louise Crenshaw Ray. ISi
Philippines were drenched in sun, The. Portrait Philippines. Alfred A. Duckett. PoNe
Philippus, for his pleadings famed afar. Horace, *tr. fr. Latin by* Francis Howes. OBVE
Philips [*or* Phillips], whose touch harmonious could remove. An Epitaph upon the Celebrated Claudy Philips, Musician, Who Died Very Poor. Samuel Johnson. NOEC; OBEC
Phillada Flouts Me. *Unknown.* HBV-1; OBEV; TrGrPo; ViBoPo
(Disdainful Shepherdess, The.) OBSC
(Oh, What a Plague Is Love!) InvP
(Phillida Flouts Me.) CoMu
(Phyllida Flouts Me.) EiL
Phillida and Coridon. Nicholas Breton. *See* Phyllida and Corydon ("In the merry month of May").
Phillida Flouts Me. *Unknown.* *See* Phillada Flouts Me.
Phillida was a fair maid. Harpalus' Complaint of Phillida's Love. *Unknown.* OBSC
Phillips! whose touch harmonious could remove. *See* Philips, whose touch harmonious could remove.
Phillis. Thomas Lodge. *See* Phyllis.
Phillis. *Unknown.* UnTE
Phillis and Corydon. Arthur Colton. HBV-1
Phillis and Corydon. Robert Greene. *See* Coridon and Phillis.
Phyllis at first seemed much afraid. Phillis. *Unknown.* UnTE
Phillis, be gentler, I advise. Song: Phillis Be Gentler. Earl of Rochester. CavP
Phillis for Shame Let Us Improve. Charles Sackville, Earl of Dorset. CavP; OBS
(Song: "Phillis for shame let us improve") SECV-2
Phillis is my only joy. Song. Sir Charles Sedley. CavP; EnLoPo; InMe; OBS; SeCV-2
Phillis kept sheep along the western plains. Coridon and Phillis [*or* Phillis and Corydon]. Robert Greene. *Fr.* Perimedes. HBV-1; OBSC
Phillis Knotting. Sir Charles Sedley. *See* Hears Not My Phillis, How the Birds.
Phillis, let's shun the common Fate. Song. Sir Charles Sedley. SeCV-2
Phillis on the new made hay. The Coy Shepherdess; or, Phillis and Amintas. *Unknown.* CoMu
Phillis; or, The Progress of Love. Swift. *See* Phyllis; or, The Progress of Love.
Phillis, though your all-powerful charms. To His Mistress. George Villiers, Duke of Buckingham. CavP
Phillis took a red rose from the tangles of her hair. Phillis and Corydon. Arthur Colton. HBV-1
Phillis was a fair maid. The Maiden's Complaint. *Unknown.* OLR
Phillis, why should [*or* shou'd] we delay. To Phillis. Edmund Waller. AnAnS-2; OAEP; SeCP
Phillis's Age. Matthew Prior. EnLoPo
(Phyllis's Age.) FaBoEE
Philocles. Leonidas of Tarentum, *tr. fr. Greek by* F. A. Wright. AWP
Philoctetes, *sel.* Lord De Tabley.
Chorus: "Throned are the gods, and in." NBM
Philoctetes. Thomas Russell. *See* Sonnet: Suppos'd to Be Written at Lemnos.
Philodendron. Helen Armstead Johnson. AmNP
Philological. John Updike. ELU
Philomel. Richard Barnfield. *See* As It Fell upon a Day.
Philomel to Corydon. William Young. AA
Philomela. Matthew Arnold. HBV-1; OAEL-2; OAEP; OBEV; PBBP; PPP; SeCeV; UnPo; VLP; WHA
Philomela. John Crowe Ransom. ChTr; CMoP; FaBoPP; MoVE; NoAM; NOBA; OBAL; OBSV; OxBA
Philomela. Sir Philip Sidney. *See* Nightingale, The.

Philomela, the Lady Fitzwater's Nightingale, *sels.* Robert Greene.
Philomela's Ode in Her Arbour. OBSC
("Sitting by a river side.") TEP
Philomela's Second Ode. OBSC
Philomela, the Nightningale, *sel.* Patrick Hannay.
"Upon the boughs and tops of trees." PBBP
Philomena Andronico. William Carlos Williams. FaBoMo
Philon [the Shepherd]. *Unknown.* NOBE; OBSC
Philonous' Paradox. Chris Gilbert. FAZ
Philosopher, A. John Kendrick Bangs. HBV-2
Philosopher, A. Sam Walter Foss. OBAL
Philosopher, The. Lao-tzŭ, *tr. by* Arthur Waley. WhC
Philosopher, The. Edna St. Vincent Millay. CMoP
Philosopher and her Father, The. Shirley Brooks. CenHV
Philosopher and the Birds, The. Richard Murphy. CIP
Philosopher and the Lover, The: To a Mistress Dying. Sir William Davenant. FaBoEn; LO; MePo; NOBE; Prf
(Lover and Philosopher.) ACP
(To a Mistress Dying.) GoBC; OBEV
Philosopher to His Mistress, The. Robert Bridges. LiTM; OAEP; PoEL-5
Philosopher, whom dost thou most affect. Epigram. Richard Garnett. HBV-1
Philosophers Have Measured Mountains. George Herbert. *See* Agonie, The.
Philosopher's Scales, The. Jane Taylor. HBV-1
Philosophic Apology, The. Samuel Greenberg. MoPo; NePA
Philosophic Flight, The. Giordano Bruno, *tr. fr. Italian by* John Addington Symonds. AWP
Philosophic Pill, The. W. S. Gilbert. GLGT
Philosophy. Paul Laurence Dunbar. BPo
Philosophy. Dorothy Parker. InMe
Philosophy Is Born. Christian Morgenstern, *tr. fr. German by* Geoffrey Grigson. FaBoNo
Philosophy the great and only heir. To the Royal Society. Abraham Cowley. AnAnS-2 (1-9); JCP (1-4)
Philosophy, the love of wisdom. On Philosophy. Jonas Goldstein. AMV-81
Phineas Pratt. Gloria MacArthur. GoYe
Phineas Within and Without. Paul Zimmer. VGW
Phlebas the Phoenician, a fortnight dead. Death by Water. T. S. Eliot. *Fr.* The Waste Land, IV. OBVE
Phoebe Dawson. George Crabbe. GoTL
"Lo! now with red rent cloak and bonnet black, " *sel.* EBEV
Phoebe in a Rosebush. Clyde Watson. NTCP
Phoebe on Latmus. Michael Drayton. *Fr.* Endimion and Phoebe. OBSC
Phoebe sate,/ Sweet she sate. Montanus' Sonnet. Thomas Lodge. *Fr.* Rosalynde. PoEL-2
Phoebe's Sonnet. Thomas Lodge. ViBoPo
Phoebus, Arise. William Drummond of Hawthornden. BSV; EIL; GoTS
(Invocation.) OBEV
(Song: "Phoebus, arise.") HBV-1; LoBV; OBS; ViBoPo
(Summons to Love.) GTBS; GTBS-P
Phoebus, art thou a god, and canst not give. Funeral Elegy on the Death of His Very Good Friend, Mr. Michael Drayton. Sir Aston Cokayne. OBS
Phoebus, farewell! A sweeter saint I serve. A Sweeter Saint I Serve. Sir Philip Sidney. *Fr.* Arcadia. SiPS
Phoebus, make haste: the day's too long; be gone. A Letter to Her Husband. Anne Bradstreet. LiTA
Phoebus, the goddess variant and changeable. Christine de Pisan, *tr. fr. French, ad. by* Joan Keefe. *Fr.* The Epistle of Othea to Hector (A Lytil Bibell of Knyghthod). PBWP
Phoebus was judge between Jove, Mars, and Love. Astrophel and Stella, XIII. Sir Philip Sidney. SiPS
Phoebus with Admetus. George Meredith. NOBE; OBEV; OBVV
Phoenix. Rose Ausländer, *tr. fr. German by* Ewald Osers. VWA
Phoenix, The. A. C. Benson. OBEV; OBVV
Phoenix, The. J. V. Cunningham. NoAM; QFR
Phoenix, The ("O blest unfabled incense tree"). George Darley. *See* O Blest Unfabled Incense Tree.
Phoenix, The ("O fast her amber blood doth flow"). George Darley. OBEV; OBRV
Phoenix, The. Robert Fisher. AmMo
Phoenix, The. Matti Megged, *tr. fr. Hebrew by* Howard Schwartz. VWA
Phoenix, The. Ogden Nash. CenHV; NePA
Phoenix, The. Howard Nemerov. LiTM; NePA
Phoenix. Carolyn M. Rodgers. JB
Phoenix, The. Siegfried Sassoon. ChTr
Phoenix, The. Theodore Spencer. CrMA
Phoenix, The, *sels.* *Unknown, tr. fr. Anglo-Saxon.*
"Lo! I have learned of the loveliest of lands," *tr. by* Charles W. Kennedy. AnOE; OAEL-1
"When the sun comes up from the salt sea, *tr. by* Peggy Munsterberg." PBBP
Phoenix and [the] Turtle, The. Shakespeare. EnRePo; FaBoEn; LiTB; LoBV; MasP; MePo; NOBE; NoP; OAEL-1; OBEV; OBSC; SeCePo; SeCeV; TEP
"Let the bird of lowdest lay," *sel.* PoEL-2
Phoenix Answered, The. Anne Ridler. ChMP
Phoenix at Fifty, A. Lawrence Ferlinghetti. NAs
Phoenix, bird of terrible pride. Sir Herbert Read. *Fr.* Mutations of the Phoenix. FaBoTw
Phoenix comes of flame and dust, The. The Phoenix. Howard Nemerov. LiTM; NePA
Phoenix in its flight, The. The Phoenix. Robert Fisher. AmMo
Phoenix of Mozart, The. Claude Vigée, *tr. fr. French by* Anthony Rudolf. VWA
Phoenix on the hot sirocco's breath. Epilogue. H. B. Mallalieu. PoA
Phoenix, phoenix in the blood. Appeal to the Phoenix. Louis Untermeyer. UnTE
Phoenix Self-born, The. Ovid, *tr. fr. Latin by* Dryden. *Fr.* Metamorphoses, XV. ChTr
Phone Call. Tom Crawford. AMV-81
Phone Call to Rutherford. Paul Blackburn. CTBA; PoM
Phone duet over the radio, A. The Louisiana Weekly #4. David Henderson. PoBA
Phone for the fish-knives, Norman. How to Get On in Society. John Betjeman. NOBL; OBSV; OxBTC
Phono, at the Boar's Head. Henri Coulette. *Fr.* The War of the Secret Agents, IX. NePoEA-2
Photo of Miners, A. Brendan Galvin. LTB
Photo of someone else's childhood, A. The Old Adam. Denise Levertov. NaP; UnPo
Photo shows me, The. The Others Hunters in the North the Cree. Jerome Rothenberg. PoM
Photograph. Quandra Prettyman. PoBA
Photograph: an empty house, the windows intact. Seizure. James E. Warren, Jr. AMV-81
Photograph at the Cloisters: April 1972. Helen Chasin. NMM
Photograph in a Stockholm Newspaper for March 13, 1910. Don Coles. NOBC
Photograph of Haymaker, 1890. Molly Holden. OxBTC
Photograph of My Father in His Twenty-second Year. Raymond Carver. WOLT
Photograph of Myself, The. Jon Anderson. AmPA
Photograph of you at the edge, A. At 85. Richard Ardinger. AMV-81
Photograph the Cat Licks, The. Beatrice Walter. NMM
Photographed at midday. To Boris Pasternak. Aleksandr Kushner, *tr. by* Dimitry Pospielovsky *and* Keith Bosley. VWA
Photographer. Philip Booth. EyDe
Photographer, The. Roger Pfingston. PoDr
Photographer, The. Louis Simpson. LCAP
Photographer Whose Shutter Died, The. William Meissner. PoDr
Photographer's Wife, The. Janet Beeler. AMV-81
Photographic Plate, Partly Spidered, Hampton Roads, Virginia, with Model T Ford Mid-Channel. Dave Smith. MAYP
Photographing the Facade—San Miguel de Allende. Betsy Colquitt. AMV-80
Photographs. William Peskett. AMV-81
Photographs. Charles Wright. HoPM
Photographs: A Vision of Massacre. Michael S. Harper. PoBA
Photos, The. Diane Wakoski. NIP
Photos from Summer Camp, The. Izora Corpman. FAZ
Photos of a Salt Mine. P. K. Page. NOBC
Phrase goes on growing in my head, The. Dark Wood. Ian Wedde. OCNZ
Phrase which was to be the axis of my poem's crystallization, The. Ars Poetica. Adam Wazyk, *tr. by* Isaac Komem. VWA
Phraseology. Jayne Cortez. BlSi
Phryne. John Donne. FaBoEE
Phyllida and Corydon ("In the merry month of May"). Nicholas Breton. *Fr.* The Honourable Entertainment Given to the Queen's Majesty in Progress at Elvetham, 1591. EIL; OAEP; SeCePo
(Pastoral, A: "In the merry month of May.") TrGrPo
(Phillida and Coridon.) HBV-1; OBEV; UnTE; ViBoPo
(Ploughman's [*or* Plowman's] Song, The.) FaBoEn; NOBE; OBSC
Phyllida and Corydon ("On a hill there grows a flower"). Nicholas Breton. *See* Pastoral, A: "On a hill there grows a flower."
Phyllida Flouts Me. *Unknown. See* Phillada Flouts Me.
Phyllida was a fair maid. Harpalus' Complaint. *Unknown.* ViBoPo
Phyllida's Love-Call [to Her Corydon, and His Replying]. *Unknown.* EIL; OBEV; OBSC
(Corydon, Arise, My Corydon.) InvP
Phyllidula. Ezra Pound. FaBoTw

Phyllis. Nicholas Breton. OBSC; TrGrPo
(Pastoral, A: "Sweet birds! that sit and sing amid the shady valleys.") ElL
Phyllis. William Drummond of Hawthornden. *See* Of Phyllis.
Phyllis, *sels.* Thomas Lodge.
"Devoide of reason, thrale to foolish ire," XXXI, *after the French of* Pierre de Ronsard. AAS
"I would in rich and golden coloured raine," XXXIV, *after the French of* Pierre de Ronsard. AAS
Love Guards the Roses of Thy Lips. ElL
(Fidelity.) OBSC
(Phillis 2.) OBEV
(To Phyllis.) ViBoPo
Ode, An: "Now I find thy looks were feigned." ElL; EnRePo; OBSC
(Song: "Now I see thy looks were feigned.") LoBV
Phillis ("My Phillis hath the morning sun"). LoBV; OBSC
(Phillis 1.) OBEV
(Phyllis.) ACP; ElL
(To Phyllis, the Fair Shepherdess.) ViBoPo
Phyllis. Thomas Randolph. BoLoP
Phyllis. Sydney King Russell. ErPo
Phyllis. *Unknown, tr. fr. Latin by* John Addington Symonds. UnTE
Phyllis Corydon clutched to him. Catullus, *tr. fr. Latin by* Peter Whigham. BoLoP
Phyllis Knotting. Sir Charles Sedley. *See* Hears Not My Phillis, How the Birds.
Phyllis; or, The Progress of Love. Swift. OAEL-1; OBSV
(Phillis; or, The Progress of Love.) PoEL-3
Phyllis! why should we delay. To Phyllis [*or* A Plea for Promiscuity]. Edmund Waller. CavP; TrGrPo; UnTE
Phyllis's Age. Matthew Prior. *See* Phillis's Age.
Phyllyp Sparowe [*or* Philip Sparrow]. John Skelton. AAS; PoEL-1
Sels.
Anathema of Cats. PCat
(Curse on the Cat, A.) EvOK
(O Cat of Carlishkind.) ChTr
Commendations of Mistress Jane Scrope, The. OBSC
("How shall I report.") ViBoPo
Funeral of Philip Sparrow, The, *abr.* ACP
"It was so prety a fole." PB
"Pla ce bo! Who is there, who?" AAS; NOBE; OAEL-1; OxBoLi, *abr.*
"When I remember again." PBBP; SeCePo
(Sparrow's Dirge, The.) FaBoCh; OBSC
Physical for My Son. Barbara Smith. AMV-80
Physical Geography. Louise Townsend Nicholl. ImOP
Physics, A. Heather McHugh. MAYP; SUW
Physiologus, *sel. Unknown, tr. fr. Anglo-Saxon.*
Whale, The. AnOE, *tr. by* Charles W. Kennedy; EBEV, *shorter vers., tr. by* Gavin Bone
("Now I will fashion the tale of a fish," *tr. by* Charles W. Kennedy.) MOS
Piano, The. Frank Davey. NOBC
Piano ("Softly, in the dusk, a woman is singing to me"). D. H. Lawrence. BLPL; CMoP; GrPl; GTBS-P; HAP; HeIP; InPK; InvP; LiTB; MoAB; MoBrPo; NIP; NoAM; NOBE; NoP; OAEL-2; OAEP; PAI; PoPle; PPP; UnPo; WeW
Piano, The ("Somewhere beneath that piano's superb sleek black"). D. H. Lawrence. WeW
Piano. Lisa Russ. PPJ
Piano, A. Gertrude Stein. *Fr.* Tender Buttons. PBWP
Piano after War. Gwendolyn Brooks. AmNP
Piano and Drums. Gabriel Okara. NIP; PBA; TTY
Piano at Evening. Palea, *tr. fr. Hawaiian by* M. K. Pukui *and* A. L. Korn. WTO
Piano di Sorrento. Robert Browning. *Fr.* The Englishman in Italy. FaBoPP
(Englishman in Italy, The ["Time for rain! for your long hot dry autumn"].) SeCePo
Piano hums, The. Effendi. Michael S. Harper. CNA; PoBA
Piano Lessons. Baron Wormser. MAYP
Piano Pieces, *sels.* Thomas W. Shapcott.
Schoenberg Op. 11. CBAP
Webern. CBAP
Piano Practice. Howard Moss. NYBP
Piano Practice. Derek Walcott. NYP
Piano Recital. Babette Deutsch. NePoAm
Piano Tuner, The. W. Atmar Smith II. AMV-80
Piano tuner spoke to me, that tenderest, The. Pyrargyrite Metal, 9. Cecília Meireles, *tr. by* James Merrill. PBWP
Piazza di Spagna. Willard M. Grimes. GoYe
Piazza di Spagna, Early Morning. Richard Wilbur. GrPl; InPS; VGW
Piazza Piece. John Crowe Ransom. AP; BoLoP; CoBMV; ErPo; HeIP; MoAB; MoAmPo; MoVE; NoAM; NOBA; NoP; OxBA; PAI; SoSe; TAP; TreFT; TrGrPo
Piazza Tragedy, A. Eugene Field. FiBHP
Piazzas. Barbara Guest. NeAP
Pibroch. Ted Hughes. FaBoMo; NePoEA-2; OAEL-2; PoCh
Pibroch of Donuil [*or* Donald] Dhu. Sir Walter Scott. EnRP; FaBoCh; HBV-2; NBM; OxBS; PoEL-4
(Gathering Song of Donald the Black.) GTBS; GTBS-P
(Gathering Song of Donuil Dhu.) GN
(Pibroch.) FaPoR
Picador Bit, The. Bink Noll. LiSp
Picasso and Matisse. Robert Francis. NePoAm
Picasso, who knows everything, will tell you. Cocteau's Opium: 2. Donald Finkel. CoPo
Picasso's Women. Olga Cabral. PoDr
Piccadilly. Thomas Burke. HBMV
Piccante. Mary Di Michele. AMV-81
Picciola. Robert Henry Newell. AA
Piccola Commedia. Richard Wilbur. GP
Piccolomini, The, *sel.* Schiller, *tr. fr. German by* Samuel Taylor Coleridge.
Thekla's Song. AWP
Pick a Bale of Cotton. *Unknown.* FSW
Pick a fern, pick a fern, ferns are high. Ezra Pound, *after the Chinese.* OBVE
Pick a quarrel, go to war. W. H. Auden. PV
Pick upon Pick. Alex Comfort. NeBP
Pickaxes, pickaxes swinging today. Bam, Bam, Bam. Eve Merriam. PDV
Pickers. Peter Brett. AMV-81
Picket Fence, The. Christian Morgenstern, *tr. fr. German by* Max Knight. GrPl
Picket-Guard, The. Ethel Lynn Beers. *See* All Quiet along the Potomac.
Picket Line Song, The. *Unknown.* FSW
Picketing Supermarkets. Tom Wayman. NIP
Picketing the Eskimo. Genocide. Nora Dauenhauer. TWSS
Pickety fence, The. David McCord. NTCP; TiPo
Picking Apples. Maurice Lindsay. BSV
Picking Grapes in an Abandoned Vineyard ("Picking grapes alone in the late autumn sun"). Larry Levis. MAYP
Picking Lilies. *Unknown.* OBET
Picking through pieces. Analyst. David Fisher. NPGG
Pick-up, The. J. V. Cunningham. UnTE
Pick-up at Chef Rizal Restaurant. Virginia Cerenio. BrSi
Pick-up clattered out of sunset, shaken, The. Mullet Snatching. Malcolm Glass. WOLT
Pickup in Tony's Hashhouse. Kenneth Pitchford. *Fr.* Good for Nothing Man. CoPo; ErPo
Pickwick Papers, The, *sel.* Charles Dickens.
Ivy Green, The, *fr. ch.* 6. BoNaP; HBV-1; HBVY
Picnic, A. Aileen Fisher. SoPo
Picnic. Hugh Lofting. GoJo; SUS
Picnic, The. John Logan. ConAP; CTBA; NCSH; NePoEA-2
Picnic. Rose Macaulay. SUMH
Picnic Day. Rachel Field. SiSoSe; SoPo; TiPo
Picnic Rhyme. *Unknown. See* Lemonade.
Picnic: the Liberated. M. Carl Holman. PoBA; PoNe
Pico della Mirandola. Mason Jordan Mason. PoNe
Pictor Ignotus. Robert Browning. CTC; TEP; VLP
Picture, The. Anacreon, *tr. fr. Greek by* Thomas Stanley. AWP; UnTE
Picture, A. D. C. Cuthbertson. PoSH
Picture, A. Dora Greenwell. EBVV
Picture, The. Robert Lowell. NoAM
(New York 1962: Fragment, *diff. version.)* NYP
Picture, The, *sel.* Phillip Massinger.
Song: "Blushing rose and purple flower, The." ViBoPo
(Song of Pleasure, A.) UnTE
Picture, A. Howard Nemerov. OxBC
Picture and book remain. An Acre of Grass. W. B. Yeats. CMoP; NoAM
Picture Framing. Bert Meyers. ELU
Picture from Life's Other Side, A. *Unknown.* FSW
Picture me at the side of an old fisherman. Night Fishing. Stephen Lewandowski. WOLT
Picture memory brings to me, A. Whittier. *Fr.* My Trust. OHIP; PGD
Picture my grandmother at sixty the year. Family Album. Lonny Kaneko. BrSi
Picture of a Castle. William Meredith. NePoEA
Picture of a Nativity. Geoffrey Hill. NoAM; OxBC
Picture of Her Mind, The. Ben Jonson. *Fr.* Elegy on the Lady Venetia Digby, Wife of Sir Kenelm Digby. GoBC
Picture of J. T. in a Prospect of Stone, The. Charles Tomlinson. PoCh; PPP
Picture of Little J. A. in a Prospect of Flowers, The. John Ashbery. ConAP; PPP

Picture of Little Letters. John Koethe. AMV-81
Picture of Little T. C. in a Prospect of Flowers, The. Andrew Marvell. AnAnS-1; HBV-1; JCP; LiTB; MeLP; MePo; NOBE; NoP; OAEL-1; OBEV; OBS; PPP; PrIm; SeCeV; SeCP; SeCV-1
Picture of Loot. Alan Sillitoe. OxBTC
Picture of Okinawa, A. Dennis Schmitz. LCAP; NPGG
Picture People. Rowena Bennett. YeAr
Picture Postcards. Miklós Radnóti, *tr. fr. Hungarian by* Emery George. VWA
Picture-Show. Siegfried Sassoon. CMoP
Picture That Is Turned toward the Wall, The. Charles Graham. TreF
Pictures. C. Fox Smith. EtS
"Pictures are my friends." Books. William Baer. AMV-81
Pictures at an Exhibition. Nathan Rosenbaum. GoYe
Pictures by Vuillard. Adrienne Rich. TwAmPo
Pictures from Brueghel, *sels.* William Carlos Williams.
Corn Harvest, The, VII. PPP
Hunters in the Snow, The, III. LCAP
Landscape with the Fall of Icarus, II. LCAP; NIP; PPP
Self-Portrait, I. LCAP
Pictures of a Gone World, *sels.* Lawrence Ferlinghetti.
"Away above a harborful," Sec. 1. BoLoP; ErPo; NMP; PoM
"Dada would have liked a day like this," Sec. 23. NeAP
"Sarolla's women in their picture hats," Sec. 8. NeAP; PoM
Pictures on the Wall. Zvi Shargel, *tr. fr. Yiddish by* Gabriel Preil *and* Howard Schwartz. VWA
Picturesque; a Fragment. John Aikin. NOEC
Pie in the Sky. *Unknown, at. to* Joe Hill. *See* Preacher and the Slave, The.
Pie Problem. Shel Silverstein. RHPC
Pie sat on a pear tree, A. Hop't She. *Unknown.* GBP; PBBP
Piece by piece I seem. Necessities of Life [*or* 33]. Adrienne Rich. CoPo; NIP; NoAM; NOBA
Piece of art, a scene, a poem, A. Silence, an Eloquent Applause. Leona Gregory. TrCP
Piece of Black Bread, A. Edward Bagritsky, *tr. fr. Russian by* C. M. Bowra. TrJP
Piece of flesh gives off, A. The Dead Shall Be Raised Incorruptible. Galway Kinnell. NOBA
Piece of green pepper, A. Haiku Ambulance. Richard Brautigan. InPK
Piece of Shrapnel, A. David Ray. NIP
Piecemeal the summer dies. Exeunt. Richard Wilbur. BoNaP; ELU; HeIP; NCSH; PoLF; Psk; TwAmPo
Pieces of memory stick together. Remembering. Judit Tóth, *tr. by* Emery George. VWA
Pied Beauty. Gerard Manley Hopkins. AWP; BiP; BrPo; CABA; CMoP; CoBMV; EaLo; EBCP; EBVV; FaBoEn; FaBoMo; FaFP; GoJo; GTBS-P; HAP; HeIP; HoPM; InPK; InPS; InvP; LiTB; LiTM; MoAB; MoBrPo; MoVE; NIP; NoAM; NOBE; NoP; OAEL-2; OAEP; OBEV; OBMV; OBNC; PAI; PoPl; PoRA; PPP; PrIm; SCV; SoSe; SOTW; TEP; TreFS; TrGrPo; TRV; ViBoPo; VLP; WeW
Pied Piper of Hamelin, The. Robert Browning. BeLS; BiP; BLPL; FaBoBe; FaBoCh; FaFP; FaPo; GN; HBV-1; HBVY; OBNV; OxBChV
Pier delle Vigne. Dante, *tr. fr. Italian by* John Ciardi. *Fr.* Divina Commedia: Inferno, XIII. HoPM
Pier-Glass, The. Robert Graves. CMoP; CoBMV; MoAB; NoAM
Piercing Chill I Feel, The. Buson, *tr. fr. Japanese by* Harold G. Henderson. InPK
Piere Vidal Old. Ezra Pound. MoAB
Pierre Falcon. Le Tombeau de Pierre Falcon. James Reaney. MoCV
Pierre of Timagami in New York. Wilson MacDonald. WhC
Pierrette in Memory ("Pierrette has gone, but it was not"). William Griffith. HBV-2
Pierrot Goes to War. Gabrielle Elliot. SUMH
Pierrot, no sentimental swain. Pantomime. Paul Verlaine, *tr. by* Arthur Symons. AWP; SyP
Piers are pummelled by the waves, The. The Fall of Rome. W. H. Auden. InPS; MAT; OAEL-2; OxBTC; UnPo
Piers Gaveston, *sel.* Michael Drayton.
"This Edward in the Aprill of his age." PeHV
Piers Plainness' Seven Years' Prenticeship, *sel.* Henry Chettle.
Aeliana's Ditty. OBSC
(Of Cupid.) EIL
Piers Plowman. William Langland. *See* Vision of Piers Plowman, The.
Pieta. David Gascoyne. *Fr.* Miserere. NeBP
Pietà. James McAuley. CBAP; PoAu-2
Pieta. Rainer Maria Rilke, *tr. fr. German by* M. D. Herter Norton. OFD
Pieta, The, Rhenish, 14th C., The Cloisters. Mona Van Duyn. Prf
Pig. Anthony Hecht. OxBC
Pig, The. Ogden Nash. DBV; FPL
Pig, The. *Unknown.* FaBoEE
Pig, The. Roland Young. RHPC
Pig, if I am not mistaken, The. The Pig. Ogden Nash. DBV; FPL
Pig Is Never Blamed, A. Babette Deutsch. RHPC
Pig is not a nervous beast, The. The Pig. Roland Young. RHPC
Pig lay on a barrow dead, The. View of a Pig. Ted Hughes. BoAnP; CABA; LiTM; MP; OxBTC; TwCP
Pig Poem. Cary Waterman. GP
Pig Song. Margaret Atwood. NoP
Pig stands squarely, The. Transubstantiation. Gary Geddes. NOBC
Pig-Tale, A. "Lewis Carroll." *Fr.* Sylvie and Bruno Concluded. WiR
(Melancholy Pig, The.) FaPON
Pig Tale, A. James Reeves. SoPo
"Pig'back" she brought me where the lake surrounded. Kineo Mountain. Celeste Turner Wright. Psk
Pigeon. Roy Fuller. PB
Pigeon. Elouise Loftin. CNA
Pigeon-Feeders in Battery Park, The. Julia Cooley Altrocchi. GoYe
Pigeons. Richard Kell. BoAnP
Pigeons. Bert Meyers. EAS
Pigeons. Lilian Moore. RHPC
Pigeons. Marianne Moore. PoA
Pigeons. Alastair Reid. MP; NePoEA; NYBP; NYP; TwCP
Pigeons. Robert F. Whisler. AMV-80
Pigeons are city folk. Pigeons. Lilian Moore. RHPC
Pigeons are cooing along the eaves. Notre Dame des Champs. John Millington Synge. SyP
Pigeons in Prison. Derek Butler. LFAC
Pigeons on the grass alas. Gertrude Stein. *Fr.* Four Saints in Three Acts. CrMA; TAP
Pigeons on the roof puzzle me. Pigeons. Robert F. Whisler. AMV-80
Pigeons that peck at the grass in Trinity Churchyard, The. Trinity Place. Phyllis McGinley. MoAmPo; SaC
Pigmeat. *Unknown.* BluL
Pigs. John Cotton. BoAnP
Pigs, The. Geoffrey Lehmann. CBAP
Pigs, The. Jane Taylor. FM
Pig's ears blossom and fold, The. Pig Poem. Cary Waterman. GP
Pigs for Circe in May, The. Joanne Kyger. PoM
Pigs o' Pelton. *Unknown.* GBP
Pigwiggen was this fairy knight. Michael Drayton. *Fr.* Nymphidia. ViBoPo
Pigwiggin Arms Himself. Michael Drayton. *Fr.* Nymphidia. MoShBr
(Arming of Pigwiggen, The.) GN
Pihsien Road. Robin Hyde. WPE
Pike, The. Edmund Blunden. LiTM; MoVE
Pike, The. John Bruce. LiSp
Pike. Ted Hughes. CMoP; FaBoMo; HAP; HeIP; LiTM; MAT; NCSH; NePoEA-2; NMP; OxBTC; SoSe; WeW
"Pikes him/ And dikes him." The English Retort. *Unknown.* OxBM
Pike's Peak. *Unknown.* BPAW; PoOw
Pike's Peakers, The. Lawrence N. Greenleaf. PoOW
Pike's Peakers! All! From whatsoever climes. Grand Opening of the People's Theatre. O. J. Goldrick. PoOW
Pile on the soil; thrust on the soil. Song of the Fairies. *Unknown, tr. by* A. H. Leahy. OnYI
Pile the bodies high at Austerlitz and Waterloo. Grass. Carl Sandburg. AWP; BLPL; FaBV; MoAB; MoAmPo; MoVE; NoAM; NOBA; NoP; OBWP; OHFP; OxBA; PoLF; PoPl; TrGrPo; WaaP; WHA
Piled deep below the screening apple-branch. The Orchard-Pit. Dante Gabriel Rossetti. EnLoPo; NBM; NCEP; OAEL-2; PoEL-5; SCV; SyP; VLP
Pilgrim, The. Bunyan. *Fr.* The Pilgrim's Progress. EvOK; GN; HBV-2
(Pilgrim Song, The.) CoMu; ELP; NOCV; OBS
(Pilgrim's Song, The.) EBCP; WiR
(To Be a Pilgrim, *sl. diff. version.*) FaPoR
("Who would true valour see.") EBEV
Pilgrim, The. Emma C. Embury. OBCA
Pilgrim, The. "E. Foxton." AA
Pilgrim, The. Richard Wightman. WGRP
Pilgrim am I, on my way, A. The Pilgrim. "E. Foxton." AA
Pilgrim and the Herdboy, The. Robert Buchanan. OBVV
Pilgrim at Rome, The. *Unknown, tr. fr. Old Irish by* Kuno Meyer. AnIL
(Word of Warning, A, *tr. by* Frank O'Connor.) KiLC
Pilgrim Cranes, The. Lord de Tabley. EBVV
Pilgrim Fathers, The. Leonard Bacon. WGRP
(O God, beneath Thy Guiding Hand, *with music.*) AH
Pilgrim Fathers, The. John Pierpont. AA; HBV-2; PAH
Pilgrim Fathers, The. Wordsworth. PAH
Pilgrim Fathers, The—where are they? The Pilgrim Fathers. John Pierpont. AA; HBV-2; PAH
Pilgrim from the East, The. Gustave Kahn, *tr. fr. French by* Jethro Bithell. TrJP
Pilgrim from the Eastern shore, A. The Miner's Progress. *At. to* Alanzo Delano. BPAW
Pilgrim of a Day, The. Thomas Campbell. OBRV

Pilgrim Song, The. Bunyan. *See* Pilgrim, The.
Pilgrim Song. Florence Earle Coates. OHIP
Pilgrimage. Austin Clarke. CIP; IPY; OxBI
Pilgrimage, The. George Herbert. AnAnS-1; ChTr; FaBoRV; PAI
Pilgrimage. Elinor Lennen. PGD
Pilgrimage, The. Sir Walter Ralegh. *See* Passionate Man's Pilgrimage, The
Pilgrimage, The. Henry Vaughan. AnAnS-1; NCEP
Pilgrimage Song. *Unknown, tr. fr. Pueblo Indian by* Mary Austin. WPE
Pilgrimage to Hennessey's. Steven Sher. AMV-81
Pilgrimage to Testour, The. Ryvel, *tr. fr. French by* Edouard Roditi. VWA
Pilgrimage towards Loves Holy Land, A. Thomas Campion. *See* What Faire Pompe.
Pilgrims. Joseph Brodsky, *tr. fr. Russian by* Dimitry Pospielovsky *and* Keith Bosley. VWA
Pilgrims. Jean Valentine. LCAP; TAP
Pilgrims Came, The. Annette Wynne. OHIP
Pilgrims in Mexico. *Unknown.* OBCP
Pilgrims landed, worthy men, The. The Pilgrims' Thanksgiving Feast. Arthur Guiterman. WhC
Pilgrims of Hope, The, *sel.* William Morris.
  Sending to the War. VLP
Pilgrims of the trackless deep. Pilgrim Song. Florence Earle Coates. OHIP
Pilgrim's Problem. C. S. Lewis. TrCP
Pilgrim's Progress, The, *sels.* Bunyan.
  Pilgrim Song, The. CoMu; ELP; NOCV; OBS
    (Pilgrim, The.) EvOK; GN; HBV-2
    (Pilgrim's Song, The.) EBCP; WiR
    (To Be a Pilgrim, *sl. diff. vers.*) FaPoR
    ("Who would true valour see.") EBEV
  Shepherd Boy Sings [in the Valley of Humiliation], The. EaLo; GN; HBV-2; HBVY; NOBE; OBEV; WGRP
    (Enough!) BLRP
    ("He that is down needs fear no fall.") EBEV
    (Shepherd Boy's Song, The.) EBCP; TRV
    (Shepherd's Song, The.) OxBoCh
    (Song of Low Degree, A.) STF
    (Song of the Shepherd in the Valley of Humiliation, The.) CavP; OBS
  "What danger is the pilgrim in." EBEV
Pilgrim's Song, The. Bible, *O.T. (Moulton, Modern Reader's Bible).* Psalms, CXXI. *See* I Will Lift Up Mine Eyes unto the Hills.
Pilgrim's Song, The. Bunyan. *See* Pilgrim, The.
Pilgrim's Song. Bernard S. Ingemann, *tr. fr. Danish by* Sabine Baring-Gould. WGRP
Pilgrims' Thanksgiving Feast, The. Arthur Guiterman. WhC
Pilgrims to St. James. *Unknown.* OxBM
Pilk lauds the verse of Jobble to the skies. Perpetuum Mobile. Edith Sitwell. HBMV
Pill, The. Austin Clarke. TW
Pillar of Cloud, The. Cardinal Newman. *See* Pillar of the Cloud, The.
Pillar of Fame, The. Robert Herrick. AnAnS-2; CaPo; JCP; NIP; SeCP
Pillar of fire by night, A. The Song of Sherman's Army. Charles Graham Halpine. PAH
Pillar of the Cloud, The. Cardinal Newman. ACP; AWP; FaFP; GoBC; HBV-2; ILwL; NBM; PoEL-5; TrCP; TrPWD; TRV; VLP; WGRP
    (Guidance.) NOCV
    (Lead, Kindly Light.) BLPL; FaBoBe; FaPoR; TreF
    (Light in the Darkness.) OBRV
    (Pillar of Cloud, The.) OBNC
Piller pearisht is whearto I lent, The. Sir Thomas Wyatt, *after the Italian of* Petrarch. AAS; OBVE
Pillory, The. Renée Vivien, *tr. fr. French by* Sandia Belgrade. PeHV
Pillow Cases. Richard Armour. WhC
Pillows wet our faces with, The. New and Old Gospel. Nate Mackey. CNA
Pilot, The. George Chapman. *Fr.* Bussy d'Ambois, I, i. EtS
Pilot, The. Russell Edson. LCAP
Pilot, The. *Unknown.* STF
Pilot Cove. C. J. Dennis. WhC
Pilot from the Carrier, A. Randall Jarrell. MoPo
Pilot in the Jungle, The. John Ciardi. MiAP
Pilot's Day of Rest, The. Lee Gerlach. HoAn
Pilots, Man Your Planes. Randall Jarrell. MoAB; MoAmPo
Pilot's Walk, The. Lee Gerlach. HoAn
Pilpul. Rodger Kamenetz. VWA
Pin, The. Ann Taylor. HBV-1; HBVY; OxBChV
Pin-swin or spine-swine, The. His Shield. Marianne Moore. DTC; LiTM; NePA; TwAmPo
Pin-up Girl. Louis O. Coxe. WaP
Pin wheels whirling round. Fourth of July Night. Dorothy Aldis. SiSoSe; TiPo
Pinay. Virginia Cerenio. BrSi
Pinball Queen of South Illinois St., The. Stephen Tietz. AMV-80
Pinch him, pinch him, black and blue. Song by Fairies [*or* A Fairy Song]. John Lyly. *Fr.* Endymion. OAEP; OBSC
Pinch of Salt, A. Robert Graves. HBMV; MoBrPo
Pindar. Antipater, *tr. fr. Greek by* John Addington Symonds. AWP
Pindar is imitable by none. The Praise of Pindar. Horace, *tr. by* Abraham Cowley. Odes, IV, 2. OAEL-1
Pindaric Ode, A. Thomas Gray. *Fr.* The Bard. SeCePo
Pindaric Ode, A. Ben Jonson. *See* To the Immortal Memory and Friendship of That Noble Pair, Sir Lucius Cary and Sir Henry Morison.
Pindaric on the Grunting of a Hog, A. Samuel Wesley. NOBL
Pindarick Elegy upon the Renowned Mr. Samuel Willard, *sel.* John Danforth.
  "In crimson flood, wave thousands to his tomb." PeD
Pindar's Revenge. Edward Sanders. PoM
Pine, The. Augusta Webster. HBV-1; OHIP
Pine at Timber-Line, The. Harriet Monroe. PoA
Pine Barrens: Letter Home. Cleopatra Mathis. TAT
Pine boat a-shift. Ezra Pound, *fr. the Chinese.* OBVE
Pine Bough, The. Richard Aldridge. NePoAm; PoSC
Pine Cones. Dave Smith. AMV-80
Pine cones on the ground of the park. Home in Indianapolis. Richard Pflum. AMV-80
Pine Gum. W. W. E. Ross. OBCV
Pine needles cover the silent ground. Woodlands. Sir Herbert Read. BrPo
Pine of Whiting Wood, The. John P. Sjolander. BPAW
Pine Point, You Are. Gordon Henry. STE
Pine to the Mariner, The, *abr.* George Turberville. EtS
Pine-trail; and all the hours are white, are long. A Walk on Snow. Peter Viereck. MiAP
Pine-tree boy breathing late-afternoon fireflies. Arkansas. Jackman Young. TAT
Pine-Tree Buoy, A. Harrison Smith Morris. AA
Pine Tree for Diana, The. Horace, *tr. fr. Latin by* Louis Untermeyer. Odes, III, 22. AWP
Pine-tree grew in the wood, The. Three Trees. C. H. Crandall. OHIP
Pine-tree standeth lonely, A. Ein Fichtenbaum steht einsam. Heine, *tr. by* James Thomson. AWP
Pine Tree Tops. Gary Snyder. NOBA; Prf
Pine-crowned hills against the sky. Christmas Eve. Catherine Parmenter. PGD
Pines, The. Julie Mathilde Lippmann. AA
Pines, The. Harriet Prescott Spofford. AA
Pines, and a blur of lithe young grasses. From a Car-Window. Ruth Guthrie Harding. HBMV
Pines and the Sea, The. Christopher Pearse Cranch. AA; HBV-1
Pines are black on Sierra's slope, The. Winter in the Sierras. Mary Austin. BPAW
Pines are white-powdered, The. New Snow. Catharine Bryant Rowles. YeAr
Pines were dark on Ramoth hill, The. My Playmate. Whittier. AP; HBV-1; NOBA; OBVV
Piney Woods. Malcolm Cowley. NYBP
Piney Woods Money Mama. *Unknown.* BluL
Pining for Love. Francis Beaumont. POL
Pink and black of silk and lace, The. Impression. Arthur Symons. SyP
Pink confused with white. The Pot of Flowers. William Carlos Williams. QFR
Pink Dominoes. Kipling. CenHV
Pink Locust, The. William Carlos Williams. PP
Pink, small and punctual. Emily Dickinson. FaBV
Pinkletinks. Grace Elisabeth Allen. GoYe
Pino the Lizard in his patent leather shoes. Four Brothers. W. S. Di Piero. MAYP
Pint of Water, A. *Unknown.* FaBoUs
Pinta, the Nina and the Santa Maria, The. John Tagliabue. AmFN
Pinto. *Unknown.* CoSo
Pinto, The. Owen Wister. BPAW
Pints and the pistols, the pike-staves and pottles, The. Song. *At. to* Winthrop Mackworth Praed. SoSe
Pinwheel's Song, The. John Ciardi. PDV; SO
Pioneer, The. Eugene Field. BPAW; PoOW
Pioneer, The. Arthur Guiterman. TiPo
Pioneer Mother, The. Ethel Romig Fuller. PGD
Pioneer Woman. Vesta Pierce Crawford. BPAW; PoOW
Pioneer Woman—in the North Country, The. Eunice Tietjens. AmFN
Pioneers. Badger Clark. FaBoBe
Pioneers. Hamlin Garland. AA
Pioneers! O Pioneers! Walt Whitman. FaBoBe; WHA, *abr.*
Pious Selinda [*or* Celinda]. Congreve. ELP; ErPo; HBV-1; NOBE; UnTE
    (Pious Celinda Goes to Prayers.) PAI

(Song: "Pious Selinda goes to prayers.") BoLoP; FaBoCo; InMe; NIP; NOEC
Pious words are but a bubble. Poem on a Slippery Sidewalk. Kenneth Porter. WhC
Pious Young Priest, The. *Unknown. See* Limerick: "There once was a pious young priest."
Pipe, The. Sir John Squire. PoPl
Pipe and Can I ("The Indian weed withered quite"). *Unknown, at. to* Robert Wisdome. *See* Religious Use of Tobacco, A.
Pipe and Can II ("When as the chill Charokko blows"). *Unknown, at. to* Thomas Bonham. *See* In Praise of Ale.
Pipe Dreams. Diana Bickston. LFAC
Pipe of Tobacco, A, *sels.* Isaac Hawkins Browne.
"Blest leaf! whose aromatic gales dispense." BXAP; Par
(In Imitation of Pope.) OBEC
"Boy! bring an ounce of Freeman's best." Par
(Boy! Bring an Ounce.) BXAP
In Imitation of Young. OBEC
Pipe of Tobacco, The. *At. to* John Usher. HBV-2
Pipe, with solemn interposing puff, The. Pernicious Weed. William Cowper. InMe; WhC
Piped a tiny voice hard by. The Chickadee. Emerson. FaPON
Piped the blackbird on the beechwood spray. Little Bell. Thomas Westwood. GN; HBV-1
Piper, The. Blake. *See* Piping Down the Valleys Wild.
Piper, A. "Seumas O'Sullivan." CH; FaPON; MoShBr; OxBI; PDV; TiPo
Piper o' Dundee, The. *Unknown.* OxBS
Piper of Arll, The. Duncan Campbell Scott. PeCV
Piper on the Hill, The. Dora Sigerson Shorter. HBV-1; HBVY; OnYI
Piper's music fills the street, The. To the Poet T. J. Mathias. Walter Savage Landor. PV
Piper's Progress, The. Francis Sylvester Mahony. FiBHP
Pipes, The. Lou Lipsitz. LTB
Pipes at Lucknow, The. Whittier. GN; HBVY
Pipes in the Sty. John Kendall. WhC
Pipes o' Gordon's Men, The. J. Scott Glasgow. HBV-2
Pipes of the misty moorlands. The Pipes at Lucknow. Whittier. GN; HBVY
Piping Down the Valleys Wild (*Introd. to* Songs of Innocence). Blake. FaBoCh; FaBV; InvP; NOBE; OBEC; OnUR; PoPle; TreFS
(Introduction: "Piping down the valleys wild.") EnRP; GoJo; HeIP; InPS; LAuP; LoBV; NIP; NOEC; NoP; OAEL-2; OAEP; OBNC; PoEL-4; RHPG; SeCeV; SoSe; TEP; TrGrPo; ViBoPo
(Introduction to "Songs of Innocence.") FaBoBe; TiPo; WHA
(Piper, The.) AWP; OxBChV; PDV; RoGo
(Reeds of Innocence.) HBV-1; HBVY; LiTB; OBEV
(Songs of Innocence: Introduction.) CABA
Piping hot, smoking hot. The Hot Pease Man. Mother Goose. OxNR
Piping Peace. James Shirley. *Fr.* The Imposture. ACP; LoBV; NOBE; OBEV
(Io.) JCP; OBS
(Song: "You virgins that did late despair.") PoEL-2
(You Virgins.) ViBoPo
Piping sharp as a reed. The Nesting Ground. David Wagoner. PoCh
Pipling. Theodore Roethke. NePA; TW
Pippa Passes, *sels.* Robert Browning.
All Service Ranks the Same with God, *fr.* Introduction. TreFT
(Service.) TrGrPo
(Song: "All service ranks the same with God.") LoBV
"Oh, what a drear dark close to my poor day!" *fr.* sc. iv. PeD
Song: "Give her but a least excuse to love me!" *fr.* sc. ii. ViBoPo
Year's at the Spring, The, *fr.* sc. i. BLPA; FaBoBc; FaBV; InPK; PAI; WGRP; YeAr
(Pippa's Song.) BLPL; EBCP; FaFP; FaPON; GoJo; LiTB; NTCP; OBEV; OBVV; OHIP; PDV; TEP; TrCP; TreF; TRV; UnPo
(Song: "Year's at the spring, The.") HBV-1; HBVY; PoPl; SoSe; TrGrPo
You'll Love Me Yet! *fr.* sc. iii. OLR
(Song: "You'll love me yet!") HBV-1
Pirate, The, *sels.* Sir Walter Scott.
Claud Halcro's Invocation, *fr. ch.* 23. NBM
Mermaids and Mermen, *fr. ch.* 16. EtS
(Song of the Mermaids and Mermen.) WSC
Song of the Reim-Kennar, The, *fr. ch.* 6. OAEL-2; OAEP; OBNC
Pirate Don Durk of Dowdee, The. Mildred Plew Meigs. OnUR; PDV; SoPo; TiPo
Pirate of High Barbary, The. *Unknown. See* Salcombe Seaman's Flaunt to the Proud Pirate, The.
Pirate Story. Robert Louis Stevenson. BeLS; FaPON; TiPo
Pirate Treasure. Abbie Farwell Brown. EtS
Pirate Wind. Mary Jane Carr. SiSoSe
Pirates. Elizabeth J. Coatsworth. EtS
Pirates' Fight, The. Joseph Schull. *Fr.* The Legend of Ghost Lagoon. CaP
Pirates of Penzance, The, *sels.* W. S. Gilbert.
Modern Major-General, The. InMe; NOBL
(I Am The Very Model of a Modern Major-General.) NoP
(Major-General's Song.) NBM
Most Ingenious Paradox, A. NAs
Policeman's Lot, A [*or* The]. NOBL; SaC; TreFT; TrGrPo
Pirithous being over hault of mynde and such a one. Philemon and Baucis. Ovid, *tr. by* Arthur Golding. *Fr.* Metamorphoses, VIII. CTC
Pirouette. Audre Lorde. NNP
Pisan Cantos, The. Ezra Pound. *See* Cantos.
Pisanello's Studies of Men Hanging on Gallows. John Wheatcroft. FAZ
Piscatorie Eclogues, *sels.* Phineas Fletcher.
Chromis, IV. LoBV
"Fisher-lad, A (no higher dares he look)," III. SeCV-1
Pisces. R. S. Thomas. OxBC
Pisces Child. Sandra McPherson. NMM
Pisgah. Willard Wattles. WGRP
Pistol Slapper Blues. *Unknown.* BluL
Piston, valves and wheels and gears. Engineers. Jimmy Garthwaite. SoPo
Pit, A—but heaven over it. Emily Dickinson. AP
Pit, pat, well-a-day. Mother Goose. OxNR
Pit Viper. N. Scott Momaday. CDW
Pit Viper. George Starbuck. NYBP; SUW
Pitch here the tent, while the old horse grazes. Juggling Jerry. George Meredith. BeLS; HBV-2; OAEP; SeCePo; VLP
Pitch Piles Up in Part, The. Desmond O'Grady. CIP
Pitch pines fade, The. The Quiet Fog. Marge Piercy. UnPo
Pitch Seven. Hamish Brown. PoSH
Pitch was lowered, slowed, decoded, The. Whale Song. Francis Maguire. BoAnP; POL
Pitcher, The. Yüan Chen, *tr. fr. Chinese by* Arthur Waley. AWP
Pitcher. Robert Francis. LiSp; NePoAm; PP; SoSe; WeW
Pitcher of Mignonette, A. H. C. Bunner. AA; HBV-1
Pitcher plant makes a living by, The. The Resident Worm. James Hayford. NePoAm-2
Pith of faith is gone, The. And as there lie. Child of Loneliness. Norman Gale. WGRP
Pithecanthropus erectus. On Evolution. John Ciardi. OBAL
Pitiful mouth, saith he, that living gavest. Henry's Lament. Samuel Daniel. *Fr.* The Complaint of Rosamond. OBSC
Pitiful the playing of the flood with dire destruction! Egan O'Rahilly, *tr. by* P. S. Dinneen *and* T. O'Donoghue. *Fr.* The Storm. OnYI
Pitiless heat from heaven pours. The Seasons. Kalidasa, *tr. by* Arthur W. Ryder. AWP
Pitt-Rivers Museum, Oxford, The. James Fenton. FaBoMo
"Pitter patter!" falls the rain. The Umbrella Brigade. Laura E. Richards. SoPo; SUS; TiPo
Pittsburgh. Witter Bynner. AmFN
Pittsburgh. Hy Sobiliff. NePA
Pity. Babette Deutsch. WHA
Pity Ascending with the Fog. James Tate. NoAM
Pity beyond all telling, A. The Pity of Love. W. B. Yeats. AnIV; CMoP; VLP
Pity for him who suffers from his waste. Suffer the Children. Audre Lorde. PoBA
Pity for Mary. *Unknown. See* Now Goeth Sonne under Wode.
Pity Me Not. Edna St. Vincent Millay. MoAB; MoAmPo; NePA; TrGrPo
("Pity me not because the light of day.") CMoP; OxBA
Pity me on my pilgrimage to Loch Derg! At Saint Patrick's Purgatory. Donnchadh Mor O'Dala, *tr. by* Sean O'Faolain. AnIL; OnYI
Pity! mourn in plaintive tone. The Death of Lesbia's Bird [*or* The Death of the Starling]. Catullus, *tr. by* Samuel Taylor Coleridge. AWP; PBBP
Pity Not. William H. Simpson. HBMV
Pity now poor Mary Ames. Mary Ames. *Unknown.* NA
Pity of It, The. Thomas Hardy. CMoP; LiTM; WaP
Pity of Love, The. W. B. Yeats. AnIV; CMoP; VLP, 2 *versions*
Pity of the Leaves, The. E. A. Robinson. AA; MoAmPo
Pity, pity, pity. A True Love Ditty. Thomas Middleton. *Fr.* Blurt, Master Constable. ElL
Pity Poor Labourers. *Unknown.* OBET
Pity poor lovers who may not do what they please. The Envy of Poor Lovers. Austin Clarke. CIP; CMoP; IPY; NMP
Pity, Religion has so seldom found. Fragment. William Cowper. WGRP
Pity, repulsion, love and anger. Poem. Roy Fuller. NeBP
Pity the Down-trodden Landlord. B. Woolf *and* Arnold Clayton. FSW
Pity the girl with crystal hair. Fable. Joan Aiken. WSC
Pity the nameless, and the unknown. The Nameless Ones. Conrad Aiken. NePA; OxBA
Pity the sorrows of a poor old man! The Beggar. Thomas Moss. NOEC
Pity This Busy Monster, Manunkind. E. E. Cummings. AmPP; AP;

CoBMV; CrMA; LiTA; LiTM; MoVE; NePA; NOBA; OxBA; PPP; TAP
Pity this girl. The Stranger. William Everson. FF
Pity this man who, slave to an affliction. The Ailing Parent. Lora Dunetz. NePoAm-2
Pity those men who from the start. A Song about Great Men. Michael Hamburger. NePoEA
Pity us not/ Because we tried to battle and to go. From Beyond. Lucia Trent. PGD
Pity, A; We Were Such a Good Invention. Yehuda Amichai, *tr. fr. Hebrew by* Assia Gutmann. BoLoP
Pity would be no more. The Human Abstract. Blake. *Fr.* Songs of Experience. BiP; EnRP; LAuP; NOEC; OAEL-2; PoEL-4; PPP
Piute Creek. Gary Snyder. CAPP; CoAP; ConAP; NaP; NOBA
Pixies, slipping, dipping, stealing. Cornish Magic. Ann Durell. FaPON
Piyyut for Rosh Hashana. Chaim Guri, *tr. fr. Hebrew by* Ruth Finer Mintz. OFD
Pizen Pete's Mistake. *At. to* Merrill Honey. BPAW
Pizza, The. Ogden Nash. RHPC
Pizza Joint in Cranston, A. Craig Weeden. BXAP
Pla ce bo. *Indexed as* Placebo.
Place a custard stand in a garden. The Invention of New Jersey. Jack Anderson. InPS; TAT; TW
Place (Any Place) to Transcend All Places. William Carlos William. NYP
Place at Albert Bay, The. Muriel Rukeyser. PoA
Place by the River, A. William Keens. TAT
Place in Thy Memory, A. Gerald Griffin. HBV-1
(Song: "Place in thy memory, dearest, A.") BLPA
Place is called the Golden Cock, The. Lunch at the Coq d'Or. Peter Davison. TwCP
Place is growing difficult, The. Flails of bramble. The Secret Garden. Thomas Kinsella. IPY; TwCP
Place is the focus. What is the language. In Defense of Metaphysics. Charles Tomlinson. MoBrPo
Place Me in the Breach. Yehuda Karni, *tr. fr. Hebrew by* Sholom J. Kahn. TrJP
Place Me under Your Wing. Hayyim Nahman Bialik, *tr. fr. Hebrew by* Gabriel Levin. VWA
Place-Names of China. Alan Bennett. FaBoPa; NOBL
Place of Backs, The. W. S. Merwin. HoPM
Place of Burial in the South of Scotland, A. Wordsworth. VLP
Place of Cupid's Fire, The. Thomas Campion. *See* Beauty, Since You So Much Desire.
Place-of-Many-Swans. Charlotte DeClue. STE; TWSS
Place of O, The. Ray A. Young Bear. VoR
Place of Pain in the Universe, The. Anthony Hecht. CrMA
Place of Peace, The. Edwin Markham. TreFT; TRV
Place of Rest, The. "Æ." WGRP
Place of the Damned, The. Milton. *Fr.* Paradise Lost, II. FaBoEn
Place of the Damned, The. Swift. FaBoEE; OBSV
Place of the Solitaires, The. Wallace Stevens. SyP
Place of V, The. Ray A. Young Bear. VoR
Place Pigalle. Richard Wilbur. HeIP
Place to Live, A. Martin Grossman. AMV-80
Place we could never enter hides away still, The. Last Visit. Robert Finch. NOBC
Place where our two gardens meet, The. The Wall. Henry Reed. LiTB
Place where soon I think to lie, The. The Wall-Flower [*or* Widcombe Churchyard]. Walter Savage Landor. OBVV
Place your hand. Love Tight. Ted Joans. CNA
Pla ce bo,/ Who is there, who? Phyllyp Sparowe [*or* Philip Sparrow *or* The Sparrow's Dirge]. John Skelton. AAS; NOBE; OAEL-1; OBSC; OxBoLi; PoEL-1
Placed on this isthmus of a middle state. Pope. *Fr.* An Essay on Man. WeW
Places and Ways to Live. Richard Hugo. GP
Places I Have Been. Joyce M. Volk. AMV-80
Places, Loved Ones. Philip Larkin. CMoP; NePoEA
Places of Nestling Green. Leigh Hunt. *Fr.* The Story of Rimini. OBRV
("Noble range it was, of many a rood, A.") EnRP
Placid Man's Epitaph, A. Thomas Hardy. MoBrPo
Placid, rotted harbour has no voice, The. Arrival and Departure. Charles Eglington. PeSA
Placing a $2 Bet for a Man Who Will Never Go to the Horse Races Any More. Diane Wakoski. UnPo
Plague is Love, a plague, A! but yet. The Little Love-God. Meleager, *tr. by* Walter Headlam. AWP
Plague of Dead Sharks. Alan Dugan. AP; LiTM; NoAM
Plague of Starlings, A. Robert Hayden. HoAn
Plague take all your pedants, say I! Sibrandus Schafnaburgensis. Robert Browning. Garden Fancies, II. CTC; EBVV; TEP
Plaidie, The. Charles Sibley. HBV-1
Plain. Miller Williams. TAT
Plain be the phrase, yet apt the verse. A Utilitarian View of the *Monitor's* Fight. Herman Melville. AmPP; AP; UnPo
Plain Dealing. Alexander Brome. OBS
Plain Dealing's Downfall. *Unknown.* OBSV
Plain Fare. Daryl Hine. CoAP
Plain Golden Band, The, 2 *vers., with music.* *At. to* Joe Scott. ShS
Plain, Humble Letters. David Vogel, *tr. fr. Hebrew by* A. C. Jacobs. VWA
Plain it is to you that I am tir'd. The Midnight March. Fred Gilbert. VLP
Plain Language from Truthful James ("Which I wish to remark"). Bret Harte. BeLS; BLPA; BPAW; CTC; FaBoBe; HBV-2; InMe; NOBL; OBAL; TreF; WhC; YaD
(Heathen Chinee, The.) FaBoCo
(That Heathen Chinee.) CenHV
Plain Language from Truthful James ("I reside at Table Mountain"). Bret Harte. *See* Society upon the Stanislaus, The.
Plain Man's Dream, A. Frederick Keppel. AA
Plain of Adoration, The. *Unknown, tr. fr. Irish* by John Montague. BIrV
Plain Sense of Things, The. Wallace Stevens. InPS; PAI
Plain Song, *sel.* Jean Cocteau, *tr. fr. French by* Wallace Fowlie.
"I have sung, to deceive the evil-sounding clock of time." PoPl
Plain Song. Benjamin Fondane, *tr. fr. French by* Matei Calinescu *and* Willis Barnstone. VWA
Plain Song Talk. Richard Eberhart. PoA
Plain Tales from the Hills, *sels.* Kipling.
By the Hoof of the Wild Goat. OBNC
(Predestination.) LoBV
"He drank strong waters and his speech was coarse." PV
Plain Talk. William Jay Smith. DBV; FiBHP; MoAmPo
Plain tilt-bonnet on her head, A. In the Days of Crinoline. Thomas Hardy. WhC
Plain truth would never serve. Take It from Me. Kenneth O. Hanson. CoAP
Plain was grassy, wild and bare, The. The Dying Swan. Tennyson. PBBP; WiR
Plain-Chant for America. Katherine Garrison Chapin. PAL
Plainer Dubliners amaze us, The. On the Use of Jayshus. Oliver St. John Gogarty. FaBoEE
Plainest lodge room in the land was over Simpkins' store, The. The Lodge Room over Simpkins' Store. Lawrence N. Greenleaf. PoOW
Plainness. Jorge Luis Borges, *tr. fr. Spanish by* Norman Thomas Di Giovanni. NYBP
Plains. W. H. Auden. NePA
Plains, The. Maynard Dixon. BPAW
Plains, The. Roy Fuller. MoPo
Plains Indians had a game, The. The Long Joke. R. T. Smith. STE
Plains of Kansas stretch out, The. Moonlit Night in Kansas. Victor Contoski. TAT
Plains of Waterloo, The. *Unknown.* OBET
Plaint. Ebenezer Elliott. OBEV, OBVV
(Land Which No One Knows, The.) HBV-2
Plaint. Charles Henri Ford. EAS; MoVE; PPON
Plaint of the Camel, The. Charles Edward Carryl. *Fr.* The Admiral's Caravan. EvOK; FaPON; HBV-2; HBVY; SoPo
(Camel's Complaint, The.) OBCA; OxBChV; RHPC
Plaint of the Wife, The. *Unknown, tr. fr. Russian by* W. R. S. Ralston. AWP
Plaintive sonnet flow'd from Milton's pen, A. Sonnet: Anniversary, February 23, 1795. William Mason. OBEC
Plainview: 3. N. Scott Momaday. CDW
Plan of Salvation, The. Milton. *Fr.* Paradise Lost, III. WGRP
Plan to Live My Life Again, A. Diana O Hehir. NPGG
Plane, The: Earth. Sun-Ra. PoBA
Plane Geometer. David McCord. NYBP
Plane Geometry. Emma Rounds. ImOP; QQQ; SpRo
Plane leaves, The. Autumn Rain. D. H. Lawrence. BrPo
Plane tilts in to Nashville, The. The Homecoming Singer. Jay Wright. PoBA
Plane wheels lurch, leave, The. Parting from My Son. Evangeline Paterson. AMV-80
Plane Wreck at Los Gatos [Deportee]. Woody Guthrie. InPK; PrIm; WTO
Planet, The. Josephine Jacobsen. GP
"Planet doesn't explode of itself, A," said drily. Earth. John Hall Wheelock. LiTM; PV; SoSe
Planet is ours, The: and the blue and the desert spaces. The Jungle. Randolph Stow. *Fr.* Thailand Railway. CBAP
Planet of Nothing fills the sky, The. The Day You Are Reading This. William Stafford. PoA
Planet on the Table, The. Wallace Stevens. HAP
Planet that we plant upon, The. Imagine Grass. Knute Skinner. GP
Planetarium. Adrienne Rich. NIP; NoAM; NOBA
Planetary Arc-Light, The. August Derleth. GoYe
Planets Line Up for a Demonstration, The. Josie Kearns. SUW

Plankton. Ruth Miller. PeSA
Planning the Perfect Evening. Rita Dove. MAYP
Plans. Helen Morgan Brooks. NNP; PoNe
Plans for Altering the River. Richard Hugo. FYAP
Planster's Vision, The. John Betjeman. PoPl
Plant a Tree. Lucy Larcom. HBVY; OHFP; PGD; WBLP
Plant the 'ahi'a and cause it to propagate. The Crawlers. Keaulumoku, *tr. by* M. W. Beckwith. *Fr.* The Kumulipo; a Creation Chant. WTO
Plant without moisture sweet, A. Rising in the Morning. Hugh Rhodes. OxBChV
Plantation Bitters. *Unknown.* FaBoUs
Plantation Ditty, A. Frank Lebby Stanton. AA; HBV-2
Planted Heel, The. Sir Arthur Quiller-Couch. EBVV
Planted Skull, The. Peter Viereck. *See* Poet.
Planter. Richard Murphy. *Fr.* The Battle of Aughrim. BIrV
Planter's Daughter, The. Austin Clarke. CIP; OxBI; OxBTC
Planticru, The. Robert Rendall. OxBS
Planting, The. Harley Elliott. NeAC
Planting a Magnolia. W. D. Snodgrass. NoAM
Planting a Tree. Nancy Byrd Turner. YeAr
Planting Flowers on the Eastern Embankment. Po Chü-i, *tr. fr. Chinese by* Arthur Waley. BoNaP
Planting of the Apple-Tree, The. Bryant. AA; GN; HBV-1; HBVY; OHIP
"Come, let us plant the apple tree," *sel.* PoSC
Planting Trees. V. H. Friedlaender. BoNaP
Planting Trout in the Chicago River. Dennis Schmitz. NPGG
Plants, The. Michael Dennis Browne. GP
Plants don't talk, people say. Rosalia de Castro, *tr. fr. Spanish by* Doris Earnshaw. WPOW
Plaque. Bruce Ruddick. CaP
Plaque in the Reading Room for My Classmates Killed in Korea, The. F. D. Reeve. GOA
Plashes the Fountain. Paul Celan, *tr. fr. German by* Michael Hamburger. OBVE
Plashes the tree-trunk lost in the river. Remember Thou Me. *Malay Oral Tradition, tr. by* R. J. Wilkinson *and* R. O. Winstedt. WTO
Plastic Jesus. *Unknown.* FSW
Platform Goodbye. H. B. Mallalieu. WaP
Platform I stood upon began to move, The. A Visit Home. Joseph Glazer. VWA
Plato, despair! Meditation on Statistical Method. J. V. Cunningham. CoAP; QFR; VGW
Plato in London. Lionel Johnson. VLP
Plato Instructs a Midwest Farmer. David Palmer. SUW
Plato to Theon. Philip Freneau. AA
Plato Told [Him]. E. E. Cummings. AmFN; AmPP; CrMA; CTC; MoVE; NoAM; NOBA; NYP; OxBA; SeCeV; WaP
Platonic Lady, The. Earl of Rochester. UnTE
Platonic Love. Abraham Cowley. *Fr.* The Mistress. NoP
(Platonick Love.) SeCV-1
Platonic Love. Coventry Patmore. *Fr.* The Angel in the House, II, xi. VLP
Platonick Love. Lord Herbert of Cherbury. AnAnS-2; OBS
Plato's Tomb. *Unknown.* *See* Spirit of Plato.
Platypus, The. Oliver Herford. FiBHP; NA
Plaudite, or End of Life, The. Robert Herrick. CaPo
Play. A. R. Ammons. PoA
Play, The. C. J. Dennis. *Fr.* The Sentimental Bloke. PoAu-1
Play, The. Charles Otis Judkins. PeD
Play, The. James B. Kenyon. HBV-2
Play About, Do. Basho, *tr. fr. Japanese by* Harold G. Henderson. SoPo
Play Ball! Robert Francis. AMV-80
Play, Beggars, Play! "A. W." *See* In Praise of a Beggar's Life.
Play I could once; but, gentle friend, you see. To His Friend, on the Untunable. Robert Herrick. CaPo
Play is done, The; the curtain drops. The End of the Play. Thackeray. *Fr.* Dr. Birch and His Young Friends. FaFP; GN; TreF
Play it once. Saturday Night. Langston Hughes. MoAmPo
Play it one more time, Bix, so I can cascade down. In a Mist. Al Young. AMV-80
Play me a march, low-toned and slow—a march for a silent tread. A Dead March. Cosmo Monkhouse. HBV-2; OBVV
Play of Opposites, A. Gray Burr. CoPo
Play of the Four P.P., The, *sel.* John Heywood.
Palmer, The. ACP
Play of the Weather, The, *sel.* John Heywood.
English Schoolboy, The. ACP
Play on the seashore. Shore. Mary Britton Miller. SUS
Play on Words, A. Eugene Field. WhC
Play, Phoebus, on thy lute. A Canticle to Apollo. Robert Herrick. CaPo
Play Song. Peter Clarke. PBA
Play that thing. Jazz Band in a Parisian Cabaret. Langston Hughes. BANP; MoAmPo
Play the St. Louis Blues. Request for Requiems. Langston Hughes. ShM
Play their offensive and defensive parts. Good Christians. Robert Herrick. LiTB
Play Time. Blake. *See* Nurse's Song ("When the voices of children are heard on the green/ And laughing").
Play was done, The. An Epilogue at Wallack's. John Elton Wayland. AA
Play was each, pleasure each. Cuchullain's Lament over Fardiad [*or* Cuchulain's Lament for Ferdiad]. *Unknown, tr. by* George Sigerson. AnIL; AnIV
Play Way, The. Seamus Heaney. NoP
Play-acting. Frances Barber. GoYe
Playboy. Richard Wilbur. FF; NoAM; NOBA; NoP; WeW
Playboy of the dawn. Gone Boy. Langston Hughes. NePoAm-2
Playboy of the Demi-World, The: 1938. William Plomer. OxBTC; PeHV; TW
Player. Stephen Dunning. FAZ
Player Piano. John Updike. WeW
Players Ask for a Blessing on the Psalteries and Themselves, The. W. B. Yeats. VLP
Playful monkey frisks with grand, A. Retinue. Paul Verlaine, *tr. by* C. F. MacIntyre. ErPo
Playgrounds. Laurence Alma-Tadema. HBV-1; HBVY
Play-House, The. Joseph Addison. APAS
Playhouse Key, The. Rachel Field. FaPON
Playing Cards, The. Pope. *Fr.* The Rape of the Lock, Canto III. ChTr
Playing Catch. Keith Moul. AMV-80
Playing House. Jack Gilbert. NPGG
Playing one day with Rhodopê at dice. A Game of Dice. *Unknown, tr. by* Louis Untermeyer. UnTE
Playing Pocahontas. Lew Blockcolski. VoR
Playing, she puts her instrument to sleep. Improvising. Louise Townsend Nicholl. NePoAm-2
Playing the Bones. Elizabeth Brewster. AMV-81
Playing the 7th. 48 Words for a Woman's Dance Song. Jerome Rothenberg. PoM
Playing upon the hill three centaurs were! The Centaurs. James Stephens. AmMo
Playmates. Lillian Everts. GoYe
Plays. Walter Savage Landor. HBV-1; NoP; OxBoLi; PV
(Alas How Soon the Hours.) EnRP
Playthings. William Cowper. WaaP
Playwright. John Woods. CoPo
Playwright, convict of public wrongs to men. On Playwright. Ben Jonson. NoP
Plaza Reál with Palmtrees. Paul Blackburn. NoAM
Plea for a Captive. W. S. Merwin. NePoEA-2; NoAM; NYBP
Plea for a Plural, A. Rudolf Chambers Lehmann. CenHV
Plea for Flood Ireson, A. Charles Timothy Brooks. PAH
Plea for Haste, A. Petronius, *tr. fr. Latin by* Louis Untermeyer. UnTE
Plea for Hope. Francis Carlin. TrPWD
Plea for Mercy, A. Kwesi Brew. PBA
Plea for Postponement, A. Petronius, *tr. fr. Latin by* Louis Untermeyer. UnTE
Plea for Promiscuity, A. Edmund Waller. *See* To Phillis.
Plea for Trigamy, A. Sir Owen Seaman. NOBL
Plea of the Midsummer Fairies, The, *sels.* Thomas Hood.
Fairy's Reply to Saturn, The. OBNC
Green Dryad's Plea, The. OBNC
Melodies of Time, The. OBNC
Shakespeare. OBRV
Shakespeare: The Fairies' Advocate. OBNC
Tender Babes. OBRV
Titania. OBRV
Plea to Boys and Girls, A. Robert Graves. GTBS-P
Plea to Eros. *Unknown, tr. fr. Greek by* Louis Untermeyer. UnTE
Plea to My Sister, A. James Cunningham. JB
Plea to Those Who Matter. James Welch. AmPA
Plead for Me. Emily Brontë. PoEL-5
(God of Visions.) TrGrPo
(O Thy Bright Eyes Must Answer Now.) BrPo
(To Imagination.) NBM
Pleaders, The. Peter Davison. NYBP
Pleading Voices. Shalom Katav, *tr. fr. Arabic by* Yoffe Berkovitz. VWA
Pleasant and Delightful. *Unknown.* OBET
Pleasant Changes. Jane Euphemia Browne. OxBChV
Pleasant Comedy of Patient Grissell [*or* Grissel *or* Grissill], The, *sels.* Thomas Dekker, *and others.*
Bridal Song, A. OBSC; TrGrPo
(Beauty, Arise!) EIL

Golden Slumbers. ELP; ViBoPo
(Cradle Song, A: "Golden slumbers kiss your eyes"), *fr.* IV, ii. OBSC; OxBChV; TrGrPo
(Golden Slumbers Kiss Your Eyes.) HBV-1
(Lullaby: "Golden slumbers kiss your eyes.") ElL; LoBV
Happy Heart, The. GTBS; GTBS-P; HBV-2
(Art Thou Poor.) ViBoPo
("Art thou poor, yet hast thou golden slumbers?") HAP; InPS; OAEP; UnPo
(Basket-Maker's Song, The.) OBSC; TrGrPo
(Sweet Content.) CH; ElL; LoBV; OBEV; TreFT; WHA
Pleasant is the theme that falls to my care. The Enchanted Fawn. *Unknown, tr. by* Edward Gwynn. *Fr.* Dinnshenchas. OnYI
Pleasant journey, little book. To the Lady with a Book. *Unknown, tr. by* Frank O'Connor. KiLC
Pleasant Life in Newfoundland, The. Robert Hayman. NOBC
Pleasant Memories, *sel.* Charles Sangster.
Meadow-Field, The. OBCV
Pleasant New Ballad of Two Lovers, A. *Unknown.* CoMu
Pleasant New Court Song, A. *Unknown.* CoMu
Pleasant smell of frying sausages, A. Mixed Feelings. John Ashbery. GP; HAP
Pleasant the House. *Unknown, tr. fr. Irish by* John Montague. BIrV
Pleasantry of the sea bells, and I talk to myself alone, The. Sea Bells. Richard Eberhart. AMV-80
Please. Ronald Koertge. GP
Please do not die now. Listen. Unsent Message to My Brother in His Pain. Leon Stokesbury. MAYP
Please excuse this letter. The Letter. Beatrice M. Murphy. PoNe
Please Excuse Typing. J. B. Boothroyd. FiBHP
Please Forward. James Welch. CDW
Please God, forsake your water and dry bread. To a Nun. John Ormond, *after the Welsh.* EBEV; FaBoTw
Please help me know it happened. Help from History. William Stafford. AMV-81
Please keep an eye on my house for a few moments. Vidya, *tr. fr. Sanskrit by* Willis Barnstone. BoWoP
Please let my hair grow, mother. *Unknown, tr. fr. Pashto by* Saduddin Shpoon. PBWP
Please Master. Allen Ginsberg. PeHV
Please open your hearts and your purses. Pity the Down-trodden Landlord. B. Woolf *and* Arnold Clayton. FSW
Please Say Something. Tomioka Taeko, *tr. fr. Japanese by* Sato Hiroaki. WPOW
Please tell me how you are not afraid. Departure. Genny Lim. BrSi
Please Tell Me Just the Fabuli. Shel Silverstein. ELU
Please to remember. *Unknown.* OxNR
Please to Ring the Belle. Thomas Hood. HBV-2
Please you, draw near.—Louder the music there! Shakespeare. *Fr.* King Lear, IV, vii. EBEV
Please your Grace, from out your store. The Beggar to Mab, the Fairy [*or* Fairie] Queen. Robert Herrick. CaPo; WSC
Pleased am I, and more than willing. The Lay of the Honeysuckle. Marie de France, *tr. by* Robin Johnson. WPE
Pleasent Delusion of a Sumpteous Citty. Sarah Kemble Knight. SCAP
Pleasing Constraint, The. Aristaenetus, *tr. fr. Latin by* Richard Brinsley Sheridan *and* Nathaniel Brassey Halhed. ErPo
Pleasing Gift, The. *Unknown.* TDH
Pleasure. *Unknown, tr. fr. German by* Louis Untermeyer. UnTE
Pleasure and pride are not, as duty knows. A Vulgar Error. J. E. Thorold Rogers. FaBoEE
Pleasure could be carried to. Pleasure. *Unknown, tr. by* Louis Untermeyer. UnTE
Pleasure It Is. William Cornish. CH; MeEL
(Gratitude.) CTC; OBSC
(Spring.) BoNaP; ChTr
Pleasure me not, for love's pleasure drained me. In the Interstices. Ruth Stone. ErPo
Pleasure of Hope, The. Pope. *See* Hope.
Pleasure of Ruins, The. J. D. McClatchy. PoA
Pleasure Reconciled to Virtue [*or* Vertue]. Ben Jonson. AnAnS-2; OAEL-1
Hymn to Comus, *sel.* ElL; OAEP
(Hymn to the Belly.) SeCePo
Pleasures. Albert Goldbarth. GeTw
Pleasures. Denise Levertov. AP; CAPP; NeAP; NoAM; NOBA
Pleasures, Beauty. John Ford. *Fr.* The Lady's Trial. ViBoPo
Pleasures I took from life, The. The Ghost of a Ghost. Brad Leithauser. MAYP
Pleasures newly found are sweet. To the Same Flower. Wordsworth. EnRP
Pleasures of Hope, The, *sel.* Thomas Campbell.
"At summer eve, when Heaven's ethereal bow." EnRP
Pleasures of Imagination, The, *sels.* Mark Akenside.
Creative Process, The, *fr.* III. NOEC
Early Influences, *fr.* IV. OBEC
Invocation to the Genius of Greece, *fr.* I. OBEC
Nature, *fr.* IV. LoBV
Nature's Influence on Man, *fr.* III. OBEC
(Creates Universe, The.) LoBV
(Love of Nature.) NOEC
Poetic Genius, *fr.* IV. NOEC
Poets, *fr.* IV. OBEC
That Delightful Time. SeCePo
"With what attractive charms this goodly frame," *fr.* I. EnRP
Pleasures of Love, The. Wilfrid Scawen Blunt. HBV-1
Pleasures of Melancholy, The. Thomas Warton, the Younger. LAuP *Sels.*
"Mother of musings, contemplation sage." EnRP
Solemn Noon of Night, The. OBEC; SeCePo
("Beneath yon ruined abbey's moss-grown piles.") NOEC
Pleasures of Merely Circulating, The. Wallace Stevens. LiTA; MAT; OBAL
Pleasures of Memory, The, *sel.* Samuel Rogers. Inscription on a Grot. OBEC
Pledge. Avraham Shlonsky, *tr. fr. Hebrew by* Francis Landy. VWA
Pledge at Spunky Point, The. John Hay. OBAL
Pleiades, The. Mary Barnard. NYBP
Pleiades, The. Elizabeth J. Coatsworth. ImOP
Pleiades are sinking calm as paint, The. Lesbos. Lawrence Durrell. EBEV
Plenary. *Unknown.* AmFP
Plenteous place is Ireland for hospitable cheer, A. The Fair Hills of Ireland. *Unknown, tr. by* Sir Samuel Ferguson. AnIV; FaBoPP; OBEV; OBVV; OnYI
Plentiful people went to the Cadillac drawing. Midweek. Josephine Miles. NoP
Plentiful sacrifice and believers in redemption. When the Saints Come Marching In. Audre Lord. NYP
Plentiful snow deepens the path to the woods. Snow. Ruth Stone. NYBP
Plexus and Nexus. Judson Jerome. AMV-81
Plight, The. James W. Thompson. BPo
Plighted. Dinah Maria Mulock Craik. HBV-1
Pliny Jane. Mildred Luton. PH
Plodder Seam, The. *Unknown.* ELP
Plot against Proteus, The. A. J. M. Smith. OBCV; PeCV
Plot against the Giant, The. Wallace Stevens. CMoP; FF; OxBA
Plot Improbable, Character Unsympathetic. Elder Olson. NePA
Plot to Assassinate the Chase Manhattan Bank, The. Carl Larsen. FF; PPON
Plough. *See also* Plow.
Plough, The. Richard Henry Horne. OBEV; OBVV
(Plow, The.) HBV-1
Plough-Horse, The. Rhoda Coghill. OnYI
Ploughboy, The. John Clare. PoEL-4
Plougher, The. Padraic Colum. GoBC; HBMV; OnYI
(Plower, The.) MoBrPo
Plough-Hands' Song, The. Joel Chandler Harris. *Fr.* Uncle Remus, His Songs and His Sayings. AA
Ploughing on Sunday. Wallace Stevens. FaPON; GoJo; NCSH; PoPl; SOTW
Ploughland has gone to bent, The. Gin the Goodwife Stint. Basil Bunting. CTC; TW
Ploughman, The. Karle Wilson Baker. WGRP
Ploughman, The. Gilbert Thomas. HBMV
Ploughman, The ("The ploughman he comes home at night"). *Unknown.* GBP
Ploughman, The ("The ploughman he's a bonnie lad"). *Unknown.* CoMu
Ploughman at the Plough. Louis Golding. HBMV; OHIP
Ploughman he comes home at night, The. The Ploughman. *Unknown.* GBP
Ploughman he's a bonnie lad, The. The Ploughman. *Unknown.* CoMu
Ploughman, in Imitation of Milton, The. Samuel Jones. NOEC
Ploughman, whose gnarly hand yet kindly wheeled. The Waving of the Corn. Sidney Lanier. AP
Ploughman's Song, The. Nicholas Breton. *See* Phyllida and Corydon ("In the merry month of May").
Plow. *See also* Plough.
Plow, The. Richard Henry Horne. *See* Plough, The.
Plow. *Unknown, tr. fr. Anglo-Saxon by* Charles W. Kennedy. *Fr.* Riddles (Exeter Book). AnOE
Plow, they say, to plow the snow, A. Plowmen. Robert Frost. SaC
Plowdens, Finns. Robert Hayden. *Fr.* Beginnings. CNA
Plower, The. Padraic Colum. *See* Plougher, The.
Plowing at Full Moon. Leo Dangel. AMV-80
Plowman, The. Burns. UnTE
Plowman. Sidney Keyes. MoAB; PoRA

Plowman, The ("All day I follow"). Raymond Knister. OBCV; PeCV
Plowman, The ("As Ralph and Nick i' th' field were plowing"). *Unknown.* APAS
Plowman plows, the fisherman dreams of fish, The. Lines on Brueghel's *Icarus.* Michael Hamburger. NIP
Plowman's Song, The. Nicholas Breton. *See* Phyllida and Corydon ("In the merry month of May").
Plowman's Song ("Turn under, plow"). Raymond Knister. CaP
Plowmen. Robert Frost. SaC
Pluck. Eva Dobell. SUMH
Pluck me ten berries from the juniper. Recipe, *parody.* A. P. Herbert. *Fr.* Two Gentlemen of Soho. WhC
Pluck the Fruit and Taste the Pleasure. Thomas Lodge. *Fr.* Robert, Second Duke of Normandy. ElL
(Carpe Diem.) OBSC
(Song: "Pluck the fruit and taste the pleasure.") EnRePo
Plucking Out a Rhythm. Lawson Fusao Inada. AmPA
Plucking the Rushes. *Unknown, tr. fr. Chinese by* Arthur Waley. BoLoP; OBVE; OLR
Plum, A. Mani Leib, *tr. fr. Yiddish by* David G. Roskies *and* Hillel Schwartz. VWA
Plum-blossom, The. Akahito. *Fr.* Manyo Shu. AWP
Plum Blossoms ("Far across hill and dale"). Basho, *tr. fr. Japanese.* SUS
Plum Blossoms ("The snow dances and the frost flies"). Chu Shu-chên, *tr. fr. Chinese by* Kenneth Rexroth *and* Ling Chung. PBWP
Plum Blossoms ("So sweet the plum tress smell!"). Ranko, *tr. fr. Japanese. See* Plum Trees.
Plum-Cake, The. Ann Taylor. HBVY
Plum Gatherer, The. Edna St. Vincent Millay. NoAM
Plum Tree, The. James Reaney. CaP
Plum Tree by the House, The. Oliver St. John Gogarty. OBEV; PoRA
Plum Trees. Ranko, *tr. fr Japanese.* FaPON
(Plum Blossoms.) SoPo
("So sweet the plum trees smell.") SUS
Plum-viewing. Haiku. Buson, *tr. by* Lucien Stryk *and* Takashi Ikemoto. FAZ
Plumber Arrives at Three Mile Island, The. Robert Stewart. AMV-81; FAZ
Plumber is icumen in. Murie Sing. A. Y. Campbell. FaBoPa
Plumber may be a poet, but a poet is not likely, A. The Difference. Stoddard King. OBAL
Plumber's price is high because he uses, A. The Plumber Arrives at Three Mile Island. Robert Stewart. AMV-81; FAZ
Plumes of love are black, The! Mad Sonnet 1. Michael McClure. PoM
Plumpuppets, The. Christopher Morley. FaPON; RHPC; TiPo
Plums are like blue pendulums, The. The Plum Tree. James Reaney. CaP
Plums on the ground. Conservancies. Josephine Miles. GP
Plunder. A. R. Ammons. NoAM
"Plunge thy right hand in St. Madron's spring." The Doom-Well of St. Madron. Robert Stephen Hawker. VLP
Plunging and labouring on in a tide of visions. In Front of the Landscape. Thomas Hardy. OBNC
Plunging downward through the slimy water. Death by Drowning. Elizabeth Brewster. NOBC
Plunging limbers over the shattered track, The. Dead Man's Dump. Isaac Rosenberg. BrPo; FaBoMo; GTBS-P; LiTM; MMA; MoPo; NoP; OBWP; TrJP; VWA; WaP
Plunging rocks, whose ravenous throats, The. Mortem, Quae Violat Suavia, Pellit Amor. William Johnson Cory. NBM
Plunging towards Phrygia over violent water. Attis. Catullus, *tr. by* Peter Whigham. OBVE
Pluralist and Old Soldier, The. John Collier. NOEC
Plus Ultra. Swinburne. VLP
Plutarch. Agathias, *tr. fr. Greek by* Dryden. AWP
Pluto's Council. Tasso, *tr. fr. Italian by* Edward Fairfax. *Fr.* Godfrey of Bulloigne. OBSC
Pluviose. Julian Bell. ChMP
Plymouth Harbor. Mrs. Ernest Radford. HBV-1
Pneumonia Blues. *Unknown.* BluL
Po' Boy, *with music. Unknown.* AS; TrAS, *diff. vers.*
(As I Set Down to Play Tin-Can, *with music, diff. vers.*) OuSiCo
Po' Boy Blues. Langston Hughes. BANP
Po Chu-i, balding old politician. As I Step over a Puddle at the End of Winter, I Think of an Ancient Chinese Governor. James Wright. CAPP; NaP
Po' Farmer, *with music. Unknown.* OuSiCo
Po' Laz'us, *with music. Unknown.* OuSiCo
Po' lil' brack sheep dat strayed away. The Little Black Sheep. Paul Laurence Dunbar. WBLP
Po' Mourner's Got a Home at Las', *with music. Unknown.* BoAN-2
Poacher, The ("In the monethe of Maye. . ."). *Unknown. Fr.* The Parlement of the Thre Ages. OxBM
Poacher, The ("When I was bound apprentice. . ."). *Unknown. See* Lincolnshire Poacher, The.
Poaching *in Excelsis.* G. K. Menzies. FaBoCo
Pobble Who Has No Toes, The. Edward Lear. AmMo; FaBoCh; FaBoCo; FaBoNo; HBV-2; HBVY; MoShBr; NA; OxBChV; WhC
Pocahontas. George Pope Morris. PAH
Pocahontas. Thackeray. AmFN; FaPON; GN; OnMSP; PAH; PAL
Pocahontas to Her English Husband, John Rolfe. Paula Gunn Allen. STE
Pocket and Steeple. M. A. DeWolfe Howe. WhC
Pocket Guide for Service Men. Hubert Creekmore. WaP
Pocket Poem. Ted Kooser. PPJ
Pockets. Howard Nemerov. NIP
Pockets of our greatcoats full of barley, The. Requiem for the Croppies. Seamus Heaney. BIrV; CIP; FaBoMo; OBWP
Pockmarked like a little moon, the golf ball. Golf Ball. John Delaney. AMV-81
Pock-marked player of the accordion, The. Wedding Party. Donald Hall. LCAP
Pocomania. Derek Walcott. NoAM
Pod of the Milkweed. Robert Frost. LiTM
Pods of summer crowd around the door. Fall Wind. William Stafford. PPJ
Poe. James Russell Lowell. *See* Poe and Longfellow.
Poe, a very sick man in Baltimore. The Poets of Hell. Karl Shapiro. NYBP
Poe and Longfellow. James Russell Lowell. *Fr.* A Fable for Critics. AmPP; AP; NOBA; OxBA
(Poe.) TAP
Poe-'em of Passion, A. Charles Fletcher Lummis. BXAP; ShM
(Cannibalee; a Po'em of Passion.) SpRo
Poem: "About the size of an old-style dollar bill." Elizabeth Bishop. FYAP
Poem: "After your death." William Knott. EAS
Poem: "Ah, I know what happiness is!" Blanche Taylor Dickinson. CDC
Poem: "And when I pay death's duty." Robin Blaser. NeAP
Poem: "As rock to sun or storm." Niall Sheridan. OnYI
Poem: "As the cat." William Carlos Williams. CABA; FaPON; InPK; InPS; InvP; NoP; PAI; PDV
Poem: "At night Chinamen jump." Frank O'Hara. NoAM; NOBA
Poem: "At your light side trees shy." William Knott. EAS
Poem: "Between rebellion as a private study and the public." Charles Donnelly. *See* Last Poem.
Poem: "By the road to the contagious hospital." William Carlos Williams. *See* Spring and All.
Poem, The: "Coming late, as always." W. S. Merwin. PP
Poem: "Country, The/ was back in the hands of the patriots." Fred Levinson. AmPA
Poem: "Day when I can not, A." James Lewisohn. LFAC
Poem: "Death walks through the mind's dark woods." Henry Treece. NeBP
Poem: "Eager note, The, on my door said, 'Call me.'" Frank O'Hara. EAS; NoAM; NOBA
Poem: "Entombed in my heart no blood flows to you." Margery Dodson. AMV-80
Poem: "Especially when the October wind." Dylan Thomas. *See* Especially When the October Wind.
Poem: "Every morning I forget how it is." Charles Simic. NNaP
Poem, A: "Father of all! in Death's relentless claim," *sel.* Oliver Wendell Holmes.
"Father of all! in Death's relentless claim." TrPWD
Poem: "For years I have heard." Robin Blaser. NeAP
Poem: "Force that through the green fuse drives the flower, The." Dylan Thomas. *See* Force That through the Green Fuse Drive the Flower, The.
Poem: "Form is the woods: the beast." Jim Harrison. VGW
Poem: "Geranium, houseleek, laid in oblong beds." John Gray. SyP
Poem: "Get your tongue." Ted Kooser. POL
Poem: "Hasten on your childhood to the hour when white." Pablo Picasso, *tr. fr. French by* David Gascoyne. EAS
Poem: "Hate is only one of many responses." Frank O'Hara. NeAP; SOTW
Poem: "He lying spilt like water from a bowl." Alison Boodson. ErPo; NeBP
Poem: "He watched with all his organs of concern." W. H. Auden. PoA
Poem: "High on a ridge of tiles." Maurice James Craig. BoAnP; NeIP
Poem: "I burn for England with a living flame." Gervase Stewart. *See* I Burn for England with a Living Flame.
Poem: "I cannot tell, not I, why she." Walter Savage Landor. GBL; OAEL-2
Poem: "I do not want only." Colleen Thibaudeau. NOBC
Poem: "I do not want to be your weeping woman." Alison Boodson. NeBP
Poem, The: "I had never heard of the whiteness." David Schloss. PoA
Poem: "I heard of a man." Leonard Cohen. ELU
Poem: "I keep feeling all space as my image." Sanders Russell. EAS

Poem: "I knew a woman, lovely in her bones." Theodore Roethke. *See* I Knew a Woman.
Poem: "I loved my friend." Langston Hughes. DFF; NTCP
Poem: "I meet Mother on the street." Lennart Bruce. POL
Poem, The: "I sing th' adventures of mine worthy wights." Thomas Morton. SCAP
Poem: "I take four devils with me when I ride." Gervase Stewart. WaP
Poem: "I walk at dawn across the hollow hills." Ruthven Todd. EAS
Poem: "I watched an armory combing its bronze bricks." Frank O'Hara. NoP
Poem: "I will always love you." Frank O'Hara. LLLT
Poem: "In its going down, the moon." Robert Hogg. MoCV
Poem: "In secret." Pablo Picasso, *tr. fr. French by* David Gascoyne. EAS
Poem: "In the corner a violet jug the bells the folds of paper." Pablo Picasso, *tr. fr. French by* David Gascoyne. EAS
Poem: "In the dark caverns of the night." Henry Treece. NeBP
Poem: "In the earnest path of duty." Charlotte Forten. BlSi
Poem: "In the stump of the old tree, where the heart has rotted out." Hugh Sykes Davies. EAS
Poem: "Is to love, this—to nurse a name." Rhoda Coghill. NeIP
Poem: "It doesn't look like a finger it looks like a feather of broken glass." Hugh Sykes Davies. EAS
Poem: "It's a dull poem." Steve Jonas. PeHV
Poem, The: "It's all in/the sound. A song." William Carlos Williams. PCP
Poem: "Khrushchev is coming on the right day!" Frank O'Hara. NeAP; PoM
Poem: "Lana Turner has collapsed!" Frank O'Hara. CAPP; VGW
Poem: "Like a deaf man meshed in his endless silence." John Wain. PoCh
Poem: "Like musical instruments." Tom Clark. *See* Like Musical Instruments.
Poem: "Little brown boy." Helene Johnson. AmNP; BANP; CDC; PoBA
Poem: "Look at me 8th." Sonia Sanchez. PoBA
Poem: "Love being what it is, full of betrayals." Ruth Herschberger. HoAn
Poem: "Maggie and Milly and Molly and May." E. E. Cummings. *See* Maggie and Milly and . . .
Poem: "Night is beautiful, The." Langston Hughes. CDC
Poem: "Nothing move thee." St. Theresa of Avila, *tr. fr. Spanish by* Arthur Symons. PBWP
Poem: "O gentle queen of the afternoon." W. S. Graham. NeBP
Poem: "O men, walk on the hills." Maxwell Bodenheim. TrJP
Poem: "O who can ever praise enough." W. H. Auden. PoA
Poem: "Old man in the crystal morning after snow." Delmore Schwartz. PoA
Poem: "On getting a card." William Carlos Williams. VGW
Poem, The: "On this hill crossed." Galway Kinnell. NaP
Poem: "One whom I knew, a student and a poet." Alex Comfort. *See* Epitaph: "One whom . . ."
Poem: "Only response, The." William Knott. InPK
Poem, A: "Out upon it! I have loved." Sir John Suckling. *See* Constant Lover, The.
Poem, The: "Painter of Dante's awful ferry-ride, The." Babette Deutsch. PoA
Poem: "Person who can do, The." Alan Dugan. ErPo; NoAM
Poem: "Pity, repulsion, love and anger." Roy Fuller. NeBP
Poem: "Process in the weather of the heart, A." Dylan Thomas. *See* Process in the Weather of the Heart, A.
Poem, The: "Rise Oedipus, and if thou canst unfould." Thomas Morton. SCAP
Poem: "Rose fades, The." William Carlos Williams. NIP
Poem: "So many pigeons at Columbus." Arthur Gregor. VGW
Poem: "So they begin. With two years gone." Boris Pasternak, *tr. fr. Russian by* C. M. Bowra. TrJP
Poem: "Some are too much at home in the role of wanderer." Denise Levertov. NeBP
Poem: "Something broke the dream." John Gill. NeAC
Poem: "There I could never be a boy." Frank O'Hara. HoAn; NNaP
Poem: "There is a wailing baby under every stone." Norman MacCaig. EAS
Poem: "These grasses, ancient enemies." Keith Douglas. NeBP
Poem: "Thing, The/ To do/ Is organize." Kenneth Koch. CAPP
Poem: "This beauty that I see." James Schuyler. PoA
Poem: "This life like no other." Gregory Orr. AmPA
Poem: "This room is very old and very wise." Sam Harrison. NeIP
Poem: "Through the dark aisles of the wood." Henry Treece. NeBP
Poem: "Time and the weather wear away." Donald Justice. *See* Houses.
Poem: "Tiny new emotions, The." Tom Clark. ConAP
Poem: "To be sad in the morning." William Pillen. VWA
Poem: "To go, to leave the classics and the buildings." Gavin Ewart. NeBP
Poem: "Upended, it crouches on broken limbs." Charles Tomlinson. CMoP
Poem: "Walls of the maelstrom are painted with trees, The." Charles Madge. EAS
Poem: "We used to float the paper boats in spring." Donald D. Olsen. PoPl
Poem, The: "What ailes Pigmalion? Is it lunacy." Thomas Morton. SCAP
Poem: "What's the balm." Alan Dugan. CAPP
Poem: "While we were walking under the top." John Ashbery. EAS
Poem: "You are ill and so I lead you away." Al Purdy. NOBC
Poem: "You can look into my face." Mike Todachine. CTBA
Poem: "You said./ don't write me/ a love poem." Pearl Cleage Lomax. CNA
Poem: "You, who in April laughed, a green god in the sun." Brenda Chamberlain. NeBP
Poem: "Your face,/so pale now it is blue." David St. John. AmPA
Poem, The/ that I chose for you. On the Margins of a Poem. Jiri Mordecai Langer, *tr. by* Gabriel Preil *and* Howard Schwartz. VWA
Poem about a Seashell. Ranice Henderson Crosby. NMM
Poem about Beauty, Blackness, Poetry, A. Linda Brown Bragg. CNA
Poem about Breasts, A. James Wright. TAP
Poem about Intelligence for My Brothers and Sisters, A. June Jordan. PAI
Poem about Love, A. G. S. Fraser. NeBP
Poem about Morning. William Meredith. NYBP
Poem about People. Robert Pinsky. NPGG
Poem about Poems about Vietnam, A. Jon Stallworthy. NoAM
Poem about Waking. David Ferry. NePoAm-2
Poem about Your Face. Nathan Alterman, *tr. fr. Hebrew by* Ruth Nevo. VWA
Poem, after A. E. Housman, A. Hugh Kingsmill. *See* What, Still Alive.
Poem after a Speech by Chief Seattle, 1855. Charles Brasher. AMV-81
Poem after Apollinaire. Ira Sadoff. AmPA
Poem against Catholics. James Fenton *and* John Fuller. OBSV
Poem against Rats, A. Fred Levinson. AmPA
Poem against the British. Robert Bly. ConAP; InPS
Poem against the Rich. Robert Bly. CAPP; NMP; NoAM; NOBA
Poem and Message. Dannie Abse. TEP
Poem as Striptease, The. Philip Dacey. PPJ
Poem at Equinox. Hilary Corke. NYBP
Poem at Thirty. Sonia Sanchez. BlSi; BPo; CNA; NMM; PoBA
Poem at Thirty. John Woods. CoPo
Poem before Departure. Jean Burden. WPE
Poem Beginning "The." Louis Zukofsky. CoPo
Poem Beginning with a Line by Pindar, A. Robert Duncan. ConAP; NeAP; NNaP; PoM
"Light foot hears you and the brightness begins, The," *sel.* NMP
Poem begins, The. Beginnings. David Rokeah, *tr. by* Robert Mezey. VWA
Poem by a Perfectly Furious Academician. *Unknown.* FiBHP
Poem by the Bridge at Ten-shin. Li Po, *tr. fr. Chinese by* Ezra Pound. OBVE
Poem by the Charles River. Robin Blaser. NeAP
Poem Called Poem. James Whitehead. GrPl
(Poem) (Chicago) (The Were-Age). William Knott. EAS
Poem Circling Hamtramck, Michigan All Night in Search of You, The. Philip Levine. NNaP
Poem Composed in Rogue River Park . . . Tom Wayman. POL
Poem Containing Some Remarks on the Present War, A. *Unknown.* PAH
Poem/ Ditty-Bop. Carolyn M. Rodgers. JB
Poem Ending with an Old Cliché. Paul Zimmer. AMV-81
Poem Entreating of Sorrow, A. Sir Walter Ralegh. SiPS
Poem Following Discussion of Brain. Stan Rice. NPGG
Poem for a Christmas Broadcast. Anne Ridler. NeBP
Poem for a "Divorced" Daughter. Horace Coleman. LTB
Poem for a Neighbor. Pat Therese Francis. AMV-81
Poem for a Poet, A. Don L. Lee. PoBA
Poem for a Poet, A. Audre Lorde. NMM
Poem for a Singer. Milton Acorn. NeAC
Poem for a Son. Heather Cadsby. AMV-80
Poem for a Suicide. George Economou. DFF
Poem for Anton Schmidt, A. William Pillen. VWA
Poem for Aretha. Nikki Giovanni. BPo; PoBA
Poem for Ben Barney. Leslie Silko. CDW; VoR
Poem for Black Boys. Nikki Giovanni. BPo
Poem for Black Hearts, A. Amiri Baraka. CAPP; IDB; PoBA; PoM; SOTW
Poem for Carroll, Descendant of Chiefs. Lance Henson. VoR
Poem for David Janssen. R. T. Smith. AMV-81
Poem for Democrats, A. Amiri Baraka. CAPP
Poem for Diane Wakoski, A. Ray A. Young Bear. CDW
Poem for Dorothy Holt. Susan Irene Rea. AMV-81
Poem for Easter. Robert Kelly. VGW
Poem for Ed "Whitey" Ford, A. Jonathan Holden. MAYP
Poem for Edie Sedgwick Who Slept in a Swimming Pool. Stewart Brisby. LFAC
Poem for Epiphany. Norman Nicholson. PoPl
Poem for Etheridge. Sonia Sanchez. BPo

Poem for Flora. Nikki Giovanni. PoBA
Poem for Friends. Quincy Troupe. PoBA
Poem for Garcia Lorca. George Woodcock. NOBC
Poem for Good Friday. D. G. Jones. PeCV
Poem for Half White College Students. Amiri Baraka. BPo; CAPP; TAP; UnPo
Poem for Hemingway & W. C. Williams. Raymond Carver. WOLT
Poem for Heroes, A. Julia Fields. CNA
Poem for Integration, A. Alvin Saxon. PoBA
Poem for J. Wendell Berry. GeTw
Poem for Jacqueline Hill. *Unknown.* BrRo
Poem for Jan. Joseph Bruchac. CDW
Poem for John My Brother. William Aberg. LFAC
Poem for L. C. Peter Klappert. AmPA
Poem for Lorry. Gerald Hausman. CTBA
Poem for Marc Chagall. Leonard Cohen. *See* Out of the Land of Heaven.
Poem for Mother's Day. Margaret Fishback. InMe
Poem for Museum Goers, A. John Wieners. NeAP
Poem for My Dead Husband. Sheila Roberts. AMV-80
Poem for My Family. June Jordan. BPo
Poem for My Father, A. Sonia Sanchez. BPo; IHMS
Poem for My Father. Annette Arkeketa West. TWSS
Poem for My Father's Ghost. Mary Oliver. Str
Poem for My Grandfather. A. C. Jacobs. VWA
Poem for My Mother. Siv Cedering Fox. Str
Poem for My Mother. Lowell Jaeger. AMV-80
Poem for My Son. John Logan. DiL
Poem for My Thirty-second Birthday. John Ciardi. MiAP
Poem for My Twentieth Birthday. Kenneth Koch. PoA
Poem for Myself and Mei: Abortion. Leslie Silko. VoR
Poem for Nana. June Jordan. BlSi
Poem for Otis Redding. Joyce Carol Thomas. CNA
Poem for Painters, A. John Wieners. NeAP; PoM
Poem for Pat. Paula Gunn Allen. TWSS
Poem for Players, A. Al Young. GP
Poem for Positive Thinkers, A. Barbara Mahone. PoBA
Poem for Some Black Women. Carolyn M. Rodgers. BlSi
Poem for Speculative Hipsters, A. Amiri Baraka. NoAM; NOBA
Poem for the Atomic Age. Emanuel Litvinov. NeBP
Poem for the Conguero in D-Yard. Raymond Ringo Fernandez. LFAC
Poem for the Creative Writing Class, Spring 1982. Merle Woo. BrSi
Poem for the Insane, A. John Wieners. NeAP; PoM
Poem for the Meeting of the American Medical Association, A. Oliver Wendell Holmes. PoEL-5
Poem for the Old Man, A. John Wieners. NeAP
Poem for the Year Twenty Twenty. Al Lee. AmPA
Poem for the Young White Man Who Asked Me How I, an Intelligent, Well-read Person, Could Believe in the War between Races. Lorna Dee Cervantes. WPOW
Poem for Thel—The Very Tops of Trees. Joseph Major. NBP
Poem for Trapped Things, A. John Wieners. NeAP; PoM
Poem for Unwed Mothers. Nikki Giovanni. OBAL
Poem for Viet Nam. Ray A. Young Bear. STE
Poem for Vladimir. G. Ripley. AMV-81
Poem for Willie Best, A. Amiri Baraka. CAPP
Poem for You. Robert Pack. NePoEA
Poem from Llanybri. Lynette Roberts. NeBP
Poem from London, 1941. George Woodcock. NeBP
Poem from the Empire State. June Jordan. BPo
Poem from "The Revolution." Ilya Rubin, *tr. fr. Russian by* Linda Zisquit. VWA
Poem, A—Good or Bad—a Thing—with One Attribute—Flat. Melech Ravitch, *tr. fr. Yiddish by* Ruth Whitman. VWA
Poem H. Vicente Rodríguez Nietzche, *tr. fr. Spanish by* Julio Marzán. InW
Poem (I Lived in the First Century). Muriel Rukeyser. UnPo
Poem, A, in Defence of the Decent Ornaments of Christ-Church, Oxon, Occasioned by a Banbury Brother, Who Called Them Idolatries, *sels.* *Unknown.*
  Beauty in Worship. OBS
  Church-Windows, The. OBS
Poem in June. Milton Acorn. WHW
Poem in May. John Hewitt. NeIP
Poem in October. Dylan Thomas. BiP; CoBMV; LiTB; MoVE; NAs; NeBP; OAEP; PoA; PoPl; PoRA; PrIm; SeCePo; SoSe
  October, *sel.* YeAr
Poem in Progress, *sel.* John Logan.
  First Prelude. Dream in Ohio; the Father. LCAP
Poem in Prose. Archibald MacLeish. PoPl
Poem in Three Parts. Robert Bly. CAPP; ConAP; NaP; NOBA; PAI
Poem in Time of War. William Abrahams. WaP
Poem in Which My Legs Are Accepted. Kathleen Fraser. AmPA; LLLT; NMM
Poem in Yellow after Tristan Tzara, A. Jerome Rothenberg. PoM
Poem Intended to Incite the Utmost Depression, A. Samuel Hoffenstein. FaBoCo
  (Cervantes, Dostoievsky, Poe.) DBV
Poem like a Grenade, A. John Haines. EAS
Poem makes truth a little more disturbing, The. Hands. Donald Finkel. CoAP; MAT
Poem may boast bravado, A. Ar(chibald')s Poetica. Alan Ribback. BXAP
Poem moves down a page, A. Richard Meltzer. POL
Poem must not charm us like a play, The. Against the False Magicians. Thomas McGrath. NePoEA; PP
Poem must resist the intelligence, The. Man Carrying Thing. Wallace Stevens. SyP
Poem near Midway Truck Stop. Lance Henson. STE
Poem, neither Hilláryous Norgay. Gardner E. Lewis. FiBHP
Poem, 1972. Syd Scroggle. PoSh
Poem (No Name No. 2). Nikki Giovanni. BOLo
Poem No. 21. Doughtry Long. CNA
Poem of a Maid Forsaken, A. *Unknown.* PBBP
Poem of Angela Yvonne Davis. Nikki Giovanni. PoBA
Poem of Broken Pieces, A. Andrew McCord Jones. LFAC
Poem of Distant Childhood. Noémia da Sousa, *tr. fr. Portuguese by* Allan Francovich *and* Kathleen Weaver. PBWP
Poem of Explanations. Dahlia Ravikovitch, *tr. fr. Hebrew by* Chana Bloch. BoWoP
Poem of Holy Madness, *sel.* Ray Bremser.
  "Let me lay it to you gently, Mr. Gone!" NeAP
Poem of Sir Walter Rawleighs, A. Sir Walter Ralegh. *See* Nature, That Washed Her Hands in Milk.
Poem of the Conscripted Warrior. "Rui Nogar," *tr. fr. Portuguese by* Dorothy Guedes *and* Philippa Rumsey. TTY
Poem of the End, *sels.* Marina Tsvetayeva, *tr. fr. Russian by* Elaine Feinstein *and* Angela Livingstone.
  "Blatant as factory buildings." PBWP
  "I didn't want this, not." OBVE
  "Single post, a point of rusting, A." BrRo
Poem of the Forty-eight States, A. Kenneth Koch. NNaP; OBAL
Poem of the Future Citizen. José Craveirinha, *tr. fr. Portuguese by* Dorothy Guedes *and* Philippa Rumsey. TTY
Poem of the Intimate Agony. Julia de Burgos, *tr. fr. Spanish by* Julio Marzán. InW
Poem of the mind in the act of finding, The. Of Modern Poetry. Wallace Stevens. CABA; InvP; NePA; NIP; NoAM; OxBA; PP; PrIm; TAP
Poem of the Mother. Myra Sklarew. AMV-80; Str
Poem of the Son. Gabriela Mistral, *tr. fr. Spanish by* Langston Hughes. PoPl
Poem on a Slippery Sidewalk. Kenneth Porter. WhC
Poem on Azure. Anna de Noailles, *tr. fr. French by* Betty L. Schwimmer. WPOW
Poem on Canada, *sels.* Patrick Anderson.
  Cold Colloquy, V. CaP; NOBC; PeCV
  Coming of the White Man, The, II. CaP; MoCV
Poem on Elijahs Translation, A. Benjamin Colman. SCAP
Poem on England's Happiness, A. *Unknown.* APAS
Poem on Hampstead Heath. Louis Adeane. NeBP
Poem on His Birthday. Dylan Thomas. NAs; SeCeV
Poem on Inter-uterine Device, A. A. Rasheed Ghazi. PeD
Poem on Our Mother, Our Mother Rachel, The. Avot Yeshurun, *tr. fr. Hebrew by* Harold Schimmel. VWA
Poem on the End of Sensation. Ken Stange. AMV-80
Poem on the Guilt, The. Avot Yeshurun, *tr. fr. Hebrew by* Harold Schimmel. VWA
Poem on the Jews, The. Avot Yeshurun, *tr. fr. Hebrew by* Harold Schimmel. VWA
Poem on the Suicide of My Teacher. Joseph Stroud. NPGG
Poem, or Beauty Hurts Mr. Vinal. E. E. Cummings. InPS; MoAB; MoAmPo; MoVE; NIP; OBAL; OxBA; PPoe
Poem out of Childhood. Muriel Rukeyser. NMM
Poem Put into My Lady Laiton's Pocket, A. Sir Walter Ralegh. SiPS
Poem Rising by Its Own Weight, The. Denise Levertov. GP
Poem Rocket. Allen Ginsberg. CoPo; VGW
Poem should be palpable and mute, A. Ars Poetica. Archibald MacLeish. AmPP; AP; AWP; BiP; CMoP; CoBMV; FPL; HAP; HeIP; HoPM; InPK; LiTA; LiTM; MoAB; MoAmPo; NIP; NOBA; NoP; OxBA; PAI; PoA; PoPl; PoRA; PP; SeCeV; SoSe; TAP; TwAmPo; WeW
Poem Some People Will Have to Understand, A. Amiri Baraka. BPo; NOBA
Poem Technology. Miroslav Holub, *tr. fr. Czech by* Stuart Friebert *and* Dana Hábová. SUW
Poem That Took the Place of a Mountain, The. Wallace Stevens. LCAP
Poem to a Mule, Dead Twenty Years. Guy Owen. BoAnP; POL
Poem to a Nigger Cop. Bobb Hamilton. TTY

Poem to a Redskin. Wendy Rose. CDW
Poem to Be Read and Sung. César Vallejo, *tr. fr. Spanish by* James Wright *and* Robert Bly. EAS
Poem to Be Read at 3 A.M. Donald Justice. HoPM
Poem to Be Said on Hearing the Birds Sing, A. Biddy Crummy, *tr. fr. Irish by* Douglas Hyde. AnIV; AWP
("Fragrant prayer upon the air, A.") WTO
Poem to Complement Other Poems, A. Don L. Lee. BPo; NoAM
Poem to Delight My Friends Who Laugh at Science-Fiction, A. Edwin Rolfe. NePA; NePoAm
Poem to Ease Birth. *Unknown, tr. fr. Nahuatl (Aztec) by* Anselm Hollo. BoWoP
Poem to Explain Everything about a Certain Day in Vermont, A. Genevieve Taggard. NYBP
Poem to Galway Kinnell, A. Etheridge Knight. NNaP
Poem to Han-shan. Joseph Stroud. NPGG
Poem to Help My Father. Norma Richman. Str
Poem to Her Daughter, *sel.* Mwana Kupona Msham, *tr. fr. Swahili.*
"Daughter, take this amulet," *tr. by* J. W. Allen, *ad. by* Deirdre Lashgari. WPOW
Poem to His Grace the Duke of Marlborough, A. Joseph Addison. *See* Blenheim.
Poem to My Death. Julia de Burgos, *tr. fr. Spanish by* Grace Schulman. BoWoP
Poem to My Father. Joseph Stroud. NPGG
Poem to My Sister, Ethel Ennis, Who Sang "The Star-spangled Banner" at the Second Inauguration of Richard Milhous Nixon. June Jordan. TAP
Poem to Negro and Whites. Maxwell Bodenheim. PoNe
Poem to the Man on My Fire Escape. Diane Wakoski. CoPo
Poem to the Memory of H. L. Mencken. Baron Wormser. MAYP
Poem to the Sun. Morty Sklar. FAZ
Poem to the Tune of "Tsui hua yin." Li Ch'ing-chao, *tr. fr. Chinese by* Marsha Wagner. WPOW
Poem to the Tune of "Yi chian mei." Li Ch'ing-chao, *tr. fr. Chinese by* Marsha Wagner. WPOW
Poem to the Tune "Riverbank Willows." Yü Hsüan-chi. *See* Composed on the Theme "Willows by the Riverside."
Poem Touching the Gestapo. William Heyen. GeTw
Poem upon the Caelestial Embassy, A. Richard Steere. SCAP
Poem upon the Death of Oliver Cromwell, A, *sel.* Andrew Marvell.
"I saw him dead, a leaden slumber lyes [*or* lies]." JCP; OBS; ViBoPo
(Cromwell Dead.) ChTr
Poem upon the Imprisonment of Mr. Calamy in Newgate, A. Robert Wild. APAS
Poem upon the Triumphant Translation of . . . Mrs. Anne Eliot, A. John Danforth. SCAP
Poem with the Answer, A. Sir John Suckling. *See* Constant Lover, The.
Poem with the Final Tune. Julia de Burgos, *tr. fr. Spanish by* Julio Marzán. InW
Poem without a Main Verb. John Wain. NePoEA-2; NMP
Poem without a Title. Charles Simic. GP; NNaP
Poem Wondering If I'm Pregnant. Kathleen Fraser. IHMS; NMM
Poem Written before Mother's Day for Mrs. Lopez from the South. R. Wayne Hardy. LFAC
Poem Written by Sir Henry Wotton, in His Youth, A. Sir Henry Wotton. AnAnS-2
Poem Written in Time of Trouble by an Irish Priest Who Had Taken Orders in France, A. *Unknown, tr. fr. Irish by* Lady Gregory. OBMV
Poem You Asked For, The. Larry Levis. AmPA
Poema Morale. Charles Gullans. NePoEA
Poems. Gary Gildner. Psk
Poems. Antonio Machado, *tr. fr. Spanish by* John Dos Passos. AWP
"Figures in the fields against the sky!"
"Frail sound of a tunic trailing, A."
"Naked is the earth."
"We think to create festivals."
Poems (I-XI). Philip O'Connor. EAS
Poems about Playmates. Ronda Davis. JB
Poems about the Moon. Vachel Lindsay. TwAmPo
Sels.
Euclid, I. ImOP; YaD
What Semiramis Said, IV. MOON
Yet Gentle Will the Griffin Be, II. MOON
Poems are bullshit unless they are. Black Art. Amiri Baraka. BPo; CAPP; NIP
Poems are made by fools like me. Atheist. E. Y. Harburg. PV
Poems are my love, my romance now. New Romance. Nellie Wong. BrSi
Poems: Birmingham 1962-1964. Julia Fields. PoBA; PoNe
Poems for My Brother Kenneth, *sel.* Owen Dodson.
"Sleep late with your dream," VII. IDB; PoBA; PoNe
(For My Brother.) BALP
Poems for My Daughter. Horace Gregory. *See* Stanzas for My Daughter.
Poems for the New. Kathleen Fraser. IHMS; NMM
Poems from a First Year in Boston. George Starbuck. NePoEA-2; TwAmPo
Aspects of Spring in Greater Boston, II. NYBP
Poems from MSS. Blake. *Poems indexed separately by titles and first lines.*
Poems from Prison, 1 ("Day after day after day"). J. J. Maloney. *See* Prison Guard, The.
Poems from Prison, 2 ("They have built us a golf course"). J. J. Maloney. FAZ
Poems from the Coalfields, *sels.* Ian Healy.
Advice from a Nightwatchman. PoAu-2
Air Shaft. PoAu-2
Poems in Praise of Practically Nothing. Samuel Hoffenstein. FiBHP
Sels.
"Only the wholesomest foods you eat." InMe; TrJP
"You buy some flowers for your table." DBV; InMe; TrJP
"You buy yourself a new suit of clothes." DBV; InMe
"You get a girl; and you say you love her." InMe
"You hire a cook, but she can't cook yet." InMe
"You leap out of bed; you start to get ready." InMe
"You meet a girl and you surrender." InMe
"You practice every possible virtue." InMe
"You take a bath, and sit there bathing." EvOK; InMe
"Your life's a wreck; you're tired of living." DBV
"You're a good girl; you're gray with virtue." InMe
"You're kind to women, children, worms." InMe
Poems of My Lambretta. Paul Goodman. NMP
Poems of Night. Galway Kinnell. NaP
Poems of Our Climate, The. Wallace Stevens. MoPo; MP; NoP; OxBA; PP; TrGrPo; TwCP
Poems of Passion, Carefully Restrained So as to Offend Nobody. Samuel Hoffentein. InMe
Poems of the Arabic, *sel. Unknown, tr. fr. Arabic by* Sir Richard Burton. *Fr.* The Thousand and One Nights.
"My soul thy sacrifice! I choose thee out." ErPo
Poems to a Brown Cricket. James Wright. NaP; NYBP
Poe's Cottage at Fordham. John Henry Boner. AA
Poet, The. Joel Benton. WGRP
Poet, The. Elizabeth Barrett Browning. VLP; WGRP
Poet, The. Bryant. AA; AP; PP; TAP
Poet, The. Witter Bynner. WGRP
Poet, The. Lucille Clifton. DFF; GP
Poet, The. W. H. Davies. DTC
Poet, The. C. Day Lewis. OxBI
Poet, The. Paul Laurence Dunbar. BPo
Poet, The, *sel.* Emerson.
"Right upward on the road of fame." PP
Poet ("To clothe the fiery thought"). Emerson. *Fr.* Quatrains. OxBA; PCP
Poet, The. Padraic Fiacc. CIP; NeIP
Poet, The. Anita Grannis. HBMV
Poet, A. Thomas Hardy. NoAM
Poet. Donald Jeffrey Hayes. AmNP; PoNe
Poet, The. Keats. PP
Poet, The. James Kirkup. PP
Poet, The. Mary Sinton Leitch. HBMV
Poet, The. Haniel Long. HBMV
Poet, The. Amy Lowell. WGRP
Poet, The. Edwin Markham. WGRP
Poet, The. Cornelius Mathews. AA
Poet, The. Angela Morgan. WGRP
"Why hast thou breathed, O God, upon my thoughts," *sel.* TrPWD
Poet, The. Yone Noguchi. WGRP
Poet. Linda Pastan. DFF
Poet, The. Thomas Randolph. POL
Poet. Karl Shapiro. CMoP; LiTM; MoAB; MoAmPo; NoAM; TwAmPo
Poet, The. Tennyson. OAEP; PP; VLP
Poet. Peter Viereck. HoPM; MiAP; MoAmPo
(Planted Skull, The.) PP
Poet, The. Sir William Watson. *Fr.* Two Epigrams. TrGrPo
Poet, The. Walt Whitman. *Fr.* By Blue Ontario's Shore. MoAmPo
Poet, The; a Rhapsody. Mark Akenside. PP
Poet and Critic. Samuel Daniel. *Fr.* Musophilus; or, Defence of All Learning. OBSC
Poet and gangster reach in the dark. The Escapade. David Ignatow. PP
Poet and Goldsmith. Vernon Watkins. PoCh
Poet and His Book, The. Edna St. Vincent Millay. MoAmPo; NePA
Poet and Lark. "Madeline Bridges." AA; HBV-2
Poet and Peasant. R. H. Long. PoAu-1
Poet and Saint! to thee alone are given. On the Death of Mr. Crashaw. Abraham Cowley. AnAnS-2; GoBC; MeLP; MePo; OBS; SeCP; SeCV-1; ViBoPo
Poet and the Butcher, The. Catherine Durning Whetham. SUMH

Poet and the Child, The. Winifred Howells. AA
Poet and the Dun, The. William Shenstone. PP
Poet and the Rose, The. John Gay. TEP
Poet and the Wood-Louse, The. Helen Parry Eden. HBV-1
Poet and the World, The. Bryon. *Fr.* Childe Harold's Pilgrimage. SeCePo
("I have not loved the world, nor the world me.") OBRV
Poet as King of Gotham, The. Charles Churchill. *Fr.* Gotham. NOEC
Poet at Fifty, The. Laurence Lerner. PeSA
Poet at Night-Fall, The. Glenway Wescott. PoA
Poet at Seven, The. Donald Justice. TwAmPo
Poet at Seven, The. Robert Lowell, *ad. fr. the French of* Arthur Rimbaud. NaP
Poet at the Breakfast Table, The, *sel.* Oliver Wendell Holmes.
Epilogue to the Breakfast-Table Series. AA
Poet at Twenty, A. Donald Hall. EAS
Poet because his hand goes first, A. Spitballer. Fred Chappell. LiSp
Poet, cast your careful eye. On Seeing a Poet of the First World War on the Station at Abbeville. Charles Causley. ChMP; LiTM; NMP
Poet Confides, The. Herbert T. J. Coleman. CaP
Poet Describes His Love, The. Robert Nathan. HBMV
Poet gathers fruit from every tree, The. The Poet. Sir William Watson. *Fr.* Two Epigrams. TrGrPo
Poet, gentle creature as he is, The. Wordsworth. *Fr.* The Prelude. PP
Poet hath the child's sight in his breast, The. The Poet. Elizabeth Barrett Browning. VLP; WGRP
Poet Haunted, The. Wendy Rose. TWSS
Poet, A!—He Hath Put His Heart to School. Wordsworth. EnRP; VLP
Poet honed, The. Lyric Barber. Liboria E. Romano. GoYe
Poet! I come to touch thy lance with mine. Wapentake. Longfellow. AA
Poet! I like not mealy fruit; give me. Walter Savage Landor. FaBoEE
Poet Imagines His Grandfather's Thoughts on the Day He Died, The. Wing Tek Lum. BrSi
Poet in a golden clime was born, The. The Poet. Tennyson. OAEP; PP; VLP
Poet in his lone yet genial hour, The. Apologia Pro Vita Sua. Samuel Taylor Coleridge. EnRP; PP
Poet in Old Age Fishing at Evening, The. Desmond O'Grady. CIP
Poet in Winter. Edward Lucie-Smith. TwCP
Poet Is Dead, The. William Everson. NoP
Poet is hunter, The. Poem prey. The Hunt of the Poem. Richard Behm. AMV-80
Poet is, or ought to be, a hater of the city, The. Rural Bliss. Anthony C. Deane. InMe
Poet is priest. Death to Van Gogh's Ear! Allen Ginsberg. CABA; NaP; VGW
Poet is the dreamer, The. Loneliness. Al Young. PoBA
Poet Laments the Coming of Old Age, The. Edith Sitwell. NoAM
Poet, let passion sleep. Art, II. Alfred Noyes. OBEV
Poet lived in Galilee, A. The Poet. Witter Bynner. WGRP
Poet Lives, The. Jacob Glatstein, *tr. fr. Yiddish by* Ruth Whitman. VWA
Poet Loosed a Wingèd Song, The. Joseph Campbell. OnYI
Poet Loves a Mistress[e] But Not to Marry, The. Robert Herrick. CaPo; CavP; ErPo
Poet Loves from Afar, The. Desmond O'Grady. NoAM
Poet of Bray, The. John Heath-Stubbs. NOBL
Poet of Earth. Stephen Henry Thayer. AA
Poet of Gardens, The. Daniel Henderson. HBMV
Poet of Nature, thou hast wept to know. To Wordsworth. Shelley. EnRP; FiP; NoP
Poet of One Mood, A. Alice Meynell. HBMV; SBG
Poet of the pulpit, whose full-chorded lyre. Bartol. Amos Bronson Alcott. AA
Poet on the Island, The. Richard Murphy. CIP; NMP
Poet Prays, The. Grace Noll Crowell. TrPWD
Poet Questions Peace, The. George Chapman. *Fr.* Euthymiae Raptus; or, The Tears of Peace. JCP
Poet Recognizing the Echo of the Voice, A. Diane Wakoski. NIP
Poet Shadwell, The. Dryden. *Fr.* MacFlecknoe. FiP
("All human things are subject to decay.") SCV; TrGrPo; ViBoPo
(Primacy of Dullness, The.) OBS
Poet Songs. Karle Wilson Baker. HBMV
Poet Speaks, The. Georgia Douglas Johnson. AmNP
Poet Speaks from the Visitors' Gallery, A. Archibald MacLeish. NYBP
Poet spilled my gin, The. Tropisms on John Berryman. Gerald Vizenor. VoR
Poet, take up your lyre. The New Song. Arthur Gordon Field. PGD
Poet Thinks, A. Lui Chi, *tr. fr. Chinese by* E. Powys Mathers. AWP
Poet to His Beloved, A. W. B. Yeats. BrPo
Poet to His Love. Maxwell Bodenheim. PoPl
Poet to the Birds, The. Alice Meynell. FM
Poet to the Sleeping Saki, The. Goethe, *tr. fr. German by* John Weiss. PeHV
Poet told me if I was serious, The. Instruction from Bly. Cynthia Macdonald. NMM
Poet-Tree. Earle Birney. OxBC
Poet Tries to Turn In His Jock, The. David Hilton. LiSp
Poet was busted by a topless judge, A. Sermonette. Ishmael Reed. NIP; PoBA
Poet, whoe'er thou art, God damn thee. Earl of Rochester. DBV; FaBoEE
Poet Woman's Mitosis; Dividing All the Cells Apart. Wendy Rose. TWSS
Poet Wondering What He Is Up To. D. J. Enright. OxBC
Poet writ a song of May, A. The First Song. Richard Burton. AA
Poeta Fit, Non Nascitur. "Lewis Carroll." FaBoNo; NBM; OBSV
Poeta Loquitur. Swinburne. OAEL-2
Poetaster, The, *sels.* Ben Jonson.
"O sacred poesie, thou spirit of artes," *fr.* II, ii. PoEL-2
Song: "If I freely may discover," *fr.* II, ii. AnAnS-2; ElL
"There is no bountie to be shew'd to such," *fr.* III, vi. PoEL-2
Poetaster, The. Samuel Rowlands. *Fr.* The Melancholy Knight. ElL
Poetess Kō Ōgimi, The. Helen Chasin. NMM
Poetess's Bouts-Rimés, The. *Unknown.* NOEC
Poeti-c Art ("The poetic cart"). Arudra, *tr. by* B. V. L. Narayana Row. PCP
Poetic Genius. Mark Akenside. *Fr.* The Pleasures of Imagination. NOEC
Poetic Land, The. William Caldwell Roscoe. OBVV
Poetic Pains. William Cowper. *Fr.* The Task, II. FiP
("There is a pleasure in poetic pains.") PP
Poetic Tale. Grace Maddock Miller. GDP
Poetic Thought. *Unknown.* FiBHP
(O Moon, When I Gaze on Thy Beautiful Face.) InPK
Poetical Commandments. Byron. *Fr.* Don Juan, I. FiP; OBRV
("If ever I should condescend to prose.") OxBoLi
(Poet's Credo.) SeCePo
Poetical Economy. Harry Graham. CenHV; FaBoCo; TreFS
Poetical Numbers. Pope. *Fr.* An Essay on Criticism. OBEC; SeCePo
("But most by numbers judge a poet's song.") FaBoUs; HAP; PP
(Sound and Sense.) NIP
Poetical Philander only thought to love. Philander. Donald Hall. ELU; ErPo
Poetics. A. R. Ammons. NoP
Poetics. André Spire, *tr. fr. French by* Edouard Roditi. VWA
Poetics against the Angel of Death. Phyllis Webb. MoCV; NOBC
Poetry. Eleanor Farjeon. RHPC
Poetry. Lucius Harwood Foote. AA
Poetry. Nikki Giovanni. NIP
Poetry. Ella Heath. HBV-2; WGRP
Poetry. Greg Kuzma. PoA
Poetry. Edwin Markham. AA
Poetry. Marianne Moore. AmPP; AP; BiP; BLPL; BoWoP; CABA; CMoP; CoBMV; FF; HAP; HeIP; LiTA; LiTM; MoAB; MoAmPo; NePA; NIP; NoAM; NOBA; NoP; OxBA; PAI; PP; SeCeV; TAP; TreFT; TwAmPo; UnPo; ViBoPo
Poetry. Carl Rakosi. GP
Poetry. Abraham Sutskever, *tr. fr. Yiddish by* Ruth Whitman. VWA
Poetry. Claude Vigée, *tr. fr. French by* Anthony Rudolf. VWA
Poetry, a Natural Thing. Robert Duncan. NoAM; NOBA
Poetry, almost blind like a camera. Imaginary Elegies, I-IV. Jack Spicer. NeAP
Poetry and Learning. George Chapman. *Fr.* The Epistle Dedicatory to Chapman's Translation of the Iliad. OBS
Poetry and Philosophy. Thomas Randolph. *Fr.* An Eclogue to Mr. Johnson. OBS
Poetry and Science. W. J. Turner. SeCePo
Poetry and the Poet. H. C. Bunner. OBAL
Poetry and Thoughts on Same. Franklin P. Adams. HBMV
Poetry Concert. Michael S. Harper. TAP
Poetry Defined. John Holmes. GrPl; PP
Poetry drives its lines into her forehead. A Young Highland Girl Studying Poetry. Iain Crichton Smith. NePoEA-2; PP
Poetry, Emily. Brief History. Olga Hampel Briggs. GoYe
Poetry for Supper. R. S. Thomas. OxBC
Poetry has opened all my pores. After Reading Nelly Sachs. Linda Pastan. VWA
Poetry Is. Bruce Bennett. AMV-81
Poetry Is a Destructive Force. Wallace Stevens. OxBA
Poetry is a projection across silence of cadences arranged to break the silence. Ten Defintions of Poetry. Carl Sandburg. MoAmPo
Poetry Is Death Cast Out. Sydney Clouts. PeSA
Poetry is easy these days. Mr. Kurtz. Robert McGovern. SOTS
Poetry Is Happiness. Wrey Gardiner. NeBP
Poetry Is in the Darkness. Aram Boyajian. NeAC
Poetry is itself a thing of God. Proem. Philip James Bailey. *Fr.* Festus. VLP
Poetry is motion graceful. Poetry. Nikki Giovanni. NIP

Poetry is no uneasy refuge, stilly centred. No Uneasy Refuge. Blanaid Salkeld. AnIV
Poetry is the supreme fiction, madame. A High-toned Old Christian Woman. Wallace Stevens. AP; CMoP; CoBMV; MoVE; NoAM; NOBA; PPP; TAP
Poetry? It's a hobby. What the Chairman Told Tom. Basil Bunting. OxBTC
Poetry of a Root Crop, The. Charles Kingsley. LoBV
Poetry of Departures. Philip Larkin. CMoP; FF; HeIP; MP; NePoEA; NMP; OxBC; PrIm; TwCP
Poetry of Earth, The. Keats. *See* On the Grasshopper and Cricket.
Poetry of one the Russians call "a broad nature," The. "Hugh MacDiarmid." *Fr.* The Kind of Poetry I Want. InPS
Poetry Paper. Andrei Codrescu. EAS
Poetry Perpetuates the Poet. Robert Herrick. FaBoEE
Poetry Reading, The. Bill Manhire. OCNZ
Poetry Reading. Vernon Scannell. NOBL
Poetry Today. John Heath-Stubbs. POL
Poetry Workshop in a Reform School. Betty Adcock. AMV-80
Poetry's a gift wherein but few excell. Nathaniel Ward. SCAP
Poetry's a tree. Yes, the Secret Mind Whispers. Al Young. PoBA
Poets. Mark Akenside. *Fr.* The Pleasures of Imagination, IV. OBEC
Poets. Hortense Flexner. HBMV
Poets. Joyce Kilmer. WGRP
Poets, The. Scudder Middleton. HBMV
Poets, The. David Wevill. PP
"Poet's age is sad, The: for why?" Prologue. Robert Browning. *Fr.* Asolando. OAEL-2; VLP
Poets Agree to Be Quiet by the Swamp, The. David Wagoner. CoAP; VGW
Poets and Linnets. Tom Hood. CenHV; HBV-1
Poets and Their Bibliographies. Tennyson. PP
Poets are singing the whole world over. Rus in Urbe. Clement Scott. HBV-1
Poets at Tea, The. Barry Pain. HBV-1; Par
Macaulay at Tea, I. CenHV
Oh! Weary Mother, VIII. NA
Poet's Bread. Sister Mary Philip. GoBC
Poet's Call, The. Thomas Curtis Clarke. WGRP
Poet's cat, sedate and grave, A. The Retired Cat. William Cowper. FM; PCat
Poet's Confidence, The. Coventry Patmore. *Fr.* The Angel in the House, I, i. VLP
Poet's Corner. Robert Graves. FaBoEE
Poet's Credo. Byron. *See* Poetical Commandments.
Poet's daily chore, The. Lens. Anne Wilkinson. MoCV; NOBC; OBCV; PeCV
Poet's Day, The. Richard Weber. CIP
Poet's Dream, The. William Dunbar. *Fr.* The Golden Targe. PoEL-1
Poet's Dream, The. Shelley. *See* On a Poet's Lips I Slept.
Poet's Epitaph, A. Kingsley Amis. DBV
Poet's Epitaph, A. Wordsworth. EnRP; OBRV
Poet's Farewell to His Teeth, The. William Dickey. DFF; GP; PoA
Poet's Fate, The. Thomas Hood. ELU; FiBHP; PV
(To the Reviewers.) TW
("What is a modern poet's fate.") FaBoEE
Poet's faults, A: some are his own. The Motives of Rhythm. Robert Conquest. PP
Poet's Final Instructions, The. John Berryman. VGW
Poet's Grace, A. Burns. TrPWD
Poets have been writing about the death of flowers. Roses, Revisited, in a Paradoxical Autumn. J. W. Cullum. AMV-81
Poets have muddied all the little fountains, The. Abla. Antara, *tr. by* E. Powys Mathers. *Fr.* The Mu'allaqât. AWP
Poets Hitchhiking on the Highway. Gregory Corso. NeAP; NoAM; PoM
Poet's Hope, A, *sel.* William Ellery Channing.
"Lady, there is a hope that all men have." AA
Poet's Household, A. Carolyn Kizer. POL
Poets in Time of War. Bertram Warr. CaP
Poet's Journal, The, *sel.* Bayard Taylor.
"God, to whom we look up blindly." TrPWD
Poet's Lament on the Death of His Wife. Raage Ugaas, *tr. fr. Somali by* B. W. Andrzejewski *and* I. M. Lewis. WTO
Poets Light But Lamps, The. Emily Dickinson. HeIP; PP
Poets like shepherds on green hills. The Shepherds. Beren Van Slyke. GoYe
Poets loiter all their leisure. The Hour Glass. Edward Quillinan. OBRV
Poets Lose Half the Praise. Edmund Waller. PP
Poet's Lot, The. Oliver Wendell Holmes. PoEL-5
Poets Love Nature. John Clare. OAEL-2
Poets make pets of pretty, docile words. Pretty Words. Elinor Wylie. HBMV; YaD
Poets may boast (as safely-vain). Of English Verse. Edmund Waller. AnAnS-2; CavP; OAEL-1; OBS; PP; SeCP
Poets may sing of their Helicon streams. The Federal Constitution. William Milns. PAH
Poets Observed. F. C. Rosenberger. AMV-80
Poets of Hell, The. Karl Shapiro. NYBP
Poets' Paradise, The. Michael Drayton. *Fr.* The Muses' Elysium. WiR
"Poets pour us wine, The." Epilogue. Robert Browning. VLP
Poet's Prayer. Adelaide Love. TrPWD
Poet's Prayer, The. Stephen Philipps. WGRP
Poet's Prayer. M. L. Sussman. AMV-80
Poet's Prayer, The. *Unknown.* OBSV
Poet's Progress, A. Michael Hamburger. NePoEA; PP
Poet's Protest. Doris Hedges. CaP
Poet's Prothalamion, The, *sel.* J. W. Scholl.
" 'How could I cheat those lips of their true food?' " PeD
Poet's Request, The. *Unknown, tr. fr. Irish by* John Montague. BIrV
Poet's Resurrection. Dryden. *Fr.* An Ode to the Pious Memory of Mrs. Anne Killigrew. WHA
Poet's Secret, The. Elizabeth Stoddard. AA
Poets Seven Years Old. Arthur Rimbaud, *tr. fr. French by* Kenneth Koch *and* Georges Guy. SOTW
Poet's Simple Faith, The. Victor Hugo, *tr. fr. French by* Edward Dowden. TRV; WGRP
Poet's Song, The. Tennyson. EBVV; ELP; FiP; VLP
Poet's Song to His Wife, The. "Barry Cornwall." HBV-1
Poet's soul has sung its way to God, A. The Dead Singer. Mary Ashley Townsend. AA
Poets survive in fame. Lector Aere Perennior. J. V. Cunningham. QFR
Poet's Terror at the Bailiffs of Exeter, The. Andrew Brice. *Fr.* Freedom; a Poem, Written in Time of Recess from the Rapacious Claws of Bailiffs. NOEC
Poet's thoughts are of the skies, The. Poet and Peasant. R. H. Long. PoAu-1
Poets to Come. Walt Whitman. FF; LiTA; TrGrPo; YaD
Poet's Use, The. Pope. *Fr.* The First Epistle of the Second Book of Horace. OBEC
("Of little use the man you may suppose.") EBEV
Poet's Voice, The. Blake. *See* Hear the Voice of the Bard.
Poet's Vow, The, *sel.* Elizabeth Barrett Browning.
Rosalind's Scroll. HBV-1
Poet's Welcome to His Love-begotten Daughter, A [*or* The]. Burns. LiTB; NAs; NOEC; OxBoLi; PoEL-4; ViBoPo
Poets, who in time of war. Poets in Time of War. Bertram Warr. CaP
Poet's Wish. Valery Larbaud, *tr. fr. French by* William Jay Smith. GrPl
Poet's Wish, The; an Ode. Allan Ramsay, *after* Horace. OBEC; OBVE
Poet's words are winged with fire, The. The Poet. Joel Benton. WGRP
Poet's yes obscenely seeing, The. Lawrence Ferlinghetti. *Fr.* A Coney Island of the Mind. LiTM
Poggio. Lawrence Durrell. OxBTC
Pogroms. André Spire, *tr. fr. French by* Stanley Burnshaw. VWA
Poh! did ever one see such a troublesome bear? Delia Very Angry. *Unknown.* NOEC
Poietes Apoietes. Hartley Coleridge. OBNC
Poinsettia petal drops, A. The rain pastes twisted flowing drapery. Family Reunion. Hollis Summers. GoYe
Point, The. John Montague. IPY
Point, The. Gary Soto. MAYP
Point, greatly enlarged, The. Thomas Kinsella. *Fr.* A Technical Supplement. IPY
Point Grey. Daryl Hine. NOBC
Point of No Return. Mari Evans. NNP
Point of No Return. Robert Graves. BIrV
Point Shirley. Sylvia Plath. NIP; NoP
Point, the Line, the Surface and Sphere, The. Claude Bragdon. *Fr.* The Beautiful Necessity. ImOP
Point where beauty and intelligence meet, The. Sonnet. Gavin Ewart. WaP
Pointed Boots. Christopher Middleton. *Fr.* Herman Moon's Hourbook. NePoEA-2
Pointed clouds have become fixed in the heaven, The. A Stormy Day. *Tr. fr. Hawaiian.* WTO
Pointed houses lean so you would swear, The. Amsterdam. Francis Jammes, *tr. by* Jethro Bithell. AWP; FaPON
Pointed People, The. Rachel Field. FaPON; WSC
Pointing, his face looked at the blackened windows. Black Fear. Elizabeth Woody. STE
Pointless old miser named Quince, A. An Old Miser Named Quince. John Ciardi. TDH
Pointless Pride of Man, The. *Unknown.* *See* With I and E.
Poised between going on and back, pulled. The Base Stealer. Robert Francis. GoJo; LiSp; NCSH; NTCP; RHPC

Poison Ivy! Katharine Gallagher. SiSoSe
Poison Tree, A. Blake. *Fr.* Songs of Experience. AWP; CABA; EnRP; FaFP; HAP; HoPM; LAuP; LiTB; NoP; OAEP; PAI; PoEL-4; PPoe; PPP; SCV; SoSe; TreFS; TrGrPo; TW; WeW
Poisoned Lands. John Montague. NMP
Poisoned Man, The. James Dickey. PAI
Poke-Pole Fishing. Dennis Schmitz. AmPA
Poker Poem. Michael Pettit. AMV-80
Poking fun at tragedy is a risky business. Reasons to Go Home. Greg Forker. LFAC
Poland, France, Judea ran in her veins. An Electric Sign Goes Dark. Carl Sandburg. HBMV
Poland/ 1931 "The Wedding." Jerome Rothenberg. PoM; Prf
Polar Bear. Gail Kredenser. RHPC
Polar DEW has just warned that, The. Your Attention Please. Peter Porter. OBWP; OxBTC
Polar Exploration. Stephen Spender. ChMP; MoAB; MoPo; NoAM
(North, The.) FaBoMo
Polar Quest, The. Richard Burton. AA
Polarities. Kenneth Slessor. CBAP
Pole/ polar. The Windy Planet. Annie Dillard. SUW
Pole Star. Archibald MacLeish. AP; CoBMV
(Pole Star for This Year.) NePA; OxBA
Pole-Vaulter, The. *Unknown.* LiSp
Poled to its environment, shored. Coyote's Daylight Trip. Paula Gunn Allen. TWSS
Poles are flying where the two eyes set, The. Discoveries. Vernon Watkins. LiTM; WaP
Poles rode out from Warsaw against the German, The. The Abnormal Is Not Courage. Jack Gilbert. CoAP; NPGG
Police are dragging for the bodies, The. Miners. James Wright. ConAP; CTBA
Police Station Ditties. Max Beerbohm. NOBL
Policeman, The. Marjorie Seymour Watts. TiPo
Policeman, A/ is a pig. Definition for Blk/Children. Sonia Sanchez. PoBA
Policeman buys shoes slow and careful, The. Psalm of Those Who Go Forth before Daylight. Carl Sandburg. MoShBr; OxBA
Policeman, policeman, don't take me. I Stole Brass. *Unknown.* ChTr
Policeman's Lot, A [*or* The]. W. S. Gilbert. *Fr.* The Pirates of Penzance. NOBL; SaC; TreFT; TrGrPo
Policemen Laughing. Ray Fraser. NeAC
Policy. Carolyn Wells. WhC
Policy of the House. Charles Stetler. GP
Politeness. A. A. Milne. PoPl
Politeness. Elizabeth Turner. HBV-1; HBVY
Politest musician that ever was seen, The. The Music of the Future. Oliver Herford. CenHV
Political Activist Living Alone. Pat Arrowsmith. BrRo
Political Despatch, A. George Canning. FaBoCo
(Dutch, The.) DBV
(Epigram: Dutch, The.) OxBoLi
Political Greatness. Shelley. EnRP
Political Intelligence. A. J. M. Smith. EAS
Political Meeting. A. M. Klein. MoCV; OBCV
Political Orlando, The. George MacBeth. NOBL
Political Poem. Amiri Baraka. CoAP; NoAM
Political Reflection. Howard Nemerov. *See* Sparrow in the Zoo, The.
Politician, A. E. E. Cummings. DBV; InPK; TW
(Politician Is an Arse Upon, A.) FaBoEE; OBAL
Politics. Tom Marshall. NOBC
Politics. W. B. Yeats. CMoP; FF; HeIP; InPS; OxBTC; POL; SCV
Politics of Rich Painters, The. Amiri Baraka. CoPo; VGW
Poll. Ed Roberson. PoBA
Poll Parrot. *Unknown.* OxNR
Polliwog, The. Arthur Guiterman. RHPC
Polly; an Opera, *sels.* John Gay.
"Sleep, O sleep," Air XXIII. ViBoPo
(Song.) FaBoEn
"Sportsmen keep hawks, and their quarry they gain, The," Air XLVIII. NOEC
Polly, from me, tho' now a love-sick youth. To a Young Lady. Richard Savage. OBEC
Polly Oliver's Rambles. *Unknown.* OBET; ViBoFo, *diff. vers., with music*
Polly Perkins. *Unknown.* DTC; ELP; OxBoLi
Polly put the kettle on. Mother Goose. OxNR
Polly Vaughn (Molly Bawn). *Unknown.* *See* Young Molly Ban.
Polly Wolly Doodle. *Unknown.* FSW; TreF; YaD
Polo Grounds. Rolfe Humphries. HoPM; LiSp
Polo Match. John Ciardi. LiSp
Polonius to Laertes. Shakespeare. *Fr.* Hamlet, I, iii. GN
("And these few precepts in thy memory.") MasP
(Polonius' Advice to His Son.) TreF
(Polonius' Advice to Laertes.) OHFP; PoPl
(This above All.) TrGrPo
(To Thine Own Self Be True.) FaFP; LiTB
Polwart on the Green. Allan Ramsay. NOEC
Polychromatic springtime's gay cadenza. Vernal Equinox. Martin Johnston. CBAP
Polyhymnia, *sel.* George Peele.
His Golden Lock[e]s [Time Hath to Silver Turned]. George Peele. ElL; EnRePo; FaBoRV; HeIP; LoBV; NoP; PPoe; ViBoPo; WHA
(Farewell to Arms, A.) HBV-1; NIP; NOBE; OBEV; OBWP; PoPle; PoRA
(Old Knight, The.) ChTr; OBSC; TrGrPo
(Sonet, A: "His golden lockes, Time hath to silver turn'd.") FaBoEn; PoEL-2
(Sonnet, A: "His golden locks time hath to silver turned.") ELP; InPS
Polyolbion, *sels.* Michael Drayton.
"And, now that every thing may in the proper place," *fr.* Fourteenth Song. FM
"Away yee barb'rous woods; how ever yee be plac't," *fr.* Third Song. OBS
Charnwood Forest, *fr.* Sixth and Twentieth Song. FaBoPP
"Duck, and Mallard first, the falconers onely sport, The," *fr.* Five and Twentieth Song. FM
(Birds in the Fens.) ChTr
Dwindling Forest of Arden, The, *fr.* Thirteenth Song. FaBoPP
"Earle Douglasse for this day doth with the Percies stand, The," *fr.* Two and Twentieth Song. OBS
Fen-Men of Lincolnshire's Holland, The, *fr.* Five and Twentieth Song. FaBoPP
Fools Gaze at Painted Courts, *fr.* Eighteenth Song. ChTr
"Forest so much fallen from what she was before, The," *fr.* Thirteenth Song. SeCePo
Lincolnshire's Holland Speaks of Her Waterfowl, *fr.* Five and Twentieth Song. FaBoPP
"My various fleets for fowl, O who is he can tell," *fr.* Fifth and Twentieth Song. PBBP
"Of all the beasts which we for our veneriall name," *fr.* Thirteenth Song. OBS
Stonehenge *fr.* Third Song. FaBoPP
"To these, the gentle South, with kisses smooth and soft," *fr.* Second Song. OBS
Trent Again, The, *fr.* Sixth and Twentieth Song. FaBoPP
"When Phoebus lifts his head out of the winter's wave," *fr.* Thirteenth Song. OBS; PBBP
"World of mightie kings and princes I could name, A," *fr.* Twentieth Song. OBS
Pomegranate, The. Louis Dudek. OBCV; PeCV
Pomegranate. Gail N. Harada. BrSi
Pomegranate speaks, The. Ezra Pound *and* Noel Stock, *fr. Egyptian hieroglyphics.* BoWoP
Pomegranate Tree in Jerusalem ("The pomegranate tree in my garden adorns itself"). Zerubavel Gilead *tr. fr. Hebrew by* Dorothea Krook. VWA
Pomona. William Morris. WiR
Pomp of the Persian I hold in aversion, The. Persicos Odi. Horace, *ad. by* Franklin P. Adams. HBMV
Pompadour, The. George Walter Thornbury. BeLS
Pompeius, best of all my comrades, you and I. Horace, *tr. by* John Wight. Odes, II, 7. WaaP
Pompeius, chief of all my friends, with whom. Horace, *tr. by* James Michie. Odes, III, 2. OBWP
Pompey and Cornelia. Lucan, *tr. fr. Latin by* Nicholas Rowe. *Fr.* Pharsalia, V. OBEC
Pomposo (insolent and loud). Charles Churchill. *Fr.* The Ghost. OBSV
Ponce de Leon. Edith M. Thomas. PAH
Ponce de León: A Morning Walk. Al Young. HoPM; NPGG
Pond, The. W. H. Davies. ChMP
Pond, The. Anthony Thwaite. MAT; NYBP
Pond. Fredrick Zydek. AMV-81
Ponder, Darling, These Busted Statues. E. E. Cummings. CMoP; NIP; NoAM; SeCeV
Ponder thy cares, and sum them all in one. Sonnet. Sir David Murray. *Fr.* Caelia. ElL
Pond'rous projectiles, hurl'd by heavy hands. The Rejected "National Hymns." "Orpheus C. Kerr." OBAL
Pondy Woods. Robert Penn Warren. MoAmPo
Ponies, The. W. W. Gibson. PH
Ponjoo. Walter de la Mare. ShM
Pont and Blyth. *Unknown.* GBP
Pont-y-Wern. Arthur Hugh Clough. *Fr.* Ambarvalia. FaBoPP
Pontoon Bridge Miracle, The. Vachel Lindsay. Every Soul Is a Circus, IV. LoBV; NePA
Pontoosuce. Herman Melville. NOBA

Pony air, wild wheat, The. The End of the Indian Poems. Stanley Plumly. GOA
Pony Blues, The. *Unknown.* BluL
Pony Express, The. Dorothy Brown Thompson. AmFN
Pony Girl. Jane P. Moreland. PH
Poodles are in the basement again so my aunt, The. Summer Visitors. Stephen Clark. AMV-81
Pooh! Walter de la Mare. FiBHP; HAP
Poohmen! Baby. Florence Kiper Frank. HBMV
Pool, The. Robert Creeley. CoAP
Pool, The. Hilda Doolittle ("H. D."). CMoP
Pool, The. E. L. Mayo. MiAP
Pool. Carl Sandburg. AP
Pool, A. Thomas Whitbread. NYBP
Pool glitters, the fishes leap in the sun, The. By Loe Pool. Arthur Symons. VLP
Pool players, The. We Real Cool. Gwendolyn Brooks. PrIm
Poolhall, The. Dan Burt. AMV-80
Poop. Gerald Locklin. Str
Poor, The. John Langhorne. *Fr.* The Country Justice. NOEC
Poor, The. William Langland. *See* Our Needy Neighbors.
Poor, The. Emile Verhaeren, *tr. fr. French by* Ludwig Lewisohn. AWP
Poor, The. William Carlos Williams. MoAB; MoAmPo; NoP; PPP
Poor, and the dazed, and the idiots, The. Hurrying Away from the Earth. Robert Bly. NaP; PoA
Poor Angels. Edward Hirsch. MAYP
Poor benighted Hindoo, The. Limerick. Cosmo Monkhouse. HBV-2
Poor [*or* Poore] bird! I do not envy thee. The Robin [*or* Ode]. George Daniel. FaBoRV; FM; OBS; PBBP
Poor Boy ("When I went down to the river, poor boy"). *Unknown.* FSW
Poor Boy Blues ("Poor boy. Poor boy. Poor boy long way from home"). *Unknown.* BluL
Poor Brother. *Unknown.* NA
Poor but Honest. *Unknown. See* She Was Poor but She Was Honest.
Poor Can Feed the Birds, The. John Shaw Neilson. PoAu-1
Poor Celia once was very fair. The Advice. Thomas Flatman. CavP
Poor Children, The. Victor Hugo, *tr. fr. French by* Swinburne. AWP
Poor Christian Looks at the Ghetto, A. Czeslaw Milosz, *tr. fr. Polish by the author.* NIP
Poor Cotton Weaver, The. *Unknown.* OBET
(Jone o' Grinfield.) VLP
Poor crawlin' bodies, sair neglectit. John Learmont. *Fr.* An Address to the Plebeians. NOEC
Poor credulous and simple maid! Phyllis. Thomas Randolph. BoLoP
Poor Crow! Mary Mapes Dodge. OBCA
Poor Dad he got five years or more as everybody knows. Stir the Wallaby Stew. *Unknown.* FaBoBa
Poor damned Catullus, here's no time for nonsense. Catullus, *tr. fr. Latin by* Horace Gregory. NAWM-1
Poor dear dead have been laid out in vain, The. Thomas Hood. FaBoEE
Poor Dear Grandpapa. D'Arcy W. Thompson. NA
Poor degenerate from the ape, A. First Philosopher's Song. Aldous Huxley. AWP; HBMV
Poor devil that I am, being so attacked. Palladas, *tr. fr. Greek by* Tony Harrison. OBVE
Poor Dick! though first thy airs provoke. Dick Hairbrain Learns the Social Graces. John Trumbull. *Fr.* The Progress of Dulness. AmPP
Poor Doctor Blow went out of church. Queen Anne's Musicians. Thomas Hennell. FaBoTw
Poor drunkards, poor drunkards, take warning by me. John Adkins' Farewell. *Unknown.* AmFP
Poor Ellen Smith. *Unknown.* AmFP
Poor Estate, The. Robert Greene. *See* Maesia's Song.
Poor fawn about to die. Image. Anna de Noailles, *tr. by* Carol Cosman. PBWP
Poor Fool. Evan V. Shute. CaP
Poor for Our Sakes. Mary Brainerd Smith. BLRP
Poor fountain, dusty, clogged with pebbles. The Fountain. Pavlos Liasides, *tr. by* Edmund Pennant. AMV-80
Poor French Sailor's Scottish Sweetheart, A. William Johnson Cory. EBVV
Poor Ghost, The. Christina Rossetti. GBL
Poor Girl's Meditation, The. *Unknown, tr. fr. Irish by* Padraic Colum. BIrV; OBMV; OLR
Poor Grandpa. R. C. O'Brien. ShM
Poor Hal caught his death standing under a spout. Fatal Love. Matthew Prior. FaBoCo
Poor have childher and to spare, The. Quantity and Quality. Winifred M. Letts. HBMV
Poor have hands, and feet, and eyes, The. The Poor Man and His Parish Church. Robert Stephen Hawker. EBVV
Poor have little, The. Enough Not One. Benjamin Franklin. TRV
Poor Henry. Walter de la Mare. HBMV
Poor Howard. Leadbelly (Huddie Ledbetter). FSW
Poor humble roach. To a Humble Bug. Linda Lyon Van Voorhis. GoYe
Poor in my youth, and in life's later scenes. On Late-acquired Wealth [*or* Riches]. *Unknown, tr. by* William Cowper. AWP; OBVE
Poor in spirit on their rosary rounds, The. Lough Derg. Denis Devlin. BIrV; CIP; IPY
Poor in wit or judgement, like all poor, The. The Envious Critick. William Wycherley. PV
Poor Is the Life That Misses. *Unknown.* ElL; UnTE
Poor is the triumph o'er the timid hare! Autumn. James Thomson. *Fr.* The Seasons. FM
Poor Jack. Charles Dibdin. BeLS; HBV-1
Poor Jane Higgins. A Pig Tale. James Reeves. SoPo
Poor john, who joined in make of wrong. Welcome the Wrath. Stanley Kunitz. VGW
Poor Johnny was bended well nigh double. Apple-Seed John. Lydia Maria Child. OHIP
Poor Kid. William Cole. OBAL; PV
Poor Kings. W. H. Davies. HBV-2
Poor Kit hath lost her key. Kit Hath Lost Her Key. *Unknown.* UnTE
Poor Kitty Popcorn, *with music. Unknown.* AS
Poor lad once and a lad so trim, A. Jean Richepin's Song. Herbert Trench. OBMV; OxBI
Poor legendary princess! The Princess of Dreams. Ernest Dowson. VLP
Poor Lil' Brack Sheep. Ethel M. C. Brazelton. BLPA
Poor little foal of an oppressèd race! To a Young Ass. Samuel Taylor Coleridge. EnRP; OBEC
Poor Little Jesus. *Unknown.* FSW
Poor Little Johnny. *Unknown.* AmFP
Poor little Nellie is weeping tonight. Why Did They Dig Ma's Grave So Deep? George Cooper. TreFS
Poor little, pretty, flutt'ring thing. Adriani Morientis ad Animam Suam. Emperor Hadrian, *tr. by* Matthew Prior. OBVE
Poor little Willie. Little Willie. Gerald Massey. PaPo
Poor lone Hannah. Hannah Binding Shoes. Lucy Larcom. GN; HBV-1
Poor Lonesome Cowboy. *Unknown.* AS, *with music*; CoSo; TiPo
Poor Lucy Lake was overgrown. Lucy Lake. Newton Mackintosh. BXAP; HBV-1; SpRo
Poor Mailie's Elegy. Burns. FM
Poor Man and His Parish Church, The. Robert Stephen Hawker. EBVV
Poor Man Blues ("And it's never mind, never mind baby"). *Unknown.* BluL
Poor Man Blues ("I never had a barrel of money"). *Unknown.* FSW
"Poor man, oh, poor man, come tell to me true." The Jolly Thresherman. *Unknown.* AmFP
Poor Man Pays for All, The. *Unknown.* OBET
(Poore Man Payes for All, The.) CoMu
Poor man went to hang himself, A. One Good Turn Deserves Another. *Unknown.* ShM
Poor Man's Pig, The. Edmund Blunden. MoBrPo
Poor Man's Province, The. John Wright. NOEC
Poor man's sins are glaring, The. Rich and Poor; or, Saint and Sinner. Thomas Love Peacock. FaBoCo; NOBE; NOBL; OBSV
Poor Man's Sunday Walk, The. Charles Mackay. EBVV
Poor Man's Work Is Never Done, A. *Unknown.* OBET
Poor Martha Snell, she's gone away. *Unknown.* WhC
Poor Matthias. Matthew Arnold. FM; PoEL-5
Poor men's God that gives them sleep, The. Overseer of the Poor. James Hayford. NePoAm-2
Poor Me. *Unknown, tr. fr. French by* Richard Beaumont. ErPo
Poor mortals that are clogged with earth below. Sir Robert Howard *and* John Dryden. *Fr.* The Indian Queen. TEP
Poor Naked Wretches. Shakespeare. *See* Take Physic, Pomp.
Poor nation, whose sweet sap and juice. The Jews. George Herbert. JCP
Poor of London, The. William Forster. CBAP
Poor of the Borough, The: Peter Grimes. George Crabbe. *See* Peter Grimes.
Poor Old Horse. David Holbrook. NePoEA-2
Poor Old Horse. *Unknown.* CH; OBET
Poor old Jonathan Bing. Jonathan Bing. Beatrice Curtis Brown. FaPON; OnMSP; PDV; RHPC; SoPo; TiPo
Poor Old Lady. *Unknown.* OBCA; RHPC; SoPo
Poor Old Man, The. J. C. Squire. HBMV
(How They Do It: Mr. W.H. Davies.) InMe
Poor Old Man, *with music. Unknown.* ShS
Poor old Mr. Bidery. Mr. Bidery's Spidery Garden. David McCord. RHPC
Poor Old Pilgrim Misery. Thomas Lovell Beddoes. *Fr.* The Bride's Tragedy. EnRP
Poor Old Prurient Interest Blues, The. John Hartford. MAT
Poor old Reuben Ranzo. Reuben Ranzo. *Unknown.* AmFP
Poor old Robinson Crusoe! Mother Goose. OxNR

Poor old Widow in her weeds, A. A Widow's Weeds. Walter de la Mare. FaBV
Poor Omie. *Unknown.* PrIm
Poor Paddy Maguire, a fourteen-hour day. Patrick Kavanagh. The Great Hunger, III. IPY
Poor Paddy Works on the Railway. *Unknown.* *See* Paddy Works on the Railway.
Poor painters oft with silly poets join. Cupid. Sir Philip Sidney. *Fr.* Arcadia. SiPS
Poor Parson, The. Chaucer. *Fr.* The Canterbury Tales: Prologue. ACP
(“Good man was ther of religioun, A.”) NOCV; PAI
(Good Parson, The, *mod. by* H.C. Leonard.) WGRP
(Poure Persoun, The.) GoBC
Poor Poll. Robert Bridges. EBEV; MoPo; OxBoLi; OxBTC
Poor Relation, A. Audrey McGaffin. NePoAm-2
Poor restless dove, I pity thee. The Captive Dove. Anne Brontë. EBVV
Poor savage, doubting that a river flows. Watching the Dance. James Merrill. NIP
Poor Scholar, The. Abraham ibn Chasdai, *tr. fr. Hebrew by* J. Chotzner. TrJP
Poor Scholar of the 'Forties, A. Padraic Colum. AnIL; GLGT; OxBI
Poor Shammes of Berditchev, The. Rochelle Ratner. VWA
Poor sheepish plaything. For Sale. Robert Lowell. ConAP
Poor slaves, how terrible this Death is to them! George Chapman. *Fr.* Caesar and Pompey. ViBoPo
Poor song. The Tape. Myra Cohn Livingston. NTCP
Poor soul, in this thy flesh what dost thou know? *See* Poore soule . . .
Poor soul sat sighing by a sycamore tree, The. Desdemona's Song. Shakespeare. *Fr.* Othello. LoBV
Poor[e] soul[e] sat[e] sighing by a sycamore [*or* sicamore] tree, The. The Green Willow [*or* The Complaint of a Lover Forsaken by His Love]. *Unknown.* CoMu; OBSC
Poor soul[e], the centre [*or* center] of my sinful[l] earth. Sonnets, CXLVI. Shakespeare. AWP; BiP; CABA; EaLo; ElL; EnRePo; FaBoEn; GoBC; GTBS; GTBS-P; HAP; HBV-1; InPK; LiTB; MasP; NIP; NOBE; NOCV; NoP; OAEL-1; OBEV; OBSC; OxBoCh; PoEL-2; PPoe; PPP; SeCeV; TreFS; TrGrPo; ViBoPo; WHA
Poor South! Her books get fewer and fewer. J. Gordon Coogler. FaBoCo; FiBHP
Poor, thick, white. Three Poems on Morris Graves' Paintings. John Logan. PoDr
Poor tired Tim! It's sad for him. Tired Tim. Walter de la Mare. FaPON; MoShBr; NTCP; RHPC; SoPo; TiPo
Poor Tom; or, The Sailor's Epitaph. Charles Dibdin. *See* Tom Bowling.
Poor turtle, thou bemoans. Madrigal. William Drummond of Hawthornden. PBBP
Poor Uncle Joe. Sartorial Solecism. R. E. C. Stringer. FiBHP
Poor vaunting earth, gloss'd with uncertain pride. George Alsop. SCAP
Poor Voter on Election Day, The. Whittier. PAL
“Poor wanderer,” said the leaden sky. The Subalterns. Thomas Hardy. CMoP; MoAB; MoBrPo; NoAM; OAEL-2; PAI; PPP; TEP; VLP
Poor Wat. Shakespeare. *Fr.* Venus and Adonis. OBSC
Poor Wayfaring Stranger. *Unknown.* AmFP; BLSo, *with music;* TrAS, *with music*
(Over Jordan, *with music.*) OuSiCo
(Wayfaring Stranger.) FSW
Poor weaver, with the hopeless brow. How Different! Ebenezer Elliott. EBEV
Poor who begs with bated breath, The. The Price of Begging. Emmanuel ben David Frances, *tr. by* A. B. Rhine. TrJP
Poor William did what could be done. William Brown. Joaquin Miller. BPAW
Poor Wolf Speaks. Poor Wolf. NU
Poor Working Girl, The, *with music.* *Unknown.* AS
Poore bird! I doe not envie thee. *See* Poor bird! I do not envy thee.
Poore Man Payes for All, The. *Unknown.* *See* Poor Man Pays for All, The.
Poore soule [*or* Poor soul], in this thy flesh what dost thou know? The Soules Ignorance in This Life and Knowledge in the Next. John Donne. *Fr.* Of the Progresse of the Soule; the Second Anniversarie. OAEL-1; OBS
Poore soule sate sighing by a sicamore tree, A. *See* Poor soul sat sighing by a sycamore tree, The.
Poore soule the center of my sinfull earth. *See* Poor soul the centre of my sinful earth.
Poore wench was sighing, and weeping amaine, A. The Bard. James Shirley. ErPo
Poore widow [*or* widwe], somedeal stape in age, A. *See* Povre widwe somdel stape in age, A.
Pop. David McFadden. NeAC
Pop bottles pop-bottles. Song of the Pop-Bottlers. Morris Bishop. FaPON; FiBHP
Pop Corn Song, A. Nancy Byrd Turner. FaPON
Pop! Goes the [*or* de] Weasel, *diff. versions.* *Unknown.* BLSo, *with music; longer version;* FaBoNo; FSW; OxNR; PoPle; PSoN, *with music;* SoPo; TreFT
(Up and Down the City Road.) EvOK
Pop my whip and I bring the blood. The Ox-Driver. *Unknown.* FSW
Popcorn peanuts clams and gum. Bar-Room Matins. Louis MacNeice. EaLo; NYBP
Pope from penance purgatorial, The. J. V. Cunningham, *after the Latin of* George Buchanan. OBVE
Pope He Leads a Happy Life, The. Charles Lever. *Fr.* Harry Lorrequer. HBV-2
Pope is dead, The. An Election. Mordecai Marcus. SOTS
Popish Plot, The. Dryden. *Fr.* Absolom and Achitophel. ACP
Poplar, The. Richard Aldington. HBMV
Poplar. Gottfried Benn, *tr. fr. German by* Christopher Middleton. PoPl
Poplar Field, The. William Cowper. CH; ChTr; ELP; FaBoPP; FaBoRV; FiP; GTBS; GTBS-P; HAP; HBV-1; LAuP; NOBE; NOEC; OBEC; PoEL-3; RoGo; SeCeV; TrGrPo; WiR
Poplar is a French tree, The. The Trees. Christopher Morley. OHIP
Poplar is a lonely tree, The. Poplars. Edward Bliss Reed. HBMV; HBVY; OHIP
Poplar Tree. Padraic Colum. NePoAm
Poplars. Henryk Grynberg, *tr. fr. Polish by* Isaac Komem. VWA
Poplars, The. Theodosia Garrison. HBMV; OHIP
Poplars. Edward Bliss Reed. HBMV; HBVY; OHIP
Poplars, The. Bernard Freeman Trotter. CaP
Poplars are fell'd [*or* felled], farewell to the shade, The. The Poplar Field. William Cowper. CH; ChTr; ELP; FaBoPP; FaBoRV; FiP; GTBS; GTBS-P; HAP; HBV-1; LAuP; NOBE; NOEC; OBEC; PoEL-3; RoGo; SeCeV; TrGrPo; WiR
Poplars are standing there still as death. Southern Mansion. Arna Bontemps. AmFN; AmNP; BALP; BANP; CNA; FB; FF; IDB; LiTM; PoBA; PoNe; TTY; WSC
Poplars in the fields of France, The. In France. Frances Cornford. HBMV
Poplar's Shadow, The. May Swenson. NYBP
Poppa left no will. Bequest. S. Gale Gilburt. AMV-81
Poppies. Sandra McPherson. GeTw
Poppies. Roy Scheele. PPJ
Poppies. Charles Weekes. OnYI
Poppies in July. Sylvia Plath. LCAP; NaP
Poppies in October. Sylvia Plath. LCAP; NoAM
Poppies in [*or* on] the Wheat. Helen Hunt Jackson. AA; BPAW
Poppies paramour the girls. Song. Haniel Long. HBMV
Poppy, The. Cid Corman. HoAn
Poppy, The. Francis Thompson. MoBrPo
Popular. Tennyson. NOBL
Popular Functionary, A. Charles Dibdin. NOEC
Popular Personage at Home, A. Thomas Hardy. FM
Popular, popular, unpopular! Popular. Tennyson. NOBL
Popular Songs of Tuscany. *Unknown, tr. fr. Italian by* John Addington Symonds. AWP
“I see the dawn e'en now begin to peer.”
“I would I were a bird so free.”
“It was the morning of the first of May.”
“On Sunday morning well I knew.”
“Passing across the billowy sea.”
“Sleeping or waking, thou sweet face.”
“Strew me with blossoms when I die.”
“What time I see you passing by.”
Popular Wobbly, The. T-Bone Slim. FSW
Popularity. Robert Browning. OAEL-2; PP
Population. George Oppen. PoA
Population Drifts. Carl Sandburg. OxBA
Porch, The. Gary Gildner. AMV-80
Porch. Alden Nowlan. NeAC
Porch, The. Philip Pain. SCAP
Porch, The. R. S. Thomas. NOCV
Porch swing and rocker, The. Radcliff, Kentucky. Thomas G. Nickens. LFAC
Porchlight coming on again, The. 1926. Weldon Kees. CoAP; NaP
Porcupine, The. Galway Kinnell. NaP; NOBA
Porcupines. Robley Wilson, Jr. AMV-81
Porgy, Maria, and Bess. DuBose Heyward. PoNe
Poring on Caesar's death with earnest eye. Julius Caesar and the Honey-Bee. Charles Tennyson Turner. FM; NBM
Poring over a book, or my sewing. The Gnomes. Beth Bentley. SaC
Pornography Box, The. Dave Smith. DiL
Pornography, Nebraska. Sandra McPherson. MAYP
Porous. William Carlos Williams. NYBP
Porphyria's Lover. Robert Browning. AWP; BeLS; CABA; HAP; HBV-1; OAEP; OBEV; PAI; TEP; TreFT; TrGrPo
Porpoise, The. Greg Pape. MAYP

Porson on German Scholarship. Richard Porson. FaBoCo
(“Germans, in Greek, The.”) FaBoEE
Porson on His Majesty's Government. Richard Porson. FaBoCo
Porson's Visit to the Continent. Richard Porson. *See* Epigram on an Academic Visit to the Continent.
Port Admiral. Frederick Marryat. MOS
Port after Stormie Seas. Spenser. *See* What If Some Little Paine the Passage Have.
Port Authority Terminal: 9 A.M. Monday. Chad Walsh. PPON
Port Bou. Stephen Spender. MoPo; MP; TwCP
Port o' Heart's Desire, The. John S. McGroarty. HBV-1
Port of Embarkation. Randall Jarrell. MiAP
Port of Holy Peter. John Masefield. OBMV
Port of Many Ships. John Masefield. MOS; OBMV
Portent, The. Herman Melville. AmPP; AP; NOBA; NoP; OBWP; OxBA; PoEL-5; PrIm; TAP; WiR
Portents, The. Lucan, *tr. fr. Latin by* Christopher Marlowe. *Fr.* Pharsalia, I. OBSC
Porter shouted, “Syracuse!” The. Reveille. Hughes Mearns. *Fr.* Later Antigonishes. InMe
Porter thoughte what to rede, The. A Lover's Stratagem. *Unknown. Fr.* Floris and Blauncheflour. OxBM
Porter to th' infernall gate is Sin, The. Sin, Despair, and Lucifer. Phineas Fletcher. *Fr.* The Locusts, or Apollyonists. OBS
Portia. Oscar Wilde. BrPo
Portia's Plea for Mercy. Shakespeare. *See* Quality of Mercy, The.
Portion of this yew. Transformations. Thomas Hardy. NoAM; PPP; TEP
Portland County Jail. *Unknown.* AS, *with music*; FSW
“Portland” Going Out, The. W. S. Merwin. NYBP
Portly he was, in carriage somewhat grand. The Bunch of Larks. Robert Leighton. EBVV
Portly prince, and goodly to the sight, A. Dryden. *Fr.* The Hind and the Panther, III. OBSV
Portly Roman Senator was sipping his Rock and Rye, A. A War Bird's Burlesque. *Unknown.* AS
Portly wood-louse, full of cares, A. The Poet and the Wood-Louse. Helen Parry Eden. HBV-1
Portoncini dei Morti. Daniel Halpern. MAYP
Portrait. George Leonard Allen. CDC
Portrait, A. Joseph Ashby-Sterry. HBV-1
Portrait. Louise Bogan. HBMV
Portrait, A. Elizabeth Barrett Browning. GN; HBV-1
Portrait. E. E. Cummings. *See* Buffalo Bill's.
Portrait, A. Walter de la Mare. NoAM
Portrait. John Lyle Donaghy. BIrV
Portrait, A. Caroline Duer. AA
Portrait. Kenneth Fearing. MoAmPo
Portrait. Gail Fox. NOBC
Portrait. Louise Glück. Str
Portrait, The. Robert Graves. CABA; CMoP
Portrait, A. Brian Hooker. HBV-1
Portrait, A. Keats. BXAP
(Spenserian Stanzas on Charles Armitage Brown.) InMe
Portrait, The. Stanley Kunitz. CTBA; DiL; GP; Psk
Portrait. Walter Savage Landor. DBV
Portrait, The. “Owen Meredith.” HBV-1
Portrait. Adèle Naudé. PeSA
Portrait. Ezra Pound. OBVV
Portrait, The (“O Lord of all compassionate control”). Dante Gabriel Rossetti. The House of Life, X. VLP
Portrait, The (“This is her picture as she was”). Dante Gabriel Rossetti. OAEP; VLP
Portrait, A. Robert Louis Stevenson. SeCePo
Portrait, The. Countess of Winchilsea. *Fr.* The Birthday of Catharine Tufton. OBEC
Portrait by a Neighbor. Edna St. Vincent Millay. FaPON; MoShBr; OBCA; PDV; TiPo
Portrait by Alice Neel. Aaron Kramer. EyDe
“Portrait de Femme.” Irving Feldman. NoAM
Portrait d'une Femme. Ezra Pound. AP; CABA; CMoP; FF; HBMV; MoAB; MoAmPo; MoVE; MP; NoAM; NOBA; NoP; PAI; PPP; TAP; TwAmPo; TwCP
Portrait in Available Light. Sara Miles. NYP
Portrait in Georgia. Jean Toomer. NoP
Portrait in the Guards, A. Laurence Whistler. GTBS-P
Portrait in Winter. Katherine Garrison Chapin. GoYe
Portrait is where you, The. Robert Creeley Also Watches. D. C. Berry. BXAP
Portrait of a Boy. Stephen Vincent Benét. HBMV
Portrait of a Child. Louis Untermeyer. HBMV
Portrait of a Cree. “Katherine Hale.” CaP
Portrait of a Florentine Lady, The. Lizette Woodworth Reese. HBMV
Portrait of a Girl. Conrad Aiken. *See* This Is the Shape of the Leaf.
Portrait of a Girl with Comic Book. Phyllis McGinley. CrMA; CTBA
Portrait of a Jew Old Country Style. Jerome Rothenberg. NNaP
Portrait of a Lady. T. S. Eliot. HBMV; MP; TwAmPo; TwCP
Portrait of a Lady. William Carlos Williams. AmPP; CMoP; NoAM; NOBA; OxBA; TwAmPo
Portrait of a Lady in the Exhibition of the Royal Academy. Winthrop Mackworth Praed. *Fr.* Every-Day Characters. NBM; PoEL-4
Portrait of a Machine. Louis Untermeyer. MoAmPo
Portrait of a Marriage. Dannie Abse. NoAM
Portrait of a Senator. Charles Norman. DBV
Portrait of a Very Old Man. Sara E. Carsley. CaP
Portrait of a Widow. Avner Strauss. VWA
Portrait of a Young Girl Raped at a Suburban Party. Brian Patten. OxBTC
Portrait of an Artist. Barbara Howes. IHMS
Portrait of an Indian. R. E. Rashley. CaP
Portrait of Brutus. Shakespeare. *Fr.* Julius Caesar, V, v. TrGrPo
(Noblest Roman, The.) FaFP; TreFS
Portrait of Caesar. Shakespeare. *Fr.* Julius Caesar, I, ii. TrGrPo
Portrait of Cressida. Shakespeare. *Fr.* Troilus and Cressida, IV, v. TrGrPo
Portrait of Helen. Shakespeare. *Fr.* Troilus and Cressida, II, ii, *and* IV, i. TrGrPo
Portrait of Henri III, A. Théodore Agrippa d' Aubigné, *tr. fr. French. Fr.* Les Tragiques. PeHV
Portrait of Henry VIII, The. Earl of Surrey. ACP
(Sardanapalus.) SiPS
(“Thassyryans king, in peas with fowle desyre.”) AAS
Portrait of Hudibras. Samuel Butler. *See* Metaphysical Sectarian, The.
Portrait of Malcolm X. Etheridge Knight. CNA; PoBA
Portrait of Milton, The. Dryden. *See* Lines Printed under the Engraved Portrait of Milton.
Portrait of My Mother on Her Wedding Day. Celia Gilbert. AMV-81; DFF
Portrait of One Dead. Conrad Aiken. *Fr.* The House of Dust. HBMV; WHA
Portrait of Prince Henry, The. Sydney Clouts. VWA
Portrait of Rudy, A. James Cunningham. CNA
Portrait of Sidrophel. Samuel Butler. *See* Sir Sidrophel, the Conjurer.
Portrait of the Artist. Dorothy Parker. WhC
Portrait of the Artist as a Prematurely Old Man. Ogden Nash. BLPL; CrMA; FaFP; LiTA; LiTM; NePA
Portrait of the Artist as an Old Man. Michael Dransfield. CBAP
Portrait of the Artist with Hart Crane. Charles Wright. GeTw
Portrait of the Autist as a New World Driver. Les A. Murray. CBAP
Portrait of the Boy as Artist. Barbara Howes. DFF; MoAmPo
Portrait of the Father. Lindy Hough. IHMS
Portrait of the Poet as Landscape. A. M. Klein. NOBC
Portrait of the Pornographer. G. W. Jones. BXAP
Portrait Philippines. Alfred A. Duckett. PoNe
Portrait; the Freedom Fighter. George Jonas. NeAC; NOBC
Portrait with Background. Oliver St. John Gogarty. OBMV
Portraits. William Carson Fagg. LFAC
Portraits, The. Anna Maria Lenngren, *tr. fr. Swedish by* C. W. Stork. WPOW
Poseidon's Law. Kipling. MOS
Posing on the sloped rock. Horned Lizard. Charles Molesworth. GrPl
Position is where you. The Window. Robert Creeley. CAPP; NoAM; NOBA; TAP; VGW
Positions of the angles, The. Billiards. Laurie Blauner. AMV-81
Positive, a Coxcomb. William Plomer. POL
Positives. Jewel C. Latimore. PoBA
Positives for Sterling Plumpp. Don L. Lee. JB; PoBA
Positivists, The. Mortimer Collins. EBVV
Positivists ever talk in s-/ Uch an epic style as Dawkins. John William Mackail. *Fr.* Balliol Rhymes. FaBoEE
Possession. Richard Aldington. MoBrPo
Possession. Lynne Lawner. ErPo
Possession. Marie Ponsot. VGW
Possession. *Unknown.* BLRP; TRV
Possessions. Ivor Gurney. FaBoPP
Possessions. Ken Smith. EAS
Possessions. Lizette Woodworth Reese. HBMV
Possessive Lover, The. Ovid. *See* To His Mistress.
Possessor. Things. W. S. Merwin. HAP
Possibilities. Peter Kane Dufault. NYBP
Possibility of New Poetry, The. Robert Bly. ConAP
Possible/ that I lift this hand. Pavane for the Passing of a Child. Laura Chester. FiCP
Possible Love Poem to the Usurer. Octavio Armand, *tr. fr. Spanish by* Carol Maier. AMV-81
Possum lay on the tracks fully dead, The. The Lull. Molly Peacock. MAYP

Possum lies curled, The. Daydreamers. Norma L. Davis. PoAu-2
Post-Boy, The. William Cowper. *See* Winter Evening, The.
Post-boy drove with fierce career, The. Alice Fell; or, Poverty. Wordsworth. BeLS; OBNV; SpRo
Post Early for Space. Peter J. Henniker-Heaton. AmFN
Post-Impressionism. Bert Leston Taylor. HBMV; InMe
Post-Meridian, *sels.* Wendell Phillips Garrison. AA
Afternoon.
Evening.
Post Mortem. Verna Loveday Harden. CaP
Post Mortem. Robinson Jeffers. MoAmPo; MoPo; TrGrPo
Post-Mortem, A. Siegfried Sassoon. DFF
Post Mortem. Shakespeare. *See* Sonnets, XXXII.
Post-Obits and the Poets. Martial, *tr. fr. Latin by* Byron. AWP
("He unto whom thou art so partial.") FaBoEE; NIP; OBVE
Post-Rail Song, *with music. Unknown.* AS
Post-Roads. Kenneth Slessor. *Fr.* The Atlas. PoAu-2
Post That Fitted, The. Kipling. CenHV; HBV-2; OnMSP
Postage Stamp Lesson, The. *Unknown.* STF
Postcard from London, 23. 10. 1972. Andrew Salkey. FAZ
Postcard from North Antrim, A. Seamus Heaney. IPY
Postcard from the Volcano, A. Wallace Stevens. AP; CABA; HAP; LiTA; WeW
Postcard from Zamboanga. Barbara J. Esbensen. PoDr
Post Card out of Panama, A. William D. Barney. LiSp
Postcard to a Foetus. Kirk Robertson. GP
Postcard to Send to Sumer, A. William Bronk. VGW
Postcards. Mark Vinz. FAZ
Postcards, The; a Triptych. Denise Levertov. PoDr
Postcards from Rotterdam. Carolyn Kizer. GP
Poster Girl, The. Carolyn Wells. BXAP; HBV-1; InMe
Poster of Our Dazzling Victory at Saarbrucken, A. Arthur Rimbaud, *tr. fr. French by* Robert Lowell. *Fr.* Eighteen-seventy. OBWP
Poster with my picture on it, The. Unwanted. Edward Field. CoPo; PPON; Psk
Posterity. Cyril Dabydeen. BrSi
Posterity. Philip Larkin. OxBC
Posterity, thy name is Samuel Johnson. A Dream of Judgement. Douglas Dunn. OxBC
Posterity will ne'er survey. An Epitaph for Castlereagh [*or* Epitaph]. Byron. DBV; FaBoEE; NIP; TW
Postern Gate, The, *sel.* Walter Rauschenbusch.
"In the castle of my soul." TRV
Posthumous. Henry Augustin Beers. AA
Posthumous Coquetry. Théophile Gautier, *tr. fr. French by* Arthur Symons. AWP
Posthumous Keats. Stanley Plumly. GeTw; SV
Posthumous Tales, *sel.* George Crabbe.
"Young Paris was the shepherd's pride," XIX. OBRV
Postilion Has Been Struck by Lightning, The. Patricia Beer. OxBC
Postlude: For Goya. Ramon Guthrie. NMP
Postman, The. Laura E. Richards. SoPo; TiPo
Postman, The. *Unknown.* FaPON
Postman Cheval. André Breton, *tr. fr. French by* David Gascoyne. EAS
Postman comes when I am still in bed, The. A Sick Child. Randall Jarrell. InvP; OxBC; SO; VGW
Postman's Bell Is Answered Everywhere, The. Horace Gregory. MoAmPo; MoVE; NYBP
Postscript. Sandra Hochman. NMM
Postscript. Mary Mills. NePoAm
Postscript. R. S. Thomas. FaBoMo; OxBC
Postscript for Gweno. Alun Lewis. BoLoP; GTBS-P
Postscript, on a Name. Stephen Ratcliffe. AMV-80
Postscript to Die Schöne Müllerin. R. P. Lister. POL
Posture of the tree, The. Lovers in Winter. Robert Graves. FaBoEE; NYBP
Postures of Love, The, *sels.* Alex Comfort. NeBP
"I saw a woman in a green field."
"In the stony night move the stars' white mouths."
"Moon fills up its hollow bowl of milk, The."
"There is a white mare that my love keeps."
(Love Poem.) ErPo
"This was Briseis' way: she was a bridge."
Posy of Thyme, The. *Unknown.* OBET
Posy Ring, The. Clement Marot, *tr. fr. French by* Ford Madox Ford. AWP
Pot and Kettle. Robert Graves. HBMV
Pot of Flowers, The. William Carlos Williams. QFR
Pot of Tea. Susan Griffin. NPGG
Pot of wine among flowers, A. Drinking Alone in the Moonlight. Li Po, *tr. by* Amy Lowell *and* Florence Ayscough. AWP
Pot Shot. Padraic Fallon. CIP
Potage au Petit Puss. Menu. Edward Lear. FaBoNo
Potato. Richard Wilbur. CAPP; CrMA; LiTA; MoAB; TrGrPo; TwAmPo
Potato Eaters, The. Frank Graziano. PoDr
Potato Harvest, The. Sir Charles G. D. Roberts. CaP; NOBC
Potato was deep in the dark under ground. The Tryst. John Banister Tabb. OBAL
Potatoes. David Donnell. NOBC
Potatoes' Dance, The. Vachel Lindsay. FaPON; SUS
Pot-bellied Anachronism, The. Ann Darr. GP
Potiphar Gubbins, C. E. Study of an Elevation, in Indian Ink. Kipling. InMe
Potomac, The. Karl Shapiro. AP; CoBMV
Potomac Town in February. Carl Sandburg. EvOK
Potpourri [*or* Pot-Pourri] from a Surrey Garden. John Betjeman. CenHV; DTC; FiBHP; NOBL; PoCh
Pots in piles of blue and white. In a V. A. D. Pantry. Alberta Vickridge. SUMH
Potter, The. *Unknown, tr. fr. Geez by* Halim El-Dabh. TTY
Potter's Song, The. Longfellow. *Fr.* Kéramos. PoEL-5
Poultries, The. Ogden Nash. CenHV
Poultry. Diana Der Hovanessian. GrPl
Pound at Spoleto. Lawrence Ferlinghetti. PoM
Pound of Flesh, The. *Unknown. Fr.* Cursor Mundi. OxBM
Pounded spise both tast and sent doth please, The. At Fotheringay [*or* Decease, Release: Dum Morior Orior]. Robert Southwell. NCEP; PoEL-2
Pour Down. John Holmes. NePoAm
Pour l'Election de Son Sepulchre. Ezra Pound. *See* E.P. Ode Pour l'Election de Son Sepulchre.
Pour, O pour that parting soul in song. Song of the Son. Jean Toomer. AmNP; CDC; NIP; PoBA
Pour out your light, O stars, and do not hold. Requiem. Ivor Gurney. FaBoEE; FaBoTw
Pour the unhappiness out. Another Weeping Woman. Wallace Stevens. MoVE
Pour Us Wine. Ibn Kolthum, *tr. fr. Arabic by* E. Powys Mathers. *Fr.* The Mu'allaqât. AWP
Pour, varlet, pour the water. The Poets at Tea, I [*or* Macaulay at Tea]. Barry Pain. CenHV; HBV-1; Par
Pour wine, and cry, again, again, again. Heliodore. Andrew Lang. OBVV
Poure Person, The. Chaucer. *See* Poor Parson, The.
Poure widwe, somdel stape in age, A. Chaucer. *See* Povre widwe . . .
Pourquoi You Greased. *Unknown.* ChTr
(Pourquoi?) GDP
Poussie, poussie, baudrons. *Unknown.* OxNR
Poussin. Louis MacNeice. EyDe
Poverty. Charles Simic. MAT
Poverty. Theognis, *tr. fr. Greek by* John Hookham Frere. AWP
Poverty. Thomas Traherne. OxBoCh; Prf; TEP; TrCP
Poverty. *Unknown, tr. fr. Sanskrit by* Arthur W. Ryder. *Fr.* The Panchatantra. AWP
Poverty, in Imitation of Milton. Samuel Jones. NOEC
Poverty in London. Samuel Johnson. *Fr.* London. ChTr; OBEC
("By numbers here from shame or censure free.") NOEC; OBSV; ViBoPo
Poverty Knock. *Unknown.* OBET; VLP, *diff. vers.*
Poverty? wealth? seek neither. Epigram. Kassia, *tr. by* Patrick Diehl. WPOW
Povre Ame Amoureuse. Louise Labé, *tr. fr. French by* Robert Bridges. AWP
Povre [*or* Poore *or* Poure] widwe [*or* widow], somdel [*or* somedeal *or* somedeel] stape in age, A. The Nun's Priest's [*or* Nonnes Preestes] Tale [*or* The Cock and the Hen]. Chaucer. *Fr.* The Canterbury Tales. NoP; OAEL-1; OBNV; PoEL-1; SeCeV; TrGrPo
Powder and scent and silence. The young dwarf. Clair de Lune. Anthony Hecht. NYBP
Power. Thomas Stephens Collier. AA
Power. Hart Crane. *Fr.* The Bridge: Cape Hatteras. MoAmPo
("Nasal whine of power whips a new universe, The.") MoAB
Power. Matthew Prior. *Fr.* Solomon. LoBV
("Pass we the ills, whid each man feels or dreads.") NOEC; POEL-3
Power. Adrienne Rich. TAP
Power above powers, O heavenly Eloquence. English Poetry [*or* Heavenly Eloquence]. Samuel Daniel. *Fr.* Musophilus; or, Defence of All Learning. NOBE; OBSC
Power and Peace. Robert Herrick. CaPo
Power and the Glory, The. Siegfried Sassoon. OBMV
Power Failure. Michael Dennis Browne. AmPA
Power Failure. Josephine Jacobsen. FAZ
Power from God. Bible, *O.T. Fr.* Isaiah. *See* They That Wait upon the Lord.
Power glides in the root. Root. Miklós Radnóti, *tr. by* Steven Polgar *and* Stephen Berg *and* S. J. Marks. VWA

Power in the People, The. Robert Herrick. CaPo
Power lies in my hand. The Sibyl. Joan LaBombard. GoYe
Power of Fancy, The. Philip Freneau. AmPP; AP
Power of Innocence, The. "C. G. H." NOEC
Power of Interval, The. Lord De Tabley. VLP
Power of Littles, The. *Unknown.* TreFT
Power of Love, The. Dryden. *Fr.* Cymon and Iphigenia. OBS
Power of Love, The. John Fletcher. *See* Hear, Ye Ladies.
Power of Love He Wants Shih (Everything), The. Rochelle Owens. NMM
Power of Malt, The. A. E. Housman. *See* Terence, This Is Stupid Stuff.
Power of Maples, The. Gerald Stern. NU
Power of Music, The. Thomas Lisle. NOBL
Power of Music, The. Shakespeare. *Fr.* The Merchant of Venice, V, i. GN
Power of Numbers, The. Abraham Cowley. *Fr.* Davideis, I. OBS
Power of Poets, The. Ben Jonson. *Fr.* Epistle to Elizabeth, Countess of Rutland. WHA
Power of Prayer, The. Samuel Johnson. *Fr.* The Vanity of Human Wishes. NOBE
(Prayer: "Where then shall hope and fear their object find.") OBEC
Power of Prayer, The. Sidney *and* Clifford Lanier. HBV-2
Power of raven be thine. Good Wish. *Unknown, tr. by* Alexander Carmichael. FaBoCh
Power of Ridicule, The. Pope. *See* Satire: "Ask you what provocation I have had?"
Power of Silence, The. W. H. Davies. BrPo
Power of the Dog, The. Kipling. BLPA; BLPL; BoAnP; GDP
Power of Thought, The. Süsskind von Trimberg, *tr. fr. Middle High German.* TrJP
Power of Time, The. Swift. FaBoEE; PV
(Shall I Repine.) NCEP
Power Station, The. James Merrill. ConAP
Power that gives with liberal hand, The. On the Religion of Nature. Philip Freneau. AmPP
Power to Change Geography, The. Diana O Hehir. NPGG
Power to the People. Howard Nemerov. POL
Power to thine elbow, thou newest of sciences. Darwinity. Herman C. Merivale. InMe; NA
Power was given at birth to me, The. One Token. W. H. Davies. BrPo
Powerful Eyes o' Jeremy Tait, The. Wallace Irwin. FiBHP
Power-house, A. Classic Scene. William Carlos Williams. OxBA
Powerline Incarnation, The. Les A. Murray. CBAP
Powers of Love, The. George Moses Horton. BALP
Powers of the Pawn, The. David Solway. AMV-81
Powhatan's Daughter. Hart Crane. *See* Bridge, The.
Powte's Complaint, The. *Unknown.* GBP
Powwow. W. D. Snodgrass. GrPl; NYBP
Powwow Remnants. Lew Blockcolski. VoR
Powwow 79, Durango. Paula Gunn Allen. STE
Pox of this fooling and plotting of late, A. The Careless Good Fellow. John Oldham. APAS; SeCV-2
Pox on't, says Time to Thomas Hearne. *Unknown.* FaBoEE
Practical Concerns. William J. Harris. PoBA
Practical Program for Monks, A. Thomas Merton. CoPo
Practical Woman, A. Thomas Hardy. NAs
"Practically all you newspaper people." The Clown. Donald Hall. NYBP
Practically everyone goes to the Petrified Forest. A Fair Warning. E. L. Mayo. FAZ
Practice of Absence, The. Robert Friend. VWA
Practice of Magical Evocation, The. Diane di Prima. PoM
Practices/ silence, they way of wind. As a Possible Lover. Amiri Baraka. AmNP
Practicing. Sonia Gernes. AMV-80
Praefatory Poem to the Little Book, Entituled, Christianus per Ignem, A. Nicholas Noyes. SCAP
Praematuri. Margaret Postgate Cole. SUMH
Praetorium Scene: Good Friday. Elinor Lennen. PGD
Prairie. Herbert Bates. AA
Prairie. K. N. Llewellyn. YeAr
Prairie, *sel.* Carl Sandburg.
Look at Six Eggs. FaPON
Prairie child,/ Brief as dew. Nancy Hanks. Harriet Monroe. OHIP
Prairie Dog, The. Arthur Guiterman. BPAW
Prairie-Dog Town. Mary Austin. BPAW; FaPON; TiPo
Prairie Fires. Hamlin Garland. OBCA
Prairie goes to the mountain. Open Range. Kathryn Jackson *and* Byron Jackson. FaPON; TiPo
Prairie Graveyard. Anne Marriott. CaP; NOBC; OBCV
Prairie Lullaby. *Unknown.* BPAW
Prairie Schooner, The. Edward Everett Dale. BPAW
Prairie Spring. Edwina Fallis. SUS
Prairie Water Colour, A. Duncan Campbell Scott. OBCV
Prairie wind blew harder than it could, The. Swallows. Thomas Hornsby Ferril. RFM
Prairie Wolves. Robert V. Carr. BPAW; PoOW
Prairies, The. Bryant. AmPP; AP; NOBA; OxBA; PoEL-4; TAP
Praise. Jane Cooper. TAP
Praise. Edith Daley. TRV
Praise. George Herbert. AnAnS-1
Praise. William Matthews. AmPA
Praise. "Seumas O'Sullivan." HBV-1
Praise. Rainer Maria Rilke, *tr. fr. German.* ChTr
Praise. Christopher Smart. OxBChV
Praise. Henry Vaughan. AnAnS-1
Praise and Love. William Brighty Rands. OBVV
Praise and Prayer. Sir William Davenant. *Fr.* Gondibert, II, vi. GoBC; OBEV
Praise be man, he is existing in milk. Chorus. Jack Kerouac. *Fr.* Mexico City Blues. NeAP
Praise be to those who gave it birth. A Soldier's Plea for the Y.M.C.A. Joseph Samuel Reed. PeD
Praise Doubt. Mark Van Doren. EaLo
Praise for an Urn. Hart Crane. AP; AWP; CMoP; CoBMV; HAP; LiTM; MoAB; MoAmPo; MoVE; NoAM; NOBA; OxBA; PPP; WeW
Praise for Mercies Spiritual and Temporal. Isaac Watts. NOEC
Praise for Sick Women. Gary Snyder. NeAP
Praise-God Barebones. Ellen Mackay Hutchinson Cortissoz. AA
Praise God, who wrought for you and me. Magnificat. Arthur Symons. UnTE
Praise, hard as that is in a world where fires. Sent Ahead. John Hay. NePoAm
Praise Hearst, from whom all blessings flow! Doxology. Bert Leston Taylor. OBAL
Praise Him Who Makes Us Happy, *with music.* Mark Van Doren. AH
Praise in Summer. Richard Wilbur. CAPP; NoP; PP
Praise is devotion fit for mighty minds. Praise and Prayer. Sir William Davenant. *Fr.* Gondibert, II, vi. GoBC; OBEV
Praise, my soul, the King of heaven. Psalm CIII: "Praise the Lord, O my soul." Henry Francis Lyte. NOCV
Praise Now Your God, *with music.* H. P. Brucker. AH
Praise, O my heart, with praise from depth and height. Adam's Song of the Visible World, *much abr.* Ridgely Torrence. TrPWD
Praise of a Child. *Yoruba Oral Tradition, tr. by* Ulli Beier *and* B. Gbadamosi. WTO
Praise of a Train. *Zulu Oral Tradition, tr. by* B. W. Vilakazi. WTO
Praise of Age, The. Robert Henryson. BSV
Praise of Amen Ra! Hymn to Amen Ra, the Sun God. *Unknown, tr. by* Frank Lloyd Griffith. WGRP
Praise of Ben Dorain, The. Duncan Ban MacIntyre, *tr. fr. Gaelic by* "Hugh MacDiarmid." GoTS
Praise of Ceres. Thomas Heywood. *Fr.* The Silver Age. ElL
Praise of Created Things. St. Francis of Assisi. FaPON
Praise of Dancing, The. Sir John Davies. *Fr.* Orchestra; or, A Poem of Dancing. NOBE
("Dancing (bright lady) then began to be.") FaBoEn; PoEL-2
Praise of Dust, The. G. K. Chesterton. MoBrPo
Praise of Earth. Elizabeth Barrett Browning. OBVV
Praise of Fionn, The. *Unknown, tr. fr. Irish by* Frank O'Connor. KiLC
Praise of His Lady, A. *At. to* John Heywood. ElL; HBV-1; OBEV; ViBoPo
(On the Princess Mary.) OBSC
Praise of His Love, Wherein He Reproveth Them That Compare Their Ladies with His, A. Earl of Surrey. *See* Give Place, Ye Lovers.
Praise of Homer. George Chapman. OBS
Praise of Ibikunle. *Yoruba Oral Tradition, tr. by* B. Awe. WTO
Praise of Industry, The. James Thomson. *Fr.* The Castle of Indolence. OBEC
Praise of Little Women. Juan Ruiz, Archpriest of Hita, *tr. fr. Spanish by* Longfellow. AWP
Praise of Mary. *Unknown, tr. fr. Old French by* Henry Sorg. ISi
Praise of meaner wits this work like profit brings, The. Another of the Same. Sir Walter Ralegh. SiPS
Praise of My Lady. William Morris. HBV-1
Praise of New England. Thomas Caldecot Chubb. GoYe
Praise of New Netherland, The. Jacob Steendam. PAH
Praise of Philip Sparrow, The. George Gascoigne. ViBoPo
(Of All the Birds.) CH
(Of All the Birds That I Do Know.) NCEP; PBBP
Praise of Pindar, The. Horace, *tr. fr. Latin by* Abraham Cowley. Odes, IV, 2. OAEL-1
Praise of Poets. William Browne. Britannia's Pastorals, II, Songs 1 *and* 2. OBS
Praise of Women. Robert Mannyng. OBEV
Praise of Zeus. Aratus of Soli, *tr. fr. Greek.* ILwL
Praise Song for King Kalakaua. *Tr. fr. Hawaiian by* N. B. Emerson. WTO

Praise the good angel doubt. Praise Doubt. Mark Van Doren. EaLo
Praise the Lord. Milton. *See* Let Us with a Gladsome Mind.
Praise the Lord and Pass the Ammunition! Frank Loesser. YaD
Praise, then, to Uriel, who in unlikely places. William Force Stead. *Fr.* Uriel, IV. OxBoCh
Praise to Light. Thomas Cole. NePoAm-2
Praise to the Holiest in the height. Chorus of Angels [*or* Fifth Choir of Angelicals]. Cardinal Newman. *Fr.* The Dream of Gerontius. GoBC; NBM; NOCV; PoEL-5
Praise we the Lord/ of Heaven's kingdom. Caedmon's Hymn. Caedmon, *tr. by* Sally Purcell. EBEV
Praise ye the Lord!/ For it is good to sing praises unto our God. Who Maketh the Grass to Grow. Bible, *O.T.* *Fr.* Psalm CXLVII. FaPON
Praise ye the Lord./Praise God in His Sanctuary. Bible, *O.T.* Psalms, CL. TRV
Praise ye the Lord./Praise ye the Lord. A Song of Praise. Bible, *O.T.* Psalms, CXLVIII. TrGrPo; TrJP
Praise ye the Lord for the avenging of Israel. The Song of Deborah and Barak. Bible, *O.T.* *Fr.* Judges. AWP
Praise Ye the Lord. O Celebrate His Fame, *with music.* Peleg Folger. AH
"Praise ye the Lord!" The psalm to-day. The Thanksgiving in Boston Harbor. Hezekiah Butterworth. AA; OHIP; PAH
Praise youth's hot blood if you will, I think that happiness. Age in Prospect. Robinson Jeffers. MoAB; MoAmPo
Praised and exalted. Alabado. *Unknown.* TrAS
Praised be Diana's fair and harmless light. Diana [*or* Homage to Diana *or* The Shepherd's Praise of Diana]. Sir Walter Ralegh. OBSC; SiPS; WiR
Praised be our Lord for our brother the sun. Thanksgiving for the Earth. Elizabeth Goudge. YeAr
Praised be the name of the Lord, who created the wine. Five Arabic Verses in Praise of Wine. *Unknown, tr. by* Hartwig Hirschfeld. TrJP
Praisers of women in their proud and beautiful poems, The. "Not Marble nor the Gilded Monuments." Archibald MacLeish. AP; BoLoP; CMoP; CoBMV; HoPM; MoAB; MP; NIP; PoRA; TwCP; ViBoPo
Praises, The. Charles Olson. VGW
Praises of a Countrie Life, The. Ben Jonson, *after* Epodes, II, *by* Horace. OBVE; SeCP
Praises of God, The. *Unknown, tr. fr. Middle Irish by* Kenneth Jackson. AnIL
Praises of Henry Francis Fynn. *Zulu Oral Tradition, tr. by* T. Cope. WTO
Praises of King George VI. A. Z. Ngani, *tr. fr. Xhosa by* Jack Cope. PeSA
Praises of the King Dingana (Vesi). *Unknown, tr. fr. Zulu.* PeSA
Praises of the King of Oyo. *Yoruba Oral Tradition, tr. by* Ulli Beier. WTO
Praises of the King Tshaka. *Unknown, tr. fr. Zulu.* PeSA
Praises of the Train. Demetrius Segooa, *tr. fr. Sotho.* PeSA
Praises, Tamalpais. Song of the Turkey Buzzard. Lew Welch. PoM
Praises to those who can wait. Zealots of Yearning. David Rokeah, *tr. by* I. M. Lask. TrJP
Praising the Poets of That Country. Howard Nemerov. PP; TwAmPo
Praties, The. *Unknown.* FSW
(Famine Song.) WTO
Praxiteles and Phryne. William Wetmore Story. AA; BeLS
Pray! Irene Arnold. BLRP; STF
Pray! Amos R. Wells. STF
Pray Billy Pitt explain thy rigs. On Mr. Pitt's Hair-Powder Tax. Burns. FaBoEE
Pray but one prayer for me 'twixt thy closed lips. Summer Dawn. William Morris. FaBoEn; LoBV; NOBE; OAEL-2; OBEV; OBNC; OBVV; ViBoPo
Pray, Christian, Pray! *Unknown.* STF
Pray! for earth has many a need. Pray! Amos R. Wells. STF
Pray for my soul. More things are wrought by prayer. Prayer. Tennyson. *Fr.* Idylls of the King. WGRP
Pray for the Dead. Arthur Wentworth Hamilton Eaton. AA
Pray—Give—Go. Annie Johnson Flint. BLRP; STF
Pray how did she look? Was she pale, was she wan? On Lady Anne Hamilton. Sheridan. FaBoEE
Pray in the early morning. Pray! Irene Arnold. BLRP; STF
Pray On! ("Pray on! Our God is on His throne"). *Unknown.* STF
Pray Remember the Poor. Christopher Smart. NOEC
Pray steal me not, I'm Mrs. Dingley's. On the Collar of Mrs. Dingley's Lap-Dog. Swift. FaBoEE; FM
Pray tell your querist if he may. Charm: Corns. *Unknown.* FaBoUs
Pray thee, take care, that tak'st my book[e] in hand. To the Reader. Ben Jonson. NoP; OAEP; SeCV-1
Pray to What Earth Does This Sweet Cold Belong. Henry David Thoreau. UnPo
Pray where would lamb and lion be. Nature Be Damned. Anne Wilkinson. NOBC; OBCV
Pray who lies here? why don't you know. Original Epitaph on a Drunkard. Royall Tyler. OBAL
Pray why are you so bare, so bare. The Haunted Oak. Paul Laurence Dunbar. BANP; UnPo
Pray without Ceasing. Ophelia Guyon Browning. *See* Sometimes, Somewhere.
Prayer, A: "Angels, where you soar." Alfred Noyes. PoPl
Prayer, A: "As I lie in bed." Joseph Seamon Cotter, Jr. BANP
Prayer: "As I walk through the streets." F. S. Flint. TrPWD
Prayer: "Be not afraid to pray—to pray is right." Hartley Coleridge. TreFT
Prayer: "Bear with me, Master, when I turn from Thee." Edith Lovejoy Pierce. TrPWD
Prayer: "Bless Thou this year, O Lord!" A. S. C. Clarke. PGD
(Prayer for a Happy New Year.) BLRP
Prayer, A: "Clother of the lily, feeder of the sparrow." Christina Rossetti. OBVV
(They Toil Not neither Do They Spin.) TrPWD
Prayer: "Dear Lord and Father of mankind." Whittier. *See* Dear Lord and Father of Mankind.
Prayer, A: "Each day I walk with wonder." Clinton Scollard. TrPWD
Prayer, A: "Eternal God, our life is but." "Yehoash," *tr. fr. Yiddish by* Isidore Goldstick. TrJP
Prayer, A: "Father in Heaven! from whom the simplest flower." Felicia Dorothea Hemans. TrPWD
Prayer, A: "Father, we thank Thee for the night." *Unknown.* SoPo
Prayer: "Fear of death disturbs me constantly, The." Gabrielle de Coignard, *tr. fr. French by* Raymond Oliver. WPOW
Prayer: "Forgive me, you whom they cast in a name." Avraham Shlonsky, *tr. fr. Hebrew by* Francis Landy. VWA
Prayer, A: "From falsehood and error." Digby Mackworth Dolben. GoBC
Prayer: "From your high bridge wave & wail." Lev Mak, *tr. fr. Russian by* Dan Jaffe. VWA
Prayer: "Give me a death like Buddha's, let me fall." Stanley Moss. GP; POL
Prayer, A: "Give me work to do." *Unknown.* PGD
Prayer, A: "Give us a good digestion, Lord." Thomas H. B. Webb. *See* Ancient Prayer, A.
Prayer: "God, although this life is but a wraith." Louis Untermeyer. *See* Prayer: "God, though this life . . ."
Prayer, A: "God, give me sympathy and sense." Margaret Bailey. TRV
Prayer, A: "God, is it sinful if I feel." Mary Dixon Thayer. HBMV; TrPWD
Prayer: "God, listen through my words to the beating of my heart." Marguerite Harmon Bro. TrPWD
Prayer: "God of light and blossom." James P. Mousley. GoYe
Prayer: "God, though [*or* although] this life is but a wraith." Louis Untermeyer. MoAmPo; TrJP; WGRP
Prayer, A: "Great Giver of the open hand." *Unknown, tr. Old Irish by* Eleanor Hull. OnYI
Prayer: "Have pity on us, Power just and severe." John Hall Wheelock, *after* St. Theresa of Avila. EaLo; NePoAm
Prayer: "I ask good things that I detest." Robert Louis Stevenson. TrPWD
Prayer: "I ask you this." Langston Hughes. CDC; EaLo
Prayer: "I had thought of putting an/ altar." Isabella M. Brown. NNP; PoNe
Prayer: "I kneel not now to pray that Thou." Harry Kemp. HBV-2; WGRP
Prayer: "I know not by what methods rare." Eliza M. Hickock. *See* This I Know.
Prayer: "I lie down with God." *Unknown, tr. by* Eleanor Hull. OnYI
Prayer, A: "I pray not for the joy that knows." Marion Franklin Ham. TrPWD
Prayer, A: "I pray Thee O Lord." Juljan Tuwim, *tr. fr. Polish by* Wanda Dynowska. TrJP
Prayer: "I rest with Thee, O Jesus." *Unknown, tr. by* Eleanor Hull. OnYI
Prayer, A: "If I dare pray for one." Vernon Watkins. PoPl
Prayer: "If I must of my senses lose." Theodore Roethke. MP; TwCP
Prayer: "If, when I kneel to pray." Charles Francis Richardson. AA
Prayer: "In the bright bay of your morning, O God." Claire Goll, *tr. fr. German by* Babette Deutsch *and* Avram Yarmolinsky. TrJP
Prayer, A: "It is my joy in life to find." Frank Dempster Sherman. TreFS
Prayer, A: "Jesus, Thy life is mine!" *Unknown.* STF
Prayer: "Keep me from fretting, Lord, today." May Carleton Lord. PGD
Prayer, A: "Let me do my work each day." Max Ehrmann. BLPA; BLPL; FaBoBe
Prayer: "Let me not know how sins and sorrows glide." James Elroy Flecker. TrPWD
Prayer, A: "Let me work and be glad." Theodosia Garrison. TrPWD
Prayer: "Let us not look upon." Witter Bynner. EaLo
Prayer: "Lo, here a little volume, but great book!" Richard Crashaw. HBV-2
(Ode Which Was Prefixed to a Prayer Booke Given to a Young Gentlewoman, An.) AnAnS-1

Prayer: "Lord, as thou wilt, bestow." Eduard Mörike, *tr. fr. German by* John Drinkwater. TrPWD
Prayer, A: "Lord, for the erring thought." William Dean Howells. *See* Thanksgiving, A.
Prayer: "Lord God of the oak and the elm." George Villiers, Duke of Buckingham. TrPWD
Prayer: "Lord I am not entirely selfish." Gavin Ewart. OxBC
Prayer, A: "Lord, let me live like a Regular Man." Berton Braley. BLPA
Prayer: "Lord, make me sensitive to the sight." Barbara Marr. TrPWD
Prayer, A: "Lord, make my childish soul stand straight." William Laird. HBMV
Prayer, A: "Lord, not for light in darkness do we pray." John Drinkwater. HBV-2; OBVV; TrPWD; WGRP
Prayer: "Lord, the newness of this day." Henry van Dyke. TRV
Prayer: "Lord, what a change within us one short hour." Richard Chenevix Trench. TRV; WBLP; WGRP
(Prevailing Prayer.) BLRP
(Sonnet.) TrPWD
Prayer: "Master, they say that when I seem." C. S. Lewis. TrCP
Prayer: "Matthew, Mark, Luke, and John." *Unknown. See* Before Sleeping.
Prayer: "More things are wrought by prayer." Tennyson. *Fr.* Morte d'Arthur. BLRP; TreF
Prayer, A: "My God (oh, let me call Thee mine)." Anne Brontë. TrPWD
Prayer, A: "Now wilt me take for Jesus' sake." Katharine Tynan. OBVV
Prayer, A: "O Earth, O dewy mother, breathe on us." Archibald Lampman. TrPWD
Prayer, A: "O for one minute hark what we are saying!" Frederic W. H. Myers. TrPWD
Prayer: "O God of earth and altar." G. K. Chesterton. *See* Hymn, A: "O God of earth and altar."
Prayer: "O God of goodness, forwardness, and fulness." Doris Hedges. GoYe
Prayer, A: "O God, our Father, if we had but truth!" Edward Rowland Sill. AA
Prayer, The: "O living will that share endure." Tennyson. *See* In Memoriam, CXXXI: "O living will."
Prayer, A: "O Lord, the hard-won miles." Paul Laurence Dunbar. TrPWD
Prayer, A: "O Love, give me a passionate heart." Irene Rutherford McLeod. TrPWD
Prayer, A: "O mighty God, Which for us men." Humphrey Gifford. OxBoCh
Prayer, A: "Often the western wind has sung to me." Alfred Bruce Douglas. TrPWD
Prayer: "Oh! that mine eye might closed be." Thomas Ellwood. WGRP
Prayer: "Omnipotent confederate of all good." Amos N. Wilder. TrPWD
Prayer, A: "Out of the deeps I cry to thee, O God!" Richard Le Gallienne. TrPWD
Prayer: "Pray for my soul. More things are wrought by prayer." Tennyson. *Fr.* Idylls of the King. WGRP
Prayer: "Prayer must be grounded on the Word." *Unknown.* STF
Prayer: "Prayer the church's [*or* churches] banquet, angels' age." George Herbert. AnAnS-1; BLPL; CABA; DTC; EBEV; ELP; InPS; JCP; MePo; NOBE; NoP; OAEL-1; OBS; OxBoCh; PoEL-2; SeCV-1; TRV
Prayer, A: "Searcher of souls, you who in heaven abide." Samuel Butler. FaBoEE
Prayer: "She cannot tell my name." Edward Bliss Reed. HBMV
Prayer: "Take from the earth its tragic hunger, Lord." Hazel J. Fowler. TrPWD
Prayer, A: "Teach me, Father, how to go." Edwin Markham. HBMV; HBVY; PGD; TrPWD; TRV; WGRP
Prayer, A: "Tend me my birds, and bring again." Norman Gale. TrPWD
Prayer: "These are the gifts I ask of thee." Henry van Dyke. *See* These Are the Gifts I Ask.
Prayer: "This evening, our Father." *Unknown.* OuSiCo
Prayer, A: "Those who love Thee may they find." George F. Chawner. BLRP
Prayer: "Three folds of cloth." *Unknown, tr. by* Eleanor Hull. OnYI
Prayer, A: "Through every minute of this day." John Oxenham. BLRP; TRV
Prayer: "Thy blessing on the boys—for time has come." Haim Guri, *tr. fr. Hebrew by* Ruth H. Lask. TrJP
Prayer, A: "To Thy continual Presence, in me wrought." William Ellery Channing. TrPWD
Prayer, A: "Until I lose my soul and lie." Sara Teasdale. HBMV; TrPWD
Prayer: "What a commanding power." Thomas Washbourne. WGRP
Prayer, A: "What weight of ancient witness can prevail." Dryden. *See* Private Judgment Condemned.
Prayer, A: "When I look back upon my life nigh spent." George Macdonald. TrPWD
Prayer: "Where then shall Hope and Fear their objects find?" Samuel Johnson. *See* Power of Prayer, The.
Prayer, The: "Wilt Thou not visit me?" Jones Very. EBCP; OxBA; TrCP; TrPWD
Prayer: "Your golden loins slake my lust for treasures." Mike Newell. AMV-80
Prayer after Illness, A. Violet Alleyn Storey. TrPWD
Prayer after World War. Carl Sandburg. VGW
Prayer against Indifference. Joy Davidman. TrPWD
Prayer—Answer. Ednah D. Cheney. *See* Larger Prayer, The.
Prayer Answered. *Unknown. See* Prayer of an Unknown Confederate Soldier.
Prayer at Dawn. Diarmuid O'Shea, *tr. fr. Irish by* Frank O'Connor. KiLC
Prayer at Dawn. Edwin McNeill Poteat. TrPWD
Prayer before Birth. Louis MacNeice. GTBS-P; LiTB; MP; NAs; OAEP; TwCP
Prayer before Execution. Mary Queen of Scots, *tr. fr. Latin by* John Fawcett. WGRP
(Prayer before Her Execution.) TRV
Prayer before Meat. Una W. Harsen. TrPWD
Prayer before Sleep. Alice Lucas. TrJP
Prayer before Study. Theodore Roethke. TrPWD
Prayer before Work. May Sarton. SaC
Prayer Brings Rain, A. Tasso, *tr. fr. Italian by* Edward Fairfax. *Fr.* Godfrey of Bulloigne. OBSC
Prayer by Moonlight. Roberta Teale Swartz. TrPWD
Prayer during Battle. Hermann Hagedorn. TrPWD
Prayer for a Happy New Year, A. A. S. C. Clarke. *See* Prayer: "Bless Thou this year, O Lord!"
Prayer for a Little Home, A. Florence Bone. BLPA; FaBoBe; FaFP
(Prayer for a Little House). TreFT
Prayer for a Marriage, A. Mary Carolyn Davies. TrPWD
Prayer for a New House. Louis Untermeyer. *See* Prayer for This House.
Prayer for a [*or* the] Pilot. Cecil Roberts. FaPON; TrPWD
Prayer for a Play House. Elinor Lennen. TrPWD
Prayer for a Preacher, A. Edward Shillito. TrPWD
Prayer for a Second Flood, A. "Hugh MacDiarmid." EBEV
Prayer for a Sleeping Child, A. Mary Carolyn Davies. OHIP
Prayer for a Very New Angel. Violet Alleyn Storey. BLPA; TreFS
Prayer for All Poets at This Time. Irwin Edman. TrPWD
Prayer for Charity, A. Edwin O. Kennedy. TrPWD
Prayer for Contentment. Edwin McNeill Poteat. TrPWD
Prayer for Dew. Eleazar ben Kalir, *tr. fr. Hebrew by* Israel Zangwill. TrJP
Prayer for Dreadful Morning. E. Merrill Root. TrPWD
Prayer for Every Day, A. Mary Carolyn Davies. BLPA; FaBoBe
Prayer for Every Day. *Unknown, tr. fr. Fanti by* Kweku Martin. PBA
Prayer for Faith, A. Michelangelo, *tr. fr. Italian by* John Addington Symonds. ILwL
Prayer for Faith, A. Alfred Norris. BLRP
Prayer for Fine Weather. Shane Leslie. POL
Prayer for Fish. Ronald Wallace. AMV-80
Prayer for Forbearance. *Unknown.* LoBV
Prayer for Good Dreams. *Unknown.* OxBM
Prayer for Indifference, A. Fanny Greville. LoBV; NOEC; OBEC
"I ask no kind return of love," *sel.* LO; OBEV
Prayer for Kafka and Ourselves. Anthony Rudolf. VWA
Prayer for Light. Stanton A. Coblentz. TrPWD
Prayer for Living and Dying. Christopher La Farge. TrPWD
Prayer for Messiah. Leonard Cohen. OBCV
Prayer for My Daughter, A. W. B. Yeats. BLPL; CABA; CMoP; CoBMV; HAP; LiTB; LiTM; LoBV; MasP; MoAB; NAs; NoAM; NoP; OxBTC; PoA; PoLF; PoRA; PrIm; TEP
"I have walked and prayed for this young child an hour," *sel.* ViBoPo
Prayer for My Son, A. Yvor Winters. CrMA; TrPWD
Prayer for My Son, A. W. B. Yeats. EBEV; NAs
Prayer for Neighborhood Evangelism. Annette Jansen. STF
Prayer for Pain. John G. Neihardt. HBV-2; TrPWD; WGRP
Prayer for Peace. Johnstone G. Patrick. TrPWD
Prayer for Peace, A. Edward Rowland Sill. TrPWD
Prayer for Peace: II. Léopold Sédar Senghor, *tr. fr. French by* John Reed *and* Clive Wake. TTY
Prayer for Pentecost, A. Catherine Bernard Brown. BLRP
Prayer for Purification, A. Michelangelo, *tr. fr. Italian by* John Addington Symonds. AWP
Prayer for Rain. Sheikh Aquib Abdullahi Jama, *tr. fr. Somali by* B. W. Andrzejewski. WTO
Prayer for Rain. *Unknown, tr. fr. Finnish.* WGRP
Prayer for Recollection, A. *Unknown, tr. fr. Irish by* Frank O'Connor. KiLC
Prayer for Redemption. *Unknown.* TrJP
Prayer for Reptiles. Patricia Hubbell. PDV
Prayer for Serenity. Reinhold Niebuhr. TreFT
Prayer for Song. Fay Lewis Noble. TrPWD
Prayer for Strength. Samuel Johnson. *See* Father, in Thy Mysterious Presence Kneeling.

Prayer for Thanksgiving, A. Joseph Auslander. TrPWD
Prayer for the Age. Myron H. Broomell. TrPWD
Prayer for the Dead. Tennyson. *Fr.* Morte d'Arthur. GoBC
("Old order changeth, yielding place to new.") TRV
Prayer for the Great Family. Gary Snyder. HAP; OFD
Prayer for the Home, *sel.* Edgar A. Guest.
"Lord, this humble house we'd keep." TRV
Prayer for the Household, A. Robert Louis Stevenson. TRV
Prayer for the Journey. *Unknown.* OxBM
Prayer for the Little Daughter between Death and Burial. Diana Scott. BrRo
Prayer for the New Year, A. Violet Alleyn Storey. TrPWD
Prayer for the New Year, A. *Unknown.* BLRP
Prayer for the Old Courage, A. Charles Hanson Towne. TrPWD
Prayer for the Pilot. Cecil Roberts. Prayer for a Pilot.
Prayer for the Self, A. John Berryman. Eleven Addresses to the Lord, VIII. PPP
Prayer for the Speedy End of Three Great Misfortunes. *Unknown, tr. fr. Irish by* Frank O'Connor. DTC; OBMV
Prayer for the Useless Days. Edith Lovejoy Pierce. TrPWD
Prayer for This Day. Hildegarde Flanner. TrPWD
Prayer for This House. Louis Untermeyer. BLPL; FaPON; PoLF
(Prayer for a New House.) TrPWD
Prayer Found in Chester Cathedral, A. Thomas H. B. Webb. *See* Ancient Prayer, An.
Prayer from 1936, A. Siegfried Sassoon. TrPWD
Prayer in a Country Church. Ruth B. Van Dusen. TrPWD
Prayer in Affliction. Violet Alleyn Storey. TrPWD
Prayer in April. Sara Henderson Hay. TrPWD
Prayer in Darkness, A. G. K. Chesterton. FPL; MoBrPo; PoLF; TrGrPo
Prayer in Late Autumn, A. Violet Alleyn Storey. TrPWD
Prayer in Mid-Passage. Louis MacNeice. EaLo
Prayer in Spring, A. Robert Frost. TrCP; TrPWD; YeAr
(Oh, Give Us Pleasure in the Flowers Today, *with music.*) AH
Prayer in the Prospect of Death, A. Burns. HBV-2; TrPWD; WGRP
Prayer in Time of Blindness, A. Clement Wood. TrPWD
Prayer in Time of War. Henry Treece. WaP
Prayer is the soul's sincere desire. What Is Prayer? James Montgomery, *also at. to* ——— Robertson. BLRP; STF; TRV; WGRP
Prayer, Living and Dying, A. Augustus Montague Toplady. *See* Rock of Ages.
Prayer Moves the Hand That Moves the World. *At. to* John A. Wallace. *See* God the Omniscient.
Prayer must be grounded on the Word. Prayer. *Unknown.* STF
Prayer of a Beginning Teacher. Ouida Smith Dunnam. TrPWD
Prayer of a Little Hope. Jean Wahl, *tr. fr. French by* Charles Guenther. VWA
Prayer of a Modern Thomas. Edward Shillito. PGD
Prayer of a Soldier in France. Joyce Kilmer. GoBC
Prayer of a Teacher. Dorothy Littlewort. TrPWD
Prayer of an Unbeliever. Lizette Woodworth Reese. TrPWD
Prayer of an Unknown Confederate Soldier. *Unknown.* TreFT
(Prayer Answered.) STF
Prayer of Beaten Men, The. William Hervey Woods. *Fr.* The House of Broken Swords. HBV-2
Prayer of Columbus. Walt Whitman. AmPP; WGRP
Sels.
"All my emprises have been fill'd with Thee." TRV
"One effort more, my altar this bleak sand." PGD
"Thou knowest my years entire, my life." TrPWD
Prayer of St. Francis of Assisi for Peace. St. Francis of Assisi. *See* Lord, Make Me an Instrument of Your Peace.
Prayer of St. Francis Xavier. Pope. TrPWD
Prayer of Thanksgiving, *with music. Unknown, tr. fr. Dutch by* Theodore Baker. BLSo
Prayer of the Cat, The. Carmen Bernos de Gasztold. PDV
Prayer of the Donkey, The. Carmen Bernos de Gasztold, *tr. fr. French by* Rumer Godden. PChr
Prayer of the Fishing Net. *Tr. fr. Hawaiian by* N. B. Emerson. WTO
Prayer of the Goldfish, The. Carmen Bernos de Gasztold. PDV
Prayer of the Little Ducks, The. Carmen Bernos de Gasztold. PDV
Prayer of the Maidens to Mary. Rainer Maria Rilke, *tr. fr. German by* Jethro Bithell. AWP
Prayer of the Mouse, The. Carmen Bernos de Gasztold. PDV
Prayer of the Old Horse, The. Carmen Bernos de Gasztold. PDV
Prayer of the Old Woman. Villon, *tr. fr. French by* J. M. Synge. MoBrPo
Prayer of the Peoples, A. Percy MacKaye. WGRP
"God of us who kill our kind!" *sel.* TrPWD
Prayer of the Young Stoic. Stephen P. Dunn. TrPWD
Prayer on Fourth of July. Nancy Byrd Turner. YeAr
Prayer on Making a Canoe. *Tr. fr. Hawaiian by* N. B. Emerson. WTO
Prayer-Poem, A. Mary S. Edgar. *See* Camp Hymn, The.
Prayer Rug, The. Sara Beaumont Kennedy. HBMV
Prayer, the church's [*or* churches] banquet, angels' age. Prayer. George Herbert. AnAnS-1; BLPL; CABA; DTC; EBEV; ELP; InPS; JCP; MePo; NOBE; NoP; OAEL-1; OBS; OxBoCh; PoEL-2; SeCV-1; TRV
Prayer to Be Said When Thou Goest to Bed, A. Francis Seager. OxBChV
Prayer to Escape from the Market Place, A. James Wright. NaP
Prayer to Go to Paradise with the Asses. Francis Jammes, *tr. fr. French by* Jethro Bithell. AWP
(Prayer to Go to Paradise with the Donkeys, A, *tr. by* Richard Wilbur.) EaLo
Prayer to God. "Placido," *tr. fr. Spanish by* Raoul Abdul. TTY
Prayer to Hermes. Robert Creeley. PoM
Prayer to Isis. Christina Walsh. BrRo
Prayer to Peace. Euripides, *tr. fr. Greek by* Moses Hadas. PoPl
Prayer to St. Helena. *Unknown.* OxBM
Prayer to St. Patrick. Ninine, *tr. fr. Old Irish by* Whitley Stokes *and* John Strachan. OnYI
Prayer to the Father of [*or* in] Heaven, A. John Skelton. HoPM; TrPWD
Prayer to the God Thot. *Unknown, tr. fr. Egyptian by* Ulli Beier. TTY
Prayer to the Holy Trinity, A. Richard Stanyhurst. PoEL-2
(Prayer to the Trinity, A.) ElL
(To the Trinity.) OxBoCh
Prayer to the Hunting Star, Canopus. *Unknown, tr. fr. Bushman by* W. H. I. Bleek *and* Jack Cope. PeSA
Prayer to the Lord Ramakrishna, A. James Wright. NNaP
Prayer to the Mountain Spirit. Mary Austin, *after Navajo Indian, tr. wr. at. to* G. W. Cronyn. BPAW; WGRP
Prayer to the Pacific. Leslie Silko. CDW; NoP; VoR
Prayer to the Sacrament of the Altar, A. *Unknown.* MeEL
Prayer to the Snowy Owl. John Haines. BoAnP
Prayer to the Trinity. James Edmeston. HBV-2
Prayer to the Trinity, A. Richard Stanyhurst. *See* Prayer to the Holy Trinity, A.
Prayer to the Trinity, A. *Unknown.* MeEL
Prayer to the Virgin. *Unknown, tr. fr. Middle Irish by* John Strachan *and* Kuno Meyer. OnYI
Prayer to the Virgin of Chartres. Henry Adams. GoBC; ISi
Prayer to the Wind, A. Thomas Carew. AnAnS-2
Prayer to the Young Moon. *Unknown, tr. fr. Bushman by* W. H. I. Bleek *and* Jack Cope. PeSA
Prayer to Venus. Spenser. *See* Address to Venus.
Prayer under the Pressure of Violent Anguish. Burns. TrPWD
Prayer unsaid, and Mass unsung. The Sea Ritual [*or* Deadman's Dirge]. George Darley. Syren Songs, V. BIrV; CH; OBNC; OBRV; OnYI; OxBI; WiR; WSC
Prayer unto Christ the Judge of the World, A. Michael Wigglesworth. SCAP
Prayerbooks return to Jerusalem. A Late Manuscript at the Schocken Institute. Gabriel Preil, *tr. by* Gabriel Levin. VWA
Prayers. Henry Charles Beeching. OBEV; OBVV
(Boy's Prayer, A.) GN
Prayers, The. Howard Schwartz. VWA
Prayers I make will then be sweet indeed, The. For Inspiration [*or* To the Supreme Being]. Michelangelo, *tr. by* Wordsworth. AWP; GoBC; TrPWD; TRV; WGRP
Prayers Must Have Poise. Robert Herrick. LiTB
Prayers of Steel. Carl Sandburg. AP; CMoP; FaPON; MoAmPo; PDV; TrCP; TrPWD; YaD
Prayers to Liberty. Anwar Shaul, *tr. fr. Arabic by* Yoffee Berkovitz. VWA
Prayerwheel: 2. David Meltzer. NeAP
Praying Mantis. Mary Ann Hoberman. RHPC
Praying Mantis, The. Ogden Nash. PV
Praying mantis doesn't pray, The. Mantis. David McCord. OBAL
Praying Mantis Visits a Penthouse, The ("The praying mantis with its length of straw"). Oscar Williams. FaFP; LiTM; NePA
Pre Domina. Jean Lipkin. PeSA
Preach wisdom unto him who understands! Che Sara Sara. Victor Plarr. HBV-1
Preacher, The. Al-Mahdi, *tr. fr. Arabic by* A. J. Arberry. TTY
Preacher and the Slave, The. *Unknown, at. to* Joe Hill. AS, *with music;* FSW; PPON; TrAS, *with music;* WTO
(Pie in the Sky.) GBP
Preacher does better, The. Stand By. *Unknown.* STF
Preacher Sought to Find Out Acceptable Words, The. Richard Eberhart. WaP
Preacher works from morn till night, The. Soft Job. William C. Summers. STF
Preachers, The. Norman Nicholson. NeBP
Preacher's Mistake, The. William Croswell Doane. BLPA
Preacher's Prayer, The. George Macdonald. TRV
Preacher's Prayer, A. *Unknown.* STF
Preacher's Vacation, The. *Unknown.* BLPA; BLPL

Preacher's Wife, The. *Unknown.* STF
Preachin' the Blues. *Unknown.* BluL
Preaching Blues. *Unknown.* BluL
Preachment for Preachers. Alexander Barclay. *Fr.* The Ship of Fools. ACP
Pre-admonisheth the writer. The Flight of the Bucket. Kipling. BXAP
Precambrian [*or* Pre-Cambrian] Shield, The. E. J. Pratt. *Fr.* Towards the Last Spike. MoCV; NOBC; OBCV
Precarious Ground. Leah Bodine Drake. GoYe
Precaution. Heine, *tr. fr. German by* Louis Untermeyer. UnTE
Precede me into this elusive country. The Caravan. Gwendolyn MacEwen. MoCV
Precept, imperfect mudra. On a Summer Day, 1972. Calvin Murry. LFAC
Precept of Silence, The. Lionel Johnson. HBV-2; MoBrPo; ViBoPo; VLP
Precepts He Gave His Folk. Elijah ben Menahem Hazaken of Le Mans, *tr. fr. Hebrew by* Israel Zangwill. TrJP
Precious Blood, The. *Unknown.* STF
Precious Child, So Sweetly Sleeping, *with music.* Anna Hoppe. AH
Precious in the Sight of the Lord. *Unknown.* BLRP
Precious Moments. Carl Sandburg. MoAmPo
Precious night-blooming cereus. Remembering Fannie Lou Hamer. Thadious M. Davis. BlSi
Precious, oh, how precious is that blessed sleep. Precious in the Sight of the Lord. *Unknown.* BLRP
"Precious!" says Mrs. Goog. And, "Love!" cries he. The Googs. Don Marquis. *Fr.* Savage Portraits. HBMV
Precious Stones. Charles Stuart Calverley. InMe
Precious Things. *Unknown.* TTY
Precious thought, my Father knoweth. God Knoweth Best [*or* Your Father Knoweth]. *Unknown.* BLRP; WBLP
Precious to me—she still shall be. Emily Dickinson. PeHV
Precise counterpart, The. The Orchestra. William Carlos Williams. HAP
Precisely down invisible threads these oak leaves. October Elegy. Margaret Gibson. FYAP
Precision, The. Yvor Winters. EAS
Precocious, impulsive young Mr., A. Nothing More than a Sister. *Unknown.* TDH
Predestination. Maurice Evan Hare. *See* Limerick: "There once was a man who said, 'Damn.' "
Predestination. Kipling. *See* By the Hoof of the Wild Goat.
Predestination. *Unknown.* DBV
Predestination and Free Will. Dryden. *Fr.* The State of Innocence. NOCV
Predicament: a corner of/ a room. Tenant at Number 9. John Blight. CBAP
Predicter of Famine, The. William Carlos Williams. VGW
Prediction, The. Mark Strand. EAS; LCAP
Preest ne monk ne yet canoun. Against Friars. *Unknown.* OxBM
Preëxistence. Frances Cornford. HBMV
Pre-Existence. Paul Hamilton Hayne. HBV-2
Preface: "Aged catch their breath, The." W. H. Auden. *Fr.* .The Sea and the Mirror. LiTA
Preface: "And did those feet in ancient time." Blake. *See* And Did Those Feet in Ancient Time.
Preface, The: "Infinity, when all things it beheld." Edward Taylor. *Fr.* Gods Determinations Touching His Elect. AmPP; AP; HAP; NOBA; OxBA; SCAP
Preface: "Mother, don't read/ my poems." Carol Shauger. AMV-80
Preface: " 'Sonja Henie,' the young girl." Theodore Weiss. NMP; VGW
Preface: "To make a start." William Carlos Williams. *Fr.* Paterson: Book One. AP; CMoP; CoBMV; NoAM; NOBA
Preface to a Twenty Volume Suicide Note. Amiri Baraka. AmNP; CABA; CAPP; InPK; InPS; NNP; PoBA; PoM; PoNe; PPP; TTY
Preface to the Memoirs, A. James Merrill. NOBA
Prefatory Poem, on . . . Magnalia Christi Americana, A. Nicholas Noyes. SCAP
Prefatory Sonnet: "Nuns fret not at their convent's narrow room." Wordsworth. *See* Nuns Fret Not at Their Convent's Narrow Room.
Prefer the cherry when the fruit hangs thick. Under the Boughs. Gene Baro. BoNaP
Preference. Langston Hughes. NOBA
Preference. Daniel Sargent. ISi
Preference Declared, The ("Persicos odi"). Horace. *See* Fie on Eastern Luxury!
Preferring "resemblance to beauty." An Esthetic of Imitation. Donald Finkel. NePoEA
Pregnancy. Sandra McPherson. BoWoP; NMM
Pregnant girl, under sorrow's sign, A. Under Sorrow's Sign. Gofraidh Fionn O'Dalaigh, *tr. by* John Montague. BIrV
Pregnant Image of "Exaggerating the Village." Nora Dauenhauer. TWSS
Pregnant Teenager on the Beach. Mary Balazs. AMV-80
Pregnant Woman. Ingrid Jonker, *tr. fr. Afrikaans by* Jack Cope *and* Uys Krige. PeSA
Prehistoric Burials. Siegfried Sassoon. MoBrPo
Pre-History Repeats. Robert J. McKent, Jr. QQQ
Prehtys whilom dwelled in oure citee, A. The Cook's Tale. Chaucer. *Fr.* The Canterbury Tales. BXAP
Preiching of the Swallow, The. Robert Henryson. OxBS
Prejudice. Georgia Douglas Johnson. AmNP; PoBA
Prejudice against the Past. Wallace Stevens. LiTM
Prelates, The. John Skelton. *Fr.* Colin Clout. TrGrPo
Preliminary Poem. John Heath-Stubbs. OxBC
Preliminary to Classroom Lecture. Josephine Miles. NoAM
Prelude, The [or, Growth of a Poet's Mind], *much abr.* Wordsworth. EnRP; OAEL-2; OAEP
Sels.
Books, *fr.* V. PoEL-4
"Gracious Spirit o'er this earth presides, A." OBRV
"On poetry and geometric truth." SyP
There Was a Boy. ChER; FaBoCh; FaBoEn; FaBoRV; OBNC; OBRV; PoEL-4
(Winander Lake.) FiP
"Twilight was coming on, yet through the gloom." SyP
Cambridge and the Alps, *fr.* VI. PoEL-4
"Brook and road, The/ Were fellow-travellers." OBRV
Imagination. FiP
Simplon Pass, The. SyP
(Alpine Descent.) WHA
"Single Tree, A/ There was," *Oxford ed.* OBRV
" 'Tis told by one whom stormy waters threw." ImOP
Childhood and School-Time, *fr.* I. FaBoEn; NOBE; NoP; OBNC; OBRV
"Dust as we are, the immortal spirit grows." SCV
"Fair seed-time had my soul, and I grew up." HAP; NoP; OBRV
(Introduction—Childhood and School-Time.) PoEL-4
(On the Solitary Fells around Hawkshead.) FaBoPP
In Patterdale. FaBoRV
"Moon was up, the lake was shining clear, The." FaBoEn
Oh There Is Blessing in This Gentle Breeze. TreFT
On Ullswater. FaBoPP
On Windermere; Bowness Bay and Belle Isle. FaBoPP
"One summer evening (led by her) I found." NU; ViBoPo
("One evening [surely I was led by her]," *Oxford ed.*) OBRV
(One Summer Evening.) FiP
"Poet, gentle creature as he is, The." PP
Skating. CH; GN
(On the Frozen Lake.) FaBoCh
(Skaters, The.) LiSp
"Wisdom and Spirit of the universe!" NOBE
(Boyhood.) WHA
(Influence of Natural Objects.) AWP; LoBV; OBRV
Wordsworth Skates on Esthwaite Water. FaBoPP
Conclusion, XIV [XIII].
Conclusion: "It was a summer's night, a close warm night." FaBoEn; OBNC; PoEL-4
"In one of these excursions, travelling then/ Through Wales on foot." EBEV
(Climb to Snowdon, The.) FaBoRV
(Snowdon Sunrise, The.) FaBoPP
"Oh! yet a few short years of useful life." OBRV
France, XI [X, *conclusion*].
"O pleasant exercise of hope and joy!" HAP; OBRV
(French Revolution, The.) FiP
(Residence in France [Continued].) PoEL-4
To Coleridge in Sicily. OBNC
Imagination and Taste, How Impaired and Restored, XII *and* XIII [XI *and* XII]. PoEL-4, XII, *abr.*
Imagination, How Impaired and Restored, *fr.* XII *and* XIII. OBNC
Oh! Mystery of Man, *fr.* XII. FiP
Residence at Cambridge, *fr.* III. FaBoPP
"Beside the pleasant mills of Trompington." OBRV
"Caverns there were within my mind, which sun." FaBoPP
"Evangelist St. John my patron was, The." HAP
(Newton's Statue.) FaBoRV
Newton. ImOP
Residence in France, IX.
"Among the band of Officers was one," *Oxford ed., incl.* Vaudracour and Julia. ChER
"To a lodge that stood," *fr.* Vaudracour and Julia. EvOK
Noble, The, 3 *ll.* ChTr
Residence in France, *fr.* X. PoEL-4
"In France, the men who for their desperate ends." OBRV
Residence in London, *fr.* VII. PoEL-4
"As the black storm upon the mountain top." HAP

Fair below Helvellyn, The. FaBoPP
"From these sights/ Take one,—that ancient festival, the Fair." HAP
"Rise up, thou monstrous ant-hill on the plain." HAP
Young Wordsworth's London, The. FaBoPP
Retrospect—Love of Nature Leading to Love of Mankind, VIII.
Shepherd, The. OBNC
School-Time, II.
"For I would walk alone." OBRV
Intimations of Sublimity. OBNC
"Our steeds remounted and the summons given." SyP
Summer Vacation, *fr.* IV. PoEL-4
Consummate Happiness. OBNC
Dedicated Spirit, A. SeCePo
"Favourite pleasure hath it been with me, A," *Oxford ed.* OBRV
"He was of stature tall." SyP
"In a throng/ A festal company of maids and youths." EBEV; OBRV
"When first I made/ Once more the circuit of our little Lake." OBRV
Prelude: "Afterwards, afterwards the wind between two mountains." David Rosenmann-Taub, *tr. fr. Spanish by* Charles Guenther. VWA
Prelude: "Along the roadside, like the flowers of gold." Whittier. *Fr.* Among the Hills. AP; OxBA; PoEL-4
Prelude: "And did those feet in ancient time." Blake. *See* And Did Those Feet in Ancient Time.
Prelude: "As one, at midnight, wakened by the call." W. W. Gibson. MoBrPo
Prelude: "England! awake! awake! awake!" Blake. *See* England! Awake! Awake! Awake!
Prelude: "Fields from Islington to Marybone, The." Blake. *Fr.* Jerusalem, II. OBNC
Prelude: "Give us another poem, he said." Patrick Kavanagh. IPY; NoAM
Prelude: "Grace comes only after the long study of choice." Traise Yamamoto. BrSi
Prelude: "How could I love you more?" Richard Aldington. BrPo
Prelude: "Hush'd is each busy shout." A. C. Benson. OBVV
Prelude: "I am the bird of the wayside." Christine Ama Ata Aidoo. PBWP
Prelude: "I saw the constellated matin choir." Edmund Clarence Stedman. AA
Prelude: "In desultory walk through orchard grounds." Wordsworth. *Fr.* Poems Chiefly of Early and Late Years. VLP
Prelude: "Lake loon paddles, A." Rokwaho. STE
Prelude: "Night and the hood." Conrad Kent Rivers. PoBA
Prelude: "Night was dark, though sometimes a faint star, The." Richard Watson Gilder. *Fr.* The New Day. HBV-1; PoLF
Prelude: "Rimbaud and Verlaine, precious pair of poets." Conrad Aiken. *See* Rimbaud and Verlaine . . .
Prelude, A: "Spirit that moves the sap in spring." Maurice Thompson. HBV-2
Prelude: "Still south I went and west and south again." J. M. Synge. AWP; BoNaP; ChTr; FaBoPP; HBMV; MoBrPo; OBMV
Prelude: "This is not you? These phrases are not you?" Conrad Aiken. Preludes for Memnon, VI. MOAB; MoAmPo
Prelude: "This is the forest primeval." Longfellow. *Fr.* Evangeline. TreF
(Primeval Forest, The.) WBLP, *abr.*
("This is the forest primeval.") SpRo
Prelude: Troops, The. Siegfried Sassoon. *See* Troops, The.
Prelude XXIII: "We are those same children who amazed." Stefan George, *tr. fr. German by* C. F. MacIntyre. WaaP
Prelude: "What makes a plenteous harvest." Virgil, *tr. fr. Latin by* Dryden. *Fr.* The Georgics. AWP
Prelude XXIX: "What shall we do—what shall we think—what shall we say?" Conrad Aiken. *Fr.* Preludes for Memnon. FaBoMo
Prelude: "Winter evening settles down, The." T. S. Eliot. *See* Preludes (I-V).
Prelude: "Woman, Woman, let us say these things to each other." Conrad Aiken. NYBP
Prelude: "You went to the verge, you say, and come back safely?" Conrad Aiken. Preludes for Memnon, XIV. FaBoMo; TwCP
("You went to the verge, you say, and came back safely?") LiTA; TwAmPo
Prelude to Akwasidae. *Unknown, tr. fr. Twi by* Halim El-Dabh. TTY
Prelude to an Evening. John Crowe Ransom. AP; CoBMV; EAS; MoAB; MoAmPo; MoPo; MoVE; NePA; OxBA; PoCh
Prelude to Commencement. Marie de L. Welch. NYBP
Prelude to "Departmental Ditties." Kipling. VLP
Prelude to Memorial Song: 100 Years Later. Phillip William George. VoR
Prelude to "Songs before Sunrise." Swinburne. VLP
Prelude to this smooth scene—mark well!, The. After Jena. Thomas Hardy. *Fr.* The Dynasts. WaaP
Preludes (I-IV). T. S. Eliot. HeIP; InPS; LiTA; MoVE; MP; NoP; OBMV; PoPl; PPP; SeCePo; SOTW; TwCP; UnPo; VGW; WeW
"Winter evening settles down, The," II. MoShBr
Preludes for Memnon; or, Preludes to Attitude, *sels.* Conrad Aiken.
"Beloved, let us once more praise the rain," VII. LiTA; TwAmPo; UnPo
"First note, simple, The; the second note, distinct," XXI. LiTA; TwAmPo
"Keep in the heart the journal nature keeps," XLII. CMoP; NePA; OxBA
"Nothing to say? Then we'll say nothing," LIII. LiTA; TwAmPo
"One star fell and another as we walked," LVII. MoAmPo
"Rimbaud and Verlaine, precious pair of poets," LVI. FaBoMo; LiTA; LiTM; MoPo; NePA; NoAM; TwAmPo; TWCP
(Prelude LVI.) FaBoMo
"Sleep: and between the closed eyelids of sleep," III. LiTA; TwAmPo
"So, in the evening, to the simple cloister," XX. LiTA; TwAmPo
(Cloister.) MoAB; MoAmPo
"Stood, at the closed door," LII. LiTM
"Then came I to the shoreless shore of silence," XXXIII. LiTA; NePA; OxBA; TwAmPo
"This is not you? These phrases are not you?" VI. MoAB; MoAmPo
"Time has come, the clock says time has come, The," XXVIII. LiTA; NePA; OxBA
"Two coffees in the Español, the last," II. FYAP; LiTA; NoAM; TwAmPo
"Watch long enough, and you will see the leaf," XIX. CMoP; NePA; OxBA
"What shall we do—what shall we think—what shall we say," XXIX. FaBoMe
"Winter for a moment takes the mind; the snow," I. LiTA; LiTM; MoPo; MoVE; OxBA; TwAmPo
"You went to the verge, you say, and came back safely," XIV. FaBoMo; LiTA; TwAmPo; TwCP
Preludes to Attitude. Conrad Aiken. *See* Preludes for Memnon.
Preludes to Definition. Conrad Aiken. *See* Time in the Rock.
Prelusive. Herman Melville. Clarel, XXXV. AmPP
Premonition. Laura Goodman Salverson. CaP
Prenegard, prenegard! My Baselard. *Unknown.* OxBM
'Prentice Boy, The. *Unknown.* AmFP
Preparation. Thomas Edward Brown. OBEV; OBVV
Preparations. Leslie Silko. VoR
Preparations. *Unknown. See* Guest, The.
Preparative, The. Thomas Traherne. AnAnS-1; OxBoCh; PoEL-2
Preparatory Meditations before My Approach to the Lord's Supper, *sels.* Edward Taylor.
First Series.
"Am I thy gold? Or purse, Lord, for thy wealth," VI. AP; LiTA; NePA; OxBA; TAP; TreP
"Deity of Love Incorporate, A," XI. TAP
"I kenning [*or* kening] through astronomy divine," VIII. AmPP; AP; LiTA; NOBA; NoP; OxBA; PoEL-3; SCAP; TAP
"Lord, art thou at the table head above," IV.
(Reflexion, The.) AmPP; AP; NePA; OxBA
"My Lord, my life, can envy ever bee," XXIII. PoEL-3
"My shattred phancy stole away from mee," XXIX. AP; SCAP
"My sin! my sin, my God, these cursed dregs," XXXIX. SCAP
"Oh, that I always breath'd in such an air," III.
(Experience, The.) AmPP
"Oh that I was the Bird of Paradise!" NOCV
"Oh! What a thing is man? Lord, who am I?" XXXVIII. AP; NOBA; OxBA
"Still I complain; I am complaining still," XL. AP; OxBA; PoEL-3
"Stupendious love! all saints astonishment," X. OxBA
"Thy grace, dear Lord's my golden wrack I find," XXXII. NoP; SCAP
"Thy human frame, my glorious Lord, I spy," VII. LiTA
"View, all ye eyes above, this sight which flings," XX. AP
"What love is this of thine, that cannot be." AmPP; AP; NOCV; PoEL-3; SCAP
Second Series.
"Like to the marigold, I blushing close," III. SCAP
"Methinks I spy Almighty holding in," LXVIII. AP; HAP
"My Blessed Lord, how doth thy Beautious Spouse," CL. SCAP
"My gracious Lord, I would thee glory doe," IV. SCAP
"Oh! Golden Rose! Oh. Glittering Lilly White," II. SCAP
"Oh! Good, good, good, my Lord. What more love yet," CXII. NOBA
"Oh leaden heeld. Lord, give, forgive I pray," I. SCAP
"Should I with silver tooles delve through the hill," LVI. OxBA; SCAP
"What shall I say, my Lord? With what begin?" XXIX. HAP
"Ye angells bright, pluck from your wings a quill," LX. PoEL-3
Prepare. Witter Bynner. PGD
Prepare for death. But how can you prepare. Speculation. Howard Nemerov. TAP
Prepare for death, if here at night you roam. Samuel Johnson. *Fr.* London: A Poem in Imitation of the Third Satire of Juvenal. OAEL-1
Prepare for Songs; He's come, He's come. The New-Yeeres Gift, or Circumcisions Song, Sung to the King in the Presence at White Hall. Robert Herrick. SeCV-1

Prepare, prepare the iron helm of war. A War Song [to Englishmen.] Blake. *Fr.* King Edward the Third. CH; OHiP; WaaP
Preparedness. Edwin Markham. FaFP; MoAmPo
Preparedness. Jean Grigsby Paxton. PGD
Pre-Positions. Jose Isaacson, *tr. fr. Spanish by* Yishai Tobin. VWA
Pre-Raphaelite, A. Christopher Morley. WhC
Presage and caveat not only seem. The Window Sill. Robert Graves. EnLoPo
Presage of Storme. George Chapman. *Fr.* Eugenia. FaBoEn
Presaging. Rainer Maria Rilke, *tr. fr. German by* Jessie Lemont. AWP; TrJP
Presbyterian Church Government. Samuel Butler. *Fr.* Hudibras, I, 3. OBS
Presbyterian Knight. Samuel Butler. *Fr.* Hudibras, I, 1. NOBE
("When civil dudgeon first grew high.") OAEL-1; ViBoPo
("When civil fury first grew high.") EBEV; SeCV-2
Presbyterian Knight and Independent Squire. Samuel Butler. *See* Metaphysical Sectarian, The.
Presbyterian Wedding, The. *Unknown.* CoMu; ErPo
Presbyterians, The. Dryden. *Fr.* The Hind and the Panther, I. OBS
Prescience. Thomas Bailey Aldrich. AA; OBVV
Prescience. Donald Jeffrey Hayes. PoNe
Prescience. Margaret Widdemer. HBMV
Prescott, press my Ascot waistcoat. Ascot Waistcoat [*or* Sportif]. David McCord. FiBHP; NYBP
Prescription of Painful Ends. Robinson Jeffers. LiTA; MoAB; MoAmPo; OxBA
Presence, The. William Everson. ErPo
Presence, The. Robert Graves. ChMP
Presence, The. Maxine W. Kumin. RFM; WPE
Presence, The. Denise Levertov. NaP; NePoEA-2
Presence, The. Dana Naone. CDW
Presence, The. Jones Very. HAP
Presence among us. Voyage to the Moon. Archibald MacLeish. MOON
Presence of an External Master of Knowledge. Wallace Stevens. NePA
Presence of Mind. Harry Graham. WhC
Presence of Snow. Melville Cane. GoYe
Presences. Zoë Karëlli, *tr. fr. Modern Greek by* Kimon Friar. PBWP
Presences Perfected. Siegfried Sassoon. MoBrPo
Present, The. Adelaide Anne Proctor. WGRP
Present. Sonia Sanchez. CNA; WPOW
Present Age, The. Arthur Cleveland Coxe. BLPA
Present Crisis, The. James Russell Lowell. OHFP
Sels.
"Careless seems the great Avenger; history's pages but record." TreFT; TRV
"Count me o'er earth's chosen heroes, they were souls that stood alone." WGRP
"New occasions teach new duties." TreFT
Once to Every Man and Nation. FaPoR, *sl. diff. sel.;* PAL; TRV
Present day we cannot spend, The. Isabella Whitney. *Fr.* A Sweet Nosegay, or Pleasant Posy. WPE
Present from the Emperor's New Concubine, A. Lady Pan, *tr. fr. Chinese by* Kenneth Rexroth. BoWoP
Present in Absence. John Hoskins. *See* Absence.
Present of Butter, A. Tadhg Dall O'Huiginn, *tr. fr. Irish by* the Earl of Longford. BIrV
Present Tense, The. Joyce Carol Oates. AMV-81
Present to a Lady, A. *Unknown.* ErPo
Presentation of Two Birds to My Son, A. James Wright. DiL; PPP
Presentation Piece. Marilyn Hacker. AmPA
Presentiment. Ambrose Bierce. AA
Presentiment—is that long shadow—on the lawn. Emily Dickinson. AP; CABA; ELU; FaBoEn; OxBA
Presently at our touch the teacup stirred. Voices from the Other World. James Merrill. GP; MP; TwCP
Presents. Marchette Chute. EvOK; SiSoSe
Presents of money, furs, and pearls. The Right Time. *Unknown, tr. by* Louis Untermeyer. UnTE
Preserve a respectful demeanor. To a Baked Fish. Carolyn Wells. FiBHP
Preserve that old kettle, so blackened and worn. My Dad's Dinner Pail. Edward Harrigan. BLPA
Preserve thy sighs, unthrifty girl[e]. The Souldier [*or* Soldier] Going to the Field [*or* Song]. Sir William Davenant. CavP; MePo; NOBE; OBWP
Preserves. Michael Waters. GeTw
President Garfield. Longfellow. PAH
President Lincoln's Grave. Caroline A. Mason. OHIP
President Ordains the Bee to Be, The. Wallace Stevens. *Fr.* Notes toward a Supreme Fiction. LiTA
President Roosevelt. *Unknown.* BluL
President Slumming, The. James Tate. OBAL
Presidents of the United States. *Unknown.* FaBoUs
Press, The. *Unknown.* PaPo
Press-Gang, The. *Unknown.* *See* Here's the Tender Coming.
Press [*or* Presse] me not to take more pleasure. The Rose. George Herbert. LiTB; PoEL-2
Press of the Spoon River *Clarion* was wrecked, The. Carl Hamblin. Edgar Lee Masters. *Fr.* Spoon River Anthology. CMoP; LiTA; LiTM; OBSV; PAI
Press often for, (nor, than at this time, more). Vox Oppressi, to the Lady Phipps. Richard Henchman. SCAP
Press Onward. *Unknown.* FaFP
Press'd [*or* Pressed] by the Moon, Mute Arbitress of Tides. Charlotte Smith. SBG
(Sonnet Written in the Church-Yard at Middleton, in Sussex.) NOEC; WPE
Presse me not to take more pleasure. *See* Press me not . . .
Pressure. Anne Waldman. PoM
Pressure of sun on the rockslide. Water. Gary Snyder. LCAP
Pressures, The. Amiri Baraka. BPo
Prest by the load of life, the weary mind. Prologue. Samuel Johnson. *Fr.* The Good-natur'd Man (*by* Goldsmith). LoBV
Presto, pronto! Two boys, two horses. Boy Riding Forward Backward. Robert Francis. LCAP; NePoAm-2
Preston. *Unknown.* GBP
Presumptuous man! the reason wouldst thou find. Pope. *Fr.* An Essay on Man, Epistle I. BiP
Pretences. Ibn Rashiq, *tr. fr. Arabic by* A. J. Arberry. TTY
Pretend you are a dragon. Things to Do If You Are a Subway. Bobbi Katz. RHPC
Pretending Not to Sleep. Ian Hamilton. NoAM
Prettiest girl, The. Sucking [*or* Sipping] Cider through a Straw. *Unknown.* AS; FSW; GBP
Prettiest Little Baby in the County-O. *Unknown.* FSW
Pretty. Stevie Smith. NoP; TEP
Pretty a Day, A. E. E. Cummings. CMoP
Pretty Ambition, A. Mary E. Wilkins Freeman. OBCA
Pretty Fair Maid, A, *with music.* *Unknown.* AS
(Broken Token, The.) AmFP
Pretty game, my girl, A. The Flirt. W. H. Davies. EnLoPo
Pretty Girl, A. J. Gordon Coogler. OBAL
Pretty Girl of Loch Dan, The. Sir Samuel Ferguson. HBV-1
Pretty girls of the fall, The. The Falls. F. D. Reeve. NYBP
Pretty good firm is "Watch & Waite," A. The Best Firm. Walter G. Doty. HBV-1; HBVY
Pretty John Watts. Mother Goose. OxNR
Pretty Lady Carenza. Tenson. Carenza *and* Iselda, *tr. by* Bridget Connelly *and* Doris Earnshaw. WPOW
Pretty lark, climbing the welkin clear. Joshua Sylvester. *Fr.* Du Bartas: His Divine Weeks and Works, the Fifth Day of the First Week. PBBP
Pretty Maid, The. Paul Fort. *See* Ballade: "Pretty maid she died, she died, in love-bed as she lay, The."
Pretty maid both kind and fair, A. The Very Pretty Maid of This Town, and the Amorous 'Squire Not One Hundred Miles from the Place. *Unknown.* CoMu
Pretty maid, pretty maid,/ Where have you been? *Unknown.* OxNR
Pretty maid she died, she died, in love-bed as she lay, The. Ballade [*or* The Pretty Maid]. Paul Fort, *tr. by* Frederick York Powell. AWP; OBMV
Pretty Maids Beware!!! *Unknown.* CoMu
Pretty Miss Apathy. Pooh! Walter de la Mare. FiBHP
Pretty party for people, A. And. Robert Creeley. LCAP
Pretty Ploughboy, The. *Unknown.* GBP
(Lark in the Morning, The.) ChTr
Pretty Polly (" 'Get up, get up, pretty Polly,' he says"). *Unknown.* UnTE
Pretty Polly ("Go get me some of your father's gold"), *with music.* *Unknown.* AS
Pretty Polly ("I courted pretty Polly the live-long night"). *Unknown.* FSW; OuSiCo, *with music*
Pretty Polly ("Pretty Polly, pretty Polly, come and go [*or* come go 'long] with me"). *See* Gosport Tragedy, The.
Pretty Polly of Topsham. *Unknown.* AmFP
Pretty prating poll. Little Miss and Her Parrot. John Marchant. OxBChV
Pretty, pretty, pretty! Sings a Bird. John Nist. AMV-80
Pretty Saro. *Unknown.* AmFP; FSW
Pretty sneaking knave I knew, A. Mr. Cromek. Blake. ChTr; FaBoEE
Pretty song, this coming spring, A. Miss Betty's Singing-Bird. John Winstanley. NOEC
Pretty Sport. William Habington. *See* Fine Young Folly.
Pretty task, Miss S——, to ask, A. I'm Not a Single Man. Thomas Hood. HBV-1
Pretty Thing, A. *Unknown.* UnTE
Pretty Twinkling Starry Eyes. Nicholas Breton. *Fr.* The Passionate Shepherd. EIL
Pretty Wantons. *Unknown.* EIL
("Pretty wantons, sweetly sing.") PBBP

Pretty white lady. Stuff. H. B. Johnson. AMV-80
Pretty Woman, A. Simon J. Ortiz. CDW
Pretty Words. Elinor Wylie. HBMV; YaD
Pretty young actress, a stammerer, A. Limerick. Eille Norwood. CenHV
Pretty young school mistress named Beauchamp, A. A Young School Mistress. *Unknown.* TDH
Pretzel Man, The. Rachel Field. SoPo
Prevailing Prayer. Richard Chenevix Trench. *See* Prayer! "Lord, what a change within us one short hour."
Prevalent Poetry. Charles Follen Adams. CenHV
Prevention of Stacy Miller, The. Peter Miller. MoCV
Prevision. Ada Foster Murray. HBV-1
Previsioning death in advance, our doom is delayed. Foresight. Lincoln Kirstein. NoAM; OBWP
Prey for us the Prince of Pees. A Song to John, Christ's Friend. *Unknown.* MeEL
Prey to Prey. David Rowbotham. CBAP
Priam and Achilles. Homer, *tr. fr. Greek. Fr.* The Iliad, XXIV. OBEC, *tr. by* Pope; OBS, *tr. by* George Chapman
Priapus and the Pool, *sels.* Conrad Aiken.
Carver, The, XVI [XIX]. HBMV
This Is the Shape of the Leaf, IV [V]. HBMV; NePA; TrGrPo; WHA
(Portrait of a Girl.) GoJo; MoAB; MoAmPo
("This is the shape of the leaf, and this of the flower.") CMoP; NOBA; OxBA
"When trout swim down Great Ormond Street," III [IV]. NoAM; NOBA
Price, The. John Davidson. EBVV
Price He Paid, The. Ella Wheeler Wilcox. WBLP
Price of a Drink. Josephine Pollard. PaPo
Price of Begging, The. Emmanuel ben David Frances, *tr. fr. Hebrew by* A. B. Rhine. TrJP
Price of Experience, The. Blake. *Fr.* Vala, or The Four Zoas. EnRP
("I am made to sow the thistle for wheat.") Prf
Price of Paper, The. Lawrence Russ. AMV-81
Price of Wisdom, The. Bible, *O.T.* Job, XXVIII. TrGrPo
("Surely there is a mine for silver.") SaC
Price seemed reasonable, location, The. Telephone Conversation. Wole Soyinka. SoSe; TTY
Prices. Louis Ginsberg. TrJP
Prick a maiden nether holly. W. J. Webster. BXAP
Pricke of Conscience, The, *sel. Unknown.*
Newly Born, The. OxBM
Prickle a lamb. Conjuring Roethke. James Tate. OBAL
Pride. Violet Jacob. OxBS
Pride, The. John Newlove. MoCV; NOBC
Pride and Hesitation. Cerise Farallon. UnTE
Pride cannot see itself by mid-day light. Barten Holyday. FaBoEE
Pride is his pity, artifice his praise. *Unknown.* FaBoEE
Pride Is the Canker. *Unknown. See* Do Not, Oh, Do Not Prize.
Pride, lust, ambition, and the people's hate. The Downfall of the Chancellor. *Unknown.* APAS
Pride of a Jew, The. Judah Halevi, *tr. fr. Hebrew by* Israel Cohen. TrJP
Pride of Ancestry. Robert Frost. OBAL
Pride of Kildare, The. *Unknown.* OBET
Pride of Ladies, A. Anne Halley. NMM
Pride of the peacock is the glory of God, The. Blake. *Fr.* The Marriage of Heaven and Hell. FF
Pride of wrights, the joy of smiths abide, The. The Junk Shop. Henri Coulette. NYBP
Pride of Youth. Dante Gabriel Rossetti. *Fr.* The House of Life. FaBoEn; OBNC
Pride of Youth, The. Sir Walter Scott. GTBS; GTBS-P
Pride, the Never-failing Vice of Fools. Pope. *Fr.* Essay on Criticism, Pt. II. TreFT
("Of all the causes which conspire to blind.") FaBoEn; NOEC; NoP; OAEP; PPoe
Priest and Pagan. Albert Durrant Watson. CaP
Priest and the Mulberry-Tree, The. Thomas Love Peacock. *Fr.* Crotchet Castle. GN; OnMSP
Priest Lake. William Stafford. PoA
Priest of Christ, The. Thomas Ken. TRV
Priest of Coloony, The. W. B. Yeats. OnYI
(Ballad of Father O'Hart.) VLP
Priest of God, unto thee I come. Absolution. Edward Willard Watson. AA
Priest or Poet. Shane Leslie. WGRP
Priest Rediscovers His Psalm-Book, The. *Unknown, tr. fr. Irish by* Frank O'Connor. KiLC
Priestcraft and Private Judgement. Dryden. *Fr.* Religio Laici. OBS
Priesthood, The. George Herbert. AnAnS-1
Priest's Chant, The. John Fletcher. *Fr.* The Faithful Shepherdess, II, i. OBS
(Evening Knell, The.) EIL
(Evening Song.) GN
(Folding the Flocks.) CH
Priest's Lament, The. Robert Hugh Benson. ACP
Priests of Apollo, sacred be the roome. The Sacrifice to Apollo. Michael Drayton. OBS
Priest's Prayer, A. Martha Dickinson Bianchi. AA
Priest's Song, A. Thomas Dekker. *Fr.* Old Fortunatus. OBSC
(Song: "Virtue's branches wither, virtue pines.") EIL; WHA
Prim old room where memories stir, A. In an Old Nursery. Patrick R. Chalmers. HBMV
Primacy of Dullness, The. Dryden. *See* Poet Shadwell, The.
Primaleon of Greece, *sel.* Anthony Munday.
Beauty Sat Bathing [by a Spring]. EIL; UnTE
(Beauty Bathing.) NOBE; OBEV
(Colin.) GTBS; GTBS-P
(To Colin Clout.) OAEP; OBSC; ViBoPo
Primary. Abbie Huston Evans. GP
Primary Education. Phyllis McGinley. GLGT
Primary Ground, A. Adrienne Rich. NNaP
Primary Lesson: The Second Class Citizens. Sun-Ra. PoBA
Primary Numbers. Edvard Kocbek, *tr. fr. Slovakian by* Herbert Kuhner *and* Peter Kersche. AMV-81
Prime. W. H. Auden. *Fr.* Horae Canonicae. CMoP
Prime. Langston Hughes. PoBA
Prime cantante! My Catbird. William Henry Venable. AA
Prime of Life, The. Walter Learned. HBV-1
Primer for Schoolchildren, A. Richard Weber. CIP
Primer Lesson. Carl Sandburg. FaPON; MoAmPo; MoShBr; PoPl
Primer Lesson. Mark Vinz. TAT
Primer of Consequences. Virginia Brasier. ShM
Primer of Plato. Jean Garrigue. MoVE; NOBA
Primer of the Daily Round, A. Howard Nemerov. NYBP; WeW
Primeval Forest, The. Longfellow. *See* Prelude: "This is the forest primeval."
Primitive, The. Don L. Lee. BPo
Primitive like an Orb, A. Wallace Stevens. NOBA
Primitive Man. Woods Night. Tom Hennen. GP
Primitive Pithecanthropus erectus, The. Heredity. Arthur Guiterman. OBAL
Primitives. Dudley Randall. BALP; BPo; CABA
Primo Vere. Giosuè Carducci, *tr. fr. Italian by* John Bailey. AWP
Primrose, The. Robert Herrick. FaBoUs (*At. to* Thomas Carew); HBV-1; OBEV; ViBoPo
Primrose Bed, The. Robert Graves. TEP
Primrose, Being at Montgomery Castle, The, [upon the Hill, on Which It Is Situate]. John Donne. FaBoPP; GBL
Primrose Dame, A. Gleason White. HBV-1
Primrose in the green forest, The. Song. Thomas Deloney. *Fr.* The Gentle Craft. TiPo; ViBoPo
Primroses. Alfred Austin. OBVV
Primrwose in the sheade do blow, The. Blackmwore Maidens. William Barnes. HBV-1
Prince, The. Edgar Bowers. ConAP
Prince Absalom and Sir Rotherham Redde. Evening. Edith Sitwell. MoBS
Prince Alfrid's Itinerary. *Unknown. See* Aldfrid's Itinerary through Ireland.
Prince, and bishop, and knight, and dame. The Losers [*or* The Pawns]. William Young. *Fr.* Wishmakers' Town. AA; HBMV
Prince Arthur. Spenser. *Fr.* The Faerie Queene, I, 7. OBSC
Prince Charming. John N. Miller. DFT
Prince Hamlet thought Uncle a traitor. Hamlet. Stanley J. Sharpless. BXAP
Prince Heathen. *Unknown.* ESPB (A *and* B *vers.*)
Prince Henry the Navigator. Sydney Clouts. PeSA
Prince leans to the girl in scarlet heels, The. Cinderella. Sylvia Plath. DFT
Prince Lucifer, *sel.* Alfred Austin.
Mother-Song. HBV-1
Prince of Life, The. John Oxenham. TrPWD
Prince of Love, The. Blake. *See* Song: "How sweet I roamed from field to field."
Prince of Peace His Banner Spreads, The, *with music.* Harry Emerson Fosdick. AH
(Prince of Peace, The.) TrPWD
Prince of Wales' Marriage. *Unknown.* CoMu
Prince Robert. *Unknown.* AmFP; ESPB (A *and* B *vers.*); OxBB
Prince Sumiya. *Mongol Oral Tradition, tr. by* C. R. Bawden. WTO
Prince Tatters. Laura E. Richards. HBV-1; HBVY
Prince, when I found you downwind of the toadstools. A Fairy Tale. Phyllis Thompson. DFT
Prince William, of the Brunswick race. The Royal Adventurer. Philip Freneau. PAH

Prince, with wonder, sees the stately tow'rs, The. Virgil, *tr. by* Dryden. *Fr.* The Aeneid, I. OBVE
Princely eagle, and the soaring hawke, The. William Wood. SCAP
Princes and kings decay and die. Stanzas. Philip Freneau. GOA
Princes of Mercia were badger and raven, The. Geoffrey Hill. Mercian Hymns, VI. HAP; NoP
Prince's Progress, The, *sel.* Christina Rossetti.
Bride Song. OBEV; OBVV; WPE
("Too late for love, too late for joy.") ViBoPo
Princes statue, or in marble carv'd, A. Poetry and Learning. George Chapman. *Fr.* The Epistle Dedicatory to Chapman's Translation of the Iliad. OBS
Prince's voice, faint at the edge of sunlight, The. The Princess in the Ivory Tower. Joy Davidman. DFT
Princess, The. Sara Henderson Hay. DFT
Princess, The, *sels.* Tennyson.
As thro' the Land at Eve, *fr.* Pt. I. LiTB; OBVV; TreFS
(Reconciliation.) HBV-1
(Song: "As thro' the land at eve we went.") OAEP
Ask Me No More [the Moon May Draw the Sea], *fr.* Pt. VI. GBL; HBV-1; LiTB; OBNC; PoEL-5; TreFT; TrGrPo; UnTE
(Song: "Ask me no more: the moon may draw the sea.") OAEP
"Come down, O maid, from yonder mountain height," *fr.* Pt. VII. CABA; EBVV; FF; GTBS-P; OAEL-2; OBNC; OBEV; OBVV; TreFT; ViBoPo; WHA
(Idyl, An.) TrGrPo
(Shepherd's Song.) LoBV
(Song: "Come down, O maid, from yonder mountain height.") FaBoEn; OAEP; SeCEV
Home They Brought Her Warrior Dead, *fr.* Pt. V. HBV-1; TreFS; TrGrPo
(Song: "Home they brought her warrior dead.") OAEP
"I loved her, one/ Not learned, save in gracious household ways," *fr.* Pt. VII. PGD
Now Sleeps the Crimson Petal [Now the White], *fr.* Pt. VII. BoLo; CABA; ChER; ChTR; EBEV; EBVV; ELP; FiP; GBL; GTBS-P; LLLT; NIP; NOBE; NoP; OBNC; OBVV; PoEL-5; PPoe; PPP; SCV; TreFT; TrGrPo; UnTE; ViBoPo
(Song: "Now sleeps the crimson petal, now the white.") BLPL; FaBoBe; LoBV; OAEP; SeCeV
(Summer Night.) OBEV; SeCePo
"Spirit haunts the year's last hours, A." InvP
(Song: "Spirit haunts the last year's hours, A.") GTBS-P; HeIP; OAEP; OBNC; PoEL-5; PoPle
Splendor Falls [on Castle Walls], The, *fr.* Pt. III. CH; EBVV; ELP; FaBoCh; FaBV; FiP; GoJo; GTBS-P; HeIP; InPK; NoP; OAEL-2; OBNC; OBVV; PoEL-5; PoPl; PrIm; RoGo; TrGrPo; ViBoPo; WSC
(Blow, Bugle, Blow.) BLPL; ChTr; FaFP; LiTB; NOBE; OBEV; UnPo; UnS; WiR
(Bugle, The.) PoPle
(Bugle Song.) FaPON; GN; HBV-1; TreF
(He Hears the Bugle at Killarney.) FaBoPP
(Song: "Splendor falls on castle walls, The.") LoBV; OAEP; PoPl
(Songs from "The Princess.") AWP
Sweet and Low [Sweet and Low], *fr.* Pt. II. BiP; BLPL; EtS; FaBoBe; FaPON; FSW; MOS; OxBChV; PoPl; TreF; TrGrPo
(Lullaby: "Sweet and low, sweet and low.") HBV-1; HBVY; PoLF
Tears, Idle Tears [I Know Not What They Mean], *fr.* Pt. IV. CABA; EBVV; ELP; FaBoRV; FaFP; FaPoR; FiP; FPL; GTBS-P; HAP; HBV-1; InPK; InPS; InvP; LiTB; MasP; NIP; NOBE; NoP; OAEL-2; OBNC; OBVV, PoEL-5; PPoe; PPP; TEP; TreF; TrGrPo; UnPo; ViBoPo; WHA
(Song: "Tears, idle tears, I know not what they mean.") FaBoEn; OAEP; PoPl; SeCeV
(Songs from the Princess.) AWP
"This world was once a fluid haze of light," 4 *ll.* ImOP
"Thy voice is heard through [*or* thro'] rolling drums," *fr.* Interlude. OBVV; TrGrPo
Princess, The. W. J. Turner. HBMV
Princess Addresses the Frog Prince, The. Elizabeth Brewster. DFT
Princess Casamassima, The. Daniel Hoffman. GLGT
Princess Elizabeth of Bohemia, as Perdita. Frank O'Hara. PoA
Princess Ida, *sel.* W. S. Gilbert.
Arac's Song. FiBHP; WhC
Princess in the Ivory Tower, The. Joy Davidman. DFT
Princess of Dreams, The. Ernest Dowson. VLP
Princess of Scotland, The. Rachel Annand Taylor. BSV; GoTS
Princess Sabbath. Heine, *tr. fr. German by* Charles Godfrey Leland. TrJP
Princess Who Fled to the Castle, The. Francis Landy. VWA
Principal and Principle. *Unknown.* FaBoUs
Principal British Writers. Edward B. Goodwin. FaBoUs
Principal pal of the principal, The. Principal and Principle. *Unknown.* FaBoUs
Principes portas tollite. The Harrowing of Hell. *Unknown.* ACP
Print, with his hand, his eye, was more than print. Hiroshige. Mark M. Perlberg. NYBP
Printed Words. Liz Sohappy Bahe. CDW
Printer's Error. P. G. Wodehouse. FiBHP
Printing Jenny ("Printing Bibles is Jenny's daily chore"). Matthew Mitchell. OxBTC
Print-out, The. Howard Nemerov. AMV-80
Prioress, The. Chaucer. *Fr.* The Canterbury Tales: Prologue. OxBM
(Madam Eglantine.) NOBE
("Ther[e] was also a Nonne, a Prioresse.") CTC, *abr.;* TrGrPo; ViBoPo
("There also was a nun, a Prioress," *mod. vers. by* Louis Untermeyer.) TrGrPo
Prioress's Tale, The. Chaucer. *Fr.* The Canterbury Tales. ACP, *mod. vers.*; GoBC, *mod. vers. by* Wordsworth; ISi, *mod. vers. by* Frank Ernest Hill; LoBV; OAEP; OxBoCh
Prior's Epitaph. Matthew Prior. *See* Epitaph on Himself.
Priory of St. Saviour, Glendalough, The. Donald Davie. OxBC
Pripet Marshes, The. Irving Feldman. NoAM; VWA
Prism, The. H. A. Pinkerton. NePoAm
Prisms. Philip Dacey. Psk
Prison. Paul David Ashley. LFAC
Prison Break. Michael Hogan. GP
Prison Cell Blues. *Unknown.* BluL
Prison Graveyard. Etheridge Knight. LFAC
Prison Guard, The. J. J. Maloney. LFAC
(Poems from Prison, 1.) FAZ
Prison House, The. Alan Paton. PeSA
Prison Letter. Michael Knoll. LFAC
Prison Moan, *with music. Unknown.* OuSiCo
Prison priorities are like Bullhead City gnats. And the Gas Chamber Drones in the Distance. Greg Forker. LFAC
Prison Song. Alan Dugan. PoA
Prison Walls—Red Brick Crevices. Terri Meyette Wilkins. LFAC
Prisoned in Windsor, He Recounteth His Pleasure There Passed. Earl of Surrey. *See* In Windsor Castle.
Prisoner, A. "Æ." *See* Terence MacSwiney.
Prisoner, The. Emily Brontë. NOBE; NoP; OAEP; OBEV; OBVV
Sels.
"He comes with western winds, with evening's wandering airs." ELP
"Still, let my tyrants know, I am not doomed to wear." ChER; OBNC
Prisoner. Marguerite George. GoYe
Prisoner, The. William Plomer. ChMP; PeSA
Prisoner, A/ lost his visits. Pacified. Thomas G. Nickens. LFAC
Prisoner aboard the S.S. *Beagle*. Calvin Murry. LFAC
Prisoner between the Panes of Glass. Silvina Ocampo, *tr. fr. Spanish by* Jason Weiss. AMV-81
Prisoner for Life, A, *with music. Unknown.* CoSo
Prisoner of Chillon, The. Byron. BeLS; DTo; EnRP; HBV-2; PoLF
Sels.
"I made a footing in the wall." OBRV
"Kind of change came in my fate, A." NOBE
"Lake Leman lies by Chillon's walls." OBRV
"Light broke in upon my brain, A." OBRV
Sonnet on Chillon, *intro. sonnet.* FiP; LiTB; LoBV; OAEP; OBRV; SeCeV; TreFS; TrGrPo
("Eternal Spirit of the chainless mind.") PoPl
(On the Castle of Chillon.) GTBS; GTBS-P
Prisoner of War. Gertrude May Lutz. GoYe
Prisoners. F. W. Harvey. MMA
Prisoners. Randall Jarrell. OxBA; WaP
Prisoners. Nancy Barr Mavity. HBMV
Prisoners, The. Stephen Spender. FaBoMo; MoAB; MoBrPo
Prisoners. *Unknown. See* Dainty Sweet Bird.
Prisoner's Prayer, A. *Unknown.* OxBM
Prisoner's Song. Horace Gregory. OLR
Prisoner's Song of Jerusalem, A. *Unknown.* ACP
Prithee die and set me free. Martial, *tr. fr. Latin by* Sir John Denham. OBVE
Prithee leave me, crafty hussy. The Cupbearer Speaks. Goethe, *tr. by* John Weiss. PeHV
Prithee, let no raindrop fall. A. M. Sayers. BXAP
Prithee, no more, how can love sail? To Her Questioning His Estate. William Hammond. JCP
Prithee now, fond fool, give o'er. A Dialogue between Strephon and Daphne. Earl of Rochester. CavP; SeCV-2
Prithee, say aye or no. The Resolute Courtier. Thomas Shipman. ErPo; GBL
Prithee tell me, Dimple-Chin. Toujours Amour. Edmund Clarence Stedman. HBV-1

Private, A. Edward Thomas. GTBS-P; MMA
Private Blair of the Regulars. Clinton Scollard. PAH
Private Devotion. Phoebe Hinsdale Brown. *See* I Love to Steal Awhile Away.
Private Dining Room, The. Ogden Nash. NYBP; PoCh
Private faces in public places. W. H. Auden. FaBoEE; PV
Private Judgement Condemned. Dryden. *Fr.* The Hind and the Panther, I. OBS
(Confessio Fidei.) NOBE
(Prayer, A: "What weight of ancient witness can prevail.") FiP
Private Letter to Brazil, A. G. C. Oden. AmNP; NNP; PoNe
Private madness has prevailed, A. O Virtuous Light. Elinor Wylie. MoAB; MoAmPo; MoPo; NePA
Private Means Is Dead. Stevie Smith. OxBC
Private Meeting Place, The. James Wright. NYBP
Private of the Buffs, The; or, the British Soldier in China. Sir Francis Hastings Doyle. HBV-2; OBEV; OBVV; PaPo; VLP
Private Pain in Time of Trouble. Kathleen Spivack. AmPA
Private Pantomime. Ruth Stone. PoA
Private Rooms. Diana O Hehir. NPGG
Private Transport. Adrian Mitchell. FaBoEE
Private Worship. Mark Van Doren. MoVE
Privately, your pencil makes. Snapshot of a Pedant. George Garrett. NePoAm-2
Privation. Hayden Carruth. FAZ
Privilege. Alejandra Pizarnik, *tr. fr. Spanish by* Yishai Tobin. VWA
Privy-Love for My Landlady. George Farewell. NOEC
Prize Cat, The. E. J. Pratt. NoAM; PeCV
Prize for Good Conduct. Kenneth Allott. OBWP
Prize of the Margaretta, The. Will Carleton. PAH
"Prize" Poem, A. Shirley Brooks. FaBoCo; FaBoNo
Prize-giving. Gwen Harwood. CBAP; PoAu-2
Prize-winning Limerick, A. R. Rhodes. FaBoUs
Pro, The. Karen Swenson. AMV-81
Pro Femina, *sels.* Carolyn Kizer.
"From Sappho to myself, consider the fate of women," I. NMM
"I take as my theme, 'The Independent Woman,'" II. MAT; NMM
"I will speak about women of letters, for I'm in the racket," III. MAT; NMM
Pro Libra Mea. Joseph I. C. Clarke. TrPWD
Pro Patria. Constance Carrier. NePoAm; NYBP; WPE, *abr.*
Pro Patria Mori. Thomas Moore. GTBS; GTBS-P
(When He Who Adores Thee.) HoPM; OBRV
Pro Sua Vita. Robert Penn Warren. MoAmPo
Probability and Birds in the Yard. Russell Atkins. CNA; FB
Probable-Possible, my black hen. Frederick Winsor. *Fr.* The Space Child's Mother Goose. QQQ
Probatioun Officeres Tale, The. Gerard Benson. BXAP
Probing my mouth as if searching for gold. Next. Tina Koyama. BrSi
Probity. David Swanger. FAZ
Problem, The. Paul Blackburn. NeAP
Problem, The. Emerson. AA; AmPP; AP; AWP; HBV-2; LiTA; NePA; NOBA; NoP; OxBA; TAP; WGRP
"Hand that rounded Peter's dome, The," *sel.* EyDe
Problem in Morals, A. Howard Moss. ErPo
Problem in Social Geometry—the Inverted Square! Ray Durem. NBP; PoBA
Problem of the Poles, The. John Kendall. WhC
Problem of Wild Horses, The. Barbara Winder. PH
Problem, surely, is to live with Here, The. Revelation. Jerald Bullis. AMV-81
Problem that confronts me here, The. Auditors In. Patrick Kavanagh. OxBI
Problem with black holes is, The. Collapsars. Sandra McPherson. LCAP
Problems. Alexander Scott. FF
Problems of a Journalist. Weldon Kees. NaP; NYP
Problems of a Writing Teacher, The. David Ray. NePoEA-2
Process, The. Robert Kelly. CoPo
Process. Charles L. O'Donnell. TrPWD
Process in the Weather of the Heart, A. Dylan Thomas. MoAB
(Poem: "Process in the weather of the heart, A.") NeBP
Process of Conception, The. Claude Quillet, *tr. fr. Latin by* George Sewell. *Fr.* Callipaedia; or, The Art of Getting Beautiful Children. FaBoUs
Process of time worketh such wonder. Sir Thomas Wyatt. SiPS
Processes of generation; deeds of settlement. Geoffrey Hill. Mercian Hymns, XXVIII. NoP
Procession, The. Margaret Widdemer. YeAr
Procession, The; a New Protestant Ballad. *Unknown.* APAS
Procession of honest men, A. Selah. R. S. Thomas. FaBoMo
Procession of the Flowers, The. Sydney Dobell. *See* Chanted Calendar, A.
Processional. William Jay Smith. NePoAm
Processionals. Alice Archer James. AA
Proclaim the Lofty Praise, *with music.* Sarah Judson. AH
Proclamation, The. Longfellow. *Fr.* John Endicott. PAH
Proclamation, A. *Unknown.* PAH
Proclamation, The. Whittier. PAH
Proclamation/ From Sleep, Arise. Carolyn M. Rodgers. JB
Procne. Peter Quennell. ChMP; LiTB; LiTM; MoBrPo
Procne, Philomela, and Itylus. Philomela. John Crowe Ransom. ChTr; CMoP; FaBoPP; MoVE; NoAM; NOBA; OBAL; OBSV; OxBA
Proconsul of Bithynia. To Petronius Arbiter. Oliver St. John Gogarty. OBMV
Procrastination. Martial, *tr. from Latin by* Abraham Cowley. AWP
("Tomorrow you will live, you always cry.") FaBoEE; NIP; OBVE
Procrastination. Edward Young. *Fr.* Night Thoughts. OBEC
Prodigal, The. Elizabeth Bishop. CoAP; InvP; LCAP; LiTM; MoAB; MP; NYBP; PPP; TwCP
Prodigal. Ellen Gilbert. GoBC
Prodigal of loves and barbecues. To the (Supposed) Patron. Geoffrey Hill. NePoEA-2
Prodigal Son, The. Bible, *N.T.* St. Luke, XV: 11-32.
("And Jesus said, A certain man had two sons.") LO
Prodigal Son, The. E. A. Robinson. MoAmPo
Prodigal Son, The. Arthur Symons. BrPo
Prodigals. Charles L. O'Donnell. HBMV
Prodigal's Return. Ralph D. Eberly. AMV-80
Prodiggus reptile! long and skaly kuss! Some Verses to Snaix. *Unknown.* NA
Prodigy, The. A. P. Herbert. EvOK
Prodigy. Charles Simic. GeTw
Produce the urn that Hannibal contains. Hannibal. Juvenal, *tr. by* William Gifford. *Fr.* Satires, X. OBVE
Proem: "I love the old melodious lays." Whittier. AA; AP; HBV-2; NePA; NoP; OxBA; TAP
Proem: "If this little world to-night." Oliver Herford. *See* If This Little World Tonight.
Proem: "Lo, thus, as prostrate, 'In the dust I write.'" James Thomson ("B.V."). *Fr.* The City of Dreadful Night. GoTS; OAEP; OxBS; ViBoPo
(City, The.) NOBE
("Lo, thus, as prostrate, 'In the dust I write.'") GoTS; ViBoPo
Proem: "Out of my own great woe." Heine, *tr. fr. German by* Elizabeth Barrett Browning. AWP
Proem: "Poetry is itself a thing of God." Philip James Bailey. *Fr.* Festus. VLP
Proem: "Snug in my easy chair." W. W. Gibson. *Fr.* Fires. HBMV
Proem: "Strong Son of God, immortal Love." Tennyson. *See* In Memoriam A. H. H.: "Strong Son of God. . ."
Proem: "There is no rhyme that is half so sweet." Madison Cawein. AA; BoNaP
Proem: To Brooklyn Bridge. Hart Crane. *See* To Brooklyn Bridge.
Proem, A: "When in my walks I meet some ruddy lad." Samuel Ward. AA
Proem to Hellenics. Walter Savage Landor. *See* On the Hellenics.
Proem to "The Kid." Conrad Aiken. *Fr.* The Kid. MoAB
Proem to the Parlement of Foules. Chaucer. *Fr.* The Parlement of Foules. FiP
("Lyf so short, the craft so long to lerne, The.") ViBoPo
Profane, The. Horace, *tr. fr. Latin by* Abraham Cowley. Odes, III, 1. AWP
("Hence ye prophane; I hate ye all.") OBVE
Professional, The. David Ignatow. NNaP
Professional prisoner. Jessica Scarbrough. LFAC
Professionals, The. Geoffrey Grigson. PoA
Professor at the Breakfast Table, The, *sels.* Oliver Wendell Holmes.
Crooked Footpath, The. HBV-2; TreF
Hymn of Trust. AA; TrPWD
(O Love Divine, That Stooped to Share, *with music.*) AH
Sun-Day Hymn. TrPWD; TRV; WGRP
(Lord of All Being, Throned Afar, *with music.*) AH
Two Streams, The. AP
Under the Violets. AA
Professor Burke's symphony, "Colorado Vistas." Cultural Notes. Kenneth Fearing. CMoP
Professor Called Chesterton, A. W. S. Gilbert. TDH
Professor Drinking Wine. Alasdair Clayre. PV
Professor Eisenbart, asked to attend. Prize-giving. Gwen Harwood. CBAP; PoAu-2
Professor Eisenbart, with grim distaste. Panther and Peacock. Gwen Harwood. CBAP; PoAu-2
Professor Gratt. Donald Hall. OBAL
Professor James Dewar, F.R.S. E. C. Bentley. *Fr.* Clerihews. PoPle
Professor Kelleher and the Charles River. Desmond O'Grady. CIP; NoAM
Professor Palamedes darts down Westow Street. News from Norwood. Christopher Middleton. FaBoMo; NePoEA-2

Professor Robinson each summer beats. Don's Holiday. G. Rostrevor Hamilton. FaBoCo
Professor strolls at dusk in the college garden, The. Processional. William Jay Smith. NePoAm
Professor Varder handles Dante. Humanities Course. John Updike. GLGT
Professor Waking, The. James Tate. FF
Professor, you've convinced me a semester of astronomy. To Harold Jacoby. Irwin Edman. InMe
Professors. Harold A. Larrabee. InMe
Professor's Song, A. John Berryman. HeIP; NoAM; NOBA; OxBC
Proffered Love Rejected. Sir John Suckling. CavP; ErPo; NCEP
(Rejected Offer, The.) UnTE
Profile. Bronwen Wallace. AMV-81
Profile on the Pillow, The. Dudley Randall. BPo; PoBA; TAP
Profiles of My Father. Rhyll McMaster. CBAP
Profit and Loss; an Elegy upon the Decease of Mrs. Mary Gerrish. John Danforth. SCAP
Progress. Ella Wheeler Wilcox. BLPA; FPL
Profound the radiance issuing. Eve. David Gascoyne. GTBS-P
Profoundest of all sensualities, The. The Deepest Sensuality. D. H. Lawrence. NoAM
Profoundly True Reflections on the Sea. A. E. Housman. *See* O Billows Bounding Far.
Progess of Poesy, The. Thomas Gray. OBEC
Prognosis. Louis MacNeice. CMoP; NOBE; OxBI
Prognostic. Samuel Yellen. NePoAm
Prognostication on Will Laud, Late Archbishop of Canterbury, A. *Unknown.* OxBoLi
Prognostication upon Cards and Dice, A. Sir Walter Ralegh. *See* On the Cards and Dice.
Progress. Edith Agnew. AmFN
Progress? W. H. Auden. SUW
Progress. Sally Belfrage. PV
Progress. Suzanne Douglass. QQQ
Progress. Felicia Lamport. QQQ
Progress. Connie Martin. PPJ
Progress. David McCord. ImOP
Progress. Peter Meinke. POL
Progress. *Unknown.* STF
Progress. Ella Wheeler Wilcox. BLPA; FPL
Progress is/ The law of life, man is not Man as yet. The Awakening of Man. Robert Browning. *Fr.* Paracelsus, V. WGRP
Progress of a Divine, The, *sel.* Richard Savage.
"Now in the patron's mansion see the wight." OBSV
Progress of Beauty, The. Swift. CABA; NCEP
Progress of Dulness, The, *sels.* John Trumbull.
Amorous Temper, An. AmPP
Dick Hairbrain Learns the Social Graces. AmPP
Harriet Simper Has Her Day. AmPP
Tom Brainless as Student and Preacher. AmPP
Progress of Evening. Walter Savage Landor. OBNC
Progress of Faust, The. Karl Shapiro. MoAB; MP; NYBP
Progress of Man, The, *sel.* George Canning.
"Mark the dark rook, on pendent branches hung." FaBoNo
Progress of Photography, The. Byron Vazakas. MoPo
Progress of Poesy, The. Matthew Arnold. PP; VLP
Progress of Poesy, The. Thomas Gray. AWP; EnRP; GTBS; GTBS-P; HBV-2; LAuP; NOEC; OAEP; OBEV; PP; ViBoPo
Progress of Poetry, The. "Christopher Caudwell." OxBTC
Progress of Poetry, The. Swift. CABA; InvP; OnYI
Progress of Sir Jack Brag, The. *Unknown.* PAH
Progress[e] of the Soul[e], The ("I sing the progress of a deathless soul"). John Donne. OxBoCh
"It quickned next a toyfull Ape, and so," *sel.* PoEL-2
Progress of the Soul, The ("Nothing could make me sooner to confess"). John Donne. *See* Of the Progress of the Soul; the Second Anniversary.
Progress of Unbelief. Cardinal Newman. GoBC
Progress Report. Charles Simic. GeTw
Progression. Francis Scarfe. NeBP
Progression of the Species. Brian W. Aldiss. FF
Prohibition, The. John Donne. ElL; MeLP; OBS
("Take heed of loving me.") GBL
Prohibition. Don Marquis. PoPl; WhC
Project, The. Gregory Orr. GeTw
Projection, A. Reed Whittemore. NePoEA
Proletarian Portrait. William Carlos Williams. OBAL; TAP
Proletarian, unlikely bird, no monarch, A. On the Death of an Emperor Penguin in Regent's Park, London. David Wright. NYBP
Prologue: "And the way goes on in the worn earth." Archibald MacLeish. *Fr.* Conquistador. NoAM
Prologue: "By landscape reminded once of his mother's figure." W. H. Auden. NoAM
Prologue: "Delusions of the days that once have been." Longfellow. *Fr.* Giles Corey of the Salem Farms. PAH
Prologue: "For who can longer hold? when every Press." John Oldham. *Fr.* Satyrs upon the Jesuits. SeCV-2
Prologue: "He says that woman speaks with nature." Susan Griffin. *Fr.* Woman and Nature. NPGG
Prologue: "I first adventure, with foolhardy might." Joseph Hall. *Fr.* Virgidemiarum. ViBoPo
Prologue: "I heard an angel speak last night." Elizabeth Barrett Browning. *Fr.* A Curse for a Nation. WPOW
Prologue: "If yet there be a few that take delight." Dryden. *Fr.* The Loyal General (*by* Nahum Tate). SeCV-2
Prologue: "In a summer season, when soft was the sun." William Langland. *Fr.* The Vision of Piers Plowman. OAEL-1, *mod. by* J. B. Trapp (B *text*)
(Field Full of Folk, The, A *text.*) OxBM
(Field of Folk, The.) PoEL-1
("In a somer seson, whan softe was the sonne.") EBEV
(On Malverne Hilles, the Place of Piers Plowman's Vision.) FaBoPP
Prologue: "In your words." Lazer Eichenrand, *tr. fr. Yiddish by* Gabriel Preil *and* Howard Schwartz. VWA
Prologue: "Lord, can a crumb of earth the earth outweigh." Edward Taylor. AP
Prologue: "Message-Bringer Woman." Carol Lee Sanchez. TWSS
Prologue: Moments in a Glade. Alan Stephens. QFR
Prologue: "Musing upon the restless bisinesse." Thomas Hoccleve. *Fr.* The Regimen of Princes. PoEL-1
Prologue: "My life is like a music-hall." Arthur Symons. *See* Prologue to "London Nights."
Prologue: "O love, the interest itself in thoughtless heaven." W. H. Auden. *See* Perhaps.
Prologue: "Of Heaven or Hell I have no power to sing." William Morris. *See* Apology, An.
Prologue: "Our author by experience finds it true." Dryden. *Fr.* Aureng-Zebe. SeCV-2
(Prologue to "Aureng-Zebe.") FiP; OBS; OxBoLi; PP; SeCeV
Prologue: "Over! the sweet summer closes." Tennyson. *Fr.* Becket. GBL
Prologue: " 'Poet's age is sad, The: for why?' " Robert Browning. *Fr.* Asolando. OAEL-2; VLP
Prologue: "Prest by the load of life, the weary mind." Samuel Johnson. *Fr.* The Good-natur'd Man (*by* Goldsmith). LoBV
Prologue: "Rawish dank of clumsy winter ramps, The." John Marston. *Fr.* Antonio's Revenge. LoBV; ViBoPo
Prologue: "See my lov'd Britons, see your Shakespeare rise." Dryden. *Fr.* Troilus and Cressida. SeCV-2
Prologue: "Self-love (which never rightly understood)." Dryden. *See* Tyrannic Love: Prologue.
Prologue: "These alternate nights and days, these seasons." Archibald MacLeish. MoAmPo
Prologue, The: "To sing of wars, of captain[e]s, and of kings." Anne Bradstreet. AP; BoWoP; NOBA; OxBA; SBG; SCAP; TAP; WPE
Prologue: "To-night we strive to read, as we may best." Longfellow. *Fr.* John Endicott. PAH
Prologue: Wanderers, The. William Morris. *Fr.* The Earthly Paradise. EBVV
Prologue: "We who with songs beguile your pilgrimage." James Elroy Flecker. *Fr.* The Golden Journey to Samarkand. BrPo; FaPoR; GoJo; OBMV; OxBTC
Prologue: "Whan that April with his showres soote." Chaucer. *See* Canterbury Tales, The.
Prologue for a Bestiary. Ronald Perry. NePoEA-2
Prologue in Heaven. Goethe, *tr. fr. German. Fr.* Faust. AWP, *tr. by* Shelley; NAWM-2, *tr. by* Louis MacNeice
(Chorus of the Archangels, The.) OBVE, *tr. by* Shelley
Prologue of Faust, *sel.* John Anster.
"Lose this day loitering, 'twill be the same story." TRV
Prologue of the Prioress's Tale, The. Chaucer. *Fr.* The Canterbury Tales. GoBC, *mod. vers. by* Wordsworth, *incl. in* The Prioress' Tale; OxBoCh, *incl. in* The Prioress's Tale
Invocation: "O mother-maid! O maiden-mother free!" *sel., mod. vers. by* Frank Ernest Hill. ISi
(Two Invocations of the Virgin, I.) ACP
Prologue Spoken [by Mr. Garrick] at the Opening of the Theatre [Royal] in Drury-Lane, 1747. Samuel Johnson. EBEV; LAuP; NOEC; NoP; OBEC; SeCeV
Prologue to a Saga. Dorothy Parker. InMe
Prologue to a Translation. John Trevisa. OxBM
Prologue to "A Word to the Wise." Samuel Johnson. FaPoR
(Prologue to Hugh Kelly's "A Word to the Wise.") EBEV
Prologue to "Aureng-Zebe." Dryden. *See* Prologue: "Our author by experience finds it true."

Prologue to Book VII, The. Gawin Douglas. *See* Prologues to the Aeneid.
Prologue to Book XIII, The. Gawin Douglas. *See* Prologues to the Aeneid.
Prologue to General Hamley, *sel.* Tennyson.
Green Sussex. FaBoPP
Prologue to Hugh Kelly's "A Word to the Wise." Samuel Johnson. *See* Prologue to "A Word to the Wise."
Prologue to "London Nights." Arthur Symons. VLP
(Prologue: "My life is like a music-hall.") BrPo
Prologue to "Love Triumphant." Dryden. *Fr.* Love Triumphant. OxBoLi
Prologue to "Rhymes and Rhythms." W. E. Henley. VLP
Prologue to "Secret-Love; or, The Maiden-Queen." Dryden. SeCV-2
Prologue to Sir Thopas. Chaucer. *Fr.* The Canterbury Tales. Par
Prologue to the Avowis of Alexander. John Barbour. *Fr.* The Buik of Alexander. OxBS
Prologue to "The Canterbury Tales." Chaucer. *See* Canterbury Tales, The.
Prologue to the First Satire. Persius, *tr. fr. Latin by* Dryden. *Fr.* Satires. AWP
Prologue to "The Lakers; a Comic Opera," *sel.* James Plumptre.
"Where Cumbria's mountains in the north arise." NOEC
Prologue to the Man of Law's Tale. Chaucer. *Fr.* The Canterbury Tales. FiP
Prologue to the Second Nun's Tale, *sels.* Chaucer. *Fr.* The Canterbury Tales.
Invocatio ad Mariam. ISi, *mod. vers. by* Frank Ernest Hill
"Thou maid and mother, daughter of thy Son." GoBC
Two Invocations of the Virgin, I. ACP
Prologue to "The Tempest." Dryden. NoP
Prologue to the University of Oxford, 1673. Dryden. OBS; PP
Prologue to the Wife of Bath's Tale, The. Chaucer. *See* Wife of Bath's Prologue, The.
Prologues are over, The. It is a question, now. Asides on the Oboe. Wallace Stevens. AP; FaBoMo; MoAB; MoAmPo
Prologues to the Aeneid, *sels.* Gavin Douglas.
Difficulties of Translation, The, *abr. fr.* Prologue to Bk. I. GoTS
"Frend, farly nocht; na caus is to complene," *fr.* Prologue to Bk. X. OxBoCh
Prologue to Book VII, The. OxBS
Evening and Morning in Winter, An. BSV
Winter. SeCePo
Prologue to Book XIII, The. OxBS
Evening and Morning in June, An. BSV
Prologues to What Is Possible. Wallace Stevens. LCAP; NePoAm
Prolonged Sonnet: In the Last Days of the Emperor Henry VII. Simone Dall' Antella, *tr. fr. Italian by* Dante Gabriel Rossetti. AWP
Prolonged Sonnet: When the Troops Were Returning from Milan. Niccolò degli Albizzi, *tr. fr. Italian by* Dante Gabriel Rossetti. AWP; OBVE
(When the Troops Were Returning from Milan.) WaaP
Promenade. David Ignatow. TrJP
Promenading their/ skirted galleons of sex. The Return to Work. William Carlos Williams. CTBA; NYBP
Prometheus. Byron. EnRP; InPS; NOBE; NoP; OAEL-2
Prometheus. Goethe, *tr. fr. German by* John S. Dwight. AWP
Prometheus. Jenny Mastoraki, *tr. fr. Modern Greek by* Nikos Germanakos. BoWoP
Prometheus Bound. Aeschylus, *tr. fr. Greek.* NAWM-1, *tr. by* Edith Hamilton
Wail of Prometheus Bound, The, *sel.* WGRP, *tr. by* Elizabeth Barrett Browning
Prometheus Unbound. A. D. Hope. OxBC
Prometheus Unbound. Shelley. EnRP; OAEL-2
Sels.
"Canst thou imagine where those spirits live," *fr.* II, ii. WSC
Chorus of Spirits: "From unremembered ages we," *fr.* I. LoBV
"Eagle so caught in some bursting cloud, An," *fr.* III, ii. PBBP
"I wandering went/ Among the haunts and dwellings of mankind," *fr.* III. FiP
Life of Life, *fr.* II, v. CH; FiP
(Chorus: "Life of Life! thy lips.") LoBV
(Hymn to the Spirit of Nature.) GTBS; GTBS-P
("Life of Life! thy lips enkindle.") LO; NOBE; OBRV; PoEL-4; ViBoPo
"Loud deep calls me home even now to feed it, The," *fr.* III, ii. ChER
"Monarch of Gods and Dæmons, and all Spirits," *fr.* I. FiP
"My coursers are fed with the lightning," *fr.* II, iv. OBRV
"My soul is an enchanted boat," *fr.* II, ii. ViBoPo
"On a battle-trumpet's blast," *fr.* I. OBRV
"On a poet's lips I slept," *fr.* I. ChER; ELP; FiP; ViBoPo
(Poet's Dream, The.) GTBS; GTBS-P
"Path through which that lonely twain, The," *fr.* II, ii. ViBoPo
"Peace! peace! A mighty Power, which is as darkness," *fr.* IV. OAEP
"Soon as the sound had ceased whose thunder filled." *fr.* III, iv. ChER
"Sphere, which is as many thousand spheres, A," *fr.* IV. ImOP
"This is the day, which down the void abysm," *fr.* IV. SeCeV
(Demogorgon's Speech.) LoBV
"There the voluptuous nightingales," *fr.* II, ii. ViBoPo
(Semichorus II: "There the voluptuous nightingales.") PBBP
"Thou, earth, calm empire of a happy soul," *fr.* IV. FaBoRV; OBRV
Who Reigns? *fr.* II, iv. SeCePo
Prometheus, with Wings. Michael Ondaatje. PeCV
Prominent lady in Brooking, A. Expert. *Unknown.* TDH
Promiscuous lovers/ Pine to have. A Problem in Morals. Howard Moss. ErPo
Promise, The. Mary B. Fowler. STF
Promise, The. Johari M. Kunjufu. BlSi
Promise, A. Sir Thomas Wyatt. *See* Lover Rejoiceth the Enjoying of His Love, The.
Promise in Disturbance, The. George Meredith. VLP
Promise Made, A. *Unknown.* FaFP
Promise of a Constant Lover, The. *Unknown.* ElL
Promise of our years was caught, The. Monody on a Century. Earle Birney. CaP
Promise of Peace. Robinson Jeffers. AP; CoBMV; LiTA; LiTM; MoAB; MoAmPo; NePA
Promise of these fragrant flowers, The. With a Spray of Apple Blossoms. Walter Learned. AA
Promise was broken too freely, The. Galway Kinnell. *Fr.* The Avenue Bearing the Initial of Christ into the New World. NaP
Promise Your Hand. Henry Rago. NMP
Promised Land. Mary Engel. AMV-80
Promised Land, The. Jessie E. Sampter. TrJP
Promised Land, The. Samuel Stennett. AmFP; TrAS, *with music*
Promises. Ruth Forbes Sherry. GoYe
Promises, *sels.* Robert Penn Warren. *sels.*
Founding Fathers, Nineteenth-Century Style, VIII. NoAM
"What was the promise that smiled from the maples at evening?" I. DiL
Promises of Freedom. *Unknown.* BPo
Promises of the World, The. Moses ibn Ezra, *tr. fr. Hebrew by* Solomon Solis-Cohen. *Fr.* The World's Illusion. TrJP
Promising a river of grass, you guided me. Everglade. Anne Chernier. AMV-81
Promissory Note, The. Bayard Taylor. BXAP; HBV-1; Par; SpRo
Promontory Moment, The. May Swenson. NYBP
Promontory Moon. Galway Kinnell. MOON; TwAmPo
Prone couple still sleeps, A. First Light. Thomas Kinsella. BIrV; CMoP; NoAM
Pronouns. Karle Wilson Baker. TreFT
Pronunciation of Erse, The. A. D. Hope. PV
Proof, The. W. H. Auden. OAEL-2
(Trial, The.) NePA
Proof. Bessie Calhoun Bird. BlSi
Proof. Ethel Romig Fuller. TRV
Proof. Brendan Kennelly. CIP
Proof. Leslie Ullman. FAZ
Proof, The. Richard Wilbur. EaLo
Proof Positive. Deems Taylor, *tr. fr. French.* UnTE
Proofs of Buddha's Existence. *Unknown.* WGRP
Prope ripam fluvii solus. Malum Opus. James Appleton Morgan. FaBoCo; NA
Proper Clay. Mark Van Doren. PoRA; TrGrPo
Proper New Ballad, Intituled The Fairies [*or* Faeryes] Farewell, A; or, God-a-Mercy Will. Richard Corbet. *See* Fairies' Farewell, The.
Proper New Song, A, *sel.* Thomas Richardson.
Take Heed of Gazing Overmuch. ElL
Proper Pride. D. H. Lawrence. FaBoEE
Proper scale would pat you on the head, The. The Scales. William Empson. CMoP; FaBoMo; LiTM
Proper Song, A, Entitled: Fain Would I Have a Pretty Thing to Give unto My Lady. *Unknown.* OAEP
("Fain would I have a pretty thing.") CoMu; ElL; InvP; ViBoPo
Proper Sonnet, How Time Consumeth All Earthly Things, A. *Unknown, at. to* Thomas Proctor. FaBoRV; OBSC
(How Time Consumeth All Earthly Things.) ChTr; ElL
(Sic Transit.) TrGrPo
Proper Study of Man [*or* Mankind], The. Pope. *Fr.* An Essay on Man, Epistle II. FiP; TreFS
Proper way to eat a fig, in society, The. Figs. D. H. Lawrence. OAEL-2
Proper way to leave a room, The. Nonsense Quatrains. Gelett Burgess. CenHV
Properte of every shire, The. The Properties of the Shires of England. *Unknown.* FaBoPP; GBP
Propertian. L. A. MacKay. *Fr.* Erotica Antiqua. PeCV
Properties of the Shires of England, The. *Unknown.* FaBoPP; GBP
Properzia Rossi. Felicia Dorothea Hemans. SBG
Prophecy, A. Allen Ginsberg. TAP

Prophecy, A. Arthur Lee. PAH
Prophecy, A. Christopher Levenson. ErPo
Prophecy. Luigi Pulci, *tr. fr. Italian. Fr.* Il Morgante Maggiore. PAH
Prophecy. Jules Supervielle, *tr. fr. French by* Jan Pallister. AMV-81
Prophecy. Tennyson. *See* For I Dipped into the Future.
Prophecy, A. Maurice Thompson. *Fr.* Lincoln's Grave. AA
"Prophecy." Gulian Verplanck. PAH
Prophecy. Elinor Wylie. BLPL; BoWoP; PrIm; VGW
Prophecy in Flame. Frances Minturn Howard. AmFN
Prophecy of Famine, The, *sels.* Charles Churchill.
"Oft have I heard thee mourn the wretched lot." OBSV
On Himself. OBEC
On His Own Poetry. NOEC
"Two boys, whose birth beyond all question springs." OBSV
Prophecy of King Tammany, The. Philip Freneau. GOA
Prophecy on Lethe. Stanley Kunitz. PoA
Prophecy Sublime, The. Frederick L. Hosmer. *See* Thy Kingdom Come, O Lord.
Prophet, The. Abraham Cowley. JCP; TrGrPo
Prophet, The, *sels.* Kahlil Gibran.
Of Love. PoLF
On Children. PoPl
On Giving. PoPl
"Then Almitra spoke, saying, We would ask now of Death." DL
Prophet, The. Pushkin, *tr. fr. Russian by* Babette Deutsch *and* Avrahm Yarmolinsky. AWP; EaLo; WGRP
Prophet, The. "Yehoash", *tr. fr. Yiddish by* Isidore Goldstick. TrJP
Prophet and Fool. Louis Golding. HBMV
Prophet digs with iron hands, The. Transfiguration. Djuna Barnes. EAS
Prophet Jeremiah and the Personification of Israel, The. *At. to* Eleazar ben Kalir, *tr. fr. Hebrew by* Nina Davis Salaman. TrJP
Prophet Lost in the Hills at Evening, The. Hilaire Belloc. OxBoCh
Prophet of the body's roving. Walt Whitman. Edwin Honig. NePA; TAP
Prophet, scourged by his own hand, progressed, The. John the Baptist. Louis Simpson. NePoEA
Prophet speaks, The. Saint Malcolm. Jewel C. Lattimore. BPo
Prophetess, The. Dorothy Livesay. MoCV
Prophetess. Whittier. *Fr.* Snow-bound. AA
Prophets, The. Richard Shelton. NYBP
Prophets at street corners, in neat grey suits. Saturday Night. Antigone Kefala. CBAP
Prophets for a New Day. Margaret Walker. BPo
Prophets, gazing toward the mountains. The Home Winner. Gene Lindberg. PoOW
Prophets have died in the desert, The. Fall. Gabriela Melinescu, *tr. by* Michael Impey *and* Brian Swann. AMV-80
Prophets, preaching in new stars. The Pontoon Bridge Miracle. Vachel Lindsay. *Fr.* Every Soul Is a Circus, IV. LoBV; NePA
Prophet's Warning or Shoot to Kill, The. Ebon Dooley. PoBA
Prophylactic, The. Russell Edson. GP
Propinquity Needed. Charles Battell Loomis. InMe
Propitious Days for Weddings. *Unknown.* FaBoUs
(Days of the Week.) TreFT
Proportion. Ben Jonson. *See* Noble Nature, The.
Proportion. Amy Lowell. BoWoP
Proportions. Joseph Stroud. NPGG
Proposal. Robert Sward. ELU
Proposal. *Unknown.* TreFS
Proposal for Recycling Wastes, A. Marge Piercy. GP
Proposition, The. Paul Blackburn. ErPo
Proposition. Nicolás Guillén, *tr. fr. Spanish by* Langston Hughes. FaPON; TTY
Propositions. Phyllis Webb. MoCV
Propped boughs are heavy with apples. In the Huon Valley. James McAuley. CBAP
Propped in a cave of pillows. 100 Year Old Woman at Christmas Dinner. Colin Style. AMV-80
Propped on a stick he viewed the August weald. The One-legged Man. Siegfried Sassoon. CMoP
Propped on the bar. Sam. St. John Adcock. WhC
Props. John Oxenham. TRV
Prorogued on prorogation—damned rogues and whores! On the Prorogation. *Unknown.* APAS
Prosaic miles of streets stretch all round. Seder-Night. Israel Zangwill. TrJP
Prose and Poesy; a Rural Misadventure. Thomas R. Ybarra. WhC
Prose for Des Esseintes. Donald Davie, *after the French of* Stéphane Mallarmé. OBVE
Prose Poem. Humphrey Jennings. EAS
Proserpina. Thomas Campion. *See* Hark, All You Ladies.
Proserpine. Algernon Charles Swinburne. *Fr.* The Garden of Proserpine. ChTr
("Pale, beyond porch and portal.") FaBoEn
Proserpine at Enna. Ronald Bottrall. SeCePo
Proserpine may pull her flowers. Song of the Stygian Naiades. Thomas Lovell Beddoes. EnRP; OAEL-2
Prosit Neujahr. George Santayana. InMe
Prospect Beach. Lou Lipsitz. VGW
Prospect of a Mountain. Andrew Young. PoSH
Prospect of Children, A. Lawrence Durrell. *Fr.* Eight Aspects of Melissa. NeBP
Prospect of Death, A. Andrew Young. DTC
Prospect of Eden, The. Milton. *Fr.* Paradise Lost, IV. PoEL-3
("O for that warning voice, which he who saw.") TEP
Prospect of Heaven Makes Death Easy, A. Isaac Watts. NOCV; NoP; OBEC
(Heaven.) WGRP
(There Is a Land.) ELP
Prospect of Swans, A. Dorothy Donnelly. HoAn
Prospect of the Future Glory of America. John Trumbull. AmPP
Prospecting. A. R. Ammons. ConAP
Prospecting Dream. *Unknown.* AmFP; FSW
Prospective Immigrants Please Note. Adrienne Rich. GOA; VGW
Prospectus. Albert Huffstickler. AMV-81
Prospectus [*incl. in* The Excursion]. Wordsworth. *Fr.* The Recluse. EnRP; NoP
("On man, on nature, and on human life.") OAEL-2; OBRV
Prospero. Shakespeare. *Fr.* The Tempest, IV, i. FiP
Prospero Dreams of Arnaud Daniel Inventing Love in the Twelfth Century. Jack Gilbert. NPGG
Prospero Ends the Revels. Shakespeare. *See* Our Revels Now Are Ended.
Prospero on the Mountain Gathering Wood. Jack Gilbert. NPGG
Prospero without His Magic. Jack Gilbert. NPGG
Prospice. Robert Browning. BiP; BLPL; DL; FaBoEn; FaBV; FiP; HBV-2; HBVY; LiTB; OAEP; OBVV; PoLF; PoRA; SeCeV; TrCP; TreFS; TrGrPo; TRV; VLP; WGRP
Prosser. Raymond Carver. GeTw
Prostration. David Semah, *tr. fr. Arabic by* Yoffee Berkovitz. VWA
Protagonist, The. Peter Hopegood. PoAu-2
Protect Me. Hans Adler. AMV-80
Protecting the Burial Grounds. Wendy Rose. TWSS
Protection of Jehovah, The. Bible, *O.T.* (*Moulton, Modern Readers' Bible*). Psalms, XXIII. WGRP
Protection of Plants, The. Erasmus Darwin. *Fr.* The Economy of Vegetation. FaBoUs
Protective Colors. William Logan. AMV-81
Protective Grigri, The. Ted Joans. PoBA
Protest. Countee Cullen. CDC
Protest, A. Sir Thomas Wyatt. OBSC
("Heaven and earth, and all that hear me plain.") SiPS
Protest in Passing. Leonora Speyer. HBMV
Protest in the Sixth Year of Ch'ien Fu, A. Ts'ao Sung, *tr. fr. Chinese by* Arthur Waley. FaBV
Protest of the Illiterate, The, *sel.* Gelett Burgess.
"I seen a dunce of a poet once, a-writin' a little book." FiBHP
Protestation, The. Thomas Carew. CavP
Prothalamion, *sel.* Robert Hillyer.
"Hills turn hugely in their sleep, The." MoAmPo
Prothalamion. Maxine W. Kumin. NYBP
Prothalamion. Michael Ryan. AmPA
Prothalamion. Delmore Schwartz. OxBA
Prothalamion. Spenser. AAS; AWP; ChTr; EBEV; ElL; EnRePo; FaBoEn; FaBoPP; GoTL; GTBS; GTBS-P; HAP; HBV-1; LiTB; LoBV; NIP; NoP; OBEV; OBSC; PPoe; PPP; SeCePo; ViBoPo; WHA
"With that I saw two swans of goodly hue," *sel.* PBBP
Prothalamion. Terence Tiller. NeBP
Prothalamion. Francis Brett Young. HBMV
Prothalamium. Donagh MacDonagh. BIrV; NeIP
Prothalamium. May Sarton. NePoAm
Prothalamium. A. J. M. Smith. CaP
Protocols. Randall Jarrell. LCAP; OxBC; VGW
Protogenes and Apelles. Matthew Prior. GoTL
Proud Aegyptian queen, her Roman guest, The. *See* Proud Egyptian queen . . .
Proud and rest-ive Chim-pan-zee, The. Having a Wonderful Time. D. B. Wyndham Lewis. FiBHP
Proud as Apollo on his forked hill. Bufo. Pope. *Fr.* Epistle to Dr. Arbuthnot. OBEC; OBSV
Proud Egyptian [*or* Aegyptian] queen, her Roman guest, The. And She Washed His Feet with Her Tear[e]s, and Wiped Them with the Hairs of Her Head [*or* The Magdalen]. Sir Edward Sherburne, *after the Italian of* Giambattista Marina. ACP; ChTr; GoBc; MeLP; OBEC; OBS; OxBoCh
Proud Engine, The. *Unknown.* TDH

Proud fountains, wave your plumes. Fountains. Sir Osbert Sitwell. MoBrPo
Proud inclination of the flesh. Villanelle. Dilys Laing. ErPo; NMP
Proud Lady, A. Elinor Wylie. SBG
Proud Lady Margaret. *Unknown. See* Proud Margret.
Proud, languid lily of the sacred Nile. The Egyptian Lotus. Arthur Wentworth Hamilton Eaton. AA
Proud Maisie. Sir Walter Scott. *Fr.* The Heart of Midlothian, *ch.* 38. BSV; CH; ChTr; EnRP; FF; GoTS; HBV-1; InPK; LoBV; NBM; OAEL-2; OAEP; OBEV; OBRV; OxBS; PoEL-4; SeCePo; SeCeV; TEP; TrGrPo; UnPo
(Madge Wildfire Sings.) OBNC
(Madge Wildfire's Death Song.) HAP
(Madge Wildfire's Song.) NOBE
(Pride of Youth.) GTBS; GTBS-P
("Proud Maisie is in the wood.") FaBoCh; PBBP
Proud Margret. *Unknown.* OxBB
(Proud Lady Margaret.) ESPB (A *and* E *vers.*)
Proud New York. John Reed. HBMV; PoA
Proud of his hump. Dromedary. François Dodat, *tr. by* Bert *and* Odette Meyers. BoAnP
Proud of my broken heart since thou didst break it. Emily Dickinson. ViBoPo
Proud of my music, let me often make. Stephane Mallarmé, *tr. by* Aldous Huxley. *Fr.* L'Après-midi d'un Faune. ErPo
Proud of my pride. A Tale Told by a Head. Lois Moyles. NYBP
Proud of you, fond of you, clinging so near to you. My Owen. Ellen Mary Patrick Downing. HBV-1
Proud old man. The Steelworker. Melvin Douglass Brown. LFAC
Proud Preston, poor people. Preston. *Unknown.* GBP
Proud Resignation. Mordecai Marcus. SOTS
Proud Song, A. Marguerite Wilkinson. HBMV
Proud Songsters. Thomas Hardy. NoAM; PB
Proud Trees, The. Walter H. Kerr. NePoAm-2
Proud who never loved, The. Sublimation. Alex Comfort. ErPo; UnTE
Proud with success, richly pleased. Alexander Jannai. C. P. Cavafy, *tr. by* Simon Chasen. TrJP
Proud Word You Never Spoke. Walter Savage Landor. *Fr.* Ianthe. OBEV; ViBoPo
("Proud word you never spoke, but you will speak.") EnLoPo; GBL
Proudest now is but my peer, The. The Poor Voter on Election Day. Whittier. PAL
"Proudly our pibroch has thrill'd in Glen Fruin." Sir Walter Scott. *Fr.* The Lady of the Lake, II. OAEP
Proudly the note of the trumpet is sounding. O'Donnell Aboo. Michael Joseph McCann. FSW; OnYI
Proust on Noah. Eisig Silberschlag. VWA
Proust's Madeleine. Kenneth Rexroth. NoAM
Provençal Lovers. Edmund Clarence Stedman. HBV-1
Proverb: "Man of words, and not of deeds, A." *Unknown. See* Man of Words, A.
Proverb: "Swarm of bees in May, A." *Unknown.* HBV-1
("Swarm of bees in May, A.") FaBoBe; OxNR
Proverb reporteth, no man can deny, The. *Unknown. Fr.* Tom Tyler and His Wife. ElL
Proverbial. John Seller Anson. AMV-80
Proverbial Philosophy: Of Reading. Charles Stuart Calverley. FaBoCo
Proverbios Morales, *sel.* Santob de Carrion.
Friend, A. TrJP
Proverbs, *sels.* Bible, *O.T.*
"As snow in summer, and as rain in harvest," XXVI. BiP
Drunkard, The, XXIII: 29-35. TrJP
Fear of the Lord, The, I: 7. TrJP
Foolish Woman, A, IX: 13-18. TrGrPo
"Go to the ant, thou sluggard: consider her ways and be wise," VI: 6-11. TreFT
(Go to the Ant, 6-8.) FaPON
(Go to the Ant, Thou Sluggard.) TrJP
(Reproof, A.) TrGrPo
Happy Is the Man That Findeth Wisdom, III: 11-18. TreF
(Happy Is the Man.) TrJP
He That Is Slow to Anger, XVI: 32. FaPON
House of Wisdom, The, IX: 1-6. TrGrPo
Legacy, The, IV: 13. TrJP
"Lord possessed me in the Beginning of His ways, The," VIII: 22-31, *Douay vers.* ISi.
(Voice of Wisdom, The.) TreFT
Neither Poverty nor Riches, XXX: 7-9. TrJP
Seven Evils, VI: 16-19. TrGrPo
She of the Impudent Face, VII: 6-27. TrJP
"Soft answer turneth away wrath, A," XV. BiP
Lips of the Wise, The, 1-5, 7-8, 15-17. TrGrPo
"Strength and honour are her clothing," XXXI: 25-29. PoSC
(Mother of the House, The.) PGD
"Who can find a virtuous woman? for her price is far above rubies," XXXI: 10-31. SaC
(Good Wife, The.) TrGrPo
(Virtuous Woman, The.) TrJP; TRV (10-12)
Word Fitly Spoken, A, XXV: 11. FaPON
Words of Agur, The, XXX: 4, 15-16, 18-19, 24-28. TrGrPo
(Four Things, 24-28.) FaPON
(Too Wonderful, 18-19.) TrJP
Proverbs. Samuel ha-Nagid, *tr. fr. Hebrew by* Israel Abrahams. TrJP
Proverbs of Alfred, The, *sel. At. to* Alfred, King of England.
Wealth and Wisdom. OxBM
Provide, Provide. Robert Frost. AmPP; CABA; CMoP; HAP; InPK; MoAB; MP; NIP; NoAM; NOBA; NoP; PPP; TAP; TwCP; UnPo; WeW
Providence. Reginald Heber. GN; HBV-2; OHIP
Province I govern is humble and remote, The. To Li Chien. Po Chü-i, *tr. by* Arthur Waley. AWP
Provincetown, *sels.* Louis Dudek. MoCV
Avant Garde.
Fishing Village.
News.
Ocean, The.
Provincetown, Mass. Harvey Shapiro. PoA
Provincia Deserta. Ezra Pound. CrMA; OxBA
Proving. Georgia Douglas Johnson. CDC
Provisions. Margaret Atwood. IHMS
Prowling the Ridge. Judith Minty. GeTw
Prowling wolf, whose shaggy skin, A. The Wolf and the Dog. La Fontaine, *tr. by* Elizur Wright. OBVE
Prows o' Reekie, The. Lewis Spence. OxBS
Prudence. Emerson. OBAL
Prudent Simplicity. William Cowper. FaBoEE
Prue, my dearest maid, is sick. Upon Prudence Baldwin Her Sickness. Robert Herrick. JCP; OAEP; SeCV-1
Pruned Tree, The. Howard Moss. NYBP
Pruners are quick and cruel, The. Knife and Sap. Kenneth Leslie. POL
Pruners: Conca di Marini ("Pruners have come again among the vineyards"). Joseph Langland. NePoEA
Pruning. John Philips. *Fr.* Cyder. FaBoUs
P's the proud Policeman. Phyllis McGinley. *Fr.* All Around the Town. SoPo; TiPo
Psalm. *See* Psalms *for all versions of the biblical Psalms.*
Psalm VI: "And on that day, upon the heavenly scarp." A. M. Klein. *Fr.* The Psalter of Avram Haktani. PeCV
(Upon the Heavenly Scarp.) PoA
Psalm: "Father/ You are the trunk." Howard Schwartz. VWA
Psalm: "Happy is the man whom Thou hast set apart." "Yehoash," *tr. fr. Yiddish by* Isidore Goldstick. TrJP
Psalm: "In the small beauty of the forest." George Oppen. NNaP
Psalm: "It's not the sun." Patricia Hooper. HoAn
Psalm: "No one kneads [*or* moulds] us again [out] of earth and clay." Paul Celan, *tr. fr. German.* OBVE, *tr. by* Michael Hamburger; VWA, *tr. by* Joachim Neugroschel
Psalm, A: "O God, in whom my deepest being dwells." Edmund Blunden. TrPWD
Psalm: "Oh Lord, I have been staring into a mirror." Eugene Heimler, *tr. fr. Hungarian by* Anthony Rudolf. VWA
Psalm: "Old ones to the side." Charles Simic. AmPA; LCAP
Psalm: "There are a very few moments when you." Avraham Ben-Yitzhak, *tr. fr. Hebrew by* A. C. Jacobs. VWA
Psalm XII: "These were the ones who thanked their God." A. M. Klein. *Fr.* The Psalter of Avram Haktani. PeCV
Psalm III: "To God: to illuminate all men. Beginning with Skid Row." Allen Ginsberg. CAPP
Psalm, The: "While Northward the hot sun was sinking o'er the trees." Robert Bridges. FaBoTw; LiTB
Psalm Concerning the Castle. Denise Levertov. TwCP; WPE
Psalm for Christmas Day. Thomas Pestel. OxBoCh
Psalm for Sunday Night, A. Thomas Pestel. OxBoCh
Psalm of Battle. *Unknown, tr. fr. Arabic by* E. Powys Mathers. *Fr.* The Thousand and One Nights. AWP
Psalm of Christ, The, *sels.* Chad Walsh. TrCP
Invocation: "Great-hearted Christ, importunate and mild."
My God, My God, Look upon Me.
There Is None to Help.
Why Hast Thou Forsaken Me?
Psalm of Life, A, *parody.* Andrew Lang. CenHV
Psalm of Life, A. Longfellow. AA; CABA; FaBoBe; FPL; HBV-2; HBVY; OBCA; OHFP; PaPo; PoLF; PoPl; PrIm; TAP; TreF; WBLP; YaD
(Tell Me Not in Mournful Numbers, *with music.*) AH

Life, *sel.* GN
Psalm of Montreal, A. Samuel Butler. *See* O God! O Montreal!
Psalm of Onan for Harp, Flute and Tambourine, A. Alden Nowlan. NeAC
Psalm of Praise, A, *sel.* Richard Baxter.
"Ye holy Angels bright." NOCV
Psalm of Praise, A. Bible, *O.T.* *See* Psalms, C.
Psalm of St. Priapus, The. James Broughton. ErPo
Psalm of the Early Buddhist Sisters, A. *Unknown.* WGRP
Psalm of the Fruitful Field. A. M. Klein. Psalter of Avram Haktani, VIII. WHW
Psalm of the Jealous God. Henry Abramovitch. VWA
Psalm of the West, *sels.* Sidney Lanier.
Land of the Wilful Gospel. PAH
Lexington. PAH; PAL
Story of Vinland, The. PAH
Triumph, The. PAH
Psalm of Those Who Go Forth before Daylight. Carl Sandburg. MoShBr; OxBA
Psalm—People Power at the Die-in. Denise Levertov. FAZ
Psalm Praising the Hair of Man's Body, A. Denise Levertov. CAPP
Psalm to My Beloved. Eunice Tietjens. ErPo
Psalm to the Holy Spirit. A. M. Sullivan. TrPWD
Psalm to the Son, A. Marguerite Wilkinson. TrPWD
Psalmodist. Mani Leib, *tr. fr. Yiddish by* David G. Roskies *and* Hillel Schwartz. VWA
Psalms, *sels.* Bible, *O.T.*
Psalm I ("Blessed is the man . . .") AWP; BiP
(Godly and the Ungodly, The.) TreF
(Happy Is the Man.) TrJP
("O blessed man, that in th' advice," *Bay Psalm Book.*) SCAP
(Tree and the Chaff, The.) WGRP
Psalm II ("Why do the heathen rage . . .").
(Psalm II: "Why do the Gentiles tumult," *paraphrased by* Milton.) OBVE
Psalm III ("Lord, how are they increased that trouble me!").
(Psalm III: "Lord how many are my foes," *paraphrased by* Milton.) OBVE
Psalm VI ("O Lord rebuke me not in thine anger . . .").
(Psalm VI: "O lord, I dred, and that I did not dred," *freely ad. and expanded by* Sir Thomas Wyatt.) OBVE
Psalm VIII ("O Lord our Lord, how excellent is thy name . . ."). AWP; NAWM-1
(How Glorious Is Thy Name.) TrJP
(O Lord, How Excellent Is Thy Name.) TreFS
(Psalm VIII: "O Lord, that rul'st the human heart," *paraphrased by* Christopher Smart.) OBVE
(Psalm VIII: "O Lorde oure governoure, howe excellent is thy name," *tr. by* Miles Coverdale.) OBVE
(What Is Man?) TrGrPo
"Lord what is man, that he should find," 4–6, *paraphrased by* Christopher Smart. TrPWD
When I Consider Thy Heavens. FaPON (3–5); ImOP (3–8)
Psalm IX ("I will praise thee, O Lord . . .").
(I Will Sing Praise.) FaPON
Psalm XI ("In the Lord put I my trust . . .").
(Psalm XI: "Since I do trust Jehova still," *paraphrased by* Sir Philip Sidney.) OBVE
Psalm XIII ("How long wilt thou forget me O Lord . . .").
(Psalm XIII: "How long, O Lord, shall I forgotten be?" *paraphrased by* Sir Philip Sidney.) OBVE
Psalm XIV ("The fool hath said in his heart . . ."). TrJP
Psalm XVI ("Preserve me, O God . . .").
I Have a Goodly Heritage, 5–9. TreFT
Psalm XVII ("Hear the right O Lord . . .").
(Psalm XVII: "My suite is just, just lord to my suite hark," *paraphrased by* Sir Philip Sidney.) OBVE
Psalm XIX ("The heavens declare the glory of God"). AWP; BiP; BLRP; NAWM-1; OBVE, *tr. by* Miles Coverdale; TreF; TRV; WBLP
(Glory of God, The.) TrJP
(God's Glory.) TrGrPo
(Heavens Above and the Law Within, The, *Moulton, Modern Reader's Bible.*) WGRP
("Heavens doe declare, The," *Bay Psalm Book.*) SCAP
(Psalm XIX: "Heavenly frame sets forth the fame, The," *paraphrased by* Sir Philip Sidney.) OBVE
(Psalm XIX: "Spacious firmament on high, The.") WGRP
God's Precepts Perfect, 7-9. BLRP
Heavens Declare the Glory of God, The, 1–4. FaPON
(Heavens, The, 1–6.) ChTr
Psalm XXII ("My God, my God . . .")
(Cry in Distress, A, 1–15.) TrGrPo
Psalm XXIII ("The Lord is my shepherd . . ."). AWP; BiP; BLPL; FaBoBe; FPL; NAWM-1; NIP; OHIP; PoPl; TrGrPo; TRV
("God of love my shepherd is, The," *paraphrased by* George Herbert.) EBCP
(Lord Is My Shepherd, The.) FaPON; PoLF; TreF; TrJP
("Lord to me a shepherd is, The," *Bay Psalm Book.*) OBCA
(Lord's My Shepherd, The, *Scottish Psalter, ad. by* Francis Rous.) AH, *with music;* TRV; WBLP
(Protection of Jehovah, The, *Moulton, Modern Reader's Bible.*) WGRP
(Psalm XXIII: "Lord my shepherd, me His sheep, The," *paraphrased by* George Sandys). JCP
(Psalm XXIII: "Lorde is my shepherde, The; therfore can I lack nothing," *tr. by* Miles Coverdale.) ILwL, *mod. version*; OBVE
(Psalm of David.) SUS
Psalm XXIV ("The Earth is the Lord's . . ."). AWP; TreFT
(Earth Is the Lord's, The.) EaLo; FaPON (1–4); TrJP
(Lift Up Your Heads.) TrGrPo
Psalm XXVII ("The Lord is my light . . .").
(Deliverance of Jehovah, The, *Moulton, Modern Reader's Bible.*) WGRP
Lord Is My Light and My Salvation, The, 1, 4, 14. TreFT
Serenity of Faith, The, 7–14, *tr. by* McFayden. BLRP
Psalm XXIX ("Give unto the Lord . . ."). AWP
Psalm XXXVII ("Fret not thyself . . .").
Psalm XXXVII: "Trust in the Lord," 1–7, *paraphrased by* Charles Frederic Sheldon. BLRP; TreFT (1–4, 7)
Psalm XXXIX ("I said: 'I will take heed to my ways' ").
(Lord, Make Me to Know Mine End.) TrJP
Psalm XLII ("As the hart panteth after the water brooks"). AWP; TRV (1–5, 7–8)
(As the Hart Panteth.) TrJP
(My Soul Thirsteth for God.) TrGrPo
(Search, The, XLII *and* XLIII, *Moulton, Modern Reader's Bible.*) WGRP
Psalm XLIII ("Judge me, O God . . .").
(Search, The, XLII *and* XLIII, *Moulton, Modern Reader's Bible.*) WGRP
Psalm XLV ("My heart is inditing a good matter . . .").
"Queen stood on thy right hand, The," 9–15, *Douay vers.*) ISi
Psalm XLVI ("God is our refuge and strength . . ."). AWP; TreFT (1–6, 10–11); TRV
(Refuge, The, *Moulton, Modern Reader's Bible.*) WGRP
(Though the Earth Be Removed.) TrGrPo
Psalm LII ("Why boastest thou thyself in mischief . . .").
(Psalm LII: "Tyrant, why swel'st thou thus," *paraphrased by* the Countess of Pembroke.) OBVE
Psalm LV ("Give ear to my prayer. . ."). AWP
(Psalm LV: Exaudi, Deus: "My God most glad to look, most prone to hear," *paraphrased by* the Countess of Pembroke.) OBVE (1–4); WPE
Wings, 6–7. FaPON
Psalm LVIII ("Do ye indeed speak righteousness . . .").
(Psalm LVIII: "Do ye indeed speak righteousness, O congregation?" *paraphrased by* the Countess of Pembroke.) NOCV
(Psalm LVIII: Si Vere Utique: "And call ye this to utter what is just," *paraphrased by* the Countess of Pembroke.) BoWoP; WPE
Psalm LXII ("Truly my soul waiteth . . .").
(Psalm LXII: "Yet shall my soule in silence still," *paraphrased by* the Countess of Pembroke.) PBWP
Psalm LXV ("Thou visitest the earth . . ."). OHIP, *abr.*
Psalm LXVII ("God be merciful unto us . . .").
(Let the Nations Be Glad.) FaPON
Psalm LXXII ("Give the king thy judgments . . .").
(Psalm LXXII: "Looke how the woods, where enterlaced trees," *paraphrased by* the Countess of Pembroke.) OBVE
Psalm LXXIV ("O God, why hast thou cast us off . . .").
(Psalm LXXIV: "O God, why hast thou cast us off for ever?" *paraphrased by* the Countess of Pembroke.) NOCV
Psalm LXXVII ("I cried unto God with my voice . . ."). AWP
"Waters saw thee, O God, The," 16–19. MOS
Psalm LXXVIII ("Give ear, O my people, to my law . . .").
(Psalm LXXVIII: "There where the deepe did show his sandy flore," *paraphrased by* the Countess of Pembroke.) OBVE
Psalm LXXIX ("O God, the heathen are come into Thine inheritance").
(Heathen Are Come into Thine Inheritance, The.) TrJP
Psalm LXXXIII ("O God, keep not Thou silence").
(Keep Not Thou Silence.) TrJP
Psalm LXXXIV ("How amiable are thy tabernacles . . ."). TRV
(Psalm LXXXIV: "How lovely are thy dwellings fair!" *paraphrased by* Milton.) TrPWD
How Lovely Are Thy Tabernacles," 1–5. TrJP
Sparrow, The, 3. FaPON
Psalm XC ("Lord, thou hast been our dwelling place in all generations"). AWP; DL
(Lord, Thou Hast Been Our Dwelling Place.) EaLo

Psalm XCI ("He that dwelleth . . ."). AWP
(Everlasting Arms, The, *Moulton, Modern Reader's Bible.*) WGRP
(Mighty Fortress, A.) TrGrPo
Psalm XCV ("O come let us sing unto the Lord"). AWP; BLRP, *abr.*; OHIP, *abr.*
Psalm XCVIII ("O sing unto the Lord . . ."). TrJP
(Floods Clap Their Hands, The.) TrGrPo
(O Sing unto the Lord a New Song.) EaLo
(Sing unto Jehovah.) BLRP
Psalm C ("Make a joyful noise . . ."). OFD; OHIP; SUS; TRV
(Be Thankful unto Him.) FaPON
(Old Hundredth, *metrical vers. by* William Kethe.) BLSo, *with music;* FaPoR; NOCV
(Old Hundred.) FSW
(Psalm of Praise, A.) SiSoSe
(Scotch Te Deum.) WGRP
Giving Thanks, 4. BLRP
Psalm CII ("Hear my prayer, O Lord . . ."). BiP
(Psalm CII: "Lord here my prayre and let my crye passe," *paraphrased by* Sir Thomas Wyatt.) OBVE
Psalm CIII ("Bless the Lord, O my soul . . ."). AWP
("O Thou my soule, Jehovah blesse," *Bay Psalm Book*). SCAP
(Psalm CIII: "Praise the Lord, O my soul," *paraphrased by* Henry Francis Lyte.) NOCV
Psalm CIV ("Bless the Lord, O my soul . . ."). NAWM-1; OHIP, *abr.*; TrJP
(Hymn of the World Without, *Moulton Modern Reader's Bible.*) WGRP
"So is this great and wide sea," 25-28. MOS
Psalm CVII ("O give thanks . . .").
("O give yee thanks unto the Lord," *Bay Psalm Book.*) SCAP
They That Go Down to the Sea. ChTr (23-31); EtS (23-30); FaPON (23-24); MOS (23-30)
(Ocean, The, 23-33, *Moulton, Modern Reader's Bible*). WGRP
Psalm CXII ("Praise ye the Lord . . .").
(Jehovah's Immovable Throne.) WGRP
Psalm CXIV ("When Israel went out of Egypt . . .").
(Psalm CXIV: "When Israel came from Egypt's coast," *paraphrased by* Christopher Smart.) OBVE
(When Israel Came Forth out of Egypt.) TrJP
Psalm CXV ("Not unto us, O Lord . . .").
(Psalm CXV: "Not unto us, O Lord, not unto us," *paraphrased by* the Countess of Pembroke.) NOCV
Psalm CXVIII ("'O give thanks unto the Lord . . .'").
(O Give Thanks.) TrJP
Psalm CXXI ("I will lift up mine eyes unto the hills"). AWP; FaPON; ILwL; TreF; TRV
("I to the hills lift up mine eyes," *Bay Psalm Book.*) OBCA
(Pilgrim's Song, The, *Moulton, Modern Reader's Bible.*) WGRP
(Song of Trust, A.) TrGrPo
Psalm CXXII ("I was glad when they said unto me . . ."). TRV
Psalm CXXIV ("If it had not been the Lord . . .").
Our Help, 8. TRV
Psalm CXXVI ("When the Lord brought back . . .").
(Like unto Them That Dream.) TrJP
Psalm CXXVII ("Except the Lord build the house . . ."). BiP; TreF; TrJP; TRV
Psalm CXXVIII ("Blessed is every one . . ."). TRV
Psalm CXXX ("Out of the depths . . .").
(De Profundis.) BLRP; TreF; WGRP
(Out of the Depths.) TrJP
(Psalm CXXX: "Ffrom depth off sinn and from a diepe dispaire," *paraphrased by* Sir Thomas Wyatt.) OBVE
(Psalm CXXX: "Out of the deep have I called unto thee, O Lord.") ILwL
(Song of Supplication, A.) TrGrPo
Psalm CXXXIII ("Behold, how good and how pleasant . . ."). AWP; TRV
(Psalm CXXXIII: "Beholde, how good and joyfull a thinge it is," *tr. by* Miles Coverdale.) OBVE
(To Dwell Together in Unity.) TrJP
(Unity of Mankind.) TreFT
Psalm CXXXIV ("Behold, bless ye the Lord . . ."). TRV
Psalm CXXXVI ("O give thanks unto the Lord; for he is good"). AWP; OHIP, *abr.*
Psalm CXXXVII ("By the rivers of Babylon . . ."). AWP; NAWM-1; OAEL-1; TrJP
(Psalm CXXXVII: "As by the streams of Babylon," *paraphrased by* Thomas Campion.) OAEL-1
(Psalm CXXXVII: "By the rivers of Babel we sate," *The Geneva Bible.*) OAEL-1
(Psalm CXXXVII: "By the waters of Babylon we sat downe and weapte," *tr. by* Miles Coverdale.) OBVE
(Psalm CXXXVII: "Nigh seated where the river flows," *paraphrased by* the Countess of Pembroke.) OAEL-1
(Psalm CXXXVII: "On the floodis of Babiloyne there we saten," *Second Wycliffite Version.*) OAEL-1
(Psalm CXXXVII: "On the proud banks of great Euphrates' flood," *paraphrased by* Richard Crashaw.) OAEL-1
(Psalm CXXXVII: "Sitting by the streams that glide," *paraphrased by* Thomas Carew.) OAEL-1
(Psalm CXXXVII: "Upon the rivers of Babylon, there we sat and wept," *The Douay-Rheims Version.*) OAEL-1
(Psalm CXXXVII: "When as we sat all sad and desolate," *paraphrased by* Francis Bacon.) OAEL-1
(Psalm CXXXVII: "When on Euphrates' banks we sate," *paraphrased by* Sir John Denham.) OAEL-1
(Psalm CXXXVII: "When we, our weary limbs to rest," *paraphrased by* Nahum Tate *and* Nicholas Brady.) OAEL-1
(Psalm CXXXVII: "Whenas we sat in Babylon," *paraphrased by* Thomas Sternhold *and* John Hopkins.) OAEL-1
(Psalme CXXXVII: "As on Euphrates shady banks we lay," *paraphrased by* George Sandys.) OBS
Song of Exile, A, 1-6. TrGrPo
Psalm CXXXVIII ("I will praise Thee . . .").
Thou Wilt Revive Me, 6-8. TreFT
Psalm CXXXIX ("O Lord, thou hast searched me . . .").
(Psalm CXXXIX: "O Lord, in me there lieth nought," *paraphrased by* the Countess of Pembroke.) NOCV; OBSC (1-6); OBVE (7-10); OxBoCh (1-6)
(Psalm CXXXIX: Domine, Probasti.) WPE
Psalm CXLV ("I will extol Thee, my God . . .").
Lord Is Good to All, The, 9. TRV
Psalm CXLVI ("Hallelujah./ Praise the Lord, O my soul").
(Hallelujah.) TrJP
Psalm CXLVII ("Praise ye the Lord").
(Psalm CXLVII: "Praise ye the Lord," *paraphrased by* the Countess of Pembroke.) NOCV
(Psalm CXLVII: "Praise ye the Lord," *paraphrased by* Christopher Smart.) NOCV
(Psalm, A, 7-9, 12.) SoPo
Who Maketh the Grass to Grow. FaPON, *greatly abr.*
Psalm CXLVIII ("Praise ye the Lord . . .").
(Praise Ye the Lord.) TrJP
(Psalm CXLVIII: "Hallelujah! kneel and sing," 1-10, *paraphrased by* Christopher Smart.) OBVE
(Song of Praise, A.) TrGrPo
Psalm CL ("O praise God in his holiness . . ."). TRV
(Laudate Dominum.) ChTr
(Psalm CL: "O praise God in his holiness; praise him," *Book of Common Prayer.*) ILwL
Psalms of Love. Peter Baum, *tr. fr. German by* Jethro Bithell. AWP
Psalter of Avram Haktani, The, *sels.* A. M. Klein.
Psalm VI: "And on that day, upon the heavenly scarp." PeCV
(Upon the Heavenly Scarp.) PoA
Psalm XII: "These were the ones who thanked their God." PeCV
Psalm of the Fruitful Field, VIII. WHW
Psalter of the Blessed Virgin Mary. St. Bonaventure, *tr. fr. Latin by* Sister Mary Emmanuel. ISi
Pshytik. Nahum Bomze, *tr fr. Yiddish by* Gabriel Preil. VWA
PSI. Melvin B. Tolson. PoBA
"Psittachus Eois Imitatrix Ales ab Indis." Sacheverell Sitwell. MoBrPo
Psss, the beard is a bit too long. Faces. D. C. Berry. BXAP
Psyche. Jones Very. AP
Psyche to Cupid: Her Ditty. James Broughton. ErPo
Psyche with the Candle. Archibald MacLeish. PCP
Psychedelic Firemen. David Henderson. NBP
Psychiatrist. Peter DeVries. OBAL
Psychiatrist works below the cliff, The. Loneliness. Sandra McPherson. AMV-80
Psychoanalysis. Gavin Ewart. NYBP
Psychoanalysts. Christopher Morley. WhC
Psychologists, psychiatrists. Basic. Ray Durem. PoNe
Psychology Today. Judson Jerome. AMV-81
Psycholophon. Gelett Burgess. CenHV; NA
Psychometrist. James Stephens. NoAM
Ptarmigan, The. *Unknown.* RHPC
Ptarmigan cries across the corrie, The. Silver in the Wind. Ian Strachan. PoSH
Ptarmigan is strange, The. The Ptarmigan. *Unknown.* RHPC
Pub. Julian Symons. LiTB; WaP
Puberty. Jon Wallace. AMV-80
Puberty Rite Dance Song. *Tr. fr. Apache Indian by* Willis Barnstone. BoWoP
Public Aid for Niagara Falls. Morris Bishop. InMe

Public Garden, The. Robert Lowell. AP; NoP; PoRA; TAP
Public haunt they found her in, A. A Girl of Pompeii. Edward Sandford Martin. AA; HBV-1
Public Holiday: Paris. Joyce Horner. GoYe
Public Library. Dannie Abse. OxBC
Public Library. Candace T. Stevenson. GoYe
Public Nuisance, A. Reginald Arkell. LiSp
Public School 168. Stewart Brisby. LFAC
Public Schools. Robert Lloyd. *Fr.* A Familiar Epistle to J. B. Esq. NOEC
Publication—is the auction. Emily Dickinson. AmPP; NoP
Publisher's Party. Phyllis McGinley. OBAL
Puck and the Fairy. Shakespeare. *See* Over Hill, over Dale.
Puck Goes to Court. Fenton Johnson. CDC
Puck of Pook's Hill, *sels.* Kipling.
  Cities and Thrones and Powers. FaBoEn; GoJo; MoVE; NOBE; OBNC; OxBTC; PoEL-5; SeCeV; VLP
  Harp Song of the Dane Women. FaBoEn; HAP; OAEP; OBNC; PoRA; SeCePo
  Puck's Song ("See you the ferny ride that steals"). FaBoCh; FaBV; OxBChV; PoPle
  Smuggler's Song, A. OxBChV; PoPle
Puck's Song. Shakespeare. *See* Now the Hungry Lion Roars.
Pudden Tame. *Unknown.* ChTr
  ("What's your name?") FaBoNo
"Pudding and pie." Greedy Jane. *Unknown.* HBVY; OxBChV
Puddle, The. Eden Phillpotts. HBMV
Puddy and the Mouse, The. *Unknown.* GBP
Pueblo Women I Watched Get Down in Brooklyn, The. Wendy Rose. TWSS
Puella Parvula. Wallace Stevens. LCAP
Puer Aeternus. Kathleen Raine. NYBP
Puer ex Jersey. *Unknown.* NA
Puerperium. Edmund Waller. JCP
Puerto Ricans in New York (I & II). Charles Reznikoff. CTBA
Puerto Rico Song. William Carlos Williams. NYBP
Puffed up with luring to her knees. The Flute. Joseph Russell Taylor. AA
Puffin, The. Robert Williams Wood. RHPC
Puk-Wudjies. Patrick R. Chalmers. HBVY
Pulkovo Meridian, The, *sel.* Vera Inber, *tr. fr. Russian by* Dorothea Prall Radin *and* Alexander Kaun.
  Leningrad: 1943. WaaP
Pull down the shades baby neighbors don want to see what you do. Crawl Blues. Vincent McHugh. ErPo
Pull in the net! Fishing Song. *Maori Oral Tradition, tr. by* A. Armstrong *and* R. Ngata. WTO
Pull me down, ladybug. Ladybug. Raymond Souster. MoCV
"Pull, men, for, lo, see there they blow!" Brand Fire New Whaling Song Right from the Pacific Ocean. *Unknown.* EtS
Pull my arm back, Seymour. Seymour and Chantelle or Un Peu de Vice. Stevie Smith. SBG
Pull my daisy. Song: Fie My Fum. Allen Ginsberg. ErPo
Pull My Daisy. Jack Kerouac. PoM
Pull up the bell-flow'rs of the spring. St. Mark. Christopher Smart. *Fr.* Hymns and Spiritual Songs. LAuP
Pulled from our ruts by the made-to-order gale. Trans Canada. F. R. Scott. PeCV
Pulled from their fathers. Marrakesh Women. Lyn Lifshin. LTB
Pulley, The. George Herbert. AWP; EaLo; EBCP; FaBoEn; HAP; HBV-1; HeIP; InPK; InPS; LiTB; MePo; NOBE; NOCV; NoP; OAEL-1; OAEP; OBEV; OBS; OxBoCh; PAI; PPP; PrIm; SeCeV; SeCP; SeCV-1; TEP; TreFT; TrGrPo; ViBoPo; WHA
  (Gifts of God, The.) GTBS; GTBS-P; TRV
Pullin me in off the corner to wash my face an. Black Jam for Dr. Negro. Mari Evans. BPo; PoBA
Pulling Out. Lyn Lifshin. NeAC
Pulling the dead sun's weight through County Meath. Cycling to Dublin. Robert Greacen. OnYI
Pulling the last tie rope taut, I pause. Getting Loaded. Jim Thomas. AMV-80
Pulling up in my car, I went into the cottage. After Five Years. Augustus Young. BIrV
Pulling Weeds. Eric Chock. BrSi
Pulpit to Be Let, A. *Unknown.* APAS
Pulse, The. Mark Van Doren. MoAmPo; PoPl
Pulverized Screen, The. Edmond Jabes, *tr. fr. French by* Anthony Rudolf. VWA
Pumas. George Sterling. BPAW
Pumberly Pott's Unpredictable Niece. Jack Prelutsky. RHPC
Pumpkin, The. Robert Graves. PDV; RHPC; WSC
Pumpkin. Robert Morgan. GeTw
Pumpkin, The. Whittier. OHIP; PoSC
Pumpkins. John Cotton. BoNaP
Puna's Fragrant Glades. Queen Lydia Liliuokalani, *tr. fr. Hawaiian by* S. H. Elbert *and* N. Mahoe. WTO
Punch, the Immortal Liar, *sel.* Conrad Aiken.
  Puppet Dreams, The. MoAmPo
Punctilio. Mary Elizabeth Coleridge. OBEV; OBVV
Punctual as bad luck. The Family Goldschmitt. Henri Coulette. CoAP; FF
Punctually at Christmas the soft plush. White Christmas. W. R. Rodgers. ChMP; LiTM; MoAB; MoBrPo; PPON; SeCePo
Punishment. Seamus Heaney. NoP
Punishment. Unknown. TDH
Punk Party (They Told Me It Was Literary. . .). Wendy Rose. TWSS
Punkin Pie. Harry Edward Mills. PeD
Punkydoodle and Jollapin. Laura E. Richards. OBCA
Punto Final. Shirley Hill Witt. TWSS
Puny child who knows he can have but little love, The. Our Lady, Help of Christians. Paul Claudel, *tr. by* Sister Mary David. ISi
Puppet Dreams, The. Conrad Aiken. *Fr.* Punch, the Immortal Liar. MoAmPo
Puppet Play, The. Padraic Colum. RoGo
Puppet Player, The. Angelina Weld Grimké. CDC
Puppets. P. K. Page. MoCV
Puppets. Paul Verlaine. *See* Fantoches.
Puppy. Aileen Fisher. *See* My Puppy.
Puppy. Fred Lape. BoAnP; GDP
Puppy and I. A. A. Milne. FaPON; OnUR; PDV; SoPo; TiPo
Purcell in many victories of his. Bounty. Josephine Miles. NoAM
Purchase of a Blue, Green, or Orange Ode. Josephine Miles. NoP
Pure air trembles, O pitiless God, The. Noon. Robinson Jeffers. MoAmPo
Pure blood domestic, guaranteed. The Prize Cat. E. J. Pratt. NoAM; PeCV
Pure Death. Robert Graves. AWP; CoBMV; GTBS-P; MoAB; MoPo
Pure fasted faces draw unto this feast. Easter Communion. Gerard Manley Hopkins. BrPo; OFD
Pure flame of one taper fall, The. Plato in London. Lionel Johnson. VLP
Pure gold, they said in her praise. Around Thanksgiving. Rolfe Humphries. OFD
Pure Heart, The. Tennyson. *Fr.* Sir Galahad. TreF
Pure is the body on the Earth. He Singeth in the Underworld. *Unknown, tr. by* Robert Hillyer. *Fr.* Book of the Dead. AWP
Pure Platonicke. George Daniel. CavP
Pure poetry, programme of the living heart. The Network. Robert Finch. CaP
Pure Products. Denise Levertov. NMP
Pure products of America, The. To Elsie. William Carlos Williams. AP; CABA; CMoP; CoBMV; InPS; NOBA; OxBA; SeCeV
Pure Simple Love. Aurelian Townshend. AnAnS-2; SeCP
Pure spite, wanting. View. Christian J. Van Gell, *tr. by* Emilie Peech *and* W. S. Di Piero. AMV-81
Pure stream, in whose transparent wave. To Leven Water. Tobias George Smollet. OBEV
Pure sun dazzled, The. The Glazier. Stéphane Mallarmé, *tr. by* Keith Bosley. OBVE
Pure? What does it mean? Fever 103°. Sylvia Plath. CMoP; NoAM; NOBA; NMP; VGW
Pure white bodies of my friends, The. Verigin 3. John Newlove. NeAC
Pure white the shields their arms upbear. The Fairy Host. *Unknown, tr. by* Alfred Perceval Graves. AnIV
Pure woman is to man a crown. The Virtuous Wife. Süsskind von Trimberg. TrJP
Purer in Heart. *Unknown.* STF
Purer than Purest Pure, *with music.* E. E. Cummings. AH
Purest soul that e'er was sent, The. Another [Epitaph on the Lady Mary Villiers]. Thomas Carew. AnAnS-2; CaPo; SeCV-1
Purgatorio. Dante. *See* Divina Commedia.
Purgatory. W. B. Yeats. CMoP
Purification, The. St. Cosmas, *tr. fr. Greek. Fr.* Menaion. ISi
Purification of the Blessed Virgin. Joseph Beaumont. ISi
Purified, I struggle. Heth. Carlos Montemayor, *tr. by* Nigel Grant Sylvester. AMV-81
Purist, The. Ogden Nash. DBV; FiBHP; GoJo; MoAmPo; MoShBr; OBCA; PV; ShM; TreFT
Purist to Her Love, The. Margaret Fishback. WhC
Puritan, The. Karl Shapiro. MoAmPo
Puritan Hacking Away at Oak, The. Todd Gitlin. AMV-80
Puritan Lady, A. Lizette Woodworth Reese. MoAmPo
Puritan on His Honeymoon, The. Robert Bly. FF; NePoEA
Puritan Sonnet. Elinor Wylie. Wild Peaches, IV. BoWoP; FPL; MoAB; MoAmPo; TrGrPo
  ("Down to the Puritan marrow of my bones.") BoWoP

Puritan Spring Beauties stood freshly clad for church, The. The Spring Beauties. Helen Gray Cone. AA
Puritan's Ballad, The. Elinor Wylie. HBMV; PoRA
Purity. Hayim Lenski, *tr. fr. Hebrew by* Pearl Grodzensky. VWA
Purity of Heart. John Keble. BLRP
Purple Blemish, The. Pär Lagerkvist, *tr. fr. Swedish by* Lennart Bruce. AMV-81
Purple blot against the dead white door, A. Monsieur Qui Passe. Charlotte Mew. SBG
Purple cloud hangs half-way down, A. Before Sunrise in Winter. Edward Rowland Sill. AA
Purple Clover. Emily Dickinson. *See* There is a flower that bees prefer.
Purple Cow, The. Gelett Burgess. FaBoCo; FaBoNo; FaFP; FaPON; FiBHP; FPL; GrPl; HBV-2; HBVY; NA; NePA; NTCP; OBAL; OBCA; PDV; PoLF; PoPl; RHPC; SoPo; TiPo; TreFS; YaD (Nonsense Quatrains.) CenHV
Purple dry buds tight to gray branches. Michelle Roberts. LFAC
Purple heather is the cloak, The. The Bog Lands. William A. Byrne. AnIV
Purple Indians pas de bourrée. Lord Fluting Dreams of America on the Eve of His Departure from Liverpool. Paul Zimmer. VGW
Purple Island, The, *sels.* Phineas Fletcher.
All-seeing Intellect, The, VI. JCP
"But ah! let me under some Kentish hill," *fr.* I. ViBoPo
Desiderium, *fr.* I. OBS
Overthrow of Lucifer, The, *fr.* XII. OBS
Purple robed, with crownèd hair. The Pawns. Frank Betts. HBMV
Purple sky, the down's long spine, The. The Novice. Edward Davison. ErPo
Purple, White and Green, The. L. E. Morgan-Browne. BrRo
Purple, yellow, red and green. *Unknown.* OxNR
Purple-blotched and red-haired. March Sound. Harry Thurston. AMV-81
Purpose. Langdon Elwyn Mitchell. *Fr.* To a Writer of the Day. AA
Purpose. John James Piatt. AA
Purpose of Altar Boys, The. Alberto Ríos. MAYP
Purpose of Fable-writing, The. Phaedrus, *tr. fr. Latin by* Christopher Smart. AWP
Purpose of the Chesapeake & Ohio Canal, The. Dave Smith. GeTW
Purse, dirk, cloak, night-cap, kerchief, shoeing-horn, buget, and shoes. Memorial Verses for Travellers. Sir Anthony Fitzherbert. *Fr.* Husbandry. FaBoUs
Purse, who'll not know you have a poet's been. A Parley with His Empty Purse. Thomas Randolph. JCP; OBS
Purse-Seine, The. Paul Blackburn. CoSo
Purse-Seine, The. Robinson Jeffers. CMoP; HAP; NoAM; NOBA; NoP; OxBA; PrIm; WeW
Pursue no more (my thoughts!) that false unkind. The Retreat. Henry King. AnAnS-2
Pursuer, eluder. While the Bells Ring. Lora Dunetz. NePoAm
Pursuit. Hilda Doolittle ("H. D."). WPE
Pursuit. Vern Rutsala. FAZ
Pursuit. Juljan Tuwim, *tr. fr. Polish by* Watson Kirkconnell. TrJP
Pursuit[e], The. Henry Vaughan. OAEP; SeCP; TrCP; TrPWD
Pursuit. Robert Penn Warren. CrMA; HAP; LiTA; MoAmPo; MoPo; MP; NePA; PPP; TwAmPo; TwCP
Pursuit from Under. James Dickey. HAP; PPP
Pursuit of Love. *Unknown. See* Art Thou Gone in Haste?
Push about the brisk bowl, 'twill enliven the heart. The Ass. Moses Mendes. *Fr.* The Chaplet. TrJP
Push hard across the sand. A Song in Time of Order 1852. Swinburne. VLP
Pushan, God of Pasture ("Pushan, God of golden day"). *Unknown, tr. fr. Sanskrit by* Romesh Dutt. *Fr.* The Rig-veda. AWP
Pushcart Row. Rachel Field. SoPo
Pushed to the Scroll. Winifred Hamrick Farrar. AMV-80
Puss and the Boots, The, *sel.* H. D. Traill.
"Put case I circumvent and kill him: good." BXAP; Par
Puss came dancing out of a barn. *Unknown.* OxNR
Pussicat, wussicat, with a white foot. *Unknown.* OxNR
Pussy. Jane Taylor. *See* I Like Little Pussy.
Pussy and the Mice. *Unknown.* MoShBr
Pussy cat ate the dumplings. Mother Goose. OxNR
Pussy cat Mole jumped over a coal. *Unknown.* OxNR
Pussy has a whiskered face. Christina Rossetti. *Fr.* Sing-Song. TiPo
Pussy sits beside the fire. Mother Goose. OxNR
Pussy-cat, Pussy-cat, where have you been? Mother Goose. FaBoBe; FaFP; HBV-1; HBVY; OxNR; SoPo; TiPo
Pussycat Sits on a Chair. Edward Newman Horn. ELU
Pussywillow's buds are soft, The. Spring Is in the Making. Nona Keen Duffy. YeAr
Put a rocket up the man in the moon. Nocturne, Central Park South. L. E. Sissman. NYP
Put a sun in Sunday, Sunday. Yet Dish. Gertrude Stein. SOTW
Put away the flutes. Song for War. W. R. Rodgers. NeBP
Put case I circumvent and kill him: good. H. D. Traill. *Fr.* The Puss and the Boots. BXAP; Par
Put Down. Léon Damas, *tr. fr. French by* Seth L. Wolitz. TTY
Put 'em up solid, they won't come down! Post-Rail Song. *Unknown.* AS
Put every tiny robe away! In Vain. Rose Terry Cooke. AA
Put Forth, O God, Thy Spirit's Might, *with music.* Howard Chandler Robbins. AH, *with music;* TrPWD
Put forth thy leaf, thou lofty plane. Arthur Hugh Clough. EBEV
Put Hannibal i'th' scale. Hannibal. Juvenal, *tr. by* Henry Vaughan. *Fr.* Satires, X. OBVE
Put his head. Odiham. John Gray. FaBoCo
Put It Through. Edward Everett Hale. PAH
Put my glad rags in a cardboard box. The Other Side of This World. Calvin Forbes. MAYP
Put My Name Down. Irwin Silber. FSW
Put off the deference that this sea compels. Beach Talk. Norman MacCaig. PoA
Put off thy bark from shore, though near the night. Frederick Goddard Tuckerman. *Fr.* Sonnets. MOS
Put on the skillet, put on the led. Short'nin' Bread. *Unknown.* BLSo
Put on your silks, and piece by piece. To His Mistresses. Robert Herrick. CaPo
Put out the candle, close the biting rose. The End of the Story. Terence Tiller. ChMP; NeBP
Put out the mourners from your heart. To One of Little Faith. Hildegarde Flanner. HBMV
Put out to sea, if wine thou wouldest make. Sent from Egypt with a Fair Robe of Tissue to a Sicilian Vinedresser. T. Sturge Moore. OBEV; OBVV
Put them aside—I hate the sight of them! Relics. George Frederick Cameron. PeCV
Put them in print? Posthumous. Henry Augustin Beers. AA
Put things in their place. The Sky Is Blue. David Ignatow. FF; NNaP
"Put up the sword!" The voice of Christ once more. Whittier. *Fr.* Disarmament. PGD
Put your/ self out. Chasm. A. R. Ammons. OBAL
Put your finger in Foxy's hole. *Unknown.* OxNR
Put your hand in the creel. Marriage. *Unknown.* GBP
Put your hand on my heart, say that you love me as. A Betrothal. E. J. Scovell. GBL
Put your head, darling, darling, darling. Dear Dark Head [*or* Cean Dubh Deelish]. *Unknown, tr. by* Sir Samuel Ferguson. AnIV; BIrV; GBL; OBVV; OnYI; OxBI; SeCePo; UnTE
Put Your Word to My Lips. Rachel Korn, *tr. fr. Yiddish by* Seymour Mayne *and* Rivka Augenfeld. VWA
Put-Down Come On, The. A. R. Ammons. NoP
Putney Hymn, *with music. Unknown.* TrAS
Putta putta putt, A. Riding in a Motor Boat. Dorothy W. Baruch. FaPON
Putting God in the nation's life. God in the Nation's Life. *Unknown.* BLRP; WBLP
Putting in the Seed. Robert Frost. ErPo; FaBoEn; NoAM; OxBA
Putting On My Shoes I Hear the Floor Cry Out beneath Me. Michael Heffernan. BXAP
Putting On the Style. *Unknown.* FSW
Putting out the candles. My Father after Work. Gary Gildner. AMV-80; Psk
Putting to Sea. Louise Bogan. LiTM; PoA
Puva . . . puva . . . puva. Lullaby. *Unknown, tr. by* Natalie Curtis. SUS
Puzzle. Arnold Spilka. RHPC
Puzzle faces in the dying elms. " 'Mystery Boy' Looks for Kin in Nashville." Robert Hayden. LCAP; NoAM
Puzzled. Langston Hughes. *See* Harlem ("Here on the edge of hell").
Puzzled. Carolyn Wells. OBCA
Puzzled Census Taker, The. John Godfrey Saxe. HBV-2
Puzzled Centipede, The. Mrs. Edward Craster.. *See* Centipede Was Happy Quite, A.
Puzzled Game Birds, The. Thomas Hardy. PBBP
Pygmalion. Hans Brockerhoff. AMV-80
Pygmalion, *sel.* Hilda Doolittle ("H.D.").
"I made god upon god." WGRP
Pygmalion. Albert G. Miller. InMe
Pygmalion seeing these to spend their times. Ovid, *tr. by* George Sandys. *Fr.* Metamorphoses, X. OAEL-1
Pygmalion thought that women were a great abomination. Pygmalion. Albert G. Miller. InMe
Pygmalion's Statue Comes to Life. Ovid, *tr. fr. Latin by* Arthur Golding. *Fr.* Metamorphoses, X. OAEL-1
"Pygmies Are Pygmies Still, Though Percht on Alps." Gwendolyn Brooks. PoNe

Pylon for some incomplete gateway. The Monadnock. John Gould Fletcher. PoA
Pylons, The. Stephen Spender. AWP; NoAM
Pyms Anarchy. *At. to* Thomas Jordan. OBS
Pyramids, first, which in Egypt were laid, The. The Seven Wonders of the Ancient World. *Unknown.* EyDe; TreFT
Pyramis; or, The House of Ascent. A. D. Hope. PoAu-2
Pyramus and Thisbe, *sel.* Laurence Dakin.
"How sweetly sings this stream," *fr.* III, iii. CaP
Pyramus and Thisbe. John Godfrey Saxe. HBV-2; OnMSP
Pyrargyrite Metal, 9. Cecília Meireles, *tr. fr. Portuguese by* James Merrill. PBWP
Pyre of My Indian Summer, The. Mani Leib, *tr. fr. Yiddish by* Keith Bosley. VWA
Pyre of Patroclus, The. Homer, *tr. fr. Greek by* Pope. *Fr.* The Iliad, XXIII. OBEC
Pyrography. John Ashbery. PoM
Pyrrha, what slender well-shap'd beau. Horace, *tr. by* Anthony Horneck. Odes, I, 5. OBVE
Pythagoras planned it. Why did the people stare? The Statues. W. B. Yeats. AnIL; NoAM; OAEL-2; WeW
Pythagorean Razzle-Dazzle. Sid Gary. QQQ
Python, The. Hilaire Belloc. EvOK; HBVY; NA; OxBChV; ShM
Python. *Yoruba Oral Tradition, tr. by* Ulli Beier. WTO
Python I should not advise, A. The Python. Hilaire Belloc. EvOK; HBVY; NA; OxBChV; ShM
Pythoness, The. Kathleen Raine. MoBrPo; ViBoPo
Pyxidanthera, The. Augusta Cooper Bristol. AA

Q

Q:dwo. E. E. Cummings. OBAL
Q is a quoter who'll cite. A Quoter. Oliver Herford. TDH
Qua Cursum Ventus. Arthur Hugh Clough. EtS; HBV-2; MOS; OAEP; OBEV; OBVV; TreFT; VLP
Qua Song. Colette Inez. FAZ
Quack! Walter de la Mare. TiPo
"Quack! Quack!" Ducks at Dawn. James S. Tippett. SiSoSe; SoPo; TiPo
Quack, quack, quack! Dumpy Ducky. Lucy Larcom. OBCA
Quadroon mermaids, Afro angels, black saints. A Ballad of Remembrance. Robert Hayden. AmNP; BPo; IDB; PoBA; PoNe
Quadrupedremian Song, A. Thomas Hood. AmMo; FaBoNo
Quaerè. George Farewell. NOEC
Quaerit Jesum Suum Maria. Richard Crashaw. ACP
Quail and rabbit hunters with tawny hounds. Hunters in the Snow: Brueghel. Joseph Langland. LiTM; NePoEA
Quail in Autumn. William Jay Smith. Psk
Quail Walk. Heather Ross Miller. BoAnP
Quake, Quake, Quake: a Leaden Treasury of English Verse. Paul Dehn. *See* Leaden Treasury of English Verse, A.
Quaker Graveyard, The. S. Weir Mitchell. AA
Quaker Graveyard in Nantucket, The. Robert Lowell. AP; CMoP; CoBMV; HAP; LiTM; MiAP; MoAB; MoPo; MOS; MoVE; NePA; NMP; NoAM; NOBA; NoP; OxBA; SeCeV; TAP; TwAmPo; UnPo; ViBoPo
Quaker Hill. Hart Crane. *Fr.* The Bridge. LiTM
Quaker Ladies. Ellen Mackay Hutchinson Cortissoz. AA
Quaker Widow, The. Bayard Taylor. AA
Quakeress Bride, The. Elizabeth Clementine Kinney. AA
Quaker's Meeting, The. Samuel Lover. CenHV; OnYI
Quaker's Song, The. *Unknown.* CoMu
Quaker's wife got up to bake, The. *Unknown.* OxNR
Quaker's Wooing, The, *with music. Unknown.* AS
Quality of Air, A. Henry Chapin. FAZ
Quality of Mercy [Is Not Strain'd], The. Shakespeare. *Fr.* The Merchant of Venice, IV, i. FaFP; LiTB; TRV
(Mercy.) OHFP; TrGrPo; WBLP
(Portia's Plea for Mercy.) TreF
Quality of these trees, green height, The. Shine, Republic. Robinson Jeffers. AmFN; GOA
Quandary. Mrs. Edward Craster. *See* Centipede Was Happy Quite, A.
Quangle Wangle's Hat, The. Edward Lear. AmMo; EBEV; OnUR
Quantity and Quality. Winifred M. Letts. HBMV
Quantocks, The. Wordsworth. FaBoPP
Quantrell, *with music. Unknown.* CoSo (A *and* B *vers.)*
Quantum. Martin Johnston. CBAP
Quantum Est Quod Desit. Thomas Moore. *See* Did Not.
Quarrel, The. Conrad Aiken. MoAB; MoAmPo; PoPl
Quarrel, The. Diane DiPrima. NMM
Quarrel, The. Eleanor Farjeon. FaPON
Quarrel. Jean McDougall. GoBC
Quarrel, The. Karen Swenson. GrPl
Quarrel. *Yoruba Oral Tradition, tr. by* Ulli Beier. WTO
Quarrel of the sparrows in the eaves, The. The Sorrow of Love. W. B. Yeats. MoAB; MoBrPo; NoAM; OAEL-2; PoEL-5; VLP
Quarrel with Fortune, A. Benjamin Colman. SCAP
Quarrelling. Isaac Watts. *See* Let Dogs Delight to Bark and Bite.
Quarrelsome Bishop, A. Walter Savage Landor. FaBoEE; OBSV
Quarrelsome Trio, The. "L. G." WBLP
Quarries in Syracuse. Louis Golding. TrJP
Quarry, The. W. H. Auden. *See* O What Is That Sound.
Quarry, The. Vassar Miller. NePoEA-2; WPE
Quarry/Rock. Paul Mariah. PeHV
Quarry Pool, The. Denise Levertov. VGW
Quarry whence thy form majestic sprung, The. Washington's Statue. Henry T. Tuckerman. AA
Quarter century ago and, A. H. S. Beeney Auction Sales. David R. Pichaske. AMV-81
Quarter horse, no rider, A. Horse. Jim Harrison. BoAnP; PH
Quarter less four,/ Half twain. *Unknown.* AmFP
Quartered/ a seed rocks. The Apple. Bruce Guernsey. PPJ
Quartermaster Store, The. *Unknown.* FSW
Quatrain: "Christ bears a thousand crosses now." Charles G. Blanden. PGD
Quatrain: "Golf links lie so near the mill, The." Sarah Cleghorn. *See* Golf Links, The.
Quatrain, A: "Hark at the lips of this pink whorl of shell." Frank Dempster Sherman. AA
Quatrain: "Jack, eating rotten cheese, did say." *Unknown, wr. at. to* Benjamin Franklin. *See* Jack and Roger.
Quatrain: "My bloodstream chokes on gall and spleen." Barend Toerien, *tr. fr. Afrikaans by author.* PeSA
Quatrain: "Oh! to be wafted away." *Unknown.* NA
Quatrain: "Sarmèd, whom they intoxicated from the cup of love." Sarmèd the Yahud, *tr. fr. Persian by* David Shea. TrJP
Quatrain: "Squeak's heard in the orchestra, A." George T. Lanigan. WhC
Quatrain: "This existence has, without the azure sphere, no reality." Sarmèd the Yahud, *tr. fr. Persian by* David Shea. TrJP
Quatrain: "Young Apollo, golden-haired, A." Frances Cornford. *See* Youth.
Quatrains. Gwendolyn B. Bennett. CDC
Quatrains, *sels.* Emerson.
Gardener. OxBA
Orator. OxBA
Poet. OxBA; PCP
Sacrifice. HBV-2; HBVY; TRV
Quatrains. Sidney Godolphin. *See* Song: "Noe more unto my thoughts appeare."
Quatrains. Salah Jahin, *tr. fr. Arabic by* Samir M. Zoghby. TTY
Quatrains. Omar Khayyám, *tr. by* Edward Fitzgerald. *Fr.* Rubáiyát of Omar Khayyám of Naishápur. SeCePo
Quatrina. Joseph Bennett. LiTA
Quavering cry, A. Screech-owl? Night, Death, Mississippi. Robert Hayden. FF; LCAP; VGW
"Quay recedes, The. Hurrah! Ahead we go!" The Colonel's Soliloquy. Thomas Hardy. OBWP
Que Bonita Bandera. *Tr. fr. Spanish.* FSW
Quebec. Eldon Grier. PeCV
Quebec Farmhouse. John Glassco. NOBC; PeCV
Quebec Liquor Commission Store. A. M. Klein. OBCV
Québec May. Earle Birney. WHW
Quebec, the grey old city on the hill. At Quebec. Jean Blewett. CaP
Queen. Dom Moraes. NePoEA-2
Queen, The. Pablo Neruda, *tr. fr. Spanish by* Donald D. Walsh. OLR
Queen, The. Kenneth Pitchford. NYBP; NYP
Queen, The. William Winter. *See* My Queen.
Queen,/ thou holdest in thine arms. To the Most Holy Mother of God. *Unknown, tr. by* Shane Leslie. ISi
Queen and Huntress. Ben Jonson. *See* Hymn to Diana.
Queen and Slave. Mortimer Collins. OBVV
Queen Anne. *Unknown.* ChTr
Queen Anne's Lace. June Jordan. TAP
Queen Anne's Lace. Mary Leslie Newton. FaPON; MoShBr
Queen Anne's Musicians. Thomas Hennell. FaBoTw
Queen-Ann's Lace. William Carlos Williams. AmPP; AP; BLPL; MoAB; MoAmPo; NoAM; NOBA; NoP; PrIm; TAP
Queen Bess was Harry's daughter. Stand forward partners all! The Looking-Glass. Kipling. EvOK; FaBoTw; OBMV
Queen Cleopatra. Conrad Aiken. Variations, X. HBMV
Queen declares, The: "The evening wears." Lullaby for an Emigrant. Benjamin Fondane, *tr. by* Keith Bosley. VWA

Queen Eleanor's Confession. *Unknown.* ESPB (A *and* B *vers.*); OBET; PrIm
Queen Elizabeth. *Unknown.* DBV
Queen has lately lost a part, The. Verses Said to Be Written on the Union. Swift. APAS
Queen is taking a drive today, The. The Queen's Last Ride. Ella Wheeler Wilcox. BLPA
Queen Jane ("Queen Jane lay in labour for six weeks and some more"). *Unknown.* *See* Death of Queen Jane, The.
Queen Jane sat at her window one day. The King's Dochter Lady Jean. *Unknown.* AmFP
Queen Jane was [*or* lay] in labor [*or* labour]. The Death of Queen Jane [*or* Queen Jane]. *Unknown.* AmFP; ESPB (A *vers.*); FSW; OBET
Queen Jeanie, Queen Jeanie, travel'd six weeks and more. The Death of Queen Jane. *Unknown.* ESPB (B *vers.*); ViBoFo
Queen lived in the South, A. Dagonet's Canzonet. Ernest Rhys. HBV-1
Queen Mab. Thomas Hood. HBV-1; HBVY
Queen Mab. Ben Jonson. *See* Mab the Mistress-Fairy.
Queen Mab. Shakespeare. *See* Mercutio's Queen Mab Speech.
Queen Mab, *sels.* Shelley.
Magic Car Moved On, The, *fr. I.* GN
War Is the Statesman's Game, *fr.* IV. FF; PPON
Queen Mother to New Queen. Robert Graves. OBSV
Queen Nefertiti. *Unknown.* RHPC
Queen of all Queens, oh! Wonder of the loveliness of women. Hymn to the Virgin Mary. Conal O'Riordan, *tr. by* Eleanor Hull. ISi
Queen of all streets, Fifth Avenue. Thompson Street. Samuel McCoy. HBMV
Queen of all streets, you stand alway. Piccadilly. Thomas Burke. HBMV
Queen of Aragon, The, *sel.* William Habington.
Fine Young Folly. CavP; OBS
(Pretty Sport.) NOBE
(Song: "Fine young folly, though you were.") FaBoEn; MePo
Queen of Cheese. James McIntyre. FiBHP; PeD
Queen of Corinth, The, *sel.* John Fletcher, *and others.*
Weep No More, *fr.* III, ii, *at. to* Fletcher. CH; EIL; OBEV; ViBoPo
(Mourn No More.) TrGrPo
Queen of Courtesy, The. *Unknown.* *Fr.* The Pearl. ACP; ISi, *mod. vers. by* Stanley Perkins Chase
Queen of Crete, The. John Grimes. HBMV
Queen of Egypt yawned and frowned, The. Events. George O'Neil. HBMV
Queen of Elfan's [*or* Elfland's] Nourice [*or* Nourrice], The. *Unknown.* ESPB
"I heard a cow low, a bonnie cow low," *sel.* FaBoCh
Queen of Fairies, The. *Unknown.* *See* Fairy Queen, The.
Queen of fragrance, lovely rose. The Rose-Bud. William Broome. LoBV; OBEC; OBEV
Queen of Hearts, The. *Unknown.* FSW; OBET
Queen of Hearts, The / She made some tarts. Mother Goose. FaBoBe; HBV-1; HBVY; OxNR
Queen of Heaven. *Unknown.* OxBM
(In Praise of Mary.) MeEL
Queen of Heaven Mausoleum. Dennis Schmitz. LCAP
Queen of Heaven, of Hell eke Emperess. To the Virgin. John Lydgate. ACP; GoBC
Queen of Horizons. Joseph Dever. ISi
Queen of Lydia, The. C. H. Sisson. OxBC
Queen of Paphos, Erycine, The. *Unknown.* EIL; GBL
Queen of Scotland, The. *Unknown.* ESPB
Queen of Seasons, The. Cardinal Newman. GoBC
Queen of the Angels, The. Boccaccio, *tr. fr. Italian by* Thomas Walsh. ISi
Queen of the heavens, we hail thee. Ave Regina Coelorum. *Unknown, tr. by* Winfred Douglas. ISi
Queen of the Nile, The. William Jay Smith. GrPl
Queen of the silver bow!—by thy pale beam. To the Moon. Charlotte Smith. MOON
Queen of the World. *Unknown.* PGD
Queen Sabbath. Hayyim Nahman Bialik, *tr. fr. Hebrew by* Jessie Sampter. TrJP
Queen sat in her balcony, The. Gil, the Toreador. Charles Henry Webb. AA
Queen she sent to look for me, The. Grenadier. A. E. Housman. OBMV; OBWP
Queen stood on thy right hand, The. Bible, *O.T.* (*Douay vers.*). Psalms, XLV, 9-15. ISi
Queen Venus wander'd away with a cry. Our Lady of the Sea. Alfred Noyes. OBVV
Queen Victoria. *Unknown.* CoMu
Queen Victoria and Me. Leonard Cohen. NoAM
Queen Virtue's Court, which some call Stella's face. Astrophel and Stella, IX. Sir Philip Sidney. SiPS
Queen was beloved by a jester, A. The Cap and Bells. W. B. Yeats. MoAB; MoBrPo
Queen was in the parlour, The. Contemporary Nursery Rhyme. *Unknown.* PV; SpRo
Queen went from me while I slept, The. Queen. Dom Moraes. NePoEA-2
Queen Yang-Se-Fu/ Has seventy great castles. Yang-Se-Fu. "Yehoash," *tr. by* Isidore Goldstick. TrJP
Queene and Huntresse. Ben Jonson. *See* Hymn to Diana.
Queene of Arragon, The. William Habington. *See* Queen of Aragon, The.
Queenie ("Queenie's strong and Queenie's tall"). Leland B. Jacobs. RHPC
Queens, The. Robert Fitzgerald. NYBP
Queens. J. M. Synge. ChTr; GBL; MoBrPo; OBMV; OnYI
Queen's Afterdinner Speech, The, *sel.* Percy French.
"'Me loving subjects,' sez she." OxBI
Queen's Chariot, The. Michael Drayton. *Fr.* Nymphidia. OBS
Queen's Last Ride, The. Ella Wheeler Wilcox. BLPA
Queen's Marie, The. *Unknown.* *See* Mary Hamilton.
Queen's Song, The. James Elroy Flecker. BrPo; HBV-2
Queen's Speech, The. Arthur Mainwaring. APAS
Queen's Wake, The, *sel.* James Hogg.
Kilmeny. HBV-2; OBEV; OBRV
(Bonny Kilmeny Gaed Up the Glen.) BSV; GoTS
Queer, The. Henry Vaughan. PoEL-2
Queer are the ways of a man I know. The Phantom Horsewoman. Thomas Hardy. CMoP; FaBoPP; LO; NOBE; PoEL-5; WSC
Queer Fellow Named Woodin, A. "Cuthbert Bede." *See* Limerick: "There was a queer fellow named Woodin."
Queer sights we every day do find. The Dandy Horse. *Unknown.* OBET
Queer Things. Emanuel Carnevali. EAS
Queer Things. James Reeves. WSC
Queer's Song. Richard Howard. *Fr.* Gaiety. ErPo
Quentin Durward, *sel.* Sir Walter Scott.
County Guy. OAEP; OBRV
(Serenade, A.) GTBS; GTBS-P
(Song: "Ah! County Guy, the hour is nigh.") CH
Query. Ebon Dooley. PoBA
Query. Mildred Weston. POL
Query, a question, A. The Water of Kane. *Tr. fr. Hawaiian by* N. B. Emerson. WTO
Quest, The. Ellen Mackay Hutchinson Cortissoz. HBV-1
Quest, The. Gladys Cromwell. HBMV
Quest. Naomi Long Madgett. BPo
Quest, The. Eliza Scudder. TrPWD
(Who by Searching Can Find Out God?) WGRP
Quest. Edmund Clarence Stedman. *Fr.* Corda Concordia. AA
Quest, The. Harold Vinal. GoYe
Quest, The. James Wright. NYBP
Quest of Silence, The, *sel.* Christopher Brennan.
"Fire in the heavens, and fire along the hills." CBAP; PoAu-1
Quest of the Sangraal, The, *sels.* Robert Stephen Hawker.
"Land is lonely now, The: Anathema." EBVV
"Then saw they that the mighty Quest was won!" VLP
Questing. Anne Spencer. CDC
Question, The. W. H. Auden. SUW
Question, The. James Beattie. FaBoCo
Question, A. William Cole. BoAnP
Question. Norma Craig. POL
Question, The. Robert Duncan. NeAP
Question, The. Norman Gale. ELU; FiBHP
Question, The. W. W. Gibson. MMA
Question, The. Karla Kuskin. NTCP; PDV
Question, A. Edna Livingston. GoYe
Question, The. F. T. Prince. BoLoP; ChMP; GTBS-P; PeSA
Question, The. Muriel Rukeyser. IHMS; WPOW
Question, The ("I dream'd that, as I wander'd by the way"). Shelley. CH; EnRP; FiP; HBV-1; OBEV; OBRV; PoPle
(Dream of the Unknown, The.) GTBS; GTBS-P
Question. May Swenson. HeIP; LiTM; NePoEA; PrIm; VGW
Question. J. M. Synge. ELU; MoBrPo; OBMV; OBVV; OxBI; OxBTC; PAI
Question, The. Rachel Annand Taylor. HBV-2
Question, The. Frederick Goddard Tuckerman. AP
Question ("Do you love me"). *Unknown.* RHPC
("Do you love me.") PoSC
Question ("If I really, really trust him"). *Unknown.* BLRP
Question ("Were the whole world as good as you—not an atom better"). *Unknown.* WBLP
Question and Answer. Samuel Hoffenstein. DBV; FiBHP; PV
Question and Answer. Langston Hughes. BPo
Question and Answer. Kathleen Raine. MoBrPo
Question Answer'd, The. Blake. *Fr.* Several Questions Answered. ELU; ErPo; FaBoEE; GBL; NoP; ViBoPo
(What Is It Men in Women Do Require.) NIP; OAEL-2
Question in a Field. Louise Bogan. NYBP; SBG

Question is, The. These Two. Howard Schwartz. VWA
Question is, The: how does one hold an apple. The Gesture. George Oppen. *Fr.* Five Poems about Poetry. NNaP
Question, Is It, The? Alfred G. Bailey. AMV-81
Question Is Proof, The. Elizabeth Bartlett. NePoAm-2
Question, lords and ladies, is, The. Percy Shelley. John Peale Bishop. ErPo
Question Mark, The. Persis Greely Anderson. WhC
Question of Form and Content, A. Jon Stallworthy. OxBC
Question of Libel, A. Pope. *Fr.* The First Satire of the Second Book of Horace. PrIm
Question then, to state it first. The. Samuel Butler. *Fr.* Hudibras. NOBL
Question to Life. Patrick Kavanagh. MoBrPo
Question to Lisetta, The. Matthew Prior. OBEV
Question was an academic one, The. Tomorrows. James Merrill. OBAL
Question Whither, The. George Meredith. HBV-2; WGRP
Question: Who am I? A Woman Defending Herself Examines Her Own Character Witness. Susan Griffin. NPGG
Questioning Faces. Robert Frost. ELU; GrPl; NCSH
Questionings. Samuel Johnson. HBV-2
Questions [1] ("Why do you love her"). Donald Hall. FF
Questions [2] ("How is it now"). Donald Hall. FF
Questions. Dagmar Hilarova, *tr. fr. Czech by* Ewald Osers. VWA
Questions, The. Robert Pinsky. NPGG
Questions and Answers. Doris Muhringer, *tr. fr. German by* Beth Bjorklund. AMV-80
Questions and Answers. Diana O Hehir. NPGG
Questions at Night. Louis Untermeyer. FaPON
Questions for the Candidate. John Holmes. PP
Questions My Son Asked Me, Answers I Never Gave Him. Nancy Willard. LCAP
Questions of Travel. Elizabeth Bishop. NOBA
Quha Is Perfyte. Alexander Scott. OxBS
Quhen [*or* Qwhen *or* When] Alexander [*or* Alysandyr] our kynge was dede. The Death of Alexander [*or* Cantus]. *Unknown.* BSV; FaBoCh; GoTS; OxBS
Quhen Flora Had O'erfret the Firth. *Unknown. See* When Flora Had Ourfret the Firth.
Quhen he wes yung, and cled in grene. Quhy Sowld Nocht Allane Honorit Be? *Unknown.* OxBS
Quhen Noye had maid his Sacrifyce. After the Flood. Sir David Lindsay. *Fr.* The Monarche. OxBS
Quhen thai him fand, and gud Wallace him saw. *See* When they him fand . . .
Quhen that I had oversene this regioun. Of the Realme of Scotland. Sir David Lindsay. *Fr.* The Dreme. OxBS
Quhen thou art careit to that cuntree. Virgil, *tr. by* Gavin Douglas. *Fr.* The Aeneid, III. OBVE
"Quhy dois your brand sae drop wi' bluid." *See* "Why does your brand sae drap wi' bluid."
Quhy Sowld Nocht Allane Honorit Be? *Unknown.* OxBS
Quhy will ye, merchantis of renoun. To the Merchantis of Edinburgh. William Dunbar. FaBoPP; OxBS
Qui Bien Aime a Tard Oublie. Chaucer. *See* Now Welcome, Somer.
Qui Laborat, Orat. Arthur Hugh Clough. TrPWD; VLP
Qui nunc dancere vult modo. A Holiday Task. Gilbert Abbot á Beckett. NA
Qui Perdiderit Animam Suam. Richard Crashaw. ACP
Quia Amore Langueo ("In a tabernacle" [*or* "Within a chamber of this toure"]). *Unknown.* ACP; ISi, *tr. fr.* Middle English *by* E. M. Clerke; MeEL
Quia Amore Langueo ("In a valley [*or* the vale *or* the vaile] of this restless mind [*or* restles mind *or* restles mynd"]). *Unknown.* LO; NOBE, *tr. by* Helen Gardner; NOCV, *tr. by* Helen Gardner; OBEV; OxBM; OxBoCh; PoEL-1
Quick, The. Sean Jennett. NeBP
Quick!/ Empty the offices. Blue Alert. Eve Merriam. PCP
Quick! a last poem before I go. On Rachmaninoff's Birthday. Frank O'Hara. CAPP; PoM
Quick and Bitter. Yehuda Amichai, *tr. fr. Hebrew by* Assia Gutmann. BoLoP
Quick and the Dead, The. Ilarie Voronca, *tr. fr. French by* Edouard Roditi. VWA
Quick-falling dew. Basho, *tr. fr. Japanese by* Curtis Hidden Page. AWP
Quick flick of a smile, The. Edwin A. Nelms. Sheryl L. Nelms. Str
Quick, for the tide is sifting down the shore. Pause. Ann Hamilton. HBMV
Quick, Henry, the Flit! James Schuyler. NoAM
Quick! Hoist the jib and cast us off, my son. Over Bright Summer Seas. Robert Hillyer. NYBP
Quick in spite I said unkind. Brazen Tongue. William Rose Benét. MoAmPo
Quick lunch! quick lunch! the neon cries, and I. Essay on Lunch. Walker Gibson. NYBP
"Quick Now, Here, Now, Always." William J. Rewak. AMV-81
Quick on my feet in those Novembers of my loneliness. A Mad Fight Song for William S. Carpenter, 1966. James Wright. LiSp
Quick, painter, quick, the moment seize. Currente Calamo. Arthur Hugh Clough. *Fr.* Mari Magno. LoBV
Quick sea shone, The/ And shivered like spread wings of angels blown. Sunrise at Sea. Swinburne. *Fr.* Tristram of Lyonesse: The Sailing of the Swallow. EtS
Quick sparks on the gorse-bushes are leaping, The. The Wild Common. D. H. Lawrence. CoBMV
Quick, woman, in your net. The Net. W. R. Rodgers. AnIL; BoLoP; CIP; ErPo; NMP; OxBI
Quickening. Christopher Morley. HBMV
Quickening, The. Stella Weston Tuttle. GoYe
Quicker/ than that can't. A Sight. Robert Creeley. NaP
Quickly and pleasantly the seasons blow. Robert Hillyer. Sonnets, I. HBMV
Quickly. What is being forgotten? What Is Being Forgotten. Eloise Klein Healy. GP
Quickness. Henry Vaughan. ELP; LoBV; MeLP; MePo; NOBE; NOCV; OBS; OxBoCh; SeCePo; SeCP; SeCV-1
Quicksands. William Zaranka. BXAP
Quicksilver lord who holds sway over thieves. To Mercury. X. J. Kennedy. SOTS
Quick-Step. Robert Creeley. VGW
Quid Non Speremus, Amantes? Ernest Dowson. HBV-1
Quid Petis, O Fily? *Unknown.* SeCeV
Quid Restat, *abr.* Lucius Beebe. RFM
Quid Sit Futurum Cras Fuge Quaerere. Matthew Prior. FaBoEE
Quid the Cynic's Song. Blake. *Fr.* An Island in the Moon. FaBoNo
Quidditie, The. George Herbert. PoEL-2
¿Quien Sabe? Madge Morris. BPAW
Quiescent, a Person Sits Heart and Soul. Ring Lardner. OBAL
Quiet. Marjorie Pickthall. NOBC; OBCV
Quiet. Ernest Radford. OBVV
Quiet. Brian Swann. AmPA
Quiet. Giuseppe Ungaretti, *tr. fr. Italian by* Allen Mandelbaum. PoPl
Quiet as are the quiet skies. A Smiling Demon of Notre Dame. Sophie Jewett. AA
Quiet by Hillsides in the Afternoon. Martha Lifson. AMV-80
Quiet deepens, The. You will not persuade. Farewell to Van Gogh. Charles Tomlinson. CMoP; GTBS-P; NMP
Quiet Desperation. Louis Simpson. SV
Quiet Enemy, The. Walter de la Mare. BrPo
Quiet-eyed Cattle, The. Leslie Norris. PChr
Quiet Fog, The. Marge Piercy. UnPo
Quiet from Fear of Evil. "S. C. M'K." BLRP
Quiet Fun. Harry Graham. DBV; ShM
Quiet Glades of Eden, The. Robert Graves. BoLoP; ErPo
Quiet Glen, The. Douglas Fraser. PoSH
Quiet his loves lay, at the bottom of his mind. We Were in the 8th Grade. John Berryman. GLGT
Quiet home had Parson Gray, A. Parson Gray. Goldsmith. NA
Quiet Hour, The. Louise Hollingsworth Bowman. BLRP
Quiet House, The. Charlotte Mew. BrRo; EBEV; SBG
Quiet Kingdom, The. Carl Busse, *tr. fr. German by* Ludwig Lewisohn. AWP
Quiet Life, The. Pope. *See* Ode on Solitude.
Quiet Life, The. *Unknown, at. to* William Byrd. EIL; GoBC; HBV-1 (Herdmen, The.) NOBE; OBSC
Quiet Light of Flies, The. Natan Zach, *tr. fr. Hebrew by* Peter Everwine *and* Shula Starkman. VWA
Quiet Mind, The. *Unknown.* OBSC
Quiet moon, immaculate of face, The. "William Baylebridge." Love Redeemed, CVII. CBAP
Quiet, my horse, be quiet. Alexander to His Horse. Eleanor Farjeon. PH
Quiet Nights, The. Katharine Tynan. HBV-2
Quiet Normal Life, A. Wallace Stevens. LCAP
Quiet now, feel the kindly pressure of darkness. Winter Solstice Poem. Diana Scott. BrRo
Quiet of the Dead, The. Mary Morison Webster. PeSA
Quiet Pilgrim, The. Edith M. Thomas. AA
Quiet Singer, The. Charles Hanson Towne. HBV-2
Quiet Soul, A. John Oldham. OBEV
Quiet Things. Grace Noll Crowell. PoLF
Quiet Tide near Ardrossan, The. Charles Tennyson Turner. FaBoPP
Quiet Town. William Stafford. MAT
Quiet Waters. Blanche Shoemaker Wagstaff. BLPA
Quiet woods in the hot Eastertide, The. Woods and Kestrel. Julian Bell. ChMP
Quiet Work. Matthew Arnold. FaBoBe; HBV-1; OAEP; TrGrPo

Quieter the people are, The. The Signboard. Robert Creeley. ConAP
Quietly. Kenneth Rexroth. ErPo
Quietly and while at rest on the trim grass I have gazed. The Air of June Sings. Edward Dorn. NeAP; PoM
Quietly as rosebuds. Love's Coming. Shaw Neilson. PoAu-1
Quietly at our side the dead. The Dead Men. Sophia de Mello Breyner Andresen, *tr. by* Allen Francovich. PBWP
Quietly the children wait. The Children. Clifford Dyment. ChMP
Quietness clings to the air. The Snow Fall. Archibald MacLeish. PoPl
Quietude of a soft wind, The. The Creditor. Louis MacNeice. EaLo
Quilled Quilt, a Needle Bed, A. Brad Leithauser. MAYP
Quills. Charlotte Gafford. AMV-81
Quilt, The. Larry Levis. MAYP
Quilt, The. Mary Effie Lee Newsome. CDC
Quilted/ patches, unlike the smooth slick loveliness. Making. Phyllis Webb. PoCh
Quinks, The. Don Marquis. *Fr.* Savage Portraits. DBV; HBMV; YaD
Quinnapoxet. Stanley Kunitz. DiL
Quinquireme of Nineveh from distant Ophir. Cargoes. John Masefield. BLPL; CMoP; FaBV; FaPo; FaPON; FaPoR; LiTM; MoAB; MoBrPo; MOS; NOBE; OBEV; OBMV; OBVV; PAI; PoRA; RoGo; SeCeV; TEP; TreF
Quintana Lay in the Shallow Grave of Coral. Karl Shapiro. VGW
Quintina of Crosses, A. Chad Walsh. TrCP
Quip, The. George Herbert. JCP; LiTB; OAEP; OBS; OxBoCh; SeCP; SeCV-1
Quire of bright Beauties in Spring did appear, A. The Lady's Song. Dryden. LoBV
"Quis pro Domino?" Robert Browning. *Fr.* The Ring and the Book, X. OAEP
Quite Apart from the Holy Ghost. Adrian Mitchell. OBSV
Quite apropos that we should visit here. Family Plot. Sarah Singer. AMV-81
Quite close to the abrupt city. Seal Rocks: San Francisco. Robert Conquest. PP
Quite Forsaken. D. H. Lawrence. BrPo
Quite horfen, fer a lark, coves on a ship. The Helbatrawss. Kingsley Amis. NOBL
Quite often, when I look out. English Train, Summer. Ralph Pomeroy. GP
Quite, quite./ Oh I agree. Restricted. Eve Merriam. TrJP
Quite rightly, we remained among the living. The Survivors. Adrienne Rich. NYBP
Quite spent with thoughts I left my cell, and lay. Vanity of Spirit. Henry Vaughan. AnAnS-1
Quite the Cheese. H. C. Waring. BXAP
Quite unexpectedly as Vasserot. The End of the World. Archibald MacLeish. AP; BLPL; CMoP; CoBMV; HoPM; InPK; LiTM; MAT; MoAB; MoAmPo; NCSH; NePA; NoAM; NOBA; OBAL; OxBA; PAI; TAP; TrGrPo; VGW
Quits. Thomas Bailey Aldrich. AA
Quits. Matthew Prior. *See* Epigram: "To John I owed great obligation."
Quitter, The. *Unknown.* BLPA; WBLP
Quitting is out of the question yet. Dispatch Number Sixty. Doug Fetherling. NeAC
Quivira. Arthur Guiterman. BPAW; PAH
Quo life, the warld is mine. The Flyting o' Life and Daith. Hamish Henderson. OxBS
Quo' the Tweed. *Unknown.* CH
Quo Vadis? Myles Connolly. TRV
Quod Dunbar to Kennedy. William Dunbar. OxBoLi
Quod Tegit Omnia. Yvor Winters. MoVE; QFR
Quoich, the Ey, the Slugain, The. The Drunken Dee. Syd Scroggie. PoSH
Quoits. Mary Effie Lee Newsome. CDC
Quondam was I in my lady's grace. Sir Thomas Wyatt. GBL
Quoniam Ego in Flagella Paratus Sum. William Habington. ACP
Quotation from Shakespeare with Slight Improvements, A. "Lewis Carroll." FaBoNo
Quotations. George Oppen. NNaP
Quoter, A. Oliver Herford. TDH
Quoth a cat to me once: "Pray relieve." Tact. Oliver Herford. TDH
Quoth Cibber to Pope, tho' in verse you foreclose. Pope. FaBoEE
Quoth he, My faith as adamantine. Samuel Butler. *Fr.* Hudibras. OBSV
Quoth he, to bid me not to love. Samuel Butler. *Fr.* Hudibras. NOBL
Quoth John to Joan. *Unknown.* CH
Quoth Rab to Kate, My sonsy dear. Marriage and the Care o't. Robert Lochore. HBV-1
Quoth Satan to Arnold: "My worthy good fellow." Epigram. *Unknown.* PAH
Quoth she, I wish I could prescribe your help. Rachel Speght. *Fr.* A Dream. WPE
Quoth the bookworm, "I don't care one bit." The Omnivorous Bookworm. Oliver Herford. TDH
Quoth tongue of neither maid nor wife. Elena's Song. Sir Henry Taylor. *Fr.* Philip van Artevelde, II. OBEV; OBRV; OBVV
Qwhen Alexander our kynge was dede. *See* Quhen Alexander our kynge was dede.

R

R. Alcona to J. Brenzaida. Emily Brontë. *See* Remembrance.
R-and-R Centre: An Incident from the Vietnam War. D. J. Enright. OxBC
RIP. Jean Balderston. SOTS
R.I.P. "Jan Struther." InMe
R is for the Restaurant. Phyllis McGinley. TiPo
R.M.S. *Titanic, sel.* Anthony Cronin.
"On the bog road the blackthorn flowers, the turf-stacks." BIrV
Rabbi Ben Ezra. Robert Browning. BLPL; FaFP; FiP; HBV-1; MasP; OAEP; OBNC; OBVV; TEP; WGRP
"Grow old along with me!" *sel.* FaBV; PoPl; TreFT; TRV
Rabbi, if a child is born with two heads. Pilpul. Rodger Kamenetz. VWA
Rabbi is before me, The. David Meltzer. *Fr.* A Midrash. GP
Rabbi of condiments. The Garlic. Bert Meyers. VWA
Rabbi Pinhas:/ From true prayers. Expounding the Torah. Louis Zukofsky. VWA
Rabbi Yom-Tob of Mayence Petitions His God. A. M. Klein. TrJP
Rabbi Yussel Luksh of Chelm. Jacob Glatstein, *tr. fr. Yiddish by* Nathan Halper. TrJP
Rabbit, The. W. H. Davies. BoAnP
Rabbit, The. Georgia Roberts Durston. SoPo
Rabbit, The. Edith King. HBMV; SoPo
Rabbit, The. Elizabeth Madox Roberts. OBCA; RHPC; SoPo; TiPo
Rabbit. Tom Robinson. FaPON
Rabbit, The. *Unknown.* DBV; FaBoCo; FiBHP
Rabbit as King of the Ghosts, A. Wallace Stevens. SOTW
Rabbit Catcher, The. Sylvia Plath. SBG
Rabbit crossed and dodged and turned, The. The Chase. J. V. Cunningham. LiSp; NoAM
Rabbit Cry. Edward Lucie-Smith. NePoEA-2
Rabbit Foot Blues. *Unknown.* BluL
Rabbit has a charming face, The. The Rabbit. *Unknown.* DBV; FaBoCo; FiBHP
Rabbit has a habit, The. The Rabbit. Georgia Roberts Durston. SoPo
Rabbit Hunter, The. Robert Frost. GDP; LiSp
Rabbits. Dorothy Baruch. SoPo; SUS; TiPo
Rabbits. Dennis Schmitz. FiCP
Rabbits' Song outside the Tavern, The. Elizabeth J. Coatsworth. SUS; TiPo
(Song of the Rabbits outside the Tavern.) OBCA
Rabble Soldier, *with music.* *Unknown.* AS
Rabia. *Unknown, tr. fr. Arabic by* James Freeman Clarke. HBV-2
Rabid or dog-dull. Let me tell you how. A Professor's Song. John Berryman. HeIP; NoAM; NOBA; OxBC
Raccoon. Kenneth Rexroth. *Fr.* A Bestiary. NNaP
(Racoon.) FiBHP
Raccoon on the Road. Joseph Payne Brennan. GoYe
Raccoon Poem. Miriam Palmer. NMM
Raccoon [*or* Racoon] wears a black mask, The. Raccoon [*or* Racoon]. Kenneth Rexroth. *Fr.* A Bestiary. FiBHP; NNaP
Raccoons. Aileen Fisher. PDV
Raccoons are selectively polygamous. Raccoon Poem. Miriam Palmer. NMM
Raccoon's Got a Bushy Tail. *Unknown.* FSW
Race of the *Oregon,* The. John James Meehan. PAH
Race Prejudice. Alfred Kreymborg. ELU
Race Question, The. Naomi Long Madgett. BPo
Race Riot, Tulsa, 1921. Sharon Olds. MAYP
Racer's Widow, The. Louise Glück. AmPA; GeTw; LiSp; NYBP
Rachel. Rachel, *tr. fr. Hebrew by* N. N. VWA
Rachel Goes to the Well for Water ("Rachel stands by the mirror and plaits"). Itzik Manger, *tr. fr. Yiddish by* Ruth Whitman. VWA
Rachelle weeping—painting 1772. Remember the Ladies. Lyn Lifshin. LTB
Rachel's Lament. Linda Zisquit. VWA
Racing Eight, A. James L. Cuthbertson. PoAu-1
Racing-Man, The. A. P. Herbert. BoAnP; FiBHP; PH; WhC
Racing, reckoning fingers flick. Palladas, *tr. fr. Greek by* Tony Harrison. OBVE
Rack upon rack of leaves all elbowing. Spring. W. R. Rodgers. OnYI
Rackets around the Blue Mountain Lake, The. *Unknown.* FSW
Rackheath. Coman Leavenworth. Norfolk Memorials, II. LiTA

Racoon. Kenneth Rexroth. *See* Raccoon.
Racoon up the 'simmon tree. The Persimmon Tree. *Unknown.* GBP
Racoon wears a black mask, The. *See* Raccoon wears a black mask, The.
Radar. Alan Ross. DFF; FF
Radcliff, Kentucky. Thomas G. Nickens. LFAC
Radiance, The. Kabir, *tr. fr. Hindi by* Robert Bly. LLLT
Radiance of Extinct Stars, The. Allan Kolski Horvitz. VWA
Radiance of that star that leans on me, The. Delay. Elizabeth Jennings. InPK; NePoEA; OxBTC
Radiant Is the World Soul. Rav Abraham Isaac Kook, *tr. fr. Hebrew by* Ben Zion Bokser. VWA
Radiant Ranks of Seraphim. Valery Bryusov, *tr. fr. Russian by* Babette Deutsch *and* Avrahm Yarmolinsky. AWP
Radiant soda of the seashore fashions, The. Far Rockaway. Delmore Schwartz. NoAM
Radiation Leak. Jody Aliesan. LTB
Radiator Lions. Dorothy Aldis. SoPo
Radical, The. Waring Cuney. CDC
Radical Creed, A. Gelett Burgess. FaBoNo
Radical in the Alligator Shirt, The. Lou Lipsitz. AMV-80
Radical Song of 1786, A. St. John Honeywood. PAH
Radical War Song, A. Macaulay. OBSV
Radio. Frank O'Hara. PoA
Radio Religion, The. William Ludlum. WBLP
Radio said, Go to your shelters, The. I'm Here. David Ignatow. GP
Radio that told me about the death of Billy the Kid, The. Billy the Kid. Jack Spicer. CoPo
Radio Under the Bed, The. Reed Whittemore. NYBP
Raftery's Dialogue with the Whiskey. Padraic Fallon. DTC
Raftsmen, The. *Unknown.* FSW
Rag Doll and Summer Birds. Owen Dodson. PoNe
Rag Time Cowboy Joe. Grant Clarke, Lewis F. Muir, *and* Maurice Abrahms. FSW
Ragas, *sels.* David Meltzer.
12th Raga: For John Wieners. NeAP
15th Raga: For Bela Lugosi. NeAP
Ragged and Dirty. *Unknown.* AmFP
Ragged and gray as the salt-cedars. Windmill in March. Katharine Privett. AMV-80
Ragged-and-Tough. Not Ragged-and-Tough. *Unknown.* ChTr; FaBoNo
Ragged Island. Edna St. Vincent Millay. NoP
Ragged Robin Opens, The. Miklos Radnoti, *tr. fr. Hungarian by* Emery George. AMV-80
Ragged, unheeded, stooping, meanly shod. The Poor Can Feed the Birds. Shaw Neilson. PoAu-1
Ragged Wood, The. W. B. Yeats. GBL
Raggedy. *Unknown.* FSW
Raggedy Man, The. James Whitcomb Riley. FaPON; HBV-1; HBVY; OBCA; OxBChV; TiPo; TreFS
Raggle, Taggle Gypsies, The. *Unknown.* *See* Wraggle Taggle Gipsies, The.
Raging Canawl. *Unknown.* AS
Ragout. William Zaranka. BXAP
Ragoût Fin de Siècle (with Reference to Certain Cafés). Erich Kästner, *tr. fr. German by* Walter Kaufman. ErPo; PeHV
Rags. Edmund Vance Cooke. BLPA
Ragwort, The. John Clare. ChTr
Ráhat, The. John Jerome Rooney. AA
Raid, The. William Everson. NoAM; PrIm
Raider, The. W. R. Rodgers. AnIL; MoBrPo
Raiders, The. Marian Allen. SUMH
Rail on, poor feeble scribbler, speak of me. The Author's Reply. Sir Carr Scroope. APAS
Railing up New Jersey. Metroliner. Jack DuVall. AMV-80
Railroad, The. Henry David Thoreau. *See* What's the Railroad to Me?
Railroad Bill. *Unknown.* AS, *with music*; FSW
Railroad Blues, The. *Unknown.* AmFP
Railroad bridge's, De. Homesick Blues. Langston Hughes. CDC; MoAmPo; PoPle
Railroad Cars Are Coming, The. *Unknown.* AmFN; AS, *with music;* BPAW; FaPON
Railroad Corral, The. *Unknown.* CoSo, *with music*; FSW; TrAS, *with music*
Railroad look so pretty. Two Hoboes. *Unknown.* WTO
Railroad Song, *sel.* Thomas Holley Chivers.
"Clitta, clatta, clatta, clatter." PeD
Railroad to Hell. *Unknown.* VLP
Railroad track is miles away, The. Travel. Edna St. Vincent Millay. FaPON; InMe; MoShBr; OBCA; PDV; RHPC; TiPo
Railroad tracks; the flight. The Old and the New. "B. M." SoPo
Railroad yard in San Jose. In Back of the Real. Allen Ginsberg. AmPP; HeIP; InPK
Railroader for Me, A. *Unknown.* AmFP
Rails pause barely to tie the horizons, The. The Depot. Lewis Turco. GrPl
Rails rise through dimness. Three Sunrises from Amtrak. Florence Dolgorukov. AMV-81
Railway Bridge of the Silvery Tay, The. William McGonagall. PeD
Railway Junction, The. Walter de la Mare. ChMP; OxBTC
Railway official at Crewe, A. The Proud Engine. *Unknown.* TDH
Railway Station. John Hay. WaP
Railway Stationery, The. Kenneth Koch. NoP
Railway Train, The. Emily Dickinson. *See* I like to see it lap the miles.
Rain. Kenneth Slade Alling. HBMV
Rain, The. Lord Bowen. *See* Rain It Raineth, The.
Rain, The. Robert Creeley. ConAP; CoAP; CAPP; VGW
Rain, The. W. H. Davies. OxBTC; TiPo
Rain. Emanuel diPasquale. InPK; POL
Rain. Haim Guir, *tr. fr. Hebrew by* Mark Elliott Shapiro. VWA
Rain. John Haines. NPAW
Rain. Sam Harrison. NeIP
Rain. W. E. Henley. SyP
Rain. Lance Henson. VoR
Rain. Anselm Hollo. PoM
Rain. Patrick F. Kirby. GoBC
Rain. Vachel Lindsay. CMoP
Rain. Sister Mary Lucina. AMV-80
Rain. Howard Moss. ErPo
Rain. Paul Murray. BIrV
Rain. Vladimir Nabokov. GrPl
Rain. "Seumas O'Sullivan." OnYI
Rain. James Whitcomb Riley. BoNaP
Rain. Peter Sears. AMV-80
Rain. Frances Shaw. HBMV
Rain. Shelley. *See* Fragment: Rain.
Rain. Robert Louis Stevenson. GoJo; NTCP; SoPo; SUS; TiPo
Rain. Adrian Stoutenberg. PDV
Rain. Edward Thomas. OBWP; OxBTC
Rain, The ("Rain on the green grass"). *Unknown.* TiPo
("Rain on the green grass.") OxNR
Rain, The (" 'Twas in Koolau I met with the rain"). *Tr. fr. Hawaiian by* N. B. Emerson. WTO
Rain. William Carlos Williams. AP; CoBMV
Rain. James Wright. NaP
Rain, / Million-footed requiem of the rain. Atavism. Richard Lake. NCSH
Rain. A heavy mane. Marina Tsvetayeva, *tr. by* Paul Schmidt. *Fr.* The Daughter of Jairus. BoWoP
Rain after a Vaudeville Show. Stephen Vincent Benét. MoAmPo
Rain all over the cornfields. Butterfly Maidens. Lahpu, *tr. by* Natalie Curtis. WTO
Rain, and a flurry of wind shaking the pear's white blossom. C. K. Stead. Twenty-one Sonnets, 2. OCNZ
Rain and wind, the rain and wind, raved endlessly, The. Melancholy. Edward Thomas. MoVE; NoP
Rain at Wildwood. May Swenson. NYBP
Rain before seven. Weather Wisdom. *Unknown.* FaBoBe; HBV-1; HBVY; OxNR; TreF
Rain begins, The. This is no summer rain. Oregon Winter. Jeanne McGahey. AmFN
Rain Chant. Louis Mertins. BPAW
Rain Clouds. Elizabeth-Ellen Long. RHPC
Rain comes in various sizes. Rain Sizes. John Ciardi. SoPo
Rain-Crow, The. Madison Cawein. AA
Rain, do not fall. Mist. Andrew Young. PoSH
Rain does down in torrents pour, The. McKinley Brook. George Calhoun. ShS
Rain Down. Mary Ellen Solt. BoWoP
Rain drifts forever in this place. The Falls of Glomach. Andrew Young. OxBS; PoSH
Rain falling on the 4th of July. Death Row. Charles Culhane. LFAC
Rain falling, what things do you grow? River Winding. Charlotte Zolotow. RHPC
Rain falls and then vanishes, The. A Green Refrain. Avraham Huss, *tr. by* Mark Elliott Shapiro. VWA
Rain falls briskly on my worn shelter-half. Inner Brother. Stephen Stepanchev. WaP
Rain falls down upon the grass, The. April Puddle. Rowena Bennett. TiPo
Rain falls in my face, The. Rain-in-the-Face. Mary Crow. PH
Rain Falls. It Dries. Miklos Radnoti, *tr. fr. Hungarian by* Emery George. AMV-81
Rain fell like grass growing, The. Rain at Wildwood. May Swenson. NYBP
Rain for Ka-waik. Paula Gunn Allen. TWSS

Rain had fallen, the Poet arose, The. The Poet's Song. Tennyson. EBVV; ELP; FiP; VLP
Rain has been reciting, The. Fishermen. Gabriel Preil, *tr. by* Betsy Rosenberg. VWA
Rain Has Fallen on the History Books. David Rosenberg. VWA
Rain has passed, The. Birth. Amir Gilboa, *tr. by* Stephen Mitchell. VWA
Rain Has Silver Sandals, The. May Justus. *See* Footwear.
Rain hits over and over. Rain. Adrian Stoutenberg. PDV
Rain imprinted the step's wet shine, The. On the Doorstep. Thomas Hardy. MoVE
Rain in my ears: impatiently there raps. Robert D. Fitzgerald. *Fr.* Essay on Memory. CBAP
Rain in Summer, *sl. abr.* Longfellow. GN
Rain in the city! City Rain. Rachel Field. SoPo; TiPo
Rain in the Desert. John Gould Fletcher. Arizona Poems, VI. BPAW; NCSH
Rain-in-the-Face. Mary Crow. PH
Rain in the Night. Amelia Josephine Burr. TiPo
Rain in the Southwest. Reeve Spencer Kelley. AmFN
Rain is due to fall, The. A Poet Thinks. Lui Chi, *tr. by* E. Powys Mathers. AWP
Rain is over, The. Birth. Amir Gilboa, *tr. by* Robert Mezey *and* Shula Starkman. OFD
Rain is plashing on my sill, The. The Unknown Dead. Henry Timrod. AP
Rain is raining all around, The. Quick, Henry, the Flit! James Schuyler. NoAM
Rain is raining all around, The. Rain. Robert Louis Stevenson. GoJo; NTCP; SoPo; SUS; TiPo
Rain is slipping, dripping down the street, The. Education. Pauline Barrington. SUMH
Rain It Raineth, The. Lord Bowen. FiBHP; NTCP; PV
(Just and Unjust.) PoPL; PoPle; WhC
(Rain, The.) FaBoCo; FaFP
("Rain it raineth on the just, The.") CenHV
Rain, it streams on stone and hillock, The. A. E. Housman. CMoP
Rain Journal: London: June 65. Lee Harwood. PeHV
Rain, lean down. Hopi Prayer. Charles Beghtol. BPAW
Rain licking the/ parched pavement. Salt Man. Annette Arkeketa West. TWSS
Rain Magic Song. *Tr. fr. Tewa Indian by* H. J. Spinden. WTO
Rain makes little cuts on the window, The. Dialogues 4 1 Voice Only. Doug Fetherling. NeAC
Rain, midnight rain, nothing but the wild rain. Rain. Edward Thomas. OBWP; OxBTC
Rain Music. Joseph S. Cotter, Jr. BANP; CDC
Rain of a night and a day and a night, The. After Rain. Edward Thomas. NCSH
Rain of London pimples, The. London Rain. Louis MacNeice. HeIP; NoP
Rain of Rites, A. Jayanta Mahapatra. PoA
Rain on a Cottage Roof. Freda Laughton. OnYI
Rain on a Grave. Thomas Hardy. CoBMV; HBV-1; OAEP
Rain on Good Friday and Easter Day. *Unknown.* FaBoUs
Rain on Rahoon falls softly, softly falling. She Weeps over Rahoon. James Joyce. ViBoPo
Rain on the Cumberlands. James Still. GrPl
Rain on the Down. Arthur Symons. *Fr.* At Dieppe. BrPo; OBNC; OBVV; SyP
Rain on the face of the sea. Commonplaces. Kipling. HBV-1
Rain on the far tip of the grove. Scattered Leaves. Lance Henson. VoR
Rain on the green grass. The Rain. *Unknown.* OxNR; TiPo
Rain on the Roof. Coates Kinney. HBV-1
Rain over a Continent. Galway Kinnell. TwAmPo
Rain patters on a sea that tilts and sighs. Absences. Philip Larkin. PoCh
Rain, Rain. Zoë Akins. HBMV
Rain! rain!/ For the growing grain. A Hopi Prayer. Harrison Conrard. BPAW
Rain, rain, and sun! a rainbow in the sky! Merlin's Riddling. Tennyson. *Fr.* Idylls of the King: The Coming of Arthur. FaBoRV
Rain, rain, go away. Mother Goose. OxNR; SoPo; TiPo
Rain, rain, go to Spain. Mother Goose. OxNR
Rain Rain on the Splintered Girl. Ishmael Reed. PoBA
Rain, rainfall, fall. Rain, Rain. Zoë Akins. HBMV
Rain rains sair on Duriesdyke, The. Duriesdyke. Swinburne. OxBB
Rain Riders. Clinton Scollard. SoPo; TiPo
Rain rins doun through Mirry-land toune, The. Sir Hugh; or, The Jew's Daughter. *Unknown.* ESPB
Rain, said the first, as it falls in Venice. Song Tournement: New Style. Louis Untermeyer. CrMA; OBAL
Rain seeps through the olives. Sabbath. Jean Burden. AMV-81
Rain set early in to-night, The. Porphyria's Lover. Robert Browning. AWP; BeLS; CABA; HAP; HBV-1; OAEP; OBEV; PAI; TEP; TreFT; TrGrPo
Rain Sizes. John Ciardi. SoPo
Rain smell comes with the wind. Love Poem. Leslie Silko. UnPo; VoR
Rain Song. Robert Loveman. *See* April Rain.
Rain Song, The. Alex Rogers. BANP
Rain-sunken roof, grown green and thin. The Barn. Edmund Blunden. MoBrPo; SeCePo
Rain That Fell upon the Height, The. Coventry Patmore. *Fr.* The Victories of Love, I, v. FaBoRV
("Your love lacks joy, your letter says.") GBL
Rain thunderstorms over the Potomac, in Georgetown. Rainscapes, Hydrangeas, Roses, and Singing Birds. Richard Eberhart. MoAmPo
Rain to the Tribe. Al-Khansa, *tr. fr. Arabic by* Willis Barnstone *and* Tony Nawfal. BoWoP
Rain Trip. Diane Wakoski. CABA
Rain was full of the freshness, The. The Dark and Falling Summer. Delmore Schwartz. NYBP
Rain was over, and the brilliant air, The. Landscapes. Louis Untermeyer. HBV-2
Rain was raining cheerfully, The. The Vulture and the Husbandman. A. C. Hilton. CenHV; FaBoCo
Rain, with a silver flail. Whale. William Rose Benét. EtS; MoAmPo
Rainbow, The. Vine Colby. HBMV
Rainbow, The. W. H. Davies. BrPo
Rainbow, The. Walter de la Mare. SoPo; TiPo
Rainbow, The. Gerard Manley Hopkins. FaBoPP
Rainbow. Robert Huff. NePoEA-2
Rainbow, The. David McCord. FaPON; SoPo
Rainbow, The. Coventry Patmore. The Angel in the House, II, iii, 2. GTBS-P
Rainbow, The. Christina Rossetti. *Fr.* Sing-Song. OxBChV; SoPo
("Boats sail on the rivers.") TiPo
Rainbow, The ("Yonder, yonder see the fair rainbow"). *Unknown, tr. fr. Hopi Indian by* Natalie Curtis. WTO
(Corn-grinding Song.) SUS
Rainbow, The. Wordsworth. *See* My Heart Leaps Up When I Behold.
Rainbow arches in the sky, The. The Rainbow. David McCord. FaPON; SoPo
Rainbow at night. Weather Wisdom. *Unknown.* FaBoBe; HBV-1; HBVY; TreF
Rainbow faded, the animals dispersed, The. Return to Ararat. Martyn Halsall. TrCP
Rainbow on the ocean, The. So Slow to Die. George Edward Woodberry. Wild Eden, XXXVIII. AA
Rainbow stands red o'er the ocean, The. *Tr. fr. Hawaiian by* N. B. Emerson. WTO
Rainbow Writing. Eve Merriam. GrPl
Rainbows all lie crumpled on these hills, The. The Painted Hills of Arizona. Edwin Curran. BPAW; HBMV
Rainbows are lovely things. The Rainbow. W. H. Davies. BrPo
Raincoats for the Dead. Albert Bellg. FAZ
Rainer,/ the man who was about to celebrate his 52nd birthday. The Death of Europe. Charles Olson. NeAP
Rainer Maria Rilke Returns from the Dead to Address the Junior Military School at Sankt Pölten. John Engman. LTB
Rainier. Jim Tollerud. VoR
Raining came with dawning. At Dawn. J. M. Synge. SyP
Raining, raining. Rain in the Night. Amelia Josephine Burr. TiPo
Rainpoem. Michael Dransfield. CBAP
Rain's all right. The boys who physic. Biography of Southern Rain. Kenneth Patchen. VGW
Rains, already old, The. Okkur Maccatti, *tr. fr. Tamil by* A. K. Ramanujan. PBWP
Rain's Already with Us, The. Salvatore Quasimodo, *tr. fr. Italian by* Allen Mandelbaum. PoPl
Rains for the Harvest. *Unknown, tr. fr. Tewa Indian by* H. J. Spinden. WTO
Rain's grey buckshot spatters the windshield. Stopped in Memphis. Steven Bauer. AMV-80
Rain's lovely gray daughter has lost her tall lover. Fog. Kenneth Patchen. NaP
Rains of Spring, The. Lady Ise, *arr. by* Olive Beaupré Miller. SUS; TiPo
Rains on the Island. Gabriel Preil, *tr. fr. Hebrew by* Robert Friend. VWA
Rainscapes, Hydrangeas, Roses, and Singing Birds. Richard Eberhart. MoAmPo
Rainuv; a Romantic Ballad from the Early Basque. Margaret Widdemer. BXAP
Rainwalkers, The. Denise Levertov. CAD; CTBA; NePoEA-2; PPP
Rainwater woman. Robin. Paula Gunn Allen. TWSS
Rainy Day, The. Longfellow. AWP; FPL; HBV-2; PoLF; PoPl; TreFT
Rainy Day Song. Violet Alleyn Storey. YeAr

Rainy mid-morning. Haiku, for Cinnamon. Lillie D. Chapin. PH
Rainy Midnight. Ivor Gurney. FaBoPP
Rainy Morning. Sotero Rivera-Avilés, *tr. fr. Spanish by* Julio Marzán. InW
Rainy morning. Don't get up. Don't even smoke. On the Hazards of Smoking. Leah Goldberg, *tr. by* Bernhard Frank. AMV-81
Rainy Mountain Cemetery. N. Scott Momaday. CDW
Rainy Night at the Writers' Colony. Josephin Jacobsen. TAP
Rainy Nights. Irene Thompson. RHPC
Rainy Pleiads Wester, The. A. E. Housman. BoLoP; NoAM
Rainy Season, The. William Meredith. NePoEA
Rainy Season Love Song. Gladys May Casely Hayford. CDC
Rainy skies, misty mountains. Fifty. Kenneth Rexroth. TAP
Rainy Song. Max Eastman. FaBoBe; HBMV
Rainy Summer, The. Alice Meynell. GoJo; MoVE; OxBTC; SBG
Rainy Summer. Ruth Pitter. MoVE
Raise a "Rucus" To-Night. *Unknown.* BPo; FSW; TAP
Raise the Cromlech high! The Lament of Maev Leith-Dherg. *Unknown, tr. by* Thomas W. H. Rolleston. OBWP; OnYI
Raise the light a little, Jim. Will Carleton. *Fr.* Johnny Rich. PeD
Raise the Shade. E. E. Cummings. VGW
Raised are the dripping oars. Matthew Arnold. *Fr.* The Youth of Nature: Wordsworth's Country. FaBoPP
Raised in a canebrake, and suckled by a lion. *Unknown.* CoSo
Raised on six-shooters till I get big enough to eat ground shot-guns. The Boasting Drunk in Dodge. *Unknown.* CoSo
Raisin, The. Donald Hall. TAP
Raisin Bread. Lee Blair. TDH
Raising of Lazarus, The. Lucille Clifton. CNA
Raising of the Dead, The. Rosemary Dobson. PoAu-2
Raising our glasses, smilingly. Libation. Denise Levertov. GP
Raising the Flag. Gerald Vizenor. VoR
Raisins and Nuts. Charles Reznikoff. VWA
Raison d'Etre. Oliver Pitcher. AmNP; NNP
Raja, my heart is mad for you. My Heart Burns for Him. *Gond Oral Tradition, tr. by* V. Elwin *and* S. Hivale. WTO
Rake. Dorothy Una Ratcliffe. BoAnP; GDP
"Rake" Windermere. Leonard Pounds. PaPo
Rakes of Mallow, The. *Unknown.* OnYI
Raking Leaves. Robert Pack. CoPo; NYBP
Raking Walnuts in the Rain. Monica Shannon. SiSoSe
Ralegh's Prizes. Robert Pinsky. MAYP
Raleigh Was Right. William Carlos Williams. NoAM; PP
Ralph Roister Doister, *sels.* Nicholas Udall.
I Mun Be Married a Sunday. ElL
Minion Wife, A. ElL
Ram came last, The. Isaac. Haim Guri, *tr. by* Naomi Tauber *and* Howard Schwartz. VWA
Ram of Darby, The. *Unknown. See* Derby Ram, The.
Ram, the Bull, the Heavenly Twins, The. The Zodiac Rhyme. *Unknown.* GBP
Ram Time. William Heyen. GeTw
Ramble of the Gods through Birmingham, *sel.* James Bisset.
"Next day they rambled round the town, and swore." NOEC
Ramble on What in the World Why. Ralph Gustafson. AMV-81
Ramble-eer, The. *Unknown.* PoAu-1
Rambling Boy, The. *Unknown.* OBET
Rambling Cowboy, The, *with music. Unknown.* CoSo
Rambling Gambler, *with music. Unknown.* CoSo
Rambling, Gambling Man. Gil Houston. FSW
Rambling Sailor, The. Charlotte Mew. HBMV; PoRA
Rambling Soldier, The. *Unknown.* OBET
Rambuncto. Margaret Widdemer. BXAP
Ramon. Bret Harte. BeLS
Ramon. E. A. Lacey. PeHV
Rampage, The. C. K. Williams. GeTw
Ram's Horn, The. John Hewitt. BIrV
Ramshackles, archipelagoes, loose constellations. The Unifying Principle. A. R. Ammons. NOBA
Ran out of tear gas and became panicky. Kent State, May 4, 1970. Paul Goodman. MAT
Rana, I know you gave me poison. Mirabai, *tr. fr. Hindi by* Willis Barnstone *and* Usha Nilsson. BoWoP
Rana, why do you treat me as your enemy? Mirabai, *tr. fr. Hindi by* Willis Barnstone *and* Usha Nilsson. BoWoP
Ranch at Twilight. *Unknown.* BPAW
Rancher, The. Keith Wilson. GP
Ranchers. Maurice Lesemann. BPAW
Ranchers are selling their wheat early this year, The. Bunch Grass #37. Robert Sund. NU
Ranching country. Crossing West Texas (1966). Kell Robertson. TAT
Randal Groveling works where I work. Song from a Two-Desk Office. Byron Buck. NYBP
Random Generation of English Sentences; or, The Revenge of the Poets. William Jay Smith. OBAL
Random Reflections on a Cloudless Sunday. John Hall Wheelock. NePoAm
Random Reflections on a Summer Evening. John Hall Wheelock. NYBP
Rang'd on the line oppos'd, Antonius brings. Virgil, *tr. by* Dryden. *Fr.* Aeneid, VIII. WaaP
Range-finding. Robert Frost. CABA; NIP; NoAM; NoP; OBWP
Range in the Desert, The. Randall Jarrell. NOBA
Range Riders, The. *Unknown.* CoSo
Range Rider's Soliloquy, The. Earl Alonzo Brininstool. PoOW
Range's filled up with farmers and there's fences ev'rywhere, The. The Old Cowboy's Lament. Robert V. Carr. BPAW; PoOW
Rank. Lincoln Kirstein. OBWP
Rank with the flesh of man and beast. The Lido. Edmund Wilson. ErPo
Rannoch, by Glencoe. T. S. Eliot. Landscapes, IV. BiP; FaBoEn; FaBoPP; PoSH
Rannoch Moor. Malcolm MacGregor. PoSH
Ransi-Tansi-Tay. *Unknown. See* Here Come Three Merchants a-Riding
Ransomed from darkness and released in Time. Edwin Muir. *Fr.* Variations on a Time Theme. NoAM
Ransomed Spirit to Her Home, The, *with music.* William B. Tappan. AH
Rant Block. Michael McClure. EAS
Rantin' Dog, the Daddie o't, The. Burns. OxBoLi; PPP
Rantin Laddie, The. *Unknown.* AmFP; BaBo (A *and* B *vers.*); ESPB
Rantin, Rovin Robin. Burns. OxBS
(Robin.) BSV
Ranting Wanton's Resolution, The; 1672. *Unknown.* CoMu
Rap Sheet. Paul D. Shiplett. LFAC
Rapacious Spain/ Follow'd her hero's triumphs o'er the main. The Lust of Gold. James Montgomery. *Fr.* The West Indies. PAH
Rape. Tom Pickard. FaBoTw
Rape. Thomas Rabbitt. MAYP
Rape. Adrienne Rich. GP
"Rape?" he says. Father of the Victim. Rae Ballard. AMV-80
Rape of Europa, The. R. P. Blackmur. CrMA
Rape of Lucrece, The, *sels.* Thomas Heywood.
Pack, Clouds, Away. ElL; GBL; GTBS; GTBS-P; PBBP; SoSe; ViBoPo; WHA
(Good Morrow.) CH
(Matin-Song.) HBV-1; OBEV
Passing Bell, The. FaBoRV
She That Denies Me [I Would Have]. ErPo; UnTE
(Valerius on Women). HBV-1
Rape of Lucrece, The. Shakespeare. BeLS
Sels.
" 'Come, Philomele, that sing'st of ravishment.' " PBBP
Midnight. OBSC
"Mis-shapen Time, copesmate of ugly Night." OAEL-1
Opportunity. LiTB; OBSC
("O opportunity, thy guilt is great.") PoEL-2
(Outcry upon Opportunity, An.) NOBE
Time's Glory. ChTr
Troy Depicted. OBSC
Rape of the Lock, The. Pope. BiP; CABA; HAP; MasP; NoP; OAEL-1; OAEP; OBNV; PoEL-3; SeCeV; TEP; TrGrPo
Sels.
"Close by those meads, for ever crowned with flow'rs," *fr.* III. FaBoPP, *shorter sel.;* FIP; OBSV, *shorter sel.;* OxBoLi, *sl. abr.*
(Ombre at Hampton Court, *abr.*) OBEC
"For lo! the board with cups and spoons is crowned," *fr.* III. ViBoPo
Lock, The, *fr.* V. MOON
"Not with more glories, in th' ethereal plain," II. EBEV; FaBoEn, *shorter sel.;* NOEC; ViBoPo, *shorter sel.;* WHA
(Voyage on the Thames, The, *shorter sel.*) NOBE
"On her white breast a sparkling Cross she wore," *fr.* II. ACP
Playing Cards, The, *fr.* III. ChTr
Toilet, The, *fr.* I. NOBE
"What dire offence from am'rous causes springs," I. NOEC
"Ye Sylphs and Sylphids, to your chief give ear!" *fr.* II. ViBoPo
Rape Poem. Marge Piercy. Psk
Raper from Passenack, The. William Carlos Williams. TW
Rapid, The. Charles Sangster. CaP; WHW
Rapid Transit. James Agee. MoAmPo
Rapidly cruising or lying on the air there is a bird. The Frigate Pelican. Marianne Moore. InvP
Rapids at Night. Duncan Campbell Scott. CaP
Rapier, lie there! and there, my hat and feather! The Poetaster. Samuel Rowlands. *Fr.* The Melancholy Knight. ElL
Rapier of Treason, A. *Tr. fr. Arabic by* Willis Barnstone. BoWoP
Rapist, The. Stephen Dunn. POL
Rapist. José Y. Terán, Jr. LFAC

Rapparees. Richard Murphy. *Fr.* The Battle of Aughrim. BIrV
Rapping Along with Ronda Davis. James Cunningham. JB
Rapture, The. Henry Baker. NOEC
Rapture, A. Thomas Carew. AnAnS-2; CaPo; CavP; ErPo; JCP; OAEL-1; SeCP; ViBoPo, *abr.*
(I Will Enjoy Thee Now.) UnTE, *abr.*
Rapture. Randolph Carlson. AMV-80
Rapture. Stefan George, *tr. fr. German by* Ludwig Lewisohn. AWP
Rapture, The. Thomas Traherne. OBS
Rapture; an Ode. Richard Watson Dixon. OxBoCh
Rapunzel. Olga Broumas. DFT
Rapunzel. Sara Henderson Hay. DFT
Rapunzel. Anne Sexton. DFT
Rapunzel. Louis Untermeyer. DFT
Rapunzel (Girl in a Tower). Eli Mandel. DFT
Rapunzel Rapunzel let down your hair. The After-Thought. Stevie Smith. OxBC
Rapunzel Song. Gerard Previn Meyer. DFT
Raquette River, Potsdam, New York, The; Lying on a Rock Drinking Scotch while My Friends Fish Upstream. Anthony Piccione. WOLT
Rarae Aves. Franklin P. Adams. WhC
Rare Moments. Charles Henry Phelps. AA
Rare music! I would rather hear cat-courtship. The Dancing Bear. Robert Southey. FM
Rare News. Nicholas Breton. NIP
Rare old bird is the pelican, A. The Pelican. *Unknown.* TreFS
Rare temples thou hast seen, I know. The Fairy Temple; or, Oberon's Chapel. Robert Herrick. CaPo
Rare Willie Drowned in Yarrow [or, The Water o Gamrie]. *Unknown.* BaBo; BSV; ESPB (A, B, *and* D *vers.*); GBP; GoTS
(Rare Willy, *with music.*) OxBB
(Willy Drowned in Yarrow.) GTBS, *longer vers.*; GTBS-P, *longer vers.*; HBV-1
Raree Show, A. Stephen College. APAS
Rarely, Rarely, Comest Thou. Shelley. *See* Song: "Rarely, rarely, comest thou."
Rash author, 'tis a vain presumptuous crime. Dryden. *Fr.* The Art of Poetry. PP
Raspberries. Laurence Lerner. EBEV
Raspberries they gave us for dessert, The. Going to Moscow. Lauris Edmond. OCNZ
Raspberry in the Pudding, The. Philip O'Connor. EAS
Rasslers, The. William D. Barney. LiSp
Rat, The. W. H. Davies. OxBTC
Rat, The. Arthur Symons. SyP
Rat-a-tat-tat. The Drummer. Anna Robinson. SUS
Rat and the Elephant, The. La Fontaine, *tr. fr. French by* Marianne Moore. OBVE
Rat is in the trap, it is in the trap, The. Song of a Rat. Ted Hughes. CMoP; NoP
Rat Riddles. Carl Sandburg. SO
Rat too has a skin (to tan), A. Sans Equity and sans Poise. Confucius, *tr. by* Ezra Pound. *Fr.* Yung Wind. CTC
Rata blooms explode, the bow-legged tomcat, The. James K. Baxter. Autumn Testament, 42. OCNZ
Ratcatcher's Daughter, The. *Unknown.* ChTr; GBP; OxBoLi
"Rather dead than spotted"; and/ believe it. Then the Ermine. Marianne Moore. NePoAm; PoA
Rather notice, mon cher. To a Solitary Disciple. William Carlos Williams. PP; VGW
Rather slender. Rather tiny. Emily Dickinson. Inger Hagerup, *tr. by* Harold P. Hanson. AMV-81
Rather than your fine hotels. Sightseers in a Courtyard. Nicolás Guillén, *tr. by* Langston Hughes. TTY
Rather Too Good, Little Peggy! Adelaide O'Keeffe. FaBoUs
Rathers. Mary Austin. FaPON
Ration Card, The. Liz Sohappy Bahe. CDW
Ration Party. John Manifold. WaP
Rats. Walter de la Mare. BoAnP
Rats Away! *Unknown.* OxBM
Rats, Ducks, Dogs, Cats, Pigs. *Unknown. See* Three Young Rats.
Rattan bed, paper netting. I wake from morning sleep. Li Ch'ing-chao, *tr. fr. Chinese by* Willis Barnstone *and* Sun Chu-chin. BoWoP
Rattler, Alert. Brewster Ghiselin. HAP; WeW
Rattler was a good old dog. Old Rattler. *Unknown.* FSW
Rattlesnake, The. Robert V. Carr. PoOW
Rattlesnake, The. Alfred Purdy. WHW
Rattlesnake, The, *with music. Unknown.* CoSo
Rattlesnake, The. Robert Wrigley. AMV-80
Rattlesnake Band, The. Robert J. Conley. STE
Rattlesnakes have begun to come out, The. Snakes. Peter Wild. AmPA; GP
Rauf Coilyear, *sel. Unknown.*
"Coilyear, gudlie in feir, tuke him be the hand, The." OxBS
Rav, The/ of Northern White Russia declined. Illustrious Ancestors. Denise Levertov. AmPP; NoAM; NOBA; VGW
Ravaged Villa, The. Herman Melville. AP; CTC; NOBA; PoEL-5
Raven, The. Samuel Taylor Coleridge. WiR
Raven. Duane Niatum. STE
Raven, The. Poe. AA; AmPP; AP; BeLS; BLPA; CH; FaBoBe; FaBoCh; FaBV; FaFP; FPL; GN; GoJo; HBV-2; LiTA; NePA; NOBA; OBCA; OBNV; OHFP; OxBA; PaPo; PoRA; RoGo; TAP; TReF; ViBoPo; WBLP; WHA
Raven, The. Adrienne Rich. NePoEA-2
Raven, The. E. A. Robinson, *after the Greek of* Nicarchus. AWP; FaBoEE; OBAL
Raven at Lemon Creek Jail. Thomas Waltner. LFAC
Raven croak'd as she sate at her meal, The. The Old Woman of Berkeley [*or* The Witch]. Robert Southey. OBRV; WiR
Raven Days, The. Sidney Lanier. NePA; OxBA
Raven/Moon. Anita Endrezze Probst. VoR
Raven sat upon a tree, A. The Sycophantic Fox and the Gullible Raven. Guy Wetmore Carryl. BLPA; CenHV; FaFP; FiBHP; HBV-1; InMe; OBCA; TreFT
Raven Visits Rawhide, The. *Unknown.* BPAW
Ravenglass Railway Station, Cumberland. Norman Nicholson. NYBP
Ravenous Time has flowers for his food. Time Eating. Keith Douglas. NeBP
Ravens. Ted Hughes. NAs
Ravens shall pick. *Unknown, tr. by* Joseph Dunn. *Fr.* The Combat of Ferdiad and Cuchulain. OnYI
Ravine, The. James Applewhite. AMV-80
Raving warre, begot. Thomas Campion. AAS
Ravings. Tom Hood. BXAP; Par
Ravin's of Piute Poet Poe. C. L. Edson. BXAP
Ravished arms. Boy in the Roman Zoo. Archibald MacLeish. NCSH
Ravished by all that to the eyes is fair. Three Poems, III. Michelangelo, *tr. by* George Santayana. AWP
Raw slopes of meat are stabbed with pikes, The. Norway. Norman Dubie. GeTw
Rawish dank of clumsy winter ramps, The. Prologue. John Marston. *Fr.* Antonio's Revenge. LoBV; ViBoPo
Ray. Otto Orban, *tr. fr. Hungarian by* Emery George. VWA
Ray Charles. Sam Cornish. CNA
Ray Charles is the black wind of Kilimanjaro. Blues Note. Bob Kaufman. CNA; NIP; PoBA
Ray John. Honky. Charles Cooper. PoBA
Raya Brenner. Pinhas Sadeh, *tr. fr. Hebrew by* Gabriel Preil *and* Howard Schwartz. VWA
"Ray-hee-nah!" Aztec Figurine. John Beecher. GP
Rays of the sun, The. The Shepherd and His Flock. Oswald Mbuyiseni Mtshali. GrPl
Raziel. Yvan Goll, *tr. fr. French by* Anthony Rudolf. VWA
Razón de Amor, *sel.* Pedro Salinas, *tr. fr. Spanish by* Linda Gutierrez *and* Lawrence Pitkethly.
"Now I love you/ as the sea loves its water." LLLT
Razor. Robert B. Smith. LFAC
Razor-Seller, The. "Peter Pindar." HBV-2; InMe
Razors pain you. Resumé [*or* Some Beautiful Letters]. Dorothy Parker. DBV; DL; HeIP; InMe; InPK; NoP; OBAL; PAI; PoPl; ShM; TrJP; WhC
Razorsharp wind, A. Valentine. Len Gasparini. NeAC
Razzle dazzle maggots are summary, The. Easter. Frank O'Hara. EAS
Re: the question of poems. Memo from the Desk of X. Donald Justice. TwCP
Reach for arrows of falling light. A man once sang. Falling Moon. Roberta Hill. CDW
Reach forth Thy hand! William Force Stead. *Fr.* Uriel, Pt. V, 1. OxBoCh
Reach like you never reached before past Night's somber robes. Tauhid. Askia Muhammad Touré. PoBA
Reach me a blue pencil of the moon. Ur Burial. Richard Eberhart. NePoAm
Reach me down my Tycho Brahe, I would know him when we meet. The Old Astronomer to His Pupil. Sarah Williams. BLPA
Reach of Silence, The. Charles Black. AMV-81
Reach, with your whiter hands, to me. To the Water Nymphs, Drinking at the Fountain. Robert Herrick. AnAnS-2; CaPo; ViBoPo
Reaching. William Carson Fagg. LFAC
Reaching down arm-deep into bright water. Shells. Kathleen Raine. ImOP
Reaching the Horizon. Robert Mezey. NaP
Re-act for Action ("Re-act to Animals"). Don L. Lee. BPo; NBP
Reactionary Poet, The. Ishmael Reed. CNA
Read about the Buddhist monk. Dilemma. Patricia Beer. OxBC

Read here,/ This is the story of Evarraman. Evarra and His Gods. Kipling. MoBrPo
Read here (sweet maid) the story of my woe. Michael Drayton. Idea's Mirrour, I. OBSC
Read in my face a volume of despairs. Samuel Daniel. To Delia, XXXIX. EnRePo
Read me a lesson, Muse, and speak it loud. Written upon the Top of Ben Nevis. Keats. PoSH
Read me no moral, priest, upon my life. The Condemned. Edward Howland. AA
Read Me, Please! Robert Graves. NYBP
Read no more of cantos Pisan. To a Young Poet. Harry M. Meacham. GoYe
Read not Milton, for he is dry; no Shakespeare. Proverbial Philosophy: Of Reading. Charles Stuart Calverley. FaBoCo
Read not this Book, in any case. Of the Incomparable Treasure of the Scriptures. *Unknown.* TRV
"Read out the names!" and Burke sat back. The Fighting Race. Joseph I. C. Clarke. AA; BLPA; BLPL; HBV-2; OnYI; PAH; YaD
Read, sweet, how others strove. Emily Dickinson. AH, *with music;* NOCV
Read the Bible Through. Amos R. Wells. STF
Read This with Gestures. John Ciardi. RHPC
Read yr/ exile. A Poem for a Poet. Don L. Lee. PoBA
Reade in these roses, the sad story. Red, and White Roses. Thomas Carew. AnAnS-2
Readen ov a Head-Stwone. William Barnes. CH; HBV-2
(Head-Stone, The.) OBVV
Reader, behold! this monster wild. Infant Innocence. A. E. Housman. FaBoNo; NOBL; WhC
Reader, beneath this turf I lie. Thomas Brown. FaBoEE
Reader, could his limbs be found. Epitaph on a Bombing Victim. Roy Fuller. NeBP
Reader! I am no poet: but I grieve! To the Reader. Urian Oakes. SCAP
Reader, I was born and cried. Epitaph on the Fart in the Parliament House. John Hoskyns. FaBoEE
Reader, I would not have thee mistake. His Own Epitaph, When He Was Sick. John Hoskyns. FaBoEE
Reader, if thou cast thine eye. Epitaph on Mris Mary Draper. Charles Cotton. CavP
Reader, pass on, nor idly waste [*or* don't waste] your time. In Peterborough Churchyard. Paulus Silentiarius, *tr. fr. Greek.* FaBoEE; NOBL; WhC
Reader, preserve thy peace: those busie eyes. An Elegie upon the Death of the Lord Hastings. Sir John Denham. SeCV-1
Reader, stay,/ And if I had no more to say. An Epitaph on Master Philip Gray. Ben Jonson. FaBoEE
Reader, we are getting ready to pull out. Epilogue: Author to Reader. Henri Coulette. *Fr.* The War of the Secret Agents, XII. NePoEA-2
Reader Writes, The. Carl Crane. PoPl; WhC
Readers and the hearers like my books, The. Critics. Martial, *tr. by* Sir John Harington. AWP
Readers of the *Boston Evening Transcript.* The *Boston Evening Transcript.* T. S. Eliot. InPK; NePA
Reading. Elizabeth Barrett Browning. *Fr.* Aurora Leigh. GN
Reading,/ weary again. After the Movement. Peter Oresick. LTB
Reading a Medal. Terence Tiller. FaBoTw; GTBS-P
Reading about the Wisconsin Weeping Willow. Song. Ruth Krauss. LLLT
Reading and Talking. Louis Zukofsky. VGW
Reading Faust. Judah Goldin. AMV-81
Reading how even the Swiss had thrown the sponge. Beyond the Alps. Robert Lowell. NOBA
Reading in bed, full of sentiment. The Bat. Ellen Bryant Voigt. MAYP
Reading in Fall Rain. Robert Bly. GP; GrPl
Reading in Li Po. After the Last Dynasty. Stanley Kunitz. NMP; TAP
Reading in Ovid the sorrowful story of Itys. Thomas Trevelyan. Edgar Lee Masters. *Fr.* Spoon River Anthology. MoPo
Reading in the Night. Roy Fuller. OxBC
Reading in War Time. Edwin Muir. WaP
Reading Indian Poetry. Ramona Wilson. VoR
Reading Lesson, The. Richard Murphy. IPY
Reading Mother, The. Strickland Gillilan. BLPA
Reading Myself. Robert Lowell. TAP
Reading Plato. Jorie Graham. MAYP
Reading Room, the New York Public Library. Richard Eberhart. GP; NYP
Reading Sign. Jack L. Anderson. LFAC
Reading the Brothers Grimm to Jenny. Lisel Mueller. DFT; NYBP
Reading the headlines in the revolutionary. The Second Man. Julian Symons. WaP
Reading the shorthand on a barber's sheet. The Barber. Roy Fuller. NoAM
Reading through your work tonight. Negative Passage. Michael Newman. PoA
Reading Time: 1 Minute 26 Seconds. Muriel Rukeyser. MoPo; NePA; PBWP
Reading Today's Newspaper. Steve Abbott. AMV-80
Reading Walt Whitman. Calvin Forbes. PoBA
Readings, Forecasts, Personal Guidance. Kenneth Fearing. MoAmPo
Readings of History. Adrienne Rich. ConAP
Ready. Phoebe Cary. PAH
Ready, Ay, Ready. Herman Charles Merivale. HBV-2
Ready she sat with one hand to turn o'er. Leigh Hunt. *Fr.* The Story of Rimini. EvOK
Ready they make hauberks Sarrazinese. *Unknown, tr. by* C. K. Scott Moncrieff. *Fr.* The Song of Roland. WaaP
Ready to seek out death in my disgrace. Henry Constable. *Fr.* Diana. OBSC
Ready we stand in San Juan town. Rain Magic Song. *Tr. fr. Tewa Indian by* H. J. Spinden. WTO
Readymade. John Perreault. EAS
Reagan, The. Richard Quick. FaBoPa
Real Deal Revelation. Raymond Ringo Fernandez. LFAC
Real Happiness. Goldsmith. *Fr.* The Traveller. OBEC
Real Life. Ted Berrigan. NoAM
Real Muse, The. Fred Muratori. AMV-81
Real Muse, The. Tom Scott. PoA
Real Old Mountain Dew. *Unknown.* FSW
Real original, I think, A. An Original Cuss. Keith Preston. WhC
Real People Loves One Another, The. Rob Penny. CNA; PoBA
Real poems are being written in outports, The. Without Benefit of Tape. Dorothy Livesay. NOBC
Real Presence: "Not on an Altar shall mine eyes behold Thee." Ivan Adair. WGRP
Real Property. Harold Monro. BoNaP
Real Question Calling for Solution, A. Robert Penn Warren. PPP
Real Story, A. Linda Pastan. Str
Real Thing, The. Ronald Wallace. AMV-81
Real was always something that came out of streets, The. The Epiphany. George Strong. GoYe
Reality. Martha Dickinson Bianchi. AA
Reality. Sir Aubrey De Vere. WGRP
Reality. Frances Ridley Havergal. WGRP
Reality. Angela Morgan. WGRP
Reality. Raymond Souster. CaP
Reality/ is like a contemporary string. Dazzled. Arthur Sze. BrSi
Realization. Anandan Acharya. WGRP
Really, what a shocking scene! A Man of Experience. Laoiseach Mac an Bhaird, *tr. by* Frank O'Connor. KiLC
Realm is here of masquing light, A. Light at Equinox. Léonie Adams. CrMA
Realm of Fancy, The. Keats. *See* Fancy.
Realm of Touching, The. Alan Bold. BSV
Reaper, The. L. H. Allen. PoAu-1
Reaper, The. Robert Duncan. CrMA
Reaper, The. John Banister Tabb. ACP
Reaper, The. Wordsworth. *See* Solitary Reaper, The.
Reaper and the Flowers, The. Longfellow. HBV-2
Reapers. Mathilde Blind. SBG; WPE
Reapers. Jean Toomer. BPo; CDC; HAP; InPK; NoAM; PoBA; PPP; WeW
Reapers, The. Lauchlan Maclean Watt. PGD
Reapers that with whetted sickles stand, The. Poetry and Philosophy. Thomas Randolph. *Fr.* An Eclogue to Mr. Johnson. OBS
Reaping. Amy Lowell. SBG
Reapings, The. Theodore Weiss. NMP
Rear Guard, The. Irene Fowler Brown. PAH
Rear-Guard, The. Siegfried Sassoon. MoBrPo; NoAM; OBWP; WaP
Rear Vision. William Jay Smith. NYBP
Rearmament. Robinson Jeffers. OxBA
Rearrange a wife's affection? Emily Dickinson. PoEL-5
Reason, The. Leonard Bacon. YaD
Reason, A. Robert Creeley. NaP
Reason. Ralph Hodgson. *See* Reason Has Moons.
Reason. Josephine Miles. InPK; NCSH; NoAM; NoP; PoCH; TAP
Reason, The. James Oppenheim. HBV-1
Reason. John Tatham. CavP
Reason. *Unknown.* TreF
Reason, The/ we got rid. Modern Romance. William J. Harris. GP
Reason and I long time known friends. Reason. John Tatham. CavP
Reason and Imagination. Blake. *Fr.* Milton. EnRP
Reason and Revelation. Dryden. *Fr.* Religio Laici. OBS
("Dim as the borrow'd beams of moon and stars.") OAEL-1; OxBoCh; ViBoPo, *br. sel.*
(Finite Reason.) LoBV
(Reason and Religion, *br. sel.*) FiP

Reason Fair to Fill My Glass, A. Charles Morris. HBV-2
Reason for Not Writing Orthodox Nature Poetry. John Wain. MP; PP
Reason for Poetry, The. Nancy Morejón, *tr. fr. Spanish by* Anita Whitney. WPOW
Reason for Skylarks, The. Kenneth Patchen. NaP
Reason for the Pelican, The. John Ciardi. PDV; PoPl; SoPo
Reason for Writing, A. Theodore Spencer. TwAmPo
Reason Has Moons. Ralph Hodgson. MoVE
(Reason.) MoBrPo
("Reason has moons, but moons not hers.") FaBoCh
Reason I Like Chocolate, The. Nikki Giovanni. RHPC
Reason I Stay on Job So Long. *Unknown.* GBP
Reason, in faith thou art well serv'd that still. Astrophel and Stella, X. Sir Philip Sidney. SiPS
Reason, tell me thy mind, if here be reason. Love and Reason. Sir Philip Sidney. *Fr.* Arcadia. SiPS
Reason, the Use of It in Divine Matters. Abraham Cowley. AnAnS-2
Reason Why, The. Thomas Lovell Beddoes. OBRV
Reason why our work is brittle, The. The Reason. Leonard Bacon. YaD
Reason with them. Speak softly. Hide your stick. 13 Ways of Eradicating Blackbirds. Mark DeFoe. BXAP
Reasonable Affliction, A. Matthew Prior. HBV-1; NOEC; NoP; ShM; TreFT; TrGrPo; WhC
Reasons. Thomas James. PoA
Reasons for and against Marrying Widows. Henricus Selyns. SCAP
Reasons for Attendance. Philip Larkin. BiP
Reasons for Drinking. Henry Aldrich. InMe; YaD
(Catch, A.) InvP; OBS
(Five Reasons, The.) FaBoCo
(Five Reasons for Drinking.) TreFT
("If all be true that I do think.") FaBoEE; FF
Reasons for Music. Archibald MacLeish. NePA
Reasons to Go Home. Greg Forker. LFAC
Reb Hanina. Paul Raboff. VWA
Reb of ruins my father. Zealot without a Face. Charles Dobzynski, *tr. by* Anita Barrows. VWA
Rebeca in a Mirror. Judith Rodriguez. CBAP
Rebecca. Joseph Eliyia, *tr. fr. Greek by* Rae Dalven. VWA
Rebecca and Rowena, *sel.* Thackeray.
Age of Wisdom, The. HBV-1; WhC
Rebecca, Who Slammed Doors for Fun and Perished Miserably. Hilaire Belloc. NOBL; SO
Rebecca's After-Thought. Elizabeth Turner. HBV-1; HBVY
(Truth the Best.) OxBChV
Rebecca's Hymn. Sir Walter Scott. *Fr.* Ivanhoe, *ch.* 39. EnRP
("When Israel of the Lord beloved.") ViBoPo
Rebecca's maid: a girl come from afar. Jacob and Esau. Else Lasker-Schüler, *tr. by* Rosemarie Waldrop. BoWoP
Rebel, The. Mari Evans. AmNP; IDB; IHMS; PoBA
Rebel, A. John Gould Fletcher. MoAmPo
Rebel. Irene Rutherford McLeod. HBMV
"Beyond the murk that swallows me," *sel.* WGRP
Rebel, The. Padraic Pearse. OnYI
Rebel, The. Innes Randolph. OBAL; OxBoLi
(Good Old Rebel, The.) FSW; TW
Rebel General, The. Chris Wallace-Crabbe. CBAP
Rebel Girl, The. Joe Hill. FSW
Rebel [*or* Rebell] Scot, The, *sels.* John Cleveland.
"Come, keen iambics, with your badger's feet." ViBoPo
("Come keen iambicks with your badger's feet.") OBS
"Lord! what a goodly thing is want of shirts." OBSV
"Nature herself doth Scotchmen beasts confess." OBSV
"Ring the bells backward; I am all on fire." PeD
Rebel Soldier, The. *Unknown.* OxBoLi
Rebellion shook an ancient dust. April Mortality. Léonie Adams. MoAB; MoAmPo
Rebellious fools that scorn to bow. The Bracelet. Thomas Stanley. AnAnS-2
Rebellious Vine, The. Harold Monro. BrPo
"Rebels." Ernest Crosby. PAH
Rebels from Fairy Tales. Hyacinthe Hill. DFT; SO
Rebirth. Kipling. LoBV; OBNC
Rebirth. Antonio Machado, *tr. fr. Spanish by* Robert Bly. NU
Rebirth. Catriona Stamp. BrRo
Re-birth. *Unknown, tr. fr. Bushman by* W. H. I. Bleek *and* Jack Cope. PeSA
Re-Birth of Venus, The. Geoffrey Hill. NePoEA
Rebolushinary X-mas. Carolyn M. Rodgers. JB
Reborn. Kingsley Amis. OxBC
Rebuff. Samuel L. Albert. NePoAm-2
Recall, The. James Russell Lowell. AP
Recall. Reed Whittemore. NYBP
Recalling War. Robert Graves. CMoP; CoBMV; LiTM; MMA; NoAM; OAEL-2; OBWP; WaP
Recapitulations, *sel.* Karl Shapiro.
"We waged a war within a war," XI. PoNe
Receipt for Stewing Veal, A. John Gay, *also at. to* Pope. FaBoUs
Receipt for the Vapours. Lady Mary Wortley Montagu. *See* Receipt to Cure the Vapours, A.
Receipt to Cure a Love Fit, A. *Unknown.* NOEC
Receipt to Cure the Vapours, A. Lady Mary Wortley Montagu. NOEC
(Receipt for the Vapours.) PBWP
Receive before you write, and write before you pay. How to Keep Accounts. *Unknown.* FaBoUs
Receive, dear friend, the truths I teach. To Licinius [*or* The Golden Mean]. Horace, *tr. by* William Cowper. Odes, II, 10. AWP; HBV-2; OBVE
Receiving Communion. Vassar Miller. NePoEA-2
Recent Dialogue, A. Thomas Moore. NBM
Recently cut she is unaccustomed. A Girl Combs Her Hair. Kimiko Hahn. BrSi
Reception, The. June Jordan. NMM
Recessional. Georgia Douglas Johnson. CDC; PoNe
Recessional. Kipling. AWP; BLPA; BLPL; BLRP; BrPo; CABA; FaBV; FaFP; FaPo; FaPoR; GN; HBV-2; HBVY; LiTB; MoBrPo; NOBE; NoP; OAEP; OBEV; OBNC; OBVV; OHFP; TreF; TrGrPo; TRV; UnPo; ViBoPo; VLP; WBLP; WGRP; WHA
Recessional. Thomas MacGreevy. CIP
Recessional, The. Sir Charles G. D. Roberts. HBV-2
Recessional. Isaac Watts. *See* O God, Our Help in Ages Past.
Recessional for the Class of 1959 of a School for Delinquent Negro Girls. Joseph R. Cowen. PoNe
Recipe. Albert Goldbarth. VWA
Recipe. A. P. Herbert. *Fr.* Two Gentlemen of Soho. WhC
Recipe. *Unknown, tr. fr. German by* Louis Untermeyer. UnTE
Recipe for a Pleasant Dinner-Party. *Unknown.* FaBoUs
Recipe for an Evening Musicale. Phyllis McGinley. WhC
(Evening Musicale.) OBAL
Recipe for an Ocean in the Absence of the Sea. Richard Howard. TAP
Recipe for Salad. Sydney Smith. *See* Salad, A.
Recipe: Gourds. Nicander, *tr. fr. Greek.* FaBoUs
Recipe: Hare. Archestratus, *tr. fr. Greek.* FaBoUs
Recipe: Onions. Philemon, *tr. fr. Greek.* FaBoUs
Recipe: Sausage. Axionicus, *tr. fr. Greek.* FaBoUs
Recipe: To Mak a Ballant. Alexander Scott. BSV
Reciprocity. John Drinkwater. PoA
Reciprocity. Vassar Miller. IHMS; NePoEA
Recital. John Updike. OBAL
Recitative. Hart Crane. FaBoMo
Recitative. Ronald McCuaig. PoAu-2
Recklessly/ I cast myself away. Izumi Shikibu, *tr. fr. Japanese by* Edwin A. Cranston. PBWP
Reckoning, The. Alice Friman. AMV-81
Reckoning, The. Theodore Roethke. PoA
Reckoning A. M. Thursday. Doris Turner. JB
Reclaimed Area. Jon Silkin. NoAM
Reclining Figure. Donald Hall. ConAP; LCAP
Recluse. Aldo Camerino, *tr. fr. Italian by* Anita Barrows. VWA
Recluse, The, *sels.* Wordsworth.
"On Man, on Nature, and on Human Life." OAEL-2; OBRV
(Prospectus [*fr.* The Excursion].) EnRP; NoP
Sunbeam Said, Be Happy, The, *fr.* I. FaBoRV
Recluses, The. Stuart Z. Perkoff. NeAP
Recognition. John White Chadwick. AA
Recognition, The. Denise Levertov. VGW
Recognition. Georgette Perry. AMV-80
Recognition, The. Frederick William Sawyer. HBV-1
Recognition of Eve, The. Karl Shapiro. *Fr.* Adam and Eve. MoAB
Recollection. Anne Reeve Aldrich. AA
Recollection. Duane Big Eagle. STE
Recollection, A. John Peale Bishop. LiTA; TwAmPo
Recollection. Amelia Walstien Carpenter. AA
Recollection, A. Frances Cornford. ELU
Recollection. Dorothy Donnelly. NCSH
Recollection. Donald D. Govan. NBP
Recollection. Marilyn R. Mumford. AMV-80
Recollection, The. Shelley. *See* To Jane: The Recollection.
Recollection in Autumn. Valentin Iremonger. *See* This Houre Her Vigill.
Recollection Long Ago: Sad Music. Robert Penn Warren. SV
Recollection of the Stone Circle near Keswick, A. Keats. *Fr.* Hyperion, II. FaBoPP
Recollections of Burgos. Richard Chenvix Trench. OBRV
Recollections of "Lalla Rookh." John Townsend Trowbridge. OBAL
Recollections of Love. Samuel Taylor Coleridge. ChER
Recollections of the Arabian Nights. Tennyson. VLP

Recompense. Nixon Waterman. HBV-2
Reconcilable Differences. Roger Sauls. AMV-81
Reconcilement, The. John Sheffield. OBEV
Reconciliation. "Æ." OBMV; OxBI; TrCP
Reconciliation. C. Day Lewis. MP; NoAM; TwCP
Reconciliation, *sel.* Elizabeth Doten.
"God of the Granite and the Rose!" TrPWD
Reconciliation. Else Lasker-Schüler, *tr. fr. German by* Robert Alter. PBWP
Reconciliation, The. Archibald MacLeish. MoAmPo
Reconciliation. Caroline Atherton Briggs Mason. AA
Reconciliation. John U. Nicolson. HBMV
Reconciliation. David Rosenmann-Taub, *tr. fr. Spanish by* Charles Guenther. VWA
Reconciliation, The. Tennyson. *See* As thro' the Land at Eve We Went.
Reconciliation. *Unknown, tr. fr. Late Middle Irish by* Kenneth Jackson. AnIL
Reconciliation. John Hall Wheelock. CrMA
Reconciliation. Walt Whitman. FaBoEn; HAP; MoAmPo; NoP; OBWP; OxBA; PAI; TrGrPo; WaaP; WeW
Reconnaissance. Arna Bontemps. AmNP; BPo
Reconsecration. Dorothy Gould. PGD
Record is nothing, and the hero great. Sonnet. Lord De Tabley. EBVV
Record Stride, A. Robert Frost. NePA
Recorder, tax collector, landlord, friends. Ode for the Burial of a Citizen. John Ciardi. LiTM; MiAP
Recorders Ages Hence. Walt Whitman. MoAmPo; NePA
Recorders in Italy. Adrienne Rich. TwAmPo
Recovery, The. Edmund Blunden. MoBrPo
Recovery. Patricia Y. Ikeda. BrSi
Recovery. F. R. Scott. CaP
Recovery, The. Thomas Traherne. AnAnS-1
Recovery Room, The: Lying-in. Helen Chasin. IHMS
Recreation. Audre Lorde. NIP; NoP
Recreation. Jane Taylor. NBM; OBRV; OxBoLi
Recrimination. Ella Wheeler Wilcox. AA
Recruit, The. Robert W. Chambers. HBV-2
Recruit, The. A. E. Housman. FaPoR
Recruit from the Slums, A. Emily Orr. SUMH
Recruited Collier, The. *Unknown. See* Jimmy's Enlisted; or, The Recruited Collier.
Recruiting Drive. Charles Causley. NePoEA; OxBTC; PPON; PrIm
Recruiting Sergeant, The. *Unknown.* OBET
Recruiting Serjeant, The, *sel.* Isaac Bickerstaffe.
Air: "What a charming thing's a battle!" NOEC
Recruits, The. Ian Hamilton. NoAM
Rectitude, and the terrible upstanding member. Washington in Love. John Berryman. LCAP
Rector's pallid neighbor at The Firs, The. The Villagers and Death. Robert Graves. HeIP
Recuerdo. Paula Gunn Allen. STE
Recuerdo. Edna St. Vincent Millay. AmFN; CTBA; EvOK; FaFP; FPL; LiTA; LiTM; NoAM; OxBA; PoA; TAP
Recuerdo, *sel.* Tennessee Williams.
Paper Lantern, The. CTBA
Recurrence, The. Edwin Muir. MoPo
Recurrences./ Coppery light hesitates. Measure. Robert Hass. GeTw
Red and blue and delicate green. *Unknown.* GBP
Red and green neon lights, the jazz hysteria. Nuit Blanche: North End. Conrad Aiken. OxBA
Red and the Green, The. Anne Wilkinson. MoCV
Red, and White Roses. Thomas Carew. AnAnS-2
Red and yellow of the Autumn salt-grass, The. At Tide Water. Sir Charles G. D. Roberts. PeCV
Red Anger. R. T. Smith. STE
Red ants in a bamboo—the passion. *Malay Oral Tradition, tr. by* R. J. Wilkinson *and* R. O. Winstedt. WTO
Red Apple Juice. *Unknown.* FSW
Red are the hands of the Reapers. The Reapers. Lauchlan Maclean Watt. PGD
Red as the guardroom lamp. Heartbreak Camp. Roy Campbell. OxBTC
Red as the lips of Rahab. The Scarlet Thread. Daniel Henderson. HBMV
Red Beauty. *Gond Oral Tradition, tr. by* V. Elwin *and* S. Hivale. WTO
Red Bird. *See* Redbird.
Red Bird Tapestry, The. May Swenson. TwAmPo
Red Book of Hergest, The, *sel. Unknown, tr. fr. Middle Welsh by* Ernest Rhys.
Lament for Urien, The. OBMV
Red brick building. The Song of a Factory Worker. Ruth Collins. SaC
Red brick [*or* bricks] in the suburbs, white horse on the wall. Ballad to a Traditional Refrain. Maurice James Craig. BIrV; SeCePo
Red brick monastery in, The/the suburbs. The Semblables. William Carlos Williams. AP; FaBoMo; NOBA
Red carpet-ing, The. While Cecil Snores: Mom Drinks Cold Milk. James Cunningham. JB
Red Clay. Linda Hogan. TWSS
Red cliffs arise. And up them service lifts. NW5 and N6. John Betjeman. SCV
Red Cloud. John G. Neihardt. BPAW
Red Cockatoo, The. Po Chü-i, *tr. fr. Chinese by* Arthur Waley. ChTr
Red Cow Is Dead, The. E. B. White. NYBP
Red-Cross Knight, The. Spenser. *Fr.* The Faerie Queene, I, 1. GoBC
("Gentle knight was pricking on the plain, A.") EBEV; OAEL-1
Red Cross Nurses. Gervase Stewart. WaP
Red dawn clouds coming up! the heavens proclaim you. Morning Light Song. Philip Lamantia. NeAP
Red Dog, The. Laura Jensen. LCAP
Red Dust. Philip Levine. NNaP
Red eyes of rabbits, The. The Springtime. Denise Levertov. CoAP; ConAP
Red fence, The. Snow Fence. Ted Kooser. PPJ
Red firelight on the Sioux tepees. Cottonwood Leaves. Badger Clark. TiPo
Red Flag, The. Jim Connell. FSW; VLP
Red Flag, The. Michael Jackson. OCNZ
Red flag is up, The. We Meet in the Lives of Animals. Peter Everwine. NNaP
Red flame flowers bloom and die, The. Nocturne. Crosbie Garstin. CH
Red fool, my laughing comrade. To a Comrade in Arms. Alun Lewis. FaBoTw; MoBrPo
Red fox, the vixen, The. Abnegation. Adrienne Rich. WPE
Red Geranium and Godly Mignonette. D. H. Lawrence. GTBS-P
Red Geraniums. Martha Haskell Clark. BLPA
Red Ghosts Chant, The. Lilian White Spencer. PoOW
Red globes of light, the liquor-green, The. William Street. Kenneth Slessor. CBAP
Red Glow in the Sky, A. Alexander Blok, *tr. fr. Russian by* Jon Stallworthy *and* Peter France. OBVE
Red-gold Rain, The. Sacheverell Sitwell. MoBrPo
Red granite and black diorite, with the blue. The Skeleton of the Future. "Hugh MacDiarmid." GoTS; MoBrPo; OBMV
Red-haired Man's Wife, The. James Stephens. HBMV; MoBrPo; OBVV
Red Hanrahan's Song about Ireland. W. B. Yeats. CMoP; FaBoCh; OnYI; OxBI
Red Harlaw. Sir Walter Scott. *See* Harlaw.
Red head, red head. Blackbird's Song. *Unknown.* GBP
Red Heart, The. James Reaney. CaP
Red-Herring. D.H. Lawrence. NoAM
Red Herring, The. George MacBeth. SO
Red Herring, The. *Unknown.* FaBoNo
Red Hugh. Thomas McGreevy. *See* Aodh Ruadh O'Domhnaill.
Red Indian Corpse. Peter Redgrove. OxBC
Red Iron Ore. *Unknown.* AS, *with music;* FSW
Red is a sunset. What Is Red? Mary O'Neill. RHPC
Red is the down which is covering me. Ankotarinya. *Unknown, tr. by* T. G. H. Strehlow. CBAP
Red Jack. Mary Durack. PoAu-1
Red Jacket. Fitz-Greene Halleck. AA
Red leaves fell upon the lake, The. Threnody. John Farrar. SUS
Red leaves flutter. Cover. Frances Frost. SUS
Red Light. Amiri Baraka. SOTW
Red Light Saloon, The, *with music. Unknown.* ShS
Red Lilies. Barbara Guest. PoM
Red lips are not so red. Greater Love. Wilfred Owen. BrPo; CMoP; EnLoPo; FaBoMo; FaBoRV; FaFP; GTBS-P; LiTB; LiTM; LO; MasP; MoAB; MoBrPo; NoAM; OAEP; SeCeV; ViBoPo; WaaP; WaP
Red lotus incense fades on/ the jewelled curtain. Li Ch'ing-chao, *tr. fr. Chinese by* Kenneth Rexroth. BoWoP
Red Man's Wife, The. *Unknown, tr. fr. Modern Irish by* Douglas Hyde. OnYI; OxBI; SeCePo
Red May. Agnes Mary Frances Robinson. HBMV
Red Men, The. Charles Sangster. CaP
Redmen come. In Autumn. Barbara Howes. LiSp
"Red o'er the Forest." John Keble. *See* November.
Red on sun sky sail. Six Eagles. Thomas Peacock. VoR
Red paths that wander through the gray, and cells. With God Conversing. Gene Derwood. LiTA; LiTM; NePA
Red quince branch. Piano. Lisa Russ. PPJ
Red, Red Rose, A. Burns. AWP; BiP; BoLoP; BSV; CABA; ChTr; FaBV; FaFP; FF; GBL; HAP; HBV-1; HeIP; InvP; LAuP; NIP; NOBE; NOEC; NoP; OAEL-1; OBEC; OBEV; OLR; OxBS; PAI; POEL-4; PoLF; PrIm; SeCeV; SoSe; TEP; ViBoPo
(My Love Is like a Red, Red Rose.) FSW; LiTB; OAEP
(My Luve.) FPL; TrGrPo

(My Luve Is [*or* My Luve's] like a Red, Red Rose.) EnRP; FaBoBe; HoPM; PoSC
(O, My Luve Is [*or* O, My Luve's] like a Red, Red Rose.) ELP; FaBoCh; GoTS; GTBS; GTBS–P; InPS; TreF; WHA
Red Riding Hood. Guy Wetmore Carryl. DFT; HBV-2; YaD
(Little Red Riding Hood.) FiBHP
Red Riding Hood and her grandmother. Happy Endings. Gail White. DFT
Red Riding Hood at the Acropolis. Myra Sklarew. DFT
Red Right Returning. Louis O. Coxe. MoVE; WaP
Red river, red river. Virginia. T. S. Eliot. Landscapes, II. BiP
Red River Shore, *with music. Unknown.* CoSo
Red River Valley. *Unknown.* AS, *with music;* BLSo, *with music*; BPAW; CoSo, *with music;* FaBoBe; FaFP; FSW; TrAS, *with music*; TreFS
Red Road, The. Nila NorthSun. STE
Red Rock Ceremonies. Anita Endrezze Probst. CDW; VoR
Red rock wilderness, The. The Wilderness. Sidney Keyes. LiTB; NeBP; OBWP
Red Room, The. Judith Berke. PoDr
Red Rose, proud Rose, sad Rose of all my days! To the Rose upon the Rood of Time. W. B. Yeats. NoAM; OAEP; TEP; VLP
Red rose whispers of passion, The. A White Rose. John Boyle O'Reilly. AA; ACP; HBV-1; OBEV; OBVV; OnYI; PoPl; SoSe
Red roses for Jerry Ford. A Bouquet for Jerry Ford. Mordecai Marcus. SOTS
Red Sea. James Agee. *Fr.* Two Songs on the Economy of Abundance. MoAmPo
Red Sea Place in Your Life, The. Annie Johnson Flint. *See* At the Place of the Sea.
Red Skins left their Agency, the Soldiers left their post, The. The Indian Ghost Dance and War. W. H. Prather. PoOW
Red Sky at Morning. Gilbert Thomas. LO; TreFS
Red sky at night. *Unknown.* OxNR
Red sky in the morning. *Unknown.* FaBoUs
Red stockings, blue stockings. *Unknown.* OxNR
Red sumac presses. On the New Road. Lyn Lifshin. NeAC
Red sun breaks through muddy lakes of haze and rifted cloud, The. The Stampede. Arthur I. Caldwell. BPAW
Red sweatshirt lies curled up, A. Still Life. Randolph Outlaw. LFAC
Red-tiled ships you see reflected, The. Five Vignettes. Jean Toomer. BALP; PoBA
Red-tiled towers of the old Chateau, The. Chateau Papineau. S. Frances Harrison. CaP
Red veins in the Gravensteins, The. Hannah Dustin. Louis O. Coxe. TwAmPo
Red Wheelbarrow, The. William Carlos Williams. BLPL; CMoP; GrPL; HeIP; HoPM; InPK; LiTA; LiTM; MoAB; MoAmPo; NIP; NoAM; NOBA; NoP; PAI; PrIm; SoSe; SOTW; TAP; UnPo; WeW
("So much depends.") HAP
(Spring and All.) EvOK
Red Whiskey. *Unknown.* AmFP
Red White & Another Ism. Harold LaMont Otey. LFAC
Red, White and Blue, The. David T. Shaw. *See* Columbia, the Gem of the Ocean.
Red, White and Red, The. *Unknown.* AmFP
Red Wig, The. *Unknown.* CoMu
Red Wine. Justin Richardson. PV
Red Bird. *Unknown.* FSW
Redbird, bluebird. They've All Gone South. Mary Britton Miller. RHPC
Redbreast, The, *sel.* Wordsworth.
"Driven in by autumn's sharpening air." PBBP
Redbreast, Early in the Morning. Emily Brontë. NCEP
Red-Breast of Aquitania, The. Francis S. Mahony. OnYI
Red-Bud, the Kentucky Tree, The. Christmas in Freelands. James Stephens. TrCP
Redbummed Sweeney bolts the gate. Sweeney, Old and Phthisic, among the Hippopotami. David Cummings. BXAP
Red-cap sang in Bishop's wood, A. Path Flower. Olive Tilford Dargan. HBMV
Rededication. Emanuel Litvinoff. WaP
Redeemer, The. "Fiona Macleod." WGRP
Redeemer, The. Siegfried Sassoon. MMA; WGRP
Redemption. Stanley Cooperman. AMV–80
Redemption. George Herbert. AnAnS–1; CABA; EaLo; EBCP; FF; HAP; InPS; JCP; LiTB; MeLP; MePo; NOBE; NOCV; NoP; OBS; PAI; SCV; SeCeV; SeCP; SeCV-1; SoSe; TEP; TrCP; WeW
Redeployment. Howard Nemerov. LiTM; NePA; OBWP; TrJP
Redesdale and Wise William. *Unknown.* ESPB
Redingote and the Vamoose, The. Richard Kendall Munkittrick. OBCA
Rediscovery. George Awoonor-Williams. TTY
Redmen. *See* Red Men.
Redoubted knights, and honorable Dames. Malbecco and Hellenore. Spenser. The Faerie Queene, III, 9 *and* 10. NoP
Redshanks, The. Julian Bell. OBMV
Redwing, The. Patric Dickinson. BoAnP
Red-Wing Blackbird, The. William Carlos Williams. DFF
Red Wing Hawk. James Applewhite. AMV–81
Red-winged blackbird, The. Bay Bank. A. R. Ammons. DFF
Redwings. James Wright. NNaP
Redwoods, The. Louis Simpson. AmFN; CoAP; PP
Reed, The. Henry Bernard Carpenter. AA
Reed, The. Caryll Houselander. ISi
Reed, The. Mikhail Yuryevich Lermontov, *tr. fr. Russian by* J. J. Robbins. AWP
Reed, A. Osip Mandelstam, *tr. fr. Russian by* James Greene. VWA
Reed-Player, The. Archibald MacLeish. HBMV
Reeds give, The. Small Song. A. R. Ammons. NoP; POL
Reeds in the Loch Sayis, The. *Unknown.* BSV; GoTS
Reeds of Innocence. Blake. *See* Piping Down the Valleys Wild.
Reedy islands. Working near Lake Traverse. Tom Hennen. FAZ
Reefing Topsails. Walter Mitchell. EtS
Reek and the Rambling Blade, The, *with music. Unknown.* OuSiCo
Reeking of unsolved crimes, the cop. Two Hookers. A. K. Redwing. VoR
Reeve, The. Chaucer. *Fr.* The Canterbury Tales: Prologue. OxBM
Reever ryves at the gullie, The. Women's Wather. T. S. Law. OxBS
Reeve's Tale, The. Chaucer. *Fr.* The Canterbury Tales. UnTE, *mod. vers. by* Frank Ernest Hill
Sels.
"At Trumpyngtoun nat fer from Cantebrigge." ViBoPo
Mill at Trumpington, The. OxBM
Reference to a Passage in Plutarch's Life of Sulla. Robinson Jeffers. CrMA
Refined Man, The. Kipling. *Fr.* Epitaphs of the War. FaBoEE; FaBoTw; MMA
Refiner's Fire, The. *Unknown.* BLRP
Reflected in a venetian mirror, heavy-framed. Soho. Joseph Brodsky, *tr. by* Alan Myers. VWA
Reflected in the pensioner's eye. Karoo Town. Robert Dederick. PeSA
Reflecting on the Aging-Process. Robert Peters. BXAP
Reflection, A. Thomas Hood. FaBoEE; PAI; PV
(Epigram: "When Eve upon the first of men," *wr. at. to* Thomas Moore.) HBV-1
Reflection. Kurt M. Stein. InMe
Reflection, The. Edward Taylor. *See* Reflexion, The.
Reflection. W. J. Turner. OBMV
Reflection. *Unknown.* STF
Reflection and Advice. Ezra Pound. OBSV
Reflection: After Visiting Old Friends. John Allison. GrPl
Reflection by a Mailbox. Stanley Kunitz. TrJP; WaP
Reflection from Rochester. William Empson. PoA
Reflection from Sea and Sky. Walter Savage Landor. FaBoEE
Reflection in a Green Arena. Gregory Corso. VGW
Reflection Kiss, one given, The. Some Kisses from *The Kama Sutra.* Hugo Williams. BoLoP
Reflection of Night, A. T. Walking Eagle Marietta. LFAC
Reflection on Babies. Ogden Nash. FaBoUs
Reflections. Anita Barrows. NMM
Reflections. Edna Becker. TRV
Reflections, *sel.* George Crabbe.
"We've trod the maze of error round." OBRV
Reflections. Antoinette Deshoulières, *tr. fr. French by* Yvor Winters. PBWP
Reflections, *sel.* Philip Freneau.
Americans! PPON
Reflections. Carl Gardner. NNP; PoBA
Reflections. Merle Molofsky. AMV–81
Reflections. David R. Pichaske. AMV–80
Reflections. Vivian Smith. CBAP
Reflections at Dawn. Phyllis McGinley. FiBHP; NOBL
Reflections in a Little Park. Babette Deutsch. ELU; NePoAm
Reflections in a Slum. "Hugh MacDiarmid." FaBoTw; NMP
Reflections in Bed. Julian Symons. WaP
Reflections of a Trout Fisherman. Andrew Demon. AMV–80
Reflections on a Womb Which Is Called "Vacant." Jeanine Hathaway. IHMS
Reflections on Having Left a Place of Retirement. Samuel Taylor Coleridge. EnRP; OBEC
Reflections on Ice-breaking. Ogden Nash. BLPL; FaBoCo; FaFP; LiTM; NePA; NoP; OBAL
Reflections on the Death of a Parrot. Jaime Jacinto. BrSi
Reflections on Water. Kenneth Pitchford. CoPo
Reflections upon a Recurrent Suggestion by Civil Defense Authorities That I Build a Bombshelter in My Backyard. Reed Whittemore. PoCh
Reflections, Written on Visiting the Grave of a Venerated Friend. Ann Plato. BlSi

Reflexes. Marvin Bell. Str
Reflexion, The. Edward Taylor. *Fr.* Preparatory Meditations. AmPP; AP; OxBA
(Reflection, The.) NePA
Reflexions on suicide, and on my father, possess me. Of Suicide. John Berryman. NoAM
Reformation of Godfrey Gore, The. William Brighty Rands. *See* Godfrey Gordon Gustavus Gore.
Reformation of Manners, *sels.* Daniel Defoe.
London. NOEC
"Search all the Christian climes from pole to pole." OBSV
"Yet Ostia boasts of her regeneration." OBSV
Reformed Drunkard. Vernon Scannell. AMV-80
Reformed Pirate, The. Theodore Goodridge Roberts. WHW
Reformer to His Father, A. James Simmons. BIrV
Re-forming the Crystal. Adrienne Rich. TAP
Refracted Lights. Celia Parker Wooley. WGRP
Refractory Gnu, The. *Unknown.* TDH
Refreshing rest, ecstatic dream. In the Grass. Annette von Droste-Hülshoff, *tr. by* James Edward Tobin. PBWP
Refrigerator, The. Howard Moss. GP
Refrigerator slams, The. Words from a Bottle. Deborah Lee. BrSi
Refrigerium. Cardinal Newman. OBNC
Refrigerium. Frederick Goddard Tuckerman. AP
Refuge. "AE." HBV-1; OnYI
Refuge. Hervey Allen. HBMV
Refuge, The. Bible, *O.T. (Moulton, Modern Reader's Bible).* Psalms, XLVI. WGRP
(Psalm XLVI: "God is our refuge . . .") AWP; TreFT; TRV
(Though the Earth Be Removed.) TrGrPo
Refuge. Archibald Lampman. PeCV
Refuge. Mabel E. McCartney. BLRP
Refuge. Lew Sarett. HBMV
Refuge. William Winter. HBV-1
Refugee. Naomi Long Madgett. PoNe
Refugee, The. Dabney Stuart. GP
Refugee Blues. W. H. Auden. LiTA
("Say this city has ten million souls.") LiTM
(Song: "Say this city has ten million souls.") NYBP
Refugee in America. Langston Hughes. AmFN; GOA
(Words like Freedom.) BPo
Refugees. Chaim Grade, *tr. fr. Yiddish by* Marc Kaminski. VWA
Refugees, The. Randall Jarrell. MoAB; MoAmPo
Refugees. Louis MacNeice. LiTB; WaP
Refugees, The. Edwin Muir. NoAM
Refugees, The. Sir Herbert Read. BrPo
Refusal, A. Barnabe Googe. EnRePo; NoP
Refusal, A. Thomas Hardy. FaBoCo; LiTB
Refusal to Mourn the Death, by Fire, of a Child in London, A. Dylan Thomas. BLPL; CABA; ChMP; CMoP; CoBMV; EBEV; FaBoEn; FaBoMo; FaFP; FF; GTBS-P; HeIP; HoPM; LiTB; LiTM; MasP; MoAB; MoBrPo; MoPo; MoVE; MP; NeBP; NoAM; NOBE; NoP; OAEL-2; OAEP; OxBTC; PAI; PoPl; SeCePo; TEP; TwCP; UnPo; WaaP
Refusals. Jon Anderson. MAYP
Refuses/ to refuse the racket. Old Tennis Player. Gwendolyn Brooks. LiSp
Refusing to fall in love with God, he gave. Didymus. Louis MacNeice. EaLo
Refusing What Would Bind You to Me Irrevocably. Ronald Koertge. GP
Regard her well—the austere face. Röntgen Photograph. Elisabeth Eybers, *tr. by* Jack Cope, Uys Krige, *and* Ruth Miller. PeSA
Regard, O reader, how it is with me. Look, in the Labyrinth of Memory. Delmore Schwartz. TrJP
Regard the capture here, O Janus-faced. Recitative. Hart Crane. FaBoMo
Regard the little needle. The Needle. Grace Cornell Tall. GoYe
Regard the motion of the villanelle. The Villanelle. Donald Harington. AMV-81; FAZ
Regarding (1) the U. S. and (2) New York. Franklin P. Adams. HBMV
Regeneration, *sel.* Walter Savage Landor.
"We are what suns and winds and waters make us." ViBoPo
Regeneration. Henry Vaughan. AnAnS-1; CABA; JCP; LoBV; MeLP; MePo; NoP; OBS
Regenesis. Ron Welburn. NBP
Regent of song! who bringest to our shore. To Rosina Pico. William Wilberforce Lord. AA
Regent's Park. Rose Fyleman. SoPo
Regent's Park Terrace. Bernard Spencer. FaBoPP
Regiment of Princes, The. Thomas Hoccleve. *See* De Regimine Principum.
Regina Angelorum G. K. Chesterton. ISi
Regina Coeli. Coventry Patmore. ISi
Regina Coeli. *Unknown, tr. fr. Latin by* Winfred Douglas. ISi
Regina Confessorum. *Unknown.* GoBC
Region desolate and wild, A. Hayeswater. Matthew Arnold. *Fr.* The Hayeswater Boat. FaBoPP
Region of life and light! The Life of the Blessed. Luis de Leon, *tr. by* Bryant. AWP
Region of our disdain. Sudan. Michael Jackson. OCNZ
Registered at the Bordello Hotel (Vienna). Larry Rubin. FAZ
Regrat. William Drummond of Hawthornden. PoEL-2
Regressing. Franz Douskey. LTB
Regret. *Malay Oral Tradition, tr. by* R. J. Wilkinson. WTO
Regret and Refusal. *Tr. fr. Tewa Indian by* H. J. Spinden. WTO
Regret not me. Thomas Hardy. MoVE; PoPle; SeCeV
Regretful Thoughts. Yü Hsüan-chi, *tr. fr. Chinese by* Geoffrey Waters. BoWoP
Regretfully, I proffer my excuses. Lines Declining a Transatlantic Dinner Invitation. Marilyn Hacker. MAYP
Regrets, *sel.* Joachim du Bellay, *tr. fr. French by* G. K. Chesterton.
Hereux Qui, comme Ulysse, A Fait un Beau Voyage, XXXI. AWP
Regulation-skirted. Emergency. Isabel Fiske Conant. HBMV
Rehabilitative Report: We Can Still Laugh. Daniel Berrigan. LFAC
Rehearsal. Cyril Dabydeen. BrSi
Rehearsal. David Fisher. NPGG
Rehearsal, The. Horace Gregory. VGW
Reid at Fayal. John Williamson Palmer. PAH
Reid in the Loch Sayis, The. *Unknown.* OxBS
Reign of Chaos, The. Pope. *See* Triumph of Dullness, The.
Reign of Peace, The. Mary Stark. WBLP
Reilly's Daughter. *Unknown.* FSW
Rein your sorry nags, boys, buckle the polished saddle. Dance on Pushback. James Still. GrPl
Reincarnating Pythagoras, say. Epigram. Ausonius. PeHV
Reincarnation [I] ("Still, passed through the spokes of an old wheel"). James Dickey. HoPM
Reincarnation [II] ("One can do one begins to one can only"). James Dickey. CAPP
Reincarnation. Mae Jackson. PoBA
Reincarnation. David Banks Sickels. *See* It Cannot Be.
Reindeer and Engine. Josephine Jacobsen. GrPl; WPE
Reindeer Report. U. A. Fanthorpe. OBCP
Reinforcements. Thomas Toke Lynch. OBVV
Reivers they stole Fair Annie, The. Fair Annie. *Unknown.* CH; HBV-2
Reject Jell-o. Lucille Day. AMV-81
Rejected Lover, The ("I once knew a little girl"). *Unknown.* AmFP
Rejected Lover, The ("The lonesome scenes of winter"). *Unknown.* AmFP
Rejected Member's Wife, The. Thomas Hardy. VLP
Rejected "National Hymns," The. "Orpheus C. Kerr." InMe, *abr.;* OBAL
Rejected Offer, The. Sir John Suckling. *See* Proffered Love Rejected.
Rejoice. Joaquin Miller. PAH
Rejoice and Be Merry. *Unknown.* EBCP
Rejoice in God, O ye tongues; give the glory to the Lord, and the Lamb. Christopher Smart. *Fr.* Jubilate Agno. LAuP
Rejoice in the Lamb. Christopher Smart. *See* Jubilate Agno.
Rejoice, Let Alleluias Ring, *with music.* Sister M. Cherubim Schaefer. AH
Rejoice, O Bridegroom! *Unknown, tr. fr. Hebrew by* Israel Abrahams. TrJP
Rejoice, O youth, in the lovely hind. Moses ibn Ezra, *tr. fr. Hebrew by* Solomon Solis-Cohen. *Fr.* Wedding Song in honor of R. Solomon ben Matir. TrJP
Rejoice, rejoice, brave patriots, rejoice! Reparation or War. *Unknown.* PAH
Rejoice, ye nations, vindicate the sway. British Commerce. John Dyer. *Fr.* The Fleece, IV. OBEC
Rejoice you sots, your idol's come again. Upon the King's Return from Flanders. Henry Hall. APAS
Rejoicing/ because we had met again. The Good Dream. Denise Levertov. NNaP
Rejoicing at the Arrival of Ch'en Hsiung. Po Chü-i, *tr. fr. Chinese by* Arthur Waley. AWP
Relapse, The. Thomas Stanley. AnAnS-2; OBEV
Relapse, The. Henry Vaughan. AnAnS-1; TrCP
Relating/ to the care of souls. Maximus, to Gloucester, Letter 19. Charles Olson. NMP
Relating to Robinson. Weldon Kees. NaP; NYP; TwAmPo
Relationship, The. Stephen Vincent. NeAC
Relationships. Mona Van Duyn. GP
Relatives are leaning over, staring expectantly, The. "The Dreadful Has Already Happened." Mark Strand. NoAM
Relativities. Louis Untermeyer. BXAP
Relativity. Kathleen Millay. QQQ
Relativity. *Unknown, at. to* Arthur Buller. FaBoCo; FaFP; ImOP
(Faster than Light.) QQQ
(Limerick: "There was a young lady named Bright.") CenH; NOBL

(Limerick: "There was a young woman named Bright.") WhC
("There was a young lady called Bright.") OxBoLi
(Young Lady Named Bright, A.) FaPON
Relaxed, nothing to do. Letting My Feelings Out. Yü Hsüan-chi, *tr. by* Geoffrey Waters. BoWoP
Relaxing all day in this tropical atmosphere. Foreign Aid. Lionel Kearns. NOBC
Relaxing here with brandy and certitude. The Epistemologist, over a Brandy, Opining. Robert Sargent. AMV-80
Relearning the Alphabet. Denise Levertov. NOBA
Release. D. H. Lawrence. CMoP
Released [*or* Releas'd] from the noise of the butcher and baker. Jinny the Just. Matthew Prior. NOBE; NOEC; OBEC; OBEV; PoEL-3
Relent, my deere, yet unkind Coelia. Coelia, XVII. William Percy. AAS
Relentless, black on white, the cable runs. T-Bar. P. K. Page. NOBC; OBCV
Reliable Service, A. Allen Curnow. OCNZ
Reliance. Henry van Dyke. FaFP
Relic, The. John Donne. CABA; EIL; EnRePo; GBL; HAP; LiTB; LoBV; NOBE; NoP; OAEL-1; PPP; SeCeV; WHA
(Relique, The.) AnAnS-1; MeLP; MePo; OAEP; OBS; PoEL-2; PoPle; SeCP; SeCV-1; ViBoPo
Relic, The. Robert Hillyer. GoYe; UnS
Relics. George Frederick Cameron. PeCV
Relics. Suzanne Gegna. AMV-81
Relics. David Wagoner. FAZ
Relief of Lucknow, The. Robert Traill Spence Lowell. HBV-2
Relief on Easter Eve, The. Thomas Pestel. OxBoCh
Relieved, I let the book fall behind a stone. Depressed by a Book of Bad Poetry. James Wright. ConAP
Relieving Guard. Bret Harte. RoGo
Religio Laici. Dryden. AnAnS-2; SeCV-2
Sels.
"But if there be a Power too just and strong." NOCV
"Dim, as the borrow'd beams of moon and stars." OAEL-1; OxBoCh; ViBoPo, *br. sel.*
(Finite Reason). LoBV
(Reason and Religion, *br. sel.*) FiP
(Reason and Revelation, *longer sel.*) OBS
Priestcraft and Private Judgement. OBS
Scriptures, The. OBS
"Thus Man by his own strength to Heaven would soar." NOCV; WGRP
Tradition. OBS
Religio Medici, *sel.* Sir Thomas Browne.
Colloquy with God, A. OBS
(Evening Hymn.) OxBoCh
Religio Novissima. Aubrey Thomas De Vere. NBM
Religion. Samuel Butler. DBV
Religion. John Donne. Satires, III. NoP
Religion. Henry Vaughan. AnAnS-1; NOCV; OAEL-1; OBS; OxBoCh
Religion and Doctrine. John Hay. WGRP
Religion and the Lower Classes. Evan Lloyd. *Fr.* The Methodist. NOEC
Religion Back Home. William Stafford. OBAL
Religion Is a Fortune I Really Do Believe, *with music.* *Unknown.* BoAN-2
Religion of Hudibras, The. Samuel Butler. *Fr.* Hudibras, I, 1. DBV; InMe
("For his religion it was fit.") LoBV; OBSV; ViBoPo
(Sir Hudibras's Religion.) FaBoEn
Religion of Sweet Jesus, The. "Onward Christian Soldiers!" Frank Marshall Davis. FB
Religious faith is a most filling vapor. Innate Helium. Robert Frost. ImOP
Religious Musings. Samuel Taylor Coleridge. WGRP
"Lovely was the death," *sel.* EnRP
Religious Use of [Taking] Tobacco, A. *Unknown, at. to* Robert Wisdome. EIL; HBV-2; OBS
(Pipe and Can, I.) OBEV
Reliquary. Hart Crane. PoA
Relique, The. John Donne. *See* Relic, The.
Reliques, *sel.* Edmund Blunden.
"And mathematics, fresh as May." ImOP
Relish honey. If you please. To a Swallow. John Peale Bishop, *after* Euenus. OBVE
Relish of the Muse, The. Sir John Beaumont. POL
Relocation. David Mura. BrSi
Reluctance. Robert Frost. CMoP; MoAB; MoAmPo; NOBA; OxBA
Reluctant Lady, The. *Unknown.* *See* Maiden's Denial, A.
Reluctant Sh Kaxwul.aat, "Being/ Troubled about Herself." Breech Birth. Nora Dauenhauer. TWSS
Relying on the disasters o' the war. March, 1941. Paul Goodman. LiTA
Remain, Ah Not in Youth Alone. Walter Savage Landor. *Fr.* Ianthe. HAP; OAEP; OBNC
Remainder. Frederika Blankner. GoYe
Remains, The. Mark Strand. NYBP; PPP
Remains of an Indian Village. Al Purdy. NOBC
Remains of blue bog children, The. Blue Bog Children. Roger Weingarten. AmPA
Remarkable Art. Gelett Burgess. FaBoNo
(Nonsense Verses: "Remarkable truly, is art!") HBV-2
Remarks from the Pup. Burges Johnson. GDP
Remarks of Soul to Body. Robert Penn Warren. NAs
Rembrandt's Late Self-Portraits. Elizabeth Jennings. EyDe
Remedies. Gary Soto. Str
Remedy Worse than the Disease, The. Matthew Prior. FaBoEE; HBV-1; TrGrPo
Remeidis of Luve. *Unknown.* OxBS
Remember. William Johnson Cory. OBVV
Remember. Joy Harjo. STE; TWSS
Remember. Georgia Douglas Johnson. PoNe
Remember. Christina Rossetti. AWP; BoLoP; CH; EnLoPo; FaBoEn; FaBV; FPL; HBV-1; NOBE; NoP; OAEL-2; OAEP; OBEV; OBNC; OBVV; PoLF; PoPle; PoRA; SBG; TreFS; TrGrPo; ViBoPo; WHA
(Sonnet: "Remember me when I am gone away.") LoBV
"But if the darkness and corruption leave," *sel.* LO
Remember. *Unknown.* BXAP
Remember a season. A Symposium: Apples. Linda Pastan. NIP
Remember Dear Mary. John Clare. WeW
Remember he was poor and country-bred. Abraham Lincoln. Mildred Plew Meigs. PAL; TiPo
Remember how it was before she came? One of the Seven Has Somewhat to Say. Sara Henderson Hay. DFT
Remember how unimportant. Milkweed. Philip Levine. LCAP
Remember it, althought you're far away. Remember. *Unknown.* BXAP
Remember man that passeth by. An Epitaph and a Reply [*or* Epitaph]. *Unknown.* TreFS; TreFT
Remember May? Rhyme for Remembrance of May. Richard Burton. HBMV
Remember Me. Keith Douglas. *See* Simplify Me When I'm Dead.
Remember me, I was a celebrity. A Voice from Out of the Night. Lisel Mueller. GP
Remember me? I was the one. Hood. C. K. Williams. InPK
Remember me when I am dead. Simplify Me When I'm Dead [*or* Remember Me]. Keith Douglas. NeBP; NePoEA; OxBTC
Remember me when I am gone away. Remember [*or* Sonnet]. Christina Rossetti. AWP; BoLoP; CH; EnLoPo; FaBoEn; FaBV; FPL; HBV-1; LoBV; NOBE; NoP; OAEL-2; OAEP; OBEV; OBNC; OBVV; PoLF; PoPle; PoRA; SBG; TreFS; TrGrPo; ViBoPo; WHA
Remember Not. Helene Johnson. BANP; PoNe
Remember now, my Love, what piteous thing. A Carrion. Baudelaire, *tr. by* Allen Tate. AWP
Remember Now Thy Creator. Bible, *O.T.* Ecclesiastes, XII: 1-7. AWP; ChTr (1-8); TreF (1-14)
("Remember now thy Creatour in the days of thy youth," 1-8.) OBVE
(Remember Then Thy Creator, 1-8.) TrJP
(Youth and Age, 1-8.) TrGrPo
Remember or Forget. Hamilton Aidé. HBV-1
"Remember Pearse," he said. The Orator. Roy McFadden. OnYI
Remember, Phyllis. Honeymoon. Samuel L. Albert. GoYe
Remember, poet, while gallivanting across the sky. Forget Me Not. Bob Kaufman. AmNP
Remember, remember/ The fifth of November. The Gunpowder Plot. *Unknown.* FaBoUs
Remember Richard, lately king of price. The Tudor Rose. Alexander Barclay. *Fr.* The Ship of Fools. ACP
Remember Sabbath Days. Larry Eigner. VWA
Remember September. May Justus. SiSoSe; YeAr
Remember, Sinful Youth, *with music.* *Unknown.* AH
Remember Suez? Adrian Mitchell. OxBTC
Remember That Country. Jean Garrigue. VGW
Remember that old love song, Daphne? Delfica. Gérard de Nerval, *tr. by* Andrew Hoyem. NU
Remember that Saturday morning. The Dirty-billed Freeze Footy. Judith Hemschemeyer. Str
Remember that we are dust. It is said. Camel. W. S. Merwin. NePA
Remember the covenant of our youth. A Dying Wife to Her Husband. Moses ibn Ezra. TrJP
Remember the Day of Judgement. *Unknown.* MeEL
Remember the day the sea turned red. Plankton. Ruth Miller. PeSA
Remember the Ladies. Lyn Lifshin. LTB
Remember the Last Things. *Unknown.* MeEL
Remember the Promise, Dakotah. Robert V. Carr. PoOW
Remember: the simplest eddy. An Angler's Vade Mecum. John Engels. WOLT
Remember the sky that you were born under. Remember. Joy Harjo. STE; TWSS

Remember the spider/ Weaving a snare. Tanist. James Stephens. OnYI
Remember the sun in the autumn, its rays. The Secret Town. Abraham Sutzkever, *tr. by* Jacob Sonntag. TrJP
Remember Thee! Remember Thee! Byron. BoLoP; ViBoPo
Remember Then Thy Creator. Bible, *O.T.* *Fr.* Ecclesiastes. *See* Remember Now Thy Creator.
Remember those wingovers and loops and spins? The Dream of Flying Comes of Age. Howard Nemerov. BiP
Remember those X-ray machines in shoe stores. On Hot Days. James Reiss. AmPA
Remember Thou Me. *Malay Oral Tradition, tr. by* R. J. Wilkinson *and* R. O. Winstedt. WTO
Remember, Though the Telescope Extend. George Dillon. ImOP
Remember, though we cannot write it, the delicate dream. Rainy Summer. Ruth Pitter. MoVE
Remember Thy Creator Now, *with music.* Peter Long. AH
Remember Times for Sandy. Carolyn M. Rodgers. JB
Remember us poor Mayers all. Song of the Mayers [*or* The Mayers' Song]. *Unknown.* CH; GBP
Remember Way Back. *Unknown.* BluL
Remember what I promised you. Way Out in Idaho [*or* Idyho]. *Unknown.* CoSo; FSW
Remember when. Among Strangers. William Stafford. NNaP
Remember when I draped. Poem for My Mother. Siv Cedering Fox. Str
Remember when I held. Javier. José Y. Terán, Jr. LFAC
Remember when you hear them beginning to say Freedom. Notes for My Son. Alex Comfort. The Song of Lazarus, VI. LiTM; MoBrPo; NeBP; SeCePo
Remember, while you are sleeping here, offshore. Evolution. John Blight. CBAP
Remember Whistling Willie's market. Whistling Willie. Kaye Starbird. QQQ
Remember Your Lovers. Sidney Keyes. WaP
Remember, youth will not last more. Advice to a Young Man (of Letters) Who Doesn't Know How to Take Care of Himself. Irwin Edman. InMe
Remembered Grace. Coventry Patmore. The Unknown Eros, XIX. OxBoCh
Remembered Melody. Andrew Lang. *See* Twilight on Tweed.
Remembered Morning. Janet Lewis. WPE
Remembered summers are the smell of nettles. Fragments. John Cotton. AMV-80
Remembering. Akjartoq, *tr. fr. Eskimo.* WTO
Remembering. Maya Angelou. PPJ
Remembering. "Michael Lewis," *after the Chinese.* *Fr.* Cherry Blossoms. UnTE
Remembering. Clarisse Nicoïdski, *tr. fr. Judezmo by* Stephen Levy. VWA
Remembering. Judit Tóth, *tr. fr. Hungarian by* Emery George. VWA
Remembering Althea. William Stafford. NYBP
Remembering Apple Times. John T. Hitchner. AMV-80
Remembering Day. Mary Wight Saunders. YeAr
Remembering Fannie Lou Hamer. Thadious M. Davis. BlSi
Remembering Fire. Rodney Jones. MAYP
Remembering Golden Bells. Po Chü-i, *tr. fr. Chinese by* Arthur Waley. AWP
Remembering Him. Joe Reccardi. AMV-80
Remembering his taste for blood. Of Baiting the Lion. Sir Owen Seaman. NA
Remembering Home. Susan Petrykewycz. AMV-80
Remembering Kevan MacKenzie. Henry Taylor. InPK
Remembering Lincoln. Frank Mundorf. GoYe
Remembering Lunch. Douglas Dunn. OxBC
Remembering Lutsky. Rayzel Zychlinska, *tr. fr. Yiddish by* Marc Kaminsky. VWA
Remembering My Father. Jonathan Holden. Str
Remembering Nat Turner. Sterling A. Brown. PoBA; PoNe
Remembering Snow. Ralph Nixon Currey. PeSA
Remembering That Island. Thomas McGrath. NePoEA; PPON
Remembering the descriptions by Wilson. Passenger Pigeons. Robert Morgan. GeTw; MAYP
Remembering the past/ And gloating at it now. What the Bones Know. Carolyn Kizer. NePoAm-2
Remembering the Strait of Belle Isle or. Large Bad Picture. Elizabeth Bishop. EyDe; MiAP; NoP; NYBP; OxBC
Remembering the 'Thirties. Donald Davie. NePoEA; OxBTC; PP
Remembering the Winter. Rowena Bennett. SiSoSe
Remembering what passed. Old Scent of the Plum Tree. Fujiwara Ietaka, *tr. by* E. Powys Mathers. AWP
Remembrance. John Henry Boner. AA
Remembrance. Emily Brontë. BLPL; BoLoP; BoWoP; CH; EBEV; EnLoPo; FaBoEn; FaFP; HAP; HBV-1; LiTB; LO; MasP; NOBE; NoP; OAEP; OBNC; OxBI; PoEL-5; TEP; TreFT; TrGrPo; VLP; WeW; WPE
(Cold in the Earth.) PBWP
(R. Alcona to J. Brenzaida.) BrRo; EBVV
Remembrance. John Clare. *See* Remembrances.
Remembrance, A. Willis Gaylord Clarke. AA
Remembrance. George Parsons Lathrop. AA
Remembrance. Shakespeare. *See* Sonnets, XXX.
Remembrance. Antoni Slonimski, *tr. fr. Polish by* Frances Notley. TrJP
Remembrance. Sir Thomas Wyatt. *See* Lover Showeth How He Is Forsaken . . .
Remembrance Day in the Dales. Dorothy Una Ratcliffe. SUMH
Remembrance of a Color inside a Forest, A. Ray A. Young Bear. CDW
Remembrance of Things Past. Horace Coleman. FAZ
Remembrancer of joys long passed away. To a Golden Heart, Worn round His Neck. Goethe, *tr. by* Margaret Fuller Ossoli. AWP
Remembrances. John Clare. NCEP
Sels.
Enclosure. NBM
"When for school o'er Little Field with its brook and wooden brig." SaC
Rememorised, Maurice Devane. Austin Clarke. Mnemosyne Lay in Dust, XVIII. CMoP; IPY
Remind you, that there was darkness in my heart. Canticle of Darkness. Wilfred Watson. MoCV
Reminder, The. Léonie Adams. MoVE
Reminder, The. Thomas Hardy. CMoP; OBCP
Reminder. *Unknown.* STF
Reminiscence. Thomas Bailey Aldrich. AA
Reminiscence, A. Anne Brontë. WPE
Reminiscence. Wallace Irwin. FiBHP; NOBL
Reminiscences of a Dancing Man. Thomas Hardy. MoVE
Reminiscent Reflection. Ogden Nash. FaBoCo
Remnant Ghosts at Dawn. Oliver La Grone. FB
Remnants and relics of a thousand years—here in a pit full of dust. The Book-burning Pit. Lo Yin, *tr. by* Edward H. Schafer. GLGT
Rémon, *with music.* *Unknown, tr. fr. French.* TrAS
Remonstrance, A. John Gerrard. NOEC
Remonstrance. Philodemos the Epicurean, *tr. fr. Greek by* Dudley Fitts. OLR
Remonstrance to the King. William Dunbar. OxBS
R-E-M-O-R-S-E. George Ade. FiBHP; OBAL; TreFT
Remorse. John Betjeman. MoBrPo
Remorse, *sel.* Samuel Taylor Coleridge.
Invocation, An. OAEP
("Hear, sweet spirit, hear the spell.") ViBoPo
(Voice Sings, A.) CH
Remorse. Richmond Lattimore. PoA
Remorse. Pierre Louÿs, *tr. fr. French by* Horace M. Brown. *Fr.* The Songs of Bilitis. UnTE
Remorse. Shelley. *See* Stanzas—April, 1814.
Remorse for Time, The. Howard Nemerov. NCSH
Remorse is memory awake. Emily Dickinson. NOBA; NOCV; NoP
Remote and ineffectual Don. Lines to a Don. Hilaire Belloc. DBV, *abr.*; FaBoCo; MoBrPo; OBSV; TW
Remote from our sordid world. Purity. Hayim Lenski, *tr. by* Pearl Grodensky. VWA
Remote music of his swans, their long. His Swans. Geoffrey Grigson. FaBoRV
Remote sky, prolonged to the sea's brim, A. For "Ruggiero and Angelica" by Ingres. Dante Gabriel Rossetti. VLP
Remote, unfriended, melancholy, slow. The Traveller. Goldsmith. BIrV; LAuP; OAEP; ViBoPo
Removal from Terry Street, A. Douglas Dunn. FaBoMo; OxBC; POL
Removal: Last Part. Carroll Arnett. VoR
Remove the decedent's refractory tripes. Undertakers. Ambrose Bierce. DBV
Removed from Europe's feuds, a hateful scene. A Warning to America. Philip Freneau. TAP
Renaissance. Robert Avrett. GoYe
Renaissance/a Triptych. John Minczeski. PoDr
Renaissance was six months old, The. A Framed Photograph. Allen Curnow. *Fr.* Trees, Effigies, Moving Objects. OCNZ
Renaming, The. Valerie Sinason. BrRo
Renaming the Evening. Eric Pankey. AMV-81
Renascence. Muredach J. Dooher. OnYI
Renascence. Edna St. Vincent Millay. FaFP; HBV-2; MoAB; MoAmPo; NePA; OHFP; TwAmPo
"All I could see from where I stood" *sel.* PDV
Rencontre. Jessie Fauset. CDC
Rend America asunder. The Ship Canal from the Atlantic to the Pacific. Francis Lieber. PAH
Render unto Cæsar. Rolfe Humphries. CrMA

Rendezvous, The. Alan Seeger. *See* I Have a Rendezvous with Death.
Rendezvous, The. Bernard Spencer. GTBS-P
Rendez-vous Manqué dans la Rue Racine. J. M. Synge. BIrV
Renegade Wants Words, The. James Welch. CDW
Renegado, The, *sel.* Philip Massinger.
"'Yet there's one scruple with which I am much.'" ACP
Renew the old stories, it is said almost every day. The Old Stories. Gene Frumkin. AMV-80
Renewal. "Michael Field." OBVV
Renewal, A. James Merrill. PoPl
Renewal, The. Theodore Roethke. VGW
Renewal by Her Element. Denis Devlin. CIP
Renewal of the cycle. The Mikveh. Blu Greenberg. AMV-80
Reno, 2 A.M. Sam Hamill. TAT
Renoir's Confidences. J. Michael Pilz. AMV-81
Renouncement. Alice Meynell. BoLoP; HBV-1; MoBrPo; NOBE; OBEV; OBMV; OBNC; OBVV; TreFT; ViBoPo; WPE
Renouncing of Love, A. Sir Thomas Wyatt. FaBoEn; GBL; OAEP
("Farewell, love, and all thy laws [*or* lawes] for ever.") AAS; LiTB; OAEL-1
(Lover Renounceth Love, The.) TrGrPo
(Sonnet: "Farewell, love, and all thy laws for ever.") SiPS
Renowned Generations, The. W. B. Yeats. OxBoLi
Renowned Spenser [*or* Spencer] lye [*or* lie] a thought more nye [*or* nigh]. Elegy on Shakespeare [*or* On Mr. Wm. Shakespeare]. William Basse. ElL; FaBoRV; OBS; ViBoPo
Rent. Jane Cooper. FYAP; TAP
Renunciants. Edward Dowden. OBVV
Renunciation. Wathen Mark Wilks Call. OBVV; WGRP
Renunciation. Emily Dickinson. *See* There came a day at summer's full.
Renunciation, A. Henry King. OBEV
Renunciation, A. Edmund de Vere, Earl of Oxford. *See* If Women Could Be Fair.
Repairman in the doorway, The. Goodbye. Chana Bloch. MAYP
Reparation. Helen Hoyt. HBMV
Reparation or War. *Unknown.* PAH
Repartée. Charles Follen Adams. OBAL
Repartee. *Unknown.* TreFT
Repast. Gertrude Tiemer-Wille. GoYe
Repeat that, repeat. The Cuckoo [*or* Fragment]. Gerard Manley Hopkins. ELU; FM; MoAB; MoBrPo; PBBP
Repeated Journey, The. Thomas McGrath. NePoEA
Repeated Pilgrimage. John Gilland Brunini. GoBC
Repeating fly, blueback, thumbthick—so gross, A. Harriet. Robert Lowell. NoP
Repent, O ye, predestinate to woe! The Conscience-Keeper. William Young. *Fr.* Wishmakers' Town. AA
Repentance. George Chapman. *Fr.* Hero and Leander, Third Sestiad. OBSC
Repentance. George Herbert. OAEP
Repentance. George Alexander Stevens. NOEC
Repetition. Wyatt Prunty. AMV-81
Repetition of Words and Weather. Ruth Stone. BoWoP
Repetitions. Carl Sandburg. HBMV
Repetitions of a Young Captain. Wallace Stevens. WaP
Repetitive Heart, The, *sels.* Delmore Schwartz.
"All clowns are masked and all *personae.*" ViBoPo
(All Clowns Are Masked.) LiTA; OxBA
For Rhoda. MoAB; MoAmPo; MoVE; OxBa
(Calmly We Walk through This April's Day.) LiTM; PrIm
(Time Is the Fire.) LiTA
"Heavy bear who goes with me, The." CrMA; LiTA; LiTM; MiAP; MoPo; MoVE; MP; NePA; NIP; NoAM; NOBA; TAP; TrJP; TwCP; UnPo
Repine not, Gray, that our weak dazzled eyes. To Mr. Gray on the Publication of His Odes. David Garrick. OBEC
Reply. Hartley Coleridge. OBRV
Reply. Sidney Godolphin. OBS
Reply, The. Philip Levine. PoA
Reply. Victoria McCabe. POL
Reply, The. Theodore Roethke. NoP; NYBP
Reply, A. *Unknown.* FaBoCo
(Answer.) PoPle
(Limerick: "Dear Sir, your astonishment's odd.") NOBL
Reply from the Akond of Swat, A. Ethel Talbot Scheffauer. FiBHP
Reply of Socrates, The. Edith M. Thomas. WGRP
Reply to a Creditor. George Harding. FaBoUs
Reply to an Imitation of the Second Ode in the Third Book of Horace, A. Richard Bentley. OBEC
(Verses: "Who strives to mount Parnassus Hill.") ViBoPo
Reply to Dipsychus. Arthur Hugh Clough. FaBoCo
Reply to "In Flanders Fields." John Mitchell. BLPA; PAL
Reply to Lines by Thomas Moore, A, *sel.* Walter Savage Landor.
"Will you come to the bower I have shaded for you?" ChTr
Reply to Marlowe's "The Passionate Shepherd to His Love." Sir Walter Ralegh. *See* Nymph's Reply to the Shepherd, The.
Reply to Marriage Proposal. Irihapeti Rangi te Apakura, *tr. fr. Maori by* Roger Oppenheim *and* Allen Curnow. PBWP
Reply to Mr. Wordsworth, *sel.* Archibald MacLeish.
"Space-time, our scientists tell us, is impervious." ImOP
Reply to Nancy Hanks, A. Julius Silberger. TiPo
Reply to the Committed Intellectual. Francis Sparshott. NOBC
Reply to the Provinces. Galway Kinnell. NYBP
Reply to the Question: "How Can You Become a Poet?" Eve Merriam. DFF
Re-plyed, extorted, oft transposed, and fleeting. Sea Voyage. William Empson. CMoP; MOS
Report, The. Jon Swan. NYBP
Report from a Planet. Richmond Lattimore. FYAP
Report from California. Lois Moyles. NYBP
Report from the Carolinas, *sel.* Helen Bevington.
"It's a debatable land. The winds are variable." AmFN
Report from the Correspondent They Fired. David McElroy. AmPA
Report of the Meeting. Weldon Kees. TwAmPo
Report on Experience. Edmund Blunden. FaBoEn; FaBoTw; GTBS-P; LO; NOBE; OBMV; OBWP
Report Song, A. Nicholas Breton. OBSC; SeCePo
(Country Song.) TrGrPo
(Report Song in a Dream, A.) GBL
(Wooing in a Dream.) NOBE
Reported Missing. Anna Gordon Keown. SUMH
Reporters, The. Newman Levy. InMe
Reportless subjects, to the quick. Emily Dickinson. NOBA
Reports Come In, The. J. D. Reed. NYBP
Reports of Midsummer Girls. Richmond Lattimore. PCP
Repose. Alfred Lichtenstein, *tr. fr. German by* Mary Zilzer. VWA
Repose of Rivers. Hart Crane. AP; AWP; CMoP; CoBMV; LiTM; MoAB; MoAmPo; NoAM; NOBA; OxBA; SeCeV
Repose they know in storefronts, The. The Village of the Presents. James McMichael. AmPA
Representing nothing on God's earth now. Lines on the Back of a Confederate Note. Samuel Alroy Jonas. BLPA
Repression. Timothy Corsellis. WaP
Repression of War Experience. Siegfried Sassoon. BrPo; CMoP; MMA; NoAM
Reprieve. Barbara Villy Cormack. CaP
Reprisall, The. George Herbert. AnAnS-1
(Second Thanksgiving, The; or, The Reprisal.) OAEP
Reprisals. W. B. Yeats. OBWP
Reproach to Julia. Robert Graves. ELU; FaBoEE
Reproduction of Life. Erasmus Darwin. *Fr.* The Temple of Nature; or, The Origin of Society, II. PBBP
Reproof, A. Bible, *O.T.* *See* Go to the Ant.
Reproof. *Unknown.* STF
Reptiles move like Navajo beadwork. Trench. Stephen Pett. GrPl
Reptilian green the wrinkled throat. Sir Gawaine and the Green Knight. Yvor Winters. MoVE; NoAM; PoRA; QFR; TwAmPo; VGW
Republic, The. Longfellow. *See* Ship of State, The.
Republic 1939, The. James Liddy. CIP
Republic of the West. On a Rhine Steamer [*or* England and America, I]. James Kenneth Stephen. InMe; NBM; NOBL; TW
Republic to Republic. Witter Bynner. PAH
Repulse, The. Thomas Stanley. AnAnS-2; MeLP; MePo; OBS
Reputedly last of his kind. The Last Moriori. Kendrick Smithyman. OCNZ
Request, The. Abraham Cowley. AnAnS-2
Request for Requiems. Langston Hughes. ShM
Request Number. G. N. Sprod. FiBHP
Request of a Dying Child. Lydia Huntley Sigourney. OBCA
Request to a Year. Judith Wright. CBAP
Requests. Digby Mackworth Dolben. *See* I Asked for Peace.
Requiem: "Breathe, trumpets, breathe." George Lunt. AA
Requiem: "Farewell my friend." Martin T. O'Connor. AMV-80
Requiem: "Hush your prayers, 'tis no saintly soul." Conal O'Riordan. HBV-2
Requiem: "I watch the roses float." Stephen Vincent. NeAC
Requiem: "Let the mountains stand forth." Hamilton Warren. GoYe
Requiem: "Mother is gone. Bird songs wouldn't let her breathe." William Stafford. NaP
Requiem, A: "My father listening to opera, that's me." David Ignatow. DiL
Requiem: "No, not far beneath some foreign sky then." "Anna Akhmatova," *tr. fr. Russian by* Robin Kemble. NAWM-2
(Requiem 1935-1940, *tr. by* Richard McKane.) BoWoP

Requiem: "Past love, past sorrow, lies this darkness." Kathleen Raine. NeBP
Requiem: "Pour out your light, O stars." Ivor Gurney. FaBoEE; FaBoTw
Requiem: "She wears, my beloved, a rose upon her head." John Frederick Matheus. CDC
Requiem: "There was a young belle of old Natchez." Ogden Nash. NoP
Requiem, A: "Thou hast lived in pain and woe." James Thomson ("B. V.") HBV-2
Requiem: "Under the wide and starry sky." Robert Louis Stevenson. BrPo; BSV; DL; EBVV; FaBV; FaPoR; FPL; GoTS; HBV-2; HBVY; MoBrPo; NOBE; OBEV; OBNC; OBVV; OHFP; PoLF; PoPl; PoRA; TreF; TrGrPo; ViBoPo; WGRP; WHA
Requiem: "When my last song is sung and I am dead." Theodore Maynard. GoBC
Requiem: "When the last voyage is ended." Joseph Lee. OHIP
Requiem: "Will they stop." Kenneth Fearing. CMoP
Requiem after Seventeen Years. Dahlia Ravikovitch, *tr. fr. Hebrew by* Chana Bloch. VWA
Requiem for a River. Kim Williams. RFM
Requiem for a Young Soldier. Florence Earle Coates. OHIP
Requiem for "Bird" Parker. Gregory Corso. PoNe
Requiem for Soldiers Lost in Ocean Transports, A. Herman Melville. PoEL-5
Requiem for Sonora. Richard Shelton. Psk
Requiem for the Croppies. Seamus Heaney. BIrV; CIP; FaBoMo; OBWP
Requiem for the Plantagenet Kings. Geoffrey Hill. NoAM
Requiem 1935-1940. "Anna Akhmatova." *See* Requiem: "No, not far beneath some foreign sky then."
Requiescat. Matthew Arnold. AWP; ELP; FiP; HBV-1; HeIP; InvP; LiTB; NOBE; OAEP; OBEV; OBVV; PoRA; TreFS; TrGrPo; ViBoPo; WHA
Requiescat. Katherine Anne Porter. HBMV
Requiescat. Frederick George Scott. OHIP
Requiescat. Rosamund Marriott Watson. HBV-1
Requiescat. Oscar Wilde. BrPo; EBVV; HBV-1; InvP; MoBrPo; OBNC; OBVV; OnYI; OxBI; TreF; TrGrPo; WHA
Required Course. Frances Stoakley Lankford. GoYe
Required of You This Night. Peter Redgrove. NMP
Requirements: "Not for me a giantess." Niarchus, *tr. fr. Greek by* Wallace Rice. ErPo
Requirements: "Not too chary, not too fast." Rufinus, *tr. fr. Greek by* Wallace Rice. ErPo
Requirements: "Not too lean, and not too fat." Rufinus, *tr. fr. Greek by* Wallace Rice. ErPo
Requirements: "Not too old, and not too young." Honestus, *tr. fr. Greek by* Wallace Rice. ErPo
Requirements: "Not too pallid, as if bleacht." Xenos Palaestes, *tr. fr. Greek by* Wallace Rice. ErPo
Rescue, The. Robert Creeley. CAPP
Rescue. Olive Tilford Dargan. GoYe
Rescue, The. John Logan. CoAP; NYBP
Rescue. Dabney Stuart. NYBP
Rescue. Ellen Bryant Voigt. NoP
Rescue the Dead. David Ignatow. ConAP; PrIm; VGW
Rescued Year, The. William Stafford. LCAP
Rescuing gate is wide, The. Like a Mourningless Child. Kenneth Patchen. MoAmPo
Resemblance. *Tr. fr. Hawaiian by* N. B. Emerson. WTO
Resembles life what once was deem'd of light. What Is Life? Samuel Taylor Coleridge. FiP
Resentments Composed because of the Clamor of Town Topers Outside My Apartment. Sarah Kemble Knight. SCAP
Reservation. David McCord. WhC
Reservation school is brown and bleak, The. Red Anger. R. T. Smith. STE
Reservation Special. Lew Blockcolski. VoR
Reserve. Richard Aldington. BrPo
Reserve. Lizette Woodworth Reese. AA
Reserve. Mary Ashley Townsend. AA
Reserved. Walter de la Mare. GTBS-P
Reservoir, The. Edward Field. GP
Residence at Cambridge. Wordsworth. *Fr.* The Prelude, III. FaBoPP
Residence in France. Wordsworth. *Fr.* The Prelude, X. PoEL-4
Residence in France (Continued). Wordsworth. *Fr.* The Prelude, XI. PoEL-4
(French Revolution as It Appeared to Enthusiasts at Its Commencement, The.) FiP
("O pleasant exercise of hope and joy!") HAP; OBRV
Residence in London. Wordsworth. *Fr.* The Prelude, VII. PoEL-4
("As the black storm upon the mountain top.") HAP
Resident Worm, The. James Hayford. NePoAm-2
Residue of Song. Marvin Bell. AmPA
Resign the rhapsody, the dream. To the Muse. Robert Louis Stevenson. EBEV
Resignation. Matthew Arnold. OAEP; VLP
If Birth Persists, *sel.* FaBoRV
Resignation. Thomas Chatterton. TrCP
Resignation. Walter Savage Landor. HBV-2; TreFT
Resignation. Longfellow. HBV-2
"There is no Death. What seems so is transition," *sel.* TRV
Resignation. Santob de Carrion, *tr. fr. Spanish by* George Ticknor. TrJP
Resignation. *Unknown.* OBSC
Resignation. Sir Thomas Wyatt. OBSC
Resignation; an Ode to the Journeyman Shoemakers, *sel.* "Peter Pindar." "Sons of Saint Crispin, 'tis in vain!" NOEC
Resignation—to Faustus. Arthur Hugh Clough. VLP
Resign'd to live, prepar'd to die. Tom Southerne's Birth-Day Dinner at LD. Orrery's. Pope. NAs
Resigning from a Job in a Defense Industry. Sandra McPherson. LCAP
Resisting poetry I am becoming a poem. Moon. Derek Walcott. NoAM
Resolute Courtier, The. Thomas Shipman. ErPo; GBL
Resolution. Ted Berrigan. OFD
Resolution. W. S. Merwin. NYBP
Resolution, The. Vassar Miller. CoPo
Resolution. Henry More. OxBoCh
Resolution. Charles L. O'Donnell. GoBC; TrPWD
Resolution. "Wiolar." InMe
Resolution and Independence. Wordsworth. CABA; ChER; EBEV; EnRP; HAP; InPS; LiTB; MasP; MAT; NOBE; NOCV; NoP; OAEL-2; OAEP; OBNC; OBRV; PoEL-4; PPP; TEP
Sels.
"I was a traveller then upon the moor." SpRo
"Now, whether it were by peculiar grace." Par
"There was a roaring in the wind all night." BoNaP
(Roaring in the Wind All Night.) TreFT
We Poets in Our Youth. FaBoRV
Resolution in Four Sonnets, of a Poetical Question Put to Me by a Friend, Concerning Four Rural Sisters. Charles Cotton. PoEL-3; Prf
Sels.
Alice. TrGrPo; UnTE
(Two Rural Sisters.) BoLoP; EnLoPo
Margaret. TrGrPo; UnTE
(Two Rural Sisters.) BoLoP; EnLoPo
Resolution of Dependence. George Barker. FaBoTw; LiTB; LiTM
Resolutions?—New and Old. Harvey E. Rolfe. STF
Resolve, The. Alexander Brome. CavP; OBEV
Resolve, The. Mary, Lady Chudleigh. OBEC; WPE
Resolve. Charlotte Perkins Gilman. WGRP
Resolve, The. Denise Levertov. RFM
Resolve, The. Henry Vaughan. AnAnS-1; NCEP
Resolve me, dearest, why two hearts in one. To His Mistresse on Her Scorne. Thomas Beedome. CavP
Resolved. Ottis Shirk. STF
Resolved to dust, intombed [*or* entombed] here lieth Love. Here Lieth Love [*or* Love's Grave]. Thomas Watson. *Fr.* Hecatompathia. EIL; OBSC
Resolving Doubts. William Dickey. ErPo
Resort. Kendrick Smithyman. OCNZ
Resound my voyse [*or* voice], ye wodes [*or* woods] that here [*or* hear] me plain. Sir Thomas Wyatt. AAS; SiPS
Resounding. Katherine Soniat. AMV-81
Respect all surfaces. The skater is. In Defense of Superficiality. Elder Olson. NYBP
Respect for the Dead. Laura Riding. LiTA
Respect the dreams of old men, said the cricket. Song for September. Robert Fitzgerald. VGW
Respectabilities. Jon Silkin. NePoEA-2; NoAM
Respectability. Robert Browning. EnLoPo; ViBoPo
Respectable Burgher, The. Thomas Hardy. CMoP; NoAM; VLP
Respectable People. Austin Clarke. CMoP; NMP
Respice Finem. Thomas Proctor. OBSC
Respice Finem. Francis Quarles. *See* Epigram: "My soul, sit thou a patient looker-on."
Respite, The. Ingeborg Bachmann, *tr. fr. German by* Michael Hamburger. WPOW
Respite, The. Maria Gowen Brooks. *Fr.* Zophiël. AA
Resplendent studs of heaven's frame. *Unknown.* SCAP
Respondez! Walt Whitman. NoAM; PoEL-5
Response. Bob Kaufman. BOLo
Response to Rimbaud's Later Manner. T. Sturge Moore. OBMV; SyP
Responses. Robert Hershon. POL
Responsibilities, *sel.* W. B. Yeats.
"Pardon, old fathers, if you still remain." PoEL-5
Responsibility. *Unknown.* FaBoUs; PV
Responsory, 1948, A. Thomas Merton. VGW

Ressaif My Saul. R. Crombie Saunders. OxBS
Rest. Mathilde Blind. SBG
Rest. Goethe. *See* True Rest.
Rest. Cardinal Newman. OBRV; OBVV
Rest, The. Ezra Pound. *Fr.* Lustra. AmPP; MoAB; MoAmPo; NoAM; NOBA; OxBA; PP
("O helpless few in my country.") PoA
Rest. Christina Rossetti. HBV-1; NOBE; OAEL-2; OBEV; OBNC; OBVV; TrGrPo
Rest. Jacob Isaac Segal, *tr. fr. Yiddish by* Seymour Mayne. VWA
Rest, and be thankful! On the verge. Adam Lindsay Gordon. *Fr.* Hippodromania; or, Whiffs from the Pipe. CBAP
Rest from Loving [and Be Living]. C. Day Lewis. CoBMV; MoBrPo; OBMV
Rest Hour. George Johnston. WHW
Rest in Peace. Wilfred J. Funk. PoLF
Rest Is Not Here. Lady Nairne. HBV-2
Rest is not quitting. True Rest [*or* Rest]. Goethe, *tr. by* John S. Dwight. TreFT; TRV; WBLP
Rest lightly O Earth upon this wretched Nearchos. Epitaph of Nearchos. Ammianus, *tr. by* Dudley Fitts. WeW
Rest, little guest. After Annunciation. Anna Wickham. MoBrPo
Rest O Sun I Cannot. Joseph Tusiani. GoYe
Rest Only in the Grave. James Clarence Mangan. BIrV
Rest! This little Fountain runs. For a Fountain [*or* Inscription for a Fountain]. "Barry Cornwall." OBEV; OBRV; OBVV
Rest ye in peace, ye Flanders dead. America's Answer. R. W. Lilliard. BLPA; PAL
Restful place, reviver of my smart, The. Sir Thomas Wyatt. SiPS
Resting Place. Jon Silkin. VWA
Restless as a Wolf. Moishe-Leib Halpern, *tr. fr. Yiddish by* Jacob Sloan. TrJP
Restless forms of living light. Address to Certain Gold Fishes. Hartley Coleridge. VLP
Restless he rolls about from whore to whore. Earl of Rochester. *Fr.* A Satire on Charles II. OBSV
Restless Heart, The. Earl of Surrey. SiPS
Restless Heart, The. *Unknown, tr. fr. Marathi.* WGRP
Restless State of a Lover, The. Earl of Surrey. GoTL
("Sonne hath twyse brought forthe the tender green, The.") AAS
("Sun hath twice brought forth his tender green, The.") SiPS
Restless, to-night, and ill at ease. In the Dark. Frances Louisa Bushnell. AA
Restless water of sound, The. War Requiem. Del Marie Rogers. LTB
Restoration. Woodridge Spears. GoYe
Restoration of Enheduanna to Her Former Station, The. Enheduanna, *tr. fr. Sumerian; ad. by* Aliki *and* Willis Barnstone. BoWoP
Restorative broth of trouts learne to make. Methods of Cooking Trout. Thomas Barker. *Fr.* The Art of Angling. FaBoUs
Restrained,/ with branch and young shoot undisclosed. Poplar. Gottfried Benn, *tr. by* Christopher Middleton. PoPl
Restricted. Eve Merriam. TrJP
Restricted. Miriam Waddington. CaP
Results of a Scientific Survey. Bruce Cutler. AMV-80; FAZ
Results of Stealing a Pin, The. *Unknown.* FaBoUs
Résumé. Dorothy Parker. DBV; DL; HeIP; InPK; NoP; OBAL; PAI; PoPl; ShM; TrJP; WhC
(Some Beautiful Letters: Résumé) InMe
Resurgam. W. Nelson Bitton. BLRP
Resurgam. Struthers Burt. HBMV
Resurgam. Emily Dickinson. *See* At last to be identified.
Resurgam. Marjorie Pickthall. OBCV; TrCP
Resurgam. *Unknown.* WGRP
Resurge San Francisco. Joaquin Miller. PAH
Resurgence. Laura Bell Everett. PGD
Resurrection. R. P. Blackmur. PoA
Resurrection, The. Jonathan Brooks. AmNP; CDC; PoNe
Resurrection. George Crabbe. OxBoCh
Resurrection. John Donne. AnAnS-1; OBS
Resurrection. Kenneth Fearing. CMoP
Resurrection. Frank Horne. OFD; PoBA
Resurrection. St. John of Damascus. *See* Day of Resurrection, The.
Resurrection. Marie Luise Kaschnitz, *tr. fr. German by* Michael Hamburger. WPOW
Resurrection. Harry Kemp. HBV-2
Resurrection. Sidney Lanier. PoEL-5
Resurrection. Robert Pack. NePoEA-2
Resurrection. Margaret Sackville. HBMV
Resurrection, The. William Edward Taylor. AMV-80
Resurrection, The. Nathaniel Wanley. LoBV
Resurrection, The, *sel.* W. B. Yeats.
Two Songs from a Play. CABA; CMoP; HAP; MoPo; NOBE; NoP; OAEL-2; PPoe; PPP; PrIm
"I saw a staring virgin stand," I. CoBMV; FaBoTw; LiTB; SeCeV
Resurrection and Immortality. Henry Vaughan. AnAnS-1
Resurrection of Arp. A. J. M. Smith. MoCV; NOBC
Resurrection of the Dead. Aliza Shenhar, *tr. fr. Hebrew by* Linda Zisquit. VWA
Resurrection of the Right Side. Muriel Rukeyser. LCAP
Resurrection Song. Thomas Lovell Beddoes. ELU; FaBoEE; InPK; NBM
Retaining its sign. The School Bus. Larry Eigner. FAZ
Retaliation. Goldsmith. LaA; OAEP; OxBoLi
Sels.
David Garrick. NOEC; OBEC; SeCeV
("Here lies David Garrick, describe him who can.") DBV
Edmund Burke. DBV; InvP; NOEC; OBEC; SeCeV
("Here lies our good Edmund, whose genius was such.") FaBoEE
Sir Joshua Reynolds. NOEC; OBEC; SeCePo
("Here Reynolds is laid and, to tell you my mind.") FaBoEE
Retarded Children Find a World Built Just for Them, The. Diana O Hehir. NPGG
Retarded Class at F. A. O. Schwarz's Celebrates Christmas, The. David Fisher. NPGG
Reticulations creep upon the slack stream's face. On Sturminster Foot-Bridge. Thomas Hardy. FaBoPP; OAEP
Retinue. Paul Verlaine, *tr. fr. French by* C. F. MacIntyre. ErPo
Retired Boxer, The. Lucilius, *tr. fr. Greek by* Tom Dodge. LiSp
Retired Cat, The. William Cowper. FM; PCat
Retired Colonel, The. Ted Hughes. NePoEA-2
Retired Farmer. David Allan Evans. Psk
Retired gardener of solitudes. N.Y. to L.A. by Jet Plane. Sonya Dorman. GOA
Retired this hour from wondering crowds. Walter Savage Landor. GBL
Retired [*or* Retyred] thoughts enjoy their own[e] delights. Look[e] Home. Robert Southwell. AnAnS-1; NOCV
Retirement, *sel.* James Beattie.
Solitude. OBEC
Retirement, The. Charles Cotton. *See* To Mr. Izaak Walton.
Retirement. William Cowper. BLPA
Sels.
Absence of Occupation. OBEC
London Suburbs. FaBoPP
Statesman in Retirement. OBEC
Retirement, The. John Norris. CavP; OBS
Retirement. Richard Chenevix Trench. OBVV
Retirement ("In youth I served my time"). *Unknown, tr. fr. Irish by* Frank O'Connor. ErPo; KiLC
Retirement, The ("Tis weak and wordly to conclude"). *Unknown.* OBEC
Retirement, an Ode, *sel.* Thomas Warton the Elder.
"Joy, rose-lipped dryad, loves to dwell." ViBoPo
Retirement of the Elephant, The. Russell Edson. AmPA
Retort, The. George Pope Morris. HBV-2
Retort Discourteous, The. Stephen Vincent Benét. HBMV
Retort on the Foregoing. John Scott of Amwell. *See* I Hate That Drum's Discordant Sound.
Retractions, *sels.* James Branch Cabell. HBMV
"Although as yet my cure be incomplete," I.
"And therefore praise I even the most high," *closing st.*
"Cry Kismet! and take heart. Erôs is gone," XII.
"I am contented by remembrances," II.
"It is in many ways made plain to us," V.
"Nightly I mark and praise, or great or small," XV.
"So, let us laugh, lest vain rememberings," XIV.
"With Love I garnered mirth, and dreams, and shame," VI.
"You ask a sonnet? Well, it is your right," *introd. st.*
Retreat. Amy Bushnell. AMV-80
Retreat. Martha Collins. AMV-80
Retreat, The. Henry King. AnAnS-2
Retreat, The. Sir Herbert Read. BrPo
Retreat[e], The. Henry Vaughan. AnAnS-1; AWP; BLPL; CABA; FaBoEn; FF; GTBS; GTBS-P; HAP; HBV-1; HeIP; InPS; InvP; JCP; LiTB; LoBV; MeLP; MePo; NIP; NOBE; NOCV; NoP; OAEL-1; OAEP; OBEV; OBS; PoEL-2; PoPle; PoRA; PPP; SBVL; SeCePo; SeCeV; SeCP; SeCV-1; TreFT; TrGrPo; ViBoPo; WHA
Retreat from Paradise, The. Milton. *Fr.* Paradise Lost, XII. PoEL-3
("He ended; and thus Adam last replied.") HeIP
Retreat of Ita Cagney, The. Michael Hartnett. CIP
Retreat to Vermont was orderly at first, The. Safe Places. Constance Urdang. GP
Retribution. Friedrich von Logau, *tr. fr. German by* Longfellow. BLPA; TreF
Retrieval System, The. Maxine W. Kumin. WeW

Retrievers run through the meadow. Exercise in a Meadow. Jean Elliot. GoYe
Retrospect. Roy Davis. WhC
Retrospect, A. Coventry Patmore. VLP
Retrospect. "An Pilibín." OnYI
Retrospect. Agnes Mary Frances Robinson. OBVV
Retrospect. Chidiock Tichborne. *See* Elegy: "My prime of youth is but a frost of cares."
Retrospection. Sir Arthur Quiller-Couch. CenHV
Return, The. Conrad Aiken. NePA
Return, The. John Peale Bishop. LiTA; MoPo; MoVE; OxBA; TwAmPo; WaP
Return, The. Arna Bontemps. CDC; PoBA; PoNe
Return, The. Bruce Bennett Brown. TAT
Return. Sterling A. Brown. BALP; CDC
Return. C. P. Cavafy, *tr. fr. Modern Greek by* John Mavrogordato. ErPo
Return, The. Eleanor Rodgers Cox. PAH
Return. Seamus Deane. BIrV
Return, The. Emily Dickinson. *See* Though I get home how late, how late!
Return! Sydney Dobell. OBVV
Return, The. Jessie Fauset. CDC
Return, The. Annie Fields. AA
Return. Robinson Jeffers. GoYe
Return, The. Kipling. MoBrPo
Return. Johari M. Kunjufu. BlSi
Return, The. George MacBeth. NYBP
Return, The. Pittendrigh Macgillivray. GoTS; OxBS
Return, The. Edna St. Vincent Millay. LiTA; MoAB; MoAmPo; MoPo; NoAM; OxBA; PoPl
Return, The. Shmuel Moreh, *tr. fr. Arabic by* Yoffee Berkovitz. VWA
Return, The. Stanley Moss. POL
Return, The ("The doors flapped open in Ulysses' house"). Edwin Muir. CMoP
Return, The ("The veteran Greeks came home"). Edwin Muir. CMoP
(Return of the Greeks, The.) NoP
Return, The. Martha Ostenso. CaP
Return, The. Ezra Pound. AmPP; AP; CMoP; CoBMV; FaBoEn; HAP; MoAB; MoAmPo; MoPo; NePA; NoAM; NOBA; OxBA; PPoe; TwAmPo; VGW; ViBoPo; WeW
Return. Earl of Rochester. *See* Song, A: "Absent from thee, I languish still."
Return, The. Theodore Roethke. PoA
Return, The. Dennis Saleh. NeAC
Return, The. Jon Silkin. NePoEA-2
Return. Theodore Spencer. PoA
Return. M. L. Sussman. AMV-81
Return, The. Swinburne. *See* Stanzas: "I will go back to the great sweet mother."
Return, The. Arthur Symons. HBMV
Return. Richard Tillinghast. MAYP
Return, The, *sels.* Margaret L. Woods.
Facing the Gulf. HBMV
"Father of Life, with songs of wonder." TrPWD
Return. Wordsworth. *Fr.* The River Duddon. HAP
Return and go again and yet return! Repeated Pilgrimage. John Gilland Brunini. GoBC
Return, dear Lord, to those who look. Jesus Return. Henry van Dyke. TRV
Return from the Wars, A. Frederick Bock. SOTS
Return, light of wing. The Cage. Avner Treinin, *tr. by* A. C. Jacobs. VWA
Return of a Popular Statesman. Vincent Buckley. CBAP
Return of a Reaper. Alan Creighton. CaP
Return of Astraea, The. Ben Jonson. NOBE
Return of Eve, The. G. K. Chesterton. ISi
Return of Napoleon from St. Helena, The. Lydia Huntley Sigourney. AA
Return of Robinson Jeffers, The. Robert Hass. AmPA
Return of the Dead, The, *sel.* Samar Attar.
"And you came back." PBWP
Return of the Goddess Artemis. Robert Graves. PoA
Return of the Greeks, The. Edwin Muir. *See* Return, The ("The veteran Greeks came home").
Return of the Native. Amiri Baraka. BPo
Return of the Native, The. Harley Matthews. PoAu-2
Return of the Prodigal Son, *sel.* Léopold Sédar Senghor, *tr. fr. French by* Ellen Conroy Kennedy.
"Elephant of Moissel, hear my pious prayer." GrPl
Return of the Sire de Nesle A. D. 16—, The. Herman Melville. NOBA
(L'Envoi: Return of the Sire de Nesle, The.) ViBoPo
Return often and take me. Return. C. P. Cavafy, *tr. by* John Mavrogordato. ErPo
Return, return! all night my lamp is burning. Return! Sydney Dobell. OBVV
Return, Return, O Shulammite. Bible, *O.T.* The Song of Solomon, VII: 1-10. TrJP
Return, sad sister, Faith. Amen. A. C. Benson. OBVV
Return, Starting Out. Daniel Halpern. MAYP
Return Thee, Hairt. Alexander Scott. BSV
(Returne The, Hairt.) OxBS
Return to a Place Lit by a Glass of Milk. Charles Simic. GeTw
Return to Ararat. Martyn Halsall. TrCP
Return to Astolat. Gail White. AMV-81
Return to Dachau. B. Z. Niditch. AMV-81
Return to Hinton. Charles Tomlinson. CMoP
Return to Lake Emily Chequamegon National Forest. Richard Behm. WOLT
Return to Lane's Island. William H. Matchett. PoPl
Return to Life. Abbie Huston Evans. NePoAm
Return to My Native Land, *sel.* Aimé Césaire, *tr. fr. French by* Emile Snyders.
"I shall not regard my swelled head as a sign of real glory." TTY
Return to Prinsengracht. Janice Blue-Swartz. AMV-81
Return to Ritual. Mark Van Doren. MoVE
Return to Spring. Florence Ripley Mastin. GoYe
Return to the most human, nothing less. Santos: New Mexico. May Sarton. EaLo
Return to the Tree of Time, A. Vesna Parun, *tr. fr. Croatian by* Vasa D. Mihailovich *and* Ronald Morgan. WPOW
Return to the Valley. Elfreida Read. AMV-80
Return to Work, The. William Carlos Williams. CTBA; NYBP
Return we to the dangers of the night. Juvenal, *tr. by* Dryden. *Fr.* Satires, III. OAEL-1
Return'd from the opera, as lately I sat. *See* Returned from the opera . . .
Returne The, Hairt. Alexander Scott. *See* Return Thee, Hairt.
Returned, a wraith from her defrauded tomb. Transformation Scene. Constance Carrier. FYAP; GoYe
Returned from college R—— gets a wife. The Discontented Student. St. George Tucker. OBAL
Returned from Mehiko he'll grab. A Hex on the Mexican X. David McCord. FiBHP
Returned [*or* Return'd] from the opera, as lately I sat. A Bon Mot. *Unknown.* ErPo; POL
Returned to Frisco, 1946. W. D. Snodgrass. AP
Returned to Say. William Stafford. ConAP; NaP
Returning. Ruth Guthrie Harding. HBV-2
Returning/ to all the unsaid. The Charge. Denise Levertov. NePoEA-2
Returning after dark, I thought. Traditional Red. Robert Huff. HoPM; NePoEA-2
Returning at Night. Jim Harrison. VGW
Returning each morning from a timeless world. Autumn 1940. W. H. Auden. LiTA
Returning from Harvest. Vernon Watkins. NYBP
Returning from its daily quest, my Spirit. To Dante [*or* Sonnet: Guido Cavalcanti to Dante]. Guido Cavalcanti, *tr. by* Shelley. AWP; OBVE
Returning, I find her just the same. Passing Visit to Helen. D. H. Lawrence. CMoP
Returning to Roots of First Feeling. Robert Duncan. PoA
Returning to Store Bay. Barbara Howes. Psk
Returning to that house. Birthplace; New Rochelle. George Oppen. DiL
Returning to the room. Margaret Atwood. *Fr.* The Circle Game. MoCV
Returning to the Town Where We Used to Live. Susan Musgrave. NOBC
Returning to the World. Laura Chester. NPGG
Returning, We Hear the Larks. Isaac Rosenberg. BrPo; FaBoMo; MMA; OAEL-2; OBWP; VWA; WaaP
Retyred thoughts enjoy their owne delights. *See* Retired thoughts enjoy . . .
Reuben and Rachel, *with music.* Harry Birch. PSoN
Reuben Bright. E. A. Robinson. MoAB; MoAmPo; NePA; NOBA; NoP; TAP; TrGrPo
Reuben, I have long been thinking. Reuben and Rachel. Harry Birch. PSoN
Reuben James. James Jeffrey Roche. PAH
Reuben Pantier. Edgar Lee Masters. *Fr.* Spoon River Anthology. GLGT
Reuben Ranzo. *Unknown.* AmFP; AmSS, *with music*; FSW; ShS, 2 *vers., with music*
Reuben, Reuben. Michael S. Harper. GeTw
Reuben, Reuben. *Unknown.* FSW
Reuben's Cabin. Robert Morgan. TAT
Reunion. Heather Cadsby. AMV-81
Reunion. Paul Dehn. PV
Reunion. Carolyn Forché. MAYP
Reunion. Judith Herzberg, *tr. fr. Dutch by* Shirley Kaufman. BoWoP
Reunion. E. A. Robinson. NoAM; NOBA
Reunion. Cyril Tawney. OBET
Reunited. Sir Gilbert Parker. OBEV; OBVV
Rev Owl. A. M. Klein. TrJP

Reve was a slendre colerik man, The. The Reeve. Chaucer. *Fr.* The Canterbury Tales: Prologue. OxBM
Reveal Thy Presence now, O Lord. A Grace. Thomas Tiplady. TrPWD; TRV
Revealed. Harry Lyman Koopman. AA
Revealed and yet dwelling hidden in the cave. *Tr. fr. Sanskrit by* Raimundo Panikkar. *Fr.* Upanishads. ILwL
Reveillé. Audrey Alexandra Brown. CaP
Reveille, The. Bret Harte. GN; HBV-2; OHIP; PAH; PAL
Reveille. A. E. Housman. A Shropshire Lad, IV. CMoP; FaFP; FPL; LiTB; LiTM; MasP; MoAB; MoBrPo; NoP; OAEP; PoLF; SoSe; TreF
Reveille. Ted Hughes. PPP
Reveille. Hughes Mearns. *Fr.* Later Antigonishes. InMe
Reveille. Michael O'Connor. AA; HBV-2
Reveille. Lola Ridge. HBMV; WPE
Reveillé. Louis Untermeyer. HBV-2
Revel, The. Bartholomew Dowling. BLPA; HBV-2; OnYI
(Our Last Toast.) YaD
(Revelry for the Dying.) AnIV
(Stand to Your Glasses.) TreF
Revel, A. Donagh MacDonagh. NeIP
Revel pauses and the room is still, The. Pannyra of the Golden Heel. Albert Samain, *tr. by* James Elroy Flecker. AWP
Revelation, *sels.* Bible, *N.T.*
Last Judgment, The, XX: 11-15; XXI: 1-7. TreF
New Jerusalem, The, XXI: 1-6, 10-12, 21, 23-25. TrGrPo
There Shall Be No Night, XXII: 1-5. TrGrPo
Revelation. Verne Bright. BLRP; WBLP
Revelation. Alice Brown. *Fr.* The Road to Castaly. WGRP
Revelation. Jerald Bullis. AMV-81
Revelation. Warren F. Cook. BLRP
Revelation. Blanche Taylor Dickinson. CDC
Revelation. Sir Edmund Gosse. OBEV; OBVV
Revelation. Carole C. Gregory. BlSi
Revelation. Nancy Keesing. PoAu-2
Revelation. Edwin Markham. WGRP
Revelation, The. Coventry Patmore. The Angel in the House, I, viii, 2. EnLoPo; GBL; GTBS-P; HAP; NBM; OBNC
("Idle poet, here and there, An.") ViBoPo
Revelation. Robert Penn Warren. LiTA; MoPo; NePA; NoAM; TwAmPo
Revelation, The. James Wright. DiL; PAI
Revelation came on Jane, A. Jump-to-Glory Jane. George Meredith. VLP
Revelations. David Meltzer. NeAP
Revelry for the Dying. Bartholomew Dowling. *See* Revel, The.
Revenant, The. Walter de la Mare. GBL
Revenant, The. Robert Siegel. GeTw
Revenge! Horace, *tr. fr. Latin by* Louis Untermeyer. Odes, IV, 13. AWP
Revenge. Lord Nugent. PV
Revenge, The. Pierre de Ronsard, *tr. fr. French by* Thomas Stanley. AWP
Revenge, The. Tennyson. BeLS; DTo; EBVV; FaBoCh; FaPo; HBV-2; OAEP; OnMSP; PoRA
(Ballad of the Fleet, A.) FaPoR
"At Flores in the Azores Sir Richard Grenville lay," *sel.* OBWP
Revenge Fable. Ted Hughes. TW
Revenge of Hamish, The. Sidney Lanier. AP; PoEL-5
Revenge of Rain-in-the-Face, The. Longfellow. BPAW; PAH
Revenge of the Hunted. R. A. D. Ford. LiSp; MoCV
Revenge to Come. Propertius, *tr. fr. Latin by* Kirby Flower Smith. Elegies, III, 25. AWP
Revenger's Tragedy, The, *sels.* Cyril Tourneur.
"Madame, his grace will not be absent long," *fr.* III, v. PoEL-2
"My study's ornament, thou shell of death," *fr.* I, i. ViBoPo
Revenue Man Blues. *Unknown.* BluL
Reverdure, *sel.* Wendell Berry.
"One thing work gives." SaC
Reverend Butler came by. Madam and the Minister. Langston Hughes. NOBA
Reverend Henry Ward Beecher, The. Limerick [*or* An Eggstravagance *or* Henry Ward Beecher]. *At. to* Oliver Wendell Holmes. CenHV; ChTr; FaBoNo; HBVY
Rev. Homer Wilbur's "Festina Lente." James Russell Lowell. *Fr.* The Biglow Papers, 2d Series. OBAL
Reverend Mr. Higginson, The. Edward Johnson. SCAP
Rev. Nicholas Noyes to the Rev. Cotton Mather, The. Nicholas Noyes. SCAP
Reverend William Winterbourne, The. Bishop Winterbourne. Walter de la Mare. FaBoNo
Reverie. Victor Hugo, *tr. fr. French by* Mary Ann Caws. NAWM-2
Reverie. Don Marquis. FPL; PoLF
Reverie, The. Egan O'Rahilly, *tr. fr. Modern Irish by* Frank O'Connor. AnIL
(Reverie at Dawn.) KiLC
Reverie of a Mum. Nancy Keesing. CBAP
Reverie of Poor Susan, The. Wordsworth. CH; EnRP; GTBS; GTBS-P; HBV-1; OxBoLi; WiR
Reverse the flight of Lucifer. The Task. Ruth Pitter. MoBrPo
Reversible Metaphor, The. "Troubadour." InMe
Reversion. Barry O. Higgs. PeSA
Reversionary. Stevie Smith. FaBoEE
Revertere. *Unknown.* PBBP
Review from Staten Island. Gloria C. Oden. NNP; PoBA; PPP
Review of a Cook Book. Louise Dyer Harris. WhC
Reviewing me without undue elation. A Choice of Weapons. Stanley Kunitz. LiTM; VGW
Reviews are gaudy shows—allowed. On the Frequent Review of the Troops. "M." NOEC
Revised Notes for a Sonnet. Edward Pygge. BXAP
Revision. Eileen Newton. SUMH
Revisiting the Field. Walter Pavlich. AMV-81
Revisiting your marble-paved sea-perfumed town. Hardy's Plymouth. Geoffrey Grigson. FaBoPP
Revival, The. Henry Vaughan. NOCV; OBS; OxBoCh; PoEL-2; PoPle; TrGrPo
(Unfold, Unfold.) ELP
Revival Hymn. Joel Chandler Harris. *Fr.* Uncle Remus and His Friends. HBV-2
Revivalist in Boston, A. Adrienne Rich. EaLo
Revive Us Again. William Paton Mackay. FSW
Revocation, A. Sir Thomas Wyatt. *See* Farewell: "What should I say."
Revolt. Rachel, *tr. fr. Hebrew by* Robert Friend. VWA
Revolt of Islam, The, *sels.* Shelley.
Child of Twelve, A, *fr.* II. GN
Ever as We Sailed, *fr.* XII. SeCePo
"I could not choose but gaze; a fascination," *fr.* I. ChER
"Islands and the mountains in the day, The," *fr.* III. ChER
"Lifting the thunder of their acclamation," *fr.* V. ChER
"Over the utmost hill at length I sped," *fr.* V. OBWP
Revolution, The. Jack Gilbert. NPGG
Revolution. Lesbia Harford. PoAu-1
Revolution. A. E. Housman. Last Poems, XXXVI. BrPo; ImOP; NoP
Revolution/ Damn you. Letter to the Revolution. Susan Griffin. NPGG
Revolution is the pod. Emily Dickinson. AP
Revolutionaries, The. R. P. Lister. NOBL
Revolutionary. James P. Friel. AMV-81
Revolutionary, The/ element remained. Mrs. Hamer. Jane Stembridge. NMM
Revolutionary Dreams. Nikki Giovanni. CNA; GP
Revolutionary Letter # 4 ("Left to themselves people"). Diane DiPrima. GP
Revolutionary Letter # 19 ("If what you want is jobs"). Diane DiPrima. IHMS
Revolutionary Letter # 29 ("Beware of those/ who say"). Diana DiPrima. GP
Revolutionary Letter # 36 ("Who is the we, who is/ the they"). Diane DiPrima. GP
Revolutionary Letter # 40 ("If the power of the word is anything, America"). Diane DiPrima. GP
Revolutionary Petunias. Alice Walker. BlSi
Revolutionary Screw, The. Don L. Lee. GP
Revolutions. Shakespeare. *See* Sonnets, LX.
Revolving Door, The. Newman Levy. ShM
Revolving doors compete with sales-day traffic. Shoplifter. Solomon Edwards. NNP
Reward of Innocent Love, The. William Habington. *See* To Castara.
Reward of Service. Elizabeth Barrett Browning. BLPA; FaBoBe
(Sweetest Lives, The.) TRV
Reward of Virtue. Arthur Guiterman. InMe
Rewards of Farming, The. *Unknown.* PoPl
Rex Mundi. David Gascoyne. ChMP
Reynard the Fox, *sels.* John Masefield.
"Cobbler bent at his wooden foot, The." ViBoPo
Fox Awakes, The. MoVE
"Fox knew well, that before they tore him, The." OBNV
"Meet was at 'The Cock and Pye,' The." OxBTC
"Ock Gurney and old Pete were there." CMoP
Reynard the Fox. *Unknown.* OnYI
Rhaicos was born amid the hills wherefrom. The Hamadryad. Walter Savage Landor. *Fr.* The Hellenics. EnRP
Rhapsodies. Cyril Dabydeen. BrSi
Rhapsody. William Stanley Braithwaite. AmNP; BALP; BANP
Rhapsody. Frank O'Hara. NoAM; NYP
Rhapsody of Old Men, A, *sel.* Dimitris Tsaloumas, *tr. fr. Greek by* Margaret Carroll.
"They brought him one morning." CBAP

Rhapsody on a Windy Night. T. S. Eliot. CMoP; HeIP
Rhapsody, Written at the Lakes in Westmorland, A: "Now sunk the sun, now twilight sunk, and Night." John Brown. NOEC
(Night.) OBEC
Rhemish Carol, A. Robert Finch, *ad. by* Bernard de la Monnoye. NAs
Rhetoric of Langston Hughes, The. Margaret Danner. BlSi; FB
Rhine is running deep and red, The. The Island of the Scots. William Edmonstoune Aytoun. VLP
Rhine was red with human blood, The. Blake. *Fr.* Jerusalem. ViBoPo
Rhino is a homely beast, The. The Rhinoceros. Ogden Nash. CenHV; FiBHP; MoAmPo; OBAL; OnUR
Rhinoceros, The. Hilaire Belloc. ChTr; FaPON
Rhinoceros. William Hart-Smith. BoAnP
Rhinoceros, The. Ogden Nash. CenHV; FiBHP; MoAmPo; OBAL; OnUR
Rhinoceros. Adrien Stoutenburg. BoAnP
Rhinoceros, your hide looks all undone. The Rhinoceros. Hilaire Belloc. ChTr; FaPON
Rhinos Purple, Hippos Green. Michael Patrick Hearn. RHPC
Rhoda Pitkin. Edgar Lee Masters. *Fr.* The New Spoon River. NoAM
Rhodanthe. Agathias, *tr. fr. Greek by* Andrew Lang. AWP
Rhode Island. William Meredith. NoP
"Rhodesia, sweaty." Black and White. Leonard Adame. SoSe
Rhododaphne, *sels.* Thomas Love Peacock. OBRV
Bacchus.
Larissa.
Rhodora, The [On Being Asked Whence Is the Flower]. Emerson. AA; AmPP; AP; AWP; BoNaP; FaBV; FaFP; GN; HBV-1; HBVY; HeIP; LiTA; NOBA; NoP; OHFP; OxBA; SeCeV; TAP; TreFS; TrGrPo; TRV; WHA
Rhoecus. James Russell Lowell.
"Hear now this fairy legend of old Greece." AA
Rhotus on Arcadia. John Chalkhill. *Fr.* Thealma and Clearchus. OBS
Rhyme: "I like to see a thunder storm." Elizabeth J. Coatsworth. RHPC
Rhyme-Beginning Fragment, A. *Unknown.* AnIL
Rhyme for a Chemical Baby. Joseph Cook. *Fr.* Boston Nursery Rhymes. InMe; QQQ; SpRo
Rhyme for a Geological Baby. Joseph Cook. *Fr.* Boston Nursery Rhymes. InMe; QQQ; SpRo
Rhyme for Astronomical Baby. Joseph Cook. *Fr.* Boston Nursery Rhymes. InMe; QQQ; SpRo
Rhyme for Botanical Baby. Joseph Cook. *Fr.* Boston Nursery Rhymes. InMe; QQQ; SpRo
Rhyme for Night. Joan Aiken. DuDa
Rhyme for Remembering How Many Nights There Are in the Month. Justin Richardson. FaBoUs
Rhyme for Remembering the Date of Easter. Justin Richardson. FaBoUs
Rhyme for Remembrance of May. Richard Burton. HBMV
Rhyme for the Child as a Wet Dog. Judith Johnson Sherwin. TAP
Rhyme from Grandma Goose. Annemarie Ewing. NePoAm
Rhyme of Joyous Garde, The, *sel.* Adam Lindsay Gordon.
"We were glad together in gladsome meads." PoAu-1
Rhyme of Life, A. Charles Warren Stoddard. HBV-2
Rhyme of One, A. Frederick Locker-Lampson. HBV-1
Rhyme of Rain. John Holmes. GrPl
Rhyme of the Chivalrous Shark, The. Wallace Irwin. ShM
(Chivalrous Shark, The.) FSW
Rhyme of the Dream-Maker Man, A. William Allen White. PoLF
Rhyme of the Fishermen's Children. *Unknown.* GBP
Rhyme of the Kipperling, The. Sir Owen Seaman. CenHV
Rhyme of the poet, The. Merlin, II. Emerson. NOBA; PoEL-4
Rhyme of the Rail[s]. John Godfrey Saxe. InMe; MoShBr; PoLF
Rhyme of the Rain Machine, The. F. W. Clarke. BoNaP
Rhyme of the Three Captains, The. Kipling. BeLS
Rhyme, the rack of finest wits. *See* Rime, the rack . . .
Rhymed Dance Calls. *Unknown.* CoSo
Rhymed Mnemonic of the Forty Counties of England. Donald Monat. FaBoUs
Rhymes (?). Henry S. Leigh. NOBL
Rhymes. Y. Y. Segal, *tr. fr. Yiddish by* Miriam Waddington. WHW
Rhymes. Frank Steele. PPJ
Rhymes and rhymers pass away. Walt Whitman. *Fr.* By Blue Ontario's Shore, XIII. InPS
Rhymes for a Modern Nursery, *sels.* Paul Dehn.
"Hey diddle diddle." FiBHP
"In a cavern, in a canyon." FiBHP; PV; ShM
"Jack and Jill went up the hill." DBV; FiBHP; PV
"Little Miss Muffet." FiBHP; ShM
"Two blind mice." FiBHP
Rhymes of a Rolling Stone, *sel.* Robert W. Service.
"Thank God! there is always a Land of Beyond." TRV
Rhymes on the Road, *sel.* Thomas Moore.
"And is there then no earthly place." OBSV
Rhymester, A. Samuel Taylor Coleridge. PV
Rhyming a Friend's Poem. Yü Hsüan-chi, *tr. fr. Chinese by* Geoffrey Waters. BoWoP
Rhyming Prophecy for a New Year. Leonard Cooper. FaBoCo
Rhyming Riddle. *Unknown.* TreFT
Rhyming Riddles, *sels.* Mary Austin.
"First I am frosted." TiPo
"I come more softly than a bird." BoNaP; SoPo; TiPo
"I have no wings, but yet I fly." SoPo; TiPo
"I never speak a word." TiPo
Rhyming with a Friend. Yü Hsüan-chi, *tr. fr. Chinese by* Geoffrey Waters. BoWoP
Rhythm, The. Robert Creeley. CoPo; LiTM
Rhythm. Jean Percival Waddell. CaP
Rhythm and blues. The Blues Today. Mae Jackson. BOLo; PoBA
Rhythm in the pulse of time. Rhythm. Jean Percival Waddell. CaP
Rhythm it is we. Spirits Unchained. Keorapetse Kgositsile. PoBA
Rib Sandwich. William J. Harris. CNA
Ribald and unbuttoned air, A. Back Lane. R. D. Murphy. PoAu-2
Ribald Romeos Less and Less Berattle. Horace, *tr. fr. Latin by* John Frederick Nims. Odes, I, 25. MAT
("Young bloods come round less often now, The," *tr. by* James Michie.) BoLoP
Ribbe ne rele ne spinne ich ne may. A Servant-Girl's Holiday. *Unknown.* OxBM
Ribbon-Fish, The. Robert Adamson. CBAP
Ribbon Two Yards Wide, A. Alfred Kreymborg. HBMV
Ribbons of iodine. Kelp. Nora Dauenhauer. TWSS
Ribh Considers Christian Love Insufficient. W. B. Yeats. TW
Ribs and Terrors, The. Herman Melville. *See* Father Mapple's Hymn.
Ribs of leaves lie in the dust, The. The Coming of the Cold. Theodore Roethke. OBCP
Rice. Carol Muske. AmPA
Rice and Mice. Edward Lear. TDH
Rice and Rose Bowl Blues. Diane Mei Lin Mark. BrSi
Rich and Poor; or, Saint and Sinner. Thomas Love Peacock. FaBoCo; NOBE; NOBL; OBSV
Rich arrived in pairs, The. The Garden Party. Hilaire Belloc. DTC; MoVE
Rich blood disturbed my thought. Arrival. John Wain. EBEV
Rich damask roses in fair cheeks do bide. Robert Tofte. *Fr.* Laura. ElL
Rich Days. W. H. Davies. BoNaP
Rich folks 'cided to take a trip, De. De Titanic. *Unknown.* AS
Rich fools there be, whose base and filthy heart. Astrophel and Stella, XXIV. Sir Philip Sidney. OAEP; SiPS
Rich in her weeping country's spoils, Versailles. The Charms of Nature. Joseph Warton. *Fr.* The Enthusiast. OBEC
Rich in the waning light she sat. Waiting. John Freeman. CH
Rich Irish Lady, A. *Unknown.* AmFP, 2 *versions*; FSW
(Irish Lady, The, *with music.*) OuSiCo
Rich king of a rainy country, The. The King in May. Michael Dennis Browne. NYBP
Rich Lazarus! richer in those gems, thy teares. Upon Lazarus His Teares. Richard Crashaw. SeCV-1
Rich Man, The. Franklin P. Adams. FiBHP; InMe; OBAL
Rich man/ Poor man. *Unknown.* SaC
Rich Man and the Kingdom of Heaven, The. Bible, *N.T.* St. Matthew, XIX:13-30. TreF
Rich Man and the Poor Man, The. *Unknown.* FSW
Rich man bought a swan and goose, A. The Swan and the Goose. Aesop, *tr. by* William Ellery Leonard. AWP; FaPON
Rich man has his motorcar, The. The Rich Man. Franklin P. Adams. FiBHP; InMe; OBAL
Rich man lay on his velvet couch, The. Mag's Song. *Unknown.* AS
Rich man, poor man, beggar-man, thief. Oberammergau. Leonora Speyer. HBMV
Rich man's son inherits lands, The. The Heritage. James Russell Lowell. HBV-1; HBVY
Rich Mine of Knowledge. George Chapman. SeCePo
Rich nights in another climate. Emblems. Douglas Dunn. FaBoMo
Rich Old Lady, The, *with music.* *Unknown.* OuSiCo
Rich Old Miser, A. *Unknown.* AmFP
Rich Statue, double-faced. To the New Yeere. Michael Drayton. PoEL-2
Rich the peace of the elements tonight on the Land-of-Joy. The Path of the Old Spells. Donald Sinclair. GoTS
Rich, voluptuous languor of dim pain, A. Vanitas Vanitatum. Israel Zangwill. TrJP
Rich Widow, The. *Unknown.* AmFP
Richard Cory. E. A. Robinson. AmPP; CMoP; DL; DTC; FaFP; FF; FPL; HAP; InPK; LiTA; LiTM; MasP; MoAB; MoAmPo; MoVE; NePA; NIP; NOBA; NoP; OxBA; PAI; PoLF; PoRA; PrIm; SoSe; TAP; TreF; TrGrPo

Richard Cory. Paul Simon. InPK
Richard Dick upon a stick. *Unknown.* OxNR
Richard Hunt's Arachne. Robert Hayden. FB
"Richard, may I ask a question? What is an episteme?" Richard Howard. *Fr.* Compulsive Qualifications. PoA
Richard on the cold roof screams, I'm the eye. In the Madness of Love. Gary Soto. NPGG
Richard Pigott, the Forger, *sel.* William McGonagall.
"For by forged letters he tried to accuse Parnell." PeD
Richard, Richard: American Fuel. Melvin Dixon. LTB
Richard Roe and John Doe. Robert Graves. CMoP
Richard II. Shakespeare. *See* King Richard II.
Richard II's Dejection. Shakespeare. *See* Death of Kings, The.
Richard Somers. Barrett Eastman. AA
Richard, thah thou be ever trichard. Against the Baron's Enemies. *Unknown.* MeEL
Richard III. Shakespeare. *See* King Richard III.
Richard III's Speech. Sir John Beaumont. *Fr.* Bosworth Field. JCP
Richard Tolman's Universe. Leonard Bacon. ImOP
"Richard, what will it be like when you ask the questions?" Richard Howard. *Fr.* Compulsive Qualifications. PoA
Riches. Blake. TrGrPo
Riches. *Unknown.* *See* On Late-acquired Wealth.
Riches and honours Buckley layes aside. Onely the Reverend Grave and Godly Mr. Buckly Remaines. Edward Johnson. SCAP
Riches I hold in light esteem. The Old Stoic. Emily Brontë. FaPoR; FPL; NOBE; OAEP; OBEV; OBNC; OBVV; OxBI; PoLF; PoPl; TreFT; TrGrPo; ViBoPo
Riches of fish whip. Dayak Man Making Fishtrap. Carol Rubenstein. WOLT
Richest realm of all the earth, The. The Poet's Confidence. Coventry Patmore. *Fr.* The Angel in the House. VLP
Richie Story. *Unknown.* BaBo; ESPB (A *and* B *vers.*)
Rick of Green Wood, The. Edward Dorn. NeAP; PoM
Riddle: "As I went over London Bridge." *Unknown.* ChTr
Riddle: "As I went over Tipple Tyne." *Unknown.* ChTr
Riddle: "At the end of my yard there is a vat." *Unknown.* ChTr
Riddle, A: "Clothes make no sound when I tread ground." *Unknown, tr. fr. Anglo-Saxon.* ChTr
Riddle: Cuckoo. *Unknown.* *See* Riddles (Exeter Book).
Riddle, The: "Down in a garden sits my dearest love." *Unknown.* UnTE
Riddle: "First it was a pretty flower, dressed in pink and white." Christina Rossetti. SoPo
Riddle: "From Belsen a crate of gold teeth." William Heyen. GP
Riddle, The: "He told himself and he told his wife." Ralph Hodgson. PoPl; WhC
Riddle: "He went to the wood and caught it." *Unknown.* GBP
("He went to the wood and caught it.") OxNR
Riddle: "Highty, tighty, paradighty, clothed in green." *Unknown.* ChTr
("Highty, tighty, paradighty, clothed in green.") OxNR
Riddle: "House full, yard full." *Unknown.* NTCP
Riddle, A: "I am just two and two, I am warm, I am cold." William Cowper. HBV-1
Riddle: "I am within as white as snow." *Unknown.* ChTr; GBP
Riddle: "I saw five birds all in a cage." *Unknown.* GBP
Riddle, A: "I walk on two legs." Cynthia Ozick. VWA
Riddle: "I washed my face in water." *Unknown.* ChTr
("I wash my face in water.") GBP
Riddle, A: "I'm a strange contradiction; I'm new, and I'm old." Hannah More. *See* Book, A.
Riddle: "I'm a strange creature, for I satisfy women." *Unknown, tr. fr. Anglo-Saxon by* Kevin Crossley-Holland. PV
Riddle: "In Mornigan's park there is a deer." *Unknown.* *See* Crescent Moon, The.
Riddle: "It has a head like a cat, feet like a cat." *Unknown.* NTCP
Riddle: "It is in the rock, but not in the stone." *Unknown.* ChTr
Riddle: Jay: *Higora.* *Unknown, tr. fr. Anglo-Saxon.* PBBP
Riddle: "Land was white, The." ChTr
("Land was white, The.") OxNR
Riddle: "Little Nancy Etticoat with a white petticoat." *See* Little Nancy Etticoat.
Riddle: "Long white barn, A." *Unknown.* ChTr
("Long white barn, A.") GBP
Riddle: Mute Swan. *Unknown.* *See* Riddles (Exeter Book).
Riddle: Nightingale. *Unknown, tr. fr. Anglo-Saxon.* PBBP
Riddle, The: "No more, no more,/ We are already pin'd." Alexander Brome. OBS
Riddle: "On yonder hill there is a red deer." *Unknown.* ChTr
("On yonder hill there is a red deer.") GBP
Riddle, A: "Once when I was very scared." Charlotte Zolotow. NTCP
Riddle: "Shoemaker makes shoes without leather, A." *Unknown.* SoPo
("Shoemaker makes shoes without leather, A.") OxNR
Riddle: "Stiff standing on the bed." *Unknown.* POL
Riddle: "Their tongues are knives, their forks are hands and feet." Adrian Mitchell. FaBoEE; GBL
Riddle, A: "There is one that has a head without an eye." Christina Rossetti. OxBChV
Riddle, A: " 'Twas whispered in Heaven [*or* " 'Twas in heaven pronounced, and], 'twas muttered in hell." Catherine M. Fanshawe. ChTr; GN
Riddle: "Two legs sat upon three legs." *Unknown.* NTCP
Riddle, A: "We are little airy creatures." Swift. *See* On the Vowels—a Riddle.
Riddle: "Wee man o' leather." *Unknown.* ChTr
Riddle: What Am I? Dorothy Aldis. SoPo
Riddle: "White bird featherless/ Flew from Paradise." *Unknown.* *See* Riddle of Snow and Sun.
Riddle: "White bird floats down through the air, A." *Unknown.* ChTr
("White bird featherless floats down through the air, A.") GBP
Riddle, The: "White men's children spread over the earth." Georgia Douglas Johnson. PoBA
Riddle, A: "Why is a pump like V-sc—nt C-stl-r—gh?" Thomas Moore. *See* What's My Thought Like?
Riddle, A: "Yon laddie wi' the gowdan pow." William Soutar. OxBS
Riddle, a riddle, as I suppose, A. Mother Goose. OXNR; TiPO
Riddle cum diddle cum dido [*or* doodle]. Kindness to Animals. Laura E. Richards. NTCP; SoPo; TiPo
Riddle me, riddle me ree. Mother Goose. OxNR
Riddle of Night. Jiri Modecai Langer, *tr. fr. Hebrew by* Gabriel Preil *and* Howard Schwartz. VWA
Riddle of Snow and Sun. *Unknown.* NCEP
(Riddle: "White bird featherless.") ChTr
("White bird featherless/ Flew from Paradise.") GBP; OxNR
Riddle of the World. Pope. *Fr.* An Essay on Man, Epistle II. FaFP
Riddle of the World, The. Whittier. TRV
Riddle Song, The. *Unknown.* BLSo; FSW
(Captain Wedderburn's Courtship, B *vers.*) ViBoFo
Riddle, A; the Vowels. Swift. *See* On the Vowels—a Riddle.
Riddle 29: The Moon and the Sun. *Unknown, tr. fr. Anglo-Saxon by* Burton Raffel. GoJo
Riddles. Patrick F. Kirby. GoBC
Riddles (Exeter Book), *sels.* *Unknown, formerly at. to* Cynewulf, *tr. fr. Anglo-Saxon by* Charles W. Kennedy.
Anchor: "Oft I must strive with wind and wave." AnOE
Book Moth: "A moth ate a word. To me it seemed." AnOE
Cuckoo: "In former days my father and mother." AnOE
(Riddle: Cuckoo.) PBBP
Fish in River: "My house is not quiet, I am not loud." AnOE
Honey-Mead: "I am valued by men, fetched from afar." AnOE
Horn: "Time was when I was weapon and warrior." AnOE
Plow: "My beak is bent downward, I burrow below." AnOE
Shield: "Lonely wanderer, wounded with iron, A." AnOE
Wild Swan: "My attire is noiseless when I tread the earth." AnOE
(Riddle: Mute Swan.) PBBP
Wind: "At times I resort, beyond man's discerning." AnOE
Riddles and Lies. Christine Zawadiwsky. AMV-80
Riddles Wisely Expounded. *Unknown.* ESPB (3 *vers.*); FaBoBa; GBP; HBV-2; ViBoFo (A *and* B *vers.*)
(Jennifer Gentle and Rosemary.) OxBoLi
(There Was a Knight.) CH
Riddling Knight, The. *Unknown.* FaBoCh; PoEL-1
"Riddling world, A!" one cried. The Two Questions. Alice Meynell. WPE
Ride a Cock Horse. Barry Pain. BXAP
Ride a cock-horse to Banbury Cross/ To buy little Johnny a galloping horse. *Unknown.* OxNR
Ride a cock-horse to Banbury Cross,/ To see a fine lady upon a white horse [*or* an old woman get up on her horse]. Mother Goose. FaBoBe; FaFP; HBV-1; HBVY; OxBoLi; OxNR; SoPo; TiPo
Ride a cock-horse to Banbury Cross/ To see what Tommy can buy. *Unknown.* OxNR
Ride away, ride away/ Johnny shall ride. Mother Goose. OxNR; TiPo
Ride-by-Nights, The. Walter de la Mare. DuDa; FaPON; SiSoSe; TiPo; WSC
Ride her up and down in your little brass wagon. Little Brass Wagon. *Unknown.* FSW
Ride 'Im Cowboy. A. L. Freebairn. PH
Ride in the swing. Tune: Crimson Lips Adorned. Li Ching-chao, *tr. by* C. H. Kwôck *and* Vincent McHugh. PBWP
Ride of Collins Graves, The. John Boyle O'Reilly. PAH
Ride On, Moses, *with music.* *Unknown.* BoAN-1
Ride round the Parapet, The. Friedrich Rueckert, *tr. fr. German by* James Clarence Mangan. AWP
Ride the Turtle's Back. Beth Brant. STE
Ride to Cherokee, The. Amelia Walstien Carpenter. AA
Ride to the Lady, The. Helen Gray Cone. AA

Rider, The. Leah Bodine Drake. NePoAm-2
Rider, The. Ann Stanford. WPE
Rider, The/ is fat. Horse & Rider. Wey Robinson. BXAP; WhC
Rider at the Gate, The. John Masefield. BrPo
Rider Victory, The. Edwin Muir. CMoP; LiTM; WaP
Riders, The. Robert Friend. GP
Riders. Linda Peavy. PH
Riders Held Back, The. Louis Simpson. ConAP
Riders of the Stars. Henry Herbert Knibbs. BPAW
Rides. Gene Derwood. LiTM; NePA
Ridiculous Excess. Shakespeare. *See* To Gild Refinèd Gold.
Ridiculous Optimist, The. *Unknown.* STF
Ridin'. Charles Badger Clark, Jr. BPAW
Riding. William Allingham. OxBChV
Riding. Harry Amoss. CaP
Riding. Florence Grossman. PH
Riding a One-eyed Horse. Henry Taylor. HeIP; PH
Riding across John Lee's Finger. Stanley Crouch. PoBA
Riding adown the country lanes. Robert Bridges. VLP
Riding against the east. To Beachey, 1912. Carl Sandburg. TiPo
Riding by there every day. Dog Hospital. Peter Wild. AmPA; GP
Riding Double. Peter Wild. AmPA
Riding Down. Nora Perry. AA; HBV-1
Riding Down from Bangor. Louis Shreve Osborne. BLPA
Riding in a Motor Boat. Dorothy W. Baruch. FaPON
Riding in an Airplane. Dorothy W. Baruch. FaPON
Riding in the Rain. Maxine W. Kumin. RFM
Riding Lesson. Henry Taylor. PH
Riding of the Kings, The. Eleanor Farjeon. YeAr
Riding Stable in Winter, The. John Tagliabue. PH
Riding the "A." May Swenson. CAD
Riding the black express from heaven to hell. Lucifer in the Train. Adrienne Rich. EaLo; NePoEA; TwAmPo
Riding the blue sapphire mountains. Mahadevi, *tr. fr. Kannada by* A. K. Ramanujan. BoWoP; PBWP
Riding the Elevator into the Sky. Anne Sexton. NYP
Riding through Ruwu swamp, about sunrise. Bête Humaine. Francis Brett Young. CH; HBMV
Riding Together. William Morris. NOBE; OAEL-2
Riding Westward. Harvey Shapiro. GP; NYP; VWA
Riding with Kilpatrick. Clinton Scollard. PAH
Rienzi to the Romans. Mary R. Mitford. TreFS
Rifled honeycomb, The. John Montague. *Fr.* The Cave of Night. CIP
"Rifleman, shoot me a fancy shot." Civil War. Charles Dawson Shanly. HBV-2; PAH
Rifleman's Song at Bennington, The. *Unknown.* PAH
(Riflemen at Bennington, The.) FSW
Rifles, The. *Unknown.* OBET
Rift Tide. Ruth M. Walsh. QQQ
Rig-Veda, The. *Unknown. See* Vedic Hymns.
Rigadoon, rigadoon, now let him fly. *Unknown.* OxNR
Rigged poker-stiff on her back. All the Dead Dears. Sylvia Plath. CAPP; IHMS
Rigger, The. Washington Jay McCormick. WhC
Righ Shemus he has gone to France. The Irish Rapparees. Charles Gavan Duffy. AnIV
Right after her birth, they crowded in. Anaesthesia. Jean Valentine. TAP
Right Apprehension. Thomas Traherne. PoEL-2
Right art thou who wouldst rather be. Platonic Love. Coventry Patmore. *Fr.* The Angel in the House. VLP
Right [*or* Ryght] as the stern [*or* star] of day begouth [*or* began] to shine [*or* schine *or* schyne]. The Golden [*or* Goldyn] Targe [*or* The Poet's Dream]. William Dunbar. BSV; OxBS; PBBP; PoEL-1
Right down the shocked street with a siren-blast. A Fire-Truck. Richard Wilbur. NCSH
"Right fresshe flowr, whos I ben have and shal. The Sorrow of Troilus. Chaucer. *Fr.* Troilus and Criseide, V. PoEL-1
Right from the start he is dressed in his best—his blacks and his whites. A March Calf. Ted Hughes. NoP
Right in the middle of the storm it was. The Storm. Elizabeth Jennings. NePoEA-2
Right Is Right. Frederick William Faber. TRV; WBLP
Right Kind of People, The. Edwin Markham. BLPA; FPL
Right Now. William Stafford. NaP
Right now it is raining in Iowa City. After Verlaine. Anselm Hollo. FAZ
Right of Way, The. William Carlos Williams. MoVE
Right-of-Way, A: 1865. William Plomer. DTC
Right on our flank the crimson sun went down. The Loss of the *Birkenhead.* Francis Hastings Doyle. HBV-2
Right On: White America. Sonia Sanchez. BOLo; PoBA
Right rigorous, and so forth! The Petition of Tom Dermody to the Three Fates in Council Sitting. Thomas Dermody. AnIV
Right so this river storms. The Course of the Tavy. William Browne. *Fr.* Britannia's Pastorals, I, Song 2. FaBoPP
Right Time, The. *Unknown, tr. fr. German by* Louis Untermeyer. UnTE
Right to Life, The. John N. Morris. AMV-80
Right True End, The. *Gond Oral Tradition, tr. by* V. Elwin *and* S. Hivale. WTO
Right under their noses, the green. The Dusk of Horses. James Dickey. AP; LiTM; NYBP
Right up under our noses, roses. Intimacy. Al Young. NPGG
Right upward on the road of fame. Emerson. *Fr.* The Poet. PP
Right Use of Prayer, The. Sir Aubrey De Vere. OBVV; WGRP
Right Way to Fish, The. *Unknown.* WhC
Right well I wote, most mighty Soveraine. The Faerie Queene, II, *induction.* Spenser. OAEL-1
Righteous Anger. James Stephens. *See* Glass of Beer, A.
Righteous Man, The. Samuel Butler. OBSV
Righteous or not, here comes an angry man. A View of the Burning. James Merrill. NePoEA-2
Rights of Woman, The. Anna Laetitia Barbauld. NOEC
Rigid Body Sings. James Clerk Maxwell. FaBoCo; FaBoPa; Par; SpRo
(In Memory of Edward Wilson.) BXAP; WhC
Rigoletto. Newman Levy. OBAL
Rigor Viris. Margaret Avison. CaP
Rigorists. Marianne Moore. NU; SBG
Rigs o' Barley, The. Burns. BSV; LiTB; LoBV; UnTE; ViBoPo
(Corn Riggs.) OxBS
(Corn Rigs Are Bonnie.) ErPo
(Song: "It was upon a Lammas night.") BoLoP
Riley. Charles Causley. SO
Rilke. Phyllis Webb. PeCV
Rilke, my river, I know your locked look of a poet. Visions. Kathleen Spivack. AmPA
Rilke Speaks of Angels. Susan Donnelly. PoDr
Rilloby-Rill. Sir Henry Newbolt. HBVY
Rillons, Rillettes. Richard Wilbur. NYBP
Rim of the desert is the Yucca land, The. In the Yucca Land. Madge Morris. BPAW
Rimbaud. W. H. Auden. SyP
Rimbaud and Verlaine, Precious Pair of Poets. Conrad Aiken. Preludes for Memnon, LVI. LiTA; LiTM; MoPo; NePA; NoAM; TwAmPo
(Prelude: "Rimbaud and Verlaine, precious pair of poets.") FaBoMo; TwCP
Rimbaud in Africa. Edgell Rickword. ChMP
Rime of the Ancient Feminist, The, *sel.* Stephanie Markman.
"They lived out in a women's house." BrRo
Rime of the Ancient Mariner, The. Samuel Taylor Coleridge. BeLS; CABA; CH; ChER; EBEV; EnRP; FaBoBe; FaBoCh; FaBV; FaFP; FiP; HAP; HBV-2; HoPM; InPS; LiTB; MasP; MOS; NOBE; NoP; OAEL-2; OAEP; OBEV; OBNC; OBNV; OBRV; PoEL-4; PrIm; RoGo; SeCeV; TEP; TreF; TrGrPo; WHA; ViBoPo
Sels.
"For when it dawn'd—they dropp'd their arms." UnS
"He prayeth best, who loveth best." FaPON; TRV
Rime of the Auncient Waggonere, The. William Maginn. BXAP
Rime of the Rood, A. Charles L. O'Donnell. GoBC
Rime [*or* Rhyme], the rack of finest wits. A Fit of Rime against Rime [*or* Rhyme against Rhyme]. Ben Jonson. AnAnS-2; InvP; MAT; OAEL-1; PoEL-2; PP; SeCP; SeCV-1; TEP
Rimrock, Where It Is. Hayden Carruth. NNaP
Rin and rout, rin and rout. The Deevil's Waltz. Sydney Goodsir Smith. FaBoTw
Rinaldo. Henry Peterson. AA
Ring, The. Paul Mariani. GeTw
Ring, The. Robert Pack. FAZ
Ring, The. Diane Wakoski. PoA
Ring-a-Ring. Kate Greenaway. FaPON; MoShBr
Ring-a-ring o' neutrons. Paul Dehn. *Fr.* A Leaden Treasury of English Verse. QQQ; SpRo
Ring-a-ring o' roses, A. Mother Goose. OxNR, 2 *vers.*; SpRo
("Ring-around-a-rosy," *sl. diff.*) SoPo; TiPo
Ring-a-ring of little boys. Ring-a-Ring. Kate Greenaway. FaPON; MoShBr
Ring and the Book, The, *sels.* Robert Browning.
"I am just seventeen years and five months old," VII. OAEP
"I have done with being judged," *fr.* VI. OAEP
"O lyric Love, half-angel and half-bird," *fr.* I. OAEP
(Lyric Love.) OBVV
(O Lyric Love.) FiP
" 'Quis pro Domino?' " *fr.* X. OAEP
"You never know what life means till you die," *fr.* XI. OAEP
Ring around a rosey. Squat Down, Josey. *Unknown.* AmFP
Ring-around-a-rosy. *See* Ring-a-ring o' roses, A.

Ring around the World. Annette Wynne. TiPo
Ring Of, The. Charles Olson. NOBA; VGW
Ring Out the Old, Ring In the New. Tennyson. *See* In Memoriam A. H. H.: "Ring out, wild bells . . ."
Ring out to the stars the glad chorus! Our Nation Forever. Wallace Bruce. OHIP
Ring out, wild bells, to the wild sky. In Memoriam A. H. H., CVI. Tennyson. BLPL; EBVV; FaFP; FaPON, 2 *sts.*; FaPoR; FiP, 7 *sts.*; HBV-2; LiTB; OFD; PGD; SBVL; SeCeV; TiPo, 2 *sts.*; TreF; TrGrPo; TRV; WBLP; WiR, 7 *sts., incl.* 2 *sts. fr.* CV
Ring Out Your Bells. Sir Philip Sidney. EIL; EnRePo; NoP; SiPS; ViBoPo
(Litany, A: "Ring out your bells.") CaBA; GBL; OBSC; UnPo
("Ring out your bells, let mourning shows be spread.") TEP
Ring Poem, The: A Husband Loses His Wedding Band as He Gestures from a Bridge. Phillip Dacey. FAZ
Ring round her! children of her glorious skies. The Foe at the Gates. John Dickson Bruns. PAH
Ring slender bells an elfin tune. Harebells in June. Annette Wynne. SUS
Ring, so worn as you behold, The. A Marriage Ring [*or* His Mother's Wedding Ring *or* His Wife's Wedding Ring *or* His Late Wife's Wedding Ring]. George Crabbe. BoLoP; EnLoPo; LO; NOBE; OBEV; OBNC; OBRV
Ring the bell! *Unknown.* HBVY; OxNR
Ring the bells backward; I am all on fire. John Cleveland. *Fr.* The Rebel Scot. PeD
Ring the bells, nor ring them slowly. Cedar Mountain. Annie Fields. PAH
Ring the bells, ring! The Dunce. *Unknown.* OxNR
Ring-ting! I wish I were a primrose. Wishing. William Allingham. FaPON; HBV-1; HBVY; OHIP; OxBChV
Ringed Plover by a Water's Edge. Norman MacCaig. OxBC
Ringers, The. John Peck. AmPA
Ringing the Bells. Anne Sexton. BiP; CAPP; FF; NMP; TAP; VGW
Ringing tire iron, A. Some Good Things to Be Said for the Iron Age. Gary Snyder. HoPM; PAI
Ringless. Diane Wakoski. Prf
Ringleted Youth of My Love. *Unknown, tr. fr. Modern Irish by* Douglas Hyde. AnIL; AnIV; OnYI; OxBI; WTO
Rings. William Barnes. NBM
Ringsend. Oliver St. John Gogarty. AnIL; OBMV; OxBTC
Rink Keeper's Sestina. George Draper. PrIm
Rino's Song. Lynne Lawner. IHMS
Rinsed with Gold, Endless, Walking the Fields. Robert Siegel. GeTw
Rintrah roars and shakes his fires in the burden'd [*or* burdened] air. The Marriage of Heaven and Hell. Blake. EnRP; LAuP; LoBV; OAEL-2
Rio Bravo—a Mexican Lament. Don Jose de Saltillo, *tr. fr. Spanish by* Charles Fenno Hoffman. PAH
Rio Grande, The. Sacheverell Sitwell. SeCePo
Rio Grande ("Heave away, Rio!"), *with music. Unknown.* ShS (2 *vers.*)
Rio Grande ("Oh, say, were you ever in Rio Grande?"), *diff. versions. Unknown.* FSW; TrAS
Río Grande de Loíza. Julia de Burgos, *tr. fr. Spanish by* Grace Schulman. InW
Riot. Gwendolyn Brooks. BPo; CAPP; PoBA; TAP
Riot, The; or, Half a Loaf Is Better than No Bread. Hannah More. NOEC
Riot Rhymes U.S.A., *sel.* Raymond R. Patterson.
"We are the same in our despair." GP
Rioting the roadsides, the fall colors. Fall Colors. Jerome Mazzaro. AMV-81
Riots and Rituals. Richard W. Thomas. PoBA
Rioupéroux. James Elroy Flecker. OBEV; OBVV
Rip. James Wright. NaP
Rip the Apple Seller Awakes; or, After 50 Years, the Great Depression (1929-79) Reawakens. Duane Ackerson. SOTS
Ripe and Bearded Barley, The. *Unknown.* BoNaP; ChTr; GBP
Ripe apples were caught like red fish in the nets. The Great Scarf of Birds. John Updike. NYBP
Ripe, Being Plunged into Fire. Friedrich Hölderlin, *tr. fr. German by* James Blair Leishman. OBVE
Ripe cherries and ripe maidens. Cherries. Zalman Schneour, *tr. by* Joseph Leftwich. TrJP
Ripe Fruit, The. *Unknown, tr. fr. Breton by* Louis Untermeyer. UnTE
Ripe Grain. Dora Reed Goodale. HBV-2
Ripeness is all; her in her cooling planet. To an Old Lady. William Empson. CoBMV; FaBoTw; GTBS-P; MoAB; MOON; NoAM; NOBE; SeCeV
Ripening. Noelle Caskey. DFT
Ripley or not. A Street in Kaufman-ville. James Cunningham. JB
Rip-off # 1: Hippie Capitalism. Geof Hewitt. NeAC
Ripper Collins' Legacy. Don Johnson. LiSp
Ripperty! Kye! Ahoo! Henry Lawson. CBAP
Ripping Trip, A. *Unknown.* CoSo
Ripple of dust panicked across, A. Ghosts. Ethna MacCarthy. NeIP
Rippling in the ocean of that darkening room. Woman at the Piano. Marya Zaturenska. MoAmPo
Riprap. Gary Snyder. NeAP; NOBA; PoM
Rise, A. Ernest McGaffey. AA
Rise and Fall of Creede, The. Cy Warman. BPAW; PoOW
Rise and Fall of Valentines. Fairfax Downey. InMe
Rise and hold up the curved glass. Pour Us Wine. Ibn Kolthum, *tr. by* E. Powys Mathers. *Fr.* The Mu'allaqát. AWP
Rise and Shine. Richmond Lattimore. NYBP
Rise and Shine. *Unknown.* FSW
Rise! arise! arise! The Sunrise Call. *Tr. by* N. Barnes. WTO
Rise at 7:15. Good Morning Love! Paul Blackburn. NMP; NoAM
Rise, brothers, rise; the wakening skies pray to the morning light. Coromandel Fishers. Sarojini Naidu. EtS
Rise, Crowned with Light. Pope. *Fr.* The Messiah. GoBC; WGRP
Rise from the waves, my rivering one. Four Poems for April, II. Louis Adeane. NeBP
Rise, happy youth, this bright machine survey. John Gay. *Fr.* The Fan. ViBoPo
Rise heart; thy Lord is risen. Sing his praise. Easter. George Herbert. AnAnS-1; SeCV-1; TrCP
Rise, Lady Mistress, Rise! Nathaniel Field. *Fr.* Amends for Ladies. EIL
(Matin Song.) HBV-1
(Song: "Rise, Lady Mistresse, rise.") OBS
"Rise, man the wall, our clarion's blast." Hymn of the Alamo. Reuben M. Potter. BPAW
Rise Me Up from Down Below, *with music. Unknown.* ShS
Rise, Mourner, Rise, *with music. Unknown.* BoAN-2
Rise, O earth, from out thy slumber. Prayer for Rain. *Unknown.* WGRP
Rise, O my Soul! *Unknown.* OxBoCh
Rise Oedipus, and if thou canst unfould. The Poem. Thomas Morton. SCAP
Rise of Man, The. John White Chadwick. AA
Rise of Shivaji, The. Zulfikar Ghose. MoBS
Rise, rise from sluggishness, fly fast my dear. The Verses of the Talkative Knight. Mary Sidney Wroth, Countess of Montgomery. *Fr.* Urania. WPE
Rise! Sleep no more! 'Tis a noble morn! The Hunter's Song. "Barry Cornwall." GN
Rise then, ere ruin swift surprize. John Trumbull. *Fr.* M'Fingal GOA
Rise thou best and brightest morning. New Year's Day. Richard Crashaw. JCP
Rise, underground sleepers, rise from the grave. Ode against St. Cecilia's Day. George Barker. PoA
Rise Up, O Men of God, *with music.* William Pierson Merrill. AH
(Festal Song.) WGRP
Rise up, rise up,/ And, as the trumpet blowing. The Trumpet. Edward Thomas. HBMV; MMA; MoBrPo; OHIP
Rise up, rise up, Jack Spratt. And you, his wife. Sonnet XIII. Winfield Townley Scott. ErPo
"Rise up, rise up, my seven brave sons [*or* you seven sleepers]." Earl Brand (The Douglas Tragedy). *Unknown.* FaBoBa; FSW; ViBoFo
"Rise up, rise up, now, Lord Douglas," she says. The Douglas Tragedy [*or* Earl Brand]. *Unknown.* ESPB; HBV-2; NoP; OxBB; TrGrPo
Rise Up, Shepherd, and Follow [*or* an' Foller]. *Unknown.* BoAN-2, *with music*; FSW
Rise up, thou monstrous ant-hill on the plain. Wordsworth. *Fr.* The Prelude, VII. HAP
Rise with the Lamb of Innocence. *Unknown.* MeEL
Rise, Ye Children, *with music.* Justus Falckner, *tr. fr. German by* Emma Frances Bevan. AH
Rise you up, my dearest dear. Shoot the Buffalo. *Unknown.* TrAS
Rise You Up, My True Love. *Unknown.* AmFP
Risen above the uncertain. To Her. Robert Mezey. NaP
Risen is the sleeper from the vaulted past. War. Georg Heym, *tr. by* Peter Viereck. AMV-80
Rises at five, just when a late moon. The Insomniac Sleeps Well for Once and. Hayden Carruth. NNaP
Risest thou thus, dim dawn, again/ And howlest, issuing out of night. In Memoriam A. H. H., LXXII. Tennyson. OBNC; PoEL-5
Risest thou thus, dim dawn, again/ So loud with voices of the birds. In Memoriam A. H. H., XCIX. Tennyson. EBVV
Rising, The. Thomas Buchanan Read. *Fr.* The Wagoner of the Alleghanies. PAH; TreFS
Rising, The/ Let me proceed by this way. Canoe-hauling Chant. *Tr. by* Apirana Ngata. WTO
Rising fondly before me. The Beloved's Image. *Tr. by* M. W. Beckwith. WTO
Rising from the pale valley, the rivers unseen from here. Oxford Commination. Paris Leary. AMV-81
Rising High Water Blues. *Unknown.* BluL

Rising hills, the slopes, The. For the Children. Gary Snyder. NoP; PAI
Rising in lamplight dying at dawn. Voices Answering Back: The Vampires. Lawrence Raab. AmPA
Rising in the Morning. Hugh Rhodes. OxBChV
Rising in the North, The. *Unknown.* ACP; ESPB
Rising moon has hid the stars. Endymion. Longfellow. AA; HBV-1
Rising of the Moon A.D. 1798, The. John Keegan Casey. OnYI
Rising of the Session, The. Robert Fergusson. OxBS
Rising Sun, The. Lawrence Durrell. *Fr.* Eight Aspects of Melissa. NeBP
Rising Sun Blues, The. *Unknown. See* House of the Rising Sun, The.
Rising Village, The, *sels.* Oliver Goldsmith, the Younger.
"How sweet it is, at first approach of morn." OBCV
"Not fifty summers yet have passed thy clime." OBCV
"What noble courage must their hearts have fired." OBCV; PeCV
(Lonely Settler, The.) NOBC
"While now the Rising Village claims a name." CaP
Rising without names today. The Survivor. Stephen Berg. *Fr.* Entering the Body. NaP
Risk, The. Anne Sexton. BoWoP
Rispetti: On the Death of a Child. Paul Heyse, *tr. fr. German by* E. H. Mueller. PoPl
Rispetto. Agnes Mary Frances Robinson. HBMV
Risposta. John Wilbye. HBV-2
Risselty-Rosselty. *Unknown.* FSW
Rissem. Sandra M. Gilbert. AMV-81
Rite, The. Peter Dale. NAs
Rite, The. Dudley Randall. HoPM
Rite of Passage. Sharon Olds. MAYP
Rite of Spring. Seamus Heaney. OxBC
Rite of Spring. Leo Kennedy. CaP
Rites for a Demagogue. Anthony Thwaite. NePoEA-2
Rites for Cousin Vit, The. Gwendolyn Brooks. *Fr.* The Womanhood. BPo; HAP; WeW; WPE
Rites of Passage. Audre Lorde. CNA; PoBA
Ritratto. Ezra Pound. PP
Ritual, The. Paul David Ashley. LFAC
Ritual, The. Joy Gwillim. AMV-80
Ritual, The. E. J. Pratt. NoAM
Ritual Not Religious. *Unknown, tr. fr. Telugu.* WGRP
Ritual of Departure. Thomas Kinsella. CIP; CMoP
Ritual of Memories, The. Tess Gallagher. GeTw
Ritual Three. David Ignatow. ConAP
Ritual to Read to Each Other, A. William Stafford. NePA
Ritualists, The. William Carlos Williams. NYBP
Rival, The. *At. to* Sir George Etherege *and to* William Walsh. *See* Rivals.
Rival, The. Sylvia Plath. PAI
Rival, The. Sylvia Townsend Warner. MoAB; MoBrPo
Rival Curates, The. W. S. Gilbert. CenHV; VLP
Rivalry. Alden Nowlan. POL
Rivals, The, *sel.* Sir William Davenant.
"My lodging it is on the cold ground." JCP
Rivals. *At. to* Sir George Etherege *and to* William Walsh. HBV-1; OBEV
(Rival, The.) CavP
(Song: "Of all the torments, all the cares.") OBEC; ViBoPo
Rivals, The. James Stephens. FaPON; InvP; MoVE; NoAM; OBEV; OBMV; PoPl
Riven Doggeries. James Tate. MAYP
Riven Quarry, The. Gloria C. Oden. PoBA
River, The. Sam Cornish. PoBA
River, The. Hart Crane. *Fr.* The Bridge: Powhatan's Daughter. AMPP; AP; CMoP; CoBMV; GOA; MoAB; MoAmPo; NoAM; NOBA; OxBA; PrIm; TwAmPo
Sels.
"Down, down—born pioneers in time's despite." TrGrPo
"You will not hear it as the sea." ViBoPo
River, The. Mary Sinton Leitch. HBMV
River. Lawrence Locke. GrPl
River, The, *sels.* Pare Lorentz.
"Black spruce and Norway pine." AmFN
"Down the Yellowstone, the Milk, the White and Cheyenne." AmFN
River, The. Patrick MacDonogh. NeIP
River, The. Roy Macnab. PeSA
River, The. Dabney Stuart. NYBP
River, The. Leo Vroman. VWA
River, The. Don Welch. Str
River Afram. Andrew Amankwa Opoku. PBA
River Again and Again, The. Linda Gregg. NPGG
River boat had loitered down its way, The. Gamesters All. DuBose Heyward. HBMV
River Boats, The. Daniel Whitehead Hicky. AmFN
River brought down, The. How We Heard the Name. Alan Dugan. CoAP; NMP; NoAM
River Compared to an Oratorical Sentence, The. Luis de Góngora, *tr. fr. Spanish by* Edward Meryon Wilson. *Fr.* The First Solitude. OBVE
River Dart, The. *Unknown.* GBP
River Don, The. *Unknown.* GBP
River Duddon, The, *sels.* Wordsworth.
After-Thought, XXXIV. EnRP; FaBoEn; OBNC; OBRV; SeCePo
(After-Thought to "The River Duddon.") OAEP
("I thought of Thee, my partner and my guide.") FaBoRV
(To the River Duddon: After-Thought.) FaBoPP
(Valediction to the River Duddon.) NOBE
(Valedictory Sonnet to the River Duddon.) OBEV
Return. HAP
River Fight, The. Henry Howard Brownell. EtS; PAH
River-Fog. Fukayabu Kiyowara, *tr. fr. Japanese by* Arthur Waley. FaPON
("Because river-fog.") AWP
River Glideth in a Secret Tongue, The. Anthony Ostroff. NePoAm-2
River God, The. John Fletcher. *Fr.* The Faithful Shepherdess, III, i. TrGrPo
River God, The. Sacheverell Sitwell. MoBrPo
River God, The. Stevie Smith. BrRo; FaBoNo; FaBoTw; PBWP
River god cries far, The. Tâo. Alfred Goldsworthy Bailey. CaP
River-God's Song, The. John Fletcher. *Fr.* The Faithful Shepherdess, III, i. FaPON; MoShBr
(Song: "Do not fear to put thy feet.") ElL; OBS
River God's Song. Anne Ridler. NYBP
River has not any care, The. Francis Thompson. *Fr.* Contemplation. FaBoEn
River, I am passing. River Afram. Andrew Amankwa Opoku. PBA
River in Asia, A. Andrew Grossbardt. FAZ
River in March, The. Ted Hughes. OxBC
River in the Meadows, The. Léonie Adams. MoAB; MoAmPo
River Is a Piece of Sky, The. John Ciardi. PDV; PoPl; SoPo
River is deep and the river is wide. Kansas City Blues. *Unknown.* FSW
River is so much mica, The. The River; North of Guelph. D. G. Jones. NOBC
River Lynher, The. Richard Carew. *Fr.* Survey of Cornwall. FaBoPP
River Map, The and We're Done. Charles Olson. *Fr.* The Maximus Poems. CoPo
River-Mates. Padraic Colum. AnIV; AWP
River Merchant's Wife, The; a Letter. Li Po, *tr. fr. Chinese by* Ezra Pound. AmPP; AWP; BoLoP; CABA; DTC; FYAP; HAP; HeIP; InPK; InPS; LiTA; MoAB; MoAmPo; MoPo; MP; NIP; NoAM; NOBA; NOBE; NoP; OBMV; OBVE; OxBA; PPoe; PPP; PrIm; SOTW; TAP; TwAmPo; TwCP; UnPo; WeW
River moans, The. River. Lawrence Locke. GrPl
River, The; North of Guelph. D. G. Jones. NOBC
River of Bees, The. W. S. Merwin. HeIP; LCAP
River of Dart, O river of Dart. The Dart. *Unknown.* GBP
River of Heaven, The. *Unknown, tr. fr. Japanese by* Lafcadio Hearn. *Fr.* Manyo Shu. AWP
River of Life, The. Thomas Campbell. BSV; FaFP; GTBS; GTBS-P; HBV-1; LiTB
River of Rivers in Connecticut, The. Wallace Stevens. HAP; NOBA; VGW
River of Stars, The. Alfred Noyes. OnMSP
River Rhyme. William Carlos Williams. PoA
River Road. Stanley Kunitz. NoAM
River Road Studio. Barbara Guest. PoM
River Roads. Carl Sandburg. VGW
River Roses. D. H. Lawrence. BrPo; CMoP; GBL; OAEL-2; ViBoPo
River Song. Elizabeth Brewster. CaP
River Song. Weldon Kees. NoAM; PPP; TwAmPo
River Swelleth More and More, The. Henry David Thoreau. NOBA
River takes the land, and leaves nothing, The. The Slip. Wendell Berry. NOCV
River That Is East, The. Galway Kinnell. NYP
River that must turn full after I stop dying. "A 11." Louis Zukofsky. *Fr.* "A." CoPo; VGW
River, that rollest by the ancient walls. Stanzas to the Po. Byron. OAEL-2
River this November afternoon, The. The Double Vision. C. Day Lewis. NoAM
River used to store up in its mouth, The. The River. Roy Macnab. PeSA
River Walk, The. Padraic Fallon. OxBI
River widens to a pathless sea, The. On a Ferry Boat. Richard Burton. AA
River Winding. Charlotte Zolotow. RHPC
Riverdale Lion. John Robert Colombo. PeCV
Riverfront, St. Louis. John Knoepfle. TAT
Riverman, The. Elizabeth Bishop. NYBP
Rivers. Thomas Storer. ElL; FaBoCh
Rivers and Mountains. John Ashbery. CoAP; NoAM; NOBA

Rivers Arise; a Fragment. Milton. ChTr
(Rivers Arise.) FaBoPP
(Rivers Arise; Whether Thou Be the Son.) InPK
Rivers Come to the Hall of Proteus for the Marriage of the Thames and the Medway, The. Spenser. *Fr.* The Faerie Queene, IV, ii. FaBoPP
Rivers of the West. "Sunset Joe." PoOW
Rivers Remember, The. Nancy Byrd Turner. AmFN
Rivers that flowed divided each from each. Chinese Poems: Arthur Waley. "C. A. Fair." PeSA
Rivers Till and Tweed, The. *Unknown. See* Tweed and Till.
"Rivers Unknown to Song." Alice Meynell. HBMV
Riverside Drive, November Fifth. Katha Pollitt. AMV-81
Rivery field spread out below, A. Let All Things Pass Away. W. B. Yeats. ChTr
Riveter, The. Mabel Watts. RHPC
Rivets. N. S. Olds. EtS
Rivulet-loving wanderer Abraham, The. Abraham. Edwin Muir. EBCP
Rivulet with rush of sound, The. Midwinter Thaw. Lenore Pratt. CaP
Rivulose. A. R. Ammons. SUW
Rizpah. Tennyson. PoEL-5; VLP
Roach, The. John Raven. BPo; HoPM
Roaches. Edward Field. NYP
Road, The. Conrad Aiken. AP; MoAmPo; PAI
Road, The. Patrick R. Chalmers. HBV-1
Road, The. John Gould Fletcher. HBMV
Road, The. Helene Johnson. AmNP; BANP; BlSi; CDC; PoNe
Road. W. S. Merwin. PPJ
Road, The. Herbert Morris. NePoAm-2
Road, The. Edwin Muir. BSV; CMoP; FaBoEn; FaFP; LiTB; LiTM; ViBoPo
Road, The. Nikolay Platonovich Ogarev, *tr. fr. Russian by* P. E. Matheson. AWP
Road, The. Christine Orr. PoSH
Road, The. Zalman Schneour, *tr. fr. Yiddish by* Joseph Leftwich. TrJP
Road, The. James Stephens. HBMV
Road along the Thumb and Forefinger, The ("The road all the way up along the coast"). Mark Hickey. AMV-81
Road at My Door, The. W. B. Yeats. Meditations in Time of Civil War, V. BlrV; LiTB; NOBE
Road at the top of the rise, The. The Middleness of the Road. Robert Frost. CrMA; LiTA; NOBA
Road Back, The. Anne Sexton. NYBP
Road beneath the giant original trees, The. Sanctuary. Judith Wright. WPE
Road can't be as sad as a shoe is sad, A. Shoe. John Perreault. EAS
Road climbs, villages, The. Going. Peter Everwine. NNaP
Road ends with the hills, The. Black Tarn. V. Sackville-West. SBG
Road from Adonoi to I Don't Know. The Three Towns. Howard Nemerov. AMV-81
Road goes ever on and on, The. The Old Walking Song. J. R. R. Tolkien. RFM
Road Hazard. Rayna Green. TWSS
Road in Kentucky, A. Robert Hayden. LCAP; NCSH
Road is left that once was trod, The. The Old Road. Jones Very. AA
Road is so rough Severn is walking, The. Posthumous Keats. Stanley Plumly. GeTw; SV
Road is wide and the stars are out and the breath of the night is sweet, The. Roofs. Joyce Kilmer. BLPL; PoLF
Road Is Wider than Long, The, *sel.* Roland Penrose.
"They breathe with the night." EAS
Road like brown ribbon, A. September. Edwina Fallis. SUS; TiPo; YeAR
Road might lead to anywhere, A. Roads. Rachel Field. FaPON; PDV; SoPo; TiPo
Road Moves On, The. Dorothy Nash. *Fr.* Kinloch. PoSH
Road Not Taken, The. Robert Frost. AmPP; AP; ChTr; CMoP; CoBMV; EvOK; FaBoCh; FaFP; FPL; HAP; HelP; LiTA; LiTM; MoAB; MoAmPo; MP; NePA; NoAM; NoP; OxBA; PoLF; PoPl; RFM; SeCeV; SoSe; TAP; TreFT; TwAmPo; TwCP
Road of Birds, The. Harry Humes. AMV-80
Road of Ireland, A. Charles L. O'Donnell. HBMV
Road of Life, The. William Morris. *Fr.* The Earthly Paradise. OBNC
Road of Remembrance, The. Lizette Woodworth Reese. HBV-1
Road outside the window was "our" road, The. Thomas McGrath. *Fr.* Letter to an Imaginary Friend. GP
Road Runner. Sharlot M. Hall. BPAW
Road runs straight with no turning, the circle, The. Black People: This Is Our Destiny. Amiri Baraka. CAPP; CNA
Road-Song of the Bandar-Log. Kipling. *Fr.* The Jungle Book. OAEP
Road that leads to Rannoch is the gangrel's royal way, The. For Summer's Here. Ratcliffe Barnett. PoSH
Road the Crows Own, The. Susan Astor. AMV-81
Road to Anywhere, The. Bert Leston Taylor. HBMV
Road to Babylon, The. Margaret Adelaide Wilson. HBMV
Road to Bologna, The. Roy Macnab. PeSA
Road to Castaly, The, *sel.* Alice Brown.
Revelation. WGRP
Road to Cook's Peak, The. *Unknown.* CoSo
Road to France, The. Daniel Henderson. HBV-2; PAH
Road to Hate, The. Patrick Kavanagh. TW
Road to Hogan's Gap, The. Andrew Barton Paterson. CBAP
Road to Nijmegen, The. Earle Birney. OBCV
Road to Pengya, The. Tu Fu, *tr. fr. Chinese by* Rewi Alley *and* Edward Field. Prf
Road to School, The. Joy M. Lane. AMV-81
Road to Texas, The. Berta Hart Nance. BPAW
Road to the Bow, The. James David Corrothers. BANP
Road to the burn, The. Roads. George Mackay Brown. PoSH
Road to the Pool, The. Grace Hazard Conkling. HBMV
Road to Vagabondia, The. Dana Burnet. PoLF
Road to Zoagli, The. Max Beerbohm. FaBoNo
Road twisted through tongues of rock, The. The Vowels of Another Language. Tom Disch. PoA
Road winds down through autumn hills, The. Tour 5. Robert Hayden. PPP
Roadmenders' Song, The. *Gond Oral Tradition, tr. by* V. Elwin *and* S. Hivale. WTO
Road-runner dodged through the chaparral, A. A California Idyl. Ernest McGaffey. BPAW
Roads. George Mackay Brown. PoSH
Roads. Rachel Field. FaPON; PDV; SoPo; TiPo
Roads Also, The. Wilfred Owen. EBEV
Road's End, The. Theodosia Garrison. HBMV
Road's End. Rolf Jacobsen, *tr. fr. Norwegian by* Robert Bly. NU
Road's End, The. John Montague. A Severed Head, I. IPY
Roads Go Ever Ever On. J. R. R. Tolkien. TiPo
("Roads go ever on and on.") FaPON
Roads go on, ending only, The. The Runner. Jerah Chadwick. AMV-81
Roads have come to their end now, The. Road's End. Rolf Jacobsen, *tr. by* Robert Bly. NU
Roads lead southward, blue, The. To Argos. Lawrence Durrell. MoPo
Roads were jammed, The. Snow in the City. Danny Siegel. VWA
Roadside Flowers. Bliss Carman. HBMV
Roadside forests here and there were touched with tawny gold, The. Mistress Hale of Beverly. Lucy Larcom. PAH
Roadside near Moscow. R. A. D. Ford. PeCV
Roadside thistle, eager, The. Basho, *tr. fr. Japanese by* Curtis Hidden Page. AWP
Roam not from pole to pole, but enter here. Swift. *Fr.* Inscription for the Sign of *The Jolly Barber,* with a Razor in One Hand, and a Pot of Beer in the Other. FaBoUs
Roan galloped, The. The Corral. Earle Thompson. STE
Roan lizard writhing on a dead leaf, A. The Translation of Verver. Mei-Mei Berssenbrugge. LTB
Roan Stallion. Robinson Jeffers. BeLS
Roarers in a Ring. Ted Hughes. NePoEA-2
Roaring alongside he takes for granted, The. Sandpiper. Elizabeth Bishop. HelP; NYBP
Roaring company that festive night, A. The Dark and the Fair. Stanley Kunitz. PoCh
Roaring Frost, The. Alice Meynell. EBVV; WPE
Roaring in the Wind All Night. Wordsworth. *See* Resolution and Independence.
Roaring Lad and the Ranting Lass, The; or, A Merry Couple Madly Met. *Unknown.* CoMu
Roaring Mad Tom. *Unknown. See* Tom o' Bedlam's Song.
Roaring of the wheels has filled my ears, The. A Cry from the Ghetto. Morris Rosenfeld, *tr. by* Charles Weber Linn. TrJP
Roast Beef of Old England, The. Henry Fielding. *Fr.* Don Quixote in England. OBEC
"Roast chestnuts, a shilling." Walking against the Wind. Jon Stallworthy. OxBC
Roasted Sucking Pig. *Unknown.* BXAP
Rob me and maim me! Why, man, take such pains. To One Who Quotes and Detracts. Walter Savage Landor. FaBoEE
Rob Roy, *sel.* Sir Walter Scott.
"Farewell to the land where the clouds love to rest." NBM
Rob Roy. *Unknown.* BaBo; ESPB (A *and* B *vers.*)
Robbed of our rights, and by such water-rats? In Defiance to the Dutch. *Unknown.* APAS
Robben Island. Robert Dederick. PeSA
Robber, The. Ivy O. Eastwick. SiSoSe
Robber, The. "Hugh MacDiarmid," *after the Cretan.* OBVE
Robber, The. W. J. Turner. MoBrPo
Robber Bridegroom, The. Allen Tate. TwAmPo

Robbers came to our house, The. *Unknown.* GBP
Robbing and Stealing Blues. *Unknown.* BluL
Robene and Makyne ("Robene [*or* Robin] sat on gude green hill"). Robert Henryson. BoLoP; BSV; GoTS
(Robin and Makin.) OAEP; PoEL-1
(Robin and Makyne.) OBEV
Robens' Promised Land. George Purdom. WTO
Robert Barnes, fellow fine. Mother Goose. OxNR
Robert Bly Finds Something in New Jersey. Carol Poster. BXAP
Robert Bly Says Something Too. Henry Taylor. BXAP
Robert Bruce's March to Bannockbum. Burns. *See* Scots Wha Hae.
Robert Burns. William Alexander. HBV-2
Robert Creeley Also Watches. D. C. Berry. BXAP
Robert Creeley Listens, Too. D. C. Berry. BXAP
Robert E. Lee. Stephen Vincent Benét. *Fr.* John Brown's Body. AmFN
Robert E. Lee. Julia Ward Howe. PAH
Robert Frost. Robert Lowell. NoAM; PAI
Robert Frost's Left-leaning *Trespassers Will Be Shot* Sign. William Zaranka. BXAP
Robert Fulton. Ann Stanford. GP
Robert G. Shaw. Henrietta Cordelia Ray. BlSi
Robert Gould Shaw. William Vaughn Moody. *Fr.* An Ode in Time of Hesitation. AA
Robert Louis Stevenson. Lizette Woodworth Reese. HBV-2
Robert Lowell. Richard O'Connell. AMV-81
Robert Lowell Is Dead. Patrick Worth Gray. SOTS
Robert of Lincoln. Bryant. FaBoBe; FaPON; HBV-1; HBVY; OBCA; WBLP, *abr.*
Robert of Sicily, brother of Pope Urbane. King Robert of Sicily. Longfellow. *Fr.* Tales of a Wayside Inn. BeLS; OHIP
Robert Rowley rolled a round roll round. Mother Goose. OxNR
Robert, Second Duke of Normandy, *sel.* Thomas Lodge.
Pluck the Fruit and Taste the Pleasure. ElL
(Carpe Diem.) OBSC
(Song: "Pluck the fruit and taste the pleasure.") EnRePo
Robert Sheridan Lowell. Robert Lowell. *Fr.* Marriage. NAs
Robert the Bruce. Edwin Muir. OxBS
Robert Whitmore. Frank Marshall Davis. BPo; NoP; PoBA; PoNe
Roberta. *Unknown.* BluL
Robertin Tush. *Unknown.* GBP
Robert's Farm. *Unknown.* FSW
Robert's Rules of Order. Robert Peterson. FAZ
Robes loosely flowing, and aspect as free. Seeing Her Dancing. Robert Heath. OBS
Robespierre and Mozart as Stage. Robert Lowell. FaBoMo
Robin. Paula Gunn Allen. TWSS
Robin. Burns. *See* Rantin, Rovin Robin.
Robin, The. George Daniel. FaBoRV; FM; OBS
(Ode: "Poor bird, I do not envy thee.") PBBP
Robin, A. Walter de la Mare. ChTr; CMoP; FaBoRV; PB
Robin, The. William Bell Scott. FM
Robin-a-bobin. Mother Goose. OxNR
Robin; a Pastoral Elegy. John Dobson. NOEC
Robin Adair. Caroline Keppel. FaBoBe; HBV-1
Robin and a robin's son, A. *Unknown.* OxNR
Robin and Gandelyn. *Unknown.* *See* Robyn and Gandeleyn.
Robin and Makin. Robert Henryson. *See* Robene and Makyne.
Robin and Richard/ Were two pretty men. Mother Goose. OxBoLi; OxNR
Robin and the red-breast, The. A Rule for Birds' Nesters. *Unknown.* HBV-1; HBVY; OxNR; PBBP
Robin and the wren, The. Four Birds [*or* Robin, Wren, Martin, Swallow]. *Unknown.* ChTr; GBP; PBBP
Robin and the wren, The. Greed. *Unknown.* OxNR
Robin at My Window. James Melville. *Fr.* The Black Bastill; or, A Lamentation of the Kirk of Scotland. BSV
Robin chants when the thrush is dumb, The. To-Morrow. Florence Earle Coates. AA
Robin dwelt in greenë wood. The Death of Robin Hood. *Unknown.* EnSB
Robin Good-Fellow ("From Oberon, in fairy land"). *Unknown.* FaBoCh; ViBoPo
Robin Goodfellow, *sels. Unknown.*
Robin Good-Fellow's Song: "Round about, little ones," *fr.* Pt. II. *Unknown.* ElL
Song: "And can the physician make sick men well?" *fr.* Pt. II. ElL; LoBV
(And Can the Physician.) ELP
Robin he's gane to the wast. The Wife Wrapt in Wether's Skin. *Unknown.* ESPB
Robin Hood. Gray Burr. NCSH
Robin Hood. Keats. AWP; EnRP
Robin Hood. Phyllis McGinley. *Fr.* Speaking of Television. OBSV
Robin Hood/ Has gone to the wood. *Unknown.* OxNR
Robin Hood and Allen [*or* Allin]-a-Dale. *Unknown.* ESPB; FaBoBe; GBP; HBV-2; MoShBr
Robin Hood and Guy of Gisborne. *Unknown.* ESPB; OAEP
Robin Hood and Little John. *Unknown.* AmFP; ESPB; ViBoFo
Robin Hood and Maid Marian. *Unknown.* ESPB
Robin Hood and Queen Katherine. *Unknown.* ESPB (A *and* B *vers.*)
Robin Hood and the Beggar, I ("Come light and listen, you gentlemen all"). *Unknown.* ESPB
Robin Hood and the Beggar, II ("Lyth and listen, gentlemen"). *Unknown.* ESPB
Robin Hood and the Bishop of Hereford. *Unknown.* ESPB
(Robin Hood and the Bishop, *sl. diff.*) ESPB
Robin Hood and the Butcher. *Unknown.* ESPB (A *and* B *vers.*)
Robin Hood and the Curtal Friar. *Unknown.* ESPB (A *and* B *vers.*)
Robin Hood and the Golden Arrow. *Unknown.* ESPB
Robin Hood and the Monk. *Unknown.* ESPB; FaBoBa; OBNV, *abr.*; ViBoFo
(In Summer.) CH
(May in the Green-Wood.) OBEV
(Robyn Hode and the Munke.) OxBB
"In somer, when the shawes be sheyne," *sel.* ViBoPo
Robin Hood and the Pedlars. *Unknown.* ESPB
Robin Hood and the Potter. *Unknown.* ESPB
Robin Hood and the Prince of Aragon. *Unknown.* ESPB
Robin Hood and the Ranger. *Unknown.* ESPB
Robin Hood and the Scotchman. *Unknown.* ESPB (A *and* B *vers.*)
Robin Hood and the Shepherd. *Unknown.* ESPB
Robin Hood and the Tanner. *Unknown.* ESPB
Robin Hood and the Three Squires. *Unknown.* *See* Robin Hood Rescuing Three Squires.
Robin Hood and the Tinker. *Unknown.* ESPB
Robin Hood and the Valiant Knight. *Unknown.* ESPB
Robin Hood and the Widow's Three Sons. *Unknown.* *See* Robin Hood Rescuing Three Squires.
Robin Hood he was [*or* hee was and] a tall young man. Robin Hood's Progress to Nottingham. *Unknown.* ESPB; OBET
Robin Hood Newly Revived. *Unknown.* ESPB
Robin Hood Rescuing Three Squires. *Unknown.* ESPB (A *and* B *vers.*); ViBoFo
(Robin Hood and the Three Squires.) EnSB
(Robin Hood and the Widow's Three Sons.) OnMSP
Robin Hood Rescuing Will Stutly. *Unknown.* ESPB
Robin Hood, Robin Hood,/ Is in the mickle wood. Mother Goose. OxNR
Robin Hood's Birth, Breeding, Valor, and Marriage. *Unknown.* ESPB
Robin Hood's Chase. *Unknown.* ESPB
Robin Hood's Death, *diff. versions. Unknown.* ESPB (A *and* B *vers.*); FaBoBa; OBET; TrGrPo; ViBoFo
(Death of Robin Hood, The.) EnSB
" 'I never hurt maid in all my time,' " *sel.* ViBoPo
Robin Hood's Delight. *Unknown.* ESPB
Robin Hood's End. *Unknown.* GoTL
Robin Hood's Funeral. Anthony Munday. *Fr.* The Death of Robert, Earl of Huntingdon. WiR
(Dirge: "Weep, weep, ye woodmen, wail.") CTC; OBSC
(Song: "Weep, weep. . . .") ElL
(Weep, Weep, Ye Woodmen.) CH
Robin Hood's Golden Prize. *Unknown.* ESPB
Robin Hood's Progress to Nottingham. *Unknown.* ESPB; OBET
Robin is a lovely lad. The Dance. *At. to* Thomas Campion. ElL; FaBoCh; LoBV
Robin is my only joe. Kind Robin Lo'es Me. *Unknown.* BSV
Robin is the one, The. Emily Dickinson. FaBV; HBVY
Robin, I've been reading Faust. Reading Faust. Judah Goldin. AMV-81
Robin on a leafless bough. Robin Redbreast. W. H. Davies. PB
Robin on my lawn, The. February. Francis Brett Young. HBMV; HBVY
Robin Redbreast. William Allingham. FaBoBe; HBV-1; HBVY; MoShBr; OxBChV; PBBP
Robin Redbreast, A, *much abr.* Blake. *Fr.* Auguries of Innocence. SiSoSe
("Robin redbreast in a cage, A.") OxBoLi, *sl. abr.*; TreFT, *much abr.*
(Three Things to Remember, *br. sel.*) FaPON; MoShBr
Robin Redbreast. W. H. Davies. PB
Robin Redbreast. George Washington Doane. AA; HBV-1; HBVY
Robin Redbreast. Stanley Kunitz. Prf
Robin Red Breast. Lula Lowe Weeden. CDC
Robin Redbreast in a cage, A. A Robin Redbreast [*or* Three Things to Remember]. Blake. *Fr.* Auguries of Innocence. FaPON; MoShBr; OxBoLi; SiSo; TreFT
Robin Redbreast's Testament. *Unknown.* GBP
Robin [*or* Robene] sat on gude green [*or* gud grene] hill. Robin [*or* Robene] and Makyne [*or* Makin]. Robert Henryson. BoLoP; BSV; GoTS; OAEP; OBEV; PoEL-1
Robin sings of willow-buds, The. Bird Song. Laura E. Richards. HBV-1

Robin skimmed into the room, A. The Bird in the Room. Rudolph Chambers Lehmann. HBMV; HBVY
Robin the Bobbin. *Unknown.* OxNR
Robin, Wren, Martin, Swallow. *Unknown.* *See* Four Birds.
Robinets and Jenny Wrens. *Unknown.* OxNR
Robin's Come. William Warner Caldwell. HBVY
Robin's Cross. George Darley. OnYI
Robin's Egg, The. Annie Charlotte Dalton. CaP
Robins in the treetop. Marjorie's Almanac. Thomas Bailey Aldrich. FaPON
Robin's Poem, A. Nikki Giovanni. AmNP
Robin's Secret. Katharine Lee Bates. AA
Robin's Song, The. C. Lovat Fraser. MoShBr
Robin's Song. E. L. M. King. TiPo
Robins wait for early worms; bees will find their clover. Birds and Bees. *Unknown, tr. by* Louis Untermeyer. UnTE
Robinson. Weldon Kees. NaP; NoAM; NYBP; TwAmPo
Robinson at cards at the Algonquin; a thin. Aspects of Robinson. Weldon Kees. CoAP; NaP; NYBP; NYP; TwAmPo
Robinson at Home. Weldon Kees. CoAP; NYBP; TwAmPo
Robinson Crusoe. Charles Edward Carryl. *Fr.* Davy and the Goblin, *ch.* 11. AA; HBV-2; HBVY; TreFT
(Robinson Crusoe's Story.) BeLS; FiBHP; InMe; PoRA
Robinson Crusoe breaks a plate on his way out. The Revolution. Jack Gilbert. NPGG
Robinson Crusoe Returns to Amsterdam. Francis Jammes, *tr. fr. French by* Jethro Bithell. *Fr.* Amsterdam. FaPON
Robinson Crusde's Story. Charles Edward Carryl. *See* Robinson Crusoe.
Robyn, A/ Joly Robyn. Sir Thomas Wyatt. AAS
Robyn and Gandeleyn. *Unknown.* ESPB; OxBB
(Robin and Gandelein) OxBM
(Robin and Gandelyn.) EnSB
Robyn Hode and the Munke. *Unknown.* *See* Robin Hood and the Monk.
Roc, The. Richard Eberhart. CMoP
Roc, The. Edward Lowbury. AmMo
Rock, The, *sels.* T. S. Eliot.
"And now you live dispersed on ribbon roads." TiPo
"Eagle soars in the summit of heaven, The," *fr.* Chorus I. OBMV
"Endless cycle of idea and action, The." TRV
"I have known two worlds." OxBoCh
"If humility and purity be not in the heart." TiPo
"In the beginning God created the world. Waste and void," *fr.* Chorus VII. OxBoCh
"Men have left God not for other gods, they say, but for no god." TRV
"O Light Invisible, we praise Thee!" *fr.* Chorus X. ILwL; OxBoCh; TrPWD
There Shall Always Be the Church. TRV
What Life Have You. EBCP
"Where My Word is unspoken." TRV
"Word of the Lord came unto me saying, The," *fr.* Chorus III. TRV
(Chorus from "The Rock.") LiTB
"World turns and the world changes, The." TiPo
Rock, The. Mary Fabilli. AMV-81
Rock, The. W. S. Merwin. NYP
Rock, *sel.* Kathleen Raine.
"There is stone in me that knows stone." ImOP
Rock, The. Wallace Stevens. AP
Rock, The. *Unknown, tr. fr. Welsh by* Geoffrey Grigson. ChTr; GBL
Rock, a leaf, mud, even the grass, A. The Concealment: Ishi, the Last Wild Indian. William Stafford. NaP
Rock About My Saro Jane. *Unknown.* FSW
Rock and Hawk. Robinson Jeffers. MoVE; NoAM; NOBA; OxBA
Rock and precipice. Landscape. Octavio Paz, *tr. by* Charles Tomlinson. OBVE
Rock away, passenger, in the Third Class. *Unknown.* CenHV
Rock, Ball, Fiddle. *Unknown.* CH; OxBoLi
("He that lies at the stock.") OxNR
Rock, Be My Dream. MacKnight Black. PoSH
Rock Carving. Douglas Stewart. SeCePo
Rock Climbing. Jane Cooper. NMM
Rock Crumbles, The. Else Lasker-Schüler, *tr. fr. German by* Ralph Manheim. TrJP
(My People, *tr. by* Michael Hamburger.) WPOW
Rock foundation of the fort was dread, The. Blockhouse. Olga Kirsch, *tr. by* Jack Cope. PeSA
Rock grows brittle, The. My People. Else Lasker-Schüler, *tr. by* Michael Hamburger. WPOW
Rock Island Line, The. *Unknown.* AmFP; FSW
Rock Leader. Dave Barthgate. PoSH
Rock-like mud unfroze a little and rills, The. The Manor Farm. Edward Thomas. SeCeV
Rock-like the souls of men. Men Fade Like Rocks. Walter James Turner. OBMV
Rock-Lily. Roland Robinson. PoAu-2
Rock Me to Sleep. Elizabeth Akers Allen. AA; BLPA; BLPL; FaBoBe; FaFP; HBV-1; OBCA; TreF; WBLP
(Rock me to Sleep, Mother.) PaPo
Rock, moon, stream. Faces. Jack L. Anderson. LFAC
Rock 'n' Row Me Over. *Unknown.* FSW
Rock-O-La plays Country and Western, The. Writing on Napkins at the Sunshine Club, Macon, Georgia 1971. David Bottoms. TAT
Rock of Ages. Augustus Montague Toplady. BLRP; BLSo, *with music;* FaFP; FaPoR; FSW; HBV-2; NOCV; OxBoCh; TreF; WGRP
(Living and Dying Prayer for the Holiest Believer in the World, A.) NOEC
(Prayer, Living and Dying, A.) OBEC
Rock of Ages, let our song. Hanukkah Hymn. *Unknown.* TreFT
Rock of Cashel, The. Sir Aubrey De Vere. NBM
Rock of My Salvation. Mordecai, *tr. fr. Hebrew by* Solomon Solis-Cohen. TrJP
Rock of Rubies, The. Robert Herrick. *See* Rubies and Pearls.
Rock Painting. Carroll Arnett. VoR
Rock Painting. Jack Cope. PeSA
Rock Pilgrim. Herbert Palmer. OxBTC
Rock, Rock, Sleep, My Baby. Clyde Watson. NTCP
Rock That Doesn't Break, she calls, The. A Piece of Shrapnel. David Ray. NIP
Rock wrinkles, folds on the near. Monastery on Athos. Richmond Lattimore. EyDe
Rock-a My Soul. *Unknown.* FSW
"Rock-a-by, baby, up in the tree-top!" In the Tree-Top. Lucy Larcom. OBCA
Rock-a-by Lady, The. Eugene Field. HBVY; TiPo
Rockaby, lullaby, bees in the clover. Lullaby. Josiah Gilbert Holland. *Fr.* The Mistress of the Manse. AA; HBV-1
Rock-a-Bye Baby, *with music.* Effie I. Canning. FSN
Rock-a-bye [*or* Hush-a-bye] baby, on [*or* in] the tree top. Mother Goose. FSW; HBVY; OxNR; TiPo
Rock-a-bye, baby, thy cradle is green. Mother Goose. FaFP; HBV-1; HBVY; OxNR
Rocked in the Cradle of the Deep. Emma Hart Willard. AA; BLPL; FaBoBe; FaFP; HBV-1; MOS; PSoN, *with music;* TreF; WBLP; WGRP
Rocket in My Pocket, A. *Unknown.* *See* I've Got a Rocket.
Rockets bubble upward and explode, The. 14 July 1956. Laurence Lerner. PeSA
Rockferns. Norman Nicholson. MoBrPo
Rocking. A. R. Ammons. GP
Rocking Chair, The. A. M. Klein. CaP; HeIP; NoP; PeCV
Rockingchair. Robert Morgan. PPJ
Rocking Hymn, A. George Wither. *See* Hymn L: Rocking Hymn, A.
Rockland. Julia Randall. WPE
Rocks. Florence Parry Heide. NTCP
Rocks and Gravel. Alan Lomax *and* W. B. Richardson. FSW
Rocks flow and the mountain shapes flow, The. The Songs of the Birds. Edward Carpenter. WGRP
Rocks have been my pillow, baby. Homeless Blues. *Unknown.* BluL
Rocks jagged in the morning mist. The Point. John Montague. IPY
Rocky Acres. Robert Graves. LiTB; NoAM; UnPo
Rocky Island, The. *Unknown.* AmFP
Rocky Mountains, The. *Unknown.* AmFP
Rocky Road to Dublin, The. *Unknown.* FaBoBa
Rococo. John Payne. OBVV
Rococo. Swinburne. HBV-1; ViBoPo
Rod light and taper, thy tackle fine, The. How to Catch Trout. Thomas Barker. *Fr.* The Art of Angling. FaBoUs
Rod of Jesse, The. Bible, *O.T.* Isaiah, XI: 1-10. AWP
(And There Shall Come Forth, XI: 1-9.) TrJP
("And there shall come forth a rod out of the stemme of Jesse," XI: 1-11.) OBVE
Rod was but a harmless wand, The. The Virtues of Sid Hamet, the Magician's Rod. Swift. APAS
Roddy M'Corley. *Unknown.* FSW
Rodeo Days. S. Omar Barker. PoOW
Rodeo rider. For Carole. Diane Burns. TWSS
Roderick Dhu. Sir Walter Scott. *Fr.* The Lady of the Lake, V. OBRV
Rodin to Rilke. Emily Grosholz. AMV-80
Rodney's Glory. Owen Roe O'Sullivan. OnYI
Rodney's Ride. *Unknown.* PAH
Roe (and my joy to name) th'art now, to go. To William Roe. Ben Jonson. OAEL-1; OBS
Roebling, his life and mind reprieved enough. Raymond Henri. *Fr.* The Bridge from Brooklyn. EyDe
Roethke Plain. John Malcolm Brinnin. NoAM; TAP

Rogation Days. Kenneth Rexroth. NaP
Roger and Dolly. Henry Carey. CoMu; NOEC
("Young Roger came tapping at Dolly's window," *st.* 1, *sl. diff.*) OxNR
Roger and Me. Anne Le Dressay. AMV-81
Roger is a friend of mine. It was his idea. Arf, Said Sandy. Charles Stetler. PPJ
Roger the Dog. Ted Hughes. RHPC
Roger Williams. Hezekiah Butterworth. PAH
Rogero's Song. George Canning, George Ellis, *and* John Hookham Frere. *See* Song: "Whene'er with haggard eyes I view."
Rogue Pearunners. R. G. Everson. PeCV
Roisin Dubh. Aubrey Thomas De Vere. AnIV
Roisin Dubh. *Unknown, tr. fr. Late Middle Irish by* Eleanor Hull. OnYI
Rokeby, *sels.* Sir Walter Scott.
Allen-a-Dale, *fr.* III. EnRP
Brignall Banks, *fr.* III. EnRP; OBEV
(Edmund's Song.) PoRA
(Outlaw, The.) GTBS; GTBS-P
(Song: "O Brignall banks are wild and fair.") HBV-2; OAEP; OBRV
Man the Enemy of Man, *fr.* III. WBLP
Song: "Weary lot is thine, fair maid, A," *fr.* III. EnLoPo; OBNC; OBRV; ViBoPo
(Rover, The.) GTBS; GTBS-P
(Rover's Adieu, The.) HBV-1; OBEV
(Rover's Farewell, The.) NOBE
(Weary Lot Is Thine, A.) BSV; CH
Rokeby Venus, The. Robert Conquest. NoAM
Roland Furious, *sel.* John Stewart of Baldynnis.
Medoro's Inscription for a Cave. BSV
Roll back, you fabulous animal. Carnal Knowledge. Gwen Harwood. CBAP
Roll-Call. Nathaniel Graham Shepherd. AA; HBV-2; OHIP
(Calling the Roll.) OBCA
Roll Call: A Land of Old Folk and Children. Isaac J. Black. CNA
Roll de Ol' Chariot Along, *with music. Unknown.* BoAN-1
Roll forth, my song, like the rushing river. The Nameless One. James Clarence Mangan. BIrV; EnRP; GoBC; HBV-2; NBM; OBEV; OBVV; OnYI; OxBI
Roll in My Sweet Baby's Arms. *Unknown.* FSW
Roll, Jordan, Roll, *diff. versions. Unknown.* AA; AH, *with music*; BoAN-1; FSW
Roll, *Julia*, Roll, *with music. Unknown.* ShS
Roll of a chariot, The. *Unknown, tr. by* Joseph Dunn. *Fr.* The Combat of Ferdiad and Cuchulain. OnYI
Roll On, Sad World! Frederick Goddard Tuckerman. Sonnets, II, xvii. AP; TreFS
(Elegy in Six Sonnets.) QFR
Roll on the Ground. *Unknown.* AmFP; FSW
Roll on, thou ball, roll on! To the Terrestrial Globe. W. S. Gilbert. FaBoNo; HBV-2; PoPl; TrGrPo; WhC
Roll On, Thou Dark Blue Ocean. Byron. *See* To the Ocean ("There is a pleasure in the pathless woods").
Roll On, Thou Deep and Dark Blue Ocean. Byron. *See* Sea, The.
Roll on, thou deep and dark blue ocean—roll! To the Ocean [*or* Address to the Ocean *or* Apostrophe to the Ocean]. Byron. *Fr.* Childe Harold's Pilgrimage. EtS; FaPON; GN; TreFS; TrGrPo; WGRP
Roll on, ye stars! exult in youthful prime. Immortal Nature. Erasmus Darwin. *Fr.* The Botanic Garden. OBEC
Roll Out, O Song. Frank Sewall. AA
Roll out ye drums, peal organs' loudest thunder. Elegy on Albert Edward the Peacemaker. *Unknown.* CoMu
Roll Over. *Unknown.* FSW
Roll the Chariot. *Unknown. See* We'll Roll the Golden Chariot Along.
Roll the Cotton Down, *diff. versions. Unknown.* AmFP; ShS, 3 *vers.*
Roll the Union On. Claude Williams *and* Lee Hays. FSW
Rolled over on Europe: the sharp dew frozen to stars. Stephen Spender. CMoP
Rolled umbrella on my wrist, The. Waterloo Bridge. Christopher Middleton. *Fr.* Herman Moon's Hourbook. NePoEA-2
Roller perched upon the wire, The. Driving Cattle to Casas Buenas. Roy Campbell. PeSA
Roller Skates. John Farrar. FaPON
Rollicking Bill the Sailor. *Unknown.* AmSS
Rollicking Mastodon, The. Arthur Macy. NA
Rolling along through Ohio. Ohio. John Updike. AMV-80
Rolling and tossing out sparkles like roses. Night Landscape. Joan Aiken. DuDa
Rolling clouds of greasy smoke. The Forest Fire. Arthur W. Monroe. BPAW; PoOW
Rolling English Road, The. G. K. Chesterton. EvOK; FaBoCh; HBMV; NOBE; NOBL; OBEV; OBMV; OxBTC; SeCeV
Rolling from St. Patrick's, The. Burial of An Irish President. Austin Clarke. BIrV
Rolling Home. Charles Mackay. AmSS, *with music*; FSW; ShS, 2 *vers., with music*
Rolling John, *sel.* A. J. Wood.
"Rolling John and night together." PoAu-2
Rolling Log Blues. *Unknown.* BluL
Rolling the Lawn. William Empson. MoBrPo
Rolling Thunder. Phyllis Wolf. STE
Rolly Trudum. *Unknown.* AmFP
(Lolly-Too-Dum.) FSW; OuSiCo, *with music*
Roly! poly! pudding and pie! The Tale of a Tart. Frederick E. Weatherley. SUS
Rom. Cap. 8 Ver. 19. Henry Vaughan. AnAnS-1
("And do they so? have they a Sense.") MeLP; OBS
Roma. Rutilius, *tr. fr. Latin by* Ezra Pound. CTC
Roma Aeterna. Adelaide Crapsey. QFR
Roman and Jew upon one level lie. In Galilee. Mary Frances Butts. AA
Roman Calendar, The. Benjamin Hall Kennedy. FaBoUs
Roman Earl, The. *Unknown, tr. fr. Irish by* Douglas Hyde. OBVE
Roman Fountain. Louise Bogan. NoP; SBG; WPOW
Roman had [*or* hired] an, A/artist, a freedman. The Jerboa. Marianne Moore. CMOP; FYAP; MoPo
Roman History in Rhyme, *sel.* Edward B. Goodwin.
"Aeneas built, in days of yore." FaBoUs
Roman host descended from the height, A. Mater Amabilis. Aubrey Thomas De Vere. ISi
Roman Mirror, A. Sir James Rennell Rodd. OBVV
Roman Numerals. *Unknown.* FaBoUs
("X shall stand for playmates ten.") OxNR
Roman Officer Writes, A. C. M. Doughty. *Fr.* The Dawn in Britain. FaBoTw
Roman Presents. Martial, *tr. fr. Latin by* James Michie. OBCP
Roman Road, The. Thomas Hardy. AWP; BrPo; FaBoPP; GoJo; MoBrPo; NOBE
Roman Roman, A. Crescenzo del Monte, *tr. fr. Judeo-Romanesque by* Barbara Garvin. VWA
Roman soldiers come ridin' at full speed. The Man of Calvary. "Sin-Killer" Griffin. AmFP; OuSiCo
Roman Stage, The. Lionel Johnson. BrPo
Roman Thank-You Letter, A. Martial, *tr. fr. Latin by* James Michie. OBCP
Roman threw us a road, a road, The. History. G. K. Chesterton. *Fr.* Songs of Education. OBSV
Roman Virgil [*or* Vergil], thou that singest Ilion's lofty temples robed in fire. To Virgil [*or* Vergil]. Tennyson. AWP; ChTr; GTBS-P; NoP; OAEL-2; PoEL-5; WHA
Roman Wall Blues. W. H. Auden. DTC
Roman Women, *sel.* Thomas Edward Brown.
"O Englishwoman on the Pincian." OBNC
Romance. W. E. Henley. In Hospital, XXI. BrPo; PAH
Romance, A. Chester Kallman. PoA
Romance. Andrew Lang. HBV-1
Romance. Poe. AmPP; AP; FaBoEn; NePA; OxBA
(Introduction: "Romance, who loves to nod and sing.") NOBA
Romance. Robert Louis Stevenson. BLPL; BSV; GoTS; HBV-1; MoBrPo; OBEV; OBVV; PoSC; TrGrPo
("I will make you brooches and toys for your delight.") BrPo; EBVV
(My Valentine.) FaPON; GrPl; OFD; SiSoSe
Romance. W. J. Turner. CH; GoJo; HBMV; HBVY; MoBrPo; NOBE; OBMV; PoRA; TrGrPo; WHA
Romance VIII. St. John of the Cross, *tr. fr. Spanish by* E. Allison Peers. ISi
Romance of the Range. Robert V. Carr. PoOW
Romance [*or* Romaunt] of the Rose, The, *sels.* Guillaume de Lorris *and* Jean de Meun, *tr. fr. French.*
Dream of the Romaunt of the Rose, The, *tr. by* Chaucer. LoBV
Garden of Amour, The, *tr. by* Chaucer. PoEL-1
"Short space my feet had traversed ere," *tr. by* F. S. Ellis. OAEL-1
"There is no place in paradise." PBBP
Romance of the Swan's Nest. Elizabeth Barrett Browning. GN
Romance, who loves to nod and sing. Romance [*or* Introduction]. Poe. AmPP; AP; FaBoEn; NePA; NOBA; OxBA
Romancer, far more coy than that coy sex. Hawthorne. Amos Bronson Alcott. AA
Romancing Poet, The. Helen Hamilton. SUMH
Romans, *sels.* Bible, *N.T.*
Duties of Man, The, XII: 3-21. TreF
To Him Be Glory, XII: 33-36. TRV
Romans Angry about the Inner World. Robert Bly. NoAM; NOBA; PPoe
Romans, countrymen, and lovers! Brutus Explains Why He Murdered Caesar. Shakespeare. Julius Caesar, *fr.* III, ii. TreFT
Romans first with Julius Caesar came, The. The English Race. Daniel Defoe. *Fr.* The True-born Englishman. OBEC

Romans in England awhile did sway, The. The Chapter of Kings. John Collins. FaBoUs
Romans, rheumatic, gouty, came. La Condition Botanique. Anthony Hecht. MP; NePoEA; NoAM
Romantic, The. Colin Ellis. POL
Romantic. George Garrett. HoPM
Romantic to Burlesque. Byron. *Fr.* Don Juan, IV. FiP
("Nothing so difficult as a beginning.") EnRP; OAEL-2
Romany Gold. Amelia Josephine Burr. HBMV
Romaunt of the Rose, The. Guillaume de Lorris *and* Jean de Meun. *See* Romance of the Rose.
Rome. Arthur Hugh Clough. *Fr.* Amours de Voyage, Canto I. FaBoPP
Rome. J. V. Cunningham, *after the Latin of* Janus Vitalis Panormitanus. OBVE
Rome. Joachim du Bellay, *tr. fr. French by* Ezra Pound. AWP
Rome. Thomas Hardy. MoAB; VLP
Rome. Milton. *Fr.* Paradise Regained, IV. OBS
Rome, by Metella's Tomb. Byron. *Fr.* Childe Harold's Pilgrimage, IV. FaBoPP
Rome, Conqueror, Conquered. Joshua Sylvester. FaBoEE
Rome did its worst; thorns platted for his brow. Praetorium Scene: Good Friday. Elinor Lennen. PGD
Rome disappoints me much,—St. Peter's, perhaps, in especial. Rome. Arthur Hugh Clough. *Fr.* Amours de Voyage, Canto I. FaBoPP
Rome disappoints me still; but I shrink and adapt myself to it. Arthur Hugh Clough. *Fr.* Amours de Voyage, Canto I, ii. EBVV
Rome has its fountains. This. Nichols Fountain. Virginia Scott Miner. FAZ
Rome Remember. Sidney Keyes. MoAB
Romeo and Juliet. H. Phelps Putnam. ErPo
Romeo and Juliet. Fred Newton Scott. InMe
Romeo and Juliet, *sels.* Shakespeare.
"But, soft! What light through yonder window breaks?" *fr.* II, ii. MOON
"Even or odd, of all days in the year," *fr.* I, iii. SCV
Friar Laurence's Cell, *fr.* II, vi. GoBC
Frost on the Flower, *fr.* IV, v. FaBoRV
"Gallop apace, you fiery-footed steeds," *fr.* III, ii. GBL
"He jests at scars that never felt a wound," *fr.* II, i. MaSP; PAI; TreF
(He Jests at Scars.) LiTB
(Living Juliet, The.) TrGrPo
"If I profane with my unworthiest hand," *fr.* I, v. BiP; SoSe
Juliet's Yearning, *fr.* III, ii. TreFS
"Lady, by yonder blessed moon I swear," *fr.* II, ii. MOON
Mercutio's Queen Mab Speech, *fr.* I, iv. LiTB; TreF
(Mercutio Describes Queen Mab.) TrGrPo
("O, then I see Queen Mab hath been with you.") WSC
(Queen Mab.) FiP; FaPON
Music's Silver Sound, *fr.* IV, v. GN
"O Romeo, Romeo! wherefore art thou Romeo?" *fr.* II, ii. WHA
Romeo and Juliet in the Orchard, *fr.* III, v. TreFT
Romeo's Last Words, *fr.* V, iii. FiP
(Everlasting Rest.) WHA
("For here lies Juliet, and her beauty makes.") FaFP
(Here Lies Juliet.) TreFS
("How oft when men are at the point of death.") DL
(Thus with a Kiss I Die.) TrGrPo
"Rome's guns are spiked; and they'll stay so." Of Rome. Herman Melville. *Fr.* Clarel. OxBA
Romira, stay. The Call. John Hall. FaBoEn; MeLP; MePo; OBS; ViBoPo
Romish Lady, The, *with music.* *Unknown.* OuSiCo
Romney, The. Harriet Monroe. HBMV
Romp. Dave Etter. WeW
Romping. John Ciardi. CTBA; NCSH
Ron Endaway, shepherd of the hills at Malvern, looked very sheepish. Come Live with Me. Naomi Marks. BXAP
Ron Mason. Hone Tuwhare. OCNZ
Ronald Wyn. Robert Bagg. MP; TwAmPo; TwCP
Ronan Robe Series, The. Jaune Quick-To-See-Smith. TWSS
Ronas Hill. Hamish Brown. PoSH
Rondeau: "By two black eyes my heart was won." *Unknown.* FaBoCo
Rondeau: "Help me to seek, for I lost it there." Sir Thomas Wyatt. *See* Help Me to Seek.
Rondeau: "Homage to change that scatters the poppy seed." Ronald Bottrall. MoVE
Rondeau: "Jenny kissed me when we met." Leigh Hunt. *See* Jenny Kiss'd Me.
Rondeau: "Lord, I'm done for: now Margot." William Jay Smith. FiBHP
Rondeau: "What no, perdie [*or* perdy]! ye may be sure!" Sir Thomas Wyatt. AAS; LoBV; OBSC
(No! Indeed.) MeEL
(What No, Perdy.) PoEL-1
Rondeau, The: "You bid me try, Blue Eyes, to write." Austin Dobson, *after the French of* Vincent Voiture. HBV-2
Rondeau for You. Mário de Andrade, *tr. fr. Portuguese by* John Nist. TTY
Rondeau Humbly Inscribed to the Right Hon. William Eden, Minister Plenipotentiary of Commercial Affairs at the Court of Versailles. *At. to* George Ellis. OBEC
Rondeau of Remorse, A. Burges Johnson. HBMV
Rondeau Redoublé. John Payne. HBV-1
Rondel: Autumn. Matt Field. AMV-80
Rondel: "Behold the works of William Morris." *Unknown.* BXAP; Par
Rondel: Beside the Idle Summer Sea. W. E. Henley. OBNC
Rondel: "Good-by, the tears are in my eyes." Villon, *tr. fr. French by* Andrew Lang. AWP
Rondel: "Kissing her hair, I sat against her feet." Swinburne. BLPL; FaBoBe; HBV-1; ViBoPo
Rondel: "Love, love, what wilt thou with this heart of mine?" Jean Froissart, *tr. by* Longfellow. AWP
Rondel: "Now that I am fifty-six." Muriel Rukeyser. FF
Rondel: "Strengthen, my Love, this castle of my heart." Charles d'Orléans, *tr. fr. French by* Andrew Lang. AWP
Rondel: "These many years since we began to be." Swinburne. HBV-1
Rondel for Middle Age. Louise Townsend Nicholl. NePoAm
Rondel for September. Karle Wilson Baker. HBMV
Rondel of Love [*or* Luve], A. Alexander Scott. BoLoP; BSV; OBEV; OxBS
Rondel of Merciless Beauty, A. Chaucer. *See* Merciles Beaute.
Rondelay: "Chloe found Amyntas lying." Dryden. CavP; ViBoPo
(Kiss Me, Dear.) UnTE
Rondo: "Did I love thee? I only did desire." George Moore. UnTE
Ronsard. Miriam Allen deFord. HBMV
Ronsard to His Mistress. Thackeray. HBV-1
Röntgen Photograph. Elisabeth Eybers, *tr. fr. Afrikaans by* Jack Cope, Uys Krige, *and* Ruth Miller. PeSA
Roof, The. Gelett Burgess. *See* Lazy Roof, The.
Roof Garden, The. Howard Moss. MAT; NYP
Roof it has a lazy time, The. The Lazy Roof [*or* The Roof]. Gelett Burgess. NA; TreFT
Roof of midnight, hushed and high, The. Nocturnal. Os Marron. NeBP
Roof of the World, The. Michael Dennis Browne. AmPA
Roofers roof from the bottom up, The. Technique. Philip Pierson. AMV-80
Roofs. Joyce Kilmer. BLPL; PoLF
Roofs are shining from the rain, The. April. Sara Teasdale. FaPON; PDV; PoSC;SoPo; TiPo; YeAr
Roofs of cars were crusted thick with frost, The. Citizen. Chris Wallace-Crabbe. CBAP
Roofs over the shops, The. Christmas Eve. Patricia Beer. OBCP
Rooftop. Willis Barnstone. FAZ
Rooftop, The. Thom Gunn. NoP
Rooftop Winter. Dwayne Thorpe. AMV-80
Roof-tops, roof-tops, what do you cover? City Roofs. Charles Hanson Towne. BLPA
Roofwalker, The. Adrienne Rich. CoAP; PPP
Rook he sells feathers, yet he still doth cry. Upon Rook: Epigram. Robert Herrick. CaPo
Rookery. Nora Dauenhauer. TWSS
Rookery at Sunrise, The. "Fiona Macleod." *Fr.* Transcripts from Nature. FM
Rookhope Ryde ("Rookhope stands in a pleasant place"). *Unknown.* ESPB
Rooks, The. Jane Euphemia Browne. OxBChV
Rooks. Charles Hamilton Sorley. HBMV; MoBrPo
Rooks, The. *Unknown.* GBP
("On the first of March.") OxNR
Rooks above the convent walls, The. The Convent. "Seumas O'Sullivan." POL
Rooks are building on the trees, The. The Rooks. Jane Euphemia Browne. OxBChV
Rook's nest do rock on the tree-top, The. Lullaby. William Barnes. VLP
Room, The. Conrad Aiken. AP; LiTM; MoAmPo; NePA; NOBA
Room, The. C. Day Lewis. PoCh
Room. Robert Finch. MoCV
Room, The. De Leon Harrison. PoBA
Room, The. Elizabeth Jennings. NePoEA-2
Room. Shirley Kaufman. NMM
Room, The. W. S. Merwin. NOBA
Room, The. Vladimir Nabokov. NYBP
Room, The. Gregory Orr. GeTw
Room, The. William Soutar. EBEV
Room. Ruth Stone. BoWoP
Room, The. Francis Webb. *Fr.* Leichhardt in Theatre. PoAu-2
Room a dying poet took, The. The Room. Vladimir Nabokov. NYBP
Room above the Square, The. Stephen Spender. ChMP; NOBE
Room above the White Rose, The. Joseph Stroud. NPGG

Room after room/ I hunt the house through. Love in a Life. Robert Browning. HBV-1; InvP; NOBE; OAEP; OBNC; OBVV
Room after room, table after table. Public Library. Candace T. Stevenson. GoYe
Room for a Jovial Tinker: Old Brass to Mend. *Unknown.* CoMu; OxBB
(Jovial Tinker, The.) UnTE
Room for a Soldier! lay him in the clover. Dirge for One Who Fell in Battle [*or* Dirge]. Thomas William Parsons. AA; GN; HBV-2; PAH
Room for all else but love. Nor House nor Heart. Elinor Lennen. PGD
Room for Jesus. Barbara H. Staples. STF
"Room for the leper! Room!" and as he came. The Leper. Nathaniel P. Willis. WGRP
Room I Once Knew, A. Henry Birnbaum. GoYe
Room in the Past, A. Ted Kooser. Str
Room in the Villa, A. William Jay Smith. NYBP
Room is already white, The. Trim it in blue. Life in the City: In Memoriam Edward Gibbon. Philip Whalen. PoM
Room is full of gold, The. Jason. Anthony Hecht. CoPo; DiL
Room is red, The. Self-Portrait with Hand Microscope. Lucille Day. SUW
Room must be warmer than, The. How the Invalids Make Love. Susan Feldman. AmPA
Room of Return. Galway Kinnell. NYP
Room on a Garden, A. Wallace Stevens. NoP
Room on room, we poke debris for fun. 1614 Boren. Richard Hugo. LCAP
Room over the Hudson. Room of Return. Galway Kinnell. NYP
Room Poems. Eli Bachar, *tr. fr. Hebrew by* Jeremy Garber. VWA
Room, room for a blade of the town. The Bully [*or* Song]. *At. to* Earl of Rochester *and to* Thomas D'urfey. InvP; SeCePo
Room! room! [*or* Roome, roome,] make room for the bouncing belly [*or* bellie]. Hymn to Comus [*or* Hymn to the Belly]. Ben Jonson. *Fr.* Pleasure Reconciled to Virtue. AnAnS-2; ElL; OAEL-1; OAEP; SeCePo
ROOM! room to turn around in, to breathe and be free. Kit Carson's Ride. Joaquin Miller. BPAW; TreFS
Room Service. John W. Moser. FAZ
Room was a, The/ red glow. We Dance like Ella Riffs. Carolyn M. Rodgers. CNA; PoBA
Room was divided by a curtain, The. The Tailor's Wedding. Louis Simpson. NNaP
Room was suddenly rich and the great bay-window was, The. Snow. Louis MacNeice. BiP; CIP; CMoP; FaBoMo; FBL; LiTM; NoAM; NOBE; OxBTC
Room where someone, A. Avenue Y. Anita Barrows. VWA
Room 000. William Stafford. GLGT
Roome, roome, make roome for the bouncing bellie. *See* Room! room! . . .
Rooming House. Ted Kooser. POL
Rooms. Charlotte Mew. PBWP
Room's Width, The. Elizabeth Stuart Phelps Ward. AA
Roosevelt and the *Antinoe,* The, *sel.* E. J. Pratt.
Burial at Sea. CaP
Roosevelt Considers Catfish Stew. R. T. Smith. WOLT
Roosevelt's in the White House, doing his best. The White House Blues. *Unknown.* OuSiCo
Roosters. Elizabeth Bishop. CrMA; LiTM; NePA
Roosters. Elizabeth J. Coatsworth. SO
Roosters Will Crow, The. Cecília Meireles, *tr. fr. Portuguese by* John Nist *and* Yolanda Leite. PBWP
Root. Miklós Radnóti, *tr. fr. Hungarian by* Steven Polgar, Stephen Berg *and* S. J. Marks. VWA
Root becomes him, the road ruts, The. Self-Portrait in 2035. Charles Wright. LCAP
Root Canal, The. Marge Piercy. DFF; HoAn
Root Cellar. Theodore Roethke. AmPP; BoNaP; HeIP; NoP; PAI; PPP
Root Hog or Die, *parody.* Floyd B. Small. PoOW
Root Hog or Die. *Unknown.* AmFP; FSW
Roots. Louis Ginsberg. TrJP
Roots. Seymour Mayne. NOBC
Roots and Branches. Robert Duncan. VGW
Roots and Leaves Themselves Alone. Walt Whitman. NePA
Roots around your soul and eyes, The. Sweating It Out on Winding Stair Mountain. Jim Barnes. CDW
Roots of mankind are tangled in my hair, The. Epitaph. Wendy Rose. CDW
Roots of Revolution in the Vegetable Kingdom, The. Constance Urdang. GP
Rope, The. Tania Van Zyl. PeSA
Rope and Drum. Robert Currie. Str
Rope for Harry Fat, A. James K. Baxter. MoBS
Ropero, so sad and so forlorn. El Ropero. Antonio di Montorio. TrJP
Rope's End. Peter F. Neumeyer. WOLT
Ropewalk, The. Longfellow. AP
Ropin' of yearlin's and tyin' 'em down. Rodeo Days. S. Omar Barker. PoOW
Rorate Coeli [*or* Celi] Desuper. William Dunbar. BSV; SBVL
(On the Nativity of Christ.) OBEV; OxBoCh
Rorschach. Laura Fargas. SUW
Rory and Liam are dead and gone. In Memoriam. Padraig de Brun. WTO
Rory of the Hill. Charles Joseph Kickham. OnYI
Rory O'More; or, Good Omens. Samuel Lover. HBV-1
Rosa ("Rosa, let us be dancing, dancing, dancing"), *with music. Unknown, tr. fr. Dutch.* TrAS
Rosa Mystica. Gerard Manley Hopkins. ACP; GoBC
Rosa Mystica. *Unknown.* GoBC; ISi
(Rose That Bore Jesu, The.) OxBM
(Two Carols to Our Lady.) ACP
Rosa Nascosa. Maurice Hewlett. OBVV
Rosa Rosarum. Agnes Mary Frances Robinson. HBMV
Rosabelle. Sir Walter Scott. *Fr.* The Lay of the Last Minstrel. BeLS; BSV; GTBS; GTBS-P; HBV-2
(Harold's Song: Rosabelle.) EnRP
Rosader's Sonnet. Thomas Lodge. *Fr.* Rosalynde; or, Euphues' Golden Legacy. OBSC
Rosalie. Washington Allston. AA
Rosalie, the Prairie Flower, *with music.* George Frederick Root. BLSo
Rosalind, in a negligee. Early Unfinished Sketch. Austin Clarke. ErPo
Rosalind; or, Euphues' Golden Legacy. Thomas Lodge. *See* Rosalynde; or, Euphues' Golden Legacy.
Rosalind's Scroll. Elizabeth Barrett Browning. *Fr.* The Poet's Vow. HBV-1
Rosalynde; or Euphues' Golden Legacy, *sels.* Thomas Lodge.
Coridon's Song. UnTE
Fancy, A. ElL; LoBV; OBSC
(Lover's Protestation, A.) GoBC
(Love's Protestation.) ACP
Montanus' Sonnet. PoEL-2
Rosader's Sonnet. OBSC
Rosalind's [*or* Rosalynd's] Madrigal[1]. ElL; EnRePo; FaBoEn; GoBC; HBV-1; InvP; LoBV; NOBE; NoP; OBEV; OBSC; PoEL-2; SeCePo; TrGrPo; UnTE; ViBoPo
Rosaline. GoBC; GTBS; GTBS-P; LiTB; OBEV; UnTE
(Rosalind [*or* Rosalynde].) ElL; TrGrPo
(Rosalind's Description.) OBSC
Rosamond's Appeal. Samuel Daniel. *Fr.* The Complaint of Rosamond. OBSC
Rosarie, The. Robert Herrick. InMe
Rosary, The, *abr.* Sister Maura. ISi
Rosary, The. Robert Cameron Rogers. AA; BLSo, *with music*; FaBoBe; FSN, *with music*; HBV-1; TreF; WBLP
Rosary of My Tears, The. Abram J. Ryan. HBV-2
Rosciad, The, *sel.* Charles Churchill.
Critical Fribble, A. OBEC
(Character of a Critic.) NOEC
(Criticaster, A.) FaBoEn
Rose, A. Arlo Bates. HBV-1
Rose, The. William Browne. *Fr.* Visions. CH; HBV-1; OBEV
("Rose, as fair as ever saw the North, A.") ViBoPo
Rose, The. Robert Creeley. AP
Rose, A. Sir Richard Fanshawe, *after the Spanish of* Luis de Góngora. *Fr.* Il Pastor Fido. CavP; HBV-1; OBEV; OBS; PoEL-2; SeCePo
(Rose of Life, The.) AWP
Rose, The. Goethe, *tr. fr. German by* James Clarence Mangan. AWP
Rose, The. William Hammond. OBS
Rose, The. George Herbert. LiTB; PoEL-2
Rose, The. Thomas Howell. ElL; OBSC
Rose, The. Thomas Lodge. *Fr.* The Life and Death of William Longbeard. OBSC
(Fancy, A.) ElL
Rose, The. Richard Lovelace. *See* To Lucasta: The Rose.
Rose. Kathleen Raine. WPE
Rose, The. Theodore Roethke. BiP; InPS; NOBA; NYBP; PPoe
Rose, The. Pierre de Ronsard, *tr. fr. French by* Andrew Lang. AWP
Rose, The. G. A. Studdert-Kennedy. EBCP
Rose, The. William Carlos Williams. NOBA
Rose, The/ was not searching for the sunrise. Casida of the Rose. Federico García Lorca, *tr. by* Robert Bly. NU
Rose aloft in sunny air, The. Rose and Root. John James Piatt. AA
Rose and God, The. Charles Wharton Stork. HBMV
Rose and grape, pear and bean. *Unknown, tr. fr. Spanish by* Willis Barnstone. BoWoP
Rose and Root. John James Piatt. AA
Rose and the Gauntlet, The. John Wilson. BeLS

Rose and the lily, the moon and the dove, The. Die Rose, die Lilie, die Taube, die Sonne. Heine, *tr. by* Richard Garnett. AWP
Rose and the Thorn, The. Paul Hamilton Hayne. AA; FaBoBe; HBV-1
Rose and the Wind, The. Philip Bourke Marston. OBVV
Rose-apple is in fruit, The. Show Me the Way. *Unknown, tr. by* U Win Pe. PBWP
Rose, as fair as ever saw the North, A. The Rose. William Browne. *Fr.* Visions. CH; HBV-1; OBEV; ViBoPo
Rose Aylmer. Walter Savage Landor. AWP; BoLoP; CABA; CH; ELP; EnRP; FaBoEn; FaFP; HAP; HBV-1; HeIP; HoPM; LiTB; LO; LoBV; NOBE; NoP; OAEP; OBEV; OBNC; OBRV; OBVV; PoEL-4; RoGo; SeCeV; TEP; TreFS; TrGrPo; UnPo; WeW; WHA
("Ah, what avails the sceptred race!") EnLoPo; ViBoPo
Rose Bay Willow Herb. Judy Ray. AMV-81; FAZ
Rose-Bud. *See* Rosebud.
Rose, but one, none other rose had I, A. Tennyson. *Fr.* Idylls of the King: Pelleas and Ettarre. PoEL-5
Rose-cheeked [*or* cheekt] Laura, Come. Thomas Campion. EnLoPo; EnRePo; InPK; InPS; InvP; LoBV; NoP; OAEL-1; OAEP; PoEL-2; SeCeV; TrGrPo; ViBoPo
(Laura.) ElL; NOBE; OBEV; OBSC; SeCePo; UnS
("Rose-cheekt Lawra, come.") AAS
Rose Connoley. *Unknown.* AmFP
Rose, die Lilie, die Taube, die Sonne, Die. Heine, *tr. fr. German by* Richard Garnett. AWP
(Love's Résumé, *tr. by* "J. F. C.") TrJP
(Rose, the Lily, the Sun and the Dove, The, *tr. by* P. G. L. Webb.) NAWM-2
Rose fades, The. Poem. William Carlos Williams. NIP
Rose Family, The. Robert Frost. NIP; OBAL; OBCA; SoSe
Rose for a young head, A. The Watcher. James Stephens. HBV-1; MoBrPo; OBEV; OBVV
Rose, harsh rose. Sea Rose. Hilda Doolittle ("H. D."). FaBoMo; NoAM; NoP
Rose in October, A. James Whitcomb Riley. OBAL
Rose in the Afternoon. Jenny Joseph. BrRo
Rose in the breast. On Waking. Alida Carey Gulick. GoYe
Rose in the Garden. *Unknown.* AmFP
Rose in the garden slipp'd her bud, The. A Fancy from Fontenelle. Austin Dobson. HBV-2; OBVV
"Rose is a mystery, The"—where is it found? Rosa Mystica. Gerard Manley Hopkins. ACP; GoBC
Rose is a rose, The. The Rose Family. Robert Frost. NIP; OBAL; OBCA; SoSe
Rose Is a Royal Lady, The. Charles G. Blanden. HBMV
Rose is fairest when 'tis budding new, The. Sir Walter Scott. *Fr.* The Lady of the Lake. ViBoPo
Rose is not the rose unless thou see, The. Hafiz, *tr. by* Richard Le Gallienne. Odes, III. AWP
Rose is red, the grass is green, The. *Unknown.* OxNR
Rose is red, the rose is white, The. *Unknown.* OxNR
Rose is red, the violet's blue, The. *Unknown.* OxNR
"Rose, it is a royal flower, The." The Peace of the Roses. Thomas Philipps. ACP
Rose kissed me to-day. A Kiss. Austin Dobson. *Fr.* Rose Leaves. CenHV; HBV-1
Rose-Leaves. Henry Austin Dobson. CenHV
Sels.
Kiss, A. HBV-1
Urceus Exit. HBV-1; OBEV
(Triolet.) PoPle
Rose o' the World, she came to my bed. The Dark Man. Nora Hopper. HBV-1
Rose of Eden, The. Susan K. Phillips. BeLS
Rose of England, The. *Unknown.* ESPB
Rose of Life, The. Sir Richard Fanshawe. *See* Rose, A.
Rose of May, The. Mary Howitt. HBV-1
Rose of Peace, The. W. B. Yeats. OBVV
Rose of Sharon, The/ I lost in the tortured night. For the New Union Dead in Alabama. Edward Dorn. PoM
Rose of Stars, The. George Edward Woodberry. Wild Eden, IX. AA; HBV-1
Rose of that Garland! fairest and sweetest. To the Most Beautiful Lady, the Lady Bridget Manners. Barnabe Barnes. EnLoPo
Rose of the World, The. John Masefield. PoRA
Rose of the World, The. Coventry Patmore. The Angel in the House, I, iv, 1. HBV-1
Rose of the World, The. W. B. Yeats. BrPo; CMoP; FaBoEn; HBV-1; MoAB; MoBrPo; OBVV
Rose of Tralee, The. *At. to* William Pembroke Mulchinock, *also at. to* C. Mordaunt Spencer. FSW; OnYI; TreFT
Rose, on this terrace fifty years ago. The Roses on the Terrace. Tennyson. VLP
Rose-red, russet-brown. A Letter to Elsa. Grace Hazard Conkling. HBMV; HBVY
Rose Red to Snow White. Joan Colby. DFT
Rose Red's hair is brown as fur. An Embroidery. Denise Levertov. DFT; NMM; NU
Rose Still Grows beyond the Wall, The. A. L. Frink. BLPA
Rose That Bore Jesu, The. *Unknown. See* Rosa Mystica.
Rose, the Lily, the Sun and the Dove, The. Heine. *See* Rose, die Lilie, die Taube, die Sonne, Die.
Rose the Red and White Lily. *Unknown.* ESPB; OxBB, *with music*
Rose to the Living, A. Nixon Waterman. HBV-1
Rose to the roseburst break of day. The Cliff Rose. Ernest Fewster. CaP
Rose Tree, The. W. B. Yeats. CMoP; ELP; OBMV
Rose upon the wall, The. The Canticle of the Rose. Edith Sitwell. NoAM
Rose was sick and smiling died, The. The Funeral[l] Rites of the Rose. Robert Herrick. AnAnS-2; CABA; CaPo; OBEV
Rose, when I remember you. To Rose. Sara Teasdale. HBV-1
Rose when shaken fragrance shed around, The. Inscription on an Ancient Bell. *Unknown, tr. by* Fr. Bridgett. ISi
Rose Will Fade, A. Dora Sigerson Shorter. HBV-1
Roseberry to his lady says. Suppertime [*or* Supper Is Na Ready]. Burns. GBP; UnTE
Rosebud. Jon Anderson. MAYP
Rose-Bud, The. William Broome. LoBV; OBEC; OBEV
Rosebud Morales, my friend. Pentecost. Ai. GeTw; LTB
Rosebush and the Trinity, The. Alfred Barrett. GoBC
Rose-Marie of the Angels. Adelaide Crapsey. HBV-1
Rosemary Lane. *Unknown.* OBET
Rosemary, Rosemary, let down your hair. A Nonsense Song. Stephen Vincent Benét. OBAL
Rosemary Spray, The. Luis de Góngora, *tr. fr. Spanish by* E. Churton. AWP
Roses. Thomas Campion. *Fr.* Lord Hay's Mask. OBSC
Roses. *At. to* Thomas Phillips. *See* I Love a Flower.
Roses. Pierre de Ronsard, *tr. fr. French by* Andrew Lang. AWP
Roses. Thomas Stanley, *after the Greek of* Anacreon. AWP
Roses and butterflies snared on a fan. A Painted Fan. Louise Chandler Moulton. AA
Roses and pinks will be strewn where you go. Song. Sir William Davenant. *Fr.* The Unfortunate Lovers. ViBoPo
Roses and Revolutions. Dudley Randall. BPo; CNA; ConAP; NIP; NoAM; PoBA; TAP
Roses are beauty, but I never see. John Masefield. *Fr.* Sonnets. HBV-2
Roses are red. Mother Goose. OxNR
Roses are red, diddle diddle, lavender's blue. The Lady's Song in Leap Year. *Unknown.* GBP
Roses at first were white. How Roses Came Red. Robert Herrick. CaPo; CavP; SoSe
Rose's crimson stain, A. Roses of Memory. A. C. Gordon. AA
Rose's Cup, The. Frank Dempster Sherman. AA
Roses Gone Wild. John Taylor. AMV-80; FAZ
Roses have been his bed so long that he. Jeremiah. Witter Bynner. CrMA
Roses in breathing forth their scent. Celia Singing. Thomas Stanley. AnAnS-2
Roses in December. G. A. Studdert-Kennedy. BLPA
Roses in my garden, The. Ballad. Maurice Baring. HBV-1
Roses (Love's delight) let's join. Roses. Thomas Stanley. AWP
Roses of Memory. A. C. Gordon. AA
Roses of Queens, The. Claire Nicholas White. NYP
Roses of Sa'adi, The. Marceline Desbordes-Valmore, *tr. fr. French.* BoWoP, *tr. by* Barbara Howes; WPOW, *tr. by* Deirdre Lashgari
Roses of yesteryear, The. At Twilight. Peyton Van Rensselaer. AA
Roses on the Breakfast Table. D. H. Lawrence. BrPo
Roses on the Terrace, The. Tennyson. VLP
Roses Only. Marianne Moore. LiTM
Roses Red. Arno Holz, *tr. fr. German by* Jethro Bithell. AWP
Roses red upon my neighbor's vine, The. My Neighbor's Roses. Abraham L. Gruber. BLPA
Roses, Revisited, in a Paradoxical Autumn. J. W. Cullum. AMV-81
Roses, rose-red and white, and green. Alleluya. Rubén Darío, *tr. by* Lysander Kemp. TTY
Rose's Scent, The. *Unknown. See* All Night by the Rose.
Roses, Their Sharp Spines. Fletcher *and* Shakespeare. *See* Bridal Song, A.
Roses with the scent bred out. In Lieu. Louis MacNeice. CMoP
Rosewood Casket. *Unknown.* FSW
Rosh Pina. Dovid Knut, *tr. fr. Russian by* Daniel Weissbort. VWA
Rosie-fingerd morne, no sooner shone, The. The Sacrifice. Homer, *tr. by* George Chapman. *Fr.* The Odyssey, III. OBS
Rosie Nell, *with music. Unknown.* AS
Rosies. Agnes I. Hanrahan. HBV-1

Roslin and Hawthornden. Henry van Dyke. AA
Ross's Poems, *sels.* Geoffrey Lehmann. CBAP
Auntie Bridge and Uncle Pat.
I Was Born at a Place of Pines.
Music Is Unevennesses.
My Father's a Still Day.
Some of Our Koorawatha Saints.
There Are Some Lusty Voices Singing.
Rostov. G. S. Fraser. WaP
Rosy Apple, Lemon or Pear. *Unknown.* CH; POL
Rosy Bosom'd Hours, The. Coventry Patmore. EnLoPo
Rosy clouds float overhead, The. The Sandman. "Margaret Vandegrift." HBV-1; HBVY
Rosy Days Are Numbered, The. Moses ibn Ezra, *tr. fr. Hebrew by* Solomon Solis-Cohen. *Fr.* Wine-Songs. TrJP
Rosy mouth and rosy toe, The. A Bunch of Roses. John Banister Tabb. HBVY
Rosy shield upon its back, A. The Dead Crab. Andrew Young. BSV; FaBoTw; FM; LoBV
Rotation. Julian Bond. FF; NIP; NNP
Rothesay, O. *Unknown.* FSW
Rothiemurchus. Colin Lamont. PoSH
Rothko. James Moore. AMV-81
Rotten Lake Elegy. Muriel Rukeyser. MoPo; NePA
Rou-cou spoke the dove. Song of Fixed Accord. Wallace Stevens. InPS; NePoAm
Rouen. May Wedderburn Cannan. OBWP; OxBTC; SUMH
Rouge Bouquet. Joyce Kilmer. HBV-2; PAH; PoPl; TreFS
Rough. Stephen Spender. *See* My Parents Kept Me.
Rough fir, hauled from the hills. The Making of the Cross. William Everson. VGW
Rough pasture where the blackberries grow! A Pasture. Frederic Lawrence Knowles. AA
Rough wind, that moanest loud. A Dirge. Shelley. CABA; ChTr; EnRP; InPK; NOBE; OAEP; PoRA; SoSe; TEP; TrGrPo; WHA; WiR
Rough Winds Do Shake. Louis Simpson. ErPo
Roughchin, the Pirate. Arthur Boswell. EtS
Roughly figured, this man of moderate habits. Life Cycle of Common Man. Howard Nemerov. NIP
Roughly-silvered leaves that are the snow. A Song from Armenia. Geoffrey Hill. FaBoMo
Roughly, so to say, you know. John William Mackail. *Fr.* Balliol Rhymes. CenHV
Round: "Everything is round." Rachel Boimwall, *tr. fr. Yiddish by* Gabriel Preil *and* Howard Schwartz. VWA
Round, A: "Hey nonny no!" *Unknown. See* Hey Nonny No!
Round, A: "Now that the spring hath filled our veins." William Browne. ViBoPo
Round, The: "Skunk cabbage, bloodroot." Philip Booth. BoNaP; GrPl; NCSH
Round: "'Wondrous life!' cried Marvell at Appleton House." Weldon Kees. CoAP; NaP; NoAm
Round: "Worlds, you must tell me." Louis Untermeyer. WhC
Round a cleft in the cliffs to come upon. Venus of the Salty Shell. Denis Devlin. BIrV
Round about, little ones, quick, quick and nimble. Robin Good-Fellow's Song. *Unknown.* ElL
Round about Me. Sappho, *tr. fr. Greek by* William Ellery Leonard. AWP
Round about, round about,/ Catch a wee mouse. *Unknown.* OxNR
Round about, round about/ In a fair ring-a. The Elves' Dance. *Unknown, at. to* John Lyly *and to* Thomas Ravenscroft. *Fr.* The Mayde's Metamorphosis. CH; FaPON
Round about, round about,/ maggotty pie. Counting Out Rhyme. *Unknown.* OxNR; PBBP; SpRo
Round about, round about, here sits the hare. *Unknown.* OxNR
Round about the cauldron go! E. O. Parrott. BXAP
Round about the cauldron go. Shakespeare. *Fr.* Macbeth, IV, i. TreFT
Round about the rosebush. *Unknown.* OxNR
Round about there/ Sat a little hare. *Unknown.* OxNR
Round among the quiet graves. Love's Resurrection Day. Louise Chandler Moulton. AA; HBV-1
Round and round. Private Transport. Adrian Mitchell. FaBoEE
Round and Round Hitler's Grave. *Unknown.* FSW
Round and round our lavatory. The Thinker. Anthony Delius. PeSA
Round and round the garden. *Unknown.* OxNR
Round and round the rugged rock. *Unknown.* OxNR
Round and sad-eyed man puffed cigars as if, The. Song of the Round Man. Michael Palmer. NPGG
Round Barrow, The. Andrew Young. SeCePo
"Round Cape Horn." *Unknown.* EtS
Round Dance, and Canticle. Robert Kelly. CoPo
Round dance of day has gone. Sitting Alone in Tulsa Three A.M. Lance Henson. VoR
Round de meadows am a-ringing. Massa's in de Cold Cold Ground. Stephen Collins Foster. AA; TreF
Round Her Neck She Wore a Yellow Ribbon. *Unknown.* FSW
Round her red garland and her golden hair. Of His Last Sight of Fiammetta. Boccaccio, *tr. fr. Italian by* Dante Gabriel Rossetti. *Fr.* Sonnets. AWP; GoBC
Round moon hangs above the rim, The. Moment Musicale. Bliss Carman. HBMV
Round moon hangs like a yellow lantern in the trees, The. The Ancient Thought. Watson Kerr. TRV; WGRP
'Round my Indiana homestead wave the cornfields. On the Banks of the Wabash, Far Away. Paul Dresser. BLSo; FSN; FSW; TreFT
Round Number, A. Keith Douglas. NeBP
Round Our Restlessness. Elizabeth Barrett Browning. TRV
Round Quebec's embattled walls. Montgomery at Quebec. Clinton Scollard. PAH
Round Song, A. Rhyll McMaster. CBAP
Round Table, The. Peggy Susberry Kenner. JB
Round Table, The. Robert Manning. ACP
Round table, holding eight, A. Recipe for a Pleasant Dinner-Party. *Unknown.* FaBoUs
Round the Bay of Mexico. *Unknown.* FSW; OuSiCo, *with music*
Round the cape of a sudden came the sea. Parting at Morning. Robert Browning. AWP; FaBoEn; FaBV; FF; FiP; HBV-1; HeIP; MOS; NOBE; OAEP; OBEV; OBNC; OBVV; PAI; SoSe; TreFT; UnPo; VLP; WiR
Round Things. William Barnes. VLP
Round Trip. Stan Rice. NPGG
Round Up in Glory, *with music. Unknown.* CoSo
Round Valley Reflections. William Oandasan. STE
Roundabout Turn, A. Robert E. Charles. MoShBr
Roundel: "Now welcome, somer, with thy sunne softe." Chaucer. *See* Now Welcom[e], Somer.
Roundel in the Rain. *Unknown.* FiBHP
Roundel of Rest, A. Arthur Symons. HBV-2
Roundelay, A: "It fell upon a holy eve." Spenser. *See* Perigot and Willye.
Roundelay, A: "Tell me, thou skilful shepherd's swain." Michael Drayton. *Fr.* The Shepherd's Garland, Eclogue IX. ElL
Roundhouse in Cheyenne is filled every night, The. The Dreary Black Hills. *Unknown.* AS
Roundhouse Voices, The. Dave Smith. AMV-80; GeTw; LiSp; MAYP
Rounding the Cape. Roy Campbell. PeSA
Rounding the Horn. John Masefield. *Fr.* Dauber. EtS; MoAB; MoBrPo; WHA
Round-up, The. Sarah Elizabeth Howard. PoOW
Roundup Cook, The. Robert V. Carr. BPAW; PoOW
Rouse, Britons! at length. A New Ballad. *Unknown.* PAH
Rouse every generous, thoughtful mind. The Blasted Herb. Mesech Weare. PAH
Rouse for Stevens, A. Theodore Roethke. OBAL
Rousecastle. David Wright. MoBS
Rousing Canoe Song, The. Hermia Harris Fraser. CaP; WHW
Rousing to rein his pad's head back. Song. Geoffrey Taylor. NeIP; OxBI
Roustabout Holler, *with music. Unknown.* OuSiCo
Rout. Phillip Booth. FAZ
Rout of San Romano, The. Jon Manchip White. NePoEA
Route 95 North: New Jersey. P. C. Bowman. AMV-80
Route of evanescence, A. Emily Dickinson. AP; NoP; PoEL-5; SoSe
Route Six. Stanley Kunitz. AMV-80
Route 29. Catharine Savage Brosman. AMV-81
Routes. Peter Everwine. FiCP; NNaP
Routine, The. Paul Blackburn. ELU
Routine. Arthur Guiterman. RHPC
Rover, The. Sir Walter Scott. *See* Song: "Weary Lot is thine, fair maid, A."
Rover killed the goat. Brave Rover. Max Beerbohm. GDP
Rover, with the good brown head. Matthew Arnold. *Fr.* Matthias. PCat
Rovers, The, *sel.* George Canning, George Ellis, *and* John Hookham Frere.
Song: "Whene'er with haggard eyes I view," *fr.* I. OBEC
(Rogero's Song). NOEC
(Song by Rogero). FaBoNo
(Song of One Eleven Years in Prison.) FiBHP
Rover's Adieu, The. Sir Walter Scott. *See* Song: "Weary lot is thine, fair maid, A."
Rover's Farewell, The. Sir Walter Scott. *See* Song: "Weary lot is thine, fair maid, A."
Roving breezes come and go, the reed-beds sweep and sway, The. The Travelling Post Office. Andrew Barton Paterson. CBAP
Roving Gambler, The, *with music. Unknown.* AS; TrAS
(Roving Gambler Blues, *diff. vers.*) FSW
Roving Shanty Boy, The. *Unknown.* AmFP

Roving Worker, The. *Unknown, tr. fr. Modern Irish by* George Sigerson. OnYI
Row after row with strict impunity. Ode to the Confederate Dead. Allen Tate. AP; CABA; FaBoMo; HeIP; LiTA; LiTM; MoAB; MoAmPo; MoPo; MoVE; NoAM; NOBA; NoP; OBWP; OxBA; PrIm; SeCeV; TAP; TwAmPo; UnPo; ViBoPo
Row between the Cages, The. Thomas Armstrong. VLP
Row, Bullies, Row, *with music. Unknown.* ShS
Row Gently Here. Thomas Moore. HBV-1
Row of Houses. John Robert Quinn. AMV-80
Row of Stalls, A, *sel.* Raymond Knister.
Nell. NOBC; OBCV
Row, Row, Row Your Boat. *Unknown.* FSW
Row us out from Desenzano, to your Sirmione row! "Frater Ave atque Vale." Tennyson. ChTr; EBVV; FaBoPP; GTBS-P; HAP; InPS; NoP
Rowan, The. Violet Jacob. PoSH
Rowan County Crew, The. *At. to* James William Day. AmFP; OuSiCo, *with music*
Rowan like a lip-sticked girl, A. Song. Seamus Heaney. IPY
Rowan Tree, The. Lady Nairne. HBV-2
Rowers, The. Laura Benét. GoYe
Rowing. Ed Ochester. Str
Rowing. Anne Sexton. BoWoP
Rowing between Pond and Western Islands. "A Loon Call." Richard Eberhart. AMV-80
Rowing, I reach'd a rock the sea was low. Gerard Manley Hopkins. *Fr.* A Vision of the Mermaids. ChTr
Rowland's Rhyme. Michael Drayton. *Fr.* The Shepherd's Garland, Eclogue II (1606 ed.). OBSC
Rows of cells are unroofed, The. The Old Prison. Judith Wright. PoAu-2
Rows of Cold Trees, The. Yvor Winters. NoAM; NOBA
Roy Bean. *Unknown.* BeLS; BPAW; CoSo, *with music*; OBAL
Royal Adventurer, The. Philip Freneau. PAH
Royal and saintly Cashel! I would gaze. The Rock of Cashel. Sir Aubrey De Vere. NBM
Royal Angler, The, *sel. Unknown.*
"Methinks I see our mighty monarch stand." OBSV
Royal Charlie's now awa. Will He No Come Back Again? *Unknown.* OBEC; OBEV
Royal Crown, The, *abr.* Solomon Ibn Gabirol, *tr. fr. Hebrew by* Israel Zangwill. AWP
My God, *tr. by* Alice Lucas, *sel.* TrJP
Royal Education. Winthrop Mackworth Praed. OBSV
Royal feast was done, The; the King. The Fool's Prayer. Edward Rowland Sill. AA; BeLS; FaBoBe; HBV-2; OHFP; OnMSP; PoLF; TreF; WBLP; WGRP
Royal Fisherman, The. *Unknown.* ChTr; GBP
Royal George, The. William Cowper. *See* On the Loss of the *Royal George.*
Royal Guest, A. *Unknown. See* Guest, The.
Royal Light Dragoon, The. *Unknown.* OBET
Royal Line, The. Leigh Hunt. FaBoUs
Royal Love Scene, The. Voltaire, *ad. by* Ernest Dowson. UnTE
Royal Mummy to Bohemia, The. Charles Warren Stoddard. AA
Royal Palace of the Highest Heaven, The. *At. to* Alexander Montgomerie. *Fr.* The Cherry and the Slae. GoTS
Royal Palm. Hart Crane. AP; CMoP; MoAB; MoAmPo; NoAM; NoP; TrGrPo
Royal [*or* Royall] Presents. Nathaniel Wanley. OBS; OxBoCh
"Instead of Incense (Blessed Lord) if wee," *sel.* TrPWD
Royal Princess, A. Christina Rossetti. BrRo
Royal Stag, The. "Hugh MacDiarmid." FaBoMo
Royal Tour, and Weymouth Amusements, The, *abr.* "Peter Pindar." OxBoli
George III and the Sailor, *sel.* NOEC
Royalist, The. Alexander Brome. CavP
Royall Presents. Nathaniel Wanley. *See* Royal Presents.
Royalties. D. J. Enright. NOBL
Royalty. Arthur Rimbaud, *tr. fr. French by* Enid Rhodes Peschal. SOTW
Roye Robert the Bruss the rayke he avowit, The. Sir Richard Holland. *Fr.* The Buke of the Howlat. OxBS
R-P-O-P-H-E-S-S-A-G-R. E. E. Cummings. AmPP; InPK; NoP; PPP
Rrrrrrrraaarghr/ We have paid you back. Fury against the Moslems at Uhud. Hind bint Utba, *tr. by* Bridget Connelly *and* Deirdre Lashgari. WPOW
Ruaumoko—the Earthquake God. Mohi Turei, *tr. fr. Maori by* A. Armstrong. WTO
Rub, A. John Bannister Tabb. OBAL
Rub a dub dub,/ Three men in a tub. Mother Goose. HBV-1; HBVY; NOBL; OxNR
Rubaiyat, The. Edwin Meade Robinson. Limericised Classics, III. HBMV
Rubáiyát of Omar Khayyám of Naishápúr, The. Omar Khayyám, *tr. fr. Persian by* Edward Fitzgerald. AWP; BiP, *abr.*; EBVV, *abr.*; FaBoBe; FaBoRV, *abr.*; FaFP; FaPOR, *abr.*; HAP, *abr.*; HeIP; LiTB; LoBV, *abr.*; MaSP; NoP; PoEL-5; PrIm, *abr.*; TrGrPo; VLP; WeW, *abr.*; WHA, *abr.*
Sels.
"Ah Love! could you and I with Him conspire." PoPl
"Ah, with the grape my fading life provide." EBEV; GTBS-P
"Awake! for morning in the bowl of night." OxBI
"Book of verses underneath the bough, A." HoPM; NOBE; OBEV; OBVV; SeCeV
(Quatrains.) SeCePo
"Come, fill the cup, and in the fire of Spring." FaBV; TEP; TreF; WGRP
"For in and out, above, about, below." TRV
"I sometimes think that never blows so red." LO
"Iram indeed is gone with all his rose." OBVE
"Myself when young did eagerly frequent." EaLo; ILwL; WGRP
"O Thou, who man of baser earth didst make." EaLo; SeCeV
"Some for the glories of this world; and some." PoPl
"They say the lion and the lizard keep." EBEV
"Think, in this batter'd caravanserai." ChTr
"Wake, for the sun, who scattered [*or* scatter'd] into flight." FF; HBV-2; OBNC; SeCeV; ViBoPo
(Wake!) FaPON
"Why, all the saints and sages who discuss'd." TRV
"Yet ah, that spring should vanish with the rose." SeCeV
Rubber penis, the wig, false breasts, The. Poggio. Lawrence Durrell. OxBTC
Rubbing a glistening circle. Aberdeen Train. Edwin Morgan. BSV
Rubens, de Vos, Memling—room after room. Antwerp: Musée Des Beaux-Arts. Alan Ross. NYBP
Rubicon, The. William Winter. HBV-2
Rubies and Pearls. Robert Herrick. HBV-1
(Rock of Rubies, The.) InMe
Rubin. Charles Cooper. PoBA
Rubinstein Staccato Etude, The. R. Nathaniel Dett. BANP
Ruby wine is drunk by knaves. Heroism. Emerson. ViBoPo
Ruddigore, *sels.* W. S. Gilbert.
Darned Mounseer, The. NOBL
Sir Roderic's Song. ShM; WhC
Ruddy poppies bend and bow, The. To Diane. Helen Hay Whitney. HBV-1
Rude architect, rich instinct's natural taste. The Mole. John Clare. SeCeV
Rude Boreas. *Unknown.* OBET
Rude mass of earth, from which moilèd hands. On a Piece of Unwrought Pipeclay. John Frederick Bryant. NOEC
Rudel to the Lady of Tripoli. Robert Browning. LoBV
Rudely blows the winter blast. Flora's Flower. *Unknown, tr. by* John Addington Symonds. UnTE
Rudely forced to drink tea, Massachusetts, in anger. Epigram. *Unknown.* PAH
Rudely thou wrongest my dear heart's desire. Amoretti, V. Spenser. EIL
Rudolph Is Tired of the City. Gwendolyn Brooks. PDV; RHPC; TiPo
Rue. *Unknown.* FSW
Rueful Lamentation [on the Death of Queen Elizabeth], A. Sir Thomas More. AAS; FaBoRV; LiTB; OBSC
Rufus Mitchell's Confession. *Unknown.* AmFP
Rufus Prays. L. A. G. Strong. MoBrPo
Rufus's Mare, *with music.* George Calhoun. ShS
Rug, The. Michael McClure. NeAP
Rugby Chapel. Matthew Arnold. OAEP; OxBoCh; PoEL-5; VLP; WGRP
Rugged forehead that with grave foresight, The. Love. Spenser. The Faerie Queene, IV, *proem.* OAEL-1; OBSC
Rugged Pyrrhus, he whose sable arm, The. Shakespeare. *Fr.* Hamlet, II, ii. Par
Ruin, The. Richard Hughes. OBMV
Ruin, The. Charles Tomlinson. NePoEA-2
Ruin, The. *Unknown, tr. fr. Anglo-Saxon.* AnOE, *tr. by* Charles W. Kennedy; EBEV, *tr. by* Gavin Bone; PrIm, *tr. by* Charles W. Kennedy
Ruin and death held sway. In Apia Bay. Sir Charles G. D. Roberts. PAH
Ruin of Bobtail Bend, The. James Barton Adams. PoOW
"Ruin seize thee, ruthless King!" The Bard [a Pindaric Ode]. Thomas Gray. EnRP; GTBS; GTBS-P; LaUP; NOBE; NOEC; OAEL-1; OAEP; OBEC
Ruined and ill, a man of two score. Remembering Golden Bells. Po Chü-i, *tr. by* Arthur Waley. AWP
Ruined Cabin, The. Alfred Castner King. PoOW
Ruined Cottage, The. Wordsworth. *See* Wanderer, The.
Ruined House, A. Richard Aldington. BrPo
Ruined Maid, The. Thomas Hardy. BoLoP; BrPo; CABA; CMoP; ErPo; FiBHP; HeIP; InPK; LiTB; NIP; NOBL; NoP; OxBTC; PAI; PPoe; SCV; SeCeV; TEP; WeW
Ruined Motel, The. Reginald Gibbons. MAYP
Ruined Nest, The. *Unknown. See* Deserted Home, The.

Ruined, time ruined, all these once good things. Rimrock, Where It Is. Hayden Carruth. NNaP
Ruins of a Great House. Derek Walcott. TwCP
Ruins of Rome, *sels.* Joachim du Bellay, *tr. fr. French by* Spenser.
"He that has seen a great oak dry and dead." FaBoPP
"Thou stranger, which for Rome in Rome here seekest." FaBoPP; OBVE
"Thou that at Rome astonished doth behold." FaBoPP
"Who list the Romane greatnes forth to figure." OBVE
Ruins of Rome, The, *sel.* John Dyer.
"Fall'n, fall'n, a silent heap; her heroes all." OBEC
Ruins of the City of Hay. Randolph Stow. CBAP; PoAu-2
Ruins under the Stars. Galway Kinnell. LCAP; NaP
"Sometimes I see them," *sel.* RFM
Rule, A. John Wesley. *See* John Wesley's Rule.
Rule, Britannia! James Thomson. *Fr.* Alfred, a Masque, II, v (*by* Thomson *and* David Mallet). FaPoR; GTBS; GTBS-P; HBV-2; NOEC; OAEP; OBEC; OBWP; TreF; WBLP
Rule for Birds' Nesters, A. *Unknown.* HBV-1; HBVY
("Robin and the red-breast, The.") OxNR; PBBP
Rule for Shooting, A. *Unknown.* FaBoUs
Rule of the Road, The. *Unknown.* FaBoUs
Rulers: Philadelphia. Fenton Johnson. AmFN
(Rulers.) PoNe
Rules. Karla Kuskin. RHPC
Rules and Lessons. Henry Vaughan. AnAnS-1
"Observe God in His works: here fountains flow," *sel.* TRV
Rules and Regulations. "Lewis Carroll." FaBoUs
Rules for Daily Life. *Unknown.* STF
Rules for the Road. Edwin Markham. TreFT
Rum Tum Tugger, The. T. S. Eliot. EvOK; FaBoNo; FaBV; FaPON; PDV; TiPo
Rumba. José Zacarías Tallet, *tr. fr. Spanish by* Sangodare Akanji. TTY
Rumba of the Three Lost Souls. Charles Madge. NeBP
Rumble of guns, A—not earthly ones. Electric Storm. Michael C. Martin. WaP
Rumble on, machines of the gold mines. In [*or* On] the Gold Mines. B. W. Vilakazi. PeSA; TTY
Rumble, rumble, rumble, goes the gloomy "L." Roller Skates. John Farrar. FaPON
Rumbling sound of man. Buzz. Jim Tollerud. VoR
Rumbling under blackened girders, Midland, bound for Cricklewood. Parliament Hill Fields. John Betjeman. FaBoTw; NOBE
Ruminant pillows! Gregarious soft boulders! The Black Faced Sheep. Donald Hall. LCAP; SV
Rumination. Richard Eberhart. LiTA; LiTM
Rummaging inside yourself. The Death of Fathers. Theodore Weiss. DiL; SV
Rummle an' dunt o' watter. Sumburgh Heid. George Bruce. OxBS
Rumoresque Senum Severiorum. Marcus Argentarius, *tr. fr. Greek by* Dudley Fitts. ErPo
Rumors. Reginald Arkell. *See* When the War Will End.
Rumors of War in Wyoming. Tom Rea. SOTS
Rumors open up. The Morning Star. Primus St. John. PoBA
Rumpelstiltskin. Anne Sexton. DFT
Rumpled river, The. River Rhyme. William Carlos Williams. PoA
Rumpled sheet, A/ of brown paper. The Term. William Carlos Williams. InvP; LiTA
Rumplestiltskin Poems, *sels.* William Hathaway. DFT
Antistrophe.
Gold Factory, The.
In Dead Air, under Furious Sun.
Liar Rumplestiltskin Loves.
Rumplestiltskin's Plan.
Rumps of horses, The. On Rears. Mary Hedin. PH
Rumpty-iddity, row, row, row. *Unknown.* OxNR
Run along, Bobby. Ego Sum. Gelett Burgess. InMe
Run Along, You Little Dogies. *Unknown. See* Run Little Dogies.
Run Come See. Blind Blake. FSW
Run from Manassas Junction, The. *Unknown.* PAH
Run Little Dogies. *Unknown.* BPAW
(Run Along, You Little Dogies, *with music.*) OuSiCo
Run, Mary, Run, *with music. Unknown.* BoAN-2
Run, Nigger, Run! *Unknown.* BPo
Run on, run on, in a way causing shaking motion on the sidewalk. Autolycus' Song [in Basic English]. Richard L. Greene. SpRo; WhC
Run out the boat, my broken comrades. Thalassa. Louis MacNeice. BIrV; FaBoMo; FaBoRV; NOBE
Run, shepherds, [*or* Runne (sheepheards)] run where Bethlehem [*or* Bethlem *or* Bethleme] blest appear[e]s. The Angels [*or* The Angels for the Nativity of Our Lord *or* The Nativitie]. William Drummond of Hawthornden. *Fr.* Flowers of Sion. GN; HBV-1; OBS; OxBoCh
Runagate Runagate. Robert Hayden. BALP; BPo; CNA; IDB; LCAP; PoBA; PoNe
Runaway. Rhoda Coghill. NeIP; OxBI
Runaway, The. Robert Frost. AWP; CH; FaBoCh; FaPON; GoJo; MoAB; MoAmPo; MP; PDV; PH; TiPo; TwCP; VGW
Runaway, The. Bobbi Katz. RHPC
Runaway. Kim Kurt. NePoAm-2
Runaway Slave, The. Walt Whitman. *Fr.* Song of Myself. PoNe
Runaway Slave at Pilgrim's Point, The. Elizabeth Barrett Browning. BrRo; PoNe; SBG
Runaways, The. Mark Van Doren. PoRA
Rune. Philip Brasfield. LFAC
Rune for C., A. Barbara Howes. NYBP
Rune of Riches. Florence Converse. SUS
Runes. Howard Nemerov. PoCh
Runes for an Old Believer. Rolfe Humphries. NYBP
Runes on Weland's Sword, The. Kipling. PoEL-5
Runilda's Chant. George Darley. *See* O'er the Wild Gannet's Bath.
Runnable Stag, A. John Davidson. BrPo; BSV; EvOK; FaPoR; FM; GoTS; HAP; HBV-1; OBEV; OBVV; OxBTC; PrIm; WiR
Runne (sheepheards) run where Bethleme blest appeares. *See* Run, shepherds, run where Bethlehem blest appears.
Runner, The. Jerah Chadwick. AMV-81
Runner, The. Gary Gildner. TAP
Runner, The. Walt Whitman. InPS; LiSp
Runner in the Skies, The. James Oppenheim. TrJP
Runner with the Lots, The. Léonie Adams. MoPo; NePA
Running. Richard Wilbur. CoAP; NCSH
Running along a bank, a parapet. The Path. Edward Thomas. BrPo; MoVE; NoAM
Running Back. Dave Smith. LiSp
Running Blind. Nancy Jones. LiSp
Running It Backward. John N. Morris. GP
Running out of town on a rail is too good for. Envoi. E. L. Mayo. FAZ
Running sweating hair wet from the shower. Captivity Narrative, September 1981. Adrian C. Louis. STE
Running the Batteries. Herman Melville. PAH
Running the Blockade. Nora Perry. PAH
Running the earth in those years of meadows. Return to the Valley. Elfreida Read. AMV-80
Running the River Lines. David Baker. MAYP
Running the Trotline. Jim Elledge. WOLT
Running through Sleep. Kathleen Norris. IHMS
Running through the thick wiry grasses to the pond. Shore. Jean Garrigue. TAP
Running to Paradise. W. B. Yeats. OxBoLi
Running under Street Lights. Christy White. AMV-80
Runoff. A. R. Ammons. PPP
Runs all day and never walks. Mother Goose. TiPo
Runs falls rises stumbles on from darkness into darkness. Runagate Runagate. Robert Hayden. BALP; BPo; CNA; IDB; LCAP; PoBA; PoNe
Runs the wind along the waste. Were-Wolf. Julian Hawthorne. AA
Rupert Brooke. W. W. Gibson. HBMV
Rural Bliss. Anthony C. Deane. InMe
Rural Dance about the Maypole, The. *Unknown.* GBP; OxBoLi
Rural Dumpheap. Melville Cane. AmFN
Rural Lass, The. Catherine Jemmat. NOEC
Rural Legend. Mary Elizabeth Osborn. NePoAm
Rural Life. George Crabbe. *Fr.* The Village. NOBE
(Truth in Poetry.) SeCePo
Rural Lines after Breughel. Norbert Krapf. PoDr
Rural Mail, The. John Glassco. MoCV
Rural Poesy. Sir Philip Sidney. *Fr.* Arcadia. EIL
Rural Route. R. T. Smith. AMV-81
Rural Sights and Sounds. William Cowper. *Fr.* The Task. NOEC
("For I have lov'd the rural walk through lanes.") EnRP
Rural Simplicity. H. J. Byron. NOBL
Rural Sports, *sels.* John Gay.
"Nor less the spaniel, skillful to betray." PBBP
"When a brisk gale against the current blows." FM
Rus in Urbe. Clement Scott. HBV-1
Rush of the *Oregon,* The. Arthur Guiterman. PAH
Rushes in a watery place. Christina Rossetti. ChTr; PDV
Rushing. Ray A. Young Bear. CDW
Rushing along on a narrow reach. The Main-Sheet Song. Thomas Fleming Day. EtS
Rushing, the brushing, the wind in your face, The. Galloping. Cordelia Chitty. PH
Rushing wind the Spirit came, A! A Prayer for Pentecost. Catherine Bernard Brown. BLRP

Rushmore ("Rushing to Rushmore, speeding as we read"). Harold Witt. TAT
Rusia en 1931. Robert Hass. MAYP
Russet leaves of the sycamore, The. The Last Days. George Sterling. HBMV
Russia. Alexander Blok, *tr. fr. Russian by* Babette Deutsch *and* Avrahm Yarmolinsky. AWP
Russia. Nathan Haskell Dole. AA
Russia. William Carlos Williams. VGW
Russia 1812. Victor Hugo, *tr. fr. French by* Robert Lowell. OBWP
Russian and Turk. Robert J. Burdette. NA
Russian Asylum. Marilyn Bowering. NOBC
Russian Cathedral. Claude McKay. CDC
(St. Isaac's Church, Petrograd.) AmNP; PoBA
Russian Cradle Song, A. David Nomberg, *tr. fr. Yiddish by* Alter Brody. TrJP
Russian Fantasy, A. Nathan Haskell Dole. AA
Russian penicillin—that was the magic. Garlic. Marvin Bell. GP
Russian sailed over the blue Black Sea, A. "Soldier, Rest!" Robert Jones Burdette. OBAL
Russian Spring Song with Minaiev, A. Thomas Walsh. GoBC
Russians. Keith Douglas. OxBTC
Rust. Mary Carolyn Davies. HBMV
Rust. Michael Hogan. LFAC
Rust, a little pile of western color, lies, The. We Continue. W. S. Merwin. CAPP
Rust destroys the wheat. The New Wife. *Gond Oral Tradition, tr. by* V. Elwin *and* S. Hivale. WTO
Rusted and without tires. 1937 Ford Convertible. Tom McKeown. PPJ
Rusted Chain, The. Yosef Damana ben Yeshaq, *tr. fr. Amharic by* Ephraim Isaac. VWA
Rusted-out skeleton, The. That Pure Place. Daniel J. Moriarty. WOLT
Rustic at the Play, The. George Santayana. HBV-2; OBVV
Rustic Childhood. William Barnes. OBNC
Rustic Song, A. Anthony C. Deane. FiBHP; InMe
Rustily creak the crickets: Jack Frost came down last night. Jack Frost. Celia Thaxter. OBCA
Rustle among bones. Only wind, the bodiless angel. Emptiness. Ray. Otto Orban, *tr. by* Emery George. VWA
Rustle of each falling leaf, The. Love. Samuele Romanelli, *tr. by* A. B. Rhine. TrJP
Rustle of whispering wind over leaves, A. Kingfisher Flat. William Everson. PoM
Rustler, The. *Unknown.* CoSo
Rustling leaves of the willow-tree. Alone in April. James Branch Cabell. HBMV
Rustling of the silk is discontinued, The. Liu Ch'e. Ezra Pound. AP; OBVE; VGW
Ruston, Louisiana: 1952. Cleopatra Mathis. AMV-80
Ruth, *sels.* Bible, *O.T.*
Intreat Me Not to Leave Thee, I: 16-17. TreF
("And Ruth said, Intreat me not to leave.") FF; PoPl
(Entreat Me Not to Leave Thee.) TRV
(Ruth to Naomi.) TrGrPo
Naomi and Ruth, I: 8-17. TrJP
Ruth. Thomas Hood. BoLoP; EnLoPo; EnRP; GN; HBV-1; LoBV; NOBE; OBEV; OBNC; OBRV; OBVV; TreFS
Ruth. Colleen J. McElroy. BlSi
Ruth. Pauli Murray. NMM
Ruth. Wordsworth. ChER; EnRP; PoEL-4
(Ruth; or, The Influences of Nature.) GTBS; GTBS-P
Ruth and Johnnie. *Unknown.* ShM
Ruth; or, The Influences of Nature. Wordsworth. *See* Ruth.
Ruth to Naomi. Bible, *O.T.* *See* Intreat Me Not to Leave Thee.
Rutherford McDowell. Edgar Lee Masters. *Fr.* Spoon River Anthology. EyDe; LiTA; OxBA
Ruthless unrest has urged slow feet. Rescue. Olive Tilford Dargan. GoYe
Ruthlessly 'twixt palm and thumb. For a Girl in Love. Florence Hynes Willette. GoBC
Ruyter the while, that had our ocean curb'd. The Dutch in the Medway. Andrew Marvell. *Fr.* Last Instructions to a Painter. OBS
Ryder. John Haines. LCAP
Rye Bread. William Stanley Braithwaite. CDC
Rye Whiskey. *Unknown.* CoSo (A *and* B *vers., with music*); FSW; OxBoLi; TrAS, *with music*
(Way Up on Clinch Mountain.) AS (A *and* B *vers., with music*)
Ryght as the stern of day begouth to schyne. *See* Right as the stern of day begouth to shine.
Ryókan. William Heyen. AMV-81

S

S & M bar, oh my dears, The. Limerick. *Unknown.* PeHV
S F. Earnest Leverett. QQQ
SM. Stanley Moss. AMV-81; NYP
SOS. Amiri Baraka. BPo; CNA; PoBA
S.P.C.A. Sermon. Stuart Hemsley. FiBHP
S. S. *City of Benares.* G. S. Fraser. NeBP
S.S.R., Lost at Sea—*The Times.* Ralph Gustafson. OBCV
S. T. Coleridge Dismisses a Caller from Porlock. Gerard Previn Meyer. GoYe
Saadabad. James Elroy Flecker. SeCePo
Saadi. Emerson. OxBA
Sabbath. John Berryman. *Fr.* Dream Songs. LCAP
Sabbath. Jean Burden. AMV-81
Sabbath. Rivka Fried. VWA
Sabbath. Jakov de Haan, *tr. fr. Dutch by* David Soetendorp. VWA
Sabbath. David Rosenmann-Taub, *tr. fr. Spanish by* Charles Guentheer. VWA
Sabbath Day Was By, The, *with music.* Howard Chandler Robbins. AH
Sabbath day was ending in a village by the sea, The. The Last Hymn. Marianne Farningham. BLPA
Sabbath, My Love. Judah Halevi, *tr. fr. Hebrew by* Solomon Solis-Cohen. TrJP
Sabbath of Rest, A. Isaac Luria, *tr. fr. Hebrew by* Nina Davis Salaman. TrJP
Sabbath Reflection. Denis Wrafter. NeIP
Sabbath, the pious carry no money. A Voice out of the Sabbaths, W.I. Derek Walcott. WeW
Sabbatical. Linda Zisquit. VWA
Sabine Farmer's Serenade, The. Francis Sylvester Mahony. HBV-2
Sable garb of darkness clothes the land, The. Night on the Prairie. Rufus B. Sage. PoOW
Sable is my throat. Negro Spiritual. Perient Trott. PoNe
Sabrina Fair. Milton. *Fr.* Comus. EBEV; ELP; FaBoCh, *much abr.;* GN; PoEL-3
(Sabrina.) CH, *abr.;* NOBE; OBEV; OBS
(Song: "Sabrina Fair.") LoBV; SeCeV; ViBoPo
Sa-cá-ga-we-a. Edna Dean Proctor. PAH
Sacco Writes to His Son. Alun Lewis. DTC
Sacco-Vanzetti. Moishe Leib Halpern, *tr. fr. Yiddish by* David G. Roskies *and* Hillel Schwartz. VWA
Sachem voices cloven out of the hills, The. Miramichi Lightning. Alfred Goldsworthy Bailey. OBCV
Sacheverell the learned. To the Tune of "Ye Commons and Peers Pray Lend Me Your Ears." *Unknown.* APAS
Sack of Deerfield, The. Thomas Dunn English. PAH
Sacrament, The. John Donne. TRV
Sacrament. Margaret Sackville. SUMH
Sacrament of Sleep, The. John Oxenham. PoLF
Sacrament of the Altar, The. *Unknown.* MeEL
Sacramental Meditations. Edward Taylor. *See* Preparatory Meditations.
Sacramento, *diff. versions. Unknown.* FSW; ShS, 3 *vers., with music;* TrAS, *with music*
(Californian, The.) AmFP
Sacraments of Nature, The. Aubrey Thomas De Vere. ACP
Sacred ape, now, children see, The. The Ape. Roland Young. PoPl; WhC
Sacred Book, The. *At. to* Zoroaster, *tr. fr. Persian by* A. V. Williams Jackson. AWP
(Zoroaster Devoutly Questions Ormazd.) WGRP
Sacred Children, The. H. R. Hays. EAS
Sacred day is this, A. Lincoln's Birthday. John Kendrick Bangs. PGD
Sacred Elegy V. George Barker. *See* Elegy V: Separation of Man from God.
Sacred Emily. Gertrude Stein. OBAL
Sacred Formula to Attract Affection. *Unknown, tr. fr. Cherokee by* James Mooney. LiTA
Sacred Formula to Destroy Life. *Unknown, tr. fr. Cherokee by* James Mooney. LiTA
(Spell to Destroy Life, A.) PAI
Sacred Grove, A. Edward Cracroft Lefroy, *after the Greek of* Theocritus. *Fr.* Echoes from Theocritus. AWP
Sacred Grove, A. Fran Winant. BrRo
Sacred Hearth, The. David Gascoyne. FaBoTw
Sacred keep of Ilion is rent, The. Homeric Unity. Andrew Lang. HBV-2
Sacred Order, The. May Sarton. ImOP
Sacred Poetry. John Wilson. WBLP
Sacred to the Memory of Maria (to Say Nothing of Jane and Martha) Sparks. "Max Adeler." FaBoCo
Sacrifice, The. Chana Bloch. VWA

Sacrifice. Emerson. *Fr.* Quatrains. HBV-2; HBVY; TRV
Sacrifice, The. George Herbert. PoEL-2
Sacrifice, The. Homer, *tr. fr. Greek by* George Chapman. *Fr.* The Odyssey, III. OBS
Sacrifice. Nana Issaia, *tr. fr. Modern Greek by* Helle Tzalopoulou Barnstone. BoWoP
Sacrifice. Thomas Kinsella. IPY
Sacrifice, The. Moshe Yungman, *tr. fr. Yiddish by* Marcia Falk. VWA
Sacrifice of a Red Squirrel. Joseph Langland. NYBP
Sacrifice of a Virgin in the Mayan Ball Court. Norman Dubie. GeTw
Sacrifice to Apollo, The. Michael Drayton. OBS
Sacrilege, The. Thomas Hardy. DTo
Sad and dismal is the tale/ I now relate to you. Invasion Song. *Unknown.* PoOW
Sad and mournful history, A. The Cabin Creek Flood. *Unknown.* AmFP
Sad Child's Song, The. Mark Van Doren. SO
Sad Day, The. Thomas Flatman. OBEV
Sad Day in Berlin. Sarah Kirsch, *tr. fr. German by* Gerda Mayer. PBWP
Sad-eyed Lady of the Lowlands. Bob Dylan. BiP
Sad for those without sweet Anglo-Saxon. The Change. David O'Bruadair, *tr. by* Austin Clarke. BIrV
Sad Green. Sylvia Townsend Warner. MoBrPo
Sad heart, the gymnast of inertia, does not count. The Sad Indian. Hart Crane. PoA
Sad Hesper o'er the buried sun. In Memoriam A. H. H., CXXI. Tennyson. NoP
Sad Indian, The. Hart Crane. PoA
Sad is our youth, for it is ever going. Human Life. Aubrey Thomas De Vere. HBV-1; OnYI
Sad Is the Seagull. Larin Paraske, *tr. fr. Finnish by* Jaakko A. Ahokas. PBWP
Sad lagoons. Film Vermouth: Six o'Clock Show. Magda Portal, *tr. by* Allan Francovich *and* Kathleen Weaver. PBWP
Sad, lost in thought, and mute I go. Medieval Norman Song. *Unknown, tr. by* John Addington Symonds. AWP
Sad Lover, The. George Crabbe. *See* Dejected Lover, The.
Sad Memories. Charles Stuart Calverley. FM
Cat, The, *sel.* ChTr
Sad music from vermilion strings. Telling My Feelings. Yü Hsüan-chi, *tr. by* Geoffrey Waters. BoWoP
Sad seamstress, The. House Guest. Elizabeth Bishop. NCSH; NYBP; TAP
Sad Shepherd, The, *sels.* Ben Jonson.
Aeglamour's Lament. CH
Karolin's Song, *fr.* I, v. LoBV; PoEL-2
(Death and Love.) NOBE
(Song: "Though I am young and cannot tell.") EnRePo; SeCP
(Though I Am Young.) ELP; OAEP
(Though I Am Young and Cannot Tell.) ELP; NoP; OAEP; TEP
Lincolnshire; from the Wolds to the Fens, *fr.* II, vii. FaBoPP
Mother Maudlin the Witch. ChTr
"Spring, now she is dead, A! of what? of thorns." GoBC
Sad Shepherd, The. W. B. Yeats. MOS; PP
Sad Song, A. Philip Massinger. *See* Death Invoked.
Sad Song about Greenwich Village, A. Frances Park. RHPC
Sad Song, The. Beaumont *and* Fletcher. *See* Away, Delights.
Sad Steps. Philip Larkin. NoP
Sad Story. Clarence Day. InMe
Sad Strains of a Gay Waltz. Wallace Stevens. OxBA
Sad Tale of Mr. Mears, The. *Unknown.* HBV-2; TreFS; YaD
Sad Thyrsis weeps till his blue eyes are dim. Thyrsis. Edward Cracroft Lefroy. *Fr.* Echoes from Theocritus. AWP
Sad to fare from the hills of Fál. A Farewell to Fál. Gerald Nugent, *tr. by* Padraic Pearse. OnYI
Sad to see the leaves abandoning. Winterscape. Jess Perlman. AMV-80
"Sad Years, The." Eva Gore-Booth. HBMV
Saddest Words, The. Whittier. *Fr.* Maud Muller. NePA
Saddle. William Haskel Simpson. BPAW
Saddle and Cell. The Three Marias, *tr. fr. Portuguese by* Helen R. Lane. BoWoP
Saddle! saddle! saddle! After the Comanches. *Unknown.* PAH
Saddled and briddled. Bonnie James Campbell. *Unknown.* ESPB
Sadie, *with music. Unknown.* AS
Sadie/ the cleaning lady. Personals. Leatrice W. Emeruwa. PCP
Sadie and Maud. Gwendolyn Brooks. NoAM; NOBA; TAP
Sadie went into the bar-room, and she ordered up a big glass of beer. Sadie. *Unknown.* AS
Sadie's Playhouse. Margaret Danner. PoBA
Sadly as some old medieval knight. My Books. Longfellow. AA
Sadly talks the blackbird here. The Deserted Home [*or* The Ruined Nest]. *Unknown, tr. by* Kuno Meyer. OnYI; OxBI
Sadly the dead leaves rustle in the whistling wind. The Church of a Dream. Lionel Johnson. OAEL-2; OBMV
Sadly unroll sleepingbag. 25:I:68. Philip Whalen. PoM
Sadness. Tennyson. FaBoEE
Sadness and Still Life. Bin Ramke. MAYP
Sadness, Glass, Theory. Roy Fuller. WaP
Sadness in the human visage stares, The. At an Exhibition of Historical Paintings, Hobart. Vivian Smith. CBAP
Sadness of the Moon, The. Baudelaire, *tr. fr. French by* F. P. Trurm. MOON
Sadness of Things for Sappho's Sickness, The. Robert Herrick. PoPle
Safari to Bwagamoyo. Bwagamoyo. Lebert Bethune. PoBA
Safari West. John A. Williams. InPS; NBP
Safe. James Walker. OBCP
Safe despair it is that raves. Emily Dickinson. AP
"Safe for Democracy." L. A. G. Strong. HBMV
Safe home, safe home in port. The Finished Course. St. Joseph of the Studium, *tr. by* John Mason Neale. WGRP
Safe in His Keeping. Edgar Cooper Mason. BLRP
Safe in their alabaster chambers. Emily Dickinson. AmPP; AP; MasP; MoPo; NIP; NOBA; NoP, 2 *vers.*; OxBA; TwAmPo; WPE
Safe Places. Constance Urdang. GP
Safe sleeping on its mother's breast. The Baby. Ann Taylor. OHIP
Safe upon the solid rock the ugly houses stand. Second Fig. Edna St. Vincent Millay. *Fr.* Figs from Thistles. FaBV; NoP; PoA
Safed. Dovid Knut, *tr. fr. Russian by* Daniel Weissbort. VWA
Safed and I. Molly Myerowitz Levine. VWA
Safely Home. *Unknown.* STF
Safety. Rupert Brooke. 1914, II. BrPo; EnLoPo; HBV-2
Safety at Forty; or, An Abecedarian Takes a Walk. L. E. Sissman. Prf
Safety of the king and's royal throne, The. The Tune to the Devonshire Cant. *Unknown.* APAS
Safety or Something. P. L. Jacobs. LFAC
Saffold's Cures. *At. to* Thomas Saffold. FaBoUs
Sag' Mir Wer Einst die Uhren Erfund. Heine. *See* Who Was it, Tell Me.
Sag', wo ist dein schönes Liebchen. Heine, *tr. fr. German by* James Thomson. AWP
Saga of Gisli, The, *sels. Tr. fr. Icelandic by* George Johnston. OBVE
"Goddess of threads gladly."
"'Wife, land of the wave fire.'"
Saga of King Olaf, The, *sels.* Longfellow. *Fr.* Tales of a Wayside Inn: The Musician's Tale.
Building of the *Long Serpent,* The, xiii. EtS
"Dawn is not distant, The," xxii. TRV
Saga of Leif the Lucky, *sel.* Hervey Allen.
"Leif was a man's name." EtS
Sagacity. William Rose Benét. MoAmPo
Sagamore. Corinne Roosevelt Robinson. HBMV
Sage Counsel. Sir Arthur Quiller-Couch. HBV-2; HBVY; NA
("Lion is a beast to fight, The.") CenHV
Sage lectured brilliantly, The. Stephen Crane. The Black Riders, III. YaD
Sagebrush. Charles Erskine Scott Wood. BPAW
Sagesse, *sel.* Hilda Doolittle ("H. D.").
"You look at me, a hut or cage contains." NOCV
Sagesse, *sels.* Paul Verlaine, *tr. fr. French.*
Chevalier Malheur, Le, *tr. by* John Gray. SyP
God Has Spoken, *tr. by* John Gray. SyP
"My God, you have wounded me with love." ILwL
"Sky is up above the roof, The," *tr. by* Ernest Dowson. AWP; FaPON; SyP
"Slumber dark and deep," *tr. by* Arthur Symons. AWP
Sagest of women, even of widows, she. Byron. *Fr.* Don Juan, I. NOBL
Sagging Bough, The. Louis Untermeyer. BXAP
Sagimusume: The White Heron Maiden. Jonny Kyoko Sullivan. WPOW
Sahara. Coventry Patmore. *Fr.* The Angel in the House. EBVV
Said ("Agatha Christie to"). George Starbuck. OBAL; PV
Said ("J. Alfred Prufrock to"). George Starbuck. OBAL; PV
Said ("President Johnson to"). George Starbuck. PV
Said/ a hip/ lip-ful. Leg-acy of a Blue Capricorn. James Cunningham. JB
Said a cat, as he playfully threw. Only Teasing. *Unknown.* TDH
Said a fellow from North Philadelphia. Church Bells. Berton Braley. TDH
Said a gabby old queer in Saint-Lô. Limerick. *Unknown.* PeHV
Said a great Congregational preacher. Limerick. *Unknown.* WhC
Said a lachrymose Labrador seal. The Feminine Seal. Oliver Herford. TDH
Said a lady beyond Pompton Lakes. The Car's in the Hall. Morris Bishop. TDH
Said a lady who wore a swell cape. Nature and Art. Oliver Herford. TDH
Said a maid, "I will marry for lucre." Money Makes the Marriage. *Unknown.* TDH

Said a saucy young skunk to a gnu. The Skunk to the Gnu. Gerard Neyroud. TDH
Said a sporty young person named Groat. A Sporty Young Person. *Unknown.* TDH
Said a woman and a dollar a bout the same. Out on Santa-Fe-Blues. *Unknown.* BluL
Said Abner, "At last thou art come! Ere I tell, ere thou speak." Saul. Robert Browning. OAEP; OxBoCh; VLP; WHA
Said active priest, "My work has increased." There Is None to Help. Chad Walsh. *Fr.* The Psalm of Christ. TrCP
Said an ancient hermit, bending. The Olive Tree. Sabine Baring-Gould. GN
Said an asp to an adder named Rhea. Serpentine Verse. Joseph S. Newman. TDH
Said Aristotle unto Plato. Owen Wister. PoPl; WhC
Said Burgoyne to his men, as they passed in review. The Progress of Sir Jack Brag. *Unknown.* PAH
Said Death to Passion. Emily Dickinson. MoVE
Said Descartes, "I extol." Theological. Clifton Fadiman. FiBHP; PV
Said Fading-leaf to Fallen-leaf. Fading-Leaf and Fallen-Leaf. Richard Garnett. OBVV
Said Folly to Wisdom. On the Road. Tudor Jenks. NA
Said God, "You sisters, ere ye go." Hope and Despair. Lascelles Abercrombie. HBV-2; OBMV
Said Hanrahan. P. J. Hartigan. PoAu-1
Said, I, Oh, give me simplicity. Rural Simplicity. H. J. Byron. NOBL
Said I to Lord & Taylor. A Father Does His Best. E. B. White. WhC
Said Jeremy Jonathan Joseph Jones. The Rhyme of the Rain Machine. F. W. Clarke. BoNaP
Said Jerome K. Jerome to Ford Madox Ford. Mutual Problem. William Cole. OBAL; POL
Said Jim X . . . Ezra Pound. *Fr.* Cantos, XII. NAs
Said lady once to lover. The Three Bushes. W. B. Yeats. DTC
Said Life to Death: "Methinks, if I were you." Recrimination. Ella Wheeler Wilcox. AA
Said Maylard to Solly one day in Glen Brittle. Doing the Dubhs. *Unknown.* PoSH
Said Mr. Smith, "I really cannot." Bones. Walter de la Mare. FiBHP; ShM
Said my landlord, white-headed Gil Gomez. Battle of the King's Mill. Thomas Dunn English. PAH
Said Old Gentleman Gay, "On a Thanksgiving Day." A Good Thanksgiving. Annie Douglas Green Robinson. PoLF
Said old Peeping Tom of Fort Lee. Limerick. Morris Bishop. WhC
Said Opie Read. Julian Street *and* James Montgomery Flagg. HBV-2 (To Be Continued.) FiBHP; InMe; PV
Said Peter the Great to a Great Dane. Peterhof. Edmund Wilson. GoJo
Said, Pull her up a bit will you, Mac, I want to unload there. Reason. Josephine Miles. InPK; NCSH; NoAM; NoP; PoCH; TAP
Said Rockefeller, senior, to his boy. Compliance. Ambrose Bierce. DBV
Said Simple Sam: "Does Christmas come." Simple Sam. Leroy F. Jackson. PoSC
Said the archangels, moving in their glory. Voice. Harriet Prescott Spofford. AA
Said the bird in search of a cage. A Bird in Search of a Cage. Robert Pack. NePoEA
Said the Birds of America. The Birds of America. James Broughton. AmFN; BoAnP
Said the Canoe. Isabella Valancy Crawford. *See* Canoe, The.
Said the Captain: "There was wire." Our Modest Doughboys. Charlton Andrews. PAH
Said the crab: "Tis not beauty or birth." The Oratorical Crab. Oliver Herford. TDH
Said the Duck to the Kangaroo. The Duck and the Kangaroo. Edward Lear. OxBChV
Said the Eagle. The Eagle's Song. Mary Austin. GOA
Said the elephant to the giraffe. The Elephant and the Giraffe. Charlotte Osgood Carter. TDH
Said the engineer, "Radio waves." Not Lost in the Stars. Bruce Bliven. QQQ
Said the Englishman: "W'at's all this bloomin' wow?" Foreigners at the Fair. Fred Emerson Brooks. OBAL
Said the father to the daughter. Our Ship She Lies in Harbour. *Unknown.* OBET
Said the first little chicken. Five Little Chickens [*or* The Chickens]. *Unknown.* FaPON; MoShBr; PDV
Said the fur-coated dame to the hairless pup. Canine Amenities. *Unknown.* GDP
Said the grave Dean of Westminster. A Refusal. Thomas Hardy. FaBoCo; LiTB
Said the Innkeeper. Myles Connolly. TRV
Said the Lion: "On music I dote." The Musical Lion. Oliver Herford. OBCA; TDH
Said the Lion to the Lioness—"When you are amber dust." Heart and Mind. Edith Sitwell. ChMP; MoPo; MP; OAEP; OxBTC; TwCP
Said the little boy, "Sometimes I drop my spoon." The Little Boy and the Old Man. Shel Silverstein. RHPC
Said the little warbling vireo. Fable of the Talented Mockingbird. Scott Bates. BoAnP
Said the mole: "You would never suppose." The Mendacious Mole. Oliver Herford. TDH
Said the monkey to the donkey. *Unknown.* FaFP
Said the mouse with scholastical hat. The Scholastic Mouse. "A. B. P." TDH
Said the Poet to the Analyst. Anne Sexton. TwAmPo
Said the Queen of the Nile. The Queen of the Nile. William Jay Smith. GrPl
Said the Raggedy Man, on a hot afternoon. The Man in the Moon. James Whitcomb Riley. HBV-1; HBVY; InMe; NA
Said the Robin to the Sparrow. Overheard in an Orchard. Elizabeth Cheney. BLRP; TRV
Said the Rose. George H. Miles. BLPA
Said the shark to the flying fish over the phone. The Flattered Flying Fish. E. V. Rieu. PDV; RHPC; ShM; SO
Said the sparrow to the robin. Feathered Faith. *Unknown.* STF
Said the spider, in tones of distress. The Eternal Feminine Oliver Herford. TDH
Said the Sword to the Ax, 'twixt the whacks and the hacks. Ned Braddock. John Williamson Palmer. PAH
Said the table to the chair. The Table and the Chair. Edward Lear. HBVY; SoPo; TreFT
Said the trout to the fluke. Johnshaven. *Unknown.* GBP
Said the very old man at the drum. Homesick Song. William Haskel Simpson. BPAW
Said the Victory of Samothrace. Overheard in the Louvre. X. J. Kennedy. ELU
Said the Whisky Flask. *Unknown.* STF
Said the wife to her husband. Rift Tide. Ruth M. Walsh. QQQ
Said the Wind to the Moon: "I will blow you out." The Wind and the Moon. George Macdonald. GoJo; HBV-1; HBVY; MoShBr; OnMSP; SUS; TreFS
Said this little fairy. The Five Little Fairies. Maud Burnham. HBVY
Said Zwingli to Muntzer. How to Start a War. Phyllis McGinley. DBV; OBSV
Saies, "Come here, cuzen Gawaine so gay." King Arthur and King Cornwall. *Unknown.* ESPB
Sail, A. Mikhail Yuryevich Lermontov, *tr. fr. Russian.* AWP, *tr. by* Max Eastman; PoPl, *tr. by* Avrahm Yarmolinsky
"Sail, A! a sail! Oh, whence away." Heart's Content. *Unknown.* HBV-2; PoLF
Sail and Oar. Robert Graves. MOS
Sail at the mast head dips from side to side, The. *Tr. fr. Aborigine by* C. H. Berndt. WTO
Sail Away. Robert Adamson. CBAP
Sail Away Ladies. *Unknown.* FSW
Sail forth—steer for the deep waters only. Walt Whitman. *Fr.* The Passage to India. TRV
Sail, Monarchs, rising and falling. Roots and Branches. Robert Duncan. VGW
Saîl of Claustra, Aelis, Azalais. The Alchemist. Ezra Pound. CMoP; LiTA; NePA; TwAmPo; WSC
Sail On, O Ship of State! Longfellow. *Fr.* The Building of the Ship. *See* Ship of State.
Sail Peacefully Home. S. Frug, *tr. fr. Yiddish.* TrJP
Sailing. Godfrey Marks. *See* Sailing Sailing.
Sailing after Lunch. Wallace Stevens. MoPo
Sailing at Dawn. Sir Henry Newbolt. EtS
Sailing from the United States. Stanley Moss. VGW
Sailing Home from Rapallo. Robert Lowell. NoAM; TAP
Sailing Homeward. Chan Fang-sheng, *tr. fr. Chinese by* Arthur Waley. AWP; FaBoCh
Sailing in Crosslight. Anita Skeen. IHMS
Sailing in the boat when the tide runs high. Rose in the Garden. *Unknown.* AmFP
Sailing of the Fleet, The. *Unknown.* PAH
Sailing of the Sword, The. William Morris. OAEP; OBVV
Sailing Pine, The; the Cedar, proud and tall. Kinds of Trees to Plant. Spenser. *Fr.* The Faerie Queene, I, i. OHIP
Sailing, Sailing. Gary Burr. CoPo; NYBP
Sailing Sailing. Godfrey Marks. FSW
(Sailing.) TreFS
Sailing to an Island. Richard Murphy. IPY; NMP
Sailing to Byzantium. W. B. Yeats. AnIL; BiP; CABA; ChMP; CMoP;

CoBMV; FaBoEn; FaFP; FF; FPL; GTBS-P; HAP; HeIP; HoPM; InPK; InPS; InvP; LiTB; LiTM; MasP; MoAB; MoBrPo; MoPo; MoVE; NIP; NoAM; NOBE; NoP; OAEL-2; OAEP; OBMV; OxBI; OxBTC; PAI; PoRA; PP; PPoe; PPP; PrIm; SeCePo; SeCeV; SoSe; TEP; TreFT; UnPo; ViBoPo; WeW
Sailing upon the River. George Crabbe. *Fr.* The Borough. OBNC
Sailor, The. William Allingham. HBV-1
Sailor. Langston Hughes. PoA
Sailor, The. Goodridge MacDonald. CaP
Sailor, The. Sylvia Townsend Warner. OBMV
Sailor and His Bride, The. *Unknown.* AmFP
Sailor and Inland Flower. Hamish Maclaren. EtS
Sailor and the Shark, The. Paul Fort, *tr. fr.* French by Frederick York Powell. OBMV
Sailor at Midnight, A. E. N. Sargent. NMM
Sailor Boy, The. Tennyson. MOS
Sailor Boy, The. *Unknown.* BaBo; ShS, *with music*
Sailor Cut Down in His Prime, The. *Unknown.* OBET
Sailor Man. H. Sewall Bailey. EtS
Sailor on Deep Blue Sea. *Unknown.* FSW
Sailor pops upon the Royal Pair, A. George III and the Sailor. "Peter Pindar." *Fr.* The Royal Tour, and Weymouth Amusements. NOEC
Sailor to His Parrot, The. W. H. Davies. BoAnP; EtS; ViBoPo
Sailor, we all stare at you. Wynyard Sailor. Ray Mathew. CBAP
Sailor, What of the Isles? Edith Sitwell. ChMP
"Sailorman, I'll give to you." The Silver Penny. Walter de la Mare. CMoP; OBMV
Sailors. Louis Simpson. NYBP
Sailors. *Unknown. See* Wrap Me Up in My Tarpaulin Jacket.
Sailors' Alphabet, The. *Unknown.* AmFP
Sailor's Apology for Bow-Legs, A. Thomas Hood. EtS; MOS
Sailor's Carol. Charles Causley. OBCP
Sailors come/ To the drum. Hornpipe. Edith Sitwell. *Fr.* Façade. FaBoMo; GTBS-P; MoVE; OAEL-2; SeCePo
Sailor's Consolation, The. William Pitt, *wr. at. to* Charles Dibdin. BeLS; EtS; FaBoCo; HBV-2; PoPle; TreFS
Sailor's Grace, The. *Unknown.* ShS
Sailor's Grave, The. Eliza Cook. BLPA
Sailor's Grave, The, *with music. Unknown, diff. vers. of song by* Eliza Cook. ShS
Sailor's Harbor [*or* Harbour]. Henry Reed. MoAB; MoBrPo; MOS
Sailor's life is a merry life, A. Sweet William. *Unknown.* OBET
Sailor's Mother, The, *sel.* Wordsworth.
"And thus continuing, she said." Par
Sailors on Leave. Owen Dodson. AmNP
Sailor's Prayer, A. George Hornell Morris. TrPWD
Sailor's Return, The. *Unknown.* OxBoLi
Sailor's Song. Thomas Lovell Beddoes. *See* To Sea, to Sea!
Sailor's Song, A. Hazel Harper Harris. EtS
Sailor's Sweetheart, The. Duncan Campbell Scott. PeCV
Sailors there are of gentlest breed. Commemorative of a Naval Victory. Herman Melville. AP; HAP; MOS; UnPo
Sailor's trade is a weary life, A. The Rocky Island. *Unknown.* AmFP
Sailor's Way, The. *Unknown.* ShS
Sailor's Wife, A. Clara Bernhardt. CaP
Sailor's Wife, The. William Julius Mickle, *also at. to* Jean Adam. BeLS; BSV; GN; GTBS; GTBS-P; HBV-1
(Mariner's Wife, The.) ViBoPo
(There's Nae Luck about the House.) NOEC; OBEC
Sailor's Woman. Annette Patton Cornell. GoYe
Sailor's Yarn, A. James J. Roche. MOS; NA
Sails. George Sterling. EtS
Sails flashing to the wind like weapons. Middle Passage. Robert Hayden. AmNP; BPo; NoAM; PoBA
Sainclaire's Defeat. *Unknown.* PAH
Saint. Robert Graves. CMoP
Saint. Stéphane Mallarmé, *tr. fr. French by* Roger Fry. NAWM-2; SyP
St. Agnes' Eve. Tennyson. GoBC; HBV-2; LiTB; OAEP; OBEV; OBVV; OxBoCh
St. Agnes' Eve—Ah, bitter chill it was! The Eve of St. Agnes. Keats. BeLS; CABA; ChER; DTo; EnRP; FiP, *abr.*; GoTL; HAP; HBV-2; HoPM; MasP; NIP; NoP; OAEL-2; OAEP; OBNC; OBNV; OBRV; PoEL-4; PoLF; SeCeV; TEP; TreF; TrGrPo; WeW; WHA
St. Andrews by the Northern Sea. Almae Matres. Andrew Lang. BSV; OBVV
St. Andrew's Voyage to Mermedonia. *Unknown, tr. fr. Anglo-Saxon by* Charles W. Kennedy. *Fr.* Andreas. AnOE
St. Anthony and His Pig; a Cantata. Frederick Forrest. NOEC
St. Anthony's Township. Gilbert Sheldon. CH
St. Asaph's. Kingsley Amis. OxBTC
St. Aubin d'Aubigne. Paul Dehn. OBWP
St. Augustine Contemplating the Bust of Einstein. Diane Ackerman. SUW
St. Benedick. *Unknown.* FaBoUs
Saint Bernard's Prayer to Our Lady. Dante, *tr. fr. Italian by* Louis How. *Fr.* Divina Commedia: Paradiso. ISi
Saint Brendan's Prophecy. *Unknown, tr. fr. Late Middle Irish by* Thomas Crofton Croker. OnYI
Saint Bridget was/ A problem child. The Giveaway. Phyllis McGinley. PoRA
Saint Called "Truth," A. William Langland, *mod. by* Donald Attwater. *Fr.* The Vision of Piers Plowman. NOCV
St. Cecilia's Day Epigram, A. Peter Porter. ELU
St. Ciaran and the Birds. Ciaran Carson. CIP
St. Columcille the Scribe. *Unknown, tr. fr. Middle Irish by* Kuno Meyer. AnIL
(Columcille the Scribe, *tr. by* Kuno Meyer.) OnYI
("My hand has a pain from writing," *tr. by* Flann O'Brien.) BIrV
St. Columcille's Island Hermitage. *Unknown, tr. fr. Middle Irish by* Kenneth Jackson. AnIL
Saint Coyote. Linda Hogan. STE
St. Crispin's Day. Shakespeare. *See* Henry V before Agincourt.
St. Cuthbert Intervenes. "Thomas Ingoldsby." NBM
St. Dunstan, as the story goes. *Unknown.* OxNR
Saint Elène, I thee pray. Prayer to St. Helena. *Unknown.* OxBM
St. Enda. Laurence Lerner. PeSA
Saint Francis. John Peale Bishop. EaLo
Saint Francis and Saint Benedight. William Cartwright. *See* House Blessing, A.
Saint Francis and the Birds. Roy McFadden. OxBI
Saint Francis and the Sow. Galway Kinnell. FYAP
Saint Francis Borgia; or, A Refutation for Heredity. Phyllis McGinley. NePoAm-2
St. Francis Einstein of the Daffodils. William Carlos Williams. MoPo
Saint Francis? No indeed, although at that. Old Man in the Park. Mary Elizabeth Osborn. NePoAm-2
St. Francis of Assisi and the Miserable Jews. Jozef Wittlin, *tr. fr. Polish by* Isaac Komen. VWA
St. Francis of the mountain cave and wattle hut. A Little Litany to St. Francis. Philip Murray. NePoAm
St. Francis' Prayer. St. Francis of Assisi. *See* Lord Make Me an Instrument of Your Peace.
St. George. Charlie Walker. AmFP
St. George he was for England. The Englishman. G. K. Chesterton. WhC
Saint Germain-en-Laye. Ernest Dowson. SyP
St. Gervais. Michael Roberts. FaBoCh
Saint Harmony my patroness. Paul Goodman. VGW
St. Helena Lullaby, A. Kipling. EBEV; FaBoCh; MoVE; OAEP; OBMV; PoEL-5
Saint . . . He Ain't, A. E. Y. Harburg. DBV
Saint-Henri Spring. Milton Acorn. NeAC
Saint Hugh. Thomas Dekker. *See* Cold's the Wind.
St. Irvyne, *sel.* Shelley.
"And the storm-fiends wild rave." PeD
St. Isaac's Church, Petrograd. Claude McKay. *See* Russian Cathedral.
Saint Ita's Fosterling. *At. to* St. Ita, *tr. fr. Old Irish by* Robin Flower. OnYI
St. James' Grove. William Carlos Williams. TwAmPo
St. James Infirmary. *Unknown.* AmFP; FSW; TreFT
(Gambler's Blues.) TrAS
(Those Gambler's Blues.) AS (A *and* B *vers., with music*)
St. James's Street. Frederick Locker-Lampson. HBV-2
Saint Jerome and his lion. Leonardo Da Vinci's. Marianne Moore. NYBP
St. John, *sels.* Bible, *N.T.*
Be of Good Cheer; I Have Overcome the World, XVI: 19–33. TreFS
"For God so loved the world," III: 16–17. LO
Good Shepherd, The, X: 7–18. TreFS
"Greater love hath no man," XV: 13–16. TreFT
I Am the Bread of Life, VI: 35–40. TreFS
"I am the true vine, and my Father is the husbandman," XV: 1–18. OBVE
Inscription on the Cross, XIX: 19–22. TreFT
Jesus and the Woman at the Well, IV: 5–26. TreFT
Jesus Answers the Parisees, VIII: 12–32. TreFS
Love One Another, XIII: 33–35. TreFT
"On the first day of the week cometh Mary Magdalene," XX: 1–17. LO
Peace of Christ, The, XIV: 1–27. TreFS
Woman Taken in Adultery, The, VIII: 2–11. TreFT
Word, The, I: 1–5. TrGrPo
("In the beginning was the Word, and the Word was with God, and the Word was God," 1–17.) TreF
Saint John, The. George Frederick Clarke. CaP
St. John. Whittier. PAH
Saint John Baptist. William Drummond of Hawthornden. *See* For the Baptist.
St. John Baptist. Arthur O'Shaughnessy. HBV-2

Saint John Damascene. The Rosebush and the Trinity. Alfred Barrett. GoBC
Saint John the Baptist. William Drummond of Hawthornden. *See* For the Baptist.
Saint Jorge, our Lady knight. For the Night-Mare. *Unknown.* OxBM
Saint Joseph, Saint Peter, Saint Paul! Prayer for Fine Weather. Shane Leslie. POL
Saint Judas. James Wright. ConAP; LCAP; NMP; NOBA; PAI
Saint-Just 1767–93 ("Saint-Just: his name seems stolen from the Missal"). Robert Lowell. FaBoMo
St. Julien's Eve. James Cunningham. JB
St. Kevin. *At. to* Samuel Lover. OnYI; WTO
St. Kilda. William Collins. *Fr.* Ode on the Popular Superstitions of the Highlands. FaBoEn
St. Lawrence and the Saguenay, The, *sels.* Charles Sangster.
"On, through the lovely Archipelago." PeCV
Thousand Islands, The. NOBC; OBCV
Saint Leger. Clinton Scollard. PAH
St. Louis/ such a colored town/ a whiskey. Nappy Edges (A Cross Country Sojourn). Ntozake Shange. BlSi
St. Louis Blues. W. C. Handy. BLSo, *with music;* FF
St. Luke, *sels.* Bible, *N.T.*
"And it came to pass in those days, that there went out a decree from Caesar Augustus," II. NAWM-1
(First Christmas, The, II: 1–19.) TreFS
"And Jesus said, A certain man had two sons," XV: 11–32. LO
(Prodigal Son, The.) TreF
"And there followed him a great company of people," XXIII: 27–44. LO
(Death of Jesus, The: 1–46.) TreF
"And there were in the same country shepherds abiding in the field," II. PChr (8–14); SoPo (8–16)
(Christmas Eve, II: 8–14.) SiSoSe
(Tidings of Great Joy, II: 8–14.) FaPON
Effective Prayer, XI: 9–13. TreFT
"Feare not, litle flocke, for it is your fathers good pleasure to give you the kingdome, " XII: 32–40. OBVE
Good Samaritan, The, X: 25–37. TreF
Jesus' Parable of the Sower, VIII: 5–15. TreFT
Lost Sheep, The, XV: 9–7. TreF
Magnificat, The, I: 46–56. BoWoP; ILwL; WGRP
("And Marie said, My soule doth magnifie the Lord.") OBVE
Nunc Dimittis, II: 29–32. WGRP
On Taking Up One's Cross, IX: 23–26. TreFT
On the Road to Emmaus, XXIV: 13–36. TreFS
"One of the Pharises desired [Jesus] that he would eat with him," VII: 36–50. LO
Pharisee and the Publican, The, XVIII: 9–14. TreFT
"Then drew near unto him all the publicans and sinners," XV. NAWM-1
Widow's Mite, The, XXI: 1–4. TreFT
Saint Luke the Painter. Dante Gabriel Rossetti. The House of Life, LXXIV. GoBC; VLP
St. Magnus control thee, that martyr of treason. Claud Halcro's Invocation. Sir Walter Scott. *Fr.* The Pirate. NBM
St. Malachy. Thomas Merton. CoPo; VGW
Saint Malcolm. Jewel C. Latimore. BPo
St. Mark, *sels.* Bible, *N.T.*
"And as soon as it was morning the chief priests," XV: 1–39. DL
"And he said, So is the kingdome of God," IV: 26–32. OBVE
Jesus and the Children, X: 13–16. TreFT
Jesus Eats with Sinners, II: 15–17. TreFT
St. Mark. Christopher Smart. *Fr.* Hymns and Spiritual Songs. LAuP
St. Martin and the Beggar. Thom Gunn. MoBS
Saint[e] Mary Magdalene; or, The Weeper. Richard Crashaw. MeLP; SeCV-1
(Weeper, The.) AnAnS-1; MePo; OAEL-1, *abr.*; OBEV; SeCP; ViBoPo, *abr.*
"And now where're he strayes," *sel.* FaBoCo; Par
St. Mary's Loch. Geoffrey Faber. PoSH
St. Matthew, *sels.* Bible, *N.T.*
Easter Morning, XXVIII: 1–10 TreF
Great Commandment, The, XXII: 34–40. TreFT
My Yoke Is Easy, XI: 28–30. TreFS
Rich Man and the Kingdom of Heaven, The, XIX: 13–30. TreF
Sermon on the Mount, The, V: 1–VII: 29. TreF
("And seeing the multitudes, he went up.") BiP; NAWM-1 (V–VII); PoPL (V: 1–10)
Beatitudes, The. TrGrPo (V: 3–10).
("Blessed are the poor in spirit.") OBVE (V: 3–10)
God Provides, VI: 26–34. BLRP
Lord's Prayer, The, VI: 9–13. EaLo; PoLF; TrGrPo; TRV
"No Man can serve two masters," VI: 24–29. OBVE
Treasures, VI: 19–21. TrGrPo
"Then one of the twelve, called Judas Iscariot," XXVI: 14–XXVII. NAWM-1
Things That Are Caesar's, The, XXII: 15–22. TreF
When the Son of Man Shall Come in His Glory, XXV: 31–46. TreF
Wise and Foolish Virgins, The, XXV: 1–13. TreF
St. Matthias. Christopher Smart. *Fr.* Hymns and Spiritual Songs. LAuP
St. Michael's Mount. John Davidson. HBV-2
Saint Nicholas. Marianne Moore. NYBP; WPE
Saint of the Golden Gate Bridge. Walking on Water. Mario Petaccia. LFAC
Saint on the pillar stands, The. Stylite. Louis MacNeice. MoPo
Saint Patrick. Henry Bennett. HBV-2
(St. Patrick Was a Gentleman.) SiSoSe
St. Patrick, *sel.* Phyllis Garlick.
"Christ with me, Christ before me, Christ behind me." TRV
Saint Patrick for Ireland, *sel.* James Shirley.
Bard's Chant. ACP
St. Patrick of Ireland, My Dear! William Maginn. InMe
Saint Patrick, slave to Milcho of the herds. The Proclamation. Whittier. PAH
St. Patrick Was a Gentleman. Henry Bennett. *See* Saint Patrick.
St. Patrick's Breastplate. *At. to* St. Patrick. *See* Deer's Cry, The.
Saint Patrick's day in 'sixty-five. Bound Down to Newfoundland. *Unknown.* ShS
St. Patrick's Day is with us. I'll Wear a Shamrock. Mary Carolyn Davies. SiSoSe; YeAr
St. Patrick's Day it is—it is. Dawn Song—St. Patrick's Day. Violet Alleyn Storey. YeAr
Saint Patrick's Day, 1973. Wendy Rose. CDW
St. Patrick's Dean, your country's pride. To Dr. Swift on His Birthday, 30th November 1721. Esther Johnson. EnLoPo
St. Patrick's Hymn before Tara[h]. James Clarence Mangan. EnRP; GoBC
Saint Paul, *abr.* F. W. H. Myers. PGD
Sels.
"Christ! I am Christ's! and let the name suffice you." TRV
Inner Light, The. HBV-2; WGRP
"Whoso has felt the Spirit of the Highest." TRV
St. Paul on Charity. Bible, *N.T.* *See* Though I Speak with the Tongues of Men and Angels.
Saint Peray. Thomas William Parsons. HBV-2
St. Peter. Christina Rossetti. NOCV
St. Peter at the Gate. Joseph Bert Smiley. BLPA
St. Peter once: "Lord, dost Thou wash my feet?" St. Peter. Christina Rossetti. NOCV
Saint Peter sat by the celestial gate. The Vision of Judgment. Byron. EnRP; MasP; OAEL-2; OBRV, *sts.* 1–6; OBSV, *sts.* 1–23; OxBoLi, *sts.* 1–15; TEP
St. Peter stood guard at the golden gate. St. Peter at the Gate. Joseph Bert Smiley. BLPA
Saint Peter's Complaint, *sel.* Robert Southwell.
Stanzas from Saint Peter's Complaint. ACP
St. Peter's Day was celebrated by St. Brendan at sea. The Fish at Mass. *Unknown, tr. by* J. F. Webb. BIrV
St Peter's Shadow. Richard Crashaw. ACP
St. Philip and St. James. Christopher Smart. Hymns and Spiritual Songs, Hymn 13. NOCV; NOEC
(Spring.) OBEC
"Now the winds are all composure," *sel.* LoBV
St. Philip in Himself. Cardinal Newman. GoBC
Saint Pumpkin. Nancy Willard. LCAP
Saint R. L. S. Sarah N. Cleghorn. HBMV
St. Roach. Muriel Rukeyser. GP
St. Saviour's, Aberdeen Park, Highbury, London, N. John Betjeman. MoVE
St. Simeon Stylites. Tennyson. OAEL-2
St. Simon and Jude, on you I intrude. *Unknown.* FaBoUs
St. Stephen and [King] Herod. *Unknown.* BaBo; *Middle English vers.*; ESPB, *Middle English vers.*; NoP, *mod. vers.*; OXBM, *Middle English vers.*; OxBoCh, *Middle English vers.*; OxBoLi, *Middle English vers.*; TrGrPo, *mod. vers.*
(Carol for St. Stephen's Day, A.) CH
(Seynt Stevyn and Herowdes.) OxBB
Saynt Stephen in San Francisco. Melvin Walker La Follette. CoPo
St. Stephen's cloistered hall was proud. Columbus. Lydia Huntley Sigourney. AA; HBV-2; PAH
St. Stephen's Day. Patric Dickinson. OBCP
St. Stephen's Word. Rayner Heppenstall. ChMP
St. Swithin. Daniel Henderson. HBMV; ShM
St. Swithin's Chair. Sir Walter Scott. WSC
St. Teresa's Book-Mark. St. Theresa of Ávila. *See* Lines Written in Her Breviary.

St. Thomas. *Unknown, at. to* Ferdinand G. Christgau. TDH
(Limerick: "Bright little maid of St. Thomas, A.") HBV-2
St. Thomas Aquinas thought. Vulture. Kenneth Rexroth. *Fr.* A Bestiary. NNaP
St. Thomas's Day is past and gone. *Unknown.* OxNR
St. Uncumber and St. Trunnion. The Palmer. John Heywood. *Fr.* The Play of the Four P.P. ACP
St. Ursanne. Michael Roberts. LiTM
St. Valentine. Pancho Aguila. LFAC
St. Valentine. Marianne Moore. NYBP; OFD
St. Valentine's Day. Wilfrid Scawen Blunt. *Fr.* The Love Sonnets of Proteus. EnLoPo; NBM; OBVV; ViBoPo
Saint Valentine's Day. Coventry Patmore. The Unknown Eros, XLIII. FaBoEn; GoBC; OBNC
Saint Valentine's Day. Shakespeare. *See* Tomorrow Is Saint Valentine's Day.
Saint Vesta! Oh thou sanctifying saint. To Vesta. Thomas Middleton. MOON
St. Vincent's. W. S. Merwin. NYP
Sainte Anne de Beaupre. Richard Eberhart. NePoAm
Sainte Mary Magdalene; or, The Weeper. Richard Crashaw. *See* Saint Mary Magdalene; or, The Weeper.
Sainte Marye Virgine. A Cry to Mary. St. Godric. MeEL
Saints, The. Robert Creeley. NMP
Saints. George Garrett. EaLo
Saints and me! Ah quit! Antoine and I Go Fishing. David Budbill. WOLT
Saints are gathering at the real, The. The Confirmers. A. R. Ammons. TAP
Saint's Bridge. Lola Ridge. WPE
Saint's Delight, The. Isaac Watts. *See* Ninety-fifth.
Saints have adored the lofty soul of you. Two Sonnets, I. Charles Hamilton Sorley. HBMV; MMA; MoBrPo
Saints, I give myself up to thee. Chorus. Jack Kerouac. *Fr.* Mexico City Blues. NeAP
Saints in Glory, The. Dante, *tr. fr. Italian by* Henry F. Cary. *Fr.* Divina Commedia: Paradiso. WGRP
Saints in Glory, We Together, *with music.* Nehemiah Adams. AH
Saints look at dirt. *Unknown, tr. fr. Pashto by* Saduddin Shpoon. PBWP
Saints Lose Back. Nancy Willard. HoAn
Saint's Parade. Robert Layzer. NePoEA
Saint's Tragedy, The, *sels.* Charles Kingsley.
Song: "Oh! that we two were Maying." HBV-1
Song: "When I was a greenhorn and young." NBM
Saints who love the Crucified, The. A Proud Song. Marguerite Wilkinson. HBMV
Sair Fyel'd, Hinny. *Unknown.* GBP
Saith the poet of nonsense. Scraps of Lear. Edward Lear. FaBoNo
Sakhara. R. A. D. Ford. NOBC
Saki, for God's love, come and fill my glass. Hafiz, *tr. by* Richard Le Gallienne. Odes, I. AWP
Sakiyeh, The. Mathilde Blind. SBG
Sal Got a Meatskin. *Unknown.* FSW
Salaam Alaikum. *Unknown.* PoLF
Salad, *sels.* Mortimer Collins.
Salad: After Browning. Par
Salad: After Swinburne. Par
Salad: After Tennyson. CenHV; Par
(King Arthur Growing Very Tired Indeed.) FaBoCo
Salad, A. Sydney Smith. HBV-2
(Recipe for Salad.) FaBoUs
Salad La Raza. Janet Campbell Hall. VoR
Salad of greens! Salad of greens! The Universal Favorite. Carolyn Wells. InMe
Salamanca Doctor's Farewell, The. *Unknown.* APAS
Salami. Philip Levine. NNaP; NOBA; TAP
Salamis. Aeschylus, *tr. fr. Greek by* G. M. Cookson. *Fr.* The Persians. WaaP
Salamis. Lawrence Durrell. NYBP
Salangadou. *Tr. fr. French Creole.* FSW; TrAS, *with music*
Salaziennes, Les, *sel.* Auguste Lacaussade, *tr. fr. French.*
"My lips from this day forgot how to smile." TTY
Salcombe Seaman's Flaunt to the Proud Pirate, The. *Unknown.* ChTr
(Pirate of High Barbary, The.) EtS
Sale. Josephine Miles. POL; WPE
Sale. Miller Williams. WeW
Sale began—young girls were there, The. The Slave Auction. Frances E. W. Harper. BPo; PoNe; TTY
Sale of Smoke, A. Roberta Spear. AmPA
Sale of the Pet Lamb, The. Mary Howitt. CH
Salem. Robert Lowell. CABA; NePoEA
Salem. Edmund Clarence Stedman. AA; PAH
Salem Witch, A. Ednah Proctor Clarke. PAH
Salesman, The. Robert Mezey. NePoEA
Salesman. Ruth Roston. AMV-80
Salesman Is an It That Stinks Excuse, A. E. E. Cummings. NoAM; OxBA; TW
(Salesman, A.) DBV; NIP
Salient point, so first is call'd the heart, The. The Circulation of the Blood. Sir Richard Blackmore. *Fr.* Creation. FaBoUs
Salisbury Plain and Stonehenge. Wordsworth. *Fr.* Guilt and Sorrow. FaBoPP
Salisbury; the Cathedral Close. Coventry Patmore. *See* Cathedral Close, The.
Sall. Inez Quilter. SUMH
Sallow waiter brings me six huge oysters, A. Storm on Fifth Avenue. Siegfried Sassoon. MoVE
Sallows like heads in Polynesia. Into the Salient. Edmund Blunden. ViBoPo
Sally and Manda. Alice B. Campbell. RHPC
Sally Ann. *Unknown.* FSW
Sally Birkett's Ale. *Unknown.* ChTr
Sally Brown. Thomas Hood. *See* Faithless Sally Brown.
Sally Brown. *Unknown.* AmFP; AmSS, *with music*; FSW; ShS, 2 *vers., with music*
Sally Free and Easy. Cyril Tawney. OBET
Sally from Coventry, The. Walter Thornbury. HBV-2
Sally Go Round the Sunshine, *with music. Unknown.* OuSiCo
("Sally go round the sun," *sl. diff.*) OxNR
Sally Goodin. *Unknown.* AmFP; FSW
Sally, having swallowed cheese. Cruel Clever Cat. Geoffrey Taylor. ChTr; FaBoEE
Sally in Our Alley. Henry Carey. AWP; BLPL; BLSO, *with music*; BoLo; CoMu; FaBoBe; FaFP; FSW; GTBS; GTBS-P; HBV-1; InMe; NOBE; OBEV; PoPle; TreF; ViBoPo
(Ballad of Sally in Our Alley.) NOEC; OBEC
"Of all the girls that are so smart," *sel.* PoSC
Sally is gone that was so kindly. Ha'nacker Mill. Hilaire Belloc. FaPoR; HBMV; MoBrPo; OxBTC
Sally is the laundress, and every Saturday. The Dolls' Wash. Juliana Horatia Ewing. OxBChV
Sally Monroe, *with music. Unknown.* ShS
Sally My Dear. *Unknown.* FSW
Sally, Sally Waters. *Unknown.* OxNR
Sally Salter, she was a young teacher who taught. The Lovers. Phoebe Cary. HBV-2
Sally Simpkin's Lament. Thomas Hood. EnRP; MOS; ShM
Sally Sweetbread. Henry Carey. CoMu
Sally's Garden. *Unknown.* AmFP
Salmon. Jorie Graham. MAYP
Salmon, The. Christian Morgenstern, *tr. fr. German by* Geoffrey Grigson. FaBoNo
Salmon and red wine. Raisins and Nuts. Charles Reznikoff. VWA
Salmon Cycle. Avner Treinin, *tr. fr. Hebrew by* Robert Friend. VWA
Salmon Draught at Inveraray. R. W. Nunley. WOLT
Salmon Drowns Eagle. Malcolm Lowry. MoCV; OBCV
Salmon Eggs. Ted Hughes. NAs
Salmon Fly Hatch on Yankee Jim Canyon of the Yellowstone. Greg Keeler. WOLT
Salmon remarked to his mate, A. Sliding Scale. Norman R. Jaffray. TDH
Salmon waiting in the amber pools, The. Salmon Draught at Inveraray. R. W. Nunley. WOLT
Salmon were just down there, The. Salmon Eggs. Ted Hughes. NAs
Salome was a dancer. *Unknown.* WTO
Salomon. Pierre Morhange, *tr. fr. French by* Edouard Roditi. VWA
Salonikan Grave. Kipling. *Fr.* Epitaphs of the War, 1914–18. OAEP
Saloon is gone up the creek, The. Hemmed-in Males. William Carlos Williams. *Fr.* A Folded Skyscraper. MAT; MoVE; PoRA
Salt. Lucille Clifton. GP
Salt. Monk Gibbon. OxBI
Salt. Ruth Stone. NMM
Salt creek mouths unflushed by the sea. The South Coast. William Everson. NeAP
Salt flakes fleck my skin. Dead Neck. Sue Standing. AMV-81
Salt Flats, The. Sir Charles G. D. Roberts. CaP
Salt Garden, The. Howard Nemerov. NePoEA
Salt Lake City. Hayden Carruth. AmFN
Salt Man. Annette Arkeketa West. TWSS
Salt of the Earth. D. H. Lawrence. NoAM
Salt Pork, The. Robert Clayton Casto. HeIP
Salt seas, mountains, deserts. Toward Climax. Gary Snyder. SUW
Salt Water Story. Richard Hugo. NoP
Salt wave sings, The. Fingernail Sunrise. Vernon Watkins. NYBP

Saltmarsh on the horizon, The. The Estuarial Republic. Douglas Dunn. FaBoMo
Salty Dog Blues. *Unknown.* FSW
Salty Dogs. *Unknown.* CoSo
Salut au Monde, *sel.* Walt Whitman.
"I see a great round wonder rolling through space." SUS
Salutamus. Sterling A. Brown. CDC
Salutation. "Æ." OnYI
Salutation. Zerea Jacob, *tr. fr. Abyssinian by* F. Baetman. ISi
Salutation. Ezra Pound. HeIP; MoAB; MoAmPo; NOBA; OxBA; TAP; VGW
Salutation, The. Thomas Traherne. AnAnS-1; InvP; NOCV; NoP; OBS; SeCP; SeCV-2
Sels.
"From Dust I rise." FaBoEn
"These little limbs." OxBoCh
Salutation of the Blessed Virgin, The. John Byrom. ISi
Salutation of the Dawn. *Unknown, at. to* Kalidasa, *ad. fr.* Sanskrit. PoLF; TreFT
Salutation the Second. Ezra Pound. NOBA; OxBA
Salutation to Jesus Christ. John Calvin. WGRP
Salutations: To Mary, Virgin. *Unknown, tr. fr. Latin by* Raymond F. Roseliep. ISi
Salute. Oliver Pitcher. PoBA
Salute. James Schuyler. FYAP; NeAP
Salute the last and everlasting day. Ascention. John Donne. AnAnS-1; OBS
Salute to Life. Dmitri Shostakovitch. FSW
Salute to the Elephant. Odeniyi Apolebieji, *tr. fr. Yoruba by* S. A. Babalola. WTO
Salute to the Modern Language Association, Convening in the Hotel Pennsylvania, December 28th-30th, A. Morris Bishop. WhC
Salute Your Partner. *Unknown.* AmFP
Salvador Dali. David Gascoyne. EAS; OxBTC
(In Defence of Humanism.) FaBoMo
Salvador Dali almost foresaw it. Nuclear Land. Ellen Tifft. AMV-81
Salvation Army lass, The. Lola Ridge. *Fr.* Ward X. WPE
Salvation comes by Christ alone. An Evening Thought. Jupiter Hammon. PoNe
Salvation of Texas Peters, The. J. W. Foley. ShM
Salvation Prospect. LeRoy Smith, Jr. NePoAm
Salvation to all that will is nigh. Annunciation. John Donne. *Fr.* La Corona. AnAnS-1; ISi; OBS; SBVL; TrCP
Salvation's not the work, but *saving*. Saving the Fish. R. T. Smith. WOLT
Salve! Thomas Edward Brown. HBV-2; OBEV; OBVV
Salve Regina. *At. to* Hermanus Contractus, *tr. fr. Latin by* Winfred Douglas. ISi
Sam. St. John Adcock. WhC
Sam. Walter de la Mare. FaBV; MoAB; MoBrPo; OnMSP; TiPo
Sam Bass. *Unknown.* AmFP; AS, *with music*; BeLS; CoSo, *with music*; FSW; ViBoFo
Sam Brown was a fellow from way down East. In the Catacombs. Harlan Hoge Ballard. YaD
Sam had spirits naught could check. Impetuous Samuel. Harry Graham. NA
Sam Hall. *Unknown.* AmFP; CoSo, *with music*; FSW; TW; UnPo; ViBoFo, *with music*
(Ballad of Sam Hall, The.) FSW; VLP
(Samuel Hall.) ChTr; DBV
Sam, Sam, the butcher man. *Unknown.* FaFP
Samantha the golden retriever. Me and Samantha. Pyke Johnson, Jr. GDP
Sambo's Right to Be Kilt. Charles Graham Halpine. AA
Same, The. Wordsworth. *See* London, 1802.
Same Dream, The. Shlomit Cohen, *tr. fr. Hebrew by* Myra Glazer Schotz. VWA
Same Gesture, The. John Montague. BIrV
Same great angel who had once, The. On the Death of Mary. Rainer Maria Rilke, *tr. by* M. D. Herter Norton. ISi
Same in Blues. Langston Hughes. *Fr.* Lenox Avenue Mural. InPS
Same leaves over and over again, The! In Hardwood Groves. Robert Frost. HAP
Same March sun that polishes St. Paul's, The. Flight 539. John Malcolm Brinnin. HoAn
Same old fable, The. On Being Told That One's Ideas Are Victorian. Sara Henderson Hay. InMe
Same Old Jazz, The. Philip Whalen. NeAP
Same old souvenirs, The. Niagara Falls Nocturne. Len Gasparini. NeAC
Same Old Story, The. James J. Montague. HBMV
Same Old Trick. William W. Pratt. QQQ
Same sequence as the night before, The. Shutting the Curtains. Bink Noll. GP
Same Side of the Canoe, The. Alda do Espírito Santo, *tr. fr. Portuguese by* Allan Francovich *and* Kathleen Weaver. PBWP
Same Tits. James Tate. FAZ
Same Train, *with music. Unknown.* BoAN-2
Samela. Robert Greene. *See* Doron's Description of Samela.
Samis Idyll. Dachine Rainer. NePoAm
Sammy Lou of Rue. Revolutionary Petunias. Alice Walker. BlSi
Samor, *sel.* Henry Hart Milman.
Beacons, The. OBRV
Sampler from Haworth. Frances Minturn Howard. WPE
Sampling the books the moderns bring. Deep Stuff. Keith Preston. WhC
Sampson Imitated. *Unknown, wr. at. to* Benjamin Franklin. *See* Jack and Roger.
Sam's World ("Sam's mother has"). Sam Cornish. CNA
Samson. Amir Gilboa, *tr. fr. Hebrew by* Stephen Mitchell. VWA
Samson, *with music. Unknown.* OuSiCo
Samson Agonistes. Milton. OAEL-1; PoEL-3
Sels.
"All is best, though we oft doubt." NOBE; OBEV; OBS; SeCeV
(All Is Best.) SeCePo
(Epilogue.) FaBoEn
Blindness of Samson, The. LiTB
"I, dark in light, exposed," 5 *ll.* TrGrPo
"But see here comes thy reverend Sire." EBEV
Death of Samson. ChTr
("Come, come, no time for lamentation now.") FiP
(No Time for Lamentation Now.) FaBoRV
Delilah. SeCePo
"Feast and noon grew high, and Sacrifice, The." EBEV
Heroic Vengeance. OBS
"Let me obtain forgiveness of thee, Samson." EBEV
"Little onward lend thy guiding hand, A." ViBoPo
"Many are the sayings of the wise." SeCeV
(Ways of God to Men, The.) OBS
O Dark, Dark, Dark. WHA
"Oh how comely it is and how reviving." NOBE; NOCV; OBEV; SeCeV
(Deliverer, The.) OBS
Samson Hath Quit Himself. LoBV
"This only hope relieves me, that the strife." TRV
"This, this is he; softly a while." UnPo
(Samson Fallen.) OBS
Transcendence of God, The. OBS
"Wilt thou then serve the Philistines with that gift." EBEV
Woman. OBS
Samson Rends His Clothes. Anadad Eldan, *tr. fr. Hebrew by* Ruth Nevo. VWA
Samson to His Delilah. Richard Crashaw. TrGrPo
Samuel. Bobbi Katz. RHPC
Samuel Allen. *Unknown.* AmFP
Samuel, Book I. Bible, *O.T. See* First Samuel.
Samuel, Book II. Bible, *O.T. See* Second Samuel.
Samuel Brown. Phoebe Cary. OBAL
Samuel Hall. *Unknown. See* Sam Hall.
Samuel Hearne in Wintertime. John Newlove. NOBC
Samuel Hoar. Franklin Benjamin Sanborn. AA
Samuel Pepys. Allan M. Laing. FiBHP
Samuel Perry Dinsmoor. In Lucas, Kansas. Jonathan Williams. FAZ
Samuel, Samuel Palmer. In a Shoreham Garden. Laurence Lerner. NePoEA-2
Samuel Sewall. Anthony Hecht. ConAP; LiTM; MP; NePoEA; PoPl; PoRA; TwCP
Samurai and Hustlers. Joe Johnson. CNA
San Diego Poem, A. Simon J. Ortiz. CDW
San Francisco. Mary Austin. BPAW
San Francisco. John Vance Cheney. PAH
San Francisco. Joaquin Miller. PAH
San Francisco. Walter Adolphe Roberts. PoNe
San Francisco Arising. Edwin Markham. BPAW
San Francisco Bay. Joaquin Miller. BPAW
San Francisco Company, The. *Unknown.* AmFP
San Francisco County Jail Cell B-6. Conyus. PoBA
San Francisco Falling. Edwin Markham. BPAW
San Francisco from the Sea. Bret Harte. BPAW
San Francisco Poem. John Logan. NNaP
San Francisco remains in grave personal danger. Jeanne Dixon's America. Gerald Costanzo. MAYP
San Juan Capistrano. Alice Cecilia Cooper. GoBC
San Lorenzo Giustiniani's Mother. Alice Meynell. HBV-2
San Marco Museum, Florence. Sister Maris Stella. GoBC
San Pedro Road. Robert Hass. GeTw; WOLT
San Quentin, sing sing, alcatraz. Bogey. Lee L. Berkson. AMV-81

San Quentin was brilliant. Within the halls. The Convicts' Ball. Ambrose Bierce. BPAW
San Ysidro, Cabezon. Paula Gunn Allen. TWSS
Sancho. William Edwin Collin. CaP
Sanct Christopher II ("Sanct Christopher's a muckle sanct and strang"). Robert Garioch, *after the Italian of* Giuseppe Belli. OBVE
Sancta Silvarum. Lionel Johnson. BrPo
"Moon labours through black cloud, The," II–IV. VLP
Sanctimonious Poets, The. Friedrich Hölderlin, *tr. fr. German by* Robert Bly. NU
Sanctimony. *Malay Oral Tradition, tr. by* R. J. Wilkinson. WTO
Sanctity. Patrick Kavanagh. BIrV; ELU
Sanctuary. J. B. Boothroyd. FiBHP
Sanctuary. Bruce Boyd. NeAP
Sanctuary. Clifford Dyment. PoA
Sanctuary, The. Ford Madox Ford. PoA
Sanctuary. Louise Imogen Guiney. AA
Sanctuary. Dorothy Hewett. CBAP
Sanctuary, The. Howard Nemerov. NePoEA
Sanctuary. Judith Wright. WPE
Sanctuary. Elinor Wylie. BoWoP; MoAB; MoAmPo
Sanctuary should exist on earth. To Any M. F. H. V. Sackville-West. SBG
Sanctum, The. T. A. Daly. TrPWD
Sanctus. David Gascoyne. *Fr.* Miserere. NeBP
Sand-between-the-Toes. A. A. Milne. TiPo
Sand Creek. Charles G. Ballard. UnPo; VoR
Sand Dunes. Robert Frost. MoAB; MoAmPo; RFM
Sand Dunes and Sea. John Richard Moreland. HBMV
Sand has the ants, clay ferny weeds for play. Possessions. Ivor Gurney. FaBoPP
Sand is a gritty flesh, The. Burial in the Sand. Nancy Sullivan. NIP
Sand Martin, The. John Clare. PBBP; TEP
Sand Painters, The. Ben Belitt. EyDe; GOA
Sand Paintings. Alice Corbin. BPAW
Sand, sand; hills of sand. The Mermaids. Walter de la Mare. BrPo
Sand: the crystalline children. Kneeling Here, I Feel Good. Marge Piercy. NeAC
Sand white as frost: the moon stayed hard and high. The Galloway Shore. Sydney Tremayne. BSV
Sandal and garment of yellow and lotus garlands upon his body of blue. Jayadeva, *tr. by* George Keyt. *Fr.* Gita Govinda. ErPo
Sandgate Girl's Lamentation, The. *Unknown.* CoMu; ELP
Sandhill Crane, The. Mary Austin. BPAW; TiPo
Sandhill People. Carl Sandburg. CMoP
Sandman, The. "Margaret Vandegrift." HBV-1; HBVY
Sandpaper, Sandpiper, Sandpit. Warren Slesinger. AMV-80
Sandpiper. Elizabeth Bishop. HeIP; NYBP
Sandpiper, The. Witter Bynner. HBMV; RHPC
Sandpiper, The. Frances Frost. RHPC
Sandpiper, The. Celia Thaxter. AA; FaBoBe; FaPON; GN; HBV-1; HBVY; OBCA; OxBChV; WBLP
Sandpipers. Helen Merrill Egerton. CaP
Sandra and that boy that's going to get her in trouble. Cora Punctuated with Strawberries. George Starbuck. NCSH; NMP
Sands of Dee, The. Charles Kingsley. *Fr.* Alton Locke, *ch.* 26. BeLS; CH; EBVV; FaBoPP; FaPON; FaPoR; GN; HBV-1; PoPle; TreF; VLP; WBLP
Sandstone. Anne Marriott. CaP
Sandstone carriage, A. For Cal. James Cunningham. JB
Sandwich in Spain now, and the duke in love. The Third Advice to a Painter. Andrew Marvell. APAS
Sandwich Man, The. Ron Padgett. ConAP
Sandy cat by the Farmer's chair, The. Summer Evening. Walter de la Mare. FM; MoAB; MoBrPo; MoShBr; TiPo
Sandy he belongs to the mill. *Unknown.* OxNR
Sandy Hook. George Houghton. AA
Sandy Kildandy. *Unknown.* OxNR
Sandy Star and Willie Gee (*Complete,* I–V). William Stanley Braithwaite. BANP
Sandy Star, V. HBMV
Sanford Barney. *Unknown.* *See* State of Arkansas, The.
Sang: "My Peggy is a young thing." Allan Ramsay. *See* My Peggy.
Sang: Recoll o Skaith. Sidney Goodsir Smith. NeBP
Sang: "There's a reid lowe in yer cheek." Robert MacLellan. OxBS
Sang of the Birth of Christ, with the Tune of Baw Lula Low, Ane, *abr.* John Wedderburn, *after the German of* Martin Luther. BSV
Sang old Tom the lunatic. Tom the Lunatic. W. B. Yeats. OnYI
Sang Solomon to Sheba. Solomon to Sheba. W. B. Yeats. CMoP; ELP
Sang the sunrise on an amber morn. An April Adoration. Sir Charles G. D. Roberts. HBV-1
Sank through easeful. The Diver. Robert Hayden. AmPP; BPo; LiSp; MOS
Sanquhar, whom this earth could scarce contain. William Drummond of Hawthornden. FaBoEE
Sans Equity and sans Poise. Confucius, *tr. fr. Chinese by* Ezra Pound. *Fr.* Yung Wind. CTC
Sans Souci. Lisel Mueller. NePoAm-2
Santa Anna [*or* Ana] came storming, as a storm might come. The Defense [*or* Defence] of the Alamo. Joaquin Miller. BeLS; BPAW; FaBoBe; HBV-2; OnMSP; PAH
Santa Anna; or, The Plains of Mexico, *with music.* *Unknown.* AmSS
(Santy Anna, *with music.*) ShS, 2 *vers.*
(Santy Anno.) FSW; OuSiCo, *longer vers., with music*
Santa Barbara. Francis Fisher Browne. AA
Santa Barbara Beach. Ridgely Torrence. HBMV
Santa Barbara Earthquake, The. *Unknown.* AmFP
Santa Caterina. Myra Glazer Schotz. VWA
Santa Claus. Walter de la Mare. PChr
Santa Claus. Christopher Hassall. OxBTC
Santa Claus. Dom Moraes. NoAM
Santa Claus. Howard Nemerov. HAP
Santa Claus ("He comes in the night!"). *Unknown.* HBVY
Santa Claus ("Little fairy snowflakes"). *Unknown.* SoPo
Santa Claus lies dead across the chair. Merry Christmas! Elder Olson. FAZ
Santa Fe Trail, The. Arthur Chapman. BPAW
Santa Fe Trail. Barbara Guest. NeAP; PoM
Santa Fe Trail, The, *with music.* *Unknown.* CoSo
Santa Fe Trail, The. Effortlessly Democratic Santa Fe Trail. Martha Baird. PoPl
Santa Lucia. Teodoro Cottrau, *tr. fr. Italian.* FSW
Santa Maria del Fiore. George Herbert Clarke. CaP
Santa Maria, well thou tremblest down the wave. The Triumph. Sidney Lanier. *Fr.* The Psalm of the West. PAH
Santa Teresa's Book-Mark. St. Theresa of Ávila. *See* Lines Written in Her Breviary.
Santiago. Thomas A. Janvier. PAH
Santo Domingo Corn Dance. R. P. Dickey. TAT
Santorin. James Elroy Flecker. FaBoTw; GoJo; OBMV
Santos: New Mexico. May Sarton. EaLo
Santy Anna [*or* Anno]. *Unknown.* *See* Santa Anna; or, The Plains of Mexico.
Saon of Acanthus. Callimachus, *tr. fr. Greek by* John Addingtion Symonds. AWP; TRV
Sap, The. Henry Vaughan. AnAnS-1
Sap rises from the sodden ditch. For Jane Myers. Louise Glück. GeTw
Saphire (Metamorpho's Chick). Joe Rosenblatt. MoCV
Sapho and Phao, *sels.* John Lyly.
"My shag-hair Cyclops, come, let's ply." EBEV
Sapho's Song. OBSC
Song in Making of the Arrows, The. LoBV; OBSC
(Vulcan's Song.) EIL
Sapientia Lunae. Ernest Dowson. HBV-2
Sappa Creek, The. Gary Snyder. NCSH
Sapper. Andrew Greig. BSV
Sapphic Dream, A. George Moore. SyP
Sapphics. D. B. Wyndham Lewis. NOBL
Sapphics. Sir Philip Sidney. *Fr.* Arcadia. SiPS
Sapphics. Swinburne. PoEL-5
Sapphics: At the Mohawk-Castle, Canada. Thomas Morris. NOEC
Sapphics: The Friend of Humanity and the Knife-Grinder. George Canning, *and* John Hookham Frere. *See* Friend of Humanity and the Knife-Grinder, The.
Sapphire, The. W. S. Merwin. PoA
Sappho, *sel.* Bliss Carman.
"When in the spring the swallows all return," XCIII. PeCV
Sappho. Catullus, *tr. fr. Latin by* William Ellery Leonard. AWP
Sappho. Jack Cope. PeSA
Sappho/ Sister/Mother. Invocation to Sappho. Elsa Gidlow. IHMS
Sappho and Phao. John Lily. *See* Sapho and Phao.
Sappho, Be Comforted. William Carlos Williams. NePoAm-2
"Sappho, if you do not come out." Sappho, *tr. fr. Greek by* Willis Barnstone. BoWoP
Sappho Rehung. LeRoy Smith, Jr. NePoAm
Sappho's Reply. Rita Mae Brown. PeHV
Sappho's Tomb. Arthur Stringer. CaP
Sara in Her Father's Arms. George Oppen. GP; NNaP
Saragossa. Henry Sambrooke Leigh. FaBoCo
Sarah. Edna Aphek, *tr. fr. Hebrew by* Yishai Tobin. VWA
Sarah. Delmore Schwartz. VWA
Sarah/ was a woman. Sarah. Edna Aphek, *tr. by* Yishai Tobin. VWA

Sarah Byng [Who Could Not Read and Was Tossed into a Thorny Hedge by a Bull]. Hilaire Belloc. CenHV; GoJo
Sarah: Cherokee Doctor. Wendy Rose. STE
Sarah Cynthia Sylvia Stout Would Not Take the Garbage Out. Shel Silverstein. OBCA
Sarah Hazard's Love Letter. John Ellis. NOEC
Sarah kissed me when we met. Osculation. Henry Sydnor Harrison. InMe
Sarah Samantha. *Unknown.* TDH
Sarah Threeneedles. Katharine Lee Bates. HBMV
Sarah T's husband shot her at the Tohatchi laundromat. The Shooting. Laura Tohe. STE
Sarai. Joseph Sherman. VWA
Sarajevo. Lawrence Durrell. GTBS-P
Sarasvati. James Stephens. NoAM
Saratoga Ending. Weldon Kees. NaP
Saratoga Song. *Unknown.* PAH
Sardanapalus. Earl of Surrey. *See* Portrait of Henry VIII, The.
Sarentino-South Tyrol. Philip Brantingham. AMV-80
Sargent's Portrait of Edwin Booth at "The Players." Thomas Bailey Aldrich. AA
Sargon is dust, Semiramis a clod. The Dust Dethroned. George Sterling. *Fr.* Three Sonnets on Oblivion. HBV-2
Saris go by me from the embassies, The. The Woman at the Washington Zoo. Randall Jarrell. AP; CoAP; HAP; LiTM; MP; NMP; OxBC; TAP; TwCP; UnPo
Sark. Swinburne. *Fr.* The Garden of Cymodoce. FaBoPP
Sarmèd, whom they intoxicated from the cup of love. Quatrain. Sarmèd the Yahud, *tr. by* David Shea. TrJP
Sarolla's women in their picture hats. Lawrence Ferlinghetti. *Fr.* Pictures of a Gone World. NeAP; PoM
Sarpedon to Glaukos. Homer, *tr. fr. Greek by* Richmond Lattimore. *Fr.* The Iliad, II. WaaP
(Sarpedon's Speech, *tr. by* George Chapman.) OBS
Sarrazine's Song to Her Dead Lover. Marie de France. *See* Song from Chartivel.
Sarsfield went out the Dutch to rout. A Ballad of Sarsfield. Aubrey Thomas De Vere. GoBC; HBV-2
Sartorial Solecism. R. E. C. Stringer. FiBHP
Sarum Primer, *sel.* *Unknown.*
God with Us. TreFT
(God Be in My Head.) EaLo; OxBoCh; TRV
(Hymnus.) ChTr; FaBoRV
Sarvent, Marster! Yes, sah, dat's me. Uncle Gabe's White Folks. Thomas Nelson Page. AA
Sasha and the Poet. Jean Valentine. VGW
Saskatchewan Dusk. C. M. Buckaway. AMV-80
Sassafras. Samuel Minturn Peck. AA
Sassafras Tea. Mary Effie Lee Newsome. CDC
Sat in the pub. The Diet. Maureen Burge. BrRo
Sat in the sun. Virginia. Elouise Loftin. PoBA
Sat there/ In a folding chair. Jim. Barbara Howes. GP
Sat up all night and lugged at the moon. Critter. W. M. Ransom. CDW
Sat Will & Kate. Those Troublesome Disguises. Jonathan Williams. NeAP
Satan ("He scarce had ceas't when . . ."). Milton. *Fr.* Paradise Lost, I. SeCePo
(Satan and the Fallen Angels.) LiTB; OBS
Satan ("He ceased; and Satan stayed not . . ."). Milton. *Fr.* Paradise Lost, II. SeCePo
(Satan Views the World.) WHA
Satan ("His pride/ Had cast him out from Heaven"). Milton. *Fr.* Paradise Lost, I. TreFT; TrGrPo
("His pride/ Had cast him out from Heaven.") PPoe
Satan and His Host. Milton. *Fr.* Paradise Lost, I. OBS
Satan and Pilate's Wife. *Unknown.* ACP
Satan and the Fallen Angels. Milton. *See* Satan ("He scarce had ceas't . . .).
Satan as Rebel-Liberator. Milton. *Fr.* Paradise Lost, I. FF
(Fall of the Angels, The.) FiP
("Is this the region, this the soil, the clime.") FF
(Satan Ponders His Fallen State.) TreFS
Satan Beholds Adam and Eve in Eden. Milton. *Fr.* Paradise Lost, IV. TW
Satan Defiant. Milton. *Fr.* Paradise Lost, I. WHA
(Fallen Angels, The.) FaBoEn
Satan from hence now on the lower stair. The Panorama. Milton. *Fr.* Paradise Lost, III. WHA
Satan in Eden "was constrain'd." Error Pursued. Helen Pinkerton. QFR
Satan is following me. *Zulu Oral Tradition, tr. by* H. Tracey. WTO
Satan Is on Your Tongue. George Barker. Secular Elegies, III. MoAB; MoBrPo
Satan Journeys to the Garden of Eden. Milton. *Fr.* Paradise Lost, IV. ChTr
Satan Looks upon Adam and Eve in Paradise. Milton. *Fr.* Paradise Lost, IV. TreFS
Satan Ponders His Fallen State. Milton. *See* Satan as Rebel-Liberator.
Satan Views the World. Milton. *See* Satan ("He ceased; and Satan stayed not . . .").
Satan's a Liah, *with music.* *Unknown.* AS
Satan's Address to the Sun. Milton. *Fr.* Paradise Lost, IV. BiP
(Scene in Paradise, A.) GN
Satan's Adjuration. Milton. *Fr.* Paradise Lost, I. FaBoEn
(What Though the Field Be Lost.) EaLo
Satan's Guile. Milton. *Fr.* Paradise Regained, I. LiTB; OBS
Satan's Legions and the Beech Leaves of the Casentino. Milton. *See* Summons, The.
Satan's Soliloquy. Milton. *Fr.* Paradise Lost, IV. LiTB
Satchmo. Melvin B. Tolson. BPo
(Lamda.) PoNe
Sathan, no woman, yet a wandring spirit. Caelica, XXI. Fulke Greville. NCEP
Sather Gate Illumination. Allen Ginsberg. NeAP
Satie, at the End of Term. Simon Curtis. NOBL
Satin-clad. Stevie Smith. OxBC
Satin Shoes, The. Thomas Hardy. CoBMV
Satire, *sel.* John Marston.
"Ambitious Gorgons, wide-mouthed Lamians," *fr.* V. ViBoPo
Satire, A, *sels.* John Oldham
"But, grant thy poetry should find success." ViBoPo
"On Butler who can think without rage." OBSV
Satire: "Ask you what provocation I have had?" Pope. *Fr.* Epilogue to the Satires. OBEC
("Ask you what provocation I have had?") OBSV
(Defence of Satire, The.) NOEC
(Power of Ridicule, The.) NOBE
Satire: "Away, thou fondling motley humorist." John Donne. Satires, I. OAEP
Satire III; "Kind pity [*or* kinde pitty] chokes my spleen[e]; brave scorn forbids. *Fr.* Satires. AnAnS-1; CABA; EBEV; JCP; OAEL-1; OBS; PoEL-2; SeCV-1
(Religion.) NoP
(Satyre: Of Religion.) MePo
(Satyre III.) MeLP
(Satyre III: On Religion.) SeCP
Seek True Religion! sel. NOBE
("Seek true religion. O where? Mirreus.") OBSV
(Truth.) SeCePo
Satire III: "Long, Dodington, in debt, I long have sought." Edward Young. *Fr.* Love of Fame, the Universal Passion. LAuP
Satire XII: Love-Sicke Poet, The. Joseph Hall. *Fr.* Virgidemarium. FaBoEn
("Great is the folly of a feeble brain.") EBEV
Satire: "Satire, my friend ('twixt me and you)." Alexander Geddes. ACP
Satire: "Sir: though (I thank God for it) I do hate." John Donne. Satires, II. ViBoPo
Satire: "Some do for pimping, some for treach'ry rise." Earl of Rochester. DBV
Satire V: "Thou shalt not laugh in this leaf, Muse, nor they." John Donne. Satires, V. OBSV
Satire 3: To Sir Francis Brian. Sir Thomas Wyatt. *Fr.* Satires. EnRePo
("Spending hand that alway powreth owte.") AAS
(To Sir Francis Brian.) SiPS
Satire: "Well, I may now receive, and die: my sin." John Donne. Satires, IV. OBSV
Satire: "Were I who to my cost already am." Earl of Rochester. *See* Satire against Mankind, A.
Satire Addressed to a Friend, A. John Oldham. *See* Satyr Address'd to a Friend That Is About to Leave the University, and come Abroad in the World, A.
Satire against [Reason and] Mankind, A. Earl of Rochester. MasP; NoP; OAEL-1; OBSV
(Homo Sapiens.) NOBE
(Satyr against Mankind.) FaBoEn, *abr.;* OBS; PoEL-3; SeCV-2
Sels.
"Were I, who to my cost already am." LiTB; SCV
Wretched Man. SeCePo
Satire against Wit, A. Sir Richard Blackmore. APAS
Satire on Charles II, A, *sel.* Earl of Rochester.
"Restless he rolls about from whore to whore." OBSV
Satire on London, A. Earl of Surrey. SiPs
(London Hast Thou Accused Me.) OAEP
("London hast thow accused me.") AAS
Satire on Old Rowley. *Unknown.* APAS
Satire on the People of Kildare, A. *Unknown, at. to* Friar Michael of Kildare, *mod. vers. by* St. John Seymour. OnYI

(Irish Satire, An, *abr.*) OxBM
Satire Septimus Contra Sollistam. William Rankins. NCEP
Satire, my friend ('twixt me and you). Satire. Alexander Geddes. ACP
Satire upon the French King, A. Thomas Brown. APAS
Satire upon the Heads. Thomas Gray. FaBoCo
Satire upon the Licentious Age of Charles II, *sel.* Samuel Butler.
"How silly were those sages heretofore." NOBL
Satires, *sels.* John Donne.
"Away thou fondling motley humorist," I. OAEP
"Kind pity [*or* kinde pitty] chokes my spleen[e]; brave scorn forbids," III. AnAnS-1; CABA; EBEV; JCP; OAEL-1; OBS; PoEL-2; SeCV-1
(Religion.) NoP
(Satyre: Of Religion.) MePo
(Satyre III.) MeLP
(Satyre III: On Religion.) SeCP
Seek True Religion! fr. III. NOBE
("Seek true religion, O where? Mirreus.") OBSV
(Truth.) SeCePo
"Sir: though (I thank God for it) I do hate," II. OBSV; ViBoPo
"Thou shalt not laugh in this leaf, Muse, nor they," V. OBSV
"Well, I may now receive, and die: my sin," IV. OBSV
Satires, *sels.* Juvenal, *tr. Fr. Latin.*
Against Women, *fr.* VI, *tr. by* Dryden. UnTE
"But of all the plagues, the greatest is untold," *fr.* VI, *tr. by* Dryden. OBSV
Celestial Wisdom, *fr.* X, *tr. by* Samuel Johnson. AWP
Faggots in Ancient Rome, *fr.* II. PeHV
"Give store of days, good Jove, give length of years," *fr.* X, *tr. by* Henry Vaughan. OBSV
Hannibal ("Produce the urn that Hannibal contains"), *fr.* X, *tr. by* William Gifford. OBVE
Hannibal ("Put Hannibal i' th' scale"), *fr.* X, *tr. by* Henry Vaughan. OBVE
Hannibal ("Throw Hannibal on the scales, how many pounds"), *fr.* X, *tr. by* Robert Lowell. OBVE
"Hear what Claudius suffered: When his wife knew he was asleep," *fr.* VI, *tr. by* Hubert Creekmore. ErPo
"In Saturn's reign, at Nature's early birth," *fr.* VI, *tr. by* Dryden. OAEL-1; OBSV; OBVE
" 'Life! length of life!' for this, with earnest cries," *fr.* X, *tr. by* William Gifford. OBVE
"Return we to the dangers of the night," *fr.* III, *tr. by* Dryden. OAEL-1
Sejanus ("How many men are killed by power, by power"), *fr.* X, *tr. by* Robert Lowell. OBVE
Sejanus ("Some ask for envy'd pow'r; which publick hate"), *fr.* X, *tr. by* Dryden. OBVE
Sejanus ("What crowds by envied power, the wish of all"), *fr.* X, *tr. by* William Gifford. OBVE
"We are led on," *fr.* X, *tr. by* L. R. Lind. PoPl
"What conscience has Venus drunk? Our inebriated beauties," *fr.* VI, *tr. by* Peter Green. PeHV
"When the last Flavius, drunk with fury, tore," *fr.* IV, *tr. by* William Gifford. OBVE
"Why do you look so gloomy, Naevolus?" *fr.* IX. PeHV
Satires, *sel.* John Oldham, *after the French of* Boileau.
"Of all the creatures, in the world, that be," *fr.* VIII. OBVE
Satires, *sel.* Persius, *tr. fr. Latin by* John Dryden. Prologue to the First Satire. AWP
Satires, *sels.* Sir Thomas Wyatt.
"My mother's maids [*or* maydes], when they did sew and spin [*or* sowe and spynne]," II. AAS; SiPS
"Myne [*or* Mine] owne John Poyntz, sins [*or* since] ye delight to know," I. AAS; OBSV; OBVE; PoEL-1; SiPS
(Mine Own John Poins.) NoP
(Of the Courtier's Life.) GoTL; OBSC
"Spending hand that alway poureth out [*or* powreth owte], A," III. AAS
(Satire 3: To Sir Francis Brian.) EnRePo
(To Sir Francis Brian.) SiPS
Satires of Circumstance, I-XV. Thomas Hardy. BrPo
Sels.
At the Altar-Rail, IX. MoAB; MoBrPo
At the Draper's, XII. MoAB; MoBrPo
By Her Aunt's Grave, III. MoAB; MoBrPo
In Church, II. DTC; MoAB; MoBrPo; SCV
In the Restaurant, XI. MoAB; MoBrPo
Satires [*or* Satyrs] upon the Jesuits, *sels.* John Oldham.
"Oh for the Swedish law enacted here!" DBV
"Once I was common wood, a shapeless log." DBV
Prologue: "For who can longer hold? when every Press." SeCV-2
Satyr III: "When shaven Crown, and hallow'd Girdle's Power." SeCV-2
Satirical [*or* Satyrical] Elegy on the Death of a Late Famous General, A. Swift. CABA; FF; HoPM; NIP; NoP; OBSV; PoEL-3; SeCeV
Satirical Poem about Drink, A, *sel.* Chimedin Jigmed, *tr. fr.* Mongol *by* C. R. Bawden
"There is drink fermented." WTO
Satirical Romance, A, *sels.* Sister Juana Ines de la Cruz, *tr. fr. Spanish by* Judith Thurman. PBWP
"Critics: in your sight."
"Ignorant men, who disclaim."
"What humour can be so rare."
Satirist, The. Harry Lyman Koopman. AA
Satisfaction. A. R. Ammons. GP
Satisfaction—is the agent. Emily Dickinson. NOBA
Satisfied. Sam V. Cole. BLRP
Satisfied. Edgar Cooper Mason. BLRP
Satisfied this morning because I saw myself. Seeing the Scenery. Leslie Scalapino. *Fr.* Hmmmm. NPGG
Satisfied Tiger, The. *At. to* Cosmo Monkhouse. *See* Limerick: "There was a young lady of Niger."
Satisfying Portion, The. *Unknown.* BLRP
Satori. Gayl Jones. BlSi
Saturday: The Small-Pox. Lady Mary Wortley Montagu. *Fr.* Six Town Eclogues. NOEC; WPE
Saturday Afternoon at the Movies. John Logan. NNaP
Saturday Afternoon, When Chores Are Done. Harryette Mullen. AMV-81
Sat., Apr. 26, 1973. A Poem to Galway Kinnell. Etheridge Knight. NNaP
Saturday Blues. *Unknown.* BluL
Saturday in the County Seat. Elijah L. Jacobs. AmFN
Saturday Market. Charlotte Mew. HBMV; WPE
Saturday Market ("In Saturday Market, there's eggs a-plenty"), *sel.* FaPON
Saturday Morning. Richard Howard. ErPo
Saturday morning. Mowing the Lawn. John Bensko. MAYP
Saturday Morning at the Laundry. Christopher Gilbert. MAYP
Saturday Night. Langston Hughes. MoAmPo
Saturday Night. Antigone Kefala. CBAP
Saturday Night. James Oppenheim. HBV-2
Saturday Night in the Parthenon. Kenneth Patchen. EAS
Saturday Night in the Village. Giacomo Leopardi, *tr. fr. Italian by* Robert Lowell. OBVE
Saturday night she comes in her little boat. Music on the Water. George Johnston. MoCV
Saturday Review, The. William Cole. PV
Saturday Review, The. Dora Greenwell. EBVV
Saturday Shopping. Katherine Edelman. SoPo
Saturday Sundae. F. R. Scott. CaP
Saturday's Child. Countee Cullen. InPK; LiTM; NAs; OFD; PAI; PoBA; SaC
Saturn. Keats. *Fr.* Hyperion; a Fragment. LoBV; OBNC; TrGrPo
Saturnian mother! why dost thou devour. Russia. Nathan Haskell Dole. AA
Saturninus. Katherine Eleanor Conway. AA
Satyr. Charles Gullans. PoA
Satyr, The, *sel.* Ben Jonson.
Queen Mab. HBV-1
(Mab.) WiR
(Mab the Mistress-Fairy.) ElL
Satyr, The. James Stephens. OnYI
(Crackling Twig, The.) ELU
Satyr III: "When shaven Crown, and hallow'd Girdle's Power." John Oldham. *Fr.* Satyrs upon the Jesuits. SeCV-2
Satyr Address'd to a Friend That Is About to Leave the University, and Come Abroad in the World, A, *sels.* John Oldham.
"If you for orders, and a gown design." OBS
"If you're so out of love with happiness." OBSV
Satyr against Mankind, A. Earl of Rochester. *See* Satire against Mankind.
Satyr on Elysium lights, A. The Tenth Nymphal. Michael Drayton. *Fr.* The Muses' Elysium. JCP
Satyre Entituled the Witch, A. *Unknown.* CoMu
Satyre: Of [*or* On] Religion. John Donne. *See* Satire III: "Kind pity chokes my spleen; brave scorn forbids."
Satyres Catch. Ben Jonson. *See* Buz, Quoth the Blue Fly.
Satyretericall Charracter of a Proud Upstart, A. John Saffin. SCAP
(March 4th Anno 1698/9; a Charracteristicall Satyre, *diff. vers.*) SCAP
Satyrical Elegy on the Death of a Late Famous General. Swift. *See* Satirical Elegy on the Death of a Late Famous General, A.
Satyrs and the Moon, The. Herbert S. Gorman. HBV-1
Satyrs' Catch, The. Ben Jonson. *See* Buz, Quoth the Blue Fly.
Satyr's Farewell, The ("Thou divinest, fairest, brightest"). John Fletcher. *Fr.* The Faithful Shepherdess, V, i. OBS
("Thou divinest, fairest, brightest.") LO
(Satyr's Leave-taking, The.) LoBV
Satyr's mouth is stained red with wine, The. Nymphs and Satyrs. Gavin Ewart. PV

Satyr's Song ("See the day begins to break"). John Fletcher. *Fr.* The Faithful Shepherdess, IV, i. OBS
Satyrs upon the Jesuits. John Oldham. *See* Satires upon the Jesuits.
Satyrs used to fall for nymphs. Love-Songs, at Once Tender and Informative. Samuel Hoffenstein. OBAL
Satyrus Peregrinans, *sel.* William Rankins.
"By this time long-gowned Lumen walked abroad." OBSV
Sauce thickens, The. I add more butter. Hollandaise. Sharon Bryan. MAYP
Saucepan of shining copper, The. How I Was Her Kitchen-Boy. Gunter Grass, *tr. by* Betty Falkenberg. AMV-81
Sauchs in the Reuch Heuch Hauch, The. "Hugh MacDiarmid." NoAM
Saucy Sailor, The. *Unknown.* OBET
Saul. Nathan Alterman, *tr. fr. Hebrew by* Dov Vardi. TrJP
Saul. Robert Browning. OAEP; OxBoCh; VLP; WHA
Sels.
"He who did most, shall bear most; the strongest shall stand the most weak," *fr.* XVIII. TRV
"I believe it! 'tis Thou God, that givest, 'tis I who receive," XVIII. ILwL
"I know not too well how I found my way home in the night," *fr.* XIX. LoBV
"Oh, the wild joys of living! the leaping from rock up to rock," *fr.* IX. FaBV
(Oh, the Wild Joy of Living.) TreFT
"Then I tuned my harptook off the lilies we twine round its chords," V-IX. FiP
"Yea, my King," XIII-XIX, *sl. abr.* WGRP
Saul. Amir Gilboa, *tr. fr. Hebrew by* Shirley Kaufman. VWA
Saul, *sels.* Charles Heavysege.
"Ah, weary! I am called the laughing devil." PeCV
Malzah's Song. OBCV
"To hunt and to be hunted make existence." CaP
Zaph Describes the Haunts of Malzah. OBCV
Saul. Else Lasker-Schüler, *tr. fr. German by* Joachim Neugroschel. VWA
Saul. Isaac Rosenberg. VWA
Saul. George Sterling. HBMV
Saul, Afterward, Riding East. John Malcolm Brinnin. HoAn; Prf
Saul did much care and diligence express. Rowland Watkyns. FaBoEE
Saul! Saul! Saul. Amir Gilboa, *tr. by* Shirley Kaufman. VWA
Saul's Progress. Harvey Shapiro. DiL
Saul's Song of Love. Shaul Tchernichovsky, *tr. fr. Hebrew by* Robert Friend. VWA
Sauntering hither on listless wings. To a Sea-Bird. Bret Harte. EtS
Sauntering in the orchard we bit the fruit. The Struggle with the Angel. Claude Vigée, *tr. by* Elizabeth Savage. VWA
Sauntering the pavement or riding the country by-road. Faces. Walt Whitman. PoEL-5
Sausage. Edgar A. Guest. OBAL
Savage, A. John Boyle O'Reilly. AA
Savage Beast, The. William Carlos Williams. TW
Savage I was sitting in my house, late, lone. The Householder. Robert Browning. LO
Savage Portraits. Don Marquis. HBMV
Quinks, The, *sel.* DBV; YaD
Savages, The. Josephine Miles. LiTM
Savage's romance, The. New York. Marianne Moore. NYP
Savannah. Alethea S. Burroughs. PAH
Savannah Mama. *Unknown.* BluL
Save by the Old Road none attain the new. Coventry Patmore. FaBoEE
Save it all; you do not know. 1915: A Pre-Raphaelite Ending, London. Richard Howard. NoAM
Save on the rare occasion when the sun. On a Sundial. Hilaire Belloc. POL
Save yourself. Run and leave me. I must go back. C. S. Lewis. *Fr.* Epigrams and Epitaphs, 6. EBEV
Saved. Maria Teresa Horta, *tr. fr. Portuguese by* Suzette Macedo. PBWP
Saved. *Unknown.* FaBoUs
Saved, But. *Unknown.* STF
Saving God, The. Fulke Greville. *Fr.* Caelica. LoBV
("Down[e] in the depth of mine iniquity.") EnRePo; PPoe; QFR
(Sonnet: "Downe in the depth of mine iniquity.") OBS
Saving the Fish. R. T. Smith. WOLT
Saving the Harvest. Geoffrey Lehmann. CBAP
Savior [*or* Saviour]! I've no one else to tell. Emily Dickinson. TrCP; TrPWD
Savior [*or* Saviour] looked on Peter, The. Ay, no word. The Look. Elizabeth Barrett Browning. TrCP; TRV
Saviour, bowed beneath his cross, climbed up the dreary hill, The. Why the Robin's Breast Was Red. James Ryder Randall. AA
Saviour came, The. With trembling lips. The Second Coming. Norman Gale. HBV-2
Saviour! I've no one else to tell. *See* Savior . . .
Saviour looked on Peter, The. Ay, no word. *See* Savior . . .
Saviour, Sprinkle Many Nations, *with music.* Arthur Cleveland Coxe. AH
Saviour, Thy Dying Love, *with music.* Sylvanus D. Phelps. AH
(Something for Jesus.) BLRP
Saviour, Who Thy Flock Art Feeding, *with music.* William Augustus Mühlenberg. AH
Saviour, Whose Love Is Like the Sun. Howard Chandler Robbins. TrPWD
Savonarola ("Savonarola looks more grim today"). Max Beerbohm. BXAP
Savonarola ("Savonarola/Declined to wear a bowler"). E. C. Bentley. OxBoLi
Saw a lamb being born. Lamb. Michael Dennis Browne. NU
Saw God Dead but Laughing. José Garcia Villa. TwAmPo
Saw Ye Bonie Lesley. Burns. *See* Bonnie Lesley.
Saw ye owt o' ma' lad. The Waggoner. *Unknown.* GBP
Saw You My Father. *Unknown.* *See* Grey Cock, The.
Saw you never in the twilight. The Adoration of the Wise Men. Cecil Frances Alexander. HBVY
Sawmill is here already, The. Progress. Connie Martin. PPJ
Sawney was Tall. Thomas D'Urfey. *Fr.* The Virtuous Wife. OAEP
Saws Were Shrieking, The. W. W. E. Ross. CaP; PeCV
Saxon Grit. Robert Collyer. HBV-2
Saxophone and subway. The Rock. W. S. Merwin. NYP
Saxophone turned into a dolphin, The. Albert Ayler: Eulogy for a Decomposed Saxophone Player. Stanley Crouch. PoBA
Saxophonetyx. Cyn Zarco. BrSi
Say/ Did you see that magnificent blonde beast. Ski Trail. Samuel Allen. FB
Say, are you she that came to me last. The Second Vision. Tadhg Dall O'Huiginn, *tr. by* the Earl of Longford. AnIL
Say "Au Revoir," but Not "Good-bye," *with music.* Harry Kennedy. FSN
Say, Billie, when yer startin' off a-nuttin with yer sack. Punkin Pie. Harry Edward Mills. PeD
"Say, bold but blessed Thief [*or* theefe]." The Thief. *Unknown.* LO; OBS; OxBoCh
Say, bud, ya got a cigarette? Refugee. Naomi Long Madgett. PoNe
Say, but did you love so long? Sir Toby Matthews. Sir John Suckling. SeCV-1
Say, crimson rose and dainty daffodil. A Nosegay. John Reynolds. OBEV
Say, darkeys [*or* darkies] hab you seen de massa. Kingdom Coming [*or* Year of Jubilo *or* The Year of Jubilee]. Henry Clay Work. BLSo; PAH; PSoN; TrAS
Say, dear Maria! is the modish life. A Familiar Epistle. Ann Murry. WPE
Say, did his sisters wonder what could Joseph see. Regina Coeli. Coventry Patmore. ISi
Say, did you go to Mae's rent party? Mae's Rent Party. Ernest J. Wilson, Jr. PoNe
Say, dwarf, for it seems to me. *Tr. fr. Icelandic by* W. H. Auden *and* Paul B. Taylor. *Fr.* The Words of the All-Wise. OBVE
Say, earth, why hast thou got thee new attire. Easter Morn. Giles Fletcher. *Fr.* Christ's Victory and Triumph. ElL; NOCV
Say father, say mother. Dove's Song in Winter. *Zulu Oral Tradition, tr. by* B. W. Vilakazi. WTO
Say, friend, if all is well still with the bowers. Vidya, *tr. by* Daniel H. H. Ingalls. *Fr.* The Wanton. PBWP
Say good-by er howdy-do. Good-by er Howdy-do. James Whitcomb Riley. CTC
Say Goodbye to Big Daddy. Randall Jarrell. LiSp; PoNe
Say goodnight to him and shut the door. Exquisite Lady. Mary Elizabeth Osborn. NePoAm-2
Say Hello to John. Sherley Anne Williams. BlSi
Say, in a hut of mean estate. The Soul of Man. Dora Read Goodale. AA
Say, is it day, is it dusk in thy bower. The Song of the Bower. Dante Gabriel Rossetti. HBV-1
Say it and cry aloud. I Am a Negro. Muhammad Al-Fītūri, *tr. by* Halim El-Dabh. TTY
Say It Now. *Unknown.* *See* If You Have a Friend.
Say it were true that thou outliv'st us all. To My Tortoise Ananke. Eugene Lee-Hamilton. OBVV
Say it's an important event like this. Off to Patagonia. Theodore Weiss. TAP
Say, lad, have you things to do? A. E. Housman. VLP
Say, Lovely Dream. Edmund Waller. OAEP
(Song: "Say lovely dream! where couldst thou find.") CavP
Say, lovely Tory, why the jest. To Miss Eleanor Ambrose on the Occasion of Her Wearing an Orange Lily at a Ball in Dublin Castle on July the 12th. Earl of Chesterfield. EnLoPo
Say Me, Wiit in the Brom. *Unknown.* OAEP
(Wight in the Broom.) OxBM
Say, mighty Love, and teach my song. Few Happy Matches. Isaac Watts. NOEC
Say, Muse, who first, who last, on foot or steed. On the Road to Anster Fair. William Tennant. *Fr.* Anster Fair. OBRV

Say my love is easy had. Fighting Words. Dorothy Parker. InMe
Say Nay. Sir Thomas Wyatt. *See* And Wilt Thou Leave Me Thus?
Say Not. Arthur Hugh Clough. *See* Say Not the Struggle Nought Availeth.
Say not of Beauty she is good. Beauty. Elinor Wylie. OxBA
Say not of me that weakly I declined. Robert Louis Stevenson. EyDe; OBNC
Say Not That Beauty. Robin Flower. HBMV; HBVY
Say Not the Struggle [Nought Availeth]. Arthur Hugh Clough. AWP; CABA; EaLo; EBVV; FaBoEn; FaBoRV; FaFP; FaPoR; GTBS-P; HBV-2; HBVY; LiTB; LoBV; NOBE; OAEL-2; OAEP; OBEV; OBNC; OBVV; SoSe; TEP; TreF; TrGrPo; TRV; ViPoBo; VLP; WaaP; WGRP
(Keeping On.) MoShBr
(Say Not.) FaBV
Say of them/ They knew no Spanish. To the Veterans of the Abraham Lincoln Brigade. Genevieve Taggard. OFD
Say over again, and yet once over again. Sonnets from the Portuguese, XXI. Elizabeth Barrett Browning. HBV-1
Say, pard, have you sighted a schooner. The Santa Fe Trail. *Unknown.* CoSo
Say, sweet, my grief and I, we may not brook. Je ne veux de personne auprès de ma tristesse. Henri de Regnier, *tr. by* "Seumas O'Sullivan." AWP
Say (sweetest) whether thou didst use me well. To Cynthia on Her Being an Incendiary. Sir Francis Kynaston. HAP; NCEP
Say That He Loved Old Ships. Daniel Whitehead Hicky. EtS
Say That I Should Say I Love Ye. Nicholas Breton. *See* Assurance, An.
Say that the men of the old black tower. The Black Tower. W. B. Yeats. CMoP
Say that thou didst forsake me for some fault. Sonnets, LXXXIX. Shakespeare. OAEP
Say That We Saw Spain Die. Edna St. Vincent Millay. SBG
Say there! P'r'aps. "Jim." Bret Harte. AA; WhC
Say there were six, say there were a dozen. Depression. Rex Burwell. AMV-80
Say this city has ten million souls. Refugee Blues [*or* Song]. W. H. Auden. LiTA; LiTM; NYBP
Say This of Horses. Minnie Hite Moody. PoLF
Say, tyrant Custom, why must we obey. The Emulation. Sarah Fyge Egerton. NOEC
Say well and do well. *Unknown.* OxNR
Say, what is love? To live in vain. What is Love? John Clare. NCEP
Say, what is the spell, when her fledglings are cheeping. A Song of Love. "Lewis Carroll." GN
Say what slim youth, with moist perfumes. Horace, *tr. by* Christopher Smart. Odes, I, 5. OBVE
Say what you will, and scratch my heart to find. Sonnet. Edna St. Vincent Millay. HBMV
Say what you will in two. Air: Sentir avec Ardeur. Marie-Françoise-Catherine de Beauveau, Marquise de Boufflers, *tr. by* Ezra Pound. CTC; WPOW
"Say, where is the maiden sweet." Sag', wo ist dein schönes Liebchen. Heine, *tr. by* James Thomson. AWP
Say who is this with silvered hair. Robert Bridges. VLP
Say, wilt thou go with me, sweet maid. Invitation [*or* Invite] to Eternity. John Clare. NBM; NCEP; PoEL-4
Say, wilt thou more of scenes so sordid know? A Slum Dwelling. George Crabbe. *Fr.* The Borough. OBNC
Say, wouldst thou guard thy son. Of Caution. Francesco da Barberino, *tr. by* Dante Gabriel Rossetti. AWP
Say you talking 'bout your red ripe tomato. T-Bone Steak Blues. *Unknown.* BluL
Say you were the kid who could not sleep. The Actor. Thomas Snapp. NYBP
Sayer. George P. Elliott. FAZ
Sayes "Christ thee saue, good Child of Ell!" Earl Brand. *Unknown.* ESPB
Saying Goodbye. Suzanne Juhasz. IHMS
Saying One Thing. Robert Long. AMV-81
Saying, "There is no hope," he stepped. A Generous Creed. Elizabeth Stuart Phelps. WGRP
Sayings from the Northern Ice. William Stafford. NU
Saylors for My Money. Martin Parker. CoMu
Sayre. Lynn Strongin. IHMS
Says A, give me a good large slice. A Curious Discourse That Passed between the Twenty-five Letters at Dinner-Time. *Unknown.* FaBoUs
Says His Grace to Will Green, whom he found in his stall. Death and the Cobbler. *Unknown.* APAS
Says I to Myself. Edward Lear. FiBHP; WhC
Says I went to Lake Michigan. Lake Michigan Blues. *Unknown.* BluL
Says my Uncle, I pray you discover. Molly Mog; or, The Fair Maid of the Inn. John Gay. CoMu
Says Phoebe Snow. The D.L. and W.'s Phoebe Snow. *Unknown.* TreF
Says Robin to Jenny, "If you will be mine." *Unknown.* PBBP
Says-so is in a woe of shuddered. Irritable Song. Russell Atkins. AmNP
Says Something Too. Samuel Hoffenstein. BXAP
Says Stonewall Jackson to "Little Phil": "Phil, have you heard the news?" Joined the Blues. John Jerome Rooney. AA
Says the auld man/ To the oak tree. Many a Long Year. *Unknown.* PoPle
Says the master to me, "Is it true, I am told." My Master and I. *Unknown.* CoMu; OBET
Says the Miner to the Mucker. *Unknown.* AmFP
Says the Pont to the Blyth. Pont and Blyth. *Unknown.* GBP
Says the window. Indoors. George Johnston. PoA
Says Tweed to Till. Tweed and Till [*or* Two Rivers *or* The Rivers Till and Tweed]. *Unknown.* BoNaP; ChTr; FaBoPP; GBP; OBEV; PV; WhC
Says William to Henry, "I cannot conceive." Henry's Secret. Dorothy Kilner. OxBChV
Says William to Phyllis, "How came you here so soon?" William and Phyllis. *Unknown.* OBET
Scala Coeli. Kathleen Raine. NYBP
Scalded cat. Night Letter. Marge Piercy. NMM
Scales, The. William Empson. CMoP; FaBoMo; LiTM
Scales of pearly cloud inlay. Holiday at Hampton Court. John Davidson. EBVV
Scales of the Eyes, The. Howard Nemerov. CMoP; NMP
"In the water cave, below the root," *sel.* NoAM
Scaling small rocks, exhaling smog. Central Park. Robert Lowell. LiTM; NYP
Scalp Dance Song. *Tr. fr. Tewa Indian by* H. J. Spinden. WTO
Scandal among the Flowers, A. Charles S. Taylor. BLPA
Scandal or two, A. Tattle. Godfrey Turner. NOBL
Scandalize My Name. *Unknown.* FSW
Scandalous man, A. Mr. Tom Narrow. James Reeves. SO
Scandalous Tale of Percival and Genevieve, The. Newman Levy. WhC
'Scaped. Stephen Crane. The Black Riders, LXV. AA
Scapegoat. W. R. Rodgers. CIP
Scapegoats. Eleanor D. Breed. PGD
Scapular of birds hung fast, A. Eclipses. Nancy Sullivan. TAP
Scar not earth's breast that I may have. The Last Camp-Fire. Sharlot M. Hall. HBV-2
Scarabs for the Living. R. P. Blackmur. TwAmPo
Sels.
In the Wind's Eye, II. CrMA
On Common Ground, III. CrMA
Too Much for One: Not Enough to Go Round, I. CrMA
Scaramouche waves a threatening hand. Fantoches [*or* Puppets]. Paul Verlaine, *tr. by* Arthur Symons. AWP; OBMV; SyP
Scarborough Fair. *Unknown.* BLSo, *with music;* FSW; OxBoLi
(Whittingham Fair.) GBP
Scarce do I pass a day, but that I hear. Meditation 8. Philip Pain. NOBA; QFR
Scarce had I seen for the first time his eyes. To Luigi del Riccio, after the Death of Cecchino Bracci. Michelangelo, *tr. by* John Addington Symonds. PeHV
Scarce images of life, one here, one there. A Recollection of the Stone Circle near Keswick. Keats. *Fr.* Hyperion, II. FaBoPP
Scarce lay the blossoms of her golden hair. Mary on Her Way to the Temple. Ruth Schaumann, *tr. by* Edwin Buers. ISi
Scarcely believe things shameful to utter which yet I shall speak of. Bernard of Cluny. *Fr.* De Contemptu Mundi. PeHV
Scarcely, I think; yet it indeed *may* by. For "An Allegorical Dance of Women" by Andrea Mantegna. Dante Gabriel Rossetti. VLP
Scare-Fire, The. Robert Herrick. HAP; NoP
Scarecrow, The. Walter de la Mare. MoBrPo; OxBTC
Scarecrow, The. H. L. Doak. OnYI
Scarecrow, The. Michael Franklin. SUS
Scarecrow, The. Andrew Young. BSV; FaBoTw
Scarecrow stood in a field one day, A. The Scarecrow. Michael Franklin. SUS
Scared?/ are responsible negros running. Concerning One Responsible Negro with Too Much Power. Nikki Giovanni. BPo
Scarlet-jewelled ashtree sighed, The—"He cometh." Autumn, 1914. Mary Webb. SUMH
Scarlet poppy smouldering in the fields, The. Narcissus. John Press. UnTE
Scarlet Tanager, The. Joel Benton. AA
Scarlet Tanager, The. Mary Augusta Mason. AA
Scarlet Thread, The. Daniel Henderson. HBMV
Scarlet tide of summer's life, The. To an Autumn Leaf. Albert Mathews. AA
Scarlet Woman, The. Fenton Johnson. BANP; PoBA; PoNe
Scarred. *Unknown.* STF
Scars Remaining, The. Samuel Taylor Coleridge. *Fr.* Christabel. OBNC
("Alas! they had been friends in youth.") OBRV
(Broken Friendship.) TreFT

Scatheless. Marguerite Wilkinson. HBMV
Scatter Seeds of Kindness. May Riley Smith. WBLP
Scattered among stiff black stalks. Grasses. Ralph J. Mills, Jr. FAZ
Scattered Leaves. Lance Henson. VoR
Scattered like flotsam on the erupting sea. The Roc. Edward Lowbury. AmMo
Scattered room, A. North Clark Street. Raymond Thompson. LFAC
Scazons. C. S. Lewis. EBEV
Scel Lem Duib. *Unknown, tr. fr. Irish.* BIrV, *tr. by* Flann O'Brien; OxBI, *tr. by* Brian O Nolan
Scenario. D. S. Savage. NeBP
Scene, The: a public square in Ruritania. The Belle of the Balkans. Newman Levy. FiBHP
Scene after Hunting at Swallowfield in Berkshire, A. Sneyd Davies. NOEC
Scene from a Dream. Janet Campbell Hale. STE
Scene from a Play, Acted at Oxford, Called "Matriculation." Thomas Moore. NBM; OBSV
Scene in a Madhouse. Aubrey Thomas De Vere. OnYI
Scene in Paradise, A. Milton. *See* Satan's Address to the Sun.
Scene is set now, The: in a silent room. Transfusion. Merrill Moore. PoA
Scene of a Summer Morning. Irving Feldman. NYBP
Scene-Shifter Death. Mary Devenport O'Neill. NeIP
Scene with Figure. Babette Deutsch. TrJP
Scenery. Ted Joans. PoBA
Scènes de la Vie de Bohème, *sel.* Arthur Symons.
Episode of a Night of May. BrPo
Scenes from Carnac. Matthew Arnold. FaBoPP
Scenes from the Life of the Peppertrees. Denise Levertov. LiTM; NeAP; NoP; PoM
Scenes of Childhood. James Merrill. CoAP; DiL
Scenes of my childhood, The, how oft I recall! My Infundibuliform Hat. Charles Follen Adams. OBAL
Scenic. John Updike. CAD
Scent of beeswax, dust, A; the empty rooms. Meeting Myself. Edward Lucie-Smith. NePoEA-2
Scent of bramble fills the air, The. Sleeping Beauty. Walter de la Mare. DFT
Scent of esparto grass, A—and again I recall. By the Weir. Wilfrid Gibson. MoVE
Scent of guava-blossoms and the smell, A. At Set of Sun. Mary Ashley Townsend. AA
Scent of ripeness from over a wall, A. Unharvested. Robert Frost. BoNaP
Scent of rotted apples, The. Late October. Sara King Carleton. GoYe
Scent of sage, The. Vision Song (Cheyenne). Lance Henson. STE
Scent of unseen jasmine on the warm night beach, The. Malaga. Pearse Hutchinson. BIrV
Scented, cool, and marble dark. Lemons. Ted Walker. NYBP
Scented Herbage of My Breast. Walt Whitman. AP
Scentless laurel a broad leaf displays, The. Walter Savage Landor. FaBoEE
Schedules ("Schedules come in different forms, all crushing"). John Dean. AMV-81
Schemmelfennig. Bret Harte. OBAL
Scherzando. W. E. Henley. London Voluntaries, III. BrPo
Schiehallion. Helen B. Cruickshank. PoSH
Schipman [*or* Shipman] was ther, wonyng fer by weste, A. The Shipman. Chaucer. *Fr.* The Canterbury Tales: Prologue. EtS; MOS
Schir, though your grace has put great order. Ane Supplication in Contemptioun of Syde Taillis, *abr.* Sir David Lyndsay. GoTS
Schir William Wallace. Henry the Minstrel. *See* Wallace, The
Schir, ye have mony servitouris. Remonstrance to the King. William Dunbar. OxBS
Schizophrenic. P. K. Page. HeIP
Schizophrenic, wrenched by two styles. Codicil. Derek Walcott. NoAM
Schlof, Bobbeli, *with music. Unknown, tr. fr. German.* TrAS
Schloss Voss, built between 1600 and 1650. Das Schloss. Lincoln Kirstein. NoAM
Schmaltztenor! M. W. Branch. FiBHP
Schoenberg Op. 11. Thomas W. Shapcott. *Fr.* Piano Pieces. CBAP
Scholar, The. Frances Cornford. BrRo
Scholar II. Seamus Deane. CIP
Scholar, The. Robert Southey. GTBS; GTBS-P
Scholar and the Cat, The. *Unknown. See* Monk and His Pet Cat, The.
Scholar Complains, The. *Unknown. See* Schoolboy's Complaint.
Scholar-Gipsy, The. Matthew Arnold. CABA; ChTr; EBEV; EBVV; FaBoEn; FiP; GoTL; HAP; HBV-2; HeIP; LoBV; MasP; NOBE; NoP; OAEL-2; OAEP; OBEV; OBNC; OBVV; PoEL-5; SeCeV; TEP; ViBoPo; VLP
"Go, for they call you, shepherd, from the hill," *sel.* FaBoPP; PoPle
Scholar in the Narrow Street, The. Tso Ssu, *tr. fr. Chinese by* Arthur Waley. AWP
Scholars. Walter de la Mare. NoAM
Scholars. *Unknown, tr. fr. Irish by* Frank O'Connor. *Fr.* Priests and Scholars. DBV; KiLC
Scholars, The. W. B. Yeats. CMoP; NoP; OAEL-2; PoA
Scholar's Life, The. Samuel Johnson. *Fr.* The Vanity of Human Wishes FaBoEn; NOBE; OBEC; SeCePo
("When first the college rolls receive his name.") OBSV
Scholar's Wife, The. Susan Mernit. VWA
Scholastic Mouse, The. "A. B. P." TDH
Scholder Indian Poem, A. Joy Harjo. TWSS
Scholfield Huxley. Edgar Lee Masters. *Fr.* Spoon River Anthology. LiTA; MoPo; TrPWD
School and Schoolfellows. Winthrop Mackworth Praed. OBRV
Schoolfellows, *sel.* NBM
School-Bell. Eleanor Farjeon. FaPON; SiSoSe
School-bell rings, The. Nine o'Clock. Katherine Pyle. *Fr.* The Wonder Clock. OBCA
School Bus, The. Larry Eigner. FAZ
School Cadets. Anne Elder. CBAP
School Children, The. Louise Glück. AmPA; WeW
School Days. Will D. Cobb. FSW; TreFT
School Days. William Stafford. LCAP
School Days in New Amsterdam. Arthur Guiterman. FaPON
School Days/Rule Days. Derek Butler. LFAC
School for Scandal, The, *sel.* Sheridan.
Let the Toast Pass, *fr.* III, iii. HBV-2; OnYI; OxBI
(Famous Toast, A.) TreF
(Here's to the Maiden.) ELP
(Song: "Here's to the maiden of bashful fifteen.") NOEC; OBEC; OxBoLi; PoRA; ViBoPo
School Girl, The. William Henry Venable. AA
School Globe, The. James Reaney. NOBC
School Is Out. Frances Frost. SiSoSe
School is over. Kate Greenaway. TiPo
School is over. It is too hot. The Lonely Street. William Carlos Williams. MP; PoA; TwCP
School of Beauty's a tavern now, The. A Street in Bronzeville: Southeast Corner. Gwendolyn Brooks. VGW
School of Desire, The. May Swenson. TwAmPo
School of Night, The. A. D. Hope. PoA
School of Sorrow, The. Harold Hamilton. BLRP
School that looks like an army barracks, A. Ecole St. Luc. Ray Fraser. NeAC
School was out. The boys were quelling Mars. A Time of Light, a Time of Shadow. Samuel Yellen. NePoAm-2
Schoolboy, The. Blake. *Fr.* Songs of Experience. BoNaP; CH; FaBoCh; GLGT
Schoolboy's Complaint, A. *Unknown.* OxBM
(Scholar Complains, The.) MeEL
Schoolboys in Winter. John Clare. InvP; NBM; PoEL-4; VLP
Schoolboy's Lot, A. *Unknown.* OxBM
Schoolboys still their morning rambles take, The. Schoolboys in Winter. John Clare. InvP; NBM; PoEL-4; VLP
Schoolfellows. Winthrop Mackworth Praed. *Fr.* School and Schoolfellows. NBM
Schoolgirl on Speech-Day in the Open Air. Iain Crichton Smith. NePoEA-2
Schoolma'am of much reputation, A. No Talking Shop. Minnie Leona Upton. TDH
Schoolmaster. George Rostrevor Hamilton. FaBoEE
Schoolmaster Abroad with His Son, The. Charles Stuart Calverley. NOBL
School-Master and the Truants, The. "John Brownjohn." OBCA
Schoolmaster, give your simple mob a break. Martial, *tr. by* Rolfe Humphries. Epigrams, X, lxii. GLGT
Schoolmaster, The. *Unknown.* GBP; GLGT
Schoolmaster's Admonition, A. *Unknown.* OxBChV
Schoolmaster's Precepts, A. John Penkethman. OxBChV
Schoolmistress, The. William Shenstone. GoTL; LaA; LAuP; NOEC
Schoolroom: 158. James E. Warren, Jr. GoYe
Schools. George Crabbe. The Borough, Letter XXIV. CTC
School's Out. W. H. Davies. OBMV
Schoolteacher his hair curled thin and gray bespectacled, A. I Promessi Sposi. Cid Corman. HoAn
Schoolyard in April. Kenneth Koch. PoA
Schooner *Blizzard*, The, *with music. At. to* Henry Burke. ShS
Schooner *Fred Dunbar*, The. Amos Hanson. AmFP
Schooner *Kandahar*, The, *with music. At. to* Sepley Collin. ShS
Schott and Willing did engage. The Duel. *Unknown.* ShM
Schreckhorn, The. Thomas Hardy. OAEL-2
Schubertiana. Tomas Tranströmer, *tr. fr. Swedish by* Robert Bly. NU
Schwiegermutterlieder. Tony Harrison. InPS
Science. Robinson Jeffers. NU; OxBA
Science as Art. Hugh Seidman. AmPA

Science, A—so the savants say. Emily Dickinson. ImOP
Science Fiction. Kingsley Amis. NePoEA-2
Science Fiction. Reed Whittemore. GP
Science finds out ingenious ways to kill. The Modern World. Colin Ellis. FaBoEE
Science for the Young. Wallace Irwin. DBV; QQQ
"Arthur with a lighted taper," *sel.* ShM
Science in God. Robert Herrick. ImOP
Science is what the world is, earth and water. The Laboratory Midnight. Reuel Denney. ImOP; NePA
Science long watched the realms of space. A World Beyond. Nathaniel Ingersoll Bowditch. AA
Science of the Night, The. Stanley Kunitz. MoAmPo; MP; TwCP; UnTE
Science takes away from the beauty of the stars? Footnote to Feynman. Jonathan V. Post. SUW
Science, that simple saint, cannot be bothered. Dr. Sigmund Freud Discovers the Sea Shell. Archibald Macleish. BiP; PPON; SoSe
Science, the agile ape, may well. Coventry Patmore. FaBoEE
Science! thou fair effusive ray. Hymn to Science. Mark Akenside. PoEL-3
Science! true daughter of Old Time thou art! Sonnet to Science. Poe. Al Aaraaf: Prologue. AmPP; AP; InPK; NePA;NoP; OxBA; PPON; TAP; TW
Scientific Proof. J. W. Foley. QQQ
Scientist, The. Janet Burroway. SoSe
Scientist has a test tube full of sheep, A. Counting Sheep. Russell Edson. FiCP; LCAP
Scientist living at Staines, A. Genius. R. J. P. Hewison. FaFP
Scientists are in terror, The. Ezra Pound. *Fr.* Cantos, CXV. FaBoMo
Scientists removed their coats and hats, The. Report of the Meeting. Weldon Kees. TwAmPo
Scientists sit long of nights, The. Astronaut's Choice. M. M. Darcy. QQQ
Scilla's Metamorphosis, *sel.* Thomas Lodge.
Earth, Late Choked with Showers, The. ElL; ViBoPo
(Melancholy). OBSC
Scintilla. William Stanley Braithwaite. AmNP; BANP; CDC
Scintillate, scintillate, globule orific. The Little Star. *Unknown.* InMe; SpRo
Scion of a noble stock! The Young American. Alexander H. Everett. PaPo
Scissor-Man. George MacBeth. FaBoMo
Scissor-Man, The. Madeline Nightingale. TiPo
Scissors and string, scissors and string. *Unknown.* OxNR
Scissors-Grinder, The. Vachel Lindsay. Poems about the Moon, V. TwAmPo
Scobble for whoredom[e] whips his wife, and cries [*or* cryes]. Upon Scobble [Epigram]. Robert Herrick. AnAnS-2; CaPo; FaBoEE; NoP; TW
Scoffers, The. Blake. *See* Mock On, Mock On, Voltaire, Rousseau.
Scolding Wives Vindication; or, An Answer to the Cuckold's Complaint, The. *Unknown.* CoMu
Scoops in the sea rock full of natural water. Bathtubs. Richmond Lattimore. NYBP
Score of years had come and gone, A. John Underhill. Whittier. PAH
Scorn me as reason, who am always there. To a Friend. Charles Gullans. NePoEA
Scorn Not the Sonnet. Wordsworth. BiP; EnRP; HBV-2; HeIP; NIP; NoP; OAEP; OBRV; PP
("Scorn not the sonnet; critic, you have frowned.") EBEV
(Sonnet.) OBEV; TrGrPo
"Scorn not the sonnet," though its strength be sapped. On a Magazine Sonnet. Russell Hillard Loines. OBAL
Scorna Boy [*or* Scorney Bwee], the Barretts' bailiff, lewd and lame. The Welshmen of Tirawley. Sir Samuel Ferguson. OBVV; OnYI
Scorne then their censure, who gave out thy wit. Jasper Mayne. *Fr.* To the Memory of Ben Johnson. OBS
Scorned. Alexander Smith. OBVV
Scorner, The. Felix TchiKaya U'Tamsi, *tr. fr. French by* Gerald Moore *and* Ulli Beier. TTY
Scorney Bwee, the Barretts' bailiff, lewd and lame. *See* Scorna Boy; the Barretts' bailiff, lewd and lame.
Scorpion, The. Hilaire Belloc. BoAnP
Scorpion, The. William Plomer. NoAM; OBMV
Scorpion. Stevie Smith. EBEV
Scorpion is black as soot, The. The Scorpion. Hilaire Belloc. BoAnP
Scot, a Welsh and an Irish Man, A. *Unknown.* GBP
Scotch Rhapsody. Edith Sitwell. MP; TwCP
Scotch Te Deum. William Kethe. *See* Old Hundredth.
Scotland. Alexander Gray. BSV; GoTS; OxBS
Scotland. William Soutar. OxBS
Scotland 1941. Edwin Muir. BSV; OxBS
Scotland Small? "Hugh MacDiarmid." PoSH
Scotland, when it is given to me. With a Lifting of the Head. "Hugh MacDiarmid." MoBrPo
Scotland Yet. Henry Scott Riddell. HBV-2
Scotland's Burning. *Unknown.* FSW
Scotland's Winter. Edwin Muir. OxBS; OxBTC
Scots in Berwick (1296), The. *Unknown.* OxBM
Scots Wha Hae [wi' Wallace Bled]. Burns. EnRP; FaPoR; OAEL-1; OAEP; OBEC; OxBS; SeCeV; TEP; WHA
(Bannockburn.) GN; TreF; WBLP
(Before Bannockburn.) FaBoCh
(Bruce to His Men at Bannockburn.) FaPo; HBV-2
(Bruce's March to Bannockburn.) TrGrPo
(Robert Bruce's March to Bannockburn.) NOBE
(Scots Wha Ha'e wi' Wallace Bled.) CABA; FSW
Scott and I bent. Heaven. Gary Soto. NPGG
Scott, your last fragments I arrange tonight. On Editing Scott Fitzgerald's Papers. Edmund Wilson. CrMA; NYBP
Scottes out of Berwik and of Abirdene. Halidon Hill. Laurence Minot. OxBM
Scottish Mountaineering Club Song, The. John G. Stott. PoSH
Scottish Proverb, A. *Unknown.* FaBoUs
Scotts, Kerrs, and Murrays, and Deloraines all, The. A Border Ballad. Thomas Love Peacock. BXAP
Scottsboro. *Unknown.* InPK
Scottsboro, Too, Is Worth Its Song. Countee Cullen. PoBA
Scourge, The. Stanley Kunitz. CrMA
Scourge deep, and quick be done. Martyr. "E." CBAP
Scourge of Folly, The, *sel.* John Davies of Hereford.
Author Loving These Homely Meats, The. ElL; FaBoNo
(Buttered Pippin-Pies.) ChTr
(Homely Meats.) FaBoCh
Scourge of Villainy [*or* Villanie], The, *sel.* John Marston.
To Everlasting Oblivion. LoBV; OBSC
To Detraction I Present My Poesie. LoBV; OBSC; TW
Scourge of wind first, to flay, The. View from My Window. Alasdair MacLean. PoSH
Scow on Cowden Shore, The, 3 *vers. with music.* Larry Gorman. ShS
Scrap Iron. Raymond Durgnat. PCP
Scrapbooks. Nikki Giovanni. CNA
Scrape no more your harmless Chins. Advice to the Old Beaux. Sir Charles Sedley. FaBoUs; SeCV-2
Scraping sound, A: The grasshopper. The Grasshopper's Song. H. N. Bialik, *tr. by* Jessie Sampter. FaPON; YeAr
Scraps. Susannah Fried, *tr. fr. Slovak by* Anthony Rudolf. VWA
Scraps of Lear. Edward Lear. FaBoNo
Scratch, The. James Dickey. AP
Scratch a Jew and you'll find a Wailing Wall. The Wall. Eve Merriam. TrJP
Scrawled in Pencil in a Sealed Railway Car. Dan Pagis, *tr. fr. Hebrew by* Anthony Rudolf. VWA
Screamer Discusses Methods of Screaming, A. James Schevill. TAP
Screams that I screamed, despairing, aching. My White Book of Poems. "Rachel," *tr. by* "N. N." VWA
Scree empties down the mountain, The. One Way Down. David Craig. PoSH
Screens. Winifred M. Letts. SUMH
Screw-Guns. Kipling. ViBoPo
Screw Spring. William M. Hoffman. FF
Scribblers, The. Walter Savage Landor. OBSV
("Why should scribblers discompose.") FaBoEE
Scribe. Paul Auster. VWA
Scribe, The. Walter de la Mare. CMoP; FaBoCh; OBMV; TrCP; TrPWD
Scribe, The. *Unknown, tr. fr. Old Irish.* AnIL, *tr. by* Kuno Meyer; OnYI, *tr. by* Whitley Stokes *and* John Strachan, *arr. by* Kathleen Hoagland
Scribe's Prayer, The. Arthur Guiterman. TrPWD
Scribe's Prayer, The. Robert W. Service. TrPWD
Scrievin. Alexander Scott. BSV
Scrim of twilight, dropping on Manhattan, A. A March with All Drums Muffled. Reuel Denney. NYP
Scrimshaw. Michael Hogan. LFAC
Scriptures, The. Dryden. *Fr.* Religio Laici. OBS
Scroll. Stanley Moss. VWA
Scroll-Section. Robert Finch. PeCV
Scroppo's Dog. May Swenson. GDP
Scrubbed pink/ They look the most naked of animals. Pigs. John Cotton. BoAnP
Scrubber. W. E. Henley. In Hospital, XIX. BrPo
Scrutiny [*or* Scrutinie], The. Richard Lovelace. AnAnS-2; BoLoP; CaPo; CavP; EnLoPo; GBL; MeLP; MePo; NoP; OBS; SeCP; TrGrPo
(Song: "Why should you swear?") InMe
(Why Should You Swear?) ELP
Sculptor first in breath and blood, A. With Metaphor. Sarah Wingate Taylor. GoYe

Sculptor, wouldst thou glad my soul. Design for a Bowl. Anacreon, *tr. by* Thomas Moore. UnTE
Sculptors, The. Alfred Purdy. PeCV
Sculpture. *Unknown.* BLPL; PoLF
Sculpture in a bare white gallery, A. The Field. Jean Valentine. LCAP
Scum o' the Earth. Robert Haven Schauffler. HBV-2
Scunner. "Hugh MacDiarmid." BSV; FaBoTw
Scurrilous Scribe, The. Philip Freneau. AA
Scurvy-grass creeps down the strand, The. January. Daniel James O'Sullivan. NeIP
Scuttle, scuttle, little roach. Nursery Rhyme for the Tender-Hearted, I. Christopher Morley. FaFP; HBMV; YaD
Scylla and Charybdis. Homer, *tr. fr. Greek by* George Chapman. *Fr.* The Odyssey, XII. OBS
Scylla and Charybdis. Thomas Kinsella. OxBTC
Scylla's Lament. Thomas Hood. *Fr.* Hero and Leander. EnRP
Scylla's Metamorphosis. Thomas Lodge. *See* Scilla's Metamorphosis.
Scyros. Karl Shapiro. HoPM; LiTA; LiTM; MoVE; NePA; SeCeV; WaP
Scythe Song. Andrew Lang. GN; HBV-1
Scythians, The. Alexander Blok, *tr. fr. Russian by* Babette Deutsch *and* Avrahm Yarmolinsky. AWP; WaaP
Sea, The. Byron. *Fr.* Childe Harold's Pilgrimage, IV. BLPL; FaBoBe; HBV-1; LiTB
(And I Have Loved Thee, Ocean!) WHA
(Apostrophe to the Ocean.) OHFP; WBLP
(Deep and Dark Blue Ocean.) ChTr
(Ocean, The.) FaBV; PoEL-4
(Roll On, Thou Deep and Dark Blue Ocean.) FiP
(There Is a Pleasure in the Pathless Woods.) TreF
("There is a pleasure in the pathless woods.") MOS; OBRV: ViBoPo
Sea, The. "Barry Cornwall." GN; HBV-1; HBVY; TreFS
Sea, The. Hart Crane. *See* Voyages, I.
Sea, The. W. H. Davies. FaBoTw
Sea, The. Lloyd Frankenberg. MOS
Sea. Don Gordon. EtS
Sea, The. D. H. Lawrence. BoNaP; MOS
Sea, The. Ken Noyle. MOS
Sea, The. Richard Henry Stoddard. AA; HBV-1
Sea, The. Swinburne. *See* Stanzas: "I will go back to the great sweet mother."
Sea, The. Francis Webb. CBAP; PoAu-2
Sea, The ("Behold the wonders of the mighty deep"). *Unknown.* NA; RHPC
Sea, The ("Look, wild and wide") *Unknown, tr. fr. Irish by* Frank O'Connor. KiLC
Sea, The/ tore a rib from its side. Water without Sound. Malka Heifetz Tussman, *tr. by* Marcia Falk. VWA
Sea and Land Victories. *Unknown.* PAH
Sea and Ourselves at Cape Ann, The. Lawrence Ferlinghetti. PoM
Sea and Shore. Harry Lyman Koopman. AA
Sea and the Eagle, The. Sydney Clouts. PeSA
Sea and the Hills, The. Kipling. FaBV; MOS
Sea and the Mirror, The, *sels.* W. H. Auden.
Alonso to Ferdinand. MoPo
Preface: "Aged catch their breath, The." LiTA
Song of the Master and Boatswain. BoLoP; DTC; MOS
(Master and Boatswain.) FaBoTw
Sea and the Skylark, The. Gerard Manley Hopkins. FM; LiTB; OBMV
Sea and the Tiger, The. Laurence Collinson. PoAu-2
Sea at evening moves across the sand, The. Soldiers Bathing. F. T. Prince. ChMP; GTBS-P; LiTB; LiTM; MoBrPo; MoVE; NOCV; OBWP; OxBTC; PeSA; WaP
Sea at this town's neat threshold spills its gloss. At the Sea's Edge. Gwen Harwood. CBAP
Sea awoke at midnight from its sleep, The. The Sound of the Sea. Longfellow. AP; EtS; MOS; TreFT
Sea Battle, The. Dryden. *Fr.* Annus Mirabilis. FiP
Sea Bells. Richard Eberhart. AMV-80
Sea Bird, The. Keith Douglas. ChMP
Sea Bird to the Wave, The. Padraic Colum. EtS; SUS
Sea-Birds. Elizabeth Akers Allen. AA; FaBoBe; HBV-1
Sea Birds, The. Van K. Brock. NYBP
Sea-Birds. Fray Angelico Chavez. ISi
Seabirds. Robert B. Smith. LFAC
Sea-Birds. James Thomson. EtS
Sea Born. Harold Vinal. HBMV
Sea-bound landsman, looking back to shore, The. John Brown. Harry Lyman Koopman. AA
Sea Boy on the Giddy Mast, A. John Clare. PPP
Sea Breeze. Stéphane Mallarmé. *See* Sea-Wind.
Sea Burial. Robina Monkman. EtS
Sea Burial from the Cruiser "Reve." Richard Eberhart. NYBP
Sea called, The. Remembering Home. Susan Petrykewycz. AMV-80
Sea Canes. Derek Walcott. HeIP
Sea-Captain, The. Gerald Gould. EtS
Sea Captain, The ("It was of a sea captain that followed the sea"). *Unknown.* ViBoFo
Sea-Captain, The ("There was a sea captain lately come to shore"). *Unknown.* BaBo
Sea Cathedral, The. E. J. Pratt. CaP
Sea Change. John Masefield. FaBoTw; MOS; OBMV
Sea-Change. Genevieve Taggard. EtS
Sea-Change, A: For Harold. Joseph Langland. LiTM
Sea-Chantey, A, *sel.* Derek Walcott.
"In the middle of the harbour." TTY
Sea-Chaplain's Petition to the Lieutenants in the Ward-Room, for the Use of the Quarter-Gallery, A. "J. T." NOEC
Sea Child, A. Bliss Carman. HBV-1
Sea-Chill. Arthur Guiterman. BXAP; FaBoPa; MOS
Sea contains a destiny, The. The Sea and the Eagle. Sydney Clouts. PeSA
Sea-cow or grey manatee, The. The Manatee. Carey Blyton. AmMo
Sea cries with its meaningless voice, The. Pibroch. Ted Hughes. FaBoMo; NePoEA-2; OAEL-2; PoCH
Sea Danceth, The. Sir John Davies. *See* Dancing Sea, The.
Sea Dawn. Francis Hackett. AnIV
Sea-Deeps, The. Thomas Miller. EtS
Sea Dialogue, A. Oliver Wendell Holmes. EtS; MOS; OBAL
Sea Dirge. Archias of Byzantium, *tr. fr. Greek by* Andrew Lang. AWP
Sea Dirge, A. "Lewis Carroll." CenHV; MOS
Sea Dirge, A. Shakespeare. *See* Ariel's Song: "Full fathom five thy father lies."
Sea-Distances. Alfred Noyes. MOS
Sea Dreams, *sel.* Tennyson.
What Does Little Birdie Say? HBV-1; HBVY
(Cradle Song.) OxBChV
Sea Eats the Land at Home, The. Kofi Awoonor. CAD
Sea Eclogue. William Diaper. Nereides; or Sea-Eclogues, X. LoBV
Sea-Elephant, The. William Carlos Williams. LiTA; NU
Sea Fever. John Masefield. EtS; FaBoBe; FaBV; FaPON; FaPoR; FPL; HBV-1; HBVY; MoAB; MoBrPo; MOS; OBVV; OHFP; OxBTC; PDV; PoLF; PoPl; TiPo; TreF; TrGoPo; WHA
Sea Flower. Mary Dorcey. BrRo
Sea Fog, The. Josephine Jacobsen. NYBP
Sea Food Thought. John W. Moser. FAZ
Sea-Games. Aliza Shenhar, *tr. fr. Hebrew by* Linda Zisquit. VWA
Sea Gipsy, The. Richard Hovey. *See* Sea Gypsy, The.
Sea gives her shells to the shingle, The. Dedication. Swinburne. VLP
Sea gleamed deep blue in the sunlight, The. Homage to Marcel Proust. Thomas MacGreevy. CIP
Sea Gods. Hilda Doolittle ("H. D."). LiTA; MOS
Sea-God's Address to Bran, The. *Unknown, tr. fr. Middle Irish by* Kuno Meyer. OnYI
Sea goes flick-flack or the light does, The. Sheep Dipping. Norman MacCaig. OxBC
Sea-Grape Tree and the Miraculous. William Pitt Root. GeTw
Sea-Grief. Dowell O'Reilly. PoAu-1
Sea guards warily its treasures, The. The Heart. Jacob Steinberg, *tr. by* Harry H. Fein. TrJP
Sea Gull. Elizabeth J. Coatsworth. RHPC
(Sea gull curves his wings, The.) TiPo
Seagull, The. Mary Howitt. OxBChV
Sea-Gull, The. Ogden Nash. FaFP; FPL; MOS; NePA
Sea-Gull, The. *Unknown.* GBP
Seagull, spreadeagled, splayed on the wind, The. George Barker. *Fr.* Pacific Sonnets. LiTM; MasP; MOS; WaP
Seagulls. Robert Francis. RFM
Seagulls. Patricia Hubbell. PDV
Sea Gulls. E. J. Pratt. EtS
Seagulls. John Updike. Psk
Seagulls inland, The. The Natural Order of Things. Harley Elliott. NeAC
Seagull's narrow sails of feather lift, The. Winged Mariner. Grace Clementine Howes. EtS
Seagulls on the Serpentine. Alfred Noyes. EtS
Sea gulls whiten and dip, The. In the Bay. Arthur Symons. *Fr.* Amorix Exsul. OBNC; PBBP
Sea Gypsy [*or* Gipsy], The. Richard Hovey. EtS; FaPON; HBV-1; HBVY; PDV; TreFS
Sea has held me, The. Cornwallis. Tony Beyer. OCNZ
Sea has it this way, The: if you see. Cormorants. John Blight. CBAP
Sea has made a wall for its defence, The. Shoreline. Mary Barnard. PoA
Sea Hath Its Pearls, The. Heine, *tr. fr. German by* Longfellow. AWP
Sea Hath Many Thousand Sands, The. *Unknown.* EIL; LiTB; OBSC; ViBoPo
(Advice to a Lover.) HBV-1

Sea hath tempered it, The; the mighty sun. The Fountain. Mu'tamid, King of Seville, *tr. by* Dulcie L. Smith. AWP
Sea-Hawk. Richard Eberhart. BoAnP
Sea here used to look, The. At Darien Bridge. James Dickey. NoP
Sea Hold, The. Carl Sandburg. MOS
Sea Holly. Conrad Aiken. AP; LiTM; NePA
Sea Horse, The. Robert Graves. FaBoMo
Sea Hunger. John Hanlon Mitchell. EtS
Sea, The—in Calm. "Barry Cornwall." EtS
Sea Irony. John Langdon Heaton. AA
Sea is a circuit of holes, The. The Coral Reef. Laurence Lieberman. CoAP
Sea is a wilderness of waves, The. Long Trip. Langston Hughes. MOS
Sea is an acre of dull glass, the land is a table, The. Lusty Juventus. Charles Madge. FaBoMo
Sea is calm tonight, The. Dover Beach. Matthew Arnold. AWP; BiP; BLPA; CABA; DTC; EaLo; EBVV; EtS; FaBoBe; FaBoEn; FaBoPP; FaBoRV; FaBV; FaFP; FF; FiP; FPL; GTBS-P; HAP; HBV-2; HeIP; HoPM; InPK; InPS; InVP; LiTB; LoBV; MasP; MAT; MOS; NIP; NOBE; NoP; NU; OAEL-2; OAEP; OBNC; OBVV; PAI; PoEL-5; PoPl; PoPle; PoRA; PPoe; PPON; PPP; Prf; PrIm; SCV; SeCePo; SeCeV; SoSe; TEP; TreFS; TrGrPo; TRV; UnPo; ViBoPo; VLP; WeW; WHA
Sea is enormous, but calm with evening, The. Whale at Twilight. Elizabeth J. Coatsworth. BoAnP
Sea is flecked with bars of grey, The. Les Silhouettes. Oscar Wilde. *Fr.* Impressions. BrPo; EBVV; MOS; SyP
Sea Is His, The. Edward Sandford Martin. EtS
Sea is large, The. The Sea Hold. Carl Sandburg. MOS
Sea is mighty, but a Mightier sways, The. A Hymn of the Sea. Bryant. MOS
Sea is never still, The. Young Sea. Carl Sandburg. MOS
Sea is obsidian, The. Fire Island. Rita Mae Brown. IHMS
Sea is wild marble waiting a stonecutter's hand, chaos crying for symmetry. Sea. Don Gordon. EtS
Sea Island Miscellany, *sels.* R. P. Blackmur. MoVE
Mirage.
"One grey and foaming day."
"Where shall I go then."
Sea-King, The. L. Frank Tooker. EtS
Sea-Lands, The. Orrick Johns. HBV-1
Sea Lavender. Louise Morey Bowman. CaP
Sea Legs. Susan Feldman. AmPA
Sea lies quieted beneath, The. After Sunset. Arthur Symons. *Fr.* At Dieppe. BrPo; SyP
Sea Limits, The. Dante Gabriel Rossetti. EtS; MOS; NBM; OAEL-2; VLP
Sea limps up here twice a day, The. Paphos. Lawrence Durrell. NYBP
Sea Love. Charlotte Mew. ELU; MoAB; MoBrPo; OxBTC; TrGrPo; ViBoPo
Sea Lullaby. Elinor Wylie. BoNaP; MOS
Sea Lyric, A. William Hamilton Hayne. EtS
Sea-Maiden, The. J. W. de Forest. EtS
Sea Marke, The. John Smith. SCAP
Sea Memories. Longfellow. *See* My Lost Youth.
Sea-Mew, The. Elizabeth Barrett Browning. HBV-1; VLP
Sea-mew on a sea-king' wrist alighting, A. Dedication to "Songs of the Springtides." Swinburne. VLP
Sea-Monster. Gertrud Kolmar, *tr. fr. German by* Henry A. Smith. VWA
Sea Monster. W. S. Merwin. WSC
Sea Monsters. Edmund Spenser. *Fr.* The Faerie Queene, II, 12. ChTr; FaBoEn
Sea-nurtured. Jean Ingelow. EtS
Sea-Nymph's Parting, The. Walter Savage Landor. *Fr.* Gebir. FaBoEn
Sea, The! O the sea! *Tr. fr. Hawaiian.* WTO
Sea of Death, The. Thomas Hood. FaBoEn; LiTB; LoBV; OBNC; PoEL-4
Sea of Death, The. *Unknown.* CH
Sea of Silence Exhales Secrets, The. Hayim Nachman Bialik, *tr. fr. Hebrew by* Gabriel Levin. VWA
Sea pearl, western star. On Leaving. Gertrudis Gomez de Avellaneda, *tr. by* Frederick Sweet. PBWP
Sea Pieces. Robert Fitzgerald. PoPl
Sea-preserved, heaped with sea-spoils. Picture of a Nativity. Geoffrey Hill. NoAM; OxBC
Sea Princess, The. Katharine Pyle. SoPo
Sea, The—quick pugilist,. Training. Herrera S. Demetrio, *tr. by* Dudley Fitts. TTY
Sea retains such images, The. Louis Dudek. Europe, XCV. OBCV; PeCV
Sea Ritual, The. George Darley. Syren Songs, V. BIrV; OBNC; OBRV; OnYI; OxBI; WiR; WSC
(Deadman's Dirge.) CH
Sea Rose. Hilda Doolittle ("H. D."). FaBoMo; NoAM; NoP
Sea-Ruck. Richard Eberhart. MOS
Sea-Sand and Sorrow. Christina Rossetti. *See* What Are Heavy?
Sea sang sweetly to the shore, The. Hymn Written for the Two Hundredth Anniversary of the Old South Church, Beverly, Massachusetts. Lucy Larcom. OHIP
Sea School. Barbara Howes. NYBP
Sea Serpant, The. Wallace Irwin. FiBHP
Sea-Serpent, The. James Robinson Planché. NA
Sea Serpent Chantey, The. Vachel Lindsay. AmMo; WSC
Sea Shanty. Clifford Dyment. POL
Sea Shell. Amy Lowell. FaPON; RHPC
Sea-Shore. Emerson. *See* Seashore.
Sea Shroud, The. Jack Kerouac. PoM
Sea Side. Robert Graves. MoPo
Sea-Sleep. Thomas Lake Harris. AA
Sea-Song, A. Allan Cunningham. *See* Wet Sheet and a Flowing Sea, A.
Sea Song, A. Digby Mackworth Dolben. EBVV
Sea Song. Norah Holland. CaP
Sea-Song from the Shore, A. James Whitcomb Riley. TiPo
Sea Sonnet. Norma Lay. GoYe
Sea-Sonnet. V. Sackville-West. SBG
Sea-Spell [for a Picture], A. Dante Gabriel Rossetti. SyP; VLP; WSC
Sea still plunges where as naked boys, The. The Grotto. Francis Scarfe. NeBP; PoA
Sea sucks in the traveller, The. The Sea and the Tiger. Laurence Collinson. PoAu-2
Sea Surface Full of Clouds. Wallace Stevens. AmPP; AP; CMoP; CoBMV; MoAB; MoAmPo; MOS; TwAmPo; VGW
Sea swings owre the slants of sand, The. The Ballad of Dead Men's Bay. Swinburne. MOS
Sea tells something, but it tells not all, The. Reserve. Mary Ashley Townsend. AA
Sea, that problem Euclid never solved, The. Sutcliffe and Whitby. William Logan. MAYP
Sea, The! the sea! the open sea! The Sea. "Barry Cornwall." GN; HBV-1; HBVY; TreFS
Sea Town. Frances Frost. EtS
Sea Turtle. Liston Pope. AMV-80
Sea-Turtle and the Shark, The. Melvin B. Tolson. *Fr.* Harlem Gallery. PoBA
Sea Violet. Hilda Doolittle ("H. D."). NoP
Sea Voyage. William Empson. CMoP; MOS
Sea-Voyage. John Hall Wheelock. EtS
Sea-Voyage from Tenby to Bristol, A. Katherine Philips. SBG; WPE
Sea was as blue as the sky, The. The Real Thing. Ronald Wallace. AMV-81
Sea was born of the earth without sweet union of love, The. Maximus, from Dogtown-I. Charles Olson. *Fr.* The Maximus Poems. CoPo
Sea-Wash. Carl Sandburg. OBCA
Sea-Way. Ellen Mackay Hutchinson Cortissoz. AA
Sea waves are green and wet. Sand Dunes. Robert Frost. MoAB; MoAmPo; RFM
Sea Weed. *See* Seaweed.
Sea-Wind. Stéphane Mallarmé, *tr. fr. French by* Arthur Symons. AWP; SyP
(Sea Breeze, *tr. by* Rober Fry.) NAWM-2
Sea Wind, The. Harry Martinson, *tr. fr. Swedish by* Robert Bly. NU
Sea Wolf, The. Violet McDougal. FaPON
Sea Words. Mary Sinton Leitch. EtS
Sea would flow no longer, The. The Frozen Ocean. Viola Meynell. CH
Sea Wrack. "Moira O'Neill." OnYI
Seaconk or Rehoboths Fate. Benjamin Tompson. SCAP
Seaconk Plain Engagement. Benjamin Tompson. SCAP
Seafarer. Archibald MacLeish. NoAM; NoP
Seafarer, The. Earl of Surrey. *See* Complaint of the Absence of Her Lover . . .
Seafarer, The. *Unknown, tr. fr. Anglo-Saxon.* AnOE, Pt. I, *tr. by* Charles W. Kennedy; AP, *tr. by* Ezra Pound; CTC, *tr. by* Ezra Pound; EtS, Pt. I, *tr. by* Charles W. Kennedy; EBEV, *tr. by* John Wain; FaBoTw, *tr. by* Ezra Pound; HeIP, *tr. by* Ezra Pound; LiTA, *tr. by* Ezra Pound; MOS, *tr. by* Charles W. Kennedy; NoP; *tr. by* Ezra Pound; OBVE, *tr. by* Michael Alexander; OxBA, *tr. by* Ezra Pound; PoRA, Pt. I, *tr. by* L. Iddings; SeCeV, *tr. by* Ezra Pound
"That man cannot know," *sel.* PBBP
Seafarer, The ("Shall I thus ever long . . .). *Unknown.* *See* Lady Prayeth the Return of Her Lover Abiding on the Seas, The.
Seafarers tell of the Eastern Isle of Bliss, The. Li Po, *tr. by* Shigeyoshi Obata. *Fr.* His Dream of the Sky-Land: A Farewell Poem. WSC
Seal, A. Oliver Herford. *Fr.* Child's Natural History. HBV-2; HBVY
Seal. William Jay Smith. GrPl; RFM; RHPC
Seal at Stinson Beach. Roberta Hill. VoR
Seal Lullaby. Kipling. *Fr.* The Jungle Book. FaPON; SoSe; TiPo
Seal of Fire. Mordecai Temkin, *tr. fr. Hebrew by* Jeremy Garber. VWA
Seal Pups. Nora Dauenhauer. TWSS

Seal Rock. Sue Baugh. AMV-81
Seal Rock. Katha Pollitt. MAYP
Seal Rocks: San Francisco. Robert Conquest. PP
Seal thou the window! Yea, shut out the light. Cloistered. Alice Brown. AA
Seal up the book, all vision's at an end. On the Death of Mr. Pope. *Unknown.* NOEC
Sealed in rainlight one. The Magic Apple Tree. Elaine Feinstein. BrRo
Sealed Orders. Richard Burton. HBV-2
Sealed with the seal of Life, thy soul and mine. The Inscription. Elsa Barker. *Fr.* The Spirit and the Bride. HBMV
Seals, The. L. A. G. Strong. LO
Seals at High Island. Richard Murphy. CIP; IPY
Seals at play off Western Isle, The. Seals, Terns, Time. Richard Eberhart. LiTM; MoAB; MoAmPo
Seals in Penobscot Bay, The. Daniel Hoffman. MP; TwCP
Seals of Love. Shakespeare. *See* Take, O Take Those Lips Away.
Seals, Terns, Time. Richard Eberhart. LiTM; MoAB; MoAmPo
Seaman's Confession of Faith, A. Harry Kemp. TrPWD
Seaman's Happy Return, The. *Unknown.* ChTr
(Valiant Seaman's Happy Return to His Love, The.) GBP
Seamark, A. Bliss Carman. PeCV
Seamen Three. Thomas Love Peacock. *See* Three Men of Gotham.
Seamy Side of Motley, The. Sir Owen Seaman. InMe
Sean Spotted Wolf examined the yellow-tinted. Winter Count of Sean Spotted Wolf. Earle Thompson. STE
Séance. William Abrahams. NYBP
Séance. Francis King. PoA
Séance. Edouard Roditi. EAS
Search. Claribel Alegria, *tr. fr. Spanish by* Aliki *and* Willis Barnstone. BoWoP
Search, The. Bible, *O.T.* *See* As the Hart Panteth.
Search, The. Kwesi Brew. PBA
Search, The. Thomas Curtis Clarke. WGRP
Search, The. Ernest Crosby. AA
Search, The. Michael Hamburger. VWA
Search, The. George Herbert. AnAnS-1
Search, The. James Russell Lowell. TRV
Search. Anne Marriott. TRV
Search. Raymond Souster. ELU; OBCV
Search, The. Henry Vaughan. AnAnS-1; SBVL; SeCP
Search. Margaret Widdemer. TrPWD
Search after Happiness, The, *sel.* Hannah More.
Solitude. WBLP
Search all the Christian climes from pole to pole. Daniel Defoe. *Fr.* Reformation of Manners. OBSV
Search for God, The, *abr.* Thomas Heywood. *Fr.* Hierarchie of the Blessed Angels. OxBoCh
("I sought thee round about, O thou my God!") WGRP
Search for Love. Henry Johnson. LFAC
Search Party, The. William Matthews. GeTw
Search. Search. Seek. Seek. A Weary Song to a Slow Sad Tune. Li Ch'ing-chao, *tr. by* Kenneth Rexroth. BoWoP
Search then the Ruling Passion: there, alone. Pope. *Fr.* Moral Essays, Epistle I. ViBoPo
Searched, we wait to fly. Sparrow in an Airport. Richard Snyder. PPJ
Searcher of souls, you who in heaven abide. A Prayer. Samuel Butler. FaBoEE
Searching, The. Alice S. Cobb. BlSi
Searching for Lambs. *Unknown.* OBET
Searching for souvenirs among some rubble. A Post-Mortem. Siegfried Sassoon. DFF
Searching for the Desert Blues. *Unknown.* BluL
Searching my heart for its true sorrow. Exiled. Edna St. Vincent Millay. EtS; MOS; PoRA
Searchlight, A/ yawns across the window. Abbreviated Rumination. P. L. Jacobs. LFAC
Seas are quiet when the winds give o'er, The. Old Age [*or* Last Verses]. Edmund Waller. *Fr.* Of the Last Verses in the Book. BLPL; NOBE; NOCV; OBEV; OxBoCh; TreFT
Sea's Last Gift, The; 1961. Milton Kessler. DiL
Sea's Spell, The. Susan Marr Spalding. AA; EtS
Sea's Voice, The. William Prescott Foster. EtS
Seascape. W. H. Auden. *See* On This Island.
Seascape. Elizabeth Bishop. MoAB; MOS; OxBC; PPP
Seascape. Stephen Spender. ChMP; CoBMV; MOS; NoP
Seascape. Francis Brett Young. OxBTC
Seascape shift, The. Distinctions. Charles Tomlinson. CMoP
Seascape with Bookends. Charles Edward Eaton. AMV-80
Seashore [*or* Sea-Shore]. Emerson. EtS; LiTA; MOS; OxBA
Seaside Golf. John Betjeman. LiSp; PoPl
Season, ending, makes no sign, but the wind. Conserves. David Mus. *Fr.* The Joy of Cooking. PoA
Season late, day late, sun just down, and the sky. Birth of Love. Robert Penn Warren. UnPo
Season, The? Not yet spring. The place? Beside. Rabbit Cry. Edward Lucie-Smith. NePoEA-2
Season of mists and mellow fruitfulness. To Autumn [*or* Ode to Autumn]. Keats. AWP; BiP; BoNaP; CABA; CH; ChER; EBEV; EnRP; FaBoEn; FaBoRV; FaBV; FF; FiP; FPL; GTBS; GTBS-P; HAP; HBV-1; HBVY; InvP; LiTB; LoBV; NIP; NOBE; NOP; NU; OAEL-2; OAEP; OBEV; OBNC; OBRV; PAI; PoEL-4; PoLF; PoPle; PPoe; PPP; Prf; PrIm; RoGo; SCV; SeCeV; SoSe; TEP; TreFS; TrGrPo; UnPo; ViBoPo; WeW; WHA
Season of Phantasmal Peace, The. Derek Walcott. NoP
Season 'Tis, My Lovely Lambs, The. E. E. Cummings. NIP; UnPo
Seasons, The. Thomas Holcroft. NOEC
Seasons, The. Rolfe Humphries. NYBP
Seasons, The. Kalidasa, *tr. fr. Sanskrit by* Arthur W. Ryder. AWP
Seasons. Christina Rossetti. YeAr
Seasons, The. Spenser. *See* Mask of Mutability, The.
Seasons, The, *sels.* James Thomson.
Autumn.
Autumn ("But see the fading many-colour'd woods"). EnRP; LoBV
"Fled is the blasted verdure of the fields." OAEP
"Here the rude clamour of the sportsman's joy." PBBP
Lavinia. OBEC
Love of Nature. OBEC
Moonlight in Autumn. OBEC
(Autumnal Moon, The, *shorter sel.*) NOBE
"Poor is the triumph o'er the timid hare." FM
Hymn on the Seasons, A. EnRP; LAuP; OxBoCh
Spring.
"As rising from the vegetable world." PoEL-3
"At length the finished garden to the view." ViBoPo
Birds in Spring. OBEC
"Lend me your song, ye nightingales! oh pour." PBBP
"Should I my steps turn to the rural seat." FM
Spring Flowers. NOBE; OBEC
Summer.
Happy Brittania. OBEC; SeCePo
(Brittania.) FaBoPP
"Still let me pierce into the midnight depth. EnRP
Storm, The. LoBV
Summer ("Home from his morning task the swain retreats"). FM
Summer Evening and Night. OBEC
Summer Morning. OBEC
" 'Tis raging noon; and, vertical, the sun." EBEV; OAEL-1
Winter. OAEP, *abr.*
Approach of Winter. OBEC
(Winter: "See Winter comes to rule the varied year.") NOEC; TEP
"Clear frost succeeds, and thro' the blew serene." FaBoEn
"Fowls of heaven, The. PBBP
Frost at Night. OBEC
(Winter Night, A.) NOBE
"Keener tempests come, The: and fuming dun." EBEV; EnRP; NoP
Winter ("As thus the snows arise, and foul and fierce.") SeCePo
Winter ("Drooping, the labourer-ox"). FM
Winter ("Now, when the cheerless empire of the sky"). BSV; OxBS
Winter ("What art thou, frost? and whence are they keen stores"). OxBS
Winter ("When from the pallid sky the sun descends"). OAEL-2; OxBS
Winter Scene, A. OBEC
Seasons/ changes moods. A Common Poem. Carolyn M. Rodgers. CNA
Season's anguish, crashing whirlwind, ice, The. Winter Garden. David Gascoyne. ChMP; GTBS-P
Seasons burn, The. The wind is dry. Earthquake. R. A. D. Ford. NOBC
Season's Greetings. Hilaire Belloc. DBV
(Lines for a Christmas Card.) TW
Season's Lovers, The. Miriam Waddington. MoCV; OBCV; PeCV
Seasons of the Soul. Allen Tate. AP; CrMA; MoPo; NePA; OxBA
Autumn, *sel.* MoVE
Seasons operate on ev'ry breast, The. About in London. John Gay. *Fr.* Trivia; or, The Art of Walking the Streets of London. FaBoPP
Seasons waiting the miracle. Farmer. Lucien Stryk. FAZ
Seat for Three, A: Written on a Settle. Walter Crane. OBVV
Seat of the soul is where the inner world, The. Aphorism. "Novalis," *tr. by* Charles E. Passage. NU
Seated on her bed legs spread open. Joyce Mansour, *tr. fr. French by* Willis Barnstone. BoWoP
Seated once by a brook, watching a child. The Brook. Edward Thomas. MoVE; OAEL-2; SeCeV

Seated one day at the organ/ I jumped as if I'd been shot. The Lost Chord. D. B. Wyndham Lewis. WhC
Seated one day at the organ/ I was weary and ill at ease. A Lost Chord. Adelaide Anne Procter. FaFP; HBV-2; PaPo; TreF; VLP; WBLP; WGRP
Seated statue of himself he seems, A. Farm Boy after Summer. Robert Francis. NCSH
Seated, the harpist waits. Marble Statuette Harpist. Sara Van Alstyne Allen. GoYe
Seattle weather: it has rained for weeks in this town. Homage to Arthur Waley. Weldon Kees. NaP
Seaward. Celia Thaxter. AA
Seaward. George Edward Woodberry. *Fr.* Wild Eden, XLI. AA
Seaward Bound. Alice Brown. TrPWD
Seaward goes the sun, and homeward by the down. The Cliffside Path. Swinburne. A Midsummer Holiday, VI. VLP
Sea-ward, White Gleaming [through the Busy Scud]. Samuel Taylor Coleridge. BiP; PBBP
Seaway. Grace Wilson. AMV-81
Sea-Weed. D. H. Lawrence. BoNaP; MOS
Seaweed. Longfellow. AP; HBV-2; MOS; OxBA; TAP
Equinox, *sel.* EtS
Sea-Weed, The. Elisabeth Cavazza Pullen. AA
Seaweed/ between rocks. Haiku. Kito, *tr. by* Lucien Stryk *and* Takashi Ikemoto. FAZ
Seaweed, seaweed, drifting, drifting. *Ad. by* Hannah Tatana, *tr. fr. Maori by* Barry Mitcalfe. WTO
Sea-weed sways and sways and swirls. Sea-Weed. D. H. Lawrence. BoNaP; MOS
Seaweeds. Sandra McPherson. AmPA
Seboyeta Chapel. Shirley Hill Witt. TWSS
Secluded from domestic strife. The Double Transformation. Goldsmith. OBNV
Second Advice to a Painter, The. Andrew Marvell. APAS
Second after, A. The Settlers. Margaret Atwood. MoCV
2nd afternoon I come, The. A Poem for the Insane. John Weiners. NeAP; PoM
Second Air Force. Randall Jarrell. AP; CMoP; CoBMV; LiTM; WaP
Second Angel, The. Philip Levine. NaP
Second Anniversary [*or* Anniversarie], The. John Donne. *See* Of the Progress of the Soule.
Second Ascension of Christ, The. John Brooks Wheelwright. *Fr.* Forty Days. NOCV
Second Asgard, The. Matthew Arnold. *Fr.* Balder Dead. FiP
Second Avenue Winter. Charles Simic. NYP
Second Best. Rupert Brooke. MoBrPo; OBVV
Second Carolina Said-Song. A. R. Ammons. OBAL
Second class is the second grade, The. Primary Lesson: The Second Class Citizens. Sun-Ra. PoBA
Second Coming, The. Dannie Abse. NoAM; NMP
Second Coming, The. Carl Clark. JB
Second Coming, The. John William Corrington. HoPM
Second Coming, The. Norman Gale. HBV-2
Second Coming, The. W. B. Yeats. BIrV; BLPL; CABA; CMoP; CoBMV; EaLo; FaBoEn; FaBoMo; FF; GTBS-P; HAP; HeIP; HoPM; InPK; InPS; LiTB; LiTM; LoBV; MasP; MAT; MoAB; MoBrPo; MoVE; NIP; NoAM; NOBE; NoP; OAEL-2; OAEP; OxBI; OxBTC; PAI; PPoe; PPP; PrIm; SBVL; SCV; SeCePo; SeCeV; SoSe; TEP; UnPo; WaP; WeW
Second Corinthians, *sel.* Bible, *N.T.*
God Was in Christ, V: 18-21. TRV
Second Crucifixion, The. Richard Le Gallienne. HBV-2; OBVV; WGRP
Second Cycle of Love Poems, *sel.* George Barker.
O Tender under Her Right Breast, II. MoAB; MoBrPo
(Love Poem.) NeBP
2nd Dance—Seeing Lines—6 February 1964. Jackson MacLow. CoPo
Second Dream, The. Jean Valentine. LCAP
Second Epistle of the Essay on Man, The. Pope. *Fr.* Essay on Man. GoTL
Second Epistle to Robert Graham. Burns. DBV
Second Epitaph, A. *Unknown.* MeEL
Second-fated, The. Robert Graves. NoAM
Second Fig. Edna St. Vincent Millay. *Fr.* Figs from thistles. FaBV; NoP; PoA
Second Generation, The. Menachem Z. Rosensaft. AMV-81
Second Glance at a Jaguar. Ted Hughes. NoAM; NYBP; PrIm
Second grade mornings. Dogskin Rug. Adrien Stoutenburg. GP
Second-hand platitudes like antique watches. Catching One Clear Thought Alive. Paula Gunn Allen. WPOW
Second-hand sights, like crumpled. Newark, for Now (68). Carolyn M. Rodgers. PoBA
Second Honeymoon. *Unknown, tr. fr. Irish by* Augustus Young. BIrV
Second Horn. W. S. Di Piero. MAYP
Second Hymn to Lenin. "Hugh MacDiarmid." OAEL-2, *abr.*
Second Hymn to the Night, The. "Novalis," *prose poem version tr. fr. German by* Robert Bly. *Fr.* Hymns to the Night. NU
Second Iron Age, The. Michael Harrington. CaP
Second Life of Lazarus, The. Gwen Harwood. CBAP
Second Life, The. Edwin Morgan. OxBS
2nd Light Poem: For Diane Wakoski. Jackson MacLow. PoM
Second Man, The. Julian Symons. WaP
Second man I love, The. Spring. Carole Gregory Clemmons. PoBA
Second Mate, The. Fitz-James O'Brien. AA
Second Molting, A. Ralph Salisbury. STE
Second Nature. Diana Chang. BrSi
Second Night, The. M. L. Hester, Jr. AMV-80
Second Nimphall, The. Michael Drayton. *Fr.* The Muses Elizium. AnAnS-2
Second Ode to Persephone. Robert Kelly. The Book of Persephone, 9. PoM
Second Pastoral, The; or, Alexis. Virgil, *tr. fr. Latin by* Dryden. PeHV
Second Poem. Peter Orlovsky. NeAP
Second Poem the Night-Walker Wrote, The. Goethe. *See* Wanderer's Night-Songs, II.
Second Quest, The. Joseph Rodman Drake. *Fr.* The Culprit Fay. AA
Second Rapture, The. Thomas Carew. CaPo; UnTE
Second Reading. Richard Beyer. AMV-81
Second Review of the Grand Army, A. Bret Harte. HBV-2; PAH
Second Samuel, *sel.* Bible, *O.T.*
David's Lament, I: 19-27. ChTr; FF; TrGrPo; TrJP
("Beauty of Israel is slaine upon thy high places, The: how are the mightie fallen!") OBVE; OBWP
(David's Lament for Saul and Jonathan,) AWP
(How Are the Mighty Fallen,) WaaP
Second Satire of the First Book of Horace Imitated, The, *sel.* Pope.
"With all a woman's virtues but the pox." OBSV
Second Seeing. Louis Golding. WGRP
Second Sermon on the Warpland, The. Gwendolyn Brooks. BPo; NOBA; PoBA
Second Shadow. Theodore Roethke. PoA
Second Shaman Song. Gary Snyder. Myths and Texts: Burning, I. NeAP; NOBA; PoM
Second Shepherds' Play, The. *Unknown.* PoEL-1
(Wakefield Second Shepherds' Play.) OAEL-1
Hail, Comly and Clene, *sel.* NAs
(Haylle, Comly and Clene.) OBEV; OxBoLi
(Shepherds at Bethlehem, The.) ChTr
Second Skins—a Peyote Song. Joseph Bruchac. CDW
Second Song. Tennyson. PBBP
Second Stanza for Dr. Johnson, A. Donald Hall. FiBHP; ShM
Second Thanksgiving, The; or, The Reprisal. George Herbert. *See* Reprisall, The.
Second Violinist's Son, The. Debora Gregor. AMV-80
Second Vision, The. Robert Herrick. UnTE
Second Vision, The. Tadhg Dall O'Huiginn, *tr. fr. Late Middle Irish by* the Earl of Longford. AnIL
Second Volume, The. Robert Mowry Bell. AA
Second Wisdom. Henry Morton Robinson. GoYe
Second Woman's Lament. Brenda Chamberlain. NeIP
(Secondary experience, nouns). Zen Buddhism and Psychoanalysis/ Psychoanalysis and Zen Buddhism. Jackson MacLow. PoM
Secrecy. Samuel Daniel. *Fr.* Hymen's Triumph. OBSC; OLR
(Eyes Hide My Love.) EIL
Secrecy Protested [*or* Secresie Protested]. Thomas Carew. *See* Fear Not, Dear Love.
Secret, The. "Æ." MoBrPo
Secret. Gwendolyn B. Bennett. BlSi; CDC
Secret, The. John Clare. GBL
Secret, The. Ralph Spaulding Cushman. STF; TRV
(His Presence Came like Sunrise.) BLRP
Secret, The. Emily Dickinson. *See* I have not told my garden yet.
Secret. Esther Hull Doolittle. YeAr
Secret. Catherine Haydon Jacobs. GoYe
Secret, The. Lonny Kaneko. BrSi
Secret, The. Denise Levertov. NaP
Secret, The. Arthur Wallace Peach. HBMV
Secret, The. James Stephens. WSC
Secret, A ("If I had wit for to indite"). *Unknown.* OBSC
Secret, The ("We have a secret"). *Unknown.* SoPo; TiPo
Secret, The. Mary Morison Webster. PeSA
Secret, The. George Edward Woodberry. Wild Eden, VI. AA; HBV-1
Secret Cavern, The. Margaret Widdemer. FaPON
Secret Garden, The. Thomas Kinsella. IPY; TwCP
Secret Garden, The. Robert Nichols. WGRP

Secret Heart, The. Robert P. Tristram Coffin. PoSC
Secret in bed the lustful with soft cries. Sonnet against the Too-Facile Mystic. Elizabeth B. Harrod. NePoEA
Secret in the Cat, The. May Swenson. DFF; GP; PAI
Secret Irish, The. Allen Hoey. AMV-81
Secret Laughter. Christopher Morley. FaBV; TreFS
Secret Love, The. "Æ." HBV-1
Secret Love. John Clare. FaBV; NBM; OBNC; PoEL-4; TrGrPo; VLP
(I Hid My Love.) GBL; MAT; NCEP
(Song: "I hid my love when young while I.") OAEL-2
Secret Love; or, The Maiden Queen, *sel.* Dryden.
I Feed a Flame Within [Which So Torments Me]. PoPle; QFR
(Hidden Flame.) OBEV
(Song: "I feed a flame within, which so torments me.") AWP
Secret Love or Two I Must Confess[e], A. Thomas Campion. AAS; ErPo
Secret Muse, The. Roy Campbell. PeSA
Secret of Poetry, The. Jon Anderson. MAYP
Secret of Song. Christine White. STF
Secret of the Deeps, The. Sidney Royse Lysaght. EtS
Secret of the polar bear, The. Polar Bear. Gail Kredenser. RHPC
Secret of the Sea, The. Longfellow. EtS
(Galley of Count Arnaldos, The.) OBEV; OBVV
Secret of these hills was stone, and cottages, The. The Pylons. Stephen Spender. AWP; NoAM
Secret People, The. G. K. Chesterton. FaPoR; OxBTC
Secret Place, The. A. A. Pollard. STF
Secret Place of Prayer, The. Georgia B. Adams. STF
Secret Pleasures. Robert Morgan. MAYP
Secret Prayer. John Cross Belle. STF
Secret Sits, The. Robert Frost. InPK; SoPo
Secret Song, The. Margaret Wise Brown. OBCA; PDV; RHPC
Secret they are, sealed, annealed, and brainless. Oystering. Richard Howard. NoAM
Secret Thoughts. Christopher Morley. *Fr.* Translations from the Chinese. EvOK
Secret Town, The. Abraham Sutzkever, *tr. fr. Yiddish by* Jacob Sonntag. TrJP
Secret was the garden. The Mistress of Vision. Francis Thompson. BrPo; Ch, *abr.;* OBVV
Secretary. Ted Hughes. ErPo; InPK
Secretary, The. Peter Redgrove. OxBTC
Secretary of State, The. Mr. Secretary. Karl Patten. SOTS
Secrets ("The secrets I keep"). Linda Pastan. AMV-80
Secrets of Angling, The, *sel.* John Dennys.
Angler's Song, The. EIL
Secrets of the Earth, The. Blake. *Fr.* The Book of Thel. NOBE
Sects. Jack Gilbert. NPGG
Secular Elegies, *sel.* George Barker.
O Golden Fleece, V. MoAB; MoBrPo
("O golden fleece she is where she lies tonight.") ErPo; LiTM; NeBP
Satan Is on Your Tongue, III. MoAB; MoBrPo
Secular Games. Richard Howard. PoA
Secular Masque, The. Dryden. PoEL-3; PrIm; SeCeV; SeCV-2
Sels.
All, All of a Piece [Throughout]. ChTr; ELP; ELU; HAP; InPS
(Chorus.) ViBoPo
(Song.) WeW
Diana's Hunting-Song. SeCePo
"With horns and with hounds I waken the day." NOBE
"Sound the trumpet, beat the drum." FaBoRV
Security. Michael Hamburger. NMP; PoCh
Security. Charles L. O'Donnell. TrPWD
Security. Lina Sandell. STF
Security. Margaret E. Sangster. BLRP
Seder, 1944. Friedrich Torberg, *tr. fr. German by* Erna Baber Rosenfeld. VWA
Seder-Night. Israel Zangwill. TrJP
Sedges, The. "Seumas O'Sullivan." AnIV
Sedge-Warbler, The. Ralph Hodgson. PB
Sedge-Warblers. Edward Thomas. PoPle
Sediment. David Ignatow. NYBP
Seduced Girl. Hedylos, *tr. fr. Greek by* Louis Untermeyer. BoLoP; ErPo
(To Venus.) UnTE
Seduction. Nikki Giovanni. NMM
Seduction. Jo Ann Hall-Evans. BlSi
Seduction, The. Suzanne Berger Rioff. NMM
Seduction of Engadu, The. *Unknown, tr. fr. Babylonian tablets by* William Ellery Leonard. *Fr.* Epic of Gilgamesh. ErPo
See/ how they trace. Birds in Snow. Hilda Doolittle ("H. D."). PoA
See/ me. A Pair of Wings. Stephen Hawes. MeEL
See a pin and pick it up. *Unknown.* FaBoBe; HBV-1; HBVY; TreF
See all the people getting off the bus. Mark Rahschulte. AMV-80
See an old unhappy bull. The Bull. Ralph Hodgson. BrPo; LiTM; MoAB; MoBrPo; MoVE; OBMV; OxBTC; WHA
See, and not see; and if thou chance t' espy. To the Generous Reader. Robert Herrick. CaPo
See, as the carver carves a rose. The Carver. Conrad Aiken. *Fr.* Priapus and the Pool. HBMV
See, as the prettiest graves will do in time. Fame. Robert Browning. PP; SoSe
See, Ben, the water. To Ben, at the Lake. Cilla McQueen. OCNZ
See, chil-dren, the fur-bear-ing seal. A Seal. Oliver Herford. *Fr.* Child's Natural History. HBV-2; HBVY
See, cold island, we stand. Clare Coast. Emily Lawless. OxBI
See columns rang'd in proud Palladian style! *Unknown.* FaBoEE
See commons, peers, and ministers of state. Edward Young. *Fr.* Love of Fame, the Universal Passion. OBSV
See dear Pater with the bills. Christmas Bills. Joseph Hatton. OBCP
See! down the red road by the brown tree. The End of Exploring. David Campbell. SeCePo
See! from the brake the whirring pheasant springs. The Shoot. Pope. *Fr.* Windsor Forest. FaBoEn; FM; PB; PoEL-3
See, from this counterfeit of him. On a Bust of Dante. Thomas William Parsons. AA; HBV-2
See her caught in the throb of a drum. Agbor Dancer. John Pepper Clark. PBA
See her come bearing down, a tidy craft! A Note on Wyatt. Kingsley Amis. WeW
See! Here, My Heart. *Unknown.* MeEL
See here, nice Death, to please his palate. Epitaph. *At. to* Pope. FaBoEE
See here the diving beetle is split. Creatures. Maxine W. Kumin. BoAnP
See, here's the grand approach. Verses on Blenheim. Martial, *tr. by* Swift. AWP
"See, here's the workbox, little wife." The Workbox. Thomas Hardy. InPK; UnPo
See how dark the night settles on my face. Nocturne. Naomi Long Madgett. BALP
See how easily our trap comes up. Crabbing. Marky Daniel. AMV-81
See how Flora smiles to see. On Clarastella Walking in Her Garden. Robert Heath. CavP; OBS
See how from far upon the eastern road. The Magi. Milton. *Fr.* On the Morning of Christ's Nativity. ChTr
See how he dives. Seal. William Jay Smith. GrPl; RFM; RHPC
See how he loves me. Generations. Joseph Awad. AMV-81
See how it flashes. In a Wine Cellar. Victor J. Daley. PoAu-1
See, how like twilight slumber falls. Song. Charles Cotton. OBS
See how she strips her lily for the sun. The Double Looking Glass. A. D. Hope. CBAP
See how the brown kelp withers in air. Landed: A Valentine. Richard Howard. PoA
See how the dolls resent us. Five Poems for Dolls, II. Margaret Atwood. NIP
See how the dying west puts forth her song. Nocturne. Richard Church. ChMP
See how the flowers, as at parade. A Garden [*or* Garden at Appleton House, The]. Andrew Marvell. HBV-1; OBEV; PoPle; TrGrPo
See how the orient dew. On a Drop of Dew. Andrew Marvell. AnAnS-1; GoBC; HAP; JCP; LiTB; MeLP; MePo; NIP; OBS; OxBoCh; SeCP; SeCV-1; TEP
See How the Rising Sun, *with music.* Elizabeth Scott. AH
See,—how the shining share. God Save the Plough. Lydia Huntley Sigourney. OBAL
See how the sky. The Moon. Louise Ayres Garnett. SiSoSe
See how the sun has somewhat not of light. El Greco. E. L. Mayo. HoPM; MiAP
See how this trim girl. Artemis. Peter Davison. ErPo
See how this violet which before. On a Violet in Her Breast. Thomas Stanley. OBS
See, I have set before thee this day life and good, and death and evil. Choose Life. Bible, *O.T.* *Fr.* Deuteronomy. TreFT
See, in the garden there, it hops and lurches about. On a Child with a Wooden Leg. Bertram Warr. OBCV
See in the Midst of Fair Leaves. Marianne Moore. MoAB
See, Lord,/ my coat hangs in tatters. The Prayer of the Old Horse. Carmen Bernos de Gasztold. PDV
See Lucifer like lightning fall. Third Sunday in Lent. John Keble. *Fr.* The Christian Year. VLP
See me with all the terrors on my roads. The Face. Edwin Muir. ChMP; GTBS-P
See, Mignonne, hath not the Rose. The Rose. Pierre de Ronsard, *tr. by* Andrew Lang. AWP
See my lov'd Britons, see your Shakespeare rise. Prologue. Dryden. *Fr.* Troilus and Cressida. SeCV-2

"See, nothing has happened to her," said my guide. Seeing Oloalok. Marilyn Bowering. NOBC
See now, dead friend. Duty to Death, LD. Dick Roberts. WaP
See on Newmarket's turf, my lord. At Newmarket. Samuel Bishop. PV
See on one hand. The Rainbow. Gerard Manley Hopkins. FaBoPP
See, one physician, like a sculler, plies. Two Heads Are Better than One. Joseph Jekyll. FaBoEE; WhC
See represented here, in light and shade. The Salutation of the Blessed Virgin. John Byrom. ISi
See, see, mine own sweet jewel. Canzonet. *Unknown.* ElL
See, see she wakes, Sabina wakes! Song. Congreve. HBV-1; NOEC
See, see the mighty hunter, fiercely bland. For the Opening of the Hunting Season. Morris Bishop. BoAnP
See, see, what shall I see? Mother Goose. OxNR
See, Sir, here's the grand approach. On Blenheim House. Abel Evans. OBEC
See! some strange comfort ev'ry [*or* every] state attend. Life's Poor Play. Pope. *Fr.* An Essay on Man, Epistle II. OBEC; SeCePo
See that brave and trembling motorman. The Dying Mine Brakeman. Orville Jenks. AmFP
See that [*or* the] building which, when my mistress living. A Well-wishing to a Place of Pleasure. *Unknown.* GBL
See That One? Robert Bagg. ErPo
See that satan pollarding a tree. Progression. Francis Scarfe. NeBP
See that señor so amorous and menacing. The Amorous Señor. Ogden Nash. TDH
See that wreck there in the gutter. The Outcast. Frank Elwood Sanford. PeD
See the chariot at hand here of Love. The Triumph of Charis [*or* Her Triumph *or* The Triumph]. Ben Jonson. *Fr.* A Celebration of Charis. AnAnS-2; CABA; CTC; EBEV; ElL; ELP; FaBoEn; GoBC; HBV-1; InPS; InvP; JCP; LiTB; LoBV; NOBE; NoP; OAEP; OBEV; PoEL-2; PoPle; PrIm; SeCeV; SeCP; SeCV-1; ViBoPo; WHA
See the Crocus' Golden Cup. Joseph Mary Plunkett. OnYI
See the day begins to break. Satyr's Song. John Fletcher. *Fr.* The Faithful Shepherdess, IV, i. OBS
See the dazzled stripling stand. Goliath and David. Louis Untermeyer. TrJP
See the fairies dancing in. The Fairies. Patricia Hubbell. WSC
See the far hills white with snow. Winter. Jean Jaszi. SoPo
See the fountain opened wide. Zion's Sons and Daughters. *Unknown.* AmFP
See the handsome hippopotamus. Hippopotamus. Joanna Cole. NTCP
See the happy moron. The Moron. *Unknown.* CenHV; TreFT; YaD
See the headlands yonder stand. Dirge Sung at Death. *Tr. fr. Maori by* John White. WTO
See the kitten on the wall. The Kitten at Play. Wordsworth. *Fr.* The Kitten and the Falling Leaves. FaPON; PCat
See the land, her Easter keeping. Easter Week. Charles Kingsley. OHIP
See the little maunderer. A Love for Patsy. John Thompson, Jr. LiTA; NePA; WaP
See the madly blowing dust. A Colorado Sand Storm. Eugene Field. PoOW
See, the pretty planet! Blowing Bubbles [*or* The Bubble]. William Allingham. GN; OnYI
See the pretty snowflakes. Falling Snow. *Unknown.* SoPo
See, the ruthless victor comes. Song for Peace. W. R. Rodgers. NeBP
See the scaffold it is mounted. Life of the Mannings. *Unknown.* FaBoBa
See, the see, the Bishop's see, The. The Bishop's See. *Unknown.* CoMu
See, the smell of my sone is as the smell of a feld. Bible, *O.T., tr. by* William Tyndale. Genesis, XXVII: 27-29. OBVE
See the smoking bowl before us. Burns. *Fr.* The Jolly Beggars. BSV; GoTS
See the Spring herself discloses. Spring. Thomas Stanley. AWP
See the star-breasted villain. Village-Born Beauty. *Unknown.* PaPo
See, the visor's pulled off and the zealots are arming. The Western Rebel. *Unknown.* APAS
See the young man I've laid out. Funeral Lament (Kommos) from Epiros. *Tr. fr. Modern Greek by* Elene Kolb. BoWoP
See them joined by strings to history. Puppets. Patricia K. Page. MoCV
See! There he stands; not brave, but with an air. Brothers. James Weldon Johnson. BANP
See, they are clearing the sawdust course. Equestrienne [*or* The Girl on the Milk-White Horse]. Rachel Field. *Fr.* A Circus Garland. OBCA; SoPo
See, they return; ah, see the tentative. The Return. Ezra Pound. AmPP; AP; CMoP; CoBMV; FaBoEn; HAP; MoAB; MoAmPo; MoPo; NePA; NoAM; NOBA; OxBA; PPoe; TwAmPo; VGW; ViBoPo; WeW
See this air, how empty it is of angels. Five for the Grace of Man. Winfield Townley Scott. VGW
See this house, how dark it is. The Empty House. Walter de la Mare. BrPo
See this seed? Food. Beggar's Song. Gregory Orr. LTB
See those cherries, how they cover. The Cherries; a Parable. Thomas Moore. OBSV
See, though the oil be low, more purely still and higher. Terence MacSwiney [*or* A Prisoner]. "Æ." AnIL; AnIV
See twilight standing on the brink. At the Edge of the Day. Clarence Urmy. HBMV
See two passenger trains, Lawd. Dey Got Each and de Udder's Man. *Unknown.* WTO
See what a clouded majesty, and eyes. To My Worthy Friend Master Peter Lely. Richard Lovelace. CaPo
See What a Lovely Shell. Tennyson. *See* Shell, The.
See what a mass of gems the city wears. Impression de Nuit; London. Lord Alfred Douglas. OBEV; OBVV
See what delights in sylvan scenes appear! Sylvan Delights. Pope. *Fr.* Pastorals: Summer. NOBE
See, when a fireship in mid ocean blazes. Surrender to Christ. Frederic William Henry Myers. OxBoCh
See where black water. Strip Mining Pit. Dan Gillespie. TAT
See where Capella with her golden kids. Edna St. Vincent Millay. Epitaph for the Race of Man, VI. CMoP; MoAB; MoAmPo
See Where My Love A-Maying Goes. *Unknown.* ElL
See where she sits upon the grassy green [*or* grassie greene]. A Ditty: In Praise of Eliza, Queen of the Shepherds. Spenser. *Fr.* The Shepheardes Calendaer: April. FaBoCh; OBEV; ViBoPo
See where the windows are boarded up. Where Are the Waters of Childhood? Mark Strand. LCAP; WeW
See, whirling snow sprinkles the starvèd fields. The Palm Willow. Robert Bridges. VLP
See who comes over the red blossomed heather. The Bold Fenian Men. *Unknown.* FSW
See, Will, 'Ere's a Go. *Unknown.* ChTr; FaBoNo
("Civile, si ergo.") WhC
See, Winter comes, to rule the vary'd [*or* varied] year. Approach of Winter [*or* Winter]. James Thomson. *Fr.* The Seasons. NoEC; OAEP; OBEC; TEP
See with what constant motion. Gratiana Dancing [*or* Dauncing] and Singing. Richard Lovelace. AnAnS-2; CaPo; CavP; JCP; LoBV; MeLP; MePo; OAEP; OBS; SeCV-1
See with what simplicity. The Picture of Little T. C. in a Prospect of Flowers. Andrew Marvell. AnAnS-1; HBV-1; JCP; LiTB; MeLP; MePo; NOBE; NoP; OAEL-1; OBEV; OBS; PPP; PrIm; SeCeV; SeCP; SeCV-1
See yonder goes old Mendax, telling lies. Mendax. *Unknown, tr. by* Gotthold Lessing. PV
See yonder hallow'd [*or* hallowed] fane! the pious work. Church and Church-Yard at Night. Robert Blair. *Fr.* The Grave. OBEC; ViBoPo
See! yonder hill the bitterns seek. Kisses. *Malay Oral Tradition, tr. by* R. J. Wilkinson *and* R. O. Winstedt. WTO
See, yonder, the belfry tower. At Midnight. Frank Dempster Sherman. AA
See yonder, where a gem of night. Es fällt ein Stern herunter. Heine, *tr. by* Richard Garnett. AWP
See you that beauteous queen, which no age tames? To Etesia Looking from Her Casement at the Full Moon. Henry Vaughan. MOON
See you the ferny ride that steals. Puck's Song. Kipling. *Fr.* Puck of Pook's Hill. FaBoCh; FaBV; OxBChV; PoPle
See young John Sutton with his Kathaleen. Speaks the Whispering Grass. Jesse Stuart. FYAP
Seed. Herman Charles Bosman. PeSA
Seed, The. Aileen Fisher. OnUR
Seed-Eaters, The. Robert Francis. NePoAm-2
Seed Growing Secretly, The. Henry Vaughan. AnAnS-1; OxBoCh; SeCV-1
Seed is dug under, A. Shekhinah. Karl Wolfskehl, *tr. by* Carol North Valhope *and* Ernst Morwitz. TrJP
Seed Journey. Gregory Corso. VGW
Seed Leaves. Richard Wilbur. BoNaP; NCSH
Seed, Lord, falls on stony ground, The. Process. Charles L. O'Donnell. TrPWD
Seed-Merchant's Son, The. Agnes Grozier Herbertson. SUMH
Seed of Nimrod, The. De Leon Harrison. PoBA
Seed of Reality, The. Max von Hartmann. AMV-80
Seed Shop, The. Muriel Stuart. BoNaP; GoTS
Seeds. Walter de la Mare. TiPo
Seeds. John Oxenham. WGRP
Seeds. Thurmond Snyder. NNP
Seeds. Augusta Webster. OBVV
Seeds clutched in my hand. Hunting. Yehoash, *tr. by* Isidore Goldstick. TrJP
Seeds I sowed, The. Seeds. Walter de la Mare. TiPo
Seeds in a dry pod, tick, tick, tick. Petit, the Poet. Edgar Lee Masters. *Fr.*

Spoon River Anthology. CMoP; InPK; MoAmPo; MoVE; NoAM; NOBA; OxBA; PPON; TAP
Seeds of Lead. Amir Gilboa, *tr. fr. Hebrew by* Stephen Mitchell. VWA
Seeds of Love, The. *Unknown, at. to* Mrs. Fleetwood Habergham. FaBoCh; GBP, *longer version;* OBET; OxBoLi, *sl. diff.;* WiR
(I Sowed the Seeds of Love.) ELP
Seeds with wings, between earth and sky. Seeds. Augusta Webster. OBVV
Seedy Henry rose up shy in de world. John Berryman. Dream Songs, LXXVII. NaP; TwCP
Seein' Things. Eugene Field. HBV-1; HBVY; TreF
Seeing. John Lyle Donaghy. NeIP
Seeing and Doing. John Dean. AMV-81
Seeing Auden Off. Philip Booth. PoA
Seeing good places/ for my hands. The Time We Climbed Snake Mountain. Leslie Silko. VoR
Seeing Her Dancing. Robert Heath. OBS
Seeing in flight along the lifting wind. Message. Dorothy M. Richardson. PoA
Seeing in the Dark. Matthew Brennan. AMV-81
"Seeing is believing." On Sir Henry Ferrett, M.P. J. B. Morton. PV
Seeing its corners, it is square. Benediction for the Felt. *Mongol Oral Tradition, tr. by* C. R. Bawden. WTO
Seeing Nellie Home (Aunt Dinah's Quilting Party). Francis Kyle. *See* When I Saw Sweet Nelly Home.
Seeing Oloalok. Marilyn Bowering. NOBC
Seeing the Plum Blossoms by the River. Lady Ise, *tr. fr. Japanese by* Etsuko Terasaki *and* Irma Brandeis. BoWoP
Seeing the Returning Geese. Lady Ise, *tr. fr. Japanese by* Etsuko Terasaki *and* Irma Brandeis. BoWoP
Seeing the Scenery. Leslie Scalapino. *Fr.* Hmmmm. NPGG
Seeing the snowman standing all alone. Boy at the Window. Richard Wilbur. NoP
Seeing them over and over each. Pickers. Peter Brett. AMV-81
Seeing thou art faire, I barre not thy false playing. Advice to a Fair Wanton. Ovid, *tr. by* Christopher Marlowe. Amores, III, 13. OBVE; UnTE
Seeing you/ in the laundromat. Thinking Twice in the Laundromat. Harley Elliott. NeAC
Seek a convenient time to take heed to thyself. Of Love of Silence and of Solitude. Thomas à Kempis. *Fr.* Imitation of Christ. TreF
Seek Flowers of Heaven. Robert Southwell. TrCP
Seek not, for thou shalt not find it, what my end, what thine shall be. To Leuconöe. Horace, *tr. by* Charles Stuart Calverley. *Fr.* Odes, I, 11. LoBV
Seek not, Leuconöe, to know how long you're going to live yet. Horace, *tr. by* Eugene Field. *Fr.* Odes, I, 11. AA
Seek not man to please, for that. Isabella Whitney. *Fr.* A Sweet Nosegay, or Pleasant Posy. WPE
Seek not the tree of silkiest bark. Song. Aubrey Thomas De Vere. OBVV
Seek not to know Love's full extent. The Ghost. W. H. Davies. BrPo
"Seek not to know" (the ghost replied with tears). Marcellus. Virgil, *tr. by* Dryden. *Fr.* The Aeneid, VI. OBS
Seek the Lord. Thomas Campion. OxBoCh; TrCP
Seek True Religion! John Donne. Satire, III. NOBE
("Seek true religion. O where? Mirreus.") OBSV
(Truth.) SeCePo
Seek ye the Lord while he may be found. For Ye Shall Go Out with Joy. Bible, *O.T. Fr.* Isaiah. TreFT
Seeke not to know my love, for shee. Song: To One That Desired To Know My Mistris. Thomas Carew. AnAnS-2; SeCP
Seeker, The. Lascelles Abercrombie. *Fr.* The Fools Adventure. WGRP
Seeker in the Marshes, The. Daniel Lewis Dawson. AA
Seeker in the Night, A. Florence Earle Coates. TrPWD
Seekers, The. John Masefield. HBV-2; WGRP
Seekers, The. Charles Hamilton Sorley. WGRP
Seekers, The. Victor Starbuck. WGRP
Seekers of Lice, The. Arthur Rimbaud. *See* Chercheuses de Poux, Les.
Seeking a Mooring. Wang Wei, *tr. fr. Chinese by* Kenneth Rexroth *and* Ling Chung. BoWoP; WPOW
Seeking, earnestly seeking in the gloom. The Creation of Man. *Maori Oral Tradition, tr. by* John White. WTO
Seeking God. Edward Dowden. WGRP
Seeking in squalor lean, elusive youth. Nightwood. William Jay Smith. PoA
Seeking the words. Poem for Jan. Joseph Bruchac. CDW
Seele im Raum. Randall Jarrell. CoBMV; LCAP
Seemingly as other men, yet always. Momist. Amy Groesbeck. GoYe
Seems lak to me de stars don't shine so bright. Sence You Went Away. James Weldon Johnson. BALP; BANP
Seems like a long time. The Partial Explanation. Charles Simic. FiCP; NoP
Seems Like We Must Be Somewhere Else. Denise Levertov. NePoEA-2
Seems not our breathing light? Renunciants. Edward Dowden. OBVV
Seen from the Quantocks. Samuel Taylor Coleridge. *Fr.* This Lime Tree Bower My Prison. FaBoPP
Seen from these cliffs the sea circles slowly. Zennor. Anne Ridler. MoVE
Seen in a Glass. Kathleen Raine. ChMP
Seen my lady home las' night. A Negro Love Song. Paul Laurence Dunbar. BANP; PoNe
Seen on the sea, no sign; no sign, no sign. The Dead Wingman. Randall Jarrell. MiAP
Seepage of time rots judgment, makes it slip. Darkened Windows. Ronald Bottrall. PoA
Seer foretold that I would love one day, A. Sonnet. Louise Labé, *tr. by* Joan Keefe *and* Richard Terdiman. PBWP
Seers have no monopoly. Communal. Mary Fullerton. PoAu-1
Sees not my love how time resumes. To a Lady in a Garden. Edmund Waller. NCEP
Seesaw, The. Oscar Williams. LiTA
See-saw, down in my lap. *Unknown.* OxNR
See-saw, Margery Daw,/ Jack[y] shall have a new master. Mother Goose. OxNR; SoPo
See-saw, Margery Daw,/ Sold her bed and lay upon straw. *Unknown.* OxNR
See-saw, Margery Daw,/ The old hen flew over the malt house. Mother Goose. OxNR
See-saw, sacradown. Mother Goose. OxNR
See'st thou not in clearest dayes. Philarete Praises Poetry. George Wither. *Fr.* The Shepherd's Hunting. OBS
"See'st thou o'er my shoulders falling." Love Song. Judah Halevi, *tr. by* Emma Lazarus. TrJP
Seething over inwardly. His Confession. "The Archpoet," *tr. by* Helen Waddell. NAWM-1
Seferis. Lawrence Durrell. EBEV
Segments of an orange, each step in a long process. Meeting at the Local. Tom Parson. SOTS
Segovia and Madrid. Rose Terry Cooke. AA
Sehnsucht. Anna Wickham. MoBrPo
Sehnsucht; or, What You Will. "Corinna." FiBHP; InMe
Seicheprey. *Unknown.* PAH
Seil o'yer face! the send has come. The Fleggit Bride. "Hugh MacDiarmid." OxBS
Seismograph. Ephraim Auerbach, *tr. fr. Yiddish by* Howard Schwartz. VWA
16 heures/L'Etoile. Two X. E.E. Cummings. FaBoMo
Seize, O seize the sounding lyre. The Hero of Bridgewater. Charles L. S. Jones. PAH
Seized with a sudden fancy for fresh meat. *Unknown, tr. by* Shelley. *Fr.* Homer's Hymn to Mercury. OBVE
Seizure. Sappho, *tr. fr. Greek by* Willis Barnstone. LLLT
Seizure. James E. Warren, Jr. AMV-81
Sejanus ("How many men are killed by power, by power"). Juvenal, *tr. fr. Latin by* Robert Lowell. *Fr.* Satires, X. OBVE
Sejanus ("Some ask for envy'd pow'r; which publick hate"). Juvenal, *tr. fr. Latin by* Dryden. *Fr.* Satires, X. OBVE
Sejanus ("What crowds by envied power, the wish of all"). Juvenal, *tr. fr. Latin by* William Gifford. *Fr.* Satires, X. OBVE
Selah. R. S. Thomas. FaBoMo
Seldom a simmer passed but him an' me. In Lythe Strathdon. Charles Murray. PoSH
Seldom "Can't." Rules of Behavior. Christina Rossetti. *Fr.* Sing-Song. HBV-1; HBVY
Seldom is the tent full, but tonight he expects the local radio. Faith Healer Come to Rabun County. David Bottoms. TAT
Seldom named. Gerda, My Husband's Wife. Eve Triem. GP
Selected Epigrams. *Unknown, tr. fr. Byzantine Greek by* Patrick Diehl. PBWP
Selective Service. Carolyn Forché. MAYP
Selestial apoley which Didest inspire. Odd to a Krokis. *Unknown.* NA
Self. Norman Henry Pritchard II. PoBA
Self Accuser, A. John Donne. FaBoEE
Self-Acquaintance. William Cowper. NOCV
Self-Analysis. Anna Wickham. MoBrPo
Self and the Weather, The. Reed Whittemore. NMP
Self-Composed Epitaph on a Doctor by the Name of I. Letsome. *Unknown. See* On Dr. Isaac Letsome.
Self-Congratulatory Ode on Mr. Auden's Election to the Professorship of Poetry at Oxford. Ronald Mason. FaBoPa
Self-Consciousness Makes All Changes Happy; Ode. Jonathan Richardson. NOEC
Self-Criticism in February. Robinson Jeffers. AmPP
Self-Deceaver, The. Thomas Stanley, *after the Spanish of* Juan Perez de Montalvan. OBVE
Self-Defense. Santob de Carrion, *tr. fr. Spanish by* George Ticknor. TrJP
Self-Dependence. Matthew Arnold. HBV-2; OAEP; TreFS; VLP; WGRP
Self Dirge. Wendy Rose. CDW

Self-Discipline. "Æ." MoBrPo
Selfe Banished, The. Edmund Waller. CavP; FaBoEn; MePo; OBS
Self-Employed. David Ignatow. NNaP
Self-Examination. *Unknown.* FaBoUs
Self-Hatred of Don L. Lee, The. Don L. Lee. BPo
Self, I want you now to be. The Thing is Violent. Gwendolyn MacEwen. MoCV; NOBC; PeCV
Self-Knowledge. Samuel Taylor Coleridge. SeCePo
Selfless now in this crucible of light. St. Augustine Contemplating the Bust of Einstein. Diane Ackerman. SUW
Self-love (which never rightly understood). Tyrannic [*or* Tyrannick] Love: Prologue. Dryden. OAEP; ViBoPo
Self-luminous as her radium granules. Marie Curie Contemplating the Role of Women Scientists in the Glow of a Beaker. Robert Frazier. SUW
Self-Pity. D. H. Lawrence. BoAnP; OxBTC
Self-Pity Is a Kind of Lying, Too. James Schuyler. PoM
Self-Portrait. Cedil Bodker, *tr. fr. Danish by* Nadia Christensen. BoWoP
Self-Portrait. Nina Cassian, *tr. fr. Rumanian by* Herbert Kuhner. VWA
Self-Portrait. Edgar Jackson. LFAC
Self-Portrait. Moses Mendelssohn, *tr. fr. German.* TrJP
Self-Portrait. Robert Pack. CoPo
Self-Portrait. R. S. Thomas. NAs
Self-Portrait. Judith Mountain Leaf Volborth. TWSS
Self-Portrait, I. William Carlos Williams. *Fr.* Pictures from Brueghel. LCAP
Self-Portrait, as a Bear. Donald Hall. SO
Self Portrait 4. Tove Ditlevsen, *tr. fr. Danish by* Ann Freeman. WPOW
Self-Portrait in 2035. Charles Wright. LCAP
Self-Portrait of the Laureate of Nonsense. Edward Lear. *See* How Pleasant to Know Mr. Lear.
Self-Portrait with Hand Microscope. Lucille Day. SUW
Self-praise is a wonderful thing! The Unawkward Singers. David Ferry. NePoAm-2
Self-Projection. A. R. Ammons. FAZ
Self-Protection. D. H. Lawrence. NoP
Self's the Man. Philip Larkin. NOBL
Selfsame Song, The. Thomas Hardy. CMoP; PBBP
Selfsame toothless voice for death or bridal, The. Bell Speech. Richard Wilbur. AP; CABA; MoAB; MoAmPo; MoVE
Self-Slaved, The. Patrick Kavanagh. MoBrPo
Self Unsatisfied Runs Everywhere, The. Delmore Schwartz. PoA
Self-Unseeing, The. Thomas Hardy. EBEV; FaBoEn; HAP; MoBrPo; NOBE; OBNC; PrIm; VLP; WeW
Selichos. Francis Landy. VWA
Sell in May. Stock Exchange Wisdom. *Unknown.* FaBoUs
Selling Ruined Peonies. Yü Hsüan-chi, *tr. fr. Chinese by* Geoffrey Waters. BoWoP
Semantic. Robert Conquest. TEP
Semblables, The. William Carlos Williams. AP; FaBoMo; NOBA
Semen. Coleman Barks. PV
Semen. Martha Paley Francescato, *tr. fr. Spanish by* Willis Barnstone. BoWoP
Semichorus II: "There the voluptuous nightingales." Shelley. *Fr.* Prometheus Unbound, II, ii. PBBP
("There the voluptuous nightingales.") ViBoPo
Seminary. Constance Carrier. NePoAm
Semi-Private Room. Alden Nowlan. NeAC
Semi-Revolution, A. Robert Frost. LiTM
Semmes in the Garden. George Marion O'Donnell. NYBP
Semphill, his hat stuck full of hooks. Trout Fisher. George Mackay Brown. OxBC
Sempronius,/ Sends greeting, warden of this Roman shore. A Roman Officer Writes. C. M. Doughty. *Fr.* The Dawn in Britain. FaBoTw
Sempstress's linnet sings, The. The Blind Linnet. Robert Buchanan. FM
Senator, A. *Unknown.* TDH
Senator said, The. Portrait of a Senator. Charles Norman. DBV
Senator Smoot (Republican, Ut.). Invocation. Ogden Nash. OBAL
Sence You Went Away. James Weldon Johnson. BALP; BANP
Send but a song oversea for us. To Walt Whitman in America. Swinburne. VLP
Send cards send. Notes on a Long Evening. David Phillips. NeAC
Send down thy truth, O God! For the Gifts of the Spirit. Edward Rowland Sill. TrPWD
Send for Lord Timothy. John Heath-Stubbs. OxBC
Send Forth, O God, Thy Light and Truth, *with music.* John Quincy Adams. AH
Send home my long-strayed [*or* strayd] eyes to me[e]. The Message. John Donne. ElL; HBV-1; MeLP; OBS; ViBoPo; WHA
Send Me. Christina Rossetti. TRV
Send me no flowers, for they will die before they leave America. Junglegrave. S. E. Anderson. PoBA
Send No Money. Philip Larkin. TW
Send soldiers again to kill you, Garcia. Lines to Garcia Lorca. Amiri Baraka. NNP
Sending to the War. William Morris. *Fr.* The Pilgrims of Hope. VLP
Send-off, The. Wilfred Owen. BrPo; InPS; LiTB; MoAB; MoBrPo; MoVE; OBWP; OxBTC
Senec. Traged. ex Thyeste Chor. 2. Seneca, *tr. by* Andrew Marvell. *Fr.* Thyestes, II. SeCV-1
("Climb at court for me that will.") OBVE
Seneca. Thomas Merton. CoPo
Senex. John Betjeman. DTC
Senex to Matt. Prior. James Kenneth Stephen. *Fr.* Two Epigrams. CenHV; FiBHP; WhC
Senile. Pat Folk. PCP
Senior Members. Sean Lucy. CIP
Senlin, a Biography, *sels.* Conrad Aiken.
Evening Song of Senlin, II, ix. HBMV
Morning Song of Senlin, II, ii. HBMV; LiTA; MoAmPo; OxBA
("It is morning, Senlin says, and in the morning.") LiTM; NoAM
(Morning Song.) CMoP; MoAB; TrGrPo
Sennacherib. Byron. *See* Destruction of Sennacherib.
Señora, it is true the Greeks are dead. Invocation to the Social Muse. Archibald MacLeish. LiTM
Sensation. Arthur Rimbaud, *tr. fr. French.* AWP, *tr. by* Jethro Bithell; SOTW, *tr. by* Kenneth Koch; SyP, *tr. by* John Gray; SyP, *tr. by* T. Sturge Moore
Sensational Relatives. Alexis Krasilovsky. AMV-80
Sensationalism. Larry Levis. MAYP
Sense and Spirit. George Meredith. WGRP
Sense of Coolness, A. Quincy Troupe. PoBA
Sense of Death, The. Helen Hoyt. HBMV
Sense of Humour, A. Vachel Lindsay. Poems about the Moon, III. TwAmPo
Sense of Smell, The. Louis MacNeice. NYBP
Sense of the Sleight-of-Hand Man, The. Wallace Stevens. AP; CABA; CoBMV; HAP; LiTM; MoAB; MoAmPo; MoPo; MP; NOBA; PoA; TwCP; WeW
Sense of the world is short, The. Eros. Emerson. FaBoBe; HBV-1
Sense with keenest edge unused. Pater Filio. Robert Bridges. CMoP; OBEV; OBVV; ViBoPo
Senseless school, where we must give, A. A Young Man's Epigram on Existence. Thomas Hardy. BrPo; NoAM
Senses' Festival, The. John Cleveland. *See* To the State of Love.
Senses loving Earth or well or ill, The. Sense and Spirit. George Meredith. WGRP
Sensibility. Louis Simpson. GP
Sensible Girl's Reply to Moore's, A. Walter Savage Landor. FaBoEE
Sensible Is the Label. Eldon Grier. MoCV
Sensitive Cat, The. Alice Brown. TDH
Sensitive Knife, The. Gerald Stern. DiL
Sensitive Man, A. Morris Bishop. TDH
Sensitive Plant, The. Shelley. EnRP; GoTL
Sels.
"In this life/ Of error, ignorance, and strife." LO
"Whether the sensitive plant, or that." OAEL-2
Sensitive, Seldom and Sad. Mervyn Peake. RHPC
Sensitive Sydney. Wallace Irwin. FiBHP
Sensitiveness. Cardinal Newman. TrCP
"Sensual will have its moment, The? The brain." Elder Tree. Conrad Aiken. AP
Sensualists, The. Theodore Roethke. ErPo; NePoAm-2
(Sensualist, The.) UnTE
Sensuality. Coventry Patmore. OBVV
Sensuous/ sloe eyed. Seduction. Jo Ann Hall-Evans. BlSi
Sensuous Latin poet, now I will go off with a thermos, A. Lynn Strongin. *Fr.* First Aspen. IHMS
Sent Ahead. John Hay. NePoAm
Sent as a present from Annam. The Red Cuckatoo. Po Chü-i, *tr. by* Arthur Waley. ChTr
Sent from Egypt with a Fair Robe of Tissue to a Sicilian Vinedresser. T. Sturge Moore. OBEV; OBVV
Sent from the Capital to Her Elder Daughter. Lady Otomo no Sakanoe, *tr. fr. Japanese by* Geoffrey Bownas *and* Anthony Thwaite. BoWoP; WPOW
Sent to a Lady, with a Seal. Robert Lloyd. FaBoUs
Sent to a Patient, with the Present of a Couple of Ducks. Edward Jenner. FaBoUs
Sent to Miss Bell H——, with a Pair of Buckles. John Cunningham. FaBoUs
Sent to Wen T'ing-yün on a Winter Night. Yü Hsüan-chi, *tr. fr. Chinese by* Geoffrey Waters. BoWoP
Sent with a Rose to a Young Lady. Margaret Deland. AA
Sentence. Witter Bynner. HBV-2

Sentence undulates, The. The End of the Parade. William Carlos Williams. NYBP
Sentences we studied are rungs upon the ladder Jacob saw, The. Luzzato. Charles Reznikoff. VWA
Sentencing goes blithely on its way, The. In a Poem. Robert Frost. PP
Sentience. Sandra McPherson. PoA
Sentiment. Thomas Chatterton. NOEC
Sentimental Bloke, The, *sel.* C. J. Dennis.
Play, The. PoAu-1
Sentimental Conversation [*or* Colloquy]. Paul Verlaine. *See* Colloque sentimental.
Sentimental Journey. "Elspeth." WhC
Sentimental Lines to a Young Man Who Favors Pink Wallpaper While I Personally Lean to the Blue. Margaret Fishback. FiBHP
Sentimentalist, The. Edward Field. PPJ
Sentimentalist sends his mauve balloon, The. The Celebration in the Plaza. Adrienne Rich. NePoEA; TwAmPo
Sentiments, The. *Unknown.* APAS
Sentiments are nice, "The Lonely Crowd." John Button Birthday. Frank O'Hara. NAs
Sentinel, The. *Unknown.* BLRP
Sentinel angel, sitting high in glory, A. A Woman's Love. John Hay. HBV-1
Sentinel Songs. Abram J. Ryan. HBV-2
Sentinel's Song, A. Rarawa Kerehoma, *tr. fr. Maori by* Barry Mitcalfe. WTO
Sentry, The. Alun Lewis. DTC
Sentry, The. Wilfred Owen. MMA
Senzangakhona. *Zulu Oral Tradition, tr. by* T. Cope. WTO
Separate Parties. Dabney Stuart. NYBP
Separate place between the thought and felt, A. The Corridor. Thom Gunn. NePoEA; PPP
Separated Lovers. *Unknown. See* One I Love Is Gone Away, The.
Separately I still recall. Portrait. Adèle Naudé. PeSA
Separation. Matthew Arnold. HBV-1
Separation. Martha Dickinson Bianchi. AA
Separation. Alice Learned Bunner. *Fr.* Vingtaine. AA
Separation, A. William Johnson Cory. OBNC
Separation. W. S. Merwin. HAP; NoP; PCP
Separation. D. S. Savage. NeBP
Separation. John L. Sweeney. TwAmPo
Separation. P. Wolny. DFF
Separation Deed, A. Sir Lewis Morris. OBVV
Separation on the River Kiang. Li Po, *tr. fr. Chinese by* Ezra Pound. SOTW; UnPo
Separations begin with placement. River Road Studio. Barbara Guest. PoM
Sephestia's Song to Her Child[e]. Robert Greene. *Fr.* Menaphon. ELP; EnRePo; LoBV; PoEL-2; TrGrPo
(Sephestia's Lullaby.) HBV-1; NOBE; OBEV
(Sephestia's Song.) OBSC
(Weep Not, My Wanton.) EIL; SeCePo; ViBoPo
Sepia Fashion Show. Maya Angelou. BlSi
Sepoy servant, Nate, the natural son, A. 1864. Richard Howard. CABA
September. George Arnold. HBV-1
September. Edwina Fallis. SUS; TiPo; YeAr
September. Marilyn Hacker. NYP
September. Ted Hughes. BoLoP; OLR
September. Aldous Huxley. EBEV
September. Helen Hunt Jackson. FaPON; FPL; GoJo; OBCA; PoLF; TiPo
(September Days Are Here.) YeAR
September. Archibald Lampman. PeCV
September. Robert Lowell, *ad. fr. the Russian of* Boris Pasternak. NaP
September. Linda Pastan. Psk
September. Edward Bliss Reed. HBMV; HBVY
(September Is Here.) YeAr
September Afternoon. Margaret Haley Carpenter. GoYe
September Butterfly. Mollie Boring. AMV-80
September Days Are Here. Helen Hunt Jackson. *See* September.
September, 1815. Wordsworth.
(Sonnet: September, 1815.) ChER
September, 1802; near Dover. Wordsworth. *See* Near Dover, September 1802.
September Evening, 1938. William Plomer. SeCePo
September evenings such as these. Watching the Moon. David McCord. YeAr
September 1, 1965. Paris Leary. CoPo
September 1, 1939. W. H. Auden. CMoP; CoBMV; LiTA; MasP; MoAB; MoBrPo; MoVE; NePA; OAEP; OxBA; PrIm; SeCeV; WaP
(1st September, 1939.) FaBoEn
September Gale, The, *sel.* Oliver Wendell Holmes.
"It chanced to be our washing day." FiBHP
September in Australia. Henry Clarence Kendall. OBVV; PoAu-1
September Is Here. Edward Bliss Reed. *See* September.
September Midnight. Sara Teasdale. PoA
Sept. 1957. Edward Marshall. CoPo
September 1957 summoned by my vision-agent. Vision of Rotterdam. Gregory Corso. NoAM
September 1913. W. B. Yeats. BrPo; CMoP; CoBMV; GTBS-P; HAP; NoAM; PoRA; PPoe
September rain falls on the house. Sestina. Elizabeth Bishop. LCAP; NoP; WeW
September 2. Wendell Berry. PoA
September 7. Ellen Bass. NMM
September six o'clock. Sea Pieces. Robert Fitzgerald. PoPl
September Song. Geoffrey Hill. NoP; OBWP
September, the First Day of School. Howard Nemerov. GLGT; OxBC
September. The gypsy and the nightingale. Autumn. Itzik Manger, *tr. by* Ruth Whitman. VWA
September 30. Dick Lourie. NeAC
September twenty-second, Sir: today. After the Surprising Conversions. Robert Lowell. AmPP; AP; CABA; ConAP; CoBMV; HAP; NePoEA; NoAM; NoP; PAI; PPP; SeCeV
September was when it began. The Coming of the Plague. Weldon Kees. NaP; VGW
Sepulcher, The. Annie Johnson Flint. STF
Sepulchre. George Herbert. AnAnS-1
Sepulchres, how thick they stand, The. Meditations on the Sepulchre in the Garden. Philip Doddridge. NOCV; NOEC
Sequaire. Godeschalk, *tr. fr. Latin by* Ezra Pound. CTC
Sequel, The. Theodore Roethke. NYBP
Sequel, The. Delmore Schwartz. LiTM
Sequel to Finality. Patrick F. Kirby. GoBC
Sequel to the Purple Cow. Gelett Burgess. *See* Ah, Yes, I Wrote "The Purple Cow."
Sequelula to "The Dynasts," A. Max Beerbohm. Par
Sequence. George Barker. PoA
Sequence. Edgar Daniel Kramer. BLRP
Sequence, A. Leslie Scalapino. NPGG
Sequence for a Young Widow Passing. Deborah Munro. IHMS
Sequence in Four Keys, A, *sel.* James Reaney.
Baby, The. NAs
Sequence of Generations, The. Hayim Be'er, *tr. fr. Hebrew by* Stephen Mitchell. VWA
Seraglio of the Sultan Bee! A Hollyhock. Frank Dempster Sherman. AA
Seraph and the Snob, The. May Kendall. CenHV
Seraph of Heaven. Shelley. *Fr.* Epipsychidion. ISi
Seravazza. Hoyt W. Fuller. PoBA
Serenade, A: "Ah! County Guy, the hour is nigh." Sir Walter Scott. *See* County Guy.
Serenade: "Ah, sweet, thou little knowest how." Thomas Hood. HBV-1
Serenade: "Awake thee, my lady-love." George Darley. *Fr.* Sylvia. HBV-1
Serenade: "Blue waves are sleeping, The." James Joseph Callanan. OnYI
Serenade: "By day my timid passions stand." Richard Middleton. HBV-1
Serenade: "Come now, and let us wake them: time." *Unknown, tr. fr. German by* Jethro Bithell. AWP
Serenade: "Frog will serenade, The." Alan Britt. FAZ
Serenade: "Hide, happy damask, from the stars." Henry Timrod. HBV-1
Serenade, A: "Look out upon the stars, my love." Edward Coote Pinkney. AA; HBV-1
Serenade: "Softly, O midnight Hours!" Aubrey Thomas De Vere. HBV-1; OBEV
Serenade: "Stars of the summer night!" Longfellow. *Fr.* The Spanish Student, I, iii. AA; FaBoBe; HBV-1; LoBV; ViBoPo
Serenade: "Thou moon, like a white Christus hanging." Kenneth Slessor. POL
Serenade: "Tin-type tune the locusts make, The." Dorothy Donnelly. NCSH
Serenade: "Western wind is blowing fair, The." Oscar Wilde. HBV-1
Serenade: "While my lady sleepeth." John Gibson Lockhart. OBRV
Serenade for Strings. Dorothy Livesay. NAs
Serenade for Two Poplars, A. Esther Raab, *tr. fr. Hebrew by* Robert Friend *and* Shimon Sandbank. VWA
Serenade of a Loyal Martyr. George Darley. *See* Song: "Sweet in her green cell the flower of beauty slumbers."
Serenade of Angels. Rina Lasnier, *tr. fr. French by* Jan Pallister. AMV-81
Serendipity of Love, A. Richard Aldridge. NePoAm-2
Serene descent, as a red leaf's descending. Epitaph. Sara Teasdale. PoA
Serene, I fold my hands [*or* arms] and wait. Waiting. John Burroughs. AA; BLPA; FaBoBe; HBV-2; OHFP; TreF; TRV; WGRP
Serene immediate silliest and whose. E. E. Cummings. MoVE

Serene, indifferent of Fate. San Francisco from the Sea. Bret Harte. BPAW
Serene, not as a prize for conflict won. On a Portrait of Mme. Rimsky-Korsakov. Kingsley Amis. NePoEA-2
Serene the silver fishes glide. At the Aquarium. Max Eastman. FaPON; HBMV; WGRP
Serene, vast head, with silver cloud of hair. A Tribute of Grasses. Hamlin Garland. AA
Serengeti Sunset. Andrew Oerke. POL
Serenity in Stones, The. Simon J. Ortiz. CDW
Serenity of Faith, The. Bible, *O.T.* Psalm XXVII: 7-14. BLRP
Serf, The. Roy Campbell. GTBS-P; LiTB; MoBrPo; OBMV
Serf's Secret, The. William Vaughn Moody. HBV-1
Sergeant, The. Don Johnson. MAYP
Sergeant Champe. *Unknown.* PAH
Sergeant, He Is the Worst of All, The, *with music. Unknown.* AS
Sgt. stands so fluently in leather, The. On a Photo of Sgt. Ciardi a Year Later. John Ciardi. MiAP
Sergeant-Major Money. Robert Graves. MMA; OBWP
Sergeant of the Lawe, war and wys, A. Chaucer. *Fr.* The Canterbury Tales: Prologue. CTC
Sergeant's Prayer, A. Hugh Brodie. PGD
Sergeant's Weddin', The. Kipling. OxBTC
Sergei's a flower. Song. Ruth Herschberger. FF
Serials are all wound up now, The. Where Are You Now Superman? Brian Patten. FF
Series 5.8, A. John Wieners. CoPo
Serio-Comic Elegy, A. Richard Whately. ShM
Serious and a Curious Night-Meditation, A. Thomas Traherne. SeCP
Serious Danger, A. R. A. Davenport. PV
Serious Merriment of Women, The. Patricia Goedicke. TAP
Serious over my cereals I broke one breakfast my fast. Breakfast with Gerard Manley Hopkins. Anthony Brode. BXAP; FaBoPa; FiBHP; NOBL; Par
Serious Poem, A. Ernest Walsh. ErPo
Serious Readers. Peter Redgrove. OxBC
Sermon, The. Richard Hughes. OBMV
Sermon, A. Margaret Sackville. HBMV
Sermon in a Churchyard. Macaulay. OBRV
Sermon in a Stocking. Ellen A. Jewett. BLPA
Sermon on Swift, A. Austin Clarke. BIrV; IPY
Sermon on the Mount, The. Bible, *N.T.* Matthew, V: 1-VII: 29. TreF
Sels.
"And seeing the multitudes, he went up." BiP (V); NAWM-1 (V-VII); PoPl (V: 1-10)
Beatitudes, The, V: 3-10. TrGrPo
("Blessed are the poor in spirit.") OBVE (V: 3-10)
God Provides, VI: 26-34. BLRP
Lord's Prayer, The, VI: 9-13. EaLo; PoLF; TrGrPo; TRV
"No man can serve two masters," VI: 24-29. OBVE
Treasures, VI: 19-21. TrGrPo
Sermon on the Warpland, The. Gwendolyn Brooks. BPo; LiTM; NOBA; PoBA
Sermon to the Birds. St. Francis of Assisi, *tr. fr. Italian by* Thomas W. Arnold. TreF
Sermonette. Ishmael Reed. NIP; PoBA
Serpent, The. Joseph Langland. MP
Serpent, The. Theodore Roethke. AmMo; RHPC
Serpent is shut out from paradise, The. Stanzas to Edward Williams. Shelley. OBNC
Serpent Knowledge. Robert Pinsky. *Fr.* An Explanation of America. NPGG
Serpent Muses, The. Peggy Henderson. NMM
Serpent of God, The. Cerise Farallon. UnTE
Serpent with a voyce, so slie and fine, The. Samuel Gorton. SCAP
Serpentine Verse. Joseph S. Newman. TDH
Serpents exploded, open balconies. Morvin. John Fuller. NePoEA-2
Serried hosts stood man to man, The. The Oranges. Abu Dharr, *tr. by* A. J. Arberry. TTY
"Serva tibi minas!" The Judge with the Sore Rump. St. George Tucker. OBAL
Servant Girl and Grocer's Boy. Joyce Kilmer. YaD
Servant-Girl's Holiday, A. *Unknown.* OxBM
Servant Man, The. *Unknown.* AmFP
Servant of the eternal Must. Pagan Epitaph. Richard Middleton. OBVV
Servant to Servants, A. Robert Frost. CMoP
Servants, The. Richard Wightman. WGRP
Servants then (commanded) soone obaid, The. Nausicaa. Homer, *tr. by* George Chapman. *Fr.* The Odyssey, VI. OBS
Serve Her Right. John Barford. PeHV
Serve in Thy Post. Arthur Hugh Clough. PGD
Service. Robert Browning. *See* All Service Ranks the Same with God.
Service. Washington Gladden. *See* O Master, Let Me Walk with Thee.
Service, The. Burges Johnson. HBMV
Service. Georgia Douglas Johnson. CDC
Service for townsman, old sailor. Orchids. Judith Minty. GeTw
Service is joy, to see or swing. Allow. Tennis. Margaret Avison. NoAM; PeCV
Service Is No Heritage. *Unknown.* OxBM
Service Man, The. Kipling. Par
Service, or Latin *sorbus*, European. The Life of Service. Donald Davie. NYBP
Service Supreme. *Unknown.* STF
Serving Girl, The. Gladys May Casely Hayford. CDC
Serving man, A. Curled my hair. Thom Gunn. *Fr.* Misanthropos. OxBC
Serving Men's Song, A. John Lyly. *Fr.* Alexander and Campaspe, I, iii. *Also in* A Mad World, My Masters (*by* Thomas Middleton). NOBE; OBSC
(Oh, For a Bowl of Fat Canary.) NoP; ViBoPo
Sesostris. Lloyd Mifflin. AA; HBV-2
Sessile, unseeing. Progress? W. H. Auden. SUW
Session[s] of the Poets, A ("A session was held the other day"). Sir John Suckling. AnAnS-2; NCEP; SeCV-1
(Wits, The.) CaPo
Sestina: Altaforte. Ezra Pound. CABA; CoBMV; FaBoTw; LiTA; MoAB; MoAmPo; NOBA; SoSe; SOTW
Sestina: "Hang it all, Ezra Pound, there is only the one sestina!" Donald Hall. NePoEA
Sestina: "I saw my soul at rest upon a day." Swinburne. VLP
Sestina: "I woke by first light in a wood." Donald Justice. NePoEA
Sestina: "Is this the object." Judith Kroll. AmPA
Sestina: "September rain falls on the house." Elizabeth Bishop. LCAP; NoP; WeW
Sestina d'Inverno. Anthony Hecht. NoP
Sestina for Cynthia, A. David Lougée. NePA
Sestina from the Home Gardener. Diane Wakoski. CABA; NoAM
Sestina in a Cantina. Malcolm Lowry. MoCV
Sestina in Time of Winter. Patrick Anderson. PoA
Sestina; of the Lady Pietra degli Scrovigni. Dante, *tr. fr. Italian by* Dante Gabriel Rossetti. AWP; OAEL-2; OBVE
Sestina of the Tramp-Royal. Kipling. BrPo; FPL; LiTB; MoBrPo; PrIm
Sestina on Her Portrait. Howard Nemerov. WaP
Sestina with Refrain. Thomas W. Shapcott. CBAP
"Set back your watches—this is Mountain Time." Continental Crossing. Dorothy Brown Thompson. AmFN
Set Down, Servant. *Unknown.* FSW
Set every stitch of canvas to woo the fresh'ning wind. The Slave Chase. *Unknown.* CoMu
"Set he that hat on his head?" Cardinal Fisher. John Heywood. ACP
Set in this stormy northern sea. Ave Imperatrix! Oscar Wilde. HBV-2
Set Love in order, thou that lovest Me. Cantica: Our Lord Christ: Of Order [*or* Of Order in Our Lord Christ]. St. Francis of Assisi, *tr. by* Dante Gabriel Rossetti. AWP; GoBC; OBVE
Set me as a seal upon thy heart. As a Seal upon Thy Heart. Bible, *O.T.* *Fr.* The Song of Solomon. BoWoP, *ad. by* Willis Barnstone; TrJP
Set me to sound for you. Ark Anatomical. Jay Macpherson. *Fr.* The Ark. NOBC
Set me where Phoebus' heat the flowers slayeth. The Last Trial. Petrarch, *tr. fr. Italian.* OBSC
Set me whereas the sun doth parch the green [*or* sunne dothe perche the grene]. A Vow to Love Faithfully, [Howsoever He Be Rewarded] [*or* Love's Fidelity *or* To His Lady]. Petrarch, *tr. by* the Earl of Surrey. Sonnets to Laura: To Laura in Life, CXIII. AAS; AWP; ElL; HAP; OBSC; SiPS; TEP; TrGrPo; ViBoPo
Set not your heart to woo that basilisk. To a Lad Who Would Wed Himself with Music. Edward Doro. TwAmPo
Set of phrases learnt by rote, A. The Furniture of a Woman's Mind. Swift. PPoe
Set of Romantic Hymns, A, *sel.* Robert Duncan.
"Fountain of forms! Life springs of unique being!" DiL
Set on this bubble of dead stone and sand. On an Engraving by Casserius. A. D. Hope. CBAP
Set silver cone to tulip flame! Inscription for a Mirror in a Deserted Dwelling. William Rose Benét. MoAmPo
Set the foot down with distrust upon the crust of the world—it is thin. Underground System. Edna St. Vincent Millay. SBG
Set up the drum. December. Maurice Kenny. STE
Set where the upper streams of Simois flow. Palladium. Matthew Arnold. FaBoEn; GTBS-P; OAEL-2; OAEP; OBNC; PPP; VLP
Set your face to the sea, fond lover. Refuge. William Winter. HBV-1
Seth Compton. Edgar Lee Masters. *Fr.* Spoon River Anthology. LiTA
Seth Compton died, and by that alone. Rhoda Pitkin. Edgar Lee Masters. *Fr.* The New Spoon River. NoAM
Setters mark the turf and run. The Hunt. Daniel Halpern. LiSp

Settin' on de Fence. *Unknown.* WBLP
Setting, The/ had no special theme. Slow Riff for Billy. James Cunningham. JB
Setting a trotline after sundown. In the Deep Channel. William Stafford. NaP
Setting of the Moon, The. Giacomo Leopardi, *tr. fr. Italian by* John Heath-Stubbs. MOON
Setting Out. W. D. Snodgrass. DiL
Setting/ Slow Drag. Carolyn M. Rodgers. JB
Setting Sun, The. George Moses Horton. BALP
Setting the Table. Dorothy Aldis. FaPON; TiPo
Settled Men, The. George M. Brady. NeIP
Settler. Stewart Lindh. PoA
Settler, The. Alfred Billings Street. AA; FaBoBe; PAH
Settler in the olden times went forth, A. Charles Harpur. *Fr.* The Creek of the Four Graves. PoAu-1
Settlers, The. Margaret Atwood. MoCV
Settlers, The. Judith Hemschemeyer. SO
Settlers, The. Laurence Housman. HBV-2; OBVV
Settlers abandoned our country long ago. Pauper Woodland. Ronald Everson. NOBC
Settler's Lament, The. *Unknown.* PoAu-1
Settling In. Floyd C. Stuart. TAT
Settling Some Old Football Scores. Morris Bishop. LiSp
Seumas Beg. James Stephens. EvOK; FaPON; GrPl; OxBTC; RoGo
Seurat. Ira Sadoff. PoDr
Seurat looked well to see these people. La Grande Jatte: Sunday Afternoon. Thomas Cole. NePoAm
Seven. Nicanor Parra, *tr. fr. Spanish by* Miller Williams. POL
Seven against Thebes, The, *sel.* Aeschylus, *tr. fr. Greek.*
  Lament for the Two Brothers Slain by Each Other's Hand, *tr. by* A. E. Housman. AWP
Seven Ages of Elf-hood, The. Rachel Field. RHPC
Seven Ages of Man, The. Shakespeare. *See* All the World's a Stage.
Seven around the moon go up. The Pinwheel's Song. John Ciardi. PDV; SO
Seven Black Friars sitting back to back. Blackfriars. Eleanor Farjeon. OxBChV
Seven Blessings of Mary, The. *Unknown. See* Joys of Mary, The.
Seven candles in silver sticks. Planter. Richard Murphy. *Fr.* The Battle of Aughrim. BIrV
Seven Cent Cotton and Forty Cent Meat. *Unknown.* FSW
Seven Days. J. R. Rowland. PAI
Seven Days, The, *sel.* Reed Whittemore.
  On First Knowing God, III. GP
Seven days he travelled. The Crowning of Dreaming John. John Drinkwater. HBMV
Seven Days of the Sun, The, *sels.* W. J. Turner. OBMV
  "Beneath a thundery glaze."
  "Dian, Isis, Artemis, whate'er thy name."
  "I had watched the ascension and decline of the moon."
  "I have seen mannequins."
  "If God kept a terrarium."
  "Spirits walking everywhere."
  "This is the last time."
  "What is the meaning of this ideal."
  "What is this tempest."
Seven dead men, Brigit. The Celtic Lyric. J. C. Squire. BXAP
Seven Deadly Sins, The. Stephen Hawes. *Fr.* The Pastime of Pleasure. PoEL-1
Seven dog-days we let pass. Queens. J. M. Synge. ChTr; GBL; MoBrPo; OBMV; OnYI
Seven Dreams. John Bayliss. EAS
Seven Evils. Bible, *O.T.* Proverbs, VI: 16–19. TrGrPo
Seven Fiddlers, The. Sebastian Evans. EBVV; OnMSP
7:v:60 (an interesting *lapsus calami*). For Kai Snyder. Philip Whalen. PoM
747 (London–Chicago). Robert Conquest. OxBC
Seven Hells of Jigoku Zoshi, The, *sels.* Jerome Rothenberg.
  Fifth Hell, The. NNaP
  Sixth Hell, The. NNaP
Seven Houses, The. George Mackay Brown. NAs
Seven hundred and a half of years. The Old Woman Remembers. Lady Gregory. OnYI
700 years ago. Slim Man Canyon. Leslie Silko. VoR
Seven lang years I hae served the King. The Whummil Bore. *Unknown.* CH; ESPB
Seven-League Boots, The. Ilarie Voronca, *tr. fr. Rumanian by* Willis Barnstone *and* Matei Calinescu. VWA
Seven Long Years in State Prison, *with music. Unknown.* AS
Seven Metal Mountains, The. Bible, Pseudepigrapha. Enoch, LII: 6–9. TrJP
Seven Mexican Children. Tom Schmidt. NeAC
Seven notes of grief. Motif for Mary's Dolors. Sister Mary Madeleva. ISi
Seven of the Clock. Roy Macnab. PeSA
Seven Old Men, The. Baudelaire, *tr. fr. French by* Roy Campbell. OBVE
Seven Pilgrims. Chaucer, *orig. and mod. vers. by* Louis Untermeyer. *Fr.* The Canterbury Tales: Prologue. TrGrPo
Seven Rainy Months. William Plomer. OxBTC
Seven Sad Sonnets. Mary Aldis. HBMV
Seven Seages, The, *sel.* John Rolland.
  "In haist ga hy thee to sum hoill." OxBS
Seven Sharp Propeller Blades. John Ciardi. QQQ
Seven Sins, The. *Unknown.* OxBM
  (Christ Complains to Sinners.) MeEL
Seven Sister Blues. *Unknown.* BluL
Seven Sleepers, The. Sir Herbert Read. SeCePo
Seven Sleepers, The. Mark Van Doren. FYAP
Seven South African Poems, *sels.* David Wright. PeSA
  "My countryman, the poet, wears a Stetson."
  "My grandfather was an elegant gentleman."
Seven Spiritual Ages of Mrs. Marmaduke Moore, The. Ogden Nash. MoAmPo
Seven Stanzas at Easter. John Updike. EaLo; EBCP; TrCP
Seven stars in the still water. The Dole of the King's Daughter. *Unknown, tr. by* Oscar Wilde. AWP
Seven sweet singing birds up in a tree. The Dream of a Girl Who Lived at Sevenoaks. William Brighty Rands. OxBChV
Seven times hath Janus ta'en new year by hand. Upon the Author's First Seven Years' Service. Thomas Tusser. ElL
Seven Times One: Exultation. Jean Ingelow. *Fr.* Songs of Seven. BLPA; FaPON; OBNC; TreF
Seven times seven/ the beads I toll. To the Queen of Dolors. Sister Mary Maura. ISi
Seven times the centuple wheels of life have whirled. The Blessing of St. Francis. Sister Maura. CaP
Seven Times the Moon Came. Jessie B. Rittenhouse. HBMV
Seven Times Three—Love. Jean Ingelow. *Fr.* Songs of Seven. PoLF
Seven Times Two—Romance. Jean Ingelow. *Fr.* Songs of Seven. GN
720 Gabriel St. Randolph Outlaw. LFAC
Seven Virgins, The. *Unknown.* CH; ChTr; GBP; OBET; OBEV; OxBoCh
Seven we were, and two are gone. Two Long Vacations: Grasmere. Arthur Gray Butler. OBVV
Seven Wealthy Towns. *Unknown.* PP
  (Cure for Poetry, A.) FaBoEE
Seven weeks of sea, and twice seven days of storm. Gibraltar. Wilfrid Scawen Blunt. ACP; HBV-2; OBEV; OBVV
Seven white peacocks against the castle wall, The. What the Orderly Dog Saw. Ford Madox Ford. CTC
Seven white roses on one tree. Seven Years Old. Swinburne. HBV-1
Seven Wonders of England, The, *sel.* Sir Philip Sidney.
  Stonehenge. FaBoPP
Seven Wonders of the Ancient World, The. *Unknown.* EyDe; TreFT
Seven Woodland Crows. Gerald Vizenor. VoR
Seven Years. Marquess of Crewe. OBVV
Seven years ago. Now or Never. Astra. BrRo
Seven years ago, almost to the month and day. Ramon. E. A. Lacey. PeHV
Seven Years at Sea, *with music. Unknown.* OuSiCo
Seven years I have kept him, dead. The Corpse-Keeper. *Unknown, tr. by* W. S. Merwin. BoWoP
Seven years I orbit around you. Sabbatical. Linda Zisquit. VWA
Seven years lived in Italy leave me convinced. The Oak and the Olive. George Barker. FaBoMo
Seven Years Old. Swinburne. HBV-1
"Seven years ye shall be a stone." The Maid and the Palmer. *Unknown.* ESPB
Seventeen. Jonathan Holden. Psk
Seventeen,/ hungry and stranded. Old Man Con. Earl Gene Box. LFAC
Seventeen Come Sunday. *Unknown.* OBET
1780 a.d. in the street they flung foam about and a young. Poems (I-XI). Philip O'Connor. EAS
17. IV. 71. Paul Blackburn. PoM
Seventeen, no great event. For Stephen. Christopher Brookhouse. AMV-80
1738. Pope. *See* Epilogue to the Satires.
Seventeen Warnings in Search of a Feminist Poem. Erica Jong. AmPA
Seventeen years ago you said. À Quoi Bon Dire. Charlotte Mew. HBMV; OxBTC
Seventeenth stanza, The. My heart aches, my tears fall. Ts'ai Yen, *tr. by* Kenneth Rexroth *and* Ling Chung. Eighteen Verses Sung to a Tatar Reed Whistle, XVII. WPOW
Seventh Day. Kathleen Raine. ChMP

Seventh Day of the First Week, The, *sel.* Joshua Sylvester. *Fr.* Du Bartas: His Divine Weeks and Works.
"There on his knee, behind a box tree shrinking." PBBP
Seventh dragon turned to his wife, The. Where Two o'Clock Came From. Kenneth Patchen. SO
Seventh Eclogue. Miklós Radnóti, *tr. fr. Hungarian by* Emery George. VWA
Seventh Georgic. George Economou. POL
Seventh Hell, The. Jerome Rothenberg. CoPo; NMP
Seventh Nimphall, The. Michael Drayton. *Fr.* The Muses Elizium. AnAnS-2
Seventh Property, The. Sir Thomas More. *Fr.* The Twelve Properties or Conditions of a Lover. EnRePo
Seventh Son. Ed Roberson. PoBA
Seventies, The. Tony Beyer. OCNZ
78 Miners in Mannington, West Virginia. Louis Philips. TAT
Seventy-five feet hoed rows equals. Gary Snyder. *Fr.* Mountains and Rivers without End: The Market. NaP
Seventy-four and Twenty. Thomas Hardy. WhC
74th Street. Myra Cohn Livingston. CTBA
Seventy-seven betrayers will stand by the road. To My Daughter. Hyam Plutzik. BiP
Seventy-six. Bryant. HBV-2; PAH
Seventy Six Trombones, *with music.* Meredith Willson. BLSo
Seventy thousand dead and gone. Bring 'Em Home. Barbara Dane *and others.* FSW
Seventy years of farming. The Deep Calling. John Rothfork. WOLT
Several months after we lost our way. The Natives. David Mura. BrSi
Several Questions Answered, Blake.
Eternity ("He who binds [*or* bends] to himself a joy"). AWP; EBEV; FaBoEE; LAuP; LoBV; NOBE; NoP; OBNC; TrGrPo
Question Answer'd, The. ELU; ErPo; FaBoEE; GBL; NoP; ViBoPo ("What is it men in women do require?") NIP; OAEL-2
Several things announced the fact to us. New Territory. Eaven Boland. CIP
Several Voices out of a Cloud. Louise Bogan. MoVE
Several years ago. A New Story. Simon J. Ortiz. STE
Severed hand flutters, The. The Persistence of Memory, the Failure of Poetry. Robert Phillips. GeTw
Severed Head, A, *sel.* John Montague.
Road's End, The, I. IPY
Severed Selves. Dante Gabriel Rossetti. The House of Life, XL. BoLoP; SyP
Severn, The. Michael Drayton. *Fr.* The Baron's War, Canto I. ChTr
Severn sweeping smooth and broad, The. At Arley. Andrew Young. FaBoPP
Seville. L. D'O. Walters. HBMV
Sev'n skunks lumbering in a row. Black and White Shuffle. Harry Elmore Hurd. WhC
Sewanee Hills of dear delight. The Hills of Sewanee. George Marion McClellan. BANP
Sex, as they harshly call it. Two Songs, I. Adrienne Rich. CABA; NIP; NOBA; TAP
Sex fingers toes. Dear John, Dear Coltrane. Michael S. Harper. AmPA; GeTw; NIP
Sex floated like a moon. A Circle, a Square, a Triangle and a Ripple of Water. Jane Cooper. TAP
Sex Play in Four Acts. Doug Fetherling. NeAC
Sex without Love. Sharon Olds. MAYP
Sexes waking, now separate and sore, The. The Martyrs. Jay Macpherson. MoCV
Sexsmith the Dentist. Edgar Lee Masters. *Fr.* Spoon River Anthology. NePA
Sext. W. H. Auden. *Fr.* Horae Canonicae. SaC
Sextant, The. A. M. Sullivan. GoBC
Sexton stood one Sabbath eve, A. Those Wedding Bells Shall Not Ring Out! Monroe H. Rosenfeld. FSN
Sextus the Usurer. Martial, *tr. fr. Latin by* Kirby Flower Smith. AWP
Sexual intercourse began. Annus Mirabilis. Philip Larkin. NIP; OBAL
Sexual Life of the Camel, The. *Unknown.* DBV
Sexual Privacy of Women on Welfare. Pinkie Gordon Lane. BlSi
Sexual Soup. Erica Jong. GP
Seymour and Chantelle; or, Un Peu de Vice. Stevie Smith. SBG
Seynt Steuyn and Herowdes ("Seynt Steuyn [*or* Stevene *or* Steuene] was a clerk . . ."). *Unknown.* *See* St. Stephen and Herod.
Seynt Valentynes Day. Chaucer. *Fr.* The Parliament of Fowls. PB ("There mighte men the royal eagle find.") PBBP
Sez Alderman Grady. Officer Brady. Robert W. Chambers. InMe
Sez Corporal Madden to Private McFadden. The Recruit. Robert W. Chambers. HBV-2
Sgoran Dhu. Nan Shepherd. PoSH
Sgurr Nan Gillean. Sorley MacLean. *Fr.* The Cuillin. PoSH
"Sh." James S. Tippett. SUS; TiPo
Shabbat Morning. Bradley R. Strahan. AMV-81
Shack, The. Nellie Burget Miller. PoOW
Shack and a few trees, The. After Work. Gary Snyder. HoPM; NNaP
Shacked Up at the Ritz. Doug Fetherling. NeAC
Shackley-Hay. *Unknown.* GBP
Shadbush. Christina Rainsford. GoYe
Shade. Theodosia Garrison. OHIP
Shade. Charles Lynch. CNA
Shade of His hand shall cover us, The. His Hand Shall Cover Us. Isaac ben Samuel of Dampière, *tr. by* Nina Davis Salaman. TrJP
Shade once swept about your boughs, The. The Fallen Tree. Andrew Young. BoNaP
Shade-Seller, The. Josephine Jacobsen. TAP
Shade, the light, the figures, the horizon as, The. October 1942. Roy Fuller. WaP
Shaded lamp and a waving blind, A. An August Midnight. Thomas Hardy. BrPo
Shaded Pool, The. Norman Gale. HBV-1; OBVV
Shades are half-drawn on classroom and hall, The. Discourse on the Real. Samuel Yellen. NePoAm
Shades of Callimachus, Coan ghosts of Philetas. Ezra Pound. *Fr.* Homage to Sextus Propertius. CMoP; HAP; MoAB; MoVE; NoAM; NOBA; OBVE; OxBA; PP
Shades of eve had crossed the glen, The. The Pretty Dan. Sir Samuel Ferguson. HBV-1
Shades of Night, The. A. E. Housman. BXAP; ChTr; FiBHP ("Shades of night were falling fast, The.) FaBoNo; SpRo
Shades of night were falling fast, The. Excelsior. Longfellow. FaPON; FaPoR; HBV-2; HBVY; OBCA; OnMSP; PaPo; PrIm; SpRo; TreF; WBLP
Shadow. Guillaume Apollinaire, *tr. fr. French by* Jessie Degen *and* Richard Eberhart. WaaP
Shadow. Richard Bruce. CDC
Shadow, The. Walter de la Mare. OnUR
Shadow. Anthony Delius. PeSA
Shadow, The. Ben Jonson. *See* That Women Are but Men's Shadows.
Shadow, The. Rose Macaulay. SUMH
Shadow. Ann Mars. GoYe
Shadow, The. Richard Henry Stoddard. AA
Shadow, The. Arthur Symons. OBVV
Shadow, A. *Unknown.* *See* I Heard a Noise and Wishèd for a Sight.
Shadow and Shade. Allen Tate. LiTA; TwAmPo; VGW; ViBoPo
Shadow and Substance. *Unknown.* *See* I Heard a Noise and Wishèd for a Sight.
Shadow and the Light, The, *sel.* Whittier.
"All souls that struggle and aspire." TrPWD
Shadow become real; follower become leader. Yellow Woman Speaks. Merle Woo. BrSi
Shadow Boat, A. Arlo Bates. HBV-1
Shadow-Bride. J. R. R. Tolkien. SO
Shadow-Child, The. Harriet Monroe. HBV-1
Shadow Dance. Ivy O. Eastwick. SoPo; TiPo
Shadow Dance, The. Louise Chandler Moulton. AA; HBV-1
Shadow Dirge. R. P. Dexter. LiSp
Shadow Evidence. Mary Mapes Dodge. AA
Shadow falls, the path I cannot trace, The. Satisfied. Sam V. Cole. BLRP
Shadow gates are swinging, The. The Gates of the Year. John Mervin Hull. STF
Shadow House of Lugh, The. "Ethna Carbery." AnIV
Shadow is floating through the moonlight, A. The Bird of Night. Randall Jarrell. DuDa; NCSH; RFM
Shadow, killer of doves. Shadow. Anthony Delius. PeSA
Shadow Life. Robert F. Reid III. AMV-81
Shadow-Love. Heine, *tr. fr. German by* Emma Lazarus. *Fr.* Songs to Seraphine. TrJP
Shadow of a Branch, The. Edith Marcombe Shiffert. WPE
Shadow of Cain, The. Edith Sitwell. CoBMV; OxBTC
Shadow of Darkness. Aquah Laluah. PBA
Shadow of her profile lay stringent, The. Woman, Gallup, N. M. Karen Swenson. NYBP
Shadow of Night, The. George Chapman. NCEP
Sels.
Hymnus in Noctem. PoEL-2
Night. OBSC
Shadow of Night, The. Coventry Patmore. *See* Night and Sleep.
Shadow of the dwarf magnolia, The. The Magnolia's Shadow. Robert Lowell. NaP
Shadow of the little fishing launch, The. The Parrot Fish. James Merrill. NOBA
Shadow of the Night, A. Thomas Bailey Aldrich. AA

Shadow of the Old City. Yehuda Amichai, *tr. fr. Hebrew by* Shirley Kaufman. VWA
Shadow of the plane, The. Looking Down on West Virginia. John Dickson. AMV-81
Shadow of the Rock, The. Frederick W. Faber. GoBC
Shadow on the Stone, The. Thomas Hardy. QFR
Shadow Remains, The. Lynette Roberts. NeBP
Shadow River. Pauline Johnson. CaP
Shadow Rose, The. Robert Cameron Rogers. AA
Shadow streamed into the wall, The. Shadow and Shade. Allen Tate. LiTA; TwAmPo; VGW; ViBoPo
Shadow to Shadow. Hervey Allen. HBMV
Shadowed by your dear hair, your dear kind eyes. The Sanctuary. Ford Madox Ford. PoA
Shadowgraphs, The. Richmond Lattimore. NYBP
Shadows. Samuel Daniel. *See* Are They Shadows?
Shadows. D. H. Lawrence. OAEP; OxBTC
Shadows, The. George Macdonald. TRV
Shadows. Richard Monckton Milnes. HBV-1
Shadows, The. Frank Dempster Sherman. AA
Shadows. *Tr. fr. Tewa Indian by* H. J. Spinden. WTO
Shadows. Yehoash, *tr. fr. Yiddish by* Elias Lieberman. TrJP
Shadows among the Ettrick Hills. William Addison. PoSH
Shadows are descending, The. Outgoing Sabbath. *Unknown, tr. by* Joseph Leftwich. TrJP
Shadows blown from trees, The. Vain Advice at the Year's End. James Wright. NYBP
Shadows do every where for substance passe. The Church-Windows. *Unknown. Fr.* A Poem, in Defence of the Decent Ornaments of Christ-Church, Oxon, Occasioned by a Banbury Brother, Who Called Them Idolatries. OBS
Shadows fall like men. Nocturne for the U.S. Congress. Victor Contoski. GP
Shadows gather round me, while you are in the sun, The. Next of Kin. Christina Rossetti. HBV-2
Shadows grazing eastwards melt. Last Meeting. Gwen Harwood. PoAu-2
Shadows in the Water. Thomas Traherne. HAP; LiTB; MePo; NoP; OAEL-1; OBS; PoEL-2; SeCP
Shadows lay along Broadway, The. Two Women [*or* Unseen Spirits]. Nathaniel Parker Willis. AA; BeLS; HBV-1; OBVV
Shadows of Chrysanthemums. E. J. Scovell. MoVE
Shadows of His Lady. Jacques Tahureau, *tr. fr. French by* Andrew Lang. AWP
Shadows of late afternoon and the odors, The. Old Dominion. Robert Hass. MAYP
Shadows of night were a-comin' down swift, The. Higher. *Unknown.* FiBHP; SpRo
Shadows of Sails. John Anderson. EtS
Shadows of the Evening Hours, The. Adelaide A. Procter. TreFS
Shadows of the rooks fly up the hill, The. Arques. Arthur Symons. Amoris Exsul, XI. VLP
Shadows of the ships, The. Sketch. Carl Sandburg. AP; HBMV
Shadows, shadows,/ Hug me round. Escape. Georgia Douglas Johnson. PoBA
Shadows slowly creeping. Prairie Lullaby. *Unknown.* BPAW
Shadow's Song, The. Yvor Winters. POL
Shadows To-day. Christina Georgina Rossetti. OxBoCh
Shadows where the Mewlips dwell, The. The Mewlips. J. R. R. Tolkien. AmMo; SO; WSC
Shadowy daughter of Urthona stood before red Orc, The. America a Prophecy. Blake. OAEL-2
Shadowy Horses, The. W. B. Yeats. *See* Michael Robartes Bids His Beloved Be at Peace.
Shadrach/ Shake the bed. *Unknown.* FaBoNo
Shadrach, Meshach, Abednego. Warm Babies. Keith Preston. FiBHP; HBMV; WhC
Shadwell Stair. Wilfred Owen. FaBoTw
Shady friend for torrid days, A. Emily Dickinson. NePA
Shady Grove. *Unknown.* FSW
Shady, Shady. T'ao Ch'ien, *tr. fr. Chinese by* Arthur Waley. AWP
Shaemus. Conrad Aiken. OxBA
Shaftesbury. Dryden. *See* Achitophel: The Earl of Shaftesbury.
Shaggy, and lean, and shrewd, with pointed ears. The Woodman's Dog. William Cowper. *Fr.* The Task, V. ELU; GDP
Shaggy Dog, A. *Unknown. See* Maggie.
Shaggy Dog Story. Frank Steele. Str
Shaka, King of the Zulus. *Unknown, tr. fr. Zulu by* A. C. Jordan. PBA; TTY
"Young viper grows as it sits, The," *tr. by* T. Cope, sel. WTO
Shake hands with Hector the Dog. Hector the Dog. Kate Barnes. GDP
Shake, Mulleary, and Go-ethe. H. C. Bunner. FiBHP; InMe
Shake off thy sloth, my drowsy soul, awake. Thomas Traherne. *Fr.* "On Christmas Day." OxBoCh
Shake Off Your Heavy Trance. Francis Beaumont. *Fr.* Masque of the Inner Temple and Gray's Inne. ELU; OBS; ViBoPo
(Fit Only for Apollo.) ChTr
(Song for a Dance.) ElL; FaBoCh
(Song from a Masque.) TrGrPo
(Three Songs, I.) GoBC
Shaken already, I know. Goodbye, Sally. James Simmons. BIrV
Shake'nbake Ballad. Peter van Toorn. NOBC
Shakespeare. Matthew Arnold. BiP; CABA; FiP; HBV-2; InvP; NoP; OAEP; OBEV; OBVV; TrGrPo; ViBoPo; WHA
Shakespeare. Henry Ames Blood. AA
Shakespeare [The Fairies' Advocate]. Thomas Hood. *Fr.* The Plea of the Midsummer Fairies. OBNC; OBRV
Shakespeare. Longfellow. AWP
Shakespeare. Swinburne. TrGrPo
Shakespeare. Sir William Watson. HBV-2
Shakespeare; an Epistle to David Garrick, Esq., *sels.* Robert Lloyd.
Critic's Rules, The. OBEC
True Genius. NOEC
Shakespeare and Milton—what third blazoned name. Tennyson. Thomas Bailey Aldrich. AA
Shakespeare Dead. Hugh Holland. ACP
Shakespeare Might Have Boiled Othello. Edwin Meade Robinson. Limericised Classics, II. HBMV
Shakespeare, Possibly, in California. Reed Whittemore. MoVE
Shakespeare: The Fairies Advocate. Thomas Hood. *See* Shakespeare.
Shakespeare would have savored his coarse, irate. "How Long Hast Thou Been a Gravemaker?" David Perkins. NCSH
Shakespearean Bear, The. Arthur Guiterman. CenHV; EvOK
Shakespearean fish swam the sea, far away from land. Three Movements. W. B. Yeats. CMoP; ELU; FaBoEE
"Shakin like the." On a Country Road. Harley Elliot. NeAC
Shaking in White streetlight in. Our Vegetable Love Shall Grow. Elaine Feinstein. POL
Shakuhachi. Jim Mitsui. BrSi
Shall a Frown [or Angry Eye]. *Unknown.* ElL; EnRePo
Shall ancient worth, or ancient fame. True Genius. Robert Lloyd. *Fr.* Shakespeare, an Epistle to David Garrick, Esq. NOEC
Shall Dumpish Melancholy spoil my Joys. On Christmas-Day. Thomas Traherne. OBS; PoEL-2
Shall Earth No More Inspire Thee? Emily Brontë. ELP
(Lines: "Shall earth no more inspire thee?") LoBV
Shall hog with holy child converse? Hog at the Manger. Norma Farber. PChr
Shall I abide this jesting? *Unknown.* GBL
Shall I be fearful thus to speak my mind. Irene Rutherford McLeod. *Fr.* Sonnets. HBMV
Shall I Be Silent? George Herbert. TRV
"Shall I be your first love, lady, shall I be your first?" Love-in-Idleness. Thomas Lovell Beddoes. ViBoPo
Shall I begin at the beginning. Yiddish. Abraham Sutskever, *tr. by* Seymour Levitan. VWA
Shall I begin by saying. Lafayette to Washington. Maxwell Anderson. *Fr.* Valley Forge. PAL
Shall I begin with *Ah,* or *Oh*? An Ode: Secundum Artem. William Cowper. PP
Shall I charge like a bull. Auvaiyar, *tr. fr. Tamil by* A. K. Ramanujan. WPOW
Shall I come, if I swim? wide are the waves, you see. Thomas Campion. EnLoPo
Shall I Come, Sweet Love, to Thee? Thomas Campion. ElL; EnRePo; FaBoEn; LoBV; OAEP; OBSC; OxBoLi; PoEL-2; ViBoPo
(Lover's Plea, A.) AAS; EBEV; GBL; HAP; NOBE
Shall I come there, or you here? Hafsa bint al-Hajj, *tr. fr. Arabic by* Michael Scott. WPOW
Shall I compare thee to a summer's day? Sonnets, XVIII. Shakespeare. AWP; BoLoP; CTC; ElL; EnLoPo; FaBoBe; FaBoEn; FaBV; FaFP; FiP; FPL; GBL; GTBS; GTBS-P; HAP; HBV-1; HeIP; InPK; InPS; InVP; LiTB; LoBV; MasP; MAT: NIP; NOBE; NoP; OAEL-1; OAEP; OBEV; OBSC; OLR; PAI; PoEL-2; PoLF; PoPl; PoRA; PPoe; PrIm; SCV; SeCePo; SeCeV; TEP; TreFT; TrGrPo; ViBoPo; WeW; WHA
Shall I complain, or not? Or shall I mask. Ovid, *tr. by* Henry Vaughan. *Fr.* De Ponto, IV, 3a. OBVE
Shall I connect for this world's eyes. The Dumb World. W. H. Davies. BoAnP
Shall I Do This. Purohit. OBMV
Shall I dwell in my shell? The Snail's Monologue. Christian Morgenstern, *tr. by* Max Knight. BoAnP
Shall I equate thee with a summer's day? New Improved Sonnet XVIII. Peter Titheradge. FaBoPa

Shall I ever see it, the Queen's River. Flyfisherman in Wartime. Leonard Bacon. FYAP
Shall I expound "whore" to you? sure, I shall. An Execration against Whores. John Webster. *Fr.* The White Devil, III, ii. TW
Shall I get drunk or cut myself a piece of cake. Cairo Jag. Keith Douglas. NePoEA
Shall I, I wonder, ever find. Peace. Irwin Edman. TrJP
Shall I (like a hermit) dwell. His Further Resolution. *Unknown.* HBV-1
Shall I Look. *Unknown.* EnRePo
(What Remains but Only Dying?) ElL
Shall I Love Again. William Browne. ViBoPo
Shall I love God for causing me to be? The Proof. Richard Wilbur. EaLo
Shall I love him. A Young Girl's Song. Paul Heyse, *tr. by* E. H. Mueller. PoPl
Shall I, mine affections slack. Answer to Master Wither's Song, "Shall I, Wasting in Despair?" Ben Jonson. InMe
Shall I pull the curtains against the coming night? If You Will. Josephine Miles. GP
Shall I Repine. Swift. *See* Power of Time, The.
Shall I say that I love you. Of Disdainful Daphne. M. H. Nowell. ElL
Shall I say that what heaven gave. Sentence. Witter Bynner. HBV-2
Shall I sonnet-sing you about myself? House. Robert Browning. OAEP; PP
Shall I spend the days of my youth in pride. God's Call. *Unknown.* STF
Shall I stray/In the middle air. John Fletcher. *Fr.* The Faithful Shepherdess. ViBoPo
Shall I strew on thee rose or rue or laurel. Ave atque Vale. Swinburne. NOBE; OAEL-2; OAEP; OBEV; OBNC; SyP; ViBoPo; VLP
Shall I tell you who [*or* what] will come. Words from an Old Spanish Carol [*or* Christmas Morn *or* On Christmas Morn]. *Unknown, tr. by* Ruth Sawyer. FaPON; OBCP; PChr; PDV
Shall I Tell You Whom I Love? William Browne. *Fr.* Brittania's Pastorals, II, Song 2. ElL
(Song: "Shall I tell you whom I Love?") HBV-1
Shall I then hope when faith is fled? Thomas Campion. AAS
Shall I then praise the heavens, the trees, the earth. Anne Bradstreet. *Fr.* Contemplations. PBWP
Shall I thus ever long, and be no whit the near? The Lady Prayeth the Return of Her Lover Abiding on the Seas [*or* To Her Seafaring Lover *or* The Seafarer]. *Unknown.* ElL; GBL; OBEV; OBSC
Shall I, Wasting in Despair [*or* Dispaire]. George Wither. *Fr.* Fidelia. ElL; LiTB; OBS; WHA
(Author's Resolution, The.) ViBoPo
(Lover's Resolution, The.) AWP; BoLoP; HBV-1; InMe; NOBE; OBEV; PoPle; TreFS
(Manly Heart, The.) FaBV; GTBS; GTBS-P
(Sonnet: "Shall I, wasting in despair.") SeCV-1
(What Care I.) TrGrPo
Shall Man, O God of Light, *with music.* Timothy Dwight. AH
Shall mine eyes behold thy glory, oh, my country! After Death. Fanny Parnell. AnIV; OBVV; OnYI; OxBI
Shall not a man sing as the night comes on? Song on Reaching Seventy. John Hall Wheelock. TwAmPo
Shall one be sorrowful because of love. De Amore. Ernest Dowson. OBNC
Shall pride a heap of sculptur'd marble raise. Epitaph on Laurence Sterne. David Garrick. FaBoEE
Shall Reason rule where Reason hath no right. To His Love, That Sent Him a Ring Wherein Was Graved, "Let Reason Rule." George Turberville. EnRePo
Shall royal praise be rhym'd by such a ribald. On the Candidates for the Laurel. Pope. FaBoEE
Shall the Dead Praise Thee? George Macdonald. TrCP
Shall these early fragrant hours. Henry Vaughan. LO
Shall they bury me in the deep. My Grave. Thomas Osborne Davis. OnYI
Shall we die, both thou and I. *Unknown.* LO
Shall We Gather at the River? Robert Lowry. *See* Beautiful River.
Shall we go dance the hay? The hay? A Report Song [in a Dream] [*or* Country Song *or* Wooing in a Dream]. Nicholas Breton. GBL; NOBE; OBSC; SeCePo; TrGrPo
Shall we go on with it? Driving ever seaward? Voyage of Discovery: 1935. Richmond Lattimore. TwAmPo
Shall we have a family born. For Walter Lowenfels. Wendy Rose. CDW
Shall we make love. *Unknown.* *Fr.* Manyo Shu. AWP
Shall we meet no more, my love, at the binding of the sheaves. Adonais. Will Wallace Harney. AA; HBV-1
Shall we not lay our holly wreath. The Fallen. Diana Gurney. SUMH
Shall we not open the human heart. Give Way! Charlotte Perkins Gilman. WGRP
Shall we send back the Johnnies their bunting. Those Rebel Flags. John H. Jewett. PAH
Shall we sit here some more. August at the Lake. David Young. AmPA
Shall we win at love or shall we lose. Hôtel Transylvanie. Frank O'Hara. NeAP; PoM
Shall you complain who feed the world? To Labor. Charlotte Perkins Stetson Gilman. PoLF
Shallo Brown, *with music. Unknown.* ShS
Shallot, A. Richard Wilbur. GP
Shallow dark but mocks the eyes. Night's Ancient Cloud. Thomas Keohler. AnIV
Shallows of the Ford, The. Henry Herbert Knibbs. BPAW
Shalom. Denise Levertov. NoAM
Shalom Aleichem. *Unknown, tr. fr. Hebrew.* TrJP
Shalom Chaverim. *Unknown, tr. fr. Hebrew.* FSW
Shaman. Will Inman. GP
Shaman. Esther M. Leiper. AMV-81
Shaman. Erika Mumford. PoDr
Shaman. Maria Sabina, *tr. fr. Spanish by* Henry Munn. WPOW
Shamash of the glade, The. The Venerable Bee. A. M. Klein. TrJP
Shambles come ready-made these years / are found. On Common Ground. R. P. Blackmur. Scarabs for the Living, III. CrMA
Shame. Coventry Patmore. OBVV
Shame. Arthur Rimbaud, *tr. fr. French by* Louise Varèse. SyP
Shame. Richard Wilbur. ConAP; FaBoMo; OxBC
Shame checks our first attempts, but then 'tis proved. Sins Loathed, and Yet Loved. Robert Herrick. LiTB
Shame He suffered left its brand, The. Scarred. *Unknown.* STF
Shame to my thoughts, how they stray from me! On the Flightiness of Thought. *Unknown, tr. by* Kuno Meyer. OnYI
Shame upon you, Robin. Song of the Milkmaid. Tennyson. *Fr.* Queen Mary. HBV-1
Shamefaced,/ I'm shunned even. No Fig. Stephen Todd Booker. LFAC
Shameful Death. William Morris. ChTr; GTBS-P; HBV-2; OAEP; OBVV; VLP
Shameful Impotence. Ovid, *tr. fr. Latin by* Christopher Marlowe. Amores, III, vii. ErPo
(Impotent Lover, The.) UnTE
Shameless thing, for ilka vileness able, A. The Octopus. "Hugh MacDiarmid." TW
Shampoo, The. Elizabeth Bishop. OxBC
Shamrock, The. Maurice Francis Egan. AA; HBV-1
Shan Van Vocht, The. *Unknown.* AnIL; AnIV; GBP; OnYI; OxBoLi
(Shan Van Voght.) FSW
Shanadore, I love your daughter. Shenandoah, *with music. Unknown.* ShS
Shancoduff. Patrick Kavanagh. BIrV; CIP; FaBoTw; IPY; NoP; OxBI
Shandon Bells, The. Francis Sylvester Mahony. *See* Bells of Shandon, The.
Shane O'Neill. Seumas MacManus. OnYI
Shane O'Neill's Cairn. Robinson Jeffers. NoAM; NOBA
Shaneen and Maurya Prendergast. Patch-Shaneen. J. M. Synge. LoBV
Shango ("Shango is an animal like the gorilla"). *Unknown, tr. fr. Yoruba by* Gbadamosi *and* Ulli Beier. PBA; TTY, *st.* 1
Shango ("Shango is the death who kills money with a big stick"). *Unknown, tr. fr. Yoruba by* Gbadamosi *and* Ulli Beier. TTY
Shankill. Eileen Shanahan. NeIP
Shannon and the *Chesapeake,* The. Thomas Tracy Bouvé. PAH
Shannon and the *Chesapeake,* The. *Unknown.* AmSS
Shantih shantih shantih. Edward Pygge. BXAP
Shanty Boys and the Pine, The. *Unknown.* AmFP
Shantyboy's Song, The. Kenneth Zwicker. ShS
Shantyman's Life, A. *Unknown.* AmFP; AS, *with music;* ShS, 2 vers., *with music*; TrAS, *diff. vers., with music*
Shao and the South, *sels.* Confucius, *tr. fr. Chinese by* Ezra Pound. CTC
" 'Chkk! chkk!' hopper-grass."
"Three stars, five stars rise over the hill."
Shapcot! to thee the Fairy State. Oberon's Feast. Robert Herrick. CaPo; SeCV-1; TrGrPo
Shape alone let others prize, The. Song. Mark Akenside. HBV-1
Shape, like folded light, embodied air, A. Aishah Schechinah. Robert Stephen Hawker. GoBC; ISi; OBNC; OxBoCh
Shape of a Bird, The. Laurence Whistler. MoVE
Shape of a Roethke, The? Theodore Roethke Foots It. D. C. Berry. BXAP
Shape of Autumn, The. Virginia Russ. GoYe
Shape of Death, The. May Swenson. TAP
Shape of the Fire, The. Theodore Roethke. CMoP; LCAP; LiTA; MiAP; MoAB
Shape of the Heart, The. Louise Townsend Nicholl. ImOP
Shape the lips to an *o*, say *a*. Ö. Rita Dove. MAYP
Shaped and vacated. The Event. T. Sturge Moore. OBMV
Shaped new to your meaure. Ark Articulate. Jay Macpherson. *Fr.* The Ark. NOBC
Shapes and Signs. James Clarence Mangan. OnYI
Shapes of Death, The. Stephen Spender. OBMV

Shapes that frowned before the eyes, The. The Eclipse of Faith. Theodore Dwight Woolsey. AA
Shapes, Vanishings. Henry Taylor. AMV-81; MAYP
Sharecropper is churning up only stones, The. Dividing the Field. William Aberg. LFAC
Share-Croppers. Langston Hughes. SaC
Shariff/ I went home for a week. Tennessee Crickets. Randolph Outlaw. LFAC
Sharing Eve's Apple. Keats. ChER; ErPo
Shark, The. J. J. Bell. RHPC
Shark, The. Lord Alfred Douglas. RHPC
Shark, The. E. J. Pratt. NOBC; WHW
Sharks, The. Denise Levertov. NeAP
Sharks. Dick Lourie. NeAC
Sharks. Ron Overton. WOLT
Sharks, Caloosahatchee River. Greg Pape. MAYP
Shark's Fin. Eithne Wilkins. NeBP
Sharks in Shallow Water. Fred Levinson. AmPA
Shark's Parlor, The. James Dickey. NYBP
Sharks tooth is perfect for biting, The. Canticle. Michael McClure. NeAP; PoM
Sharon Will Be No/Where on Nobody's Best-selling List. Sharon Scott. JB
Sharp air folds like giftwrap. Thirst of the Dragon. Dianne Hai-Jew. BrSi
Sharp is the night, but stars with frost alive. Winter Heavens. George Meredith. CABA; NoP
Sharp Ridge, The. Robert Graves. FaBoEE
Sharp ridges of clear blue windows, The. I Am a Dangerous Woman. Joy Harjo. TWSS
Sharp smoke drifts, A. Landscape with Figures. Theodore Enslin. CoPo
Sharpbreasted Snake, The. Louis (LittleCoon) Oliver. STE
Sharpening grandpa's scythe. David Martinson. *Fr.* Nineteen Sections from a Twenty Acre Poem. TAT
Sharpeville Inquiry. Anne Welsh. PeSA
Shash, The. *Unknown.* APAS
Shasta. Witter Bynner. BPAW
"Shatnes" or Uncleanliness. Eliezer Steinbarg, *tr. fr. Yiddish by* Seth L. Wolitz. VWA
Shattered Sabbath. Roberta B. Goldstein. AMV-81
Shattered water made a misty din, The. Once by the Pacific. Robert Frost. BPAW; CMoP; CoBMV; HAP; HeIP; LiTA; LiTM; MoAB; MoAmPo; MOS; NePA; NOBA; PrIm; VGW; WeW
Shattering of Love, The. *Gond Oral Tradition, tr. by* V. Elwin *and* S. Hivale. WTO
Shaving. Charles David Wright. AMV-81
Shavings, fall from the carved stick. Working Song. Buluguru, *tr. by* E. A. Worms. CBAP
Shawls, The. Monk Gibbon. NeIP; OxBI
She. *See also* Shee.
She. Zinaida Gippius, *tr. fr. Russian by* Dianne Levitin. WPOW
She. Theodore Roethke. BoLoP; ErPo; NIP
She. Richard Wilbur. AmPP; ConAP; CoPo; NIP
She. Manfred Winkler, *tr. fr. Hebrew by* Mary Zilzer. VWA
She/ not to be confused with she, a dog. Lady Tactics. Anne Waldman. PoM
She/ wore/ her flossiest smile. Movie Queen. James P. Vaughn. NNP
She always leaned to watch for us. The Watcher [*or* Mother]. Margaret Widdemer. HBMV; OHIP; STF
She always played Mother as a child. Child Bearing. Charles Ghigna. AMV-81
She and He. Sir Edwin Arnold. HBV-2
(He and She.) BLPA
She appeared before me that night: the vanquished one. The Ancient Law. André Spire, *tr. by* Stanley Burnshaw. VWA
She, as a veil down to the slender waist. Before the Fall. Milton. *Fr.* Paradise Lost, IV. ErPo; NIP
She asked brown eyes, "Burn me loose." Seal at Stinson Beach. Roberta Hill. VoR
She asked him why he'd never wed. Misogynist. Richard Conniff. DBV
She Asks for New Earth. Katherine Tynan. HBMV
She: At His Funeral. Thomas Hardy. VLP
She Attempts to Refute the Praises That Truth, Which She Calls Passion, Inscribed on a Portrait of the Poet. Sister Juana Ines de la Cruz, *tr. fr. Spanish by* Willis Barnstone. BoWoP
("This coloured counterfeit that thou beholdest," *tr. by* Samuel Beckett.) PBWP
She bade me follow to her garden, where. Snap-Dragon. D. H. Lawrence. ErPo
She beat the happy pavement. Gratiana Dancing. Richard Lovelace. OBEV
She Being Brand. E. E. Cummings. ErPo; NOBA; OxBA; UnTE
She Bewitched Me. Thomas Burbidge. EnLoPo
She bites into the red skin. My Love Eats an Apple. Ralph Gustafson. MoCV
She bounded o'er the graves. Anna Playing in a Graveyard. Caroline Gilman. OBCA
She brings that breath, and music too. The Visitor. W. H. Davies. GBL
She brought a drinking-cup to him. Two. Hugo von Hofmannsthal, *tr. by* Jethro Bithell. TrJP
She brought us a month noisy with rain. Full Moon in Malta. Asphodel. BrRo
She Called Him Mr. *Unknown.* FaPON
She came among the gathering crowd. Common Sense. Thomas Field. AA
She came among us from the south. Enrica, 1865. Christina Rossetti. TEP
She came and stood in the Old South Church. In the "Old South." Whittier. AA
She Came and Went. James Russell Lowell. AA; HBV-1; ViBoPo
She came and went as comes and goes. Under the Red Cross. Chauncey Hickox. AA
She came every morning to draw water. A Drink of Water. Seamus Heaney. OxBC
She came in from the snowing air. Ice. Stephen Spender. FaBoMo; GTBS-P; SeCePo
She came on Earth soon after the creation. The Fairy Maimounè. John Moultrie. OBRV
She Came Out of the Frost. Alexander Blok, *tr. fr. Russian by* Avrahm Yarmolinsky. PoPl
She came to me in hidden guise. Mater Incognita. Sister Mary Benvenuta. ISi
She came to the village church. Tennyson. *Fr.* Maud, VIII. EBVV
She can be as wise as we. Marian. George Meredith. HBV-1
She cannot tell my name. Prayer. Edward Bliss Reed. HBMV
She casts a spell, oh, casts a spell! My Love, Oh, She Is My Love. *Unknown, tr. by* Douglas Hyde. AnIV
She clasps a jewel. Words. David Phillips. NeAC
She clasps the cup with both her hands. In a Café. Rosemary Dobson. CBAP
She climbed the ladder looking over the wall at the party. Jim Harrison. *Fr.* Ghazals. InPS
She coaxes her fat in front of her. New Day. Naomi Long Madgett. BlSi
She combed her long hair at the window. The Woman Who Combed. Rush Rankin. FAZ
She comes like the hush and beauty of the night. Poetry. Edwin Markham. AA
She Comes Majestic with Her Swelling Sails. Robert Southey. MOS
(Homeward Bound.) EtS
She comes not: in the summer night. O Ubi? Nusquam. R. W. Dixon. LO
She Comes Not When Noon Is on the Roses. Herbert Trench. HBMV; OBEV; OBVV
She comes on at night. From St. Luke's Hospital. Madeleine L'Engle. CTBA
She comes on drenched in a perfume called Self Satisfaction. Mae West. Edward Field. FYAP
She comes—the spirit of the dance! A Dancing Girl. Frances Sargent Osgood. AA
She comes up the walk toward her back door. Longing for the Persimmon Tree. Millen Brand. TAT
She Contrasts with Herself Hippolyta. Hilda Doolittle ("H. D."). SBG
She cooked all day. Brooklyn Summer. Lou Lipsitz. LTB
She could die laughing. Minnie and Mrs. Hoyne. Kenneth Fearing. PoRA
She coulda been somethin. Ho. Al Young. GP; NPGG
She curls her darkened lashes; manicures. The Minority: 1917. May O'Rourke. SUMH
She danced, near nude, to tom-tom beat. Zalka Peetruza. Ray Garfield Dandridge. BANP; PoBA
She dances,/ And I seem to be. Perdita. Florence Earle Coates. AA
She dealt her pretty words like blades. Emily Dickinson. HAP
She-Devil. Douglas Goldring. HBMV
She Didn't Even Wave. Ai. MAYP
She didn't know she was beautiful. On Getting a Natural. Dudley Randall. FB; PoBA
She died after the beautiful snow had melted. In Memorial. J. Gordon Coogler. OBAL
She Died in Beauty. Charles Doyne Sillery. HBV-2
She died in the upstairs bedroom. Death in Leamington. John Betjeman. NoP; PoPl
She died,—this was the way she died. Vanished. Emily Dickinson. AA
She died turning aside from the sink. Another Death. D. E. Borrell. FF
She dismisses me in late sunbeams. Dismissal. Peter Redgrove. NMP
She does not know. No Images. Waring Cuney. AmNP; BANP; CDC; MAT; TTY

She does not talk. Floor: Five. Stephen Vincent. *Fr.* Elevator Landscapes. NeAC
She doesn't say a word, concentrating on one thing only. Balgu Song. *Unknown, tr. by* Clancy McKenna. CBAP
She doesn't wear/ costume jewelry. Gwendolyn Brooks. Don L. Lee. NoAM
She dreamed along the beaches of this coast. Palo Alto; the Marshes. Robert Hass. NPGG
She dreams her girl lover steals toward her. Dream. Stephen Dobyns. MAYP
She dreams of Love upon the temple stair. A Sleeping Priestess of Aphrodite. Robert Cameron Rogers. AA
She dreams of swimming the Platte. Calamity Jane Greets Her Dreams. Kathleen Lignell. AMV-80
She drew back; he was calm. The Subverted Flower. Robert Frost. CMoP; HAP; NoAM; NOBA; OxBA; WeW
She dwells, pale midnight sun, beyond the river. Une Idole du Nord. Francis Stuart. NeIP
She Dwelt among the Untrodden Ways. J. C. Squire. BXAP
She Dwelt among the Untrodden Ways. Wordsworth. *Fr.* Lucy. AWP; BoLoP; CABA; ELP; EnLoPo; EnRP; FF; HBV-1; HBVY; HAP; HeIP; LiTB; NIP; NoP; OAEL-2; OAEP; OBEV; OBRV; PAI; PPP; PrIm; SpRo; TEP; TrGrPo; UnPo; ViBoPo; WeW; WHA
(Lost Love, The.) GTBS; GTBS-P
(Lucy.) BLBA; FaBoEn; FaBV; FPL; LoBV; OBNC; TreF
She Employed the Familiar "Tu" Form. Doug Fetherling. NeAC
She entered, and passionately, the eyes half closed. Desire. Pierre Louÿs, *tr. by* Horace M. Brown. *Fr.* The Songs of Bilitis. UnTE
She enters the bus demurely. Puerto Ricans in New York, I. Charles Reznikoff. CTBA
She even thinks that [*or* She thinks that even] up in heaven. For a Lady I Know. Countee Cullen. Four Epitaphs, 4. CDC; HeIP; IDB; InPK; MoAmPo; NIP; OBAL; PoNe; ShM; TAP; TRV
She fears him, and will always ask. Eros Turannos. E. A. Robinson. AP; CMoP; CoBMV; CrMA; GBL; HAP; LiTA; LiTM; MoAB; MoAmPo; MoPo; MoVE; NePA; NoAM; NOBA; NoP; OxBA; PoA; PPoe; QFR; TAP; TwAmPo
She fell asleep on Christmas Eve. My Sister's Sleep. Dante Gabriel Rossetti. LoBV; OAEP; SeCeV; VLP
She fell away in her first ages spring. An Elegy. Spenser. *Fr.* Daphnaïda. OBEV; PoPle
She felt, I think, but as a wild-flower can. An Irish Wild-flower. Sarah Morgan Bryan Piatt. AA
She finds grief, her meat. Hyena. Carol Muske. AmPA
She fled in anguish; he pursued desire. First Love. Charles Gullans. NePoEA
She floats/ in a white shell. Riddle of Night. Jiri Mordecai Langer, *tr. by* Gabriel Preil *and* Howard Schwartz. VWA
She flourished in the 'Twenties, "hectic" days of peace. Mews Flat Mona. William Plomer. FaBoTw
She fluted with her mouth as when one sips. Beauty and the Bird. Dante Gabriel Rossetti. FM
She follows their races and climbings. Crippled Child at the Window. Melissa Cannon. AMV-80
She found herself no less. Snow White. Robert Gillespie. DFT
She Found Me Roots. R. W. Ransford. BXAP
She frowned and called him Mr. She Called Him Mr. *Unknown.* FaPON
She gamboll'd on the greens. Olivia. Tennyson. *Fr.* The Talking Oak. GN
She glows against. The Pro. Karen Swenson. AMV-81
She goes but softly, but she goeth sure. Upon the Snail [*or* a Snail]. Bunyan. ChTr; OxBChV
She goes with her pot for water. Who Can Tell? *Gond Oral Tradition, tr. by* V. Elwin *and* S. Hivale. WTO
She got off, according to the diary. The Arrival of My Mother. Keith Wilson. DFF; GP
She grew ninety years through sombre winter. Epitaph on a Fir-Tree. Richard Murphy. FaBoTw
She grew up in bedeviled southern wilderness. The Ballad of Sue Ellen Westerfield. Robert Hayden. AmPP; NoAM
She had a little time to think. Leda Reconsidered. Mona Van Duyn. NMM
She had a name among the children. A Cat. Edward Thomas. BoAnP; BrPo
She had always loved to read, even. White Autumn. Robert Morgan. Str
She had been reading, that much we know. Folds of a White Dress/Shaft of Light. Deborah Keenan. PoDr
She had corn flowers in her ear. Gipsy Jane. William Brighty Rands. FaPON; SoPO; TiPo
She had green eyes, that excellent seer. Bast. William Rose Benét. HBMV
She had no business doin' it, but she come o' the East. The Peeler's Lament. *Unknown.* CoSo; WTO
She had not held her secret long enough. The Visitation. Elizabeth Jennings. MoBS
She Had Some Horses. Joy Harjo. STE; TWSS
She had thought the studio would keep itself. Living in Sin. Adrienne Rich. FF; IHMS; NePoEA; NoP; NYBP; SoSe; TAP; UnPo
She handles bones, dull gray or ivory hued. On Hearing a Beautiful Young Woman Describe Her Class in Physical Anthropology. A. J. Hovde. AMV-81
She has a bright and clever mind. A Disagreeable Feature. Edwin Meade Robinson. HBMV
She has a husband, he a wife. Modern Love. J. V. Cunningham. POL
She has a primrose at her breast. A Primrose Dame. Gleason White. HBV-1
"She has beauty, but [still] you must keep your heart cool." Dear Fanny. Thomas Moore. HBV-1; InMe
She has been bleeding. Wounds. Judith Minty. GeTw
She has been condemned to death by hanging. Marrying the Hangman. Margaret Atwood. NOBC
She has begun to see men invite themselves. The Professional. David Ignatow. NNaP
She has calld to her her bower-maidens. Young Hunting. *Unknown.* ESPB
She has finished and sealed the letter. Parting, without a Sequel. John Crowe Ransom. DTC; MoAB; MoAmPo; MoVE; OxBA; SoSe
She has gone out, she is far from me, but I see her. Absence. Pierre Louÿs, *tr. by* Horace M. Brown. *Fr.* The Songs of Bilitis. UnTE
She has gone,—she has left us in passion and pride. Brother Jonathan's Lament for Sister Caroline. Oliver Wendell Holmes. HBV-2; PAH
"She has gone to be with the angels." The Vision of the Snow. Margaret Junkin Preston. AA
She has gone to the bottom! the wrath of the tide. The *Alabama.* Maurice Bell. PAH
She has laughed as softly as if she sighed. A Woman's Shortcomings. Elizabeth Barrett Browning. BLPA; HBV-1
She has left me, my pretty. Song. Sylvia Townsend Warner. MoAB; MoBrPo
She has no need to fear the fall. Portrait. Louise Bogan. HBMV
She has not found herself a hard pillow. To Clarissa Scott Delany. Angelina Weld Grimké. AmNP
She has taken a woman lover. Carol, in the Park, Chewing on Straws. Judy Grahn. The Common Woman, IV. PeHV; WPOW
She has that quality of innocence. Virgin Country. Roy McFadden. NeIP
She has the immaculate look of the new. Chinese Baby Asleep. Dorothy Donnelly. NCSH
She has the strange sweet grace of violets. Elizabeth. George Brandon Saul. HBMV
She has tightened her cinch by another inch. Over the Hills with Nancy. Gelett Burgess. WhC
She heard the sounds of a couple having intercourse. A Sequence. Leslie Scalapino. NPGG
She heard with patience all unto the end. Prince Arthur. Spenser. *Fr.* The Faerie Queene, I, 7. OBSC
She held his head of close hard hair. All One. Millen Brand. GP
She hid herself in the soirée kettle. A Ballade of the Nurserie. John Twig. NA
She hissed in my ear. Lilith. Donald Finkel. VWA
She hovered hooded, blue-eyed. Catechism, 1958. W. M. Ransom. CDW
She Hugged Me and Kissed Me. *Unknown.* BPo
She hung away her years, her eyes grew young. Waiting for the Bus. D. J. Enright. OxBTC
She I loved so much will not appear again. Farewell and Good. Denis Devlin. IPY
She, in dowdy dress and dumpy. Still Life: Lady with Birds. Quandra Prettyman. CAD; PoBA
She in whose lipservice. The Goddess. Denise Levertov. AP; LiTM; NeAP; NOBA; PoCh; PoM
She is a black crow being driven out of sight. Drinking the Wind. Tan Ying, *tr. by* Kenneth Rexroth *and* Ling Chung. WPOW
She is a reed,/ straight and simple. The Reed. Caryll Houselander. ISi
She is a rich and rare land. My Land. Thomas Osborne Davis. HBV-2; PAL
She is a winsome wee thing. My Wife's a Winsome Wee Thing. Burns. HBV-1
She is all so slight. After Two Years. Richard Aldington. HBV-1; MoBrPo; PoPl; WHA
She is all there. For My Lover, Returning to His Wife. Anne Sexton. IHMS; NMM; UnPo; WPE
She is as in a field a silken tent. The Silken Tent. Robert Frost. AmPP; BLPL; CABA; InPK; MoPo; MP; NePA; NOBA; SoSe; TAP; TwCP
She is bravest and best of a cursed race. Chipeta. Eugene Field. PoOW
She is committed to the earth and the earth. Canaan. Muriel Spark. NYBP
She is dead. Birthdays. Hilde Domin, *tr. by* Tudor Morris. BoWoP

"She is dead!" they said to him. "Come away." She and He [*or* He and She]. Sir Edwin Arnold. BLPA; HBV-2
She is devout and plump, but not happy. A Baroque Gravure. Thomas Merton. CoPo
She Is Far from the Land. Thomas Moore. AnIL; DTC; EnRP; FaBoNo; HBV-1; OBNC; WiR
She is first seen dancing which is a figure. The Origin of Cities. Robert Hass. NPGG
She is free of the trap and the paddle. The Half-Breed Girl. Duncan Campbell Scott. CaP
She is gentil and al so wise. That Ever I Saw. *Unknown.* TrGrPo
She is gone, she is lost, she is found, she is ever fair. My Woe Must Ever Last. Sir Walter Ralegh. ElL
She is gone! The occasion for ever is past! Lines Written Immediately after Parting from a Lady. Sir Samuel Egerton Brydges. NOEC
She is in full color. The Girl/The Girlie Magazine. Pat Gray. AMV-81
She is like pearls, of course, and rubies, and other. Valentine. Hollis Summers. GoYe
She Is More to Be Pitied than Censured. William B. Gray. BeLS; BLPA; FSN, *with music;* FSW; TreF
She is most fair. The Unknown. Edward Thomas. GBL
She Is My Dear. *Unknown, tr. fr. Irish by* Frank O'Connor. KiLC
She is named Melissa. Melissa. Carolyn D. Redl-Hlus. AMV-80
She Is Not Fair [to Outward View]. Hartley Coleridge. *See* Song: "She is not fair to outward view."
She Is Not for Me. *Gond Oral Tradition, tr. by* V. Elwin *and* S. Hivale. WTO
She is not of the fireside. Revolution. Lesbia Harford. PoAu-1
She is not old, she is not young. The Woman with the Serpent's Tongue. Sir William Watson. HBV-1
She is not yet; but he whose ear. The Dominion of Australia. Brunton Stephens. PoAu-1
She is now water and air. Sea Burial from the Cruiser "Reve." Richard Eberhart. NYBP
She is older than the rocks among which she sits. Mona Lisa. Walter Pater. OBMV
She Is Overheard Singing. Edna St. Vincent Millay. InMe
She is purposeless as a cyclone; she must move. Cubist Portrait. Marjorie Allen Seiffert. PoA
She is shameless, despicable, vile. She. Zinaida Gippius, *tr. by* Dianne Levitin. WPOW
She is so proper and so pure. My Sweet Sweeting. *Unknown.* CH
She is so young, and never never before. Sonnet. Edward Davison. ErPo
She is standing on my lids. Lady Love. Paul Eluard, *tr. by* Samuel Beckett. OBVE
She is still, she is cold. Shelley. *Fr.* Ginevra. ChER
She is submarine, she is an octopus. Ezra Pound. *Fr.* Cantos, XXIX. MoPo
She is teck'wi. The Taboo Woman. *Tr. fr. Zuni Indian by* K. Kennedy. WTO
She is the dark sister. Iscah. Howard Schwartz. VWA
She is the fairies' midwife, and she comes. Mercutio Describes Queen Mab. Shakespeare. *Fr.* Romeo and Juliet, I, iv. TrGrPo
She is the knife-thrower's lady. On a Professional Couple in a Side-Show. Alan Dugan. GP
She is the one you call sister. The Mirror in Which Two Are Seen as One. Adrienne Rich. NNaP
She is the Rose, the glorie of the day. Lament for Daphnaida. Spenser. FiP
She is the woman hanging from the 13th floor. The Woman Hanging from the 13th Floor Window. Joy Harjo. TWSS
She is touching the cycle—her tender tread. Tennessee. Virginia Fraser Boyle. PAH
She is tougher than me, harder. For My Mother. Iain Crichton Smith. OxBS
She is washed by white-water, white if she looked up. Fish. Daniel Halpern. AmPA
She kept finding arrowheads. Madonna of the Hills. Paula Gunn Allen. TWSS
She kept her secret well, oh, yes. My Angeline. Harry B. Smith. InMe
She kept her songs, they took so little space. Love Songs in Age. Philip Larkin. PPP
She kissed me on the forehead. Windle-Straws. Edward Dowden. HBV-1
She kneeled before me begging. Confession. Donald Jeffrey Hayes. CDC
She kneeled before the dead lamb weeping. Synekdechestai. C. M. Schmid. GoYe
She knew it not:—most perfect pain. The Mirror. Dante Gabriel Rossetti. SyP
She knew that she was growing blind. Blind Louise. George Washington Dewey. AA
She knew the grades of all her neighbors' children. Elegy for a Woman Who Remembered Everything. David Wagoner. DFF
She laid it where the sunbeams fall. Motherhood. Charles Stuart Calverley. FM
She Lay All Naked [in Her Bed]. *Unknown.* BoLoP; ErPo; UnTE
She lay, and serving-men her lithe arms took. Abishag. Rainer Maria Rilke, *tr. by* Jethro Bithell. AWP
She lay as if at play. Emily Dickinson. LiTA
She lay in her girlish sleep at ninety-six. Castoff Skin. Ruth Whitman. InPK
She lay there in the stone folds of his life. Private Worship. Mark Van Doren. MoVE
She Lay Wrapped. Gail Fox. NOBC
She leaned her back unto a thorn. The Cruel Mother. *Unknown.* ESPB; ViBoFo
She leaned her cheek upon her hand. The Ballad of Oriskany. Obadiah Cyrus Auringer. AA
She leaned her head upon her hand. Vashti. Frances E. W. Harper. BlSi
She leans across a golden table. For Amy Lowell. Countee Cullen. PoA
She left me at the silent time. Lines Written in the Bay of Lerici. Shelley. OAEL-2
She let her golden ball fall down the well. The Frog and the Golden Ball. Robert Graves. DFT; NoP
She lies far inland, and no stick nor stone of her. Inland City. John Crowe Ransom. CMoP
She lies in silence. She Walks. Joseph Joel Keith. ISi
She lies on her left side her flank golden. Landscape as a Nude. Archibald MacLeish. Frescoes for Mr. Rockefeller's City, I. AmPP; CMoP; UnPo
She lies upon the cold stone of her cell. The Nun. Arthur Symons. BrPo
She, like the morning, is still fresh and fair. Her Praises. Anthony Scoloker. ElL
She listen'd to the music of the spheres. Leirioessa Kalyx. Maurice Baring. OBVV
She lived beside the Anner. The Irish Peasant Girl. Charles Joseph Kickham. AnIV
She lived in storm and strife. That the Night Come. W. B. Yeats. CoBMV; PoEL-5
She lives by Cherry Hill where the dirt road. The Chosen. Carl Dennis. AMV-81
She lives in a garret. A Sad Song about Greenwich Village. Frances Park. RHPC
She lives in light, not shadow. Of One Who neither Sees nor Hears. Richard Watson Glider. AA
She lives in the porter's room; the plush is nicotined. Bitter Sanctuary. Harold Monro. FaBoMo; LiTB; OBMV
She looked over his shoulder. The Shield of Achilles. W. H. Auden. EBEV; FaBoMo; GTBS-P; HAP; NePA; NOBE; NOCV; NoP; OAEP; PoA; SeCeV; WeW
She looked to east, she looked to west. Mater Dei. Katharine Tynan. ISi
She looks out in the blue morning. The Window. Conrad Aiken. CMoP
She Lost Her Sheep. J. Moyr Smith. FaBoNo
She loved the Autumn, I the Spring. Spirit of Sadness. Richard Le Gallienne. HBV-2
She loves, and she confesses too. Honour. Abraham Cowley. BoLoP
She loves him . . . and what small child could deny. Americanized. Bruce Dawe. CBAP
She loves the wind. The Old One and the Wind. Clarice Short. IHMS
She made a little shadow-hidden grave. The Dead Faith. Fanny Heaslip Lea. HBV-2; WGRP
She makes thee seek, yet fear to find. Love's Servile Lot. Robert Southwell. ACP
She married him because. Because. Paul Johnson. AMV-81
She may be old, ninety years. Bottle Up and Go. *Unknown.* FSW
She May Have Seen Better Days, *with music.* James Thornton. FSN
She met a lion face to face. A Cautionary Tale. Anne Wilkinson. OBCV; PeCV
She met me, Stranger, upon life's rough way. True Love. Shelley. *Fr.* Epipsychidion. LoBV
She might have borne them had they come. Breaking Point. Sylvia Auxier. GoYe
She might have chosen cities, but the man. Droving Man. Thea Astley. PoAu-2
She might have known it in the earlier spring. Feminine. H. C. Bunner. AA
She might have stolen from his arms. Solitary Confinement. X. J. Kennedy. NePoEA-2
She might, so noble from head. A Thought from Propertius. W. B. Yeats. OAEL-2
She Moved through the Fair. Padraic Colum. BIrV; InvP
She moved through the garden in glory, because. Marigold. Richard Garnett. PCat
She moves in tumult; round her lies. The Teresian Contemplative. Robert Hugh Benson. ACP

She must have been kicked unseen or brushed by a car. Dog's Death. John Updike. Psk
She naked lies asleep beside the wine. From Titian's "Bacchanal" in the Prado at Madrid. T. Sturge Moore. QFR
She never climbed a mountain. Farm Wife. John Hanlon Mitchell. CaP
She never could sleep in the earth, in the cold dark grave. Fire Burial. Edgar McInnis. CaP
She never told her love. Love Concealed [*or* Patience on a Monument]. Shakespeare. *Fr.* Twelfth Night, II, iv. TreFS; TrGrPo
She never was quite one of us. Sleep-Walking Child. Elisabeth Eybers, *tr. by* Jack Cope, Uys Krige, *and* Adèle Naudé. PeSA
She of the Impudent Face. Bible, *O.T.* Proverbs, VII: 6-27. TrJP
She often lies with her hands behind her head. For My Daughter. Ronald Koertge. GP; Str
She only knew the birth and death. At Dawn. Arthur Symons. OBNC
She only lit the closet and the bathroom. The Disordering. Lynda Yates. AMV-81
She only said she wished there was a place. What She Wished. Marilyn Throne. AMV-81
She opens her mouth, a switchblade falls out. Lower Court. Carolyn Baxter. LFAC
She paced the silent hall. Sleep. Robert Eyres Landor. *Fr.* The Impious Feast. OBRV
She packs the flower beds with leaves. For Fran. Philip Levine. FF; PoCh
She passed away like morning dew. Early Death. Hartley Coleridge. HBV-2; OBEV; TreFS
She pauses in the act of dressing. Chamber Music. John Ditsky. AMV-81
She Plans Her Funeral. Louise Morey Bowman. CaP
She played me false, but that's not why. Our Photograph[s]. Frederick Locker-Lampson. DBV; NOBL
She played upon her music-box a fancy air by chance. Her Polka Dots. Peter Newell. NA
She pops their flanks with a rawhide whip. Pony Girl. Jane P. Moreland. PH
She practices a fugue, though it can matter. Suburban Sonnet. Gwen Harwood. CBAP
She Promised She'd Meet Me, *with music.* *Unknown.* AS
She Proves the Inconsistency of the Desires and Criticism of Men Who Accuse Women of What They Themselves Cause. Sister Juana Ines de la Cruz, *tr. fr. Spanish by* Aliki *and* Willis Barnstone. BoWoP
She put him on a snow-white shroud. The Little Shroud. Letitia E. Landon. PaPo
She reads the paper. Two People. Eve Merriam. RHPC
She Rebukes Hippolyta. Hilda Doolittle ("H. D."). SBG
She remembers the episode taking place at night. Night. Joyce Carol Oates. GeTw
She returned from the clinic. Unhappy Diary Days. Gerald Vizenor. VoR
She rides a broom and curses God. The Subversive. Merle Woo. BrSi
She rides the last few minutes. Squeal. Heather McHugh. GeTw
She rises clear to memory's eye. Red Jack. Mary Durack. PoAu-1
She rose among us where we lay. The Vampire. Conrad Aiken. HBMV
She rose from her untroubled sleep. Chamber Scene. Nathaniel Parker Willis. HBV-1
She rose to his requirement, dropped [*or* dropt]. Emily Dickinson. CABA; FaBoEn
She roves through shadowy solitudes. Tacita. James Benjamin Kenyon. AA
She Said . . . Jonathan Henderson Brooks. PoNe
She Said. Walter de la Mare. ELP
She said, "I cannot come." The Cenci's Curse upon His Daughter. Shelley. *Fr.* The Cenci, IV, i. TW
She said, "I was not born to mope at home in loneliness." The Ride round the Parapet. Friedrich Rueckert, *tr. by* James Clarence Mangan. AWP
She said, "I will come back again." She Said. Walter de la Mare. ELP
She said, if tomorrow my world were torn in two. The 5:32. Phyllis McGinley. *Fr.* I Know a Village. NMM; WPE
She said, "Not only music; brave men marching." She Said . . . Jonathan Henderson Brooks. PoNe
She said, "Now give me flesh to eat." Cherry. Gene Baro. ErPo
She said the Jehovah Witness man. 3-31-70. Gayl Jones. *Fr.* Journal. BlSi
She Said the Same to Me, *with music.* *Unknown.* AS
She said: The world is empty that we loved. Eternal. Agnes Foley Macdonald. CaP
She said, "They gave me of their best." After Aughrim. Emily Lawless. OBEV; OxBI
She said to me, He lay there sleeping. The Watchers. Muriel Rukeyser. NMP
She said to one: "How glows." Subalterns. Elizabeth Daryush. OBWP; SUMH
She sang beyond the genius of the sea. The Idea of Order at Key West. Wallace Stevens. AP; CMoP; CoBMV; FF; HAP; HeIP; MoAB; MoAmPo; MoPo; MOS; NIP; NoAM; NOBA; NoP; OxBA; PP; PPP; PrIm; SeCeV; TAP
She Sang, Dear Son, Lullay. *Unknown.* *See* This Yonder Night I Sawe a Sighte.
She sang her little bedtime air. Evening Prayer. Hermann Hagedorn. GoBC
She sang of lovers met to play. A Casual Song. Roden Noel. HBV-1
She sat across from me and her eyes. Parting. Gabriel Preil, *tr. by* Laya Firestone. VWA
She sat and sang alway. Song. Christina Rossetti. GBL
She sat and wept beside His feet; the weight. "Multum Dilexit." Hartley Coleridge. EnRP; HBV-2
She sat down below a thorn. The Cruel Mother *Unknown.* ESPB; FaBoBa; InPK; OxBB
She sat on a shelf. Motherhood. May Swenson. CoAP
She sate upon her Dobie. The Cummerbund. Edward Lear. CenHV
She Saw Me in Church. *Unknown.* MeEL
She saw the bayonets flashing in the sun. Memorial Day. Richard Watson Gilder. OHIP
She says how/ is it when you. John Knoepfle. *Fr.* The Ten-Fifteen Community Poems. MAT
She says "How was you?" Kissing. "Come on in." Unrecorded Speech. Anna Adams. BrRo
She seemed an angel to our infant eyes! A Mother's Picture. Edmund Clarence Stedman. OHIP
She seems to come by wing. 2nd Dance—Seeing Lines—6 February 1964. Jackson MacLow. CoPo
She Sees Another Door Opening. Firman Houghton. Par
She sees her image in the glass. The Shadow Dance. Louise Chandler Moulton. AA; HBV-1
She sends me news of bluejays, frost. A Letter from Home. Mary Oliver. Str
She served love well. Elegy, Montreal Morgue. Goodridge MacDonald. CaP
She Sews Fine Linen. Julia Johnson Davis. HBMV
She shakes in the take-off lounge. The Frightened Flier Goes North. Judith Kazantzis. BrRo
She sharpened her knife both sharp and keen. Young Hunting. *Unknown.* OxBoLi
She, she is dead; she's dead: when thou knowest this. John Donne. *Fr.* An Anatomy of the World; the First Anniversary. JCP
She shifts her pelvis to the tune of muted bells. The Pinball Queen of South Illinois St. Stephen Tietz. AMV-80
She should have died hereafter. Tomorrow and Tomorrow and Tomorrow. Shakespeare. *Fr.* Macbeth, V, v. DL; FaBoRV; FiP; SoSe
"She should have had. . .," I said, and there I stopped. After Speaking of One Dead a Long Time. Padraic Colum. GoYe
She should have had the state. Requiescat. Katherine Anne Porter. HBMV
She should never have looked at me. Cristina. Robert Browning. OAEP
She sidled up to me coyly and said. Sea Food Thought. John W. Moser. FAZ
She sings her wild dirges, and smiles 'mid the strain. Scene in a Madhouse. Aubrey Thomas De Vere. OnYI
She sinks/ into the tub of herself. A Life. Chana Bloch. MAYP
She sits beside him. Renoir's Confidences. J. Michael Pilz. AMV-81
She sits in her glass garden. The One Whose Reproach I Cannot Evade. George Hitchcock. EAS
She sits in Sarras, delicate and strange. Our Lady with Two Angels. Wilfred Rowland Childe. ISi
She sits in the park. Her clothes are out of date. In the Park. Gwen Harwood. CBAP
She sits in the tawny vapour. A Wife in London. Thomas Hardy. OBWP
She sits on the floor. Letters. Charles Bukowski. GP
She sits on tumulus Savoor, and stares. Flax. Ivan Bunin, *tr. by* Babette Deutsch *and* Avrahm Yarmolinsky. AWP
She sits underneath. A Child of Hers. T. Walking Eagle Marietta. LFAC
She sits upon her Bulbul. Edward Lear. FaBoNo
She sits with one hand poised against her head. Dialogue. Adrienne Rich. TAP
She sits within the white oak hall. Helen. Edward A. U. Valentine. AA
She slid past. And She Was Bad. Marvin Wyche, Jr. AmNP
She slipped. Heels over head she landed. Portrait. Gail Fox. NOBC
She smil'd, and more of pleasure than disdain. The Sea-Nymph's Parting. Walter Savage Landor. *Fr.* Gebir. FaBoEn
She smiled behind a lawny cloud. Fancy Dress. Dorothea MacKellar. PoAu-1
She Smiled like a Holiday. *Unknown.* OxBoLi
She smiles and smiles, and will not sigh. Urania. Matthew Arnold. HBV-1
She softly droops here maiden eyes. A Russian Spring Song with Minaiev. Thomas Walsh. GoBC

She sought him east, she sought him west. Rare Willie Drowned in Yarrow; or, The Water o Gamrie. *Unknown.* ESPB
She sought the Studios, beckoning to her side. Heiress and Architect. Thomas Hardy. VLP
She speaks always in her own voice. The Portrait. Robert Graves. CABA; CMoP
She Speaks the Morning's Filigree. Philip Lamantia. VGW
She spent her time recalling. Play-acting. Frances Barber. GoYe
She spent three hundred and sixty four days a year. Grandmother Jackson. David Jackson. OBCP
She spoke no English. Eureka. Ruth O. Maunders. AMV-80
She spoke to me gently with words of sweet meaning. Song. Patrick MacDonogh. NeIP
She springs from the ground-clinging thicket, her face. Veneris Venefica Agrestis. Charles Tomlinson, *after* Lucio Piccolo. OBVE
She stands/ In the quiet darkness. Troubled Woman. Langston Hughes. CTBA; PCP
She stands as pale as Parian statues stand. A Soul. Christina Rossetti. WPOW
She stands beside me, stands away. Like Rousseau. Amiri Baraka. PoA
She stands full-throated and with careless pose. The Onondaga Madonna. Duncan Campbell Scott. PeCV
She stands in the dead center like a star. The Mother. S. S. Gardons. NePoEA-2
She stares from out the wagon as/ It trails the dimming road. The Woman in the Wagon. Clyde Robertson. PoOW
She stay'd not for her robes, but straight arose. Christopher Marlowe. *Fr.* Hero and Leander. UnTE
She stole his eyes because they shone. The Kleptomaniac. Leonora Speyer. HBMV
She stole my pencil-case, red leather. The Thief. Josephine Jacobsen. WPE
She stood/ apart from the grazing herd. The Death of an Elephant. Gianfranco Pagnucci. NU
She stood alone amidst the April fields. The Spring Is Late. Louise Chandler Moulton. HBV-2
She stood at the bar of justice. "Guilty or Not Guilty?" *Unknown.* BeLS; BLPA
She stood breast high amid the corn. Ruth. Thomas Hood. BoLoP; EnLoPo; EnRP; GN; HBV-1; LoBV; NOBE; OBEV; OBNC; OBVV; TrePS
She stood hanging wash before sun. Ghetto Lovesong—Migration. Carole Gregory Clemmons. NBP; NMM; PoBA
She Stoops to Conquer, *sel.* Goldsmith.
Song: "Let school-masters puzzle their brain," *fr.* I, ii. BIrV; OAEP; ViBoPo
(Three Jolly Pigeons, The.) PoRA
(Three Pigeons, The.) ELP
She straddles me like this. The Minotaur. Robert Gibb. FAZ
She stroked molten tones. Yonosa House. R. T. Smith. STE; Str
She strolls in the valley, alone. Madwoman at Rodmell. Michele Roberts. BrRo
She suffers like a red stone, small as a carat. Sisters. Sandra McPherson. AmPA
She suns on grass, my dark, my gifted mistress. Nude. Harold Witt. ErPo
She swam smiling in the river. Waiting to Be Fed. Ray A. Young Bear. CDW
She sweeps with many-colored brooms. Emily Dickinson. SaC
She talks about the law. The Unteaching. Carol Oles. SOTS
She talks not, plays not, visits not, in bed. *Unknown.* FaBoEE
She Tells Her Love while Half Asleep. Robert Graves. BoLoP; EBEV; FaBoTw; GBL; NOBE; OxBTC
She tells me with claret she cannot agree. Drinking Song. *Unknown.* NOBL
She tells us an interminable story, from television. The Somerset Dam for Supper. John Holmes. NYBP
She that but little patience knew. On a Political Prisoner. W. B. Yeats. OAEL-2; OBMV
She That Denies Me [I Would Have]. Thomas Heywood. *Fr.* The Rape of Lucrece. ErPo; UnTE
(Valerius on Women.) HBV-1
She that holds me under the laws of love. Sir Arthur Gorges. GBL
She that I pursue, still flies me. Les Amours. Charles Cotton. HBV-1
She That Is Memory's Daughter. Vernon Watkins. NYBP
She, the sensual creature, the green singer. Slow Dancer That No One Hears but You. Duane Niatum. CDW
She—the woman whom I loved. The Avenger. James Wright. TwAmPo
She thinks that even up in heaven. *See* She even thinks that up in heaven.
She thus; when I had great desire to prove. Homer, *tr. by* George Chapman. *Fr.* The Odyssey, XI. OBVE
She Tied Up Her Few Things. John Clare. HAP
She, to Him. Thomas Hardy. OBEV; OBVV; OxBTC
She told how they used to form for the country dances. One We Knew. Thomas Hardy. VLP
She Told Me. James C. Kilgore. SOTS
She told the story, and the whole world wept. Harriet Beecher Stowe. Paul Laurence Dunbar. BPo
She, too, the voyaging in doors and Keys. This Alice. Herbert Morris. PoRA
She took her name beneath according skies. The Ritual. E. J. Pratt. NoAM
She took the bone from her arm. The Empress. Diane Wakoski. CoPo
She took the dappled partridge flecked [*or* fleckt] with blood. Sonnet. Tennyson. CABA; FM
She tosses and rumples alone on the double bed. Flying Fox. Thomas W. Shapcott. CBAP
She touches me. Her fingers nibble gently. In Love. David Wevill. MoCV
She transplanted each spruce, blue as the. Spruce. Phillip William George. VoR
She tripped and fell against a star. Innocence. Anne Spencer. CDC
She truly needs good character. Women. *Yoruba Oral Tradition, tr. by* Ulli Beier. WTO
She turned in the high pew, until her sight. A Church Romance. Thomas Hardy. FaBoTw; NOBE; OxBTC; VLP
She turns and calls him by name. His Wife. Rachel, *tr. by* Sholom J. Kahn. WPOW
She turns the pillow, smoothes the rumpled bed. Rites for a Demagogue. Anthony Thwaite. NePoEA-2
She used to let her golden hair fly free. Petrarch, *tr. by* Morris Bishop. Sonnets to Laura: To Laura in Life, LXIX. NAWM-1
She wadna bake, she wadna brew. The Wife Wrapt in Wether's Skin. *Unknown.* BaBo; ESPB
She Waited. Tania Van Zyl. PeSA
She waited on the 7th floor. Frank Albert and Viola Benzena Owens. Notzake Shange. BlSi
She wakes long before he does. A fierce shock. Aubade. Mekeel McBride. MAYP
She walked along the crowded street. Revelation. Blanche Taylor Dickinson. CDC
She Walked Unaware. Patrick MacDonogh. BoLoP; ErPo; FaBoTw; NeIP; OnYI; OxBI
She Walks. Joseph Joel Keith. ISi
She walks down the road. Girl with the Green Skirt. Dana Naone. CDW
She Walks in Beauty. Byron. AWP; BLPA; BoLoP; CABA; ChER; ELP; EnRP; FaBoBe; FaBoEn; FaFP; FF; FiP; FPL; HBV-1; HBVY; HeIP; InPS; LiTB; LoBV; NIP; NOBE; NoP; OAEP; OBEV; OBNC; OBRV; PoEL-4; PrIm; RoGo; SeCeV; TreF; TrGrPo; WHA
("She walks in beauty like the night.") GTBS; GTBS-P
She walks—the lady of my delight. The Shepherdess [*or* The Lady of the Lambs]. Alice Meynell. ACP; AWP; GoBC; HBV-1; HBVY; MoBrPo; OBEV; OBVV; PeD; SBG; TreFS
"She Wandered after Strange Gods." Laura Benét. HBMV
She wanders in the April woods. Agatha. Alfred Austin. HBV-1
She wanders up and down the main. Derelict. Elisabeth Cavazza Pullen. AA
She wanted rain. Dust. Kathleen Spivack. BoWoP
She wanted to be a dancer. Palace Dancer, Dancing at Last. Rayna Green. TWSS
She wanted to depict man and woman. An Artist Draws a Peach. Patricia Hampl. PoDr
She wants what no clerk in the city can bring her. At the Millinery Shop. Daniel Mark Epstein. MAYP
She Warns Him. Frances Cornford. EnLoPo
She Was a Beauty. H. C. Bunner. AA; HBV-1
She was a city of patience; of proud name. Ypres. Laurence Binyon. MMA
She was a gently shaking chandelier. Denials 1. Jane Somerville. AMV-80
She was a high-class bitch and a dandy. Epitaph. Theodore Spencer. LiTA
She was a maid of high degree. He Took Her. Tom Masson. OBAL
She Was a Phantom of Delight. Wordsworth. BLPL; EnRP; FaBoBe; FaBV; FaFP; GTBS; GTBS-P; HeIP; LiTB; LoBV; NoP; OAEL-2; OAEP; OBRV; OHFP; PoEL-4; PoPl; TrGrPo; ViBoPo
(Perfect Woman.) HBV-1; OBEV; TreF
She Was a Pretty Horse. Joy Harjo. TWSS
She Was a Pretty Little Girl. Ramon Perez de Ayala, *tr. fr. Spanish by* Alida Malkus. FaPON
She was a queen of noble Nature's crowning. The Solitary-Hearted. Hartley Coleridge. HBV-1
She was a quiet little body. Silence. Winifred Welles. HBMV
She was a sweet country lassie. Blackpool Breezes. *Unknown.* CoMu
She was a Virgin of austere regard. Giles Fletcher. *Fr.* Christ's Victory and Triumph. ViBoPo
She was a weaver. Arachne. Jody Aliesan. LTB

She was a woman peerless in her station. On Mistress Nicely, a Pattern for Housekeepers. Thomas Hood. OBRV
She was afraid of men. Chicken-Licken. Maya Angelou. FF
She was all around me. The Blue Wing. Donald Hall. ConAP
She Was All That You Loved. Halldór Laxness, *tr. fr. Icelandic by* Magnús Á. Árnason. PoPl
She was as lovely as a flower. Dream Tryst. Richard Le Gallienne. HBMV
She was beautiful that evening and so gay. An Escape. Abu Nuwas, *tr. by* E. Powys Mathers. ErPo
She Was Bred in Old Kentucky, *with music.* Harry Braisted. FSN
She was built for the hard voyage. Tanker. Christopher Middleton. NMP
She was careerish in a gentle way. Domestic: Climax. Merrill Moore. ErPo
She was cleaning—there is always. Black Silk. Tess Gallagher. MAYP
She was generous, helpful, went out of her way. Epitaph on a Career Woman. William Cole. PV
She was in her orange Volks waiting. Hell Hath No Fury. Charles Bukowski. GP
She was in the garden, sequestered behind bushes, as night came. The Garden. Susan Griffin. *Fr.* Woman and Nature. NPGG
She was just a parson's daughter. It's the Syme the Whole World Over. *Unknown.* FSW
She was lyin face down in her face. Song. William Knott. MAT
She was my staff and I am blind. Jana Bai, *tr. fr. Marathi by* Willis Barnstone. BoWoP
She was never a dog that had much sense. Of an Ancient Spaniel in Her Fifteenth Year. Christopher Morley. GDP
She was newly betrothed, and. Cornelia's Window. Julie Kane. AMV-81
She was not as pretty as women I know. My Kate. Elizabeth Barrett Browning. OBVV; OHFP; WBLP
She was not so sweet as you would think. What the Animals Said. Peter Serchuk. HoAn
She was only a woman, famished for loving. A Tragedy. Théophile Marzials. HBV-1
She Was Poor but She Was Honest. *Unknown.* ErPo; FaBoCo; FiBHP; GBP; NOBL
(It's the Same the Whole World Over, *diff. vers.*) UnTE
(Poor but Honest.) OxBoLi
She was seated of her goodness on my knee. The Snake. Hilary Corke. PV
She was skilled in music and the dance. Alas! Poor Queen. Marion Angus. BSV; GoTS; OxBS
She was so aesthetic and culchud. The Cultured Girl Again. Ben King. FiBHP; OBAL
She was so little—little in her grave. The Mother Who Died Too. Edith M. Thomas. AA
She was so small and pretty. Art's Variety. David McFadden. NeAC
She was still upset. Bubba Esther, 1888. Ruth Whitman. AMV-81
She was the daughter of Glubstein the Glover. Villanelle of a Villainess. Edwin Meade Robinson. HBMV
She was the human chalice. Venite Adoremus. Margery Cannon. GoBC
She was urgent to speak of the moon: she offered delight. An Old Woman Speaks of the Moon. Ruth Pitter. WPE
She was wearing the coral taffeta trousers. Full Moon. V. Sackville-West. MoShBr
She Was Young and Blithe and Fair. Harold Monro. HBV-1
She wasn't the least bit pretty. The Factory Girl. J. A. Phillips. SaC
She wears her middle age like a cowled. From a Correct Address in a Suburb of a Major City. Helen Sorrells. PAI; WPE
She wears, my beloved, a rose upon her head. Requiem. John Frederick Matheus. CDC
She wears trousers. Mary Ackerman, 1938. Diane Glancy. STE
She Weeps over Rahoon. James Joyce. ViBoPo
She welcomes him with pretty impatience. The Visit. Ogden Nash. FiBHP
She went about accustomed tasks. Loss. Julia Johnson Davis. HBMV
She went along the road. Hagar. Francis Lauderdale Adams. OxBS
She went away from us upon a snow-white/ steed. The Dwarf. Gerard Locklin. DFT; GP
She Went to Stay. Robert Creeley. OBAL
She went up the mountain to pluck wild herbs. Old and New. *Unknown, tr. by* Arthur Waley. AWP
She went upstairs to make her bed. The Butcher's Boy. *Unknown.* FSW
She Wept, She Railed. Stanley Kunitz. ErPo; VGW
She, who could neither rest nor sleep. Alas! Sadi, *tr. by* L. Cranmer-Byng. *Fr.* The Gulistan. AWP
She who has no love for women. Calliope in the Labour Ward. Elaine Feinstein. BrRo
She who has power to call her man. An Unsaid Word. Adrienne Rich. NMM
She who hath felt a real pain. John Gay. EnLoPo
She who is always in my thoughts prefers. Bhartrihari, *tr. fr. Sanskrit by* John Brough. BoLoP; DBV
She, who so long has lain. New Love, New Life. Amy Levy. OBVV
She who to Heaven more Heaven doth annex. On a Virtuous Young Gentlewoman That Died Suddenly. William Cartwright. OBEV
She who usually feeds us. Teeth. Susan Griffin. NPGG
She who was burned more than half her body. The Praises. Charles Olson. VGW
She who was easy for any chance lover. Effie. Sterling A. Brown. BANP
She who with innocent and tender hands. The Monstrous Marriage. William Carlos Williams. MoPo
She whose matchless beauty staineth. *Unknown.* OBSC
She wishes her eyes did not sting mornings. Fish. Sandra Witt. AMV-80
She with his sight made breathless haste to meet him. Homer, *tr. by* George Chapman. *Fr.* The Iliad, VI. ViBoPo
She woke at length, but not as sleepers wake. The Death of Haidée. Byron. *Fr.* Don Juan, IV. FiP
She Wolf, The. Muriel Spark. NYBP
She wore a new "terra-cotta" dress. A Thunderstorm in Town. Thomas Hardy. BoLoP; EnLoPo; GBL
She Wore a Wreath of Roses. Thomas Haynes Bayly. BeLS
She Would if She Could, *sel.* Sir George Etherege.
To Little or No Purpose. UnTE
She wouldn't believe. Magical Eraser. Shel Silverstein. WSC
Sheaf, The. Andrew Young. ChTr
Sheaf-Tosser. Eric Rolls. PoAu-2
Sheafe of snakes used heretofore to be, A. To Mr. George Herbert. John Donne. OBVE
Shear your sheep in May. *Unknown.* FaBoUs
Shearer's Song, The. *Unknown.* PoAu-1
Shearer's Wife, The. Louis Esson. PoAu-1
Shearing, as the gardener. That's All? Anna Hajnal, *tr. by* Jascha Kessler. PBWP
Shearing Grass. Peter Redgrove. NePoEA-2
Sheath and Knife. *Unknown.* CH; ESPB (A *and* E *vers.*); ViBoFo
Sheaves, The. E. A. Robinson. AP; AWP; CMoP; CoBMV; FaBV; HAP; MoAB; MoAmPo; NePA; NoAM; NOBA; OxBA; TAP; WHA
Sheba, now let down your hair. The Puppet Dreams. Conrad Aiken. *Fr.* Punch, the Immortal Liar. MoAmPo
Shechem. David Shevin. VWA
Shed, The. Charles L. O'Donnell. ISi
Shed a tear for Twickham Tweer. Twickham Tweer. Jack Prelustky. RHPC
Shed in blue-grey weatherboard with a high, A. Hillside. Alexander Craig. PoAu-2
Shed no tear! O, shed no tear! Fairy [*or* Faery] Song. Keats. CH; FaPON; HBV-1
She'd Say. Frank Davey. NOBC
Shee brought her to her joyous paradize. The Garden of Adonis. Spenser. *Fr.* The Faerie Queene, III, 6. PoEL-1
Shee is dead; and all which die. The Dissolution. John Donne. OAEP; SeCV-1
Shee with whom troopes of Bustuary slaves. A Satyre entituled the Witch. *Unknown.* CoMu
Sheep. W. H. Davies. LiTM; MoBrPo
Sheep. Robert Francis. LCAP
Sheep. Samuel Hoffenstein. TrJP
Sheep, The. "Seumas O'Sullivan." OxBI
Sheep. Hal Porter. PoAu-2
Sheep, The. Ann *or* Jane Taylor. OxBChV
Sheep!/ Unhappy connotation. Bleat of Protest. Mildred Weston. FiBHP
Sheep and Lambs. Katharine Tynan. AnIV; HBV-2; OBEV; OBVV; OnYI; OxBI
Sheep and the Goat, The. George Macdonald. EBVV
Sheep are coming home in Greece, The. The Homecoming of the Sheep. Francis Ledwidge. HBMV
Sheep Beezness, The. S. Omar Barker. BPAW
Sheep Child, The. James Dickey. CAPP; GP; NoAM; NOBA; Prf; TAP
Sheep Country. Peggy Pond Church. BPAW
Sheep Dipping. Norman MacCaig. OxBC
Sheep Fair, A. Thomas Hardy. Prf
Sheep get up and make their many tracks, The. Sheep in Winter. John Clare. BoAnP
Sheep in Fog. Sylvia Plath. LCAP; NaP
Sheep in the Rain. James Wright. AMV-80
Sheep in the Sheade. William Barnes. FM
Sheep in Winter. John Clare. BoAnP
Sheep is blind, The; a passing owl. The Blind Sheep. Randall Jarrell. NYBP; OBAL
Sheep Ranching. Owen Wister. BPAW
Sheep Shearing. *Unknown.* OBET
Sheepbells. Edmund Blunden. BrPo

Sheepdog Trials in Hyde Park. C. Day Lewis. NoAM; NoP; OxBTC
Sheepfol', De. Sarah Pratt McLean Greene. AA; HBV-2
Sheepheards Daffadill, The. Michael Drayton. *See* Gorbo and Batte.
Sheep-Herder, The. Charles Badger Clark, Jr. BPAW
Sheepherder, The. Lew Sarett. AmFN; FaPON
Sheepherder Blues. Luci Tapahonso. STE
Sheep-Herder's Lament, The. Arthur Chapman. BPAW
Sheeprancher Named John, A. Gretel Ehrlich. MAYP
Sheep's in the meadow, The. Bonny at Morn. *Unknown.* GBP
Sheepstor. L. A. G. Strong. HBMV
Sheer Joy. Ralph Spaulding Cushman. TRV
Sheet of water which reflects the house, The. Ornamental Water. Louise Townsend Nicholl. NePoAm
Sheet of writing paper, The. The Alchemist. Richard Church. OxBTC
Sheeted in steel, embedded face to face. At a Low Mass for Two Hot-Rodders. X. J. Kennedy. Psk
Sheets are exposed like film, The. Finding an Old Newspaper in the Woods. Robert Morgan. WeW
Sheets of night mist travel a long valley, The. Mist Forms. Carl Sandburg. CMoP; HBMV
Sheets were frozen hard, and they cut the naked hand, The. Christmas at Sea. Robert Louis Stevenson. BLPL; BrPo; CH; EBVV; EtS; FaBoBe; FaBV; HBV-1; MOS; OBVV
Sheffield Apprentice, The. *Unknown.* OBET
(Sheffield 'Prentice, The, *diff. version.*) AmFP
Sheffield grinder's a terrible blade, The. The Grinders; or, The Saddle on the Right Horse. *Unknown.* GBP
Sheffield 'Prentice, The. *Unknown.* *See* Sheffield Apprentice, The.
Sheiling, The. Edward Thomas. PoSH
Shekhina[h]. Karl Wolfskehl, tr. fr. German. TrJP, *tr by* Carol North Valhope *and* Ernst Morwitz; VWA, *tr. by* Erna Baber Rosenfeld
Shekhina and the Kiddushim. Edouard Roditi. VWA
Shelby County, Ohio. November 1974. G. E. Murray. FAZ
Shell, The. James Stephens. BoNaP; CH; CMoP; MoAB; MoBrPo; MOS; MoShBr; MoVE
Shell, The. Tennyson. *Fr.* Maud. GN
(See What a Lovely Shell.) BoNaP; GoJo; PoEL-5
She'll Be Comin' Round the Mountain. *Unknown.* AS (A *and* B *vers., with music*); BLSo, *with music*; FSW
She'll come at dusky first of day. August. Francis Ledwidge. OxBI
She'll Do It. Burns. *See* Muirland Meg.
Shellbrook William Barnes. OBNC; VLP, 2 *vers.*
Shelley. Robert Browning. *Fr.* Pauline. OBRV
("Sun-treader—life and light be thine for ever.") VLP
Shelley and jazz and lieder and love and hymn-tunes. Louis MacNeice. *Fr.* Autumn Journal. NOBL
Shelley, madman, made his rhymes. Wiser Than the Children of Light. Monk Gibbon. NeIP
"Shelley? Oh yes, I say him often then." The General Public. Stephen Vincent Benét. GLGT
Shelley! whose song so sweet was sweetest here. To Shelley. Walter Savage Landor. ViBoPo
Shelley's "Arethusa" Set to New Measures. Robert Duncan. CMoP
Shelley's loves. For a Little Lady. Fred Saidy. InMe
Shelley's Skylark. Thomas Hardy. CoBMV; FaBV; PBBP; VLP
Shell-less, on your slimey trail. After Tempest. Percy MacKaye. FYAP
Shellpicker, The. Ronald Perry. NePoEA-2
Shells. Medb Mahony. AMV-80
Shells. T. Sturge Moore. SeCePo
Shells. Kathleen Raine. ImOP
Shell's Song, The. Keats. EtS
Shelly. James McIntyre. FiBHP
Shelly crawlers each returning year, The. William Diaper. *Fr.* Halieutica. FM
Shelter. Gene Derwood. NePA
Shelter this candle from the wind. To the Wife of a Sick Friend. Edna St. Vincent Millay. SBG
Sheltered from the falling snow, inside the stable. Chekhov Comes to Mind at Harvard. William T. Freeman. AMV-81
Sheltered from the spring wind by/ A silver screen. The Old Anguish. Chu Shu-chen, *tr. by* Kenneth Rexroth. BoWoP
Shelving slimy river Don, The. The River Don. *Unknown.* GBP
Shema. Primo Levi, *tr. fr. Italian by* Ruth Feldman *and* Brian Swann. VWA
Shema Yisrael. *Unknown.* TrJP
Shemuel. Edward Ernest Brown. HBV-2
Shenandoah, *sel.* Delmore Schwartz.
Let Us Consider Where the Great Men Are. MoAB; MoAmPo
Shenandoah. *Unknown.* AmSS, *with music*; AmFN; BLSo, *with music*; FSW; ShS, *with music*; TrAS, with music; TreFT
(Wide Mizzoura, The.) AS
Shep lies long-bodied upon the auburn grass. February's Forgotten Mitts. Raymond Knister. NOBC
Shepeheards boye, A (no better doe him call). January Eclogue. Spenser. *Fr.* The Shepheards Calender. FiP
Shep'erd Bwoy, The. William Barnes. EBVV
Sheperd upon a hill he satt, The. *Unknown.* *See* Can I Not Sing.
Shephard loveth thow me vell? Song. Jean Passerat, *tr. by* William Drummond of Hawthornden. OBVE
Shepheard and the Milkmaid, The. *Unknown.* CoMu
Shepheard Paris bore the Spartan bride, The. Theocritus, *tr. by* Dryden. Idylls, XXVII. OBVE
Shepheardes [*or* Shepeards *or* Shepherd's] Calender, The, *sels.* Spenser.
Aprill. PoEL-1
Ditty, A: In Praise of Eliza, Queen of the Shepherds. OBEV
(Ditty, A: "See where she sits upon the grassy green.") FaBoCH
("See where she sits upon the grassy green," 2 *sts.*) ViBoPo
Elisa ("Ye dainty nymphs, that in this blessed brook"). OBSC
(Lay to Eliza, The.) NOBE
August. OAEP
Perigot and Willye. LoBV
(It Fell upon a Holy Eve.) InvP
(Roundelay, A: "It fell upon a holy eve.") EIL
February.
Oak and the Brere, The. OBSC
January Eclogue. FiP
November. PoEL-1
Dido My Dear, Alas, Is Dead. ChTr
October. OAEL-1
(Contempt of Poetry, The.) OBSC
(October Eclogue.) PP
Shepheards, The. Henry Vaughan. AnAnS-1
(Shepheards, The.) SBVL
Shepheards Calendar, The. John Clare. *See* Shepherd's Calendar, The.
Shepheards Hunting, The. George Wither. *See* Shepherd's Hunting, The.
Shepheards Sirena, The. Michael Drayton. *See* Shepherd's Sirena, The.
Shepherd, The. Blake. *Fr.* Songs of Innocence. EnRP; HBV-1; LoBV; OBEC; TiPo
Shepherd. Edmund Blunden. HBMV
Shepherd, The. Mary Gilmore. PoAu-1
Shepherd. William Stafford. PoA
Shepherd, The. *Unknown.* UnTE
Shepherd, The. Wordsworth. *Fr.* The Prelude, VIII. OBNC
Shepherd and His Flock, The. Oswald Mbuyiseni Mtshali. GrPl
Shepherd and Shepherdess. Nicholas Breton. *Fr.* The Passionate Shepherd. OBSC
(Happy Countryman, The.) CH
(Merry Country Lad, The.) EIL; LoBV
(Pastoral.) ELP
Shepherd and Shepherdess. Thomas Hennell. FaBoTw
Shepherd and the Milkmaid, The. *Unknown.* UnTE
Shepherd and the Nymph, The. Walter Savage Landor. *See* Tamar's Wrestling.
Shepherd and the Shepherdess, The. *Unknown.* OBET
Shepherd Boy, The. Edward J. O'Brien. HBMV
Shepherd-Boy and the Wolf, The. Aesop, *tr. fr. Greek by* William Ellery Leonard. AWP
Shepherd Boy Sings [in the Valley of Humiliation], The. Bunyan. *Fr.* The Pilgrim's Progress. EaLo; GN; HBV-2; HBVY; NOBE; OBEV; WGRP
(Enough!) BLRP
("He that is down needs fear no fall.") EBEV
(Shepherd Boy's Song, The.) EBCP; TRV
(Shepherd's Song, The.) OxBoCh
(Song of Low Degree, A.) STF
(Song of the Shepherd in the Valley of Humiliation, The.) CavP; OBS
Shepherd Boys, The. Nicolas Saboly, *tr. fr. Provençal.* OHIP
Shepherd Boy's Song, The. Bunyan. *See* Shepherd Boy Sings, The.
Shepherd: Echo, I ween, will in the wood reply. A Gentle Echo on Woman. Swift. FiBHP
Shepherd Kept Sheep on a Hill So High, A. Thomas D'Urfey. CoMu; ErPo
Shepherd Left Behind, The. Mildred Plew Meigs. TrCP
Shepherd, Ned Vaughan, A. Ned Vaughan. Walter de la Mare. FaBoEE
Shepherd of King Admetus, The. James Russell Lowell. HBVY
Shepherd of Meriador, The. Wilfred Rowland Childe. HBMV
Shepherd on his journey heard when nigh, The. The Fox. John Clare. BoAnP
Shepherd sat 'neath a tree one day, A. The Shepherd. *Unknown.* UnTE
Shepherd set him under a thorn, A. The Merry Bagpipes. *Unknown.* CoMu
Shepherd, Shepherd, Hark. Saint Teresa, *tr. fr. Spanish by* Arthur Symons. AWP
Shepherd, Show Me How to Go, *with music.* Mary Baker Eddy. AH
Shepherd shrieves in Egyptian light, De. Pocomania. Derek Walcott. NoAM
Shepherd Song. Sir Philip Sidney. *Fr.* Arcadia. SiPS

Shepherd Speaks, The. John Erskine. TrCP
Shepherd stands at one end of the arena, A. Sheepdog Trials in Hyde Park. C. Day Lewis. NoAM; NoP; OxBTC
Shepherd to His Love, The. Christopher Marlowe. *See* Passionate Shepherd to His Love, The.
Shepherd upon a [*or* the] Hill, The. *Unknown.* *See* Can I Not Sing.
Shepherd, what's love, I pray thee tell? The Shepherd's Description of Love. Sir Walter Ralegh. ViBoPo
Shepherd, who can pass such wrong. Song. Jorge de Montemayor, *tr. by* Bartholomew Young. *Fr.* Diana. ElL
Shepherd Who Stayed, The. Theodosia Garrison. OHIP; PChr
Shepherd, wilt thou take counsel of the bird. Philomel to Corydon. William Young. AA
Shepherdess. Norman Cameron. Three Love Poems, III. GBL; GTBS-P; OxBS
Shepherdess, The. Alice Meynell. ACP; AWP; GoBC; HBV-1; HBVY; MoBrPo; OBVV; PeD; SBG; TreFS
(Lady of the Lambs, The.) OBEV
Shepherdess and the Sailor, The. *Unknown.* OBET
Shepherdess' Valentine, *sel.* Francis Andrewes.
"I bear, in sign of love." OFD
Shepherds, The. Beren Van Slyke. GoYe
Shepherds, The. Henry Vaughan. *See* Shepheards, The.
Shepherds all, and maidens fair. The Priest's Chant [*or* The Evening Knell *or* Evening Song *or* Folding the Flocks]. John Fletcher. *Fr.* The Faithful Shepherdess, II, i. CH; ElL; GN; OBS
Shepherds armed with staff and sling. Carol of Patience. Robert Graves. OBCP
Shepherds at Bethlehem, The. *Unknown.* *See* Hail, Comly and Clene.
Shepherd's [*or* Shepheards] Calendar, The, *sels.* John Clare.
February. NOBE; OBNC
(February: A Thaw.) NCEP
"Milkmaid singing, The," *sel.* OBRV
"Loud is the summer's busy song," *fr.* July. OBRV
October Eclogue. PP
"Or, trying simple charms and spells." FaBoUs
Shepherds' Carol. Norman Nicholson. OBCP
Shepherd's Coat, A. Lilian Bowes Lyon. ChMP
Shepherd's Complaint, A. Richard Barnfield. OBSC
Shepherd's Complaint, The, *sel.* John Dickenson.
Tityrus to His Fair Phyllis. ElL
Shepherd's Daffodil, The. Michael Drayton. *See* Gorbo and Batte.
Shepherd's daughter watching sheep, A. The Knight and the Shepherd's Daughter. *Unknown.* AmFP
Shepherd's Description of Love, The. Sir Walter Ralegh. ViBoPo
Shepherd's Despair, The. Thomas Dermody. OnYI
Shepherd's Dirge, The. George Peele. *See* Dirge, The: "Welladay, welladay, poor Colin, thou art going to the ground."
Shepherd's Dochter, The. *Unknown.* *See* Knight and Shepherd's Daughter, The.
Shepherd's Dog, The. Leslie Norris. OBCP
Shepherd's Garland, The, *sels.* Michael Drayton.
Batte's Song: "What is love but the desire," *fr.* Eclogue VII (1606 ed.) LoBV
Cassamen and Dowsabell, *fr.* Eclogue VIII (1593 ed.). OBSC
(Ballad of Dowsabell, The.) LoBV
(Dowsabell.) UnTE
Eclogue: "Late 'twas in June," *fr.* Eclogue IX (1606 ed.). OBSC
Gorbo and Batte, *fr.* Eclogue IX (1606 ed.). LoBV
("Gorbo, as thou cam'st this way.") ViBoPo
(Ninth Eclogue.) OAEP
(Sheepheard's Daffadil, The.) FaBoEn
(Shepherd's Daffodil, The.) ElL
Roundelay, A: "Tell me, thou skilful shepherd's swain," *fr.* Eclogue IX (1606 ed.). ElL
Rowland's Rhyme, *fr.* Eclogue II (1606 ed.). OBSC
Song to Beta: "O thou fair silver Thames," *fr.* Eclogue III (1593 ed.). OBSC
Tenth Eclogue, The. JCP
Shepherd's Gift, A. Anytes, *tr. fr. Greek by* John William Burgon. AWP
Shepherd's Gratitude, The. Virgil, *tr. fr. Latin by* Charles Stuart Calverley. Eclogues, I. AWP
Shepherds Had an Angel, The. Christina Rossetti. OHIP
Shepherd's Holiday. Elinor Wylie. CrMA; HBMV
Shepherd's Home, The. William Shenstone. GN
Shepherd's House, The, *sel.* Alfred de Vigny, *tr. fr. French by* Robert Bly.
"Eva, I agree to love, among creation, all the creatures!" NU
Shepherd's Hunting, The, *sels.* George Wither.
Fourth Eglogue, The, *abr.* SeCV-1
Philarete Praises Poetry, *fr.* Eclogue IV. OBS
Shepherd's Hut, The. Andrew Young. DTC; GrPl; OxBTC
Shepherds' Hymn, The ("Gloomy night embraced the place"). Richard Crashaw. *Fr.* In the Holy Nativity of Our Lord God. NOBE
("Gloomy night embraced the place.") ViBoPo
(Hymn Sung As by the Shepherds, A.) GoBC
(Verses from the Shepherd's Hymn.) OBEV
Shepherd's Hymn, The ("We saw Thee in Thy balmy nest"). Richard Crashaw. *Fr.* In the Holy Nativity of Our Lord. ACP; TrGrPo
Shepherd's Lament, The. Goethe, *tr. fr. German by* Bayard Taylor. AWP
Shepherd's Ode, The. Robert Greene. *Fr.* Tullie's Love. OBSC
Shepherds on old hills, with robber. Gallery Shepherds. Patricia Beer. OxBC
Shepherd's Pipe, The, *sel.* William Browne.
Dawn of Day. ElL
Shepherd's Play (Townley cycle), *sel.* *Unknown.*
"It is sayde full ryfe." FaBoUs
Shepherd's Plea, The. Christopher Marlowe. *See* Passionate Shepherd to His Love, The.
Shepherd's Praise of Diana, The. Sir Walter Ralegh. *See* Diana.
Shepherds sing, The; and shall I silent be. Shall I Be Silent? George Herbert. TRV
Shepherd's Sirena, The, *sel.* Michael Drayton.
Trent, The. FaBoPP
(Jovial Shepheard's Song, The.) PoEL-2
(Sirena.) OBEV
Shepherd's Song, The. John Bunyan. *See* Shepherd Boy Sings, The.
Shepherd's Song. Tennyson. *See* Come Down, O Maid.
Shepherd's Song at Christmas. Langston Hughes. PChr
Shepherds' Song, Sung before Queen Anne, on the Wiltshire Downs, 11 June 1613, The, *sel.* George Ferebe.
Houseless Downs, The. FaBoPP
Shepherd's star with trembling glint, The. En Bateau. Paul Verlaine, *tr. by* Arthur Symons. AWP
Shepherd's Tale, The. James Kirkup, *after the French of* Raoul Ponchon. OBCP
Shepherd's Tale, A. Sir Philip Sidney. *Fr.* Arcadia. SiPS
Shepherds that on this mountain ridge abide. Cleitagoras. Leonidas of Tarentum, *tr. by* William M. Hardinge. AWP
Shepherd's Week, The, *sels.* John Gay.
Blouzelinda's Funeral, *fr.* Friday; or, The Dirge. OBEC
Thursday; or, The Spell. PoEL-3
"Last May-day fair I search'd to find a snail." FaBoUs
"When first the year, I heard the cuckoo sing." PBBP
Tuesday; or, The Ditty. NOEC
(Ditty, The.) LoBV
Wednesday; or, The Dumps. OAEL-1
Shepherds went their hasty way, The. A Christmas Carol. Samuel Taylor Coleridge. ISi; OxBoCh
Shepherd's Wife's Song, The. Robert Greene. *Fr.* Greene's Mourning Garment. ElL; HAP; HBV-1; LoBV; OBSC; ViBoPo
Sheridan. Robert Lowell. DiL
Sheridan at Cedar Creek. Herman Melville. LiTA; PAH
Sheridan's Ride. Thomas Buchanan Read. BeLS; FaBoBe; FaBV; FaFP; GN; HBV-2; HBVY; OHFP; OHIP; PAH; TreF; WBLP; YaD
Sheriff. Ambrose Bierce. DBV
Sheriff followed hard and fast, a muy hombre he, The. *Unknown.* CoSo
Sheriff's Report, The. Arthur Chapman. BPAW
Sherman. Richard Watson Gilder. AA
Sherman Cyclone, The. *Unknown.* AmFP
Sherman's in Savannah. Oliver Wendell Holmes. PAH
Sherman's March to the Sea. Samuel H. M. Byers. PAH
(Song of Sherman's March to the Sea.) HBV-2
Sherpa gasped out as they mounted the slope, The. Poem, Neither Hilláryous Norgay. Gardner E. Lewis. FiBHP
Sherwood in the twilight, is Robin Hood awake? A Song of Sherwood. Alfred Noyes. FaPON; HBV-2; HBVY; MoBrPo; TiPo
She's a copperheaded waitress. Ella, in a Square Apron, along Highway 80. Judy Grahn. *Fr.* The Common Woman. NMM
She's a saucy fast packet and a packet of fame. The *Dreadnought, vers.* II. *Unknown.* ShS
She's All My Fancy Painted Him. "Lewis Carroll." CenHV; FaBoNo; NA
She's an enchanting little Israelite. Orientale. W. E. Henley. PeD
She's bin out here a-teachin' fer this winter now a-past. Romance of the Range. Robert V. Carr. PoOW
She's bitter to her country: hear me, Paris. Helen of Troy. Shakespeare. *Fr.* Troilus and Cressida, IV, i. TreFT
She's Free! Frances E. W. Harper. BlSi
She's Gone Blues. *Unknown.* BluL
She's gone. She was my love, my moon or more. Complaint. James Wright. NOBA; TAP; VGW
She's had a Vassar education. An American Girl. Brander Matthews. AA
She's Hoy'd Me Out o' Lauderdale. *Unknown.* CoMu

She's learned to hold her gladness lightly. A Lesson in Detachment. Vassar Miller. NePoEA-2
She's like the Swallow. *Unknown.* FSW
She's little and she's low she's right down on the ground. She's Mine. *Unknown.* BluL
She's loveliest of the festal throng. The Rose and the Thorn. Paul Hamilton Hayne. AA; FaBoBe; HBV-1
She's My Love. Augustus Young, *tr. fr. Irish.* CIP
She's not a faultless woman; no! James Kenneth Stephen. *Fr.* After the Golden Wedding. EBVV
She's somewhere in the sunlight strong. Song. Richard Le Gallienne. HBV-1; OBEV; OBVV
She's tall and gaunt, and in her hard, sad face. Scrubber. W. E. Henley. In Hospital, XIX. BrPo
She's taught me that I mustn't bark. Remarks from the Pup. Burges Johnson. GDP
She's the camera. Judy-One. Don L. Lee. TAP
She's up there—Old Glory—where lightnings are sped. Our Flag Forever. Frank L. Stanton. PGD
Sheskinbeg. Elizabeth Shane. HBMV
Shetland, Hill Dawn. Robin Munro. PoSH
Shetland Pony. Maurice Lindsay. BSV
Shew! Fly, Don't Bother Me. *Unknown. See* Shoo Fly, Don't Bother Me.
Shew me thy feet; shew me thy legs, thy thighes. *See* Show me thy feet . . .
Shi King, *sels. Unknown, tr. fr. Chinese.*
  How Goes the Night? *tr. by* Helen Waddell. AWP
  I Wait My Lord, *tr. by* Helen Waddell. AWP
  Maytime, *tr. by* L. Cranmer-Byng. AWP
  Morning Glory, The, *tr. by* Helen Waddell. AWP
  Pear-Tree, The, *tr. by* Allen Upward. AWP
  Under the Pondweed, *tr. by* Helen Waddell. AWP
  Woman, *tr. by* H. A. Giles. AWP
  You Will Die, *tr. by* H. A. Giles. AWP
Shield from every dart, The. What Christ Is to Us. *Unknown.* BLRP
Shield: "Lonely wanderer, wounded with iron, A." *Unknown, tr. fr. Anglo-Saxon by* Charles W. Kennedy. *Fr.* Riddles (Exeter Book). AnOE
Shield of Achilles, The. W. H. Auden. EBEV; FaBoMo; GTBS-P; HAP; NePA; NOBE; NOCV; NoP; OAEP; PoA; SeCeV; WeW
Shield of War, The. Thomas Sackville. *See* Vision of War, A.
Shift, here, in town, not meanest among squires. On Lieutenant Shift. Ben Jonson. OBSV
Shifting his position to relieve a cramped limb. Christ. Daniel Hoffman. CoPo
Shiftless and shy, gentle and kind and frail. An Epitaph. J. C. Squire. HBMV
Shifty limpet on his rocky shore, The. Every Earthly Creature. John Malcolm Brinnin. LiTA
Shih Ching, *sels. Unknown, tr. fr. Chinese by* Arthur Waley.
  "Very handsome gentleman, A." BoWoP
  Widow's Lament. BoWoP
Shillin' a Day. Kipling. OAEP; ViBoPo
Shilling life will give you all the facts, A. Who's Who. W. H. Auden. CABA; CoBMV; MoAB; MoBrPo; NoAM
Shiloh; a Requiem. Herman Melville. AmFN; AP; FF; LiTA; NCEP; NOBA; NoP; OBWP; OxBA; PAL; SCV; ViBoPo; WiR
"Shimmer of Evil, The." Theodore Roethke. NePoAm-2
Shine alone, shine nakedly, shine like bronze. Nuances of a Theme by Williams. Wallace Stevens. CMoP
Shine forth into the night, O flame. Give Our Conscience Light. Aline B. Carter. TrPWD
Shine Just Where You Are. *Unknown.* STF
Shine, O sun! tenderly on my skin. Love Dirge. *Tr. fr. Maori by* John White. WTO
Shine, O thou sacred shepherds' star. The Houseless Downs. George Ferebe. *Fr.* The Shepherds' Song, Sung before Queen Anne, on the Wiltshire Downs, 11 June 1613. FaBoPP
Shine, "O world!" don't weary the gulping Pole. Frank O'Hara. *Fr.* Life on Earth. UnPo
Shine On, *with music. Unknown.* TrAS
Shine on me, moon. A Sentinel's Song. Rarawa Kerehoma, *tr. by* Barry Mitcalfe. WTO
Shine on me, oh, you gold, gold sun. Vacation Song. Edna St. Vincent Millay. YeAr
Shine on Me, Secret Splendor. Edwin Markham. TrPWD
Shine Out, Fair Sun [with All Your Heat]. *At. to* George Chapman. *Fr.* The Masque of the Twelve Months. ChTr; ELP
  (Song: "Shine out, fair sun, with all your heat.") ElL
Shine, Perishing Republic. Robinson Jeffers. CMoP; FF; LiTA; LiTM; MAT; MoAB; MoVE; NePA; NoAM; NOBA; NoP; OxBA; PAI; PrIm; TAP; UnPo; VGW; ViBoPo
  "And boys, be in nothing so moderate as in love of man," *sel.* TRV
Shine, Republic. Robinson Jeffers. AmFN; GOA
Shining. Kathleen Spivack. AMV-81
Shining children in the fog. The Swimming Lesson. Robert Hershon. NeAC
Shining daggers of the harbor lights, The. Evening on the Harbor. Virginia Lyne Tunstall. HBMV
Shining Eye of Horus cometh, The. He Kindleth a Fire. *Unknown, tr. by* Robert Hillyer. *Fr.* Book of the Dead. AWP
Shining neutral summer has no voice, The. In Memoriam: Ernst Toller. W. H. Auden. NYBP
Shining Night or Dick Daring, the Poacher, A. *Unknown.* CoMu
Shining pins that dart and click. Socks. Jessie Pope. SUMH
Shining waters rise and swell, The. The Drowning of Conaing. *Unknown, tr. by* Frank O'Connor. AnIL
Shiny coach squeaks and crawls over arid, The. Amtrak. Elliot Fried. PPJ
Shiny Little House, The. Nancy M. Hayes. SUS
Shiny record albums scattered over. As You Leave Me. Etheridge Knight. ConAP; FF; NNaP
Ship, The. Louise A. Doran. EtS
Ship, The. J. F. Hendry. NeBP
Ship, The. Charles Mackay. BLPA
Ship, The. Lloyd Mifflin. AA
Ship, The. J. C. Squire. CH
Ship, The. *Unknown.* PoLF
Ship, an Isle, a Sickle Moon, A. James Elroy Flecker. BrPo; FaBoRV; SyP
Ship Bottom. Richmond Lattimore. NePoAm-2
Ship-broken Men Whom Stormy Seas Sore Toss. William Fowler. BSV; GoTS
Ship-Builders, The. Whittier. EtS
Ship-Building Emperors Commanded. Peter Levi. NePoEA-2
Ship Burning and a Comet All in One Day, A. Richard Eberhart. NYBP
Ship Canal from the Atlantic to the Pacific, The. Francis Lieber. PAH
Ship Comes In, A. Oliver Jenkins. EtS
Ship from Thames. Rex Ingamells. PoAu-2
Ship goes sailing down the bay, The. Goodbye, My Lover, Goodbye. *Unknown.* FSW
Ship I have got in the North Country, A. The *Golden Vanity*. *Unknown.* FaBoCh; PoPle
Ship is floating in the harbour now, A. Shelley. *Fr.* Epipsychidion. OBRV
Ship, leaving or arriving, of my lover. After a Passage in Baudelaire. Robert Duncan. CMoP; PoA
Ship moves, The. 4th of July. William Carlos Williams. PoA
Ship near Shoals. Anna Wickham. HBMV
Ship of Death, The. D. H. Lawrence. CMoP; DTC; FaBoRV; FaBoTw; GTBS-P; LiTB; LoBV; MasP; MoAB: MoBrPo; MOS; NoAM; NoP; OAEL-2; OAEP; PrIm; ViBoPo
Ship of Earth, The. Sidney Lanier. MOS
Ship of Fools, The, *sels.* Alexander Barclay
  Ballade to Our Lady. ISi
  Geographers. ACP
  Preachment for Preachers. ACP
  Star of the Sea. ACP
  Tudor Rose, The. ACP
Ship of Rio, The. Walter de la Mare. CenHV; EtS; MOS; PDV; PoPle; TiPo
Ship of State, The. Horace, *tr. fr. Latin by* William Ewart Gladstone. Odes, I, 14. AWP
Ship of State, The. Longfellow. *Fr.* The Building of the Ship. FaBoBe; HBVY; OHIP; PAL
  (O Ship of State.) FaFP
  (Republic, The.) AA; PAH; WGRP
  (Sail On, O Ship of State.) FaPON; TreF
  ("Thou, too, sail on, O Ship of State.") MOS; PGD; YaD
Ship *Rambolee*, The, *with music. Unknown.* ShS
Ship That Never Returned, The, *with music. Unknown, diff. vers. of song by* Henry Clay Work. AS
Ship That Never Returned, The. Henry Clay Work. BLPA; FSW
Ship was built in Glasgow, and oh, she looked a daisy, A. In Prize. Cicely Fox Smith. WhC
Ship with shields before the sun, A. Near Avalon. William Morris. OAEL-2
Shiperd-boy, what is yer trade? The Beggar-Laddie. *Unknown.* ESPB
Shipman, The ("A Schipman was ther, wonyng fer by weste"). Chaucer. *Fr.* The Canterbury Tales: Prologue. EtS
  ("Shipman was ther, woning fer by weste, A.") MOS
Shipman, The ("The Parson him answered, 'Benedicte!' "). Chaucer, *mod. Fr.* The Canterbury Tales: Prologue to the Shipman's Tale. ACP
Shipmates, if you'll listen to me. Can't They Dance the Polka! *with music. Unknown.* ShS
Shipmen, The. William Hunnis. OBSC
Shipment to Maidanek. Ephim G. Fogel. OBWP; TrJP
Ships. Nancy Byrd Turner. SoPo; SUS

Ships are fitted, and the convoy sails, The. Convoy. William Jay Smith. WaP
Ships are lying in the bay, The. The Wanderer. Zoë Akins. HBMV
Ships at Sea. Barry Gray. EtS
Ship's Cook, a Captive Sings, The. Hugo von Hofmannsthal, *tr. fr. German by* Charles Wharton Stork. TrJP
Ships in Harbour. David Morton. EtS
Ship's master:/ before him, in the waist and before it. David Jones. *Fr.* The Anathemata. FaBoTw
Ships of Arcady, The. Francis Ledwidge. EtS
Ships of Saint John, The. Bliss Carman. EtS
Ships of Yule, The. Bliss Carman. CaP; HBVY; WHW
Ships That Pass in the Night. Paul Laurence Dunbar. BANP; CDC; MOS
Ships That Pass in the Night. Longfellow. *Fr.* Tales of a Wayside Inn: The Theologian's Tale. EtS; MOS
(Ocean of Life, The.) TreFT
Ships with Your Silver Nets. Wade Oliver. EtS
Shipwreck, The. Byron. *Fr.* Don Juan, II. OBRV; WHA
Shipwreck, The, *sels.* William Falconer.
All Hands Unmoor! *fr.* I. EtS
"As the proud horse with costly trappings gay," *fr.* II. MOS
(Shortening Sail.) EtS
"But now Athenian mountains they descry," *fr.* III. GoTL
"Four hours the sun his high meridian throne," *fr.* II. MOS
"In vain the cords and axes were prepared," *fr.* III. OBEC
Shipwreck, The. E. H. Palmer. NA
Shir Ma'alot/ A Song of Degrees. Richard Flantz. VWA
Shira. Howard Schwartz. VWA
Shires, The. *Unknown.* OxBM
Shirley Temple. Cyril R. Michael. PeD
Shirt, The. Hilda Morley. AMV-81
Shirt, The. Jon Silkin. NoAM
Shirt races in the meadow, A. Storm. Agnes Nemes Nagy, *tr. by* Laura Schiff. PBWP
Shirts, The. Tess Gallagher. MAYP
Shitty. Kingsley Amis. OxBC; TW
Shiva. Robinson Jeffers. NoAM; NOBA
Shlof Mayn Kind, Shlof Keseyder (Sleep My Child). *Unknown, tr. fr. Yiddish.* FSW
Shlup, shlup, the dog. Denise Levertov. Six Variations, III. HeIP; InPK
Shock, The. Larry Eigner. CoPo
Shocked that she missed the footbridge! The Suicide. V. R. Laing. PoA
Shocking Rape and Murder of Two Lovers. *Unknown.* CoMu
Shock's fate I mourn; poor Shock is now no more. An Elegy on a Lap-Dog. John Gay. HBV-1
Shoe. John Perreault. EAS
Shoe a little horse. *Unknown.* OxNR
Shoe Factory, The. Ruth Harwood. HBMV
Shoe Shop. Barton Sutter. SoSe
Shoe the colt, shoe the colt. Mother Goose. OxNR
Shoe the steed with silver. Sheridan at Cedar Creek. Herman Melville. LiTA; PAH
Shoe-tying, The. Robert Herrick. CaPo
Shoemaker, The ("As I was a-walking the other day"). *Unknown.* FaPON; SoPo
Shoemaker, The ("I am a shoemaker by my trade"), *with music. Unknown.* TrAS
Shoemaker makes shoes without leather, A. Riddle. *Unknown.* OxNR; SoPo
Shoemaker's Holiday, The, *sels.* Thomas Dekker.
Cold's the Wind, *fr.* V, iv. ViBoPo
(Drinking Song.) TrGrPo
(Hey Derry Derry.) SeCePo
(Saint Hugh.) OBSC
(Troll the Bowl!) ElL
Oh, the Month of May! *fr.* III, v. ElL; ViBoPo
(May.) OBSC
(Maytime.) TrGrPo
(Song: "O the month of May, the merry month of May.") PBBP
Shoemakker, The. *Unknown.* OBET
Shoes. Tom Robinson. SoPo; TiPo
Shoes are made to fit the feet. *Gond Oral Tradition, tr. by* V. Elwin *and* S. Hivale. WTO
Shoes fall on their feet. How Things Fall. Donald Finkel. VWA
Shoes instead of slippers down the stairs. The Couple Upstairs. Hugo Williams. POL
Shoes, secret face of my inner life. My Shoes. Charles Simic. CoAP
Shoichi brushed the black. Awakening. Lucien Stryk. SV
Sholom Aleichem. Elias Lieberman. TrJP
Sholto Peach Harrison you are no son of mine. Correspondence between Mr. Harrison in Newcastle and Mr. Sholto Peach Harrison in Hull. Stevie Smith. FaBoNO; OxBC
Shon a Morgan. *Unknown.* GBP
("Little Johnny Morgan.") OxNR
Shoo Fly, Don't Bother Me. *Unknown.* FSW
(Shew! Fly, Don't Bother Me, *longer version, with music, at. to* Billy Reeves *and to* T. Brigham Bishop.) PSoN
Shoo over! *Unknown.* PBBP
Shoofly, The. Felix O'Hare. AmFP
Shoogy-Shoo, The. Winthrop Packard. HBV-1
Shoon-a-shoon/ I sing no psalm/ Little Man. The Virgin's Slumber Song. Francis Carlin. ISi; YeAr
Shoot, The. Pope. *Fr.* Windsor Forest. PB
("See! from the brake the whirring pheasant springs.") FaBoEn; FM; PoEL-3
Shoot down the rebelsmen who dare. "Rebels." Ernest Crosby. PAH
Shoot, false Love, I care not. *Unknown.* OBSC
Shoot the Buffalo, *with music. Unknown.* TrAS
Shooter's Hill, *sel.* Robert Bloomfield.
"Health! I seek thee; dost thou love." OBNC
Shootin' with Rasputin. *Unknown.* FSW
Shooting, The. Robert Pack. CoPo
Shooting, The. Laura Tohe. STE
Shooting at the Moon. Kim Yo-sop, *tr. by* Ko Won. MOON
Shooting Ducks in South Louisiana. Richard Tillinghast. MAYP
Shooting Gallery. Martin Galvin. AMV-80
Shooting of Dan McGrew, The. Robert W. Service. BeLS; FaBoBe; FaFP; FPL; PoLF; PoRA; TreF; WHW
Shooting of His Dear. *Unknown. See* Young Molly Ban.
Shooting of John Dillinger outside the Biograph Theater, July 22, 1934, The. David Wagoner. CoAP; FYAP
Shooting of the Cup, The. John G. Neihardt. *Fr.* The Song of Three Friends. PoOW
Shooting of Werfel, The. Vernon Watkins. WaP
Shooting Song, A. William Brighty Rands. OxBChV
Shooting Whales. Mark Strand. LCAP
Shop. Robert Browning. VLP
Shop and Freedom. *Unknown.* PAH
Shop Talk. Roy Fuller. OxBC
Shop Windows. Rose Fyleman. SoPo; TiPo
Shopkeepers. Mani Leib, *tr. fr. Yiddish by* Richard Fein. AMV-81
Shoplifter. Solomon Edwards. NNP
Shoplifters. Maura Stanton. MAYP
Shopman, The. Eleanor Farjeon. HBVY
Shopping. Jane Chance Nitzche. AMV-80
Shopping Day. Orrick Johns. InMe
Shopping for Meat in Winter. Oscar Williams. LiTA; LiTM; NePA
Shopping for Midnight. G. E. Murray. MAYP
Shops, the streets are full of old men, The. Talk. Roo Borson. NOBC
Shore. Jean Garrigue. TAP
Shore. Mary Britton Miller. SUS
Shore. Diana O Hehir. NPGG
Shore, The. David St. John. LCAP; MAYP
Shore Birds. Vi Gale. GoYe
Shore-lark soars to his topmost flight, The. Ecstasy. Duncan Campbell Scott. CaP
Shore Leave Lorry. Roy Fuller. NoAM
Shore looked wild, without a trace of man. Byron. *Fr.* Don Juan, II. HAP
Shore of Life, The. Robert Fitzgerald. VGW
Shore Roads of April. Bill Adams. EtS
Shore Scene. John Logan. NMP
Shore Tullye. Robert Rendall. OxBS
Shore wind is cold on my travel clothes, the. Abutsu the Nun, *tr. by* Edwin O. Reischauer. The Diary of the Waning Moon. PBWP
Shoreham: Twilight Time. Samuel Palmer. NBM; OAEL-2
(Twilight Time.) FaBoPP
Shoreline. Mary Barnard. PoA
Shores are crown'd with people, The. Luis Vaz de Camoëns, *tr. by* Sir Richard Fanshawe. *Fr.* The Lusiads. OBVE
Shores of anguish. Madga Portal, *tr. fr. Spanish by* Allan Francovich *and* Kathleen Weaver. PBWP
Shores of my native land. Farewell. Isaac Toussaint L'Ouverture, *tr. by* Edna Worthley Underwood. TTY
Shores of Styx are lone for evermore, The. Idle Charon. Eugene Lee-Hamilton. OBVV
Shoring up the ocean. A railroad track. Blood-Sister. Adrienne Rich. NoP
Short and sweet, and we've come to the end of it. Da Capo. H. C. Bunner. HBV-1
Short cut home lay through the cemetery, The. The Mistress. Joan Barton. OxBTC
Short day has grown, A. The Place of V. Ray A. Young Bear. VoR
Short direction, A. Rules and Regulations. "Lewis Carroll." FaBoUs
Short Eulogy. Zali Gurevitch, *tr. fr. Hebrew by* Gabriel Levin. VWA

Short grass and the hillside, a level road. Paths They Kept Barren. John Garmon. AMV-81
Short Haired Woman. *Unknown.* BluL
Short History of British India, A. Geoffrey Hill. OxBC
Short History of the Better Life, A. Tess Gallagher. LTB
Short History of the Teaching Profession, A. Sister Maura. AMV-80
Short History of Twentieth-Century Scholarship. John Wain. GLGT
Short Hymne to Venus, A. Robert Herrick. CavP
Short Is My Rest. *Unknown.* EnRePo
Short Lay of Sigurd, The. *Unknown. See* Lay of Sigurd, The.
Short Night, The. Buson, *tr. fr. Japanese by* Harold G. Henderson. MOON
Short Order. Charles Bukowski. HoPM
Short Prayer to Mary, A. *Unknown.* MeEL
Short seemed the space 'twixt sunset and the night. Nineveh. Robert Eyres Landor. *Fr.* The Impious Feast. OBRV
Short Sermon. *Unknown, ad. fr. German by* Louis Untermeyer. TiPo
Short Short Story. Josephine Jacobsen. NePoAm-2
Short Song of Congratulation, A. Samuel Johnson. CABA; EBEV; ELP; HAP; InPK; InPS; InvP; LAuP; LoBV; NOBE; NOEC; NoP; OBEC; OBSV; PoEL-3; TEP
(One-and-Twenty.) OBEV; PoPle
(To a Young Heir.) UnPo
Short space my feet had traversed ere. Guillaume de Lorris *and* Jean de Meun, *tr. by* F. S. Ellis. *Fr.* The Romance of the Rose. OAEL-1
Short Winter Tale, A. Natan Zach, *tr. fr. Hebrew by* Peter Everwine *and* Shula Starkman. VWA
Shortening Sail. William Falconer. *Fr.* The Shipwreck, II. EtS
("As the proud horse with costly trappings gay.") MOS
Shortest fight, The. The Knockout. Lillian Morrison. RHPC
Shortness and Misery of Life, The. Isaac Watts. NOCV
Short'nin' Bread, *with music. Unknown.* BLSo
Shorty George. *Unknown.* FSW
Sho-shó-ne Sa-cá-ga-we-a—captive and wife was she. Sa-cá-ga-we-a. Edna Dean Proctor. PAH
Shot at Random, A. D. B. Wyndham Lewis. FaBoCo; FaFP; FiBHP
Shot, A: from crag to crag. Hunting Season. W. H. Auden. LiSp
Shot in the Park, A. William Plomer. MP
Shot? So Quick, So Clean an Ending? A. E. Housman. A Shropshire Lad, XLIV. PeHV
Shot Who? Jim Lane! Merrill Moore. MoAmPo
Should all our churchmen foam in spite. At Farringford. Tennyson. *Fr.* To the Rev. F. D. Maurice. FaBoPP
Should all the world so wide to atoms fall. Our Insufficiency to Praise God Suitably for His Mercy. Edward Taylor. LiTA
Should any ask me on His form to dwell. He Hath No Parallel. Sadi, *tr. by* L. Cranmer-Byng. *Fr.* The Gulistan. AWP
Should auld acquaintance be forgot. Auld Lang Syne. Burns. AWP; BiP; BLPL; BLSo; BSV; EnRP; FaFP; FSW; GoTS; HBV-1; LAuP; LiTB; NOBE; OAEP; OBEC; OBEV; OxBS; PoLF; TEP; TreF
Should Dennis print how once you robb'd your brother. On Dennis. Pope. FaBoEE
Should he upon an evening ramble fare. Keats. *Fr.* Epistle to George Keats. ChER
Should I Be a Rabbi? Hayyim Nahman Bialik, *tr. fr. Hebrew by* Grace Goldin. TrJP
Should I believe you, e'en my oaths are witty. *Unknown.* FaBoEE
Should I get married? Should I be good? Marriage. Gregory Corso. CABA; CoAP; InPS; LiTM; NeAP; NoAM; NoP; OBAL; PPP; PrIm; TAP
Should I know this room. Locale. Penelope Shuttle. BrRo
Should I my steps turn to the rural seat. Spring. James Thomson. *Fr.* The Seasons. FM
Should I not be ashamed. The Ending. Paul Engle. NYBP
Should I say, my people? I turned stone. Maratea Porto: Saying Goodbye to the Vitolos. Richard Hugo. MAT
Should I sigh out my dayes in griefe. Song. Matthew Stevenson. CavP
Should I thee ranke with Radamanthus fell. A Satyretericall Charracter of a Proud Upstart [*or* March 4th Anno 1698/9; a Charracteristicall Satyre]. John Saffin. SCAP, 2 *vers.*
Should I with silver tooles delve through the hill. Edward Taylor. Preparatory Meditations: Second Series, LVI. OxBA; SCAP
Should I worry about choosing. Begging on North Main. Dabney Stuart. AMV-81
Should no man write, say you, but such as do excel? That No Man Should Write but Such as Do Excel. George Turberville. EnRePo
Should not the glowing lilies of the field. In His Steps. Katharine Lee Bates. PGD
Should old acquaintance be forgot. Old-Long-Syne. *Unknown.* OBS
Should some ill painter, in a wild design. Horace, *tr. by* John Oldham. *Fr.* The Art of Poetry. OBVE
Should the building totter, run for an archway! The Fallen Tower of Siloam. Robert Graves. WaP
Should the cold Muscovit, whose furre and stove. To the Right Honourable the Countesse of C. William Habington. AnAnS-2; SeCP
Should the shade of Plato. On Installing an American Kitchen in Lower Austria. W. H. Auden. NYBP
Should the wide world roll away. Stephen Crane. The Black Riders, X. AmPP; BiP
Should they not have the best of both worlds? Mules. Paul Muldoon. CIP
Should Thy Love Die. George Meredith. ELP
Should we go now a-wand'ring, we should meet. London in 1646. Henry Vaughan. FaBoPP
Should We Legalize Abortion? Frank O'Hara. NoAM
Should we our sorrows in this method range. An Elegy upon My Best Friend. Henry King. AnAnS-2
Should you ask me, whence these stories? The Song of Hiawatha: Introduction. Longfellow. NOBA
Should You Go First. A. K. Rowswell. BLPL; PoLF
Should you meet a little saint. Identity. Sister Mary Helen. GoBC
Should you, my lord, while you pursue my song. Phillis Wheatley. *Fr.* To the Right Honorable William, Earl of Dartmouth. BPo; TTY
Should you revisit us. New Approach Needed. Kingsley Amis. OxBTC; PPON
Shoulder of rock, A. High Island. Richard Murphy. CIP
Shoulder up your gun and call your dog. Ground Hog. *Unknown.* TrAS
Shouldering shapes of the skies of Broceliande. Taliessin's Song of the Unicorn. Charles Williams. FaBoTw
Shout for Joy. *Unknown.* AmFP
Shout for the mighty men. Leonidas. George Croly. HBV-2
Shout, Little Lulu. *Unknown.* AmFP
Shout, shout, up with your song! The March of the Women. Cicely Hamilton. BrRo
Shouting Song. *Unknown.* AmFP
Shovel-gnats gnaw at the open wound, The. On the Edge of the Copper Pit. Pauline Henson. GoYe
Shovel Man, The. Carl Sandburg. HAP
Shovelling Iron Ore. *Unknown.* AS, *with music*; GBP
Show, The. Wilfred Owen. LiTB; LiTM; MoAB; MoBrPo; NoAM; OxBTC; WaaP; WaP
Show is not the show, The. Emily Dickinson. AmPP
Show me again the time. Lines: To a Movement in Mozart's E-Flat Symphony. Thomas Hardy. ELP
Show me dear[e] Christ, thy spouse, so bright and clear. John Donne. Holy Sonnets, XVIII. AnAnS-1; MasP; MeLP; NoP; OAEP; OBS
"Show Me More Love." *Unknown.* OxBoCh
Show Me the Way. *Unknown, tr. fr. Burmese by* U Win Pe. PBWP
Show [*or* Shew] me thy feet: show [*or* shew] me thy legs, thy thighs[e]. To Dianeme. Robert Herrick. AnAnS-2; CaPo; POL; UnTE
Show Me Thyself. Margaret E. Sangster. TrPWD
Show the runner coming through the shadows. The Runner. Gary Gildner. TAP
Shower, A. Izembō, *arr. by* Olive Beaupré Miller. SUS; TiPo
Shower, The. Henry Vaughan. BoNaP; ChTr; FaBoPP; LiTB; OBS; ViBoPo
(Showre, The.) AnAnS-1; MePo; SeCP
Shower, a sprinkle, A. Summer Rain. Eve Merriam. PDV
Shower hath past, ere it hath well begun, The. After the Shower. Archibald Lampman. CaP
Shower of green gems on my apple-tree, A. May Garden. John Drinkwater. HBMV
Showing Off. *Unknown, tr. fr. Irish by* Frank O'Connor. KiLC
Showman comes with his box of dolls, The. The Puppet Play. Padraic Colum. RoGo
Showre, The. Henry Vaughan. *See* Shower, The.
Shredded sunset, The. Night Interpreted. Everett Hoagland. NBP
Shrew, The. Ogden Nash. CenHV
Shriek said the saw smile said the mice. To the Age's Insanities. Marie Ponsot. VGW
Shrieks in dark leaves. The rumpled owl. Hunger and Thirst. John Peale Bishop. PoA
Shrill, glass-clear notes—"Titmouse!" I sighed, enchanted. Tat for Tit. Walter de la Mare. FM
Shrill the fife, kettle the drum. Baldy Bane. W. S. Graham. NePoEA
Shrilling locust slowly sheathes, The. The Beetle. James Whitcomb Riley. *Fr.* The Beetle. FaPON
Shrimp, The, *sel.* Moses Browne.
"Shrimp, A! Black thing as widow's crape." NOEC
Shrimping boats are late today, The. Nocturne: Georgia Coast. Daniel Whitehead Hicky. AmFN
Shrine, The. Digby Mackworth Dolben. GoBC; HBV-1
Shrine in Nazareth. Sister Mary St. Virginia. ISi
Shrine to What Should Be. Mari Evans. NNP
Shrinking to enter, did. Your heart. Part of the Vigil. James Merrill. NoAM

Shropshire Lad, A. John Betjeman. MoBS
Shropshire Lad, A. A. E. Housman. *Poems indexed separately by titles and first lines.*
Shropshire Lad, A. *Unknown.* ChTr
Shropshire Lad's Cousin, The. Samuel Hoffenstein. BXAP
Shrouded Stranger, The. Allen Ginsberg. NeAP
Shrouding of the Duchess of Malfi. John Webster. *See* Hark, Now Everything Is Still.
Shrouds and Away. Alfred G. Bailey. PeCV
Shrovetide's Countenance. Rabelais, *tr. fr. French by* Sir Thomas Urquhart. FaBoNo
Shrubbery, The. William Cowper. FaBoEn; FaBoRV; NCEP; NOBE; OBEC
Sh-Ta-Ra-Dah-Dey, *with music. Unknown.* AS
Shtil Di Nacht (Silent Is the Night). Hirsh Glik, *tr. fr. Yiddish.* FSW
Shubble, The. Walter de la Mare. FaBoNo; TDH
Shudder, The. Donald Hall. NYBP
Shuddring the Spectre howls, his howlings terrify the night. Blake. *Fr.* Jerusalem. OAEL-2
Shuffle and shudder of Autumn, The. Autumn Imagined. Donald Davie. PoA
Shuffling along in her broken shoes from the slums. Douglas Stewart. *Fr.* Lady Feeding the Cats. BoAnP
Shui Shu, *sels. Tr. fr. Japanese by* Arthur Waley.
"Because river-fog." Kiyowara Fukuyabu. AWP
("Because river-fog.") AWP
"Deer which lives, The." Onakatomi Yoshinobu. AWP
(Deer on Pine Mountain, The, *tr. by* Kenneth Rexroth.) PAI
"If it were not for the voice." Nakatsukasa. AWP
"Time I went to see my Sister, The." Tsurayuki. AWP
"When,/ Halting in front of it, I look." Hitomaro. AWP
"Winter has at last come." Minamoto no Shigeyuki. AWP
Shulamit in Her Dreams. Marcia Falk. VWA
Shule, Agrah! "Fiona Macleod." OBVV
Shu-lin was a parrot who sat on the shoulder. Deprecating Parrots. Beulah May. EtS
Shun delays, they breed remorse. Loss in Delay. Robert Southwell. OBSC
Shut in from all the world without. Firelight. Whittier. *Fr.* Snow-bound. AA; OBCP
Shut not so soon; the dull-eyed night. To Daisies, Not to Shut So Soon[e]. Robert Herrick. CaPo; CH; ELP; GBL; HBV-1; InPK; OBEV; OBS; SeCV-1; TrGrPo
Shut Not Your Doors. Walt Whitman. NOBA; OxBA
Shut Out. Christina Rossetti. VLP
Shut Out That Moon. Thomas Hardy. BrPo; CMoP; MoVE; NoAM; NOBE; ViBoPo
Shut, shut the door, good John! Epistle to Dr. Arbuthnot [*or* An Epistle from Mr. Pope, to Dr. Arbuthnot]. Pope. CABA; HoPM; InPS; LoBV; NOEC; NoP; OAEL-1; OAEP; OxBoLi; PoEL-3; WHA
Shut the Seven Seas against Us. George Barker. Third Cycle of Love Poems, II. MoAB; MoBrPo
Shut Up, I Said. Peggy Bennett. ELU
Shut up. Shut up. There's nobody here. The Beast in the Space. W. S. Graham. FaBoTw; PoA
Shutter of time darkening ceaselessly, The. August. Louis MacNeice. FaBoEn; LiTM; PoPle
Shutters unhinge the bat, and brazen sun. Praise to Light. Thomas Cole. NePoAm-2
Shutting the Curtains. Bink Noll. GP
Shuttles of trains going north, going south, drawing threads of blue. Morning Sun. Louis MacNeice. MoAB; MoBrPo; MP; TwCP
Shy and timid, Gloom to me. The Outcast. James Stephens. MoBrPo
Shy Geordie. Helen B. Cruickshank. BSV; GoTS; OxBS
Shy in their herding dwell the fallow deer. Deer. John Drinkwater. CH
Shy midwinter sun. Seboyeta Chapel. Shirley Hill Witt. TWSS
Shy one, shy one. To an Isle in the Water. W. B. Yeats. AWP
Shylock's Defense. Shakespeare. *Fr.* The Merchant of Venice, III, i. TreFS
Shyly the silver-hatted mushrooms make. May. Shaw Neilson. PoAu-1
Si Hubbard, *with music. Unknown.* AS
Si Jeunesse Savait! Edmund Clarence Stedman. AA
Si Me Quieres Escribir (If You Want to Write Me). *Unknown, tr. fr. Spanish.* FSW
Si monumentum requiris . . . the church in which we are sitting. In Memory of George Whitby, Architect. John Betjeman. EyDe
Si, señor, is halligators here, your guidebook say it. Sinalóa. Earle Birney. CABA; MoCV; OxBC
Siamese twins: one, maddened by. Twins. Robert Graves. FaBoEE; PV
Siasconset Song. Philip Booth. NePoAm
Siberia. James Clarence Mangan. BIrV; NBM; RoGo
Sibilla's Dirge. Thomas Lovell Beddoes. *See* Dirge: "We do lie beneath the grass."
Sibrandus Schafnaburgensis. Robert Browning. Garden Fancies, II. CTC; EBVV; TEP
Sibyl, The. Joan LaBombard. GoYe
Sibyl. Joseph Stroud. NPGG
Sibyl of the Waters. Ruth Fainlight. VWA
Sibylline Prophecy, The. Virgil, *tr. fr. Latin by* Thomas Walsh. *Fr.* Eclogues, IV. ISi
Sibyl's Song, The. Michele Roberts. BrRo
Sic a Wife as Willie Had. Burns. GoTS
Sic 'Em Dogs On. *Unknown.* BluL
Sic et Non. Sir Herbert Read. FaBoTw
Sic Itur. Arthur Hugh Clough. EBVV; NCEP
Sic Transit. Joseph Mary Plunkett. ACP
Sic Transit. *Unknown. See* Proper Sonnet, How Time Consumeth All Earthly Things.
Sic Transit Gloria Mundi. James Wreford Watson. CaP
Sic Transit Gloria Scotia. "Hugh MacDiarmid." CMoP
Sic Vita. William Stanley Braithwaite. BANP
Sic Vita. Henry King. AnAnS-2; ELP; HBV-2; MePo; NOBE; OBS; PAI; SeCePo; SeCP
("Like to the falling of a star.") FF
(Of Human Life.) TrGrPo
(On the Life of Man, *wr. at to* Francis Beaumont.) GoBC; WHA
Sic Vita. Henry David Thoreau. *See* I Am a Parcel of Vain Strivings Tied.
Siccine separat amara mors? Knowledge after Death. Henry Charles Beeching. OBVV
Sicelides, *sel.* Phineas Fletcher.
Woman's Inconstancy. EIL
Sicilian Cyclamens. D. H. Lawrence. ChMP; MoVE
Sicilian Muse, begin a loftier strain! The Messiah. Virgil, *tr. by* Dryden. Eclogues, IV. AWP
Sicilian Muse, I Would Try Now a Somewhat Grander Theme. Virgil, *tr. fr. Latin by* C. Day Lewis. Eclogues, IV. NAs
Sicilian Muse, thy voice and subject raise. The Golden Age. *Unknown.* APAS
Sicilian Muses, sing we greater things. Virgil, *tr. by* Sir John Beaumont. Eclogues, IV. OBVE
Siciliana: The Landings at Gela. G. Stanley Koehler. NePoAm-2
Sicilian's Tale, The. Longfellow. *See* Monk of Casal-Maggiore, The.
Sick Child, A. Randall Jarrell. InvP; OxBC; SO; VGW
Sick Child, The. Robert Louis Stevenson. CH; PoSC
Sick Image of My Father Fades, The. John Horder. TEP
Sick Love. Robert Graves. BoLoP; CMoP; EBEV; GTBS-P; HAP; NoAM; NOBE; OAEL-2
(O Love in Me.) FaBoMo
Sick man, though, had wit who thought you up, The. For Two Girls Setting Out in Life. Peter Viereck. MiAP
Sick Nought, The. Randall Jarrell. OxBA
Sick of pale European beauties spoiled. Black Marble. Arthur O'Shaughnessy. SyP
Sick of the day's heat, of noise. The Underground Gardens. Robert Mezey. NaP
Sick of the piercing company of women. A Country Walk. Thomas Kinsella. CIP; CMoP; NMP
Sick of thy northern glooms, come, shepherd, seek. Philip Freneau. *Fr.* The Beauties of Santa Cruz. AmPP
Sick Rose, The. Blake. *Fr.* Songs of Experience. AWP; BoLoP; CABA; ChER; ChTr; EnLoPo; FaBoEn; HAP; HeIP; InPK; InPS; LAuP; LoBV; NIP; NOBE; NOEC; NoP; OAEL-2; OAEP; OBNC; PAI; PoEL-4; PPP; PrIm; SeCeV; SoSe; TrGrPo; ViBoPo; WeW
(O Rose, Thou Art Sick!) ELP
Sick Shark, The. Morris Bishop. TDH
Sick Stockrider, The. Adam Lindsay Gordon. CBAP; OBVV; PoAu-1
Sick unto Death of Love. *Malay Oral Tradition, tr. by* R. J. Wilkinson *and* R. O. Winstedt. WTO
Sickens my gut, Yellow Bittern. The Yellow Bittern. *Tr. fr. Irish by* Tom MacIntyre. CIP
Sickle Pears. Owen Dodson. AmNP
Sickles sound. Harvest Song. Ludwig Heinrich Christoph Hölty, *tr. by* Charles T. Brooks. AWP
Sickness, The. Frederick Seidel. CoPo
Sickness and death, you are but sluggish things. A Winged Heart. Henry Vaughan. *Fr.* Of Life and Death. FaBoRV
Sickness, intending my love to betray. Sir John Davies. *Fr.* Sonnets to Philomel. SiPS
Sickness of Adam, The. Karl Shapiro. *Fr.* Adam and Eve. AP; CoBMV; MoAB
Sickness of desire, that in dark days, The. Melancholia. Robert Bridges. CMoP
Sickness of Friends, The. Henri Coulette. NYBP
Sickness, 'tis true. Samuel Taylor Coleridge. *Fr.* A Tombless Epitaph. OBRV

Side by side on the narrow bed. That Room. John Montague. CIP
Side by side, their faces blurred. An Arundel Tomb. Philip Larkin. HeIP; NePoEA-2; PPP
Side by side through the streets at midnight. April Midnight. Arthur Symons. SyP
Sidewalk joins the concrete wall around the vacant lot, The. Where or When. Philip Whalen. PoM
Sidewalk Orgy. Richard O'Connell. PV
Sidewalk Racer, The; or, On the Skateboard. Lillian Morrison. NTCP; RHPC
Sidewalks of New York, The. James W. Blake. BLPA; BLSo; *with music*; FaBoBe; FSN; *with music;* FSW; TreFS; YaD
Sidewinder, The. Charles F. Lummis. BPAW
Siding near Chillicothe, A. Richmond Lattimore. AmFN
Sidney, according to report, was kindly hearted. Various Ends. Ruthven Todd. NeBP; SeCePo
Sidney Godolphin. Clinton Scollard. AA
Sidrophel, the Rosicrucian Conjurer. Samuel Butler. *Fr.* Hudibras. OxBoLi
Siege, The. Sir John Suckling. *See* 'Tis Now, Since I Sat Down Before.
Siege and the assault being ceased at Troy, The. Sir Gawain and the Green Knight. *Unknown, tr. by* Brian Stone. OAEL-1
Siege at Stony Point. Horace Gregory. FAZ
Siege of Belgrade, The. *Unknown. See* Austrian Army, An.
Siege of Chapultepec, The. William Haines Lytle. PAH
Siege of Corinth, The. Byron. GoTL
Siege of Valencia, The, *sel.* Felicia Dorothea Hemans.
Dirge: "Calm on the bosom of thy God." HBV-2; OBEV
(Death-Hymn, A.) OBRV
Siegfried. Randall Jarrell. MiAP
Siena. Swinburne. VLP
"Siena Mi Fe'; Disfecemi Maremma." Erza Pound. *Fr.* Hugh Selwyn Mauberley. MoAmPo
Sierra. Alfonsina Storni, *tr. fr. Spanish by* Rachel Benson. PBWP
Sierra Kid, *sel.* Philip Levine.
He Faces the Second Winter. PoA
Sierran Vigil. Ewart Milne. NeIP
Siesta, The. *Unknown, tr. fr. Spanish by* Bryant. AWP
Siesta of a Hungarian Snake. Edwin Morgan. InPK
Sifting. Victor E. Beck. GoYe
Sigh. Stéphane Mallarmé, *tr. fr. French by* Arthur Symons. AWP; SyP
Sigh, A. Harriet Prescott Spofford. AA; HBV-1
Sigh, The. Nathaniel Wanley. OBS; OxBoCh
Sigh as It Ends. John Berryman. WeW
Sigh, heart, and break not; rest, lark, and wake not! Nuptial Song. Lord De Tabley. GTBS-P; OBVV
Sigh, in the wind fall flowers, their petals dance. Selling Ruined Peonies. Yü Hsüan-chi, *tr. by* Geoffrey Waters. BoWoP
Sigh no more, dealers, sigh no more. Much Ado about Nothing in the City. *Unknown.* FaBoPa
Sigh No More, Ladies [Sigh No More]. Shakespeare. *Fr.* Much Ado about Nothing, II, iii. AWP; CTC; ElL; ELP; FF; HBV-1; InMe; LiTB; OAEP; PAI; SeCeV; TreFS; TrGrPo; ViBoPo
(Balthasar's Song.) OBSC
(Song: "Sigh no more, ladies, sigh no more.") FiP; PoEL-2
Sigh of Silence, The. Keats. *See* I Stood Tiptoe.
Sigh that heaves the grasses, The. A. E. Housman. MoVE
Sigh, wind in the pine. Glencoe. Douglas Stewart. CBAP
Sighed a dear little shipboard divinity. Conrad Aiken. OBAL
Sighing, and sadly sitting by my Love. Richard Barnfield. Sonnets, XI. PeHV
Sighing high and/ again a sigh! Weaving at the Window. Wang Chien, *tr. by* William H. Nienhauser. SaC
Sighing Time, The. Edmund Blunden. BrPo
Sighs and Grones. George Herbert. PoEL-2
Sighs are my food, drink are my tears. Epigram. Sir Thomas Wyatt. SiPS
Sight, A. Robert Creeley. NaP
Sight. Sir John Davies. LoBV
Sight. W. W. Gibson. MoBrPo
Sight and Insight. Eleanor Slater. TrPWD
Sight in Camp [in the Daybreak Gray and Dim], A. Walt Whitman. AA; AmPP; AP; BiP; LO; NoAM; OFD; OxBA; PAI; PoEL-5; TAP; TRV
Sight of his guests filled Lord Cray, The. Lord Cray. Edward Gorey. RHPC
Sight of the English is getting me down, The. Hiraeth in N.W.3. Wynford Vaughan-Thomas. NOBL
Sight Unseen. Kingsley Amis. ErPo; NePoEA-2
Sighted a black tornado of. Comments. Peggy Susberry Kenner. JB
Sighted Sub. *Unknown.* WhC
Sighting down the silver barrel. The League of Selves. Alvin Toffler. AMV-80
Sightings I. Jerome Rothenberg. CoPo
Sightseer Named Sue, A. *Unknown.* TDH
Sightseers in a Courtyard. Nicolás Guillén, *tr. fr. Spanish by* Langston Hughes. TTY
Sigil. Hilda Doolittle ("H. D."). VGW
Sigismonda and Guiscardo, *sel.* Dryden.
Ave atque Vale. OBS
Sigismundo. Linda Gregg. AmPA
Sigmund Freud. Howard Nemerov. PoA
Sign, The. Paul Blackburn. TAT
Sign for anger could be a felled pine tree, The. Learning to Type. Diana O Hehir. NPGG
Sign for My Father, Who Stressed the Bunt. David Bottoms. MAYP
Sign of the Bonny Blue Bell, The. *Unknown.* OBET
Sign of the Cross, The. Cardinal Newman. GoBC
Signal, The. David Ignatow. NNaP
Signal, deep within the inconsistent clocking, radiates. Hookerlumps in the Love Canal. William Sylvester. SOTS
Signal Fire, The. Aeschylus, *tr. fr. Greek by* Dallam Simpson. *Fr.* Agamemnon. CTC
Signal, The; or, A Satire against Modesty, *sel.* Francis Hawling.
Author Consults a Critic and Sells His Manuscript, The. NOEC
Signals. Jewel C. Latimore. PoBA
Signals. Keith Waldrop. AMV-81
Signals spelled summer but for me it was spring, The. Evergreen. Ewart Milne. OxBI
Signature. Hannah Kahn. IHMS
Signature. Dorothy Livesay. OBCV
Signature. Larry Mollin. NeAC
Signature. Carol Orlock. AMV-81
Signature II ("All morning he lay in the tight, dark room"). Joseph Stroud. NPGG
Signature III ("Tsangyang Gyatso was twelve years old"). Joseph Stroud. NPGG
Signature for Tempo. Archibald MacLeish. MoVE; VGW
Signature of All Things, The. Kenneth Rexroth. NNaP; NU
"When I dragged the rotten log," *sel.* BoNaP
Signatures. Daniel Hoffman. VGW
Signatures. Candace Thurber Stevenson. AmFN
Signboard, The. Robert Creeley. ConAP
Significance of a Veteran's Day, The. Simon J. Oritz. GP
Significant Fevers. Alison Fell. BrRo
Signpost. Robinson Jeffers. GoYe; ViBoPo
Sign-Post, The. Edward Thomas. ViBoPo
Signs. Gjertrud Schnackenberg. PoA
Signs everywhere of birds nesting, while. William Carlos Williams. MoVE
Signs of Christmas. Edwin Lees. OHIP
Signs of Love. Petrarch, *tr. fr. Italian by* C. B. Cayley. Sonnets to Laura: To Laura in Life, CLXXXVIII. AWP
Signs of Rain. Edward Jenner. BLPA; BoNaP; FaBoUs
Signs of the Zodiac, The. Ebenezer Cobham Brewer. FaBoUs
Signs of wear. Monogram 29. Martina Werner, *tr. by* Rosemarie Waldrop. BoWoP
Signs of Winter. John Clare. BoNaP; PoSC; WiR
"Cat runs races with her tail, The," *sel.* OAEL-2
Signum Cui Contradicetur. Sister Mary Angelita. GoBC
Sigurd of yore. The Lay of Sigurd. *Unknown, tr. by* William Morris *and* Eirikur Magnusson. *Fr.* The Elder Edda. AWP
Sigurd Rideth to the Glittering Heath. William Morris. *Fr.* The Story of Sigurd the Volsung, II. PoEL-5
Sigurd's Ride. William Morris. *Fr.* The Story of Sigurd the Volsung, II. NBM
Siilenboor. *Mongol Oral Tradition, tr. by* C. R. Bawden. WTO
Sila. Robert Penn Warren. NoP
Silence. Bella Akhmadulina, *tr. fr. Russian by* Daniel Halpern. BoWoP
Silence. Robert Bly. NaP
Silence. E. E. Cummings. CMoP
Silence. Susan Griffin. *Fr.* Woman and Nature. NPGG
Silence. Samuel Miller Hageman. TRV
Silence. Thomas Hood. CH; EBEV; EnRP; FaBoEn; NOBE; OBEV; OBRV; PoEL-4; ViBoPo
(Sonnet: Silence.) OBNC
Silence, The. Archibald MacLeish. HBMV
Silence. Edgar Lee Masters. MoAmPo
Silence. Marianne Moore. CMoP; FaBoEn; FaBoMo; LiTA; NOBA; PAI; SBG; ViBoPo
Silence. T. Sturge Moore. QFR; SyP
Silence. James Herbert Morse. AA
Silence. Gregory Orr. GeTw
Silence. John Lancaster Spalding. AA
Silence. Charles Hanson Towne. TRV; WGRP
Silence. W. J. Turner. MoBrPo
Silence. Winifred Welles. HBMV

Silence. John Hall Wheelock. LiTM
Silence all flesh, your selves prepare. A Judicious Observation of That Dreadful Comet. Ichabod Wiswall. SCAP
Silence, an Eloquent Applause. Leona Gregory. TrCP
Silence—and a muted bell rings. Consecration. Patrick F. Kirby. GoBC
Silence, and a starry night. Shtil Di Nacht (Silent Is the Night). Hirsh Glik, *tr. fr. Yiddish.* FSW
Silence and solitude may hint. An Uninscribed Monument on One of the Battle-Fields of the Wilderness. Herman Melville. AA
Silence and Stealth of Day[e]s! Henry Vaughan. AnAnS-1; JCP; MePo; SeCV-1; WHA
Silence augmenteth grief, writing increaseth rage. Epitaph on [*or* upon the Right Honorable] Sir Philip Sidney [*or* Elegy on the Death of Sidney]. *At. to* Fulke Greville *and to* Sir Edward Dyer. EnRePo; LiTB; LoBV; OBSC; Prf
Silence beside the Pacific. The Reach of Silence. Charles Black. AMV-81
Silence Concerning an Ancient Stone. Rosario Castellanos, *tr. fr. Spanish by* George D. Schade. PBWP
Silence here bears gunfire in its breath. Cozzo Grillo. H. B. Mallalieu. WaP
Silence holds for it, taut and true, The. Click o' the Latch. Nancy Byrd Turner. HBMV
Silence hovers over the earth, A. A Late Spring Day in My Life. Robert Bly. NCSH
Silence in Court. "Lewis Carroll." *See* Evidence Read at the Trial of the Knave of Hearts.
Silence in the classroom, The. Poem for the Creative Writing Class, Spring 1982. Merle Woo. BrSi
Silence, in truth, would speak my sorrow best. Tears at the Grave of Sir Albertus Morton. Sir Henry Wotton. AnAnS-2; SeCP
Silence instead of thy sweet song, my bird. Lament of a Mocking-Bird. Frances Anne Kemble. AA; HBV-1
Silence Invoked. Richard Flecknoe. GoBC
Silence is first, The. Still water. Demolition. Philip Raisor. AMV-81
Silence of our watching, waiting springs, A. A View. Beverly Quint. NYBP
Silence rules in the home. The Convoy. Juan Antonio Corretjer, *tr. by* Julio Marzán. InW
Silence slipping around like death, A. A Winter Twilight. Angelina Weld Grimké. CDC; PoBA; PoNe
Silence Spoke with Your Voice. Ryah Tumarkin Goodman. GoYe
Silence. The man defined. The Hand at Callow Hill Farm. Charles Tomlinson. NePoEA-2
Silence was envious of the only voice. Robert Underwood Johnson. *Fr.* The Voice of Webster. AA
Silence, with its ragged edge of lost communication, The. Barbed Wire. Eithne Wilkins. NeBP
Silences. Arthur O'Shaughnessy. OBNC; VLP
Silences. E. J. Pratt. NOBC; OBCV; PoCh
Silences; a Dream of Governments. Jean Valentine. LCAP
Silent, about-to-be-parted-from house. Invocation. Denise Levertov. PoA
Silent alone, where none or saw, or heard. Anne Bradstreet. *Fr.* Contemplations. PBWP
Silent amidst unbroken silence deep. India. Florence Earle Coates. AA
Silent are the woods, and the dim green boughs are. On Eastnor Knoll. John Masefield. CH
Silent at last, beneath the silent ground. On the Death of Echo. Hartley Coleridge. BoAnP; GDP
Silent bivouac of the dead, we say, A. Decorating the Soldiers' Graves. Minot J. Savage. OHIP
Silent fell the rain. Fallen Rain. Richard Watson Dixon. NBM
Silent Generation, The. Louis Simpson. NePoAm-2
Silent girl, The. In the Library. Ed Ochester. Psk
Silent girl at the spindle, The. The Spinning Girl. Nathan Alterman, *tr. by* Ruth Nevo. VWA
Silent Hour. Rainer Maria Rilke, *tr. fr. German by* Jessie Lemont. AWP
Silent I gaze at the cataract. By the Waterfall. Friedrich Adler, *tr. by* Jethro Bithell. TrJP
Silent Icicles, The. Samuel Taylor Coleridge. *Fr.* Frost at Midnight. FaBoRV
Silent in America. Philip Levine. NaP
Silent is the dark. Hope's Song. Francis Carlin. HBMV
Silent is the house: all are laid asleep. The Visionary. Emily Brontë. BLPL; BrRo; CH; ELP; LiTB; LO; LoBV; NOBE; OAEP; OBNC; PBWP; SCV
Silent Love. John Clare. EnRP
Silent Love, A. Sir Edward Dyer. BoLoP; NOBE
  (Love is Love.) TrGrPo
  (Lowest Trees Have Tops, The.) ElL; EnRePo; HAP; PoEL-1; PoRA; WeW
  ("Lowest trees have tops, the ant her gall, The.") EBEV; FaBoEn
  (Modest Love, A.) OBSC
Silent Lover, The. Sir Walter Ralegh. ElL; OBEV, *abr.;* ViBoPo
  (Sir Walter Ralegh to the Queen.) AAS; OAEP
  (To His Mistress.) SiPS
  (To the Queen.) OBSC
  Sels.
  Passion, *st.* 1. PoPle
  (Silent Lover, The.) LiTB
  Wrong Not, Sweet[e] Empress of My Heart. HBV-1; OBS, *sl. diff., at. to* Sir Robert Ayton
  (Merit of True Passion, The.) LiTB
Silent Movies. Pedro Juan Pietri. InW
Silent, my jaws working, I knew. The Lesson. Paul Mariani. MAYP
Silent Night! [Holy Night!] Joseph Mohr, *tr. fr. German.* FaFP; FSW; TreF
Silent Noon. Dante Gabriel Rossetti. The House of Life, XIX. ELP; HAP; NoP; OAEP; OBNC; PoEL-5; TrGrPo; VLP; WHA
Silent nymph, with curious eye! Grongar Hill. John Dyer. *Fr.* Looking Back. ChTr; EnRP; FaBoPP; GoTL; LAuP; LoBV; NOEC; NoP; OBEC; PoEL-3
Silent, O Moyle, be the roar of thy water. The Song of Fionnuala. Thomas Moore. AnIL; BIrV; OnYI
Silent One, The. Ivor Gurney. MMA; OBWP
Silent Poem. Robert Francis. FiCP; LCAP
Silent Pool, The. Harold Monro. BrPo
Silent Ranges, The. Stephen Moylan Bird. HBMV
Silent Room, The. Kingsley Amis. OxBC
Silent room, the heavy creeping shade, The. Fabien Dei Franchi. Oscar Wilde. BrPo
Silent Slain, The. Archibald MacLeish. *See* Too-late Born, The.
Silent Snake, The. *Unknown.* FaPON; TiPo
Silent tepees stand like shocked corn, The. Always the Melting Moon Comes. Margot Osborn. CaP
Silent Testimony. Catherine Parmenter. PGD
Silent Tower of Bottreaux, The. Robert Stephen Hawker. GoBC; OBRV
Silent Town, The. Richard Dehmel, *tr. fr. German by* Jethro Bithell. AWP
"Silent upon a peak in Darien." Darien. Edwin Arnold. PAH
Silent Walls, The. Ian Strachan. PoSH
Silent, with her eyes. Blind Girl. W. S. Merwin. NePoEA-2
Silent Woman, The. Ben Jonson. *See* Epicoene; or, The Silent Woman.
Silent, you say, I'm grown of late. Walter Savage Landor. GBL
Silentium. Fyodor Tyutchev, *tr. fr. Russian by* Avrahm Yarmolinsky. PoPl
Silently my wife walks on the still wet furze. Berry Picking. Irving Layton. MoCV; NoP
Silently, slowly falls the snow from an ashen sky. Snowfall. Giosuè Carducci, *tr. by* Romilda Rendel. AWP
Silenus in Proteus. Thomas Lovell Beddoes. EnRP
Silesian Weavers, The. Heine, *tr. fr. German by* Aaron Kramer. NAWM-2
Silet. Erza Pound. MoAB; MoAmPo
Silhouette. Annette M'Baye, *tr. fr. French by* Kathleen Weaver. PBWP
Silhouette/ On the face of the moon. Shadow. Richard Bruce. CDC
Silhouette in Sepia. Robert V. Carr. PoOW
Silhouettes, they lean against a ringed moon. Paiute Ponies. Jim Barnes. CDW
Silica Carbonate Rock. Fred Berry. NU
Silk,/ Satin. *Unknown.* OxNR
Silk I have for you, Madonna—you shook your small dear head. Needs. Elizabeth Rendall. HBMV
Silk Merchant's Daughter, The, 2 *vers., with music. Unknown.* ShS
Silk Weaver's Daughter, The. *Unknown.* AmFP
Silken-sheathed Angelica, The. Daily Paradox. Sara Henderson Hay. InMe
Silken Tent, The. Robert Frost. AmPP; BLPL; CABA; InPK; MoPo; MP; NePA; NOBA; SoSe; TAP; TwCP
Silkie o' Sule Skerrie, The. *Unknown. See* Great Silkie of Sule Skerry, The.
Silkweed. Philip Henry Savage. AA
Silkworms, The. Douglas Stewart. CBAP; PoAu-2
Siller Croun, The. Susanna Blamire. HBV-1
Silly. All giggles and ringlets and never. Romping. John Ciardi. CTBA; NCSH
Silly boy, there is no cause. Song. Thomas Pestel. ElL
Silly boy, 'tis full moon yet, thy night as day shines clearly. First Love. Thomas Campion. GBL; OxBoLi
Silly country maiden went, A. Leda in Stratford, Ont. Anne Wilkinson. MoCV
Silly Dog. Myra Cohn Livingston. GDP
Silly Fool, The. W. H. Auden. OBMV
Silly girl! Yet morning lies. To a Pretty Girl. Israel Zangwill. TrJP
Silly Old Man, The. *Unknown.* CoMu; TW
Silly swain whose love breeds discontent, The. Tityrus to His Fair Phyllis. John Dickenson. *Fr.* The Shepherd's Complaint. ElL
Silly Sweetheart. *Unknown.* CH
Silly Willy. "R. L. B." ShM

Silly young cricket, accustomed to sing, A. The Ant and the Cricket. *Unknown.* HBV-1; HBVY
Silly young fellow named Hyde, A. Limerick. *Unknown.* ShM; WhC
Silly zebras don't know, The. Zoo Dream. David Barker. GP
Silver. A. R. Ammons. NoP
Silver. Walter de la Mare. BoNaP; FaPON; MoAB; MoBrPo; PoPl; PoRA; RHPC; SiSoSe; SUS; TiPo; TreF
Silver Age, The, *sel.* Thomas Heywood.
Praise of Ceres. EIL
Silver bark of beech, and sallow. Counting-out Rhyme. Edna St. Vincent Millay. GoJo; MoShBr
Silver birch is a dainty lady, The. Child's Song in Spring. Edith Nesbit. HBV-1; OHIP; OxBChV
Silver birch-tree like a sacred maid, A. Recollection. Amelia Walstien Carpenter. AA
Silver Bird of Herndyke Mill, The. Edmund Blunden. GoTL
Silver Bowl, The, *sel.* Joseph Ezobi, *tr. fr. Spanish by* D. I. Friedmann.
Barren Soul, A. TrJP
Silver Dagger, The. *Unknown.* AmFP; BaBo
Silver dust. Pear Tree. Hilda Doolittle ("H. D."). AP; BoWoP; CMoP; HBMV; MoAmPo; NOBA; UnPo
Silver Herring Throbbed Thick in My Seine, The. Kenneth Leslie. *Fr.* By Stubborn Stars. ErPo; OBCV; PeCV
(Sonnet.) NOBC
Silver in the Wind. Ian Strachan. PoSH
Silver Jack's Religion. John P. Jones. BPAW
(Silver Jack, *sl. diff.*) CoSo
Silver jet, A. Sitting Down, Looking Up. A. R. Ammons. PCP
Silver key of the fountain of tears. Music. Shelley. TrGrPo
Silver Lantern, A. Karle Wilson Baker. HBMV
Silver Leaf, The. John Hay. NePoAm
Silver Lucifer, A. Lunar Baedeker. Mina Loy. VGW
Silver moon's enamored beam, The. Kate of Aberdeen. John Cunningham. HBV-1
Silver Penny, The. Walter de la Mare. CMoP; OBMV
Silver Question, The. Oliver Herford. NA
Silver Racer, The. Joseph Colin Murphey. AMV-80
Silver-scaled Dragon with jaws flaming red, A. The Toaster. William Jay Smith. GrPl; RHPC; SoPo
Silver Sheep. Anne Blackwell Payne. SiSoSe
Silver Ships. Mildred Plew Meigs. FaPON; TiPo
Silver Swan, The. *Unknown.* ChTr; EIL; ELP; EnRePo; FaBoCh; HAP; HeIP; InPK; NIP; NoP; OAEP; PAI; PoPle (*at. to* Orlando Gibbons)
("Silver swan[ne], who living had no note, The.") PBBP; PoEL-2
Silver Tassie, The. Burns. NOBE; OBEC; PoPle
(Farewell, A.) GTBS; GTBS-P
(My Bonnie [or Bonie] Mary.) BSV; HBV-1; OBEV; ViBoPo
Silver that shies off the silver-leaf maple, The. The Silver Leaf. John Hay. NePoAm
Silver Threads among the Gold. Eben Eugene Rexford. BLSo, *with music*; FaFP; FSW; PSoN, *with music*; TreF
Silver-vested monkey trips, A. Cortège. Paul Verlaine, *tr. by* Arthur Symons. AWP; OBVE
Silver Wedding. Ralph Hodgson. HBMV; OxBTC; TrGrPo
Silverthorn Bush. Robert Finch. NOBC
Silvery the olives on Ravello's steeps. Above Salerno. Ada Foster Murray. HBV-2
Silvery Tide, The. *Unknown.* AmFP
Silvia. Sir George Etherege. CavP
Silvia. Shakespeare. *See* Who Is Sylvia?
Silvia, let us from the crowd retire. To Silvia. Countess of Winchelsea. *Fr.* The Cautious Lovers. HBV-1
Sim Ines. Jane Stubbs. FiBHP
Simchas Torah. Morris Rosenfeld, *tr. fr. Yiddish.* TrJP
Simfunny of Thee Hold Whorl. Charles Lynch. LTB
Simhat Torah. Judah Leib Gordon, *tr. fr. Hebrew by* Alice Lucas *and* Helena Frank. TrJP
Similar Cases. Charlotte Perkins Stetson Gilman. HBV-1; PoLF
Simile. N. Scott Momaday. CDW
Simile, A. Matthew Prior. FaBoEn; NOEC
Simile for Her Smile, A. Richard Wilbur. HoPM; InPK; MiAP; OLR
Similes. Edward Moxon. OBRV
Similes. *Unknown.* HBVY
Similes for Two Political Characters of 1819. Shelley. InPS; TW
Similia Similibus. John Hunt Morgan. ShM
Simmer's a pleasant time. Ay Waukin O. Burns. NOEC; PoEL-4
Simón,/ we knew him as la Zorrauncouth but. Aquellos Vatos. Tino Villanueva. FIA
Simon and Susan. *Unknown.* OxBoLi
Simon and the Tarantula. James Wright. NNaP
Simon Danz Longfellow. *See* Dutch Picture, A.
Simon Gerty. Elinor Wylie. OBAL
Simon Lee. Wordsworth. EnRP
(Simon Lee the Old Huntsman.) GTBS; GTBS-P
Simon Legree—a Negro Sermon. Vachel Lindsay. The Booker Washington Trilogy, I. HBMV; InMe; LiTA; MoVE; NePA; TAP
(Negro Sermon, A: Simon Legree.) MoAmPo
Simon my son, son of my Nuptiall knot. A Lamentation on My Dear Son Simon. John Saffin. SCAP
Simon the Cyrenean. Lucy Lyttleton. HBV-2
Simon the Cyrenian Speaks. Countee Cullen. AmNP; BPo; HAP; MoAmPo; TrCP; TTY
Simple. Naomi Long Madgett. FB; PoBA
Simple and fresh and fair from winter's close emerging. The First Dandelion. Walt Whitman. NePA
Simple Autumnal. Louise Bogan. MoAB; MoAmPo; QFR
Simple child, A. We Are Seven. Wordsworth. BLPA; BLPL; EnRP; GN; HBV-1; OxBChV; SpRo; TEP; TreF; WBLP
Simple Faith. William Cowper. *Fr.* Truth. OBEC
Simple flick of the switch, A. Running It Backward. John N. Morris. GP
Simple-hearted child was He, A. The Little Child. Albert Bigelow Paine. AA
Simple-minded interstates have it now, The. Western Ways. Richmond Lattimore. AMV-80
Simple Nature. George John Romanes. HBV-1
Simple nosegay, A! was that much to ask? The Troll's Nosegay. Robert Graves. PoCh
Simple Pastoral, A. George Alexander Stevens. NOEC
Simple Ploughboy, The. *Unknown.* FaBoCh
Simple Purification, The. Kabir, *ad. fr. Hindi by* Robert Bly. NU
Simple Sam. Leroy F. Jackson. PoSC
Simple Simon. Harriet S. Morgridge. AA
Simple Simon met a pieman. Mother Goose. FaBoBe; HBV-1; HBVY; OxNR; PoPl; SoPo
Simple-Song. Marge Piercy. CTBA; LLLT
Simple soul, who so early in the morning. Charles Reznikoff. *Fr.* Depression. CTBA
Simple Verses, *sels.* José Martí, *tr. fr. Spanish by* Seymour Resnick. TTY
"I am a sincere man."
"I grow a white rose."
Simpler Thing, a Chair, A. Robert Mezey. NePoEA
Simples. Gladys Cardiff. TWSS
Simples. James Joyce. HBMV; PoPl
Simplex Munditiis. Ben Jonson. *See* Still to Be Neat.
Simplicity ("Persicos odi"). Horace. *See* Fie on Eastern Luxury!
Simplicity. Carl Rakosi. *See* Americana XV: Simplicity.
Simplicity. Louis Simpson. InPS; Prf
Simplicity Aims Circularly. Anna Walters. VoR
Simplicity sings it and 'sperience doth prove. Simplicity's Song. Robert Wilson. *Fr.* Three Ladies of London. CTC; OBSC
Simplicity so graven hurts the sense. So Graven. Josephine Miles. NoAM
Simplicity's Song. Robert Wilson. *Fr.* Three Ladies of London. CTC; OBSC
Simplification, A. Richard Wilbur. CMoP
Simplify Me When I'm Dead. Keith Douglas. NePoEA; OxBTC
(Remember Me.) NeBP
Simplon Pass, The. Wordsworth. *Fr.* The Prelude, VI. SyP
(Alpine Descent.) WHA
Simply. Laura Chester. NPGG
Simply to breathe. An Emblem of Two Foxes. Barry Spacks. HoPM
Simpson's Rest. George S. Simpson. PoOW
Simultaneously. David Ignatow. GrPl; NCSH; POL; TwCP
Simultaneously, as soundlessly. Prime. W. H. Auden. CMoP
Simultaneously, five thousand miles apart. Simultaneously. David Ignatow. GrPl; NCSH; POL; TwCP
Sin. George Herbert. NoP; ViBoPo
Sin!/ O only fatal Woe. Thomas Traherne. AnAnS-1
Sin and Death. Milton. *Fr.* Paradise Lost, II. OBNV
(Meanwhile the adversary of God and man.") DL; EBEV
Sin and Its Cure. *Unknown.* STF
Sin, Despair, and Lucifer. Phineas Fletcher. *Fr.* The Locusts, or Apollyonists. OBS
Sin of Omission, The. Margaret E. Sangster. BLPA; HBV-2; TreFS; TRV
Sin [*or* Sinne] of self-love possesseth al[l] mine eye [*or* eie]. Sonnets, LXII. Shakespeare. EBEV; EnRePo; PoEL-2
Sin-satiate, and haggard with despair. Tannhäuser. William Morton Payne. AA
Sin that I have a nounparall maistress. A Mistress without Compare. Charles d'Orléans. MeEL
Sin! wilt Thou vanquish me! The Recovery. Thomas Traherne. AnAnS-1
Sinalóa. Earle Birney. CABA; MoCV; OxBC
Since. W. H. Auden. InPS
Since/ Malcolm died. Aardvark. Julia Fields. BOLo; CNA; OFD

Since all our keys are lost or broken. An Art of Poetry. James McAuley. NOCV
Since all that I can ever do for thee. The Last Wish. "Owen Meredith." OBVV
Since all the riches of this world. Blake. OAEL-2
Since as in night's deck-watch ye show. Herman Melville. *Fr.* John Marr. ViBoPo
Since Bonny-Boots Was Dead. *Unknown.* NCEP; PoEL-2
(Madrigal: "Since Bonny-boots was dead, that so divinely.") OxBoLi
Since born. Since beginning. Since dawn. Since When As Ever More. Lawson Inada. BrSi
Since brass, nor stone, nor earth, nor boundless sea. Sonnets, LXV. Shakespeare. AWP; CABA; EnRePo; FaFP; FF; FiP; GTBS; GTBS-P; HAP; InPS; LiTB; MasP; NOBE; NoP; PoRA; SeCeV; UnPo
Since Brunswick's smile has authoris'd my muse. Edward Young. *Fr.* The Instalment. FaBoCo
Since bundling very much abounds. A New Bundling Song. *Unknown.* ErPo
Since by just flames the guilty piece is lost. Advice to the Painter. Matthew Prior. APAS
Since cast-iron has got all the rage. Humphrey Hardfeature's Descriptions of Cast-Iron Inventions. *Unknown.* OBET
Since Christmas they have lived with us. Balloons. Sylvia Plath. NCSH
Since clarity suggests simplicity. The Counterpart. Elizabeth Jennings. LiTM
Since Cleopatra Died. Thomas Wentworth Higginson. AA
Since counterfeit plots have affected this age. A Ballad upon the Popish Plot. John Gadbury. CoMu
Since earth has put you away, O sons of Barmak. Abu Nowas for the Barmacides. *Unknown, tr. by* E. Powys Mathers. *Fr.* The Thousand and One Nights. AWP
Since every quill is silent to relate. A Monumental Memorial of Marine Mercy. Richard Steere. SCAP
Since fate commands me hence, and I. The Farewell. Thomas Stanley. CavP
Since Feeling Is First. E. E. Cummings. BiP; MoAB; MoAmPo; NoP; PrIm
Since First I Saw Your Face. *Unknown.* ELP; LiTB; OBEV
("Since first I saw your face, I resolved to honour and renown ye.") OBSC
Since first you knew my am'rous smart. Epigram. Robert, Earl Nugent. NOEC
Since fortune's wrath envieth the wealth. Earl of Surrey. SiPS
Since God's eye is on the sparrow. God's Eye Is on the Sparrow. Bertha Meyer. STF
Since Hanna Moved Away. Judith Viorst. RHPC
Since his death, nothing removes my fear. The Weasel. Robert Pack. CoPo
Since honour from the honourer proceeds. Of Books. John Florio. ElL
Since I am coming [*or* comming] to that holy room[e]. Hymn[e] to God My God, In My Sickness[e]. John Donne. AnAnS-1; CABA; ChTr; DTC; EBEV; EnRePo; FaBoEn; GoBC; HeIP; LoBV; MasP; MeLP; MePo; NIP; NoP; OAEL-1; OAEP; OBS; OxBoCh; PoEL-2; PPP; SeCP; SeCV-1; TrPWD
Since I am convinced. Saigyo Hoshi, *tr. fr. Japanese by* Arthur Waley. AWP
Since I believe in God the Father Almighty. Johannes Milton, Senex. Robert Bridges. CMoP; LiTB; PoEL-5; PoPl
Since I care naught for what is pale and cold. To a Brown Girl. Ossie Davis. PoNe
Since I do trust Jehova still. Bible, *O.T. paraphrased by* Sir Philip Sidney. Psalm XI. OBVE
Since I emerged that day from the labyrinth. The Labyrinth. Edwin Muir. CMoP; MoBrPo; NoAM
Since I entered the inner rooms. Written on a Leaf. *Unknown, tr. by* Geoffrey Waters. BoWoP
Since I have been so quickly done for. On an Infant Eight Months Old. *Unknown.* WhC
Since I have felt the sense of death. The Sense of Death. Helen Hoyt. HBMV
Since I have lacked the comfort of that light. Amoretti, LXXXVIII. Spenser. EnRePo
Since I have seen a bird one day. The Truth. W. H. Davies. FaBoTw
Since I have set my lips to your full cup, my sweet. More Strong Than Time. Victor Hugo, *tr. by* Andrew Lang. AWP
Since I heard. Mitsune, *tr. by* Arthur Waley. *Fr.* Kokin Shu. AWP
Since I keep only what I give away. Sonnet. George Hetherington. NeIP
Since I must love your north. To My Mountain. Kathleen Raine. OxBS; PoPl
Since I must needs into thy school[e] return[e]. A Lady's [*or* Ladies] Prayer to Cupid. Thomas Carew, *after* Giovanni Battista Guarini. CaPo; OBVE
Since I no longer speak I. Silent in America. Philip Levine. NaP
Since I noo mwore do zee your feace. The Wife a-Lost. William Barnes. BoLoP; EBVV; ELP; EnLoPo; HAP; OBEV; OBVV
Since I was a little child. Rebel. Irene Rutherford McLeod. HBMV
Since I was in Syracuse is a month ago. Quarries in Syracuse. Louis Golding. TrJP
Since I was ten I have not been unkind. The Final Word. Dom Moraes. NePoEA-2
Since I'm a girl. *Unknown, tr. fr. Spanish by* Willis Barnstone. BoWoP
Since I'm completely drunk. Epigram. *Unknown, tr. fr. Greek by* Peter Jay. PeHV
Since in a land not barren still. Love and Discipline. Henry Vaughan. TrPWD
Since in religion all men disagree. To Caelia. *Unknown.* FaBoEE
Since I've felt this pain. Ono no Komachi, *tr. fr. Japanese by* Rob Swigart. WPOW
Since Just Disdain. *Unknown.* EnRePo
Since last September I've been trying to describe. Edward Lear in February. Christopher Middleton. TwCP
Since last the tutelary hearth. Christmas Family Reunion. Peter De Vries. NOBL
Since laws were made for ev'ry degree. Air. John Gay. *Fr.* The Beggar's Opera. NOEC
Since life is nothing in your philosophy. Nothing. Julia de Burgos, *tr. by* Aliki *and* Willis Barnstone. BoWoP
Since, Lord, to thee/ A narrow way and little gate. Holy [*or* H.] Baptism[e]. George Herbert. HBV-2; PoEL-2; SeCV-1
Since love is such that as ye wot. Sir Thomas Wyatt. SiPS
Since love will needs that I shall love. Sir Thomas Wyatt. SiPS
Since lovers' joys then leave so sick a taste. Henry King. *Fr.* Paradox: That Fruition Destroys Love. ErPo
Since man has been articulate. Every Thing. Harold Monro. MoBrPo
Since Man's a little world, to make it great. An Epigram on Woman. Philip Ayres. FaBoEE
Since Maria left me to go to another star. Autumn Complaint. Stéphane Mallarmé, *tr. by* George Moore. SyP
Since me and Jesus got: married. Jesus Make Up My Dying Bed. *Unknown.* BluL
Since men grow diffident at last. Youth Sings a Song of Rosebuds. Countee Cullen. BANP; PoLF; PoNe
Since more than half my hopes came true. Contented at Forty. Sarah N. Cleghorn. HBMV
Since most sharks have no flotation bladders and must swim. Nurse Sharks. William Matthews. FiCP
"Since mountains sink to vales, and valleys die." The Bathos. Richard Porson. FaBoEE
Since my life's been spent. Côte d'Azur. Katherine Hoskins. NYBP
Since my old friend is grown so great. A Dialogue. Pope. POL
Since naturally black is naturally beautiful. Naturally. Audre Lorde. BlSi; CNA
Since Nature's works be good, and death doth serve. Why Fear to Die? Sir Philip Sidney. *Fr.* Arcadia. OAEP; SiPS
Since Nothing Is Impossible. Michael Waters. WOLT
Since nought avails, let me arise and leave. Love's Last Resource. Sadi, *tr. by* L. Cranmer-Byng. *Fr.* The Gulistan. AWP
Since now I dare not ask. The Sharp Ridge. Robert Graves. FaBoEE
Since now in every public place. The Sea Horse. Robert Graves. FaBoMo
Since now my Silvia is as kind as fair. The Happy Night. John Sheffield, Duke of Buckingham and Normanby. UnTE
Since ocean rolled and ocean winds were strong. Sonnets on the Sea's Voice. George Sterling. EtS
Since o'er thy footstool here below. Heaven's Magnificence. William August Muhlenberg. AA
Since of no creature living the last breath. Edna St. Vincent Millay. VGW
Since one anthologist put in his book. Anthologistics. Arthur Guiterman. InMe; WhC
Since reverend doctors now declare. The Respectable Burgher. Thomas Hardy. CMoP; NoAM; VLP
Since Robin Hood. *Unknown.* NCEP
Since, Señora, you torment me. The Challenge. *Unknown, tr. by* Louis Untermeyer. UnTE
Since she must go, and I must mourn, come night. His Parting from Her. John Donne. Elegies, XII. EBEV; OBS
Since she whom[e] I lov'd hath payd [*or* paid] her last debt. Holy Sonnets, XVII. John Donne. AnAnS-1; JCP; MasP; MePo; OAEP
Since Shylock's book has walk'd the circles here. To a Noisy Politician. Philip Freneau. TAP
Since, Sir, you have made it your study to vex. The Lady's Receipt for a Beau's Dress. *Unknown.* CoMu
Since So Mine Eyes. Sir Philip Sidney. *Fr.* Arcadia. SiPS
Since so ye please to hear me plain. Sir Thomas Wyatt. SiPS

Since succour to the feeblest of the wise. Remembered Grace. Coventry Patmore. The Unknown Eros, XIX. OxBoCh
Since that night/ I cannot know myself. Izumi Shikibu, *tr. fr. Japanese by* Willis Barnstone. BoWoP
Since that this thing we call the world. An Epicurean Ode. John Hall. MeLP; MePo
Since the Conquest none of us. The Conquest. Oliver St. John Gogarty. OBMV
Since the instant exists I sing. Motive. Cecilia Meireles, *tr. by* Don Wilson. AMV-81
Since the night is dark. *Unknown, tr. fr. Spanish by* Willis Barnstone. BoWoP
Since "the pillow knows all." Lady Ise, *tr. fr. Japanese by* Kenneth Rexroth *and* Ikuko Atsumi. WPOW
Since the storm two nights ago. The Recognition. Denise Levertov. VGW
Since the wise men have not spoken, I speak that am only a fool. The Fool. Padraic Pearse. OnYI
Since Then. Yehuda Amichai, *tr. fr. Hebrew by* Shlomo Vinner *and* Howard Schwartz. VWA
Since Then. D. J. Enright. OBSV
Since, then, constrain'd, we must expel the flock. How to Build a Ha-ha. William Mason. *Fr.* The English Garden. FaBoUs
Since there's no help, come, let them kiss and part. The Limited. Robert Penn Warren. PoA
Since there's no help[e], come let us kiss[e] and part. Idea, LXI [*or* Farewell to Love *or* Love's Farewell *or* The Parting *or* Sonnet]. Michael Drayton. AAS; AWP; BLPL; BoLoP; CABA; EIL; EnLoPo; EnRePo; FaBoEn; GBL; GTBS; GTBS-P; HAP; HBV-1; HeIP; InPK; InPS; JCP; LiTB; LoBV; NOBE; NoP; OAEL-1; OAEP; OBEV; OBSC; PAI; PoEL-2; PoPle; PPoe; PrIm; SCV; SeCePo; SeCeV; SoSe; TEP; TreFS; TrGrPo; ViBoPo; WHA
Since They Have Died. May Wedderburn Cannan. SUMH
Since they were morose in August. The Branch. Stanley Moss. DiL
Since this is to be ceremonial. Homage to Marian Pyszko. Richard Snyder. SOTS
Since Those We Love and Those We Hate. W. E. Henley. OBMV
Since thou art gone, my friend, I seek in vain for peace. On Parting with Moses ibn Ezra. Judah Halevi, *tr. by* Solomon Solis-Cohen. TrJP
Since Thou Hast Given Me This Good Hope, O God. Robert Louis Stevenson. TrPWD
Since thou hast view'd some Gorgon, and art grown. Sonnet: The Double Rock. Henry King. AnAnS-2; SeCP
Since thou wou'dst needs, bewitcht with some ill charms. To One Married to an Old Man. Edmund Waller. FaBoEE; SeCP
Since through vertue encreaseth dignity. Good Counsel. James I, King of Scotland. ACP
Since thy third curing of the French infection. Against an Old Lecher. Sir John Harington. FaBoEE
Since Time began, such alphabets begin. From a Cheerful Alphabet. John Updike. FaBoCo
Since to obtaine thee, nothing me will sted. His Remedie for Love. Michael Drayton. *Fr.* Idea. AAS
Since tonight the wind is high. The Viking Terror. *Unknown, tr. by* Frank O'Connor. KiLC
Since we agreed to let the road between us. No Road. Philip Larkin. EBEV; MoBrPo
Since we are born in blood to be convinced. La Ci Darem la Mano. John Frederick Nims. MiAP
Since we are told it we believe it's true. Surprise. Anthony Cronin. CIP
Since we can die but once, what matters it. Sentiment. Thomas Chatterton. NOEC
Since we had [*or* we'd] always sky about. Can. Lit. Earle Birney. CABA; NOBC
Since we had changed. Message. Allen Ginsberg. ConAP; NeAP; VGW
Since We Loved. Robert Bridges. VLP
Since We Parted. "Owen Meredith." HBV-1
Since we'd always sky about. *See* Since we had always sky about.
Since When As Ever More. Lawson Inada. BrSi
Since, when you die, delight. Modern Love Poems. *Somali Oral Tradition, tr. by* B. W. Andrzejewski *and* M. Laurence. WTO
Since without Thee we do no good. Hymn. Elizabeth Barrett Browning. TrPWD
Since ye delight to know. Sir Thomas Wyatt. SiPS
Since you all will have singing, and won't be said nay. The King's Own Regulars. *Unknown.* PAH
Since you ask, most days I cannot remember. Wanting to Die. Anne Sexton. ConAP; IHMS; NoAM; TAP
Since you have come thus far. Chorus. C. Day Lewis. *Fr.* Noah and the Waters. OAEP
Since you have gone. Three Moments. Susan Sherman. DFF
Since you have turned unkind. To a Lady Friend. W. H. Davies. MoBrPo
Since you must go, and I must bid farewell. An Elegy. Ben Jonson. EnRePo; LoBV
"Since you refuse to communicate by telephone." Survivors. Mordecai Marcus. AMV-81
Since you remember Nimmo, and arrive. Nimmo. E. A. Robinson. HBMV
Since you walked out on me. Lady of Miracles. Nina Cassian, *tr. by* Laura Schiff. WPOW
Since you will needs that I shall sing. Sir Thomas Wyatt. SiPS
Since you wrote a poem. What Color Is Lonely. Carolyn M. Rodgers. BPo
Since Youth Is All for Gladness. Glenn Ward Dresbach. HBMV
Since youth is wise, and cannot comprehend. Inscription for Arthur Rackham's Rip Van Winkle. James Elroy Flecker. BrPo
Sincere Flattery of R. B. James Kenneth Stephen. FaBoPa; NOBL; Par
(Imitation of Robert Browning.) InMe
Sincere Flattery of W. W. (Americanus). James Kenneth Stephen. HBV-1; NOBL; Par; SpRo
(Imitation of Walt Whitman.) FaBoPa
(Of W. W. [Americanus].) FiBHP; WhC
(Sincere Flattery, The.) InMe
Sincere Praise, *sel.* Isaac Watts.
"Almighty Maker God!" TrPWD
Sincerest critic of my prose, or rhyme. Letter to Viscount Cobham. Congreve. LoBV
Sindhi Woman. Jon Stallworthy. OxBC
Sinew of Our Dreams, The. Edgar Jackson. LFAC
Sinfonia Domestica. Jean Starr Untermeyer. HBMV; MoAmPo
Sinfonia Eroica. Alice Archer James. AA
Sinful to Flirt. *Unknown.* AmFP
Sing a little as the feet unwearied. Voyageur. R. E. Rashley. CaP
Sing a song o' sixpence. Song of Sixpence. *Unknown.* OxBoLi
Sing a song of critics. Valentine. Ernest Hemingway. OBAL; TW
Sing a Song of Juniper. Robert Francis. NCSH
Sing a song of laughter. The Giraffe and the Woman. Laura E. Richards. PDV
Sing a song of monkeys. The Monkeys. Edith Osborne Thompson. TiPo
Sing a Song of Moonlight. Ivy O. Eastwick. SiSoSe
Sing a Song of People. Lois Lenski. RHPC
Sing a song of picnics. Picnic Day. Rachel Field. SiSoSe; SoPo; TiPo
Sing a song of pop corn. A Pop Corn Song. Nancy Byrd Turner. FaPON
Sing a song of rockets. Fourth of July Song. Lois Lenski. SiSoSe
Sing a song of scissor-men. The Scissor-Man. Madeline Nightingale. TiPo
Sing a song of sixpence. Mother Goose. FaBoBe; HBV-1; HBVY; OxNR; PoPl; SoPo; SpRo; TiPo
Sing a Song of Sixpence, *parody.* Frank Sidgwick. WhC
Sing a song of Spring-time. A Song of the Seasons. Cosmo Monkhouse. HBV-1
Sing a Song of Subways. Eve Merriam. RHPC
Sing a Song of Sunshine. Ivy O. Eastwick. SiSoSe
Sing a Song of the Cities. Morris Bishop. CAD; WhC
Sing a Song of War-Time. Nina Macdonald. SUMH
Sing a song of whisky. A Whisky Song. *Unknown.* STF
Sing a song of winter. A Sledding Song. Norman C. Schlichter. FaPON
Sing again the song you sung. Egyptian Serenade. George William Curtis. HBV-1
Sing and heave, and heave and sing. The Banks of the Sacramento. *Unknown.* AmSS
Sing, ballad-singer, raise a hearty tune. The Ballad-Singer. Thomas Hardy. At Castlebridge Fair, I. BoLoP; OLR; VLP
Sing, bird, on green Missouri's plain. The Death of Lyon. Henry Peterson. PAH
Sing, Brothers, Sing! W. R. Rodgers. MoAB; MoBrPo
Sing Cuccu. *Unknown. See* Cuckoo Song, The.
Sing for the Garish Eye. W. S. Gilbert. NA
Sing Heigh-Ho! Charles Kingsley. HBV-1
Sing hey diddle diddle, the cat and the fiddle. *See* Hey diddle diddle.
Sing hey! for bold George Washington. George Washington. Rosemary *and* Stephen Vincent Benét. FaPON
Sing, hey! Sing, hey!/ For Christmas Day. Christmas Greeting [*or* An Old Christmas Greeting]. *Unknown.* FaPON; PChr; SiSoSe; TiPo
Sing his praises that doth keep. Hymn to Pan. John Fletcher. *Fr.* The Faithful Shepherdess, I, ii. NOBE; OBEV; OBS; ViBoPo
Sing ho! for a brave and a gallant ship. Ten Thousand Miles Away. *Unknown.* FSW
Sing; how 'a would sing! Julie-Jane. Thomas Hardy. MoVE
Sing I for a brave and gallant barque, and a stiff and a rattling breeze. Ten Thousand Miles Away. *Unknown.* AS
Sing jigmijole the pudding-bowl. Kissing of My Dame. *Unknown.* GBP; OxNR
Sing, Little Bird. Maria Hastings. SoPo

Sing low, my heart, lest we be overheard. The Heart Has Its Reasons. *Unknown.* GoBC
Sing lullaby, as women do[e]. The Lullaby [*or* Lullabie] of a Lover [*or* Gascoigne's Lullaby *or* A Lover's Lullaby]. George Gascoigne. AAS; EBEV; ElL; EnRePo; HAP; HBV-1; InvP; NoP; OAEP; OBEV; PoEL-1; QFR; TrGrPo
Sing, magnarello, merrily. The Leaf-Picking. Frédéric Mistral, *tr. by* Harriet Waters Preston. AWP
Sing me a hero! Quench my thirst. Tray. Robert Browning. FM
Sing Me a New Song. John Henrik Clarke. PoBA
Sing me a song of a lad that is gone. Over the Sea to Skye [*or* A Lad That Is Gone]. Robert Louis Stevenson. BrPo; EtS; HBV-1; MOS; NOBE
Sing Me a Song of Teapots and Trumpets. N. M. Bodecker. RHPC
Sing me a sweet, low song of night. A Song. Hildegarde Hawthorne. FaBoBe; HBV-1
Sing me the men ere this. He Would Have His Lady Sing. Digby Mackworth Dolben. EBEV; GoBC
Sing, My Soul, *with music.* *Unknown.* AH
Sing, my tongue, the Saviour's glory. Hymn. St. Thomas of Aquinas. WGRP
Sing, O goddess, the wrath, the ontamable dander of Keitt. The Fight over the Body of Keitt. *Unknown.* PAH
Sing of the brave and the miracles they wrought. Song of the Brave. Laurence Altgood. PAL
Sing On, Blithe Bird. William Motherwell. GN; HBV-1; HBVY
Sing out, my soul, thy songs of joy. Songs of Joy. W. H. Davies. MoBrPo; OBVV
Sing out pent souls, sing cheerfully. The Vintage to the Dungeon. Richard Lovelace. CaPo; SeCV-1
Sing, sing,/ What shall I sing? Mother Goose. OxNR
Sing, Sing for Christmas. J. H. Egar. OHIP
Sing Song. Robert Creeley. NMP
Sing song/ Tag along. Tag Along. Nina Payne. RHPC
Sing-Song: A Nursery Rime Book. Christina Rossetti. *Poems indexed separately by titles and first lines.*
Sing-Song of Old Man Kangaroo, The. Kipling. FaPON
Sing-Song Rhyme. *Unknown.* SiSoSe
Sing the old song, amid the sound dispersing. Song. Aubrey Thomas De Vere. HBV-1
Sing to Apollo, God of Day. Song of Apollo. John Lyly. *Fr.* Midas. OBSC
Sing to Ashtaroth and Bel. To Ashtaroth and Bel. Saul Tchernichowsky, *tr. by* L. V. Snowman. TrJP
Sing to the Lord, for what can better be. Psalm CXLVII: "Praise ye the Lord." Countess of Pembroke. NOCV
Sing to the Lord Most High, *with music.* Timothy Dwight. AH
Sing to whom a hallelujah? Whom endorse? The Umbrella, the Cane, and the Broom. Eliezer Steinbarg, *tr. by* Curt Leviant. VWA
Sing unto Jehovah. Bible, *O.T.* *See* Floods Clap Their Hands, The.
Sing unto the Lord with thanksgiving. Bible, *O.T.* Psalm CXLVII. OHIP; *abr.;* SoPo
Sing we all merrily. A Catch by the Hearth. *Unknown.* OHIP
Sing We and Chant It. *Unknown.* EBEV; EnRePo; OBSC (To Live in Pleasure.) TrGrPo
Sing we for love and idleness. An Immorality. Ezra Pound. CMoP; GoJo; GrPl; HBV-1; LiTM; MoAB; MoAmPo; NePA; NOBA; OBAL; OLR; PoPl
Sing we the two lieutenants, Parer and M'Intosh. The Flight. C. Day Lewis. *Fr.* A Time to Dance. MoVE
Sing We Yule. *Unknown.* MeEL
Sing while you may, O bird upon the tree! Dark Wings. James Stephens. PoA
Sing with Your Body. Janice Mirikitani. WPOW
Singe we alle and say we thus. My Purse. *Unknown.* EBEV; OxBM
Singee a songee sick a pence. Nursery Song in Pidgin English [or Song]. *Unknown.* BXAP; SpRo; WhC
Singer, The. Anna Wickham. HBMV; MoBrPo
Singer Asleep, A. Thomas Hardy. OAEP
Singer in the Prison, The. Walt Whitman. BeLS
Singer of One Song, The. Henry Augustin Beers. AA
Singer within the little streets. Song. Monk Gibbon. NeIP
Singers, The. George Bruce. OxBS
Singers are gone from the Cornmarket-place, The. After the Fair. Thomas Hardy. At Casterbridge Fair, VII. CMoP; HAP; VLP
Singer's House, The. Seamus Heaney. CIP; EBEV
Singers in a Cloud, The. Ridgely Torrence. HBMV
Singers in the Snow, The. *Unknown.* OHIP
Singers of serenades, The. Mandoline. Paul Verlaine, *tr. by* Arthur Symons. AWP; OBMV
Singer's Prelude, The. William Morris. *See* Apology, An.
Singers, sing! The hoary world. The Servants. Richard Wightman. WGRP
Singers to Come. Alice Meynell. WPE
Singin' Wid a Sword in Ma Han', *with music.* *Unknown.* BoAN-1
Singing. Robert Louis Stevenson. SUS
Singing Aloud. Carolyn Kizer. IHMS
Singing and shouting they swept to the treacherous forest. The Lost Army. Margery Lawrence. SUMH
Singing Bones, The. Randolph Stow. CBAP
Singing Cat, The. Stevie Smith. OxBTC; PCat
Singing Death. Stan Rice. FYAP
Singing in the Dark. Irma Wassall. PoNe
Singing Leaves, The. James Russell Lowell. GN
Singing-Lesson, The. Jean Ingelow. HBV-1
Singing Lesson, A. Swinburne. HBV-2
Singing Maid, The. *Unknown.* *See* Now Springs the Spray.
Singing Man, The. Josephine Preston Peabody. HBV-2
Singing my days. Passage to India. Walt Whitman. AmPP; PoEL-5
Singing of Niagara, and the Huron squaws. The Possibility of New Poetry. Robert Bly. ConAP
Singing on the Moon. Ted Hughes. WSC
Singing robes fly onto your body, The. The Poem Rising by Its Own Weight. Denise Levertov. GP
Singing. Singing. Winter Song. Juan Ramón Jiménez, *tr. by* H. R. Hays. WSC
Singing the Reapers Homeward Come. *Unknown.* OHIP
Singing through the forests. Rhyme of the Rail[s]. John G. Saxe. InMe; MoShBr; PoLF
Singing-Time. Rose Fyleman. SiSoSe; TiPo
Singing Water. Rudolph Chambers Lehmann. HBMV
Singing-Woman from the Wood's Edge, The. Edna St. Vincent Millay. HBMV
Single-eyed to child and sunbeam. Blue-eyed Mary. Mary E. Wilkins Freeman. OBCA
Single flow'r he sent me, since we met, A. One Perfect Rose. Dorothy Parker. FiBHP; NIP; NoP; OBAL; OLR
Single Girl, The. *Unknown.* FSW; TrAS, *with music*
Single-handed, and surrounded by Lecompton's black brigade. Lecompton's Black Brigade. Charles Graham Halpine. PAH
Single man stands like a bird-watcher, A. The Mouth of the Hudson. Robert Lowell. AmFN; CAD; CoPo; NaP; NYP
Single naked wire at ground level, A. George Jonas. *Fr.* To Christian Montpelier. NeAC
Single post, a point of rusting, A. Marina Tsvetayeva, *tr. by* Elaine Feinstein. *Fr.* The Poem of the End. BrRo
Single-Rhyme Alphabet, A. *Unknown.* FaBoUs
Single roar, A. The Lone Biker. R. Wayne Hardy. LFAC
Single tree, A/ There was. Wordsworth. *Fr.* The Prelude, VI. OBRV
Single Woman, The. Frances Cornford. ELU
Singles. Michael Waters. GeTw; MAYP
Sings a Bird. John Nist. AMV-80
Sing-Song. *See* Sing Song.
Singular Indeed. David McCord. OBCA
Singular Metamorphosis, A. Howard Nemerov. ConAP
Singular Sangfroid of Baby Bunting, The. Guy Wetmore Carryl. NA
Singular Singulars, Peculiar Plurals. Willard R. Espy. FaBoUs
Singularly and in pairs the decade has been ripped by bullets. Lines. Herbert Martin. PoBA
Sinister presence changed life in a twelvemonth, A. Mountain Convent. Laura Benét. GoYe
Sink the world! Can that dismay us? A Pair. Karl Gjellerup, *tr. by* Charles Wharton Stork. PoPl
Sinkholes. Janet Reed McFatter. GrPl
Sinking of the Mendi, The. S. E. K. Mqhayi, *tr. fr. Xhosa by* C. M. Mcanyangwa *and* Jack Cope. PeSA
Sinking of the *Merrimac,* The. Lucy Larcom. PAH
Sinks the sun below the desert. Cleopatra Dying. Thomas Stephens Collier. BLPA; BLPL; FaBoBe; TreFT
Sinless Child, The, *sel.* Elizabeth Oakes Smith.
"Her ways were gentle while a babe." AA
Sinne of selfe-love possesseth al mine eie. *See* Sin of self-love possesseth all mine eye.
Sinner, Is Thy Heart at Rest? *with music.* Jared B. Waterbury. AH
Sinner Man. *Unknown.* FSW
Sinner man sat on the gates of hell, A. No Hiding Place Down There. *Unknown.* GBP
Sinner, Please Don't Let Dis Harves' Pass, *with music.* *Unknown.* BoAN-2
Sinner-Saint, The. Wilfrid Scawen Blunt. ACP
Sinners. D. H. Lawrence. ViBoPo
Sinners, abhor the Fiend. Charles Wesley. *Fr.* The Horrible Decree. NOCV
Sinner's Lament, A. Lord Herbert of Cherbury. SeCP
Sinners, Will You Scorn the Message? *with music.* Jonathan Allen. AH
Sinnes Heavie Loade. Robert Southwell. AnAnS-1
Sins Loathed, and Yet Loved. Robert Herrick. LiTB

Sins of Kalamazoo, The. Carl Sandburg. VGW
Sins of Youth, The. Thomas, Lord Vaux. ACP
Sins' Round. George Herbert. LoBV
Sion. George Herbert. AnAnS–1
Sion Lies Waste [and Thy Jerusalem]. Fulke Greville. *Fr.* Caelica. EnRePo; NoP; OxBoCh
("Syon lyes waste, and thy Jerusalem.") PoEL–1
Sion the son of Evan sang. Microcosmos, XLVI. Nigel Heseltine. NeBP
Sion, thy bridal-bower prepare. The Purification. Saint Cosmas. *Fr.* Menaion. ISi
Sioux, The. Eugene Field. FiBHP; GoJo
Sioux, The. *Unknown.* TDH
Sioux Indians, The. *Unknown.* AmFP; CoSo, *with music*
Sip a little. Baby's Drinking Song. James Kirkup. NTCP
Sipping a Schlitz. Bullfrogs. David Allan Evans. Psk
Sipping Cider through a Straw. *Unknown.* *See* Sucking Cider through a Straw.
Sipping judiciously, he saw come near. Narcissus in a Cocktail Glass. Frances Minturn Howard. GoYe
Sipping whiskey and gin. Analysands. Dudley Randall. BPo; CABA
Sipsop's Song. Blake. *Fr.* An Island in the Moon. FaBoNo
Sir,/ Ere you pass this threshold, stay. To the King, at His Entrance into Saxham: By Master John Crofts. Thomas Carew. CaPo
Sir/ I read of late. Four Questions Addressed to His Excellency, the Prime Minister. James Vaughn. AmNP
Sir/ Our times are much degenerate from those. To His Noble Friend, Mr. Richard Lovelace, upon His Poems. Andrew Marvell. PP
Sir, after you have wip'd the eyes. A Consolatory Poem Dedicated unto Mr. Cotton Mather. Nicholas Noyes. SCAP
Sir Aldingar. *Unknown.* ESPB (A, B, *and* C *vers.*); OxBB
Sir Andrew Bar[t]ton. *Unknown.* AmFP, 2 *vers.*; EnSB; ESPB; OxBB; ViBoFo
Determination ("Sir Andrew Barton said, I'm hurt"), 4 *ll.* TreFT
Sir, as your mandate did request. The Inventory, in Answer to the Usual Mandate Sent by a Surveyor of the Taxes, Requiring a Return of the Number of Horses, Servants, Carriages, etc. Kept. Burns. FaBoUs
Sir—awaiting you. Waiting for the Emperor Tenji. Princess Nukada, *tr. by* Cid Corman *and* Susumu Kamaike. PBWP
Sir Bedivere Bors. Frederick B. Opper. TDH
Sir Beelzebub. Edith Sitwell. *Fr.* Façade. BoWoP; CoBMV; HoPM; MoAB; MoBrPo; OxBTC; PrIm
(When Sir Beelzebub.) FaBoMo
Sir Bumper was a baron bold. The Lover's Leap; a Tale. Andrew Macdonald. NOEC
Sir Cawline. *Unknown.* ESPB
Sir Christopher Wren. E. C. Bentley. *Fr.* Clerihews. CenHV; FaBoCo; FiBHP; InMe; InPK; MoShBr; PV; WhC
Sir Colin, *with music.* *Unknown.* OxBB
Sir Dilberry Diddle, Captain of Militia. *Unknown.* NOEC
Sir Drake, whom well the worlds end knew. Epigram: On Sir Francis Drake. *Unknown.* OBS
Sir Edward, that was by este tho mid power gret ynow. Town against Gown at Oxford. Robert of Gloucester. *Fr.* Chronicle. OxBM
Sir Eggnogg. Bayard Taylor. BXAP
Sir Eglamour. Samuel Rowlands. *Fr.* The Melancholy Knight. ElL; FaBoCh; FaBoNo; InvP
Sir Egrabell had sonnes three. Sir Lionel. *Unknown.* ESPB
Sir Eustace Grey, *sels.* George Crabbe.
Frenzy. NOBE
"Peace, peace, my friend; these subjects fly." PoEL–4
"Then those ill-favour'd Ones, whom none." ELP
Sir Francis Bacon. Ambrose Bierce. DBV
Sir Francis Drake, *sel.* Charles Fitzgeffry.
Bee, The. ElL
Sir Francis Drake; or, Eighty-eight. *Unknown.* GBP
("Some years of late, in eighty-eight.") FaBoCh
Sir Francis, Sir Francis, Sir Francis is come. Upon Sir Francis Drake's Return [from His Voyage about the World, and the Queen's Meeting Him]. *Unknown.* CoMu; ElL; FaBoCh
Sir Galahad. Tennyson. HBV–2; OBVV
Pure Heart, The, *sel.* TreF
Sir Gawain and the Green Knight. *Unknown, tr. fr. Middle English by* Brian Stone. OAEL–1
Sels.
Gawain and the Lady of the Castle, *orig. and mod. English prose.* OxBM
("Thus laykes this lorde by lynde-wodes eves.") EBEV, *orig. only*
Passage of a Year, The. PoEL–1
Sir Gawayn Goes to Receive His Return Blow from the Green Knight. FaBoPP
Temptation of Sir Gawain, The. ACP
Sir Gawain Encounters Sir Priamus. *Unknown.* *Fr.* Morte d'Arthur. PoEL–1
Sir Gawaine and the Green Knight. Yvor Winters. MoVE; NoAM; PoRA; QFR; TwAmPo; VGW
Sir Gawayn Goes to Receive His Return Blow from the Green Knight. *Unknown, tr. fr. Middle English.* *Fr.* Sir Gawain and the Green Knight. FaBoPP
Sir Geoffrey Chaucer. Robert Greene. *See* Description of Sir Geoffrey Chaucer, The.
Sir George Prevost, with all his host. The Battle of Plattsburg. *Unknown.* PAH
Sir Halewyn. Alexander Gray. OxBB
Sir Helmer Blaa and His Bride's Brothers. *Unknown.* BaBo
Sir Henry Clinton's Invitation to the Refugees. Philip Freneau. PAH
Sir Hudibras, His Passing Worth. Samuel Butler. *Fr.* Hudibras, I, Argument. EBEV; OAEL–1; SeCV–2
Sir Hudibras, His Passing Worth ("He was in logick a great critic"). Samuel Butler. *See* Metaphysical Sectarian, The.
Sir Hudibras's Religion. Samuel Butler. *See* Religion of Hudibras, The.
Sir Hudson Lowe, Sir Hudson *Low.* To Sir Hudson Lowe. Thomas Moore. OBSV
Sir Hugh; or, The Jew's Daughter. *Unknown.* AmFP; CH; ESPB (A, B, C, *and* N *vers.*); FaBoBa; ViBoFo (A, B, *and* C *vers.*)
(Hugh of Lincoln.) ACP; EnSB; OxBB
Sir Humphrey Gilbert. Longfellow. EtS; HBV–2; HBVY; PAH
Sir Humphry Davy. E. C. Bentley. *Fr.* Clerihews. CenHV; FaBoCo; ImOP
Sir, I admit your general rule. Epigram. Pope, *also at. to* Matthew Prior *and to* Samuel Taylor Coleridge. FaBoEE; FiBHP; HBV–1; LiTB; TreF
Sir, I encountered Death. Incident in a Rose Garden. Donald Justice. NCSH
Sir Isaac Newton. *Unknown.* WeW
Sir J. S. Sir John Suckling. *See* Constant Lover, The.
Sir James the Rose. *Unknown.* ESPB
Sir John addressed the Snake-god in his temple. Grotesque. Robert Graves. DTC
Sir John Barleycorn. *Unknown.* FaBoBa
Sir John Butler. *Unknown.* ESPB
Sir John Graeme and Barbara Allan. *Unknown.* *See* Barbara Allen.
Sir Joseph's Song. W. S. Gilbert. *See* First Lord's Song, The.
Sir Joshua Reynolds. Blake. ELU; FaBoCo; FiBHP; OxBoLi
("When Sir Joshua Reynolds died.") FaBoEE; TW
Sir Joshua Reynolds. Goldsmith. *Fr.* Retaliation. NOEC; OBEC; SeCePo
("Here Reynolds is laid and, to tell you my mind.") FaBoEE
Sir Lancelot beside the mere. Lancelot and Guinevere. Gerald Gould. HBV–2
Sir Lark and King Sun; a Parable. George Macdonald. *Fr.* Adela Cathcart, *ch.* 16. GN; HBV–1; HBVY
Sir Launfal, *sel.* John Moultrie.
"But here, at starting, I must just premise." OBRV
Sir Launfal and the Leper. James Russell Lowell. *Fr.* The Vision of Sir Launfal. GN
Sir Lionel. *Unknown.* AmFP; ESPB (A, B, *and* C *vers.*)
Sir Marmaduke's Musings. Theodore Tilton. AA
Sir Menenius Agrippa, the Friend of the People. Robert Brough. VLP
Sir Moses, Sir Aaron, Sir Jamramajee. A New Order of Chivalry. Thomas Love Peacock. CenHV
Sir Nameless, once of Athelhall, declared. The Children and Sir Nameless. Thomas Hardy. NoP
Sir, no man's enemy, forgiving all. Petition. W. H. Auden. CMoP; CoBMV; LiTB; MoPo; OAEP
Sir, now unravelled is the Golden Fleece. To Dr. F. B. on His Book of Chess. Richard Lovelace. CaPo
Sir Olaf. Johann Gottfried von Herder, *tr. fr. German by* Elizabeth Craigmyle. AWP
Sir Oluf he rideth over the plain. The Elected Knight. *Unknown, tr. by* Longfellow. AWP
Sir, or Madam, choose you whether. Upon an Hermaphrodite. John Cleveland. AnAnS–2
Sir Orfeo. *Unknown.* OxBM
Sir Patient Fancy, *sel.* Aphra Behn.
"What has poor Woman done, that she must be," *fr.* Epilogue. WPOW
Sir Patrick Spens [*or* Spence]. *Unknown.* AmFP; AWP; BiP; BSV; CABA; CH; EBEV; ELP; EnRP; EnSB; ESPB (A, B, *and* G *vers.*); FaBoBa; FaBoCh; FaPoR; FF; GN; GoJo; HAP; HBV–2; HoPM; InPK; InPS; InvP; LiTB; LoBV; MOS; NIP; NOBE; NoP (A *vers.*); OAEL–1, *with music*; OAEP; OBEV; OxBB, *with music;* PAI; PoEL–1; PoRA; PPP; PrIm; SeCeV; TreF; TrGrPo; UnPo; ViBoFo (A *vers., with music;* B *vers.*); ViBoPo; WeW; WHA
(Ballad of Sir Patrick Spens, The.) EtS; RoGo
Sir Rider Haggard. W. H. Auden. FaBoCo
Sir Robert Bolton had three sons. Sir Lionel. *Unknown.* ESPB
Sir Roderic's Song. W. S. Gilbert. *Fr.* Ruddigore. ShM; WhC
Sir Roland; a Fragment. Robert Merry. NOEC

Sir, say no more. Dramatic Fragment. Trumbull Stickney. ELU; InPK; OxBA
Sir Sidrophel, the Conjuror. Samuel Butler. *Fr.* Hudibras, II, 3. FaBoEn (Portrait of Sidrophel.) PoEL-3
Sir, since the last Elizabethan died. A Letter to a Live Poet. Rupert Brooke. BrPo
Sir Smasham Uppe. E. V. Rieu. RHPC
Sir T. J.'s Speech to his Wife and Children. *Unknown.* CoMu
Sir, the night is darker now. A Nightly Deed. Charles Madge. NeBP
Sir Thomas Armstrong's Last Farewell to the World. *Unknown.* APAS
Sir Thomas, stark green until he crept acurl. A Contempt for Dylan Thomas. Wilfred Watson. PeCV
Sir Thopas. Chaucer. *Fr.* The Canterbury Tales. Par (Tale of Sir Thopas, The.) BXAP
Sir, though (I thank God for it) I do hate. John Donne. Satires, II. OBSV; ViBoPo
Sir Toby Matthews. Sir John Suckling. SeCV-1
Sir Tristram was a Bear, in listed field. Tristram and Isolt. Don Marquis. HBMV
Sir Tristrem, *sel.* *At. to* Thomas of Erceldoune.
Tristrem and the Hunters. OxBS
Sir Walter Ralegh to His Son. Sir Walter Ralegh. *See* Wood, the Weed, the Wag, The.
Sir Walter Ralegh to the Queen. Sir Walter Ralegh. *See* Silent Lover, The.
Sir Walter Raleigh. E. C. Bentley. *Fr.* Clerihews. CenHV
Sir Walter Raleigh Sailing in the Low-lands. *Unknown.* *See* Golden Vanity, The.
Sir Walter Rauleigh His Lamentation. *Unknown.* CoMu
Sir Walter Scott at the Tomb of the Stuarts in St. Peter's. Richard Monckton Milnes. EBVV
Sir Walter Scott's Tribute. Sir Walter Scott. *See* Book of Books, The.
Sir, whatsoever you are pleas'd to do. Dedications [of Orchestra], II: To the Prince. Sir John Davies. SiPS
Sir! when I flew to seize the bird. Beau's Reply. William Cowper. FaBoCh
Sir, when you say. 15th Raga: For Bela Lugosi. David Meltzer. *Fr.* Ragas. NeAP
Sir William Dyer, Knight, *sel.* Lady Catherine Dyer.
Epitaph on the Monument of Sir William Dyer at Colmworth, 1641. BoLoP; EnLoPo; NIP
Sir William of Deloraine at the Wizard's Tomb. Sir Walter Scott. *See* Melrose Abbey.
Sir, you should [shall, *wr.*] notice me: I am the Man. Epitaph. Lascelles Abercrombie. MoBrPo; ViBoPo
Sir, you were a credit to whatever. To a Teacher of French. Donald Davie. OxBC
Sire. W. S. Merwin. CoAP; NaP; VGW
Sire of the rising day. Ode. Lord De Tabley. OBVV
Siren Chorus. George Darley. *See* Mermaiden's Vesper-Hymn, The.
Siren sang, and Europe turned away, A. To the Western World. Louis Simpson. CoAP; ConAP; GOA; LiTM; NePoAm-2; NePoEA-2; NOBA; PoPl; TAP
Siren Song. Margaret Atwood. *Fr.* Songs of the Transformed. HAP; PoA; WeW
Sirena. Michael Drayton. *See* Trent, The.
Sirens, The, *sel.* Laurence Binyon.
"Mystery of Dawn, ere yet the glory streams." GoTL
Sirens. Elliott Coleman. FAZ
Sirens, The. Donald Finkel. NePoEA
Sirens, The. Lou Lipsitz. LTB
Sirens, The. John Manifold. LiTB; LiTM; MoBrPo; WaP
Sirens in Bad Weather. Sherod Santos. MAYP
Sirens' Song, The. William Browne. *Fr.* Inner Temple Masque. EtS; NOBE; OBEV; PoPle
(Song of the Sirens.) ElL
(Song of the Syrens.) ChTr; OBS
("Steer hither, steer your winged pines.") ViBoPo
(Syrens' Song, The.) GBL
Sirius/ what mystery is this? Hilda Doolittle ("H. D."). *Fr.* The Walls Do Not Fall. PBWP
Sirmio. Catullus, *tr. fr. Latin by* Charles Stuart Calverley. AWP
Sirmio, thou dearest dear of strands. Catullus, *tr. fr. Latin by* Thomas Hardy. OBVE
Sirocco at Deyá. Robert Graves. MoVE
Sirs—though we fail you—let us live. To Men. Anna Wickham. MoBrPo
Sirventes. Paul Blackburn. NeAP; PoM
Sis Joe, *with music.* *Unknown.* OuSiCo
Sisiphus is he, whom noise and strife, The. The Fear of Death. Lucretius, *tr. by* Dryden. *Fr.* De Rerum Natura, III. LoBV
Siskins, The. Theodore Roethke. PB
Sisseton Indian Reservation, The. Richard Lyons. TAT
Sister. Gabriela Mistral, *tr. fr. Spanish by* Langston Hughes. BoWoP
Sister. Whittier. *Fr.* Snow-bound. AA
Sister and mother and diviner love. To the One of Fictive Music. Wallace Stevens. AP; CoBMV; MoAB; MoAmPo; MoVE; NoP; TwAmPo
Sister Anne, Sister Anne. Perspectives Are Precipices. John Peale Bishop. LiTA; MoVE; NePA
Sister, Awake! *Unknown.* CH; ElL; HBV-1; NOBE; OBEV; PoPle; PoSC
Sister Bernardo. Heather Wilde. FAZ
Sister Helen. Dante Gabriel Rossetti. BeLS; OAEP; VLP
Sister, it will be necessary. Mother Superior. George MacBeth. NMP
Sister Lou. Sterling A. Brown. AmNP; PoBA; PoNe
Sister Nell. *Unknown.* FaPON
Sister once of weeds & a dark water that held still. Family Romance. Larry Levis. MAYP
Sister Pharaoh. Ruth Whitman. MAT
Sister Rose. Richard Martin. AMV-81
"Sister, sister, go to bed!" Brother and Sister. "Lewis Carroll." ChTr; FaBoNo; ShM
Sister Songs, *sels.* Francis Thompson.
"But lo! at length the day is lingered out." OBMV
We Poets Speak. FaBV
Sister Veronica's class. A tall nun with a pale. Change of School. Elizabeth Smither. OCNZ
Sister was wedged beside the wicker basket. The Burned Bridge. Ruth Stone. WPE
Sister Zahava. Edith Bruck, *tr. fr. Italian by* Anita Barrows. VWA
Sistern and Brethren, *with music.* *Unknown.* TrAS
Sisters, The. Roy Campbell. BoLoP; ChMP; ErPo; FaBoTw; MoVE; OBMV
Sisters. Eleanor Farjeon. FaPON
Sisters, The. Nicki Jackowska. BrRo
Sisters, The. Amy Lowell. SBG
Sisters. Sandra McPherson. AmPA
Sisters. Adrienne Rich. IHMS
Sisters. Dorothy Roberts. CaP
Sisters, The. John Banister Tabb. AA
Sisters, The. Tennyson. InvP; PAI
Sisters, The. Whittier. AWP
Sisters/ Snow White and Rose Red. Breasts. Barbara Unger. DFT
Sisters,/ The Blue Nun has eloped with one. With a Bottle of Blue Nun to All My Friends. Madeline DeFrees. GP
Sisters are always drying their hair. Triolet against Sisters. Phyllis McGinley. OBCA
Sisters, listen to my story. The Kent State Massacre. Jack Warshaw *and* Barbara Dane. FSW
Sisyphus. Robert Garioch. BSV; PoSH
Sisyphus. Josephine Miles. NYBP
Sisyphus Angers the Gods of Condescension. Calvin Murry. LFAC
Sit down by the side of your mother, my boy. Mother's Advice. *Unknown.* AmFP
Sit Down, Sad Soul. Bryan Waller Procter. TreFT
Sit further, and make room for thine own fame. To His Worthy Friend Doctor Witty upon His Translation of the Popular Errors. Andrew Marvell. GLGT; PP
Sit-in, The. Darwin T. Turner. BALP
Sit on the bed. I'm blind, and three parts shell. A Terre. Wilfred Owen. LiTM; MMA; OxBTC; PAI; WaP
Sit quiet in my lap while solemnly. Evensong. Carleton Drewry. GoYe
Sit tight, little hills, little valleys. Dame Liberty Reports from Travel. Dorothy Cowles Pinkney. GoYe
Sitalkas. Hilda Doolittle ("H. D."). ViBoPo
Site of Ambush, *sel.* Eilean Ni Chuilleanain.
"At alarming bell daybreak, before." CIP
Sith fortune favors not and all things backward go. A Refusal. Barnabe Googe. EnRePo; NoP
Sith, in dark speech, Carvilios hymn unfolds. Hymn to the Sun. C. M. Doughty. *Fr.* The Dawn in Britain. FaBoTw
Sith my life from life is parted. Marie Magdalens Complaint at Christs Death. Robert Southwell. AnAnS-1; MePo
Sith sickles and the shearing scythe. Hawking for the Partridge. Thomas Ravenscroft. NCEP; OxBoLi
Sith Venus had her mole, Helen her stain. Against Proud Poor Phryna. John Davies of Hereford. FaBoEE
Sits at the window, waits the threatened steel. Medusa. Vincent O'Sullivan. PAI
Sits by a fireplace, the seducer talks. Sonnet. Leonard Wolf. ErPo
Sitter Bitter. Miss Bitter. N. M. Bodecker. NTCP
Sitters on the mead-bench, quaffing among questions. An Exeter Riddle. Gavin Ewart. OxBC
Sitteth alle stille and herkneth to me. The Song of Lewes [*or* Against the Baron's Enemies]. *Unknown.* MeEL; OxBM; OxBoLi
Sittin' on the Porch. Edgar A. Guest. TreFS
Sitting. Susan Griffin. NPGG

Sitting alone (as one forsook). The Vision. Robert Herrick. AnAnS-2; CaPo; ErPo; JCP; SeCP; UnTE
Sitting Alone in Tulsa Three A.M. Lance Henson. VoR
Sitting at a window. *See* Sitting at her window.
Sitting at evening in the warm grass. For My Wife. Julian Symons. NeBP; WaP
Sitting at her table, she serves. Nani. A. A. Rios. GP
Sitting at her [*or* a] window/ in her cloak and hat. Mother Tabbyskins. Elizabeth Anna Hart. CenHV; OxBChV
Sitting at Night on the Front Porch. Charles Wright. LCAP
Sitting at table, or. Dialectique. Hugh Maxton. CIP
Sitting Bard, The. Sir Owen Seaman. NOBL
Sitting between the sea and the buildings. The Painter. John Ashbery. NOBA; NoP; SOTW
Sitting Bull's Will versus the Sioux Treaty of 1868 and Monty Hall. A. K. Redwing. VoR
Sitting by a river [*or* river's] side. Philomela's Ode in Her Arbour. Robert Greene. *Fr.* Philomela, the Lady Fitzwater's Nightingale. OBSC; TEP
Sitting by the roadside on a summer day. Goober Peas. *Unknown.* FSW; PSoN
Sitting by the streams that glide. Bible, *O.T., paraphrased by* Thomas Carew. Psalm CXXXVII. OAEL-1
Sitting down near him in the shade. The Smoker. Robert Huff. GP; NePoEA-2
Sitting in Bib Overalls, Workshirt, Boots on the Monument to Liberty in the Center of the Square, Jacksonville, Illinois. Louis Daniel Brodsky. AMV-81
Sitting in the disorder of my silence. Fulfillment. Vassar Miller. NePoEA-2
Sitting in the shelter of this porch, I struggle. The Origins of Escape. Charles P. R. Tisdale. AMV-81
Sitting in the Woods: A Contemplation. W. R. Moses. NCSH
Sitting in this garden you cannot escape symbols. The Phoenix Answered. Anne Ridler. ChMP
Sitting, legs crossed, copper-toned old man. My Song. King D. Kuka. VoR
Sitting naked together. Rain Journal: London: June 65. Lee Harwood. PeHV
Sitting Pretty. Margaret Fishback. PoLF
Sitting straightbacked, a modest Irish miss. A Lesson in Love. Philip Hobsbaum. OxBTC
Sitting under the mistletoe. Mistletoe. Walter de la Mare. SO
Sitting upright in the 2 a.m. blackness, off-balance. Too Many Miles of Sunlight between Us. Jack Myers. AMV-80
Situation. Langston Hughes. OBAL
Situation Normal. Hank Chernick. WhC
Six!/ Such different minds and faces! Mistresses. *Unknown, tr. by* Frank O'Connor. KiLC
Six Badgers, The. Robert Graves. GoJo; GrPl; WSC
Six beds in a square room: you give your name. Wait. Timothy Steele. PoA
Six children dear, God, died out in this waste. Beyond Feith Buidhe. Hamish Brown. PoSH
Six Days. Mario Petaccia. LFAC
Six disorderly bears. Bad Example. Isabella Fey. BoAnP
Six Divine Circles. Gail Ghai. AMV-81
Six Dukes Went a-Fishing. *Unknown.* FaBoBa; OBET
Six Eagles. Thomas Peacock. VoR
Six Epigrams, *sel.* Gerard Manley Hopkins.
"No, they are come; their horn is lifted up." SeCePo
Six feet beneath. Jerry Jones. *Unknown.* ShM
Six Feet of Earth. *Unknown.* BLPA
Six Feet Under. Janet Campbell Hale. VoR
Six-foot nest of the sea-hawk, The. Sea-Hawk. Richard Eberhart. BoAnP
Six foot two in his moccasins. Alibi. Zoe A. Tilghman. BPAW
Six-forty-two Farm Commune Struggle Poem. Jay Leifer. MAT
Six Haiku for Graham V. Phillips Who First Said the First One. Robert Phillips. GrPl
Six-Horse Limited Mail, The. Ethel Romig Fuller. BPAW
Six hundred dark feet from the cliffs. "But Still in Israel's Paths They Shine." Carter Revard. VoR
Six hundred stalwart warriors of England's pride the best. Balaclava. *Unknown.* OBET
Six Hundred Thousand Letters, The. Harvey Shapiro. VWA
Six Jolly Wee Miners. *Unknown.* CoMu
Six kilos of cat! Fat Cat. John Ronan. AMV-81
Six little mice sat down to spin. Mother Goose. HBV-1; OxNR
Six month child, The. Slippery. Carl Sandburg. FaPON; TiPo
Six Movements on a Theme. David Ignatow. NNaP
Six o'Clock. Owen Dodson. PoNe
Six o'Clock. Trumbull Stickney. NCEP; OxBA; PPoB
Six o'clock and/ the sun rises across the river. Love Poem. Miller Williams. MAT
Six o'clock, the morning still and. The Names. Lauris Edmond. OCNZ
Six of Cups. Diane Wakoski. CoPo
Six Periods of Creation, The. *Maori Oral Tradition, tr. by* Richard Taylor. WTO
Six Poets in Search of a Lawyer. Donald Hall. NYBP
Six-Quart Basket, The. Raymond Souster. MoCV; PeCV
Six Reasons for Drinking. Vernon Scannell. OxBC
Six Religious Lyrics, *sel.* Karl Shapiro.
"I sing the simplest flower," I. CMoP
Six street-ends come together here. Blue Island Intersection. Carl Sandburg. MoAmPo
Six Sunday. Hart Leroi Bibbs. NBP
Six Ten Sixty-nine. Conyus. PoBA
Six times faster than the fool can weep. The Peasant. Leonard Wolf. NYBP
Six to Six. *Unknown, tr. fr. Xhosa by* A. C. Jordan. PBA
Six Town Eclogues, *sel.* Lady Mary Wortley Montagu.
Saturday: The Small-Pox. NOEC; WPE
Six Variations. Denise Levertov. AmPP; ConAP; CoPo; LCAP
"Shlup, shlup, the dog," III. HeIP; InPK
Six Week Old Blues. *Unknown.* BluL
Six Weeks Old. Christopher Morley. RHPC
Six Winter Privacy Poems. Robert Bly. LCAP
Six Winters. Ruthven Todd. NeBP
Six wives I've had and they're all dead. The Fox and the Hare. *Unknown.* OBET
Six-Year-Old Marjory Fleming Pens a Poem. Marjory Fleming. *See* Melancholy Lay, A.
Six Years. Alice Bloch. PeHV
Six years ago in Ohio we argued free will. On the Lawn at Ira's. Gregory Orr. GeTw
Six Years Later. Joseph Brodsky, *tr. fr. Russian by* Richard Wilbur. AMV-80
Six Young Men. Ted Hughes. OBWP
"Sixpence a week," says the girl to her lover. By Her Aunt's Grave. Thomas Hardy. *Fr.* Satires of Circumstance. MoAB; MoBrPo
Sixt Nimphall, The. Michael Drayton. *See* Fine Day, A.
Sixteen Dead Men. Dora Sigerson Shorter. ACP; OnYI
Sixteen Dead Men. W. B. Yeats. OBWP
16/53. Marge Piercy. NeAC
1614 Boren. Richard Hugo. LCAP
16. ix. 65. James Merrill. NAs
Sixteen years ago I built this house. A World within a War. Sir Herbert Read. MoPo
Sixteen years old and beautiful. Girl. A. W. Purdy. NoAM
Sixth Book of the Aeneis, The, *sel.* Virgil, *tr. fr. Latin by* Dryden.
"Let others better mold the running Mass." SeCV-2
Sixth Day, The. Betty Adcock. LiSp
Sixth Hell, The. Jerome Rothenberg. *Fr.* The Seven Hells of Jigoku Zoshi. NNaP
Sixth Song: "O you that hear this voice." Sir Philip Sidney. *See* Astrophel and Stella: Sixth Song.
Sixth was August, being rich arrayed, The. August. Spenser. *Fr.* The Faerie Queene, VII, 7. GN
Sixties, The. Thomas Listmann. AMV-80
Sixties, I think, were not a total loss, The. January 15 as a National Holiday. Carter Revard. VoR
Sixty-eighth Birthday. James Russell Lowell. PCP; PoEL-5
61. Charlotte DeClue. TWSS
Sixty-one years. Money in the Bank. W. D. Ehrhart. FAZ
Size of a cavern for men to crouch in, The. Dawn Hippo. Sydney Clouts. PeSA
Skaian Gate, The, *sel.* Geoffrey Scott.
"Hector, the captain bronzed, from simple fight." OBMV
Skater, The. Sir Charles G. D. Roberts. NOBC
Skaters, The. John Gould Fletcher. MoAmPo
Skaters, The. John Williams. LiSp; NePoAm-2
Skaters, The. Wordsworth. *See* On the Frozen Lake.
Skater's Valentine, A. Arthur Guiterman. SiSoSe
Skater's Waltz, A. Gray Burr. CoPo
Skating. Herbert Asquith. FaPON; SoPo; SUS; TiPo
Skating ("And in the frosty season, when the sun"). Wordsworth. *See* On the Frozen Lake.
Skating ("So through the darkness and the cold we flew"). Wordsworth. *Fr.* The Prelude, I. CH
'Skeeter and Peter, The. Marie Bruckman MacDonald. TDH
'Skeeters am a hummin' on de honeysuckle vine. Kentucky Babe. Richard Henry Buck. AA; FSN; HBV-1
Skein, The. Carolyn Kizer. PrIm; VGW
Skeleton, The. G. K. Chesterton. FaBoTw

Skeleton at the Feast, The. James Jeffrey Roche. AA
Skeleton in Armor, The. Longfellow. AA; AmPP; AP; AWP; BeLS; BLPL; FaBoBe; HBV-2; HBVY; PAH; TreF
Skeleton in the Cupboard, The. Frederick Locker-Lampson. HBV-1
Skeleton is hiding in the closet as it should, The. Everything in Its Place. Arthur Guiterman. OBAL
Skeleton Key. John Hollander. InPK; NoP
Skeleton of the Future, The. "Hugh MacDiarmid." GoTS; MoBrPo; OBMV
Skeleton Once in Khartoum, A. *Unknown.* ShM
Skeleton Parade. Jack Prelutsky. NTCP
Skelton Laureate, Defender, against Lusty Garnesche, Well-beseen Christopher, Challenger. John Skelton. TW
Skeltoniad, A. Michael Drayton. PoEL-2; PP
Skeptic, The. Robert Service. PV
Skerryvore. Robert Louis Stevenson. EyDe
Sketch, A. Byron. OBRV
(Sketch from Private Life, A.) OBNC
Sketch. "Seumas O'Sullivan." AnIV
Sketch, A. Christina Rossetti. GTBS-P
Sketch. Carl Sandburg. AP; HBMV
Sketch for a Job Application Blank. Jim Harrison. AmPA; NoAM
Sketch for a Morning in Muncie, Indiana. G. E. Murray. MAYP
Sketch from Private Life, A. Byron. *See* Sketch, A.
Sketch of His Own Character. Thomas Gray. LAuP
Sketch of Lord Byron's Life. Julia A. Moore. OBAL
" 'Lord Byron' was an Englishman," *sel.* FiBHP
Sketches of Harlem. David Henderson. CABA; NNP; PoNe
Skew-Ball Black, The. *Unknown.* CoSo
Ski Trail. Samuel Allen. FB
Skier. Robert Francis. LiSp; NCSH; RFM
Skiers. Robert Penn Warren. *Fr.* In the Mountains. LiSp
Skies are low, the winds are slow, The. Under the Blue. Francis Fisher Browne. AA
Skies contain still groves of silver clouds, The. Spring 1943. Roy Fuller. LiTB; LiTM; WaP
Skies have sunk, and hid the upper snow, The. Les Vaches. Arthur Hugh Clough. OAEP; PeD
Skies is different than they was, The. A Spring Lay. Oliver Opdyke. InMe
Skies they were ashen and sober, The, *parody.* The Willows. Bret Harte. BXAP; InMe
Skies they were ashen and sober, The. Ulalume. Poe. AA; AmPP; AP; AWP; BLPL; LiTA; NePA; NOBA; OxBA; TAP; TreF; ViBoPo; WHA
Skies to the West are stained with madder. Gloaming. Robert Adger Bowen. HBV-1
Skiing on Russian Christmas. Nora Dauenhauer. TWSS
Skilful Listener, The. John Vance Cheney. AA
Skilful Spearman, A! *Tr. fr. Hawaiian.* WTO
Skill'd to deceive our ears and eyes. The County Member. Winthrop Mackworth Praed. *Fr.* The County Ball. OBNC
Skilled in each art that can adorn the fair. The Modern Fine Lady. Soame Jenyns. NOEC
Skilled to pull wires, he baffles Nature's hope. The Boss. James Russell Lowell. OBAL; SaC
Skimbleshanks: The Railway Cat. T. S. Eliot. FaBoCo; NOBL
Skimmers. Ted Walker. NYBP
Skimming/ an asphalt sea. The Sidewalk Racer; or, On the Skateboard. Lillian Morrison. NTCP; RHPC
Skimming lightly, wheeling still. Shiloh; a Requiem. Herman Melville. AmFN; AP; FF; LiTA; NCEP; NOBA; NoP; OBWP; OxBA; PAL; SCV; ViBoPo; WiR
Skin. Philip K. Jason. AMV-81
Skin-and-Bone Lady, The. *Unknown.* AmFP
Skin Divers, The. George Starbuck. NYBP
Skin Diving in the Virgins. John Malcolm Brinnin. NYBP; TAP
Skin-flakes, repetitions, erosions. Ezra Pound. *Fr.* Cantos, XV. MoPo
Skin Man. *Unknown.* BluL
Skin of my mouth, chewed raw, tastes good, The. The Expectant Father. Ai. GeTw
Skin of the sea, The. In Sylvia Plath Country. Erica Jong. IHMS
Skin pulsates. Diary. Charlotte DeClue. TWSS
Skin quickens to noises, The. One Eyed Black Man in Nebraska. Sam Cornish. PoBA
Skin ripples over my body like moon-wooed water, The. Prison Song. Alan Dugan. PoA
Skin that is a closed curtain. Poll. Ed Roberson. PoBA
Skin the Goat's Curse on Carey. *Unknown.* BlrV; TW
Skinful of bowls, he bowls them. Second Glance at a Jaguar. Ted Hughes. NoAM; NYBP; PrIm
Skinning-the-Cat. Dennis Schmitz. NPGG
Skinny Girl, The. Anne Hébert, *tr. fr. French by* Willis Barnstone. BoWoP
Skinny Mrs. Snipkin. Mrs. Snipkin and Mrs. Wobblechin. Laura E. Richards. OxBChV; SoPo; TiPo
Skinny waterfalls, footpaths, The. Lastness. Galway Kinnell. NNaP
Skins. Elizabeth Spires. MAYP
Skip-Scoop-Anellie. Tom Prideaux. FiBHP
Skip to My Lou. *Unknown.* AmFP; FSW; TrAS, *with music*
Skipper-Hermit, The. Hiram Rich. EtS
Skipper Ireson's Ride. Whittier. AA; AP; BeLS; HBV-2; InMe; NOBA; OBAL; OBCA; OxBA; PAH; PoLF; TreFS; YaD
Skipping Along Alone. Winifred Welles. SoPo; TiPo
Skirt Dance. Ishmael Reed. FF
Skirting the river road (my forenoon walk, my rest). The Dalliance of the Eagles. Walt Whitman. AA; AmPP; BiP; BoAnP; CABA; FaBoEn; FM; HAP; HeIP; InPK; NoP; POL; PPoe; PPP; PrIm; TAP
Skittery two-year-olds. Morgans in October. Suzanne Brabant. PH
Skreak and skritter of evening gone, The. Autumn Refrain. Wallace Stevens. LiTA
Skull, The. Ian Young. NeAC
Skull in the Desert, The. Alison A. Trimpi. AMV-81
Skull of a Neandertal. Michael Cadnum. SUW
Skull stark. The Strath of Kildonan. Betty Morris. PoSH
Skunk, The. Dorothy Baruch. SoPo
Skunk, The. Robert P. Tristram Coffin. FaPON; TiPo
Skunk, The. Philip Dow. BXAP
Skunk, The. Seamus Heaney. OxBC
Skunk cabbage, bloodroot. The Round. Philip Booth. BoNaP; GrPl; NCSH
Skunk Hour. Robert Lowell. AmPP; AP; BiP; CAPP; CMoP; CoAP; ConAP; FaBoMo; HAP; HeIP; InPK; LCAP; MoAmPo; NIP; NMP; NoAM; NOBA; NoP; OxBC; PAI; PPP; PrIm; SCV; TAP; WeW
Skunk to the Gnu, The. Gerard Neyroud. TDH
Skunks, *sel.* Robinson Jeffers.
"We have little animals here." BoAnP
Sky, The. Elizabeth Madox Roberts. MoAmPo
Sky, The. Richard Henry Stoddard. AA
Sky, The. *Unknown, tr. fr. Ewe by* Ulli Beier. TTY
Sky a black sphere, The. Lighthouse in the Night. Alfonsini Storni, *tr. by* Aliki *and* Willis Barnstone. BoWoP
Sky, a dome of glaring brass, The. 112 at Presidio. Virginia Long. AMV-80
Sky a shock, the gingkos yellow fever, The. Riverside Drive, November Fifth. Katha Pollitt. AMV-81
Sky above London, The. London Night. Kathleen Raine. NeBP
Sky at night is like a big city, The. The Sky. *Unknown, tr. by* Ulli Beier. TTY
Sky can't get in, The. Room. Shirley Kaufman. NMM
Sky ceases. There is only. Michael Dransfield. Geography, VI. CBAP
Sky Clears, The. *Tr. fr. Chippewa Indian by* Frances Densmore. OBVE
Sky Diver. Adrien Stoutenburg. LiSp
Sky Diving. Richmond Lattimore. LiSp
Sky grew darker with each minute, The. Before the Storm. Richard Dehmel, *tr. by* Ludwig Lewisohn. AWP
Sky hangs heavy tonight, The. Negro Woman. Lewis Alexander. CDC; PoBA
Sky has been dark, The. The Youngest Daughter. Cathy Song. MAYP
Sky in its lucent splendor lifted. A Tropical Morning at Sea. Edward Rowland Sill. EtS
Sky in red mist. *Unknown.* FaBoUs
Sky is a dead fish, The. The Plaque in the Reading Room for My Classmates Killed in Korea. F. D. Reeve. GOA
Sky is a drinking-cup, The. The Sky. Richard Henry Stoddard. AA
Sky Is Blue, The. David Ignatow. FF; NNaP
Sky is changed, The!—and such a change! Oh night. Sky, Mountains, River! Byron. *Fr.* Childe Harold's Pilgrimage. WHA
Sky is cold as pearl, The. Ancient. "Æ." SeCePo
Sky is dark and the hills are white, The. Norse Lullaby. Eugene Field. SUS
Sky is dotted like th' unleavened bread, The. Haggadah. Abraham M. Klein. TrJP
Sky is gray with rain that will not fall, The. At the Zoo. Israel Zangwill. TrJP
Sky is haywire alive with fire, The. Weeding in January. Louis Daniel Brodsky. AMV-80
Sky is heavy, it is raining stars, The. The Cannibal Hymn. *Unknown, tr. by* Samuel A. B. Mercer. TTY
Sky is hid in a snowy shroud, The. The Snowstorm. Frederick George Scott. PeCV
Sky is his ceiling, grass is his bed. Speaking of Cowboy's Home. *Unknown.* CoSo
Sky is low, the clouds are mean, The. Emily Dickinson. AA; BoNaP; ELU; FaBoEn; FaBV; MoAmPo; OxBA; PoEL-5
Sky is overcast, The. A Night-Piece. Wordsworth. EnRP; MOON

Sky is perfectly clear, The. Maximian Elegy V. Kenneth Rexroth. CrMA
Sky is ruddy in the east, The. The Ship-Builders. Whittier. EtS
Sky is such a softness, is such dark. No Moon, No Star. Babette Deutsch. NYBP
Sky Is Up above the Roof, The. Paul Verlaine, *tr. fr. French by* Ernest Dowson. *Fr.* Sagesse. AWP; FaPON; SyP
Sky, lazily disdaining to pursue, The. Georgia Dusk. Jean Toomer. AmNP; BPo; CDC; NoAM; NoP; PoBA
Sky, The—like a lunatic's dream. Landscape. Abraham Sutskever, *tr. by* Ruth Whitman. VWA
Sky links cloud waves, links dawn fog. Li Ch'ing-chae, *tr. fr. Chinese by* Willis Barnstone *and* Sun Chu-chin. BoWoP
Sky, Mountains, River! Byron. *Fr.* Childe Harold's Pilgrimage, III. WHA
Sky of gray is eaten in six places, The. Broken Sky. Carl Sandburg. PCP
Sky of Late Summer, A, *sel.* Henry Rago.
"Fountains of fire, The." NMP
Sky Pair, A. Robert Frost. MoAB; MoAmPo
Sky Patterns. Jeannette Maino. AMV-80
Sky Pictures. Mary Effie Lee Newsome. CDC
Sky, reading our thoughts, The. Tornado Watch, Bloomington, Indiana. Gary Young. SUW
Sky sags low with convoluted cloud, The. Rain. W. E. Henley. SyP
Sky seemed so small that winter day, The. Two Illustrations That the World Is What You Make of It. Wallace Stevens. NePoAm
Sky so pale, and the trees, such frail things, The. A la Promenade. Paul Verlaine, *tr. by* Arthur Symons. AWP; OBVE
Sky the color of a wrens breath, A. At Chadwicks Bar and Grill. Lance Henson. STE
Sky turns, The. Numbers. Harley Elliott. LTB
Sky unfolding its blankets to free, The. Morning Workout. Babette Deutsch. LiSp; NePoAm-2
Sky was battened down, The. On Galveston Beach. Barbara Howes. MoAmPo
Sky was blue, so blue, that day, The. For the Candle Light. Angelina Weld Grimké. BlSi; CDC; PoNe
Sky was gold in those days, The. In the Beginning. Valerie Sinason. BrRo
Sky was low, the sounding rain was falling dense and dark, The. The Late Passenger. C. S. Lewis. EBCP; TrCP
Sky was on the hill, The. When You Reach the Hilltop the Sky Is on Top of You. Etta Blum. GoYe
Sky where the white clouds stand in prayer. Easter. Mary Carolyn Davies. OHIP
Sky widens to Cornwall, The. A sense of sea. In Memoriam: A. C., R.J.O., K.S. John Betjeman. NYBP
Sky with clouds was overcast, The. Washing Day. *Unknown.* CoMu
Skycoast. Samuel Hazo. GrPl
Skye. John Gawsworth. PoSH
Skye, *sel.* W. W. Gibson.
Witch, The. PoSH
Skye Summer ("Skye rasps the mind"). Islay Murray Donaldson. PoSH
Skyhook. Gary Allan Kizer. LFAC
Skyjacker, The. Stan Rice. NPGG
Skykomish River Running. Richard Hugo. PoA
Skylark, The. James Hogg. GN; HBV-1; HBVY; PBBP
Skylark, The. Frederick Tennyson. GN; HBV-1
Sky-lark hath perceived his prison-door, The. On a Picture by J. M. Wright, Esq. Robert Southey. FM
Skylarks. Ted Hughes. HAP
Skylarks are far behind that sang over the down, The. Good-Night. Edward Thomas. NoP
Skylark's Nest, The. R. H. Long. PoAu-1
Sky-Lark's Song, The. John Bennett. *Fr.* Master Sky-Lark. AA
Skylights. Tess Gallagher. MAYP
Skylike limpid eyes, The. Brennbaum. Erza Pound. *Fr.* Hugh Selwyn Mauberley. MoAmPo
Skyline of New York does not excite me, The. Review from Staten Island. Gloria C. Oden. NNP; PoBA; PPP
Sky's a faded blue and taut-stretched flag, The. Jardin du Palais Royal. David Gascoyne. MoPo
Sky's as blue and black as ink, The. Calligram, 15 May 1915. Guillaume Apollinaire, *tr. by* O. Bernard. OBWP
Sky's lip and the sea's lip shut in peace, The. Lines on the Sea. Dilys Bennett Laing. NYBP
Sky's unresting cloudland, that with varying play, The. Robert Bridges. *Fr.* The Testament of Beauty. EBEV; MoVE
Skyscraper. Carl Sandburg. PoPl
Skyscrapers. Rachel Field. FaPON
"Slack your rope, hangs-a-man." The Maid Freed from the Gallows [*or* Hangsaman]. *Unknown.* AS; TrAS
Slacker Apologizes, The. Peter Viereck. MiAP
Slain. T. W. H. Crosland. OBWP
Slain Lamb of God, *with music.* Nicolaus L. Zinzendorf, *tr. fr. German by* Sheema Z. Buehne. AH
Slainthe! Patrick MacGill. AnIV
(Dedication: "I speak with a proud tongue.") OnYI
Slant of Sun on Dull Brown Walls, A. Stephen Crane. War Is Kind, XIV. LiTM
(Hymn: "Slant of sun on dull brown walls, A.") MoAmPo
Slant sheen/ wrinkled silver. Letters to Walt Whitman, II. Ronald Johnson. VGW
Slant-windowed belt-footed enormously long-boomed, A. Bucyrus. John Holmes. CrMA; NePoAm
Slashed clouds leak gold. Along the slurping wharf. Fishing Harbour towards Evening. Richard Kell. CIP
Slaughter of the Innocents by Order of King Herod, The. Caelius Sedulius, *tr. fr. Latin by* George Sigerson. *Fr.* Carmen Paschale. OnYI
Slaughter of the Laird of Mellerstain, The. *Unknown.* ESPB
Slaughter-House, The. Alfred Hayes. LiTA
Slaughterhouse Boys, The. William Meissner. AMV-81
Slave. Langston Hughes. LiTM
Slave, The. James Oppenheim. TrJP
Slave, The. Jones Very. AP; TAP
Slave and the Iron Lace, The. Margaret Danner. AmNP; BPo
Slave Auction, The. Frances E. W. Harper. BPo; PoNe; TTY
Slave Chase, The. *Unknown.* CoMu
Slave Marriage Ceremony Supplement. *Unknown.* BPo; POL; TAP
Slave Quarters. James Dickey. CAPP; NYBP
Slave Singing at Midnight, The. Longfellow. GOA
Slave Story. Hodding Carter. PoNe
Slavery Chain Done Broke at Last. *Unknown.* FSW
(Slav'ry Chain, *with music.*) TrAS
Slaves. James Grainger. *Fr.* The Sugar Cane. NOEC
Slaves. James Russell Lowell. *Fr.* Stanzas on Freedom. TRV; WBLP
(Commitment.) TreFT
(On Freedom.) PAL
(Stanza on Freedom, A.) AA
Slaves Cannot Breathe in England. William Cowper. *Fr.* The Task, II. OBEC
Slave's Dream, The. Longfellow. FaPoR; OBVV; PoNe
Slaves to London. Peter Anthony Motteux. *Fr.* Love's a Jest. OAEP
Slav'ry Chain. *Unknown. See* Slavery Chain Done Broke at Last.
Slay fowl and beast; pluck clean the vine. Cavalier. Richard Bruce. CDC
Slayer of winter, art thou here again? March. William Morris. HBV-1
Slaying of multitudes should be mourned with sorrow, The. *Unknown. Fr.* Tao Teh King. TRV
Sledburn Fair. *Unknown.* CH
Sledding Song, A. Norman C. Schlichter. FaPON
Sleek and lax as a slug in the grass. The Sun-Bather. Kim Kurt. NePoAm-2
Sleek as a lizard at round of a stone. Penetration and Trust. George Meredith. VLP
Sleep. Thomas Bailey Aldrich. AA
Sleep. Beaumont *and* Fletcher. *See* Come, Sleep.
Sleep. Mei-mei Berssenbrugge. LTB
Sleep. Alice Brown. AA
Sleep, The. Elizabeth Barrett Browning. HBV-2; TRV; WGRP
Sleep. Abraham Cowley. ChTr
Sleep M. R. Doty. AMV-80
Sleep, A. Larry Eigner. CoPo
Sleep. Bartholomew Griffin. *Fr.* Fidessa, More Chaste than Kind. OBSC
("Care-charmer sleep, sweet ease in restless misery.") NIP
("Care-charmer sleepe, sweet ease in restles miserie.") AAS
Sleep. Bravig Imbs. EAS
Sleep. William Knott. EAS
Sleep. Robert Eyres Landor. *Fr.* The Impious Feast. OBRV
Sleep. Ada Louise Martin. HBV-2
Sleep. Dana Naone. CDW
Sleep. Del Marie Rogers. LTB
Sleep. Thomas Sackville. *Fr.* The Induction to "The Mirror for Magistrates." WHA
Sleep. Shakespeare. *Fr.* Macbeth, II, ii. TreFS
Sleep ("Come, sleep, O sleep, the certain knot of peace"). Sir Philip Sidney. *See* Astrophel and Stella, XXXIX.
Sleep, ("Lock up, fair lids"). Sir Philip Sidney. *Fr.* Arcadia. OBSC; SiPS
(Sonnet: "Lock up, fair lids, the treasure of my heart.") ElL
Sleep. Charles Simic. CoAP
Sleep. Statius, *tr. fr. Latin by* W. H. Fyfe. AWP
Sleep. Lewis Frank Tooker. AA
Sleep. Theophile de Viau, *tr. fr. French by* Sir Edmund Gosse. AWP
Sleep. Yvor Winters. POL
Sleep/ Now the charge is won. Taps. Lizette Woodworth Reese. OHIP
Sleep a little, a little little. The Sleep Song of Diarmaid and Grainne [*or* The Sleep-Song of Grainne over Dermiud]. *Unknown.* AnIV; OnYI

Sleep after Toil. Spenser. *Fr.* The Faerie Queene, I, 9. ChTr
("He there does now enjoy eternall rest.") MOS
Sleep: and between the closed eyelids of sleep. Conrad Aiken. Preludes for Memnon, III. LiTA; TwAmPo
Sleep and His Brother Death. William Hamilton Hayne. AA
Sleep and Poetry. Keats. EnRP; PP
Sels.
"Could all this be forgotten? Yes, a schism." ChER
"O for ten years, that I may overwhelm." OAEL-2
"Stop and consider! life is but a day." OBRV; SeCePo; TreFT
Sleep, Angry Beauty. Thomas Campion. EnRePo; ErPo; HBV-1; NCEP; TrGrPo
(Sleep, Angry Beauty, Sleep.) FF
("Sleep, angry beauty, sleep and fear me not!") ElL
Sleep at noon. Window blind. Hurricane. Archibald MacLeish. NCSH
Sleep at Sea. Christina Rossetti. MOS; NBM; PoEL-5
Sleep, Baby Boy. *Unknown.* FaPON
Sleep, baby mine, Desire, nurse Beauty singeth. Sir Philip Sidney. NOBE
Sleep, Baby, Sleep ("Sleep baby sleep!/ Thy father watches the sheep"). *Unknown.* FaPON
Sleep, Baby, Sleep. George Wither. HBV-1
Sleep Brings No Joy. Emily Brontë. ViBoPo
Sleep, calm winter sleep, the rides are woollen. Calm Winter Sleep. Hilary Corke. MP; NYBP
Sleep Close to Me. Gabriela Mistral, *tr. fr. Spanish by* D. M. Pettinella. PBWP
Sleep, comrades, sleep and rest. Decoration Day. Longfellow. OHIP; PoSC
Sleep enfold thee,/ Jesukin. Cradle Song. James L. Duff. ISi
Sleep evades me, there's no light. Verses Written during a Sleepless Night. Pushkin, *tr. by* Babette Deutsch. PoPl
Sleep, gray brother of death. On Waking. Joseph Campbell. AnIV
Sleep in the Heat. Laura Jensen. AmPA
Sleep in the Mojave Desert. Sylvia Plath. NoP
Sleep in your silent glory. The Cliff Dwelling. Arthur W. Monroe. PoOW
Sleep is a country of water. Country of Water. Bernice Ames. WPE
Sleep is a god too proud to wait in palaces. Sleep. Abraham Cowley. ChTr
Sleep Is a Reconciling. *Unknown.* *See* Weep You No More.
Sleep is 20. 20. Barbara Guest. PoM
Sleep, King Jesus. Mary's Song. Charles Causley. OBCP
Sleep late with your dream. For My Brother. Owen Dodson. Poems for My Brother Kenneth, VII. BALP; IDB; PoBA; PoNe
Sleep-Learning. Ruth Fainlight. NMM
Sleep, little Baby, sleep;/ The holy angels love thee. Holy Innocents. Christina Rossetti. HBV-1; HBVY
Sleep, little baby, sleep and rest. Lullaby. Elinor Chipp. HBMV
Sleep, little one, sleep. Schlof, Bobbeli. *Unknown.* TrAS
Sleep, little one, sleep for me. Response. Bob Kaufman. BOLo
Sleep, love, sleep! Watching. "Fanny Forester." AA
Sleep, love, sleep. Lullaby. Quandra Prettyman. BOLo
Sleep, Madame, Sleep. Annemarie Ewing. NePoAm
Sleep, McKade. Evening Song. Kenneth Fearing. EAS
Sleep, Motley, with the great of ancient days. In Memory of John Lothrop Motley. Bryant. AA
Sleep, mouseling, sleep. Lullaby. Elizabeth J. Coatsworth. SiSoSe
Sleep, Mr. Speaker! it's surely fair. Stanzas to the Speaker Asleep [*or* Stanzas on Seeing the Speaker Asleep in His Chair]. Winthrop Mackworth Praed. EnRP; NBM; OBSV; VLP
Sleep, my babe, lie still and slumber. *See* Sleep, my child, and peace attend thee.
Sleep, my baby, little elf. For Little Boys Destined for Big Business. Samuel Hoffenstein. DBV
Sleep, my baby, while I sing. Bed-Time Song. Emilie Poulsson. HBV-1; HBVY
Sleep, My Child. Sholom Aleichem, *tr. fr. Yiddish by* Alter Brody. TrJP
Sleep, my child [*or* babe *or* love], and peace attend thee [*or* lie still and slumber]. All through the Night. Harold Boulton, *also at. to* David Owen. FaPON; FSW; TreFS
Sleep, my child, my little daughter. Cradle Song. *Unknown, tr. by* Joseph Leftwich. TrJP
Sleep my child, sleep. Shlof Mayn Kind, Shlof Keseyder (Sleep My Child). *Unknown.* FSW
Sleep, my child—sleep, it is late! Lullaby for Miriam. Richard Beer-Hofmann, *tr. by* Jonathan Griffin. VWA
Sleep, my darling, sleep. Cradle Song. Louis MacNeice. OxBI; PoPl
Sleep, my little baby, sleep. Lullaby. Samuel Hoffenstein. TrJP
Sleep, my love, and peace attend thee. *See* Sleep, my child, and peace attend thee.
Sleep Not, Dream Not. Emily Brontë. LoBV
Sleep now. Lullaby. Shlomo Vinner, *tr. by* Laya Firestone. VWA
Sleep now, O sleep now. James Joyce. GBL
Sleep, O sleep. Song. John Gay. Polly, Air XXIII. FaBoEn; ViBoPo
Sleep of the Brave, The. William Collins. *See* How Sleep the Brave.
Sleep of the late afternoon, The. Resounding. Katherine Soniat. AMV-81
Sleep of this night deepens, The. Under Stars. Tess Gallagher. GeTw; MAYP
Sleep on, and dream of Heaven awhile. The Sleeping Beauty. Samuel Rogers. GTBS; GTBS-P; HBV-1
Sleep on, beloved, sleep and take thy rest. The Christian's "Good-Night." Sarah Doudney. BLPA
Sleep on, dear, now. The Dead Child. Ernest Dowson. BrPo
Sleep on, I lie at heaven's high oriels. Nirvana. John Hall Wheelock. HBMV; MoAmPo
Sleep on, my Love, in thy cold bed. Henry King. *Fr.* The Exequy. CH; PoPle; TrGrPo
Sleep on that short summer. Six Days. Mario Petaccia. LFAC
Sleep on the Fraser. Patrick Lane. NeAC
Sleep only with strangers. George Jonas. NeAC
Sleep, our lord, and for thy peace. Night Song for a Child. Charles Williams. OBEV
Sleep, Silence' Child [Sweet Father of Soft Rest]. William Drummond of Hawthornden. BSV; HBV-2
(Sonnet: "Sleep[e], Silence' child, sweet father of soft rest.") ElL; OBS
(Sonet to Sleepe.) OxBS
Sleep, sleep, beauty bright. Cradle Song. Blake. EnRP; FPL; HBV-1; HBVY; OBEC; OBEV; PoLF; PoPl
Sleep, sleep mine Holy One! The Virgin Mary to the Child Jesus, *abr.* Elizabeth Barrett Browining. ISi
Sleep, sleep, sleep/ In thy folded waves, O Sea! Sea-Sleep. Thomas Lake Harris. AA
Sleep, sleep, sweetly sleep. Lady Day in Harvest. Sheila Kaye-Smith. ISi
Sleep softly . . . eagle forgotten . . . under the stone. The Eagle That Is Forgotten. Vachel Lindsay. AWP; CMoP; HBV-2; LiTA; MoAB; MoAmPo; NePA; NOBA; OxBA; TwAmPo; ViBoPo; WHA
Sleep Song of Diarmaid and Grainne, The. *Unknown, tr. fr. Late Middle Irish by* Eoin MacNeill. OnYI
(Sleep-Song of Grainne over Dermiud, The, *tr. by* Eleanor Hull.) AnIV
Sleep sound, O soldier, through the night. Pillow Cases. Richard Armour. WhC
Sleep Sweet. Ellen M. Huntington Gates. BLPA; BLRP; FaBoBe
Sleep sweetly in your humble graves. Ode [*or* At Magnolia Cemetery *or* Ode Sung on the Occasion of Decorating the Graves of the Confederate Dead *or* Ode to the Confederate Dead]. Henry Timrod. AA; AH; AP; GOA; HBV-2; NOBA; OxBA; PAL; TAP; TreFT
Sleep That Like the Couchèd Dove. Gerald Griffin. OnYI
Sleep, Thou little Child of Mary. Song of a Shepherd Boy at Bethlehem. Josephine Preston Peabody. OHIP
Sleep upon the World. Alcman, *tr. fr. Greek by* Thomas Campbell. ChTr
Sleep was only a dream. Chicago: Near West-Side Renewal. Dennis Schmitz. AmPA
Sleep Watch. Lance Henson. VoR
Sleep, Wayward Thoughts. *Unknown.* *See* So Sleeps My Love.
Sleeper, The. Sydney Clouts. PeSA; VWA
Sleeper, The. Walter de la Mare. MoAB; MoBrPo; SeCeV
Sleeper, The. Edward Field. LiSp
Sleeper, The. Sara Henderson Hay. DFT
Sleeper, The. Isobel Hume. HBMV
Sleeper, The. Poe. AA; AmPP; AP; LiTA; NePA; NOBA; OBVV; OxBA; PoEL-4; TAP; TrGrPo
Sleeper, The. Clinton Scollard. HBV-2
Sleeper, The. *Unknown, tr. fr. Arabic by* E. Powys Mathers. *Fr.* The Thousand and One Nights. AWP
Sleeper from the Amazon, A. Limerick. *Unknown.* WhC
Sleeper Hood-winked, The. John Skelton. *See* My Darling Dear, My Daisy Flower.
Sleeper in the Valley, The. Rimbaud, *tr. fr. French.* OBWP, *tr. by* Robert Lowell; WaaP, *tr. by* Selden Rodman
(Sleeper of the Valley, The, *tr. by* Ludwig Lewisohn.) AWP
Sleeper Rise. *Gond Oral Tradition, tr. by* V. Elwin *and* S. Hivale. WTO
Sleeper, the palm-trees drink the breathless noon. The Sleeper. *Unknown, tr. by* E. Powys Mathers. *Fr.* The Thousand and One Nights. AWP
Sleepers, The. William Aberg. LFAC
Sleepers, The. F. W. Harvey. MMA
Sleepers, The. Peter Kocan. CBAP
Sleepers, The. Randolph Stow. *Fr.* Thailand Railway. CBAP
Sleepers, The. Walt Whitman. AmPP
Sleepin' at the Foot o' the Bed. Luther Patrick. BLPA
Sleeping, The. Lynn Emanuel. MAYP
Sleeping Alone. Kurt J. Fickert. AMV-80
Sleeping at Last. Christina Rossetti. HeIP; TrGrPo
Sleeping at the Beach. Lucile Burt. AMV-81
Sleeping-bag, The. Herbert George Ponting. CenHV
Sleeping Beauty, The. Leonard Cohen. DFT

Sleeping Beauty. Walter de la Mare. DFT
Sleeping Beauty, The. Sara de Ford. DFT
Sleeping Beauty, The. Mary Hutton. DFT
Sleeping Beauty. Charles Johnson. DFT
Sleeping Beauty, The. Robert Layzer. NePoEA
Sleeping Beauty, The. E. L. Mayo. DFT
Sleeping Beauty. Howard Nemerov. DFT
Sleeping Beauty, The. Wilfred Owen. DFT
Sleeping Beauty, A. James Whitcomb Riley. DFT
Sleeping Beauty, The. Samuel Rogers. GTBS; GTBS-P; HBV-1
Sleeping Beauty. Laurie Sheck. DFT
Sleeping Beauty. Jane Shore. DFT
Sleeping Beauty, The, *sels.* Edith Sitwell.
"In the great gardens, after bright spring rain." OxBTC
(Innocent Spring, The.) NOBE
"When we come to that dark house." MoVE; OBMV
Sleeping Beauty, A. Evelyn M. Watson. DFT
Sleeping Beauty. Elinor Wylie. DFT
Sleeping Beauty: August. Douglas Knight. DFT
Sleeping Beauty, The: Variation of the Prince. Randall Jarrell. DFT; PoA
Sleeping Beauty without her hedge of thorns? Ripening. Noelle Caskey. DFT
Sleeping butterfly, A. The Butterfly. Kikaku, *tr. by* Harold G. Henderson. SoPo
Sleeping Fury, The. Louise Bogan. IHMS; LiTM
Sleeping Giant, The. Donald Hall. GrPl; MP; NCSH; NePoEA; NYBP; PAI; Psk; TwCP
Sleeping Gypsy, The. Nick Johnson. PoDr
Sleeping Heroes. Edward Shanks. OBMV
Sleeping House, The. Tennyson. *Fr.* Maud. FaBoEn; OBNC
Sleeping in a Cave. Naomi Shihab Hye. AMV-81
Sleeping in fever, I am unfit. For God While Sleeping. Anne Sexton. CABA; CAPP; NePoEA-2
Sleeping in the Forest. Mary Oliver. NU
Sleeping on Fists. Alberto Ríos. DiL
Sleeping on Her Couch. Richard Leigh. FaBoEn; MePo
(Thus Lovely Sleep.) ELP
Sleeping on the Ceiling. Elizabeth Bishop. MiAP
Sleeping on the Wing. Frank O'Hara. SOTW
"Sleeping or waking, thou sweet face." Popular Songs of Tuscany. *Unknown, tr. by* John Addington Symonds. AWP
Sleeping Peasants. Phyllis Janik. PoDr
Sleeping Pill. Diana O Hehir. AMV-81
Sleeping Priestess of Aphrodite, A. Robert Cameron Rogers. AA
Sleeping Saint, The. Melvin Walker La Follette. CoPo
Sleeping They Bear Me. Alfred Mombert, *tr. fr. German by* Jethro Bithell. AWP
Sleeping Together. Katherine Mansfield. Two Nocturnes, II. HBMV
Sleeping, turning in turn like planets. Adrienne Rich. Twenty-one Love Poems, XII. PeHV
Sleeping with Foxes. Roberta Hill. CDW
Sleeping with One Eye Open. Mark Strand. NYBP
Sleeping with Someone Who Came in Secret. Lady Ise, *tr. fr. Japanese by* Burton Watson. *Fr.* Eleven Tanka. LLLT
Sleeping with Women. Kenneth Koch. NoAM; PoM
Sleeping woman dreams she wakes, A. Nightmare. Isabella Gardner. CoAP
Sleeping Youth, A. Keats. *Fr.* Endymion. SeCePo
Sleepless. Al-Khansa, *tr. fr. Arabic by* Willis Barnstone. BoWoP
Sleepless at Crown Point. Richard Wilbur. WeW
Sleepless, by the windowpane I stare. Verses at Night. Dannie Abse. MP
Sleepless Dreams. Dante Gabriel Rossetti. The House of Life, XXXIX. OAEP
Sleepless ghost perpetually striving, The. Eros Out of the Sea. Dilys Bennett Laing. PoA
Sleepless hours who watch me as I lie, The. Hymn of Apollo. Shelley. EnRP; HBV-1; OAEL-2; OAEP; OBRV
Sleepless Night, A. Egan O'Rahilly, *tr. fr. Modern Irish by* Frank O'Connor. AnIL; KiLC
Sleepless on a Summer Night. Umberto Saba, *tr. fr. Italian by* Keith Bosley. VWA
Sleeplessness of Our Time. R. A. D. Ford. AMV-81
Sleepmonger,/ deathmonger. The Addict. Anne Sexton. CTBA
Sleeps tranquilly the lake—a slender throat. Bohernabreena. Leslie Daiken. OnYI
Sleepwalker, The. Nelly Sachs, *tr. fr. German by* Michael Hamburger. BoWoP; NYBP
Sleepwalkers. Bella Akhmadulina, *tr. fr. Russian by* Barbara Einzig. BoWoP
Sleepwalkers' Ballad. Federico García Lorca, *tr. fr. Spanish by* John Frederick Nims. WeW
Sleep-Walking Child. Elisabeth Eybers, *tr. fr. Afrikaans by* Jack Cope, Uys Krige, *and* Adèle Naudé. PeSA
Sleepy Betsy from her pillow. The Bedpost. Robert Graves. SO
Sleepy Dog, The. Josephine Daskam Bacon. SUS
Sleepy Giant, The. Charles Edward Carryl. OnUR
Sleepy Man Blues. *Unknown.* BluL
Sleepy vines on the chalk-white houses. Sancho. William Edwin Collin. CaP
Sleepyhead. Walter de la Mare. TiPo
Sleepytown Express, The. James J. Montague. HBMV
Sleet. Norman MacCaig. OBCP
Sleet Storm. James S. Tippett. SiSoSe
Sleet Storm on the Merritt Parkway. Robert Bly. ConAP; NOBA
Sleigh Bells at Night. Elizabeth J. Coatsworth. SiSoSe
Sleighing Song. John Shaw. AA
Sleighride. Patrick Anderson. CaP; OBCV
Slender Fingers ("Slender, delicate, soft jade"). Chao Luan-luan, *tr. fr. Chinese by* Kenneth Rexroth *and* Ling Chung. BoWoP
Slender I saw her stand, stooped a little, her arms akimbo. The White Sand. Edmund Wilson. NePoAm
Slender Maid. Joseph Eliyia, *tr. fr. Modern Greek by* Rae Dalven. VWA
Slender man in jogging duds. Running Blind. Nancy Jones. LiSp
Slender one, white one. Alcibiades to a Jealous Girl. Arthur Davison Ficke. HBMV
Slender pine skirts walls now silent, The. The Silent Walls. Ian Strachan. PoSH
Slepynge Long in Greet Quiete Is Eek a Greet Norice to Leccherie. John Hollander. ErPo
Slice of Wedding Cake, A. Robert Graves. BoLoP; NOBE; OxBTC
Sliced with shade and scarred with snow. Inverberg. J. F. Hendry. NeBP
Slicing my head off shaving I think of Charles I. Notes for a Revised Sonnet. Edward Pygge. BXAP
Slick. Daniel Hoffman. SOTS
Slide at the Empire Mine, The. Harriet L. Wason. PoOW
Slide, Kelly, Slide. J. W. Kelly. FaFP; TreFS
Slides. Jennifer Maiden. CBAP
Sliding. Marchette Chute. TiPo
Sliding. Myra Cohn. SiSoSe
Sliding Scale. Norman R. Jaffray. TDH
Sliding step unlocks a hero's cure, A. Oedipus, Pentheus. David Bromwich. AMV-81
Sliding Trombone. Georges Ribemont-Dessaignes, *tr. fr. French by* David Gascoyne. EAS
Slieve Gua. *Unknown, tr. fr. Old Irish.* ChTr
Slievenamon. *Unknown, tr. fr. Irish by* Frank O'Connor. KiLC
Slight as thou art, thou art enough to hide. To a Daisy. Alice Meynell. MoBrPo; WGRP
Slight-boned animal, young, A. Small Colored Boy in the Subway. Babette Deutsch. PoNe
Slight Confusion, A. James Reiss. AmPA
Slight unpremeditated words are borne. Love's Witness. Aphra Behn. BoWoP
Slightly before the middle of Congressman Pudd. E. E. Cummings. FaBoEE; OBAL
Sligo and Mayo. Louis MacNeice. *See* County Sligo.
Slim and singing copper girl, A. Early Copper. Carl Sandburg. HeIP
Slim Cunning Hands. Walter de la Mare. ELU; FaBoEE; NIP; SeCePo
Slim dragonfly. Arthur Mitchell. Marianne Moore. PoNe
Slim Greer ("Listen to the tale"). Sterling A. Brown. BALP; BANP
Slim in Hell ("Slim Greer went to heaven"). Sterling Brown. BPo; FB
Slim Man Canyon. Leslie Silko. VoR
Slim sentinels. Trees at Night. Helene Johnson. BlSi
Slimy obscene creatures, insane. The Nigga Section. Welton Smith. BPo
Sling me under the sea. Bones. Carl Sandburg. MOS
Slioch and Sgurr Mor. Loch Luichart. Andrew Young. PoSH
Slip, The. Wendell Berry. NOCV
Slipped it under a mothering. Beautiful Poultry. Ian Wedde. OCNZ
Slippery. Carl Sandburg. FaPON; TiPo
Slipping in blood, by his own hand, through pride. To an Artist, to Take Heart. Louise Bogan. GrPl; NYBP; PAI
Slipping Out of Intensive Care. Florence Trefethen. AMV-80
Sliprails and the Spur, The. Henry Lawson. PoAu-1
Slithergadee, The. Shel Silverstein. AmMo; OnUR; RHPC
(Not Me.) NTCP
("Slithergadee has crawled out of the sea, The.) WSC
Slog brute streets with rebel tramping! Our March. Vladimir Mayakovsky, *tr. by* Babette Deutsch *and* Avrahm Yarmolinsky. AWP
Slogan, The. Paul Blackburn. PoM
Sloops in the Bay. James Tate. MAYP
Slopping like sphagnum, battered, baptised in cloud. Discomfort in High Places. Sydney Tremayne. PoSH
Sloth, The. Isabella Gardner. BoAnP
Sloth, The. Theodore Roethke. FiBHP; NePA; NePoAm; OBAL; OBCA; RHPC

Sloth, The. George J. Romanes. FM
Slouches over four-bit beers. The Linebacker at Forty. Jon Wallace. AMV-81
Slough. John Betjeman. DBV; MoBrPo
Slough of Despond, The. Robert Lowell. SyP
Slovenly Peter. Heinrich Hoffmann. *Poems indexed separately by titles and first lines.*
Slow are the years of light. Lachrymae. David Gascoyne. *Fr.* Miserere. NeBP
Slow bells at dawn. Bells. Duncan Campbell Scott. CaP
Slow bleak awakening from the morning dream. Living. Harold Monro. LiTB; SeCePo
Slow burn, A. Pit Viper. George Starbuck. NYBP; SUW
Slow, cold breathing, The. The Marsh, New Year's Day. Peter Everwine. NNaP
Slow Dance. David St. John. AmPA; LCAP
Slow Dancer That No One Hears but You. Duane Niatum. CDW
Slow Death. Lorri Martinez. LFAC
Slow Drag Dead. Alcide Pavageau. Miller Williams. TAT
Slow freight wriggles along, The. The Freight Train. Rowena Bastin Bennett. PDV
Slow, groping giant, whose unsteady limbs. Doubt. Robert Cameron Rogers. AA
Slow heave of the sleeping sea, The. A Dead Calm and Mist. "Fiona Macleod." SyP
Slow, horses, slow. Night of Spring. Thomas Westwood. OBVV; SoSe
Slow lines lay down the curve, curve. Mother in the 45¢ Bottle. Paul Blackburn. NYP
Slow Mama Slow. *Unknown.* BluL
Slow May. Spring in These Hills. Archibald MacLeish. NCSH
Slow Me Down. *Unknown.* STF
Slow Me Down, Lord! Orin L. Crane. TreFT
Slow Movement. William Carlos Williams. PoA
Slow moves the acid breath of noon. Field of Autumn. Laurie Lee. LiTM; NCSH
Slow Oxen. Ilya Rubin, *tr. fr. Russian by* Linda Zisquit. VWA
Slow Pacific Swell, The. Yvor Winters. HeIP; MOS; NoAM; NOBA; QFR
Slow pass the hours—ah, passing slow! Ballade Tragique à Double Refrain. Max Beerbohm. OBSV
Slow Rain. Gabriela Mistral, *tr. fr. Spanish by* Gunda Kaiser *and* James Tipton. PBWP
Slow Riff for Billy. James Cunningham. JB
Slow sinks, more lovely ere his race be run. Summer [*or* Sunset over the Aegean]. Byron. *Fr.* The Corsair, III. OBNC; OBRV
Slow, Slow, Fresh Fount. Ben Jonson. *Fr.* Cynthia's Revels, I, ii. ChTr; ElL; ELP; NOP; OBS; PrIm; SeCeV; WHA
(Echo's Lament for Narcissus.) CH
(Echo's [*or* Eccho's] Song.) JCP; LoBV; SeCV-1; TrGrPo
("Slow, slow, fresh fount, keep time with my salt tears.") InPK; OAEL-1; OAEP
(Song: "Slow, slow fresh fount, keep time with my salt tears.") AnAnS-1; EnRePo; FaBoEn; PoEL-2; SeCP; ViBoPo
(Song of Echo.) GoBC
Slow Summer Twilight. John Hall Wheelock. LiTM
Slow the Kansas sun was setting o'er the wheat fields far away. Towser Shall Be Tied Tonight. *Unknown.* BLPA; BoAnP
Slow the moon rises, wraith of a moon long drowned. Fog-Horn. George Herbert Clarke. CaP
Slow to Come, Quick a-Gone. William Barnes. VLP
Slow to resolve, but in performance quick. King James II. Dryden. *Fr.* The Hind and the Panther. ACP
Slow to wake, often I catch. Nystagmus. Joseph Matuzak. SUW
Slow turns the water by the green marshes. Virginiana. Mary Johnston. HBMV
Slow Waker. Thom Gunn. Str
Slow wand'ring came the sightless sire and she. Antigone and Oedipus. Henrietta Cordelia Ray. BlSi
Slowly a hundred miles through the powerful rain. You Drive in a Circle. Ted Hughes. NYBP
Slowly, as one who bears a mortal hurt. La Mort d'Arthur. William Edmonstoune Aytoun. FaBoPa
Slowly, by day, in the cold sun of autumn. The Stone Orchard. Joyce Carol Oates. GeTw
Slowly by God's hand unfurled. Evening Hymn [*or* The Light of Stars]. William Henry Furness. AA; AH, *with music*; FaBoBe; HBV-2; TrPWD
Slowly England's sun was setting o'er the hilltops far away. Curfew Must Not Ring Tonight. Rose Hartwick Thorpe. BeLS; BLPA; BLPL; FaBoBe; FaPON; HBV-2; PaPo
Slowly flutters the snow from ash-coloured heavens in silence. Snowfall. Giousè Carducci, *tr. by* G. A. Greene. PoPl
Slowly he rode home at the end of day. The Captain. Jon Manchip White. NePoEA
Slowly he sways that head that cannot hear. Rattler, Alert. Brewster Ghiselin. HAP; WeW
Slowly he turns himself round and round. The Dancing Bear. Rachel Field. NTCP
Slowly I mount the stairs to have/ my picture taken. The Progress of Photography. Byron Vazakas. MoPo
Slowly, my lords, go slowly. The Case of Thomas More. Sister Mary St. Virginia. GoBC
Slowly, O so slowly, longing rose up. Christ Walking on the Water. W. R. Rodgers. AnIL; MoAB; NoAM; OxBI
Slowly, silently, now the moon. Silver. Walter de la Mare. BoNaP; FaPON; MoAB; MoBrPo; PoPl; PoRA; RHPC; SiSoSe; SUS; TiPo; TreF
Slowly, Slowly Wisdom Gathers. Mark Van Doren. PoA
Slowly the daylight left our listening faces. Early Chronology. Siegfried Sassoon. GLGT
Slowly the mist o'er the meadow was creeping. Lexington. Oliver Wendell Holmes. PAH
Slowly the Moon her banderoles of light. A Battle. Isabella Valancy Crawford. NOBC
Slowly the moon is rising out of the ruddy haze. Aware. D. H. Lawrence. BoNaP; MoBrPo
Slowly the muddy pool becomes a river. Let the Dead Depart in Peace. *Yoruba Oral Tradition, tr. by* Ulli Beier. WTO
Slowly the night blooms, unfurling. Flowers of Darkness. Frank Marshall Davis. AmNP; IDB; NoP; PoBA; PoNe
Slowly the poison the whole blood stream fills. Missing Dates. William Empson. ChMP; CMoP; CoBMV; FaBoEn; HAP; LiTB; LiTM; MoAB; MoBrPo; MoPo; NoAM; NOBE; NoP; OAEL-2; UnPo; ViBoPo
Slowly the ponderous doors of lead imponderous. Sleep. Bravig Imbs. EAS
Slowly the roses bleed into the water. The Vase. Terence Tiller. ChMP
Slowly the salt of the earth becomes salt of the sea. Salt of the Earth. D. H. Lawrence. NoAM
Slowly the sea is parted from the sky. North of Berwick. Sydney Tremayne. BSV
Slowly the thing comes. Panic. Archibald MacLeish. *Fr.* Panic. MoAmPo
Slowly the vision grows. Lakeside Incident. Robin Skelton. NOBC
Slowly the women file to where he stands. Faith Healing. Philip Larkin. NoAM
Slowly the world contracts about my ears. The Flagpole Sitter. Donald Finkel. CoAP
Slowly they pass. The Sheep. "Seumas O'Sullivan." OxBI
Slowly thy flowing tide. The Ebb Tide. Robert Southey. OBNC
Slowly ticks the big clock. The Big Clock. *Unknown.* SoPo; TiPo
Slowly upwards past the girdles. The Escalator. Alex Glasgow. OBET
Slowly with bleeding nose and aching wrists. The Hero. Robert Graves. PCP
Slug. Gwen Head. GP
Slug. Theodore Roethke. CABA
Slug in Woods. Earle Birney. CaP; NOBC; OBCV; PeCV
Sluggard, The. W. H. Davies. OBMV
Sluggard, The. Isaac Watts. CH; HAP; HBV-1; HBVY; MoShBr; NOEC; OBEC; OxBChV; OxBoLi; PaPo; Par; PoEL-3; SpRo; TreFS
Sluggish morn[e] as yet undrest, The. Upon Phillis Walking in a Morning before Sun-Rising. John Cleveland. AnAnS-2; MeLP
Sluice gates of sleep are open wide, The. Viaticum. Ethna MacCarthy. NeIP
Slum Dwelling, A. George Crabbe. *Fr.* The Borough. OBNC
Slumber dark and deep. Paul Verlaine, *tr. by* Arthur Symons. *Fr.* Sagesse. AWP
Slumber Did My Spirit Seal, A. Wordsworth. *Fr.* Lucy. AWP; BiP; BLPL; CABA; ELP; EnLoPo; EnRP; FaBoCh; FaBoEn; GTBS; GTBS-P; HAP; HBV-1; HeIP; InPK; InPS; InvP; LiTB; NIP; NOBE; NoP; OAEL-2; OAEP; OBEV; OBNC; OBRV; PAI; PoEL-4; PoPle; PoRA; PPP; PrIm; SCV; SeCeV; TEP; TreFS; TrGrPo; UnPo; ViBoPo; WeW
(Lines.) LoBV
Slumber, Jesu, lightly dreaming. Lullaby. *Unknown, tr. by* Raymond R. Roseliep. ISi
Slumber, Small One. Though She Slumbers. Joseph Joel Keith. ISi
Slumber Song. Louis V. Ledoux. FaPON; HBMV
Slump. Vassar Miller. BoWoP
Slung between the homely poplars at the end. Ursa Major. James Kirkup. ImOP
Slurped/ and waters moved. Lee-ers of Hew. James Cunningham. JB
Slushy snow splashes and sploshes, The. Mary Ann Hoberman. TiPo

Sly merchants plotted newer, greater gains. Renaissance. Robert Avrett. GoYe
Smack in School, The. William Pitt Palmer. HBV-2
Small, The. Theodore Roethke. GrPl; SO
Small, The. Don Welch. WOLT
Small Aircraft. Bella Akhmadulina, *tr. fr. Russian by* Daniel Halpern. BoWoP
Small and Early. Tudor Jenks. AA
Small and emptied woman, you lie here a thousand years dead. In the Museum. Isabella Gardner. ELU; NYBP
Small and flat. Tumor. Lucille Day. SUW
Small April sobbed. April Fool. Eleanor Hammond. SoPo
Small as a fox and like. Our Lucy (1956-1960). Paul Goodman. GDP
Small babe, tell me. The Baby. James Reaney. *Fr.* A Sequence in Four Keys. NAs
Small bird/ tracks. Rain. Lance Henson. VoR
Small Birds. Peter Quennell. MoVE
Small birds and turtle doves. Arise and Pick a Posy. *Unknown.* OBET
Small Bird's Nest Made of White Reed Fiber, A. Robert Bly. NNaP
Small birds play in the ivy. A Spring Day on Campus. Gilbert Schedler. AMV-80
Small birds swirl around, The. The Small. Theodore Roethke. GrPl; SO
Small black birds. Coots. Joseph Bruchac. FAZ
Small black blobs on the beach are the heads, The. The Class. Josephine Jacobsen. GP
Small black wedge, the shepherd, A. In the Cheviots. Maurice Lindsay. PoSH
Small blond girl brings a dark haired woman, A. Trellis. Laura Chester. NPGG
Small Bones Ache. Moshe Dor, *tr. fr. Hebrew by* Ruth Fainlight. VWA
Small Boy, Dreaming, A. Albert Herzing. NYBP
Small boy drove the shaggy ass, The. Turf Carrier on Aranmore. John Hewitt. PoRA
Small boy has thrown a stone at a statue, A. The Statue. Robert Finch. OBCV; PeCV
Small bundles of rotting vines smoke beside. Evening Refrain. Sherod Santos. MAYP
Small, busy flames play through the fresh-laid coals. To My Brothers. Keats. NAs; TEP
Small Celandine, The. Wordsworth. *See* Lesson, A.
Small child of a wind, A. Requiem for Sonora. Richard Shelton. Psk
Small Colored Boy in the Subway. Babette Deutsch. PoNe
Small Comment. Sonia Sanchez. NBP
Small Country. Claribel Alegria, *tr. fr. Spanish by* Aliki *and* Willis Barnstone. BoWoP
Small Dark Song. Philip Dacey. PPJ
Small dawn, sailor, A. First light glints. Here, but Unable to Answer. Richard Hugo. DiL
Small Dragon, A. Brian Patten. AmMo
Small dragon, phoenix, centaur, A. Monster Alphabet. Robert Fisher. AmMo
Small ears prick on the bushes, The. The Common Living Dirt. Marge Piercy. GeTw
Small Elegy, A. Jiri Orten, *tr. fr. Czech by* Lyn Coffin. AMV-81
Small Elegy, A. Richard Snyder. PCP
Small eyes water on the branch. Another Face. Ray A. Young Bear. CDW
Small Faculty Stag for the Visiting Poet, A. Earle Birney. OxBC
Small Farm, A. Michael Hartnett. CIP
Small Fountains. Lascelles Abercrombie. *Fr.* Emblems of Love, Epilogue. CH
Small Frogs Killed on the Highway. James Wright. NNaP
Small girl, I knelt, A. Woman Painter of Mithila. Erika Mumford. PoDr
Small girls on trikes. Christmas Day. Roy Fuller. OBCP
Small gnats that fly. Song: One Hard Look. Robert Graves. MoAB; MoBrPo
Small gray cloudy louse that nests in my beard, The. James K. Baxter. Jerusalem Sonnets, 1. NoP; OCNZ
Small have always talked well about fishing, The. The Small. Don Welch. WOLT
Small Hotel, The. Michael Longley. CIP
Small house with a pointed roof, A. Epiphany. Eileen Shanahan. NeIP
Small Lady, The. Stevie Smith. TEP
Small lights pirouette. Peterhead in May. Burns Singer. OxBS
Small Lizard, The. Linda Gregg. MAYP
Small man suffers the indignities of childhood, The. Paul Klee. Ruthven Todd. EAS
Small Moon. Howard Nemerov. PCP
Small moon. Prayer to the Young Moon. *Unknown, tr. by* W. H. I. Bleek *and* Jack Cope. PeSA
Small nests/ On branches up high. A Bird's Nest. Erez Biton, *tr. by* Judith Katz. VWA
Small Paths. Henriette Roland-Holst, *tr. fr. Dutch by* Jonathan Crewe. WPOW
Small Perfect Manhattan. Peter Viereck. MiAP
Small Poem about the Hounds and the Hares. Lisel Mueller. GP
Small Prayer. Weldon Kees. PoA; VGW
Small procession waddles single file, A. Ducks. Phoebe Hesketh. BoAnP
Small Quiet Song. Robert Paul Smith. CAD
Small Registry of Births and Deaths, A, *sel.* C. K. Stead.
All Night It Bullied You. NAs
Small room with one table and one chair, A. Poet in Winter. Edward Lucie-Smith. TwCP
Small Sad Song. Alastair Reid. NYBP
Small-scale Reflections on a Great House. A. K. Ramanujan. OxBC
Small service is true service while it lasts. To a Child [*or* In a Child's Album *or* Written in the Album of a Child]. Wordsworth. GN; HBV-1; HBVY; OBRV; OxBChV
Small shining drop, no lady's ring. For a Dewdrop. Eleanor Farjeon. HBVY
Small Silver-coloured Bookworm, The. Thomas Parnell. OnYI
Small Song. A. R. Ammons. NoP; POL
Small Song. Luci Shaw. EBCP
Small space. Two Tile Beaks. Maria Amalia Fonte Boa, *tr. by* Willis Barnstone *and* Nelson Cerqueira. BoWoP
Small speckled visitor, A. Ladybug. Joan Walsh Anglund. RHPC
Small Square, The. Sophia de Mello Breyner Andresen, *tr. fr. Portuguese by* Alexis Levitin. WPOW
Small Town. William Joyce. FAZ
Small Town: The Friendly. Stephen Dunn. POL
Small Towns. Alejandro Murguía. FIA
Small traveler from an unseen shore. To a New-born Child. Cosmo Monkhouse. HBV-1
Small type of great ones, that do hum. A Fly Caught in a Cobweb. Richard Lovelace. CaPo; SeCP
Small voice is fretting my house in the night, A. The Smallish Son. Hayden Carruth. DiL
Small wasp lies in state, The. Dead Wasp. Kenneth Slade Alling. NePoAm
Small wheel, A. Watch Repair. Charles Simic. NoP
Small White House. Robert Penn Warren. *Fr.* Notes on a Life to Be Lived. NoAM
Small Woman on Swallow Street. W. S. Merwin. CoAP; ConAP
Smaller role for peanut butter, A. Being Adult. Bill Zavatsky. POL
Smallest breath. Two Clouds. Lawrence Raab. AMV-80
Smallish Son, The. Hayden Carruth. DiL
Smart. Shel Silverstein. RHPC
Smart and stylish girl and you see, A. Ta-Ra-Ra Boom-De-Ay! *Unknown.* FSN; VLP
Smart Little Bear, The. Mark Fenderson. TDH
Smart man was Bishop Colenso, A. Colenso Rhymes for Orthodox Children. Bret Harte. OBAL
Smash myself against a wall. Thoughts. David Ignatow. FAZ
Smear of blue peat smoke, The. The Shepherd's Hut. Andrew Young. DTC; GrPl; OxBTC
Smell. William Carlos Williams. MoAB; MoAmPo; TAP
Smell My Fingers. David G. Axelrod. Str
Smell of cigar smoke, Sunday, after dinner. Cigar Smoke, Sunday, after Dinner. Louise Townsend Nicholl. FYAP; NePoAm
Smell of death is so powerful, The. Marguerite de Navarre, *tr. fr. French by* Aline Allard. PBWP
Smell of death was in the air, The. Farewell. John Press. PoRA
Smell of Fish, The. William Meissner. WOLT
Smell of Old Newspapers Is Always Stronger after Sleeping in the Sun, The. Mike Lowery. Psk
Smell of potatoes just taken out of the earth, The. The Chilean Elegies: 5. The Interior. Tom Wayman. NOBC
Smell of sage, The. Church Poem. Joyce Carol Thomas. CNA
Smell of snow, stinging in nostrils as the wind lifts it from a beach, The. The Crystal Lithium. James Schuyler. PoM
Smell of the heat is boxwood, The. To Daphne and Virginia. William Carlos Williams. CrMA
Smell of woodyards in the rain is strong, The. Woodyards in the Rain. Anne Marriott. CaP
Smell on the Landing, The. Peter Porter. NMP
Smell the recorders buried here. Cedar. Robert Morgan. GeTw
Smelling or feeling of the several holes. Dishonor. Edwin Denby. ErPo
Smelling the End of Green July. Peter Yates. ChMP
Smells. Kathryn Worth. RHPC
Smells—how many. The Sense of Smell. Louis MacNeice. NYBP
Smells (Junior). Christopher Morley. TiPo
Smile, The. Blake. OBRV
("There is a smile of love.") TEP

Smile, The. Anthony Euwer. *See* Limerick: "No matter how grouchy you're feeling."
Smile. D. M. Thomas. AMV-81
Smile, A ("Let others cheer"). *Unknown.* BLPA; WBLP
Smile ("Like a bread"). *Unknown.* BLPA; WBLP
Smile, The/ A. One gull wing flying alone. Forehead Dead-Ends Half-Way through the Poem. D. C. Berry. BXAP
Smile/ to see the lake. Lorine Niedecker. VGW
Smile and Never Heed Me. Charles Swain. HBV-1
Smile, and the world smiles with you. Hustle and Grin. *Unknown.* WBLP
Smile at Me. Musa Moris Farhi. VWA
Smile at us, pay us, pass us; but do not quite forget. The Secret People. G. K. Chesterton. FaPoR; OxBTC
Smile, Death. Charlotte Mew. WPE; WPOW
Smile fell in the grass, A. The Night Dances. Sylvia Plath. LCAP
Smile is already there, The. Smile. D. M. Thomas. AMV-81
Smile is quite a funny thing, A. Growing Smiles. *Unknown.* PoLF
Smile, Massachusetts, smile. A Song. *Unknown.* PAH
Smile of iceboxes annihilates me, The. An Appearance. Sylvia Plath. CAPP
Smile of the Goat, The. Oliver Herford. FiBHP
Smile of the Walrus, The. Oliver Herford. FiBHP
(Two Smiles.) PV
Smile, smile/ Blest isle! A Lilliputian Ode on Their Majesties' Accession. Henry Carey. NOEC
Smile then, children, hand in hand. Epithalamion. James Elroy Flecker. BrPo
Smiles of the Bathers, The. Weldon Kees. NaP
Smiling Demon of Notre Dame, A. Sophie Jewett. AA
Smiling girls, rosy boys. Mother Goose. OxNR
Smiling morn, the breathing spring, The. The Birks of Endermay. David Mallet. OBEC
Smiling Mouth and Laughing Eyen Grey, The. Charles d'Orléans. HAP
(Smiling Mouth, The.) NoP
Smiling, sweet girl, this proffered toy approve. To a Lady, with a Present of a Fan. *Unknown.* FaBoUs; NOEC
Smith at the organ is like an anvil being. The Sound of Afroamerican History Chapt II. S. E. Anderson. PoBA
Smith makes me, A/ To betray my Man. The Runes on Weland's Sword. Kipling. PoEL-5
Smith's Song. George Sigerson, *ad. fr. the Irish.* OnYI
Smoke. Henry David Thoreau. *Fr.* Walden, *ch.* 13. AA; AWP; HeIP; NoP; OxBA
(Light-winged Smoke.) ViBoPo
(Light-winged Smoke, Icarian Bird.) AP; NOBA; TAP
Smoke. Charles Wright. NYBP
Smoke and Steel, *sel.* Carl Sandburg.
"Smoke of the fields in spring is one." MoAmPo
Smoke Animals. Rowena Bastin Bennet. PDV
Smoke beshags. History: Madness. Stan Rice. NPGG
Smoke-blackened Smiths. *Unknown. See* Blacksmiths, The.
Smoke-blue Plains, The. Badger Clark. YaD
Smoke from the train-gulf hid by hoardings blunders upward. Birmingham. Louis MacNeice. CMoP; MoAB; MoBrPo
Smoke of the fields in spring is one. Carl Sandburg. *Fr.* Smoke and Steel. MoAmPo
Smoke, shadowy deep smoke. Masks. Brian Swann. AMV-81
Smoke snakes. Indian Camp. Janet Reed McFatter. GrPl
Smoke when the sun fell and when it rose. Peter Levi. *Fr.* Life Is a Platform. FaBoTw
Smoked Herring, The. Charles Cros, *tr. fr. French by* A. L. Lloyd. GrPl
Smoker, The. Robert Huff. GP; NePoEA-2
Smokestack Lightnin'. *Unknown.* BluL
Smokey the Bear Sutra. *Unknown.* MAT
Smokin' my pipe on the mountings. Screw-Guns. Kipling. ViBoPo
Smoking all that much has got her eyes. He Records a Little Song for a Smoking Girl. James Whitehead. GP
Smoking Drugs with Strangers. George Bowering. NeAC
Smoking Flax. Mary Josephine Benson. CaP
Smoky blue of evening wreathes from fields, The. Living. D. S. Savage. NeBP
Smoky rain riddles the ocean plains, A. My Father Paints the Summer. Richard Wilbur. DiL; NCSH; NOBA
Smoky sunset, A. I dab my eyes. Required of You This Night. Peter Redgrove. NMP
Smoldering dry fern. And What of Me? Liz Sohappy Bahe. CDW
Smooth between Sea and Land. A. E. Housman. MoPo
Smooth-bottomed fellow named Fritz, A. Limerick. *Unknown.* PeHV
Smooth Divine, The. Timothy Dwight. *Fr.* The Triumph of Infidelity. AA; PPON; WGRP
Smooth smell of Manhattan taxis, The. Dance of the Infidels. Al Young. PoBA
Smooth was the water, calm the air. Song. Sir Charles Sedley. SeCV-2
Smooth-worn coin and threadbare classic phrase, The. Andromeda. Thomas Bailey Aldrich. AA
Smoothing a cypress beam. The Builder. Willard Wattles. HBMV
Smothered Fires. Georgia Douglas Johnson. BlSi
Smothered streams of love, which flow. The Atlantides. Henry David Thoreau. *Fr.* A Week on the Concord and Merrimack Rivers. ViBoPo
Smothering dark engulfs relentlessly, The. A Child's Winter Evening. Gwen John. CH
Smudged eyeballs. Breakfast in a Bowling Alley in Utica, New York. Adrienne Rich. CoPo
Smudging. Diane Wakoski. AmPA; PrIm
Smuggler, The. *Unknown.* WhC
Smugglers, The. Owen Wister. BPAW
Smuggler's Song, A. Kipling. *Fr.* Puck of Pook's Hill. OxBChV; PoPle
Snack, The. L. L. Zeiger. BXAP
Snacks. Ronald P. Tanaka. BrSi
Snail, The ("The frugal snail with forecast of repose"). Vincent Bourne, *tr. fr. Latin by Charles Lamb. See* Housekeeper, The
Snail, The ("To grass, or leaf, or fruit, or wall"). Vincent Bourne, *tr. fr. Latin by* William Cowper. HBV-1; HBVY; OBVE
Snail, The. Grace Hazard Conkling. SUS
Snail. John Drinkwater. GoJo; OnUR; SoPo
Snail. Elisabeth Eybers, *tr. fr. Afrikaans by* Elisabeth Eybers. PeSA
Snail, The. A. P. Herbert. BoAnP
Snail. Langston Hughes. FaPON; TiPo
Snail, The. Richard Lovelace. CaPo; OAEL-1
(Snayl, The.) PoEL-3
Snail ("The snail crawls over blackness"). Shinkichi Takahashi, *tr. fr. Japanese by* Lucien Stryk *and* Takashi Ikemoto. NU
Snail gives off stillness, The. Evening. Charles Simic. GeTw
Snail is very odd and slow, The. The Snail. Grace Hazard Conkling. SUS
Snail moves like a, The. Hedgehog. Paul Muldoon. BIrV
Snail pushes through a green, The. Considering the Snail. Thom Gunn. GrPl; LiTM; MP; NePoEA-2; TwCP
Snail, snail, put out your horns. *Unknown.* OxNR
Snail upon the wall. Snail. John Drinkwater. GoJo; OnUR; SoPo
Snail, who had a way, it seems, A. The Snail's Dream. Oliver Herford. RHPC
Snails. E. D. Blodgett. NOBC
Snails. Liagarang, *tr. fr. Dharlwangu dialect by* Ronald M. Berndt. CBAP; WTO
Snail's Derby, A. Eugene Lee-Hamilton. FM
Snail's Dream, The. Oliver Herford. RHPC
Snails have made a garden of green lace, The. After Rain. P. K. Page. NOBC
Snail's Monologue, The. Christian Morgenstern, *tr. fr. German by* Max Knight. BoAnP
Snake, The. Wendell Berry. GeTw
Snake, The. Hilary Corke. PV
Snake, A. Emily Dickinson. *See* Narrow fellow in the grass, A.
Snake. D. H. Lawrence. BrPo; CMoP; CoBMV; FaBoMo; GoTL; HeIP; HoPM; LiTB; LiTM; LoBV; MoAB; MoPo; MoVE; NoAM; NOBE; NoP; NU; OAEL-2; OAEP; PAI; PoRA; PPP; PrIm; SeCeV; SOTW
Snake, The. Thomas Moore. HBV-1
Snake. Theodore Roethke. NOBA; NYBP; PoPl; RFM
Snake, The. Andrew Suknaski. NOBC
Snake came to my water-trough, A. Snake. D. H. Lawrence. BrPo; CMoP; CoBMV; FaBoMo; GoTL; HeIP; HoPM; LiTB; LiTM; LoBV; MoAB; MoPo; MoVE; NoAM; NOBE; NoP; NU; OAEL-2; OAEP; PAI; PoRA; PPP; PrIm; SeCeV; SOTW
Snake-Charmer, The. Thomas Gordon Hake. VLP
Snake-Charmer, The. Sarojini Naidu. PBWP
Snake Doctor Blues. *Unknown.* BluL
Snake emptied itself into the grass, A. Monsoon. David Wevill. NYBP
Snake Eyes. Amiri Baraka. VGW
Snake fence—peace sign—"Poodle Pups." Learning to Count. Alberta Turner. LCAP
Snake Handling Religious Service. Charles Wright. *Fr.* Tattoos. GP
Snake Hill. Jay Parini. AMV-81; MAYP
Snake Hunt. David Wagoner. GP
Snake It Was That Died, The. Demodocus, *tr. fr. Greek by* J. H. Merivale. DBV
Snake tooth pinches his own mail, The. Remorse. Richmond Lattimore. PoA
Snake Trying, The. W. W. E. Ross. MoCV; NOBC; OBCV
Snakecharmer. Sylvia Plath. NePoEA-2; PP
Snakes. Peter Wild. AmPA; GP
Snakes, Mongooses, Snake-Charmers and the Like. Marianne Moore. CMoP
Snakes of September, The. Stanley Kunitz. AMV-81
Snakeskin and Stone. Keith Douglas. NePoEA

Snap back the canopy. Parachute Descent. David Bourne. WaP
Snap Judgement on the Llama, A. Peggy Bennett. ELU
Snap-Dragon. D. H. Lawrence. ErPo
Snapdragon. Cardinal Newman. GoBC
Snapper, The. William Heyen. AmPA; MAYP; PCP
Snapping gunshot cold. The Women in Old Parkas. Mary TallMountain. STE
Snaps for Dinner, Snaps for Breakfast, and Snaps for Supper. George Moses Horton. OBAL
Snaps its twig-tethermounts. A Dove. Ted Hughes. OxBC
Snapshot. John Fuller. NePoEA-2
Snapshot: Ambassadress. George Garrett. NePoAm-2
Snapshot for Miss Bricka Who Lost in the Semifinal Round of the Pennsylvania Lawn Tennis Tournament at Haverford, July, 1960, A. Robert Wallace. LiSp
Snapshot of a Pedant. George Garrett. NePoAm-2
Snapshot of Hue. Daniel Halpern. MAYP
Snapshot of Uig in Montana, A. Richard Hugo. NPAW
Snapshot: Politician. George Garrett. NePoAm-2
Snapshots, *sel.* X. J. Kennedy.
Birth Report. NAs
Snapshots of a Daughter-in-Law. Adrienne Rich. NIP; NMM; NoP
"You, once a belle in Shreveport," I, *sel.* NCSH
Snapshots of the Cotton South. Frank Marshall Davis. PoBA
Snare, The. Edward Davison. ViBoPo
Snare, The. Patrick MacDonogh. NeIP
Snare, The. James Stephens. CH; CMoP; HBMV; OxBI; PDV; TiPo
Snarleyyow; or, The Dog Fiend, *sel.* Frederick Marryat.
Captain Stood on the Carronade, The. Ets; HBV-2; MOS
(Old Navy, The.) PaPo
Snatch the departing mood. To a Town Poet. Lizette Woodworth Reese. AA
Snaw, snaw, coom faster. Snow. *Unknown.* GBP
Snayl, The. Richard Lovelace. *See* Snail, The.
Sneaked about here. By the Road. Geoffrey Grigson. OxBTC
Sneaky Bill. William Cole. RHPC
Sneeze, The. Anthony Euwer. *Fr.* The Limeratomy. HBMV
Sneeze on a Monday, you [*or* you'll] sneeze for danger. Mother Goose. EvOK; HBV-1; HBVY; TreF
Sneezing. Marie Louise Allen. SoPo
Sneezing. Leigh Hunt. HBV-2
Sniff. Frances Frost. SiSoSe; TiPo
Sniffed, dilating my nostrils. Elvin's Blues. Michael S. Harper. BPo
Snitterjipe, The. James Reeves. AmMo
Snore in the foam: the night is vast and blind. Tristan da Cunha. Roy Campbell. MoBrPo; MoVE; PeSA; RoGo
Snoring. Aileen Fisher. SoPo
Snoring Bedmate, The. *Unknown, tr. fr. Irish by* John V. Kelleher. BIrV
Snorting his pleasure in the dying sun. Landscape, Deer Season. Barbara Howes. GoJo; LiSp; POL
Snow. Dorothy Aldis. TiPo
(On a Snowy Day.) PDV
Snow. Elizabeth Akers Allen. HBV-1
Snow. Mary Austin. *Fr.* Rhyming Riddles. GrPl
("I come more softly than a bird.") BoNaP; SoPo; TiPo
Snow. Margaret Avison. NOBC
Snow. Fay Chiang. BrSi
Snow. Elizabeth J. Coatsworth. SiSoSe
Snow. Adelaide Crapsey. QFR
Snow, The. Robert Creeley. AP
Snow. Walter de la Mare. OnUR
Snow, The. Emily Dickinson. *See* It sifts from leaden sieves.
Snow, The. Clifford Dyment. MoVE
Snow. Nan Fry. PPJ
Snow, The. Donald Hall. NePoEA-2; NMP
Snow. John Kelleher. ELU
Snow, The. Sidney Keyes. NeBP
Snow. Archibald Lampman. PeCV
Snow. Louis MacNeice. BiP; CIP; CMoP; FaBoMo; FPL; LiTM; NoAM; NOBE; OxBTC
Snow. David Malouf. CBAP
Snow. Ralph Pomeroy. Psk
Snow. W. R. Rodgers. LiTM
Snow. Ruth Stone. NYBP
Snow. Edward Thomas. FaBoTw; MoVE
Snow. *Unknown.* GBP
Snow David Wevill. MoCV
Snow. Alice Wilkins. TiPo
Snow. Charles Wright. LCAP
Snow/ is an anthology. Snow Anthology. Arthur S. Bourinot. GoYe
Snow air in the wind. It stings out lunch sacks. Dog Lake with Paula. Richard Hugo. WOLT
Snow and stars, the same as ever. Age. William Winter. HBV-1
Snow Anthology. Arthur S. Bourinot. GoYe
Snow-Ball, The. Soame Jenyns, *after the Latin of* Petronius Afranius. OBVE
Snow-Ball, The. Thomas Stanley. CavP
Snow by Morning. May Swenson. NYBP
Snow came down last night like moths, The. First Snow in Alsace. Richard Wilbur. AP; NoP; OBWP
Snow can come as quietly, A. Snow. Elizabeth J. Coatsworth. SiSoSe
Snow cannot melt too soon for the birds left behind, The. Rag Doll and Summer Birds. Owen Dodson. PoNe
Snow Country. Dave Etter. AmFN
Snow Country Weavers. James Welch. CDW
Snow Crystals on Meall Glas. Elizabeth A. Wilson. PoSH
Snow Curlew, The. Vernon Watkins. NYBP
Snow curls in on the cold wind. Courtyard in Winter. John Montague. IPY
Snow dances and the frost flies, The. Plum Blossoms. Chu Shu-chên, *tr. by* Kenneth Rexroth *and* Ling Chung. PBWP
Snow dissolv'd no more is seen, The. Horace, *tr. by* Samuel Johnson. Odes, IV, 7. LAuP; OBVE
Snow-dust driven over the snow. Winter Noon. Sara Teasdale. YeAr
Snow Fall. *See* Snowfall.
Snow falling. Snowfall. Artis Bernard. NTCP
Snow falling and night falling fast, oh, fast. Desert Places. Robert Frost. AmPP; AP; BiP; CABA; CMoP; CoBMV; MoAB; MoAmPo; MoVE; NCSH; NoAM; NOBA; OxBA; PPP; TAP; TwAmPo; UnPo
Snow falling outside, The. Written on a Paper Napkin. Len Gasparini. NeAC
Snow falls/ flake on flake. Winter in the Wood. Ivy O. Eastwick. YeAr
Snow falls deep, The; the forest lies alone. Gipsies [*or* Gypsies *or* The Gipsy Camp]. John Clare. CH; ChTr; NBM; NoP; PoEL-4; PrIm
Snow falls in a hush under night lights, lampposts. Snow. Fay Chiang. BrSi
Snow falls on the cars in Doctors' Row and hoods the [*or* and] headlights. Doctors' Row. Conrad Aiken. AP; HAP; NYP; PoPl
Snow falls, stops, starts again. A House by the Tracks. Dave Etter. TAT
Snow fell/ on the smiling of the sheep. Christmas Morning. Steven Lautermilch. AMV-80
Snow fell, and its power was multiplied, The. Russia 1812. Victor Hugo, *tr. by* Robert Lowell. OBWP
Snow fell as for Wenceslas. Roarers in a Ring. Ted Hughes. NePoEA-2
Snow fell slowly over the long sweep, The. Landscape. Alfred W. Purdy. CaP
Snow fell softly all the night, The. Snow. Alice Wilkins. TiPo
Snow Fell with a Will. Richard Gillman. NePoAm-2
Snow Fence. Ted Kooser. PPJ
Snow-filled Nest, The. Rose Terry Cooke. OBCA
Snow Geese in the Wind. Philip Dow. NPGG
Snow-Girl. Yunna Moritz, *tr. fr. Russian by* Elaine Feinstein. VWA
Snow-Gum, The. Douglas Stewart. PoAu-2
Snow had begun in the gloaming, The. The First Snowfall. James Russell Lowell. BLPA; BLPL; FaBoBe; FaPON; HBV-1; PoSC; TAP; TreF; WBLP
Snow had fallen many nights and days, The. The End of the World. Gordon Bottomley. BrPo; CH; MoBrPo; MoVE
Snow Harvest. Andrew Young. BoNaP
Snow has come back to make of weeds. Annunciation. D. G. Jones. PeCV
Snow has covered the next line of tracks. Looking at New-fallen Snow from a Train. Robert Bly. NaP
Snow has fallen all night. The Snow Curlew. Vernon Watkins. NYBP
Snow has left [*or* is gone from] the cottage top[s], The. February. John Clare. *Fr.* The Shepherd's Calendar. NCEP; NOBE; OBNC
Snow has melted now, The. January. Douglas Gibson. OBCP
Snow-hills all about. Ice-Skaters. Elder Olson. LiSp
Snow in Jerusalem, A. Hayim Naggid, *tr. fr. Hebrew by* Shlomo Vinner *and* Howard Schwartz. VWA
Snow in New York. May Swenson. NYP
Snow in October. Alice Dunbar Nelson. BlSi; CDC
Snow in Spring. Ivy O. Eastwick. PDV
Snow in the City. Rachel Field. TiPo
Snow in the City. Danny Siegel. VWA
Snow in the Suburbs. Thomas Hardy. BoNaP; CMoP; GoJo; MoAB; MoBrPo; OAEL-2; OBMV; OxBTC; PPP
Snow is a strange white word. On Receiving News of the War. Isaac Rosenberg. MMA; MoBrPo; OBWP
Snow is fast descending, The. The Orphan Boy. *Unknown.* OBET
Snow is gone from cottage tops, The. *See* Snow has left the cottage top, The.
Snow is in the oak. The Snow. Donald Hall. NePoEA-2; NMP
Snow is lying on my roof. Lullabye. Kathryn Stripling. AMV-80
Snow is lying very deep, The. Convention. Agnes Lee. HBMV
Snow is out of fashion. Snow in the City. Rachel Field. TiPo

Snow is sick, The. The pure. March Snow. Don McKay. NOBC
Snow-Leopard, The. Randall Jarrell. LiTM; MoPo; MP; TwCP
Snow, less intransigent [*or* intransigeant] than their marble, The. At the Grave of Henry James. W. H. Auden. LiTA; MoPo; NoP
Snow lies deep, The: nor sun nor melting shower. Winter at Tomi. Ovid, *tr. by* F. A. Wright. AWP
Snow lies in claws. At Liberty. Anne S. Perlman. SUW
Snow Lies Sprinkled on the Beach, The. Robert Bridges. NoAM
Snow Line. John Berryman. Dream Songs, XXVIII. PoA
("It was wet & white & swift and where I am.") NaP
Snow makes whiteness where it falls. First Snow. Marie Louise Allen. RHPC; SoPo; TiPo
Snow Man. *See* Snowman.
Snow may come as quietly, A. January. Elizabeth J. Coatsworth. PoSC
Snow on Saddle Mountain, The. Kenji Miyazawa, *tr. fr. Japanese by* Gary Snyder. NoAM; NOBA; PAI
Snow Party, The. Derek Mahon. CIP; OxBC
Snow Queen's Portrait. Ruth Berman. PoDr
Snow-Shower, The. Bryant. HBV-1
Snow, Snow. Marge Piercy. AMV-81
Snow, snow faster. *Unknown.* OxNR; PBBP
Snow squall comes down, A. High Field—First Day of Winter. Gary Eddy. AMV-80
Snow Storm. *See* Snowstorm.
Snow toward Evening. Melville Cane. PDV; SUS; TiPo
Snow Train. Louise Erdrich. TWSS
Snow was falling soft and slow, The. Winter Night. Boris Pasternak, *tr. by* Eugene M. Kayden. PoPl
Snow White. Olga Broumas. DFT
Snow White. Robert M. Chute. DFT
Snow White. Robert Gillespie. DFT
Snow White. Ed Ochester. GP
Snow White and the Seven Dwarfs. Roald Dahl. DFT
Snow White and the Seven Dwarfs. Anne Sexton. DFT
Snow wind-whipt to ice. Winter. Richard Hughes. OBMV
Snowbanks North of the House. Robert Bly. LCAP
Snow-Bird, The. Frank Dempster Sherman. SiSoSe; SoPo; TiPo
Snow-Bound; a Winter Idyl. Whittier. AmPP; AP; GN, *sels.*; NOBA; OxBA; TAP; WiR
Sels.
Firelight. AA
("Shut in from all the world without.") OBCP
Mother. AA; OHIP
Prophetess. AA
Sister. AA
Storm, The. FaBV
(Winter Day.) TrGrPo
World Transformed, The. AA
Snowbound City, The. John Haines. EAS
Snow-bound mountains, snow-bound valleys. Carol of the Russian Children. *Unknown, tr. fr. Russian.* OHIP
Snowdon Sunrise, The. Wordsworth. *See* Climb to Snowdon, The.
Snowdrop, The. Anna Bunston de Bary. HBMV
Snowdrop. Ted Hughes. FaBoMo
Snowdrop, A, *abr.* Harriet Prescott Spofford. GN
Snowdrop. William Wetmore Story. HBV-1
Snowdrop of dogs, with ear of brownest dye. Sonnet: To Tartar, a Terrier Beauty. Thomas Lovell Beddoes. FM; OBNC
Snowdrop, who, in habit white and plain, The. The Poet as King of Gotham. Charles Churchill. *Fr.* Gotham. NOEC
Snowdrops. George MacBeth. OBCP
Snowdrops, lift your timid heads. Easter Song. Mary A. Lathbury. OHIP
Snowfall. Artis Bernard. NTCP
Snowfall. Giosuè Carducci, *tr. fr. Italian.* AWP, *tr. by* Romilda Rendel; PoPl, *tr. by* G. A. Greene
Snowfall, A. Richard Eberhart. FiCP
Snowfall, The. Donald Justice. NePoEA-2; VGW
Snow Fall, The. Archibald MacLeish. PoPl
Snowfall. W. S. Merwin. NNaP
Snowfall. Hone Tuwhare. OCNZ
Snowfall. "I. V. S. W." InMe
Snowfall; a Poem about Spring. James Wright. LCAP
Snowfall: Four Variations. George Amabile. NYBP
Snowfall in the Afternoon. Robert Bly. CAPP; EAS; NMP; NOBA
Snowfish, The. Edward Field. GrPl
Snowflake, The. Walter de la Mare. NCSH; RHPC
Snowflake on asphodel, clear ice on rose. Conrad Aiken. CMoP
Snowflake Which Is Now and Hence Forever, The. Archibald MacLeish. NoP
Snowflakes. Alice Behrend. GoYe
Snowflakes. Marchette Chute. PDV
Snowflakes. Mary Mapes Dodge. AA; HBVY
Snow-Flakes. Longfellow. AP; ChTr; FaBoRV; FPL; NOBA; NoP; PoEl-5; TAP; UnPo; WiR
Snowflakes. Howard Nemerov. PCP
Snowflakes. Clive Sansom. OBCP
Snowgoose. Paula Gunn Allen. TWSS
Snowing of the Pines, The. Thomas Wentworth Higginson. AA; GN
Snow-Man, The. "Marian Douglas." OBCA
Snowman. Andrew McCord Jones. LFAC
Snowman, The. P. K. Page. NOBC
Snow Man, The. Wallace Stevens. AP; CABA; CMoP; CoBMV; CrMA; GoJo; HAP; HeIP; InPK; MAT; NoP; NU; PAI; PrIm; QFR; SoSe; WeW
Snowman's Resolution, The ("The snowman's hat was crooked"). Aileen Fisher. SoPo
Snows are fled away, leaves on the shaws, The. Diffugere Nives. Horace, *tr. by* A. E. Housman. Odes, IV, 7. OBVE
Snows have fled, the hail, the lashing rain, The. Diffugere Nives, 1917. Maurice Baring. HBMV
Snows have joined the little streams and slid into the sea, The. One Morning When the Rain-Birds Call. Lloyd Roberts. CaP
Snows of Yester-Year, The. Villon. *See* Ballad of Dead Ladies, The.
Snowstorm. John Clare. BoNaP; WiR
Snowstorm, The. Pearl Riggs Crouch. BPAW; PoOW
Snow-Storm, The. Emerson. AA; AmPP; AP; BLPL; BoNaP; FaBoBe; GN; LiTA; NePA; NOBA; NoP; OHFP; OxBA; PoEL-4; PoLF; Prf; TAP; TreFT; TrGrPo; UnPo; WiR
"Announced by all the trumpets of the sky," *sel.* TiPo
Snow Storm. Sister Mary Madeleva. GoBC
Snow Storm, The. Edna St. Vincent Millay. PoA
Snow Storm. Kenneth Rexroth. NaP
Snowstorm, The. Frederick George Scott. PeCV
Snowy Egret. Bruce Weigl. MAYP
Snowy, Flowy, Blowy. The Twelve Months. "Gregory Gander." TreFT
Snowy Heron. John Ciardi. WeW
Snowy Night. John Haines. NCSH
Snowy path for squirrel and fox, A. The Brook in February. Sir Charles G. D. Roberts. BoNaP; OBCV; WHW
Snub nose, the guts of twenty mules are in your cylinders/ and transmission. New Farm Tractor. Carl Sandburg. FaPON
Snug at the club two fathers sat. The Fathers. Siegfried Sassoon. NoAM
Snug in my easy chair. Proem. W. W. Gibson. *Fr.* Fires. HBMV
So. *See also* Soe.
So? Alvin Greenberg. FAZ
So? James P. Vaughn. AmNP
So/ Went this little pig from the mainland to the market. Archibald MacLeish Suspends the Five Little Pigs. Louis Untermeyer. *Fr.* Mother Goose Up-to-Date. MoAmPo
So Abram rose, and clave the wood, and went. The Parable of the Old Man and the Young. Wilfred Owen. FaBoRV; PAI
So active they seem passive, little sheep. Grace. Richard Wilbur. LiTA
So advised, did you laugh and forget. Before the Statue of a Laughing Man. William C. Bowie. AMV-81
So all day long the noise of battle roll'd. Morte d'Arthur. Tennyson. DL; DTo; FaBoBe; FaBoRV; FiP; HBV-2; NIP; OAEL-2; OAEP; OBNV; PoEL-5; SeCeV; VLP; WHA
So all day long the noise of battle rolled, *parody.* The Passing of Arthur. J. C. Squire. BXAP
So all men come at last to their Explorer's Tree. Burke and Wills. Ken Barratt. PoAu-2
So am I as the rich, whose blessed key. Sonnets, LII. Shakespeare. OBSC
So an age ended, and its last deliverer died. Sonnets from China, X. W. H. Auden. CMoP
So-and-So Reclining on Her Couch. Wallace Stevens. AmPP; LiTM; NOBA
So, April, here thou art again. Lady April. Richard Le Gallienne. YeAr
So are you to my thoughts as food to life. Sonnets, LXXV. Shakespeare. PoEL-2
So as they traveild, lo they gan espy. The Cave of Despair. Spenser. *Fr.* The Faerie Queene, I, 9. LoBV
So as they travelled, the drouping night. Spenser. *Fr.* The Faerie Queene, IV, 5. OAEL-1
So, back again? To a Dog. Josephine Preston Peabody. BLPA; WGRP
So bandit-eyed, so undovelike a bird. Blue Jay. Robert Francis. ELU; LCAP; PCP
So be it. I am. Hayden Carruth. VGW
So Be My Passing. W. E. Henley. *See* Margaritae Sorori.
So Beautiful Is the Tree of Night. Pauline Hanson. TAP
So Beautiful You Are, Indeed. Irene Rutherford McLeod. HBMV
So beautiful—God himself quailed. The Woman. R. S. Thomas. OxBC
So Big! Max Fatchen. AmMo
So, bored with dragons, he lay down to sleep. Beowulf. Kingsley Amis. FaBoCo; OxBC

So! breakers of broncos! With miles of jagged wire. Breakers of Broncos. Lew Sarett. BPAW
"So careful of the type?" but no. In Memoriam A. H. H., LVI. Tennyson. FF; HAP; HBV-2; LoBV; NoP; OBNC; SeCeV
So, circling about my head, a fly. For Mao Tse-tung; a Meditation on Flies and Kings. Irving Layton. NOBC
So Close Should Be Our Love. *Gond Oral Tradition, tr. by* V. Elwin *and* S. Hivale. WTO
So cold the first Thanksgiving came. The First Thanksgiving. Nancy Byrd Turner. YeAr
So cool and so composed. Song of the Intruder. Maria Jacobs. AMV-81
So crewell prison, howe could betyde, alas. *See* So cruel prison . . .
So Crow found Proteus—steaming in the sun. Truth Kills Everybody. Ted Hughes. InPS
So cruel [*or* cruell *or* crewell] prison how could betide [*or* howe coulde betyde], alas. In Windsor Castle [*or* Prisoned in Windsor, He Recounteth His Pleasure There Passed]. Earl of Surrey. AAS; EnRePo; FaBoEn; HAP; NOBE; NoP; OAEP; OBSC; SeCePo; SiPS
So Cynthia seems star chamber's president. Cynthia. Edward Benlowes. *Fr.* Theophila; or, Love's Sacrifice. MOON
So Davies wrote: "This leaves me in the pink." "In the Pink." Siegfried Sassoon. CMoP
So detached and cool she is. The Mask. Clarissa Scott Delany. CDC; PoNe
So died John So. On John So. *Unknown.* FaBoEE
So different, this man. Marriage. William Carlos Williams. PoA
So does the sun withdraw his beames. On His Mistress Going from Home. *Unknown.* OBS
So down the silver streams of Eridan. Christ's Triumph over Death. Giles Fletcher. *Fr.* Christ's Victory and Triumph, III. LoBV
So dream thy sails, O phantom bark. The Phantom Bark. Hart Crane. CMoP
So dry and clean. The Skull in the Desert. Alison A. Trimpi. AMV-81
So earnest with thy God, can no new care. Of His Majesties Receiving the News of the Duke of Buckingham's Death. Edmund Waller. SeCV-1
So earth's inclined toward the one invisible. Winter Scene. Marguerite Young. NU; WPE
So fair, so dear, so warm upon my bosom. The Firstborn. John Arthur Goodchild. HBV-1
So Fair, So Sweet, Withal So Sensitive. Wordsworth. EnRP; NoP
So faire a church as this, had Venus none. Love at First Sight. Christopher Marlowe. *Fr.* Hero and Leander. FaBoEn
So faith is strong. The Tide of Faith. "George Eliot." *Fr.* A Minor Prophet. TRV; WGRP
So fallen! so lost! the light withdrawn. Ichabod. Whittier. AA; AP; HBV-1; LiTA; NOBA; OxBA; PAH; PoEL-4; TAP
So far as I can see. Meditations of a Tortoise Dozing under a Rosetree Near a Beehive at Noon While a Dog Scampers About and a Cuckoo Calls from a Distant Wood. E. V. Rieu. FiBHP
So far as our story approaches the end. A Light Woman. Robert Browning. HBV-1; VLP
So Far, So Near. Christopher Pearse Cranch. TrPWD
So fare ye well, my darlin', so fare ye well, my dear. Fare Ye Well, My Darlin'. *Unknown.* OuSiCo
So Fast Entangled. *Unknown.* TrGrPo
"So fleet the works of men, back to the earth again." The Curtain (Old Tabor Grand Opera House). Jean Milne Gower. PoOW
So flies love's meteor to her shroud of winds. The Dead Words. Vernon Watkins. LiTM
So, forth issued the Seasons of the year. The Mask of Mutability [*or* The Seasons]. Spenser. *Fr.* The Faerie Queene, VII, 7. GN; OBSC
So forth she comes, and to her coche does clyme. Spenser. *Fr.* The Faerie Queene, I, 4. OAEL-1
So free, so bright, so beautiful and fair. Pentecost. John Bennett. EBCP
So, friend, your shop was all your house! Shop. Robert Browning. VLP
So frisky and fit. Simchas Torah. Morris Rosenfeld. TrJP
So from the ground we felt that virtue branch. The Transfiguration. Edwin Muir. MasP; OxBS
So from the years their gifts were showered: each. Sonnets from China, I. W. H. Auden. CMoP
So from this life, male in its first motion. Vittoria Colonna. Roy Marz. PoA
So gentle Ellen now no more. Samuel Taylor Coleridge. *Fr.* The Three Graves. ChER
So glad I done done. I Done Done What Ya' Tol' Me to Do. *Unknown.* BoAN-1
So good luck came, and on my roof did light. The Coming of Good Luck. Robert Herrick. ELU; FaBoEE; JCP
So goodbye, Mrs. Brown. On Leaving Mrs. Brown's Lodgings [*or* To-Day I Leave Mrs. Brown's Lodgings]. Sir Walter Scott. FaBoEE; NBM
So Graven. Josephine Miles. NoAM
So great the pain. On Love. Kyōgoku Tamekane, *tr. by* Burton Watson. *Fr.* Twenty-three Tanka. LLLT
So Handy, Me Boys, So Handy. *Unknown.* AmFP
(So Handy, *with music.*) ShS
So hard for women to believe each other. Apron Strings. Marge Piercy. TAP
So hath he fallen, the Endymion of the air. Chavez. Mildred McNeal Sweeney. HBV-2
So have I seen a little silly fly. A Quarrel with Fortune. Benjamin Colman. SCAP
"So Have I Spent on the Banks of Ysca Many a Serious Hour." Thomas Vaughan. FaBoPP
So having ended, silence long ensewed. Nature's Reply to Mutability. Spenser. *Fr.* The Faerie Queene, VII, 7. NOBE
So having said, Aglaura him bespake. Colin Clout at Court. Spenser. *Fr.* Colin Clout's Come Home Again. OBSC
So he came to write again. Burning Hills. Michael Ondaatje. NOBC; NoP
So he said then: I will make the poem. The Maker. R. S. Thomas. ELU
So he sat down and slowly, slowly. Foreclosure. Mark Van Doren. CrMA
So he sits down. His host will play for him. Concert Scene. John Logan. NePoEA-2
So he that saileth in this world of pleasure. Anne Bradstreet. *Fr.* Contemplations. WPOW
So he won't talk to me when we meet? Confucius, *tr. by* Ezra Pound. *Fr.* Songs of Cheng. CTC
So Hector spake; the Trojans roar'd applause. Night Encampment outside Troy. Homer, *tr. by* Tennyson. *Fr.* The Iliad, VIII. OBVE; RoGo
So help me God, I couldn't choose between. Catullus, *tr. fr. Latin by* James Michie. DBV
So here hath been dawning. To-Day. Thomas Carlyle. GN; HBV-2; HBVY; WGRP
So here I sit behind my nasty desk. Any Man to His Secretary. Hilary Corke. ErPo
So here is my desert and here am I. In Paris. Thomas MacDonagh. OnYI
So here the great man stood. On the Porch at the Frost Place, Franconia, NH. William Matthews. MAYP
So, here we meet—after long seeking. Linota Rufescens. Lyle Donaghy. OnYI
So he's got there at last, been received as a partner. Security. Michael Hamburger. NMP; PoCh
So huge a burden to support. Ill Luck. Baudelaire, *tr. by* Roy Campbell. *Fr.* The Flowers of Evil. PoPl
So humble things thou hast borne for us, O God. Veni Creator. Alice Meynell. ILwL; WPE
So I am your "darling girl"! Remonstrance. Philodemos the Epicurean, *tr. by* Dudley Fitts. OLR
So I came down the steps to Lenin. Dorothy Wellesley. *Fr.* Lenin. OBMV
So I cut my hair; so I'm shorn. Song of the Strange Young Duckling. Deborah Munro. IHMS
So I decided watching an old woman like her, who could rise so easily. Leslie Scalapino. *Fr.* Hmmmm. NPGG
So I have killed my black goat. I Have Got to Stop Loving You. Ai. GeTw
So I have known this life. Lollingdon Downs. John Masefield. LiTB
So, I have seen a man killed! An experience that, among others! Arthur Hugh Clough. Amours de Voyage, II, vii. EBVV
So I Let Her Go, 2 *versions. Unknown.* AmFP
So I may gain thy death, my life I'll give. Qui Perdiderit Animam Suam. Richard Crashaw. ACP
So I possess a perfect thing. A Bed of Campanula. "John Crichton." CaP
So I Said I Am Ezra. A. R. Ammons. NoAM; NOBA; NoP; PAI
So I, who love, with all this outward. The Meaning. Ralph Gustafson. OBCV
So I would hear out those lungs. Buckdancer's Choice. James Dickey. NoAM; NOBA; NoP; NYBP; PoNe
So in a one man Europe I sit here. George Barker. NeBP
So in Love, *with music.* Cole Porter. BLSo
So in Pieria, from the wedded bliss. In Memory of Bryan Lathrop. Edgar Lee Masters. PoA
So, in the evening, to the simple cloister. Cloister. Conrad Aiken. Preludes for Memnon, XX. LiTA; MoAB; MoAmPo; TwAmPo
So, in the midst of Neptune's angry tide. The Halcyon's Nest. Giles Fletcher. *Fr.* Christ's Victory and Triumph. FaBoPP
So in the sinful streets, abstracted and alone. Easter Day. Arthur Hugh Clough. OAEP
So innocent, so quiet—yet. The Pond. W. H. Davies. ChMP
So is it not with me as with that muse. Sonnets, XXI. Shakespeare. InvP; OBSC
So is the child slow stooping beside him. Gardeners. David Ignatow. PCP
So is this great and wide sea. Bible, *O.T.* Psalm CIV: 25-28. MOS
So it begins. Adam is in his earth. James Agee. Sonnets, I. MoAmPo

So it comes to this, then. Winter Watch. Jeff Daniel Marion. AMV-80
So It Happens. Irving Feldman. GP
So it is, my dear. Even So. Dante Gabriel Rossetti. NOBE; OBNC; VLP
So it is true. Elastic air could fill. Ash. George MacBeth. NMP
So it was./ I broke the copious curls upon my head. Elizabeth Barrett Browning. *Fr.* Aurora Leigh. GLGT
So I've come south this time. Tracks. Brad Lee Shurmantine. AMV-81
So large a morning, so itself, to lean. Song. W. H. Auden. NePoAm-2
So Late into the Night. Byron. *See* So We'll Go No More a-Roving.
So Late Removed from Him She Swore. Walter Savage Landor. OBRV
So late, so late, so haunting. On the Threshold. Karl Kraus, *tr. by* Albert Bloch. TrJP
So lay the youth with Mary in his arms. J. C. Squire. *Fr.* Country Wooing. BXAP
So leave her, and cast care from thy heart. His Camel. Alqamah, *tr. by* Sir Charles Lyall. *Fr.* The Mufaddaliyat. AWP
So, let us laugh—lest vain rememberings. James Branch Cabell. Retractions, XIV. HBMV
So light no one noticed. The Song. Edward Dorn. CoPo; VGW
So like a queen she moves/ among the rabble. Our Lady on Calvary. Sister Michael Marie. ISi
So Little and So Much. John Oxenham. BLRP
So Little Wanted. Cid Corman. GP
So live, that when thy summons comes to join. Bryant. *Fr.* Thanatopsis. TRV
So lonely am I. Ono no Komachi, *tr. fr. Japanese by* David Keene. BoWoP; PBWP
So lonely he'd kiss maggots from the mouth. Rumplestiltskin's Plan. William Hathaway. *Fr.* Rumplestiltskin Poems. DFT
So Long. Jayne Cortez. BoWoP
So Long. William Stafford. PPJ
So Long Ago. Morris Rosenfeld, *tr. fr. Yiddish by* Elbert Aidline. TrJP
So long as Time & Space are the stars. Michael Silverton. PV
So long as you live and move. Teach Us to Mark This, God. Franz Werfel, *tr. by* Jacob Sloan. TrJP
So Long Folks, Off to the War. Anthony Ostroff. NePoAm-2; PoPl
So long had I travelled the lonely road. Home. W. W. Gibson. HBMV
So long had life together been that now. Six Years Later. Joseph Brodsky, *tr. by* Richard Wilbur. AMV-80
So long I sat and conned. The Elm Beetle. Andrew Young. LoBV
So Long Solon. Jack Myers. AmPA
So Long? Stevens. John Berryman. HAP; NOBA
So long you wandered on the dusky plain. To His Friend in Elysium. Joachim du Bellay, *tr. by* Andrew Lang. AWP
So Look the Mornings. Robert Herrick. ELP
So looks Anthea, when in bed she lyes. To Anthea Lying in Bed. Robert Herrick. SeCP
So Love, emergent out of Chaos, brought. Love. Ben Jonson. UnTE
So Love is dead that has been quick so long. Hic Jacet. Louise Chandler Moulton. AA
So lucky I was in being born. Yankee Cradle. Robert P. Tristram Coffin. EvOK
So luminous around them lay the air. Oystercatchers. Christopher Middleton. FaBoTw
So make your impassive passage to the act. Poem in Time of War. William Abrahams. WaP
So, Man? Gene Derwood. NePA
So many cares to vex the day. Summer Magic. Leslie Pinckney Hill. BANP
So many damp hanks of hair and feathers. Dirge for Small Wilddeath. Judith Moffett. LTB
So many evenings, on the red-tiled terrace. Lost Garden. "Katherine Hale." CaP
So Many Feathers. Jayne Cortez. BlSi
So many girls vague in the yielding orchard. The Greenhouse. James Merrill. TwAmPo
So many little flowers. Cycle. Langston Hughes. FaPON
So Many Monkeys. Marion Edey *and* Dorothy Grider. SoPo; TiPo
So many moral matters, and so little used. John Skelton. *Fr.* Speak, Parrot. ViBoPo
So many new crimes since then! Since Then. D. J. Enright. OBSV
So many pigeons at Columbus. Poem. Arthur Gregor. VGW
So many stories written here. Written in a Copy of "The Earthly Paradise," Dec. 25, 1870. William Morris. *Fr.* The Earthly Paradise. VLP
So many things happen. The War of the Worlds. Vern Rutsala. Psk
So many thousands for a house. On a Certain Lord Giving Some Thousand Pounds for a House. David Garrick. FaBoEE; PV
"So many unlived lives," she said; and idle. An Idyl in Idleness. Robert Pack. NePoEA
So many wagons they have cut that good road down. Chock House Blues. *Unknown.* BluL
So many worlds, so much to do. In Memoriam A. H. H., LXXIII. Tennyson. HBV-2
So many years I've seen the sun. The Mystery of Life. John Gambold. NOEC
So may the auspicious Queen of Love. To the Ship on Which Virgil Sailed to Athens. Horace, *tr. by* Dryden. Odes, I, 3. AWP
So men, who once have cast the truth away. Leaving Me, and Then Loving Many. Abraham Cowley. AnAnS-2
So Might is Right, you say; I fight in vain. "Might Is Right." Israel Zangwill. TrJP
So Might It Be. John Galsworthy. BLPL; PoLF
So Miss Myrtle is going to marry? The Charming Woman. Helen Selina Sheridan. OBRV; WPE
So moping flat and low our valleys lie. Winter in the Fens. John Clare. BoNaP
So much depends. The Red Wheelbarrow [*or* Spring and All]. William Carlos Williams. BLPL; CMoP; EvOK; GrPl; HAP; HeIP; HoPM; InPK; LiTA; LiTM; MoAB; MoAmPo; NIP; NoAM; NOBA; NoP; PAI; PrIm; SoSe; SOTW; TAP; UnPo; WeW
So much have I forgotten in ten years. Flame-Heart. Claude McKay. AmNP; BALP; BANP; CDC; PoNe
So much is parchment where I gloom. The Black Mesa. James Merrill. PoA
So much to tell you. 2 Variations: All About Love. Philip Whalen. NeAP
So near to death yourself. For a Very Old Man, on the Death of His Wife. Jane Cooper. NePoEA-2
So neck to stubborn neck, and obstinate knee to knee. Antaeus; a Fragment. Wilfred Owen. PeHV
So nigh is grandeur to man. Cook. YaD
So nigh is grandeur to our dust. Duty. Emerson. *Fr.* Voluntaries, III. FaFP; GN; HBV-1; HBVY; TreF; TreFS; TRV; YaD
So. None crows to this April field. Crows. Philip Booth. DFF
So Not Seeing I Sung. Arthur Hugh Clough. *Fr.* Amours de Voyage. OBNC
("Tibur is beautiful, too, and the orchard slopes, and the Anio.") GTBS-P
(Valley and Villa of Horace, The.) FaBoPP
So now I have confessed that he is thine. Sonnets, CXXXIV. Shakespeare. InvP
So now is come our joyful'st [*or* joyful] feast. A Christmas Carol [*or* Our Joyful Feast] George Wither. OBS; OHIP; SiSoSe; ViBoPo
So now my summer task is ended, Mary. To Mary. Shelley. EnRP
So now the very bones of you are gone. Doricha. Poseidippus, *tr. by* E. A. Robinson. AWP; FaBoEE; OBVE
So now, this poet, who forsakes the stage. Prologue to "Love Triumphant." Dryden. *Fr.* Love Triumphant. OxBoLi
So oft as I her beauty do behold. Amoretti, LV. Spenser. HBV-1; TrGrPo
So oft as I with state of present time. Spenser. *Fr.* The Faerie Queene, V, *proem.* OAEL-1
So oft our hearts, belovèd lute. Dream and the Song. James David Corrothers. BANP
So often we praise our mothers here and merit all their ways. Dear Old Dad. Eva Gilbert Shaver. STF
So on a night when a heavy full moon was low. On the Eve of a Birthday. Geoffrey Grigson. NAs
So on he pricked, and loe, he gan espy. Ride a Cock Horse. Barry Pain. BXAP
So on his Nightmare through the evening fog. Nightmare. Erasmus Darwin. *Fr.* The Botanic Garden. NOEC
So, on the bloody sand, Sohrab lay dead. Sohrab Dead. Matthew Arnold. *Fr.* Sohrab and Rustum. GTBS-P; NOBE
So once again, hearing the tired aunts. In the House of the Dying. Jane Cooper. NMM
So open was his mind, so wide. The Independent. Phyllis McGinley. FaBoEE
So Paradise was brightened, so 'twas blest. To Philomela. Benjamin Colman. SCAP
So pass my days. But when nocturnal shades. The Thirsty Poet. John Philips. OBEC
So passed the morning away. The Church Scene. Longfellow. *Fr.* Evangeline. TreF
So passed they naked on, nor shunned the sight. Adam and Eve. Milton. *Fr.* Paradise Lost, IV. SeCePo
So Pleasant It Is to Have Money. Arthur Hugh Clough. *See* As I Sat at the Café.
So poor old Prunes has cashed in—too bad. Me and Prunes. Rupe Sherwood. PoOW
So, praise the gods, at last he's away! From a Letter from Lesbia. Dorothy Parker. DBV
So prayis me as ye think caus quhy. Remeidis of Luve. *Unknown.* OxBS
So proud she was to die. Emily Dickinson. NOBA

So prudent and so young a wife! To Geron. Hildebrand Jacob. NOEC
So, pure and dutiful, she sought that place. *Unknown. Fr.* The Mahabharata. DL
So put your nightdress on. Bedtime. Ian Hamilton Finlay. BSV
So Quick, So Hot. Thomas Campion. NCEP
("So quicke, so hot, so mad is thy fond sute.") PoEL-2
So Quietly. Leslie Pinckney Hill. BANP; IDB; PoBA
So rare, so mere. Presence of Snow. Melville Cane. GoYe
So restless Cromwell could not cease. Andrew Marvell. *Fr.* A Horatian Ode upon Cromwell. ViBoPo
So Runs Our Song. Mary Eva Kitchel. PGD
So sang I in the springtime of my years. Thysia, XXXVI. Morton Luce. HBV-1
So sang the hierarchies: meanwhile the Son. The First Day of Creation. Milton. *Fr.* Paradise Lost, VII. OxBoCh
So Satan spake, and him Beelzebub. The Council of Satan. Milton. *Fr.* Paradise Lost, I. PoEL-3
So saying, light-foot Iris passed away. Homer, *tr. by* Tennyson. *Fr.* The Iliad, XVIII. OBVE
So several factions from this first ferment. Achitophel: The Earl of Shaftsbury. Dryden. *Fr.* Absalom and Achitophel, Pt. I. NOBE
So shall I live, supposing thou art true. Sonnets, XCIII. Shakespeare. InvP; MasP
So shall it ever be. As Thy Days. Grant Colfax Tullar. BLRP
So shalt thou come to a court as clear as the sun. The Palace of Truth. William Langland. *Fr.* The Vision of Piers Plowman. ACP
So she became a bird and bird-like danced. Procne. Peter Quennell. ChMP; LiTB; LiTM; MoBrPo
So she took up a number twelve crewel needle. Agatha. Nadine Major. POL
So she went into the garden. The Great Panjandrum [Himself]. Samuel Foote. FaBoCh; FaBoCo; MoShBr; Par; PoLF; WhC
So shoots a star as doth my mistress glide. Sonnet. John Davies of Hereford. EIL
So short the road from Bethlehem. "The Way." Leslie Savage Clark. PGD
So Shuts the Marigold Her Leaves ("Marina's gone, and now sit I"). William Browne. *See* Celadyne's Song.
So shuts the marigold her leaves. Memory. William Browne. *Fr.* Britannia's Pastorals, III, Song 1. OBEV; ViBoPo
So, since your heart is set on those sweet fields. To Colman Returning. *At. to* Colman, *tr. by* Helen Waddell. BIrV
So sleep undoes itself and I arrive. For My Twenty-fifth Birthday in Nineteen Forty-one. John Ciardi. WaP
So Sleeps My Love. *Unknown.* TrGrPo
(Sleep, Wayward Thoughts.) EnRePo
So Slow to Die. George Edward Woodberry. Wild Eden, XXXVIII. AA
So small are the flowers of Seamu. Ezra Pound *and* Noel Stock, *fr. Egyptian hieroglyphics.* BoWoP; PBWP
So smell those odours that do rise. To the Most Fair and Lovely Mistress Anne Soame, Now Lady Abdie. Robert Herrick. CaPo; NOBE; ViBoPo
So smile the heavens upon this holy act. Friar Laurence's Cell. Shakespeare. *Fr.* Romeo and Juliet, II, vi. GoBC
So smooth and clear the fountain was. To a Lady Sitting before Her Glass. Elijah Fenton. OBEC
So smooth, so sweet, so silv'ry is thy voice. Upon Julia's Voice. Robert Herrick. CABA; InPK; JCP; NOBE; SeCeP; SeCP; SoSe
So, So. William Clerke. ELP
So, so, break[e] off this last lamenting kiss[e]. The Expiration. John Donne. EiL; MeLP; MePo; SeCP
So, So. It is an old man sleeping here. In the Forest. Pinhas Sadeh, *tr. by* Harris Lenowitz. VWA
So soft in the hemlock wood. Pastoral. Robert Hillyer. MoAmPo
So soft streams meet, so springs with gladder smiles. The Welcome to Sack. Robert Herrick. AnAnS-2; CaPo; SeCP; SeCV-1
So, some tempestuous morn in early June. Matthew Arnold. *Fr.* Thyrsis. PoPle
So soon as day, forth dawning from the East. Artegall and Radigund. Spenser. *Fr.* The Faerie Queene, V, 5. OBSC
So soon grown old! Hast thou been six years dead. The Anniverse; an Elegy. Henry King. JCP
So soon my body will have gone. Immortal. Sara Teasdale. WGRP
So spake our Mother Eve, and Adam heard. The Banishment [*or* The Exit from Eden]. Milton. *Fr.* Paradise Lost, XII. FaBoRV; NOBE; OBS
So spake the enemy of mankind, enclosed. Milton. *Fr.* Paradise Lost, IX. FM
So squeezed, wince you I scream? I love you & hate. John Berryman. *Fr.* Homage to Mistress Bradstreet. FF
So: standing in the front yard in January in the evening. So? Alvin Greenberg. FAZ
So stick up ivy and the bays. The True Christmas. Henry Vaughan. SBVL
So still the night swinging. Mariners' Carol. W. S. Merwin. EaLo
So stood the holy Christ. Whittier. *Fr.* The Healer. PGD
So stretched out huge in length the Arch-Fiend lay. Milton. *Fr.* Paradise Lost, I. TEP
So summer comes in the end to these few stains. The Beginning. Wallace Stevens. VGW
So Sweet a Kiss. Shakespeare. *Fr.* Love's Labour's Lost, IV, iii. EIL; InvP
So Sweet Is She. Ben Jonson. *See* So White, So Soft, So Sweet.
So Sweet Love Seemed. Robert Bridges. FaBV; HBV-1
So sweet, so sweet the roses in their blowing. In June. Nora Perry. YeAr
So sweet the plum trees smell! Plum Trees [*or* Plum Blossoms]. Ranko, *tr. fr. Japanese.* FaPON; SoPo; SUS
So swete a kis yistrene fra thee I reft. To His Maistres [*or* Mistress]. Alexander Montgomerie. GBL; OxBS
So swift to bloom, so soon to pass, Love's flower! Ulysses Returns, II. Roselle Mercier Montgomery. HBMV
So take a happy view. A Happy View. C. Day Lewis. CMoP
So take my vows and scatter them to sea. Sonnet for the End of a Sequence. Dorothy Parker. DBV
So tall she is, and slender, and so fair. The Poet Describes His Love. Robert Nathan. HBMV
So tall was a cowboy called Slouch. Tall. *Unknown.* TDH
So tame, so languid looks this drowsing sea. Calm. Stanton A. Coblentz. EtS
So that a colony will breed here. We Must Make a Kingdom of It. Gregory Orr. MAYP
So that each person may quickly find that. Johann Joachim Quantz's Five Lessons. W. S. Graham. FaBoMo
So That Even a Lover. Louis Zukofsky. CoPo
So that soldierly legend is still on its journey. Kearny at Seven Pines. Edmund Clarence Stedman. AA; HBV-2; HBVY; PAH
So that the vines burst from my fingers. Ezra Pound. Cantos, XVII. LoBV; OBMV
So that's my role—the professional defendant. Ovid, *tr. by* Guy Lee. Amores, II, 7. NAWM-1
So That's Who I Remind Me Of. Ogden Nash. BLPL; PoLF
So, the All-Great, were the All-Loving too. Robert Browning. *Fr.* An Epistle. TRV
So the church Christ was hit and buried. Le Christianisme. Wilfred Owen. BrPo
So the committee met again, and again. The Committee. C. Day Lewis. BiP; CMoP
So the distances are Galatea. The Distances. Charles Olson. NeAP; NoP
So the man spread his blanket on the field. A Tall Man Executes a Jig. Irving Layton. MoCV; NOBC; PoCh
So, the powder's low, and the larder's clean. The Last Cup of Canary. Helen Gray Cone. AA
So the red Indian, by Ontario's side. Lords of the Wilderness. John Leyden. OBRV
So the sky wounded you, jagged at the heart. Daylights. Rosanna Warren. MAYP
So the soldier replied to the poet. The Volunteer's Reply to the Poet. Roy Campbell. *Fr.* Talking Bronco. ViBoPo
So the tide forgets, as morning. The Shore. David St. John. LCAP; MAYP
So, the year's done with! Love. Robert Browning. EnLoPo
So then, at last, let me awake this sleep. Purpose. Langdon Elwyn Mitchell. *Fr.* To a Writer of the Day. AA
So Then, I Feel Not Deeply! Walter Savage Landor. EnRP
So then naturally/ This Count Rainuv I speak of. Rainuv; a Romantic Ballad from the Early Basque. Margaret Widdemer. BXAP
So, then, we were no new device at all. America. Donald G. Babcock. NePoAm
"So then you won't fight?" Dooley Is a Traitor. James Michie. NePoEA-2; OxBTC
So there stood Matthew Arnold and this girl. The Dover Bitch. Anthony Hecht. BXAP; CABA; MAT; NePoEA-2; NIP; NOBA; NOBL; OBAL; PP; PPP; UnPo; VGW
"So there we were stuck." The Life of . . . Theodore Weiss. NYBP
So, there, when sunset made the downs look new. Charles Hamilton Sorley. *Fr.* Marlborough. WGRP
So these two faced each other there. A Portrait in the Guards. Laurence Whistler. GTBS-P
So they begin. With two years gone. Poem. Boris Pasternak, *tr. by* C. M. Bowra. TrJP
So they came. The Animals' Arrival. Elizabeth Jennings. PBWP
So they carried the dead man out of the fighting. Patroclus' Body Saved. Homer, *tr. by* E. R. Dodds. *Fr.* The Iliad, XVII. WaaP
So they in Heav'n their odes and vigils tun'd. The Messiah. Milton. *Fr.* Paradise Regained, I. OBS

So they rode/ Into a land of wells and gardens, where. Sir Edwin Arnold. *Fr.* The Light of Asia, I. VLP
So they went, leaving a picnic-litter of talk. The Party. W. R. Rodgers. BlrV
So they were married, and lived/ Happily for ever? Marriage of Two. C. Day Lewis. ChMP
So, they will have it! Sumter. Henry Howard Brownell. PAH
So This Is Autumn. W. W. Watt. PoPl
So this is it. At the Western Wall. Barbara F. Lefcowitz. VWA
So this is life, the ranger said. Optimism. Blanaid Salkeld. NeIP
So this is love. Squid. Michael Blumenthal. MAYP
So This Is Middle Age! Francis Whiting Hatch. WhC
So this is Monday. The Art of Holding On. Dwight Okita. BrSi
So This Is Our Revolution. Sonia Sanchez. GP
So this is the dust that passes through porcelain. The Iron Lung. Stanley Plumly. AmPA; GeTw; LCAP
So Thomas Edison. Lines to Be Embroidered on a Bib; or, The Child Is Father of the Man, but Not for Quite a While. Ogden Nash. FaBoUs
So thou art come again, old black-winged Night. To Night. Thomas Lovell Beddoes. LoBV
So through that unripe day you bore your head. Philip Larkin. NoAM
So through the darkness and the cold we flew. Skating. Wordsworth. *Fr.* The Prelude, I. CH
So through the sun-laced woods they went. The Sphere of Glass. John Lehmann. ChMP
So thus he sorrowed till it was day. King Pellam's Launde. David Jones. In Parenthesis, IV. NoAM
So Tir'd Are All My Thoughts. Thomas Campion. LoBV
So, to begin with, ghosts of rain arise. The Dance of Dust. Louis Untermeyer. BXAP
So to Tell the Truth. Janet Dubé. BrRo
So to the sea we came; the sea, that is. Her Heards Be Thousand Fishes. Spenser. *Fr.* Colin Clout's Come Home Again. ChTr
So Touch Our Hearts with Loveliness, *with music.* Gail Brook Burket. AH
So unwarely was never no man caught. Sir Thomas Wyatt. SiPS
So up and up they journeyed, and ever as they went. Sigurd's Ride. William Morris. *Fr.* Story of Sigurd the Volsung. NBM
So vile was poor Wat, such a miscreant slave. Burns. FaBoEE
So Wags the World. Ellen Mackay Hutchinson Cortissoz. AA
So warm I may melt. Sunday Morning. Christina Jenkins. BrRo
So was it even then. So soundlessly. A Trysting. Richard Dehmel, *tr. by* Jethro Bithell. AWP
So wayward is the wind to-night. The Wind. Harold Monro. OBVV
So, we are ghosts of angels. Ghazal. Philip Dow. NPGG
So we are taking off our masks, are we, and keeping. Homosexuality. Frank O'Hara. NYP; PeHV; PoA; TAP
"So we diverted the river," he said. Requiem for a River. Kim Williams. RFM
So we must say goodbye, my darling. Goodbye. Alun Lewis. BoLoP; OBWP; OxBTC
So we reveal our status. Hilda Doolittle ("H. D."). *Fr.* The Walls Do Not Fall. NoAM
So we ride, and ride through milked heaven. Rides. Gene Derwood. LiTM; NePA
So we, who've supped the self-same cup. After the Quarrel. Paul Laurence Dunbar. CDC
So We'll Go No More a-Roving. Byron. AWP; BLPL; BoLoP; ELP; EnRP; FaBoEn; FaFP; FF; FiP; HAP; HeIP; LiTB; LoBV; NOBE; NoP; OAEL-2; OAEP; OBRV; OLR; OxBS; PAI; PoEL-4; PoPle; PoRA; PrIm; SeCeV; TreFS; ViBoPo; WeW; WHA
(So Late into the Night.) Wir
(Song.) EnLoPo
(We'll Go No More a-Roving.) CH; FaBV; FaPoR; HBV-1; MOON; OBEV; PoLF; TrGrPo
So [*or* Soe] well I love thee as without thee I. Verses Made the Night before He Died [*or* Last Verses]. Michael Drayton. EnRePo; FaBoEn; GBL; NOBE
So, we're estranged again—how it goes on! Drought. David Holbrook. OxBTC
So We've Come at Last to Freud. Alice Walker. IHMS
So What. Philip Appleman. BXAP
So what if Lowry got spooked by sea-birds and volcanoes crossing. Imperfect Sestina. Phyllis Webb. NOBC
So what said the others and the sun went down. Mrs. Alfred Uruguay. Wallace Stevens. AP; InPS; MoPo; MP; NePA; TwCP
So, When I Swim to the Shore. Molly Peacock. MAYP
So When the Hammers of the Witnesses of Heaven Are Raised All Together. Edward Brathwaite. *Fr.* Cherries. NAs
So when the shadows laid asleep. The Kingfisher. Andrew Marvell. *Fr.* Upon Appleton House. FaBoEn; PB
So where have you been, my good old man? Where Have You Been, My Good Old Man? *Unknown.* OuSiCo
So while the blear-eyed pimp beside me walked. Easter Day II, *earlier version.* Arthur Hugh Clough. VLP
So white I was, he would have me cry. The Dead Bride. Geoffrey Hill. TW
So White, So Soft, So Sweet. Ben Jonson. *Fr.* A Celebration of Charis: The Triumph of Charis. TrGrPo; UnTE
("Have you seen but a bright lily grow.") FaBoCh
(So Sweet Is She.) GN
So wild yet candle-calm. The Grave's Cherub. Sydney Clouts. PeSA
So winter closed its fist. Rite of Spring. Seamus Heaney. OxBC
So without sediment. The Hill Burns. Nan Shepherd. PoSH
So ye're runnin' fer Congress, mister? Le' me tell ye 'bout my son. Whisperin' Bill. Irving Bacheller. PoLF
So you are gone, and are proved bad change, as we had always known. Address Not Known. John Heath-Stubbs. ChMP
So you are married, girl. It makes me sad. Epithalamium. Roy McFadden. NeIP
So you beg for a story, my darling, my brown-eyed Leopold. How He Saved St. Michael's. Mary A. P. Stansbury. BLPA
So you came/ with a hyacinth, a poem and a thousand kisses. Meeting. Sam Harrison. NeIP
So you have swept me back. Eurydice. Hilda Doolittle ("H. D."). VGW
So you met him in a magic place? Tam Lin's Lady. Liz Lochhead. BSV
So you said you'd go home to work on your father's farm. To a Young Poet Who Died. John Logan. CAPP
So you trust like the birds. The Way It Happens. Philip Dacey. LTB
So, you want a lot of money.—The way. The Accountings. Albert Goldbarth. GeTw
So you want me to be your mistress. From the Commonwealth. Sandra Maria Esteves. LTB
So you were David's father. In Memoriam, Private D. Sutherland. Ewart Alan Mackintosh. BSV
So Young ane King. Sir David Lindsay. SeCePo
So you're going away. Good Bye, My Lady Love. Joseph E. Howard. FSN
So youre playing. Identities. Al Young. NPGG
So, you've come to the tropics, heard all you had to do. Down and Out. Clarence Leonard Hay. BeLS; BLPA
So zestfully canst thou sing? The Blinded Bird. Thomas Hardy. BiP; CMoP; EaLo; LiTM; NoAM
Soap. Martin Gardner. RHPC
Soap (II). Jerome Rothenberg. NNaP
Soap Suds. Louis MacNeice. FaBoMo; NoP; SCV
Soap, the Oppressor. Burges Johnson. PoLF
Soaping Down for Saint Francis of Assisi: The Canticle of Sister Soap. Gibbons Ruark. MAYP
Soaps. Harold Witt. SOTS
Soapship went a-rocking, A. The Voyage of Jimmy Poo. James A. Emanuel. AmNP; NNP
Soar up, my soul, unto thy rest. Seek Flowers of Heaven. Robert Southwell. TrCP
Soaring. Cal Clothier. PoSh
Soaring hawk from fist that flies, The. The Lover Compareth Himself to the Painful Falconer. *Unknown.* PBBP
Sob, Heavy World. W. H. Auden. DTC
Sob of fall, and song of forest, come you here on haunting quest. The Trail to Lillooet. Pauline Johnson. CaP
Sober, he thinks of her; so he gets drunk. Man and Woman. Robert Conquest. OxBTC
Sober laverock, warbling wild, The. Burns. *Fr.* The Humble Petition of Bruar Water to the Noble Duke of Athole. PBBP
Soccer. Andrei Voznesensky, *tr. fr. Russian by* Anselm Hollo. LiSp
Social Future, The. John Kells Ingram. OnYI
Social Note. Dorothy Parker. *Fr.* Some Beautiful Letters. FaBoUs; InMe
"Social Science." Thomas Edward Brown. PeD
Social Studies. Mary Neville. POL
Society has quite forsaken all her wicked courses. Anglicized Utopia. W. S. Gilbert. OBSV
Society upon the Stanislaus, The. Bret Harte. AA; BeLS; BPAW; HBV-2; InMe; OBAL
(Plain Language from Truthful James.) FaBoCo
Sockeye Salmon. Ronald Hambleton. CaP; OBCV
Socks. Jessie Pope. SUMH
Socrates' Ghost Must Haunt Me Now. Delmore Schwartz. LiTM; TwAmPo
Socrates Snooks. Fitz Hugh Ludlow. BLPA
Socratic. Hilda Doolittle ("H. D."). HoPM
Sod-Breaker, The. Arthur Stringer. CaP
Sodenly afraid, half waking, half sleeping. A Woman Sat Weeping [*or* Suddenly Afraid]. *Unknown.* NCEP; OxBM
Sodger laddie's socht a hoose, A. Under the Greenwood Tree. "Hugh MacDiarmid," *after the Cretan.* OBVE

Sodom. Chaim Grade, *tr. fr. Yiddish by* Joseph Leftwich. TrJP
Sodom. Herman Melville. Clarel, XXXVI. AmPP
Sodom; or, The Quintessence of Debauchery, *sel.* *At. to* the Earl of Rochester.
"To Love and Nature all their rights restore." PeHV
Sodom's Sister City. Yehuda Amichai, *tr. fr. Hebrew by* Shirley Kaufman. VWA
Soe, Mistress Anne, faire neighbour myne. Salem. Edmund Clarence Stedman. AA; PAH
Soe well I love thee, as without thee I. *See* So well I love thee . . .
Sofa, The. William Cowper. The Task, I. LAuP; OAEP, *abr.*
"For I have lov'd the rural walk through the lanes," *sel.* EnRP
Soft/ The stars are melting. Sopranosound, Memory of John. Sharon Bourke. CNA
Soft and pure fell the snow. Infant Spring. Fredegond Shove. HBMV
Soft answer turneth away wrath, A. The Lips of the Wise. Bible, *O.T.* *Fr.* Proverbs. BiP; TrGrPo
Soft Answers. Robert Bagg. FF; UnTE
Soft as the voice of an angel. Whispering Hope. Septimus Winner. PSoN
Soft as the wind your hair. Love Song. Adam Drinan. NeBP
Soft-boiled Egg. Russell Hoban. NTCP
(Egg Thoughts.) RHPC
Soft child of love, thou balmy bliss. To a Kiss. "Peter Pindar." HBV-1
Soft crying of the dawn while cockatoos. 'Morning, Morning. Ray Mathew. PoAu-2
Soft Day, A. Winifred M. Letts. AnIV; OnYI
Soft fall the February snows, and soft. Bereavement of the Fields. William Wilfred Campbell. CaP
Soft, gray buds on the willow. The Turn of the Road. Alice Rollit Coe. HBV-1
Soft gray hands of sleep, The. Forgotten Dreams. Edward Silvera. PoNe
Soft grey ghosts crawl up my sleeve. Remembering. Maya Angelou. PPJ
Soft grey mist, A. July 1st, 1916. Aimee Byng Scott. SUMH
Soft grey of the distant hills, The. Dawn. Constance Ortmayer. SaC
Soft Job. William C. Summers. STF
Soft Landings. Howard Sergeant. OnUR
Soft lights, the companionship, the beers, The. The Pick-Up. J. V. Cunningham. UnTE
Soft little hands that stray and clutch. Little Hands. Laurence Binyon. HBV-1
Soft, lovely, rose-like lips, conjoined with mine. Barnabe Barnes. *Fr.* Parthenophil and Parthenophe. EnLoPo
Soft new grass is creeping o'er the graves, The. By the Potomac. Thomas Bailey Aldrich. PAH
Soft o'er the fountain. Juanita. Caroline Norton. FSW
Soft on the sunset sky. Ashes of Roses. Elaine Goodale Eastman. AA; HBV-1
Soft on the wave the oars at distance sound. Netley Abbey; Midnight. William Sotheby. NOEC
Soft petals fell out of a brooding air. Flemish Primitive. G. S. Fraser. BSV
Soft rainsqualls on the swells. Oil. Gary Snyder. LCAP
Soft-sandalled twilight, handmaid of the night. Winter Twilight. George Tracy Elliot. AA
Soft she was, young. Dead Girl. Anna Hajnal, *tr. by* Jascha Kessler. VWA
Soft Snow. Blake. FF; SoSe
("I walked abroad on a snowy day.") TEP
Soft songs, like birds, die in poison air. Apology for Apostasy? Etheridge Knight. NeAC
Soft sounds and odours brim up through the night. Guided Missiles Experimental Range. Robert Conquest. OxBC
Soft-throated South, breathing of summer's ease. South-Wind. George Parsons Lathrop. AA
Soft White. Lee Harwood. EAS
Soft Wood. Robert Lowell. LiTM
Soft you; a word or two before you go. Death of Othello [*or* Othello's Farewell]. Shakespeare. *Fr.* Othello, V, ii. FiP; TreFS
Softened by time's consummate plush. Emily Dickinson. NOBA
Softening of her face which comes, The. At Only That Moment. Alan Ross. ErPo
Softer than silence, stiller than still air. The Snowing of the Pines. Thomas Wentworth Higginson. AA; GN
Softly!/ She is lying/ With her lips apart. Dirge. Charles Gamage Eastman. AA
Softly along the road of evening. Nod. Walter de la Mare. HBMV; MoAB; MoBrPo; OxBTC
Softly and gently, dearly-ransom'd soul. Angel. Cardinal Newman. *Fr.* The Dream of Gerontius. OxBoCh
Softly and humbly to the Gulf of Arabs. Beach Burial. Kenneth Slessor. CBAP; PoAu-2
Softly blow lightly. Nocturne. Donald Jeffrey Hayes. CDC
Softly croons the radiogram, loudly hoot the owls. Invasion Exercise on the Poultry Farm. John Betjeman. NOBL
Softly, drowsily. Walter de la Mare. *Fr.* A Child's Day. SoPo; SUS
Softly Fades the Twilight Ray, *with music.* Samuel Francis Smith. AH
Softly I closed the book as in a dream. The Book. Winfred Ernest Garrison. TRV
Softly, in the dusk, a woman is singing to me. Piano. D. H. Lawrence. BLPL; CMoP; GrPl; GTBS-P; HAP; HeIP; InPK; InvP; LiTB; MoAB; MoBrPo; NIP; NoAM; NOBE; NoP; OAEL-2; OAEP; PAI; PoPle; PPP; UnPo; WeW
Softly now the burn is rushing. Lullaby. Seumas MacManus. AnIV
Softly now the light of day. Evening Contemplation [*or* Evening]. George Washington Doane. AA; AH; BLPA; BLPL; FaBoBe; HBV-2; TreFS
Softly, O midnight Hours! Serenade. Aubrey Thomas De Vere. HBV-1; OBEV
Softly rustled the oaks, whispered low in my ear. The Graveyard. Hayyim Nahman Bialik, *tr. by* Bertha Beinkinstadt. TrJP
Softly sailing emerald lights. Fireflies. "Fiona Macleod." *Fr.* Transcripts from Nature. FM
Softly sighs the April air. Bel m'es quan lo vens m'alena. Arnaut Daniel, *tr. by* Harriet Waters Preston. AWP
Softly Softly. Richard Shelton. NPAW
Softly the car goes with the music in it. Mollesse. Josephine Jacobsen. NePoAm-2
Softly the crane's foot crumples a star. Recollection. Dorothy Donnelly. NCSH
Softly the dead stir, call, through the afternoon. A Cemetery in New Mexico. A. Alvarez. VWA
Softly the Evening. W. H. Mallock. BXAP
Softly the Night. *Unknown.* OBET
Softly the waters ripple. Ares. Albert Ehrenstein, *tr. by* Babette Deutsch *and* Avram Yarmolinsky. TrJP
Softly through the Mellow Starlight. *Unknown.* OHIP
Softly, White and Pure. Dorothy R. Fulton. AMV-80
Softly Woo Away Her Breath. "Barry Cornwall." HBV-2
Soggarth Aroon. John Banim. GoBC
Soho. Joseph Brodsky, *tr. fr. Russian by* Alan Myers. VWA
Sohrab and Rustum. Matthew Arnold. DTo; OBNV; VLP
Sels.
Death of Sohrab, The ("He spoke; and Sohrab smiled on him, and took"). FiP
"So, on the bloody sand, Sohrab lay dead." GTBS-P
(Sohrab Dead.) NOBE
Sohrab's Death ("He spoke, and Sohrab kindled at his taunts"). WHA
"Then Sohrab with his sword smote Rustum's helm." OBWP
Soil is quick with dust of men, The. What Far Kingdom. Arthur S. Bourinot. CaP
Soil now gets a rumpling soft and damp, The. The Strong Are Saying Nothing. Robert Frost. CMoP
Soil of man's escape, The. Suburbia. Maurice Martinez. PoNe
Soil Searcher. J. Joyce. CTBA
Soil was deep and the field well-sited, The. A Failure. C. Day Lewis. NOBE
Soil ysowpit into water wak, The. Winter. Gavin Douglas. SeCePo
Soirée. Ezra Pound. DTC
Sois sage o ma douleur. Baudelaire. *See* Peace, Be at Peace, O Thou My Heaviness.
Sojourn in the Whale. Marianne Moore. SBG
Sojourner Truth. Robert Hayden. *Fr.* Stars. CNA
Sojourning through a southern realm in youth. The Sleeping Beauty. Wilfred Owen. DFT
Sokoya, I said, looking through. There Is No Word for Goodbye. Mary TallMountain. STE
Sol, Bronze Age came first Sol. The Windows of Waltham. John Wieners. CoPo
Solace. Clarissa Scott Delany. AmNP; CDC; PoBA; PoNe
Solace in Age. Sir Richard Maitland. OxBS
Solar Creation. Charles Madge. FaBoMo; OBMV; OxBTC
Solar Myth. Genevieve Taggard. MoAmPo
Solar Signals. L. Pearl Schuck. AMV-81
Soldier, The, *sels.* Conrad Aiken.
I. Wars, The. WaaP
II. Unknown Soldier, The. WaaP; WaP
Soldier, The. Rupert Brooke. 1914, V. BrPo; FaBoEn; FaBV; FaFP; FaPoR; FF; FPL; HBV-2; HeIP; LiTB; LiTM; MoBrPo; MoVE; NIP; NOBE; OBEV; OBWP; OxBTC; PoA; PoLF; PoPl; PoRA; TEP; TreF; TrGrPo; ViBoPo; WaP; WHA
Soldier, A. Robert Frost. MoPo; NePA; OFD; SeCeV; WaaP; WaP
Soldier, The. Gerard Manley Hopkins. WaaP
Soldier, The. Uys Krige, *tr. fr. Afrikaans by the author.* PeSA
Soldier, A. Sir John Suckling. SeCV-1
Soldier, The. J. Y. Watson. BXAP

"Soldier an' Sailor Too." Kipling. MOS
Soldier and a Sailor, A. Congreve. *Fr.* Love for Love. CoMu
(Buxom Joan.) InMe
(Souldier and a Sailor, A.) OAEP
Soldier and a Sailor, A. John Gay. *Fr.* The Beggar's Opera, I, i. TEP
(Air: "Fox may steal your hens, sir, A.") NOEC
Soldier and a Scholar, A, *sel.* Swift.
"Thus spoke to my lady the knight full of care." OBEC
Soldier and singer of Erin. In Memoriam: Francis Ledwidge. Norreys Jephson O'Conor. HBMV
Soldier and statesman, rarest unison. Ours, and All Men's [*or* Washington]. James Russell Lowell. *Fr.* Under the Old Elm. GN; OHIP; PAL; PGD
Soldier and the Sailor, The, *with music.* *Unknown.* ShS
Soldier Boy for Me. *Unknown.* AmFP
Soldier brave, sailor true. *Unknown.* OxNR
Soldier from the Wars Returning. A. E. Housman. LiTB; OBMV
Soldier Going to the Field, The. Sir William Davenant. NOBE; OBWP
(Souldier Going to the Field, The.) MePo
Soldier, A: His Prayer. Gerald Kersch. TreFS
Soldier in the Park, The. Elizabeth Riddell. CBAP
Soldier is, The/ all alone. Glove Glue. Ken Belford. NeAC
Soldier Is Home, The. Shaw Neilson. CBAP
Soldier Loves His Rifle, The. W. H. Auden. TEP
Soldier maimed and in the beggars' list, A. The Pluralist and Old Soldier. John Collier. NOEC
Soldier of the Cromwell stamp, A. Heredity. Thomas Bailey Aldrich. AA
Soldier of the Legion lay dying in Algiers, A. Bingen on the Rhine. Caroline Norton. BeLS; BLPA; HBV-2; TreF; WBLP
Soldier of Weight, A. John Kendall. WhC
Soldier, oh soldier, a-coming from the plain. The Bold Soldier. *Unknown.* FSW
Soldier passed me in the freshly fallen snow, A. To a Conscript of 1940. Sir Herbert Read. ChMP; LiTB; LiTM; OBWP; WaP
Soldier Poet, A. Rossiter Johnson. AA
"Soldier, Rest!" Robert Jones Burdette. OBAL
Soldier, Rest! [Thy Warfare O'er]. Sir Walter Scott. *Fr.* The Lady of the Lake, I. AWP; GN; HBV-2; HBVY; MoShBr; NOBE; PoRA; TreFS; TrGrPo
(Song: "Soldier, rest! thy warfare o'er.") OAEP; OBNC; OBRV
Soldier, Soldier, Won't You Marry Me? *Unknown.* Soldier, Won't You Marry Me?
Soldier (T. P.). Randall Jarrell. WaP
Soldier That Has Seen Service, The. *Unknown.* NOEC
Soldier, There Is a War between the Mind. Wallace Stevens. *Fr.* Notes toward a Supreme Fiction. LiTM; NePA
Soldier: Twentieth Century. Isaac Rosenberg. ChMP; MMA
Soldier Walks under the Trees of the University, The. Randall Jarrell. OxBA; PoPl; WaP
Soldier, Won't You Marry Me? *Unknown.* AmFP; OLR; OxBoLi
(Soldier, Soldier, Won't You Marry Me?) FSW
Soldiers. *Unknown.* FaBoEE; GBP
Soldiers/ Sailors/ Marines. The Gray Oak Twilight. James C. Kilgore. SOTS
Soldiers are citizens of death's grey land. Dreamers. Siegfried Sassoon. BrPo; HBMV; MoBrPo; NoAM
Soldiers are marching over the pontoon bridge. Nike. Adam Wazyk, *tr. by* Isaac Komem. VWA
Soldiers, as we come to lay. More than Flowers We Have Brought. Nancy Byrd Turner. SiSoSe
Soldiers Bathing. F. T. Prince. ChMP; GTBS-P; LiTB; LiTM; MoBrPo; MoVE; NOCV; OBWP; OxBTC; PeSA; WaP
("Sea at evening moves across the sand, The.") ChMP
Soldiers came, brewed tea in Snoddy's field, The. After the War. Douglas Dunn. OxBC
Soldier's Death, A. Cyril. Tourneur. *Fr.* The Atheist's Tragedy. SeCePo
Soldier's Dove. James Forsyth. WaP
Soldier's Dream, The. Thomas Campbell. BeLS; EnRP; FaPoR; GTBS; GTBS-P; HBV-2; RoGo; TreFS
Soldier's Dream. Wilfred Owen. ILwL
Soldier's Farewell to Manchester, The. *Unknown.* CoMu
Soldiers' Friend, The. George Canning *and* John Hookham Frere. OBEC; Par
Soldiers fuzz the city in khaki confusion. Habana. Julian Bond. NNP
Soldier's Grave, A. John Albee. AA
Soldier's Grave, The. Henry D. Muir. OHIP
Soldiers have to fight and swear. Unequal Distribution. Samuel Hoffenstein. TrJP
Soldiers never do die well. Champs d'Honneur. Ernest Hemingway. PoA
Soldiers of Christ, arise. The Whole Armour of God. Charles Wesley. NOCV
Soldier's Plea for the Y.M.C.A., A. Joseph Samuel Reed. PeD
Soldier's Prayer, A. Robert Freeman. TrPWD
Soldier's Song. Goethe, *tr. fr. German by* Bayard Taylor. *Fr.* Faust. AWP
Soldier's Song, The. Peadar Kearney. OnYI
Soldier's Song. Sir Walter Scott. *Fr.* The Lady of the Lake, VI. NBM; ViBoPo
Soldier's Song. *Unknown.* WiR
Soldiers suddenly struck by love, The. In Postures That Call. Oscar Williams. WaP
Soldiers who wish to be a hero. Soldiers. *Unknown.* FaBoEE; GBP
Soldier's Wife, The. George Canning *and* John Hookham Frere. Par
Soldier's Wife, The. Robert Southey. OBEC
Soldier's Wooing, The, 2 *versions.* *Unknown.* AmFP
Soldier's Wound, The. Wallace Stevens. WaaP
Sole-hungering Camel. Oliver Herford. TDH
Sole Lord of Lords and very King of Kings. Sesostris. Lloyd Mifflin. AA; HBV-2
Sole positive of night. Ne Plus Ultra. Samuel Taylor Coleridge. OAEL-2
Sole true something—This! In Limbo's den, The. Limbo. Samuel Taylor Coleridge. OAEL-2
Sole watchman of the flying stars, guard me. Eleven Addresses to the Lord, III. John Berryman. UnPo
Solemn and slow they move. The Sod-Breaker. Arthur Stringer. CaP
Solemn he paced upon that schooner's deck. The Captain. John G. C. Brainard. EtS
Solemn Hour. Rainer Maria Rilke, *tr. fr. German by* C. F. MacIntyre. PoPl; TrJP
Solemn Meditation, A. Ruth Pitter. OxBoCh
Solemn Meditation, A. William Shenstone. NOEC
Solemn Noon of Night, The. Thomas Warton, the Younger. *Fr.* The Pleasures of Melancholy. OBEC; SeCePo
("Beneath yon ruined abbey's moss-grown pile.") NOEC
Solemn pastors. The MJQ. Joyce Carol Thomas. CNA
Solemn plain-faced child stands gazing there, A. A Portrait. Walter de la Mare. NoAM
Solemn Rondeau. Charles Dent Bell. OBVV
Solemn whip-poor-will, The. The Queens. Robert Fitzgerald. NYBP
Solemnly, mournfully,/ Dealing its dole. Curfew. Longfellow. AA; OxBA
Solemnly swearing, to swear as an oath to you. Vera from My Childhood. Judy Grahn. The Common Woman, VII. GP
Soles Occidere et Redire Possunt, *sel.* Aldous Huxley.
" 'Misery,' he said, 'to have no chin.' " ViBoPo
Solid citizens, The. Undertow. Langston Hughes. LiTM
Solid houses in the mist, The. New Year's. Charles Reznikoff. VGW
Solid Mountain. George Bowering. NeAC
Solidarity Forever. Ralph Chaplin. FSW
Soliloquy. Frederick E. Laight. *See* Drought.
Soliloquy. Francis Ledwidge. HoPM
Soliloquy by the Shore. Martin Scholten. GoYe
Soliloquy from "Hamlet." Shakespeare. *See* To Be, or Not to Be.
Soliloquy in a Motel. Walker Gibson. GrPl
Soliloquy in an Air-Raid. Roy Fuller. PoA
Soliloquy in the Suburbs, A. Charles Jenner. *Fr.* Eclogue IV: The Poet. NOEC
Soliloquy of a Tortoise on Revisiting the Lettuce Beds after an Interval of One Hour While Supposed to Be Sleeping in a Clump of Blue Hollyhocks. E. V. Rieu. FiBHP; RHPC
Soliloquy of a Turkey. Paul Laurence Dunbar. BPo
Soliloquy of One of the Spies Left in the Wilderness, A. Gerard Manley Hopkins. TrCP
Soliloquy of the Returned Gold Adventurer. "Syntax." PoOW
Soliloquy of the Spanish Cloister. Robert Browning. CABA; DTo; FaBoCo; InPK; LiTB; NIP; NOBL; NoP; OAEL-2; OAEP; PAI; SeCeV; TEP; TrGrPo; TW
Soliloquy on Death. F. K. Fiawoo. PBA
Soliloquy on Sleep. Shakespeare. *See* Cares of Majesty, The.
Soliloquy I. Richard Aldington. BrPo
Soliloquy to Absent Friends. Douglas G. Jones. MoCV
Soliloquy II. Richard Aldington. BrPo; MMA
Solitaire. Amy Lowell. MoAmPo
Solitariness (3 *sonnets*). Sir Philip Sidney. *Fr.* Arcadia. OBSC; SiPS
(Delight of Solitariness, The.) LiTB
(Dorus's Song.) LoBV
(O Sweet Woods.) FaBoRV; PoEL-1
Solitary, The. Mary Barnard. FAZ
Solitary, The. Nietzsche, *tr. fr. German by* Ludwig Lewisohn. AWP
Solitary. Sharon Olds. SOTS
Solitary, The. Rainer Maria Rilke, *tr. fr. German by* C. F. MacIntyre. TrJP
Solitary, The. Sara Teasdale. MoAmPo; WHA
Solitary, The, *sel.* Wordsworth. The Excursion, II.
"I could not, ever and anon, forbear." EnRP
Solitary bird of night, The. Ode to Wisdom. Elizabeth Carter. OBEC
Solitary Canto to Chloris the Disdainful, A. John Smith. NOEC

Solitary Confinement. X. J. Kennedy. NePoEA-2
Solitary egret, The. Early Morning. Philip Dow. DFF
Solitary-Hearted, The. Hartley Coleridge. HBV-1
Solitary invalid in a fuchsia garden, A. The Philosopher and the Birds. Richard Murphy. CIP
Solitary Life, A. William Drummond of Hawthornden. *See* Thrice Happy He.
Solitary Lyre, The. George Darley. LiTB; OBEV
(Enchanted Lyre, The.) OBNC
(Wherefore, Unlaurelled Boy.) FaBoRV; NOBE; OBRV
Solitary prospector, A. Sunstrike. Douglas Livingstone. PeSA
Solitary Reaper, The. Wordsworth. AWP; BLPL; CABA; CH; ChER; EnRP; FaBoCh; FaBoEn; FaPoR; FiP; GN; HAP; HBV-1; InPS; LiTB; LoBV; NOBE; NoP; OAEL-2; OAEP; OBEV; OBNC; OBRV; PAI; PoEL-4; PoPle; PoRA; PPP; RoGo; SCV; SeCeV; SoSe; TEP; TreF; TrGrPo; UnPo; WeW; WHA
(Reaper, The.) GTBS; GTBS-P
Solitary Song. *Unknown, tr. fr. Eskimo.* WTO
Solitary Visions of a Kaufmanoid. James Cunningham. JB
Solitary wayfarer! Hoopoe. George Darley. *Fr.* Nepenthe. OBNC; OBRV; PBBP
Solitary Woodsman, The. Sir Charles G. D. Roberts. CaP; OBCV
Solitude. James Beattie. *Fr.* Retirement. OBEC
Solitude. John Clare. EnRP
Solitude. Walter de la Mare. CMoP; FaBoEn
Solitude. Babette Deutsch. HBMV
Solitude, *abr.* James Grainger. OBEC
(Ode to Solitude.) ViBoPo
Solitude. Keats. EnRP
Solitude. Archibald Lampman. BoNaP; OBCV; PeCV
Solitude, A. Denise Levertov. NePoEA-2
Solitude. Mary Mollineux. CavP
Solitude. Harold Monro. BSV; MoBrPo; TrGrPo
Solitude. Hannah More. *Fr.* The Search after Happiness. WBLP
Solitude. Frederick Peterson. AA
Solitude. Pope. *See* Ode on Solitude.
Solitude. Rainer Maria Rilke, *tr. fr. German by* C. F. MacIntyre. TrJP
Solitude. Philip Henry Savage. AA
Solitude. Charles Simic. GP
Solitude. Thomas Traherne. OBS
"I do believ," *sel.* FaBoEn
Solitude. Ella Wheeler Wilcox. FaFP; FPL; HBV-2; OHFP; PaPo; PoLF; YaD
(Way of the World, The.) TreF; WBLP
Solitude and Reason, in the Village. Abraham Cowley. *Fr.* Of Solitude. FaBoPP
Solitude and the Lily. Richard Henry Horne. OBVV
Solitude is like rain. Solitude. Rainer Maria Rilke, *tr. by* C. F. MacIntyre. TrJP
Solitude Late at Night in the Woods. Robert Bly. BiP; VGW
Solitude of Alexander Selkirk, The. William Cowper. *See* Verses Supposed to be Written by Alexander Selkirk . . .
Solitude that unmakes me one of men. Compensation. Robinson Jeffers. MoAB; MoAmPo
Solo for Bent Spoon. Donald Finkel. NePoEA-2
Solo for Ear-Trumpet. Edith Sitwell. MoAB; MoBrPo
Solo Native. Thomas Lux. LCAP
Solomon. Hermann Hagedorn. GoBC
Solomon. Heine, *tr. fr. German by* Emma Lazarus. TrJP
Solomon, *sel. Unknown, tr. fr. Greek by* J. Rendel Harris.
Inspiration, VI. WGRP
To Truth, XXXVIII. WGRP
Solomon and Morolph, Their Last Encounter. Oscar Levertin, *tr. fr. Swedish by* Richard Burns *and* Göran Printz-Pahlson. VWA
Solomon and the Bees. John Godfrey Saxe. GN
Solomon and the Witch. W. B. Yeats. NoAM
Solomon Grundy. Mother Goose. HBV-1; HBVY; OxBoLi; OxNR; RHPC; TreFT
Solomon Grundy. Frederick Winsor. *Fr.* The Space Child's Mother Goose. QQQ
Solomon Judges between Two Women Disputing over a Child. Bible, *O.T.* First Kings, III: 16-27. TreFT
Solomon on the Vanity of the World, *sels.* Matthew Prior.
"Fix thy corporeal, and internal eye." FM
Love and Reason. OBEC
"Pass we the ills, which each man feels or dreads," *fr.* Bk. III. NOEC; PoEL-3
(Power.) LoBV
Solomon Pease. *Unknown.* WhC
Solomon to Sheba. W. B. Yeats. CMoP; ELP
Solomon! where is thy throne? It is gone in the wind. Gone in the Wind. James Clarence Mangan. ACP; GoBC; OBVV; OnYI; OxBI; SeCePo
Solsequium, The. Alexander Montgomerie. GoTS; NoP; OxBS
Solstice. Emery George. HoAn
Solstice. Charles Weekes. OnYI
Solstitium Saeculare. Robert Fitzgerald. MoVE
Soluble Noughts and Crosses; or, California, Here I Come. Roger Roughton. EAS
Solution. Emerson. OBAL
Solution, The. Brian Merriman, *tr. fr. Modern Irish by* Arland Ussher. *Fr.* The Midnight Court. BIrV
Solutions. David Barton. AMV-81
Solway wind, The. On Ellson Fell. William Landles. PoSH
Som tyme this world was so stedfast and stable. Lak of Stedfastnesse. Chaucer. AWP
"Sombra?" The Shade-Seller. Josephine Jacobsen. TAP
Sombre [*or* Somber] and rich, the skies. By the Statue of King Charles at Charing Cross. Lionel Johnson. BrPo; FaBoRV; HBV-2; MoBrPo; NBM; NOBE; OBEV; OBMV; OBNC; OBVV; PoEL-5; RoGo; VLP
Sombre the night is. Returning, We Hear the Larks. Isaac Rosenberg. BrPo; FaBoMo; MMA; OAEL-2; OBWP; VWA; WaaP
Some act of Love's bound to reherse. Why I Write Not of Love. Ben Jonson. OAEP
Some ages hence, for it must not decay. Under a Lady's Picture. Edmund Waller. EnLoPo
Some are bewildered in the maze of schools. Pope. *Fr.* An Essay on Criticism. OBSV
Some Are Born. Stevie Smith. FaBoCo
Some are in prison; some are dead. The Chumbs. Theodore Roethke. NoAM
Some are plain lucky—we ourselves among them. A Lost Soul. Jay Macpherson. NOBC
Some are sick for Spring and warm winds blowing. The Hound. Babette Deutsch. HBMV
Some are stout. Professors. Harold A. Larrabee. InMe
Some are teethed on a silver spoon. Saturday's Child. Countee Cullen. InPK; LiTM; NAs; OFD; PAI; PoBA; SaC
Some are too difficult to win. Dinah. A. R. Ammons. PV
Some are too much at home in the role of wanderer. Poem. Denise Levertov. NeBP
Some are waiting, some can't wait. Lines. Heather McHugh. MAYP
Some ask for envy'd pow'r; which publick hate. Sejanus. Juvenal, *tr. by* Dryden. *Fr.* Satires, X. OBVE
Some asked me where the rubies grew. Rubies and Pearls [*or* The Rock of Rubies]. Robert Herrick. HBV-1; InMe
Some autumn leaves a painter took. The Sumach Leaves. Jones Very. NOBA
Some awful. Sounds. Robert Creeley. GP
Some beauties yet no precepts can declare. Pope. *Fr.* An Essay on Criticism. HAP
Some Beautiful Letters, *sels.* Dorothy Parker.
Comment. InMe; NIP; OBAL
Interview. InMe
News Item. FaBoUs; InMe; OBAL; TreF; YaD
Observation. FiBHP; InMe
Résumé. DBV; DL; HeIP; InMe; InPK; NoP; OBAL; PAI; PoPl; ShM; TrJP; WhC
Social Note. FaBoUs; InMe
Some beetle trilling. Continuum. Denise Levertov. LCAP
Some Bird. *Unknown.* STF
Some Blesseds. John Oxenham. WGRP
Some blind themselves, 'cause possibly they may. Reason, the Use of It in Divine Matters. Abraham Cowley. AnAnS-2
Some bloodied sea-bird's hovering decay. The Lie. Howard Moss. LiTM; MoAB; NePoAm
Some books are lies frae end to end. Death and Doctor Hornbook. Burns. OxBS
Some Boys. Chuck Ortleb. PeHV
Some Boys. John Penkethman. OxBChV
Some Brave, awake in you to-night. Fancy Dress. Siegfried Sassoon. BrPo
Some broken/ Iroquois adze. A State of Nature. John Hollander. NIP
Some by their friends, more by themselves thought wise. Dryden. *Fr.* Absalom and Achitophel, Pt. I. OBSV
Some, by their monarch's fatal mercy grown. Lord Shaftesbury. Dryden. *Fr.* Absalom and Achitophel, Pt. I. LoBV
Some can gaze and not be sick. A. E. Housman. FaBoEE; OBSV
Some candle clear burns somewhere I come by. The Candle Indoors. Gerard Manley Hopkins. LiTB; LiTM; OxBoCh; PoEL-5
Some clouds are rainclouds. On the Pole. Uri Zvi Greenberg, *tr. by* Robert Mezey *and* Ben Zion Gold. VWA
Some Contemplations of the Poor, and Desolate State of the Church at Deerfield. John Williams. SCAP
Some Cook. John Ciardi. PDV
Some cowpoke named her Nevada. Nevada. Stanley Noyes. PH

Some cry up Haydn, some Mozart. Free Thoughts on Several Eminent Composers. Charles Lamb. DBV; FaBoCo; OBRV; OxBoLi
Some curse that traitor Judas life and limb. Francis Quarles. FaBoEE
Some Day. *See also* Someday.
Some Day. Medora C. Addison. HBMV
Some Day. Shel Silverstein. PH
Some day. What Someone Said When He Was Spanked on the Day before His Birthday. John Ciardi. RHPC
Some day, all unawares, alone in the deep forest. My Death. Carl Zuckmayer, *tr. by* E. B. Ashton. TrJP
Some day I will go to Aarhus. The Tollund Man. Seamus Heaney. BIrV; EBEV; FaBoMo; IPY; NoP; TEP
Some day I'm going to have a store. General Store. Rachel Field. SoPo; SUS
Some Day of Days. Nora Perry. HBV-1
Some day perhaps I too may speak your name. Some Day. Medora C. Addison. HBMV
Some Day, Some Day. Cristobal de Castillejo, *tr. fr. Spanish by* Longfellow. AWP; ViBoPo
Some day, some day of days, threading the street. Some Day of Days. Nora Perry. HBV-1
Some day, some happy day. The Reign of Peace. Mary Starck. WBLP
Some day, when trees have shed their leaves. After the Winter. Claude McKay. BANP; IDB; PoBA; PoNe
Some Days/ Out Walking Above. De Leon Harrison. PoBA
Some days a road streams back, a road you took. Other Lives. Patricia Hooper. AMV-81; HoAn
Some days are fairy days. The minute that you wake. Sometimes. Rose Fyleman. SiSoSe
Some days, I'm sorely tempted to throw out the baby. Lamentations of an Au Pair Girl. Susan Feldman. AmPA
Some days my thoughts are just cocoons—all cold, and dull and blind. Days. Karle Wilson Baker. TiPo
Some days the tick of two protestant clocks. Greystone Cottage. Richard Hugo. NPAW
Some days, you say, are good days. Warp and Woof. Harry Halbisch. BLRP
Some die too late and some too soon. The Lost Occasion. Whittier. BLPL; NOBA
Some do for pimping, some for treach'ry rise. Satire. Earl of Rochester. DBV
Some dogs are brats. For a Good Dog. Arthur Guiterman. GDP
Some Dreams They Forgot. Elizabeth Bishop. NoAM
Some dreams we have are nothing else but dreams. The Haunted House. Thomas Hood. EBEV
Some Eyes Condemn. Edward Thomas. NoAM
Some farms have graveyards tucked upon a knoll. Horse Graveyard. Fred Lape. PH
Some Feelings. Michael Benedikt. ConAP
Some find love late, some find him soon. When Will Love Come? Pakenham Beatty. HBV-1
Some Fishy Nonsense. Laura E. Richards. SoPo; TiPo
Some Flowers o' the Spring. Shakespeare. *Fr.* The Winter's Tale, IV, iii. ChTr
Some folks are drunk, yet do not know it. An English Ballad, on the Taking of Namur by the King of Great Britain, 1695. Matthew Prior. PoEL-3
Some folks as can afford. Under a Wiltshire Apple Tree. Anna de Bary. CH
Some folks jump up and down all night and d-a-n-c-e. It's G-L-O-R-Y to Know I'm S-A-V-E-D. *Unknown.* FSW
Some food, some sun. Human Needs. *Unknown.* POL
Some fools keep ringing the dumb waiter bell. Chant Royal of the Dejected Dipsomanic. Don Marquis. HBMV
Some for everyone. Snow by Morning. May Swenson. NYBP
Some for the Glories of this World; and some. Omar Khayyám, *tr. by* Edward Fitzgerald. *Fr.* The Rubáiyát of Omar Khayyám of Naishápúr. PoPl
Some Foreign Letters. Anne Sexton. MoAmPo; PoCh
Some Frenchmen. John Updike. FaBoCo
Some Geese. Oliver Herford. *Fr.* Child's Natural History. FiBHP; NA (Geese.) HBV-2
Some girls wear short dresses. Nehi Blues. *Unknown.* BluL
Some Good Things to Be Said for the Iron Age. Gary Snyder. HoPM; PAI
Some Gypsies are like her. The Ballad of Adam's First. Leland Davis. HBMV
Some had in Courts been Great, and thrown from thence. The Earl of Shaftesbury. Dryden. *Fr.* Absalom and Achitophel. FaBoEn
Some hae meat and [*or* that] canna eat. A Child's Grace. Burns. FaBoCh; FaPON; MoShBr
Some hand, that never meant to do thee hurt. On Finding a Small Fly Crushed in a Book. Charles Tennyson Turner. FM
Some hang above the tombs. On Such a Day. Mary Elizabeth Coleridge. LO; MoVE
Some Harvard men, stalwart and hairy. Edward Gorey. OBAL
Some hearts there are of deeper sort. Lyon. Herman Melville. PeD
Some in the Godspeed, the Susan C. Enough. Marianne Moore. NOBA
Some in the Town go betimes to the Downs. The Hunt. *Unknown.* CoMu
Some in their harts their mistris colours bears. Chloris, XXIX. William Smith. AAS
Some Indian Uses of History on a Rainy Day. A. K. Ramanujan. OxBC
Some innocent girlish kisses by a charm. Wild Rose, *abr.* William Allingham. GN
Some keep the Sabbath [*or* Sunday] going to church. Emily Dickinson. MoAB; MoAmPo; PAI; SoSe; WGRP
Some Kind of Giant. Sheila Pritchard. BoAnP
Some Kisses from "The Kama Sutra." Hugo Williams. BoLoP
Some Knots. Edwin Honig. NoAM
Some Lamb. Stan Rice. NPGG
Some lasses are nice and strange. The Innocent Country-Maid's Delight; or, A Description of the Lives of the Lasses of London. *Unknown.* CoMu
Some Last Questions. W. S. Merwin. CAPP
Some Late Lark Singing. W. E. Henley. *See* Margaritae Sorori.
Some leaders lead too far ahead. Leaders. *Unknown.* WBLP
Some like drink. Not I. Robert Louis Stevenson. NA
"Some likes picturs o' women," said Bill, "an' some likes 'orses best." Pictures. C. Fox Smith. EtS
Some Lines in Three Parts. Peter Viereck. MiAP
Some Litanies. Michael Benedikt. CoAP; TwCP
Some Little Bug. Roy Atwell. PoLF
"In these days of indigestion," *sel.* ShM
Some long forgotten prisoner. Rune. Philip Brasfield. LFAC
Some lovers speak, when they their Muses entertain. Astrophel and Stella, VI. Sir Philip Sidney. SiPS
Some lucky day each November great waves awake and are drawn. November Surf. Robinson Jeffers. CrMA; MoPo; OxBA
Some Magic. James Koller. PoM
Some Magnetism in the Sea. Rodney Hall. *Fr.* The Owner of My Face. CBAP
Some make potteries. Womanwork. Paula Gunn Allen. TWSS
Some Me of Beauty. Carolyn M. Rodgers. CNA
Some men break your heart in two. Experience. Dorothy Parker. InMe; PoPl; WhC
Some men marriage do commend. De Se. John Weever. FaBoEE
Some men sayen that I am blac. The Dark Lady. *Unknown.* OxBM
Some men, some men. Chant for Dark Hours. Dorothy Parker. SBG
Some men, 'tis said, prefer a woman fat. Nathaniel Parker Willis. *Fr.* The Lady Jane: A Humorous Novel in Rhyme. OBAL
Some Modern Good Turns. Dennis Dibben. FAZ
Some modest windfalls from the Tree. Vacation Trip. Donald G. Babcock. NePoAm
Some months ago a journalist. "The Banquet of the Century" in Persepolis. Alamgir Hashmi. SOTS
Some morning I shall rise from sleep. The Last Voyage. Katherine Tynan. HBMV
Some morning, while you and I are dozing. Intruder. Susan Feldman. AmPA
Some Murmur When Their Sky Is Clear. Richard Chevenix Trench. HBVY
Some must delve when the dawn is nigh. The King of Dreams. Clinton Scollard. HBV-2
Some must employ the scythe. The Dedicated. Philip Larkin. OxBC
Some names there are of telling sound. The *Cumberland.* Herman Melville. PAH
Some ne'er advance a judgment of their own. Pope. *Fr.* An Essay on Criticism. OBSV
Some Negatives: X. at the Chateau. James Merrill. NePoEA-2
Some nights the moon is the curve of a comb. The Window Frames the Moon. Laureen Mar. BrSi
Some nights when you're asleep. Dawn Walk. Edward Hirsch. MAYP
Some nights when you're off. The Avenues. David St. John. AMV-80; MAYP
Some nine hundred fifty circlings of my moon. Birthday. Earle Birney. NAs
Some nine years gone, as we dwelt together. Dedication. Swinburne. VLP
Some nineteen German planes, they say. Reprisals. W. B. Yeats. OBWP
Some of my best friends are white boys. Friends. Ray Durem. PoBA
Some of our dead are famous, but they would not care. W. H. Auden. *Fr.* Commentary. MoPo
Some of Our Koorawatha Saints. Geoffrey Lehmann. *Fr.* Ross's Poems. CBAP
Some of the girls are playing jacks. Narcissa. Gwendolyn Brooks. GrPl; NTCP
Some of the grandest have chosen marble. Gravestones. Floyd C. Stuart. AMV-80

Some of the hurts you have cured. Borrowing. Emerson. WhC
Some of the roofs are plum-color. Not Three—But One. Esther Lilian Duff. HBMV
Some of the sky is grey and some of it is white. Moving. Randall Jarrell. DFF
Some of the time, going home, I go. Looking for the Buckhead Boys. James Dickey. LiSp
Some of their chiefs were princes of the land. Zimri. Dryden. *Fr.* Absalom and Achitophel, Pt. I. AWP; EBEV; SCV
Some of us/ these days. Resurrection. Frank Horne. OFD; PoBA
Some of Us Are Exiles from No Land. Diana O Hehir. NPGG
Some of Wordsworth. Walter Savage Landor. ChTr
Some of your hurts you have cured. Needless Worry. Emerson. TreFT
Some officers take them away: good guard. Lear and Cordelia. Shakespeare. *Fr.* King Lear, V, iii. FiP
Some "old Robin Down" they call me. Ibby Damsel. *Unknown.* AmFP
Some One. *See* Someone.
Some Opposites. Richard Wilbur. OBCA
Some Painful Butterflies Pass Through. Tess Gallagher. MAYP
Some part of us lives. The Fourth Dimension. Leonard Nathan. AMV-81
Some People. Rachel Field. FaPON; NTCP; PDV; RHPC
Some people,/ no matter what you give them. Adam's Complaint. Denise Levertov. BoWoP; NNaP
Some people admire the work of a fool. Blake. OAEL-2
Some people cannot endure. Going the Rounds; a Sort of Love Poem. Anthony Hecht. BoLoP
Some people grow chalky dust on their skin. For My Mother, Feeling Useless. Paula Rankin. MAYP
Some people hang portraits up. A Likeness. Robert Browning. CTC; InPS; VLP
Some People I Know. Jack Prelutsky. RHPC
Some people know how to love. Poem of Explanations. Dahlia Ravikovitch, *tr. by* Chana Bloch. BoWoP
Some people long to have plenty money. Ease It to Me Blues. *Unknown.* BluL
Some people, now, like mountains, where the shafts. Horizontal World. Thomas Saunders. CaP
Some people say the world's all a stage. The Gate at the End of Things. *Unknown.* BLPA
Some people see only you. The Couple. Ana Blandiana, *tr. by author and* William M. Murray. WPOW
Some people shave before bathing. And Three Hundred and Sixty-six in Leap Year. Ogden Nash. NePA
Some people stop hunting because they get tired. On Dressing to Go Hunting. *Unknown.* PH
Some people talk and talk. People. Charlotte Zolotow. RHPC
Some people talk in a telephone. Thoughts on Talkers. Walter R. Brooks. RHPC
Some people tell me God takes care of old folks and fools. Fool's Blues. *Unknown.* BluL
Some people think I think I'm good. Oh, If They Only Knew! Edith L. Mapes. BLRP; WBLP
Some people understand all about machinery. Up from the Wheelbarrow. Ogden Nash. FaBoBe
Some Pieces. Calvin Forbes. MAYP
Some pimps wear summer hats. What? Langston Hughes. OBAL
Some pretty face remembered in our youth. Fragment. John Clare. VLP
Some primal termite knocked on wood. The Termite. Ogden Nash. CenHV; OBCA; PoPl; ShM; WhC
Some Questions to Be Asked of a Rajah, Perhaps by the Associated Press. Preston Newman. FiBHP
Some reckon their age by years. The Rosary of My Tears. Abram J. Ryan. HBV-2
Some Refrains at the Charles River. Peter Viereck. PoCh
Some Ruthless Rhymes, *sel.* Graham.
  Tender-heartedness, II. DBV; FaFP; NA; RHPC; TreFT; WhC
  (Billy.) FaBoCo
  ("Billy, in one of his nice new sashes.") CenHV
Some San Francisco Poems. George Oppen. NNaP
Some say/ it was a pear. Pears. Linda Pastan. VWA
Some say cavalry and others claim. Sappho, *tr. fr. Greek by* Willis Barnstone. BoWoP
Some say, compar'd to Bononcini. Epigram on [the Feuds between] Handel and Bononcini. John Byrom. FaBoEE; NOBL; NOEC; OBEC
Some say kissin's ae [*or* that kissing's a] sin. Kissin' [*or* Kissing's No Sin]. *Unknown.* FiBHP; HBV-1; TreF; UnTE
Some say love. Menaphon's Song. Robert Greene. *Fr.* Menaphon. LoBV; OBSC
Some say my love has proved unfaithful. The Weeping Willow. *Unknown.* AmFP
Some say that ever 'gainst that season comes. Christmas [*or* The Bird of Dawning *or* The Gracious Time]. Shakespeare. *Fr.* Hamlet, I, i. ChTr; FaBoRV; GN; OFD; PChr
Some say that kissing's a sin. *See* Some say kissin's ae sin.
Some say the dead are lonely where they lie. Sonnets to My Mother. Arthur S. Bourinot. CaP
Some say the deil's deid. *Unknown.* FaBoCh
Some say the nightmare is. Nightmares. Siv Cedering Fox. WSC
Some say the Phoenix dwells in Aethiopia. The Phoenix. Siegfried Sasson. ChTr
Some say the sun is a golden earring. Natalia M. Belting. PDV
Some say the world will end in fire. Fire and Ice. Robert Frost. AmPP; BiP; CABA; CMoP; CoBMV; FaBoEE; FaFP; FaPo; FF; FPL; HBMV; HeIP; HoPM; InPK; LiTA; LiTM; MoAB; MoAmPo; MoVE; NePA; NoAM; NOBA; OxBA; PAI; PoPl; PPP; PrIm; SoSe; TAP; TreFS; TrGrPo; TW; TwAmPo; ViBoPo; WHA
Some say you dye your hair. But I deny it. To Chloe. *Unknown, tr. by* Louis Untermeyer. UnTE
Some Scribbles for a Lumpfish. Thomas Johnson. AMV-80
Some seek for ecstasies of joy. The One Thing Needful. Max Isaac Reich. BLRP
Some Semblance of Order. Charles David Wright. FAZ
Some shapes cannot be seen in a glass. Holding the Mirror Up to Nature. Howard Nemerov. PoA
Some silent movie star. The Flicker. Lew Blockcolski. VoR
Some sit and stare. The Common Grave. James Dickey. CoAP
Some Small Shells from the Windward Islands. May Swenson. FYAP
Some sort of fire leaped out of the dirty and poor and merciless city. Hymn. Otto Orban, *tr. by* Emery George. VWA
Some Sound Advice from Singapore. John Ciardi. GrPl
Some space beyond the garden close. The Hollyhocks. Craven Langstroth Betts. AA
Some steerage. In a Dream Ship's Hold. Suzanne Bernhardt. VWA
Some Stories of the Beauty Wapiti. Ebbe Borregaard. NeAP
Some Syrian rainmaker. Assumption. Padraic Fallon. BIrV
Some talk of Alexander, and some of Hercules. The British Grenadiers. *Unknown.* FSW; HBV-2; OBEC; OxBoLi
Some talk of Ganymede th' Idalian boy. Sonnet. Richard Barnfield. Sonnets, XII. PeHV
Some tell us 'tis a burnin' shame. Sambo's Right to Be Kilt. Charles Graham Halpine. AA
Some ten or twelve old friends of yours and mine. A Gentleman of Fifty Soliloquizes. Don Marquis. HBMV
Some ten or twenty times a day. Ballade of a Friar. Clément Marot, *tr. by* Andrew Lang. HBV-1
Some that have deeper digged love's mine than [*or* myne then] I. Love's Alchemy [*or* Alchemie]. John Donne. AnAnS-1; CABA; MePo; NoP; OAEL-1; OAEP; SeCP; SUW; ViBoPo
Some that reporte great Alexanders life. Thomas Watson. *Fr.* Hekatompathia. AAS
Some, the great Adepts, found it. The Adepts. Lawrence Durrell. *Fr.* Eight Aspects of Melissa. ErPo; NeBP
Some—the ones with fish names—grow so north. Wildflower. Stanley Plumly. LCAP
Some there are as fair to see to. Her Commendation [*or* Madrigal]. Francis Davison. EIL; OBSC
Some there are who are present at such occasions. On the Suicide of a Friend. Reed Whittemore. ConAP; NMP
Some there are who say that the fairest thing seen. Sappho, *tr. fr. Greek by* Richmond Lattimore. WPOW
Some they will talk of bold Robin Hood. Robin Hood and the Bishop of Hereford. *Unknown.* ESPB
Some thing is lost in me. Man Thinking about Woman. Don L. Lee. CNA; NoAM; PAI
Some things are blessedly alyrical. Give Us This Day Our Daily Day. Robert J. Levy. AMV-81
Some things are very dear to me. Sonnets, II. Gwendolyn B. Bennett. AmNP; BANP; CDC; PoBA; PoNe
Some Things Don't Make Any Sense at All. Judith Viorst. RHPC
Some things I do not profess. The Abduction. Stanley Kunitz. SV
Some things persist by suffering change, others. Homage to the Philosopher. Babette Deutsch. ImOP; TrJP
Some Things That Easter Brings. Elsie Parrish. SoPo
Some things that fly there be. Emily Dickinson. OxBA
Some things will never change although. Far Trek. June Brady. QQQ; RHPC
Some Things You Cannot Will to Men. Walter E. Isenhour. STF
Some think that in the Christian scheme. Mutual Subjection [*or* Consideration for Others]. Christopher Smart. Hymns for the Amusement of Children, Hymn 26. NOCV; OxBChV
Some think the world is made for fun and frolic. Funiculi, Funicula. Luigi Denza. TreFT
Some thirty inches from my nose. W. H. Auden. FaBoEE

Some thought it mounted to the Lunar sphere. The Lock. Pope. *Fr.* The Rape of the Lock. MOON
Some thousands in England are starving. An Appeal by Unemployed Ex-Service Men. *Unknown.* OBET
Some three, or five, or seven, and thirty years. Lady-Probationer. W. E. Henley. In Hospital, IX. BrPo
Some time. *See also* Sometime.
Some time ago from Rome, in smart array. The Cudgelled but Contented Cuckold. La Fontaine. UnTE
Some time ago—two weeks or more. The Cowboy at Church. *Unknown.* CoSo
Some Time at Eve. Elizabeth Clark Hardy. HBV-2; PoLF
Some time in the dark hours. Snowfall. W. S. Merwin. NNaP
Some time now past in the autumnal tide. Contemplations. Anne Bradstreet. AmPP; AP; PoEL-3, *abr.*; SCAP; WPE, *abr.*
Some time there ben a lyttel boy. The Lyttel Boy. Eugene Field. AA
Some Time We'll Understand. Maxwell N. Cornelius. BLRP; WBLP
Some time when the river is ice ask me. Ask Me. William Stafford. FiCP; NPAW
Some Tips on Watching Birds. Deatt Hudson. NYBP
Some to extinguish, others to prevent. The Dangers of Sexual Excess. John Armstrong. *Fr.* The Art of Preserving Health. FaBoUs
Some Trees. John Ashbery. CAPP; ConAP
Some twenty years of marital agreement. J. V. Cunningham. POL
Some tyme I fled the fyre that me brent. Sir Thomas Wyatt. AAS
Some Uses for Poetry. Eve Merriam. PCP
Some vast amount of years ago. Gemini and Virgo. Charles Stuart Calverley. WhC
Some Verses to Snaix. *Unknown.* NA
Some Verses upon the Burning of Our House, July 10th, 1666. Anne Bradstreet. AP; NOBA; TAP
(Here Follow[e]s Some Verses upon the Burning of Our House.) BoWoP; NoP; SCAP
(Upon the Burning of Our House, July 10th, 1666.) OxBA; PAI; WPE
(Verses upon the Burning of Our House.) SBG
Some vex their souls with jealous pain. On One Who Died Discovering Her Kindness. John Sheffield, Duke of Buckingham and Normanby. LO; OBEV
Some want a vault, some want a grave. Madrigal Macabre. Samuel Hoffenstein. ShM
Some we see no more, Tenements of Wonder. Emily Dickinson. MoVE
Some were for setting up a king. Samuel Butler. *Fr.* Hudibras, III, 2. EBEV
Some were unlucky. Blown a mile to shoreward. Moonlight Night on the Port. Sidney Keyes. DTC
Some whirled scythes through the thick oats. The Farm Hands. Dilys Laing. SaC
Some who are uncertain compel me. They fear. At This Moment of Time. Delmore Schwartz. TwAmPo
Some Who Do Not Go to Church. *Unknown.* WBLP
Some will tell. The Old Man Said. Carroll Arnett. STE
Some winter night, shut snugly in. Ronsard to His Mistress. Thackeray. HBV-1
Some winters, taking leave. A Storm in April. Richard Wilbur. LCAP; NoP
Some women marry houses. Housewife. Anne Sexton. NMM
Some words clink. Feelings about Words. Mary O'Neill. RHPC
Some wretched creature, savior take. Emily Dickinson. MoVE
Some years ago, ere time and taste. The Vicar. Winthrop Mackworth Praed. *Fr.* Every-Day Characters. EnRP; HBV-1; InMe; NBM; OBEV; OBNC; OBRV; OBVV; PoEL-4
Some years ago you heard me sing. Sarah Byng [Who Could Not Read and Was Tossed into a Thorny Hedge by a Bull]. Hilaire Belloc. CenHV; GoJo
Some years back I worked a strip mine. Lester Tells of Wanda and the Big Snow. Paul Zimmer. FAZ
Some years of late, in 'eighty-eight, as I do well remember-a. Sir Francis Drake; or, Eighty-eight. *Unknown.* FaBoCh; GBP
Somebodies walked the woods. The North. Barry McKinnon. NOBC
Somebody. Burns. BSV
Somebody. Tennyson. NOBL
("Somebody being a nobody.") FaBoEE
Somebody ("Och hon for somebody!"). *Unknown.* OxBS
Somebody ("Somebody did a golden deed"). *Unknown.* FaFP
Somebody ("Somebody loves you deep and true"). *Unknown.* RHPC
Somebody ("Somebody's tall and handsome"), *with music.* *Unknown.* AS
Somebody,/ Cut his hair. Young Poet. Myron O'Higgins. PoBA; PoNe
Somebody almost walked off wid alla my stuff. Ntozake Shange. WPOW
Somebody being a nobody. Somebody. Tennyson. FaBoEE; NOBL
Somebody Call. Carolyn M. Rodgers. JB
Somebody did a golden deed. Somebody. *Unknown.* FaFP
Somebody has given my. Proust's Madeleine. Kenneth Rexroth. NoAM
Somebody has got to tell me something real. Runaway. Rhoda Coghill. NeIP
Somebody just keep on calling me. Stocking Feet Blues. *Unknown.* BluL
Somebody left a mirror. Twenty Foolish Fairies. Nancy Byrd Turner. SUS
Somebody left the world last night, I felt it. Elegy. Olga Broumas. LTB
Somebody loses whenever somebody wins. Crapshooters. Carl Sandburg. VGW
Somebody loves you deep and true. Somebody. *Unknown.* RHPC
Somebody Prayed. *Unknown.* STF
Somebody Said That It Couldn't Be Done, *parody.* *Unknown.* FiBHP
Somebody said that it couldn't be done. It Couldn't Be Done. Edgar A. Guest. BLPA; FaBoBe; FaFP; FPL; STF; TreFS; WBLP; YaD
Somebody said wrecks. The Drowned. Norman MacCaig. OxBC
Somebody stole my myths. Song to the Tune of "Somebody Stole My Gal." X. J. Kennedy. CoPo
Somebody told me I wouldn't know how to choose. Song: Paper. Keith Waldrop. MAT
Somebody up in the rocky pasture. The Ant Village. Marion Edey *and* Dorothy Grider. FaPON; TiPo
Somebody who should have been born. The Abortion. Anne Sexton. CAPP; IHMS; MAT; NMM; VGW
Somebody's Child. Louise Chandler Moulton. HBV-1
Somebody's Darling. Marie Ravenel de la Coste. BLPA; HBV-2; TreF; UnPo; WBLP
Somebody's Gone. Charles Henri Ford. EAS
Somebody's in there. Saint Pumpkin. Nancy Willard. LCAP
Somebody's knockin' at th' door. The Collier's Wife. D. H. Lawrence. OxBTC
Somebody's Knockin' at Yo' Do', *with music.* *Unknown.* BoAN-1
Somebody's Mother. Mary Dow Brine. BeLS; BLPA; FaFP; TreF; WBLP
Somebody's Sweetheart I Want to Be, *with music.* Will D. Cobb. FSN
Somebody's tall and handsome. Somebody. *Unknown.* AS
Someday. *See also* Some Day.
Someday Baby. *Unknown.* BluL
Someday I'd like to climb the Puig. Balearic Idyll. Frederick Packard. FiBHP
Somedays now/ I can squash a cockroach. Wendy G. Rickert. NMM
Somehow/ I cannot think of god. Hypnopompic Poem. William Cole. POL
Somehow/ I had come to the desert. Abraham in Egypt. Howard Schwartz. VWA
Somehow, but God knows how, we'll meet again. Somehow, Somewhere, Sometime. Winifred M. Letts. HBMV
Somehow come to the calm of this present, a Sunday in summer. To Lighten My House. Alastair Reid. NePoEA
Somehow it should have been. Masks. Elizabeth Fenton. NMM
Somehow, Somewhere, Sometime. Winifred M. Letts. HBMV
Someone [*or* Some One]. Walter de la Mare. FaPON; MoBrPo; MoShBr; PDV; RHPC; SoPo; SUS; TiPo
Someone approaches to say his life is ruined. The Dream. David Ignatow. CoAP; MAT; NNaP; PAI
Someone Asked the Publisher. J. B. Morton. *Fr.* When We Were Very Silly. FaBoPa
Someone came knocking. Someone [*or* Some One]. Walter de la Mare. FaPON; MoBrPo; MoShBr; PDV; RHPC; SoPo; SUS; TiPo
Someone Could Certainly Be Found. Anne Hébert, *tr. fr. French by* F. R. Scott. CaP
Someone else/ looked at the sky. Izumi Shikibu, *tr. fr. Japanese by* Willis Barnstone. BoWoP
Someone fits a flute to his lips, and. Deception. Alfred Corn. PoA
Someone Gave Him Some Plastic Flowers Once. Dennis Shady. LFAC
Someone had been walking in and out. The Origin of Baseball. Kenneth Patchen. LiSp
Someone has built a dirigible in my parlor. Zeppelin. Andrew Glaze. WeW
Someone has got to tell me something real. Runaway. Rhoda Coghill. OxBI
Someone has idly set a record turning. In a Liberal Arts Building. Ruth Stone. TwAmPo
Someone has left a light on at the boathouse. Fishing on a Lake at Night. Robert Bly. LCAP
Someone has left a stack. The Stack. Stanley Snaith. ChMP
Someone has lived here where twin chimneys. The Grapevine. Zoe Kincaid Brockman. GoYe
Someone has opened and undone. Beyond the Tapestries. Norma Farber. GoYe
Someone has remembered to dry the dishes. Red Lilies. Barbara Guest. PoM
Someone has shut the shining eyes, straightened and folded. Beside the Bed. Charlotte Mew. MoAB; MoBrPo; TrGrPo; WPE

Someone here, listen to your pulse and. For a Plaque on the Door of an Isolated House. William Stafford. FAZ
Someone, I tell you,/ will remember us. Sappho, *tr. fr. Greek by* Willis Barnstone. BoWoP
Someone in a prayer-shawl is walking over your ramparts. Vilna. Moishe Kulbak, *tr. by* Joachim Neugroschel. VWA
Someone in the next apartment. Room. Ruth Stone. BoWoP
Some one is always sitting there. The Little Green Orchard. Walter de la Mare. EvOK
Someone is breathing in the room. Waking. Hugh Maxton. BIrV; CIP
Someone is dead. Lament. Anne Sexton. ConAP; WPE
Someone is smoking in the darkness. First Star. Dave Smith. AMV-81
Someone Knocks. Peter Everwine. NNaP
Someone like No One Else. Forugh Farrokhzad, *tr. fr. Farsi by* Deirdre Lashgari. WPOW
Someone painted pictures on my. Jack Frost. Helen Bayley Davis. SoPo
Someone passes. Lady Murasaki Shikibu, *tr. fr. Japanese by* Kenneth Rexroth. BoWoP; OLR
Someone said dead men make islands in the sea. Fishermen, Drowned beyond the West Coast. Vivian Smith. CBAP
Someone Sits at the Harp. Jon Lang. AMV-81
Some one started the whole day wrong—was it you? Was It You? Stewart I. Long. WBLP
Someone stole a winter from my life. The Groundhog Foreshadowed. Steven Sher. AMV-80
Someone Talking. Joy Harjo. TWSS
Someone walks my father's way. On the Way. Mordechai Husid, *tr. by* Seymour Mayne *and* Rivka Augenfeld. VWA
Someone who well knew how she'd toss her chin. Loose Woman. X. J. Kennedy. WeW
Someone's been up here nights. In a Country Cemetery in Iowa. Ted Kooser. DFF
Someone's youngest daughter. The Vietnamese Girl in the Madhouse. David Fisher. NPGG
Someplace Else. Marge Piercy. NeAC
Somersault. Dorothy Aldis. SoPo
Somersby, Lincolnshire; after Leaving the Rectory. Tennyson. *See* In Memoriam A. H. H.: "Unwatch'd, the garden bough shall sway."
Somerset Dam for Supper, The. John Holmes. NYBP
Somerset Maugham said a professional was someone who could do his best. Churchyard. Robert Hass. NPGG
Somerset Wassail. *Unknown.* OBET
Somethin' Else and/ *Kind of Blue*. Cannon Arrested. Michael S. Harper. CNA; FAZ
Something. Robert Creeley. NaP
Something. Jared Smith. AMV-81
Something/ holds up two or three leaves. In One Place. Robert Wallace. Psk
Something about It, *sel.* John Hollander.
  Its Lunch. GP
Something about the idea. Abandonment of Autos. Bruce Dawe. CBAP
Something about your smile is more than you. Becoming Is Perfection. Tom Johnson. AMV-81
Something always remains a mystery. A Classical Idyll. Avraham Huss, *tr. by* Mark Elliott Shapiro. VWA
Something befell. At the Bottom of the Well. Louis Untermeyer. GoJo
Something broke the dream. Poem. John Gill. NeAC
Something broken something. Nightbreak. Adrienne Rich. IHMS
Something calls and whispers, along the city street. Song. Georgiana Goddard King. *Fr.* The Way of Perfect Love. HBV-1
Something Childish, but Very Natural. Samuel Taylor Coleridge. *See* If I Had But Two Little Wings.
Something disturbs your big pale limbs among. For Delphine. James Simmons. POL
Something fallen out of the air, some. A Difference. Tom Clark. HoAn
Something far off buried deep and free. The Flash. James Dickey. LCAP
Something for Jesus. Sylvanus D. Phelps. *See* Saviour, Thy Dying Love.
Something for My Russian Friends. Edmund Wilson. OBAL
Something for Supper. Carroll Arnett. VoR
Something forgotten for twenty years: though my fathers. A Map of the Western Part of the County of Essex in England. Denise Levertov. CoAP; ConAP
Something goes wrong with my synthetic brain. The Case for the Miners. Siegfried Sassoon. SaC
Something hangs in back of me. The Wings. Denise Levertov. CAPP
Something happened the other day that never happened before. Shovelling Iron Ore. *Unknown.* AS; GBP
Something has ceased to come along with me. Death of a Son. Jon Silkin. FF; GTBS-P; NePoEA; NoAM; OxBTC; VWA
Something Has Fallen. Philip Levine. LCAP
Something has happened to my name. Catalogue Army. Naomi Shihab Nye. MAYP
Something I saw or thought I saw. On the Heart's Beginning to Cloud the Mind. Robert Frost. CMoP
Something I want to communicate to you. With the Door Open. David Ignatow. CTBA
Something immense and lonely. Foreboding. John Haines. ConAP
Something in the climate of a hammer. Because Going Nowhere Takes a Long Time. Kenneth Patchen. NaP
Something in the darkness. An Overture. Michael Knoll. LFAC
Something inspires the only cow of late. The Cow in Apple Time. Robert Frost. CABA; MoAB; MoAmPo; PoLF
Something Is Bound to Happen. W. H. Auden. *See* Wanderer, The.
Something is dead. Prologue to "Rhymes and Rhythms." W. E. Henley. VLP
Something Is Dying Here. Thomas McGrath. TAT
Something is tearing, tearing a hole. Good Friday. Arlene De Bevoise. AMV-81
Something Is There. Lilian Moore. RHPC; WSC
Something massively large has slept. Something. Jared Smith. AMV-81
Something more than the lilt of the strain. Poetry. Lucius Harwood Foote. AA
Something occurred after the operation. Surgical Ward: Men. Robert Graves. FaBoMo
Something of glass about her, of dead water. Circe. Louis MacNeice. OBMV
Something of how the homing bee at dusk. Southern Gothic. Donald Justice. NIP; TwAmPo
Something old and tyrannical burning there. A Coal Fire in Winter. Thomas McGrath. NU
Something one day occurr'd about a bill. George Crabbe. *Fr.* Tales of the Hall. Par
Something startles me where I thought I was safest. This Compost. Walt Whitman. AWP; CABA; LiTA; MoAmPo
Something steps from leaf to leaf. At Night. Alan Proctor. FAZ
Something tapped at my window-pane. April. Theodosia Garrison. HBMV
Something that was not there before. The Beast. Brian Patten. AmMo
Something there is that doesn't love a wall. Mending Wall. Robert Frost. AmFN; AmPP; AP; CMoP; CoBMV; FaBV; FaFP; FPL; HAP; HBV-2; HeIP; HoPM; InPS; LiTA; LiTM; MoAB; MoAmPo; MoVE; NePA; NoAM; NOBA; NoP; OHFP; OxBA; PAI; PrIm; SCV; SeCeV; SoSe; TAP; VGW; ViBoPo; WeW; WHA
Something there is, whose veiled creation was. Lao Tzu, *tr. by* Raymond B. Blakney. *Fr.* Tao Teh King. ILwL
Something to do with territory makes them sing. Birds All Singing. Norman MacCaig. ChMP
Something to live for came to the place. Only. Harriet Prescott Spofford. HBV-1
Something Told the Wild Geese. Rachel Field. NTCP; OBCA; OnUR; PDV; PoSC; RHPC; SiSoSe; SoPo; TiPo; YeAr
Something vague waxes or wanes. Lines for a Friend Who Left. John Logan. DFF
Something was whispered. Accusation. Utahania, *tr. fr. Eskimo.* WTO
Something went crabwise. The Presence. Maxine W. Kumin. RFM; WPE
Something You Can Do. *Unknown.* STF
Something you said—I found it written down. A Postcard to Send to Sumer. William Bronk. VGW
Sometime. *See also* Some time.
Sometime. May Riley Smith. BLPA; HBV-2
Sometime ago there was a rich old codger. The Miller's Tale. Chaucer, *mod. vers. by* Nevill Coghill. *Fr.* The Canterbury Tales. TEP
Sometime during eternity. Lawrence Ferlinghetti. *Fr.* A Coney Island of the Mind. CAPP; NoAM
Sometime, I feel, I'll hear. Duke of Parma's Ear. Eli Siegel. ELU
Sometime I Loved. *Unknown.* OxBM
Sometime I sigh, sometime I sing. Sir Thomas Wyatt. SiPS
Sometime in Fraunce dwelled a plowman. How the Ploughman Learned His Paternoster. *Unknown.* OxBM
Sometime in the night I stir, rain. Loft. Michael Dransfield. CBAP
Sometime, It May Be. Arthur Colton. *See* Faustine.
Sometime Lively Gerald. Richard Stanyhurst. NCEP
Sometime, Somewhere. Ophelia Guyon Browning. BLRP; STF
  (Pray without Ceasing.) BLPA; BLPL
Sometime, when all life's lessons have been learned. Sometime. May Riley Smith. BLPA; HBV-2
Sometimes. Annie Johnson Flint. STF
Sometimes. Rose Fyleman. SiSoSe
Sometimes. Hermann Hesse, *tr. fr. German by* Robert Bly. NU; WSC
Sometimes. Thomas S. Jones, Jr. HBV-1; TreFT; TRV
Sometimes. Greg Kuzma. Psk
Sometimes/ I cool out. Spacin. Ronda Davis. JB
Sometimes/ I help my dad. Automobile Mechanics. Dorothy Baruch. FaPON; SoPo; TiPo

Sometimes/ the poems. Sharon Scott. JB
Sometimes a child is washed from that warm room. Verse for Vestigials. Elizabeth Allen. AMV-80
Sometimes a huge wave of thought. Song for a Day. Francisco Arriví, *tr. by* Julio Marzán. InW
Sometimes a lantern moves along the night. The Lantern out of Doors. Gerard Manley Hopkins. CMoP; LiTB; OxBoCh; TrCP; VLP
Sometimes a light surprises. Joy and Peace in Believing. William Cowper. NOCV; TRV
Sometimes a rain comes. A Rain of Rites. Jayanta Mahapatra. PoA
Sometimes a right white mountain. Sky Pictures. Mary Effie Lee Newsome. CDC
Sometimes a wild thing. Yours Truly. Leonard Nathan. AMV-80
Sometimes after the break of a bone. Painlessly out of Ourselves. William Page. AMV-81
Sometimes, apart in sleep, by chance. The Trance. Stephen Spender. ChMP; CoBMV
Sometimes, as if forewarned, before we die. Views of Boston Common and Nearby. R. P. Blackmur. MoVE
Sometimes at night when the heart stumbles and stops. Caesura. Kenneth Mackenzie. CBAP
Sometimes before great events a person will try. Things That Happen. William Stafford. NNaP
Sometimes, childishly watching a beetle, thrush or trout. Clarence Mangan. Thomas Kinsella. CIP
Sometimes goldfinches one by one will drop. Goldfinches. Keats. *Fr.* I Stood Tip-Toe. GN; PBBP
Sometimes he roars among the leafy trees. The Wind. William Henry Davies. SeCePo
Sometimes he was cool like an eternal. Lester Young. Ted Joans. AmNP
Sometimes Heaven Is a Mean Machine. William Pitt Root. MAYP
Sometimes I. Song of the Thunders. *Tr. by* Frances Densmore. OBVE
Sometimes I am a Tapster new. The Jolly Trades-Men. *Unknown.* CoMu
Sometimes I am a young child. World within a World. Debra Woolard Bender. AMV-80
Sometimes I call X nostalgia. Little Ode for X. Maura Stanton. MAYP
Sometimes I can believe. Valediction. Lawrence Raab. AMV-81
Sometimes I catch a glimpse of it. The Presence. Dana Naone. CDW
Sometimes I envy those. The Mole. John Haines. NCSH
Sometimes I Feel like a Motherless Child. *Unknown.* BLSo, *with music*; BoAN-2, *with music*; FSW
Sometimes I feel like I will never stop. To Satch [*or* American Gothic]. Samuel Allen. AmNP; CTBA; IDB; LiSp; NIP; PAI; PoBA; PoNe; SoSe; TTY
Sometimes I get the feeling that I have been here before. Reincarnation. Mae Jackson. PoBA
Sometimes I Go to Camarillo and Sit in the Lounge. K. Curtis Lyle. PoBA
Sometimes I have supposed seals. Soft Wood. Robert Lowell. LiTM
Sometimes I have to cross the road. Bobby Blue. John Drinkwater. FaPON; SoPo
Sometimes, I know not why, nor how, nor whence. Inspirations. William James Dawson. WGRP
Sometimes I know the way. Absence. Charlotte Mew. ChMP; MoAB; MoBrPo
Sometimes I like to go. Memorandum. Rudy Bee Graham. PoNe
Sometimes I see reflections on bits of glass on sidewalks. Wonder Woman. Genny Lim. BrSi
Sometimes I see them. Galway Kinnell. *Fr.* Ruins under the Stars. RFM
Sometimes I see them coming. Benediction. Myra Sklarew. VWA
Sometimes I seem to see gliding the green. Nilotic Elegy. G. S. Fraser. WaP
Sometimes I stare into an awning of spirit. Sometimes I Go to Camarillo and Sit in the Lounge. K. Curtis Lyle. PoBA
Sometimes I Think of Maryland. Jodi Braxton. CNA
Sometimes I think that my body is a vase. A Chinese Vase. Edward Hirsch. AMV-80
Sometimes I think that nothing. Small-scale Reflections on a Great House. A. K. Ramanujan. OxBC
Sometimes I walk in the shadow. Walking with God. *Unknown.* BLRP
Sometimes I walk where the deep water dips. Frederick Goddard Tuckerman. *Fr.* Sonnets. NOBA
Sometimes I Want to Go Up. Rachel Korn, *tr. fr. Yiddish by* Ruth Whitman. VWA
Sometimes I wish that I his pillow were. Richard Barnfield. Sonnets, VIII. PeHV
Sometimes I wish that I might do. Patience. G. A. Studdert-Kennedy. TrPWD
Sometimes I write with the stub of a pencil. The Poet Confides. Herbert T. J. Coleman. CaP
Sometimes I'm happy. MANICdepressant. Kim Dammers. POL
Sometimes I'm happy: la la la la la la la. Joy Sonnet in a Random Universe. Helen Chasin. HeIP; NIP
Sometimes—I'm sorry—but sometimes. Yawning. Eleanor Farjeon. RHPC
Sometimes in bonnet that she. Heart-summoned. Jesse Stuart. GoYe
Sometimes, in morning sunlights by the river. Resurrection. Sidney Lanier. PoEL-5
Sometimes in summer months, the gestate [*or* matrix] earth. Summer Idyll. George Barker. FaBoMo; MoPo
Sometimes in the fast food kitchen. Song. Randy Lane. FAZ
Sometimes in the hills. Burma Hills. Bernard Gutteridge. WaP
Sometimes in the over-heated house, but not for long. Fame. Charlotte Mew. BrRo; PBWP; SBG
Sometimes, in the palpitating chrysalis of night. Listening-Post. Martin C. Rosner. AMV-80
Sometimes in the summer. Sprinkling. Dorothy Mason Pierce. SUS; TiPo
Sometimes in the winter mountains. Buffalo Trace. Robert Morgan. GeTw
Sometimes in weariness I stop. Years. Jon Anderson. AmPA
Sometimes in winter you see one. Porcupines. Robley Wilson, Jr. AMV-81
Sometimes it happens. The Porch. Gary Gildner. AMV-80
Sometimes it is inconceivable that I should be the age I am. The Child. W. S. Merwin. NoAM
Sometimes it is like a beast. A Trucker. Thom Gunn. PCP
Sometimes it seems. The Children. Susan MacDonald. IHMS
Sometimes it seems as though some puppet player. The Puppet Player. Angelina Weld Grimké. CDC
Sometimes late at night dozing over a book. Flying. Henry Carlile. AMV-80
Sometimes Love Poem, A. George Leong. BrSi
Sometimes my mind is like a house where no one lives. The Visit. Jim Gauer. AMV-81
Sometimes, old pal, in the morning. Is It Really Worth the While? *Unknown.* BLPA
Sometimes on My Way Back Down to the Block. Victor Hernandez Cruz. BOLo
Sometimes she is a child within mine arms. Heart's Haven. Dante Gabriel Rossetti. The House of Life, XXII. OAEP
Sometimes she is like sherry, like the sun through a vessel of glass. Polarities. Kenneth Slessor. CBAP
Sometimes that promised glory haunts my sleep. Descent. Helen Frazee-Bower. Two Married, II. HBMV
Sometimes the frugal matron seems in haste. William King. *Fr.* The Art of Making Puddings. FaBoUs
Sometimes the light falls here too as at Florence. The Old Age of Michelangelo. F. Templeton Prince. PeSA
Sometimes the lions' mouths are shut. Sometimes. Annie Johnson Flint. STF
Sometimes the night echoes to prideless wailing. Sonnet. John Berryman. NoAM
Sometimes the pencil, in cool airy halls. James Thomson. *Fr.* The Castle of Indolence. PoEL-3
Sometimes the road was a twisted riddle. The Road's End. Theodosia Garrison. HBMV
Sometimes the sea lays. Dragging in Winter. David McElroy. AmPA
Sometimes the weather goes on for days. The Mystery of Emily Dickinson. Marvin Bell. LCAP
Sometimes the wind is all I need. Fickle in the Arms of Spring. Susie Fry. AMV-81
Sometimes they smear the evening on the air. Bat Angels. Larry Levis. AmPA
Sometimes this quiet settles in like a stone. A Letter from a Friend. Carolyn Maisel. IHMS
Sometimes those crazy drunks on the corner. Houston and Bowery, 1981. Diane Burns. TWSS
Sometimes thou seem'st not as thyself alone. Heart's Compass. Dante Gabriel Rossetti. The House of Life, XXVII. WHA
Sometimes, tired, I imagine your death. To L. B. S. Winfield Townley Scott. DFF
Sometimes to think about age. Age. Rae Desmond Jones. CBAP
Sometimes waking, sometimes sleeping. Nestus Gurley. Randall Jarrell. MP; TwCP
Sometimes walking down these halls. Green Haven Halls. Charles Culhane. LFAC
Sometimes walking late at night. Butcher Shop. Charles Simic. AmPA; LCAP; NNaP
Sometimes we get down to loneliness. Refusals. Jon Anderson. MAYP
Sometimes we get up. Resurrection. Marie Luise Kaschnitz, *tr. by* Michael Hamburger. WPOW
Sometimes we're bound to New York town and others we're bound to France. Heave Away, *vers.* II. *Unknown.* ShS
Sometimes, what is most real shimmers, a dark. To Speak of Chile. Margaret Gibson. MAYP

Sometimes, when a bird cries out. Sometimes. Hermann Hesse, *tr. by* Robert Bly. NU; WSC
Sometimes when a man is old. Passages. David Walker. AMV-80
Sometimes, when after spirited debate. Change. William Dean Howells. AA
Sometimes when alone. The Outcast. "Æ." LO; OxBI
Sometimes when clouds float. At the Edge of Town. William Stafford. NNaP
Sometimes when fragrant summer dusk comes in with scent of rose and musk. Night for Adventures. Victor Starbuck. HBV-1
Sometimes when I/ am walking down the street. New York in the Spring. David Budbill. CAD
Sometimes when I dance. Balinda's Dance. Louise Erdrich. TWSS
Sometimes when I hold. The School Globe. James Reaney. NOBC
Sometimes when I see the bare arms of trees in the evening. The Bare Arms of Trees. John Tagliabue. Psk
Sometimes When I Sit Musing All Alone. Agnes Mary Frances Robinson. WHA
Sometimes when I think of things. Evidence. Arthur Kober. InMe
Sometimes when I wake up I lie. Roughchin, the Pirate. Arthur Boswell. EtS
Sometimes when I walk across the yard at night. The Two Coyotes. T. Walking Eagle Marietta. LFAC
Sometimes when I'm lonely. Hope. Langston Hughes. OBCA
Sometimes when it is bedtime. The Critic. John Farrar. SoPo
Sometimes when my eyes are red. My Sad Self. Allen Ginsberg. NoAM; UnPo
Sometimes, when Nature falls asleep. Night Mists. William Hamilton Hayne. AA
Sometimes When Night. V. Sackville-West. SBG; WPE
Sometimes when on night-herd I'm ridin', and the stars are a-gleam in the sky. The Range Rider's Soliloquy. Earl Alonzo Brininstool. PoOW
Sometimes when the boy was troubled he would go. The Cave. Glenn W. Dresbach. RFM
Sometimes when you are gone. Suite from Catullus. Vincent McHugh. ErPo
Sometimes when you watch the fire. Long Distance. William Stafford. ELU; SO; WSC
Sometimes, when you're called a bastard. When Something Happens. James A. Randall, Jr. BPo
Sometimes wind and sometimes rain. Children's Song. Ford Madox Ford. HBV-1
Sometimes with One I Love. Walt Whitman. GBL
Sometimes you feel/ alone within your ribs. What Is Needed. Marcos Rodríguez Frese, *tr. by* Julio Marzán. InW
Sometimes you hear, fifth-hand. Poetry of Departures. Philip Larkin. CMoP; FF; HeIP; MP; NePoEA; NMP; OxBC; PrIm; TwCP
Sometimes your medulla. Living in the Present. Clarinda Harriss Lott. AMV-81
Somewhat apart from the village, and nearer the Basin of Minas. Evangeline in Acadie. Longfellow. *Fr.* Evangeline. AA
Somewhat back from the village street. The Old Clock on the Stairs. Longfellow. HBV-2; WBLP
Somewhere. Robert Creeley. NoAM
Somewhere. Walter de la Mare. FaPON
Somewhere/ a niche. Wish. Lance Henson. CDW
Somewhere/ near the center of things. Black Holes. James A. Perkins. SOTS
Somewhere/ she is waiting. I'm Coming I'm Coming. Edgar Jackson. Three Songs, II. LFAC
Somewhere a forest, every. These Leaves. William Stafford. NNaP
Somewhere afield here something lies. Shelley's Skylark. Thomas Hardy. CoBMV; FaBV; PBBP; VLP
Somewhere along the road. The Meeting. Gerald Costanzo. MAYP
Somewhere beneath that piano's superb sleek black. The Piano. D. H. Lawrence. WeW
Somewhere beneath the sun. Amaturus. William Johnson Cory. HBV-1
Somewhere between our nervousness and. "Portrait de Femme." Irving Feldman. NoAM
Somewhere cities burn. April 68. Sam Cornish. CNA
Somewhere Down below Me Is a Street. J. J. Maloney. LFAC
Somewhere Else. Paula Rankin. MAYP
Somewhere Farm. Guy Rotella. AMV-81
Somewhere he failed me, somewhere he slipt away. The Lost Shipmate. Theodore Goodridge Roberts. CaP
"Somewhere," he mused, "its dear enchantments wait." The Land of Heart's Desire. Emily Huntington Miller. HBV-1
Somewhere his number must have been betrayed. The Common Man. A. J. M. Smith. NOBC
Somewhere I Chanced to Read. Gustav Davidson. HBMV
Somewhere I Have Never Travelled [Gladly Beyond]. E. E. Cummings. AP; BoLoP; CoBMV; FaBoEn; InPS; LiTA; LiTM; MoAB; MoAmPo; MoPo; MP; NoP; SOTW; TrGrPo; TwAmPo; TwCP; VGW
Somewhere, I think in Dakota. A Sound from the Earth. William Stafford. NNaP; RFM
Somewhere in a foxhole. Cancel My Subscription. J. A. Hines. LFAC
Somewhere in a hungry muzzle rooted. Design for Mediæval Tapestry. A. M. Klein. CaP
Somewhere in Chelsea, early summer. Relating to Robinson. Weldon Kees. NaP; NYP; TwAmPo
Somewhere—in desolate wind-swept space. Identity. Thomas Bailey Aldrich. AA
"Somewhere in France," upon a brown hillside. The First Three. Clinton Scollard. PAH
Somewhere in India, upon a time. An Oriental Apologue. James Russell Lowell. PoEL-5
Somewhere in the field. The Field. Douglas Lawder. PH
Somewhere in the world. Shekhina. Karl Wolfskehl, *tr. by* Erna Baber Rosenfeld. VWA
Somewhere inside me. Coming Back Home. Ray A. Young Bear. CDW
Somewhere Is Such a Kingdom. John Crowe Ransom. CMoP; LiTA
Somewhere lost in the haze. Lord Dunsany. Songs from an Evil Wood, II. HBV-2
Somewhere near here a new-loosed creek sloughs down. A Walk in March. Tim Reynolds. MAT
Somewhere near Phu Bai. Yusef Komunyakaa. MAYP
Somewhere near the end of a snowshoe trail. A Baby Ten Months Old Looks at the Public Domain. William Stafford. NYBP
Somewhere now she takes off the dress I am putting. Palindrome. Lisel Mueller. IHMS; WeW
Somewhere nowhere in Utah, a boy by the roadside. Utah. Anne Stevenson. NCSH
Somewhere on his travels the strange child. Santa Claus. Howard Nemerov. HAP
Somewhere on these bare rocks in some bare hall. For a College Yearbook. J. V. Cunningham. NoAM
Somewhere or Other. Christina Rossetti. NOBE
Somewhere out on the blue seas sailing. When My Ship Comes In. Robert J. Burdett. FaFP
Somewhere out past the high walls. The Edge of Town. William Clamurro. AMV-81
Somewhere outside your window. A Sense of Coolness. Quincy Troupe. PoBA
Somewhere she waits to make you win, your soul in her firm, white hands. The Woman Who Understands. Everard Jack Appleton. PoLF
Somewhere, sometime, in an April twilight. Dedicatory. Willa Cather. WPE
Somewhere, somewhen I've seen. The Parrots. W. W. Gibson. CH; RoGo
Somewhere the Equation Breaks Down. Daniel Berrigan. NYBP
Somewhere the sun is shining. Beautiful Isle of Somewhere. Jessie B. Pounds. FSN; TreFT
Somewhere the world has a place for you. Take Your Place. *Unknown.* STF
Somewhere, then—the bottom. There. William Harmon. AMV-80
Somewhere there is Grace, Lord. Latter Day Psalms. Cliff Ashby. NOCV
Somewhere there waiteth in this world of ours. Destiny. Sir Edwin Arnold. PoLF
Somewhere this dusk. Kissing the Toad. Galway Kinnell. DFT
Somewhere to the east. A River in Asia. Andrew Grossbardt. FAZ
Somewhere upon a battlefield. In Memory of Two Sons. Russell Stellwagon. STF
Somewhere we should sit down and rest. Just a While. Frantisek Gottlieb, *tr. by* Ewald Osers. VWA
Somewhere West. Andrew McCord Jones. LFAC
Somewhere You Exist. Manfred Winkler, *tr. fr. Hebrew by* Mary Zilzer. VWA
Somewhere you have been. To His Love in Middle-Age. Edwin Brock. AMV-80
Somewhile before the dawn I rose, and stept. A Memory. Rupert Brooke. BrPo
Somnolent through landscapes and by trees. The Permanent Tourists. P. K. Page. LiTM; NOBC
Son. James A. Emanuel. PoNe
Son, A. Kipling. *Fr.* Epitaphs of the War. ChMP; FaBoEE
Son, The. R. S. Thomas. NAs
Son, The. Ridgely Torrence. HBMV; InvP; WHA
Son/ I didn't rest while home. 720 Gabriel St. Randolph Outlaw. LFAC
"Son,"/ my father used to say. Father and I in the Woods. David McCord. SO
Son, a son, a son, A! I wanted a son of yours and mine. Poem of the Son. "Gabriela Mistral," *tr. by* Langston Hughes. PoPl
Son and Father. C. Day Lewis. EaLo
Son and Surf. Julia Hurd Strong. GoYe

Son, Condemned, The. Larry Rubin. GP
Son Cotton! these light idle brooks. Izaac Walton, Cotton, and William Oldways. Walter Savage Landor. NBM; PoEL-4
Son David. *Unknown.* OxBB, *with music*; OxBS
Son just born, A. Mary Britton Miller. TiPo
Son, my son! Lament of a Man for His Son. *Unknown, tr. by* Mary Austin. AWP; BPAW; DL
Son of a Gambolier, The, *with music.* *Unknown.* AS
Son of a Gun. *Unknown.* CoSo
Son of a mystic race, he came. Heinrich Heine. Ludwig Lewisohn. TrJP
Son of a Scots manse though you were. Curse. Robert Greacen. TW
Son of Enops, Thestor next he smote, The. Homer, *tr. by* William Cowper. *Fr.* The Iliad, XVI. OBVE
Son of Erebus and Night. William Browne. *Fr.* The Inner Temple Masque. ViBoPo
Son of God Goes Forth to War, The. Reginald Heber. HBV-2; TreFS (Who Follows in His Train?) WGRP
Son, of great fortune have I none. Christine to Her Son. Christine de Pisan, *tr. by* Barbara Howes. BoWoP
Son of Lamech let a black raven, The. *Unknown.* *Fr.* Genesis. PBBP
Son of the King of Moy, The. *Unknown, tr. fr. Old Irish.* AnIL, *tr. by* Myles Dillon; BIrV, *tr. by* John Montague
Son of the ocean isle! England's Dead. Felicia Dorothea Hemans. HBV-2
Son of the old moon-mountains African! To the Nile. Keats. OBRV
Son of the righteous one, he who thunders on the ground. Praises of the King Tshaka. *Unknown.* PeSA
Son of the Romanovs, A. Louis Simpson. OxBC
Son of the Sea, A. Bliss Carman. EtS
Son of the Thundercloud. Song of the Thunder. *Unknown.* PeSA
Son replied, The, "For all your good advice." To His Father on Praising the Honest Life of the Peasant. Parvin E'tesami, *tr. by* Deirdre Lashgari. WPOW
"Son," said my mother. The Ballad of the Harp-Weaver. Edna St. Vincent Millay. WSC
Son with a Future, A. Charles Reznikoff. *Fr.* Five Groups of Verse. DiL
Sonatina in Yellow. Donald Justice. DiL; LCAP
Son-Dayes. Henry Vaughan. SeCP
Sonet: "Fra bank to bank [*or* banc to banc], fra wood to wood [*or* wod to wod] I rin." Mark Alexander Boyd. *See* Fra Bank to Bank . . .
Sonet, A: "His golden lockes, Time hath to silver turn'd." George Peele. *See* His Golden Locks . . .
Sonet to Sleepe. William Drummond of Hawthornden *See* Sleep, Silence' Child.
Sonet Written in Prayse of the Browne Beautie, A. George Gascoigne. AAS
Sonetto XXXV: To Guido Orlando. Guido Cavalcanti, *tr. fr. Italian by* Ezra Pound. CTC
Sonetto VII: "Who is she that comes, making turn every man's eye." Guido Cavalcanti. *See* Sonnet: Rapture Concerning His Lady, A.
Song: "A ho! A ho!/ Love's horn doth blow." Thomas Lovell Beddoes. ChER
Song, A: "Absent from thee, I languish still." Earl of Rochester. BoLoP; CavP; ELP; EnLoPo; FaBoEn; GBL; LoBV; MePo; OBS; SeCePo; SeCV-2; ViBoPo (Return.) NOBE; OBEV
Song: "Adieu, farewell earths blisse." Thomas Nashe. *See* Adieu, Farewell Earth's Bliss.
Song: "Ae fond kiss, and then we sever." Burns. *See* Ae Fond Kiss.
Song: "After the pangs of a desperate Lover." Dryden. *See* After the Pangs of a Desperate Lover.
Song: "Afternoon cooking in the fall sun." Robert Hass. AmPA
Song: "Again rejoicing Nature sees." Burns. BoNaP; HBV-1
Song: "Ah Chloris! that I now could sit." Sir Charles Sedley. *See* Child and Maiden.
Song: "Ah! County Guy, the hour is nigh." Sir Walter Scott. *See* County Guy.
Song: "Ah fading joy, how quickly art thou past?" Dryden. *See* Ah, Fading Joy.
Song: "Ah false Amyntas, can that hour." Aphra Behn. *Fr.* The Dutch Lover. WPE
Song, A: "Ah how sweet it is to love." Dryden. *See* Ah How Sweet It Is to Love.
Song: "Ah stay! ah turn! ah whither would you fly." Congreve. *Fr.* The Fair Penitent (*by* Nicholas Rowe.) LoBV; OBEC
Song: "Ah, vale of woe, of gloom and darkness moulded." Rachel Morpurgo, *tr. fr. Hebrew by* Nina Davis Salaman. TrJP
Song: "All, all of a piece throughout." Dryden. *See* All, All of a Piece.
Song: "All in green went my love riding." E. E. Cummings. *See* All in Green Went My Love Riding.
Song: "All joy to mortals, joy and mirth." Aphra Behn. *Fr.* Emperor of the Moon. WPE
Song: "All service ranks the same with God." Robert Browning. *See* All Service Ranks the Same with God.
Song: "All the flowers of the spring." John Webster. *See* All the Flowers of the Spring.
Song: "And can the physician make sick men well?" *Unknown.* *See* And Can the Physician.
Song: "And will he not come again?" Shakespeare. *See* And Will He Not Come Again?
Song: "April, April,/ Laugh thy girlish laughter." Sir William Watson. HBV-1; HBVY; OBEV; OBVV; PoSC; TreF; TrGrPo (April.) FaBV (Song to April.) GN
Song: "Are they shadowes that we see?" Samuel Daniel. *See* Are They Shadows?
Song, A: "As Chloris [*or* Cloris] full of harmless thoughts." Earl of Rochester. ErPo; UnTE ("As Chloris full of harmless thoughts.") TEP
Song: "As I walked out one evening." W. H. Auden. *See* As I Walked Out One Evening.
Song: "As thro' the land at eve we went." Tennyson. *See* As thro' the Land at Eve We Went.
Song: "Ask me no more: the moon may draw the sea." Tennyson. *See* Ask Me No More.
Song, A: "Ask me no more where Jove bestows." Thomas Carew. *See* Ask Me No More Where Jove Bestows.
Song: "At setting day and rising morn." Allan Ramsay. HBV-1
Song: "Awake thee, my Bessy, the morning is fair." James Joseph Callanan. OnYI
Song: "Balkis was in her marble town." Lascelles Abercrombie. *See* Balkis.
Song: "Because I know deep in my own heart." Pauli Murray. BlSi
Song: "Because the rose must fade." Richard Watson Gilder. HBV-2
Song: "Bee to the heather, The." Sir Henry Taylor. OBVV
Song: "Before the barn-door crowing." John Gay. *See* Before the Barn-Door Crowing.
Song: "Before we shall again behold." Sir William Davenant. *See* Endimion Porter and Olivia.
Song: "Bells of Sunday rang us down, The." John Ciardi. WaP
Song: "Belovèd, it is morn!" Emily Henrietta Hickey. *See* Belovèd, It Is Morn.
Song: "Bird in my bower, A." Francis Howard Williams. AA
Song: "Blow, blow, thou winter wind." Shakespeare. *See* Blow, Blow, Thou Winter Wind.
Song: "Blushing rose and purple flower, The." Philip Massinger. *Fr.* The Picture. ViBoPo (Song of Pleasure, A.) UnTE
Song, A: "Boast no more fond Love, thy power." Thomas D'Urfey. CavP
Song: "Boat is chafing at our long delay, The." John Davidson. OBEV; OBVV; PoPle
Song: "Bone-aged is my white horse." Brenda Chamberlain. NeIP (Song—Talysarn.) NeBP
Song: "Bring from the craggy haunts of birch and pine." John Todhunter. OBVV (O Mighty, Melancholy Wind.) OnYI
Song, A: "Calm was the even, and cleer was the sky [*or* skie]." Dryden. *Fr.* An Evening's Love. CavP; SeCV-2 (Calm Was the Even [and Clear Was the Sky].) FF; OAEP
Song: "Can Life be a blessing." Dryden. *See* Can Life Be a Blessing.
Song: "Can love be controll'd by advice?" John Gay. *Fr.* The Beggar's Opera. LoBV
Song: "Care charming sleep, thou easer of all woes." John Fletcher. *See* Care-charming Sleep.
Song, A: "Celia, that I once was blest." Dryden. *Fr.* Amphitrion. CavP
Song, A: "Celimena, of my heart." Dryden. *Fr.* An Evening's Love. CavP (Damon and Celimena.) InvP
Song: "Celinda, by what potent art." Thomas Stanley. CavP
Song: "Child, is thy father dead?" Ebenezer Elliott. SaC
Song: "Chloris! farewell. I now must go." Edmund Waller. CavP (Chloris Farewell.) OBS
Song: "Chloris, forbear a while." Henry Bold. GBL
Song, A: "Chloris, when I to thee present." *Unknown.* OBS
Song: "Choose now among this fairest number." William Browne. GBL
Song: "Christ keep the Hollow Land." William Morris. *Fr.* The Hollow Land. NBM; PoEL-5 ("Christ keep the Hollow Land.") ChTr
Song: "Cloris, it is not thy disdaine." Sidney Godolphin. *See* To the Tune of, In Fayth I Cannot Keepe My Father's Sheepe.
Song: "Closes and courts and lanes." John Davidson. BrPo; HBV-2
Song: "Come away, come away death." Shakespeare. *See* Come Away, Come Away, Death
Song: "Come, Celia, let's agree at last." John Sheffield. HBV-1
Song, A: "Come, cheer up, my lads, like a true British band." *Unknown.* PAH
Song: "Come down, O maid, from yonder mountain height." Tennyson. *See* Come Down, O Maid.

Song: "Come live with me and be my love." C. Day Lewis. *See* Come, Live with Me and Be My Love.
Song: "Come my Celia, let us prove." Ben Jonson. AnAnS-2
Song: "Come unto these yellow sands." Shakespeare. *See* Ariel's Song: "Come unto these yellow sands."
Song: "Curse upon that faithless maid, A." Aphra Behn. *Fr.* Emperor of the Moon. WPE
Song: "Daughter of Egypt, veil thine eyes!" Bayard Taylor. AA
Song: "Day will rise and the sun from eastward." George Campbell Hay. OxBS
Song: "Deftly, admiral, cast your fly." W. H. Auden. GTBS-P
Song: "Delicious beauty that doth lie." John Marston. *See* Delicious Beauty.
Song: "Desire for a woman took hold of me in the night." *Unknown, tr. fr. Azande.* LLLT
Song: "Dew on the bamboos." *Unknown, tr. fr. Sanskrit by* E. Powys Mathers. LLLT
Song: "Do I venture away too far." Keith Douglas. NePoEA
Song: "Do not fear to put thy feet." John Fletcher *See* River-God's Song, The.
Song: "Don't Tell Me What You Dreamt Last Night." Franklin P. Adams. FiBHP
Song: "Dorinda's sparkling wit, and eyes." Charles Sackville. CavP; OBS; SeCV-2
(Dorinda.) OBEV; SeCePo
(On the Countess of Dorchester.) APAS
Song: "Down the dimpled green-sward dancing." George Darley. OnYI
Song: "Dressed up in my melancholy." M. Carl Holman. AmNP; PoNe
Song, The: "Drinke and be merry, merry, merry boyes." Thomas Morton. SCAP
Song: "Earl March looked on his dying child." Thomas Campbell. *See* Maid of Neidpath, The.
Song: Endimion Porter and Olivia. Sir William Davenant. *See* Endimion Porter and Olivia.
Song: "Fain would I change that note." *Unknown. See* Fain Would I Change That Note.
Song: "Fair Iris I love, and hourly I die." Dryden. *Fr.* Amphitryon. AWP
(Fair Iris and Her Swain.) ViBoPo
(Hourly I Die.) UnTE
(Mercury's Song to Phaedra.) PoEL-3; SeCV-2
Song: "Fair is the night, and fair the day." William Morris. The Earthly Paradise. HBV-1
Song, A: "Fair, sweet and young, receive a prize." Dryden. OBS
Song: "Fall, leaves, fall; die, flowers, away." Emily Brontë. *See* Fall, Leaves, Fall.
Song: "False though she be to me and love." Congreve. *See* False Though She Be.
Song, A: "Fame let thy trumpet sound." Joel Barlow. AmPP
Song: "Farewell, adieu, that court-like life!" John Pickering. *See* Haltersick's Song.
Song, A: "Farewell ungratefull traytor [*or* traitor]." Dryden. *See* Farewell, Ungrateful Traitor.
Song: "Fear no more the heat o' the sun." Shakespeare. *See* Fear No More the Heat o' the Sun.
Song: "Feathers of the willow, The." Richard Watson Dixon. BoNaP; CH; FaBoCh; GTBS-P; LoBV; NOBE; OBNC; OBVV; YeAr
(Willow.) OBEV
Song: Fie My Fum. Allen Ginsberg. ErPo
Song: "Fine young folly, though you were." William Habington. *See* Fine Young Folly.
Song: "Fire, fire." Henry Bold. GBL
Song: "First month of his absence, The." Alun Lewis. ChMP; LiTM; OBWP; WaaP
Song: "Fish in the unruffled lakes." W. H. Auden. *See* Fish in the Unruffled Lakes.
Song: "Flame at the core of the world." Arthur Upson. HBV-1
Song: "Flowers that in thy garden rise, The." Sir Henry Newbolt. FaBoTw
Song: "Fly hence, shadows, that do keep." John Ford. *See* Fly Hence, Shadows.
Song: "Follow thy fair sun, unhappy shadow!" Thomas Campion. *See* Follow Thy Fair Sun.
Song: "Fond affection, hence, and leave me!" Robert Parry. *Fr.* The Mirror of Knighthood. ElL
Song: "Fond men! whose wretched care the life soon ending." Phineas Fletcher. *Fr.* Brittain's Ida. ElL
Song: "Fool, take up thy shaft again." Thomas Stanley. EnLoPo
Song: "Fooles, they are the onely nation." Ben Jonson. *See* Fools, They Are the Only Nation.
Song: For A' That and A' That. Burns. *See* For A' That and A' That.
Song: "For her gait, if she be walking." William Browne. *See* Complete Lover, The.
Song: "For me the jasmine buds unfold." Florence Earle Coates. *See* World Is Mine, The.
Song, A: "For Mercy, Courage, Kindness, Mirth." Laurence Binyon. HBMV; MoBrPo
Song: "For the tender beech and the sapling oak." Thomas Love Peacock. *Fr.* Maid Marian. OHIP
(For the Slender Beech and the Sapling Oak.) EnRP
Song: "Four arms, two necks, one wreathing." *Unknown.* ElL
Song: "Fresh from the dewy hill, the merry year." Blake. EnRP
Song: "Fringèd vallance of your eyes advance, The." Thomas Shadwell. ViBoPo
Song: "From whence cometh song?" Theodore Roethke. NCSH
Song: "Full fadom five thy father lies." Shakespeare. *See* Ariel's Song: "Full fathom five thy father lies."
Song: "Gather kittens while you may." Oliver Herford. SpRo
Song: "Give her but a least excuse to love me!" Robert Browning. *Fr.* Pippa Passes. ViBoPo
Song: "Give me more love or more disdain." Thomas Carew. *See* Mediocrity in Love Rejected.
Song: "Glories of our blood and state, The." James Shirley. *See* Glories of Our Blood and State, The.
Song, A: "Glories, pleasures, pomps, delights, and ease." John Ford. *See* Glories, Pleasures.
Song: "Go and catch a falling star." John Donne. AWP; CABA; EBEV; ElL; ELP; EnRePo; FaFP; FPL; HAP; HBV-1; HeIP; InMe; InPK; InPS; JCP; LoBV; NIP; NOBE; NoP; OBEV; PAI; PoPle; PPoe; PPON; SeCeV; SoSe; TrGrPo; ViBoPo; WHA
(Go and Catch a Falling Star.) BiP; FaBV; LiTB
(Goe and Catche a Falling Starre.) TreFT
(Song: "Goe and catche a falling starre.") AnAnS-1; HoPM; MeLP; MePo; OAEP; PoEL-2; PoPl; SeCP; SeCV-1
Song: "Go lovely rose." Edmund Waller. *See* Go, Lovely Rose.
Song, A: "Go tell Amynta gentle swain." Dryden. *Fr.* Sylvoe. CavP
Song: "Go with your tauntings, go." John Clare. OBRV
Song: "Goe, and catche a falling starre." John Donne. *See* Song: "Go and catch a falling star."
Song: "Goe lovely Rose." Edmund Waller. *See* Go, Lovely Rose.
Song: "Going down the old way." Margaret Widdemer. HBMV
Song: "Gold wings across the sea!" William Morris. *See* Song of Jehane du Castel Beau, The.
Song: Good Counsel to a Young Maid. Thomas Carew. *See* Good Counsel to a Young Maid.
Song: "Good morrow, 'tis St. Valentine's day." Shakespeare. *Fr.* Hamlet, IV, v. SiSoSe
Song, A: "Good neighbour, why do you look awry?" *Unknown.* TW
Song: Green Grow the Rashes. Burns. *See* Green Grow the Rashes.
Song: "Gross sun squats above, The." Dom Moraes. NePoEA-2
Song: "Had I a heart for falsehood framed." Sheridan. *Fr.* The Duenna, I. HBV-1; OBEC
Song: "Hang sorrow, cast away care." *Unknown.* OBS
Song: Hark, Hark ("Hark, hark!/ Bow-wow./ The watch-dogs bark"). Shakespeare. *Fr.* The Tempest. SoSe
Song, A: "Hark! 'tis freedom that calls, come, patriots, awake!" *Unknown.* PAH
Song: "Hark! hark! the lark at heaven's gate sings." Shakespeare. *See* Hark! Hark! the Lark.
Song: "Has summer come without the rose." Arthur O'Shaughnessy. HBV-1
Song, A: "Hast thou seen the down in the air." Sir John Suckling. *See* Song to a Lute.
Song: "He came unlook'd for, undesir'd." Sara Coleridge. *See* He Came Unlook'd For.
Song: "He that will court a wench that is coy." *Unknown.* ErPo
Song: "Heap cassia, sandal-buds and stripes." Robert Browning. *Fr.* Paracelsus. OBEV; OBRV; WHA
Song: "Heare ye ladies that despise." Beaumont *and* Fletcher. *Fr.* The Tragedy of Valentinian. PoEL-2
Song: "Hears not my Phillis how the birds." Sir Charles Sedley. *See* Hears Not My Phillis, How the Birds.
Song: "Help me now." Emmett Jarrett. NeAC
Song: "Hence all you vaine delights." Beaumont *and* Fletcher. *Fr.* The Nice Valour. PoEL-2
Song: "Here's to the maiden of bashful fifteen." Sheridan. *See* Let the Toast Pass.
Song: "Heron is harsh with despair." Brenda Chamberlain. NeBP; NeIP
Song: "Home they brought her warrior dead." Tennyson. *See* Home They Brought Her Warrior Dead.
Song: How Can I Care? Robert Graves. GBL
Song: "How can that tree but withered be." *Unknown.* ElL
Song: "How delicious is the winning." Thomas Campbell. *See* Freedom and Love.
Song: "How do I love you?" Irene Rutherford McLeod. HBV-1

Song: "How happy were my days, till now." Isaac Bickerstaffe. *Fr.* Love in a Village. OBEC
Song: "How many times do I love thee, dear?" Thomas Lovell Beddoes. *Fr.* Torrismond. LiTB; NBM; OBRV; PoEL-4; TrGrPo; ViBoPo
(How Many Times?) ELP
(How Many Times Do I Love Thee, Dear?) EnRP
Song: "How pleasant it is that always." Florence Smith. BLPA
Song: "How should I your true love know." Shakespeare. *See* How Should I Your True Love Know.
Song: "How sweet I roam'd from field to field." Blake. CABA; CH; ChER; ChTr; EnLoPo; EnRP; FaBoEn; LiTB; NOEC; NoP; OAEL-2; OAEP; OBEC; OBNC; OLR; PoEL-4; SeCeV; TrGrPo; ViBoPo; WHA
(How Sweet I Roam'd.) TreFT
(How Sweet I Roamed from Field to Field.) SeCePo
(Prince of Love, The.) NOBE
Song: "I am weaving a song of waters." Gwendolyn B. Bennett. BlSi
Song: "I came to the door of the House of Love." Alfred Noyes. HBV-1
Song: "I can't be talkin' of love, dear." Esther Mathews. FaFP; NePA
Song: "I could make you songs." Dorothy Dow. HBMV
Song: "I feed a flame within, which so torments me." Dryden. *Fr.* Secret Love. AWP
(Hidden Flame.) OBEV
(I Feed a Flame Within [Which So Torments Me].) PoPle; QFR
Song: "I had a dove and the sweet dove died." Keats. *See* I Had a Dove.
Song: "I have loved flowers that fade." Robert Bridges. *See* I Have Loved Flowers.
Song: "I hid my love when young while I." John Clare. *See* Secret Love.
Song: "I kept neat my virginity." Glyn Jones. NeBP
Song: "I know that any weed can tell." Louis Ginsberg. TrJP
Song: "I lately vow'd, but 'twas in haste." John Oldmixon. *See* I Lately Vowed, but 'Twas in Haste.
Song: "I love my lady's eyes." Robert Bridges. VLP
Song: "I love you, Mrs. Acorn. Would your husband mind." Kath Fraser. PeHV
Song: "I made another garden, yea." Arthur O'Shaughnessy. HBV-1; OBEV; OBVV
Song: "I make my shroud but no one knows." Adelaide Crapsey. HBV-2
Song, The: "I met a ragged man." Theodore Roethke. AP; CrMA
Song: "I once had a sweet little doll, dears." Charles Kingsley. *See* Lost Doll, The.
Song: "I peeled bits of straw and I got switches too." John Clare. *See* Bits of Straw.
Song: "I placed my dream in a boat." Cecilia Meireles, *tr. fr. Portuguese by* Eloah F. Giacomelli. WPOW
Song: "I prithee [*or* prethee] let my heart alone." Thomas Stanley. AnAnS-2; ViBoPo
Song: "I prithee send me back my heart." *At. to* Henry Hughes *and also to* Sir John Suckling. HBV-1; JCP; ViBoPo
Song: I Promised Sylvia. Earl of Rochester. CavP
(Song: "I promised Sylvia to be true.") SeCePo
Song: "I saw the day's white rapture." Charles Hanson Towne. HBV-1
Song: "I try to knead and spin, but my life is low the while." Louise Imogen Guiney. *See* In Leinster.
Song: "I walk'd in the lonesome evening." William Allingham. EnLoPo
Song: "I was so chill, and overworn, and sad." Anna Wickham. MoBrPo
Song: "I went to her who loveth me no more." Arthur O'Shaughnessy. *See* Enchainment.
Song: "I who love you bring." Theodore Spencer. TwAmPo
Song, A: "I will not tell her that she's fair." Matthew Coppinger. CavP
Song: "I would not feign a single sigh." John Clare. GBL
Song: "I'd much rather sit there in the sun." Ruth Krauss. RHPC; SO
Song: "If any wench Venus's girdle wear." John Gay. *Fr.* The Beggar's Opera, I, i. PoEL-3
Song, A: "If for a woman I would die." Countess of Winchilsea. ViBoPo
Song: "If I freely may discover." Ben Jonson. *Fr.* Poetaster, II, ii. AnAnS-2; ElL
Song: "If I had only loved your flesh." V. Sackville-West. HBMV
Song: "If love were but a little thing." Florence Earle Coates. HBMV
Song: "If once I could gather in song." W. W. Gibson. OBVV
Song: "If she be not as kind as fair." Sir George Etherege. *Fr.* The Comical Revenge. CavP
Song: "If the scorn of your bright eyne." Shakespeare. *Fr.* As You Like It, IV, iii. CTC
Song: "If thou art sleeping, maiden." Gil Vicente, *tr. fr. Spanish by* Longfellow. AWP
Song, A: "If Wine and Musick have the Pow'r." Matthew Prior. LoBV
Song: "If you love God, take your mirror between your hands and look." Mahmud Djellaladin Pasha, *tr. fr. Turkish by* E. Powys Mathers. ErPo
Song: "In crystal towns and turrets richly set." Geffrey Whitney. *See* Content.
Song, A: "In her fair cheeks two pits do lie." Thomas Carew. UnTE
Song: "In his last bin[n] Sir Peter lies." Thomas Love Peacock. *See* In His Last Binn Sir Peter Lies.
Song, A: "In the air there are no coral-/ Reefs or ambergris." Duncan Campbell Scott. PeCV
Song, A: In the Name of a Lover, to His Mistress; Who Said, She Hated Him for His Grey Hairs, Which He Had at Thirty. William Wycherley. SeCV-2
Song: "In vain you tell your parting lover." Matthew Prior. HBV-1
Song: "Indeed, my Caelia, 'tis in vain." Sir John Henry Moore. LO; OBEC
Song: Inviting the Influence of a Young Lady upon the Opening Year. Hilaire Belloc. *See* Song: "You wear the morning like your dress."
Song: "Is it dirty." Frank O'Hara. CAD
Song: "It Autumnne was, and on our hemispheare." William Drummond of Hawthornden. OBS
Song: "It is all one in Venus' wanton school." John Lyly. SeCePo
Song, A: "It is not beauty I demand." George Darley. *See* It Is Not Beauty I Demand.
Song: "It is the miller's daughter." Tennyson. *See* Miller's Daughter, The.
Song: "It was a friar of orders free." Thomas Love Peacock. *Fr.* Maid Marian. ViBoPo
Song: "It was a lover and his lass." Shakespeare. *See* It Was a Lover and His Lass.
Song: "It was upon a Lammas night." Burns. *See* Rigs o' Barley, The.
Song: "I've taught thee Love's sweet lesson o'er." George Darley. *Fr.* Sylvia; or, The May Queen. OBRV
Song: "Join once again, my Celia, join." Charles Cotton. ViBoPo
Song (2): "Keep the dream alive and growing always." Edwin Rolfe. TrJP
Song: "Know, Celadon, in vain you use." "Ephelia." CavP
Song: "Know then, my brethren, heaven is clear." *Unknown. Fr.* The Song of Anarchus. FaBoCo
Song: "Ladies, though to your conquering eyes." Sir George Etherege. *Fr.* The Comical Revenge, V, iii. HBV-1; OBS
Song: "Lady, you are with beauties so enriched." Francis Davison. ElL
Song: "Lake and a fairy boat, A." Thomas Hood. HBV-1
Song: Landskip, The. William Shenstone. OBEC
(Landscape, The.) SeCePo
Song: "Lark now leaves his wat'ry nest, The." Sir William Davenant. *See* Lark Now Leaves His Wat'ry Nest, The.
Song XI: "Lay your sleeping head, my love." W. H. Auden. *See* Lullaby: "Lay your sleeping head, my love."
Song: "Let it be forgotten, as a flower is forgotten." Sara Teasdale. *See* Let It Be Forgotten.
Song: "Let my voice ring out and over the earth." James Thomson ("B.V."). Sunday up the River, XVII. HBV-1; OBVV; TreFT
Song: "Let not the sluggish sleep." William Byrd. ACP; GoBC
("Let not the sluggish sleep.") OxBoCh
Song: "Let school-masters puzzle their brain." Goldsmith. *Fr.* She Stoops to Conquer. BIrV; OAEP; ViBoPo
(Three Jolly Pigeons, The.) PoRA
(Three Pigeons, The.) ELP
Song: "Let's sing a song together once." Louis Simpson. NePoAm
Song: "Life with her weary eyes." Marya Zaturenska. NMP
Song: Lift Boy. Robert Graves. DTC
Song: "Light of spring, The." Alice Duer Miller. AA
Song: "Like violets pale i' the Spring o' the year." James Thomson ("B. V."). Sunday up the River, IX. OBVV
Song: "Linnet in the rocky dells, The." Emily Brontë. HAP; HBV-1; OAEP; OBNC
(Linnet in the Rocky Dells, The.) BrRo; VLP
(My Lady's Grave.) OBVV
Song: "Little onion lay by the fireplace, A." Nicholas Moore. EAS
Song: "Lo! here we come a-reaping, a-reaping." George Peele. *Fr.* The Old Wife's Tale. OBSC
Song, A: "Lord, when the sense of Thy sweet grace." Richard Crashaw. SeCeV; TrPWD; ViBoPo
(Song of Divine Love, A.) GoBC
Song: "Love a woman! y'are an ass." Earl of Rochester. GBL; NOBL; PeHV; TW
(Love a Woman.) CavP
("Love a woman! y'are an ass.") TEP
Song: "Love and harmony combine." Blake. EnRP
Song: Love Arm'd. Aphra Behn. *See* Song: "Love in fantastic triumph sate."
Song: "Love, by that loosened hair." Bliss Carman. HBV-1
Song: "Love for such a cherry lip." Thomas Middleton. *Fr.* Blurt, Master Constable. ElL
(Lips and Eyes.) HBV-1
(Love for Such a Cherry Lip.) ViBoPo
Song: "Love in fantastic [*or* fantastique] triumph sate [*or* sat]." Aphra Behn. *Fr.* Abdelazer. HBV-1; NOBE; OBEV; TrGrPo; ViBoPo; WPE
(Love Arm'd) SBG
(Love in Fantastic Triumph Sat.) OAEP

(Song: Love Arm'd.) CaVP; OBS; PAI; WeW
Song: "Love in her eyes sits playing." John Gay. *See* Love in Her Eyes Sits Playing.
Song: "Love is a sickness full of woes." Samuel Daniel. *See* Love Is a Sickness.
Song: "Love is cruel, Love is sweet." Thomas MacDonagh. ACP
Song: "Love laid his sleepless head." Swinburne. TrGrPo
Song: Love Lives beyond the Tomb. John Clare. NoP; OBVV
(Love.) ChTr
(Love Lives Beyond [the Tomb].) FaBoEn; FaBoRV; NOBE; OBNC
Song: "Love, love today, my dear." Charlotte Mew. MoBrPo
Song: "Love still has something of the sea." Sir Charles Sedley. CavP; FaBoEn; GBL; HBV-1; NOBE; OBS; SeCV-2; ViBoPo
(Love Still Has Something of the Sea.) EtS; LoBV
Song: "Love took my life and thrill'd it." Sir Lewis Morris. OBVV
(Surface and the Depths, The.) HBV-1
Song: "Love was true to me." John Boyle O'Reilly. ACP
Song: "Lovely hill-torrents are." W. J. Turner. GoJo; MoBrPo
Song: "Lovers in ladies' magazines." Thomas McGrath. VGW
Song: "Love's on the highroad." Dana Burnet. HBV-1
Song: "Lying is an occupation." Laetitia Pilkington. WPE
Song: "Make this night loveable." W. H. Auden. TW
Song: Mary Morison. Burns. *See* Mary Morison.
Song: "Master, the swabber, the boatswain, and I, The." Shakespeare. *Fr.* The Tempest, II, ii. NOBL
("Master, the swabber, the boatswain and I, The.") DBV; FF; MOS; PoPle; ViBoPo
(Stephano's Song.) WhC
Song: "Me Cupid made a happy slave." Sir Richard Steele. OBEC
Song: Mediocrity in Love Rejected. Thomas Carew. *See* Mediocrity in Love Rejected.
Song: "Memory, hither come." Blake. PoEL-4
Song: "Merchant, to secure his treasure, The." Matthew Prior. *See* Ode, An: "Merchant, to secure his treasure, The."
Song: "Methinks the poor town has been troubled too long." Charles Sackville. CavP; SeCV-2
Song: "Misty and dim, a bush in the wilds of Kapa'a." Kaiama, *tr. fr. Hawaiian by* N. B. Emerson. WTO
Song: "Morning opened/ Like a rose." Donald Justice. DFF; NCSH
Song: "Mother Mother shave me." *Tr. fr. Nyasa by* Ulli Beier. BoWoP
Song: "Moth's kiss, first, The!" Robert Browning. *See* Moth's Kiss, First, The.
Song: Murdring Beautie. Thomas Carew. AnAnS-2; SeCP
(Murdering Beauty.) OAEP
Song: "My cabinets are oyster-shells." Margaret Cavendish, Duchess of Newcastle. *Fr.* The Convent of Pleasure. WPE
Song: "My dark-headed Käthchen, my spit-kitten darling." John Manifold. DTC
Song, A: "My dear mistress has a heart." Earl of Rochester. HBV-1; LoBV; SeCV-2
Song, A: "My head on moss reclining." *Unknown.* NOEC
Song: "My love bound me with a kiss." *At. to* Thomas Campion. *See* Kisses.
Song: "My love is the flaming sword." James Thomson ("B. V."). Sunday up the River, XVI. OBVV
Song: "My luve is like a red, red rose." Burns. *See* Red, Red, Rose, A.
Song, A: "My name is sweet Jenny, my age is sixteen." *Unknown.* POL
Song: "My silks and fine array." Blake. EnRP; FaBoEn; HBV-1; LAuP; LoBV; OAEP; OBEC; OBNC; TrGrPo
(My Silks and Fine Array.) ChTr; ELP; GBL; TEP; UnPo
Song: "My spirit like a shepherd boy." V. Sackville-West. HBMV
Song: "My straying thoughts, reduced stay." Anne Collins. WPE
Song: "Nay but you, who do not love her." Robert Browning. HBV-1; TrGrPo; ViBoPo
Song: "Never seek to tell thy love." Blake. *See* Never Seek to Tell Thy Love.
Song, A: "Night her blackest sables wore, The." Thomas D'Urfey. CavP
Song: "Night is darkening round me, The." Emily Brontë. *See* Night Is Darkening round Me, The.
Song: "No, no, fair heretic[k], it needs must be." Sir John Suckling. *Fr.* Aglaura, IV, i. AnAnS-2; CaPo; CABA; LoBV; OBS; PrIm
Song: "No, no, no, no, I cannot hate my foe." Sir Philip Sidney. SiPS
Song: "No, no, poor suff'ring heart no change endeavour." Dryden. *See* No, No, Poor Suffering Heart.
Song: Noble Name of Spark, The. *At. to* the Earl of Rochester *and to* Thomas D'Urfey. *See* Bully, The.
Song: "Noe more unto my thoughts appeare." Sidney Godolphin. MeLP; MePo
(Quatrains.) OBS
Song: "Not, Celia, that I juster am." Sir Charles Sedley. *See* To Celia.
Song: "Not from the whole wide world I chose thee." Richard Watson Gilder. *Fr.* The New Day. AA
Song: "Now and then there will arise." *Tr. fr. Chippewa Indian by* Frances Densmore. OBVE
Song: "Now I see thy looks were feigned." Thomas Lodge. *See* Ode: "Now I find thy looks were feigned."
Song: "Now in golden glory goes." Lionel Johnson. VLP
Song: "Now sleeps the crimson petal, now the white." Tennyson. *See* Now Sleeps the Crimson Petal.
Song: "Now that Fate is dead and gone." Edith Sitwell. MoAB; MoBrPo
Song: "Nymphs and shepherds dance no more." Milton. *Fr.* Arcades. FiP; ViBoPo
(Nymphs and Shepherds.) ELP
Song: "O Bird, thou dartest to the sun." Maria White Lowell. AA
Song: "O, Brignal banks are wild and fair." Sir Walter Scott. *See* Brignall Banks.
Song: "O come, soft rest of cares! come, Night!" George Chapman. *See* Bridal Song ("O! Come . . .").
Song: "O, do not wanton with those eyes." Ben Jonson. *See* Song, A: "Oh do not wanton with those eyes."
Song: "O fair! O sweet! when I do look on thee." Sir Philip Sidney. SiPS
Song: "O fair sweet face, O eyes celestial bright." John Fletcher. *See* Song: "Oh, fair sweet face . . ."
Song: "O fly not, Pleasure, pleasant-hearted Pleasure." Wilfrid Scawen Blunt. *See* Song: "Oh fly not, Pleasure . . ."
Song: "O harmless feast." Barten Holyday. *Fr.* Technogamia. EIL
Song: "O, Inexpressible as sweet." George Edward Woodberry. *See* O, Inexpressible as Sweet.
Song: "O, it was out by Donnycarney." James Joyce. Chamber Music, XXXI. MoBrPo; OBVV
Song: "O lady, when the tipped cup of the moon blessed you." Ted Hughes. LLLT
Song: "O, let the solid ground." Tennyson. Maud, I, xi. HBV-1
Song: "O, like a queen's her happy tread." Sir William Watson. HBV-1
Song: "O Love, how strangely sweet." John Marston. EIL
Song: "O lovely April, rich and bright." Gustave Kahn, *tr. fr. French by* Ludwig Lewisohn. TrJP
Song: "O memory! thou fond deceiver." Goldsmith. *See* Memory.
Song: "O mistress mine, where are you roaming?" Shakespeare. *See* O Mistress Mine, Where Are You Roaming?
Song: "O, no more, no more, too late." John Ford. *See* Song: "Oh, no more, no more, too late."
Song: "O ruddier than the cherry!" John Gay. *See* O Ruddier than the Cherry.
Song: "O sing unto my roundelay." Thomas Chatterton. *See* Minstrel's Song.
Song: "O Sorrow,/ Why dost borrow." Keats. *See* Song of the Indian Maid.
Song: "O sweet delight, O more than human bliss." *See* O Sweet Delight.
Song: "O, that joy so soon should waste!" Ben Jonson. *Fr.* Cynthia's Revels, IV, iii. ViBoPo
(Kiss, The.) HBV-1; UnTE
Song: "O the month of May, the merry month of May." Thomas Dekker. *See* O, the Month of May.
Song: " 'O Where Are You Going?' said reader to rider." W. H. Auden. *See* O Where Are You Going?
Song: "O whistle, and I'll come to ye, my lad." Burns. *See* Whistle, and I'll Come to Ye, My Lad.
Song: "O'er desert plains, and rushy meers." William Shenstone. FaBoEn
Song: "O'er [*or* O're] the smooth enameled green." Milton. *Fr.* Arcades. LoBv; TrGrPo; ViBoPo
("O're the smooth enameld green.") OBEV
Song: "O'er the waste of waters cruising." Philip Freneau. PAH
Song: "Of all the torments, all the cares." *At. to* Sir George Etherege and to William Walsh. *See* Rivals
Song: "Of thee, (kind boy), I ask no red and white." Sir John Suckling. *See* Sonnet: "Of thee (kind boy) . . ."
Song: "Often I have heard it said." Walter Savage Landor. HBV-1
Song: "Oh, bid my tongue be still." Richard Watson Dixon. VLP
Song, A: "Oh do[e] not wanton with those eyes." Ben Jonson. AnAnS-2; HBV-1; OBS; SeCP
Song: "Oh fair [*or* O faire] sweet face, oh eyes celestial[l] bright." John Fletcher. *Fr.* Women Pleased, III, iv. OBS; PoEL-2
Song: "Oh [*or* O] fly not, Pleasure, pleasant-hearted Pleasure." Wilfrid Scawen Blunt. OBVV; ViBoPo
Song: "Oh, let us howl some heavy note." John Webster. *See* Madman's Song, The.
Song: "Oh! Love, that stronger art than wine." Aphra Behn. *Fr.* The Lucky Chance. WPE; WPOW
Song: " 'Oh! Love,' " they said, 'is King of Kings.' " Rupert Brooke. HBV-1
Song, A: "Oh [*or* O], no more, no more, too late." John Ford. *Fr.* The Broken Heart, IV, iii. LoBV; OBS; SeCePo
(Love's Martyrs.) NOBE

(Oh No More, No More.) ELP; ViBoPo
("Oh no more, no more, too late.") GBL; LO; PoEL-2
Song: "Oh roses for the flush of youth." Christina Rossetti. GTBS-P; LoBV; ViBoPo
(Oh Roses for the Flush of Youth.) ELP
Song: "Oh! say not woman's love is bought." Isaac Pocock. The Heir of Vironi. HBV-1
Song: "Oh! that we two were Maying." Charles Kingsley. The Saint's Tragedy. HBV-1
Song: "Oh the charming month of May!" Joseph Addison. NOEC
Song: "Old Adam, the carrion crow." Thomas Lovell Beddoes. *Fr.* Death's Jest-Book, V, iv. ChER; EBEV; LiTB; OAEL-2; OBRV; PBBP; PoEL-4
(Carrion Crow, The.) TrGrPo; Wir
(Old Adam.) ELP
(Old Adam, the Carrion Crow.) EnRP
(Wolfram's Song.) OBVV
Song: "Old England is eaten by knaves." Alexander McLachlan. *Fr.* The Emigrant. NOBC; OBCV
Song: "Old Farmer Oats and his son Ned." John Jay Chapman. PoEL-5
Song: Old Rowley the King. *Unknown.* APAS
Song: "On the side of the road." Edmond Jabès, *tr. fr. French by* Anthony Rudolf. VWA
Song: "Once my heart was a summer rose." Edith Sitwell. ChMP
Song: "One day the god of fond desire." James Thomson. EnLoPo
Song: One Hard Look. Robert Graves. MoAB; MoBrPo
Song: "Only a little while since first we met." Brian Hooker. HBMV
Song: "Only tell her that I love." John Cutts. HBV-1
Song: "Only the wanderer." Ivor Gurney. FaBoPP
Song: "Or love me less [*or* mee lesse], or love me more." Sidney Godolphin. CavP; JCP; MePo; OBS
Song: "O're the smooth enamel'd green." Milton. *See* Song: "O'er the smooth . . ."
Song: "Orpheus with his lute made trees." *At. to* John Fletcher. *See* Orpheus with His Lute.
Song: "Out upon it, I have lov'd." Sir John Suckling. *See* Constant Lover, The.
Song: "Over hill, over dale." Shakespeare. *See* Over Hill, over Dale.
Song: "Over the sea our galleys went." Robert Browning. *See* Wanderers, The.
Song: Owl, The. Tennyson. *See* Owl, The.
Song: "Owl is abroad, The." Ben Johnson. *See* Witches' Charms, The.
Song: Paper. Keith Waldrop. MAT
Song: "Pardon, goddess of the night." Shakespeare. *Fr.* Much Ado about Nothing, V, iii. CTC
(Claudio's Lament.) OBSC
("Pardon, goddess of the night.") ViBoPo
Song: "Peasant sun went crushing grapes, The." Laurence Dakin. *Fr.* Tancred, I, i. CaP
Song: Persuasions [*or* Perswasions] to Enjoy. Thomas Carew. *See* Persuasions to Enjoy.
Song: "Phillis, be gentler I advise [*or* advice]." Earl of Rochester. CavP
Song: "Phillis, for shame let us improve." Charles Sackville. *See* Phillis for Shame Let Us Improve.
Song: "Phillis is my only joy." Sir Charles Sedley. CavP; EnLoPo; InMe; OBS; SeCV-2
Song: "Phillis, let's shun the common fate." Sir Charles Sedley. SeCV-2
Song: "Phoebus arise." William Drummond of Hawthornden. *See* Phoebus, Arise.
Song: "Pints and the pistols, the pike-staves and pottles, The." *At. to* Winthrop Mackworth Praed. SoSe
Song: "Pious Selinda goes to prayers." Congreve. *See* Pious Selinda
Song: "Place in thy memory, dearest, A." Gerald Griffin. *See* Place in Thy Memory, A.
Song: "Pluck the fruit and taste the pleasure." Thomas Lodge. *See* Pluck the Fruit and Taste the Pleasure.
Song: "Poppies paramour the girls." Haniel Long. HBMV
Song: "Primrose in the green forest, The." Thomas Deloney. *Fr.* The Gentle Craft. TiPo; ViBoPo
Song: "Rarely, rarely comest thou." Shelley. EnRP; HBV-2; OAEP; OBNC; OBRV; TrGrPo
(Invocation: "Rarely, rarely, comest thou.") GTBS; GTBS-P
("barely, rarely, comest thou.") CH; TEP
Song: "Reading about the Wisconsin Weeping Willow." Ruth Krauss. LLLT
Song: "Rise Lady Mistresse, rise." Nathaniel Field. *See* Rise, Lady Mistress, Rise!
Song: "Roses and pinks will be strewn where you go." Sir William Davenant. *Fr.* The Unfortunate Lovers. ViBoPo
Song: "Rousing to rein his pad's head back." Geoffrey Taylor. NeIP; OxBI
Song: "Rowan like a lip-sticked girl, A." Seamus Heaney. IPY
Song: "Sabrina fair." Milton. *See* Sabrina Fair.
Song: "Say, lovely dream! where couldst thou find." Edmund Waller. *See* Say, Lovely Dream.
Song: "Say this city has ten million souls." W. H. Auden. *See* Refugee Blues.
Song: "See, how like twilight slumber falls." Charles Cotton. OBS
Song: "See, see, she wakes! Sabina wakes." Congreve. HBV-1; NOEC
Song: "Seek not the tree of silkiest bark." Aubrey Thomas De Vere. OBVV
Song: "Sergei's a flower." Ruth Herschberger. FF
Song: "Shall I tell you whom I love?" William Browne. *See* Shall I Tell You Whom I Love?
Song: "Shape alone let others prize, The." Mark Akenside. HBV-1
Song: "She has left me, my pretty." Sylvia Townsend Warner. MoAB; MoBrPo
Song: "She is not fair to outward view." Hartley Coleridge. EnRP; HBV-1; OBEV; OBRV; OBVV; TreFS; ViBoPo
(She Is Not Fair.) FaBV
(She Is Not Fair to Outward View.) GTBS, GTBS-P
Song: "She sat and sang alway." Christina Rossetti. GBL
Song: "She spoke to me gently with words of sweet meaning." Patrick MacDonogh. NeIP
Song: "She was lyin face down in her face." William Knott. MAT
Song: "Shephard loveth thow me vell?" Jean Passerat, *tr. fr. French by* William Drummond of Hawthornden. OBVE
Song: "Shepherd, who can pass such wrong." Jorge de Montemayor. *See* Nymph Selvagia, The, Her Song.
Song: "She's somewhere in the sunlight strong." Richard Le Gallienne. HBV-1; OBEV; OBVV
Song: "Shine out, fair Sun, with all your heat." *Unknown.* *See* Shine Out, Fair Sun.
Song: "Should I sigh out my dayes in griefe." Matthew Stevenson. CavP
Song: "Sigh no more, ladies, sigh no more." Shakespeare. *See* Sigh No More, Ladies.
Song: "Silly boy, there is no cause." Thomas Pestel. EIL
Song, A: "Sing me a sweet, low song of night." Hildegarde Hawthorne. FaBoBe; HBV-1
Song: "Sing the old song, amid the sound dispersing." Aubrey Thomas De Vere. HBV-1
Song: "Singee songee sick a pence." *Unknown.* *See* Nursery Song in Pidgin English.
Song: "Singer within the little streets." Monk Gibbon. NeIP
Song: "Sleep, O sleep." John Gay. Polly, Air XXIII. FaBoEn
("Sleep, O Sleep.") ViBoPo
Song: "Slow, slow, fresh fount, keep time with my salt tears." Ben Jonson. *See* Slow, Slow Fresh Fount.
Song, A: "Smile, Massachusetts, smile." *Unknown.* PAH
Song: "Smooth was the water, calm the air." Sir Charles Sedley. SeCV-2
Song: "So large a morning, so itself, to lean." W. H. Auden. NePoAm-2
Song, The: "So light no one noticed." Edward Dorn. CoPo; VGW
Song: "So, we'll go no more a-roving." Byron. *See* So We'll Go No More a-Roving.
Song: " 'Soldier, rest! thy warfare o'er.' " Sir Walter Scott. *See* Soldier, Rest!
Song: "Something calls and whispers, along the city street." Georgiana Goddard King. *Fr.* The Way of Perfect Love. HBV-1
Song: "Sometimes in the fast food kitchen." Randy Lane. FAZ
Song, A: "Song, A/ That seemed so brief at first." Howard Schwartz. VWA
Song: "Song is so old." Hermann Hagedorn. HBV-1
Song, A: "Song of grass, A,/ A song of earth." "Yehoash," *tr. fr. Yiddish by* Isidore Goldstick. TrJP
Song, The: "Song, The! the song!" Hemda Roth, *tr. fr. Hebrew by* Mariana Potasman. VWA
Song: Souldier going to the Field, The. Sir William Davenant. *See* Souldier Going to the Field, The.
Song: "Soules joy, now I am gone." *Unknown, at. to* the Earl of Pembroke. AnAnS-1; OBS
Song: "Spirit haunts the year's last hours, A." Tennyson. GTBS-P; HeIP; OAEP; OBNC; PoEL-5; PoPle
(Spirit Haunts the Year's Last Hours, A.) InvP
Song: "Splendor falls on castle walls, The." Tennyson. *See* Splendor Falls, The.
Song: Spring and Winter. Shakespeare. *See* When Daisies Pied and Violets Blue.
Song: "Spring lights her candles everywhere." Fredegond Shove. HBMV
Song: "Star that bids the shepherd fold, The." Milton. *See* Star That Bids the Shepherd Fold, The.
Song: "Stay Phoebus, stay." Edmund Waller. AnAnS-2; SeCP
Song: "Stay, stay at home, my heart, and rest." Longfellow. *See* Home Song.
Song: "Still to be neat, still to be drest." Ben Jonson. *See* Still to Be Neat.
Song: Stop all the Clocks. W. H. Auden. MoBrPo
Song: "Stranger, you who hide my love." Stephen Spender. FaBoTw

Song: "Streams that wind among the hills, The." George Darley. *Fr.* Sylvia; or, The May Queen. NBM
Song: "Strew not earth with empty stars." Thomas Lovell Beddoes. *Fr.* The Second Brother. ViBoPo
Song: "Sun in mine, The." Robert Hogg. WHW
Song: "Sunny shaft did I behold, A." Samuel Taylor Coleridge. *See* Glycine's Song.
Song: "Sweet are the charms of her I love." Barton Booth. OBEC
Song: "Sweet are the thoughts that savour of content." Robert Greene. *See* Maesia's Song.
Song: "Sweet beast, I have gone prowling." W. D. Snodgrass. LLLT; MoAmPo; NYBP
Song: "Sweet Cupid, ripen her desire." *Unknown. See* Sweet Cupid, Ripen . . .
Song: "Sweet Echo, sweetest nymph, that liv'st unseen." Milton. *Fr.* Comus. LoBV; SeCeV; ViBoPo
(Echo.) OBEV; OBS
(Lady Sings, The.) NOBE
(Lady's Song.) TrGrPo
(Sweet Echo, Sweetest Nymph.) ELP
Song: "Sweet in her green cell the flower of beauty slumbers." George Darley. OBEV; OBVV
(Flower of Beauty.) HBV-1
(Serenade of a Loyal Martyr.) NOBE; OBNC; OBRV; OnYI
Song: "Sweetest love, I do not go[e]." John Donne. AnAnS-1; AWP; BoLoP; ElL; ELP; EnRePo; FaBoEn; HeIP; InvP; JCP; MeLP; MePo; NOBE; NoP; OAEL-1; OAEP; OBS; PAI; PoEL-2; SeCP; SeCV-1; ViBoPo
(Sweetest Love, I Do Not Go.) BiP; TEP; TreFT; TrGrPo
Song: "Sylvia the fair, in the bloom of fifteen." Dryden. EBEV; ErPo; ViBoPo
(Sylvia the Fair.) UnTE
Song: "Take it, love!" Richard Le Gallienne. HBV-1
Song: "Take, O take those lips away." Shakespeare. *See* Take, O Take Those Lips Away.
Song: "Tears, idle tears, I know not what they mean." Tennyson. *See* Tears, Idle Tears.
Song: "Tell me no more I am deceived." Sir George Etherege. CavP
Song: "Tell me not, sweet, I am unkind." Richard Lovelace. *See* To Lucasta, Going to the Wars.
Song, A: "Tell me, where is fancy bred." Shakespeare. *See* Tell Me Where Is Fancy Bred.
Song, The: "That day, in the slipping of torsos and straining flanks." Lola Ridge. WPE
Song: That Women Are but Men's Shadows. Ben Jonson. *See* That Women Are but Men's Shadows.
Song, A: "There is a blue sky." Edward Dorn. ConAP
Song: "There is many a love in the land, my love." Joaquin Miller. HBV-1
Song: "There is no joy in water apart from the sun." Ralph Nixon Currey. PeSA
Song: "There stands a lonely pine-tree." Heine, *tr. fr. German by* Emma Lazarus. TrJP
Song: "There was a jolly miller once." Isaac Bickerstaffe. *See* There Was a Jolly Miller.
Song: "There's a barrel of porter at Tammany Hall." Fitz-Greene Halleck. OBAL
Song: "There's one great bunch of stars in heaven." Theophile Marzials. OBVV
Song: "Think of dress in ev'ry light." John Gay. *See* Think of Dress in Every Light.
Song: "This is the song of those who live alone." William Justema. NYBP
Song: "This peach is pink with such a pink." Norman Gale. HBV-1
Song: "Those rivers run from that land." Robert Creeley. VGW
Song, A: "Thou art the soul of a summer's day." Paul Laurence Dunbar. AmNP
Song: "Though I am young, and cannot tell." Ben Jonson. *See* Karolin's Song.
Song: "Though regions farr devided." Aurelian Townshend. *See* Though Regions Far Divided.
Song: "Though richer swains thy love pursue." Joanna Baillie. *Fr.* The Country Inn. OBRV
Song: "Three little maidens they have slain." Maurice Maeterlinck, *tr. by* Jethro Bithell. AWP
Song: "Thus when the swallow, seeking prey." John Gay. *Fr.* The Beggar's Opera, II, ii. PoEL-3
Song: "Thy face I have seen as one seeth." Sophie Jewett. AA
Song: "Thy fingers make early flowers of all things." E. E. Cummings. MoAmPo
Song: "Thyrsis, when we parted, swore." Thomas Gray. OAEP
Song: " 'Tis affection but dissembled." Sidney Godolphin. JCP
Song: " 'Tis said that absence conquers love!" Frederick William Thomas. AA; HBV-1
Song: " 'Tis sweet to hear the merry lark." Hartley Coleridge. HBV-1
Song: "To all you ladies now at land." Charles Sackville. SeCV-2
(Song: Written at Sea, in the First Dutch War, 1665, the Night before an Engagement.) EnLoPo; HBV-1; NOBE; OBEV; OBS; OBWP
(Song Written at Sea.) CoMu
Song: To Amarantha, That She Would Dishevel Her Hair. Richard Lovelace. *See* To Amarantha, That She Would Dishevel Her Hair.
Song: To Celia ("Come, my Celia, let us prove"). Ben Jonson. *See* Come, My Celia.
Song: To Celia ("Drink to me only with thine eyes"). Ben Jonson. *See* To Celia ("Drink to me, only . . .").
Song: To Celia ("Kiss me, sweet; the wary lover"). Ben Jonson. *See* To Celia ("Kiss me, sweet . . .").
Song: To Cynthia. Ben Jonson. *See* Hymn to Diana.
Song: To Her Againe, She Burning in a Feaver. Thomas Carew. AnAnS-2; SeCP
Song: To Lucasta, Going to the Wars. Richard Lovelace. *See* To Lucasta, Going to the Wars.
Song: To My Inconstant Mistress. Thomas Carew. *See* To My Inconstant Mistress.
Song: To My Mistris, I Burning in Love. Thomas Carew. AnAnS-2
(To My Mistris, I Burning in Love.) SeCP
Song: to One That Desired to Know My Mistris. Thomas Carew. AnAnS-2; SeCP
Song: To the Masquers Representing Stars. Thomas Campion. *Fr.* The Lords' Mask. LoBV
(Stars Dance, The.) OBSC
Song: "To the ocean now I fly." Milton. *See* To the Ocean now I fly.
Song: "Tomorrow is Saint Valentine's day". Shakespeare. *See* Tomorrow Is St. Valentine's Day.
Song: "Too late, alas! I must confess." Earl of Rochester. HBV-1
Song: "Trip it Gipsies, trip it fine." Thomas Middleton *and* William Rowley. *See* Trip It Gipsies, Trip It Fine.
Song: "Turn, turn thy beauteous face away." Beaumont *and* Fletcher. *Fr.* Love's Cure. PoEL-2
Song: "Under a southern wind." Theodore Roethke. CrMA
Song: Under the Bronze Leaves. "St.-J. Perse," *tr. fr. French by* T. S. Eliot. *Fr.* Anabasis. PoPl
Song: "Under the greenwood tree." Shakespeare. *See* Under the Greenwood Tree.
Song: "Under the winter, dear." Eugene Lee-Hamilton. OBVV
Song: "Victorious men of Earth, no more." James Shirley. *See* Victorious Men of Earth.
Song: "Violet in her lovely hair, A." Charles Swain. HBV-1
Song: "Virtue's branches wither, virtue pines." Thomas Dekker. *See* Priest's Song, A.
Song: "Wait but a little while." Norman Gale. HBV-1
Song: "Wake all the dead!" Sir William Davenant. *See* Wake All the Dead.
Song: " 'Wake not, but hear me, love!' " Lew Wallace. *Fr.* Ben Hur. AA
Song: "We break the glass, whose sacred wine." Edward Coote Pinkney. AA; HBV-1
Song: "We came to Tamichi in 1880." Scott Judy *and* "Doc" Hammond. PoOW
Song: "We have bathed, where none have seen us." Thomas Lovell Beddoes. *See* Bridal Song to Amala.
Song: "We only ask for sunshine." Helen Hay Whitney. HBV-2
Song: "We raise de wheat." *Unknown.* BPo; PAI
(We Raise de Wheat.) TAP
Song: "We sail toward evening's lonely star." Celia Thaxter. AA
Song: "Weary lot is thine, fair maid, A." Sir Walter Scott. *Fr.* Rokesby, III. EnLoPo; OBNC; OBRV; ViBoPo
(Rover, The.) GTBS; GTBS-P
(Rover's Adieu, The.) HBV-1; OBEV
(Rover's Farewell, The.) NOBE
(Weary Lot is Thine, A.) BSV; CH
Song: "Weep, weep, ye woodmen, wail!" Anthony Munday. *See* Robin Hood's Funeral.
Song: "Were I laid on Greenland's coast." John Gay. *Fr.* The Beggar's Opera, I, i. OBEC: OxBoLi; PoEL-3; SeCeV
(Macheath and Polly.) LoBV; NOEC
(Over the Hills and Far Away.) BLSo, *with music*; NOBE; PrIm
(Were I Laid on Greenland's Coast.) EnLoPo
Song: "Westron wynde when wyll thou blow." *Unknown. See* Western Wind.
Song: "What binds the atom together." Philip Dow. NPGG
Song: "What bird so sings, yet so does wail?" John Lyly. PBBP
Song: "What I took in my hand." Robert Creeley. NoP; PoA
Song: "What is there hid in the heart of a rose." Alfred Noyes. CH
Song: "What shall he have that kill'd the deer?" Shakespeare. *Fr.* As You Like It, IV, ii. CTC
(Amiens's Song.) OBSC
("What shall he have that kill'd the deer?") ViBoPo

Song: "What think you of this age now." *Unknown.* APAS
Song: "Whaur yon broken brig hings owre." William Soutar. GoTS; OxBS
Song: "When as the rye reach to the chin." George Peele. *See* Whenas the Rye.
Song: "When daffodils begin to peer." Shakespeare. *See* When Daffodils Begin to Peer.
Song: "When daisies pied, and violets blue." Shakespeare. *See* When Daisies Pied and Violets Blue.
Song: "When, dearest, I but think of thee." *At. to* Sir John Suckling *and to* Owen Felltham. *See* When, Dearest, I but think of Thee.
Song: "When Delia on the plain appears." George Lyttelton. *See* Tell Me, My Heart, If This Be Love.
Song: "When I am dead, my dearest." Christina Rossetti. AWP; BiP; BoLoP; CH; DL; EBEV; FaFP; FF; FPL; GBL; HBV-1; NOBE; NoP; OAEL-2; OAEP; OBEV; OBVV; PoLF; PoRA; SCV; SoSe; TreFS; ViBoPo; VLP; WHA; WPE
(When I Am Dead [My Dearest].) ELP; LiTB; TrGrPo
Song: "When I lie burning in thine eye." Thomas Stanley. CavP; ViBoPo
Song: "When I was a greenhorn and young." Charles Kingsley. *Fr.* The Saint's Tragedy. NBM
Song: "When icicles hang by the wall." Shakespeare. *See* When Icicles Hang by the Wall.
Song: "When love at first did move." Ben Jonson. *Fr.* The Masque of Beauty. GoBC
Song: "When love on time and measure makes his ground." *At. to* John Lilliat. *See* False Love.
Song: "When lovely woman, prone to folly." *Unknown.* FaBoPa
Song: "When lovely woman stoops to folly." Goldsmith. *Fr.* The Vicar of Wakefield, *ch.* 24. AWP; BoLoP; LAuP; NOBE; NOEC; OBEC; PoPl; SeCePo; TrGrPo; ViBoPo
(Stanzas on Woman.) ELP; OnYI; OxBI
(When Lovely Woman Stoops to Folly.) GTBS; GTBS-P; HAP; HBV-1; HeIP; NoP; PAI; PrIm; SeCeV; TreF; UnPo
(Woman.) FPL; LiTB; OBEV
Song: "When maidens are young, and in their spring." Aphra Behn. *Fr.* The Emperor of the Moon. FF
Song: "When o'er the wold the heedless lamb." Thomas Holcroft. NOEC
Song: "When that I was and a little tiny boy." Shakespeare. *See* When That I Was and a Little Tiny Boy.
Song: "When the echo of the last footstep dies." E. W. Mandel. MoCV; OBCV
Song: "When thy beauty appears." Thomas Parnell. OBEC; OBEV; UnTE
Song: "When working blackguards come to blows." Ebenezer Elliott. EBEV; NBM
Song: "Whenas the rye reach to the chin." George Peele. *See* Whenas the Rye.
Song: "Whene'er with haggard eyes I view." George Canning, George Ellis, *and* John Hookham Frere. *Fr.* The Rovers, I. OBEC
(Rogero's Song.) NOEC
(Song by Rogero.) FaBoNo
(Song of One Eleven Years in Prison.) FiBHP
Song: "Whenever, Chloe, I begin." Earl of Chesterfield. NOEC
Song: "Where did you come from, baby dear?" George Macdonald. *See* Baby, The.
Song: "Where I walk out." Yvor Winters. BoAnP; POL
Song: "Where in blind files." Eavan Boland. CIP
Song: "Where is the nymph, whose azure eye." Thomas Moore. EnLoPo
Song: "Where shall Celia fly for shelter." Christopher Smart. EnLoPo
Song: "Where shall the lover rest." Sir Walter Scott. *See* Where Shall the Lover Rest.
Song, A: "While a thousand fine projects are planned ev'ry day." *Unknown.* NOEC
Song: "While Morpheus thus doth gently lay." Henry Killigrew. CH
Song, A: "Whil'st Alexis lay prest." Dryden. *See* Whilst Alexis Lay Prest.
Song: "Whipped by sorrow now." Miklós Radnóti, *tr. fr. Hungarian by* Steven Polgar *and* Stephen Berg *and* S. J. Marks. VWA
Song: "Who can say." Tennyson. FaBoCh
Song: "Who has robbed the ocean cave." John Shaw. AA; HBV-1
Song: "Who hath his fancy pleasèd." Sir Philip Sidney. *See* Who Hath His Fancy Pleasèd.
Song: "Who is Silvia? what is she." Shakespeare. *See* Who Is Silvia?
Song: "Who tames the lion now?" Thomas Lovell Beddoes. *See* Lord Alcohol.
Song: "Why art thou slow, thou rest of trouble, Death." Philip Massinger. *See* Death Invoked.
Song: "Why do the houses stand." George Macdonald. OBVV
Song: "Why fadest thou in death." Richard Watson Dixon. ChTr
Song: "Why, lovely charmer, tell me why." Sir Richard Steele. ViBoPo
(Why, Lovely Charmer.) HBV-1
Song: "Why should a foolish marriage vow." Dryden. *See* Why Should a Foolish Marriage Vow.
Song: "Why should you swear I am forsworn." Richard Lovelace. *See* Scrutiny, The.
Song: "Why so pale and wan, fond lover?" Sir John Suckling. *See* Why So Pale and Wan?
Song, A: "Widow bird sate mourning for her love, A." Shelley. *Fr.* Charles the First. FaBoEn; LoBV; NOBE; OBNC; PoEL-4; PoPle
(Widow Bird, A.) CH; FaPON
("Widow bird sate mourning for her love, A.") ELP; GTBS; GTBS-P; LO; OBRV; SeCeV
Song: Willing Prisoner to His Mistress, The. Thomas Carew. CaPo
Song: Wit and Beauty. Robert Gould. CavP
Song, A: "With Love among the haycocks." Ralph Hodgson. GoJo
Song: "With my frailty don't upbraid me." Congreve.
Song: "With whomsoever I share the spring." Jan Burroway. NePoAm-2
Song: "Woman sits on her porch." Earle Thompson. STE
Song: "Woman's beauty is like a white, A." W. B. Yeats. *Fr.* The Only Jealousy of Emer. MoAB
Song: "Woman's face is full of wiles, A." Humfrey Gifford. ElL
Song: "World is full of loss, The; bring, wind, my love." Muriel Rukeyser. MiAP
Song, A: "World is young today, The." Digby Mackworth Dolben. LoBV; OBNC
Song: Written at Sea, in the First Dutch War (1665), the Night before an Engagement. Charles Sackville. *See* Song: "To all you ladies now at land."
Song, A: "Ye happy swains, whose hearts are free." Sir George Etherege. HBV-1; ViBoPo
Song: "Year's at the spring, The." Robert Browning *See* Year's at the Spring, The.
Song: "Years have flown since I knew thee first." Richard Watson Gilder. *Fr.* The New Day, Pt. IV, Song VII. AA
Song: "You are as gold." Hilda Doolittle ("H. D."). LiTA; LiTM; MoAmPo; TwAmPo
Song, A: "You charm'd me not with that fair face." Dryden. *Fr.* An Evening's Love. CavP; SeCV-2
Song: "You spotted snakes with double tongue." Shakespeare. *See* You Spotted Snakes.
Song: "You virgins that did late despair." James Shirley. *See* Piping Peace.
Song: "You wear the morning like your dress." Hilaire Belloc. OBEV
(Song: Inviting the Influence of a Young Lady upon the Opening Year.) OBVV
Song: "You wrong me, Strephon, when you say." "Ephelia." CavP
Song: "You'll love me yet! and I can tarry." Robert Browning. *See* You'll Love Me Yet.
Song: "Young flowers were whispering in melody." Poe. *Fr.* Al Aaraaf. NOBA
Song: "Young Philander woo'd me long." *Unknown.* ErPo
Song: "Your hay it is mow'd, and your corn is reap'd." Dryden. *See* Harvest Home.
Song: "Your heart is a music-box, dearest!" Frances Sargent Osgood. AA
Song: "You're wondering if I'm lonely." Adrienne Rich. PBWP
Song: "Youth's the season made for joys." John Gay. *See* Youth and Love.
Song, A/ That seemed so brief at first. A Song. Howard Schwartz. VWA
Song about Charleston, A. *Unknown.* PAH
Song about Great Men, A. Michael Hamburger. NePoEA
Song about Major Eatherly, A. John Wain. OxBTC
Song about My Father. Elizabeth Smither. OCNZ
Song about Myself. Keats. InvP; PoEL-4
(There Was a Naughty Boy.) FaBoCh; FaBoCo, *st.* 4; LiTB; MoShBr; OnUR; OxBChV, *sts.* 1 *and* 4; PP
(Verses from a Letter.) EBEV
Song about Singing, A. Anne Reeve Aldrich. AA
Song about Whiskers. P. G. Wodehouse. FiBHP
Song against Broccoli. Roy Blount, Jr. *See* Against Broccoli.
Song against Grocers, The. G. K. Chesterton. CenHV; DBV; FaBoCo
Song against Women. Willard Huntington Wright. HBV-1
Song and Science. Milicent Washburn Shinn. AA
Song as Yet Unsung, A. "Yehoash," *tr. fr. Yiddish by* Isidore Goldstick. TrJP
Song at Easter, A. Charles Hanson Towne. BLRP
Song at Morning, A. Edith Sitwell. CMoP
Song at Night. Norman Nicholson. FaBoTw
Song at Santa Cruz. Francis Brett Young. HBMV
Song at the Beginning of Autumn. Elizabeth Jennings. OxBTC
Song at the Feast of Brougham Castle. Wordsworth. EnRP
Song at the Moated Grange, A. Shakespeare. *See* Take, O Take Those Lips Away.
Song at the Ruin'd Inn. Tennyson. *Fr.* The Vision of Sin. PoEL-5
Song at the Skirts of Heaven. Uri Zvi Greenberg, *tr. fr. Hebrew by* Zvi Jagendorf. VWA
Song at the Well, The. George Peele. *Fr.* The Old Wives' Tale. SeCeV
(Celanta at the Well of Life.) LoBV

(Fair Maiden.) PoEL-2
(Gently Dip.) ELP
("Gently dip, but not too deep.") InPS
(Voice from the Well [of Life Speaks to the Maiden], The.) ChTr; FaBoEn; NOBE
(Voice Speaks from the Well, A.) FaBoCh; OBSC; OxBoLi
Song Ballet (I Was Sixteen Years of Age). *Unknown.* AmFP
Song Be Delicate. Shaw Neilson. PoAu-1
Song before Action, *sel.* Kipling
O Mary Pierced with Sorrow. ISi
Song before Grief, A. Rose Hawthorne Lathrop. AA
Song between two silences Life sings, A. The Silence. Archibald MacLeish. HBMV
Song-birds, The? are they flown away? Flight. Madison Cawein. AA
Song by Fairies. John Lyly. *Fr.* Endymion. OAEP
(Fairy Song, A.) OBSC
Song by Isbrand. Thomas Lovell Beddoes. *Fr.* Death's Jest Book. OBNC; PrIm
("Squats on a toad-stool under a tree.") InvP
Song by Mr. Cypress. Thomas Love Peacock. *See* There Is a Fever of the Spirit.
Song by Rogero [the Captive]. George Canning, George Ellis *and* John Hookham Frere. *See* Song: "Whene'er with haggard eyes I view."
Song by the Wavering Nymph. Aphra Behn. SBG
Song Called "His Hide Is Covered with Hair," The. Hilaire Belloc. FaBoNo; FM
Song for a Birth or a Death. Elizabeth Jennings. EBEV
Song for a Blue Roadster. Rachel Field. FaPON; TiPo
Song for a Camper. John Farrar. YeAr
Song for a Child. Helen B. Davis. SoPo
Song for a Country Wedding. William Jay Smith. GrPl
Song for a Cracked Voice. Wallace Irwin. InMe
Song for a Dance. Francis Beaumont. *See* Shake off Your Heavy Trance.
Song for a Dance. Abraham Sutskever, *tr. fr. Yiddish by* Ruth Whitman. VWA
Song for a Dancer. Kenneth Rexroth. TAP
Song for a Dark Girl. Langston Hughes. AmPP; CDC; IDB; PoBA
Song for a Day, *sel.* Francisco Arriví, *tr. fr. Spanish by* Julio Marzán.
"Sometimes a huge wave of thought." InW
Song for a Departure. Elizabeth Jennings. NMP
Song for a Girl. Dryden. ErPo; ELP
(Sung by a Young Girl.) UnTE
Song for a Girl on Her First Menstruation. *Tr. fr. Papuan by* Joe Prentuo. BoWoP
Song for a Jewess. Iwan Goll, *tr. fr. French by* Joseph T. Shipley. TrJP
Song for a Listener, *sel.* Leonard Feeney.
Because of Her Who Flowered So Fair. ISi
Song for a Little Cuckoo Clock. Elizabeth J. Coatsworth. SiSoSe
Song for a Little House. Christopher Morley. FaPON; TreF
Song for a Lost Art. Virginia Brasier. AMV-81
Song for a Lyre. Louise Bogan. LiTA
Song for a New Generation. Gertrude May Lutz. AMV-80
Song for a Proud Relation. Patrick MacDonogh. OnYI
Song for a Suicide. Langston Hughes. PoNe
Song for a Transformation, *sel.* Francisco Arriví, *tr. fr. Spanish by* Julio Marzán.
"This tree/ growing out of me." InW
Song for All Seas, All Ships. Walt Whitman. CH; FaBoBe; HBV-1; MOS; NePA
Song for an Allegorical Play. John Ciardi. PoCh
Song for Apollo. Matthew Arnold. *See* Song of Callicles, The.
Song for Autumn. Andrew Young. GBL
Song for "Buvez les Vins du Postillion"—Advt. Jean Garrigue. TAP
Song for December Thirty-first. Frances Frost. YeAr
Song for Dov Shamir. Dannie Abse. VWA
(Song of a Hebrew.) WTO
Song for Fine Weather. *Unknown, tr. fr. Haida Indian by* Constance Lindsay Skinner. AWP
Song for Healing. Roberta Hill. CDW
Song for Ireland. Phil *and* June Colclough. OBET
Song for Ishtar. Denise Levertov. NaP; NMM; NoAM; PoM
Song for Lexington, A. Robert Kelley Weeks. AA
Song for Memorial Day. Clinton Scollard. OHIP
Song for Midsummer Night. Elizabeth J. Coatsworth. YeAr
Song for Mother's Day. T. S. Matthews. ELU
Song for Music. G. S. Fraser. ChMP
Song for My Father. Jessica Hagedorn. BrSi
Song for My Lady. A. Godwin. OxBoLi
(Absent Lover, An.) OxBM
(Now Wolde.) CH
(Song in His Lady's Absence, A.) MeEL
Song for My Little Friends. Leonard Adame, *tr. fr. Spanish by* Toni Empringham. FIA
Song for My Mother, A: Her Hands. Anna Hempstead Branch. *Fr.* Songs for My mother. OHIP
Song for My Mother, A: Her Stories. Anna Hempstead Branch. *Fr.* Songs for My Mother. OHIP
Song for My Mother, A: Her Words. Anna Hempstead Branch. *Fr.* Songs for My Mother. OHIP; SiSoSe; TiPo; YeAr
Song for My Name. Linda Hogan. STE; TWSS
Song for Naomi. Irving Layton. WHW
Song for New Orleans, A. George Keithley. NPGG
Song for Our Flag, A. Margaret E. Sangster. FaFP
Song for Past Midnight. Geoffrey Lehmann. CBAP
Song for Peace. W. R. Rodgers. NeBP
Song for St. Cecilia's Day. W. H. Auden. FaBoTw; MP; TwCP
Song for St. Cecilia's Day, 1687, A. Dryden. AWP; BiP; CABA; FaBoEn; FaBoTw; GoBC; GTBS; GTBS-P; HAP; HBV-2; InPS; LiTB; MasP; OAEL-1; OAEP; OBEV; PoEL-3; PPP; SeCV-2; TEP; TreFT; TrGrPo; UnS
Fife and Drum, 8 *ll.* GN
Song for September. Robert Fitzgerald. VGW
Song for Seven Parts of the Body, *sels.* Maxine W. Kumin. POL
"I have a life of my own," III.
"These nubbins/ these hangers-on," VII.
"They have eyes that see not," V.
Song for Simeon, A. T. S. Eliot. EaLo; EBCP; LiTB; NAs; NOCV; OxBoCh
Song for the Asking, A. Francis Orrery Ticknor. AA
Song for the Clatter-Bones. F. R. Higgins. AnIL; LiTB; OBMV; OnYI; OxBI
Song for the Dead, III. *Unknown, tr. by* Frances S. Herskovits. TTY
Song for the Greenwood Fawn. I. L. Salomon. GoYe
Song for the Heroes. Alex Comfort. MoBrPo; NeBP
Song for the Infant Judas. Thomas Blackburn. NAs
Song for the Last Act. Louise Bogan. NePoAm; NoP; NYBP; UnPo; WPE
Song for the Lute. Thomas Campion. *See* Thrice Toss These Oaken Ashes in the Air.
Song for the Middle of the Night, A. James Wright. WeW
Song for the Newborn. *Unknown, tr. fr. Grande Pueblo Indian by* Mary Austin. OFD; WPE
Song for the Old Ones. Maya Angelou. SaC
Song for the Passing of a Beautiful Woman. *Unknown, tr. fr. Paiute by* Mary Austin. LiTA
Song for the Pike's Peaker. *Unknown.* PoOW
Song for the Ragged Schools of London, A. Elizabeth Barrett Browning. SBG
Song for the Seasons, A. "Barry Cornwall." HBV-1
Song for the Sick Emperor. John Fletcher. *See* Care-charming Sleep.
Song for the Spanish Anarchists, A. Herbert Read. ChMP
Song for the Spinning Wheel. Wordsworth. OBRV
Song for the Squeeze-Box. Theodore Roethke. NePoAm
Song for the Sun That Disappeared behind the Rainclouds. *Unknown, tr. fr. Hottentot by* Ulli Beier. TTY
Song for the unsung heroes who rose in the country's need, A. The Unsung Heroes. Paul Laurence Dunbar. BPo
Song for These Days. Patrick F. Kirby. GoBC
Song for Thrift Week. Mildred Weston. WhC
Song for Tomorrow. Lucia Trent. PGD
Song for Unbound Hair. Genevieve Taggard. PoRA
Song for War. W. R. Rodgers. NeBP
Song Form. Amiri Baraka. CTBA; SOTW
Song from a Country Fair. Léonie Adams. GoJo; GrPl
Song from a Drama. Edmund Clarence Stedman. AA
Song from a Two-Desk Office. Byron Buck. NYBP
Song from "Al Aaraaf." Poe. *Fr.* Al Aaraaf. AmPP; NePA; OxBA
Song from "April." Irene Rutherford McLeod. SUS
Song from Armenia, A. Geoffrey Hill. FaBoMo
Song from Chartivel. Marie de France, *tr. fr. French by* Arthur O'Shaughnessy. AWP
("Hath any loved you well, down there.") EnLoPo; WPOW
(Sarrazine's Song to Her Dead Lover.) HBV-1
Song from Fragment of an Eccentric Drama. Henry Kirke White. OBRV
Song from "Maud". Tennyson. *See* Come into the Garden, Maud.
Song from "Ogier the Dane." William Morris. *Fr.* The Earthly Paradise. OAEP
("In the white-flowered hawthorn brake.") ViBoPo
Song from Shakespeare's "Cymbeline," A ("To fair Fidele's grassy tomb"). William Collins. EnRP; LAuP; NOEC; OAEP
(Dirge in "Cymbeline.") ELP; HBV-2; NOBE; OBEC; SeCePo; ViBoPo
(Fidele.) OBEV

Song from Sylvan, A. *At. to* Elizabeth Barrett Browning *and to* Louise Imogen Guiney. *See* Out in the Fields with God.
Song from the Bride of Smithfield. Sylvia Townsend Warner. MoBrPo
Song from the Italian, A. Dryden. *Fr.* The Kind Keeper. SeCV-2
Song from the Maker of Totems. Duane Niatum. STE
Song from the Ship. Thomas Lovell Beddoes. *See* To Sea, to Sea!
Song from the Unfinished Man. Paul David Ashley. LFAC
Song from the Waters. Thomas Lovell Beddoes. *See* Dirge: "Swallow leaves her nest, The."
Song gives birth to. Round Valley Reflections. William Oandasan. STE
Song gives birth to. The Song of Ancient Ways. William Oandasan. STE
Song, *Hamlet.* John Poole. BXAP
Song I sing of my sea-adventure, A. The Seafarer. *Unknown, tr. fr. Anglo-Saxon by* Charles W. Kennedy. AnOE; EtS; MOS
Song I sing of sorrow unceasing, A. The Wife's Lament. *Unknown, tr. by* Charles W. Kennedy. AnOE
Song in a Siege. Robert Heath. CavP; OBS
Song in a windless night, A. The Toad. Tristan Corbière, *tr. by* Vernon Watkins. SyP
Song in His Lady's Absence, A. A. Godwin. *See* Song for My Lady.
Song in Making of the Arrows, A. John Lyly. *Fr.* Sapho and Phao. LoBV; OBSC
(Vulcan's Song.) EIL
Song in March. William Gilmore Simms. AA; HBV-1
Song in Passing, A. Yvor Winters. VGW
Song in Praise of a Beggar's Life, A. "A. W." *See* In Praise of a Beggar's Life.
Song in Praise of Old English Roast Beef, A. Richard Leveridge. OBEC
Song in Praise of Paella. C. W. V. Wordsworth. FiBHP
Song in Spite of Myself. Countee Cullen. BALP
Song in Spring. Louis Ginsberg. YeAr
Song in the Cold Season. Samuel French Morse. PoA
Song in the Dell, The. Charles Edward Carryl. AA
Song in the Front Yard, A. Gwendolyn Brooks. IDB; NoAM; NOBA; PoBA
Song in the valley of Nemea, A. Nemea. Lawrence Durrell. ChMP; FaBoTw; GTBS-P
Song in the Wood. John Fletcher. *Fr.* The Little French Lawyer. EIL
Song in Time of Order 1852, A. Swinburne. VLP
Song in Time of Plague. Thomas Nashe. *See* Adieu, Farewell Earth's Bliss.
Song in Time of Revolution 1860, A. Swinburne. VLP
Song in White. Anne Le Dressay. AMV-80
Song is not singing. Kissing the Dancer. Robert Sward. CoPo
Song is so old. Song. Hermann Hagedorn. HBV-1
Song IV: Sudden Light. Dante Gabriel Rossetti. *See* Sudden Light.
Song made by F. B. P., A. *Unknown.* *See* New Jerusalem, The.
Song-Maker. Anita Endrezze-Danielson. STE
Song-Maker, The. Anna Wickham. MoBrPo
Song Making. Sara Teasdale. WGRP
Song My. Susan Griffin. NMM; WPOW
Song My Paddle Sings, The. E. Pauline Johnson. BPAW; CaP; FaPON; HBV-1
Song of a Common Lover. Flavien Renaivo, *tr. fr. French by* Alan Ryder. TTY
Song of a Factory Girl. Marya Zaturenska. HBMV
Song of a Factory Worker, The. Ruth Collins. SaC
Song of a Happy Rising, The. John Thewlis. ACP
Song of a Heathen, The. Richard Watson Gilder. AA; TRV; WGRP
Song of a Hebrew. Dannie Abse. *See* Song for Dov Shamir.
Song of a Jewish Boy. "M. J.," *tr. fr. Polish by* A. Glanz-Leyeles. TrJP
Song of a Man about to Die in a Strange Land. *Unknown, tr. fr. Chippewa Indian by* Mary Austin. DL
Song of a Man Who Has Come Through. D. H. Lawrence. ChMP; CMoP; CoBMV; FaBoMo; GTBS-P; InPS; LiTM; MoPo; NoAM; OxBTC; SeCeV; ViBoPo
Song of a Passionate Lover. *Unknown.* *See* Come Not Near My Songs.
Song of a Rat. Ted Hughes. CMoP; NoP
Song of a Second April. Edna St. Vincent Millay. CMoP; OxBA
Song of a Shepherd Boy at Bethlehem. Josephine Preston Peabody. OHIP
Song of a Sick Child. *Malay Oral Tradition, tr. by* R. J. Wilkinson *and* R. O. Winstedt. WTO
Song of a Train. John Davidson. BrPo
Song of a Woman Abandoned by the Tribe. *Unknown, tr. fr. Shoshone Indian by* Mary Austin. BPAW; WPE
Song of a Young Lady to Her Ancient Lover, A. Earl of Rochester. BoLoP; CavP; EBEV; ErPo; GBL; MePo
Song of Abuse. *Yoruba Oral Tradition, tr. by* Ulli Beier *and* B. Gbadamosi. WTO
Song of Accius and Silena. John Lyly. *See* O Cupid! Monarch over Kings.
Song of Albert Graeme. Sir Walter Scott. *Fr.* The Lay of the Last Minstrel, IV. EnRP
("It was an English ladye bright.") OBRV
Song of Ale, A. *At. to* William Stevenson. *See* Back and Side Go Bare, Go Bare.
Song of Amergin. *Unknown.* *See* Alphabet Calendar of Amergin.
Song of Anarchus, The, *sel.* *Unknown.*
Song: "Know then, my brethren, heaven is clear." FaBoCo
Song of Ancient Ways, The. William Oandasan. STE
Song of Angiola in Heaven, A. Austin Dobson. HBV-2
Song of Apelles. John Lyly. *See* Cards and Kisses.
Song of Apollo. John Lyly. *Fr.* Midas. OBSC
Song of Autumn, A. Sir Rennell Rodd. HBV-1
Song of Autumn I. Baudelaire, *tr. fr. French by* C. F. McIntyre. NAWM-2
Song of Basket-weaving. Constance Lindsay Skinner. BPAW
Song of Battle. Bertrans de Born. *See* Well Pleaseth Me the Sweet Time of Easter.
Song of Bekotsidi, The. *Tr. fr. Navajo Indian by* Washington Matthews. OBVE
Song of Black Cubans. Federico García Lorca, *tr. fr. Spanish by* William B. Logan. SOTW
Song of Bliss. Spenser. *Fr.* The Faerie Queene, II, 12. FF
(Gather the Rose.) EIL
("Whiles some one did chaunt this lovely lay, The.") OBVE
Song of Braddock's Men, The. Stephen Tilden. PAH
Song of Breath, A. Stephen Vincent Benét. MoVE
Song of Breath. Peire Vidal, *tr. fr. French by* Ezra Pound. AWP
Song of Callicles, The ("Far, far from here"). Matthew Arnold. *See* Cadmus and Harmonia.
Song of Callicles, The ("Through the black, rushing smoke-burst"). Matthew Arnold. *Fr.* Empedocles on Etna, II. NOBE; OAEL-2; OBEV; OBVV
(Callicles' Song.) ChTr; LoBV
(Not Here, O Apollo.) FaBoRV
(Song for Apollo.) FiP
(Song of the Muses, The.) WiR
Song of canaries, The. The Canary. Ogden Nash. DFF; FiBHP; RHPC
Song of Caribou, Musk Oxen, Women, and Men Who Would Be Manly. *Tr. fr. Eskimo.* WTO
"Glorious it is/ to see long-haired winter caribou," *sel.* RFM
Song of Carroll's Sword, The. *At. to* Dallan MacMore, *tr. fr. Middle Irish by* Kuno Meyer. OnYI
(Carroll's Sword, *tr. by* Frank O'Connor.) KiLC
Song of Chess, The. *At. to* Abraham ibn Ezra, *tr. fr. Hebrew by* Nina Davis Salaman. TrJP
Song of Clover, A. Helen Hunt Jackson. GN
Song of Coridon and Melampus. George Peele. *Fr.* The Hunting of Cupid. OBSC
Song of Cove Creek Dam, The. *Unknown.* AmFP
Song of Cradle-making. Constance Lindsay Skinner. CaP
Song of Creation, The. *Unknown.* *See* Brahma, the World Idea.
Song of Crede, Daughter of Gooary, The. *Unknown, tr. fr. Middle Irish by* Kuno Meyer. OnYI
(Song of Crede, *tr. by* Alfred Perceval Graves.) BIrV
Song of Dalliance, A. William Cartwright. ErPo; JCP
Song of Daphne to the Lute, A. John Lyly. *Fr.* Midas. OBSC
Song of David, The. Christopher Smart. *See* Song to David.
Song of Deborah [and Barak], The. Bible, *O.T.* *Fr.* Judges. AWP; BoWoP; PBWP; WPOW
(Then Sang Deborah and Barak.) TrJP
Song of Degrees. Paul Auster. VWA
Song of Degrees, A. W. P. Ker. PoSH
Song of Derivations, A. Alice Meynell. WGRP
Song of Desire, A. Frederick Lawrence Knowles. HBV-1
Song of Despair. Rangiaho, *tr. fr. Maori by* Barry Mitcalfe. WTO
Song of Diana's Nymphs, A. John Lyly. *See* Cupid's Indictment.
Song of Diligence, A. Helen Frazee-Bower. HBMV
Song of Divine Love, A. Richard Crashaw. *See* Song, A: "Lord, when the sense of Thy sweet grace."
Song of Doubt, A. Josiah Gilbert Holland. WGRP
Song of Duke William. Hilaire Belloc. FaBoNo
Song of Dust, A. Lord De Tabley. EnLoPo
Song of Early Autumn, A. Richard Watson Gilder. HBV-1
Song of Echo. Ben Jonson. *See* Slow, Slow Fresh Fount.
Song of Egla. Maria Gowen Brooks. AA
Song of Emptiness to Fill up the Empty Pages Following, A. Michael Wigglesworth. SCAP
Song of Eros. George Edward Woodberry. *Fr.* Agathon. AA; HBV-1
Song of Exile, A. Bible, *O.T.* Psalm CXXXVII: 1-6. TrGrPo
Song of Exile, *sel.* Antônio Gonçalves Dias, *tr. fr. Portuguese by* Frances Ellen Buckland.
"There are palm trees in my homeland." TTY
Song of Expectancy. George Hitchcock. EAS
Song of Fairies Robbing an Orchard. Thomas Randolph, *tr. by* Leigh Hunt. *Fr.* Amyntas. OBRV
(Fairy Song.) HBV-1

Song of Faith, A. Josiah Gilbert Holland. WGRP
Song of Farewell. Nellie Wong. BrSi
Song of Finis, The. Walter de la Mare. MoBrPo
Song of Finn, The. *Unknown. See* In Praise of May.
Song of Fionnuala, The. Thomas Moore. AnIL; BlrV; OnYI
Song of Fixed Accord. Wallace Stevens. InPS; NePoAm
Song of Fleet Street, A. Alice Werner. HBV-2
Song of Four Priests Who Suffered Death at Lancaster, A. *Unknown.* ACP
Song of Freedom, A. Alice Milligan. AnIV; OnYI
Song of Glenann, A. "Moira O'Neill." HBV-2
Song of grass, A,/ A song of earth. A Song. "Yehoash," *tr. by* Isidore Goldstick. TrJP
Song of Greatness, A. *Tr. fr. Chippewa by* Mary Austin. AmFN; FaPON; TiPo
Song of Gwythno. Thomas Love Peacock. *Fr.* The Misfortunes of Elphin. OBRV
Song of Handicrafts, A. Annie Matheson. OBVV
Song of Hannah, The. Bible, *O.T.* First Samuel. *See* Hannah's Song of Thanksgiving.
Song of Hate. Jacob ben David Frances, *tr. fr. Hebrew by* A. B. Rhine. TrJP
Song of Hate for Eels. Arthur Guiterman. OBAL
Song of Hiawatha, The, *sels.* Longfellow.
  As Brothers Live Together, *fr.* I. TreFT
  Death of Minnehaha, The, *fr.* XX. AA
  "From his pouch he took his colors." EyDe
  "From his wanderings far to eastward," *fr.* XXI. GOA
  Ghosts, The, XIX. LoBV
  Hiawatha's Canoe. OHIP
  Hiawatha's Childhood, *fr.* III. FaBV; FaPON; OHFP; TiPo; TreF; WBLP
    (Old Nokomis Sings.) SpRo
  Hiawatha's Wooing, *fr.* X. BeLS; TreFS
    ("As the bow unto the cord is.") TRV
  Introduction: "Should you ask me, whence these stories?" NOBA
  Little Hiawatha, The, *fr.* III. OnUR
  "When he heard the owls at midnight," *fr.* III. FM
Song of Honor [*or* Honour], The. Ralph Hodgson. LiTB; MoBrPo
  "I heard the hymn of being sound," *sel.* LO
Song of Hope. Mary Artemisia Lathbury. BLPA
Song of Impossibilities, A. Winthrop Mackworth Praed. InMe; NA
Song of Ithamore, The. Christopher Marlowe. *Fr.* The Jew of Malta, IV. WHA
Song of January. Gerta Kennedy. PoPl
Song of Jed Smith, The, *sel.* John Neihardt.
  "One more rendezvous." FYAP
Song of Jehane du Castel Beau, The. William Morris. *Fr.* Golden Wings. ChTr
  (Song: "Gold wings across the sea!") LoBV
Song of Joy. Uvavnuk. *See* Great Sea, The.
Song of Lazarus, The, *sel.* Alex Comfort.
  Notes for My Son, VI. LiTM; MoBrPo; NeBP; SeCePo
Song of Lewes, The. *Unknown.* OxBM; OxBoLi
  (Against the Baron's Enemies.) MeEL
Song of Liberty, A. Blake. EnRP
Song of Liberty, *sel.* Louise Ayres Garnett.
  "Lead on, lead on, America." PGD
Song of Life, A. Franz Werfel, *tr. fr. German by* Edith Abercrombie Snow. TrJP
Song of Living, A. Amelia Josephine Burr. HBV-2
Song of Lo-fu, The. *Unknown, tr. fr. Chinese by* Arthur Waley. AWP
Song of Loneliness. Judah Halevi, *tr. fr. Hebrew by* Nina Davis Salaman. TrJP
Song of Longing. *Gond Oral Tradition, tr. by* V. Elwin *and* S. Hivale. WTO
Song of Longing. *Tr. fr. Maori by* John White. WTO
Song of Love, A. "Lewis Carroll." GN
Song of Love, The. Rainer Maria Rilke, *tr. fr. German by* Ludwig Lewisohn. AWP
Song of Love and Death, The. Tennyson. Idylls of the King: Lancelot and Elaine. OBNC
  (Elaine's Song.) FaBoEn
Song of Love for Jesus, A. Richard Rolle. MeEL
Song of Low Degree, A. Bunyan. *See* Shepherd Boy Sings, The.
Song of Maelduin. Thomas William Rolleston. HBMV
Song of Marion's Men. Bryant. HBV-2; HBVY; PAH; TreF
Song of Mary the Mother of Christ, The. *At. to* Henry Walpole. ISi
Song of May Morning. Milton. *See* Song on May Morning.
Song of Mehitabel, The. Don Marquis. FiBHP; TreFS
Song of Milkanwatha, The, *parody, sel.* George A. Strong.
  Modern Hiawatha, The. FaBoCo; FaBoPa; FaFP; FaPON; FiBHP; HBV-1; InMe; MoShBr; NA; Par; RHPC; SpRo; TreFS; WhC; YaD
  (Hiawatha Revisited.) BXAP
Song of Mr. Toad, The. Kenneth Grahame. *Fr.* The Wind in the Willows. FaPON; FiBHP; GoJo; NOBL
Song of Moses and the Lamb, The. *Unknown. See* O Lord, Almighty God.
Song of My Soul. Ralph Chubb. PeHV
Song of Myself. Walt Whitman. AmPP; AP; LiTA; MoAmPo, *abr.*; NOBA; OxBA; SOTW, *much abr.*; TAP; TrGrPo, *abr.*; WHA, *much abr.*
  Sels.
  "Alone far in the wilds and mountains I hunt," X. SeCeV
  Battle of the *Bonhomme Richard* and the *Serapis,* XXXV-XXXVI. MOS; UnPo
    (John Paul Jones, *fr.* XXXV.) PAL
    (Old-Time Sea-Fight, An, XXXV.) OnMSP
    ("Would you hear of an old-time sea-fight," XXXV-XXXVI.) SeCeV
  "Child said, A, *What is the grass?*," VI. NoP
    (Grass.) BLPL; NePA
    (Leaves of Grass, *fr.* VI *and* XX.) AA
  Drayman, The, *fr.* XIII. PoNe
  Encountering God, *fr.* XLVIII. TreFT
  Has Any One Supposed It Lucky to Be Born? NAs
  Heroes, fr. XXXIII *and* XXXV. AA
    ("I understand the large heart of heroes," fr. XXXIII.) InPS
  "Houses and rooms are full of perfumes," *fr.* II. UnPo
  Hub for the Universe, A, XLVIII. FaFP
  "I Am He that Aches with Love." LLLT
  "I am the poet of the Body and I am the poet of the Soul," XXI. BiP; SeCeV; WeW
  "I believe a leaf of grass is no less than the journey-work of the stars," *fr.* XXXI. InPS; PDV; SeCeV; TiPo; TRV
  "I believe in the flesh and the appetites," *fr.* XXIV. Prf
  "I believe in you my soul," V. BiP; Prf
  "I celebrate myself and sing myself," I. AA; BiP; NoP; PP; ViBoPo
    (I Celebrate Myself.) NePA
    (Myself.) BLPL; FaBoBe
  "I hear and behold God in every object, yet understand God not in the least," *fr.* XLVIII. WGRP
  "I know I have the best of time and space," XLVI. BiP
  "I think I could turn and live awhile with the animals," *fr.* XXXII. HAP; NU; PDV; WeW; WGRP
    (Animals.) FaFP; NePA; PAI; POL; PoPl; PPON
    (Beasts, The.) HBV-2; OBVV
  Infinity, *fr.* XLIV-XLV. AA
  My Barbaric Yawp, LII. NePA
    ("Spotted hawk swoops by and accuses me, The.") BiP; NoP; PP
  "My signs are a rain-proof coat, good shoes, a staff cut from the woods," *fr.* XLVI. Prf
  "Now I will do nothing but listen," XXVI. HoPM
  "Oxen that rattle the yoke and chain or halt in the leafy shade." FM
  Runaway Slave, The, *fr.* X. PoNe
  Stallion, The, *fr.* XXXII. PH
    ("Gigantic beauty of a stallion, fresh and responsive to my caresses, A.") PDV
  Swiftly Arose. TrCP
  "These are really the thoughts of all men in all ages and lands," XVIII. BiP
  "Trippers and askers surround me," *fr.* IV. InPS; UnPo
  "Twenty-eight young men bathe by the shore," XI. HAP; NoP
  "Walt Whitman, a kosmos, of Manhattan the son," *fr.* XXIV. NoP; SCV
  Wounded Person, The, *fr.* XXXIII. PoNe
Song of Napalm. Bruce Weigl. MAYP
Song of Nature. Emerson. HBV-1
Song of Nezahualcoyotl. *Unknown, tr. fr. Aztec.* DL
Song of Nidderdale, The. Dorothy Una Ratcliffe. HBMV
Song of Nuns, A. James Shirley. *See* O Fly My Soul.
Song of Nu-Numma-Kwiten, The. *Unknown, tr. fr. Bushman.* PeSA
Song of Occident. Claude Vigée, *tr. fr. French by* Anthony Rudolf. VWA
Song of Oenone and Paris. George Peele. *See* Fair and Fair.
Song of One Eleven Years in Prison. George Canning, George Ellis *and* John Hookham Frere. *See* Song: "Whene'er with haggard eyes I view."
Song of O'Ruark, Prince of Breffni, The. Thomas Moore. OnYI
Song of Panama, A. Damon Runyon. PAH
Song of Parting, A. Compton Mackenzie. HBV-1; OBVV
Song of Perfect Propriety. Dorothy Parker. DBV; InMe
Song of Pleasure, A. Phillip Massinger. *See* Song: "Blushing rose and purple flower."
Song of Poverty. *Gond Oral Tradition, tr. by* V. Elwin *and* S. Hivale. WTO
Song of Praise, A. Bible, *O.T.* Psalms, CXLVIII. TrGrPo
Song of Praise, A. Countee Cullen. BiP
Song of Praise for an Ox. Abraham Sutskever, *tr. fr. Yiddish by* Ruth Whitman. VWA
Song of Quoodle, The. G. K. Chesterton. GoJo
Song of Renunciation, A. Sir Owen Seaman. CenHV

Song of Resignation. Yehuda Amichai, *tr. fr. Hebrew by* Assia Gutmann. NYBP
Song of Returnings. William Pitt Root. GeTw
Song of Riches, A. Katharine Lee Bates. AA
Song of Roland, The. *Unknown, tr. fr. Old French by* Dorothy L. Sayers. NAWM-1, *abr.*
Sels.
"In wrath and grief away the Paynims fly," *tr. by* Dorothy L. Sayers. OBWP
Ready They Make Hauberks Sarrazinese, *tr. by* C. K. Scott Moncrieff. WaaP
Song of Sack, A. *At. to* Charles Cotton. OBS
(Ode: "Come, let us drink away the time.") CavP
Song of Samuel Sweet, The. Charles Causley. OBNV
Song of Satisfaction on Completing an Overhauling of Fishing Tackle, A. Leslie P. Thompson. WhC
Song of Seyd Nimetollah of Kuhistan. Emerson. NOBA
Song of Shadows, The. Walter de la Mare. MoBrPo; TrGrPo
(Song of the Shadows, The.) CMoP
Song of Sherman's Army, The. Charles Graham Halpine. PAH
Song of Sherman's March to the Sea. Samuel H. M. Byers. *See* Sherman's March to the Sea.
Song of Sherwood, A. Alfred Noyes. FaPON; HBV-2; HBVY; TiPo
(Sherwood.) MoBrPo
Song of Sickness, A. Hine Tangikuku, *tr. fr. Maori by* Barry Mitcalfe. WTO
Song of Sitting Bull. *Unknown.* GOA
Song of Sixpence. *Unknown.* OxBoLi
Song of Slaves in the Desert. Whittier. OBVV; OxBA;
Song of Snow-white Heads. Cho Wen-chün, *tr. fr. Chinese by* Arthur Waley. BoWoP
Song of Solomon, The. Bible, *O.T.*
(Song of Songs, The.) AWP; TrGrPo; UnTE
Sels.
"Awake! Oh, north wind," IV: 16. SUS
(Awake!) FaPON
As a Seal upon Thy Heart, VIII: 6–7. TrJP
("Set me as a seal on your heart," *ad. by* Willis Barnstone.) BoWoP
"Behold, thou art fair," IV. BiP (1–16); TrJP (1–7)
"For, lo, the winter is past," II: 11–12. PDV; SUS; TiPo
(For, Lo, the Winter Is Past, 10–13.) TreF
(Lo, the Winter Is Past, 11–12.) FaPON
(Winter Is Past, The, 11–12.) SoPo; YeAr
Hark! My Beloved! II: 8–13. TrJP
("Voice of my beloved, The! behold he.") PoPl
("Voice of my darling, The," 8–14, *ad. by* Willis Barnstone.) BoWoP
"I am come into my garden, my sister, my spouse," V. OBVE
I Am My Beloved's, VII: 11–14. TrJP
("I am my lover's and he desires me," *ad. by* Willis Barnstone.) BoWoP
"I am the flower of the field," II: 1, 2, 14, *Douay vers.* (Canticle of Canticles). ISi
"I am the rose of Sharon, and the lily of the valleys," II. BiP; BoLoP; FF; GBL; LLLT; OBVE
(I Am the Rose of Sharon.) ChTr
(Song of Songs.) OLR
I Sleep, but My Heart Waketh, V: 2–16; VI: 1–3. TrJP
("I sleep but my heart is awake," 2–18, *ad. by* Willis Barnstone.) BoWoP
"My love has gone down to his garden," *ad. by* Willis Barnstone. BoWoP
"My love is white and ruddy," *ad. by* Willis Barnstone. BoWoP
On My Bed I Sought Him, III: 1–5. TrJP
("In my bed at night," *ad. by* Willis Barnstone.) BoWoP
Return, Return, O Shulammite, VII: 1–10. TrJP
"Song of songs, which is Solomon's, The," I. OBVE
"Thou art beautiful, O my love," VI: 3, 8, 9, *Douay vers.* (Canticle of Canticles). ISi
"Turning to him, who meets me with desire," VII: 10–13, *tr. by* Marcia Falk. PBWP
"Under the quince tree," VIII: 5, *tr. by* Marcia Falk. PBWP
"Yes, I am black! and radiant," I: 5–6, *tr. by* Marcia Falk. PBWP
Song of Songs, The. Bible, *O.T.* *See* Song of Solomon, The.
Song of Songs, The. Heine, *tr. fr. German by* Louis Untermeyer. UnTE
Song of Sukkaartik, the Assistant Spirit. Ajukutooq, *tr. fr. Eskimo.* WTO
Song of sunshine through the rain, A. Calvary and Easter [*or* An Easter Song]. "Susan Coolidge." BLRP; PGD; TRV; WBLP
Song of Supplication, A. Bible, *O.T.* *See* De Profundis.
Song of Switzerland. Stoddard King. WhC
Song of Texas. William Henry Cuyler Hosmer. PAH
Song of Thanatos. Thomas Lovell Beddoes. NBM
Song of Thanks, A. Edward Smyth Jones. BANP
Song of Thanksgiving. John Richard Moreland. PGD
Song of the Ancient People, The. Edna Dean Proctor. AA
Song of the Answerer, *sel.* Walt Whitman.
"Indications and tally of time, The." PP
Song of the Argonauts. William Morris. *Fr.* The Life and Death of Jason, IV. EtS
Song of the Arrow, The. Isabella Valancy Crawford. *Fr.* Gisli, the Chieftain. OBCV; PeCV
Song of the Ballet. J. B. Morton. DBV; FiBHP
Song of the Banjo, The. Kipling. FaBoCh; PrIm; VLP
Song of the Blue-Corn Dance. *Tr. fr. Hopi Indian by* Natalie Curtis. WTO
Song of the Border. Gordon W. Norris. BPAW
Song of the Borderguard, The. Robert Duncan. NeAP; PoM
Song of the Bow, The. Sir Arthur Conan Doyle. *Fr.* The White Company. HBV-2
Song of the Bower, The. Dante Gabriel Rossetti. HBV-1
Song of the Bowmen of Shu. Ezra Pound, *after the Chinese.* OBVE
Song of the Brave. Laurence Altgood. PAL
Song of the Breed. Carroll Arnett. STE
Song of the Bride. Susan Mernit. VWA
Song of the Broad-Ax, *sel.* Walt Whitman.
Broad-Ax, The. MoAmPo
Song of the Builders. Jessie Wilmore Murton. AmFN
Song of the Bush-Shrike. *Unknown, tr. fr. Zulu.* PeSA
Song of the Camels. Elizabeth J. Coatsworth. FaPON
Song of the Camp, The. Bayard Taylor. AA; BeLS; GN; HBV-2; HBVY; WBLP
Song of the Cape of Good Hope. Christian Schubart, *tr. fr. German by* Alfred Baskerville, *ad. by* Robert Bly. NU
Song of the Captured Woman. James Devaney. PoAu-1
Song of the Cauld Lad of Hylton. *Unknown.* *See* Cauld Lad of Hilton, The.
Song of the Chattahoochee. Sidney Lanier. AA; AmFN; AP; BoNaP; FaBoBe; FaBV; HBV-1; LiTA; NePA; OHFP; TreF; YaD
Song of the Christmas Tree, The. Blanche Elizabeth Wade. OHIP
Song of the Closing Service. Aliza Shenhar, *tr. fr. Hebrew by* Linda Zisquit. VWA
Song of the Clouds. Aristophanes, *tr. fr. Greek by* Oscar Wilde. *Fr.* The Clouds. AWP
Song of the Colorado, The. Sharlot M. Hall. HBV-2
Song of the Corsairs. Byron. EtS
Song of the Creatures, The. St. Francis of Assisi. *See* Canticle of the Sun.
Song of the Dark Ages. Francis Brett Young. HBMV
Song of the Demented Priest, The. John Berryman. MoPo
Song of the Derelict, The. John McCrae. EtS
Song of the Dew. *Unknown, tr. fr. Hebrew by* Solomon Solis-Cohen. TrJP
Song of the Elfin Steersman. George Hill. AA
Song of the Emigrants [in Bermuda]. Andrew Marvell. *See* Bermudas.
Song of the Exposition, *sel.* Walt Whitman.
Muse in the New World, The. MoAmPo
("Come, Muse, migrate from Greece and Ionia.") PP
Song of the Factory Girls. *Unknown.* SaC
Song of the Fairies. *Unknown, tr. fr. Middle Irish by* A. H. Leahy. OnYI
Song of the Fallen Deer. *Tr. fr. Piman Indian by* Frank Russell. OBVE
Song of the Farmworker. T. R. Jahns. AMV-80
Song of the Fisherman's Lover. Roseann Lloyd. WOLT
Song of the Fishes. *Unknown.* *See* Blow Ye Winds Westerly.
Song of the Flags, The. S. Weir Mitchell. PAH
Song of the Flea. Judah al-Harizi, *tr. fr. Hebrew.* TrJP
Song of the Flume, The. *At. to* Anna M. Fitch. BPAW
Song of the Forest Ranger, The. Herbert Bashford. HBV-1; OHIP
Song of the Forest Trees. *Unknown, tr. fr. Middle Irish by* Standish Hayes O'Grady. OnYI
Song of the Four Seasons, A. Austin Dobson. HBV-1
Song of the Four Winds, The. Thomas Love Peacock. *Fr.* The Misfortunes of Elphin. OBRV; WiR
Song of the Fucked Duck. Marge Piercy. BoWoP; NMM
Song of the Full Catch. Constance Lindsay Skinner. CaP
Song of the Galley, The. *Unknown, tr. fr. Spanish by* John Gibson Lockhart. AWP
Song of the Galley-Slaves. Kipling. ChTr; GTBS-P; HAP; PoEL-5
Song of the Ghost, The. Alfred Perceval Graves. AnIV
Song of the Good Samaritan, The. Vernon Watkins. LiTM
Song of the GPO, A. Gerry Hamill. NOBL
Song of the Graves, The. *Unknown, tr. fr. Welsh by* Ernest Rhys. *Fr.* The Black Book of Carmarthen. OBMV
Song of the Gulf Stream. Francis Alan Ford. EtS
Song of the Hanged. Eléni Vakaló, *tr. fr. Modern Greek by* James Damaskos. PBWP
Song of the Happy Shepherd, The. W. B. Yeats. NoAM; VLP
Song of the Harlot. Bible, *O.T.* Isaiah, XXIII: 16. TrJP
Song of the Harvest. Henry Stevenson Washburn. OHIP
Song of the Hatteras Whale, A. *Unknown.* EtS
Song of the Heads, The. *Unknown, tr. fr. Irish by* Frank O'Connor. KiLC
Song of the Hesitations. Paul Blackburn. NMP

Song of the Highest Tower. Arthur Rimbaud, *tr. fr. French by* Edgell Rickword. AWP
Song of the Hill. Edith Lodge. GoYe
Song of the Horse. *Unknown, tr. fr. Navaho Indian by* Natalie Curtis. AWP
Song of the Hunt, The. John Bennett. *Fr.* Master Sky-Lark. AA
Song of the Ill-Married. *Unknown, tr. fr. French by* Patricia Terry. BoWoP
Song of the Indian Maid, The ("Beneath my palm-trees, by the riverside"). Keats. *Fr.* Endymion. NOBE
("Beneath my palm-trees, by the riverside.") ViBoPo
Song of the Indian Maid. ("O Sorrow,/ Why dost borrow"). Keats. *Fr.* Endymion, IV. OAEP; OBEV
(O Sorrow! *abr.*) CH
(Song: "O Sorrow," *shorter sel.*) LoBV
("To Sorrow/ I bade Good Morrow," *shorter sel.*) OBRV
Song of the Intruder. Maria Jacobs. AMV-81
Song of the Invisible Corpse in the Field. Gregory Orr. LTB
Song of the Jellicles, The. T. S. Eliot. FaBoCh; FaBoNo; OxBChV; PCat; PoPle
Song of the King's Minstrel, The. Richard Middleton. HBV-1
Song of the Last Jewish Child. Edmond Jabès, *tr. fr. French by* Anthony Rudolf. VWA
Song of the Leadville Mine Boss. Don Cameron. PoOW
Song of the Lilies, The. Lucy Wheelock. OHIP
Song of the Lioness for Her Cub. *Tr. fr. Hottentot by* Thomas Hahn. BoWoP
Song of the Lotos-Eaters. Tennyson. *See* Choric Song: "There is sweet music here that softer falls."
Song of the Love of Jesus, A. Richard Rolle of Hampole. *See* Love Is Life.
Song of the Lower Classes, The. Ernest Charles Jones. CoMu; OBVV; VLP
Song of the Mad Prince, The. Walter de la Mare. EBEV; FaBoCh; GoJo; MoVE; NoAM; NOBE; OAEP; OxBChV
Song of the Mariner's Needle. C. R. Clarke. EtS
Song of the Master and Boatswain. W. H. Auden. *Fr.* The Sea and the Mirror. BoLoP; DTC; MOS
(Master and Boatswain.) FaBoTw
Song of the Mayers. *Unknown.* CH
(Mayers' Song, The.) GBP
Song of the Mean Mary Jean Machine, The. James Baker Hall. FiCP; TAT
Song of the Mermaids. George Darley. *See* Mermaidens' Vesper-Hymn, The.
Song of the Mermaids and Mermen. Sir Walter Scott. *See* Merrmaids and Mermen. WSC
Song of the Micmac, The. Joseph Howe. CaP
Song of the Militant Romance, The. Wyndham Lewis. FaBoTw; OxBTC
Song of the Milkmaid. Tennyson. *Fr.* Queen Mary. HBV-1
Song of the Mischievous Dog, The. Dylan Thomas. FaFP; FPL; GrPl
Song of the Moderns. John Gould Fletcher. AWP
Song of the Moon, A. Claude McKay. PoNe
Song of the Murdered Child. *Unknown.* GBP
(Milk-white Dove, The.) ChTr
Song of the Muses, The. Matthew Arnold. *See* Song of Callicles, The.
Song of the Narcissus, The. *Unknown, tr. fr. Arabic by* E. Powys Mathers. *Fr.* The Thousand and One Nights. AWP
Song of the Navajo. Albert Pike. PoOW
Song of the Negro Boatman. Whittier. *Fr.* At Port Royal. GN
Song of the New World. Angela Morgan. HBMV; HBVY
Song of the Night at Daybreak. Alice Meynell. CH
Song of the Ogres. W. H. Auden. RHPC
Song of the Old Love. Jean Ingelow. Supper at the Mill. HBV-1
Song of the Old Mother, The. W. B. Yeats. AnIV; MoBrPo
Song of the Old Woman. *Tr. fr. Eskimo by* Paul Emile Victor, *ad. by* Armand Schwerner. BoWoP
Song of the Open Road. Ogden Nash. FaBoCo; FPL; OBAL; PPJ; TreFS; WhC
Song of the Open Road, A. *Unknown, tr. fr. Latin by* John Addington Symonds. AWP
Song of the Open Road. Walt Whitman. FaFP; NePA; NOBA; WHA
"Afoot and light-hearted I take to the open road," *sel.* HBVY; RFM; TiPo; TreFT; ViBoPo
Song of the Outlaws. Joanna Baillie. *See* Outlaw's Song, The.
Song of the Owl, The. Richard Kendall Munkittrick. OBCA
Song of the Palm. Tracy Robinson. AA
Song of the Passion, A. Richard Rolle of Hampole. OxBoCh
Song of the Pen, The. Judah al-Harizi, *tr. fr. Hebrew by* J. Chotzner. TrJP
Song of the Pilgrims, The, *sel.* Rupert Brooke.
"O Thou/ God of all long desirous roaming." TrPWD
Song of the Pilgrims. Thomas Cogswell Upham. PAH
Song of the Pixies. Samuel Taylor Coleridge. OBEC
Song of the Poor Man. *Unknown, tr. by* Anselm Hollo. TTY
Song of the Pop-Bottlers. Morris Bishop. FaPON; FiBHP
Song of the Queen Bee. E. B. White. NYBP
Song of the Rabbits outside the Tavern. Elizabeth J. Coatsworth. *See* Rabbits' Song outside the Tavern, The.
Song of the Rain. Hugh McCrae. CBAP; PoAu-1
Song of the Rain Chant. *Unknown, tr. fr. Navaho Indian by* Natalie Curtis. AWP
Song of the Redwood-Tree. Walt Whitman. AmPP
Song of the Reed Sparrow, The. *Unknown.* OxBChV
Song of the Reim-Kennar, The. Sir Walter Scott. *Fr.* The Pirate. OAEL-2; OAEP; OBNC
Song of the Rejected Woman. Kibkarjuk, *tr. fr. Eskimo into Danish by* Knud Rasmussen; *tr. into English by* Tom Lowenstein. WPOW
Song of the Riders. Stephen Vincent Benét. *Fr.* John Brown's Body. MoAmPo
Song of the River Thames, A. Dryden. *Fr.* Albion & Albanius. FaBoEn
Song of the Road, A. Robert Louis Stevenson. BrPo
Song of the Robin, The. Beatrice Bergquist. SUS
Song of the Round Man. Michael Palmer. NPGG
Song of the Sabbath. Kadia Molodowsky, *tr. fr. Yiddish by* Jean Valentine. PBWP; WPOW
Song of the Satyrs. Ben Jonson. *See* Buz, Quoth the Blue Fly.
Song of the saw, The. Busy Carpenters. James S. Tippett. SoPo
Song of the Screw. *Unknown.* NA
Song of the Sea. Richard Burton. EtS
Song of the Sea. *At. to* Rumann MacColmain, *tr. fr. Middle Irish by* Kuno Meyer. OnYI
Song of the sea-adventurers, that never were known to fame, The. The Pageant of Seamen. May Byron. HBV-2
Song of the Seasons. Blanche De Good Lofton. YeAr
Song of the Seasons, A. Cosmo Monkhouse. HBV-1
Song of the Seaweed, *sel.* Eliza Cook.
"Many a lip is gaping for drink." FiBHP
Song of the Settlers. Jessamyn West. FaPON
Song of the Shadows, The. Walter de la Mare. *See* Song of Shadows, The.
Song of the Sheet. *Unknown.* BXAP
Song of the Shepherd in the Valley of Humiliation, The. Bunyan. *See* Shepherd Boy Sings, The.
Song of the Shirt, The. Thomas Hood. EBVV; EnRP; FaPoR; HBV-2; OBVV; PaPo; PPON, *abr.*; SaC; TEP; TreF; VLP; WBLP
Song of the Silent Land. Johann Gaudenz von Salis-Seewis, *tr. fr. German by* Longfellow. AWP; HBV-2
Song of the Sirens. William Browne. *See* Sirens' Song, The.
Song of the Ski, The. Wilson MacDonald. CaP
Song of the Sky Loom. *Unknown, tr. fr. Tewa Indian by* Herbert J. Spinden. WTO
Song of the Smoke, The. W. E. B. DuBois. PoBA; UnPo
Song of the Son. Jean Toomer. AmNP; CDC; NIP; PoBA
Song of the Spanish Main, The. John Bennett. HBV-2
Song of the Spirits, The. Joseph Sheridan Le Fanu. *Fr.* The Legend of the Glaive. OnYI
Song of the Springbok Does. *Unknown, tr. fr. Bushman by* W. H. I. Bleek. PeSA
Song of the Strange Ascetic, The. G. K. Chesterton. HBMV
Song of the Strange Young Duckling. Deborah Munro. IHMS
Song of the Stygian Naiades. Thomas Lovell Beddoes. EnRP; OAEL-2
Song of the Syrens. William Browne. *See* Sirens' Song, The.
Song of the Taste. Gary Snyder. LCAP
Song of the Three Holy Children, The. Bible, Apocrypha. ILwL
Song of the Three Hundred Thousand Drunkards in the United States, *sel.* William B. Tappan.
"We come! we come! to fill our graves." PeD
Song of the Three Minstrels. Thomas Chatterton. *Fr.* Aella. TrGrPo
("Budding floweret blushes at the light, The.") ViBoPo
(Mynstrelles Songe.) EnRP
Song of the Thunder. *Unknown, tr. fr. Hottentot.* PeSA
Song of the Thunders. *Tr. fr. Chippewa Indian by* Frances Densmore. OBVE
Song of the Toad, The. John Burroughs. FaPON
Song of the Tortured Girl, The. John Berryman. CoAP
Song of the Train. David McCord. FaPON; NTCP; SoPo
Song of the Trees. *Tr. fr. Chippewa Indian by* Frances Densmore. OBVE
Song of the Trees of the Black Forest. Edmond Jabès, *tr. fr. French by* Anthony Rudolf. VWA
Song of the Trout Fisher, The. Ikinilik, *tr. fr. Eskimo.* WTO
Song of the Truck. Doris Frankel. AmFN
Song of the Turkey Buzzard. Lew Welch. PoM
Song of the Turnkey, The. Harry Bache Smith. AA
Song of the Turtle and Flamingo. James Thomas Fields. *See* Turtle and the Flamingo, The.
Song of the Ungirt Runners, The. Charles Hamilton Sorley. HBMV; MoBrPo; OBEV; TreFT
Song of the Universal. Walt Whitman. PGD

Song of the Unloved. *Unknown, tr. fr. Sotho by* Jack Cope *and* Dan Kunene. PeSA
Song of the Unsuccessful, The. Richard Burton. WGRP
Song of the Valkyries, The. *Unknown, tr. fr. Norse by* Lee M. Hollander. WaaP
Song of the Virgin Mother, A. Lope de Vega, *tr. fr. Spanish by* Ezra Pound. AWP
Song of the Vivandière. Heine, *tr. fr. German by* Louis Untermeyer. UnTE
Song of the Wave, A. George Cabot Lodge. EtS
Song of the Weaving Woman. Yüan Chen, *tr. fr. Chinese by* Wu-chi Liu. SaC
Song of the Well. Bible, *O.T.* Numbers, XXI: 17–18. TrJP
Song of the Western Men, The. Robert Stephen Hawker. EnRP; FaPoR; GoBC; HBV-2; OBNC; OBRV; OBVV; PaPo; RoGo
(And Shall Trelawny Die?) EvOK
Song of the White Lady of Avenel. Sir Walter Scott. *Fr.* The Monastery. NBM
Song of the Wind and the Rain. Solomon ibn Gabirol, *tr. fr. Hebrew by* Solomon Solis-Cohen. TrJP
Song of the Wise Men. Edith Lovejoy Pierce. PGD
Song of the Witches. Shakespeare. *Fr.* Macbeth, IV, i. RHPC
Song of the Woman-Drawer, The. Mary Gilmore. PoAu-1
Song of the Zambra Dance. Dryden. *See* Beneath a Myrtle Shade.
Song of This House, The. Stephen Vincent. NeAC
Song of Three Friends, The, *sel.* John G. Neihardt.
Shooting of the Cup, The. PoOW
Song of Three Smiles. W. S. Merwin. CoAP; NOBA; VGW
Song of Thyrsis. Philip Freneau. *Fr.* Female Frailty. AA; LiTA; ViBoPo
Song of Troylus, The. Chaucer, *after the Italian of* Petrarch. *Fr.* Troilus and Criseyde. AWP
("If no love is, O God, what fele I so"). FF; OAEL-1
Song of Trust, A. Bible *O.T.* *See* I Will Lift Up Mine Eyes Unto the Hills.
Song of Twilight, A. *Unknown.* HBV-1
Song of Two Angels, A. Laura E. Richards. AA
Song of Two Wanderers, A. Marguerite Wilkinson. HBMV
Song of Venus. Dryden. *Fr.* King Arthur. LoBV; OxBoLi; PoEL-3; SeCeV
Song of Waking, A. Katharine Lee Bates. OHIP
Song of Wandering Aengus, The. W. B. Yeats. BrPo; CABA; CH; CMoP; FaBoCh; GoJo; MAT; MoAB; MoBrPo; PoEL-5; PoRA; SOTW; TiPo; VLP; WSC
Song of Welcome. Hermia Harris Fraser. CaP
Song of Winter, A. *Unknown, tr. fr. Middle Irish by* Kuno Meyer. AnIL; CH; OnYI
Song on a Young Lady Who Sung Finely. Wentworth Dillon, Earl of Roscommon. CavP
Song on King William III, A. *Unknown.* *See* As I Walked by Myself.
Song on May Morning. Milton. BoNaP; CH; GN; HBV-1; HBVY; TrGrPo
(May Morning.) YeAr
(Song of May Morning.) PoPl
Song on Reaching Seventy. John Hall Wheelock. TwAmPo
Song, on Reading That the Cyclotron Has Produced Cosmic Rays, *sel.* Samuel Hoffenstein.
"Be gay, be merry, and don't be wary of milking the modest minute." ShM
Song on the South Sea, A. Countess of Winchilsea. NOEC
Song on the Water. Thomas Lovell Beddoes. *Fr.* Death's Jest Book. FaBoCh
Song Set by John Farmer. *Unknown.* CTC
("Take time while time doth last.") OBSC
Song Set by Nicholas Yonge. *Unknown.* *See* Brown Is My Love.
Song soars from a sordid city street, A. A Street Melody. Belle Cooper. GoBC
Song—Talysarn. Brenda Chamberlain. *See* Song: "Bone-aged is my white horse."
Song that I'm going to sing, The. The Crafty Farmer. *Unknown.* BaBo; ESPB
Song that she sang was all written, The. The Moon of Mobile. Thomas Holley Chivers. OBAL
Song the Body Dreamed in the Spirit's Mad Behest, The. William Everson. ErPo
Song the Grass Sings, A. Charles G. Blanden. HBV-1
Song the Oriole Sings, The. William Dean Howells. HBV-1
Song—the Owl. Tennyson. *See* Owl, The.
Song-Throe, The. Dante Gabriel Rossetti. The House of Life, LXI. VLP
Song thumbed down a cruiser for a ride, A. James Cunningham. *Fr.* The Narrator's Trance. JB
Song, 'tis my will that thou do seek out Love. Dante, *tr. by* Dante Gabriel Rossetti. La Vita Nuova, V. AWP
Song to a Fair Young Lady, Going Out of [the] Town in the Spring. Dryden. CABA; HBV-1; OBEV; OBS
Song to a Lover. *Tr. fr. Amharic by* Willis Barnstone. BoWoP
Song to a Lute. Sir John Suckling. CaPo; TrGrPo
(Song: "Hast thou seen the down in the air.") AnAnS-2; EnLoPo
Song to a Tree. Edwin Markham. FaPON
Song to Amoret, A. Henry Vaughan. HBV-1; ViBoPo
Song to April. Sir William Watson. *See* Song: "April, April,/ Laugh thy girlish laughter."
Song to Be Sung by the Father of Infant Female Children. Ogden Nash. MoAmPo
Song to Beta. Michael Drayton. *Fr.* The Shepherd's Garland, Eclogue III (1593 ed.). OBSC
Song to Celia ("Come my Celia, let us prove"). Ben Jonson. *See* Come, My Celia, Let Us Prove.
Song to Celia ("Drink to me only with thine eyes"). Ben Jonson. *See* To Celia.
Song to Celia. Sir Charles Sedley. *See* To Celia.
Song to Cloris, A. Earl of Rochester. ErPo
Song to David, A. Christopher Smart. ChTr; GoTL; LaA; LAuP; LoBV, *abr.*; MasP; NOBE, *abr.*; OAEL-1; OBEC; PoEL-3; TrGrPo, *abr.*
Sels.
Adoration. FaBoEn
Beauteous, Yea Beauteous More Than These. EaLo
"Glorious the sun in mid career." FaBoCh
"He sang of God—the mighty source." TRV
(Catholic Amen, The.) GoBC
Man of Prayer, The. 3 *sts.* LiTB
"O David, highest in the list," 38 *sts.* NOEC; OxBoCh
"O servant of God's holiest charge." ViBoPo
"O Thou, that sit'st upon a throne." EBEV
"Strong is the lion—like a coal." HAP
"Sublime—invention ever young." HBV-2; OBEV
"Tell them, I AM, Jehovah said." WGRP
Song to His Cynthia. Fulke Greville. *See* Of His Cynthia.
Song to His Purse for the King, A. Chaucer. *See* Complaint of Chaucer to His Purse, The.
Song to Imogen. Shakespeare. *See* Hark! Hark! the Lark.
Song to Imogen (in Basic English.) Richard L. Greene. BXAP; WhC
Song to John, Christ's Friend, A. *Unknown.* MeEL
Song to Mary, A. *At. to* William of Shoreham. *See* Hymn to the Virgin.
Song to My Love. Laurence McKinney. InMe
Song to Promote Growth. *Tr. fr. Navajo Indian by* Washington Matthews. OBVE
Song to Silvia. Shakespeare. *See* Who Is Silvia?
Song to Sleep. John Fletcher. *See* Care-Charming Sleep.
Song to the Evening Star. Thomas Campbell. *See* To the Evening Star.
"Song to the Gods, Is Sweetest Sacrifice." Annie Fields. AA
Song to the Men of England. Shelley. EnRP; FiP; InPS; PAI; SaC; SeCeV; TrGrPo; ViBoPo
Song to the Mountains. *Unknown, tr. fr. Pawnee Indian by* Alice C. Fletcher. AWP
Song to the oak, the brave old oak, A. The Brave Old Oak. Henry Fothergill Chorley. FaBoBe; HBV-1
Song to the Runaway Slave. *Unknown.* BPo
Song to the Tune of "Somebody Stole My Gal." X. J. Kennedy. CoPo
Song to the Virgin, A. *Unknown.* *See* Hymn to the Virgin, A.
Song to the Wind, A. Taliessin, *tr. fr. Welsh by* A. P. Graves. FaBoCh
Song Tournement [*or* Tournament]: New Style. Louis Untermeyer. CrMA; OBAL
Song Turning Back into Itself, The, *sel.* Al Young. CNA; NPGG
"Ocean Springs Mississippy," 3. CNA; NPGG
Song unto liberty's brave buccaneer, A. Paul Jones. *Unknown.* PAH
Song, A! What songs have died. A Song for the Asking. Francis Orrery Ticknor. AA
Song will deceive you, the scent will incite you to sing, The. You Cannot Go Down to the Spring. Shaw Neilson. CBAP
Song with a Discord, A. Arthur Colton. AA
Song with Words. James Agee. MoAmPo
Song, Written at Sea, in the First Dutch War. Charles Sackville. *See* Song: "To all you ladies now at land."
Song you sang you will not sing again, The. Local Places. Howard Moss. NePoEA-2
Song, Youth, and Sorrow. William Cranston Lawton. AA
Songe betwene the Quenes majestie and Englande, A. William Birche. CoMu
Songs, The. Martin Bell. FF
Songs. Babette Deutsch. HBMV
Songs ("How are songs begot and bred?"). Richard Henry Stoddard. AA
Songs, The. *Tr. fr. Zuni Indian by* K. Kennedy. WTO
Songs Ascending. Witter Bynner. HBV-1
Songs at Amala's Wedding. Thomas Lovell Beddoes. *See* Bridal Song to Amala.
Song's Eternity. John Clare. FaBoCh; NCEP

Songs for a Colored Singer. Elizabeth Bishop. MiAP; PoNe
Songs for a Three-String Guitar. Léopold Sédar-Senghor, *tr. fr. French by* Miriam Koshland. PBA
Songs for Fragoletta. Richard Le Gallienne. HBV-1
Songs for My Mother, *sels.* Anna Hempstead Branch.
Song for My Mother: Her Hands. OHIP
Song for My Mother: Her Stories. OHIP
Song for My Mother: Her Words. OHIP; SiSoSe; TiPo; YeAr
Songs for the Cisco Kid; or, Singing for the Face. K. Curtis Lyle. PoBA
Songs for the Cisco Kid; or, Singing: Song # 2. K. Curtis Lyle. PoBA
Songs for the Four Parts of the Night. Owl Woman (Juana Manwell), *tr. fr. Papago by* Frances Densmore. PBWP
Songs from a Masque. Francis Beaumont. *See* Shake Off Your Heavy Trance *and* Ye Should Stay Longer.
Songs from an Evil Wood. Lord Dunsany. HBV-2
Songs from Cyprus, *sels.* Hilda Doolittle ("H. D."). MoAmPo
"Gather for festival," I.
"Where is the nightingale," II.
Songs from the Masque of the Gentlemen of Gray's-Inne and the Inner-Temple. Francis Beaumont. *See* Masque of the Inner Temple and Gray's Inne, The.
Songs from the Princess. Tennyson. *See* Splendor Falls, The *and* Tears, Idle Tears.
Songs I Sing, The. Charles G. Blanden. HBV-2
Songs in Absence, *sel.* Arthur Hugh Clough.
Where Lies the Land [to Which the Ship Would Go?], VII. FaBoRV; HBV-2; MOS
Songs in Flight, *sel.* Ingeborg Bachmann, *tr. fr. German.*
"Instructed in love," *tr. by* Daniel Huws. WPOW
Songs in the Turtle Dance at Santa Clara. *Tr. fr. Tewa Indian by* H. J. Spinden. WTO
Songs My Mother Taught Me. David Wagoner. Str
Songs of Bilitis, The, *sels.* Pierre Louÿs, *tr. fr. French by* Horace M. Brown. UnTE
Absence.
Bilitis.
Desire.
Despairing Embrace, The.
Endearments.
Kiss, The.
Little House, The.
Remorse.
Songs of Ch'en, *sels.* Confucius, *tr. fr. Chinese by* Ezra Pound. CTC
Aliter.
"Marsh bank, lotus rank."
Songs of Cheng, *sels.* Confucius, *tr. fr. Chinese by* Ezra Pound. CTC
"Be kind, good sir, and I'll lift my sark."
"Hep-Cat Chung, 'ware my town."
"In chariot like an hibiscus flower at his side."
"So he won't talk to me when we meet?"
Songs of Divorce. Jane Green, *tr. fr. Ojibwa Indian by* Frances Densmore. WPOW
Songs of Education, *sels.* G. K. Chesterton.
For the Crèche. FaBoCo
Geography. HBMV; OBSV
History. OBSV
Songs of Experience, *sels.* Blake.
Ah, Sunflower. AWP; CABA; ELP; ELU; EnRP; FaBoRV; HAP; LAuP; NIP; NOEC; NOP; OAEL-2; OAEP; OBEC; OBNC; PoEL-4; PoPle; PPP; PrIm; SeCeV; TEP; UnPo; ViBoPo; WeW
("Ah Sun-flower! weary of time.") EBEV
(Sunflower, The.) ChTr; TrGrPo
Angel, The. CH; EnRP; LAuP; LiTB
Chimney Sweeper, The ("A little black thing among the snow"). CABA; LAuP; NOEC; OAEL-2; PPoe; PPP; SaC; TEP
Clod and the Pebble, The. CABA; EBCP; EnLoPo; EnRP; FaBoEn; FaBV; InPS; LAuP; LoBV; NOBE; NoP; OAEP; OBEC; OBNC; PAI; PrIm; SCV; TEP; TrGrPo; ViBoPo
Divine Image, A ("Cruelty has a Human heart"). ChTr; NoP; OBNC; TEP
Earth's Answer. EnRP; InPS; LAuP; NOEC; OAEL-2
Fly, The. FM; LAuP; TrGrPo
Garden of Love, The. AWP; CABA; EnLoPo; EnRP; FABV; GBL; HAP; LAuP; LiTB; LO; LoBV; MAT; NIP; NoP; OAEP; PAI; PPoe; SeCeV; SoSe; TEP; ViBoPo
Hear the Voice of the Bard, *Introd.* EBEV; ELP; NOBE; NU; OBEC
(Bard, The.) TRV; WGRP
(Hear the Voice.) OBEV
(Introduction: "Hear the voice of the bard!") CABA; EnRP; HAP; InPS; LAuP; LoBV; NOEC; NoP; OAEL-2; OAEP; PoEL-4; TEP
(Poet's Voice, The.) ChTr
Holy Thursday ("Is this a holy thing to see"). EnRP; FF; InPS; LAuP; NOEC; NoP; OAEL-2; OAEP; TEP
Human Abstract, The. BiP; EnRP; LAuP; NOEC; OAEL-2; PoEL-4; PPP
Infant Sorrow. FaBoEn; InPS; LAuP; NAs; OBNC; PAI; PoEL-4; PoPle
Little Boy Lost, A: ("Nought loves another as itself"). EnRP; OAEP; PAI; ViBoPo
Little Vagabond, The. OBSV; SeCeV
London ("I wander thro' each charter'd street"). AWP; CABA; ChER; ChTr; EnRP; FaBoEn; FaBoPP; FF; HAP; HeIP; InPK; InPS; LAuP; LiTB; MAT; NIP; NOBE; NOEC; NoP; OAEL-2; OBNC; PAI; PoEL-4; PPON; PrIm; SCV; SeCePo; SeCeV; TEP; UnPo; ViBoPo; WeW
My Pretty Rose Tree. BoLoP; LAuP
Nurse's Song ("When the voices of children are heard on the green/ And whisp'rings are in the dale"). CABA; EnRP; FF; LAuP
Poison Tree, A. AWP; CABA; EnRP; FaFP; HAP; HoPM; LAuP; LiTB; NoP; OAEP; PAI; PoEL-4; PPoe; PPP; SCV; SoSe; TreFS; TrGrPo; TW; WeW
Schoolboy, The. BoNaP; CH; FaBoCh; GLGT
Sick Rose, The. AWP; BoLoP; CABA; ChER; ChTr; EnLoPo; FaBoEn; HAP; HeIP; InPK; InPS; LAuP; LoBV; NIP; NOBE; NOEC; NoP; OAEL-2; OAEP; OBNC; PAI; PoEL-4; PPP; PrIm; SeCeV; SoSe; TrGrPo; ViBoPo; WeW
(O Rose, Thou Art Sick!) ELP
Tiger, The. AWP; ChTr; FaBoBe; FaFP; FaPON; FaPoR; FPL; GN; HBV-1; ILwL; InPS; LiTB; NIP; NOBE; NOEC; OAEP; OBEC; OBEV; PAI; PoLF; PoPl; PoPle; PoRA; PrIm; RoGo; SoSe; SpRo; TEP; TreF; TRV; UnPo; ViBoPo; WGRP; WHA
(Tyger, The.) BiP; CABA; CH; EaLo; EnRP; FaBoCh; FaBoEn; FaBV; FF; FM; HAP; HeIP; HoPM; InPK; LAuP; LoBV; MasP; NoP; OAEL-2; OBNC; PoEL-4; PPoe; PPP; SCV; SeCePo; SeCeV; TrGrPo; WeW
To Tirzah. EnRP; LO; NOBE; OAEL-2; OxBoCh
Songs of Guthrum and Alfred, The. G. K. Chesterton. *Fr.* The Ballad of the White Horse. HBV-2
Songs of Innocence, *sels.* Blake.
Blossom, The. GoJo; PB; PBBP
Chimney Sweeper, The ("When my mother died I was very young"). CH; EnRP; FF; HeIP; InPK; LAuP; NOEC; OAEL-2; OxBChV; PAI; PPoe; PPP; SaC; SoSe; TEP
Cradle Song, A: "Sweet dreams form a shade." EnRP; LAuP; OAEP; OBCP; SBVL; ViBoPo
Divine Image, The ("To mercy pity peace and love"). EBCP; EnRP; FaBoEn; LAuP; NOBE; NOEC; NoP; OAEL-2; OAEP; OBEC; OBNC; OxBoCh; PoEL-4; PPP; TEP; TRV; ViBoPo; WGRP
("To Mercy Pity Peace and Love.") LO
Dream, A. CH; EnRP; LAuP; PoPle
Echoing [*or* Ecchoing] Green, The. CABA; CH; LAuP; OBEC; POSC; UnPo; WiR
Holy Thursday (" 'Twas on a Holy Thursday, their innocent faces clean"). CH; EnRP; HBV-1; InPS; LAuP; NOBE; NOEC; NoP; OAEL-2; OAEP; OBEC; OFD; SCV; TEP; TrCP
Infant Joy. FaPON; GoJo; HBV-1; HBVY; LAuP; LOBV; NAs; PoLF; SiSoSe; TEP; ViBoPo
Lamb, The. BLPL; CABA; CH; EaLo; EBCP; EnRP; FaBoBe; FaBoCh; FaPON; GoJo; HBV-1; HeIP; InPS; LAuP; LiTB; LoBV; NIP; NOEC; NoP; OAEL-2; OAEP; OBEC; OxBoCh; OxBChV; PAI; PoPl; SBVL; SeCeV; SoSe; SUS; TEP; TrCP; TreF; TrGrPo; TRV; UnPo; WGRP; WHA
Laughing Song. EnRP; GoJo; LAuP; OxBChV; PoSC; SoPo; SUS; TiPo
(When the Green Woods Laugh.) CH
Little Black Boy, The. AWP; BiP; CABA; CH; EnRP; HBV-1; HeIP; InPK; LAuP; NOEC; NoP; OAEL-2; OAEP; OBEC; OBEV; OBNC; OxBChV; OxBoCh; PoEL-4; PoNe; SeCeV; TreFS; TrGrPo
Little Boy Found, The. EnRP; LAuP; NoP
Little Boy Lost, The ("Father, father, where are you going?"). EnRP; LAuP; NoP; TiPo
Night. BLPL; BoNaP; CH; EnRP; FaBoBe; FaPoN; HBV-1; HBVY; OBEC; OBEV; OxBChV; OxBoCh; PoLF; TreFT; WiR
Nurse's Song ("When the voices of children are heard on the green/ And laughing"). AWP; BLPL; CH; EnRP; FaBoBe; HBV-1; HBVY; LAuP; OBEC; OxBChV
(Play Time.) FaPON
On Another's Sorrow. AWP; EBCP; EnRP; FaBV; PoEL-4; ViBoPo
Piping Down the Valleys Wild. FaBoCh; FaBV; HeIP; InvP; NIP; NOBE; OBEC; OnUR; PoPle; TreFS
(Introduction: "Piping down the valleys wild.") CABA; EnRP; GoJo; InPS; LAuP; LOBV; NOEC; NoP; OAEL-2; OAEP; OBNC; PoEL-4; RHPC; SeCeV; SoSe; TEP; TrGrPo; ViBoPo
(Introduction to "Songs of Innocence.") FaBoBe; TiPo; WHA
(Piper, The.) AWP; OxBChV; PDV; RoGo

(Reeds of Innocence.) HBV-1; HBVY; LiTB; OBEV
Shepherd, The. EnRP; HBV-1; LoBV; OBEC; TiPo
Spring. FaBoCh; FaPON; MoShBr; PoPl; SUS; YeAr
Songs of Joy. W. H. Davies. MoBrPo; OBVV
Songs of Kabir. Kabir, *tr. fr. Hindi by* Rabindranath Tagore. WGRP
Songs of Labor, *sel.* Whittier.
Dedication: "I would the gift I offer here." OxBA
Songs of Maximus, The. Charles Olson. *Fr.* The Maximus Poems. NeAP
Sels.
"All/ wrong," II. NoAM
"Colored pictures," I. NoAM
"I have seen faces of want," V. PAI
"I know a house made of mud & wattles," IV. PAI
"This morning of the small snow," III. PAI; PPP
"You sing, you," VI. PAI
Songs of Seven. Jean Ingelow. HBV-1
Sels.
Longing for Home. WGRP
Maternity. OHIP
Seven Times One—Exultation. BLPA; FaPON; OBNC; TreF
Seven Times Three—Love. PoLF
Seven Times Two—Romance. GN
Songs of shepherds and rustical roundelays. The Hunting of the Gods. *Unknown.* OxBoLi
Songs of T'ang, *sel.* Confucius, *tr. fr. Chinese by* Ezra Pound.
Alba. CTC
Songs of the Birds, The. Edward Carpenter. WGRP
Songs of the Common Day, *sels.* Sir Charles G. D. Roberts.
Flight of the Geese, The. PeCV
Herring Weir, The. NOBC; PeCV
Pea-Fields, The. NOBC; OBCV; PeCV
Songs of the Ghost Dance. *Unknown, tr. fr. Paiute Indian.* WSC
Songs of the Greenwood. Shakespeare. *Fr.* As You Like It, II, v. TrGrPo
Songs of the People, *sels.* Hayyim Nahman Bialik, *tr. fr. Hebrew by* Maurice Samuel. AWP
"Two steps from my garden rail," I.
"On a hill there blooms a palm," II.
Songs of the Priestess. Malka Heifetz Tussman, *tr. fr. Yiddish by* Marcia Falk. VWA
Songs of the Sea-Children, *sels.* Bliss Carman. OBCV
"I see the golden hunter go," LIV.
"What is it to remember?" LXVI.
Songs of the Soul in Rapture at Having Arrived at the Height of Perfection, Which Is Union with God by the Road of Spiritual Negation. St. John of the Cross. *See* Dark Night, The.
Songs of the Squatters. Robert Lowe. PoAu-1
Songs of the Transformed, *sel.* Margaret Atwood.
Siren Song. HAP; PoA; WeW
Songs of Travel, *sels.* Robert Louis Stevenson. OBNC
"Bright is the ring of words."
If This Were Faith.
To S. R. Crockett.
Songs on the Voices of Birds, *sel.* Jean Ingelow.
Child and Boatman. FM
Songs, so old and bitter, The. The Coffin. Heine, *tr. by* Louis Untermeyer. AWP
Songs to a Lady Moonwalker. Abraham Sutskever, *tr. fr. Yiddish by* Ruth Whitman. VWA
Songs to Seraphine, *sels.* Heine, *tr. fr. German by* Emma Lazarus. TrJP
Shadow-Love.
Waves Gleam in the Sunshine, The.
Songs to Survive the Summer. Robert Hass. AmPA
Song's Worth, A. Susan Marr Spalding. AA
Sonic Boom. John Updike. QQQ
"Sonja Henie," the young girl. Preface. Theodore Weiss. NMP; VGW
Sonne, The. George Herbert. SeCP
Sonne hath twyse brought forthe the tender grene, The. *See* Sun hath twice brought forth the tender green, The.
Sonnet. *See also* Sonet *and* Sonetto.
Sonnet XVI: "After an age when thunderbolts and hail." Louise Labé, *tr. fr. French by* Willis Barnstone. BoWoP
Sonnet: "After dark vapours have oppress'd our plains." Keats. *See* After Dark Vapours.
Sonnet XIX: "After having slain very many beasts." Louise Labé, *tr. fr. French by* Willis Barnstone. BoWoP
Sonnet: "Afterwards there are dogends in." Maureen Duffy. PeHV
Sonnet: "Against my Love shall be, as I am now." Shakespeare. *See* Sonnets, LXIII.
Sonnet: Age. Richard Garnett. OBVV
Sonnet: "Ah no; nor I myselfe: though my pure love." Richard Barnfield. Sonnets, XIX. PeHV
Sonnet: "Ah, sweet Content! where is thy mild abode?" Barnabe Barnes. *See* Content.
Sonnet: "Ah wherefore with infection should he live." Shakespeare. *See* Sonnets, LXVII.
Sonnet: "Alas, 'tis true I have gone here and there." Shakespeare. *See* Sonnets, CX.
Sonnet: "Alexis, here she[e] stayed; among these pines." William Drummond of Hawthornden. *See* Spring Bereaved 3.
Sonnet: "All we were going strong last night this time." John Berryman. FaBoMo
Sonnet: "Altarwise by owl-light in the halfway-house." Dylan Thomas. *See* Altarwise by Owl-Light.
Sonnet XIV: "Although I cry and though my eyes still shed." Louise Labé, *tr. fr. French by* Willis Barnstone. BoWoP
(Sonnet: "As long as I continue weeping," *tr. by* Joan Keefe *and* Richard Terdiman.) PBWP
Sonnet, A: "Amazing thing happened to me, An." Daniil Kharms, *tr. fr. Russian by* George Gibian. FaBoNo
Sonnet: "And change with hurried hand has swept these scenes." Frederick Goddard Tuckerman. *See* Sonnets.
Sonnet: "And faces, forms and phantoms, numbered not." Frederick Goddard Tuckerman. *See* Sonnets.
Sonnet: "And me my winter's task is drawing over." Frederick Goddard Tuckerman. *See* Sonnets.
Sonnet: "And then I sat me down, and gave the rein." Gustav Rosenhane, *tr. fr. Swedish by* Sir Edmund Gosse. AWP
Sonnet: "And you as well must die, belovèd dust." Edna St. Vincent Millay. *See* And You as Well Must Die, Beloved Dust.
Sonnet: Anniversary, February 23, 1795. William Mason. OBEC
Sonnet: Army Surgeon, The. Sydney Thompson Dobell. NCEP
Sonnet: "As an unperfect actor on the stage." Shakespeare. *See* Sonnets, XXIII.
Sonnet: "As due by many titles I resigne." John Donne. *See* Holy Sonnets.
Sonnet: "As in a duskie and tempestuous night." William Drummond of Hawthornden. FaBoEn; OBS
Sonnet: "As long as I continue weeping." Louise Labé. *See* Sonnet XIV: "Although I cry and though my eyes still shed."
Sonnet IX: "As soon as I lie down in my soft bed." Louise Labé, *tr. fr. French by* Willis Barnstone. BoWoP
Sonnet: "As when, to one who long hath watched, the morn." John Codrington Bampfylde. NOEC
Sonnet: At Dover Cliffs. William Lisle Bowles. *See* At Dover Cliffs.
Sonnet: At Ostend. William Lisle Bowles. NOEC; OBEC
(Bells of Ostend, The.) EnRP
Sonnet: "At the round earths imagin'd corners, blow." John Donne. *See* Holy Sonnets.
Sonnet: "Avenge, O Lord, thy slaughtered saints, whose bones." Milton. *See* On the Late Massacre in Piedmont.
Sonnet: "Azured vault, the crystal circles bright, The." James I, King of England. *See* Heaven and Earth.
Sonnet: Barren Spring. Dante Gabriel Rossetti. *See* Barren Spring.
Sonnet: "Batter my heart, three-personed God; for you." John Donne. *See* Holy Sonnets.
Sonnet: "Beatrice is gone up into high heaven." Dante, *tr. fr. Italian by* D. G. Rossetti. *Fr.* La Vita Nuova. GoBC
Sonnet: "Beauty [*or* Beautie], sweet Love, is like the morning dew[e]." Samuel Daniel. *See* To Delia: "Beauty, sweet love . . ."
Sonnet: "Because mine eyes can never have their fill." Dante. *See* Ballata: He Will Gaze upon Beatrice.
Sonnet: "Because my grief seems quiet and apart." Robert Nathan. TrJP
Sonnet: "Beckie, my luve!—What is't, ye twa-faced tod?" George Campbell Hay. OxBS
Sonnet: "Being your slave, what should I do[e] but tend." Shakespeare. *See* Sonnets, LVII.
Sonnet: "Beshrew that heart that makes my heart to groan." Shakespeare. *See* Sonnets, CXXXIII.
Sonnet: "Bible says Sennacherib's campaign was spoiled, The." C. S. Lewis. TrCP
Sonnet: "Black pitchy night, companion of my woe." Michael Drayton. *Fr.*Idea's Mirrour. LoBV
("Black pitchy night, companion of my woe.") OBSC
Sonnet: "Breeze is sharp, the sky is hard and blue, The." Frederick Goddard Tuckerman. *See* Sonnets.
Sonnet: "Bright star! would I were steadfast as thou art." Keats. *See* Bright Star! Would I Were . . .
Sonnet: "But be contented: when that fell arrest." Shakespeare. *See* Sonnets, LXXIV.
Sonnet: "But love whilst that thou may'st be loved again." Samuel Daniel. *See* To Delia: "But love whilst that thou may'st be loved again."
Sonnet: "But now my Muse toyled with continuall care." Richard Barnfield. Sonnets, XX. PeHV

Sonnet: "But unto him came swift calamity." Frederick Goddard Tuckerman. *See* Sonnets.
Sonnet: "But we are set to strive to make our mark." Frederick Goddard Tuckerman. *See* Sonnets.
Sonnet X: "But where began the change; and what's my crime?" George Meredith. *See* Modern Love: "But where began . . ."
Sonnet: "But wherefore do not you a mightier waie." Shakespeare. *See* Sonnets, XVI.
Sonnet I: "By this he knew she wept with waking eyes." George Meredith. *See* Modern Love: "By this he knew. . . "
Sonnet: "By this low fire I often sit to woo." Frederick Goddard Tuckerman. *See* Sonnets.
Sonnet: "By what glass of resemblance may we see." William Alabaster. SBVL
Sonnet: "Caelica, I overnight was finely used." Fulke Greville. *Fr.* Caelica. JCP
("Caelica, I overnight was finely used.") AAS; EnRePo
Sonnet: "Captain or colonel, or knight in arms." Milton. *See* When the Assault Was Intended to the City.
Sonnet: "Care-charmer sleep[e], son[ne] of the sable night." Samuel Daniel. *See* Care-Charmer Sleep.
Sonnet: Cell, The. John Thelwall. NOEC
Sonnet: "Cherry-lipt Adonis in his snowie shape." Richard Barnfield. Sonnets, XVII. PeHV
Sonnet: "Chloris, whilst thou and I were free." Charles Cotton. ViBoPo
Sonnet, XXV: "Cleare moving cristall, pure as the Sunne beames." Earl of Stirling. *Fr.* Aurora. OxBS
Sonnet, A: "Cold are the crabs that crawl on yonder hills." Edward Lear. *See* Cold Are the Crabs.
Sonnet: "Come, Sleep! O Sleep, the certain knot of peace." Sir Philip Sidney. *See* Astrophel and Stella, XXXIX.
Sonnet VI: "Coming of that limpid star is twice, The." Louise Labé, *tr. fr. French by* Willis Barnstone. BoWoP
Sonnet: Common Grave, The. Sydney Thompson Dobell. NCEP
Sonnet: "Companions were we in the grove and glen!" Frederick Goddard Tuckerman. *See* Sonnets.
Sonnet: Composed after a Journey across the Hamilton Hills, Yorkshire. Wordsworth. ChER
Sonnet: Composed by the Side of Grasmere Lake. Wordsworth. ChER
Sonnet: Composed While the Author Was Engaged in Writing a Tract Occasioned by the Convention of Cintra. Wordsworth. ChER
Sonnet: Content and Resolute. William Drummond of Hawthornden. JCP
Sonnet: Corpse, The. George Moore. SyP
Sonnet: "Could then the babes from yon unshelter'd cot." Thomas Russell. OBEC
Sonnet: "Crumbled rock of London is dripping under, The." Roy Fuller. PoA
Sonnet: "Cry, crow." Hayden Carruth. NNaP
Sonnet: "Cyriack, whose grandsire on the royal bench." Milton. *See* To Cyriack Skinner ("Cyriack, whose grandsire").
Sonnet: Dante Alighieri to Guido Cavalcanti. Dante. *See* Sonnet: To Guido Cavalcanti.
Sonnet: "Daughter to that good Earl, once President." Milton. *See* To the Lady Margaret Ley.
Sonnet: "Dead men of 'ninety-two, also of 'ninety-three." Arthur Rimbaud, *tr. fr. French by* Norman Cameron. WaaP
Sonnet, A: "Dear, if you love me, hold me most your friend." Alice Duer Miller. AA
Sonnet: "Dear quirister, who from those shadows sends." William Drummond of Hawthornden. ViBoPo
(To the Nightingale.) HBV-1
Sonnet: "Dear to my soul! then leave me not forsaken!" Henry Constable. *Fr.* Diana. EIL
("Dear to my soul, then leave me not forsaken!") OBSC
Sonnet: "Dear, why should you command me to my rest." Michael Drayton. *See* Idea: "Dear, why should you command me . . . "
Sonnet: "Death be not proud, though some have called thee." John Donne. *See* Holy Sonnets.
Sonnet: "Death is all metaphors, shape in one history." Dylan Thomas. Altarwise by Owl-Light, II. MoAB
("Death is all metaphors, shape in one history.") CMoP; NoAM
Sonnet: Death Is Not without but within Him. Cino da Pistoia, *tr. fr. Italian by* Dante Gabriel Rossetti. AWP
Sonnet: Death Warnings. Francisco de Quevedo y Villegas, *tr. fr. Spanish by* John Masefield. AWP
Sonnet: Death's Last Will. William Drummond of Hawthornden. JCP
Sonnet: "Deem not, because you see me in the press." George Santayana. *See* Sonnets: "Deem not . . . "
Sonnet: "Deem not, devoid of elegance, the sage." Thomas Warton the Younger. *See* Sonnet: Written in a Blank Leaf of Dugdale's "Monasticon."
Sonnet: "Deep in a vale where rocks on every side." Gustav Rosenhane, *tr. fr. Swedish by* Sir Edmund Gosse. AWP
Sonnet: "Deere, why should you commaund me to my rest." Michael Drayton. *See* Idea: "Dear, why should you command me . . . "
Sonnet: "Devouring Time, blunt thou the lion's paws [*or* lyons pawes]." Shakespeare. *See* Sonnets, XIX.
Sonnet: "Did not the heavenly rhetoric of thine eye." Shakespeare. *See* Did Not the Heavenly Rhetoric of Thine Eye.
Sonnet: "Divers doth use (as I have heard and know)." Sir Thomas Wyatt. *See* Divers Doth Use . . .
Sonnet: Dolce Stil Novo. Gavin Ewart. GrPl
Sonnet XXIV: "Don't blame me, ladies, if I've loved. No sneers." Louise Labé, *tr. fr. French by* Willis Barnstone. BoWoP
(Sonnet: "Don't scold me, ladies, if I have loved," *tr. by* Carol Cosman.) PBWP
Sonnet: "Do'st see how unregarded now." Sir John Suckling. AnAnS-2; CaPo; ELP
Sonnet: Double Rock, The. Henry King. AnAnS-2; SeCP
Sonnet: "Downe in the depth of mine iniquity." Fulke Greville. *See* Saving God, The.
Sonnet VII: "Dull day darkens to its close, The . The sheen." "Fiona Macleod." SyP
Sonnet: "Each man me telleth I change most my devise." Sir Thomas Wyatt. SiPS
Sonnet: "Earth with thunder torn, with fire blasted, The." Fulke Greville. *Fr.* Caelica. JCP
("Earth with thunder torn[e], with fire blasted, The.) AAS; EnRePo; QFR
Sonnet: England in 1819. Shelley. *See* England in 1819.
Sonnet: "England! the time is come when thou shouldst wean." Wordsworth. ViBoPo
Sonnet: "Eternall Truth, almighty, infinite." Fulke Greville. *Fr.* Caelica. OBS
("Eternal truth, almighty, infinite.") EnRePo; OxBoCh
Sonnet: "Euclid alone has looked on Beauty bare." Edna St. Vincent Millay. *See* Euclid Alone Has Looked on Beauty Bare.
Sonnet: "Even as a lover, dreaming, unaware." Frederick Goddard Tuckerman. *See* Sonnets.
Sonnet: "Evening, as slow thy placid shades descend." William Lisle Bowles. NOEC
Sonnet: "Evil spirit, your beauty haunts me still, An." Michael Drayton. Idea, XX. LoBV
("Evil spirit, your beauty haunts me still, An.") AAS; EIL; GBL; HBV-2; NOBE; OAEP; OBSC
Sonnet: "Expense of spirit in a waste of shame, The [*or* Th']." Shakespeare. *See* Sonnets, CXXIX.
Sonnet: "Fair[e] is my love, and cruel[l] as she is fair[e]." Samuel Daniel. *See* Fair is My Love.
Sonnet: "Fair is my love, for April is her face." Robert Greene. *See* Fair Is My Love for April's in Her Face.
Sonnet: "Fair[e] is my love that feeds among the lilies." Bartholomew Griffin. Fidessa, More Chaste than Kind, XXXVII. EIL; ErPo
("Fair is my love that feeds among the lilies.") GBL; ViBoPo
(Faire Is My Love.) PoEL-2
(My Love.) TrGrPo
Sonnet: "Farewell, love, and all thy laws for ever." Sir Thomas Wyatt. *See* Renouncing of Love, A.
Sonnet: "Farewell! thou art too dear for my possessing." Shakespeare. *See* Sonnets, LXXXVII.
Sonnet: "Father, part of his double interest." John Donne. *See* Holy Sonnets.
Sonnet: "Flesh, I have knocked at many a dusty door." John Masefield. *See* Flesh, I Have Knocked at Many a Dusty Door.
Sonnet: "For Nature daily through her grand design." Frederick Goddard Tuckerman. *See* Sonnets.
Sonnet: "For shame! deny that thou bear'st love to any." Shakespeare. *See* Sonnets, X.
Sonnet: "Forward violet thus did I chide, The." Shakespeare. *See* Sonnets, XCIX.
Sonnet: "Fra banc to banc, fra wod to wod, I rin." Mark Alexander Boyd. *See* Fra Bank to Bank . . .
Sonnet: French and the Spanish Guerillas, The. Wordsworth. *See* French and the Spanish Guerillas, The.
Sonnet: "Fresh morning gusts have blown away all fear." Keats. EnRP
Sonnet: "From fairest creatures we desire increase." Shakespeare. *See* Sonnets, I.
Sonnet IV: "From that first flash when awful Love took flame." Louise Labé, *tr. fr. French by* Willis Barnstone. BoWoP
Sonnet: "From you have I been absent in the spring." Shakespeare. *See* Sonnets, XCVIII.
Sonnet: "Full many a glorious morning have I seen[e]." Shakespeare. *See* Sonnets, XXXIII.

Sonnet: "Gertrude and Gulielma, sister-twins." Frederick Goddard Tuckerman. *See* Sonnets.
Sonnet: "Give me the darkest corner of a cloud." R. W. Dixon. LO
Sonnet: "Go from me. Yet I feel that I shall stand." Elizabeth Barrett Browning. *See* Sonnets from the Portuguese, "Go from me . . . "
Sonnet: "Go you, O winds that blow from north to south." Alexander Craig. EIL
Sonnet: "God and man, though in this amphitheatre." William Alabaster. SBVL
Sonnet: Guido Cavalcanti to Dante. Guido Cavalcanti. *See* To Dante.
Sonnet: He Argues His Case with Death. Cecco Angiolieri da Siena, *tr. fr. Italian by* Dante Gabriel Rossetti. AWP
Sonnet: "He came in silvern armor, trimmed with black." Gwendolyn B. Bennett. AmNP; CDC; PoBA; PoNe
Sonnet: He Compares All Things with His Lady, and Finds Them Wanting. Guido Cavalcanti, *tr. fr. Italian by* Dante Gabriel Rossetti. AWP
Sonnet: He Craves Interpreting of a Dream of His. Dante da Maiano, *tr. fr. Italian by* Dante Gabriel Rossetti. AWP
Sonnet: He Is Out of Heart with His Time. Guerzo di Montecanti, *tr. fr. Italian by* Dante Gabriel Rossetti. AWP
Sonnet: He Is Past All Help. Cecco Angiolieri da Siena, *tr. fr. Italian by* Dante Gabriel Rossetti. AWP
Sonnet: He Jests Concerning His Poverty. Bartolomeo di Sant' Angelo, *tr. fr. Italian by* Dante Gabriel Rossetti. AWP
Sonnet: He Rails against Dante, Who Had Censured His Homage to Becchina. Cecco Angiolieri da Siena, *tr. fr. Italian by* Dante Gabriel Rossetti. AWP
Sonnet: He Speaks of a Third Love of His. Guido Cavalcanti, *tr. fr. Italian by* Dante Gabriel Rossetti. AWP
Sonnet: He Will Not Be Too Deeply in Love. Cecco Angiolieri da Siena, *tr. fr. Italian by* Dante Gabriel Rossetti. AWP
Sonnet: He Will Praise His Lady. Guido Guinicelli, *tr. fr. Italian by* Dante Gabriel Rossetti. AWP
Sonnet: "Here hold this glove (this milk-white cheveril glove)." Richard Barnfield. Sonnets, XIV. PeHV
Sonnet: "Here in the self is all that men can know." John Masefield. *Fr.* Lollingdon Downs. AWP
Sonnet XVIII: "Here Jack and Tom are paired with Moll and Meg." George Meredith. *See* Here Jack and Tom Are Paired with Moll and Meg.
Sonnet: "Highway, since you my chief Parnassus be." Sir Philip Sidney. *See* Astrophel and Stella, LXXXIV.
Sonnet, A: "His golden locks time hath to silver turned." George Peele. *See* His Golden Locks . . .
Sonnet: "His heart was in his garden; but his brain." Frederick Goddard Tuckerman. *See* Sonnets.
Sonnet: "How can I then return in happy plight." Shakespeare. *See* Sonnets, XXVIII.
Sonnet: "How do I love thee? Let me count the ways." Elizabeth Barrett Browning. *See* Sonnets from the Portuguese: "How do I love thee . . ."
Sonnet: "How like a winter hath my absence been[e]." Shakespeare. *See* Sonnets, XCVII.
Sonnet: "How many paltry, foolish, painted things." Michael Drayton. *See* Idea: "How many paltry, foolish, painted things."
Sonnet: "How most unworthy, echoing in mine ears." Frederick Goddard Tuckerman. *See* Sonnets.
Sonnet: "How oft, when thou, my music, music play'st." Shakespeare. *See* Sonnets, CXXVIII.
Sonnet: "How soon hath time, the subtle thief of youth." Milton. *See* How Soon Hath Time.
Sonnet: "How sweet and lovely dost thou make the shame." Shakespeare. *See* Sonnets, XCV.
Sonnet: "How that vast heaven intitled First is rolled." William Drummond of Hawthornden. EIL
Sonnet: "I abide and abide and better abide." Sir Thomas Wyatt. SiPS
("I abide and abide and better abide.") EnLoPo; BoLoP
Sonnet: "I am a little world made cunningly." John Donne. *See* Holy Sonnets.
Sonnet XLI: "I, being born a woman and distressed." Edna St. Vincent Millay. *See* I, Being Born a Women and Distressed.
Sonnet: "I envy not Endymion now no more." Earl of Stirling. *Fr.* Aurora. EIL
Sonnet: "I fear to me such fortune be assign'd." William Drummond of Hawthornden. NCEP
Sonnet: "I find no peace, and all my war is done." Petrarch. *See* Description of the Contrarious Passions . . .
Sonnet XVII: "I flee the city, temples, and each place." Louise Labé, *tr. fr. French by* Willis Barnstone. BoWoP
Sonnet: "I had no thought of violets of late." Alice Dunbar Nelson. BANP; BlSi; CDC; PoBA; PoNe
Sonnet: "I have not spent the April of my time." Bartholomew Griffin. Fidessa, More Chaste than Kind, XXXV. AAS; EIL
(Youth.) OBSC
Sonnet: "I hereby swear that to uphold your house." Elinor Wylie. *See* I Hereby Swear That to Uphold Your House.
Sonnet: "I know I am but summer to your heart." Edna St. Vincent Millay. HBMV
Sonnet: "I know that all beneath the moon decays." William Drummond of Hawthornden. *See* I Know That All beneath the Moon Decays.
Sonnet VIII: "I live, I die, I burn myself and drown." Louise Labé, *tr. fr. French by* Willis Barnstone. BoWoP
Sonnet: "I must not grieve my Love, whose eyes would read." Samuel Daniel. *See* To Delia: "I must not grieve my love . . ."
Sonnet: "I never see the red rose crown the year." John Masefield. *Fr.* Sonnets ("Long, long ago"). GoYe
Sonnet: "I on my horse, and Love on me, doth try." Sir Philip Sidney. *See* Astrophel and Stella, XLIX.
Sonnet: "I saw magic on a green country road." Michael Hartnett. BIrV
Sonnet: "I saw the object of my pining thought." Thomas Watson. EIL
Sonnet 21: "I start awake at night afraid of death." Paul Goodman. VGW
Sonnet XX: "I was foretold that on a certain day." Louise Labé, *tr. fr. French by* Willis Barnstone. BoWoP
(Sonnet: "Seer foretold that I would love one day, A," *tr. by* Joan Keefe *and* Richard Terdiman.) PBWP
Sonnet: "I watched the sea for hours blind with sun." Winfield Townley. Scott. MiAP
Sonnet: "Idly she yawned, and threw her heavy hair." George Moore. ErPo
Sonnet: "If ever Sorrow spoke from soul that loves." Henry Constable. *Fr.* Diana. EIL
Sonnet: "If faithfull soules be alike glorifi'd." John Donne. *See* Holy Sonnets.
Sonnet XIII: "If I could linger on his lovely chest." Louise Labé, *tr. fr. French by* Aliki *and* Willis Barnstone. BoWoP
Sonnet: "If it must be; if it must be, O God!" David Gray. *Fr.* In the Shadows. BSV; OxBS
Sonnet: "If poysonous mineralls, and if that tree." John Donne. *See* Holy Sonnets
Sonnet: "If their bee nothing new, but that which is." Shakespeare. *See* Sonnets, LIX.
Sonnet: "If thou must love me, let it be for naught." Elizabeth Barrett Browning. *See* Sonnets from the Portuguese: "If thou must love me . . ."
Sonnet: "If thou survive my well-contented day." Shakespeare. *See* Sonnets, XXXII.
Sonnet, XXVI: "Ile give thee leave my love, in beauties field." Earl of Stirling. *Fr.* Aurora. OxBS
Sonnet: In Absence from Becchina. Cecco Angiolieri da Siena, *tr. fr. Italian by* Dante Gabriel Rossetti. AWP
Sonnet: "In every dream thy lovely features rise." William Barnes. BoLoP
Sonnet: "In faith I do[e] not love thee with mine eyes." Shakespeare. *See* Sonnets, CXLI.
Sonnet: "In minds pure glasse when I my selfe behold." William Drummond of Hawthornden. OBS
Sonnet: "In truth, O Love, with what a boyish kind." Sir Philip Sidney. *See* Astrophel and Stella, Sonnets, XI.
Sonnet: "Ingratitude, how deadly is the smart." Anna Seward. NOEC
Sonnet: "Innumerable Beauties, thou white haire." Lord Herbert of Cherbury. PoEL-2
Sonnet XI: "Is God invisible? This very room." Adele Greeff. GoYe
Sonnet: "Is it for fear to wet a widow's eye." Shakespeare. *See* Sonnets, IX.
Sonnet: "Is it thy wil, thy Image should keepe open." Shakespeare. *See* Sonnets, LXI.
Sonnet: "Is there a great green commonwealth of Thought." John Masefield. *See* Is There a Great Green Commonwealth of Thought.
Sonnet: It Is a Beauteous Evening [Calm and Free]. Wordsworth. *See* It Is a Beauteous Evening.
Sonnet: "It is as true as strange, else trial feigns." John Davies of Hereford. EIL
Sonnet: "It is not death, that sometime in a sigh." Thomas Hood. LoBV; OBNC; ViBoPo
(Death.) OBEV
(It Is Not Death.) OBRV
Sonnet: "It is not to be thought of that the Flood." Wordsworth. *See* It Is Not to Be Thought Of.
Sonnet XLV: "It is the season of the sweet wild rose." George Meredith. *Fr.* Modern Love. GBL; NBM; PoEL-5
Sonnet: "It shall be said I died for Coelia!" William Percy. *Fr.* Coelia. EIL
("It shall be sayd I dy'de for Coelia.") AAS
Sonnet: "Jesus is born. Peace, such high words forbear." William Alabaster. SBVL
Sonnet: "Keen, fitful gusts are whisp'ring here and there." Keats. *See* Keen, Fitful Gusts.
Sonnet XVIII: "Kiss me again, re-kiss and kiss me whole." Louise Labé, *tr. fr. French by* Raymond Oliver. WPOW

(Sonnet XVIII: "Kiss me again, rekiss, kiss me more," *tr. by* Willis Barnstone.) BoWoP
Sonnet: Lady Laments for Her Lost Lover, by Similitude of a Falcon, A. *Unknown, tr. fr. Italian by* Dante Gabriel Rossetti. AWP
Sonnet: "Lamp of heaven's crystal hall that brings the hours." William Drummond of Hawthornden. JCP
Sonnet: "Last All Saints' holy-day, even now gone by." Dante. *See* Sonnet: Of Beatrice de' Portinari, on All Saints Day.
Sonnet: "Lawrence of vertuous father vertuous son." Milton. *See* To Mr. Lawrence.
Sonnet: "Leave me, all sweet refrains my lip hath made." Luis de Camoes, *tr. fr. Spanish by* Richard Garnett. AWP
Sonnet: Leaves. William Barnes. *See* Leaves.
Sonnet: "Let me confess that we two must be twain." Shakespeare. *See* Sonnets, XXXVI.
Sonnet: "Let me not to the marriage of true mind[e]s." Shakespeare. *See* Sonnets, CXVI.
Sonnet: "Let others of the world's decaying tell." Earl of Stirling. *Fr.* Aurora. EIL
Sonnet: "Let others sing of knights and paladins." Samuel Daniel. *See* To Delia: "Let others sing . . ."
Sonnet: "Let those who are in favour with their stars." Shakespeare. *See* Sonnets, XXV.
Sonnet: "Let us leave talking of angelic hosts." Elinor Wylie. *Fr.* One Person. OxBA
Sonnet: "Lift not the painted veil which those who live." Shelley. EnRP; FaBoEn; OBNC; SyP
Sonnet: "Like as the fountain of all light created." William Alabaster. *See* Incarnatio Est Maximum Donum Dei.
Sonnet: "Like as the waves make towards the pebbled shore." Shakespeare. *See* Sonnets, LX.
Sonnet: "Like as, to make our appetites more keen." Shakespeare. *See* Sonnets, CXVIII.
Sonnet: "Like Memnon's rock, touched with the rising sun." Giles Fletcher the Elder. Licia, XLVII. AAS; EIL; FF
Sonnet: "Like to an hermit poor, in place obscure." *At. to* Sir Walter Ralegh. *See* Like to a Hermit Poor.
Sonnet: "Lo, as a careful housewife runs to catch." Shakespeare. *See* Sonnets, CXLIII.
Sonnet: "Lock up, fair lids, the treasure of my heart." Sir Philip Sidney. *See* Sleep.
Sonnet: "Long time a child, and still a child, when years." Hartley Coleridge. *See* Long Time a Child.
Sonnet: "Look, Delia, how we esteem the half-blown rose." Samuel Daniel. *See* To Delia: "Look, Delia, how we esteem the half-blown rose."
Sonnet: "Look in thy glass, and tell the face thou viewest." Shakespeare. *See* Sonnets, III.
Sonnet: "Looking into the windows that doom has broken." George Woodcock. NeBP
Sonnet: "Lord, what a change within us one short hour." Richard Chevenix Trench. *See* Prayer: "Lord, what a change . . ."
Sonnet: "Love is not all: it is not meat nor drink." Edna St. Vincent Millay. MasP
("Love is not all: it is not meat nor drink.") CMoP; FPL; HAP; NoAM; OxBA; PrIm; TAP
Sonnet: "Love is the peace, whereto all thoughts do strive." Fulke Greville. *Fr.* Caelica. JCP
("Love is the peace whereto all thoughts doe strive.") AAS
Sonnet: "Love is too young to know what conscience is." Shakespeare. *See* Sonnets, CLI.
Sonnet: Lovesight. Dante Gabriel Rossetti. *See* Lovesight.
Sonnet XII: "Lute, companion of my calamity." Louise Labé, *tr. fr. French by* Aliki *and* Willis Barnstone. BoWoP
Sonnet: Lyke as a Ship. Spenser. *See* Amoretti, XXXIV.
Sonnet: "Madam, 'tis true, your beauties move." Sidney Godolphin. JCP
Sonnet: "Man, dream[e] no more of curious mysteries." Fulke Greville. *Fr.* Caelica. JCP; MePo; OBS; QFR
("Man, dream[e] no more of curious mysteries.") EnRePo; QFR
Sonnet XLIII: "Mark where the pressing wind shoots javelin-like." George Meredith. *See* Modern Love: "Mark where the pressing . . ."
Sonnet: "Master and the slave go hand in hand, The." E. A. Robinson. PP
Sonnet: "Men call you fair, and you do credit it." Spenser. *See* Amoretti, LXXIX.
Sonnet: "Men, that delight to multiply desire." Fulke Greville. *Fr.* Caelica. OBS
Sonnet: "Methought I saw my late espoused saint." Milton. *See* On His Deceased Wife.
Sonnet: "Milton! thou shouldst be living at this hour." Wordsworth. *See* London, 1802.
Sonnet: "Mine eyes beheld the blessed pity spring." Dante, *tr. fr. Italian by* Dante Gabriel Rossetti. La Vita Nuova, XXIII. PoPl
Sonnet: Morning comes, The; not slow, with reddening gold." Frederick Goddard Tuckerman. *See* Sonnets.
Sonnet: "Most glorious Lord of Life, that on this day." Spenser. *See* Amoretti, LXVIII.
Sonnet: "Most men know love but as a part of life." Henry Timrod. HBV-2
Sonnet: "Muses that sing Love's sensual empery [emperie]." George Chapman. *Fr.* A Coronet for His Mistress Philosophie. EIL; LoBV
(Love and Philosophy.) OBSC; SeCePo
Sonnet: "Music[k] to hear[e], why hear'st thou music[k] sadly?" Shakespeare. *See* Sonnets, VIII.
Sonnet: "My Anna! though thine earthly steps are done." Frederick Goddard Tuckerman. *See* Sonnets.
Sonnet: "My Anna! When for her my head was bowed." Frederick Goddard Tuckerman. *See* Sonnets.
Sonnet: "My dream a drink with Lonnie Johnson." Ted Berrigan. NoAM
Sonnet: "My duchess was the werst she laffed she bitte." Ernest Walsh. ErPo
Sonnet: "My galley charged with forgetfulness." Sir Thomas Wyatt. SiPS
Sonnet: "My glass shall not persuade me I am old." Shakespeare. *See* Sonnets, XXII.
Sonnet: "My God, where is that ancient heat towards thee." George Herbert. AnAnS-1; OAEL-1
Sonnet: "My lady's presence makes the roses red." Henry Constable. *Fr.* Diana. EIL
Sonnet: "My Love, I cannot thy rare beauties place." William Smith. *See* My Love, I Cannot Thy Rare Beauties Place.
Sonnet: "My love is as a fever, longing still." Shakespeare. *See* Sonnets, CXLVII.
Sonnet: "My love is strengthen'd, though more weak in seeming." Shakespeare. *See* Sonnets, CII.
Sonnet: "My love took scorn my service to retain." Sir Thomas Wyatt. SiPS
Sonnet: "My lute, be as thou wast when thou didst grow." William Drummond of Hawthornden. EIL; LoBV; OBS; ViBoPo
Sonnet: "My mistress' eyes are nothing like the sun." Shakespeare. *See* Sonnets, CXXX.
Sonnet: "My simple heart, bred in provincial tenderness." G. S. Fraser. NeBP
Sonnet: "My soul surcharged with grief now loud complains." Rachel Morpurgo, *tr. fr. Hebrew by* Nina Davis Salaman. TrJP
Sonnet: "My true Love hath my heart, and I have his." Sir Philip Sidney. *See* My True Love Hath My Heart.
Sonnet: "No longer mourn for me when I am dead." Shakespeare. *See* Sonnets, LXXI.
Sonnet: "No more be grieved at that which thou hast done." Shakespeare. *See* Sonnets, XXXV.
Sonnet: "No, Time, thou shalt not boast that I do change." Shakespeare. *See* Sonnets, CXXIII.
Sonnet: "No worst, there is none. Pitched past pitch of grief." Gerard Manley Hopkins. *See* No Worst, There Is None.
Sonnet: "Not from the stars do I my judgement pluck." Shakespeare. *See* Sonnets, XIV.
Sonnet: "Not, I'll not, carrion comfort, Despair, not feast on thee." Gerard Manley Hopkins. *See* Carrion Comfort.
Sonnet: "Not marble, nor the gilded monuments." Shakespeare. *See* Sonnets, LV.
Sonnet: "Not mine own fears, nor the prophetic soul." Shakespeare. *See* Sonnets, CVII.
Sonnet I: "Not Ulysses, no, nor any other man." Louise Labé, *tr. fr. Italian by* Willis Barnstone. BoWoP
Sonnet: "Not with libations, but with shouts and laughter." Edna St. Vincent Millay. HBMV
(Not with Libations.) WHA
Sonnet: "Not with vain tears, when we're beyond the sun." Rupert Brooke. BrPo
Sonnet: "Not wrongly moved by this dismaying scene." William Empson. LiTM; WaP
Sonnet: "Now keep that long revolver at your side." George Hetherington. NeIP
Sonnet: "Now the bat circles on the breeze of eve." Anne Radcliffe. WPE
Sonnet I: "Now there is a love of which Dante does not speak unkindly." Robert Duncan. GP
Sonnet: "Nuns fret not at their convent's narrow room." Wordsworth. *See* Nuns Fret Not . . .
Sonnet: Nuptial Sleep. Dante Gabriel Rossetti. *See* Nuptial Sleep.
Sonnet: "Nurse-life wheat within his green husk growing, The." Fulke Greville. *See* Youth and Maturity.
Sonnet XXII: "O blazing Sun, how happy you are there." Louise Labé, *tr. fr. French by* Willis Barnstone. BoWoP
Sonnet XI: "O eyes clear with beauty, O tender gaze." Louise Labé, *tr. fr. French by* Willis Barnstone. BoWoP

Sonnet: "O false and treacherous Probability." Fulke Greville. *Fr.* Caelica. OBS
("O false and treacherous Probability.") AAS; OxBoCh
Sonnet II: "O handsome chestnut eyes, evasive gaze." Louise Labé, *tr. fr. French by* Willis Barnstone. BoWoP
Sonnet: "O hard endeavor, to blend in with these." Frederick Goddard Tuckerman. *See* Sonnets.
Sonnet: "O how much more doth beauty beauteous seem." Shakespeare. *See* Sonnets, LIV.
Sonnet III: "O interminable desires, O futile hope." Louise Labé, *tr. fr. French by* Willis Barnstone. BoWoP
Sonnet, A: "O lovely O most charming pug." Marjory Fleming. *See* Sonnet on a Monkey, A.
Sonnet: "O me! what eyes hath love put in my head." Shakespeare. *See* Sonnets, CXLVIII.
Sonnet: "O might those sighs and tears returne again." John Donne. *See* Holy Sonnets.
Sonnet: "O my black soule! now thou art summoned." John Donne. *See* Holy Sonnets.
Sonnet: "O, never say that I was false of heart." Shakespeare. *See* Sonnets, CIX.
Sonnet: "O nightingale, that on yon bloomy spray." Milton. *See* To the Nightingale.
Sonnet: "O shady vales, O fair enriched meads." Thomas Lodge. *Fr.* A Margarite of America. ElL; OBSC
Sonnet: "O! that you were yourself; but, love, you are." Shakespeare. *See* Sonnets, XIII.
Sonnet: "O time! who knows't a lenient hand to lay." William Lisle Bowles. *See* Time and Grief.
Sonnet: "O world, thou choosest not the better part!" George Santayana. *See* Sonnets: "O world, thou choosest . . ."
Sonnet: Of All He Would Do. Cecco Angiolieri da Siena, *tr. fr. Italian by* Dante Gabriel Rossetti. AWP
Sonnet: Of an Ill-Favored Lady. Guido Cavalcanti, *tr. fr. Italian by* Dante Gabriel Rossetti. AWP
Sonnet: Of Beatrice de' Portinari, on All Saints' Day. Dante, *tr. fr. Italian by* Dante Gabriel Rossetti. AWP
(Sonnet: "Last All Saints' holy-day, even now gone by.") GoBC
Sonnet: Of Beauty and Duty. Dante, *tr. fr. Italian by* Dante Gabriel Rossetti. AWP
Sonnet: Of Becchina in a Rage. Cecco Angiolieri da Siena, *tr. fr. Italian by* Dante Gabriel Rossetti. AWP
Sonnet: Of Becchina, the Shoemaker's Daughter. Cecco Angiolieri da Siena, *tr. fr. Italian by* Dante Gabriel Rossetti. AWP
Sonnet: Of His Lady in Heaven. Jacopo da Lentino, *tr. fr. Italian by* Dante Gabriel Rossetti. AWP
Sonnet: Of His Lady's Face. Jacopo da Lentino, *tr. fr. Italian by* Dante Gabriel Rossetti. AWP
Sonnet: Of His Pain from a New Love. Guido Cavalcanti, *tr. fr. Italian by* Dante Gabriel Rossetti. AWP
Sonnet: Of Love, in Honor of His Mistress Becchina. Cecco Angiolieri da Siena, *tr. fr. Italian by* Dante Gabriel Rossetti. AWP
Sonnet: Of Love in Men and Devils. Cecco Angiolieri da Siena, *tr. fr. Italian by* Dante Gabriel Rossetti. AWP
Sonnet: Of Moderation and Tolerance. Guido Guinicelli, *tr. fr. Italian by* Dante Gabriel Rossetti. AWP
Sonnet: Of the Eyes of a Certain Mandetta. Guido Cavalcanti, *tr. fr. Italian by* Dante Gabriel Rossetti. AWP
Sonnet: Of the Grave of Selvaggia, on the Monte della Sambuca. Cino da Pistoia, *tr. fr. Italian by* Dante Gabriel Rossetti. AWP
Sonnet: Of the Making of Master Messerin. Rustico di Filippo, *tr. fr. Italian by* Dante Gabriel Rossetti. AWP
Sonnet: Of the 20th of June 1291. Cecco Angiolieri da Siena, *tr. fr. Italian by* Dante Gabriel Rossetti. AWP
Sonnet: "Of thee (kind boy) I ask no red and white." Sir John Suckling. AnAnS-2; CaPo; MeLP; MePo; NoP; OBS; OxBoLi; SeCP; SeCV-1
(Song: "Of thee (kind boy) I ask no red and white.") LoBV
Sonnet: Of Virtue. Folgore da San Geminiano, *tr. fr. Italian by* Dante Gabriel Rossetti. AWP
Sonnet: Of Why He Is Unhanged. Cecco Angiolieri da Siena, *tr. fr. Italian by* Dante Gabriel Rossetti. AWP
Sonnet: Of Why He Would Be a Scullion. Cecco Angiolieri da Siena, *tr. fr. Italian by* Dante Gabriel Rossetti. AWP
Sonnet: "Oft I have seen at some cathedral door." Longfellow. *See* Oft I Have Seen at Some Cathedral Door.
Sonnet: Oft o'er My Brain. Samuel Taylor Coleridge. ChER
Sonnet: "Oh! Death will find me, long before I tire." Rupert Brooke. MoBrPo
(Oh! Death Will Find Me.) HBV-1; PoRA
Sonnet: "Oh for a poet—for a beacon bright." E. A. Robinson. *See* Oh for a Poet—for a Beacon Bright.
Sonnet: "Oh! for some honest lover's ghost." Sir John Suckling. AnAnS-1; FaBoEn; JCP; MeLP; MePo; OBS; PoEL-3; SeCP; SeCV-1
(Actuality.) LoBV
(Doubt of Martyrdom, A.) BoLoP; CaPo; HBV-1; NOBE: OBEV; PoPle
("O! for some honest lover's ghost.") BXAP; Par
Sonnet: "Oh for the face and footstep!—Woods and shores!" Frederick Goddard Tuckerman. *See* Sonnets.
Sonnet: "Oh, how much more doeth beauty beauteous seem." Shakespeare. *See* Sonnets, LIV.
Sonnet: "Oh, if thou knew'st how thou thyself dost harm." Earl of Stirling. *See* To Aurora.
Sonnet: "Oh, my belovèd, have you thought of this." Edna St. Vincent Millay. HBMV
Sonnet: "Oh, never say that I was false of heart." Shakespeare. *See* Sonnets, CIX.
Sonnet: "Oh that you were yourself! But, love, you are." Shakespeare. *See* Sonnets, XIII.
Sonnet: "Oh, think not I am faithful to a vow!" Edna St. Vincent Millay. *See* Oh, Think Not I Am Faithful to a Vow.
Sonnet: "Oh, to vex me, contraryes meet in one." John Donne. Holy Sonnets, XXIX. AnAnS-1; MasP; OAEL-1; PoEL-2
(Devout Fits.) SeCePo
Sonnet: On a Picture of Leander. Keats. EnRP
Sonnet: On First Looking into Chapman's Homer. Keats. *See* On First Looking into Chapman's Homer.
Sonnet: On His Blindness. Milton. *See* On His Blindness.
Sonnet: On His Having Arrived at the Age of Twenty-three. Milton. *See* How Soon Hath Time.
Sonnet: On the Detection of a False Friend. Guido Cavalcanti, *tr. fr. Italian by* Dante Gabriel Rossetti. AWP
Sonnet: On the Late Massacre in Piedmont. Milton. *See* On the Late Massacre in Piedmont.
Sonnet: On the 9th of June 1290. Dante, *tr. fr. Italian by* Dante Gabriel Rossetti. AWP
Sonnet: On the Religious Memorie of Mrs. Catherine Thomason My Christian Friend Deceas'd Decem. 1646. Milton. OBS
Sonnet: On the Sea. Keats. *See* On the Sea.
Sonnet: "One day I wrote her name upon the strand." Spenser. *See* Amoretti, LXXV.
Sonnet: "One still dark night, I sat alone and wrote." Frederick Goddard Tuckerman. *See* Sonnets.
Sonnet: "Open wound which has been healed anew, An." Richard Chenevix Trench. TrPWD
Sonnet: "Or I shall live your epitaph to make." Shakespeare. *See* Sonnets, LXXXI.
Sonnet: "Orgasm completely, The." Tom Clark. CoAP
Sonnet: Ozymandias. Shelley. *See* Ozymandias.
Sonnet: "Passing glance, a lightning long the skies, A." William Drummond of Hawthornden. ViBoPo
Sonnet: "Patience, hard thing! the hard thing but to pray." Gerard Manley Hopkins. FaBoEn; OBNC
(Patience, Hard Thing!) CoBMV; Prf
Sonnet: "Perhaps a dream; yet surely truth has beamed." Frederick Goddard Tuckerman. *See* Sonnets.
Sonnet: "Point where beauty and intelligence meet, The." Gavin Ewart. WaP
Sonnet: "Ponder thy cares, and sum them all in one." Sir David Murray. *Fr.* Caelia. ElL
Sonnet: "Poor soul, the center of my sinful earth." Shakespeare. *See* Sonnets, CXLVI.
Sonnet: Rapture Concerning His Lady, A. Guido Cavalcanti, *tr. fr. Italian by* Dante Gabriel Rossetti. AWP
(Sonnet [*or* Sonetto] VII: "Who is she that comes, makyng turn every man's eye," *tr. by* Ezra Pound.) CTC; OBVE
Sonnet: "Record is nothing, and the hero great." Lord De Tabley. EBVV
Sonnet: "Remember me when I am gone away." Christina Rossetti. *See* Remember.
Sonnet XIII: "Rise up, rise up, Jack Spratt. And you, his wife." Winfield Townley Scott. ErPo
Sonnet: "Roll on, sad world! Not Mercury or Mars." Frederick Goddard Tuckerman. *See* Sonnets.
Sonnet: "Saints have adored the lofty soul of you." Charles Hamilton Sorley. *See* Two Sonnets.
Sonnet: "Say that thou didst forsake me for some fault." Shakespeare. *See* Sonnets, LXXXIX.
Sonnet: "Say what you will, and scratch my heart to find." Edna St. Vincent Millay. HBMV
Sonnet: "Scorn not the sonnet; critic, you have frown'd." Wordsworth. OBEV; TrGrPo
Sonnet: "Seer foretold that I would love one day, A." Louise Labé. *See* Sonnet XX: "I was foretold that on a certain day."

Sonnet: September, 1802. Wordsworth. *See* Near Dover, September 1802.
Sonnet: September, 1815. Wordsworth. *See* September, 1815.
Sonnet: September 1, 1802. Wordsworth. ChER
Sonnet: "Shall I compare thee to a summer's day?" Shakespeare. *See* Sonnets, XVIII.
Sonnet 4: "Shall I wasting in Dispaire." George Wither. *See* Shall I, Wasting in Despair.
Sonnet: "She is so young, and never never before." Edward Davison. ErPo
Sonnet: "She took the dappled partridge flecked with blood." Tennyson. CABA
("She took the dappled patridge fleckt with blood.") FM
Sonnet: "Show me deare Christ, thy spouse, so bright and clear." John Donne. *See* Holy Sonnets.
Sonnet: "Sighing, and sadly sitting by my Love." Richard Barnfield. Sonnets, XI. PeHV
Sonnet: Silence. Thomas Hood. *See* Silence.
Sonnet: "Silver herring throbbed thick in my seine, The." Kenneth Leslie. *See* Silver Herring Throbbed . . .
Sonnet: "Sin of self-love possesseth all mine eye." Shakespeare. *See* Sonnets, LXII.
Sonnet: "Since brass, nor stone, nor earth, nor boundless sea." Shakespeare. *See* Sonnets, LXV.
Sonnet: "Since I keep only what I give away." George Hetherington. NeIP
Sonnet: "Since she whom I lov'd hath payd her last debt." John Donne. *See* Holy Sonnets.
Sonnet: "Since there's no help, come let us kiss and part." Michael Drayton. *See* Idea: "Since there's no help . . ."
Sonnet: "Sits by a fireplace, the seducer talks." Leonard Wolf. ErPo
Sonnet: "Sleep, Silence' child, sweet father of soft rest." William Drummond of Hawthornden. *See* Sleep, Silence' Child.
Sonnet: "So am I as the rich, whose blessed key." Shakespeare. *See* Sonnets, LII.
Sonnet: "So are you to my thoughts as food to life." Shakespeare. *See* Sonnets, LXXV.
Sonnet: "So is it not with me as with that Muse." Shakespeare. *See* Sonnets, XXI.
Sonnet: "So now I have confessed that he is thine." Shakespeare. *See* Sonnets, CXXXIV.
Sonnet: "So shall I live, supposing thou art true." Shakespeare. *See* Sonnets, XCIII.
Sonnet: "So shoots a star as doth my mistress glide." John Davies of Hereford. ElL
Sonnet: "Some talk of Ganymede th' Idalian boy." Richard Barnfield. Sonnets, XII. PeHV
Sonnet II: "Some things are very dear to me." Gwendolyn B. Bennett. AmNP; BANP; CDC; PoBA; PoNe
Sonnet: "Sometimes I wish that I his pillow were." Richard Barnfield. Sonnets, VIII. PeHV.
Sonnet: "Sometimes the night echoes to prideless wailing." John Berryman. NoAM
Sonnet, The: "Sonnet is a fruit which long hath slept, The." John Addington Symonds. HBV-2
Sonnet, A [*or* The]: "Sonnet is a moment's monument, A." Dante Gabriel Rossetti. The House of Life, *introd.* HBV-2; HeIP; NoP; VLP
(Sonnet Is a Moment's Monument, A.) OAEP; PP; ViBoPo
Sonnet, The: "Sonnet, she told the crowd of bearded, The." Daniel Hoffman. GP
Sonnet: "Spit in my face you Jewes, and pierce my side." John Donne. *See* Holy Sonnets.
Sonnet: "Sporting at fancie, setting light by love." Richard Barnfield. Sonnets, I. PeHV
Sonnet: "Still pressing through these weeping solitudes." Frederick Goddard Tuckerman. *See* Sonnets.
Sonnet: "Such, such is Death: no triumph: no defeat." Charles Hamilton Sorley. *See* Two Sonnets.
Sonnet: Superscription, A. Dante Gabriel Rossetti. *See* Superscription, A.
Sonnet: Suppos'd to Be Written at Lemnos. Thomas Russell. FaBoEn; NOEC; OBEC
(Philoctetes.) LoBV
Sonnet: "Sure Lord, there is enough in thee to dry." George Herbert. AnAnS-1
Sonnet: Surprised by Joy. Wordsworth. *See* Surprised by Joy.
Sonnet: "Sweet corrall lips, where Nature's treasure lies." Richard Barnfield. Sonnets, VI. PeHV
Sonnet: "Sweet love, renew thy force, be it not said." Shakespeare. *See* Sonnets, LVI.
Sonnet: "Sweet poets of the gentle antique line." John Hamilton Reynolds. OBRV
Sonnet: "Sweet semi-circled Cynthia played at maw." John Taylor. *See* Mockado, Fustian, and Motley.
Sonnet: "Sweet soul, which in the April of thy years." William Drummond of Hawthornden. JCP
Sonnet: "Sweet Spring, thou turn'st with all thy goodly [*or* goodlie] train[e]." William Drummond of Hawthornden. *See* Spring Bereaved 2.
Sonnet: "Sweet Thames I honour thee, not for thou art." Richard Barnfield. Sonnets, VII. PeHV
Sonnet: "Take all my loves, my Love, yea, take them all." Shakespeare. *See* Sonnets, XL.
Sonnet, A: "Take all of me,—I am thine own, heart, soul." Amélie Rives. AA
Sonnet: "Tell me[e] no more how fair[e] she[e] is." Henry King. AnAnS-2; CavP; EnLoPo; MeLP; MePo; OBS; SeCP; ViBoPo
(That Distant Bliss.) TrGrPo
Sonnet: "That learned Graecian (who did so excell)." William Drummond of Hawthornden. OBS
Sonnet: "That thou hast her, it is not all my grief." Shakespeare. *See* Sonnets, XLII.
Sonnet: "That time of year mayst in me behold." Shakespeare. *See* Sonnets, LXXIII.
Sonnet: "That you were once unkind befriends me now." Shakespeare. *See* Sonnets, CXX.
Sonnet: "Then hate me when thou wilt; if ever, now. Shakespeare. *See* Sonnets, XC.
Sonnet: "Then let not winter's ragged hand deface." Shakespeare. *See* Sonnets, VI.
Sonnet: "Then whilst that Latmos did contain her bliss." Earl of Stirling. Aurora, XXVIII. ViBoPo
Sonnet: There Is a Bondage Worse. Wordsworth. ChER
Sonnet: "There, on the darkened deathbed, dies the brain." John Masefield. EBEV
(There, on the Darkened Deathbed.) DL; LiTB
Sonnet: "There was an Indian, who had known no change." J. C. Squire. *See* Discovery, The.
Sonnet: "They may suppose, because I would not cloy your ear." John Berryman. NoP
Sonnet: "They say that shadow[e]s of deceased ghosts." Joshua Sylvester. ElL; OBS
Sonnet: "They that have power to hurt, and will do none." Shakespeare. *See* Sonnets, XCIV.
Sonnet: "Thine eyes I love, and they, as pitying me." Shakespeare. *See* Sonnets, CXXXII.
Sonnet: "This infant world has taken long to make." George Macdonald. OBVV
Sonnet: "This is my playes last scene, here heavens appoint." John Donne. *See* Holy Sonnets.
Sonnet: "This is the garden: colours come and go." E. E. Cummings. *See* This Is the Garden.
Sonnet: "This is the golden book of spirit and sense." Swinburne. SyP
Sonnet XV: "This is the way we say it in our time." Winfield Townley Scott. ErPo
Sonnet: "This virgin, beautiful and lively day." Stéphane Mallarmé, *tr. fr. French by* Roger Fry. NAWM-2; PoPl
Sonnet: "Those hours, that with gentle work did frame." Shakespeare. *See* Sonnets, V.
Sonnet: "Those petty wrongs that liberty commits." Shakespeare. *See* Sonnets, XLI.
Sonnet: "Thou blind fool, Love, what dost thou to mine eyes." Shakespeare. *See* Sonnets, CXXXVII.
Sonnet: "Thou hast made me. And shall thy worke decay?" John Donne. *See* Holy Sonnets.
Sonnet: Thought of a Briton on the Subjugation of Switzerland. Wordsworth. *See* Thought of a Briton on the Subjugation of Switzerland.
Sonnet: "Three silences made him a single word." R. P. Blackmur. PoA
Sonnet: "Three things there be in Mans opinion deare." Fulke Greville. *See* Three Things There Be.
Sonnet: "Thus ends my love, but this doth grieve me most." Lord Herbert of Cherbury. *See* Loves End.
Sonnet: "Thus is his cheek the map of days outworn." Shakespeare. *See* Sonnets, LXVIII.
Sonnet L: "Thus piteously Love closed what he begat." George Meredith. *See* Modern Love: "Thus piteously Love closed . . ."
Sonnet: "Thus was my love, thus was my Ganymed." Richard Barnfield. Sonnets, X. PeHV
Sonnet: "Thy baby, too, the child that was to be." Frederick Goddard Tuckerman. *See* Sonnets.
Sonnet: "Thy bosom is endeared with all hearts." Shakespeare. *See* Sonnets, XXXI.
Sonnet: "Thy glass will show thee how thy beauties wear." Shakespeare. *See* Sonnets, LXXVII.
Sonnet: "Time and the mortal will stand never fast." Luis de Camoes, *tr. fr. Spanish by* Richard Garnett. AWP
Sonnet: "Tired [*or* Tir'd] with all these, for restful death I cry." Shakespeare. *See* Sonnets, LXVI.

Sonnet: " 'Tis better to be vile than vile esteemed." Shakespeare. *See* Sonnets, CXXI
Sonnet: To ———. Wordsworth. ChER
Sonnet: To a Friend. Hartley Coleridge. *See* To a Friend.
Sonnet: To a Friend Who Does Not Pity His Love. Guido Cavalcanti, *tr. fr. Italian by* Dante Gabriel Rossetti. AWP
Sonnet: To Brunetto Latini. Dante, *tr. fr. Italian by* Dante Gabriel Rossetti. AWP
Sonnet: To Certain Ladies; When Beatrice Was Lamenting Her Father's Death. Dante, *tr. fr. Italian by* Dante Gabriel Rossetti. AWP
Sonnet: To Dante Alighieri (He Commends the Work of Dante's Life). Giovanni Quirino, *tr. fr. Italian by* Dante Gabriel Rossetti. AWP
Sonnet: To Dante Alighieri (He Writes to Dante, Then in Exile at Verona, Defying Him as No Better Than Himself). Cecco Angiolieri da Siena, *tr. fr. Italian by* Dante Gabriel Rossetti. AWP
Sonnet: To Dante Alighieri (On the Last Sonnet of the Vita Nuova). Cecco Angiolieri da Siena, *tr. fr. Italian by* Dante Gabriel Rossetti. AWP
Sonnet: To Guido Cavalcanti. Dante, *tr. fr. Italian by* Shelley. AWP
(Sonnet: Dante Alighieri to Guido Cavalcanti.) OBVE
Sonnet: To His Lady Joan, of Florence. Guido Cavalcanti, *tr. fr. Italian by* Dante Gabriel Rossetti. AWP
Sonnet: To Homer. Keats. *See* To Homer.
Sonnet XV: "To honor the return of sparkling sun." Louise Labé, *tr. fr. French by* Willis Barnstone. BoWoP
Sonnet: To Love, in Great Bitterness. Cino da Pistoia, *tr. fr. Italian by* Dante Gabriel Rossetti. AWP
Sonnet: "To me, fair friend, you never can be old." Shakespeare. *See* Sonnets, CIV.
Sonnet: To Mr. H. Lawes, on His Aires. Milton. *See* To Mr. H. Lawes. . . .
Sonnet: "To one who has been long in city pent." Keats. *See* To One Who Has Been Long in City Pent.
Sonnet: To Oxford. Thomas Russell. OBEC
Sonnet: "To rail or jest, ye know I use it not." Sir Thomas Wyatt. SiPS
Sonnet: To Science. Poe. *See* Sonnet to Science.
Sonnet: To Tartar, a Terrier Beauty. Thomas Lovell Beddoes. FM; OBNC
Sonnet: To the Asshole. Arthur Rimbaud *and* Paul Verlaine, *tr. fr. French by* J. Murat *and* W. Gunn. PeHV
Sonnet: To the Critic. Michael Drayton. Idea, XXXI. LoBV
Sonnet: To the Departing Spirit of an Alienated Friend: "Behold him now his genuine colours wear." Anna Seward. PeHV
Sonnet: To the Lady Beaumont. Wordsworth. ChER
Sonnet: To the Lady Pietra degli Scrovigni. Dante, *tr. fr. Italian by* Dante Gabriel Rossetti. AWP
Sonnet: To the River Lodon [*or* Loddon]. Thomas Warton, the Younger. NOEC; OBEC; ViBoPo
Sonnet: To the River Otter. Samuel Taylor Coleridge. ChER; OAEL-2
Sonnet: To the Same Ladies; with Their Answer. Dante, *tr. fr. Italian by* Dante Gabriel Rossetti. AWP
Sonnet: "To travel like a bird, lightly to view." C. Day Lewis. *Fr.* O Dreams, O Destinations. ChMP; GTBS-P
Sonnet: To Valclusa. Thomas Russell. OBEC
Sonnet: Trance of Love, A. Cino da Pistoia, *tr. fr. Italian by* Dante Gabriel Rossetti. AWP
Sonnet: True Ambition. Benjamin Stillingfleet. OBEC
Sonnet: "Two loves I have of comfort and despair." Shakespeare. *See* Sonnets, CXLIV.
Sonnet: "Two stars there are in one faire firmament." Richard Barnfield. Sonnets, IV. PeHV
Sonnet, A: "Two voices are there: one is of the deep." James Kenneth Stephen. BXAP; DBV; FaBoCo; FaBoPa; FiBHP; NOBL; Par; SpRo; WhC
(Sonnet on Wordsworth, A.) CenHV
(Wordsworth.) HBV-1
Sonnet: "Tyr'd with all these for restfull death I cry." Shakespeare. *See* Sonnets, LXVI.
Sonnet: "Under the mountain, as when first I knew." Frederick Goddard Tuckerman. *See* Sonnets.
Sonnet: "Understanding of a medical man, The." Rex Warner. ChMP
Sonnet: "Unlike are we, unlike, O princely Heart!" Elizabeth Barrett Browning. *See* Sonnets from the Portuguese: "Unlike are we . . ."
Sonnet XII: "Virgins terrify too many men." Winfield Townley Scott. ErPo
Sonnet: "Was it the proud full sail of his great verse." Shakespeare. *See* Sonnets, LXXXVI.
Sonnet VII: "We see each living thing finally die." Louise Labé, *tr. fr. French by* Willis Barnstone. BoWoP
Sonnet: "We will not whisper, we have found the place." Hilaire Belloc. MoBrPo
Sonnet: "Weary with toil, I haste me to my bed." Shakespeare. *See* Sonnets, XXVII.
Sonnet: "Weary year his race now having run, The." Spenser. *See* Amoretti, LXII.
Sonnet: "Were I as base as is the lowly plain." *At. to* Joshua Sylvester. *See* Were I as Base as Is the Lowly Plain.
Sonnet XXX: "What are we first? First, animals; and next." George Meredith. *See* Modern Love: "What are we . . ."
Sonnet: "What doth it serve to see sun's burning face." William Drummond of Hawthornden. ElL
Sonnet XXIII: "What good is it to me if long ago." Louise Labé, *tr. fr. French by* Willis Barnstone. BoWoP
Sonnet XXI: "What grandeur makes a man seem venerable?" Louise Labé, *tr. fr. French by* Willis Barnstone. BoWoP
Sonnet: "What if this present were the worlds last night?" John Donne. *See* Holy Sonnets.
Sonnet, The: "What is a sonnet? 'Tis the pearly shell." Richard Watson Gilder. AA; HBV-2
Sonnet: "What is your substance, whereof are you made." Shakespeare. *See* Sonnets, LIII.
Sonnet: "What lips my lips have kissed, and where, and why." Edna St. Vincent Millay. *See* What Lips My Lips Have Kissed.
Sonnet: "What potions have I drunk of siren tears." Shakespeare. *See* Sonnets, CXIX.
Sonnet: "What riches have you that you deem me poor?" George Santayana. *See* Sonnets: "What riches have you . . ."
Sonnet: "When as man's life, the light of human lust." Fulke Greville. *Fr.* Caelica. MePo; OBS
("Whenas [*or* When as] man's life, the light of human[e] lust.") LiTB; OxBoCh; PoEL-1
Sonnet: "When forty winters shall besiege thy brow." Shakespeare. *See* Sonnets, II.
Sonnet: "When, from the tower whence I derive love's heaven." *Unknown. Fr.* Zephereria. ElL
Sonnet: "When I catch sight of your fair head." Louise Labé. *See* Sonnet X: "When I perceive your blond and graceful head."
Sonnet: "When I consider every thing that grows." Shakespeare. *See* Sonnets, XV.
Sonnet: "When I consider how my light is spent." Milton. *See* On His Blindness.
Sonnet: "When I do count the clock that tells the time." Shakespeare. *See* Sonnets, XII.
Sonnet: "When I entreat, either thou wilt not hear." Henry King. AnAnS-2
Sonnet: "When I have fears that I may cease to be." Keats. *See* When I Have Fears.
Sonnet: "When I have seen by Time's fell hand defac'd." Shakespeare. *See* Sonnets, LXIV.
Sonnet X: "When I perceive your blond and graceful head." Louise Labé, *tr. fr. French by* Willis Barnstone. BoWoP
(Sonnet: "When I catch sight of your fair head," *tr. by* Joan Keefe *and* Richard Terdiman.) PBWP
Sonnet: "When I was marked for suffering, Love forswore." Miguel de Cervantes, *tr. fr. Spanish by* Sir Edmund Gosse. AWP
Sonnet: "When in disgrace with fortune and men's eyes." Shakespeare. *See* Sonnets, XXIX.
Sonnet: "When in the chronicle of wasted time." Shakespeare. *See* Sonnets, CVI.
Sonnet: "When men shall find thy flower, thy glory, pass." Samuel Daniel. *See* To Delia: "When men shall find thy flower . . ."
Sonnet: "When my love swears that she is made of truth." Shakespeare. *See* Sonnets, CXXXVIII.
Sonnet: "When our two souls stand up erect and strong." Elizabeth Barrett Browning. *See* Sonnets from the Portuguese: "When our two souls . . ."
Sonnet: "When Phoebe form'd a wanton smile." William Collins. EnLoPo
Sonnet: "When to the sessions of sweet silent thought." Shakespeare. *See* Sonnets, XXX.
Sonnet XXVIII: "When we are old and these rejoicing veins." Edna St. Vincent Millay. ErPo; VGW
Sonnet: "Where are we to go when this is done?" Alfred A. Duckett. AmNP; PoBA; PoNe
Sonnet: "Where art thou, Muse, that thou forget'st so long." Shakespeare. *See* Sonnets, C.
Sonnet: Where Lies the Land. Wordsworth. *See* Where Lies the Land to Which Yon Ship Must Go?
Sonnet V: "White Venus limpid wandering in the sky." Louise Labé, *tr. fr. French by* Aliki *and* Willis Barnstone. BoWoP
Sonnet VII: "Who is she that comes, makyng turn every man's eye." Guido Cavalcanti. *See* Sonnet: Rapture Concerning His Lady, A.
Sonnet: "Who will believe my verse in time to come." Shakespeare. *See* Sonnets, XVII.
Sonnet: "Whoever hath her wish, thou hast thy Will." Shakespeare. *See* Sonnets, CXXXV.
Sonnet: "Whoso list to hunt, I know where is an hind." Sir Thomas Wyatt. *See* Whoso List to Hunt.

Sonnet: "Why are wee by all creatures waited on?" John Donne. *See* Holy Sonnets.
Sonnet: "Why didst thou promise such a beauteous day." Shakespeare. *See* Sonnets, XXXIV.
Sonnet: "Why is my verse so barren of new pride." Shakespeare. *See* Sonnets, LXXVI.
Sonnet: Wild Duck's Nest, The. Wordsworth. *See* Wild Duck's Nest, The.
Sonnet: "Wilt thou love God, as he thee! then digest." John Donne. *See* Holy Sonnets.
Sonnet: "Wind has blown the rain away and blown, A." E. E. Cummings. MoAB; MoAmPo
Sonnet: "Winter deepening, the hay all in, The." Richard Wilbur. PoPl
Sonnet: "With how sad steps, O Moon, thou climb'st the skies!" Sir Philip Sidney. *See* Astrophel and Stella, XXXI.
Sonnet: "With sighs my bosom always laboureth." Dante, *tr. fr. Italian by* Dante Gabriel Rossetti. *Fr.* La Vita Nuova. GoBC
Sonnet: "Woman's face with nature's own hand painted, A." Shakespeare. *See* Sonnets, XX.
Sonnet: "Women have loved before as I love now." Edna St. Vincent Millay. PoA
Sonnet: "Wonderfully out of the beautiful form." Dante, *tr. fr. Italian by* Dante Gabriel Rossetti. *Fr.* La Vita Nuova. GoBC
Sonnet: "World is too much with us, The; late and soon." Wordsworth. *See* World Is Too Much with Us, The.
Sonnet: "World's a stage, The. The light is in one's eyes." Hilaire Belloc. DBV
Sonnet: "World's bright comforter, whose beamsome light, The." Barnabe Jones. *See* World's Bright Comforter, The.
Sonnet: Written after Seeing Wilton-House. Thomas Warton, the Younger. Sonnets, V. OBEC
Sonnet: Written at the End of "The Floure and the Lefe." Keats. EnRP
Sonnet: Written in a Blank Leaf of Dugdale's "Monasticon." Thomas Warton, the Younger. Sonnets, III. OBEC
(Sonnet: "Deem not, devoid of elegance, the sage.") SeCePo
Sonnet: Written in January, 1818. Keats. *See* When I Have Fears.
Sonnet: Written in London, September, 1802. Wordsworth. *See* Written in London, September, 1802.
Sonnet: Written on the Day That Mr. Leigh Hunt Left Prison. Keats. ChER
Sonnet: "You that in love find luck and abundaunce." Sir Thomas Wyatt. SiPS
(May Time.) OBSC
("You that in love finde lucke and habundance.") AAS
Sonnet: "You waken slowly. In your dream you're straying." William Bell. NePoEA
Sonnet: "You were born; must die; were loved; must love." Stephen Spender. MoAB; MoBrPo
Sonnet against the Too-Facile Mystic. Elizabeth B. Harrod. NePoEA
Sonnet and Limerick. Morris Bishop. FiBHP
Sonnet Composed upon Westminster Bridge, September 3, 1802. Wordsworth. *See* Composed upon Westminster Bridge, September 3, 1802.
Sonnet Ending with a Film Subtitle. Marilyn Hacker. MAYP
Sonnet Entitled How to Run the World. E. E. Cummings. NePA
Sonnet for a Loved One. Dorothy Joslin. AMV-80
Sonnet for a Picture. Swinburne. *Fr.* Heptalogia. BXAP; FaBoNo; OAEL-2; OAEP
Sonnet for My Father. Donald Justice. DFF
(Sonnet to My Father.) DiL
Sonnet for My Son. Melanie Gordon Barber. GoYe
Sonnet for the End of a Sequence. Dorothy Parker. DBV
Sonnet Found in a Deserted Madhouse. *Unknown.* FaBoCo; FaBoNo; InvP; NA
Sonnet from "One Person." Elinor Wylie. *Fr.* One Person. MoAmPo
Sonnet in a Pass of Bavaria. Richard Chenevix Trench. OBRV
Sonnet in Autumn. Donald Petersen. NePoEA-2
Sonnet in the Mail Coach. Henry Taylor. TEP
Sonnet is a fruit which long hath slept, The. The Sonnet. John Addington Symonds. HBV-2
Sonnet is a moment's monument, A. A [*or* The] Sonnet. Dante Gabriel Rossetti. *Fr.* The House of Life, *introd.* HBV-2; HeIP; NoP; OAEP; PP; ViBoPo; VLP
Sonnet is a sleek iambic beast, The. Sonnet Sonnet. John D. Engle, Jr. AMV-81
Sonnet July 18th 1787. William Lisle Bowles. *See* Time and Grief.
Sonnet Made on Isabella Markham, A. John Harington. ElL; OBSC
Sonnet Made upon the Groves near Merlou Castle. Lord Herbert of Cherbury. JCP
Sonnet of Black Beauty. Lord Herbert of Cherbury. AnAnS-2; MePo
Sonnet of Fishes. George Barker. FaBoMo
Sonnet of the Moon, A. Charles Best. CH; HBV-1
(Looke How the Pale Queene.) EtS
(Moon, The.) OBSC
(Of the Moon.) ElL; MOON
Sonnet of the Mountain, The. Mellin de Saint-Gelais, *tr. fr. French by* Austin Dobson. AWP
Sonnet on a Family Picture. Thomas Edwards. NOEC; OBEC
Sonnet on a Monkey, A. Marjory Fleming. FaFP; FiBHP
(Sonnet, A: "O lovely O most charming pug.") FaBoCo
Sonnet on a Still Night. J. V. Cunningham. PoA
Sonnet on Chillon. Byron. The Prisoner of Chillon, *introd. sonnet.* EnRP; FiP; LiTB; LoBV; OAEP; OBRV; SeCeV; TreFS; TrGrPo
("Eternal Spirit of the chainless Mind!") BeLS; HBV-2; PoPl
(On the Castle of Chillon.) GTBS; GTBS-P
Sonnet on Death. William Walsh. ViBoPo
Sonnet on Hearing the *Dies Irae* Sung in the Sistine Chapel. Oscar Wilde. TrPWD
Sonnet on His Blindness. Milton. *See* On His Blindness.
Sonnet on His Deceased Wife. Milton. *See* On His Deceased Wife.
Sonnet on Life. Sir Brooke Boothby. ViBoPo
Sonnet on Stewed Prunes. William F. Kirk. WhC
Sonnet on the Crimean War. William Forster. CBAP
Sonnet on the Death of [Mr.] Richard West. Thomas Gray. EnRP; LAuP; NOEC; NoP; OAEP; OBEC; PeHV; PoEL-3; SeCePo; ViBoPo
(On the Death of [Mr.] Richard West.) NOBE; TrGrPo
Sonnet on the Sea. Keats. *See* On the Sea.
Sonnet on Wordsworth, A. James Kenneth Stephen. *See* Sonnet, A: "Two voices are there: one is of the deep."
Sonnet or Dittie: "Mars in a fury gainst love's brightest Queen." Robert Greene. *See* Mars and Venus.
Sonnet Reversed. Rupert Brooke. NOBL
Sonnet Sequence. Darwin T. Turner. BALP
Sonnet, she told the crowd of bearded, The. The Sonnet. Daniel Hoffman. GP
Sonnet—Silence. Poe. AP; NOBA
Sonnet Sonnet. John D. Engle, Jr. AMV-81
Sonnet Supposed to Be Written at Lemnos. Thomas Russell. *See* Sonnet: Supposed . . .
Sonnet to ———. John Hamilton Reynolds. OBRV
Sonnet to a Clam. John Godfrey Saxe. BoAnP
Sonnet to a Friend Who Asked, How I Felt When the Nurse First Presented My Infant to Me. Samuel Taylor Coleridge. EnRP
Sonnet to a Negro in Harlem. Helene Johnson. AmNP; BANP; CDC; NIP
Sonnet to a Tyrant. Mary Anne Ellis. AMV-80
Sonnet to Ailsa Rock. Keats. *See* To Ailsa Rock.
Sonnet to Be Written from Prison. Robert Adamson. CBAP
Sonnet to Britain. William Edmonstoune Aytoun. FaBoCo
Sonnet to Gath. Edna St. Vincent Millay. BoWoP; CMoP; MoAB; MoAmPo
Sonnet to Heavenly Beauty, A. Joachim du Bellay, *tr. fr. French by* Andrew Lang. AWP; CTC
Sonnet to Mrs. Unwin. William Cowper. *See* To Mary Unwin.
Sonnet to My Father. Donald Justice. *See* Sonnet for my Father.
Sonnet to My Friend, with an Identity Disc. Wilfred Owen. PeHV
Sonnet to My Mother. George Barker. FaFP; LiTB; MoAB; SeCePo; ViBoPo; WaP
(To My Mother.) DTC; FaBoMo; FF; LiTM; MP; NCSH; OxBTC; TWCP
Sonnet to My Mother, A. Heine. *See* To My Mother.
Sonnet to Negro Soldiers. Joseph Seamon Cotter, Jr. PoBA
Sonnet to Opium, A; Celebrating Its Virtues. "Orestes." NOEC
Sonnet to Science. Poe. *Fr.* Al Aaraaff: Prologue. AmPP; AP; InPK; NePA; NoP; OxBA; PPON; TAP; TW
Sonnet to Seabrook. David Ray. AMV-80
Sonnet to Sleep. Keats. *See* To Sleep.
Sonnet to the Moon. Yvor Winters. TwAmPo
Sonnet, to the Noble Lady, the Lady Mary Worth, A. Ben Jonson. AnAnS-2
Sonnet to the River Lodon [*or* Loddon]. Thomas Warton, the Younger. *See* Sonnet: To the River Lodon.
Sonnet to the Sea Serpent. John G. C. Brainard. EtS
Sonnet to the Virgin. Wordsworth. *See* Virgin, The.
Sonnet to Vauxhall. Thomas Hood. PoEL-4
Sonnet to William Wilberforce, Esq. William Cowper. OAEP
Sonnet with a Different Letter at the End of Every Line. George Starbuck. OBAL
Sonnet with her Mona Lisa smile, The. Sonnet and Limerick. Morris Bishop. FiBHP
Sonnet Written at the Close of Spring. Charlotte Smith. OBEC
(Elegiac Sonnet.) FaBoEn
Sonnet Written in the Church-Yard at Middleton, in Sussex. Charlotte Smith. *See* Press'd by the Moon, Mute Arbitress of Tides.
Sonnet Written in Tintern Abbey, Monmouthshire. Edmund Gardner. NOEC

Sonneteering Made Easy. S. B. Botsford. NYBP
Sonnets, *sels.* James Agee. MoAmPo
"Now stands our love on that still verge of day," XX.
"Our doom is in our being. We began," II.
"So it begins. Adam is in his earth," I.
"Those former loves wherein our lives have run," XIX.
Sonnets, *sels.* Richard Barnfield. PeHV
"Ah no; nor I myselfe: though my pure love," XIX.
"But now my Muse toyled with continuall care," XX.
"Cherry-lipt Adonis in his snowie shape," XVII.
"Here hold this glove (this milk-white cheveril glove)," XIV.
"Sighing, and sadly sitting by my Love," XI.
"Some talk of Ganymede th' Idalian boy," XII.
"Sometimes I wish that I his pillow were," VIII.
"Sporting at fancie, setting light by love," I.
"Sweet corrall lips, where Nature's treasure lies," VI.
"Sweet Thames I honour thee, not for thou art," VII.
"Thus was my love, thus was my Ganymed," X.
"Two stars there are in one faire firmament," IV.
Sonnets, *sel.* Hilaire Belloc. Because My Faltering Feet, *XVII.* OxBoCh
(Her Faith.) GoBo
Sonnets, *sels.* Boccaccio, *tr. fr. Italian* by Dante Gabriel Rossetti.
Inscription for a Portrait of Dante. AWP; GoBC
Of Fiammetta Singing. AWP; GoBC
Of His Last Sight of Fiammetta. AWP; GoBC
Of Three Girls and of Their Talk. AWP
To Dante in Paradise, after Fiammetta's Death. AWP; GoBC
To One Who Had Censured His Public Exposition of Dante. AWP; GoBC
Sonnets, *sel.* George Henry Boker.
To My Lady. AA
Sonnets, *sel.* Bartholomew Griffin.
"Fair is my love that feeds among the lilies." ViBoPo
Sonnets, *sels.* Robert Hillyer. HBMV
"Even as love grows more, I write the less," XVI.
"Golden spring redeems the withered year, The," II.
"I will fling wide the windows of my soul," XII.
"Let all men see the ruins of the shrine," XIV.
"Over the waters but a single bough," XXIII.
"Quickly and pleasantly the seasons blow," I.
"Then judge me as thou wilt, I cannot flee," III.
Sonnets, *sels.* Muna Lee. HBMV
"Along my ways of life you never came," XII.
"I have a thousand pictures of the sea," IV.
"I make no question of your right to go," III.
"It will be easy to love you when I am dead," XI.
"Life of itself will be cruel and hard enough," V.
"What other form were worthy of your praise," *foreword.*
Sonnets ("Long long ago"), *sels.* John Masefield.
Flesh, I Have Knocked at Many a Dusty Door. LiTM
"How many ways, how many times." WGRP
(How Many Ways.) LiTB
"I could get within this changing I." WGRP
"I never see the red rose crown the year." GoYe
"If I could come again to that dear place." HBV-2
"Is there a great green commonwealth of Thought." LiTM; MoBrPo
"Let that which is to come be as it may." HBV-2
"Long, long ago, when all the glittering earth." HBV-2
"O little self, within whose smallness lies." HBV-2; WGRP
"Roses are beauty, but I never see." HBV-2
"There is no God, as I was taught in youth." CMoP; HBV-2; WGRP
What Am I, Life? ImOP
Sonnets, *sels.* Irene Rutherford McLeod. HBMV
"Between my love and me there runs a thread."
"In heaven there is a star I call my own."
"Shall I be fearful thus to speak my mind."
"Sweet, when I think how summer's smallest bird."
"When sane men gather in to talk of Love."
Sonnets, *sels.* George Santayana.
After Grey Vigils, XLIX. WHA
"Deem not, because you see me in the press," XI. TrGrPo
"O world, thou choosest not the better part!" III. HBV-2; TrGrPo
(Faith.) WGRP
(O World.) FPL
"What riches have you that you deem me poor?" XXIV. HBV-2; TrGrPo
Sonnets, *sels.* Shakespeare.
I. "From fairest creatures we desire increase." CTC; FaBoEn; LiTB; MasP; OAEP; OBSC; TrGrPo
II. "When forty winters shall besiege thy brow." BLPL; FF; LiTB; OBSC; TEP
III. "Look in thy glass, and tell the face thou viewest." CABA; EnRePo; LiTB; MasP; OBSC
V. "Those hours, that with gentle work did frame." TEP
VI. "Then let not winter's ragged hand deface." MasP
VIII. "Music[k] to hear[e], why hear'st thou music[k] sadly?" PoEL-2; ViBoPo
IX. "Is it for fear to wet a widow's eye." MasP
X. "For shame! deny that thou bear'st love to any." MasP
XII. "When I do count the clock that tells the time." AWP; ElL; EnRePo; InPS; MasP; NoP; OAEL-1; OBSC; TEP; ViBoPo
(When I Do Count the Clock.) FaFP
XIII. "Oh [*or* O]! that you were yourself! but, love, you are." OAEP; TEP
XIV. "Not from the stars do I my judgement pluck." MasP
XV. "When I consider everything that grows." AWP; BLPL; MasP; OAEP; OBSC; TEP; TrGrPo
XVI. "But wherefore do not you a mightier waie." FaBoEn
XVII. "Who will believe my verse in time to come." OBSC
XVIII. "Shall I compare thee to a summer's day?" AWP; BoLoP; CTC; ElL; EnLoPo; FaBoBe; FaBoEn; FaBV; FaFP; FiP; FPL; GBL; HAP; HBV-1; HeIP; InPK; InPS; InvP; LiTB; LoBV; MasP; MAT; NIP; NOBE; NoP; OAEL-1; OAEP; OBEV; OBSC; OLR; PAI; PoEL-2; PoLF; PoPl; PoRA; PPoe; PrIm; SCV; SeCePo; SeCeV; TEP; TreFT; TrGrPo; ViBoPo; WeW; WHA
(To His Love.) GTBS; GTBS-P
XIX. "Devouring Time, blunt thou the lion's paws [lyons pawes]." AWP; ChTr; EBEV; MAT; OAEL-1; OBSC; PoEL-2; TrGrPo; WHA
XX. "Woman's face with nature's own hand painted, A." ErPo; InvP; MasP; OAEL-1; PeHV
XXI. "So is it not with me as with that muse." InvP; OBSC
XXII. "My glass shall not persuade me I am old." OBSC
XXIII. "As an unperfect actor on the stage." BiP; HBV-1; InvP; OAEP
XXIV: "Mine eye hath play'd the painter, and hath steel'd." EyDe
XXV. "Let those who are in favour with their stars." OBSC
XXVII. "Weary with toil, I haste me to my bed." OBSC
XXVIII. "How can I then return in happy plight." OBSC
XXIX. "When, in disgrace with fortune and men's eyes." AWP; CTC; EBEV; ElL; FaBoEn; FaBoRV; FaBV; GBL; HAP; HBV-1; HeIP; InvP; LiTB; LoBV; MasP; NOBE; NoP; OAEL-1; OAEP; OBEV; OBSC; PeHV; PoEL-2; PoPl; PoRA; PPoe; PPP; Prf; PrIm; SCV; SeCeV; TEP; TreF; TrGrPo; TRV; ViBoPo; WeW; WHA
(Consolation, A.) GTBS; GTBS-P
XXX. "When to the sessions of sweet silent thought." AWP; BiP; CABA; CTC; EBEV; ElL; EnRePo; FaBoEn; FaBoRV; FaBV; FF; FPL; GBL; HAP; HBV-1; InPS; LiTB; LoBV; MasP; NOBE; NoP; OAEL-1; OAEP; OBEV; OBSC; PAI; PoEL-2; PoLF; PoPle; PoRA; PPP; PrIM; SeCeV; TEP; TreFS; TrGrPo; ViBoPo; WHA
(Remembrance.) FaFP; GTBS; GTBS-P; TRV
XXXI. "Thy bosom is endeared with all hearts." NOBE; OBEV; OBSC; PoEL-2
XXXII. "If thou survive my well-contented day." ElL; HBV-1; OBSC; PP
(Post Mortem.) GTBS; GTBS-P
XXXIII. "Full many a glorious morning have I seen[e]." AWP; EBEV; ElL; FaBoEn; HAP; HBV-1; LiTB; LoBV; NoP; OAEL-1; OAEP; OBSC; PoRA; PPP; SeCePo; SeCeV; TEP; TreFS; TrGrPo; ViBoPo; WeW
(Full Many a Glorious Morning.) FaFP
XXXIV. "Why didst thou promise such a beauteous day." OBSC
XXXV. "No more be grieved at that which thou hast done." CABA; PeHV; TEP; UnPo
XXXVI. "Let me confess that we two must be twain." OAEP; PeHV
XL. "Take all my loves, my Love, yea, take them all." InvP; OBSC
XLI. "Those petty wrongs that liberty commits." InvP
XLII. "That thou hast her, it is not all my grief." InvP
XLVI: "Mine eye and heart are at a mortal war." EyDe
XLVII: "Betwixt mine eye and heart a league is took." EyDe
LII. "So am I as the rich, whose blessed key." OBSC
LIII. "What is your substance, whereof are you made." CTC; EBEV; ElL; EnRePo; LiTB; MasP; OAEL-1; OAEP; OBEV; OBSC; PeHV; ViBoPo
(What Is Your Substance.) FaFP
LIV. "O [*or* Oh], how much more doth beauty beauteous seem." AWP; ElL; OBEV; OBSC; ViBoPo
LV. "Not marble, nor the gilded monuments." AWP; BLPL; CABA; CTC; EnRePo; FaBoEn; FaFP; FF; HeIP; InPK; LiTB; LoBV; MasP; NIP; NOBE; NoP; OAEL-1; OAEP; OBSC; PAI; PeHV; PoEL-2; PoRA; PPoe; SeCeV; TEP; TrGrPo; ViBoPo
LVI. "Sweet love, renew thy force, be it not said."
(Sweet Love, Renew Thy Force.) PoLF
LVII. "Being your slave, what should I do[e] but tend." HAP; OBEV; PeHV; PoEL-2; ViBoPo
(Absence.) GTBS; GTBS-P
LIX. "If their bee nothing new, but that which is." FaBoEn
LX. "Like as the waves make towards the pebbled shore." ChTr; EBEV; ElL; EnRePo; FaBoEn; FPL; HBV-1; LiTB; LoBV; NIP; NOBE; OBSC; PeHV; PoRA; SeCeV; TEP; UnPo; ViBoPo

(Like as the Waves.) FaFP
(Revolutions.) GTBS; GTBS-P
LXI. "Is it thy wil, thy Image should keepe open." PoEL-2
LXII. "Sin [*or* Sinne] of self-love [*or* selfe-love] possesseth all mine eye [*or* eie]." EBEV; EnRePo; PoEL-2
LXIII. "Against my Love shall be, as I am now." OBSC
LXIV. "When I have seen by Time's fell hand defaced." AWP; BLPL; CABA; ElL; EnLoPo; EnRePo; HAP; HeIP; LiTB; LO; NOBE; NoP; OAEL-1; OBSC; PoRA; PPoe; SeCeV; ViBoPo
(Time and Love, I.) GTBS; GTBS-P
(When I Have Seen by Time's Fell Hand.) FaFP
LXV. "Since brass, nor stone, nor earth, nor boundless sea." AWP; CABA; EnRePo; FF; FiP; HAP; InPS; LiTB; MasP; NOBE; NoP; PoRA; SeCeV; UnPo
(Since Brass, Nor Stone, Nor Earth.) FaFP
(Time and Love, II.) GTBS; GTBS-P
LXVI. "Tired [*or* Tyr'd] with all these, for restful death I cry." AWP; CTC; EBEV; FaFP; HAP; InPS; LiTB; NOBE; OAEL-1; OBSC; PoEL-2; SeCeV; TrGrPo; ViBoPo; WeW; WHA
(Tired with All These.) FaFP
(World's Way, The.) GTBS; GTBS-P
LXVII. "Ah wherefore with infection should he live." PeHV
LXVIII. "Thus is this cheek the map of days outworn." OBSC
LXXI. "No longer mourn for me when I am dead." AWP; EBEV; ElL; EnRePo; FaBoRV; GBL; HAP; HBV-1; LiTB; LO; NoP; OAEP; OBSC; PAI; PoRA; PPoe; SeCeV; TEP; TreFT; TrGrPo; ViBoPo; WHA
(Triumph of Death, The.) GTBS; GTBS-P
LXXII. "O, lest your true love may seem false in this." LO
LXXIII. "That time of year thou may'st [*or* maist] in me behold." AWP; BiP; BoLoP; CABA; ChTr; CTC; EBEV; ElL; EnLoPo; EnRePo; FaBoEn; FaBoRV; FaBV; FF; FiP; GBL; GTBS; GTBS-P; HAP; HBV-1; HeIP; HoPM; InPK; InPS; InvP; LiTB; LoBV; MasP; NIP; NOBE; NoP; OAEL-1; OAEP; OBEV; OBSC; OHFP; PAI; PoEL-2; PoPle; PoRA; PPP; PrIm; QFR; SeCeV; SoSe; TEP; TrGrPo; UnPo; ViBoPo; WeW; WHA
LXXIV. "But be contented: when that fell arrest." OBSC
LXXV. "So are you to my thoughts as food to life." PoEL-2
LXXVI. "Why is my verse so barren of new pride." EBEV; InvP; PP
LXXVII. "Thy glass will show thee how thy beauties wear." EnRePo; QFR
LXXXI. "Or I shall live your epitaph to make." OAEP; OBSC
LXXXVI. "Was it the proud full sail of his great verse." InvP; OAEL-1; OAEP; TEP
LXXXVII. "Farewell! Thou art too dear [*or* deare] for my possessing." EBEV; ElL; GTBS; GTBS-P; InPS; InvP; LiTB; MasP; NOBE; OAEL-1; OAEP; OBEV; OBSC; PeHV; PoEL-2; QFR; TrGrPo; ViBoPo
LXXXIX. "Say that thou didst forsake me for some fault." OAEP
XC. "Then hate me when thou wilt; if ever, now." AWP; EBEV; ElL; NOBE; OBEV; OBSC; PoEL-2; WHA
XCIII. "So shall I live, supposing thou art true." InvP; MasP
XCIV. "They that have power to hurt, and will do none." BLPL; CABA; ElL; FaBoEn; InPS; LiTB; MasP; NOBE; NoP; OAEL-1; OBEV; PeHV; PoEL-2; PPoe; PPP; SCV; TEP; TrGrPo; ViBoPo
(Life without Passion.) GTBS; GTBS-P
XCV. "How sweet and lovely dost thou make the shame." MasP; TrGrPo
XCVII. "How like a winter hath my absence been[e]." AWP; CABA; ElL; EnLoPo; EnRePo; FaBoEn; GTBS; GTBS-P; NOBE; OAEL-1; OBEV; OBSC; PoRA; TEP; TrGrPo
XCVIII. "From you have I been absent in the spring." AWP; ChTr; EBEV; ElL; LiTB; NOBE; OBEV; OBSC; PoPle; TEP; ViBoPo
XCIX. "Forward violet thus did I chide, The." OAEP; OBSC
C. "Where art thou, Muse, that thou forget'st so long." OBSC
CII. "My love is strengthen'd, though more weak in seeming." AWP; ElL; OAEP; OBEV; OBSC; ViBoPo
CIV. "To me, fair[e] friend, you never can be old." ElL; EnRePo; FaBoEn; FPL; GBL; GTBS; GTBS-P; HBV-1; HeIP; OAEP; OBEV; OBSC; PeHV; Prf; ViBoPo
CVI. "When in the chronicle of wasted time." AWP; BLPL; CTC; ElL; EnLoPo; EnRePo; FaBoCh; FaBoEn; FaBV; FiP; HBV-1; LiTB; LoBV; MasP; NOBE; NoP; OAEP; OBEV; OBSC; PoRA; PPoe; SeCeV; TEP; TreFT; TrGrPo; ViBoPo; WHA
(To His Love.) GTBS; GTBS-P
CVII. "Not mine own fears nor the prophetic soul." AWP; CABA; CTC; EBEV; FiP; HAP; LiTB; LoBV; MasP; NoP; OAEL-1; OAEP; OBSC; PPoe; SeCeV
CIX. "O [*or* Oh]! Never say that I was false of heart." ElL; HBV-1; NOBE; OBEV; OBSC
(Unchangeable, The.) GTBS; GTBS-P
CX. "Alas, 'tis true I have gone here and there." EBEV; OAEP; OBSC; PeHV; ViBoPo
CXVI. "Let me not to the marriage of true minds." AWP; CABA; ElL; EnLoPo; EnRePo; FaBoEn; FaBV; FaFP; FPL; GBL; HAP; HBV-1; HeIP; InPK; InPS; InvP; LiTB; LoBV; MasP; NiP; NOBE; NoP; OAEL-1; OAEP; OBEV; OBSC; PAI; PeHV; PoEL-2; PoPl; PoRA; PPoe; PPP; PrIm; SCV; SeCePo; SeCeV; SoSe; TEP; TrGrPo; TRV; UnPo; ViBoPo; WeW; WHA
(Love's Not Times Fool.) TreF
(True Love.) GoBC; GTBS; GTBS-P
CXVIII. "Like as, to make our appetities more keen." CABA
CXIX. "What potions have I drunk of siren tears." WHA
CXX. "That you were once unkind befriends me now." InvP
CXXI. " 'Tis better to be vile than vile esteemed." InvP; OAEL-1; PoEL-2
CXXIII. "No, Time, thou shalt not boast that I do change!" OAEP; OBSC; TrGrPo
CXXVIII. "How oft, when thou, my music, music play'st." ElL
CXXIX. "Expense of spirit in a waste of shame, The [*or* Th']." AWP; BiP; CABA; EBEV; EnRePo; ErPo; FaBoEn; GBL; HAP; HeIP; InPS; LiTB; LoBV; MasP; NIP; NOBE; NoP; OAEL-1; OBEV; OBSC; PAI; PoEL-2; PPoe; PPP; QFR; SCV; SeCePo; SeCeV; TEP; TrGrPo; UnPo; WeW; WHA
CXXX. "My mistress' eyes are nothing like the sun." AWP; BiP; BoLoP; CABA; EBEV; FF; HAP; HBV-1; HoPM; InPK; InPS; InvP; LiTB; NIP; NoP; OAEL-1; OAEP; PAI; PoPle; PP; PPP; PrIm; SeCeV; SoSe; TEP; WeW
CXXXII. "Thine eyes I love, and they, as pitying me." OAEP; OBSC
CXXXIII. "Beshrew that heart that makes my heart to groan." InvP
CXXXIV. "So now I have confessed that he is thine." InvP
CXXXV. "Whoever hath her wish, thou hast thy Will." OAEL-1
CXXXVII. "Thou blind fool, Love, what dost thou to mine eyes." WeW
CXXXVIII. "When my love swears [*or* sweares] that she is made of truth." AWP; BiP; CABA; EBEV; NoP; OAEL-1; OAEP; PAI; PoEL-2; PPP; SoSe; TEP; TrGrPo; ViBoPo
CXLI. "In faith, I do[e] not love thee with mine eyes." PoEL-2; TrGrPo
CXLIII. "Lo, as a careful housewife runs to catch." BiP; InPK; OAEP
CXLIV. "Two loves I have of comfort and despair." CABA; EBEV; InvP; LoBV; NIP; OAEL-1; OAEP; PeHV; PoEL-2
CXLVI. "Poor[e] soul[e], the centre of my sinful[l] earth." AWP; BiP; CABA; EaLo; ElL; EnRePo; FaBoEn; HAP; HBV-1; InPK; LiTB; MasP; NIP; NOBE; NOCV; NoP; OAEL-1; OBEV; OBSC; OxBoCh; PoEL-2; PPoe; PPP; SeCeV; TrGrPo; ViBoPo; WHA
(Death of Death, The.) TreFS
(Soul and Body.) GoBC; GTBS; GTBS-P
CXLVII. "My love is as a fever [*or* feaver], longing still." EBEV; HoPM; PoEL-2; TEP
CXLVIII. "O me! what eyes hath love put in my head." (Blind Love.) GTBS; GTBS-P
CLI. "Love is too young to know what conscience is." BiP; EBEV; HeIP; PoEL-2
Sonnets, *sels.* Frederick Goddard Tuckerman.
"And change with hurried hand has swept these scenes," II, xviii. HAP; NOBA; QFR; TAP
"And faces, forms and phantoms, numbered not," II, xix. QFR
"And me my winter's task is drawing over," V, xiv. QFR
"Breeze is sharp, the sky is hard and blue, The," II, xiv. AP
"But unto him came swift calamity," II, ix. AP
"But we are set to strive to make our mark," III, xv. TrCP
"By this low fire I often sit to woo," I, xxv. AP
"Companions were we in the grove and glen!" II, viii. AP
"Even as a lover, dreaming, unaware," II, xiii. AP
"For Nature daily through her grand design," I, xxvi. AP
"Gertrude and Gulielma, sister-twins," II, xv. AP; HAP; QFR
"Hast thou seen reversed the prophet's miracle," IV, x. NOBA
"Here, where the red man swept the leaves away," IV, ix. NOBA; TAP
"His heart was in his garden; but his brain," II, vii. AP
"How most unworthy, echoing in mine ears," II, xii. AP
"Morning comes, The; not slow, with reddening gold," I, xxii. AP
"My Anna! though thine earthly steps are done," II, xxxiv. AP
"My Anna! When for her my head was bowed," II, xxxi. AP
"Not the round natural world, not the deep mind," I, xxviii. NoP
"O hard endeavor, to blend in with these," II, xx. QFR
"Oh for the face and footstep!—Woods and shores!" II, xxxii. AP
"One dark still night, I sat alone and wrote," II, xxxiii. AP
"Perhaps a dream; yet surely truth has beamed," I, xxiv. AP
"Put off thy bark from shore, though near the night." MOS
"Roll on, sad world! Not Mercury or Mars," II, xvii. AP; QFR; TreFS
"Sometimes I walk where the deep water dips," III, x. NOBA
"Still pressing through these weeping solitudes," II, xi. AP; NOBA
"Thin little leaves of wood fern, ribbed and toothed," III, iv. TAP
"Thy baby, too, the child that was to be," II, x. AP
"Under the mountain, as when first I knew," II, xvi. AP; HAP; QFR; TAP

"Upper chamber in a darkened house, An," I, x. NOBA; NoP; TAP
"Yes: though the brine may from the desert deep," II, iii. HAP
Sonnets—Actualities, *sel.* E. E. Cummings.
I Like My Body When It Is with Your Body. BoLoP; ErPo; LLLT; UnTE; VGW
Sonnets after the Italian, *sels.* Richard Watson Gilder. HBV-1
"I know not if I love her overmuch."
"I like her gentle hand that sometimes strays."
Sonnets are full of love, and this my tome. To My First Love, My Mother. Christina Rossetti. OHIP
Sonnets at Christmas (I-II). Allen Tate. AP; HAP; LiTA; LiTM; NePA; NoAM; NOBA; OxBA; VGW
"Ah, Christ, I love you rings to the wild sky," II. PoNe
Sonnets for a Dying Man, *sels.* Burns Singer. NePoEA-2
"Christ comes to mind and comes across the mind," XXXIX.
"I promise you by the harsh funeral," XLVIII.
"Old man dozed, The. The hospital quietened," XV.
"Those flaming Christians with their hygienic rose," XXXIII.
"To see the petrel cropping in the farmyard," XXX.
Sonnets for Pictures: "Our Lady of the Rocks." Dante Gabriel Rossetti. *See* For "Our Lady of the Rocks" by Leonardo da Vinci.
Sonnets from China, *sels.* W. H. Auden.
"Chilled by the present, its gloom and its noise," XVIII. PPP
"Far from a cultural centre he was used," XIII. CMoP
"He stayed, and was imprisoned in possession," IV. CMoP
"He was their servant (some way he was blind)," VII. CMoP
"He watched the stars and noted birds in flight," VI. CMoP
"Here war is harmless like a monument, XII." OBWP
"His care-free swagger was a fine invention," V. CMoP
"So an age ended, and its last deliverer died," X. CMoP
"So from the years their gifts were showered: each," I. CMoP
"They wondered why the fruit had been forbidden," II. CMoP
Sonnets from Greece, *sel.* Trumbull Stickney.
Mount Lykaion. MoVE; NePA; OxBA; TrGrPo
Sonnets from the Portuguese, *sels.* Elizabeth Barrett Browning.
"And wilt thou have me fashion into speech," XIII. BrRo
"And yet, because thou overcomest so," XVI. OAEP
"Belovéd, my Belovéd, when I think," XX. OAEP; WPE
"Belovéd, thou hast brought me many flowers," XLIV. EBVV; OAEP; OBNC; WPE
"Can it be right to give what I can give?" IX. CTC; HBV-1
"Face of all the world is changed, I think, The," VII. CTC; HBV-1; OAEP; VLP
"First time he kissed me, he but only kissed," XXXVIII. BLPA; BLPL; CTC; FaBoBe; HBV-1; PoPl; ViBoPo
"First time that the sun rose on thine oath, The," XXXII. ViBoPo; WPE
"Go from me. Yet I feel that I shall stand," VI. BLPL; HBV-1; OBEV; OBVV; TreFS; TrGrPo; ViBoPo
"How do I love thee? Let me count the ways," XLIII. BoLoP; CTC; EBVV; FaBoBe; FaBV; FaFP; FF; FPL; HBV-1; HeIP; HoPM; InPS; LiTB; NIP; NoP; OAEP; OLR; PoLF; PoPl; PoRA; TEP; TreF; TrGrPo; TRV; UnPo; ViBoPo; WHA; WPE
"I lived with visions for my company," XXVI. OAEP
"I never gave a lock of hair away," XVIII. EBVV; HAP; HBV-1
"I thought once how Theocritus had sung," I. EBVV; GBL; HBV-1; NOBE; NoP; OAEP; OBEV; OBNC; TreFT; ViBoPo; WPE
"If I leave all for thee, wilt thou exchange," XXXV. ViBoPo
"If thou must love me, let it be for nought," XIV. CTC; FaFP; HBV-1; HeIP; LiTB; OBEV; OBNC; OBVV; TreFS; TrGrPo; ViBoPo; WHA
"Indeed this very love which is my boast," XII. HBV-1
"Let the world's sharpness like a clasping knife," XXIV. VLP
"My letters! all dead paper, mute and white," XXVIII. HAP; HBV-1; ViBoPo
"My poet, thou canst touch on all the notes," XVII. BrRo; HBV-1; VLP; WHA
"Say over again, and yet once over again," XXI. HBV-1
"Unlike are we, unlike, O princely heart!" III. HBV-1; OAEP; OBEV; OBVV; TrGrPo
"What can I give thee back, O liberal," VIII. HBV-1; OBVV
"When our two souls stand up erect and strong," XXII. BoWoP; HBV-1; NOBE; OAEP; OBEV; OBVV; SBG; TreFT; TrGrPo; ViBoPo; VLP; WHA; WPE
"Yet, love, mere love, is beautiful indeed," X. CTC; HBV-1; VLP
Sonnets from the Series Relating to Edgar Allan Poe, *sels.* Sarah Helen Whitman. AA
"If thy sad heart, pining for human love," VI.
"Oft since thine earthly eyes have closed on mine," III.
"On our lone pathway bloomed no earthly hopes," V.
"When first I looked into thy glorious eyes," II.
Sonnets in Quaker Language, *sels.* Hildegarde Flanner. WPE
"Hearing a sound that may be thy return," VI.
"Thee sets a bell to swinging in my soul," II.
Sonnets of a Portrait Painter, *sels.* Arthur Davison Ficke. HBMV
April Moment, XI.
Her Pedigree, IX.
Spring Landscape, XII.
Summons, XIV.
Troubadours, X.
View from Heights, XIII.
Sonnets of the Blood, *sels.* Allen Tate. PoA
"Fire I praise was once perduring flame, The," VII.
"Near to me as my flesh, my flesh and blood," II.
"Not power nor the storied hand of God," IX.
"Times have changed, there is not left to us, The," IV.
"What is this flesh and blood compounded of," I.
Sonnets of the Months. Folgore da San Geminiano, *tr. fr. Italian by* Dante Gabriel Rossetti. AWP
August, *sel.* CTC
Sonnets of the Triple-headed Manichee, *sel.* George Barker.
"Keelhauled across the star-wrecked death of God," II. PoA
Sonnets on the Divina Commedia. Longfellow. *See* Divina Commedia (*poems introductory to Longfellow's tr. of the* Divine Comedy).
Sonnets on the Sea's Voice. George Sterling. EtS
Sonnets on the War, *sel.* Sydney Dobell
"I saw the human millions as the sand." VLP
Sonnets—Realities, *sels.* E. E. Cummings.
Cambridge Ladies Who Live in Furnished Souls, The. AmPP; HeIP; InPK; MoVE; NoAM; NOBA; NoP; OBAL; OxBA; PAI; PPON; TAP; ViBoPo
"My girl's tall with hard long eyes." UnTE
Sonnets to Aurelia, *sels.* Robert Nichols. OBMV
"But piteous things we are—when I am gone."
"Come, let us sigh a requiem over love."
"Though to your life apparent stain attach."
"When the proud World does most my world despise."
Sonnets to Delia. Samuel Daniel. *See* To Delia.
Sonnets to Diana. Henry Constable. *See* Diana.
Sonnets to Idea. Michael Drayton. *See* Idea.
Sonnets to Karl Theodore German, *sels.* August, Graf von Platen. PeHV
"How shall I still mankind's good will retrieve," XXII.
"When shall I master this anxiety," I.
Sonnets to Laura, *sels.* Petrarch, *tr. fr. Italian.*
To Laura in Death.
"Eyes that drew from me such fervent praise, The," XXIV, *tr. by* Edwin Morgan. NAWM-1; PAI
"First day she passed up and down through the Heavens, The," LXXV, *tr. by* J. M. Synge. OBMV
"Go, grieving rimes of mine, to that hard stone," LX, *tr. by* Morris Bishop. NAWM-1
"Great is my envy of you, earth, in your greed," XXXII, *tr. by* Edwin Morgan. NAWM-1
"In the years of her age the most beautiful," *tr. by* J. M. Synge. OBMV
"My flowery and green age was passing away," XLVII, *prose tr. by* J. M. Synge. OBMV
(He Understands the Great Cruelty of Death.) BIrV
Nightingale, The, XLIII, *tr. by* Thomas LeMesurier. PoPl
"What a grudge I am bearing the earth," XXXIII, *tr. by* J. M. Synge.
(Translation from Petrarch, A.) MoBrPo
To Laura in Life.
"Blest be the day, and blest the month and year," XLVII, *tr. by* Joseph Auslander. NAWM-1
("Father in heaven, after each lost day," *tr. by* Bernard Bergonzi.) NAWM-1
Heart on the Hill, The, CCV, *tr. by* C.B. Cayley. AWP
"I find [*or* fynde] no peace and all my war[r] is done," CIV, *tr. by* Sir Thomas Wyatt. AAS; OAEL-1 OBVE; PPoe
(Description of the Contrarious Passions in a Lover.) FF; OAEP; TrGrPo
If It Be Destined, XI, *tr. by* Edward Fitzgerald. AWP
(I Find No Peace.) LiTB
(Sonnet: "I find no peace . . .") SiPS
"It was the morning of that blessed day," III, *tr. by* Joseph Auslander. NAWM-1
Last Trial, CXIII, *tr. Unknown.* OBSC
"Long[e] love that in my thought doth harbour, The," CIX, *tr. by* Sir Thomas Wyatt. CABA; OAEL-1; OBVE
(Long Love That in My Thought Doth Harbour, The.) NoP
(Lover for Shamefastnesse Hideth His Desire within His Faithfull Hart, The.) AAS, 2 *versions*
Love, That Doth Reign and Live Within My Thought, *tr. by* Earl of Surrey. HeIP; NoP; OAEL-1
(Complaint of a Lover Rebuked.) AWP; CABA; TrGrPo
("Love that doth raine and live within my thought.") AAS; OBVE
("Love that liveth and reigneth in my thought.") SiPS

"My galley [*or* galy] charged with forgetfulness," CLVI, *tr. by* Sir Thomas Wyatt. AAS; BiP; CABA; HAP; NoP; OAEL-1; OBVE; PPP
(Galley, The.) OBSC
(Lover Compareth His State to a Ship in Perilous Storm Tossed on the Sea, The.) EIL; GBL; HeIP; PoEL-1
(Lover Like to a Ship Tossed on the Sea.) EtS
(My Galley.) MOS
(Sonnet.) SiPS
"Set me whereas the sun doth parch the green [*or* sonne dothe perche the grene]," CXIII, *tr. by* the Earl of Surrey. AAS; HAP; SiPS
(Love's Fidelity.) AWP
(To His Lady.) OBSC
(Vow to Love Faithfully, Howsoever He Be Rewarded, A.) TrGrPo; ViBoPo
"She used to let her golden hair fly free," LXIX, *tr. by* Morris Bishop. NAWM-1
Signs of Love, CLXXXVIII, *tr. by* C.B. Cayley. AWP
Songs.
Canzone VIII, *tr. by* Helen Lee Peabody.
(Ode to the Virgin.) ISi
Visions, The. To Laura in Death, Canzone III, *tr. by* Spenser. AWP
I saw a Phoenix in the Wood Alone, *sel.* ChTr
Sonnets to Miranda, *sels.* Sir William Watson.
"Daughter of her whose face, and lofty name," I. HBV-1
"I cast these lyric offerings at your feet," V. HBV-1
"I dare but sing of you in such a strain," III. HBV-1
"I move amid your throng, I watch you hold," VI. HBV-1
"If I had never known your face at all," VIII. FaBoBe; HBV-1
"If you had lived in that more stately time," II. HBV-1
Sonnets to My Mother. Arthur S. Bourinot. CaP
Sonnets to Orpheus, *sels.* Rainer Maria Rilke, *tr. fr. German.*
"Full, ripe apple, pear and banana," *tr. by* Christopher Hawthorne. SOTW
"Mirrors, no one yet has really described," *tr. by* Christopher Hawthorne. SOTW
"Spring has come again. The earth," *tr. by* Christopher Hawthorne. SOTW
"This is the creature there has never been," Pt. II, IV, *tr. by* James Blair Leishman. OBVE
"Torn apart by us ever and again," ILwL
"Tree ascending there, O pure transcension, A!" *fr.* I, i, *tr. by* James Blair Leishman. UnS
"Wait . . . that tastes good . . . already it is on the wing," *tr. by* Christopher Hawthorne. SOTW
"Where, in what ever-blissfully watered gardens," Pt. II, XVII, *tr. by* James Blair Leishman. OBVE
("Where, in whatever happily watered garden, on what trees," *tr. by* Christopher Hawthorne.) SOTW
Sonnets to Philomel, *sels.* Sir John Davies. SiPS
"If you would know the love which I you bear."
"Oft did I hear our eyes the passage were."
"Once did my Philomel reflect on me."
"Sickness, intending my love to betray."
Sonnets to the Fairest Coelia. William Percy. *See* Coelia.
Sonnets to the Seasons, *sel.* Hartley Coleridge.
November, XII. LoBV; OBNC; OBRV
Sonnets—Unrealities, *sel.* E. E. Cummings.
"It may not always be so; and I say." BoLoP
(It May Not Always Be So.) FaBV
Sonnets upon the Punishment of Death, *sels.* Wordsworth.
Apology. VLP
"Ye brood of Conscience—Spectres! that frequent." PeD
Sonnet's Voice, The. Theodore Watts-Dunton. EtS; HBV-2
Sonnets Written in the Fall of 1914. George Edward Woodberry. HBV-2; PAH
Sonnets Written in the Orillia Woods, *sels.* Charles Sangster.
"Blest Spirit of Calm that dwellest in these woods!" PeCV
"Our life is like a forest, where the sun," *fr.* VII. NOBC
Sons. Jack Cope. PeSA
Sons. Don Polson. AMV-81
Sons, my sons. Black Star Line. Henry Dumas. PoBA
Sons of freedom, listen to me, and ye daughters, too, give ear. James Bird. *Unknown.* AmFP
Sons of Indolence. James Thomson. *Fr.* The Castle of Indolence. OBEC
Sons of Levi, The. *Unknown.* AmFP
Sons of Martha, The ("The sons of Mary seldom bother, for they have inherited that good part"). Kipling. HBV-2; WGRP
Sons of New England, in the fray. Treason's Last Device. Edmund Clarence Stedman. PAH
Sons of Our Sons, The. Ilya Ehrenburg, *tr. fr. Russian by* Babette Deutsch. TrJP
Sons of Saint Crispin, 'tis in vain! "Peter Pindar." *Fr.* Resignation; an Ode to the Journeyman Shoemakers. NOEC
Sons of the Empire, bond and free. The Hands-across-the-Sea Poem. J. C. Squire. HBMV
Sons of the prophet are brave men [*or* hardy *or* valiant] and bold, The. Abdul A-Bul-Bul A-Mir [*or* Abdullah Bulbul Amir; or, Ivan Petrofsky Skovar *or* Abdul, the Bulbul Ameer]. *Unknown.* AS; BLPA; FPL; FSW; TreF
Sons of valor, taste the glories. Off from Boston. *Unknown.* PAH
Sons of War sometimes are known, The. Evan Lloyd. *Fr.* The Methodist. OBSV
Sonship. John C. Rezmerski. FAZ
Soo Line, Reading, Pacific Fruit. The Other Side. Thomas Reiter. AMV-80
Soomtyme liv'lye Girald in grave now liv'les is harbourd. Sometime Lively Gerald. Richard Stanyhurst. NCEP
Soon as/ you stop. Cleavage. A. R. Ammons. OBAL
Soon as the day begins to waste. The Constant Swain and Virtuous Maid. *Unknown.* HBV-1
Soon as the dismal news came down. Oxford Barber's Verses on the Queen's Death. *Unknown.* APAS
Soon as the father saw the rosy morn. Ovid, *tr. by* Joseph Addison. *Fr.* Metamorphoses. OBVE
Soon as the harvest hath laid bare the plains. Stephen Duck. *Fr.* The Thresher's Labour. NOEC
Soon as the sound had ceased whose thunder filled. Shelley. *Fr.* Prometheus Unbound, III, iv. ChER
Soon as the sun forsook the eastern main. An Hymn to the Evening. Phillis Wheatley. WPE
Soon at Last My Sighs and Moans. Louis Ginsberg. TrJP
Soon I shall be in tears this birthday morning. A Birthday in Hospital. Elizabeth Jennings. NAs
Soon I will climb the hill to the sunlight. From the Rain Forest. Desirée Flynn. BrRo
Soon I will let myself back into the street. Proof. Leslie Ullman. FAZ
Soon One Mornin' Death Come Creepin', *with music.* *Unknown.* OuSiCo
Soon one mornin', was mistin' rain. The Wreck on the Somerset Road. *Unknown.* OuSiCo
Soon shall thy arm, unconquer'd steam! afar. Steam Power. Erasmus Darwin. *Fr.* The Botanic Garden. OBEC
Soon, summer's drum will shake the earth no longer. Fall of Leaves. D. S. Savage. PoA
Soon the night in mantle dark. The Ploughboy. John Clare. PoEL-4
Soon we entered in the woods. The Arrival. Alexander McLachlan. *Fr.* The Emigrant. NOBC
Soon we shall plunge into the chilly fogs. Song of Autumn I. Baudelaire, *tr. by* C. F. McIntyre. NAWM-2
Soon with the Lilac Fades Another Spring. Patrick MacDonogh. OxBI
Sooner I may some fixed statue be. On the Duke of Buckingham, Slain by Felton, the 23rd August, 1628. Owen Felltham. JCP
Sooner or Later. Sam Cornish. CNA
Sooner or Later. John Digby. EAS
Sooner or later I will forget. No Difference. Beverly Lawn. AMV-81
Soonest Mended. John Ashbery. Prf
Soot on the cassies, The. And Happy Am I. Syd Scroggie. PoSH
Soote Season, The. Earl of Surrey, *after* Petrarch. AAS; EnRePo; HeIP; NIP; NoP
(Description of Spring.) LiTB; LOBV
(Description of Spring, Wherein Each Thing Renews Save Only the Lover.) EIL; OAEP; OBEV; SeCePo; SeCeV
("Soote season, that bud and blome furth bringes, The.") OBVE; SiPS
(Spring.) NOBE; OBSC
(Summer Is Come.) AWP
Soothd by the murmurs of a plaintive streame. A Wild Romantic Dell. William Julius Mickle. *Fr.* The Concubine. OBEC
Soothing sigh of the night wind, the whine of a coyote's call, The. Ranch at Twilight. *Unknown.* BPAW
Soothsay. William Carlos Williams. TwAmPo
Sooth-Sayer, The. Sadi, *tr. fr. Persian by* Sir Edwin Arnold. *Fr.* The Gulistan. AWP
Sootie Joe. Melvin B. Tolson. FAZ
Sooty, swart smiths, smattered with smoke. The Blacksmiths. *Unknown.* TW
Sophia, her age between. Wisdom of the Gazelle. George P. Solomos. GoYe
Sophia Nichols. Robin Blaser. CoPo
Sophisticate. Barbara Young. SiSoSe
Sophisticated, worldly-wise. I Found God. Mary Afton Thacker. TRV
Sophistication. Vassar Miller. NCSH
Sopolis. Callimachus, *tr. fr. Greek by* William M. Hardinge. AWP
Sopranosound, Memory of John. Sharon Bourke. CNA
Sops of Light. Fredegond Shove. ChMP
Soraidh Slan Don Oidhche Areir. Niall Mor MacMuireadach, *tr. fr. Irish by* Maire Cruise O'Brien. BIrV

Sorcerer, The. A. J. M. Smith. PeCV
Sorcerer, Mr. Wells, The, *sel.* W. S. Gilbert.
Oh! my name is John Wellington Wells. WSC
Sorceress, The! Vachel Lindsay. PDV; WSC
Sorceress, The. Eugène Marais, *tr. fr. Afrikaans by* Jack Cope *and* Uys Krige. PeSA
Sorrow. Chu Shu-chen, *tr. fr. Chinese by* Kenneth Rexroth. BoWoP
Sorrow. Samuel Daniel. *See* Had Sorrow Ever Fitter Place.
Sorrow. Aubrey Thomas De Vere. BLPA; GoBC; HBV-2; WGRP; WiR
Sorrow. Emily Dickinson. WGRP
Sorrow. D. H. Lawrence. CMoP; GTBS-P; OBMV
Sorrow. Marie Tello Phillips. GoYe
Sorrow. George Santayana. WGRP
Sorrow. Katrina Trask. AA
Sorrow. *Unknown, tr. fr. Russian by* W. R. S. Ralston. AWP
Sorrow can wait. Folded Power. Gladys Cromwell. HBMV
Sorrow has a harp of seven strings. The Harp of Sorrow. Ethel Clifford. HBV-2; WGRP
Sorrow heaped on sorrow, ruin on disaster. On My Sorrowful Life. Moses ibn Ezra, *tr. by* Solomon Solis-Cohen. TrJP
Sorrow how high it is. Dark Song. A. R. Ammons. MAT
Sorrow Humanize Our Race. Jean Ingelow. WGRP
Sorrow is my own yard. The Widow's Lament in Springtime. William Carlos Williams. AP; CMoP; CoBMV; HAP; LiTM; NoAM; NOBA; TAP
Sorrow is my stock in trade. Reunion. Cyril Tawney. OBET
Sorrow is over the fields. The Land War. "Seumas O'Sullivan." OxBI
Sorrow Is the Only Faithful One. Owen Dodson. AmNP; BALP, *at. to* William Stanley Braithwaite; IDB; PoBA
Sorrow lay upon my breast more heavily than winter clay. "Desolation Is a Delicate Thing." Elinor Wylie. MoAmPo
Sorrow, my friend. A Song before Grief. Rose Hawthorne Lathrop. AA
Sorrow of Kodio, The. *Unknown, tr. fr. Baule by* Miriam Koshland. PBA
Sorrow of Love, The. W. B. Yeats. MoAB; MoBrPo; NoAM; OAEL-2; PoEL-5; TEP; VLP
Sorrow of Mydath. John Masefield. MoBrPo
Sorrow of Troilus, The. Chaucer. *Fr.* Troilus and Criseide, V. PoEL-1
Sorrow of Unicume, The. Sir Herbert Read. BrPo; ChMP
Sorrowing nymph, oh why display. On a Statue of Sir Arthur Sullivan. G. Rostrevor Hamilton. FaBoCo
Sorrows of my heart enlarged are, The. Some Contemplations of the Poor, and Desolate State of the Church at Deerfield. John Williams. SCAP
Sorrows of Sunday, The; an Elegy, *sel.* "Peter Pindar."
"Susan, the constant slave to mop and broom." NOEC
Sorrows of Werther. Thackeray. BLPA; CenHV; FaBoCo; FiBHP; FPL; HBV-1; InMe; NA; NBM; NOBL; PoPle; ShM; TreF; VLP
Sorry I am, my God, sorry I am. Sins' Round. George Herbert. LoBV
Sorry world is sighing now, The. Fin de Siècle. Newton Mackintosh. NA
Sort of a Song, A. William Carlos Williams. BiP; FAZ; HoPM; NoP; PP; SeCeV; TAP
Sort of Elegy, A. Blanche Farley. SOTS
Sort of extra hunger, A. Poet Wondering What He Is Up To. D. J. Enright. OxBC
Sorting out letters and piles of my old. Mementos, 1. W. D. Snodgrass. CABA; FF; HeIP; MoAmPo; NePoEA-2; PPP; UnPo
Sorting, Wrapping, Packing, Stuffing. James Schuyler. NoAM
Sory beuerech it is and sore it is abouth, A. Christ's Prayer in Gethsemane. *Unknown.* SeCePo
So-shu dreamed. Ancient Wisdom, Rather Cosmic. Ezra Pound. NOBA
Sospetto d'Herode. Giambattista Marini, *tr. fr. Italian by* Richard Crashaw. *Fr.* La Strage degli Innocenti. SeCV-1
Sought by the world, and hath the world disdained. Love's Ending. *Unknown.* OBSC
Soul, The. George Barlow. OBVV
Soul. Austin Black. NBP
Soul, The. Madison Cawein. AA
Soul, The. Abraham Cowley. AnAnS-2
Soul. D. L. Graham. PoBA
Soul, A. Randall Jarrell. CMoP
Soul, A. Christina Rossetti. WPOW
Soul, The. *Unknown.* STF
Soul and Body. Shakespeare. *See* Sonnets, CXLVI.
Soul and Body. Samuel Waddington. OBVV
Soul and Body of John Brown, The. Muriel Rukeyser. MoAmPo
Spring Song. Shakespeare. *See* When Daisies Died and Violets Blue.
Soul and race. Here Where Coltrane Is. Michael S. Harper. CNA; PoBA
Soul and Sense. Hannah Parker Kimball. AA
Soul and the Body, The. Sir John Davies. *See* In What Manner the Soule Is United to the Body.
Soul, art thou sad again. Triumphalis. Bliss Carman. HBMV
Soul before God, The. Cardinal Newman. *Fr.* The Dream of Gerontius. OxBoCh
Soul, do you hear the trumpets down in the valley. Reveillé. Audrey Alexandra Brown. CaP
Soul-Drift. Mathilde Blind. SBG
Soul has many motions, body one, The. The Motion. Theodore Roethke. SeCeV
Soul, heart, and body, we thus singly name. Love's Trinity. Alfred Austin. OBVV
Soul in the Body, The. Edith M. Thomas. AA
Soul is a region without definite boundaries, The. Terrain. A. R. Ammons. ConAP
Soul Is Form. Spenser. *See* Beauty.
Soul is lonely, The. La Selva. Cid Corman. VGW
Soul Lifted. Albert Durrant Watson. CaP
Soul lonely comes and goes; for each our theme. Lachesis. Kathleen Raine. NYBP
Soul Longs to Return Whence It Came, The. Richard Eberhart. CMoP
Soul must have, for its great need, The. Neoplatonic Soliloquy. Donald G. Babcock. NePoAm
Soul of a coconut can't live, The. Coconut. Mario Satz, *tr. by* Willis Barnstone. VWA
Soul of a tree ungrown, new life out of God's life proceeding. Yosemite. Milicent Washburn Shinn. *Fr.* Yosemite. AA
Soul of Dante, The. Michelangelo, *tr. fr. Italian by* John Addington Symonds. GoBC
Soul of Jesus Is Restless, The. Cyprus R. Mitchell. TrCP
Soul of Lincoln, The. Chauncey R. Piety. PGD
Soul of Man, The. Dora Read Goodale. AA
Soul of mine, pretty one, flitting one. Emperor Hadrian's Dying Address to His Soul. *Unknown.* TreFT
Soul of my child, Princess Splendid! Invocation before the Rice Harvest. *Malay Oral Tradition, tr. by* R. O. Winstedt. WTO
Soul of the World, The. Ernest Crosby. AA
Soul of Time, The. Trumbull Stickney. LiTA; NePA
Soul Remembers, The. Richard Burdick Eldridge. GoYe
Soul selects her own society, The. Emily Dickinson. AmPP; AP; AWP; BLPL; BoWoP; CABA; CMoP; InPK; InPS; MoAB; MoAmPo; NePA; NoAM; NOBA; NoP; OxBA; PAI; PoEL-5; SBG; TAP; TreFT; TrGrPo; UnPo; WHA; WPE
Soul-Severance. St. John Hankin. FaBoPa
Soul shall burst her fetters, The. The Soul. George Barlow. OBVV
Soul-Sickness. Jones Very. AP
Soul-soothing drug! your virtues let me laud. A Sonnet to Opium; Celebrating Its Virtues. "Orestes." NOEC
Soul Speaks, The. Edward H. Pfeiffer. HBMV
Soul unto Soul Glooms Darling. Charles Leonard Moore. AA
Soul, Wherefore Fret Thee? "Stuart Sterne." AA
Soul wherein God dwells, The. The Cherubic Pilgrim. "Angelus Silesius. WGRP
Soul Winner's Prayer, The. Eugene M. Harrison. STF
Souldier and a Sailor, A. Congreve. *See* Soldier and a Sailor, A.
Souldier Going to the Field, The. Sir William Davenant. *See* Soldier Going to the Field, The.
Souldiers Farewel to His Love, The. *Unknown.* CoMu
Soules Ignorance in This Life and Knowledge in the Next, The. John Donne. *Fr.* Of the Progresse of the Soule; the Second Anniversarie. OBS
("Poor soul, in this thy flesh what dost thou know?") OAEL-1
Soules joy, now I am gone. Song. *Unknown, at. to.* the Earl of Pembroke. AnAnS-1; OBS
Soulfolk, think a minute. To Soulfolk. Margaret Goss Burroughs. BlSi
Souling Song. *Unknown. See* Christmas Carol: "God bless the master of this house."
Souls. Fannie Stearns Gifford. HBMV
Souls. Paul Wertheimer, *tr. fr. German by* Jethro Bithell. TrJP
Soul's Beauty. Dante Gabriel Rossetti. The House of Life, LXXVII. OAEP; OBEV; OBVV; VLP
Soul's Bitter Cry, The. *Unknown, tr. fr. Tamil.* WGRP
Soul's Calm Sunshine, The. Pope. *Fr.* An Essay on Man, IV. FaBoRV
Soul's Dark Cottage, The. Edmund Waller. *Fr.* Of The Last Verses in the Book. ChTr
Soul's Defiance, The. Lavinia Stoddard. AA
Soul's Desire, The. *Unknown, tr. fr. Irish by* Eleanor Hull. OxBI
Soul's Errand, The. Sir Walter Ralegh. *See* Lie, The.
Soul's Expression, The. Elizabeth Barrett Browning. VLP
Soul's Garment, The. Margaret Cavendish, Duchess of Newcastle. OxBoCh; SeCePo; WPE
Souls Groan to Christ for Succour, The. Edward Taylor. *Fr.* God's Determinations. PAI; PoEL-3
Soul's joy, bend not those morning stars from me. Astrophel and Stella, XLVIII. Sir Philip Sidney. NoP; SiPS
Souls joy, when thou art gone. A Parodie. George Herbert. AnAnS-1; OBS
Soul's Kiss. Samuel Greenberg. LiTA

Souls Lake. Robert Fitzgerald. MoPo; MP; TwCP
Soul's Liberty. Anna Wickham. MoBrPo
Souls of men! why will ye scatter. Come to Jesus [*or* God Our Father]. Frederick William Faber. VLP; WGRP
Souls of poets dead and gone. Lines on the Mermaid Tavern [*or* The Mermaid Tavern]. Keats. AWP; BLPL; EnRP; FaBoBe; GTBS; GTBS-P; HBV-2; InMe; InvP; LoBV; OAEP; OBRV; PORA; PP; SeCeV; TreFS; ViBoPo
Souls of the patriot dead. The Kidnapping of Sims. John Pierpont. PAH
Souls of the Slain, The. Thomas Hardy. CMoP; LiTB; PoEL-5
Souls of Women at Night, The. Wallace Stevens. CMoP
Soul's shining place, The. About the Heavenly Life. Luis de Léon, *tr. fr. Spanish.* ILwL
Soul's Soliloquy, A. Wenonah Stevens Abbott. BLPA
Soul's Travelling, the, *sel.* Elizabeth Barrett Browning.
"God, God!/ With a child's voice I cry." ILwL
Sound. Jim Harrison. VGW
Sound, The. Robert Kelly. PoM
Sound Advice. *Unknown.* FaBoUs
Sound and Sense ("But most by numbers judge a poet's song"). Pope. *See* Poetical Numbers
Sound and Sense ("True ease in writing comes from art, not chance"). Pope. *Fr.* An Essay on Criticism, Pt. II. SoSe; UnPo
("True ease in writing comes from art, not chance"). HAP; PrIm; TrGrPo
Sound came booming through the air, A. The Philosopher and Her Father. Shirley Brooks. CenHV
Sound Country Lass, The. *Unknown.* CoMu; ErPo
Sound from the Earth, A. William Stafford. NNaP; RFM
Sound like I can hear this morning. Death Bells. *Unknown.* BluL
Sound-Noise. Memory as Memorial in the Last. Edward Marshall. CoPo
Sound not the depths for anchorage, but ways. Seaway. Grace Wilson. AMV-81
Sound of Afroamerican History Chapt I, The ("The history of blacklife is put down in the motions"). S. E. Anderson. PoBA
Sound of Afroamerican History Chapt II, The ("Smith at the organ is like an anvil being"). S. E. Anderson. PoBA
Sound of Breaking. Conrad Aiken. AWP
Sound of happy laughter leap with shadows on the walls. Taos Winter. Patty L. Harjo. VoR
Sound of many waters, A!—now I know. Sonnet in a Pass of Bavaria. Richard Chenevix Trench. OBRV
Sound of Morning in New Mexico, The. Reeve Spencer Kelley. AmFN
Sound of Night, The. Maxine W. Kumin. BoNaP; DFF; WPE
Sound of Rain, The. Bella Akhmadulina, *tr. fr. Russian by* Daniel Halpern *and* Albert Todd. BoWoP
Sound of rain on the roof was too loud, The. The Gold Country, The; Hotel Leger, Mokelumne Hill, Revisited. Joseph Stroud. NPGG
Sound of snails—crying. Snails. Liagarang *tr. by* Ronald M. Berndt. CBAP; WTO
Sound of the Drum, The. *Unknown.* OBET
Sound of the Horn, The. Alfred de Vigny, *tr. fr. French by* Wilfred Thorley. AWP
Sound of the Sea, The. Longfellow. AP; EtS; MOS; TreFT
Sound of the Sea, The. John Hall Wheelock. EtS
Sound of the Trees [*or* of Trees], The. Robert Frost. NoAM; OxBA; TwAmPo
Sound of the Wind, The. Christina Rossetti. *Fr.* Sing-Song. OnUR
("Wind has such a rainy sound, The.") TiPo
Sound of thy sweet name, my dearest treasure, The. Madrigal. Francis Davison. ElL
Sound of Trees, The. Robert Frost. *See* Sound of the Trees, The.
Sound of Water. Mary O'Neill. NTCP
Sound of water running, The. Civilization. Tom Schmidt. NeAC
Sound of your lips beating, The. Thoughts for My Grandmother. Laya Firestone. VWA
Sound out, proud trumpets. Osbert Sitwell. *Fr.* England Reclaimed. ViBoPo
Sound, Sound the Clarion. Thomas Osbert Mordaunt, *formerly at. to* Sir Walter Scott. *Fr.* Verses Written during the War, 1756-1763; 4 *ll.* In Old Mortality (*by* Scott), *ch.* 34. FaBoEE; FaPoR; NOBE
(Call, The.) OBEV
(One Crowded Hour.) TrGrPo
("Sound, sound the clarion, fill the fife!") OAEP
(Sound the Clarion.) TreFS
Sound the deep waters. Sleep at Sea. Christina Rossetti. MOS; NBM; PoEL-5
Sound the flute! Spring. Blake. *Fr.* Songs of Innocence. FaBoCh; FaPON; MoShBr; PoPl; SUS; YeAr
Sound the Loud Timbrel. Thomas Moore. GoBC
Sound the trumpet, beat the drum. Dryden. *Fr.* The Secular Masque. FaBoRV
Sound variegated through beneath lit. Gyre's Galax. Norman Henry Pritchard II. PoBA
Soundest of all literary legal tenders. Old Bill's Memory Book. William Rose Benét. InMe
Sounding, The. Conrad Aiken. CrMA
Sounding. Doris Ferne. CaP
Sounding. David Jauss. Str
Sounding cataract, The/ Haunted me like a passion. Wordsworth. *Fr.* Lines Composed a Few Miles above Tintern Abbey. FaBoEn; WGRP
Sounding Fog, The. Susan Nichols Pulsifer. PDV
Sounding Portage, The. Annie Charlotte Dalton. CaP
Soundless, The/ light drifts over. The Light of the World. B. Alquit, *tr. by* Howard Schwartz. VWA
Soundless the moth-flit, crisp the death-watch tick. Maerchen. Walter de la Mare. CoBMV
Soundlessly, a tide at the ear. Awakening. John Haines. EAS
Sounds. Paul David Ashley. LFAC
Sounds. Robert Creeley. GP
Sounds are heard too high for ears. Watching Television. Robert Bly. BiP; CoAP
Sounds in the Morning, The. Eleanor Farjeon. SUS
Sounds like big. Waking from a Nap on the Beach. May Swenson. NTCP; PCP; RFM
Sounds of Ireland, The. Windharp. John Montague. CIP
Soup. Carl Sandburg. NOBE; OBCA
Soup of Venus, The. James Tate. AmPA
Soup on a Cold Day. Nellie Hill. AMV-81
Soup Song. Maurice Sugar. FSW
Soupy, soupy, soupy, without a single bean. Words for Army Bugle Calls: Mess Call. *Unknown.* TreF
Sour daylight cracks through my sleep-caked lids, The. The Distant Winter. Philip Levine. VGW
Sour fiend, go home and tell the Pit. Ghoul Care. Ralph Hodgson. MoBrPo
Source, The. Jon Stallworthy. NoP
Source immaterial of material naught. The Rejected "National Hymns." "Orpheus C. Kerr." InMe; OBAL
Source of News. *Unknown.* TreF
Sources of Good Counsel. Peter Idley. OxBChV
Sourdough french bread and pinot chardonnay. Maps. Robert Hass. NPGG
Sourdough mountain called a fire in. Gary Snyder. Myths and Texts: Burning, XVII. NaP; NoP
Sourdough Mountain Lookout. Philip Whalen. NeAP; PoM
Sourwood Mountain. *Unknown.* AmFP; AS, *with music;* FSW; GBP; TrAS, *with music*
Sourwood sprouts are long, The. Secret Pleasures. Robert Morgan. MAYP
Sousa. Edward Dorn. CoPo
Souster. Ray Fraser. NeAC
South, The. Wang Chien, *tr. fr. Chinese by* Arthur Waley. AWP
South African Bloodstone. Quincy Troupe. CNA
South African Broadsheets, *sel.* David Wright.
"Under the African lintel, Table Mountain." PeSA
South and west winds joined, and, as they blew, The. The Storm, *abr.* John Donne. EtS
South Atlantic clouds rode low, The. Safari West. John A. Williams. InPS; NBP
South Australia. *Unknown.* FSW; ShS, *with music*
South Carolina, The. *Unknown.* PAH
South Carolina to the States of the North. Paul Hamilton Hayne. PAH
South Coast, The. William Everson. NeAP
South Coast Idyll, A. Rosamund Marriott Watson. OBVV
South Country, The. Hilaire Belloc. ACP; GoBC; HBV-2; MoBrPo; OBVV
South Country. Kenneth Slessor. CBAP
South End. Conrad Aiken. CMoP; HoPM; MoVE; OxBA
South-Folk in Cold Country. Ezra Pound, *after the Chinese.* CrMA; OBVE
South, in the town, the sun had spread. The Brothers. John Holloway. NMP
South Inlet. Greg Kuzma. WOLT
South is green with coming spring, The. The Trial. Muriel Rukeyser. PoNe
South of Guardafui with a dark tide flowing. The Dhows. Francis Brett Young. EtS
South of My Days. Judith Wright. PoAu-2; WPE
South of success and east of gloss and glass are. The Wall. Gwendolyn Brooks. PoNe
South of the Border. Virginia Real Nicholas. AMV-80
South of the border and north of the sea. Song of the Border. Gordon W. Norris. BPAW
South of the Bridge on Seventeenth. Fifteen. William Stafford. CAD

South of the fabled pillars of Hercules. Volubilis, North Africa. Ralph Nixon Currey. PeSA
South of the Great Sea. *Unknown, tr. fr. Chinese by* Arthur Waley. OLR
South of the Line, inland from far Durban. A Christmas Ghost-Story. Thomas Hardy. OBWP
South Shore Line. John Schlesinger. AMV-80
South Street. Francis E. Falkenbury. EtS
South Street. Edward S. Silvera. CDC
South Wind, The. Robert Bridges. OBNC
South-Wind. George Parsons Lathrop. AA
South Wind. Nathan Yonathan, *tr. fr. Hebrew by* Richard Flantz. VWA
South-wind brings, The. Threnody. Emerson. AA; AP
South wind brings wet weather, The. *Unknown. Fr.* Weather Wisdom. FaBoUs; HBV-1; HBVY; TreF
South Wind laid his moccasins aside, The. Isabella Valancy Crawford. *Fr.* Malcolm's Katie. OBCV
South-wind strengthens to a gale, The. Low Barometer. Robert Bridges. CMoP; CoBMV; LiTB; LoBV; QFR; NoAM; NOCV
South wind's molded by a spine of hill, The. Another Kind of Burning. Ruth Fox. NYBP
Southbound on the Freeway. May Swenson. AmFN; NTCP; NYBP
Southeast, and storm, and every weathervane. Hatteras Calling. Conrad Aiken. BoNaP; NoAM; NOBA; TAP
Southeast Arkanasia. Maya Angelou. SaC
Southeast at low tide. Skiing on Russian Christmas. Nora Dauenhauer. TWSS
Southeast Ramparts of the Seine, The. Judit Tóth, *tr. fr. Hungarian by* Emery George. VWA
Souther, wind, souther! Rhyme of the Fishermen's Children. *Unknown.* GBP
Southerly Wind, *with music. Unknown.* ShS
Southern Blues. *Unknown.* BluL
Southern Cop. Sterling Brown. SoSe
Southern Cross, The. Robert Stephen Hawker. *See* Mystic Magi, The.
Southern Cross. Herman Melville. LiTA
Southern Exposures. G. E. Murray. AMV-81
Southern Girl, A. Samuel Minturn Peck. AA
Southern Gothic. Donald Justice. NIP; TwAmPo
Southern Mansion. Arna Bontemps. AmFN; AmNP; BALP; BANP; CNA; FB; FF; IDB; LiTM; PoBA; PoNe; TTY; WSC
Southern Pines. John Peale Bishop. GOA
Southern Road. Sterling A. Brown. BALP; BANP; BPo; FB; PoBA
Southern Road, The. Dudley Randall. CNA; NNP; PoBA
Southern Season. Alice Moser Claudel. TAT
Southern Ships and Settlers. Rosemary *and* Stephen Vincent Benét. AmFN
Southern Snow-Bird, The. William Hamilton Hayne. AA
Southern Summer. Francis Stuart. NeIP
Southerner, The. Karl Shapiro. NYBP; PoNe
Southey and Wordsworth. Byron. *See* Dedication: "Bob Southey! You're a poet—poet-laureate."
Southey Looks out of the Window at Greta Hill. Southey. *Fr.* A Vision of Judgement. FaBoPP
Southrons, hear your country call you! Dixie. Albert Pike. AA; HBV-2; PAH
Southward Bound. J. F. A. Burt. PoSH
Southward Sidonian Hanno. Hervey Allen. EtS
Southward through Eden went a river large. Milton. *Fr.* Paradise Lost, IV. ViBoPo
Southward with fleet of ice. Sir Humphrey Gilbert. Longfellow. EtS; HBV-2; HBVY; PAH
Southwest Passage. Dudley Fitts. PoA
Southwest wind blows in from the sea unceasing, The. Return to Life. Abbie Huston Evans. NePoAm
South-west wind, how pleasant in the face, The. Beans in Blossom. John Clare. VLP
Soutine the Sour. A Story of Soutine. James Schevill. PoCh
Souvenir. Alfred de Musset, *tr. fr. French by* George Santayana. AWP
Souvenir. E. A. Robinson. NoAM
Souvenirs. Dudley Randall. BPo
Sou'wester whips the day awake, The. Bruce Beaver. Letters to Live Poets, X. CBAP
Soverayne [*or* Sovereign] beauty which I doo admyre, The. Amoretti, III. Spenser. HBV-1; OAEP; PoEL-1
Sovereign and Transforming Grace, *with music.* Frederic Henry Hedge. AH
Sovereign beauty which I do admire. *See* Soverayne beauty which I do admyre, The.
Sovereign Poet, The. Sir William Watson. WGRP
Sovereign Poets. Lloyd Mifflin. *See* Sovereigns, The.
Sovereign Queen. Padeshah Khatun, *tr. fr. Farsi by* Deirdre Lashgari. WPOW
Sovereigns, The. Lloyd Mifflin. AA; HBV-2
(Sovereign Poets.) WGRP
Sovereignty, His. Kalonymos ben Moses of Lucca, *tr. fr. Hebrew by* Nina Davis Salaman. TrJP
Sow beans in the mud. *Unknown.* FaBoUs
Sow Came In, The. *Unknown.* NOBL
Sow came in with the saddle, The. Mother Goose. OxNR
Sow of Feeling, The. Robert Fergusson. NOEC
Sow thin. *Unknown.* FaBoUs
Sow Took the Measles, The. *Unknown.* FSW
Sow ye by all waters. Fear Not. J. Bullock. STF
Sower, The. Laurence Binyon. MMA
Sower, The. Mathilde Blind. SBG; WPE
Sower, The. William Cowper. SaC
Sower, The. R. Olivares Figueroa, *tr. fr. Spanish by* Dudley Fitts. FaPON
Sower, The. Sir Charles G. D. Roberts. CaP; OBCV
Sower a Singer, The. Cotton Mather. *See* When the Seed of Thy Word Is Cast.
Sower went out to sow his seed, A. Jesus' Parable of the Sower. Bible, *N.T. Fr.* St. Luke TreFT
Sower's Song, The. Thomas Carlyle. OBVV
Sowing. Edward Thomas. HBMV
Sowing in the morning, sowing seeds of kindness. Bringing in the Sheaves. Knowles Shaw. FSW
Sowing on the Mountain. *Unknown.* FSW
Sowing Season. Evening. Victor Hugo, *tr. fr. French by* Mary Ann Caws. NAWM-2
Sow's Ear, A. Theodore Weiss. NoAM
Soyer is gone! Then be it said. On the Death of the Great Chef Alexis Soyer. *Unknown.* FaBoEE
Space. William Hart-Smith. *Fr.* Christopher Columbus. PoAu-2
Space. X. J. Kennedy. MOON
Space and Dread and the Dark. W. E. Henley. WHA
Space, and the twelve clean winds of heaven. The Most-Sacred Mountain. Eunice Tietjens. HBMV
Space and Time. Syd Scroggie. PoSH
Space beats the ruddy freedom of their limbs. Daughters of War. Isaac Rosenberg. BrPo
Space Being (Don't Forget to Remember) Curved. E. E. Cummings. NoAM
Space between the hysterical squeals, The. Space for Colour. Alan Bold. BSV
Space Child's Mother Goose, The, *sels.* Frederick Winsor.
"Hydrogen Dog and the Cobalt Cat, The." QQQ; ShM
"Little Bo-Beep." QQQ
"Probable-Possible, my black hen." QQQ
"Solomon Grundy." QQQ
"This little pig built a spaceship." QQQ; RHPC
Space Eater Camps at Fifth Lake, The. Reg Saner. GP
Space Fiction. Norman MacCaig. TEP
Space for Colour. Alan Bold. BSV
Space in the Air, A. Jon Silkin. NePoEA; TrJP
Space is too full. Did nothing happen here? American Farm, 1934. Genevieve Taggard. VGW
Space-man, space-man. Soft Landings. Howard Sergeant. OnUR
Space Shuttle. Diane Ackerman. MAYP; SUW
Space-Suit Sammy. Going Up. John Travers Moore. RHPC
Space-time, our scientists tell us, is impervious. Archibald MacLeish. *Fr.* Reply to Mr. Wordsworth. ImOP
Space Travel. Jane W. Krows. SoPo
Space-Wanderer's Homecoming. Peter Viereck. AMV-80
Space we feel inside us, The. After. Michael Ryan. MAYP
Spaces await their people. Homage to Robert Bresson. Jon Anderson. MAYP
'Spacially Jim. Bessie Morgan. HBV-2
Spacin. Ronda Davis. JB
Spacious Firmament on High, The. Joseph Addison. BLPA; EaLo; ELP; FaBoBe; FaPoR; FPL; GN; HBV-2; HBVY; NIP; PoEL-3; TreFT
(Hymn: "Spacious firmament on high, The.") AWP; OBEV
(Hymn to the Creation.) OHIP
(Ode: "Spacious firmament on high, The.") HeIP; ILwL; NOCV; NOEC; OBEC; OxBoCh
(Psalm XIX.) WGRP
Spade, A! a rake! a hoe! The Lay of the Labourer. Thomas Hood. SaC
Spade-bearded grandfather, squat Lenin. Summer Pogrom. Fay Zwicky. CBAP
Spade Is Just a Spade, A. Walter Everette Hawkins. PoBA
Spade Scharnweber. Don Welch. Psk
Spades take up leaves. Gathering Leaves. Robert Frost. VGW
Spading earth. Animal Kingdom. Sydney Clouts. PeSA
Spaewife, The. Robert Louis Stevenson. BrPo; OxBS
Spain. W. H. Auden. *See* Spain 1937.
Spain. Dorothy Livesay. NOBC
Spain drew us proudly from the womb of night. Full Cycle. John White Chadwick. PAH

Spain 1937. W. H. Auden. LiTB; OBWP
(Spain.) WaP
Spain. The wild dust, the whipped corn. Teresa of Avila. Elizabeth Jennings. NePoEA-2
Spain's Last Armada. Wallace Rice. PAH
Spake full well, in language quaint and olden. Flowers. Longfellow. HBV-1
Spake the Lord Christ—"I will arise." An Easter Hymn. Richard Le Gallienne. OHIP
Span of Life, The. Robert Frost. GDP; HoPM; LiTM; SoSe
Spangled Pandemonium, The. Palmer Brown. AmMo; RHPC; TiPo
Spaniel, Beau, that fares like you, A. On a Spaniel Called Beau Killing a Young Bird. William Cowper. FaBoCh
Spaniel's Sermon. Colin Ellis. PV
Spanish Armada met its fate, The. *Unknown.* FaBoUs
Spanish Blue. Herbert Morris. NYBP
Spanish Curate, The, *sels.* John Fletcher.
Dearest, Do Not You Delay Me, *fr.* II, iv. ViBoPo
"Let the bells ring, and let the boys sing," *fr.* III, ii. OBS
Spanish Descent, The. Daniel Defoe. APAS
"Word's gone out, and now they spread the main, The," *sel.* OBWP
Spanish expression, The, *Cuando yo era muchacho.* Habla Usted Español? James Reiss. AmPA
Spanish Folk Songs. Antonio Machado, *tr. fr. Spanish by* Havelock Ellis. AWP
"Let the rich man fill his belly."
"My father was a sailor."
Spanish Friar [*or* Fryar], The, *sel.* Dryden.
Farewell, Ungrateful Traitor. BoLoP; CavP; ELP; EnLoPo; FaBoEn; HAP; LiTB; NOBE; PoPle; ViBoPo
(Love's Despair.) ACP
(Song: "Farewell ungrateful[l] traytor [*or* traitor].") CavP; FaBoEn; FiP; OBS; SeCV-2
" 'Twere well your judgments but in plays did range," *fr.* prologue. OBSV
Spanish Gipsy [*or* Gypsy], The, *sel.* Thomas Middleton *and* William Rowley.
Trip It Gipsies, Trip It Fine, *fr.* III, i. OAEP
(Song: "Trip it Gipsies, trip it fine.") OBS
Spanish Girls, The. Iván Argüelles. FIA
Spanish Gypsy, The, *sel.* "George Eliot."
I Am Lonely. GN; HBV-1
Spanish Gypsy, The. Thomas Middleton *and* William Rowley. *See* Spanish Gipsy, The.
Spanish heavens spread their brilliant starlight. Freiheit (Freedom). Karl Ernst *and* Peter Daniel, *tr. fr. German.* FSW
Spanish Is the Loving Tongue. *Unknown.* FSW
Spanish is the tongue of lovers. Mi Corazón. Gordon W. Norris. BPAW
Spanish Johnny. Willa Cather. BPAW; FaPON; HBMV
Spanish Ladies. *Unknown.* AmSS, *with music*; FaBoCh
Spanish Lions, The. Phyllis McGinley. NYBP
Spanish noon is a blaze of azure fire, and the dusty pilgrims, The. The Exodus (August 3, 1492). Emma Lazarus. *Fr.* By the Waters of Babylon. WPE
Spanish Song. Charles Divine. HBMV
Spanish Student, The, *sel.* Longfellow.
Serenade: "Stars of the summer night!" AA; FaBoBe; HBV-1; LoBV; ViBoPo
Spanish War, The. "Hugh MacDiarmid." CMoP; NMP
Spanish Waters. John Masefield. BeLS; FaPON; OnMSP
Sparafucile fought his peasant war. Dead Fly. Eilean Ni Chuilleanain. CIP
Spare!/ There is one, yes, I have one. The Golden Echo. Gerard Manley Hopkins. *Fr.* Leaden Echo and the Golden Echo, The. MoAB; MoBrPo
Spare, gen'rous [*or* generous] victor, spare the slave. To a Lady: She Refusing to Continue a Dispute with Me, and Leaving Me in the Argument. Matthew Prior. NoP; WHA
Spare Professor, grave and bald, The. At a Reading. Thomas Bailey Aldrich. OBAL
Spare Quilt, The. John Peale Bishop. GOA
Spare then the person, and expose the vice. Pope. *Fr.* Epilogue to the Satires. OBSV
Spare Us, O Lord, Aloud We Pray, *with music.* Isaac Watts. AH
"Spare us of dying beauty," cries out Youth. Of Dying Beauty. Louis Zukofsky. PoA
Spare us this silence after the guns. Map Reference T994724. John Pudney. WaP
Spared by a car- or airplane-crash or. Accidents of Birth. William Meredith. NoP
Sparhawk [*or* Sparrow-hawk] proud did hold in wicked jail, A. A Sparrow-Hawk. *Unknown.* CH; EBEV; PBBP
Spark, The. Joseph Plunkett. AnIV; AWP
Spark of Laurel, A. Stanley Kunitz. NoAM
Sparkles from the Wheel. Walt Whitman. AP; BiP; FaBoEn
Sparkling and Bright. Charles Fenno Hoffman. AA; HBV-2
Sparkling sunset, oranged to gold, A. First Frost. Edwin Curran. HBMV
Sparkling Water. Richard Schaaf. TAT
Sparks showering off the paint, The. Second Horn. W. S. Di Piero. MAYP
Sparrow, The. William Carlos Williams. DiL; InPS; LCAP; PrIm; VGW
Sparrow, The. Bible, *O.T.* Psalms, LXXXIV. FaPON
Sparrow and Diamond, The. Matthew Green. FM; PBBP
Sparrow dips in his wheel-rut bath, The. The Five Students. Thomas Hardy. CMoP; GTBS-P; PoEL-5
Sparrow hath found an house, The. The Sparrow. Bible, *O.T.* *Fr.* Psalm LXXXIV. FaPON
Sparrow Hawk, The. Russell Hoban. RHPC
Sparrow-Hawk, A. *Unknown.* CH, 1 *st.*
("Sparrow-hawk proud did hold in wicked jail, A." EBEV; PBBP
Sparrow-Hawk's Complaint, The. *Unknown.* OxBM
("In what state that ever I be.") PBBP
(Timor Mortis.) FF; NoP
Sparrow Hills. Robert Lowell, *ad. fr. the Russian of* Boris Pasternak. NaP
Sparrow in an Airport. Richard Snyder. PPJ
Sparrow in the Dust, A. Ruth Domino, *tr. fr. Italian by* Daniel Hoffman *and* Jerre Mangione. BoWoP
Sparrow in the Zoo, The. Howard Nemerov. NoAM
(Epigram: Political Reflection.) NIP
(Political Reflection.) ELU
Sparrow in Winter. Shinkichi Takahashi, *tr. fr. Japanese by* Lucien Stryk *and* Takashi Ikemoto. NU
Sparrow lights, A. Abandoned House in Late Light. Chase Twichell. MAYP
Sparrow told it to the robin, The. Early News. Anna M. Pratt. AA
Sparrows among Dry Leaves ("The sparrows/ by the iron fence post"). William Carlos Williams. NYBP
Sparrows at the Airport, The. Anthony Ostroff. NePoAm-2
Sparrow's Dirge, The ("Placebo, /Who is there? Who?"). John Skelton. Fr. Phyllyp Sparowe. OBSC
Sparrow's Dirge, The ("When I remember again"). John Skelton *Fr.* Phyllyp Sparowe. FaBoCh
("When I remember again.") PBBP; SeCePo
Sparrow's Feather, A. George Barker. NYBP
Sparrows in College Ivy. Edgar Wolfe. AMV-81
Sparrows in gossip outside the bedroom eaves. Come Not Near. Mary Elizabeth Osborn. NePoAm-2
Sparrow's Nest, The. Wordsworth. EnRP
Sparrows quarreled outside our window. Waking an Angel. Philip Levine. NaP
Sparrow's Skull, The. Ruth Pitter. EaLo
Sparrow's Song, The. *Unknown.* STF
Sparrows were feeding in a freezing drizzle. Because You Asked about the Line between Prose and Poetry. Howard Nemerov. WeW
Sparse mists of moonlight hurt our eyes. Festubert: The Old German Line. Edmund Blunden. MMA
Spartan Wrestler, The. Damagetus, *tr. fr. Greek by* Tom Dodge. LiSp
Spassky at Reykjavik. David Fisher. AMV-81
Spate in Winter Midnight. Norman MacCaig. GTBS-P; PoSH
Spatial depths of being survive. The Lost Dancer. Jean Toomer. BALP; PoBA
Spattering of the rain upon pale terraces, The. John Gould Fletcher. Irradiations, I. TwAmPo
Spawn of fantasies. Love Songs. Mina Loy. VGW; WPE
Spawn of Slums, The. James W. Thompson. BPo
Spawning in Northern Minnesota. David McElroy. AmPA
Speak. Bea Opengart. AMV-80
Speak! Wordsworth. *See* Why Art thou Silent.
Speak. James Wright. HAP; TAP; WeW
Speak and tell us, our Ximena, looking northward far away. The Angels of Buena Vista. Whittier. BeLS; PAH
Speak Gently. David Bates. PaPo; Par; SpRo
Speak gently, Spring, and make no sudden sound. Four Little Foxes. Lew Sarett. FaPON; PDV; PoSC; RFM; RHPC; YeAr
Speak gently to the herring and kindly to the calf. Kindness to Animals. Joseph Ashby-Sterry. InMe; NA
Speak, gracious Lord, oh speak; Thy servant hears. A Paraphrase on Thomas à Kempis. Pope. GoBC; OBEC; TrPWD
Speak like Rain. Jerred Metz. VWA
Speak low to me, my Saviour, low and sweet. Comfort. Elizabeth Barrett Browning. HBV-2; TRV
Speak no evil today, for we honour Cornutus' birth. Dicamus Bona Verba. Tibullus, *tr. by* Constance Carrier. NAs
Speak not ill of womankind. Against Blame of Woman. Gerald, Earl of Desmond, *tr. by* the Earl of Longford. AnIL; BIrV

“Speak not of niceness, when there's chance of wreck.” Sir Walter Scott. *Fr.* Peveril of the Peak. FaBoEE; NBM
Speak not—whisper not. The Sunken Garden. Walter de la Mare. HBMV
Speak of this to no one. Sleeping with Someone Who Came in Secret. Lady Ise, *tr. by* Burton Watson. *Fr.* Eleven Tanka. LLLT
Speak Out for Jesus. *Unknown.* STF
Speak [*or* speke], Parrot, *sels.* John Skelton.
Parrot's Soliloquy. PoEL-1
(“My name is Parrot, a byrd of paradyse.”) OxBoLi
(Parrot, The.) ACP
“So many moral matters, and so little used.” ViBoPo
Speak Roughly to Your Little Boy. “Lewis Carroll.” *Fr.* Alice's Adventures in Wonderland. FaBoCh; FaBoCo; Par
(Duchess's Lullaby, The.) FaBoNo; SpRo
(Lullaby, A.) RHPC
Speak, Satire, for there's none can tell like thee. The True-born Englishman. Daniel Defoe. APAS
“Speak! speak! thou fearful guest!” The Skeleton in Armor. Longfellow. AA; AmPP; AP; AWP; BeLS; BLPL; FaBoBe; HBV-2; HBVY; PAH; TreF
Speak the speech, I pray you, as I pronounced it to you. Hamlet's Instructions to the Players. Shakespeare. *Fr.* Hamlet, III, ii. TreFS
Speak This Kindly to Her. Robert Bagg. NePoAm-2
Speak Thou and Speed. Sir Thomas Wyatt. EnRePo
Speak, thou jaded heart, defective heart. To a Bad Heart. Tim Reynolds. TW
Speak to her heart! Ars Amoris. J. V. Cunningham. QFR
Speak to me. Take my hand. What are you now? Effort at Speech between Two People. Muriel Rukeyser. FYAP; MoAB; MoAmPo; MP; PAI; TrGrPo; TrJP; TwCP; WeW
Speak to the Sun. Dedie Huffman Wilson. GoYe
Speak to us who/ are also split. Tiresias. George Garrett. NePoAm-2
Speak when you're spoken to,/ Come for one call. Mother Goose. OxNR
Speak when you're spoken to,/ Do as you're bid. *Unknown.* CenHV
Speak with the Sun. David Campbell. SeCePo
Speake gentle heart, where is thy dwelling place? Thomas Watson. *Fr.* Hekatompathia. AAS
Speaker, The. Charles G. Ballard. VoR
Speakers, Columbus Circle. Raymond Souster. CaP
Speakin' in general, I 'ave tried 'em all. Sestina of the Tramp-Royal. Kipling. BrPo; FPL; LiTB: MoBrPo; PrIm
Speaking. Michael Ryan. AmPA
Speaking: The Hero. Felix Pollak. CTBA
Speaking as a woman who has thought. Cosmetic. Gretchen Herbkersman. AMV-80
Speaking for Them. Hayden Carruth. GP
Speaking like wind. Swimmer. Gladys Cardiff. CDW
Speaking of Cowboy's Home. *Unknown.* CoSo
Speaking of Joe, I should have said. Fred. David McCord. TiPo
Speaking of marvels, I am alive. Alive Together. Lisel Mueller. IHMS
Speaking of Poetry. John Peale Bishop. LiTA; OxBA; PP; TwAmPo
Speaking of Television, *sel.* Phyllis McGinley.
Robin Hood. OBSV
Speaking of wine. The Grapes of Wrath. Christopher Morley. WhC
Speaking Tree, The. Muriel Rukeyser. VGW
Speaks the Whispering Grass. Jesse Stuart. FYAP
Spearmen heard the bugle sound, The. Beth Gêlert. William Robert Spencer. BeLS; BLPA; GDP; OBNV; TreFS
Special Bulletin. Langston Hughes. PoBA
Special Delivery. John Montague. CIP; IPY
Special Jurymen of England! who admire your country's laws. Damages, Two Hundred Pounds. Thackeray. OBSV
Special Moment, A. Frank Lamont Phillips. FAZ
Special Rider Blues. *Unknown.* AmFP
Specialist, The. Anne S. Perlman. SUW
Specialist. Theodore Roethke. PV
Speck of protoplasm in a finch's egg, The. Birdsong. James Burns Singer. FaBoTw
Speck of Sand, A. Paul Celan, *tr. fr. German by* Joachim Neugroschel. VWA
Speck that would have been beneath my sight, A. A Considerable Speck. Robert Frost. MoAB; MoAmPo; OBAL; PPP; WhC
Speckle-black Toad and freckle-green Frog. George Darley. *Fr.* Thomas à Becket, a Dramatic Comedy. FM
Speckled cat and a tame hare, A. Two Songs of a Fool. W. B. Yeats. CMoP
Speckled horse is bucking, The. *Mongol Oral Tradition, tr. by* C. R. Bawden. WTO
Speckled sky is dim with snow, The. Midwinter. John Townsend Trowbridge. AA; GN; HBV-1
Speckled Trout/ worked in a greasy spoon. The Dirt Doctor. Melvin Douglass Brown. LFAC
Speckled with glints of star and moonshine. Mr. Walter de la Mare Makes the Little Ones Dizzy. Samuel Hoffenstein. Par; SpRO
Spectacle of Truth, The. John Hewitt. CIP
Spectator ab Extra. Arthur Hugh Clough. FaBoCo; GTBS-P; OxBoLi
Sels.
As I Sat at the Café, *also in* Dipsychus. ELP; FaBoCo; FiBHP; GTBS-P; NBM
(How Pleasant It Is to Have Money.) NOBE; OAEL-2
(So Pleasant It Is to Have Money.) SeCePo
“Come along, 'tis the time, ten or more minutes past.” OBSV
“I cannot but ask, in the park and the streets.” III. NBM
Spectator's Guide to Contemporary Art, *sels.* Phyllis McGinley.
On the Farther Wall, Marc Chagall. OBSV
Squeeze Play. DBV; FaBoEE; OBSV
Spectators only on this bustling stage. Charles Churchill. *Fr.* Night; an Epistle to Robert Lloyd. OBSV
Specter, The. Ernst Hardt, *tr. fr. German by* Jethro Bithell. AWP
Spectra, *sel.* Witter Bynner.
“If I were only dafter,” Opus 6. InPK
Spectral Attitudes, The. André Breton, *tr. fr. French by* David Gascoyne. EAS
Spectral Lovers. John Crowe Ransom. GBL; HeIP
Spectre, The. Walter de la Mare. WhC
Spectre is haunting America—the spectre of hoodooism, A. Black Power Poem. Ishmael Reed. BPo
Spectre is haunting Europe, with no name, A. Manifesto. Paris Leary. CoPo
Spectre Ship, The. Thomas Stephens Collier. EtS
Spectrum. William Dickey. ELU
Spectrum. Mari Evans. BPo
Speculation. Howard Nemerov. TAP
Speculative Evening. Marguerite Young. LiTA
Speculators, The. Thackeray. OBSV
Speech. Henry Taylor. MAT
Speech after long silence; it is right. After Long Silence. W. B. Yeats. BoLoP; CMoP; ELU; EnLoPo; HeIP; HoPM; LiTM; OAEL-2; OBMV; PoPl; PPP; PrIm; UnPo
Speech for the Repeal of the McCarran Act. Richard Wilbur. CMoP; GOA; NePoAm
Speech of the Dead, The. Anne Ridler. ChMP
Speech of the Salish Chief. Earle Birney. *Fr.* Damnation of Vancouver. OBCV
“Speech, or dark cities screaming.” Johnie Scott. *Fr.* The American Dream. NBP
Speech to a Crowd. Archibald MacLeish. MoAB; MoAmPo; NePA
Speech to Those Who Say Comrade. Archibald MacLeish. OxBA
Speechless [Upon the Marriage of Two Deaf and Dumb Persons]. Philip Bourke Marston. EBVV; VLP
Speechless Sorrow sat with me. The Guest. Harriet McEwen Kimball. AA
Speechless tree and animal and bird. A Lesson from Van Gogh. Howard Moss. MoAB
Speechless upon the Marriage of Two Deaf and Dumb Persons. Philip Bourke. *See* Speechless.
Speed of Darkness, The. Muriel Rukeyser. LCAP
Speed on, speed on, good master! The Walker of the Snow. Charles Dawson Shanly. OnYI
Speke, Parrot. John Skelton. *See* Speak, Parrot.
Spell, The. Medora C. Addison. HBMV
Spell, A. Dryden. *See* Incantation to Oedipus.
Spell. Robert Francis. GP
Spell, The. Robert Herrick. CaPo; WSC
Spell, The. Henry Martyn Hoyt. HBMV
Spell, A. George Peele. ChTr
Spell, The. Michelle Roberts. LFAC
Spell against Sorrow. Kathleen Raine. PBWP
Spell against Spelling, The. George Starbuck. FYAP
Spell before Winter, A. Howard Nemerov. LiTM
Spell Eva back and Ave shall you find. Our Lady's Salutation. Robert Southwell. ISi
Spell is past, the dream is o'er, The. We Never Speak As We Pass By. *Unknown.* TreFS
Spell It. *Unknown.* TDH
Spell o' the Hills, The. Douglas Fraser. PoSH
Spell of Creation. Kathleen Raine. FaBoCh; OxBS
Spell of Invisibility, A. *At. to* Christopher Marlowe. ChTr
Spell of the Yukon, The. Robert W. Service. BLPA; BLPL; FaBoBe; FaFP; PoPl; TreF
Spell to Destroy Life, A. *Unknown.* *See* Sacred Formula to Destroy Life.
Spellbound. Emily Brontë. *See* Night Is Darkening round Me.
Spelling. Margaret Atwood. NoP
Spelling of Elliot, The. *Unknown.* FaBoUs

Spelling reformer indicted, A. Ambrose Bierce. *Fr.* The Devil's Dictionary. OBAL
Spelt from Sibyl's Leaves. Gerard Manley Hopkins. BrPo; CMoP; CoBMV; FaBoMo; LiTM; MoPo; OAEL-1; PrIm
Spencer the Rover. *Unknown.* OBET
Spend the years of learning squandering. Gnome. Samuel Beckett. BIrV
Spending beyond their income on gifts for Christmas. Christmas Shopping. Louis MacNeice. OBCP
Spending hand that alway poureth out [*or* powreth owte], A. Satire 3: To Sir Francis Brian. Sir Thomas Wyatt. Satires, III. AAS; EnRePo; SiPS
Spendor. Shin Shalom, *tr. fr. Hebrew by* Abraham Birman. VWA
Spendthrift. I. A. Richards. PoPl
Spenserian Stanzas on Charles Armitage Brown. Keats. *See* Portrait, A.
Spenser's Ireland. Marianne Moore. LiTA; LiTM; MasP; NePA; NoAM; NOBA; OxBA; TAP
Spent purpose of a perfectly marvellous, The. In Favor of One's Time. Frank O'Hara. NeAP; PoA
Sphere of Glass, The. John Lehmann. ChMP
Sphere of pure chance, free agent of no cause. Calvin in the Casino. Turner Cassity. NIP
Sphere, which is as many thousand spheres, A. Shelley. *Fr.* Prometheus Unbound. ImOP
Sphinx, The. Henry Howard Brownell. AA
Sphinx, The. Emerson. AmPP; AP; NOBA; OxBA
Sphinx, The, *sel.* Oscar Wilde.
"How subtle-secret is your smile! Did you love none then? Nay, I know." MoBrPo; UnTE
Sphinx Speaks, The. Francis Saltus Saltus. AA
Sphinx with lion's feet, The. The Phoenix. Theodore Spencer. CrMA
Sphinxes Inclined to Be. Olga Orozco, *tr. fr. Spanish by* Leslie Keffer. WPOW
Spicewood. Lizette Woodworth Reese. MoAmPo
Spider, The. Robert P. Tristram Coffin. ImOP
Spider. Thomas Cole. PoA
Spider. Padraic Colum. RoGo
Spider, The. Richard Eberhart. PoA
Spider, The. Loren Eiseley. SUW
Spider. Norma Farber. PChr
Spider, The. Hannah F. Gould. OBCA
Spider. Richmond Lattimore. PP
Spider, The. Edward Littleton. NOEC
Spider, The. Kenneth Mackenzie. BoAnP
Spider, The. Walt Whitman. WiR
Spider and the Fly, The. Mary Howitt. BeLS; FaFP; FaPON; HBV-1; HBVY; OHFP; OnUR; OxBChV; Par; TreFS; WBLP
Spider and the Ghost of the Fly, The. Vachel Lindsay. VGW
Spider bite the size of a dinner plate, A. Into the Dark. Paul Monette. AmPA
Spider Crystal Ascension. Charles Wright. GeTw; LCAP
Spider Danced a Cozy Jig, A. Irving Layton. WHW
Spider expects the cold of winter, The. The Spider. Richard Eberhart. PoA
Spider, from his flaming sleep. Little City. Robert Horan. CrMA; NePA
Spider holds a silver ball, The. Emily Dickinson. FM; WPOW
Spider in the bath, A. The image noted. The Image. Roy Fuller. ChMP; GTBS-P; OxBTC
Spider, juiced crystal and Milky Way, drifts on his web through the night sky, The. Spider Crystal Ascension. Charles Wright. GeTw; LCAP
Spider, put outside the world, A. The Cross Spider. May Swenson. SUW
Spider Reeves. Henry Carlile. Psk
Spider, Sir Spider. Spider. Padraic Colum. RoGo
Spider! thou need'st not run in fear about. To a Spider. Robert Southey. FM
Spider weaves his silver wire, The. Of a Spider. Wilfrid Thornley. FaPON; PDV
Spider web pulled tight between two stones, A. Winter Sign. Loren Eiseley. SUW
Spider works across the wall, The. The Huntress. George Johnston. WHW
Spiders. Diane Ackerman. MAYP
Spiders. David Wevill. MoCV
Spiders are spinning their webs. Mid-August. Louise Driscoll. YeAr
Spider's Nest, The. George MacBeth. NMP
Spiders started out to go with the wind on its pilgrimage, The. The Broken. W. S. Merwin. LCAP
Spider's web, The. Special Delivery. John Montague. CIP; IPY
Spiel of the Three Mountebanks. John Crowe Ransom. MoAB; MoAmPo
Spies, you are lights in state, but of base stuff. On Spies. Ben Jonson. NoP
Spike Driver Blues. *Unknown.* *See* Take This Hammer.
Spikenard. Laurence Housman. TrPWD
Spikes of new smell driven up nostrils. Gary Snyder. Myths and Texts: Burning, XIII. NaP
Spilled into the cup. Bubbling Wine. Abu Zakariya, *tr. by* A. J. Arberry. TTY
Spilled Milk. John Haines. GP
Spin a coin, spin a coin. Queen Nefertiti. *Unknown.* RHPC
Spin, a hardy spin, and here's the globe, A. A Small Boy, Dreaming. Albert Herzing. NYBP
Spin cheerfully. Leave the Thread with God. *Unknown.* BLRP
Spin, Dame, spin. *Unknown.* OxNR
"Spin, oh my darling daughter, I'll give you a hat." Spinning Song. *Unknown, tr. by* Louis Untermeyer. UnTE
Spin the ball! I reel, I burn. Song of Seyd Nimetollah of Kuhistan. Emerson. NOBA
Spindrift. Galway Kinnell. NaP; NYBP
Spined and gullet shaped. Free me. Oh Bright Oh Black Singbeast Lovebeast Catkin Sleek. Michael McClure. CoPo
Spinner, The. "Madeline Bridges." AA
Spinner, The. Charles L. O'Donnell. GoBC; ISi
Spinners at Willowsleigh. Marya Zaturenska. HBMV
Spinning. Helen Hunt Jackson. HBV-2
Spinning. Al Purdy. NOBC
Spinning Girl, The. Nathan Alterman, *tr. fr. Hebrew by* Ruth Nevo. VWA
Spinning in April. Josephine Preston Peabody. HBV-1
Spinning Song. Edith Sitwell. MoAB; MoBrPo
Spinning Song. *Unknown, tr. fr. German by* Louis Untermeyer. UnTE
Spinning Wheel, The. A. M. Klein. CaP
Spinning Wheel, The. John Francis Waller. AnIV; ChTr
Spinning Woman, The. Leonidas of Tarentum, *tr. fr. Greek by* Andrew Lang. AWP
Spinoza/ Collected curiosa. Clerihew. *Unknown.* NOBL
Spinster Song. Virginia Lyne Tunstall. HBMV
Spinsterish/ silver/ Before the shuttered window. Men Walked To and Fro. Blanaid Salkeld. NeIP
Spinster's Lullaby. Vassar Miller. BoWoP; NMM
Spiral, The. John Holmes. MiAP
Spiralwise it spins. Time. Ralph Hodgson. BrPo; GTBS-P
Spire cranes, The. Its statue is an aviary. Dylan Thomas. PoA
Spires, firm on their monster feet rose light and thin, The. Denis Devlin. *Fr.* The Heavenly Foreigner. CIP
Spires of Oxford, The. Winifred M. Letts. FaFP; HBV-2; OHFP; OnYI; PoLF; PoRA; TreF; WGRP
Spirit, The. Doug Turner. AMV-81
Spirit and the Bride, The, *sels.* Elsa Barker. HBMV
Caresses.
Confession.
Consummation.
Fulfilment.
Inscription, The.
Love's Immortality.
Spirit breathes upon the Word, The. The Light and Glory of the World [*or* The Spirit's Light]. William Cowper. BLRP; TRV
Spirit came in Childhood, The. The Four Calls. Lydia Hadley. STF
Spirit Craft, The. Charles G. Ballard. VoR
Spirit Epiloguizes, The. Milton. *See* To the Ocean now I fly.
Spirit Flowers. Della Burt. BlSi
Spirit from Perfecter Ages, A. Arthur Hugh Clough. *Fr.* Amours de Voyage. OBNC
("Is it illusion? or does there a spirit from perfecter ages.") EBEV
Spirit from Whom Our Lives Proceed. Howard Chandler Robbins. TrPWD
Spirit Haunts the Year's Last Hours, A. Tennyson. *See* Song: "Spirit haunts the year's last hours, A." InvP
Spirit in Our Hearts, The, *with music.* Henry Ustic Onderdonk. AH
Spirit Lake, Iowa, this January morning is ten below. Tea. Ann Struthers. AMV-80
Spirit Land, The. Jones Very. HAP
Spirit-like before Light. Arthur Gregor. VWA
Spirit moves, The. A Light Breather. Theodore Roethke. NoP
Spirit of Earth with still, restoring hands, The. The Last Furrow. Edwin Markham. AA
Spirit of "Fire and dew." To O. S. C. Annie Eliot Trumbull. AA
Spirit of Freedom, Thou Dost Love the Sea. Henry Nehemiah Dodge. EtS
Spirit of Life, in This New Dawn, *with music.* Earl B. Marlatt. AH
Spirit of Night, The. Thomas Rogers. EIL
Spirit of Plato. *Unknown, tr. fr. Greek by* Shelley. AWP; OBVE
(Plato's Tomb.) FaBoCh
Spirit of Poetry, The. Longfellow. PP
Spirit of Sadness. Richard Le Gallienne. HBV-2
Spirit of song, whose shining wings have borne. Song and Science. Milicent Washburn Shinn. AA
Spirit of the Birch, The. Arthur Ketchum. OHIP
Spirit of the *Bluenose,* The. Claire Harris MacIntosh. CaP

Spirit of the Cairngorms, The. Axel Firsoff. PoSH
Spirit of the Fall, The. Danske Bedinger Dandridge. AA
Spirit of the *Maine,* The. Tudor Jenks. AA; PAH
Spirit of the Time-to-be, The. Resurgence. Laura Bell Everett. PGD
Spirit of the Wheat, The. Edward A. U. Valentine. AA
Spirit of 34th Street, The. Peggy Shriver. AMV-80
Spirit of twilight, through your folded wings. Twilight. Olive Custance. HBV-1
Spirit of Wine, The. W. E. Henley. HBV-2
Spirit of Wrath, The. William Heyen. AmPA; WOLT
Spirit seems to pass, A. Lausanne. Thomas Hardy. FaBoRV; FaBoTw
Spirit, Silken Thread. Margot Ruddock. OBMV
Spirit Song. *Tr. fr. Eskimo.* WTO
Spirit that breathest through my lattice, thou. The Evening Wind. Bryant. AA; AP
Spirit that moves the sap in spring. A Prelude. Maurice Thompson. HBV-2
Spirit who sweepest the wild Harp of Time! Ode to the Departing Year. Samuel Taylor Coleridge. EnRP
Spirits. Robert Bridges. *See* Angel Spirits of Sleep.
Spirits. Victor Hernandez Cruz. PoBA; WSC
Spirits and illusions have died. Life from the Lifeless. Robinson Jeffers. CMoP
Spirits and Men, *sel.* Ebenezer Elliott.
"I sing of men and angels, and the days." OBRV
Spirits, Dancing. Arthur Gregor. NYBP; VGW
Spirit's Epochs, The. Coventry Patmore. The Angel in the House, I, viii, 3. EBEV; GBL; GoBC
Spirits Everywhere. Ludwig Uhland, *tr. fr. German by* James Clarence Mangan. AWP
Spirit's Grace, The. Janie Screven Heyward. HBMV
Spirit's Light, The. William Cowper. *See* Light and Glory of the World, The.
Spirit's Odyssey, The. M. Krishnamurti. PeD
Spirits of well-shot woodcock, partridge, snipe. "New King Arrives in His Capital by Air . . ."—Daily Newspaper [*or* Death of King George V]. John Betjeman. NOBE; OxBoLi; WhC
Spirit's Song. Louise Bogan. NYBP
Spirit's Song, The. Arthur Hugh Clough. *See* "There Is No God," the Wicked Saith.
Spirits Unchained. Keorapetse Kgositsile. PoBA
Spirits walking everywhere. Walter James Turner. *Fr.* The Seven Days of the Sun. OBMV
Spiritual, A. Paul Laurence Dunbar. BPo
Spiritual Isolation. Isaac Rosenberg. TrJP
Spiritual Love. William Caldwell Roscoe. OBVV
Spiritual Passion. George Barlow. OBVV
Spiritual, the carnal, are one, The. Dorothy Wellesley. *Fr.* Matrix. OBMV
Spirituality. Samuel Greenberg. LiTA
Spirk Troll-Derisive. James Whitcomb Riley. *See* Craqueodoom.
Spiro, thou shouldst be humble at this hour. Proud Resignation. Mordecai Marcus. SOTS
Spit. Charles Kenneth Williams. VWA
Spit in my face you Jewes, and pierce my side. John Donne. Holy Sonnets, XI. AnAnS-1; JCP; MasP; OBS
Spitballer. Fred Chappell. LiSp
Spite hath no power to make me sad. Sir Thomas Wyatt. SiPS
Spite o' the tempests a-blowin'. "Tollable Well!" Frank L. Stanton. FaFP
Spite of Thy Godhead, Powerful Love. Anne Wharton. CavP
Spits of glitter in lowgrade ore. Conserving the Magnitude of Uselessness. A. R. Ammons. NoAM
Spittal wives are no' very nice. The Wives of Spittal. *Unknown.* GBP
Spitting/ on this platform. Underground Poetry. Pedro Pietri. NYP
Spitting on Ira Rosenblatt. Robert Hershon. NeAC
Spiv Song. Royston Ellis. PeHV
Splashing along the boggy woods all day. Together. Siegfried Sassoon. BrPo
Splat of bare feet on wet tile, The. Women's Locker Room. Marilyn Waniek. MAYP
Spleen LXXVI ("I have more memories than if I had lived a thousand years"). Baudelaire, *tr. fr. French by* Anthony Hecht. NAWM-2
Spleen LXXVII ("I'm like the king of a rain-country, rich"). Baudelaire, *tr. fr. French by* Robert Lowell. NAWM-2
Spleen LXXV ("Old Pluvius, month of rains, in peevish mood"). Baudelaire, *tr. fr. French by* Kenneth O. Hanson. NAWM-2
Spleen LXXVIII ("When the low heavy sky weighs like a lid"). Baudelaire, *tr. fr. French by* Sir John Squire. NAWM-2
(Spleen ["When the dull dire sky weighs a heavy cover"], *tr. by* Arthur Symons.) SyP
Spleen ("I was not sorrowful"). Ernest Dowson. BrPo; MoBrPo; NCEP; SyP
Spleen, The, *sels.* Matthew Green.
"But now more serious let me grow." PoEL-3
Cure for the Spleen, A. OBEC
Epistle, An: "And may my humble dwelling stand." LoBV
"First know, my friend, I do not mean." NOEC
In Praise of Water-Gruel. FaBoUs
On Even Keel. OBEC
Spleen ("Around were all the roses red"). Paul Verlaine, *tr. fr. French by* Ernest Dowson. AWP; SyP
Splendid and Terrible. "Seumas O'Sullivan." HBMV
Splendid burns the huge house with bronze. An Armoury. Alcaeus, *tr. by* Gilbert Highet. WaaP
Splendid fellow in the grass, A. Feathered Friends. Robert Peters. BXAP
Splendid Lover, The. John Richard Moreland. PGD
Splendid paper palace, The. The Mask and the Poem. Alejandra Pizarnik, *tr. by* Alina Rivero. VWA
Splendid Shilling, The. John Phillips. BXAP; OAEL-1, *abr.*; Par
Sels.
"Happy the man, who, void of cares and strife." NOEC
"Thus while my joyless hours I lingring spend." FaBoPa
Splendid Spur, The. Sir Arthur Quiller-Couch. HBVY
Splendid Village, The, *sels.* Ebenezer Elliott.
Bailiff, The. NBM
"Village! thy butcher's son, the steward now." OBSV
(Steward, The.) NBM
Splendidis Longum Valedico Nugis. Sir Philip Sidney. *See* Leave Me, O Love.
Splendor Falls, The. Tennyson. *Fr.* The Princess. CH; EBVV; ELP; FaBoCh; FaBV; FiP; GoJo; GTBS-P; HeIP; InPK; NoP; OAEL-2; OBNC; OBVV; PoEL-5; PoPl; PrIm; RoGo; TrGrPo; ViBoPo; WSC
(Blow, Bugle, Blow.) BLPL; ChTr; FaFP; LiTB; NOBE; OBEV; UnPo; WiR
(Bugle, The.) PoPle
(Bugle Song.) FaPON; GN; HBV-1; TreF
(He Hears the Bugle at Killarney.) FaBoPP
(Song: "Splendor falls on castle walls, The.") LoBV; OAEP; PoPl
(Songs from "The Princess.") AWP
Splendor of Thine Eyes, The. Moses ibn Ezra, *tr. fr. Hebrew by* Solomon Solis-Cohen. TrJP
Splendour falls on castle walls. Behold the fatal day arrive! Swift. *Fr.* On the Death of Doctor Swift. ViBoPo
Splendour of my Spring I destroy here, The. Not knowing. Abishag. Jacob Fichman, *tr. by* Sholom J. Kahn. TrJP
Splendour recurrent. Fraternitas. Confucius, *tr. by* Ezra Pound. *Fr.* Deer Sing. CTC; OBVE
Splendours of this passing world, The. "Peace Is the Tranquillity of Order." Robert Wilberforce. GoBC
Splinter. Carl Sandburg. FaPON; OBCA; SoSe; SUS; TiPo
Splinter, The. James Kenneth Stephen. CenHV
Splinters of information, stones of information. Minerals of Cornwall, Stones of Cornwall. Peter Redgrove. FaBoMo
Splish splosh, February-fill-the-dike. February. John Heath-Stubbs. OBCP
Split the lark—and you'll find the music. Emily Dickinson. AP
Spoiling daylight inched along the bar-top, The. The Mill. Richard Wilbur. Psk; SoSe
Spoils. Robert Graves. HAP; WeW
(Spoils of Love, The.) NYBP
Spoils of War, The. Vernon Watkins. WaP
Spokane Falls 1874. Phillip William George. VoR
Spoken by Venus on Seeing Her Statue Done by Praxiteles. *Unknown, tr. fr. Greek.* EyDe; FaBoEE
Spoken Extempore. Earl of Rochester. SeCePo
Spoken Extempore on the Death of Mr. Pope. *Unknown.* NOEC
Spoken through Glass. Eithne Wilkins. NeBP
Sponge out nostrils—ugh!—and eyes. More to It than Riding. J. A. Lindon. PH
Spontaneous Me. Walt Whitman. OxBA
Spontaneous Requiem for the American Indian. Gregory Corso. MAT; PoM
Spooks. Nathalia Crane. ShM
Spool of Thread, A. Sophie E. Eastman. PAH
Spoon, The. Charles Simic. NNaP
Spoon River Anthology, *sels.* Edgar Lee Masters.
Aaron Hatfield. LiTA
Alfonso Churchill. GLGT
Amanda Barker. NoAM
Anne [*or* Ann] Rutledge. AmFN; CMoP; FaFP; FaPo; HAP; LiTA; LiTM: MoAmPo; MoVE; NePA; NoAM; NoBA; OFD; OHFP; OxBA; PoPl; PoSC; TrGrPo
("Out of me unworthy and unknown.") PAI
Arlo Will. LiTA

"Butch" Weldy. NePA; SaC
Carl Hamblin. CMoP; LiTA; LiTM; OBSV; PAI
Cassius Hueffer. NoAM; OxBA
Circuit Judge, The. FaBoEE
Cooney Potter. CTBA; SaC
Daisy Fraser. CMoP; HAP; MoVE
Davis Matlock. LiTA; LiTM
Dora Williams. HAP
Editor Whedon. CMoP; CrMA; FaBoEE; NoAM; NOBA; OBSV; OxBA
Edmund Pollard. ErPo
Elliott Hawkins. OxBA
Elsa Wertman. NoAM; OxBA; PAI
Emily Sparks. GLGT
English Thornton. OxBA
Father Malloy. OxBA
Fiddler Jones. CMoP; LiTA; NoAM; OxBA; TAP; TrGrPo
Frank Drummer. NoAM
Hamilton Greene. NoAM; OxBA; PAI
Harry Wilmans. PPON
Henry C. Calhoun. LiTA; LiTM
Herman Altman. OxBA
Hill, The. CMoP; FYAP; LiTA; LiTM; NePA; NoAM; NOBA; OxBA: SeCeV; TAP; ViBoPo
J. Milton Miles. CrMA
Jacob Godbey. LiTA
John Horace Burleson. CrMA
Jonathan Houghton. OxBA
Jonathan Swift Somers. OBAL
Judge Somers. FaBoEE; OBSV
Julia Miller. MoVE
Knowlt Hoheimer. OxBA
Lucinda Matlock. CMoP; FaBV; FF; HAP; LiTA; LiTM; MoAmPo; MoVE; NoAM; NOBA; OxBA
Perry Zoll. CrMA
Petit, the Poet. CMoP; InPK; MoAmPo; MoVE; NoAM; NOBA; OxBA; PPON; TAP
Reuben Pantier. GLGT
Rutherford McDowell. EyDe; LiTA; OxBA
Scholfield Huxley. LiTA; MoPo; TrPWD
Seth Compton. LiTA
Sexsmith the Dentist. NePA
Spooniad, The. OBAL
Thomas Trevelyan. MoPo
Village Atheist, The. EaLo; LiTA
William Jones. ImOP
Spoon River Anthology. Edwin Meade Robinson. *Fr.* Limericised Classics, V. HBMV
Spoonmeat at Bill Porter's in the Hall. After Tennyson. Edward Lear. FaBoNo
Sport, an adventitious sprout, A. Perspective. Margaret Avison. OBCV; PeCV
Sportif. David McCord. *See* Ascot Waistcoat.
Sporting Acquaintances. Siegfried Sassoon. OxBTC
Sporting at fancie, setting light by love. Richard Barnfield. Sonnets, I. PeHV
Sporting Cowboy, The, *with music. Unknown.* OuSiCo
Sporting Life Blues. *Unknown.* FSW
Sports and gallantries, the stage, the arts, the antics of dancers. Boats in a Fog. Robinson Jeffers. MOS; NoP; OxBA
Sports Field. Judith Wright. LiSp
Sportsman, The. David McCord. LiSp
Sportsmen keep hawks, and their quarry they gain, The. Air. John Gay. *Fr.* Polly; an Opera. NOEC
Sporty Young Person, A. *Unknown.* TDH
Sporus. Pope. *Fr.* Epistle to Dr. Arbuthnot. AWP; ChTr; NOBE; OBSV; TW
("Let Sporus tremble—'What? That thing of silk.' ") DBV; SCV
Spot-Check at Fifty. Vernon Scannell. NAs
Spotless Maid, The. Vincent McNabb. ISi
Spotlights had you covered, The. A Poem about Poems about Vietnam. Jon Stallworthy. NoAM
Spots of Blood. Phyllis Webb. NOBC
Spots on black skin. Blind Old Woman. Clarence Major. PoBA
Spotted hawk swoops by and accuses me, The. My Barbaric Yawp. Walt Whitman. *Fr.* Song of Myself, LII. BiP; NePA; NoP; PP; TrGrPo
Spouse I Do Hate, A. William Wycherley. *Fr.* Love in a Wood. OAEP
Spouse! Sister! Angel! Pilot of the Fate. Shelley. *Fr.* Epipsychidion. ChER
Spouse to the Beloved, The. William Baldwin. *See* Christ, My Beloved.
Sprawled/ on our faces in the spring. The Hen Flower. Galway Kinnell. NNaP
Sprawled, like park derelicts, about. The Sleepers. Peter Kocan. CBAP
Sprawled on the crates [*or* bags] and sacks [*or* crates] in the rear of the truck. Green, Green Is El Aghir. Norman Cameron. FaBoTw; MoBS; OBWP; OxBTC
Spray. D. H. Lawrence. BoNaP
Spray of Honeysuckle, A. Mary Emily Bradley. AA
Spray sprang up across the cusps of the moon, The. Once at Swanage. Thomas Hardy. FaBoPP
Spraying the Potatoes. Patrick Kavanagh. BIrV; IPY; NoP; OxBI
Spread on the roadway. The Cyclists. Amy Lowell. WPE
Spread the board with linen snow. Invitation to the Dance. Sidonius Apollinaris, *tr. by* Howard Mumford Jones. AWP
Spread thy close curtain, love-performing night. Juliet's Yearning. Shakespeare. *Fr.* Romeo and Juliet, III, ii. TreFS
Spreading and low, unwatered, concentrate. The California Oaks. Yvor Winters. GOA
Spreeng ees com', Da; but oh, da joy. Da Leetla Boy. T. A. Daly. HBV-1
Sprig of Lime, The. Robert Nichols. GTBS-P
Sprig of Rosemary, A. Amy Lowell. PeHV
Sprin' Fevah. Ray Garfield Dandridge. BANP
Spring, The. William Barnes. BoNaP; HBV-1
Spring. Harry Behn. TiPo
Spring. Blake. *Fr.* Songs of Innocence. FaBoCh; FaPON; MoShBr; PoPl; SUS; YeAr
Spring, The. Thomas Carew. AnAnS-2; CaPo; CavP; FaBoEn; GN; NoP; PoEL-3; PPoe; SeCV-1; TEP; TrGrPo; WiR
(Now That the Winter's Gone.) PoSC
Spring. Catullus, *tr. fr. Latin by* L. R. Lind. PoPl
Spring. Marchette Chute. TiPo
Spring. Carole Gregory Clemmons. PoBA
Spring. William Cornish. *See* Pleasure It Is.
Spring, The. Abraham Cowley. *Fr.* The Mistress. HAP; JCP; MeLP; OBS
Spring. Aubrey Thomas De Vere. *Fr.* The Year of Sorrow. OBNC
Spring. Frederick Feirstein. AMV-81
Spring, The. Rose Fyleman. FaPON
Spring. Caroline Giltinan. HBMV
Spring. Thomas Gisborne. *Fr.* Walks in a Forest. PBBP
Spring. Giovanni Battista Guarini, *tr. fr. Italian by* Leigh Hunt. AWP
Spring. Michael Hogan. LFAC; TAT
Spring. Gerard Manley Hopkins. BoNaP; BrPo; EBCP; EBVV; FaBoEn; FaBV; HAP; InvP; LiTM; MoAB; MoBrPo; MoVE; NoAM; NOBE; OAEL-2; OAEP; OBMV; OBNC; OxBoCh; SoSe; TrCP; VLP
("Nothing is so beautiful as spring.") LO
Spring, *sel.* Richard Hovey.
Stein Song, A. HBV-2
Spring. Orrick Johns. InMe
Spring. Moishe Kulbak, *tr. fr. Yiddish by* Ruth Whitman. VWA
Spring. Karla Kuskin. PDV; RHPC
Spring. Philip Larkin. MoBrPo
Spring. James Russell Lowell. *Fr.* The Biglow Papers; Sunthin' in the Pastoral Line. FaBV
Spring, The. John Lyly. *See* Trico's Song.
Spring. Vladimir Mayakovsky, *tr. fr. Russian by* Babette Deutsch. CAD
Spring. Linda McCarriston. AMV-81
Spring. Meleager, *tr. fr. Greek by* William M. Hardinge. AWP
Spring. W. S. Merwin. NaP
Spring. Edna St. Vincent Millay. BoWoP; MoAB; MoAmPo; NePA; NoP
Spring, *sel.* William Miller.
"Spring comes linking and jinking through the woods, The." PoSC
Spring. Thomas Nashe. *See* Spring, the Sweet Spring.
Spring. Charles d'Orleans, *tr. fr. French by* Andrew Lang. AWP; CTC
Spring. Lola Ridge. WPE
Spring. W. R. Rodgers. AnIL; OnYI
Spring. Isaac Rosenberg. TrJP
Spring. Christina Rossetti. OBNC
Spring. V. Sackville-West. *Fr.* The Land. PeHV
Spring. Shakespeare. *See* Daisies Pied and Violets Blue.
Spring. Princess Shikishi, *tr. fr. Japanese by* Hiroaki Sato. PBWP
Spring. Edith Sitwell. OAEP
Spring. Christopher Smart. *Fr.* Hymns and Spiritual Songs: St. Philip and St. James. OBEC
("Now the winds are all composure.") LoBV
Spring. André Spire, *tr. fr. French by* Jethro Bithell. AWP
Spring. Thomas Stanley, *after the Greek of* Anacreon. AWP
Spring. James Still. GrPl
Spring. Earl of Surrey. *See* Soote Season, The.
Spring ("Dip down upon the northern shore.") Tennyson. *See* In Memoriam: "Dip down upon . . ."
Spring ("Now fades the last long streak of snow"). Tennyson. *See* In Memoriam A. H. H.: "Now fades the last . . ."
Spring. James Thomson. *Fr.* The Seasons. LAuP
Sels.
"As rising from the vegetable world." PoEL-3

"At length the finished garden to the view." ViBoPo
Birds in Spring. OBEC
"Lend me your song, ye nightingales! oh pour." PBBP
"Should I my steps turn to the rural seat." FM
Spring Flowers. NOBE; OBEC
Spring. Henry Timrod. AP; HBV-1
Spring ("Lenten is come with love to towne"). *Unknown. See* Lenten Is Come.
Spring ("When from her winter-prison"). *Unknown, tr. fr. Japanese.* SUS
Spring. Paul Verlaine, *tr. fr. French by* Roland Grant *and* Paul Archer. ErPo; PeHV
Spring, The. Ellen Bryant Voigt. MAYP
Spring. Ruth Whitman. IHMS
Spring. Oscar Williams. LiTA
Spring; a Formal Ode. Fyodor Tyuchev, *tr. fr. Russian by* Charles Tomlinson. FaBoRV
Spring Again. Ronald Wallace. PPJ
Spring again. Out of Mourning. Anthony S. Abbott. AMV-81
Spring Air. Gene Derwood. FaFP
Spring all the Graces of the age. Chorus. Ben Jonson. *Fr.* Neptune's Triumph. OBS
Spring, and a new pair of moccasins! Sunflower Moccasins. Phillip William George. VoR
Spring and All. Grace Bauer. PPJ
Spring and All: ("By the road to the contagious hospital"). William Carlos Williams. AP; CABA; CMoP; CoBMV; HAP; LiTM; MoVE; NoAM; NOBA; PPoe; QFR; TAP
("By the road to the contagious hospital.") OxBA
(Poem: "By the road to the contagious hospital"). MoAB; MoAmPo; UnPo
Spring and All ("So much depends"). William Carlos Williams. *See* Red Wheelbarrow, The.
Spring and Autumn. William James Linton. EBVV
Spring and Death. Gerard Manley Hopkins. BrPo; SyP
Spring and Fall. Gerard Manley Hopkins. BiP; BrPo; CMoP; EBEV; ELP; FaBoUs; FF; GTBS-P; HAP; HeIP; HoPM; InPK; InPS; LiTM; MAT; MoPo; MoVE; NIP; NOBE; NoP; OAEP; PAI; PoEL-5; PoPle; PPoe; PPON; PPP; SCV; SOTW; TEP; VLP; WeW
(Spring and Fall: To a Young Child.) ChTr; GoJo; LiTB; MoAB; PoPl; SeCeV
Spring, and the Blind Children. Alfred Noyes. OxBTC
Spring! and the buds against the sky. Spring. Caroline Giltinan. HBMV
Spring appears, in which the earth, The. The Vigil of Venus. *Unknown, tr. by* Thomas Stanley. AWP
Spring approaches blowing east. On the Eve of Our Anniversary. Gary Margolis. Str
Spring Arithmetic. *Unknown.* FiBHP
Spring at Fort Okanogan. Ramona Wilson. VoR
Spring at her height on a morn at prime. Ballade of Youth and Age. W. E. Henley. VLP
Spring Beauties, The. Helen Gray Cone. AA
Spring Bereaved 1 ("That zephyr every year"). William Drummond of Hawthornden. OBEV
Spring Bereaved 2 ("Sweet Spring, thou turn'st with all thy goodly train"). William Drummond of Hawthornden. OBEV
(Sonnet.) ElL; FaBoEn
Spring Bereaved 3 ("Alexis, here she stay'd; among these pines"). William Drummond of Hawthornden. OBEV
(Alexis, Here She Stayed.) HBV-1
(Sonnet.) ElL; OBS
Spring blew trumpets of color, The. Blind. Harry Kemp. HBMV
Spring Burning. Patrick Roland. PeSA
Spring bursts to-day. An Easter Carol. Christina Rossetti. OHIP
Spring came earlier on, The. A Song for Lexington. Robert Kelley Weeks. AA
Spring came with tiny lances thrusting. Blossom Time. Wilbur Larremore. AA
Spring Catch. Greg Keeler. WOLT
Spring Cellar. Gladys McKee. GoYe
Spring Cleaning. Phillip William George. VoR
Spring comes early to the gardens. Green Jade Plum Trees in Spring. Ou-yang Hsiu, *tr. by* Kenneth Rexroth. NaP
Spring comes hurrying. Hello! Louise Ayres Garnett. SiSoSe
Spring comes in with all her hues and smells, The. A Spring Morning. John Clare. GBL
Spring comes laughing down the valley. New Life. Amelia Josephine Burr. HBV-1
Spring comes linking and jinking through the woods, The. William Miller. *Fr.* Spring. PoSC
Spring comes: the flowers learn their coloured shapes. A Vision. Maria Konopnicka, *tr. by* Jerzy Peterkiewicz *and* Burns Singer. WPOW
Spring Comes to Murray Hill. Ogden Nash. FiBHP
Spring Coming. A. R. Ammons. HeIP; InPK
Spring Cricket. Frances Rodman. FaPON; SiSoSe
Spring Day. John Ashbery. NOBA
Spring day in the weeds, A. Dog Yoga. Charles Wright. LCAP
Spring Day on Campus, A. Gilbert Schedler. AMV-80
Spring day the teen on his bike slanted his caucasian eyes, The. Woodtick. Joy Kogawa. BrSi
Spring Death. Russell Marano. AMV-81
Spring Doggerel. Rhoda Coghill. NeIP
Spring Drawing II. Robert Hass. MAYP
Spring Ecstasy. Lizette Woodworth Reese. MoAmPo
Spring Equinox, The. Anne Ridler. NeBP
Spring Festival on the River, The. John Peck. AmPA
Spring Floods. Gregory Orr. GeTw
Spring Flowers. James Thomson. *Fr.* The Seasons: Spring. NOBE; OBEC
Spring flowers and autumn moon enter poems. For Hidden Mist Pavilion. Yü Hsüan-chi, *tr. by* Geoffrey Waters. BoWoP
Spring Flowers from Ireland. Denis Florence MacCarthy. ACP; GoBC
Spring, for Julian, was amber in the hand. In the Henry James Country. William Abrahams. WaP
Spring-gazing Song. Hsüeh T'ao, *tr. fr. Chinese by* Carolyn Kizer. BoWoP
Spring Goeth All in White. Robert Bridges. BoNaP; ChTr; HBMV
Spring Grass. Carl Sandburg. FaPON
Spring has come again. The earth. Rainer Maria Rilke, *tr. by* Christopher Hawthorne. *Fr.* Sonnets to Orpheus. SOTW
Spring has come and the snow has gone. Captive. Peretz Hirshbein, *tr. by* Joseph Leftwich. TrJP
Spring has come to the pass. Two Springs. Li Ch'ing-chao, *tr. by* Kenneth Rexroth. BoWoP
Spring Has Come to Town with Love. *Unknown. See* Lenten Is Come.
Spring has darkened with activity, The. Time and the Garden. Yvor Winters. MoAmPo; NoAM; QFR; VGW
Spring hath her own bright days of calm and peace. Robert Bridges. The Growth of Love, XXIV. VLP
Spring Hawks. Jim Thomas. AMV-81
Spring hides scars of Dickens Street but the old cottages. C. K. Stead. Twenty-one Sonnets, 6. OCNZ
Spring I remember wild canaries. Saint-Henri Spring. Milton Acorn. NeAC
Spring in England. Charles Buxton Going. HBMV
Spring in Hiding. Frances Frost. YeAr
Spring in New Hampshire. Claude McKay. BANP; BPo; PoNe
Spring in the Desert. Arthur Truman Merrill. BPAW
Spring in the Old World. Philip Levine. FAZ
Spring in the Students' Quarter. Henri Murger, *tr. fr. French by* Andrew Lang. AWP
Spring in These Hills. Archibald MacLeish. NCSH
Spring in Virginia. Ramona Wilson. VoR
Spring in War-Time. Edith Nesbit. SUMH
Spring in War-Time. Sara Teasdale. OHIP; SUMH
Spring in Washington. James Den Boer. TAT
Spring Is. Bobbi Katz. RHPC
Spring is a recurring astonishment—like poetry. C. K. Stead. Twenty-one Sonnets, 9. OCNZ
Spring is a requiem rehearsed. Spring Song. LeRoy Smith, Jr. NePoAm
Spring Is at Work with Beginnings of Things. Greta Leora Rose. CaP
Spring is coming by a many signs, The. Young Lambs. John Clare. TrGrPo
Spring is hard on us. *Unknown.* ErPo; PV
Spring is in her eyes. A Little Girl. Charles Angoff. GoYe
Spring Is in the Making. Nona Keen Duffy. YeAr
Spring Is Late, The. Louise Chandler Moulton. HBV-2
Spring is like a Perhaps Hand. E. E. Cummings. AmPP; NePA; NoP; SOTW; TAP; VGW
Spring is passing and. Empress Jito, *tr. fr. Japanese by* Cid Corman *and* Susumu Kamaike. PBWP
Spring is past and over these many days. September. Aldous Huxley. EBEV
Spring is short. Yosano Akiko, *tr. fr. Japanese by* Geoffrey Bownas *and* Anthony Thwaite. BoWoP; PBWP
Spring is showery, flowery, bowery. Mother Goose. FaBoUs; RHPC; SoPo; TiPo
Spring is the morning of the year. The Golden Rod. Frank Dempster Sherman. FaPON
Spring is the period. Emily Dickinson. TAP
Spring is when. Spring Is. Bobbi Katz. RHPC
Spring Journey, A. Alice Freeman Palmer. HBV-1
Spring-Joy Praising God; Praise of the Sun. Catharina Regina von Greiffenberg, *tr. fr. German by* George C. Schoolfield. WPOW
Spring Landscape. Arthur Davison Ficke. Sonnets of a Portrait Painter, XII. HBMV
Spring Landscape. Melvin Walker La Follette. NePoEA-2

Spring Lay, A. Oliver Opdyke. InMe
Spring lights her candles everywhere. Song. Fredegond Shove. HBMV
Spring Lilt, A. *Unknown.* HBV-1
Spring made little promise. Portrait of an Indian. R. E. Rashley. CaP
Spring Market. Louise Driscoll. HBMV; HBVY
Spring Memorandum, A. Robert Duncan. PoA
Spring Morning, A. John Clare. GBL
Spring morning! Galante Garden: I. Juan Ramón Jiménez, *tr. by* H. R. Hays. PoPl
Spring Morning. D. H. Lawrence. BrPo; CMoP; MoAB; MoBrPo
Spring Morning—Santa Fe. Lynn Riggs. BPAW
Spring Morning: Waking. Emily Seelbinder. AMV-81
Spring Mountain Climb. Richard Eberhart. GoYe; LiSp
Spring, my dear, The. Out of Tune. W. E. Henley. MoBrPo
Spring Night. Richard Aldridge. NePoAm
Spring Night. "Rana Mukerji." UnTE
Spring Night. Su Tung-p'o, *tr. fr. Chinese by* Burton Watson. Prf
Spring Night. Sara Teasdale. BLPL; FaBoBe; HBMV; LiTA; MoAmPo
Spring Night in Shokoku-ji, A. Gary Snyder. *Fr.* Four Poems for Robin. VGW
Spring night—one hour worth a thousand gold coins. Spring Night. Su Tung-p'o, *tr. by* Burton Watson. Prf
Spring 1940. W. H. Auden. OAEP
Spring 1943. Roy Fuller. LiTB; LiTM; WaP
Spring 1942. Roy Fuller. LiTM; NeBP; OxBTC; WaaP
Spring 1974. C. K. Stead. Twenty-one Sonnets, 1. OCNZ
Spring MCMXL. David Gascoyne. MoVE
Spring Nocturne. Abraham Liessin, *tr. fr. Yiddish.* TrJP
Spring, now she is dead, A! of what? of thorns. Ben Jonson. *Fr.* The Sad Shepherd. GoBC
Spring Oak. Galway Kinnell. BoNaP; ELU; NePoAm
Spring of Joy Is Dry, The. *Unknown.* ElL; EnRePo
Spring of the Thief. John Logan. BiP; CAPP; NNaP
Spring of the Year, The. Allan Cunningham. HBV-2
(Gone Were But the Winter Cold.) CH
Spring Offensive. Wilfred Owen. BrPo; GTBS-P; LiTB; MoVE
Spring Offensive, 1941. Maurice Biggs. PoAu-2
Spring Offensive of the Snail, The. Marge Piercy. TAP
Spring Omnipotent Goddess. E. E. Cummings. OxBA
Spring on the Ochils. J. Logie Robertson. OBVV
Spring once said to the nightingale. The Birds' Ball. C. W. Bardeen. BLPA
Spring over the City. Anne Hébert, *tr. fr. French by* Kathleen Weaver. PBWP
Spring Passion. Joel Elias Springarn. HBV-1
Spring Poem. Bin Ramke. AMV-81
Spring Poem. Julian Symons. NeBP
Spring Pools. Robert Frost. AmPP; MoAB; NoAM; NOBA; NoP; OxBA
Spring Quiet. Christina Rossetti. BoNaP; CH; GTBS-P; LoBV; PoEL-5; WPE
Spring Rain. Harry Behn. TiPo
Spring Rain. Marchette Chute. RHPC; TiPo
Spring Rain. William Hawkins. MoCV
Spring rain. Haiku. Kaga no Chiyo, *tr. by* R. H. Blyth. PBWP
Spring rain is soft rain, The. Rainy Day Song. Violet Alleyn Storey. YeAr
Spring Returns, The. Charles Leonard Moore. HBV-1
Spring rides down, The; from Judith and the Larb. A Missouri Traveller Writes Home: 1830. Robert Bly. NePoEA
Spring Rites. Martin Robbins. AMV-81
Spring, St. Stephen's Green. Leslie Daiken. OnYI
Spring Scene. Taniguchi Buson, *tr. fr. Japanese by* Harold G. Henderson. PoPl
Spring Sequence. Judith Minty. AMV-80
Spring shakes the windows; doors whang to. A Spring Wind. Bernard Spencer. GTBS-P
Spring shall rouse my buried Lord, The. Easter Poem. Kathleen Raine. LiTB
Spring Signs. Rachel Field. InMe
Spring Song. Bliss Carman. HBV-1; HBVY, *abr.*
Spring Song. Hilda Conkling. PoSC
Spring Song. Donald Finkel. NYBP
Spring Song. Rayner Heppenstall. NeBP
Spring Song. Hermann Hesse, *tr. fr. German by* Ludwig Lewisohn. AWP
Spring Song. Rod McKuen. CAD
Spring Song. Nahum, *tr. fr. Hebrew by* Emma Lazarus. TrJP
Spring Song. Katharine O'Brien. GoYe
Spring Song. George Brandon Saul. GoYe
Spring Song. Shakespeare. *See* When Daisies Died and Violets Blue.
Spring Song. LeRoy Smith, Jr. NePoAm
Spring Song. Theodore Spencer. TwAmPo
Spring Song ("As my eyes search the prairie"). *Unknown. tr. fr. Chippewa Indian by* Frances Densmore. OBVE
Spring Song ("Lenten is come with love to towne"). *Unknown. See* Lenten Is Come.
Spring Song, A ("Old Mother Earth woke up from her sleep"). *Unknown.* PoLF
Spring Song in the City. Robert Buchanan. HBV-1
Spring Song of a Super-Blake. Louis Untermeyer. HBMV
Spring Song of Aspens. Lilian White Spencer. PoOW
Spring Song of the Birds. James I, King of Scotland. OBEV
Spring Song of Tzu-yeh, A. Hsiao Yen, *tr. fr. Chinese by* Jan W. Walls. LLLT
Spring Stops Me Suddenly. Valentin Iremonger. OnYI
Spring Street Bar. Mei-Mei Berssenbrugge. WPOW
Spring Street in '58. Derek Walcott. NYP
Spring Sunday on Quaker Street. Tom Bass. FAZ
Spring: the first morning when that one true block of sweet,/laminar, complex scent arrives. From My Window. C. K. Williams. SV
Spring: The Lover and the Birds. William Allingham. OBNC
(Lover and the Birds, The.) OBVV
Spring, the Sweet Spring. Thomas Nashe. *Fr.* Summer's Last Will and Testament. CH; HeIP; LiTB; NIP; NoP; ViBoPo
(Spring.) BoNaP; ElL; GTBS; GTBS-P; HBV-1; NOBE; OBEV; OBSC; OnUR; TrGrPo; WiR
Spring Thoughts. Huang-fu Jan, *tr. fr. Chinese by* Witter Bynner. OFD
Spring Thoughts Sent to Tzu-an. Yü Hsüan-chi, *tr. fr. Chinese by* Geoffrey Waters. BoWoP
Spring thunder. Story Tellers Summer, 1980. Nia Francisco. STE
Spring to Winter. George Crabbe. *Fr.* The Ancient Mansion. ChTr
(In Suffolk.) FaBoPP
Spring too, very soon! Harbingers. Bashō, *tr. by* Harold G. Henderson. PoPl
Spring Trip of the Schooner *Ambition*, The, *with music. Unknown.* ShS
Spring under a Thorn, The. *Unknown.* MeEL
(Virgin, The.) GBP
Spring up, O well—sing ye unto it. Song of the Well. Numbers, Bible, *O.T.* TrJP
Spring Waters, *sels.* "Ping Hsin," *tr. fr. Chinese by* Kai-yu Hsu.
"Falling star, The." PBWP
"In shaping the snow into blossoms." BoWoP; WPOW
"O, Lord/ If in life eternal," *tr. by* Kai-yu Hsu. WPOW
Spring we went into the heat of lilacs. For My Father. Philip Schultz. DiL
Spring Whistles. Lucy Larcom. OBCA
Spring Will Come, The. H. D. Lowry. BoNaP
Spring Wind, A. Bernard Spencer. GTBS-P
Spring Wind. Nancy Byrd Turner. SiSoSe
Spring wind on the Bowery, A. Spring. Lola Ridge. WPE
Spring with its thrusting leaves and jargling birds is here again. Unpredictable but Providential. W. H. Auden. SUW
Spring, with that nameless pathos in the air. Spring. Henry Timrod. AP; HBV-1
Spring Workman. Alan Creighton. CaP
Springboard, The. Louis MacNeice. ChMP; PoA
Springbok. *Unknown, tr. fr. Hottentot.* PeSA
Springbok doe mothers sang, The. Song of the Springbok Does. *Unknown, tr. by* W. H. I. Bleek. PeSA
Springer Mountain. James Dickey. CAPP
Springfield Calibre Fifty, The. Joseph Mills Hanson. PoOW
Springfield Mountain. *Unknown.* AmFP; BaBo; BLSo, *with music*; FSW; TrAS, *with music*; ViBoFo (A, B, C, *and* B *vers.*)
Springful of larks in a rolling, A. October. Dylan Thomas. *Fr.* Poem in October. YeAr
Springs, The. Wendell Berry. GP
Spring's Arrival. *Unknown.* FaPON
Spring's Delights. Joseph Ashby Sterry. CenHV
Spring's Welcome. John Lyly. OBEV
Spring-Tide. *Unknown. See* Lenten Is Come.
Springtime, The. Denise Levertov. CoAP; ConAP
Springtime in Cookham Dean. Cecil Roberts. HBMV
Springtime is a green time. Four Seasons. Rowena Bennett. SiSoSe; TiPo
Springtime of the earth has come, The. Isaiah Shembe, *tr. fr. Zulu by* B. G. M. Sundkler. WTO
Springtime, Summer and Fall: days to behold a world. In Due Season. W. H. Auden. Prf
Sprinkler twirls, The. August. John Updike. *Fr.* A Child's Calendar. OBCA; RHPC
Sprinkling. Dorothy Mason Pierce. SUS; TiPo
Spritely Dead, The. Oscar Williams. *Fr.* Variations on a Theme. LiTA; NePA
Spruce. Phillip William George. VoR
Spruce and limber yellow-hammer, The. Fragment. Samuel Taylor Coleridge. FM; PBBP

Spruce Is Standing Lonely, A. Heine, *tr. fr. German by* Max Knight *and* Joseph Fabry. NAWM-2
Spruce Macaronis, and pretty to see. The Maryland Battalion. John Williamson Palmer. AA; HBV-2; PAH
Sprung from a race that had long till'd the soil. The Adventures of Simon Swaugum, a Village Merchant. Philip Freneau. PoEL-4
Spry, wry, and grey as these March sticks. Among the Narcissi. Sylvia Plath. FaBoMo; SCV
Spur, The. W. B. Yeats. ELU; WeW
Spur is red upon the briar, The. An Outdoor Litany. Louise Imogen Guiney. TrPWD
Spurgeon would daub designs on flowerpots. John Beecher. *Fr.* To Live and Die in Dixie. GP
Sputter, city! Bead with fire. To Chicago at Night. Mildred Plew Meigs. HBMV
Spy bears his bald intent like a maniac, The. John Tranter. *Fr.* Crying in Early Infancy. CBAP
Squabbling Blues. *Unknown.* BluL
Squalid, empty-headed hen, A. Hen under Bay-Tree. Ruth Pitter. OxBTC
Squalid village set in wintry mud, A. Born without a Chance. Edmund Vance Cooke. BLPA
Squalid with wounds, and many a gaping sore. The Wounded Man and the Swarm of Flies. William Somerville. FM
Squall. John Moore. NCSH
Squall. Stanley Moss. CoAP
Square at Dawn, The. James Tate. NoAM
Square-Cap. John Cleveland. AnAnS-2
Square figures climb off and on. On the "Sievering" Tram. Bernard Spencer. NAs
Square-heeled boat sets off for the Statue, The. To the Statue. May Swenson. GOA; NYP
Square of the hypotenuse of the right triangle, The. Pythagorean Razzle-Dazzle. Sid Gary. QQQ
Square sheets—they saw the marble into. Island Quarry. Hart Crane. CrMA; PPP
Square, squat room (a cellar on promotion), A. Waiting. W. E. Henley. In Hospital, II. BrPo; NBM; VLP
Square-toed Princes. Robert P. Tristram Coffin. AmFN
Square, with gravel paths and shabby lawns, The. Charleville. Arthur Rimbaud, *tr. by* John Gray. SyP
Squares. Michael Hamburger. FF
Squaring the Circle. Louis O. Coxe. NYBP
Squash in Blossom. Robert Francis. FYAP
Squat Down, Josey. *Unknown.* AmFP
Squat, granular skinned. Toad. John Cotton. BoAnP
Squat in swamp shadows. Second Shaman Song. Gary Snyder. *Fr.* Myths and Texts: Burning. NeAP; NOBA; PoM
Squats on a toad-stool under a tree. Song by Isbrand. Thomas Lovell Beddoes. *Fr.* Death's Jest Book. InvP; OBNC; PrIm
Squatter's Children. Elizabeth Bishop. NePoAm-2; NoP
Squatting under the weight. 527 Cathedral Parkway. Rika Lesser. NYP
Squeak the fife, and beat the drum. Independence Day. Royall Tyler. PAH
Squeak's heard in the orchestra, A. Quatrain. George T. Lanigan. WhC
Squeal. Heather McHugh. GeTw
Squeal. Louis Simpson. BXAP; FiBHP; Par; UnPo
Squeal of car wheels braking, The. The Accident. Raymond Richard Patterson. CAD
Squealing under city stone. Rapid Transit. James Agee. MoAmPo
Squeeze Play. Phyllis McGinley. *Fr.* Spectator's Guide to Contemporary Art. DBV; FaBoEE; OBSV
Squid. Michael Blumenthal. MAYP
Squid-jiggin' Ground, The. *Unknown.* FSW
Squinting against neon signs. Eclipse. Anita Endrezze Probst.
Squire, a squire, he lived in the woods, A. The Broomfield Wager. *Unknown.* OBET
Squire Adam had two wives, they say. Ballade of My Lady's Beauty. Joyce Kilmer. HBV-1
Squire and Milkmaid; or, Blackberry Fold. *Unknown.* CoMu; InPK; OxBB (Blackberry Fold.) OBET
Squire he had whose name was Ralph, A. Independent Squire. Samuel Butler. *Fr.* Hudibras, I, 1. NOBE
Squire her hent in arms two, The. Medieval Mirth. *Unknown.* *Fr.* The Squire of Low Degree. ACP
Squire is in his library, The. He is rather worried. Send for Lord Timothy. John Heath-Stubbs. OxBC
Squire Meldrum at Carrickfergus. Sir David Lindsay. *Fr.* The Historie of Squyer William Meldrum. OxBS
Squire of Alsatia, The, *sel.* Thomas Shadwell.
Expostulation, The. OAEP
Squire [*or* Squyer] of Low[e] Degre[e], The, *sels.* *Unknown.*
Diversions for an Unhappy Princess. OxBM
Medieval Mirth. ACP
"On every branch sat birdes three." PBBP
Squirrel, The. Ogden Nash. CenHV
Squirrel, The ("Squirrel he's a funny little thing"). *Unknown.* FSW
Squirrel, The ("Whisky Frisky). *Unknown.* FaPON; PDV; SoPo; SUS; TiPo
Squirrel in Sunshine. William Cowper. BoAnP
Squirrel near Library. Genevieve Taggard. WPE
Squirrel to some is a squirrel, A. The Squirrel. Ogden Nash. CenHV
Sri Rama's Raiment. *Malay Oral Tradition, tr. by* R. O. Winstedt. WTO
Stab, The. Will Wallace Harney. AA
Stab incision below nipple. Debridement: Operation Harvest Moon: *On Repose.* Michael S. Harper. GeTw
Stabat Mater. Sam Hunt. OCNZ
Stabat Mater [*or* Stabat Mater Dolorosa]. *At. to* Jacopone da Todi, *tr. fr. Latin.* HBV-2, *tr. by* Abraham Coles; ISi, *tr. by* Aubrey Thomas De Vere; TreFS, *tr. by* Richard Mant *and* Edward Caswell; WGRP, *tr. by* Richard Mant *and* Edward Caswell
Stabilities. Anne Stevenson. NCSH
Stable, The. Jill Hoffman. PH
Stable Cat, The. Leslie Norris. PChr
Stable-lamp is lighted, A. A Christmas Hymn. Richard Wilbur. CoPo; OBCP; OFD; PChr; TrCP
Stable-Talk. Raymond Knister. CaP
Stable yields a stercoraceous heap, The. How to Grow Cucumbers. William Cowper. *Fr.* The Task, III. FaBoUs
Staccato! Staccato! The Rubinstein Staccato Etude. R. Nathaniel Dett. BANP
Stack, The. Stanley Snaith. ChMP
"Stack Arms!" Joseph Blynth Alston. PAH
Stack o' Dollars. *Unknown.* BluL
Stacked houses on either side, The. The Languages We Are. F. J. Bryant. NBP
Stacking Up. Rita Rosenfeld. AMV-81
Stadium, The. William Heyen. LiSp
Staff and Scrip, The. Dante Gabriel Rossetti. OAEP
Staff is now greased, The. The Hag. Robert Herrick. CaPo
Staff-Nurse: New Style. W. E. Henley. In Hospital, X. BrPo; NBM
Staff-Nurse: Old Style. W. E. Henley. In Hospital, VIII. BrPo
Staff of Aesculapius, The. Marianne Moore. ImOP
Staff slips from the hand, The. Outward. Louis Simpson. NYBP
Stafford in Kansas. James B. Hall. BXAP
Stag does not lay his side to sleep. Grania. *Unknown, tr. by* Frank O'Connor. KiLC
Stag-Hunt. *Unknown.* OxBM
Stage is about to be swept of corpses, The. Horatian Epode to the Duchess of Malfi. Allen Tate. FaBoMo
Stage is lighted, the first act half over, The. Third Row, Centre. William Rose Benét. WhC
Stage is set in darkness, The. A table, small, oval. The Chandelier as Protagonist. William Virgil Davis. AMV-80
Stage Love. Swinburne. NIP; PoEL-5
Stage-road runs on the sunrise plain, The. Laguna Perdida. Maynard Dixon. BPAW
Stages on a Journey Westward. James Wright. CABA; LCAP; NaP
Staggering down the road at midnite. The Encounter. Paul Blackburn. NeAP
Stagolee. *Unknown.* BaBo (A *and* B *vers.*); FSW; MAT; OxBoLi; TTY; ViBoFo (A *and* B *vers.*)
Stags. William Montgomerie. PoSH
Staid schizophrenic named Struther, A. Limerick. *Unknown.* NIP
Stained Glass. Willis Barnstone. AMV-81
Stained Glass Man, The. Cynthia Macdonald. FiCP
Stained with blood from a hare. Fleadh. Michael Longley. CIP
Stains. Theodosia Garrison. HBV-2; WGRP
Stair-carpet is Turkey red, The. On the Staircase. Eleanor Farjeon. SiSoSe
Staircase, The. Samuel Allen. PoBa
Staircase with a Hundred Steps, The. Benjamin Péret, *tr. fr. French by* David Gascoyne. EAS
Stairs. Oliver Herford. FiBHP; InMe; WhC
Stairs mount to his eternity, The. The Staircase. Samuel Allen. PoBa
Stairway is not, The. The Jacob's Ladder. Denise Levertov. AmPP; CoPo; PoM; PPP
Stalagmites and Stalactites. *Unknown.* FaBoUs
Stalin stood committed to peasant hunger. Reply to the Committed Intellectual. Francis Sparshott. NOBC
Stalks of Wild Hay. H. L. Davis. PoA
Stall so tight he can't raise heels or knees, The. Bronco Busting, Event #1. May Swenson. LiSp; PH
Stalled before my metal shaving mirror. Notes for a Sonnet. Edward Pygge. BXAP

Stalled on the sidelines we must hope and wait. We Who Build Visions. Stanton A. Coblentz. PGD
Stallion, The. Boynton Merrill, Jr. PH
Stallion, The. Alan Porter. PH
Stallion, The. Walt Whitman. *Fr.* Song of Myself, XXXII. PH
("Gigantic beauty of a stallion, fresh and responsive to my caresses, A.") PDV
Stammerers, The. Margaret Kent. AMV-80
Stamm'ring cuckoo, whose lewd voice doth grieve, The. Ingratitude. Francis Thynne. PBBP
Stamp Blues. *Unknown.* BluL
Stampede, The. Earl Alonzo Brininstool. PoOW
Stampede, The. Arthur I. Caldwell. BPAW
Stampede, The. Wallace D. Coburn. PoOW
Stampede, The. Freeman E. Miller. BPAW
Stampede, The. *Unknown.* CoSo
Stan' Still Jordan, *with music. Unknown.* BoAN-1
Stance. Theodore Enslin. CoPo
"Stand aside." Sun and Cloud. Melville Cane. PoPl
Stand at my window. Apology for Youth. Sister Mary Madeleva. PoPl
Stand back, make way, you mindless scum. Dr. Joseph Goebbels. W. D. Snodgrass. *Fr.* The Führer Bunker. TW
Stand By. *Unknown.* STF
Stand by the Flag. John Nichols Wilder. GN; PGD
Stand close around, ye Stygian set. Dirce. Walter Savage Landor. *Fr.* Pericles and Aspasia. AWP; ChTr; CTC; EBEV; EnRP; FaBoEE; FaBoEn; GBL; HAP; LiTB; LoBV; NOBE; NoP; OAEL-2; OAEP; OBEV; OBNC; OBRV; PAI; PoEL-4; PoPle; PoRA; SeCeV; TreFT; TrGrPo; ViBoPo; VLP; WeW; WHA; WhC
Stand forth, Seithenyn: winds are high. Song of Gwythno. Thomas Love Peacock. *Fr.* The Misfortunes of Elphin. OBRV
Stand here by my side and turn, I pray. The Snow-Shower. Bryant. HBV-1
Stand: knees slightly. Dance Instructions for a Young Girl. Kimiko Hahn. BrSi
Stand Not Uttering Sedately. Victor Plarr. *See* Epitaphium Citharistriae.
Stand off, and let me take the air. A Fair Nymph Scorning a Black Boy Courting Her. John Cleveland. AnAnS-2
Stand on the highest pavement of the stair. La Figlia Che Piange. T. S. Eliot. FaBoTw; GBL; HeIP; LiTA; MAT; OxBTC; PoA; UnPo; VGW; ViBoPo
Stand, Stately Tavie. *Unknown.* ErPo; PV
Stand still, and I will read to thee. A Lecture upon the Shadow. John Donne. AnAnS-1; AWP; CABA; EnRePo; InPK; OBS; SeCP; TEP; UnPo
Stand still. The trees ahead and bushes beside you. Lost. David Wagoner. GP; PoA
Stand still, true poet that you are! Popularity. Robert Browning. OAEL-2; PP
Stand still, you floods, do[e] not deface. On Sight of a Gentlewoman's Face in the Water. Thomas Carew. CaPo; SeCV-1
Stand straight. Rules for the Road. Edwin Markham. TreFT
Stand! the ground's your own, my braves! Warren's Address at Bunker Hill [*or* to the American Soldiers]. John Pierpont. AA; FaBoBe; GN; GOA; HBV-2; HBVY; PAH; PAL; TreF; WBLP
Stand this way—more near the window. My Picture. Adelaide Anne Proctor. PeD
Stand-to, The. C. Day Lewis. OBWP
Stand-to: Good Friday Morning. Siegfried Sassoon. FaBoTw
Stand To Your Glasses. Bartholomew Dowling. *See* Revel, The.
"Stand to your guns, men!" Morris cried. On Board the *Cumberland.* George Henry Boker. PAH
Stand Up! D. H. Lawrence. OxBTC
Stand up and rejoice! a great day is here! Hallelujah, I'm a-Travelin'. Harry Raymond. FSW
Stand up, but not for Jesus. Stand Up! D. H. Lawrence. OxBTC
Stand Up for Jesus. George Duffield, Jr. TreFS
(Stand Up! Stand Up for Jesus.) AH
"Stand up, stand up, thou May Janet." May Janet. Swinburne. VLP
Stand wel, moder, under roode. At the Crucifixion. *Unknown.* OxBM
Stand Whoso List. Seneca, *tr. fr. Latin by* Sir Thomas Wyatt. *Fr.* Thyestes. NoP
("Stand [*or* Stond] whoso list, upon the slipper top.") AAS; OBVE; PoEL-1; SiPS
Stand with thy nose against. Of One That Had a Great Nose. George Turberville. FaBoEE
Stand ye calm and resolute. Shelley. *Fr.* The Masque of Anarchy. LoBV
Standards of the king go forth, The. Venantius Fortunatus, *tr. fr. Latin by* Helen Waddell. NAWM-1
Standin' on the Walls of Zion, *with music. Unknown.* AS
Standing aloof in giant ignorance. To Homer [*or* Sonnet: To Homer]. Keats. CABA; ChER; EBEV; NCEP; NoP; OBRV
Standing at my writing desk. Difficult Times. Bertolt Brecht, *tr. by* Martin Esslin. ELU
Standing at the edge of the warped dock. The Crane's Ascent. Nick Bozanic. AMV-81
Standing at the portal. At the Portal. Frances Ridley Havergal. BLRP
Standing at the station. Depot Blues. *Unknown.* BluL
Standing between the sun and moon preserves. Einstein. Archibald MacLeish. MoPo; TwAmPo
Standing corn is green, the wild in flower, The. Nunc Viridant Segetes. Sedulius Scottus, *tr. by* Helen Waddell. BIrV; NAWM-1
Standing guests, a grotesque glade, The. The Party. Margaret Avison. PoA
Standing high on the shoulders of all things, all things. The Place at Albert Bay. Muriel Rukeyser. PoA
Standing in the hall against the/ wall. Listening to Grownups Quarreling. Ruth Whitman. NTCP
Standing on Earth. Milton. *Fr.* Paradise Lost, VII. ChTr
Standing on my head makes. Ingestion. Barry McDonald. POL
Standing on 127th the. Langston. Mari Evans. BOLo; CNA
Standing on the Corner. Philip Levine. NNaP
Standing on the mountaintop. Lost Silvertip. J. D. Reed. NYBP
Standing on Tiptoe. George Frederick Cameron. CaP; OBCV; PeCV
Standing on top of the hay. The Farm. Donald Hall. LiTM
Standing there they began to grow skins. Pilgrims. Jean Valentine. LCAP; TAP
Standing under the fobbed. Send No Money. Philip Larkin. TW
Standing up on lifted, folded rock. By Frazier Creek Falls. Gary Snyder. GOA
Standing upon the margent of the Main. The Tempest. Charles Cotton. SeCePo
Standing uptight in books against the wall. Stained Glass. Willis Barnstone. AMV-81
Standing with raised arms before. Edwardian Hat. Betty Parvin. POL
Stands for Gnu, whose weapons of Defense. G. Hilaire Belloc. FiBHP
Stane-chack! Malison of the Stone-chat. *Unknown.* GBP
Stanes. Duncan Glen. PoSH
Stanley Matthews. Alan Ross. LiSp; OxBTC
Stanley Meets Mutesa. James D. Rubadiri. PBA
Stans Puer ad Mensam. Sir Walter Raleigh. WhC
Stanza: "Often rebuked, yet always back returning." *At. to* Emily Brontë. *See* Stanzas: "Often rebuked, yet always back returning."
Stanza from an Early Poem. Christopher Pearse Cranch. *See* Gnosis.
Stanza on Freedom, A. James Russell Lowell. *See* Slaves.
Stanza Put on Westminster Hall Gate, A. *Unknown.* APAS
Stanzas, *sel.* Charles Newton.
Wild Nature ("Fresh were the breathings of the nightborn gale.") NOEC
Stanzas: "Away! the moor is dark beneath the moon." Shelley. *See* Stanzas—April, 1814.
Stanzas: "Black absence hides upon the past." John Clare. EnLoPo
Stanzas: "Could love for ever." Byron. HBV-1; ViBoPo, *3 sts.*
Stanzas: "How smooth that lake expands its ample breast!" Anne Radcliffe. WPE
Stanzas: "I thought I woke: the midnight sun." Paul Goodman. PoA
Stanzas: "I will go back to the great sweet mother." Swinburne. *Fr.* The Triumph of Time. HBV-1; OAEP
(Return, The.) EtS
(Sea, The.) TrGrPo
Stanzas: "I'll not weep that thou art going to leave me." Emily Brontë. LoBV; WPE
Stanzas: "In a drear-nighted December." Keats. *See* In a Drear-nighted December.
Stanzas: "Mighty thought of an old world, The." Thomas Lovell Beddoes. *See* Mighty Thought of an Old World, The.
Stanzas: "My life is like the summer rose." Richard Henry Wilde. *See* My Life Is like the Summer Rose.
Stanzas: "Often rebuked, yet always back returning." *At. to* Emily Brontë, *also at. to* Charlotte Brontë. ChER; FaBoEn; HBV-2; LiTB; LoBV; OAEL-2; OAEP; OBNC; OBVV; PBWP
(Stanza.) OBEV
Stanzas: "Princes and kings decay and die." Philip Freneau. GOA
Stanzas: "When a man hath no freedom to fight for at home." Byron. *See* When a Man Hath No Freedom . . .
Stanzas: "Where forlorn sunsets flare and fade." W. E. Henley. *See* Over the Hills and Far Away.
Stanzas: "With tears thy grief thou dost bemoan." Solomon ibn Gabirol, *tr. fr. Hebrew by* Emma Lazarus. TrJP
Stanzas—April, 1814. Shelley. ChER; EnRP; FiP; OAEP; OBNC
(Remorse.) OBEV
(Stanzas: "Away! the moor is dark beneath the moon.") LoBV
Stanzas Concerning Love. Stefan George, *tr. fr. German by* Ludwig Lewisohn. AWP
Stanzas, for Music ("There be none of Beauty's daughters"). Byron. AWP;

ChER; DTC; EnRP; FiP; HBV-1; NoP; OAEL-2; OAEP; OBRV; PoRA; TrGrPo
(For Music.) PoPle
("There be none of Beauty's daughters.") ELP; GTBS; GTBS-P; LiTB; LoBV
Stanzas for Music ("There's not a joy the world can give like that it takes away"). Byron. EnRP; HAP; HBV-1; OAEP
(Youth and Age.) GTBS; GTBS-P
Stanzas for My Daughter. Horace Gregory. MoVE
(Poems for My Daughter.) MoAmPo
Stanzas from "Child Harold." John Clare. *Fr.* Child Harold. OBNC
(In Epping Forest.) FaBoPP
Stanzas from Saint Peter's Complaint. Robert Southwell. *Fr.* Saint Peter's Complaint. ACP
Stanzas from the Grande Chartreuse. Matthew Arnold. EBVV; OAEL-2; OAEP; PoEL-5; TEP; VLP
"For rigorous teachers seized my youth," *sel.* ViBoPo
Stanzas from the Ivory Gate. Thomas Lovell Beddoes. EnRP
Stanzas in Meditation, *sels.* Gertrude Stein.
"Full well I know that she is there." PoA
"How I wish I were able to say what I think." PBWP
Stanzas in Memory of the Author of "Obermann." Matthew Arnold. VLP
Stanzas Occasioned by the Ruins of a Country Inn, Unroofed and Blown Down in a Storm. Philip Freneau. OxBA
(On The Ruins of a Country Inn.) AA
Stanzas on Freedom. James Russell Lowell. GN, 2 *sts.*; OHIP; PGD, *abr.*; PoNe
Slaves, *last st.* TRV; WBLP
(Commitment.) TreFT
(On Freedom.) PAL
(Stanza on Freedom, A.) AA
Stanzas on Mutability. Hugo von Hofmannsthal, *tr. fr. German by* Jethro Bithell. AWP; TrJP
Stanzas on Seeing the Speaker Asleep in His Chair. Winthrop Mackworth Praed. *See* Stanzas to the Speaker Asleep.
Stanzas on the Emigration to America, and Peopling the Western Country. Philip Freneau. *See* On the Emigration to America.
Stanzas on Woman. Goldsmith. *See* Song: "When lovely woman stoops to conquer."
Stanzas Subjoined to the Yearly Bill of Mortality of the Parish of All Saints, Northampton; for the Year 1787. William Cowper. NOCV
Stanzas to ——— ("Well, some may hate, and some may scorn"). Emily Brontë. LoBV; WPE
Stanzas to a Lady, with the Poems of Camoëns. Byron. FaBoUs
Stanzas to Augusta. Byron. EnRP
Stanzas to Edward Williams. Shelley. OBNC
Stanzas to Mr. Bentley. Thomas Gray. NoP
Stanzas to the Po. Byron. OAEL-2
Stanzas to the Speaker Asleep. Winthrop Mackworth Praed. NBM; OBSV; VLP
(Stanzas on Seeing the Speaker Asleep in His Chair.) EnRP
Stanzas Written in Dejection near Naples. Shelley. CABA; ChER; EnRP; FaBV; FiP; GTBS; GTBS-P; NoP; OAEP; OBRV; PoRA; TEP; ViBoPo; WHA
Stanzas Written in My Pocket Copy of Thomson's "Castle of Indolence." Wordsworth. EnRP
Stanzas Written on Battersea Bridge during a Southwesterly Gale. Hilaire Belloc. GoBC
Stanzas Written on the Road between Florence and Pisa. Byron. EnRP; HBV-1; OBRV
(All for Love.) GTBS; GTBS-P; TreFT
Staoineag. Leen Volwerk. PoSH
Star, The. Grace Hazard Conkling. HBMV
Star. Gene Derwood. NePA; TwAmPo
Star, A. George MacBeth. NYBP
Star, The. Beatrice Redpath. CaP
Star, The. Marion Couthouy Smith. PAH
Star, The. William Soutar. NeBP
Star, The. Jane Taylor. FaBoBe; FaFP; FaPON; HBV-1; HBVY; NTCP; OxBChV; RHPC; SoPo; SpRo; TiPo; TreF
Star, The. Willoughby Weaving. HBMV; HBVY
Star. Joanie Whitebird. GP
Star,/ If you are. A Christmas Tree. William Burford. NePA; SoSe
Star & Garter Theater. Dennis Schmitz. LCAP; NPGG
Star Blanket. Ray A. Young Bear. CDW
Star Child Suite. Paula Gunn Allen. TWSS
Star crashes in a small plaza and a bird loses its eyes, A. The Things I Say Are True. Blanca Varela, *tr. by* Donald Yates. BoWoP
Star-crowned cliffs seem hinged upon the sky, The. Glencoe. G. K. Chesterton. PoSH
Star Drill. T. Inglis Moore. PoAu-2
Star Dust, *with music.* Mitchell Parish. BLSo
Star-dust and vaporous light. Noel. Richard Watson Gilder. AA
Star-face Lightfoot, sired by the Fox. Monologue of the Rating Morgan in Rutherford County. C. F. MacIntyre. PH
Star-filled seas are smooth tonight, The. The Isle of Portland. A. E. Housman. A Shropshire Lad, LIX. MoBrPo
Star is gone, A! a star is gone! The Fallen Star. George Darley. HBV-2; OBEV
Star Journey. Naomi Long Madgett. BPo
Star light, star bright. Star Wish [*or* Wishing Poem]. *Unknown.* HBVY; NTCP; OxNR; SoPo; TiPo
Star looks down at me, A. Waiting Both. Thomas Hardy. MoAB; MoBrPo; OxBoLi; WHA
Star Morals. Nietzsche, *tr. fr. German by* Ludwig Lewisohn. AWP
Star must cease to burn with its own light, The. Et Mori Lucrum. John Lancaster Spalding. *Fr.* God and the Soul. AA
Star-nosed Mole, The. Robert Wallace. BoAnP
Star of Calvary, The. Nathaniel Hawthorne. AA
Star of Columbia. Timothy Dwight. *See* Columbia.
Star of Empire poets say, The. Ho! Westward Ho! Ossian E. Dodge. BLSo
Star of Eternal Possibles and Joy. Peter Yates. ChMP
Star of Ethiopia. Lucian B. Watkins. BANP
Star of my mishap imposed this pain, The. To Delia, XXXI. Samuel Daniel. OBSC
Star of ocean fairest. Ave Maris Stella. *Unknown.* ISi
Star of Sangamon, The. Lyman Whitney Allen. PGD
Star of the East. Eugene Field. PGD
Star of the Evening. James M. Sayles. Par; SpRo
Star of the Nativity. Boris Pasternak, *tr. fr. Russian by* Eugene M. Kayden. PoPl
Star of the North! though night winds drift. The Fugitive Slave's Apostrophe to the North Star. John Pierpont. AA
Star of the Sea. Alexander Barclay. *Fr.* The Ship of Fools. ACP
Star of the Sea. Richard Webb Sullivan. ISi
Star of the Western Skies. *Unknown.* BPAW
Star over all. Christmas Tree. Laurence Smith. OBCP
Star Quilt. Roberta Hill Whiteman. CDW; TWSS
Star Song. Robert Underwood Johnson. HBV-1
Star-Song, The; a Carol to the King; sung at White-Hall. Robert Herrick. OxBoCh
(Star Song, The.) GN
Star Song of the Bushman Women. *Unknown, tr. fr. Bushman by* W. H. I. Bleek. PeSA
Star-spangled Banner, The. Francis Scott Key. AA; BLPA; BLSo, *with music*; FaBoBe; FAFP; FaPo; FaPON; FaPoR; FSW; HBV-2; HBVY; NePA; PAH; PAL; TAP; TreF; WBLP; YaD
Star-Splitter, The. Robert Frost. ImOP
Star, star, shining bright. Star. Gene Derwood. NePA; TwAmPo
"Star stood over where the young child was, The." A Christmas Prayer. Molly Anderson Haley. PGD
Star-Talk. Robert Graves. BoNaP; GoJo; HBMV; MoBrPo; OxBTC
Star That Bids the Shepherd Fold, The. Milton. *Fr.* Comus. FaBoCh; OBEV; PPoe; ViBoPo, *longer sel.*; WHA
(Comus' Invocation to His Readers.) TrGrPo
(Comus Speaks.) NOBE
(Invocation of Comus, The.) OBS, *longer sel.*
(Mask, A.) FiP
(Song: "Star that bids the shepherd fold, The.") SeCeV, *longer sel.*
Star that bringest home the bee. To the Evening Star [*or* Song to the Evening Star]. Thomas Campbell. GTBS; GTBS-P; HBV-1; TRV
Star There Fell, A. Zalman Schneour, *tr. fr. Hebrew by* Harry H. Fein. TrJP
Star Watcher, The. Peter Davison. TwCP
Star Wish. *Unknown.* HBVY
("Star light, star bright.") OxNR; SoPo
(Wishing Poem.) NTCP
Stare at the monster: remark. Famous Poet. Ted Hughes. LiTM
Stare at the stars, the stars say. Look at me. Ego. Norman MacCaig. GTBS-P
Stared, astonied all. È, the Feasting Florentines. Daniel Hoffman. VGW
Stare's Nest by My Window, The. W. B. Yeats. Meditations in Time of Civil War, VI BIrV; GTBS-P; LiTB; NOBE
Starfish, The. Robert P. Tristram Coffin. ImOP
Starfish. Winifred Welles. FaPON; SiSoSe
Star-Gazer. Louis MacNeice. NoP
Stargazer, The. *Unknown.* OxBChV
Staring at the mud turtle's eye. Concepts and Their Bodies (The Boy in the Field Alone). Pattiann Rogers. MAYP
Staring corpselike at the ceiling. Suicide. W. E. Henley. In Hospital, XXIV. BrPo
Staring into the past and at. Into & At. Edmund Pennant. SOTS

Stark by the Eastern gate. Two Men in Armour. John Heath-Stubbs. NeBP
Stark County Holidays. Mary Oliver. Str
Stark in the pasture on the skull-shaped hill. Pieta. David Gascoyne. *Fr.* Miserere. NeBP
Starless and chill is the night. A Night by the Sea. Heine, *tr. by* Howard Mumford Jones. *Fr.* The North Sea. AWP
Starlight. John White Chadwick. AA
Starlight. William Meredith. NePoEA
Starlight like Intuition Pierced the Twelve. Delmore Schwartz. MiAP; NMP; PoCh; TwAmPo
(Starlight's Intuitions Pierced the Twelve, The.) MoPo; NePA
Starlight Night, The. Gerard Manley Hopkins. ACP; BrPo; GoBC; GTBS-P; InPS; LiTM; MoAB; MoBrPo; MoVE; OBVV; OxBoCh; PoPle; PPP; SeCePo; ViBoPo; VLP; WSC
Starlight Scope Myopia. Yusef Komunyakaa. MAYP
Starlighter, The. Arthur Guiterman. SiSoSe
Starlight's Intuitions Pierced the Twelve, The. Delmore Schwartz. *See* Starlight like Intuition Pierced . . .
Starling, The. Robert Buchanan. FM
Starling and a Willow-Wren, A. W. H. Auden. FaBoMo
Starling Lake, The. "Seumas O'Sullivan." AnIV; AWP
(My Sorrow.) HBV-2
Starlings. Laura Jensen. AMV-81
Starlings. Norman MacCaig. BoAnP
Starlings. Ted Olson. PV
Starling's Spring Rondel, A. James Cousins. HBV-1; HBVY
Starre, The. George Herbert. AnAnS-1
Starre, The. Henry Vaughan. AnAnS-1; MePo
Starred Mother, The. Robert Whitaker. PGD
Starry Host, The. John Lancaster Spalding. *Fr.* God and the Soul. AA; HBV-2
Starry hosts whose far-flung cohorts gleam, The. Human Greatness. Edwin Barclay. PBA
Starry Night, The. Anne Sexton. NMP; NoAM
Starry Night, The. George Starbuck. NYBP
Starry Sky. Charles Simic. POL
Starry Sky. *Unknown, tr. fr. Old Irish by* Sean O'Faolain. AnIL
Stars. George Mackay Brown. OxBS
Stars, The. Mary Mapes Dodge. AA
Stars. Robert Hayden. LCAP
Sojourner Truth, *sel.* CNA
Stars. Howard Moss. HoAn
Stars. Alden Nowlan. POL
Stars, The, *sels.* "Ping Hsin," *tr. fr. Chinese by* Kai-yu Hsu.
"Builder of continents, The." WPOW
"Fragile blades of grass." WPOW
Stars, The, *sel.*. Christopher Smart.
"Stars of the superior class." ChTr
Stars. Sara Teasdale. FaPON; HBMV; TiPo
Stars and atoms have no size. Measurement. A. M. Sullivan. RHPC
Stars are circles of children. Everything Is Round. Gabriela Mistral, *tr. by* D. M. Pettinella. PBWP
Stars are dimly seen among the shadows of the bay, The. Barcarolle. Arthur William Edgar O'Shaughnessy. NBM
Stars are dropping thick as stones into the twiggy. Stars over the Dordogne. Sylvia Plath. PoA
Stars are everywhere to-night, The. Daisies. Andrew Young. GoJo
Stars are forth, the moon above the tops, The. Byron. *Fr.* Manfred: A Dramatic Poem, III, iv. OAEL-2
Stars Are Glittering in the Frosty Sky, The. Charles Heavysege. CaP; PeCV
(Winter Galaxy.) NOBC; OBCV
Stars are gone out spark by spark, The. At Cockcrow. Lizette Woodworth Reese. TrPWD
Stars Are Lit, The. Hayyim Nahman Bialik, *tr. fr. Hebrew by* Florence L. Friedman. TrJP
Stars are old, that stood for me, The. Emily Dickinson. PeHV
Stars are only a backdrop for, The. Notes on a Life to Be Lived. Robert Penn Warren. NYBP
Stars are pale, The. Break of Day. Shaw Neilson. PoAu-1
Stars are pinned against the sky, The. It Is the Stars That Govern Us. Michael Magee. PoA
Stars are shining/ the eyes of men are closed. Rabi'a al-Adawiyya, *tr. fr. Arabic by* Margaret Smith; *ad. by* Deirdre Lashgari. WPOW
Stars are thundering in the sky, The. *Gond Oral Tradition, tr. by* V. Elwin *and* S. Hivale. WTO
Stars Are with the Voyager, The. Thomas Hood. EnRP
Stars at their zenith, more tranquil than you, The. The Stars on Shabbat. Avraham Shlonsky, *tr. by* Francis Landy. VWA
Stars began to peep, The. The Little Ghost. Katherine Tynan. HBV-1
Stars Begin to Fall. *Unknown.* AA
Stars catch my eyes, The. A Thought for My Love. Bruce Williamson. NeIP
Stars Climb Girders of Light. Bert Meyers. MAT
Stars Dance, The. Thomas Campion. *See* Song: To the Masquers Representing Stars.
Stars Fade. Peretz Hirshbein, *tr. fr. Yiddish by* Joseph Leftwich. TrJP
Stars Go By, The. Lilian Bowes Lyon. ChMP
Stars Go over the Lonely Ocean, The. Robinson Jeffers. LiTA; LiTM; NePA; WaP
Stars had the look of dogs to him sometimes. The Star Watcher. Peter Davison. TwCP
Stars have given me a hard fate, The. Gaspara Stampa, *tr. fr. Italian by* Lynne Lawner. PBWP
Stars Have Not Dealt Me, The. A. E. Housman. ELU; OxBoLi; SeCeV
("Stars have not dealt me the worst they could do, The.") EBEV; GTBS-P
Stars have not yet retired, and the sky is still dark, The. Women Transport Corps. *Unknown, tr. by* Kai-yu Hsu. WPOW
Stars have their glory and, or near or far. The Sun Men Call It. John Hall Wheelock. NePoAm-2
Stars have ways I do not know. I Look into the Stars. Jane Draper. HBMV
Stars, I Have Seen Them Fall. A. E. Housman. ChTr; NoP
Stars in Apple Cores. Luci Shaw. TrCP
Stars in the sky are as big as coins. *Turkish Love Songs, tr. by* Reza Baraheni *and* Zahra-Soltan Shokoohtaezeh. BoWoP
Stars in your face, The. In Missing. Ray A. Young Bear. CDW
Stars, it is the end. Ducks Down in the Meadow. William Stafford. NPAW
Stars know a secret, The. Force. Edward Rowland Sill. AA
Stars lie broken on a lake. Reflections. Edna Becker. TRV
Stars never had any mystery for me, The. Sailor and Inland Flower. Hamish Maclaren. EtS
Stars of night contain the glittering day, The. The Dying Words of Stonewall Jackson. Sidney Lanier. PAH
Stars of the morn, The/ On our banner borne. The Flag of the *Constellation.* Thomas Buchanan Read. EtS
Stars of the summer night! Serenade. Longfellow. *Fr.* The Spanish Student. AA; FaBoBe; HBV-1; LoBV; ViBoPo
Stars of the superior class. Christopher Smart. *Fr.* The Stars. ChTr
Stars on Shabbat, The. Avraham Shlonsky, *tr. fr. Hebrew by* Francis Landy. VWA
Stars over snow. Night. Sara Teasdale. FaPON; SoPo; SUS; TiPo
Stars over the Dordogne. Sylvia Plath. PoA
Stars shine down, The. Rosh Pina. Dovid Knut, *tr. by* Daniel Weissbort. VWA
Stars Shine So Faithfully. Jane Flanders. AMV-80
Stars Stand Up in the Air, The. *Unknown, tr. fr. Irish by* Thomas Macdonagh. AnIV; BIrV
Stars, the stars everlasting are fugitives also, The. Emerson. POL
Stars trembling o'er us and sunset before us. In Our Boat. Dinah Maria Mulock Craik. HBV-1
Stars walk downhill. Concert. Robert Sward. VGW
Stars Wheel in Purple. Hilda Doolittle ("H. D."). *Fr.* Let Zeus Record. NOBA; TAP
(Stars wheel in purple, yours is not so rare.) MoAmPo
Stars wheel past the windows, The. For the New Year. Norman Nicholson. NeBP
Stars Which See, Stars Which Do Not See. Marvin Bell. LCAP
Starscape, A. John Bellenden. ACP
Starshine on the Arch is silver white, The. Villanelle of Washington Square. Walter Adolphe Roberts. PoNe
Starship. David McAleavey. AMV-81
Start not—or deem my spirit fled. Lines Inscribed upon a Cup Formed from a Skull. Byron. InPK
Start with a simple room. Plucking Out a Rhythm. Lawson Fusao Inada. AmPA
Starting again. A Dark Country. Derek Mahon. BIrV
Starting at Dawn. Sun Yün-feng, *tr. fr. Chinese by* Kenneth Rexroth *and* Ling Chung. PBWP
Starting Early from the Ch'u-ch'êng Inn. Po Chü-i, *tr. fr. Chinese by* Arthur Waley. OBVE
Starting from Paumanok, *sels.* Walt Whitman.
"Dead poets, philosophs, priests." InPS
"Starting from fish-shape Paumanok where I was born." ViBoPo
Starting from San Francisco. Lawrence Ferlinghetti. BiP; CAPP
Starting Over. Shirley Kaufman. VWA
Startled/ By a single scream. Saigyo Hoshi, *tr. fr. Japanese by* Arthur Waley. AWP
Startled stag, the blue-grey night, A. The Dark Stag. Isabella Valancy Crawford. NOBC; PeCV

Starvation Camp near Jaslo. Wislawa Szymborska, *tr. fr. Polish by* Jan Darowski. WPOW
Starved lost frozen. La Belle Saison. Jacques Prévert, *tr. by* Lawrence Ferlinghetti. CAD
Starved old gelding, blind and lamed, A. An Irish Marriage Night. Brian Merriman, *tr. by* Frank O'Connor. *Fr.* The Midnight Court. BIrV
Starved, scarred, lenten, amidst ash of air. The Sugaring. A. M. Klein. OBCV
Starving of Bangladesh, The. Encounter with Hunger. Brian Vanderlip. AMV-81
Starving, savage, I aspire. The Tiger of Desire. Tom MacInnes. OBCV
Starving to Death on a Government Claim. *Unknown.* AmFP; BPAW; FSW; OBAL
(Lane County Bachelor, The, *with music.*) AS
Stasis in darkness. Ariel. Sylvia Plath. CABA; CMoP; HeIP; InPK; LCAP; NMP; NoAM; NOBA; NoP; PBWP
State, The. Randall Jarrell. LiTM; MiAP
State Fair Pigs. Roger Pfingston. TAT
State of Arkansas, The. *Unknown.* CoSo, *with music;* FSW; TrAS, *with music*
(Sanford Barney, *diff. vers.*) AmFP
State of Innocence, The, *sels.* Dryden.
Death the Consequence of the Fall. NOCV
Predestination and Free Will. NOCV
State of Nature, A. John Hollander. NIP
State Prison 5:00 P.M. ("The count bell rings"). Thomas G. Nickens. LFAC
State Prison 4:00 P.M. ("Groups of me"). Thomas G. Nickens. LFAC
State School. Paul D. Shiplett. LFAC
State set its whole official will, The. To the Carp, and Those Who Hunt Her. James Hazard. AMV-80
State Street is lonely today. Aunt Jane Allen. Fenton Johnson. IDB; PoBA; PoNe
State the alternative preferred. F. H. Townsend. PV
State with the prettiest name, The. Florida. Elizabeth Bishop. MP; TwCP
Stately Homes of England, The. Noël Coward. FaBoPa
Stately Homes of England, The, *parody.* E. V. Knoz. WhC
Stately homes of England, The. The Homes of England. Felicia Dorothea Hemans. FaPoR; PaPo; SBG; WhC; WPE
Stately, kindly, lordly friend. To a Cat. Swinburne. PCat
Stately rainbow came and stood, A. The Rainbow. Coventry Patmore. *Fr.* The Angel in the House, II, iii. GTBS-P
Stately Southerner, The. *Unknown. See* Yankee Man-of-War, The.
Stately state that wise men count their good, The. Barmenissa's Song. Robert Greene. FaBoRV
Stately Structure of This Earth, The, *with music.* Martha Brewster. AH
Stately the feast, and high the cheer. The Grave of King Arthur. Thomas Warton. EnRP; GoTL
Stately Verse. *Unknown.* FaPON; TiPo
Statement on Our Higher Education. W. M. Ransom. CDW
States when they black out and lie there rolling, The. Falling. James Dickey. LCAP; NYBP
Statesboro Blues. *Unknown.* BluL
Statesman, The. Hilaire Belloc. NOBE
Statesman in Retirement, The. William Cowper. *Fr.* Retirement. OBEC
Statesman's Holiday, The. W. B. Yeats. CMoP; OxBTC
Static. Barton Sutter. AMV-81
Static Autumn. Yvor Winters. PoA
Stationed Scout, The. Lyman H. Sproull. PoOW
Stationmaster is garrulous in, The. Daphne Stillorgan. Denis Devlin. CIP
Stationmaster's Lament, The. Jerome Rothenberg. CoPo
Stations. Ted Hughes. NoAM
Stations of the Cross, The. Padraic Colum. GoBC
Statistics. Stephen Spender. MoBrPo
Statue, The. Kenneth Allott. EAS
Statue, The. Hilaire Belloc. ACP; MoVE; POL
Statue, The. John Berryman. NYP
Statue, The. Robert Creeley. LCAP
Statue, The. Robert Finch. OBCV; PeCV
Statue, The. John Fuller. NePoEA-2
Statue, The. Roy Fuller. NOBE
Statue against a Clear Sky. Wallace Stevens. *Fr.* New England Verses. EyDe
Statue and Birds. Louise Bogan. EyDe; MoAB; MoAmPo
Statue and the Bust, The. Robert Browning. OAEP
Statue and the Perturbed Burghers, The. Denis Devlin. OnYI
Statue in a Garden, A. Agnes Lee. HBMV
Statue of a rich industrialist, The. In the City of Bogotá. Greg Pape. MAYP
Statue of Liberty, The. Sheila Jane Crooke. YaD
Statue of Liberty, The. Edward Field. TAT
Statue of Liberty, The. Thomas Hardy. LiTB
Statue of Lorenzo de' Medici, The. James Ernest Nesmith. AA
Statue of Medusa, The. William Drummond of Hawthornden. EyDe
Statue of Shadow, The. John Peale Bishop. LiTA
Statue stood, The/ Of Newton with his prism and silent face. Newton. Wordsworth. *Fr.* The Prelude, III. ImOP
Statue, tolerant through years of weather, The. The Statue. John Berryman. NYP
Statues, The. Laurence Binyon. OBEV; OBVV
Statues. Kathleen Raine. NYBP
Statues. Richard Wilbur. EyDe
Statues, The. W. B. Yeats. AnIL; NoAM; OAEL-2; WeW
Statues in the Public Gardens, The. Howard Nemerov. ConAP; EyDe
Statuette: Late Minoan. C. Day Lewis. OxBI
Status Quo. Binga Dismond. PoNe
Status Symbol. Mari Evans. IDB
Status Symbols. Anne Sostrom. SOTS
Stavin' Chain, *with music. Unknown.* OuSiCo
Stavro's dead. A truant vine. Epitaph. Lawrence Durrell. FaBoCo
Stay All Night, Stay a Little Longer. *Unknown.* AmFP
Stay beautiful/ but dont stay down underground too long. For Poets. Al Young. CNA; DFF; PoBA; RFM
Stay, Christmas! Ivy O. Eastwick. SiSoSe
Stay here, fond youth, and ask no more, be wise. Against Fruition. Sir John Suckling. CaPo
Stay, June, Stay! Christina Rossetti. *Fr.* Sing-Song. YeAr
("Days are clear, The.") TiPo
"Stay, lady, stay, for mercy's sake." The Orphan Boy's Tale. Amelia Opie. PaPo
Stay near me—do not take thy flight! To a Butterfly. Wordsworth. EnRP
Stay near me. Speak my name. Oh, do not wander. Midcentury Love Letter. Phyllis McGinley. ViBoPo
Stay now with me, and listen to my sighs. Dante, *tr. by* Dante Gabriel Rossetti. La Vita Nuova, XX. AWP
Stay, Nymph. *Unknown.* EnRePo
Stay, O sweet, and do not rise! Break of Day [*or* Aubade *or* Daybreak]. *Unknown, at. to* John Donne. BoLoP; EIL; NOBE; OBEV; TrGrPo
Stay Phoebus, stay. Song. Edmund Waller. AnAnS-2; SeCP
Stay, shade of my shy treasure! Oh, remain. Sister Juana Inés de la Cruz, *tr. fr. Spanish by* Alice Stone Blackwell. WPOW
Stay, ship from Thames, with fettered sails. Ship from Thames. Rex Ingamells. PoAu-2
Stay silent/ keep away from sharks. Anticipation of Sharks. Diane Wakoski. MAT
Stay, speedy time; behold, before thou pass. Michael Drayton. Idea, XVII. EnRePo; OBSC
Stay, Spring. Andrew Young. FaBoTw
Stay, stay at home, my heart, and rest. Home Song [*or* Song]. Longfellow. GN; HBV-2
Stay, Thames, to heare my Song, thou great and famous Flood. Michael Drayton. *Fr.* The Third Eclogue. PoEL-2
Stay, Time. James Wreford Watson. CaP
Stay weary traveler, stay! The Fountain at the Tomb. Nicias, *tr. by* Charles Merivale. AWP
Stay with me, God. The night is dark. A Soldier: His Prayer. Gerald Kersch. TreFS
Stay yet, pale flower, though coming storms will tear thee. On a Rose in December. Ebenezer Elliott. FaBoEE
Stay your rude steps, or e'er your feet invade. John Hookham Frere. *Fr.* The Loves of the Triangles. FaBoNo
Stayed where he was. The Boar. Robert Kelly. CoPo
Staying Ahead. Malcolm Glass. AMV-81; FAZ
Staying Alive. David Wagoner. BoNaP; CABA; CoAP; NYBP; RFM; WeW
Staying here, we turn inflexible. Setting Out. W. D. Snodgrass. DiL
Staying in the Mountains in Summer. Yü Hsüan-chi, *tr. fr. Chinese by* Geoffrey Waters. BoWoP
Staying Up on Jack's Fork near Eminence, Missouri. Albert Salsich. AMV-80
Stays shut. My Mouth. Arnold Adoff. RHPC
Steadfast Cross. *Unknown.* OxBM
(Holy Cross.) ACP
(Hymn to the Cross, A.) MeEL
Steadfastness. Sir Thomas Wyatt. *See* Forget Not Yet.
Steady heart, which in its steadiness, The. Angina Pectoris. W. R. Moses. LiTA; NCSH
Steady Rain. Lynn Merrill. AMV-80
Steady time of being unknown, The. Consider a Move. Michael Ryan. MAYP
Steal Away to Jesus. *Unknown.* BoAN-1, *with music;* BPo; FSW
(Steal Away.) TrGrPo
Steal not this book for fear of shame. *Unknown.* FaBoUs
Stealin', Stealin'. *Unknown.* FSW

Stealing. James Russell Lowell. TreF
(International Copyright.) AA; PV
Stealing Trout. Ted Hughes. NYBP
Stealing white from the withered moon. Halloween. Myra Cohn Livingston. OFD
Stealthy the silent hours advance, and still. On a Sundial. Hilaire Belloc. MoVE
Steam, *sel.* Ebenezer Elliott.
"No; there he moves, the thoughtful engineer," VII *and* VIII. VLP
Steam Engine, The; or, The Power of Flame, *sels.* Thomas Baker.
Electric Telegraph, The. FaBoUs
"I dream'd I walked in raptures high." BXAP
Means of Propulsion for Steam-Ships. FaBoUs
Watt's Improvements to the Steam Engine. FaBoUs
Steam in Sacrifice. Robert Herrick. CaPo
Steam Power. Erasmus Darwin. *Fr.* The Botanic Garden. NOEC; OBEC
Steam Shovel. Charles Malam. NTCP; RHPC
Steam Song. Gwendolyn Brooks. GP
Steam Threshing-Machine, The. Charles Tennyson Turner. OBNC; VLP
Steamboat Bill. *Unknown.* FSW
Steamboat is a slow poke, The. Boats. Rowena Bastin Bennett. SoPo; TiPo
Steamboats, Viaducts, and Railways. Wordsworth. VLP
Steddefast [*or* Steadfast] cross[e], inmong [*or* among] alle [*or* all] other. Steadfast Cross [*or* Holy Cross *or* A Hymn to the Cross]. *Unknown.* ACP; MeEL; OxBM
Steed, a steed of matchless[e] speed, A! The Cavalier's Song. William Motherwell. GN; HBV-2
Steed bit his master, The. On a Clergyman's Horse Biting Him. *Unknown.* FaBoCo; FaBoEE; OxBoLi; TreFT; WhC
Steeds. Paul Hiebert. WHW
Steekit, consecrat, fou o fire but fuel. Douglas Young, *after the French of* Paul Valéry. *Fr.* The Kirkyaird by the Sea. OBVE
Steel fibrous slant & ribboned glint, The. The Turncoat. Amiri Baraka. NeAP
Steele Glas, The. George Gascoigne. AAS
Steelworker, The. Melvin Douglass Brown. LFAC
Steel worker on the girder, The. The Building of the Skyscraper. George Oppen. GOA
Steely train in the stupid green, The. Train: Abstraction. Genevieve Taggard. WPE
Steeped in ecstasies of perfume. Spring Nocturne. Abraham Liessin. TrJP
Steepies for the bairnie. Supper. William Soutar. OxBS
Steeple-Jack, The. Marianne Moore. *Fr.* Part of a Novel, Part of a Poem, Part of a Play. AP; BoWoP; CMoP; CoBMV; CrMA; FaBoMo; HAP; MoPo; NoAM; NOBA; NoP; OxBA; PBWP; SBG; TwAmPo; WeW; WPE
Steer, Bold Mariner, On! Schiller, *tr. fr. German.* PAH
Steer[e] hither, steer[e], your winged pines. The Sirens' Song [*or* Song of the Sirens *or* Song of the Syrens]. William Browne. *Fr.* Inner Temple Masque. ChTr; EIL; EtS; GBL; NOBE; OBEV; OBS; PoPle; ViBoPo
Steer on, courageous sailor! Columbus. Schiller, *tr. by* Erika Gathmann Koessler. OFD
Stein Song, A. Richard Hovey. *Fr.* Spring. HBV-2
Stella. Charles Henry Crandall. AA
Stella at Wood-Park. Swift. BIrV
Stella is sick, and in that sick-bed lies. Astrophel and Stella, CI. Sir Philip Sidney. SiPS
Stella oft sees the very face of woe. Astrophel and Stella, XLV. Sir Philip Sidney. SiPS
Stella, since thou so right a princess art. Astrophel and Stella, CVII. Sir Philip Sidney. HBV-1; NoP; SiPS
Stella Sleeping. Sir Philip Sidney. Astrophel and Stella, Second Song. SiPS
Stella, the fullness of my thoughts of thee. Astrophel and Stella, L. Sir Philip Sidney. SiPS
Stella, the only planet of my light. Astrophel and Stella, LXVIII. Sir Philip Sidney. OBSC; SiPS
Stella, think not that I by verse seek fame. Astrophel and Stella, XC. Sir Philip Sidney. OBSC; SiPS
Stella this day is thirty-four. Stella's Birth-day, 1718/19 [*or* On Stella's Birthday, 1719]. Swift. EnLoPo; InPk; NAs; NIP; OAEL-1
Stella, whence doth these new assaults arise. Astrophel and Stella, XXXVI. Sir Philip Sidney. SiPS
Stella, while now by Honour's cruel might. Astrophel and Stella, XCI. Sir Philip Sidney. SiPS
Stella's Birthday; March 13, 1726/27 ("This day, whate'er the fates decree"). Swift. LoBV; NAs; NoP; OAEL-1; OBEC; PoEL-3
Stella's Birth-day; 1718/19 ("Stella this day is thirty-four"). Swift. EnLoPo; NAs
(On Stella's Birthday [1719].) InPK; NIP; OAEL-1
Stella's Birth-day, 1720 ("All travellers at first incline"). Swift. OxBI; PoEL-3
Stella's Birthday, 1725 ("As when a beauteous nymph decays"). Swift. NOEC
Stenka Razin. *Unknown, tr. fr. Russian.* FSW
Stenographers, The. P. K. Page. CaP; HeIP; LiTM; NoP; OBCV; PeCV
Step aside, you ornery tenderfeet. I'm an Old Cowhand. Johnny Mercer. OBAL
Step Away from Them, A. Frank O'Hara. ConAP; HoAn; NYP; VGW
Step by Step. Barbara C. Ryberg. STF
Step in, young man, I know your face. The Gaol Song. *Unknown.* GBP
Step into my room tonight. People Trying to Love. Stephen Berg. NaP
Step It Up and Go. *Unknown.* FSW
Step lightly on this narrow spot! Emily Dickinson. NePA
Step on His Head. James Laughlin. VGW
Step on it, said Aunt Alice, for God's sake. The Ascension: 1925. John Malcolm Brinnin. Str
Step on the path, A. Ireland Lake. Robert Hershon. NeAC
Step to the garden from the cool-roomed house. Weekend Stroll. Frances Cornford. BoNaP
Stepfather: A Girl's Song. Yusef Komunyakaa. Str
Stepfather Blues. *Unknown.* BluL
Stepfathers. David Donnell. NOBC
Stephano's Song. Shakespeare. *See* Song: "Master, the swabber, the boatswain and I, The."
"Stephen Smith, University of Iowa sophomore, burned what he said was his draft card." Of Late. George Starbuck. VGW
Stepney Green. John Singer. WaP
Stepping gingerly. Cat in the Snow. Aileen Fisher. NTCP
Stepping Outside. Tess Gallagher. AmPA
Stepping Stones, The. Conrad Aiken. CrMA
Stepping Westward. Denise Levertov. CAPP; NMM; VGW
Stepping Westward. Wordsworth. CH; EnRP; HBV-1; OBRV; PoEL-4; SeCeV
Steps. Roberta Hill. VoR
Steps. Frank O'Hara. CAPP; ConAP
Steps out/ from a lily. Woman. Carl Rakosi. TAP
Stereo. Don L. Lee. AmNP; POL
Sterile these stones. The Corner Stone. Walter de la Mare. BrPo
Sterkfontein. Ruth Miller. PeSA
Stern be the pilot in the dreadful hour. To Abraham Lincoln. John James Piatt. AA
Stern daughter of the voice of God! Ode to Duty. Wordsworth. AWP; BiP; EnRP; FPL; GTBS; GTBS-P; HBV-2; HBVY; NoP; OAEL-2; OBEV; OBRV; TreFS; TRV; WGRP
Stern eagle of the far north-west. The Song of the Reim-Kennar. Sir Walter Scott. *Fr.* The Pirate. OAEL-2; OAEP; OBNC
Stern Master Munchem, rod in hand, stole out of school one day. The School-Master and the Truants. "John Brownjohn." OBCA
Stern Parent, The. Harry Graham. Some Ruthless Rhymes, I. ChTr; TreFT
("Father heard his children scream.") CenHV
Stethoscope, The. Dennis Abse. SUW
Stethoscope tells what everyone fears, The. Academic. Theodore Roethke. CrMA; ELU; FaBoEE; MiAP; OBAL
Stevedore. Leslie M. Collins. AmNP
Steven, your birth brought. For My Son, Born during an Ice Storm. David Jauss. Str
Steveston, *sel.* Daphne Marlatt.
Imagine; a Town. NOBC
Stew Meat Blues. *Unknown.* BluL
Steward, The. Ebenezer Elliott. *Fr.* The Splendid Village. NBM
("Village! thy butcher's son, the steward now.") OBSV
Stewball. *Unknown.* FSW
Sticheron for Matins, Wednesday of Holy Week. Kassia, *tr. fr. Greek by* Patrick Diehl. WPOW
Stick, The. Bruce Bennett. LTB
Stick, The. May O'Rourke. HBMV
Stick the finger inside. Black Mail. Alice Walker. AmPA
Stick to It. Edgar A. Guest. FaFP
Stick was almost a staff, The. Hebrew Letters in the Trees. J. Rutherford Willems. VWA
Stick your patent name on a signboard. The River: Powhatan's Daughter. Hart Crane. *Fr.* The Bridge. AmPP; AP; CMoP; CoBMV; GOA; MoAB; MoAmPo; NoAM; NOBA; OxBA; PrIm; TwAmPo; ViBoPo
Stickball. Virginia Schonborg. RHPC
Sticks-in-a-drowse droop over sugary loam. Cuttings. Theodore Roethke. LCAP; NoAM; NOBA; TAP; UnPo
Sticky inside their winter suits. Thaw. Margaret Avison. NOBC
Stiff are the warrior's muscles. Lines Written after a Battle. *Unknown.* InMe

Stiff as the icicles in their beards, the Ice Kings. The Labors of Thor. David Wagoner. GP
Stiff in a white coat. A Child's Visit to the Biology Lab. Kathleen Spivack. AmPA
Stiff spokes of this wheel, The. July in Washington. Robert Lowell. LCAP; NaP; Prf
Stiff standing on the bed. *Unknown.* GBL; POL
Stiff wind off the channel, A. Wet Thursday. Weldon Kees. NaP; NYBP
Stigmata. Patrick Lane. NOBC
Stigmata. Charles Warren Stoddard. TrPWD
Stiles. John Pudney. NYBP
Still. Lucille Clifton. InPS
Still. Aila Meriluoto, *tr. fr. Finnish by* Jaakko A. Ahokas. PBWP
Still,/ I would leap too. Small Frogs Killed on the Highway. James Wright. NNaP
Still a bare, silent, solitary glen. Thalaba and the Banquet. Robert Southey. *Fr.* Thalaba the Destroyer. SeCePo
Still a bit dazed. Saul, Afterward, Riding East. John Malcolm Brinnin. HoAn; Prf
Still, after all, the kelp remain. At the Western Shore. Sarah Youngblood. IHMS
"Still alive" the message ran. The Emergency Maker. David Wagoner. NePoEA-2
Still am I haunting. Come Down. George Macdonald. TrPWD
Still and All. Burns Singer. NePoEA-2; OxBS
Still and blanched and cold and lone. The Mountains. Walter de la Mare. BrPo
Still and calm. The Blue Ridge. Harriet Monroe. HBMV
Still and dark along the sea. Twilight on Sumter. Richard Henry Stoddard. PAH
Still are there wonders of the dark and day. To Keep the Memory of Charlotte Forten Grimké. Angelina Weld Grimké. BlSi
Still as I move thou movest. Her Shadow. Elisabeth Cavazza Pullen. AA
Still as of Old. Hester H. Cholmondeley. *See* Betrayal.
Still Birth. Catherine Rutan. AMV-81
Still blue stones. Park Pigeons. Melville Cane. CAD
Still by meadow and stream. The Whisperer. Arthur Bullen. HBMV
Still, Citizen Sparrow. Richard Wilbur. AmPP; AP; CMoP; HoPM; LiTM; MiAP; MoAB; MoPo; NePA; NoAM
"Still Do I Keep My Look, My Identity . . ." Gwendolyn Brooks. PoA
Still do the stars impart their light. Falsehood. William Cartwright. OBEV
Still drifting together. The Unpossessed. Adèle Naudé. PeSA
Still explosions on the rocks, The. The Shampoo. Elizabeth Bishop. OxBC
Still Falls the Rain. Edith Sitwell. BoWoP; ChMP; CoBMV; DTC; EBCP; FaBoEn; LiTM; MoAB; MoBrPo; MoPo; MP; NoAM; NOBE; OBWP; SBVL; SeCePo; TEP; TrGrPo; TwCP; WaaP
Still fettered, still unconquered, still in pain. Prometheus Unbound. A. D. Hope. OxBC
Still glowing from the red-lipped kiss of noon. Twilight. Virginia McCormick. HBMV
Still Growing. *Unknown. See* Trees They Do Grow High, The.
Still Gyte, Man? George Campbell Hay. BSV
Still He Sings. Allan Taylor. OBET
Still-Heart. Frank Pearce Sturm. OBMV
Still heavy with may, and the sky ready to fall. Before Invasion, 1940. John Betjeman. MoVE
Still Here. Langston Hughes. BPo
Still I complain; I am complaining still. Edward Taylor. Preparatory Meditations, XL. AP; OxBA; PoEL-3
Still I Rise. Maya Angelou. BlSi
Still I'm for upper. Satisfaction. A. R. Ammons. GP
Still in an amorphous world she moves. The Idiot. Adèle Naudé. PeSA
Still in her native glory, unsubdued. Babylon. Robert Eyres Landor. *Fr.* The Impious Feast. OBRV
Still in October, the woodcock. On the Mountain. Ruth Stone. BoWoP
Still, in some hidden towns of our Dispersion. The Talmud Student. Hayyim Nahman Bialik, *tr. by* Helena Frank. TrJP
Still, it is dear defiance now to carry. Flags. Gwendolyn Brooks. AmNP
Still let me pierce into the midnight depth. James Thomson. *Fr.* The Seasons: Summer. EnRP
"Still, let my tyrants know, I am not doomed to wear." Emily Brontë. *Fr.* The Prisoner. ChER; NOBE; NoP; OBEV; OBNC; OBVV
Still let us go the way of beauty; go. A Prayer for the Old Courage. Charles Hanson Towne. TrPWD
Still Life. Regina M. Austin. AMV-80
Still Life. Betsy Bering. PoDr
Still-Life. Elizabeth Daryush. QFR; WPE
Still Life. Walter de la Mare. EyDe
Still-Life. Ted Hughes. NYBP
Still Life, A. Jascha Kessler. HoAn
Still Life. Randolph Outlaw. LFAC
Still-Life. Ronald Perry. NePoEA-2
Still Life. Kathleen Raine. NeBP
Still Life. Vivian Smith. AMV-80; AMV-81
Still Life. Reed Whittemore. CoAP; ConAP
Still Life: Lady with Birds. Quandra Prettyman. CAD; PoBA
Still like his Master, known by breaking bread. Epitaph on a Worthy Clergyman. Benjamin Franklin. TRV
Still Lives. Emilie Buchwald. PoDr
Still night. The old clock ticks. Last Night in Calcutta. Allen Ginsberg. NoAM
Still, no one has paid much tribute to the man. Cocteau's Opium: 1. Donald Finkel. CoPo
Still, O Lord, for Thee I Tarry. Charles Wesley. OxBoCh
Still on my cheeks I feel their fondling breath. Stanzas on Mutability. Hugo von Hofmannsthal, *tr. by* Jethro Bithell. AWP; TrJP
Still on the spot Lord Marmion stay'd. Edinburgh from the Pentland Hills. Sir Walter Scott. *Fr.* Marmion, IV. FaBoPP
Still on the tower stood the vane. The Letters. Tennyson. HBV-1
Still, passed through the spokes of an old wheel. Reincarnation (I). James Dickey. HoPM
Still playing. In the Cabinet. Shlomo Vinner, *tr. by* Laya Firestone *and* Howard Schwartz. VWA
Still Poem 9. Philip Lamantia. NeAP
Still Pond, No More Moving. Howard Moss. NYBP
Still Pool, The. Kathleen Raine. MoAB
Still pressing through these weeping solitudes. Frederick Goddard Tuckerman. Sonnets, II, xi. AP; NOBA
Still round thy towers descend the fertile rain! Cordova. Ibn Zaydun, *tr. by* H. A. R. Gibb. AWP
Still salt pool, locked in with bars of sand, A. Lincolnshire Shores. Tennyson. *Fr.* The Palace of Art. FaBoPP
Still scene scintillates, The. Glass World. Dorothy Donnelly. NCSH
Still shall the tyrant scourge of Gaul. Ode to the Inhabitants of Pennsylvania. Longfellow. PAH
Still sits the school-house by the road. In School-Days. Whittier. AA; BLPA; FaBoBe; FaPON; FPL; GLGT; OBCA; OxBChV; PoPl; TreF
Still sleeps the unknown soldier. Memorial. Mae Winkler Goodman. PGD
Still Small Voice, The. A. M. Klein. OBCV; PeCV
Still small voice spake unto me, A. The Two Voices. Tennyson. MasP
Still south I went and west and south again. Prelude. J. M. Synge. AWP; BoNaP; ChTr; FaBoPP; HBMV; MoBrPo; OBMV
Still, still my eye will gaze long fixed on thee. The Columbine. Jones Very. AP; NOBA
Still, Still, with Thee. Harriet Beecher Stowe. AH, *with music;* BLRP
(When I Awake I Am Still with Thee.) TrPWD
Still tell me no, my God, and tell me no. Though He Slay Me. Vassar Miller. NePoEA-2
Still the ghost of Joseph Alston. Theodosia Burr. Myra Burnham Terrell. GoYe
Still the Mind Smiles. Robinson Jeffers. CMoP
Still the same function, still the same habit come. Conrad Aiken. *Fr.* Time in the Rock. TwAmPo
Still the Wonder Grew. Goldsmith. *Br. sel. fr.* The Deserted Village. TreF
Still thirteen years: 'tis autumn now. Palinode. James Russell Lowell. AA
Still Thou Art Question. *Unknown.* PGD
Still Though the One I Sing. Walt Whitman. AA
Still to Be Neat [Still to Be Drest (*or* Dressed)]. Ben Jonson, *tr. fr. the Latin of* Jean Bonnefons. *Fr.* Epicoene; or, The Silent Woman, I, i. CABA; EIL; FF; GBL; HAP; HeIP; InPS; JCP; NIP; NoP; OAEP; PAI; PoPle; PrIm; SeCePo; TEP; TreFT; WeW; WHA
(Clerimont's Song.) InPS; LoBV; OAEL-1; PPP; SeCP; SeCV-1; TrGrPo
(Simplex Munditiis.) AWP; GoBC; HBV-1; HoPM; NOBE; OBEV
(Song: "Still to be neat, still to be dressed [*or* drest].") AnAnS-2; EnRePo; OBS; ViBoPo
Still to one end they both so justly drew. David and Jonathan. Abraham Cowley. *Fr.* Davideis, II. PeHV
Still unable to pronounce the months. Ice Cream. Peter Wild. Psk
Still Voice of Harlem, The. Conrad Kent Rivers. CNA; IDB; NNP; PoBA
Still was the night, serene and bright. The Day of Doom. Michael Wigglesworth. SCAP
Still wilt thou sigh, and still in vain. The Expostulation. Thomas Shadwell. *Fr.* The Squire of Alsatia. OAEP
Still Wrestling. Phil Boiarski. AMV-81
Stillborn Silence, thou that art. Silence Invoked. Richard Flecknoe. GoBC
Stilled is the quarrel over his bones. At Dante's Grave. Ezra Zussman, *tr. by* D. Shnayorson. VWA
Stillness. James Elroy Flecker. BrPo; CH; GoJo; MoBrPo; SyP
Stillness, The/ of the wood. The Figures. Robert Creeley. UnPo
Stillness and moonlight, with. Loneliness. Hayden Carruth. FiCP

Stillness and splendour of the night. Canticle. James McAuley. PoAu-2
Stillness in the grove, not a rustling sound. Moscow Nights. M. Matusovskii *and* V. Solovyov-Sedoi, *tr. fr. Russian.* FSW
Stillness of the Austral noon, The. The Bell-Bird. "Fiona Macleod." *Fr.* Australian Transcripts. FM
Stillness of the Poem, The. Ron Loewinsohn. NeAP; PoM
Stillness of the rose, The. The Rose. William Carlos Williams. NOBA
Sting of Death, The. Frederick George Scott. OBCV; PeCV
Stinger and Gonoph and Peterman. Another Villon-ous Variation. Don Marquis. HBMV
Stingier your suppers, The. Karl Marx. Al Lee. AmPA
Stinginess, sin, stupidity, shall determine. To the Reader. Baudelaire, *tr. by* Arthur Symons. SyP
Stinging/ gold swarms. Sunset. E. E. Cummings. MoAmPo
Stinging Nettle. Gwen Head. GP
Stingo! to thy bar-room skip. Anacreontic to Flip. Royall Tyler. OBAL
Stings. Sylvia Plath. NaP
Stir Me. *Unknown.* STF
Stir not the sand too much, for there lies Stuyvesant. Epitaph for Peter Stuyvesant. Henricus Selyns. NYP; SCAP
Stir not, whisper not. The River. Patrick MacDonogh. NeIP
Stir the Wallaby Stew. *Unknown.* FaBoBa
Stirling's Hotel. *Unknown.* AmFP
Stirring as among, A/ cattle. Snow. David Malouf. CBAP
Stirring porch pots up with green-fingered witchcraft. Aspects of Spring in Greater Boston. George Starbuck. Poems from a First Year in Boston, II. NYBP
Stirring suddenly from long hibernation. Mid-Winter Waking. Robert Graves. MoAB
Stirrup Cup, The. Douglas Ainslie. GoTS
Stirrup Cup, The. John Hay. AA; HBV-2
Stirrup-Cup, The. Sidney Lanier. AA; AmPP; WHA
"Stirrups, leggings, a stainless." Love Medley: Patrice Cuchulain. Michael S. Harper. GeTw
Stitches over and over. Lesbia Sewing. Harold Vinal. HBMV
Stock Exchange Wisdom. *Unknown.* FaBoUs
Stock whom Cromwell planted here, The. Lines Written in a Country Parson's Orchard. Leslie Daiken. OnYI
Stockdove, The. Ruth Pitter. SeCePo
Stockdoves, The. Andrew Young. BoAnP
Stocking and Shirt. James Reeves. OnUr
Stocking Fairy. Winifred Welles. FaPON; SoPo; TiPo
Stocking Feet Blues. *Unknown.* BluL
Stocking Song on Christmas Eve. Mary Mapes Dodge. OHIP
Stockton Lake; Stockton, Missouri. Mark Sanders. WOLT
Stocky, cocky little man, A. Instamatic. Edwin Morgan. FF
Stocky woman at the door, The. The Last Day and the First. Theodore Weiss. TwCP; VGW
Stockyard, The. J. C. Squire. OxBTC
Stoic. Lawrence Durrell. NYBP
Stoic, The: for Laura von Courten. Edgar Bowers. CoAP; NePoEA; QFR
Stoklewath; or, The Cumbrian Village, *sel.* Susanna Blamire.
"From where dark clouds of curling smoke arise." NOEC
Stolen Child, The. W. B. Yeats. CMoP; NoP; OnYI; OxBI; WSC
Stolen Fifer, The. Padraic Fiacc. NeIP
Stolen Kiss, A. George Wither. *Fr.* Fair Virtue, the Mistress of Philarete. HBV-1
(Kiss, The.) UnTE
Stolen kisses, wary eyes. Epigram. Strato. PeHV
Stolen Pleasure. William Drummond of Hawthornden. EnLoPo
Stomach. Kathleen Norris. OBAL
Stomach in my throat. Coasting toward Midnight at the Southeastern Fair. David Bottoms. AMV-81
Stomach of goat, crushed. Salami. Philip Levine. NNaP; NOBA; TAP
"Stond well, moder, under Rode." The Mother and Her Son on the Cross. *Unknown.* MeEL
Stond [*or* Stand] who so list upon the slipper toppe. Stand Whoso List. Seneca, *tr. by* Sir Thomas Wyatt. *Fr.* Thyestes. AAS; NoP; OBVE; PoEL-1; SiPS
Stone, The. Paul Blackburn. NYBP; NYP
Stone. Juliet Chayat. AMV-80
Stone, A. Richard Eberhart. NePoAm-2
Stone, The. W. W. Gibson. MoBrPo
Stone. E. L. Mayo. FAZ
Stone. Charles Simic. NU
Stone, The. Thomas Vaughan. OBS
Stone/ cold/ daylight. Poem for Etheridge. Sonia Sanchez. BPO
Stone, The/ would like to be. Evolution. May Swenson. TrGrPo
Stone, a Leaf, a Door, A. Thomas Wolfe. PoPl
Stone and Rock. Webster Ross. Naomi Mitchison. PoSH
Stone and the Blade of Grass in the Warsaw Ghetto, The. David Scheinert, *tr. fr. French by* Edouard Roditi. VWA
Stone and the Obliging Pond. Felix Pollak. POL
Stone Angel. Anne Ridler. EaLo
Stone, bronze, stone, steel, stone, oakleaves, horses' heels. Triumphal March. T. S. Eliot. *Fr.* Coriolan. OBWP; WaaP
Stone Canyon Nocturne. Charles Wright. LCAP
Stone cries from the wall, The. Epitaph. *Unknown.* TrJP
Stone Diary, A. Pat Lowther. NOBC
Stone Face is the likeness of all lovers. Buster Keaton & the Cops. George Keithley. NPGG
Stone-flake and salmon. Gary Snyder. Myths and Texts: Burning, XV. NaP
Stone Fleet, The. Herman Melville. EtS
Stone found me in bright sunlight, The. The Stone. Paul Blackburn. NYBP; NYP
Stone from the Gods. Irma Wassall. GoYe
Stone from which I carved you. A Speck of Sand. Paul Celan, *tr. by* Joachim Neugroschel. VWA
Stone Garden, The. Richard Shelton. NPAW
Stone Giant. Joseph Bruchac. CDW
Stone goes straight, The. Washington Monument by Night. Carl Sandburg. CMoP; FaPON; OFD; OHIP; PoSC
Stone-gray roses by the desert's rim, The. The Princess. W. J. Turner. HBMV
Stone Gullets. May Swenson. InPK
Stone Hammer Poem. Robert Kroetsch. NOBC
Stone Horse Shoals. Malcolm Cowley. NYBP; TwAmPo
Stone jug and a pewter mug, A. The Kavanagh. Richard Hovey. HBV-2
Stone Orchard, The. Joyce Carol Oates. GeTw
Stone Song (Zen Rock) the Seer & the Unbeliever. Karoniaktatie. STE
Stone the size of man was my stone, A. A Stone. Richard Eberhart. NePoAm-2
Stone Too Can Pray. Conrad Aiken. EaLo
Stone Trees. John Freeman. BoNaP
Stone Troll, The. J. R. R. Tolkien. SO
Stone Venus, fixed and still. The Venus of Bolsover Castle. Sacheverell Sitwell. HBMV
Stone Walls. Julie Mathilde Lippmann. AA
Stone Words for Robert Lowell. Richard Eberhart. AMV-80
Stonecarver. Carole Oles. Str
Stone-cutters fighting time with marble, you foredefeated. To the Stone-Cutters. Robinson Jeffers. AmPP; MoAB; MoAmPo; NIP; NOBA; NoP; OxBA; PAI; PoCH; PoPl; PoRA; PP; PrIm; TrGrPo
Stoned dogs crawl back through the blood, The. The Contours of Fixation. Weldon Kees. NaP
Stonehenge. Michael Drayton. *Fr.* Polyolbion. FaBoPP
Stonehenge. Sir Philip Sidney. *Fr.* The Seven Wonders of England. FaBoPP
Stonehouse. Jeff Tagami. BrSi
Stones, The. Wendell Berry. GP
Stones. William Jeffrey. OxBS
Stones, The. Sylvia Plath. CAPP; SBG
Stones (a miracle to mortal view), The. Ovid, *tr. by* Dryden. *Fr.* Metamorphoses, I. OBVE
Stones: Avesbury. Daisy Aldan. PoA
Stones in Jordan's stream, The. Stones. William Jeffrey. OxBS
Stones in My Passway. *Unknown.* BluL
Stones of Sleep, The. E. L. Mayo. FAZ
Stones of the desert town, The. The Lodging. George Mackay Brown. BSV
Stones only, the *disjecta membra* of this Great House. Ruins of a Great House. Derek Walcott. TwCP
Stones rattle on the hillside, The. My Cow. Howard McCord. GP
Stones surpass the silence. Another Stone Poem. Philip Dacey. AMV-81
Stonetalk. Jacques Hamelin, *tr. fr. French by* Ria Leigh-Louhuizen. AMV-80
Stonewall Jackson. Henry Lynden Flash. AA; PAH
Stonewall Jackson's Way. John Williamson Palmer. AA; HBV-2; PAH
Stoney Ridge Dance Hall. Alden Nowlan. MoCV
Stony Brook Tavern. J. D. Reed. NeAC
Stony Grey Soil. Patrick Kavanagh. CIP
Stony Lonesome. Langston Hughes. NOBA
Stood, at the closed door. Conrad Aiken. Preludes for Memnon, LII. LiTM
Stood straight/ holding the choker high. Gary Snyder. Myths and Texts: Logging, III. NaP; NMP; NOBA
Stood the afflicted mother weeping. Stabat Mater Dolorosa. Jacopone da Todi, *tr. by* Abraham Coles. HBV-2
Stood there then among. Stars. Robert Hayden. LCAP
Stood-up. Bruce Byfield. AMV-80
Stool Ball. *Unknown.* CH
Stoop on the log-house is brown with sweet rain-rot, The. Joan Finnigan. *Fr.* May Day Rounds: Renfrew County. WPE

Stop! Lee Blair. TDH
Stop. Richard Wilbur. LCAP
Stop a Minute! *Unknown.* STF
Stop all the clocks, cut off the telephone. Song: Stop All the Clocks. W. H. Auden. MoBrPo
Stop and consider! life is but a day. Keats. *Fr.* Sleep and Poetry. OBRV; SeCePo; TreFT
Stop, Christian passer-by!—Stop, child of God. Epitaph [on Himself *or* O, Lift One Thought]. Samuel Taylor Coleridge. CH; EnRP; FiP; NOCV; NoP; OAEL-2; OAEP; OBRV; OxBoCh
Stop! Don't touch me. *Unknown, tr. fr. Spanish by* Willis Barnstone. BoWoP
Stop! for thy tread is on an empire's dust! Byron. *Fr.* Childe Harold's Pilgrimage. InPS
Stop—Go. Dorothy W. Baruch. FaPON; TiPo; SUS
Stop: if you're racing at night. Happy at 40. Peter Meinke. GP
Stop Kicking My Dog Around. *Unknown.* GDP
Stop, let me have the truth of that! Dîs Aliter Visum; or, Le Byron de Nos Jours. Robert Browning. VLP
Stop look listen. Crossing. Philip Booth. AmFN; GOA
Stop!—not to me, at this bitter departing. Separation. Matthew Arnold. HBV-1
Stop on the Appian Way. On the Campagna. Elizabeth Stoddard. AA
Stop playing, poet! May a brother speak? Transcendentalism: A Poem in Twelve Books. Robert Browning. PP; VLP
Stop playing with your melancholy. Goethe, *tr. by* Walter Kaufmann. *Fr.* Faust. DL
Stop, Science—Stop! A. P Herbert. FiBHP
Stop still on the stair. Sops of Light. Fredegond Shove. ChMP
"Stop, stop!" The Maid Freed from the Gallows. *Unknown.* ViBoFo
Stop, stop and listen for the bough top. The Blackbird of Derrycairn. *Unknown, tr. by* Austin Clarke. BIrV; NeIP
Stop the Alabama bus I don't wanna ride. Alabama Bus. *Unknown.* BluL
Stop there, old one, within your haven. Lament for Apirana Ngata. Arnold Reedy, *tr. by* Barry Mitcalfe. WTO
"Stop thief!" dame Nature call'd to Death. On William Graham, Esq., of Mossknowe. Burns. DBV
Stoplights edged the licorice street with ribbon. Leap in the Dark. Roberta Hill. WPOW
Stopped. Allen Polite. NNP
Stopped clocks, The. On the Porch of the Antique Dealer. Paul Ramsey. FAZ
Stopped in Memphis. Steven Bauer. AMV-80
Stopping at an otel with an Ibernian. Dropping Your Aitches. Joseph Warren Beach. NYBP
Stopping by Shadows. Robin Fulton. PoSH
Stopping by Woods on a Snowy Evening. Robert Frost. AmPP; AP; BiP, BoNaP; CABA; CMoP; CoBMV; FaBoCh; FaBV; FaFP; FaPON; FF; FPL; GoJo; GrPl; HAP; HBMV; HeIP; HoPM; InPK; InPS; LiTA; LiTM; MasP; MoAB; MoAmPo; MoShBr; MoVE; MP; NePA; NIP; NoAM; NOBA; NoP; NTCP; OBCA; OxBA; PAI; PDV; PoRA; PoSC; PrIm; RHPC; SCV; SiSoSe; SoSe; SUS; TAP; TiPo; TreFS; TrGrPo; TwAmPo; TwCP; UnPo; ViBoPo; WHA
"Woods are lovely, dark and deep, The," *sel.* TRV
Stopping near Highway 80. David Ray. TAT
Stopping on the Green. The Stories in the Light. Michael Waters. GeTw
Stopping the Heart. Murray Edmond. OCNZ
Stopwatch and an Ordnance Map, A. Stephen Spender. MoBS
Store cattle from Nelanjie! The mob goes feeding past. From the Gulf. Will H. Ogilvie. PoAu-1
Store in Havana, The. José Kozer, *tr. fr. Spanish by* David Unger. VWA
Store-House, A. Louis Dudek. CaP
Stores and filling stations prefer a roof. Christmas Tree. Stanley Cook. OBCP
Stories from Kansas. William Stafford. RFM
Stories in the Light, The. Michael Waters. GeTw
Stories of Snow. P. K. Page. NOBC; NoP; OBCV; PoA
Stories Relate Life. Dennis Shady. LFAC
Stork questioned the swan whose moving song, The. Aria Senza da Capo. Robert Finch. MoCV
Storks like elbows had a fit of falling, The. There's No Place to Sleep in This Bed, Tanguy. Charles Henri Ford. EAS
Storm, The. Alcaeus, *tr. fr. Greek by* John Hermann Merivale. AWP
Storm, The. Elizabeth J. Coatsworth. OBCA
Storm, The. Robert David Cohen. NYBP
Storm, The. Emily Dickinson. *See* There came a wind like a bugle.
Storm, The. John Donne. *See* Storme, The.
Storm. Hilda Doolittle ("H.D."). TiPo
Storm, The. John Hay. AMV-81
Storm, The. Heine, *tr. fr. German by* Louis Untermeyer. AWP
Storm, The. George Herbert. AnAnS-1
Storm, The. Elizabeth Jennings. NePoEA-2
Storm. Agnes Nemes Nagy, *tr. fr. Hungarian by* Laura Schiff. PBWP
Storm, The, *sel.* Egan O'Rahilly, *tr. fr. Modern Irish by* P. S. Dinneen *and* T. O'Donoghue.
"Pitiful the playing of the flood with dire destruction!" OnYI
Storm, The. Coventry Patmore. EnLoPo
Storm, The. Theodore Roethke. NCSH
Storm, The. Edward Shanks. BoNaP
Storm, The. James Thomson. *Fr.* The Seasons: Summer. LoBV
Storm, The. Henry Vaughan. AnAnS-1; FaBoPP
Storm, The. Robert Wallace. NYBP
Storm, The. Whittier. *Fr.* Snowbound. FaBV
(Winter Day, *shorter sel.*) TrGrPo
Storm, The. William Carlos Williams. PCP; PPJ
Storm. Judith Wright. PoAu-2; WPE
Storm and Quiet. Richard Eberhart. AMV-81
Storm and unconscionable winds once cast. The Wreck. Walter de la Mare. MOS
Storm at Sea. Sir William Davenant. RoGo
Storm at Sea, A. John Donne. *Fr.* The Storm. NOBE
("But when I waked, I saw that I saw not.") PoPle
Storm at Sea. *Malay Oral Tradition, tr. by* R. O. Winstedt. WTO
Storm at Sea, A. *Unknown, tr. fr. Irish.* AnIL, *tr. by* Robin Flower; KiLC *tr. by* Frank O'Connor.
Storm-beaten old watch-tower, A. Symbols. W. B. Yeats. OBMV
Storm broke, and it rained, The. Frogs. Louis Simpson. BoAnP; InPS
Storm came home too blind to stand. One A.M. X. J. Kennedy. ELU
Storm came up so very quick, The. Spring Rain. Marchette Chute. RHPC; TiPo
Storm-Child, The. May Byron. HBV-1
Storm-Cock's Song, The. "Hugh MacDiarmid." OxBTC
Storm Cone, The. Kipling. ChMP; OxBTC
Storm cries every night, The. Spring Song. Hermann Hesse, *tr. by* Ludwig Lewisohn. AWP
Storm-dances of gulls, the barking game of seals, The. Divinely Superfluous Beauty. Robinson Jeffers. HeIP; MoAmPo; PoPl
Storm Fear. Robert Frost. CMoP; HBV-1; OxBA; ViBoPo
Storm from the East, A. Reed Whittemore. NYBP; PoPl
Storm had strong intention in its flow, The. Cleavage. Louise Townsend Nicholl. NePoAm
Storm House, The. Elizabeth Jennings. WPE
Storm in April, A. Richard Wilbur. LCAP; NoP
Storm in Summer, A. Wilfrid Scawen Blunt. FaBoTw
Storm in the Distance, A. Paul Hamilton Hayne. AA
Storm Is Over, The. Robert Bridges. LiTB; LiTM (rev. ed.); MoPo; OBMV
("Storm is over, the land hushes to rest, The.") BrPo; GTBS-P
Storm lasted all night, The. The Complaisant Friend. Pierre Louys. *Fr.* Chansons de Bilitis. PeHV
Storm not, brave Friend, that thou hast never yet. To Scilla. Sir Charles Sedley. FaBoEE; PV
Storm of Love, A. Hilary Corke. NYBP
Storm on Fifth Avenue. Siegfried Sassoon. MoVE
Storm on the Island. Seamus Heaney. NCSH
Storm Song. Bayard Taylor. EtS; HBV-1
Storm that needed a mountain, A. Found in a Storm. William Stafford. RFM
Storm Tide on Mejit. *Unknown, tr. fr. Micronesian by* Augustin Krämer *and* Willard Trask. RFM
Storm Warning. Alice Bardsley. AMV-80
Storm Warnings. Adrienne Rich. NIP
Storm was coming, that was why it was dark, A. Sudden Things. Donald Hall. EAS
Storm-Wind, The. William Barnes. NOBE
Storm Windows. Howard Nemerov. ConAP
Storm winds carry snow. Deer Song. Leslie Silko. VoR
Stormalong, *with music. Unknown.* AmSS; ShS
Storme, The. John Donne. MOS
(Storm, The, *abr.*) EtS
"But when I waked, I saw that I saw not," *sel.* PoPle
(Storm at Sea, A.) NOBE
Storming of Stony Point, The. Arthur Guiterman. PAH
Stormpetrel. Richard Murphy. IPY
Storms Are on the Ocean, The. *Unknown.* FSW
Storms are past, the clouds are overblown, The. Bonum Est Mihi Quod Humiliasti Me, *abr.* Earl of Surrey. SiPS
Storms come and sorrows come. Security. Margaret E. Sangster. BLRP
Storms lend you wings, destroyer of the lands. Inanna and Enlil. Enheduanna, *ad. by* Aliki *and* Willis Barnstone. BoWoP
Storms once hurled my howls about. The Lighthouse Keeper's Offspring. James Broughton. CrMA
Stormy Day. W. R. Rodgers. LiTB
Stormy Day, A. *Unknown, tr. fr. Hawaiian.* WTO

Stormy Hebrides, The. William Collins. *Fr.* An Ode on the Popular Superstitions. NOBE
Stormy March is come at last, The. March. Bryant. GN
Stormy Night. W. R. Rodgers. OxBI
Stormy Night in Autumn. Chu Shu-chen, *tr. fr. Chinese by* Kenneth Rexroth. BoWoP
Stormy Nights. Robert Louis Stevenson. BrPo
Stormy Petrel, The. "Barry Cornwall." EtS; HBV-1
Stormy Scenes of Winter, The, 2 *versions. Unknown.* AmFP
Stormy sea, A! Waves dashing high! He Shall Speak Peace unto the Nations. Lila V. Walters. WBLP
Stormy the night and the waves roll high. Asleep in the Deep. Arthur J. Lamb. FSN; TreFT
Story, A. Margaret Avison. MoCV
Story. Dorothy Parker. InMe
Story. Dennis Saleh. NeAC
Story, The. Charles Simic. NNaP
Story, A. William Stafford. NNaP; RFM
Story, a story, A! Rowing. Anne Sexton. BoWoP
Story, a story, a story anon, A. The Bishop of Canterbury. *Unknown.* AmFP
Story, a story to you I will tell, A. The Cunning Cobbler Done Over. *Unknown.* CoMu
Story about Chicken Soup, A. Louis Simpson. LCAP; NMP; NNaP; NoAM; TAP
Story about Indians, A. The Climate of Paradise. Louis Simpson. NOBA
Story about the Body, A. Robert Hass. GeTw; NPGG
Story, as now we see, was over-written, The. Thermopylae. Michael Thwaites. PoAu-2
Story for a Child, A. Bayard Taylor. HBV-1; HBVY
(Night with a Wolf, A.) GN
Story from Another World. Paul Petrie. AMV-81
Story from Bear Country. Leslie Silko. STE
Story from Russian Author. Peter Redgrove. NePoEA-2
Story haunts this tribe that cannot wipe from its eyes, The. Isaac. Stanley Burnshaw. VWA
Story I shall tell today, The. The Nightingale. Marie de France, *tr. by* Patricia Terry. BoWoP
Story in the Snow, A. Pearl Riggs Crouch. SoPo; TiPo
Story of a Hotel Room. Rosemary Tonks. OxBTC
Story of a Stowaway, The. Clement Scott. PaPo
Story of a Well-made Shield, The. N. Scott Momaday. CDW; GrPl
Story of Abraham and Hagar, The. Edna Aphek, *tr. fr. Hebrew by* Yishai Tobin. VWA
Story of Augustus, Who Would Not Have Any Soup, The. Heinrich Hoffmann, *tr. fr. German.* FaBoUs; GoJo; HBV-1; HBVY; MoShBr; OxBChV; RHPC; ShM; SpRo; TiPo
Story of Cruel Psamtek, The. *Unknown.* NA
Story of Fidgety Philip, The. Heinrich Hoffmann, *tr. fr. German.* OxBChV
Story of Flying Robert, The. Heinrich Hoffmann, *tr. fr. German.* SpRo
Story of Frederick Gowler, The. The King of Canoodle-Dum. William Schwenck Gilbert. CenHV
Story of Good, The. Phyllis Janik. IHMS
Story of How a Wall Stands, A. Simon Ortiz. MAYP
Story of Isaac. Leonard Cohen. VWA
Story of Johnny Head-in-Air, The. Heinrich Hoffman, *tr. fr. German.* OxBChV; TiPo
Story of Lava, The. David Allan Evans. Psk
Story of Little Suck-a-Thumb, The. Heinrich Hoffman, *tr. fr. German.* EvOK; HBV-1; HBVY; SpRo
Story of Macha, The. *Unknown, tr. fr. Middle Irish by* Sir Samuel Ferguson. *Fr.* Dinnshenchas. OnYI
Story of My Life, The. Carroll Arnett. VoR
Story of Phoebus and Daphne Applied, Etc., The. Edmund Waller. InvP; OBS
Story of Ponce de Leon, A. The Fountain of Youth. Hezekiah Butterworth. PAH
Story of Prince Agib, The. W. S. Gilbert. FaBoCo; InMe; NA
Story of Pyramid Thothmes, The. *Unknown.* NA
Story of Rimini, The, *sels.* Leigh Hunt.
"Noble range it was, of many a rood, A," *fr.* III. EnRP
(Places of Nestling Green.) OBRV
"Ready she sat with one hand to turn o'er." EvOK
Story of Sigurd the Volsung, *sels.* William Morris.
Brooding of Sigurd, The. SeCePo
Sigurd Rideth to the Glittering Heath, *fr.* II. PoEL-5
Sigurd's Ride, fr. II. NBM
Story of Soutine, A. James Schevill. PoCh
Story of the Baby Squirrel, The. Dorothy Aldis. TiPo
Story of the Flowery Kingdom. James Branch Cabell. HBMV; OnMSP
Story of the Gadsbys, The, *sel.* Kipling.
Winners, The. BLPA; FaPoR; FPL
(L'Envoi: "What is the moral? Who rides may read.") MoBrPo; TrGrPo
Story of the Pot and the Kettle, The. Charles Montagu. APAS
Story of the Rose, The, *with music.* "Alice." FSN
Story of the Shepherd, The. *Unknown, tr. fr. Spanish.* OHIP
Story of the Wild Huntsman, The. Heinrich Hoffman, *tr. fr. German.* NA
Story of the Zeros, The. Victor Hernandez Cruz. PoBA
Story of Ug, The. Edwin Meade Robinson. HBMV; YaD
Story of Uriah, The. Kipling. BrPo; SCV
Story of Vinland, The. Sidney Lanier. *Fr.* The Psalm of the West. PAH
Story-Teller, The. Mark Van Doren. CTBA
Story Tellers Summer, 1980. Nia Francisco. STE
Story That Could Be True, A. William Stafford. NTCP
Story to you I'll tell of little Omie Wise, A. Poor Omie. *Unknown.* PrIm
Story was always the same, The. The Migrations of People. Dorothy Leiser. AMV-80
Story went that once someone, an unbeliever, The. Face. Robert Morgan. GeTw
Storys to rede ar delitabill. John Barbour. *Fr.* The Bruce. OxBS
Stout Affirmation. Kenneth Burke. TwAmPo
Stout poet tiptoes, The. A Poet's Household. Carolyn Kizer. POL
Stove. Ken Belford. NeAC
Stove. Philip Booth. FYAP
Stowaway. Bill Adams. EtS
Stowaway in a fold. The Witnesses. X. J. Kennedy. PChr
Stowed away in a Montreal lumber room. O God! O Montreal! [*or* A Psalm of Montreal]. Samuel Butler. DTC; FaBoCo; NBM; OBSV; OxBoLi
Stradivarius, *sel.* "George Eliot."
Working with God. TRV
Strage degli innocenti, La, II, *sel.* Giambattista Marini, *tr. fr. Italian by* Richard Crashaw.
Sospetto d'Herode. SeCV-1
Stragglers. Pietro Aretino, *tr. fr. Italian by* Samuel Putnam. ErPo
Strahan, Tonson, Lintot of the times. To Mr. Murray. Byron. FaBoCo
Straight and swift the swallows fly. Rococo. John Payne. OBVV
Straight flagged road, laid on the rough earth, A. Field Ambulance in Retreat. May Sinclair. SUMH
Straight from a mighty bow this truth is driven. The Arrow. Clarence Urmy. HBMV
Straight-jacketing sprang to every lock. Austin Clarke. Mnemosyne Lay in Dust, II. CMoP; IPY
Straight Road, The. Ellen Hooper. HBV-2
Straight, the swift, the debonair, The. Magnets. Countee Cullen. BALP
Straight to Syr Martins hall the hunters bend. Sunset. William Julius Mickle. *Fr.* The Concubine. OBEC
Straight up away from this road. Achieving Perspective. Pattiann Rogers. MAYP
Strain, strain thine eyes, this parting is for aye! Lohengrin. William Morton Payne. AA
Strains of Sight. Robert Duncan. CMoP; NMP
Strampin' the bent, like the Angel o' Daith. Molecatcher. Albert D. Mackie. GoTS
Strand, The. Louis MacNeice. AnIV
Strand at Lough Beg, The. Seamus Heaney. NoP; OBWP
Strand on the Green. *Unknown.* GBP
Strand-Thistle. Gustav Falke, *tr. fr. German by* Jethro Bithell. AWP
Stranded in My Ontario. Ronald Everson. NOBC
Stranded on the moon. Moon-Man. Dorothy Hewett. CBAP
Stranded Whales, The. Geoffrey Dutton. CBAP
Strange. Stanley Burnshaw. TrJP
Strange. Kirby Doyle. NeAP
Strange,/ That in this nigger place. Esthete in Harlem. Langston Hughes. BANP; BPo
Strange, All-absorbing Love. Digby Mackworth Dolben. GoBC; TrPWD
Strange and unnatural! lets stay and see. Destinie. Abraham Cowley. MeLP
Strange are the feelings arising within me. The Love of Hell. Abraham Burstein. TrJP
Strange—as I sat brooding here. Lucy. Walter de la Mare. CMoP
Strange as it seems, the smallest mammal. The Shrew. Ogden Nash. CenHV
Strange atoms unto ourselves. Lovelight. Georgia Douglas Johnson. AmNP
Strange beauty, eight-limbed and eight-handed. Octopus. A. C. Hilton. BXAP; CenHV; FaBoCo; FaBoPa; Par
Strange bed, whose recurrent dream we are, The. Hotel de l'Univers et Portugal. James Merrill. MoAB; NePoAm; NePoEA-2; PoA
Strange bird/ His song remains secret. Youth. James Wright. DiL; NaP; NoP
Strange, but he cheats his master. Man of the World. Michael Hamburger. NePoEA-2

Strange but true is the story. The Sea-Turtle and the Shark. Melvin B. Tolson. *Fr.* Harlem Gallery. PoBA
Strange creeper. The Creeper. Tom Schmidt. NeAC
Strange, dear, but true, dear. So in Love. Cole Porter. BLSo
Strange, fantastic claims abound. Christ Alone. Shel Helsley. STF
Strange Fits of Passion Have I Known. Wordsworth. EBEV; EnRP; GBL; LiTB; LO; NOBE; OAEL-2; OAEP; OBRV; PPP; TEP; ViBoPo
(Lucy.) FiP; HBV-1; OBEV; OBNC; TrGrPo
Strange Fortunes of Two Excellent Princes, The, *sel.* Nicholas Breton.
His Wisdom. OBSC
(I Would Thou Wert Not Fair [or I Were Wise].) ElL; InvP
Strange Fruit. Randolph Stow. PoAu-2
Strange grows the river on the sunless evenings! Vesperal. Ernest Dowson. OBMV
Strange Guest, The. Itzik Manger, *tr. fr. Yiddish by* Stephen Garrin. VWA
Strange Hells. Ivor Gurney. OxBTC
Strange, Is It Not. Edward D. Kennedy. HBMV
Strange is it not if scholars yell. Scholars. *Unknown, tr. by* Frank O'Connor. DBV; KiLC
Strange Kind (II). J. D. Reed. MOON
Strange Lands. Laurence Alma-Tadema. HBVY
Strange Legacies. Sterling A. Brown. CNA; PoBA; TTY
Strange lesson taught by war. Lessons. Helen Weber. PGD
Strange little tune, so thin and rare. To a Scarlatti Passepied. Robert Hillyer. HBMV
Strange Love. Moses ibn Ezra, *tr. fr. Hebrew by* Solomon Solis-Cohen. TrJP
Strange Man, The. *Unknown.* FaPON
Strange Meeting. Wilfred Owen. BrPo; ChMP; CMoP; CoBMV; DTC; FaBoEn; FaBoMo; FaBoRV; GTBS-P; HeIP; HoPM; LiTB; LoBV; MMA; MoAB; MoBrPo; MoPo; MoVE; NoAM; NOBE; NoP; OAEL-2; OAEP; OBWP; SCV; SeCeV; TreFT; TrGrPo; WaaP; WaP
Strange Meetings, *sels.* Harold Monro.
Birth. PoA
Flower Is Looking, A. MoBrPo
If Suddenly a Clod of Earth. MoBrPo
Strange Monsters. Rowland Watkyns. FaBoEE
Strange news! a cittie full? will none give way. Upon Christ His Birth. Sir John Suckling. NCEP
Strange now to think of you, gone without corsets & eyes. Kaddish. Allen Ginsberg. NeAP; NOBA; PoM; VWA
Strange [*or* Straunge] Passion of a Lover, A. George Gascoigne. AAS; EnRePo
Strange People, The. Louise Erdrich. TWSS
Strange pie that is almost a passion. A Melton Mowbray Pork Pie. Richard Le Gallienne. BXAP; Par
Strange spirit with inky hair. The Lion. W. J. Turner. MoBrPo
Strange that I did not know him then. An Old Story. E. A. Robinson. HBMV; MoAmPo; TreFS
Strange, that such horror and such grace. To [*or* Of] a Fair Lady Playing with a Snake. Edmund Waller. EBEV; HoPM; NCEP; PoEL-3
Strange that we should sit here like this. Baseball Pitcher. Mabel M. Kuykendall. LiSp
Strange the formation of the eely race. Eels and Tortoises. William Diaper, *after the Greek of* Oppian. *Fr.* Halieutica. NOEC; OBVE
Strange to be torn away from your embrace. Strange. Stanley Burnshaw. TrJP
Strange Tree. Elizabeth Madox Roberts. BoNaP; FaPON; GrPl; WSC
Strange Visitor, The. *Unknown.* ChTr; FaBoCh; GBP
Strange walkers! See their professional. The Mushroom Gatherers. Donald Davie. NePoEA-2
Strange wares are handled on the wharves of sleep. The Wharf of Dreams. Edwin Markham. HBV-2
Strange was the wooing! Lullaby of the Catfish and the Crab. William Rose Benét. WhC
Strange Western town at the round edge of night. Western Town. Karl Shapiro. NYBP
Strange wind off the night, A. The Face. Philip Levine. DiL
Strangely/ my mother's sad eyes. X-Ray. David Ray. NePoEA-2
Strangely assorted, the shape of song and the bloody man. The Military Harpist. Ruth Pitter. FaBoTw; MoVE
Strangeness of Heart. Siegfried Sassoon. TrJP
Stranger, The. Baudelaire, *tr. fr. French by* Arthur Symons. SyP
Stranger, The. John Clare. OxBoCh
Stranger, The. Walter de la Mare. BrPo; MoVE; OAEP; OxBTC
Stranger, The. William Everson. FF
Stranger, The. Jean Garrigue. LiTA; LiTM; MP; NOBA; TwCP
Stranger, The. Juan Gelman, *tr. fr. Spanish by* Yishai Tobin. VWA
Stranger, The. Daniel Henderson. HBMV
Stranger, A. Lionel Johnson. VLP
Stranger. Thomas Merton. EaLo
Stranger, The. Adrienne Rich. CoPo; NNaP
Stranger. Elizabeth Madox Roberts. MoAmPo
Stranger! Approach this spot with gravity! A Dentist [*or* Epitaph on a Dentist]. *Unknown.* FaBoCo; FaBoEE; OxBoLi; TreFS; TreFT; WhC
Stranger arrives at her door, A. The Widow. Susan Ludvigson. MAYP
Stranger! awhile upon this mossy bank. Inscription for a Tablet on the Banks of a Stream. Robert Southey. OBEC
Stranger Call This Not. *Unknown.* ShM
Stranger came one night to Yussouf's tent, A. Yussouf. James Russell Lowell. BeLS; BLPA; BLPL; FaBoBe
Stranger came to the door at eve, A. Love and a Question. Robert Graves. MoBS
Stranger, if thou hast learned a truth which needs. Inscription for the Entrance to a Wood. Bryant. AmPP; AP; BiP; OxBA; TAP
Stranger, if you passing meet me and desire to speak to me. To You. Walt Whitman. BiP
Stranger in his own element. Penguin on the Beach. Ruth Miller. PeSA
Stranger in my gates, The—lo! that am I. Omnia Exeunt in Mysterium. George Sterling. WGRP
Stranger in the Pumpkin, The. John Ciardi. NTCP
Stranger in This Land, A. Cliff Ashby. NOCV
Stranger it was never meant for, A. Mine. Frank Polite. NYBP
Stranger Not Ourselves, The. William Stafford. NNaP
Stranger, pause and drop a tear. Sacred to the Memory of Maria (To Say Nothing of Jane and Martha) Sparks. Max Adeler. FaBoCo
Stranger! Tell the people of Spoon River two things. Unknown Soldiers. Edgar Lee Masters. *Fr.* The New Spoon River. NoAM; TAP
Stranger than the Worst. Babette Deutsch. WPE
Stranger, the bark you see before you says. The Yacht. Catullus, *tr. by* John Hookham Frere. AWP; OBVE
Stranger walks into the dark room, The. Seance. Edouard Roditi. EAS
Stranger walls, that shell no violent presence. Zimbabwe. F. D. Sinclair. PeSA
Stranger, when you come to/ Lakedaimon. Simonides, *tr. fr. Greek by* Kenneth Rexroth. OBVE
Stranger, whoe'er thou art, whose ling'ring feet. Sonnet Written in Tintern Abbey, Monmouthshire. Edmund Gardner. NOEC
Stranger! whoe'er thou art, whose restless mind. Verses Copied from the Window of an Obscure Lodging-House, in the Neighbourhood of London. *Unknown.* ViBoPo
Stranger, Why Do You Wonder So? K. B. Jones-Quartey. PBA
Stranger with the pile of luggage proudly labelled for Portree. At Euston. A. M. Harbord. PoSH
Stranger, wond'ring, stalks, and stares upon, The. Rome, Conqueror, Conquered. Joshua Sylvester. FaBoEE
Stranger, you freeze to this: there ain't no kinder gin-palace. Home, Sweet Home, with Variations, II. H. C. Bunner. CenHV
Stranger, you who hide my love. Song. Stephen Spender. FaBoTw
Strangers, The. Audrey Alexandra Brown. WHW
Strangers. William Stafford. NNaP
Strangers. R. S. Thomas. NMP
Strangers, The. Jones Very. OxBA
Strangers Are We All upon the Earth. Franz Werfel, *tr. fr. German by* Edith Abercrombie Snow. TrJP
"Strangers are we and pilgrims here!" At a Friends' Meeting. Mary Elizabeth Coleridge. WPE
Strangers ask. The Tower. Philip Booth. NePoEA-2
Strangers' eyes don't see. Memorial Poem. Jacob Glatstein, *tr. by* Ruth Whitman. VWA
Stranger's Grave, The. Emily Lawless. OnYI
Strangers on a train. Travels with the Band-Aid Army. Lance Henson. VoR
Stranger's Song, The. Thomas Hardy. BrPo
Strangers! your eyes are on that valley fixed. The Field of the Grounded Arms. Fitz-Greene Halleck. PoEL-4
Strangling women in the suburban bush. Das Kapital. Amiri Baraka. PoM
Strappado for the Devil, A, *sel.* Richard Brathwaite.
Of Maids' Inconstancy. ElL
Strapped at the center of the blazing wheel. A Pilot from the Carrier. Randall Jarrell. MoPo
Strapped helpless, monarchs and prelates, round they swung. The Wheel of Fortune. Thom Gunn. OxBC
Strapped to my seat, I turn. Above It All. Philip Levine. NOBA
Strapped to the roof rack of her. The Song of the Mean Mary Jean Machine. James Baker Hall. FiCP; TAT
Strapping young stockman lay dying, A. The Dying Stockman. *Unknown.* PoAu-1; ViBoFo
Strategies. Welton Smith. NBP; PoBA
Strath of Kildonan, The. Betty Morris. PoSH
Stratton Water. Dante Gabriel Rossetti. OxBB
Straunge Passion of a Lover, A. George Gascoigne. *See* Strange Passion of a Lover, A.
Straus Park. Gerald Stern. NYP

Straw, The. Robert Graves. MoVE; OxBTC
Straw bonnet, The. Southern Season. Alice Moser Claudel. TAT
Straw Men, The. Charles Culhane. LFAC
Strawberries. Judith Hemschemeyer. DFF
Strawberries. Dorothy Hughes. AMV-81
Strawberries. Edwin Morgan. BoLoP; LLLT
Strawberries in Mexico. Ron Padgett. EAS
Strawberries in November. Shaw Neilson. PoAu-1
Strawberries mit Cream. Rochelle Owens. CoPo
Strawberries that in gardens grow. Wild Strawberries. Robert Graves. FaBoCh
Strawberry Fair. *Unknown.* OBET
Strawberry Jam. May Justus. FaPON
Strawberry Roan, The. Curley W. Fletcher. BPAW; FSW
Strawberry Shrub, The. Edna St. Vincent Millay. CMoP
Straws. Elisabeth J. Coatsworth. AmFN
Straws like tame lightnings lie about the grass. Summer Farm. Norman MacCaig. BSV; OxBTC
Stray Animals. James Tate. NoAM
Stray Dog. Charlotte Mish. PoLF
Stray Dog, near Écully, Valley of the Rhône. Margaret Avison. OBCV (Stray Dog, near Ecully.) PoA
Strayed Reveller, The. Matthew Arnold. LoBV; OAEL-2; VLP
Strayed Reveller to Ulysses, The, *sel.* OBEV
Straying Student, The. Austin Clarke. AnIL; BIrV; CIP; IPY; MoAB; NeIP; OxBI
Streak of car paint, A. Uptown. Paul Zweig. NYP
Streak of Sappho, it is said, A. Mould of Castile. Jack Clemo. NOCV
Streaked and fretted with effort, the thick. The Street. Robert Pinsky. MAYP
Stream, The. Lula Lowe Weeden. CDC
Stream, The/ piles out of the pile. The Crossing. Paul Blackburn. NYBP
Stream descends on Meru mountain, A. Robert Southey. *Fr.* The Curse of Kehama. OBRV
Stream flowing steadily over a stone does not wet its core, A. An Elder's Reproof to his Wife. 'Abdillaahi Muuse, *tr. by* B. W. Andrzjewski *and* I. M. Lewis. TTY; WTO
Stream has taken its shred of sound, The. Winter Night, Cold Spell. Howard Nelson. AMV-81
Stream is frozen hard, The. Going by. Antenora. "Hugh MacDiarmid." SeCePo
Stream of Faith, The. William Channing Gannett. *See* From Heart to Heart.
Stream of tender gladness, A. Shadow River. Pauline Johnson. CaP
Stream sorrow, eyes. Elegy for Her Brother, Sakhr. Al-Khansa, *tr. by* Bridget Connelly. WPOW
Stream swirls, The. The wind moans in. Jade Flower Palace. Tu Fu, *tr. by* Kenneth Rexroth. NaP
Stream to mingle with your favorite Dee, A. To Lady Eleanor Butler and the Honourable Miss Ponsonby, Composed in the Grounds of Plas-Newydd, Llangollen. Wordsworth. PeHV
Stream was smooth as glass, The, we said, "Arise and let's away." The Ballad of the Boat. Richard Garnett. HBV-2
Streamlined Stream-Knowledge. Arthur W. Bell. WhC
Streams fall down and through the darkness bear, The. Spate in Winter Midnight. Norman MacCaig. GTBS-P; PoSH
Streams of Bunclody, The. *Unknown.* BIrV
Streams of Lovely Nancy, The. *Unknown.* FaBoBa; OBET; OxBoLi
Stream's Song, The. Lascelles Abercrombie. OBMV
Streams that wind among the hills, The. Song. George Darley. *Fr.* Sylvia; or, The May Queen. NBM
Street, The. Gene Baro. NYBP
Street. George Oppen. GP
Street, The. Octavio Paz, *tr. fr. Spanish by* Willis Knapp Jones. FF
Street, The. Robert Pinsky. MAYP
Street, The. Gary Soto. NPAW; NPGG
Street blood throbbing. Disco Chinatown. Yuri Kageyama. BrSi
Street Car Blues. *Unknown.* BluL
Street climbs upward steeply, The. The Street. Gene Baro. NYBP
Street comes to him, The. The Blind Man. James Lewisohn. LFAC
Street Corner College. Kenneth Patchen. MoAmPo
Street Demonstration. Margaret Walker. BPo; CNA
Street Fight. Harold Monro. FaBoTw
Street Fire. Daniel Halpern. AmPA; NYP
Street in April, A. Louis Dudek. OBCV
Street in Bronzeville, A: Southeast Corner. Gwendolyn Brooks. VGW
Street in Kaufman-ville, A. James Cunningham. JB
Street is no river, The. For slouching. The Dogchain Gang. Stan Rice. NPGG
Street is quiet, The. Where the Blue Horses. Raymond Souster. PeCV
Street is very long and filled with silence, The. The Street. Octavio Paz, *tr by* Willis Knapp Jones. FF
Street Kid. Duane Niatum. STE
Street Lanterns. Mary Elizabeth Coleridge. PoRA
Street light, The/ On its lonely arm. Late Corner. Langston Hughes. NePoAm-2
Street Melody, A. Belle Cooper. GoBC
Street of Named Houses, The. Robert David Cohen. NYBP
Street Performers, 1851. Terence Tiller. GTBS-P
Street Preacher. Norman MacCaig. BSV
Street Scene. Robert Mezey. LiTM
Street Scene, A. Lizette Woodworth Reese. OBCA
Street Scene—1946. Kenneth Porter. PoNe
Street Song. Thom Gunn. HeIP; NoP; OxBC
Street Song. Edith Sitwell. CMoP; CoBMV; MoPo; MoVE
Street Sounds to the Soldiers' Tread, The. A. E. Housman. PPP
Street there is in Paris famous, A. The Ballad of Bouillabaisse. Thackeray. HBV-1; InMe; OBEV; OBVV; ViBoPo
Street Window. Carl Sandburg. PCP
Streets. Douglas Goldring. HBMV
Streets. Amy Lowell. SBG
Streets also have eyes, The. The Messiah. Moshe Yungman, *tr. by* David G. Roskies *and* Hillel Schwartz. VWA
Streets are a bit confused, The. Drunken Streets. Malka Locker, *tr. by* Jeremy Garber. VWA
Streets of Air, The. Malcolm Cowley. *Fr.* Blue Juniata. PoA
Streets of Baltimore. *Unknown.* BLPA
Streets of Cairo; or, The Poor Little Country Maid, *with music.* James Thornton. FSN
Streets of Forbes, The. *Unknown.* CBAP
Streets of Glory. *Unknown.* FSW
Streets of Laredo, The. Louis MacNeice. ChTr; MoBS; OBWP
Streets of Laredo, The. *Unknown. See* Cowboy's Lament, The.
Streets of New York, The, *with music.* Henry Blossom. FSN
Streets of the roaring town. On a Soldier Fallen in the Philippines. William Vaughn Moody. AP; HBV-2; NOBA; PAH
Streets outside have ice on them, The. My Grandfather Always Promised Us. Liam Rector. AMV-80
Streets that slept all afternoon in sun, The. Camptown. John Ciardi. WaP
Street-Walker in March. Samuel L. Albert. NePoAm-2
Strength and dignity [*or* honour] are her clothing. The Mother of the House. Bible, *O.T.* Proverbs, XXXI: 25-29. PGD; PoSC, *sl. diff. vers.*
Strength leaves the hand I lay on this beech bole. The Beech. Andrew Young. BoNaP
Strength, Love, Light. Robert II, King of France. WGRP
Strength of Fate, The. Euripides, *tr. fr. Greek by* A. E. Housman. *Fr.* Alcestis. AWP
Strength through Joy. Kenneth Rexroth. FYAP; VGW
Strength to War. Stephen Stepanchev. WaP
Strengthen, my Love, this castle of my heart. Rondel. Charles d'Orleans, *tr. by* Andrew Lang. AWP
Strengthened to live, strengthened to die for. In Distrust of Merits. Marianne Moore. AP; CoBMV; EaLo; LiTA; LiTM; MoAB; MoAmPo; NePA; OBWP; OxBA; SeCeV; TreFT; TrGrPo; ViBoPo; WaaP; WaP
Strephon. John Smyth. UnTE
Strephon kissed me in the spring. The Look. Sara Teasdale. HBV-1
Stress of his anger set me back. The Revelation. James Wright. DiL; PAI
Stretch forth! stretch forth! from the south to the north! The Anglo-Saxon Race; a Rhyme for Englishmen. Martin Tupper. PeD
Stretched in the shadow of the broad beech. The Shepherd's Gratitude. Virgil, *tr. by* Charles Stuart Calverley. Eclogues, I. AWP
Stretching her head toward the stars. Pliny Jane. Mildred Luton. PH
Strew lightly o'er the soldier's grave. The Soldier's Grave. Henry D. Muir. OHIP
"Strew me with blossoms when I die." Popular Songs of Tuscany. *Unknown, tr. by* John Addington Symonds. AWP
Strew not earth with empty stars. Song. Thomas Lovell Beddoes. ViBoPo
Strew on her roses, roses. Requiescat. Matthew Arnold. AWP; ELP; FiP; HBV-1; HeIP; InvP; LiTB; NOBE; OAEP; OBEV; OBVV; PoRA; TreFS; TrGrPo; ViBoPo; WHA
Stricken Deer, The. William Cowper. *See* I Was a Stricken Deer, That Left the Herd.
Stricken Deer, The. Thomas Moore. *See* Come, Rest in This Bosom.
Stricken South to the North, The. Paul Hamilton Hayne. PAH
Strict hairshirt of circumstance tears the flesh. The Veterans. Donagh MacDonagh. CIP; OnYI
Strictly for Posterity. Charles Simic. NNaP
Strictly Germ-proof. Arthur Guiterman. BLPA; HBV-2; TreF; TrJP; YaD
Strictures on the Economy of Nature. George Outram. FaBoCo
Strife is grown between Virtue and Love, A. Astrophel and Stella, LII. Sir Philip Sidney. NoP; SiPS
Strike, The. *Unknown.* OBET
Strike a match. Within Us, Too. R. H. Grenville. AMV-80

Strike among the Poets, A. *Unknown.* FaBoCo; FiBHP; PP
Strike down into my breast, O sun, and cleanse my soul. Hymn to the Sun. William Alexander Percy. TrPWD
Strike It Up, Tabor. *Unknown.* NCEP
Strike the Blow. *Unknown.* PAH
Strike the concertina's melancholy string! The Story of Prince Agib. W. S. Gilbert. FaBoCo; InMe; NA
Strike up, you lusty gallants, with music [*or* musick] and sound of drum. Captain Ward and the *Rainbow.* *Unknown.* BaBo; ESPB; OBET
Strike ye our land. Buffalo Dance. Alice Corbin, *after the Chippewa Indian.* BPAW
Striking. Charles Stuart Calverley. CenHV
Striking like lightning to the quick of the real world. Duns Scotus. Thomas Merton. CoPo
Striking Times. *Unknown.* OBET
String. Dennis Schmitz. LCAP
String-chewing bass players. Mingus. Bob Kaufman. PoBA
String of My Ancestors, The. Nina Nyhart. Str
String Stars for Pearls. John U. Nicolson. HBMV
String vibrates, The. The steel string vibrates. The skin. The calfskin. Acoustics. Susan Griffin. *Fr.* Woman and Nature. NPGG
Stringer, The. James Brasfield. AMV-81
Strings' Excitement, The. W. H. Auden. MoAB; MoBrPo
Strings/Himo. Yuri Kageyama. BrSi
Strings in the Earth. James Joyce. Chamber Music, I. HBMV; MoBrPo
(Strings in the Earth and Air.) OnYI
Strings lay all about. The Disconnection. Rita Mae Brown. IHMS
Strip Me Naked, or Royal Gin for Ever; a Picture. *Unknown.* NOEC
Strip Mining Pit. Dan Gillespie. TAT
Strip of Blue, A. Lucy Larcom. AA; HBV-1; WGRP
Strip off your clothes and give them to a man. The Visiting Hour. David Wagoner. HoPM
Strip to the waist and have a seat. The doctor. Words. Miller Williams. AMV-81
Striped blouse in a clearing by Bazille, A. Ceremony. Richard Wilbur. CoAP; MiAP; NoAM; PP
Stripped/ you're beginning to float free. November 1968. Adrienne Rich. NMM
Stripped almond of the plane is gone, The. Between Two Worlds. Rosemary Thomas. NYBP
Stripper, The. Anita Endrezze Probst. CDW
Stripping off another yard of line. Casting at Night. Allen Hoey. AMV-80; WOLT
Stripping the green tissue from the flowers. Bridesmaid. Robley Wilson, Jr. AMV-80
Strive Not, Vain Lover, to Be Fine. Richard Lovelace. OAEP
Stroke. Mike Lowery. Psk
Strokes. William Stafford. ConAP; PCP
Strolling Player, The. Arthur Rimbaud, *tr. fr. French by* William Jay Smith. GrPl
Strolling vaguely after luncheon through the streets of Amsterdam. Belle de Jour. George Melly. FaBoPa
Strong, The. John Vance Cheney. AA
Strong am I among mortals, not without a name. Hippolytus. Euripides, *tr. by* Rex Warner. NAWM-1
Strong and slippery, built for the midnight grass-party confronted by four cats. Peter. Marianne Moore. CMoP; NoP; OxBA
Strong ankled, sun burned, almost naked. Vitamins and Roughage. Kenneth Rexroth. NoAM
Strong Are Saying Nothing, The. Robert Frost. CMoP
Strong as Death. H. C. Bunner. HBV-1
Strong Bond, The. Juana de Ibarbourou, *tr. fr. Spanish by* Linda Scheer. PBWP
Strong, but with gentleness. Variations on a Medieval Theme. Geoffrey Dutton. PoAu-2
Strong City, The. Alfred Noyes. *Fr.* The Last Voyage, Dedication. GoBC
Strong Feeling for Poultry, A. Roy Blount, Jr. TDH
Strong God which made the topmost stars. The Prophet Lost in the Hills at Evening. Hilaire Belloc. OxBoCh
Strong Hand, A. Aaron Hill. HBV-1
Strong Heroic Line, The. Oliver Wendell Holmes. AA
Strong in a dream of perfect bloom. To the Brave Soul. Wilbur Underwood. WGRP
Strong in thy steadfast purpose, be. Purpose. John James Piatt. AA
Strong is the horse upon his speed. The Man of Prayer. Christopher Smart. *Fr.* A Song to David. LiTB
Strong is the lion—like a coal. Christopher Smart. *Fr.* A Song to David. HAP
Strong man, a fair woman, A. Sun and Moon. Jay Macpherson. SoSe
Strong Men. Sterling A. Brown. BANP; BPo; CNA; FB; PoBA; TTY
Strong men keep coming on, The. Upstream. Carl Sandburg. HBMV; MoAB; MoAmPo
Strong Men, Riding Horses. Gwendolyn Brooks. PoBA
Strong-minded Lady, A. Morris Bishop. TDH
Strong rods for scepters to bear sway. On the Decease of the Religious and Honourable Jno Haynes Esqr. John James. SCAP
Strong-shouldered mole. A Dead Mole. Andrew Young. FM; GTBS-P
Strong sob of the chafing stream, The. Orara. Henry Kendall. CBAP; PoAu-1
Strong Son of God, Immortal Love. In Memoriam A. H. H., Proem. Tennyson. EBVV; HAP; HBV-2; LiTB; OAEL-2; OAEP; SeCeV; TreF; TrGrPo; TrPWD; TRV; VLP; WGRP; WHA
(Strong Son of God.) EaLo; OxBoCh; TrCP
Strong song tows, A. Coda. Basil Bunting. *Fr.* Briggflatts. OAEL-2
Strong sun across the sod can make. Song for the Passing of a Beautiful Woman. *Unknown, tr. by* Mary Austin. LiTA
Strong Swimmer, The. William Rose Benét. PoNe
Strong Wind, A. Austin Clarke. BoNaP
Stronger than alcohol, more great than song. Ted Berrigan. EAS
Strongest, The. "Yehoash," *tr. fr. Yiddish by* Marie Syrkin. TrJP
Strongest and the noblest argument, The. Dedication II. Sir John Davies. *Fr.* Nosce Teipsum. SiPS
Strongest creature for his size, The. Weary Will. A. B. Paterson. BoAnP
Strop, the lunge, lunge, lunge, The. Razor. Robert B. Smith. LFAC
Struck dumb at arm's length. A Child's Nativity. John N. Morris. GP
Struck with huge Love, of what to be possest. A Prefatory Poem, on . . . *Magnalia Christi Americana.* Nicholas Noyes. SCAP
Structural Study of Myth, The. Jerome Rothenberg. PoM
Struggle. Sidney Lanier. LiTA; OxBA
Struggle, The. Sully-Prudhomme, *tr. fr. French by* Arthur O'Shaughnessy. AWP; PoPl
Struggle is over, the boys are defeated, The. Bold Robert Emmet. Tom Maguire. OnYI
Struggle is strong and splendid, The. Sounding. Doris Ferne. CaP
Struggle with the Angel, The. Claude Vigée, *tr. fr. French by* Elizabeth Savage. VWA
Strumming your melodic hair. Mouth of the Amazon. R. P. Gira. AMV-80
Strung Out with Elgar on a Hill, *sel.* Jonathan Williams.
"All you ask is." GP
Strut for Roethke, A. John Berryman. NOBA
Stuart Howard-Jones. Where He Takes Tea with Cromwell. *Unknown.* DBV
Stubborn Spring pushed through the cold twigs. The Boarder. Frederick Feirstein. NYP
Stud Groom. John Glassco. OBCV
Studded with flies. State Fair Pigs. Roger Pfingston. TAT
Student. Cheng Min, *tr. fr. Chinese by* Kenneth Rexroth *and* Ling Chung. PBWP
Student. Josephine Miles. NoP
Student, The. Marianne Moore. MP; TwCP
Student, The. *Unknown, tr. fr. Early Modern Irish by* Frank O'Connor. AnIL; KiLC; OBMV
Student came from Oxford town also, A. Chaucer, *mod. vers. by* Louis Untermeyer. *Fr.* The Canterbury Tales: Prologue. TrGrPo
Student Courting, A. *Unknown.* OxBM
Student, do the simple purification. The Simple Purification. Kabir, *ad. by* Robert Bly. NU
Students. Florence Wilkinson Evans. HBV-1
Students groan, The. Etudes. Laurence W. Thomas. AMV-80
Student's life is pleasant, The. The Student. *Unknown, tr. by* Frank O'Connor. AnIL; KiLC; OBMV
Students, like students, form and fly. "When the Students Resisted, a Minor Clash Ensued." David Knight. MoCV
Students of Justice, The. W. S. Merwin. NaP
Student's Tale, The. Longfellow. *Fr.* Tales of a Wayside Inn, III. AmPP
Studies at Delhi, *sels.* Sir Alfred Comyn Lyall.
Badminton. OBVV
Hindu Ascetic, The. OBVV
Studies from Life. Martha Dickey. FAZ
Studios Photographic, The, *sel.* Paul Shivell.
In God's Eternal Studios. HBV-2
Study horror?—without a doubt. Pisanello's Studies of Men Hanging on Gallows. John Wheatcroft. FAZ
Study in Aesthetics, A. Robert Peters. BXAP
Study in Aesthetics, The. Ezra Pound. CMoP; InPS; NOBA; NoP
Study No. X. Pierre Coupey. PeCV
Study of a Spider, The. Lord De Tabley. VLP
Study of an Elevation, in Indian Ink. Kipling. InMe
Study of Reading Habits, A. Philip Larkin. NOBL; PPP; SoSe; TW
Study of Two Pears. Wallace Stevens. AP; InPK; InPS; NU; OxBA
Study Peace. Amiri Baraka. PoBA
Study this violent and trembling woman. How Music's Made. Dilys Laing. ELU

Study War No More. *Unknown.* *See* Ain' Go'n to Study War No Mo'.
Stuff. H. B. Johnson. AMV-80
Stuff of Dreams, The. Shakespeare. *See* Our Revels Now Are Ended.
Stuff of the moon. Nocturne in a Deserted Brickyard. Carl Sandburg. MoAmPo
Stuffed Owl, The, *sel.* Wordsworth.
"While Anna's peers and early playmates tread." Par
Stuffed owls drum in my heart. Fear. Thomas Love Peacock. VoR
Stuffy chill of clouded Summer, crowdsmell, booksmell. Supervising Examinations. Sean Lucy. CIP
Stumbling. Dick Lourie. NeAC
Stumbling over fallen logs. Lost in a Blizzard. Arthur W. Monroe. PoOW
Stump Is Not the Tombstone, The. Ralph W. Seager. AMV-81
Stumpfoot on 42nd Street. Louis Simpson. NNaP; NYP; UnPo; VGW
Stumptown Attends the Picture Show. David Bottoms. GP
Stun. James Schuyler. MAT
Stunned cabin boy, A. Miscarriage. Michael Longley. POL
Stunned in that first estrangement. What We Said. W. D. Snodgrass. GP
Stunned in the stone light, laid among the lilies. Ophelia. Vernon Watkins. MoVE
Stuntman. Lionel Kearns. MoCV
Stupendious love! All saints astonishment! Edward Taylor. Preparatory Meditations: First Series, X. OxBA
Stupendous God! how shrinks our bounded sense. Robert Montgomery. *Fr.* The Omnipresence of the Deity. VLP
Stupid Old Body, The. Edward Carpenter. WGRP
Stupid Old Myself. Russell Hoban. RHPC
Stupidity. "E." CBAP
Stupidity Street. Ralph Hodgson. BrPo; CH; HBV-2; LiTM; MoAB; MoBrPo; OxBTC; PDV; SiSoSe; TreFS
Sturdiest of forest trees, The. The Holly. Walter de la Mare. CMoP
Sturdy Conq'ror, politic, severe, The. The Royal Line. Leigh Hunt. FaBoUs
Sturdy ploughman doth the soldier see, The. Joseph Hall. *Fr.* Virgidemiarum. OBSV
Stutterer. Alan Dugan. CAPP; NYBP
Stwuns that built Gaarge Ridler's oven, The. George Ridler's Oven. *Unknown.* OBET
Style. Charles Bukowski. HoPM
Style. Howard Nemerov. NoAM
Style is the answer to everything. Style. Charles Bukowski. HoPM
Stylite. Louis MacNeice. MoPo
Suave and paltry man, my enemy, A. In the Tail of the Scorpion. Genevieve Taggard. VGW
Suave Mari Magno. Lucretius, *tr. fr. Latin by* W. H. Mallock. *Fr.* De Rerum Natura. AWP
Sub-average *Time* Reader, The. Ernest Wittenberg. FiBHP
Sub Specie Aeternitatis. Robert Hayden. AmPP
Subalterns. Elizabeth Daryush. OBWP; SUMH
Subalterns, The. Thomas Hardy. CMoP; MoAB; MoBrPo; NoAM; OAEL-2; PAI; PPP; TEP; VLP
Subaltern's Love-Song, A. John Betjeman. BoLoP; ChMP; EvOK; HAP; LiSp; MP; NOBL; OxBTC; TwCP
Subject. Marie Ponsot. VGW
Subject chosen for tonight's discussion, The. An Evening of Russian Poetry. Vladimir Nabokov. NYBP
Subject of Heroic Song, The. Milton. *Fr.* Paradise Lost, IX. OBS
("No more of talk where God or angel guest.") NoP
Subject to All Pain. *Unknown.* MeEl
Subject today, my friends, is stinted praise, The. "The Art of Our Necessities Is Strange." Forrest Izard. WhC
Subject was put to bed at midnight, The. Operative No. 174 Resigns. Kenneth Fearing. NYBP
Subjectivity at Sestos. P. M. Hubbard. NYBP
Sublimation. Alex Comfort. ErPo; UnTE
Sublime—invention ever young. Christopher Smart. *Fr.* A Song to David. HBV-2; OBEV
Submarine Bed, The. John Peale Bishop. LiTA
Submarine Mountains. Cale Young Rice. EtS
Submerged city, The. Cologne. Hilde Domin, *tr. by* Tudor Morris. VWA
Submerged, silent, rooted in water. Foetus. Phyllis Haring. PeSA
Submission. George Herbert. JCP
Submission. *Unknown, tr. fr. Siamese by* E. Powys Mathers. ErPo
Submission and Rest. Anna Temple Whitney. *See* Kneeling Camel, The.
Submission in Affliction. *Unknown.* STF
Submission to Afflictive Providences. Isaac Watts. NOCV
Submite submitted to her heavenly king. *Unknown.* WhC
Submitting to a sentry's fate. Common Dawn. Guy Butler. PeSA
Subsiding from those heavenly wings the air. Hymn for the Feast of the Annunciation. Aubrey Thomas De Vere. ISi
Substance and Shadow. Cardinal Newman. GoBC
Substantiations, *sel.* Vidya, *tr. fr. Sanskrit by* Daniel H. H. Ingalls.
"One born to hardship in his place and station." PBWP
Substitution. Elizabeth Barrett Browning. WGRP
Substitution. Anne Spencer. BlSi; CDC
Subterranean Homesick Blues. Bob Dylan. InPK
Subtle almost beyond thought are these dim colours. Dun-Colour. Ruth Pitter. FM; MoVE; PoRA
Subtle chain of countless rings, A. Nature. Emerson. AWP
Subtle tracery of the leafless bough, The. Ad Matrem in Coelis. Linda Lyon Van Voorhis. GoBC
Suburb. Harold Monro. HBV-1
Suburb, The. Anne Stevenson. NMM
Suburb Hilltop. Richard Moore. NYBP
Suburban Dream. Edwin Muir. OxBTC
Suburban Dusk. Bert Meyers. EAS
Suburban Song. Elizabeth Riddell. CBAP
Suburban Sonnet. Gwen Harwood. CBAP
Suburban villas, highway-side retreats. London Suburbs. William Cowper. *Fr.* Retirement. FaBoPP
Suburban Wife's Song. Robert Hutchinson. NYBP
Suburbia. Maurice Martinez. PoNe
Suburbs is a Fine Place, The. *Unknown.* CoMu
Suburbs on a Hazy Day. D. H. Lawrence. OBMV
Subversive, The. Merle Woo. BrSi
Subverted Flower, The. Robert Frost. CMoP; HAP; NoAM; NOBA; OxBA; WeW
Subway, The. Allen Tate. AP; NoAM; NOBA; NYP
Subway from New Britain to the Bronx, The. Randall Jarrell. NYP
Subway messes me up, The. Tubes. Larry Mollin. NeAC
Subway Psalm. Alden Nowlan. Str
Subway Witnesses, The. Lorenzo Thomas. PoBA
Success! Berton Braley. WBLP
Success. Rupert Brooke. OxBTC
Success. Emily Dickinson. *See* Success is counted sweetest.
Success. William Empson. OxBTC
Success. Edgar A. Guest. TreF
Success. Emma Lazarus. SBG
Success. *Unknown.* FaFP
Success is counted sweetest. Emily Dickinson. AP; CABA; CMoP; FPL; GoJo; InPS; LiTA; LiTM; MoAB; MoAmPo; NOBA; OxBA; PoRA; SBG; TAP; TreFT; WaaP; WPE
(Success.) AWP
Success is like some horrible disaster. After Publication of *Under the Volcano.* Malcolm Lowry. FaBoTw
Success is speaking words of praise. Success. *Unknown.* FaFP
Success Story. Bruce Bennett. LTB
Success to the Newport Railway. The Newport Railway. William McGonagall. PeD
Succession, The. Frances Laughton Mace. AA
Succession of the Four Sweet Months, The. Robert Herrick. *See* Four Sweet Months, The.
Succubi. John Newlove. NeAC
Succubus, The. Robert Graves. OAEL-2
Succubus, The. Harriet Rose. BrRo
Succumbing. Paul Eaton Reeve. ErPo
Such a beast is the Hipporhinostricow. Hipporhinostricow. Spike Milligan. AmMo
Such a calmness. Rest. Jacob Isaac Segal, *tr. by* Seymour Mayne. VWA
Such a fine pullet ought to go. A Blue Ribbon at Amesbury. Robert Frost. NePA
Such a fool as I am you had better ignore. The Usk. C. H. Sisson. NOCV
Such a hubbub in the nests. Freaks of Fashion. Christina Rossetti. FM
Such a merry suburb! Dachau. John Malcolm Brinnin. GP
Such a morning it is when love. Day of These Days. Laurie Lee. BoNaP; MoVE
Such a Parcel of Rogues in a Nation. Burns. OxBS
Such a Pleasant Familee. Wallace Irwin. ShM
Such a prelate, I trow. John Skelton. *Fr.* Why Come Ye Not to Court. OBSV
Such a sad celebration. A Grain of Moonlight. Asya, *tr. by* Gabriel Preil *and* Howard Schwartz. VWA
Such a strong color on the late chrysanthemums. Two Drinking Songs, 2. T'ao Yuan-ming, *ad. by* Robert Bly. NU
Such a time of it they had. Stanley Meets Mutesa. James D. Rubadiri. PBA
Such as in God the Lord Do Trust, *with music.* William Kethe. AH
Such as it is. Such as two men. The Clothing's New Emperor. Donald Finkel. NePoEA
Such as to himself eternity's changed him. The Tomb of Edgar Poe. Stéphane Mallarmé, *tr. by* Roger Fry. NAWM-2
Such as unto himself at last Eternity changes him. The Tomb of Edgar Poe. Stéphane Mallarmé, *tr. by* author. NAWM-2

Such beautiful, beautiful hands. Beautiful Hands [*or* My Mother's Hands]. *Unknown, at. to* Ellen M. H. Gates. TreF; TreFS
Such brazen slatterns. Dandelions. Gerda Mayer. POL
Such Comfort as the Night Can Bring to Us. Peter Cooley. MAYP
Such darkness as when Jesus died! San Francisco. Joaquin Miller. PAH
Such dubious nomenclatures crowding in. Basic Communication. Thomas Hornsby Ferril. NePoAm-2
Such easy, easy hours. Moon as Medusa. Vinnie-Marie D'Ambrosio. IHMS
Such fame as I have drops from me in a flash. The Perturbations of Uranus. Roy Fuller. ErPo
Such Foolish Old Dames. Sam S. Stinson. TDH
Such glorious faith as fills your limpid eyes. Verse for a Certain Dog. Dorothy Parker. GDP
Such hap as I am happed in. Sir Thomas Wyatt. SiPS
Such hints as untaught Nature yields! Nature: The Artist. Frederic Lawrence Knowles. AA
Such ills attend. Advice to Lovers. John Armstrong. *Fr.* The Oeconomy of Love; a Poetical Essay. NOEC
Such Is Holland! Petrus Augustus de Genestet, *tr. fr. Dutch by* Adriaan Barnouw. POL
Such Is the Death the Soldier Dies. Robert Burns Wilson. AA; HBV-2
Such is the Mode of these censorious Days. On Mr. Hobbs, and His Writings. John Sheffield, Duke of Buckingham and Normanby. PoEL-3
Such is the secret union, when we feel. The Creative Process. Mark Akenside. *Fr.* The Pleasures of Imagination. NOEC
Such is the way of the world. "St.-J. Perse," *tr. by* T. S. Eliot. Anabasis, IV. OBVE
Such light is in sea-caves. Musica No. 3. Richard Duerden. NeAP
Such little, puny things are words in rhyme. Quickening. Christopher Morley. HBMV
Such majestic rhythms, such tiny disturbances. A Grain of Rice. F. R. Scott. PeCV
Such marvellous ways to kill a man! The Bofors A.A. Gun. Gavin Ewart. WaP
Such moving sounds from such a careless touch. Of [*or* On] My Lady Isabella Playing on the Lute. Edmund Waller. HAP; MePo; SeCP
Such natural debts of love our Oxford knows. Martyr's Memorial. Louise Imogen Guiney. AA
Such natural love twixt beast and man we find. Eden's Courtesy. C. S. Lewis. EBCP
Such pictures of the heavens were never seen. The Invisible. Richard Watson Gilder. WGRP
Such poor folk as to law do go. Isabella Whitney. *Fr.* A Sweet Nosegay, or Pleasant Posy. WPE
Such shameless bards we have; and yet 'tis true. Pope. *Fr.* An Essay on Criticism. OBSV
Such should this day be, so the sun should hide. On the Marriage of T. K. and C. C., the Morning Stormy. Thomas Carew. BoLoP
Such skill, matcht with such courage as he had. Spenser. *Fr.* Astrophel. OBWP
Such special sweetness was about. That Day You Came. Lizette Woodworth Reese. HBV-1
Such splendid icecaps and hard rills, such weights. Piano Practice. Howard Moss. NYBP
Such Stuff as Dreams. Franklin P. Adams. FiBHP; SpRo
Such Stuff as Dreams Are Made of. Thomas Wentworth Higginson. AA
Such Stuff as Dreams Are Made On. Shakespeare. *See* Our Revels Now Are Ended.
Such subtile filigranity and nobless of construccion. "Wellcome, to the Caves of Artá!" Robert Graves. NOBL; NYBP
Such, such is Death: no triumph: no defeat. Two Sonnets, II. Charles Hamilton Sorley. HBMV; MMA; MoBrPo
Such times as windy moods do stir. The Spirit of the Wheat. Edward A. U. Valentine. AA
Such Tophet was; so looked the grinning fiend. Tophet. Thomas Gray. FaBoEE; NOEC. *See also* Thus Etough looked; so grinned the brawling fiend.
Such walls, like honey, and the old are happy. Luss Village. Iain Crichton Smith. BSV
Such was he, our Martyr-Chief. Our Martyr-Chief. James Russell Lowell. OHIP
Such was old Chaucer. Such the placid mien. For a Statue of Chaucer at Woodstock. Mark Akenside. SeCePo
Such was the Boy—but for the growing Youth. Wordsworth. *Fr.* The Excursion, I. OBRV
Such[e] wayward[e] ways [*or* wais] hath love, that most[e] part[e] in discord[e]. Earl of Surrey. AAS; SiPS
Such were the notes, thy once-lov'd poet sung. To Robert Earl of Oxford and Earl Mortimer. Pope. OBEC
Suck the bare sob out of the heart. Microcosmos, X. Nigel Heseltine. NeBP
Sucking Cider through a Straw. *Unknown.* AS, *with music;* GBP
(Sipping Cider through a Straw.) FSW
Sucking on hard candy. A Real Story. Linda Pastan. Str
Sucking soup out of a spoon. On a Wednesday. Jody Aliesan. AMV-80
Suction's Anthem. Blake. *Fr.* An Island in the Moon. FaBoNo
Sudan. Michael Jackson. OCNZ
Sudbury Fight, The. Wallace Rice. PAH
Sudden amid the slush and rain. In the City. Israel Zangwill. WGRP
Sudden Assertion. Kenneth Leslie. BoAnP; GDP; POL
Sudden autumn winds, like hounds, The. Mary Gilmore. *Fr.* The Disinherited. PoAu-1
Sudden blow, A: the great wings beating still. Leda and the Swan. W. B. Yeats. AnIL; CABA; ChMP; CMoP; CoBMV; EBEV; ErPo; FaBoEn; FF; FPL; GTBS-P; HAP; HelP; InPK; LiTM; MoAB; MoBrPo; MoVE; NIP; NoAM; NOBE; NoP; OAEL-2; OAEP; PAI; PBBP; PPoe; PPP; PrIm; SCV; SeCeV; SoSe; TEP; TrGrPo; WeW
Sudden Frost. David Wagoner. PoPl
Sudden Light. Dante Gabriel Rossetti. BoLoP; ELP; FaBoEn; FPL; LO; LoBV; NBM; NOBE; NoP; OAEL-2; OAEP; OBNC; PoLF; TrGrPo; VLP
(Song IV: Sudden Light.) CTC
Sudden night is here at once, The. Poppies. Charles Weekes. OnYI
Sudden refreshment came upon the school. Physical Geography. Louise Townsend Nicholl. ImOP
Sudden Shower. John Clare. OBRV; PoSC
Sudden the desert changes. Bridge-Guard in the Karroo. Kipling. OBWP
Sudden Things. Donald Hall. EAS
Sudden thrust of speech is no mean test, The. The Fire i' the Flint. Lucy Catlin Robinson. AA
Sudden upriseth from her stately place. Spenser. *Fr.* The Faerie Queene, I, 4. PPP
Sudden wakin', a sudden weepin', A. Man's Days. Eden Phillpotts. HBV-2; OBEV; OBVV; OxBTC
Suddening one day by myself. The Fence. Heather McHugh. GeTw
Suddenly. Robin Blaser. PoM
Suddenly/ in middle age. Icons. Miriam Waddington. NOBC
Suddenly,/ out of the faint gray smother. White Fox. Elizabeth Alsop Shepard. GoYe
Suddenly Afraid. *Unknown. See* Woman Sat Weeping, A.
Suddenly, after the quarrel, while we waited. The Quarrel. Conrad Aiken. MoAB; MoAmPo; PoPl
Suddenly all the fountains in the park. The Fountains. W. R. Rodgers. MoVE; POL
Suddenly everything stops. Slump. Vassar Miller. BoWoP
Suddenly half in jest. Album Leaf. Stéphane Mallarmé, *tr. by* Keith Bosley. OBVE
Suddenly her breast has never been larger. Impotence. Marvin Bell. AmPA
Suddenly his mouth filled with sand. Death of a Poet. Charles Causley. OxBTC
Suddenly his poor body. Stations. Ted Hughes. NoAM
Suddenly I remember the holes. The Holes. Stephen Berg. NaP; NYBP
Suddenly I saw the cold and rook-delighting heaven. The Cold Heaven. W. B. Yeats. AWP; CTC; GTBS-P; HAP; MoVE; NoAM; OAEL-2; OAEP; TEP; WeW
Suddenly in October the morning air. What I Have. Susan North. AMV-81
Suddenly in the midnight on mortal men. The Last Judgment. *Unknown, tr. by* Charles W. Kennedy. *Fr.* Christ 3. AnOE
Suddenly it was quiet as a Sunday. The Wave. Daryl Hine. Prf
Suddenly it's autumn, I think, as I look in the garden. Last Sheet. Roy Fuller. TEP
Suddenly night crushed out the day and hurled. The Unreturning. Wilfred Owen. MoBrPo
Suddenly, out of dark and leafy ways. Tenants. W. W. Gibson. HBV-2
Suddenly, out of my darkness, shines Thy beauty, O Brother. A Psalm to the Son. Marguerite Wilkinson. TrPWD
"Suddenly she slapped me, hard across the face." Elizabeth in Italy [*or* In Memoriam, II.]. Richard Weber. BoLoP; ErPo
Suddenly the old fancy has me! Battery Park, High Noon. Ben Belitt. NYP
Suddenly the sky turned gray. Snow toward Evening. Melville Cane. PDV; SUS; TiPo
Suddenly there was a dress. White Notes. Donald Justice. LCAP
Suddenly they are there as I. The Windows. Ron Loewinsohn. GP
Suddenly they came flying, like a long scarf of smoke. The Thing. Theodore Roethke. CMoP
Suddenly to become John Benbow, walking down William Street. Metempsychosis. Kenneth Slessor. ViBoPo

Sudds launders bands in piss[e]; and starches them. Upon Sudds, a Laundress[e]. Robert Herrick. AnAnS-2; DBV
Sueños. James Reiss. FiCP
Suet Dumpling, The. *Unknown.* BXAP
Suez Crisis, The. *Somali Oral Tradition, tr. by* B. W. Andrzejewski. WTO
Suffenus, whom so well you know. To Varus. Catullus, *tr. by* Walter Savage Landor. AWP
Suffenus whom you know, the witty. Catullus, *tr. fr. Latin by* Matthew Prior. OBVE
Suffer, Poor Negro! David Diop, *tr. fr. French by* Langston Hughes. PBA
Suffer the Children. Audre Lorde. PoBA
Sufferance of her race is shown, The. "Formerly a Slave." Herman Melville. PoNe; TAP
Suffering. Albert Ehrenstein, *tr. fr. German by* Babette Deutsch. TrJP
Suffering has settled like a sly disguise. A Korean Woman Seated by a Wall. William Meredith. NePoEA
Sufficed not, madame, that you did tear. Sir Thomas Wyatt. SiPS
Sufficeth it to you [*or* yow] my joys [*or* joyes] interred. The 11th and Last Book of the Ocean to Cynthia [*or* The Ocean's Love to Cynthia]. Sir Walter Ralegh. NCEP; OBSC *and* SiPS, *sl. abr.*
Suffolk. Swinburne. *Fr.* By the North Sea, III. FaBoPP
Suffolk Miracle, The. *Unknown.* AmFP (2 *vers.*); BaBo (A *and* B *vers.*); ESPB
Suffolk Shore, The. George Crabbe. *Fr.* The Borough, Letter XXIII. FaBoPP
Sufi Quatrain. Rabi'a bint Isma'il of Syria, *tr. fr. Arabic by* Deirdre Lashgari. WPOW
Sugar-Candy Bird, A. Ian Young. NeAC
Sugar Cane, The, *sels.* James Grainger.
  Compost. NOEC
  How to Exterminate Rats. FaBoUs
  How to Fertilize Soil. FaBoUs
  Slaves. NOEC
Sugar-cane is just a cubit high, The. Love Songs (Dadaria). *Gond Oral Tradition, tr. by* V. Elwin *and* S. Hivale. WTO
Sugar Daddy. Elizabeth Smither. OCNZ
Sugar dripping into your vein, The. Firstborn. Charles Wright. DiL; GP
Sugar in the Cane. Tennessee Williams. OBAL
Sugar Lady, The. Frank Asch. RHPC
Sugar-Plum Tree, The. Eugene Field. FaFP; HBV-1; HBVY; OxBChV; SoPo; TreF
Sugar Weather. Peter McArthur. CaP
Sugarfields. Barbara Mahone. CNA; PoBA
Sugaring, The. A. M. Klein. OBCV
Suggested by a Picture of the Bird of Paradise. Wordsworth. VLP
Suggestion Made by the Posters of the *Globe,* A. J. E. Thorold Rogers. FaBoEE
Suicide. W. E. Henley. In Hospital, XXIV. BrPo
Suicide, A. Tom Kryss. NeAC
Suicide, The. V. R. Laing. PoA
Suicide. Louis MacNeice. DTC
Suicide, The. Joyce Carol Oates. Psk
Suicide. Alice Walker. FF
Suicide in [the] Trenches. Siegfried Sassoon. BrPo; MMA
Suicide of the night—ah, flotsam. Strange Fruit. Randolph Stow. PoAu-2
Suicide off Egg Rock. Sylvia Plath. NMP; PPP
Suicide Pond. Kathy McLaughlin. PoA
Suicides, The. George MacBeth. NoAM
Suicide's Grave, The. W. S. Gilbert. *Fr.* The Mikado, II. TreF; VLP; WhC
  (Ko-Ko's Song.) FaFP
  (Ko-Ko's Winning Song.) LiTB
  (Titwillow.) NoP
Suicide's Note. Langston Hughes. CDC; DFF
Suicides of the Rich, The. Victor Contoski. FAZ
Suicid/ing(ed) Indian Women. Paula Gunn Allen. TWSS
Suilven. Andrew Young. OxBS
Suilven and the Eagle, *sel.* Gordon Bottomley.
  Eagle Song. MoBrPo
Suit of Nettles, A, *sels.* James Reaney.
  Branwell's Sestina. MoCV
  Drunken Preacher's Sermon, The. PeCV
  January. OBCV
  November. OBCV
Suit of sheep's clothing, A. Policy. Carolyn Wells. WhC
Suite for Celery and Blind Date. Philip Dow. BXAP
Suite for Marriage, A. David Ignatow. NNaP
Suite from Catullus. Vincent McHugh. ErPo
Suite of Six Pieces for Siskind, A. John Logan. LCAP
Suite to Fathers. Jim Harrison. AmPA; DiL
Suits hang half a year in. Tyburn and Westminster. John Heywood. ACP
Sukey, you shall by my wife. *Unknown.* OxNR
Sukkot. Sol Lachman. VWA
Sulk. Felice Holman. RHPC
Sulk when you're spoken to. *Unknown.* CenHV
Sulkily the sticks burn, and though they crackle. Under the Pot. Robert Graves. FaBoEE
Sulky witch and a surly cat, A. Hallowe'en Indignation Meeting. Margaret Fishback. PoSC
Sullen and dark [*or* dull], in the September day. The Last Reservation. Walter Learned. AA; PAH
Sullen Sullom Voe. Ronas Hill. Hamish Brown. PoSH
Sullenly a gale. Red Cloud. John G. Neihardt. BPAW
Sullivan arrived at the very lowest Heaven. John L. Sullivan Enters Heaven. Robert Frost. BXAP
Sulphur-yellow chord of the eleventh, A. On Hearing Prokofieff's Grotesque for Two Bassoons, Concertina and Snare-Drums. Louis Untermeyer. BXAP
Sultan, The. *Unknown.* TDH
Sultan's Harem, The. *Unknown.* TreFT
Sultry air, the smoke of shavings. A Night in a Village. Ivan Savvich Nikitin, *tr. by* P. E. Matheson. AWP
Sultry and brazen was the August day. Saint R. L. S. Sarah N. Cleghorn. HBMV
Sultry, summer evening, the children playing jacks, A. Death of a Cat. James Schevill. NMP
Sum. James Nolan. Str
Sum, Es, Est ("Sum—I am a gentleman"). *Unknown.* ChTr
Sum of Life, The. Ben King. *See* Pessimist, The.
Sum speiks of lords, sum speiks of lairds. Johnie Armstrang. *Unknown.* ESPB; OxBB; ViBoFo
Sumach Leaves, The. Jones Very. NOBA
Sumburgh Heid. George Bruce. OxBS
Sumer is comen and winter gon. An Easter Song. *Unknown.* OxBM
Sumer Is Icumen In. *Unknown.* *See* Cuckoo Song.
Summa contra Gentiles. Paris Leary. CoPo
Summa is i-cumen in. Baccalaureate. David McCord. BXAP; OBAL; SpRo; WhC
Summah night an' sighin' breeze. Lover's Lane. Paul Laurence Dunbar. BANP
Summary. Sonia Sanchez. BPo
Summary of the Distance between the Bomber and the Objective. Walter Benton. WaP
Summer. Conrad Aiken. NoAM
Summer. Frank Asch. NTCP; RHPC
Summer. Robert Bloomfield. *Fr.* The Farmer's Boy. PBBP
Summer. Byron. *Fr.* The Corsair, III. OBRV
  (Sunset over the Aegean.) OBNC
Summer. John Clare. BoNaP
Summer. Douglas Crase. NoP
Summer. John Davidson. BoNaP
Summer. Moishe Kulbak, *tr. fr. Yiddish by* Ruth Whitman. VWA
Summer. Bill Manhire. OCNZ
Summer. Tom Marshall. NOBC
Summer. Josephine Miles. WPE
Summer. P. K. Page. PeCV
Summer. Christina Rossetti. BoNaP; ELP; NBM; PoPle
Summer. Gary Soto. WeW
Summer. Spenser. *Fr.* The Faerie Queene, VII, 7. GN
Summer. James Thomson. *Fr.* The Seasons. FM
  Sels.
  Happy Britannia. OBEC; SeCePo
  (Britannia.) FaBoPP
  "Still let me pierce into the midnight depth." EnRP
  Summer Evening and Night. OBEC
  Summer Morning. OBEC
Summer. Diane Wakoski. VGW
Summer. Ramona Wilson. VoR
Summer/ The earth is warm, the sun's ablaze. The Four Seasons. Jack Prelutsky. RHPC
Summer!/ the painting is organized. The Corn Harvest. William Carlos Williams. *Fr.* Pictures from Brueghel. PPP
Summer Acres. Anne Wilkinson. CaP
Summer Afternoon. Elizabeth B. Harrod. NePoEA
Summer Afternoon. Raymond Souster. BoNaP
Summer again. Margaret Atwood. *Fr.* The Circle Game. MoCV
Summer and autumn had been so wet, The. God's Judgment on a Wicked Bishop [*or* Bishop Hatto and the Rats]. Robert Southey. ChTr; EnRP; HBV-1; HBVY; OBNV; OBRV; OnMSP; PaPo
Summer, and noon, and a splendour of silence, felt. A Nympholept. Swinburne. VLP
Summer and spring the lovely rose. Not Quite Fair. H. S. Leigh. InMe
Summer and Winter. Shelley. BoNaP

Summer as it passes owes to night, The. Incense. Louise Townsend Nicholl. NePoAm-2
Summer Band Concert. Vivian Smith. CBAP
Summer Beach. Frances Cornford. BrRo; ChMP
Summer, betray this tree again! Misericordia. Margaret Mead. PoA
Summer Christmas in Australia, A. Douglas Sladen. OBCP
Summer cloud in summer blue, The. Cloud and Flame. John Berryman. AP
Summer Comes. Edith Agnew. SiSoSe
Summer comes/ The ziczac hovers. Magalu. Helene Johnson. BlSi; CDC; PoBA; PoNe
Summer comes October, the green becomes the brown. The Long and Lonely Winter. Dave Goulder. OBET
Summer Commentary, A. Yvor Winters. LiTM; QFR
Summer Concert. Reed Whittemore. AmFN
Summer Countries, The. Henry Rago. VGW
Summer Dawn. William Morris. FaBoEn; LoBV; NOBE; OAEL-2; OBEV; OBNC; OBVV; ViBoPo
Summer Day, A. Alexander Hume. LoBV
(Of the Day Estivall.) BSV; NOCV; OxBS
(Midsummer Day in France, *diff. vers.*) FaBoPP
Summer Day in Old Sicily, A. Edward Cracroft Lefroy. *Fr.* Echoes from Theocritus. OBVV
Summer day is full of ease, A. Joyful. Rose Burgunder. RHPC
Summer day suffocates, smothers, pants, The. Poem on Azure. Anna de Noailles, *tr. by* Betty L. Schwimmer. WPOW
Summer Days. Wathen Mark Wilks Call. EBVV
Summer Days. Roy Daniells. CaP
Summer days are come again, The. Samuel Longfellow. TRV
Summer days moved with the pace of a caged lion, The. July in the Jardin des Plantes. Claire McAllister. NePA
Summer Ending, The. Glenway Wescott. PoA
Summer ends now; now, barbarous in beauty, the stooks arise. Hurrahing in Harvest. Gerard Manley Hopkins. BiP; BoNaP; BrPo; ChTr; CMoP; EBCP; FaBoPP; InvP; LO; MoAB; MoBrPo; MoPo; MoVE; VLP
Summer Evening. Charles Cotton. *See* Evening.
Summer Evening. Walter de la Mare. FM; MoAB; MoBrPo; MoShBr; TiPo
Summer Evening, A. Archibald Lampman. PeCV
Summer Evening and Night. James Thomson. *Fr.* The Seasons: Summer. OBEC
Summer Farm. Norman MacCaig. BSV; OxBTC
Summer flows in golden waves, The. Invasion Weather. Douglas Newton. NeBP
Summer Garden. "Anna Akhmatova," *tr. fr. Russian by* Stephen Stepanchev. BoWoP
Summer Gone, A. Howard Moss. NePoEA
Summer hangs. The Death of the Bronx. Chana Bloch. MAYP
Summer harvest day begun, The. July. *At. to* Whittier. YeAr
Summer Harvest Spreads the Fields, The, *with music.* Nathan Strong. AH
Summer Has Come. *Unknown, tr. fr. Middle Irish by* Kuno Meyer. OnYI
Summer holds me here, The. The Aspen's Song. Yvor Winters. POL
Summer holds, The: upon its glittering lake. Chorus. W. H. Auden. *Fr.* The Dog beneath the Skin. OxBTC
Summer Holiday. Robinson Jeffers. CrMA; MoAmPo; MoVE; OxBA
Summer Holidays. W. R. Rodgers. LiTB
Summer Home. Seamus Heaney. IPY
Summer Idyll. George Barker. FaBoMo; MoPo
Summer Images. John Clare. ChTr; OBNC
"Green lane now I traverse, where it goes, The," *sel.* OBRV
Summer in a Small Town. Linda Gregg. MAYP
Summer in England, 1914. Alice Meynell. BrRo; SBG; SUMH; WPE
Summer in the Tehachapi Mountains. Naming. Joseph Stroud. NPGG
Summer Interlude. Lionel Stevenson. CaP
Summer Invocation. William Cox Bennett. *See* Invocation to Rain in Summer.
Summer is, The/ coming. The Cure All. Don L. Lee. CAD
Summer is a chartreuse hell in the mountains. Old Roadside Resorts. Molly Peacock. MAYP
Summer is all a green air. Summer Music. May Sarton. NCSH; NePoAm
Summer Is Come. Earl of Surrey. *See* Soote Season, The.
Summer is come, and evening spreads its gold. Return. Theodore Spencer. PoA
Summer Is Coming, The. Bryan Guinness. OxBI
"Summer is coming, summer is coming." The Throstle. Tennyson. BoNaP; FaPON; HBV-1; HBVY; PBBP; PoSC
Summer Is Ended, The. Christina Rossetti. HBV-2
Summer is fading; the broad leaves that grew. Farewell to Summer. George Arnold. AA
Summer Is Gone. *Unknown, tr. fr. Old Irish.* AnIL *tr. by* Sean O'Faolain; FaBoCh *tr. by* Kuno Meyer; OnYI, *tr. by* Kuno Meyer; PoPl, *tr. by* Sean O'Faolin
Summer is gone and all the merry noise. Autumn. John Clare. SaC
Summer is gone with all its roses. Bitter for Sweet. Christina Rossetti. GBL
Summer Is Icumen [*or* a-Coming] In. *Unknown. See* Cuckoo Song.
Summer is over, The. October. Rose Fyleman. SiSoSe; TiPo
Summer is over, the old cow said. Moo! Robert Hillyer. OBAL; WhC
Summer is the perfect metaphysics. Manitou. Ron Ikan. PPJ
Summer is y-comen in. *Unknown. See* Cuckoo Song.
Summer Island. William Logan. MAYP
Summer journeys. Manhattan. Lorenz Hart. OBAL
Summer Landscape, The; or, The Dragon's Teeth. Rolfe Humphries. NYBP
Summer Lightning. Horatio Colony. TwAmPo
Summer Lightning. T. Sturge Moore. BrPo; SyP
Summer, like a dread disease. Thredbo River. Sydney Jephcott. PoAu-1
Summer Longings. Denis Florence MacCarthy. HBV-1
Summer Magic. Leslie Pinckney Hill. BANP
Summer Malison, The. Gerard Manley Hopkins. CMoP; NoAM; PoEL-5
Summer Mansions. Ruth Herschberger. HoAn
Summer Matures. Helene Johnson. BlSi; CDC; PoNe
Summer Morning. John Clare. PoSC
Summer Morning, A. Rachel Field. PDV; SoPo; SUS; TiPo
Summer Morning. James Thomson. *Fr.* The Seasons: Summer. OBEC
Summer Morning, A. Richard Wilbur. FaBoMo
Summer morning—five o'clock. In the Courtyard. Miriam Ulinover, *tr. by* Seth L. Wolitz. VWA
Summer Music. May Sarton. NCSH; NePoAm
Summer near the River. Carolyn Kizer. CoAP; VGW
Summer nests uncovered by autumn wind, The. Birds' Nests. Edward Thomas. HeIP
Summer Night, A. Matthew Arnold. OAEP; SeCePo; SeCeV
Summer Night, A. W. H. Auden. FaBoRV
Summer Night. Hayim Nachman Bialik, *tr. fr. Hebrew by* Robert Friend. VWA
Summer Night, A. Elizabeth Stoddard. AA
Summer Night. Tennyson. *Fr.* The Princess. *See* Now Sleeps the Crimson Petal.
Summer night, a woman rests. Window. Anne Cherner. AMV-80
Summer Night in the Beehive, A. Charles Tennyson Turner. FM
Summer nights. The Way I Was. Carol Lee Sanchez. TWSS
Summer, 1970. Daniel Halpern. AmPA
Summer 1970. Lindiwe Mabuza. WPOW
Summer, 1960, Minnesota. Robert Bly. InPS
Summer Noon at Sea, A. Epes Sargent. EtS
Summer Noon: 1941. Yvor Winters. CrMA
Summer of nineteen eighteen, The. The Bad Old Days. Kenneth Rexroth. NNap; NoAM; PAI
Summer of sixty-eight. A Day in a Long Hot Summer. Yuri Kageyama. BrSi
Summer of 'sixty-three, sir, and Conrad was gone away. Kentucky Belle. Constance Fenimore Woolson. BeLS; BLPA; FaBoBe; PAH; PH
Summer on the Great American Desert. Rufus B. Sage. BPAW; PoOW
Summer Oracle. Audre Lorde. BlSi; PoBA
Summer Palace burnt, the Winter Palace, wherever it was, The. 10:X:57, 45 Years Since the Fall of the Ch'ing Dynasty. Philip Whalen. NeAP; PoM
Summer pipers have flickered, The. In the Rut. Hamish Brown. PoSH
Summer Pogrom. Fay Zwicky. CBAP
Summer Rain. Hartley Coleridge. VLP
Summer Rain. Laurie Lee. MoVE
Summer Rain. Eve Merriam. PDV
Summer Rain. Sir Herbert Read. LiTM
Summer Rain. Richard Tillinghast. MAYP
Summer Rentals, The. Daniel Halpern. DiL; MAYP
Summer Resort. P. K. Page. CaP
Summer Sabbath. Jessie E. Sampter. TrJP
Summer Sanctuary, A. John Hall Ingham. AA
Summer season at Tyne Dock, The. Tyne Dock. Francis Scarfe. NeBP
Summer set lip to earth's bosom bare. The Poppy. Francis Thompson. MoBrPo
Summer Shower. Emily Dickinson. *See* Drop fell on the apple tree, A.
Summer sits wilting like a lilac woman. The Garden. Marvin Solomon. NePoAm
Summer Sky. Ruth McKee Gordon. TiPo
Summer slams the tropic sun, The. A Country Club Romance. Derek Walcott. OxBC
Summer Solstice, *sel.* George Bowering.
"I am slowly dying, water evaporating." NOBC
Summer Song. E. Nesbit. PoSC
Summer Song, A. George Peele. *See* When as the Rye.
Summer Song. W. W. Watt. FiBHP; QQQ
Summer Song I. George Barker. ChMP

Summer Stars. Carl Sandburg. RFM; YeAr
Summer still plays across the street. Dying: An Introduction. L. E. Sissman. NYBP
Summer Storm. Lionel Johnson. BrPo
Summer Storm. Richard B. Kent. AMV-80
Summer Storm. John Montague. IPY
Summer Storm. Louis Simpson. ErPo; OxBC
Summer Storm. Louis Untermeyer. UnTE
Summer Storm, A. Charles Whitehead. OBRV
Summer Story, The. John Lehmann. MP
Summer Street. Ana Ilce, *tr. fr. Spanish by* Steven White. AMV-81
Summer Sun. Robert Louis Stevenson. MoBrPo
Summer Sunday morning, A. A Battle Ballad. Francis Orrery Ticknor. PAH
Summer Sunshine. Mary A. Lathbury. YeAr
Summer that I was ten, The. The Centaur. May Swenson. GrPl; MP; NePoAm-2; NMM; PH; SO; TwAmPo; TwCP
Summer, this is our flesh. Seasons of the Soul. Allen Tate. AP; CrMA; MoPo; NePA; OxBA
Summer Twilight, A. Charles Tennyson Turner. OBRV
Summer Vacation. Wordsworth. *Fr.* The Prelude, IV. PoEL-4
Summer Visitors. Stephen Clark. AMV-81
Summer voice. Musketaquit, The. Two Rivers. Emerson. AmPP
Summer was dry, dry the garden. On the Debt My Mother Owed to Sears Roebuck. Edward Dorn. ConAP
Summer was over, the season unkind, The. The Colliers' March. John Freeth. OBET
Summer was sauntering by. Austin Clarke. Mnemosyne Lay in Dust, XVII. IPY
Summer Wind. Bryant. AP; PoEL-4
Summer Wish. Louise Bogan. TwAmPo
Summer Wish, A. Christina Rossetti. OBNC
Summer Wooing, A. Louise Chandler Moulton. HBV-1
Summer Words of a Sistuh Addict. Sonia Sanchez. BPo
(Summer Words for a Sister Addict.) BlSi; UnPo
Summerhouse. Melvin Walker La Follette. NePoEA
Summers and summers have come, and gone with the flight of the swallow. The Tantramar Revisited. Sir Charles G. D. Roberts. CaP; NOBC; OBCV
Summer's Day, A. Alexander Hume. CH
Summer's Dream, A. Elizabeth Bishop. OxBC
Summer's Early End at Hudson Bay. Hayden Carruth. NYBP
Summer's gone brown, and, with it. Me to You. Alastair Reid. NYBP
Summer's last half moon waning high. 16. ix. 65. James Merrill. NAs
Summer's Last Will and Testament, *sels.* Thomas Nashe.
Adieu, Farewell, Earth's Bliss[e] CH; EBEV; ElL; ELP; HAP; HeIP; InvP; LoBV; OAEP; PPoe; QFR; TEP; ViBoPo; WeW
(Death's Summons.) HBV-2
(Dust Hath Closed Helen's Eye.) SeCePo
(In a Time of Pestilence.) HoPM; OBEV; TrGrPo
(In Plague Time.) FaBoCh; FaPoR; OBSC
(In Time of Pestilence.) DTC; NOBE; PoPle
(In Time of Plague.) EnRePo
(Litany in Time of Plague, A.) CABA; DL; NIP; NoP; OAEL-1; PAI; PoRA; PPP; PrIm
(Lord, Have Mercy on Us.) ChTr
(Song: "Adieu, farewell earth's blisse.") FaBoEn; PoEL-2
(Song in Time of Plague.) SCV
A-Maying, a-Playing. ElL
(Clownish Song, A.) OBSC
Autumn. ElL; LoBV; OAEL-1; OBSC; TrGrPo
(Autumn Hath All.) QFR
(Autumn Hath All the Summer's Fruitful Treasure.) EnRePo
Fair Summer Droops. ElL; LoBV
(Waning Summer.) OBSC
Harvest. OBSC
Spring, the Sweet Spring. CH; HeIP; LiTB; NIP; NoP; ViBoPo
(Spring.) BoNaP; ElL; GTBS; GTBS-P; HBV-1; NOBE; OBEV; OBSC; OnUR; TrGrPo; WiR
Summer's Farewell. PoEL-2
Summer's morning sun creeps up the blue, The. Sunrise in Summer. John Clare. FaBoPP
Summer's pleasures they are gone like to visions every one. Remembrances. John Clare. NCEP
Summer's residue, The. Lines with a Gift of Herbs. Janet Lewis. QFR
Summer's sun is warm and bright. Pleasant Changes. Jane Euphemia Browne. OxBChV
"Summertime and the Living." Robert Hayden. BPo; NCSH; PoBA; PPP; TwCP
Summery Windermere, sweet lake! From Four Lakes' Days. Richard Eberhart. MiAP
Summing-Up, The. Stanley Kunitz. ELU; OBAL; PoPl
Summing Up, A. Gabriel Preil, *tr. fr. Hebrew by* Jeremy Garber. VWA
Summing Up, The. James Simmons. POL
Summing Up in Italy. Elizabeth Barrett Browning. VLP
Summit, The. Kathleen Raine. Beinn Naomh, IV. OxBS
Summit Lake. Mark Thalman. AMV-81
Summits and vales, slim cypresses and pines. Santa Maria del Fiore. George Herbert Clarke. CaP
Summoned. Diana O Hehir. NPGG
Summoned by Bells, *sels.* John Betjeman.
"Afternoons, The/ Brought coconut smell of gorse". FaBoPP
Back Again for the Holidays. FaBoPP
"My dear deaf father, how I loved him then." OxBTC
Summoned by love and heat and God knows what. News from the Court. David Wagoner. NePoAm-2; NePoEA-2
Summoned by the frantic powers. Summoned. Diana O Hehir. NPGG
Summonee's Tale, The. Stanley J. Sharpless. BXAP; FaBoPa
Summons, The. James Dickey. LiSp
Summons. Arthur Davison Ficke. Sonnets of a Portrait Painter, XIV. HBMV
Summons, The. James Laughlin. LiTA
Summons, The. Elizabeth Roberts MacDonald. CaP
Summons, The. Milton. *Fr.* Paradise Lost, I. WHA
(Satan's Legions and the Beech Leaves of the Casentino.) FaBoPP
Summons, The. W. W. E. Ross. CaP
Summons to Execution. John Webster. *See* Hark, Now Everything Is Still.
Summons to Love. William Drummond of Hawthornden. *See* Phoebus, Arise.
Summum Bonum. Robert Browning. ELU; HBV-1; OHFP
Sumter. Henry Howard Brownell. PAH
Sumter. Edmund Clarence Stedman. PAH
Sumter—A Ballad of 1861. *Unknown.* PAH
Sumter's Band. J. W. Simmons. PAH
Sun, The. John Davis. NA
Sun. James Dickey. CAPP
Sun, The. John Drinkwater. FaPON; NTCP; SoPo; TiPo
Sun, The. Andrew Oerke. PoA
Sun. Henry Rowe. OBEV
Sun, The. Anne Sexton. NYBP; PBWP
Sun, The. Francis Thompson. *Fr.* Ode to the Setting Sun. MoAB; MoBrPo
Sun, The. W. J. Turner. MoBrPo
Sun, The, *sel.* Vidya, *tr. fr. Sanskrit by* Daniel H. H. Ingalls.
"I praise the disk of the rising sun." PBWP; WPOW
Sun, The/ Is warm to-day. Roma Aeterna. Adelaide Crapsey. QFR
Sun/ proud Bessemer. World Winter. Earle Birney. GrPl
Sun and Cloud. Melville Cane. PoPl
Sun and I. Ken Mammone. AMV-81
Sun and Moon. Jay Macpherson. SoSe
Sun and moon at the same time. On Certain Days of the Year. Nancy Simpson. AMV-81
Sun and Moon So High and Bright, The, *with music. Unknown.* AH
Sun and moon, that ceaselessly obey, The. Immortal Israel. Judah Halevi, *tr. by* Solomon Solis-Cohen. TrJP
Sun and Rain and Dew from Heaven. Adam Lindsay Gordon. *Fr.* Ye Wearie Wayfarer. PoLF
Sun and rain at work together. The Red-Gold Rain. Sacheverell Sitwell. MoBrPo
Sun and softness. Sun Song. Langston Hughes. CNA
Sun and the Moon and Fear of Loneliness, The. *Tr. fr. Eskimo.* WTO
Sun and Wind, The. Owen Felltham. CavP
Sun appeared so smug and bright, The. The Silver Question. Oliver Herford. NA
Sun appearing, The: a pendant. Plainview: 3. N. Scott Momaday. CDW
Sun, as hot as he was bright, The. In Search of the Picturesque. William Combe. *Fr.* Dr. Syntax in Search of the Picturesque. OBRV
Sun at noon to higher air, The. March. A. E. Housman. FaBoCh
Sun became a small round moon, The. Climbing in Glencoe. Andrew Young. LiSp
Sun blazes over empty. Volleyball Teacher Ends the Game. José Y. Terán, Jr. LFAC
Sun blazing slowly in its last hour, The. An Evening. Robert Mezey. NaP
Sun blooms in our bodies. Summer. Tom Marshall. NOBC
Sun breaks over the eucalyptus. Marin-An. Gary Snyder. TAT
Sun, bright lemon from the blinds, The. Morning Light. Louis Dudek. AMV-80
Sun burns on its sultry wick, The. Elegy Written on a Frontporch. Karl Shapiro. MoPo
Sun burns out, The. The Last Fire. Moishe Steingart, *tr. by* Gabriel Preil. VWA
Sun Came, The. Etheridge Knight. NeAC; PoBA
Sun Came Out in April, The. C. Day Lewis. MoBS

Sun came up, The. Rain Rain on the Splintered Girl. Ishmael Reed. PoBA
Sun cheers us for a pin-point, flicks, then westers. Mating Answer. Ronald Bottrall. PoA
Sun Children. Leslie Silko. VoR
Sun claims these streets. Following Van Gogh (Avignon, 1982). Marla Puziss. PoDr
Sun comes up and the sun goes down, The. The Fallow Field. Julia Caroline Ripley Dorr. AA
Sun cracks down on Cambridge like a voice, The. Winter Term. John Malcolm Brinnin. GLGT
Sun dazzle and black shadow. Mending the Adobe. Hayden Carruth. EyDe; Psk
Sun descending in the west, The. Night. Blake. *Fr.* Songs of Innocence. BLPL; BoNaP; CH; EnRP; FaBoBe; FaPON; HBV-1; HBVY; OBEC; OBEV; OxBChV; OxBoCh; PoLF; TreFT; WiR
Sun does arise, The. The Echoing [*or* Ecchoing] Green. Blake. *Fr.* Songs of Innocence. CABA; CH; LAuP; OBEC; PoSC; UnPo; WiR
Sun drew off at last his piercing fires, The. Witchcraft: New Style. Lascelles Abercrombie. MoBrPo
Sun drops below the elms. Routes. Peter Everwine. FiCP; NNaP
Sun Drops Red, The. Nellie Burget Miller. PoOW
Sun finds your eye, The. Aubade after the Party. Tom O'Grady. FAZ
Sun from the east tips the mountains with gold, The. Hunting Song. Paul Whitehead. *Fr.* Apollo and Daphne. OBEC; OxBoLi
Sun gas coughed, A. A million miles of flame. In the Year of Many Conversions and the Private Soul. John Ciardi. MiAP
Sun God, The. Aubrey Thomas De Vere. ACP; OBVV
Sun, God's eye, The. The Nature of Love. James Kirkup. EaLo
Sun goes down, and over all, The. Low Tide on Grand Pré. Bliss Carman. CaP; NOBC; OBCV; PeCV
Sun goes down for hours, taking more of her along, The. The Lady in the Pink Mustang. Louise Erdrich. TWSS
Sun goes lime in a throng of oak. First Reader. Paris Leary. CoPo
Sun Gonna Shine in My Door Some Day, *with music. Unknown.* OuSiCo
Sun had begun in the gloaming, The. The First Snow-fall. James Russell Lowell. AA
Sun had clos'd the winter-day, The. The Vision. Burns. BSV, 5 *sts.*; OxBS
Sun had long since in the lap, The. Godly Casuistry. Samuel Butler. *Fr.* Hudibras, II, 2. OBS
Sun had set, The;/ The leaves with dew. Keenan's Charge. George Parsons Lathrop. AA; HBV-2; PAH
Sun had sunk beneath the west, The. The Ocean-Fight. *Unknown.* PAH
Sun has come, I know, The. The Sun. W. J. Turner. MoBrPo
Sun has gone down o'er the lofty Benlomond, The. Jessie, the Flower o' Dunblane. Robert Tannahill. HBV-1
Sun has kissed the violet sea, The. Betrayal. Sidney Lanier. *Fr.* The Jaquerie. AA
Sun Has Long Been Set, The. Wordsworth. YeAr
Sun has risen on the eastern brim of the world, The. The Song of Lo-fu. *Unknown, tr. by* Arthur Waley. AWP
Sun Has Set, The. Emily Brontë. UnPo; ViBoPo
("Sun has set, and the long grass now, The.") VLP
Sun has set, the stars are still, The. The Fair-Haired Girl. *Unknown, tr. by* Sir Samuel Ferguson. OnYI
Sun has sucked and beat the encircling hills, The. In Hospital: Poona, II. Alun Lewis. DTC
Sun [*or* Sonne] hath twice [*or* twyse] brought forth[e] the [*or* his] tender green, The. The Restless State of a Lover. Earl of Surrey. AAS; GoTL; SiPS
Sun Heals, A. Jewel C. Latimore. JB
Sun, his journey ending in the west, The. Henry Constable. *Fr.* Diana. OBSC
Sun in Capricorn, The. Joyce Mansour, *tr. fr. French by* Carol Cosman. PBWP
Sun, in clownish yellow, but not a clown, The. Wallace Stevens. *Fr.* Esthétique du Mal. NOBA
Sun is a gold coin slipping into, The/ an envelope of sea. Mediterranean. Ruth Whitman. VWA
Sun is a huntress young, The. An Indian Summer Day on the Prairie. Vachel Lindsay. BPAW; RFM; SoPo
Sun is a rose window. To a Butterfly. L. Pearl Schuck. AMV-80
Sun is always in the sky, The. Breakfast Time. James Stephens. SUS
Sun is blue and scarlet on my page, The. Falling Asleep over the Aeneid. Robert Lowell. AP; CoBMV; CrMA; MoAmPo; NoAM; OxBA; TwAmPo
Sun is clear of bird and cloud, The. Alulvan. Walter de la Mare. MoVE
Sun is eclipsed, The; and one by one. Poetry Today. John Heath-Stubbs. POL
Sun is folding, cars stall and rise, The. The New World. Amiri Baraka. NoAM; NoP
Sun is going down, The. Aranda Song. *Unknown, tr. by* T. G. H. Strehlow. CBAP
Sun is gray and without a rim, The. Father Fisheye. Peter Balakian. MAYP
Sun is high, The. Young Saxons shouldering oars. North Shore. Peter Davison. CoPo
Sun is in the sky, mother, the flowers are springing fair, The. The Biter Bit. William Edmondstoune Aytoun. InMe
Sun is lord and god, sublime, serene, The. The Lake of Gaube. Swinburne. OAEL-2; VLP
Sun is low, to say the least, The. The Sunset. Gelett Burgess. FaBoNo; HBVY
Sun is mine, The. Song. Robert Hogg. WHW
Sun is nigh the verge, The. Soon we must part. A Walk. Hedwig Lachmann, *tr. by* Jethro Bithell. TrJP
Sun is not abed, when I, The. The Sun's Travels. Robert Louis Stevenson. FaPON
Sun is not in love with us, The. The Isles of Greece. Demetrios Capetanakis. GTBS-P
Sun is rising, The. Healing Song. *Tr. by* Frances Densmore. OBVE
Sun is sad, The. Tree. Harold LaMont Otey. LFAC
Sun is set, The; the swallows are asleep. Evening; Ponte al Mare, Pisa. Shelley. SyP
Sun is shining in my backdoor, The. Myself When I Am Real. Al Young. CNA; PoBA
Sun is sinking over hill and sea, The. At Night. George Edgar Montgomery. AA
Sun is the blind eyes of statues gilded, The. The Sun. Andrew Oerke. PoA
Sun is the center of the universe, The. Nicholas Copernicus (1473-1543). Siv Cedering. *Fr.* Letters from the Astronomers. SUW
Sun is warm, the sky is clear, The. Stanzas Written in Dejection near Naples. Shelley. CABA; ChER; EnRP; FaBV; FiP; GTBS; GTBS-P; NoP; OAEP; OBRV; PoRA; TEP; ViBoPo; WHA
Sun itself was cheering, so they said, The. Independence. Roy McFadden. OxBI
Sun like an orange mousse through the trees. Dog Day Vespers. Charles Wright. LCAP
Sun looked from his everlasting skies, The. My Old Counselor. Gertrude Hall. AA
Sun makes music as of old, The. Prologue in Heaven [*or* The Chorus of the Archangels]. Goethe, *tr. by* Shelley. *Fr.* Faust. AWP; OBVE
Sun makes my skin burn, The. Tryst. Derek Butler. LFAC
Sun may be visible or not, The. Drawings by Children. Lisel Mueller. PoDr
Sun May Set, The. Sir Walter Ralegh, *after the Latin of* Catullus. FaBoRV (Lines from Catullus.) EnRePo; SiPS
("Sun [*or* Sunne] may set and rise, The.") FaBoEE; OBVE
Sun Men Call It, The. John Hall Wheelock. NePoAm-2
Sun, moon, and tides. The Kitchen Cupboard. Allen Curnow. *Fr.* Trees, Effigies, Moving Objects. OCNZ
Sun Moon Kelp Flower or Goat. Linda Gregg. NPGG
Sun now darts his fervid rays, The. Lines Written in the Dog-Days. William Woty. NOEC
Sun Now Risen, The, *with music.* Johann Conrad Beissel. AH
Sun of Grace, The. *Unknown.* OxBM
Sun of [*or* on] Ivera, The/ No longer shines brightly. Dirge of [*or* The Lament for] O'Sullivan Bear[e]. *Unknown, tr. by* Jeremiah [*or* James] Joseph Callanan. AnIV; NBM
Sun of July beats down on the small white house, The. Small White House. Robert Penn Warren. *Fr.* Notes on a Life to Be Lived. NoAM
Sun of life has crossed the line, The. Equinoctial. Adeline D. T. Whitney. HBV-1
Sun of My Perfection Is a Glass, The. Attar, *tr. fr. Persian.* ILwL
Sun of the Center. Robert Kelly. CoPo
Sun of the moral world; effulgent source. Freedom. Joel Barlow. PAL
Sun of the Sleepless! Byron. MOON
Sun of the stately day. The National Ode. Bayard Taylor. PAH
Sun, of whose terrain we creatures are, The. Solar Creation. Charles Madge. FaBoMo; OBMV; OxBTC
Sun on his face wakes him. Morning Song. Gregory Orr. MAYP
Sun on Ivera, The. *See* Sun of Ivera, The.
Sun on the tree-tops no longer is seen, The. Queen Sabbath. Hayyim Nahman Bialik, *tr. by* Jessie Sampter. TrJP
Sun over the horizon, The. Morning Once More. Joy Harjo. TWSS
Sun revolving on his axis turns, The. The Copernican System. Thomas Chatterton. FaBoUs
Sun rises, The. In Fields of Summer. Galway Kinnell. BoNaP; RFM; VGW
Sun Rises Bright in France, The. Allan Cunningham. BSV; HBV-2; OBRV
Sun [*or* Sunne] Rising, The. John Donne. AnAnS-1; BiP; BoLoP; CABA; EnRePo; FF; GBL; HAP; HeIP; InPS; InvP; JCP; LiTB; LoBV; MeLP;

MePo; NIP; NOBE; NoP; OAEL-1; OAEP; PAI; PoEL-2; PoPle; PPP; SCV; SeCePo; SeCeV; SeCP, SeCV-1; SoSe; TEP; TrGrPo; UnTE; WeW
Sun rose over a mound of corpses, The. I Hear a Voice. H. Leivick, *tr. by* David G. Roskies. VWA
Sun rushed up the sky, The; the taxi flew. Parting as Descent. John Berryman. LiTA; MoAmPo
Sun saw on that widening shore, The. Sainte Anne de Beaupre. Richard Eberhart. NePoAm
Sun scanned the river with its lidless, The. The Breakdown. Sherod Santos. MAYP
Sun Set. Umberto Aridjis, *tr. fr. Spanish by* Eliot Weinberger. AMV-81
Sun Set, and Up Rose the Yellow Moon, The. Byron. *Fr.* Don Juan, I. MOON
Sun set, but set not his hope, The. Character. Emerson. AA; LiTA
Sun sets in the cold without friends, The. Dusk in Winter. W. S. Merwin. NaP
Sun sets on a bright blameless wall a barrage of rays. In Impressions of Hawk Feathers Willow Leaves Shadow. Elizabeth Woody. STE
Sun sets, The. The wind moans. Ts'ai Yen, *tr. by* Kenneth Rexroth *and* Ling Chung. Eighteen Verses Sung to a Tatar Reed Whistle, VII. BoWoP; WPOW
Sun shines, The. Tommies in the Train. D. H. Lawrence. MMA
Sun shines bright in the [*or* on my *or* in our] old Kentucky home, The. My Old Kentucky Home. Stephen Collins Foster. AA; BLSo; FaBoBe; FaBV; FaFP; FSW; HBV-2; PoLF; PSoN; TrAS; TreF; TrGrPo
Sun shines high on yonder hill, The. The False Lover [Won Back]. *Unknown.* ESPB; OxBB
Sun Shines over the Mountain, The. *Unknown.* AmFP
Sun shines warm on seven old soldiers, The. The Oldest Soldier. Robert Graves. DTC
Sun shone in my hut, The. He Who Has Lost All. David Diop, *tr. by* Anne Atik. TTY
Sun sinks softly to his ev'ning post, The. The Rejected "National Hymns." "Orpheus C. Kerr." InMe; OBAL
Sun, slicing near the edge, The. Meeting Halfway. R. Wayne Hardy. LFAC
Sun Song. Langston Hughes. CNA
Sun sought thy dim bed and brought forth light, The. Africa. Claude McKay. BALP
Sun sounds, according to ancient custom, The. The Chorus of the Archangels. Goethe, *tr. by* Shelley. *Fr.* Faust. OBVE
Sun Spirit, The, *sel.* Ralph Chubb.
"At the time of puberty I had obsessions." PeHV
Sun streaked the coffee urn. The Deaths of Paragon, Indiana. John Woods. CoPo
Sun strikes gold the dirty street, The. Brest Left Behind. John Chipman Farrar. PAH
Sun strikes those windows blind. The Library. Mary Mills. NePoAm
Sun struts over the asphalt world, The. Noon of the Sunbather. Marge Piercy. NMM
Sun, stun me, sustain me. On Looking into Henry Moore. Dorothy Livesay. OBCV
Sun, that brave man, The. The Brave Man. Wallace Stevens. SOTW
Sun that brief December day, The. Snow-Bound; a Winter Idyl. Whittier. AmPP; AP; FaBV; GN; NOBA; OxBA; TAP; TrGrPo; WiR
Sun that in Breadalbane's lake doth fall, The. The Botanist's Vision. Sydney Dobell. VLP
Sun, the moon, the stars, the seas, the hills and the plains, The. The Higher Pantheism. Tennyson. HBV-2; SpRo; TRV; VLP; WGRP
Sun, the rose, the lily, the dove, The. Love's Résumé. Heine, *tr. by* J. F. C. TrJP
Sun-treader—life and light be thine for ever. Shelley. Robert Browning. *Fr.* Pauline. OBRV; VLP
Sun-up in March. Abbie Huston Evans. NePoAm
Sun upon the lake is low, The. Datur Hora Quieti. Sir Walter Scott. GTBS; GTBS-P
Sun upon the Weirdlaw Hill, The. The Dreary Change. Sir Walter Scott. BSV; FaBoPP; OAEL-2; OBNC
Sun Used to Shine, The. Edward Thomas. FaBoTw
Sun was bright when we went in, The. At the Theater. Rachel Field. FaPON
Sun was down, and twilight grey, The. In the Room. James Thompson. OBVV
Sun was now withdrawn, The. Damon and Cupid. John Gay. EnLoPo; SeCeV
Sun was shining on the sea, The. The Walrus and the Carpenter. "Lewis Carroll." *Fr.* Through the Looking-Glass. BeLS; BLPA; FaBoBe; FaBoCo; FaBoNo; FaBV; FaFP; FaPON; FiBHP; FPL; GN; HBV-2; HBVY; InMe; LiTB; NA; NOBL; OxBChV; PoRA; SoPo; TEP; TreF
Sun was sinking in the west, The. The Dying Ranger [*or* Soldier]. *Unknown.* CoSo; ShS
Sun was sinking when we reached the glen, The. On Walking Back to the Bus. Alan Gardner. PoSH
Sun Was Slumbering in the West, The. Thomas Hood. FiBHP
Sun was warm but the wind was chill, The. Early April. Robert Frost. YeAr
Sun went down behind yon hill, The. The Farmer's Boy. *Unknown.* OBET
Sun which doth the greatest comfort bring[e], The. Mr. Francis Beaumont's Letter [from the Country] to Ben Jonson [*or* A Letter to Ben Jonson]. Francis Beaumont. LoBV; OBS; SeCP; ViBoPo
Sun Wields Mercy, The. Charles Bukowski. MAT
Sun-Witch to the Sun, The. George Howe. NYBP
Sun, with his great eye, The. Daisy's Song. Keats. BoNaP
Sun woke me this morning loud, The. A True Account of Talking to the Sun at Fire Island. Frank O'Hara. NNaP; SOTW
Sun, yon glorious orb of day, The. The Sun. John Davis. NA
Sun-Bather, The. Kim Kurt. NePoAm-2
Sunbather, The. Vernon Watkins. MoPo; MoVE
Sunbeam, The. *Unknown.* NA
Sunbeam Said, Be Happy, The. Wordsworth. *Fr.* The Recluse, I. FaBoRV
Sun-beames in the East are spred, The. Epithalamion Made at Lincolnes Inne. John Donne. OBS; SeCP
Sunbeams streamed without, The. In the Morgue. Israel Zangwill. TrJP
Sunburst cabbage in grey light. Return. Richard Tillinghast. MAYP
Sunday. Elizabeth J. Coatsworth. AmFN
Sunday. George Herbert. OBS; SeCV-1; TrCP
Sunday. Josephine Miles. PoA
Sunday. Lawrence R. Rungren. AMV-80
Sunday. Vern Rutsala. DFF
Sunday Afternoon. Denise Levertov. ConAP; IHMS; PAI
Sunday Afternoon. Philip Levine. NaP
Sunday afternoon/ and couples walk the breakwater. Veracruz. Robert Hayden. AmNP
Sunday afternoon and the water. Fording the River. Seamus Deane. CIP
Sunday Afternoon in Italy. D. H. Lawrence. BrPo
Sunday Afternoon Service in St. Enodoc Church, Cornwall. John Betjeman. MoVE; NOCV
Sunday Afternoons. Anthony Thwaite. OxBTC
Sunday and sunlight ashen on the Square. The Self Unsatisfied Runs Everywhere. Delmore Schwartz. PoA
Sunday at Hampstead, *sel.* James Thomson ("B.V.").
"As we rush, as we rush in the train." ViBoPo
(In the Train.) OBEV
Sunday at the End of Summer. Howard Nemerov. BoNaP
Sunday Crappies. Jim Thomas. WOLT
Sunday Evening. Barbara Guest. NeAP
Sunday Evening in the Common. John Hall Wheelock. HBV-2; MoAmPo
Sunday evening. The thick-lipped men binoculared. Merthymawr. George Woodcock. NeBP
Sunday Evenings. John Hollander. NYBP; NYP
Sunday Funnies. Anna Keiter. DFF
Sun-Day Hymn, A. Oliver Wendell Holmes. *Fr.* The Professor at the Breakfast Table. TrPWD; TRV; WGRP
(Lord of All Being, Throned Afar, *with music.*) AH
Sunday in Cambridge, A. Eddie Linden. PeHV
Sunday in Glastonbury. Robert Bly. ConAP
Sunday in Old England. *Kearsarge.* S. Weir Mitchell. PAH
Sunday in South Carolina. Robert Parham. AMV-80
Sunday in the Country. May Swenson. NePoAm-2
Sunday in the Park. William Carlos Williams. *Fr.* Paterson. CrMA
Sunday is the dullest day, treating. Sweeney in Articulo. "Myra Buttle." *Fr.* The Sweeniad. BXAP; FaBoPa; Par
Sunday, July 14th; a Fine Day at the Baths. Julian Symons. WaP
Sunday lamb cracks in its fat, The. Mary's Song. Sylvia Plath. FaBoMo
Sunday Morning. James Grahame. OBRV
Sunday Morning. Christina Jenkins. BrRo
Sunday Morning. Louis MacNeice. CoBMV; FaBoMo; HeIP; LiTB; MoAB; MoBrPo; MoVE; NIP
Sunday Morning. Wayne Moreland. PoBA
Sunday Morning. Wallace Stevens. AmPP; AP; BiP; BLPL; CABA; CMoP; CoBMV; CrMA; FaBoEn; HAP; HeIP; LiTA; LiTM; MasP; MoAB; MoAmPo; MoVE; NePA; NIP; NOBA; NoP; OxBA; PoA, *early version*; PPoe; QFR; SeCeV; TAP; TwAmPo; WeW
Sunday Morning. L. A. G. Strong. WhC
Sunday morning and her mother's hands. Birmingham 1963. Raymond R. Patterson. CNA; GP; PoBA
Sunday morning, blues on the radio. Morning After. Mark Vinz. PPJ
Sunday morning just at nine. Down Went McGinty. Joseph Flynn. FSN; TreF; YaD
Sunday Morning, King's Cambridge. John Betjeman. EaLo
Sunday morning restlessness. Second Reading. Richard Beyer. AMV-81
Sunday: New Guinea. Karl Shapiro. AmFN; PoPl

Sunday Night in Santa Rosa. Dana Gioia. GrPl
Sunday Night Walk. Raymond Souster. CaP
Sunday on Hampstead Heath. George Woodcock. NeBP
Sunday: Outskirts of Knoxville, Tennessee. James Agee. ErPo
Sunday Rain. John Updike. DFF
Sunday Review Section. Baron Wormser. MAYP
Sunday School Teacher Speaks, A. *Unknown.* STF
Sunday Service. Michael Heffernan. BXAP
Sunday shuts down on this twentieth-century evening. Boy with His Hair Cut Short. Muriel Rukeyser. InPK; LiTM; MoAB; MP; PoPl; RoGo; TwAmPo; TwCP; VGW; WPE
Sunday Stroll. Michael Pettit. MAYP
Sunday strollers along a sewage-choked Schuylkill. To Some Millions Who Survive Joseph E. Mander, Sr. Sarah E. Wright. PoBA
Sunday the only day we don't work. A Walk. Gary Snyder. NoAM; NOBA
Sunday the sea made morning worship, sang. Half-Tide Ledge. R. P. Blackmur. MOS; TwAmPo
Sunday, the shout of hosannas. His Last Week. Elinor Lennen. PGD
Sunday up the River, *sels.* James Thomson. ("B.V.")
Bridge, The, II. OBVV
"Church bells are ringing, The," IV. OAEP
Gifts, XV. HBV-1; OBEV; OBVV; TreF
"I looked out into the morning," I. OAEP; ViBoPo
Song: "Let my voice ring out and over the earth," XVII. HBV-1; OBVV; TreFT
Song: "Like violets pale i' the spring o' the year." IX. OBVV
Song: "My love is the flaming sword," XVI. OBVV
"Were I a real Poet, I would sing," X. OAEP
"Wine of Love is music, The," XVIII. OBEV; OBVV; ViBoPo
(Vine, The.) HBV-1
Sundays. Marieve Rugo. AMV-81
Sundays too my father got up early. Those Winter Sundays. Robert Hayden. CNA; CTBA; DFF; DiL; FF; GP; GrPl; HAP; HoAn; IDB; LCAP; NoAM; NoP; PoBA; PPP; SoSe; UnPo; WeW
Sundays Visiting. Alberto Rios. Str
Sundays when the wind blows. Sunday. Lawrence R. Rungren. AMV-80
Sunder me from my bones, O sword of God. The Sword of Surprise. G. K. Chesterton. MoBrPo
Sundered. John Barford. PeHV
Sundered. Israel Zangwill. TrJP
Sundew, The. Swinburne. ELP; NoP; OBNC; VLP
Sun-dial, The. Thomas Love Peacock. *Fr.* Melincourt. OBNC; OBRV
Sundown. Léonie Adams. MoAB; MoAmPo; TrGrPo; TwAmPo
Sundown at Darlington 1878. Lance Henson. VoR
Sundowner, The. Shaw Neilson. CBAP; PoAu-1
Sunflakes. Frank Asch. NTCP
Sunflower, The. Blake. *See* Ah! Sun-Flower.
Sun-Flower, The. Dora Greenwell. WPE
Sunflower. Rolf Jacobsen, *tr. fr. Norwegian by* Robert Bly. NU
Sunflower. John Updike. BoNaP; CrPl
Sunflower ain't de daisy, De. Doan't You Be What You Ain't. Edwin Milton Royle. BLPA
Sunflower Moccasins. Phillip William George. VoR
Sunflower, of flowers. Sunflower. John Updike. BoNaP; GrPl
Sunflower Rock. Paul Blackburn. NoAM
Sunflower Sutra. Allen Ginsberg. AmPP; CoAP; MAT; NeAP; NOBA
Sunflower to the Sun, The. Mary Elizabeth DeWitt Stebbins. AA
Sunflowers. Clinton Scollard. HBMV
Sunflowers, The. Douglas Stewart. POL
Sunflowers and Saturdays. Melba Joyce Boyd. BlSi
Sung by a Young Girl. Dryden. *See* Song for a Girl.
Sung on a Sunny Morning. Jean Starr Untermeyer. TrPWD
Sunglare and sea pale as tears. Blackfish Poem. Milton Acorn. NeAC
Sungrazer. Alvin Greenberg. FAZ
Sunk earlier in the silence of gray cashmere. Slepynge Long in Greet Quiete Is Eek a Greet Norice to Leccherie. John Hollander. ErPo
Sunk Lyonesse. Walter de la Mare. CoBMV; FaBoCh; LiTM
Sunken Evening [in Trafalgar Square]. Laurie Lee. LiTM; NYBP
Sunken Garden, The. Walter de la Mare. HBMV
Sunken Gold. Eugene Lee-Hamilton. EtS; NCEP
Sunlicht still on me, you row'd in clood, The. At My Father's Grave. "Hugh MacDiarmid." ELU; GTBS-P
Sunlight. Joseph Bruchac. AMV-80
Sunlight. Seamus Heaney. *See* Mossbawn: Two Poems in Dedication.
Sunlight and Sea. Alfred Noyes. MOS
Sunlight and summer wind are never sure. The Attic. Charles Bruce. *Fr.* The Flowing Summer. CaP
Sunlight drawing from shadow, up and down the street. Passages. Larry Eigner. NeAP
Sunlight falls happily upon this sea. Tranquil Sea. Claire Aven Thomson. EtS
Sunlight folds back pages of quiet shadows. At Hans Christian Andersen's Birthplace, Odense, Denmark. Maurice Lindsay. BSV
Sunlight from the sky's own heart. A Song of Handicrafts. Annie Matheson. OBVV
Sunlight glints off the chrome of many cars. Family Reunion. Jim Wayne Miller. Str
Sunlight in a Cafeteria. Criss E. Cannady. PoDr
Sunlight in the house. Maritimes. Penelope Shuttle. BrRo
Sunlight lies along my table. The Weather of Six Mornings. Jane Cooper. IHMS; NYBP
Sunlight, moonlight. Dream-Song. Walter de la Mare. PoPle
Sunlight on the Garden, The. Louis MacNeice. BiP; CMoP; CoBMV; EBEV; GTBS-P; HAP; LiTB; MoPo; MP; NoAM; NOBE; NoP; OAEP; OxBI; OxBTC; PPoe; PrIm; TwCP
Sunlight passes through the mountain as if the stone. Sunlight. Joseph Bruchac. AMV-80
Sunlight pillars through glass, probes each desk. The Play Way. Seamus Heaney. NoP
Sunlight speaks, and its voice is a bird, The. The Hummingbird. Harry Hibbard Kemp. FaPON; HBMV
Sunlight that pulls itself over the roof-tops looks vacant, The. Inertia. Kirti Chaudhari, *tr. by* Leonard Nathan. WPOW
Sunlight the tall women may never have seen. Children, the Sandbar, That Summer. Muriel Rukeyser. LCAP
Sunlit Vale, The. Edmund Blunden. ChMP; MoVE
Sunne begins uppon my heart to shine, The. William Alabaster. AnAnS-1
Sunne may set and rise, The. *See* Sun May Set, The.
Sunne Rising, The. John Donne. *See* Sun Rising, The.
Sunning. James S. Tippett. GDP; RHPC; SiSoSe; SUS; TiPo
Sunny. Robert Vander Molen. FAZ
Sunny Bank. *Unknown.* *See* As I Sat on a Sunny Bank.
Sunny hair and eyes of wonder. A Little Person. Brian Hooker. HBMV
Sunny Prestatyn. Philip Larkin. CABA; NoAM
Sunny shaft did I behold, A. Glycine's Song. Samuel Taylor Coleridge. *Fr.* Zapolya. CH; OBEV; PBBP; PoPl; PoSC
Sunrise. Frank Asch. RHPC
Sunrise. Rowena Bennett. TiPo
Sunrise. Sidney Lanier. *Fr.* Hymns of the Marshes. AA; PoEL-5
"Tide's at full, The: the marsh with flooded streams," *sel.* FaBoEn
Sunrise. Margaret E. Sangster. TRV
Sunrise. Jim Tollerud. VoR
Sunrise and Sunset. Emily Dickinson. *See* I'll tell you how the sun rose.
Sunrise at Sea. Edwin Atherstone. EtS
Sunrise at Sea. Epes Sargent. EtS
Sunrise at Sea. Swinburne. *Fr.* Tristram of Lyonesse: The Sailing of the Swallow. EtS
Sunrise Call, The. *Tr. fr. Pueblo Indian by* N. Barnes. WTO
Sunrise in Summer. John Clare. FaBoPP
Sunrise of the Poor, The. Robert Burns Wilson. AA
Sunrise on Mansfield Mountain. Alice Brown. HBV-1
Sunrise on Rydal Water. John Drinkwater. HBV-1; LiTM
Sunrise on the Sea. Shakespeare. *Fr.* A Midsummer Night's Dream, III, ii. ChTr
Sunrise tints the dew, The. Crocuses. Jōsa. TiPo
Sunrise Trumpets. Joseph Auslander. TrJP
Sun's a bright-haired shepherd boy, The. Silver Sheep. Anne Blackwell Payne. SiSoSe
Sun's a roaring dandelion, hour by hour. In the Field Forever. Robert Wallace. PPJ
Sun's Darling, The, *sels.* Thomas Dekker.
Country Glee. OBSC
Haymakers, Rakers. ELP; ViBoPo
Sun's gone dim, and, The. Two-Volume Novel. Dorothy Parker. InMe
Suns in a skein, the uncut stones of night. Roy Fuller. Mythological Sonnets, VIII. GTBS-P
Sun's low light splinters in a plastic gleam, The. On a Scooter. D. A. Greig. PeSA
Sun's noon throne is hid in hazy cloud, The. A View of the Present State of Ireland. Edmund Blunden. BrPo
"Sun's Over the Foreyard, The." Christopher Morley. EtS
Sun's Perpendicular Rays, The. William Lort Mansel. ChTr; FaBoEE
Suns, planets, stars, in glorious array. Victor J. Daley. *Fr.* Night. PoAu-1
Sun's snow, conversing, lowly slides from limbs. To a Young Lady Swinging Upside Down on a Birch Limb over a Winter-swollen Creek. James H. Koch. GoYe
Sun's Travels, The. Robert Louis Stevenson. FaPON
Sunset. Arthur Bayldon. PoAu-1
Sunset. Hayyim Nahman Bialik, *tr. fr. Hebrew by* Helena Frank. TrJP
Sunset, The. Gelett Burgess. FaBoNo; HBVY
Sunset. E. E. Cummings. MoAmPo
Sunset. David Allan Evans. PPJ

Sunset, A. Victor Hugo, *tr. fr. French by* Francis Thompson. *Fr.* Feuilles d'Automne. AWP
Sunset. William Julius Mickle. *Fr.* The Concubine. OBEC
Sunset/ molten bronze. Tune: Endless Union. Li Ching-chao, *tr. by* C. H. Kwôck *and* Vincent McHugh. PBWP
Sunset, a huge flower, wilts on the horizon, The. Flowers. Roo Borson. NOBC
Sunset after Rain. W. S. Merwin. PoA
Sunset and evening star. Crossing the Bar. Tennyson. BiP; BLRP; CABA; DL; EBVV; EtS; FaBoEn; FaBoRV; FaBV; FaFP; FaPoR; FF; FiP; FPL; HBVY; HBV-2; HeIP; InPK; LiTB; MOS; NOBE; NoP; OAEL-2; OAEP; OBEV; OBNC; OBVV; OHFP; PAI; PoLF; PoRA; SoSe; TEP; TrCP; TreF; TrGrPo; TRV; ViBoPo; VLP; WBLP; WGRP; WHA
Sunset and silence! A man: around him earth savage, earth broken. The Plougher [*or* The Plower]. Padraic Colum. GoBC; HBMV; MoBrPo; OnYI
Sunset and Sunrise. Emily Dickinson. *See* I'll tell you how the sun rose.
Sunset; and the mountain tops are afire. Mountain Evenings. Jamie Sexton Holme. PoOW
Sunset at Les Éboulements, A. Archibald Lampman. OBCV
Sunset City, The. Henry Sylvester Cornwell. HBV-2
Sunset—God's face from which grief radiates. Sodom. Chaim Grade, *tr. by* Joseph Leftwich. TrJP
Sunset Horn. Myron O'Higgins. AmNP; PoNe
Sunset in the Sea. Tom Hood. FaBoNo
Sunset is always disturbing. Afterglow. Jorge Luis Borges, *tr. by* Norman Thomas di Giovanni. NYBP
Sunset is golden on the steep. The Flock at Evening. Odell Shepard. HBMV
Sunset of the City, A. Gwendolyn Brooks. PBWP
Sunset over the Ægean. Byron. *See* Summer.
Sunset Song. *Tr. fr. Pueblo Indian by* N. Barnes. WTO
Sunset Wings. Dante Gabriel Rossetti. FM; HBV-2
Sunsets. Carl Sandburg. MoAmPo
Sunset's kiss, with lingering desire, The. The Wind in the Elms. J. Corson Miller. HBMV
Sunset's mounded cloud, A. An Evening. William Allingham. EnLoPo
Sunshade, The. Thomas Hardy. OxBTC
Sunshine, come softly here. Prayer for a Play House. Elinor Lennen. TrPWD
Sunshine let it be or frost. After St. Augustine. Mary Elizabeth Coleridge. TrPWD; TRV
Sunshine of Paradise Alley, The, *with music.* Walter H. Ford. FSN
Sunshine of the Gods, The, *sel.* Bayard Taylor.
"Ah, moment not to be purchased." AA
Sunshine of thine eyes, The. George Parsons Lathrop. AA
Sunshiny shower, A. Weather Wisdom. *Unknown.* FaBoBe; HBV-1; HBVY; OxNR; TreF
Sunstrike. Douglas Livingstone. PeSA
Sunstruck spray sifts back breakwater waves, A. The Pavilion on the Pier. Byron Vazakas. NePA
Sunt Leones. Stevie Smith. SBG
Sun-tanned men and women, toiling there together. Reapers. Mathilde Blind. SBG; WPE
Sunthin' in the Pastoral Line. James Russell Lowell. *Fr.* The Biglow Papers. AP
Super-cool/ ultrablack. But He Was Cool; or, He Even Stopped for Green Lights. Don L. Lee. AmNP; BPo; NoAM; PoBA
Super Flumina Babylonis. Swinburne. OBVV; PoEL-5; VLP
Super-Suburbia of the Southern Seas. Farewell to New Zealand. Wynford Vaughan-Thomas. DBV; NOBL
Superb and sole, upon a plumèd spray. The Mocking Bird. Sidney Lanier. AA
Superballs. Tom Clark. EAS
Superbull. Harold Witt. FAZ
Supercilious nabob of the East, A. A Modest Wit. Selleck Osborn. BLPA; HBV-1
Superfluous Saddle, The. La Fontaine, *tr.fr. French.* UnTE
Superintindint wuz Flannigan. Finnigin to Flannigan. Strickland W. Gillilan. FaBoBe; HBV-2; TreF; YaD
Superior Nonsense Verses. *Unknown.* NA
Superliminare. George Herbert. AnAnS-1; SeCP
Superman. John Updike. LiSp
Supermarket. Felice Holman. QQQ
Supermarket in California, A. Allen Ginsberg. AmPP; CoAP; ConAP; HAP; HeIP; LiTM; NaP; NeAP; NOBA; PoM; PrIm; SOTW; TAP; TwCP; UnPo
Superscription, A. Dante Gabriel Rossetti. The House of Life, XCVII. FaBoEn; GTBS-P; HBV-1; NOBE; NoP; OAEL-2; OBNC; PoEL-5; SeCePo; VLP; WHA
(Sonnet: A Superscription.) EBVV
Supersensual. Evelyn Underhill. WGRP
Superstition. Minji Karibo. WPOW
Superstitious Ghost, The. Arthur Guiterman. ShM
Supervising Examinations. Sean Lucy. CIP
Supper. Walter de la Mare. NYBP
Supper. William Soutar. OxBS
Supper after the Last, The. Galway Kinnell. NOBA; PoCH; TwAmPo
Supper Is Na Ready. Burns. *See* Suppertime.
Supper is over, the hearth is swept, The. Sermon in a Stocking. Ellen A. Jewett. BLPA
Suppertime. Burns. UnTE
(Supper Is Na Ready.) GBP
Supplement, A. Benjamin Tompson. SCAP
Suppliant. Florence Earle Coates. TrPWD
Suppliant, The. Georgia Douglas Johnson. BALP; CDC; PoBA; PoNe
Suppliant. Alan Sullivan. CaP
Supplication, A. Nicholas Breton. OBSC
Supplication. Joseph Seamon Cotter, Jr. BANP; CDC; PoNe
Supplication, A. Abraham Cowley. *Fr.* Davideis. GTBS; GTBS-P
Supplication. Josephine Johnson. TrPWD
Supplication. Edgar Lee Masters. TrCP; TrPWD
Supplication. Edith Lovejoy Pierce. TrPWD
Supplication. Louis Untermeyer. HBMV
Supplication, A. Sir Thomas Wyatt. *See* Forget Not Yet.
Supplication of the Black Aberdeen. Kipling. BLPA
Support Your Local Police Dog. Carter Revard. VoR
Suppose. Anne Reeve Aldrich. HBV-1
Suppose. Phoebe Cary. BLPA; BLPL
Suppose. Lewis Horne. AMV-81
Suppose—/ Ah well, suppose. Above the Wall. Susannah P. Malarkey. AMV-80
Suppose a Man. R. T. Smith. WOLT
Suppose he had been tabled at thy teats. Luke XI: Blessed Be the Paps Which Thou Hast Sucked. Richard Crashaw. BXAP; CABA; JCP; PeD
Suppose in Perfect Reason. Howard Griffin. CrMA
Suppose it, for the last time, in that moment. The Coming of the White Man. Patrick Anderson. *Fr.* Poem on Canada. MoCV
Suppose it is nothing but the hive. Davis Matlock. Edgar Lee Masters. *Fr.* Spoon River Anthology. LiTA; LiTM
Suppose me dead; and then suppose. Swift. *Fr.* Verses on the Death of Doctor Swift. NOBE
Suppose, my little lady. Suppose. Phoebe Cary. BLPA; BLPL
Suppose some peddler offered. The Market Economy. Marge Piercy. GeTw
Suppose that you have seen. Shakespeare. King Henry V, *fr.* III, *prologue.* MOS
Suppose the ceiling went outside. The Ceiling. Theodore Roethke. EyDe
Suppose the dead could crown their wit. A Responsory, 1948. Thomas Merton. VGW
Suppose the little cowslip. Deeds of Kindness. Epes Sargent, *sometimes at. to* Fanny Crosby. HBV-1; HBVY
Suppose the ruler used to mark our days. Suppose. Lewis Horne. AMV-81
Suppose they had cheated me out of my. Remember Times for Sandy. Carolyn M. Rodgers. JB
Suppose This Moment Some Stupendous Question. Alden Nowlan. NOBC
Suppose those/ who made/ wars. Nigerian Unity/ or Little Niggers Killing Little Niggers. Don L. Lee. NeAC
Suppose we are standing together a minute. April. Jean Valentine. TAP
Suppose You Met a Witch, *sel.* Ian Serailler.
"Suppose you met a witch . . . There's one I know." WSC
Suppose you screeve? or go cheap-jack? Villon's Straight Tip to All Cross Coves. W. E. Henley, *after* Villon. AWP; CenHV; FaBoCo; HBV-1; InMe; InvP; NA; SeCePo
Suppose you were dreaming about your family. Benign Neglect/ Mississippi, 1970. Primus St. John. PoBA
Suppose you're a solo native here. Solo Native. Thomas Lux. LCAP
Supposed Confessions of a Second-rate Sensitive Mind. Tennyson. VLP
Supposed of Phamphylax the Antiochene. A Death in the Desert. Robert Browning. GoTL; OxBoCh
Suppositions. Margherita Faulkner. AMV-80
Suppressed. *Unknown.* TDH
Supremacy. E. A. Robinson. NoAM
Supremacy of Bacteria, The. Robert Frazier. SUW
Supreme Death. Douglas Dunn. FaBoMo
Supreme Fiction. Howard Winn. SOTS
Supreme Fortune Falls Soonest. Robert Herrick. CaPo
Supreme Sacrifice, The. John S. Arkwright. WGRP
Supremer Sacrifice, The. "Furnley Maurice." CBAP
Supremes done gone, The. Memorial. Sonia Sanchez. BlSi
Sur le Pont d'Avignon (On the Bridge at Avignon). *Tr. fr. French.* FSW

Surcease. Patrick Lane. NeAC
Surcharged with discontent. *Unknown.* PBBP
Sure a Poor Man. *Tr. fr. Hawaiian by* M. K. Pukui *and* A. L. Korn. WTO
Sure an' twas a/ fine st. patrick's day. Saint Patrick's Day, 1973. Wendy Rose. CDW
Sure and exact, the master's quiet touch. The Dead Player. Robert Burns Wilson. AA
Sure as hell. Blueline. Ken Belford. NeAC
Sure as Hell, the Devil. Another One for the Devil. David C. Childers. AMV-80
Sure, deck your lower limbs in pants. What's the Use. Ogden Nash. PoPl
Sure, I am a wild young Irish boy and from Dub-a-lin town I came. I Am a Wild Young Irish Boy, *Unknown.* ShS
Sure, It was so. Man in those early days. Corruption. Henry Vaughan. AnAnS-1; FaBoEn; JCP; NOCV; OAEL-1; OBS; OxBoCh; Prf; SeCP; SeCV-1
Sure Lord, there is enough in thee to dry. Sonnet. George Herbert. AnAnS-1
Sure maybe ye've heard the storm-thrush. Birds. "Moira O'Neill." HBV-1
Sure never was picture drawn more to the life. The Virginia Song. *Unknown.* PAH
Sure Sign, A. Nancy Byrd Turner. SoPo; TiPo
Sure the night was smooth. The Night Was Smooth. James Bertolino. POL
Sure there are poets which did never dream. Cooper's Hill. Sir John Denham. AnAnS-2; SeCP; SeCV-1
Sure, There's a Tie of Bodies! Henry Vaughan. NCEP
Sure, this world is full of trouble. Ain't It Fine Today [*or* It's]! Douglas Malloch. BLPA; WBLP
Sure thou didst flourish once! and many springs. The Timber. Henry Vaughan. FaBoRV, *abr.*; NoP; OBEV; SeCP; SeCV-1
Sure 'twas by Providence design'd. On a Beautiful Youth Struck Blind with Lightning. Goldsmith. OAEP
Sure You Can Ask Me a Personal Question. Diane Burns. STE
Surely a dead moth's. Funeral. Bert Meyer. PCP
Surely A-flat may be forgiven. Lois in Concert. Charles Moorman. AMV-81
Surely among a rich man's flowering lawns. Ancestral Houses. W. B. Yeats. Meditations in Time of Civil War, I. ChMP; LiTB; MoVE; OAEL-2
Surely in my eyes that light is now lost. The Photograph of Myself. Jon Anderson. AmPA
Surely it is death to come here. Tlanusi' Yi, the Leech Place. Gladys Cardiff. CDW; STE; TWSS
Surely most signs pass me by unnoticed. Driving North from Savannah on My Birthday. Paul Zimmer. AMV-81
Surely My Soul. Jacob Cohen, *tr. fr. Hebrew by* I. M. Lask. TrJP
Surely one of my finest days, I'd just. Extract from Memoirs. Howard Nemerov. OxBC
Surely that is not a man. Acrobat. Rachel Field. *Fr.* A Circus Garland. SoPo
Surely that moan is not the thing. Fog-Horn. W. S. Merwin. NMP
Surely the day will come. Guns. John Woods. GP
Surely the finger of God that governs the stars. Yeats' Tower. Vernon Watkins. NeBP
Surely the saints you loved visibly came. Joyce Kilmer. Amelia Josephine Burr. HBMV
Surely there is a vein for the [*or* mine for] silver. The Price of Widsom. Bible, *O.T.* Job, XXVIII. SaC; TrGrPo
Surely You Remember. Dahlia Ravikovitch, *tr. fr. Hebrew by* Chana Bloch. VWA
Surely you would not ask me to have known. Question to Life. Patrick Kavanagh. MoBrPo
Surf. Lillian Morrison. NTCP
Surf-casting. W. S. Merwin. NOBA
Surface and the Depths, The. Sir Lewis Morris. *See* Song: "Love took my life and thrill'd it."
Surface of the pond was mostly green, The. The Lotus Flowers. Ellen Bryant Voigt. MAYP
Surfaces. David Madden. AMV-80
Surfaces. Jane Mayhall. NYP
Surfaces. Peter Meinke. Str
Surfer, The. Judith Wright. WPE
Surfers at Santa Cruz. Paul Goodman. FF; LiSp
Surgeon and the Ape, The ("The surgeon once owned a big ape"). *Unknown.* TDH
Surgeons must be very careful. Emily Dickinson. ImOP; TAP
Surgery. Carol Burbank. SUW
Surgical Ward: Men. Robert Graves. FaBoMo
Surging sea of human life forever onward rolls, The. A Hundred Years from Now. Mary A. Ford. BLPA
Surnames to be Avoided in Marriage. *Unknown.* FaBoUs
Surprise. Harry Behn. TiPo
Surprise. Anthony Cronin. CIP
Surprise, The. *Unknown, tr. fr. Greek by* Louis Untermeyer. UnTE
Surprise. Harold Witt. AMV-81
Surprise at Ticonderoga, The. Mary A. P. Stansbury. PAH
Surprise, surprise, they're flying in today. Surprise. Harold Witt. AMV-81
Surprised by Evening. Robert Bly. CAPP; NaP; VGW
Surprised by Joy [Impatient as the Wind]. Wordsworth. BoLoP; EnRP; HAP; LiTB; LO; NOBE; NoP; OAEL-2; OBRV; PoPle; SeCeV; TEP
(Desideria.) BLPL; GTBS; GTBS-P; OBEV
(Sonnet: Surprised by Joy.) CheR; ViBoPo
(To Catherine Wordsworth 1808-1812.) FaBoEn; OBNC
Surprised by Me. Walter Darring. NYBP
Surprises. *Unknown.* STF
Surprises: ("Surprises are round"). Jean Conder Soule. RHPC
Surprising my dupe by his egg of Oedipus. Dirge for Three Trumpets. *Unknown.* EAS
Surrender. Amelia Josephine Burr. HBV-1
Surrender. Angelina Weld Grimké. CDC
Surrender. Ruth Guthrie Harding. HBMV
Surrender, The. Henry King. AnAnS-2; BoLoP; EBEV; JCP; MePo; TrGrPo
Surrender at Appomattox, The. Herman Melville. PAH
Surrender of Cornwallis, The. *Unknown.* PAH
Surrender of New Orleans, The. Marion Manville. PAH
Surrender of Spain, The. John Hay. AA
Surrender to Christ. Frederic William Henry Myers. OxBoCh
Surrounded by beakers, by strange coils. The Naked World. Sully-Prudhomme, *tr. by* William Dock. ImOP
Surrounded by scientists in a faculty. Homage to the New World. Michael Harper. LCAP
Surrounded by tigers. The Life of the Wolf. Gary Gildner. AmPA
Surrounded by unnumbered foes. His Banner over Me. Gerald Massey. HBV-2; WGRP
Surrounded by Walls Am I. Ronald James Dessus. LFAC
Surrounding woods are burning with subdued fire, The. Treason. Lora Dunetz. NePoAm
Survey. Paul Lawson. GP
Survey of Cornwall, *sel.* Richard Carew.
River Lynher, The. FaBoPP
Survey of Literature. John Crowe Ransom. FaBoCh; LiTA; MP; OBAL; TAP; TwCP; VGW
Survey of the Amphitheatre, A. Moses Browne. NOEC
Survey our progress from our birth. John Webster. LO
Surveyor. Guy Butler. PeSA
Surview. Thomas Hardy. ChMP
(Surview: Cogitavi Vias Meas.) LO
Survival, The. Edmund Blunden. OBEV; OBMV
Survival. Florence Earle Coates. AA
Survival, I know how this way. Survival This Way. Simon J. Ortiz. CDW; STE
Survival in a Stone Maze. George Rachow. LFAC
Survival Kit. Robert Slater. FAZ
Survival of the Fittest, The. Sarah N. Cleghorn. HBMV
Survival This Way. Simon J. Ortiz. CDW; STE
Surviving. James Welch. CDW; STE
Surviving a Poetry Circuit. William Stafford. FAZ
Survivor, The. Stephen Berg. *Fr.* Entering the Body. NaP
Survivor, The. Robert Graves. CMoP; MoVE
Survivor. Archibald MacLeish. NCSH; PrIm
Survivor. Judy Dothard Simmons. CNA
Survivor, The. R. S. Thomas. FaBoTw
Survivor sole, and hardly such, of all. Yardley Oak. William Cowper. LaA; NCEP; NOEC
Survivors. Elaine Feinstein. VWA
Survivors, The. Daryl Hine. TwCP
Survivors. Michael Hogan. FAZ
Survivors. Mordecai Marcus. AMV-81
Survivors, The. Adrienne Rich. NYBP
Survivors, The. Robert Slater. FAZ
Survivors, The. Miriam Waddington. VWA
"Susaddah!" exclaimed Ibsen. E. C. Bentley. *Fr.* Clerihews. PV
Susan. Robin Magowan. EAS
Susan ("Susan poisoned her grandmother's tea".) *Unknown.* NA
Susan, the constant slave to mop and broom. "Peter Pindar." *Fr.* The Sorrows of Sunday; an Elegy. NOEC
Susan to Diana. Frances Cornford. MoVE
Susan, we meet in late fall. The Meeting. Kathleen Spivack. NMM
Susanna and the Elders. Adelaide Crapsey. WPE
Susanna and the Elders. Jack Gilbert. NPGG
Susannah and the Elders. *Unknown.* ErPo; OLR
Susannah Prout. Walter de la Mare. FaBoEE
Susannah the fair. Susannah and the Elders. *Unknown.* ErPo; OLR

Sushi-Okashi and Green Tea with Mitsu Yashima. Al Robles. BrSi
Susiana, *with music. Unknown.* ShS
Susie Asado. Gertrude Stein. SOTW; TAP
Susie Wong Doesn't Live Here. Diane Mei Lin Mark. BrSi
Susie's galoshes. Galoshes. Rhoda W. Bacmeister. NTCP; SoPo; TiPo
Suspecting hollow trees, the barn to be. Playwright. John Woods. CoPo
Suspended in a moving night. Corner Seat. Louis MacNeice. MoVE
Suspended Moment. Mariana B. Davenport. GoYe
Suspense. Emily Dickinson. *See* Elysium is as far to.
Suspense. D. H. Lawrence. MoBrPo
Suspiria. Longfellow. ViBoPo
Suspiria. *Unknown.* OBEV
Suspition upon His Over-much Familiarity with a Gentlewoman, The. Robert Herrick. CavP
Sussyissfriin, *sel.* Philip Dow.
"My son & I, between *Fu-Sang* and/ Cathay." NPGG
Sutcliffe and Whitby. William Logan. MAYP
Sutra Blues; or, This Pain Is Bliss. Jody Aliesan. LTB
Sutter's Fort, Sacramento. Lucius Harwood Foote. BPAW
Suzanne Takes You Down. Leonard Cohen. BiP; InPK; NIP; NoP
Suzie's Enzyme Poem. Paul Zimmer. PPJ
Suzie's New Dog. John Ciardi. GDP
Swaggering prince. Python. *Yoruba Oral Tradition, tr. by* Ulli Beier. WTO
Swahili Love Song. *Unknown, tr. fr. Swahili by* Jan Knappert. LLLT
Swain, give o'er your fond pretension. Hildebrand Jacob. FaBoEE
Swallow, The. Lucy Aikin. OxBChV
Swallow, The. Abraham Cowley, *after the Greek of* Anacreon. *Fr.* Anacreontics. EBEV; FM; PBBP
(Anacreontics: The Swallow.) OBEV
Swallow, The, *sel.* J. C. Squire.
"Birds, trees and flow'rs they bring to me." BXAP
Swallow, The. Thomas Stanley, *after the Greek of* Anacreon. AWP
Swallow, for a moment seen, The. Thomas Warton, the Younger. *Fr.* Ode: The First of April. PBBP
Swallow has come again, The. The Children's Song. *Unknown.* FaPON
Swallow has set her six young on the rail, The. In the Doorway. Robert Browning. *Fr.* James Lee's Wife. NCEP
Swallow is flying over, The. Tears in Spring. William Ellery Channing. AA
Swallow leaves her nest, The. Dirge [*or* A Voice from the Waters]. Thomas Lovell Beddoes. *Fr.* Death's Jest-Book, I. LoBV; NOBE; OBNC; OBRV; OBVV; PoEL-4
Swallow, my sister, O sister swallow. Itylus. Swinburne. ChTr; HBV-1; WHA
Swallow-shell that eases birth, The. Gary Snyder. Myths and Texts: Hunting, IV. NaP
Swallow sings "Dawn," The. Ezra Pound *and* Noel Stock, *fr. Egyptian hieroglyphics.* BoWoP
Swallow Song. Majorie Pickthall. CaP
Swallow Tails. Tom Robinson. FaPON
Swallow, that on rapid wing. The Swallow. Lucy Aikin. OxBChV
Swallow the Lake. Clarence Major. PoBA
Swallowing. Harold Bond. AMV-81
Swallows, The. Patric Dickinson. ChMP
Swallows. Thomas Hornsby Ferril. RFM
Swallows flap in waves against the house, The. Late Spring: A Heaving, a Turning. John Gill. NeAC
Swallows flew in the curves of an eight, The. Overlooking the River Stour. Thomas Hardy. FaBoPP
Swallow's Flight, The. Louis Levy, *tr. fr. Danish by* Martin S. Alwood *and* Sanford Kaufman. TrJP
Swallows hide, The. From Life. Lazer Eichenrand, *tr. by* Gabriel Preil *and* Howard Schwartz. VWA
Swallows in their torpid state, The. To the Rev. Mr. Newton. William Cowper. LoBV
Swallows nest. Return to Lake Emily Chequamegon National Forest. Richard Behm. WOLT
Swallows Over the Camp. Uys Krige, *tr. fr. Afrikaans by the author and* Jack Cope. PeSA
Swallows travel to and fro. Robert Louis Stevenson. EBVV
Swam too far out: the swell took him. Elegy for a School-Friend. Augustus Young. BIrV
Swamp. Roberta Hill. VoR
Swamp Fox, The. William Gilmore Simms. AA; BeLS; FaBoBe; PAH
Swamp reeds murmur the song, The. Marsh Leaf. David Wagoner. PoA
Swampstrife and spatterdock. The Marsh. W. D. Snodgrass. BoNaP; NePoEA
Swampy State of Illinois, The. Excelsior. *Unknown.* BXAP
Swan, The. Baudelaire, *tr. fr. French by* F. P. Sturm. SyP
Swan, The. Edmund Gosse. SyP
Swan. Donald Hall. LCAP
Swan. D. H. Lawrence. CMoP
Swan. Edward Lowbury. GTBS-P
Swan, The. Jay MacPherson. PeCV
Swan, The. Stéphane Mallarmé, *tr. fr. French by* T. Sturge Moore. SyP
Swan, The. W. R. Rodgers. NeBP; NMP; NoAM
Swan, The. Theodore Roethke. VGW
Swan, The. *Unknown.* ChTr; FaPON
("Swan swam over the sea.") OxNR
Swan and Shadow. John Hollander. NoP; PoA
Swan and the Goose, The. Aesop, *tr. fr. Greek by* William Ellery Leonard. AWP; FaPON
Swan Bathing, The. Ruth Pitter. BoAnP; MoBrPo
Swan Song of Parson Avery, The. Whittier. AA
Swan swam over the sea. The Swan. *Unknown.* ChTr; FaPON; OxNR
Swan Swims So Bonny, The. *Unknown.* OBET
Swan, The—Vain Pleasures. George Moses Horton. BALP
Swank, The. V. C. Vickers. AmMo
Swannanoa Tunnel. *Unknown.* FSW
Swans. Lawrence Durrell. MoBrPo; SeCePo
Swans, The. Clifford Dyment. BoAnP; MoVE
Swans, The. Edith Sitwell. CMoP; MoVE; WPE
Swans. Leonora Speyer. FYAP
Swans. Wordsworth. *Fr.* An Evening Walk. OBEC
Swans at Night, *sel.* Mary Gilmore.
"Within the night, above the dark." PoAu-1
Swan's Feet, The. E. J. Scovell. OxBTC
Swans of Vadstena, The. Ralph Gustafson. MoCV
Swans of Worcester with their lifted wings, The. Depression. "Michael Field." SyP
Swans rise up with their wings in day, The. The Boy and the Geese. Padraic Fiacc. NeIP
Swans Sing [before They Die]. Samuel Taylor Coleridge. *See* On a Bad Singer.
Swans, whose pens as white as ivory, The. Robert Greene. *Fr.* A Madrigal. ViBoPo
Swansea Town, *with music. Unknown.* ShS
Swansong. Carol Muske. AmPA
Swapping yarns, two Mountain Men/ Chewed and spat in the fire. Mountain Liars. Ann Woodbury Hafen. PoOW
Swarm, The. Richard Moore. SUW
Swarm of bees in May, A. Proverb. *Unknown.* FaBoBe; HBV-1; OxNR
Swarming, A. A Sheeprancher Named John. Gretel Ehrlich. MAYP
Swarming Bees, The. James Laughlin. VGW
Swarms of minnows show their little heads. Minnows. Keats. FaPON
Swarte-smeked smethes, smatered with smoke. Smoke-blackened Smiths. *Unknown.* MeEL. *See also* Blacksmiths, The.
Swarthmore Phi Beta Kappa Poem, The. Richmond Lattimore. GLGT
Swarthy bee is a buccaneer, The. A More Ancient Mariner. Bliss Carman. OBAL
Swarthy little statue, The. Naked War. Michael Heffernan. BXAP
Swart-smeked Smithes. *Unknown. See* Blacksmiths, The.
Swashbuckler's Song, The. James Stuart Montgomery. HBMV
Swathe Uncut, The. John Hewitt. NeIP
Sway song. Eye of God. Jim Tollerud. VoR
Swear by what the sages spoke. Under Ben Bulben. W. B. Yeats. AnIV; CMoP; CoBMV; HAP; LiTM; LoBV; NoAM; NoP; OxBI; OxBTC
Swearing. Henry Fitzsimon. ACP
Sweat, The. Nila NorthSun. STE
Sweat like drops of blood run down, The. Dark Was the Night. *Unknown.* AmFP
Sweat Song. Peter Blue Cloud. STE; VoR
Sweater, The. Gregory Orr. PPJ
Sweating It Out on Winding Stair Mountain. Jim Barnes. CDW
Swedenborg's Skull. Vernon Watkins. FaBoTw
Swedes. Edward Thomas. BrPo; MoVE; OAEL-2
Swedish Angel. Winfield Townley Scott. LiTM
Sweeney Agonistes, *sels.* T. S. Eliot.
"Under the bamboo." UnPo
"You'll be my little seven stone missionary!" UnPo
Sweeney among the Nightingales. T. S. Eliot. AmPP; AP; CABA; ChMP; CMoP; CoBMV; FaBoMo; HAP; HeIP; InPK; InvP; LiTA; LiTM; MoVE; NePA; NoAM; NOBA; NOBE; NoP; OAEP; OBMV; OxBA; PPP; SeCeV; TwAmPo; WeW
Sweeney Erect. T. S. Eliot. OxBTC; VGW
Sweeney in Articulo. "Myra Buttle." *Fr.* The Sweeniad. BXAP; Par
("Sunday is the dullest day, treating.") FaBoPa
Sweeney, Old and Phthisic, among the Hippopotami. David Cummings. BXAP
Sweeney the Mad, *sels. Unknown, tr. fr. Middle Irish by* J. G. O'Keefe.
"'He came to me in his swift course.'" OnYI
"Man by the wall snores, The." AnIL
Sweeney to Mrs. Porter in the Spring. L. E. Sissman. NYBP

Sweeniad, The, *sel.* "Myra Buttle."
Sweeney in Articulo. BXAP; Par
("Sunday is the dullest day, treating.") FaBoPa
Sweep the house clean. Love Song. William Carlos Williams. MoAB; MoAmPo
Sweep thy faint strings, Musician. The Song of [the] Shadows. Walter de la Mare. CMoP; MoBrPo; TrGrPo
Sweeper, The. Agnes Lee. HBMV; QFR
Sweepers, The. William Whitehead. NOEC
Sweeping the Skies. Elizabeth Anna Hart. CenHV
Sweet, The. Ai. GP
Sweet, a delicate white mouse, A. The Waltzer in the House. Stanley Kunitz. ErPo; NYBP; RHPC
Sweet, acidulous, down-reaching thrill, A. Ode on [*or* to] a Jar of Pickles. Bayard Taylor. BXAP; FaBoPa; SpRo
Sweet Adeline. Richard H. Gerard. FSN, *with music*; FSW; TreFT
Sweet Adon, darest not glance thine eye. Infida's Song. Robert Greene. *Fr.* Never Too Late. OBSC
Sweet after showers, ambrosial air. Tennyson. In Memoriam A. H. H., LXXXVI. EBVV
Sweet Afton. Burns. *See* Afton Water.
Sweet Amarillis, by a spring's. Upon Mistress Elizabeth Wheeler under the Name of Amarillis. Robert Herrick. CaPo; PBBP
Sweet and Low. Tennyson. *Fr.* The Princess. BiP; BLPL; EtS; FaBoBe; FaPON; FSW; MOS; OxBChV; PoPl; TreF; TrGrPo
(Lullaby: "Sweet and low, sweet and low.") HBV-1; HBVY; PoLF
Sweet and Sour. Spenser. *See* Amoretti, XXVI.
Sweet-and-Twenty. Shakespeare. *See* O Mistress Mine, Where Are You Roaming.
Sweet antidote to sorrow, toil and strife. To a Segar. Samuel Low. OBAL
Sweet Apple. James Stephens. CMoP
Sweet are the charms of her I love. Song. Barton Booth. OBEC
Sweet are the thoughts that savo[u]r of content. Maesia's Song [*or* A Mind Content *or* The Poor Estate]. Robert Greene. *Fr.* Farewell to Folly. CTC; ElL; HBV-2; OBSC; PoEL-2; TrGrPo; UnPo; ViBoPo
Sweet are the ways of death to weary feet. Chorus. Lord De Tabley. *Fr.* Medea. NBM; OBEV; OBVV
Sweet are the whispers of yon pine that makes. The Death of Daphnis. Theocritus, *tr. by* Charles Stuart Calverley. *Fr.* Idylls. AWP
Sweet Armida tooke this charge on hand, The. Tasso, *tr. by* Edward Fairfax. *Fr.* Godfrey of Bulloigne; or, The Recoverie of Jerusalem, IV. OBVE
Sweet as violets to a weary heart. The Pleiades. Elizabeth J. Coatsworth. ImOP
Sweet, at this morn I chanced. Buen Matina. Sir John Salusbury. ElL
Sweet Auburn! loveliest village of the plain. The Deserted Village [*or* Sweet Auburn]. Goldsmith. BeLS; EnRP; FaFP; GoTL; HBV-2; LaA; LAuP; LiTB; LoBV; MasP; NOBE; NOEC; NoP; OAEL-1; OAEP; OBEC; OnYI; OxBI; PoEL-3; SeCePo; TEP; TreFS; TrGrPo; ViBoPo
Sweet Auburn! parent of the blissful hour. Blest Retirement. Goldsmith. *Fr.* The Deserted Village. EBEV; OBEC
Sweet babe! a golden cradle holds thee. The Fairy Nurse. Edward Walsh. OnYI
Sweet baby sleep: what ail[e]s my dear? A Lullaby [*or* A Rocking Hymn] Hymn L. George Wither. *Fr.* Haleluiah or, Britan's Second Remembrancer. OxBChV; OxBoCh; SeCV-1
Sweet baked apple dappled cinnamon speckled sin of mine. Love Child—a Black Aesthetic. Everett Hoagland. BPo
Sweet basil. Having Replaced Love with Food and Drink. Diane Wakoski. NAs
Sweet, be not proud of those two eyes. To Dianeme. Robert Herrick. CaPo; FaBoEn; GTBS; GTBS-P; HBV-1; JCP; LoBV; NOBE; OBEV; OBS; PoPle; SeCV-1; TrGrPo; ViBoPo
Sweet beast, I have gone prowling. Song. W. D. Snodgrass. LLLT; MoAmPo; NYBP
Sweet beats of jazz impaled on slivers of wind. Walking Parker Home. Bob Kaufman. PoBA
Sweet bell of Stratford, tolling slow. The Passing Bell at Stratford. William Winter. AA
Sweet Be'mi'ster, that bist a-bound. Be'mi'ster. William Barnes. EBVV
Sweet Benedict, whilst thou art young. To His Little Son Benedict from the Tower of London. John Hoskyns. OxBChV
Sweet Betsy from Pike. *Unknown.* AmFP, *with music*; AS, *with music*; BLSo, *with music*; BPAW; CoSo, *with music*; FaBoBa; FSW; OBAL; OxBoLi, *with music*; TrAS, *with music*; TreFT; ViBoPo, *with music*
(Betsy from Pike.) BaBo
Sweet bird that shunn'st the noise of folly. Milton. *Fr.* Il Penseroso. CH
Sweet bird, that sing'st away the early howres. To a Nightingale. William Drummond of Hawthornden. OBS
Sweet birds! that sit and sing amid the shady valleys. Phyllis [*or* A Pastoral]. Nicholas Breton. ElL; OBSC; TrGrPo
Sweet boy, gentle boy. Pushkin, *tr. fr. Russian by* Valery Pereleshin. PeHV
"Sweet boy," she says, "this night I'll waste in sorrow." Shakespeare. *Fr.* Venus and Adonis. ErPo
Sweet-breathed and young. A Woman's Execution. Edward King. AA
Sweet brother, if I do not sleep. For My Brother. Thomas Merton. TreFS
Sweet By and By. Sanford Filmore Bennett. *See* In the Sweet Bye-and-Bye.
Sweet caresses that I give to you, The. Caresses. Elsa Barker. *Fr.* The Spirit and the Bride. HBMV
Sweet Caroline. *Unknown.* PoPle
Sweet Chance, that led my steps abroad. A Great Time. W. H. Davies. LiTB; MoBrPo; MoVE; WHA
Sweet child of April, I have found thy place. The Pyxidanthera. Augusta Cooper Bristol. AA
Sweet Clover. Wallace Rice. HBV-1
Sweet Content. Thomas Dekker. *Fr.* The Pleasant Comedy of Patient Grissell, I, i. CH; ElL; LoBV; OBEV; TreFT; WHA
("Art thou poor, yet hast thou golden slumbers?") HAP; InPS; OAEP; UnPo; ViBoPo
(Basket-Maker's Song, The.) OBSC; TrGrPo
(Happy Heart, The.) GTBS; GTBS-P; HBV-2
Sweet corrall lips, where Nature's treasure lies. Richard Barnfield. Sonnets, VI. PeHV
Sweet Country Life, A. *Unknown.* OBET
Sweet Cupid, Ripen Her Desire. *Unknown.* EnRePo; OBSC; ViBoPo
(Song.) LoBV
Sweet cyder is a great thing. Great Things. Thomas Hardy. GTBS-P; MoVE; NOBE; TreFT
Sweet Cynthia, take the book away. To Cynthia, Not to Let Him Read the Ladies' Magazines. P. M. Hubbard. FiBHP
Sweet day, so cool, so calm, so bright. Virtue [*or* Vertue]. George Herbert. AnAnS-1; AWP; CABA; CH; ELP; FaBoEn; FaBoRV; HAP; HBV-2; HeIP; InvP; JCP; LoBV; MeLP; MePo; NOBE; NOCV; NoP; OAEL-1; OBEV; OBS; PAI; PoPle; PoRA; PPP; SeCeV; SeCeV-1; SeCP; SoSe; TEP; TreFT; TrGrPo; ViBoPo; WGRP; WHA
Sweet, deep sense of mystery filled the wood, A. In Cool, Green Haunts. Mahlon Leonard Fisher. WeW
Sweet Diane. George Barlow. CNA
Sweet dimness of her loosened hair's downfall. Love-Sweetness. Dante Gabriel Rossetti. *Fr.* The House of Life. OAEP
Sweet disorder in the dress, A. Delight in Disorder [*or* Sweet Disorder]. Robert Herrick. AnAnS-2; AWP; BiP; BLPL; CABA; CaPo; CavP; EBEV; EnLoPo; ErPo; FaBoEn; FaBV; FF; GTBS; GTBS-P; HAP; HBV-1; HeIP; InMe; InPK; InPS; JCP; LiTB; LoBV; NIP; NOBE; NoP; OAEL-1; OAEP; OBEV; OBS; PAI; PoPle; PoRA; PP; PPoe; PPP; PrIm; SeCePo; SeCeV; SeCP; SeCV-1; TEP; TreFS; TrGrPo; ViBoPo; WeW; WHA
Sweet Dreams. Ogden Nash. OnUR
Sweet dreams, form a shade. A Cradle Song. Blake. *Fr.* Songs of Innocence. EnRP; LAuP; OAEP; OBCP; SBVL; ViBoPo
Sweet dreams, sweet memories, sweet taste of earth. Cemetery Nights. Stephen Dobyns. SV
Sweet earth, he ran and changed his shoes to go. Arrangements with Earth for Three Dead Friends. James Wright. NIP
Sweet Echo, Sweetest Nymph. Milton. *See* Song: "Sweet Echo, sweetest nymph, that livest unseen."
Sweet Emma Moreland of yonder town. Edward Gray. Tennyson. OBVV
Sweet empty sky of June without a stain. Epochs. Emma Lazarus. SBG
Sweet Ethel. Linda Piper. BlSi
Sweet Evelina. *Unknown.* FSW
Sweet, exclude me not, nor be divided. Bar Not the Door. Thomas Campion. UnTE
Sweet eyes by sorrow still unwet. Wonderland. Harry Thurston Peck. AA
Sweet father I have shrunk a bit. Father Father Son and Son. Jon Swan. NYBP
Sweet flower, that art so fair and gay. Medieval Norman Song. *Unknown, tr. by* John Addington Symonds. AWP
Sweet floweret, pledge o' meikle love. On the Birth of a Posthumous Child, Born in Peculiar Circumstances of Family Distress. Burns. NAs
Sweet for a little even to fear, and sweet. Erotion. Swinburne. PoEL-5
Sweet gem of infant fairy-flowers! To an Infant Daughter. John Clare. NAs
Sweet Genevieve. George Cooper. FSW; BLSo, *with music;* PSoN, *with music*; TreFS
Sweet girl graduate, lean as a fawn, A. Nancy Hanks, Mother of Abraham Lincoln. Vachel Lindsay. CMoP
Sweet hand! the sweet yet cruel bow thou art. Love's Franciscan. Henry Constable. ACP; GoBC
Sweet, harmles[s] livers [*or* livers]! (on whose holy leisure). The Shepherds [*or* Shepheards]. Henry Vaughan. AnAnS-1; SBVL
Sweet have I known the blossoms of the morning. Because of You. Sophia Almon Hensley. HBV-1
Sweet heart,/ A morning, climbing in its brass. Letter from an Island. John Malcolm Brinnin. TAP

Sweet Highland Girl, a very shower. To the [or a] Highland Girl [of Inversneyde]. Wordsworth. EnRP; GTBS; GTBS-P; LoBV; TreFT
Sweet Hour of Prayer. William W. Walford. BLRP; TreFT; WBLP
Sweet if thou wilt be. Come Turn to Mee, Thou Pretty Little One. *Unknown.* CoMu
Sweet, if you like and love me still. His Farewell to His Unkind and Unconstant Mistress. Francis Davison. ElL; OBSC
Sweet in goodly fellowship. There's No Lust like to Poetry [*or* Wine and Love and Lyre]. *Unknown, tr. by* John Addington Symonds. AWP; UnTE
Sweet in her green dell [*or* cell] the Flower of Beauty slumbers. Song [*or* Serenade of a Loyal Martyr *or* The Flower of Beauty]. George Darley. HBV-1; NOBE; OBEV; OBNC; OBRV; OBVV; OnYI; UnTE
Sweet in the heat of summer is cool water for one's thirst. Sweetest of All. *Unknown, tr. by* Louis Untermeyer. UnTE
Sweet infancy! The Rapture. Thomas Traherne. OBS
Sweet Innisfallen. Thomas Moore. HBV-2; OBNC
Sweet Is Childhood. Jean Ingelow. TreFS
Sweet is the breath of Morn, her rising sweet. The World Beautiful. Milton. *Fr.* Paradise Lost, IV. GN
Sweet Is the Budding Spring of Love, *with music.* John Hippisley. BLSo
Sweet is the rose, but grows upon a brier [*or* brere]. Sweet and Sour. Spenser. Amoretti, XXVI. ElL; HBV-2
Sweet is the swamp with its secrets. A Snake. Emily Dickinson. TwAmPo
Sweet is the time for joyous folk. Hora Christi. Alice Brown. HBV-2; TrPWD; WGRP
Sweet is the voice that calls. September. George Arnold. HBV-1
Sweet is true love tho' given in vain, in vain. The Song of Love and Death [*or* Elaine's Song]. Tennyson. *Fr.* Idylls of the King: Lancelot and Elaine. FaBoEn; OBNC
Sweet it is to see the sun. Every Day Thanksgiving Day. Harriet Prescott Spofford. OHIP
Sweet Jane. *Unknown.* AmFP
Sweet Jesu. *Unknown. See* Swete Ihesu King of Blisse.
Sweet Jesus. Friar Michael of Kildare, *mod. vers. by* Russell K. Alspach. OnYI
Sweet Jesus with Thy Mother mild. England's Prayer. William Blundell. GoBC
Sweet kiss, thy sweets I fain would sweetly indite. Astrophel and Stella, LXXIX. Sir Philip Sidney. SiPS
"Sweet land"/ at last! St. Francis Einstein of the Daffodils. William Carlos Williams. MoPo
Sweet land of song, thy harp doth hang. The War Ship of Peace. Samuel Lover. PAH
Sweet, Let Me Go! *Unknown.* ElL; InvP; PV; TrGrPo; UnTE; ViBoPo
Sweet, let us love enjoy. Love Play. William Cavendish, Duke of Newcastle. ErPo
Sweet little bell. The Church Bell in the [*or* at] Night. *Unknown.* AnIL, *tr. by* Kuno Meyer; OnYI, *tr. by* Howard Mumford Jones
Sweet little maid with winsome eyes. The Other One. Harry Thurston Peck. AA
Sweet love has twined his fingers in my hair. Love's Prisoner. Mariana Griswold Van Rensselaer. HBV-1
Sweet Love, mine only treasure. Where His Lady Keeps His Heart. "A. W." CTC; ElL; OBSC
Sweet love, renew thy force, be it not said. Sonnets, LVI. Shakespeare. PoLF
Sweet Loving Friendship. Peter Bellamy. OBET
Sweet Lullaby, A. Nicholas Breton. ElL; OBSC; ViBoPo
Sweet Lydia take this maske, and shroud. A Maske for Lydia. Thomas Randolph. AnAnS-2
Sweet maid, if thou wouldst charm my sight. A Persian Song of Hafiz. Hafiz, *tr. by* Sir William Jones. AWP; OBEC
Sweet maiden of Passamaquoddy. Lines to Miss Florence Huntingdon [*or* The Maiden of Passamaquoddy] *Unknown, at. to* James De Mille. NA; WhC; WHW
Sweet Marie. Cy Warman. TreFS
Sweet Mary was a servant girl. Young Edwin in the Lowlands Low. *Unknown.* BaBo
Sweet Meat Has Sour Sauce; or, The Slave-Trader in the Dumps. William Cowper. NOEC; OBSV
Sweet mermaid of the incomparable eyes. The Mermaid. Ben King. OBAL
Sweet mouth, that send'st a musky-rosed breath. Joshua Sylvester. EnLoPo
"Sweet Muse." Isaac Watts. OxBoCh
(Sweet Muse, Descend.) NOBE
Sweet Music, sweeter far. A Carol. Edmund Bolton. OxBoCh
Sweet Music's Power. *At. to* John Fletcher. *See* Orpheus with His Lute.
Sweet my musings used to be. Mot eran dous miei cossir. Arnaut Daniel, *tr. by* Harriet Waters Preston. AWP
Sweet 'n Sour. Genny Lim. BrSi
Sweet names, the rosary of my evening prayer. Love's Rosary. George Edward Woodberry. AA
Sweet Nea!—for your lovely sake. Because. Edward Fitzgerald. HBV-1
Sweet "No! no!" with a sweet smile beneath, A. A Love-Lesson. Clement Marot, *tr. by* Leigh Hunt. AWP
Sweet Nosegay, A, or Pleasant Posy, *sels.* Isabella Whitney. WPE
"Do not account that for thine own."
"Gold savours well, though it be got."
"In loving, each one hath free choice."
"Little gold in law will make, A."
"Present day we cannot spend, The."
"Seek not man to please, for that."
"Such poor folk as to law do go."
Sweet notes in dimensionless clusters. The X of the Unknown. Tom Clark. LiSp
Sweet nymph, come to thy lover. *Unknown.* PBBP
Sweet nymphs, if, as ye stray. Madrigal: Love Vagabonding. William Drummond of Hawthornden. LoBV
Sweet o' the Year, The. George Meredith. BoNaP
Sweet Patuni. *Unknown.* BluL
Sweet peace, where dost thou dwell? I humbly crave. Peace. George Herbert. AnAnS-1; AWP; ChTr; ELP; NOCV; OxBoCh; SeCeV; TEP
Sweet Peas. Keats. GN
Sweet Peril. George Macdonald. BLPA; FaBoBe; TreFS
Sweet Phillis, if a silly swain. A Supplication. Nicholas Breton. OBSC
Sweet Philomel in groves and deserts haunting. *Unknown.* PBBP
Sweet Phosphor tricks to a smile the brow of heaven. All's Right with the World. Gerald Massey. EBVV
Sweet Pity, Wake. *Unknown.* ElL
Sweet poets of the gentle antique line. Sonnet. John Hamilton Reynolds. OBRV
Sweet pretty fledgelings, perched on the rail arow. Flycatchers. Robert Bridges. MoVE
Sweet procession, rose-blue. Seems Like We Must Be Somewhere Else. Denise Levertov. NePoEA-2
Sweet Reader. E. B. White. ImOP
Sweet Riley. *Unknown.* BaBo (B *vers. of* Willie Riley)
Sweet Rivers of Redeeming Love, *with music.* John A. Granade. AH
Sweet Robin, I have heard them say. Robin Redbreast. George Washington Doane. AA; HBV-1; HBVY
Sweet Robinette. *Unknown.* CoMu
Sweet Rose, Fair Flower. Shakespeare. *Fr.* The Passionate Pilgrim. ElL
Sweet rose [*or* Sweit rois] of virtue [*or* vertew] and of gentleness [*or* gentilnes]. To a Lady[e]. William Dunbar. BSV; EBEV; GBL; GoBC; MeEL; OAEP; OBEV; OxBS
Sweet Rosie O'Grady, *with music.* Maude Nugent. FSN
Sweet Saint, thou better canst declare to me. To Saint Mary Magdalen. Henry Constable. ACP
Sweet saint! whose rising dawned upon the sight. Ariana. Franklin Benjamin Sanborn. AA
Sweet season, that bud and bloom forth brings, The. *See* Soote Season.
Sweet secrecy, what tongue can tell thy worth? Michael Drayton. Idea's Mirrour, XLVI. ViBoPo
Sweet semi-circled Cynthia played at maw. Mockado, Fustian, and Motley [*or* Sonnet]. John Taylor. *Fr.* Odcomb's Complaint. ElL; FaBoNo
Sweet September. George Arnold. GN
Sweet serene sky-like Flower. To Lucasta: The Rose [*or* The Rose]. Richard Lovelace. AnAnS-2; HBV-1; SeCV-1; ViBoPo
Sweet she was, as kind a love. She Smiled like a Holiday. *Unknown.* OxBoLi
Sweet singer of the Spring, when the new world. On a Thrush Singing in Autumn. Sir Lewis Morris. OBVV
Sweet sixteen is shy and cold. Growing Old. Walter Learned. HBV-1
Sweet Slug-a-Bed. *Unknown.* FaBoCo
Sweet, Smiling Village. Goldsmith. *Fr.* The Deserted Village. PPON
Sweet Solitude, thou placid queen. Solitude. Hannah More. *Fr.* The Search after Happiness. WBLP
Sweet soul, which in the April of thy years. Sonnet. William Drummond of Hawthornden. JCP
Sweet sounds, oh, beautiful music, do not cease! On Hearing a Symphony of Beethoven. Edna St. Vincent Millay. LiTA; LiTM; MasP; MoAB; MoAmPo; NePA; TrGrPo; TwAmPo
Sweet spouse, you must presently troop and be gone. An Imitation of Martial, Book II Ep. 105. "Captain H——." NOEC
"Sweet spring is your." E. E. Cummings. NCSH
Sweet Spring, thou turn'st with all thy goodly [*or* goodlie] train[e]. Spring Bereaved 2 [*or* Sonnet]. William Drummond of Hawthornden. ElL; FaBoEn; OBEV
Sweet Stay-at-Home. W. H. Davies. CH; HBMV
Sweet stream, that dost with equal pace. On His Mistress Drown'd. Thomas Spratt. EnLoPo
Sweet stream, that winds through [*or* thro'] yonder glade. To a Young Lady

[*or* Addressed to a Young Lady]. William Cowper. EnRP; GTBS; GTBS-P; HBV-1
Sweet Suffolk Owl. *Unknown, at. to* Thomas Vautor. CH; ChTr; EBEV; ElL; EnRePo; FaBoRV; HBV-1; PBBP
Sweet summer breeze, whispering trees. Kiss Me Again. Henry Blossom. BLSo; TreFT
Sweet Swan of Avon! what a sight it were. Ben Jonson. *Fr.* To the Memory of My Beloved; the Author Mr. William Shakespeare. ChTr
Sweet, sweet Caroline. Sweet Caroline. *Unknown.* PoPle
Sweet sweet Robinette all the shepherds do declare. Sweet Robinette. *Unknown.* CoMu
Sweet, sweet, sweet,/ Is the wind's song. Harvest. Ellen Mackay Hutchinson Cortissoz. AA; HBV-1
Sweet, sweet, sweet, let me go. *Unknown.* GBL
Sweet sweet sweet sweet sweet tea. Susie Asado. Gertrude Stein. SOTW; TAP
Sweet Teviot! on thy silver tide. A Father's Notes of Woe. Sir Walter Scott. *Fr.* The Lay of the Last Minstrel. OBNC; OBRV
Sweet Thames I honour thee, not for thou art. Richard Barnfield. Sonnets, VII. PeHV
Sweet Thing, *diff. vers.* *Unknown.* FSW; OuSiCo, *with music*
"Sweet, thou art pale." The Three Enemies. Christina Rossetti. TrCP; VLP
Sweet thought—sweet model—that gloweth for all. The Opponent Charm Sustained. Samuel Greenberg. MoPo
Sweet timber land. Homing. Arna Bontemps. CDC
Sweet trees who shade this mould. *Unknown, tr. fr. Spanish by* James Mabbe. GBL
Sweet Trinity, The. *Unknown.* *See* Golden Vanity, The.
Sweet Tuxedo girl you see, A. Ta-ra-ra Boom-der-é. Henry J. Sayers. BLSo; FSW
Sweet twining hedgeflowers wind-stirred in no wise. The Lovers' Walk. Dante Gabriel Rossetti. *Fr.* The House of Life. OAEP
Sweet Unsure. Sir Walter Ralegh. SiPS
Sweet upland, to whose walks, with fond repair. To Hampstead. Leigh Hunt. EnRP
Sweet upland! where, like hermit old. In Mortem Venerabilis Andreae Prout Carmen. Francis Sylvester Mahony. NBM
Sweet Violets. *Unknown.* NoP
(Sweet Violets, Love's Paradise.) ElL
(Violets and Roses.) OBSC
Sweet waft their rounds those tuneful brothers five. Balsham Bells. Kenrick Prescot. NOEC
Sweet Was the Song. Walter Savage Landor. ViBoPo
Sweet Was the Song. *Unknown.* NOCV; PoSC
Sweet was the sound when oft at evening's close. Goldsmith. *Fr.* The Deserted Village. FaBoEn
Sweet were the dayes, when thou didst lodge with Lot. Decay. George Herbert. AnAnS-1; SeCP; SeCV-1
Sweet were the joys that both might like and last. Sweet Unsure. Sir Walter Ralegh. SiPS
Sweet [*or* Swete] were the sauce would please e[a]ch kind of tast[e]. In Commendation of George Gascoigne's Steel Glass [*or* Walter Rawley of the Middle Temple, in Commendation of Steele Glasse]. Sir Walter Ralegh. AAS; SiPS
Sweet western wind, whose luck it is. To the Western Wind. Robert Herrick. CaPo; HBV-1; OBEV; SeCV-1
Sweet, when I think how summer's smallest bird. Irene Rutherford McLeod. *Fr.* Sonnets. HBMV
Sweet Wild April. William Force Stead. HBV-1; HBVY
Sweet William ("A sailor's life is a merry life"). *Unknown.* OBET
Sweet William ("It was in the merry, merry month of May"), *with music. Unknown.* OuSiCo
Sweet William and May Margaret. *Unknown.* *See* Sweet William's Ghost.
Sweet William he married a wife. The Wife Wrapt [*or* Wrapped] in Wether's Skin. *Unknown.* AmFP; ESPB; ViBoFo
Sweet William he would a wooing ride. *See* Sweet William would. . .
Sweet William rode up to the old man's gate. Earl Brand. *Unknown.* AmFP
Sweet William would [*or* he would] a wooing ride. Fair Margaret and Sweet William. *Unknown.* ESPB; OBET; ViBoFo
Sweet William's Farewell to Black-eyed Susan. John Gay. BeLS; BoLoP; NOEC; OBEC
(All in the Downs, *folk version.*) AmFP
(Black-eyed Susan.) EtS; GTBS; GTBS-P; HBV-1; MOS; RoGo; TreFS
Sweet William's Ghost. *Unknown.* AWP; ESPB (A, B, F, *and* G *vers.*); ViBoFo (A *and* B *vers.*)
(Sweet William and May Margaret.) CH; HBV-2
Sweet William's gone over seas. Lord William; or, Lord Lundy. *Unknown.* BaBo; ESPB
Sweet Willie. *Unknown.* OxBB
Sweet Willie was a widow's son. Willie and Lady Margerie [*or* Maisry]. *Unknown.* ESPB; OxBB
Sweet Willie's ta'en him o'er the faem. Sweet Willie. *Unknown.* OxBB
Sweet wooded way in life, forgetful Sleep! To Sleep. Maybury Fleming. AA
Sweet World, if you will hear me now. Envoy. Sarah Morgan Bryan Piatt. AA
Sweeter Far Than the Harp, More Gold than Gold. "Michael Field." OBMV
Sweeter Saint I Serve, A. Sir Philip Sidney. *Fr.* Arcadia. SiPS
Sweeter than honey and the honeycomb. The Shed. Charles L. O'Donnell. ISi
Sweeter than sour apples flesh to boys. Ted Berrigan. EAS
Sweetes' Li'l' Feller. Frank L. Stanton. FaFP; TreFS
(Mighty Lak' a Rose.) BLSo; FSN
Sweetest bud of beauty, may. To a Very Young Lady. Sir George Etherege. ViBoPo
Sweetest Home, The. *Unknown.* STF
Sweetest Jesus, gracious, free. Sweet Jesus. Friar Michael of Kildare, *mod. vers. by* Russell K. Alspach. OnYI
Sweetest li'l' feller, ev'rybody knows. *See* Sweetes' Li'l' Feller.
Sweetest lives are those to duty wed, The. Reward of Service [*or* The Sweetest Lives]. Elizabeth Barrett Browning. BLPA; FaBoBe; TRV
Sweetest Love, I Do Not Go. John Donne. *See* Song: "Sweetest love, I do not go."
Sweetest of All. *Unknown, tr. fr. Greek by* Louis Untermeyer. UnTE
Sweetest of all childlike dreams. The Vanishers. Whittier. AA
Sweetest of sweets, I thank you: when displeasure. Church-Musick. George Herbert. AnAnS-1; SeCV-1; UnS
Sweetest Saviour, if my soul. A Dialogue. George Herbert. MePo; OBEV; OBS; SeCV-1
Sweetest Story Ever Told, The. R. M. Stults. BLSo, *with music*; FSN, *with music*; TreFS
Sweetest Thing, The. *Unknown, tr. fr. Susu by* Ulli Beier. TTY
Sweethairt, Rejoice in Mind. Alexander Montgomerie. BSV
Sweetheart in the Army, A. *Unknown.* BaBo (A *and* B *vers.*)
Sweetly-favored face, The. Canzonetta: Of His Lady in Absence. Giacomino Pugliesi, *tr. by* Dante Gabriel Rossetti. AWP
Sweetly (my Dearest) I left thee asleep. John Saffin. SCAP
Sweetness. *Unknown, tr. fr. Irish by* John Montague. BIrV
Sweetness of Nature, The. *Unknown, tr. fr. Irish by* Frank O'Connor. KiLC
Sweetness of poverty like this, The. Aspiration. Mário de Andrade, *tr. by* John Nist. TTY
Sweets That Die. Langdon Elwyn Mitchell. AA
Sweit rois of vertew and of gentilnes. *See* Sweet rose of virtue . . .
Swell the Anthem, Raise the Song, *with music.* Nathan Strong. AH
Swell'd with our late successes on the foe. Dryden. *Fr.* Annus Mirabilis. EBEV
Swell's Soliloquy. *Unknown.* FiBHP
Swept by the hot wind, stark, untrackable. Mohammed and Seid. Harrison Smith Morris. AA
Swerve, The. William Stafford. GP
"Swerve to the left, son Roger," he said. The Judgement of God. William Morris. OBVV
Swerving east, from rich industrial shadows. Here. Philip Larkin. CMoP
Swet Jesus/ Is cum to us. Welcome! Our Messiah. *Unknown.* MeEL
Swete Ihesu King of Blisse. *Unknown.* OxBoCh
(Sweet Jesu.) OxBM
Swete were the sauce would please ech kind of tast. *See* Sweet were the sauce would please each kind of taste.
Swetnam, the Woman-Hater, *sel.* *Unknown.*
Ding Dong. ElL
Swich fyn hath, lo, this Troilus for love! Chaucer. *Fr.* Troilus and Criseyde. NOCV
Swift, *sel.* Thomas Caulfield Irwin.
"It was a dim October day." BIrV
Swift. Delmore Schwartz. PoA
Swift across the palace floor. Little Guinever. Annie Fields. AA
Swift as a spirit hastening to his task. The Triumph of Life. Shelley. ChER; MasP; OAEL-2; PoEL-4
Swift boomerang, come get! December 18th. Anne Sexton. *Fr.* Eighteen Days without You. CAPP
Swift Bullets, The. Carolyn Wells. ShM
Swift cries answering back. Evening Ride. Jill Hoffman. PH
Swift fleet the billowy clouds along the sky. Charlotte Smith. *Fr.* Montalbert. BoWoP; WPE
Swift Floods. Kata Szidónia Petröczi, *tr. fr. Hungarian by* Laura Schiff. WPOW
Swift had pains in his head. January 1940 [*or* War Poet]. Roy Fuller. HoPM; LiTM; PP; SeCePo; WaP
Swift had sailed into his rest. Swift's Epitaph. W. B. Yeats. CMoP; OBVE

Swift is't in pace, light poiz'd, to look in clear. Description of a New England Spring. John Josselyn. SCAP
Swift Love, Sweet Motor. Hildegarde Flanner. WPE
Swift o'er the sunny grass. Shadow Evidence. Mary Mapes Dodge. AA
Swift red flesh, a winter king, The. The Dance. Hart Crane. *Fr.* The Bridge: Powhatan's Daughter. LiTM; MoAB; MoAmPo; OxBA; SeCeV; TwAmPo
Swift shot the curlew 'thwart the rising blast. Ode on Lord Macartney's Embassy to China. William Shepherd. NOEC
Swift through some trap mine eyes have never found. The Harlequin of Dreams. Sidney Lanier. AA; AP
Swift through the yielding air I glide. The Lark. *Unknown.* OBS
Swift to the western bounds of this wide land. On the Completion of the Pacific Telegraph. Jones Very. AP; TAP
Swift was sweet on Stella. Us Poets. Franklin P. Adams. PoPl; WhC
Swiftly Arose. Walt Whitman. *Fr.* Song of Myself. TrCP
Swiftly turn the murmuring wheel! Song for the Spinning Wheel. Wordsworth. OBRV
Swiftly walk o'er [*or* over] the western wave. To the Night [*or* Night]. Shelley. AWP; CH; ChER; EnRP; FPL; GTBS; GTBS-P; HBV-1; HBVY; LoBV; NoP; OAEL-2; OAEP; OBEV; OBNC; OBRV; PoLF; PoRA; SeCeV; TEP; TreFS; TrGrPo; ViBoPo; WHA; WiR
Swift's Epitaph. W. B. Yeats. CMoP; OBVE
Swim in Ohuira Bay, A. Robert Peterson. NeAC
Swimmer. Gladys Cardiff. CDW
Swimmer. Robert Francis. CrMA; DFF; LiSp; NePoAm; WeW
Swimmer, The. Irving Layton. PeCV
Swimmer, The. Roden Noel. OBVV
Swimmer in the Rain. Robert Wallace. FiCP; LiSp
Swimmer of Nemi, The. "Fiona Macleod." SyP
Swimmer whose clothing was strewed, A. Limerick. *Unknown.* NIP
Swimmers. Paul D. Shiplett. LFAC
Swimmers, The. Allen Tate. AP; InPS; MoAmPo; MoVE; NOBA
Swimmer's Moment, The. Margaret Avison. NOBC
Swimming. Byron. *Fr.* The Two Foscari. GN
Swimming. Clinton Scollard. FaPON
Swimming. Swinburne. *Fr.* Tristram of Lyonesse. GN
Swimming by Night. James Merrill. NYBP; VGW
Swimming Chenango Lake. Charles Tomlinson. FaBoMo; NoAM
Swimming down to us. Moon Man. Jean Valentine. MOON
Swimming in the Pacific. Robert Penn Warren. AMV-80
Swimming is a gift. Let Go: Once. Gerald Fleming. AMV-81
Swimming Lady, The: or, A Wanton Discovery. *Unknown.* ErPo; UnTE
Swimming Lesson, The. Robert Hershon. NeAC
Swimming Pool, The. Jonathan Holden. MAYP
Swimming Pool. Maria Teresa Horta, *tr. fr. Portuguese by* Suzette Macedo. PBWP
Swine com jingling doun Pelton lonin, The. Pigs o' Pelton. *Unknown.* GBP
Swineherd. Eilean Ni Chuilleanain. BIrV; CIP; WPOW
Swineherd, let us make for the moorland. The Wry Rowan. *Unknown, tr. by* Eoin MacNeill. OnYI
Swing, The. Robert Louis Stevenson. FaBoBe; FaFP; GoJo; NTCP; PDV; SoPo; SUS; TEP; TiPo; TreF
Swing dat hammer—hunh. Southern Road. Sterling A. Brown. BALP; BANP; BPo; FB; PoBA
Swing Low, Sweet Chariot ("I ain't never been to heaven"). *Unknown.* GBP
Swing Low, Sweet Chariot ("I looked over Jordan and what did I see"). *Unknown.* AmFN; BLSo, *with music*; BoAN-1, *with music*; FaPON; FSW; UnPo
Swing Low, Sweet Chariot ("Oh, de good ole chariot swing so low"). *Unknown.* AA
Swing on the Corner, *with music. Unknown.* TrAS
Swing One, Swing All. George Bradley. AMV-80
Swing out, oh bells. The Bells of Peace. Aileen Fisher. SiSoSe
Swing Song, A. William Allingham. FaPON; MoShBr; SUS
Swinging Chick. Ern Alpaugh *and* Dewey G. Pell. InPK
Swinging mill bell changed its rate, The. A Lone Striker. Robert Frost. SaC
Swirl of water dominated the plain, The. The Blue-Hole. Charles G. Bell. GrPl
Swirl sleeping in the waterfall! Chomei at Toyama. Basil Bunting. OxBTC
Swirling spring. Young Girl. Ricarda Huch, *tr. by* Janine Canan *and* Deirdre Lashgari. WPOW
Swiss Air. Bret Harte. NA
Swiss Peasant, The. Wordsworth. OBEC
Swiss they are a hardy race, The. Song of Switzerland. Stoddard King. WhC
Switch Blade, The; or, John's Other Wife. Jonathan Williams. NeAP
Switch Cut in April, A. Clifford Dyment. MoVE
Switchback. Edith Sitwell. PBWP
Switzerland. Matthew Arnold. OAEP
Sels.
Farewell, A: "My horse's feet beside the lake," III. VLP
Isolation: To Marguerite, IV. EBVV; TEP; VLP
(Isolation.) TreFT
Meeting, I. ELP; VLP
Parting, II. VLP
Terrace at Berne, The, VII. VLP
To Marguerite—Continued, V. BoLoP; EBEV; EBVV; ELP; FaBoEn; FiP; GTBS-P; HBV-1; MOS; NOBE; NoP; OAEL-2; OBEV; OBNC; PoEL-5; PPP; PrIM; SeCeV; TEP; VLP
(Isolation.) OBVV
Swollen river sang through the green hole, The. The Sleeper in the Valley. Arthur Rimbaud, *tr. by* Robert Lowell. *Fr.* Eighteen-Seventy. OBWP
Swollen to bursting like a pod, her ripeness. Beets. Alden Nowlan. PeCV
Swooning swim to less and less. Buddha. Herman Melville. HeIP
Sword, The. Abu Bakr, *tr. fr. Arabic by* A. J. Arberry. TTY
Sword, A. Karin Boye, *tr. fr. Swedish by* Joanna Bankier. WPOW
Sword, a sword, and a sword, A. Which Sword? Jason Noble Pierce. PGD
Sword and the Sickle, The. Blake. *Fr.* Gnomic Verses. ChTr
("Sword sang on the barren heath, The.) FaBoEE; TrGrPo
Sword fell down, The: I heard a knell. The Leader. Hilaire Belloc. ACP
Sword in a Cloud of Light, A. Kenneth Rexroth. NMP
Sword in length a reaping-hook amain. King Harald's Trance. George Meredith. VLP
Sword of light is unsheathed from the cloud, A. Parting. Shlomo Vinner, *tr. by* Laya Firestone *and* Howard Schwartz. VWA
Sword of Surprise, The. G. K. Chesterton. MoBrPo
Sword of Tethra, The. William Larminie. *Fr.* Moytura. OnYI
Sword sang on the barren heath, The. The Sword and the Sickle. Blake. *Fr.* Gnomic Verses. ChTr; FaBoEE; TrGrPo
Sword was sheathed, The: in April's sun. The Vow of Washington. Whittier. PAH
Swords crossed, but not in strife! The Crossed Swords. Nathaniel Langdon Frothingham. AA
Swordy Well. John Clare. WHA
Sybilla's Dirge. Thomas Lovell Beddoes. *See* Dirge: "We do lie beneath the grass."
Sycamore Tree, The. *Unknown.* AmFP
Sycophantic Fox and the Gullible Raven, The. Guy Wetmore Carryl. BLPA; CenHV; FaFP; FiBHP; HBV-1; InMe; OBCA; TreFT
Sydney? It's a building site now, says Kevin. Telling the Cousins. Les A. Murray. AMV-81
Sylla declares the world shall know. A Serious Danger. R. A. Davenport. PV
Syl La Ble Speaks En Erg y/Sound, The. Carol Lee Sanchez. TWSS
Syllables disintegrate ingrate alphabets. Phyllis Webb. *Fr.* The Kropotkin Poems. NOBC
Syllables of grief are small, The. Text for Today. Phyllis McGinley. WhC
"Sylphs! on each oak-bud wound the wormy galls." The Protection of Plants. Erasmus Darwin. *Fr.* The Economy of Vegetation. FaBoUs
Sylvae, *sel.* Statius, *tr. fr. Latin.*
"Too harsh the man who setting bounds to grief." PeHV
Sylvan Delights. Pope. *Fr.* Pastorals: Summer. NOBE
Sylvan meant savage in those primal woods. Woods. W. H. Auden. NePA; NePoAM
Sylvan Muses, can ye sing. Aglaia. Nicholas Breton. *Fr.* The Passionate Shepherd. OBSC
Sylvan Revel, A. Edward Cracroft Lefroy, *after the Greek of* Theocritus. *Fr.* Echoes from Theocritus. AWP
Sylvester Vermicelli was a conscientious clerk. Ballad of the Faithful Clerk. Albert Stillman. DBV; InMe
Sylvester's Dying Bed. Langston Hughes. NoAM; UnPo
Sylvia. Samuel Croxall. NOEC
Sylvia. Robert Lowell, *ad. fr. the Italian of* Giacomo Leopardi. NaP
Sylvia. Shakespeare. *See* Who Is Silvia?
Sylvia, do you remember the minutes. Sylvia. Robert Lowell. NaP
"Sylvia, hush!" I said, "come here." Dove's Nest. Joseph Russell Taylor. HBV-1
Sylvia; or, The May Queen, *sels.* George Darley.
Chorus of Spirits. OnYI
Dirge: "Wail! wail ye o'er the dead!" OBRV
Serenade: "Awake thee, my lady-love." HBV-1
Song: "I've taught thee Love's sweet lesson o'er." OBRV
Song: "Streams that wind among the hills, The." NBM
Sylvia the fair, in the bloom of Fifteen. Song. Dryden. ErPo; EBEV; UnTE; ViBoPo
Sylvie and Bruno, *sels.* "Lewis Carroll."
He Thought He Saw. HBVY
("He thought he saw a Banker's clerk.") NA

Mad Gardener's Song, The. BLPL; FaBoCo; FaBoNo; FiBHP; NBM; OnUR, 4 *sts.*; OxBChV; TreFS; WiR
(Gardener's Song, The.) EvOK; HBV-2
Sylvie and Bruno Concluded, *sels.* "Lewis Carroll."
King-Fisher Song, The. FaBoNo
Little Birds. FaBoNo; WhC
Little Birds Are Playing, *sel.* OxBoLi
Pig-Tale, A. WiR
(Melancholy Pig, The.) FaPON
Sylvius, your hands near my mouth are heady flowers. Marguerite Burnat-Provins, *tr. fr. French by* Cassia Berman. BoWoP
Sylvoe, *sel.* Dryden.
Song, A: "Go tell Amynta gentle swain." CavP
Sym of Lyntoun, be the ramis horn. King Berdok. *Unknown.* OxBS
Symbol. David Morton. HBMV
Symbol from the first, of mastery, A. The Staff of Aesculapius. Marianne Moore. ImOP
Symbol of star or lily of the snows. The Cloud of Carmel. Jessica Agnes Powers. ISi
Symbol of war, a war, The. All That Is Perfect in Woman. William Carlos Williams. BiP
Symbols. John Richard Moreland. PGD
Symbols. Harry Roskolenko. FAZ
Symbols. Christina Rossetti. VLP
Symbols. Vance Thompson. AA
Symbols. W. B. Yeats. OBMV
Symmetrical Poem. Michael Palmer. NPGG
Symon's Lesson of Wisdom for All Manner of Children. *Unknown.* OxBChV
Sympathizers, The. Josephine Miles. CrMA
Sympathy. Emily Brontë. OAEP
Sympathy. Paul Laurence Dunbar. AmNP; CDC; IDB; PoBA; PoNe
Sympathy. Althea Gyles. HBV-1
Sympathy. Reginald Heber. BeLS
Sympathy, a Welcome, A. John Berryman. GrPl; NYBP
Symphony. Alfred Dorn. AMV-80
Symphony. Frank Horne. AmNP
Symphony, The. Sidney Lanier. AmPP; AP; LiTA
"I speak for each no-tonguèd tree," *sel.* ViBoPo
Symphony in Blue. Raymond F. Roseliep. ISi
Symphony in Yellow. Oscar Wilde. EBVV; FaBoPP; MoBrPo; SyP
Symphony No. 3, in D Minor. Jonathan Williams. *Fr.* Mahler. VGW
Symposium, The, *sel.* Leah Goldberg, *tr. fr. Hebrew by* Robert Alter.
"Outside the cats are wailing." PBWP
Symposium, A: Apples. Linda Pastan. NIP
Symptom Recital. Dorothy Parker. SBG
Symptoms of Love. Robert Graves. BoLoP
Synekdechestai. C. M. Schmid. GoYe
Synge's Grave. Winifred Letts. AnIV
Synnöve's Song. Björnstjerne Björnson, *tr. fr. Norwegian by* Charles Wharton Stork. PoPl
Synods are whelps of th' Inquisition. Presbyterian Church Government. Samuel Butler. *Fr.* Hudibras, I, 3. OBS
Synthesizing Several Abstruse Concepts with an Experience. Carol Poster. BXAP
Syon lyes waste, and thy Jerusalem. *See* Sion Lies Waste.
Syren Songs, *sels.* George Darley.
Mermaidens' Vesper-Hymn, The, VI. FaBoEn; GBL; LoBV; OBNC; OBRV; PoEL-4
(Chorus of Sirens.) NBM
(Siren Chorus.) BIrV; FaBoRV; OxBI; ViBoPo; WSC
Sea-Ritual, The, V. BIrV; OBNC; OBRV; OnYI; OxBI; WiR; WSC
(Deadman's Dirge.) CH
Syrens' Song, The. William Browne. *See* Sirens' Song, The.
Syrinx. John Lyly. *See* Pan's Song.
System. Robert Louis Stevenson. TEP
Systole and Diastole. Conrad Aiken. CrMA
Systolic city noise denies the thrush. Rural Legend. Mary Elizabeth Osborn. NePoAm

T

T. A. H. Ambrose Bierce. AA; YaD
T. B. Blues. Leadbelly (Huddie Ledbetter). BluL
T-Bar. P. K. Page. NOBC; OBCV
T-Bone Steak Blues. *Unknown.* BluL
T. E. Lawrence Poems, The, *sels.* Gwendolyn MacEwen.
There Is No Place to Hide. NOBC
Void, The. NOBC
T. R. Donald Hall. PoA
T. S. Eliot. W. H. Auden. OBAL
T. S. Eliot. Robert Lowell. NoAM; NOBA
TV. John Forbes. CBAP
TV echoes, The. Nights Primarily III. Ed Lipman. LFAC
T.V.A., The, *with music.* *Unknown.* TrAS
T was a tidy young tapir. A Tidy Young Tapir. Carolyn Wells. TDH
Ta wa nee ta wa nee—i softly call into the gentle night. Ronald James Dessus. LFAC
Tabernacle of Peace. Hayim Be'er, *tr. fr. Hebrew by* Stephen Mitchell. VWA
Tabernacle Thought, A. Israel Zangwill. TrJP
Tabernacles. Gerrit Lansing. CoPo
Table, The. Michael Heffernan. PoA
Table and the Chair, The. Edward Lear. HBVY; SoPo; TreFT
Table-Birds. Kenneth MacKenzie. PoAu-2
Table for One. John Holmes. WhC
Table Manners. Gelett Burgess. OBCA; RHPC
Table Manners. James Montgomery Flagg. TDH
Table Richly Spread, A. Milton. *Fr.* Paradise Regained, II. FaBoCh
Table Rules for Little Folks. *Unknown.* FaBoUs; OxBChV
Table Talk, *sel.* William Cowper.
"I know the mind that feels indeed the fire." PP
Table Talk. Donald Mattam. FiBHP
Table Talk. Wallace Stevens. NoP
Table was filled with many objects, The. The "Utopia." Lee Harwood. EAS
Tableau. Countee Cullen. AmFN; BANP; PoBA
Tableau. Judith Wright. CBAP
Tableau at Twilight. Ogden Nash. FiBHP
Tableau Vivant. Tess Gallagher. GeTw
Tablerock. Darryl Wally. AMV-81
Tables. Naomi Clark. AMV-80
Table's long and gleaming, The. The Board Meets. John Gloag. FiBHP
Tables Turned, The. Wordsworth. EnRP; HBV-1; OAEL-2; OAEP; OBRV
Taboo to Boot. Ogden Nash. FiBHP
Taboo Woman, The. *Tr. fr. Zuni Indian by* K. Kennedy. WTO
Taborer beat/ Your little drum. Jig for Sackbuts. D. B. Wyndham Lewis. ErPo
Tacita. James Benjamin Kenyon. AA
Tacking Ship off Shore. Walter Mitchell. AA; EtS; FaBoBe; GN; HBV-1
Tact. Oliver Herford. TDH
Tact. Paul Pascal. PV; WeW
Tact. E. A. Robinson. NoAM
Taddeo Gaddi built me. I am old. The Old Bridge at Florence. Longfellow. EyDe
Tadhg sat up on his hills. Senior Members. Sean Lucy. CIP
Tadlow. Abel Evans. FaBoCo
Tadoussac. Charles Bancroft. BLPA
Tae be wan o them Kings. Stars. George Mackay Brown. OxBS
Tae titly. *Unknown.* OxNR
Taedium Vitae. Oscar Wilde. SyP
Taffy, the topaz-coloured cat. In Honour of Taffy Topaz. Christopher Morley. TiPo
Taffy was a Welshman, Taffy was a thief. Mother Goose. GBP; OxNR
Taffy was born. *Unknown.* OxNR
Tag Along. Nina Payne. RHPC
Tagus, Farewell. Sir Thomas Wyatt. EnRePo; QFR
(In Spain.) OBSC; SeCePo
(Of His Returne from Spain.) FaBoEn
("Tagus, fare well, that westward with thy stremes.") AAS
Tahiti, Tahiti. Vor a Gauguin Picture zu Singen. Kurt M. Stein. FiBHP
Tahola. Richard Hugo. WOLT
Tail behind, a trunk in front, A. The Elephant, or the Force of Habit. A. E. Housman. FaBV; NOBL; PV; WhC
Tail of the See, A. Elizabeth T. Corbett. OBCA
Tail toddle, tail toddle. Tommie Makes My Tail Toddle. Burns. ErPo
Taill of the Foxe, That Begylit the Wolf, in the Schadow of the Mone, The. Robert Henryson. OxBS
Taill of the Uponlandis Mous and the Burges Mous, The. Robert Henryson. *See* Tale of the Upland Mouse and the Burgess Mouse, The.
Tailor, The. "S. Ansky," *tr. fr. Yiddish by* Joseph Leftwich. TrJP
Tailor, The. Thomas Lovell Beddoes. *See* Oviparous Tailor, The.
Tailor. Eleanor Farjeon. OxBChV
Tailor, The. Patricia Garfinkel. AMV-80
Tailor, The. Joseph Leftwich. TrJP
Tailor Called Sorrow, A. Betti Alver, *tr. fr. Estonian by* Willis Barnstone *and* Felix Oinas. BoWoP
Tailor of Bicester. *Unknown.* OxNR
Tailor That Came from Mayo, The. Denis A. McCarthy. OnYI
Tailor's Wedding, The. Louis Simpson. NNaP

Tailspinning from the shelves of sky. Jubilo. Allen Tate. WaP
Tain't Nobody's Business. *Unknown.* BluL
Taisigh Agat Fein Do Phog. *Unknown, tr. fr. Irish by* Maire Cruise O'Brien. BIrV
Tak for Sidst. Babette Deutsch. PoA
Tak tyme in tym, or tym will not be tane. A Description of Tyme. Alexander Montgomerie. OxBS
Tak' Your Auld Cloak about Ye. *Unknown.* OxBS
Takamura Kotaro/ speaks. On Writing Asian-American Poetry. Geraldine Kudaka. BrSi
Take a blessing from my heart to the land of my birth. The Fair Hills of Eiré, O. James Clarence Mangan. OBVV
Take a chair. (This is going to take some time.) Chairs. Henry Petroski. PoDr
Take a common little bronco. The Cowboy Up to Date. Charles F. Thomas, Jr. CoSo
Take a dainty paradox. Finale. A. P. Herbert. *Fr.* Perseverance; or, Half a Coronet. InMe
Take a Drink on Me. *Unknown.* FSW
Take a father's admonition, from a heart disturbed. A Father's Testament. Judah ibn Tibbon, *tr. by* Israel Abrahams. TrJP
Take a golden comb. This Earthen Body. *Gond Oral Tradition, tr. by* V. Elwin *and* S. Hivale. WTO
Take a harp. Song of the Harlot. Bible, *O.T. Fr.* Isaiah. TrJP
Take a knuckle of veal. A Receipt for Stewing Veal. John Gay, *also at. to* Pope. FaBoUs
Take a large olive, stone it and then stuff it. A Dish for a Poet. *Unknown.* OBCP
Take a look, i/ sd. For Kelley. Ken Belford. NeAC
Take a model of the world so big. The Rescued Year. William Stafford. LCAP
Take a recipe now for that clot of inanity. Gilbertian Recipe for a Politician. J. A. Lindon. DBV
Take a statement: the same as yesterday's dictation. Vowel Movements. Daryl Hine. PoA
Take a strip of white paper, turn. Farolita. Mei-Mei Berssenbrugge. BrSi
Take a trip with me in nineteen thirteen. The 1913 Massacre. Woody Guthrie. FSW
Take a Walk around the Corner. *Unknown.* BluL
Take a Whiff on Me. Leadbelly (Huddie Ledbetter). FSW
Take a Whiff on Me. *Unknown.* NOBA
Take all my loves, my love, yea, take them all. Sonnets, XL. Shakespeare. InvP; OBSC
Take all of me, I am thine own, heart, soul. A Sonnet. Amélie Rives. AA
Take as a gift. Giving and Taking. James Kirkup. EaLo
Take Away. Margot Ruddock. OBMV
Take away the stuff! Dry. Samuel Hoffenstein. BXAP
Take away your soft hair and your softer lips. Supplication. Louis Untermeyer. HBMV
Take Back the Heart. Charlotte Alington Barnard. TreFT
Take Back the Virgin Page. Thomas Moore. HBV-1; OBNC
Take Back Your Gold. Louis W. Pritzkow. FSN, *with music*; TreF
Take care, O wisp of a moon. To the Afternoon Moon, at Sea. Cale Young Rice. EtS
Take care when you speak to me. When You Speak to Me. Tess Gallagher. LTB
Take Down the Fiddle, Karl! Shaw Neilson. CBAP
Take, for instance, a woman at a desk in a white room. Absence. Kathy Mangan. AMV-81
Take fortune as it falls, as one adviseth. The Author, of His Own Fortune. Sir John Harington. FaBoEE
Take Frankincense, O God. Charles Fitz-Geffry. *Fr.* Holy Transportations. ChTr
Take from the earth its tragic hunger, Lord. Prayer. Hazel J. Fowler. TrPWD
Take hand[s] and part with laughter. Rococo. Swinburne. HBV-1; ViBoPo
Take Heart. Edna Dean Proctor. HBV-2
Take heart, monsieur, four-fifths of this province. For Jean Vincent d'Abbadie, Baron St.-Castin. Alden Nowlan. NOBC
Take heart, Prytherch. Aside. R. S. Thomas. OxBC
Take heart, the journey's ended. In the Town, *tr. by* Eleanor Farjeon. *Unknown.* OBCP; PChr
Take heed betime, lest ye be spied. Sir Thomas Wyatt. SiPS
Take Heed of Gazing Overmuch. Thomas Richardson. *Fr.* A Proper New Song. ElL
Take heed of loving me[e]. The Prohibition. John Donne. ElL; GBL; MeLP; OBS
Take heed of this small child of earth. The Poor Children. Victor Hugo, *tr. by* Swinburne. AWP
Take Him away, he's dead as they die. Obituary. Kenneth Fearing. VGW
Take him up tendahly. Parody on Thomas Hood's "The Bridge of Sighs." *Unknown.* FiBHP
Take home Thy prodigal child, O Lord of Hosts! Birthday Sonnet. Elinor Wylie. MoAB; MoAmPo
Take I, 4:11:58. Philip Whalen. NeAP
Take It from Me. Kenneth O. Hanson. CoAP
Take it from me kiddo. Poem, or Beauty Hurts Mr. Vinal. E. E. Cummings. InPS; MoAB; MoAmPo; MoVE; NIP; OBAL; OxBA; PPoe
Take it, love! Song. Richard Le Gallienne. HBV-1
Take it, my dear. Keep it beneath your pillow. Gift of a Mirror to a Lady. David Wagoner. NePoAm-2
Take me as I drive alone. White Blossoms. Robert Mezey. NaP; VWA
Take me away, and in the lowest deep. The Soul before God. Cardinal Newman. *Fr.* The Dream of Gerontius. OxBoCh
Take me back to Arizona as it was in early days. Back to Arizona. Earl Alonzo Brininstool. BPAW
Take me back to old Montana. Way Out West. *Unknown.* CoSo
Take Me in Your Arms, Miss Moneypenny-Wilson. Patrick Barrington. WhC
Take Me Out to the Ball Game. Jack Norworth. OBAL
Take me upon thy breast. O Sleep. Grace Fallow Norton. HBV-2
Take my hand. There are two of us in this cave. The Blind Leading the Blind. Lisel Mueller. IHMS
Take My Heart. St. Augustine, *tr. fr. Latin.* TRV
Take My Life and Let It Be. Frances Ridley Havergal. BLRP; TreFT
Take my share of Soul Food. High on the Hog. Julia Fields. CNA
Take note, passers-by, of the sharp erosions. The Circuit Judge. Edgar Lee Masters. *Fr.* Spoon River Anthology. FaBoEE
Take Nothing for Granite. Nate Salsbury. InMe
Take, O take the cream away. Breakfast Song in Time of Diet. Stoddard King. OBAL
Take, O Take Those Lips Away. Shakespeare. *Fr.* Measure for Measure, IV, i; *also given, with add. st., in* The Bloody Brother (*by* John Fletcher, *and others*). AWP; BiP; EBEV; ElL; ELP; EnLoPo; EnRePo; FaBV; GBL; HBV-1; HeIP; InPS; LiTB; NoP; OAEL-1; OAEP; OBEV; SeCeV; ViBoPo; WHA
(At the Moated Grange.) NOBE
(Love Song: "Take, o take those lips away.") FaBoEn
(Madrigal: "Take, o take those lips away.") GTBS; GTBS-P
(Seals of Love.) TrGrPo
(Song: "Take, O take those lips away.") FiP; PoEL-2
(Song at the Moated Grange, A.) OBSC
Take of me what is not my own. Envoi. Kathleen Raine. NeBP; NOBE
Take off your hat. Pass Office Song. *Unknown, tr. by* Peggy Rutherford. PBA; TTY; WTO
Take One Home for the Kiddies. Philip Larkin. ELU; OxBTC
Take Physic, Pomp. Shakespeare. *Fr.* King Lear, III, iv. TrGrPo
(Poor Naked Wretches.) PPON
Take *quantum sufficit* of meadows and trees. To Make a Pastoral; a Receipt. *Unknown.* FaBoUs
Take strands of speech, faded and broken. Maker of Songs. Hazel Hall. HBMV
Take the back off the watch. Time Piece. William Cole. ELU; GrPl; PPJ
Take the cloak from his face, and at first. After. Robert Browning. TrGrPo
Take the cloak of all my love. Song for a Jewess. Iwan Goll, *tr. by* Joseph T. Shipley. TrJP
Take the Crust. Sadi, *tr. fr. Persian by* L. Cranmer-Byng. *Fr.* The Gulistan. AWP
Take the leaf of a tree. Reply to the Question: "How Can You Become a Poet?" Eve Merriam. DFF
Take them, O Death! and bear away. Suspiria. Longfellow. ViBoPo
Take, then your paltry Christ. To the Christians. Francis Lauderdale Adams. OxBS; WGRP
Take these flowers which, purple waving. To a Lady with Flowers from the Roman Wall. Sir Walter Scott. OAEP
Take these stripes from, stripes from around my shoulder, huh! Lord, It's All, Almost Done. *Unknown.* OuSiCo
Take these who will as may be: I. Permit Me Voyage. James Agee. MoAmPo
Take this blessing. Benediction. William Freedman. VWA
Take this flyswatter and exterminate the angels. Adolph Hitler Meditates on the Jewish Problem. Oscar Hahn, *tr. by* James Hoggard. AMV-81
Take This Hammer. *Unknown.* FSW, *sl. diff. version*; OuSiCo, *with music*
(Spike Driver Blues.) BluL
Take this kiss upon the brow! A Dream within a Dream. Poe. AmPP; AP; BLPL; GBL; NOBA; OxBA; SyP; TAP; TrGrPo
Take this old man with the soldierly straight back. Louis MacNeice. *Fr.* The Kingdom. LiTM
Take this stabbing or that rape. Monologue through Bars. Nelson Hubbell. AMV-81

Take Thou Our Minds, Dear Lord, *with music.* William H. Foulkes. AH
Take Thy Bliss, O Man. Blake. *Fr.* Visions of the Daughters of Albion. EnRP
Take time, my dear, ere Time takes wing. Fading Beauty. *Unknown.* FaBoEE
Take Time to Be Holy. W. D. Longstaff. BLRP
Take Time to Talk with God. Helen Frazee-Bower. STF
Take time to work. Old English Prayer. *Unknown.* TreFT
Take time while time doth last. Song Set by John Farmer. *Unknown.* CTC; OBSC
Take Tools Our Strength. Gerald L. Simmons, Jr. NBP
Take two-o coo, Taffy! *Unknown.* PBBP
Take up the oxen, boys, and harness up the mules. The Gold Seeker's Song. *Unknown.* PoOW
Take up the pen and write a text. *Malay Oral Tradition, tr. by* R. J. Wilkinson *and* R. O. Winstedt. WTO
Take what is at hand. Ode on a Decision to Settle for Less. William Pillen. VWA
Take you my brushes, child of light, and lay. Spring Landscape. Arthur Davison Ficke. Sonnets of a Portrait Painter, XII. HBMV
Take Your Accusation Back! Kittaararter, *tr. fr. Eskimo.* WTO
Take Your Fingers Off It. *Unknown.* FSW
Take your meals, my little man. The Little Gentleman. *Unknown. Fr.* Little Derwent's Breakfast. HBV-1; HBVY
Take Your Place. *Unknown.* STF
Take your pleasure, dance and play. Invitation to Youth. *Unknown, tr. by* John Addington Symonds. UnTE
Take your time kind mama I'm gonna do it just as slow as I can. Slow Mama Slow. *Unknown.* BluL
Take 25 basic convict students. Basic Writing 702. John Paul Minarik. LFAC
Taken from the. The Primitive. Don L. Lee. BPo
Takes All Kinds. R. P. Dickey. POL
Taking a charity. Confession in Holy Week. Christopher Morley. HBMV
Taking a Walk with You. Kenneth Koch. CABA; CAPP
Taking between them/ A specially straight willow tree. Eulogy to the Bow and Arrow. *Mongol Oral Tradition, tr. by* C. R. Bawden. WTO
Taking Care of It. Deborah Lee. BrSi
Taking Ford's dictation on Samuel Butler. Ford Madox Ford. Robert Lowell. OxBC
Taking, giving back their lives. The Field Hospital. Paul Muldoon. CIP
Taking Leave of a Friend. Li Po, *tr. fr. Chinese by* Ezra Pound. SOTW; TwAmPo
Taking Long Views. May Kendall. CenHV
Taking me into your body. The Source. Jon Stallworthy. NoP
Taking Off. Mary McB. Green. TiPo
Taking Off. *Unknown.* SoPo
Taking Off My Clothes. Carolyn Forché. AmPA
Taking pity on this scrag-end of the city. One Kingfisher and One Yellow Rose. Eileen Brennan. NeIP
Taking the air rifle from my son's hand. Cain. Irving Layton. MoCV; PeCV
Taking the Train Home. William Matthews. GeTw
Taking to the Woods. Henry Taylor. MAYP
Taking us by and large, we're a queer lot. The Sisters. Amy Lowell. SBG
Talbragar. Henry Lawson. PoAu-1
Tale, A. Edward Thomas. ChTr
Tale for Husbands, A. Sir Philip Sidney. *Fr.* Arcadia. SiPS
Tale half told and hardly understood, A. Exodus for Oregon. Joaquin Miller. BPAW
Tale I frame shall be found to tally, The. The Seafarer. *Unknown, tr. by* Michael Alexander. OBVE
Tale is every time the same, The. Fable. Maurice James Craig. NeIP
Tale is told of a doomed planet whose, The. Easier. James Harrison. AMV-80
Tale of a Pony, The. Bret Harte. OBNV
Tale of a Tart, The. Frederick E. Weatherley. SUS
Tale of Custard the Dragon, The. Ogden Nash. FaPON; OBCA; PoPl; PoRA; TiPo
(Custard the Dragon.) OnUR
Tale of Drury Lane, A. Horace Smith. FaBoCo
Tale of Genji, The, *sels.* Murasaki Shikibu, *tr. fr. Japanese by* Kenneth Rexroth *and* Ikuko Atsumi.
"Lady Murasaki says." BoWoP
"Troubled waters, The/ are frozen fast." WPOW
Tale of Genji. Hugh Seidman. AmPA
Tale of Jorkyns and Gertie, The; or, Vice Rewarded. R. P. Lister. NYBP
Tale of Lord Lovell, The. *Unknown. See* Lord Lovel.
Tale of Sigemund, The. *Unknown, tr. fr. Anglo-Saxon by* Charles W. Kennedy. *Fr.* Beowulf. AnOE
Tale of Sir Thopas, The. Chaucer. *See* Sir Thopas.
Tale of the Dixie-Belle, The. Frank Chase. InMe
Tale of the times of old, A! The deeds of days of other years! Carthon; a Poem. James Macpherson. EnRP
Tale of the Upland Mouse and the Burgess Mouse, The, *abr.* Robert Henryson. OBNV
(Taill of the Uponlandis Mous and the Burges Mous, The.) BSV
(Two Mice, The.) OxBM
Tale the Hermit Told, The. Alastair Reid. NePoEA-2
Tale Told by a Head, A. Lois Moyles. NYBP
Talent is what they say. For the Young Who Want To. Marge Piercy. Psk
Talented Man, The. Winthrop Mackworth Praed. EnRP; FiBHP; HBV-1; NOBL
"Talents Differ." Laura E. Richards. TiPo
Tales, *sels.* George Crabbe.
"Grave Jonas Kindred, Sybil Kindred's sire." OBRV
Jonas Kindred's Household. FaBoEn; OBNC, *longer sel.*
Tales and talismans I have chronicled. The Task. Robert Bhain Campbell. MoPo
Tales from a Family Album. Donald Justice. NePoEA-2; TwAmPo
Tales of a Wayside Inn, *sels.* Longfellow.
Birds of Killingworth, The (The Poet's Tale), *fr.* Pt. I. OnMSP; OxBA
"Do you ne'er think what wondrous beings these?" 2 *sts.* WBLP
King Robert of Sicily (The Sicilian's Tale), *fr.* Pt. I. BeLS; OHIP
Monk of Casal-Maggiore, The (The Sicilian's Tale), *fr.* Pt. III. AmPP; OxBA
(Sicilian's Tale, The.) AP
Paul Revere's Ride (The Landlord's Tale), *fr.* Pt. I. BeLS; BLPA; FaBoBe; FaBoTw; FaBV; FaFP; FaPo; FaPON; FaPoR; FPL; HBV-2; HBVY; OBAL; OBCA; OBNV; OHFP; PAH; TreF; TrGrPo; WBLP; YaD
(Midnight Ride of Paul Revere.) PaPo
Saga of King Olaf, The (The Musician's Tale), *fr.* Pt. I.
(Building of the *Long Serpent,* The, xiii.) EtS
("Dawn is not distant, The," xxii.) TRV
Ships That Pass in the Night (The Theologian's Tale), *fr.* Pt. III. EtS; MOS
(Ocean of Life, The.) TreFT
Student's Tale, The, *fr.* Pt. III. AmPP
Tales of Shatz. Dannie Abse. OxBC; VWA
Tales of the folk? Long may their creeds inspire. Tellers of Tales. Chester Kallman. DFT
Tales of the Hall, *sels.* George Crabbe.
Dejected Lover, The. FaBoEn
(Sad Lover, The.) OBNC
East Anglian Fen. FaBoPP
"Something one day occurr'd about a bill." Par
Tales of the Islands. Derek Walcott. OxBTC
Tales of witches warned me. Blemishes. James Hart. AMV-81
Tales Told of the Fathers. John Hollander. DiL
Taliesin, *sel.* Richard Hovey.
"Here falls no light of sun nor stars." AA
Taliessin's Song of the Unicorn. Charles Williams. FaBoTw
Talisman, A. Marianne Moore. GoJo; MoAB; MoAmPo; NCSH; ViBoPo
Talisman, The, *sel.* Sir Walter Scott.
"You talk of gayety and innocence," *fr. ch.* 13. NBM
Talk. Roo Borson. NOBC
Talk. Philip A. Stalker. FiBHP
Talk about de lates', de lates' of this song. The Ballet of the Boll Weevil. *Unknown.* ViBoFo
Talk about killing. In a life. A Sow's Ear. Theodore Weiss. NoAM
Talk about the shade of the sheltering palms. Under the Anheuser Bush. Andrew B. Sterling. OBAL
Talk about your harbor girls around the corner, Sally. Haul Away, My Rosy. *Unknown.* AmFP
Talk happiness. The world is sad enough. Optimism. Ella Wheeler Wilcox. BLPA; BLPL; FaBoBe
Talk of passion is a winter thing. The Kiss. Ned O'Gorman. FYAP
"Talk of pluck!" pursued the sailor. Romance. W. E. Henley. In Hospital, XXI. BrPo; PAH
Talk of the Greeks at Thermopylae! A Ballad of Redhead's Day. Richard Butler Glaenzer. PAH
Talk of the Town, The. Ed Fisher. FiBHP
Talk to Me, Talk to Me. Hedva Harkavi, *tr. fr. Hebrew by* Tova Weizman. VWA
Talk to Me Tenderly. Vivian Yeiser Laramore. HBMV
Talk was of too much, too, The. Zürich, zum Storchen. Paul Celan, *tr. by* Joachim Neugroschel. VWA
Talk with a Poet. Helen Bevington. SaC
Talked to my father again in a dream he seemed happy. Le Jazz Hot. Anselm Hollo. PoM
Talker, The. Benjamin Appel. TrJP
Talker, The. Mona Van Duyn. POL
Talking across Kansas. Paula Kwon. AMV-80

Talking along in this not quite prose way. Near. William Stafford. ConAP
Talking Blues. *Unknown.* FSW
Talking Bronco, *sel.* Roy Campbell.
Volunteer's Reply to the Poet, The. ViBoPo
Talking Designs. Liz Sohappy Bahe. CDW
Talking Drums, The. Kojo Gyinaye Kyei. PBA
Talking Fish, The. Ruth Stone. BoWoP
Talking his cock, talking. Mr. Muscle-On. Faye Kicknosway. GeTw
Talking in Bed. Philip Larkin. BoLoP; NoP
Talking in Their Sleep. Edith M. Thomas. BoNaP; OHIP
Talking Myself to Sleep in the Mountain. Gibbons Ruark. MAYP
Talking Nothin'. *Unknown.* FSW
Talking Oak, The, *sel.* Tennyson.
Olivia. GN
Talking oak, The/ To the ancients spoke. Be Different [*or* Deferent] to Trees. Mary Carolyn Davies. FaPON; HBMV; HBVY; OHIP
Talking of Ezra Pound and long-dead pantos. Robert Nichols. *Fr.* Fisbo. OBSV
Talking of sects quite late one eve. No Sect [*or* Sects] in Heaven. Elizabeth H. Jocelyn Cleaveland. BLPA; TreFS
Talking to Animals. Barbara Howes. GrPl
Talking to Her. Vincent O'Sullivan. OCNZ
Talking to her, he knew it was the end. Hector. Valentin Iremonger. CIP; NeIP; OxBI
Talking to Myself, *sel.* Vincent McHugh.
"I am very fond of the little ribs of women." ErPo
Talking to Myself. *Unknown.* BluL
Talking to the Moon. Joy Harjo. TWSS
Talking to the Moon #002. Joy Harjo. TWSS
Talking to the Mule. Laura Jensen. AmPA
Talking to the Townsfolk in Ideal, Georgia. Isaac J. Black. CNA
Talking Union. Lee Hays, Millard Lampell, *and* Pete Seeger. FSW
Talking Union: 1964. L. E. Sissman. TW
Talking with Soldiers. W. J. Turner. ChMP; MoBrPo
Tall. *Unknown.* TDH
Tall/ Poetic/ Loud. Washiri (Poet). Kattie M. Cumbo. BOLo
Tall Ambrosia. Henry David Thoreau. PoEL-4
Tall and clothed in samite. A White Iris. Pauline B. Barrington. PoLF
Tall and fair. Death of a Fair Girl. Alpheus Butler. PeD
Tall and great-bearded: black and white. Anachronism. Oliver St. John Gogarty. FYAP
Tall and singularly dark you pass among the breakers. Louis Zukofsky. NoAM
Tall Atlas, Jupiter, Hercules, Thor. Deities and Beasts. John Updike. ELU
Tall Braunighrindas left her bed. A Legend of Camelot. George Du Maurier. CenHV
Tall buildings darken the sidewalks like a blight. Promised Land. Mary Engel. AMV-80
Tall camels of the spirit, The. "A World without Objects Is a Sensible Emptiness." Richard Wilbur. ConAP; LiTM; MoAmPo; NoAM; NOBA; PoA
Tall candles, tapered waxes scent the air. Guyana. Fern Pankratz Ruth. AMV-80
Tall chestnuts keep away the sun and moon. Concordance. Paul Violi. AMV-81
Tall dancer dances, The. The Dancer. Joseph Campbell. OBMV; OxBI
Tall ears. What Is It? Marie Louise Allen. TiPo
Tall elm, The. The Connecticut Elm. Emma Swan. PoPl
Tall, handsome, tweeded Dr. Leeper. Austin Clarke. Mnemosyne Lay in Dust, IV. IPY
Tall Hat. Victor Daley. CBAP
Tall Man Executes a Jig, A. Irving Layton. MoCV; NOBC; PoCh
Tall Men Riding. S. Omar Barker. BPAW
Tall Nettles. Edward Thomas. BrPo; ChTr; ELU; FaBoTw; HBMV; MoAB; MoBrPo
Tall Oaks from Little Acorns Grow. David Everett. FaFP; TreF
(Boy Reciter, The.) BLPA
Tall palm tree sixty feet high, The. Prayer to the God Thot. *Unknown, tr. by* Ulli Beier. TTY
Tall people, short people. People. Lois Lenski. FaPON; SoPo
Tall Poets, The. William Jay Smith. SOTS
Tall poles leaned like dust-bowl fences. Absence. Jeannette Barnes. AMV-80
Tall Sky, The. Arthur Ball. PoSH
Tall, somber, grim, against the morning sky. Aspects of the Pines. Paul Hamilton Hayne. AA; HBV-1
Tall Tale God. Mark Van Doren. CrMA
Tall Tale, A; or, A Moral Song. Phyllis Webb. OBCV
Tall timber stood here once. Improved Farm Land. Carl Sandburg. RFM
Tall Toms, The. Edwin Honig. NePA
Tall Trees by Still Waters. James Tate. MAYP
Tall unpopular men. Dedication. Oliver St. John Gogarty. OBMV
Tall Windows. Robert Hass. NPGG
Tallahassee, *sel.* Andrew Merkel.
"Ann stood and watched the combers race to shore." CaP
Taller to-day, we remember similar evenings. W. H. Auden. CMoP
Tallest poet for his height. Arroyo. Tom Weatherly. PoBA
Tall-topped acacia, you, full of branches. Elephant. *Unknown.* PeSA
Tally. Josephine Miles. NoAM
Tally Stick, The. Jarold Ramsey. NIP
Tallyho! Tallyho!/ Echo faints far astray. The Hunt. Walter de la Mare. BoAnP
Tallyho-Hum. Ogden Nash. PH
Talmud, *sels.* *Tr. fr. Hebrew.* TrJP
God to Man.
Good Man, The.
Why?
Talmud, The. S. Frug, *tr. fr. Yiddish by* Alice Stone Blackwell. TrJP
Talmud Student, The. Hayyim Nahman Bialik, *tr. fr. Hebrew by* Helena Frank. TrJP
Talmudist. Stanley Burnshaw. VWA
Tam Glen. Burns. AWP; BSV; OAEP; OBEC; OxBS
Tam i' the Kirk. Violet Jacob. BSV; GBL; GoTS; HBMV
Tam Lin. *Unknown.* BSV; ESPB; FaBoBa; NOBE; OBEV; OBNV; OxBB, *with music*; OxBS; ViBoFo
(Tamlane.) WSC
Tam Lin's Lady. Liz Lochhead. BSV
Tam o' Shanter. Burns. BeLS; BSV; EnRP; GoTL; GoTS; HBV-2; NoP; OAEL-1; OAEP; OBEC; OBNV; OxBS; SeCePo; TrGrPo, *sl. abr.*; ViBoPo; WHA
Tam o' the linn cam up the gait. *Unknown.* FaBoCh
Tam Pierce. *Unknown.* FSW
Tam Samson's Elegy. Burns. PoEL-4
Tamales. "O. Henry." BPAW
Tamarack. Eugene McCarthy. GrPl
Tamaracks swing light away. Swamp. Roberta Hill. VoR
Tamar's Wrestling. Walter Savage Landor. *Fr.* Gebir. EnRP
(Shepherd and the Nymph, The.) OBNC
Tambour. István Vas, *tr. fr. Hungarian by* Jascha Kessler. VWA
Tambourine. James Cunningham. JB
Tambourine song for Soldiers Going into Battle. Hind bint Utba, *tr. by* Bridget Connelly *and* Deirdre Lashgari. WPOW
Tamburlaine the Great, *sels.* Christopher Marlowe.
"And ride in triumph through Persepolis!" *fr.* Pt. I, Act II. TrGrPo; WHA
Beauty, *fr.* Pt. I, Act V. TrGrPo
Bloody Conquests of Mighty Tamburlaine, The, *fr.* Pt. II, Act IV. ChTr
(Emperor of the Threefold World.) TrGrPo
("Forward, then, ye jades!") ViBoPo
"Disdains Zenocrate to live with me?" *fr.* Pt. I, Act I. ViBoPo
(Tamburlaine to Zenocrate.) WHA
Divine Zenocrate, *fr.* Pt. II, Act II. WHA
("Black is the beauty of the brightest day.") ViBoPo
(To Entertain Divine Zenocrate.) ChTr
Fair Is Too Foul an Epithet, *fr.* Pt. I, Act V. LiTB
("Ah, fair Zenocrate, divine Zenocrate.") EBEV; PoEL-2; ViBoPo
If All the Pens That Ever Poets Held, *fr.* Pt. I, Act V. ChTr; TrGrPo
Nature That Framed Us of Four Elements, *fr.* Pt. I, Act II. PoEl-2; TrGrPo
(Perfect Bliss and Sole Felicity.) SeCePo
Now Clear the Triple Region of the Air, *fr.* Pt. I, Act IV. TrGrPo
Overreacher, The, *fr.* Pt. I, Act I. NIP
"Thirst of reign and sweetness of a crown, The," *fr.* Pt. I, Act II. ViBoPo
"Those wallèd garrisons will I subdue," *fr.* Pt. I, Act III. ViBoPo
Tame Cat. Ezra Pound. ELU; OBAL
Tamed by Miltown, we lie on Mother's bed. Man and Wife. Robert Lowell. AmPP; BoLoP; ConAP
Tameless in his stately pride, along the lake of islands. The Loon. Alfred Billings Street. AA
Tamer and Hawk. Thom Gunn. FaBoTw; NePoEA
Tamerlane. Victor J. Daley. PoAu-1
Tamerlane. Poe. AP
Tamerton Church-Tower; or, First Love, *sel.* Coventry Patmore.
Devonshire Scenes. FaBoPP
Taming of the Shrew, The, *sel.* Shakespeare.
Petruchio Is Undaunted by Katharina, *fr.* I, ii. TreFT
Tamlane. *Unknown.* *See* Tam Lin.
Tammuz. Nathan Alterman, *tr. fr. Hebrew by* Robert Friend. VWA
Tammuz. Rayner Heppenstall. WaP
Tammy Messer. *Unknown.* FaBoEE
Tampico. Grace Hazard Conkling. HBMV
Tamping Ties ("Tamp 'em up solid"). *Unknown.* AmFP
"Tan Ta Ra, Cries Mars. . ." David Wagoner. NePoAm-2

Tan Ta Ra Ran Tan Tant: Cries Mars on Bloody Rapier. *Unknown.* NCEP
Tanagra! think not I forget. Corinna, from Athens, to Tanagra [*or* Corinna to Tanagra]. Walter Savage Landor. *Fr.* Pericles and Aspasia. NOBE; OBEV; OBNC; OBRV; OBVV; ViBoPo
Tancred, *sels.* Laurence Dakin. CaP
"All night I raced the moon," *fr.* II, i.
"How gently sings my soul and whets its wings," *fr.* III, i.
Song: "Peasant sun went crushing grapes, The," *fr.* I, i.
Tandaradei. Walther von der Vogelweide. *See* Under the Lindens.
Tang! tang! went the gong's wild roar. Night Quarters. Henry Howard Brownell. GN
Tangere. Theodore Enslin. CoPo
Tangle of iron rods and spluttered beams, A. Les Halles d'Ypres. Edmund Blunden. MMA
Tangled [*or* Tanglid] I was [*or* was I] in Love's snare. The Lover Rejoiceth [*or* Liberty]. Sir Thomas Wyatt. AAS; OBSC; SiPS; TrGrPo
Tangled web indeed we weave, A. Women's Degrees. A. D. Godley. GLGT; NOBL
Tanglid I was yn loves snare. *See* Tangled I was in love's snare.
Tangmalangaloo. P. J. Hartigan. PoAu-1
Tango. Elena Jordana, *tr. by* Kathrine Jason. AMV-80
Tanist. James Stephens. OnYI
Tank, The. Roland Robinson. PoAu-2
Tank Town. John Atherton. NYBP
Tanka (I–VIII). Lewis Alexander. CDC
Tanker. Christopher Middleton. NMP
Tanks. Rhyll McMaster. CBAP
Tanned blonde, The. The Once-over. Paul Blackburn. ErPo; NeAP; PoM
Tannhäuser, *sel.* Heine, *tr. fr. German by* Emma Lazarus.
Best Religion, The. TrJP
Tannhauser. Newman Levy. OBAL
Tannhäuser. William Morton Payne. AA
Tansy for August. Theodore Enslin. CoPo
Tant' Amare. *Unknown, tr. fr. Mozarabe by* Paul Blackburn. ErPo
Tantalos. Paulus Silentiarius, *tr. fr. Greek by* Dudley Fitts. ErPo
Tantalus—Texas. *Unknown, at. to* Joaquin Miller. HBV-1
(Llano Estacado, The.) CoSo
Tantanoola Tiger, The. Max Harris. MoBS; PoAu-2
Tantivee, tivee, tivee, tivee, high and low. Brother Solon's Hunting Song. Thomas D'Urfey. *Fr.* The Marriage-Hater Match'd. CavP
Tantramar Revisited. Sir Charles G. D. Roberts. CaP; NOBC; OBCV
Tanya. Jay Parini. AMV-80
Tâo. Alfred Goldsworthy Bailey. CaP
Tao in the Yankee Stadium Bleachers. John Updike. LiSp
Tao Teh King, *sels. Unknown, at. to* Lao Tzu, *tr. fr. Chinese.*
He Walks in Peace. TRV
"Slaying of multitudes should be mourned with sorrow." TRV
"Something there is, whose veiled creation was," *tr. by* Raymond B. Blakney. ILwL
Taos Drums. William Haskel Simpson. BPAW
Taos Winter. Patty L. Harjo. VoR
Tape, The. Myra Cohn Livingston. NTCP
Taped to the wall of my cell are 47 pictures: 47 black. The Idea of Ancestry. Etheridge Knight. BALP; BPo; CNA; ConAP; LFAC; NIP; NNaP; PoBA; PPoe; SV
Tapering stars glint cool. Challengers. Alfred Dorn. GoYe
Tapers in the great God's hall, The. By Night. Philip Jerome Cleveland. TRV
Tapestry, The. Howard Nemerov. Prf
Tapestry. Charles Simic. LCAP
Tapestry Trees. William Morris. BoNaP; FaPON; OHIP
Tapestry Weavers, The. Anson G. Chester. BLPA; BLRP; WBLP
Tappster, fill another ale. Drinking Song. *Unknown.* OxBM
Taps. Lizette Woodworth Reese. OHIP
Tapwater. Laura Jensen. LCAP
Tar. C. K. Williams. GeTw
Tara. *Unknown, tr. fr. Middle Irish by* Edward Gwynn. *Fr.* Dinnshenchas. OnYI
Tara Is Grass. *Unknown, tr. fr. Irish by* Padraic Pearse. AnIL; AnIV; POL
Tarantella. Hilaire Belloc. CH; FaBoCh; GoBC; MoBrPo; MoShBr; OBMV; SpRo
Tarantula. Diana O Hehir. NPGG
Tarantula, The. Reed Whittemore. CoAP
Tarantula or the Dance of Death. Anthony Hecht. CoAP
Tarantula rattling at the lily's foot, The. O Carib Isle! Hart Crane. AP; MoPo; NePA; NoAM; PoA; VGW
Ta-ra-ra Boom-der-é, *with music.* Henry J. Sayers. BLSo; FSW
(Ta-Ra-Ra Boom-De-Ay!, *diff. version.*) FSN; VLP (*At. to* Richard Morton)
Tardy Epithalamium for E. and N., A. Ralph Pomeroy. PeHV
Tardy George. *Unknown.* PAH
Target of the hunting shepherd boys. Zebra Stallion. *Unknown.* PeSA
Target Practice. Donald Finkel. NePoEA-2
Target shudders in the layered heat, The. Technique on the Firing Line. Turner Cassity. PoA
Tarpauling Jacket. *Unknown.* DTC; OxBoLi
Tarquin and Tullia. Arthur Mainwaring. APAS
Tarry a moment, happy feet. The Statues. Laurence Binyon. OBEV; OBVV
Tarry Flynn, *sel.* Patrick Kavanagh.
"On an apple-ripe September morning." IPY
"Tarry," said the Master, "till the power." "Tarry Ye." *Unknown.* STF
Tarry with Me, O My Saviour, *with music.* Caroline Sprague Smith. AH
"Tarry Ye." *Unknown.* STF
Tarsier worked as a waiter, A. The Contrary Waiter. Edgar Parker. RHPC
Tartar. Solyman Brown. *Fr.* Dentologia; a Poem on the Diseases of the Teeth and Their Proper Remedies. FaBoUs
Tartary. Walter de la Mare. HBMV; OxBChV
Tartuffe; or, The Impostor. Molière, *tr. fr. French by* Richard Wilbur. NAWM-2
Tarye no lenger; toward thyn herytage. Vox Ultima Crucis. John Lydgate. OBEV; OxBoCh
Tashkent Breaks into Bloom. "Anna Akhmatova," *tr. fr. Russian by* Richard McKane. BoWoP
Task, The. Robert Bhain Campbell. MoPo
Task, The, *sels.* William Cowper.
Ease, *fr.* I. TEP
England, *fr.* II. FiP; OBEC
(Love of England.) LoBV
God Made the Country, *fr.* I. FiP; PoEL-3
(Town and Country.) FaBoEn
"Groans of nature in this nether world, The," *fr.* VI. NoP
Hatred and Vengeance, My Eternal Portion. FaBoRV
How to Grow Cucumbers, *fr.* III. FaBoUs
"I say the pulpit (in the sober use)," *fr.* II. TRV
"I was a stricken deer, that left the herd," *fr.* III. EnRP; FaBoRV; OAEP; OxBoCh; PAI
(Stricken Deer, The.) FiP; LoBV
"Lord of all, himself through all diffused, The," *fr.* VI. OAEL-1
"Night was winter in his roughest mood, The," *fr.* VI. EnRP; TEP
(Winter Scene.) OBEC
"No noise is here, or none that hinders thought." BoAnP
"Oh for a lodge in some vast wilderness," *fr.* II. EnRP; OAEP
(Against Slavery.) NOEC
Poetic Pains, *fr.* II. FiP
("There is a pleasure in poetic pains.") PP
Rural Sights and Sounds, *fr.* I. NOEC
("For I have lov'd the rural walk through lanes.") EnRP
Slaves Cannot Breathe in England, *fr.* II. OBEC
Sofa, The, I. LAuP; OAEP, *abr.*
"Whose freedom is by suff'rance, and at will," *fr.* V. EnRP
Winter, *fr.* IV. OBEC
Winter Evening, The, *fr.* IV. NOEC; OAEP; SeCePo
(Evening.) OBEC
(Post-Boy, The.) FiP
Winter Morning Walk, The, V. LAuP
"Tis morning; and the sun with ruddy orb." PoEL-3
(Frosty Morning, A, *shorter sel.*) NOEC
Winter Walk at Noon, A, *fr.* VI. TEP
Woodman's Dog, The, *fr.* V. ELU; GDP
"Would I describe a preacher, such as Paul," *fr.* II. TRV
Task, The. Ruth Pitter. MoBrPo
Task That Is Given to You, The. Edwin Markham. WBLP
Taste. Christopher Smart. Hymns for the Amusement of Children, Hymn 15. NOCV
Taste. John Updike. AMV-81
Taste of peaked champagne. This Night. Dianne Hai-Jew. BrSi
Taste of Prayer, The. Ralph W. Seager. TrPWD
Taste of Purple. Leland B. Jacobs. RHPC
Taste of Space, The. A. J. M. Smith. PV
Tat for Tit. Walter de la Mare. FM
Tatar chief forced me to become his wife, A. Ts'ai Yen, *tr. by* Kenneth Rexroth *and* Ling Chung. Eighteen Verses Sung to a Tatar Reed Whistle, II. WPOW
Tattle. Godfrey Turner. NOBL
Tattoo. Wallace Stevens. LiTA
Tattooed. William Plomer. ChMP
Tattooed Man, The. Harry B. Smith. *Fr.* The Idol's Eye. InMe
Tattoos, *sels.* Charles Wright.
Janitor, The; Kindergarten, Corinth. GP
Snake Handling Religious Service. GP
Taught early that his mother's skin was the sign of error. Mr. Z. M. Carl Holman. SoSe

Taught to Be Polite. Virginia Brady Young. AMV-81
Tauhid. Askia Muhammad Touré. PoBA
Taunt. *Malay Oral Tradition, tr. by* R. J. Wilkinson *and* R. O. Winstedt. WTO
Taut on the leash, at last I have my way. Moving: New York—New Haven Line. Alfred Corn. MAYP
Tawny are the leaves turned, but they still hold. Antique Harvesters. John Crowe Ransom. AP; CoBMV; CrMA; FaBoEn; MoAB; MoAmPo; NoP; OxBA
Tawny gleam in the sunlight, A. The First Robin. Lilian Leveridge. CaP
Tawny in a pasture by the true sea. The Forgotten Rock. Richard Eberhart. NePA
Tawny iris, Theoh! the slim-necked swan. Flowers. Stéphane Mallarmé, *tr. by* John Gray. SyP
Tax-Gatherer, The. John Banister Tabb. GN
Tax not the royal Saint with vain expense. Inside of [*or* Within] King's College Chapel, Cambridge. Wordsworth. *Fr.* Ecclesiastical Sonnets. EnRP; GoBC; GTBS; GTBS-P; OAEP; OBNC; OBRV; OxBoCh
Tax Return. *Unknown.* FaBoUs
Taxes. Don L. Lee. BOLo
Taxi, The. Amy Lowell. BoWoP; MoAmPo; PBWP
Taxi halts before a pale museum, The. Letter to Statues. John Malcolm Brinnin. EyDe
Taxi Suite, *sel.* Lew Welch.
After Anacreon. NeAP; PoM
Taxi-cab whore out at Iver, A. Limerick. Victor Gray. NOBL
Taxicabs scuttle by on the wet streets. Whaddaya Do for Action in This Place? George Starbuck. NePoEA-2
Taxis. Rachel Field. FaPON; SoPo; TiPo
Taxis, The. Louis MacNeice. OxBTC
Tay Bridge Disaster, The. William McGonagall. EvOK; PeD
Te Deum. Gertrud von Le Fort, *tr. fr. German.* ILwL
Te Deum. Charles Reznikoff. TrJP; VWA
Te Deum, The. *Unknown, tr. fr. Latin by* Dryden. AWP
Te Deum Laudamus. *Unknown, tr. fr. Latin.* WGRP
Te Deum of the Commonplace, A, *sel.* John Oxenham.
"For all the wonders of this wondrous world." PGD
"Te Judice." Frederick George Scott. PeCV
Te Martyrum Candidatus. Lionel Johnson. ACP; HBV-2; OBMV; OxBoCh
Tea. Jacqueline Embry. HBMV; YaD
Tea. Wallace Stevens. CABA
Tea. Ann Struthers. AMV-80
Tea at the Palaz of Hoon. Wallace Stevens. FaBoMo; PoA
Tea by the Sea. Edward Lear. TDH
Tea for Two, *with music.* Irving Caesar. BLSo
Tea garden shows you how, A. Bridge. A. R. Ammons. CoAP
Tea party at Le Cannet, The. Bonnard; a Novel. Richard Howard. CoAP; NYBP
Tea Poems. George Mackay Brown. OxBC
Tea-rose tea-gown, etc., The. Ezra Pound. *Fr.* Hugh Selwyn Mauberley. MoAmPo; NOBE
Tea Shop, The. Ezra Pound. HeIP
Teach me, Father, how to go. A Prayer. Edwin Markham. HBMV; HBVY; PGD; TrPWD; TRV; WGRP
Teach Me How to Repent. John Donne. *See* Holy Sonnets, VII.
Teach me, life. Only the Heart. Marjorie Freeman Campbell. CaP
Teach me, my God and King. The Elixir. George Herbert. AnAnS-1; FaBoCh; GN; NoP; OHIP; SeCV-1; TrGrPo; WGRP
Teach me the ritual that runs beyond. Worship. Robert Whitaker. TrPWD
Teach me the secret of thy loveliness. To a Wind-Flower. Madison Cawein. AA; HBV-1
Teach me to live! 'Tis easier far to die. The Harder Task. *Unknown.* BLRP
Teach me to love? Go, teach thyself more wit. The Prophet. Abraham Cowley. JCP; TrGrPo
Teach not thy parent's mother to extract. *Unknown.* WhC
Teach us, good Lord, to serve Thee as Thou deservest. Teach Us to Serve Thee, Lord. St. Ignatius of Loyola. TRV
Teach Us to Mark This, God. Franz Werfel, *tr. fr. German by* Jacob Sloan. TrJP
Teach Us to Serve Thee, Lord. St. Ignatius of Loyola, *tr. fr. Latin.* TRV
Teacher, The. Helen Bevington. GLGT
Teacher. Sonya Dorman. GLGT
Teacher, The. David Fisher. NPGG
Teacher, The. Leslie Pinckney Hill. BANP; PoNe; TrPWD
Teacher, A. Reed Whittemore. GLGT; NCSH
Teacher, The. Virginia Brady Young. GoYe
Teacher Bruin said, "Cub, bear in mind." The Smart Little Bear. Mark Fenderson. TDH
Teacher Sees a Boy, The. Margaret Morningstar. STF
Teacher should impart what's true, A. Flower for a Professor's Garden of Verses. Irwin Edman. DBV; InMe
Teacher Taught Me, A. Anna Walters. VoR
Teacher to Heloise, The (After Waddell). Daniel Burke. AMV-81
Teacher's Dream, The. William Henry Venable. BeLS
Teacher's Prayer, A. Frances Ridley Havergal. BLRP; TRV
For Every Day, *1 st.* BLRP
Teaching about Arthropods. Miroslav Holub, *tr. fr. Czech by* Stuart Friebert *and* Dana Hábová. SUW
Teaching assistant hands it over, The. Skull of a Neandertal. Michael Cadnum. SUW
Teaching Penguins to Fly. Barry Spacks. GP
Teaching Poetry. Cyn Zarco. BrSi
Teaching Swift to Young Ladies. William Dickey. PoA
Teaching the Ape to Write Poems. James Tate. GP
Teahouse. Nicholas Rinaldi. AMV-81
Teak Forest, The, *sel.* "Laurence Hope."
For This Is Wisdom. PoLF; TreFT
Team, The. "Furnley Maurice." CBAP
Team of Budweiser horses, The. 8-Ball at the Twilite. David Baker. MAYP
Teams, The. Henry Lawson. CBAP; PoAu-1
Teamster's Song, *with music. Unknown.* TrAS
Teapots and Quails. Edward Lear. GoJo
Tear, The. Byron. *See* Hours of Idleness.
Tear [*or* Teare], The. Richard Crashaw. LiTB; MasP; OAEP; SeCP
Tear. Thomas Kinsella. IPY
Tear down the Ivory Tower! Bring Torches. A. M. Stephen. CaP
Teare, The. Richard Crashaw. *See* Tear, The.
Tearing at my package like a child. Eczema. David Slavitt. TW
Tears. Elizabeth Barrett Browning. WPE
Tears. Khansa, *tr. fr. Arabic by* R. A. Nicholson. AWP
Tears. "Owen Meredith." *Fr.* Glenaveril. EBVV
Tears. Lizette Woodworth Reese. AA; HBV-2; HBVY; MoAmPo; TreFS; WGRP; WHA
Tears. Edith Sitwell. CMoP; MoPo
Tears. Edward Thomas. GTBS-P; LiTB; PoPle
Tears. *Unknown. See* Weep You No More.
Tears. Walt Whitman. NePA
Tears at the Grave of Sir Albertus Morton. Sir Henry Wotton. AnAnS-2; SeCP
Tears, ere thy death, for many a one I shed. Tears. Khansa, *tr. by* R. A. Nicholson. AWP
Tears fall within mine heart. Il pleut doucement sur la ville. Paul Verlaine, *tr. by* Ernest Dowson. AWP; BrPo; SyP
Tears, Flow No More. Lord Herbert of Cherbury. AnAnS-2; ElL; OBS; SeCP
Tears for Sale. Leonora Speyer. HBMV
Tears, Idle Tears [I Know Not What They Mean]. Tennyson. *Fr.* The Princess. CABA; EBVV; ELP; FaBoRV; FaFP; FaPoR; FiP; FPL; GTBS-P; HAP; HBV-1; InPK; InPS; InvP; LiTB; MasP; NIP; NOBE; NoP; OAEL-2; OBNC; OBVV; PoEL-5; PPoe; PPP; TEP; TreF; TrGrPo; UnPo; ViBoPo; WeW; WHA
(Song: "Tears, idle tears, I know not what they mean.") FaBoEn; PoPl; SeCeV
(Songs from "The Princess.") AWP
Tears in my heart that weeps. Paul Verlaine, *tr. fr. French by* Arthur Symons. SyP
Tears in Spring. William Ellery Channing. AA
Tears in the eyes of the surgeon. To My Friends. Peter De Vries. FiBHP
Tears of Scotland, The; Written in the Year 1746. Tobias Smollett. NOEC; OBEC
Tears of the Poplars, The. Edith M. Thomas. AA
Tears of the widower, when he sees. In Memoriam A. H. H., XIII. Tennyson. PeHV
Tears of the World. Mu'tamid, King of Seville, *tr. fr. Arabic by* Dulcie L. Smith. AWP
Tears on the Death of Moeliades, *sel.* William Drummond of Hawthornden.
Lament: "Chaste maids which haunt fair Aganippe's well." LoBV
Tears! tears! tears! Tears. Walt Whitman. NePA
Tears that never quite touched earth. White Violets. Benjamin R. C. Low. HBMV
Tears will betray all pride, but when ye mourn him. Parnell [*or* Parnell's Memory]. Thomas Kettle. AnIV
Teased and titillated by the need. Beyond Biology. Robert Francis. NePoAm
Teasers, The. William Empson. OxBTC
Teasing Lovers, The. Horace, *tr. fr. Latin by* Louis Untermeyer. Odes, III, 9. UnTE
Teasing; or, I Was Only, Only Teasing You, *with music.* Cecil Mack. FSN
Teasing Song. Princess Magogo, *tr. fr. Zulu by* D. K. Rycroft. WTO

Technical Supplement, A, *sels.* Thomas Kinsella.
"It is hard to beat a good meal." CIP
"Point, greatly enlarged, The." IPY
Technicalities for Jack Spicer. Philip Whalen. PoM
Technically they were all the same. The Art of Love. Richard Grossman. AMV–81
Technique. Burnham Eaton. GoYe
Technique. Langdon Elwyn Mitchell. *Fr.* To a Writer of the Day. AA
Technique. Philip Pierson. AMV–80
Technique on the Firing Line. Turner Cassity. PoA
Technogamia, *sel.* Barten Holyday.
Song: "O harmless feast." ElL
Technologies. George Starbuck. NYBP
Tecumseh, *sels.* Charles Mair.
"I love you better than I love my race." NOBC
"Once we were strong." PeCV
"Tell me more of those unrivalled wastes," *fr.* IV, iv. CaP
"There was a time on this fair continent." NOBC; OBCV
"We left/ The silent forest." OBCV
Ted & marge had been married eight years. Wasp Sex Myth (Two). Anselm Hollo. PoM
Teddy Bear. A. A. Milne. OnUR
Teddy Bear, Teddy Bear. *Unknown.* NTCP
Tee Roo, *with music.* *Unknown.* OuSiCo
Te-ell me milkcow. Milkcow's Calf Blues. *Unknown.* BluL
Teemothy Hatch. Wilson MacDonald. WhC
Teen-Ager, A. W. D. Snodgrass. TW
Teeney and Weeney together are going. Green Grass and White Milk. Winifred Welles. TiPo
Teeth. Susan Griffin. NPGG
Teeth. Miroslav Holub, *tr. fr. Czech by* David Young *and* Dana Hábová. SUW
Teeth Mother Naked at Last, The. Robert Bly. NNaP
"Excellent Roman knives slip along the ribs," *sel.* GP
Teeth of flowers, hairnet of dew. I Am Going to Sleep (Suicide Poem). Alfonsina Storni, *tr. by* Aliki *and* Willis Barnstone. BoWoP
Teeth on the saw. Piney Woods. Malcolm Cowley. NYBP
Teeth you see up here, The. Oisin. *Unknown, tr. by* Frank O'Connor. KiLC
Teevee. Eve Merriam. QQQ
Tee-Vee Enigma. Selma Raskin. QQQ
Tefillin: phylacteries. The Journey with Hands and Arms. Benjamin Saltman. VWA
Telegram. Dick Lourie. NeAC
Telegram. William Wise. TiPo
Telegram One. Adrian Mitchell. PV
Telélestai. Conrad Aiken. LiTM; PrIm
Telemachus and the Bow. Randall Colaizzi. AMV–81
Telephone, The. Hilaire Belloc. MoVE
Telephone, The. Edward Field. CAD; PPJ
Telephone, The. Robert Frost. HBV–1; SO; SoSe
Telephone. Robin Shectman. AMV–81
Telephone Arguin' Blues. *Unknown.* BluL
Telephone Conversation. Wole Soyinka. SoSe; TTY
Telephone Directory. Harry Crosby. EAS
Telephone Ghosts. Robert Frazier. SUW
Telephone-installer was interested, The. Moving In. Josephine Miles. NoP
Telephone line goes cold, A. The Farm on the Great Plains. William Stafford. HAP; PoCh; VGW
Telephone Lineman. Ernest Kroll. AMV–81
Telephone Operator, The. Pat-Therese Francis. AMV–80
Telephone Poles. John Updike. FYAP; Psk; SaC
Telephone poles, The. Crossing Kansas by Train. Donald Justice. NYBP
Telephoning It. Murray Edmond. OCNZ
Telephonist. Janet Frame. WPE
Television/ radio sunday benevolent sunday. They Are Killing All the Young Men. David Henderson. PoBA
Television aerials, Chinese characters. On Roofs of Terry Street. Douglas Dunn. OxBTC
Tell a wise person, or else keep silent. The Holy Longing. Goethe, *tr. by* Robert Bly. NU
Tell all my mourners. Wake. Langston Hughes. OBAL; ShM
Tell all the truth but tell it slant. Emily Dickinson. AmPP; AP; HBVY; HeIP; LiTA; NePA; NoAM; NOBA; NoP; PPP; TAP; UnPo; WeW
Tell All the World. Harry Kemp. HBMV
Tell Freedom, *sel.* Peter Abrahams.
Me, Colored. PBA
Tell her I love. Stanzas [*or* Poems] for My Daughter. Horace Gregory. MoAmPo; MoVE
Tell him it's all [*or* the tale is] a lie. A Learned Mistress. *Unknown, tr. by* Frank O'Connor. KiLC; OBMV
Tell Him, O Night. *Unknown, tr. fr. Arabic by* E. Powys Mathers. *Fr.* The Thousand and One Nights. AWP
Tell Him So. *Unknown.* BLPA; BLPL; WBLP
Tell him the tale is a lie! *See* Tell him it's all a lie.
Tell it to the forest fire, tell it to the moon. John Berryman. Dream Songs, XLIV. NaP
Tell Jesus. *Unknown.* STF
Tell Me. Edith M. Thomas. *Fr.* The Inverted Torch. AA
Tell me,/ Was Venus more beautiful. Venus Transiens. Amy Lowell. PoA
"Tell me a story." Bedtime Stories. Lilian Moore. NTCP
"Tell me a story, father, please." The Natives of America. Ann Plato. BlSi
Tell me a story, Father, please do. Request Number. G. N. Sprod. FiBHP
Tell me, abandoned miscreant, prithee tell. Upon the Author of a Play Called *Sodom.* John Oldham. TW
Tell me about that harvest field. Real Property. Harold Monro. BoNaP
Tell me about yourself they. A Word in Edgeways. Charles Tomlinson. NOBL
Tell Me Again. Nigâr Hanim, *tr. fr. Turkish by* Tâlat S. Halman. PBWP
Tell me Beatrice. The Van Gogh Influence. Shel Silverstein. ELU
Tell me, dear, in terms laconic. The Conservative Shepherd to His Love. Jack D'arcy. InMe
Tell Me, Dearest, What Is Love? John Fletcher. *Fr.* The Captain. ElL; ViBoPo
(What Is Love?) HBV–1
Tell me, Dorinda, why so gay. On the Countess of Dorchester. Charles Sackville. APAS; CavP
Tell me, Echo fair! Lover and Echo. Carrol O'Daly, *tr. by* George Sigerson. OnYI
"Tell me, good dog, whose tomb you guard so well." The Tomb of Diogenes. *Unknown, tr. by* John Addington Symonds. AWP
Tell me, good Hobbinoll, what garres thee greete? Aprill. Spenser. *Fr.* The Shepheardes Calender. PoEL–1
Tell me, hair of her head, where I should lie. The Hair's-Breadth. Nicholas Moore. NeBP
Tell me if it is too far for you. Elegy for N. N. Czeslaw Milosz. SV
Tell me, is there among you one. The Sleeping Beauty. Mary Hutton. DFt
Tell me is there anything lovelier. Greenness. Angelina Weld Grimké. CDC
Tell me, is there sovereign cure. Tell Me. Edith M. Thomas. *Fr.* The Inverted Torch. AA
Tell me it was just a dream. Julia. Wendy Rose. STE; TWSS
Tell me, lovely, loving pair! On the Friendship betwixt Two Ladies. Edmund Waller. PeHV
Tell Me Man Blues. *Unknown.* BluL
Tell me more of those unrivalled wastes. Charles Mair. *Fr.* Tecumseh, IV, vi. CaP
Tell Me, My Heart, if This Be Love. George Lyttleton. HBV–1
(Song: "When Delia on the plain appears.") OBEC
Tell me (my love) since Hymen ty'de. An Hymeneall Dialogue. Thomas Carew. AnAnS–2; SeCP
Tell me, my patient friends, awaiters of messages. Speech to a Crowd. Archibald MacLeish. MoAB; MoAmPo; NePA
Tell Me No More. William Drummond of Hawthornden. TrGrPo
Tell me[e] no more how fair[e] she[e] is. Sonnet [*or* That Distant Bliss]. Henry King. AnAnS–2; CavP; EnLoPo; MeLP; MePo; OBS; SeCP; TrGrPo; ViBoPo
Tell me no more I am deceived. Song. Sir George Etherege. CavP
Tell me no more I am deceived. The Better Bargain. Congreve. UnTE
Tell me no more of constancy. Against Constancy. Earl of Rochester. GBL
Tell me no more of minds embracing minds. No Platonic [*or* Platonique] Love. William Cartwright. CABA; ErPo; GBL; InvP; JCP; LiTB; OAEL–1; PAI; PoEL–2
Tell me no secret, friend. The Burden. Francesca Yetunde Pereira. PBA
Tell Me Not Here [It Needs Not Saying]. A. E. Housman. ChMP; CoBMV; ELP; FaBoEn; GTBS–P; LiTM; MoPo; MoVE; NOBE; OAEL–2; OBNC; OxBTC; PoPle; SCV
Tell me not in joyous numbers. Stephen Crane. OBAL
Tell me not, in mournful numbers. A Psalm of Life. Longfellow. AA; AH; CABA; FaBoBe; FPL; HBV–2; HBVY; OBCA; OHFP; PaPo; PoLF; PoPl; PrIm; TAP; TreF; WBLP; YaD
Tell me not, O Soul that slumbers. A Psalm of Life. Andrew Lang. CenHV
Tell me not of a face that's fair. The Resolve. Alexander Brome. CavP; OBEV
Tell me not of joy; there's none. The Dead Sparrow [*or* Lesbia on Her Sparrow]. William Cartwright. BoAnP; CavP; CH
Tell me not, Sweet, I am unkind. Lines Where Beauty Lingers. Franklin P. Adams. OBAL
Tell me not, Sweet, I am unkind. To Lucasta, Going to the Wars [*or*

Warres]. Richard Lovelace. AnAnS-2; AWP; CABA; CaPo; CavP; ELP; EnLoPo; FaBoEn; FaBV; FaFP; FF; FPL; GBL; GTBS; GTBS-P; HAP; HBV-1; HeIP; HoPM; InPK; InPS; JCP; LiTB; LoBV; MeLP; MePo; NIP; NOBE; NoP; OAEL-1; OAEP; OBEV; OBS; OBWP; PAI; PoEL-3; PoPl; PoRA; SCV; SeCePo; SeCeV; SeCP; SeCV-1; TreF; TrGrPo; ViBoPo; WeW; WHA
Tell me not the good and wise. And There Will I Be Buried. Thomas Davidson. BSV
Tell me not what too well I know. On Catullus. Walter Savage Landor. OBEV; ViBoPo
Tell Me Now. Wang Chi, *tr. fr. Chinese by* Arthur Waley. FaBoCh
Tell me now in what hidden way is. The Ballad[e] of Dead Ladies [*or* The Snows of Yester-Year]. Villon, *tr. by* Dante Gabriel Rossetti. AWP; CTC; FaFP; GoBC; HBV-1; OBVE; PoRA; PrIm; ViBoPo; WiR
"Tell me now, what should a man want." Tell Me Now. Wang Chi, *tr. by* Arthur Waley. FaBoCh
"Tell me, O Muse of the shifty, the man who wandered afar." Jubilee before Revolution. Andrew Lang. BXAP
Tell me, O Octopus, I begs. The Octopus. Ogden Nash. MOS; NePA; SoPo; TiPo
Tell me, O Swan, your ancient tale. Songs of Kabir. Kabir, *tr. by* Rabindranath Tagore. WGRP
Tell me, O tell, what kind[e] of thing is wit. Ode: Of Wit. Abraham Cowley. AnAnS-2; MeLP; MePo; OAEL-1; OAEP; OBS; SeCP; SeCV-1
Tell me, Oh Muse (for thou, or none canst tell). The Power of Numbers. Abraham Cowley. *Fr.* Davideis, I. OBS
Tell me once, dear, how it does prove. To the Unconstant Cynthia. Sir Robert Howard. CavP
Tell me, Perigot, what shalbe the game. August. Spenser. *Fr.* The Shepheardes Calender. OAEP
Tell me, Praise, and tell me, Love. Praise and Love. William Brighty Rands. OBVV
Tell Me Pretty Maiden; or, English Girls and Clerks, *with music.* Owen Hall. FSN
Tell me, Pyrrha, what fine youth. Another to the Same. Horace, *tr. by* William Browne. Odes, I, 5. OAEL-1; WiR
Tell me, shepherd, tell me, pray. Country Gods. Cometas, *tr. by* T. F. Higham. FaBoCh
Tell me, some pitying angel, quickly say. The Blessed Virgin's Expostulation. Nahum Tate. ISi
Tell Me, Tell Me. Emily Brontë. *See* Tell Me, Tell Me, Smiling Child.
Tell Me, Tell Me. Marianne Moore. LiTM; NYBP
"Tell me, tell me,/ Unknown stranger." The Galliass. Walter de la Mare. FaBoTw
Tell me, tell me everything! Curiosity. Harry Behn. SoPo
Tell me, tell me, gentle Robin. The Cat and the Bird. George Canning. ChTr
Tell Me, Tell Me, Smiling Child. Emily Brontë. OAEP; TEP; VLP
(Tell me, Tell Me.) ViBoPo
Tell me that the snow is red. Belief. Ruth Fitch Bartlett. InMe
Tell me the auld, auld story. The Parrot Cry. "Hugh MacDiarmid." OxBS
Tell me the tales that to me were so dear. Long, Long Ago. Thomas Haynes Bayly. BLSo; FSW; PSoN; TreF
Tell me, thou skilful shepherd's swain. A Roundelay. Michael Drayton. *Fr.* The Shepherd's Garland, Eclogue IX. EIL
Tell me, thou soul of her I love. Ode. James Thomson. OBEC
Tell me, thou Star, whose wings of light. The World's Wanderers. Shelley. ViBoPo
Tell me though safest end of all our woe. On Death. Anne Killigrew. BoWoP
Tell me today, when all my tides are gone. Sea Sonnet. Norma Lay. GoYe
Tell me was a glorie ever seen. Loch Leven. Sydney Goodsir Smith. BSV
Tell me what is that only thing. Women's Longing. John Fletcher. *Fr.* Women Pleased. HBV-1
Tell Me What Month Was My Jesus Born In. *Unknown.* FSW
Tell me what sail the seas. Under the Stars. Wallace Rice. AA; OHIP
Tell me what shapes your mind. The light grows less. Autumnal. Louis O. Coxe. TwAmPo
Tell me what time do the trains come through your town. Black Horse Blues. *Unknown.* BluL
"Tell me what you're doing over here, John Gorham." John Gorham. E. A. Robinson. MoAB; MoAmPo; NoAM
Tell me whaur, in whit countrie. Ballat o the Leddies o Langsyne. Villon, *tr. by* Tom Scott. OBVE
Tell me, where doth Whiteness grow. Whiteness, or Chastity. Joseph Beaumont. LoBV
Tell Me Where Is Fancy [*or* Fancie] Bred. Shakespeare. *Fr.* The Merchant of Venice, III, ii. CH; EIL; ELP; EnRePo; LiTB; OAEL-1; OAEP; SeCeV; ViBoPo; WHA
(Casket Song, A.) OBSC
(Fancy.) FaPON; TreFS; TrGrPo
(Love.) OBEV
(Madrigal.) GTBS; GTBS-P
(Song, A.) CTC; PoEL-2
Tell me where thy lovely love is. Heine, *tr. by* Ezra Pound. *Fr.* Die Heimkehr. AWP
Tell me whither, maiden June. The Reaper. John Banister Tabb. ACP
Tell me, wide wandering soul, in all thy quest. But Once. Theodore Winthrop. AA
Tell me you/ That sing in the black-thorn. You That Sing in the Blackthorn. Alfred Noyes. *Fr.* The Last Voyage, II. GoBC
Tell me[e], you anti-saint[e]s, why glass[e]. Upon Fairford Windows [*or* Upon Faireford Windowes]. Richard Corbett. AnAnS-2; EyDe
Tell Me You Wandering Spirits. *Unknown.* OBS
Tell mee no more how faire shee is. *See* Tell me no more how fair she is.
Tell my priests, when I am gone. The Bishop's Last Directions. *Unknown.* DBV; WhC
Tell, O Tell. Thomas Campion. *See* When Thou Must Home.
Tell Old Bill. *Unknown.* FSW
(Dis Mornin', Dis Evenin', So Soon, *with music.*) AS
Tell Our Daughters. Besmilr Brigham. IHMS
Tell, tell our fortune, Mirabel. Fortune for Mirabel. Horace Gregory. TwAmPo
Tell the random pilgrims. Eve's Advice to the Children of Israel. Joachim Neugroschel. VWA
Tell the story to your sons. The Fight of the *Armstrong* Privateer. James Jeffrey Roche. PAH
Tell them, I am, Jehovah said. Christopher Smart. *Fr.* Song to David. WGRP
Tell Them I'm Struggling to Sing with Angels. David Meltzer. VWA
Tell them in Lacedaemon [*or* Lakedaimon], passer-by. At Thermopylae [*or* On the Army of Spartans, Who Died at Thermopylae]. Simonides. ChTr; FaBoEE; WaaP
Tell them, O Sky-born, when I die. Farewell. Harry Kemp. HBMV
Tell them to go away. Insomnia. Ethna MacCarthy. NeIP
Tell them, when you are home again. Love's Caution. W. H. Davies. ChMP
Tell this to ladies: how a hero man. Man without Sense of Direction. John Crowe Ransom. LiTM; OxBA
Tell thou the world, when my bones lie whitening. The Nameless One. James Clarence Mangan. ACP
Tell us, old man. Old Man. David E. Stern. AMV-81
"Tell us, streaming lady." History. James Liddy, *tr. fr. Irish.* CIP
Tell us, tell us, holy shepherds. Flowers for the Altar. Digby Mackworth Dolben. GoBC
Tell us, thou clear and heavenly tongue. The Star-Song; a Carol to the King; Sung at White-Hall. Robert Herrick. GN; OxBoCh
Tell Us, Ye Servants of the Lord, *with music.* William Staughton. AH
Tell you? ha! who. Maximus, to Gloucester, Letter 2. Charles Olson. *Fr.* The Maximus Poems. NoAM
Tell you I chyll. The Tunnyng [*or* Tunning] of Elynour [*or* Elinour] Rummyng [*or* Rumming]. John Skelton. AAS; TrGrPo
Tell you what I like the best. Knee-deep in June. James Whitcomb Riley. OHFP
Tell your son, my son. Message. Renata Pallottini, *tr. by* Monique *and* Carlos Altschul. WPOW
Tellers of Tales. Chester Kallman. DFT
Telling It. Nancy Sullivan. TAP
Telling My Feelings. Yü Hsüan-chi, *tr. fr. Chinese by* Geoffrey Waters. BoWoP
Telling the Bees. Lizette Woodworth Reese. AA
Telling the Bees. Whittier. AP; AWP; BLPL; HBV-1; NOBA; TAP
Telling the Cousins. Les A. Murray. AMV-81
Tellus. William Reed Huntington. AA
Tèma con Variazioni. "Lewis Carroll." FaBoNo; SpRo
Temagami. Archibald Lampman. OBCV
Temair noblest of hills. Tara. *Unknown, tr. by* Edward Gwynn. *Fr.* Dinnshenchas. OnYI
Temeraire, The. Herman Melville. WaaP
Temper. Rose Fyleman. OxBChV
Temper, The. George Herbert. AnAnS-1; MePo; NOCV; NoP; OBS; OxBoCh; PoEL-2; WHA
Temper my spirit, O Lord. The Passionate Sword. Jean Starr Untermeyer. HBMV; TrJP; TrPWD
Temper of Aristippus, The. John Gilbert Cooper. *Fr.* Epistles to His Friends in Town. PBBP
Temperament. Martial, *tr. fr. Latin by* Joseph Addison. AWP; ELU
Temperaments, The. Ezra Pound. BoLoP; ErPo; NoAM; NOBA; PAI
Temperance. *Unknown.* ACP
Temperance and Virginity. Milton. *Fr.* Comus. OBS
Temperance Billiards Rooms, The. P. J. Kavanagh. OxBTC

Temperance Note: and Weather Prophecy. James Agee. *Fr.* Two Songs on the Economy of Abundance. MoAmPo
Temperance or the Cheap Physitian upon the Translation of Lessius. Richard Crashaw. SeCV-1
Temperance Song. *Unknown.* FaBoUs
Temperature. Gerard Malanga. NYBP
Tempered, annealed, the hard essence of autumn metals. Needle and Thread. Pan Chao, *tr. by* Richard Mather *and* Rob Swigart. WPOW
Tempest, The. Charles Cotton. SeCePo
Tempest, The. James Thomas Fields. *See* Ballad of the Tempest.
Tempest, The. Shakespeare. OAEL-1, *with music*
Sels.
Ariel's Song: "Come unto these yellow sands," *fr.* I, ii. CTC; FaBoCh; GN; GoJo; LoBV; NOBE; TEP
("Come unto these yellow sands.") CH; ElL; HBV-1; HeIP; OBEV; OBSC; PoPle; SpRo; ViBoPo
(Song: "Come unto these yellow sands.") PoEL-2
Ariel's Song: "Full fathom [*or* fadom] five thy father lies," *fr.* I, ii. FaBoEn; GN; LoBV; NOBE; OBSC; SeCePo; TreFT
(Ariel's Dirge.) EvOK; GoJo
("Full fathom [*or* fadom] five thy father lies.") AWP; BiP; ChTr; EBEV; ElL; ELP; FaBoCh; HAP; HeIP; HoPM; InPK; InPS; LiTB; MOS; NoP; OAEP; OBEV; PAI; PoPle; PoRA; PPoe; SeCeV; TEP; ViBoPo; WHA
(Sea Dirge, A.) EtS; GTBS; GTBS-P; HBV-2; TrGrPo
(Song: "Full fathom [*or* fadom] five thy father lies.") PoEL-2
Ariel's Song: "Where the bee sucks, there suck I," *fr.* V, i. GN; NOBE; OBSC; PDV
(Fairy Songs: "Where the bee sucks, there suck I.") HBVY
(Fairy's Life, A.) PoPl
("Where the bee sucks, there suck I.") AWP; CABA; CH; CTC; ElL; EnRePo; FaBV; HBV-1; HeIP; NoP; OBEV; SeCeV; TiPo; TreFT; ViBoPo; WHA
Brave New World, *fr.* V, i. TrGrPo
Caliban, *fr.* III, ii. FiP
(To Dream Again.) TrGrPo
"Cloud-capp'd towers, the gorgeous palaces, The," *fr.* IV, i. PoPl
Epilogue: "Now my charms are all o'erthrown," *fr.* V, i. CTC
"Honour, riches, marriage—blessing," *fr.* IV, i. PoPle
"I saw him beat the surges under him," *fr.* II, i. MOS
"Master, the swabber, the boatswain, and I, The," *fr.* II, ii. DBV; MOS; ViBoPo
(Song: "The master, the swabber, the boatswain and I.") FF; NOBL; PoPle
(Stephano's Song.) WhC
"No more dams I'll make for fish," *fr.* II, ii. ViBoPo
Our Revels Now Are Ended, *fr.* IV, i. LiTB; WHA
(Prospero Ends the Revels.) TreF
(Stuff of Dreams, The.) FaBV
(Such Stuff as Dreams Are Made On.) TrGrPo
Prospero, *fr.* IV, i. FiP
Song: Hark, Hark! *fr.* I, ii. SoSe
"Ye elves of hill, brooks, standing lakes, and groves," *fr.* V, i. EBEV; SCV
(Magic.) AWP
"You nymphs, call'd Naiads, of the windring brooks," *fr.* IV, i. ViBoPo
Tempest, The. William Jay Smith. MoAmPo
Tempest, The ("Cease rude Boreas blust'ring railers"). *Unknown.* AmFP
Tempest, The. Henry Vaughan. AnAnS-1
Tempest, The. Marya Zaturenska. MoAmPo
Tempest cracked on the theatre, A. Quickly. Repetitions of a Young Captain. Wallace Stevens. WaP
Tempest on the great seaborders! A Storm at Sea. *Unknown, tr. by* Robin Flower. AnIL
Tempest on the plain of Lir. Storm at Sea. *Unknown, tr. by* Frank O'Connor. KiLC
Temple. John Donne. AnAnS-1; OBS
Temple, The. Clifford Dyment. ChMP
Temple, The. Robert Herrick. CaPo
Temple, The. Gustave Kahn, *tr. fr. French by* Edouard Roditi. VWA
Temple, A. Kenneth Patchen. EAS
Temple, The. Po Chü-i, *tr. fr. Chinese by* Arthur Waley. OBMV
Temple, The. C. H. Sisson. OxBTC
Temple at Segesta, The. Raymond Henri. GLGT
Temple Garlands. Agnes Mary Frances Robinson. HBV-1
Temple is full of blood, The. Salvador Villanueva, *tr. fr. Spanish by* Julio Marzán. InW
Temple of Fame, The, *sel.* Pope.
Honest Fame. OBEC
Temple of Infamy, The, *sel.* Charles Harpur.
"But hark! What hubbub now is this that comes." PoAu-1
Temple of Nature, The; or, The Origin of Society, *sels.* Erasmus Darwin.
" 'How few,' the Muse in plaintive accents cries," *fr.* IV. FM
Reproduction of Life, *fr.* II. PBBP
Temple of the Animals, The. Robert Duncan. NOBA
Temple of the Muses. Beth Bentley. EyDe
Temple of the Trees, The. J. D. C. Pellow. PGD
Temple of Venus, The. Soame Jenyns. NOEC
Temple of Venus, The. Spenser. *Fr.* The Faerie Queene, IV, 10. WHA
Temple to Friendship, A. Thomas Moore. BeLS; HBV-1
Temple tree grew in our garden in Ceylon, A. Coppersmith. Richard Murphy. IPY
Templeogue. Blanaid Salkeld. NeIP
Tempora Acta. "Owen Meredith." OBVV
Tempora Mutantur. James Russell Lowell. HAP
Temporal. George Jonas. NOBC
Temporary Problems. Larry Rubin. AMV-80
Tempt Me No More. C. Day Lewis. *Fr.* The Magnetic Mountain. MoAB; MoBrPo; OAEP; OBMV; PoA; PoPl
Temptation. Robert Herrick. LiTB
Temptation. *Unknown.* ELU
Temptation and Fall of Man, The. *Unknown, tr. fr. Anglo-Saxon by* Charles W. Kennedy. *Fr.* Genesis. AnOE
Temptation of Saint Anthony, The. Arthur Symons. BrPo
Temptation of Sir Gawain, The. *Unknown. Fr.* Sir Gawain and the Green Knight. ACP
Temptation, temptation, temptation. Temptation. *Unknown.* ELU
Temptations still nest in it like basilisks. Dead Hand. W. S. Merwin. CAPP; InPK
Tempted. Edward Rowland Sill. AA
Tempted and tried, we're oft made to wonder. Farther Along. *Unknown.* FSW
Ten bloody years with this quill lying. Invocation. Valentin Iremonger. BIrV
Ten Commandments, Seven Deadly Sins, and Five Wits. *Unknown.* ChTr; FaBoEE
Ten Commandments, The ("Have thou no other gods but me"). *Unknown.* FaBoUs; OxBChV
Ten Commandments, The. Bible, *O.T.* Exodus, XX: 3-17. TreF; WBLP
Ten cuckolds slain without confession. Ballad of Don Juan Tenorio and the Statue of the Comendador. Roy Campbell. PeSA
Ten dancers glide. Ballad of the Ten Casino Dancers. Cecilia Meireles, *tr. by* James Merrill. BoWoP
Ten Days Leave. W. D. Snodgrass. MoAmPo; Psk; UnPo
Ten Definitions of Poetry. Carl Sandburg. MoAmPo
Ten-fifteen Community Poems, The, *sel.* John Knoepfle.
"She says how/ is it when you." MAT
Ten Kinds. Mary Mapes Dodge. RHPC
Ten Little Indian Boys. M. M. Hutchinson. SoPo
Ten Little Injuns. Septimus Winner. OBAL
Ten little nigger boys went out to dine. *Unknown.* OxNR
Ten men will dress in white, The. The Hunters of the Deer. Dale Zieroth. NOBC
Ten months after Florimel happen'd to wed. Another True Maid. Matthew Prior. FaBoEE
Ten more minutes! Say yer prayers. Over the Top. Sybil Bristowe. SUMH
Ten o'clock train to New York, The. Winter. Ruth Stone. BoWoP
Ten of the night is Talavera tolling. The Field of Talavera. Thomas Hardy. *Fr.* The Dynasts. CMoP
10 p.m., the river thinking. Weldon Kees. Larry Levis. FAZ
Ten pound hammer kill John Henry. John Henry. *Unknown.* ViBoFo
Ten Sonnets for Today. Phil Stanway. AMV-80
Ten South Sea Island boys. Fun with Fishing. Eunice Tietjens. FaPON
10:X:57, 45 Years Since the Fall of the Ch'ing Dynasty. Philip Whalen. PoM
(Forty-five Years Since the Fall of the Ch'ing Dynasty.) NeAP
Ten thousand bees in the backyard. Bees inside Me. Laura Chester. NPGG
Ten Thousand Cattle. Owen Wister. BPAW
Ten Thousand Cattle, *with music. Unknown.* CoSo
Ten thousand flakes about my window blow. Fame. Walter Savage Landor. FaBoEE; PV
Ten Thousand God-damn Cattle, *with music. Unknown.* CoSo
Ten Thousand Miles. *Unknown.* AmFP
Ten Thousand Miles Away. *Unknown.* FSW
Ten Thousand Miles Away, *with music. Unknown.* AS
Ten Thousand Miles Away from Home, *with music. Unknown.* AS
Ten thousand times ten thousand. Henry Alford. VLP
Ten Types of Hospital Visitor. Charles Causley. OxBC
Ten Week Wife. Rhoda Donovan. Str
Ten years/ and will you be/ a footnote. Return to Hinton. Charles Tomlinson. CMoP
Ten years ago it seemed impossible. In Progress. Christina Rossetti. BoWoP; WPE

Ten Years and More. Miriam Waddington. NOBC
Ten years being enough of copra, he souvenired a. Trader's Return. Sylvia Lawson. PoAu-2
Ten years together without yet a cloud. Firelight. E. A. Robinson. NoAM
Ten years Villon lived in a small village. Exile. Joseph Stroud. NPGG
Ten years!—and to my waking eye. The Terrace at Berne. Matthew Arnold. Switzerland, VII. OAEP; VLP
Tenancy, The. Mary Gilmore. CBAP; PoAu-1
Tenant at Number 9. John Blight. CBAP
Tenant Farmer. Robert Ward. AMV-81
Tenantry. George Scarbrough. TAT
Tenants. W. W. Gibson. HBV-2
Tend me my birds, and bring again. A Prayer. Norman Gale. TrPWD
Tended by Faustina. Faustina, or Rock Roses. Elizabeth Bishop. FaBoMo; NMP
Tender Babes. Thomas Hood. *Fr.* The Plea of the Midsummer Fairies. OBRV
Tender Buttons, *sels.* Gertrude Stein. PBWP
Blue Coat, A.
More.
Nothing Elegant.
Piano, A.
Water Raining.
Tender fingers ran up my ankle. "Can I Tempt You to a Pond Walk?" James Schuyler. PoA
Tender-handed stroke a nettle. A Strong Hand. Aaron Hill. HBV-1
Tender, semi-/ articulate flickers. For My Mother: Genevieve Jules Creeley. Robert Creeley. PoM
Tender, Slow. *Unknown, tr. fr. Greek by* Wallace Rice. ErPo
Tender softness, infant mild. To an Infant Expiring the Second Day of Its Birth. Hetty Wright. NOEC
Tender, the young auburn woman. Spring. Paul Verlaine, *tr. by* Roland Grant *and* Paul Archer. ErPo; PeHV
Tenderfoot, The. *Unknown.* AS, *with music*; FSW
Tender-heartedness. Harry Graham. Some Ruthless Rhymes, II. DBV; FaFP; NA; RHPC; TreFT; WhC
(Billy.) FaBoCo
("Billy, in one of his nice new sashes.") CenHV
Tenderly as a/ barber. For the Barbers. Joel Oppenheimer. CoPo
Tenderly as a bee that sips. Escalade. Arthur Symons. UnTE
Tenderly, day that I have loved, I close your eyes. Day That I Have Loved. Rupert Brooke. FPL; PoLF
Tenderness, ache on me, and lay your neck. James Dickey. *Fr.* The Zodiac. TAP
Tenderness and resolution! Reliquary. Hart Crane. PoA
Tenderness of dignity of souls, The. Peter Viereck. *Fr.* Crass Times Redeemed by Dignity of Souls. HoPM
Tenderness so hard to swallow, The. View from a Window. Eldon Grier. PeCV
Tending. Paula Rankin. AMV-81
Tenebrae. Paul Celan, *tr. fr. German by* Joachim Neugroschel. VWA
Tenebrae. Austin Clarke. AnIL; BIrV; CIP; IPY; NeIP
Tenebrae. David Gascoyne. *Fr.* Miserere. NeBP
Tenebrae. Denise Levertov. CABA; NoP
Tenebris. Angelina Weld Grimké. CDC; PoBA; PoNe
Tenebris Interlucentem. James Elroy Flecker. MoBrPo
Teneriffe, *sel.* Frederic William Henry Myers.
"Atlantid islands, phantom-fair." OBVV
Tennessee. Virginia Fraser Boyle. PAH
Tennessee. *Unknown.* AmFP
Tennessee Crickets. Randolph Outlaw. LFAC
Tennis. Margaret Avison. NoAM; PeCV
Tennis. Nina Nyhart. AMV-81
Tennis Court Oath, The. John Ashbery. NoAM; TAP
Tennis Pro. Lawrence Jay Dessner. AMV-81
Tennyson. Thomas Bailey Aldrich. AA
Tennyson. Alan Ansen. CoAP
Tennyson. Florence Earle Coates. AA
Tennyson. Thomas Henry Huxley. HBV-2
Tennyson. Henry van Dyke. AA
Tenour, The/ which my life holds. Wordsworth. *Fr.* The Excursion, III. OBRV
Tension in the tendons of her wing, The. Soldier's Dove. James Forsyth. WaP
Tenson. Carenza *and* Iselda, *tr. fr. Provençal by* Bridget Connelly *and* Doris Earnshaw. WPOW
Tent-lights glimmer on the land, The. At Port Royal. Whittier. PAH
Tent that is pitched at the base, A. War. Edgar Wallace. OBWP
Tentacled for food. In the Sea of Tears. Naomi Replansky. BrRo; GP
Tentative Description of a Dinner to Promote the Impeachment of President Eisenhower. Lawrence Ferlinghetti. CoPo
Tenth Armistice Day, The. S. Gertrude Ford. SUMH
10th Dance—Coming On as a Horn—20 February 1964. Jackson MacLow. CoPo
Tenth Eclogue, The. Michael Drayton. *Fr.* The Shepherd's Garland. JCP
Tenth Elegy: Elegy in Joy. Muriel Rukeyser. MiAP
Tenth Nimphall [*or* Nymphal], The. Michael Drayton. *Fr.* The Muses Elizium. AnAnS-2; JCP
Tenth Reunion. Edward Steese. GoYe
Tenth Symphony. John Ashbery. NOBA
Tenting on the Old Camp Ground. Walter Kittredge. FSW; PSoN, *with music;* TreFS
(Tenting Tonight, *with music.*) BLSo; TrAS
(We're Tenting Tonight.) PAL
Tenuous and Precarious. Stevie Smith. FaBoNo; OxBTC
Tenzone. Ezra Pound. *Fr.* Contemporania. PoA
Tequila. Elizabeth Spires. MAYP
Terce. James McMichael. PoA
Terence, if I could return. To Myself, after Forty Years. T. H. White. NYBP
Terence MacSwiney. "Æ." AnIV
(Prisoner, A.) AnIL
Terence McDiddler. *Unknown.* OxNR
Terence, This Is Stupid Stuff. A. E. Housman. A Shropshire Lad, LXII. BiP; CABA; CMoP; CoBMV; HeIP; InPK; LiTB; LiTM; MasP; NIP; NoAM; NoP; OAEP; PP; PrIm; SeCeV; VLP
(Epilogue: "Terence, this is stupid stuff.") MoAB; MoBrPo; TrGrPo
Power of Malt, The, *sel.* HBV-2
("Why, if 'tis dancing you would be.") WHA
Terenure. Blanaid Salkeld. NeIP
Teresa of Avila. Elizabeth Jennings. NePoEA-2
Teresa was God's familiar. She often spoke. Conversation in Avila. Phyllis McGinley. EaLo
Teresian Contemplative, The. Robert Hugh Benson. ACP
Teresina's Face. Margaret Widdemer. HBMV
Term, The. William Carlos Williams. InvP; LiTA
Term of Death, The. Sarah Morgan Bryan Piatt. AA
Terminal Theater. Robert Sward. CoPo
Terminal Vision. Diana O Hehir. NPGG
Terminus. Emerson. AA; AmPP; AP; AWP; FPL; HBV-1; NOBA; OxBA; PoEL-4; PoLF; TAP
Termite, The. Ogden Nash. CenHV; OBCA; PoPl; ShM; WhC
Termites. Charles G. Bell. NePoAm-2
Termites. Eric Chock. BrSi
Terms of all kinds mellow with time, growing. Their Speech, Compared with Wisdom and Poetry. Robert Pinsky. *Fr.* Essay on Psychiatrists. PoA
Ternarie of Littles, upon a Pipkin of Jelly [*or* Jellie] Sent to a Lady, A. Robert Herrick. FaBoCh; FaBoUs; GoJo; HBV-1; HBVY; PoEL-3; WhC
Ternissa! You Are Fled. Walter Savage Landor. *Fr.* The Hellenics. LoBV; PoEL-4; SeCeV
(On Ternissa's Death.) ELP
(Ternissa.) FaBoEn; NOBE; OBNC
Terpsichore looks kindly on me. Korinna, *tr. fr. Greek by* John Dillon. PBWP
Terra Cotta. K. Curtis Lyle. CNA
Terrace, The. Richard Wilbur. MiAP
Terrace at Berne, The. Matthew Arnold. Switzerland, VII. OAEP; VLP
Terrace in the Snow, The. Su Tung-p'o. *tr. fr. Chinese by* Kenneth Rexroth. NaP
Terrace is empty, which shows how flat it is, The. Heron Weather. Douglas Crase. NoP
Terraces rise and fall, The. Going to Sleep in the Country. Howard Moss. DFF; PoCh
Terra-cotta house in the moonlight, The. Birth of a Country. Agnes Gergely, *tr. by* Emery George. VWA
Terrain. A. R. Ammons. ConAP
Terrapin War. *Unknown.* PAH
Terraplane Blues. *Unknown.* BluL
Terrestrial Cuckoo, A. Frank O'Hara. SOTW
Terrible/ a horse at night. Lawrence Ferlinghetti. HoPM
Terrible/ is the soft sound of a hardboiled egg. Late Rising. Jacques Prévert, *tr. by* Selden Rodman. CAD
Terrible and splendid trust, A. Ways of War. Lionel Johnson. AnIV
Terrible Beauty. Kingsley Amis. ErPo; NePoEA-2; PV
Terrible childbed hast thou had, my dear, A. Shakespeare. *Fr.* Pericles, III, i. EBEV
Terrible Door, The. Harold Monro. BoLoP; EnLoPo; FaBoTw
Terrible Dread, The. Mary Carolyn Davies. HBMV
Terrible Infant, A. Frederick Locker-Lampson. FiBHP; HBV-1; InMe; TreFS; WhC
Terrible is my plight this night. Wolves for Company. *Unknown.* BIrV
Terrible is the price. The Price. John Davidson. EBVV

Terrible lodgings. In the frightful lodgings. Lodgers. Julian Tuwin, *tr. by* Isaac Komem. VWA
Terrible oldness, The. The Fisherman. Sam G. Harrison. AMV-80
Terrible People, The. Ogden Nash. NePA; TAP
Terrible Robber Men, The. Padraic Colum. HBMV
Terrible Sonnets, The. Gerard Manley Hopkins.
See Carrion Comfort; I Wake and Feel the Fell of Dark, Not Day; *and* No Worst, There Is None.
Terrible sons of the mighty race, The. The Terrible Sons. Eleazar ben Kalir, *tr. by* Israel Zangwill. TrJP
Terrible Sons, The. Eleazar ben Kalir, *tr. fr. Hebrew by* Israel Zangwill. TrJP
Terrible Thought, A. Eliezer Steinberg, *tr. fr. Yiddish by* Joseph Leftwich. TrJP
Terribly for mystery or glory my dawns have arisen. Dawns I Have Seen. Ivor Gurney. FaBoPP
Terrifying are the attent sleek thrushes on the lawn. Thrushes. Ted Hughes. FaBoMo; GoYe; NePoEA-2
Territory. Susan Wood-Thompson. AMV-81
Terror. Thomas O'Brien. NeIP
Terror. Robert Penn Warren. MoPo; NePA; PoA; WaP
Terror. "Yehoash," *tr. fr. Yiddish by* Isidore Goldstick. TrJP
Terror by Night, The. Giacomo Leopardi, *tr. fr. Italian by* John Heath-Stubbs. MOON
Terror Conduction. Philip Lamantia. NeAP
Terror does not belong to open day. Counterpoint. Owen Dodson. PoNe
Terror of Death, The. Keats. *See* When I Have Fears.
Terror strikes lightly your stillness. Spider. Thomas Cole. PoA
Terror swoops down on his heart like a vulture. Ezekiel. A. N. Stencl, *tr. by* Joseph Leftwich. VWA
Terrorless, I awake. To a Wasp Caught in the Storm Sash at the Advent of the Winter Solstice. Peter Cooley. MAYP
Terrors are to come. The earth. To My Children, Fearing for Them. Wendell Berry. Str
Terry is sitting in the kafeneion writing letters to all his friends. Human Relations. Emmett Jarrett. NeAC
Tess's Lament. Thomas Hardy. FaBoTw; TEP
Test, The. Emerson. AA; OBAL; PP
Test, The. Robert Friend. GP
Test, The. Walter Savage Landor. HBV-1
Test, The. Rachel McAlpine. OCNZ
Test of Competence, A. Greg Forker. LFAC
Test of Manhood, The, *sel.* George Meredith.
"In fellowship Religion has its founts." WGRP
Test of Men, The. Bible, Apocrypha. Ecclesiasticus, XXVI: 5-8. TrJP
Testament. Lucille Clifton. GeTw
Testament. Langston Hughes. NePoAm-2
Testament, A. *Unknown.* OBSC
Testament, The, *abr.* Villon, *tr. fr. French by* Galway Kinnell. NAWM-1
Testament of a Man Forbid, The, *sel.* John Davidson. I Haunt the Hills That Overlook the Sea. BSV
Testament of Beauty, The, *sels.* Robert Bridges.
Ethick, *fr.* IV. OxBTC
"How was November's melancholy endear'd to me," *fr.* II. MoVE
Introduction: " 'Twas late in my long journey, when I had clomb to where." MoVE
"Sky's unresting cloudland, that with varying play, The," *fr.* I. EBEV; MoVE
" 'Twas at that hour of beauty when the setting sun," *fr.* III. MoVE; OxBoCh
Testament of Cathaeir Mor, The. *Unknown, tr. fr. Middle Irish by* James Clarence Mangan. *Fr.* Book of Rights. OnYI
Testament of Cresseid, The Robert Henryson. GoTS; OxBS
Sels.
"Ane doolie season to ane careful dyte!" BSV
Assembly of the Gods, The. PoEL-1
Cresseid's Complaint against Fortune. MeEL
Cressida's Leprosy. SeCePo
"I mend the fyre and beikit me about." EBEV
"This duleful sentence Saturn took on hand." BSV
Testament of John Davidson, The, *sel.* John Davidson.
Last Journey, The. BSV; GoTS; PoSH
Testament of Mr. Andro Kennedy, The. William Dunbar. OxBS
Testament of Perpetual Change, The. William Carlos Williams. GOA
Testimonies. Weldon Kees. NYP
Testimony. Carolyn M. Rodgers. BPo
Testimony to an Inquisitor. William Stafford. NePoAm-2
Testing Ground. Karla M. Hammond. AMV-81
Testing, Testing. Dan Dillon. PV
Testing-Tree, The. Stanley Kunitz. FYAP; MAT; UnPo
Testubicles spill blood across the page. Crossedroads. Martin Staples Shockley. FF
Tête-à-Tête. Edwin Honig. NoAM
Tetélestai. Conrad Aiken. LiTA; MoAB; MoAmPo
Tethys' Festival, *sel.* Samuel Daniel.
Are They Shadows [That We See]? CH; ElL; InvP; LoBV; NoP; SeCeV
(Shadows.) NOBE; OBSC
(Song: "Are they shadowes that we see?") PoEL-2
Tetrachordon, *sel.* Milton.
Whom Do We Count a Good Man. NCEP
Teuton sang the "Wacht am Rhein," The. "Il Est Cocule Chef de Gare!" H. S. Mackintosh. WhC
Tewkesbury Road. John Masefield. TreFT
Texas. James Daugherty. TiPo
Texas. Amy Lowell. AmFN; BPAW
Texas. Whittier. PAH
Texas Cowboy, The ("Oh, I am a Texas cowboy"). *Unknown.* AmFP
Texas Cowboy, The ("Oh, I am a Texas cowboy, far away from home"), *with music. Unknown.* CoSo
Texas Cowboy [lay down] on a barroom floor, A. The Hell-bound Train. *Unknown.* BeLS; BLPA; BPAW; CoSo
Texas Cowboys, The ("It's of those Texas cowboys a story"). *Unknown.* CoSo
Texas Ranger, The. Margie B. Boswell. BPAW
Texas Rangers, The *(diff. versions). Unknown.* BPAW; CoSo, *with music*; FSW; OuSiCo, *with music*
Texas Song, The. *Unknown.* CoSo
Texas Trains and Trails. Mary Austin. SoPo; TiPo
Texas Types—"The Bad Man." William Lawrence Chittenden. PoOW
Texas, you swagger in our veins. Driving North from Kingsville, Texas. Naomi Shihab. TAT
Texian Boys, The, *with music. Unknown.* CoSo
Text. Audrey Wurdemann. FYAP
Text. Aaron Zeitlin, *tr. fr. Yiddish by* Ruth Whitman. VWA
Text for These Distracted Times, A. Rodney Hall. CBAP
Text for Today. Phyllis McGinley. WhC
Textile Mills and Prison Reform. George Rachow. LFAC
Th' have left Thee naked, Lord, O that they had. *See* They have left thee naked, Lord . . .
Thaba Bosio. S. D. R. Sutu, *tr. fr. Sotho by* Dan Kunene *and* Jack Cope. PeSA
Thack church and a wooden steeple, A. Legsby, Lincolnshire. *Unknown.* GBP
Thaddeus Stevens. Phoebe Cary. PAH
Thaddeus Stevens was a burning scandal. Old Thad Stevens. Kenneth Porter. NePoAm-2
Thai passit in thare pilgramage. *Unknown. Fr.* Golagros and Gawane. OxBS
Thailand Railway, *sels.* Randolph Stow. CBAP
Jungle, The.
Sleepers, The.
Thair is nocht ane Winche. *Unknown.* OxBS
Thais. Newman Levy. FiBHP; InMe
Thalaba the Destroyer, *sels.* Robert Southey. SeCePo
Thalaba and the Banquet.
Thalaba and the Magic Thread.
Thalamos. Peter Kane Dufault. ErPo
Thalassa. Louis MacNeice. BlrV; FaBoMo; FaBoRV; NOBE
Thalassius. Swinburne. VLP
Thalatta. Willis Boyd Allen. EtS
Thalatta! Thalatta! Joseph Brownlee Brown. AA; HBV-2
Thalia. Thomas Bailey Aldrich. AA; HBV-1; InMe
Thames, The. Sir John Denham. *Fr.* Cooper's Hill. FaBoEn
Thames from Cooper's Hill, The. Sir John Denham. *Fr.* Cooper's Hill. OBS; SeCePo
("My eye descending from the hill, surveys.") OAEL-1; ViBoPo
Thames Head Wassailers' Song. *Unknown.* OBET
Thames nocturne of blue and gold, The. Impression du Matin. Oscar Wilde. BrPo; CABA; EBVV; MoBrPo; SyP; VLP
Thames, the most lov'd of all the Oceans sons. The Thames Sir John Denham. *Fr.* Cooper's Hill. FaBoEn
Thammuz. William Vaughn Moody. AP
Thamuris Marching. Robert Browning. OAEL-2
Than (By Yon Sunset's Wintry Glow). E. E. Cummings. VGW
Than this great universe no less. Rowland's Rhyme. Michael Drayton. *Fr.* The Shepherd's Garland, Eclogue II (1606 ed.). OBSC
Thanatopsis. Bryant. AA; AmPP; AP; AWP; BLPL; BoNaP; DL; FaBoBe; FaFP; HBV-2; HBVY; LiTA; NePA; NOBA; OBEV; OBRV; OBVV; OHFP; OxBA; TAP; TreF; TrGrPo; ViBoPo; WBLP; WGRP; WHA
"So live, that when thy summons comes to join," *sel.* TRV
Thank God. Joseph Rolnik, *tr. fr. Yiddish by* Joseph Leftwich. TrJP
Thank God, a man can grow! Per Aspera. Florence Earle Coates. HBMV

Thank God, bless God, all ye who suffer not. Tears. Elizabeth Barrett Browning. WPE
Thank God for Life. *Unknown.* PGD
Thank God for sleep! The Sacrament of Sleep. John Oxenham. PoLF
Thank God! for that lovely spirit. Wondrous Motherhood. *Unknown.* PGD
Thank God for the Country! Mrs. Major Arnold. WBLP
Thank God my brain is not inclined to cut. The Menagerie. William Vaughn Moody. AP; YaD
Thank God our liberating lance. The Road to France. Daniel Henderson. HBV-2; PAH
Thank God, thank God, we do believe. A Christmas Carol. Christina Rossetti. PChr
Thank God that God shall judge my soul, not man. The Eternal Justice. Anne Reeve Aldrich. AA
Thank God! there is always a Land of Beyond. Robert W. Service. *Fr.* Rhymes of a Rolling Stone. TRV
Thank God we do not live by bread alone. Twice Fed. A. A. Bassett. HBV-2
Thank God who seasons thus the year. The Fall of the Leaf. Henry David Thoreau. AP
Thank Goodness, the moving is over. "When the World Was in Building." Ford Madox Ford. CTC
Thank Heaven! the crisis. For Annie. Poe. AmPP; AP; BLPL; HBV-1; LiTA; LO; NePA; NOBA; OBEV; OBVV; OxBA; TreFS
Thank heav'n! I'm safely landed frae Ostend. To the Memory of Gavin Wilson (Boot, Leg and Arm Maker). George Galloway. NOEC
Thank Thee, Lord. Georgia B. Adams. STF
Thank Thee, O Giver of life, O God! Thanksgiving. Angela Morgan. TrPWD; TRV
Thank You. Kenneth Koch. NeAP; PoM
Thank You/ for all my hands can hold. Thanksgiving. Ivy O. Eastwick. RHPC
Thank You for the Valentine. Diane Wakoski. HoPM
Thank you for your recent letter. Dear Mother. Emmett Jarrett. NeAC
Thank you, my children, my students. As I Grow Older and Fatten on Myself. Joseph Carson. AMV-80
Thank you, pretty cow, that made. The Cow. Ann *or* Jane Taylor. HBV-1; HBVY; OxBChV
Thank you, thank you, lovely plant. Have You Thanked a Green Plant Today. Don Anderson. QQQ
Thankful Acknowledgment of God's Providence, A. John Cotton. SCAP
Thankful Country Lass, The; or, The Jolly Batchelor Kindly Entertained. *Unknown.* CoMu
Thankful Heart. F. W. Davis. STF
Thankfulness. Adelaide Anne Procter. TrPWD
Thankless for favours from on high. On a Similar Occasion for the Year 1792. William Cowper. NOCV
Thanks and a Plea to Mary. *Unknown. See* Lady, I Thank Thee.
Thanks Be to God. Janie Alford. PGD
Thanks, fair Urania; to your scorn. The Indifference. Sir Charles Sedley. SeCV-2
Thanks for Everything. Helen Isabella Tupper. *See* For Everything Give Thanks.
Thanks from Earth to Heaven. John Hall Wheelock. HBMV
"Holy Poet, I have heard," *sel.* TrPWD
Thanks, Gentle Moon, for Thy Obscured Light. *Unknown.* NCEP
Thanks, I will. Phono, at the Boar's Head. Henri Coulette. *Fr.* The War of the Secret Agents, IX. NePoEA-2
Thanks Just the Same. *Unknown.* PoLF
Thanks to God. J. A. Hultman. STF
Thanks to Industrial Essex. Donald Davie. OxBTC
Thanks to Saint Matthew, who had been. Comrade Jesus. Sarah N. Cleghorn. HBMV; WGRP
Thanksgiving. Susie M. Best. TrPWD
Thanksgiving. Philip Booth. Str
Thanksgiving. Alice Williams Brotherton. PGD
Thanksgiving. Florence Earle Coates. TrPWD
Thanksgiving. Louise Driscoll. YeAr
Thanksgiving. Ivy O. Eastwick. RHPC
Thanksgiving, The. George Herbert. AnAnS-1
Thanksgiving. Robert Herrick. LiTB; OFD
Thanksgiving, A. William Dean Howells. HBV-2; TrPWD
(Prayer, A: "Lord, for the erring thought.") WGRP
Thanksgiving. Arthur Ketchum. STF
Thanksgiving. Kenneth Koch. VGW
Thanksgiving, A. Lucy Larcom. OHIP
"For the rosebud's break of beauty," *sel.* TrPWD
Thanksgiving. David Abenatar Melo, *tr. fr. Spanish by* Henry Hart Milman. TrJP
Thanksgiving. Angela Morgan. TrPWD; TRV
Thanksgiving. John N. Morris. OFD
Thanksgiving, A. Cardinal Newman. TrPWD
Thanksgiving. Robert Nichols. MMA
Thanksgiving. Gene H. Osborne. PGD
Thanksgiving. John Oxenham. BLRP; WBLP
Thanksgiving. Margaret E. Sangster. BLRP; TRV
Thanksgiving. A. B. Simpson. STF
Thanksgiving. *Unknown, at. to* Emerson. SoPo
(Father in Heaven, *sl. diff.*) TreFT
Thanksgiving. "Yehoash," *tr. fr. Yiddish by* Isidore Goldstick. TrJP
Thanksgiving after Communion. *Tr. from Gaelic by* Douglas Hyde. WTO
Thanksgiving at Snake Butte. James Welch. STE
Thanksgiving Day. John Kendrick Bangs. TrPWD
Thanksgiving Day. Robert Bridges. OHIP
Thanksgiving Day. Lydia Maria Child. FaPON; NTCP; OHIP; RHPC; SiSoSe; TreFS
(New-England Boy's Song about Thanksgiving Day, The.) OBCA
Thanksgiving Day. Annette Wynne. OHIP
Thanksgiving Day I like to see. Thanksgiving Magic. Rowena Bastin Bennett. RHPC; SiSoSe; TiPo
Thanksgiving for a former, doth invite. Thanksgiving. Robert Herrick. LiTB; OFD
Thanksgiving for a Habitat. W. H. Auden. NYBP
"From gallery-grave and the hunt of a wren-king," *sel.* EyDe
Thanksgiving for America, The. Hezekiah Butterworth. PAH
Thanksgiving for the Body. Thomas Traherne. ImOP
Thanksgiving for the Earth. Elizabeth Goudge. YeAr
Thanksgiving Hymn. *Unknown.* PAH
Thanksgiving in Boston Harbor, The. Hezekiah Butterworth. AA; OHIP; PAH
Thanksgiving Magic. Rowena Bastin Bennett. RHPC; SiSoSe; TiPo
Thanksgiving, 1963. Molly Kazan. TreFT
Thanksgiving. They have/ taken a sample. 78 Miners in Mannington, West Virginia. Louis Philips. TAT
Thanksgiving Time. *Unknown.* SoPo
Thanksgiving to God, for His House, A. Robert Herrick. AnAnS-2; BLBL; ChTr; FaBoBe; HAP; HBV-2; OBS; OFD; OHIP; PGD; PoRA; SeCeV; SeCP; SeCV-1; TrCP; TreFT; TrPWD; ViBoPo; WGRP
Thanksgiving to the gods! The Seeker in the Marshes. Daniel Lewis Dawson. AA
Thanksgiving Wishes. Arthur Guiterman. PoSC
Thanksgivings for the Beauty of His Providence. Thomas Traherne. FaBoCh
Thanksliving. Chauncey R. Piety. PGD
Thar's More in the Man than Thar Is in the Land. Sidney Lanier. AP; NOBA
Thar's no respect fer youth er age. Californy Stage. *Unknown.* BPAW
Thass a funny title, Mr. Bones. April Fool's Day, or, St. Mary of Egypt. John Berryman. Dream Songs, XLVII. NaP
Thassyryans king, in peas with fowle desyre. *See* Assyrian King in peace, with foul desire, The.
That after horror that was us. Emily Dickinson. MoPo
That aged woman with the bass voice. The Great-Grandmother. Robert Graves. DTC
That all should change to ghost and glance and gleam. The Transmutation. Edwin Muir. FaBoEn
That All Things Are as They Are Used. George Turberville. EnRePo
That all things should be mine. Amendment. Thomas Traherne. SeCV-2
That amazing holiday. The Unscarred Fighter Remembers France. Kenneth Slade Alling. HBMV
That American Poet's future. The Line of an American Poet. Reed Whittemore. MoVE; PPON
That angel whose charge was Eiré sang thus. The Three Woes. Aubrey Thomas De Vere. AnIV
That any thing should be. Axle Song. Mark Van Doren. MoPo
That autumn when the partridges called in the stubble. Microcosmos, XLI. Nigel Heseltine. NeBP
That balmy eve, within a trellised bower. The Marriage of Pocahontas. M. M. Webster. PAH
That Beauty I Ador'd Before. Aphra Behn. *See* Westminster Drollery, 1671.
That Black Snake Moan. *Unknown.* BluL
That boat has killed three people. Building her. Unlucky Boat. George Mackay Brown. NePoEA-2
That bony potbellied arrow, wing-pumping along. The Cormorant in Its Element. Amy Clampitt. SUW
That Bright Chimeric Beast. Countee Cullen. AmNP
That Brings Us to the Woodstove in the Wilds, at Night. Walter Hall. AMV-81
That broken star. David McCord. *Fr.* A Christmas Package. PChr
That bull-necked blotch-faced farmer from Drumlore. Ghosts' Stories. Alastair Reid. NePoEA-2

That came through our town. I Never Saw the Train. Jean Roberts. AMV-80
That Cat. Ben King. FiBHP
That child will never lie in me, and you. The Unknown Child. Elizabeth Jennings. PBWP
That childish thoughts such joys inspire. The Approach. Thomas Traherne. AnAnS-1; OxBoCh
That Chinese restaurant was a joke. The Will to Change. Adrienne Rich. NMM
That civilisation may not sink. Long-legged Fly. W. B. Yeats. CMoP; FaBoEn; FaBoMo; FaBoTw; InPK; InPS; LiTM; NoAM; NOBE; NOP; PAI; PPoe; TEP
That conversation we were always on the edge. Adrienne Rich. *Fr.* Twenty-one Love Poems. BoWoP
"That cop was powerful mean." The Idiot. Dudley Randall. BPo
That Corner. Blanaid Salkeld. OnYI; OxBI
That corner of the earth. Aware Aware. Tram Combs. MP; TwCP
That crackle is well worth hearing. Mr. T. S. Eliot Cooking Pasta. József Tornai, *tr. by* Richard Wilbur. GrPl
That "Craning of the Neck." Isabella Gardner. NePA; WPE
That Crawling Baby Blues. *Unknown.* BluL
That crazed girl improvising her music. The Crazed Girl. W. B. Yeats. InPS
That Crazy War. *Unknown.* FSW
That creepycrawly traversing the stone. Close-ups of Summer. Norman MacCaig. OxBC
That dark brown rabbit, lightness in his ears. John Berryman. Dream Songs, LXII. TwCP
That dark form lies in a cumulus tower. Vancouver Island. Joan Swift. DFT
That Dark Other Mountain. Robert Francis. LiSp; NCSH
That Day. David Kherdian. SaC
That Day. John Leax. TrCP
That Day. Anne Sexton. BoWoP; ConAP
That Day. Mark Van Doren. WaP
That day began with a shower. The Day Duke Raised. Quincy Troupe. LTB
That day everything went wrong. Poetry Defined. John Holmes. GrPl; PP
That day in the Interpreter's house, in one of his Significant Rooms. Christiana. Peter Redgrove. OxBC
That day, in the slipping of torsos and straining flanks. The Song. Lola Ridge. WPE
That Day of Wrath, That Direful Day. Thomas of Celano. *See* Dies Irae.
That day, someone died down the beach. Hard Strain in a Delicate Place. Janet Sylvester. MAYP
That day the/ words. That Day. John Leax. TrCP
That day the eggshell of appearance split. Transfigured Bird. James Merrill. MoAB
That day the sunlight lay on the farms. On Heaven. Ford Madox Ford. CTC
That day we brought our Beautiful One to lie. Two Days. W. E. Henley. VLP
That day when oats were reaped, and wheat was ripe. When Oats Were Reaped. Thomas Hardy. OxBTC
That Day You Came. Lizette Woodworth Reese. HBV-1
That death may not be casual. Epilogue. James Singer Burns. FaBoTw
That Death should thus from hence our Butler catch. In Obitum Promi. Henry Parrot. FaBoCo
That Delightful Time. Mark Akenside. *Fr.* The Pleasures of Imagination. SeCePo
"That Did in Luve So Lively Write." Georgine M. Adams. InMe
That Distant Bliss. Henry King. *See* Sonnet: "Tell me no more how fair she is."
That dog was always a dizzy blond. Dame. Susan Astor. AMV-80
That dog with daisies for eyes. The Dog of Art. Denise Levertov. NoAM
That dolphin-torn, that gong-tormented face. The Death of Yeats. George Barker. LiTB
That duck, bobbing up. Joso, *tr. fr. Japanese by* Harry Behn. WSC
That Each Thing Is Hurt of Itself. *Unknown.* EIL
That enraged and frightened woman of Goya. La Pesadilla. Gerde Penfold. GP
That Eureka of Archimedes out of his bath. Voluptuaries and Others. Margaret Avison. MoCV
That evening/ after Scotty and his mother moved out. Zoe and the Ghosts. Dieter Weslowski. PPJ
That evening all in fond discourse was spent. The Dejected Lover [*or* The Sad Lover]. George Crabbe. *Fr.* Tales of the Hall. FaBoEn
That evening, when the fire was lit. The Dream. Helen Spalding. ChMP
That Ever I Saw. *Unknown.* TrGrPo
That Everything Moves Its Bowels. David R. Slavitt. BXAP
That face which no man ever saw. Sargent's Portrait of Edwin Booth at "The Players." Thomas Bailey Aldrich. AA
That famous old pederast, Wilde. Limerick. *Unknown.* PeHV
That final newsreel of the war. A Welcoming Party. John Montague. IPY
That firewood pale with salt and burning green. Gigha. W. S. Graham. NeBP
"That First Gulp of Air We All Took When First Born." Nancy Paddock. PoDr
That first September day was blue and warm. The Artist on Penmaenmawr. Charles Tennyson Turner. FaBoPP
That flattering glass whose smooth face wears. A Looking-Glass. Thomas Carew. CaPo
That flower unseen, that gem of purest ray. In a Churchyard. Richard Wilbur. HeIP
That for seven lustres [*or* lusters] I did never come. To the Reverend Shade of His Religious Father. Robert Herrick. AnAnS-2; CaPo; JCP; OBS; SeCV-1
That force is lost. Snake Eyes. Amiri Baraka. VGW
That frantic error I adore. The Apostasy of One and But One Lady. Richard Lovelace. CaPo
That girl from the sun is bathing in the creek. The Dosser in Springtime. Douglas Stewart. ErPo
That girl has borne too much. The Girl Who Had Borne Too Much. John Woods. GP
That girl this summer reading Dante. Audiences. Robert Hollander. GLGT
That God of ours, the Great Geometer. Grace to Be Said at the Supermarket. Howard Nemerov. SoSe
That grave small face, but twelve hours here. The Chart. Walter de la Mare. CoBMV
That great ox, built just right! The Frog Who Would Be an Ox. La Fontaine, *tr. by* Marianne Moore. NAWM-2
That grey morning I left you asleep. Mysterious Britain. Amy Clampitt. AMV-81
That gusty spring, each afternoon. Love's Calendar. William Bell Scott. HBV-1
That Harp You Play So Well. Marianne Moore. HBMV; MoAB; MoAmPo; PoA
That haughty tyranny of thine. Love Song. Luís De León, *tr. by* Thomas Walsh. TrJP
That He Findeth Others as Fair, but Not So Faithful as His Friend. George Turberville. EIL
That he to his unmeasur'd mightie acts. Praise of Homer. George Chapman. OBS
That he was born it cannot be denied. On a Certain Alderman. John Cunningham, *after* Simonides. FaBoEE
That he would never have any rest this side of his death. Hagiograph. Rayner Heppenstall. NeBP
That Heathen Chinee. Brett Harte. *See* Plain Language from Truthful James.
That her serene influence should spread. Two Loves. Richard Eberhart. CMoP
That Hill. Blanche Taylor Dickinson. CDC
That hobnailed goblin, the bobtailed Hob. Country Dance. Edith Sitwell. NoAM
That hollow space, where now in living rowes. Fairies. Thomas Tickell. *Fr.* Kensington Garden. OBEC
That holy night when stars shone bright. A Child Is Born. *Unknown.* STF
That Holy Thing. George Macdonald. *Fr.* Paul Faber, Surgeon. HBV-2; OBEV; OBVV; TrPWD; TRV; WGRP
That horse whose rider fears to jump will fall. Masters. Kingsley Amis. NePoEA; PoPl
That hoür-glass, which there ye see. The Hour-Glass. Robert Herrick. CaPo
That house, a stone's throw from the shell-strewn shore. Boat-Haven, Co. Mayo. Geoffrey Taylor. NeIP
That houses forme within was rude and strong. The House of Richesse. Spenser. *Fr.* The Faerie Queene, II, 7. CH
"That humble, simple duty of the day." Serve in Thy Post. Arthur Hugh Clough. PGD
That hump of a man bunching chrysanthemums. Old Florist. Theodore Roethke. CTBA; NCSH; PCP; SaC
That Hypocrite. *Unknown.* BPo
That I have felt the rushing wind of Thee. The Poet's Prayer. Stephen Philipps. WGRP
That I have often been in love, deep love. Ode. "Peter Pindar." NOEC
That I should have a joyous life. A Gift of God. *Unknown.* STF
That I went to warm my self in Lady Betty's Chamber. To Their Excellencies the Lords Justices of Ireland, the Humble Petition of Frances Harris, Who Must Starve, and Die a Maid if It Miscarries. Swift. NOEC; Par; PoEL-3
That Idiot, Wordsworth. Byron. *Fr.* English Bards and Scotch Reviewers. DBV
("Next comes the dull disciple of thy school.") OBRV; PP

That insect, without antennae, over its. The Crane. Charles Tomlinson. MoBrPo
That Is All I Heard. "Yehoash," *tr. fr. Yiddish by* Isidore Goldstick. TrJP
"That is important. I do not watch the birds." He Said the Facts. Merrill Moore. CrMA
That is no country for old men. Sailing to Byzantium. W. B. Yeats. AnIL; BiP; CABA; ChMP; CMoP; CoBMV; FaBoEn; FaFP; FF; FPL; GTBS-P; HAP; HeIP; HoPM; InPK; InPS; InvP; LiTB; LiTM; MasP; MoAB; MoBrPo; MoPo; MoVE; NiP; NoAM; NOBE; NoP; OAEL-2; OAEP; OBMV; OxBI; OxBTC; PAI; PoRA; PP; PPoe; PPP; PrIm; SeCePo; SeCeV; SoSe; TEP; TreFT; UnPo; ViBoPo; WeW
That Is Not Indifference. Howard G. Hanson. AMV-81
That is what they say, who were broken off from love. Children's Elegy. Muriel Rukeyser. *Fr.* Eighth Elegy. LCAP
That it should end in an Albert Pick hotel. At the End of the Affair. Maxine W. Kumin. TAP
That it will never come again. Emily Dickinson. NOBA
That June before the judge gave. Seventeen. Jonathan Holden. Psk
"That just reminds me of a yarn," he said. The Jester in the Trench. Leon Gellert. PoAu-1
That Justice is a blind goddess. Justice. Langston Hughes. BPo
That knot in the wood if wood. The Man with the Hollow Breast. Tania Van Zyl. PeSA
That labor/ a face to remember in wonder. Sappho, *tr. fr. Greek by* Guy Davenport. OBVE
That lady of all gentle memories. Dante, *tr. by* Dante Gabriel Rossetti. La Vita Nuova, XXII. AWP
That lamb. Some Lamb. Stan Rice. NPGG
That learned Græcian (who did so excell). Sonnet. William Drummond of Hawthornden. OBS
That lifted blade transformed our jangling clans. James Russell Lowell. *Fr.* Under the Old Elm. GOA
That 'lil girl that Daddy loved. Ted Kooser. *Fr.* Themes for Country-Western Singers. POL
That Little Black Cat. D'Arcy Wentworth Thompson. OxBChV
That Little Hatchet. C. Butler-Andrews. PeD
That Little Lump of Coal. *Unknown.* AmFP
That Lonesome Train Took My Baby Away. *Unknown.* BluL
That love is all there is. Emily Dickinson. NOBA
That love which once was nearest to my heart. Vetus Flamma. Robert Mezey. PoA
That lovely spot which thou dost see. Upon a Mole in Celia's Bosom[e]. Thomas Carew. AnAnS-2; CaPo
That lover of a night. Crazy Jane on God. W. B. Yeats. CMoP; EBEV; MoAB; OxBTC
That Love,—whose power and sovranty we own. The Creation of My Lady. Francesco Redi, *tr. by* Sir Edmund Gosse. AWP
That man. Night Song for Two Mystics. Paul Blackburn. NeAP
That man cannot know. *Unknown. Fr.* The Seafarer. PBBP
That man entered through my eyes. Dream of the Forgotten Lover. Lucia Fox, *tr. by* R. Maghan. BoWoP
That Man in Manhattan. Shannon Keith Kelley. AMV-80
That man must be more patient than a cow. In Camus Fields. L. A. G. Strong. DBV
That man over there say. Ain't I a Woman? Sojourner Truth. BlSi
That man's a fool who tries by art and skill. Woman's Will. *Unknown.* HBV-1
That mare stood in the field. All through the Rains. Gary Snyder. ConAP
That matter of the murder is hushed up. The Cenci. Shelley. EnRP
That May Morning. Leland B. Jacobs. RHPC
That me alone you lov'd, you once did say. Catullus, *tr. fr. Latin by* Richard Lovelace. OBVE
That memory like a derelict plane. Payments. Diana O Hehir. NPGG
That Men Should Fear. Shakespeare. *See* Death of Cowards, The.
That mirror/ Which makes of men a transparency. Moments of Vision. Thomas Hardy. OAEL-2
That Moment. Ted Hughes. FF
That moment now embalmed in decrepitude. The Resurrection. William Edward Taylor. AMV-80
That month he was broke. Whiplash. William Matthews. MAYP
That morn which saw me made a bride. Upon a Maid That Died [*or* Dyed] the Day She Was Married [*or* Marryed]. Meleager, *tr. by* Robert Herrick. AWP; NIP; OBVE
That morning, after the storm. After the Storm. Elizabeth Bartlett. GoYe
That morning I walked out. Leaving Raiford. Mario Petaccia. LFAC
That mountain there. Pilgrimage Song. *Unknown, tr. by* Mary Austin. WPE
That Mulberry Wine. Janet Sylvester. MAYP
That my old bitter heart was pierced in this black doom. A Grey Eye Weeping. Egan O'Rahilly, *tr. by* Frank O'Connor. AnIL; KiLC; OBMV; OxBI
That Nature Is a Heraclitean Fire and of the Comfort of the Resurrection. Gerard Manley Hopkins. BiP; BrPo; CABA; CoBMV; FaBoMo; GTBS-P; LiTB; MoAB; MoPo; MoVE; NoP; OAEL-2; OAEP; PoEL-5; TEP; VLP
That neither fame nor love might wanting be. To Sir Henry Cary. Ben Jonson. NoP
That night I think that no one slept. The Last Fight. Lewis Frank Tooker. AA; FaBoBe
That night in the barn. Rope and Drum. Robert Currie. Str
That night my angel stooped and strained. My Angel. Jonathan Henderson Brooks. PoNe
That night she felt those searching hands. Mary, Mother of Christ. Countee Cullen. PChr
That night the moon drifted over the pond. The Prediction. Mark Strand. EAS; LCAP
That night, when I woke suddenly, was sweet. Conversation with Rain. Louise D. Gunn. GoYe
That Night When Joy Began. W. H. Auden. OxBTC; PAI; SoSe
That night when October played. Concert. Michael Arvey. AMV-81
That night, when storms were spent and tranquil heaven. John Addington Symonds. *Fr.* Ithocles. PeHV
That night, when through the mooring-chains. The Ballad of Fisher's Boardinghouse. Kipling. PoRA
That night your great guns, unawares. Channel Firing. Thomas Hardy. BiP; BrPo; CABA; CMoP; CoBMV; EBEV; HAP; HeIP; InPK; LiTB; MoPo; NIP; NoAM; NoP; OAEL-2; OAEP; OxBTC; PAI; PoEL-5; PoRA; PPON; PrIm; SeCeV; SoSe; UnPo; WaaP
That nightingale, whose strain so sweetly flows. The Nightingale. Petrarch, *tr. by* Thomas LeMesurier.
Sonnets to Laura: To Laura in Death, XLIII. PoPl
That no fair woman will, wonder not why. Catullus, *tr. fr. Latin by* Richard Lovelace. OBVE
That No Man Should Write but Such as Do Excel. George Turberville. EnRePo
That none beguiled be by time's quick flowing. Love's Clock. Sir John Suckling. CaPo; PoEL-3
That nose is out of drawing. With a gasp. Sonnet for a Picture. Swinburne. *Fr.* The Heptalogia. BXAP; FaBoNo; OAEL-2; OAEP
That Nova was a moderate star like our good sun. Nova. Robinson Jeffers. CMoP; HAP
That ocean you of late surveyed. To Mr. Newton on His Return from Ramsgate. William Cowper. NOEC
That odyssey? We three left Amherst late. To My Fellow-Mariners, March, '53. Thomas Whitbread. NYBP
That old 'Frisco train left a mile a minute. 'Frisco Town. *Unknown.* BluL
That "old last act"! Two Songs, II. Adrienne Rich. CABA; NIP
That old man at the farm near Norman's Lane. The Farm near Norman's Lane. Mary Finnin. PoAu-2
That old monk confined in his cell. Monasteries. Charles David Webb. NePoAm-2
That Old Sauna High. Anselm Hollo. PoM
That on her lap she casts her humble eye. On the Blessed Virgin's Bashfulness. Richard Crashaw. HAP; ISi; OAEP
That once this life was really mine. A Song of Life. Franz Werfel, *tr. by* Edith Abercrombie Snow. TrJP
That once which pained to think of. The Forgiven Past. Laura Riding. NoAM; PBWP
That one bird, one star. In Praise of Creation. Elizabeth Jennings. PAI
That one small boy with a face like pallid cheese. Incendiary. Vernon Scannell. OxBC
That orbèd maiden with white fire laden. Orbed Maiden. Shelley. *Fr.* The Cloud. MOON
That Orpheus Calliops sonne who stayde the running brooke. Seneca, *tr. by* John Studley. *Fr.* Medea, III. OBVE
That our earth mother may wrap herself. Our Earth Mother. *Tr. fr. Zuni Indian by* R. Bunzel. WTO
That overnight a rose could come. Overnight, a Rose. Caroline Giltinan. HBMV
That pair of great blue herons. Fishing Blue Creek. Roy Scheele. PPJ
That Poem. Juan Sáez Burgos, *tr. fr. Spanish by* Julio Marzán. InW
That poets are far rarer births than kings. To Elizabeth, Countess of Rutland. Ben Jonson. NoP
That praying mantis over there. Praying Mantis. Mary Ann Hoberman. RHPC
That Priapus with his big divining rod. To Bellinus. *Unknown.* PeHV
That prudent Prince who ends Shakespearian plays. Elizabethan Tragedy; a Footnote. Howard Moss. NePoEA
That Pure Place. Daniel J. Moriarty. WOLT
That raft we rigged up, under the water. A Distance from the Sea. Weldon Kees. NoAM
That ragged/ leaking raft held. Ireland. Richard Ryan. CIP
"That rake up near the rafters, why leave it there so long?" Rory of the Hill. Charles Joseph Kickham. OnYI

That Rama whom the Indian sung. Of Rama. Herman Melville. LiTA
That Reminds Me. Ogden Nash. FiBHP
That resigned look! Here I am. Self-Portrait. R. S. Thomas. NAs
That Room. John Montague. CIP
That row of icicles along the gutter. Beyond Words. Robert Frost. TW; WeW
That same look. Leslie. Marvin Wyche, Jr. AmNP
That sculptor we know, the passionate-eyed son of a quarryman. An Artist. Robinson Jeffers. VGW
That scything wind has cut the rich corn down. John Knox. Iain Crichton Smith. OxBS
That sea was greater than we knew. The Voyage. Edwin Muir. LiTM
That season when the leaf deserts the bole. October 1. Karl Shapiro. MoAB; MoAmPo; PoA
That seat of Science, Athens. Free America. Joseph Warren. PAH
That second time they hunted me. The Italian in England. Robert Browning. OAEP; OBNV
That selfsame tongue which first did thee entreat. The Constancy of a Lover. George Gascoigne. EnRePo; QFR
That sensualist Rodin, who used his mouth. Rodin to Rilke. Emily Grosholz. AMV-80
That Sharp Knife. Thomas Wolfe. NCSH
That she adored me as the most. Elegy on Any Lady by George Moore. Max Beerbohm. FaBoEE
That she hath gone to Heaven suddenly. Dante, *tr. by* Dante Gabriel Rossetti. *Fr.* La Vita Nuova, XIX. CTC
That single whitethroat, he that lives nearby. Dissonance. Cedric Whitman. AMV-80
That smoke/ would remain. If It All Went Up in Smoke. George Oppen. VWA
That soldier with a machinegun bolted. Two Summers in Moravia. Roger McDonald. CBAP
That somebody, my own special one. Shadows *Tr. fr. Tewa Indian by* H. J. Spinden. WTO
That son of Italy who tried to blow. Austerity of Poetry [*or* Jacopone da Todi]. Matthew Arnold. GoBC; OAEP; OBVV
That song it sing the sweetness. Steam Song. Gwendolyn Brooks. GP
That song there I borrow. Take Your Accusation Back! Kittaararter, *tr. fr. Eskimo.* WTO
That sound like the scratch. One, The Other, And. Wendy Wieber. NMM
That sovereign thought obscured? That vision clear. On a Great Man Whose Mind Is Clouding. Edmund Clarence Stedman. AA
That spot of blood on the drawing room wall. The Conversation in the Drawing Room. Weldon Kees. EAS; TwAmPo
That spring day. My Happiness. Greg Pape. MAYP
That story which the bold Sir Bedivere. The Passing of Arthur. Tennyson. *Fr.* Idylls of the King. OBNC
That Strain Again. Ronald Hambleton. CaP
That strange flower, the sun. Gubbinal. Wallace Stevens. SOTW
That such have died enables us. Emily Dickinson. AA
That Summer. Judith Hemschemeyer. PPJ
That Summer. Henry Treece. NYBP
That summer nothing would do. Herbert Scott. POL
That summer, the red may and the white may made. That Summer. Henry Treece. NYBP
That summer we saw the Blue Horse. The Blue Horse. Melvin Walker La Follette. NePoEA
That summer, you were game for anything. Lupine Dew. Jarold Ramsey. NIP
That Summer's Shore. John Ciardi. ErPo
That Sunday morning, at half past ten. The Ballad of Longwood Glen. Vladimir Nabokov. NYBP
That Sunday, on my oath, the rain was a heavy overcoat. Mary Hynes. Padraic Fallon, *after the Irish of* Anthony Raftery. AnIV; OxBI
That Sunday was like an unfinished dream. A Sunday in Cambridge. Eddie Linden. PeHV
That tea is not the most benign of latter-day beverages. Peter Titheradge. Teatime Variations: After Algernon Charles Swinburne. FaBoPa
That teacher gave me a new name . . . again. Name Giveaway. Phillip William George. VoR
That the glass would melt in heat. The Glass of Water. Wallace Stevens. AP; CABA; CoBMV; MoAB; MoAmPo; MoPo; OxBA; TAP
That the high sheen of death could blot. Midsummer. James Scully. MP; NYBP; TwCP
That the neighborhood might be covered. Larry Eigner. PoM
That the Night Come. W. B. Yeats. CoBMV; PoEL-5
That the poet "does not number the streaks of the tulip." To Hugh MacDiarmid. Edwin Morgan. FaBoTw
That the Traylee's the best cigarette. A Prize-winning Limerick. R. Rhodes. FaBoUs
That the war would be over before they got to you. When You Have Forgotten Sunday: The Love Story. Gwendolyn Brooks. WPOW
That there is falsehood in his looks. The Parson's Looks. Burns. OxBoLi
That Things Are No Worse, Sire. Helen Hunt Jackson. OHIP
That Thou Art Nowhere to Be Found. George Macdonald. *Fr.* Diary of an Old Soul. TrCP
That thou hast her, it is not all my grief. Sonnets, XLII. Shakespeare. InvP
That thou mayst injure no man, dove-like be. Prudent Simplicity. William Cowper. FaBoEE
That time/ in the sun. When Sun Came to Riverwoman. Leslie Silko. VoR
That time/ we all heard it. Paul Robeson. Gwendolyn Brooks. CNA; PoBA
That time of evening, weightless and disparate. Blackwater Mountain. Charles Wright. GeTw
That time of revolution being come. Reflections in Bed. Julian Symons. WaP
That time of year thou mayst [*or* maist] in me behold. Sonnets, LXXIII. Shakespeare. AWP; BiP; BoLoP; CABA; ChTr; CTC; EBEV; EIL; EnLoPo; EnRePo; FaBoEn; FaBoRV; FaBV; FF; FiP; GBL; GTBS; GTBS-P; HAP; HBV-1; HeIP; HoPM; InPK; InPS; InvP; LiTB; LoBV; MasP; NIP; NOBE; NoP; OAEL-1; OAEP; OBEV; OBSC; OHFP; PAI; PoEL-2; PoPle; PoRA; PPP; PrIm; QFR; SeCeV; SoSe; TEP; TrGrPo; UnPo; ViBoPo; WeW; WHA
That time of year you may in me behold. The Winter Twilight, Glowing Black and Gold. Delmore Schwartz. NoAM
That time that mirth did steer my ship. Sir Thomas Wyatt. SiPS
That time we went to Suffolk Downs to see. The Beautiful Horses. Donald Hall. NePoAm-2
That tremor rising. Snow Geese in the Wind. Philip Dow. NPGG
That trumpet tongue which taught a nation. The Demagogue. Phyllis McGinley. FaBoEE
"That turn'll get her," I said. Toujours la Politesse. Ezra Pound, *after the Chinese.* OBVE
That vengeaunce I ask and cry. O Cat of Carlish Kind. John Skelton. *Fr.* Philip Sparrow. ChTr
That very time I saw, but thou couldst not. Love-in-Idleness. Shakespeare. *Fr.* A Midsummer Night's Dream, II, ii. TrGrPo
That war should bankrupts make of merchants is no wonder. Upon the Bankruptcy of a Physician. Henricus Selyns. SCAP
That was a brave old epoch. The Battle of La Prairie. William Douw Schuyler-Lighthall. PAH
That was a shocking day. Beasts. Paul Engle. PoCh
That was a year of suddenness. Initial Response. Katherine Soniat. AMV-80
That was her beginning, an apparition. First Love. Laurie Lee. ChMP
That Was Summer. Marci Ridlon. NTCP
That was the chirp of Ariel. Wind on the Lyre. George Meredith. NBM
That was the day they killed the Son of God. The Killing. Edwin Muir. ChMP; PoPl
That was the night, Love, Bird came back and blew. Ballade of the Session after Camarillo. David Galler. NMP
That was the proverb. Let my mistress be. Long and Lazy. Robert Herrick. FaBoEE
That was the year. A Poem to Delight My Friends Who Laugh at Science-Fiction. Edwin Rolfe. NePa; NePoAm
That Was Then. Isabella Gardner. FAZ; GP
That Way. Anne Welsh. PeSA
That way look, my infant, lo! The Kitten and the Falling Leaves. Wordsworth. HBVY
That way the moonflower and the sunflower this. Morning Dialogue. Conrad Aiken. NoAM
That We Head Towards. Stephany Fuller. BPo
That week the fall was opulent. Vendanges. 1956. Daniel G. Hoffman. PoCh
That which brings death upon you. Amen. Alvaro Mutis, *tr. by* James Normington. AMV-81
That which hath made them drunk hath made me bold. The Murderers. Shakespeare. *Fr.* Macbeth, II, ii. WHA
"That Which Hath Wings Shall Tell." Linda Lyon Van Voorhis. GoBC
That which her slender waist confined. On a Girdle. Edmund Waller. AnAnS-2; AWP; BLPL; CABA; CavP; FF; GTBS; GTBS-P; HBV-1; HeIP; InMe; InPK; LiTB; LoBV; NoP; OAEP; OBEV; OBS; PoRA; SeCePo; SeCV-1; TreFS; TrGrPo; UnTE; ViBoPo; WHA
That which I should have done. A Common Light. Steve Orlen. Str
That which is, being the only answer. Question and Answer. Kathleen Raine. MoBrPo
That which is, for example. The Bicycle. Stan Rice. NPGG
That which is marred at birth Time shall not mend. Gertrude's Prayer. Kipling. FaBoEn
That which shall last for aye can have no birth. Or Ever the Earth Was. Charles Leonard Moore. AA
That Which We Call a Rose. Michael Dransfield. CBAP

That which we dare invoke to bless. In Memoriam A. H. H., CXXIV. Tennyson. NOCV; WGRP
That Which You Call "Love Me." Luis Rosales, *tr. from Spanish by* Lynn C. Jacox. AMV-81
That Whitsun, I was late getting away. The Whitsun Weddings. Philip Larkin. FaBoMo; NePoEA-2; NoAM; NoP; OxBTC
That Wind. Emily Brontë. CH
That winter love spoke and we raised no objection, at. Jig. C. Day Lewis. OxBI
That winter, the dead could not be buried. Leningrad Cemetery, Winter of 1941. Sharon Olds. NIP
That with this bright believing band. The Impercipient. Thomas Hardy. EBVV; OAEP; PrIm; TrGrPo; ViBoPo; WGRP
That wolf, shivering by the palisade. Colonial Set. Alfred Goldsworthy Bailey. OBCV
That woman down there beneath the sea. *Unknown, tr. fr. Eskimo.* WSC
"That woman there is almost dead." The Rat. W. H. Davies. OxBTC
That woman, vacuum in her mouth. The Great Nebula in Andromeda. Hugh Seidman. AmPA
That woman who to me seems most a woman. Sonnet: Dolce Stil Novo. Gavin Ewart. GrPl
That Women Are but Men's Shadows. Ben Jonson. ElL; InPS; OBS; ViBoPo
(Shadow, The.) NOBE; OBEV
(Song: That Women Are but Men's Shadows.) FaBoEn; HBV-1; SeCP
(Women Men's Shadows.) WBLP
That wooded face of cliffs and shadows. Remembering Lincoln. Frank Mundorf. GoYe
That year no wondering shepherds came. Christmas, the Year One, A.D. Sara Henderson Hay. PoRA
That year of the cloud, when my marriage failed. River Road. Stanley Kunitz. NoAM
That year the end of winter stood under a sign. The Comet. Michael Palmer. NPGG
That year they fought in the snow. Rostov. G. S. Fraser. WaP
That year we hardly slept, waking like inmates. Getting Out. Cleopatra Mathis. MAYP
That year? Yes, doubtless I remember still. The World Well Lost. Edmund Clarence Stedman. AA
That you were once unkind befriends me now. Sonnets, CXX. Shakespeare. InvP
That your honour's petitioners (dealers in rhymes). To the Right Hon. Henry Pelham. Edward Moore. OBSV
That zephyr every year. Spring Bereaved. William Drummond of Hawthornden. OBEV
Thatched roof rings like heaven where mice, The. Byre. Norman MacCaig. BoAnP; BSV
Thatcher. Seamus Heaney. IPY
Thatcher, The. Brendan Kennelly. CIP
Thatcher of Thatchwood went to Thatchet a-thatching, A. *Unknown.* OxNR
That's All? Anna Hajnal, *tr. fr. Hungarian by* Jascha Kessler. PBWP
That's Ethan Allen on the monument. Green Mountain Boy. Florida Watts Smyth. GoYe
That's Faith. S. N. Leitner. STF
That's his saddle across the tie-beam, an' them's his spurs up there. My Mate Bill. G. H. Gibson. PoAu-1
That's Jack. Jack. Charles Henry Ross. OxBChV; RHPC
That's July. Mary F. Butts. YeAr
That's June. Mary F. Butts. YeAr
That's Life? Alan Bold. FF
That's me, second from the left. Perpetuum Immobile. Bruce Dawe. CBAP
That's my grandpa behind the meatcase. The Age of the Butcher. Stuart Friebert. AMV-80
That's my house with the red door, and all those steps. Taking Care of It. Deborah Lee. BrSi
That's my last duchess painted on the wall. My Last Duchess. Robert Browning. AWP; BeLS; BiP; CABA; EBVV; FaBoEn; FaFP; FF; FiP; FPL; GTBS-P; HAP; HBV-1; HeIP; HoPM; InPS; LiTB; MasP; MAT; NIP; NOBE; NoP; OAEL-2; OAEP; OBNC; PAI; PoEL-5; PoLF; PoPle; PPP; PrIm; SCV; SeCeV; SoSe; TEP; TreFS; TrGrPo; VLP; WeW; WHA
That's No Way to Get Along. *Unknown.* BluL
That's not any old six-foot rabbit. Nearly Everybody Loves Harvey Martin. William D. Barney. LiSp
That's Our Lot. Moishe Leib Halpern, *tr. fr. Yiddish by* Kathryn Hellerstein. VWA
That's somebody's child. Houston Street, N. Y. Carolyn Baxter. LFAC
That's the cuckoo, you say. I cannot hear it. The Cuckoo. Edward Thomas. BrPo
That's the queer life, *said the chair.* Chair, Dog, and Clock. Hilary Corke. NYBP
That's what misery is. Poetry Is a Destructive Force. Wallace Stevens. OxBA
That's What We'd Do. Mary Mapes Dodge. OBCA
Thaw. Margaret Avison. NOBC
Thaw. T. Alan Broughton. AMV-81
Thaw. Walker Gibson. ELU; NePoAm
Thaw. Edward Thomas. EBEV; ELU; FaBoTw; FM; GTBS-P; MoAB; MoBrPo; OxBTC
Thaw in the City. Lou Lipsitz. MAT; NCSH
Thay walkit furth so derk oneith they wist. The Entrance to Hell. Virgil, *tr. by* Gavin Douglas. *Fr.* The Aeneid, VI. GoTS
The/ Voice of Jesus I. Rush singing. Poem Beginning "The." Louis Zukofsky. CoPo
Thealma and Clearchus, *sel.* John Chalkhill.
Rhotus on Arcadia. OBS
Theater Hat, The. Carolyn Wells. TDH
Theatre, The. Horace Smith *and* James Smith. Par
Theatre is still, and Duse speaks, The. Eleonora Duse as Magda. Laurence Binyon. SyP
Thebes of the Seven Gates. Sophocles, *tr. fr. Greek by* Dudley Fitts *and* Robert Fitzgerald. *Fr.* Antigone. WaaP
Thee entirely I have loved. George Wither. *Fr.* Philarete to His Mistress. PeD
Thee, Father, first they sung Omnipotent. Milton. *Fr.* Paradise Lost, III. ILwL
Thee finds me in the garden, Hannah. The Quaker Widow. Bayard Taylor. AA
Thee for my recitative. To a Locomotive in Winter. Walt Whitman. AmPP; AP; FaBV; InPK; MoAmPo; NoAM; NoP; PoEL-5; TAP
Thee, God, I come from, to thee go. Gerard Manley Hopkins. VLP
"Thee, Mary, with this ring I wed." To His Wife on the Fourteenth Anniversary of Her Wedding-Day, with a Ring [*or* To Mary]. Samuel Bishop. HBV-1; ViBoPo
Thee, May and Mother, I entreat. Author's Entreaty for His Lay. Eysteinn Asgrímsson, *tr. by* Eirik Magnusson. *Fr.* Lilya. ISi
Thee Pompey thy past deeds by turns infest. Lucan, *tr. by* Nicholas Rowe. *Fr.* Pharsalia, I. OBVE
Thee sets a bell to swinging in my soul. Hildegarde Flanner. *Fr.* Sonnets in Quaker Language. WPE
Thee, Sovereign God, our grateful accents praise. The Te Deum. *Unknown, tr. by* Dryden. AWP
Thee, the son of God most high. Delphic Hymn to Apollo. Swinburne. VLP
Thee, Thee, Only Thee. Thomas Moore. GBL; OBNC
Thee too, modest tressèd maid. Moon. Henry Rowe. OBEV
Thee too the years shall cover; thou shalt be. Swinburne. *Fr.* Anactoria. ViBoPo
Thefts of the Morning. Edith M. Thomas. AA
Theh Thet Hi Can Wittes Fule-Wis. *Unknown.* HAP
Their ardour kindless all the Grecian pow'rs. Homer, *tr. by* Pope. *Fr.* The Iliad, XII. OBVE
Their attendant nuns spare the tourists well. Bathing the Aged. Paul Monette. AmPA
Their auburn or black hair, curly hair. Just This. István Vas, *tr. by* Jascha Kessler. VWA
Their Banishment. Milton. *Fr.* Paradise Lost, XII. SeCePo
Their barbarism did not assuage the grief. The Retreat of Ita Cagney. Michael Hartnett. CIP
Their Beginning. C. P. Cavafy, *tr. fr. Greek by* John Mavrogordato. PeHV
Their belongings were buried side by side. The Drawer. George MacBeth. NePoEA-2
Their black truck rattled up the dusty hill. The Diviners. Mary Oliver. WPE
Their boughs curve upward in praise. White Pines. Barry Silesky. AMV-80
Their brown, harmless flack. The Sparrows at the Airport. Anthony Ostroff. NePoAm-2
Their calendars are based on rice. Rice. Carol Muske. AmPA
Their chains are/ polished. Punk Party (They Told Me It Was Literary. . .) Wendy Rose. TWSS
Their cheeks are blotched for shame, their running verse. The Bards [*or* Lust in Song]. Robert Graves. DTC; FaBoMo; OxBI; SeCePo. *See also* Bards falter in shame, their running verse, The.
Their Cone-like Cabins. Charles G. Ballard. VoR
Their duffle-bags sprawl like a murder. Words without Music. Irving Layton. CaP
Their eyelids are drooping, no tears lie beneath. Weavers. Heine. TrJP
Their eyes had known the quiet color blue. Prisoner of War. Gertrude May Lutz. GoYe

Their faces, safe as an interior. The Middle-aged. Adrienne Rich. NePoEA-2
Their feet on London, their heads in the grey clouds. Whit Monday. Louis MacNeice. NYBP; OAEL-2
Their fingers numb in thimbles. You Owe Them Everything. John Allman. SaC
Their ground they stil made good. Homer, *tr. by* George Chapman. *Fr.* The Iliad, V. OBVE
Their hair, pomaded, faces jaded. Sepia Fashion Show. Maya Angelou. BlSi
Their hands/ passing thru the darkness. Healing. Charlotte DeClue. TWSS
Their hands should minister unto the flame of life. Women at Munition Making. Mary Gabrielle Collins. SUMH
Their hearts are filled with Pity's mead. A Gaelic Christmas. Liam P. Clancy. ISi
Their heels slapped their bumping mules. Merchants from Cathay. William Rose Benét. HBMV; MoAmPo
Their height in heaven comforts not. Emily Dickinson. NePA
Their house faces east, is protected by trees. A Storm from the East. Reed Whittemore. NYBP; PoPl
Their life, collapsed like unplayed cards. Moving in Winter. Adrienne Rich. DFF
Their lips upon each other's lips are laid. Speechless [upon the Marriage of Two Deaf and Dumb Persons]. Philip Bourke Marston. EBVV; VLP
Their little room grew light with cries. Proper Clay. Mark Van Doren. PoRA; TrGrPo
Their Lonely Betters. W. H. Auden. GoJo
Their memories behind them. Salvation Prospect. LeRoy Smith, Jr. NePoAm
Their minds are so frail the least squeak upsets them. Dismissing Progress and Its Progenitors. George Reavey. EAS
Their mockery brought him double force. Blind Samson. William Plomer. PeSA
Their Mouths Full. David Ignatow. GP
Their mouths have drunken Death's eternal wine. The Night of Gods. George Sterling. *Fr.* Three Sonnets on Oblivion. HBV-2; WHA
Their noonday never knows. Fame. John Banister Tabb. AA
Their Party, Our House. Jon Swan. NYBP
Their pink mouths opened wide. After the Deformed Woman Is Made Correct. Robert Lietz. AMV-80
Their poet, a sad trimmer, but no less. Byron. *Fr.* Don Juan, III. OAEP
Their rugs are sodden, their heads are down. Gun Teams. Gilbert Frankau. OxBTC
Their scrape and clink together of musical coin. Some Small Shells from the Windward Islands. May Swenson. FYAP
Their sense is with their senses all mixed in. Modern Love, XLVIII. George Meredith. OAEL-2; OAEP; NoP
Their shoulders you shook. The Preacher. Al-Mahdi, *tr. by* A. J. Arberry. TTY
Their spare, fanatic sentry comes. Ants and Others. Adrien Stoutenburg. BoAnP; FYAP; NYBP
Their Speech, Compared with Wisdom and Poetry. Robert Pinsky. *Fr.* Essay on Psychiatrists. PoA
Their time past, pulled down. Burning the Christmas Greens. William Carlos Williams. AP; CoBMV; LiTM; MoPo; NePA; NoAM; NOBA; TwAmPo
Their tongues are knives, their forks are hands and feet. Riddle. Adrian Mitchell. FaBoEE; GBL
Their verdure dare not show. Valediction. Louis MacNeice. AnIL; MoVE
Their voices heard, I stumble suddenly. One More New Botched Beginning. Stephen Spender. CMoP; NoAM; NYBP
Their war-boots said big shots to the plank floor. Behold, One of Several Little Christs. Kenneth Patchen. NaP
Their Wedded Love. Milton. *Fr.* Paradise Lost, IV. SeCePo
("Hail wedded love, mysterious law, true source.") BiP
(Wedded Love.) OBS
Their wings beat the floor. Angels in the House. Jerred Metz. VWA
Theirs is a gesture of sorrow, infinite and taut. Snails. E. D. Blodgett. NOBC
Theirs is a white and a green life, a smooth. Red Cross Nurses. Gervase Stewart. WaP
Theirs is the house whose windows—every pane. On the Asylum Road. Charlotte Mew. MoBrPo
Their's is yon house that holds the parish poor. The Parish Poor-House. George Crabbe. *Fr.* The Village. OBEC
Thekla's Song. Schiller, *tr. fr. German by* Samuel Taylor Coleridge. *Fr.* The Piccolomini. AWP
Thel's Motto. Blake. *Fr.* The Book of Thel. ChTr (4 *ll.*)
Them ez wants, must choose. A Baker's Duzzen uv Wize Sawz. Edward Rowland Sill. FaBoBe; FaFP; HBV-1; HBVY; InMe; TreFS
Theme. Carl Spitteler, *tr. fr. German by* Margarete Münsterberg. PoPl
Theme and Variation. Peter De Vries. NYBP
Theme and Variations. W. P. Ker. PoSH
Theme and Variations. Edna St. Vincent Millay. SBG
Theme Brown Girl. Elton Hill. NBP
Theme for English B. Langston Hughes. BALP; NoAM; NOBA; NoP
Theme in Yellow. Carl Sandburg. TiPo; YeAr
Theme no poet gladly sung. Prudence. Emerson. OBAL
Theme of morning was the sound of rain, The. Rain. Sam Harrison. NeIP
Theme One: The Variations. August Wilson. PoBA
Theme Song for a Songwriters' Union. Al Graham. WhC
Theme tune occurs again, The! Das Liebesleben. Thom Gunn. ErPo
Themes for Country-Western Singers, *sel.* Ted Kooser.
"That 'lil girl that Daddy loved." POL
Themes of love and death I have rehearsed, The. Judges, Judges. Gene Baro. NePoEA-2
Then. Rose Terry Cooke. HBV-1
Then. Gary Gildner. FiCP
Then. John Morgan. AMV-81
Then. Edwin Muir. CMoP; PoA
Then. Muriel Rukeyser. LCAP
Then a partridge-shaped cloud over dust storm. Ezra Pound. *Fr.* Cantos, CXIII. NYBP
Then Achilles/ Before all the Danaans. The Funeral Games for Patroclus: Wrestling to a Draw. Homer, *tr. by* Ennis Rees. *Fr.* The Iliad, XXIII. LiSp
Then after Eden. New World. Derek Walcott. OxBC
Then Ag'in. Sam Walter Foss. HBV-1
Then all became silent. White Bird. Matti Megged, *tr. by* Howard Schwartz. VWA
Then all the nations of birds lifted together. The Season of Phantasmal Peace. Derek Walcott. NoP
Then Almitra spoke, saying, We would ask now of Death. Kahlil Gibran. *Fr.* The Prophet. DL
Then and Now. Charles Frederick Johnson. AA
Then and Now. Anne B. Murray. PoSH
Then and Now. Kath Walker. IHMS
Then as to Feasting. Oliver Wendell Holmes. WhC
Then, blessing all, "Go, children of my care!" The Triumph of Dulness. Pope. *Fr.* The Dunciad. NOEC
Then bold Robin Hood to the north he would go. Robin Hood and the Scotchman. *Unknown.* ESPB
Then call me traitor if you must. To Certain Critics. Countee Cullen. BPo
Then came fair May, the fairest maid on ground. May. Spenser. *Fr.* The Faerie Queene, VII, 7. GN
Then came I to the shoreless shore of silence. Conrad Aiken. Preludes for Memnon, XXXIII. LiTA; NePA; OxBA; TwAmPo
Then came jolly Summer, being dight. Summer. Spenser. *Fr.* The Faerie Queene, VII, 7. GN
Then came old January, wrapped well. Old January. Spenser. *Fr.* The Faerie Queene, VII, 7. YeAr
Then came the Autumn all in yellow clad. Autumn. Spenser. *Fr.* The Faerie Queene, VII, 7. GN
Then came the cry of "Call all hands on deck!" Rounding the Horn. John Masefield. *Fr.* Dauber. EtS; MoAB; MoBrPo; WHA
Then came there two women, that were harlots. Solomon Judges between Two Women Disputing over a Child. Bible, *O.T. Fr.* First Kings. TreFT
Then comes the Winter, like a hale old man. Winter. James Hurnard. PoSC
Then cometh he to a city of Samaria. Jesus and the Woman at the Well. Bible, *N.T. Fr.* St. John. TreFT
Then Constantine, mindful of the Holy Cross. Helena Embarks for Palestine. Cynewulf, *tr. by* Charles W. Kennedy. *Fr.* Elene. AnOE
Then, day by day, her broidered gown. The Earth in Spring. Judah Halevi, *tr. by* Edward G. King. TrJP
Then did Siddartha raise his eyes, and see. The End Which Comes. Sir Edwin Arnold. *Fr.* The Light of Asia. LoBV
Then drew near unto him all the publicans and sinners. Bible, *N.T.* St. Luke, XV. NAWM-1
Then first he form'd th' immense and solid shield. Homer, *tr. by* Pope. *Fr.* The Iliad, XVIII. OBVE
Then fled, O brethren, the wicked juba. The Ballad of Nat Turner. Robert Hayden. BALP; BPo; VGW
Then forth issewed (great goddesse) great Dame Nature. Dame Nature. Spenser. *Fr.* The Faerie Queene, VII, 7. PoEL-1
Then from the sea the dawning 'gan arise. Dido's Hunting. Virgil, *tr. by* the Earl of Surrey. *Fr.* The Aeneid, IV. OBSC
Then from their poverty they rose. The Ordinary Women. Wallace Stevens. OxBA
Then has a man less might than a beste. The Newly Born. *Unknown. Fr.* The Pricke of Conscience. OxBM

Then hate me when thou wilt; if ever, now. Sonnets, XC. Shakespeare. AWP; EBEV; EIL; NOBE; OBEV; OBSC; PoEL-2; WHA
Then He summoned an archangel. Romance VIII. St. John of the Cross, *tr. by* E. Allison Peers. ISi
Then Hrothgar's minstrel rehearsed the lay. The Lay of Finn. *Unknown, tr. by* Charles W. Kennedy. *Fr.* Beowulf. AnOE
Then I heard a voice celestial. John Lydgate. *Fr.* Devotions of the Fowls. PBBP
Then I said to the elegant ladies. Sappho, *tr. fr. Greek by* Willis Barnstone. BoWoP
Then I tuned my harp—took off the lilies we twine round its chords. Robert Browning. *Fr.* Saul. FiP
Then I was sealed, and like the wintering tree. Alas, Kind Element. Léonie Adams. MoVE
Then, if you say you do not know. *Unknown.* FaBoUs
Then I'll Believe. B. W. Vilakazi, *tr. fr. Zulu by* Jack Cope. PeSA
Then is our charter, Pollexfen, quite lost? The Great Despair of the London Whigs. *Unknown.* APAS
Then it came to pass that a pestilence fell on the city. The Finding of Gabriel. Longfellow. *Fr.* Evangeline. AA
Then it was dusk in Illinois, the small boy. First Song. Galway Kinnell. BiP; CTBA; GoJo; GrPl; LiTM; MP; NCSH; NePoAm; NoP; TwCP
Then it's a hooraw, and a hooraw. Standin' on the Walls of Zion. *Unknown.* AS
Then Job answered and said. Not Flesh of Brass. Bible, *O.T.* *Fr.* Job. TrJP
Then Job arose, and rent his mantle. The Lord Gave. Bible, *O.T.* *Fr.* Job. TreF
Then judge me as thou wilt, I cannot flee. Robert Hillyer. Sonnets, III. HBMV
Then, lady, at last thou art sick of my sighing? The West-Country Lover. Alice Brown. HBV-1
Then, land! then, England! oh, the frosty cliffs. Elizabeth Barrett Browning. *Fr.* Aurora Leigh. FaBoPP
Then Laugh. Bertha Adams Backus. BLPA; TreFT; WBLP; YaD
Then lay I lax. Circe. William Gibson. PoA
Then leave old regret. A Moral Poem. J. V. Cunningham. VGW
Then Lelex rose, an old experienced man. Baucis and Philemon. Ovid, *tr. by* Dryden. *Fr.* Metamorphoses. AWP; OBVE
Then let not winter's ragged hand deface. Sonnets, VI. Shakespeare. MasP
Then let the chill Sirocco blow. The Winter Glass. Charles Cotton. HBV-2
Then let us boast of ancestors no more. Daniel Defoe. *Fr.* The True-born Englishman. OBSV
Then, like a miracle, the violets came out. Bay Violets. Sister Maris Stella. GoBC
Then Lose in Time Thy Maidenhead. *Unknown.* ErPo
Then Mahoney, standing in the surf. Mahoney. Seán Jennett. NeIP
Then Margery Milk-Duck. John Skelton. *Fr.* The Tunning of Elinor Rumming. EBEV; OAEL-1
Then Mercury 'gan bend him to obey. Virgil, *tr. by* the Earl of Surrey. *Fr.* The Aeneid, IV. ViBoPo
Then Milton rose up from the heavens of Albion ardorous! Blake. *Fr.* Milton. OAEL-2
Then next a merry Woodsman, clad in green. The Green Dryad's Plea. Thomas Hood. *Fr.* The Plea of the Midsummer Fairies. OBNC
Then one of the twelve, called Judas Iscariot. Bible, *N.T.* St. Matthew, XXVI: 14-XXVIII. NAWM-1
Then out at Shellbrook, roun' by stile an' tree. Shellbrook [Dorset]. William Barnes. VLP
Then out-streamed a Light/ Brightest that of beaming pillars! Death of Saint Guthlac. Cynewulf. *Fr.* Guthlac. ACP
Then ran ther a route of ratones, as it were. Belling the Cat. William Langland. *Fr.* The Vision of Piers Plowman. OxBM
Then rising in his rage above the shores. Homer, *tr. by* Pope. *Fr.* The Iliad, XXI. OBVE
Then roll the swag and blanket up. The Golden Gullies of the Palmer. *Unknown.* PoAu-1
Then 'round the Bay of Mexico. Round the Bay of Mexico. *Unknown.* FSW; OuSiCo
Then said Almitra, Speak to us of Love. Of Love. Kahlil Gibran. *Fr.* The Prophet. PoLF
Then said Jesus unto them again, Verily, verily, I say unto you, I am the door of the sheep. The Good Shepherd. Bible, *N.T.* *Fr.* St. John. TreFS
Then said that royall Pere in sober wise. Spenser. *Fr.* The Faerie Queene, I, 12. OAEL-1
Then saith another, "We are kindly things." Tender Babes. Thomas Hood. *Fr.* The Plea of the Midsummer Fairies. OBRV
Then saith the timid Fay—"Oh, mighty Time!" The Fairy's Reply to Saturn. Thomas Hood. *Fr.* The Plea of the Midsummer Fairies. OBNC
Then Sang Deborah and Barak. Bible, *O.T.* *Fr.* Judges. *See* Song of Deborah, The.
Then Sang Moses. Bible, *O.T.* Exodus, XV: 1-18. TrJP
("Then sang Moses and the children of Israel this song unto the Lord.") OBWP
(Triumphal Chant, 1-13, 18.) TrGrPo
Then Saturn thus: "Sweet is the merry lark." The Melodies of Time. Thomas Hood. *Fr.* The Plea of the Midsummer Fairies. OBNC
Then saw I, with gray eyes fulfilled of rest. In Hades. Anna Callender Brackett. AA
Then saw they that the mighty Quest was won! Robert Stephen Hawker. *Fr.* The Quest of the Sangraal. VLP
Then, say, was I or nature in the wrong. *Unknown.* *Fr.* Don Leon. PeHV
Then see it! in distressing. The Last Turn. William Carlos Williams. NYP
Then seek your job with thankfulness and work till further orders. The Glory of the Garden. Kipling. EBCP
Then sent the King Constantine. The Pound of Flesh. *Unknown.* *Fr.* Cursor Mundi. OxBM
Then shall the kingdom of heaven be likened unto ten virgins. The Wise and Foolish Virgins. Bible, *N.T.* *Fr.* St. Matthew. TreF
Then Shall We See. Charles Leonard Moore. AA
Then sing, ye Birds, sing, sing a joyous song! The Gladness of the May. Wordsworth. YeAr
Then Sings My Soul. Paul Mariani. GeTw; MAYP
Then Sohrab with his sword smote Rustum's helm. Matthew Arnold. *Fr.* Sohrab and Rustum. OBWP
Then spake Jesus again unto them, saying, I am the light of the world. Jesus Answers the Pharisees. Bible, *N.T.* *Fr.* St. John. TreFS
Then sprang up first the golden age, which of itself maintained. Ovid, *tr. by* Arthur Golding. *Fr.* Metamorphoses, I. OAEL-1
Then step by step walks Autumn. Autumn's Processional. Dinah Maria Mulock Craik. GN
Then that dread angel near the awful throne. Fiat Lux. Lloyd Mifflin. AA
Then the air was perfect. And his descent. The Parachutist. Jon Anderson. AmPA; LiSp; NYBP
Then the Ermine. Marianne Moore. NePoAm; PoA
Then the golden hour. Length of Moon. Arna Bontemps. CDC; LiTM; PoNe
Then the knee of the wave. Reclining Figure. Donald Hall. ConAP; LCAP
Then the little Hiawatha. The Little Hiawatha. Longfellow. *Fr.* The Song of Hiawatha. OnUR
Then the long sunlight lying on the sea. The Insusceptibles. Adrienne Rich. ConAP; HeIP; InPK
Then the Lord Answered. Bible, *O.T.* Job, XXXVIII: 2-XXXIX. AWP
(God Replies, XXXVIII: 2-41.) TrGrPo
("Then the Lord answered Job out of the whirlewind, and sayd," XXXVIII.) OBVE
Then the Lord answered Job out of the whirlwind. . ./Do you give the horse his might. The War Horse. Bible, *O.T.* Job, XXXIX:19-25. PH
Then the Lord God spoke and said unto Noah. Noah's Flood. *Unknown, tr. by* Charles W. Kennedy. *Fr.* Genesis. AnOE
Then the Master With a gesture. Longfellow. *Fr.* The Building of the Ship. OHFP
Then the Northmen fled in their nailed ships. *Unknown.* *Fr.* The Battle of Brunanburh. PBBP
Then the pair followed Pa to Manhasset. Limerick. *Unknown.* TreF
Then the Provost he uprose. William Edmonstoune Aytoun. *Fr.* Edinburgh after Flodden. OBWP
Then the son of Weohstan, stalwart in war. The Funeral Pyre. *Unknown, tr. by* Charles W. Kennedy. *Fr.* Beowulf. AnOE
Then there is this civilising love of death, by which. Ignorance of Death. William Empson. CMoP; CoBMV; LiTM; NoAM
"Then there shall be signs in Heaven." The Fifteen Days of Judgement. Sebastian Evans. NBM
Then there was the guy. Free Enterprise. Charles Stetler. GP
Then there were the grapes turned purple in the sun. Grapes. Sister Maris Stella. GoBC
Then they paraded Pompey's urn. Jenny Mastoraki, *tr. fr. Modern Greek by* Nikos Germanakos. BoWoP; PBWP
Then they saw/ Forth and forward faring. The Approach of Pharoah. Cædmon. *Fr.* Genesis. ACP; WaaP
Then they took whole stones according to the law. Bible, Apocrypha. *Fr.* First Maccabees. OFD
Then thick as locusts black'ning all the ground. Carnations and Butterflies. Pope. *Fr.* The Dunciad. NOEC
Then this poor woman's blind. Oh Oh Blues. *Unknown.* BluL
Then those ill-favour'd Ones, whom none. George Crabbe. *Fr.* Sir Eustace Grey. ELP
Then thus we have beheld. Chorus. Samuel Daniel. *Fr.* Cleopatra. OBSC

Then to the bar, all they drew near. Michael Wigglesworth. *Fr.* The Day of Doom. OBCA
Then to the bees one said. The Bees. Monk Gibbon. OnYI
"Then tooke they seate, and forth our passage strooke." Homer, *tr. by* George Chapman. *Fr.* The Odyssey, XII. MOS
Then touch the park; the leaves are stained to lure you. Counter-Serenade: She Invokes the Autumn Instant. Peter Viereck. CrMA
Then up aloft this yard must go. A Long Time Ago, *vers.* VI. *Unknown.* ShS
Then up I rose, and make no more delay. Elizabeth Melvill, Lady Culross. *Fr.* A Godly Dream. WPE
Then Urizen wept & thus his lamentation poured forth. Urizen's Curse upon His Children. Blake. *Fr.* Vala; or, The Four Zoas. TW
Then was I cast from out my state. Frenzy. George Crabbe. *Fr.* Sir Eustace Grey. NOBE
Then was there heard a most celestial sound. The Rivers Come to the Hall of Proteus for the Marriage of the Thames and the Medway. Spenser. *Fr.* The Faerie Queene, IV, 2. FaBoPP
Then watching the unposed beggars pose. Et Quid Amabo Nisi Quod Aenigma Est. Stephen Sandy. NYBP
Then we descended, as into a labyrinth. Fear. Aldo Camerino, *tr. by* Anita Barrows. VWA
Then wear the gold hat, if that will move her. Epitaph from *The Great Gatsby.* F. Scott Fitzgerald. ELU
"Then, we'll go through with the journey." Jansenist Journey. Denis Devlin. IPY
Then we'll sing of Lydia Pinkham. Lydia Pinkham. *Unknown.* AS
Then went the Pharisees, and took counsel. The Things That Are Caesar's. Bible, *N.T.* *Fr.* St. Matthew. TreF
Then were there brought unto him little children. The Rich Man and the Kingdom of Heaven. Bible, *N.T.* *Fr.* St. Matthew. TreF
Then what is the answer?—Not to be deluded by dreams. The Answer. Robinson Jeffers. CMoP; GoYe
Then When I Am Thy Captive, Talk of Chains. Milton. *Fr.* Paradise Lost, IV. WHA
Then When the Ample Season. Richard Wilbur. MiAP
Then, when the child was gone. The Empty House. Stephen Spender. NYBP; PCP
Then whilst that Latmos did contain her bliss. Sonnet. Earl of Stirling. ViBoPo
Then will a quiet gather round the door. Beyond Wars. David Morton. PAH
Then you'll see our oars with feathered spray. In Measure Time We'll Row. *Unknown.* ShS
Thence forward by that painfull wa they pas. Spenser. *Fr.* The Faerie Queene, I, 10. OAEL-1
Thence passing forth, they shortly do arruve. The Bower of Bliss. Spenser. *Fr.* The Faerie Queene, II, 12. FiP
Thenot Protests. "C. N. S." InMe
Theobald James. J. B. Morton. *Fr.* When We Were Very Silly. FaBoPa
Theocritus. Annie Fields. AA
Theocritus. Oscar Wilde. HBV-2; NOBE; OxBI
Theodor Herzl. Israel Zangwill. TrJP
Theodore Roethke. Morton Paley. AMV-81
Theodore Roethke Foots It. D. C. Berry. BXAP
Theodosia Burr. Myra Burnham Terrell. GoYe
Theodosia Burr: The Wrecker's Story. John Williamson Palmer. PAH
Theologians. Walter de la Mare. EaLo
Theological. Clifton Fadiman. FiBHP; PV
Theological Limerick. T. Lindsay. FaBoCo
Theology. Paul Laurence Dunbar. TRV
Theology. Ted Hughes. FaBoMo; NoAM; PAI
Theology of Bongwi, the Baboon, The. Roy Campbell. PeSA
Theology of John Edwards, The. Phyllis McGinley. MoAmPo
"Theon to his father Theon greetings. Another." To Theon from His Son Theon. C. A. Trypanis. NCSH
Theophany. Evelyn Underhill. WGRP
Theophila; or, Love's Sacrifice, *sels.* Edward Benlowes.
 Cynthia. MOON
 Evening Prayer. FaBoEn
 Life and Death. FaBoEn
Theophilus Thistledown, the successful thistle sifter. *Unknown.* OxNR
Theoretikos. Oscar Wilde. BrPo; VLP
Theory. Dorothy Parker. SBG
Theory of Poetry. Archibald MacLeish. AP; DFF
Theory of the Flower, The. Michael Palmer. NPGG
Theory of Wind, A. Albert Goldbarth. MAYP
Ther is no rose of swich vertu. *See* There is no rose of such virtue.
Ther mighte men the royal egle finde. *See* There mighte men the royal eagle find.
Ther was a knight, a worthy for the chaffre. Portrait of the Pornographer. G. W. Jones. BXAP
Ther was a lady fair an rear. The Kitchie-Boy. *Unknown.* ESPB
Ther was also a Nonne, a Prioresse. *See* There was also a nun, a Prioress.
Ther was also a povre closet queane. Lost Lines from Chaucer's Prologue to "The Canterbury Tales." *Unknown.* PeHV
Ther was in Asye, in a greet citee. *See* There was in Asia, in a great city.
Therapeutist, The. Beth Bentley. AMV-80
Therapy. Ken Poyner. AMV-81
There. Mary Elizabeth Coleridge. EBCP
There. William Harmon. AMV-80
There. Robert Mezey. NaP
There/ is someone I can bear. W. S. Landor. Marianne Moore. OBAL
There ain' no liars there. In My Father's House. *Unknown.* AS
There aince was a very pawky duke. The Pawky Duke. David Rorie. BSV; GoTS
There ain't but three men who really can spend my dough. Three Men. *Unknown.* BluL
There Ain't No Bugs on Me. *Unknown.* FSW
There ain't no more cane on this Brazos. Ain't No More Cane on This Brazos. *Unknown.* FSW
There all the golden codgers lay. News for the Delphic Oracle. W. B. Yeats. CMoP; CoBMV; FaBoMo; LiTB; LiTM; MoPo; NoAM; OAEP
There also was a nun, a Prioress. Chaucer, *mod. version by* Louis Untermeyer. *Fr.* The Canterbury Tales: Prologue. TrGrPo
There always is a noise when it is dark! In the Night. James Stephens. OBMV
There Ance Was a May. Lady Grisell Baillie. BSV
 (Werena My Heart Licht Wad Dee.) OBEV
There are/ two methods. In the Case of Lobsters. Petra von Morstein, *tr. by* Rosemarie Waldrop. BoWoP
There are a few things I shall not forget. 1917-1919. Henry Martyn Hoyt. HBMV
There are a number of us creep. Horace Paraphrased. Isaac Watts. LoBV
There are a very few moments when you. Psalm. Avraham Ben-Yitzhak, *tr. by* A. C. Jacobs. VWA
There are abandoned corners of our Exile. The Mathmid. Hayyim Nahman Bialik, *tr. by* Maurice Samuel. AWP
There are always shadows among the hills. Shadows among the Ettrick Hills. William Addison. PoSH
There Are Bad Times Just around the Corner. Noel Coward. DBV; NOBL
There Are Big Waves. Eleanor Farjeon. OnUR
There are blind eyes. A Prayer in Time of Blindness. Clement Wood. TrPWD
There are brightest apples on those trees. The Fertile Muck. Irving Layton. NOBC; OBCV; PeCV
There are caverns/ under our feet. Shirley Kaufman. BoWoP
There are cemeteries that are lonely. Nothing but Death. Pablo Neruda, *tr. by* Robert Bly. EAS
There are certain things—as, a spider, a ghost. A Sea Dirge. "Lewis Carroll." CenHV; MOS
There Are Children in the Dusk. Bertram Warr. PeCV
There are days to which God. The Days. Paul Blocklyn. AMV-80
There are days when housework seems the only. Coast to Coast. Adrienne Rich. NIP
There are dealers in pictures named Agnew. Tom Agnew, Bill Agnew. Dante Gabriel Rossetti. ChTr; FaBoEE
There Are Delicacies. Earle Birney. NoP
There are different ways of dying without. After the Revolution. Marilyn Hacker. AmPA
"There are dreams that need rest." Okay. Sharon Scott. JB
There are fairies at the bottom of our garden! Fairies. Rose Fyleman. FaPON; HBMV; HBVY; OxBChV; SoPo
There are figures like the dark figures. Microcosmos, XXXII. Nigel Heseltine. NeBP
There are fixed points. Lauris Edmond. Wellington Letter, XI. OCNZ
There are flowers of Zait in the garden. Ezra Pound *and* Noel Stock, *fr. Egyptian hieroglyphics.* BoWoP; PBWP
There are four men mowing down by the Isar. A Youth Mowing. D. H. Lawrence. MoAB; MoBrPo; NoAM; TrGrPo
There are four vibrators, the world's exactest clocks. Four Quartz Crystal Clocks. Marianne Moore. AmPP; ImOP; MP; TwCP
There are gains for all our losses. The Flight of Youth. Richard Henry Stoddard. AA; HBV-1
"There are gains for all our losses." An Old Song Reversed. Richard Henry Stoddard. AA
There Are Gods. C. L. Riley. PoSH
There are half-naked men who stand. The Glass Eaters. George Jonas. NeAC
There are harps that complain to the presence of the night. Music of the Night. John Neal. AA
There are hermit souls that live withdrawn. The House by the Side of the Road. Sam Walter Foss. BLPA; BLPL; FaBoBe; FaFP; HBV-2; HBVY; OHFP; TreF; TRV; WBLP; WGRP

There are (I scarce can think it, but am told.) The First Satire of the Second Book of Horace. Pope. OAEL-1; OBSV; PPP; PrIm
There are in our existence spots of time. Imagination and Taste, How Impaired and Restored. Wordsworth. *Fr.* The Prelude, XII. PoEL-4
There are in Paradise. The Shepherd Who Stayed. Theodosia Garrison. OHIP; PChr
There Are in Such Moments. David I. Silverstein. AMV-80
There are lions and roaring tigers, and enormous camels and things. At the Zoo. A. A. Milne. FaPON; TiPo
There are little eyes upon you, and they're watching night and day. To Any Daddy. *Unknown.* STF
There are lonely hearts to cherish. While the Days Are Going By. George Cooper. BLRP; STF; WBLP
There are loved ones who are missing. The Blessings That Remain. Annie Johnson Flint. BLRP
There are loyal hearts, there are spirits brave. Life's Mirror. "Madeline Bridges." BLPA; FaBoBe; TreF; WBLP
There are many cumbersome ways to kill a man. Five Ways to Kill a Man. Edwin Brock. DL
There are many dead in the brutish desert. First Elegy [for the Dead in Cyrenaica]. Hamish Henderson. ChMP; OxBS
There are many desert places. Missions. *Unknown.* STF
There are many like him here, without epitaph, without a mound. The Grave. Saul Tchernichowsky, *tr. by* Robert Mezey *and* Shula Starkman. VWA
There are many like him there—unsymbolled heap. A Grave in Ukraine. Saul Tchernichowsky, *tr. by* L. V. Snowman. TrJP
There are many monsters that a glassen surface. The Octopus. James Merrill. CoAP; GP; TwAmPo
There are many Washingtons. Which Washington? Eve Merriam. NTCP
There are many ways to die. History among the Rocks. Robert Penn Warren. *Fr.* Kentucky Mountain Farm. GOA; MoAmPo; MoVE
There are many who go to the Vineyard. The Vineyard. *Unknown.* STF
There are many who say that a dog has his day. The Song of the Mischievous Dog. Dylan Thomas. FaFP; FPL; GrPl
There are many who think of Quintia in terms of beauty. Catullus, *tr. fr. Latin by* Horace Gregory. NAWM-1
There are men in the village of Erith. Erith, on the Thames [*or* The Village of Erith]. *Unknown.* ChTr; FaBoPP; GBP; WSC
There are men making death together in the wood. The Delta. Michael Dennis Browne. NYBP
There are miracles that happen. Breaking Silence. Janice Mirikitani. BrSi
There are moments a man turns from us. Drowning with Others. James Dickey. CoPo
There are moments. Snow Crystals on Meall Glas. Elizabeth A. Wilson. PoSH
There are more stars than people. The Astrologer Argues Your Death. Charles deGravelles. AMV-81
There are no angels yet. Gabriel. Adrienne Rich. VGW
There are no bells in all the world. Sleigh Bells at Night. Elizabeth J. Coatsworth. SiSoSe
There are no crosses. A Death in the Desert. Charles Tomlinson. FF
There are no dry bones. The Bones of My Father. Etheridge Knight. DiL
There are no fairy-folk in our Southwest. Western Magic. Mary Austin. AmFN
There Are No Gods. Euripides, *tr. fr. Greek by* John Addington Symonds. *Fr.* Bellerophon. EaLo
There are no heroes. Dead Heroes. Karoniaktatie. STE
There are no hollows any more. Ironic: LL.D. William Stanley Braithwaite. BANP
There are no nightmares now. Only when memory settles. Seravezza. Hoyt W. Fuller. PoBA
There are no red leaves in yellow Oxford. Views of the Oxford Colleges. Paris Leary. CoPo
There are no roads but the frost. Old Age Compensation. James Wright. NNaP
There are no rocks. Geography; a Song. Howard Moss. CAD; PV
There are no stars to-night. My Grandmother's Love Letters. Hart Crane. BLPL; CMoP; FaBoBe; MoAB; NoAM; NOBA; NoP
There are no stars which fell on Alabama. Elements of Grammar. Calvin C. Hernton. NBP
There are no trenches dug in the park, not yet. Nightmare at Noon. Stephen Vincent Benét. OxBA
There are no upper hands in love. After You, Madam. Alex Comfort. ErPo; UnTE
There Are No Wolves in England Now. Rose Fyleman. HBMV
There Are Oceans. Joy Harjo. TWSS
There are one or two things I should just like to hint. To His Countrymen. James Russell Lowell. *Fr.* A Fable for Critics. AA
There are only two things now. New Year's Eve. D. H. Lawrence. BoLoP; ErPo
There are palm trees in my homeland. Antônio Gonçalves Dias, *tr. by* Frances Ellen Buckland. *Fr.* Song of Exile. TTY
There are people after Jesus. How to Hide Jesus. Steve Turner. EBCP
There are people go to Carmel. At Carmel. Mary Austin. AmFN
There are people, I know, to be found. Drinking Song. James Kenneth Stephen. NOBL
"There are people so dumb," my father said. Plain Talk. William Jay Smith. DBV; FiBHP; MoAmPo
There are, perhaps, whom passion gives a grace. The Aged Lover Discourses in the Flat Style. J. V. Cunningham. NoAM
There are pines that are tall enough. An Elegy Is Preparing Itself. Donald Justice. HoPM
There Are Places. Myra Von Riedemann. OBCV
There are portraits and still-lifes. Paring the Apple. Charles Tomlinson. CMoP; NePoEA-2; NMP; OxBTC
There are pumpkins in the field. Fall Days. Marion Conger. SiSoSe
There are questions that must be asked. Incidents in Playfair House. Nicholas Moore. ErPo; NeBP
There are records. Do not. Buying a Record. Robert Peters. BXAP
There are rivers. Wilderness Rivers. Elizabeth J. Coatsworth. AmFN
There are rock-rooted ranges to dominate. Rex Ingamells. *Fr.* Memory of Hills. CBAP
There Are Roughly Zones. Robert Frost. CMoP; PPP
There are seeds within the tide. City. Joseph Bruchac. CDW
There are seven hills. The Windy Bishop. Wilfred Watson. OBCV
There are seventy times seven kinds of loving. Veterans. George Johnston. NOBC
There are several attitudes towards Christmas. The Cultivation of Christmas Trees. T. S. Eliot. OFD
"There are sixteen lang miles, I'm sure." The Bent Sae Brown. *Unknown.* ESPB
There are so many lies in nature. Degas. Paul Monette. AmPA
There Are So Many Ways of Going Places. Leslie Thompson. FaPON; SoPo
There are some/ secrets. July 31. Norman Jordan. PoBA
There are some birds in these valleys. The Decoys. W. H. Auden. CMoP; SyP
There are some days the happy ocean lies. Seascape. Stephen Spender. ChMP; CoBMV; MOS; NoP
There are some hearts like wells, green-mossed and deep. Living Waters. Caroline Spencer. HBV-2
There are some heights in Wessex, shaped as if by a kindly hand. Wessex Heights. Thomas Hardy. CMoP; EBVV; FaBoEn; FaBoPP; OAEL-2; OBNC; PoEL-5
There Are Some Lusty Voices Singing. Geoffrey Lehmann. *Fr.* Ross's Poems. CBAP
There are some qualities—some incorporate things. Sonnet—Silence. Poe. AP; NOBA
There are some quiet crossings in his city. Water Color. Stephen Mooney. NYBP
There are some quiet ways. The Wayside. James Herbert Morse. AA
There are some that love the Border-land and some the Lothians wide. The Road. Christine Orr. PoSH
There are some things which, left unsaid, are true. Paradox. Benjamin K. Bennett. POL
There are some tiny obvious details in human life. Against Surrealism. James Wright. LCAP
There are some who believe the Bible. Believe the Bible. A. B. Simpson. STF
There are spaces. Old Maps and New. Norman MacCaig. OxBC
There are statues moving into a war. The War. W. S. Merwin. LCAP
There are strange hells within the minds war made. Strange Hells. Ivor Gurney. OxBTC
There are strange things done in the midnight sun. The Cremation of Sam McGee. Robert W. Service. BLPL; FaFP; NOBC; OBNV; PoLF; ShM; TreF
There are sunsets who whisper a goood-by. Sunsets. Carl Sandburg. MoAmPo
There Are Sweet Flowers. Walter Savage Landor. EnRP
There are that love the shades of life. The Evening Primrose. John Langhorne. OBEC
There are the Alps. What is there to say about them? On the Fly-Leaf of Pound's Cantos. Basil Bunting. FaBoTw; NoAM; OxBTC
There are the fair-limbed nymphs o' the woods. Leigh Hunt. *Fr.* The Nymphs. OBNC; OBRV
There are the many red birds holding a document. Sacrifice of a Virgin in the Mayan Ball Court. Norman Dubie. GeTw
There are things/ Feet know. Feet. Dorothy Aldis. SUS
There are things/ Hands do. Hands. Dorothy Aldis. SUS
There are things/ you could have said. The Final Fall. Alexandre L. Amprimoz. AMV-81
There are things a man does. Being with Men. Linda Gregg. NPGG

There are things to be said. No doubt. Cid Corman. VGW
There are things you almost see. Almost. Rachel Field. SUS
There are things you have words for. Two Words; a Wedding. B. P. Nichol. NOBC
There are thirteen months in all the year. Robin Hood and the Three Squires. *Unknown.* EnSB
There are those fish that swim ever in the dim. Pearl Perch. John Blight. CBAP
There are those to whom place is unimportant. The Rose. Theodore Roethke. BiP; InPS; NOBA; NYBP; PPoe
There Are Three Bones in the Human Ear. Anita Endrezze-Danielson. STE
There are three central figures preoccupied by toplighting. Composition for a Nativity. John Ciardi. MiAP
There are three Cezannes. Three Cezannes. George Whipple. AMV-80
There are three green eggs in a small brown pocket. At Little Virgil's Window. Edwin Markham. TRV
There are three names. National Security. Archibald MacLeish. GOA
There are three preachers, ever preaching. The Three Preachers. Charles Mackay. EBVV
There are three things which are too wonderful for me. Too Wonderful. Bible, *O.T.* *Fr.* Proverbs. TrJP
There are three ways in which men take. The Music Grinders. Oliver Wendell Holmes. WhC
There are too many heart-shaped words for one. Too Much for One: Not Enough to Go Round. R. P. Blackmur. Scarabs for the Living, I. CrMA
There are too many waterfalls here. Questions of Travel. Elizabeth Bishop. NOBA
There are trails that a lad may follow. Silver Ships. Mildred Plew Meigs. FaPON; TiPo
There are truths you Americans need to be told. American Literature. James Russell Lowell. *Fr.* A Fable for Critics. OBSV
There are twelve months in all the year. Robin Hood Rescuing Three Squires [*or* Robin Hood and the Widow's Three Sons]. *Unknown.* ESPB; OnMSP; ViBoFo
There are twenty dead who're sleeping near the slopes of Bud Dajo. The Fight at Dajo. Alfred E. Wood. PAH
There are two births; the one when light. William Cartwright. *Fr.* To Chloe, Who Wished Herself Young Enough for Me. OBEV
There are two different kinds, I believe, of human attraction. Arthur Hugh Clough. *Fr.* Amours de Voyage. GTBS-P
There are two facing peacocks. Chenille. James Dickey. NoAM
There are two kinds of people on earth today. Lifting and Leaning. Ella Wheeler Wilcox. BLPA; WBLP
There are two kinds of rat. The Migratory Rats. Heine, *tr. by* Ernst Feise. NAWM-2
There are two landscapes. A July Storm: Johnson, Nemaha County, Nebraska. Steve Hahn. AMV-81
There are two Mays. Emily Dickinson. NOBA
There are two miseries in human life. Walter Savage Landor. FaBoEE
There are two ways now. Progress. Edith Agnew. AmFN
There are two women; one I love, and one. Twins. "Owen Meredith." ErPo
There are veils that lift, there are bars that fall. Song of Maelduin. Thomas William Rolleston. HBMV
There are veins in the hills where jewels hide. The Best Treasure. John J. Moment. TRV
There are voices of pain. Lost in a Norther. Hamlin Garland. BPAW
There are voices, voices. Light's dying. Birds have quit. John Berryman. *Fr.* Dream Songs. CAPP
There are white moon daisies in the mist of the meadow. Summer Song. E. Nesbit. PoSC
There are wolves in the next room waiting. The Wolves. Allen Tate. LiTA; LiTM; NoAM; NOBA; OxBA; PoA
There are women of many descriptions. The Rebel Girl. Joe Hill. FSW
There are words like freedom. Refugee in America [*or* Words like Freedom]. Langston Hughes. AmFN; BPo; GOA
There are words that can only be said on paper. Words. Robert Finch. PoA
There are wrongs done in the fair face of heaven. The Deeds That Might Have Been. Wilfrid Scawen Blunt. *Fr.* In Vinculis. TrGrPo
There are youngsters now. Furniture. Phyllis Harris. NYBP
There arent. Untitled Requiem for Tomorrow. Conyus. PoBA
There, as she sewed, came floating through her head. Past. Winifred Howells. AA
There at the top of the world. Harlem in January. Julia Fields. CAD; CNA
There be four things which are little upon the earth. Four Things. Bible, *O.T.* *Fr.* Proverbs. FaPON
There be many kinds of partingyes, I know. Separation. Martha Dickinson Bianchi. AA
There be none of Beauty's daughters. Stanzas for Music. Byron. AWP; ChER; DTC; ELP; EnRP; FiP; GTBS; GTBS-P; HBV-1; LiTB; LoBV; NoP; OAEL-2; OAEP; OBRV; PoPle; PoRA; TrGrPo
There be three badgers on a mossy stone. The Three Badgers. "Lewis Carroll." FaBoNo
There be three hundred different ways and more. Tears. "Owen Meredith." *Fr.* Glenaveril. EBVV
There be three things seeking my death. Prayer for the Speedy End of Three Great Misfortunes. *Tr. by* Frank O'Connor. DTC; OBMV
There be two men of all mankind. Two Men. E. A. Robinson. WhC
There beams no light from thy hall to-night. The Dark Palace. Alice Milligan. AnIV
There between the riverbank. Angel. Brad Leithauser. FYAP; MAYP
There Blooms No Bud in May. Walter de la Mare. MoAB; MoBrPo
There blows a cold wind today, today. To Keep the Cold Wind Away. *Unknown.* OxBM
There breathes a sense of Spring in the boon air. Accidia. Henry Charles Beeching. OBVV
There calleth me ever a marvelous horn. Home-Sickness. Justinus Kerner, *tr. by* James Clarence Mangan. AWP
There cam' seven Egyptians on a day. The Gypsy Countess. *Unknown.* PoPle
There came a bird out o' a bush. Lady Isabel and the Elf-Knight. *Unknown.* ESPB
There came a day at summer's full. Emily Dickinson. AP; NoAM; NOBA (Renunciation.) MoAmPo
There came a ghost to Margret's door. Sweet William's Ghost [*or* Sweet William May Margaret]. *Unknown.* AWP; CH; ESPB; HBV-2; ViBoFo
There came a gray owl at sunset. *Unknown.* WSC
There came a satyr creeping through the wood. The Satyr [*or* The Crackling Twig]. James Stephens. ELU; OnYI
There came a seaman up from the sea. The Drowned Seaman. Maude Goldring. HBMV
There came a wind like a bugle. Emily Dickinson. CMoP; FaBoEn; LoBV; MoAB; NePA; NoAM; NOBA; OxBA
(Storm, The.) TwAmPo
There came a youth upon the earth. The Shepherd of King Admetus. James Russell Lowell. HBVY
There came an ancient man and slow. The Call to a Scot. Ruth Guthrie Harding. HBV-2
There came an earl a-riding by. The Gypsy Countess. *Unknown.* OBET
There came an image in Life's retinue. Death-in-Love. Dante Gabriel Rossetti. The House of Life, XLVIII. SyP; VLP
There came, for lack of sleep. New York in August. Donald Davie. NMP
There came from Normandy an old. The Two Lovers. Marie de France, *tr. by* Patricia Terry. BoWoP
There came three men from out of the west. Sir John Barleycorn. *Unknown.* FaBoBa
There came to port last Sunday night. The New Arrival. George Washington Cable. AA; HBV-1
There came to the beach a poor exile of Erin. Exile of Erin. Thomas Campbell. HBV-2
There came two gentlemen. The Cock. Ewa Lipska, *tr. by* Peter Jay *and* Geri Lipschultz. VWA
There came unto me yesterday. A Bob-tailed Flush. John R. Painter. BPAW
There Came You Wishing Me. José Garcia Villa. TwAmPo
There can be no explanation. His Side/ Her Side. Jeffrey Skinner. AMV-81
There can be no power in a square. Lines. Brian Swann. AMV-81
There can be no songs for dead children. Kindertotenlieder. Michael Longley. CIP
There chanced to be a pedlar bold. The Bold Pedlar and Robin Hood. *Unknown.* ESPB
There Charon stands, who rules the dreary coast. Virgil, *tr. by* Dryden. *Fr.* The Aeneid, VI. OBVE
There comes a moment late in Summer. Prognostic. Samuel Yellen. NePoAm
There comes a moment when to believe is not enough. Action. James Oppenheim. TrJP
There comes a time when everything is laced. The Imagination of Necessity. Andrei Codrescu. EAS
There comes a wail of anguish. A Cry for Light. *Unknown.* BLRP
There comes Emerson first, whose rich words, every one. Emerson. James Russell Lowell. *Fr.* A Fable for Critics. AmPP; AP; NOBA; OxBA; PP; TAP
There comes Poe, with his raven, like Barnaby Rudge. Poe and Longfellow. James Russell Lowell. *Fr.* A Fable for Critics. AmPP; AP; NOBA; OxBA; TAP
There died a myriad. Ezra Pound. *Fr.* Hugh Selwyn Mauberley. DBV; FF; MoAmPo; NIP; NOBE; PAI; WaaP

There dwelt a fair maid in the West. James Harris (The Daemon Lover). *Unknown.* BaBo; ESPB
There dwelt a man in fair[e] Westmoreland [*or* Westmerland]. Johnie Armstrong. *Unknown.* BiP; ESPB; FaBoBa; HoPM; NoP; TrGrPo; ViBoFo
There dwelt a miller, hale and bold. The Miller of [the] Dee. *At. to* Charles Mackay. GBP; HBV-2
There dwelt the Man, the flower of human kind. Mount Vernon, the Home of Washington. William Day. OHIP
There exists no proof as. E. C. Bentley. *Fr.* Clerihews. NOBL
There falls with every wedding chime. Walter Savage Landor. *Fr.* The Last Fruit Off an Old Tree. SeCePo
There fared a mother driven forth. The House of Christmas. G. K. Chesterton. GoBC; HBV-1; HBVY; MoBrPo
There Faunus and Sylvanus keep their courts. Sir John Denham. *Fr.* Cooper's Hill. JCP
There fell red rain of spears athwart the sky. Last Judgment. John Gould Fletcher. AWP
There flames the first gay daffodil. Daffodils. Ruth Guthrie Harding. HBMV
There flourished once a potentate. The King of Yvetot. Pierre Jean de Béranger, *tr. by* William Toynbee. AWP
There Goes a Girl Walking. Dodie Meeks. AMV-81
There goes the clock; there goes the sun. Epitaph for John and Richard. Karl Shapiro. TwAmPo
There goes the dog of the mind. Soliloquy by the Shore. Martin Scholten. GoYe
There goes the grandson, run off to the beach! The Grandson. James Scully. NYBP
There goes the Wapiti. The Wapiti. Ogden Nash. MoShBr
There Gowans Are Gay. *Unknown.* GBP
There grew a goodly tree him faire beside. Balme. Spenser. *Fr.* The Faerie Queene, I, 11. CH
There grew a lowly flower by Eden-gate. Eden-Gate. Sydney Dobell. OBVV
There grew an aged tree on the green. The Oak and the Brere. Spenser. *Fr.* The Shepheardes Calender: February. OBSC
There grew two olives, closest of the grove. Homer, *tr. by* Pope. *Fr.* The Odyssey, V. OBVE
There grows no rootless flower. The First Reader. Winfield Townley Scott. PoA
There had been portents. The Black Death. Philip Dacey. GP
There had been years of passion—scorching, cold. "And There Was a Great Calm." Thomas Hardy. ChTr; CMoP; FaBoRV; LiTM; OAEL-2
There hang three crosses at thy door. To the Landlord. Swift. DBV
There hangs this bellied pear, let no rake doubt. The Pear. Ruth Stone. TwAmPo
There hartes ware so roted in the popes lawes. Fragment of an Anti-Papist Ballad. *Unknown.* CoMu
There has been a light snow. In a Train. Robert Bly. CAPP; NaP; POL
There has been a play on T.V. Lesbian Play on T.V. Caroline Gilfillan. PeHV
There has been no change. Autumn. Princess Shikishi, *tr. by* Hiroaki Sato. PBWP
There has been. To W. C. W. M. D. Alfred Kreymborg. PoA
There has something gone wrong. Keep a Stiff Upper Lip. Phoebe Cary. FaFP
There Has to Be a Jail for Ladies. Thomas Merton. VGW
There hath a question been of late. Up-Tails All. *Unknown.* UnTE
There hath come an host to see Thee. Lullaby in Bethlehem. Henry Howarth Bashford. HBV-1; HBVY
There have always been dolls. Five Poems for Dolls, III. Margaret Atwood. NIP
There have been three storms in my heart. Summerhouse. Melvin Walker La Follette. NePoEA
There have been times when I well might have passed and the ending have come. Thomas Hardy. In Tenebris, III. OAEL-2
There he is crawling stomach and elbows. The Mad Farmer Stands Up in Kentucky for What He Thinks Is Right. James Baker Hall. TAT
"There he is, woman!" The Seduction of Engadu. *Unknown, tr. by* William Ellery Leonard. *Fr.* Epic of Gilgamesh. ErPo
There he moved, cropping the grass at the purple canyon's lip. The Horse Thief. William Rose Benét. BPAW; HBMV; MoAmPo; OnMSP
There he stands. see? Two Jazz Poems. Carl Wendell Hines, Jr. AmNP
There he was—having spent. "Yes, But. . ." Theodore Weiss. TAP
There headlong into the calm black night. Orestes Pursued. Charles David Webb. NePoAm-2
There I could never be a boy. Poem. Frank O'Hara. HoAn; NNaP
There in a bare place, in among the rocks. The Little Lough. John Hewitt. NeIP
There in his room, whene'er the moon looks in. Ode for a Master Mariner Ashore. Louise Imogen Guiney. AA; GoBC
There, in that other world, what waits for me? There. Mary Elizabeth Coleridge. EBCP
There in the bracken was the ominous spoor mark. The Tantanoola Tiger. Max Harris. MoBS; PoAu-2
There, in the corner, staring at his drink. Docker. Seamus Heaney. NoAM; TW
There, in the earliest and chary spring, the dogwood flowers. Sunday: Outskirts of Knoxville, Tennessee. James Agee. ErPo
There in the fane a beauteous creature stands. Woman. Kalidasa. HBV-1
There in the flower garden. *Unknown, tr. fr. Spanish by* Willis Barnstone. BoWoP
There in the hard light. An Irish Lake. W. R. Rodgers. BIrV
There, in the market, with Mrs. Peters. Journal of the Storm. Greg Kuzma. AmPA
There Is. Louis Simpson. ConAP
There is/ A welcome at the door to which no one comes? Angel Surrounded by Paysans. Wallace Stevens. LCAP; PPP
There is/ One great society alone on earth. The Noble. Wordsworth. *Fr.* The Prelude, IX. ChTr
There is a bale of hay. Beside the Road. Ken Belford. NeAC
There is a balm in Gilead, to make the wounded whole. Balm in Gilead. *Unknown.* FSW
There is a big artist named Val. Dante Gabriel Rossetti. FaBoEE
There is a bird in the poplars. Metric Figure. William Carlos Williams. MoAB; MoAmPo
There is a bird that comes and sings. The Song the Oriole Sings. William Dean Howells. HBV-1
There is a bird who, by his coat. The Jackdaw. Vincent Bourne, *tr. by* William Cowper. HBV-1; HBVY; PB; PBBP
There is a black dog in my painting. Joan Brown, about Her Painting. Kathleen Fraser. NPGG
There is a blue sky. A Song. Edward Dorn. ConAP
There is a blue star, Janet. Baby Toes. Carl Sandburg. FaPON; SUS
There is a bondage worse, far worse, to bear. Sonnet: There Is a Bondage Worse. Wordsworth. ChER
There Is a Box. Uri Zvi Greenberg, *tr. fr. Hebrew by* Robert Mezey *and* Ben Zion Gold. VWA
There is a bridge, whereof the span. The Unseen Bridge. Gilbert Thomas. HBMV
There is a careful look. Existence. Sheila Moon. AMV-80
There is a change—and I am poor. A Complaint. Wordsworth. NOBE; OBRV; PoEL-4
There is a charm I can't explain. The Big Sunflower. Bobby Newcomb. BLSo
There Is a Charming Land. Adam Oehlenschlager, *tr. fr. Danish by* Robert Hillyer. AWP; FaPON
There Is a City. "The Jewish Sibyl," *tr. fr. Greek by* Bohn. *Fr.* The Fourth Book of Sibylline Oracles. TrJP
There is a city, builded by no hand. Paradisi Gloria. Thomas William Parsons. AA
There is a city, Chaldean Ur. There Is a City. "The Jewish Sibyl," *tr. by* Bohn. *Fr.* The Fourth Book of Sibylline Oracles. TrJP
There is a clouded city, gone to rest. The Aztec City. Eugene Fitch Ware. AA; HBV-2
There is a club for boys where they. To G. R. Samuel Elsworth Cottam. PeHV
There is a coarseness. Jungle Taste. Edward S. Silvera. CDC
There is a conflict of jurisdictions here. Intersection. Florence Dolgorukov. AMV-80
There is a cool river. Detroit. Donald Hall. AmFN
There is a cop who is both prowler and father. Rape. Adrienne Rich. GP
There is a country full of wine. Two Voices. Alice Corbin. HBMV
There is a creator named God. On the Painter Val Prinsep. Dante Gabriel Rossetti. FaBoEE
There is a crying in the world. End of the World. Else Lasker-Schüler, *tr. by* Willis Barnstone *and* Michael Gillespie. BoWoP
There is a dale in Ida, lovelier. *See* There lies a vale in Ida, lovelier.
There is a dark planet striking against us. Invisible. The Dark Planet. John Heath-Stubbs. OAEL-2
There is a deep brooding. My Arkansas. Maya Angelou. BlSi
There is a desert island of the heart. "What Five Books Would You Pick to Be Marooned with on a Desert Island?" Paris Leary. CoPo
There is a destiny that makes us brothers. A Creed. Edwin Markham. BLPA; BLPL; FaBoBe; FaFP; PoPl; TreFS
There is a dish to hold the sea. Imagination. John Davidson. *Fr.* New Year's Eve. MoBrPo
There Is a Dream Dreaming Us. Norman Dubie. GeTw
There is a dream of eternal warmth. Overcoats. Larry Kramer. AMV-80
There is a drear and lonely tract of hell. Supremacy. E. A. Robinson. NoAM
There is a drunk on Main Avenue, slumped. Song-Maker. Anita Endrezze-Danielson. STE

There is a face, a woman's face, coming up. Lost in Yucatan. Tom McKeown. HoAn
There is a far country where there is a hall for dreams. The Far Country. Robert Greacen. NeIP
"There is a fashion in this land." The Knight's Ghost. *Unknown.* ESPB
"There is a feast in your father's house." Leesome Brand. *Unknown.* ESPB
There Is a Fever of the Spirit. Thomas Love Peacock. *Fr.* Nightmare Abbey, *ch.* 11. OBRV
(Song by Mr. Cypress.) OAEL-2; OBNC; Par
There is a fine stuffed chavender. A False Gallop of Analogies. Warham St. Leger. CenHV; FaBoCo; FiBHP; WhC
There is a fish so large. Night Fishing. Michael Waters. WOLT
There is a flashpacket, 'n' a packet of fame. The *Dreadnought, vers.* I. *Unknown.* ShS
There is a flower, a little flower. A Field Flower. James Montgomery. HBV-1
There is a flower blossoming out of season. Flower Ensnarer of Psalms. Rossana Ombres, *tr. by* I. L. Salomon. BoWoP
There is a flower I wish to wear. Hearts-Ease. Walter Savage Landor. EnRP
There is a flower that bees prefer. Emily Dickinson. MoAmPo
There is a flower, the Lesser Celandine. A Lesson [*or* The Small Celandine]. Wordsworth. GTBS; GTBS-P; HBV-1; OBRV
There is a flower within my heart. Daisy Bell; or, A Bicycle Built for Two. Harry Dacre. BLSo; FSN; FSW; TreF
There is a flowr sprung of a tree. The Fairest Flower. John Audelay. OxBM
There Is a Garden. Thomas Campion. *See* There Is a Garden in Her Face.
There is a garden enclosed. Wild Eden, III. George Edward Woodberry. HBV-2
There Is a Garden in Her Face. Thomas Campion. AAS; BiP; CABA; EIL; EnRePo; FaBoEn; GoJo; HeIP; InPK; NIP; NoP; OAEL-1, *with music*; OAEP; OBSC; PAI; PoEL-2; PrIm; TrGrPo; ViBoPo; WHA
(Cherry-ripe.) BoLoP; CH; GTBS; GTBS-P; HBV-1; LiTB; NOBE; OBEV; PPoe; SeCeV; TreFT
(There Is a Garden.) ELP
There is a garden where lilies. Eutopia. Francis Turner Palgrave. EBVV; OBVV
There is a garden, which I think He loves. The Garden. Digby Mackworth Dolben. GoBC
There is a general idiom to all rime. Karl Shapiro. *Fr.* Essay on Rime. PP
There is a gentle nymph not far from hence. Sabrina. Milton. *Fr.* Comus. OBS
There is a ghost. Ghost. Christian Morgenstern, *tr. by* W. D. Snodgrass *and* Lore Segal. WSC
There is a girl you like so you tell her. Courtship. Mark Strand. GP
There is a gray enameled sky. Private Rooms. Diana O Hehir. NPGG
There is a great amount of poetry in unconscious/ fastidiousness. Critics and Connoisseurs. Marianne Moore. AmPP; CMoP; NePA; NoAM; NOBA; OxBA
There is a great river this side of Stygia. The River of Rivers in Connecticut. Wallace Stevens. HAP; NOBA; VGW
There Is a Green Hill [Far Away]. Cecil Frances Alexander. BLRP; HBV-2; OxBChV; WGRP
There is a grey thing that lives in the tree-tops. Stephen Crane. WSC
There is a growth that hurts the child. An Age. Laura Jensen. LCAP
There is a halo around the moon. Debt. *Gond Oral Tradition, tr. by* V. Elwin *and* S. Hivale. WTO
There is a harp set above us. Harp in the Rigging. Hamish Maclaren. EtS
There is a hawk that is picking the birds out of our sky. Shiva. Robinson Jeffers. NoAM; NOBA
There is a heaven, for ever, day by day. Theology. Paul Laurence Dunbar. TRV
There is a heigh-ho in these glowing coals. Heigh-ho on a Winter Afternoon. Donald Davie. NePoEA-2; OxBTC
There Is a High Place, *with music.* Edwin Markham. AH
There Is a Hill. Robert Bridges. OAEP
("There is a hill beside the silver Thames.") BrPo
There is a hill and on that hill is a stone. The Heart of the World. Nahman of Bratzlav, *tr. by* Joseph Leftwich. TrJP
There is a hill beside the silver Thames. Robert Bridges. BrPo
There is a hornet in the room. Buried at Springs. James Schuyler. CoAP; PoM
There is a house in New Orleans. The House of the Rising Sun [*or* The Rising Sun Blues]. *Unknown.* FSW; OuSiCo
There is a house with ivied walls. Architectural Masks. Thomas Hardy. EyDe
There is a hush this golden afternoon. Classroom in October. Elias Lieberman. GoYe
There is a jewel which no Indian mines. Risposta. John Wilbye. HBV-2
There is a joyful night in which we lose. When the Dumb Speak. Robert Bly. CAPP; NoAM; NOBA
There is a kind of lace laid over the city, a lightness. The Serious Merriment of Women. Patricia Goedicke. TAP
There Is a Lady ("There is a lady conquering with glances"). Walther von der Vogelweide, *tr. fr. German by* Jethro Bithell. AWP
There Is a Lady [Sweet and Kind]. *At. to* Thomas Ford. CH; EBEV; EIL; ELP; FaFP; GBL; GoBC; HeIP; HBV-1; LiTB; NoP; OAEP; OBEV; OBS; TreFS; TrGrPo
(Passing By, *abr.*) NOBE
There Is a Land. James Montgomery. PAL; PGD
There Is a Land. Isaac Watts. *See* Prospect of Heaven Makes Death Easy, A.
There is a land called Lost. Two Chorale-Preludes. Geoffrey Hill. OxBC
There Is a Land Mine Eye Hath Seen, *with music.* Gurdon Robins. AH
There is a land of Dream. Dream Fantasy. "Fiona Macleod." WGRP
There is a land, of every land the pride. There Is a Land. James Montgomery. PAL; PGD
There is a land of pure delight. A Prospect of Heaven Makes Death Easy [*or* Heaven *or* There Is a Land]. Isaac Watts. ELP; NOCV; NoP; OBEC; WGRP
There is a language in a naval log. E. J. Pratt. *Fr.* Behind the Log. MoCV
There is a languor of the life. Emily Dickinson. BoWoP
There is a litany. Compline. Debora Greger. AMV-81
There is a little lightning in his eyes. Of Robert Frost. Gwendolyn Brooks. NoAM; NOBA
There is a little lonely grave. The Unknown Grave. Letitia Elizabeth Landon. VLP
There is a little man. The Merry Man of Paris. Stella Mead. SUS
There is a lonely mountain-top. Jephthah's Daughter. "Yehoash," *tr. by* Alter Brody. TrJP
There is a loud noise of Death. To Dear Daniel. Samuel Greenberg. LiTA; MoPo
There Is a Love. Philip Jerome Cleveland. TRV
There is a magic melting pot. The Melting Pot. Dudley Randall. BALP; BPo
There is a magic. Light Baggage. Alice Walker. LTB
There Is a Man on the Cross. Elizabeth Cheney. PGD; TRV
There is a meadow. Last Light. Robert Kelly. VGW
There is a memory stays upon old ships. Old Ships. David Morton. EtS
There is a middleaged man, Tim Flanagan. The Middleaged Man. Louis Simpson. NNaP
There is a moment country children know. Village before Sunset. Frances Cornford. BoNaP
There is a moment in midsummer when the earth. Midsummer Pause. Fred Lape. PoSC
There is a morn by men unseen. Emily Dickinson. OxBA
There is a mountain everyone must climb. The Mountain. Robert Finch. CaP
There is a mystery too deep for words. Silence. John Hall Wheelock. LiTM
There is a mystic borderland that lies. The Mystic Borderland. Helen Field Fischer. WBLP
There is a niche provided. For Every Man. Max I. Reich. STF
There is a niland on a river lying. Collusion between a Alegaiter and a Water-Snaik. J. W. Morris. NA
There is a pain—so utter. Emily Dickinson. BoWoP; NOBA
There is a panther caged within my breast. The Black Panther. John Hall Wheelock. FF; HBMV; LiTM
There is a party tonight. The Party at the Contessa's House. Brian Robertson. AMV-80
There is a people mighty in its youth. Tribute to America. Shelley. PAL
There is a pity in forgotten things. The Triumph of Forgotten Things. Edith M. Thomas. HBV-1
There Is a Place. Alma Hoellein. STF
There is a place in Montana where the grass stands up two feet. Rosebud. Jon Anderson. MAYP
There is a place of peace and rest. There Is a Place. Alma Hoellein. STF
There is a place that some men know. The Cross. Allen Tate. AP; AWP; MoAmPo; MoVE; OxBA
There is a place where contrarieties are equally true. The Vision of Beulah. Blake. *Fr.* Milton, II. OAEL-2
There is a place where goblins dwell. Where Goblins Dwell. Jack Prelutsky. RHPC
There is a place where thou canst touch the eyes. The Secret Place. A. A. Pollard. STF
There is a place where, wisdom won, right recorded. Elegy for Our Dead. Edwin Rolfe. WaP
There is a plan far greater than the plan you know. There Is No Death. *Unknown.* BLPA; FPL
There is a pleasure in poetic pains. Poetic Pains. William Cowper. *Fr.* The Task, II. FiP; PP

There is a pleasure in the pathless woods. The Sea [*or* And I Have Loved Thee, Ocean *or* Apostrophe to the Ocean *or* Roll On, Thou Deep and Dark Blue Ocean]. Byron. *Fr.* Childe Harold's Pilgrimage, IV. BLPL; ChTr; FaBoBe; FaBV; FIP; HBV-1; LiTB; MOS; OBRV; OHFP; PoEL-4; TreF; ViBoPo; WBLP; WHA
There Is a Pool on Garda. Clinton Scollard. HBV-2
There is a poor sneak called Rossetti. On Himself. Dante Gabriel Rossetti. FaBoEE
There is a pretty piece of work. The Naughty Lord and the Gay Young Lady Damages, $10,000. *Unknown.* CoMu
There is a private tension that endears. The Crack. Michael Goldman. NYBP
There is a quality of air. A Quality of Air. Henry Chapin. FAZ
There is a quest that calls me. The Mystic. Cale Young Rice. WGRP
There is a question one woman. Child of Blue. Michael Hogan. LFAC
There is a quiet kingdom's strand. The Quiet Kingdom. Carl Busse, *tr. by* Ludwig Lewisohn. AWP
There is a quiet spirit in these woods. The Spirit of Poetry. Longfellow. PP
There is a Reaper, whose name is Death. The Reaper and the Flowers. Longfellow. HBV-2
There is a river clear and fair. Fragment in Imitation of Wordsworth [*or* An Imitation of Wordsworth]. Catherine Fanshawe. BXAP; FaBoNo; FaBoPa; HBV-1; NA; Par
There is a road that turning always. The Road. Edwin Muir. BSV; CMoP; FaBoEn; FaFP; LiTB; LiTM; ViBoPo
There is a rumour hereabout of summer. The Overgrown Back Yard. John Holmes. CrMA; NePoAm
There is a sad carnival up the valley. Are They Dancing. Edward Dorn. NeAP; PoM
There is a secret laughter. Secret Laughter. Christopher Morley. FaBV; TreFS
There is a secret room. The Same Gesture. John Montague. BIrV
There is a selfhood in my nothingness. Al-Hallaj, *tr. fr. Persian.* ILwL
There is a sentinel before the gate. The City Church. "E. H. K." WGRP
There is a serpent in perfection tarnished. True Vine. Elinor Wylie. LiTA
There is a shame of nobleness. Emily Dickinson. NePA
There is a sheeling hidden in the wood. The Lay of Prince Marvan. *Unknown, tr. by* Eleanor Hull. AnIV
There is a shrine whose golden gate. The Shrine. Digby Mackworth Dolben. GoBC; HBV-1
There is a silence where hath been no sound. Silence [*or* Sonnet: Silence]. Thomas Hood. CH; EBEV; EnRP; FaBoEn; NOBE; OBEV; OBNC; OBRV; PoEL-4; ViBoPo
There is a singer everyone has heard. The Oven Bird. Robert Frost. AmPP; AP; AWP; CoBMV; CrMA; HeIP; NoAM; NOBA; NoP; OxBA; PPP; TAP; TwAmPo
There is a small store-house of knowledge in which I sit sometimes on hard wooden cases. A Store-House. Louis Dudek. CaP
There is a smile of love. The Smile. Blake. OBRV; TEP
There is a soldier on the battlefield. *Unknown, tr. fr. Chinese by* Geoffrey Waters. BoWoP
There is a solitude of space. Emily Dickinson. AP
There is a sorcerer in Lachine. The Sorcerer. A. J. M. Smith. PeCV
There is a soul above the soul of each. Humanity. Richard Watson Dixon. OBVV
There is a sound I would not hear. Fear. Langdon Elwyn Mitchell. AA
There is a sound that's dear to me. The Lay of the Levite. William Edmondstoune Aytoun. HBV-2
There is a space for winter here. Heron's Bay. Martin Galvin. AMV-81
There is a special privacy on stage. Gig at Big Al's. Heather McHugh. GeTw
There Is a Spell, for Instance. Hilda Doolittle ("H. D."). *Fr.* The Walls Do Not Fall. MoPo; NoAM
There is a stane in yon water. Burd Isabel and Earl Patrick. *Unknown.* BaBo; ESPB
There is a star that runs very fast. Moon Song. Hilda Conkling. TiPo
There is a story so true, so becoming, so full of duty. Window. Bruce Smith. DiL
There is a stream, I name not its name. A Highland Glen near Loch Ericht. Arthur Hugh Clough. *Fr.* The Bothie of Tober-na-Vuolich. BoNaP; FaBoPP; VLP
There is a stream that flowed before the first beginning. Kathleen Raine. *Fr.* Water. ImOP
There is a stream which rises. Joseph Bruchac. CDW
There is a Supreme God in the ethnological section. Homage to the British Museum. William Empson. CMoP; FaBoMo; LiTM; MoAB; MoBrPo
There is a tall long-sided dame. Samuel Butler. *Fr.* Hudibras, II, 1. OBSV
There Is a Tavern in the Town. *Unknown, at. to* William H. Hills. BLSo, *with music*; FaFP; FSW; PSoN, *with music*; TreF; YaD
There is a temple in my heart. Temple Garlands. Agnes Mary Frances Robinson. HBV-1
There is a thing which in the light. A Candle. Sir John Suckling. ErPo
There is a Thorn—it looks so old. The Thorn. Wordsworth. EnRP
There is a through-otherness about Armagh. Armagh. W. R. Rodgers. NoAM
There Is a Tide [in the Affairs of Men]. Shakespeare. *Fr.* Julius Caesar IV, iii. PoPl; TRV
(Time to Strike, The.) TreFS
There is a time, we know not when. The Doomed Man [*or* The Hidden Line]. Joseph Addison Alexander. BLPA; TRV
There is a time wherein eternity. The Last Communion. Leo Ward. GoBC
There is a tiny wind in our room. Loving. Shirley Kaufman. VWA
There is a train inside this iris. Iris. David St. John. LCAP
There is a Treasure. God's Treasure. "A. M. N." STF
There is a tree, by day. Tenebris. Angelina Weld Grimké. CDC; PoBA; PoNe
There is a tree grows upside down. The Winds. Jack Clemo. EBCP
There is a tree native in Turkestan. Note on Local Flora. William Empson. FaBoMo; MoVE
There is a two-headed goat, a four-winged chicken. Believe It. John Logan. LCAP
There is a wailing baby under every stone. Poem. Norman MacCaig. EAS
There is a walled garden where the flowers never pale or turn dark. Paradise. E. N. Sargent. NYBP
There is a way of seeing that is not seeing. Trompe L'Œil. Daryl Hine. MoCV
There is a way, that sages tell. The Advantage of the Outside. Richard Eberhart. NePA
There is a well, a willow-shaded spot. The Cherwell Waterlily. Frederick W. Faber. GoBC
There is a white mare that my love keeps. Love Poem. Alex Comfort. *Fr.* The Postures of Love. ErPo; NeBP
There is a wild flower growing. Jean. Paul Potts. NeBP
There is a willow grows aslant a brook. Ophelia's Death. Shakespeare. *Fr.* Hamlet, V, i. ChTr
There is a wind where the rose was. Autumn. Walter de la Mare. OxBTC
There is a window stuffed with hay. The Hay Hotel. Oliver St. John Gogarty. BIrV
There is a wolf in me . . . fangs pointed for tearing gashes. Wilderness. Carl Sandburg. AP
There is a woman climbing a glass hill. Two Women. Naomi Replansky. NMM
There is a woman in our town. William Carlos Williams. *Fr.* Paterson. CMoP
There Is a Woman in This Town. Patricia Parker. BlSi
There is a woman like a seed. Another Generation. J. C. Squire. HBMV
There is a woman running. The Joining. Gerda Norvig. VWA
There is a word at heart for the next of death. Written in Exile. Kathleen Raine. TrCP; WPE
There is a world of pain beyond the heart. Sonnet for a Loved One. Dorothy Joslin. AMV-80
There is a world of wonder in this rose. The Rose. G. A. Studdert-Kennedy. EBCP
There is a yew tree, pride of Lorton Vale. Yew Trees. Wordsworth. CABA; EnRP; UnPo
There is a young lady, whose nose. Edward Lear. OxBChV
There is a young Muslim Chinese. Taunt. *Malay Oral Tradition, tr. by* R. J. Wilkinson *and* R. O. Windstedt. WTO
There is always a first flinging. Variations on a Theme. Anne Wilkinson. MoCV
There is always a journey. Water. Judith McPheron. AMV-81
There is an aggression of fact. After Jericho. R. S. Thomas. OxBC
There is an air for which I would disown. An Old Tune. Gérard de Nerval, *tr. by* Andrew Lang AWP; HBV-1
There is an evening coming in. Going. Philip Larkin. CMoP
There is an exquisite torture in living with dull people. Always Battling. Thomas O'Brien. NeIP
There is an Eye that never sleeps. God the Omniscient [*or* Prayer Moves the Hand That Moves the World]. *At. to* James Cowden Wallace, *also at. to* John A. Wallace. BLRP; STF; WGRP
There is an eye, there was a slit. Sabbath. John Berryman. *Fr.* Dream Songs. LCAP
There Is an Hour of Peaceful Rest. William Bingham Tappan. *See* Hour of Peaceful Rest, The.
There is an inevitability. Fable. Norman Harris. NYBP
There is an island in a far-off sea. Where the Single Men Go in Summer. Nina Bourne. FiBHP
There is an ode in every swaying tree. Reflection. Kurt M. Stein. InMe
There is an old and very cruel god. Vicarious Atonement. Richard Aldington. WGRP
There Is an Old City. Karl Bulcke, *tr. fr. German by* Ludwig Lewisohn. AWP

There is an old cook house not far away. Old Soldiers Never Die. *Unknown.* FSW
There is an old he-wolf named Gambart. Limerick. Dante Gabriel Rossetti. CenHV; FaBoEE
There is an old lady who lives down the hall. The Sugar Lady. Frank Asch. RHPC
There is an Order by a northern sea. Religio Novissima. Aubrey Thomas de Vere. NBM
There is another kind of sleep. Hematite Lake. James Galvin. AMV-80
There is another world above this one. Through the Smoke Hole. Gary Snyder. PoA; PoM
There is blood on thy desolate shore. Apostrophe to the Island of Cuba. James Gates Percival. PAH
There is bound to be a certain amount of. Trouble. Don Marquis. *Fr.* Archy and Mehitabel. TreFT
There is bright light. Its Name Is Known. Daniel Lawrence Kelleher. NeIP
There is Bryant, as quiet, as cool, and as dignified. Bryant. James Russell Lowell. *Fr.* A Fable for Critics. AP; NOBA; TAP
There is but one great sorrow. The Shadow. Richard Henry Stoddard. AA
There is but one May in the year. Christina Rossetti. *Fr.* Sing-Song. TiPo
There is dark. Trying to Sleep. Ralph Pomeroy. ELU
There is death enough in Europe without these. Dead Ponies. Brenda Chamberlain. NeBP; WPE
There is death in this river. To the Spirit of Monahsetah. Charlotte DeClue. STE; TWSS
There is delight in singing, though [*or* tho'] none hear. To Robert Browning. Walter Savage Landor. EnRP; NoP; OAEP; ViBoPo
There is drink fermented. Chimedin Jigmed, *tr. by* C. R. Bawden. *Fr.* A Satirical Poem about Drink. WTO
There is Earth. Out of Question & Mind. Noah Mitchell. LFAC
There is fear in/ Turning the mind away. The Sun and the Moon and Fear of Loneliness. *Tr. fr.* Eskimo. WTO
There is fire in the lower hold. Fire Down Below. *Unknown.* FSW
"There is frost in the air." Schoenberg Op. 11. Thomas W. Shapcott. *Fr.* Piano Pieces. CBAP
There Is Good News. Josephine Jacobsen. AMV-80
There is great mystery, Simone. Hair. Remy de Gourmont, *tr. by* Jethro Bithell. AWP; ErPo
There is grey in your hair. The Aged Woman to Her Sons. Babette Deutsch. AMV-81
There Is Hallelujah Hannah. A. E. Housman. WhC
There is hardly a mouthful of air. Nelson Street. "Seumas O'Sullivan." OxBI
There is Hawthorne, with genius so shrinking and rare. Hawthorne. James Russell Lowell. *Fr.* A Fable for Critics. AmPP; AP; NOBA; OxBA; TAP
There is health in thy gray wing. To a Marsh Hawk in Spring. Henry David Thoreau. PB; PoEL-4
There is heard a hymn when the panes are dim. The Feast of the Snow. G. K. Chesterton. HBV-1
There is in human closeness a sacred boundary. "Anna Akhmatova," *tr. fr. Russian by* Dianne Levitin. WPOW
There is in this world something. The Sweetest Thing. *Unknown, tr. by* Ulli Beier. TTY
There is interest in being able to feel what you see. Symmetrical Poem. Michael Palmer. NPGG
There is joy. Welcome Morning. Anne Sexton. PAI
There is joy in/ Feeling the warmth. Eskimo Chant. *Unknown, tr. by* Knud Rasmussen. RFM; WHW
There is little in afternoon tea. On Drawing-Room Amenities. Gelett Burgess. FaBoNo
There is Lowell, who's striving Parnassus to climb. Lowell. James Russell Lowell. *Fr.* A Fable for Critics. AA; AmPP; AP; NOBA; OxBA; TAP
There is many a love in the land, my love. Song. Joaquin Miller. HBV-1
There is many a slipton. Sir Thomas Johnstone. WhC
There is many a wild Canadian boy who leaves his happy home. Harry Dunne, *vers.* II. *Unknown.* ShS
There is more than one rain. Rain. Peter Sears. AMV-80
There is more to this meadow under the mountains. Meadow Grass. Michael Mott. AMV-80
There is much to be said. Mac Diarmod's Daughter. Francis Carlin. HBMV
There is much to be said for the portrait painted in winter. Portrait in Winter. Katherine Garrison Chapin. GoYe
There is much work to be done before we leave. Moving Out. Joyce Carol Oates. AMV-81
There is music in me, the music of a peasant people. The Banjo Player. Fenton Johnson. BANP; PoNe
There is my country under glass. At the Tourist Center in Boston. Margaret Atwood. NoP
There is naught for thee by thy haste to gain. The Created. Jones Very. NOCV; QFR
There Is Never a Day So Dreary. *At. to* Lilla M. Alexander. BLRP
(Consolation.) STF
There is never an open door to the wild beasts' home. The Uninvited. William D. Mundell. NYBP
There Is No. Faye Kicknosway. GeTw
There is no answer. We do here what we will. The Usurpers. Edwin Muir. CMoP
There Is No Balm in Birmingham. Ann Deagon. NIP
There is no balm on earth. Invocation. Gilbert Thomas. TrPWD
There is no bountie to be shew'd to such. Ben Jonson. *Fr.* The Poetaster, III, vi. PoEL-2
There is no chance, no destiny, no fate. Will. Ella Wheeler Wilcox. BLPA; FPL
There is no chapel on the day. Oscar Wilde. *Fr.* The Ballad of Reading Gaol. EBVV; OxBI
There Is No Country. Juljan Tuwim, *tr. fr. Polish by* Watson Kirkconnell. TrJP
There is no cut rock. Climbing Zero Gully. David J. Morley. PoSH
There is no dearer lover of lost hours. Idleness. S. Weir Mitchell. AA
There Is No Death. John Luckey McCreery. BLPA; FaBoBe; HBV-2; TreF; WBLP
There Is No Death. *Unknown.* BLPA; FPL
There is no death, O child divine. The Great Victory. R. V. Gilbert. BLRP
There is no death! The stars go down. There Is No Death. John Luckey McCreery. BLPA; FaBoBe; HBV-2; TreF; WBLP
There is no Death. What seems so is transition. Longfellow. *Fr.* Resignation. TRV
There is no difference between being raped. Rape Poem. Marge Piercy. Psk
There is no end to the/ Deception of quiet things. The Chinese Banyan. William Meredith. NePoEA
There is no escape by the river. At the End of the Day. Richard Hovey. HBVY
There is no fire of the crackling boughs. Glenaradale. Walter Chalmers Smith. OBEV; OBVV
There is no fitter end than this. In Memoriam S.C.W., V.C. Charles Sorley. MMA
There is no flock, however watched and tended. Resignation. Longfellow. HBV-2
There is no form but shape! Rant Block. Michael McClure. EAS
There is no frigate like a book. Emily Dickinson. FPL; GoJo; MoAmPo; NIP; OBCA; PoLF; PoPl; SiSoSe; SoSe; TAP; TrGrPo; YeAr
(Book, A.) FaPON; TreFS
There Is No God. Arthur Hugh Clough. *See* "There Is No God," the Wicked Saith.
There is no God, as I was taught in youth. John Masefield. *Fr.* Sonnets ("Long long ago"). CMoP; HBV-2; WGRP
"There is no God," the foolish saith. Convinced by Sorrow. Elizabeth Barrett Browning. *Fr.* The Cry of the Human. BLRP; WBLP
"There Is No God," the Wicked Saith. Arthur Hugh Clough. *Fr.* Dipsychus. NBM; TreFS
(Spirit's Song, The.) LoBV
(There Is No God.) BLPL; NOBE
There is no great and no small. The Informing Spirit. Emerson. AWP
There is no happy life. Love's Matrimony. William Cavendish. SeCePo
There is no Job but cries to God and hopes. A Copy of Verses. John Wilson. SCAP
There is no joy in water apart from the sun. Song. Ralph Nixon Currey. PeSA
There is no light in any path of Heaven. The Dark Road. Ethel Clifford. HBV-2
There is no Lover hee or shee. A Paradox. Aurelian Townshend. AnAnS-2; SeCP
There is no memorial site. For Brother Malcolm. Edward S. Spriggs. CAD
There is no more good water. No More Good Water. *Unknown.* BluL
There is no music now in all Arkansas. Variations for Two Pianos. Donald Justice. NYBP
There is no music that man has heard. A Sea Lyric. William Hamilton Hayne. EtS
There Is No Name So Sweet on Earth, *with music.* George W. Bethune. AH
(Blessed Name, The.) BLRP
There is no one in the picture. Painting of a White Gate and Sky. Louise Erdrich. TWSS
There Is No Opera like "Lohengrin." John Wheelwright. NYBP; WhC
There is no page or servant, most or least. The Seventh Property. Sir Thomas More. *Fr.* The Twelve Properties or Conditions of a Lover. EnRePo
There is no peace with you. Enigma. Jessie Redmond Fauset. PoNe

"There is no permanence," you sagely said. Two Sonnets for a Lost Love, I. Samuel A. DeWitt. GoYe
There Is No Place. Aleksander Wat, *tr. fr. Polish by* Isaac Komem. VWA
There is no place in paradise. Guillaume de Lorris *and* Jean de Meun. *Fr.* The Romance of the Rose. PBBP
There Is No Place to Hide. Gwendolyn MacEwen. *Fr.* The T. E. Lawrence Poems. NOBC
"There is no place to turn," she said. The Sensualists. Theodore Roethke. ErPo; NePoAm-2; UnTE
There is no point in work. Work. D. H. Lawrence. OBMV
There is no portrait. Robert Creeley Listens, Too. D. C. Berry. BXAP
There is no power to change. Permanence. Francis Meynell. HBMV
There is no quenching of the other thirst. Hagar. Elisabeth Eybers, *tr. by author.* PeSA
There Is No Reason Why Not to Look at Death. Robert Sward. CoPo
There is no rest for her, and sleep has left her bed. *Gond Oral Tradition, tr. by* V. Elwin *and* S. Hivale. WTO
There is no rhyme that is half so sweet. Proem. Madison Cawein. AA; BoNaP
There is no roof in all the world. Waiting for the Morning. *Unknown.* STF
There [*or* Ther] is no rose of such virtue [*or* swich vertu]. Rosa Mystica [*or* The Rose That Bore Jesu *or* Two Carols to Our Lady]. *Unknown.* ACP; GoBC; ISi; OxBM
There is no sense in asking those who fought. Anabasis. Eithne Wilkins. NeBP
There is no siding for the brain. Listening to a Broadcast. John Manifold. WaP
There is no silence in the earth—so silent. Emily Dickinson. FaBoEE
There is no silence in their going down. New Year, 1916. Ada M. Harrison. SUMH
There is no silence upon the earth or under the earth like the silence under the sea. Silences. E. J. Pratt. NOBC; OBCV; PoCh
There is no silk nor worm to spin it. There Is No. Faye Kicknosway. GeTw
There is no sky today. Echoes of birds. Counterparts. Stephen Dobyns. PoA
There is no sorrow. Away. Walter de la Mare. NoP
There is no sorrow anywhere. Homeward Bound. L. Frank Tooker. EtS
There is no surrealist blood. The Blood Supply in New York City Is Low. Terry Stokes. NYP
There is no sweeter sight, I swear, in Heaven. The Crimson Cherry Tree. Henry Treece. WaP
There is no thing in all the world but love. The Camel-Rider. *Unknown, tr. by* Wilfrid Scawen Blunt. AWP
There Is No Unbelief. Elizabeth York Case. HBV-2; TreFS; WBLP; WGRP
(Faith, *wr. at. to* Edward Bulwer-Lytton.) TRV
There is no vacancy in this house. Jessica Scarbrough. LFAC
There is no vacant chair. The loving meet. Afterward. Elizabeth Stuart Phelps Ward. HBV-2
There Is No Word for Goodbye. Mary TallMountain. STE
There is no worldly pleasure here below. The Exercise of Affection. Sir Robert Ayton. BSV
There is no wrath in the stars. Lord Dunsany. Songs from an Evil Wood, I. HBV-2
There Is None like Her. Tennyson. *Fr.* Maud. FaBoEn; OBNC
There Is None, O None but You. Thomas Campion. EIL; HBV-1; OBSC
There Is None to Help. Chad Walsh. *Fr.* The Psalm of Christ. TrCP
There is not a grand inspiring thought. Mother. Emily Taylor. PGD
There is not a poem in sight. Writing while My Father Dies. Linda Pastan. PCP
There is not half so warm a fire. Against Fulfillment of Desire. *Unknown.* TrGrPo
There is not in the wide world a valley so sweet. The Meeting of the Waters. Thomas Moore. AnIL; NBM; OxBoLi; PoEL-4
There Is Nothin' like a Dame. Oscar Hammerstein II. OBAL
There is nothing as sweet as independence. Independence. Adebayo Faleti, *tr. by* Bakare Gbadamosi *and* Ulli Beier. PBA
There Is Nothing False in Thee. Kenneth Patchen. PoPl
There Is Nothing New in New York. Muguel Piñero. NYP
There is nothing to save, now all is lost. Nothing to Save. D. H. Lawrence. SOTW
There is one flower. Fleshflower. William Pitt Root. GeTw
There is one form of life to which I unconditionally surrender. Oh, Please Don't Get Up! Ogden Nash. NePA
There is one grief worse than any other. Daughter. Ellen Bryant Voigt. AMV-80
There is one Mind, one omnipresent Mind. Religious Musings. Samuel Taylor Coleridge. WGRP
There is one sin: to call a green leaf gray. Ecclesiastes. G. K. Chesterton. MoBrPo
There is one story and one story only. To Juan at the Winter Solstice. Robert Graves. CMoP; CoBMV; EBEV; FaBoMo; LiTB; LiTM; MoBrPo; MoPo; MP; NoAM; OAEL-2; SeCeV; TwCP
There is one sure way. The Fourth Option. Henry Rasof. AMV-80
There is one that has a head without an eye. A Riddle. Christina Rossetti. OxBChV
There is one who sits in his room. The Ancestors. Anita Barrows. VWA
There is only one love. Sappho, Be Comforted. William Carlos Williams. NePoAm-2
There Is Only One of Everything. Margaret Atwood. NOBC
There Is Pleasure in the Pathless Woods. Byron. *See* Sea, The.
There is pleasure in the wet, wet clay. The Lie. Kipling. NOBL
There Is Power. Joe Hill. FSW
There is red/ on the clown-lady's lips. Toulouse Lautrec. Astrid Tollefsen, *tr. by* Nadia Christensen. PBWP
There is silence that saith, "Ah, me!" Golden Silence. Christina Rossetti. NBM
There Is Snowdrift on the Mountain. W. P. Ker. PoSH
There is so much good in the worst of us. Charity [*or* Good and Bad]. *At. to* Edward Wallis Hoch. BLPA; TreFS
There is so much loveliness gone out of the world. The Triumph of Doubt. John Peale Bishop. EaLo
There is some beauty in sorrow. Placing a $2 Bet for a Man Who Will Never Go to the Horse Races Any More. Diane Wakoski. UnPo
There is some demon turning me into an old man. The Banjo. Robert Winner. FF
There is some great sensitivity I want to rip. Nightmares: Part Three. Lynn Moskowitz. AMV-81
There is some that like the city. Ridin'. Charles Badger Clark, Jr. BPAW
There is some will talk of lords and knights. Robin Hood's Delight. *Unknown.* ESPB
There is someone naked flying alongside the airplane. Centerfold Reflected in a Jet Window. Sandra McPherson. GeTw; MAYP
There Is Something. Deborah Pope. AMV-81
There is something about a Martini. A Drink with Something in It. Ogden Nash. PoPl
There is something between us. Breasts. Donald Hall. OBAL
There Is Something I Want to Say. Alex Kuo. BrSi
There is something in the autumn that is native to my blood. A Vagabond Song. Bliss Carman. FaPON; GN; HBV-1; HBVY; PoSC
There is something of every good-bye in this. There Is Something. Deborah Pope. AMV-81
There is somewhere a Secret Garden, which none hath seen. The Secret Garden. Robert Nichols. WGRP
There is sorrow enough in the natural way. The Power of the Dog. Kipling. BLPA; BLPL; BoAnP; GDP
There is stone in me that knows stone. Kathleen Raine. *Fr.* Rock. ImOP
There Is Strength in the Soil. Arthur Stringer. OHIP
There Is Sweet Music Here. Tennyson. *See* Choric Song: "There is sweet music here that softer falls."
There is that whispering gallery where. Letter to a Young Poet. George Barker. ChMP
There is the caw of a crow. Jonathan Houghton. Edgar Lee Masters. *Fr.* Spoon River Anthology. OxBA
There is the loneliness of peopled places. Solitude. Babette Deutsch. HBMV
There is the moon, there is the sun. The Universe. Mary Britton Miller. RHPC
There is the morning shuffle of traffic confined. City Walk-up, Winter 1969. Carolyn Forché. MAYP
There is the prayer of the father. The Prayers. Howard Schwartz. VWA
There is the star bloom of the moss. Forest. Jean Garrigue. LiTM; NOBA
There is this cave. The Jewel. James Wright. CAPP; CoAP
There is this distance between me and what I see. Still Poem 9. Philip Lamantia. NeAP
There is, this moment, a man who knows. Prisoner Aboard the S.S. Beagle. Calvin Murry. LFAC
There is unknown dust that is near us. Surprised by Evening. Robert Bly. CAPP; NaP; VGW
There is Whittier, whose swelling and vehement heart. Whittier. James Russell Lowell. *Fr.* A Fable for Critics. AmPP; AP; NOBA; OxBA
There is wisdom in the Bible. The Bible. Dorothy Conant Stroud. STF
There is wonder past all wonder. The Ways of Living Things. Jack Prelutsky. RHPC
There Is Yet Time. Arvel Steece. PGD
There isn't anything that you won't do. Aerosol. Harold Witt. SOTS
There Isn't Enough Bread. Charles Culhane. LFAC
There isn't much a man can do. The Jellyfish. William Pitt Root. BoAnP
There Isn't Time. Eleanor Farjeon. FaPON
"There it is!/ You play beside a death-bed like a child." Elizabeth Barrett Browning. *Fr.* Aurora Leigh. BrRo

There it is again! I'd wondered. Paper Words. William Franklin. LFAC
There it is, the jagged sprawl of the familiar. Return, Starting Out. Daniel Halpern. MAYP
There it lies. The Foundered Tram. Harold Monro. BrPo
There it was, word for word. The Poem That Took the Place of a Mountain. Wallace Stevens. LCAP
There leeft a may, an a weel-far'd may. Katharine Jaffray. *Unknown.* ESPB
There leeved a wee man at the fit o yon hill. Get Up and Bar the Door. *Unknown.* ESPB
There Let Thy Bleeding Branch Atone. Emily Brontë. SeCePo
There leviathan/ Hugest of living creatures. Leviathan. Milton. *Fr.* Paradise Lost, VII. AmMo
There lies a city inaccessible. The Unknown City. Sir Charles G. D. Roberts. CaP
There lies a cold corpse upon the sands. Death Song. Robert Stephen Hawker. OBNC; OBRV; OBVV
There lies a little city in the hills. Home. Edward Rowland Sill. HBV-2
There lies a lone isle in the tropic seas. Easter Island. Frederick George Scott. OBCV
There lies a somnolent lake. In the Past. Trumbull Stickney. NOBA; OxBA
There lies a vale [*or* There is a dale] in Ida, lovelier. Oenone. Tennyson. OAEP; OBRV; ViBoPo; VLP
There lies afar behind a western hill. The Town without a Market. James Elroy Flecker. MoBrPo
There lies the port; the vessel puffs her sail. Tennyson. *Fr.* Ulysses. EtS
There! little girl, don't cry! A Life-Lesson. James Whitcomb Riley. AA; FPL; HBV-1; PoLF; TreFS
There liv'd a lady in Lauderdale. She's Hoy'd Me Out o' Lauderdale. *Unknown.* CoMu
There livd a laird down into Fife. The Wife Wrapt in Wether's Skin. *Unknown.* ESPB
There livd a lass in yonder dale. *See* There lived a lass . . .
There livd a lord on yon sea-side. Fair Annie. *Unknown.* ESPB
There liv'd a man in yonder glen. Johnie Blunt. *Unknown.* OxBB
There liv'd, as authors tell, in days of yore. The Nun's Priest's Tale. Chaucer, *mod. version by* Dryden. *Fr.* The Canterbury Tales. OBVE
There liv'd of late in Luteners Lane. A Westminster Wedding; or, Like unto Like, Quoth the Devil to the Collier. *Unknown.* CoMu
There lived a carl in Kellyburnbraes. Kellyburnbraes. *Unknown.* OxBB
There lived a fat old lady, in London she did dwell. The Old Lady of London. *Unknown.* AmFP
There Lived a King. W. S. Gilbert. *Fr.* The Gondoliers. FiBHP; PoPle; WhC
(King Goodheart.) InMe
There Lived a Lady in Milan. William Rose Benét. HBMV
There lived [*or* livd] a lass in yonder dale. Katharine Jaffray. *Unknown.* BaBo; ESPB; ViBoFo
There lived a man at the foot of a hill. Get Up and Bar the Door. *Unknown.* EnSB
There lived a Puddy in a well. The Puddy and the Mouse. *Unknown.* GBP
There lived a sage in days of yore. A Tragic Story. Adelbert von Chamisso, *tr. by* Thackeray. FaPON; HBV-2; HBVY; MoShBr; OnMSP
There lived a small hermaphrodite beside the silver Brent. The Waif. Walter de la Mare. FaBoNo
There lived a wife at Usher's Well. The Wife of Usher's Well. *Unknown.* AWP; BSV; CH; ChTr; EBEV; EnRP; EnSB; ESPB; FaBoBa; GoTS; HBV-2; LiTB; LoBV; NOBE; NoP; OAEL-1; OAEP; OBEV; OnMSP; OxBS; PoEL-1; PrIm; SeCeV; TreF; TrGrPo; ViBoFo
There Lived among the Untrodden Ways. Hartley Coleridge. BXAP; SpRo
There lived an old man in the Kingdom of Tess. The New Vestments. Edward Lear. RHPC
There lived an old woman at Lynn. *Unknown.* OxBChV
There lived in ancient Scribbletown a wise old writer-man. Puzzled. Carolyn Wells. OBCA
There lives a good-for-nothing cat. The Lazy Pussy. Palmer Cox. OBCA
There lives a maid down under yon brae. Katherine Jaffray. *Unknown.* OxBB
There lives a man in Rynie's land. Lang Johnny More. *Unknown.* ESPB
There lives a pig in Georgia's far land. Pipes in the Sty. John Kendall. WhC
There lives in/ my childhood street. Self Portrait 4. Tove Ditlevsen, *tr. by* Ann Freeman. WPOW
There may be a basement to the Atlantic. Somebody's Gone. Charles Henri Ford. EAS
There may be agony in furnished rooms. The Room. Francis Webb. *Fr.* Leichhardt in Theatre. PoAu-2
There [*or* Ther] mighte men the royal eagle find. Seynt Valentynes Day. Chaucer. *Fr.* The Parliament of Fowls. PB; PBBP
There mounts in squalls a sort of rusty mire. The Exile's Return. Robert Lowell. AmPP; AP; MiAP; NePA; OxBA
There mournful cypress grew in greatest store. The Garden of Proserpina. Spenser. *Fr.* The Faerie Queene, II, 7. ChTr
There must be fairy miners. Buttercups. Wilfrid Thorley. FaPON; HBV-1; HBVY; OBVV
There must be magic. Otherwise. Aileen Fisher. SoPo; SUS
There must be something that links them all. The Obsession. Rosy Liggett. AMV-80
There, my blessing with thee! To Thine Own Self Be True. Shakespeare. *Fr.* Hamlet, I, iii. FaFP; LiTB
There, my lad, lie the Articles. Scene from a Play, Acted at Oxford, Called "Matriculation." Thomas Moore. NBM; OBSV
There never breathed a man, who, when his life. Epitaphs, IV. Gabriello Chiabrera, *tr. by* Wordsworth. AWP
There never shall be the strange beauties of Vignettes. The Ideal. Baudelaire, *tr. by* Arthur Symons. SyP
There never yet was honest man. Loving and Beloved. Sir John Suckling. CaPo; FaBoEn; OBS
There never yet was woman made. Woman's Constancy. Sir John Suckling. AnAnS-2; CaPo
There now, where the first crumb. Solitude. Charles Simic. GP
There on his knee, behind a box tree shrinking. Joshua Sylvester. *Fr.* Du Bartas: His Divine Weeks and Works, the Seventh Day of the First Week. PBBP
There, on the Darkened Deathbed. John Masefield. *See* Sonnet: "There, on the darkened deathbed, dies the brain."
"There, on the left!" said the colonel. Marthy Virginia's Hand. George Parsons Lathrop. PAH
There on the sea sails wandered. The Names of Georgian Women. Bella Akhmadulina, *tr. by* Stanley Noyes *and* Olga Carlisle. BoWoP
There on the top of the down. June Bracken and Heather. Tennyson. EnLoPo; PPoe
There once the walls. A Tale. Edward Thomas. ChTr
There once was a bonnie Scotch laddie. Limerick. *Unknown.* WhC
There once was a cow with a double udder. The Cow. Theodore Roethke. FiBHP; OBAL; OBCA
There once was a Dormouse who lived in a bed. The Dormouse and the Doctor. A. A. Milne. WhC
There once was a fastidious yak. The Fastidious Yak. Oliver Herford. TDH
There once was a girl of New York. Limerick. Cosmo Monkhouse. NA
There once was a girl of Pitlochry. Limerick. *Unknown.* CenHV
There once was a guy named Othello. Shakespeare Might Have Boiled Othello. Edwin Meade Robinson. Limericised Classics, II. HBMV
There once was a happy hyena. The Happy Hyena. Carolyn Wells. TDH
There once was a kind armadillo. The Kind Armadillo. Oliver Herford. TDH
There once was a man from Nantucket. Limerick. *Unknown.* TreF
There once was a man, named Power. Clock Time by the Geyser. John White. ShM
There once was a man of Bengal. Limerick [*or* Bengal]. *Unknown.* CenHV; OnUR
There once was a man of Calcutta. Limerick. *Unknown.* WhC
There once was a man [*or* There was a young man] who said, "Damn!" Limerick [*or* Determinism *or* Predestination]. Maurice Evan Hare. CenHV; FaBoCo; NOBL; OxBoLi; PoPle
There once was a man who said, "God." Limerick [*or* Idealism]. Ronald Arbuthnott Knox. FaBoCo; NOBL; OxBoLi; PoPle
There once was a man who said, "How." Limerick. *Unknown.* NA
There once was a man who said, "Oh." The Disobliging Bear. Carolyn Wells. TDH
There once was a Master of Arts. Master of Arts. Cosmo Monkhouse. TDH
There once was a noble ranger. Mustang Gray. *Unknown.* CoSo
There once was a painter named Scott. Limerick. Dante Gabriel Rossetti. CenHV
There once was a peach on a tree. The Peach. Abbie Farwell Brown. TDH
There once was a person of Benin. Limerick. Cosmo Monkhouse. NA
There once was a pious young priest. Limerick [*or* The Pious Young Priest]. *Unknown.* NIP; TDH
There Once Was a Puffin. Florence Page Jaques. NTCP; SoPo; TiPo
There once was a Renaissance man. Limerick. *Unknown.* PeHV
There once was a sensitive cat. The Sensitive Cat. Alice Brown. TDH
There once was a spinster of Ealing. Limerick. *Unknown.* NIP
There once was a Union maid. Union Maid. Woody Guthrie. FSW
There once was a warden of Wadham. Limerick. *Unknown.* PeHV
There once was a wicked young minister. Conrad Aiken. OBAL
There once was a Willow, and he was very old. The Willow-Man. Juliana Horatia Ewing. OxBChV

There once was a woman named Jacqueline Gray. Jacqueline Gray. Kenneth Pitchford. *Fr.* Good for Nothing Man. CoPo
There once was a wonderful wizard. Limerick. Conrad Aiken. FaBoNo
There once was a wood, and a very thick wood. The First Tooth. William Brighty Rands. HBV-1; HBVY
There Once Was a Young Man Named Hall. *Unknown.* ShM
There once was an old man of Blackheath. Limerick. *Unknown.* CenHV
There once was an old man of Lyme. Limerick. *At. to* Edward Lear, *also at. to* Cosmo Monkhouse. NA
There once was an old sailor my grandfather knew. The Old Sailor. A. A. Milne. CenHV
There once were some people called Sioux. The American Indian. *Unknown.* FaBoCo; FiBHP
There once were three brothers from merry Scotland. Sir Andrew Barton. *Unknown.* AmFP
There once were two cats of Kilkenny. *See* There wanst was two cats of Kilkenny.
There ought to be capital punishment for cars. Thoughts on Capital Punishment. Rod McKuen. InPK
There our murdered brother lies. The Wake of William Orr. William Drennan. OnYI; OxBI
There out of hell the Old One bellows. Lamentations of the Fallen Angels. *Unknown, tr. by* Charles W. Kennedy. *Fr.* Christ and Satan. AnOE
There, pay it, James! 'tis cheaply earned. Vers de Société. H. D. Traill. Par
There piped a piper in the wood. The Magic Piper. E. L. Marsh. SiSoSe
There pipes the wood-lark, and the song thrush there. Fragment. Thomas Gray. FM
There rolls the deep where grew the tree. In Memoriam A. H. H., CXXIII. Tennyson. FaBoRV; HAP; NOBE; SeCePo; SeCeV
There sat a happy fisherman. The Reed. Mikhail Yuryevich Lermontov, *tr. by* J. J. Robbins. AWP
There sat an old man on a rock. Too Late. Fitz Hugh Ludlow. PoLF
There sat down, once, a thing on Henry's heart. John Berryman. *Fr.* Dream Songs. CAPP; HAP; NMP; NoP
There sat two glasses filled to the brim. The Two Glasses. Ella Wheeler Wilcox. BLPA; BLPL
There sat upon the linden tree. The Linden Tree. Dietmar von Aist, *tr. by* Edgar Taylor. PoPl
There sate the seniors of the Trojan Race. Homer, *tr. by* Pope. *Fr.* The Iliad, III. OBVE
There set out, slowly, for a different world. A War. Randall Jarrell. DFF
There Shall Always Be the Church. T. S. Eliot. *Fr.* The Rock. TRV
There shall be beds full of light odours blent. The Lovers' Death. Baudelaire, *tr. by* "Michael Field." SyP
There shall be no more songs. Black Power. Alvin Saxon. PoBA
There Shall Be No Night. Bible, *N.T.* Revelation, XXII: 1-5. TrGrPo
There shall come from out this noise of strife and groaning. Sir Lewis Morris. *Fr.* Brotherhood. PGD
There She Blows! *Unknown.* EtS
There She Is. Linda Gregg. NPGG
There she is. The Nike of Samothrace. Hilda Morley. FAZ
There she is, out in the rain. Silly Dog. Myra Cohn Livingston. GDP
There she sits a'-smokin'. Motorcycle Irene. Skip Spence. MAT
There she sits in her Island-home. England. Gerald Massey. HBV-2
There She Stands a Lovely Creature. *Unknown.* AmFP; OLR
There should be no despair for you. Sympathy. Emily Brontë. OAEP
There shouldn't be a North. The Carolinas. David Ray. TAT
There sits a bird on every tree. Sing Heigh-Ho! Charles Kingsley. HBV-1
There sits a fair couple courting. The Jealous Brothers. *Unknown.* AmFP
There sits a piper on the hill. The Piper on the Hill. Dora Sigerson Shorter. HBV-1; HBVY; OnYI
There smiled the smooth Divine, unused to wound. The Smooth Divine. Timothy Dwight. *Fr.* The Triumph of Infidelity. AA; PPON; WGRP
There souls of men are bought and sold. London. Blake. *Fr.* The Human Image. ChTr
There, spring lambs jam the sheepfold. In air. Watercolor of Grantchester Meadows. Sylvia Plath. LCAP; NYBP; SBG
There stand three mills on Manor Water. Manor Water. *Unknown.* GBP
There stands a lady on a mountain. Kiss in the Ring. *Unknown.* OxBoLi
There stands a lonely pine-tree. Song. Heine, *tr. by* Emma Lazarus. TrJP
There stood an unsold captive in the mart. Parrhasius. Nathaniel Parker Willis. AA
There sunk the greatest, nor the worst of men. Napoleon. Byron. *Fr.* Childe Harold's Pilgrimage, III. OBRV
There the black river, boundary to hell. The Southern Road. Dudley Randall. CNA; NNP; PoBA
There the companions of his fall, o'erwhelmed. Immortal Hate. Milton. *Fr.* Paradise Lost, I. NOBE
There the most daintie Paradise on ground. Spenser. *Fr.* The Faerie Queene, II, 12. EBEV
"There the Parthenon, & there." Slides. Jennifer Maiden. CBAP
There the voluptuous nightingales. Semichorus II. Shelley. *Fr.* Prometheus Unbound, II, ii. PBBP; ViBoPo
There, there is no mountain within miles. Nebraska. Jon Swan. RFM
There, there where those black spruces crowd. Ragged Island. Edna St. Vincent Millay. NoP
There they are/ Thirty at the corner. The Blackstone Rangers. Gwendolyn Brooks. BALP; CAD; NoAM; PoBA
There they are in the billiard room of the faculty club. The Modern Chinese History Professor Plays Pool Every Tuesday and Thursday. James Baker Hall. TAT
There they are, my fifty men and women. One Word More. Robert Browning. FiP; HBV-1; OAEP; PoEL-5; ViBoPo; VLP
There they are now. Three Sentences for a Dead Swan. James Wright. NaP; NoAM; NOBA
There they dismounting, drew their weapons bold. Britomart in the House of Busirane. Spenser. *Fr.* The Faerie Queene, III, 11-12. FiP
There they go. Seed Journey. Gregory Corso. VGW
There they go marching all in step so gay! Joining the Colours. Katharine Tynan. SUMH
There they stand, on their ends, the fifty faggots. Fifty Faggots. Edward Thomas. BrPo; MoAB; MoBrPo
There they were. A Day at the Races. Louis Phillips. PH
There they were, as if our memory hatched them. Triptych. Seamus Heaney. CIP
There they were many, O God, so many. They. Mani Leib, *tr. by* David G. Roskies *and* Hillel Schwartz. VWA
There 'tis the Shepherd's task the winter long. The Shepherd. Wordsworth. *Fr.* The Prelude, VIII. OBNC
There used to be a picket fence. The Picket Fence. Christian Morgenstern, *tr. by* Max Knight. GrPl
There used to be gods in everything, and now they're gone. The Companions. Howard Nemerov. NYBP
There walked on Plover's shady banks. Driving Saw-Logs on the Plover. *Unknown.* AS
There wanst was [*or* once were] two cats of Kilkenny. The Kilkenny Cats [*or* Limerick]. *Unknown.* CenHV; FaFP; ShM; TreF
There was a bad poet named Clough. On Arthur Hugh Clough. Swinburne. FaBoEE
There was a battle in her face. The Battle. W. H. Davies. BrPo
There was a battle in the north. Geordie. *Unknown.* BaBo; ESPB; FaBoBa; OxBB
There was a blacksmith in my breast. The Dead Sheep. Andrew Young. FM
There Was a Boy. Wordsworth. *Fr.* The Prelude, V. ChER; FaBoCh; FaBoEn; FaBoRV; OBNC; OBRV; PoEL-4
(Winander Lake.) FiP
There was a Boy bedded in bracken. Carol. John Short. DTC; FaBoCh; FaBoTw
There was a boy of other days. Lincoln. Nancy Byrd Turner. FaPON; RHPC; TiPo
There was a boy whose name was Jim. Jim, Who Ran Away from His Nurse, and Was Eaten by a Lion. Hilaire Belloc. CenHV; ChTr; EvOK; HBMV; OxBChV; ShM
There was a boy whose name was Phinn. A Fishing Song. William Brighty Rands. CenHV
There was a Boy, ye knew him well, ye Cliffs. There Was a Boy [*or* Winander Lake]. Wordsworth. *Fr.* The Prelude, V. ChER; FaBoCh; FaBoEn; FaBoRV; FiP; OBNC; OBRV; PoEL-4
There was a brave girl of Connecticut. Benjamin. Ogden Nash. NePA
There was a brave knight of Lorraine. A Brave Knight. Mary Mapes Dodge. TDH
There was a bridge that Rozinante would not cross. The Bridge of Heraclitus. George Reavey. BIrV
There was a bright and happy tree. The Happy Tree. Gerald Gould. WGRP
There was a bright fellow named Peter. The 'Skeeter and Peter. Marie Bruckman MacDonald. TDH
There was a brightness in the branches. The Leaves. Ron Loewinsohn. GP
There Was a Brisk Girle. *Unknown.* CoMu
(Brisk Girl, The, *shorter vers.*) UnTE
There was a captain-general who ruled in Vera Cruz. El Capitan-General. Charles Godfrey Leland. AA; HBV-2; YaD
There was a chap—I forget his name. The Gemlike Flame. R. P. Lister. DBV; FiBHP
There Was a Child Went Forth. Walt Whitman. AmPP; AWP; BiP; InPS; OxBA; SoSe; TAP
"There was a child went forth every day," *sel.* RFM
There was a clever skipper, in Akron he did dwell. The Clever Skipper. *Unknown.* AmFP
There was a composer named Bong. Hit Tune. *Unknown.* TDH
There Was a Crimson Clash of War. Stephen Crane. UnPo

There was a crooked man, and he went [*or* walked] a crooked mile. Mother Goose. FaBoBe; FaFP; HBV-1; HBVY; OxBoLi; OxNR; SoPo
There Was a Dance, Sweetheart. Joy Harjo. TWSS
There was a dark and awful wood. Wood. Thomas Hornsby Ferril. PoRA
There Was a Darkness in This Man. John Gould Fletcher. *Fr.* Lincoln. OFD; PAL
There was a dear lady of Eden. Limerick. *Unknown.* NA
There was a desperado from the wild and woolly West. The Desperado. *Unknown.* FSW
There was a devil and his name was I. Malzah's Song. Charles Heavysege. *Fr.* Saul. OBCV
There was a difference of opinion. The Poem as Striptease. Philip Dacey. PPJ
There was a duck egg as green as the evening sky. Ulinda. David Campbell. CBAP
There was a duke's daughter lived in York. The Cruel Mother. *Unknown.* ESPB
There was a fair lady far crossed in love. The Fair Maid by the Seashore. *Unknown.* BaBo
There was a fair maiden who lived on the shore. The Fair Maid by the Shore. *Unknown.* AmFP
There was a fair young creature who lived by the seaside. The Silvery Tide. *Unknown.* AmFP
There was a faith-healer of Deal. Limerick [*or* Mind and Matter *or* Faith-Healer]. *Unknown.* CenHV; FaBoCo; FaFP; WhC
There was a farmer had a dog. Bingo. *Unknown.* FSW
There was a farmer had two sons. Bohunkus. *Unknown.* YaD
There was a farmer's son kept sheep upon a hill. Blow Away the Morning Dew. *Unknown.* FSW
There was a fat canon of Durham. Limerick. *Unknown.* WhC
There was a feeling, I know. A Still Life. Jascha Kessler. HoAn
There was a frank lady of Dedham. A Limerick of Frankness. "X. Y. Z." TDH
There was a Friar, a wanton one and merry. Chaucer, *mod. version by* Nevill Coghill. *Fr.* The Canterbury Tales: Prologue. BiP
There Was a Frog. *Unknown.* NA
There was a frozen tree that I wanted to paint. Vegas. Charles Bukowski. NoP
There was a gallant lady all in her tender youth. Canada-I-O. *Unknown.* AmFP
There was a gallant ship, and a gallant ship was she. The Golden Vanity [*or* The Sweet Trinity]. *Unknown.* CH; ESPB; ViBoFo
There was a gay damsel of Lynn. Limerick. *Unknown.* NA
There was a gay maiden lived down by the mill. The Ferry. George Henry Boker. AA
There was a gentle hostler. Gates and Doors. Joyce Kilmer. HBV-1; HBVY
There was a giant by the Orchard Wall. In the Orchard. James Stephens. RoGo; SO; WSC
There was a giant in times of old. The Dorchester Giant. Oliver Wendell Holmes. FaPON; OnMSP
There was a gifted Mexican who came up here to paint. Sad Story. Clarence Day. InMe
There was a girl in our town. *Unknown.* HBV-1; HBVY; OxNR
There was a good Canon of Durham. Limerick. William Ralph Inge. CenHV
There was a gray rat looked at me. Rat Riddles. Carl Sandburg. SO
There was a great commotion. The Lollypops. Cordia Thomas. SoPo
There was a great white wallbare, bare, bare. The Smoked Herring. Charles Cros, *tr. by* A. L. Lloyd. GrPl
There was a guy in utah. 8:00 A. M. Monday Morning. William Welsh. SOTS
There was a hag who kept two chambermaids. The Hag and the Slavies. La Fontaine, *tr. by* Edward Marsh. AWP; OBVE
There was a Jewish bandit who lived in a wood. Bandit. A. M. Klein. WHW
There was a jolly beggar, and a begging he was born. The Jolly Beggar. *At. to* James V, King of Scotland. CoMu; OxBB
There was a jolly blade that married a country maid. Dumb, Dumb, Dumb. *Unknown.* OnYI
There was a jolly fat frog that did in the river swim O. The Frog and the Crow. *Unknown.* GBP
There Was a Jolly Miller. Isaac Bickerstaff. *Fr.* Love in a Village, I. HBV-1; ViBoPo
(Song: "There was a jolly miller once," *st.* 1.) OBEC; OnYI
("There was a jolly miller once," *st.* 1.) OxNR
There was a jolly student with a medical degree. Similia Similibus. John Hunt Morgan. ShM
There was a jury sat at Perth. The Earl of Errol. *Unknown.* ESPB
There was a kind Curate of Kew. Limerick. *Unknown.* CenHV
There was a kind Lady called Gregory. James Joyce. FaBoEE
There Was a King. *Unknown.* OxBoLi
("There was a king, and he had three daughters.") OxNR
There was a king, and a very great king. Lady Diamond. *Unknown.* BaBo; ESPB
There was a King in Brentford, of whom no legends tell. The King of Brentford. Thackeray. HBV-1
There was a king met a king. *Unknown.* OxNR
There was a king of the north countree. The Twa Sisters. *Unknown.* ViBoFo
There was a knicht riding frae the east. Riddles Wisely Expounded [*or* Jennifer Gentle and Rosemary *or* There Was a Knight]. *Unknown.* CH; ESPB; FaBoBa; GBP; HBV-2; OxBoLi; ViBoFo
There was a Knight, a most distinguished man. Persons of the Prologue. Chaucer, *mod. version by* Nevill Coghill. *Fr.* The Canterbury Tales: Prologue. BiP
There was a knight, an he had a daughter. Erlinton. *Unknown.* ESPB
There was a knight and a lady bright. The Broomfield Hill. *Unknown.* ESPB; OxBB; ViBoFo
There Was a Knight, and He Was Young. *See* Baffled Knight, The.
There was a knight, in a summer's night. The Bonny Birdy. *Unknown.* ESPB
There was a lad was born in Kyle. Rantin, Rovin Robin [*or* Robin]. Burns. BSV; OxBS
There was a lady all skin and bone. The Skin-and-Bone Lady. *Unknown.* AmFP
There was a lady fair and gay. The Wife of Usher's Well. *Unknown.* ESPB; ViBoFo
There was a lady fine and gay. Willie o Winsbury. *Unknown.* ESPB
There was a lady in the north. The Dowie Dens of Yarrow. *Unknown.* FSW
There was a lady in this land. The Tinker. *Unknown.* CoMu
There was a lady lived at Leith. The Irishman and the Lady. William Maginn. HBV-2
There was a lady lived in a hall. Two Red Roses across the Moon. William Morris. EBVV; VLP
There was a lady lived in York. The Cruel Mother. *Unknown.* AmFP; FSW; OBET
There Was a Lady Loved a Swine. *Unknown.* *See* Lady Who Loved a Swine, The.
There was a lady of beauty rare. The Wife of Usher's Well. *Unknown.* AmFP
There was a lady of the North Country. Riddles Wisely Expounded. *Unknown.* ESPB
There was a lame soldier in time of the war. The Lame Soldier. *Unknown.* OuSiCo
There was a lass and a bonnie lass. The Nut-gathering Lass. Burns. UnTE
There was a Lass of Islington. The Lass of Islington [*or* The Fair Lass of Islington]. *Unknown.* CoMu; OxBB
There was a lily and rose sea-maiden. The Sea-Maiden. J. W. de Forest. EtS
There was a little boy and a little girl. Mother Goose. OxNR
There was a little boy went into a barn. *Unknown.* OxNR
There was a little, Elvish man. The Man Who Hid His Own Front Door. Elizabeth MacKinstry. FaPON; TiPo
There was a little family. The Little Family. *Unknown.* BaBo
There Was a Little Girl. *St.* 1, Mother Goose; *sts.* 2 *and* 3, *unknown, at. to* Longfellow. BLPA, *st.* 1; EvOK; FaFP; HBV-1; HBVY; NA; OxBChV, *st.* 1; RHPC, *st.* 1; TreF; YaD, *st.* 1
(Jemima, *diff. vers.*) FaBoCh
(Little Girl, The.) OxNR
There was a little guinea-pig. The Guinea-Pig [*or* A Guinea-Pig Song]. *Unknown.* NA; OxBChV; OxNR
There was a little lawny islet. The Isle. Shelley. SyP
There was a little maid, and she was afraid. *Unknown.* OxNR
There was a little man,/ And he had a little gun. Mother Goose. FaFP; HBV-1; HBVY; OxNR
There was a little man,/ and he wooed a little maid. Mother Goose. OxNR
There was a little man and he had a little can. No More Booze [*or* Fireman Save My Child]. *Unknown.* AS; OBAL; TrAS; TreF
There was a little one-eyed gunner. *Unknown.* OxNR
There was a little postage stamp. The Postage Stamp Lesson. *Unknown.* STF
There was a little rill of water, near the den. The Coyote. Carter Revard. VoR
There was a little ship in South Amerikee. The Sweet Trinity. *Unknown.* AmFP
There was a little turtle. The Little Turtle. Vachel Lindsay. FaPON; GoJo; NTCP; OBAL; OBCA; PDV; SoPo; SUS; TiPo
There was a little woman,/ As I have heard tell. *See* There was an old woman, as I've heard tell.

There was a lofty ship, and she put out to sea. The Golden Vanity. *Unknown.* FSW
There was a Lord in London town. Lady Isabel and the Elf Knight. *Unknown.* FSW
There was a lord of worthy fame. The Lady Isabella's Tragedy. *Unknown.* GBP
There was a lovely lady Gnu. The Gnu Wooing. Burges Johnson. HBVY
There Was a Maid. *Unknown. See* Maid of Kent, A.
There was a maid, richly arrayd. Blancheflour and Jellyflorice. *Unknown.* ESPB
There Was a Maid Went to the Mill. *Unknown.* GBP
There Was a Man. Stephen Crane. *See* There Was a Man with a Tongue of Wood.
There was a man,/ And his name was Dob. *Unknown.* OxNR
There was a man/ who collected facts. Introduction of the Shopping Cart. Gerald Costanzo. MAYP
There was a man/ Whose name was Pete. The Tragedy of Pete. Joseph S. Cotter, Sr. CDC
There was a man a-coming from the south. Trooper and Maid. *Unknown.* AmFP
There was a man and he had nought. Mother Goose. OxNR
There Was a Man and He Was Mad. *Unknown.* GBP
There was a man from Singapore. Some Sound Advice from Singapore. John Ciardi. GrPl
There was a man, he went mad. *Unknown.* OxNR
There was a man in Arkansaw. Tuscaloosa Sam. "Orpheus C. Kerr." OBAL
There was a man in Denver. The Man Who Thought He Was a Horse. Thomas Hornsby Ferril. NePoAm-2
There was a man in olden times. Dives and Lazarus. *Unknown.* AmFP
There was a man in our town. It Happens, Often. Edwin Meade Robinson. HBMV
There was a man in the land of Uz whose name was Job. Bible, *O.T. Fr.* Job. NAWM-1
There was a man lived in the moon. Aiken Drum. *Unknown.* FaBoCh; FaBoNo; OxNR
There was a man lived in the west. Dandoo. *Unknown.* TrAS
There was a man lived under the hill. The Devil and the Farmer's Wife. *Unknown.* TrAS
There was a man made a thing. *Unknown.* GBP
There was a man named Johnny Sands, who married Betty Hague. Johnny Sands. *Unknown.* AmFP
There was a man, now please take note. The Goat [*or* Bill Groggin's Goat]. *Unknown.* BLPL; FSW; OnUR; PoLF
There was a man of double deed. *Unknown.* GBP; InPK; OxNR
There was a man of our town. Mother Goose. FaFP; HBV-1; HBVY
There was a man of Thessaly. The Man of Thessaly. *Unknown.* FaBoCo; FaBoNo; OxNR
There was a man rode through our town. *Unknown.* OxNR
There was a man that lived in England. Lord Bateman. *Unknown.* FSW
There was a man who dwelt alone. Shadow-Bride. J. R. R. Tolkien. SO
There was a man who found two leaves. The Fall. Russell Edson. LCAP
There was a man who had a clock. The Sad Tale of Mr. Mears. *Unknown.* HBV-2; TreFS; YaD
There was a man who had no eyes. *Unknown.* OxNR
There was a man who married a maid. She laughed as he led her home. I Love My Love. Helen Adam. NeAP; NMM; WPOW
There was a man who watched the river flow. The Cranes of Ibycus. Emma Lazarus. AA
There was a man whom Sorrow named his friend. The Sad Shepherd. W. B. Yeats. MOS; PP
There Was a Man with a Tongue of Wood. Stephen Crane. War Is Kind, XVI. LiTA; NePA
(There Was a Man.) MoAmPo
There was a man within our tenement. The Spritely Dead. Oscar Williams. *Fr.* Variations on a Theme. LiTA; NePA
There was a man, don't mind his name. The Deserter. Winifred M. Letts. SUMH
"There was a marriage in Cana of Galilee. . .And both." The Bridegroom of Cana. Marjorie Pickthall. TrCP
There Was a Monkey. *Unknown.* NA
("There was a monkey climbed a tree.") OxNR
There was a naked greatness in those times. The Festival. Robert Eyres Landor. *Fr.* The Impious Feast. OBRV
There Was a Naughty Boy. Keats. *See* Song about Myself.
There was a perfect tree. 229. José Garcia Villa. PoPl
There was a person. Revenge Fable. Ted Hughes. TW
There was a Pig that sat alone. A Pig-Tale [*or* The Melancholy Pig]. "Lewis Carroll." *Fr.* Sylvie and Bruno Concluded. FaPON; WiR
There was a piper had a cow. Mother Goose. OxNR
There was a pond on which we learned to skate. A Skater's Waltz. Gray Burr. CoPo
There was a pond we'd fish. Thirteen, Full of Life. Graham Everett. WOLT
There was a poor chap called Rossetti. Limerick. Dante Gabriel Rossetti. CenHV
There was a powder the druggist had. Reflexes. Marvin Bell. Str
There Was a Presbyterian Cat. *Unknown.* FaBoCh
(Auld Seceder Cat, The.) FaBoCo
There was a princess of Bengal. Limerick. *At. to* Walter Parke. NA
There was a professor called Chesterton. A Professor Called Chesterton. W. S. Gilbert. TDH
There was a professor of Beaulieu. Materialism. C. E. M. Joad. FaBoCo
There was a queen that fell in love with a jolly sailor. The Sailor and the Shark. Paul Fort, *tr. by* Frederick York Powell. OBMV
There was a queer fellow named Woodin. Limerick [*or* A Queer Fellow Named Woodin]. "Cuthbert Bede." CenHV; TDH
There was a rat, for want of stairs. *Unknown.* OxNR
There was a rich Dutchman. Villkins and His Dinah. *Unknown.* BaBo
There was a rich lady, from England she came. The Brown Girl (B *vers.*). *Unknown.* BaBo
There was a rich lady, from London she came. A Rich Irish Lady. *Unknown.* AmFP
There was a rich lord, and lived in Forfar. Bonnie Annie. *Unknown.* ESPB
There was a rich man and he lived in Jerusalem. The Rich Man and the Poor Man. *Unknown.* FSW
There was a rich old rancher who/ lived in the country by. The Rambling Cowboy. *Unknown.* CoSo
There was a road ran past our house. The Unexplorer. Edna St. Vincent Millay. MoShBr; PoA; SUS
There was a roaring in the wind all night. Wordsworth. *Fr.* Resolution and Independence. BoNaP; CABA; ChER; EBEV; EnRP; HAP; InPS; LiTB; MasP; MAT; NOBE; NOCV; NoP; OAEL-2; OAEP; OBNC; OBRV; PoEL-4; PPP; TEP; TreFT
There was a Romish lady brought up in popery. The Romish Lady. *Unknown.* OuSiCo
There was a roof over our heads. Lost on September Trail, 1967. Alberto Ríos. FYAP
There was a rover from a western shore. Mother England. Edith M. Thomas. AA; HBV-2
There was a Russian came over the sea. Russian and Turk. Robert J. Burdette. NA
There was a sea captain lately come to shore. The Sea-Captain. *Unknown.* BaBo
There was a serpent who had to sing. The Serpent. Theodore Roethke. AmMo; RHPC
There was a shadow on the moon; I saw it poise and tilt, and go. The Shadow. Rose Macaulay. SUMH
There was a shepherd's dochter [*or* daughter]. The Knight and Shepherd's Daughter [*or* The Shepherd's Dochter]. *Unknown.* ESPB; OxBB; ViBoFo
There was a shepherd's son. Blow the Winds, I-Ho. *Unknown.* GBP; OxBoLi
There was a ship, and a ship of fame. William Glen. *Unknown.* BaBo
There was a ship called *The Golden Vanitie.* The Golden Vanitie. *Unknown.* EnSB
There was a ship of Rio. The Ship of Rio. Walter de la Mare. CenHV; EtS; MOS; PDV; PoPle; TiPo
There was a ship sailed from the North Countree. The Golden Vanity. *Unknown.* WiR
There was a sick man of Tobago. *Unknown.* OxBChV
There was a sightseer named Sue. A Sightseer Named Sue. *Unknown.* TDH
There was a slumbrous silence in the air. Richard Henry Horne. *Fr.* Orion. VLP
There was a small boy of Quebec. *See* There was a young boy of Quebec.
There was a small maiden named Maggie. Maggie [*or* A Shaggy Dog]. *Unknown.* OnUR; TDH
There was a snake that dwelt in Skye. The Fastidious Serpent. Henry Johnstone. HBV-2; HBVY
There was a sound of hunting in the mountains. Incident on a Front Not Far from Castel di Sangro. Harry Brown. NYBP
There was a sound of revelry by night. Waterloo [*or* The Eve of Waterloo *or* The Battle of Waterloo]. Byron. *Fr.* Childe Harold's Pilgrimage, III. BeLS; EBEV; FaBoBe; FaBoCh; FaBoEn; FaBV; FaFP; FiP; GN; HBV-2; NOBE; OBNC; OBRV; OBWP; TreF; TrGrPo; ViBoPo; WaaP; WBLP; WHA
There was a squire lived in this town. The Suffolk Miracle. *Unknown.* BaBo
There was a strange and unknown race. The New World. Paul Engle. AmFN
There was a strife 'twixt man and maid. Kipling. PV

There was a stunted handpost just on the crest. Near Lanivet, 1872. Thomas Hardy. AWP; CMoP; LoBV; NoAM
There was a sudden croon of lilies. The Martyrdom of St. Teresa. A. D. Hope. CBAP
There was a sunlit absence. Mossbawn: Two Poems in Dedication [*or* Sunlight]. Seamus Heaney. BIrV; CIP; NoP
There was a thing a full month old. *Unknown.* OxNR
There Was a Time. Edward Thomas. MMA
There was a time. Somewhere West. Andrew McCord Jones. LFAC
There was a time for discoveries. Voyage West. Archibald MacLeish. VGW
There was a time, O Lesbia, when you said Catullus was the only man. Catullus, *tr. fr. Latin by* Horace Gregory. NAWM-1
There was a time on this fair continent. Charles Mair. *Fr.* Tecumseh. NOBC; OBCV
There was a time (such songs begin this way). Inflation. Charles O. Hartman. PoA
There was a time when Death and I. Beyond Recall. Mary Emily Bradley. AA
There was a time when death was terror. New Fashions. George Moses Horton. OBAL
There was a time when I could fly, I swear it. I, Icarus. Alden Nowlan. NCSH
There was a time when I was very small. Childhood. Jens Baggesen, *tr. by* Longfellow. AWP
There was a time when meadow, grove, and stream. Ode: Intimations of Immortality from Recollections of Early Childhood. Wordsworth. AWP; BiP; BLPL; CABA; ChER; EnRP; FaBoRV; FaFP; FiP; GTBS; GTBS-P; HAP; HBV-1; HeIP; InvP; LiTB; LoBV; MasP; NAs; NOBE; NoP; OAEL-2; OAEP; OBEV; OBNC; OBRV; OHFP; PAI; PoEL-4; PPoe; PPP; PrIm; TEP; TreF, *abr.*; TrGrPo; SeCeV; ViBoPo; WHA
There was a time when Mother Nature made. First Miracle. Genevieve Taggard. HBMV
There was a time when the stars fell like rain. Tauhindauli. STE
There was a time when this poor frame was whole. There Was a Time. Edward Thomas. MMA
There was a tinker liv'd of late. The Jovial Tinker; or, The Willing Couple. *Unknown.* CoMu
There was a tree stood in the ground. The Green Grass Growing All Around. *Unknown.* HBVY; MoShBr
There was a troop of merry gentlemen. The Broom of Cowdenknows. *Unknown.* ESPB
There was a tumult in the city. Independence Bell—July 4, 1776 [*or* Liberty and Independence]. *Unknown.* BLPA; FaBoBe; FPL; PAL; TreFS
There was a vital scorn of all. Byron. *Fr.* Lara. OBRV
There was a way out of here. The Elaboration. Bill Manhire. OCNZ
There was a wealthy merchant/ in London still did dwell. The Wars of Santa Fe. *Unknown.* AmFP
There was a wealthy merchant/ in London's town did dwell. Lily Munro. *Unknown.* OuSiCo
There was a weasel lived in the sun. The Gallows. Edward Thomas. ChMP; FM; InPS; LiTB; MoAB; MoBrPo; NoAM; PAI; UnPo
There Was a Wee Bit Mousikie. *Unknown.* MoShBr
(Cheetie-Poussie-Cattie, O.) FaBoCh
There was a wee bit wifie. *Unknown.* OxNR
There was a wee cooper who lived in Fife. The Wife Wrapt [*or* Wrapped] in Wether's Skin [*or* The Wee Cooper of Fife]. *Unknown.* BaBo; FSW; ViBoFo
There was a whispering in my hearth. Miners. Wilfred Owen. BrPo; MoAB; MoBrPo; NOBE
There was a widow-woman lived in far Scotland. The Wife of Usher's Well. *Unknown.* ESPB; ViBoFo
There was a Wife from Bath, a well-appearing. Chaucer, *mod. version by* Louis Untermeyer. *Fr.* The Canterbury Tales: Prologue. TrGrPo
There was a wild colonial boy, Jack Dollin was his name. The Wild Colonial Boy. *Unknown.* OuSiCo
There was a wild Montana boy, Jack Nolan was his name. The Wild Montana Boy. *Unknown.* CoSo
There was a winter. Alba after Six Years. Christopher Middleton. NePoEA-2
There was a witch. Two Witches. Alexander Resnikoff. RHPC
There was a wood, a witches' wood. The Witches' Wood. Mary Elizabeth Coleridge. PBWP
There Was a Wyly Ladde. *Unknown.* ErPo
There was a yellow pumpkin. Coach. Eleanor Farjeon. DFT
There was a young bard of Japan. Limerick. *Unknown.* CenHV
There was a young belle of old Natchez. Requiem. Ogden Nash. NoP
There was a young [*or* small] boy [*or* man] of Quebec. The Boy of Quebec [*or* Limerick]. *At. to* Kipling. FaBoCo; FaBoNo; HBV-2; HBVY
There was a young critic of King's. Limerick. Arthur Clement Hilton. CenHV
There was a young curate of Hants. Limerick. E. V. Knox. CenHV
There was a young curate of Kidderminster. A Young Curate of Kidderminster. *Unknown.* TDH
There was a young curate of Salisbury. *Unknown.* FaBoCo
There was a young doctor, from London he came. The Fair Damsel from London. *Unknown.* AmFP
There was a young fellow called Crouch. Limerick. Victor Gray. NOBL
There was a young fellow called Green. Limerick. *Unknown.* CenHV
There was a young fellow from Boise. A Young Fellow from Boise. John Straley. TDH
There was a young fellow named Hall. Limerick [*or* A Fellow Named Hall]. *Unknown, at. to* J. F. Wilson. TDH; WhC
There was a young fellow named Nutz. Limerick. *Unknown.* PeHV
There was a young fellow named Shear. A Young Fellow Named Shear. John Ciardi. TDH
There was a young fellow named Tait. Limerick. *At. to* Carolyn Wells. HBV-2; HBVY
There was a young fellow named West. Suppressed. *Unknown.* TDH
There was a young Fellow of Caius. Limerick. *Unknown.* NOBL
There was a young fellow of Ceuta. Limerick. *Unknown.* CenHV
There was a young Fellow of King's. Limerick. *Unknown.* NOBL
There was a young fellow of Perth. Limerick. *Unknown.* WhC
There was a young Fellow of Wadham. Limerick. *Unknown.* NOBL
There was a young fir-tree of Bosnia. The Fir-Tree of Bosnia. Dante Gabriel Rossetti. FaBoNo
There was a young genius of Queens'. Limerick. Frederick Edward Weatherley. CenHV
There was a young girl of Asturias. A Young Girl of Asturias. *Unknown.* TDH
There was a young girl of Lahore. Limerick. Cosmo Monkhouse. HBV-2
There was a young gourmand of John's. Limerick. Arthur Clement Hilton. CenHV
There was a young hopeful named Sam. Jammy. Elizabeth Ripley. TDH
There was a young lady called Bright. *See* There was a young lady named Bright.
There was a young lady called Starky. Limerick. *Unknown.* CenHV
There was a young lady from Cork. A Young Lady from Cork. Ogden Nash. TDH
There was a young lady from Del. A Young Lady from Delaware. *Unknown.* TDH
There was a young lady in white. Limerick. Edward Lear. NBM
There was a young lady [*or* woman] named Bright. Relativity [*or* Faster than Light *or* Limerick *or* A Young Lady Named Bright]. *At. to* Arthur Buller. CenHV; FaBoCo; FaFP; FaPON; ImOP; NOBL; OxBoLi; QQQ; WhC
There was a young lady named Sue. A Young Lady Named Sue. *Unknown.* TDH
There was a young lady of Corsica. Limerick. Edward Lear. CenHV; FaBoNo
There Was a Young Lady of Crete. *Unknown.* OnUR
(Young Lady of Crete, A.) TDH
There was a young lady of Ealing. Limerick [*or* A Young Lady of Ealing]. *Unknown.* CenHV; TDH
There was a young lady of Flint. Limerick. *Unknown.* CenHV
There was a young lady of Hull. Limerick. Edward Lear. MoShBr
There was a young lady of Kent. Limerick. *Unknown.* CenHV
There was a young lady of Limerick. Limerick. Andrew Lang. CenHV
There was a young lady of Lynn. Limerick [*or* The Young Lady of Lynn]. *Unknown.* CenHV; ChTr; RHPC; SoSe
There was a young lady of Milton. Limerick. *Unknown.* NA
There was a young lady of Munich. A Young Lady of Munich. *Unknown.* TDH
There Was a Young Lady of Niger. *At. to* Cosmo Monkhouse. *See* Limerick: "There was a young lady of Niger."
There Was a Young Lady of Norway. Edward Lear. EBEV; TiPo
(Young Lady of Norway, A.) FaPon
There Was a young lady of Oakham. A Young Lady of Oakham. *Unknown.* TDH
There Was a Young Lady of Portugal. Edward Lear. OxBoLi
There was a young lady of Rheims. Moonshine. Walter de la Mare. FiBHP; TDH
There was a young lady of Riga. Limerick. *Unknown.* CenHV; FaBoCo
There Was a Young Lady of Rome. Ogden Nash. QQQ
There was a young lady of Russia. Limerick. Edward Lear. MoShBr
There Was a Young Lady of Ryde. *Unknown.* *See* Limerick: "There was a young lady of Ryde/ Who ate a green apple and died."
There was a young lady of Ryde/ Whose shoe-strings were seldom untied. Limerick. Edward Lear. OxBoLi; WhC
There was a young lady of Spain. *Unknown.* FaBoCo
There was a young lady of station. Limerick. "Lewis Carroll." CenHV
There was a young lady of Sweden. Edward Lear. EBEV
There was a young lady of Tottenham. *Unknown.* WeW
There was a young lady of Twickenham. Limerick. Oliver Herford. WhC

There was a young lady of Tyre. The Young Lady of Tyre. Edward Lear. TDH
There was a young lady of Wales. Limerick. *Unknown.* NA
There was a young lady of Wilts. Limerick [*or* A Young Lady of Wilts]. *Unknown.* HBV-2; TDH
There was a young lady of Woosester. Limerick. *Unknown.* WhC
There was a young lady whose bonnet. Edward Lear. EBEV
There was a young lady whose chin. Edward Lear. SoPo; TiPo
There was a young lady whose dream. Food for a Cat. David Starr Jordan. TDH
There was a young lady whose eyes. Limerick. Edward Lear. EBEV; GoJo
There Was a Young Lady Whose Nose. Edward Lear. EBEV; FaPON
There was a young maid who said, "Why." Limerick. *Unknown.* NA; SoSe
There was a young man from Elnora. Lenora. *Unknown.* TDH
There was a young man from the city. The "Kitty." *Unknown.* TreFT
There Was a Young Man from Trinity. *Unknown.* ImOP
There was a young man named Achilles. How Homer Should Have Written the Iliad. Edwin Meade Robinson. Limericised Classics, I. HBMV
There was a young man of Bengal. *Unknown.* OxBoLi
There was a young man of Cohoes. Limerick. Robert J. Burdette. NA
There was a young man of Devizes. Limerick. *Unknown, at. to* Archibald Marshall. CenHV; WhC
There was a young man of Japan. *Unknown.* FaBoCo
There was a young man of Madrid. Limerick. *Unknown.* WhC
There was a young man of Mauritius. Theological Limerick. T. Lindsay. FaBoCo
There Was a Young Man of Montrose. Arnold Bennett. FaBoNo; OxBoLi
(It Pays.) FaFP
(Limerick: "There was a young man of Montrose.") CenHV
There was a young man of Quebec. *See* There was a young boy of Quebec.
There was a young man of Sid. Sussex. Limerick. Arthur C. Hilton. WhC
There was a young man of St. Bees. *Unknown, at. to* W. S. Gilbert. FaBoCo
There was a young man of the Clyde. Just for the Ride. *Unknown.* FaFP
There was a young man on a plain. A Young Man Who Loved Rain. William Jay Smith. TDH
There was a young man so benighted. Limerick. *Unknown.* HBV-2
There was a young man who said, "Damn!" *See* There once was a man who said, "Damn!"
There was a young man who was bitten. Limerick. *At. to* Walter Parke. NA
There was a young man with a beard. Beatnik Limernik. Norman R. Jaffray. TDH
There was a young monk of Siberia. Limerick. *Unknown.* TreFT
There was a young person named Crockett. Crockett. William Jay Smith. TDH
There was a young person named Tate. Limerick. Carolyn Wells. WhC
There was a young person of Crete. Limerick. Edward Lear. FaBoNo
There Was a Young Person of Smyrna. Edward Lear. *See* Limerick: "There was a young person of Smyrna."
There was a young poet of Thusis. *Unknown.* OxBoLi
There was a young puppy called Howard. The Young Puppy [*or* Howard]. A. A. Milne. GDP; TDH
There was a young soldier called Edser. Edser. Spike Milligan. TDH
There was a young waitress named Myrtle. A Mock Miracle. Oliver Herford. TDH
There was a young woman, and what do you think? A Lost Illusion. George Du Maurier. CenHV
There was a young woman, as I've heard tell. Ripperty! Kye! Ahoo! Henry Lawson. CBAP
There was a young woman called Starkie. Mendelian Theory [*or* Limerick]. *Unknown.* FaBoCo; NOBL
There was a young woman from Aenos. The Young Woman from Aenos. *Unknown.* OBAL
There was a young woman named Bright. *See* There was a young lady named Bright.
There was a young woman named Plunnery. Edward Gorey. OBAL
There was a youth[e], and a well belovd [*or* well-belovéd] youth[e]. The Bailiff's Daughter of Islington. *Unknown.* ESPB; FaBoBa; FSW; GN; HBV-2; OAEP; OBET; OxBB; OxBoLi; ViBoFo
There was airy music and sport at the fair. The Fair at Windgap. Austin Clarke. OnYI; OxBTC; SeCePo
There [*or* Ther] was also a nun [*or* Nonne], a Prioress[e]. The Prioress [*or* Madam Eglantine]. Chaucer. *Fr.* The Canterbury Tales: Prologue. CTC, *abr.*; NOBE; OxBM; ViBoPo
There was always the river or the train. Grandmother Watching at Her Window. W. S. Merwin. PrIm; VGW
There was an ancient carver that carved of a saint. The Figure-Head. Crosbie Garstin. EtS
There was an ancient craftsman once, who made. The Leaf-Makers. Harold Stewart. PoAu-2
There was an ancient Grecian boy. A Tiger's Tale [*or* A Tiger Tale]. John Bennett. OBCA; TiPo
There was an ancient spring inside the glacier. Found. Carol Muske. AmPA
There was an Archbishop named Tait. Archbishop Tait. *Unknown.* ChTr; FaBoNo
There was an Archdeacon who said. *Unknown.* OxBoLi
There was an Auchtergaven mouse. A Whigmaleerie. William Soutar. OxBS
There was an auld birkie ca'ed Milton. Limerick. Andrew Lang. CenHV
There was an earthquake. The Earthquake. *Tr. fr. Zuni Indian by* K. Kennedy. WTO
There was an ease of mind that was like being alone in a boat at sea. Prologues to What Is Possible. Wallace Stevens. LCAP; NePoAm
There was an emptiness. The Day You Are Born. Cathy Song. BrSi
There was an exclusive old oyster. The Exclusive Old Oyster. Laura A. Steel. TDH
There Was an Indian. J. C. Squire. *See* Discovery, The.
There was an old bear that lived near a wood. The Bear and the Squirrels. Christopher Pearse Cranch. OBCA
There was an old cat named Macduff. The Genial Grimalkin. J. G. Francis. TDH
There was an old crow. *Unknown.* OxNR
There was an old dragon under grey stone. The Dragon's Hoard. J. R. R. Tolkien. AmMo
There was an old farmer in Sussex did dwell. The Farmer's Curst Wife. *Unknown.* BaBo; ESPB; ViBoFo
There was an old Fellow of Trinity. Limerick. *Unknown, at. to* Arthur Clement Hilton. CenHV; WHC
There was an old Fox. The Owl and the Fox. *Unknown.* BLPA
There was an old grocer of Goring. Green. Walter de la Mare. FaBoNo
There was an old lady/ Who had three faces. Godmother. Phyllis B. Morden. RHPC; SoPo
There Was an Old Lady Named Crockett. William Jay Smith. ShM
There was an old lady of Chertsey. Edward Lear. OxBChV
There was an old lady of Dover. The Old Lady from Dover. Carolyn Wells. TDH
There was an old lady of Harrow. An Old Lady of Harrow. *Unknown.* TDH
There was an old lady who lived in Dundee. A Long Time Ago, *vers.* V. *Unknown.* ShS
There was an old looney of Rhyme. An Old Looney. *Unknown.* TDH
There was an old man,/ And he had a calf. *Unknown.* OxNR
There was an old-man and a jolly old-man. The Old Man and Young Wife. *Unknown.* CoMu
There was an old man and he lived [out] in a wood. Broom, Green Broom [*or* Green Broom]. *Unknown.* CH, *diff. vers.*; LiTB; OxBoLi; PoRA
There was an old man at the foot of the hill. The Farmer's Curst Wife. *Unknown.* AmFP
There was an old man by Salt Lake. An Old Man by Salt Lake. William Jay Smith. TDH
There was an old man from Darjeeling. Old Man from Darjeeling. *Unknown.* NTCP
There was an old man from Peru/ Who dreamed he was eating his shoe. *See* There was an old man of Peru/ Who dreamt he was eating his shoe.
There was an old man in a Barge. Edward Lear. EBEV
There was an old man in a boat. Limerick [*or* The Floating Old Man]. Edward Lear. EBEV; FaBoNo; HBV-2; WiR
There was an old man in a pew. Limerick. Edward Lear. MoShBr
There Was an Old Man in a Tree. Edward Lear. *See* Limerick: "There was an old man in a tree."
There was an old man in a trunk. Limerick [*or* Ultimate Reality]. Ogden Nash. CenHV; FaBoCo
There was an old man in a velvet coat. Mother Goose. OxNR
There was an old man in the North Countrie. The Two [*or* Twa] Sisters. *Unknown.* PrIm; ViBoFo (D *vers.*)
There was an old man lived out in the wood. *See* There was an old man and he lived in a wood.
There was an old man lived under the hill/ As you may plainly see, see. Father Grumble. *Unknown.* ViBoFo
There was an old man lived over the hill/ If he ain't moved away he's living there still. The Devil and the Farmer's Wife. *Unknown.* FSW
There was an old man named Michael Finnigan [*or* Finnegan]. Michael Finnigan. *Unknown* FSW; TiPo
There was an old man of Bengal. Limerick. "F. Anstey." CenHV
There was an old man of Blackheath. Limerick. *Unknown.* PDV
There was an old man of Bohemia. Edward Lear. PAI
There Was an Old Man of Boulogne. *Unknown.* *See* Limerick: "There was an old man of Boulogne."
There was an old man of Calcutta. Arthur. Ogden Nash. FiBHP; NoP

There was an old man of Cape Horn. Edward Lear. EBEV
There was an old man of Cape Race. *Unknown.* FaBoCo
There Was an Old Man of Dumbree. Edward Lear. *See* Limerick: "There was an old man of Dumbree."
There was an old man of Dunblane. Edward Lear. EBEV
There was an old man of Dundee. Limerick. Edward Lear. FaBoNo
There was an old man of El Hums. Limerick. Edward Lear. FaBoNo
There was an old man of Girgenti. Limerick. Edward Lear. FaBoNo
There was an old man of Hawaii. An Old Man of Hawaii. *Unknown.* TDH
There was an old man of high feather. A What-Is-It. Ruth McEnery Stuart *and* Albert Bigelow Paine. TDH
There Was an Old Man of Hong Kong. Edward Lear. *See* Limerick: "There was an old man of Hong Kong."
There was an old man of Ibreem. Edward Lear. EBEV
There was an old man of Kamschatka. Limerick. Edward Lear. NA; NOBL
There Was an Old Man of Khartoum. *Unknown, at. to* W. R. Inge. *See* Limerick: "There was an old man of Khartoum."
There was an old man of Leghorn. Limerick. Edward Lear. NA
There was an old man of Madras. Limerick. Edward Lear. FaBoNo
There was an old man of Nantucket. Limerick. *Unknown, at. to* Dayton Voorhees. HBV-2
There was an old man of [*or* from] Peru/ Who dreamt [*or* dreamed] he was eating his shoe. Limerick [*or* An Old Man from Peru]. *Unknown.* CenHV; FaFP; NTCP; OnUR; PDV; SoSe; TDH
There was an old man of Peru/ Who never knew what he should do. Edward Lear. EBEV
There was an old man of Peru/ Who watched his wife making a stew. A Fatal Mistake. Edward Lear. EBEV; TDH
There was an old man of Spithead. Limerick. Edward Lear. FaBoNo
There Was an Old Man of St. Bees. W. S. Gilbert. InvP
There was an old man of Tarentum. Limerick. *Unknown.* HBV-2; WhC
There was an old man of the coast. Limerick. Edward Lear. CenHV; MoShBr
There was an old man of the Dargle. Limerick. Edward Lear. ChTr
There was an old man of the Dee. Limerick. Edward Lear. FaBoNo
There was an old man of the East. Edward Lear. EBEV
There was an old man of The Hague. Limerick [*or* The Old Man of The Hague]. Edward Lear. EvOK; TDH
There was an old man of the Nile. An Old Man of the Nile. Edward Lear. TDH; VLP
There was an old man of the West. Edward Lear. EBEV
There was an old man of Thermopylae. Limerick. Edward Lear. EBEV; EvOK; FaBoNo; NA; NBM; NOBL
There was an old man of Three Bridges. Limerick. Edward Lear. FaBoNo
There was an old man of Toulon. An Old Man of Toulon. William Jay Smith. TDH
There was an old man of Vesuvius. Limerick. Edward Lear. FaBoNo; GLGT
There was an old man of West Dumpet. Edward Lear. EBEV
There was an old man of Whitehaven. Limerick. Edward Lear. EBEV; NBM; VLP
There was an old man on the Border. Limerick. Edward Lear. CenHV; EBEV
There Was an Old Man, on Whose Nose. Edward Lear. SoPo
There was an old man said, "I fear." The Shubble. Walter de la Mare. FaBoNo; TDH
There was an old man that lived in a wood. *See* There was an old man who lived in the wood.
There was an old man who had a kite for a son. An Old Man's Son. Russell Edson. LCAP
There was an old man who lived [*or* liv'd] in Middle Row. The Five Hens. *Unknown.* GBP; OxNR
There was an old man who lived in the West. The Wife Wrapt in Wether's Skin (C *vers.*). *Unknown.* BaBo
There was an old man who [*or* that] lived in the [*or* a] wood [*or* woods]. Father Grumble [*or* Old Man in the Wood *or* The Old Man Who Lived in the Woods.] *Unknown.* AmFP; FSW; MoShBr; OnUR
There was an old man who made his will. The Dishonest Miller. *Unknown.* AmFP
There was an old man who owned a small farm. The Farmer's Curst Wife. *Unknown.* BaBo
There Was an Old Man Who Said: "How." Edward Lear. *See* Limerick: "There was an old man who said 'How.' "
There Was an Old Man Who Said, "Do." *Unknown.* FaPON; ImOP
(Limerick: "There was an old man who said 'Do.') NA
There was an old man who said, "Hush!" Limerick. Edward Lear. FaBoCo; GoJo; HBV-2; NA; NBM; NOBL; OxBChV; OxBoLi; TEP
There was an old man who screamed out. Edward Lear. EBEV
There Was an Old Man Who Supposed. Edward Lear. *See* Limerick: "There was an old man who supposed."
There was an old man whose despair. Limerick. Edward Lear. FaBoNo; VLP
There Was an Old Man with a Beard. Edward Lear. *See* Limerick: "There was an old man with a beard."
There was an old man with a gong. Limerick [*or* The Old Man with a Gong]. Edward Lear. GoJo; TDH
There was an old man with a gun. Miss Pheasant. Walter de la Mare. FaBoNo
There was an old man with a poker. Limerick. Edward Lear. HBV-2
There was an old man with a ribbon. Limerick. Edward Lear. FaBoNo
There was an old man who lived on a common. The Wonderful Old Man. *Unknown.* NA
There was an old miller and he lived all alone. The Miller. *Unknown.* FSW
There was an old miser at Reading. *Unknown.* OxBChV
There was an old Monk of great renown. The Monk of Great Renown. *Unknown.* CoMu
There was an old owl lived in an oak. *Unknown.* CenHV
There Was an Old Party of Lyme. *At. to* Edward Lear, *also at. to* Cosmo Monkhouse. FaBoCo; FF; OxBoLi
(Limerick: "There once was an old man of Lyme.") NA
(Limerick: "There was an old person of Lyme.") CenHV
There was an old person of Anerley. Limerick. Edward Lear. FaBoCo
There was an old person of Bar. Limerick. Edward Lear. FaBoNo
There was an old person of Basing. Edward Lear. EBEV; PAI
There was an old person of Blythe. Edward Lear. EBEV
There was an old person of Bow. Edward Lear. EBEV; VLP
There was an old person of Bromley. Limerick. Edward Lear. NBM
There was an old person of Brussels. Limerick. Edward Lear. FaBoNo
There was an old person of Buda. Edward Lear. PAI
There was an old person of Burton. Edward Lear. EBEV
There was an old person of Cassel. Edward Lear. EBEV
There was an old person of Cromer. An Old Person of Cromer. Edward Lear. TDH
There was an old person of Crowle. Limerick. Edward Lear. FaBoNo
There was an old person of Dean. Limerick. Edward Lear. MoShBr
There was an old person of Diss. Limerick. Edward Lear. GoJo
There was an old person of Dover/ Who called on his sister in Deal. The Eel. Walter de la Mare. ShM
There was an old person of Dover/ Who rushed through a field of blue clover. Limerick. Edward Lear. FaBoNo
There was an old person of Dutton. Edward Lear. EBEV
There was an old person of Ewell. Rice and Mice. Edward Lear. TDH
There was an old person of Grange. Limerick. Edward Lear. FaBoNo
There Was an Old Person of Gretna. Edward Lear. OxBChV; VLP
(Limerick: "There was an old person of Gretna.") ChTr
There was an old person of Harrow. Limerick. Edward Lear. FaBoNo
There was an old person of Hove. Limerick. Edward Lear. FaBoNo
There was an old person of Ickley. Limerick. Edward Lear. EvOK
There was an old person of Leeds. Limerick. *Unknown.* WhC
There was an old person of Lyme. *See* There Was an Old Party of Lyme.
There was an old person of Philae. Limerick. Edward Lear. FaBoNo
There was an old person of Prague. Edward Lear. EBEV
There was an old person of Putney. Tea by the Sea. Edward Lear. TDH
There was an old person of Rhodes. Edward Lear. EBEV
There was an old person of Shoreham. Limerick. Edward Lear. NBM
There was an old person of Skye. Limerick. Edward Lear. ChTr
There was an old person of Tring. Limerick [*or* An Old Person of Tring]. *Unknown.* TDH; WhC
There was an old person of Twickenham. Limerick. Edward Lear. FaBoNo
There Was an Old Person of Ware. Edward Lear. *See* Limerick: "There was an old person of Ware."
There was an old person of Wick. Limerick. Edward Lear. FaBoNo; NA
There was an old person of Woking. Limerick. Edward Lear. NA
There was an old person who said. The Oil Lamp. William Jay Smith. TDH
There Was an Old Person Whose Habits. Edward Lear. *See* Limerick: "There was an old person whose habits."
There was an old skinflint of Hitching. Buttons. Walter de la Mare. DTC; FaBoNo
There Was an Old Soldier. *Unknown.* AS, *with music*; FSW, *sl. diff. vers.*; TrAS, *with* Old Zip Coon
There was an old soldier of Bicester. *Unknown.* FaBoNo; OxBChV
There was an old stump of an old tree standing. The New View. John Holmes. MiAP
There was an old stupid who wrote. Limerick [*or* A Person of Note]. *At. to* Walter Parke. NA; TDH
There was an old tailor of Bicester. Limerick. *Unknown.* CenHV
There was an old vicar of Sinder. J. J. Walter de la Mare. FaBoNo
There was an old villain. Oh, How He Lied. *Unknown.* FSW

There was an old wife and she lived all alone. The Old Wife and the Ghost. James Reeves. PDV; ShM
There was an old woman/ And nothing she had. *Unknown.* OxNR
There was an old woman/ Lived down in a dell. Was She a Witch? Laura E. Richards. PDV; SoPo
There was an old woman/ Lived under a hill/ And if she's not gone. *Unknown.* OxNR
There was an old woman/ Lived under a hill/ She put a mouse in a bag. Mother Goose. OxNR
There was an old woman/ Sold puddings and pies. *Unknown.* OxNR
There was an old woman/ Went blackberry picking. Berries. Walter de la Mare. MoBrPo; TiPo
There was an old woman/ Who lived in Dundee. *Unknown.* OxNR
There was an old woman and she lived in a shoe. The Old Woman Who Lived in a Shoe. *Unknown.* OxBoLi
For Mother Goose *vers., see* There was an old woman who lived in a shoe.
There was an old woman, and what do you think? Mother Goose. FaBoCh; HBV-1
There was an old [*or* little] woman, as I've heard tell. Mother Goose. InvP; MoShBr; OnMSP; OxNR; PoSC; TiPo
There was an old woman as ugly as sin. An Old Woman. Charles Henry Ross. OxBChV
There was an old woman called Nothing-at-all. Mother Goose. OxNR
There was an old woman had three cows. *Unknown.* OxNR
There was an old woman, her name was Peg. *Unknown.* OxNR
There was an old woman in Ireland, in Ireland she did dwell. The Wife of Kelso. *Unknown.* ShS
There was an old woman in our town. Eggs and Marrowbone. *Unknown.* FSW
There was an old woman in Surrey. Mother Goose. OxBChV
There was an old woman lived on the seashore. The Two Sisters. *Unknown.* AmFP; FSW
There was an old woman lived under a hill. Mother Goose. HBV-1; HBVY
There was an old woman lived under the hill. The Trooper's Horse. *Unknown.* OBET
There was an old woman named Towl. Mistress Towl. *Unknown.* FaBoNo; OxBChV
There was an old woman of Harrow. Old Woman of Harrow. *Unknown.* FaBoNo
There was an old woman sat spinning. Mother Goose. OxNR
There was an old woman tossed up in a basket [*or* blanket]. Mother Goose. EvOK; OxNR; PDV; SoPo
There was an old woman who lived in a shoe. Mother Goose. FaBoBe; FaFP; HBV-1; HBVY; OxNR; TiPo *See also* There was an old woman and she lived in a shoe.
There was an ould man down by Killyburn brae. Killyburn Brae. *Unknown.* OnYI
There was an owd yowe wi' only one horn. The One-horned Ewe. *Unknown.* GBP
There was an owl lived in an oak. *Unknown.* OxNR
There was an young lady of Corsica. Limerick. Edward Lear. ChTr
There was blood on the saddle. Blood on the Saddle [*or* Trail End]. *Unknown.* CoSo; FSW
There was Dai Puw. He was no good. On the Farm. R. S. Thomas. OxBTC
There was fire & the people were yelling. running crazy. Urban Dream. Victor Hernandez Cruz. NBP
There was great beauty by the Tree. Eve. Arthur J. Bull. UnPo
There was heat lightning out west. Last Night in Sisseton, S. D. Mary Goose. STE
There was Hep and Texas an' Bronco Jack. Campfire and Bunkhouse. *Unknown.* CoSo
There was in Arll a little cove. The Piper of Arll. Duncan Campbell Scott. PeCV
There [*or* Ther] was in Asia, in a great city. The Prioress's Tale. Chaucer. *Fr.* The Canterbury Tales. ACP; ISi, *mod. vers. by* Frank Ernest Hill; LoBV.
There was in danger desperate delight. The Aging Poet, on a Reading Trip to Dayton, Visits the Air Force Museum and Discovers There a Plane He Once Flew. Richard Snyder. Psk
There was, in the village of Patton. Good Thinking. *Unknown.* TDH
There was little important. An American Boyhood. Jonathan Holden. Psk
There was little mignonette in life. War Poem. Ilya Ehrenburg, *tr. by* Leonard Opalov. AMV-81
There was monie a braw noble. Glenlogie. *Unknown.* GN
There was movement at the station, for the word had passed around. The Man from Snowy River. A. B. Paterson. CBAP; PH; PoAu-1
There was music in the air. Music in the Air. Ronald McCuaig. ErPo
There was never a leaf on bush or tree. A Winter Morning. James Russell Lowell. *Fr.* The Vision of Sir Launfal. GN
There was never a sound beside the wood but one. Mowing. Robert Frost. BLPL; CMoP; HBMV; HoPM; LiTA; NOBA; OxBA; PPP; TwAmPo; VGW
There was never nothing more me pained [*or* payned]. Sir Thomas Wyatt. AAS; GBL; SiPS
There was no ceremony. Lion. Mary Fullerton. PoAu-1
There was no change in the summer wind. In the Flowering Season. Michael Roberts. FaBoTw
There was no hunted one. The Baying Hounds. Mary Gilmore. PoAu-1
There was no land, they used to tell. At the Grave of a Land-Shark. Ernest G. Moll. DBV; WhC
There was no one like 'im, 'Orse or Foot. "Follow Me 'Ome." Kipling. OAEP
There was no one. The water—no one? Galente Garden: II. Juan Ramón Jiménez, *tr. by* H. R. Hays. WSC
"There Was No Place Found." Mary Elizabeth Coleridge. OxBoCh
There was no repose. Hero Song. Robert Duncan. CrMA
There was no road at all to that high place. The Grove. Edwin Muir. LiTM; MoPo
There Was No Room on the Cross. *Unknown.* GoBC
There was no song nor shout of joy. The Ship. J. C. Squire. CH
There was no sound at all, no crying in the village. A Memory. Margaret Sackville. SUMH
There was no trace of Heaven. Bivouac. Alun Lewis. ChMP
There was no union in the land. Gettysburg. James Jeffrey Roche. PAH
There was once a boat on a billow. Longing for Home. Jean Ingelow. WGRP
There was once a considerate crocodile. The Considerate Crocodile. Amos R. Wells. OBCA
There was once a dear little gnome. Gnome Matter. Carolyn Wells. TDH
There was once a Filipino hombre. A Filipino Hombre. *Unknown.* AS
There was once a high wall, a bare wall. The Red Herring. George MacBeth. SO
There was once a hog theater where hogs performed. A Performance at Hog Theater. Russell Edson. AmPA
There was once a little animal. Similar Cases. Charlotte Perkins Stetson Gilman. HBV-1; PoLF
There was once a maiden of Siam. Limerick. *Unknown.* TreFT
There was once a maiden who loved a cheese. Quite the Cheese. H. C. Waring. BXAP
There was once a man who smiled. The Ridiculous Optimist. *Unknown.* STF
There was once a man with a beard. Limerick. Edward Lear. NA
There was once a pious young priest. *See* There once was a pious young priest.
There was once a pirate, greedy and bold. A Message of Peace. John Boyle O'Reilly. OnYI
There was once a swing in a walnut tree. The Walnut Tree. David McCord. OBCA
There was once a young lady of Ryde. Limerick. *Unknown.* EvOK
There was once a young man of Oporta. "Lewis Carroll." FaBoNo
There was once two Irish labouring men; to England they came over. How Paddy Stole the Rope. *Unknown.* BLPA
There was once upon a time a man who lost the. Doctor Bill Williams. Ernest Walsh. InvP
There was one among us who rose. Death of a Friend. Pauli Murray. PoBA
There Was One I Met upon the Road. Stephen Crane. EaLo
There was one little Jim. Dirty Jim. Jane Taylor. HBV-1; HBVY
There was rebellion, Father, and the door was slammed. Father. Robert Lowell. DiL
There was silence in heaven, as if for half an hour. Mary's Assumption. Alfred J. Barret. ISi
There was six jovial tradesmen, they all sat down to drinking. When Jones's Ale Was New. *Unknown.* AmFP
There was some jolly drivers on the Denver City Line. Root Hog or Die. Floyd B. Small. PoOW
There was such speed in her little body. Bells for John Whiteside's Daughter. John Crowe Ransom. AP; CMoP; CoBMV; CrMA; DTC; FF; HAP; HeIP; HoPM; InPK; InPS; LiTA; LiTM; MoAB; MoAmPo; MoVE; NePA; NIP; NoAM; NOBA; NoP; OxBA; PAI; PPON; PPP; PrIm; SoSe; TAP; TreFT; TwAmPo; UnPo; VGW; WeW
There was that fall the fall of desire. Two. Winfield Townley Scott. NYBP
There was the battle stricken weill. The Battle of Bannockburn. John Barbour. *Fr.* The Bruce. BSV
There was the buffalo blowing. Composition. Peter Blue Cloud. VoR
There was the sonne of Ampycus of great forecasting wit. Meleager. Ovid, *tr. by* Arthur Golding. *Fr.* Metamorphoses, VIII. CTC
There was this empty bird cage in the garden. A Sparrow's Feather. George Barker. NYBP
There was this gym-teacher. Epigram. Strato, *tr. by* Teddy Hogge. PeHV
There was this hayfield. Water Tap. Norman MacCaig. BSV

There was this road. The Legs. Robert Graves. LiTB; LiTM; NoAM
There was this time in Boston. The Wedding Night. Anne Sexton. PoA
There was three crows sat on a tree. Blow the Man Down, *vers.* IV. *Unknown.* ShS
There was three kings into the east. *See* There were three kings into the east.
There was three ladies play'd at the ba'. The Cruel Brother. *Unknown.* ESPB; OxBB; ViBoFo
There was three travelers, travelers three. The Three Travelers. *Unknown.* UnTE
There was three worms on yonder hill. Died of Love. *Unknown.* OBET
There was, 'tis said, and I believe, a time. George Crabbe. *Fr.* The Parish Register: Burials. OAEL-1
There was tumult in the city. *See* There was a tumult in the city.
There was twa sisters in a bow'r [*or* bower]. The Twa Sisters. *Unknown.* ESPB; FaBoBa; HBV-2; NoP; OxBS; ViBoFo
There was two little boys going to the school. The Twa Brothers. *Unknown.* ESPB; ViBoFo
There went out in the dawning light. A Pastoral. *Unknown, tr. by* John Addington Symonds. AWP; UnTE
There went three children down to the shore. The Black Pebble. James Reeves. PDV
There Were an Old and Wealthy Man. *Unknown.* AmFP
There were bees about. From the start I thought. Shore Scene. John Logan. NMP
There were blood spots on the skirt. James Cunningham. *Fr.* The Narrator's Trance. JB
There were estrangements on the road of love. The Altar. Jean Starr Untermeyer. HBMV
There Were Fierce Animals in Africa. Alvin Aubert. GP
There were five of us within the room. I Come to Bury Caesar. Sydney Justin Harris. PoA
There were flowers all summer long. Wind Flowers. Margo Lockwood. DFF
There were four of us about that [*or* the] bed. Shameful Death. William Morris. ChTr; GTBS-P; HBV-2; OAEP; OBVV; VLP
There were four red apples on the bough. August. Swinburne. WiR
There were ghosts that returned to earth to hear his phrases. Large Red Man Reading. Wallace Stevens. HAP; LCAP
There were hours when life was bitter. Now and Then. Margaret E. Sangster. TRV
There were ladies, they lived in a bower. Mary Hamilton. *Unknown.* ESPB
There were miners from Bisbee. Tramp Miner's Song. *Unknown.* AmFP
There were never strawberries. Strawberries. Edwin Morgan. BoLoP; LLLT
There Were Ninety and Nine. Elizabeth A. Clephane. *See* Ninety and Nine, The.
There were no antelope on the balcony. Midnight Special. Kenneth Patchen. VGW
There were no men and women then at all. Then. Edwin Muir. CMoP; PoA
There were no undesirables or girls in my set. Commander Lowell. Robert Lowell. DiL; VGW
There were no witnesses when you saw. To a Victim of Radiation. Arturo Vivante. FAZ
There were old women. Calling Myself Home. Linda Hogan. TWSS
There were once two cats of Kilkenny. The Cats of Kilkenny. *Unknown.* RHPC
There were only Adam and Eve. From the Dust. Elaine Dallman. VWA
There were saddened hearts in Mudville for a week or even more. Casey's Revenge. James Wilson. BLPA; OnMSP; TreFS
There were some dirty plates. The Last Words of My English Grandmother. William Carlos Williams. SOTW
There were some kings, in number three. Jumbo Jee. Laura E. Richards. SUS
There were some pines, a canal, a piece of sky. Landscape with Little Figures. Donald Justice. LCAP
There Were Some Summers. Thomas Lux. LCAP
There were sparkles on the windowpane and sparkles in the sky. The Waits. Madeleine Nightingale. SUS
There were ten in the bed. Roll Over. *Unknown.* FSW
There were the roses, in the rain. The Act. William Carlos Williams. ELU; SOTW; VGW
There were the starlings hunched against the sky. Rooftop Winter. Dwayne Thorpe. AMV-80
There were the whales, six of them. The Stranded Whales. Geoffrey Dutton. CBAP
There were three brothers in merry Scotland. Henry Martin [*or* Martyn]. *Unknown.* FSW; ViBoFo (B *vers.*)
There were three cherry trees once. The Three Cherry Trees. Walter de la Mare. CMoP
There were three cooks of Colebrook. Three Cooks. *Unknown.* OxNR
There were three crows sat on a tree. *See* There were three ravens sat on a tree.
There were three gipsies a-come to my door. The Wraggle [*or* Raggle] Taggle Gipsies [*or* Gypsies]. *Unknown.* CH; EvOK; FaPON; FSW; TiPo; WiR
There were three hills that stood alone. The Three Hills. J. C. Squire. HBMV
There were three in the meadow by the brook. The Code. Robert Frost. InPS; OBNV; PoA; UnPo
There were three jovial huntsmen. Three Jovial Huntsmen. *Unknown.* NA
There Were Three Jovial Welshman. *Unknown.* *See* Three Jovial Welshmen, The.
There were three kings cam' frae the East. The Kings from the East. Heine, *tr. by* Alexander Gray. GoTS
There were [*or* was] three kings into the east. John Barleycorn. Burns. FaBoCh; HBV-2; SeCeV
There were three ladies [*or* maids] lived in a bower [*or* barn]. Babylon [*or* Baby Lon]; or, The Bonnie Banks o' Fordie. *Unknown.* AmFP; ESPB; OxBB; SeCePo
There were three maidens who loved a king. Three Loves. Lucy H. Hooper. BeLS
There were three men came out of the west. John Barleycorn. *Unknown.* OBET
There were three men of Gotham. The Three Wise Men of Gotham. *Unknown.* FaBoNo
There were three ravens [*or* rauens *or* crows] sat on a tree. The Three Ravens [*or* Billy Magee Magaw]. *Unknown.* AmFP; CABA; ChTr; ESPB; FaBoBa; FSW; GBP; HBV-2; HeIP; InPK; NoP; OAEL-1; OAEP; OBET; OBEV; OxBB; PAI; PoEL-1; SeCeV; TrGrPo; UnPo; ViBoFo; ViBoPo
There were three sailors of Bristol city. Little Billee [*or* The Three Sailors]. Thackeray. CenHV; EtS; FaBoCh; FaBoCo; HBV-2; HBVY; MOS; NA; NOBL; OxBB; PoPle; ShM; TreFS
There were three sisters fair and bright. The Riddling Knight. *Unknown.* FaBoCh; PoEL-1
There were three sisters in a hall. *Unknown.* OxNR
There were three young women of Birmingham. Limerick. Cosmo Monkhouse. HBV-2
There were twa brethren in the North. The Twin [*or* Twa] Brothers. *Unknown.* CH; EBEV; ESPB; OxBB; ViBoFo
There were twa knights in fair Scotland. The Twa Knights. *Unknown.* ESPB
There were twa sisters sat in a bower [*or* bour *or* bowr]. Binnorie; or, The Two Sisters [*or* The Twa Sisters of Binnorie]. *Unknown.* BSV; CH; EnSB; OBEV; PoPle; TrGrPo; WHA
There were two birds sat on a stone. Mother Goose. OxNR
There were two blackbirds sitting on a hill. Mother Goose. HBV-1; HBVY
There were two great trees. Laly, Laly. Mark Van Doren. SO
There were two little girls, neither handsome nor plain. Jane and Eliza. Ann Taylor. HBV-1; HBVY
There were two lofty ships from old England came. High Barbaree [*or* Barbary]. *Unknown.* AmSS; BaBo; FSW; OuSiCo; ViBoFo
There were two sisters sat in a bour. The Cruel Sister. *Unknown.* OxBB
There were two sisters, they went playing. The Twa Sisters. *Unknown.* ESPB; ViBoFo
There were two, small one replacing large one. Kitchen Tables. David Huddle. Str
There were two wrens upon a tree. *Unknown.* OxNR
There weren't any other cars. At the Scenic Drive-in. David McAleavey. SUW
There when the water was not potable. Chloride of Lime and Charcoal. Louis Zukofsky. CoPo
There where he sits, in the cold, in the gloom. The Hidden Weaver. Odell Shepard. WGRP
There, where it was, we never noticed how. The Sagging Bough. Louis Untermeyer. BXAP
There where the course is. At Galway Races. W. B. Yeats. LiSp
There where the deepe did show his sandy flore. Bible, *O.T.* Psalms, LXXVIII, *paraphrased by* Countess of Pembroke. OBVE
There where the hackles of the Rocky Mountains. Observe the Whole of It. Thomas Wolfe. TreFT
There where the rusty iron lies. Rooks. Charles Hamilton Sorley. HBMV; MoBrPo
There where the sottish ignoraunt adore. Satire Septimus Contra Sollistam. William Rankins. NCEP
There, where the sun shines first. The Azalea. Coventry Patmore. *Fr.* The Unknown Eros. ELP; GBL; GoBC
There will be a rusty gun on the wall, sweetheart. A. E. F. Carl Sandburg. CMoP; HBMV; MoAB; MoAmPo; WaaP
There will be bluebells growing under the big trees. Bluebells for Love. Patrick Kavanagh. IPY
There will be butterflies. Butterflies. Haniel Long. HBMV

There will be no examination in Long Term Suffering. Long Term Suffering. Richard Eberhart. GLGT; GP
There will be no Holyman crying out this year. Jitterbugging in the Streets. Calvin C. Hernton. PoBA
There will be no more cats. Mort aux Chats. Peter Porter. OxBC
There Will Be No Peace. W. H. Auden. NePoAm-2
There will be no speech from. No Speech from the Scaffold. Thom Gunn. OxBTC
There Will Be Peace. Margaret Miller Pettengill. PGD
There will be rose and rhododendron. Elegy before Death. Edna St. Vincent Millay. CMoP; LiTA; LiTM
There will be the cough before the silence, then. Dictum: For a Masque of Deluge. W. S. Merwin. AP; NoAM
There Will Come Soft Rains. Sara Teasdale. LiTA; SUMH
There will greet you at the end, Vasco. Wine from the Cape. Turner Cassity. AMV-81
There Won't Be Another. Diane Glancy. STE
There, wrapped in his own roars, the lone airman. The Raider. W. R. Rodgers. AnIL; MoBrPo
There you are once more near me. Shadow. Guillaume Apollinaire, *tr. by* Jessie Degen *and* Richard Eberhart. WaaP
There you go, a four-year-old. Good-by, Steer. Robert V. Carr. BPAW
There you go, it's everywhere. Shopping for Midnight. G. E. Murray. MAYP
There you sit. Shelley Silverstein. PoSC
There you were in my dreams last night. Stepfathers. David Donnell. NOBC
There'd Be an Orchestra. F. Scott Fitzgerald. *Fr.* Thousand-and-First Ship. ELU; GoJo
There'd ha'e to be nae warnin'. Times ha'e changed. Prayer for a Second Flood. "Hugh MacDiarmid." EBEV
Therefore I will not refrain my mouth. Bible, *O.T.* *Fr.*Job. PAI
Therefore Is the Name of It Called Babel. Sir Osbert Sitwell. MMA
Therefore let pass, as they are transitory. Milton. *Fr.* Paradise Regained, IV. OAEL-1
Therefore Philippi saw once more the Roman battalions. We Have Paid Enough Long Since in Our Own Blood. Virgil, *tr. by* Richmond Lattimore. *Fr.* Georgics. WaaP
Therefore the Lord Himself/ Shall Give You a Sign. Bible, *O.T. (Douay vers.).* Isaias, VII: 14-15. ISi
Therefore, to be possess'd with double pomp. Shakespeare. *Fr.* King John, IV, ii. TreFT
Therefore We Preserve Life. Shen Ch'üan, *tr. fr. Chinese by* William C. White. TrJP
Therefore, We Thank Thee, God. Reuben Grossman, *tr. fr. Hebrew by* L. V. Snowman. TrJP
Therefore, when thou wouldst pray, or dost thine alms. The Right Use of Prayer. Sir Aubrey De Vere. OBVV; WGRP
Therefore your halls, your ancient colleges. Lines on Cambridge of 1830. Tennyson. GLGT
There'll Be a Hot Time. Joe Hayden. *See* Hot Time in the Old Town.
There,—my blessing with you! Polonius' Advice to Laertes. Shakespeare. *Fr.* Hamlet, I, iii. OHFP; PoPl
There's a band of men who roam this land. Ballad of Badmen. Owen Dodson. FB
There's a barrel of porter at Tammany Hall. Song. Fitz-Greene Halleck. OBAL
There's a barrel-organ caroling across a golden street. The Barrel-Organ. Alfred Noyes. BLPL; FaBV; HBV-2; MoBrPo; PoRA; TreF, *sl. abr.*
There's a bear in the Truro woods. The Truro Bear. Mary Oliver. SoSe
There's a beautiful island away in the West. The Land of the Evening Mirage. *Unknown, tr. by* A. M. Bede. WGRP
There's a big difference. Face in a Mirror. Jack L. Anderson. LFAC
There's a big hollow tree down the road here from me. Mountain Dew. *Unknown.* FSW
There's a big ship sailing on the il-li-al-lay oh. A Big Ship Sailing. *Unknown.* FSW
There's a bird perched on my shoulder. Bird. Agnes Nemes Nagy, *tr. by* Bruce Berlind. BoWoP
There's a bit of sky across the street. My "Patch of Blue." Mary Newland Carson. BLPA
There's a bower of roses by Bendemeer's stream. Bendemeer's Stream [*or* Bendemeer]. Thomas Moore. FSW; OBRV
There's a brand new wind a-blowin' down that Lincoln Road. A New Wind a-Blowin'. Langston Hughes. TrAS
There's a breathless hush in the Close tonight. Vitaï Lampada. Sir Henry Newbolt. BLPA; FaPoR; OBWP; PaPo; TreF
There's a breathless hush on the freeway tonight. Wild Dreams of a New Beginning. Lawrence Ferlinghetti. GP
There's a brief spring in all of us and when it finishes. To S. T. C. on His 179th Birthday, October 12th, 1951. Maurice Carpenter. FaBoTw
There's a brown 'cross town and she's. Deceitful Brownskin Blues. *Unknown.* BluL
There's a Catholic church on the corner. Young Buck's Sunday Blues. Kenneth Pitchford. *Fr.* Good for Nothing Man. CoPo
There's a certain slant of light. Emily Dickinson. AmPP; AP; BLPL; BoWoP; CABA; CMoP; HAP; HeIP; LiTM; MasP; MoAB; MoAmPo; MoPo; NePA; NoAM; NOBA; NoP; OxBA; PoEl-5; PPP; QFR; SBG; TreFT; WPE
(Certain Slant of Light, A.) LiTA
There's a certain young lady. A Certain Young Lady. Washington Irving. FaBoBe; HBV-1
There's a charming Irish lady with a roguish winning way. Bedelia. William Jerome. FSN
There's a church in the valley by the wildwood. Little Brown Church in the Vale. William S. Pitts. TreFT
There's a circus in the sky. Winter Circus. Aileen Fisher. YeAr
There's a city that lies in the Kingdom of Clouds. The Sunset City. Henry Sylvester Cornwell. HBV-2
There's a colleen fair as May. Pearl of the White Breast. *Unknown, tr. by* George Petrie. AnIV; OnYI
There's a combative Artist named Whistler. Limerick. Dante Gabriel Rossetti. CenHV
There's a comforting thought at the close of the day. Touching Shoulders. *Unknown.* BLPA
There's a crackle of brown on the leaf's crisp edge. Romany Gold. Amelia Josephine Burr. HBMV
There's a craze among us mortals that is cruel hard to name. The Other Fellow's Job. Strickland Gillilan. WBLP
There's a day we feel gay. On a Sunday Afternoon. Andrew B. Sterling. FSN
There's a dear little plant that grows in our isle. The Green Little Shamrock of Ireland. Andrew Cherry. HBV-2
There's a death-dealing custom,/ Abroad in the land. Drilling Missed Holes. Don Cameron. PoOW
There's a deep secret place, dark in the hold of this ship. Down Below. Joan Aiken. WSC
There's a dusky, husky maiden in the Arctic. When the Iceworms Nest Again. Robert W. Service. FSW
There's a faerie at the bottom of my garden. My Garden. Janice Appleby Succorsa. HoPM
There's a fairmer up in Cairnie. Drumdelgie. *Unknown.* GBP
There's a family nobody likes to meet. The Grumble Family. *Unknown.* WBLP
There's a famous seaside place called Blackpool. The Lion and Albert. Marriott Edgar. OBNV
There's a Feeling. Marcia Bullwinkle. AMV-80
There's a feeling comes a stealing. You're a Grand Old Flag. George M. Cohan. FSN
There's a feeling gathering inside me. There's a Feeling. Marcia Bullwinkle. AMV-80
There's a flash packet, a flash packet of fame. The Dreadnought. *Unknown.* AmSS
There's a fortune to be made in just about everything. My Great Great etc. Uncle Patrick Henry. James Tate. GP; OBAL
There's a Friend for little children. Albert Midlane. *Fr.* Above the Bright Blue Sky. OxBChV
There's a game much in fashion—I think it's called Euchre. The Game of Life. John Godfrey Saxe. BLPA; BLPL
There's a gathering in the village, that has never been outdone. The Country Doctor. Will M. Carleton. BLPA
There's a girl in these parts. No Names. *Unknown, tr. by* Frank O'Connor. KiLC
There's a glade [*or* glen] in Aghadoe, Aghadoe, Aghadoe. Aghadoe. John Todhunter. AnIL; AnIV; OBVV; OxBI
There's a good time coming, boys. The Good Time Coming. Charles Mackay. PaPo; VLP
There's a Grandfather's Clock in the Hall. Robert Penn Warren. NoP
There's a grass-grown road from the valley. Threnody. Ruth Guthrie Harding. HBV-1
There's a graveyard near the White House. The Unknown Soldier. Billy Rose. BLPA; FPL; PAL
There's a great mystery. Diddie Wa Diddie. *Unknown.* BluL
There's a green hollow where a river sings. The Sleeper of the Valley. Arthur Rimbaud, *tr. by* Ludwig Lewisohn. AWP
There's a grey wind wails on the clover. Numerous Celts. J. C. Squire. BXAP; SpRo
There's a grim one-horse hearse in a jolly round trot. The Pauper's Drive. Thomas Noel. PaPo
There's a house in Baltimore. Goodbye 'Liza Jane. *Unknown.* FSW
There's a humming in the sky. Aeroplane. Mary McBride Green. SoPo; TiPo

There's a knack in living with you. Living with You. Angela Langfield. FF
There's a Lady in Washington Heights. Morris Bishop. QQQ
There's a land bears a well-known name. The Englishman. Eliza Cook. PaPo
There's a Land That Is Fairer than Day. Sanford Fillmore Bennett. *See* In the Sweet Bye-and-Bye.
There's a Light upon the Mountains. Henry Burton. TRV
There's a little black train a-comin' [*or* a-coming]. The Little Black Train. *Unknown.* AmFP; OuSiCo
There's a little grey friar in yonder green bush. The Grey Linnet. James McCarroll. CaP
There's a little rosewood casket. Little Rosewood Casket. *Unknown.* FSW
There's a little secret. Keep Sweet. A. B. Simpson. STF
There's a little side street such as often you meet. The Sunshine of Paradise Alley. Walter H. Ford. FSN
There's a lonely green valley by the old Kentucky shore. *See* There's a low green valley on the old Kentucky shore.
There's a lonely stretch of hillocks. Anzac Cove. Leon Gellert. PoAu-1
There's a lot of music in 'em—the hymns of long ago. The Old Hymns. Frank L. Stanton. BLRP
There's a low [*or* lonely] green valley on [*or* by] the old Kentucky shore. Darling Nelly Gray. Benjamin Russel Hanby. BLSo; FSW; PSoN; TrAS; TreFS
There's a Man Goin' 'Round Takin' Names. *Unknown.* FSW
(Angel of Death, The.) AmFP
(Man Goin' Roun', *with music.*) AS
There's a man I really believe's in heaven. Sappho, *tr. fr. Greek by* John Frederick Nims. WeW
There's a man with a nose. Ambrose Bierce. *Fr.* The Devil's Dictionary. OBAL
There's a mean black snake been suckin' my rider's tongue. Black Snake. *Unknown.* BluL
There's a mellower light just over the hill. Morning Song. Karle Wilson Baker. HBMV
There's a merry brown thrush sitting up in the [*or* a] tree. The Brown Thrush. Lucy Larcom. FaPON; HBV-1; HBVY; OBCA
There's a new grave up on Boot Hill, where we've planted Rowdy Pete. Pete's Error. Arthur Chapman. BPAW
There's a nice green little gully on the Numerella shore. The Numerella Shore. "Cockatoo Jack." PoAu-1
There's a notable [*or* wonderful] family named [*or* called] Stein. Limerick. *Unknown.* DBV; NOBL
There's a one-eyed yellow idol to the north of Khatmandu. The Green Eye of the Yellow God. J. Milton Hayes. BLPA; PaPo
There's a package. The Package. Aileen Fisher. SoPo
There's a palace in Florence, the world knows well. The Statue and the Bust. Robert Browning. OAEP
There's a part o' the sun in an apple. Each a Part of All. Augustus Wright Bamberger. WBLP
There's a patch of old snow in a corner. A Patch of Old Snow. Robert Frost. CMoP; WeW
There's a path that leads to Nowhere. The Path that Leads [to] Nowhere. Corinne Roosevelt Robinson. BLPA; HBMV
There's a pathos in the solemn desolation. The Ruined Cabin. Alfred Castner King. PoOW
There's a piping wind from a sunrise shore. Off to the Fishing Ground. L. M. Montgomery. CaP
There's a place the man always say. Where? Kenneth Patchen. LiTM
There's a plump little chap in a speckled coat. Bob White. George Cooper. HBVY
There's a Portuguese person named Howell. Limerick. *At. to* Dante Gabriel Rossetti *and to* James Abbott McNeill Whistler. CenHV; DBV
There's a pretty fuss and bother both in country and in town. A New Song on the Birth of the Prince of Wales. *Unknown.* CoMu; FaBoBa; VLP
There's a pretty spot in Ireland I always claim for my land. Where the River Shannon Flows. James I. Russell. FSN
There's a puckle lairds in the auld house. The Auld House. William Soutar. OxBS
There's a quaint little place they call Lullaby Town. Lullaby Town. John Irving Diller. BLPA
There's a race of men that don't fit in. The Men That Don't Fit In. Robert W. Service. BLPA; BLPL
There's a red light on the track for Bolsum Brown. Bolsum Brown. *Unknown.* AS
There's a reid lower in yer cheek. Sang. Robert MacLellan. OxBS
There's a road to heaven, a road to hell. My Road. Oliver Opdyke. HBV-1
There's a rosie-show in Derry. Rosies. Agnes I. Hanrahan. HBV-1
There's a saucy, wild packet and a packet of fame. The *Dreadnought.* *Unknown.* AmFP
There's a schooner out from Kingsport. Arnold, Master of the *Scud.* Bliss Carman. EtS
There's a sensitive man in Toms River. A Sensitive Man. Morris Bishop. TDH
There's a small café off the Avenue. Wardour Street. Humbert Wolfe. OxBTC
There's a snake on the western wave. The Sea Serpent Chantey. Vachel Lindsay. AmMo; WSC
There's a Song in the Air. Josiah Gilbert Holland. *See* Christmas Carol, A.
There's [*or* Dere's] a star in the East [*or* de Eas'] on Christmas morn. Rise Up, Shepherd, and Follow [*or* an' Foller]. *Unknown.* BoAN-2; FSW
There's a stir among the trees. The Christmas Trees. Mary F. Butts. OHIP
There's a stone deer in that garden, plus two or three nude. A Floridian Museum of Art. Reed Whittemore. EyDe
There's a street in Trieste where I see my reflection. Three Streets. Umberto Saba, *tr. by* Anita Barrows. VWA
There's a sweet old story translated for man. The Gospel According to You. *Unknown.* BLRP
There's a sweetness in surrender. The Blessings of Surrender. Mary J. Helphingtine. STF
There's a three-penny Lunch on Dover Street. Eat and Walk. James Norman Hall. BLPA
There's a time each year that we always hold dear. In the Good Old Summer Time. Ren Shields. BLSo; FSN; FSW; TreF
There's a town called Don't-You-Worry. The Town of Don't-You-Worry. I. J. Barlett. BLPA; WBLP
There's a trade you all know well. The Overlander. *Unknown.* PoAu-1
There's a tramping of hoofs in the busy street. The Troop of the Guard. Hermann Hagedorn. OHIP
"There's a tree in father's garden, lovelye William," says she. Lovelye William. *Unknown.* AmFP
There's a valley in Spain called Jarama. Jarama Valley. *Unknown.* FSW
There's a vaporish maiden in Harrison. A Vaporish Maiden [*or* Limerick]. Morris Bishop. TDH; WhC
There's a very funny insect that you do not often spy. The Triantiwontigongolope. C. J. Dennis. AmMo
There's a vile old man. Limeraiku. Ted Pauker. NOBL
There's a whisper down the field where the year has shot her yield. The Long Trail [L'Envoi]. Kipling. FaBV; HBV-1; MOS; OBEV; OBVV; ViBoPo
There's a whisper down the line at 11:39. Skimbleshanks: The Railway Cat. T. S. Eliot. FaBoCo; NOBL
There's a whisper of life in the grey dead trees. The White Canoe. Alan Sullivan. CaP
There's a Wideness in God's Mercy. Frederick William Faber. TRV; WBLP
(All-embracing, The.) BLRP; TRV, *sl. diff.*
(Hymn.) NBM, *sl. diff.*
There's a woman in the earth, sitting on/ her heels. Orbiter 5 Shows How Earth Looks from the Moon. May Swenson. SUW
There's a woman like a dew-drop, she's so purer than the purest. Earl Mertoun's Song. Robert Browning. *Fr.* A Blot in the 'Scutcheon. HBV-1; OBEV; PoPle; UnTE
There's a wonderful family called Stein. *See* There's a notable family named Stein.
There's a yellow rose of Texas that I am going to see. The Yellow Rose of Texas. *Unknown.* BLSo; FSW; PSoN; TreFT
There's all of pleasure and all of peace. A Friend of Two. Wilbur D. Nesbit. PoLF
There's all sorts of fowl and fish. An Invitation to Lubberland. *Unknown.* FaBoNo; GBP
There's an ancient party. Old Brown's Daughter. *Unknown.* OBET
There's an Irishman, Arthur O'Shaughnessy. Limerick. Dante Gabriel Rossetti. CenHV
There's antimony, arsenic, aluminium, selenium. The Elements. Tom Lehrer. FaBoUs
There's Asia on the avenue. Manhattan. Morris Abel Beer. AmFN
There's beauty in the deep. The Deep. John Gardiner Calking Brainard. AA; EtS
There's been a death in the opposite house. Emily Dickinson. InPS; NCEP; SoSe
"There's been an accident," they said. Mr. Jones [*or* Common Sense]. Harry Graham. CenHV; FaBoCo; FaFP; FiBHP
There's black grief on the plains, and a mist on the hills. Roisin Dubh. *Unknown, tr. by* Eleanor Hull. OnYI
There's blood between us, love, my love. The Convent Threshold. Christina Rossetti. MasP; NoP; PoEL-5
There's combative artist named Whistler. Dante Gabriel Rossetti. FaBoEE
There's definitely been a mistake. An Unraveled Thought. Shlomit Cohen, *tr. by* Myra Glazer Schotz. VWA

There's folks that like the good dry land, an' folks that like the sea. When the Drive Goes Down. Douglas Malloch. AmFN
There's four square miles of timber, mostly oak. Wild Pigs. Ted Kooser. TAT
There's good cooks and there's bad ones. The Roundup Cook. Robert V. Carr. BPAW; PoOW
There's Gowd in the Breast. James Hogg. HBV-1
There's half a god in many a man. Inspiration. Mary Fullerton. PoAu-1
There's heaven above, and night by night. Johannes Agricola in Meditation. Robert Browning. OAEL-2; OBVV
There's Holmes, who is matchless among you for wit. Holmes. James Russell Lowell. *Fr.* A Fable for Critics. NOBA
There's in my mind a woman. In Mind. Denise Levertov. InPS; NMM
"There's just one Book!" cried the dying sage. Just One Book. *Unknown.* BLRP
There's Life in a Mussel; a Meditation. George Farewell. NOEC
There's light in the west, o'er the rims of the walnut. By the Turnstile. John Francis O'Donnell. NBM
There's little in taking or giving. Coda. Dorothy Parker. DBV; InMe; SBG; TreFS
There's little joy in life for me. On the Death of Anne Brontë. Charlotte Brontë. ViBoPo; WPE
There's little wildness in my city head. The Wind Blows. Donagh MacDonagh. NeIP
There's lots of funny goings-on the public don't suspect. Montgomery. H. A. C. Evans. GDP
"There's machinery in the butterfly." The Horrid Voice of Science. Vachel Lindsay. PoA
There's Many a Man Killed on the Railroad, *with music.* *Unknown.* AS
There's many a young Canadian boy leaves home and friends so dear. Harry Dunne. *Unknown.* ShS
There's moaning somewhere in the dark. Voice in Darkness. Richard Dehmel, *tr. by* Margarete Münsterberg. AWP
There's Money in Mother and Father. Morris Bishop. FiBHP
There's more in words than I can teach. Loving and Liking. Dorothy Wordsworth. OxBChV
There's More Pretty Girls than One. *Unknown.* AmFP
There's much afoot in heaven and earth this year. The Rainy Summer. Alice Meynell. GoJo; MoVE; OxBTC; SBG
There's Music in the Air, *with music.* Fanny Crosby. BLSo
There's nae lark loves the lift, my dear. A Lyric. Swinburne. HBV-1
There's Nae Luck about the House. William Julius Mickle. *See* Sailor's Wife, The.
There's naught but care on every hand. *See* There's nought but care on ev'ry han'.
There's naught (thou say'st) but one eternal flux. The Infidel Reclaimed. Edward Young. *Fr.* The Complaint; or, Night Thoughts on Life, Death and Immortality, VII. NOEC
There's never enough whiskey or rain. Wishing Africa. Marilyn Bowering. NOBC
"There's no a bird in a' this foreste." Johnie Cock. *Unknown.* ESPB
There's no a muir in my ain land but's fu' o' sang the day. The Comin' o' the Spring. Lady John Scott. BSV
There's no Avenging Angel. The Tree of Life Is Also a Tree of Fire. Gerda Norvig. VWA
There's no badger in this sandbox. Explaining about the Dachshund. John Stone. NIP
There's no better dog nor Hardcastle's Rake. Rake. Dorothy Una Ratcliffe. BoAnP; GDP
There's no dew left on the daisies and clover. Seven Times One [*or* Seven Times One: Exultation]. Jean Ingelow. *Fr.* Songs of Seven. BLPA; FaPON; HBV-1; OBNC; TreF
There's no end to wisdom, no mask for folly. To the Elephants. Nathan Alterman, *tr. by* Ruth Nevo. VWA
There's no fleeing the cry-bird. This evening. The Cry-Bird Journey. Stan Rice. NPGG
There's no hiding here in the glare of the desert. Desert Song. Glenn Ward Dresbach. BPAW
There's no hiding place down here. *See* Dere's No Hidin' Place Down Dere.
There's No Lust like to Poetry. *Unknown, tr. fr. Latin by* John Addington Symonds. AWP
(Wine and Love and Lyre.) UnTE
There's no more to be done, or feared, or hoped. After the Last Breath. Thomas Hardy. VLP
There's No Place to Sleep in This Bed, Tanguy. Charles Henri Ford. EAS
There's no respect for youth or age. The California Stage Company. *Unknown.* CoSo
"There's no sense of going further—it's the edge of cultivation." The Explorer. Kipling. WHA
There's no smoke in the chimney. The Deserted House. Mary Elizabeth Coleridge. CH; MoVE
There's no track. NN 616410. Bill Tulloch. PoSH
There's no way out. In the Suburbs. Louis Simpson. ELU; MAT
There's no Xmas leave for us scullions. Christmas, 1916. M. Winifred Wedgwood. SUMH
There's nobody here. A Woman. Denis Johnson. MAYP
There's not a joy the world can give like that it takes away. Stanzas for Music [*or* Youth and Age]. Byron. EnRP; GTBS; GTBS-P; HAP; HBV-1; OAEP
There's not a nook within this solemn Pass. The Trosachs. Wordsworth. HBV-1; OBEV; OBRV; SeCePo
There's not a pair of legs so thin, there's not a head so thick. The Job That's Crying to Be Done. Kipling. TRV
There's not a spider in the sky. A Love-Song by a Lunatic. *Unknown.* NA
There's not a tear that brims thine eye unshed. Faithless. Louis Lavater. PoAu-1
There's not on earth a thing more vile and base. A Prayer for Faith. Michelangelo, *tr. by* John Addington Symonds. ILwL
There's nothing gentle where Aphrodite was. Trying to Believe. Linda Gregg. NPGG
There's nothing grieves me, but that age should haste. Michael Drayton. *Fr.* Idea. AAS; OAEL-1
There's nothing left to say. Slow Death. Lorri Martinez. LFAC
There's Nothing like the Sun. Edward Thomas. FaBV
"There's nothing mysterious about the skull." The Scientist. Janet Burroway. SoSe
There's Nothing Polite about a Tank. John Paul Minarik. LFAC
There's nothing you can say to a man who drinks. The Drunken Man. Stephen Orlen. MAYP
There's nought [*or* naught] but care on ev'ry han'. Green Grow the Rashes, O. Burns. FSW; HBV-1; LAuP; PPP
There's old Molly Hogan who cooks from a book. Stirling's Hotel. *Unknown.* AmFP
There's one great bunch of stars in heaven. Song. Theophile Marzials. OBVV
There's one joins sweetly in the quavering hymn. Sunday Morning. L. A. G. Strong. WhC
There's one joins sweetly in the quavering hymn. Sunday P Is for Paleontology. Milton Bracker. WhC
There's one rides very sagely on the road. Upon the Horse and His Rider. Bunyan. OxBChV
There's one thing I like about that gal of mine. One Way Gal. *Unknown.* BluL
There's part of the sun in an apple. Out of the Vast. Augustus Wright Bamberger. TRV
There's pleasure, sure, in being clad in green. A Scene after Hunting at Swallowfield in Berkshire. Sneyd Davies. NOEC
There's raw meat for the tiger cub. Song for the Infant Judas. Thomas Blackburn. NAs
There's recompense to balm your spirit's ire. Da Silva Gives the Cue. Walter Hart Blumenthal. TrJP
There's room for most things: Tropic seas. A Sermon. Margaret Sackville. HBMV
There's room in the bus. Jittery Jim. William Jay Smith. RHPC
There's scarce a point whereon mankind agree. On the Phrase, "To Kill Time." Voltaire. PV
There's snakes on the mountain. Wanderin'. *Unknown.* AS
There's snow in every street. Winter. J. M. Synge. OBMV; OxBTC; POL
There's some is born with their legs straight by natur. A Sailor's Apology for Bow-Legs. Thomas Hood. EtS; MOS
"There's someone at the door," said gold candlestick. Green Candles. Humbert Wolfe. HBMV; MoBrPo; RHPC; SO
There's Somethin'. Adam Small, *tr. fr. Afrikaans.* PeSA
There's something in a noble boy. The Torn Hat. Nathaniel Parker Willis. AA
There's something in a noble tree. The Trees. Samuel Valentine Cole. OHIP
There's something in a stupid ass. Epilogue. Byron. Par
"There's something in the air," he said. Two Voices. Edmund Blunden. OBWP
There's something in the air. The Coming of Spring [*or* the Spring]. Nora Perry. HBVY; SoPo; YeAr
There's somewhat on my breast, father. The Confession. "Thomas Ingoldsby." FiBHP
There's Tap o' Noth, the Buck, Ben Newe. Bennachie. Charles Murray. PoSH
There's teuch sauchs growin' i' the Reuch Heuch Hauch. The Sauchs in the Reuch Heuch Hauch. "Hugh MacDiarmid." NoAM
There's the field. I can see it. The Word. Neil Weiss. NYBP
There's the gals at the bar, there's the beer. The Homeward Bound. Bill Adams. EtS
There's the girl who clips your ticket for the train. War Girls. Jessie Pope. SUMH

There's the Irishman Arthur O'Shaughnessy. On the Poet O'Shaughnessy. Dante Gabriel Rossetti. ChTr
There's the story of me sitting in the grass in the dark. In the Dead of the Night. Norman Dubie. AmPA
There's the wonderful love of a beautiful maid. Love. *Unknown.* SoSe
There's thik wold hag, Moll Brown, look zee, jus' past! A Witch. William Barnes. VLP
There's three fair maids went to play at ball. The Cruel Brother. *Unknown.* AmFP
There's trampling of hoofs in the busy street. A Troop of the Guard. Hermann Hagedorn. HBV-2
There's two white horses in a line. Two White Horses in a Line. *Unknown.* BluL
There's Wisdom in Women. Rupert Brooke. HBV-1
Theresa. John Pass. AMV-81
Therese. Alden Nowlan. NeAC
Theresienstadt Poems, *sel.* Robert Mezey.
"In your watercolor, Nely Silvínová." NaP; VWA
Theris the old, the waves that harvested. The Fisherman. Leonidas of Tarentum, *tr. by* Andrew Lang. AWP
Thermal Stair, The. W. S. Graham. FaBoMo
Thermometer Wine. Robert Morgan. SUW
Thermopylae. Simonides. *See* On the Spartan Dead at Thermopylae.
Thermopylae. Michael Thwaites. PoAu-2
Thermopylae Ode, The. Simonides, *tr. fr. Greek by* Richmond Lattimore. WaaP
Therwith, when he was ware and gan beholde. Troilus Laments Criseyde's Absence. Chaucer. *Fr.* Troilus and Criseyde, V. OxBM
Thesaurus Nightmare, A. J. Willard Ridings. WhC
These. William Carlos Williams. AP; CoBMV; MoAB; MoAmPo; NoAM; NOBA; NoP; OxBA
These acres, always again lost. Lost Acres. Robert Graves. NoAM
These acres breathe my family. Summer Acres. Anne Wilkinson. CaP
These all their care expend on outward show. Edward Young. *Fr.* Love of Fame, the Universal Passion. OBSV
These alternate nights and days, these seasons. Prologue. Archibald MacLeish. MoAmPo
These apartment acres, good only. Instructions for a Park. Brad Walker. AMV-80; AMV-81
These Apple Trees. Valentin Iremonger. NeIP
These are also/ The war victims. "O. D." Zack Gilbert. CNA
These are amazing: each. Some Trees. John Ashbery. CAPP; ConAP
These are arrows that murder sleep. The Song of Crede, Daughter of Gooary. *Unknown, tr. by* Kuno Meyer. OnYI
These are men! the gaunt, unforesold, the vocal. Ol' Bunk's Band. William Carlos Williams. NOBA
These are my legs. I don't have to tell them, legs. Walter Jenks' Bath. William Meredith. HoPM
These are my murmur-laden shells that keep. On Some Shells Found Inland. Trumbull Stickney. LiTA; NCEP; NePA; TwAmPo
These Are My People. Lucia Trent. PGD
These are my scales to weigh reality. Reality. Martha Dickinson Bianchi. AA
These are my thoughts on realising. Anniversary. John Wain. MP; NePoEA-2
These are not dewdrops, these are tears. Epitaph on a Free but Tame Redbreast. William Cowper. PBBP
These are not my sentiments. Louis Zukofsky. *Fr.* Light. NoAM
These are not words set down for the rejected. A Communication to Nancy Cunard. Kay Boyle. PoNe
These are notes to lightning in my bedroom. Star Quilt. Roberta Hill. CDW; TWSS
These are really the thoughts of all men in all ages and lands. Walt Whitman. Song of Myself, XVIII. BiP
These are the arrows that murder sleep. The Song of Crede. *Unknown, tr. by* Alfred Perceval Graves. BIrV
These are the beds. Sylvia Plath. *Fr.* The Bed Book. RHPC
These are the best of him. On a Fly-Leaf of Burns's Songs. Frederic Lawrence Knowles. HBV-2
These Are the Chosen People. Robert Nathan. TrJP
These are the days of falling leaves. Autumn Song. Elizabeth-Ellen Long. SiSoSe
These are the days of our youth, our days of glory and honor. The Days of Our Youth. *Unknown, tr. by* Wilfrid Scawen Blunt. AWP
These are the days when birds come back. Emily Dickinson. AP; FF (Indian Summer.) HBV-1; MoAmPo
These are the desolate, dark weeks. These. William Carlos Williams. MoAB; MoAmPo; OxBA
These are the dog days. Songs to Survive the Summer. Robert Hass. AmPA
These are the fellows who smell of salt to the prairie. Words Are Never Enough. Charles Bruce. CaP; OBCV
These are the fields of light, and laughing air. The Pea-Fields. Sir Charles G. D. Roberts. *Fr.* Songs of the Common Day. NOBC; OBCV; PeCV
These are the gardens of the Desert, these. The Prairies. Bryant. AP; NOBA; OxBA; PoEL-4; TAP
These Are the Gifts I Ask. Henry van Dyke. FaBoBe; TreFT (Prayer.) WGRP
These are the green paths trodden by patience. The Rural Mail. John Glassco. MoCV
These are the kinds of injury that. Horn, Mouth, Pit, Fire. William Dickey. AMV-81
These are the nights when the geese. A Gaggle of Geese, a Pride of Lions. John Moore. DuDa
These are the ones who escape. Ice Horses. Joy Harjo. TWSS
These are the saddest of possible words. Baseball's Sad Lexicon. Franklin P. Adams. FaFP; InMe; TreFS
These are the signs in which my days endure. Museum Piece. Lawrence P. Spingarn. GoYe
These are the sins for which they cast out angels. Annotation for an Epitaph. Adrienne Rich. TwAmPo
These are the small hours when. Epithalamion. Michael Longley. CIP
These are the stone paths. Breakfast. Robin Shectman. AMV-80
These are the things I prize. The Things I Prize. Henry van Dyke. TreFT
These are the words. Stone from the Gods. Irma Wassall. GoYe
These are the words that leap. Words. Jean Burden. AMV-81
These are thy glorious works, parent of good. Morning Hymn of Adam [*or* Morning Hymn of Adam and Eve *or* Adam's Morning Hymn]. Milton. *Fr.* Paradise Lost, V. OxBoCh; TrPWD; WGRP
These, as they change, Almighty Father, these. A Hymn on the Seasons. James Thomson. *Fr.* The Seasons. EnRP; LAuP; OxBoCh
These attempts to drink coffee. The New Formalists. Marvin Bell. AMV-81
These August evenings in Hatteras. August Evenings in Hatteras. Gabriele Glang. WOLT
These barrows of the century-darkened dead. Prehistoric Burials. Siegfried Sassoon. MoBrPo
These be/ Three silent things. Triad. Adelaide Crapsey. PoPle; WPE
These beds of bracken, climax of the summer's growth. Bracken Hills in Autumn. "Hugh MacDiarmid." NoP
These being the haunts of those. The Death of Friends. Adele Levi. GoYe
These birds frequent the rolling plains. The Moon Bird. V. C. Vickers. AmMo
These birds were born singing for joy. Another Song of the Same Woman, to Some Partridges, Sent to Her Alive. Florencia del Pinar, *tr. by* Julie Allen. BoWoP
These branches. Haiku. Joso, *tr. by* Lucien Stryk *and* Takashi Ikemoto. FAZ
These bright colors of red. Ode to a Homemade Coffee Cup. Marine Robert Warden. AMV-81
These buildings are too close to me. Rudolph Is Tired of the City. Gwendolyn Brooks. PDV; RHPC; TiPo
These butterflies, in twos and threes. Flying Blossoms. W. H. Davies. BrPo
These carved and glowing crowds. Chartres. Raymond Henri. View of the Cathedral, I. EyDe
These caverns yield. The Bats. Robert Hillyer. GoYe
These children playing at statues fill. Statues. Richard Wilbur. EyDe
These children—with their careless hair. The Collector. Richard Behm. AMV-81
These chill pillars of fluted stone. Winter Homily on the Calton Hill. Douglas Young. OxBS
These clouds are soft fat horses. Clouds. James Reaney. WHW
These Crossings, These Words. Quincy Troupe. LTB
These Damned Trees Crouch. Jim Barnes. CDW
These Days. Robert Jones. AMV-81
These Days. William Stafford. NNaP
These days I get up with the birches. Days in White. Ingeborg Bachmann, *tr. by* Daniel Huws. BoWoP
These days in prison seem a decayed time where. Decayed Time. Jean Wahl, *tr. by* Charles Guenther. VWA
These days of disinheritance, we feast. Cuisine Bourgeoise. Wallace Stevens. LiTA
These Days the Papers in the Street. Charles Reznikoff. VGW
These days the river. These Days. Robert Jones. AMV-81
These dead astronauts cannot decay. The Everlasting Astronauts. Tom Buchan. BSV
These discords and these warring tongues are gales. A Solemn Meditation. Ruth Pitter. OxBoCh
These dried-out paint brushes which fell from my lips. Sestina from the Home Gardener. Diane Wakoski. CABA; NoAM
These errors loved no less than the saint loves arrows. Elegy V: Separation

of Man from God [*or* Elegy *or* Sacred Elegy V]. George Barker. FaBoTw; LiTB; MoPo
These evenings,/ out where the Lackawanna boxcars. Winter Twilight. Jeff Schiff. AMV-81
These exquisite rags carry. A Box for Tom. James Tate. FiCP
These eyes, dear [*or* deare] Lord, once brandons of desire. For the Magdalene. William Drummond of Hawthornden. LoBV; PoEL-2
These fallen boughs now never more will weave. The Fallen Tree. Patrick Maybin. NeIP
These February days, though few. Lent Tending. J. Barrie Shepherd. AMV-80
These fell miasmic rings of mist, with ghoulish menace bound. Prejudice. Georgia Douglas Johnson. AmNP; PoBA
These few precepts in thy memory. Polonius' Advice to His Son. Shakespeare. *Fr.* Hamlet, I, iii. TreF
These flowers are I, poor Fanny Hurd. Voices from Things Growing in a Churchyard. Thomas Hardy. OxBTC
"These foreigners with strange and avid faces." Immigrants. Nancy Byrd Turner. AmFN
These fought in any case. Ezra Pound. *Fr.* Hugh Selwyn Mauberley. FF; HeIP; MoAmPo; NOBE; OBWP; PPoe; VGW; WaaP
These fresh beauties, we can prove. Why Flowers Change Color. Robert Herrick. HAP
These germs are medusan: a touch. Isolation Ward. Robert L. Koenig. AMV-81
These going home at dusk. French Peasants. Monk Gibbon. NeIP; OxBI
These golden heads, these common suns. Dandelions. Howard Nemerov. DFF; NePA; TwAmPo
"These Gothic windows, how they wear me out." The Young Glass-Stainer. Thomas Hardy. CTC; EyDe; SaC
These grand and fatal movements toward death. Rearmament. Robinson Jeffers. OxBA
These grasses, ancient enemies. Poem. Keith Douglas. NeBP
These great brown hills move in herds, humped like bison. Among the Finger Lakes. Robert Wallace. GrPl
These green painted park benches are. In a Season of Unemployment. Margaret Avison. MoCV; NOBC
These Green-going-to-Yellow. Marvin Bell. FYAP; LCAP
These had been together from the first. Leolin and Edith. Tennyson. *Fr.* Aylmer's Field. GN
These have forsaken other lives and ways. The Monks at Ards. Patrick Maybin. NeIP
These have no Christ to spit and stoop. Black Magdalens. Countee Cullen. BANP
These hearts were woven of human joys and cares. The Dead. Rupert Brooke. 1914, IV. BrPo; CH; HBV-2; LiTB; MMA; PoA; SeCeV
These Horses Came. Ray A. Young Bear. CDW
These hours of spring are jolly. The Lover and the Nightingale. *Unknown, tr. by* John Addington Symonds. UnTE
These I have loved with passion, loved them long. Quiet Things. Grace Noll Crowell. PoLF
These immigrant houses. Mineral Point. Robert Dana. FAZ
These, in the day when heaven was falling. Epitaph on an Army of Mercenaries. A. E. Housman. Last Poems, XXXVII. BrPo; CMoP; CoBMV; MMA; MoAB; MoVE; NoAM; NOBE; NIP; OBEV; OBWP; OxBTC; PrIm; PPP; SaC; UnPo; ViBoPo; WaaP
These Indians explain away their hair. A Night at the Napi in Browning. Richard Hugo. TAT
These Indians once imitated life. The Only Bar in Dixon. James Welch. AmPA; FF
These jewel-coloured walls, gemmed Salomè. "L'Apparition" of Gustave Moreau. Gordon Bottomley. BrPo
These Labdanum Hours. Kathleen Fraser. NPGG
These labouring wits, like paviours, mend our ways. Edward Young. *Fr.* Epistles to Mr. Pope. OBSV
These Lacustrine Cities. John Ashbery. CAPP; PoM; UnPo
These larger-than-life comic characters. Homage to Our Leaders. Julian Symons. NeBP
These Leaves. William Stafford. NNaP
These lines/ are the truth. Survival Kit. Robert Slater. FAZ
These lines are a discipline he would avoid. Notes on a Child's Coloring Book. Robert Patrick Dana. PoPl
These little firs to-day are things. A Young Fir-Wood. Dante Gabriel Rossetti. GN
These little limbs [*or* limmes]. The Salutations. Thomas Traherne. AnAnS-1; InvP; NOCV; NoP; OBS; OxBoCh; SeCP; SeCV-2
These locks on doors have brought me happiness. Locks. Kenneth Koch. CoAP
These locusts by day, these crickets by night. Wallace Stevens. PoA
These lodge in London in Lent and at other times too. The Civil Service. William Langland, *mod. by* Donald Attwater. *Fr.* The Vision of Piers Plowman. NOCV
These London wenches are so stout. The Sound Country Lass. *Unknown.* CoMu; ErPo
These lovely groves of fountain-trees that shake. Golden Bough. Elinor Wylie. MoAmPo; PBWP
These lover's inklings which our loves enmesh. Counsel to Unreason. Léonie Adams. PoA
These Magicians. Sarah Provost. AMV-81
These magnificent senses. A Hymn of Touch. Gordon Bottomley. BrPo
These many years since we began to be. Rondel. Swinburne. HBV-1
These market-dames, mid-aged, with lips thin-drawn. Former Beauties. Thomas Hardy. *Fr.* At Casterbridge Fair. FaBoEn; NoAM; OBMV; OBNC
These massacres of the superior peoples. John Berryman. *Fr.* Dream Songs. CAPP
These Men. Philip Booth. GLGT
These Men. Leon Gellert. PoAu-1
These men were kings, albeit they were black. Black Majesty. Countee Cullen. PoBA; VGW
These native angles of decay. Deserted Buildings under Shefford Mountain. John Glassco. OBCV
These never knew or had a hint. Bones of a French Lady in a Museum. Richard Gillman. NePoAm
These new night. Ivory Masks in Orbit. Keorapetse Kgositsile. PoBA
These nights we fear the aspects of the moon. Full Moon; New Guinea. Karl Shapiro. MiAP
These nubbins/ these hangers-on. Maxine W. Kumin. *Fr.* Song for Seven Parts of the Body. POL
These nymphs I would perpetuate. The Afternoon of a Faun: Eclogue. Stéphane Mallarmé, *tr. by* Roger Fry. NAWM-2; SyP
These Obituaries of Rattlesnakes Being Eaten by the Hogs. Roger Weingarten. AmPA
These panting damsels, dancing for their lives. The Mother's Choice. *Unknown.* OxBoLi
These Past Years, Passages 10. Robert Duncan. PoM
These pearls of thought in Persian gulfs were bred. In a Copy of Omar Khayyám. James Russell Lowell. AA
These people have not heard your name. In a Cathedral City. Thomas Hardy. EnLoPo; FaBoPP
These people with their illegible diplomas. Metamorphoses. Howard Nemerov. EyDe
These pines, these fall oaks, these rocks. After Drinking All Night with a Friend, We Go Out in a Boat at Dawn to See Who Can Write the Best Poem. Robert Bly. NaP
These plaintive verse, the posts [*or* postes] of my desire. Samuel Daniel. *Fr.* To Delia. AAS; OBSC
These Poems, She Said ("These poems, these poems"). Robert Bringhurst. NOBC
These pools that, though in forests, still reflect. Spring Pools. Robert Frost. AmPP; MoAB; NoAM; NOBA; NoP; OxBA
These populous slopes. The Quantocks. Wordsworth. FaBoPP
These pretty little birds see how. Humaine Cares. Nathaniel Wanley. OBS
These Purists. William Carlos Williams. OBAL
These rioteres [*or* riotoures] three of which I tell[e]. Death and the Three Revellers [*or* Three Revellers Search for Death]. Chaucer. *Fr.* The Canterbury Tales: The Pardoner's Tale. OBNV; OxBM
These rioters, of whom I make my rime. Chaucer. *Fr.* The Canterbury Tales: The Pardoner's Tale. WHA, *mod. vers.*
These royall kinges, that reare up to the skye. Thomas Sackevyll in Commendation of the Worke to the Reader. Thomas Sackville. AAS
These set a crown of glory on their land. On the Lacedaemonian Dead at Plataea. Simonides, *tr. by* Richard Eberhart. WaaP
These seven houses have learned to face one another. On a Painting by Patient B of the Independence State Hospital for the Insane. Donald Justice. CoAP; ConAP; NePoEA-2
These sheets primeval doctrines yield. On Barclay's Apology for the Quakers. Matthew Green. NOEC
These six things doth the Lord hate. Seven Evils. Bible, *O.T. Fr.* Proverbs. TrGrPo
These souls, my lord, assembled at the bar. The Parish Poor-Officers. Edward Ward. *Fr.* A Journey to Hell; or, A Visit Paid to the Devil. NOEC
These spectres resting on plastic stools. Cafe in Warsaw. Allen Ginsberg. HAP
These Stoic Romans had a flair for dying. In the Annals of Tacitus. Philip Murray. NePoAm
These suggestions by Asians are not taken seriously. Asian Peace Offers Rejected without Publication. Robert Bly. CAPP; NaP; NoAM
These summer-birds did with thy master stay. To His Maid Prew. Robert Herrick. OBS
These sweeter far than lilies are. Thanksgivings for the Beauty of His Providence. Thomas Traherne. FaBoCh

These ten-year-olds all want other names. Lunch with Girl Scouts. Sharon Bryan. MAYP
These the assizes: here the charge, denial. Epigraph from *The Judge Is Fury.* J. V. Cunningham. QFR
These the dread days which the seers have foretold. The Death of Justice. Walter Everette Hawkins. PoBA
These Things I Do Remember. Solomon Ephraim ben Aaron of Lenczicz, *tr. fr. Hebrew by* Nina Davis Salaman. TrJP
These things I wish you for our friendship's sake. Wishes for William. Winifred M. Letts. OnYI
These Things Shall Be. John Addington Symonds. TRV
(Church Triumphant, The.) WBLP
(Human Outlook, The.) WGRP
These thoughts of mine. Thoughts. Duncan Campbell Scott. PeCV
These tiny Mexican mosquitoes are like lost souls. Baja. Gerald Stern. SV
These to His Memory—since he held them dear. Dedication. Tennyson. *Fr.* Idylls of the King. CABA; VLP
These, to you now, O, more than ever now. Epilogue to Rhymes and Rhythms. W. E. Henley. ViBoPo
These tracings from a world that's dead. To Violet [with Prewar Poems]. Basil Bunting. FaBoMo; PoA
These Trees Are. Susan Strayer Deal. AMV-81
These Trees Are No Forest of Mourners. D. G. Jones. NOBC
These Trees Stand. W. D. Snodgrass. NIP; NoAM; PPP
These truly are the Brave. The Negro Soldiers. Roscoe Conkling Jamison. BANP
These Two. Howard Schwartz. VWA
These umbered cliffs and gnarls of masonry. Rome. Thomas Hardy. VLP
These unshaped islands, on the sawyer's bench. New Zealand. James K. Baxter. NoP
These walls, so full of monument and bust. The Abbey Church at Bath. Henry Harington. FaBoEE
These walls they knew those shadows. Wall Shadows. Carl Sandburg. WSC
These were our fields. Dust Bowl. Robert A. Davis. IDB
These were the ones who thanked their God. Psalm XII. A. M. Klein. *Fr.* The Psalter of Avram Haktani. PeCV
These were the sounds that dinned upon his ear. Dream of Winter. George Mackay Brown. FaBoTw
These white-clay pits of Byfield. The Byfield Rabbit. Katherine Hoskins. SaC
These Women All. —— Heath. *See* Women.
These women have no language and so they chatter. Lines for Those to Whom Tragedy Is Denied. Joyce Carol Oates. IHMS
These wonderful things. A Last World. John Ashbery. PoM
These woods are one of my great lies. The Owl. W. S. Merwin. PPP
These Words I Write on Crinkled Tin. Lynette Roberts. ChMP
These words spake Don Henriquez. The Last Words of Don Henriquez. Zalman Schneour, *tr. by* Joseph Leftwich. TrJP
These words the poet heard in Paradise. President Garfield. Longfellow. PAH
These words were composed by Spencer the Rover. Spencer the Rover. *Unknown.* OBET
Theseus: A Trilogy. Yvor Winters. NOBA
Theseus and Ariadne. Robert Graves. HAP
Theseus and Ariadne. Lloyd Mifflin. AA
Thesis. William Walter De Bolt. AMV-80
Thesis. Edward Dorn. NOBA
Thesis, Antithesis and Nostalgia. Alan Dugan. CAD; PCP
Thesmophoriazusae, The, *sel.* Aristophanes, *tr. fr. Greek by* B. B. Rogers.
Women Speak Out in Defense of Themselves, The. TreFT
Thespian in Jerusalem. Myra Glazer Schotz. VWA
Thespians at Thermopylae, The. Norman Cameron. ChMP; GTBS-P
Thessalian. Winifred Bryher. PoA
Thetis is the moon-goddess. Hilda Doolittle ("H. D."). *Fr.* Helen in Egypt. MOON
They. Donald Finkel. GP
They. Mani Leib, *tr. fr. Yiddish by* David G. Roskies *and* Hillel Schwartz. VWA
"They." Siegfried Sassoon. CMoP; HBMV; OBSV; OBWP
They. R. S. Thomas. OxBTC
They/ say/ you/ went/ abroad. Incidental Pieces to a Walk. James Cunningham. JB
They, after the slow building of the house. Asmodai [*or* Asmodeus]. Geoffrey Hill. FaBoTw; NePoEA
They aint no use a-telling, boy, what's for you to do. Dan Ellis's Boys. *Unknown.* AmFP
They all are riders: Spring on a two-year-old. The Seasons. Rolfe Humphries. NYBP
They all array before my eyes. Muscae Volitantes. Lewis B. Horne. HoAn
They all arrived, and then with generous show. The Wedding Feast. Luis de Góngora, *tr. by* Edward Meryon Wilson. *Fr.* The First Solitude. OBVE
They All Belong to Me. Eliza Cook. PGD
They all climbed up on a high board-fence. The Nine Little Goblins. James Whitcomb Riley. OBCA
They All Love Jack, *with music. Unknown.* ShS
They all see the same movies. Powwow. W. D. Snodgrass. GrPl; NYBP
They All Want to Play Hamlet. Carl Sandburg. NOBA
They all were looking for a king. That Holy Thing. George Macdonald. *Fr.* Paul Faber, Surgeon. HBV-2; OBEV; OBVV; TrPWD; TRV; WGRP
They alone are left me; they alone still faithful. My Dead. Rachel, *tr. by* Robert Mezey. VWA
They Also Stand. Merrill Moore. CrMA
They amputated/ Your thighs off my hips. A Pity; We Were Such a Good Invention. Yehuda Amichai, *tr. by* Assia Gutmann. BoLoP
They Answer Back: To His Ever-worshipped Will from W. H. "Francis." FiBHP
They are able, with science, to measure. C Stands for Civilization. Kenneth Fearing. TrJP
They are all dying. Death as History. Jay Wright. PoBA
They Are All Gone. Henry Vaughan. *See* They Are All Gone into the World of Light.
They are all gone away. The House on the Hill. E. A. Robinson. AA; FaPON; GoJo; HBMV; MoAmPo; PrIm; TreFT; TrGrPo; WHA
They Are All Gone into the World of Light. Henry Vaughan. AnAnS-1; ChTr; FaBoRV; InPS; JCP; MePo; NOBE; NoP; OAEL-1; OAEP; OBS; OxBoCh; PoEL-2; SeCP; SeCV-1
(Ascension Hymn.) MeLP; NOCV; SeCeV
(Departed Friends.) AWP; TreFS
(Friends Departed.) FaBoEn; HBV-2; OBEV
(They Are All Gone.) BLPL; HeIP; LiTB; SeCePo; ViBoPo; WHA
(World of Light, The.) CH; WGRP
They are all outline, uniformly gray. Those before Us. Robert Lowell. LCAP
They are always living. The Animal's Christmas. Philip Dacey. GP
They are at rest. Rest [*or* Refrigerium]. Cardinal Newman. OBNC; OBRV; OBVV
They are bringing him down. Casualty. Robert Nichols. MMA
They are by nature lonely things. Ideal Angels. John Robert Colombo. MoCV
They are chanting now the service of All the Dead. All Souls. D. H. Lawrence. FaBoRV
They are crying salt tears. Repetitions. Carl Sandburg. HBMV
They are cutting down the great plane-trees at the end of the gardens. The Trees Are Down. Charlotte Mew. BoNaP; BrRo; MoAB; MoBrPo; TrCP; WPE; WPOW
They are disturbed even by my hair. My Strawlike Hair. Asya, *tr. by* Gabriel Preil *and* Howard Schwartz. VWA
They are dreaming of children. Torrential. Nocturne in the Women's Prison. Maria Beneyto, *tr. by* Catherine Rodriguez-Nieto. WPOW
They are 18 inches long. Trees at the Arctic Circle. Al Purdy. NoP
They are eternal as angels and demons. Photographing the Facade—San Miguel de Allende. Betsy Colquitt. AMV-80
They are formidable under any feather. The Murmurers. Josephine Jacobsen. GrPl
They are gathered, astounded and disturbed. The Last Supper. Rainer Maria Rilke, *tr. by* M. D. Herter Norton. OFD
They are gathering round. Concert Party. Siegfried Sassoon. MMA
They are given to. Knee Lunes. Robert Kelly. CoPo
They are heard as a choir of seven. The Pleiades. Mary Barnard. NYBP
They are immortal, voyagers like these. Flight. Harold Vinal. FaPON
They are in the forest. In the Forest. George Bowering. NOBC
They are inspecting hearts again. A Glimpse of the Body Shop. Stephen Berg. NaP
They Are Killing All the Young Men. David Henderson. PoBA
They are lang deid, folk that I used to ken. Elegy. Robert Garioch. OxBS
They are left alone in the dear old home. They Two. Mrs. Frank A. Breck. WBLP
They are like tightrope walkers, unable to fall. The People at the Party. Lisel Mueller. NePoAm-2
They are making a crèche at the Saturday morning classes. The Crib. Robert Finch. OBCP
They are moving inwards; the circle is closing. Man Meeting Himself. Howard Sergeant. EAS
They are my laddie's hounds. My Laddie's Hounds. Marguerite Elizabeth Easter. AA
They are my secret food. The Children's Letters. Dorothy Livesay. NOBC
They are no substitutes for gas masks. Newspaper Hats. Jim Howard. AMV-81; FAZ
They are not automobiles. The Cherokee Dean. Norman H. Russell. STE

They are not dead, the soldiers fallen here. On a World War Battlefield. Thomas Curtis Clark. PGD
They are not given much to laughter. Hill People. Harriet Gray Blackwell. AmFN
They are not here. And we, we are the Others. The Absent. Edwin Muir. NoAM
They are not long, the weeping and the laughter. Vitae Summa Brevis Spem Nos Vetat Incohare Longam [*or* Envoy *or* They Are Not Long]. Ernest Dowson. AWP; BrPo; ChTr; EBVV; FaBoRV; HAP; HBV-2; LoBV; MoBrPo; NOBE; NoP; OBEV; PCP; PoRA; TreFT; TrGrPo; ViBoPo; VLP; WGRP; WHA
They are not silent like workhorses. Donkeys. Edward Field. BoAnP
They are not those who used to feed us. The Puzzled Game Birds. Thomas Hardy. PBBP
They are ordinary men like you and me. The Reporters. Newman Levy. InMe
They Are Ours. A. B. Magil. PoNe
They are rattling breakfast plates in basement kitchens. Morning at the Window. T. S. Eliot. AWP; CABA; CAD; NePA; PoA
They are rebuilding/ the old bridge, the Nagara. Lady Ise, *tr. fr. Japanese by* Etsuko Terasaki *and* Irma Brandeis. BoWoP
They are remembering forests where they grew. Wooden Ships. David Morton. EtS
They are rhymes rudely strung with intent less. A Dedication. Adam Lindsay Gordon. CBAP; PoAu-1
They are riding bicycles on the other side. Snapshot of Hue. Daniel Halpern. MAYP
They are slaves who fear to speak. A Stanza on Freedom [*or* Commitment *or* On Freedom *or* Slaves]. James Russell Lowell. *Fr.* Stanzas on Freedom. AA; PAL; TreFT; TRV; WBLP
They are sleeping—dreams came to them. The Sleepers. William Aberg. LFAC
They are so like. Dolls. David St. John. LCAP
They are so moving in. The Love of Older Men. James Kirkup. PeHV
They are the angels of that watery world. Goldfish. Harold Monro. BrPo
They are the flesh we feed upon come from the depths. The Ribbon-Fish. Robert Adamson. CBAP
They are the last romantics, these candles. Candles. Sylvia Plath. NMM
They are the oldest living captive race. Ginkgoes in Fall. Howard Nemerov. GP
They are the slums of great cities, with narrow streets. In the Ghetto. Hugo Sonnenschein, *tr. by* Edouard Roditi. VWA
They are there on the other side of the hill. The Stammerers. Margaret Kent. AMV-80
They are unholy who are born. Wild Plum. Orrick Johns. HBMV
They are waiting on the shore. The Old. Roden Noel. OBVV
They are with us always, but they have the wit. The Distances They Keep. Howard Nemerov. BoAnP
They argued on till dead of night. Theologians. Walter de la Mare. EaLo
They ask me to handle bronzes. Bronzes. Carl Sandburg. EyDe
They ask me where I've been. Back. W. W. Gibson. TreFT
They asked for bread. For Our Soldiers Who Fell in Russia. Franco Fortini, *tr. by* Ruth Feldman. VWA
They bade me cast the thing away. Doubt. Helen Hunt Jackson. WGRP
They bade me to my spinning. The Warrior Maid. Anna Hempstead Branch. HBV-2
They bear him to his resting-place. She: At His Funeral. Thomas Hardy. VLP
They bear no laurels on their sunless brows. Failures. Arthur W. Upson. HBV-2; WGRP
They beat the tom-tom, they plucked the guitar. Fandango. "Stanley Vestal." BPAW
They began to sway to the. When These Old Barns Lost Their Inhabitants. David Kherdian. TAT
They borrowed a bed to lay His head. The Cross Was His Own [*or* "Borrowed"]. *Unknown.* BLPA; BLRP
They bowed to him: "O man of God." The Prophet. "Yehoash," *tr. by* Isidore Goldstick. TrJP
They breathe with the night. Roland Penrose. *Fr.* The Road Is Wider than Long. EAS
They bring me gifts, they honour me. If They Honoured Me, Giving Me Their Gifts. "Michael Field." OBMV
They bring me in two eggs and a slice of bacon. James K. Baxter. How to Fly by Standing Still, 3. OCNZ
They brought him in on a stretcher from the world. Grandfather. Derek Mahon. OxBC
They brought him one morning. Dimitris Tsaloumas, *tr. by* Margaret Carroll. *Fr.* A Rhapsody of Old Men. CBAP
They brought it along and they slipped it in. Heart Burial. Geoffrey Grigson. POL
They brought me ambrotypes. Rutherford McDowell. Edgar Lee Masters. *Fr.* Spoon River Anthology. EyDe; LiTA; OxBA
They built the front, upon my word. The Building [*or* On the Building] of a New Church. *Unknown.* EyDe; FaBoEE
They call all experiences of the senses *mystic*, when the experience is considered. Mystic. D. H. Lawrence. PAI
They call it regional, this relevance. Lake Chelan. William Stafford. BiP; NaP
They call me and I go. Complaint. William Carlos Williams. QFR
They call me cruel. Do I know if mouse or songbird feels? The Cat. Charles Stuart Calverley. *Fr.* Sad Memories. ChTr
They call me Hanging Johnny. Hanging Johnny. *Unknown.* AmSS; GBP
They call streets "boulevards" and build them huge. Big Crash Out West. Peter Viereck. PoPl
They call thee rich; I deem thee poor. Treasure. Lucillius, *tr. by* William Cowper. AWP
They call us aliens, we are told. On Behalf of Some Irishmen Not Followers of Tradition. "Æ." AnIL
They call you "drunk with words"; but when we drink. A Poet's Epitaph. Kingsley Amis. DBV
They call your name in vain. St. Francis of Assisi and the Miserable Jews. Josef Whittlin, *tr. by* Isaac Komem. VWA
They called her "Angel," sardonic. "Angel." Robin Skelton. NMP
"They called it Annandale—and I was there." How Annandale Went Out. E. A. Robinson. AP; CoBMV; HBMV; MoAB; MoAmPo; NoAM; NOBA
They called me to the window, for. Emily Dickinson. MoVE
They called my love a poor blind maid. On a Blind Girl. Baha Ad-din Zuhayr, *tr. by* E. H. Palmer. AWP
They called the place Lookout Farm. Memoirs of a Spinach-Picker. Sylvia Plath. GrPl
They called them shadblow or service bush. Those Trees That Line the Northway. Ellen Perreault. AMV-81
They came back, a well known face. This Beach Can Be Dangerous. Allen Curnow. OCNZ
They came hurrying across the mountain highway. Monkeys on Mt. Hiei. Edith Marcombe Shiffert. WPE
They came in to the little town. We Are Going. Kath Walker. CBAP
They came on to fish-hook Gettysburg in this way, after this fashion. The Battle of Gettysburg. Stephen Vincent Benét. *Fr.* John Brown's Body. BeLS
They came out of the sun undetected. The Raid. William Everson. NoAM; PrIm
They came running over the perilous sands. 1945. Sir Herbert Read. OxBTC
They Came This Evening. Léon Damas, *tr. fr. French by* Seth L. Wolitz. TTY
They Came to the Wedding. Babette Deutsch. NePoAm
They can have your thighs. M. A. P. Calvin Forbes. MAYP
They cannot contain the death. After the Murder of Jimmy Walsh. Joan Murray. LTB
They cannot wholly pass away. The Departed. John Banister Tabb. AA
They Can't Do That. *Unknown.* WTO
"They carry on." Floodtide. Askia Muhammad Touré. PoBA; PoNe
They cast lots on the day of Azazel. Lament for Azazel. Francis Landy. VWA
They Cast Their Nets in Galilee, *with music.* William A. Percy. AH
They catch your eye early, those rising black. For Stephen Drawing Birds. Pattiann Rogers. MAYP
They chained her fair young body to the cold and cruel stone. Andromeda. James Jeffrey Roche. AA; HBV-2
They changed her name. Nechama. Shirley Kaufman. LCAP
They chose me from my brothers. Riddle: What Am I? Dorothy Aldis. SoPo
They claim no guard of heraldry. Aristocrats of Labor. W. Stewart. PGD
They Clapped. Nikki Giovanni. WPOW
They Closed Her Eyes. Gustavo Adolfo Becquer, *tr. fr. Spanish by* John Masefield. AWP
They cloud the mirror, when I put them on. In Grandfather's Glasses. Patricia Peters. Str
They come/ each one. Circus Maximus. George Bowering. PeCV
They come again, those monsters of the sea. Icebergs. William Prescott Foster. EtS
They come as a boon and a blessing to men. The Waverley Pen. *Unknown.* FaBoUs
They come, beset by riddling hail. Albuera. Thomas Hardy. *Fr.* The Dynasts. WaaP
They come down. Deer in the Bush. Chana Bloch. MAYP
They come from beds of lichen green. The Assembling of the Fays. Joseph Rodman Drake. The Culprit Fay. GN
They come in from the street. Inebriates. Philip Brasfield. LFAC
They come in search of front porch. Tourism. Lillie D. Chaffin. TAT
They come into. Feeding the Lions. Norman Jordan. BOLo; CTBA; NBP; PoBA

They come not within the tall woods. To One Elect. S. I. Hayakawa. PoA
They come!—they come!—the heroes come. Evacuation of New York by the British. *Unknown.* PAH
They come, they come, with fife and drum. The Palace. Charles Stuart Calverley. EBVV
They come with, ah, fell footfall. Fêtes, Fates. John Malcolm Brinnin. LiTA
They could not shut you out of heaven. To ——. Katharine Morse. HBMV
They cross the frontier as their names cross your pages. The New Emigration. Kay Boyle. WPE
They cross the yard. Dedication to Hunger. Louise Glück. GeTw
They Crucified My Lord ("They nailed my Saviour to the cross"). *Unknown.* STF
They crucified my Lord, an' He never said a mumbalin' word. Crucifixion. *Unknown.* BoAN-1; BPo; TAP; TrGrPo
"They cut it in squares." Socratic. Hilda Doolittle ("H. D."). HoPM
They deployed military troops. White Weekend. Quincy Troupe. NBP
They did it George. They did it. Conversation with Washington. Myra Cohn Livingston. OFD
They did not know that the moon had shone. Moon-Madness. Victor Starbuck. HBMV
They did not know this face. Job. Elizabeth Sewell. EaLo
They didn't have much trouble. Teaching the Ape to Write Poems. James Tate. GP
They didn't hire him. Hitch Haiku. Gary Snyder. InPK; LCAP
They dither softly at her bedroom door. Cover Her Face. Thomas Kinsella. CIP; IPY
They do but grope in learning's pedant round. Substance and Shadow. Cardinal Newman. GoBC
They do me wrong who say I come no more. Opportunity. Walter Malone. BLPA; BLPL; FaBoBe; HBV-2; WBLP; YaD
They do neither plight nor wed. The City of the Dead. Richard Burton. HBV-2
They do not care, the dying, whether it be dawn or dusk or daylight full and clear. Illi Morituri. Mary Morison Webster. PeSA
They do not come with furred caps. Barbarians. John Fowles. POL
They do not live in the world. The Animals. Edwin Muir. CMoP; EBCP; EBEV; HeIP; MoBrPo; NoP
They do zay that a travellen chap. The Leane. William Barnes. EBVV
They dogged him all one afternoon. On the Way to the Mission. Duncan Campbell Scott. CaP; NOBC
They done took Cordelia. Stony Lonesome. Langston Hughes. NOBA
They don't build houses like that any more. Verandahs. R. F. Brissenden. CBAP
They don't get anywhere. The Couple Overheard. William Meredith. HoPM; NoAM; TW
They don't hold grudges. First Monday Scottsboro Alabama. Tom Weatherly. PoBA
They don't like strangers. Stoney Ridge Dance Hall. Alden Nowlan. MoCV
They Don't Speak English in Paris. Ogden Nash. OBAL
They dragged you from [the] homeland. Strong Men. Sterling A. Brown. BANP; BPo; CNA; FB; PoBA; TTY
They Dream Only of America. John Ashbery. CAPP; EAS
They dressed us up in black. The Funeral. Walter de la Mare. CMoP; MoVE
They drift away. Ah, God! they drift for ever. Drifting Away. Charles Kingsley. OxBoCh
They droop like sad fuchsias from our bodies. The Grief of Our Genitals. Henry Carlile. GP
They drop with periodic regularity. The Preacher Sought to Find Out Acceptable Words. Richard Eberhart. WaP
They dropped like flakes, they dropped like stars. Emily Dickinson. AA; OHIP
They drove the hammered nails into His hands. Sequel to Finality. Patrick F. Kirby. GoBC
"They dug ten streets from that there hole," he said. Millom Old Quarry. Norman Nicholson. ChMP
They eat beans mostly, this old yellow pair. The Bean Eaters. Gwendolyn Brooks. BlSi; CAPP; GrPl; HAP; HeIP; MAT; NoP; PoBA; PrIm; TAP; TTY; WeW
They Eat Out. Margaret Atwood. NoP
("In restaurants we argue.") NeAC
They ended parle, and both addressed for fight. Milton. *Fr.* Paradise Lost, VI. OBWP
They enter the bare wood, drawn. The Novices. Denise Levertov. NaP
They erect gallows in the prison yard. The Condemned. Edmond Jabès, *tr. by* Jack Hirschman. VWA
They Feed They Lion. Philip Levine. LCAP; MAT; NNaP; NoAM; NOBA; Prf
They feel the calm delight, and thus proceed. The Suffolk Shore. George Crabbe. *Fr.* The Borough, Letter XXIII. FaBoPP
They find the way who linger where. The Way. Sidney Henry Morse. HBV-2
They fished and they fished. The Fish with the Deep Smile. Margaret Wise Brown. PDV
They Flee [*or* Fle] from Me That Sometime Did Me Seek [*or* Seke]. Sir Thomas Wyatt. *See* Lover Showeth How He Is Forsaken. . .
They fling their flags upon the morn. Spain's Last Armada. Wallace Rice. PAH
They flow forth. Stories Relate Life. Dennis Shady. LFAC
They flutter out of white, and run. Bathers. Terence Tiller. ChMP; NeBP
They fly in their own time. Pigeons in Prison. Derek Butler. LFAC
They fought last year by the upper valley of Son-Kan. The Long War. Li Po, *tr. by* Cheng Yu Sun. WaaP
They fought south of the Castle. Fighting South of the Castle. *Unknown, tr. by* Arthur Waley. AWP; WaaP
They found a taxi. He took her home. The Moral Taxi Ride. Erich Kästner, *tr. by* Jerome Rothenberg. ErPo
They Found Him Sitting in a Chair. Horace Gregory. MoAmPo
They found it in her hollow marble bed. A Roman Mirror. Sir James Rennell Rodd. OBVV
They framed him once. The Hills of *Tsa la gi.* Robert Jo Conley. STE
They gathered around and told him not to do it. Noah. Roy Daniells. PeCV; WHW
They gave him an overdose. Loyal. William Matthews. MAYP
They gave him his orders at Monroe, Virginia. The Wreck of the Old 97. *Unknown.* ViBoFo
They gave me the wrong name, in the first place. Her Story. Naomi Long Madgett. IHMS; PoBA
They gave my father a television. Death. Howard Byatt. FF
They gave us the mysterious deep warehouse. The Ajax Samples. Laura Jensen. LCAP
They glare—those stony eyes! The Sphinx. Henry Howard Brownell. AA
They go along the graveled walks. Seminary. Constance Carrier. NePoAm
They go before the fog lifts, looking for light. The Beekeeper's Dream. Katharine Auchincloss Lorr. SUW
They go by, go by, love, the days and the hours. Teresa de Jesús, *tr. fr. Spanish by* Maria A. Proser, Arlene Scully, *and* James Scully. WPOW
They go in different ways. No One Talks about This. Carl Rakosi. GP
They got him in the end, of course. Walt Whitman at the Reburial of Poe. Nicholas Christopher. MAYP
They Got You Last Night. Aaron Kurtz. *Fr.* Behold the Sea. PPON
They grew and charcoal bundle shakes itself. Brothers. Solomon Edwards. NNP
They grew in beauty side by side. The Graves of a Household. Felicia Dorothea Hemans. FaPoR; HBV-2; VLP; WBLP; WPE
They Grow Up Too Fast, She Said. Diana O Hehir. NPGG
They guided birds and came to hear their story. Of History More like Myth. Jean Garrigue. NYBP
They had a pocketful of stories that they told. A High Place. Eithne Wilkins. NeBP
They had a tale on which to gloat. No Miracle. Daniel Corkery. AnIV
They had been there a month; the water had begun to tear them apart. A Negro Soldier's Viet Nam Diary. Herbert Martin. PoBA
They had brought in such sheafs of hair. The Last Bowstrings. Edward Lucas White. AA
They had chiseled on my stone the words. *See* They have chiseled . . .
They had dragged for hours. These Trees Are No Forest of Mourners. D. G. Jones. NOBC
They had me laid out in a white. April Fools' Day. Yusef Komunyakaa. MAYP
They had pulled her out of the river. She was dead. Along the River. D. J. Enright. DFF
They had secured their beauty to the dock. The Crowd. John Masefield. OxBTC
They hadn't noticed her coming, too busy with loud. An Aftermath. Thomas Blackburn. NMP
They hail you as their morning star. Men. Dorothy Parker. DBV
They hand it to you, a slot. Christ. Greg Forker. LFAC
They hanged Jeff Buckner from a sycamore tree. Jeff Buckner. Frank Beddo. WTO
They hanged the King of Ai at eventide. The King of Ai. Hyam Plutzik. LiTM; VWA
They have been with us a long time. Telephone Poles. John Updike. FYAP; Psk; SaC
They have built us a golf course. Poems from Prison, 2. J. J. Maloney. FAZ
They have carried the mahogany chair and the cane rocker. Mourning Picture. Adrienne Rich. CoAP
They have [*or* had] chiseled on my stone the words. Cassius Hueffer. Edgar Lee Masters. *Fr.* Spoon River Anthology. NoAM; OxBA

They have come by carloads. Surfers at Santa Cruz. Paul Goodman. FF; LiSp
They have connived at those jewelled fascinations. Auspice of Jewels. Laura Riding. LiTA; NoAM
They have dreamed as young men dream. Old Black Men. Georgia Douglas Johnson. CDC; PoBA; PoNe
They have eyes that see not. Maxine W. Kumin. *Fr.* Song for Seven Parts of the Body. POL
They have fenced in the dirt road. Burial. Alice Walker. AmPA; PrIm
They have given the gorilla language. Koko. Ann Downer. SUW
They have gone/ into the green hill. Apples. Donald Hall. LCAP
They have laid the penthouse scenes away. Elegy in a Theatrical Warehouse. Kenneth Fearing. NYBP
They have left bread on the table. Bread. Gabriela Mistral, *tr. by* Allan Francovich *and* Kathleen Weaver. WPOW
They have [*or* They've *or* Th' have] left Thee naked, Lord, O that they had! Upon the Body of Our Blessed Lord, Naked and Bloody [*or* On Our Crucified Lord Naked and Bloody]. Richard Crashaw. ACP; CABA; HoPM; InvP; OAEL-1; OAEP; OBS; PAI; SeCP; SeCV-1; TrCP
They have left us, all the summer's mornings. Classical Autumn. Robert Clayton Casto. AMV-81
They have made for Leonora this low dwelling in the ground. Leonora. E. A. Robinson. NePA
They have met at last—as storm-clouds. Manassas. Catherine M. Warfield. PAH
They have no word for conscience. Carrier Indians. Ken Belford. NOBC
They have not gone from us. O no! they are. Our Dead. Robert Nichols. WGRP
They have said evil of my dear. Medieval Norman Song. *Unknown, tr. by* John Addington Symonds. AWP
They have said, "too risky." To Words. Ralph Pomeroy. CoPo
They have sed. Hospital/Poem. Sonia Sanchez. BPo; PoBA
They have slain you, Sean MacDermott. Lament for Sean MacDermott. "Seumas O'Sullivan." AnIV
They Have Taken It from Me. Timothy Corsellis. WaP
They have taken the gable from the roof of clay. Swedes. Edward Thomas. BrPo; MoVE; OAEL-2
They have taken the maps and spread them out. Still Pond, No More Moving. Howard Moss. NYBP
They have turned, and say that I am dying. That. I Substitute for the Dead Lecturer. Amiri Baraka. NOBA
They Have Turned the Church Where I Ate God. Gary Gildner. GP
They have vanished, the immortal horses of Achilles. The Deathless Ones. Eleanor Glenn Wallis. NePoAm
They Have Yarns. Carl Sandburg. *Fr.* The People, Yes. AmFN; LiTA; MoAmPo
They haven't got no noses. The Song of Quoodle. G. K. Chesterton. GoJo
They head the list. Horses. Richard Armour. PoPl; WhC
They heard the South wind sighing. The Crocuses. Frances E. W. Harper. BlSi
They held her South to Magellan's mouth. The Rush of the *Oregon.* Arthur Guiterman. PAH
They hire you for the silk to line their budgets. Advice from Euterpe. Carter Revard. VoR
They hold their hands over their mouths. The Poets Agree to Be Quiet by the Swamp. David Wagoner. CoAP; VGW
They howled 'til Pilate. Crucifixion. Waring Cuney. BANP
They hunch their heads against the fable of the night. The Dolls Play at Hansel and Gretel. William Dickey. DFT
They hunt chameleon worlds with cameras. Adina. Harold Milton Telemaque. TTY
They hunt, the velvet tigers in the jungle. India. W. J. Turner. MoBrPo; PDV
They hurt no one. They rove the North. In Fur. William Stafford. RFM
They journeyed,/ When the darkness of night. Ode. Ibn al-Arabi, *tr. by* R. A. Nicholson. AWP
They kill me for the death within them. Mihailovich. Roy McFadden. NeIP
They killed you and didn't tell us where they. Epitaph for the Tomb of Adolfo Baez Bone. Ernesto Cardenal, *tr. by* Janet Brof. POL
They knew the conjugations of the flesh. Emeritus, n. Henri Coulette. FF
They knew they were fighting our war. As the months grew to years. Pershing at the Tomb of Lafayette. Amelia Josephine Burr. PAH
They know not of their mission from above. Cowper's Three Hares. Charles Tennyson Turner. FM
They know the lion's power. Killed in Action. Terence Tiller. NeBP
They know the time to go! Time to Go. "Susan Coolidge." GN
They laughed at me as "Prof. Moon." Alfonso Churchill. Edgar Lee Masters. *Fr.* Spoon River Anthology. GLGT
They lean against the cooling car, backs pressed. The Discovery of the Pacific. Thom Gunn. HeIP
They lean over the path. Orchids. Theodore Roethke. CMoP; NMP; PPoe
They lean upon their windows. It is late. Ladies by Their Windows. Donald Justice. TwAmPo
They leave their love-lorn haunts. Wedded. Isaac Rosenberg. FaBoEn; PoPle
They leave us so to the way we took. In Neglect. Robert Frost. VGW
They leave us—artists, singers, all. When London Calls. Victor Daley. CBAP
They left behind the insistent strain. Retrospect. Roy Davis. WhC
They left him hanging for the deed. Once the Wind. Mark Van Doren. TwAmPo
They left the primrose glistening in its dew. Spring, and the Blind Children. Alfred Noyes. OxBTC
They left the vine-wreathed cottage and the mansion on the hill. The Women of the West. G. Essex Evans. PoAu-1
They left their Babylon bare. The Destruction of Jerusalem by the Babylonian Hordes. Isaac Rosenberg. VWA
They lie in the Sunday street. The Dead. C. Day Lewis. MP; TwCP
They lie on beaches and are proud to tan. Summer Resort. P. K. Page. CaP
They lie, the men who tell for reasons of their own. Faces in the Street. Henry Lawson. CBAP
They lie who say that love must be. No Sufferer for Her Love. *Unknown, tr. by* Robin Flower. AnIL
They lied about. Strange Kind (II). J. D. Reed. MOON
They lied, those lying traitors all. Medieval Norman Song. *Unknown, tr. by* John Addington Symonds. AWP
They lined the long perches like a living color spectrum. The Finches. Philip Murray. NePoAm
They Live. Randall Swingler. WaP
They live alone. Neighbors. David Allan Evans. Psk
They live by [*or* lived in] the Lakes, an appropriate quarter. The Lake Poets [*or* On the Lake Poets]. Charles Townsend. DBV; FaBoEE
They Live in Parallel Worlds. William J. Harris. CNA
They live in their country. Restricted. Miriam Waddington. CaP
They live 'neath the curtain. Puk-Wudjies. Patrick R. Chalmers. HBVY
They lived alone. The Romney. Harriet Monroe. HBMV
They lived in the Lakes, an appropriate quarter. *See* They live by the Lakes . . .
They lived out in a women's house. Stephanie Markman. *Fr.* The Rime of the Ancient Feminist. BrRo
They look up with their pale and sunken faces. Elizabeth Barrett Browning. *Fr.* The Cry of the Children. NBM
They looked at me all ghosts. Mellisandra. Harriet Rose. BrRo
They looked so good. The Young Fenians. Padraic Fallon. BlrV
They looked soft floating down. Invasion North. Richard Hugo. GP
They made a myth of you, professor. Mr. Attila. Carl Sandburg. ImOP
"They made her a grave too cold and damp." The Lake of the Dismal Swamp. Thomas Moore. BLPA
"They made impudent inspection of our coast." Rex Ingamells. *Fr.* The Great South Land. CBAP
They made the chamber sweet with flowers and leaves. Meeting. Christina Rossetti. Monna Innominata. HBV-1
They made them idols in the elder days. Idols. Richard Burton. TrPWD
They made them ready and we saw them go. The Travellers. Mark A. De Wolfe Howe. AA
They make a pretty pair of debauchees. Catullus, *tr. fr. Latin by* James Michie. DBV
They marched,/ That sun-gold summer day. Via Dolorosa. Phoebe Smith. PGD
They May Rail at This Life. Thomas Moore. NBM; PoEL-4
They may suppose, because I would not cloy your ear. Sonnet. John Berryman. NoP
They may talk of love in a cottage. Love in a Cottage. Nathaniel Parker Willis. HBV-1
They meet but with unwholesome Springs. Against Them Who Lay Unchastity to the Sex of Women. William Habington. *Fr.* Castara, II. AnAnS-2; JCP; MePo; OBS; SeCP
They meet over water. 3rd Dance—Making a Structure with a Roof or Under a Roof—6-7 February 1964. Jackson MacLow. CoPo
They met in passion; Satyrs of the glade. Once. George Ives. PeHV
They met inside the gateway that gives the view. Wind and Mist. Edward Thomas. BrPo
They might not need me, but they might. Emily Dickinson. TRV
They more than we are what we are. Statues. Kathleen Raine. NYBP
They mouth love's language. Gnash. A Memory of the Players in a Mirror at Midnight. James Joyce. InvP; NoAM; ViBoPo
They move on tracks of never-ending light. The Master Singers. Rhys Carpenter. WGRP
They moved like rivers in their mended stockings. The Grandmothers. Mary Oliver. WPE

They must be shown as about to taste of the tree. Adam and Eve. C. H. Sisson. FaBoTw
They must to keep their certainty accuse. The Leaders of the Crowd. W. B. Yeats. EBEV; MoAB; MoBrPo
They nailed my Saviour to the cross. They Crucified My Lord. *Unknown.* STF
They named it Aultgraat—Ugly Burn. The Black Rock of Kiltearn. Andrew Young. FaBoTw
They named the huge one Grendel. Grendel. *Unknown, tr. by* Burton Raffel. *Fr.* Beowulf. NU
They nearly strike me dumb. My Mistress's Boots. Frederick Locker-Lampson. HBV-1
They need them the most. Raincoats for the Dead. Albert Bellg. FAZ
They never feel they can be well in the water. Lament for the Non-Swimmers. David Wagoner. DFF
They never knew or never cared to know. Coach into Pumpkin. Dorothy E. Reid. DFT
They Never Quite Leave Us. Margaret Elizabeth Sangster. WBLP
They never seem to be far away. Within the Veil. Margaret E. Sangster. BLRP
They nicknamed me Mririda. Mririda. Mririda n'Ait Attik, *tr. by* René Euloge; *English vers. by* Daniel Halpern *and* Paula Paley. WPOW
They nod at me and I at stems. Open. Larry Eigner. NeAP
They opn our mail petulantly. Th Wundrfulness uv th Mountees Our Secret Police. Bill Bissett. NOBC
They paddle with staccato feet. Pigeons. Richard Kell. BoAnP
They paper the walls of their world. The Recluses. Stuart Z. Perkoff. NeAP
They pass like a warning of snow. The Insects. Nancy Willard. LCAP
They pass so close, the people on the street. Footsteps. Hazel Hall. HBMV
They pass too fast. Ships, and there's time for sighing. Earth Has Shrunk in the Wash. William Empson. CMoP
They pity me./ "Look at him, see." Lonely. André Spire, *tr. by* Jethro Bithell. AWP; TrJP
They played till the dusk of summer in the wood. Coogan's Wood. Francis Stuart. NeIP
They pointed me out on the highway, and they said. The Traveller. John Berryman. PoA; VGW
They possessed nothing. The Inheritors. Gary Geddes. NOBC
They Pray the Best Who Pray and Watch, *with music.* Edward Hopper. AH
They pull any hints of light. Fishermen at Dawn. William Meissner. WOLT
They put him here because God came at night. Dementia Praecox. Morris Bishop. PoA
They put the screens around his bed. Screens. Winifred M. Letts. SUMH
They put up big wooden gods. Manufactured Gods. Carl Sandburg. WGRP
They put us far apart. Emily Dickinson. AP
They ran through the streets of the seaport town. A Greyport Legend. Bret Harte. Ets; GN; MOS
They rear'd their lodges in the wilderness. The First Fathers. Robert Stephen Hawker. OBVV
They renounce the very idea. The Parents of Psychotic Children. Marvin Bell. SUW
They Return. Jay MacPherson. *Fr.* The Way Down. NOBC; PoA
They rise like sudden fiery flowers. Fireworks. James Reeves. OnUR; PoSC
They rise to mastery of wind and snow. Pioneers. Hamlin Garland. AA
They roamed between/ Delicious dells. Prose and Poesy; a Rural Misadventure. Thomas R. Ybarra. WhC
They rode from the camp at morn. Sidney Godolphin. Clinton Scollard. AA
They rode north. Blackie Thinks of His Brothers. Stanley Crouch. PoBA
They rose up in a twinkling cloud. The Stockdoves. Andrew Young. BoAnP
They roused him with muffins—they roused him with ice. The Baker's Tale. "Lewis Carroll." *Fr.* The Hunting of the Snark. EBEV
They said, It will be like snow falling. The Snow. Sidney Keyes. NeBP
They said, It will be like snow falling. Variations On a Theme by Sidney Keyes. Eithne Wilkins. NeBP
They said the furnaces were cold. The Factory Olga Cabral. GP
They said, "The Master is coming." Unawares. Emma A. Lent. PoLF
They said the moon wasn't going to rise no no. August 18. Joanne Kyger. PoM
They said this mystery shall never cease. Blake. *Fr.* Gnomic Verses. TrGrPo
They said, "Wait." Well, I waited. Alabama Centennial. Naomi Long Madgett. BALP; BPo
They said, "You are no longer a lad." Battle Won Is Lost. Phil George. GrPl
They sat by the water. The fine women. Stars Which See, Stars Which Do Not See. Marvin Bell. LCAP
They sat. They stood about. Of Commerce and Society. Geoffrey Hill. NePoEA-2; PPoe
They sate to meat, and Satyrane his chaunce. Spenser. *Fr.* The Faerie Queene, III, 9. OAEL-1
They saw the sun looke pale, and cast through aire. Presage of Storme. George Chapman. *Fr.* Eugenia. FaBoEn
They Say. Ella Wheeler Wilcox. WBLP
They say a maiden conceived. Christmas Carols. Patricia Beer. OxBC
They say a tropic river threads the seas. The Gulf Stream. Henry Bellamann. EtS
They say, God wot! On the Death of the Giraffe. Thomas Hood. FaBoEE
They say: He lives with colours. Sons. Jack Cope. PeSA
They say He was a serious child. The Gentlest Lady. Dorothy Parker. ISi
They say, his strange, large eyes. Father. Margit Kaffka, *tr. by* Laura Schiff. PBWP
They say ideal beauty cannot enter. Hiram Powers' "Greek Slave." Elizabeth Barrett Browning. SBG; VLP
They say I'm crazy got no sense. I Don't Care. Jean Lenox. FSN
They say its's better to be poor. Rain Has Fallen on the History Books. David Rosenberg. VWA
They say La Jac Brite Pink Skin Bleach avails not. Government Injunction. Josephine Miles. PoNe
They say my mother is a witch. Johannes Kepler (1571-1630). Siv Cedering. *Fr.* Letters from the Astronomers. SUW
They Say My Verse Is Sad: No Wonder. A. E. Housman. NoAM; PAI
They say no one died. Celebration 1982. Terri Meyette Wilkins. LFAC
They say, old man, your horse will die. The Dead Horse. *Unknown.* AmSS; AS
They say one good shot deserves another. Fools. Glenn Hardin. AMV-81
They say Revis found a flatrock. Mountain Bride. Robert Morgan. GeTw; GP; MAYP
They say "Son." Old Black Men Say. James A. Emanuel. PoBA
They say that, afar in the land of the west. The Green Isle of Lovers. Robert Charles Sands. AA
They say that blood is salt. Gifts. Leon Stokesbury. GP
They say that dead men tell no tales! Dead Men Tell No Tales. Haniel Long. HBMV
They say that every idle word. Idle Words. Walter Savage Landor. OBSV
They say that freedom is a constant struggle. Freedom Is a Constant Struggle. *Unknown.* FSW
They say that God lives very high! A Child's Thought of God. Elizabeth Barrett Browning. FaPON; TRV
They say that I was in my youth. Limerick. *Unknown.* CenHV
They Say That in the Unchanging Place. Hilaire Belloc. *Fr.* Dedicatory Ode. PoLF
They say that man is mighty. What Rules the World. William Ross Wallace. OHIP
They say that old age. Unbeliever. Dorothy Dow. HBMV
They say that plants don't talk, nor do. Rosalia de Castro, *tr. fr. Spanish by* Aliki *and* Willis Barnstone. BoWoP
They say that Richard Cory owns. Richard Cory. Paul Simon. InPK
They say that shadow[e]s of deceased ghosts. Sonnet. Joshua Sylvester. EIL; OBS
They say that "Time assuages." Sorrow. Emily Dickinson. WGRP
They say that when they burned young Shelley's corpse. The Fishes and the Poet's Hands. Frank Yerby. AmNP; PoNe
They say the experimental. Nothing. Burns Singer. OxBS
They say the Lion and the Lizard keep. Omar Khayyám, *tr. by* Edward Fitzgerald. *Fr.* The Rubáiyát of Omar Khayyám. EBEV
They say the men are. The Men Are Coming Back! Barry Cole. OxBTC
They say the most of mothers. My Mother. *Unknown.* STF
They say the Phoenix is dying, some say dead. News of the Phoenix. A. J. M. Smith. ELU; MoCV; PeCV
They say the sea is cold, but the sea contains. Whales Weep Not! D. H. Lawrence. CMoP; MOS; NU; PPoe
They Say the Sea Is Loveless. D. H. Lawrence. MOS
They say the Spanish ships are out. The Dragon of the Seas. Thomas Nelson Page. PAH
They say the war is over. But water still. Redeployment. Howard Nemerov. LiTM; NePA; OBWP; TrJP
They say the wells. Winter News. John Haines. PPJ
They say the windows were welded. A Dangerous Music. Michael Knoll. LFAC
They say the world is round, and yet. Life's Scars. Ella Wheeler Wilcox. BLPA
They say there is a land. Idaho. *Unknown.* BPAW; GBP
They say there is a sweeter air. A Carriage from Sweden. Marianne Moore. HAP; LiTA; LiTM; MoAB; MP; NePA; TwCP; WeW
They say there is no hope. Sea Gods. Hilda Doolittle ("H. D."). LiTA; MOS

They say there's a high windless world and strange. Mutability. Rupert Brooke. BrPo
They say this is His mother. Fourth Station. Ruth Schaumann, *tr. by* William J. Brell. ISi
They say 'tis sinful to flirt. Sinful to Flirt. *Unknown.* AmFP
They say Tom Starr. Tom Starr. Robert J. Conley. STE
They say we devour our men. To the Man Who Watches Spiders. Siv Cedering Fox. LTB
They say you were made to your father's image. Frog Prince. Phoebe Pettingell. DFT
They say you're in love with that keck-eyed lad. Braggart! Denis Wrafter. OnYI
They see Gods wonders that are call'd. Roger Williams. SCAP
They seemed, to those who saw them meet. Shadows. Richard Monckton Milnes. HBV-1
They sell good beer at Haslemere. West Sussex Drinking Song. Hilaire Belloc. MoBrPo
They sent him back to her. The letter came. Not to Keep. Robert Frost. CMoP; OxBA
They served tea in the sandpile, together with. The Party. Reed Whittemore. CAD; CoAP; ConAP; NCSH
They set the fish upon the table. Pesci Misti. Leonard Aaronson. FaBoTw
They set the slave free, striking off his chains. The Slave. James Oppenheim. TrJP
They shall come in the black weathers. The Waiting Watchers. Henry Treece. NeBP
They shall go down unto life's borderland. Sonnet to Negro Soldiers. Joseph Seamon Cotter, Jr. PoBA
"They shall not die in vain," we said. Dedication. Ralph Gustafson. CaP
They shall not return to us, the resolute, the young. Mesopotamia. Kipling. MMA
They shall sink under water. The Cities. "Æ." OBMV
They shook the green leaves down. Magic Fox. James Welch. CDW
They shot him on the Nine-Stane Rig. Barthram's Dirge. *Unknown.* FaBoRV
They shot young Windebank just here. Young Windebank. Margaret L. Woods. HBV-2; HBVY
They should never have built a barn there, at all. The Barn. Edward Thomas. EyDe
They shut me up in prose. Emily Dickinson. InPS; NOBA; SBG
They shut the road through the woods. The Way Through the Woods. Kipling. CH; FaBoCh; FaPON; MoVE; NOBE; OBEV; OBNC; OBVV; OxBChV; OxBTC; PoPle; RFM; SeCeV; VLP
They sin who tell us love can die. Love Indestructible. Robert Southey. *Fr.* The Curse of Kehama. OBNC; OBRV
They Sing. Theodore Roethke. NYBP
They sing their dearest songs. During Wind and Rain. Thomas Hardy. CMoP; ELP; GTBS-P; HAP; InPK; NIP; OAEL-2; OxBTC; PoPle; PPP; QFR; SeCeV; TEP
They sit and smoke on the esplanade. At a Watering Place. Thomas Hardy. CMoP
They sit at home and they dream and dally. The Adventurers. May Byron. HBV-2
They sit in a glass egg. Dead Embryos. Judit Tóth, *tr. by* Laura Schiff. WPOW
They sit in the roots. The Lost Tribe. Robert Finch. CaP
They sit on the wall at the square. The Old Men. Cid Corman. PCP
They slept on the field which their valor had won. Beyond the Potomac. Paul Hamilton Hayne. PAH
They slew a god in a valley. Gluskap's Hound. T. G. Roberts. WHW
They slew by night. The Pentecost Castle. Geoffrey Hill. HAP
They slip on to the bus, hair piled up high. The Young Ones. Elizabeth Jennings. OxBTC
They sneaked into the limbo of time. Ancestral Faces. Kwesi Brew. PBA
They Sometimes Call Me. Wendy Rose. CDW
They speak not of torment. Flowers in the Ward. Shaw Neilson. CBAP
They Speak o' Wiles. William Thom. HBV-1
They speak of time, as if the hour were split. Madaket Beach. Isabel Harriss Barr. GoYe
They spent my life plotting against me. Possessions. Ken Smith. EAS
They splayed him scientifically on the rock. Prometheus, with Wings. Michael Ondaatje. PeCV
They spoke/ of the queen at night growing. Short Eulogy. Zali Gurevitch, *tr. by* Gabriel Levin. VWA
They spoke of the horse alive. The Horse. Philip Levine. CoAP
They spoke the loveliest of languages. History of World Languages. D. J. Enright. OxBC
They sprint eight feet and. Ringed Plover by a Water's Edge. Norman MacCaig. OxBC
They stand in a row like chimneys. Poplars. Henry Grynberg, *tr. by* Isaac Komem. VWA
They stand like penitential Augustines. Gothic Landscape. Irving Layton. TrJP
They step from the high plane and begin to tumble. Sky Diving. Richmond Lattimore. LiSp
They still vibrate with the sound. The Drowned. Stephen Spender. MOS
They stole little Bridget. Up the Airy Mountain. William Allingham. FaFP
They stood above the world. Yes. Richard Doddridge Blackmore. HBV-1
They stood among many others. The Window of the Tobacco Shop. C. P. Cavafy, *tr. by* Edmund Keeley *and* Philip Sherrard. PeHV
They stood on the bridge at midnight. How Often. Ben King. HBV-1
They stood—rain pelting at window, shrouded sea. In the Local Museum. Walter de la Mare. HAP
They strolled down the lane together. A Farmer's Boy. *Unknown.* PoPle
They suck and whisper it in mercury. The Break-up. A. M. Klein. NOBC
They sucked at the sweat on his forehead. Motive for Mercy. Ken Milburn. PoSH
They sung how God spoke out the worlds vast ball. The Creation. Abraham Cowley. *Fr.* Davideis, I. OBS
They swing across the screen in brave array. At the Movies. Florence Ripley Mastin. SUMH
They take it from me. Wulf. Bill Manhire. OCNZ
They teeter with an inane care among the skewbald stones. Sheep. Hal Porter. PoAu-2
They tell me I am beautiful: they praise my silken hair. Sad Memories. Charles Stuart Calverley. FM
They Tell Me I Am Lost. Maurice Kenny. STE
They tell me I have to exercise to lose weight. Amen Jaime Sabines, *tr. by* Steve Kowit AMV-81
They tell me, Liberty! that in thy name. Liberty for All. William Lloyd Garrison. AA
They tell me she is beautiful, my city. Dusk. DuBose Heyward. HBMV
They tell me thou art rich, my country: gold. America's Prosperity. Henry van Dyke. PGD
They tell me 'tis decided; you depart. Byron. *Fr.* Don Juan. ViBoPo
They tell of a hunter named Shephard. A Hunter Named Shephard. *Unknown.* TDH
They tell that I must not love. Love Unsought. Emma Catharine Embury. AA
They tell us of an Indian tree. To My Mother. Thomas Moore. OHIP
They tell you Lincoln was ungainly, plain? His Face. Florence Earle Coates. OHIP
They tell you that Death's at the turn of the road. The Unillumined Verge. Robert Bridges (1858-1941). AA
They That Go Down to the Sea. Bible, *O.T.* *Fr.* Psalm CVII. ChTr; EtS; FaPON; MOS
(Ocean, The, *Moulton, Modern Reader's Bible.*) WGRP
They that have power [*or* powre] to hurt, and will do[e] none. Sonnets, XCIV. Shakespeare. BLPL; CABA; ElL; FaBoEn; GTBS; GTBS-P; InPS; LiTB; MasP; NOBE; NoP; OAEL-1; OBEV; PeHV; PoEL-2; PPoe; PPP; SCV; TEP; TrGrPo; ViBoPo
They that in play can do the thing they would. The Growth of Love, I. Robert Bridges. NoAM
They that never had the use. An Apology [*or* Apologie] for Having Loved Before. Edmund Waller. MePo; OAEP
They That Wait upon the Lord. Bible, *O.T.* Isaiah, XL: 28-31. TRV
(Power from God.) TreFT
They that wash on Monday. Mother Goose. FaBoBe; HBV-1; HBVY; TreF
They think/ I am stronger than I am. Naming Power. Wendy Rose. TWSS
They think I like it here, I guess. Comanche Gary Gildner. PH
They think it's easy to be dead, those. Tableau Vivant. Tess Gallagher. GeTw
They threw a stone, you threw a stone. After the Martyrdom. Scharmel Iris. HBV-2
They throw in Drummer Hodge, to rest. Drummer Hodge. Thomas Hardy. AWP; BrPo; CoBMV; EBEV; GTBS-P; HAP; InPS; NoAM; NoP; OBWP; PAI; SeCeV; VLP; WeW
They tied my mother's legs when I was born. Years Later. Laurence Lerner. NAs; PeSA
They tinkle laughter at the solemn hills. Spring Song of Aspens. Lilian White Spencer. PoOW
They Toil Not neither Do They Spin. Christina Rossetti. *See* Prayer, A: "Clother of the lily, feeder of the sparrow."
They told her she had hair the color. Daphne. Hildegarde Flanner. HBMV
They told me/ I smile prettier with my mouth closed. Witch. Jean Tepperman. NMM
They told me/ When I came. The Shoe Factory. Ruth Harwood. HBMV
They told me first she was a tree. Girl. Dom Moraes. NePoEA-2
They told me, Heraclitus, they told me you were dead. Heraclitus. William

Johnson Cory, *paraphrased fr. the Greek of* Callimachus. AWP; EBVV; ELU; FaBoEE; FaPoR; HBV-2; InPK; NOBE; OBEV; OBNC; OBVV; PeHV; PoRA; SeCePo; TreF; ViBoPo; VLP
They told me I was heir: I turned in haste. My Legacy. Helen Hunt Jackson. HBV-2
They told me that Life could be just what I made it. Life. Nan Terell Reed. BLPA
They told me this story a long time ago. Sleeping Beauty. Howard Nemerov. DFT
They told me you had been to her. Evidence Read at the Trial of the Knave of Hearts. "Lewis Carroll." *Fr.* Alice's Adventures in Wonderland. FaBoCo; FaBoNo; FaFP; GTBS-P; NBM; OxBoLi
They told us/ Our mothers told us. Cornfields in Accra. Ama Ata Aidoo. WPOW
They told us that the King was coming up to see the base. The Inspection. Frederick B. Watt. CaP
They took John Henry to the steep hillside. If I Die a Railroad Man. *Unknown.* AS
They took me from the white sun and they. "A Little Boy Lost." Jerome Rothenberg. CoPo
They took me out. Ku Klux. Langston Hughes. BPo
They took their time to die, this dynasty. The Last of the Princes. A. K. Ramanujan. OxBC
They tore down the toll-gate. The Toll-Gate Man. Wilson MacDonald. CaP
They trace their ancestry. The Legend of Paper Plates. John Haines. GP
They travelled like a blue pencil against the stars. In Praise of Antonioni. Stephen Holden. NYBP
They tried to evolve a sphere. Succumbing. Paul Eaton Reeve. ErPo
They trod the streets and squares where I now tread. London Poets. Amy Levy. OBVV
They Two. Mrs. Frank A. Breck. WBLP
They unfold before the sky. Doors. Therese Plantier, *tr. by* Willis Barnstone *and* Elene Kolb. BoWoP
They uprooted an ancient cave. Archaeologists. Real Faucher. AMV-80
They used to meet one night a week at a place on top of Telegraph Hill. The Harbor at Seattle. Robert Hass. NPGG; SV
They used to tell me I was building a dream. Brother, Can You Spare a Dime? E. Y. Harburg. SaC
They vacuum. Nova. Charles Levendosky. SOTS
They wait all day unseen by us, unfelt. The Stars. Mary Mapes Dodge. AA
They wait like darkness not becoming stars. The New Pietà: For the Mothers and Children of Detroit. June Jordan. PoBA
They walk dangerously. The Home. Susan Axelrod. NMM
They walk on the edge of the world. Vanguardia. Sandra Maria Esteves. LTB
They walk with surer step the paths of men. Motherhood. Karl M. Chworowsky. PGD
They walked in straitened ways. The Old Ladies. Colin Ellis. OxBTC
They warned Our Lady for the Child. Our Lord and Our Lady. Hilaire Belloc. GoBC; HBMV; ISi
They was a lawyer from Fredericton came. Perigoo's Horse. *At. to* George Calhoun *or* John Calhoun. ShS
They was twenty men on the Cabbage Rose. The Fate of the Cabbage Rose. Wallace Irwin. FiBHP
They watch the glittering moon. Someone Talking. Joy Harjo. TWSS
They watch us always. Always We Watch Them. Paul Mariah. LFAC
They wear air. Naked in Borneo. May Swenson. NYBP
They wear their evening light as women wear. Fields at Evening. David Morton. HBMV
They wear white scarves and shawls. The Madwomen of the Plaza de Mayo. Eli Mandel. NOBC
They weave a slow andante as in sleep. The Andante of Snakes. Arthur Symons. VLP
They went/ along the Camino Real. O California. Alejandro Murguía, *tr. by* Toni Empringham. FIA
They Went Forth to Battle but They Always Fell. Shaemas O'Sheel. HBV-2; WaaP; WGRP
They Went Home. Maya Angelou. IHMS
They went off on the buckboard in the rain. Ranchers. Maurice Lesemann. BPAW
They went to sea in a sieve, they did. The Jumblies. Edward Lear. BLPL; ChTr; EBEV; EvOK; FaBoBe; FaBoNo; FaFP; GoJo; HBV-2; HBVY; LiTB; MOS; NA; OnMSP; OxBChV; OxBoLi; PoRA; SeCeV; SoPo; TEP; TiPo; WiR
They went with axe and rifle, when the trail was still to blaze. Western Wagons. Rosemary *and* Stephen Vincent Benét. BPAW
They went with songs to the battle. Laurence Binyon. *Fr.* For the Fallen. ViBoPo
They Were All like Geniuses. Horace Gregory. *See* Lunchroom Bus Boy Who Looked like Orson Welles, The.
They were alone once more; for them to be. Byron. *Fr.* Don Juan, IV. EBEV
They were approaching the region where reigns perpetual summer. Longfellow. *Fr.* Evangeline. FaBoEn
They were at play, she and her cat. Femme et Chatte. Paul Verlaine, *tr. by* Arthur Symons. AWP; OBVE
They were beautiful, the old books, beautiful I tell you. The Old Books. Vernon Scannell. OxBC
They were both still. Lamentations. Louise Glück. BoWoP; MAYP
They were buying . . . your name maybe. An Open Letter-Poem-Note to Vincent van G. Bernadine. LTB
They were coming across the prairie, they were galloping hard and fast. The Cattle Thief. Pauline Johnson. WPOW
They were dancing as if. Glass. Takake Uchino Lento. BoWoP
They were fishing two centuries or more. Georges Bank. Julia Older. WOLT
They were hopeful of a curtain raiser. Because in This Sorrowing Statue of Flesh. Kenneth Patchen. NaP
They were human, they suffered. Founding Fathers, Nineteenth-Century Style. Robert Penn Warren. *Fr.* Promises. NoAM
They were just meant as covers. My Mother Pieced Quilts. Teresa Palomo Acosta. FIA; WPOW
They were like fish meal. Lead. Jayne Cortez. PoBA
They were met in the Last Inn's tap-room, where the road strikes hands with the sea. Wayfarers. Dana Burnet. EtS
They were not good. Those Who Come What Will They Say of Us. John Knoepfle. FAZ
They were sitting on the thin mattress. Wavelength. David St. John. SUW
They were so mean they could not between them. As in Their Time. Louis MacNeice. POL
They were the people, those who. The Broken String. *Unknown, tr. by* W. H. I. Bleek. PeSA
They were the Thompsons. I Wasn't No Mary Ellen. Linda King. GP
They were walking in the woods along the coast. The Apple Trees at Olema. Robert Hass. NPGG
They were women then. Women. Alice Walker. GOA; WPOW
They wheel'd me up the snow-clear'd garden way. Elfin Skates. Eugene Lee-Hamilton. OBVV
They whisted all, with fixèd face attent. *See* They wished all . . .
They who create rob death of half its stings. The Sovereigns [*or* Sovereign Poets]. Lloyd Mifflin. AA; HBV-2; WGRP
They who have best succeeded on the stage. Epilogue. Dryden. *Fr.* The Conquest of Granada, Pt. II. FiP; SeCV-2
They who in folly or mere greed. Where Are the War Poets? C. Day Lewis. FaBoMo; OBWP; OxBTC
They Who Possess the Sea. Marguerite Janvrin Adams. EtS
They Who Tread the Path of Labor. Henry van Dyke. TRV
They Who Wait. Charles Buxton Going. HBMV
They whose life is given utterly over to valor. Epitaph: Inscription from Anticyra. *Unknown, tr. by* Richmond Lattimore. WaaP
They will be telling you soon who you are. Arsenic. Howard Moss. CoAP; NYBP
They will bury that fair body and cover you. Epitaph on a Young Child. Ivor Gurney. FaBoEE
They will bury you at last. At Last. Syd Scroggie. PoSH
They will catch me. On Hearing the Airlines Will Use a Psychological Profile to Catch Potential Skyjackers. Stephen Dunn. AmPA
They will come for you in morning. Whispers. Roberta Hill. CDW
They Will Look for a Few Words. Nancy Byrd Turner. AmFN
They will never die on that battlefield. Uccello. Gregory Corso. FF; NeAP; PoM
They will soon be down. For the Last Wolverine. James Dickey. LiSp
They will take us from the moorings, they will tow us down the Bay. Homeward Bound. D. H. Rogers. EtS
They will win, I thought once. Politics. Tom Marshall. NOBC
They wind a thousand soldiers round the king. A Ribbon Two Yards Wide. Alfred Kreymborg. HBMV
They wished [*or* whisted] all, with fixèd face attent. Virgil, *tr. by* the Earl of Surrey. *Fr.* The Aeneid, II. LiTB; SiPS
They wondered why the fruit had been forbidden. Sonnets from China, II. W. H. Auden. CMoP
They won't come to you. These nights, you could sit for a year. Seal Rock. Katha Pollitt. MAYP
They wore it walking Sunday, three small men. Spanish Blue. Herbert Morris. NYBP
They wore light dresses and their arms were bare. A Pride of Ladies. Anne Halley. NMM
They would be shamed to see back at us. The Shirts. Tess Gallagher. MAYP
They would have fought again,/ Had not the Major stepped between the men.

The Shooting of the Cup. John G. Neihardt. *Fr.* The Song of Three Friends. PoOW
They wove for me a little cloak. Codes. Lois Seyster Montross. HBMV
They wrapped Big Frank in plaster. Because Our Past Lives Every Day. Ed Lipman. LFAC
They'd gone shopping. Alone in their apartment. Dream Fishing. Jim Thomas. WOLT
They'd learn more playing stickball in the street. Ghetto Summer School. Douglas Worth. FF
They'll come again to the apple tree. The Building of the Nest. Margaret E. Sangster. HBV-1; HBVY
They'll None of 'Em Be Missed. W. S. Gilbert. *See* Ko-Ko's Song.
They'll Tell You about Me. Ian Mudie. PoAu-2
They'll walk no longer to Mass on Sunday. The Shawls. Monk Gibbon. NeIP; OxBI
They're altogether otherworldly now. Grandparents. Robert Lowell. LiTM
They're beautiful, really, three. To My Sister, from the Twenty-seventh Floor. Michael Knoll. AMV-81
They're big. Grownups. William Wise. TiPo
They're building a skyscraper. Building a Skyscraper. James S. Tippett. OnUR
They're Calling. Felice Holman. RHPC
They're changing guard at Buckingham Palace. Buckingham Palace. A. A. Milne. OxBChV; PDV
They're changing partners again, safely unseen. Perpetual Motion. David Lehman. SUW
They're dancing. two step. Club 82: Lisa. Cynthia Kraman Genser. NYP
They're Dying Just the Same in Station Homesteads. Rodney Hall. *Fr.* Black Bagatelles. CBAP
They're dying off, the kerchiefed. Elegy for Bella, Sarah, Rosie, and All the Others. Sonya Dorman. GOA
They're like the valentines from old schoolmates. Butchery. Sandra McPherson. LCAP
They're more beautiful than the angels of heaven. Lennox Island. David McFadden. NOBC
They're Moving Father's Grave. *Unknown. See* They're Shifting Father's Grave.
They're out of sorts in Sunderland. There Are Bad Times Just around the Corner. Noel Coward. DBV; NOBL
They're out of the dark's ragbag, these two. Blue Moles. Sylvia Plath. BiP; NePoEA-2
They're putting Man-Fix on my hair. Wanting Out. Gavin Ewart. EAS
They're rioting in Africa. The Merry Minuet. Sheldon Harnick. DBV
They're selling postcards of the hanging. Desolation Row. Bob Dylan. InPS
They're selling tickets to the sundance. Indian America. Mah-do-ge Tohee. STE
They're Shifting Father's Grave. *Unknown.* CoMu
(They're Moving Father's Grave, *sl. diff.*) FSW
They're still my grown-ups. We Interrupt This Broadcast. Judith Hemschemeyer. Str
They're taking down a tree at the front door. Learning by Doing. Howard Nemerov. HAP; TwCP; WeW
They're taking me to the gallows, mother—they mean to hang me high. Death-doomed. Will Carleton. PaPo
They're Tearing Down a Town. Jud Strunk. QQQ
They're tunin' up the orchestray down at old Bill Haller's. Bill Haller's Dance. Robert V. Carr. PoOW
They've All Gone South. Mary Britton Miller. RHPC
They've Come. Alfonsina Storni, *tr. fr. Spanish.* BoWoP, *tr. by* Aliki *and* Willis Barnstone; WPOW, *tr. by* Marti Moody
They've got a brand-new organ, Sue. The New Church Organ. Will Carleton. PoLF
They've killed you. Martyrdom. Richard W. Thomas. PoBA
They've left Thee naked, Lord; O that they had. *See* They have left thee naked . . .
They've opened up a road in the jungle and found. 2976. Julia Uceda, *tr. by* Willis Barnstone. BoWoP
They've paid the last respects in sad tobacco. Padraic O'Conaire—Gaelic Storyteller. F. R. Higgins. OBMV; OnYI; OxBI
They've putten her into prison strang. Sir Aldingar. *Unknown.* ESPB
They've turned at last! Good-by, King George. Haarlem Heights. Arthur Guiterman. PAH
Th'have left thee naked, Lord, O that they had! *See* They have left thee naked . . .
Thick and stormy was the night. My Delight. Gamaliel Bradford. HBMV
Thick in its glass. Poor Henry. Walter de la Mare. HBMV
Thick lay the dust, uncomfortably white. Summer Rain. Hartley Coleridge. VLP
Thick lids of night closed upon me, The. The Souls of the Slain. Thomas Hardy. CMoP; LiTB; PoEL-5
Thick now with sludge from the years of suburbs, with toys. The Purpose of the Chesapeake & Ohio Canal. Dave Smith. GeTW
Thick water laps. The Fisherman. Dabney Stuart. LiSp
Thick wool is muslin to-night, and the wire. A Cold Night. Bernard Spencer. WaP
Thickness of paint or flesh cannot deface. Sestina on Her Portrait. Howard Nemerov. WaP
Thief became the rabbi, The. The Structural Study of Myth. Jerome Rothenberg. PoM
Thief in me is running a, The/ round in circles. Zapata & the Landlord. Alfred B. Spellman. NNP; PoBA
Thief is dying in the moonlit night, The. Dying Thief. Itzik Manger, *tr. by* Stephen Garrin. VWA
Thief, The. Abraham Cowley. *Fr.* The Mistress. JCP; OAEP; WHA
Thief, The. Josephine Jacobsen. WPE
Thief, The. Stanley Kunitz. MoAmPo; VGW
Thief, The. *Unknown.* LO; OBS; OxBoCh
Thief's Niece, The. George Keithley. NPGG
Thiepval Wood. Edmund Blunden. MMA
Thieves, The. Robert Graves. BoLoP; CMoP; GTBS-P; LiTM; OAEL-2; OxBI
Thieves' Anthology, The, *sel.* Theodore Martin.
"I met a cracksman coming down the Strand." FaBoPa
Thieves gave more to blue. Detroit City. Jill Witherspoon Boyer. CNA
Thieves of Love, The. R. A. D. Ford. PeCV
Thieving hands poke around where. Mother. Aldo Camerino, *tr. by* Anita Barrows. VWA
Thighs were awkward at first, The. The Harvest. William Aberg. LFAC
Thin air I breathe and birds use for flying. Air. Edwin Denby. CrMA
Thin, erect and silent. Alone. Elsie Laurence. CaP
Thin Façade for Edith Sitwell, A. John Malcolm Brinnin. FiBHP; NYBP
Thin feet are caught. The Wanderer. Claude Vigée, *tr. by* Anthony Rudolf. VWA
Thin filaments of/ seasons bind us. On Linden Street. Shelley Ehrlich. AMV-80
Thin fox, A/ sidled by with his stingy shadow. Dead Center. Ruth Whitman. NYBP
Thin ice/ Free advice. David McCord. TiPo
Thin ill-natured ghost that haunts the king, A. The Nine. John Sheffield, Duke of Buckingham and Normanby. APAS
Thin in beard, and thick in purse. On Tom-o-Combe. *Unknown.* FaBoEE
Thin lip, it is said, A. The Trumpet Shall Sound. John V. Hicks. AMV-81
Thin little leaves of wood fern, ribbed and toothed. Frederick Goddard Tuckerman. Sonnets, III, iv. TAP
Thin mask of my sleep, The. Lament for the European Exile. A. L. Strauss, *tr. by* A. C. Jacobs. VWA
Thin Potomac scarcely moves, The. The Potomac. Karl Shapiro. AP; CoBMV
"Thin Rain, whom are you haunting." Wraith. Edna St. Vincent Millay. WSC
Thin rank at regular intervals lines, A. The Proud Trees. Walter H. Kerr. NePoAm-2
Thin snow, and the first small pools of dusk. Faeryland. Robert Pinsky. MAYP
Thin steel in paired lines, forever mated, cuts. North Philadelphia, Trenton, and New York. Richmond Lattimore. NYBP
Thin wet sky, that yellows at the rim, A. Marshlands. Pauline E. Johnson. NOBC
Thin wickedly intricate, The. Dark Area. Russell Atkins. FB
Thin wind seemed uneasy, The. The Gallows Tree. Frederick Robert Higgins. OnYI
Thin woman from her porch hears, The. A Death in the Streets. Mario Petaccia. LFAC
Thine be those motions strong and sanative. To Coleridge in Sicily. Wordsworth. *Fr.* The Prelude, XI. OBNC
Thine elder that I am, thou must not cling. Sweeter Far than the Harp, More Gold than Gold. "Michael Field." OBMV
Thine eyes I love, and they, as pitying me. Sonnets, CXXXII. Shakespeare. OAEP; OBSC
Thine eyes shall see the light of distant skies. To Cole, the Painter, Departing for Europe. Bryant. AmPP; AP; TAP
Thine Eyes Still Shined. Emerson. NOBA
Thine is a strain to read amongst the hills. To the Poet Wordsworth. Felicia Dorothea Hemans. BrRo
Thine old-world eyes—each one a violet. On a Miniature. Henry Augustin Beers. AA
Thing, The. Theodore Roethke. CMoP
Thing, The/ To do/ Is organize. Poem. Kenneth Koch. CAPP
Thing about a shark is—teeth, The. About the Teeth of Sharks. John Ciardi. OBCA

Thing could barely stand, The. Yet taken. The Bull Calf. Irving Layton. InPK; OBCV; PeCV
Thing Dylan Thomas once said, A. Talk with a Poet. Helen Bevington. SaC
Thing Is Sex, Ben, The. Edgar Lee Masters. *Fr.* Tomorrow Is My Birthday. NAs
Thing Is Violent, The. Gwendolyn MacEwen. MoCV; NOBC; PeCV
Thing itself was rough and crudely done, The. The Knight in the Wood. Lord De Tabley. NCEP; VLP
Thing, loved one, A. The 29th Month. Stan Rice. NPGG
Thing Made Real, The. Ron Loewinsohn. NeAP
Thing of Beauty [Is Joy a Forever], A. Keats. *Fr.* Endymion, I. BLPL; CTC; EnRP; FaBV; FaFP; FiP; LiTB; NIP; OAEP; OBNC; OBRV; PoPl; PrIm; TreF; TrGrPo; TRV; ViBoPo
Thing Poem. Petra von Morstein, *tr. fr. German by* Rosemarie Waldrop. BoWoP
Thing Remembered, A. *Unknown, tr. fr. Arabic by* E. Powys Mathers. ErPo
Thing that goes the farthest toward making life worth while, The. Let Us Smile. Wilbur D. Nesbit. WBLP
Thing to do is try for that sweet skin, The. Catch What You Can. Jean Garrigue. VGW
Thing which fades, A. Ono no Komachi, *tr. fr. Japanese by* Arthur Waley. *Fr.* Kokin Shu. AWP; BoWoP; PBWP
Things, The. Conrad Aiken. HAP; WeW
Things. Walter de la Mare. PoA
Things. Dorothy Dow. HBMV
Things. W. S. Merwin. HAP
Things. Louis Simpson. OxBC
Things. William Jay Smith. TiPo
Things/ do not know their collective name. Workaday Morning. Astrid Tollefsen, *tr. by* Nadia Christensen. PBWP
Things About Comin' My Way. *Unknown.* FSW
Things are the mind's mute looking-glass. Things. Walter de la Mare. PoA
Things begin again. Return. Johari M. Kunjufu. BlSi
Things being what they are do not imply necessity. Theodore Enslin. *Fr.* Forms, LXXVII. CoPo
Things come from nothing. Metaphysical Shock while Watching a TV Cartoon. Stan Rice. NPGG
Things concentrate at the edges; the pond-surface. Marginalia. Richard Wilbur. CMoP; NMP; PoA
Things Dead. Marcel Schwob, *tr. fr. French by* William Brown Meloney. TrJP
Things did not vibrate so when I was young. Lines Written in a Moment of Vibrant Ill-Health. Morris Bishop. WhC
Things Going out of My Life. Robert Adamson. CBAP
Things I do not understand. Knowledge. Harold M. Grutzmacher. AMV-81
Things I Miss, The. Thomas Wentworth Higginson. TrPWD
Things I Prize, The. Henry van Dyke. TreFT
Things I Say Are True, The. Blanca Varela, *tr. fr. Spanish by* Donald Yates. BoWoP
Things I Used to Do, *with music. Unknown.* AS
Things I'm told, I could raise your hair, The. The Old Man's Tale. Brian Merriman, *tr. by* David Marcus. *Fr.* The Midnight Court. BIrV
Things Kept. William Dickey. NYBP
Things long forgotten. Haiku. Masaoka Shiki, *tr. by* Lucien Stryk *and* Takashi Ikemoto. FAZ
Things Lovelier. Humbert Wolfe. TrJP
Things Men Have Made. D. H. Lawrence. NoAM; PCP
Things Native sweetly grew. Thomas Traherne. *Fr.* Christendom. FaBoEn
Things never get lost. Like Children of the Summertime Playing at Cards. Julie Herrick White. AMV-80
Things Not of This Union. Linda Gregg. NPGG
Things of every day are all so sweet, The. Life's Common Things. Alice E. Allen. WBLP
Things of Late. David Phillips. NeAC
Things of the North, The. Rennie McOwan. PoSH
Things of the Spirit. Mason Jordan Mason. PoNe
Things start to happen. This is not. To Sherrie. Joseph Matuzak. AMV-81
Things That Are Caesar's, The. Bible, *N.T.* St. Matthew, XXII: 15-22. TreF
Things that are going out of my life remain, The. Things Going out of My Life. Robert Adamson. CBAP
Things that are lovely. Things. Dorothy Dow. HBMV
Things That Are More Excellent, The. Sir William Watson. OHFP
Things That Are Worse than Death. Sharon Olds. MAYP
Things that can bless a life, and please. Contentment. Owen Felltham. CavP
Things That Cause a Quiet Life, The. Martial. *See* Happy Life, The.
Things That Endure. Ted Olson. WBLP
Things That Go Bump in the Night. *Unknown. See* Litany for Halloween.
Things That Happen. William Stafford. NNaP
Things that make a life to please, The. A Happy Life. Martial, *tr. by* Sir Richard Fanshawe. OBVE
Things that Make a Soldier Great, The. Edgar A. Guest. NIP
Things that make the happier life, are these, The. Martial, *tr. fr. Latin by* Ben Jonson. FaBoEE; OBVE
Things That Matter, The. Edith Nesbit. OxBTC
Things That Might Have Been. Jorge Luis Borges, *tr. fr. Spanish by* Alastair Reid. AMV-80
Things that were not spiritual, The. Waiting for God. Harry Roskolenko. *Fr.* Baguio Poems. FAZ
Things the way they are. Saturday Morning at the Laundry. Christopher Gilbert. MAYP
Things to Do around a Lookout. Gary Snyder. CAPP; NaP; TAP
Things to Do around a Ship at Sea. Gary Snyder. CAPP
Things to Do around Kyoto. Gary Snyder. NaP
Things to Do If You Are a Subway. Bobbi Katz. RHPC
Things to Do in New York (City). Ted Berrigan. NoAM
Things We Dreamt We Died For. Marvin Bell. CoAP
Things we'll donate to the world. Poem H. Vincente Rodríguez Nietzche, *tr. by* Julio Marzán. InW
Think. Charles Weekes. AnIV; OnYI
"Think as I Think." Stephen Crane. *Fr.* The Black Riders, XLVII. WeW
Think back now to that cleft. The Power Station. James Merrill. ConAP
Think before You Act. Mary Elliott. HBVY
Think from how many trees. The Compost Heap. Vernon Watkins. NYBP
Think how some excellent, lean torso hugs. The Cost. Anthony Hecht. OxBC
Think, in this batter'd Caravanserai. Omar Khayyám, *tr. fr. Persian by* Edward FitzGerald. *Fr.* The Rubáiyát of Omar Khayyám. ChTr
Think It Over. *Unknown.* STF
Think me not unkind and rude. The Apology. Emerson. AmPP; AP
Think no evil, have no fear. Phyllis. *Unknown, tr. by* John Addington Symonds. UnTE
Think no more, lad; laugh, be jolly. A. E. Housman. CABA; CMoP
Think not by rigorous judgment seized. Three Epitaphs on John Hewet and Sarah Drew, I. Pope. NIP
Think not 'cause men flattering say. *See* Thinke not cause men flatt'ring say.
Think not I may not know thee kneeling there. Dusk. Archibald MacLeish. HBMV
Think not my Phebe, cause a cloud. To His Mistris Confined. James Shirley. OBS
Think not, nor for a moment let your mind. Edna St. Vincent Millay. VGW
Think not this paper comes with vain pretense. Epistle from Mrs. Yonge to Her Husband. Lady Mary Wortley Montagu. NoP
Think Not When You Gather to Zion, *with music.* Eliza R. Snow. AH
Think, O my soul. Phaedra. Hilda Doolittle ("H. D."). SBG
Think of/ Stepping on shore, and finding it Heaven! Heaven. *Unknown.* PoLF
Think of all the people. The World's So Big. Aileen Fisher. SoPo
Think of Dress in Every Light. John Gay. *Fr.* Achilles. InvP
(Song: "Think of dress in every light.") OBEC
Think of gentleness, as when. Motherhood. Susan Ludvigson. AMV-81
Think of it little, a fib. The Lie. Al Lee. AmPA
Think of only now, and how this pencil. The Promontory Moment. May Swenson. NYBP
Think of sweet and chocolate. The Anniad. Gwendolyn Brooks. BlSi
Think of the shark's tiny brain. In a Museum in the Capital. William Stafford. LCAP
Think of the storm roaming the sky uneaslly. Little Exercise [at 4 A.M.]. Elizabeth Bishop. CoAP; CrMA; MoAB; MoAmPo; NCSH; NYBP; UnPo
Think on St. Francis' feathered friends, dear heart. "That Which Hath Wings Shall Tell." Linda Lyon Van Voorhis. GoBC
Think on These Things. Bible, *N.T.* Philippians, IV: 8. TreFT
Think on Yesterday. *Unknown.* OxBM
Think Tank. Eve Merriam. QQQ
Think that this world against the wind of time. Signature for Tempo. Archibald MacLeish. MoVE; VGW
Think, the ragged turf-boy urges. Think. Charles Weekes. AnIV; OnYI
Think then, my soul, that death is but a groom. *See* Thinke then, my soule, that death is but a groome.
Think thinktank THINK. Think Tank. Eve Merriam. QQQ
Think thou and act; to-morrow thou shalt die. The Choice, 3. Dante Gabriel Rossetti. *Fr.* The House of Life, LXXIII. GTBS-P; HBV-2; OBEV; OBVV; WHA
Think what you like, but. You and It. Mark Strand. NYBP
Think ye the joys that fill our early day. Life. George Crabbe. OBEC

Think you I am not fiend and savage too? To the White Fiends. Claude McKay. BANP; PoBA
Think you the dead are lonely in that place? The Dead. David Morton. PAH
Thinke [*or* Think] not cause men flatt'ring say. To A. L.: Perswasions [*or* Persuasions] to Love. Thomas Carew. AnAnS-2; CaPo; SeCP
Thinke [*or* Think] then, my soule, that death is but a groome. Contemplation of Our State in Our Deathbed. John Donne. *Fr.* Of the Progresse of the Soule; the Second Anniversarie. OBS; OxBoCh
Thinker, The. Berton Braley. BLPA; WBLP
Thinker, The. Anthony Delius. PeSA
Thinkers and airmen—all such. To Poets and Airmen. Stephen Spender. WaP
Thinking. Walter D. Wintle. WBLP
(Man Who Thinks He Can, The.) PoLF; SoSe
Thinking hard, hunting rhymes, humming by my lamp. Sent to Wen T'ing-yün on a Winter Night. Yü Hsüan-chi, *tr. by* Geoffrey Waters. BoWoP
Thinking is not a smile. For Mattie and Eternity. Sterling D. Plumpp. CNA
Thinking myself in a warm country. Six Movements on a Theme. David Ignatow. NNaP
Thinking of Bookshops. James Liddy. CIP
Thinking of her had saddened me at first. Celandine. Edward Thomas. OxBTC
Thinking of Hölderlin. Christopher Middleton. NePoEA-2
Thinking of painters, musicians, poets. Orgy. Norman MacCaig. OxBC
Thinking of rain clouds that rose over the city. St. Vincent's. W. S. Merwin. NYP
Thinking of Tents. Reed Whittemore. TAP
Thinking of "The Autumn Fields." Robert Bly. NNaP
Thinking of the Lost World. Randall Jarrell. NoAM; NOBA
Thinking of those who walked here long ago. On the Ridgeway. Andrew Young. FaBoPP
Thinking of words that would save him. Finding Them Lost. Howard Moss. CoAP; NYBP
Thinking of You. Dick Lourie. NeAC
Thinking of you, I think of the *coureurs de bois*. Coureurs de Bois. Douglas Le Pan. CaP; MoCV; NOBC
Thinking on my life under. It Says. Jon Silkin. VWA
Thinking to take on the power. The Wives of Mafiosi. Erica Jong. AmPA
Thinking Twice in the Laundromat. Harley Elliott. NeAC
Thinking we were safe—insanity! Story of a Hotel Room. Rosemary Tonks. OxBTC
Think'st Thou that this Love can stand. Ametas and Thestylis Making Hay-Ropes. Andrew Marvell. CavP; InvP; SeCP
Think'st Thou to Seduce Me Then. Thomas Campion. BiP; ElL
Thin-legged, thin-chested, slight unspeakably. Apparition. W. E. Henley. In Hospital, XXV. BrPo; TrGrPo
Thinner now/ we are together. Air Is. John Michael Brennan. MAT
Thinning Out the Grove. Judith Neeld. SOTS
Thir Lenterne Dayis Ar Luvely Lang. *At. to* William Stewart. OxBS
Thir riveris and thir watteris kepit war. Virgil, *tr. by* Gavin Douglas. *Fr.* The Aeneid, VI. OBVE
Third Advice to a Painter, The. Andrew Marvell. APAS
Third Alley Blues. *Unknown.* BluL
Third and Fourth. Keidrych Rhys. NeBP
Third Avenue in Sunlight. Anthony Hecht. CoAP; NePoEA-2; NYP; PPP
Third Century, The, *sels.* Thomas Traherne.
News. MePo; NOBE; OBEV; PoPle; SeCV-2
(On News.) AnAnS-1; FaBoEn; QFR
"Will you see the Infancy of this sublime." AnAnS-1
Third Cycle of Love Poems, *sel.* George Barker.
Shut the Seven Seas against Us, II. MoAB; MoBrPo
3rd Dance—Making a Structure with a Roof or under a Roof—6-7 February 1964. Jackson MacLow. CoPo
Third Degree. Langston Hughes. BPo
Third Dimension, The. Denise Levertov. NeAP; NoAM
Third Eclogue, The, *sel.* Michael Drayton.
"Stay, Thames, to heare my Song, thou great and famous Flood." PoEL-2
Third Enemy Speaks. C. Day Lewis. *Fr.* The Magnetic Mountain. EaLo
Third Eye, The. Jay Macpherson. MoCV
Third-grade angels, two by two, The. Christmas Pageant. Margaret Fishback. PoSC
Third in our Borough's list appears the sign. The Caroline. George Crabbe. *Fr.* The Borough. SeCePo
Third Limick. Ogden Nash. NePA
Third Madrigal. Gene Derwood. NePA
Third Ode to Persephone. Robert Kelly. The Book of Persephone, 14. PoM
Third Row, Centre. William Rose Benét. WhC
Third Sermon on the Warpland, The. Gwendolyn Brooks. BPo
Third Sunday after Easter and the first dominical day of the white month of Mary, The. Ave Maria. Henriette Charasson, *tr. by* Frederic Thompson. ISi
Third Sunday in Lent. John Keble. *Fr.* The Christian Year. VLP
Third Voice, The. "Lewis Carroll." *Fr.* The Three Voices. VLP
Third Wonder, The. Edwin Markham. FYAP
Thirsis a youth of the inspired train. The Story of Phoebus and Daphne Applyed. Edmund Waller. OBS
Thirst. Emily Dickinson. *See* We thirst at first—'tis nature's act.
Thirst. Musa Moris Farhi. VWA
Thirst of reign and sweetness of a crown, The. Christopher Marlowe. *Fr.* Tamburlaine the Great. ViBoPo
Thirst of the Dragon. Dianne Hai-Jew. BrSi
Thirsty earth soaks up the rain, The. Drinking [*or* The Thirsty Earth *or* Anacreontic on Drinking]. Abraham Cowley, *after the Greek of* Anacreon. BLPL; CABA; FF; HBV-2; HeIP; LoBV; MePo; NOBE; OBEV; OBVE; PAI; PoPle; SeCePo; SeCP; SeCV-1; TrGrPo; WhC; WiR
Thirsty Island. Jim Tollerud. VoR
Thirsty Poet, The. John Philips. OBEC
Thirteen, Full of Life. Graham Everett. WOLT
Thirteen pieces of silver means bad luck. Digging Out the Roots. Duane Niatum. STE
Thirteen Sisters, The. Stephen Vincent Benét. *Fr.* John Brown's Body, I. TreF
13 Ways of Eradicating Blackbirds. Mark DeFoe. BXAP
Thirteen Ways of Looking at a Blackbird. Wallace Stevens. AP; BLPL; CABA; CMoP; CoBMV; HeIP; InPK; LiTM; NoAM; NOBA; NoP; PAI; SOTW; TAP; TwAmPo
Thirteen will attend. Another Meeting. Lawrence A. Lucas. AMV-80
Thirteen's no age at all. Thirteen is nothing. Portrait of a Girl with Comic Book. Phyllis McGinley. CrMA; CTBA
Thirteenth Station. William A. Donaghy. ISi
Thirtieth of November, The. Toward the Solstice. Adrienne Rich. NoP
Thirtieth of November last, eighteen hundred and thirty, The. The Owslebury Lads. *Unknown.* OBET
Thirty Bob a Week. John Davidson. BSV; EBEV; EBVV; FaBoTw; FaFP; InPS; LiTB; NBM; NoAM; NOBE; OAEL-2; OBNC; OxBS; OxBTC; VLP
"I step into my heart and there I meet," *sel.* ELU
Thirty candles and one. The Birthday. Philip Dacey. AmPA
Thirty Childbirths. Millen Brand. AMV-80
Thirty days hath November. The Months of the Year. Richard Grafton. FaBoUs
Thirty days hath September, *sl. diff. versions.* Mother Goose. FaBoBe; FaBoUs; HBV-1; HBVY; OxNR; SoPo; TreFT
Thirty days in jail with my back turned to the wall. Jailhouse Blues. *Unknown.* BluL
.38, The. Ted Joans. NNP; WeW
Thirty-eight. Charlotte Smith. SBG; WPOW
Thirty eighth year, The. Lucille Clifton. AmPA
31st day of August 1914, The. The Little Car. Guillaume Apollinaire, *tr. by* Ron Padgett *and others.* SOTW
34 Blues. *Unknown.* BluL
Thirty miles or so south of L. A. View from an Institution. Franz Wright. AMV-81
Thirty-one Camels, The. Rachel Korn, *tr. fr. Yiddish by* Howard Schwartz. VWA
Thirty-one nights hath December. Rhyme for Remembering How Many Nights There Are in the Month. Justin Richardson. FaBoUs
37th Dance—Banding—22 March 1964. Jackson MacLow. CoPo
36 just men. The Lamed-Vov. Rose Ansländer, *tr. by* Ewald Osers. VWA
"Thirty," the doctor said, "three grains, each one." Felo de Se. Thomas Blackburn. OxBTC
33. Adrienne Rich. *See* Necessities of Life, The.
Thirty today, I saw. A Birthday Candle. Donald Justice. NYBP
Thirty-two years since, up against the sun. Zermatt: To the Matterhorn. Thomas Hardy. OBNC
Thirty white horses upon a red hill. Mother Goose. HBV-1; HBVY; NTCP; OxNR; SoPo; TiPo
Thirty years ago. Builder Kachina; Home-going. Wendy Rose. TWSS
This:/ That is my straight-flying fury. Witch Hazel. Theodore Enslin. CoPo
This above All. Shakespeare. *See* Polonius' Advice to Laertes.
This above All Is Precious and Remarkable. John Wain. LiTM
This act reminds me, ge'men, under favour. Four Epigrams on the Naturalization Bill. John Byrom. NOBL
This ae nighte [*or* ean night], this ae nighte. The [*or* A *or* The Cleveland] Lyke-Wake Dirge [*or* Final Dirge]. *Unknown.* ACP; CH; ChTr; EaLo; EnSB; EvOK; FaBoCh; FaBoRV; GBP; GoBC; HAP; HBV-2; HoPM; LoBV; NOBE; NoP; OBEV; OxBoCh; PoEL-1; SeCeV; WeW
This Afternoon. Juan Sáez Burgos, *tr. fr. Spanish by* Julio Marzán. InW
This afternoon. Migration as a Passage in Time. Judy Bolz. SUW

This afternoon as I sat. Elegy for Jack Bowman. Joseph Bruchac. CDW
This afternoon, darling, when you were here. Letter from a Death Bed. John Ciardi. NCSH
This afternoon I swam with a school of fish. Sea School. Barbara Howes. NYBP
This afternoon in loud Jerusalem. Fourth Station. William A. Donaghy. ISi
This afternoon, my love, speaking to you. In Which She Satisfies a Fear with the Rhetoric of Tears. Sister Juana Inés de la Cruz, *tr. by* Aliki *and* Willis Barnstone. BoWoP
This age it is the same with less remembered. The Rape of Europa. R. P. Blackmur. CrMA
This ain't Torquemada. Dialect Quatrain. Marcus B. Christian. AmNP
This Alice. Herbert Morris. PoRA
This almost bare tree is racing. November through a Giant Copper Beech. Edwin Honig. NoAM; NYBP
This Amber Sunstream. Mark Van Doren. GoYe; LiTA; MoPo; MoVE
This America is an ancient land. Edgar Lee Masters. *Fr.* The New World. AmFN
This anchorage will do. A Diary of the Sailors of the North. David Shulman. VWA
This ancient hag. Mexican Market Woman. Langston Hughes. SaC
This ancient silver bowl of mine, it tells of good old times. On Lending a Punch-Bowl. Oliver Wendell Holmes. AA
This and That. Florence Boyce Davis. FaPON
This animal, this sleek and beautiful ox ambling along the pleasant road. The Ox. Mary Morison Webster. PeSA
This autumn rainfall. November Rain. Maud E. Uschold. YeAr
This Be Our Revenge. Saul Tchernichowsky, *tr. fr. Hebrew by* Shalom Spiegel. TrJP
This Beach Can Be Dangerous. Allen Curnow. OCNZ
This bears the seal of immortality. The Living Book. Charlotte Fiske Bates. AA
This Beast That Rends Me. Edna St. Vincent Millay. PrIm
("This beast that rends me in the sight of all.") VGW
This beauty made me dream there was a time. Sedge-Warblers. Edward Thomas. PoPle
This beauty that I see. Poem. James Schuyler. PoA
"This beginning of miracles did." Cana. Thomas Merton. TrCP
This being a fair and peaceful day. Benediction for the Tent. *Mongol Oral Tradition, tr. by* C. R. Bawden. WTO
This being a minimum security facility, it feels more like being on a reservation. Visiting Day. Al Young. NPGG
This biplane is the shape of human flight. The Wrights' Biplane. Robert Frost. WeW
This black life. Spring Rain. William Hawkins. MoCV
This black scrap from Viet Nam. Nocturn at the Institute. David McElroy. Psk
This black "Yeyhoo" said he's Seminole. Indian Macho. Louis (LittleCoon) Oliver. STE
This Blatant Beast was finally overcome. Saint. Robert Graves. CMoP
This Blessed Christ of Calvary. *Unknown.* STF
This Blessed Plot . . . This England. Shakespeare. *See* This England ("This royal throne of kings; this sceptered isle").
This blue-washed, old, thatched summerhouse. The Old Summerhouse. Walter de la Mare. CMoP; FaBoPP; FaBoRV; GTBS-P; MoPo
This body of my mother, pierced by me. Epithalamium. Leo Kennedy. OBCV
This body offers to carry us for nothing—as the ocean. Finding the Father. Robert Bly. DiL
This bond of the prelates I pray you revoke. Now God Stand Up for Bastards. Brian Merriman, *tr. by* Arland Ussher. *Fr.* The Midnight Court. BIrV
This book is all that's left me now. My Mother's Bible. George Pope Morris. AA; BLRP; PaPo; WBLP
This book is mine. *Unknown.* FaBoUs
This book is one thing. *Unknown.* FaBoUs
This book was written in order to change the world. Foreword to New Numbers. Christopher Logue. OxBTC
This bookplate, that thou here seest put. Book and Bookplate. John Masefield. WhC
This bouillabaisse a noble dish is. Thackeray. *Fr.* A Ballad of Bouillabaisse. FaBoUs
This brand of soap has the same smell as once in the big. Soap Suds. Louis MacNeice. FaBoMo; NoP; SCV
This Bread I Break Was Once the Oat. Dylan Thomas. FaBoTw
This bread is rock, not wheat. The Bread of Our Affliction. Martin Grossman. VWA
This brief common youth I was once in dread for it. Youth. Blanaid Salkeld. OxBI
This bronze doth keep the very form and mold. On the Life-Mask of Abraham Lincoln. Richard Watson Gilder. AA; HBV-2
This brown woman's voice. Nina Simone. Lance Jeffers. CNA
This burly son of a bitch. Not Just Yet. Carter Revard. VoR
This burning in the eyes, as we open doors. In Danger from the Outer World. Robert Bly. CAPP
This cankered earth, this murrain'd patch of land. King Ethelred the Unready. Bill Greenwell. BXAP
This cannon cannot shoot again; but sits, a relic in the park. Cannon Park. Mark St. Germain. PCP
This cat was bought upon the day. The Family Cat. Roy Fuller. OxBC; TEP
This celestial seascape, with white herons got up as angels. Seascape. Elizabeth Bishop. MoAB; MOS; OxBC; PPP
This chair I trusted, lass, and I looted the leaves. Aristotle to Phyllis. John Hollander. PoCh
This Chauntecleer stood hye up-on his toos. Chaucer. *Fr.* The Canterbury Tales: The Nonne Preestes Tale. FiP
This Child ("This child, exile of hope"). Norman Rosten. TrJP
This Child Is the Mother. Gloria C. Oden. BlSi
This child that God has given you. A Sunday School Teacher Speaks. *Unknown.* STF
This, children, is the famed mon-goos. The Mon-goos. Oliver Herford. *Fr.* Child's Natural History. AA; HBV-2
This city and this country has brought forth many mayors. Good English Hospitality [*or* The Mayors]. Blake. *Fr.* An Island in the Moon. CH; CoMu
This city is made of stone, of blood, and fish. Anchorage. Joy Harjo. STE; TWSS
This city is the child of France and Spain. Vieux Carré. Walter Adolphe Roberts. PoNe
This claw remains alive. Painting of a Lobster by Picasso. Hy Sobiloff. NePA; TwAmPo
This cluck of water in the tangles. The Voices of Nature. Thomas Edward Brown. PeD
This Cold Nothing Else. Dara Wier. MAYP
This coloured counterfeit that thou beholdest. Sister Juana Inés de la Cruz, *tr. fr. Spanish by* Samuel Beckett. PBWP
This commonwealth's capitol's corridors view. Commonwealth. Ambrose Bierce. DBV
This Compost. Walt Whitman. AWP; CABA; LiTA; MoAmPo
This conduit stream that's tangled here and there. Zillebeke Brook. Edmund Blunden. MMA
This consciousness that is aware. Emily Dickinson. AP
This cool night is strange. Nocturne. Gwendolyn Bennett. BANP
This Corruptible. Elinor Wylie. MoAB; MoAmPo
This, could I paint my inward sight. Lines for a Drawing of Our Lady of the Night. Francis Thompson. ISi
This country/ people in it in their cars. Us. David Ignatow. PPJ
This country might have. Right On: White America. Sonia Sanchez. BOLo; PoBA
This country needs a few. Dragon Lesson. James Hearst. AMV-80
This creature kneeling. November. Margaret Atwood. NOBC
This cross section, here incorrectly titled. Robert Fulton. Ann Stanford. GP
This Cross-Tree Here. Robert Herrick. OFD
This cruising caballero of the deep. Flying Fish. J. Corson Miller. EtS
This cup has touched. The Wine Cup. Meleager, *tr. by* Dudley Fitts. OLR
This damsel was brought up to read and to write. The Female Warrior. *Unknown.* ShS
This darksome burn, horseback brown. Inversnaid. Gerard Manley Hopkins. ACP; BLPL; BrPo; CABA; CMoP; FaBoPP; GTBS-P; InPK; LiTB; LiTM; LoBV; MoAB; MoBrPo; NoAM; OAEL-2; PoRA; PoSH; UnPo
This dawn when the mountain-cherry lifts. Easter in the Woods. Frances Frost. SiSoSe
This Day. Hildegarde Flanner. WPE
This Day. Lawrence Raab. NoP
This Day Be with Me. George Macdonald. *Fr.* Diary of an Old Soul. TrCP
This day day dawes. The Lily-white Rose. *Unknown.* MeEL
This day for our new navigation. The New Navigation. John Freeth. OBET
This day is called the feast of Crispian. Henry V before Agincourt [*or* St. Crispin's Day]. Shakespeare. King Henry V, *fr.* IV, iii. FaPoR; FF
This day is for Israel light and rejoicing. A Sabbath of Rest. Isaac Luria, *tr. by* Nina Davis Salaman. TrJP
This Day is Thine. Verna Whinery. BLRP
This day of all our days has done. Byron. FaBoEE
This day relenting God. Lines Written after the Discovery by the Author of the Germ of Yellow Fever. Sir Ronald Ross. ImOP
This day the children of Speakthunder. In My Lifetime. James Welch. CDW; STE
This Day, under My Hand. David Malouf. CBAP

This day upon the bitter tree. Good Friday. A. J. M. Smith. CaP
This day, whate'er the Fates decree. Stella's Birthday; March 13, 1726-27. Swift. LoBV; NAs; NoP; OAEL-1; OBEC; PoEL-3
This day when I lay my hope aside. This Day. Hildegarde Flanner. WPE
This day will be remembered by America's noble sons. The Battle of Bull Run. *Unknown.* AmFP
This day writhes with what? The Ultimate Poem Is Abstract. Wallace Stevens. PoA
This daylit doll, this dim divinity. Neo-Classical Poem. William Jay Smith. WaP
This Decoration. Hayden Carruth. NNaP
This decorous, nineteenth-century. Croquet. David Huddle. Str
This definition poetry doth fit. Thomas Randolph. FaBoEE
This delightful young man. Heine, *tr. by* Ezra Pound. *Fr.* Die Heimkehr. AWP
This desert still remembers Eden. Indian. Jeanne Doriot. AMV-81
This Dim and Ptolemaic Man. John Peale Bishop. CrMA; ImOP; LiTA; LiTM; NePA
This dirty little heart. Emily Dickinson. PoEL-5
This divine October afternoon I would like. Pain. Alfonsina Storni, *tr. by* Merrilee Antrim. WPOW
This Do in Remembrance of Me. Horatius Bonar. STF
"Here, O my Lord, I see Thee face to face," *sel.* TrPWD
This dog barking at me now. Dog, Midwinter. Raymond Souster. GDP
This dread is like a calm. Winter Holding off the Coast of North America. N. Scott Momaday. CDW
This dreadful, dark and dismal day. Frankie Silvers. Frances Silvers. AmFP
This dream won't fit. Adolescence. Dennis Schmitz. FAZ
This drop of ink chance leaves upon my pen. A Drop of Ink. Joseph Ernest Whitney. AA
This dry night nothing unusual. The War Horse. Eavan Boland. BIrV; CIP
This duleful sentence Saturn took on hand. Robert Henryson. *Fr.* The Testament of Cresseid. BSV
This dumbell bee must be working. How the Laws of Physics Love Chocolate. Reg Saner. GP
This dust was Timas. The Dust of Timas. Sappho, *tr. by* E. A. Robinson. AWP
This ean night, this ean night. *See* This ae nighte, this ae nighte.
This earth is not the steadfast place. William Vaughn Moody. *Fr.* Gloucester Moors. WGRP
This earth Pythonax and his brother hides. On Two Brothers. Simonides, *tr. by* W. H. D. Rouse. AWP
This Earthen Body. *Gond Oral Tradition, tr. by* V. Elwin *and* S. Hivale. WTO
This Easter, Arthur Winslow, less than dead. In Memory of Arthur Winslow. Robert Lowell. AP; MiAP; MP; TwCP
This Edward in the Aprill of his age. Michael Drayton. *Fr.* Piers Gaveston. PeHV
This egle, of which I have you told. Jove's Eagle Carries Chaucer into Space. Chaucer. *Fr.* The House of Fame. OxBM
This endless gray-roofed city, and each heart. London Despair. Frances Cornford. OBMV
This Endris Night. *Unknown.* EBEV; NOCV
(Lullay, By-by, Lullay.) OxBM
This England ("This royal throne of kings, this sceptered isle"). Shakespeare. King Richard II, *fr.* II, i. TreF; TrGrPo
(John of Gaunt Speaks.) FaPoR
(John of Gaunt's Dying Speech, *longer sel.*) FiP
(John of Gaunt's Speech.) FaBoPP
(This Blessed Plot . . . This England.) FaBV
This Englishwoman is so refined. Stevie Smith. FaBoEE
This evening holds her breath. Winter Night. C. Day Lewis. PoA
This evening I prepared Wardance Soup. Wardance Soup. Phillip William George. VoR
This evening, my love, even as I spoke vainly. Sister Juana Inés de la Cruz, *tr. fr. Spanish by* Judith Thurman. PBWP
This evening, our Father. Prayer. *Unknown.* OuSiCo
This evening the cuckoo and the corncrake. Seamus Heaney. Glanmore Sonnets, III. IPY
This Evening, without Blinking. Pattiann Rogers. AMV-80
This Excellent Machine. John Lehmann. OxBTC
This existence has, without the azure sphere, no reality. Quatrain. Sarmèd the Yahud, *tr. by* David Shea. TrJP
This face had no use for light, took none of it. Made Shine. Josephine Miles. NoAM
This fairest lady, who, as well I wot. Sonnet: Death Is Not without but within Him. Cino da Pistoia, *tr. by* Dante Gabriel Rossetti. AWP
This fairest one of all the stars, whose flame. Ballata: One Speaks of the Beginning of His Love. *Unknown, tr. by* Dante Gabriel Rossetti. AWP
This Fall ("This fall the japanese maple turned coral red"). Jody Aliesan. AMV-81
This far from Chicago and Natchez, Mississippi. Richard, Richard: American Fuel. Melvin Dixon. LTB
This far you have slid. My Childhood's Bedroom. Charles Tisdale. AMV-80
This fat woman in canvas knickers. Tourist Time. F. R. Scott. PoPl; WhC
This feast-day of the sun, his altar there. The Hill Summit. Dante Gabriel Rossetti. The House of Life, LXX. NoP; VLP
This Feast of the Law. *Unknown, tr. fr. Hebrew by* Israel Zangwill. TrJP
This February in Berkeley. Outside Every Window Is a Flowering Thing. Anita Skeen. AMV-81
This field-grass brushed our legs. In the Field. Richard Wilbur. NYBP
This figure, that thou here seest put. On the Portrait of Shakespeare Prefixed to the First Folio Edition, 1623 [*or* To The Reader]. Ben Jonson. EnRePo; HBV-2
This finde I write in poesie. Ceix and Alceone. John Gower. *Fr.* Confessio Amantis, IV. OxBM
This first Sunday in June, this green. Decoration Day. Bennie Lee Sinclair. TAT
This first year/ Of the atom. There Is Yet Time. Arvel Steece. PGD
This flattering glass, whose smooth face wears. On His Mistress Looking in a Glass. Thomas Carew. CaPo
This Flock So Small, *with music.* Anna Nitschmann, *tr. fr. German by* Sheema Z. Buehne AH
This flying angel's torrent cry. Eastern Tempest. Edmund Blunden. MoBrPo
This Form of Life Needs Sex. Allen Ginsberg. NNaP
This fountain sheds her flowery spray. The Fountain. A. J. M. Smith. CaP
This Fresshe Flour. Chaucer. *Fr.* The Legend of Good Women. SeCePo
This from that soul incorrupt whom Athens had doomed to the death. The Reply of Socrates. Edith M. Thomas. WGRP
This fugue must be hummed, found. Dumb Dick. Leslie A. Fiedler. ErPo
This gang who protect me. Wulf and Eadwacer. Richard Ryan. CIP
This garden does not take my eyes. The Garden. James Shirley. CavP; OBS
This garden is outlandish. The Women's Jail. Miriam Waddington. NOBC
This garden needs you. Between its walls. The Deserted Garden. Ann Stanford. AMV-81
This garden too pleasant. Concert. Helen Quigless. NBP
This gentle and half melancholy breeze. An Autumn Breeze. William Hamilton Hayne. AA
This gentleman the charming duck. A Trueblue Gentleman. Kenneth Patchen. SO
This girlchild was born as usual. Barbie Doll. Marge Piercy. DFF; NIP
This gives support to insects. 12th Dance—Getting Leather by Language—21 February 1964. Jackson MacLow. CoPo
This Golden Summer. Robert Lowell. NoP
This "good plan, fleshed in childhood"; these fruits. Jerusalem. Jon Silkin. VWA
This grandson of fishes holds inside him. Evolution from the Fish. Robert Bly. NoAM; NOBA
This grave-yard with its umbrella pines. The Island Cemetery. W. H. Auden. NePoAm-2
This ground once was consecrated. Cry for a Disused Synagogue in Booysens. Mannie Hirsch. VWA
This grove is too secret: one thinks of murder. The Grove Beyond the Barley. Alden Nowlan. MoCV
This guy on t.v. The Electric Cop. Victor Hernandez Cruz. PoBA
This handless clock stares blindly from its tower. A Clock in the Square. Adrienne Rich. HeIP; NIP
This Happy Day. Harry Behn. TiPo
This harpie with dry red curls. Red Dust. Philip Levine. NNaP
This has little to do with the flower. The Night-blooming Cactus. John Bensko. MAYP
This having learnt, thou hast attaind the summe. Milton. *Fr.* Paradise Lost, XII. SCV
This He was then. The Carpenter. Mary Brent Whiteside. TrCP
This Heart That Flutters near My Heart. James Joyce. AnIV
This heaven is too clear and bright. Macrocosm. Philip Child. CaP
This helmet, I suppose. Arac's Song. W. S. Gilbert. *Fr.* Princess Ida. FiBHP; WhC
This Heritage to the Race of Kings. Joseph Mary Plunkett. AnIV
(Our Heritage.) OnYI
This high-caught hooded Reason broods upon my wrist. The Falcon and the Dove. Sir Herbert Read. BrPo; FaBoMo
This high-way. March of the Three Kings. *Unknown, tr. fr. French.* OHIP
This hill indents my soul. Champ de Manœuvres. Sir Herbert Read. BrPo
This hinder yeir I hard be tald. The Bludy Serk. Robert Henryson. OxBoCh

This holy night in open forum. Office Party. Phyllis McGinley. OBSV
This Hour. Oliver La Grone. NNP; PoNe
This hour was set the time for heaven's descent. Twilit Revelation. Léonie Adams. MoAB; MoAmPo
This Houre Her Vigill. Valentin Iremonger. CIP; OxBI; OxBTC
(Elizabeth.) NeIP
(Recollection in Autumn.) OnYI
This House. Ray A. Young Bear. CDW
This house cannot be handed down. Usufruct. Austin Clarke. IPY
This house has been far out at sea all night. Wind. Ted Hughes. SoSe
This house is built within a sheltering. Back Road Farm. Charles Bruce. CaP
This house is floored with water. The Water Below. Fleur Adcock. PAI
This house is haunted, this house is haunted. Calliope. *Unknown.* AS
This house of flesh was never loved of me! Protest in Passing. Leonora Speyer. HBMV
This house that has been our home has been condemned. Packing a Photograph from Firenze. William H. Matchett. NePoEA
This House Where Once a Lawyer Dwelt. William Erskine. TreF; WhC
(Epigram: "This house where once a lawyer dwelt.) HBV-1
This huge and purged trust I have. My Love behind Walls. Heather Spears. OBCV
This Humanist whom no beliefs constrained. Epigram. J. V. Cunningham. ELU; VGW
This I admit, Death is terrible to me. Pure Death. Robert Graves. AWP
This I ask Thee—tell it to me truly, Lord! The Sacred Book [*or* Zoroaster Devoutly Questions Ormazd]. *At. to* Zoroaster, *tr. by* A. V. Williams Jackson. AWP; WGRP
This I beheld, or dreamed it in a dream. Opportunity. Edward Rowland Sill. BLPA; GN; HBV-2; HBVY; OHFP; TreFS; WGRP; YaD
This I Can Do. H. T. Lefevre. STF
This I would like to be—braver and bolder. Lord, Make a Regular Man out of Me. Edgar A. Guest. BLPA; BLPL
This idol with black eyes and yellow hair. Arthur Rimbaud, *tr. by* T. Sturge Moore. *Fr.* Illuminations: Childhood. SyP
This, if Japanese. Thyme Flowering among Rocks. Richard Wilbur. LCAP
This ignorance upon my tongue. On Reading Aloud My Early Poems. John Williams. WeW
This indecent procession of the undead. Mannequins. Daniel Mark Epstein. MAYP
This Indian weed, that once did grow. Tobacco. Philip Freneau. TAP
This infant world has taken long to make. Sonnet. George Macdonald. OBVV
This institution,/ perhaps one should say enterprise. Marriage. Marianne Moore. NOBA
This instrument. Telephone. Robin Shectman. AMV-81
This involves more than just the water standing. Country Landscape. Sherod Santos. AMV-80
This is a breath of summer wind. On Reading a Poet's First Book. H. C. Bunner. AA
This is a country where there are no mountains. Morning on the St. John's. Jane Cooper. NYBP
This is a damned inhuman sort of war. Unseen Fire. R. N. Currey. OBWP; OxBTC
This is a decade of insomnia. Sleeplessness of Our Time. R. A. D. Ford. AMV-81
This is a dream I needed. Old Man. Philip Booth. AMV-80
This is a fair in Magh Eala of the king. The Headless Phantoms. *Unknown, tr. by* Eoin MacNeill. AnIL
This is a fearful thing to bear. Horror. Peter Baum, *tr. by* Jethro Bithell. AWP
This is a glove. The Village of Reason. Michael Palmer. NPGG
This is a legend from Siskiyou Bar. Coyote and the Star. Arthur Guiterman. BPAW
This is a lie. Adam and Eve at the Garden Gate. Marsha Pomerantz. VWA
This is a morning of/ white parakeets. Morning Poem. Jennivien-Diana Beenen. AMV-81
This is a morning to say something. A Morning to Remember; or, E Pluribus Unum. Edward Dorn. NoAM
This is a new sort of poem. Buy One Now. D. J. Enright. NOBL
This is a nice vase that's so very Greek. Ode on a Grecian Urn. E. O. Parrott. BXAP
This is a night to be out. Street-Walker in March. Samuel L. Albert. NePoAm-2
This Is a Photograph of Me. Margaret Atwood. NoP
This is a piece too fair. What Is the World? Dryden. *Fr.* To My Honor'd Friend Sir Robert Howard. TRV
This is a place of ease. Pastoral. Marion Strobel. PoA
This is a poem for a woman doing dishes. Three Poems for Women. Susan Griffin. NPGG
This Is a Poem for the Dead. Michael Ryan. AmPA; DiL
This Is a Poem for the Fathers and for Michael Ryan. Thomas Lux. AmPA
(This Is a Poem for the Fathers.) DiL
This is a poem. Take it. Pack it up. Notes to the Reader. Robert Bringhurst. NOBC
This Is a Poem to My Son Peter. Peter Meinke. DFF; GP
This is a pool which bears deep looking into. A Pool. Thomas Whitbread. NYBP
This is a quiet sector of a quiet front. A Letter from Aragon. John Cornford. OBWP
This is a room with a death. The Death Watchers. Alice Ryerson. AMV-80
This is a rune I ravelled in the still. The Cow. Bernard O'Dowd. PoAu-1
This is a salt steep-cobbled town. Sea Town. Frances Frost. EtS
This is a silence. Arabesque. Fred Johnson. PoBA
This is a simple poem. Since Nothing Is Impossible. Michael Waters. WOLT
This Is a Sin-trying' World, *with music. Unknown.* TrAS
This is a song to be sung at night. The Middle of the Night. Karla Kuskin. RHPC
This is a song to celebrate banks. Bankers Are Just like Anybody Else, except Richer. Ogden Nash. LiTA
This is a spray the bird clung to. Misconceptions. Robert Browning. OBEV; OBVV
This is a story my father told to me. *Tsa'lagi* Council Tree. Gladys Cardiff. TWSS
This is a stray donkey wearing. Driving Home. Jonathan London. AMV-81
This is a tale of the body, its inert. Case. Phyllis Janowitz. AMV-81
This is a tale that the coachman told. The Coachman's Yarn. E. J. Brady. PoAu-1
This is a theme for muted coronets. The Plot against Proteus. A. J. M. Smith. OBCV; PeCV
This is a white. Imperial Thumbprint. Tom Weatherly. PoBA
This is a wild land, country of my choice. Rocky Acres. Robert Graves. LiTB; NoAM; UnPo
This is a wrong that needs not my bespeaking. New Testament; Revised Edition. Sister Mary Catherine. ISi
This is about the stillness in moving things. Runes. Howard Nemerov. PoCh
This is about the summer and the wheels of sleep. The Salt Pork. Robert Clayton Casto. HeIP
This is about the women of that country. The Women in Vietnam. Grace Paley. NMM
This Is after All Vacation. Louis Zukofsky. CoPo
This is all flummery, a feast of sham. The Rasslers. William D. Barney. LiSp
This is all we ever say. Christopher Morley. WhC
This Is America. Thomas Curtis Clark. PGD
This Is an African Worm. Margaret Danner. BPo
This is an ancient pattern on these hills. American Vineyard. Mildred Cousens. GoYe
This is an easy poem to make. An Easy Poem. Terry Kennedy. AMV-80
This is an evening for a hallowed landfall. Pattern of Saint Brendan. Francis MacManus. AnIV; OxBI
This is an old and very cruel god. Vicarious Atonement. Richard Aldington. MoBrPo
This is Avram the cello-mender. A Son of the Romanovs. Louis Simpson. OxBC
This is Campidojo, whaur Titus ran. Campidoglio. Robert Garioch, *after* Guiseppe Belli. OBVE
This is Cherry running for her life. 12 Photographs of Yellowstone. Ronald Koertge. GP
This is earthquake. Today. Langston Hughes. VGW
This is enchanted country, lies under a spell. Bonac. John Hall Wheelock. MoVE
This is everyone's marriage. Nesting. Dennis Saleh. NeAC
This is Flag Day. Hang Out the Flags. James S. Tippett. SiSoSe
This is God's house—the blue sky is the ceiling. In the Woods. Frederick George Scott. CaP
This Is Halloween. Dorothy Brown Thompson. RHPC; TiPo; YeAr
This is her picture as she was. The Portrait. Dante Gabriel Rossetti. OAEP; VLP
This is Hill 49, an arena for bad dreams. The Tin Woodsman. Paulette Jiles. NOBC
This is how forever is. Lineage. Reba Terry. AMV-81
This is how it happens. Chance Meeting. Susan Griffin. NPGG
This is how the flowers grow. How the Flowers Grow. "Gabriel Setoun." SoPo
This is how the page must feel: it doesn't. A Theory of Wind. Albert Goldbarth. MAYP
This is how to come in. Welcome. Harvey Feinberg. POL

This Is Indeed the Blessed Mary's Land. Longfellow. *Fr.* The Golden Legend. ISi
This is Independence Day. Stephen Vincent Benét. *Fr.* Listen to the People: Independence Day, 1941. PoSC
This is just the weather, a wet May and blowing. A Memory. Katherine Tynan. OxBI
This Is Just to Say. William Carlos Williams. FF; GoJo; HoPM; InPK; InPS; NIP; NOBA; NoP; PAI; RHPC; SOTW; SpRo; TAP
This is like a place. Snowy Night. John Haines. NCSH
This is Mab, the mistress-fairy. Mab the Mistress-Fairy [*or* Queen Mab]. Ben Jonson. *Fr.* The Satyr. EIL; HBV-1; WiR
This is Mister Beers. Mister Beers. Hugh Lofting. FaPON
This Is My Beloved, *sels.* Walter Benton. UnTE
"I saw autumn today . . . incipiently, on the sunset."
"It was like something done in fever, when nothing fits."
"White full moon like a great beautiful whore, The."
This is my Carnac, whose unmeasured dome. Henry David Thoreau. EyDe
This is my country, all this golden plain. The Greater Country. Grace V. Watkins. AMV-80
This is my curse, Pompous, I pray. Epigram. J. V. Cunningham. HAP; PV
This Is My Death-Dream. Ralph Salisbury. STE
This Is My Father's World. Malthie D. Babcock. AH, *with music*; BLRP; TRV
This Is My Hour. Zoë Akins. HBV-1
This is my last cry. For Stephen Dixon. Zack Gilbert. PoBA
This is my legacy. Folklore. Cyril Dabydeen. BrSi
This is my letter to the world. Emily Dickinson. AmPP; AP; NoAM; NOBA; OxBA; SCV; TAP; TreFT; WPE
This Is My Love for You. Grace Fallow Norton. HBV-1
This Is My Play's [*or* Playes] Last Scene, Here Heavens Appoint. John Donne. Holy Sonnets, VI. AnAnS-1; EBEV; JCP; LoBV; MasP; MeLP; NIP; OAEP; OBS; OxBoCh; PAI; SeCP; TEP
This is my return to Czechoslovakia. My Return to Czechoslovakia. Murray Edmond. OCNZ
This is my rock. David McCord. FaPON; NTCP; PDV; SiSoSe; SoPo; TiPo
This is my wolf. He sits. The Appointment. Maxine W. Kumin. NMM
This is Nevada, near the end of one. You Are on U.S. 40 Headed West. Vera White. AmFN
This is no book. To a Poet. Sister Mary Angelita. GoBC
This is no country for hedonists. The Mirrors of Jerusalem. Barbara F. Lefcowitz. AMV-80; VWA
This is no green bird, but gray with bright red. The Gossip. Daniel Halpern. SO
"This is no place for a tree," said the sour black soil. The Mountain Tree. Hugh Connell. NeIP
This is no place for lovers. Advice from a Nightwatchman. Ian Healy. *Fr.* Poems from the Coalfields, II. PoAu-2
This is no poet's heaven. Colophon for Lan-t'ing Hsiu-hsi. John Peck. AmPA
This is no time for fear, for doubts of good. Challenge. Thomas Curtis Clark. PGD
This is no wood for me to walk. Forest. Harriet Gray Blackwell. GoYe
This is not all I would have said. Arlington Cemetery Looking toward the Capitol. Winthrop Palmer. GoYe
This Is Not Death. Humbert Wolfe. MoBrPo
This is not hell. Loss. Richard Aldington. BrPo
This is not poetry, he said. Some Tips on Watching Birds. Deatt Hudson. NYBP
This is not real: this is the shape of a dream spun. Grant Wood's American Landscape. Winfield Townley Scott. GOA
This is not sorrow, this is work: I build. The Tomb of Lt. John Learmonth, A.I.F. John Manifold. CBAP; PoAu-2
This is not the classic torso. All the Farewells. Byron Vazakas. MoPo
This is not the man that women choose. Act of Love. Vernon Scannell. ErPo
This is not the way to die. In Memoriam. Dave Gingell. PoSH
This is not you? These phrases are not you? Prelude VI. Conrad Aiken. *Fr.* Preludes for Memnon. MoAB; MoAmPo
This is now—this was erst. A Mathematical Problem. Samuel Taylor Coleridge. FaBoUs
This is of green—unclassic shade. The Final Green. Leah Bodine Drake. NePoAm
This Is of Two Worlds. Christopher Dewdney. NOBC
This is one of those Tuesdays. Temporal. George Jonas. NOBC
This is our lot if we live so long and labour unto the end. The Old Men. Kipling. OBSV
This is our love, these wheels and chains. The Night Loves Us. Louis Adeane. NeBP
This Is Our Music. George Leong. BrSi
This is Palm Sunday: mindful of the day. To a Young Girl Dying. Thomas William Parsons. AA
This Is Pioneer Weather. William Carlos Williams. NePoAm-2
This is really the story of a/ sista. The House of Desire. Sherley Anne Williams. BlSi
This is Scotch William Wallace. William Wallace. Francis Lauderdale Adams. OxBS
This is that blessèd Mary, pre-elect. Mary's Girlhood. Dante Gabriel Rossetti. GoBC; WGRP
This is that month, Elizabeth. George Barker. NeBP
This is the age. Time of the Mad Atom. Virginia Braiser. QQQ
This is the Arsenal. From floor to ceiling. The Arsenal at Springfield. Longfellow. AmPP; AP; HBV-2; WaaP
This is the autumn and our harvest. Charles Reznikoff. *Fr.* New Year's. OFD
This is the beauty of being alone. Stray Animals. James Tate. NoAM
This is the best world that we live in. The Best and the Worst. *Unknown.* TreFT
This is the birthday of our land. Prayer on Fourth of July. Nancy Byrd Turner. YeAr
This is the black day when. The Dark Morning. Thomas Merton. PoA
This is the black sea-brute bulling through wave-wrack. Leviathan. W. S. Merwin. ConAP; NePoEA; NoAM; NOBA
This is the blessed Mary, pre-elect. Mary's Girlhood. Dante Gabriel Rossetti. ISi
This is the breed that followed the tails. Nantucket Whalers. Daniel Henderson. EtS
This is the bricklayer; hear the thud. Sanctuary. Elinor Wylie. BoWoP; MoAmPo; MoAB
This is the cave of which I spoke. The Caves. Michael Roberts. ChMP
This is the Chapel: here, my son. Clifton Chapel. Sir Henry Newbolt. OBEV; OBVV
This is the city where men are mended. The Stones. Sylvia Plath. CAPP; SBG
This is the country of the Norman tower. A Warning to Conquerors. Donagh MacDonagh. CIP; OxBI
This is the creature there has never been. Rainer Maria Rilke, *tr. by* James Blair Leishman. Sonnets to Orpheus, Pt. II, iv. OBVE
This is the day His hour of life draws near. Sonnets at Christmas, I. Allen Tate. AP; HAP; LiTA; LiTM; NePA; NoAM; NOBA; OxBA; VGW
This is the day the circus comes. Parade. Rachel Field. *Fr.* A Circus Garland. OBCA; SoPo
This is the day the prophets have foretold. Without Regret. Lilith Lorraine. PGD
This is the day when all through the town. Sunday. Elizabeth J. Coatsworth. AmFN
This is the day, which down the void abysm. Demogorgon's Speech. Shelley. *Fr.* Prometheus Unbound. LoBV; SeCeV
This is the dead fiddle. Look where the wood. The Dead Fiddle. Humbert Wolfe. TrJP
This is the death by water. This is dying. Dead Marine. Louis O. Coxe. WaP
This is the debt I pay. The Debt. Paul Laurence Dunbar. AmNP; BANP; CABA; CDC; SoSe; TRV
This is the desk I sit at. That Day. Anne Sexton. BoWoP; ConAP
This is the dragon's country, and these his own streams. Dragon Country: To Jacob Boehme. Robert Penn Warren. PPP
This is the easy time, there is nothing doing. Wintering. Sylvia Plath. NMM
This is the end of him, here he lies. Epitaph. Amy Levy. TrJP
This is the end of the book. Written at the End of a Book. Langdon Elwyn Mitchell. AA
This is the end of the line. End of the Line. John Taylor. FAZ
"This is the end": the anguished word. The End. Walter de la Mare. OAEP
This is the factory. The Old Maid Factory. Constance Urdang. GP
This is the feast-time of the year. The Feast-Time of the Year. *Unknown.* OHIP
This is the female form. Whitman. *Fr.* I Sing the Body Electric. ErPo
This is the field where the battle did not happen. At the Un-National Monument along the Canadian Border. William Stafford. HeIP; HAP
This is the first year. The Poet Imagines His Grandfather's Thoughts on the Day He Died. Wing Tek Lum. BrSi
This is the football hero's moment of fame. Settling Some Old Football Scores. Morris Bishop. LiSp
This is the forest primeval. The murmuring pines and the hemlocks. Evangeline. Longfellow. BeLS; SpRo; TreF; WBLP
This is the forest primeval. To What Base Uses! *parody.* Bert Leston Taylor. WhC
This is the form my passion takes. A Form of Passion. David McFadden. NOBC

This is the foul fiend Flibbertigibbet: he begins at. Shakespeare. *Fr.* King Lear, III, iii. WSC
This Is the Garden. E. E. Cummings. MoAmPo
(Sonnet: "This is the garden: colours come and go.") MoAB
This is the gay cliff of the nineteenth century. Brooklyn Heights. John Wain. LiTM; NYP; OxBTC
This is the golden book of spirit and sense. Sonnet. Swinburne. SyP
This is the golden goddess; friend is she. Aphrodite Pandemos. *Unknown, tr. by* Louis Untermeyer. UnTE
This is the gospel of labor. The Gospel of Labor. Henry van Dyke. WBLP
This is the grave of Mike O'Day. Mike O'Day [*or* On Mike O'Day]. *Unknown.* FaBoEE; TreFT; WhC
This is the hand. At Cambridge. Audrey McGaffin. NePoAm
This Is the Hay That No Man Planted. Elizabeth J. Coatsworth. OBCA
This is the height of our deserts. Deservings. *Unknown.* HBV-2
This is the hero; he is black or white. Fairy Tale. John Frederick Nims. MiAP
This is the hidden place that hiders know. Stephen Vincent Benét. *Fr.* John Brown's Body. ViBoPo
This is the horrible tale of Paul. The Revolving Door. Newman Levy. ShM
This is the horror that, night after night. Gerald Gould. OxBTC
This is the hour of magic, when the Moon. The Hour of Magic. W. H. Davies. MoBrPo
This is the hour that we must mourn. Tenebrae. Austin Clarke. AnIL; BlrV; CIP; IPY; NeIP
This is the house of Bedlam. Visits to St. Elizabeths. Elizabeth Bishop. CoAP; VGW
This is the house of Circe, queen of charms. Circe. Lord De Tabley. VLP
This is the house. On one side there is darkness. Portrait of One Dead. Conrad Aiken. *Fr.* The House of Dust. HBMV; WHA
This is the house that Jack built. Mother Goose. HBV-1; HBVY; OxNR; SoPo; SpRo
This is the house we used to know so well. I. M. H. Maurice Baring. ACP
This is the house where Jesse White. Lowery Cot. L. A. G. Strong. MoBrPo
This is the huge dream of us that we are heroes. The Flowers of Politics, I. Michael McClure. NeAP
This Is the Key. *Unknown.* CH; FaBoCh; FaFP; MoShBr; OxBoLi; Prf; TreFS
("This is the key of the kingdom.") OxNR
This is the key to it. The Breast. Anne Sexton. CABA
This is the key to the playhouse. The Playhouse Key. Rachel Field. FaPON
This is the kind/ of marriage they live in. The Way Sun Keeps Falling Away from Every Window. Lyn Lifshin. NeAC
This is the knife with a handle of horn. The House That Jack Built. *Unknown.* OxBoLi
This is the land our fathers came to find. New World. Brewster Ghiselin. MoVE
This is the land where hate should die. The Land Where Hate Should Die. Denis A. McCarthy. PGD
This is the Landlords' Circle, built by me. Inferno: A New Circle. Frank Ormsby. CIP
This is the landscape of the Cambrian age. Coastline. Elaine Feinstein. BrRo
This Is the Last. Gilbert Waterhouse. PGD
This is the last day of the world. On the river docks. Downwards. C. K. Williams. GeTw
This is the last hotel. Irish Hotel. David Wevill. NYBP
This is the last stroke my toungs clock must strike. Summer's Farewell. Thomas Nashe. *Fr.* Summer's Last Will and Testament. PoEL-2
This is the last time. W. J. Turner. *Fr.* The Seven Days of the Sun. OBMV
This is the law of the Yukon, and ever she makes it plain. The Law of the Yukon. Robert W. Service. CaP; HBV-2; TreFS
This is the lay of Ike. The Lay of Ike. John Berryman. *Fr.* Dream Songs. LCAP
This Is the Life. Louis MacNeice. NoAM
This is the light of the mind, cold and planetary. The Moon and the Yew Tree. Sylvia Plath. CoAP; FaBoMo; MOON; NaP; NYBP; PPP; VGW; WPE; WPOW
This is the light we dream in. Negatives. Charles Wright. PoA
This is the loggia Browning loved. Browning at Asolo. Robert Underwood Johnson. AA
This is *The Making of America in Five Panels.* Empire Builders. Archibald MacLeish. OxBA
This is the meadow of the mind. A Way of Keeping. Nancy Willard. IHMS
This is the metre Colombian. The Metre Colombian. *Unknown.* BXAP; Par; SpRo
This is the Mexican. Tamales. "O. Henry." BPAW
This is the midnight—let no star. The Storm Cone. Kipling. ChMP; OxBTC
This is the month, and this the happy morn. On [*or* Ode on] the Morning of Christ's Nativity. Milton. GoTL; GTBS; GTBS-P; HBV-1; LiTB; MasP; MeLP; NAs; NOCV; NoP; OBS; OxBoCh; PoEL-3; SBVL; SeCeV; WGRP
This is the month of the Thunder Moon. The Month of the Thunder Moon. Marion Doyle. YeAr
This is the month the nightingale, clod-brown. The Nightingale. John Clare. EBVV
This is the month when hills turn white. The Long Night Moon: December. Frances Frost. YeAr
This is the morning. The Charge. Jay Wright. DiL; FB
This is the most ridiculous womb! Womb Song. Susan Fromberg Schaeffer. IHMS
This is the mouth-filling song of the race/ that was run by a Boomer. The Sing-Song of Old Man Kangaroo. Kipling. FaPON
This is the night mail crossing the border. The Night Mail. W. H. Auden. ChTr; GrPl; OxBTC
This Is the Non-existent Beast. Cid Corman. GP
This is the old way. New Year. Gail N. Harada. BrSi
This is the one song everyone. Siren Song. Margaret Atwood. *Fr.* Songs of the Transformed. HAP; PoA; WeW
This is the only thing that clarifies my life. Days of 1978. Gerald Stern. AMV-81
This is the only way it can be. Twilight. Tenant Farmer. Robert Ward. AMV-81
This is the pathway where she walked. Amy. James Matthew Legaré. AA
This is the Pentagon building. Pentagonia. G. E. Bates. SpRo
This is the place/ Where far from the unholy populace. In a Meadow. John Swinnerton Phillimore. OBEV; OBVV
This is the place/ you would rather not know about. Notes towards a Poem That Can Never Be Written. Margaret Atwood. NOBC
This is the place, as wild as summer snow. The Track into the Swamp. Samuel French Morse. CrMA
This is the place: be still for a while, my high-pressure steamboat! Nauvoo. Bayard Taylor. OBAL
This is the place I love. Here I belong. Mountain Creed. Medora Addison Nutter. GoYe
This Is the Place to Wait. Horace Gregory. *Fr.* The Passion of M'Phail. MoAmPo
This is the plaza of Paradise. Marigold. John Haines. POL; PPJ
This is the poetry reading. Before the Poetry Reading. Louis Simpson. OxBC
This is the pool that Plato visited. The Pool. E. L. Mayo. MiAP
This is the prettiest motion. To a Lady That Desired Me I Would Bear My Part with Her in a Song. Richard Lovelace. CaPo
This is the rain on Mozart's grave. Lives of the Saints. Jon Anderson. FiCP
This is the realm no man dares. The World Looks On. Louis Newman. PoNe
This is the ring my father gave me. The Alexandrite Ring. Margaret Ryan. AMV-81
This is the river that had to be dammed. Pentagonia. G. E. Bates. NYBP
This is the road I tread today. The Death of Moses. *Unknown, tr. by* Alice Lucas. TrJP
This is the safest prayer to pray. Thy Will Be Done. Annie Johnson Flint. STF
This is the shack where the old man died. Post Mortem. Verna Loveday Harden. CaP
This Is the Shape of the Leaf. Conrad Aiken. Priapus and the Pool, IV. HBMV; NePA; TrGrPo; WHA
(Portrait of a Girl.) GoJo; MoAB; MoAmPo
("This is the shape of a leaf, and this of a flower.") CMoP; NOBA; OxBA
This is the ship of pearl, which, poets feign. The Chambered Nautilus. Oliver Wendell Holmes. *Fr.* The Autocrat of the Breakfast Table, *Ch.* 4. AA; AmPP; AP; EtS; FaBoBe; FaFP; FPL; GN; HBV-2; HBVY; HoPM; LiTA; MOS; NePA; NOBA; NoP; OBVV; OHFP; PoEL-5; PoLF; PrIm; TreF; WGRP
This is the sin against the Holy Ghost. The Unpardonable Sin. Vachel Lindsay. BiP; CMoP; NePA
This is the song I rested with. Mammy Hums. Carl Sandburg. PoNe
This is the song of mehitabel. The Song of Mehitabel. Don Marquis. *Fr.* Archy and Mehitabel. FiBHP; TreFS
This is the song of the wave! The mighty one! A Song of the Wave. George Cabot Lodge. EtS
This is the song of those who live alone. Song. William Justema. NYBP

This is the song that the night birds sing. Tall Men Riding. S. Omar Barker. BPAW
This is the song that the truck drivers hear. Song of the Truck. Doris Frankel. AmFN
This is the sorrowful story. The Legends of Evil I. Kipling. MoShBr
This is the south. I look for evidence. New Orleans. Joy Harjo. STE; TWSS
This is the southeast section of town now. The Southeast Ramparts of the Seine. Judit Tóth, *tr. by* Emery George. VWA
This is the stagnant hour. Drunken Lover. Owen Dodson. AmNP
This is the story/ of a beautiful. Reading Plato. Jorie Graham. MAYP
This is the story of a coal miner's child. The Coal Miner's Child. *Unknown.* OuSiCo
This is the sugar. At the Long Island Jewish Geriatric Home. Jorie Graham. NPGG
This is the summer storm. For My Daughter. Ed Ochester. Str
This is the surest death. Mortality. Naomi Long Madgett. NNP; PoBA; PoNe
This is the tale from first to last. Simon the Cyrenean. Lucy Lyttleton. HBV-2
This is the tale of Ephraim. Ephraim the Grizzly. Arthur Guiterman. BPAW
This is the tale of the man. Ticonderoga; a Legend of the West Highlands. Robert Louis Stevenson. OBNV
This is the tale that Cassidy told. The Mornin's Mornin'. Gerald Brennan. BLPA
This is the tale that was told to me. A Sailor's Yarn. James Jeffrey Roche. MOS; NA
This is the terminal: the light. At the San Francisco Airport. Yvor Winters. HeIP; InPK; NIP; NOBA; QFR
This is the time lean woods shall spend. Sundown. Léonie Adams. MoAB; MoAmPo; TrGrPo; TwAmPo
This is the time of the crit, the creeple, and the makeiteer. Five Men against the Theme "My Name Is Red Hot. Yo Name Ain Doodley Squat." Gwendolyn Brooks. CNA
This is the time of wonder, it is written. It Rolls On. Morris Bishop. ImOP
This is the time of year. The Armadillo [*or* The Armadillo—Brazil]. Elizabeth Bishop. NoAM; NOBA; NoP; NYBP; TAP; VGW
This is the time when bit by bit. Turn o' the Year. Katharine Tynan. HBV-1
This is the time when larks are singing loud. The End of April. Robert Fuller Murray. CenHV
This is the toll of the desert. The Toll of the Desert. Arthur W. Monroe. BPAW; PoOW
This is the truth sent from above. The Truth from Above. *Unknown.* OBET
This is the truth what I now tell you. The Miramichi Fire. *Unknown.* AmFP
This is the twilight of the summer dead. George Moore. *Fr.* A Parisian Idyl. SyP
This is the urgency: Live! The Second Sermon on the Warpland. Gwendolyn Brooks. BPo; NOBA; PoBA
This Is the Violin. Trumbull Stickney. NCEP
This is the voice of high midsummer's heat. The Mowing. Sir Charles G. D. Roberts. NOBC; OBCV
This is the way a tree: from the rain down. From the Rain Down. Rhina P. Espaillat. GoYe
This is the way it is. We see. Ingmar Bergman's "Seventh Seal." Robert Duncan. NMP
This is the way it must have been in the first dusk. Invisible Landscape. Charles Wright. LCAP
This is the way it was at Uncle Rob's. History Lesson for My Son. Ted Kooser. POL
This is the way the baby slept. The Way the Baby Slept. James Whitcomb Riley. AA
This is the way the ladies are. Cantata for Two Lovers. Helga Sandburg. UnTE
This is the way the ladies ride. Mother Goose. OxNR; TiPo
This is the way we come. Riding in the Rain. Maxine W. Kumin. RFM
This is the way we say it in our time. Sonnet XV. Winfield Townley Scott. ErPo
This is the weather the cuckoo likes. Weather[s]. Thomas Hardy. CH; EvOK; FaBoCh; FaBV; MoAB; MoBrPo; OBMV; PoPle; SeCePo; WHA
This is the week when Christmas comes. In the Week When Christmas Comes. Eleanor Farjeon. PChr; PDV; SiSoSe
This is the Wheel of Dreams. Carriers of the Dream Wheel. N. Scott Momaday. CDW
This is the Wild Huntsman that shoots the hares. The Story of the Wild Huntsman. Heinrich Hoffman. NA
This is the wisdom of the ape. The Theology of Bongwi, the Baboon. Roy Campbell. PeSA
This is the Word whose breaking heart. Mathematics or the Gift of Tongues. Anna Hempstead Branch. ImOP
This is the world we wanted. Gretel in Darkness. Louise Glück. AmPA; DFT; GP
This is the yak, so neg-li-gee. The Yak. Oliver Herford. *Fr.* Child's Natural History. HBV-2; HBVY
This is the year Europe looks up in sublime disregard. Berlin Interior with Jews, 1939. Lynn Emanuel. MAYP
This is their image: the desert and the wild. Pyramis; or, The House of Ascent. A. D. Hope. PoAu-2
This is their third parting. Now she goes. The Adventurers. John Thompson. PoAu-2
This is Thomas Jones's book. Thomas Jones. FaBoUs
This is thy hour O Soul, thy free flight into the wordless. A Clear Midnight. Walt Whitman. HAP
This is to let you know. A Message to the Photographer Whose Prints I Purchased. Beryle Williams. PoDr
This is to say, my dear Augusta. King William's Dispatch to Queen Augusta. Coventry Patmore. FaBoEE
This is Tongue River, where lovers lie down. Tongue River Psalm. Gary Gildner. FAZ
This is true Love, by that true Cupid got. The Dance of Love. Sir John Davies. *Fr.* Orchestra; or, A Poem of Dancing. EIL; SeCePo
This is what I want to happen. Offering. *Unknown, ad. by* Robert Bly. NU
This is what it was like? God on a donkey. The Palms. David Knight. MoCV
This Is What the Watchbird Sings, Who Perches in the Lovetree. Bruce Boyd. NeAP
This is what we really want. By Fiat of Adoration. Oscar Williams. LiTM; NePA
This is what you changed me to. Pig Song. Margaret Atwood. NoP
This is where/ the light sleeps. Lullaby. Sue Owen. AMV-80
This is where he finds you. February. Over the phone. Over the Phone. Mekeel McBride. MAYP
This is where poor Percy died. The Murder. Gwendolyn Brooks. DBV
This is where the scarlet lords-and-ladies. Under the Cliff. Geoffrey Grigson. WaP
This is where the serpent lives, the bodiless. The Auroras of Autumn. Wallace Stevens. CMoP
This is where we're at the gate. Photograph at the Cloisters: April 1972. Helen Chasin. NMM
This is why in the wormpaths. Toward the Splendid City. Ed Ochester. LTB
This is Willy Walker, and that's Tam Sim. *Unknown.* OxNR
This is winter, this is night, small love. By Candlelight. Sylvia Plath. SBG
This island, garlanded with wild woods. Archilochus, *tr. fr. Latin by* Guy Davenport. OBVE
This island is the world's end. The Island. Seán Jennett. NeIP; SeCePo
This Italian square. Dancers at the Moy. Paul Muldoon. BIrV
This Journey. Ingrid Jonker, *tr. fr. Afrikaans by* Jack Cope *and* William Plomer. BoWoP
This Kansas boy who never knew the sea. Kansas Boy. Ruth Lechlitner. AmFN
This kind o' sogerin' aint a mite like our October trainin'. A Letter. James Russell Lowell. *Fr.* The Biglow Papers, 1st series, No. II. OxBA
This kiss kissed by death. Hershey Kiss. Patti Renner-Tana. SOTS
This kiss upon your fan I press. What He Said. Harrison Robertson. *Fr.* Two Triolets. HBV-1
This knot I knit. To Know Whom One Shall Marry. *Unknown.* GBP
This lady, curled like a shell. The Shellpicker. Ronald Perry. NePoEA-2
This Lady She Wears a Dark Green Shawl. *Unknown.* AmFP
This lake was clean (we used to swim in it once). The Moorhen Pond. Tom Earley. BoAnP
This land grows the oldest living things. Karl Shapiro. *Fr.* California Winter. AmFN
This land is your land. Is This Land Your Land? *Unknown.* FSW
This land like a mirror turns you inward. Dark Pines under Water. Gwendolyn MacEwen. NOBC
This land whose streams seem as the lives of men. The Connecticut River. Reuel Denney. TwAmPo
This land won't lie down. Driving to Sauk City. Warren Woessner. TAT
This landscape demands: open vowels. Campi Flegrei. Barend Toerien, *tr. by author*. PeSA
This last generation. Last Generation. Michelle Roberts. LFAC
This last October working to a day of sun. Voyage. John Lyle Donaghy. OxBI
This Last Pain. William Empson. ChMP; CMoP; CoBMV; EBEV; FaBoMo; GTBS-P; LiTM; MoAB; MoBrPo; MoVE; NoAM; OAEL-2; SeCePo; SeCeV

This last soft lie. Almost. December Sunset. Jonathan Holden. FAZ
This lay, a favorite of mine. Honeysuckle (Chevrefoil). Marie de France, *tr. by* Patricia Terry. BoWoP
This legend is told of me. Actaeon. Rayner Heppenstall. FaBoTw
This legendary house, this dear enchanted tomb. Monticello. May Sarton. GOA
This let me further add, that nature knows. Of the Pythagorean Philosophy. Ovid, *tr. by* Dryden. *Fr.* Metamorphoses, XV. OBVE
This level reach of blue is not my sea. Fair Weather. Dorothy Parker. SBG
This Life. Rita Dove. AmPA
This Life. William Drummond of Hawthornden. *See* Madrigal: "This life, which seems so fair."
This Life. *Unknown. See* Life of This World, The.
This Life a Dream and Shadow. Sir Thomas More. *Fr.* The Twelve Weapons of Spiritual Battle. EnRePo
This life a theatre we well may call. Palladas, *tr. fr. Greek by* Robert Bland. NIP
This Life Is All Chequer'd with Pleasures and Woes. Thomas Moore. ELP
This life is but a game of cards. Life's a Game. *Unknown.* BLPA
This life is not a circus where. Lawrence Ferlinghetti. *Fr.* A Coney Island of the Mind. PPP
This life like no other. Poem. Gregory Orr. AmPA
This life, which seems [*or* seemes] so fair [*or* faire]. Madrigal. William Drummond of Hawthornden. CH; EIL; GTBS; GTBS-P; OAEL-1; OBS; SeCePo; TrGrPo
This life's a hollow bubble. Fin de Siècle. Edmund Vance Cooke. BLPA
This light is loss backward; delight by hurt and by bias gained. March Twilight. Louise Bogan. NePoAm-2
This lilac loses its leaves. Vertigos or Contemplation of Something That Is Over. Alejandra Pizarnik, *tr. by* Yishai Tobin. VWA
This Lime-Tree Bower My Prison. Samuel Taylor Coleridge. EnRP; HeIP; LoBV; NIP; PoEL-4
Seen from the Quantocks, *sel.* FaBoPP
This little book, my God and King. Dedication. Sir James Chamberlayne. CavP
This Little Bride and Groom Are. E. E. Cummings. AmPP
This little child, so white, so calm. Challenge. Kenton Foster Murray. HBV-1
This Little House Is Sugar. Langston Hughes. NTCP
This Little Light of Mine. *Unknown.* FSW
This Little Pig Built a Spaceship. Frederick Winsor. *Fr.* The Space Child's Mother Goose. QQQ; RHPC
This little pig had a rub-a-dub. *Unknown.* OxNR
This little pig went to market. Mother Goose. HBV-1; HBVY; OxNR; SoPo; TiPo
This little talent goes to market. Rhyme from Grandma Goose. Annemarie Ewing. NePoAm
This little vault, this narrow room. An Epitaph on the Lady Mary Villiers [*or* An Other]. Thomas Carew. AnAnS-2; CaPo; OBEV; SeCP; SeCV-1
This Little Vigil. Charles G. Bell. NePoAm
This Living Hand [Now Warm and Capable]. Keats. BoLoP; CABA; HAP; InPK; InPS; NoP; OAEL-2; PAI; SyP
(Lines Supposed to Have Been Addressed to Fanny Browne.) ChER; ELU; NCEP; OBNC
(To Fanny Brawne.) NOBE
This Loneliness for You Is like the Wound. Dunstan Thompson. WaaP; WaP
This lonely figure of not much fun. Absent-minded Professor. Howard Nemerov. ELU
This lonely following in the old town. Lines for a Young Wanderer in Mexico. John Logan. PoA
This long and lonely month. The Lonely Month. Ruthven Todd. NeBP
This, Lord, was an anxious brother and. Funeral Oration for a Mouse. Alan Dugan. AP; HAP; NoAM; PPP
This love is a rich cry over. A Black Wedding Song. Gwendolyn Brooks. CNA
This lovely flower fell to seed. For My Grandmother. Countee Cullen. Four Epitaphs, 1. AmNP; CDC; MoAmPo; PoBA; VGW
This lovely little life whose toes. With the Shell of a Hermit Crab. James Wright. NoP
This loving attention to the details. At a Private Showing in 1982. Maxine W. Kumin. SV
This Lunar Beauty. W. H. Auden. MoAB; MoBrPo; OBMV; OxBTC; SOTW
This luxury they call the Flesh. Phineas Pratt. Gloria MacArthur. GoYe
This lyfe, I see, is but a cheyre feyre. A Cherry Fair. *Unknown. Fr.* Farewell, This World. ChTr
This mad carnival of loving. Heine, *tr. by* Emma Lazarus. *Fr.* To Angélique. TrJP
This maiden hight Mary, she was full mild. She Sang, Dear Son, Lullay. *Unknown.* SBVL
"This making of bastards great." Song: Old Rowley the King. *Unknown.* APAS
This man contrived (but yet no glory won). Epigram on the Unknown Inventor of Scissors. L. E. Jones. POL
This man escaped the dirty fates. Flyer's Fall. Wallace Stevens. CABA; MoAB
This man is o so. Item. E. E. Cummings. MoAB; MoAmPo
This man, this poet, said. A Spark of Laurel. Stanley Kunitz. NoAM
This man, this stranger in my arms. Indian Summer. Barbara Howes. IHMS
This man, who his own fatherland forgets. He Is My Countryman. Antoni Slonimski, *tr. by* Frances Notley. TrJP
This man whose homely face you look upon. Abraham Lincoln. Richard Henry Stoddard. GN; OHIP; PGD
This massive, carved medieval harp of Irish oak. The Library. John Logan. AMV-80
This mast, new-shaved, through whom I rive the ropes. Choosing a Mast. Roy Campbell. FaBoTw; PeSA
This May Be Your Captain Speaking. C. K. Stead. OCNZ
This Measure. Léonie Adams. MoAmPo; MoAB
This menopause of mine. Bloody Pause. Astra. BrRo
This midnight breathing. A House Divided. Michael Ondaatje. MoCV
This might be nature—twenty stories high. The Picture [*or* New York 1962: Fragment]. Robert Lowell. NoAM; NYP
This might have been a place for sleep. Thistledown. Harold Monro. BrPo; OxBTC
This mighty empire hath but feet of clay. Theoretikos. Oscar Wilde. BrPo; VLP
This mild September mist recalls the soul. The Origin of Centaurs. Anthony Hecht. NePoEA
This miracle in me I scan. William Baylebridge. Life's Testament, VIII. PoAu-1
This mist has followed on an all-day rain. Spring Night. Richard Aldridge. NePoAm
This Moment. Annie Johnson Flint. BLRP
This moment is precious. Urgency. Sarah E. Wright. PoNe
This month of May, one pleasant eventide. Medieval Norman Song. *Unknown, tr. by* John Addington Symonds. AWP
This Monument Will Outlast. Horace, *tr. fr. Latin by* Ezra Pound. Odes, III, 30. CTC
This morn a young squire shall be made a knight. On Knighthood. Folgore da San Geminiano, *tr. by* John Addington Symonds. AWP
This morn, ere yet had rung the matin peal. On a Frightful Dream. John Codrington Bampfylde. NOEC
This morn my friend Al mentioned his wife had taken a job. The Day of the Pancreas. David McFadden. NeAC
This Morning. Lucille Clifton. GLGT
This Morning. Javier Gálvez. FF
This Morning. Muriel Rukeyser. BoWoP; NMM
This Morning. Jon Stallworthy. NoP
This Morning. Jay Wright. NNP
This morning/ being rather young and foolish. Little Johnny's Confession. Brian Patten. CAD
This morning/ My child dances naked. Variations on a Theme. Mark Vinz. Psk
This morning/ With a class of girls outdoors. In a Spring Still Not Written Of. Robert Wallace. BoNaP; PP
This morning a cat got. Dad and the Cat and the Tree. Kit Wright. OnUR
This morning Amanda. Amanda Dreams She Has Died and Gone to the Elysian Fields. Maxine W. Kumin. GP
This morning, as I walked to school. A Story in the Snow. Pearl Riggs Crouch. SoPo; TiPo
This morning, because the snow swirled deep. Oatmeal Deluxe. Stephen Dobyns. AMV-81
This morning blue vast clarity of March sky. Birth of Rainbow. Ted Hughes. NAs
This morning came down. Four Fawns. Barbara Howes. AMV-80
This morning, flew up the lane. *See* This morning, there flew up the lane.
This morning he studied the dead wasps. Holding On. Richard Jackson. AMV-80
This morning I come to the water again. Going to the Water. Geary Hobson. STE
This morning I do not despair. The Vestal in the Forum. James Wright. AMV-81
This morning I fight against the silence. Against the Silences to Come. Ron Loewinsohn. PoM
This morning I held Harriet in my head. True Love. Joe Johnson. CNA
This morning I threw the windows. This Morning. Jay Wright. NNP

This Morning I Wakened among Loud Cries of Seagulls. Patrick MacDonogh. NeIP
This morning I wanted to bring you roses. The Roses of Saadi. Marceline Desbordes-Valmore, *tr. by* Deirdre Lashgari. WPOW
This morning I woke/ to an impatient scratching on the window. Apricot Tree. Magda Isanos, *tr. by* Willis Barnstone *and* Matei Calinescu. BoWoP
This morning I wrote a poem. Akriel's Consolation. William Pillin. AMV-80
This morning, in Assisi, I woke. In Assisi. Michael Blumenthal. MAYP
This morning, in my garden. November Garden. Louise Driscoll. YeAr
This morning kelp is drying on the dockside. Homage to Hart Crane. Peter Balakian. MAYP
This morning of my birthday, rain is starting to fall. Bar Mitzvah. Steve Orlen. GP
This morning of the small snow. The Songs of Maximus, III. Charles Olson. *Fr.* The Maximus Poems. PAI; PPP
This morning on the beach where the last wash of spray. The Wedding. Sandra Kohler. AMV-80
This morning, on the opposite shore of the river. Fire. William Carpenter. Psk
This morning saw I, fled the shower. Contemplation. Francis Thompson. BrPo; LoBV
This morning take a holiday from unhappiness because. First Cycle of Love Poems (I-V). George Barker. MoPo
This morning, the memory of you. Inertia. Vivienne Finch. BrRo
This morning the overhanging clouds are piecrust. Overhanging Cloud. Robert Lowell. *Fr.* Marriage. NAs
This Morning the Sun. Olga Cabral. *Fr.* Another Late Edition. PPON
This morning, there flew up the lane. Lady Lost. John Crowe Ransom. MoAB; MoAmPo; TrGrPo; TwAmPo; UnPo
This morning they are putting away the whales. Autumn. William Carpenter. Psk
This morning, timely rapt [*or* wrapt] with holy fire. On Lucy Countess[e] of Bedford. Ben Jonson. AnAnS-2; EnRePo; OAEP; OBS; SeCP; SeCV-1
This Morning Tom Child, the Painter, Died. Samuel Sewall. SCAP
This morning trimming ivy in. Not Blindly in the Dark. Robert M. Stanley. AMV-81
This morning we found him. Bushed. Charles Lillard. NOBC
This morning we shall spend a few minutes. Money. Howard Nemerov. OxBC; WeW
This morning, when he looked at me. Black All Day. Raymond Richard Patterson. BOLo; PoBA
This morning when I awoke,/ I found the enemy had invaded. Bella Ciao. *Unknown, tr. fr. Italian.* FSW
This morning, when I had to kill. Circle of Struggle. William Pitt Root. NYBP
This morning, when I heard the crows. The Crows. David McCord. MoAmPo
This morning with a blue flame burning. A Poem for Trapped Things. John Wieners. NeAP; PoM
This morning your hairs hurt with disuse, stiff. Ghazal: Japanese Paintbrush. Randy Mott. PoDr
This mossie [*or* mossy] bank they prest [*or* press'd]. A Pastorall Dialogue. Thomas Carew. AnAnS-2; CaPo; GBL; SeCP
This moth caught in the room tonight. Lying Awake. W. D. Snodgrass. HoPM; MoAmPo; NYBP
This mound the Achaeans reared—Achilles' tomb. Epitaph on Achilles. *Unknown, tr. by* William M. Hardinge. AWP
This much, O heaven—if I should brood or rave. A Prayer in Darkness. G. K. Chesterton. FPL; MoBrPo; PoLF; TrGrPo
This mud, my genesis. Ascent. Wendell Berry. AP
This my father taught. Four Things Choctaw. Jim Barnes. STE
This my heart, so flowing and so simple. Poem of the Intimate Agony. Julia de Burgos, *tr. by* Julio Marzán. InW
This Narrow Stage. Theodore Weiss. NoAM
This never-ended searching for the eyes. Egg-and-Dart. Robert Finch. OBCV
This new Daks suit, greeny-brown. Metamorphosis. Peter Porter. OxBTC
This New Day, *with music.* Vail Read. AH
This new Diana makes weak men her prey. Diana. Ernest Rhys. OBVV
This Night. Nathan Alterman, *tr. fr. Hebrew by* Ruth Nevo. VWA
This Night. Dianne Hai-Jew. BrSi
This Night. William Heyen. MAYP
This Night. Osip Mandelstam, *tr. fr. Russian by* Daniel Weissbort. VWA
This night cast iron over flat land. The Unreal Song of the Old. James Koller. PoM
This night is pure and clear as thrice refinèd silver. Fountains. Sacheverell Sitwell. MoBrPo
This night of no moon. Ono no Komachi, *tr. fr. Japanese by* Donald Keene. PBWP
This night presents a play, which publick rage. Prologue to Hugh Kelly's "A Word to the Wise." Samuel Johnson. EBEV; FaPoR
This Night Sees Ireland [*or* Eire] Desolate. Aindrais MacMarcuis, *tr. fr. Irish by* Robin Flower. BIrV
(Flight of the Earls, The.) AnIL
"This night shall thy soul be required of thee." Scorpion. Stevie Smith. EBEV
This night talk is godless. From Which War. Phillip Yellowhawk Minthorn. STE
This night there is a child born. Three Christmas Carols, III. *Unknown.* ACP
This night, while sleep begins with heavy wings. Astrophel and Stella, XXXVIII. Sir Philip Sidney. SiPS
This night's calm water. Whatever Is, Is Right. Frank Gaik. AMV-81
This nine-pound hammer is a little too heavy. Nine-Pound Hammer. *Unknown.* FSW
This noiseless ball and top so round. Philocles. Leonidas of Tarentum, *tr. by* F. A. Wright. AWP
This nycht befoir the dawing cleir. Followis How Dumbar Wes Desyrd to Be Ane Freir. William Dunbar. OAEP
This, O my stomach, is a painting. American Heritage. Robert Sward. OBAL
This old crabbed man, with his wrinkled, fusty clothes. Old Crabbed Men. James Reeves. ChMP; ErPo
This old hammer killed John Henry. John Henry. *Unknown.* ViBoFo
This Old Man. *Unknown.* FSW; SoPo
This old soul, you know, time she left Chicago. The Panama Limited. *Unknown.* BluL
This Olympian pug you see now, Sir, once possessed. Boxer Loses Face and Fortune. Lucilius, *tr. by* Tom Dodge. LiSp
This on thy posy-ring I've writ. The Posy Ring. Clement Marot, *tr. by* Ford Madox Ford. AWP
This one deceives her husband with her eyes. Hostia. Irving Layton. PV
This One Heart-shaken. Sister Maris Stella. GoBC
This One Is About the Others. Dan Jaffe. FAZ
This one request I make to him that sits the clouds above. Love and Debt Alike Troublesome. *At. to* Sir John Suckling. AnAnS-2; CavP
This one was put in a jacket. Counting the Mad. Donald Justice. ConAP; FF; NePoEA; NIP; PAI; PPON; UnPo
This one's for you, Uncle Bill. Papio. Eric Chock. BrSi
This One's on Me. Phyllis Gotlieb. MoCV; NOBC
This onion-dome holds all intricacies. Greenwich Observatory. Sidney Keyes. MoAB; MoBrPo
This Only Grant Me. Abraham Cowley. *Fr.* A Vote. TreFT
(Of Myself.) OAEP; OBS
This only hope relieves me, that the strife. Milton. *Fr.* Samson Agonistes. TRV
This Other Night. *Unknown.* ISi
This other speaks of bones, blood wet. Fair/ Boy Christian Takes a Break. Jim Harrison. NoAM
This Pacific ocean. This Earth. Phillip Yellowhawk Minthorn. STE
This page I send you, sir, your Newgate fate. A Poem upon the Imprisonment of Mr. Calamy in Newgate. Robert Wild. APAS
This Page My Pigeon ("This page is my pigeon sailing"). Earle Birney. PeCV
This Pardoner had hair as yellow as wax. Chaucer, *mod. vers. by* Nevill Coghill. *Fr.* The Canterbury Tales: Prologue. SCV
This Particular Christian. Louis Johnson. OCNZ
This peach is pink with such a pink. Song. Norman Gale. HBV-1
This pennant new. Poems of My Lambretta. Paul Goodman. NMP
This perspex model is what you might call a perfect replica. Naming of Private Parts. John Lloyd Williams. BXAP; FaBoPa
This picnic tea. Peter Titheradge. *Fr.* Teatime Variations: After Walter de la Mare. FaBoPa
This pig got in the barn. *Unknown.* OxNR
This pit is Hell where through thou now must go. Elizabeth Melvill, Lady Culross. *Fr.* A Godly Dream. WPE
This Place in the Ways. Muriel Rukeyser. MiAP
This place is cold. Three Poems for the Indian Steelworkers. Joseph Bruchac. CDW
This place moves from me. Poem before Departure. Jean Burden. WPE
This place (quoth she) they say's enchanted. Samuel Butler. *Fr.* Hudibras, II, 1. NOBL
This Place Rumord to Have Been Sodom. Robert Duncan. NeAP; NOBA; PoM; PPP
This pleasant tale is like a little copse. Sonnet: Written at the End of "The Floure and the Lefe." Keats. EnRP
This ploughman dead in battle slept out of doors. A Private. Edward Thomas. GTBS-P; MMA
This poem I write to teach the reader. Writing in England Now. Philip O'Connor. OxBTC

This poem is about the strength and sadness of potatoes. Potatoes. David Donnell. NOBC
This poem is an erection. Erotic Suite. José Luis Vega, *tr. by* Julio Marzán. InW
This poem is concerned with language on a very plain level. Paradoxes and Oxymorons. John Ashbery. NoP
This Poem Is for Bear. Gary Snyder. Myths and Texts: Hunting, VI. NOBA; NU
("Bear down under the cliff, A.") NaP
This Poem Is for Deer. Gary Snyder. Myths and Texts: Hunting, VIII. CAPP; NOBA
("'I dance on all the mountains.'") NaP
This poem is for my wife. Poem in Prose. Archibald MacLeish. PoPl
This poem is written in an ancient form. Poem Called Poem. James Whitehead. GrPl
This Poem Will Never Be Finished. Raymond Souster. CaP
This poet is. Meeting Mick Jagger. Robert Peters. BXAP
This poetry gets bored of being alone. Living Poetry. Hugo Margenat, *tr. by* Julio Marzán. InW
This pool, the quiet sky. March Evening. L. A. G. Strong. MoBrPo
This poring over your *Grand Cyrus.* On a Romantic Lady. Mary Monck. NOEC
This porthole overlooks a sea. Bendix. John Updike. NYBP
This portrait painter boasted twenty sons. The Artist as Cuckold. *Unknown, tr. by* Louis Untermeyer. UnTE
This portrait which I treasure so. Epigram: The Likeness. Martial, *tr. by* Brian Hill. PeHV
This pretty bird, oh, how she flies and sings! Upon the Swallow. Bunyan. OxBChV
This Pretty Woman. *Unknown.* OxBM
This prophecy came by mail. Requiem for "Bird" Parker. Gregory Corso. PoNe
This queen of prey (now prey to you). A Lady with a Falcon on Her Fist. Richard Lovelace. CaPo
This Quiet Dust. John Hall Wheelock. MoAmPo; WHA
This quiet dust was gentlemen and ladies. Emily Dickinson. AP; CMoP; DL; OxBA; ViBoPo
(Cemetery, A.) MoAB; MoAmPo
This quiet morning light. To Mark Anthony in Heaven. William Carlos Williams. NOBA
This quiet mound beneath. Corporal Pym. Walter de la Mare. FaBoEE
This Quintus, Corydon, for whom you lust. Panormitanus, *tr. fr. Latin.* PeHV
This racer of the watry plain. Catullus, *tr. fr. Latin.* OBVE
This rain like silver corn, this northern rain. Count Orlo in England. Jon Manchip White. NePoEA
This rain that has come from far away, like breath. Lifelines. T. R. Hummer. AMV-80
This ration card, once shocking pink. The Ration Card. Liz Sohappy Bahe. CDW
This realm is sacred to the silent past. In a Garret. Elizabeth Akers Allen. AA
This red nun on my left hand leans away. Red Right Returning. Louis O. Coxe. MoVE; WaP
This Relative of mine. To My Grandmother. Frederick Locker-Lampson. HBV-1; InMe; OBVV
This revelation, the retreat of tide. Liberation. Diane Mei Lin Mark. BrSi
This reverend shadow cast that setting sun. Upon Bishop Andrewes His Picture before His Sermons. Richard Crashaw. OBS
This rich marble doth enter. An Epitaph on the Marchioness of Winchester. Milton. CavP; OBS
This rite perform'd, all inly pleas'd and still. A Wondrous Show. James Thomson. *Fr.* The Castle of Indolence. OBEC
This road ends in a field of grain. Documentation. Michael Palmer. NPGG
This road is like a tomb. On Passing Two Negroes on a Dark Country Road Somewhere in Georgia. Conrad Kent Rivers. IDB; NNP
This road is so fuzzy. Cinéma Vérité. Dorothy Walters. IHMS
This road isn't passable. Warning. Jesse Douglas. WhC
This road winds smooth. The Belly of the Land. Luci Tapahonso. STE
This room holds. The Spell. Michelle Roberts. LFAC
This room I know so well becomes. The Room. Elizabeth Jennings. NePoEA-2
This room is very old and very wise. Poem. Sam Harrison. NeIP
This room need not speak of her. The Glove. Andrew Greig. BSV
This root of bog-oak the sea dug up she found. Trouvaille. Richard Murphy. CIP; IPY
This rose tree is not made to bear. Envy. Charles *and* Mary Lamb. OxBChV
This Royal Infant. Shakespeare. King Henry VIII, *fr.* V, iv. NAs
This royal throne of kings, this sceptered isle. This England [*or* John of Gaunt's Speech *or* This Blessed Plot . . . This England]. Shakespeare. King Richard II, *fr.* II, i. FaBoPP; FaBV; FaPoR; TreF; TrGrPo
This rudely sculptured porter-pot. Undying Thirst. Antipater, *tr. by* Robert Bland. AWP
This rule in gardening ne'er forget. *Unknown.* FaBoUs
This Runner. Francis Webb. CBAP
This rusty mound of cans. Rural Dumpheap. Melville Cane. AmFN
This sadness could only be a color. When You Leave. Kimiko Hahn. BrSi
This said; he (begging) gather'd clouds from land. Ulysses in the Waves. Homer, *tr. by* George Chapman. *Fr.* The Odyssey, V. OBS
This said; he high Olympus reacht, the king then left his coach. Priam and Achilles. Homer, *tr. by* George Chapman. *Fr.* The Iliad, XXIV. OBS
This said, he reacht to take his sonne. Homer, *tr. by* George Chapman. *Fr.* The Iliad, VI. OBVE
This said, he turned about his steed. Sidrophel, the Rosicrucian Conjurer. Samuel Butler. *Fr.* Hudibras. OxBoLi
This sailor knows of wondrous lands afar. The Child and the Mariner. W. H. Davies. CH
This saying good-by on the edge of the dark. Good-by and Keep Cold. Robert Frost. CMoP
This sea will never die, neither will it ever grow old. Middle of the World. D. H. Lawrence. HAP
This second night. The Second Night. M. L. Hester, Jr. AMV-80
This seems, in a world where love must take its chances. Mona Van Duyn. Footnotes to "The Autobiography of Bertrand Russell," II. HAP
This sentence have I left behind. A Nameless Epitaph. Matthew Arnold. FaBoEE
This shade-bestowing pear-tree, thou. The Pear-Tree. *Unknown, tr. by* Allen Upward. *Fr.* Shi King. AWP
This shadow at my shoulder doesn't shed. Climbing. Jennifer Maiden. CBAP
This shadow flesh of risen man. Night. Glyn Jones. NeBP
This shall be called the laying on of hands. A Necessary Miracle. Eda Lou Walton. NYBP
This Shall Be Sufficient. Kenneth Rexroth. CAD
This shell, this slender spiral in the hand. The Enduring Music. Harold Vinal. EtS
This ship is the ship of butchery and increase. Songs for the Cisco Kid: or Singing: Song #2. K. Curtis Lyle. PoBA
This Shirt. Arturo Trías, *tr. fr. Spanish by* Julio Marzán. InW
This silken wreath, which circles in mine arm[e]. Upon a Ribband. Thomas Carew. AnAnS-2; CaPo; OAEL-1
This sky is to be opened. Hermetic Bird. Philip Lamantia. VGW
This slender girl/ sprawled on th buffalo grass. Celebrant. David Mitchell. OCNZ
"This small lodge is now." Old Man, the Sweat Lodge. Phil George. GrPl
This Smoking World. Graham Lee Hemminger. *See* Tobacco.
This Solitude of Cataracts. Wallace Stevens. LCAP
This song is of no importance. Evensong. Conrad Aiken. HBMV
This song of late autumn. Autumn. Itzig Manger, *tr. by* Joseph Leftwich. TrJP
This song of mine sets my soul free. Vusumzi's Song. L. T. Manyase, *tr. by* C. M. Mcanyangwa *and* Jack Cope. PeSA
This song of mine will wind its music around. My Song. Rabindranath Tagore. OHIP
This Song Shows Me Pictures; Morningside Drive, New York City 1950–1960. Richard Oyama. BrSi
This soup is cold. The Soup of Venus. James Tate. AmPA
This sparrow/ who comes to sit at my window. The Sparrow. William Carlos Williams. DiL; InPS; LCAP; PrIm; VGW
This speech all Trojans did applaud; who from their traces loos'd. The Trojans outside the Walls. Homer, *tr. by* George Chapman. *Fr.* The Iliad, VIII. OBS; OBVE
This spoke, a huge wave tooke him by the head. Homer, *tr. by* George Chapman. *Fr.* The Odyssey, V. MOS; OBVE
This spoonful of chocolate tapioca. Thinking of the Lost World. Randall Jarrell. NoAM; NOBA
This Spot [Is the Sweetest I've Seen in My Life]. *Unknown.* ShM; WhC
(From a Churchyard in Wales.) FiBHP
This spring as it comes bursts up in bonfires green. The Enkindled Spring. D. H. Lawrence. NoAM
This Spring of Love. Shakespeare. *Fr.* The Two Gentlemen of Verona, I, iii. ChTr
This spring, you'd swear it actually gets dark earlier. Turning Thirty. Katha Pollitt. WeW
This starry world, and I in it. Death. James Oppenheim. WGRP
This statue of Liberty, busy man. The Statue of Liberty. Thomas Hardy. LiTB
This steaming night in Vientiane. A filthy room. The Room above the White Rose. Joseph Stroud. NPGG
This still life is still life after all. Still Life. Vivian Smith. AMV-80; AMV-81

This Stone. *Unknown, tr. fr. Greek by* Goldwin Smith. AWP
This stone. Stone Hammer Poem. Robert Kroetsch. NOBC
This story goes on a long time. My Children's Book. John N. Morris. AMV-80
This story's strange, but altogether true. "R. B." SCAP
This strange thing must have crept. Fork. Charles Simic. AmPA; GP; LCAP; PCP
This sturdy squire, he had, as well. Samuel Butler. *Fr.* Hudibras. ViBoPo
This sudden cockerel who stood. Cock-Crow. Ralph Nixon Currey. PeSA
This Summer and Last. Thomas Hardy. OxBTC
This summer is your perfect summer. Never will the skies. To a Child before Birth. Norman Nicholson. ChMP; NAs
This Sun Is Hot. *Unknown.* BPo
This sunlight shames November where he grieves. Autumn Idleness. Dante Gabriel Rossetti. *Fr.* The House of Life. GBL; OAEL-2
This sycamore, oft musical with bees. Inscription for a Fountain on a Heath. Samuel Taylor Coleridge. OAEP
This talking of death in itself is getting over. Vincent O'Sullivan. Brother Jonathan, Brother Kafka, 9. OCNZ
This tempest sweeps the Atlantic!—Nevasink. Night Storm. William Gilmore Simms. EtS; MOS
This that I give you now. Bread. Stanley Burnshaw. TrJP
This that is washed with weed and pebblestone. The Figurehead. Léonie Adams. WPE
This the house that Jack built. The House That Jack Built. *Unknown.* FaBoBe
This, the last ornament among the peers. Hilaire Belloc. OBSV
This the law of all war through all ages. The Waste of War. William L. Stidger. PGD
This the true sign of ruin to a race. The Decay of a People. William Gilmore Simms. AA
This, the twentieth day of March. A Letter to Three Irish Poets. Michael Longley. BIrV
This they know well: the Goddess yet abides. In Her Praise. Robert Graves. BIrV
This thin elastic stick was plucked. A Switch Cut in April. Clifford Dyment. MoVE
This, this is he; softly a while. Samson Fallen. Milton. *Fr.* Samson Agonistes. OBS; UnPo
This tiger is not Blake's tiger burning bright. The Wooden Tiger. Samuel Yellen. NePoAm
This time/ in the darkness. Stuntman. Lionel Kearns. MoCV
This time, I mean it. A Little Tumescence. Jonathan Williams. ErPo; NeAP; PoM
This time of autumn. Lilies for Neal. James Minor. WOLT
This time the snow came fiercely down. Of Snow. Norman Brick. WaP
This time you're with me. Barbara's Land Revisited—August 1978. Geary Hobson. STE
This to the crown and blessing of my life. A Letter to Daphnis [*or* Dafnis]. Countess of Winchilsea. EnLoPo; SBG
This Tokyo. Gary Snyder. CAPP; NeAP
This told, strange Teras touched her lute, and sung. The Wedding of Alcmane and Mya. George Chapman. *Fr.* Hero and Leander, Fifth Sestiad. OBSC
This tomb, by loving hands up-piled. At the Lincoln Tomb. John H. Bryant. PGD
This too is an experience of the soul. Isis Wanderer. Kathleen Raine. OxBS
This, Too, Shall Pass Away. Lanta Wilson Smith. BLPA
(This Too Will Pass Away.) STF
This Town. James Paul. HoAn
This town has a spire. This Town: Winter Morning. William Stafford. NPAW
This town has docks where channel boats come sidling. Arrivals, Departures. Philip Larkin. MoBrPo
This Town: Winter Morning. William Stafford. NPAW
This tragical tale, which, they say, is a true one. Pyramus and Thisbe. John Godfrey Saxe. HBV-2; OnMSP
This Train ("This train is bound for glory, this train"). *Unknown.* FSW; OxBoLi
(This Train Don't Carry No Gamblers.) AmFP
This tree/ growing out of me. Song for a Transformation. Francisco Arriví, *tr. by* Julio Marzán. InW
This tree, here fall'n, no common birth or death. On the Site of a Mulberry-Tree [Planted by William Shakespeare, Felled by the Rev. F. GastrellPiatt. Dante Gabriel Rossetti. NCEP; TW
This tree is like the man. Thinning Out the Grove. Judith Neeld. SOTS
This tree outside my window here. On Not Saying Everything. C. Day Lewis. NoP
This Troilus, with blisse of that supprysed. Chaucer. *Fr.* Troilus and Criseyde, III. EBEV
This truly wonderful steed. Title of a Swift Horse. *Mongol Oral Tradition, tr. by* C. R. Bawden. WTO
This tuft that thrives on saline nothingness. The Air Plant. Hart Crane. MoAB; MoAmPo; NoP; PAI
This twilight of two yeares, not past nor next. To the Countesse of Bedford, on New-Yeares Day. John Donne. OBS
This ultimate austerity. Desert Claypan. Frederick T. Macartney. PoAu-1
This unheated star is not the kind to take in pious babble. Computer. Otto Orban, *tr. by* Emery George. VWA
This Unimportant Morning. Lawrence Durrell. BoLoP; NeBP; OxBTC
This urge, wrestle, resurrection of dry sticks. Cuttings [Later]. Theodore Roethke. AP; LCAP; NoAM; NOBA; PPoe; TAP; UnPo
This vale of teargas. Unlawful Assembly. D. J. Enright. OxBTC
This valley wood is hedged. An English Wood. Robert Graves. BrPo
This vast web, of Nature's weaving. The Cosmic Fabric. Yakov Polonsky, *tr. by* Avrahm Yarmolinsky *and* Cecil Cowdery. EaLo
This vegetable body drops. Cinderella. Feroz Ahmed-ud-Din. DFT
This verse be thine, my friend, nor thou refuse. To Mr. Jervas, with Fresnoy's Art of Painting, Translated by Mr. Dryden. Pope. OBEC
This Version of Love. Dorothy Hewett. CBAP
This very day, a little while ago, you lived. Dead on the War Path. *Tr. fr. Tewa Indian by* H. J. Spinden. WTO
This Very Hour. Lizette Woodworth Reese. HBMV
This very remarkable man. On Monsieur Coué. Charles Inge. FaFP
This virgin, beautiful and lively day. Sonnet. Stéphane Mallarmé, *tr. by* Roger Fry. NAWM-2; PoPl
This votive pledge of fond esteem. Stanzas to a Lady, with the Poems of Camoëns. Byron. FaBoUs
This wall-paper has lines that rise. Missing My Daughter. Stephen Spender. GTBS-P; Str
"This warning, Gallus, for thy love I send." Hylas. Propertius, *tr. by* F. A. Wright. Elegies, I, 20. AWP
This was a love in which there was always. Brief Farewell. Anthony Delius. PeSA
This was a man bivouacked in wool. The Magistrate's Escape. Alice Fulton. PoDr
This was a man of mighty mould. On a Bust of Lincoln. Clinton Scollard. OHIP
This was a mouse who played around. Tracks in the Snow. Marchette Chute. SiSoSe
This was a poet—it is that. Emily Dickinson. AmPP; AP; NOBA; PP
This was Briseis' way: she was a bridge. Alex Comfort. *Fr.* The Postures of Love. NeBP
This was decreed by superior powers. Tower of Ivory. Leonard Bacon. WhC
"This was Mr. Bleaney's room. He stayed." Mr. Bleaney. Philip Larkin. HoPM; InPS; NePoEA-2; OxBC; PPoe
"This was Mr. Strugnell's room," she'll say. Mr. Strugnell. Wendy Cope. FaBoPa
This Was My Brother. Mona Gould. CaP
This was my dream: I saw a forest. Robert Browning. Bad Dreams, III. OAEL-2; VLP
This was that mystery of clearest light. The Statue of Shadow. John Peale Bishop. LiTA
This was the color of coolness. Spring Cellar. Gladys McKee. GoYe
This was the crucifixion on the mountain. Altarwise by Owl-Light, VIII. Dylan Thomas. CMoP; NoAM
This was the end and yet, another start. Merlin in the Cave: He Speculates without a Book. Thom Gunn. NePoEA
This was the first world, where the wild dove cries. Creation. Louise Townsend Nicholl. GoYe
This was the hand that knew to swing. The Hand of Lincoln. Edmund Clarence Stedman. PGD
This was the hawk's way. This was the hawk. Hawk's Way. Ted Olson. HoPM
This was the man God gave us when the hour. George Washington. John Hall Ingham. AA; OHIP; PAH; PAL
This was the moment when Before. BC:AD. U. A. Fanthorpe. OBCP
This was the noblest Roman of them all. Portrait of Brutus [*or* The Noblest Roman]. Shakespeare. *Fr.* Julius Caesar, V, v. FaFP; TreFS; TrGrPo
This was the summer when the tired girls. Now Kindness. Peter Viereck. LiTA
This was the woman; what now of the man? Modern Love, III. George Meredith. HBV-1
AA; HBV-1
This was your very first wall, your crib against. Comes Winter, the Sea Hunting. Norman Dubie. MAYP
This watchful nurse and bundled boy at play. A Matter of Life and Death. Richard Aldridge. NePoAm
This water is so clear. The Fisherman Writes a Letter to the Mermaid. Joan Aiken. WSC

This water, sad and fearful. Slow Rain. Gabriela Mistral, *tr. by* Gunda Kaiser *and* James Tipton. PBWP
This way from the north. Corn-grinding Song. *Tr. fr. Tewa Indian.* WTO
This Way Only. Lesbia Harford. PoAu-1
This way, this way, come and hear. Song in the Wood. John Fletcher. *Fr.* The Little French Lawyer. ElL
This wet sack, wavering slackness. MacDuff. Charles Tomlinson. NAs; OxBC
This is what it was. The Meat Epitaph. Michael Benedikt. FiCP
This while we are abroad. An Ode Written in the Peak[e]. Michael Drayton. FaBoPP; OBS
This whirlwind sounds a larger dissonance. Mid-Century. Mary Elizabeth Osborn. NePoAm
This White and Slender Body. Heine, *tr. fr. German by* Louis Untermeyer. UnTE
This wight all mercenary projects tries. Sir Samuel Garth. *Fr.* The Dispensary. OBSV
This wild night, gathering the washing as if it were flowers. From the Roof. Denise Levertov. NoP
"This will not do," he said. If It Offend Thee. Horace Gregory. NMP
This will really try you. Mamma! Frank Horne. BPo
This Wind. Tom Kryss. NeAC
This window frames an alien climate. The Documentary on Brazil. Alfred Corn. MAYP
This wine-press is call'd war on earth. Blake. *Fr.* Milton, I. EBEV
This winter day, we build our fire. The Fire. William Burford. NePA
This winter the ocean rushes west. Lovely Girls with Flounder on a Starry Night. Anselm Parlatore. SUW
This winter's morning, turning the other way. Turning. Robert Finch. MoCV; OBCV
This Winter's Weather It Waxeth Cold *Unknown.* *See* Old Cloak, The.
This woman is getting on her last bus. Poem for Jacqueline Hill. *Unknown.* BrRo
This woman vomiten her. Present. Sonia Sanchez. CNA; WPOW
This woman with a dead face. A Cold Front. William Carlos Williams. NAs
This worker is a fearless one. The Riveter. Mabel Watts. RHPC
This World. Abbie Huston Evans. NePoAm
This world/ is amazingly flat. Natalya Gorbanyevskaya, *tr. fr. Russian by* Barbara Einzig. BoWoP
This world a vale of soul-making. In Cemeteries. D. J. Enright. OxBC
This World and This Life Are So Scattered, They Try Me. Heine, *tr. fr. German by* Charles Godfrey Leland. ELU
(Zu fragmentarisch ist Welt und Leben.) AWP
This World Fares as a Fantasy. *Unknown.* OxBM
This World Is All a Fleeting Show. Thomas Moore. HBV-2
This world is gradually becoming a place. John Berryman. *Fr.* Dream Songs. NoAM; NOBA
This world is not conclusion. Emily Dickinson. EaLo
This world is not my home, I'm just a-passing through. I Can't Feel at Home in This World Anymore. *Unknown.* FSW
This world is very odd we see. Reply to Dipsychus. Arthur Hugh Clough. FaBoCo
This world of strange creations, so prodigal in wastefulness of life. Of Curious Questions. Martin Farquhar Tupper. VLP
This world was not. The Golden Age. Ernest Francisco Fenollosa. AA
This world was once a fluid haze of light. Tennyson. *Fr.* The Princess. ImOP
This worlde is full of variaunce. The Duplicity of Women. John Lydgate. MeEL
This World's Joy. *Unknown.* *See* Winter Wakeneth All My Care.
This would be spring, if seasons could be found. Perhaps the Best Time. William Meredith. NePoEA
This wretched life, the trust and confidence. This Life a Dream and Shadow. Sir Thomas More. *Fr.* The Twelve Weapons of Spiritual Battle. EnRePo
This Year. Joseph Hutchison. AMV-81
This year,/ I'm raising the emotional ante. These Green-going-to-Yellow. Marvin Bell. FYAP; LCAP
This year,/ Next year. *Unknown.* OxNR
This year I intended children. Margaret Atwood. NeAC
"This year she has changed greatly"—meaning you. Change. Robert Graves. OxBTC
This year (so I hear). A Year without Seasons. Mance Williams. NNP
This year, till late in April, the snow fell thick and light. The Nineteenth of April. Lucy Larcom. PAH
This year we are making/ nothing but elegies. Dufferin, Simcoe, Grey. Margaret Atwood. AMV-81
This yellow velvet visitor. Caterpillar. R. E. Rashley. CaP
This Yonder Night I Sawe a Sighte. *Unknown.* NAs
(She, Sang, Dear Son, Lullay.) SBVL
This yonge fresshe wenche, wel loking honey-swete. The Hicche-Hykeres Tale. W. F. N. Watson. BXAP
Thisbe. Helen Gray Cone. AA
Thise olde gentil Britons in hir dayes. The Franklin's Prologue. Chaucer. *Fr.* The Canterbury Tales. OAEL-1
Thistle and darnell and dock grew there. Nicholas Nye. Walter de la Mare. HBMV; HBVY
Thistle whips spitefully across brown thigh. Judean Summer. Fay Lipshitz. VWA
Thistle, Yarrow, Clover. Kenneth Porter. NePoAm
Thistle-Down. Clara Doty Bates. AA
Thistledown. James Merrill. UnPo
Thistledown. Harold Monro. BrPo; OxBTC
Thistledown. Lizette Woodworth Reese. YeAr
Thistledown blows over the poisoned fields. The Martyred Earth. Ewart Milne. BIrV
Thistledown's flying, though the winds are all still, The. Autumn. John Clare. BoNaP; HAP; NBM; NU; PoEL-4; WeW
Thistles. Ted Hughes. NoAM; OxBTC
THISTRIOLET. A Cubic Triolet. *Unknown.* PV
Tho'. *See also* Though.
Tho' [*or* Though] grief and fondness in my breast rebel. London. Samuel Johnson. GoTL; LAuP; PoEL-3; TEP
Tho' grief had nipp'd her early bloom. The Maniac. Thomas Russell. OBEC
Tho he is young. The Red Road. Nila NorthSun. STE
Tho' I can not your cruelty constrain. Sir Thomas Wyatt. SiPS
Tho I die on a distant strand. The Cool, Grey City of Love. George Sterling. BPAW
Tho' I my party long have chose. Moderation. Christopher Smart. Hymns for the Amusement of Children, Hymn 9. NOCV
Tho' ill at ease, a stranger and alone. Thoughts on Pausing at a Cottage near the Paukataug River. Sarah Kemble Knight. SCAP
Tho' I'm no Catholic. The Catholic Bells. William Carlos Williams. CMoP; NOBA; OxBA
Tho' my verse is exact. Hence These Rimes. Bert Leston Taylor. FiBHP
Tho' truths in manhood darkly join. The Word. Tennyson. In Memoriam A. H. H., XXXVI. GoBC
Tho We All Speak. Daniel Ort. AMV-80
Tho when as chearelesse night ycovered had. Spenser. *Fr.* The Fairie Queene, III, 12. OAEL-1
Tho' You May Boast You're Fairer. *Unknown.* OBS
Thocht, The. William Soutar. NeBP
Thocht raging stormes movis us to schaik. The Reid in the Loch Sayis. *Unknown.* OxBS
Thocht that this warld be verie strange. Solace in Age. Sir Richard Maitland. OxBS
Thomas à Becket, a Dramatic Comedy, *sel.* George Darley.
"Speckle-black Toad and freckle-green Frog." FM
Thomas à Kempis. Richard Rogers Bowker. AA
Thomas à Kempis. Lizette Woodworth Reese. AA
Thomas a Tattamus took two T's. Riddles. *Unknown.* HBV-1; HBVY
Thomas and Charlie. Peter Wild. AmPA
Thomas at Chickmauga. Kate Brownlee Sherwood. PAH
Thomas Carlyle. *Unknown.* FiBHP
Thomas Cromwell. *Unknown.* ESPB
Thomas Dudley, Ah! Old Must Dye. *Unknown.* SCAP
Thomas Gray's View of Nature. William Mason. *Fr.* The English Garden, III. NOEC
Thomas Hardy. Walter de la Mare. NoAM
Thomas Hardy in the stars. Winter's Dregs. George Bowering. PeCV
Thomas Hood. E. A. Robinson. HBMV
Thomas in the Fields. Lois Moyles. NYBP
Thomas Iron-Eyes. Marnie Walsh. WPOW
Thomas Jefferson [1743–1826]. Rosemary *and* Stephen Vincent Benét. FaPON; PoPl; TiPo
Thomas lay on the Huntlie bank. Thomas the Rimer [*or* Thomas Rymer]. *Unknown.* EnSB; ESPB
Thomas Logge. Walter de la Mare. FaBoEE
Thomas MacDonagh. Francis Ledwidge. *See* Lament for Thomas MacDonagh.
Thomas More to Them That Seek Fortune. Sir Thomas More. EnRePo
Thomas o Yonderdale. *Unknown.* ESPB
Thomas Rhymer. *Unknown.* *See* Thomas the Rhymer.
Thomas Rymer [and the Queen of Elfand]. *Unknown.* *See* Thomas the Rhymer.
Thomas Sackevyll in Commendation of the Worke to the Reader. Thomas Sackville. AAS
Thomas Shadwell the Poet. John Dryden *and* Nahum Tate. *Fr.* Absalom and Achitophel, Pt. II. ChTr
Thomas Stuart was a lord. Lord Thomas Stuart. *Unknown.* BaBo; ESPB
Thomas the Rhymer. *Unknown.* BSV; ELP; FaBoCh; GoTS; HBV-2;

InPS; LiTB; NOBE; OAEL-1, *with music;* OBEV; OnMSP; OxBB, *with music;* Prf; SeCeV; ViBoPo
(Thomas Rhymer.) PAI
(Thomas Rymer [and the Queen of Elfland].) CH; ChTr; ESPB (A *and* C *vers.*); FaBoBa; HAP; OAEP; ViBoFo
(Thomas the Rimer.) EnSB; InPK
(True Thomas.) OxBS; TrGrPo
Thomas, the vagrant piper's son. John Masefield Relates the Story of Tom, Tom, the Piper's Son. Louis Untermeyer. *Fr.* Mother Goose Up-to-Date. MoAmPo
Thomas Trevelyan. Edgar Lee Masters. *Fr.* Spoon River Anthology. MoPo
Thomas Winterbottom Hance. W. S. Gilbert. InMe
Thompson Street. Samuel McCoy. HBMV
Thoralf and Synnöv. Hjalmar Hjorth Boyesen. AA
Thorberg Skafting, master-builder. The Building of the *Long Serpent.* Longfellow. *Fr.* Tales of a Wayside Inn: The Musician's Tale, Pt. I. EtS
Thoreau. Amos Bronson Alcott. AA
Thoreau. Rodney Jones. MAYP
Thoreau,/ grabbing on, hard. The Distances to the Friend. Jonathan Williams. NeAP
Thoreau, you've come into your own. To Henry David Thoreau. Irwin Edman. WhC
Thoreau's Flute. Louisa May Alcott. AA; HBV-2
Thorn, The. Wordsworth. EnRP
Sels.
"And they had fixed the wedding day." EvOK
"High on a mountain's highest ridge." Par
Thorn Forever in the Breast, A. Countee Cullen. BiP
Thorn Leaves in March. W. S. Merwin. MP; TwCP
Thorn Piece. Amy Lowell. PeHV
Thorn tree, pale and sharp, The. The Tree of Hatred. Shmuel Moreh. VWA
Thorns have whitened along the way, The. Do Not Accompany Me. Shimon Halkin, *tr. by* Ruth Nevo. VWA
Thoroughbred Horse, The. Oliver Herford. TDH
Those animals that follow us in dream. Lupus in Fabula [*or* Xochitepec]. Malcolm Lowry. MoCV; NOBC; OBCV; PeCV
Those awful words "Till death do part." Early Thoughts of Marriage. Nathaniel Cotton. FaBoUs; OxBChV
Those Beauteous Maids. Moses ibn Ezra, *tr. fr. Hebrew by* Solomon Solis-Cohen. TrJP
Those before Us. Robert Lowell. LCAP
Those Being Eaten by America. Robert Bly. CoAP; NaP
Those Betrayed at Dawn. Stanislaw Wygodski, *tr. fr. Polish by* Isaac Komem. VWA
Those blessèd structures, plot and rhyme. Epilogue. Robert Lowell. NoP
Those Boys That Ran Together. Lucille Clifton. CNA; PoBA
Those calm swamp-green eyes. Pisces Child. Sandra McPherson. NMM
Those Cambridge generations, Russell's, Keynes'. On Bertrand Russell's "Portraits from Memory." Donald Davie. FaBoTw
Those charming eyes within whose starry sphere. On the Death of Catarina de Attayda. Luis de Camoes, *tr. by* R. F. Burton. AWP
Those Chu Lai priests who raised me as a boy. A Viet Cong Sapper Dies. Stephen Sossaman. AMV-81
Those clarities detached us, gave us form. The Tourist and the Town. Adrienne Rich. NePoEA-2
Those dabbing hens I ferociously love. Cock before Dawn. Norman MacCaig. OxBC
Those dark mountains face to face. Dark Mountains. Milton Lockyer, *tr. by* Frank Wordick. CBAP
Those days we spent on Lebanon. On Lebanon. David Gray. AA
Those days when it was all right. Letter to E. Franklin Frazier. Amiri Baraka. BPo; PoBA
Those Denver evenings I'd drag myself. Going to Press. Judith Moffett. AMV-80
Those dreams that on the silent night intrude. On Dreams. Swift. BIrV
Those earlier men that owned our earth. The After-Comers. Robert Traill Spence Lowell. AA
Those envied places which do know her well. A Day of Love. Dante Gabriel Rossetti. The House of Life, XVI. VLP
Those eyes (dear Lord) once brandons of desire. On Mary Magdalene. William Drummond of Hawthornden. OAEL-1
Those eyes still shine which promised that behind. Pygmalion. Hans Brockerhoff. AMV-80
Those eyes that [*or* which] set my fancy on a fire. Conquest [*or* His Lady's Might]. Philippe Desportes. AWP; OBSC
Those famous men of old, the Ogres. Ogres and Pygmies. Robert Graves. CABA; CMoP; FaBoMo; LiTB; LiTM; NoAM; SeCePo; SeCeV
"Those fantastic forms, fang-sharp." City without Walls. W. H. Auden. NYBP; NYP
Those flaming Christians with their hygienic rose. Burns Singer. Sonnets for a Dying Man, XXXIII. NePoEA-2
Those Flapjacks of Brown's. Bert Leston Taylor. OBAL
Those flaxen locks, those eyes of blue. To My Son. Byron. NAs
Those former loves wherein our lives have run. James Agee. Sonnets, XIX. MoAmPo
Those four black girls blown up. American History. Michael S. Harper. BPo
Those Gambler's Blues. *Unknown. See* St. James Infirmary.
Those gathered by heartache in alien lands. Beyond Memory. Monny de Boully, *tr. by* Aleksander Nejgebauer. VWA
Those graves, with bending osier bound. A Night-Piece on Death. Thomas Parnell. SeCePo
Those great rough ranters, Branns. A Simplification. Richard Wilbur. CMoP
Those great sweeps of snow that stop suddenly six feet from the house. Snowbanks North of the House. Robert Bly. LCAP
Those greetings! those goodbyes! Kennedy Airport. Aaron Kramer. AMV-80
Those groans men use. The Mutes. Denise Levertov. IHMS; NaP; NOBA
Those Guyana Nights. Richard Foerster. SOTS
Those hands, which you so clapped, go now and wring. Shakespeare Dead. Hugh Holland. ACP
Those hours, that with gentle work did frame. Sonnets, V. Shakespeare. TEP
Those Hours When Happy Hours Were My Estate. Edna St. Vincent Millay. PrIm
Those houses haunt in which we leave. Ghosts. Elizabeth Jennings. NePoEA-2; PPJ
Those I Love. Victor Contoski. GP
Those Images. W. B. Yeats. CMoP; PP
Those in the vegetable rain retain. Stories of Snow. P. K. Page. NOBC; NoP; OBCV; PoA
Those joys that us'd to flatter me. Corydon's Complaint. Samuel Pordage. CavP
Those Last, Late Hours of Christmas Eve. Lou Ann Welte. PChr
Those lathered horses galloping past. The Horsemen. Gene Baro. NePoEA-2
Those long uneven lines. MCMXIV. Philip Larkin. EBEV; OBWP
Those looks, whose beams be joy, whose motion is delight. Astrophel and Stella, LXXVII. Sir Philip Sidney. SiPS
Those lumbering horses in the steady plough. Horses. Edwin Muir. CMoP; FaBoCh; MoVE; OAEL-2; PoPle; SeCePo
Those lustrous eyes but tell me this. Fred Emerson Brooks. *Fr.* Kissing. PeD
Those make thunder though taking pigs somewhere. 13th Dance—Matching Parcels—21 February 1964. Jackson Mac Low. CoPo
Those moon-gilded dancers. The Gay. "Æ." OBMV
Those mornings in green mountains. Virginia Beach. Stanley Plumly. AMV-81
Those mothers down there off the hill. Seventh Son. Ed Roberson. PoBA
Those my friendships most obtain. Contentment. Nathaniel Cotton. OxBChV
Those nights lit by the moon and the moon's nimbus. Nights in Hackett's Cove. Mark Strand. GeTw
Those nights we said "Goodbye! goodbye!" and then. Decent Burial. Lois Seyster Montross. HBMV
Those Not Confused Are Prisoners of War. Noah Mitchell. LFAC
Those Not Elect. Léonie Adams. MoVE
Those occasions involving the veering of axles. Munich Elegy No. 1. George Barker. SeCePo; WaP
Those of Pure Origin. Roy Fuller. FaBoMo
Those old tunes take me back. I used to go. Her Dancing Days. Anna Adams. BrRo
Those Old Zen Blues. James Broughton. GP
Those paths on the mountainside. Circumambulation of Mt. Tamalpais. Andrew Hoyem. PoA
Those petty wrongs that liberty commits. Sonnets, XLI. Shakespeare. InvP
Those petulant capricious sects. Religion. Samuel Butler. DBV
Those quaint old worn-out words! Antiques. Walter de la Mare. PoA
Those ravens black that rested. Heavy-hearted. Judah al-Harizi. TrJP
Those Rebel Flags. John H. Jewett. PAH
Those reckless hosts rush to the wells. Elegy. Baruch of Worms. TrJP
Those red men you offended were my brothers. In My First Hard Springtime. James Welch. AmPA; CDW
Those rivers run from that land. Song. Robert Creeley. VGW
Those roman stones. Dan, the Dust of Masada Is Still in My Nostrils. Ruth Whitman. VWA
Those scraps of paper. Scraps. Susannah Fried, *tr. by* Anthony Rudolf. VWA

Those ships which left. Saigyo Hoshi, *tr. fr. Japanese by* Arthur Waley. AWP
Those snooty boys in all their purple drag! Epigram. Strato, *tr. by* Tony Harrison. PeHV
Those souls that of His own good life partake. Eternal Life. Henry More. TRV
Those stopped by the barrage. Dirge; for the Barrel-Organ of the New Barbarism. Louis Aragon, *tr. by* Selden Rodman. WaaP
Those that can give, open their hands this day. A New Year's Sacrifice: To Lucinda. Thomas Carew. CaPo
Those trackless deeps, where many a weary sail. The Trackless Deeps. Shelley. *Fr.* The Daemon of the World, Pt. II. EtS
Those Trees That Line the Northway. Ellen Perreault. AMV-81
Those Troublesome Disguises. Jonathan Williams. NeAP
Those two bad shepherds, hunched above their sheep. Buachaille Etive Mor and Buachaille Etive Beag. Naomi Mitchison. PoSH
Those Two Boys. Franklin P. Adams. FiBHP; TrJP
Those two young men, dancing quietly together in a corner. Gay Boys. James Kirkup. PeHV
Those upon whom Almighty doth intend. The Frowardness of the Elect in the Work of Conversion. Edward Taylor. SCAP
Those Various Scalpels. Marianne Moore. LoBV
Those villages stricken with the melancholia of Sunday. Sabbaths, W.I. Derek Walcott. WeW
Those vitreous vivariums. Ode of Odium on Aquariums. Arthur Guiterman. BoAnP
Those wallèd garrisons will I subdue. Christopher Marlowe. *Fr.* Tamburlaine the Great, Pt. I. ViBoPo
Those we have loved the dearest. The Fallen. Duncan Campbell Scott. TrPWD
Those we love truly never die. Forever. John Boyle O'Reilly. HBV-2; OnYI; WGRP
Those Wedding Bells Shall Not Ring Out! *with music.* Monroe H. Rosenfeld. FSN
Those were countries simple to observe, difficult. Report from a Planet. Richmond Lattimore. FYAP
Those were good times, in olden days. Written on a Fly-Leaf of Theocritus. Maurice Thompson. AA
Those were the conquered, still too proud to yield. The Battle-Field. Lloyd Mifflin. PAH
Those Were the Days. *Zulu Oral Tradition, tr. by* H. Tracey. WTO
Those who cannot love the heavens or the earth. The Chaff. W. S. Merwin. PPP
Those Who Come What Will They Say of Us. John Knoepfle. FAZ
Those who favor our plan to alter the river. Plans for Altering the River. Richard Hugo. FYAP
Those who fling off, toss head. Meeting Together of Poles & Latitudes: In Prospect. Margaret Avison. NOBC; OBCV
Those who have chosen to pass the night. Violent Storm. Mark Strand. NYBP
Those who have laid the harp aside. To Wordsworth. Walter Savage Landor. OAEL-2
Those who live in country places. Epiphany. Eileen Duggan. ISi
Those who lived here are gone. A Ruined House. Richard Aldington. BrPo
Those Who Lost Everything. David Diop, *tr. fr. French by* Langston Hughes. PBA
Those who love cats which do not even purr. Cats. Francis Scarfe. BoAnP; NeBP; PCat
Those who love Thee may they find. A Prayer. George F. Chawner. BLRP
Those who loved me. Memento Vivendi. Eva Brudne. VWA
Those who said God is praised. For the New Railway Station in Rome. Richard Wilbur. NePoEA
"Those who speak know nothing." The Philosopher. Lao-tzu, *tr. by* Arthur Waley. WhC
Those who split wood know. To a Young Poet. Paula Bennett. AMV-81
Those Winter Sundays. Robert Hayden. CNA; CTBA; DFF; DiL; FF; GP; GrPl; HAP; HoAn; IDB; LCAP; NoAM; NoP; PoBA; PPP; SoSe; UnPo; WeW
Those Zionists. Crescenzo del Monte, *tr. fr. Judeo-Romanesque by* Barbara Garvin. VWA
Those—dying then. Emily Dickinson. CABA; NoP
Thothmes, who loved a pyramid. The Story of Pyramid Thothmes. *Unknown.* NA
Thou alive on earth, sweet boy. Epitaph. Francis Davison. OBSC
Thou are great, and compared with Thy greatness. The Royal Crown, V. Solomon Ibn Gabirol, *tr. by* Israel Zangwill. AWP
Thou are Light celestial, and the eyes of the pure shall behold Thee. The Royal Crown, VII. Solomon Ibn Gabirol, *tr. by* Israel Zangwill. AWP
Thou are not, Penshurst, built to envious show. *See* Thou art not, Penshurst . . .
Thou art as a lone watcher on a rock. England. Richard Edwin Day. AA
Thou art beautiful, O my love. Bible, *O.T. (Douay vers.) Fr.* The Song of Solomon. ISi
Thou art come at length. Sitalkas. Hilda Doolittle ("H. D."). ViBoPo
Thou Art Coming! Frances Ridley Havergal. WGRP
Thou Art Coming to a King. John Newton. TRV
Thou art God, and all things formed are Thy servants and worshipers. The Royal Crown, VIII. Solomon Ibn Gabirol, *tr. by* Israel Zangwill. AWP
Thou art God's sky. Mary. Robert Farren. ISi
Thou Art Indeed Just, Lord, If I Contend. Gerard Manley Hopkins. AWP; BrPo; CABA; CMoP; CoBMV; EaLo; EBVV; GTBS-P; HAP; HoPM; LiTM; LoBV; MoAB; MoBrPo; MoVE; NoAM; NOBE; NoP; OAEL-2; OAEP; OxBoCh; PAI; TrPWD; UnPo; VLP
(Justus Quidem Tu Es, Domine.) EBEV
Thou art King of Israel and of Davides kunne. A Palm-Sunday Hymn. William Herebert. MeEL
Thou art like to a flower. The Translated Way. Franklin P. Adams. FiBHP
Thou art lost to me forever!—I have lost thee, Isadore! The Widowed Heart. Albert Pike. AA
Thou art mine, thou hast given thy word. Song from a Drama. Edmund Clarence Stedman. AA
Thou art my God, sole object of my love. Prayer of St. Francis Xavier. Pope. TrPWD
Thou art my Hiding Place. My Hiding Place. Kathryn T. Bowsher. STF
Thou art not dead, although the spoiler's hand. Africa. Lewis Alexander. CDC
Thou art not dead, my Prote! thou art flown. To Prote. Simmias of Thebes, *tr. by* John Addington Symonds. AWP
Thou Art Not Fair. Thomas Campion. EIL; EnRePo; InvP; ViBoPo
("Thou art not fair for all thy red and white.") AAS; EnLoPo; OBSC
Thou art [*or* are] not, Penshurst, built to envious show. [To] Penshurst. Ben Jonson. AnAnS-2; AWP; CABA; FaBoPP; JCP; LoBV; NIP; NoP; OAEL-1; OBS; PoEL-2; PPP; SeCP; SeCV-1; TEP
Thou art not so black, as my heart. A Jeat Ring Sent. John Donne. PoEL-2
Thou Art, O God. Thomas Moore. *See* Glory of God in Creation, The.
Thou Art, O God, the God of Might, *with music.* Emily Swan Perkins. AH
Thou art, O God, the life and light. The Glory of God in Creation [*or* Thou Art, O God]. Thomas Moore. OHIP; TrPWD
Thou Art of All Created Things. Pedro Calderón de la Barca, *tr. fr. Spanish.* WGRP
Thou art One, the first of every number, and the foundation. The Royal Crown, II. Solomon Ibn Gabirol, *tr. by* Israel Zangwill. AWP
Thou art so fair, and young [*or* yong] withal. Youth and Beauty. Aurelian Townsend. AnAnS-2; GBL; MePo; SeCP
Thou art the essence of all created things. Thou Art of All Created Things. Pedro Calderón de la Barca. WGRP
Thou art the rock of empire, set mid-seas. At Gibraltar, II. George Edward Woodberry. GN
Thou Art the Sky. Rabindranath Tagore. *Fr.* Gitanjali. OBMV
Thou art the soul of a summer's day. A Song. Paul Laurence Dunbar. AmNP
Thou art the source that causes our river to flow. Jalal al-Din Rumi, *tr. fr. Persian.* ILwL
Thou art the Star, blazing with beames bright. Star of the Sea. Alexander Barclay. *Fr.* The Ship of Fools. ACP
Thou Art the Tree of Life, *with music.* Edward Taylor. AH
Thou Art the Way, *with music.* George Washington Doane. AH
Thou art the Way. "I Am the Way." Alice Meynell. ACP; EBCP; GoBC; OBMV; TRV
Thou art the wind and I the lyre. Wind and Lyre. Edwin Markham. TRV
"Thou art! Thou art!" Lavater says. "Thou art!!" On Lavater's Song of a Christian to Christ. Goethe, *tr. by* Walter Kaufmann. ELU
Thou art to all lost love the best. To the Willow-Tree. Robert Herrick. CaPo; HBV-1; OBEV
Thou art weary, weary. weary. A Witch's Chant. James Hogg. BSV
Thou art wise. And wisdom is the fount of life and from Thee it welleth. The Royal Crown, IX. Solomon Ibn Gabirol, *tr. by* Israel Zangwill. AWP
Thou barren waste; unprofitable strand. Winter in Lower Canada. Standish O'Grady. *Fr.* The Emigrant. NOBC; OBCV
Thou beauteous off-spring of a syre as fair. On a Sunbeam. Thomas Heyrick. MePo
Thou Beautiful Sabbath. *Unknown, tr. fr. Yiddish by* Isidore Myers. TrJP
Thou bleedest, my poor Heart! and thy distress. On a Discovery Made Too Late. Samuel Taylor Coleridge. EnRP
Thou Blind Man's Mark. Sir Philip Sidney. *Sometimes considered Sonnet CIX of* Astrophel and Stella; *also in* Certain Sonnets. CABA; EnRePo; ErPo; HeIP; PPP; ViBoPo
(Desire.) LiTB; MasP; NOBE; OBSC; SiPS; TrGrPo
Thou blossom bright with autumn dew. To the Fringed Gentian. Bryant.

AA; AP; AWP; FaBoBe; FPL; GN; HBV-1; NePA; NoP; OBRV; PoLF; TAP; TreFT
Thou booby, say'st thou nothing but cuckoo? Of the Cuckoo. Bunyan. PBBP
Thou, born to sip the lake or spring. On a Honey Bee [*or* To a Honey Bee]. Philip Freneau. AA; AP; TAP; YaD
Thou brown, bare-breasted, voiceless mystery. To the Colorado Desert. Madge Morris. BPAW
Thou burden of all songs the earth hath sung. Autumn. Sir William Watson. OBVV
Thou canst not die whilst any zeal abound. To Delia, XL. Samuel Daniel. OAEP; OBSC
Thou canst not prove that thou art body alone. The Ancient Sage. Tennyson. WGRP
Thou cheat'st us Ford, mak'st one seem two by art. Upon Ford's Two Tragedies, "Loves Sacrifice" and "The Broken Heart." Richard Crashaw. OBS
Thou Christ, my soul is hurt and bruised! The Doubter. Richard Watson Gilder. TrPWD
Thou comest, Autumn, heralded by the rain. Autumn. Longfellow. OBVV
Thou comest by. 10th Dance—Coming On as a Horn—20 February 1964. Jackson MacLow. CoPo
Thou comest, much wept for: such a breeze. Tennyson. In Memoriam A. H. H., XVII. EBVV
Thou comest to me, thou exultest, seeing my beauty. Hymn of Victory: Thutmose III. Amon-Re, *tr. by* James Henry Breasted. WaaP
Thou cursed cock, with thy perpetual noise. On a Cock at Rochester. Sir Charles Sedley. FaBoEE; POL; TW
Thou dancer of two thousand years. The Dancing Faun. Robert Cameron Rogers. AA
Thou dear and mystic semblance. Lines to the Blessed Sacrament. James Joseph Callanan. OnYI
Thou, Death, alone art kind, helpest men give. To Azrael. Baudelaire, *tr. by* T. Sturge Moore. SyP
Thou Didst Delight My Eyes. Robert Bridges. ELP; MoAB; MoBrPo
Thou Didst Say Me. Miriam Waddington. OBCV; PeCV
Thou divinest, fairest, brightest. The Satyr's Farewell [*or* The Satyr's Leave-taking]. John Fletcher. *Fr.* The Faithful Shepherdess, V, i. LO; LoBV; OBS
Thou dome, where Edward first enroll'd. An Ode Inscribed to the Earl of Sunderland at Windsor. Thomas Tickell. OBEC
Thou dreamer with the million moods. A Song of Desire. Frederick Lawrence Knowles. HBV-1
Thou, Earth, calm empire of a happy soul. Shelley. *Fr.* Prometheus Unbound, IV. FaBoRV; OBRV
Thou Easer of All Woes. John Fletcher. *See* Care-charming Sleep.
Thou enemy of love, how slow you creep. Dawn. *Unknown, tr. by* Louis Untermeyer. UnTE
Thou ever young! Persephone but gazes. To Demeter. Maybury Fleming. AA
Thou existest, but hearing of ear cannot reach Thee. The Royal Crown, III. Solomon Ibn Gabirol, *tr. by* Israel Zangwill. AWP
Thou fair-hair'd [*or* haired] angel of the evening. To the Evening Star. Blake. BoNaP; CH; ChER; ChTr; EnRP; FaBoRV; FaBV; FPL; LAuP; LoBV; NOEC; NoP; OAEL-2; OAEP; PoLF; PPP; TEP; TrGrPo; WiR
Thou fool profane, be silent! Epigram II. *Unknown. Fr.* Duel with Verses over a Great Man. TrJP
Thou foolish bird, of feathers proud. On a Peacock. Thomas Heyrick. PB
Thou for whose birth the whole creation yearned. The Rise of Man. John White Chadwick. AA
Thou foul-mouthed wretch! The Sailor to His Parrot. W. H. Davies. BoAnP; EtS; ViBoPo
Thou from th' enthroned martyrs blood-stain'd line. Henry King. *Fr.* An Elegy upon the Most Incomparable King Charles the First. OBS
Thou gallant Chief whose glorious name. Washington. Denis O'Crowley. OHIP
Thou gav'st me leave to kiss. Chop-Cherry. Robert Herrick. EnLoPo; UnTE
Thou glorious mocker of the world! I hear. To the Mocking-Bird. Albert Pike. AA
Thou God of all, whose presence dwells. Hymn. John Haynes Holmes. TrPWD
Thou God of This Great Vast, Rebuke These Surges. Shakespeare. *Fr.* Pericles, III, i. MOS; NAs
Thou God, whose high, eternal Love. Wedding-Hymn. Sidney Lanier. TrPWD
Thou goest more and more. Ode on Advancing Age. Richard Watson Dixon. NBM
Thou goest; to what distant place. Farewell. John Addington Symonds. HBV-1
Thou Grace Divine, Encircling All, *with music.* Eliza Scudder. AH
Thou Great God. *Unknown, tr. fr. Xhosa by* A. C. Jordan. PBA
Thou great Supreme, whom angel choirs adore. Unseen. Fanny Crosby. TrPWD
Thou green and blooming, cool and shaded hill. The Heart on the Hill. Petrarch, *tr. by* C. B. Cayley. Sonnets to Laura: To Laura in Life, CCV. AWP
Thou grimmest far o grusome tykes. To a Hedgehog. Samuel Thompson. BIrV
Thou Guide to doubt, be silent evermore. Epigram I. *Unknown. Fr.* Duel with Verses over a Great Man. TrJP
Thou half-unfolded flower. The Blossom of the Soul. Robert Underwood Johnson. AA
Thou happiest thing alive. To the Boy. Elizabeth Clementine Kinney. AA
Thou, happy creature, art secure. On the Death of a Lady's Dog. Wentworth Dillon, Earl of Roscommon. CavP
Thou happy, happy elf! A Parental Ode to My Son, Aged Three Years and Five Months [*or* To My Son]. Thomas Hood. FaPON; FiBHP; HBV-1; PoLF
Thou has clothed thy steepest hillsides. To Pikes Peak. Elijah Clarence Hills. PoOW
Thou has come from the old city. The Old City. Ruth Manning-Sanders. CH
Thou Has Wounded the Spirit That Loved Thee. Mrs. David Porter. BLPA
Thou hast beauty bright and fair. Hermione. "Barry Cornwall." OBVV
Thou hast been very tender to the Moon. Malvolio. Walter Savage Landor. Par
Thou Hast Diamonds. Heine, *tr. fr. German by* Emma Lazarus. *Fr.* Homeward Bound. TrJP
Thou hast done evil. The Judgment. Dora Read Goodale. AA
Thou hast given so much to me. A Heart to Praise Thee. George Herbert. TRV
Thou hast lived in pain and woe. A Requiem ("B. V."). James Thomson. HBV-2
Thou hast made me, and shall thy work [*or* worke] decay? John Donne. Holy Sonnets, I. AnAnS-1; EBEV; EnRePo; FaBoEn; MasP; MeLP; NOBE; NOCV; NoP; OAEP; OBS; OxBoCh; PoEL-2; SeCP; TEP
Thou hast made me endless, such is thy pleasure. Rabindranath Tagore. *Fr.* Gitanjali. ILwL
Thou Hast Made Us for Thyself. St. Augustine, *tr. fr. Latin.* TRV
Thou hast not drooped thy stately head. Savannah. Alethea S. Burroughs. PAH
Thou hast not left the rough-barked tree to grow. I Was Sick and in Prison. Jones Very. NOBA
Thou hast not rais'd, Ianthe, such desire. Walter Savage Landor. *Fr.* Ianthe. GBL
Thou hast on earth a Trinity. To the Christ. John Banister Tabb. TrPWD
Thou hast stirred. Song of Cradle-making. Constance Lindsay Skinner. CaP
Thou hast thine eyrie in the lifted lands. Colorado. John D. Dillenback. PoOW
Thou hast thy ponds, that pay thee tribute fish. Ben Jonson. *Fr.* To Penshurst. FaBoEn
Thou hearest the nightingale begin the song of spring. The Vision of Beulah [*or* The Birds *or* The Choir of Day *or* Nightingale and Flowers]. Blake. *Fr.* Milton, II. EnRP; FaBoEn; LoBV; NOBE; OBNC; OBRV; PB; PBBP; WiR
Thou heavenly quivering beneath the deathlike above! To a Lark in War-Time. Franz Werfel, *tr. by* Edith Abercrombie Snow. TrJP
Thou heaven-threat'ning Rock, gentler then she! Echo to a Rock. Lord Herbert of Cherbury. PoEL-2
Thou, heedless Albion, what, alas, the while. England, Unprepared for War. Mark Akenside. *Fr.* An Ode to the Country Gentlemen of England. OBEC
Thou hermit, haunter of the lonely glen. The Sand Martin. John Clare. PBBP; TEP
Thou hidden love of God, whose height. Hymn. John Wesley. NOEC; OBEC
Thou ill-formed offspring of my feeble brain. The Author to Her Book. Anne Bradstreet. AmPP; AP; InPK; NePA; NOBA; NoP; OxBA; SCAP; TAP
Thou in this wide cold church art laid. On the Dead. Walter Savage Landor. NBM
Thou inmost, ultimate. To the Body. Alice Meynell. ACP
"Thou jestedst when thou swor'st that thou betrothedst." Tudor Aspersions. R. A. Piddington. FiBHP
Thou Joy'st, Fond Boy. Thomas Campion. OAEP
Thou Knowest. Katharine Lee Bates. TrPWD
Thou knowest, love, I know that thou dost know. Love's Entreaty. Michelangelo, *tr. by* John Addington Symonds. AWP; PeHV
Thou knowest my years entire, my life. Walt Whitman. *Fr.* Prayer of Columbus. TrPWD

Thou knowest, Thou who art the soul of all. Thou Knowest. Katharine Lee Bates. TrPWD
Thou knowest what is best. Trust and Obedience. *Unknown.* BLRP
Thou know'st, my Julia, that it is thy turn. To Julia, the Flaminica Dialis, or Queen-Priest. Robert Herrick. CaPo
Thou large-brained woman and large-hearted man. To George Sand: [I.] A Desire. Elizabeth Barrett Browning. BoWoP; TEP
Thou leanest to the shell of night. James Joyce. EBEV
Thou Light of Ages. Rolland W. Schloerb. TrPWD
Thou lily-leaf, thou roseal-bud. To Mary. Gottfried Von Strasburg, *tr. by* E. M. Sweetman. ISi
Thou Lingering [*or* Ling'ring] Star. Burns. EnRP; OBEC
(To Mary in Heaven.) HBV-1; OAEP
Thou little bird, thou dweller by the sea. The Little Beach-Bird. Richard Henry Dana. AA; EtS; HBV-1
Thou livest, but not from any restricted season nor from any known period. The Royal Crown, IV. Solomon Ibn Gabirol, *tr. by* Israel Zangwill. AWP
Thou Livest, O Soul! Charles Leonard Moore. AA
Thou Long Disowned, Reviled, Oppressed, *with music.* Eliza Scudder. AH
Thou, Lord, Hast Been Our Sure Defense, *with music.* John Hopkins. AH
Thou Lord of Hosts, Whose Guiding Hand, *with music.* Octavius Brooks Frothingham. AH
Thou lovely and belovèd, thou my love. Mid-Rapture. Dante Gabriel Rossetti. The House of Life, XXVI. BLPL; FaBoBe; HBV-1; OAEP
Thou maid and mother, daughter of thy Son. Chaucer. *Fr.* The Canterbury Tales: Prologue to the Second Nun's Tale. GoBC
Thou mastering me. The Wreck of the *Deutschland.* Gerard Manley Hopkins. BrPo; CMoP; CoBMV; FaBoMo; LiTB; LiTM; MasP; MoVE; NoAM; NOBE; OAEP; OBNC; OxBoCh; PoEL-5; SeCeV; TEP; VLP
Thou mayst retire, but think of me. To a Departing Favorite. George Moses Horton. BALP
Thou mercenary renagade, thou slave. To Mr. Bays. Charles Sackville. APAS
Thou mighty gulf, insatiate cormorant. To Everlasting Oblivion. John Marston. *Fr.* The Scourge of Villainy. LoBV; OBSC
Thou moon, like a white Christus hanging. Serenade. Kenneth Slessor. POL
Thou Moon, that aidest us with thy magic might. A Charm. Dryden. ChTr
Thou more than most sweet glove. The Glove. Ben Jonson. ElL; GBL
Thou most absurd of all absurdities. The Sloth. George J. Romanes. FM
Thou Mother with Thy Equal Brood, *sel.* Walt Whitman.
"Thou wonder world yet undefined, unform'd." PeD
Thou must be true thyself. Be True [*or* Honesty]. Horatius Bonar. FaBoBe; GN; HBV-2; HBVY; TRV
Thou ne're wutt [*or* nere wilt] riddle, neighbour Jan. A Devonshire Song. *Unknown, at. to* William Strode. PoEL-2
Thou One in All, Thou All in One, *with music.* Seth Curtis Beach. AH
Thou, Our Elder Brother. Whittier. ILwL
Thou, paw-paw-paw; thou, glurd; thou, spotted. Adam's Task. John Hollander. NIP; NoP; PPP
Thou perceivest the flowers put forth their precious odors. The Wild Thyme. Blake. *Fr.* Milton. WiR
Thou, proud man, look upon yon starry vault. Man's Littleness in Presence of the Stars. Henry Kirke White. WBLP
Thou Remainest. Annie Johnson Flint. BLRP
Thou rob'st [*or* robb'st] my days of bus'ness [*or* business] and delights. The Thief. Abraham Cowley. *Fr.* The Mistress. JCP; OAEP; WHA
Thou saidst that I alone thy heart cou'd move. Catullus, *tr. fr. Latin by* William Walsh. OBVE
Thou sai'st I swore I lov'd thee best. The Variety. John Dancer. CavP
Thou saist Love's dart. To Oenone. Robert Herrick. CaPo
Thou saist my lines are hard. To My Ill Reader. Robert Herrick. CaPo
Thou seemest like a flower. Heine, *tr. by* Emma Lazarus. *Fr.* Homeward Bound. TrJP
Thou seest me, Lucia, this year droop. Crutches. Robert Herrick. CaPo
Thou seest the hills candied with snow. To Thaliarchus. Horace, *tr. by* Sir Richard Fanshawe. Odes, I, 9. OBVE
Thou seest the under side of every leaf. Omniscience. Blanche Mary Kelly. TrPWD
Thou seest this world is but a thoroughfare. Eternal Reward, Eternal Pain. Sir Thomas More. *Fr.* The Twelve Weapons of Spiritual Battle. EnRePo
Thou sent [*or* sent'st] to me [*or* mee] a heart was crowned [*or* crown'd]. Upon a Diamond Cut in Form[e] of a Heart . . . Sent in a New Year's Gift. Sir Robert Ayton. ElL; OBS; PoPle
Thou shalt have no other gods before me. The Ten Commandments. Bible, *O.T. Fr.* Exodus. WBLP
Thou shalt have one God only; who. The Latest Decalogue. Arthur Hugh Clough. BiP; CABA; ChTr; DBV; EBEV; EBVV; FaBoCo; FaBoEE; FF; GTBS-P; HAP; HoPM; InMe; LoBV; NBM; NIP; NOBE; OAEL-2; OAEP; OBNC; OBSV; OBVV; PAI; PPP; TreFT; TRV; ViBoPo; VLP; WeW; WGRP
Thou Shalt Not. Malka Heifetz Tussman, *tr. fr. Yiddish by* Marcia Falk. VWA
Thou shalt not covet thy friend's wife. Covet. Ambrose Bierce. DBV
Thou shalt not covet thy neighbour's wife. Addendum to the Ten Commandments. *Unknown.* DBV
Thou shalt not laugh in this leaf, Muse, nor they. Satires, V. John Donne. OBSV
Thou shalt say to the eye of the strange woman: Be the water. In Egypt. Paul Celan, *tr. by* Joachim Neugroschel. VWA
"Thou shalt seek the beach of sand." The Fay's Sentence. Joseph Rodman Drake. *Fr.* The Culprit Fay. GN
Thou Ship of Earth, with Death, and Birth, and Life, and Sex aboard. The Ship of Earth. Sidney Lanier. MOS
"Thou Shouldst Be Living at This Hour!" Kenyon West. PGD
Thou should'st be living at this hour. Heathcote William Garrod. CenHV
Thou, Sibyl rapt! whose sympathetic soul. Margaret Fuller. Amos Bronson Alcott. AA
Thou simple bird what mak'st thou here to play? Upon the Lark and the Fowler. Bunyan. CH; PBBP
Thou Sleepest Fast. *Unknown.* ElL
Thou snowy farm with thy five tenements! Elinda's [*or* Ellinda's] Glove. Richard Lovelace. CaPo; OBS
Thou, so far, we grope to grasp thee. So Far, So Near. Christopher Pearse Cranch. TrPWD
Thou sorrow, venom elfe. Upon a Spider Catching a Fly. Edward Taylor. AmPP; AP; NePA; NOBA; NoP; OxBA; PoEL-3; SCAP; TAP
Thou spark of life that wavest wings of gold. Ode to a Butterfly. Thomas Wentworth Higginson. AA; FaBoBe; HBV-1
Thou speakest always ill of me. To an Acquaintance. *Unknown.* FaFP
Thou stately stream that with the swelling tide. The Lover to the Thames of London, to Favour His Lady Passing Thereon. George Turberville. ChTr; ElL; NoP; OBSC
Thou still unravished bride of quietness. Ode on a Grecian Urn. Keats. AWP; BiP; CABA; ChER; EBEV; EnRP; FaBoBe; FaBoEn; FaFP; FF; FiP; FPL; HAP; HBV-2; HBVY; HeIP; HoPM; InPK; InPS; LiTB; LoBV; MasP; NIP; NOBE; NoP; OAEL-2; OAEP; OBEV; OBNC; OBRV; OHFP; PAI; PoEL-4; PPoe; PPP; PrIm; SeCeV; SoSe; TEP; TreF; TrGrPo; UnPo; ViBoPo; WHA
Thou stranger, which for Rome in Rome here seekest. Joachim du Bellay, *tr. by* Spenser. Ruins of Rome, I. FaBoPP; OBVE
Thou swear'st thou'lt drink no more; kind Heaven send. To Julius [*or* The Mistaken Resolve]. Martial, *tr. by* Sir Charles Sedley. FaBoEE; PV
Thou sweetly-smelling fresh red rose. Dialogue: Lover and Lady. Ciullo d'Alcamo, *tr. by* Dante Gabriel Rossetti. AWP
Thou that art by Fates degree. New Canaans Genius; Epilogus. Thomas Morton. SCAP
Thou that art wise, let wisdom minister. Sonnet: He Craves Interpreting of a Dream of His. Dante da Maiano, *tr. by* Dante Gabriel Rossetti. AWP
Thou that at Rome astonished doth behold. Joachim du Bellay, *tr. by* Spenser. Ruins of Rome, VII. FaBoPP
Thou that didst grant the wise King his request. The Sins of Youth. Thomas, Lord Vaux. ACP
Thou that didst leave the ninety and the nine. Missing. John Banister Tabb. TrPWD
Thou that from the heavens art. Wanderer's Night-Songs, I. Goethe, *tr. by* Longfellow. AWP
Thou that has given so much to me. Our Prayer. George Herbert. PGD
Thou that hast a daughter. The Sailor. William Allingham. HBV-1
Thou that in prayeres hes bene lent. Rise with the Lamb of Innocence. *Unknown.* MeEL
Thou that sellest the word of God. Against the Friars. *Unknown.* OxBM
Thou the faint beams of reason's scattered light. Solitude and Reason, in the Village. Abraham Cowley. *Fr.* Of Solitude. FaBoPP
Thou to wax fierce. The Zeal of Jehu. Cardinal Newman. OBRV
Thou, to whom my name bears witness. Be Not Silent. David ben Meshullam. TrJP
Thou, to whom the World unknown. Ode to Fear. William Collins. LAuP; NOEC; OAEP; TrGrPo
Thou too art gone, thou loved and lovely one! To Eddleston. Byron. *Fr.* Childe Harold's Pilgrimage. PeHV
Thou too hast travelled [*or* traveled], little fluttering thing. To a Swallow Building under Our Eaves. Jane Welsh Carlyle. HBV-1; OBRV
"Thou, too, my Lancelot," ask'd the King, "my friend." Lancelot and the Grail. Tennyson. *Fr.* Idylls of the King. GoBC
Thou, too, O bronze-eyed darling of the feast. In an Autumn Wood. William Alexander Percy. HBMV
Thou, too, sail on, O Ship of State! The Ship of State [*or* O Ship of State *or* Sail On, O Ship of State *or* The Republic]. Longfellow. *Fr.* The

Building of the Ship. AA; FaBoBe; FaFP; FaPON; HBVY; MOS; OHIP; PAH; PAL; PGD; TreF; WGRP; YaD
Thou tool of faction, mercenary scribe. Upon the Anonymous Author of Legion's Humble Address to the Lords. Thomas Brown. APAS
Thou tryant, whom I will not name. Wedlock; a Satire. Hetty Wright. NOEC
Thou two-faced year, Mother of Change and Fate. 1492. Emma Lazarus. WPE
Thou unrelenting Past! The Past. Bryant. AA
Thou vague dumb crawler with the groping head. To My Tortoise Chronos. Eugene Lee-Hamilton. FM
Thou visitest the earth, and waterest it. Bible, *O.T.* Psalms, LXV, *abr.* OHIP
Thou wast all that [*or* that all] to me, love. To One in Paradise. Poe. *Fr.* The Assignation. AA; AmPP; AP; BLPL; BoLoP; HBV-1; LiTA; LO; NePA; OBEV; OBRV; OBVV; OxBA; PoLF; TAP; TrGrPo; ViBoPo; WHA
Thou wast not born for death, immortal Bird! Magic Casements. Keats. *Fr.* Ode to a Nightingale. FaBV
Thou water turn'st to Wine (faire friend of Life). To Our Lord, upon the Water Made Wine. Richard Crashaw. MePo
Thou wert the morning star among the living. To Stella [*or* Morning and Evening Star]. Plato, *tr. by* Shelley. AWP; EnLoPo; FaBoEE; LO; OBVE; ViBoPo
Thou which art I, ('tis nothing to be soe). The Storme. John Donne. MOS
Thou who art clothed in silk, who drawest on. Man Is a Weaver. Moses ibn Ezra, *tr. by* Emma Lazarus. TrJP
Thou who art Lord of the wind and rain. A Hymn of Thanksgiving. Wilbur Dick Nesbit. OHIP
Thou Who Createdst Everything. *Unknown, tr. fr. Middle English by* Donald Davie. NOCV
Thou who didst hang upon a barren tree. Long Barren. Christina Rossetti. PBWP; TrCP; VLP
Thou, who didst lay all other bosoms bare. To Shakespeare. Richard Edwin Day. AA
Thou, who dost dwell alone. Desire. Matthew Arnold. WGRP
Thou, who dost feel Life's vessel strand. Edmund Clarence Stedman. *Fr.* The Ordeal by Fire. WGRP
Thou who hast slept all night upon the storm. To the Man-of-War-Bird. Walt Whitman. AA; AmPP; BoAnP; EtS; FaBoBe; FM; HBV-1; NePA
Thou who on Sin's wages starvest. Barnfloor and Winepress. Gerard Manley Hopkins. ACP
Thou, who on some dark mountain's brow. Captain Jones' Invitation. Philip Freneau. MOS
Thou who ordainest, for the land's salvation. God Save the Nation. Theodore Tilton. AA
Thou who stealest fire. Ode to Memory. Tennyson. VLP
Thou Who Taught the Thronging People. Henry S. Minde. TRV
Thou who, when fears attack. Ode to Tobacco. Charles Stuart Calverley. FaBoCo; FiBHP; HBV-2; InMe; WhC
Thou who wilt not love, doe [*or* do] this. Upon Some Women. Robert Herrick. AnAnS-2; CaPo; DBV
Thou who wouldst see the lovely and the wild. Monument Mountain. Bryant. BeLS
Thou, who wouldst wear the name. The Poet. Bryant. AA; AP; PP; TAP
Thou, Whom rich and poor adore. An Offer. Arthur Guiterman. DBV; TrJP
Thou, whom the former precepts have. Superliminare. George Herbert. AnAnS-1; SeCP
Thou whose birth on earth. Swinburne. *Fr.* Christmas Antiphones. PGD; TrPWD; TRV
Thou, whose diviner soul hath caus'd thee now. To Mr. Tilman after He Had Taken Orders. John Donne. EBEV
Thou—whose endearing hand once laid in sooth. Invocation. Edmund Clarence Stedman. AA
Thou, whose sad heart, and weeping head lyes low. Easter-Day. Henry Vaughan. AnAnS-1
Thou, whose sweet youth and early hopes inhance. The Church-Porch. George Herbert. AnAnS-1
Thou whose thrilling hand in mine. George Darley. *Fr.* Nepenthe. OBRV
Thou, whose unmeasured temple stands. Dedication [*or* How Amiable Are Thy Tabernacles]. Bryant. BLRP; TrPWD; TRV
"Thou wilt forget me." "Love has no such word." Spring and Autumn. William James Linton. EBVV
Thou wilt keep him in perfect peace. Perfect Peace. Bible, *O.T.* *Fr.* Isaiah. TRV
Thou wilt not look on me? A Farewell. Alice Brown. HBV-1
Thou wilt remember. Thou art not more dear. Robert Browning. *Fr.* Pauline. OAEL-2
Thou Wilt Revive Me. Bible, *O.T.* Psalms, CXXXVIII: 6-8. TreFT
Thou winst thy wealth by war. To the Roving Pirate. George Turberville. EnRePo
Thou, with thy looks, on whom I look full oft. The Looks of a Lover Enamoured. George Gascoigne. ElL; SeCePo
Thou wommon boute fere. The Devout Man Prays to His Relations. William Herebert. MeEL
Thou wonder of the Atlantic shore. To Aaron Burr, under Trial for High Treason. Sarah Wentworth Morton. PAH
Thou wonder world yet undefined, unform'd. Walt Whitman. *Fr.* Thou Mother with Thy Equal Brood. PeD
Thou wouldst be greate and to such height wouldst rise. Greatness. *Unknown.* OBS
Thou youngest virgin-daughter of the skies. To [*or* Ode to] the Pious Memory of the Accomplished Young Lady, Mrs. Anne Killigrew. Dryden. HBV-2; LoBV; OAEL-1; OBEV; PoEL-3; SeCV-2
Thou, Zion, old and suffering. David Levi, *tr. by* Mary A. Craig. *Fr.* The Bible. TrJP
Though. *See also* Tho'.
Though a Fool. Robert Francis. GP
Though a soldier at present, a doctor of yore. Sir Thomas More. DBV
Though All the Fates Should Prove Unkind. Henry David Thoreau. AP; HAP
Though Amaryllis Dance in Green. *Unknown.* ElL; NIP; OAEP
Though art be on vacation. Leonard Feeney. WhC
Though authors are a dreadful clan. I Missed His Book, I Read His Name. John Updike. OBAL
Though aware of our rank and alert to obey orders. Ode: To My Pupils [*or* Which Side Am I Supposed to Be On?]. W. H. Auden. MoBrPo
Though beauty [*or* beautie] be the mark of praise. An Elegy [*or* Elegie]. Ben Jonson. EnRePo; NoP; OBEV; QFR; SeCV-1
Though Bodies Are Apart. C. Day Lewis. *Fr.* From Feathers to Iron. NAs
Though brave your beauty be, and feature passing fair. The Lover Exhorteth His Lady to Take Time, While Time Is. George Turberville. EnRePo
Though buds still speak in hints. Field-Glasses. Andrew Young. ChMP; GTBS-P
Though by thy bounteaous favor I be in. The Examination of His Mistress' Perfections. Francis Beaumont. GoBC
Though Christ a thousand times. In Thine Own Heart. "Angelus Silesius." TRV
Though clasp'd and cradled in his nurse's arms. William Cowper. *Fr.* Hope. PoEL-3
Though clock,/ To tell how night drawes hence, I've none. His Grange, or Private Wealth. Robert Herrick. AnAnS-2; CaPo; FM; GoJo; OAEP; SeCV-1
Though come down in the world to. Camel. Jon Stallworthy. BoAnP
Though conscience void of all offence. Praise. Christopher Smart. OxBChV
Though countless as the grains of sand. Boethius, *tr. by* Samuel Johnson. The Consolation of Philosophy, II, 2. OBVE
Though day is just breaking. Angling, a Day. Galway Kinnell. WOLT
Though dusty wits dare scorn Astrology. Astrophel and Stella, XXVI. Sir Philip Sidney. OAEL-1; SiPS
Though earth and man were gone. Emily Brontë. *Fr.* Last Lines. TRV
Though fast youth's glorious fable flies. Lone Founts. Herman Melville. LiTA; ViBoPo
Though Fatherland Be Vast, *with music.* Allen Eastman Cross. AH
Though folks no more go Maying. The May Day Garland. Edmund Blunden. HBMV
Though frost and snow locked [*or* lock'd *or* lockt] from mine eyes. To Saxham. Thomas Carew. AnAnS; JCP; NoP; OBS
Though gifts like thine the fates gave not to me. To Hafiz. Thomas Bailey Aldrich. AA
Though good things answer many good intents. Crosses. Robert Herrick. CaPo
Though grief and fondness in my breast rebel. *See* Tho' grief . . .
Though he hung dumb upon her wall. And One Shall Live in Two. Jonathan Henderson Brooks. PoNe
Though He Slay Me. Vassar Miller. NePoEA-2
Though he that, ever kind and true. Verses Written in 1872. Robert Louis Stevenson. BLPA; BLPL
Though heart grows faint and spirits sink. The Word of God. Annie Johnson Flint. BLRP
Though her mother told her/ Not to go a-bathing. Leda and the Swan. Oliver St. John Gogarty. AnIL; HAP; OnYI
Though here it is already hot. Blackberry Winter. Peter Huggins. AMV-81
Though he's turned forty, they call him Idiot Boy. Idiot Boy. Rowland M. Hill. AMV-81
Though I am dark. *Unknown, tr. fr. Spanish by* Willis Barnstone. BoWoP
Though I am humble, slight me not. The Moss Supplicateth for the Poet. Richard Henry Dana. AA

Though I am Laila of the Persian romance. Princess Zeb-un-Nissa, *tr. fr. Persian by* Willis Barnstone. BoWoP
Though I am native to this frozen zone. Reminiscence. Thomas Bailey Aldrich. AA
Though I am to-day against the breast of battle. Knightsbridge of Libya. Sorley Maclean. NeBP
Though I Am Young and Cannot Tell. Ben Jonson. *See* Karolin's Song.
Though I be foul, ugly, lean, and mis-shape. Death. Sir Thomas More. EnRePo
Though I be wooden Priapus (as thou see'st). Epigrams on Priapus. *Unknown.* ErPo
Though I get home how late, how late! The Return. Emily Dickinson. MoAmPo
Though I have an admiration for your charming resignation. Not Tonight, Josephine. Colin Curzon. ErPo
Though I have given. Lines Written in a Mausoleum. Lillian Grant. GoYe
Though I have not seen the milk snake. Five Serpents. Charles Burgess. NePoAm-2
Though I have twice been at the doores of death. To Sir William Alexander. William Drummond of Hawthornden. OBS; PoEL-2
Though I met her in the summer. The Ballad of Cassandra Brown. Helen Gray Cone. InMe
Though I must live here, and by force. To My Mistresse in Absence. Thomas Carew. AnAnS-2; CaPo
Though I regarded not. Earl of Surrey. AAS; SiPS
Though I Should Seek, *with music.* Henry Ustic Onderdonk. AH
Though I Speak with the Tongues of Men and Angels. Bible, *N.T.* First Corinthians, XIII. BiP; LO; OAEL-1
(Greatest of These, The.) TrGrPo, *abr.*
(Love.) TRV
(St. Paul on Charity.) TreF
Though I Thy Mithridates Were. James Joyce. NoAM
Though I was born a Londoner. Oak and Olive. James Elroy Flecker. HBMV
Though I with strange desire. Kisses Desired. William Drummond of Hawthornden. EnLoPo
Though I would take comfort against sorrow. The Cry of the Daughter of My People. Bible, *O.T.* *Fr.* Jeremiah. TrJP
Though it is only February, turned. Letter from Germany. Emily Grosholz. AMV-81
Though it's true we were young girls when we met. For Jan, in Bar Maria. Carolyn Kizer. VGW
Though I've a Clever Head. *Unknown.* HAP
Though joy is better than sorrow, joy is not great. Joy. Robinson Jeffers. CMoP
Though knowledge must be got with pain. For Scholars and Pupils. George Wither. OxBChV
Though leaves are many, the root is one. The Coming of Wisdom with Time. W. B. Yeats. FaBoEE; PAI; POL; SoSe
Though little be the god of love. Love's Victories. James Shirley. *Fr.* Cupid and Death. GoBC
Though loath to grieve. Ode Inscribed to W. H. Channing. Emerson. AmPP; AP; HAP; NOBA; NoP; OxBA; PPON; TAP
"Though logic-choppers rule the town." Tom O'Roughley. W. B. Yeats. CMoP
Though love repine and reason chafe. Sacrifice. Emerson. *Fr.* Quatrains. HBV-2; HBVY; TRV
Though love's my daily and my nightly theme. To Emma, Extempore; Hyaena, off Gambia, June 4, 1779. Edward Thompson. NOEC
Though many a year above his dust. His Living Monument. Minna Irving. PGD
Though marriage by some folks. My Three Wives. *Unknown, after* Etienne Pasquier. FaBoEE
Though mild clear weather. There Will Be No Peace. W. H. Auden. NePoAm-2
Though Mine Eye Sleep Not. *Unknown, tr. fr. Hebrew by* Theodor H. Gaster. *Fr.* The Dead Sea Scrolls. TrJP
Though much a little map unfolds, more still. The River Compared to an Oratorical Sentence. Luis de Góngora, *tr. by* Edward Meryon Wilson. *Fr.* The First Solitude. OBVE
Though my interest in viands is easy to whet up. Tirade on Tea. Phyllis McGinley. InMe
Though my soul may set in darkness, it will rise in perfect light. Sarah Williams. *Fr.* The Old Astronomer. TRV
Though My Thoughts, *with music.* Francis Daniel Pastorius, *tr. fr. German by* Sheema Z. Buehne. AH
Though naked trees seem dead to sight. Hopeless Desire Soon Withers and Dies. "A. W." OBSC
Though naughty flesh will multiply. No Mean City. Patrick MacDonogh. BIrV
Though never in the wards of the hospital for/ Disabled servicemen at Erskine. Warriors. Douglas Dunn. OxBC
Though no kin to those fine glistening. Christening-Day Wishes for My God-Child. Robert P. Tristram Coffin. OFD
Though now 'tis neither May nor June. Love's Nightingale. Richard Crashaw. LoBV
Though one with all that sense or soul can see. Transcendence. Richard Hovey. TRV; WGRP
Though pain and care are everywhere. Vita Brevis. *Unknown, tr. by* Louis Untermeyer. UnTE
Though pleasures still can touch my soul. How Singular. Tom Hood. FaBoNo
Though prejudice perhaps my mind befogs. I Think I Know No Finer Things than Dogs. Hally Carrington Brent. BLPA
Though raging stormes movis us to shake. The Reeds in the Loch Sayis. *Unknown.* BSV; GoTS
Though Regions Far Divided. Aurelian Townshend. LoBV
(Constant Lover, The.) OxBoLi
(Song: "Though regions farr divided.") MePo
("Though regions far [*or* farr] divided.") JCP; PoEL-2
Though richer swains thy love pursue. Song. Joanna Baillie. *Fr.* The Country Inn. OBRV
Though riders be thrown in black disgrace. *Unknown, tr. fr. Irish by* Douglas Hyde. BIrV
Though Shakespeare's Mermaid, ocean's mightiest daughter. On a Prohibitionist Poem. G. K. Chesterton. ViBoPo
Though She Slumbers. Joseph Joel Keith. ISi
Though short her strain nor sung with mighty boast. Erinna. Antipater, *tr. by* A. J. Butler. AWP
Though singing but the shy and sweet. Content. Norman Gale. HBV-1
Though somewhat large, exuberant, and truculent. Byron. *Fr.* Don Juan, IX. OAEL-2
Though the barn is so warm. The Palomino Stallion. Alden Nowlan. BoAnP; PH; POL
Though the bee. In Him. James Vila Blake. WGRP
Though the Clerk of the Weather insist. Pebbles. Herman Melville. AP
Though the cover is worn. My Old Bible. *Unknown.* BLRP; STF
Though the crocuses poke up their heads in the usual places. Vernal Sentiment. Theodore Roethke. ELU; MiAP
Though the day be never so long. Evensong. George Tankervil. TRV
Though the day of my destiny's over. Stanzas to Augusta. Byron. EnRP
Though the Earth Be Removed. Bible, *O.T.* Psalms, XLVI. *See* Refuge, The.
Though the evening comes with slow steps and has signalled for all songs to cease. The Bird. Rabindranath Tagore. PoPl
Though the great song return no more. The Nineteenth Century and After. W. B. Yeats. FaBoEE
Though the great waters sleep. Emily Dickinson. EaLo
Though the house had burned years ago. The Two Old Gentlemen. Robert Wallace. DFF
Though the long seasons seem to separate. Harvest. Eva Gore-Booth. HBMV
Though the Lord be high, yet hath he respect unto the lowly. Thou Wilt Revive Me. Bible, *O.T.* Psalms, CXXXVIII: 6-8. TreFT
Though the midnight found us weary. Sunrise. Margaret E. Sangster. TRV
Though the mills of God grind slowly. Retribution. Friedrich von Logau, *tr. by* Longfellow. BLPA; TreF
Though the moon beaming matronly and bland. To Lucia at Birth. Robert Graves. NAs
Though the Muse be gone away. Persistency of Poetry. Matthew Arnold. VLP
Though the music of love is Schubérty. Limerick. *Unknown.* PeHV
Though the pale white within your cheeks compos'd. The Green-Sickness Beauty. Lord Herbert of Cherbury. AnAnS-2
Though the rough, bitter-sweet haw of pioneering. American History. W. R. Moses. LiTA
Though the roving bee, as lightly. The Bridal Pair. William Young. *Fr.* Wishmakers' Town. AA
Though the times be dark and dreary. Bide a Wee! John Oxenham. TRV
Though the tough cough and hiccough plough me through. Ways of Pronouncing "Ough." *Unknown.* FaBoUs
Though the world has slipped and gone. Lullaby. Edith Sitwell. ChMP; CMoP; LiTM; SBVL; WaP
Though there are distances between us. Desert Warfare. Michael Longley. CIP
Though there are wild dogs. Orpheus and Eurydice. Geoffrey Hill. NePoEA-2
Though there was nothing final then. The Parting. Elizabeth Jennings. NePoEA-2
Though they have loved me as the gentle roebuck. Deirdre and the Poets. Ewart Milne. NeIP

Though this the port, and I thy servant true. Sir Thomas Wyatt. SiPS
Though thou, indeed, hast quite forgotten ruth. Ballata: Of a Continual Death in Love. Guido Cavalcanti, *tr. by* Dante Gabriel Rossetti. AWP
Though thou, my ring, be small. To His Ring, Given to His Lady, Wherein Was Graven This Verse, "My Heart Is Yours." George Turberville. EIL
"Though three men dwell on Flannan Isle." Flannan Isle. W. W. Gibson. CH; GoTL; MoVE; OBVV; PoRA
Though thy constant love I share. To M. T. Bayard Taylor. AA
Though to good breeding she made no pretence. On a Gentleman Marrying His Cook. Colin Ellis. FaBoEE
Though to strangers' approach. Paired Lives. W. R. Rodgers. CIP
Though to talk too much of Heaven. Japanese Fan. Margaret Veley. NBM
Though to think/ Rejoiceth me. Love Song. Margot Ruddock. OBMV
Though to your life apparent stain attach. Robert Nichols. *Fr.* Sonnets to Aurelia. OBMV
Though truth and falsehood be. Seek True Religion! John Donne. *Fr.* Satires, III. NOBE
Though tuneless, stringless, it lies there in dust. The Old Violin. Maurice Francis Egan. AA
Though Virtue be the same when low she stands. To the Lady Lucy, Countess of Bedford. Samuel Daniel. OBSC
Though we boast of modern progress as aloft we proudly soar. A Paradox. *Unknown.* ShM
Though we lived in the same lane. Answering Li Ying Who Showed Me His Poems about Summer Fishing. Yü Hsüan-chi, *tr. by* Geoffrey Waters. BoWoP
Though we may waver, He remaineth steadfast. The Everlasting Love. Annie Johnson Flint. BLRP
Though when I loved thee thou wert fair. A Deposition from Beauty. Thomas Stanley. HBV-1
Though, when other maids stand by. Smile and Never Heed Me. Charles Swain. HBV-1
Though Winter come with dripping skies. A Song with a Discord. Arthur Colton. AA
Though with the North we sympathize. Shop and Freedom. *Unknown.* PAH
Though wolves against the silver moon do bark. To the Detracted. John Andrews. *Fr.* The Anatomy of Baseness. EIL; LO
Though ye were hard-hearted. To Mistress Gertrude Statham. John Skelton. *Fr.* The Garlande of Laurell. OAEP
Though you are a continent and two seasons away. Cape Coast Castle Revisted. Jo Ann Hall-Evans. BlSi
Though You Are Young. Thomas Campion. EnRePo; OBSC
Though you be absent here, I needs must say. The Spring. Abraham Cowley. *Fr.* The Mistress. HAP; JCP; MeLP; OBS
Though you desire me I will still feign sleep. Reserve. Richard Aldington. BrPo
Though you Diana-like have liv'd still chaste. Lutea Allison. Sir John Suckling. ErPo
Though you regret it. Out of Your Hands. Theodore Weiss. CoPo
Though you serve richest wines. Martial, *tr. fr. Latin.* DBV
Though you should build a bark of dead men's bones. Cancelled Stanza of the Ode on Melancholy. Keats. SyP
Though you tear the medals. Nightmare Inspection Tour for American Generals. Gibbons Ruark. TW
Though your eyes with tears were blind. A Leader. "Æ." HBMV
Though your prerogative is to disdain. To His Coy Mistress. Peter Scupham. BXAP
Though your strangenesse frets my hart. Thomas Campion. AAS
Thought. Christopher Pearse Cranch. *See* Gnosis.
Thought, A. W. H. Davies. MoShBr
Thought. Emerson. AmPP
Thought, The. Lord Herbert of Cherbury. AnAnS-2; InvP; LoBV
Thought, A. Mikhail Yuryevich Lermontov, *tr. fr. Russian by* Max Eastman. AWP
Thought, The. William Brighty Rands. OBEV; OBVV
Thought, A. Margaret E. Sangster. TRV
Thought, A. James Kenneth Stephen. FiBHP
Thought and the Poet. Peter Yates. ChMP
Thought beneath so slight a film, The. Emily Dickinson. AmPP; OxBA
Thought Eternal, The. Goethe, *tr. fr. German by* Ludwig Lewisohn. AWP
Thought for a New Year. Gail Brook Burket. PGD
Thought for My Love, A. Bruce Williamson. NeIP
Thought for the Winter Season. Mary Elizabeth Osborn. NePoAm
Thought-Fox, The. Ted Hughes. FaBoMo; HeIP; NCSH; NePoEA-2; NoAM; NoP; NYBP; SCV
Thought from Propertius, A. W. B. Yeats. OAEL-2
Thought I heard the wind. Spring at Fort Okanogan. Ramona Wilson. VoR
Thought in Time, A. Robert Hillyer. NYBP
Thought is deeper than all speech. Gnosis [*or* Stanza from an Early Poem *or* Thought]. Christopher Pearse Cranch. AA; HBV-2; WGRP
Thought is false happiness: the idea. Crude Foyer. Wallace Stevens. LiTM; NePA
Thought looking out on thought. Opening of Eyes. Laura Riding. NoAM
Thought [*or* Thoughts] of a Briton on the Subjugation of Switzerland. Wordsworth. EnRP; OBRV; SeCeV; SpRo
(England and Switzerland 1802.) GTBS; GTBS-P
(Sonnet: Thought of a Briton on the Subjugation of Switzerland.) ChER
Thought of Death, A. Thomas Flatman. OBS
Thought of Marigolds, A. Janice Farrar. GoYe
Thought of the Nile, A. Leigh Hunt. *See* Nile, The.
Thought of what America would be like, The. Cantico del Sole. Ezra Pound. OBAL
Thought of writing came to me today, The. W. H. Auden. *Fr.* Letter to Lord Byron. NOBL
Thought rattles along the empty railings. Respectable People. Austin Clarke. CMoP; NMP
Thought Suggested by the New Year, A. Thomas Campbell. OBNC
Thought went up my mind today, A. Emily Dickinson. AmPP
Thought, with good cause thou likest so well the night. Astrophel and Stella, XCVI. Sir Philip Sidney. SiPS
Thought: Zero. Fell at his feet wanted to eat him right up. The Knife. Jean Valentine. LCAP
Thoughtful little Willie Frazer. Science for the Young. Wallace Irwin. DBV; QQQ
Thoughts. Michael Benedikt. ConAP
Thoughts. Roy Davis. WhC
Thoughts. David Ignatow. FAZ
Thoughts. Duncan Campbell Scott. PeCV
Thoughts about the Person from Porlock. Stevie Smith. FaBoCo; NoP
Thoughts are broken in my memory, The. Dante, *tr. by* Dante Gabriel Rossetti. La Vita Nuova, VIII. AWP
Thoughts at the Museum. Eileen Brennan. OnYI
Thoughts during an Air Raid. Stephen Spender. MoBrPo; ViBoPo
Thought's End. Léonie Adams. MoAB; MoAmPo
Thoughts for My Grandmother. Laya Firestone. VWA
Thoughts for St. Stephen. Christopher Morley. ShM; WhC
Thoughts for You (When She Came Back from the Mountains). Ranice Henderson Crosby. NMM
Thoughts from a Bottle. Carl Clark. JB
Thoughts from Abroad. Patrick Maybin. NeIP
Thoughts in a Garden. Andrew Marvell. *See* Garden, The ("How vainly men themselves amaze").
Thoughts in Separation. Alice Meynell. ACP; GoBC
Thoughts in the Gulf Stream. Christopher Morley. EtS
Thoughts like an empty cage. The Cage. Elizabeth Bartlett. NePoAm-2
Thoughts of a Briton on the Subjugation of Switzerland. Wordsworth. *See* Thought of a Briton . . .
Thoughts of a Little Girl. María Enriqueta, *tr. fr. Spanish by* Emma Gutiérrez Suárez. FaPON
Thoughts of a Young Girl. John Ashbery. ConAP; TAP; VGW
Thoughts of Chairman Mao. David Young. AmPA
Thoughts of God. *Tr. from Gaelic by* Douglas Hyde. WTO
Thoughts of Loved Ones. Margaret Fishback. FiBHP
Thoughts of Men appear, The. Consummation. Thomas Traherne. SeCV-2
Thoughts of Phena [at News of Her Death]. Thomas Hardy. EBVV; NoP; OxBTC
Thoughts of Thomas Hardy. Edmund Blunden. PoCh
Thoughts on Being Invited to Dinner. Christopher Morley. HBMV
Thoughts on Capital Punishment. Rod McKuen. InPK
Thoughts on Editors. Thomas Moore. WhC
Thoughts on One's Head. William Meredith. HAP
Thoughts on Pausing at a Cottage near the Paukataug River. Sarah Kemble Knight. SCAP
Thoughts on Talkers. Walter R. Brooks. RHPC
Thoughts on the Christian Doctrine of Eternal Hell. Stevie Smith. PPON
Thoughts on the Commandments. George Augustus Baker. AA; HBV-1
Thoughts on the Cosmos. Franklin P. Adams. HBMV
Thoughts on the Shape of the Human Body. Rupert Brooke. BrPo
Thoughts on the Sight of the Moon. Sarah Kemble Knight. SCAP
Thoughts That Move the Heart of Man, The. Ebenezer S. Oakley. TrPWD
Thoughts upon a Walk with Natalie, My Niece, at Houghton Farm. Harold Trowbridge Pulsifer. HBMV
Thou'lt fight, if any man call Thebe whore. To Sergius. Sir Charles Sedley. FaBoEE
Thou'rt more inconstant than the wind or sea. The Hypocrite. John Caryll. APAS
Thou's welcome, wean! Mischanter fa' me. A Poet's Welcome to His Love-begotten Daughter. Burns. LiTB; NAs; NOEC; OxBoLi; PoEL-4; ViBoPo

Thousand-and-First Ship, *sel.* F. Scott Fitzgerald.
There'd Be an Orchestra. ELU; GoJo
Thousand and One Nights, The, *sels.* *Unknown, tr. fr. Arabic by* E. Powys Mathers.
Abu Nowas for the Barmacides. AWP
Birds. AWP
Dates. AWP; FaPON
Death. AWP
Haroun al-Rachid for Heart's-Life. AWP
Haroun's Favorite Song. AWP
Her Rival for Aziza. AWP
Inscription on a Chemise. ErPo
Inscriptions at the City of Brass. AWP; WaaP, 3 *sts.*
Love. AWP
Of Women. ErPo; PV
("Women: that is to say.") DBV
Poems of the Arabic, *tr. by* Sir Richard Burton.
"My soul thy sacrifice! I choose thee out." ErPo
Psalm of Battle. AWP
Sleeper, The. AWP
Song of the Narcissus, The. AWP
Tell Him, O Night. AWP
To Lighten My Darkness. AWP
Tumadir al-Khansa for Her Brother. AWP
(For Her Brother.) PBWP
Wazir Dandan for Prince Sharkan. AWP
Thousand and Second Night, The. James Merrill. NYBP
Thousand burdened burrows [*or* burros] filled, A. The Rise and Fall of Creede. Cy Warman. BPAW; PoOW
Thousand deaths a day, A. Resurrection of the Dead. Aliza Shenhar, *tr. by* Linda Zisquit. VWA
Thousand doors ago, A. Young. Anne Sexton. NCSH
Thousand guileless sheep have bled, A. Song from the Bride of Smithfield. Sylvia Townsend Warner. MoBrPo
Thousand Hairy Savages, A. Spike Milligan. OnUR; PV; RHPC
Thousand Islands, The. Charles Sangster. *Fr.* The St. Lawrence and the Saguenay. NOBC; OBCV
Thousand Killed, A. Bernard Spencer. OBWP
Thousand knights have rein'd their steeds, A. Calais Sands. Matthew Arnold. OAEP
Thousand Martyrs I Have Made, A. Aphra Behn. CavP; SBG
Thousand men then came thronging together, A. A Saint Called "Truth." William Langland, *mod. by* Donald Attwater. *Fr.* The Vision of Piers Plowman. NOCV
Thousand miles from land are we, A. The Stormy Petrel. "Barry Cornwall." EtS; HBV-1
Thousand silent years ago, A. Praxiteles and Phryne. William Wetmore Story. AA; BeLS
Thousand sounds, and each a joyful sound, A. Omnipresence. Edward Everett Hale. TRV; WGRP
Thousand streets of London gray, The. The Sheep and the Goat. George Macdonald. EBVV
Thousand Things, The. Christopher Middleton. NePoEA-2
Thousand times have I herd men telle, A. Old Books. Chaucer. *Fr.* The Legend of Good Women: Prologue. OxBM
Thousand times you've seen that scene, A. Country Burying (1919). Robert Penn Warren. LiTM
Thousand years from now, A. The Extermination of the Jews. Marvin Bell. VWA
Thousand Years Have Come, A. Thomas T. Lynch. BLRP
Thousand years now had his breed, A. E. J. Pratt. *Fr.* The Cachalot. MoCV; OBCV
Thousand years, you said, A. Parting. Lady Heguri, *tr. by* Geoffrey Bownas *and* Anthony Thwaite. BoLoP; OLR
Thousands/ of weird little figurines. Semen. Coleman Barks. PV
Thousands and Three. Paul Verlaine, *tr. fr. French by* François Pirou. PeHV
Thousands strong,/ they march. Funeral of Rufino Contreras. Ruth Wildes Schuler. SOTS
Thouzandz of thornz there be. The Bees' Song. Walter de la Mare. WhC
Thracian Filly, The. Anacreon, *tr. fr. Greek by* Tom Dodge. LiSp
Thracian Wonder, The, *sels.* *Unknown, at. to* John Webster *and* William Rowley.
Art Thou Gone in Haste? *fr.* I, i. ElL; ELP; OxBoLi
(Chase, The.) CH
(Love Pursued.) GBL
(Pursuit of Love.) ChTr
Love Is a Law, *fr.* I, i. ElL; GBL
"Whither shall I go," *fr.* II, i. GBL
Thraldome, The. Abraham Cowley. *Fr.* The Mistress. SeCV-1
Thrash away, you'll hev to rattle. A Letter [*or* Mr. Hosea Biglow Speaks]. James Russell Lowell. *Fr.* The Biglow Papers, 1st series, No. I. AmPP; OxBA; PAH
Thraw oot your shaddaws. Moonlight among the Pines. "Hugh MacDiarmid." OAEL-2
Thrawn water? Aye, owre thrawn to be aye thrawn! By Wauchopeside. "Hugh MacDiarmid." EBEV
Thre Prestis of Peblis, The, *sel.* *At. to* John Reid of Stobo.
"In Peblis town sum tyme, as I heard tell." OxBS
Thread, A/ of meaning. Meaning light. The Dead Lady Canonized. Amiri Baraka. CAPP
Thread of Life, The, *sel.* Christina Rossetti.
Aloof, I. OBEV; OBVV; TrGrPo
("Irresponsive silence of the land, The.") FaBoEn; NOBE; OBNC
Thread of silver marks along the sand, A. The Lost Continent. Jenny Joseph. BrRo
Thread Suns. Paul Celan, *tr. fr. German by* Michael Hamburger. OBVE
Thread the nerves through the right holes. Resurrection Song. Thomas Lovell Beddoes. ELU; FaBoEE; InPK; NBM
Threading the palm, a web of tiny lines. Signs. Gjertrud Schnackenberg. PoA
Threads spiral toward a center. Notes for Albuquerque. Roberta Hill Whiteman. STE
Threatened ("Threatened by my rising need"). Alice Walker. LTB
Thredbo River. Sydney Jephcott. PoAu-1
Three. John N. Morris. GP
3 A.M. Lauris Edmond. OCNZ
Three a.m.—a far bell. December. Gary Snyder. InPS
3 a.m. in New York. Jean Valentine. NYP
Three accomplishments well regarded in Ireland: a clever. *Unknown, tr. by* Thomas Kinsella. *Fr.* The Triads of Ireland. OxBI
Three Acres of Land. *Unknown.* NA
("My father left me three acres of land.") OxNR
Three American Women and a German Bayonet. Winfield Townley Scott. NMP
Three ancient men in Bethlehem's cave. The Mystic Magi [*or* The Southern Cross]. Robert Stephen Hawker. ChTr; OBCP; OxBoCh
Three anti-depressants and one diuretic a day. Bruce Beaver. Letters to Live Poets, XII. CBAP
Three around the Old Gentleman. John Berryman. AP
Three Arrows, The. Edward Fitzgerald. OBVV
Three Badgers, The. "Lewis Carroll." FaBoNo
Three Ballate. Angelo Poliziano, *tr. fr. Italian by* John Addington Symonds. AWP
"I found myself one day all, all alone," I.
"He who knows not what thing is Paradise," II.
"I went a roaming, maidens, one bright day," III.
Three Barrows Down. Jocelyn Brooke. ChMP
Three Bells, The. Whittier. EtS
Three Best Things, The, *sel.* Henry van Dyke.
Let Me But Live from Year to Year. TreFT
(Zest of Life, The.) WBLP
Three black boys. Panther. Sam Cornish. PoBA
Three blind mice, see how they run! Mother Goose. FaBoNo; FSW; OxNR
Three blind mice, three blind mice,/ Dame Julian, Dame Julian. *Unknown.* OBS
Three bold brothers of merrie Scotland. Henry Martyn (E *vers.*). *Unknown.* ESPB
Three boys, American, in dungarees. February 22. John Updike. GOA
Three brothers in old Scotland did dwell. Henry Martyn (A *vers.*). *Unknown.* ViBoFo
Three Brown Girls Singing. M. Carl Holman. NIP
Three Bushes, The. W. B. Yeats. DTC
Lady's Third Song, The, *sel.* FaBoTw
Three Captains, The. *Unknown, tr. fr. French by* Andrew Lang. AWP
Three Car Poems. Richard Jones. FAZ
Three Cezannes. George Whipple. AMV-80
Three Cheers for the Black, White and Blue. Ruth Pitter. BoAnP
Three Cherry Trees, The. Walter de la Mare. CMoP
Three Children. *Unknown, at. to* John Gay. NA; NOBL
("Three children sliding on the ice.") OxNR
Three children dancing around an orange tree. Coins and Coffins under My Bed. Diane Wakoski. CoPo
Three children dash in the dim dooryard. Tree Tag. Mary E. Caragher. GoYe
Three Children near Clonmel, The. Eileen Shanahan. OnYI; OxBI
Three Christmas Carols. *Unknown.* ACP
"Babe is born all of a May, A," I.
"Man, be merry, I thee rede," II.
"This night there is a child born," III.
Three City Cantos. Charles A. Wagner. GoYe
Three clear days. January. Robert Hass. NPGG

Three Colts Exercising in a Six-Acre. Joseph Campbell. BoAnP; OnYI
Three 'coons come at his garbage. He be cross. John Berryman. *Fr.* Dream Songs. LCAP
Three Cottage Girls, The. Wordsworth. HBV-1
Three counties blacken and vanish. L'Aurore Grelottante. Peter Levi. NePoEA-2
Three crests against the saffron sky. Twilight on Tweed [*or* Remembered Melody]. Andrew Lang. BSV; EBVV; OBVV; POSH
Three crooked cripples went through Cripplegate. Mother Goose. OxNR
Three cups of wine a prudent man may take. The Benefits and Abuse of Alcohol. Eubulus, *tr. by* Richard Cumberland. FaBoUs
Three damsels in the queen's chamber. A Christmas Carol. Swinburne. SBVL
Three dark maids, I loved them when. Villancico. *Unknown, tr. by* Thomas Walsh. AWP
Three Darks Come Down Together. Robert Francis. LCAP
Three days ago I found my love, and it's not so long. I'll Give My Love a Light and Friendly Kiss. *Unknown.* OuSiCo
Three days I dreamed her. Proposal. Robert Sward. ELU
Three days of ocean riding. Incident at Mossel Bay. Mary Balzs. AMV-81
Three days of rain: indoors. Rainpoem. Michael Dransfield. CBAP
Three days of rest. The Sun in Capricorn. Joyce Mansour, *tr. by* Carol Cosman. PBWP
Three days through sapphire seas we sailed. The Bay Fight. Henry Howard Brownell. PAH
Three Dead and the Three Living, The. George Barker. LiTB
Three decades of my life had passed. Hebrew Lesson. Max Brod, *tr. fr. German.* AMV-80
Three Dreams. James Michie. NePoEA-2
Three Elements. Stephen Vincent Benét. *Fr.* John Brown's Body. EaLo
Three Enemies, The. Christina Rossetti. TrCP; VLP
Three Epigrams. J. V. Cunningham.
"Here lies New Critic who would fox us." MoAmPo; OBAL
"I had gone broke, and got set to come back." MoAmPo
"I married in my youth a wife." MoAmPo; TW
(Epigram.) PV
Three Epitaphs. Countee Cullen. *See* Four Epitaphs.
Three Epitaphs on John Hewet and Sarah Drew. Pope.
"Here lie two poor lovers, who had the mishap," III. FaBoEE; NIP
"Think not by rigorous judgment seized," I. NIP
"When Eastern lovers feed the fun'ral fire," II. NIP
Three excellent qualities in narration. Triads. *Unknown, tr. by* Thomas Kinsella. BIrV
Three-faced, The. Robert Graves. FaBoEE
Three faces. . ./mirrored in the muddy streams of living. For Andy Goodman—Michael Schwerner—and James Chaney. Margaret Walker. BPo
Three fallen leaves chase. Threes. Henry Chapin. FAZ
3 fat trout hang. Poem for Hemingway & W. C. Williams. Raymond Carver. WOLT
Three Fates, The. Rosemary Dobson. BoWoP
Three fellows were marching over the Rhine. The Hostess' Daughter. Ludwig Uhland, *tr. by* Margarete Münsterberg. AWP
Three figures rise into a dirty gold field. What I Saw in October. Warren Carrier. PoDr
Three Fishers, The. Charles Kingsley. BeLS; EBVV; EtS; FaPoR; HBV-1; OnMSP; PoLF; TreF; WBLP
Three Fitts. Stewart Parker. CIP
Three flutes, two oboes, English horn, violins. Guide to the Symphony. Weldon Kees. VGW
Three folds of the cloth. *Unknown, tr. by* Eleanor Hull. *Fr.* Four Prayers. OnYI
3 for 25. William Jay Smith. WaP
Three Found Poems. George Hitchcock. OBAL
Three Foxes, The. A. A. Milne. GoJo; GrPl; MoShBr; OxBChV
Three Friends. *Unknown, tr. fr. Yoruba by* Ulli Beier. BoWoP; PBA
Three Gates. Beth Day, *after the Arabic.* BLPA; TreFS
Three Ghostesses. *Unknown.* RHPC
("Three little ghostesses.") OxNR
Three ghosts on the lonesome road, The. Stains. Theodosia Garrison. HBV-2; WGRP
Three Girls on a Buttress. Eilidh Nisbet. PoSH
Three Graves, The, *sel.* Samuel Taylor Coleridge.
"So gentle Ellen now no more." ChER
Three Green Trees. Angela Morgan. HBMV
Three Green Windows. Anne Sexton. NYBP
Three grey boys tracked us to an old house. In One Battle. Amiri Baraka. BPo
Three grey geese in a green field grazing. *Unknown.* OxNR; PBBP
Three halves of you are elsewhere. How to Reach the Moon. Marsha Pomerantz. VWA
Three-handed Fugue. Phyllis Gotlieb. NOBC
Three hand-spike raps on the forward hatch. Reefing Topsails. Walter Mitchell. EtS
Three Helpers in Battle. Mary Elizabeth Coleridge. EaLo
Three Hermits, The. W. B. Yeats. CMoP
Three Hills, The. J. C. Squire. HBMV
Three Holy Kings from Morgenland. Heine, *tr. fr. German by* Herman Eichenthal. PChr
Three horsemen galloped the dusty way. On the Road to Chorrera. Arlo Bates. AA
Three hot-eyed kids hard on a fix's heels. The Death of Professor Backwards. X. J. Kennedy. SOTS
Three hours ago he blundered up the trench. A Working Party. Siegfried Sassoon. CMoP; MMA
Three hugest dinosaurs do not outweigh. The Blue Whale. Robert Watson. MAT
Three hundred from one village. 1867: Last Sounds. Gerry O'Egan. POL
300,000,000. What Happened Here Before. Gary Snyder. NNaP
Three Hundred Thousand More. James Sloan Gibbons. PAH
Three Huntsmen, The. *Unknown.* *See* Three Jovial Welshmen, The.
Three images of dying stick in my mind like morbid tranfers. Bruce Beaver. Letters to Live Poets, V. CBAP
Three jolly gentlemen. The Huntsmen. Walter de la Mare. CenHV; DuDa; HBMV; PH; SiSoSe; TiPo
Three Jolly Pigeons, The. Goldsmith. *See* Song: "Let school-masters puzzle their brain."
Three Jovial Gentlemen. Daniel Hoffman. MoBS
Three Jovial Huntsmen. *Unknown.* *See* Three Jovial Welshmen, The.
Three Jovial Welshmen, The. *Unknown.* HBVY
(There Were Three Jovial Welshmen.) GBP; OxNR
(Three Huntsmen, The.) OnMSP; OxBoLi
(Three Jovial Huntsmen.) NA
(Three Welshmen, The.) MoShBr
Three Khalandeers, The. James Clarence Mangan. OBVV
Three Kingdoms of Nature, The. Gotthold Lessing, *tr. fr. German by* Alfred Baskerville, *ad. by* Robert Bly. NU
Three Kings, The. Rubén Darío, *tr. fr. Spanish by* Lysander Kemp. PChr
Three Kings, The. Eugene Field. GN
Three Kings, The. Longfellow. GN; HBV-1; HBVY; OnMSP
Three Kings. James P. Vaughn. NNP; PoNe
Three Kings Came. Thomas W. Shapcott. PoAu-2
Three Kings came riding from far away. The Three Kings. Longfellow. GN; HBV-1; HBVY; OnMSP
Three Kings stepped out of my body. Poem for Epiphany. Norman Nicholson. PoPl
Three kings stood before the manger. The Gifts. John Heath-Stubbs. OxBC
Three kings went down to the soul of the sea. Three Kings. James P. Vaughn. NNP; PoNe
Three Knights from Spain. *Unknown.* CH; PoPle
(We Are Three Brethren Come from Spain.) GBP
("We are three brethren out of Spain.") OxNR
Three Ladies, The. Robert Creeley. NeAP
Three Ladies of London, The, *sels.* Robert Wilson.
New Brooms. EIL
(Conscience's Song.) OBSC
Simplicity's Song. CTC; OBSC
Three Lads, The. Elizabeth Chandler Forman. SUMH
Three Landscapes, *sel.* Jerome Rothenberg.
"Dark bull quartered in my eye." CoPo
Three little children sitting on the sand. All, All a-Lonely. *Unknown.* ChTr; OxBoLi
Three little fellows sing to the wind. Tohub. Jakov van Hoddis, *tr. by* Charles Guenther. VWA
Three little ghostesses. Three Ghostesses. *Unknown.* OxNR; RHPC
Three Little Girls. Richard Aldington. BrPo
Three Little Kittens, The ("Three little kittens, they lost their mittens"). *Unknown, at. to* Eliza Cook *and to* Eliza Lee Follen. FaPON; OBCA; OxNR; SoPo; TreFS
Three little lads were seated one day. Her Eyes Don't Shine like Diamonds. David Marion. FSN
Three little maidens they have slain. Song. Maurice Maeterlinck, *tr. by* Jethro Bithell. AWP
Three Little Maids from School. W. S. Gilbert. *Fr.* The Mikado. TreFT
Three little mice sat down to spin. Pussy and the Mice. *Unknown.* MoShBr
Three little ones splash in the shallows along the beach. The Hot Day and Human Nature. Gordon Johnston. AMV-81
Three Little Pigs, The. Sir Alfred Scott Gatty. OxBChV
Three Little Puffins. Eleanor Farjeon. TiPo
Three little words you often see. Grammar in a Nutshell [*or* Grammar in

Rhyme *or* The Parts of Speech]. *Unknown.* FaBoUS; HBV-1; HBVY; TreFS
Three long nights, an' three long days. Walk, Mary, down de Lane. *Unknown.* BoAN-2
Three Love Poems. Norman Cameron. FaBoTw; GTBS-P
From a Woman to a Greedy Lover, I. ELU; FaBoEE
In the Queen's Room, II. OxBTC
Shepherdess, III. GBL; OxBS
Three lovely notes he whistled, too soft to be heard. The Unknown Bird. Edward Thomas. DTC; FaBoEn
Three lovely sisters working were. The Parcae; or, Three Dainty Destinies: The Armillet. Robert Herrick. CaPo
Three Loves. Lucy H. Hooper. BeLS
Three Maids a-Milking Would Go. *Unknown.* CoMu
Three Memorial Sonnets. George Barker. *See* Pacific Sonnets.
Three Men. *Unknown.* BluL
Three men came talking up the road. Night Piece. John Manifold. LiTM; MoBrPo; WaP
Three men coming down the winter hill, The. Winter Landscape. John Berryman. AP; LiTA; LiTM; MoAmPo; MP; PoPl; TwCP
Three men in a limousine travelling westward. The Three Dead and the Three Living. George Barker. LiTB
Three Men of Gotham. Thomas Love Peacock. *Fr.* Nightmare Abbey. FaBoCh; OBEV
(Catch, A.) ViBoPo
(Men of Gotham, The.) CH
(Seamen Three.) OBRV; WiR
(Wise Men of Gotham, The.) BXAP; FaBoNo; LoBV
Three Migrations. Ralph Salisbury. STE
Three miles extended around the fields of the homestead. Frithiof's Homestead. Esaias Tegner, *tr. by* Longfellow. *Fr.* Frithiof's Saga. AWP
Three million times your bones have swept around. Love Song to Lucy. Helen Ehrlich. SUW
Three Mirrors, The. Edwin Muir. NoAM
Three Modes of History and Culture. Amiri Baraka. NoAM
Three Moments. Susan Sherman. DFF
Three Monkeys ("Three monkeys once dining in a cocoanut tree"). *Unknown.* STF
Three Movements, The. Donald Hall. NePoEA-2
Three Movements. W. B. Yeats. CMoP; ELU; FaBoEE
Three Moves. John Logan. CAPP
Three Musicians, The. Aubrey Beardsley. VLP
Three Nights Drunk. *Unknown.* *See* Our Goodman.
3/19—"just a day's march." Conquistador. Georgia Lee McElhaney. CoPo
Three of us/ in the bar. Jazz. Carolyn M. Rodgers. JB
Three of us afloat in the meadow by the swing. Pirate Story. Robert Louis Stevenson. BeLS; FaPON; TiPo
Three of us went to the top of the city. Poem from the Empire State. June Jordan. BPo
3 of Washingtons heads. George Washington Goes to a Girlie Movie. Aram Boyajian. NeAC
Three Old Brothers. Frank O'Connor. OnYI
Three old hermits took the air. The Three Hermits. W. B. Yeats. CMoP
Three old men in the corner. Jailhouse Lawyers. Robert B. Smith. LFAC
Three outas from the bleak Karoo. Christmas Carol. D. J. Opperman, *tr. by* Anthony Delius. PeSA
Three Part Invention. Paul Blackburn. CoPo
Three Phases of Africa. Francis Ernest Kobina Parkes. PBA
Three Pigeons, The. Goldsmith. *See* Song: "Let school-masters puzzle their brain."
Three pigeons down-swing. Possibilities. Peter Kane Dufault. NYBP
Three Poems, *sel.* "Ping Hsin," *tr. fr. Chinese by* Julia C. Lin.
"Fishing boats have returned, The!" PBWP
Three Poems. Michelangelo, *tr. fr. Italian by* George Santayana. AWP
"Haven and last refuge of my pain, The," II.
"I know not if from uncreated spheres," I.
"Ravished by all that to the eyes is fair," III.
Three Poems about Children. Austin Clarke. CIP
Three Poems for the Indian Steelworkers. Joseph Bruchac. CDW
Three Poems for Women. Susan Griffin. NPGG
Three Poems for Your Eyes. Rachel McAlpine. OCNZ
Three Poems of the Atomic Bomb, *sel.* Edith Sitwell.
Dirge for the New Sunrise. CMoP; EaLo; MoAB; MoBrPo; SeCePo
Three Poems on Morris Graves' Paintings. John Logan. PoDr
Three poets, in three distant ages born. Lines Printed under the Engraved Portrait of Milton [*or* Lines on Milton *or* Under the Portrait of Milton *or* Epigram on Milton]. Dryden. ACP; HBV-2; HeIP; InPK; OAEL-1; SeCeV; SeCV-2; TrGrPo; WHA
Three Poplars, The. Philip Francis Little. OxBI
Three Portraits. George Hitchcock. VGW
Three practical farmers from back of the dale. Shepherds' Carol. Norman Nicholson. OBCP
Three Preachers, The. Charles Mackay. EBVV
Three Presidents. Robert Bly. LCAP
Three Ravens, The ("As I was walking all alane"). *Unknown.* *See* Twa Corbies, The.
Three Ravens, The ("There were three ravens [*or* crows] sat on a tree"). *Unknown.* AmFP; CABA; ChTr; ESPB; FaBoBa; FSW; GBP; HBV-2; HeIP; InPK; NoP; OAEL-1, *with music;* OAEP; OBET; OBEV; OxBB; PAI; PoEL-1; SeCeV; TrGrPo; UnPo; ViBoFo (A, B, *and* C *vers.*); ViBoPo
Three Revellers Search for Death. Chaucer. *See* Death and the Three Revellers.
Three roads were shadowy and the sky over. Vanessa Vanessa. Ewart Milne. BIrV; NeIP
Three Roundels of Love Unreturned. Chaucer. *See* Merciless Beaute.
Three Sailors, The. Thackeray. *See* Little Billee.
Three sang of love together. A Triad. Christina Rossetti. PBWP; VLP
Three Sayings from Highlands, North Carolina. Jonathan Williams. OBAL
Three score and ten! The tumult of the world. Life's Evening. Dudley Foulke. WGRP
Three Seamstresses, The. Isaac Leibush Peretz, *tr. fr. Yiddish by* Joseph Leftwich. TrJP
Three Seasons. Christina Rossetti. HBV-1
Three Seasons. Francis Sparshott. NOBC
Three Sentences for a Dead Swan. James Wright. NaP; NoAM; NOBA
Three Sermons to the Dead. Laura Riding. LiTA
Nor Is It Written, III.
Not All Immaculate, II.
Way of the Air, The, I.
Three Shades of Light on the Windowsill. Susan Griffin. NPGG
Three Shadows. Dante Gabriel Rossetti. HBV-1; ViBoPo
Three ships of war had Preble when he left the Naples shore. Reuben James. James Jeffrey Roche. PAH
Three silences made him a single word. Sonnet. R. P. Blackmur. PoA
Three Singing Birds, The. James Reeves. PDV
Three Sisters. Walter de la Mare. FaBoEE
Three Sisters, The. Arthur Davison Ficke. HBV-1
3:16 and One Half. Charles Bukowski. GP
Three slender things that best support the world. *Unknown, tr. by* Kuno Meyer. *Fr.* The Triads of Ireland. OnYI
Three Songs, *sel.* Hart Crane. *Fr.* The Bridge.
National Winter Garden. ErPo
Three Songs. Edgar Jackson. LFAC
Already I Feel the Emptiness, III.
I'm Coming I'm Coming, II.
In the Mountains, I.
Three Songs from the Haida. Constance Lindsay Skinner. BPAW
Bear's Song, The, *sel.* AWP
Three Songs from the Temple. Don Domanski. NOBC
Three Songs of Mary, *sel.* Madeleine L'Engle.
O Simplicitas. EBCP; OBCP; PChr
Three Songs to Mark the Night. Judith Mountain Leaf Volborth. TWSS
Three Sonnets, *sel.* Hartley Coleridge.
How Shall a Man Fore-doomed, II. NCEP
Three Sonnets. Leigh Hunt. *See* Fish, the Man, and the Spirit, The.
Three Sonnets on Oblivion. George Sterling.
Dust Dethroned, The. HBV-2
Night of Gods, The. HBV-2; WHA
Oblivion. HBV-2
Three Sonnets on the Divina Commedia. Longfellow. *See* Divina Commedia.
Three sortes of teares doe from myne eies distraine. William Alabaster. AnAnS-1
Three sorts of serpents do resemble thee. Michael Drayton. Idea, XXX. EnRePo
Three spirits came to me. April. Ezra Pound. CMoP
Three Spring Notations on Bipeds. Carl Sandburg. AWP
3 Stanzas about a Tree. Marvin Bell. Prf
Three Star Final. Conrad Aiken. OxBA
Three stars, five stars rise over the hill. Confucius, *tr. by* Ezra Pound. *Fr.* Shao and the South. CTC
Three steps and I reach the door. Fate. Louis James Block. AA
Three strange men came to the inn. A Lady Comes to an Inn. Elizabeth J. Coatsworth. MoAmPo; SO
Three Streets. Umberto Saba, *tr. fr. Italian by* Anita Barrows. VWA
Three strings, a neck of almond, and the heart. Balalaika. Norman Dubie. AmPA
Three students once tarried over the Rhine. From the German of Uhland. James Weldon Johnson. CDC
Three Summers since I chose a maid. The Farmer's Bride. Charlotte Mew. BoLoP; ErPo; HBMV; MoAB; MoBrPo; OxBTC; SBG; TrGrPo; WPE

Three Sunrises from Amtrak. Florence Dolgorukov. AMV-81
Three Sweethearts. Heine, *tr. fr. German by* Louis Untermeyer. UnTE
Three Tall Men, The. *Unknown.* OBET
Three then came forward out of darkness, one. The Road. Conrad Aiken. AP; MoAmPo; PAI
Three thinges there bee that prosper up apace. *See* Three things there be that prosper up apace.
Three Things. Joseph Auslander. HBMV; TrJP
Three Things. May Sarton. AMV-80
Three Things. W. B. Yeats. DTC; FaBoEn; OBMV
Three things filled this day for me. Three Things. Joseph Auslander. HBMV; TrJP
Three Things Jeame Lacks. *Unknown.* MeEL
Three things must a man possess if his soul would live. The New Trinity. Edwin Markham. PGD
Three things must epigrams, like bees, have all. Epigram. *Unknown.* NIP
Three things remind me of you. Meditation. Carl Rakosi. VWA
Three things seek my death. Inheritance. *Unknown, tr. by* Frank O'Connor. DBV; KiLC; TW
Three things the Master hath to do. Pray—Give—Go. Annie Johnson Flint. BLRP; STF
Three things there are more beautiful. The Beautiful. W. H. Davies. ELU
Three things there are, worth living for. The Swashbuckler's Song. James Stuart Montgomery. HBMV
Three Things There Be [in Man's Opinion Dear]. Fulke Greville. *Fr.* Caelica. LiTB; NOCV; PoEL-1
(Sonnet: "Three things there be in mans opinion deare.") OBS
Three things [*or* thinges] there be that prosper up [*or* all] apace. The Wood, the Weed, the Wag [*or* To His Son]. Sir Walter Raleigh. EnRePo; InPS; NoP; PoEL-2; PPoe; SiPS; TrGrPo
Three Things to Remember. Blake. *See* Robin Redbreast, A.
3-31-70. Gayl Jones. *Fr.* Journal. BlSi
Three Thousand Dollar Death Song. Wendy Rose. TWSS
Three thousand for my brand new car. A Dollar I Gave. *Unknown.* STF
Three times a day my prayer is. *Unknown.* OBSC
Three times he crossed our way where with me went. Old Man Pondered. John Crowe Ransom. MoAmPo
Three times round the cuckoo waltz. Cuckoo Waltz. *Unknown.* AS
Three times we heard it calling with a low. The Ground-Swell. E. J. Pratt. CaP
Three Tiny Songs. Cid Corman. HoAn
"I have come far to have found nothing," *sel.* VGW
Three-toed Sloth. Dorothy Donnelly. HoAn
Three Towns, The. Howard Nemerov. AMV-81
Three Travelers, The. *Unknown.* UnTE
Three Trees. C. H. Crandall. OHIP
Three Troopers, The. George Walter Thornbury. BeLS; HBV-2
Three Turkeys fair their last have breathed. A Melancholy Lay [*or* Six-Year-Old Marjory Fleming Pens a Poem]. Marjory Fleming. FaBoCh; FiBHP; TreFT
Three Variations. Boris Pasternak, *tr. fr. Russian by* Babette Deutsch. TrJP
Three viands in three different courses served. Oyster-Crabs. Carolyn Wells. BXAP
Three Voices, The. "Lewis Carroll." BXAP
Third Voice, The, *sel.* VLP
Three Warnings, The. Hester Thrale. BeLS; HBV-2
Three weeks, and now I hear! My Olson Elegy. Irving Feldman. Prf
Three weeks gone and the combatants gone. Vergissmeinnicht. Keith Douglas. ChMP; FaBoMo; GTBS-P; InPS; NePoEA; OBWP; OxBTC; SoSe
Three Welshmen, The. *Unknown.* *See* Three Jovial Welshmen, The.
Three White Birds of Angus. Eleanor Rogers Cox. HBMV
Three Wise Couples, The. Elizabeth T. Corbett. BLPA
Three Wise Kings. William E. Brooks. PGD
Three wise men of Gotham. Mother Goose. FaBoBe; FaBoNo; FaFP; HBV-1; HBVY; OxNR
Three Wise Men of Gotham, The ("There were three men of Gotham"). *Unknown.* FaBoNo
Three Wise Monkeys, The. Florence Boyce Davis. WBLP
Three Wise [Old] Women. Elizabeth T. Corbett. BLPA; OBCA; OxBChV
Three without slumber ride from afar. Five Carols for Christmastide, III. Louise Imogen Guiney. ISi
Three Woes, The. Aubrey Thomas De Vere. AnIV
Three Women. Alan Dienstag. ErPo
Three Women. Lauris Edmond. OCNZ
Three Women. Sylvia Plath. NAs
Three women/ on a marriage bed. Snow White. Olga Broumas. DFT
Three Women Blues. *Unknown.* BluL
Three words fall sweetly on my soul. Mother, Home, Heaven. William Goldsmith Brown. FaBoBe; HBV-2
Three Years She Grew [in Sun and Shower]. Wordsworth. *Fr.* Lucy. EnRP; FiP; GN; HAP; HBV-1; HBVY; LoBV; NOBE; NoP; OAEL-2; OAEP; OBEV; OBNC; OBRV; PoEL-4; SeCeV; TreFS; TrGrPo
(Education of Nature, The.) GTBS; GTBS-P
Three Young Rats ("Three young rats with black felt hats"). *Unknown.* ChTr; FaBoNo; InvP; OxBoLi; OxNR; PoPle
(Rats, Ducks, Dogs, Cats, Pigs.) GBP
Three youths went a-fishing. The Banished Duke of Grantham. *Unknown.* EnSB
Threefold terror of love, The; a fallen flare. The Mother of God. W. B. Yeats. SBVL
Threes. Henry Chapin. FAZ
Threes. Carl Sandburg. CMoP; OxBA; PoLF
Threescore and Ten. Richard Henry Stoddard. HBV-1
Threescore o' nobles rade to the king's ha'. Glenlogie. *Unknown.* HBV-1
Threnody: "Let happy throats be mute." Donald Jeffrey Hayes. AmNP
Threnody: "Lilacs blossom just as sweet." Dorothy Parker. InMe
Threnody: "Mother, in my unwanted suffering, I turn to you." David Ignatow. FAZ
Threnody: "No sunny ray, no silver night." Thomas Lovell Beddoes. EnRP
Threnody: "Only quiet death." Waring Cuney. AmNP; BANP
Threnody. "Red leaves fall upon the lake, The." John Farrar. SUS
Threnody: "South-wind brings, The." Emerson. AA; AP
Threnody: "There's a grass-grown road from the valley." Ruth Guthrie Harding. HBV-1
Threnody: "Truth is a golden sunset far away." I. O. Scherzo. HoPM
Threnody, A: "What, what, what/ What's the news from Swat?" George Thomas Lanigan. AA; FiBHP; HBV-2; InMe; NA; PeCV; WHW
(Ahkoond of Swat, The.) CaP; TreFS
(Threnody on the Ahkoond of Swat, A.) CenHV
Threnody for a Poet. Bliss Carman. CaP
Threshed corn lay piled like grit of ivory. The Barn. Seamus Heaney. HAP
Thresher's Labour, The, *sel.* Stephen Duck.
"Soon as the harvest hath laid bare the plains." NOEC
Threshing Machine, The. Alice Meynell. SeCePo; WPE
Threshold. Edmund Blunden. HBMV
Threshold. Charles David Webb. NePoAm-2
Threw a woman's shoe. My Atlas Poet. George Bowering. NeAC
Thrice, and above, blest, my soul's half [*or* my soules halfe], art thou. A Country Life: To His Brother, Master Thomas Herrick. Robert Herrick. CaPo; SeCP; SeCV-1
Thrice at the huts of Fontenoy the English column failed. Fontenoy. Thomas Osborne Davis. HBV-2; OnYI
Thrice Blest the Man, *with music.* John Barnard. AH
Thrice cruel fell my fate. In Rebellion. J. M. Synge. SyP
Thrice-cruel maid, may Heaven frown on thee. The Elusive Maid. Abraham ibn Chasdai, *tr. by* J. Chotzner. TrJP
Thrice hail, thou prince of jovial fellows. An Ode to Myself. Thomas Dermody. OnYI
Thrice happy authors, who with little skill. A Soliloquy in the Suburbs. Charles Jenner. *Fr.* Eclogue IV: The Poet. NOEC
Thrice happy days! in rural business past. Blest Winter Nights. John Armstrong. *Fr.* The Art of Preserving Health, III. OBEC
Thrice Happy He. William Drummond of Hawthornden. BoNaP; HBV-1
(Solitary Life, A.) OBS
Thrice happy maid; supremely blest. The Wedding Night. Johannes Secundus, *tr. by* George Ogle. *Fr.* Epithalamium. UnTE
Thrice happy, who free from ambition and pride. The Fire Side; a Pastoral Soliloquy. Isaac Hawkins Browne. *Fr.* The Foundling Hospital for Wit. NOEC; OBEC
Thrice he came. Malacoda. Samuel Beckett. CIP
Thrice Holy. Reginald Heber. *See* Holy, Holy, Holy.
Thrice the age of a dog is that of a horse. The Age of Animals. *Unknown.* FaBoUs
Thrice the Brinded Cat Hath Mewed. Shakespeare. *Fr.* Macbeth, IV, i. InvP; OFD; WSC
(Charm, The.) ElL
Thrice the crested cock has crowed. The Glory of Early Rising. Frank Sidgwick. WhC
Thrice Toss [*or* Tosse] These Oaken Ashes in the Air [*or* Ayre]. Thomas Campion. EBEV; ElL; EnLoPo; FaBoCh; HAP; LoBV; MAT; OAEL-1; OBSC; PoEL-2; PoRA; ViBoPo; WeW; WSC
(Love-Charms.) NOBE
(Song for the Lute.) PoPle
Thrice Welcome First and Best of Days, *with music.* Isaac Chanler. AH
Thrice welcome to the Norther. Ode to the Norther. William Lawrence Chittenden. BPAW
Thrice with her lips she touch'd my lips. Parting [*or* For Ever]. William Caldwell Roscoe. HBV-1; OBVV
Thriftles thred which pampred beauty spinnes, The. A Sonet Written in Prayse of the Browne Beautie. George Gascoigne. AAS
Thrifty Elephant, The. John Holmes. NYBP

Thrifty Soprano, A. Ogden Nash. TDH
Thrifty Young Fellow, A. *Unknown.* TDH
Thrippsy pillivinx. A Letter to Evelyn Baring. Edward Lear. FaBoNo
Thro'. *See also* Through.
Thro elm and maple and syringa branches. Commencement. Constance Carrier. WPE
Thro' Grief and Thro' Danger. Thomas Moore. AnIV
Thro' the hush'd air the whitening shower descends. A Winter Scene. James Thomson. *Fr.* The Seasons: Winter. OBEC
Thro' the night of doubt and sorrow. Pilgrim's Song. Bernard S. Ingemann, *tr. by* Sabine Baring-Gould. WGRP
Throat of thunder, a tameless heart, A. A Cyclone at Sea. William Hamilton Hayne. AA
Throb, throb, throb . . . the tall ship. Night Boat. Audrey Alexandra Brown. CaP
Throbs the Night with Mystic Silence. Hayyim Nahman Bialik, *tr. fr. Hebrew by* Bertha Beinkinstadt. TrJP
Thron'd in the sun's descending car. Benevolence. Mark Akenside. *Fr.* Against Suspicion. OBEC
Throne of the Lily-King, The ("The throne was reared upon the grass"). Joseph Rodman Drake. *Fr.* The Culprit Fay. GN
Throned are the gods, and in. Chorus. Lord De Tabley. *Fr.* Philoctetes. NBM
Throng of eyes. Covenant. Paul Auster. VWA
Thronged boughs of the shadowy sycamore, The. The Day-Dream. Dante Gabriel Rossetti. SyP
Throstle, The. Tennyson. BoNaP; FaPON; HBV-1; HBVY; PBBP; PoSC;
Through a Glass Eye, Lightly. Carolyn Kizer. BoWoP
Through a green gorge the river like a fountain. The Sleeper in the Valley. Arthur Rimbaud, *tr. by* Selden Rodman. WaaP
Through a mist of tears I watch the years. The Covered Wagon. Lena Whittaker Blakeney. BPAW
Through a square sealed-off with. A Word about Freedom and Identity in Tel Aviv. Jon Silkin. VWA
Through a wild midnight all my mountainous past. The Monster. Henry Rago. PoA
Through a window in the attic. Burglar Bill. "F. Anstey." CenHV; FiBHP
Through all my youth/ I followed my lusts. It's Just the Same to Me. Hermann Hesse. ILwL
Through all the employments of life. The Employments of Life. John Gay. PV
Through all the frozen winter. Smells. Kathryn Worth. RHPC
Through all the wind-blown aisles of May. A Benedictine Garden. Alice Brown. HBV-1
Through All the World, *with music. Unknown.* TrAS
Through All Your Abstract Reasoning. Brian Patten. FaBoTw
Through Alpine meadows soft-suffused. Stanzas from the Grande Chartreuse. Matthew Arnold. EBVV; OAEL-2; OAEP; PoEL-5; TEP; VLP
Through and through the inspired leaves. The Book-Worms. Burns. ChTr; ELU; FaBoEE; FiBHP
Through autumn evening, water whirls thin blue. The Castle of Thorns. Yvor Winters. NoAM
Through Baltimore. Bayard Taylor. PAH
Through Binoculars. Charles Tomlinson. OAEL-2
Through broken arches moonbeams softly shine. San Juan Capistrano. Alice Cecilia Cooper. GoBC
Through brush and love-vine, well blooded by blackberry thorn. Boy Wandering in Simm's Valley. Robert Penn Warren. DFF; SoSe
Through bushes and through briars I lately took my way. Bushes and Briars. *Unknown.* OBET
Through calm and storm the years have led. Centennial Hymn. Bryant. PAH
Through Dangly Woods the aimless Doze. The Doze. James Reeves. AmMo
Through darkening pines the cavaliers. The Legend of Waukulla. Hezekiah Butterworth. PAH
Through Death to Love. Dante Gabriel Rossetti. The House of Life, XLI. SyP
Through every age, eternal God. Isaac Watts. AmFP
Through every minute of this day. A Prayer. John Oxenham. BLRP; TRV
Through every night we hate. Mothers, Daughters. Shirley Kaufman. BoWoP; GP; NMM
Through Fire in Mobile Bay. *Unknown.* PAH
Through frost and snow locked from mine eyes. To Saxham. Thomas Carew. CaPo
Through grass, through amber'd cornfields, our slow Stream. Meadowsweet. William Allingham. OBNC
Through grief and through danger thy smile hath cheered my way. The Irish Peasant to His Mistress. Thomas Moore. ACP
Through his million veins are poured. William Bull Wright. *Fr.* The Brook. AA
Through ignorance we arrived late. Gate. David McAleavey. SUW
Through it/ over young women's abdomens tense. The Stethoscope. Dennis Abse. SUW
Through jaggedy cliffs of snow, along sidewalks of glass. Party in Winter. Karl Shapiro. PCP
Through lane or black archway. The Young Woman of Beare. Austin Clarke. NoAM
Through life's dull road, so dim and dirty. On My Thirty-third Birthday. Byron. FaBoEE; NAs; OBRV
Through love to light! O, wonderful the way. After-Song. Richard Watson Gilder. AA; TrPWD
Through meadow-ways as I did tread. A May Burden. Francis Thompson. HBV-1
Through most that sets the hills on fire. Dundonnel Mountains. Andrew Young. PoSH
Through my small town I roamed, a taunting ghost. Rimbaud in Africa. Edgell Rickword. ChMP
Through or over the deathless feud. Pacific Door. Earle Birney. PeCV
Through our laced and latticed windows. Shacked Up at the Ritz. Doug Fetherling. NeAC
Through rain falling on us no faster. Goodbye to Serpents. James Dickey. NYBP
Through random doors we wandered. Exits and Entrances. Naomi Long Madgett. BlSi
Through reedy banks. The Nima. Jorge Isaacs, *tr. by* Alice Jane McVan. TrJP
Through Ruddy Orchards. Mary Oliver. WPE
Through salt marsh, grassy channel where the shark's. Tide Turning. John Frederick Nims. FYAP
Through sepia air the boarders come and go. The Landlady. P. K. Page. CaP; SoSe
Through some strange sense of sight or touch. Death. Madison Cawein. AA
Through storm and fire and gloom, I see it stand. The Celtic Cross. Thomas D'Arcy McGee. OnYI
Through storm and wind. *Unknown.* OxNR
Through storms you reach them and from storms are free. The Enviable Isles. Herman Melville. AA; FaBoBe
Through swamps and alligators I wend my weary way. On the Lakes of Ponchartrain. *Unknown.* AmFP
Through that pure virgin-shrine. The Night. Henry Vaughan. AnAnS-1; EBEV; LiTB; MeLP; MePo; NOBE; NOCV; NoP; OAEL-1; OBEV; OBS; OxBoCh; PoEL-2; SeCeV; SeCV-1
Through that window—all else being extinct. The Room. Conrad Aiken. AP; LiTM; MoAmPo; NePA; NOBA
Through the Ages. Margaret Hope. PGD
Through the ample open door of the peaceful country barn. A Farm Picture. Walt Whitman. InPS; PPoe
Through the Appalachian valleys, with his kit a buckskin bag. A Ballad of Johnny Appleseed. Helmer O. Oleson. SiSoSe; TiPo
Through the Barber Shop Window. Violet Anderson. CaP
Through the black pockets. Train to Reflection. Lawrence T. O'Neill. AMV-80
Through the black, rushing smoke-bursts. The Song of Callicles [*or* Callicles' Song *or* The Song of the Muses *or* Song for Apollo *or* Not Here, O Apollo]. Matthew Arnold. *Fr.* Empedocles on Etna II. ChTr; FaBoRV; FiP; LoBV; NOBE; OAEL-2; OBEV; OBVV; WiR
Through the bound cable strands, the arching path. Atlantis. Hart Crane. *Fr.* The Bridge. LiTM; MoPo; NePA; NYP; TwAmPo
Through the clangor of the cannon. Defeat and Victory. Wallace Rice. PAH
Through the dark aisles of the wood. Poem. Henry Treece. NeBP
Through the Dark the Dreamers Came, *with music.* Earl B. Marlatt. AH
Through the deep woods, at peep of day. The Canadian Herd-Boy. Susanna Moodie. OBCV
Through the dim window, I could see. In Passing. Roy Helton. HBMV
Through the faintest filigree. The Ships of Arcady. Francis Ledwidge. EtS
Through the fierce fever I nursed him, and then he said. Little Wild Baby. "Margaret Vandegrift." AA; HBV-1
Through the fires. Birthsong. Jessica Scarbrough. LFAC
Through the first days of Lent. The Street. Gary Soto. NPGG
Through the forest have I gone. Shakespeare. *Fr.* A Midsummer Night's Dream, II, ii. CTC
Through the forest the boy wends all day long. The Boy and the Flute. Björnstjerne Björnson, *tr. by* Sir Edmund Gosse. AWP; PoPl
Through the garden of shadow-/ flowers. The Boy and the Lantern. Evaristo Ribera Chevremont, *tr. by* Julio Marzán. InW
Through the great sinful streets of Naples as I past. Easter Day; Naples, 1849. Arthur Hugh Clough. OAEP; VLP

Through the green boughs I hardly saw thy face. Saint Germain-en-Laye. Ernest Dowson. SyP
Through the green tassels of the weeper tree. Triumphal Ode MCMXXXIX. George Barker. LiTB; WaP
Through the hill by the Rite Nite Motel. A Water Glass of Whisky. X. J. Kennedy. CoPo
Through the House ("Through the house give glimmering light"). Shakespeare. *See* Oberon and Titania to the Fairy Train.
Through the house what busy joy. The First Tooth. Charles *and* Mary Lamb. OxBChV; RHPC
Through the light rain I think I see them going. The Burial in Flanders. Robert Nichols. PeHV
Through the long death of the moon. The Death of the Moon. David Wagoner. PoA
Through the Long Night. Edward Carpenter. *Fr.* Towards Democracy. PeHV
Through the long ward the gramophone. Gramophone Tunes. Eva Dobell. SUMH
Through the long winter. And Fall Shall Sit in Judgment. Audre Lorde. NNP
Through the Looking-Glass, *sels.* "Lewis Carroll."
Humpty Dumpty's Recitation, *fr. ch.* 6. ChTr; FaBoCo; FaBoNo; FiBHP; NBM
(Humpty Dumpty's Song.) GTBS-P; OnMSP; OxBChV; OxBoLi
("In winter, when the fields are white.") EBEV
Jabberwocky, *fr. ch.* 1. AmMo; BiP; CABA; EBEV; EBVV; FaBoBe; FaBoCo; FaBoNo; FaBV; FaFP; FaPON; FF; FiBHP; FPL; GoJo; HBV-2; HeIP; HoPM; InPK; InPS; LiTB; NA; NBM; NIP; NOBE; NOBL; NoP; NTCP; OAEL-2; OxBChV; PoPl; PoRA; PPoe; PPP; RHPC; SeCeV; SpRo; TEP; TiPo; TreF; TrGrPo; VLP; WhC
"To the Looking-Glass world it was Alice that said," *fr. ch.* 9. Par
Walrus and the Carpenter, The, *fr. ch.* 4. BeLS; BLPA; FaBoBe; FaBoCo; FaBoNo; FaBV; FaFP; FaPON; FiBHP; FPL; GN; HBV-2; HBVY; InMe; LiTB; NA; NOBL; OxBChV; PoRA; SoPo; TEP; TreF
" 'Time has come, The,' the Walrus said," 1 *st.* TiPo
White Knight's Song, The, *fr. ch.* 8. FaBoCh; FaBoCo; InPS; NOBE; NOBL; NoP; OAEL-2
(Aged, Aged Man, The.) BXAP; FaBoPa; OxBChV; SpRo
(A-Sitting on a Gate.) PoRA
(I'll Tell Thee Everything I Can.) InvP; Par
(Ways and Means.) FiBHP; NA
(White Knight's Ballad.) FaBoNo; HAP; VLP
Through the Maze. *Unknown.* BLRP
Through the Metidja to Abd-el-Kadr. Robert Browning. PeD
Through the Night of Doubt and Sorrow. Sabine Baring-Gould. FaPoR
Through the night on fire with my blood. She Speaks the Morning's Filigree. Philip Lamantia. VGW
Through the night, through the night. The Sea. Richard Henry Stoddard. AA; HBV-1
"Through the Open Door." Patrick Kavanagh. AnIV
Through the open French window the warm sun. Still-Life. Elizabeth Daryush. QFR; WPE
Through the Parklands, through the Parklands. The Parklands. Stevie Smith. MoBS
Through the "Philadelphy" college he went in a week. The New Doctor. "Parmenas Mix." DBV
Through the pregnant universe rumbles life's terrific thunder. Exhortation: Summer, 1919. Claude McKay. CDC
Through the purple dusk on this pathless heath. The Heath. Thomas Boyd. OnYI
Through the rain forests, up a long river. The Deceptive Grin of the Gravel Porters. Gavin Ewart. FaBoMo
Through the revolving door. Alligator on the Escalator. Eve Merriam. SO
Through the shine, through the rain. Twilight Song. E. A. Robinson. HBV-2
Through the shrubs as I can crack[e]. Doron's Jigge [*or* A Jig]. Robert Greene. *Fr.* Menaphon. ElL; PoEL-2
Through the silver mist. A Spring Lilt. *Unknown.* HBV-1
Through the Smoke Hole. Gary Snyder. PoM
"There is another world above this one," *sel.* PoA
Through the soft pulp. Hand Saw. Erica Funkhouser. AMV-81
Through the starred Judean night. Mary Tired. Marjorie Pickthall. PeCV
Through the street as I trot when the weather is hot. Midsummer Fantasy. Newman Levy. PoSC
Through the stricken air, through the buttonwood balls. Rain on the Cumberlands. James Still. GrPl
Through the thick morning steam they took shape. A Papuan Shepherd. Francis Webb. *Fr.* A Drum for Ben Boyd. PoAu-2
Through the trees outside small. Departure. George Hitchcock. GP
Through the trees, with the moon underfoot. The Owl King [*or* The Call]. James Dickey. CoPo; NePoEA-2
Through the vague morning, the heart preoccupied. Bombers. C. Day Lewis. CMoP; MoAB
Through the viridian (and black of the burnt match). Virgo Descending. Charles Wright. LCAP
Through the Waters. Annie Johnson Fint. *See* Passing Through.
Through the Whole Long Night. H. Leivick, *tr. fr. Yiddish by* Ruth Whitman. VWA
Through the windmills. Fairy Wings. Winifred Howard. SUS
Through the Year. Julian S. Cutler. BLPA
Through these green Parthenons. In the Redwood Forest. Ralph Pomeroy. CoPo
Through These Pale Cold Days. Isaac Rosenberg. TrJP
Through thick Arcadian woods a hunter went. Atalanta's Race. William Morris. DTo
Through this most difficult country, this world we had known. Travelling Light. David Wagoner. NPAW
Through this our city of delight. Chiffons! William Samuel Johnson. HBV-1
Through this toilsome world, alas! I Shall Not Pass This Way Again. *Unknown.* BLPA; FPL; TreFS
Through throats where many rivers meet, the curlews cry. In the White Giant's Thigh. Dylan Thomas. LiTB
Through time their sharp features. The Indians on Alcatraz. Paul Muldoon. CIP
Through Unknown Paths. Frederick L. Hosmer. TrPWD
Through verdant banks where Thames's branches glide. The Assault on the Fortress. Timothy Dwight. PAH
Through Warmth and Light of Summer Skies, *with music.* Austin Faricy. AH
Through water, his own waterfall. Cold Fire. George Starbuck. NYBP
Through weary days and sleepless nights. One Gift I Ask. Virginia Bioren Harrison. HBV-2
Through what long heaviness, assayed in what strange fire. Carthusians. Ernest Dowson. VLP
Through what rock-strewn tunnels, O companions. The D Minor. E. L. Mayo. MiAP
Through Willing Heart and Helping Hand, *with music.* Frederick Lucian Hosmer. AH
Through winter-time we call on spring. The Wheel. W. B. Yeats. GTBS-P; MoVE
Through woods, Mme Une Telle, a trifle ill. Autumn Chapter in a Novel. Thom Gunn. FaBoMo; OxBTC
Through years of Irish history. Mr. Gunman. Vin Garbutt. OBET
Through You. Edwin Honig. TAP
Through your eyes' round and perfect pupils. Narrative. Louis Dudek. CaP
Through your grey eyes evasive heaven. Four Poems for April, III. Louis Adeane. NeBP
Throughe a forest as I can ryde. Crow and Pie. *Unknown.* ESPB
Throughout a garden greene and gay. The Rose of England. *Unknown.* ESPB
Throughout Australian history no tongue or pen can tell. The Death of Morgan. *Unknown.* FaBoBa
Throughout the day we are able to ban the voices. Henriëtte Roland-Holst, *tr. fr. Dutch by* Manfred Wolf. PBWP
Throughout the field I find no grain. Winter in Durnover Field. Thomas Hardy. MoBrPo
Throughout the soft and sunlit day. The Pines. Julie Mathilde Lippmann. AA
Throughout the World [If It Were Sought]. Sir Thomas Wyatt. ELU; MAT
(Honesty.) OBSC
Throw Away the Flowers. Elizabeth Daryush. PBWP
Throw away Thy rod. Discipline. George Herbert. FPL; HBV-2; LiTB; LoBV; MeLP; MePo; NOBE; NOCV; NoP; OBEV; OBS; OxBoCh; PAI; PoLF; SeCePo; SeCeV; TrGrPo; ViBoPo
Throw Hannibal on the scales, how many pounds. Hannibal. Juvenal, *tr. by* Robert Lowell. *Fr.* Satires, X. OBVE
Throw Him Down M'Closkey. John W. Kelly. FSN, *with music;* TreF
Throw Out the Lifeline. Edward Smith Ufford. TreF
Throw something to the gulls, any old scrap. Writing on the Wall. Padraic Fallon. NeIP
Throwing a bomb is bad. Ethics for Everyman. Roger Woddis. DBV; NOBL
Thrown. Ralph Hodgson. HBMV
Thrown Away. Kipling. *See* Horses.
Thrown backwards first, head over heels in the wind. To My Friend Whose Parachute Did Not Open. David Wagoner. TwAmPo
Thrown suddenly into a corner of the world. Exodus 1940. Alfred Wolfenstein, *tr. by* Erna Baber Rosenfeld. VWA
Thrush, The. Alfred Austin. TEP
Thrush, The. Laura Benét. HBMV
Thrush, The. Timothy Corsellis. WaaP; WaP

Thrush before Dawn, A. Alice Meynell. HBMV; MoBrPo; WPE
Thrush in February, The. George Meredith. OBNC
"Love born of knowledge, love that gains," *sel.* FaBoEn
Thrush is tapping a stone, A. Dawn. Gordon Bottomley. MoBrPo
Thrush, linnet, stare and wren. In Glencullen. J. M. Synge. ELU; FM; OBMV; OxBI
Thrushes. Ted Hughes. FaBoMo; GoYe; NePoEA-2
Thrushes flying under the lake. Nightingales singing underground. Pewter. Jack Gilbert. NPGG
Thrushes sing as the sun is going, The. Proud Songsters. Thomas Hardy. NoAM; PB
Thrush's Nest, The. John Clare. BoAnP; GoJo; PB
Thrush's Song, The. *Unknown, tr. fr. Gaelic by* William MacGillivray. CH
Thrust of the dragon's tight bone, The. The Dream Feast (Three Poems). Anita Endrezze Probst. VoR
Thrustararorum. Henry Nehemiah Dodge. EtS
Thrusting glance grows dim, The. Portrait of a Very Old Man. Sara E. Carsley. CaP
Thrusting its armoury of hot delight. Descartes and the Stove. Charles Tomlinson. FaBoMo
Thrusting of It, The. Burns. *See* Duncan Gray.
Thu sikest sore. Christ's Tear Breaks My Heart. *Unknown.* MeEL
Thule, the Period of Cosmography. *Unknown. See* Wonders.
Thumb. Philip Dacey. POL; PPJ
Thumb, The. Dennis Saleh. MAT; NeAC
Thumb bold. *Unknown.* OxNR
Thumb, for a summer's promise, The. The Sand Painters. Ben Belitt. EyDe; GOA
Thumb he. *Unknown.* OxNR
Thumb, loose tooth of a horse. Bestiary for the Fingers of My Right Hand. Charles Simic. AmPA; LCAP
Thumbikin, Thumbikin, broke the barn. *Unknown.* OxNR
Thumbing Old Magazines. Gerald Vizenor. VoR
Thumbkin says, I'll dance. *Unknown.* OxNR
Thumbprint. Celeste Turner Wright. Psk
"Thumbs in the thumb-place." The Mitten Song. Marie Louise Allen. NTCP; SoPo; SUS; TiPo
Thumpin' sound o' hosses' hoofs, the clack o' runnin' cows, The. Hot Ir'n! S. Omar Barker. PoOW
Thumping old tunes give a voice to its whereabouts. Fairground. W. H. Auden. NYBP
Thunder. Walter de la Mare. BoNaP
Thunder/ The Gallop of innumerable Walkyrie. Barrage. Richard Aldington. BrPo
Thunder clouds are sweeping, shrouding. A Russian Cradle Song. David Nomberg, *tr. by* Alter Brody. TrJP
Thunder in the Garden. William Morris. VLP
Thunder moved in sleep. Seven Days. J. R. Rowland. PAI
Thunder of riotous hoofs over the quaking sod. The Maid. Theodore Goodridge Roberts. HBV-2; MoShBr
Thunder of the Rain God. A House in Taos. Langston Hughes. CDC
Thunder our thanks to her—guns, hearts, and lips. *Mayflower.* John Boyle O'Reilly. AA; PAH
Thunder over Earth. Horatio Colony. TwAmPo
Thunder, the flesh quails, and the soul bows down. John Webster. Swinburne. InvP
Thunderer, The. Phyllis McGinley. EaLo
Thundering sound, A/ He hears. All Hands Unmoor! William Falconer. *Fr.* The Shipwreck, I. EtS
Thunderlight on the split logs: big raindrops. Seamus Heaney. Glanmore Sonnets, VII. IPY
Thunder-Storm, A. Emily Dickinson. *See* Wind began to rock the grass, The.
Thunderstorm, A. Archibald Lampman. CaP; NOBC
Thunderstorm in South Dakota. Kay Boyle. WPE
Thunderstorm in Town, A. Thomas Hardy. BoLoP; EnLoPo; GBL
Thunderstorms. W. H. Davies. HBV-2
Thurn, A. John Berryman. NOBA
Thursday. Edna St. Vincent Millay. InMe; PoA
Thursday; or, The Spell. John Gay. *Fr.* The Shepherd's Week. PoEL-3
"When first the year, I heard the cuckoo sing," *sel.* PBBP
Thursday was baking day in our house. Baking Day. Rosemary Joseph. Str
Thus all is here in motion, all is life. The Wool Trade. John Dyer. *Fr.* The Fleece, III. OBEC; SeCePo
Thus at the panting dove a falcon flies. Homer, *tr. by* Pope. *Fr.* The Iliad, XXII. OBVE
Thus been they parted, Arthur on his way. The Cave of Despair. Spenser. *Fr.* The Faerie Queene, I, 9. OBNV
Thus being entered, they behold around. Spenser. *Fr.* The Faerie Queene, II, 12. OAEL-1
Thus Bonny-Boots the Birthday Celebrated. *Unknown.* NCEP
Thus briefly sketch'd the sacred Rights of Man. To a Republican. Philip Freneau. AmPP
Thus by himself compell'd [*or* compelled] to live each day. Peter Grimes. George Crabbe. *Fr.* The Borough, Letter XXII. FaBoEn; NOBE; OBNC; SeCePo
Thus, by the way, to human loves interring. George Chapman. *Fr.* Euthymiae Raptus; or, The Tears of Peace. LoBV
Thus charg'd he; nor Argicides denied. Homer, *tr. by* George Chapman. *Fr.* The Odyssey, V. OBVE
Thus chydand with her drery desteny. Cressida's Leprosy. Robert Henryson. *Fr.* The Testament of Cresseid. SeCePo
Thus Crosslegged on Round Pillow Sat in Space. Allen Ginsberg. NNaP
Thus deaths hand clos'd his eyes. The Death of Hector. Homer, *tr. by* George Chapman. *Fr.* The Iliad, XXII. OBS
Thus down a lone valley with cedars o'er spread. Columbia. *Unknown.* AmFP
Thus draif they out that dear night with dances full noble. William Dunbar. *Fr.* The Twa Mariit Wemen and the Wedo. BSV
Thus ends my Love, but this doth grieve me most. Loves End [*or* Sonnet]. Lord Herbert of Cherbury. AnAnS-2; SeCP; ViBoPo
Thus ere another noon they emerged from the shades. The Lakes of the Atchafalaya. Longfellow. *Fr.* Evangeline. PoEL-5
Thus Etough looked; so grinned the brawling fiend. Tophet. Thomas Gray. NCEP *See also* Such Tophet was; so looked the grinning fiend.
Thus Eve to Adam. Milton. *Fr.* Paradise Lost, IV. FaBV
Thus far the Lord hath led us on—in darkness and in day. Light Shining Out of Darkness. Jane Borthwick. BLRP
Thus far, with rough and all-unable pen. Epilogue. Shakespeare. *Fr.* King Henry V. CTC
Thus fell the King, who yet surviv'd the state. Virgil, *tr. by* Sir John Denham. *Fr.* The Aeneid, II. OBVE
"Thus grief still treads upon the heels of pleasure."Congreve. *Fr.* The Old Bachelor, V, iii. TreF
Thus Harriet, rising on the stage. Harriet Simper Has Her Day. John Trumbull. *Fr.* The Progress of Dulness. AmPP
Thus have I back again[e] to thy bright name. An Apology for the Foregoing Hymn. [*or* An Apologie for the Precedent Hymnes on Teresa]. Richard Crashaw. AnAnS-1; JCP
Thus have I shunned the fire for fear of burning. Shakespeare. *Fr.* The Two Gentlemen of Verona, I, iii. GBL
Thus having passed all peril, I was come. The Happy Isle. Spenser. *Fr.* The Fairie Queene, IV, 10. OBSC
Thus I/ Pass by. Upon His Departure Hence. Robert Herrick. FaBoRV; QFR
Thus I awaked and wrote what I had dreamed. The Vision of Jesus. William Langland. *Fr.* The Vision of Piers Plowman. ACP
Thus I awakede, wot God, when I wonede in Cornehille. Long Will in London. William Langland. *Fr.* The Vision of Piers Plowman. OxBM
Thus I come to you. Author Unknown. William Montgomerie. OxBS
Thus I would walk abroad when gentle night. Walking at Night. Henry Treece. WaP
Thus is his cheek the map of days outworn. Sonnets, LXVIII. Shakespeare. OBSC
Thus it befell upon a night. Medea's Magic. John Gower. *Fr.* Confessio Amantis, V. OxBM
Thus Kitty, beautiful and young. The Female Phaeton. Matthew Prior. HBV-1
Thus laykes this lorde by lynde-wodes [*or* lunde-wodes] eves. Gawain and the Lady of the Castle. *Unknown. Fr.* Sir Gawain and the Green Knight. EBEV; OxBM
Thus Lovely Sleep. Richard Leigh. *See* Sleeping on Her Couch.
Thus man by his own strength to Heaven would soar. Dryden. *Fr.* Religio Laici. NOCV; WGRP
Thus much be sung of picking—next succeeds. How to Cure Hops and Prepare Them for Sale. Christopher Smart. *Fr.* The Hop-Garden. FaBoUs
Thus much the fates have allotted me. Turning Aside from Battles. Sextus Propertius, *tr. by* Ezra Pound. WaaP
Thus, near the gates conferring as they drew. Ulysses and His Dog. Homer, *tr. by* Pope. *Fr.* The Odyssey, XVII. FiP; OBEC
Thus piteously Love closed what he begat. Modern Love, L. George Meredith. EBEV; EnLoPo; FaBoEn; GTBS-P; HAP; HBV-1; LoBV; NBM; NOBE; NoP; OAEL-2; OAEP; OBNC; PoEL-5; SeCePo; SeCeV; TreFT; TrGrPo; ViBoPo; WHA
Thus queth Alfred. Wealth and Wisdom. *At. to* Alfred, King of England. *Fr.* The Proverbs of Alfred. OxBM
Thus reader, by our astrologick art. Almanac Verse. *Unknown.* SCAP
Thus re-inforc'd, against the adverse fleet. The Fourth Day's Battle. Dryden. *Fr.* Annus Mirabilis. OBS
Thus sadly I thought/ As that bird unsought. L'Envoy to W. L. H. Ainsworth, Esq. Francis Sylvester Mahony. OnYI

Thus safely low, my friend, thou can'st not fall. To the Reverend Mr. Murdoch. James Thomson. OBEC
Thus said the Lord in the Vault above the Cherubim. The Last Chantey. Kipling. EtS; FaBoCh; MoBrPo; MOS; OBVV
Thus said The Lord in the Vault above the Cherubim. The Last Chantey. Kipling. OBVV
Thus saith my Chloris bright. Giovanni Battista Guarini, *tr. fr. Italian.* GBL
Thus saith the great god Thoth. He Is Declared True of Word. *Unknown, tr. by* Robert Hillyer. *Fr.* Book of the Dead. AWP
Thus saith the Lord. I Return unto Zion. Bible, *O.T. Fr.* Zechariah. TrJP
Thus saith the Ruler of the Skies. The Passion and Exaltation of Christ. Isaac Watts. NOCV
Thus saying, from her Husbands hand her hand. The Fall. Milton. *Fr.* Paradise Lost, IX. PoEL-3
Thus saying, from her side the fatal key. Milton. *Fr.* Paradise Lost, II. EBEV
Thus she had lain. Africa. Maya Angelou. NIP
Thus should have been our travels. Over 2000 Illustrations and a Complete Concordance. Elizabeth Bishop. LCAP; NoAM
Thus, some tall tree that long hath stood. On the Death of Benjamin Franklin. Philip Freneau. PAH
Thus spake the Lord. The Word of the Lord from Havana. Richard Hovey. HBV-2; PAH
Thus Spake the Saviour, *with music.* Jeremy Belknap. AH
Thus Speak the Slain. Carl Holliday. PGD
Thus Speaketh Christ Our Lord. *Unknown.* PGD
Thus spoke Priam's shining son with words supplicating. Achilles to Lycaon. Homer, *tr. by* Richmond Lattimore. *Fr.* The Iliad, XXI. WaaP
Thus spoke the lady underneath the tree. Colonel Fantock. Edith Sitwell. MoAB; MoBrPo; MoVE; OBMV
Thus spoke the Lord to Israel. Amalek. Friedrich Torberg, *tr. by* Erna Baber Rosenfeld. VWA
Thus spoke to my lady the knight full of care. Swift. *Fr.* A Soldier and a Scholar. OBEC
Thus Sung Orpheus to His Strings. *Unknown.* GBL; NCEP
Thus systole addressed diastole. Systole and Diastole. Conrad Aiken. CrMA
Thus talking hand in hand alone they pass'd. Milton. *Fr.* Paradise Lost, IV. EBEV
Thus the Mayne Glideth. Robert Browning. *Fr.* Paracelsus. OBEV
Thus the old men lamented. Pogroms. André Spire, *tr. by* Stanley Burnshaw. VWA
Thus the poor bird, by some disast'rous fate. Time's Balm. Cuthbert Shaw. *Fr.* Monody to the Memory of a Young Lady. OBEC
Thus, therefore, he who feels the fiery dart. The Nature of Love. Lucretius, *tr. by* Dryden. *Fr.* De Rerum Natura. UnTE
Thus they in heav'n, above the starry sphear. Milton. *Fr.* Paradise Lost, III. EBEV
Thus, thus, begin the yearly rites. Pans Anniversarie. Ben Jonson. AnAnS-2; OBS
Thus, thus I steer my bark, and sail. On Even Keel. Matthew Green. *Fr.* The Spleen. OBEC
Thus to Glaucus spake/ Divine Sarpedon. Homer, *tr. by* Sir John Denham. *Fr.* The Iliad, XII. OBVE
Thus was my love, thus was my Ganymed. Sonnets, X. Richard Barnfield. PeHV
Thus was this place. Eden. Milton. *Fr.* Paradise Lost, IV. FaBoEn
Thus when the swallow, seeking prey. Song. John Gay. *Fr.* The Beggar's Opera. PoEL-3
Thus while he spoke, each eye grew big with tears. The Pyre of Patroclus. Homer, *tr. by* Pope. *Fr.* The Iliad, XXIII. OBEC
Thus while I ape the measure wild. Sir Walter Scott. *Fr.* Marmion, *Introd. to* III. OBRV
Thus while my joyless hours I lingring spend. John Philips. *Fr.* The Splendid Shilling. FaBoPa
Thus will despair/ In ecstasy of nightmare. The Succubus. Robert Graves. OAEL-2
Thus will I have the woman of my dream. Dawn of Womanhood. Harold Monro. HBV-1
Thus with a Kiss I Die. Shakespeare. *See* Here Lies Juliet.
"Thus with Hermetic art the adept combines." The Action of Invisible Ink. Erasmus Darwin. *Fr.* The Economy of Vegetation. FaBoUs
Thus with imagin'd wing our swift scene flies. Shakespeare. King Henry V, *fr.* III, Prologue. EBEV
Thus writeth Meer Djafrit. To the Ingleezee Khafir, Calling Himself Djann Bool Djenkinzun. James Clarence Mangan. OnYI
Thwart the sunrise of our western day, A. Achilles. Ernest Myers. OBVV
Thy arms with bracelets I will deck. Homage. Gustave Kahn, *tr. by* Jethro Bithell. TrJP
Thy azure robe, I did behold. Julia's Petticoat [*or* Upon Julia's Petticoat]. Robert Herrick. AnAnS-2; CaPo; UnTE
Thy baby, too, the child that was to be. Frederick Goddard Tuckerman. Sonnets, II, x. AP
Thy beard and head are of a different dye. To a Rogue. Joseph Addison. PV
Thy Beauty Fades. Jones Very. AP
Thy beauty haunts me heart and soul. The Moon. W. H. Davies. BrPo; MoBrPo; MoVE
Thy beauty, O Israel, upon thy high places is slain! David's Lament. Bible, *O.T. Fr.* Second Samuel. TrJP
Thy blessing on the boys—for time has come. Prayer. Haim Guri, *tr. by* Ruth H. Lask. TrJP
Thy Blood was shed for me. In My Place. Esther Archibald. STF
Thy blue waves, Patapsco, flow'd soft and serene. Fort McHenry. *Unknown.* PAH
Thy bosom is endearèd [*or* indeared] with all hearts. Sonnets, XXXI. Shakespeare. NOBE; OBEV; OBSC; PoEL-2
Thy braes were bonny [*or* bonnie], Yarrow stream. The Braes of Yarrow. John Logan. BSV; GTBS; GTBS-P; HBV-1; OBEC
"Thy breath is far sweeter than honey." Far Sweeter than Honey. Abraham ibn Ezra, *tr. by* Israel Abrahams. TrJP
Thy Brother's Blood. Jones Very. AP; NOBA; PoEL-4; QFR; TAP
Thy byrth, thy beautie, nor thy brave attyre. Farewell with a Mischeife. George Gascoigne. AAS
Thy copp's, too, nam'd of Gamage, thou hast there. Ben Jonson. *Fr.* To Penshurst. FM
Thy country, Wilberforce, with just disdain. Sonnet to William Wilberforce, Esq. William Cowper. OAEP
Thy cruise is over now. Mr. Merry's Lament for "Long Tom." John Gardiner Calking Brainard. AA
Thy dawn, O Ra, opens the new horizon. Adoration of the Disk by King Akhnaten and Princess Nefer Neferiu Aten. *Unknown, tr. by* Robert Hillyer. *Fr.* Book of the Dead. AWP
Thy error, Frémont, simply was to act. To John C. Frémont. Whittier. PAH
Thy eyes and eyebrows I could spare. *Unknown.* FaBoEE
Thy eyes are sparks, Lycines, god-like made. Epigram. Strato, *tr. by* Sydney Oswald. PeHV
Thy face I have seen as one seeth. Song. Sophie Jewett. AA
Thy Faithful Sons. Eleazar, *tr. fr. Hebrew.* TrJP
Thy filed words that from thy mouth did flow. Of Mistress D. S. Barnabe Googe. EnRePo
Thy fingers make early flowers of/ all things. Song. E. E. Cummings. MoAmPo
Thy flattering picture, Phryne, is like thee. Phryne. John Donne. FaBoEE
Thy forests, Windsor! and thy green retreats. Pope. *Fr.* Windsor Forest. NOEC
Thy friend, whom thy deserts to thee enchaine. To Mr. C.B. John Donne. AnAnS-1
Thy [*or* Your] friendship oft has made my heart to ache [*or* ake]. To William Hayley [*or* To Hayley]. Blake. FaBoCo; FaBoEE; FF; TrGrPo
Thy functions are ethereal. On the Power of Sound. Wordsworth. VLP
Thy Garden. Mu'tamid, King of Seville, *tr. fr. Arabic by* Dulcie L. Smith. AWP
Thy garden, orchard, fields. Francis Daniel Pastorius. SCAP
Thy glass will show thee how thy beauties wear. Sonnets, LXXVII. Shakespeare. EnRePo; QFR
Thy grace, dear Lord's my golden wrack I find. Edward Taylor. Preparatory Meditations, First Series, XXXII. NoP; SCAP
Thy Heart ("Thy heart is like some icy lake"). *Unknown.* NA
Thy hue, dear pledge, is pure and bright. To a Lock of Hair. Sir Walter Scott. GTBS; GTBS-P
Thy human frame, my glorious Lord, I spy. Meditation Seven. Edward Taylor. *Fr.* Sacramental Meditations. LiTA
Thy husband to a banquet goes with me. The Possessive Lover. Ovid, *tr. by* Christopher Marlowe. Amores, I, 4. UnTE
Thy Kingdom Come ("Thy kingdom come—on bended knee"). Frederick L. Hosmer. WGRP
Thy Kingdom Come, O Lord. Frederick L. Hosmer. WGRP (Prophecy Sublime, The.) TrPWD
Thy Kingdom, Lord, We Long For. Vida Scudder. WGRP
Thy kisses dost thou bid me count. To Lesbia. Catullus, *tr. by* George Lamb. UnTE
Thy knights, O Queen, ride forth by east and west. Regina Confessorum. *Unknown.* GoBC
Thy laugh's a song an oriole trilled. Kitty's Laugh. Arlo Bates. *Fr.* Conceits. AA
Thy leopard legs and python thighs. The Zoo of You. Arthur Freeman. ErPo
Thy little footsteps on the sands. To William Shelley. Shelley. ChER

Thy Loving Kindness, Lord, I Sing, *with music.* George Barrell Cheever. AH
Thy Mercies, Lord, to Heaven Reach, *with music.* William Kethe. AH
Thy merits, Wolfe, transcend all human praise. The Death of Wolfe. *Unknown.* PAH
Thy Mother Was like a Vine. Bible, *O.T.* Ezekiel, XIX: 10–14. TrJP
Thy nags (the leanest things alive). Epigram. Matthew Prior. FaBoEE
Thy Nail-pierced Hands. Kathryn Bowsher. STF
Thy Name We Bless and Magnify. John Power. BLRP
Thy need is great. For the Earth God. *Unknown, tr. by* Frances Herskovits. EaLo
Thy nights moan into my days. Psalms of Love. Peter Baum, *tr. by* Jethro Bithell. AWP
Thy one white leaf is open to the sky. To a Cherokee Rose. William Hamilton Hayne. AA
Thy Praise, O God, in Zion Waits, *with music.* Jacob Kimball. AH
Thy praise, O Lord, will I proclaim. Palms and Myrtles. Eleazar ben Kalir, *tr. by* Alice Lucas. TrJP
Thy praise or dispraise is to me alike. To Fool, or Knave. Ben Jonson. FaBoEE; NoP; SoSe
Thy restless feet now cannot go. Christ Crucified. Richard Crashaw. GoBC; OBEV
Thy Rising Is Beautiful. Akhnaton (Amenhotep IV), *tr. fr. Egyptian.* ILwL
Thy Sea So Great. Winfred Ernest Garrison. TrPWD
Thy shades, thy silence, now be mine. Solitude. James Beattie. *Fr.* Retirement. OBEC
Thy skin is like an unwasht carrot's. Portrait. Walter Savage Landor. DBV
Thy sooty godhead I desire. To Vulcan. Robert Herrick. CaPo
Thy sorrow, and the sorrow of the sea. Ireland. Lionel Johnson. HBV-2
Thy soul/ Grown delicate with satieties. O Atthis. Ezra Pound. PoA
Thy soul is not enchanted by the moon. The Lilies of the Field. Compton Mackenzie. OBVV
Thy soul within such silent pomp did keep. A Quiet Soul. John Oldham. OBEV
Thy span of life was all too short. To a Withered Rose. John Kendrick Bangs. AA
Thy spirit, Independence, let me share! Independence. Tobias Smollett. OBEC
Thy stricken daughter, now, O Lord, prepares. Hymn for the Eve of the New Year. Abraham Gerondi, *tr. by* Solomon Solis-Cohen. TrJP
Thy summer voice, Musketaquit. Two Rivers. Emerson. AP; NOBA; OxBA; TrGrPo
Thy Sun Posts Westward. William Drummond of Hawthornden. SeCePo
(No Trust in Time.) LoBV
Thy trivial harp will never please. Merlin. Emerson. AmPP; AA; AP; NOBA; OxBA
Thy tu whits are lulled, I wot. Second Song. Tennyson. PBBP
Thy various works, imperial queen, we see. On Imagination. Phillis Wheatley. AmPP; BlSi; PoNe
Thy victory is in the heart. Victoria. Henry van Dyke. TRV
Thy voice, as tender as the light. To a Friend. James Fenimore Cooper. PeHV
Thy voice is heard through [*or* thro'] rolling drums. Tennyson. *Fr.* The Princess. OBVV; TrGrPo
Thy voice is hovering o'er my soulit lingers. To Constantia Singing. Shelley. EnRP
Thy voice is on the rolling air. In Memoriam A. H. H., CXXX. Tennyson. HBV-2; NoP; PeHV; TRV
Thy vowes are heard, and thy Castara's fame. His Muse Speakes to Him. William Habington. AnAnS-2
Thy Way, Not Mine. Horatius Bonar. OxBoCh; TrPWD; TRV
Thy Will Be Done. Annie Johnson Flint. STF
Thy Will Be Done. John Hay. *See* Not in Dumb Resignation.
Thy Will Be Done. Hugh Thomson Kerr. BLRP
Thy Will Be Done. Albert Simpson Reitz. STF
Thy Will is best for me. God's Will Is Best. *Unknown.* BLRP
Thy will, O God, is best. Thy Will Be Done. Hugh Thomson Kerr. BLRP
Thy wisdom and Thy might appear. The Burning Bush. Henry van Dyke. TRV
Thy wisdom speak in me, and bids me dare. Shelley. *Fr.* Epipsychidion. OAEL-2
Thy words are compounded of sweet-smelling myrrh. Words Wherein Stinging Bees Lurk. Judah Halevi, *tr. by* Nina Davis Salaman. TrJP
Thyestes, *sels.* Seneca, *tr. fr. Latin.*
"O yee, whome lorde of lande and waters wyde," *fr.* III, *tr. by* Jasper Heywood. OBVE
"Stond [*or* Stand] who so list upon the slipper toppe," *fr.* II, *tr. by* Sir Thomas Wyatt. AAS; NoP; OBVE; PoEL-1; SiPS
("Climb at court for me that will," *tr. by* Andrew Marvell.) OBVE
("Let him that will, ascend the tottering seat," *tr. by* Sir Matthew Hale.) OBVE
("Let who so lyst with might mace to raygne," *tr. by* Jasper Heywood.) OBVE
(Senec. Traged. ex Thyeste Chor. 2, *tr. by* Andrew Marvell.) SeCV-1
("Upon the slippery tops of humane state," *tr. by* Abraham Cowley.) OBVE
Thyme. *Unknown.* AmFP
Thyme Flowering among Rocks. Richard Wilbur. LCAP
Thyrsis. Matthew Arnold. FiP; NOBE; NoP; OAEP; OBEV; OBNC; OBVV; VLP
Sels.
"How changed is here each spot man makes or fills!" FaBoPP
"So, some tempestuous morn in early June," *sts.* 6-7. PoPle
Thyrsis. Edward Cracroft Lefroy, *after the Greek of* Theocritus. *Fr.* Echoes from Theocritus. AWP
Thyrsis, a youth of the inspired train. The Story of Phoebus and Daphne Applied, etc. Edmund Waller. InvP
Thyrsis and Milla, arm in arm together. *Unknown.* GBL
Thyrsis, Sleep'st Thou? *Unknown.* InvP; OBSC
Thyrsis, when we parted, swore. Song. Thomas Gray. OAEP
Thys Endris Nygth. *Unknown.* *See* Christmas Carol, A: "Thys ender nyght."
Thysia, *sels.* Morton Luce.
"Bow down, my song, before her presence high," III. HBV-1
"Comes the New Year; wailing the north winds blow," XVI. HBV-1
"Hear, O Self-Giver, infinite as good," XXXVII. HBV-1
"How shall I tell the measure of my love," XLV. HBV-1
"I watch beside you in your silent room," VII. HBV-1
"Like some lone miser, dear, behold me stand," XXIII. HBV-1
"So sang I in the springtime of my years," XXXVI. HBV-1
"Twin songs there are, of joyance, or of pain," II. HBV-1
Tiare Tahiti. Rupert Brooke. BrPo; SeCeV
Tibur is beautiful, too, and the orchard slopes, and the Anio. So Not Seeing I Sung [*or* The Valley and Villa of Horace]. Arthur Hugh Clough. *Fr.* Amours de Voyage. FaBoPP; GTBS-P; OBNC
Tic-tic-tic!/ The sound of the sleet. Sleet Storm. James S. Tippett. SiSoSe
Tichborne's Elegy. Chidiock Tichborne. *See* Elegy: "My prime of youth is but a frost of cares."
Tick Picking in the Quetico. Don Johnson. MAYP
"Tick-tock! Tick-tock!" Sings the great time-clock. The Time-Clock. Charles Hanson Towne. HBMV
Tick-a-lock rock-a-bye. Child's Game. Judson Jerome. DuDa
Ticket Agent, The. Edmund Leamy. HBMV
Ticket, The, said: to SFO. Man of Letters. Warren Knox. QQQ
Ticking Clocks. Rachel Field. TiPo
Tickle Rhyme, The. Ian Serraillier. NTCP; OnUR; RHPC; SoPo
Tickled,/ my thoughts wander. Celebration for My Mother. Wendy Rose. CDW
Tickly, tickly, on your knee. *Unknown.* OxNR
Ticonderoga. V. B. Wilson. PAL
Ticonderoga; a Legend of the West Highlands. Robert Louis Stevenson. OBNV
Tiddle liddle lightum. *Unknown.* OxNR
Tide, The. Longfellow. *See* Tide Rises, the Tide Falls, The.
Tide be runnin' the great world over. Sea Love. Charlotte Mew. ELU; MoAB; MoBrPo; OxBTC; TrGrPo; ViBoPo
Tide, high tide of golden air, A. Homage to the Weather. Michael Hamburger. NMP
Tide in the river, The. Eleanor Farjeon. TiPo
Tide of Faith, The. "George Eliot." *Fr.* A Minor Prophet. TRV; WGRP
Tide of Life, The, *sel.* Watson Kirkconnell.
"Ah, Flood of Life on which I am a wave." CaP
Tide Pools. Dave Smith. AMV-81
Tide Rises, the Tide Falls, The. Longfellow. AA; AmPP; AP; BLPL; ChTr; FaFP; MOS; NePA; NOBA; OxBA; PAI; PoRA; TAP; TreFT
(Tide, The.) WiR
Tide River, The. Charles Kingsley. *Fr.* The Water Babies. BoNaP; HBV-1; OxBChV
(Clear and Cool.) GN
Tide slips up the silver sand, The. Sea-Way. Ellen Mackay Hutchinson Cortissoz. AA
Tide Turning. John Frederick Nims. FYAP
Tide Will Win, The. Priscilla Leonard. TRV
Tides, The. Paul Blackburn. PoM
Tides. Will H. Blackwell. AMV-80
Tides, The. Bryant. TAP
Tide's at full, The: the marsh with flooded streams. Sidney Lanier. *Fr.* Sunrise. FaBoEn
Tides in my eyes are heavy, The. Thanksgiving. Philip Booth. Str
Tides of Love, The. T. A. Daly. InMe; PoPl; WhC; YaD
Tides shape the sides of the agate mountain. On Visiting My Son, Port Angeles, Washington. Duane Niatum. CDW
Tidewash . . . Memories. Lament of the Flutes. Christopher Okigbo. PBA

Tidewater born he was, and ever. The Rivers Remember. Nancy Byrd Turner. AmFN
Tidings of Great Joy. Bible, *O.T. Fr.* St. Luke. *See* First Christmas, The.
Tidy Young Tapir, A. Carolyn Wells. TDH
Tidying Up. Nancy Weber. AMV-80
Tie a bandage over his eyes. A Rebel. John Gould Fletcher. MoAmPo
Tie one end of a rope fast over a beam. A Receipt to Cure a Love Fit. *Unknown.* NOEC
Tie the moccasin, bind the pack. Young Washington. Arthur Guiterman. FaPON; OHIP; PoSC
Tie the strings to my life, my Lord. Emily Dickinson. TrCP
Tie your own noose if you want to be. The Advice of an Efficiency Expert. Augustus Young. CIP
Tie Your Tongue, Sir? Robert Paul Smith. CAD
Tiempo Muerto. Ricardo Alonso. SaC
Ties. Raymond Souster. MoCV; OBCV
Ties. Dabney Stuart. GrPl; LiSp
Tiffany, Tiffany. Captain Kelly Lets His Daughter Go to Be a Nun. Thomas Butler Feeney. PoPl
Tiger, The. Hilaire Belloc. MoBrPo
Tiger, The. Blake. *Fr.* Songs of Experience. AWP; ChTr; FaBoBe; FaFP; FaPON; FaPoR; FPL; GN; HBV-1; ILwL; InPS; LiTB; NIP; NOBE; NOEC; OAEP; OBEC; OBEV; PAI; PoLF; PoPl; PoPle; PoRA; PrIm; RoGo; SoSe; SpRo; TEP; TreF; TRV; UnPo; ViBoPo; WGRP; WHA
(Tyger, The.) BIP; CABA; CH; EaLo; EnRP; FaBoCh; FaBoEn; FaBV; FF; FM; HAP; HeIP; HoPM; InPK; LAuP; LoBV; MasP; NoP; OAEL-2; OBNC; PoEL-4; PPoe; PPP; SCV; SeCePo; SeCeV; TrGrPo; WeW
Tiger, The. Robert Creeley. GP
Tiger. A. D. Hope. OxBC
Tiger. Claude McKay. BPo
Tiger. *Yoruba Oral Tradition, tr. by* B. King. WTO
Tiger at Play. Joanna Baillie. PCat
Tiger-Cat Tim. Edith Newlin Chase. SoPo; TiPo
Tiger Christ unsheathed his sword. For the One Who Would Take Man's Life in His Hands. Delmore Schwartz. LiTA; LiTM; MiAP; MoAB; MoAmPo; MoVE; NePA; NoAM; VGW; WaP
Tiger in the tiger-pit, The. Lines for an Old Man. T. S. Eliot. FaBoTw; TW
Tiger-Lilies. Thomas Bailey Aldrich. GN
Tiger Lily. David McCord. GoJo; PDV
Tiger of Desire, The. Tom MacInnes. OBCV
Tiger, on the other hand, is kittenish and mild, The. The Tiger. Hilaire Belloc. MoBrPo
Tiger People. Geary Hobson. STE
Tiger stalking in the night, The. Edward Newman Horn. ELU
"Tiger, strolling at my side." Triumph of Sensibility. Sylvia Townsend Warner. MoAB; MoBrPo
Tiger Tale, A. John Bennett. *See* Tiger's Tale, A.
Tiger! Tiger! [*or* Tyger! Tyger!] burning bright. The Tiger [*or* Tyger]. Blake. *Fr.* Songs of Experience. AWP; BiP; CABA; CH; ChTr; EaLo; EnRP; FaBoBe; FaBoCh; FaBoEn; FaBV; FaFP; FaPON; FaPoR; FF; FM; FPL; GN; HAP; HBV-1; HeIP; HoPM; ILwL; InPK; InPS; LAuP; LiTB; LoBV; MasP; NIP; NOBE; NOEC; NoP; OAEL-2; OAEP; OBEC; OBEV; OBNC; PAI; PoEL-4; PoLF; PoPl; PoPle; PoRA; PPoe; PPP; PrIm; RoGo; SCV; SeCePo; SeCeV; SoSe; SpRo; TEP; TreF; TrGrPo; TRV; UnPo; ViBoPo; WeW; WGRP; WHA
Tiger, when a man goes by, The. The Dignity of Man—Lesson #1. Walter H. Kerr. NePoAm-2
Tiger's Tale, A. John Bennett. TiPo
(Tiger Tale, A.) OBCA
Tiggady Rue. David McCord. TiPo; WSC
Tight,—proof, unavailable. Falling Out. Helen Chasin. IHMS
Tight Rope. Amiri Baraka. CNA
Tight scrimmage of blankets in the dark. Ward Two. Francis Webb. CBAP
Tight-sphinctered and inhibited. Peace Delegate. Douglas Livingstone. PeSA
Tightly-folded bud. Born Yesterday. Philip Larkin. NAs
Tightrope Walker. Vernon Scannell. NCSH
Till Christ. *Unknown. Fr.* The Gude and Godlie Ballatis. OxBS
Till dawn the wind drove round me. It is past. Dawn on the Night-Journey. Dante Gabriel Rossetti. NCEP
Till dawn the winds' insuperable throng. In Extremis. George Sterling. HBV-2
Till Death Do Us Part. Leila Miccolis, *tr. fr. Portuguese by* Willis Barnstone *and* Nelson Cerqueira. BoWoP
Till Eve was brought to Adam, he. Nearest the Dearest. Coventry Patmore. *Fr.* The Angel in the House. HBV-1
Till I shall come again, let this suffice. A Panegyric to Sir Lewis Pemberton. Robert Herrick. CaPo
Till now the doubtful dusk reveal'd. Tennyson. *Fr.* In Memoriam A. H. H., XCV. GTBS-P
Till now your indiscretion sets us free. Eves Apologie. Emilia Lanier. BoWoP
Till one dawn,/ Above the green bloom of a gleaming lawn. The Death of Urgan. Swinburne. *Fr.* Tristram of Lyonesse. WHA
Till the Sea Runs Dry. *Malay Oral Tradition, tr. by* R. J. Wilkinson. WTO
Till the slow daylight pale. The Sun-Flower. Dora Greenwell. WPE
Till they tangled and seemed to trip and lie down. His Legs Ran About. Ted Hughes. LLLT
Till thinking had worn out my enterprise. Spring Mountain Climb. Richard Eberhart. GoYe; LiSp
Till you've earned. Mahádéviyakka, *tr. fr. Kannada by* A. K. Ramanujan. PBWP
Tillie. Walter de la Mare. TiPo
Tilt. Wilt. Snow. Ralph Pomeroy. Psk
Tilth. Robert Graves. FaBoEE; OBSV
Tim, an Irish Terrier. Winifrid M. Letts. GDP
Tim Evans was a prisoner. Go Down You Murderers. Ewan MacColl. FSW
Tim Finnegan [*or* Finnigin *or* Finigan] liv'd in Walkin [*or* lived in Walker] Street. Finnegan's [*or* Finigan's] Wake. *Unknown.* BLPA; FaBoBa; FSW; TrAS
Tim the Dragoon. Sir Arthur Quiller-Couch. WhC
Tim, the Fairy. Florence Randal Livesay. CaP
Tim tryeth truth convicting all that strive. T. Street. SCAP
Tim Turpin. Thomas Hood. WiR
Timber, *with music. Unknown.* AS
Timber, The. Henry Vaughan. FaBoRV, *abr.*; NoP; OBEV; SeCP; SeCV-1
Timber (Jerry the Mule). *Unknown.* FSW
Timber Line Trees. Jamie Sexton Holme. PoOW
Timbers heaving to heaven we sailed at seven. Crabbing. Norman Levine. CaP; OBCV
Time. Bhartrihari, *tr. fr. Sanskrit by* Paul Elmer More. AWP
Time. Thomas Stephens Collier. AA
Time. Robert Creeley. LCAP
Time. Giles Fletcher the Elder. *See* Licia: "In time the strong and stately turrets fall."
Time, The. G. S. Fraser. WaP
Time. Robert Graves. LiTM
Time. George Herbert. TEP
Time. Ralph Hodgson. BrPo; GTBS-P
Time. Avraham Huss, *tr. fr. Hebrew by* Mark Elliott Shapiro. VWA
Time. Jasper Mayne. OBEV
Time. Sir Thomas More. EnRePo
Time. Shelley. FaBoRV; FPL; MOS; Par; PoLF
(Unfathomable Sea.) EtS
Time. Allan Taylor. OBET
Time. *Unknown.* TreFT
Time. Thomas Watson. *Fr.* Hecatompathia. FaBoRV; OBSC
Time. John Huddlestone Wynne. OxBChV
Time allowed for sleep at length elapsed, The. Thomas Cole. *Fr.* The Life of Hubert. NOEC
Time and again/ the world heals itself. Cathedrals. W. S. Doxey. AMV-80
Time and again I've longed for adventure. All the Things You Are. Oscar Hammerstein II. BLSo
Time and Eternity. Bunyan. WiR
Time and Eternity. Fulke Greville. *Fr.* Caelica. OBSC
("You that seek what life is in death.") EnRePo
Time and Eternity. Stephen Hawes. *Fr.* The Pastime of Pleasure. PoEL-1
Time and Grief. William Lisle Bowles. HBV-2; OBEV
(Influence of Time on Grief.) EnRP
("O time! who know'st a lenient hand to lay.") LO
(Sonnet: "O time! who know'st a lenient hand to lay.") OBEC
(Sonnet July 18th 1787.) FaBoEn
Time and Love ("Since brass, nor stone, nor earth, nor boundless sea"). Shakespeare. *See* Sonnets, LXV.
Time and Love ("When I have seen by Time's fell hand defaced"). Shakespeare. *See* Sonnets, LXIV.
Time and the Garden. Yvor Winters. MoAmPo; NoAM; QFR; VGW
Time and the mortal will stand never fast. Sonnet. Luis de Camoes, *tr. by* Richard Garnett. AWP
Time and the weather wear away. Houses [*or* Poem]. Donald Justice. EyDe; PoA; PPJ
Time and the World, whose magnitude and weight. Epitaph. Robert Southey. OBNC
Time and Tide. Hazel Washington Lamarre. PoNe
Time & time again the laughter after the footsteps. The Jungle. Diane di Prima. PoM
Time as something concrete, like the wash of a wave. Passage. Richard Eberhart. FAZ

Time bagged you at last. Poem for Vladimir. G. Ripley. AMV-81
Time breaks our passion but the Virgin smiles. Our True Beginnings. Wrey Gardiner. NeBP
Time brings not death, it brings but changes. A Comrade Rides Ahead. Douglas Malloch. HBMV
Time can [*or* will] say nothing but I told you so. Villanelle [*or* If I Could Tell You]. W. H. Auden. LiTA; MoAB; MoBrPo; PAI
Time cannot age thy sinews, nor the gale. Albatross. Charles Warren Stoddard. AA; EtS
Time cannot break the bird's wing from the bird. To a Young Poet. Edna St. Vincent Millay. CrMA
Time-Clock, The. Charles Hanson Towne. HBMV
Time, cruel Time, come and subdue that brow. To Delia, XIII. Samuel Daniel. OBSC
Time demands a rolling eye, The. The Time. G. S. Fraser. WaP
Time Does Not Bring Relief. Edna St. Vincent Millay. FaBV
Time draws near the birth of Christ, The. In Memoriam A. H. H., XXVIII. Tennyson. FaBoRV; NOCV; PChr; PGD
Time draws near the birth of Christ, The. In Memoriam A. H. H., CIV. Tennyson. SBVL
Time drops in decay. The Moods. W. B. Yeats. CTC; VLP
Time Eating. Keith Douglas. NeBP
Time ends when vision sees its lapse in/ liberty. Beata l'Alma. Sir Herbert Read. FaBoMo
Time Exposures. Muriel Rukeyser. PoA
Time flies. On an Old Sun Dial. *Unknown.* TreFT
Time flits away, time flits away, lady. Variation on Ronsard. T. Sturge Moore. OBMV
Time for Building, A. Myra Cohn Livingston. PDV
Time for Everything, A. Bible, *O.T. Fr.* Ecclesiastes. *See* To Everything There Is a Season.
Time for rain! for your long hot dry autumn. Piano di Sorrento. Robert Browning. *Fr.* The Englishman in Italy. FaBoPP; SeCePo
Time for toil is past, and night has come, The. Bringing Our Sheaves. Elizabeth Akers Allen. HBV-2
Time for Us to Leave Her, *with music. Unknown.* ShS
Time goes, you say? Ah, no! The Paradox of Time. Pierre de Ronsard, *tr. by* Austin Dobson. AWP; HBV-1
Time had come to kill himself, he said, The. Epitaph on a Madman's Grave. Morris Gilbert. YaD
Time has a magic wand! On an Old Muff. Frederick Locker-Lampson. CenHV
Time has an end, they say. Hilda Doolittle ("H. D."). *Fr.* Good Frend. NOBA; VGW
Time has been that these wild solitudes, The. A Winter Piece. Bryant. AmPP; AP; OxBA
Time has come for a wench to wed, The. Ballad of the Double Bed. Eve Merriam. UnTE
Time has come for us to part, The. I'm Through with You. *Unknown.* WTO
Time Has Come, the Clock Says Time Has Come, The. Conrad Aiken. Preludes for Memnon, XXVIII. NePA; OxBA
"Time has come, The," the Walrus said. "Lewis Carroll." *Fr.* The Walrus and the Carpenter. TiPo
Time has its ends and its beginnings. The Jungle. Louis Dudek. PeCV
Time has no flight—'tis we who speed along. Time. Thomas Stephens Collier. AA
Time has pulled up a chair, dashed. Ron Mason. Hone Tuwhare. OCNZ
Time Hath Been, The. Joseph Skipsey. VlP
Time hath, my Lord, a wallet at his back. Ulysses Advises Achilles. Shakespeare. *Fr.* Troilus and Cressida, III, iii. LiTB
Time heals not: it extends a sorrow's scope. Epigram. J. V. Cunningham. VGW
Time holds no purring hour-glass to your face. The Day. George M. Brady. NeIP
Time I dropped your almost body down, The. The Lost Baby Poem. Lucille Clifton. BlSi; InPK; WPE
Time I went to church I sat, The. Mr. Rockefeller's Hat. Helen Bevington. OBAL
Time I went to see my sister, The. Tsurayuki, *tr. by* Arthur Waley. *Fr.* Shui Shu. AWP
Time in the Rock [or, Preludes to Definition], *sels.* Conrad Aiken.
"And there I saw the seed upon the mountain," I. TwAmPo
"And you who love, you who attach yourselves," XX. ViBoPo
"Bird flying past my head said previous previous, The," LXII. VGW
"But no, the familiar symbol, as that the," XCII. VGW
"Mysticism, but let us have no words," XI. VGW
"On that wild verge in the late light he stood," XXXIX. TwAmPo
"Or else, in an afternoon of minor reflection," XCIII. MoVE
"Still the same function, still the same habit come," XLV. TwAmPo
"What face she put on it, we will not discuss," LXXXIV. VGW
"What without speech we knew and could not say," XLVI. TwAmPo
"Where we were walking in the day's light, seeing," XXXVII. VGW
Time in the Sun. Louise Townsend Nicholl. NePoAm-2
Time is, The. Anger. Robert Creeley. CoPo; NaP
Time is/ Too slow for those who wait. Time. *Unknown.* TreFT
Time is a fox on quick, velvet feet. Earthly Illusion. Louise Leighton. GoYe
Time is a heavy legend to be told. French Clock. Hortense Flexner. HBMV
Time is a thing. Epilogue. Stephen Spender. MoBrPo
Time is a treasure. New Time. *Unknown.* BLRP
Time is after dinner, The. Cigarettes. The Boarder. Louis Simpson. PoPl
Time is come to speak, I think, The. Mrs. Golightly. Gertrude Hall. AA
Time is divided into. Time Is the Mercy of Eternity. Kenneth Rexroth. VGW
Time is God's tenderness. Time. Marguerite Wilkinson. HBMV
Time is moving, people move up and down. The Parade. Ashton Greene. NePoAm
Time is never wasted, listening to the trees. The Trees. Lucy Larcom. OHIP
Time is not remote when I, The. Swift. *Fr.* Verses on the Death of Doctor Swift. EBEV; NOBE; NOBL; OBEC; OxBoLi; ViBoPo
Time is of the essence. This is a highly skilled. Polo Grounds. Rolfe Humphries. HoPM; LiSp
Time Is Swiftly Rolling On, The. Berryman Hicks. AH, *with music*
(Dying Father's Farewell, The, *diff. version.*) AmFP
Time is the feather'd thing. Time. Jasper Mayne. OBEV
Time Is the Fire. Delmore Schwartz. *See* For Rhoda.
Time Is the Mercy of Eternity. Kenneth Rexroth. VGW
Time is the root of all this earth. Time. Bhartrihari, *tr. by* Paul Elmer More. AWP
Time Is Today, The. John Farrar. GoYe
Time it took he could have, The. The Invention of the Telephone. Peter Klappert. AmPA; PPJ
Time I've Lost in Wooing, The. Thomas Moore. EnRP; HBV-1; HoPM; OAEP; OnYI; TreF
Time like an Ever-rolling Stream. P. G. Wodehouse. FiBHP
Time like the receptions of a child's piano. The Reconciliation. Archibald MacLeish. MoAmPo
Time Long Past. Shelley. HBV-1
Time of Change, A. Egan O'Rahilly, *tr. fr. Irish by* Eavan Boland. BIrV
Time of Creation Has Come, The. *Yoruba Oral Tradition, tr. by* Ulli Beier. WTO
Time of Day. Selden Rodman. PoA
Time of Fish Dying. Gabriela Melinescu, *tr. fr. Rumanian by* Stavros Deligiorgis. BoWoP
Time of grease beginneth at Midsummer day. Julians Barnes. *Fr.* Book of Hunting. WPE
Time of Light, a Time of Shadow, A. Samuel Yellen. NePoAm-2
"Time of Man, The." Phyllis Webb. MoCV
Time of Night, A. David Ignatow. FAZ
Time of Nobody, The. Winter over Nothing. Elliot Coleman. FAZ
Time of Roses. Thomas Hood. OBEV; OBVV
(It Was Not in the Winter.) ELP
(It Was the Time of Roses.) CH
Time of the Barmecides, The. James Clarence Mangan. EnRP; RoGo
Time of the Mad Atom. Virginia Braiser. QQQ
Time of Turquoise, A. Judith Mountain Leaf Volborth. TWSS
Time of Waiting. Geoffrey Dutton. CBAP
Time of Waiting in Amsterdam. Ingrid Jonker, *tr. fr. Afrikaans by* Jack Cope *and* William Plomer. BoWoP
Time Out. Frances Westgate Butterfield. GoYe
Time Out. Donald Finkel. HoPM
Time Out. Oliver Jenkins. GoYe
Time Out. John Montague. BoAnP
Time out of mind I have stood. The Old Grey Wall. Bliss Carman. CaP
Time Passes. R. P. Lister. NYBP
Time Passing, Beloved ("Time passing, and the memories of love"). Donald Davie. BoLoP; NePoEA-2
Time Piece. William Cole. ELU; GrPl; PPJ
Time Poem. Quentin Hill. NBP
Time present and time past. Burnt Norton. T. S. Eliot. *Fr.* Four Quartets. CMoP; LiTM; MoAB; MoAmPo; MoPo; TwAmPo
Time quietly compiling us like sheaves. Seferis. Lawrence Durrell. EBEV
Time, Real and Imaginary. Samuel Taylor Coleridge. EnRP; NOBE; OBEV; OBRV
Time Recover'd. Thomas Stanley, *after the Italian of* Girolamo Casone. OBVE
Time Reminded Me. Julia Uceda, *tr. fr. Spanish by* Willis Barnstone. BoWoP
Time rolls his ceaseless course. The race of yore. The Gathering. Sir Walter Scott. *Fr.* The Lady of the Lake. OBNC; ViBoPo
Time runs wild on the hilltops. Wild Thyme. Eleanor Farjeon. SiSoSe

Time seems not now beneath his years to stoop. Dryden. *Fr.* To His Sacred Majesty, a Panegyrick on His Coronation, 1661. OBS
Time-Servers. Judah Halevi, *tr. fr. Hebrew by* Solomon Solis-Cohen. TrJP
Time sitting on the throne of Memory. October XXIX, 1795. William Stanley Braithwaite. CDC
Time soaked anachronism. Public School 168. Stewart Brisby. LFAC
"Time stands still." The Unbeseechable. Frances Cornford. MoBrPo
Time stands still, with gazing on her face! *Unknown.* EnLoPo
Time taken by the forelock as he flies. Bluebell. Geoffrey Taylor. NeIP
Time that bringes all things to light. Epitaph. Thomas Morton. SCAP
Time that brings children from the wizard den. Clock Symphony. John Frederick Nims. MiAP
Time that is moved by little fidget wheels. Five Bells. Kenneth Slessor. CBAP; PoAu-2; PoRA; SeCePo
Time, the Faithless. Valentin Iremonger. *See* While the Summer Trees Were Crying.
Time there was—as one may guess. Before Life and After. Thomas Hardy. FaBoRV
Time they misdirected themselves to a wake, The. The Continuance. William Bronk. GP
Time ticks away the centre of my pride. The Empty Glen. R. Crombie Saunders. OxBS
Time time said old King Tut. Don Marquis. FiBHP
Time to Be Wise. Walter Savage Landor. HBV-1; InMe
(Yes: I Write Verses.) EnRP
Time to Choose a Lover. Horace. *See* To Chloe.
Time to Dance, A, *sel.* C. Day Lewis.
Flight. MoVE
Time to Die. Ray Garfield Dandridge. BANP; PoBA
Time to get. It's Nation Time. Amiri Baraka. NoP
Time to Go. "Susan Coolidge." GN
Time to Leave Her, *with music.* *Unknown.* AmSS
Time to Myself. Paulette Jiles. NOBC
Time to put off the world and go somewhere. Beggar to Beggar Cried. W. B. Yeats. CMoP; NoAM
Time to Rise. Robert Louis Stevenson. OxBChV; SiSoSe
Time to Strike, The. Shakespeare *See* There Is a Tide.
Time to Talk, A. Robert Frost. NCSH
Time to tell you things are well, A. Snow Country Weavers. James Welch. CDW
Time to Tickle a Lizard, The. The Lizard. Theodore Roethke. GrPl; RHPC
Time to Trust, The. *Unknown.* BLRP
Time-Travel. Sharon Olds. AMV-80
Time was. Pati Hill. FAZ
Time was, an Englishman would join. James Cawthorn. *Fr.* Of Taste; an Essay. NOEC
Time was, and that was termed the time of gold. The Olden Days. Joseph Hall. *Fr.* Virgidemiarum. OBSC; OBSV
Time was away and somewhere else. Meeting Point. Louis MacNeice. ChMP
Time was he sang the British brute. Ballade of Expansion. Hilda Johnson. PAH
Time was, I shrank from what was right. Sensitiveness. Cardinal Newman. TrCP
Time was I was a plowman driving. Plowman. Sidney Keyes. MoAB; PoRA
Time was, no archer with impunity. Archers of the King. Sister Mary Genoveva. GoBC
Time was upon/ The wing, to flie away. Upon Time. Robert Herrick. OBS
Time was when his half million drew. Bewick Finzer. E. A. Robinson. AP; CMoP; CoBMV; MoAB; MoAmPo; PPP
Time was when I was weapon and warrior. Horn. *Unknown, tr. by* Charles W. Kennedy. *Fr.* Riddles (Exeter Book). AnOE
Time was when once upon a time, such toys. Epigram. Glaukos, *tr. by* Peter Jay. PeHV
Time wasted and time spent. The Times. Charles Madge. OBMV
Time wasteth years, and months, [and days], and hours. Time. Thomas Watson. *Fr.* Hecatompathia. FaBoRV; OBSC
Time We Climbed Snake Mountain, The. Leslie Silko. VoR
"Time! where didst thou those years inter." William Habington. OxBoCh
Time will assuage. To the Reader. J. V. Cunningham. NoAM; QFR
Time will come when, looking in a glass, The. The Frailty of Beauty. "J. C." *Fr.* Alcilia. ElL
Time will not be mastered, he will do just as he please. Time. Allan Taylor. OBET
Time Will Not Grant. Sidney Keyes. SeCePo
Time will say nothing but I told you so. *See* Time can say nothing . . .
Time Will Surely Come, The, *with music.* Robert T. Daniel. AH
Time winnows beauty with a fiery wind. The Harvest of Time. Harold Trowbridge Pulsifer. HBMV
Time-worn, the soldier lays aside the steel. Propertian. L. A. MacKay. *Fr.* Erotica Antiqua. PeCV
Time would not wait on me. Time and Tide. Hazel Washington Lamarre. PoNe
Time, wouldst thou hurt us? Never shall we grow old. The Double Fortress. Alfred Noyes. GoBC
Time, You Old Gypsy Man. Ralph Hodgson. BrPo; CH; FaPON; HBV-2; LiTM; MoAB; MoBrPo; MoShBr; SiSoSe; TreF; TrGrPo; ViBoPo
Time you won your town the race, The. To an Athlete Dying Young. A. E. Housman. A Shropshire Lad, XIX. BiP; BLPL; BrPo; CABA; CMoP; DL; HAP; HeIP; InPK; LiSp; LiTB; LiTM; MasP; MoAB; MoBrPo; NBM; NIP; NoAM; OAEP; PAI; PoEL-5; PoPl; PoRA; PPoe; PrIm; SeCeV; SoSe; TEP; TreF; TrGrPo; UnPo; VLP; WeW; WHA
Time Zones for Forty-four. Donald A. Stauffer. WaP
Timely blossom, infant fair. To Miss Charlotte Pulteney in Her Mother's Arms [*or* To Charlotte Pulteney]. Ambrose Philips. ELP; FaBoEn; GTBS; GTBS-P; HBV-1; NOEC; OBEC
Timepiece, The, *sel.* William Cowper. The Task, II.
"Oh for a lodge in some vast wilderness." EnRP; OAEP
(Against Slavery.) NOEC
Timepiece, A. James Merrill. HoPM; NePoEA-2; NoAM
Timers. Flora J. Arnstein. GoYe
Times, The, *sels.* Charles Churchill.
"Go where we will, at ev'ry time and place." PeHV
"Is a son born into this world of woe?" OBSV
Times, The. Charles Madge. OBMV
Times, The. *Unknown.* PAH
Time's a circumference. The Soul of Time. Trumbull Stickney. LiTA; NePA
Times ain't now nothing like they used to be, The. James Alley. *Unknown.* BluL
Time's an hand's-breadth; 'tis a tale. Time. John Huddlestone Wynne. OxBChV
Times Are Getting Hard. *Unknown.* FSW
Times are swiftly drawing nigh. When You and I Must Part. *Unknown.* AmFP
Time's Balm. Cuthbert Shaw. *Fr.* Monody to the Memory of a Young Lady. OBEC
Time's Bright Sand. Robert Finch. CaP
Time's Changes. James Bramston. *Fr.* The Art of Politics. NOEC
Times come round again, The. To a Military Rifle, 1942. Yvor Winters. MoAmPo; WaP
"Time's Conscience!" cried the allerion. For-ever Morning. Laura Riding. LiTA
Time's Dedication. Delmore Schwartz. VGW
Time's Fool. Ruth Pitter. ChMP; MoBrPo; OxBTC; PoRA; WPE
Time's Fool. John Updike. DBV
Time's fool, but not heaven's: yet hope not for any return. Time's Fool. Ruth Pitter. ChMP
Times Gettin' Hard, Boys, *with music.* *Unknown.* AS
Time's Glory. Shakespeare. *Fr.* The Rape of Lucrece. ChTr
Times Go [*or* Goe] by Turns. Robert Southwell. ACP; ElL; GoBC; HBV-2; LiTB; OBSC; OxBoCh; PoEL-2
(Tymes Goe By Turnes.) FaBoEn
Times Have Altered, The. *Unknown.* CoMu
Times have changed. Anything Goes. Cole Porter. OBAL
Times have changed, there is not left to us, The. Allen Tate. *Fr.* Sonnets of the Blood. PoA
Time's Mutability. Bertolt Brecht, *tr. fr. German by* Martin Esslin. ELU
Times o' Year. William Barnes. BoNaP
Time's Revenge. Walter Learned. HBV-1
Time's Revenges. Sir Owen Seaman. FaBoUs
Time's sea hath been five years at its slow ebb. To ———. Keats. SyP
Times she'll sit quiet by the hearth, and times. The Woodcutter's Wife. William Rose Benét. AWP
Time's Song. Winthrop Mackworth Praed. EnRP; NBM
Times Square Parade. Robert Watson. NYP
Time's Times Again. A. R. Ammons. SUW
Times wherein old Pompion was a Saint, The. New-Englands Crisis. Benjamin Tompson. SCAP
Time's winged chariot (poets say). To His Not-so-coy Mistress. Wynford Vaughan-Thomas. BXAP; NOBL
"Times without Number Have I Pray'd." Charles Wesley. OxBoCh
Timid child with heart oppressed, A. Buffalo Creek. J. Le Gay Brereton. PoAu-1
Timid Gazelle, The. Kasmuneh, *tr. fr. Arabic.* TrJP
Timid Hortense. Peter Newell. NA
Timid Lover. Countee Cullen. BANP
Timocreon. Simonides, *tr. fr. Greek by* H. W. Garrod. DBV
Timon Curses Athens and Mankind. Shakespeare. *Fr.* Timon of Athens, IV, i. TW
Timon of Archimedes. Charles Battell Loomis. NA

Timon of Athens, *sels.* Shakespeare.
Timon Curses Athens and Mankind, *fr.* IV, i. TW
Timon's Epitaph, *fr.* V, iv. AWP
"Warr'st thou 'gainst Athens?" *fr.* IV, iii. EBEV
Timon Speaks to a Dog. Philip Hobsbaum. TW
Timon's Villa. Pope. *See* Moral Essays.
Timor Mortis. *Unknown. See* Sparrow-Hawk's Complaint, The.
Timor Mortis Conturbat Me. William Dunbar. *See* Lament for the Makaris.
Timoshenko. Sidney Keyes. OBWP
Timothy Boon. Ivy O. Eastwick. SoPo; TiPo
Timothy Tiggs and Tomothy Toggs. Some Fishy Nonsense. Laura E. Richards. SoPo; TiPo
Timothy Tim was a very small cat. Tiger-Cat Tim. Edith Newlin Chase. SoPo; TiPo
Timothy Titus took two ties. *Unknown.* OxNR
Tin Cup Blues. *Unknown.* BluL
Tin Frog, The. Russell Hoban. RHPC
Tin-Ore. *Malay Oral Tradition, tr. by* W. W. Skeat. WTO
Tin shack, where my baby sleeps on his back. Everything: Eloy, Arizona, 1956. Ai. AmPA; FF
Tin-type tune the locusts make, The. Serenade. Dorothy Donnelly. NCSH
Tin Woodsman, The. Paulette Jiles. NOBC
Tinder, The. Thomas Carew. CaPo
Tinged with the blood of Aztec lands. El Vaquero. Lucius Harwood Foote. AA
Tingling, misty marvel, A. November Morning. Evaleen Stein. YeAr
Tiniest of turtles! Ladybird. Clive Sansom. GrPl
Tinker,/ Tailor. *Unknown.* OxNR; SaC
Tinker, The ("There was a lady in this land"). *Unknown.* CoMu
Tinkers, The. Joseph Campbell. OnYI
Tinker's Moon. Ewart Milne. OnYI
Tinker's Wife. Patrick Kavanagh. CIP; NoAM
Tint I cannot take is best, The. Emily Dickinson. MoAmPo
Tintadgel bells ring o'er the tide. The Silent Tower of Bottreaux. Robert Stephen Hawker. GoBC; OBRV
Tintern Abbey. Wordsworth. *See* Lines Composed a Few Miles above Tintern Abbey.
Tintock. *Unknown.* GBP
Tiny ant at night you would be seeking, The. The Disdainful Mistress. *Malay Oral Tradition, tr. by* R. J. Wilkinson *and* R. O. Winstedt. WTO
Tiny baby, you're ugly. King D. Kuka. VoR
Tiny bell the tree-toad has, A. The Tree-Toad. Orrick Johns. HBMV
Tiny children. Love Song. Yityangu Ejong, *tr. by* Frank Wordick. CBAP
Tiny fish enjoy themselves, The. Little Fish. D. H. Lawrence. OxBTC; SOTW
Tiny fleece of my own flesh. Close to Me. Gabriela Mistral, *tr. by* Langston Hughes. PoPl
Tiny fly fell down on my page, A. A Death to Us. Jon Silkin. NePoEA
Tiny green birds skate over the surface of the room. Saturday Night in the Parthenon. Kenneth Patchen. EAS
Tiny island, A. Ladybug. François Dodat, *tr. by* Bert *and* Odette Meyers. BoAnP
Tiny moon as small and white as a single jasmine flower, A. A White Blossom. D. H. Lawrence. MoBrPo
Tiny new emotions, The. Poem. Tom Clark. ConAP
Tiny nut, a bit of tasteless betel, A. Carved on an Areca Nut. Ho Xuan Huong, *tr. by* Nguyen Ngoc Bich. PBWP
Tiny slippers of gold and green. To a Pair of Egyptian Slippers. Sir Edwin Arnold. HBV-1; OBVV
Tiny snow of the stunningly cold black day. In the Snowfall. Gwerfyl Mechain, *tr. by* Willis Barnstone. BoWoP
Tiny spill of bird-things in a swirl, A. The Finches. Thomas W. Shapcott. BoAnP; PoAu-2
Tip-of-the-Single-Feather. Velema, *tr. fr. Fijian by* B. H. Quain. WTO
Tipperary Recruiting Song. *Unknown.* OnYI
Tiptoe. Karla Kuskin. PDV
Tiptoe Night. John Drinkwater. SiSoSe
Tip-Toe Tail. Dixie Willson. NTCP
Tiptoeing twilight. Twilight. Hazel Hall. HBMV
Tir-Nan-Og. J. F. Hendry. NeBP
Tirade on Tea. Phyllis McGinley. InMe
Tir'd nature's sweet restorer, balmy sleep! *See* Tired nature's sweet restorer . . .
Tir'd with all these, for restful death I cry. *See* Tired with all these . . .
Tired. Fenton Johnson. BANP; IDB; PAI; PoBA; PoLF; PoNe; TTY
Tired air groans as the heavies swing over, The. Thiepval Wood. Edmund Blunden. MMA
Tired and bloodshot. Abraham Sutskever. Seymour Mayne. VWA
Tired and thirsty, weary of the way. After the Hunt. Detlev von Liliencron, *tr. by* Ludwig Lewisohn. AWP
Tired and Unhappy, You Think of Houses. Delmore Schwartz. LiTM; MoAB; MoAmPo; NePA
Tired as I Can Be. *Unknown.* BluL
Tired brain, there is a place of rest. Quiet. Ernest Radford. OBVV
Tired cattle stumbled on the dusty trail. Babies of the Pioneers. Eunice W. Luckey. BPAW
Tired Man, The. Anna Wickham. HBMV; ViBoPo
Tired Mothers. May Riley Smith. HBV-1
Tired [*or* Tir'd] nature's sweet restorer, balmy sleep! Night. Edward Young. Night Thoughts, I. EnRP; LAuP; NOEC; OBEC; SeCePo
Tired of Eating Kisses. Edward Vincent Swart. PeSA
Tired of lips and gums. The Palace for Teeth. Abigail Luttinger. AMV-80
Tired of play! Tired of play! On the Picture of a "Child Tired of Play." Nathaniel Parker Willis. HBV-1
Tired of the bitter repose where my idleness hurts. Stéphane Mallarmé, *tr. fr. French by* Roger Fry. NAWM-2
Tired of Towns. Andrew Lang. EBVV
Tired Petitioner, The, *sel.* George Wither.
"It may be 'tis observ'd, I want Relations." SeCV-1
Tired Tim. Walter de la Mare. FaPON; MoShBr; NTCP; RHPC; SoPo; TiPo
Tired [*or* Tir'd *or* Tyr'd] with all these, for restful death I cry. Sonnets, LXVI. Shakespeare. AWP; CTC; EBEV; FaFP; GTBS; GTBS-P; HAP; InPS; LiTB; NOBE; OAEL-1; OBSC; PoEL-2; SeCeV; TrGrPo; ViBoPo; WeW; WHA
Tired with books and rolling on the bed. The New River Head, a Fragment. E. Dower. NOEC
Tired with dull grief, grown old before my day. 1916 Seen from 1921. Edmund Blunden. MMA
Tired with its dogs and doves. Summer Band Concert. Vivian Smith. CBAP
Tired with the noisome follies of the age. Earl of Rochester. *Fr.* Farewell to the Court. TrGrPo
Tired Woman, The. Anna Wickham. MoBrPo
Tired Worker, The. Claude McKay. BANP; BPo
Tireless budding and flowering of women. Image in a Lilac Tree. Terence Tiller. NeBP
Tireless flight of a pursuing gull, The. A Christmas Dawn at Sea. Evan Morgan. EtS
Tirelessly the stream licks the world until. Elk Ghosts: A Birth Memory. Dave Smith. GeTw
Tires on my bike are flat, The. Since Hanna Moved Away. Judith Viorst. RHPC
Tires revolve, blurring, The. Night Driving. Sharyn November. AMV-80
Tiresias, *sel.* Austin Clarke.
"My mother wept loudly." CIP
Tiresias. George Garrett. NePoAm-2
Tiresias. Tennyson. VLP
Tiresias' Lament. Ellen de Young Kay. NePoEA
Tiring of rest, of plain and fruitless toil. The Dreamer. Dorothy Gould. PGD
Tirocinium; or, A Review of Schools, *sels.* William Cowper.
"Father, who designs his babe a priest, The." OBSV
"To you, then, tenants of life's middle state." OBSV
"Would you your son should be a sot or dunce." OBSV
'Tis a dull sight. Old Song [*or* The Meadows in Spring]. Edward Fitzgerald. GN; HBV-1; OBEV; OBVV
" 'Tis a hundred years," said the bosun bold. The Whale. *Unknown.* EtS
'Tis a lesson you should heed. Try, Try Again. *Unknown, at. to* T. H. Palmer. FaFP; FaPON; TreF
'Tis a new life;—thoughts move not as they did. The New Birth. Jones Very. AP; NOBA
'Tis a sad land, that in one day. Death. Henry Vaughan. NCEP
'Tis a soft Rogue, this Lycias. Lycias. Earl of Rochester. ErPo
'Tis a world of silences. I gave a cry. Silences. Arthur O'Shaughnessy. OBNC; VLP
'Tis advertised in Boston, New York and Buffalo. Blow Ye Winds in the Morning. *Unknown.* AmFP; AmSS; FSW
'Tis affection but dissembled. Song. Sidney Godolphin. JCP
'Tis all a myth that Autumn grieves. Autumn's Mirth. Samuel Minturn Peck. GN
'Tis all the way to Toe-town. Foot Soldiers. John Banister Tabb. HBV-1; HBVY; OBAL
'Tis an act of the priest to give patience a test. Matrimony. John Williams. NOEC
'Tis an old maxim in the schools. Flattery. Swift. *Fr.* Cadenus and Vanessa. PV; TreFT
'Tis bad enough in man or woman. On Inclosures [*or* Epigram: On Inclosures *or* On Enclosures]. *Unknown.* FaBoCo; FaBoEE; OxBoLi
'Tis bedtime; say your hymn, and bid "Good-night." Bedtime. Francis Robert St. Clair Erskine. HBV-1; HBVY; OBVV

'Tis better to be vile than vile esteemed. Sonnets, CXXI. Shakespeare. InvP; OAEL-1; PoEL-2
Tis braul I cudgel, ranters, Quakers braul. Claudius Gilbert. John Wilson. SCAP
'Tis but a foil at best, and that's the most. Emblem. Francis Quarles. Emblems, II, 14. LoBV
'Tis but a Little Faded Flower. Ellen Clementine Howarth. AA; HBV-2
'Tis but a Wanton Trick. *See* Wanton Trick, The.
Tis clear, Great Dane, thy barque's worse than thy bite. King Canute. Stanley J. Sharpless. BXAP
'Tis curiosity's benefit night. Her Fancy Ball. Thomas Hood. *Fr.* Miss Kilmansegg and Her Precious Leg. VLP
'Tis day, my crystal Usk: now the sad night. "So Have I Spent on the Banks of Ysca Many a Serious Hour." Thomas Vaughan. FaBoPP
'Tis dead night round about: Horror [*or* Horrour] doth creep[e]. The Lamp[e]. Henry Vaughan. AnAnS-1; QFR
'Tis done, the edict past, by Heaven decreed. Ode to the Fourth of July. Daniel George. TrAS
'Tis "Done"—the wondrous thoroughfare. The Pacific Railway. C. R. Ballard. PAH
'Tis down in the valley my father does dwell. The Only Daughter. *Unknown.* OBET
'Tis easy enough to be twenty-one. Responsibility. *Unknown.* FaBoUs; PV
'Tis education forms the common mind. As the Twig Is Bent. Pope. Moral Essays, 2 *ll. fr.* Epistle I. TreF
'Tis eight o'clock—a clear March night. The Idiot Boy. Wordsworth. OBNV
'Tis evening: the black snail has got on his track. Evening. John Clare. VLP
'Tis fine to play/ In the fragrant hay. A Boy's Summer Song. Paul Laurence Dunbar. SiSoSe
'Tis fine to see the Old World, and travel up and down. America for Me. Henry van Dyke. BLPA; BLPL; FaFP; HBVY; OHFP; PAL; SoSe; TreFS; WBLP
'Tis from high life high characters are drawn. The Gem and the Flower. Pope. *Fr.* Moral Essays, Epistle I. OBEC
'Tis God that girds our armor on. The American Soldier's Hymn. *Unknown.* PAH
'Tis gone, that bright and orbèd blaze. Evening. John Keble. TrPWD; VLP
'Tis goodbye then to last night. Soraidh Slan Don Oidhche Areir. Niall Mor MacMuireadach, *tr. by* Maire Cruise O'Brien. BIrV
'Tis Hard to Find God. Robert Herrick. LiTB
'Tis hard to find in life. True Friendship. *Unknown, tr. by* Arthur W. Ryder. *Fr.* The Panchatantra. AWP
'Tis hard to say, if greater want of skill. An Essay on Criticism. Pope. CABA; FaBoEn; FiP; HAP; OAEL-1; OAEP; PoEL-3; PP; WHA
'Tis highly rational, we can't dispute. Epigram. Richard Garnett. HBV-1
'Tis human fortune's happiest height, to be. Epigram. Sir William Watson. TreFT
'Tis I Go Fiddling, Fiddling. Nora Hopper. *See* Fairy Fiddler, The.
'Tis in the spirit that attire. Elegance. Christopher Smart. Hymns for the Amusement of Children, Hymn 13. NOCV
'Tis known, at least it should be, that throughout. Beppo; a Venetian Story. Byron. NOBL; OBNV; OBSV
'Tis Late and Cold. John Fletcher. *See* Dead Host's Welcome, The.
'Tis late; the astronomer in his lonely height. The Appointment. Sully Prudhomme, *tr. by* Arthur O'Shaughnessy. OxBI
'Tis life in a half-breed shack. Life in a Half-breed Shack. *Unknown.* CoSo
'Tis like stirring living embers when, at eighty, one remembers. Grandmother's Story of Bunker-Hill Battle. Oliver Wendell Holmes. PAH
'Tis little I can give you, yet I can give you these. Oblation. A. Newberry Choyce. HBMV
T'is madnesse to give Physicke to the dead. Upon Castara's Absence. William Habington. AnAnS-2
'Tis Merry in Greenwood. Sir Walter Scott. *Fr.* Harold the Dauntless. FaPON; OHIP
'Tis Midnight. *Unknown.* NA; NTCP
'Tis Midnight and on Olive's Brow. William B. Tappan. AH, *with music* (Gethsemane.) STF
'Tis Midnight, and the setting sun. 'Tis Midnight. *Unknown.* NA; NTCP
'Tis midnight o'er the dim mere's lonely bosom. Midnight. Tennyson. VLP
'Tis mirth that fills the veins with blood. Mirth [*or* Laugh and Sing]. Beaumont *and* Fletcher. *Fr.* The Knight of the Burning Pestle. EIL; TrGrPo
'Tis more than Spaniel's place is worth. Spaniel's Sermon. Colin Ellis. PV
'Tis morning; and the sun with ruddy orb. The Winter Morning Walk [*or* A Frosty Morning]. William Cowper. The Task, V. LAuP; NOEC; PoEL-3
'Tis mute, the word they went to hear on high Dodona mountain. The Oracles. A. E. Housman. HAP; OAEP; RoGo
'Tis Nancy's birth-day—raise your strains. On My Wife's Birth-Day. Christopher Smart. NAs
'Tis never or but seldom known. Power and Peace. Robert Herrick. CaPo
'Tis nigh two thousand years. Lewis Morris. *Fr.* Christmas 1898. TrPWD
'Tis noonday by the buttonwood, with slender-shadowed bud. The Minute-Men of Northboro'. Wallace Rice. PAH
'Tis not a year or two shows us a man. Shakespeare. *Fr.* Othello, III, iv. DBV
'Tis not by brooding on delight. Marcus Curtius. Oliver St. John Gogarty. OBMV
'Tis not by guilt the onward sweep. Edward Rowland Sill. *Fr.* The Fool's Prayer. TrPWD
'Tis not enough for one that is a wife. Lady Elizabeth Carey. *Fr.* Mariam, III. WPE
'Tis not enough that Christ was born. Day Dawn of the Heart. *Unknown.* PGD
'Tis not ev'ry day that I. Not Every Day Fit for Verse. Robert Herrick. PoRA
'Tis not for the unfeeling, the falsely refined. The Farmer of Tilsbury Vale. Wordsworth. EBEV
'Tis not great, what I solicit. John Clare. *Fr.* Address to Plenty. OBRV
'Tis not her birth, her friends, nor yet her treasure. Why I Love Her. Alexander Brome. HBV-1
'Tis not how witty, nor how free. Upon Kinde and True Love. Aurelian Townshend. CavP; MeLP; MePo; OBS
'Tis not in blood that Liberty inscribes her civil laws. True Freedom. Charles MacKay. PGD
'Tis not my ladies face that makes me love her. Love's without Reason. Alexander Brome. OBS
'Tis not on the face displayed. The Bedlamite. Thomas Mozeen. NOEC
'Tis not so much, these men more forms survey. Charles Lloyd. *Fr.* An Essay on the Genius of Pope. OBRV
'Tis not that both my eyes are black. The Penalties of Baldness. Sir Owen Seaman. FiBHP
'Tis not that dying hurts us so. Emily Dickinson. BoWoP
'Tis not that I am weary grown. Upon [His] Leaving His Mistress. Earl of Rochester. EnLoPo; GBL; TEP; TrGrPo; UnTE; ViBoPo
'Tis not that I design to rob. An Epistle to Robert Lloyd, Esq. William Cowper. FiP
'Tis not that love is less or sorrow more. Fear Has Cast Out Love. Wilfrid Scawen Blunt. The Love Sonnets of Proteus, XXXVI. VLP
'Tis not the babbling of a busy world. Conscience. Charles Churchill. *Fr.* The Conference. OBEC
'Tis not the gaudy stream of rosy flame. Self-Consciousness Makes All Changes Happy; Ode. Jonathan Richardson. NOEC
'Tis not the President alone. McKinley. *Unknown.* PAH
'Tis not your beauty can engage. To Flavia. Edmund Waller. HBV-1
'Tis now clear[e] day: I see a rose. The Search. Henry Vaughan. AnAnS-1; SBVL; SeCP
'Tis now since I began to dy. Upon Absence. Katherine Philips. PBWP
'Tis Now, Since I Sat[e] Down Before. Sir John Suckling. AnAnS-2; CavP; PoEL-3; SeCV-1
(Besieged Heart, The.) TrGrPo
(Love's Siege.) CaPo; JCP
(Siege, The.) OxBoLi; SeCP; ViBoPo
'Tis now the very witching time of night. The Witching Time of Night. Shakespeare. *Fr.* Hamlet, III, ii. TreFT
'Tis now we'd want to be wary, boys. Tipperary Recruiting Song. *Unknown.* OnYI
'Tis of a blind beggar who a long time was blind. The Blind Beggar. *Unknown.* AmFP
'Tis of a brave young highwayman. Brennan on the Moor. *Unknown.* FSW
'Tis of a brisk young Farmer, in Derbyshire did dwell. The Frolicsome Farmer. *Unknown.* CoMu; UnTE
'Tis of a fearless Irishman. Brennan on the Moor. *Unknown.* BaBo
'Tis of a gallant Yankee ship that flew the stripes and stars. The Yankee Man-of-War. *Unknown.* AA; AmSS; Ets; FaBoBe; PAH; PaPo
'Tis of a handsome female as you may understand. The Handsome Cabin Boy. *Unknown.* FSW
'Tis of a jolly soldier that lately came from war. The Jolly Soldier. *Unknown.* AmFP
'Tis of a lady both fair and handsome. The Servant Man. *Unknown.* AmFP
'Tis of a little drummer. The Little Drummer. Richard Henry Stoddard. PAH
'Tis of a pedlar, a pedlar trim. The Bold Pedlar and Robin Hood. *Unknown.* AmFP

'Tis [*or* Oh! 'tis] of a rich merchant who in London did dwell. Villikins [*or* Vilikins] and His Dinah. *At. to* Edward Laman Blanchard; *also at. to* Sam Cowell. FSW; VLP
'Tis of a sad and dismal story that happened off the fatal rock. The Loss of the *New Columbia. Unknown.* AmFP
'Tis of a silk merchant in London I write. The Silk Merchant's Daughter, *vers.* II. *Unknown.* ShS
'Tis of a stately Southerner who flew the Stripes and Stars. The Stately Southerner. *Unknown.* ShS
'Tis of a wild Colonial boy, Jack Doolan [*or* Dulan] was his name. The Wild Colonial Boy. *Unknown.* FaBoBa; FSW; PoAn-1; ViBoFo
'Tis of my country that I would endite. Ezra Pound. *Fr.* L'Homme Moyen Sensuel. OBSV
'Tis of the Father Hilary. World's Worth. Dante Gabriel Rossetti. GoBC; VLP
'Tis oft I'm tired of an old man. An Old Man He Courted Me. *Unknown.* OBET
'Tis on Eilanowen. The Faëry Reaper. Robert Buchanan. OBVV
'Tis only a half truth the poet has sung. Crowded Ways of Life. Walter S. Gresham. BLPA
'Tis pleasing to be schooled in a strange tongue. Byron. *Fr.* Don Juan. ViBoPo
'Tis queer, it is, the ways o' men. The Ways o' Men. Angelina Weld Grimké. CDC
'Tis raging noon; and vertical, the sun. James Thomson. *Fr.* The Seasons: Summer. EBEV; OAEL-1
'Tis religion that can give. The Satisfying Portion. *Unknown.* BLRP
'Tis right for her to sleep between. In Memoriam. Richard Monckton Milnes. HBV-2
'Tis sad to see the sons of learning. He That Never Read a Line. *Unknown, tr. by* Robin Flower. AnIL
'Tis said, as Cupid danced among. How Roses Came Red. Robert Herrick. ChTr
'Tis said that absence conquers love! Song. Frederick William Thomas. AA; HBV-1
'Tis Said That Some Have Died for Love. Wordsworth. EnRP; LO
'Tis said that the gods on Olympus of old. The Mint Julep. Charles Fenno Hoffman. AA
'Tis said the Gods lower down that chain above. George Alsop. SCAP
'Tis so much joy! 'tis so much joy! Emily Dickinson. NOCV
'Tis solemn darkness; the sublime of shade. Night. Charles Heavysege. OBCV
'Tis something from that tangle to have won. Icarus. Harry Lyman Koopman. AA
'Tis Sorrow Builds the Shining Ladder Up. James Russell Lowell. WGRP
'Tis spring; come out to ramble. The Lent Lily. A. E. Housman. A Shropshire Lad, XXIX. OHIP; PoSC
'Tis spring, warm glows the south. Birds' Nests. John Clare. OAEL-2; VLP
'Tis still observ'd, that Fame ne'er sings. Fame. Robert Herrick. FaBoEE
'Tis Strange. Eugene Field. TDH
'Tis strange how my head runs on! 'tis a puzzle to understand. The City Clerk. Thomas Ashe. EBVV; OBVV
'Tis strange, the miser should his cares employ. To Richard Boyle, Earl of Burlington [*or* Of the Use of Riches]. Pope. Moral Essays, Epistle IV. OAEL-1; PoEL-3; PPP
'Tis Strange to Me. Hartley Coleridge. NCEP
(From Country to Town.) OBRV
'Tis summer time on Bredon. Hugh Kingsmill. FaBoCo; NOBL
. . .'Tis sweet to hear,/At midnight on the blue and moonlit deep. Byron. *Fr.* Don Juan, I. ViBoPo
'Tis sweet to hear of heroes dead. The Great Adventure. Henry David Thoreau. HBV-2; OBVV
'Tis sweet to hear the merry lark. Song. Hartley Coleridge. HBV-1
'Tis sweet to hear the watch-dog's honest bark. First Love. Byron. *Fr.* Don Juan, I. OBRV
'Tis Sweet to Rest in Lively Hope. *Unknown.* AmFP
'Tis Sweet to Roam. *Unknown.* NA
'Tis sweet to trace the setting sun. The Setting Sun. George Moses Horton. BALP
'Tis sweet to view, from half-past five to six. The Theatre. Horace Smith *and* James Smith. Par
'Tis the Arabian bird alone. The Chaste Arabian Bird. Earl of Rochester. ErPo
'Tis the blithest, bonniest weather for a bird to flirt a feather. Robin's Secret. Katharine Lee Bates. AA
'Tis the Gift to Be Simple, *with music. Unknown.* AH
'Tis the great art of life to manage well. Madness. John Armstrong. *Fr.* The Art of Preserving Health. NOEC
'Tis the hour of fairy ban and spell. Fairy Dawn. Joseph Rodman Drake. *Fr.* The Culprit Fay. GN
'Tis the hour when white-horsed Day. Morning. Charles Stuart Calverley. FiBHP; NBM
'Tis the human touch in this world that counts. The Human Touch. Spencer Michael Free. BLPA; FaBoBe
'Tis the Last Rose of Summer. Thomas Moore. BLPA; BoNaP; ELP; FPL; HBV-1; PoEL-4; PoPl; TreF; WBLP; WHA
(Last Rose of Summer, The.) FaBoBe; FaFP; FSW; OnYI; OxBoLi
'Tis the laughter of pines that swing and sway. The Phantom Light of the Baie des Chaleurs. Arthur Wentworth Hamilton Eaton. CaP
'Tis the merry Nightingale. Samuel Taylor Coleridge. *Fr.* The Nightingale. OBRV
'Tis the middle of night by the castle clock. Christabel. Samuel Taylor Coleridge. CH; EnRP; FiP; GoTL; OAEL-2; OAEP; OBRV; SeCePo; WHA
"Tis the Octoroon ball! And the halls are alight!" Ballade des Belles Milatraisses. Rosalie Jonas. BlSi
'Tis the terror of tempest. The rags of the sail. A Vision of the Sea. Shelley. MOS
'Tis the voice of a sluggard; I heard him complain. *See* 'Tis the voice of the sluggard . . .
'Tis the voice of the Lobster: I heard him declare. Alice's Recitation [*or* The Lobster *or* The Voice of the Lobster]. "Lewis Carroll." *Fr.* Alice's Adventures in Wonderland, *ch.* 10. EvOK; FaBoCo; FaBoNo; NOBL; OxBChV; Par; SpRo
'Tis the voice of the [*or* a] sluggard; I heard him complain. The Sluggard. Isaac Watts. CH; HAP; HBV-1; HBVY; MoShBr; NOEC; OBEC; OxBChV; OxBoLi; PaPo; Par; PoEL-3; SpRo; TreFS
'Tis the week before Christmas and every night. For the Children or the Grown-ups? *Unknown.* OBCP
'Tis the white anemone, fashioned so. "Owen Meredith." *Fr.* The White Anemone. GN
'Tis the White Plum Tree. Shaw Neilson. PoAu-1
'Tis the witching hour of night. Keats. TEP
'Tis the year's [*or* yeares] midnight, and it is the day's [*or* dayes]. A Nocturnal[l] upon Saint Lucy's [*or* S. Lucies] Day, Being the Shortest Day. John Donne. AnAnS-1; EBEV; EnRePo; FaBoEn; GBL; JCP; LiTB; MeLP; MePo; NOBE; NoP; OAEL-1; OBS; PoEL-2; PoPle; PPP; SeCP; SeCV-1; TEP
'Tis these that free the small entangled fly. Shakespeare: The Fairies' Advocate. Thomas Hood. *Fr.* The Plea of the Midsummer Fairies. OBNC
'Tis time, I think, by Wenlock town. Wenlock Edge. A. E. Housman. A Shropshire Lad, XXXIX. FaBoPP; PoPle; SeCePo
'Tis time this heart should be unmoved. On This Day I Complete My Thirty-sixth Year. Byron. CABA; EnRP; FiP; HBV-1; NAs; NoP; OAEL-2; OAEP; OBWP; TreFT; ViBoPo
'Tis to yourself I speak; you cannot know. Yourself. Jones Very. AA; NePA; NOBA; OxBA; PoEL-4
'Tis told by one whom stormy waters threw. Wordsworth. *Fr.* The Prelude, VI. ImOP
Tis true (deare Ben:) thy just chastizing hand. To Ben Jonson [*or* Johnson]. Thomas Carew. AnAnS-2; CaPo; MePo
'Tis true, fair Celia, that by thee I live. Against Platonick Love. *Unknown.* OBS
'Tis true I write and tell me by what rule. The Appology. Countess of Winchilsea. SBG
'Tis true, I'm broke! Vowes, oathes, and all I had. An Elegie. Ben Jonson. AnAnS-2
'Tis true, no Lover has that Pow'r. The Art of Love. Samuel Butler. *Fr.* Hudibras. FaBoEn
'Tis true, one half of woman's life is hope. Her Horoscope. Mary Ashley Townsend. AA
'Tis true, 'tis day; what though it be? Break[e] of Day. John Donne. CABA; EnRePo; ErPo; LiTB
'Tis true—then why should I repine. In Sickness [Written Soon after the Author's Coming to Live in Ireland, upon the Queen's Death, October 1714]. Swift. NOEC; OBEC
'Tis true—they shut me in the cold. Emily Dickinson. SBG
'Tis weak and worldly to conclude. The Retirement. *Unknown.* OBEC
'Tis well; 'tis something; we may stand. Tennyson. In Memoriam A. H. H., XVIII. EBVV
'Tis what they say. The Red Man's Wife. *Unknown, tr. by* Douglas Hyde. OnYI; OxBI; SeCePo
'Tis Winter Now, *with music.* Samuel Longfellow. AH
'Tis with our judgments as our watches, none. Pope. *Fr.* An Essay on Criticism. ViBoPo
Tissue. Susan Griffin. NPGG
Tit for Tat; a Tale. John Aikin. OxBChV
Tit, tat, toe. *Unknown.* OxNR
Titan! to whose immortal eyes. Prometheus. Byron. EnRP; InPS; NOBE; NoP; OAEL-2
Titania. Thomas Hood. *Fr.* The Plea of the Midsummer Fairies. OBRV

Titanic, The, *sels.* E. J. Pratt.
Final Moments, The. NOBC
"Out on the water was the same display." PeCV
Titanic, De, *with music. Unknown.* AS
Titanic, The ("It was on one Monday morning . . ."). *Unknown.* AmFP; ViBoFo (A *vers.*)
Titanic, The ("Oh they built the ship *Titanic* . . ."). *Unknown.* FSW
Titanic Blues ("Early in the morning just about four o'clock"). *Unknown.* BluL
Titans, The. Betti Alver, *tr. fr. Estonian by* Willis Barnstone *and* Felix Oinas. BoWoP
Tithe, The: To the Bride. Robert Herrick. CaPo
Tithonus. Tennyson. CABA; FaBoEn; HAP; LiTB; LoBV; NOBE; NoP; OAEL-2; OAEP; OBNC; PAI; PoEL-5; PoPle; PPP; TEP; VLP; WHA
Title divine—is mine! Emily Dickinson. AP; NOBA; ViBoPo
Title of a Swift Horse. *Mongol Oral Tradition, tr. by* C. R. Bawden. WTO
Titmouse. Walter de la Mare. BrPo
Tittery-Irie-Aye. *Unknown.* AmFP
Titty cum tawtay. *Unknown.* OxNR
Titus and Berenice. John Heath-Stubbs. GTBS-P
Titus reads neither prose nor rhyme. The Writer. Hildebrand Jacob. FaBoCo
"Titus, Son of Rembrandt: 1665." Richard J. Lyons. AMV-81
Titwillow. W. S. Gilbert. *See* Suicide's Grave, The.
Tityrus to His Fair Phyllis. John Dickenson. *Fr.* The Shepherd's Complaint. ElL
Tlanusi' Yi, the Leech Place. Gladys Cardiff. CDW; STE; TWSS
Tlingit Concrete Poem. Nora Dauenhauer, *after the German of* Reinhold Döhl. TWSS
To ("A child (a boy) bouncing"). William Carlos Williams. OBAL
To ———: "All good things have not kept aloof." Tennyson. OBRV
To ———: "Asleep within the deadest hour of night." Robert Nichols. HBMV
To ———: "Half in the dim light from the hall." William Stanley Braithwaite. BALP; PoBA
To ———: "I fear thy kisses, gentle maiden." Shelley. *See* I Fear Thy Kisses, Gentle Maiden.
To ———?: "I have baptized the Withy, because of thy slender lambs." Richard Dehmel, *tr. fr. German by* Jethro Bithell. AWP
To ———in Church. Alan Seeger. HBV-1
To ———: "Music, when soft voices die." Shelley. *See* Music, When Soft Voices Die.
To ———: "One word is too often profaned." Shelley. BoLoP; ELP; EnRP; FaBoEn; FaBV; HBV-1; LoBV; NOBE; OAEP; OBEV; OBNC; PoLF; PPP; TrGrPo; ViBoPo
(Love.) FiP
(One Word Is Too Often Profaned.) BLPL; GTBS; GTBS-P; LiTB; OBRV; TreFT; WHA
To ———: "They could not shut you out of heaven." Katharine Morse. HBMV
To ———: "Time's sea hath been five years at its slow ebb." Keats. SyP
To ———: "We met but in one giddy dance." Winthrop Mackworth Praed. HBV-1
To ———: "What can I do to drive away." Keats. OAEL-2
To ———: "When I loved you, I can't but allow." Thomas Moore. *See* When I Loved You.
To ———: "When passion's trance is overpast." Shelley. EnRP
To ———, with an Ivory Hand-Glass. Lord Alfred Douglas. FaBoUs
To ———: With the Following Poem. Tennyson. *Introd. poem to* The Palace of Art. VLP
To a Bad Heart. Tim Reynolds. TW
To a Baked Fish. Carolyn Wells. FiBHP
To a Baseball. *Unknown.* LiSp
To a Bed of Tulips. Robert Herrick. CaPo
To a Bicycle. *Unknown.* BXAP
To a Bird after a Storm. Henry Vaughan. *See* Bird, The.
To a Blossoming Pear Tree. James Wright. HAP
To a Blue Flower. Shaw Neilson. PoAu-1
To a Blue Hippopotamus. Ellen de Young Kay. NePoEA
To a Book. Elinor Wylie. LiTA
To a Boon Companion. Oliver St. John Gogarty. OBMV
To a Boy. *Unknown, tr. fr. Irish by* Frank O'Connor. KiLC
To a Boy-Poet of the Decadence. Sir Owen Seaman. CenHV; FiBHP
To a Brown Girl. Ossie Davis. PoNe
To a Bull-Dog. J. C. Squire. FM
To a Butterfly. W. H. Davies. FM
To a Butterfly. L. Pearl Schuck. AMV-80
To a Butterfly. Wordsworth. EnRP; FM; HBV-1; SeCeV
To a Cactus Seller. Anwar Shaul, *tr. fr. Arabic by* Yoffee Berkovitz. VWA
To a Calvinist in Bali. Edna St. Vincent Millay. NoAM
To a Candle. Walter de la Mare. ChMP; ELP
To a Captain in Sinai. Ada Aharoni. AMV-81
To a Captious Critic. Paul Laurence Dunbar. BPo
To a Cat. Hartley Coleridge. FM
To a Cat. Keats. FaBoCh; PCat
(On Mrs. Reynolds's Cat.) FM
To a Cat. Swinburne. PCat
To a Caty-did. Philip Freneau. AA; TAP
To a Certain Lady, in Her Garden. Sterling A. Brown. CDC
To a Certain Most Certainly Certain Critic. David McCord. OBAL
To a Chameleon. Marianne Moore. GoYe; PoPl
To a Cherokee Rose. William Hamilton Hayne. AA
To a Child. S. S. Gardons. NePoEA-2
To a Child, *sel.* Longfellow.
"By what astrology of fear or hope." FaBoEn
To a Child. George Edgar Montgomery. AA
To a Child. Christopher Morley. HBMV
To a Child. Norreys Jephson O'Conor. *See* To a Child (With a Copy of the Author's "Hansel and Gretel").
To a Child. Wordsworth. HBV-1; HBVY; OxBChV
(In a Child's Album.) GN
(Written in the Album of a Child.) OBRV
To a Child before Birth. Norman Nicholson. ChMP; NAs
To a Child Born in Time of Small War. Helen Sorrells. WPE
To a Child Five Years Old. Nathaniel Cotton. OxBChV
To a Child in Death. Charlotte Mew. MoAB; MoBrPo
To a Child of Fancy. Lewis Morris. HBV-1
To a Child of Quality [Five Years Old, the Author Supposed Forty]. Matthew Prior. GN; HBV-1; LiTB; NiP; NOBE; NOEC; OBEC; OBEV; PoEL-3; SeCeV
To a Child Running with Outstretched Arms in the Canyon de Chelly. N. Scott Momaday. CDW
To a Child Trapped in a Barber Shop. Philip Levine. InPK; NoAM; NOBA; PAI; TAP; VGW
To a Child Who Inquires. Olga Petrova. BLPA
To a Child (With a Copy of the Author's "Hansel and Gretel"). Norreys Jephson O'Conor. DFT
(To a Child.) HBMV
To a Christmas Two-Year-Old. Luci Shaw. TrCP
To a Common Prostitute. Walt Whitman. MoAmPo; ViBoPo
To a Comrade in Arms. Alun Lewis. FaBoTw; MoBrPo
To a Conscript of 1940. Sir Herbert Read. ChMP; LiTB; LiTM; OBWP; WaP
To a Contemporary Bunkshooter. Carl Sandburg. WGRP
To a Courtesan a Thousand Years Dead. Paul Eldridge. PoA
To a Covetous Churl. Edward May. FaBoEE
To a Cricket. William Cox Bennett. GN; HBV-1
To a Crow. Robert Burns Wilson. AA
To a Crucifix. Anna Wickham. MoBrPo
To A. D. W. E. Henley. *See* Blackbird, The.
To a Daisy. Alice Meynell. MoBrPo; WGRP
To a Dark Girl. Gwendolyn B. Bennett. BANP; BlSi; CDC; PoBA
To a Daughter with Artistic Talent. Peter Meinke. Psk
To a Dead Elephant. Douglas Livingstone. PeSA
To a Dead Journalist. William Carlos Williams. QFR
To a Deaf and Dumb Little Girl. Hartley Coleridge. PoEL-4; VLP
To a Defeated Saviour. James Wright. NePoEA
To a Departing Favorite. George Moses Horton. BALP
To a Depraved Lying Woman. Sorley Maclean. NeBP
To a Dictatorial Sultan. *Somali Oral Tradition, tr. by* B. W. Andrzejewski. WTO
To a Distant Friend. Wordsworth. *See* Why Art Thou Silent.
To a Dog. Josephine Preston Peabody. BLPA; WGRP
To a Dog Injured in the Street. William Carlos Williams. LCAP; LiTM; MoAB; NePoAm; PP; SeCeV
To a Fair Lady Playing with a Snake. Edmund Waller. EBEV; HoPM; NCEP
(Of a Fair Lady Playing with a Snake.) PoEL-3
To a Faithless Friend. Salaan Arrabey, *tr. fr. Somali by* M. Laurence. WTO
To a Faithless Lover. Robert Greacen. OnYI
To a Fat Lady Seen from the Train. Frances Cornford. BLPA; ELU; GoJo; MoBrPo; OBMV; SpRo; WeW
To a Field Mouse. Burns. *See* To a Mouse.
To a Fighter Killed in the Ring. Lou Lipsitz. LiSp
To a Fine Young Woman. William Wycherley. TW
To a Fish. Leigh Hunt. *Fr.* The Fish, the Man, and the Spirit. FiBHP; MOS; NOBL
To a Flea in a Glass of Water. D. A. Greig. PeSA
To a Fly, Taken out of a Bowl of Punch. "Peter Pindar." NOEC
To a Foreign Friend. Leonard Nathan. GP
To a Friend. Matthew Arnold. OAEP
To a Friend. Hartley Coleridge. HBV-2; OBRV; PoLF
(Friendship.) OBEV
(Sonnet: To a Friend.) OBNC

To a Friend. James Fenimore Cooper. PeHV
To a Friend. Grace Stricker Dawson. BLPA
To a Friend. Charles Gullans. NePoEA
To a Friend. Amy Lowell. FPL; PoLF
To a Friend Concerning Several Ladies. William Carlos Williams. VGW
To a Friend Going on a Journey. Mahammed Abdille Hassan, *tr. fr. Somali by* M. Laurence. WTO
To a Friend in Love during the Riots. William Parsons. NOEC
To a Friend in the Country. Oliver St. John Gogarty. OnYI
To a Friend, Inviting Him to a Meeting upon Promise. William Habington. AnAnS-2
To a Friend, on Her Examination for the Doctorate in English. J. V. Cunningham. TwAmPo; VGW
To a Friend on His Marriage. F. T. Prince. LiTM
To a Friend Whose Work Has Come to Nothing. W. B. Yeats. AWP; BiP; LiTM; MoAB; MoBrPo; OAEL-2; OBMV; PoA
To a Friend's Child. Aliki Barnstone. BoWoP
To a Gentleman and Lady on the Death of the Lady's Brother and Sister, and a Child of the Name Avis, Aged One Year. Phillis Wheatley. BlSi
To a Gentleman, Who Desired Proper Materials for a Monody. *Unknown.* NOEC
To a Gentlewoman Objecting to Him His Grey Hairs. Robert Herrick. CaPo; JCP
(Age Not to Be Rejected.) OBS
To a Girl. Horace. *See* To Pyrrha.
To a Girl. Edmund Waller. *See* To a Very Young Lady.
To a Gnat. *Unknown, tr. fr. Greek by* Louis Untermeyer. UnTE
To a God Unknown. David Eller. VWA
To a Golden Heart, Worn round His Neck. Goethe, *tr. fr. German by* Margaret Fuller Ossoli. AWP
To a Golden-haired Girl in a Louisiana Town. Vachel Lindsay. MoAmPo
To a Gone Era. Irma McClaurin. BlSi
To a Good Physician. William Wycherley. ACP
To a Goose [*or* Gosse]. Robert Southey. BXAP; FM; NOBL
To a Greek Girl. Austin Dobson. HBV-1
To a Greek Ship in the Port of Dublin. William Bedell Stanford. NeIP
To a Hedgehog. Samuel Thompson. BIrV
To a Hero Dead at al-Safra. Hind bint Uthatha, *tr. fr. Arabic by* Bridget Connelly *and* Deirdre Lashgari. WPOW
To a Highland Girl. Wordsworth. EnRP; LoBV; TreFT, *abr.*
(To the Highland Girl of Inversneyde.) GTBS; GTBS-P
To a History Professor. *Unknown, tr. by* Louis Untermeyer. UnTE
To a Honey Bee. Philip Freneau. *See* On a Honey Bee.
To a Horse. Jill Hoffman. PH
To a Human Skeleton. Richard Armour. WhC
To a Humble Bug. Linda Lyon Van Voorhis. GoYe
To a Hurt Child. Grace Denio Litchfield. AA
To a Husband. Maya Angelou. IHMS
To a Jack Rabbit. S. Omar Barker. BPAW
To a Jilt. Martin Armstrong. FaBoEE
To a June Breeze. H. C. Bunner. AA
To a Junior Waiter. A. P. Herbert. FiBHP
To a king who had. King Rufus. Y. Y. Segal, *tr. by* A. M. Klein. WHW
To a Kiss. "Peter Pindar." HBV-1
To A. L.: Perswasions [*or* Persuasions] to Love. Thomas Carew. AnAnS-2; CaPo; SeCP
To a Lad Who Would Wed Himself with Music. Edward Doro. TwAmPo
To a Lady. Franklin P. Adams. FiBHP
To a Lady [*or* Ladye]. William Dunbar. BSV; EBEV; GBL; GoBC, *mod. vers. by* Belle Cooper; OAEP; OBEV; OxBS
(Sweet Rose of Virtue.) MeEL
To a Lady. John Gay. OBEV
To a Lady. J. B. Morton. POL
To a Lady. Thomas William Parsons. AA
To a Lady. John James Piatt. AA
To a Lady across the Way. E. B. White. InMe
To a Lady Asking Him How Long He Would Love Her. Sir George Etherege. HBV-1; LoBV; OBEV; ViBoPo
To a Lady Friend. W. H. Davies. MoBrPo
To a Lady Holding the Floor. Mildred Weston. FiBHP
To a Lady in a Garden. Edmund Waller. NCEP
To a Lady; of the Characters of Women. Pope. *See* Moral Essays.
To a Lady on Her Passion for Old China. John Gay. FaFP; LiTB; LoBV; OBEC
To a Lady on Her Marriage. William Bell. NePoEA
To a Lady on Reading Sherlock "Upon Death". Earl of Chesterfield. *See* Verses Written in a Lady's Sherlock upon Death.
To a Lady on the Death of Her Husband. Phillis Wheatley. TAP
To a Lady: She Refusing to Continue a Dispute with Me, and Leaving Me in the Argument. Matthew Prior. NoP; WHA
To a Lady Sitting before Her Glass. Elijah Fenton. OBEC
To a Lady That Desired I Would Love Her. Thomas Carew. AnAnS-2; CaPo; CavP; LoBV; MeLP; MePo; OBS; SeCV-1
To a Lady That Desired Me I Would Bear My Part with Her in a Song. Richard Lovelace. CaPo
To a Lady That Forbade to Love before Company. Sir John Suckling. CaPo
To a Lady to Answer Directly with Yea or Nay. Sir Thomas Wyatt. *See* Madame, withouten Many Words.
To a Lady Troubled by Insomnia. Franklin P. Adams. InMe
To a Lady Who Did Sing Excellently. Lord Herbert of Cherbury. AnAnS-2; OBS; SeCP
To a Lady Who Sent Me a Copy of Verses at My Going to Bed. Henry King. PP
To a Lady, with a Compass. George Napier. FaBoUs
To a Lady, with a Guitar. Shelley. *See* With a Guitar, to Jane.
To a Lady, with a Present of a Fan. *Unknown, at. to* Charles Brandling. FaBoUs; NOEC
To a Lady, with a Present of a Walking-Stick. John Hookham Frere. FaBoUs
To a Lady with Flowers from the Roman Wall. Sir Walter Scott. OAEP
To a Ladye. William Dunbar. *See* To a Lady.
To a Lark in War-Time. Franz Werfel, *tr. fr. German by* Edith Abercrombie Snow. TrJP
To a Lily. James Matthew Legaré. AA
To a Linnet in a Cage. Francis Ledwidge. OnYI; RoGo
To a Little Boy Learning to Fish. Robert D. Hoeft. AMV-81
To a Little Boy, Who Had Destroyed a Nest of Young Birds. *Unknown.* FaBoUs
To a Little Girl. Helen Parry Eden. HBV-1
To a Little Girl. Gustav Kobbé. HBV-1
To a Little Girl, One Year Old, in a Ruined Fortress, *sel.* Robert Penn Warren.
"It rained toward day. The morning came sad and white." MoVE
(Colder Fire.) LiTM
To a Lock of Hair. Sir Walter Scott. GTBS; GTBS-P
To a Locomotive in Winter. Walt Whitman. AmPP; AP; FaBV; InPK; MoAmPo; NoAM; NoP; PoEL-5; TAP
To a lodge that stood. Wordsworth. *Fr.* Vaudracour and Julia. EvOK
To a Lofty Beauty, from Her Poor Kinsman. Hartley Coleridge. OBVV
To a Lost Sweetheart. Don Marquis. POL
Sels.
"I oft stand in the snow at dawn." FiBHP
"When Whistler's Mother's Picture's frame." FiBHP
To a Loudmouth Pontificator. Ray Mizer. TW
To a Louse [on Seeing One on a Lady's Bonnet at Church]. Burns. BLPA; EnRP; FaFP; InvP; LiTB; NOEC; OAEP; OxBS; PrIm; SeCeV; TreF; ViBoPo
To a Madonna. John Gray, *after the French of* Baudelaire. SyP
To a Magnolia Flower in the Garden of the Armenian Convent at Venice. S. Weir Mitchell. AA
To a man eating a pear. Please Say Something. Tomioka Taeko, *tr. by* Sato Hiroaki. WPOW
To a Man in a Picture Window Watching Television. Mildred Weston. ELU
To a Maple Seed. Lloyd Mifflin. AA
To a Marsh Hawk in Spring. Henry David Thoreau. PB; PoEL-4
To a Mayflower. William E. Marshall. CaP
To a' men living be it kend. The Rising of the Session. Robert Fergusson. OxBS
To a Midge. Eilidh Nisbet. PoSH
To a Military Rifle, 1942. Yvor Winters. MoAmPo; WaP
To a Millionaire. Archibald Lampman. NOBC
To a Mistress Dying. Sir William Davenant. *See* Philosopher and the Lover, The: To a Mistress Dying.
To a Mountain Daisy [on Turning One Down with the Plough, in April 1786]. Burns. EnRP; GN; HBV-1; OAEP; PoLF; WBLP
(Daisy, The.) BoNaP
To a Mouse [on Turning Her Up in Her Nest, with the Plough, November 1785]. Burns. BiP; BSV; EnRP; FaFP; FF; FM; GoTS; HAP; HBV-1; HBVY; HeIP; InPS; LAuP; LoBV; NOEC; NoP; OAEL-1; OAEP; OBEC; OxBS; PoLF; PPP; PrIm; SeCeV; TEP; TreFS; TrGrPo; WHA
(To a Field Mouse.) GTBS; GTBS-P
To a Musician. George Wither, *wr. at. to* William Austin. OxBoCh
To a Negro Boy Graduating. Eugene T. Maleska. PoNe
To a New York Shop-Girl Dressed for Sunday. Anna Hempstead Branch. HBV-2
To a New-born Baby Girl. Grace Hazard Conkling. HBV-1
To a New-born Child. Cosmo Monkhouse. HBV-1
To a Nightingale. William Drummond of Hawthornden. OBS
To a Nightingale. Keats. *See* Ode to a Nightingale.
To a Noisy Politician. Philip Freneau. TAP

To a Nun. John Ormond, *after the Welsh.* EBEV; FaBoTw
To a Painted Lady. Alexander Brome. CavP
To a Pair of Egyptian Slippers. Sir Edwin Arnold. HBV-1; OBVV
To a Passer-by. Baudelaire, *tr. fr. French by* C. F. MacIntyre. NAWM-2; SyP
To a Persistent Phantom. Frank Horne. AmNP; BANP; CDC
To a Phoebe-Bird. Witter Bynner. HBMV
To a Photograph. Parker Tyler. NePA
To a Plagiarist. Moses ibn Ezra, *tr. fr. Hebrew by* Solomon Solis-Cohen. TrJP
To a Poet. Sister Mary Angelita. GoBC
To a Poet a Thousand Years Hence. James Elroy Flecker. ChTr; FaBoRV; HBV-2; MoBrPo; PoRA
To a Poet a Thousand Years Hence. John Heath-Stubbs. OxBC
To a Poet I Knew. Jewel C. Latimore. PoBA
To a Poet, Who Would Have Me Praise Certain Bad Poets, Imitators of His and Mine. W. B. Yeats. CTC; DBV; FaBoEE; PV
To a Poor Old Woman. William Carlos Williams. OBAL; SOTW; TAP
To a Pope. Pier Paolo Pasolini, *tr. by* James Kirkup. PeHV
To a Portrait of Lermontov. Margarita Aliger, *tr. fr. Russian by* Elaine Feinstein. VWA
To a Portrait of Whistler in the Brooklyn Art Museum. Eleanor Rogers Cox. HBMV
To a Post-Office Inkwell. Christopher Morley. PoLF
To a President. Witter Bynner. OBAL
To a Pretty Girl. Israel Zangwill. TrJP
To a Print of Queen Victoria. James K. Baxter. OxBC
To a Publisher. . .Cut-out. Amiri Baraka. NeAP
To a Race Horse at Ascot. Jennie M. Palen. PH
To a Red-headed Do-good Waitress. Alan Dugan. CAPP
To a Republican. Philip Freneau. AmPP
To a Republican Friend: Continued. Matthew Arnold. VLP
To a Republican Friend, 1848. Matthew Arnold. VLP
To a Reviewer Who Admired My Book. John Ciardi. OBAL
To a River in the South. Sir Henry Newbolt. CH
To a Rogue. Joseph Addison. PV
To a Roman. J. C. Squire. HBMV
To a Rose. Frank Dempster Sherman. AA
To a Sacred Cow. *Unknown, tr. fr. Toda by* W. E. Mashiel. WGRP
To a Salesgirl, Weary of Artificial Holiday Trees. James Wright. NYBP
To a Scarlatti Passepied. Robert Hillyer. HBMV
To a School-Girl. Shaw Neilson. PoAu-1
To a Scottish Poet. G. S. Fraser. BSV
To a Sea-Bird. Bret Harte. EtS
To a Sea Eagle. "Hugh MacDiarmid." MoBrPo
To a Seaman Dead on Land. Kay Boyle. PoA
To a Seamew. Swinburne. EtS; VLP
To a Segar. Samuel Low. OBAL
To a Severe Nun. Thomas Merton. CoPo
To a Shade. W. B. Yeats. AnIL; LiTB; PoEL-5
To a Sicilian Boy. Theodore Wratislaw. PeHV
To a Single Shadow without Pity. Sam Cornish. NBP; PoBA
To a Skeleton. Anna Jane Vardhill. BLPA
To a Skull. Joshua Henry Jones. BANP
To a Skylark. Shelley. BoAnP, *abr.*; EnRP; FaBoBe; FaBV; FaFP; FaPON; FPL; GN; GTBS; GTBS-P; HAP; HBV-1; HBVY; InPS; InvP; LiTB; LoBV; NoP; OAEL-2; OAEP; OBEV; OBNC; OBRV; OHFP; PB; PBBP; PoLF; RoGo; TEP; TreFS; TrGrPo; WHA
(Ode to a Skylark.) NOBE
To a Skylark ("Ethereal minstrel! pilgrim of the sky!"). Wordsworth. EnRP; HBV-1; HBVY; OAEP; PBBP; TrGrPo
(To the Skylark.) FaFP; GTBS; GTBS-P
To a Skylark ("Up with me! up with me into the clouds!"). Wordsworth. FPL; HBV-1
To a Sleeping Friend. Jean Cocteau, *tr. fr. French.* PeHV
To a Small Boy Standing on My Shoes While I Am Wearing Them. Ogden Nash. DBV; FiBHP
To a Snail. Marianne Moore. CMoP; FaBoMo
To a Snowflake. Francis Thompson. BoNaP; EBCP; FaBV; HBV-1; ImOP; LoBV; MoAB; MoBrPo; PoPl; SeCePo; TrGrPo
To a Solitary Disciple. William Carlos Williams. PP; VGW
To a Spaniel. Walter Savage Landor. FM
To a Spanish Poet. Stephen Spender. OAEP
To a Sparrow. Francis Ledwidge. HBMV
To a Spider. Robert Southey. FM
To a Squirrel at Kyle-na-no. W. B. Yeats. FaPON; FM; PDV; RHPC
To a Steam Roller. Marianne Moore. BoWoP; CMoP; FaBoMo; MoAB; MoAmPo; OxBA; PP; VGW
To a Stranger. Walt Whitman. NoAM; NOBA
To a Swallow. John Peale Bishop, *after the Greek of* Euenus. OBVE
To a Swallow Building under Our Eaves. Jane Welsh Carlyle. HBV-1; OBRV
To a Talkative Hairdresser. Phyllis McGinley. DBV
To a Teacher of French. Donald Davie. OxBC
To a "Tenting" Boy. Charles Tennyson Turner. OBNC
To a Thesaurus. Franklin P. Adams. BLPL; PoPl; WhC
To a Town Poet. Lizette Woodworth Reese. AA
To a Traveler [*or* Traveller]. Lionel Johnson. MoBrPo; NBM
To a Traveler. Su Tung p'o, *tr. fr. Chinese by* Kenneth Rexroth. HoPM
To a Tyrant. Joseph Brodsky, *tr. fr. Russian by* Alan Myers. VWA
To a Vagabond. Constance Davies Woodrow. CaP
To a Very Beautiful Lady. Ruthven Todd. BSV; NeBP
To a Very Wise Man. Siegfried Sassoon. BrPo
To a Very Young Lady. Sir George Etherege. ViBoPo
To a Very Young Lady. Edmund Waller. AnAnS-2; OBS; SeCP; TrGrPo; ViBoPo
(To a Girl.) WiR
(To My Young Lady, Lucy Sidney.) MePo; OAEP
To a Victim of Radiation. Arturo Vivante. FAZ
To a Vine-clad Telegraph Pole. Louis Untermeyer. MoAmPo
To a Visiting Poet in a College Dormitory. Carolyn Kizer. PoA
To a Wall of Flame in a Steel Mill, Syracuse, New York, 1969. Larry Levis. AMV-81; DiL; MAYP
To a Wanton. William Habington. AnAnS-2; SeCP
To a Wasp Caught in the Storm Sash at the Advent of the Winter Solstice. Peter Cooley. MAYP
To a Waterfowl. Bryant. AA; AmPP; AP; AWP; BLPL; CH; EBCP; FaBoBe; FaBoEn; FaFP; GN; HBV-1; HBVY; HoPM; LiTA; NePA; NOBA; NoP; OBRV; OHFP; OxBA; PB; PoEL-4; PoLF; PrIm; SeCeV; SoSe; TAP; TreF; TrGrPo; TRV; WBLP; WGRP
To a Waterfowl. Donald Hall. OBAL
To a Weak Gamester in Poetry. Ben Jonson. JCP
To a Western Bard Still a Whoop and a Holler Away from English Poetry. William Meredith. PP
To a Wind-Flower. Madison Cawein. AA; HBV-1
To a Withered Rose. John Kendrick Bangs. AA
To a Witty Man of Wealth and Quality; Who, after His Dismissal from Court, Said, He Might Justly Complain of It. William Wycherley. SeCV-2
To a woman that I knew. Her Eyes. John Crowe Ransom. LiTM; NePA; OBAL; PoPl
To a Woman Who Wants Darkness and Time. Gerald W. Barrax. PoBA
To a Wood-Violet. John Banister Tabb. HBV-1
To a Worm Which the Author Accidentally Trode Upon. William Hawkins. FM
To a Writer of the Day, *sels.* Landgon Elwyn Mitchell.
Purpose. AA
Technique. AA
To a Young Ass. Samuel Taylor Coleridge. EnRP; OBEC
To a Young Beauty. W. B. Yeats. CMoP
To a Young Brother. Maria Jane Jewsbury. OxBChV
To a Young Child. Eliza Scudder. AA
To a Young Friend, *sel.* Samuel Taylor Coleridge.
"And haply, bason'd in some unsunn'd cleft." ChER
To a Young Gentleman in Love; a Tale. Matthew Prior. TEP
To a Young Gentle-Woman, Councel Concerning Her Choice. Richard Crashaw. OBS
To a Young Girl. David Rosenmann-Taub, *tr. fr. Spanish by* Charles Guenther. VWA
To a Young Girl. W. B. Yeats. EBEV; OLR
To a Young Girl Dying. Thomas William Parsons. AA
To a Young Girl Leaving the Hill Country. Arna Bontemps. CDC
To a Young Heir. Samuel Johnson. *See* Short Song of Congratulation, A.
To a Young Lady. William Cowper. GTBS; GTBS-P; HBV-1
(Addressed to a Young Lady.) EnRP
To a Young Lady. Richard Savage. OBEC
To a Young Lady. Wordsworth. EnRP
To a Young Lady on Her Leaving the Town after the Coronation. Pope. *See* Epistle to Miss Blount, on Her Leaving the Town after the Coronation.
To a Young Lady Swinging Upside Down on a Birch Limb over a Winter-swollen Creek. James H. Koch. GoYe
To a Young Lady, with Some Lampreys. John Gay. FaBoUs; NOEC
To a Young Leader of the First World War. Stefan George, *tr. fr. German by* E. B. Ashton. WaaP
To a Young Poet. Paula Bennett. AMV-81
To a Young Poet. Harry M. Meacham. GoYe
To a Young Poet. Edna St. Vincent Millay. CrMA
To a Young Poet Who Fled. John Logan. CAPP
To a Young Wretch. Robert Frost. OFD
To Aaron Burr, under Trial for High Treason. Sarah Wentworth Morton. PAH
To Aberdein. William Dunbar. FaBoPP
To Abraham Lincoln. John James Piatt. AA

To Adam, His Scribe. Chaucer. OAEL-1; OxBM
To Adhiambo. Gabriel Okara. PBA
To Aenone. Robert Herrick. HBV-1
(To Oenone.) OBEV
To Age. Walter Savage Landor. EnRP; HBV-1; TreFS
To Ailsa Rock. Keats. EnRP; OBNC
(Sonnet to Ailsa Rock.) MOS
To Alan. Douglas Fraser. PoSH
To Alexander Meiklejohn, *sel.* John Beecher.
"I read your testimony and I thought." GOA
To Alexander Neville. Barnabe Googe. EnRePo; NoP
To Alfred Tennyson. Walter Savage Landor. *Sel* I Entreat You, Alfred Tennyson.
To All Angels and Saints. George Herbert. SeCV-1
To All Brothers. Sonia Sanchez. BPo
To All Sisters. Sonia Sanchez. PoBA
To all who carve their love on a picnic table. Open Letter from a Constant Reader. Mona Van Duyn. GP; PoA
To all you ladies now at Bath. Farewell to Bath. Lady Mary Wortley Montagu. WPE
To all you ladies now at land. Song [Written at Sea in the First Dutch War (1665), the Night before an Engagement]. Charles Sackville. CauP; CoMu; EnLoPo; HBV-1; NOBE; OBEV; OBS; OBWP; SeCV-2
To all young men that love to wooe. To Chuse a Friend, but Never Marry. *At. to* the Earl of Rochester. CoMu
To Allegra Florence in Heaven, *sel.* Thomas Holly Chivers.
"As an egg, when broken, never." BXAP; PeD
To Althea, from Prison. Richard Lovelace. AnAnS-2; AWP; BiP; BLPA; CABA; CaPo; CavP; FaBoBe; FaBoEn; FPL; GBL; GTBS; GTBS-P; HAP; HBV-1; HeIP; InPS; JCP; LiTB; LoBV; MeLP; MePo; NOBE; NoP; OAEP; OBEV; OBS; PoPle; PoRA; SeCeV; SeCP; SeCV-1; SoSe; TEP; TreF; TrGrPo; ViBoPo; WHA
To Amanda. James Thomson. BSV
To Amarantha, That She Would Dishevel[l] Her Hair[e]. Richard Lovelace. AnAnS-2; HBV-1; HoPM; MePo; NIP; NoP; OBEV; SeCP; SeCV-1, *longer vers.*; TrGrPo
(Song: To Amarantha, That She Would Dishevel Her Hair.) CaPo
(To Amarantha.) UnTE; ViBoPo
To America. Alfred Austin. GN; HBV-2
(Britannia to Columbia.) PAH
To America, on Her First Sons Fallen in the Great War. E. M. Walker. PAH
To Amine. James Clarence Mangan. OBEV; OBVV
To Amoret [Gone from Him]. Henry Vaughan. EnLoPo; MeLP; OBS; SeCP
To Amoret. Edmund Waller. SeCV-1
To amuse His Royal Majesty he will change water into wine. Zito the Magician. Miroslav Holub, *tr. by* Ian Milner *and* George Theiner. SUW
To Amy. J. Gordon Coogler. OBAL
To an Acquaintance. *Unknown.* FaFP
To an Adolescent Weeping Willow. Marvin Bell. DiL
To an Aging Charioteer. Leontius Scholasticus, *tr. fr. Greek by* Tom Dodge. LiSp
To an Alcoholic. Sandra McPherson. MAYP
To an Ambitious Friend. Horace, *tr. fr. Latin by* Matthew Arnold. Odes, II, 11. AWP
To an American Poet Just Dead. Richard Wilbur. NoP
To an Anti-poetical Priest. Giolla Brighde MacNamee, *tr. fr. Middle Irish by* the Earl of Langford. AnIV
To an Artful Theatre Manager. Lorenzo da Ponte, *tr. fr. Italian by* John Mazzinghi. *Fr.* Il Capriccio Dramatico. TrJP
To an Artist. Burns. EyDe
To an Artist, to Take Heart. Louise Bogan. GrPl; NYBP; PAI
To an Athlete Dying Young. A. E. Housman. A Shropshire Lad, XIX. BiP; BLPL; BrPo; CABA; CMoP; DL; HAP; HeIP; InPK; LiSp; LiTB; LiTM; MasP; MoAB; MoBrPo; NIP; NoAM; NoP; OAEP; PAI; PoEL-5; PoPL; PoRA; PPoe; PrIm; SeCeV; SoSe; TEP; TreF; TrGrPo; UnPo; VLP; WeW; WHA
To an Athlete Turned Poet. Peter Meinke. LiSp
To an Author. Philip Freneau. AmPP; NOBA; OxBA
To an Autumn Leaf. Albert Mathews. AA
To an Avenue Sport. Helen Johnson Collins. PoNe
To an Aviator. Daniel Whitehead Hicky. RHPC
To an Early Primrose. Henry Kirke White. HBV-1; OBNC; OBRV
To an ebbing tide, all sail apeak. A Song of the Hatteras Whale. *Unknown.* EtS
To an Egyptian Boy. H. W. Berry. WhC
To an Elder Poet. William Carlos Williams. PoA
To an Enemy. Maxwell Bodenheim. TrJP
To an Estranged Wife. Gary Young. AMV-81
To an Icicle. Blanche Taylor Dickinson. CDC
To an Imaginary Father. Wendy Rose. CDW
To an Imperilled Traveller. Nathan Haskell Dole. AA
To an Inconstant [Mistress *or* One]. Sir Robert Ayton. *See* I Loved Thee Once.
To an Indian Poet. Patty L. Harjo. VoR
To an Indian Skull, *sel.* Alexander McLachlan.
"And art thou come to this at last." CaP
To an Infant Daughter. John Clare. NAs
To an Infant Expiring the Second Day of Its Birth. Hetty Wright. NOEC
To an Insect. Oliver Wendell Holmes. HBV-1; HBVY; TreF
To an Irish Blackbird. James MacAlpine. HBMV; HBVY
To an Isle in the Water. W. B. Yeats. AWP
To an Oak Tree. Sir Walter Scott. *Fr.* Waverley. OBNC
To an Obscure Poet Who Lives on My Hearth. Charles Lotin Hildreth. AA
To an Old Danish Song-Book. Longfellow. OBVV
To an Old Gentlewoman, Who Painted Her Face. George Turberville. EnRePo
To an Old Lady. William Empson. CoBMV; FaBoTw; GTBS-P; MoAB; MOON; NoAM; NOBE; SeCeV
To an Old Lady Dead. Siegfried Sassoon. PoPle
To an Old Philosopher in Rome. Wallace Stevens. AP; NoAM; NOBA
To an Old Poet. Walter Savage Landor. DBV
To an Old Tenor. Oliver St. John Gogarty. WhC
To an Old Tune. William Alexander Percy. HBMV
To an open house in the evening. Home at Last. G. K. Chesterton. TRV; WGRP
To an Oriole. Edgar Fawcett. HBV-1
To an Unborn Pauper Child. Thomas Hardy. CoBMV; FaBoRV; GTBS-P; LiTB; NAs; ViBoPo
To an Ungentle Critic. Robert Graves. HBMV; InMe
To an Unknown Neighbor at the Circus. Rosemary Benét. DBV; InMe
To and fro in the city I go. A City Flower. Austin Dobson. TEP
To and on Other Intellectual Poets on Reading That the U.S.A.F. Had Sent a Team of Scientists to Africa. Ramon Guthrie. NMP
To Angélique, *sel.* Heine, *tr. fr. German by* Emma Lazarus.
"This mad carnival of loving." TrJP
To Anne. William Stirling-Maxwell. HBV-1
To Antenor. Katherine Philips. SBG
To Anthea ("Ah, my Anthea! must my heart still break?"). Robert Herrick. CaPo
(What Shame Forbids to Speak.) UnTE
To Anthea ("If deare Anthea, my hard fate it be"). Robert Herrick. OBS
To Anthea ("Now is the time, when all the lights wax dim"). Robert Herrick. OAEP; OBS; PoEL-3
To Anthea Lying in Bed. Robert Herrick. SeCP
To Anthea, Who May Command Him [in] Anything. Robert Herrick. AnAnS-2; CaPo; CavP; GTBS; GTBS-P; HBV-1; JCP; LoBV; NOBE; OAEL-1; OAEP; OBEV; OBS; SeCP; SeCV-1; TrGrPo; ViBoPo
To Anthea, Who May Command Him Anything (New Style.). Alfred Cochrane. HBV-1
To Any Daddy. *Unknown.* STF
To Any M. F. H. V. Sackville-West. SBG
To Any Member of My Generation. George Barker. LiTM; ViBoPo; WaP
To Aphrodite; with a Mirror. Aline Kilmer. HBMV
To Apollo and Diana. Horace, *tr. fr. Latin by* Branwell Brontë. Odes, I, 21. OBVE
To Arcady. Charles Buxton Going. HBV-1
To Archaeanassa, on whose furrow'd brow. On Archaeanassa. Plato, *tr. by* Thomas Stanley. AWP
To Archinus. Callimachus, *tr. fr. Greek by* F. A. Wright. AWP
To Argos. Lawrence Durrell. MoPo
To Ariake Kambara. Norman Rosten. NYBP
To Aristius Fuscus. Horace, *tr. fr. Latin by* Samuel Johnson. Odes, I, 22. OBVE
To Arms. Park Benjamin. PAH
To arms, to arms! my jolly grenadiers. The Song of Braddock's Men. Stephen Tilden. PAH
To Arolilia, *sel.* Herbert Trench.
"Ay, since beyond these walls no heavens there be." LO
To Art. Dante Gabriel Rossetti. POL
To Arthur's court, when men began. A Scot, a Welsh and an Irish Man. *Unknown.* GBP
To Ashtaroth and Bel. Saul Tchernichowsky, *tr. fr. Hebrew by* L. V. Snowman. TrJP
To Ask for All Thy Love. *Unknown.* EIL
To assassinate the Chase Manhattan Bank. The Plot to Assassinate the Chase Manhattan Bank. Carl Larsen. FF; PPON
To Atalanta. Dorothy Dow. HBMV
To Auden on His Fiftieth. Richard Eberhart. GLGT; NAs
To Augustus, *sels.* Pope.
Court of Charles II, The. OBEC
Poet's Use, The. OBEC

To Aunt Rose. Allen Ginsberg. CABA; LiTM; NoP; PAI; VGW
To Aurora. Earl of Sterling. Aurora, XXXIII. FaFP; GTBS; GTBS–P
(Sonnet: "Oh, if thou knew'st how thou thyself dost harm.") ElL
To Ausonius. Paulinus of Nola, *tr. fr. Latin by* Helen Waddell. PeHV
To Autumn. Blake. BoNaP; WiR
To Autumn. Keats. AWP; BiP; BoNaP; CH; ChER; EBEV; EnRP; FaBoEn; FaBoRV; FiP; FF; FPL; HAP; HBV–1; HBVY; InvP; LiTB; NIP; NOBE; NOP; NU; OAEL–2; OAEP; OBEV; OBNC; OBRV; PAI; PoEL–4; PoLF;PoPle; PPoe; PPP; Prf; PrIm; RoGo; SCV; SeCeV; SoSe; TEP; TreFS; UnPo; ViBoPo; WeW; WHA
(Ode to Autumn.) CABA; FaBV; GTBS; GTBS–P; LOBV; TrGrPo
To 'ave a garden in fettle. Michael Hyde. BXAP
To Avisa. Henry Willoby. *Fr.* Willobie His Avisa. ElL
To Azrael. Baudelaire, *tr. fr. French by* T. Sturge Moore. SyP
To B. C. Sir John Suckling. CaPo
To banish your shape from my mind. Exorcism. Oliver St. John Gogarty. AnIL
To Barba. Edward May. FaBoEE
To Bary Jade. Charles Follen Adams. OBAL
To be a birth there must be a begetting. Begetting. Dorothea Spears. PeSA
To be a giant and keep quiet about it. Trees. Howard Nemerov. BoNaP; Psk
To Be a Jew in the Twentieth Century. Muriel Rukeyser. *Fr.* Letter to the Front. TrJP
To Be a Master in Your House. Natan Zach, *tr. fr. Hebrew by* Peter Everwine *and* Shula Starkman. VWA
To be a mistress. Kiyoko Tsuda, *tr. fr. Japanese by* Edith Marcombe Shiffert *and* Yuki Sawa. BoWoP
To be a Negro in a day like this. At the Closed Gate of Justice. James David Corrothers. BANP
To Be a Pilgrim. Bunyan. *See* Pilgrim, The.
To Be a Pilgrim. Robert Conquest. OxBC
To be a poet and not know the trade. Sanctity. Patrick Kavanagh. BIrV; ELU
To be a poet is to be vanquished. Ars Poetica. Victor van Vriesland, *tr. by* Adriaan J. Barnouw. TrJP
To be a successful and competent vet. The Vet. Guy Boas. BoAnP
To be a whore, despite of grace. Madrigal. Charles Cotton. FaBoEE
To be able/ and not to do it. To an Elder Poet. William Carlos Williams. PoA
To be able to see every side of every question. Editor Whedon. Edgar Lee Masters. *Fr.* Spoon River Anthology. CMoP; CrMA; FaBoEE; NoAM; NOBA; OBSV; OxBA
To be alive in such an age! Today. Angela Morgan. BLPA; TRV
To be an orphan. The Orphan. *Unknown, tr. by* Arthur Waley. PoA
To Be Answered in Our Next Issue. *Unknown.* RHPC
To Be Black, to Be Lost. Hannah Kahn. GoYe
To Be Carved on a Stone at Thoor Ballylee. W. B. Yeats. FaBoEE; NoAM; NoP
To Be Continued. Julian Street *and* James Montgomery Flagg. *See* Said Opie Read.
To Be Engraven on a Dial. Samuel Sewall. SCAP
To be forever young. Immortality. Frank Horne. BANP
To be homeless is a pride. A Jealous Man. Robert Graves. CMoP
To Be Honest, to Be Kind. Robert Louis Stevenson. *Fr.* A Christmas Sermon. PoLF
To be in a place for spring and not have lived its winter. Vincent O'Sullivan. Brother Jonathan, Brother Kafka, 13. OCNZ
To Be in Love. Gwendolyn Brooks. IHMS; OLR
To be in love is like going out. The Business. Robert Creeley. CAPP
To Be in Love while in Prison. John Paul Minarik. LFAC
To be married. The Relationship. Stephen Vincent. NeAC
To be moved comes of want, though want be complete. 1892–1941. Louis Zukofsky. PoA
To be my own Messiah to the. The Rows of Cold Trees. Yvor Winters. NoAM; NOBA
To be near/ Yet not to wake. Spell. Robert Francis. GP
To Be of Use. Marge Piercy. GeTw; HoAn
To Be or Not to Be, *parody.* William H. Edmunds. FaBoPa
To Be or Not to Be. Spenser. *See* Cave of Despair, The.
To Be or Not to Be ("I sometimes think I'd rather crow"). *Unknown.* FaBoCo; FaFP; MoShBr; RHPC
To be, or not to be; that is the bare bodkin. Samuel Clemens. BXAP
To Be, or Not to Be [That Is the Question]. Shakespeare. *Fr.* Hamlet, III, i. BiP; FaFP; FF; FiP; HoPM; LiTB; MasP; PAI; PoPl; TreFT; TrGrPo; WHA
(Hamlet Contemplates Suicide.) TreF
(Hamlet's Soliloquy.) WBLP
(Soliloquy from "Hamlet.") OHFP
To be, or not to be: that is the question. To Be or Not to Be, *parody.* William H. Edmunds. FaBoPa
To be, or not to be, that is the question./ Whether to suffer with mental anguish. Plantation Bitters. *Unknown.* FaBoUs
To be put on the train and kissed and given my ticket. Observation Car. A. D. Hope. NoAM
To Be Quicker. Don L. Lee. JB
To Be Recited to Flossie on Her Birthday. William Carlos Williams. VGW
To be sad in the morning. Poem. William Pillen. VWA
To Be Said at the Seder. Karl Wolfskehl, *tr. fr. German by* Carol North Valhope *and* Ernst Morwitz. TrJP
To Be Sung. Peter Viereck. FaBV
To Be Sung on the Water. Louise Bogan. MoVE; PrIm; VGW
To be ten and skinny. Exodus. Anita Endrezze Probst. CDW
To be unloved brings sweet relief. Lovers. Mary Fullerton. PoAu-1
To Beachey, 1912. Carl Sandburg. TiPo
To Beatrice Stuart Wortley: Aetat 2. Alfred Austin. PeD
To Bed, to Bed. Beaumont *and* Fletcher. *Fr.* The Maid's Tragedy. UnTE
To Begin. Fran Winant. BrRo
To Begin the Day. *Unknown.* BLRP
To begin with a light as vivid and warm. Matisse. Edward Hampl. PoDr
To begin with he was a beautiful object. Louis MacNeice. *Fr.* The Death of a Cat. PCat
To begin with she wouldn't have fallen in. Our Silly Little Sister. Dorothy Aldis. EvOK; FaPON
To Bellinus. *Unknown, tr. fr. Latin.* PeHV
To Ben, at the Lake. Cilla McQueen. OCNZ
To Ben Jonson [*or* Johnson]. Thomas Carew. AnAnS–2; CaPo; MePo
To Bert Campaneris. Tom Clark. LiSp
To Bethlehem town in the long ago. Three Wise Kings. William E. Brooks. PGD
To Bethlehem's silly shed, methinks I see. The Bee. Henry Hawkins. ACP
"To Bethlem did they go, the shepherds three." Masters, in This Hall. William Morris. ChTr
To Betsey-Jane, on Her Desiring to Go Incontinently to Heaven. Helen Parry Eden. HBMV
To biographers, in rebuttal. Lives of the Poet. Ron Miles. AMV-81
To Blok/ words that had stuck together. Blok: Let Me Learn the Poem. Aram Boyajian. NeAC
To Blossoms. Robert Herrick. BoNaP; CaPo; GTBS; GTBS–P; HBV–1; JCP; LoBV; OBEV; OBS; SeCP; SeCV–1
To Bobby Seale. Lucille Clifton. CNA; PoBA
To Borglum's Seated Statue of Abraham Lincoln. Charlotte B. Jordan. OHIP
To Boris Pasternak. Aleksander Kushner, *tr. fr. Russian by* Dimitry Pospielovsky *and* Keith Bosley. VWA
To Boston. John Collins Bossidy. *See* Boston Toast, A.
To Bran in his coracle it seems. The Sea-God's Address to Bran. *Unknown, tr. by* Kuno Meyer. OnYI
To brave and to know the unknown. The Unknown. John Davidson. MoBrPo
To break bolt and bar. Christmas Amnesty. Edith Lovejoy Pierce. PGD
To Bring Spring. George Keithley. NPGG
To Bring the Dead to Life. Robert Graves. MoBrPo
To Brooklyn Bridge. Hart Crane. *Fr.* The Bridge. AP; BLPL; CABA; CoBMV; CrMa; EyDe; FaBoEn; HAP; InPS; LiTA; LiTM; MoAB; MoAmPo; MoPo; NePA; NOBA; NYP; OxBA; PoPl; PrIm; SeCeV
(Proem: To Brooklyn Bridge.) AmFP; CMoP; HeIP; NoAM; NoP; TAP; WeW
To build the trout a crystal stair. The Whole Duty of Berkshire Brooks. Grace Hazard Conkling. HBMV; HBVY
To Bülow. August, Graf von Platen, *tr. fr. German by* Reginald Bancroft Cooke. PeHV
To burn is surely bad, to be. House of Fire. Theodore Weiss. CoPo
To Butterfly. William Alexander Percy. HBMV
To buy, or not to buy; that is the question. Investor's Soliloquy. Kenneth Ward. FaFP; FPL
To C———/ her lover. Love-Letter One. *Unknown.* PeHV
To C.W.S. *Unknown.* OxBC
To C. F. H. on Her Christening-Day. Thomas Hardy. NAs
To Caelia. *Unknown.* FaBoEE
To call our sight Vision. I Am Not a Camera. W. H. Auden. EyDe
To Calliope. Robert Graves. CMoP
To Cara, after an Interval of Absence. Thomas Moore. PeD
To Carry on Living. Yehuda Amichai, *tr. fr. Hebrew by the author.* LLLT
To Carry the Child. Stevie Smith. NoAM; NYBP
To Castara ("Doe not their prophane orgies heare"). William Habington. AnAnS–2
To Castara ("Give me a heart where no impure"). William Habington. AnAnS–2
To Castara ("We saw and woo'd each others eyes"). William Habington. *Fr.* Castara, II. CavP; LoBV
(Reward of Innocent Love, The.) ACP
To Castara, of True Delight. William Habington. AnAnS–2

To Castara, upon an Embrace. William Habington. AnAnS-2
To Castara, upon Beautie. William Habington. *Fr.* Castara, II. AnAnS-2; SeCP
To Castara, Ventring to Walke Too Farre in the Neighbouring Wood. William Habington. AnAnS-2
To catch some fragment from her hands. Beauty. Kenneth Slade Alling. HBMV
To Catherine Wordsworth 1808–1812. Wordsworth. *See* Surprised by Joy.
To Cattraeth's vale in glitt'ring row. Aneirin, *tr. by* Thomas Gray. *Fr.* The Gododdin. OBVE
To cause accord or to agree [*or* aggre]. Sir Thomas Wyatt. AAS; SiPS
To celebrate this season I must find. Forsythia Is the Color I Remember. Joseph Cherwinski. AMV-80
To Celia. Charles Cotton. HBV-1
(To Coelig.) OBEV
To Celia ("Come my Celia, let us prove"). Ben Johnson. *See* Come, My Celia, Let Us Prove.
To Celia ("Drink[e] to me, on[e]ly, with thine eyes"). Ben Jonson. AnAnS-2; BoLoP; EnLoPo; FaBoBe; FaBoEn; FaBV; FaFP; FPL; GTBS; GTBS-P; HBV-1; InPK; LiTB; MasP; NOBE; OBEV; OBS; OBVE; PoLF; SeCeV; TrGrPo; ViBoPo; WHA
(Drink to Me Only with Thine Eyes.) BiP; BLSo, *with music*; FSW; TEP
(Song: To Celia.) AWP; CABA; EIL; ELP; EnRePo; GBL; HeIP; OAEL-1; NoP; PAI; PoEL-2; PoPl; PrIm; SeCP; SeCV-1; TreF
To Celia ("Kiss me, sweet; the wary lover"). Ben Jonson. AWP; EnRePo; LoBV
("Kiss me, sweet; the wary lover."). BiP; OBVE; UnTE
(Song: To Celia.) EIL; JCP
(To the Same.) AnAnS-2; OAEL-1; SeCP; SeCV-1
To Celia. Sir Charles Sedley. AWP; NOBE; OBEV
("Not, Celia, that I juster am.") GTBS; GTBS-P
(Song: "Not, Celia, that I juster am.") FaBoEn; ViBoPo
(Song to Celia.) CavP; OBs; SeCeP
To Celia Pleading Want of Merit. Thomas Stanley. *See* To One That Pleaded Her Own Want of Merit.
To Celia, upon Love's Ubiquity. Thomas Carew. AnAnS-2
To Certain Critics. Countee Cullen. BPo
To change the name, and not the letter. Surnames to Be Avoided in Marriage. *Unknown.* FaBoUs
To Charles Cowden Clarke. Keats. EnRP
"Oft have you seen a swan superbly frowning," *sel.* PBBP
To Charlotte Corday. Sir Osbert Sitwell. ChMP
To Charlotte Pulteney. Ambrose Philips. *See* To Miss Charlotte Pulteney in Her Mother's Arms.
To Chaucer. Thomas Hoccleve. *Fr.* De Regimine Principum. ACP
To Cheer Our Minds. William Ronksley. OxBChV
To Cherry-Blossomes. Robert Herrick. SeCV-1
To Chicago at Night. Mildred Plew Meigs. HBMV
To "Chick." Frank Horne. *Fr.* Letters Found near a Suicide. BPo
To Children. Lawrence McGaugh. PoBA
To Chloe. William Cartwright. *See* To Chloe, Who Wished Herself Young Enough for Me.
To Chloe. Earnest Albert Hooten. UnTE
To Chloe ("Vitas hinnuleo"). Horace, *tr. fr. Latin.* Odes, I, 23. AWP, *tr. by* Austin Dobson; OBVE, *tr. by* Branwell Brontë
(Time to Choose a Lover, *tr. by* Branwell Brontë.) UnTE
To Chloe. *Unknown, tr. fr. Greek by* Louis Untermeyer. UnTE
To Chloe Jealous. Matthew Prior. *See* Answer to Cloe Jealous.
To Chloe, Who Wished Herself Young Enough for Me. William Cartwright. JCP; MePo; OBS; ViBoPo
(To Chloe.) LiTB
(To Chloe Who for His Sake Wished Herself Younger.) HBV-1, OBEV, 2 *sts.*
To Chloris. Charles Cotton. CavP
To Chloris. Sir Charles Sedley. *See* Child and Maiden.
To Christ. John Donne. *See* Hymn to God the Father, A.
To Christ Our Lord. Galway Kinnell. InPK; MP; NIP; PrIm; RFM; TwCP
To Christian Montpelier, *sel.* George Jonas.
"Single naked wire at ground level, A." NeAC
To Christopher North. Tennyson. EvOK; FaBoEE; FiBHP
To Christopher Smart. Joseph Stroud. NPGG
To church! I heard a sermon once in spring. God. Harold Monro. *Fr.* Dawn. WGRP
To Chuse a Friend, but Never Marry. *At. to* the Earl of Rochester. CoMu
To claim, at a dead party, to have spotted a grackle. Lying. Richard Wilbur. SV
To Clarastella on St. Valentines Day Morning. Robert Heath. OBS
To Clarissa. Robert, Earl Nugent. NOEC
To Clarissa Scott Delany. Angelina Weld Grimké. AmNP
To clean fish you need a sharp knife. A Fish Story. Charles Fishman. WOLT
To Clelia. Matthew Coppinger. CavP
To climb a hill that hungers for the sky. Fulfillment. Helene Johnson. CDC; PoNe
To Clio, from Rome. John Dyer. NOEC
To Cloe. George Granville. PV
("Cloe's the wonder of her sex.") FaBoEE (*At. to* Charles Sackville), POL
To Cloe. Hildebrand Jacob. NOEC
To Cloe. Martial. *See* Abnegation.
To Cloe Jealous, a Better Answer. Matthew Prior. *See* Answer to Cloe Jealous.
To Cloris ("Cloris, I cannot say your eyes"). Sir Charles Sedley. BoLoP
To clothe the fiery thought. Poet. Emerson. *Fr.* Quatrains. OxBA; PCP
To Coelia. Charles Cotton. *See* To Celia.
To Cole, the Painter, Departing for Europe. Bryant. AmPP; AP; TAP
To Coleridge in Sicily. Wordsworth. *Fr.* The Prelude, XI. OBNC
To Colin Clout. Anthony Munday. *See* Beauty Sat Bathing.
To Colman Returning. *At. to* Colman, *tr. fr. Medieval Latin by* Helen Waddell. BIrV
To Columbus. Rubén Darío, *tr. fr. Spanish by* Lysander Kemp. TTY
To come back from the sweet South, to the North. Italia, Io Ti Saluto. Christina Rossetti. OBVV; WPE
To come to the river. The Resolve. Denise Levertov. RFM
To Constantia Singing. Shelley. EnRP
To Cordelia. Joseph Stansbury. CaP; NOBC
To covet and resist for years. The Gash. William Everson. GP
To: Coymistress/ From: Marvell. Telegram One. Adrian Mitchell. PV
To Crinog. *Unknown, tr. fr. Middle Irish by* Kuno Meyer. AnIL; OnYI
To Critics. Robert Herrick. CaPo; PV
To Critics. Walter Learned. AA; HBV-1
To Crown It. Robert Herrick. CaPo
To Cupid. Francis Davison. OBSC
To Cupid. Michael Drayton. EIL
To Cynthia. *At. to* George Clifford. *See* My Thoughts Are Winged with Hopes.
To Cynthia; a Song. Thomas D'Urfey. CavP
(Born with the Vices.) OBS
To Cynthia, not to let him read the ladies' magazines. P. M. Hubbard. FiBHP
To Cynthia, on Concealment of Her Beauty. Sir Francis Kynaston. CavP; HBV-1; MeLP; MePo; NOBE; OBS; ViBoPo
To Cynthia on Her Being an Incendiary. Sir Francis Kynaston. HAP; NCEP
To Cynthia, on Her Changing. Sir Francis Kynaston. MePo
To Cynthia, on Her Embraces. Sir Francis Kynaston. NCEP
To Cyriack Skinner ("Cyriack, this three years' day"). Milton. *See* To Mr. Cyriack Skinner upon His Blindness.
To Cyriack Skinner ("Cyriack, whose grandsire"). Milton. GTBS; GTBS-P; OBEV
(Cyriack, Whose Grandsire.) NoP
(Sonnet: "Cyriack, whose grandsire on the royal bench.") LoBV; OBS
To D——, Dead by Her Own Hand. Howard Nemerov. PoA
To Daffodils [*or* Daffadills]. Robert Herrick. AnAnS-2; AWP; BoNaP; CaPo; ELP; EvOK; FaBoCh; FaBoEn; GN; GoJo; GTBS; GTBS-P; HBV-1; HBVY; InPS; JCP; LiTB; LoBV; NOBE: NoP; OAEP; OBEV; OBS; PoEL-3; PoRA; PPP; QFR; SeCeV; SeCP; SeCV-1; TrGrPo; UnPo; ViBoPo; WHA
To Daisies. Francis Thompson. HBV-1
To Daisies, Not to Shut So Soon[e]. Robert Herrick. CaPo; CH; ELP; GBL; HBV-1; InPK; OBEV; OBS; SeCV-1; TrGrPo
To D'Annunzio: Lines from the Sea. Robert Nichols. OBMV
To Dante. Vittorio Alfieri, *tr. fr. Italian by* Lorna De' Lucchi. AWP
To Dante. Guido Cavalcanti, *tr. fr. Italian by* Shelley. AWP
(Sonnet: Guido Cavalcanti to Dante.) OBVE
To Dante Alighieri. Guido Cavalcanti, *tr. fr. Italian by* Dante Gabriel Rossetti. AWP
To Dante Alighieri: He Conceives of Some Compensation in Death. Cino da Pistoia, *tr. fr. Italian by* Dante Gabriel Rossetti. AWP
To Dante Alighieri: He Interprets Dante Alighieri's Dream. Dante da Maiano, *tr. fr. Italian by* Dante Gabriel Rossetti. AWP
To Dante Alighieri: He Interprets Dante's Dream. Cino da Pistoia, *tr. fr. Italian by* Dante Gabriel Rossetti. AWP
To Dante Alighieri: He Mistrusts the Love of Lapo Gianni. Guido Cavalcanti, *tr. fr. Italian by* Dante Gabriel Rossetti. AWP
To Dante Alighieri: He Reports, in a Feigned Vision, the Successful Issue of Lapo Gianni's Love. Guido Cavalcanti, *tr. fr. Italian by* Dante Gabriel Rossetti. AWP
To Dante in Paradise, after Fiammetta's Death. Boccaccio, *tr. fr. Italian by* Dante Gabriel Rossetti. *Fr.* Sonnets. AWP; GoBC (*in* Fiammetta)
To Daphne. Walter Besant. HBV-1

To Daphne and Virginia. William Carlos Williams. CrMA
To Dark Eyes Dreaming. Zilpha Keatley Snyder. RHPC
To David, about His Education. Howard Nemerov. DiL
To Dean Bourn, a Rude River in Devon [by Which Sometimes He Lived]. Robert Herrick. AnAnS-2; CaPo; FaBoPP
(Dean-bourn, a Rude River in Devon.) SeCV-1
To Dear Daniel. Samuel Greenberg. LiTA; MoPo
To Death. Oliver St. John Gogarty. FaBoEE; OBMV
To Death. Padraic Pearse, *tr. fr. Modern Irish by* Thomas MacDonagh. AnIV
To Death. Countess of Winchilsea. HBV-2
To Death, Castara Being Sicke. William Habington. AnAnS-2
To Death, of His Lady. Villon, *tr. fr. French by* Dante Gabriel Rossetti. AWP
To deities of gauds and gold. Ad Patriam. Clinton Scollard. PAH
To Delia, *sels.* Samuel Daniel.
"And yet I cannot reprehend the flight." HBV-1; OAEP; OBEV
"Beauty, sweet love, is like the morning dew." EnRePo; HBV-1; NOBE; OBEV; OBSC; ViBoPo
(Sonnet: "Beauty, sweet love, is like the morning dew.") ElL
(Sonnet: "Beautie, sweet love, is like the morning dew.") FaBoEn
"But love whilst that thou mayst be loved again." ElL; NoP; OBSC
"Care charmer sleep, son of the sable night." AAS; EnRePo; GTBS; GTBS-P; HBV-1; InPS; LiTB; LoBV; NIP; NOBE; NoP; OAEL-1; OAEP; OBSC; TreFS; TrGrPo
(Sonnet: "Care charmer sleep[e], son[ne] of the sable night.") ElL; FaBoEn; PoEL-2; ViBoPo
"Fair is my love, and cruel as she's fair." AAS; EnRePo; HBV-1; NOBE: NoP; OAEP; OBSC; TEP; TrGrPo
(Beauty, Time and Love.) OBEV
(Fair Is My Love.) LiTB
(Sonnet: "Fair is my love, and cruel as she's fair.") ElL; HoPM; ViBoPo
"I must not grieve my love, whose eyes would read." HBV-1; OBEV; PoPle
("Sonnet: I must not grieve my love, whose eyes would read.") ElL
"I once may see when yeares shall wreck my wrong." AAS
"If it so hap, this of-spring of my care." AAS
"If this be love, to draw [*or* drawe] a weary [*or* wearie] breath." AAS; GBL; OBSC; TrGrPo
"Let others sing of knights and paladins [*or* palladines]." AAS; HBV-1; NOBE; NoP; OAEP; OBEV; OBSC
(Sonnet: "Let others sing of knights and paladin[e]s.") ElL; FaBoEn
"Like as the lute delights or else dislikes." OAEP
"Look, Delia, how we esteem the half-blown rose." HBV-1; HeIP; NoP; OBSC; WHA
(Half-blown Rose, The.) SeCePo
(Sonnet: "Look, Delia, how we esteem the half-blown rose.") ElL
"My spotless love hovers, with purest wings." HBV-1; OBEV; OBSC
(Most Unloving One, The.) SeCePo
"My cares draw on mine everlasting night." OBSC
"None other fame mine unambitious muse." AAS
"Read in my face a volume of despairs." EnRePo
"Star of my mishap imposed this pain, The." OBSC
"These plaintive verse, the posts of my desire." AAS; OBSC
"Thou canst not die whilst any zeal abound." OAEP; OBSC
"Time, cruel time, come and subdue that brow." OBSC
"Unto the boundless ocean of thy beauty." LoBV; OAEP; OBSC
"When men shall find thy flower, thy glory, pass." HBV-1; NOBE: NoP; OBEV; OBSC; TrGrPo
(Sonnet: "When men shall find thy flower, thy glory, pass.") ElL
"When winter snows upon thy sable hairs." CTC; EnRePo; OBSC; TEP
To Delmore Schwartz. Robert Lowell. NoAM; NMP
To Demeter. Maybury Fleming. AA
To demolish it. All Splendor on Earth. Karin Kiwus, *tr. by* Almut McAuley. BoWoP
To Desi as Joe as Smoky the Lover of 115th Street. Audre Lorde. CNA
To Destiny. *Unknown, tr. fr. Dahomean song by* Frances Herskovits. EaLo
To destroy or deride Creation's task. Kashrut. Edouard Roditi. VWA
To Detraction [I Present My Poesie]. John Marston. *Fr.* The Scourge of Villainy. LoBV; OBSC; TW
To Diane. Helen Hay Whitney. HBV-1
To Dianeme ("Dear, though to part it be hell"). Robert Herrick. CaPo
To Dianeme ("Give me one kiss"). Robert Herrick. CaPo; FaBoBe
To Dianeme ("Show me thy feet; show me thy legs, thy thighs"). Robert Herrick. AnAnS-2; CaPo; POL
(Show Me Thy Feet.) UnTE
To Dianeme ("Sweet, be not proud of those two eyes"). Robert Herrick. CaPo; FaBoEn; GTBS; GTBS-P; HBV-1; JCP; LoBV; NOBE; OBEV; OBS; PoPle; SeCV-1; TrGrPo; ViBoPo
To die be given us, or attain! Resignation. Matthew Arnold. OAEP; VLP
To die old. Ancient of Days. Anthony Rudolf. VWA
To die with a forlorn hope, but soon to be raised. The Survivor. Robert Graves. CMoP; MoVE
To Dinah Washington. Etheridge Knight. PoBA
To Disraeli. Shirley Brooks. NOBL
To dive for the nimbus on the sea-floor. Nimbus. Douglas Le Pan. MoCV; OBCV; PeCV
To Dives. Hilaire Belloc. HBMV; OBSV
To Doctor Bale. Barnabe Googe. EnRePo
To Doctor Empirick [*or* Empiric]. Ben Jonson. DBV; FaBoEE; NoP; SeCP
To Donnybrook steer, all you sons of Parnassus. The Humours of Donnybrook Fair. *Unknown.* OnYI
To Dorothy. Marvin Bell. Psk
To Dorothy on Her Exclusion from the *Guinness Book of World Records.* X. J. Kennedy. Psk
To Dr. Arbuthnot. Pope. *See* Epistle to Dr. Arbuthnot.
To Dr. Delaney, *sel.* Ben Jonson.
"How oft am I for rhyme to seek?" PP
To Dr. F. B. on His Book of Chess. Richard Lovelace. CaPo
To Dr. Kipling. Richard Porson. FaBoCo
To Dr. Swift on His Birthday, 30th November 1721. Esther Johnson. EnLoPo
To draw no envy, Shakespeare, on thy name. To the Memory of My Beloved Master [*or* the Author, Mr.] William Shakespeare [and What He Hath Left Us]. Ben Jonson. AnAnS-2; CABA; EnRePo; GoTL; HAP; HBV-2; HeIP; JCP; LiTB; NoP; OAEL-1; OAEP; OBS; PoEL-2; PP; SeCeV; SeCP; SeCV-1; TreFS; TrGrPo; ViBoPo; WHA
To draw, or not to draw, that is the question. *Unknown.* BXAP
To Dream Again. Shakespeare. *See* Caliban.
To dream of love, and, waking, to remember you. Dreams. Arthur Symons. PoA
To dream the impossible dream. The Impossible Dream. Joe Darion. BLSo
To dreamy languors and the violet mist. Dogwood Blossoms. George Marion McClellan. BANP
To Drift Down. Janet Carncross Chandler. AMV-81
To drift with every passion till my soul. Hélas. Oscar Wilde. AnIV; BrPo; MoBrPo; TEP; UnTE; VLP
To Drink. Gabriela Mistral, *tr. fr. Spanish by* Gunda Kaiser. NU
To drink a toast. The Man for Galway. Charles James Lever. OnYI
To drink in moderation, and to smoke. Party Knee. John Updike. FiBHP
To drive the kine one summer's morn. The Cow-Chace. John André. PAH
To drum-beat and heart-beat. Nathan Hale. Francis Miles Finch. PAH; PAL
To Duty. Thomas Wentworth Higginson. AA
To Dwell Together in Unity. Bible, *O.T.* Psalms, CXXXIII, TrJP
(Psalm CXXXIII.) AWP; TrV
(Unity of Mankind.) TreFT
To E. Fitzgerald. Tennyson. *See* To Edward Fitzgerald.
To E. M. O. Thomas Edward Brown. WhC
To Each His Own. Margaret Root Garvin. HBV-2
To each his suffering; all are men. Where Ignorance Is Bliss. Thomas Gray. *Fr.* On a Distant Prospect of Eton College. TreF
To each one is given a marble to carve for the wall. The Task That Is Given to You. Edwin Markham. WBLP
To Earth. James Applewhite. PoA
To Earthward. Robert Frost. AP; BiP; BLPL; CABA; CoBMV; HBMV; LiTA; MoAB; MoAmPo; MoPo; MoVE; NePA; NoAM; NOBA; NoP; OxBA; PPoe; TAP; TwAmPo
To eastward ringing, to westward winging, o'er mapless miles of sea. When the Great Gray Ships Come In. Guy Wetmore Carryl. EtS; FaBoBe; HBV-2; PAH
To eat pain like bread is a condition. Ruth Miller. *Fr.* Cycle. PeSA
To Eddleston. Byron. *Fr.* Childe Harold's Pilgrimage, II. PeHV
To Edom. Heine, *tr. fr. German.* TrJP
To Edward Allen. Ben Jonson. OAEP; OBS
To Edward Fitzgerald. Robert Browning. DBV; TW
To Edward Fitzgerald. Tennyson. LoBV
(To E. Fitzgerald.) PoEL-5
To Edward Thomas. Alun Lewis. WaP
To Egypt. Gloria Davis. NBP
To E.L., on His Travels in Greece. Tennyson. SeCePo
To Electra ("I dare not ask a kiss"). Robert Herrick. BLPL; CaPo; CavP; HBV-1; HoPM; LoBV; OBEV; OBS; SeCV-1
To Electra ("I'll come to thee in all those shapes"). Robert Herrick. *See* I've Come to Thee.
To Eliza, Duchess of Dorset. Joseph Bennett. LiTA; NePA
To Elizabeth, Countess of Rutland. Ben Jonson. NoP
To Elizabeth she came. The Visitation. Calvin Le Compte. ISi
To Ellen. Charles Stetler. PPJ
To Elsie. William Carlos Williams. AP; CABA; CMoP; CoBMV; InPS; NOBA; SeCeV

To Emily. Arthur Gregor. AMV-80
To Emily Dickinson. Hart Crane. CMoP; NoAM; NOBA; NoP; TAP
To Emma, Extempore; Hyaena, off Gambia, June 4, 1779. Edward Thompson. NOEC
To employ her. Europe. John Ashbery. CoPo
To End Her Fear. John Freeman. OBMV
To end it all, the people elected a thumb. The Thumb. Dennis Saleh. MAT; NeAC
To England. George Henry Boker. AA; HBV-2
To England. Byron. *Fr.* Childe Harold's Pilgrimage, IV. WHA
To England. Charles Leonard Moore. AA
To English Connoiseurs. Blake. OxBoLi
To Entertain Divine Zenocrate. Chistopher Marlowe. *See* Divine Zenocrate.
To escape from internal dragons. Modern Architecture. Norman Nathan. AMV-81
To Etesia Looking from Her Casement at the Full Moon. Henry Vaughan. MOON
To Evan. Richard Eberhart. DFF
To Evening. William Collins. *See* Ode to Evening.
To Everlasting Oblivion. John Marston. *Fr.* The Scourge of Villainy. LoBV; OBSC
To every action, they say. Newton's Third. Jake T. W. Hubbard. AMV-80
To every Class we have a School assign'd. Schools. George Crabbe. The Borough, Letter XXIV. CTC
"To every Form of being is assigned." Discourse of the Wanderer, and an Evening Visit to the Lake. Wordsworth. *Fr.* The Excursion, IX. EnRP
To every heart which the sweet pain doth move. Dante, *tr. by* Dante Gabriel Rossetti. La Vita Nuova, I. AWP
To every man. The Treehouse. James A. Emanuel. AmNP; BPo; NNP; PoBA
To every man there openeth. The Ways. John Oxenham. HBMV; PoLF; TRV
To Everything There Is a Season. Bible, *O. T.* Ecclesiastes, III: 1-8. FF; NAWM-1 (1-22); OBVE; PoPl (1-11)
(Time for Everything, A.) TrGrPo
To explain the nature of fishes in craft of verse. The Whale. *Unknown, tr. by* Gavin Bone. EBEV
To F. C. Mortimer Collins. HBV-1; TreFS
To F. C. in Memoriam Palestine. G. K. Chesterton. HBMV
To failing strength a stick is given. The Stick. May O'Rourke. HBMV
To fair Fidele's grassy tomb. A Song from Shakespeare's "Cymbeline" [*or* Dirge in "Cymbeline" *or* Fidele]. William Collins. ELP; EnRP; HBV-2; LAuP; NOBE; NOEC; OAEP; OBEC; OBEV; SeCePo; ViBoPo
To fall in love, though classically human. Advice to Colonel Valentine. Robert Graves. NYBP
To fall, like an apple, no mind. In the Emptied Rest Home. Bella Akhmadulina, *tr. by* Jean Valentine *and* Olga Carlisle. BoWoP
To Fancy. Keats. *See* Fancy.
To Fanny. Keats. EBEV; EnRP; TrGrPo; UnTE
(I Cry Your Mercy.) BoLoP; PPP
To Fanny. Thomas Moore. HBV-1
To Fanny Brawne. Keats. *See* This Living Hand, Now Warm and Capable.
To farther this, Achitophel unites. The Malcontents. Dryden. *Fr.* Absalom and Achitophel, I. OBS
To Favonius. Edmund Bolton. OBSC
To feel and speak the astonishing beauty of things. The Beauty of Things. Robinson Jeffers. PoA
To Felicity Who Calls Me Mary. Frances Chesterton. HBMV
To Fez Cobra. Ted Joans. GP
To fight aloud is very brave. Emily Dickinson. AP; LiTA; WPE
To find the Western path. Morning. Blake. FaBoCh; LoBV; OAEL-2; OBRV
To Finde God. Robert Herrick. WGRP
To Fine Grand. Ben Jonson. JCP
To Fine Lady Would-Be. Ben Jonson. FaBoEE; JCP; NoP
To fish for pearls in Lethe. The Great Magicians. C. Day Lewis. EaLo
To Flavia. Edmund Waller. HBV-1
To Flaxman. Blake. FaBoEE; OxBoLi
To flee from memory. Emily Dickinson. FaBoEE
To fleece the Fleece from golden sheep. The Scales of the Eyes. Howard Nemerov. CMoP; NMP
To Fletcher Reviv'd. Richard Lovelace. OBS
To fling my arms wide. Dream Variation [*or* Variations]. Langston Hughes. AmNP; BALP; CDC; HAP; IDB; NOBA; PoBA; PoNe; PoPl; WeW
To Flood Stage Again. James Wright. NOBA; Prf
To Flossie. William Carlos Williams. NePoAm-2
To fly off, a ripe pear in a storm. Definition of the Soul. Boris Pasternak, *tr. fr. Russian by* Babette Deutsch. TrJP
To Fool, or Knave. Ben Jonson. FaBoEE; NoP; SoSe
To Ford Madox Ford in Heaven. William Carlos Williams. AmPP; NoAM; NOBA
To Forget Me. Theodore Weiss. CoAP
To forgive enemies Hayley does pretend. Blake. FaBoEE
To Form a Just and Finish'd Piece. Swift. *Fr.* Directions for Making a Birth-Day Song. NAs
To Fortune. Robert Herrick. SeCV-1
To Fortune. Sir Thomas More. ACP
To Fortune. James Thomson. BSV
("For ever, Fortune, wilt thou prove.") GTBS; GTBS-P
To France. Ralph Chaplin. HBMV
To Francelia. Thomas Duffett. CavP
To Francis Beaumont. Ben Jonson. OAEP; OBS
To Frankfort I on *Schobbas* came. The Best Religion. Heine, *tr. by* Emma Lazarus. *Fr.* Tannhäuser. TrJP
To free me from domestic strife. At Hadleigh, Suffolk. *Unknown.* FaBoCo
To free the ball the chief now turns his mind. Victory on the Last Green. Thomas Mathison. *Fr.* The Goff; an Heroi-comical Poem. NOEC
To freight cars in the air. The Descent of Winter (Section 10/30). William Carlos Williams. InPK
To Friend and Foe. *Unknown.* CoMu
To Friends Who Have Also Considered Suicide. Phyllis Webb. NOBC
To Frighten a Storm. Gladys Cardiff. CDW; STE
To Fuscus Aristus. Horace, *tr. fr. Latin by* Abraham Cowley. Epistles I, 10. AWP
To G, her one and only rose. Love-Letter Two. *Unknown.* PeHV
To G. K. Chesterton. Joseph Mary Plunkett. OnYI
To G. R. Samuel Elsworth Cottam. PeHV
To gallop off to town post-haste. Friar Lubin. Clement Marot, *tr. by* Longfellow. AWP; DBV
To "Garryowen" upon an organ ground. In the Dials. W. E. Henley. BrPo
To gather flowers Sappha went. The Apron of Flowers. Robert Herrick. CaPo; SeCV-1
To George Barker. Gene Derwood. NePA
To George Pulling Buds. Adelaide O'Keeffe. FaBoUs
To George Sand: A Desire. Elizabeth Barrett Browning. BoWoP; TEP
To George Sand: A Recognition. Elizabeth Barrett Browning. BoWoP; SBG; TEP
To Germany. Charles Hamilton Sorley. MoBrPo
To Geron. Hildebrand Jacob. NOEC
To get betimes in Boston town I rose this morning early. A Boston Ballad. Walt Whitman. OBAL
To get off the ground has always been difficult. Dialectics of Flight. John Hall Wheelock. NePoAm-2
To Gild Refinèd Gold. Shakespeare. *Fr.* King John, IV, ii. LiTB
(Ridiculous Excess). TreFT
To Giotto. Wesley Trimpi. NePoEA
To Giulia Grisi. Nathaniel Parker Willis. AA
To give up everything. Huck Finn at Ninety, Dying in a Chicago Boarding House Room. James Schevill. TAP
To give—and forgive. Short Sermon. *Unknown.* TiPo
To go in the dark with a light is to know the light. To Know the Dark. Wendell Berry. GP
To go, to leave the classics and the buildings. Poem. Gavin Ewart. NeBP
To go to Rome. The Pilgrim at Rome [*or* A Word of Warning]. *Unknown.* AnIL; KiLC
To God. Blake. OAEL-2
To God. Robert Herrick. AnAnS-2; TrPWD; TRV; WGRP
To God alone, the only donour. Francis Daniel Pastorius. SCAP
To God, on His Sickness. Robert Herrick. OxBoCh
To God Our Strength Shout Joyfully, *with music.* Henry Ainsworth. AH
To God, the Architect. Harry Kemp. *See* God, the Architect.
To God, the everlasting, who abides. An Invocation. John Addington Symonds. WGRP
To God the Father. Henry Constable. GoBC
To God the Son. Henry Constable. OBSC
To God: to illuminate all men. Beginning with Skid Road. Psalm III. Allen Ginsberg. CAPP
"To God, Ye Choir Above." Philip Skelton. OxBoCh
To God's anointed and his chosen flock. "Christo et Ecclesiae" 1700. Oliver Wendell Holmes. *Fr.* Two Sonnets: Harvard. AP
To grasp it; say that you have seized that hour. César Franck. Joseph Auslander. HBMV
To grass, or leaf, or fruit, or wall. The Snail. Vincent Bourne, *tr. by* William Cowper. HBV-1; HBVY; OBVE
To Greet a Letter-Carrier. William Carlos Williams. OBAL
To Grosphus. Godfrey the Satirist, *tr. fr. Latin.* PeHV
To Groves. Robert Herrick. CaPo
To Grow Older. "Jan Struther." LO
To grow unguided at a time when none. A Tough Generation. David Gascoyne. LiTM

To H. Blake. *See* To William Hayley.
To H. C. Wordsworth. ChER; EnRP; OBRV; PoEL-4
(To Hartley Coleridge.) HBV-1
To Hafiz. Thomas Bailey Aldrich. AA
To Hampstead. Leigh Hunt. EnRP; OBRV
To Harold Jacoby. Irwin Edman. InMe
To Hartley Coleridge. Wordsworth. *See* To H. C.
To Hasekawa. Walter Conrad Arensberg. HBV-2
To have it out or not? that is the question. "C. A. W." BXAP
To have known him, to have loved him. Monody. Herman Melville. AP; LiTA; NCEP; PoEL-5
To have liv'd eminent in a degree. Upon the Death of My Ever Desired Friend Doctor Donne Dean of Pauls. Henry King. AnAnS-2; SeCP
To Haydn. Thomas Holcroft. NOEC
To Hayley. Blake. *See* To William Hayley.
To heal you Hieronymus I had brought you. Bear's Blood. Ileana Malancioiu, *tr. by* Stavros Deligiorgis. BoWoP
To hear a dripping water tap in a house. Betweens. Norman MacCaig. EAS
To hear an oriole sing. Emily Dickinson. AP; PB; PoEL-5
To Hear My Head Roar. Henry Taylor. MAYP
To Heaven. Ben Jonson. AnAnS-2; EnRePo; HAP; ILwL; JCP; LiTB; LoBV; NOCV; OBS; PPoe; QFR; SeCeV; SeCP; TrPWD; UnPo
(Good and Great God!) OxBoCh
To Helen. Poe. AA; AmPP; AP; AWP; BoLoP; CABA; CH; ChTr; FaBoBe; FaBoEn; FaBV; FaFP; FaPo; FPL; GBL; HAP; HBV-1; HBVY; HeIP; HoPM; InPS; InvP; LiTA; LoBV; NePA; NIP; NOBE; NoP; OBEV; OBRV; ONVV; OxBA; PAI; PoEL-4; PoLF; PoRA; PrIm; SeCeV; TAP; TreF; TrGrPo; ViBoPo; WeW; WHA
To Helen. Winthrop Mackworth Praed. HBV-1; LoBV
To Helen Frankenthaler. Anne Cherner. PoDr
To Helen in a Huff. Nathaniel Parker Willis. OBAL
To Helen of Troy (N.Y.) Peter Viereck. WeW
To Hell with Commonsense. Patrick Kavanagh. CIP; FaBoTw
To Hell with It. Frank O'Hara. NeAP
To Hell with Your Fertility Cult. Gary Snyder. NAs; TW
To Henrietta, on Her Departure for Calais. Thomas Hood. OxBChV
To Henry Constable and Henry Keir. Alexander Montgomerie. OxBS
To Henry David Thoreau. Irwin Edman. WhC
To Henry Reynolds, of Poets and Poesy, *sel.* Michael Drayton. Christopher Marlowe. ChTr
To Henry Vaughan. A. J. M. Smith. OBCV
To Henry Wright of Mobberley, Esq. on Buying the Picture of Father Malebranche. John Byrom. NOEC
To Her. Robert Mezey. NaP
To Her Body, against Time. Robert Kelly. CoPo
To Her Dead Mate: Montana, 1966. Elizabeth Libbey. AmPA
To Her Eyes. Lord Herbert of Cherbury. JCP; OBS
To Her in Absence; a Ship. Thomas Carew. CaPo
To Her Love. Edward May. FaBoEE
To Her Questioning His Estate. William Hammond. JCP
To Her Sea-faring Lover. *Unknown. See* Lady Prayeth the Return of Her Lover Abiding on the Seas, The.
To Her—Unspoken. Amelia Josephine Burr. HBV-1
To Hero nightly, wet and rather cold. Subjectivity at Sestos. P. M. Hubbard. NYBP
To hide her ordure, claws the cat. A Quarrelsome Bishop. Walter Savage Landor. FaBoEE; OBSV
To Him Be Glory. Bible, *N.T.* Romans, XII: 33-36. TRV
To Him be praise who made. Deus Noster Ignis Consumens. Laurence Housman. HBMV
To him who felt a human sea. Ballad of the Common Man. Alfred Kreymborg. PAL
To him who in the love of Nature holds. Thanatopsis. Bryant. AA; AmPP; AP; AWP; BLPL; BoNaP; DL; FaBoBe; FaFP; HBV-2; HBVY; LiTA; NePA; NOBA; OBEV; OBRV; OBVV; OHFP; OxBA; TAP; TreF; TrGrPo; ViBoPo; WBLP; WGRP; WHA
To Him Who Is Feared. Eleazar ben Kalir, *tr. fr. Hebrew by* Lady Katie Magnus. TrJP
To Himself. Richard Aldridge. NePoAm
To Himself. Catullus, *tr. fr. Latin by* William Ellery Leonard. AWP
To Himselfe and the Harpe, *abr.* Michael Drayton. OBS
To His Book[e] ("To read my book, the virgin shy"). Martial, *tr. fr. Latin by* Robert Herrick. AnAnS-2; AWP
("To read my booke, the virgin shie.") OBVE
To His Book ("Go thou forth, my book, though late"). Robert Herrick. CaPo
To His Book ("Have I not blessed thee? Then go forth; nor fear"). Robert Herrick. CaPo
To His Booke ("Who with thy leaves shall wipe at need"). Robert Herrick. FaBoUs; JCP
(Another.) AnAnS-2
To His Booke. Martial. *See* To His Book.
To His Books. Henry Vaughan. QFR
To his book's end this last line he'd have placed. Robert Herrick. CaPo
To his Castle Lord Fothergay bore his young bride. High-Life Low-Down. Justin Richardson. PV
To His Chi Mistress. George Starbuck. NYBP
To His Child. William Bullokar. OxBChV
To His Children in Darkness. James Dickey. DiL
To His Conscience. Robert Herrick. AnAnS-2; NoP; OxBoCh; PoEL-3
To His Countrymen. James Russell Lowell. *Fr.* A Fable for Critics. AA
To His Coy Love. Michael Drayton. EIL; ErPo; HBV-1; OBEV; OBS; ViBoPo
(I Pray Thee Leave, Love Me No More.) ELP; InvP
To His Coy Mistress, *parody.* Edward Bird. BXAP; FaBoPa
To His Coy Mistress, *parody.* John Flood. BXAP; FaBoPa
To His Coy Mistress, *parody.* Gerry Hamill. BXAP
To His Coy Mistress. Andrew Marvell. AnAnS-1; AWP; BiP; BoLoP; CABA; CavP; EBEV; ELP; EnLoPo; ErPo; FaBoEn; FaBV; FaFP; FF; FPL; GBL; HAP; HBV-1; HeIP; HoPM; InPK; InPS; InvP; JCP; LiTB; LoBV; MAT; MasP; MeLP; MePo; NIP; NOBE; NoP; OAEL-1; OAEP; OBEV; OBS; PAI; PoEL-2; PoLF; PoPl; PoPle; PoRA; PPoe; PPP; PrIm; SCV; SeCePo; SeCeV; SeCP; SeCV-1; SoSe; TEP; TreFT; TrGrPo; UnPo; UnTE; ViBoPo; WeW; WHA
To His Coy Mistress, *parody.* Peter Scupham. BXAP
To His Coy Mistress, *parody.* Stanley J. Sharpless. BXAP
To His Coy Mistress, *parody.* W. J. Webster. BXAP
To His Darrest Freind. John Steward of Baldynneis. OxBS
To His Dead Body. Siegfried Sassoon. NoAM
To His Dear Friend, Bones. Jay Parini. MAYP
To His Dying Brother, Master William Herrick. Robert Herrick. CaPo; OAEP; PoPle; SeCV-1
To His Ever-loving God. Robert Herrick. AnAnS-2; TrPWD
To His Ever-worshipped Will from W.H. "Francis." ErPo
To His Excellency George Washington. Phillis Wheatley. OFD; SBG; WPE
(His Excellency General Washington.) PoNe
To His Excellency Joseph Dudley. John Saffin. SCAP
To His Father. Robinson Jeffers. DiL
To His Father on Praising the Honest Life of the Peasant. Parvin E'tesami, *tr. fr. Persian by* Deirdre Lashgari. WPOW
To His Flocks. *At. to* Henry Constable *and to* Henry Chettle. FM
To His Forsaken Mistress. Sir Robert Ayton. EIL; ErPo; HBV-1; OBEV; OBS; SeCePo
(Inconstancy Reproved.) BSV; GBL
To His Friend. George Turberville. *See* To His Friend, Promising That Though Her Beauty Fade . . .
To His Friend ———. Henry Vaughan. PP
To his Friend Ben. Johnson, of his Horace made English. Lord Herbert of Cherbury. AnAnS-2
To His Friend in Absence. Walafrid Strabo, *tr. fr. Latin by* Helen Waddell. PeHV
To His Friend in Elysium. Joachim du Bellay, *tr. fr. French by* Andrew Lang. AWP
To His Friend J. H. Alexander Brome. CavP
To His Friend Master R. L., in Praise of Music and Poetry. Richard Barnfield. EIL; UnS
("If musique [*or* music] and sweet poetrie [*or* poetry] agree.") AAS; ViBoPo
To His Friend, on the Untunable Times. Robert Herrick. CaPo
To His Friend, Promising That Though Her Beauty Fade, Yet His Love Shall Last. George Turberville. OBSC
(To His Friend.) CTC
To His Girl. Martial, *tr. fr. Latin by* Louis Untermeyer. UnTE
To His Godson Gerald C. A. Jackson. A. E. Housman. WhC
To His Heart. Sir Thomas Wyatt. OBSC
("Ah! my heart, ah! what aileth thee.") SiPS
To His Honoured and Most Ingenious Friend, Master Charles Cotton. Robert Herrick. CaPo
To His Inconstant Mistress. Thomas Carew. *See* To My Inconstant Mistress.
To His Kinsman, Master Thomas Herrick, Who Desired to Be in His Book. Robert Herrick. CaPo
To His Kinswoman, Mistress Penelope Wheeler. Robert Herrick. CaPo
To His Lady. Sir John Davies. SiPS
To His Lady. Fulke Greville. *See* More than Most Fair.
To His Lady. Henry VIII, King of England. CTC; EBEV; OBSC
To His Lady. Petrarch. *See* Vow to Love Faithfully.
To His Lady. Sir Thomas Wyatt. *See* Madame, withouten Many Words.
To His Lady, Who Had Vowed Virginity. Walter Davison. OBSC
To His Late Majesty Concerning the True Form of English Poetry. Sir John Beaumont. JCP; OBS
"He makes sweet music who, in serious lines," *sel.* PP

To His Little Son Benedict from the Tower of London. John Hoskyns. OxBChV
To His Love. Ivor Gurney. MMA; OBWP
To His Love. *At. to* John Dowland. *See* Come Away, Come, Sweet Love.
To His Love ("Shall I compare thee to a summer's day?"). Shakespeare. *See* Sonnets, XVIII.
To His Love ("When in the chronicle of wasted time"). Shakespeare. *See* Sonnets, CVI.
To His Love in Middle-Age. Edwin Brock. AMV–80
To His Love, That Sent Him a Ring Wherein Was Graved, "Let Reason Rule." George Turberville. EnRePo
To His Lovely Mistresses. Robert Herrick. CaPo; CTC; OAEP; SeCP
To His Lute. William Drummond of Hawthornden. GTBS; GTBS–P
To His Lute. Sir Thomas Wyatt. *See* Lover Complaineth the Unkindness . . .
To His Maid Prew. Robert Herrick. OBS
To His Maistres. Alexander Montgomerie. *See* To His Mistress.
To His Mistress[e] ("Choose me your valentine"). Robert Herrick. OFD; ViBoPo
To His Mistress [*or* Maistres]. Alexander Montgomerie. GBL; OxBS
To His Mistress. Ovid, *tr. fr. Latin by* Dryden. BoLoP; ErPo
(Possessive Lover, The, *tr. by* Christopher Marlowe.) UnTE
("Your husband? Going to the same dinner as us?" *tr. by* Guy Lee.) NAWM–1
To His Mistress. Sir Walter Ralegh. *See* Silent Lover, The.
To His Mistress. Earl of Rochester. OBEV
To His Mistress. George Villiers, Duke of Buckingham. CavP
To His Mistress Desiring to Travel with Him as His Page. John Donne. *See* On His Mistress.
To His Mistress for Her True Picture. Lord Herbert of Cherbury. AnAnS–2; SeCP
To His Mistress Going to Bed. John Donne. *See* Going to Bed.
To His Mistress in Absence. Tasso, *tr. fr. Italian by* Thomas Stanley. AWP
To His Mistress Objecting to Him neither Toying or Talking. Robert Herrick. FaBV
To His Mistress, the Queen of Bohemia. Sir Henry Wotton. ELP
To His Mistresse. Robert Herrick. *See* To His Mistress.
To His Mistresse on Her Scorne. Thomas Beedome. CavP
To His Mistresses ("Help me! Help me! now I call"). Robert Herrick. CaPo; ErPo; SeCP; UnTE
To His Mistresses ("Put on your silks, and piece by piece"). Robert Herrick. CaPo
To His Mistris Confined. James Shirley. OBS
To His Mistris Going to Bed. John Donne. *See* Going to Bed.
To His Mother. John Banister Tabb. *Fr.* The Child. AA
To His Mother, C. L. M. John Masefield. *See* C. L. M.
To His Muse. Nicholas Breton. OBSC
To His Muse. Robert Herrick. OAEP
To His Noble Friend, Mr. Richard Lovelace, upon His Poems. Andrew Marvell. PP
To His Not-so-coy Mistress. Wynford Vaughan-Thomas. BXAP; NOBL
To His Pen. Sir Thomas Wyatt. OBSC
To His Reader. Samuel Daniel. *See* To the Reader.
To His Retired Friend, an Invitation to Brecknock, *sels.* Henry Vaughan.
"Come! leave this sullen state, and let not wine." ViBoPo
Winter's Frosty Pangs. FaBoRV
To His Ring, Given To His Lady, Wherein Was Graven This Verse, "My Heart Is Yours." George Turberville. ElL
To His Sacred Majesty, a Panegyrick on His Coronation, 1661, *sel.* Dryden.
"Time seems not now beneath his years to stoop." OBS
To His Saviour, a Child; a Present, by a Child. Robert Herrick. OxBoCh; SeCP; TrCP
(Child's Present to His Child-Saviour, A.) OHIP; OxBChV
To His Son. Sir Walter Ralegh. *See* Wood, the Weed, the Wag, The.
To His Son Bennet. John Hoskyns. FaBoEE
To His Son [*or* Sonne], Vincent Corbet[t] [on His Birth-Day, November 10, 1630]. Richard Corbet. AnAnS–2; FaBoCh; OBS; OxBChV
(To His Son, Vincent.) TrGrPo
To His Soul. Emperor Hadrian. *See* Hadrian's Address to His Soul When Dying.
To His Tomb-Maker. Robert Herrick. SeCV–1
To His Unconstant Friend. Henry King. AnAnS–2
To His Valentine. Michael Drayton. PoEL–2
To His Verse. Walter Savage Landor. OBVV
To His Watch. Gerard Manley Hopkins. MoAB; MoBrPo
To His Watch, When He Could Not Sleep. Lord Herbert of Cherbury. JCP; MePo; NOBE; PoEL–2
To His Wife. Ausonius, *tr. fr. Latin by* Terrot Reaveley Glover. AWP
To His Wife on the Fourteenth Anniversary of Her Wedding-Day, with a Ring. Samuel Bishop. ViBoPo
(To Mary.) HBV–1
To His Worthy Friend Doctor Witty upon His Translation of the "Popular Errors." Andrew Marvell. GLGT; PP
To His Young Mistress. Anacreon, *tr. fr. Greek by* Abraham Cowley. UnTE
To His Young Mistress. Pierre de Ronsard, *tr. fr. French by* Andrew Lang. AWP
To hold my own hand in some secret place. Knee Deep. Ted Joans. GP
To Homer. Keats. CABA; EBEV; NCEP; NoP; OBRV
(Sonnet: To Homer.) ChER
To honor the return of sparkling sun. Sonnet XV. Louise Labé, *tr. by* Willis Barnstone. BoWoP
To Hope. Helen Maria Williams. OBEC
To hope is good, but with such wild applause. Hope. Sir Richard Fanshawe. *Fr.* Il Pastor Fido. OBS
To Houston at Gonzales town, ride, Ranger, for your life. The Men of the Alamo. James Jeffrey Roche. BPAW; PAH
To Hugh MacDiarmid. Edwin Morgan. FaBoTw
To Hunt. Blake. OxBoLi
To hunt and to be hunted make existence. Charles Heavysege. *Fr.* Saul. CaP
To hurt the Negro and avoid the Jew. University. Karl Shapiro. LiTA; OxBA
To I. Lavrentevaya. Natalya Gorbanyevskaya, *tr. fr. Russian by* Daniel Weissbort. BoWoP
To Ianthe. Byron. *Fr.* Childe Harold's Pilgrimage, *dedication.* FaBoEn
(Dedication: To Ianthe.) OBNC
To Ianthe ("You smiled, you spoke, and I believed"). Walter Savage Landor. *See* You Smiled . . .
To Ianthe ("Past ruined Ilion Helen lives"). Walter Savage Landor. *See* Past Ruined Ilion . . .
To Ibn Zaidun. Wallada, *tr. fr. Arabic by* James Monroe *and* Deirdre Lashgari. WPOW
To Imagination ("When weary with long day's care"). Emily Brontë. VLP
To Imagination ("O [*or* Oh] thy bright eyes must answer now"). Emily Bronte. *See* Plead for Me.
To Imagination. Edith M. Thomas. AA
To Inez Milholland. Edna St. Vincent Millay. WPE
To Insure Survival. Simon J. Ortiz. CDW
To Ireland in the Coming Times. W. B. Yeats. NoAM; OxBI
(Apologia Addressed to Ireland in the Coming Days.) BrPo
To Iron-Founders and Others. Gordon Bottomley. OBEV; OBMV; OBVV
To Italy. Giacomo Leopardi, *tr. fr. Italian by* Romilda Rendel. AWP
To J. S. Collis. Ruth Pitter. OxBoCh
To James. Frank Horne. *Fr.* Letters Found near a Suicide. BPo
To James Smith. *See* Epistle to James Smith.
To Jane: The Invitation. Shelley. *See* Invitation, The.
To Jane: The Keen Stars Were Twinkling. Shelley. NoP
To Jane: The Recollection. Shelley. ChER; OBNC; OBRV
(Recollection, The.) GTBS; GTBS–P
"We wandered to the pine forest," *sel.* CH
To Janet. Ralph Pomeroy. NYBP
To Jann, in Her Absence. C. J. Driver. PeSA
To Jessie's Dancing Feet. William De Lancey Ellwanger. AA
To Jesus of Nazareth. Frederic Lawrence Knowles. TrPWD
To Jesus on His Birthday. Edna St. Vincent Millay. TrCP; TrGrPo
To J.F.K. 14 Years After. Roger Weaver. AMV–80
To Joan. Lucille Clifton. GeTw
To John C. Frémont. Whittier. PAH
To John Donne ("Donne, the delight of Phoebus, and each Muse"). Ben Jonson. AnAnS–2; OAEP; OBS; SeCV–1
To John Donne ("Who shall doubt, Donne, where I a poet bee"). Ben Jonson. AnAnS–2; JCP; NoP; SeCP; SeCV–1
To John Greenleaf Whittier. William Hayes Ward. AA
To John I ow'd [*or* owed] great obligation. Epigram [*or* Quits]. Martial, *tr. by* Matthew Prior. AWP; FaBoCo; FaBoEE; FaFP; OBVE
To John Keats, Poet, at Springtime. Countee Cullen. BANP; CDC
To John Taylor. Robert Burns. WhC
To join the ages they have gone. Seven Years. Marquess of Crewe. OBVV
To Juan at the Winter Solstice. Robert Graves. CMoP; CoBMV; EBEV; FaBoMo; LiTB; LiTM; MoBrPo; MoPo; MP; NoAM; OAEL–2; SeCeV; TwCP
To Judith Asleep. John Ciardi. LiTM; MiAP
To Julia ("How rich and pleasing thou, my Julia, art"). Robert Herrick. CaPo
To Julia ("Julia, when thy Herrick dies"). Robert Herrick. CaPo
To Julia de Burgos. Julia de Burgos, *tr. fr. Spanish by* Grace Schulman. BoWoP; PBWP
To Julia in Shooting Togs. Sir Owen Seaman. BXAP
To Julia, the Flaminica Dialis, or Queen-Priest. Robert Herrick. CaPo
To Julia under Lock and Key. Sir Owen Seaman. BXAP; FaBoPa
To Julius. Martial, *tr. fr. Latin by* Sir Charles Sedley. FaBoEE
(Mistaken Resolve, The.) PV

To justify the quiver in my quill. Poet's Prayer. M. L. Sussman. AMV-80
To K. H. Thomas Edward Brown. OBNC
To Kalòn. Ezra Pound. PoA
To Kate, Skating Better than Her Date. David Daiches. CTBA; FiBHP; NYBP
To K[atharine] de M[attos]. Robert Louis Stevenson. OBNC
To Keep a True Lent. Robert Herrick. AnAnS-2; HBV-2; TrCP; TRV (True Lent, A.) OFD; OHIP
To keep my health! Resolve. Charlotte Perkins Gilman. WGRP
To Keep the Cold Wind Away. *Unknown.* OxBM
To Keep the Memory of Charlotte Forten Grimké. Angelina Weld Grimké. BlSi
To keep your marriage brimming. A Word to Husbands. Ogden Nash. POL
To kill a bat is easy. Easy as a Bat. *Gond Oral Tradition*, tr. by V. Elwin *and* S. Hivale. WTO
To kill its enemies and cheat its friends. International Conference. Colin Ellis. FaBoEE
To kinder skies, where gentler manners reign. France. Goldsmith. *Fr.* The Traveller. OBEC
To King James. Ben Jonson. OAEP
To kiss a fan! What She Thought. Harrison Robertson. *Fr.* Two Triolets. HBV-1
To kiss my Celia's fairer breast. On Snow-Flakes Melting on His Lady's Breast. William Martin Johnson. AA
To Know All Is to Forgive All. Nixon Waterman. BLPA; TreFT
To know just how He suffered would be dear. Emily Dickinson. InvP
To Know the Dark. Wendell Berry. GP
To know the inhabiting reasons. For the Rebuilding of a House. Wendell Berry. EyDe
To know there are rhododendrons on the slopes of the Himalayas. Nearer. Judith Herzberg, *tr. by* Shirley Kaufman. BoWoP; VWA
To know thy bent and then pursue. Ella Wheeler Wilcox. CenHV
To Know Whom One Shall Marry. *Unknown.* GBP
To Krishna Haunting the Hills. Andal, *tr. fr. Tamil by* Willis Barnstone. BoWoP
To Kurnos. Theognis, *tr. fr. Greek by* G. Lowes Dickinson. PeHV
To Kyris. Strato, *tr. fr. Greek by* Teddy Hogge. PeHV
To L. Julianne Perry. PoBA
To L. B. C. L. M. Robert Bridges. *See* I Love All Beauteous Things.
To L. B. S. Winfield Townley Scott. DFF
To L. C. Lucy Hawkins. HBMV
To L. H. B. Katherine Mansfield. HBMV
To Labor. Charlotte Perkins Stetson Gilman. PoLF
To Laddie. Anna Robinson. SUS
To Ladies' Eyes. Thomas Moore. OxBoLi; PoEL-4
To Lady Anne Fitzpatrick, When about Five Years Old, with a Present of Shells, 1772. Horace Walpole. NOEC; OBEC
To Lady Eleanor Butler and the Honourable Miss Ponsonby, Composed in the Grounds of Plas-Newydd, Llangollen. Wordsworth. PeHV
To Lake Aghmoogenegamook. The American Traveller. "Orpheus C. Kerr." FaBoCo; OBAL; WhC
To Landrum Guy, Beginning to Write at Sixty. James Dickey. PP
To Larr. Robert Herrick. CaPo; SeCV-1
To Laura Phelan: 1880-1906. Leon Stokesbury. MAYP
To Laura W——, Two Years Old. Nathaniel Parker Willis. HBV-1
To Laurels. Robert Herrick. CaPo; SeCV-1
To learn the transport by the pain. Emily Dickinson. NOCV
To leave the earth was my wish, and no will stayed my rising. A Temple. Kenneth Patchen. EAS
To leave the world and serve God. Compiuta Donzella, *tr. fr. Italian by* Laura Stortoni. WPOW
To Leigh Hunt, Esq. Keats. EnRP
(Dedication: To Leigh Hunt, Esq.) OBNC
(Dedication to Leigh Hunt.) ViBoPo
To Lesiba ("I hate, and yet I love thee too"). Catullus, *tr. by* Abraham Cowley.. *See* Odi et Amo.
To Lesiba ("Thy kisses dost thou bid me count"). Catullus, *tr. fr. Latin by* Geogre Lamb. UnTE
To Lesbia. John Godfrey Saxe. HBV-1; UnTE
To Lesbia. Thomas Campion. *See* My Sweetest Lesbia.
To Leuconöe. Horace, *tr. fr. Latin.* *Fr.* Odes, I, 11. AA, *tr. by* Eugene Field; LoBV, *tr. by* Charles Stuart Calverley
To Leven Water. Tobias Smollet. OBEV
To Li Chien. Po Chü-i, *tr. fr. Chinese by* Arthur Waley. AWP
To Li Po from Tu Fu. Carolyn Kizer. GP
To Licinius. Horace, *tr. fr. Latin by* William Cowper. Odes, II, 10. AWP
(Golden Mean, The.) HBV-2
("Receive, dear friend, the truths I teach.") OBVE
To lie at the edge of the forest. In Memory of Francois Rabelais. Yunna Moritz, *tr. by* Elaine Feinstein. VWA
To Liebig ("Longing for that true comrade of my need"). August, Graf von Platen, *tr. fr. German by* Reginald Bancroft Cooke. PeHV
To Liebig ("Who feels a growing hunger for fair eyes"). August, Graf von Platen, *tr. fr. German by* Reginald Bancroft Cooke. PeHV
To Life I Said Yes. Chaim Grade, *tr. fr. Yiddish by* Joseph Leftwich. TrJP
To Lighten My Darkness. *Unknown, tr. fr. Arabic by* E. Powys Mathers. *Fr.* The Thousand and One Nights. AWP
To Lighten My House. Alastair Reid. NePoEA
To Ligurinus. Horace, *tr. fr. Latin by* Sir Edward Sherburne. Odes, IV, 10. CavP
To Lillian Russell. Bert Leston Taylor. WhC
To Lindsay. Allen Ginsberg. ConAP
To Little or No Purpose. Sir George Etherege. *Fr.* She Would if She Could. UnTE
To Little Renée on First Seeing Her Lying in Her Cradle. William Aspenwall Bradley. HBV-1
To Live and Die in Dixie, *sels.* John Beecher. GP
"Confederate veterans came to town."
"Old Maggie's sweat would drip and sizzle."
"Spurgeon would daub designs on flowerpots."
To live illusionless, in the abandoned mine. Double Monologue. Adrienne Rich. NePoEA-2
To live in/ myself. Drifting. Kathleen Spivack. IHMS
To Live in Hell, and Heaven to Behold. Henry Constable. Diana, LXII. AAS; HBV-1; InvP; OBSC
To Live in Pleasure. *Unknown. See* Sing We and Chant It.
To live in Wales is to be conscious. Welsh Landscape. R. S. Thomas. FaBoMo
To Live Merrily, and to Trust to Good Verses. Robert Herrick. AnAnS-2; AWP; CaPo; InvP; LoBV; OBS; PP; SeCP; SeCV-1
To live within a cave—it is most good. Salve! Thomas Edward Brown. HBV-2; OBEV; OBVV
To live's a gift, to dye's a debt that we. The Porch. Philip Pain. SCAP
To Lizbie Browne. Thomas Hardy. DTC; ELP
To London once my stepps [*or* steps] I bent. London Lickpenny. *Unknown.* GoTL; OxBM
To Look at Any Thing. John Moffitt. RFM
To look from the Acrocorinth. Mycenae. David Fisher. NPGG
To look in my son's eyes. Address. William Carlos Williams. DiL
To loosen with all ten fingers held wide and limber. Moss-gathering. Theodore Roethke. CoBMV; RFM; VGW
To lose it all at once. Marina Tsvetayeva, *tr. by* Paul Schmidt. *Fr.* The Daughter of Jairus. BoWoP
To Love and Nature all their rights restore. *At. to* Earl of Rochester. *Fr.* Sodom; or, The Quintessence of Debauchery. PeHV
"To love is to give," said the crooked old man. Cupidon. William Jay Smith. NePoEA
To love November, a turned joy. Late in Fall. Ramona Wilson. VoR
To love one woman, or to sit. Woman and Tree. Robert Graves. ErPo
To love somebody/ Who doesn't love you. Lady Kasa, *tr. fr. Japanese by* Kenneth Rexroth. WPOW
To love someone/ Who does not return that love. Lady Kasa, *tr. fr. Japanese by* Harold P. Wright. PBWP
To love thee brings me sadness, for I know. The Waning of Love. "Arthur Lyon Raile." PeHV
To Love Unlovit. Alexander Scott. *See* To Luve Unluvit.
To Lovers of Earth: Fair Warning. Countee Cullen. CDC
To Lucasta ("Ah, Lucasta, why so bright"). Richard Lovelace. AnAnS-2; CaPo
To Lucasta ("I laugh and I sing but cannot tell"). Richard Lovelace. OBS
To Lucasta, from Prison. Richard Lovelace. AnAnS-2; CaPo
To Lucasta: Her Reserved Looks. Richard Lovelace. CaPo; SeCV-1
To Lucasta, [on] Going beyond the Seas. Richard Lovelace. AnAnS-2; CaPo; FaBoEn; GTBS; GTBS-P; HBV-1; LiTB; LoBV; MeLP; MOS; OAEP; OBEV; OBS; PoPle; SeCP; SeCV-1; TreFT; ViBoPo
To Lucasta, [on] Going to the Wars [*or* Warres]. Richard Lovelace. AnAnS-2; AWP; CABA; CaPo; CavP; ELP; EnLoPo; FaBoEn; FaBV; FaFP; FF; FPL; GBL; GTBS; GTBS-P; HAP; HBV-1; HeIP; HoPM; InPK; InPS; LiTB; LoBV; MeLP; MePo; NIP; NOBE; NoP; OAEP; OBEV; OBWP; PAI; PoEL-3; PoPl; PoRA; SCV; SeCePo; SeCeV; SeCP; SeCV-1; TreF; TrGrPo; ViBoPo; WeW; WHA
(Going to the Warres.) OBS
(Song: "Tell me not, sweet, I am unkind.") OAEL-1
(Song: To Lucasta, Going to the Wars.) JCP
"To Lucasta, on Going to the Wars." Edwin Meade Robinson. Limericised Classics, IV. HBMV
To Lucasta: The Rose. Richard Lovelace. AnAnS-2; SeCV-1
(Rose, The.) HBV-1; ViBoPo
To Lucia at Birth. Robert Graves. NAs
To Lucy, Countesse of Bedford, with Mr. Donnes Satyres. Ben Jonson. AnAnS-2; OBS; SeCV-1

To Luigi del Riccio, after the Death of Cecchino Bracci. Michelangelo, *tr. fr. Italian by* John Addington Symonds. PeHV
To Luve Unluvit. Alexander Scott. GoTS; OxBS
(To Love Unlovit.) BSV
To Lydia. Horace, *tr. fr. Latin by* Philip Francis. Odes, I, 25. OBVE
To "Lydia Languish." Austin Dobson. NBM; VLP
To Lydia, with a Coloured Egg, on Easter Monday. John Jones. FaBoUs
To M. E. W. G. K. Chesterton. HBV-2
To M. Henry Lawes, the Excellent Composer, of His Lyrics. Robert Herrick. *See* To Master Henry Lawes, the Excellent Composer of Lyrics.
To M. T. Bayard Taylor. AA
To Mackinnon of Strath. Iain Lom, *tr. fr. Gaelic.* GoTS
To Madame A. V. Pletneff. Karolina Pavlova, *tr. fr. French by* Paul Schmidt. PBWP
To Maecenas. Horace, *tr. fr. Latin.* Odes, III, 29. AWP, *tr. by* Dryden; OBVE, *tr. by* Thomas Flatman
("Descended of an ancient line," *tr. by* Dryden.) OBVE
(Horat. Ode 29. Book 3. Paraphras'd in Pindarique Verse, *tr. by* Dryden.) SeCV-2
To mak a ballant. Recipe: To Mak a Ballant. Alexander Scott. BSV
To Make a Bridge. Charles Madge. NeBP
To make a final conquest of all me. The Fair Singer. Andrew Marvell. CavP; EnLoPo; MeLP; MePo; NOBE; NoP; PoEL-2; PoPle
To make a Juju of my own. A Juju of My Own. Lebert Bethune. InPS; PoBA; PoNe
To Make a Pastoral; a Receipt. *Unknown.* FaBoUs
To make a prairie it takes a clover and one bee. Emily Dickinson. BoWoP; HBVY; HeIP; OBCA; OxBA; PoPl
To make a resurrection there must be a death. Twin. Phyllis Haring. PeSA
To make a start. Preface. William Carlos Williams. *Fr.* Paterson, I. AP; CMoP; CoBMV; NoAM; NOBA
To make me do the thing I will, I won't. The Human Animal. Jane Mayhall. TAP
To make quick way I'll leap o'er heavy blocks. Dryden. *Fr.* Absalom and Achitophel, Pt. II. OBSV
To make some bread you must have dough. One, Two, Three—Gough! Eve Merriam. NTCP
To Make the People Happy. Victor Hugo, *tr. fr. French.* PPON
To make the vapor bath. That Old Sauna High. Anselm Hollo. PoM
To make this condiment, your poet begs. A Salad [*or* Recipe for Salad.]. Sydney Smith. FaBoUs; HBV-2
To make this scene I climb miles. The Space Eater Camps at Fifth Lake. Reg Saner. GP
To make your candles last for aye. Mother Goose. OxNR
To Man Who Goes Seeking Immortality. Adelaide Crapsey. QFR
To Manon, as to His Choice of Her. Wilfrid Scawen Blunt. The Love Sonnets of Proteus, VIII. HBV-1
(As to His Choice of Her.) ViBoPo
To Manon, Comparing Her to a Falcon. Wilfrid Scawen Blunt. The Love Sonnets of Proteus, II. OBVV
(Falcon, The.) ACP
To Manon, on Her Lightheartedness. Wilfrid Scawen Blunt. The Love Sonnets of Proteus, XI. NBM
To Margot Heinemann. John Cornford. *See* Huesca.
To Marguerite ("Yes! in the sea of life enisled"). Matthew Arnold. *Fr.* Switzerland. ELP; FaBoEn; FiP; HBV-1; NOBE; NoP; OBEV; OBNC; PoEL-5; PrIm; SeCeV
(To Marguerite—Continued.) BoLoP; EBEV; EBVV; GTBS-P; MOS; OAEL-2; OAEP; PPP; TEP; VLP
To Maria Gisborne in England, from Italy. Shelley. *Fr.* Letter to Maria Gisborne. NOBE
To Marie. *Unknown.* NA
To Mark Anthony in Heaven. William Carlos Williams. NOBA
To Mark Rothko. Anne Cherner. PoDr
To market, to market/ To buy a plum bun. Mother Goose. OxNR
To market, to market. Saturday Shopping. Katherine Edelman. SoPo
To market, to market. The Cost-of-Living Mother Goose. Dow Richardson. QQQ
To market, to market, to buy a fat pig. Mother Goose. FaBoBe; FaFP; HBV-1; HBVY; OxNR; SoPo; TiPo
To Mars. *Unknown, tr. fr. Greek by* George Chapman. LoBV
To Mary. Samuel Bishop. *See* To His Wife on the Fourteenth Anniversary of Her Wedding-Days with a Ring.
To Mary. John Clare. *See* To Mary: I Sleep with Thee, and Wake with Thee.
To Mary. William Cowper. EnLoPo; EnRP; FiP; LAuP; NOEC; OAEP; OBEC
(My Mary.) OBEV; TreFS
(To the Same.) GTBS; GTBS-P
To Mary. Shelley. EnRP
To Mary. Gottfried von Strasburg, *tr. fr. German by* E. M. Sweetman. ISi
To Mary. Charles Wolfe. HBV-1; LO; OBEV; OBRV; ViBoPo
To Mary: At the Thirteenth Station. Raymond F. Roseliep. ISi
To Mary: I Sleep with Thee, and Wake with Thee. John Clare. GBL
(To Mary.) EnLoPo
To Mary: It Is the Evening Hour. John Clare. BoLoP; ChTr; GBL
(Mary.) EnLoPo; FaBoEn
To Mary at Christmas. John Gilland Brunini. ISi
To Mary in Heaven. Burns. *See* Thou Lingering Star.
To Mary Lady Wroth. Ben Jonson. OBS
To Mary our Queen, that flower so sweet. The Marigold. William Forrest. ACP
To Mary Unwin. William Cowper. GTBS; GTBS-P; HBV-1; OBEV; TrGrPo
(Sonnet to Mrs. Unwin.) OAEP; OBEC
To Master Davenant for Absence. Sir John Suckling. CaPo
To Master Denham, on His Prospective Poem. Robert Herrick. AnAnS-2
To Master Edward Cobham. Barnabe Googe. EnRePo
To Master Henry Lawes, the Excellent Composer of Lyrics. Robert Herrick. CaPo
(To Henry Lawes, the Excellent Composer, of His Lyrics.) OAEP
To Maynard on the Long Road Home. W. D. Ehrhart. LTB
To Maystres Isabell Pennell. John Skelton. *See* To Mistress Isabel Pennell.
To Maystres Jane Blenner-Haiset. John Skelton. *Fr.* The Garlande of Laurell. AAS
To Maystres Margaret Hussey. John Skelton. *See* To Mistress Margaret Hussey.
To Me. William Barnes. NBM; PoEL-4
To me, fair[e] Friend, you never can be old. Sonnets, CIV. Shakespeare. ElL; EnRePo; FaBoEn; FPL; GBL; GTBS; GTBS-P; HBV-1; HeIP; OAEP; OBEV; OBSC; PeHV; Prf; ViBoPo
To me he seems like a god. Sappho, *tr. fr. Greek by* Willis Barnstone. BoWoP
To me, one silly task is like another. Cassandra. Louise Bogan. HAP; MoAmPo; MoVE; PBWP; SBG; VGW
To me that man equals a god. Seizure. Sappho, *tr. by* Willis Barnstone. LLLT
To me the earth once seemed to be. Then and Now. Charles Frederick Johnson. AA
To me, whom in their lays the shepherds call. Inscription for a Grotto [*or* For a Grotto]. Mark Akenside. NOEC; OBEC; PoEL-3; SeCePo
To Meadows. Robert Herrick. AWP; CaPo; CH; HBV-1; JCP; LoBV; NOBE; OBEV; QFR; ViBoPo
(To Meddowes.) FaBoEn; OBS; PoEL-3; SeCP; SeCV-1
To meake up rhymes, my mind wer zoo a-vire. The Young Rhymer Snubbed. William Barnes. VLP
To Meath of the pastures. A Drover. Padraic Colum. AnIL; AnIV; AWP; HBV-1; MoBrPo; OBMV; OxBI; ViBoPo
To Meddowes. Robert Herrick. *See* To Meadows.
To meditate the marvel of mixed media. Mixed Media. James Schevill. AMV-81
"To meet and then to part," and that is all. The Close of Day. Wesley Curtwright. CDC
To meet the fountain of true life I run. Longing. Judah Halevi, *tr. by* Nina Davis Salaman. TrJP
To Meets or Otherwise. Thomas Hardy. OBNC
To Melancholy. Countess of Winchilsea. WPE
To Melody. George Leonard Allen. CDC
To Men. Anna Wickham. MoBrPo
To mend their every hurt, to heal all their ills. Mountain Medicine. Elizabeth-Ellen Long. AmFN
To Mercury. X. J. Kennedy. SOTS
To Mercy, Pity, Peace, and Love. The Divine Image. Blake. *Fr.* Songs of Innocence. EBCP; EnRP; FaBoEn; LAuP; LO; NOBE; NOEC; NoP; OAEL-2; OAEP; OBEC; OBNC; OxBoCh; PoEL-4; PPP; TEP; TRV; ViBoPo; WGRP
To Midnight; an Epitaph. *Unknown.* CoSo
(To Midnight.) BPAW
To Miguel de Cervantes Saavadra. Richard Kendall Munkittrick. AA
To Milk in the Valley Below. *Unknown.* OBET
To Milton. Wordsworth. *See* London, 1802.
To Milton. Oscar Wilde. BrPo
To mine own self I am a wilderness. Stéphane Mallarmé, *tr. by* Arthur Symons. *Fr.* Hérodiade. SyP
To Minerva. Thomas Hood. ChTr; FaBoCo; FaBoNo; FiBHP; HBV-2; InMe; NOBL; OxBoLi; WhC
To Miss ——: On Her Playing upon the Harpsichord. Samuel Johnson. CABA
To Miss —— on the Death of Her Goldfish. Mr. Meredyth. FM
To Miss Arundell. Walter Savage Landor. OBVV
To Miss Charlotte Pulteney in Her Mother's Arms. Ambrose Philips. ELP; FaBoEn; NOEC; OBEC
(To Charlotte Pulteney.) GTBS; GTBS-P; HBV-1

To Miss Eleanor Ambrose on the Occasion of Her Wearing an Orange Lily at a Ball in Dublin Castle on July the 12th. Earl of Chesterfield. EnLoPo
To Miss L. F. on the Occasion of Her Departure for the Continent. J. C. Squire. BXAP
To Miss Laetitia Van Lewen. Constantia Grierson. WPE
To Miss Lucy F——, with a New Watch. George Lyttelton. FaBoUs
To Mr. ———, an Unlettered Poet, on Genius Unimproved. Ann Yearsley. NOEC
To Mr. Alexander Ross. James Beattie. OxBS
To Mr. Bays. Charles Sackville. APAS
To Mr. C. B. ("Thy friend, whom thy deserts to thee enchaine"). John Donne. AnAnS-1
To Mr. Cyriack Skinner upon His Blindness. Milton. OBS
(To Cyriack Skinner.) TrGrPo
To Mr. Gay, Who Wrote Him a Congratulatory Letter on the Finishing of His House. Pope. NOEC
To Mr. George Herbert. John Donne. OBVE
To Mr. Gray on the Publication of His Odes. David Garrick. OBEC
To Mr. H. Lawes on His Airs. Milton. AWP; LoBV; NoP
(Sonnet: To Mr. H. Lawes, on His Aires.) OBS
To Mr. Henry Lawes. Katherine Philips. SBG; WPE
To Mr. Henry Lawes, Who Had Then Newly Set a Song of Mine in the Year 1635. Edmund Waller. AnAnS-2; CTC; PP; SeCP; SeCV-1
To Mr. Hobbes [*or* Hobs]. Abraham Cowley. LoBV; SeCV-1
To Mr. I. L. John Donne. SeCP
To Mr. Izaak Walton, *sel.* Charles Cotton.
"Farewell; thou busy world, and may." ViBoPo
(Retirement, The.) FaBoPP; HBV; OBS
To Mr. Jervas, with Fresnoy's Art of Painting, Translated by Mr. Dryden. Pope. OBEC
To Mr. Lawrence. Milton. AWP; GTBS; GTBS-P; OBEV
("Lawrence, of virtuous father virtuous son.") CABA
(Sonnet.) OBS
To Mr. Murray. Byron. FaBoCo
To Mr. Newton on His Return from Ramsgate. William Cowper. NOEC
To Mr. Rowland Woodward. John Donne. AnAnS-1; MePo
To Mr. R. W. ("Kindly I envy the songs perfection"). John Donne. AnAnS-1
To Mr. S. T. Coleridge. Anna Laetitia Barbauld. NOEC
To Mr. T. W. John Donne. PP
To Mr. Tilman after He Had Taken Orders. John Donne. EBEV
To Mrs. Ann Flaxman. Blake. OBRV
To Mistress Anne. John Skelton. EnRePo
To Mistress Anne Cecil, upon Making Her a New Year's Gift. William Cecil, Lord Burghley. ElL; OBSC
To Mrs. Diana Cecyll. Lord Herbert of Cherbury. AnAnS-2
To Mistress Gertrude Statham. John Skelton. *Fr.* The Garlande of Laurell. OAEP
To Mistress [*or* Maystres] Isabell Pennell. John Skelton. *Fr.* The Garlande of Laurell. AAS; NAs; NOBE; OAEP; OBEV; OBSC; OxBoLi; PoEL-1; TrGrPo
(In Praise of Isabel Pennell.) CH
To Mistress Katherine Bradshaw the Lovely, That Crowned Him with Laurel. Robert Herrick. CaPo
To Mrs. M. B. on Her Birth-Day [*or* Birthday]. Pope. EnLoPo; FaBoEn; OBEC
To Mistress [*or* Maystres] Margaret Hussey. John Skelton. *Fr.* The Garlande of Laurell. AAS; ACP; EBEV; EnLoPo; GN; GoBC; GoJo; HBV-1; HelP; HoPM; LoBV; NOBE; NoP; OAEL-1; OAEP; OBEV; OBSC; PoEL-1; PoRA; PPoe; PPP; SCV; SeCeV; TreFT; TrGrPo; ViBoPo
(Mistress Margaret Hussey.) FaBoCh
To Mistress Margaret Tilney. John Skelton. *Fr.* The Garlande of Laurell. MeEL
To Mistress Margery Wentworth. John Skelton. *Fr.* The Garlande of Laurell. EBEV; EnLoPo; EnRePo; LoBV; NOBE; OBEV; OBSC; TrGrPo; ViBoPo
To Mrs. Thrale on Her Thirty-fifth Birthday. Samuel Johnson. FaBoEE
(To Mrs. Thrale.) NAs
To Modigliani to Prove to Him That I Am a Poet. Max Jacob, *tr. fr. French by* Wallace Fowlie. TrJP
To Mollidusta. James Robinson Planché. NA
To Monsieur de la Mothe le Vayer. Molière, *tr. fr. French by* Austin Dobson. AWP
To Morfydd. Lionel Johnson. AnIV; MoBrPo; OAEL-2; OBMV
To Morning. Blake. EnRP
To Morris Louis. Anne Cherner. PoDr
To mortal men Peace giveth these good things. Peace on Earth. Bacchylides, *tr. by* John Addington Symonds. AWP
To Mother. Frank Horne. *Fr.* Letters Found near a Suicide. BPo
To Mother and Steve. Mari Evans. BPo; PoBA
To Mother Fairie. Alice Cary. OBCA
To Mother Nature. Frederic Lawrence Knowles. HBV-1
To move over shifting borders. Eeva-Liisa Manner, *tr. by* Jaakko A. Ahokas. *Fr.* Cambrian. PBWP
To Music. William Kean Seymour. HBMV
To Music ("Begin to charm, and as thou strok'st mine ears"). Robert Herrick. CaPo
(To Musick.) UnS
To Music; a Song. Robert Herrick. CaPo
To Music [*or* Musicke] Bent Is My Retired Mind. Thomas Campion. AAS; EnRePo; NOCV; OxBoCh; UnS
(To Musicke Bent.) TrPWD
To Music, to Becalm a Sweet-sick Youth. Robert Herrick. CaPo
To Music, to Becalm his Fever. Robert Herrick. CaPo; HBV-2; OBEV; QFR
(To Musique, to Becalme His Fever.) GoJo; OBS; SeCV-1
"Charm me asleep, and melt me so," *sel.* UnS
To Musick. Robert Herrick. *See* To Music.
To Musicke Bent. Thomas Campion. *See* To Music Bent Is My Retired Mind.
To mute and to material things. Nelson, Pitt, Fox [*or* Patriotism, II]. Sir Walter Scott. *Fr.* Marmion. OBEV
To my/ Aye. Paddy Doyle. *Unknown.* AmSS
To My Blood Sister. Christine E. Hemp. Str
To My Body. Nancy Sullivan. TAP
To My Book[e]. Ben Jonson. AnAnS-2; OAEP; SeCV-1
To My Brother. Louise Bogan. NYBP
To My Brother. Vera Brittain. SUMH
To My Brother George. Keats. EnRP
To My Brothers. Keats. NAs; TEP
To My Cat. Rosamund Marriott Watson. PCat
To My Child. Abraham Sutskever, *tr. fr. Yiddish by* David G. Roskies *and* Hillel Schwartz. VWA
To My Child Carlino. Walter Savage Landor. NoP; OBRV
To My Children, Fearing for Them. Wendell Berry. Str
To My Children Unknown, Produced by Artificial Insemination. James Kirkup. NAs
To My Cosen Mrs. Ellinor Evins. George Alsop. SCAP
To My Country. "Rahel," *tr. fr. Hebrew by* Diane Mintz. PBWP
To My Cousin (C. R.) Marrying My Lady (A.). Thomas Carew. AnAnS-2; SeCP
To My Cousin Mary, for Mending My Tobacco Pouch. Francis Scott Key. OBAL
To My Daughter. Hyam Plutzik. BiP
To My Daughter. Stephen Spender. DFF
To My Daughter Betty, the Gift of God. Thomas M. Kettle. HBMV; OnYI
To My Daughter the Junkie on a Train. Audre Lorde. CNA
To My Dead Father. Frank O'Hara. DiL
To My Dead Friend Ben: Johnson. Henry King. AnAnS-2; SeCP
To My Dear and Loving Husband. Anne Bradstreet. AmPP; AP; BLPL; BoWoP; FF; HAP; HeIP; NePA; NOBA; NOCV; OxBA; PoEL-3; PoLF; PrIm; SBG; SCAP; TAP; WeW; WPE
To My Dear and Most Worthy Friend, Mr. Isaac Walton. Charles Cotton. FaBoEn
To My Dear Friend Mr. Congreve [on His Comedy Called "The Double-Dealer"]. Dryden. EBEV; FiP; OAEL-1; OBS; PoEL-3; SeCV-2
To my dear wife. A Last Will and Testament. John Winstanley. OBSV
To My Distant Beloved. Alois Jeitteles, *tr. fr. German by* the Reverend Dr. Troutbeck. TrJP
To My Dog "Blanco." Josiah Gilbert Holland. PoLF
To My Ever-honoured Cousin W. R. Esquire, *sel.* Phineas Fletcher.
Lines Written at Cambridge, to W. R., Esquire. ElL
To My Excellent Lucasia, on Our Friendship. Katherine Philips. CavP; MeLP; OBS; PeHV; SBG; WPE; WPOW
To My Father. Tony Curtis. AMV-81
To My Father. Susannah Fried, *tr. fr. Slovak by* Anthony Rudolf. VWA
To My Father. W. S. Graham. FaBoTw
To My Father. Ralph Pomeroy. DFF
To My Father. Henrietta Cordelia Ray. BlSi
To My Father. Iris Tree. HBMV
To My Fellow-Mariners, March, '53. Thomas Whitbread. NYBP
To My First Love, My Mother. Christina Rossetti. OHIP
To my firstborn land, in the south. The Firstborn Land. Ingeborg Bachmann, *tr. by* Daniel Huws. BoWoP
To My Friend. Francis Thompson. PoA
To My Friend, behind Walls. Carolyn Kizer. NePoAm-2
To My Friend Butts I Write. Blake. EnRP
To My Friend, Dr. Charleton, on His Learned and Useful Works; and More Particularly This of Stone-Heng, by Him Restored to the True Founders. Dryden. SeCV-2
To My Friend G. N. from Wrest. Thomas Carew. AnAnS-2; CaPo
To My Friend, Grown Famous. Eunice Tietjens. HBMV
To My Friend Whose Parachute Did Not Open. David Wagoner. TwAmPo

To My Friends. Stephen Berg. NaP; NYBP
To My Friends. Peter De Vries. FiBHP
To My Friends. Peter Levi. NePoEA-2
To My Friends. Schiller, *tr. fr. German by* James Clarence Mangan. AWP
To My Generation. Benyamin Galai, *tr. fr. Hebrew by* Jacob Sonntag. TrJP
To My God. George Macdonald. TrPWD; TRV
To My God in His Sickness. Philip Levine. NNaP
To My Grandmother. Frederick Locker-Lampson. HBV-1; InMe; OBVV
To My Hairdresser. Warham St. Leger. CenHV
To My Honor'd Friend Sir Robert Howard, *sel.* Dryden.
What Is the World? TRV
To My Honour'd Kinsman, John Driden, of Chesterton. Dryden. OBS, *abr.*
"No porter guards the passage of your door," *sel.* EBEV
To My Honoured Friend Mr. George Sandys. Henry King. AnAnS-2
To My Honoured Patron Humphery Davie. Benjamin Tompson. SCAP
To My Ill Reader. Robert Herrick. CaPo
To My Inconstant Mistress [*or* Mistris]. Thomas Carew. EnLoPo; HBV-1; LoBV; MeLP; MePo; NOBE; OBS; SeCePo; SeCV-1; TrGrPo
(Song: To My Inconstant Mistress.) AnAnS-2; CaPo; CavP; GBL; JCP; NoP; SeCP
(To His Inconstant Mistress.) OBEV
To My Infant Daughter. Yvor Winters. VGW
To My Ingenious and Worthy Friend William Lowndes, Esq. John Gay. OBSV
To My Lady. George Henry Boker. *Fr.* Sonnets. AA
To My Lady Mirriel Howard. John Skelton. *Fr.* The Garlande of Laurell. LoBV
To My Lady Rogers, the Authors Wives Mother, How Doctor Sherwood Commended Her House in Bathe. Sir John Harington. EyDe
To My Least Favorite Reviewer. Howard Nemerov. TW
To My Little Son. Julia Johnson Davis. HBMV
To My Love. John Godfrey Saxe. HBV-1
To My Lucasia, in Defence of Declared Friendship. Katherine Phillips. MeLP
To My Mistress[e] in Absence. Thomas Carew. AnAnS-2; CaPo
To My Mistress [*or* Mistris] Sitting by a River's Side; an Eddy. Thomas Carew. AnAnS-2; CaPo
To My Mistris, I Burning in Love. Thomas Carew. *See* Song: To My Mistris, I Burning in Love.
To My Most Dearly-loved Friend, Henry Reynolds, Esquire, of Poets and Poesy. Michael Drayton. AnAnS-2; OAEP; OBS
Sels.
First Steps up Parnassus. NOBE
"For from my cradle you must know that I." PP
To My Mother. George Barker. *See* Sonnet to My Mother.
To My Mother. Edwin Brock. NMP
To My Mother. Louis Ginsberg. PoSC
To My Mother. Heine, *tr. fr. German by* Matilda Dickson. AWP
(Sonnet to My Mother, A, *tr. by* Emma Lazarus) TrJP
To My Mother. Thomas Moore. OHIP
To My Mother. Poe. AP; NePA; OxBA
To My Mother at 73. Elizabeth Jennings. NAs
To My Mountain. Kathleen Raine. OxBS; PoPl
To My Mouse-colored Mare. Tristan Corbière, *tr. fr. French by* C. F. MacIntyre. ErPo
To My Native Land. James Clarence Mangan. AnIL
To My New Mistress. Beverly Bowie. PoPl
To My Ninth Decade [I Have Tottered On]. Walter Savage Landor. EnRP; NAs
(On His Ninth Decade.) TrGrPo
To My Noble Kinsman, Thomas Stanley, Esquire, on His Lyric Poems Composed by Master John Gamble. Richard Lovelace. CaPo
To My Nose. Alfred A. Forrester. BLPA
To My Old Schoolmaster. Whittier. NOBA
To my parents I am/ a thick layer of innovation. Houses, Past and Present. Eli Bachar, *tr. by* Jeremy Garber. VWA
To My People. Edwin Seaver. TrJP
To my people it's as though he gave them a sacrifice. Eadwacer. *Unknown.* WPE
To my prowd foe thus, sister, humblie saye. Virgil, *tr. by* the Earl of Surrey. *Fr.* The Aeneid, II. OBVE
To my quick ear the leaves conferred. Emily Dickinson. TwAmPo
To my revenge and to her desperate fears. The Bubble; a Song. Robert Herrick. CaPo
To My Reverend Dear Brother, M. Samuel Stone. John Cotton. SCAP
To My Setter, Scout. Frank H. Seldon. BLPA
To My Sister. Olga Berggolts, *tr. fr. Russian by* Daniel Weissbort. BoWoP
To My Sister. Wordsworth. EnRP; OAEL-2; OBRV
To My Sister, from the Twenty-seventh Floor. Michael Knoll. AMV-81
To My Son, *sel.* George Barker.
"My darkling child the stars have obeyed," I. MP; TwCP
To My Son. Byron. NAs
To My Son. Margaret Johnston Grafflin. SoSe
(Like Mother, like Son.) BLPA
To My Son, *sel.* Helen Selina Sheridan.
Love Hath a Language. HBV-1
To My Son. *Unknown.* PoLF
To My Son, Aged Three Years and Five Months. Thomas Hood. *See* Parental Ode to My Son, A.
To My Son, Not Yet Born. William Virgil Davis. AMV-81
To My Son Parker, Asleep in the Next Room. Bob Kaufman. PoBA; TwCP; VGW
To My Soul. Phineas Fletcher. OxBoCh
To My Tortoise Ananke. Eugene Lee-Hamilton. OBVV
To My Tortoise Chronos. Eugene Lee-Hamilton. FM
To my true king I offered free from stain. A Jacobite's Epitaph [*or* Epitaph on a Jacobite]. Macaulay. EBEV; FaPoR; NOBE; OBEV; OBNC; OBVV; ViBoPo
To My Truly Valiant, Learned Friend, Who in His Book Resolved the Art Gladiatory into the Mathematics. Richard Lovelace. CaPo; PoEL-3
To my twin who lives in a cruel country. The Dual Site. Michael Hamburger. MP; NePoEA-2; TwCP
To My Unborn Son. Cyril Morton Thorne. BLPA
To My Valentine. *Unknown.* SoPo
To my village fair no lass can compare. The Lovely Village Fair; or, I Dont Mean to Tell You Her Name. *Unknown.* CoMu
To My Wife. James Forsyth. WaP
To My Wife. Robert Louis Stevenson. *See* My Wife.
To My Wife Asleep. Edward Tick. AMV-80
To My Worthy Friend Master Geo. [*or* George] Sands [on His Translation of the Psalmes]. Thomas Carew. AnAnS-2; CaPo; JCP; MePo; SeCV-1
(To My Worthy Friend Mr. George Sandys.) MeLP; OBS
To My Worthy Friend Master Peter Lely. Richard Lovelace. CaPo
To My Worthy Friend, Mr. James Bayley. Nicholas Noyes. SCAP
To My Young Lady, Lucy Sidney. Edmund Waller. *See* To a Very Young Lady.
To My Youngest Kinsman, R. L. Abraham Chear. OxBChV
To Myra. Fulke Greville. *See* Myra.
To Myself, after Forty Years. T. H. White. NYBP
To Myself, Late, in a Myrtle Grove. Robert Peterson. NeAC
To N. V. de G. S. Robert Louis Stevenson. BrPo
To Naples. H. B. Mallalieu. WaP
To Naso. Catullus, *tr. fr. Latin by* Jack Lindsay. ErPo
("Naso, you're all men's man, yet few," *tr. by* James Michie.) DBV
To Natalie. Morrie Ryskind. HBMV
To Nature. Samuel Taylor Coleridge. OAEL-2
To Nature, in her shop on day, at work compounding simples. Filling an Order. John Townsend Trowbridge. OBAL
To Nature Seekers. Robert W. Chambers. MoShBr
To Nearly Everybody in Europe To-Day. "Hugh MacDiarmid." DBV
To Ned. Herman Melville. MOS; NOBA; PoEL-5; ViBoPo
To New Haven. Frederick Scheetz Jones. *See* On the Democracy of Yale.
To New Haven and Boston. Walter Foster Angell. TreFS
To New York. Léopold Sédar Senghor. *See* New York.
To Night. Thomas Lovell Beddoes. LoBV
To Night. Shelley. AWP; ChER; EnRP; FPL; HBV-1; HBVY; LoBV; NoP; OAEL-2; OAEP; OBNC; OBRV; PoLF; PoRA; SeCeV; TEP; TreFS; TrGrPo; ViBoPo; WHA; WiR
(Night.) OBEV
(To the Night.) CH; GTBS; GTBS-P
To Night. *Unknown.* *See* O Jealous Night.
To Night. Joseph Blanco White. EBEV; GoBC; HBV-1; OBEV; OBRV; RoGo; TreFS; ViBoPo; WGRP
To night, grave sir, both my poore house, and I. *See* Tonight, grave sir . . .
To Night; to Judith. George Mosby, Jr. LFAC
To no one Muse does she her glance confine. On a Squinting Poetess. Thomas Moore. FaBoCo
To Nobodaddy. Blake. OAEL-2
To Noel. Gabriela Mistral, *tr. fr. Spanish by* Doris Dana. PChr
To Noël Coward. Noël Coward. FaBoPa
To nothing fitter can I thee compare. Michael Drayton. Idea, X. EIL; OBSC; TrGrPo; ViBoPo
To Nowhere. David Ignatow. CAD; NCSH
To Nysus. Sir Charles Sedley. FaBoEE; OBSV
To O. E. A. Claude McKay. BANP; BPo
To O. S. C. Annie Eliot Trumbull. AA
To Oenone ("Thou saist Love's dart"). Robert Herrick. CaPo
To Oenone ("What conscience, say, is it in thee"). Robert Herrick. *See* To Aenone.
To Olive. Lord Alfred Douglas. OBEV; OBVV
To Oliver Cromwell. Milton. *See* To the Lord General Cromwell.
To Olivia. Francis Thompson. MoBrPo
To One Admiring Herself [*or* Her Selfe] in a Looking Glass. Thomas Randolph. AnAnS-2; ViBoPo

To One Being Old. Langdon Elwyn Mitchell. AA
To One Elect. S. I. Hayakawa. PoA
To one fair Lady out of Court. The Challenge. Pope. PoEL-3
To One Far Away, Dancing. C. Stephen Finley. AMV-81
To one full sound and silently. The Man with Three Friends. Dora Greenwell. OBVV
To One in Bedlam. Ernest Dowson. ACP; BrPo; MoBrPo; OBMV; VLP; WHA
To One in Paradise. Poe. *Fr.* The Assignation. AA; AmPP; AP; BLPL; BoLoP; HBV-1; LiTA; LO; NePA; OBEV; OBRV; OBVV; OxBA; PoLF; TAP; TrGrPo; ViBoPo; WHA
To one kneeling down no word came. In a Country Church. R. S. Thomas. FaBoMo
To One Married to an Old Man. Edmund Waller. FaBoEE; SeCP
To One of Little Faith. Hildegarde Flanner. HBMV
To One Older. Marion M. Boyd. HBMV
To One on Her Waste of Time. Wilfrid Scawen Blunt. *Fr.* The Love Sonnets of Proteus. ViBoPo
To One Persuading a Lady to Marriage. Katherine Philips. *See* Answer to Another Persuading a Lady to Marriage, A.
To One That Had Little Wit. George Turberville. EnRePo
To One That Pleaded Her Own Want of Merit. Thomas Stanley. OBS
(To Celia Pleading Want of Merit.) MeLP
To One Who Denies the Possibility of a Permanent Peace. Margaret Sackville. HBMV
To One Who Died in Autumn. Virginia McCormick. HBMV
To One Who Had Censured His Public Exposition of Dante. Boccaccio, *tr. fr. Italian by* Dante Gabriel Rossetti. *Fr.* Sonnets. AWP; GOBC (*in* A Tribute to Dante)
To One Who Has Been Long in City Pent. Keats. EnRP; HBV-1; LiTB; SeCeV; TreFT; TrGrPo
(Sonnet: "To one who has been long in city pent.") BLPA; FaBoBe; FPL; LoBV
To One Who Quotes and Detracts. Walter Savage Landor. FaBoEE
To One Who Would Make a Confession. Wilfrid Scawen Blunt. The Love Sonnets of Proteus, LXII. HBV-1; ViBoPo
To onpreise women[e] it were a shame. A Woman Is a Worthy Thing [*or* Women Are Worthy]. *Unknown.* FaBoCo; MeEL
To other eyes and ears you are a great. Bernard O'Dowd. *Fr.* The Bush. CBAP
To Our Blessed Lady. Henry Constable. ACP; GoBC; ISi; OBSC
To Our Blessed Lord upon the Choice of His Sepulchre. Richard Crashaw. ACP
(Upon Our Saviour's Tomb Wherein Never Man Was Laid.) OAEL-1
To Our Daughter. Jennifer Armitage. BrRo
To Our Friends. Lucian B. Watkins. BANP
To Our House-Dog Captain. Walter Savage Landor. NBM; PoEL-4
To Our Ladies of Death. James Thomson. GoTS
To Our Lady. Robert Henryson. ACP
To Our Lady. Mary Dixon Thayer. TreFS
To Our Lady, the Ark of the Covenants. Raymond E. F. Larsson. ISi
To Our Lord, upon the Water Made Wine. Richard Crashaw. MePo
To our ruined vineyard come. Love Song for the Future. Vassar Miller. NCSH
To our theme—The man who has stood on the Acropolis. Byron. *Fr.* Don Juan, XI. InPS; OBSV
To outer senses there is peace. La Fuite de la Lune. Oscar Wilde. *Fr.* Impressions. SyP
To own nothing, but to be. Words Spoken Alone. Dannie Abse. NYBP
To Oxford. Gerard Manley Hopkins. BrPo; FaBoPP
To Paint a Water Lily. Ted Hughes. PP
To paint without a palette. Some Uses for Poetry. Eve Merriam. PCP
To Pan. John Fletcher. *See* God of Sheep, The.
To Paris that was once her owne though now it be not so. Ovid, *tr. by* George Turberville. *Fr.* Heroides. OBVE
To Pass the Place Where Pleasure Is. *Unknown.* CoMu
To Paths Unknown. Whittier. *See* At Last.
To Paul Eluard. Jorie Graham. AMV-80
To Pensacola town we'll bid adieu. Homeward Bound. *Unknown.* AmSS
To Penshurst. Ben Jonson. AnAnS-2; AWP; CABA; JCP; LoBV; NIP; NoP; OAEL-1; OBS; PoEL-2; PPP; SeCP; SeCV-1; TEP
Sels.
"Thou hast thy ponds, that pay thee tribute fish." FaBoEn
"Thy copp's, too, nam'd of Gamage, thou hast there." FM
To people who allege that we. The Uses of Ocean. Sir Owen Seaman. FiBHP
To Perilla. Robert Herrick. AnAnS-2; CaPo; OBS; SeCP; SeCV-1
To Pertinax Cob. Ben Jonson. JCP
To Pete Atkin: A Letter from Paris, *sel.* Clive James.
"Weather's cleared, The. We're filming at Versailles." OBSV
To Petronilla Who Has Put Up Her Hair. Henry Howarth Bashford. HBV-1
To Petronius Arbiter. Oliver St. John Gogarty. OBMV
To Phidyle. Horace, *tr. fr. Latin by* Austin Dobson. Odes, III, 23. AWP
To Phillis. Edmund Waller. AnAnS-2; OAEP; SeCP
(Plea for Promiscuity, A.) UnTE
(To Phyllis.) CavP; TrGrPo
To Phillis [*or* Phyllis], to Love and Live with Him. Robert Herrick. CaPo; CavP; OAEP
To Philomela. Benjamin Colman. SCAP
To Phoebe. W. S. Gilbert. InMe; OLR
To Phyllis. Eugene Field. InMe
To Phyllis. Thomas Lodge. *See* Love Guards the Roses of Thy Lips.
To Phyllis. Edmund Waller. *See* To Phillis.
To Phyllis, the Fair Shepherdess. Thomas Lodge. *See* Phyllis.
To Phyllis, to Love and Live with Him. Robert Herrick. *See* To Phillis . . .
To Phylocles, Inviting Him to Friendship. "Ephelia." WPE
To Pikes Peak. Elijah Clarence Hills. PoOW
To Ping-ku, Asleep. Lawrence Durrell. ChMP; NeBP
To Pius IX. Whittier. TW
To place one's little boy—just so. Archery. Walter de la Mare. FaBoNo
To plant a seed and see it grow. Lesson. Harry Behn. TiPo
To plant a tree! How small the twig. Arbor Day. Dorothy Brown Thompson. SiSoSe
To plant three roses for you each one only a dollar. Third Ode to Persephone. Robert Kelly. The Book of Persephone, 14. PoM
To Plautia. Sir Aston Cokayne. CavP
To Pledge or Not to Pledge. *Unknown.* STF
To Poem. Lyn Lifshin. NeAC
To Poesy. Tennyson. VLP
To Poets. Walter Savage Landor. FaBoEE; ViBoPo
To Poets and Airmen. Stephen Spender. WaP
To popularize the mule, its neat exterior. The Labors of Hercules. Marianne Moore. OxBA
To praise men as good, and to take them for such. Charity in Thought. Samuel Taylor Coleridge. WhC
To praise the blue whale's crystal jet. The Whale, His Bulwark. Derek Walcott. OxBC; TTY
To praise thy life or wail thy worthy death. Epitaph on Sir Philip Sidney. *At. to* Sir Walter Ralegh. SiPS
To pray for an easy heart is no prayer at all. James K. Baxter. Autumn Testament, 22. OCNZ
To Primroses Fill'd [*or* Filled] with Morning-Dew. Robert Herrick. AnAnS-2; HBV-1; OBS; PoPl; SeCV-1; ViBoPo
To prinke me up and make me higher plaste. George Gascoigne. AAS
To print, or not to print—that is the question. Hamlet's Soliloquy Imitated. Richard Jago. BXAP; FaBoCo; FaBoPa
To print our poems the propulsive cause. Fame Makes Us Forward. Robert Herrick. CaPo
To Promise Is One Thing, to Perform Is Another. La Fontaine, *tr. fr. French.* UnTE
To Prote. Simmias of Thebes, *tr. fr. Greek by* John Addington Symonds. AWP
To prove himself no plagiary, Moore. On J. M. S. Gent. Pope. FaBoEE
To Psyche. Keats. *See* Ode to Psyche.
To Puck. Beatrice Llewellyn Thomas. HBMV
To purge what I am pleased to call my mind. Ataraxia. Bert Leston Taylor. HBMV; InMe
To Purity and Truth. *Unknown, tr. fr. Chinese by* William C. White. TrJP
To put new shingles on old roofs. A Little Brother of the Rich. Edward Sanford Martin. AA; HBV-1
To Pyrrha ("Quis multa gracilis"). Horace, *tr. fr. Latin by* Milton. Odes, I, 5. AWP
(Fifth Ode of Horace, The.) EnLoPo; PoEL-3
(To a Girl.) WiR
("What slender youth bedewed with liquid odours.") EBEV; OBVE
To Queen Elizabeth. Sir John Davies. *See* Dedication I: "To that clear majesty which in the north."
To R. B. Gerard Manley Hopkins. CMoP; CoBMV; GTBS-P; InvP; OAEL-2; VLP
To R. Hudson. Alexander Montgomerie. OxBS
To R. K. James Kenneth Stephen. BXAP; CenHV; FaBoCo; FaBoEE; FaBoPa; NBM; NOBL; Par; VLP; WhC
To rack and torture thy unmeaning brain. On the Supposed Author of a Late Poem "In Defense of Satire." Earl of Rochester. APAS
To rage I/ gravitate. Field. Susan Griffin. NPGG
To rail or jest, ye know I use it not. Sonnet. Sir Thomas Wyatt. SiPS
To raise an iron tree. A Calder. Karl Shapiro. EyDe
To Rathlin's Isle I chanced to sail. The Enchanted Island. Luke Aylmer Conolly. OBRV
To reach it. Waterfall. Anne Welsh. PeSA
To read my book[e], the virgin shy [*or* shie]. To His Book[e]. Martial, *tr. by* Robert Herrick. AnAnS-2; AWP; OBVE
To Redouté. John Ashbery. PoA

To Remain. C. P. Cavafy, *tr. fr. Modern Greek.* BoLoP, *tr. by* Nikos Stangos *and* Stephen Spender; ErPo, *tr. by* John Mavrogordato
To remember is not always to go back to what was. Time Reminded Me. Julia Uceda, *tr. by* Willis Barnstone. BoWoP
To reply, in face of a bad season. The Ill Wind. Jay Macpherson. MoCV
To Retirement. Luís de León, *tr. fr. Spanish by* Thomas Walsh. TrJP
To Richard Boyle, Earl of Burlington: Of the Use of Riches. Pope. Moral Essays, Epistle IV. OAEL-1; PPP
(Of the Use of Riches.) PoEL-3
To Richard Wright. Conrad Kent Rivers. AmNP; CABA; IDB; PoBA
To ride piggy-back. Slave. Langston Hughes. LiTM
To robbers furious, and to lovers tame. Samuel Johnson, *after the Latin of* Joachim du Bellay. FaBoEE
To Robert Browning. Walter Savage Landor. EnRP; NoP; OAEP; ViBoPo
To Robert Earl of Oxford and Earl Mortimer. Pope. OBEC
To Robert Louis Stevenson. W. E. Henley. MoBrPo
To Robert Lowell and Osip Mandelstam. Frederick Seidel. AMV-81
To Robin Redbreast. Robert Herrick. OBS; PBBP; TrGrPo
To Rose. Sara Teasdale. HBV-1
To Rosemond [*or* Rosamond]. Chaucer. CABA; NoP
(Ballade to Rosamund.) MeEL
(To Rosemounde.) OAEL-1
To Roses in the Bosom[e] of Castara. William Habington. *Fr.* Castara, Pt. I. AnAnS-2; CavP; EnLoPo; GoBC; HBV-1; LoBV; MeLP; NIP; OBEV; SeCP; UnTE; ViBoPo
To Rosina Pico. William Wilberforce Lord. AA
To Rotenham. August, Graf von Platen, *tr. fr. German by* Reginald Bancroft Cooke. PeHV
To Russia. Joaquin Miller. AA
To S. A. T. E. Lawrence. PeHV
To S. M. a Young African Painter, on Seeing His Work. Phillis Wheatley. BlSi
To S. R. Crockett. Robert Louis Stevenson. *See* Blows the Wind To-Day.
To S. T. C. on His 179th Birthday, October 12, 1951. Maurice Carpenter. FaBoTw
To safeguard man from wrongs, there nothing must. Distrust. Robert Herrick. CaPo
To Saffold's Customers. *At. to* John Case. FaBoUs
To Saint Catherine. Henry Constable. GoBC
To Saint Margaret. Henry Constable. ACP; GoBC
To Saint Mary Magdalen. Henry Constable. ACP; LoBV; PoEL-2
To St. Mary Magdalen. Benjamin Dionysius Hill. AA
To Sally. Horace, *tr. fr. Latin by* John Quincy Adams. Odes, I, 22. AA; AWP; OBAL
To San Francisco. S. J. Alexander. PAH
To Satch. Samuel Allen. AmNP; CTBA; LiSp; NIP; PAI; PoBA; PoNe; SoSe; TTY
(American Gothic.) IDB
To save your world, you asked this man to die. Epitaph for the Unknown Soldier. W. H. Auden. FaBoCo
To Saxham. Thomas Carew. AnAnS-2; CaPo; JCP; NoP; OBS
To say it once held daisies and bluebells. The Broken Bowl. James Merrill. PoA
To Schmidlein. August, Graf von Platen, *tr. fr. German by* Reginald Bancroft Cooke. PeHV
To School! Stevie Smith. FaBoEE
To Scilla. Sir Charles Sedley. FaBoEE; PV
To Scott. Winifred Letts. PoLF
To Sea, to Sea! Thomas Lovell Beddoes. *Fr.* Death's Jest-Book, I, i. EtS
(Mariners' Song.) OBVV
(Sailor's Song.) HBV-1
(Song from the Ship.) OBRV
(To Sea.) CH
To search for love is futile in this den. Search for Love. Henry Johnson. LFAC
To Search Our Souls. Jane McKay Lanning. TRV
To see a strange [*or* quaint] outlandish fowl. The Bounty of Our Age. Henry Farley. FaBoCh; FaBoEE; SeCePo; ViBoPo
To see a [*or* the] world in a grain of sand. Auguries of Innocence. Blake. BiP; BLPL; CABA; EBEV; EnRP; FaBoCh; FaBoEn; FaBV; FaFP; FaPoR; FM; ImOP; InPK; LAuP; LiTB; LoBV; MasP; OAEL-2; OAEP; OBNC; OBRV; PoEL-4; PPoe; RHPC; SeCeV; TreFS; TrGrPo; TRV; ViBoPo; WGRP; WHA
To see both blended in one flood. Upon the Infant Martyrs. Richard Crashaw. NoP; OAEL-1; PAI
To See God's Bleedin' Lam', *with music.* *Unknown.* BoAN-2
To see her is a picture. Emily Dickinson. PeHV
To See Him Again. Gabriela Mistral, *tr. fr. Spanish by* Doris Dana. OLR
To see my coat hanging there limp as a scarecrow's. On the Couch. Oscar Williams. WaP
To see my father. Golden State. Frank Bidart. DiL
To see such dainty ghosts as you appear. On Meeting a Gentlewoman in the Dark. *Unknown.* FaBoEE
To see the anemones, urchins, and crabs. Open Casket. Sandra McPherson. GeTw
To See the Cross at Christmas. Roger Cooper. TrCP
To see the Kaiser's epitaph. The Laughing Willow. Oliver Herford. HBV-2
To see the Lord the shepherds. We Would See Jesus. *Unknown.* STF
To see the petrel cropping in the farmyard. Burns Singer. Sonnets for a Dying Man, XXX. NePoEA-2
To see the world in a grain of sand. *See* To see a world in a grain of sand.
To see the world the way a painter must. Conversing with Paradise. Howard Nemerov. PoDr
To see them coming headstrong. In Love with the Bears. Greg Kuzma. NYBP
To see them go by drowning in the river. Eli, Eli. Judith Wright. CBAP
To seek each where where man doth live. Sir Thomas Wyatt. SiPS
To seeke new worlds, for golde, for prayse, for glory. Sir Walter Ralegh. *Fr.* The Last Booke of the Ocean to Scinthia. FaBoEn
To Seem the Stranger Lies My Lot. Gerard Manley Hopkins. BrPo; CoBMV
To Sergius. Sir Charles Sedley. FaBoEE
To Sextus. Martial, *tr. fr. Latin by* Sir Charles Sedley. FaBoEE
To Shades of Underground. Thomas Campion. *See* When Thou Must Home.
To shaggy Pan, and all the Wood-Nymphs fair. A Shepherd's Gift. Anytes, *tr. by* John William Burgon. AWP
To Shakespeare. Richard Edwin Day. AA
To shave, or not to shave? that is the question. T. F. Dillon Crocker. BXAP
To Shelley. Walter Savage Landor. ViBoPo
To Shelley. John Banister Tabb. AA
To Sherrie. Joseph Matuzak. AMV-81
To Shimá Sání. Laura Tohe. STE
To shoot, to shoot, would be my delight. A Shooting Song. William Brighty Rands. OxBChV
To Show How Humble, *with music.* *Unknown.* AH
To show that Africa is more than breadth. The Giraffe. Marvin Solomon. NePoAm-2
To show the lab'ring bosom's deep intent. To S. M. a Young African Painter, on Seeing His Work. Phillis Wheatley. BlSi
To show their love, the neighbours far and near. Blouzelinda's Funeral. John Gay. *Fr.* The Shepherd's Week. OBEC
To shred them: a narrow labor, and simply toss. Destruction of Letters. Babette Deutsch. WPE
To Signora Cuzzoni. Ambrose Philips. LoBV; OBEC
To Silence. T. Sturge Moore. BrPo
To Silvestre Revueltas of Mexico, in His Death. Pablo Neruda, *tr. fr. Spanish by* Harry Thomas. AMV-81
To Silvia. Countess of Winchilsea. *Fr.* The Cautious Lovers. HBV-1
To sin, unshamed, to lose, unthinking. Russia. Alexander Blok, *tr. by* Babette Deutsch *and* Avrahm Yarmolinsky. AWP
To sing of wars, of captains [*or* captaines], and of kings. The Prologue. Anne Bradstreet. AP; BoWoP; NOBA; OxBA; SBG; SCAP; TAP; WPE
To sin's a vice in nature, and we find. Daniel Defoe. *Fr.* More Reformation. OBSV
To Sir Edward Herbert at Julyers. John Donne. SeCV-1
To Sir Francis Brian. Sir Thomas Wyatt. *See* Satire 3: To Sir Francis Brian.
To Sir H. W. at His Going Ambassador to Venice. John Donne. MeLP
(Letter to Sir H. Wotton at His Going. . .) OBS
To Sir Henrie Savile [upon His Translation of Tacitus]. Ben Jonson. OBS; SeCV-1
To Sir Henry Cary. Ben Jonson. NoP
To Sir Henry Vane the Younger. Milton. OBS
To Sir Hudson Lowe. Thomas Moore. OBSV
To Sir Philip Sidney's Soul. Henry Constable. *See* On the Death of Sir Philip Sidney.
To Sir Robert Wroth. Ben Jonson. SeCV-1
To Sir Thomas Egerton. Samuel Daniel. OBSC
To Sir Toby. Philip Freneau. AP; NoP; TAP
To Sir William Alexander. William Drummond of Hawthornden. OBS
[To Sir W. A.] PoEL-2
To Sir William Davenant: Upon His Two First Books of Gondibert. Abraham Cowley. AnAnS-2; SeCV-1
To sit composing like a sunlit ghost. The Table. Michael Heffernan. PoA
To Sit in Solemn Silence. W. S. Gilbert.. *Fr.* The Mikado. FiBHP; WhC
To sit on a shelf in the cabin across the lake. What Good Poems Are For. Tom Wayman. NoP
To Sleep. Giovanni della Casa, *tr. fr. Italian by* John Addington Symonds. AWP

To Sleep. Barbara Fialkowski. AMV-81
To Sleep. Maybury Fleming. AA
To Sleep. John Fletcher. *See* Care-charming Sleep.
To Sleep. Robert Graves. MoVE
To Sleep. Keats. ChTr; EnRP; FaBoRV; LoBV; NIP; OAEP; OBEV; OBRV; PoEL-4; PrIm; TEP; WHA
(Sonnet to Sleep.) ViBoPo
To Sleep. Percy MacKaye. HBMV
To Sleep. Frances Sargent Osgood. AA
To Sleep. Sir Philip Sidney. *See* Astrophel and Stella, Sonnets, XXXIX.
To Sleep. Charlotte Smith. WPE
To Sleep. Wordsworth. EnRP; GTBS; GTBS-P; HBV-2; OBRV; TrGrPo; ViBoPo
To sleep easy all night. *Unknown.* OxNR
To smash the simple atom. Atomic Courtesy. Ethel Jacobson. FaFP; QQQ; ShM
To Soar in Freedom and in Fullness of Power. Walt Whitman. RFM
To So-kin of Rakuyo, ancient friend, Chancellor of Gen. Exile's Letter. Li Po, *tr. by* Ezra Pound. CTC; FaBoMo; OxBA; SeCeV
To Some Few Hopi Ancestors. Wendy Rose. TWSS
To Some Millions Who Survive Joseph E. Mander, Sr. Sarah E. Wright. PoBA
To some, the pattering raindrops on the roof. Reprieve. Barbara Villy Cormack. CaP
To Someone Who Insisted I Look Up Someone. X. J. Kennedy. PV
To Song. Olga Berggolts, *tr. fr. Russian by* Daniel Weissbort. BoWoP
To Song. Thomas S. Jones, Jr. HBV-2
To Sorrow,/ I bade good-morrow. Keats. *Fr.* Endymion, IV. OBRV
To Soulfolk. Margaret Goss Burroughs. BlSi
To Spain—a Last Word. Edith M. Thomas. PAH
To speak in a flat voice. Speak. James Wright. HAP; TAP; WeW
To speak in summer in a lecture hall. Lecture Hall. Patrick Kavanagh. FaBoTw; NoAM
To Speak of Chile. Margaret Gibson. MAYP
To speak of everyday things with ease. The Shadow Remains. Lynette Roberts. NeBP
"To Speak of Woe That Is in Marriage." Robert Lowell. CAPP; NoAM
To speak out clean. Telling It. Nancy Sullivan. TAP
To speke of an unkinde man. Adrian and Bardus. John Gower. *Fr.* Confessio Amantis, V. OxBM
To spend uncounted years of pain. Arthur Hugh Clough. OBNC
To Spring. Blake. BLPL; BoNaP; EnRP; HBV-1; LAuP; NOEC; OAEL-2; OBEC; OBEV; PoEL-4; PoLF; PPP; WiR
To Spring. Charlotte Smith. WPE
To spring belongs the violet, and the blown. A Petition. Thomas Bailey Aldrich. AA
To Spring: On the Banks of the Cam. William Stanley Roscoe. OBVV
To stab my youth with desperate knives, to wear. Taedium Vitae. Oscar Wilde. SyP
To stand here in the wings of Europe. On a Return from Egypt. Keith Douglas. NeBP; NePoEA
To stand on common ground. A Common Ground. Denise Levertov. PoM
To Stand Up Straight. A. E. Housman. OAEL-2
To stand within a gently gliding boat. The Haunts of the Halcyon. Charles Henry Luders. AA
To starve, or not to starve? that is the question. W. H. Ireland. BXAP
To Stella. Hester Chapone. OBEC
To Stella. Plato, *tr. fr. Greek by* Shelley. EnLoPo; FaBoEE; OBVE; ViBoPo
(Morning and Evening Star.) AWP
("Thou wert the morning star among the living.") LO
To Stella: "Doubt you to whom my Muse these notes intendeth." Sir Philip Sidney. *See* Astrophel and Stella: First Song.
To Stella. Swift. NOEC
To Stephen Spender. Timothy Corsellis. WaP
To Stew a Rump-Steak. *Unknown.* FaBoUs
To stones trust not your monument. To W. B. Yeats Who Says That His Castle of Ballylee Is His Monument. Oliver St. John Gogarty. AnIL
To stop time, a twig spinning. A Juggle of Myrtle Twigs. Edward Codish. VWA
To Strike for Night. Lebert Bethune. NBP
To stub an oar on a rock where none should be. Basking Shark. Norman MacCaig. BoAnP
To Summer. Blake. LAuP; WiR
To Summer. Alan Nadel. AMV-80
To sup with thee thou didst me home invite. The Invitation. Robert Herrick. CaPo; OAEP
To Switzerland, right up the Rhine. The Salmon. Christian Morgenstern, *tr. by* Geoffrey Grigson. FaBoNo
To Sycamores. Robert Herrick. CaPo
To T. H., a Lady Resembling My Mistress[e]. Thomas Carew. AnAnS-2; CaPo
To T. S. Eliot. Emanuel Litvinoff. VWA
To T. A. R. H. Stephen Spender. PeHV
To take things as they be. A Philosopher. John Kendrick Bangs. HBV-2
To talk with God. Wait On! *Unknown.* STF
To Tan Ch'iu. Li Po, *tr. fr. Chinese by* Arthur Waley. AWP
To teach the grey earth like a child. The Happy Man. G. K. Chesterton. EBCP
To tell strange feats of deamons, here I am. To the Much Honoured R. F. Esq. Richard Chamberlain. SCAP
To tell the truth, I really am. The All-Night Waitress. Maura Stanton. AmPA
To Teresa. Iván Silén, *tr. fr. Spanish by* Julio Marzán. InW
To Terraughty, on His Birth-Day. Burns. NAs
To Thaliarchus. Horace, *tr. fr. Latin.* Odes, I, 9. AWP, *tr. by* Dryden; OBVE, *tr. by* Sir Richard Fanshawe
("Behold yon mountains hoary height," *tr. by* Dryden.) CaVP; OBVE
To that clear majesty which in the north. Dedication I [*or* To Queen Elizabeth]. Sir John Davies. *Fr.* Nosce Teipsum. OBSC; SiPS
To That Most Senseless Scoundrel, the Author of Legion's Humble Address to the Lords. Thomas Brown. APAS
To the Accuser Who Is the God of This World. Blake. *See* Epilogue: "Truly, my Satan, thou art but a dunce."
To the Afternoon Moon, at Sea. Cale Young Rice. EtS
To the Age's Insanities. Marie Ponsot. VGW
To the Anxious Mother. Valente Malangatana, *tr. fr. Portuguese by* Dorothy Guedes *and* Philippa Rumsey. PBA
To the Archbishop of Tuam. *Unknown.* FaBoEE
To the Archdeacon. George Farewell. NOEC
To the Authoress of "Aurora Leigh." Sydney Dobell. PeD
To the Avon River above Stratford, Canada. James Reaney. MoCV
To the banks of the Moldau River. How They Made the Golem. John Robert Colombo. MoCV
To the Bell-Ringer. Robert Farren. OnYI
To the Blacksmith with a Spade. Owen O'Sullivan, *tr. fr. Irish by* Frank O'Connor. KiLC
To the Blessed Sacrament. Henry Constable. ACP
To the Blessed Virgin Mary. Gerald Griffin. OnYI
To the Body. Alice Meynell. ACP
To the Body. Coventry Patmore. The Unknown Eros, XL. GoBC; OAEL-2; OxBoCh; PoEL-5; VLP
To the Borrower of This Book. Samuel Showell, Jr. FaBoUs
To the Boston Women. *Unknown.* PAH
To the Boy. Elizabeth Clementine Kinney. AA
To the brave all homage render. Ashby. John Reuben Thompson. AA
To the Brave Soul. Wilbur Underwood. WGRP
To the Cambro-Britons and Their Harp, His Ballad of Agincourt. Michael Drayton. *See* Agincourt.
To the Canary Bird. Jones Very. AP
To the Carp, and Those Who Hunt Her. James Hazard. AMV-80
To the Child Jesus. Henry van Dyke. TrPWD
To the Christ. John Banister Tabb. TrPWD
To the Christians. Francis Lauderdale Adams. OxBS; WGRP
To the Christians. Blake. *Fr.* Jerusalem, *prologue to ch.* 4. EnRP; WGRP
(Epigraph.) OBNC
("I give you the end of a golden string.") OBRV
To the City of London. William Dunbar. ChTr; EBEV; FaBoPP
(In Honour of the City of London.) OBEV
To the cold peak without their careful women. The Climbers. Elizabeth Jennings. NePoEA
To the Colorado Desert. Madge Morris. BPAW
To the Contemporary Muse. Edgar Bowers. ELU
To the Countesse of Bedford ("Honour is so sublime perfection"). John Donne. MeLP
To the Countesse of Bedford, on New-Yeares Day. John Donne. OBS
To the Countesse of Salisbury. Aurelian Townshend. AnAnS-2; MePo; OBS; SeCP
(Loves Victory.) MeLP
To the Cowpens riding proudly, boasting loudly, rebels scorning. The Battle of the Cowpens. Thomas Dunn English. PAH
To the Cuckoo. Michael Bruce, *revised by* John Logan. BSV; HBV-1; OBEV; ViBoPo
(Ode: To the Cuckoo.) NOEC; OBEC; PBBP
To the Cuckoo. F. H. Townsend. ChTr; FaBoNo
To the Cuckoo. Wordsworth. ELP; EnRP; FaFP; FiP; GTBS; GTBS-P; HBV-1; LoBV; OBRV; PB; PBBP; PoLF; TreFT; TrGrPo
To the Daisy ("Bright Flower! whose home is everywhere"). Wordsworth. EnRP
To the Daisy ("In youth from rock to rock I went"). Wordsworth. EnRP
To the Daisy ("With little here to do or see"). Wordsworth. GTBS; GTBS-P; HBV-1; HBVY

To the Dandelion. James Russell Lowell. AP; HBV-1; HBVY
"Dear common flower, that grow'st beside the way," *sel.* FaPON, 2 *sts.*; GN
To the Dead of '98. Lionel Johnson. HBV-2
To the Defenders of New Orleans. Joseph Rodman Drake. PAH
To the Detracted. John Andrews. *Fr.* The Anatomy of Baseness. EIL, *longer sel.;* LO
To the dim light and the large circle of shade. Sestina, of the Lady Pietra degli Scrovigni. Dante, *tr. by* Dante Gabriel Rossetti. AWP; OAEL-2; OBVE
To the Divine Neighbor. Judah Leib Teller, *tr. fr. Yiddish by* Gabriel Preil *and* Howard Schwartz. VWA
To the Driving Cloud. Longfellow. ChTr; FaBoEn; FaBoRV; PoEL-5
To the Earl of Dorset. Ambrose Philips. *See* Winter-Piece, A.
To the Earl of Oxford, Late Lord Treasurer. Swift, *after the Latin of* Horace. OBVE
To the Earl of Warwick on the Death of Mr. Addison. Thomas Tickell. HBV-2; NOEC; OBEC
To the Elephants. Nathan Alterman, *tr. fr. Hebrew by* Ruth Nevo. VWA
To the End. John E. Bode. BLRP
To the Eternal Feminine. Tristan Corbière, *tr. fr. French by* C. F. MacIntyre. ErPo
To the Etruscan Poets. Richard Wilbur. OxBC
To the Evening. John Codrington Bampfylde. NOEC
To the Evening Star. Mark Akenside. PoEL-3
To the Evening Star. Blake. BoNaP; CH; ChER; ChTr; EnRP; FaBoRV; FaBV; FPL; LAuP; LoBV; NOEC; NoP; OAEL-2; OAEP; PoLF; PPP; TEP; TrGrPo; WiR
To the Evening Star ("Gem of the crimson-colour'd even"). Thomas Campbell. GTBS; GTBS-P
(Caroline, II: To the Evening Star.) OBNC
To the Evening Star ("Star that bringest home the bee"). Thomas Campbell. GTBS; GTBS-P; TRV
(Song to the Evening Star.) HBV-1
To the Evening Star: Central Minnesota. James Wright. NaP
To the Excellent Pattern of Beauty and Virtue, Lady Elizabeth, Countess of Ormond. James Shirley. GoBC
To the Fair Clarinda, Who Made Love to Me, Imagin'd More than Woman. Aphra Behn. SBG
To the fairest! Winchester. Lionel Johnson. OBVV
To the Federal Convention. Timothy Dwight. PAH
To the fence posts leaning. Go Home. Janet Reed McFatter. GrPl
To the field I carried my milking pail. I Want to Be Married and Cannot Tell How. *Unknown.* OnYI
To the Field Mice. Richard Eberhart. BoAnP
To the figures bathing at the river. A Bodhisattva Undoes Hell. Jerome Rothenberg. CoPo
To the Film Industry in Crisis. Frank O'Hara. CAPP; NoAM; NOBA; OBAL; SOTW
To the First of August. Ann Plato. BlSi
To the first of my lovers. The First of My Lovers. Sydney Carter. OBET
To the Five Members of the Honourable House of Commons. Sir John Denham. NCEP
To the Fly in My Drink. David Wagoner. DFF
To the Fountain of Bandusia. Horace, *tr. fr. Latin by* Eugene Field. Odes, III, 13. AA; AWP
To the Four Courts, Please. James Stephens. BIrV; HBMV; MoAB; MoBrPo; UnPo
To the French of the Second Empire. Arthur Rimbaud, *tr. fr. French by* Robert Lowell. *Fr.* Eighteen-seventy. OBWP
To the Fringed Gentian. Bryant. AA; AP; AWP; FaBoBe; FPL; GN; HBV-1; NePA; NoP; OBRV; PoLF; TAP; TreFT
To the Frivolous Muse. George Meason Whicher. InMe
To the Garden the World. Walt Whitman. AP
To the Gardener at Nuneham. Horace Walpole. FaBoEE
To the gaunt House of Art which lacks for naught. Athanasia. Oscar Wilde. BrPo
To the Generous Reader. Robert Herrick. CaPo
To the Ghost of a Kite. James Wright. NePoEA
To the Ghost of John Milton. Carl Sandburg. PP
To the Ghost of Martial. Ben Jonson. OAEP
To the Girls of My Graduating Class. Irving Layton. ErPo
To the God of all sure mercies let my blessing rise to-day. Cassandra Southwick. Whittier. PAH
To the God of Love. E. V. Knox. HBMV; NOBL
To the Grasshopper and the Cricket. Leigh Hunt. EnRP; GN; HBV-1; OBNC
To the Greek Anthologists. George Rostrevor Hamilton, *after the Greek of* Satyros. FaBoEE
To the green wood where I found my love. These Words I Write on Crinkled Tin. Lynette Roberts. ChMP
To the Hand. W. S. Merwin. EAS
To the Harbormaster. Frank O'Hara. CoAP; MOS; PoM
To the hard-working miner whose dangers are great. The Hard-working Miner. *Unknown.* AmFP
To the Harpies. Arthur Davison Ficke. HBV-2
To the Heart. Tadeusz Rozewicz, *tr. fr. Polish by* Victor Contoski. POL
To the Heavens above us. An Astrologer's Song. Kipling. MoBrPo
To the Highland Girl of Inversneyde. Wordsworth. *See* To a Highland Girl.
To the Holy Spirit. Yvor Winters. MoAmPo; MoVE; QFR; VGW
To the house on the grassy hill. The Presence. Denise Levertov. NaP; NePoEA-2
To the Immortal[l] Memory [*or* Memorie] and Friendship of That Noble Pair[e], Sir Lucius Cary and Sir Henry Morrison. Ben Jonson. AnAnS-2; NOBE; NoP; OAEL-1; OBS; PoEL-2; SeCP; SeCV-1
Noble Nature, The, *sel.* GN; GoBC; GTBS; GTBS-P; HBV-2; HBVY; TreFT
(It Is Not Growing like a Tree.) CABA; ChTr; HeIP; LiTB
(Oak and Lily.) TrGrPo
(Part of an Ode, A.) OBEV
(Proportion.) FaBoEn
To the Immortal Memory of the Halibut on Which I Dined This Day [Monday, April 26, 1784]. William Cowper. MOS; SeCePo
To the Infant Martyrs ("Go, smiling souls, your new-built cages break"). Richard Crashaw. NoP; PAI; SeCV-1
To the Ingleezee Khafir, Calling Himself Djann Bool Djenkinzun. James Clarence Mangan, *after the Persian.* OnYI
To the Jews in Poland. Jozef Wittlin, *tr. fr. Polish by* Isaac Komem. VWA
. . .to the King./ Thou art the wall-stone the workers rejected. Advent Lyrics, I. *Unknown, tr. by* Charles W. Kennedy. *Fr.* Christ 1. AnOE
To the King, at His Entrance into Saxham: By Master John Crofts. Thomas Carew. CaPo
To the King, upon His Com[m]ing with His Army into the West. Robert Herrick. AnAnS-2; CaPo
To the King, upon his Welcome to Hampton-Court. Robert Herrick. AnAnS-2
To the King's Most Excellent Majesty. Phillis Wheatley. TAP
To the Ladies. Mary Lee, Lady Chudleigh. NOEC; WPE; WPOW
To the Ladies. Arnold Kenseth. PPON
To the Lady in the Chemisette with Black Buttons. Nathaniel Parker Willis. OBAL
To the Lady Lucy, Countess of Bedford. Samuel Daniel. OBSC
To the Lady Margaret, Countess[e] of Cumberland. Samuel Daniel. LoBV; OBSC
"Knowing the heart of man is set to be," *sel.* FaBoEn
To the Lady Margaret Ley. Milton. GTBS; GTBS-P; OBEV
(Sonnet: "Daugher to that good Earl, once President.") OBS
To the Lady May. Aurelian Townsend. GBL; MePo
To the Lady Portrayed by Margaret Dumont. John Hollander. OBAL
(For the Passing of Groucho's Pursuer.) PoA
To the Lady Radegunde, with Violets. Venantius Fortunatus, *tr. fr. Latin by* Helen Waddell. NAWM-1
To the Lady with a Book. *Unknown, tr. fr. Irish by* Frank O'Connor. KiLC
To the Laggards. Joseph Bovshover, *tr. fr. Yiddish by* Joseph Bovshover. TrJP
To the Landlord. Swift. DBV
To the last moment of his breath. Hope. Goldsmith. *Fr.* The Captivity. OBEC
To the Last Wedding Guest. Horace Gregory. NYBP
To the Leanán Shee. Thomas Boyd. OnYI
To the Learned and Reverend Mr. Cotton Mather, on His Excellent Magnalia. Grindall Rawson. SCAP
To the Learned Critic. Ben Jonson. PP
To the Leaven'd Soil They Trod. Walt Whitman. AP
To the Liffey with the Swans. Oliver St. John Gogarty. AnIL; OxBI
To the Lighted Lady Window. Marguerite Wilkinson. ISi
To the Little House. Christopher Morley. HBMV
To the Looking-Glass world it was Alice that said. "Lewis Carroll." *Fr.* Through the Looking-Glass. Par
To the Lord Chancellor, *sels.* Shelley.
"May the strong curse of crushed affections light." DBV
"Oh, let a father's curse be on thy soul." ViBoPo
To the Lord General[l] Cromwell, May 1652. Milton. CABA; NoP; OBS; TrGrPo; ViBoPo
(To Oliver Cromwell.) SeCeV
To the Lord Love. "Michael Field." OBMV
To the Lords of Convention 'twas Claver'se who spoke. Bonny [*or* Bonnie] Dundee. Sir Walter Scott. *Fr.* The Doom of Devorgoil. EnRP; FaBoCh; HBV-2; OBRV; OxBoLi; OxBS; Par; SeCeV
To the lucky now who have lovers or friends. Alexandria. Lawrence Durrell. MoVE
To the Maiden in the East. Henry David Thoreau. OxBA

To the Maids Not to Walk in the Wind. Oliver St. John Gogarty. AnIL; ErPo
To the Man after the Harrow. Patrick Kavanagh. CIP; GTBS-P
To the Man I Live With. Ann Menebroker. IHMS
To the Man Who Sidled Up to Me and Asked: "How Long You In Fer, Buddy?" Etheridge Knight. NeAC
To the Man Who Watches Spiders. Siv Cedering Fox. LTB
To the man-in-the-street, who, I'm sorry to say. Note on Intellectuals. W. H. Auden. FiBHP; PoPl
To the Man-of-War-Bird. Walt Whitman. AA; AmPP; BoAnP; EtS; FaBoBe; FM; HBV-1; NePA
To the Marchesana of Pescara. Michelangelo, *tr. fr. Italian by* Wordsworth. CTC
(Love's Justification.) AWP
("Yes! hope may with my strong desire keep pace.") OBVE
To the Marquis of Graham on His Marriage. *Unknown.* OBSV
To the Memory of a Lady, *abr.* George Lyttelton. OBEC
To the Memory of a Young Man. *Unknown.* WhC
To the Memory of Abraham Lincoln. Bryant. *See* Death of Lincoln, The.
To the Memory of Ben Johnson, *sel.* Jasper Mayne.
"Scorne then their censure, who gave out thy wit." OBS
To the Memory of Gavin Wilson (Boot, Leg and Arm Maker). George Galloway. NOEC
To the Memory of J. Horace Kimball. "Ada." BlSi
To the Memory of Lord Halifax, *sel.* Ambrose Philips.
"Weeping o'er the sacred urn." FaBoCo
To the Memory of Mr. Oldham. Dryden. AWP; CABA; EBEV; FaBoEn; FiP; HAP; HeIP; InPK; InPS; LoBV; NIP; NOBE; NoP; OAEL-1; OBS; PAI; PoEL-3; PP; PPoe; PPP; Prf; SeCeV; SeCV-2; ViBoPo
To the Memory of My Beloved Master William Shakespeare [and What He Hath Left Us]. Ben Jonson. GoTL; HBV-2; TreFS; TrGrPo; WHA
(To the Memory of My Beloved, the Author Mr. [*or* Master] William Shakespeare [and What He Hath Left Us].) AnAnS-2; CABA; HAP; HeIP; JCP; LiTB; NoP; OAEL-1; OAEP; OBS; POEL-2; PP; SeCP; SeCeV; SeCV-1; ViBoPo
(To the Memory of My Beloved William Shakespeare and What He Hath Left Us.) EnRePo
Sels.
"I, therefore, will begin. Soul of the age!" NOBE
"Sweet Swan of Avon! what a sight it were." ChTr
To the Memory of Sir Isaac Newton, *sel.* James Thomson.
"All-intellectual eye, our solar round." ImOP; NOEC
To the Memory of the Brave Americans. Philip Freneau. AmPP; AP; PAL; PoLF;
(Eutaw Springs.) AA; BeLS; PAH
To the Memory of the Learned and Reverend, Mr. Jonathan Mitchell. Francis Drake. SCAP
To the Men of Kent. Wordsworth. OBWP
To the Men Who Lose. George L. Scarborough. BLPA
To the Merchantis of Edinburgh. William Dunbar. FaBoPP; OxBS
To the Mercy Killers. Dudley Randall. DL
To the Milkweed. Lloyd Mifflin. AA
To the Minister Liu. Yü Hsüan-chi, *tr. fr. Chinese by* Geoffrey Waters. BoWoP
To the Mocking-Bird. Albert Pike. AA
To the Mocking-Bird. Richard Henry Wilde. AA; BoAnP
To the Modern Man. John Hall Wheelock. HBMV
To the Moon. George Darley. MOON
To the Moon. Babette Deutsch. MOON
To the Moon. Goethe, *tr. fr. German by* John Frederick Nims. MOON
To the Moon. Thomas Hardy. BoNaP; ChTr
To the Moon. Pierre de Ronsard, *tr. fr. French by* Andrew Lang. AWP
To the Moon. Shelley. BoNaP; ChER; GTBS; GTBS-P; LoBV; MOON; PPP; TrGrPo; ViBoPo
(Fragment: To the Moon.) EnRP
To the Moon. Charlotte Smith. MOON
To the Moon. Yvor Winters. HeIP
To the Moon and Back. William Plomer. MOON
To the Moonflower. Craven Langstroth Betts. AA
To the Most Beautiful Lady, the Lady Bridget Manners. Barnabe Barnes. EnLoPo
To the Most Excellent and Learned Shepheard Collin Cloute. William Smith. Chloris: Dedication. AAS
To the Most Fair and Lovely Mistress Anne Soame, Now Lady Abdie [*or* Abdy]. Robert Herrick. CaPo; NOBE; ViBoPo
To the Most Holy Mother of God. *Unknown, tr. fr. Greek by* Shane Leslie. ISi
To the Most Learned, Wise, and Arch-Antiquary, M. John Selden. Robert Herrick. SeCV-1
To the Most Virtuous Mistress Pot, Who Many Times Entertained Him. Robert Herrick. CaPo
To the Mother of Christ, the Son of Man. Alice Meynell. ISi
To the Mothers. Ernst Toller, *tr. fr. German by* E. Ellis Roberts. TrJP
To the Mountains. Henry David Thoreau. PoEL-4
To the Much Honoured R. F. Esq. Richard Chamberlain. SCAP
To the much-tossed Ulysses, never done. Ulysses. Robert Graves. ChMP; CMoP; FaBoTw; NoAM; OxBI; PrIm
To the Muse. Robert Louis Stevenson. EBEV
To the Muse. Philip Whalen. PoM
To the Muse. James Wright. NNaP; NoP
To the Muses. Blake. ChER; ChTr; EnRP; HAP; HBV-2; HeIP; LAuP; LiTB; LoBV; NOBE; NOEC; NoP; OAEL-2; OAEP; OBEC; OBEV; SeCeV; TrGrPo; ViBoPo; WHA
To the Mutable Fair. Edmund Waller. AnAnS-2; SeCP
To the Name above Every Name, the Name of Jesus, a Hymn. Richard Crashaw. SeCV-1
(On the Name of Jesus.) AnAnS-1
To the New Annex to the Detroit County Jail. Richard W. Thomas. PoBA
To the new wick/ Of freedom's torch. My Thread. David Hofstein, *tr. by* Joseph Leftwich. TrJP
To the New Year. Thomas Carew. CaPo
To the New Yeere. Michael Drayton. PoEL-2
To the Newborn. Judit Tóth, *tr. fr. Hungarian by* Laura Schiff. WPOW
To the Night. Shelley. *See* To Night.
To the Nightingale. Sir John Davies. *Fr.* Hymns of Astraea. OBSC; PBBP; TrGrPo
To the Nightingale. William Drummond of Hawthornden. *See* Sonnet: "Dear quirister, who from those shadows sends."
To the Nightingale. Milton. HBV-1
(O Nightingale.) SeCePo
(O Nightingale, That on Yon Bloomy Spray.) PB
(Sonnet: "O Nightingale. . .") OAEL-1; OBS; PBBP; ViBoPo
To the Nightingale. Countess of Winchilsea. SBG; WPE
To the Nile. Keats. OBRV
To the Nile. Shelley. OBRV
To the Noble Woman of Llanarth Hall. Evan Thomas, *tr. fr. Welsh by* Anthony Conran. PV
To the Noblest and Best of Ladies [*or* Ladyes], the Countess [*or* Countesse] of Denbigh. Richard Crashaw. JCP; MeLP
(Against Irresolution.) OxBoCh
(Letter to the Countess of Denbigh.) SeCP
(Letter to the Countess of Denbigh against Irresolution and Delay in Matters of Religion.) MePo
To the Oaks of Glencree. J. M. Synge. ELU; MoBrPo; OxBI
To the Ocean. Byron. *Fr.* Childe Harold's Pilgrimage, IV. GN; WGRP
(Address to the Ocean.) TreFS
(Apostrophe to the Ocean.) EtS
(Ocean.) TrGrPo
(Roll On, Thou Dark Blue Ocean.) FaPON
To the Ocean Now I Fly. Milton. *Fr.* Comus. OBEV; OBS; ViBoPo
(Farewell of the Attendant Spirit.) TrGrPo
(Song: "To the ocean now I fly.") SeCeV
(Spirit Epiloguizes, The.) NOBE
To the Old Masters. Wing Tek Lum. BrSi
To the One God. *Tr. fr. Sanskrit by* Raimundo Panikkar. *Fr.* Vedic Hymns. ILwL
To the One I Love Most. *Unknown.* MeEL
(Lines from Love Letters, I.) OBEV
To the One of Fictive Music. Wallace Stevens. AP; CoBMV; MoAB; MoAmPo; MoVE; NoP; TwAmPo
To the Painter Preparing to Draw M. M. H. James Shirley. CavP
To the Parotid Gland. ——— Schlesinger. WhC
To the Parted One. Goethe, *tr. fr. German by* Christopher Pearse Cranch. AWP
To the Pay Toilet. Marge Piercy. GP
To the pines, to the pines. *Unknown.* WTO
To the Pious Memory of the Accomplished [*or* Accomplisht] Young Lady, Mrs. Anne Killigrew. Dryden. HBV-2; LoBV; OAEL-1
(Ode to the Pious Memory of the Accomplished Young Lady, Mrs. Anne Killigrew.) OBEV
(To the Pious Memory of the Accomplisht Young Lady, Mrs. Anne Killegrew, Excellent in the Two Sister-Arts of Poesie and Painting.) PoEL-3; SeCV-2
Poet's Resurrection, *sel.* WHA
To the Poet T. J. Mathias. Walter Savage Landor. PV
To the Poet Wordsworth. Felicia Dorothea Hemans. BrRo
To the Poets. Keats. *See* Bards of Passion and of Mirth.
To the Polyandrous Lydia. Franklin P. Adams, *after the Latin of* Horace. HBMV
To the Portrait of "A Gentlemen." Oliver Wendell Holmes. InMe
To the Postmaster General. Peter Redgrove. AMV-81
To the Queen. Blake. *See* Door of Death, The.
To the Queen. Lord Darnley. OxBS
To the Queen. Sir Walter Ralegh. *See* Silent Lover, The.

To the Queen ("O loyal to the royal in thyself"). Tennyson. Idylls of the King: Dedication. VLP
To the Queen[e], Entertain'd at Night by the Countess[e] of Anglesey. Sir William Davenant. FaBoEn; MeLP; MePo; OBS
To the Queen of Dolors. Sister Mary Maura. ISi
To the Queen of Hearts goes [*or* is] the Ace of Sorrow. The Queen of Hearts. *Unknown.* FSW; OBET
To the quick brow Fame grudges her best wreath. The Guerdon. John James Piatt. AA
To the Rainbow. Thomas Campbell. HBV-1
To the Reader. Baudelaire, *tr. fr. French by* Arthur Symons. SyP
To the Reader. J. V. Cunningham. NoAM; QFR
To the Reader. Samuel Daniel. PP
(To His Reader.) OBSC
To the Reader ("Pray thee, take care, that tak'st my book in hand"). Ben Johnson. NoP; OAEP; SeCV-1
To the Reader ("This figure, that thou here seest put"). Ben Jonson. EnRePo
(On the Portrait of Shakespeare Prefixed to the First Folio Edition, 1623.) HBV-2
To the Reader. Denise Levertov. AmPP; CoPo; PoM; VGW
To the Reader. Urian Oakes. SCAP
To the Reader of Master William Davenant's Play "The Wits." Thomas Carew. CaPo
To the Reader of These Sonnets. Michael Drayton. *See* Idea: "Into these loves, who but for passion looks."
To the Respective Judges. *Unknown.* APAS
To the Returning Brave. Robert Underwood Johnson. PAH
To the Rev. F. D. Maurice. Tennyson. GTBS-P; VLP
At Farringford, *sel.* FaBoPP
To the Rev'd Mr. Jno. Sparhawk on the Birth of His Son. Samuel Sewall. SCAP
To the Reverend Mr. Murdoch. James Thomson. OBEC
To the Rev. Mr. Newton. William Cowper. LoBV
To the Revd. Mr. ——— on His Drinking Sea-Water. John Winstanley. NOEC
To the Reverend Shade of His Religious Father. Robert Herrick. AnAnS-2; CaPo; JCP; OBS; SeCV-1
To the Reverend W. L. Bowles. Samuel Taylor Coleridge. EnRP
To the Reviewers. Thomas Hood. *See* Poet's Fate, The.
To the Right Hon. Henry Pelham. Edward Moore. OBSV
To the Right Honourable the Countesse of C. William Habington. AnAnS-2; SeCP
To the Rt. Hon. the Lady C. Tufton. Countess of Winchilsea. SBG
To the Right Honourable William, Earl of Dartmouth. Phillis Wheatley. AmPP; SBG
Sels.
"No more, America, in mournful strain." WPOW
"Should you, my lord, while you pursue my song." BPo; TTY
To the Right Person. Robert Frost. GLGT
To the Right Worthy Knight Sir Fulke Greville. Samuel Daniel. EnRePo
To the River Duddon: After-Thought. Wordsworth. *See* After-Thought.
To the River Isca. Henry Vaughan. FaBoPP
To the River Itchin, near Winton. William Lisle Bowles. OAEL-2
To the Rose. Sir John Davies. *Fr.* Hymns of Astraea. OBSC
To the Rose; a Song. Robert Herrick. HBV-1
(To the Rose.) SeCP
(To the Rose: Song.) OBS
To the Rose upon the Rood of Time. W. B. Yeats. NoAM; OAEP; TEP; VLP
To the Roving Pirate. George Turberville. EnRePo
To the Royal Society. Abraham Cowley. AnAnS-2
"Philosophy, the great and only heir," *sel.* JCP
To the Rulers. Howard Nemerov. OxBC
To the Sad Moon. Sir Philip Sidney. *See* Astrophel and Stella, Sonnets, XXXI.
To the sagging wharf. A Summer's Dream. Elizabeth Bishop. OxBC
To the Same. William Cowper. *See* to Mary.
To the Same. Ben Jonson. *See* To Celia ("Kiss me, sweet").
To the Same Flower. Wordsworth. EnRP
To the Same Purpos[e]. Thomas Traherne. NoP; SeCV-2
To the sea they came. Pure Products. Denise Levertov. NMP
To the sea-shell's spiral round. Appreciation. Thomas Bailey Aldrich. AA
To the Ship on Which Virgil Sailed to Athens. Horace, *tr. fr. Latin by* Dryden. Odes, I, 3. AWP
To the Shore. May Swenson. NePoAm-2
To the Sister of Elia. Walter Savage Landor. HBV-2
To the Sistine Madonna. Cornelia Otis Skinner. ISi
To the Skylark. Wordsworth. *See* To a Skylark.
To the Small Celandine. Wordsworth. EnRP; HBV-1; OBRV
To the Snake. Denise Levertov. AmPP; LiTM; NePoEA-2; NMM; PAI; PoA
To the Snipe. John Clare. NCEP; OBNC
To the Soul. John Collop. TrGrPo
To the Sour[e] Reader. Robert Herrick. AnAnS-2; NoP; OAEP; SeCP
To the South. Brewster Ghiselin. LiTA; NePA
To the Spirit Great and Good. Leigh Hunt. TrPWD
To the Spirit of Monahsetah. Charlotte DeClue. STE; TWSS
To the Spring. Sir John Davies. *Fr.* Hymns of Astraea. ElL
To the Spring Sun. Freda Laughton. NeIP
To the State of Love; or, The Senses' Festival. John Cleveland. MePo; PeD
(Senses Festival, The.) AnAnS-2
To the States. Walt Whitman. CTC
To the Statue. May Swenson. GOA; NYP
To the Stone-Cutters. Robinson Jeffers. AmPP; MoAB; MoAmPo; MoVE; NIP; NOBA; NoP; OxBA; PAI; PoCh; PoPl; PoRA; PP; PrIm; TrGrPo
To the Street Piano, *sel.* John Davidson.
Labourer's Wife, A. EBVV
To the suburban house you return again. Portrait of a Marriage. Dannie Abse. NoAM
To the Sun. Ingeborg Bachmann, *tr. fr. German by* Michael Hamburger. BoNaP
To the Sun. Roy Campbell. *Fr.* Mithraic Emblems. EaLo
To the Sun/ Who has shone. Last Song. James Guthrie. PDV; TiPo
To the Sun from a Flower. Guido Gezelle, *tr. fr. Flemish by* Jethro Bithell. FaPON
To the (Supposed) Patron. Geoffrey Hill. NePoEA-2
To the Supreme Being. Michelangelo. *See* For Inspiration.
To the Swallow. William Cowper, *after the Greek of* Euenus. OBVE
To the Terrestrial Globe. W. S. Gilbert. FaBoNo; HBV-2; PoPl; TrGrPo; WhC
To the Thawing Wind. Robert Frost. OxBA
To the Thirty-ninth Congress. Whittier. PAH
To the Thoughtful Reader. William Meredith. NoAM
To the Translation of Palingenius. Barnabe Googe. EnRePo
To the Translator of Lucan's Pharsalia (1614). Sir Walter Ralegh. SiPS
To the Trinity. Richard Stanyhurst. *See* Prayer to the Holy Trinity.
To the Tune of, In Fayth I Cannot Keepe My Father's Sheepe. Sidney Godolphin. OBS
(Song: "Cloris, it is not thy disdaine.") MeLP
To the Tune of the Coventry Carol. Stevie Smith. FaBoTw
To the Tune of "Ye Commons and Peers Pray Lend Me Your Ears." *Unknown.* APAS
To the Tune "Red Embroidered Shoes." Huang O, *tr. fr. Chinese by* Kenneth Rexroth *and* Ling Chung. PBWP; WPOW
To the Tune "Soaring Clouds." Huang O, *tr. fr. Chinese by* Kenneth Rexroth *and* Ling Chung. PBWP; WPOW
("You held my lotus blossom.") BoWoP
To the Tune "The Fall of a Little Wild Goose." Huang O, *tr. fr. Chinese by* Kenneth Rexroth *and* Ling Chung. WPOW
To the Tune "The Phoenix Hairpin." T'ang Wan, *tr. fr. Chinese by* Kenneth Rexroth *and* Ling Chung. WPOW
To the Tune "The River Is Red." Ch'iu Chin, *tr. fr. Chinese by* Kenneth Rexroth *and* Ling Chung. PBWP
("How many wise men and heroes.") BoWoP
To the Unconstant Cynthia. Sir Robert Howard. CavP
To the United States of America. Robert Bridges. HBV-2; PAH
To the University of Cambridge, in New-England. Phillis Wheatley. AmPP; BALP; SBG; TAP
To the University of Oxford, 1674: Epilogue. Dryden. *See* Epilogue Spoken by Mrs. Boutell.
To the Unknown Eros. Coventry Patmore. The Unknown Eros, II. LO; OxBoCh; PoEL-5
To the Unknown God. Friedrich Nietzsche, *tr. fr. German.* ILwL
To the Unknown Light. Edward Shanks. TrPWD
To the Unknown Warrior. G. K. Chesterton. MMA
To the Veterans of the Abraham Lincoln Brigade. Genevieve Taggard. OFD
To the Virgin. John Lydgate. ACP; GoBC
To the Virginian Voyage. Michael Drayton. EnRePo; HAP; HBV-2; NOBE; OAEP; OBEV; OBS; PAH; PoEL-2; SeCePo; TEP; ViBoPo
(Virginian Voyage, The.) LoBV
To the Virgins, to Make Much of Time. Robert Herrick. AnAnS-2; AWP; BLPA; BoLoP; CABA; CaPo; CavP; ChTr; ELP; EnLoPo; FaBoEn; FaBV; FaFP; FF; FPL; GBL; HAP; HeIP; HBV-1; InMe; InPK; InPS; JCP; LiTB; LoBV; MaSP; NIP; NOBE; NoP; OAEL-1; OAEP; OBEV; OBS; OLR; PAI; PoEL-3; PoPL; PPoe; PrIm; QFR; SCV; SeCeV; SeCP; SeCV-1; SoSe; SpRo; TreFS; TrGrPo; ViBoPo; WHA
(Counsel to Girls.) GTBS; GTBS-P
("Gather ye rosebuds while ye may.") TEP
(To the Virgins to Make Much of Their Time.) ErPo
(To Virgins, to Make Much of Time.) SCV
To the wall of the old green garden. A Yellow Pansy. Helen Gray Cone. HBMV

To the Water Nymphs, Drinking at the Fountain. Robert Herrick. AnAnS-2; CaPo; ViBoPo
To the Wayfarer. *Unknown.* SiSoSe
To the Western Wind. Judah Halevi, *tr. fr. Hebrew by* Solomon Solis-Cohen. TrJP
To the Western Wind. Robert Herrick. CaPo; HBV-1; OBEV; SeCV-1
To the Western World. Louis Simpson. CoAP; ConAP; GOA; LiTM; NePoAm-2; NePoEA-2; NOBA; PoPl; TAP
To the White Fiends. Claude McCay. BANP; PoBA
To the white-mantled maidens. Corinna, *tr. fr. Greek by* Richmond Lattimore. WPOW
To the Wife of a Sick Friend. Edna St. Vincent Millay. SBG
To the wild wild beat of a tom tom tom. Reversion. Barry O. Higgs. PeSA
To the Willow-Tree. Robert Herrick. CaPo; HBV-1; OBEV
To the Wind at Morn. W. H. Davies. ELU
"To the winds give our banner!" St. John. Whittier. PAH
To the Woman in Bond Street Station. Edward Weismiller. LiTA; NePA; WaP
To the World; a Farewell for a Gentlewoman, Virtuous and Noble. Ben Jonson. EnRePo; JCP; QFR; SeCP
To the World, the Perfection of Love. William Habington. AnAnS-2; JCP
To the Yew and Cypress to Grace His Funeral. Robert Herrick. QFR
To the Young Man Jesus. Annie Charlotte Dalton. CaP
To the Young Rebels. E. L. Mayo. FAZ
To Thee, Eternal Soul, Be Praise, *with music.* Richard W. Gilder. AH
To thee, fair freedom! I retire. Written at [*or* in] an Inn at Henley. William Shenstone. AWP; HBV-2; LoBV; NOBE; NOEC; OBEC; OBEV; ViBoPo
To thee now, Christes dere derling. A Song to John, Christ's Friend. *Unknown.* MeEL
To Thee, O God, *with music.* Abiel Holmes. AH
To Thee, O God, the Shepherd Kings, *with music.* John G. C. Brainard. AH
To thee obeyeth all the East as far as Ganges goes. Ovid, *tr. by* Arthur Golding. *Fr.* Metamorphoses, IV. OBVE
To thee, sweet Fop, these lines I send. Bounce to Fop; an Heroick Epistle from a Dog at Twickenham to a Dog at Court. Pope. FM
To Thee the Tuneful Anthem Soars, *with music.* Mather Byles. AH
To Thee, Then, Let All Beings Bend, *with music.* Nathaniel Evans. AH
To thee, whose cautious step and specious air. Annabella Plumptre. *Fr.* Ode to Moderation. NOEC
To Their Excellencies the Lords Justices of Ireland, the Humble Petition of Frances Harris [Who Must Starve, and Die a Maid if It Miscarries]. Swift. NOEC; Par; PoEL-3
(Mrs. Frances Harris's Petition.) OxBI
To their long home the greatest princes go. Upon a Funeral. Sir John Beaumont. FaBoRV
To them who crossed the flood. Inscription for Marye's Heights, Fredericksburg. Herman Melville. UnPo
To Theodora. *Unknown.* OxBChV
To Theon from His Son Theon. C. A. Trypanis. NCSH
To these I turn, in these I trust. The Kiss. Siegfried Sassoon. MMA
To these, the gentle South, with kisses smooth and soft. Michael Drayton. *Fr.* Polyolbion, Second Song. OBS
To these whom death again did wed. An Epitaph upon Husband and Wife [*or* a Young Married Couple] Who Died and Were Buried Together. Richard Crashaw. EBEV; ELP; FaBoEE; FaBoEn; LO; NIP; NOBE; OAEP; OBEV; OBS; PAI; SeCePo; SeCP; TreFS; TrGrPo; WHA
To Thine Eternal Arms, O God, *with music.* Thomas Wentworth Higginson. AH
To Thine Own Self Be True. Shakespeare. *See* Polonius to Laertes.
To think I once saw grocery shops. Counters. Elizabeth J. Coatsworth. SoPo; SUS
To think of it! He knows me. And Yet. Arthur B. Rhinow. BLRP
To Think of Time. Walt Whitman. BLPL; LiTA
"To think of time . . . . to think through the retrospection," *sel.* AP
To Think That Two and Two Are Four. A. E. Housman. ImOP
To think to know the country and not know. A Hillside Thaw. Robert Frost. CMoP
To This Hill Again. James Macmillan. PoSH
To this khan, and from this khan. The World; a Ghazel. James Clarence Mangan. OBVV
To this man, to his boned shoulders. The Sympathizers. Josephine Miles. CrMA
To this room—it was somewhere at the palace's. The Room. C. Day Lewis. PoCh
To this the Panther, with a scornful smile. Dryden. *Fr.* The Hind and the Panther, Pt. III. SeCV-2
To Thomas Lord Chancellor. Ben Jonson. OBS
To Thomas Moore. Byron. EnRP; OAEP; TreFT
To Those Who Sing America. Frank Marshall Davis. FB
To throw away the key and walk away. Chorus [*or* The Walking Tour]. W. H. Auden. *Fr.* Paid on Both Sides. CMoP; MoBrPo
To Thy continual Presence, in me wrought. A Prayer. William Ellery Channing. TrPWD
To thy lover. Out of the Italian; a Song. Richard Crashaw. SeCV-1
To Time. "A. W." ElL
To Tirzah. Blake. *Fr.* Songs of Experience. EnRP; LO; NOBE; OAEL-2; OxBoCh
To Toma[u]s Costello at the Wars. *At. to* Tomas O'Higgins, *tr. fr. Irish by* Frank O'Connor. AnIV; KiLC
To Tommaso de' Cavalieri ("Why should I seek to ease intense desire"). Michelangelo, *tr. fr. Italian by* John Addington Symonds. PeHV
To Tommaso de' Cavalieri ("With your fair eyes a charming light I see"). Michelangelo. *See* Love, the Light-Giver.
To Tony (Aged 3). Marjorie Wilson. SUMH
To touch all points in the past. Reflection: After Visiting Old Friends. John Allison. GrPl
To touch the cup with eager lips and taste, not drain it. Living. *Unknown.* BLPA; FaBoBe; TreFS
To Toussaint L'Ouverture. Wordsworth. EnRP; InPK; LoBV; NOBE; OAEP; OBNC; OBRV; PoNe; PoRA; PPP; TrGrPo; TRV
To travel like a bird, lightly to view. Sonnet. C. Day Lewis. *Fr.* O Dreams, O Destinations. ChMP; GTBS-P
To treat the thing directly, Ezra Pound. A High-toned Old Fascist Gentleman. William Zaranka. BXAP
To tremble, when I touch her hands. Divine Awe. George Edward Woodberry. Wild Eden, XVI. AA
To true roses uplifted on the bilious tide of evening. To Redouté. John Ashbery. PoA
To Trust. Antonia Pozzi, *tr. fr. Italian by* Lynne Lawner. PBWP
To Truth. *Unknown, tr. fr. Greek by* J. Rendel Harris. *Fr.* Solomon. WGRP
To Turn Back. John Haines. BoNaP; ConAP
To Turn from Love. Sarah Webster Fabio. BlSi
To Tzu-an. Yü Hsüan-chi, *tr. fr. Chinese by* Geoffrey Waters. BoWoP
To Urania. Benjamin Colman. SCAP
To Usward. Gwendolyn B. Bennett. BlSi
To Vanity. Darwin T. Turner. PoNe
To Varus. Catullus, *tr. fr. Latin by* Walter Savage Landor. AWP
("Suffenus whom you know, the witty.") OBVE
To Venus. Hedylos. *See* Seduced Girl.
To Venus. Horace, *tr. fr. Latin by* Ben Jonson. Odes, IV, 1. AWP; OBVE
To Vera Thompson. John Haines. LCAP
To Vergil. Tennyson. *See* To Virgil.
To Verse Let Kings Give Place. Ovid, *tr. fr. Latin by* Christopher Marlowe. Elegies, XV. ChTr
To Vesta. Thomas Middleton. MOON
To Victor Hugo. Swinburne. OBVV
To Vietnam. Charlie Cobb. PoBA
To Vineyarders in cold Korea. Pinkletinks. Grace Elisabeth Allen. GoYe
To Violet [with Prewar Poems]. Basil Bunting. FaBoMo; PoA
To Violets. Robert Herrick. CaPo; HBV-1; JCP; OBEV; OBS; SeCP; TrGrPo; ViBoPo
To Virgil. Tennyson. ChTr; GTBS-P; NoP; OAEL-2; PoEL-5; WHA
(To Vergil.) AWP
To Virgins. Robert Herrick. CaPo; UnTE; ViBoPo
To Virgins, to Make Much of Time. Robert Herrick. *See* To the Virgins, to Make Much of Time.
To Vittoria Colonna. Michelangelo, *tr. fr. Italian by* Longfellow. AWP
To Vulcan. Robert Herrick. CaPo
To W. B. Yeats Who Says That His Castle of Ballylee Is His Monument. Oliver St. John Gogarty. AnIL
To W. C. W. M. D. Alfred Kreymborg. PoA
To W. J. M. "G. G." PeHV
To W. L. G. on Reading His "Chosen Queen." Charlotte Forten. BlSi
To W.M. Alice Meynell. *See* At Night.
To W. P., *sel.* George Santayana.
"With you a part of me hath passed away." TrGrPo
To W. R. W. E. Henley. *See* Madam Life's a Piece in Bloom.
"To wade the sea mist, then to wade the sea." Stone Horse Shoals. Malcolm Cowley. NYBP; TwAmPo
To Waken a Small Person. Donald Justice. NYBP
To Waken an Old Lady. William Carlos Williams. HAP; InPK; NoP; PAI; QFR; WeW
To Walk Abroad. Thomas Traherne. ELP
(Walking.) EBEV; TrGrPo
To Walk in Warm Rain. David McCord. RHPC
To Walt Whitman. Tom MacInnes. CaP
To Walt Whitman in America. Swinburne. VLP
To watch the tipsy cripples on the beach. After Tennyson. Edward Lear. FaBoNo
To wear the arctic fox. The Arctic Ox. Marianne Moore. NYBP

To weary hearts, to mourning homes. The Angel of Patience. Whittier. WGRP
To wed, or not to wed? That is the question. *Unknown.* BXAP
To western woods and lonely plains. On the Emigration to America [and Peopling the Western Country]. Philip Freneau. GDA; PAH; TAP
To wet your eye withouten tear. Sir Thomas Wyatt. SiPS
To what a cumbersome unwieldinesse. Love's Diet. John Donne. OAEP
To What Base Uses! *parody.* Bert Leston Taylor. WhC
To what dark purpose was the will employed. Sea-Voyage. John Hall Wheelock. EtS
To what intent or purpose was Man made. As Concerning Man. Alexander Radcliffe. OBSV
To what new fates, my country, far. Unmanifest Destiny. Richard Hovey. AA; HBV-2; HBVY; PAL; TRV; WGRP
To what purpose, April, do you return again? Spring. Edna St. Vincent Millay. BoWoP; MoAB; MoAmPo; NePA; NoP
To What Strangers, What Welcome. J. V. Cunningham. NoAM
Miramar Beach, *sel.* PoA
To Whistler, American. Ezra Pound. PoA
To Whom Else? Robert Graves. FaBoMo
To whom I owe the leaping delight. A Dedication to My Wife. T. S. Eliot. BoLoP; FF
To Whom It May Concern. J. V. Cunningham. FYAP
To Whom It May Concern. Adrian Mitchell. OBWP
To whom none ever said scat. Epitaph for Bathsheba. Whittier. PCat
To whom now, Pyrrha, art thou kind? Catullus, *tr. by* Abraham Cowley. Odes, I, 5. OBVE
To whom our Saviour calmly thus reply'd [*or* replied]. True and False Glory. Milton. *Fr.* Paradise Regained, III. LiTB; OBS
To whom shall I this dancing poem send. Dedications [of Orchestra], I: To His Very Friend, Master Richard Martin. Sir John Davies. SiPS
To Whom Shall the World Henceforth Belong? John Oxenham. WBLP
To Whom Shall They Go? *Unknown.* STF
To whom should I speak today? A Dispute over Suicide. *Unknown, tr. by* T. Eric Peet. TTY
To whom should you entrust your son. Martial, *tr. by* Rolfe Humphries. Epigrams, V, 56. GLGT
To whom thus also th' angel last replied. Milton. *Fr.* Paradise Lost, XII. FiP
To William Allen White. Edna Ferber. InMe
To William Blake. Olive Tilford Dargan. HBMV
To William Camden. Ben Jonson. AnAnS-2; AWP; JCP; OBS; SeCV-1
To William Carlos Williams. Galway Kinnell. NePoAm
To William Earle of Pembroke. Ben Jonson. SeCP
To William Hayley. Blake. FaBoCo
(To H.) FF
(To Hayley.) FaBoEE; TrGrPo
To William Lloyd Garrison. Whittier. PAH
To William Roe. Ben Jonson. OAEL-1; OBS; SeCV-1
To William Sharp. Clinton Scollard. HBV-2
To William Shelley. Shelley. ChER
To William Simpson, Ochiltree. Burns. OxBS
(Epistle to William Simpson, Ochiltree.) BSV
To William Stanley Braithwaite. Georgia Douglas Johnson. BALP
To William (Whom We Have Missed.) P. G. Wodehouse. NOBL
To William Wordsworth. Samuel Taylor Coleridge. EnRP; OAEL-2
To William Wordsworth from Virginia. Julia Randall. NMM; WPE
To win our fight and our demands. The Picket Line Song. *Unknown.* FSW
To win the love of women one should first discover. Kenneth Koch. The Art of Love, Pt. I. NNaP
To Winter. Blake. WiR
To wish, and want, and not obtain. Sir Thomas Wyatt. SiPS
To Woman. Byron. HBV-1
"Woman! experience might have told me," *sel.* ViBoPo
To Women. Richard Hugo. NIP
To Women, as Far as I'm Concerned. D. H. Lawrence. InPS; WeW
To Women, to Hide Their Teeth, if They Be Rotten or Rusty. Robert Herrick. FaBoUs
To Words. Ralph Pomeroy. CoPo
To Wordsworth. John Clare. OAEL-2
To Wordsworth. Walter Savage Landor. OAEL-2
To Wordsworth. Shelley. EnRP; FiP; NoP
To write as your sweet mother does. Advice. Walter Savage Landor. HBV-1
To write in verse has been my pleasing choice. To the Rt. Hon. the Lady C. Tufton. Countess of Winchilsea. SBG
To Wystan Auden. Geoffrey Grigson. NAs
To Xanadu, Which Is Beth Shaul. Arye Sivan, *tr. fr. Hebrew by* Anthony Rudolf *and* Natan Zach. VWA
To yon fause stream that, by the sea. The Mermaid. *Unknown.* CH
To You. Frank Horne. *Fr.* Letters Found near a Suicide. BPo
To You. Kenneth Koch. CAPP
To You. Walt Whitman. BiP
To you/ the ocean was an old mother, saying. For a Man Who Learned to Swim When He Was Sixty. Diane Wakoski. FAZ
To You Building the New House. Nelly Sachs, *tr. fr. German by* Keith Bosley. VWA
To you, holding in spent hands all seasons' memories. To a Faithless Lover. Robert Greacen. OnYI
To you, morning and evening. Prayers to Liberty. Anwar Shaul, *tr. by* Yoffee Berkovitz. VWA
To you, my lordis, that standis by. So Young Ane King. Sir David Lindsay. SeCePo
To you [*or* yow], my purse [*or* purs], and to non [*or* no *or* noon] other wight. The Complaint [*or* Compleint] of Chaucer to His [Empty] Purse. Chaucer. CABA; GoBC; GP; InPK; MeEL; NoP; OAEL-1; OxBM; TrGrPo, 2 *vers.*; ViBoPo; WHA
The Complaint [*or* Compleint] of Chaucer to His [Empty] Purse.
To You on the Broken Iceberg. Tess Gallagher.
To you, then, tenants of life's middle state. William Cowper. *Fr.* Tirocinium; or, A Review of Schools. OBSV
To you this little village is dear as the moon. Dear as the Moon. *Gond Oral Tradition, tr. by* V. Elwin *and* S. Hivale. WTO
To you, troop so fleet. Hymn to the Winds. Joachim du Bellay, *tr. by* Andrew Lang. AWP
To You Who Wait. John Pudney. WaP
To you whose groves protect the feathered choirs. The Goldfinches. Richard Jago. PBBP
To you, whose temperate pulses flow. On the Fly-Leaf of Manon Lescaut. Walter Learned. AA
To Your Question. Duane Niatum. CDW
To Youth. Walter Savage Landor. EnRP; HBV-1
To youths, who hurry thus away. On a Painted Woman. Shelley. FaBoCo
To Yvor Winters, 1955. Thom Gunn. GTBS-P
To zig-zag with the ant. Summer Afternoon. Raymond Souster. BoNaP
To Zion. Judah Halevi, *tr. fr. Hebrew by* Maurice Samuel. AWP
Toad, A. Elizabeth Akers Allen. OBCA
Toad, The. Tristan Corbière, *tr. fr. French by* Vernon Watkins. SyP
Toad. John Cotton. BoAnP
Toad, The. Gerald Locklin. GP
Toad, The. Robert S. Oliver. RHPC
Toad beneath the harrow knows, The. Pagett, M. P. Kipling. BrPo
Toad-Eater, The. Burns. *See* Addressed to a Gentleman at Table, Who Kept Boasting of the Company He Kept.
Toad Suck Ferry. H. R. Stoneback. TAT
Toad that lived on Albury Heath, A. A Roundabout Turn. Robert E. Charles. MoShBr
Toad the power mower caught, A. The Death of a Toad. Richard Wilbur. AP; BiP; CABA; CMoP; LiTM; MiAP; MoVE; NMP; NoAM; NoP; PoA; TwAmPo
Toads. Philip Larkin. CMoP; NePoEA; NMP; NoAM; NOBL; OxBTC; PAI; SoSe
Toads Revisited. Philip Larkin. CMoP; NOBL; SaC
Toadstool Wood, The. James Reeves. DuDa; WSC
Toast, A. John Byrom. *See* Jacobite Toast, A
Toast. Frank Horne. BANP; PoNe
Toast, A. Charles Stetler. GP
Toast, A ("Here's to ye absent lords"). *Unknown.* WhC
Toast, A ("Here's to you and here's to me"). *Unknown.* PV
Toast ("Up to my lips and over my gums"). *Unknown.* CoSo
Toast to Our Native Land, A. Robert Bridges. PAH; PAL
Toast to that lady over the fireplace, A. Drinking Song. Anthony Hecht. NMP
Toast to the Flag, A. John Daly. PAL; PoLF
Toaster, The. William Jay Smith. GrPl; RHPC; SoPo
Tobacco. Philip Freneau. TAP
Tobacco. Graham Lee Hemminger. FPL; PoLF; WhC
(This Smoking World.) InMe
Tobacco is a filthy weed. *Unknown.* FaBoEE
Tobacconist of Eighth Street, The. Richard Eberhart. MiAP; NYP
Tobit, *sel.* Bible, Apocrypha.
Blessed Is God, XIII, *tr. fr. Greek by* D. C. Simpson. TrJP
Toccata of Galuppi's, A. Robert Browning. EBVV; GTBS-P; HAP; HBV-2; LiTB; LoBV; NCEP; NOBE; NoP; OAEL-2; OAEP; TEP; WHA
Today. Mary Frances Butts. TreFT; TRV
To-Day. Thomas Carlyle. GN; HBV-2; HBVY; WGRP
Today. Langston Hughes. VGW
To-Day. Benjamin R. C. Low. HBV-1
To-Day. Sister Mary Philip. GoBC
Today. Angela Morgan. BLPA; TRV
To-Day. John Boyle O'Reilly. OnYI
Today. Jones Very. TAP

Today. Margaret Walker. FB
To-Day. Lydia Avery Coonley Ward. HBV-2
Today:/ Hark! Heaven sings! On Christmas Day [to My Heart]. Clement Paman. OBS; OxBoCh
Today/ I am 24. January 3, 1970. Mae Jackson. PoBA
Today/ I lost my temper. For Witches. Susan Sutheim. NMM
Today, a candle in a glass. Poem for My Grandfather. A. C. Jacobs. VWA
To-day a rude brief recitative. Song for All Seas, All Ships. Walt Whitman. CH; FaBoBe; HBV-1; MOS; NePA
To-Day a Shepherd. St. Theresa of Avila, *tr. fr. Spanish by* Arthur Symons. AWP
Today a silver coffin guards St. Agnes'. Catacombs. István Vas, *tr. by* Jascha Kessler. VWA
To-day a wind from the West out over the hills came blowing. A Wind from the West. Lauchlan MacLean Watt. PoSH
To-day, all day, I rode upon the Down. St. Valentine's Day. Wilfrid Scawen Blunt. *Fr.* The Love Sonnets of Proteus. EnLoPo; NBM; OBVV; ViBoPo
To-Day and Thee. Walt Whitman. NePA
Today and tomorrow are the same day. School Days/Rule Days. Derek Butler. LFAC
Today, as I rode by. The Falling Leaves. Margaret Postgate Cole. SUMH
Today at the Gateway. Butter. Tom Schmidt. NeAC
Today beneath Benignant Skies, *with music.* Denis Wortman. AH
Today between skirmishes. For Alan Blanchard. John Oliver Simon. NeAC
Today Blackness. For Muh' Dear. Carolyn M. Rodgers. CNA
Today, Day of the Dead, procession of shadows. Pentachromatic. Julia de Burgos, *tr. by* Julio Marzán. InW
Today, dear heart, but just today. Her Answer. John Bennett. AA; BLPA
Today ees com' from Eetaly. Da Boy from Rome. T. A. Daly. FaPON
Today for the first time. A New Dress. Rachel Korn, *tr. by* Ruth Whitman. VWA
Today I Am Envying the Glorious Mexicans. Michael Blumenthal. MAYP
Today I am walking alone in a bare place. Late November in a Field. James Wright. CAPP; NNaP
Today I cleared out the kitchen with Dougie so Hedley could sand the kitchen floor. A Day in the Life. . . Stef Pixner. BrRo
Today I get this letter from you and the sun. You (III). Tom Clark. EAS
Today I have grown taller from walking with the trees. Good Company. Karle Wilson Baker. FaPON; HBV-1; WGRP
Today I have seen all I wish. At the Water Zoo. E. V. Knox. BoAnP
Today I Have Touched the Earth. William Jay Smith. WaP
To-Day I Leave Mrs. Brown's Lodgings. Sir Walter Scott. *See* On Leaving Mrs. Brown's Lodgings.
To-day I saw a butterfly. Teresa Hooley. TiPo
Today I saw a picture of the cancer cells. The Cancer Cells. Richard Eberhart. HAP; LiTM; MiAP
Today I saw a place no one has seen. Iron Heaven. Betti Alver, *tr. by* Willis Barnstone *and* Felix Oinas. BoWoP
Today I saw a thing of arresting poignant beauty. Snow in October. Alice Dunbar Nelson. BlSi; CDC
Today I saw a woman plowing a furrow. Sister. Gabriela Mistral, *tr. by* Langston Hughes. BoWoP
Today I saw a woman wrapped in rags. At the Slackening of the Tide. James Wright. CABA; MOS; UnPo; VGW
To-Day I Saw Bright Ships. Eloise Robinson. HBMV
To-day I saw the shop-girl go. To a New York Shop-Girl Dressed for Sunday. Anna Hempstead Branch. HBV-2
Today I think of a boy in the Transvaal. Remembering Snow. Ralph Nixon Currey. PeSA
Today I think. Digging. Edward Thomas. MoAB; MoBrPo; OxBTC
Today I thought I'd call home. Cuento. Carlos Cumpian. FIA
Today I trade my last unwise. How It Goes On. Maxine W. Kumin. FAZ; FiCP
Today I want/ everything. The Greed Song. Albert Goldbarth. AMV-80
Today I was awakened by the moon. Remembering Lutsky. Rayzel Zychlinska, *tr. by* Marc Kaminsky. VWA
Today I was pleased by the image. Tune. Carl Rakosi. GP
Today, I will see some empty spaces. Today: The Idea Market. Michael Nicholas. NBP
Today I'll draw/ A line in the dust. Adam's Death. Gabriel Levin. VWA
Today in Peru, this first day of summer. Pastoral. Lawrence Raab. AmPA
Today in the middle of Missouri. The Porpoise. Greg Pape. MAYP
Today Is a Day of Great Joy. Victor Hernandez Cruz. TTY
Today is a holiday in the Western heart. Today Is Armistice, a Holiday. Delmore Schwartz. TrJP
Today is a thought, a fear is tomorrow. Dirge Written for a Drama. Thomas Lovell Beddoes. EnRP
Today Is Armistice, a Holiday. Delmore Schwartz. TrJP
Today Is Ours. Abraham Cowley. *See* Epicure, The ("Fill the bowl with rosy wine").
Today Is Sun. Arnold Adoff. CAD
Today, lonely for my father, I saw. My Father's Wedding. Robert Bly. DiL
To-day my heart is heavy. Cologne. John Bate. NeBP
Today my mother and sisters. They've Come. Alfonsina Storni, BoWoP, *tr. by* Aliki *and* Willis Barnstone; WPOW, *tr. by* Marti Moody
Today my mother's letter said. Not to March. Kris Hackleman. AMV-80
To-day my thoughts/ Are swift and cool. To-Day. Sister Mary Philip. GoBC
To day old Janus opens the new yeare. A New-Yeares-Gift Sung to King Charles, 1635. Ben Jonson. SeCP
Today, Prison Won. Jessica Scarbrough. LFAC
Today, should you let fall a glass it would. Tramontana at Lerici. Charles Tomlinson. GTBS-P
Today six slender fruit trees stand. Planting Trees. V. H. Friedlaender. BoNaP
Today, the angels are all writing postcards. Saying One Thing. Robert Long. AMV-81
Today, the first dead leaf in the hall. A Dead Leaf. Howard Moss. NYBP; NYP
Today: The Idea Market. Michael Nicholas. NBP
Today the jailbird maple in the yard. For My Son on the Highways of His Mind. Maxine W. Kumin. MAT
Today the journey is ended. A Soul's Soliloquy. Wenonah Stevens Abbott. BLPA
Today the leaves cry, hanging on branches swept by wind. The Course of a Particular. Wallace Stevens. PPoe; QFR
Today the light will be as the darkness; our dreams. Equinox. Gary Young. SUW
To-day the lot caved in upon me. Page from a Diary. Desmond O'Grady. NoAM
Today the peace of autumn pervades the world. Autumn. Rabindranath Tagore. WGRP
Today the self-destroying anger. Bruce Beaver. Letters to Live Poets, XXX. CBAP
Today the trees are only blazed with paint. The Wilderness. Maura Stanton. MAYP
Today, the Twenty-sixth of February. George Barker. *Fr.* The True Confession of George Barker. NAs
To-day the woods are trembling through and through. Corn. Sidney Lanier. AP
Today the world unwrapped itself again. Summer. Moishe Kulbak, *tr. by* Ruth Whitman. VWA
Today there are holes in. Parole Denial. J. Charles Green. LFAC
To-day they laid him in the earth's cold colour. For Angus MacLeod. Iain Crichton Smith. OxBS
Today upon a bus, I saw. Forgive Me When I Whine. *Unknown.* STF
Today we carted home the last brown sheaf. Load. John Hewitt. OnYI
To-day we have naming of parts. Naming of Parts. Henry Reed. Lessons of the War, I. DTC; FF; GoJo; HeIP; HoPM; InPK; InPS; LiTB; LiTM; MoAB; MoBrPo; MoVE; MP; NOBE; NoP; OBWP; OxBTC; PAI; PoPl; PoRA; PrIm; SeCePo; SeCeV; SoSe; TrGrPo; UnPo; ViBoPo; WaP
Today we saw a tiger. The Tiger. Robert Creeley. GP
Today we think of that great man. For February Twelfth. Muriel M. Gessner. YeAr
Today we went to see the summer rentals. The Summer Rentals. Daniel Halpern. DiL; MAYP
Today we will speak in megatons. How Do You Spell "Missile"?: Preliminary Instructions in the Nuclear Age. George Uba. BrSi
Today when I heard. Retrospect. "An Pilibín." OnYI
To-day you shall have but little song from me. John Gould Fletcher. Irradiations, X. TwAmPo
To-day's house makes to-morrow's road. The Survival. Edmund Blunden. OBEV; OBMV
Todd. Stewart Conn. BSV
Todlen Butt, and Todlen Ben. *Unknown.* OBS
Todlin' Hame. *Unknown.* HBV-2
Tod's Hole, The. *Unknown.* GBP
Toe sticking out from under the hem, The. On a Fifteenth-Century Flemish Angel. David Ray. NePoEA-2
Toe tipe. *Unknown.* OxNR
Toe, trip and go. *Unknown.* OxNR
Toe upon [*or* after] toe, a snowing flesh. Nude Descending a Staircase. X. J. Kennedy. CoAP; ConAP; HeIP; HoAn; HoPM; NePoEA; NIP; PoA; POL
Toe'osh; a Laguna Coyote Story. Leslie Silko. CDW; STE; VoR
Together. Paul Engle. RHPC
Together. Maxine W. Kumin. BoWoP; NMM
Together. Ludwig Lewisohn. HBMV; TrJP

Together. Siegfried Sassoon. BrPo
Together Again. William Stafford. LCAP
Together, fourteen years older. In the Cathedral. Patricia Beer. OxBC
Together how many hours. Tant' Amare. *Unknown, tr. by* Paul Blackburn. ErPo
Together in infinite shade. Too Much Coffee. E. A. Robinson. MoAmPo
Together we laughed and talked in the warm lit room. November. Laurence Binyon. SyP
Together we looked down. Wedding Procession. James A. Emanuel. NNP
Tohub. Jakov van Hoddis, *tr. fr. German by* Charles Guenther. VWA
Toil and grow rich. The Witch. W. B. Yeats. ELU
Toil Away. John Jay Chapman. HBMV
Toil of the Trail, The. Hamlin Garland. HBV-1
Toil on, poor muser, to attain that goal. The Ideal. Francis Saltus Saltus. AA
Toiler, The, *sel.* Edwin Markham.
"Behold, O world, the toiling man." PGD
Toilet Bowl Congregation. Carolyn Baxter. LFAC
Toilet, The. Pope. *Fr.* The Rape of the Lock, I. NOBE; OBEC
Toiling fisher here is tewing of his net, The. The Fen-Men of Lincolnshire's Holland. Michael Drayton. *Fr.* Polyolbion, Song XXV. FaBoPP
Toiling of Felix, The, *sels.* Henry van Dyke.
Angler's Reveille, The. GN
Envoy: "Legend of Felix is ended, the toiling of Felix is done, The." BLPA
Toils Are Pitched, The. Sir Walter Scott. *See* Hunter's Song.
Token. Peggy Bacon. PV
Token, A. Robert Creeley. VGW
Token, The. F. T. Prince. FaBoTw; OxBTC
Token of Attachment, A. J. Adair Strawson. TDH
Tokens. William Barnes. NBM; PoEL-4; VLP
Tokens of Love, The ("I had four brothers over the sea"). *Unknown.* GBP
Tokens of Love, The ("I have a yong suster"). *Unknown. See* I Have a Young Sister.
Tokyo West. Alfred Corn. NYP
Told by Seafarers. Galway Kinnell. NePoAm-2
Toledo. Roy Campbell. MoBrPo
Tolerance. Sir Lewis Morris. OBVV
Tolerance of Crows, The. Charles Donnelly. CIP
Toleration. John Barford. PeHV
Toll-a-Winker, *with music. Unknown.* OuSiCo
Toll for the brave! On the Loss of the *Royal George* [*or* Loss of the *Royal George*]. William Cowper. EBEV; EtS; FaPoR; FiP; GN; GTBS; GTBS-P; HBV-2; NOBE; OAEP; OBEC; RoGo; TrGrPo; WHA
Toll-Gate Man, The. Wilson MacDonald. CaP
Toll no bell for me, dear Father, dear Mother. The Changeling. Charlotte Mew. CH
Toll of the Desert, The. Arthur W. Monroe. BPAW; PoOW
Toll! Roland, toll! The Great Bell Roland. Theodore Tilton. PAH
Toll the bell, fellow. The Red Cow Is Dead. E. B. White. NYBP
Toll the Bell for Damon. Maxwell Anderson. InMe
"Tollable Well!" Frank L. Stanton. FaFP
Tolling. Lucy Larcom. OHIP
Tolling from St. Patrick's, The. Burial of an Irish President. Austin Clarke. IPY
Tollund Man, The. Seamus Heaney. BIrV; EBEV; FaBoMo; IPY; NoP; TEP
Tom-a-Bedlam's Poem. *Unknown. See* Tom o' Bedlam's Song.
Tom Agnew, Bill Agnew. Dante Gabriel Rossetti. ChTr
("There are dealers in pictures named Agnew.") FaBoEE
Tom Ball's Barn. Ted Kooser. GP
Tom Bolyn[n], *with music. Unknown.* OuSiCo; TrAS
Tom Bowling. Charles Dibdin. EtS; HBV-1
(Poor Tom.) NOEC
(Poor Tom; or, The Sailor's Epitaph.) OBEC; OxBoLi
(Tom Bowline, *with music.*) AmSS
Tom Brainless as Student and Preacher. John Trumbull. *Fr.* The Progress of Dulness. AmPP
Tom Brainless, at the close of last year. An Amorous Temper. John Trumbull. *Fr.* The Progress of Dulness. AmPP
Tom Brown. *Unknown.* FSW
Tom Brown's two little Indian boys. *Unknown.* OxNR
Tom-Cat, The. Don Marquis. BoAnP; PoRA
Tom Cat Blues. *Unknown.* FSW
Tom Child had often painted Death. This Morning Tom Child, the Painter, Died. Samuel Sewall. SCAP
Tom Dixon, *with music. Unknown.* ShS
Tom done buck and Bill won't pull. Whoa Back, Buck. Leadbelly (Huddie Ledbetter). FSW
Tom Dooley. *Unknown.* AmFP; BLSo, *with music*; FSW; ViBoFo
Tom Dunstan; or, The Politician. Robert Buchanan. HBV-2
Tom Farley. Colin Thiele. PoAu-2
Tom Fool at Jamaica. Marianne Moore. AP; NYBP
Tom Gage's Proclamation. *Unknown.* PAH
Tom—garlanded with squat and surly steel. Tom's Garland: Upon the Unemployed. Gerard Manley Hopkins. BrPo; VLP
Tom, He Was a Piper's Son. *Unknown.* GBP; OxNR
Tom Hight is my name, an old bachelor I am. Greer County. *Unknown.* CoSo
Tom Joad, *with music.* Woody Guthrie. TrAS
Tom Jones's Plum Tree. *Unknown.* AmFP
Tom Long. *Unknown.* EBEV
Tom o' Bedlam's Song (*diff. versions*). *Unknown.* ChTr; EvOK; InvP; LiTB; MOON; PoEL-2; SeCeV; TrGrPo; ViBoPo, *at. to* Giles Earle
(Loving Mad Tom.) EnSB; HAP; NOBE; WeW
(Roaring Mad Tom.) WiR
(Tom-a-Bedlam's Poem.) HBV-2
(Tom o' Bedlam.) CH, *much abr.*; EBEV; FaBoCh; OAEL-1; OxBoLi; PoRA
"Moon's my constant mistress, The," *sel.,* 5 *ll.* PoPle
Tom on the Beach. George Bruce. BSV
Tom O'Roughley. W. B. Yeats. CMoP
"Tom Pearse, Tom Pearse, lend me your gray mare." Widdecombe [*or* Widdicombe] Fair. *Unknown.* CH; MoShBr; PH
Tom Potts. *Unknown.* ESPB
Tom Pringle. Louis Simpson. NePoAm-2
Tom Southerne's Birth-Day Dinner at LD. Orrery's. Pope. NAs
Tom Starr. Robert J. Conley. STE
Tom Sucklebat, in dressing-gown, without his teeth. An Administrator. Geoffrey Grigson. FaBoEE
Tom Tatter's Birthday Ode. Thomas Hood. LoBV
Tom the Lunatic. W. B. Yeats. OnYI
Tom the Porter. John Byrom. NOEC
Tom Thomson. Arthur S. Bourinot. CaP
Tom Thumbkin. *Unknown.* OxNR
Tom Thumb's Alphabet. *Unknown.* HBV-1; HBVY
("A was an archer, who shot at a frog.") FaBoUs; OxBChV; OxNR
Tom Tiler; or, The Nurse. *Unknown.* APAS
Tom told his dog called Tim to beg. Tom's Little Dog. Walter de la Mare. GDP; TiPo
Tom, Tom, the piper's son. Mother Goose. OxNR
Tom, Tom, the Piper's Son. John Crowe Ransom. ViBoPo
Tom Tyler and His Wife, *sel.* Unknown.
"Proverb reporteth, no man can deny, The." EIL
Tom Wedgewood Tells. Brian W. Aldiss. NOBL
Tomah Stream, *with music.* Larry Gorman. ShS
Tomato Juice. A. P. Herbert. WhC
Tomb. David Semah, *tr. fr. Arabic by* Yoffee Berkovitz. VWA
Tomb/ A hollow hateful word. Agamemnon's Tomb. Sacheverell Sitwell. LiTB; OBMV
Tomb of Akr Çaar, The. Ezra Pound. TwAmPo
Tomb of Crethon, The. Leonidas of Tarentum, *tr. fr. Greek by* John Hermann Merivale. AWP
Tomb of Diogenes, The. *Unknown, tr. fr. Greek by* John Addington Symonds. AWP
Tomb of Edgar Poe, The. Stéphane Mallarmé, *tr. fr. French.* NAWM-2, 2 *versions, tr. by* Roger Fry *and by author*
Tomb of Honey Snaps Its Marble Chains, The. Derek Stanford. NeBP
Tomb of Lt. John Learmonth, A.I.F., The. John Manifold. CBAP; PoAu-2
Tomb of Michael Collins, The. Denis Devlin. OxBI
Tomb of the Brave, The. Joseph Hutton. PAH
Tomb of the Kings, The. Anne Hébert, *tr. fr. French.* BoWoP, *tr. by* Aliki *and* Willis Barnstone; PBWP, *tr. by* Kathleen Weaver
Tombe, The. Thomas Stanley. OBS
Tombless Epitaph, A, *sel.* Samuel Taylor Coleridge.
"Sickness, 'tis true." OBRV
Tomboy, The. William Burford. NePA
Tombstone. Lucia M. *and* James L. Hymes, Jr. RHPC
"Tombstone" Johnson, head of the school board. Catherine Ogg. Edgar Lee Masters. *Fr.* The New Spoon River. GLGT
Tombstone told when she died, The. Dylan Thomas. OxBTC
Tombstones in the Starlight: The Fisherwoman. Dorothy Parker. NIP
Tombstones in the Starlight: The Very Rich Man. Dorothy Parker. NIP
Tomlinson. Kipling. BeLS
Tommie Makes My Tail Toddle. Burns. ErPo
Tommies in the Train. D. H. Lawrence. MMA
Tommy. Kipling. BrPo; CABA; EBEV; FaBV; FaPoR; MoBrPo; NoP; OBWP; OxBTC; TreFS
Tommy for his evening game. *Unknown.* WhC
Tommy kept a chandler's shop. *Unknown.* OxNR
Tommy O'Linn was a Scotsman born. *Unknown.* OxNR
Tommy Tibule. *Unknown.* OxNR
Tommy Trot, a man of law. *Unknown.* OxNR
Tommy was a silly boy. Kate Greenaway. TiPo

"Tommy" you was when it began. The Service Man. Kipling. Par
Tommy's Dead. Sydney Dobell. HBV-2
Tommy's Gone to Hilo. *Unknown.* AmSS, *with music;* FSW; ShS, *with music*
Tommy's tears and Mary's fears. Mother Goose. HBV-1; HBVY
To-morowe ye shall on hunting fare. Diversions for an Unhappy Princess. *Unknown. Fr.* The Squyer of Lowe Degre. OxBM
To-Morrow. Florence Earle Coates. AA
Tomorrow. John Collins. GTBS; GTBS-P; HBV-1; TreFT
Tomorrow. Kenneth Fearing. CMoP
Tomorrow. Della Adams Leitner. STF
To-Morrow. Lope de Vega, *tr. fr. Spanish by* Longfellow. AWP; TrPWD
Tomorrow. John Masefield. MoBrPo; TrGrPo
Tomorrow. Mark Strand. PPJ
Tomorrow, and Tomorrow, and Tomorrow. Shakespeare. *Fr.* Macbeth, V, v. FaBoRV; FaFP; FF; LiTB; MasP; PoPl; TrGrPo; TRV; WHA
(Macbeth Learns of His Wife's Death.) TreF
(Out, Out, Brief Candle.) ChTr
("She should have died hereafter.") DL; FiP; SoSe
Tomorrow, at Daybreak. Victor Hugo, *tr. fr. French by* Mary Ann Caws. NAWM-2
Tomorrow I will rise most probably. To Night; to Judith. George Mosby, Jr. LFAC
Tomorrow Is a Birthday. Gwendolen Haste. GoYe
Tomorrow Is My Birthday, *sel.* Edgar Lee Masters.
Thing Is Sex, Ben, The. NAs
Tomorrow Is Saint Valentine's Day. Shakespeare. *Fr.* Hamlet, IV, v. EnLoPo; OFD; PV; ViBoPo
(Ophelia's Song.) UnTE
(Saint Valentine's Day.) LiTB
(Song.) FaPON, NTCP
(Song: "Good morrow, 'tis . . .") SiSoSe
Tomorrow Is the Marriage Day. *Unknown.* NCEP
"Tomorrow" it said. A Letter from When. Bernadine. LTB
Tomorrow, Julia, I betimes must rise. The Perfume. Robert Herrick. CaPo
Tomorrow let loveless, let lover tomorrow make love. The Vigil of Venus. *Unknown, tr. by* Allen Tate. GBL
"Tomorrow morn I'll be sixteen, and Billy Grimes the rover." Billy Grimes. *Unknown.* AmFP
Tomorrow morning, some poet will wake up. Modern Poetry. Anita Skeen. IHMS
To-morrow shall be my dancing day. My Dancing Day. *Unknown.* OxBoLi; PoEL-1
Tomorrow the Heroes. A. B. Spellman. CNA; PoBA
Tomorrow, tomorrow's the circus parade! The Circus Parade. Olive Beaupré Miller. SoPo
Tomorrow when the farm boys find this. The Two-headed Calf. Laura Gilpin. FYAP
Tomorrow you will live, you always cry. Proscrastination. Martial, *tr. by* Abraham Cowley. AWP; FaBoEE; NIP; OBVE
Tomorrows. James Merrill. OBAL
Tomorrow's the Fair. *Unknown.* GBP; RHPC
Tom's Garland: Upon the Unemployed. Gerard Manley Hopkins. BrPo; VLP
Tom's Little Dog. Walter de la Mare. GDP; TiPo
Tom's sickness did his morals mend. Epigram. Matthew Prior. FaBoEE
Tomtit, The. Walter de la Mare. FM
Tom-tom, c'est moi. The blue guitar. Wallace Stevens. The Man with the Blue Guitar, XII. CMoP
Tone's Grave. Thomas Osborne Davis. OnYI
Tongue, The. Phillips Burrows Strong. TreFT; WBLP
Tongue River Psalm. Gary Gildner. FAZ
Tongue that mothered such a metaphor, The. Hogwash. Robert Francis. LCAP
Tongues. Sharon Berg. AMV-80
Tongues. T. Sturge Moore. HBMV
Tongues of Dying Men, The. Shakespeare. King Richard II, *fr.* II, i. FaBoRV
Tongues of Fire. Jorge Plescoff, *tr. fr. Spanish by* Yishai Tobin. VWA
Tongues there are that naught can say. Tongues. T. Sturge Moore. HBMV
Tonight. Franklin P. Adams. FiBHP
To-Night. Louise Chandler Moulton. AA
To-Night. Edward Thomas. PoPle
Tonight/ when the moon comes out. Proposition. Nicolás Guillén, *tr. by* Langston Hughes. FaPON; TTY
Tonight a blackout. Twenty years ago. Christmas Eve under Hooker's Statue. Robert Lowell. AP; CAPP; ConAP; FF; NePA; OxBA
Tonight and forever I shall be yours so says the oleo king. Some Stories of the Beauty Wapiti. Ebbe Borregaard. NeAP
Tonight, at Least, My Sinner. *Gond Oral Tradition, tr. by* V. Elwin *and* S. Hivale. WTO
Tonight, at the bar. The Leather Bar. Ralph Pomeroy. PeHV
Tonight, early August. At Camino. Timothy Sheehan. SUW
Tonight Everyone in the World Is Dreaming the Same Dream. Susan Litwack. VWA
To-night from deeps of loneliness I wake in wistful wonder. Bluebells. Lucia Clark Markham. HBMV
Tonight, grave sir, both my poor[e] house and I. Inviting a Friend to Supper. Ben Jonson, *after* Martial. AnAnS-2; AWP; BiP; EnRePo; JCP; LiTB; LoBV; NIP; NOBE; NoP; OAEL-1; OAEP; OBS; OxBoLi; PAI; PoEL-2; PPP; SeCP; SeCV-1
Tonight I can write the saddest line. Pablo Neruda, *tr. fr. Spanish by* W. S. Merwin. BoLoP; OLR
Tonight I could die as easily as the grass. In the Soul Hour. Robert Mezey. AmPA; NaP
Tonight I disentangle. Wakepick I. Kristjana Gunnars. NOBC
To-night I do not come to conquer thee. Anguish. Stéphane Mallarmé, *tr. by* Arthur Symons. AWP; SyP
Tonight I find the/ Calendar with its days. Angel. Gary Soto. AMV-80
Tonight I have a date. A Serenade for Two Poplars. Esther Raab, *tr. by* Robert Friend *and* Shimon Sandbank. VWA
Tonight I looked at the pale northern sky. Back. Robert Mezey. AmPA
Tonight I saw so many windows. Little Political Poem. Edward Hirsch. AMV-81
To-night I saw three maidens on the beach. Ibant Obscuræ. Thomas Edward Brown. OBNC
Tonight I want to say something wonderful. For the Sleepwalkers. Edward Hirsch. FYAP; MAYP
Tonight I watch my father's fair. Two Postures beside a Fire. James Wright. GP
Tonight in Chicago. *Unknown.* AmFN
Tonight in Fort Morgan. Anthropology in Fort Morgan, Colorado. Sam Hamod. TAT
To-night in million-voicèd London I. The Telephone. Hilaire Belloc. MoVE
Tonight in our secret town. Right Now. William Stafford. NaP
Tonight is the night. Hallowe'en. Harry Behn. FaPON; PDV; PoSC; SiSoSe; TiPo; YeAr
Tonight is the one. A Way of Speaking. Gretel Ehrlich. MAYP
Tonight I've watched. Sappho, *tr. fr. Greek by* Mary Barnard. MOON
Tonight my children hunch. "It Out-Herods Herod. Pray You, Avoid It." Anthony Hecht. CoAP; NCSH; NIP; NoAM; NOBA; OxBC
Tonight, not far from where Jefferson Davis. Night Fishing for Blues. Dave Smith. GeTw; WOLT
Tonight, on a bank line strung. Running the River Lines. David Baker. MAYP
Tonight, on the deck, the lights. Two Stories. Charles Wright. FYAP
Tonight our cat, Tahi, who lately lost. The Buried Stream. James K. Baxter. OxBC
To-night retir'd the queen of heaven. Ode to the Evening Star [*or* The Nightingale *or* To the Evening Star]. Mark Akenside. HBV-1; OBEC; OBEV; PoEL-3; PBBP
Tonight the Christmas landscape of the skull. Carol for His Darling on Christmas Day. Derek Stanford. NeBP
Tonight the City. R. L. Cook. AMV-81
Tonight the Famous Psychiatrist. Louis Simpson. OxBC
Tonight, the first snow. November Song. Mark Vinz. Psk
To-night, the gaudy auditorium. After the Show. Sam Harrison. NeIP
Tonight the moon is high, to summon all. Elegy. William Bell. FaBoTw
Tonight the moths. Tyranny of Moths. Gerald Vizenor. VoR
Tonight the rain sheets down. After an hour. Cheshire Cat. Kenneth Allott. NeBP
Tonight the Sabbath dreams stalk. Sabbath. Rivka Fried. VWA
Tonight the schools disperse. On the Breaking-up of a School. Tadhg O'g O'Huiginn, *tr. by* Osborn Bergin. AnIL
Tonight the spirit of an elder. Havdolah Susan Litwack. VWA
To-night the very horses springing by. Winter Evening. Archibald Lampman. NOBC; OBCV; PeCV
Tonight the waves march. Moonlight Night; Carmel. Langston Hughes. MOS
Tonight the wind gnaws. Christmas Landscape. Laurie Lee. OBCP
To-night the winds begin to rise. In Memoriam A. H. H., XV. Tennyson. BiP; EBVV; FaBoEn; GTBS-P; LiTB; NOBE; OBNC; PoEL-5
To-night this sunset spreads two golden wings. Sunset Wings. Dante Gabriel Rossetti. FM; HBV-2
To-night, to-night,/ The pillow fight. End of Term. *Unknown.* PoPle
Tonight ungather'd [*or* ungathered] let us leave. In Memoriam A. H. H., CV. Tennyson. EBVV; SBVL
Tonight we sat,/ telly dead. Old Man. Alan J. Carr. AMV-80
To-night we strive to read, as we may best. Prologue. Longfellow. *Fr.* John Endicott. PAH

Tonight when the hoar frost falls on the wood. Christmas in the Wood. Frances Frost. TrCP
Tonight When You Leave. Gayle Elen Harvey. AMV-81
Tonight you broke into my dreams. For Anne, Who Doesn't Know. Gail Fox. IHMS
To-night's a moonlit cup. The Offensive. Keith Douglas. NeBP
Tonio told me at catechism. The Purpose of Altar Boys. Alberto Ríos. MAYP
Tonite, thriller was. Beware: Do Not Read This Poem. Ishmael Reed. BPo; CNA; NCSH; NIP; NoP; PAI; PoBA; WSC
Tonopah Bill was a desert rat who had traveled the gold. The Ballad of Tonopah Bill. *Unknown.* BPAW
Tonsilectomy. James W. Rivers. AMV-81
Tonto. Ronald Koertge. GP
Tonversation with Baby, A. Morris Bishop. FiBHP; WhC
Tony/ To be casual and have the wish to heal. The Book of Gawain. Jack Spicer. *Fr.* The Holy Grail. PoM
Tony Baloney ("Tony Baloney is fibbing again"). Dennis Lee. RHPC
Tony Get the Boys. D. L. Graham. PoBA
Tony O! Colin Francis. CH; FaBoCo; PV
Tony said: "Boys are better!" Girls Can, Too! Lee Bennett Hopkins. RHPC
Tony shot his Delia. Delia's Gone. Blind Blake (Blake Alphonso Higgs). FSW
Tony the Turtle. E. V. Rieu. SO
Too Bright a Day. Norman MacCaig. GTBS-P
Too Busy. Paul Laurence Dunbar. *See* Get Somebody Else.
Too Busy ("Too busy this morning"). *Unknown.* STF
Too Busy ("Too busy to read a chapter a day"). *Unknown.* STF
Too Candid by Half. John Godfrey Saxe. HBV-1
Too cold this night for Hugh Maguire. Hugh Maguire. Eochy O'Hussey, *tr. by* Frank O'Connor. AnIL; KiLC
Too Dark. Mark McCloskey. PoA
Too dearly had I bought my green and youthful years. Earl of Surrey. SiPS
Too dense to have a door. The Haystack. Andrew Young. POL
Too elementary. Reply. Victoria McCabe. POL
Too fair, I may not call thee mine. Parting. Gerald Massey. HBV-1
Too far afield thy search. Nay, turn. Nay, turn. To Man Who Goes Seeking Immortality. Adelaide Crapsey. QFR
Too garrulous minion, stop. Be dumb. To a Talkative Hairdresser. Phyllis McGinley. DBV
Too green the springing April grass. Spring in New Hampshire. Claude McKay. BANP; BPo; PoNe
Too happy time dissolves itself. Emily Dickinson. NOBA
Too harsh the man who setting bounds to grief. Statius. *Fr.* Sylvae. PeHV
Too honest for a Gipsy, too lazy for a farmer. Shepherd's Holiday. Elinor Wylie. CrMA; HBMV
Too Late. Dinah Maria Mulock Craik. *See* Douglas, Douglas, Tender and True.
Too Late. Emily Dickinson. *See* Delayed till she had ceased to know.
Too Late. Rachel Korn, *tr. fr. Yiddish by* Seymour Mayne *and* Rivka Augenfeld. VWA
Too Late. Fitz Hugh Ludlow. PoLF
Too Late. Philip Bourke Marston. OBNC
Too Late? Longfellow. *See* It Is Too Late.
Too Late. R. S. Thomas. NMP
Too Late, *with music. Unknown.* BoAN-2
Too late, alas! I must confess. Song. Earl of Rochester. HBV-1
Too-late Born, The. Archibald MacLeish. GoJo; MoAB; MoAmPo; OxBA; SeCeV; TwAmPo; WaP
(Silent Slain, The.) CABA; CMoP; CoBMV; LiTM; MoVE; NePA; POL
Too late for love, too late for joy. Bride Song. Christina Rossetti. *Fr.* The Prince's Progress. OBEV; OBVV; ViBoPo; WPE
Too late, too late, sinnah. Too Late. *Unknown.* BoAN-2
Too late? Why, no; I, that do speak a word. Man New Made. Shakespeare. *Fr.* Measure for Measure, II, ii. GoBC
Too Literal Pupil, The. Martial, *tr. fr. Latin by* Louis Untermeyer. UnTE
Too little/ has been said. The Door. Charles Tomlinson. PoA
Too long outside your door I have shivered. The Terrible Door. Harold Monro. BoLoP; EnLoPo; FaBoTw
Too Many Daves. "Dr. Seuss." OBCA; RHPC
Too Many Miles of Sunlight between Us. Jack Myers. AMV-80
Too many of the dead, some I knew well. In the Backs. Frances Cornford. BrRo
Too many summers out of the way of a trowel. The Lawn Roller. Robert Layzer. NePoEA
Too Much. Edwin Muir. LiTB
Too Much. *Unknown.* TDH
Too Much Coffee. E. A. Robinson. MoAmPo
Too Much for One: Not Enough to Go Round. R. P. Blackmur. Scarabs for the Living, I. CrMA
Too much good luck no less than misery. Joy May Kill. Michelangelo, *tr. by* John Addington Symonds. AWP
Too Much Sex. *Unknown.* MeEL
Too much thought. Day-Dreamer. *Unknown.* TiPo
Too new in town, we're told. Being Refused Local Credit. Paula Rankin. MAYP
Too poor for a bribe, and too proud to importune. Sketch of His Own Character. Thomas Gray. LAuP
Too powerful a drug is Hope. "Bottle Should Be Plainly Labeled 'Poison.'" Sara Henderson Hay. GoYe
Too proud, too delicate to tell her wants. With a China Chamberpot, to the Countess of Hillsborough. Lord Holland. FaBoUs
Too proud you are. Gladioli for My Mother. Harriet Bernstein. AMV-81
Too solemn for day, too sweet for night. William Sidney Walker. OBEV
Too Soon the Lightest Feet. Amanda Benjamin Hall. HBMV
Too soon to be out of me bed. On a Monday Morning. Cyril Tawney. OBET
"Too tame, too pretty," you said. At Staufen. Michael Hamburger. VWA
Too tight, it is running over. Fence Wire. James Dickey. NYBP; VGW
Too warm, my friend, your anger waxes. The Peace. Henry Luttrell. *Fr.* Advice to Julia. OBRV
Too Wonderful. Bible, *O.T.* Proverbs, XXX: 18-19. TrJP
Too Young for Love. Horace, *tr. fr. Latin by* Louis Untermeyer. UnTE
Took Bladyn then his crowth, anew, and toucht. Bladyn's Song of Cloten. Charles M. Doughty. *Fr.* The Dawn in Britain. PoEL-5
Tool of Fate, The. "Yehoash", *tr. fr. Yiddish by* Isidore Goldstick. TrJP
Toot! Toot! *Unknown.* RHPC
Tooten Out Blues. *Unknown.* BluL
Toothless Satires. Joseph Hall. *See* Virgidemiarum.
Top Hand. *Unknown.* CoSo
Top of a hill, The. How to Tell the Top of a Hill. John Ciardi. SoPo
Tophet. Thomas Gray. NCEP; NOEC
("Such Tophet was; so looked the grinning fiend.") FaBoEE
Toplight hammered down by shadowless noon. Fire: The People. Alfred Corn. MAYP
Tops of the spruces here have always done, The. Jefferson Valley. John Hollander. PPP
Topsy-turvy Land. H. E. Wilkinson. SoPo
Topsy-turvy World. William Brighty Rands. OxBChV
Tor House. Robinson Jeffers. LoBV
Tora's Song. Knut Hamsun, *tr. fr. Norwegian by* Charles Wharton Stork. PoPl
Torch, The. Greg Forker. LFAC
Torch, The. Theodosia Garrison. BLPA
Torch-Bearers, The, *sel.* Arlo Bates.
America. AA; PAL
("America, last hope of man and truth.") PGD
Torch of love dispels the gloom, The. Walter Savage Landor. GBL
Torches surrounded by butterflies, The. The Mutilated Soldier. David Fisher. NPGG
Torch-Light in Autumn. John James Piatt. AA
Tories' flag is deepest blue, The. The Blue Flag. Chris Miller. FaBoPa
Tormented with incessant pains. To Stella. Swift. NOEC
Tormenting Virgin. *Unknown, tr. by* Louis Untermeyer. UnTE
Torn apart by us ever and again. Rainer Maria Rilke. *Fr.* Sonnets to Orpheus. ILwL
Torn between griefs, which grief shall I lament. Sophocles, *tr. by* Ezra Pound. *Fr.* Women of Trachis. OBVE
Torn book we burn, and the dead tree, The. The Broken One. John Holmes. MiAP
Torn Hat, The. Nathaniel Parker Willis. AA
Torn into light, you woke wriggling. How Much Earth. Philip Levine. NNaP
Torn Nightgown, The. Joel Oppenheimer. CoPo
Torn upon Thy wheel. Out of the Depths. Frederic Lawrence Knowles. TrPWD
Tornado, The. Charles de Kay. EtS
Tornado, The. Norman H. Russell. STE
Tornado. William Stafford. NaP
Tornado Soup. A. K. Redwing. VoR
Tornado Watch. Paul Shuttleworth. AMV-80
Tornado Watch, Bloomington, Indiana. Gary Young. SUW
Toro. W. S. Merwin. NePA
Toroi Bandi. *Mongol Oral Tradition, tr. by* C. R. Bawden. WTO
Torrent, The. E. A. Robinson. NePA
Torrent, A/ of cobalt bullets. Lacrimas or There Is a Need to Scream. K. Curtis Lyle. PoBA
Torrismond, *sel.* Thomas Lovell Beddoes.
Song: "How many times do I love thee, dear?" *fr.* sc. iii. LiTB; NBM; OBRV; PoEL-4; TrGrPo; ViBoPo
(How Many Times?) ELP
(How Many Times Do I Love Thee, Dear?) EnRP

Torso, The: Passages 18. Robert Duncan. GP
Tortoise, The. Cid Corman. InPK; VGW
Tortoise. Joanne de Longchamps. BoAnP
Tortoise Family Connections. D. H. Lawrence. BrPo; ChMP
Tortoise Gallantry. D. H. Lawrence. CMoP; NoAM
Tortoise in Eternity, The. Elinor Wylie. FaPON; ImOP
Tortoise Shell. D. H. Lawrence. CMoP; FM; OAEL-2
Tortoiseshell Cat, The. Patrick Reginald Chalmers. BoAnP; CenHV; PCat
Tortoise Shout. D. H. Lawrence. LiTM; NoAM
Torture scene developed under a glass bell, The. Heirloom. Leonard Cohen. NOBC
Tortured body, lie at rest alone. Unknown Man in the Morgue. Merrill Moore. MoAmPo
Tortured Heart, The. Arthur Rimbaud, *tr. fr. French.* PeHV
Tory Pledges. Thomas Moore. FaBoCo; OBSV
Toss me a kiss, and take your leave with laughter. No Madam Butterfly. Louise Hajek. AMV-80
Toss your gay heads. At April. Angelina Weld Grimké. BlSi
Tossed in a troubled sea of griefs, I float. To Her in Absence; a Ship. Thomas Carew. CaPo
Tossed on a Sea of Trouble. Archilochus, *tr. fr. Greek by* William Hay. PoPl
Tossing his mane of snows in wildest eddies and tangles. Earliest Spring [*or*]. In Earliest Spring. William Dean Howells. AA; FaBoBe; OBEV; OBVV
To-ta Ti-om. Peter Blue Cloud. STE
Total Influence or Outcome of the Matter, The: The Sun. Marge Piercy. WPOW
Totem. Nissim Ezekiel. VWA
T'other day, as I was twining. Cupid Drowned. Leigh Hunt. HBV-1
T'other eb'ning eb'ryting was still, Oh! babe. Mister Johnson. Ben Harney. OBAL
Tottingham Frolic. *Unknown.* UnTE
Toucan, The. Pyke Johnson, Jr. NTCP
Toucannery. Jack Prelutsky. OnUR
Touch. Thom Gunn. CMoP
Touch. Octavio Paz, *tr. fr. Spanish by* Charles Tomlinson. BoLoP
Touch/ is what the eyes do, sometimes. From a Brother Dreaming in the Rye. James Cunningham. JB
Touch but thy lire [*or* lyre] (my Harrie) [*or* Harry] and I hear[e]. To M. [*or* Master] Henry Lawes, the Excellent Composer, of [His] Lyrics. Robert Herrick. CaPo; OAEP
Touch It. Robert Mezey. NaP
Touch it: it won't shrink like an eyeball. A Life. Sylvia Plath. NOBA
Touch me, touch me. Grass Fingers. Angelina Weld Grimké. CDC
Touch my hand as though it were an old coin. Sailing in Crosslight. Anita Skeen. IHMS
Touch of cold in the autumn night, A. Autumn. T. E. Hulme. FaBoMo; LoBV; MOON; SeCePo; ViBoPo
Touch of the Master's Hand, The. Myra Brooks Welch. BLPA; STF; TRV
Touch once more a sober measure. Lament for Captain Paton. John Gibson Lockhart. OBRV
Touch Thou Mine Eyes, *with music.* Marion Franklin Ham. AH
Touché. Jessie Redmond Fauset. BlSi; CDC
Touching. Christopher Gilbert. MAYP
Touching books. For Gabriel. Laya Firestone. VWA
Touching Ezekiel his workman's hand. Jesus. James McAuley. CBAP
Touching Shoulders. *Unknown.* BLPA
Touching your goodness, I am like a man. The Illiterate. William Meredith. NoP
Touch-Stone, The. Samuel Bishop. HBV-1
Touchstone, The, *sels.* Kalonymos ben Kalonymos, *tr. fr. Hebrew by* J. Chotzner. TrJP
  Hypocrite, The.
  Unfortunate Male, The.
  Yoke, The.
Touchstone. James Worley. AMV-80
Tough Captain Spud and his First Mate, Spade. Captain Spud and His First Mate, Spade. John Ciardi. OBCA
Tough Cuss from Bitter Creek, A. James Barton Adams. PoOW
Tough Generation, A. David Gascoyne. LiTM
Tough guy. Star of David. The Cabdriver's Smile. Denise Levertov. NYP
Tough hand closes gently on the load, The. Man Carrying Bale. Harold Monro. BrPo; MoBrPo
Tough Ones, The. Errol Miller. AMV-80
Toughest gal I ever did see. Kissie Lee. Margaret Walker. BlSi; NMM
Toujours Amour. Edmund Clarence Stedman. HBV-1
Toujours la Politesse. Ezra Pound, *after the Chinese.* OBVE
Toulouse Lautrec. Astrid Tollefsen, *tr. fr. Norwegian by* Nadia Christensen. PBWP
Tour de Force. Peter Kane Dufault. ErPo
Tour 5. Robert Hayden. PPP
Tour Guide: La Maison des Esclaves. Melvin Dixon. LTB
Touring. David Morton. TrPWD
Touring the old miles again. Baldpate Pond. E. F. Weisslitz. NYBP
Tourism. Lillie D. Chaffin. TAT
Tourist, The. Garret Keizer. AMV-81
Tourist. Mark Van Doren. NePoAm-2
Tourist and the Town, The. Adrienne Rich. NePoEA-2
Tourist came in from Orbitville, A. Southbound on the Freeway. May Swenson. AmFN; NTCP; NYBP
Tourist from Syracuse, The. Donald Justice. TwCP
Tourist Guide: How You Can Tell for Sure When You're in South Dakota. Jim Heynen. GP
Tourist, spare the avid glance. The Attic Landscape. Herman Melville. NOBA; OBAL
Tourist Time. F. R. Scott. PoPl; WhC
Tourists. Howard Moss. FiBHP; NYBP
Tourists arrive, swarming, The. Spring in Washington. James Den Boer. TAT
Tournament of Man, The. Ernest Crosby. PGD
Tournament of Tottenham, The. *Unknown.* OxBoLi
Tours. Stephen Shu Ning Liu. AMV-80
Toussaint L'Ouverture. E. A. Robinson. PoNe
Toussaint, the most unhappy man of men! To Toussaint L'Ouverture. Wordsworth. EnRP; InPK; LoBV; NOBE; OAEP; OBNC; OBRV; PoNe; PoRA; PPP; TrGrPo; TRV
"Towanda Winooski? Gowanda!" Sing a Song of the Cities. Morris Bishop. CAD; WhC
Toward a Theory of Instruction. Danny Rendleman. SUW
Toward a True Peace. Lucia Trent *and* Ralph Cheyney. PGD
Toward Climax. Gary Snyder. SUW
Toward Lesbos. Renée Vivien, *tr. fr. French by* Sandia Belgrade. PeHV
Toward Myself. Leah Goldberg, *tr. fr. Hebrew by* Robert Friend. VWA
Toward Tenses Two Moons. George Rachow. LFAC
Toward the end. On the Death of Ho Chi Minh. Eli Mandel. NIP
Toward the last in the morning she could not. Old Dog. William Stafford. BoAnP; GDP
Toward the sea turning my troubled eye. The Huge Leviathan. Spenser. *Fr.* Visions of the World's Vanity. ChTr
Toward the Solstice. Adrienne Rich. NoP
Toward the Splendid City. Ed Ochester. LTB
Toward world's end, through the bare. The Magi. Louise Glück. PoA
Towards a City That Sings. June Jordan. NYP
Towards Democracy, *sel.* Edward Carpenter.
  Through the Long Night. PeHV
Towards nightfall when the wind. Winter Mask. Allen Tate. NePA; OxBA; Prf
Towards not being/ anyone else's center. Movement. Denise Levertov. LLLT
Towards the end he sailed into an extraordinary mildness. Herman Melville. W. H. Auden. LiTA; NePA; OAEP; OxBA
Towards the evening of her splendid day. The Fragment. Hilaire Belloc. POL
Towards the Last Spike, *sels.* E. J. Pratt.
  Gathering, The. MoCV; OBCV
  Precambrian Shield, The. MoCV; NOBC; OBCV
Towards the Source, *sels.* Christopher Brennan. PoAu-1
  I Saw My Life as Whitest Flame.
  Let Us Go Down, the Long Dead Night Is Done.
Towart the evyn, amyd the symmyris heit. The Prologue to Book XIII. Gawin Douglas. *Fr.* Prologues to the Aeneid. OxBS
T'owd pig's got mezzles an' she's deead, poor thing. The Dead Pig. *Unknown.* FaBoNo
Tower, The. Philip Booth. NePoEA-2
Tower, The. Dan Pagis, *tr. fr. Hebrew by* Stephen Mitchell. VWA
Tower, The. Mark Van Doren. MoPo
Tower, The. W. B. Yeats. CMoP; CoBMV; LiTB; LiTM; MoPo; NoAM; OAEP; SeCeV
  "It is time I wrote my will," III. MoVE
Tower of Babel, The. Nathaniel Crouch. OxBChV
Tower of Ivory. Leonard Bacon. WhC
Tower of Refuge is our God, A! Ein feste Burg ist unser Gott. Martin Luther, *tr. by* M. Woolsey Stryker. CTC
Tower of the Dream, The, *sel.* Charles Harpur.
  "Yes, wonderful are dreams: and I have known." PoAu-1
Towery city and branchy between towers. Duns Scotus's Oxford. Gerard Manley Hopkins. EBEV; EyDe; FaBoPP; GTBS-P; NoAM; OBMV; PoEL-5; VLP
Town, The. David Rowbotham. PoAu-2
Town and Country. William Cowper. *See* God Made the Country.
Town against Gown at Oxford. Robert of Gloucester. *Fr.* Chronicle. OxBM
Town Betrayed, The. Edwin Muir. CMoP

Town Called Providence, Its Fate, The. Benjamin Tompson. SCAP
Town Clerk's Views, The. John Betjeman. CMoP
Town does not exist, The. The Starry Night. Anne Sexton. NMP; NoAM;
Town Dump, The. Howard Nemerov. BiP; CMoP; MAT; NIP
Town froze, close as a fist, The. Operation. A. Alvarez. NMP
Town Ghost. Lauris Edmond. OCNZ
Town has opened to the sun, The. Bombardment. D. H. Lawrence. MMA
Town I Left. Helen Sorrells. IHMS
Town I Was Born In, The. Yehuda Amichai, *tr. fr. Hebrew by* A. C. Jacobs. VWA
Town lies in the valley, A. The Silent Town. Richard Dehmel, *tr. by* Jethro Bithell. AWP
Town Meeting. John Hay. NePoAm
Town might abort, A. How the Death of a City Is Never More than the Sum of the Deaths of Those Who Inhabit Its Spaces. Victor Coleman. NOBC
Town Mouse and the Country Mouse, The. Matthew Prior. BXAP
Town of Don't-You-Worry, The. I. J. Bartlett. BLPA; WBLP, *st.* 1
Town of Hay, The. Sam Walter Foss. AA
Town of Hill, The. Donald Hall. FiCP; TAP
Town of Nogood, The. W. E. Penny. BLPA
Town of Passage, The. *Unknown.* OxBoLi
Town of Passage is both large and spacious, The. The Attractions of a Fashionable Irish Watering-Place. Francis Sylvester Mahony. FaBoPP; NBM
Town or poem, I don't care how it looks. Old woman. White Center. Richard Hugo. NoP
Town Owl. Laurie Lee. PB
Town-Rakes, The. *At. to* P. A. Motteux. CoMu
Town Rat and the Country Rat, The. La Fontaine, *tr. fr. French by* Marianne Moore. NAWM-2
(City Rat and the Country Rat, The, *tr. by* Elizur Wright.) OBVE
Town remembers no such plenty, The. Lancashire Winter. Tony Connor. OxBTC
Town without a Market, The. James Elroy Flecker. MoBrPo
Townsman on his yielding bed, The. Michael Hamburger. *Fr.* The Note-Book of a European Tramp. NePoEA
Tow'rds the lofty walls of Balbi, lo! Durand of Blonden hies. Durand of Blonden. Ludwig Uhland, *tr. by* James Clarence Mangan. AWP
Towser Shall Be Tied Tonight, *parody. Unknown.* BLPA; BoAnP
Toy, The. Cid Corman. GP
Toyland, *with music.* Glen MacDonough. BLSo; FSN
Toy-Maker, The. Padraic Colum. SaC
Toys, The. Coventry Patmore. The Unknown Eros, I, x. ACP; BeLS; EBEV; EBVV; FaFP; GoBC; HBV-1; OBEV; OBVV; SoSe; TreFS; TrGrPo; TrPWD; TRV; ViBoPo
Toys. Abraham Sutskever, *tr. fr. Yiddish by* Seymour Levitan. VWA
Toys I bought for you, The. Gill Boy. Dennis Schmitz. NPGG
Toys Talk of the World, The. Katherine Pyle. OBCA
Tracer of wind's contour by line of flight. The Butterfly. Gray Burr. CoPo
Track, The. Nicholas Christopher. MAYP
Track. Tomas Tranströmer, *tr. fr. Swedish by* Robert Bly. EAS
Track into the Swamp, The. Samuel French Morse. CrMA
Track-lining Song. *Unknown.* AmFP
Track of a broad rattler, dragged over dust at dawn, The. The Catch. Brewster Ghiselin. HAP
Tracking deep signals given off. Homing. Reg Saner. NPAW
Tracking Rabbits: Night. Jim Barnes. CDW
Tracking the Sled, Christmas 1951. Jeanne Murray Walker. AMV-81
Trackless Deeps, The. Shelley. *Fr.* The Daemon of the World, Pt. II. EtS
Tracks. Elaine Schwager. CAD
Tracks. Brad Lee Shurmantine. AMV-81
Tracks. Joseph Torain. FAZ
Tracks in the Snow. Marchette Chute. SiSoSe
Tract. William Carlos Williams. AP; BiP; BLPL; CoBMV; DL; FF; LiTA; LiTM; MoAB; MoAmPo; MP; NePA; NoAM; NOBA; PAI; TAP; TrGrPo; TwAmPo; TwCP; VGW
Traction: November 22, 1963. Howard Moss. AmFN
Tractor. John L. Sellers. LFAC
Tractor now is an essential, A. Horatian Variation. Leonard Bacon. NYBP
"Trade" Rat. Eleanor Glenn Wallis. NePoAm
Trade Winds. John Masefield. FaBoCh; OBMV
Traded by my father in a drunken rage. Poem to a Mule, Dead Twenty Years. Guy Owen. BoAnP; POL
Trader. Jim Harrison. NoAM
Trader I am to the African shore, A. Sweet Meat Has Sour Sauce; or, The Slave-Trader in the Dumps. William Cowper. NOEC; OBSV
Trader's Return. Sylvia Lawson. PoAu-2
Trading Chicago. Charles O. Hartman. AMV-80
Tradition. Dryden. *Fr.* Religio Laici. OBS
Tradition. Arthur Guiterman. DBV
Tradition of Conquest. Sarah Morgan Bryan Piatt. AA
Traditional Funeral Songs. *Tr. fr. Modern Greek by* Willis Barnstone *and* Elene Kolb. BoWoP
Traditional Grammarian as Poet, The. Ted Hipple. POL
Traditional Red. Robert Huff. HoPM; NePoEA-2
Traditions. Seamus Heaney. FaBoMo
Trafalgar. Thomas Hardy. *See* Night of Trafalgar, The.
Trafalgar. Francis Turner Palgrave. BeLS; FaBoBe
Traffic light, Mexico, cactus, A. Tugs. José Y. Terán Jr. LFAC
Traffic Lights. Lina Kasdaglis, *tr. fr. Modern Greek by* Edmund *and* Mary Keeley. BoWoP
Trafique is earth's great Atlas, that supports. George Alsop. SCAP
Tragedie of Philotas, The, *sel.* Samuel Daniel.
Chorus: "How dost thou wear and weary out thy days." OBSC
Tragedies that entertained the burghers of antiquity, The. The New Hellas. Irwin Edman. InMe
Tragedy. "Æ." MoBrPo
Tragedy, A. Théophile Marzials. HBV-1; PeD
Tragedy, A. Tom Masson. OBAL
Tragedy. Howard Moss. NePoEA
Tragedy, A. Edith Nesbit. HBV-1
Tragedy. Jill Spargur. BLPA
Tragedy. Mark Van Doren. NePoAm-2
Tragedy of Dido, The, *sel.* Christopher Marlowe.
I Have an Orchard, *fr.* IV, v. ChTr
Tragedy of Pete, The. Joseph S. Cotter, Sr. CDC
Tragedy of Pompey the Great, The, *sel.* John Masefield.
"Man is a sacred city built of marvelous earth." WGRP
Tragedy of the Leaves, The. Charles Bukowski. HoPM
Tragedy of Valentinian, The, *sels.* John Fletcher.
Care-charming Sleep [Thou Easer of All Woes], *fr.* V, ii. ELP; FaBoRV; OAEP; TrGrPo
(Into Slumbers.) SeCePo
(Invocation to Sleep.) WHA
(Song: "Care-charming sleep, thou easer of all woes.") LoBV; OBS; PoEL-2
(Song for the Sick Emperor.) FaBoEn
(Song to Sleep.) OxBoLi
(Thou Easer of All Woes.) TreFT
(To Sleep.) PoRA
God Lyaeus, Ever Young, *fr.* V, viii. OBEV; ViBoPo
Hear, Ye Ladies [That Despise], *fr.* II, v. ElL; ELP; NOBE; OBEV; PoEL-2; ViBoPo
(Mighty Love.) TrGrPo
(Power of Love.) UnTE
Love's Emblems *fr.* II, v. BoLoP; ElL; HBV-1; NIP; NOBE; UnTE
(Love Song: "Now the lusty Spring is seen.") FaBoEn
(Now the Lusty Spring.) ELP; ErPo; FF; ViBoPo
Tragic Guilt. Keidrych Rhys. WaP
Tragic Love. W. J. Turner. LO; OBMV
Tragic Mary Queen of Scots, The, I ("Ah me, if I grew sweet to man"). "Michael Field." EnLoPo; OBMV
Tragic Mary Queen of Scots, The, II ("I could wish to be dead!"). "Michael Field." OBMV
Tragic, said I. Oh, Tragicker, says she. Noël Tragique. Ramon Guthrie. ErPo
Tragic Story, A. Adelbert von Chamisso, *tr. fr. German by* Thackeray. FaPON; HBV-2; HBVY; MoShBr; OnMSP
Tragic Verses. *Unknown.* CoMu
Tragical History of Doctor Faustus. Christopher Marlowe. *See* Doctor Faustus.
Tragi-Comedy of Titus Oates, The. *Unknown.* APAS
Tragiques, Les, *sel.* Théodore Agrippa d' Aubigné, *tr. fr. French.*
Portrait of Henri III, A. PeHV
Trail, The. Edward Weismiller. WaP
Trail All Your Pikes. Countess of Winchilsea. WPE
Trail beside the River Platte, The. William Heyen. GOA
Trail Breakers. James Daugherty. AmFN
Trail climbing/ you have to watch your footing. Finding a Poem. Eve Merriam. RFM
Trail climbs in zig-zags, The. The Trail up Wu Gorge. Sun Yün-feng, *tr. by* Kenneth Rexroth *and* Ling Chung. BoWoP; PBWP
Trail End. *Unknown. See* Blood on the Saddle.
Trail Herd, The, *Unknown.* BPAW
Trail Horse, The. David Wagoner. PH
Trail into Kansas, The. W. S. Merwin. GOA
Trail of the Bird, The. William John Courthope. HBVY
Trail to Lillooet, The. Pauline Johnson. CaP
Trail to Mexico, The, *diff. versions. Unknown.* AmFP; AS, *with music*; BPAW; CoSo, *with music*; FSW

Trail up Wu Gorge, The. Sun Yün-feng, *tr. fr. Chinese by* Kenneth Rexroth *and* Ling Chung. BoWoP; PBWP
Trailing her father, bearing his hand axe. Goose. Richard Emil Braun. NoAM
Train, The. Alan Brownjohn. OxBTC
Train, The. Emily Dickinson. *See* I like to see it lap the miles.
Train. Ken Smith. EAS
Train, The. *Unknown, tr. by* D. F. van der Merwe. TTY
Train/ run off/ nine mile, The. Chain Gang Trouble. *Unknown.* BluL
Train: Abstraction. Genevieve Taggard. WPE
Train at night, A. Night Train. Adrien Stoutenburg. PDV
Train Blues. Paul Zimmer. PPJ
Train Butcher, The. Thomas Hornsby Ferril. GoYe
Train Dogs, The. E. Pauline Johnson. GDP; WHW
Train from out the castle drew, The. Marmion and Douglas. Sir Walter Scott. *Fr.* Marmion, VI. OHFP
Train has come to rest and ceased its creaking, The. La Máquina a Houston. Edward Dorn. PoM
Train has stopped for no apparent reason, The. En Route. Duncan Campbell Scott. NOBC; OBCV
Train has stopped running, The. South Shore Line. John Schlesinger. AMV-80
Train is a dragon that roars through the dark, A. A Modern Dragon. Rowena Bastin Bennett. PDV; SoPo; TiPo
Train Is Off the Track, The. *Unknown.* AmFP
Train Journey. Judith Wright. PBWP
Train moves, The. Landscape with Minute Wildflowers. Hugh Maxton. CIP
Train of Religion, The, *sel.* Martin Farquhar Tupper.
"How beautiful their feet." FaBoCo
Train Out, The. Sydney Lea. MAYP
Train Ride. John Wheelwright. MoPo; TwAmPo; VGW
Train Runs Late to Harlem, The. Conrad Kent Rivers. IDB; PoBA
Train shot through the dark, The. Return. Seamus Deane. BIrV
Train Song. Diane Siebert. RHPC
Train Stops at Healy Fork, The. John Haines. TAT
Train, The! The twelve o'clock for paradise. Week-End, 1. Harold Monro. BSV; MoBrPo
Train through the night of the town, The. City Nights: In the Train. Arthur Symons. SyP; VLP
Train to Glasgow, The. Wilma Horsburgh. OnUR
Train to Reflection. Lawrence T. O'Neill. AMV-80
Train Tune. Louise Bogan. NePoAm
Train will come tomorrow year, The. The Train. Alan Brownjohn. OxBTC
Train Window. Robert Finch. OBCV; PeCV
Training. Herrera S. Demetrio, *tr. fr. Spanish by* Dudley Fitts. TTY
Training on the Shore. Shlomo Vinner, *tr. fr. Hebrew by* Laya Firestone *and* Howard Schwartz. VWA
Trains. James S. Tippett. FaPON; SoPo; SUS; TiPo
Trains are for going. Things. William Jay Smith. TiPo
Trains are not coming as often now, The. Tracks. Elaine Schwager. CAD
Trains at Night. Frances M. Frost. TiPo
Train's french horn sighs, sheds a few tears, The. To I. Lavrentevaya. Natalya Gorbanyevskaya, *tr. by* Daniel Weissbort. BoWoP
Trains Made of Stone. Ray A. Young Bear. CDW
Trains of thought, The. La Bête Humaine. James Kirkup. NeBP
Trains ran through the eleven, The. The Dance of the Elephants. Michael Harper. LCAP
Trainwrecked Soldiers. John Frederick Nims. MiAP
"Tra la la la—See me dance the polka." Neptune—Polka. Edith Sitwell. NOBE
Trala Trala Trala La-le-la. William Carlos Williams. OFD
Tra-La-Larceny. Oliver Herford. TDH
Tramontana at Lerici. Charles Tomlinson. GTBS-P
Tramp, The. Joe Hill. FSW
Tramp. Richard Hughes. MoBrPo
Tramp Miner's Song. *Unknown.* AmFP
Tramp, Tramp, Tramp, Keep on a-Tramping. *Unknown.* AS
Tramp! Tramp! Tramp! or, The Prisoner's Hope. George Frederick Root. BLSo, *with music;* FSW; PSoN, *with music;* TreFS
Tramping the right-of-way. Beaver Sign. Kenneth Porter. NePoAm
Trample! trample! went the roan. The Cavalier's Escape. Walter Thornbury. FaBoBe; GN; HBV-2
Tramplings tumultuous and a charge of sound! A Vision. "Michael Field." SyP
Tramp's Song, The. Mary Devenport O'Neill. AnIV
Trampwoman's Tragedy, A. Thomas Hardy. BeLS; HBMV; MoVE; OBNC; OBNV; VLP
Trance, The. Stephen Spender. ChMP; CoBMV
Trance of Time, The. Cardinal Newman. OxBoCh
Tranquil Sea. Claire Aven Thomson. EtS
Tranquility as his breath, his eye a camera. Observation Car and Cigar. William Stafford. LCAP
Trans Canada. F. R. Scott. PeCV
Transaction. A. R. Ammons. PoA
Transandean Railway, The. Thomas Kretz. AMV-80
Transcendence. Richard Hovey. TRV; WGRP
Transcendence of God, The. Milton. *Fr.* Samson Agonistes. OBS
Transcendentalism. *Unknown.* NA
Transcendentalism; a Poem in Twelve Books. Robert Browning. PP; VLP
Transcripts from Nature, *sels.* "Fiona Macleod." FM
Eagle, The.
Fireflies.
Rookery at Sunrise, The.
Wasp, The.
Transferring my ashes from the urn. The Burial. Mark Thalman. AMV-80
Transfiguration. Djuna Barnes. EAS
Transfiguration, The. Robert Herrick. CaPo
Transfiguration, The. Edwin Muir. MasP; OxBS
Transfiguration of Beauty, The. Michelangelo, *tr. fr. Italian by* John Addington Symonds. AWP
Transfigured. Sarah Morgan Bryan Piatt. AA
Transfigured Bird. James Merrill. MoAB
Transfigured Life. Dante Gabriel Rossetti. The House of Life, LX. VLP
Transfigured Night. Ralph Gustafson. MoCV
Transformation. Lewis Alexander. CDC; PoNe
Transformation. Jessie B. Rittenhouse. HBMV
Transformation. Quincy Troupe. CNA
Transformation Scene. Constance Carrier. FYAP; GoYe
Transformations. Thomas Hardy. NoAM; PPP; TEP
Transformed. D. Weston Gates. STF
Transfusion. Merrill Moore. PoA
Transience. John Armstrong. *Fr.* The Art of Preserving Health. NOEC
Transient Americans. Gifts. Karen Snow. FYAP
Transient as a Rose. John Lydgate. MeEL
Transient city, marvellously fair, A. Buffalo. Florence Earle Coates. PAH
Transit. Adrienne Rich. NoP
Transit. Richard Wilbur. LCAP
Transition. May Sarton. NePoAm
Translated into language it is something like this. The Voice. Judith Herzberg, *tr. by* Shirley Kaufman. VWA
Translated Way, The. Franklin P. Adams. FiBHP
Translated, won't the operatic word. Opera in English? Benjamin M. Steigman. WhC
Translating. Ruth Whitman. VWA
Translation. Roy Fuller. ChMP; NOBE; OxBTC
Translation. Rika Lesser. PoA
Translation. Anne Spencer. BANP
Translation From, A. Fred Levinson. AmPA
Translation from Petrarch ("Mine old dear enemy, my froward master"). Petrarch, *tr. fr. Latin by* Sir Thomas Wyatt. SiPS
Translation from Petrarch ("What a grudge I am bearing"). Petrarch, *tr. fr. Latin by* J. M. Synge. *Fr.* Sonnets to Laura: To Laura in Death, XXXII. MoBrPo
Translation from the Ancient British. *Unknown.* *See* Winifreda.
Translation from Walter von der Vogelweide, A ("I never set my two eyes"). Walter von der Vogelweide, *tr. fr. German by* J. M. Synge. MoBrPo
Translation into the Original. Jack Gilbert. NPGG
Translation is man's deep, continual task. Required Course. Frances Stoakley Lankford. GoYe
Translation of Lines by Benserade. Samuel Johnson, *after the French of* Isaac Benserade. CABA
("In bed we laugh, in bed we cry.") FaBoEE
Translation of Verver, The. Mei-Mei Berssenbrugge. LTB
Translations. Patricia Y. Ikeda. BrSi
Translations. Wing Tek Lum. BrSi
Translations. Adrienne Rich. WPOW
Translations from the Chinese, *sels.* Christopher Morley. EvOK
He Comforts Himself.
Human Instinct, A.
Man with the Rake, The.
Secret Thoughts.
Translations from the English. George Starbuck. VGW
Translator attempted to bare things unsaid, The. A Lesson in Translation. Gabriel Preil, *tr. by* Howard Schwartz. VWA
Translator to Translated. Ezra Pound. FaBoEE
Translucent green on the wall, a dance of leaves. The Green Afternoon. Henry Rago. VGW
Transmutation, The. Edwin Muir. FaBoEn
Transparence of November, The. Roo Borson. PPJ
Transparent Man, The. Anthony Hecht. FYAP
Transplantitis. Lester A. Sobel. QQQ

Transport. William Meredith. WaP
Transport of Wounded in Mesopotamia, 1917. Margery Lawrence. SUMH
Transportation Problem. Richard Armour. WhC
Transubstantiation. Gary Geddes. NOBC
Trap I am setting to catch a tribe, The. James K. Baxter. Jerusalem Sonnets, 35. OCNZ
Trapped Fly, A. Robert Herrick. *See* Amber Bead, The.
Trapped me in ice. No, not one chink is gaping. Ennui. Peter Viereck. NYBP
Trapping fairies in West Virginia. Gelett Burgess. FaBoNo
Trappist Abbey, The: Matins. Thomas Merton. PoPl
Traps. Mary Carolyn Davies. HBMV
Tras Os Montes, *sel.* L. E. Sissman.
"Whether the rivals for a wife and mother can." DiL
Trash. Earl Gene Box. LFAC
Trash Men, The. Charles Bukowski. NoP
Traubel, Traubel, boil and bubble. I Like to Sing Also. John Updike. FiBHP
Traümerei at Ostendorff's. William Laird. HBMV
Travail of Passion, The. W. B. Yeats. TrCP
Travel. Edna St. Vincent Millay. FaPON; InMe; MoShBr; OBCA; PDV; RHPC; TiPo
Travel. Robert Louis Stevenson. BrPo; FaBoCh; FaPON; MoShBr; TiPo
Travel Bureau, The. Ruth Comfort Mitchell. HBMV
Travel Song. Hugo von Hofmannsthal, *tr. fr. German by* Charles Wharton Stork. TrJP
Traveller, The. W. H. Auden. SyP
Traveller, The. John Berryman. PoA; VGW
Traveler, The. David Bottoms. AMV-80
Travel[l]er, The, *sels.* Goldsmith. LAuP; OAEP
Britain. NOEL
First, Best Country, The. GN
France. OBEC
Happiness Dependent on Ourselves. OBEC
Real Happiness. OBEC
"Remote, unfriended, melancholy, slow." BrIV; ViBoPo
Traveler, The. Vachel Lindsay. MoAmPo
Traveller, A. J. R. Rowland. CBAP
Traveller, The. Allen Tate. LiTM
Traveller, A ("Into the dusk and snow"). *Unknown.* WGRP
Traveller, The ("I'm trav'ling to my grave"). *Unknown.* AmFP
Traveller for many long years I have been, A. The Widow That Keeps the Cock Inn. *Unknown.* CoMu
Traveller Has Regrets, The. G. S. Fraser. BSV
Traveler on a dusty road, A. Little and Great. Charles Mackay. HBV-2; HBVY; PoLF
Traveller on the skirt of Sarum's Plain, A. Salisbury Plain and Stonehenge. Wordsworth. *Fr.* Guilt and Sorrow. FaBoPP
Traveler, pluck a stem of moly. Moly. Edith M. Thomas. HBV-1
Travel[l]er take heed for journeys undertaken in the dark of the year. October Journey. Margaret Walker. AmNP; IDB; PoBA; PoNE
Traveller wended the wilds among, A. The Quaker's Meeting. Samuel Lover. CenHV; OnYI
Traveller who walks a temperate zone, A. Against Romanticism. Kingsley Amis. NePoEA; NoAM
Travellers, The. Mark A. De Wolfe Howe. AA
Travelers, The. James Reeves. POL
Travel[l]er's Curse after Misdirection. Robert Graves, *tr. fr. Welsh.* BrPo; CMoP; DBV; DTC; FiBHP; HoPM; LiTM; MoAB; MoBrPo; NCSH; TW
Traveller's Ditty. Miriam Allen deFord. HBMV
Traveller's Guide to Antarctica. Adrien Stoutenburg. NYBP
Traveller's Hope. Charles Granville. HBV-2; OBVV
Travel[l]er's Rest. Ogden Nash. DBV; InMe
Travellers Turning Over Borders. Basil Ransome. BXAP
Travelers who came that day to Pisa's Baptistry. Echo. Elizabeth Stanton Hardy. GoYe
Travelin' Blues. *Unknown.* BluL
Travelling,/ where darkness hauls the world. Tanks. Rhyll McMaster. CBAP
Traveling America. "Jan Struther". AmFN
Travelling Backward. Gene Baro. NYBP
Traveling Boy. William Meredith. NoAM
Travelling Companions. Richard Armour. GrPl
Travelling eye has seen its many birds, The. Many Birds. Anne Welsh. PeSA
Traveling for days to reach you. Journey. Diane Wakoski. IHMS
Travelling Light. David Wagoner. NPAW
Traveling North. John Woods. POL
Traveling on My Knees. Sandra Goodwin. STF
Travel[l]ing Out, The. Lucile Adler. IHMS; NYBP
Travelling Post Office, The. Andrew Barton Paterson. CBAP
Traveling Riverside Blues. *Unknown.* BluL
Traveling sky goes landward, the blind mass, The. Headland. Brewster Ghiselin. PoA
Travelling Song. Thomas McGrath. FAZ
Travelling south, leaves overflow the farms. The Puritan on His Honeymoon. Robert Bly. FF; NePoEA
Traveling through the Dark. William Stafford. BiP; BoAnP; CABA; CoAP; ConAP; GrPl; HAP; HeIP; InPK; LCAP; LiTM; NCSH; NMP; NoP; PAI; SoSe; WeW
Traveling up the lonesome trail. Doney-Gal. *Unknown.* BPAW
Travelogue, A: Clovelly. Carolyn Wells. InMe
Travelogue for Exiles. Karl Shapiro. MoAmPo; TrJP; TwAmPo
Travels with the Band-Aid Army. Lance Henson. VoR
Traverse City Zoo. Jim Harrison. BoAnP
Traverse not the globe for lore! Advice against Travel. James Clarence Mangan. OBVV
Travis, the Kid Was All Heart. Terry Stokes. AmPA
Tray. Robert Browning. FM
Tray, The. Thomas Cole. NePoAm
Tray's Epitaph. "Peter Pindar." TreFS
Treacherous monster is the shark, A. The Shark. Lord Alfred Douglas. RHPC
Tread back—and back, the lewd and lay! Horace, *tr. by* Gerard Manley Hopkins. Odes, III, 1. OBVE
Tread lightly here, for here, 'tis said. An Epitaph on a Robin Redbreast. Samuel Rogers. FaBoEE; FM; PBBP
Tread lightly, she is near. Requiescat. Oscar Wilde. BrPo; EBVV; HBV-1; InvP; MoBrPo; OBNC; OBVV; OnYI; OxBI; TreF; TrGrPo; WHA
Tread softly; bid a solemn music sound. Epitaph. J. B. Morton. FaBoEE
Treading a field I saw afar. Death on a Live Wire. Michael Baldwin. MoBS
Treading pigeon arcs his wings, The. The Ivory Bed. Winfield Townley Scott. ErPo
Treadmill prisoner of that century, The. Scene with Figure. Babette Deutsch. TrJP
Treason. Lora Dunetz. NePoAm
Treason doth never prosper [*or* Treason never prospers]; what's the reason? Of Treason [*or* Treason *or* Treason Never Prospers *or* Epigram *or* On Treason]. Sir John Harington. ELU; FaBoCo; FaBoEE; FF; FiBHP; HBV-1; InPK; NIP; OxBoLi
Treason of Sand. Hemda Roth, *tr. fr. Hebrew by* Mariana Potasman. VWA
Treason's Last Device. Edmund Clarence Stedman. PAH
Treasure. Lucillius, *tr. fr. Greek by* William Cowper. AWP
Treasure, A. Reed Whittemore. NePoEA
Treasure Hunt. Robert Penn Warren. NoP
(Fairy Story.) NYBP
Treasure not so the forlorn days. Behind the Line. Edmund Blunden. ChMP
Treasure-like, I found her in a field. The Meeting. Pierre Louys. *Fr.* Chansons de Bilitis. PeHV
Treasures. Mary Dixon Thayer. SoPo
Treasures. Bible, *N.T.* St. Matthew, VI; 19-21. TrGrPo
Treat the woman tenderly, tenderly. *Unknown.* POL
Treatise of the Subtle Body, A. Salamis. Lawrence Durrell. NYBP
Treatment by old Mr. Mears, The. Limerick. *Unknown.* PeHV
Treaty-Trip from Shulus Reservation. Patrick Lane. NeAC
Trebetherick. John Betjeman. CMoP; EvOK
Tree, The. Björnstjerne Björnson, *tr. fr. Norwegian.* FaPON; OHIP; PoSC
Tree, The. Ilya Ehrenburg, *tr. fr. Russian by* Babette Deutsch. TrJP
Tree, The. Alfred Kreymborg. HBMV; PoPl
Tree. Harold LaMont Otey. LFAC
Tree, The. Ezra Pound. CMoP; TwAmPo
Tree, The. Joel Sloman. VGW
Tree, The. Jones Very. GN; HBV-1; OHIP; PoSC
Tree, The. Countess of Winchilsea. OBEC
Tree and the Chaff, The. Bible, *O.T.* Psalms, I. *See* Godly and the Ungodly, The.
Tree and the Lady, The. Thomas Hardy. MoAB; MoBrPo
Tree ascending there, O pure transcension, A! Ranier Maria Rilke, *tr. by* J. B. Leishman. Sonnets to Orpheus, I, i. UnS
Tree at My Window. Robert Frost. BLPL; BoNaP; FaBoBe; FaBoEn; InPK; MoAB; MoAmPo; MoVE; NePA; NoAM; OxBA; TAP; TrGrPo
Tree beside the synagogue atones, A. Yom Kippur. Linda Pastan. VWA
Tree Birthdays. Mary Carolyn Davies. OHIP
Tree-building. Franklin Cable. PGD
Tree Design, A. Arna Bontemps. CDC
Tree Feelings. Charlotte Perkins Stetson. PGD
Tree Felling. George Woodcock. NeBP
Tree Frog, The. John Travers Moore. RHPC
Tree has entered my hands, The. A Girl. Ezra Pound. MoAB; MoAmPo

Tree I know where a love-bird's lighted, A. Open the Door. *Malay Oral Tradition, tr. by* R. J. Wilkinson *and* R. O. Winstedt. WTO
Tree in December. Melville Cane. MoAmPo
Tree in the Wood, The. *Unknown.* AmFP
Tree is built of many things, A. Tree-building. Franklin Cable. PGD
Tree Is Father to the Man, The. Lou Lipsitz. NCSH
Tree is more than a shadow, A. A Tree Design. Arna Bontemps. CDC
Tree is such a sacred thing, A. The Cross and the Tree. William L. Stidger. PGD
Tree-leaves labour up and down. Nobody Comes. Thomas Hardy. BiP; MoVE
Tree Man. Rennie McQuilkin. AMV-81
Tree of Death, The. Claude Vigée, *tr. fr. French by* J. R. Le Master *and* Kenneth L. Beaudoin. VWA
Tree of deepest root is found, The. The Three Warnings. Hester Thrale. BeLS; HBV-2
Tree of Diana, The. Alejandra Pizarnik, *tr. fr. Spanish by* Yishai Tobin. VWA
Tree of Faith its bare dry boughs must shed, The. Adjustment. Whittier. WGRP
Tree of Hatred, The. Shmuel Moreh, *tr. fr. Arabic by author.* VWA
Tree of intense, The. Ode to the Watermelon. Pablo Neruda, *tr. by* Robert Bly. EAS; NU
Tree of Knowledge. Edward Lowbury. VWA
Tree of Life Is Also a Tree of Fire, The. Gerda Norvig. VWA
Tree of Rivelin, The. Ebenezer Elliott. VLP
Tree of Silence, The. Vassar Miller. NePoEA-2
Tree Party. Louis MacNeice. OxBTC
Tree-planting. Samuel Francis Smith. OHIP
Tree Planting. *Unknown.* OHIP
Tree Poem on My Wife's Birthday. Tom Hanna. FAZ
Tree Sleeps in the Winter, The. Norman H. Russell. STE
Tree Stands Very Straight and Still, The. Annette Wynne. SoPo; SUS
Tree still bends over the lake, The. Winter. Sheila Wingfield. EnLoPo
Tree Tag. Mary E. Caragher. GoYe
Tree to Flute. Anna Hajnal, *tr. fr. Hungarian by* Jascha Kessler. VWA
Tree-Toad, The. Orrick Johns. HBMV
Tree Toad, The ("The tree Toad is a creature neat "). Monica Shannon. FaPON
Tree Toad ("A tree toad loved a she-toad"). *Unknown, ad. by* Stephanie Calmenson. NTCP
Tree, too, wants to bend over, The. 3 Stanzas about a Tree. Marvin Bell. Prf
Tree, Tree. Federico García Lorca, . *tr. fr. Spanish.* PoPl
Treehouse, The. James A. Emanuel. AmNP; BPo; NNP; PoBA
Treehouse. Ted Kooser. PPJ
Trees. Harry Behn. SiSoSe; SoPo; TiPo; YeAr
Trees. Bliss Carman. OHIP
Trees. Thomas Curtis Clark. PGD
Trees, The. Samuel Valentine Cole. OHIP
Trees. Sara Coleridge. OHIP; OxBChV; RHPC
Trees. Walter de la Mare. OHIP
Trees. Ted Hughes. NYBP
Trees. Joyce Kilmer. BLPA; FaBoBe; FaFP; FaPON; FPL; HBV-1; HBVY; OHFP; TreF; WBLP; WGRP
Trees, The. Lucy Larcom. OHIP
Trees. W. S. Merwin. GP; PPJ
Trees, The. Christopher Morley. OHIP
Trees. Howard Nemerov. BoNaP; Psk
Trees, The. Adrienne Rich. CoAP; CoPo; NOBA; WPE
Trees/ and the wind. The Hand. Brian Fawcett. NOBC
Trees across the street have loved me, The. Midwinter Stars. Roberta Hill Whiteman. STE
Trees along our city streets, The. City Trees. Vere Dargan. PGD
Trees along this city street, The. City Trees. Edna St. Vincent Millay. FaPON
Trees and brown squares. The Clearing. Amiri Baraka. CoPo
Trees and Cattle. James Dickey. NePoEA-2
Trees and Evening Sky. N. Scott Momaday. CDW
Trees are afraid to put forth buds, The. A Backward Spring. Thomas Hardy. PPP
Trees are a'ivied, the leaves they are green, The. The Bonnie Laddie's Lang a-Grouwin'. *Unknown.* OxBS
Trees Are Down, The. Charlotte Mew. BoNaP; BrRo; MoAB; MoBrPo; TrCP; WPE; WPOW
Trees are God's great alphabet, The. A B C's in Green. Leonora Speyer. HBMV; HBVY; OHIP
Trees are growing, The. The Princess Who Fled to the Castle. Francis Landy. VWA
Trees are in their autumn beauty, The. The Wild Swans at Coole. W. B. Yeats. BoAnP; CABA; ChTr; CMoP; FaBoPP; FaBoRV; FM; HeIP; MoAB; MoBrPo; MoVE; NoAM; NoP; OAEP; OnYI; PB; PBBP; PPP; SoSe; SOTW; TEP; UnPo; WHA
Trees are tall, but the moon small, The. Hide and Seek. Robert Graves. NTCP
Trees are the kindest things I know. Trees. Harry Behn. SiSoSe; SoPo; TiPo; YeAr
Trees are tracing in the waning haze, The. Evening. Victor van Vriesland, *tr. by* Adrian J. Barnouw. TrJP
Trees ask me, The. Who Am I? Felice Holman. RFM
Trees at Night. Helene Johnson. BlSi
Trees at the Arctic Circle. Al Purdy. NoP
Trees both in hills and plaines, in plenty be. William Wood. SCAP
Tree's early leaf-buds were bursting their brown, The. The Tree. Björnstjerne Björnson, *tr. fr. Norwegian.* FaPON; OHIP; PoSC
Trees, Effigies, Moving Objects, *sels.* Allen Curnow. OCNZ
Framed Photograph, A.
Kitchen Cupboard, The.
Trees file along curbs. Shrub-faces. Bell Weather. Lewis Turco. AMV-80
Tree's green explains what a light means, The. Notes for Echo Lake 5. Michael Palmer. NPGG
Trees have been born. In Memoriam Paul Celan. Gad Hollander. VWA
Trees in groves,/ Kine in droves. Saadi. Emerson. OxBA
Trees in Sherwood forest are old and good, The. Sonnet to ———. John Hamilton Reynolds. OBRV
Trees in the Garden. D. H. Lawrence. CMoP; MoAB; MoBrPo; NoP
Trees in the Garden Rained Flowers, The. Stephen Crane. War Is Kind, XXVI. LiTM; PrIm
Trees in the old days used to stand. Carentan O Carentan. Louis Simpson. CoAP; MoBS; NMP; NOBA; OBWP; PrIm
Trees in the river. Big Grave Creek. Cid Corman. HoAn
Trees in the Road, The. James Still. GrPl
Trees inside are moving out into the forest, The. The Trees. Adrienne Rich. CoAP; CoPo; NOBA; WPE
Trees learn music from the birds they hold, The. Wood Music. Ethel King. GoYe
Tree's leaves may be ever so good, A. Leaves Compared with Flowers. Robert Frost. NOBA
Trees, like great jade elephants, The. John Gould Fletcher. Irradiations, III *or* VII [X]. MoAmPo; NePA; TwAmPo
Trees Lose Parts of Themselves inside a Circle of Fog. Francis Ponge, *tr. fr. French by* Robert Bly. NU
Trees of Life, The. Jones Very. NOBA
Trees of the elder lands, The. St. Anthony's Township. Gilbert Sheldon. CH
Trees on the Calais Road. Edmund Blunden. BrPo
Trees Once Walked and Stood. Joshua Tan Pai, *tr. fr. Hebrew by* Yishai Tobin. VWA
Trees shake gentle skaters out. Cadenza. Miriam Waddington. CaP
Trees So High, The. *Unknown.* OxBoLi
Trees they are tall and the leaves they are green, The. Daily Growing. *Unknown.* FSW
Trees They Do Grow High, The. *Unknown.* OBET
(Still Growing.) FaBoBa; InPK, *with music*
Trees turn, The. Leaflight. Dorothy Donnelly. NCSH
Trees were taller than the night, The. The Robber. W. J. Turner. MoBrPo
Tress Who Are Distant. Bertram Warr. CaP
Treetalk and windsong are. Sugarfields. Barbara Mahone. CNA; PoBA
Tree-Top Road, The. May Riley Smith. HBV-2
Tree-topped Hill. *Unknown.* NOEC
Treetops. Marvin Bell. AmPA; DiL
Tregardock. John Betjeman. FaBoPP
Treizaine. Sir Thomas Wyatt. *See* If in the World There Be More Woe.
Trelawny Lies by Shelley. Charles L. O'Donnell. HBMV
Trellie. Lance Jeffers. CNA; FB
Trellis. Laura Chester. NPGG
Trembling. Aliza Shenhar, *tr. fr. Hebrew by* Linda Zisquit. VWA
Trembling before Thine Awful Throne, *with music.* Augustus L. Hillhouse. AH
(Forgiveness of Sins a Joy Unknown to Angels.) AA
Trembling November winds. Nocturnal Sounds. Kattie M. Cumbo. BlSi
Trembling old men are stamm'ring. Lines on Carmen Sylva. Emma Lazarus. TrJP
Trembling, sand-dollar. Grunion. Wendy Rose. CDW
Trembling train clings to the leaning wall, The. Moonrise in the Rockies. Ella Higginson. AA
Tremendous pleasure lurking in my skin. Incident. Harvey Shapiro. FAZ
Tremor, like magnitude, shook the world, A. Coup d'Etat. Ruth Herschberger. LiTA
Tremulous distance, A. Stance. Theodore Enslin. CoPo
Trench. Stephen Pett. GrPl
Trench Blues, *with music.* *Unknown.* OuSiCo
Trench Poets. Edgell Rickword. DBV

Trendy young girl from St. Paul, A. Limerick. *Unknown.* NIP
Trent Again, The. Michael Drayton. *Fr.* Polyolbion, Sixth and Twentieth Song. FaBoPP
Trent, The. Michael Drayton. *Fr.* The Shepherd's Siren. FaBoPP
(Jovial Shepheard's Song, The.) PoEL-2
(Sirena.) OBEV
Trenton and Princeton. *Unknown.* PAH
Tresco. Goeffrey Grigson. FaBoPP
Trespass. Robert Frost. FaBV
Trestle Bridge, The. Carolyne Wright. AMV-80
Tretis of the Tua Mariit Wemen and the Wedo, The. William Dunbar. GoTS; OxBS
Sels.
"Bot of ane bowrd in to bed I sall yow breif yit." EBEV
"Thus draif they out that dear night with dances full noble." BSV
"Upon the midsummer even, merriest of nichtis." BSV
Triad. Adelaide Crapsey. PoPl; WPE
Triad. Donald Foster. AMV-80
Triad, A. Christina Rossetti. PBWP; VLP
Triad of Things Not Decreed, The. Alice Furlong. AnIV
Triads of Ireland, The, *sels. Unknown, tr. fr. Old Irish.*
"Three accomplishments well regarded in Ireland: a clever," *tr. by* Thomas Kinsella. OxBI
"Three slender things that best support the world," *tr. by* Kuno Meyer. OnYI
Triads ("Three excellent qualities in narration"), *tr. by* Thomas Kinsella. BIrV
Trial, The. W. H. Auden. *See* Proof, The.
Trial, A. Alan Dugan. NoAM
Trial, The. Longfellow. *Fr.* Giles Corey of the Salem Farms. PAH
Trial, The. Muriel Rukeyser. PoNe
Trial, The. Gershom Scholem, *tr. fr. German by* Jonathan Griffin. VWA
Trials. Grace E. Troy. STF
Trials of a Tourist. Anne Tibble. FaBoCo
Triangle Ladies, The. Carol Artman Montgomery. AMV-80
Triangles are commands of God. The Starfish. Robert P. Tristram Coffin. ImOP
Triangular Field, The. Stephen Dobyns. MAYP
Triantiwontigongolope, The. C. J. Dennis. AmMo
Tribal Chant. Carol Lee Sanchez. TWSS
Tribal Memories. Robert Duncan. *Fr.* Passages. NOBA
Tribal Stumps ("Tribal mixed bloods"). Gerald Vizenor. VoR
Tribe Searching, A. Shlomo Reich, *tr. fr. French by* Mira Reich. VWA
Tribes, The. Roy Fuller. LiTM
Tribulations of an Uneducated Poet in the 1760's, The. James Woodhouse. *Fr.* The Life and Lucubrations of Crispinus Scriblerus. NOEC
Tribute, The. Coventry Patmore. The Angel in the House, I, iv. EBEV; HBV-1; OBNC
Tribute, A. *Unknown.* PGD
Tribute of Grasses, A. Hamlin Garland. AA
Tribute to America. Shelley. PAL
Tribute to Dante, A. Boccaccio. *See* Inscription for a Portrait of Dante *and* To One Who Had Censured His Public Exposition of Dante.
Tribute to Grass. John James Ingalls. WBLP
Tribute to Henry Ford. Richard Kostelanetz. TAP
Tribute to Kafka for Someone Taken. Alan Dugan. CAPP; NoAM
Tribute to the Angels, *sels.* Hilda Doolittle ("H. D.").
"Invisible, indivisible Spirit." BoWoP
"Not in our time, O Lord." NOBA
"We have seen her/ the world over." VGW
Tribute to the Founder, A. Kingsley Amis. DBV; NePoEA-2
Tribute to the Memory of the Same Dog. Wordsworth. FM
Tribute to Washington. *Unknown.* OHIP
Tribute to Wyatt. Earl of Surrey. *See* Wyatt Resteth Here.
Trick, The. W. H. Davies. ChMP
Trick for Tyburn, A; or, A Prison Rant. *Unknown.* APAS
Trick Is Consciousness, The. Paula Gunn Allen. TWSS
Trick is, to live your days, The. Advice to My Son. J. Peter Meinke. PAI; Psk
Trick that everyone abhors, A. Rebecca, Who Slammed Doors for Fun and Perished Miserably. Hilaire Belloc. NOBL; SO
Tricked Again. Ridhiana. NBP
Trickle Drops. Walt Whitman. PeD
Trickle of water from, A. Hard Way to Learn. James Hearst. AMV-80
Tricks of Imagination, The. Shakespeare. *See* Lunatic, the Lover, and the Poet, The.
Tricksters. William Rose Benét. HBMV
Tri-colored Ribbon, The. Peadar Kearney. OnYI
Trico's Song: "What bird so sings, yet so does wail?" John Lyly. *Fr.* Alexander and Campaspe, V, i. OBSC; TrGrPo
(Song: "What bird so sings.") PBBP
(Spring, The.) CH
(Spring's Welcome.) OBEV
(Welcome to Spring.) NOBE
(What Bird So Sings.) ElL; ViBoPo
Trifle. Georgia Douglas Johnson. AmNP
Trifle, A. Henry Timrod. HBV-1
Trifle for Trafalgar Day, A. Ted Pauker. NOBL
Trifles. *Unknown.* HBV-2
Trifling Women. *Unknown.* AmFP
Trilby. Alice Brown. AA
Trilby, *sel.* George Du Maurier.
Little Work, A, *fr.* Pt. VIII. FaBoBe; HBV-2; PoLF
(Little Work, a Little Play, A.) TreFS
Trilobite, grapholite, nautilus pie. Rhyme for a Geological Baby. Joseph Cook. *Fr.* Boston Nursery Rhymes. InMe; QQQ; SpRo
Trilogy for X, *sels.* Louis MacNeice.
"And love hung still as crystal over the bed," II. CIP; GBL
(And Love Hung Still.) MoBrPo
"When clerks and navvies fondle," I. ErPo
(For X.) BoLoP; EnLoPo
Trim the lamp; polish the lens; draw, one by one, rare coins. Geoffrey Hill. Mercian Hymns, XIII. FaBoMo
Trimdon Grange Explosion, The. Tommy Armstrong. OBET
Trimming the Sails. Vassar Miller. NMM
Trinidad, 1958. Bob Mondy. WOLT
Trinity, The. William Langland. *Fr.* The Vision of Piers Plowman. OxBM
Trinity, The. Marian Osborne. CaP
Trinity, The. *Unknown.* ACP
Trinity [*or* Trinitee] blessed, deity [*or* deitee] coequal. A Prayer to the [Holy] Trinity [*or* To the Trinity]. Richard Stanyhurst. ElL; OxBoCh; PoEL-2
Trinity Churchyard. Muriel Rukeyser. NYP
Trinity Place. Phyllis McGinley. MoAmPo; SaC
Trinity Place. Carl Sandburg. NYP
Trio for Two Cats and a Trombone. Edith Sitwell. PBWP
Triolet: "All women born are so perverse." Robert Bridges. HBV-1; PV; SeCePo; TW
Triolet: "Child is father to the man, The." Gerard Manley Hopkins. *See* "Child Is Father to the Man, The."
Triolet: "I intended an ode." Austin Dobson. *See* Urceus Exit.
Triolet: "I love you, my Lord!" Paul T. Gilbert. PV
Triolet: "When first we met we did not guess." Robert Bridges. BrPo
Triolet against Sisters. Phyllis McGinley. OBCA
Triolet on a Dark Day. Margaret Fishback. PoSC
Triolet on a Downhill Road. Margaret Fishback. WhC
Triolets Ollendorfiens. James Kenneth Stephen. WhC
Trip, The. Emmett Jarrett. NeAC
Trip, The. William Stafford. PCP
Trip: San Francisco. Langston Hughes. AmFN
Trip and go, heave and ho! A-Maying, a-Playing [*or* A Clownish Song]. Thomas Nashe. *Fr.* Summer's Last Will and Testament. ElL; OBSC
Trip down to Bangor, the Fourth of July, A. The Red Light Saloon *Unknown.* ShS
Trip It Gipsies, Trip It Fine. Thomas Middleton *and* William Rowley. *Fr.* The Spanish Gipsy, [*or* , III, i. OAEP
(Song: "Trip it gipsies, trip it fine.") OBS
Trip on the Staten Island Ferry, A. Audre Lorde. CNA
Trip to Four or Five Towns, A. John Logan. CoAP; ConAP; NNaP
"In New York I got drunk, to tell the truth," *sel.* NMP
Trip to the Grand Banks, A. Amos Hanson. AmFP; ShS, *with music*
Trip trap in a gap. *Unknown.* GBP
Trip upon trenchers, and dance upon dishes. Mother Goose. NOBL; OxNR
Tripart. Gayl Jones. BlSi
Tripe. J. B. Morton. InMe
Triphammer Bridge. A. R. Ammons. NOBA
Triple-decker and the double-cone, The. Saturday Sundae. F. R. Scott. CaP
Triple Feature. Denise Levertov. FF; NoP
Triple Fool, The. John Donne. GBL; OAEP; PP
Triple Mirror, The. Gloria C. Oden. IHMS
Trippers and askers surround me. Walt Whitman. *Fr.* Song of Myself, IV. InPS; UnPo
Tripping down the Field-Path. Charles Swain. HBV-1
(Field Path, The.) OBVV
Trips to Farmington were a special treat. It Was a Special Treat. Luci Tapahonso. STE
Triptych. Seamus Heaney. CIP
Tristan and Isolda. Newman Levy. InMe
Tristan da Cunha. Roy Campbell. MoBrPo; MoVE; PeSA; RoGo
Tristium, *sels.* Ovid, *tr. fr. Latin.*
"And here I wish my soul died with my breath," *fr.* III, 3a, *tr. by* Henry Vaughan. OBVE

"And on this day, which poets unto thee," *fr.* V, 3, *tr. by* Henry Vaughan. OBVE
"Look, he is superfluous—for of what use was it to be born?" XIII, *tr. by* L. R. Lind. XIII. NAs
Tristram and Isolt. Don Marquis. HBMV
Tristram lies sick to death. Tristram's End. Laurence Binyon. OBMV
Tristram of Lyonesse, *sels.* Swinburne.
Death of Urgan, The. WHA
Sunrise at Sea, *br. sel. fr.* The Sailing of the Swallow. EtS
Swimming. GN
Tristram's End. Laurence Binyon. OBMV
Tristram's Song. Tennyson. *Fr.* Idylls of the King: The Last Tournament. FaBoRV
Tristrem and the Hunters. *At. to* Thomas of Erceldoune. *Fr.* Sir Tristrem. OxBS
Trit trot to market to buy a penny doll. *Unknown.* OxNR
Trite usages in tamest style. Thomas Hardy. *Fr.* A Jog-Trot Pair. PeD
Triumph, The. Ben Jonson. *See* Triumph of Charis, The.
Triumph, The. Sidney Lanier. *Fr.* The Psalm of the West. PAH
Triumph. John Crowe Ransom. HBMV
Triumph. L. D. Stearns. BLRP
Triumph may be of several kinds, A. Emily Dickinson. NePA
Triumph of Bacchus and Ariadne. Lorenzo de' Medici, *tr. fr. Italian by* Richard Aldington. *Fr.* Carnival Songs. CTC
Triumph of Beautie Song, The, *sel.* James Shirley.
"Heigh-ho, what shall a Shepheard doe." ErPo
Triumph of Charis, The. Ben Jonson. *Fr.* A Celebration of Charis. CABA; ELP; GoBC; InPS; LiTB; LoBV; NOBE; NoP; PoPle; SeCeV; WHA
(Her Triumph.) AnAnS-2; CTC; EBEV; ElL; FaBoEn; HBV-1; JCP; OAEP; PoEL-2; PrIm; SeCP; SeCV-1; ViBoPo
("See the chariot at hand here of Love.") InvP
(Triumph, The.) OBEV
So White, So Soft, So Sweet, *sel.* TrGrPo; UnTE
("Have you seen but a bright lily grow.") FaBoCh
(So Sweet Is She.) GN
Triumph of Chastity, The. Barbara Howes. NePoAm-2
Triumph of Death, The. Barbara Howes. MoAmPo; NePoAm-2
Triumph of Death, The. Shakespeare. *See* Sonnets, LXXI.
Triumph of Doubt, The. John Peale Bishop. EaLo
Triumph of Dullness [*or* Dulness], The. Pope. *Fr.* The Dunciad, IV. EBEV; NOBE; NOEC; NoP; OBEC
(Chaos.) LoBV
("In vain, in vain—the all-composing hour.") EBEV; SCV; ViBoPo
(Reign of Chaos, The.) FiP
Triumph of Forgotten Things, The. Edith M. Thomas. HBV-1
Triumph of Infidelity, The, *sel.* Timothy Dwight.
Smooth Divine, The. AA; PPON; WGRP
("Here stood Hypocrisy, in sober brown.") NOCV
Triumph of Life, The. Shelley. ChER; MasP; OAEL-2; PoEL-4
Triumph of Love. John Hall Wheelock. MoAmPo
Triumph of Sensibility. Sylvia Townsend Warner. MoAB; MoBrPo
Triumph of the Whale, The. Charles Lamb. EtS; OBRV
"Io! Paean! Io! sing," *sel.* ImOP
Triumph of Time, The. Swinburne. VLP
Sels.
"I have put my days and dreams out of mind." ViBoPo
Stanzas: "I will go back to the great sweet mother." HBV-1
("I will go back to the great sweet mother.") OAEP
(Return, The.) EtS
(Sea, The.) TrGrPo
Triumph of Vice, The. Pope. *Fr.* Epilogue to the Satires. NOBE
("Virtue may choose the high or low degree.") OBSV
Triumphal arch, that fill'st the sky. To the Rainbow. Thomas Campbell. HBV-1
Triumphal Chant. Bible, *Fr.* Exodus. *See* Then Sang Moses. TrGrPo
Triumphal March. T. S. Eliot. *Fr.* Coriolan. OBWP; WaaP
Triumphal Ode MCMXXXIX. George Barker. LiTB; WaP
Triumphalis. Bliss Carman. HBMV
Triumphant Demons stand, and Angels start. The Heart's Abysses. Walter Savage Landor. FaBoEE; OBSV
Triumphs of Owen, The. Thomas Gray. EnRP; PoEL-3
Trivia; or, The Art of Walking the Streets of London, *sels.* John Gay.
About in London. FaBoPP
"Experienced men, inured to city ways," *fr.* II. OAEL-1
Great Frost, The. OBEC; SeCePo, *shorter sel.*
"Let due civilities be strictly paid," *fr.* II. OAEL-1
London at Night. FaBoPP
"Where the mob gathers, swiftly shoot along," *fr.* III. OAEL-1
"Who can the various city frauds recite," *fr.* III. OAEL-1
"Winter my theme confines; whose nitry wind." *fr.* II. NOEC
Triviality, A. Waring Cuney. CDC
Troades, *sel.* Seneca, *tr. fr. Latin by* the Earl of Rochester.
"After death nothing is, and nothing death," *fr.* II. EBEV; OBVE
Trochee trips from long to short. Metrical Feet [Lessons for a Boy]. Samuel Taylor Coleridge. FaBoUs; HBV-2; NIP; OxBChV; SoSe
Troia Fuit. Reginald Wright Kauffman. HBV-1
Troika, The. Louis Simpson. NoAM; NOBA
Troilus and Cressida, *sels.* Dryden.
"Can life be a blessing?" SeCePo; ViBoPo
(Song: "Can life be a blessing.") NoP; SeCV-2
Prologue: "See my lov'd Britons, see your Shakespeare rise." SeCV-2
Troilus and Cressida, *sels.* Shakespeare.
Helen of Troy, *fr.* IV, i. TreFT
Order and Degree *fr.* I, iii. NIP
("Heavens themselves, the planets and this center, The.") ImOP; PAI
Portrait of Cressida, *fr.* IV, v. TrGrPo
Portrait of Helen, *fr.* II, ii, *and* IV, i. TrGrPo
Ulysses Advises Achilles, *fr.* III, iii. LiTB
Troilus and Criseyde [*or* Criseide], *sels.* Chaucer.
At the Gate. SeCePo
Complaint of Troilus, The, *fr.* V. NOBE; OBEV
Criseyde Sees Troilus Return from Battle, *fr.* II. OxBM
Despair of Troilus, The, IV. LoBV
Go, Little Book ("Go, litel book, go litel myn tragedy"), *fr.* V. OAEL-1; OxBM; ViBoPo
(Envoy, The.) FiP
"If no love is, O God, what fele I so," *fr.* I. FF; OAEL-1
(Song of Troylus, The.) AWP
Love Unfeigned, *fr.* V. NOBE; OBEV
("O yonge fresshe folkes, he or she.") LO; OxBM
"Out of thise blake wawes for to saile." PP
Sorrow of Troilus, The, *fr.* V. PoEL-1
"Swich fyn hath, lo, this Troilus for love!" NOCV
"This Troilus, with blisse of that supprysed," *fr.* III. EBEV
Troilus Laments Criseyde's Absence, *fr.* V. OxBM
Wooing of Criseide, The, III. PoEL-1
Trojan Horse, The. William Drummond of Hawthornden. EyDe
Trojans outside the Walls, The. Homer, *tr. fr. Greek by* George Chapman. *Fr.* The Iliad, VIII. OBS
("This speech all Trojans did applaud.") OBVE
Troll, The. Jack Prelutsky. RHPC
Troll Chanting. Anselm Hollo. *Fr.* Out of the "Kalevala." WSC
Troll sat alone on his seat of stone. The Stone Troll. J. R. R. Tolkien. SO
Troll the Bowl! Thomas Dekker. *See* Cold's the Wind.
Troll's Nosegay, The. Robert Graves. PoCh
Trompe L'Œil. Daryl Hine. MoCV
Troop home to silent grots and caves! The Mermaidens' Vesper-Hymn [*or* Chorus of Sirens *or* Song of the Mermaids *or* Siren Chorus]. George Darley. Syren Songs, VI. BIrV; ChTr; FaBoEn; FaBoRV; GBL; LoBV; NBM; OBNC; OBRV; OxBI; PoEL-4; ViBoPo; WSC
Troop of the Guard, A. Hermann Hagedorn. HBV-2; OHIP
Troop Train. Karl Shapiro. OxBA; WaaP; WaP
Trooper and Maid, *diff. versions.* *Unknown.* AmFP, 2 *versions*
(Trooper and the Maid, The.) BaBo; FSW
Trooper's Horse, The. *Unknown.* OBET
Troops, The. Siegfried Sassoon. CMoP
(Prelude: The Troops.) ChMP
Troops exulting sate in order round, The. Homer, *tr. by* Pope. *Fr.* The Iliad, VIII. OBVE
Troopship, The. Lionel Johnson. EBVV
Troopship for France, War II. George Bogin. FAZ
Troopship in the Tropics. Alun Lewis. WaP
Trophy, The. Edwin Muir. LiTM
Tropic of ice. Cape Ann; a View. John Malcolm Brinnin. NYBP
Tropic tonight, burning, filled with fast trains. At the Band Concert. John Malcolm Brinnin. PoA
Tropical Morning at Sea, A. Edward Rowland Sill. EtS
Tropical Town. Salomòn de la Selva. HBV-2
Tropical Weather. Epes Sargent. EtS
Tropics in New York, The. Claude McKay. AmNP; NoAM; PoBA; PoNe; TTY
Tropisms on John Berryman. Gerald Vizenor. VoR
Trosachs, The. Wordsworth. HBV-1; OBEV; OBRV; SeCePo
Trot Along, Pony. Marion Edey *and* Dorothy Grider. SoPo; TiPo
Trot, and a canter, a gallop, and over, A. *Unknown.* OxNR
Trot, Trot! Mary F. Butts. HBV-1; HBVY
Troubador. J. Edgar Simmons. TAT
Troubadour of God, The. Charles Wharton Stork. WGRP
Troubadours. Arthur Davison Ficke. Sonnets of a Portrait Painter, X. HBMV
Trouble. Philip Brasfield. LFAC
Trouble. David Keppel. FaFP; FPL; PoLF; TreF, WBLP
Trouble. Don Marquis. *Fr.* Archy and Mehitabel. TreFT

Trouble. James Wright. FF; InPK
Trouble in the "Amen Corner." Thomas Chalmers Harbaugh. BLPA
Trouble is, it's getting harder. Wild West. Mark Vinz. Psk
Trouble, not of clouds, or weeping rain, A. On the Departure of Sir Walter Scott from Abbotsford, for Naples. Wordsworth. EBEV; EnRP
Trouble, Trouble, *with music. Unknown.* OuSiCo
Trouble was, The. Trouble. Philip Brasfield. LFAC
Trouble was too much, The. Indian Love Song. Lew Blockcolski. VoR
Trouble with a kitten is, The. The Kitten. Ogden Nash. DFF; FaPON; MoShBr; WhC
Trouble with you is, The. Denunciation; or, Unfrock'd Again. Philip Whalen. NeAP
Trouble with you is, The. Love in a Warm Room in Winter. James Wright. OBAL
Troubled Jesus. Waring Cuney. BANP
Troubled Soldier, The, *with music. Unknown.* AS
Troubled was a house in Ealing. The Widow's Plot; or, She Got What Was Coming to Her. William Plomer. NoAM
Troubled waters, The/ are frozen fast. Murasaki Shikibu, *tr. by* Kenneth Rexroth *and* Ikuko Atsumi. *Fr.* The Tale of Genji. WPOW
Troubled Woman. Langston Hughes. CTBA; PCP
Troubles of the Day. William Barnes. GTBS-P
Trouble-shooting. William Stafford. AMV-80
Troupial, A. Milton Bracker. TDH
Trousers first of ancient fabric. Sri Rama's Raiment. *Malay Oral Tradition, tr. by* R. O. Winstedt. WTO
Trousers of Wind. *Unknown, tr. fr. Amharic by* Sylvia Pankhurst. PBA; TTY
Trout. Seamus Heaney. CIP
Trout. Norman Hindley. WOLT
Trout, The. Daryl Hine. CoAP
Trout, The. John Montague. BoAnP; IPY; NMP
Trout Fisher. George Mackay Brown. OxBC
Trout Fishing; a Sign. Richard Behm. WOLT
Trout Fishing in Virginia. Michael Beirne McMahon. AMV-80
Trouvaille. Richard Murphy. CIP; IPY
Troy. Robin Flower. SeCePo
Troy. Edwin Muir. CMoP
Troy. Thomas Sackville. *Fr.* Induction to "A Mirror for Magistrates." SeCePo
Troy Depicted. Shakespeare. *Fr.* The Rape of Lucrece. OBSC
Troynovant ("Troynovant is now no more a city"). Thomas Dekker. *Fr.* Entertainment to James. ChTr; LoBV; OBSC
Truant, The. E. J. Pratt. NoAM; NOBC; NoP; OBCV
Truants, The. Walter de la Mare. MoBrPo
Truce, gentle love, a parley now I crave. Idea, LXIII. Michael Drayton. NoP
Truck Drivers. Terri Haag. CTBA
Trucker, A. Thom Gunn. PCP
Trucks. James S. Tippett. FaPON
Trudge, Body. Robert Graves. MoAB
True Account of Talking to the Sun at Fire Island, A. Frank O'Hara. NNaP; SOTW
True and Faithful Inventory of the Goods Belonging to Dr. Swift, Vicar of Laracor, A; upon Lending His House to the Bishop of Meath, till His Palace Was Rebuilt. Swift. FaBoUs
True and False. Isabella Valancy Crawford. PeCV
True and False Glory. Milton. *Fr.* Paradise Regained, III. LiTB; OBS
True and Joyful News. *Unknown.* APAS
True Apostolate, The. Ruby T. Weyburn. BLRP
True Aristocrat, The. W. Stewart. WBLP
True as the church clock hand the hour pursues. John Clare. *Fr.* The Cottager. OBRV
True Ballad of the Great Race to Gilmore City, The. Phil Hey. Psk
True Beauty. Francis Beaumont. EIL; HBV-1
True Beauty, The. Thomas Carew. *See* Disdain Returned.
True Brahmin, in the morning meadows wet. Gardener. Emerson. *Fr.* Quatrains. OxBA
True Brotherhood. Ella Wheeler Wilcox. WBLP
True Cat, A. Anna Seward. PCat
True Child ("True Child of God, stand innocently awed"). Marion Hodge. AMV-81
True Christian hearts cease to lament. The Song of a Happy Rising. John Thewlis. ACP
True Christmas, The. Henry Vaughan. SBVL
True Confession, A. Jon Stallworthy. NoAM
True Confession of George Barker, The, *sels.* George Barker.
"I see the young bride move among." ErPo
"I sent a letter to my love." FaBoTw
"Today, the Twenty-sixth of February." NAs
True Confessional. Lawrence Ferlinghetti. NAs
True daughters of Lilith, night demons. Summer Night. Hayyim Nahman Bialik, *tr. by* Robert Friend. VWA
True ease in writing comes from art, not chance. Sound and Sense. Pope. *Fr.* An Essay on Criticism. HAP; PrIm; SoSe; TrGrPo; UnPo
True Englishmen, drink a good health to the miter. A New Catch in Praise of the Reverend Bishops. *Unknown.* APAS
True Enough: To the Physicist (1820). Goethe, *tr. fr. German by* Michael Hamburger. SUW
True Facts of the Case, The. Anthony Euwer. OBAL
True faith discovered was, The. Wisdom. W. B. Yeats. TrCP
True Freedom. Charles MacKay. PGD
True Friendship. *Unknown, tr. fr. Sanskrit by* Arthur W. Ryder. *Fr.* The Panchatantra. AWP
True friendship unfeigned. Of Perfect Friendship. Henry Cheke. EIL
True Genius. Robert Lloyd. *Fr.* Shakespeare, an Epistle to David Garrick, Esq. NOEC
True genius, but true woman! dost deny. To George Sand: A Recognition. Elizabeth Barrett Browning. BoWoP; SBG; TEP
True Heaven, The. Paul Hamilton Hayne. WGRP
True Hymn, A. George Herbert. InvP; NOCV; OxBoCh
True Import of Present Dialogue, Black vs. Negro, The. Nikki Giovanni. BPo; PoBA
True is it that Ambrosio Salinero. Epitaphs, V. Gabriello Chiabrera, *tr. by* Wordsworth. AWP
True Knight, The. Stephen Hawes. *Fr.* The Pastime of Pleasure. ACP; OBEV
(True Knighthood.) TrGrPo
True Knight, The. Ella Wheeler Wilcox. PeD
True Knowledge. Panatattu, *tr. fr. Sanskrit.* WGRP
True Lent, A. Robert Herrick. *See* To Keep a True Lent.
True Love. *Also see* Truelove.
True Love. Waring Cuney. CDC
True Love, A. Nicholas Grimald. EIL; OBEV
(Truelove, A.) OBSC
True Love. Joe Johnson. CNA
True Love. Shakespeare. *See* Sonnets, CXVI.
True Love. Shelley. *Fr.* Epipsychidion. LoBV
True Love. Sir Philip Sidney. *See* My True Love Hath My Heart.
True Love. *Unknown, tr. fr. Greek by* Louis Untermeyer. UnTE
True Love Ditty, A. Thomas Middleton. *Fr.* Blurt, Master Constable. EIL
True Love in this differs from gold and clay. Shelley. *Fr.* Epipsychidion. OBNC
True love is sweet and true love is pleasant. William Hall. *Unknown.* AmFP
True love, true love, don't lie to me. In the Pines (Where Did You Sleep Last Night?) Leadbelly (Huddie Ledbetter). FSW
True love, true love, what have I done. In the Pines. *Unknown.* AmFP
True Lovers Bold, The. *Unknown.* AmFP
True Lover's Farewell, The *Unknown. See* Lass of Lochroyan, The.
True love's own talisman, which here. A Footnote to a Famous Lyric. Louise Imogen Guiney. AA
True love's the gift which God has given. Sir Walter Scott. *Fr.* The Lay of the Last Minstrel, V. OBRV
True Maid, A. Matthew Prior. ErPo; FaBoCo; FaBoEE; NIP; NOEC; PV
True Martyr, The. Thomas Wade. OBVV
True Mexican or not, let's open our shirts. Kearney Park. Gary Soto. NPGG
True mirth resides not in the smiling skin. Mirth. Robert Herrick. LiTB
True Night. René Char, *tr. fr. French by* Jackson Mathews. PoPl
True or False. Catullus, *tr. fr. Latin by* Walter Savage Landor. AWP
("None could ever say that she.") OBVE
True Paddy's Song, The, *with music. Unknown.* OuSiCo
True Picture Restored, A. Vernon Watkins. NoAM
True poesy is not in words. Pastoral Poesy. John Clare. OAEL-2
True Rest. Goethe, *tr. fr. German by* John S. Dwight. TRV; WBLP
(Rest.) TreFT
True Riches. Bessie June Martin. STF
True Riches. Isaac Watts. OBEC
True Romance, The. Herbert Jones. HBMV
True Son of God, Eternal Light, *with music.* P. J. Cormican. AH
True Story, A. Marvin Bell. SV
True Story of Mary and Her Little Lamb, The. *Unknown.* DBV
True Tale of Robin Hood, A. *Unknown.* ESPB
True, the Good and the Beautiful, The. Delmore Schwartz. MiAP
True, the time, to one who does not love farce. A Little Scraping. Robinson Jeffers. NoAM
True Thomas. *Unknown. See* Thomas the Rhymer.
True Thomas lay o'er yond grassy [*or* on Huntlie] bank. Thomas the Rhymer [*or* Thomas Rymer *or* True Thomas]. *Unknown.* BSV; CH; ChTr; ELP; ESPB; FaBoBa; FaBoCh; GoTS; HAP; HBV-2; InPK; InPS; LiTB; NOBE; OAEL-1; OAEP; OBEV; OnMSP; OxBB; OxBS; PAI; Prf; SeCeV; TrGrPo; ViBoFo; ViBoPo

True to a Dream. Donald Petersen. NePoEA-2
True to your might [*or* Truth to your mighty] winds on dusky shores. On the Death of William Edward Burghardt Du Bois by African Moonlight and Forgotten Shores. Conrad Kent Rivers. NBP; PoBA
True Vine. Elinor Wylie. LiTA
True, we are the children. The Second Generation. Menachem Z. Rosensaft. AMV-81
True, we must tame our rebel will. Courage. Matthew Arnold. OAEL-2
True Weather for Women, The. Louis Simpson. NePoAm
True Wisdom. *Unknown.* STF
True wit is nature to advantage dressed. Pope. *Fr.* An Essay on Criticism. HAP
True worth is in being, not seeming. Nobility. Alice Cary. OHFP; WBLP
Trueblue Gentleman, A. Kenneth Patchen. SO
True-born Englishman, The. Daniel Defoe. APAS
Sels.
"Breed's described, The: Now, Satire, if you can," *fr.* II. OBSV
English Race, The. OBEC
"In their religion they are so unev'n," *fr.* II. OBSV
"Labouring poor, in spite of double pay," *fr.* II. NOBL; SaC
"Then let us boast of ancestors no more," *conclusion.* OBSV
"Wherever God erects a house of prayer," *fr.* I. NOBL; OBSV; TreF
Truelove. *Unknown, tr. fr. German by* Jethro Bithell. AWP
Truelove, A. Nicholas Grimald. *See* True Love, A.
Truest Poetry Is the Most Feigning, The; or, Ars Poetica for Hard Times. W. H. Auden. NYBP
Truisms, The. Louis MacNeice. NOBE; OBSV
Truly buzzards/ Around my sky are circling! Glyph. *Unknown, tr. by* Mary Austin. LiTA
Truly Great. W. H. Davies. HBV-1; OBMV; OBVV
Truly in the east/ The white bean. Song to Promote Growth. *Tr. by* Washington Matthews. OBVE
Truly, my Satan, thou art but a dunce. Epilogue [*or* To the Accuser Who Is the God of this World]. Blake. *Fr.* The Gates of Paradise. CABA; FaBoEn; HAP; NoP; OAEL-2; OBNC; TrGrPo; ViBoPo; WeW
Truly the light is sweet. The Light Is Sweet. Bible, *O.T.* *Fr.* Ecclesiastes. FaPON
Truly, the light is sweet. A Man's Bread. Josephine Preston Peabody. YeAr
Truly these women are like birds; they take. Birds. "Seumas O'Sullivan". OxBI
Trump hath blown, The. The Lonely Bugle Grieves. Grenville Mellen. *Fr.* Ode on the Celebration of the Battle of Bunker Hill, June 17, 1825. AA
Trumpet, The. Ilya Ehrenburg, *tr. fr. Russian by* Y. Hornstein. TrJP
Trumpet, The, *sel.* Robinson Jeffers.
Grass on the Cliff, V. PoA
Trumpet, The. Edward Thomas. HBMV; MMA; MoBrPo; OHIP
Trumpet, A/ A trumpet. Lewis Has a Trumpet. Karla Kuskin. PDV
Trumpet of Liberty, The. John Taylor. NOEC
Trumpet Player. Langston Hughes. TTY
Trumpet Shall Sound, The. John V. Hicks. AMV-81
Trumpeter, The. *Unknown.* CoMu
Trumpeter of Fyvie, The, *with music.* *Unknown.* OxBB
(Andrew Lammie.) ESPB
Trumpeter swan's neck was curved, The. At the Smithsonian. Vanessa Haley. AMV-81
Trumpets. A valley opens and beyond. Drums in Scotland. Richard Hugo. LCAP
Trumpet's loud clangor, The. Fife and Drum. Dryden. *Fr.* A Song for St. Cecilia's Day, 1687. GN
Trumpets sound and steeples ring. A Trick for Tyburn; or, A Prison Rant. *Unknown.* APAS
Trumpet's voice, loud and authoritative, The. Reasons for Attendance. Philip Larkin. BiP
Trundled from/ the strangeness of the sea. The Sea-Elephant. William Carlos Williams. LiTA; NU
Trunk of cherry-tree without bark or flowers. Materia Nupcial. Pablo Neruda, *tr. by* Clayton Eshleman. ErPo
Trunk won't budge, The; I open it. Calvin in the Attic Cleans. Craig Weeden. AMV-81
Truro Bear, The. Mary Oliver. SoSe
Trus' an' Smile. B. Y. Williams. BLRP
Trust. Lizette Woodworth Reese. AA
Trust a woman. Kitchen Song. Jeannine Dobbs. Str
Trust and Obedience. *Unknown.* BLRP
Trust Him. *Unknown.* STF
Trust in God and Do the Right. Norman Macleod. PaPo
Trust in God, *sel.* BLRP; TreFT
Trust in Me, *with music.* *Unknown.* AH
Trust in the Lord: so shalt thou dwell. Bible, *O.T.* Psalms, XXXVII: 1-7. BLRP
Trust in Women. *Unknown.* NA
"When sparrows build churches and steeples high," *sel.* PBBP
Trust not his wanton tears. Of Cupid [*or* Aeliana's Ditty]. Henry Chettle. *Fr.* Piers Plainness' Seven Years' Prenticeship. ElL; OBSC
Trust not the treason of those smiling looks. Amoretti, XLVII. Spenser. TrGrPo
Trust not too much, fair youth, unto thy feature. White Primit Falls. *Unknown.* ChTr
Trust Only Yourself. *Unknown.* MeEL
Trust-Song, A. Eben E. Rexford. BLRP
Trust the Great Artist. Thomas Curtis Clark. WBLP
Trust Thou Thy Love. John Ruskin. OBEV; OBVV
Trustful curator has left me alone, The. Museum of Man. Earle Birney. OxBC
Trusty, Dusky, Vivid, True. Robert Louis Stevenson. *See* My Wife.
Truth. "Æ." AnIL; MoBrPo
Truth. Chaucer. *See* Balade de Bon Conseyl.
Truth, *sels.* William Cowper.
"Man on the dubious waves of error toss'd." NOCV
Simple Faith. OBEC
Truth, The. W. H. Davies. FaBoTw
Truth. John Donne. *See* Seek True Religion.
Truth, The. Randall Jarrell. DiL; OxBC
Truth, The. Ted Joans. BOLo; TTY
(Voice in the Crowd.) AmFP
Truth, The. Archibald Lampman. CaP
Truth. Cecil Francis Lloyd. CaP
Truth. John Masefield. WGRP
Truth. Claude McKay. BPo
Truth, A. Noah Mitchell. LFAC
Truth. Howard Nemerov. HoPM; LiTM; MoVE
Truth. Jessica Nelson North. HBVY
Truth. Coventry Patmore. *See* Magna Est Veritas.
Truth. Susan Fromberg Schaeffer. IHMS
Truth. *Unknown.* OxBM
Truth: So the frontlet's older legend ran. Veritas. Oliver Wendell Holmes. *Fr.* Two Sonnets: Harvard. AP
Truth about B. F., The. Albert Stillman. InMe
Truth about Horace, The. Eugene Field. InMe
Truth about My Sister and Me, The. Anita Endrezze Probst. CDW
Truth, be more precious to me than the eyes. Invocation. Max Eastman. WGRP
Truth, Beauty, Love, in these are formed a ring. The Trinity. Marian Osborne. CaP
Truth Brought to Light, or Murder Will Out. Stephen College. APAS
Truth, crushed to earth, shall rise again. Truth, the Invincible. Bryant. *Fr.* The Battle-Field. TreF; TRV
Truth Doth Truth Deserve. Sir Philip Sidney. *Fr.* Arcadia. HBV-1
(Advice to the Same.) SiPS
Truth from Above, The. *Unknown.* OBET
Truth Has Perished. Ulma Seligman, *tr. fr. Yiddish by* Joseph Leftwich. TrJP
Truth I do not stretch or shove, The. The Dog. Ogden Nash. GDP
Truth I pursued, as Fancy sketch'd the way. Samuel Taylor Coleridge. FaBoEE
Truth in Poetry ("Fled are those times"). George Crabbe. *Fr.* The Village. OBEC
Truth in Poetry ("I grant indeed that fields and flocks have charms"). George Crabbe. *See* Rural Life.
Truth is a golden sunset far away. Threnody. I. O. Scherzo. HoPM
Truth is a native, naked beauty; but. Roger Williams. SCAP
Truth is as old as God. Emily Dickinson. MoAmPo
"Truth Is Blind, The." David Gascoyne. EAS
Truth is love and love is truth. Mendacity. A. E. Coppard. OBMV
Truth Is Quite Messy, The. William J. Harris. BOLo
Truth is that there comes a time, The. Sad Strains of a Gay Waltz. Wallace Stevens. OxBA
Truth Kills Everybody. Ted Hughes. InPS
Truth, like a mysterious, silken cat. Open Your Hand. Dorothy R. Fulton. AMV-81
Truth like the Belly of a Woman Turning, The. Gary Synder. NNaP
Truth-loving Persians do not dwell upon. The Persian Version. Robert Graves. CMoP; FaBoCo; LiTB; LiTM; NoAM; NOBL; OBWP; WeW
Truth Never Dies. *Unknown.* WBLP
Truth Shall Set You Free. Chaucer. *See* Balade de Bon Conseyl.
Truth, so far, in my book; the truth which draws. Elizabeth Barrett Browning. *Fr.* Aurora Leigh. WGRP
Truth the Best. Elizabeth Turner. *See* Rebecca's After-Thought.
Truth the Dead Know, The. Anne Sexton. MoAmPo; NePoEA-2; NIP; NoAM; PBWP; TAP
Truth, the Invincible. Bryant. *Fr.* The Battle-Field. TreF
("Truth, crushed to earth, shall rise again.") TRV

Truth, the whole truth always, The. A True Confession. Jon Stallworthy. NoAM
Truth to your mighty winds on dusky shores. *See* True to your might winds on dusky shores.
Truthful James. Bret Harte. *See* Further Language from Truthful James.
Truthful man, that's me, A. Guantanamera. Jose Marti, *ad. by* Pete Seeger *and* Hector Angulo. FSW
Truth's Complaint over England. Thomas Lodge. ACP
Truxton's Victory. *Unknown.* PAH
Try. Philip Appleman. BXAP
Try first this figure 2. A Lesson in Handwriting. Alastair Reid. NYBP
Try Smiling. *Unknown.* BLPA; FaFP; WBLP
Try the Uplook. *Unknown.* BLRP
Try This Once. *Unknown.* WBLP
Try Topic. Genevieve Taggard. MoAmPo
Try, Try Again. *Unknown, at. to* T. H. Palmer. FaFP; FaPON; TreF
Try wading in sand. Try. Philip Appleman. BXAP
Trying. Leonard Nathan. Str
Trying beforehand to make out. Beforehand. Witter Bynner. HBMV
Trying to Believe. Linda Gregg. NPGG
Trying to chop mother down is like. She Went to Stay. Robert Creeley. OBAL
Trying to fall asleep. Night Thought. Gerald Jonas. NYBP
Trying to open locked doors with a sword, threading. Sojourn in the Whale. Marianne Moore. SBG
Trying to say. Susan Griffin. *Fr.* Nineteen Pieces for Love, #15. LLLT
Trying to scrape the burned soup from my only pot. The Lives of Famous Men. Jack Gilbert. NPGG
Trying to Sleep. Ralph Pomeroy. ELU
Trying to Stay. Diana Chang. PoDr
Trying to Talk with a Man. Adrienne Rich. NIP
Trying to write. Jessy. Nora Dauenhauer. TWSS
Tryptych for Jan Bockelson, A. John Oliver Simon. NeAC
Tryst. Derek Butler. LFAC
Tryst, The. Knox. CenHV
Tryst. Eve Merriam. NMM
Tryst, The. Christopher Morley. HBMV
Tryst, A. Louise Chandler Moulton. HBV-1
Tryst, The. William Soutar. BSV; EBEV; ErPo; GoTS; NeBP; OxBS
 (Trysting Place, The.) BoLoP
Tryst, The. John Banister Tabb. OBAL
Tryst after Death, The, *abr.* *Unknown, tr. fr. Old Irish by* Kuno Meyer. OnYI
Tryst in Brobdingnag, A. Adrienne Rich. NYBP
Tryste Noël. Louise Imogen Guiney. HBV-1; OBVV
 (Five Carols for Christmastide, I.) IS
Trysting, A. Richard Dehmel, *tr. fr. German by* Jethro Bithell. AWP
Trysting Bush, The. Joanna Baillie. WPE
Trysting Place, The. William Soutar. *See* Tryst, The.
Ts'ai Chi'h. Ezra Pound. NoP
Tsa'lagi Council Tree. Gladys Cardiff. TWSS
Tsangyang Gyatso was twelve years old. Signature III. Joseph Stroud. NPGG
Ts'eekkaayah. Mary TallMountain. STE; WTSS
Tsigane's Canzonet, The. Edward King. AA
Tu Du,/ Skies blue. Thomas Holley Chivers. *Fr.* Chinese Serenade for the Ut-Kam and Tong-Koo. PeD
"Tu Non Se' in Terra, Si Come Tu Credi." Kathleen Raine. NeBP; WPE
Tu-Whit To-Who. Shakespeare. *See* When Icicles Hang by the Wall.
Tubal Cain. Charles Mackay. WBLP
Tubby or not tubby—there's the rub. F. C. Burnand. BXAP
Tuberose. Louis James Block. AA
Tubes. Larry Mollin. NeAC
Tuck the earth, fold the sod. Dirge. William Alexander Percy. HBMV
Tucking in yellow curls, she poises, set. The Diver. Leonard E. Nathan. ErPo
Tucking the Baby In. Curtis May. HBV-1
Tudor Aspersions. R. A. Piddington. FiBHP
Tudor indeed is gone and every rose. Ezra Pound. *Fr.* Cantos, LXXX. FaBoTw
Tudor Portrait. Richmond Lattimore. EyDe
Tudor Rose, The. Alexander Barclay. *Fr.* The Ship of Fools. ACP
Tuesday. Zishe Landau, *tr. fr. Yiddish by* Ruth Whitman. VWA
Tuesday afternoons in the cave of our basement. Making Music. Judith Minty. GeTw
Tuesday; or, The Ditty. John Gay. *Fr.* The Shepherd's Week. NOEC
 (Ditty, The.) LoBV
Tuesday, 5 March (Morning) 1963. Pier Paolo Pasolini, *tr. fr. Italian by* Nigel Thompson. AMV-81
Tuft of Flowers, The. Robert Frost. AP; AWP; CoBMV; GoYe; HBV-2; HBVY; LiTA; MoAB; MoAmPo; OxBA; SeCeV
Tuft of Kelp, The. Herman Melville. ChTr; FaBoEE; FaBoRV; MOS
Tug pulls, tightening the steel strand, The. From Le Havre. Charles G. Bell. NePoAm
Tugs. José Y. Terán Jr. LFAC
Tugs. James S. Tippett. FaPON
Tulip. Robert Wallace. PPJ
Tulip. Humbert Wolfe. MoBrPo
Tulip Tree. Sacheverell Sitwell. MoBrPo
Tulips. Padraic Colum. ImOP
Tulips. Sylvia Plath. HAP; NaP; NoP; NYBP; PAI; PPP; WeW; WPE
Tulips and Addresses. Edward Field. NYBP; Psk
Tulips are too excitable, it is winter here, The. Tulips. Sylvia Plath. NaP; NoP; NYBP; PAI; WeW
Tulips charge the grazing dikes, and I walk. Dutch April. Daniel Halpern. GrPl
Tulips from Their Blood. Edwin Brooks. NBP
Tulips now are pushing up, The. April. Eunice Tietjens. SoPo; YeAr
Tullie's Love, *sels.* Robert Greene.
 Mars and Venus. OBSC
  (Sonnet or Ditties: "Mars in a fury 'gainst love's brightest queen.") LoBV
 Shepherd's Ode, The. OBSC
Tullochgorum. John Skinner. BSV; GoTS; OBEC; OxBS
Tully, the queen of beauty's boast. Molly Moor. George Farewell. NOEC
Tumadir Al-Khansa for Her Brother. *Unknown, tr. fr. Arabic by* E. Powys Mathers. *Fr.* The Thousand and One Nights. AWP
 (For Her Brother.) PBWP
Tumbalalaika. *Tr. fr. Yiddish.* FSW
Tumble, The. Ann Taylor. HBVY
Tumble me down, and I will sit. To Fortune. Robert Herrick. SeCV-1
Tumble of arms and legs led to this, A. Sleeping Peasants. Phyllis Janik. PoDr
Tumbleweed. David Wagoner. BoNaP
Tumbling. *Unknown.* OxBChV
Tumbling among its stones. The Ladder. Gene Baro. NePoEA-2
Tumbling Mustard. Malcolm Cowley. AmFN
Tumbling, pausing, leaping, knocking together. Metaphysic of Snow. Donald Finkel. PoA
Tummy Ache. Aileen Fisher. SoPo
Tumor. Lucille Day. SUW
Tumor Virus workshop is finished, The. Cancer Research. Anselm Parlatore. SUW
Tumult. Charles Enoch Wheeler. PoNe
Tumult in a Syrian town had place, A. The Great Physician. Sadi, *tr. by* Sir Edwin Arnold. *Fr.* The Bustan. AWP
Tumult of death, dizziness hath seized me, The. Elegy (for Himself). Moses Rimos of Majorca, *tr. by* Israel Abrahams. TrJP
Tumult of my fretted mind, The. Self-Analysis. Anna Wickham. MoBrPo
Tumult, weeping, many new ghosts. Snow Storm. Kenneth Rexroth. NaP
Tumultuous sea, whose wrath and foam are spent. Eumares. Asclepiades, *tr. by* Richard Garnett. AWP
Tunbridge Wells. Earl of Rochester. FaBoPP; OBSV
Tundra, The. John Haines. ConAP
Tune. Carl Rakosi. GP
Tune, A. Arthur Symons. BoLoP; OBNC
Tune: Butterfly Woos the Blossoms, The. Li Ching-chao, *tr. fr. Chinese by* C. H. Kwôck *and* Vincent McHugh. PBWP
Tune: Crimson Lips Adorned. Li Ching-chao, *tr. fr. Chinese by* C. H. Kwôck *and* Vincent McHugh. PBWP
 ("After kicking on the swing," *tr. by* Kenneth Rexroth *and* Ling Chung.) BoWoP
Tune: Endless Union. Li Ching-chao, *tr. fr. Chinese by* C. H. Kwôck *and* Vincent McHugh. PBWP
Tune: Magnolia Blossom. Li Ching-chao, *tr. fr. Chinese by* C. H. Kwôck *and* Vincent McHugh. PBWP
Tune beyond us as we are, A. Wallace Stevens. The Man with the Blue Guitar, VI. CMoP
Tune for a Lonesome Fife. Donald Justice. NYBP
Tune in to a raga. Assassination Raga. Lawrence Ferlinghetti. CAPP
Tune is cowboy, The; the words, sentimental crap. D-Y Bar. James Welch. CDW; STE
Tune me for life again, oh, quiet Musician. A Prayer after Illness. Violet Alleyn Storey. TrPWD
Tune Me, O Lord, into One Harmony. Christina Rossetti. TrPWD
Tune on my pipe the praises of my Love. In Praise of His Daphnis. Sir John Wotton. ElL
Tune on my pipe the praises of my Love. Of His Mistress. Robert Greene. *Fr.* Menaphon. ElL
Tune Thou My Harp. Amy Carmichael. TRV
Tune thy music[ke] to thy heart [*or* hart]. Heart's Music. *Unknown, at. to* Thomas Campion. AAS; OBEV
Tune to the Devonshire Cant, The. *Unknown.* APAS

Tuneful Hipponax rests him here. Epitaph of Hipponax. Theocritus, *tr. by* Charles Stuart Calverley. FaBoEE
Tuneful poet, Britain's glory. The Mutual Congratulations of the Poets Anna Seward and Hayley. Richard Porson. FaBoEE; OBSV
Tunes fainter on winds waywarder than others. Graves Are Made to Waltz On. Peter Viereck. PoA
Tuning myself by morning coffee. May Morn. Michael McClure. EAS
Tunnel, The. Hart Crane. *Fr.* The Bridge. AP; CMoP; MAT; MoAB; MoAmPo; MoVE: NePA; NYP; OxBA
Tunnel, The. Mark Strand. HeIP; TwCP; WeW
Tunnyng [*or* Tunning] of Elynour [*or* Elinor] Rummyng [*or* Rumming], The. John Skelton. AAS
Sels.
"Tell you I chyll." TrGrPo
"Then Margery Milkduck." EBEV; OAEL-1
Tupelo Destruction, The. *Unknown.* AmFP
Turf Carrier on Aranmore. John Hewitt. PoRA
Turf-Stacks. Louis MacNeice. *See* Among These Turf-Stacks.
Turin beneath, on the green banks of the Po. At the Tombs of the House of Savoy. William Jay Smith. NePoAm-2
Turista. Mark Osaki. BrSi
Turkey and the Ant, The. John Gay. *Fr.* Fables. PBBP
Turkey in the Straw. *Unknown, wr. at. to* Robert Farrell *or* George Washington Dixon. AS, *with music;* BLSo, *with music*; FaFP; FSW; GBP; TrAS, *with music;* TreFS; YaD
Turkish Bakery, The. *Unknown, tr. fr. Korean by* Peter H. Lee. PBWP
Turkish Legend, A. Thomas Bailey Aldrich. GN; HBV-2; HBVY
Turkish Trench Dog, The. Geoffrey Dearmer. GDP
Turn, The. Robert Creeley. LCAP
Turn (a Poem in 4 Parts). Ken Belford. NOBC
Turn Again. *Unknown.* OxBM
Turn Again to Life. Mary Lee Hall. BLPL; PoLF
Turn again, turn again, turn once again. Carrousel Tune. Tennessee Williams. OBAL
Turn All Thy Thoughts. Thomas Campion. ViBoPo
Turn Back, O Man. Clifford Bax. NOCV; TRV
Turn back. Turn, young lady dear. The Robber Bridegroom. Allen Tate. TwAmPo
Turn Back, You Wanton Flyer. Thomas Campion. UnTE
Turn Blind. Paul Celan, *tr. fr. German by* Joachim Neugroschel. VWA
Turn from that girl. I Shall Laugh Purely. Robinson Jeffers. CrMA; LiTA; LiTM; WaP
Turn I my looks unto the skies. Rosader's Sonnet. Thomas Lodge. *Fr.* Rosalynde. OBSC
Turn inward on the brain. What the Emanation of Casey Jones Said to the Medium. Arthur James Marshall Smith. MoCV
Turn like a top, spin on your dusty axis. Instead of a Journey. Michael Hamburger. NYBP
Turn Me to My Yellow Leaves. William Stanley Braithwaite. BANP
Turn not aside, Shepherd, to see. Help, Good Shepherd. Ruth Pitter. OxBoCh
Turn not to the prophet's page, O Son! For the Holy Family by Michelangelo. Dante Gabriel Rossetti. GoBC
Turn o' the Year. Katharine Tynan. HBV-1
Turn o'er thy outward man, and judge aright. The Outward Man Accused. Edward Taylor. LiTA
Turn of the Moon. Robert Graves. TEP
Turn of the Road, The. Alice Rollit Coe. HBV-1
Turn of the Road, The. Fannie Stearns Gifford. HBMV
Turn of the Road, The. James Stephens. SO; WSC
"Turn on the anvil twice or thrice." To an Old Poet. Walter Savage Landor. DBV
Turn on the Footlights: The Perils of Pedagogy. John Marshall Carter. AMV-80
Turn on Your Side and Bear the Day to Me. George Barker. OxBTC
Turn out more ale, turn up the light. Dum Vivimus Vigilamus. Charles Henry Webb. AA
Turn Right Next Corner. Wichita Vortex Sutra. Allen Ginsberg. CAPP
Turn the Glasses Over. *Unknown.* FSW
Turn the Key Deftly. Edwin Brock. POL
Turn the page of stone and there. Eeva-Liisa Manner, *tr. by* Jaakko A. Ahokas. *Fr.* Cambrian. PBWP
"Turn to me in the darkness." Titus and Berenice. John Heath-Stubbs. GTBS-P
Turn to right, turn to left. Witches' Spells. Madeleine Edmondson. NTCP
Turn to the Left. Deems Taylor, *tr. fr. French.* UnTE
Turn, turn, my wheel! Turn round and round. The Potter's Song. Longfellow. *Fr.* Kéramos. PoEL-5
Turn, turn thy beauteous face away. Song. Beaumont and Fletcher. *Fr.* Love's Cure. PoEL-2
Turn, Turn, Unhappy Souls, Return, *with music.* Henry Alline. AH
Turn under, plow. Plowman's Song. Raymond Knister. CaP
"Turn, Willie Macintosh." Willie Macintosh [*or* Burning of Auchindown]. *Unknown.* ESPB; OxBB; OxBoLi; ViBoFo
Turn with me from the city's clamorous street. Thomas à Kempis. Richard Rogers Bowker. AA
Turnaround for Higherground, The. Pancho Aguila. LFAC
Turncoat, The. Amiri Baraka. NeAP
Turner's Camp on the Chippewa. *Unknown.* AmFP
Turners Dish of Lentten Stuffe; or, A Galymaufery. William Turner. CoMu
Turner's Sunrise. Helen Bevington. EyDe
Turning, The. Philip Booth. NePoAm-2
Turning. Robert Finch. MoCV; OBCV
Turning, The. Philip Levine. VGW
Turning, The. Philip Murray. NePoAm
Turning and turning in the widening gyre. The Second Coming. W. B. Yeats. BIrV; BLPL; CABA; CMoP; CoBMV; EaLo; FaBoEn; FaBoMo; FF; GTBS-P; HAP; HeIP; HoPM; InPK; InPS; LiTB; LiTM; LoBV; MasP; MAT; MoAB; MoBrPo; MoVE; NIP; NoAM; NOBE; NoP; OAEL-2; OAEP; OxBI; OxBTC; PAI; PPoe; PPP; PrIm; SBVL; SCV; SeCePo; SeCeV; SoSe; TEP; UnPo; WaP; WeW
Turning Aside from Battles. Sextus Propertius, *tr. fr. Latin by* Ezra Pound. WaaP
Turning Away from Lies. Robert Bly. LCAP
Turning deer flesh over. Blood. Barney Bush. STE
Turning Fifty. Judith Wright. NAs
Turning, following the arrows through. The House of Madam Juju. Kanai Mieko, *tr. by* Christopher Drake. BoWoP
Turning from Plato to the rocky sergeant. Apocalypse. John Frederick Nims. MiAP
Turning from Shelley's sculptured face aside. On a Grave in Christchurch, Hants. Oscar Fay Adams. AA
Turning Into. Robert Duncan. EAS
Turning it over, considering, like a madman. John Berryman. Dream Songs, LXXV. NaP; NoAM
Turning of the Leaves, The. Vernon Watkins. NeBP
Turning Point. W. L. Holshouser. AMV-81
Turning, returning on world winds that know. Angel Eye of Memory. John Malcolm Brinnin. PoA
Turning the secrets from her pack of cards. A Fortune-Teller. Witter Bynner. HBMV
Turning Thirty. W. D. Ehrhart. AMV-81
Turning Thirty. Katha Pollitt. WeW
Turning through a collection. Wes Hardin: From a Photograph. Raymond Carver. GeTw
Turning to him, who meets me with desire. Bible, *O.T.* The Song of Solomon, VII: 10-13. PBWP
Turnip Crier [*or* Seller], The. Samuel Johnson. *See* If the Man Who Turnips Cries.
Turnstile, The. William Barnes. CH; OBVV
Turris Eburnea. *Unknown.* GoBC
Turtle. Robert Lowell. LCAP
Turtle, The. Ogden Nash. FaFP; FiBHP; NePA; NIP; NoP; OBAL; SoSe; TAP; WhC
(Autres Bêtes, Autres Moeurs.) TreFS
Turtle, The. *Unknown.* PAH
Turtle, The. Diane Wakoski. *Fr.* Greed. NoAM
Turtle and the Flamingo, The. James Thomas Fields. HBV-2
(Song of the Turtle and Flamingo, The.) GN
Turtle and the Sparrow, The, *sel.* Matthew Prior.
"Behind an unfrequented glade." PBBP
Turtle Dove, The. Geoffrey Hill. FaBoTw; NePoEA
Turtle Dove ("Now don't you see a little turtle dove"). *Unknown.* FSW
Turtle-Dove, The ("Oh, don't you see the turtle dove"). *Unknown.* OxBoLi
Turtle-Doves' Nest, The. *Unknown.* HBVY
Turtle Lake. Richard Hugo. NPAW
Turtle lives 'twixt plated decks, The. The Turtle [*or* Autres Bêtes, Autres Moeurs]. Ogden Nash. FaFP; FiBHP; NePA; NIP; NoP; OBAL; SoSe; TAP; TreFS; WhC
Turtle Mountain Reservation. Louise Erdrich. TWSS
Turtle, old as earth. Red Clay. Linda Hogan. TWSS
Turtle on yon withered bough, The. Song of Thyrsis. Philip Freneau. *Fr.* Female Frailty. AA; LiTA; ViBoPo
Turtle Soup. "Lewis Carroll." *Fr.* Alice's Adventures in Wonderland, *ch.* 10. FaBoNo; InMe; RHPC; SpRo
("Beautiful soup, so rich and green.") Par
Turtle swims slowly, The. The Turtle. Diane Wakoski. *Fr.* Greed. NoAM
Turtle thus with plaintive crying, The. John Gay. PBBP
Turtle's Belly, The. Ellen Pearce. IHMS
Turtle's Song, The. *Unknown.* BPo
Turvey Top. William Sawyer. NA
Tuscaloosa Sam. "Orpheus C. Kerr." OBAL
Tuscan cypresses. Cypresses. D. H. Lawrence. FaBoPP

Tuscan Life. Elizabeth Barrett Browning. *Fr.* Aurora Leigh, VII. FaBoPP
Tuscan, that wanderest through the realms of gloom. Dante. Longfellow. AA
Tuskegee. Leslie Pinckney Hill. BANP; PoNe
Tusks of Blood, The. Samuel Greenberg. MoPo
Tusks that clashed in mighty brawls, The. On the Vanity of Earthly Greatness. Arthur Guiterman. BXAP; HeIP; HOPM; InPK; NIP; OBCA; PAI; PoPl; PV; TrJP; WhC
Tuslag. T. A. Robertson. OxBS
Tusser, they tell me when thou wert alive. Ad Tusserum. *Unknown.* FaBoUs
Tut! Bah! we take as another case. The Poets at Tea, V. Barry Pain. Par
Tutankhamen. William Dickey. Psk
Tutelage, The. Robert Mowry Bell. AA
Tutivillus, the Devil. *Unknown.* MeEL
(Chatterers in Church.) OxBM
("Tutivillus, the devil of hell.") EBEV
Tutor [Who Tooted a Flute], A. Carolyn Wells. *See* Limerick: "Tutor who tooted a flute, A."
Tutto è Sciolto. James Joyce. OBMV; OxBI;
Twa Books, The. Allan Ramsay. OxBS
Twa Brothers, The. *Unknown.* CH; EBEV; ESPB (A *and* B *vers.*); OxBB; ViBoFo (A *and* B *vers.*)
Twa Corbies, The. *Unknown.* AWP; BSV; CABA; CH; ELP; EnSB; ESPB; FaBoBa; FaBoCh; GoTS; GTBS; GTBS-P; HAP; HBV-2; InPK; NoP; OBEV; OxBS; PAI; PoPle; PPP; SeCePo; SeCeV; UnPo
(Three Ravens, The, B *vers.*) BaBo; ViBoFo
Twa Knights, The. *Unknown.* ESPB
Twa Magicians, The. *Unknown.* ESPB; GBP; OxBB
(Two Magicians, The.) ChTr; OAEL-1; OxBoLi
Twa Mariit Wemen and the Wedo, The. William Dunbar. *See* Tretis of the Tua Mariit Wemen and the Wedo, The.
Twa Sisters, The. *Unknown.* *See* Two Sisters, The.
Twain that were foes, while Mary lived, are fled. His Lady's Death. Pierre de Ronsard, *tr. by* Andrew Lang. AWP
'Twas a balmy summer evening, and a goodly crowd was there. The Face upon [*or* on] the Floor. H. Antoine D'Arcy. BeLS; BLPA; FaBoBe; FaFP; FPL; HBV-2; PaPo; TreF; YaD
'Twas a balmy summer morning. The Dawning of the Day. James Clarence Mangan. GoBC
'Twas a busy day in the courtroom, and a curious crowd was there. The Bank Thief. J. R. Farrell. BeLS; BLPA
'Twas a calm and peaceful evening in a camp called Arapahoe. Buckskin Joe. *Unknown.* CoSo
'Twas a calm, still night. Lilly Dale. H. S. Thompson. BLSo
'Twas a dangerous cliff, as they freely confessed. A Fence or an Ambulance. Joseph Malins. BLPA
'Twas a Friday morn when we set sail, and we were not far from the land. The Mermaid. *Unknown.* TreF
'Twas a grand display was the prince's ball. Baron Renfrew's Ball. Charles Graham Halpine. PAH
'Twas a Jacqueminot rose. A Rose. Arlo Bates. HBV-1
'Twas a jolly old pedagogue, long ago. The Jolly Old Pedagogue. George Arnold. HBV-1; TreFS
'Twas a new feeling—something more. Did Not [*or* Quantum Est Quod Desit]. Thomas Moore. BoLoP; EnLoPo; ErPo; NBM
'Twas a pleasant summer's morning. As I'd Nothing Else to Do. Herbert Fry. TreFS
'Twas a stylish congregation, that of Theophrastus Brown. Trouble in the "Amen Corner." Thomas Chalmers Harbaugh. BLPA
'Twas a Sunday morning, quite serene the air. A City Eclogue. "W. J." NOEC
'Twas a sunny day in June. Dear Old Girl. Richard Henry Buck. FSN
'Twas a wonderful brave fight! The Fight at Sumter. *Unknown.* PAH
'Twas after a supper of Norfolk brawn. Turvey Top. William Sawyer. NA
'Twas after dread Pultowa's day. Mazeppa. Byron. EnRP
'Twas all along the Binder Line. Sensitive Sydney. Wallace Irwin. FiBHP
'Twas all on board a ship down in a southern sea. The Golden Vanity. *Unknown.* BaBo
'Twas an evening in November. *Unknown.* CenHV
'Twas at that sober hour when the light of the day is receding. Southey Looks out of the Window at Greta Hill. Robert Southey. *Fr.* A Vision of Judgement. FaBoPP
'Twas at thatt hour of beauty when the setting sun. Robert Bridges. *Fr.* The Testament of Beauty. MoVE; OxBoCh
'Twas at the Cimarron Crossing. Oliver Wiggins. "Stanley Vestal." BPAW
'Twas at the landing-place that's just below Mount Wyse. Port Admiral. Frederick Marryat. MOS
'Twas at the Matin Hour. *Unknown.* OHIP
'Twas at the Pictures, Child, We Met. A. P. Herbert. WhC
'Twas at the royal feast, for Persia won. Alexander's Feast; or, The Power of Music [*or* Musique]. Dryden. ACP; FaPo; FaPoR; FiP; GN; GoBC; GTBS; GTBS-P; HBV-2; LiTB; LoBV; NOBE; OAEL-1; OAEP; OBS; SeCeV; SeCV-2; TrGrPo; WHA; WiR
'Twas at the silent, solemn hour. William and Margaret. David Mallet. NOEC; OBEC
'Twas August, and the fierce sun overhead. East London. Matthew Arnold. OAEP; WGRP
'Twas autumn and 'round me the leaves were descending. The Banks of Champlain. *Unknown.* AmFP
'Twas battered and scarred, and the auctioneer. The Touch of the Master's Hand. Myra Brooks Welch. BLPA; STF; TRV
'Twas Bedford Special Assize, one daft mid-summer's day. Ned Bratts. Robert Browning. VLP
'Twas brillig, and the slithy toves. Jabberwocky. "Lewis Carroll." *Fr.* Through the Looking-Glass. AmMo; BiP; CABA; EBEV; EBVV; FaBoBe; FaBoCo; FaBoNo; FaBV; FaFP; FaPON; FF; FiBHP; FPL; GoJo; HBV-2; HeIP; HoPM; InPK; InPS; LiTB; NA; NBM; NIP; NOBE; NOBL; NoP; NTCP; OAEL-2; OxBChV; PoPl; PoRA; PPoe; PPP; RHPC; SeCeV; SpRo; TEP; TiPo; TreF; TrGrPo; VLP; WhC
'Twas Brillo, and the G.E. Stoves. Jabber-Whacky. Isabelle Di Caprio. QQQ
'Twas but a single Rose. Upon a Virgin Kissing a Rose. Robert Herrick. SeCP; SeCV-1
'Twas Captain Church, bescarred and brown. King Philip's Last Stand. Clinton Scollard. PAH
'Twas Christmas Eve, the month was May. A Tragedy. Tom Masson. OBAL
'Twas Christmas Eve, the snow lay deep. When the Christ Child Came. Frederick E. Weatherly. OHIP
'Twas down at Aunty Jackson's. Walking for That Cake. Ed Harrigan. BLSo
'Twas down at Dan McDevitt's at the corner of this street. Throw Him Down M'Closkey; or, M'Closkey's Great Fight. John W. Kelly. FSN; TreF
'Twas down by Brannigan's Corner, one morning I did stray. Johnson's Motor Car. *Unknown.* FSW
'Twas early in the month of May. Barbara Allen. *Unknown.* OBET
'Twas early in the springtime of the year. Early in the Springtime. *Unknown.* OBET
'Twas early on a May morning. Lady Isabel. *Unknown.* BaBo; ESPB
'Twas early one morning a fair maid arose. A Kiss in the Morning Early. *Unknown.* GBP
'Twas early one morning by the break of the day. All Jolly Fellows That Follow the Plough. *Unknown.* OBET
'Twas earlye, earlye in the spring. Earlye, Earlye, in the Spring. *Unknown.* AmFP
'Twas Euclid, and the theorem pi. Plane Geometry. Emma Rounds. ImOP; QQQ; SpRo
'Twas evening, though not sun-set, and spring-tide. Tamar's Wrestling [*or* The Shepherd and the Nymph]. Walter Savage Landor. *Fr.* Gebir. EnRP; OBNC
'Twas Ever Thus. Henry S. Leigh. FaBoCo; FaBoPa; HBV-1; SpRo
'Twas Ever Thus. *Unknown.* BXAP
'Twas ever thus from childhood's hour! Disaster. Charles Stuart Calverley. CenHV; FM; HBV-1; SpRo
'Twas Friday morn: the train drew near. Through Baltimore. Bayard Taylor. PAH
'Twas Friday morn when we set sail. The Mermaid. *Unknown.* FSW; ViBoFo
'Twas going to snow—'twas snowing! Curse his luck! The Drove-Road. W. W. Gibson. OxBTC
'Twas good to live when all the range. Way Out West. *Unknown.* CoSo
'Twas Goosey Goosey Gander. Goosey Goosey Gander—by Various Authors (Macaulay's Version). William Percy French. CenHV
'Twas homeward bound one night on the deep. Lady Franklin's Lament, *vers.* II. *Unknown.* ShS
'Twas hurry and scurry at Monmouth town. Molly Pitcher. Kate Brownlee Sherwood. PAH
'Twas in a basement table d'hote. Reverie. Don Marquis. FPL; PoLF
'Twas in eighteen hundred and fifty-three. The Greenland Whale Fishery [*or* Greenland Fisheries]. *Unknown.* FSW; ViBoFo
'Twas in heaven pronounced, and 'twas muttered in hell. *See* 'Twas whispered in heaven . . .
'Twas in Koolau I met with the rain. The Rain. *Tr. by* N. B. Emerson. WTO
'Twas in Rosemary Lane, sirs. Neddy Nibble'm and Biddy Finn. *Unknown.* GBP
'Twas in that island summer where. He Loves and He Rides Away. Sydney Dobell. OBNC
'Twas in the days of the Revolution. Emily Geiger. *Unknown.* BLPL; PAL; PoLF;
'Twas in the merry month of May. Barbara Allen. *Unknown.* TrAS

'Twas in the middle of the night. Mary's Ghost. Thomas Hood. FiBHP
'Twas in the month of August, or the middle of July. She Said the Same to Me. *Unknown.* AS
'Twas in the moon of winter time when all the birds had fled. Jesous Ahatonhia [*or* The Huron Carol]. Jesse Edgar Middleton. CaP; OBCP
'Twas in the prime of summer time. The Dream of Eugene Aram [the Murderer]. Thomas Hood. BeLS; EnRP; HBV-2
'Twas in the reign of George the Third. A New Song Called the Gaspee. *Unknown.* PAH
'Twas in the schooner *Kandahar.* The Schooner *Kandahar* *At. to* Sepley Collin. ShS
'Twas in the town of Jacksboro in the spring [*or* year] of seventy-three. The Buffalo Skinners. *Unknown.* AS; BaBo
'Twas in the year '92, in the merry month of June. The Girl on the Greenbriar Shore. *Unknown.* FSW
'Twas in the year of forty-nine. The [Greenland] Whale. *Unknown.* ChTr; GBP
'Twas in the year of 1898, and on the 21st of June. The Albion Battleship Calamity. William McGonagall. BXAP; PeD
'Twas in the year two thousand and one. The Last Man. Thomas Hood. OBRV; VLP
'Twas Jolly, Jolly Wat. C. W. Stubbs. OHIP
'Twas Juet spoke—the Half Moon's mate. The Death of Colman. Thomas Frost. PAH
'Twas June on the face of the earth, June with the rose's breath. The Eve of Bunker Hill. Clinton Scollard. PAH
'Twas just before the last fierce charge. The Last Fierce Charge. *Unknown.* ViBoFo
'Twas late, and the gay company was gone. The Declaration. Nathaniel Parker Willis. OBAL
'Twas late in my long journey, when I had clomb to where. Introduction. Robert Bridges. *Fr.* The Testament of Beauty. MoVE
'Twas like a maelstrom, with a notch. Emily Dickinson. CABA; CMoP; LiTM; SeCeV
(Final Inch, The.) LiTA; NePA
'Twas May upon the mountains, and on the airy wing. The Surprise at Ticonderoga. Mary A. P. Stansbury. PAH
'Twas mercy brought me from my pagan land. On Being Brought from Africa to America. Phillis Wheatley. BALP; FF; GOA; HeIP; NOBA; NOEC; SBG; TAP; TTY; WPE
'Twas midnight on the ocean. The Dying Fisherman's Song. *Unknown.* TreFT
'Twas midnight—Donna Julia was in bed. Byron. *Fr.* Don Juan, I. BiP; UnTE
'Twas midnight—every mortal eye was closed. The Helmets; a Fragment. Thomas Penrose. NOEC
'Twas midsummer: cooling breezes all the languid forests fanned. The Death of Jefferson. Hezekiah Butterworth. PAH
'Twas more than a million years ago. Annabel Lee. Stanley Huntley. SpRo
'Twas my pleasure to walk in the river meadows. The Midnight Court. Brian Merriman, *tr. by* Frank O'Connor. AnIL
'Twas my wont to wander beside the stream. The Midnight Court. Brian Merriman, *tr. by* Arland Ussher. OnYI
'Twas Night. *Unknown.* OBS
'Twas night; the noise and bustle of the day. Bologna, and Byron. Samuel Rogers. *Fr.* Italy. OBRV
'Twas night upon the Darro. The Thanksgiving for America. Hezekiah Butterworth. PAH
'Twas noontide of summer. Evening Star. Poe. AP
'Twas not as lonesome as it might have been. The Cricket Kept the House. Edith M. Thomas. OBCA
'Twas not enough, Ben Johnson, to be thought. To His Friend Ben. Johnson, of His Horace Made English. Lord Herbert of Cherbury. AnAnS-2
'Twas not my wish. About the Shelleys. *Unknown.* WhC
" 'Twas not so in my time," surly Grumio exclaims. Epigram. Samuel Bishop. NOEC
'Twas not the brown of chestnut boughs. Gwendoline. Bayard Taylor. BXAP
'Twas November the fourth, in the year of ninety-one. Sainclaire's Defeat. *Unknown.* PAH
'Twas of a brisk young sailor, as I have heard it said. Johnny German. *Unknown.* AmFP
" 'Twas of a gay young cavalier." Riddles Wisely Expounded. *Unknown.* ViBoFo
'Twas of a lovely creature who dwelled by the seaside. Mary in the Silvery Tide. *Unknown.* OBET
'Twas of a maiden both young and fair. The Dark-eyed Sailor. *Unknown.* ShS
'Twas of a nobleman's daughter. Caroline and Her Young Sailor Bold. *Unknown.* AmFP
'Twas of a shepherd's son. Blow Away the Morning Dew. *Unknown.* OBET
'Twas of a young brickster a-going from his work. The Brickster. *Unknown.* OBET
'Twas on a holy Thursday, their innocent faces clean. Holy Thursday. Blake. *Fr.* Songs of Innocence. CH; EnRP; HBV-1; InPS; LAuP; NOBE; NOEC; NoP; OAEL-2; OAEP; OBEC; OFD; SCV; TEP; TrCP
'Twas on a lofty vase's side. Ode on [*or* On] the Death of a Favourite Cat, Drowned in a Tub of Gold Fishes [*or* On a Favourite Cat Drowned . . . *or* The Cat and the Fish]. Thomas Gray. BeLS; EBEV; FaBoBe; FaBoCo; FM; FPL; GN; GTBS; GTBS-P; HBV-1; HoPM; InMe; InvP; LAuP; LiTB; NOBE; NOBL; NOEC; NoP; OAEL-1; OAEP; OBEC; OBEV; PCat; PoEL-3; PoLF; PoPle; PoRA; PPP; SeCeV; TEP; WiR
'Twas on a longstone lighthouse there dwelt an English maid. Grace Darling. *Unknown.* OBET
'Twas on a Monday morning. Charlie, He's [*or* Is] My Darling. Burns. HBV-2; ViBoPo
'Twas on a Monday morning, just at the break of day. Maggie Mac. *Unknown.* AmFP
'Twas on a Monday morning, the first I saw my darling. Hanging Out the Linen Clothes. *Unknown.* AS
'Twas on a night, an evening bright. Proud Lady Margaret. *Unknown.* ESPB
'Twas on a pleasant mountain. The Battle of King's Mountain. *Unknown.* PAH
'Twas on a simmer's afternoon. The Lass o' Gowrie. Lady Nairne. HBV-1
'Twas on a summer noon, in Stainsford mead. My Ox Duke. John Dyer. NOEC
'Twas on a summer's day—the sixth of June. Byron. *Fr.* Don Juan, I. PPP
'Twas on a windy night. The Sabine Farmer's Serenade. Francis Sylvester Mahony. HBV-2
'Twas on an evening fair I went to take the air. Willie's Fatal Visit. *Unknown.* BaBo; ESPB
'Twas on board the sloop of war *Wasp,* boys. The *Wasp*'s Frolic. *Unknown.* PAH
'Twas on Lake Erie's broad expanse. John Maynard. Horatio Alger, Jr. BeLS; BLPA; FaBoBe
'Twas on one dark and cheerless night to the south'ard of the Cape. The Flying Dutchman. *Unknown.* ShS
'Twas on the eighth of January, just at the dawn of day. The Battle of New Orleans. *Unknown.* AmFP
'Twas on the field of Antietam where many's the soldier fell. The Battle of Antietam Creek. *Unknown.* AmFP
'Twas on the first of February from Lunenburg we set sail. The *Donzella* and the *Ceylon.* *At. to* Daniel Smith. ShS
'Twas on the fourteenth day of April we sailed from the land. The Bold *Princess Royal, vers.* II. *Unknown.* ShS
'Twas on the glorious day. The Death of General Pike. Laughton Osborn. PAH
'Twas on the shores that round our coast. The Yarn of the *Nancy Bell.* W. S. Gilbert. BeLS; BLPA; CenHV; EtS; EvOK; FaBoBe; FaBoCh; FaBoCo; FaBV; FaFP; HBV-2; HoPM; InMe; MOS; MoShBr; NOBL; OnMSP; TreFS; TrGrPo; VLP
'Twas on the twelfth of April. Sumter—a Ballad of 1861. *Unknown.* PAH
'Twas one October mornin'. Bigerlow. *Unknown.* AS
'Twas one of the charmed days. The Heart of All the Scene. Emerson. *Fr.* Woodnotes. AA
'Twas one of those dark, cloudy days. Emily Brontë. VLP
'Twas only a cheerful, radiant smile. Life's Little Things. *Unknown.* STF
'Twas out upon mid ocean that the San Jacinto hailed. Death of the Lincoln Despotism. *Unknown.* PAH
'Twas over hills and over dales. Locks and Bolts. *Unknown.* OBET
'Twas silent below on the desert. Death Valley. Jack H. Lee. BPAW
'Twas so, I saw thy birth: that drowsy [*or* drowsie] lake. The Shower [*or* Showre]. Henry Vaughan. AnAnS-1; FaBoPP; LiTB; MePo; SeCP; ViBoPo
'Twas spring, and dawn returning breathed new-born. Idyll of the Rose. Ausonius, *tr. by* John Addington Symonds. AWP
'Twas summer, and the spot a cool retreat. A Dream. Elizabeth Clementine Kinney. AA
'Twas summer, and the sun had mounted high. The Wanderer [*or* The Ruined Cottage]. Wordsworth. The Excursion, I. EnRP, *abr.*; NoP; OAEL-2
'Twas sung of old in hut and hall. Birthday Verses Written in a Child's Album. James Russell Lowell. OxBChV
'Twas sure a luckless planet. Out of Luck. Abraham ibn Ezra, *tr. by* Solomon Solis-Cohen. TrJP
'Twas the body of Judas Iscariot. The Ballad of Judas Iscariot. Robert Buchanan. HBV-2

'Twas the dead of the night. By the pine-knot's red light. New England's Chevy Chase. Edward Everett Hale. HBV-2; HBVY; PAH; PAL; YaD
'Twas the deep mid-watch of the silent night. The Cid's Rising. Felicia Dorothea Hemans. OBRV
'Twas the dream of a God. Ireland. Dora Sigerson Shorter. OBEV; OBVV; OxBI
'Twas the end of round-up, the last day of June. Whose Old Cow? *Unknown.* CoSo
'Twas the eve before Christmas. "Good night," had been said. Annie and Willie's Prayer. Sophia P. Snow. BeLS; BLPA
'Twas the gray of early morning when the dreadful cry of "Fire!" The Milwaukee Fire. *Unknown.* AmFP
'Twas the heart of the murky night, and the lowest ebb of the tide. Wayne at Stony Point. Clinton Scollard. PAH
'Twas the lean coyote told me, baring his slavish soul. The Desert. Henry Herbert Knibbs. BPAW
'Twas the night before Christmas, when all through the house. A Visit from St. Nicholas [*or* The Night before Christmas]. Clement Clarke Moore. AA; BeLS; BLPA; FaBoBe; FaBV; FaFP; FaPo; FaPON; FPL; HBV-1; HBVY; NTCP; OBAL; OBCA; OBCP; OHFP; OnMSP; OxBChV; PaPo; PChr; PoPl; RHCP; SiSoSe; TiPo; TreF; WBLP; YaD
'Twas the proud Sir Peter Parker came sailing in from the sea. The Boasting of Sir Peter Parker. Clinton Scollard. PAH
'Twas the soul of Judas Iscariot. Judas Iscariot. Robert Buchanan. OBVV; OxBoCh
'Twas the spring in the air. Danny's Wooing. David McKee Wright. PoAu-1
'Twas the very verge of May. Dewey at Manila. Robert Underwood Johnson. HBV-2; PAH
'Twas the year of the famine in Plymouth of old. Five Kernels of Corn. Hezekiah Butterworth. PAH
'Twas twilight, and the sunless day went down. The Shipwreck. Byron. *Fr.* Don Juan, II. OBRV; WHA
'Twas warm—at first—like us. Emily Dickinson. CMoP; LiTA; QFR; SoSe
'Twas when bright Cynthia with her silver car. A Night-Piece; or, Modern Philosophy. Christopher Smart. NOEC
Twas when fleet Snowball's head was waxen gray. Sir Walter Scott. *Fr.* The Fortunes of Nigel, *ch.* 15. NBM
'Twas when Tacita hushed the noisy world. The Dream. "Brian Bendo." NOEC
'Twas when the friendly shade of night. To Clarissa. Robert, Earl Nugent. NOEC
'Twas when the rain fell steady an' the Ark was pitched and ready. The Legends of Evil II. Kipling. MoShBr
'Twas When the Seas Were Roaring. John Gay. *See* Ballad: "'Twas when the seas were roaring."
'Twas when the spousal time of May. Coventry Patmore. *Fr.* The Angel in the House, II, vii. GBL
'Twas whispered in Heaven [*or* in heaven pronounced, and], 'twas muttered in hell. A Riddle. Catherine M. Fanshawe. ChTr; GN
'Twas wond'rous, then, a bardling should be found. The Tribulations of an Uneducated Poet in the 1760's. James Woodhouse. *Fr.* The Life and Lucubrations of Crispinus Scriblerus. NOEC
'Twas yesterday He made me and tomorrow I shall die. Song of the Gulf Stream. Francis Alan Ford. EtS
Tweed and Till. *Unknown.* BoNaP; FaBoCh; FaBoPP; GBP; PV
(Rivers Till and Tweed.) WhC
(Two Rivers, The.) ChTr; OBEV
Tweedle-Dum and Tweedle-Dee. Mother Goose. NA; NOBL; OxNR
"Tweet" pipes the robin as the cat creeps by. The Firetail's Nest. John Clare. EnRP
12th Dance—Getting Leather by Language—21 February 1964. Jackson MacLow. CoPo
Twelfth day of Christmas, The. The Twelve Days of Christmas. *Unknown.* OxBoLi
Twelfth Night. Philip Booth. NePoEA
Twelfth Night. Peter Scupham. OBCP
Twelfth Night, *sels.* Shakespeare.
Come Away, Come Away, Death, *fr.* II, iv. ElL; ELP; GBL; NOBE; NoP; OAEP; PoPle; ViBoPo; WHA
(Clown's Song, The.) CTC
(Come Away, Death.) PoRA; SeCeV
(Dirge: "Come away, come away, death.") OBEV
(Dirge of Love.) GTBS; GTBS-P
(Love's Despair.) TrGrPo
(Song: "Come away, come away, death.") FiP; PoEL-2
Food of Love, The, *fr.* I, i. TrGrPo
(Music.) TreFS
Love Concealed, *fr.* II, iv. TreFS
(Patience on a Monument.) TrGrPo
O Mistress Mine, Where Are You Roaming? *fr.* II, iii. AWP; BiP; ElL; ELP; EnRePo; GBL; HAP; InPS; LoBV; NOBE; OAEL-1; OAEP; OLR; ViBoPo; WHA
(Carpe Diem.) GTBS; GTBS-P
(Clown's Song: "O Mistris mine where are you roming?") FaBoEn
(Feste's Song.) BoLoP; OBSC
(O [*or* Oh] Mistress Mine.) CTC; FaBV; FaFP; HeIP; InMe; LiTB; NoP; OxBoLi; PoRA; SeCeV; TreFT; TrGrPo
(Song: "O mistress mine! where are you roaming?") FiP; GoJo; HBV-1
(Sweet-and-Twenty.) OBEV
"Once more, Cesario," *fr.* II, iv. SCV
"What is love? 'tis not hereafter," *fr.* II, iii. TreFT
When That I Was and a Little Tiny Boy, *fr.* V, i. CH; EBEV; ElL; EnRePo; FaBoCh; HBV-1; HeIP; LiTB; LoBV; NOBE; NoP; OAEL-1; OAEP; PoRA; PPoe; ViBoPo
(Feste's Song.) OBSC; OxBoLi
(Song: "When that I was and a little tiny boy.") FiP; PoEL-2
(Wind and the Rain, The.) WiR
12th Raga: For Jon Wieners. David Meltzer. NeAP
Twelve, The, *sel.* Alexander Blok, *tr. fr. Russian.*
"Black Night./ White snow," *tr. by* Babette Deutsch *and* Avrahm Yarmolinsky. AWP
Twelve and ugly. Dresses. Kathleen Fraser. NMM
Twelve Articles. Swift. InMe
Twelve Bells/ Benny's on the ropes. The Memory of Boxer Benny (Kid) Paret. Frank Lima. PoNe
Twelve Days of Christmas, The. *Unknown.* AmFP; FaFP; FSW; OxBoLi; OxNR; PChr; TreFT
Twelve elements in slow orbit, The. Upon Looking at a Book of Astrology. David McFadden. NeAC
Twelve-Elf raises his left hand, The. Christian Morgenstern, *tr. fr. German by* W. D. Snodgrass *and* Lore Segal. WSC
Twelve Gates to the City. Nikki Giovanni. IHMS; PoBA
Twelve Gates to the City. *Unknown.* FSW
Twelve good friends. Peter and John. Elinor Wylie. HBMV; MoAB; MoAmPo; MoBS
"Twelve herds of oxen, no lesse flockes of sheepe." Homer, *tr. by* George Chapman. *Fr.* The Odyssey, XIV. CTC
Twelve hundred million men are spread. Kipling. PV
Twelve Lines about the Burning Bush. Melech Ravitch, *tr. fr. Yiddish by* Ruth Whitman. VWA
Twelve Months, The. "Gregory Gander." TreFT
Twelve o'clock./ Along the reaches of the street. Rhapsody on a Windy Night. T. S. Eliot. CMoP; HeIP
12 O'Clock News. Elizabeth Bishop. GP; OxBC
12 October. Myra Cohn Livingston. NTCP; RHPC
12 Oct. Allen Planz. WOLT
Twelve Oxen, The. *Unknown. See* I Have Twelve Oxen.
Twelve pears hanging high. Mother Goose. OxNR
12 Photographs of Yellowstone. Ronald Koertge. GP
Twelve Properties or Conditions of a Lover, The, *sels.* Sir Thomas More. EnRePo
Eleventh Property, The.
First Property, The.
Seventh Property, The.
Twelve snails went walking after night. The Haughty Snail-King. Vachel Lindsay. SO
Twelve stars upon the bow of her. Our Lady of the Skies. James M. Hayes. ISi
Twelve Weapons of Spiritual Battle, The, *sels.* Sir Thomas More.
Eternal Reward, Eternal Pain. EnRePo
Peace of a Good Mind, The. EnRePo; FaBoRV
This Life a Dream and Shadow. EnRePo
Twelve years ago I made a mock. School and Schoolfellows. Winthrop Mackworth Praed. OBRV
Twelve years ago I was twelve. From. Richard Terrill. AMV-81
Twelve years denied me. This dusk. Seabirds. Robert B. Smith. LFAC
Twelve years old, my father put. Harvest Time. G. A. Watermeyer, *tr. by* Guy Butler, Uys Krige, *and* Jack Cope. PeSA
Twentieth century, The/ crawls to the side. Deeper in the Tank—the Last Middle East Crisis, 1972. Eugene Ruggles. SOTS
Twentieth-Century Blues. Kenneth Fearing. CMoP
Twentieth year is well-nigh past, The. To Mary [*or* My Mary *or* To the Same]. William Cowper. EnLoPo; EnRP; FiP; GTBS; GTBS-P; LAuP; NOEC; OAEP; OBEC; OBEV; TreFS
20. Barbara Guest. PoM
Twenty abreast down the Golden Street ten thousand riders marched. Riders of the Stars. Henry Herbert Knibbs. BPAW
Twenty Below. R. A. D. Ford. CaP; NOBC
Twenty below. It is too cold. Prayer for Fish. Ronald Wallace. AMV-80
Twenty bracelets and a cackle later. Janis Joplin and the Folding Company. Bayla Winters. AMV-80

Twenty brothers of Eynhallow, The. Our Lady of the Waves. George Mackay Brown. NePoEA-2
28 VIII 69. Laura Chester. IHMS
Twenty-eight young men bathe by the shore. Song of Myself, XI. Walt Whitman. HAP; NoP
25 December 1960. Ingrid Jonker, *tr. fr. Afrikaans by* Jack Cope *and* Uys Krige. PeSA
25:I:68. Philip Whalen. PoM
25 Spontaneous Lines Greeting the World. Jim Tyack. AMV-80
Twenty-fifth Year of His Life, The. C. P. Cavafy, *tr. fr. Greek by* Edmund Keeley *and* Philip Sherrard. PeHV
Twenty Foolish Fairies. Nancy Byrd Turner. SUS
Twenty-four Years. Dylan Thomas. CMoP; MAT; MoAB; NAs; NoAM;
Twenty Golden Years Ago. James Clarence Mangan. NBM, *abr.*; OnYI
Twenty lost years have stol'n their hours away. Alone in an Inn at Southampton, April the 25th, 1737. Aaron Hill. NOEC
Twenty men crossing a bridge. Metaphors of a Magnifico. Wallace Stevens. SOTW
Twenty men stand watching the muckers. Muckers. Carl Sandburg. CTBA; SaC
29 (A Dream in Two Parts). Ai. MAYP
2976. Julia Uceda, *tr. fr. Spanish by* Willis Barnstone. BoWoP
Twenty nine years of stale cake and flat ale. The Gorilla at Twenty Nine Years. J. D. Reed. NeAC
29th Dance—Having an Instrument—22 March 1964. Jackson MacLow. CoPo
29th Month, The. Stan Rice. NPGG
Twenty-one Love Poems, *sels.* Adrienne Rich.
"Across a city from you, I'm with you," XVI. PeHV
"I come home from you through the early light of spring," IV. BoWoP
"Sleeping, turning in turn like planets," XII. PeHV
"That conversation we were always on the edge," XX. BoWoP
"Wherever in this city, screens flicker," I. PeHV
Twenty-one Sonnets, *sels.* C. K. Stead. OCNZ
"Rain, and a flurry of wind shaking the pear's white blossom," 2.
"Spring hides scars of Dickens Street but the old cottages," 6.
Spring 1974, 1.
Twenty-one Years. *Unknown.* AmFP
Twenty-second of August, The. The Cruise of the Fair American. *Unknown.* PAH
Twenty-second of December, The. Bryant. GN
Twenty-seven Bums Give a Prostitute the Once. E. E. Cummings. OBAL
Twenty Stars to Match His Face. William Stanley Braithwaite. HBMV
Twenty-third Flight. Earle Birney. HeIP; OxBC; SoSe
Twenty-third Psalm, The. George Herbert. EBCP
Twenty-third Street Runs into Heaven. Kenneth Patchen. ErPo
Twenty-three Tanka, *sel.* Kyōgoku Tamekane, *tr. fr. Japanese by* Burton Watson
On Love. LLLT
22 Miles. José Angel Gutiérrez. FIA
Twenty-two Minutes. Lorri Martinez. LFAC
Twenty white horses on a red hill. *Unknown.* PrIm
Twenty-Year Marriage. Ai. BoWoP; GP; MAYP
Twenty Years After. Evan V. Shute. CaP
Twenty Years Ago. *Unknown, at. to* A. J. Gault *and also to* Dill Armor Smith. *See* Forty Years Ago.
Twenty years are gone. Palinode. Oliver St. John Gogarty. OBMV
Twenty Years Hence. Walter Savage Landor. TrGrPo; ViBoPo
("Twenty years hence my eyes may grow.") GBL
'Twer May, but ev'ry leaf wer dry. A Wife a-Prais'd. William Barnes. EBVV
'Twer where the zun did warm the lewth. The Bean Vield. William Barnes. VLP
'Twere a dree night, a dree night, as the squire's end drew nigh. The Dree Night. *Unknown.* ChTr
'Twere folly if ever/ The Whigs should endeavor. A New Ballad. *Unknown.* APAS
'Twere time that I died too, now she is dead. The Lady Venetia Digby. Ben Jonson. GoBC
'Twere well your judgments but in plays did range. Dryden. *Fr.* The Spanish Friar, *prologue.* OBSV
Twice. Ian Hamilton Finlay. BSV
Twice. Christina Rossetti. GBL; NOBE; OBEV; OBNC; OBVV; TrCP; ViBoPo; VLP
Twice a week. Visit. Randolph Outlaw. LFAC
Twice a Week the Winter Thorough. A. E. Housman. LiSp
Twice a year. Alma Mater, Forget Me. William Cole. FiBHP
Twice Fed. A. A. Bassett. HBV-2
Twice happy violets! that first had birth. Violets in Thaumantia's Bosome. Sir Edward Sherburne. OBS
"Twice have I sought Clan-Alpine's glen." Roderick Dhu. Sir Walter Scott. *Fr.* The Lady of the Lake, V. OBRV
Twice I have written you that I am unhappy. A Letter to Her Father. Inib-sarri, *tr. by* Willis Barnstone. BoWoP
Twice nineteen years, dear Nancy, on this day. On Our Thirty-ninth Wedding Day. Jonathan Odell. CaP
Twice or thrice had I loved thee. Air[e] and Angels. John Donne. AnAnS-1; EnRePo; JCP; MeLP; MePo; OAEL-1; OBS; Prf; SeCP; SeCV-1
Twice recently young girls have/ given me the finger. Finger of Necessity. Coleman Barks. TW
Twice Shy. Seamus Heaney. NCSH; TwCP
Twice thirty centuries and more ago. The First Spousal. Coventry Patmore. *Fr.* The Unknown Eros. OBVV
Twice Times Then Is Now. Ibn Hazm Al-Andalusi, *tr. fr. Persian by* Omar Pound. OBVE
Twice upon a time. Duality. Dannie Abse. NoAM
Twickenham Ferry. Theophile Marzials. HBV-1
Twickham Tweer. Jack Prelustky. RHPC
Twicknam Garden. John Donne. AnAnS-1; EBEV; EnLoPo; FaBoPP; MeLP; MePo; OBS; PoEL-2; SeCP
(Twickenham Garden.) LoBV; TEP
Twig turned in her hand and the diviner said, The: "Water." The Water-Witch. Martha Eugenie Perry. CaP
Twilight. Olive Custance. HBV-1
Twilight. Hazel Hall. HBMV
Twilight. Heine, *tr. fr. German by* Louis Untermeyer. AWP
Twilight. D. H. Lawrence. OBMV
Twilight. Longfellow. CH
Twilight. John Masefield. OxBTC
Twilight. Virginia McCormick. HBMV
Twilight. Agnes Mary Frances Robinson. HBV-1
Twilight: and pine trees keep the blessed enclosure. Convent Cemetery, Mount Carmel. Sister Mary St. Virginia. GoBC
Twilight, a timid fawn, went glimmering by. Refuge. "Æ." HBV-1; OnYI
Twilight at Sea. Amelia B. Welby. AA; HBV-1
Twilight at the Heights. Joaquin Miller. AA
Twilight at the Zoo. Alex Rodger. NCSH
Twilight. By now the genial sea of dusk. Half Past Four, October. Anna Hajnal, *tr. by* Daniel Hoffman. BoWoP
Twilight Calm. Christina Rossetti. BoNaP; OBNC
Twilight Comes. Hayden Carruth. NNaP
Twilight comes, The; the sun. June Twilight. John Masefield. GoYe
Twilight falls on the hill. Vespers. Odell Shepard. TrPWD
Twilight glitters on the fragmented glass. Judeebug's Country. Joe Johnson. PoBA
Twilight had fallen, austere and grey. The Tomtit. Walter de la Mare. FM
Twilight has fallen and the candled gloom. Peter Titheradge. Teatime Variations: After John Keats. FaBoPa
Twilight hours like birds flew by, The. Twilight at Sea. Amelia B. Welby. AA; HBV-1
Twilight in California. Philip Dow. AmPA
Twilight in Middle March, A. Francis Ledwidge. BIrV; OnYI; OxBI; WHA
Twilight is here, soft breezes bow the grass. In Exile. Emma Lazarus. SBG
Twilight is sad and cloudy, The. Twilight. Longfellow. CH
Twilight is spacious, near things in it seem far. Miracles. Conrad Aiken. HBMV; MoAmPo
Twilight it is, and the far woods are dim, and the rooks cry. Twilight. John Masefield. OxBTC
Twilight leaned mirrored in a pool. The Old Angler. Walter de la Mare. GoTL; OAEP
Twilight of Disquietude, The, *sels.* Christopher Brennan. PoAu-1
My Heart Was Wandering in the Sands.
Years That Go to Make Me Man, The.
Twilight of Earth, The. "Æ." AnIL
Twilight of Freedom. Osip Mandelstam, *tr. fr. Russian by* Andrew Glaze. VWA
Twilight on Sumter. Richard Henry Stoddard. PAH
Twilight on Tweed. Andrew Lang. BSV; EBVV; OBVV
(Remembered Melody, *much abr.*) PoSH
Twilight People, The. "Seumas O'Sullivan." OnYI
Twilight. Red in the west. The Wild Duck. John Masefield. BrPo
Twilight Shadows round Me Fall, The, *with music.* Ernest Edwin Ryden. AH
Twilight Song. John Hunter-Duvar. *Fr.* De Roberval. WHW
Twilight Song. E. A. Robinson. HBV-2
Twilight Thoughts in Israel. Melech Ravitch, *tr. fr. Yiddish by* Seymour Levitan. VWA
Twilight Time. Samuel Palmer. *See* Shoreham: Twilight Time.
Twilight twiles in the vernal vale, The. In the Gloaming. James C. Bayles. NA

Twilight was coming on, yet through the gloom. Wordsworth. *Fr.* The Prelude, V. SyP
Twilighted reek in a blood-rugged hall. Stood-up. Bruce Byfield. AMV-80
Twilights. James Wright. LCAP; NaP
Twilight's Last Gleaming. Arthur W. Monks. OFD
Twilit Revelation. Léonie Adams. MoAB; MoAmPo
" 'Twill take some getting." "Sir, I think 'twill so." Man and Dog. Edward Thomas. FM
Twin. Phyllis Haring. PeSA
Twin Aces. Keith Wilson. Psk
Twin songs there are, of joyance, or of pain. Thysia, II. Morton Luce. HBV-1
Twin stars through my purpling pane. Dusk. Angelina Weld Grimké. CDC
Twin streaks twice higher than cumulus. Vapor Trails. Gary Snyder. CAPP
Twine then the rays. Psycholophon. Gelett Burgess. CenHV; NA
Twined together and, as is customary. Never Such Love. Robert Graves. BoLoP; FaBoEn
"Twiner," A. J. A. Lindon. DBV
Twinings Orange Pekoe. Judith Moffett. PoA
Twink Drives Back, in a Bad Mood, from a Party in Massachusetts. George Amabile. NYBP
Twinkle of twilight. Rapture. Randolph Carlson. AMV-80
Twinkle, twinkle, little bat. The Mad Hatter's Song. "Lewis Carroll." *Fr.* Alice's Adventures in Wonderland. FaBoNo; NOBL; Par; SpRo; WhC
Twinkle, twinkle, little star. Paul Dehn. SpRo
Twinkle, twinkle, little star. The Star. Jane Taylor. FaBoBe; FaFP; FaPON; HBV-1; HBVY; NTCP; OxBChV; OxNR; Par; RHPC; SoPo; SpRo; TiPo; TreF
Twinkling Earn, The. John Davidson. *Fr.* Winter in Strathearn. PoSH
Twinkum, twankum, twirlum, twitch. The Little Creature. Walter de la Mare. EvOK
Twins, The. Berton Braley. TDH
Twins. Robert Graves. FaBoEE; PV
Twins, The. Henry Sambrooke Leigh. CenHV; FaPON; HBV-2; HBVY; PoPl; RHPC; ShM; TiPo
Twins. William Matthews. MAYP
Twins. "Owen Meredith." ErPo
Twins, The. Elizabeth Madox Roberts. TiPo
Twins, The. Karl Shapiro. MiAP; MoAmPo; TrJP; TwAmPo
Twins, The. Mona Van Duyn. GP
Twins, The. Judith Wright. PoAu-2
Twirling your blue skirts, travel[l]ing the sward. Blue Girls. John Crowe Ransom. ChTr; CMoP; GBL; LiTA; MoAB; MoAmPo; MoVE; NoAM; PrIm; TAP; TreFT; TwAmPo; VGW; WeW
Twist about, turn about. *Unknown.* OxNR
Twist me a crown of windflowers. A Crown of Windflowers. Christina Rossetti. OxBChV
Twist-Rime on Spring. Arthur Guiterman. PoSC
Twist thou and twine! in light and gloom. Featherstone's Doom. Robert Stephen Hawker. OBNC
Twist Ye, Twine Ye! Even So. Sir Walter Scott. *Fr.* Guy Mannering, *ch.* 4. EnRP
Twisted apple, with rain and magian fire, The. June Morning. Hugh McCrae. PoAu-1
Twister Twisting Twine. John Wallis. ChTr
("When a twister a-twisting will twist with a twist.") FaBoNo; OxNR
Twitched strings, the clang of metal, beaten drums. Javanese Dancers. Arthur Symons. VLP
Twitching in the cactus. Deathwatch. Michael S. Harper. AmPA; PoBA
Twittingpan seized my arm, though I'd have gone. The Encounter. Edgell Rickword. OxBTC
'Twixt Carrowbrough Edge and Settlingstones. Old Skinflint. W. W. Gibson. OBMV
'Twixt clouded heights Spain hurls to doom. The *Brooklyn* at Santiago. Wallace Rice. PAH
'Twixt Cup and Lip. Mark Hollis. FiBHP
Twixt devil and deep sea, man hacks his caves. Arachne. William Empson. InvP; MoVE; OBMV
'Twixt East and West a giant shape she grew. Sonnet on the Crimean War. William Forster. CBAP
'Twixt failure and success the point's so fine. Don't Give Up. *Unknown.* FaFP
'Twixt handkerchief and nose. A Rub. John Banister Tabb. OBAL
Twixt nature and Pygmalion there might appear great strife. *Unknown.* OAEL-1
Twixt optimist and pessimist. Optimist and Pessimist. *At. to* McLandburgh Wilson. TreFT
'Twixt the coastline and the border lay the town of Grog-an'-Grumble. Grog-an'-Grumble Steeplechase. Henry Lawson. PH
Twixt the Girthhead and Langwoodend. The Lads of Wamphray. *Unknown.* ESPB
'Twixt the seas and the deserts. Just California. John S. McGroarty. BPAW
Two. Margarita Aliger, *tr. fr. Russian by* Elaine Feinstein. VWA
Two. Robert Canzoneri. HoPM
Two. Hugo von Hofmannsthal, *tr. fr. German.* AWP, *tr. by* Ludwig Lewisohn; TrJP, *tr. by* Jethro Bithell
Two. Moishe Kulbak, *tr. fr. Yiddish by* Ruth Whitman. VWA
Two. Winfield Townley Scott. NYBP
2 a.m./December, and still no moon. Late Moon. Philip Levine. LCAP
2 AM: moonlight. The train has stopped. Track. Tomas Tranströmer, *tr. by* Robert Bly. EAS
Two against One. *Unknown, tr. fr. Greek by* Louis Untermeyer. UnTE
Two aldermen, three lawyers, five physicians. Of a Zealous Lady. Sir John Harington, *after* Martial. FaBoEE
Two-an'-Six. Claude McKay. BANP
Two Anchors, The. Richard Henry Stoddard. BeLS
Two and One Are a Problem. Ogden Nash. FiBHP
Two and thirty is the ploughman. Etching. W. E. Henley. In Hospital, XII. BrPo
Two Angels. Richard Monckton Milnes. OBRV
Two Angels, The. Whittier. AA
Two angels came through the gate of Heaven. A Song of Two Angels. Laura E. Richards. AA
Two angels from the North. Charm: Burns. *Unknown.* FaBoUs
Two Animals, One Flood. Diane Glancy. STE
Two Appeals to John Harralson, Agent, Nitre and Mining Bureau, C.S.A. *Unknown.* OBAL
Two apples, a book. Autumn Eve. Amelia Andriello. SiSoSe
Two April Mornings, The. Wordsworth. EBEV; EnRP; GTBS; GTBS-P; HBV-2
Two Are Together. Geoffrey Grigson. GBL
Two Argosies. Wallace Bruce. AA
Two Armies. Stephen Spender. ChMP; CoBMV; OBWP; OxBTC; SeCeV; WaP
Two armies covered hill and plain. Music in Camp. John R. Thompson. AA; BLPA; HBV-2
Two at a Fireside. Edwin Markham. TRV
Two at Showtime. Suzanne Brabant. PH
Two baths in one day! Man and Woman. Don L. Lee. NeAC
Two bells to pealing through my age. Harald, the Agnostic Ale-loving Old Shepherd Enemy of the Whisky-drinking Ploughmen and Harvesters, Walks over the Sabbath Hill to the Shearing. George Mackay Brown. NePoEA-2
Two Birds. Kathleen Linnell. AMV-81
Two birds within one nest. Home. Dora Greenwell. HBV-1
Two Bits. Sharlot M. Hall. BPAW
Two black heifers and a red. Drinking Time. D. J. O'Sullivan. OnYI
Two blind mice. Paul Dehn. *Fr.* Rhymes for a Modern Nursery. FiBHP
Two bloated bodies in rotted rags. War. Sulamith Ish-Kishor. GoYe
Two blue glasses of neat. Living in the Moment. Marilyn Hacker. NYP
Two bodies have I. *Unknown.* OxNR
Two books a prayer shawl and one glass eye. Formations. William Freedman. VWA
Two-boots in the forest walks. The Intruder. James Reeves. OnUR; PDV
Two Boys, The. Mary Lamb. OBRV
Two boys uncoached are tossing a poem together. Catch. Robert Francis. HeIP; InPK; LiSp; NCSH; PP
Two boys, whose birth beyond all questions springs. Charles Churchill. *Fr.* The Prophecy of Famine. OBSV
Two bronzes, but they were passing bronze before. Two Wrestlers. Robert Francis. LiSp
Two Brothers, The. *Unknown.* AmFP
Two brothers we are. *Unknown.* OxNR
Two brown heads with tossing curls. Katie Lee and Willy [*or* Willie] Grey. *Unknown, at. to* Josie R. Hunt *and to* J.H. Pixley. BeLS; BLPA
Two Bums Walk Out of Eden. Robert Francis. PPON
Two Burdens, The. Philip Bourke Marston. VLP
Two Campers in Cloud Country. Sylvia Plath. NYBP
Two Captains, The. William Johnson Cory. *See* Ballad for a Boy, A.
Two Carols to Our Lady. *Unknown.* *See* I Sing of a Maiden and Rosa Mystica.
Two caterpillars crawling on a leaf. Immortality. Joseph Jefferson. BLPA
Two Cats/ One up a tree. Diamond Cut Diamond. Ewart Milne. FaBoCh; NeIP; PCat
Two-Cent Coal. *Unknown.* AmFP
Two centuries ago Linnaeus said "nose frightful, tears pitiful" of you. The Sloth. Isabella Gardner. BoAnP
Two Childhood Memories. Al Zolynas. LTB
Two Children, The. Emily Brontë. PoEL-5
(A.E.) NBM

Two Chorale Preludes. Geoffrey Hill. OxBC
Two Christs were at Golgotha. Early Lynching. Carl Sandburg. MoAmPo
Two Chronometers. Kenneth Slessor. *Fr.* Five Visions of Captain Cook. SeCePo
Two Clouds. Lawrence Raab. AMV-80
Two coffees in the Español, the last. Conrad Aiken. Preludes for Memnon, II. FYAP; LiTA; NoAM; TwAmPo
Two college sophs of Cambridge growth. Cassinus and Peter. Swift. OAEL-1; PPP
Two Communist Poets. Irving Layton. AMV-81
Two Countries. José Martí, *tr. fr. Spanish by* Mona Hinton. TTY
Two cows stand transfixed. Blurry Cow. Chase Twichell. MAYP
Two Coyotes, The. T. Walking Eagle Marietta. LFAC
Two Days. W. E. Henley. VLP
Two days ago the sky was. Autumn Rain. Kenneth Rexroth. NU
Two days she miss'd her dove, and then alas! Minnie and Her Dove. Charles Tennyson Turner. FM
Two Decisions. Vernon Watkins. OxBTC
Two Dedications. Gwendolyn Brooks.
  Chicago Picasso, The. BPo; EyDe; LiTM
  Wall, The. PoBA
Two Deserts, The. Coventry Patmore. BoNaP
Two Dogs ("Two dogs on Bournemouth beach: a mongrel, one"). John Davidson. FM
Two Dogs Have I. Ogden Nash. GDP
Two Drinking Songs. T'ao Yuan-ming, *ad. by* Robert Bly.
  "I built my hut near where people live," 1. NU
  (I Built My Hut, *tr. by* Arthur Waley.) AWP
  "Such a strong color on the late chrysanthemums," 2. NU
Two drummers sat at dinner, in a grand hotel one day. My Mother Was a Lady; or, If Jack Were Only Here. Edward B. Marks. FSN; TreF; YaD
Two dykes went their separate routes. Limerick. *Unknown.* PeHV
Two Egrets. John Ciardi. PoPl
Two empires by the sea. International Hymn. George Huntington. PoLF
Two Englishmen. Douglas Stewart. CBAP
Two Epigrams. James Kenneth Stephen.
  Cynicus to W. Shakspere. CenHV; WhC
  Senex to Matt. Prior. CenHV; FiBHP; WhC
Two Epigrams. Sir William Watson. TrGrPo
  Love.
  Poet, The.
Two evils, monstrous either one apart. Winter Remembered. John Crowe Ransom. AP; HAP; MoAB; NOBA; OxBA; PrIm; UnPo; VGW
Two Families. Charles G. Bell. FAZ
Two Figures. Molly Peacock. AMV-81
Two figures in deep water. Walking to Bellrock. Michael Ondaatje. NOBC
Two Figures in Dense Violet Light. Wallace Stevens. MoAB; MoAmPo;
Two Fires, The. Judith Wright. MoBrPo
Two Fishermen. Stanley Moss. CoAP; VWA
  (Fisherman.) DiL
Two fleets have sailed from Spain. The one would seek. The Sailing of the Fleet. *Unknown.* PAH
Two foals sleep back to back, The. The Absent Ones. Maxine W. Kumin. PAI
Two forms inseparable in unity. Robert Southey. *Fr.* The Curse of Kehama. OBRV
Two forms move among the dead, high sleep. The Owl in the Sarcophagus. Wallace Stevens. FaBoMo
Two Foscari, The, *sel.* Byron.
  Swimming. GN
Two Friends, The. Charles Godfrey Leland. AA
Two friends talked of dark politics in light. Night Out. R. A. Simpson. PoAu-2
Two Fusiliers. Robert Graves. MMA
Two Garden Scenes. Charles Burgess. NePoAm-2
Two Gardens. Arlene De Bevoise. AMV-80
Two gates unto the road of life there are. The Road of Life. William Morris. *Fr.* The Earthly Paradise. OBNC
Two Generations. L. A. G. Strong. OBMV
Two Gentlemen of Soho, *parody, sel.* A. P. Herbert.
  Recipe. WhC
Two Gentlemen of Verona, The, *sels.* Shakespeare.
  My Thoughts Do Harbour, *fr.* III, i. CTC
  This Spring of Love, *fr.* I, iii. ChTr
  "Thus have I shunned the fire for fear of burning," *fr.* I, iii. GBL
  Who Is Silvia [*or* Sylvia]? *fr.* IV, ii. BLPL; ElL; EnRePo; FaBoBe; FaFP; GN; LiTB; OAEL-1; SeCeV; TreF; TrGrPo; WHA
  (Silvia [*or* Sylvia].) HBV-1; OBEV
  (Song: "Who Is Silvia.") ViBoPo
  (Song to Silvia.) OBSC
  ("Who is Silvia? What is she?") OAEP
Two German officers crossed the Rhine, parlee-voo. Hinky Dinky, Parlee-Voo. *Unknown.* AS
Two Gifts. *Unknown, tr. fr. Catalan by* Willis Barnstone. BoWoP
Two girls barefoot walking in the rain. On Growing Old in San Francisco. Jack Gilbert. NPGG
Two girls discover. The Secret. Denise Levertov. NaP
Two girls of twelve or so at a table. Charles Reznikoff. PCP
Two Girls Singing. Iain Crichton Smith. BSV
Two Glasses, The. Ella Wheeler Wilcox. BLPA; BLPL
Two Graces. Robert Herrick. *See* Grace for a Child *and* Grace for Children, A.
Two Graces. *Unknown.*
  "Hurly, hurly, roon the table." FaBoCh
  "Some hae meat that canna eat." FaBoCh
  (Child's Grace, A, *at. to Burns.*) *FaPON; MoShBr*
Two gray-winged farmers of the sea, they ride. Maine Sea Gulls. Russell Hoban. BoAnP
Two Gretels, The. Robin Morgan. DFT
Two Handfuls of *Waka* for Thelonious Sphere Monk (d. Feb. 1982). Walter Lew. BrSi
Two hands lie still, the hairy and the white. Love for a Hand. Karl Shapiro. CoAP; NYBP
Two hands upon the breast. Now and Afterwards. Dinah Maria Mulock Craik. HBV-2; PoLF; WGRP
Two Hangovers. James Wright. LCAP
Two-headed Calf, The. Laura Gilpin. FYAP
Two Heads Are Better than One. Joseph Jekyll. WhC
  ("See, one physician, like a sculler, plies.") FaBoEE
Two hearts: two blades of grass I braid together. Weaving Love-Knots 2. Hsüeh T'ao, *tr. by* Carolyn Kizer. BoWoP
Two Heavens. Leigh Hunt. GN
Two heavy trestles, and a board. My Table. W. B. Yeats. Meditations in Time of Civil War, III. LiTB
Two Heroes. Harriet Monroe. *Fr.* Commemoration Ode. OHIP
Two Hoboes. *Unknown.* WTO
Two honder year ago de worl' is purty slow. Two Hundred Years Ago. William Henry Drummond. HBV-2
Two Hookers. A. K. Redwing. VoR
Two Hopper. Ron Ikan. Str
Two Horses. Joy Harjo. TWSS
Two Horses. W. S. Merwin. NePA; TwAmPo
Two horses in yellow light. August. Adrienne Rich. NNaP; PBWP
Two hours, or more, beyond the prime of a blithe April day. The Battle of Charleston Harbor. Paul Hamilton Hayne. PAH
Two Houses. Edward Thomas. ChMP; FaBoCh
Two hummingbirds as evanescent as. Vision. Richard Eberhart. NYBP
Two Hundred Girls in Tights & Halters. Daniel Hoffman. ELU
225 days under grass. For Jane. Charles Bukowski. HoPM
224 Stoop. Victor Hernandez Cruz. BOLo
229. José Garcia Villa. PoPl
Two hundred wagons, rolling out to Oregon. The Oregon Trail. Arthur Guiterman. BPAW; FaPON
Two Hundred Years Ago. William Henry Drummond. HBV-2
Two Illustrations That the World Is What You Make of It. Wallace Stevens. NePoAm
Two in August. John Crowe Ransom. AWP; MoPo; NePA; OxBA; PPP
Two in Bed. Abram Bunn Ross. FaPON; NTCP; SoPo; TiPo
Two in the Campagna. Robert Browning. EBEV; EBVV; ELP; FaBoEn; GTBS-P; HBV-1; NOBE; NoP; OAEL-2; OAEP; OBNC; PoEL-5; SeCePo; SeCeV; TrGrPo; VLP; WHA
Two infants vis-à-vis. Bleecker Street. Jean Garrigue. NYP; TAP
Two Invocations of Death. Kathleen Raine.
  "Death, I repent," I. OxBTC
  (Invocation of Death.) MoAB
  "From a place I came," II. OxBTC
Two Invocations of the Virgin, I ("Within the cloister blissful of thy sides"). Chaucer. *Fr.* The Canterbury Tales: The Second Nun's Tale. ACP
Two Invocations of the Virgin, II ("O mother maid, O maiden mother free!"). Chaucer. *See* Invocation: "O mother-maid, O maiden mother free!"
Two ivory women by a milky sea. The Bathers. Hart Crane. SyP
Two Jays at St. Louis. Ferdinand G. Christgau. TDH
Two Jazz Poems. Carl Wendell Hines, Jr.. AmNP
Two Jerusalems rise up. Jerusalem. Ruben Kanalenstein, *tr. by* Yishai Tobin. VWA
Two Kitchen Songs. Edith Sitwell. CMoP
Two Ladies Bidding Us "Good Morning." James P. Vaughn. NNP
Two ladies sit in the spotless driveway. Garage Sale. Karl Shapiro. Psk
Two ladies to the summit of my mind. Sonnet: Of Beauty and Duty. Dante, *tr. by* Dante Gabriel Rossetti. AWP
Two ladies with high social aims. Such Foolish Old Dames. Sam S. Stinson. TDH

Two Lean Cats. Myron O'Higgins. PoBA; PoNe
Two leaps the water from its race. A Mill. William Allingham. FaBoEE; NBM; POL; SeCePo
Two legs sat upon three legs. Mother Goose. HBV-1; HBVY; NTCP; OxNR
Two lengths has every day. Emily Dickinson. MoPo
Two Letters from Chang-kan. Li Po, *tr. fr. Chinese by* Shigeyoshi Obata. OLR
Two liddle niggers all dressed in white. Raise a "Rucus" To-Night. *Unknown.* BPo; TAP
Two Limericks. Carolyn Wells. YaD
"Canner, exceedingly canny, A," I.
"Tutor who tooted a flute, A," II.
Two Lines from the Brothers Grimm. Gregory Orr. AmPA
Two Lips. Thomas Hardy. BoLoP
Two little arabs adult and arabesque. Hans Arp, *tr. fr. French by* Harriet Watts. FaBoNo
Two little children one morning. You Tell Me Your Dream, I'll Tell You Mine. Seymour Rice *and* Albert H. Brown. FSN
Two little creatures. Monkeys. Padraic Colum. OxBTC
Two little dicky birds. *Unknown.* OxNR
Two little dogs/ Sat by the fire. *Unknown.* OxNR
Two little feet, so small that both may nestle. Little Feet. Elizabeth Akers Allen. HBV-1
Two little girls are better than one. One and One. Mary Mapes Dodge. HBV-1; HBVY
Two little girls, one fair, one dark. The Lost Children. Randall Jarrell. CoAP; PrIm; TAP
Two Little Kittens. *Unknown.* OBCA; OxBChV
Two Little Miss Lloyds, The. Elizabeth Turner. OxBChV
Two little ships were sailing by. Upon a Christmas Morning. *Unknown.* AmFP
2 little whos. E.E. Cummings. OLR
Two Lives, *sel.* William Ellery Leonard.
Indian Summer. HBMV
Two Lives and Others. Winfield Townley Scott. PoPl
Two lofty ships of Eng-e-land set sail. The Wild Barbaree. *Unknown.* AmFP
Two Long Vacations: Grasmere. Arthur Gray Butler. OBVV
Two Look at Two. Robert Frost. AP; CoBMV; CrMA; MoAB; MoAmPo; NU
Two Lovers. "George Eliot." HBV-1
Two Lovers, The. Richard Harvey. HBV-1
Two Lovers, The. Marie de France, *tr. fr. French by* Patricia Terry. BoWoP
Two Lovers Discoursing, *with music. Unknown.* ShS
Two lovers sitting on a tomb. Pati Hill. FAZ
Two Loves. Lord Alfred Douglas. PeHV
Two Loves. Richard Eberhart. CMoP
Two Loves, The. Laurence Housman. HBMV
Two loves had I. Now both are dead. Dead Love. Mary Mathews Adams. AA
Two loves I have of comfort and despair [*or* dispaire]. Sonnets, CXLIV. Shakespeare. CABA; EBEV; InvP; LoBV; NIP; OAEL-1; OAEP; PeHV; PoEL-2
Two low whistles, quaint and clear. Guild's Signal. Bret Harte. PaPo
Two Lyrics. Lorenzo de' Medici, *tr. fr. Italian by* John Addington Symonds. AWP
"How can I sing light-souled and fancy-free." II.
"Into a little close of mine I went," I.
Two Magicians, The. *Unknown. See* Twa Magicians, The.
Two Magpies Sat on a Garden Rail. D'Arcy W. Thompson. MoShBr
Two magpies under the cypresses, The. What Birds Were There. William Everson. NoAM
Two Maidens [*or* Maids] Went Milking [*or* a-Milking] One Day. *Unknown.* FSW; UnTE
Two main diseases. A Trial. Alan Dugan. NoAM
Two Married, (I-IV). Helen Frazee-Bower. HBMV
Two Masks Unearthed in Bulgaria. William Meredith. EyDe
Two Men. E. A. Robinson. WhC
Two Men in Armour. John Heath-Stubbs. NeBP
Two men wrote a lexicon, Liddell and Scott. *Unknown.* CenHV
Two Mice, The. Robert Henryson. *See* Tale of the Upland Mouse and the Burgess Mouse, The.
Two minutes' rest till the next man goes in! A Cricket Bowler. Edward Cracroft Lefroy. OBVV
Two mites, two drops (yet all her house and land). The Widow's Mites. Richard Crashaw. OxBoCh
Two Mornings. Lawrence McGaugh. PoBA
Two Mornings and Two Evenings. Elizabeth Bishop. PoA
Two Mothers, The. Shane Leslie. ISi
Two Mountains Men Have Climbed. Pauline Starkweather. GoYe
Two murders this month. October. Greg Pape. AmPA
Two Musics. Norman McCaig. NeBP
Two Mysteries, The. Mary Mapes Dodge. AA; HBV-2; TrCP; WGRP
Two Neighbours, The. George Campbell Hay. OxBS
Two never-ever-will-be lovers each. Mathematics of Encounter. Isabella Gardner. ErPo
Two nights in Manchester: nothing much to do. Mr. Cooper. Anthony Thwaite. OxBTC
Two nights running I was out there. The Mummies. Maxine W. Kumin. Psk
Two Noble Kinsmen, The, *sels.* Fletcher *and* Shakespeare.
Bridal Song, A, *fr.* I, i. ElL; NOBE; OBEV; OBSC
(Roses Their Sharp Spines.) ViBoPo
"Hail Sovereign Queen of secrets, who hast power," *fr.* V, i. PoEL-2
Urns and Odours Bring Away! *fr.* I, v. ElL
(Dirge of the Three Queens.) OBEV
(Funeral Song.) ChTr; OBS
Two Nocturnes. Katherine Mansfield. HBMV
Arabian Shawl, The, I.
Sleeping Together, II.
Two nudists of Dover. Third Limick. Ogden Nash. NePA
Two o'Clock. Katherine Pyle. *Fr.* The Wonder Clock. OBCA
209 Canal. Richard Howard. NYP; TAP
Two of a Trade. Samuel Willoughby Duffield. AA
Two, of course there are two. Death and Co. Sylvia Plath. CMoP; ConAP; FF; LCAP; PrIm
Two of Cups, The. Emmett Jarrett. NeAC
Two of far nobler shape, erect and tall. Satan Looks upon Adam and Eve in Paradise. Milton. *Fr.* Paradise Lost, IV. TreFS
Two of Thy children one summer day worked in their garden, Lord. The Garden. Rose Parkwood. WGRP
Two of us roof my house, The. Ed Shreckongost. Ed Ochester. TAT
Two Old Bachelors, The. Edward Lear. BeLS; FiBHP; ShM
Two Old Crows. Vachel Lindsay. FaBoNo; OBAL
Two Old Gentlemen, The. Robert Wallace. DFF
Two Old Kings, The. Lord De Tabley. OBEV; OBVV
Two Old Ladies. Siegfried Sassoon. OxBTC
Two Old Lenten Rhymes. *Unknown.* ACP
"Lenten stuff is come to the town," I.
"Lenten has brought us, as I understand," II.
Two Old Women of Mumbling Hill, The. James Reeves. ShM
Two-ones is the name for it, The. The Twins. Elizabeth Madox Roberts. TiPo
Two opponents, The. Hokusai's Wave. Olga Cabral. PoDr
Two or Three; a Recipe [*or* Receipt] to Make a Cuckold. Pope. BoLoP; FaBoEE
Two or three lines across; the black ones, down. Crayon House. Muriel Rukeyser. EyDe
Two Paintings by Gustav Klimt. Jorie Graham. SV
Two pairs of hands go round. Korf's Clock. Christian Morgenstern, *tr. by* Geoffrey Grigson. FaBoNo
Two pairs of mallards, tandem. Nearing Winter. Ernest Sandeen. NYBP
Two Parents, The. "Hugh MacDiarmid." FaBoTw; OxBTC
Two Parodies. *Unknown.* CoSo
Two parts lye, and one part quicklime. Mr. Cherry. Paul Baker Newman. AMV-81
Two Paths. Julia Caroline Ripley Dorr. AA
Two People. Eve Merriam. RHPC
Two People ("Two people live in Rosamund"). E. V. Rieu. RHPC
Two people in a room, speaking harshly. Novella. Adrienne Rich. PPP
Two people live side by side. Two. Moishe Kulbak, *tr. by* Ruth Whitman. VWA
Two Pewits. Edward Thomas. CH; FM
Two Pictures. *Unknown.* BeLS; BLPA; FaBoBe
Two Pictures of a Leaf. Marvin Bell. LCAP
Two Pieces after Suetonius. Robert Penn Warren. *See* Apology for Domitian.
Two pilgrims, broiling in the sun. Beware of Dogmas. Ebenezer Elliott. FaBoEE
Two Poems. Robert J. Abrams. NNP
"For my unborn son," II.
"I do not want to turn away," I.
Two Poems. Edward Marshall. CoPo
Two Poems about President Harding. James Wright. CoAP; NoAM
Two Poems (after A. E. Housman). Hugh Kingsmill. NOBL
Two Poems Based on Fact. Frank J. Lepkowski. AMV-81
2 Poems for Black Relocation Centers. Etheridge Knight. NNaP; NoAM
Two Poems on the Catholic Bavarians. Edgar Bowers. PoCh
"Fierce and brooding holocaust of faith, The," I.
"I know a wasted place high in the Alps," II.
Two Poets, The. Alice Meynell. OBVV
Two Points of View. Lucian B. Watkins. BANP
Two policemen laughed, The. Policemen Laughing. Ray Fraser. NeAC

Two Postures beside a Fire. James Wright. GP
Two Prayers. Andrew Gillies. BLRP; TRV
Two Prayers. Charlotte Perkins Gilman. WGRP
Two Presentations. Robert Duncan. InPS
Two Puritans. *Unknown.* UnTE
(Off a Puritane.) CoMu
Two purple pigeons circle a London square. The Exiled Heart. Maurice Lindsay. OxBS
Two Pursuits. Christina Rossetti. WPE
Two-quart virgin in my lap, A. The Aged Wino's Counsel to a Young Man on the Brink of Marriage. X. J. Kennedy. FF
Two Questions. William Stanley Braithwaite. BALP
Two Questions, The. Alice Meynell. WPE
Two Rats, The. *Unknown.* PoPle
(What Became of Them?) OBCA; OxBChV
Two Red Roses across the Moon. William Morris. EBVV; VLP
Two Refugees. Mordecai Marcus. VWA
Two respectable rhymes. Rhymes. Y. Y. Segal, *tr. by* Miriam Waddington. WHW
Two Rivers. Emerson. AmPP; AP; NOBA; OxBA; TrGrPo
Two Rivers, The. *Unknown. See* Tweed and Till.
Two roads diverged in a yellow wood. The Road Not Taken. Robert Frost. AmPP; AP; ChTr; CMoP; CoBMV; EvOK; FaBoCh; FaFP; FPL; HAP; HeIP; LiTA; LiTM; MoAB; MoAmPo; MP; NePA; NoAM; NoP; OxBA; PoLF; PoPl; RFM; SeCeV; SoSe; TAP; TreFT; TwAmPo; TwCP
Two Roads, etc. Dorothy Walters. IHMS
Two rows of foolish faces blent. Bored. Horatio Brown. PeHV
Two Rural Sisters. Charles Cotton. *See* Resolution in Four Sonnets, of a Poetical Question, Concerning Four Rural Sisters.
Two sculptors. Four Translations from the English of Robert Hershon. Robert Hershon. NeAC
Two Selves, The. Margaret Avison. NoAM
Two separate divided silences. Severed Selves. Dante Gabriel Rossetti. The House of Life, XL. BoLoP; SyP
Two shall be born, the whole wide world apart. Fate. Susan Marr Spalding. AA; BLPA; HBV-1
Two Shapes. Arthur Gregor. TAP
Two shots down and I'm exalted. Alan Dugan. GP
Two Sides of War. Grantland Rice. TreFT
Two Sisters, The. *Unknown.* AmFP; FSW; MAT; PrIm; TrGrPo
(Binnorie.) BSV; OBEV; PoPle; WHA
(Cruel Sister, The.) OxBB, *with music*
(Twa Sisters, The.) CH; EnSB; ESPB (A *and* B *vers.*); FaBoBa; HBV-2; NoP (B *vers.*); OxBS; ViBoFo (A, B, *and* D *vers.; vers.; with music*)
Two Smiles. Oliver Herford. *See* Smile of the Walrus, The.
Two Societies, The. John Hall Wheelock. PoCh
Two Solitudes. Evelyn Ames. GoYe
Two Somewhat Different Epigrams. Langston Hughes. NePoAm-2
Two Songs. C. Day Lewis. HAP; NoAM
Come, Live with Me and Be My Love. BoLoP; CoBMV; OBMV
(Song: "Come, live with me and be my love.") NIP; NoP
I've Heard Them Lilting at Loom and Belting. OBMV
Two Songs [Written to Irish Airs]. C. Day Lewis. OAEP
Love Was Once Light as Air.
Oh Light Was My Head.
Two Songs. Adrienne Rich. CABA; NIP; NOBA; TAP
Two Songs from a Play. W. B. Yeats. *Fr.* The Resurrection. CABA; CMoP; CoBMV; FaBoTW; HAP; LiTB; MoPo; NOBE; NoP; OAEL-2; PPoe; PPP; PrIm; SeCeV
Two Songs of a Fool. W. B. Yeats. CMoP
Two Songs on the Economy of Abundance. James Agee. MoAmPo
Red Sea.
Temperance Note: and Weather Prophecy.
Two Sonnets. John Ashbery.
Dido. CAPP; VGW
Idiot, The. VGW
Two Sonnets. Charles Hamilton Sorley. HBMV; MMA; MoBrPo
"Saints have adored the lofty soul of you," I.
"Such, such is Death: no triumph: no defeat," II.
Two Sonnets: Harvard. Oliver Wendell Holmes. AP
"Christo et Ecclesiae" 1700.
Veritas.
Two Sonnets for a Lost Love. Samuel A. DeWitt. GoYe
"If I were less the man, I might have kept," II.
" 'There is no permanence,' you sagely said," I.
Two Sonnets on Fame. Keats.
"Fame, like a wayward girl, will still be coy," I. EnRP
(On Fame.) CABA
"How fever'd is the man who cannot look," II. EnRP
(On Fame.) NCEP
Two Sonnets. David P. Berenberg. HBMV
"Antigone and Helen—would they laugh."
"Or is it all illusion? Do the years."
Two Sorrows. David St. John. SUW
Two Souls. Marjorie Pickthall. NOBC
Two souls diverse out of our human sight. On the Deaths of Thomas Carlyle and George Eliot. Swinburne. HBV-2
Two Spirits, The. James Benjamin Kenyon. AA
Two Spirits, The; an Allegory. Shelley. CH; OAEL-2; Prf; WiR
Two spoons of sherry. The Witch's Work Song. T. H. White. FaBoNo
Two Springs. Li Ch'ing-chao, *tr. fr. Chinese by* Kenneth Rexroth. BoWoP
Two springs she saw—two radiant Tuscan springs. Eugene Lee-Hamilton. Mimma Bella, II. HBV-1
Two Stars, The. W. H. Davies. MoBrPo
Two stars alone of primal magnitude. Washington and Lincoln. Wendell Phillips Stafford. PGD
Two stars there are in one faire firmament. Richard Barnfield. Sonnets, IV. PeHV
Two statesmen met by moonlight. What the Moon Saw. Vachel Lindsay. CrMA; FaBoEE
Two steps from my garden rail. Hayyim Nahman Bialik, *tr. by* Maurice Samuel. Songs of the People, I. AWP
Two Stories. Charles Wright. FYAP
Two Strange Worlds. Francesca Yetunde Pereira. PBA
Two Streams, The. Oliver Wendell Holmes. *Fr.* The Professor at the Breakfast Table. AP
Two Streams, The. Thomas Moore. *Fr.* Evenings in Greece, First Evening. GoBC
Two stubborn beaks. Argument. Mildred Weston. WhC
Two Summers in Moravia. Roger McDonald. CBAP
Two summers since, I saw at Lammas fair. Phoebe Dawson. George Crabbe. GoTL
Two Surprises. R. W. McAlpine. PoLF
Two Swans, The. Thomas Hood. CH
Two sweeter babes you nare did see. *Unknown.* FaBoEE
Two tapsters traded on Thames's side. Ballad of the Two Tapsters. Vernon Watkins. MoBS
Two Temples. Hattie Vose Hall. BLPA
Two that could not have lived their single lives. Two in August. John Crowe Ransom. AWP; MoPo; NePA; OxBA; PPP
Two that through windy nights kept company. The Two Neighbours. George Campbell Hay. OxBS
Two Things. Donald G. Babcock. NePoAm
Two things have I asked of Thee. Neither Poverty nor Riches. Bible, *O.T. Fr.* Proverbs. TrJP
Two things have set the world a-twist. Foxgloves and Snow. Marion Angus. PoSH
Two things make woman slow, we find. Good Reasons. Keith Preston. WhC
"Two things," said Kant, "fill me with breathless awe." The Third Wonder. Edwin Markham. FYAP
Two things there are with Memory will abide. Memories. Thomas Bailey Aldrich. AA
Two things were set. Two Things. Donald G. Babcock. NePoAm
Two thousand days. South Inlet. Greg Kuzma. WOLT
Two thousand feet beneath our wheels. Cockpit in the Clouds. Dick Dorrance. FaPON; RHPC; TiPo
2001: The Tennyson/Hardy Poem. Gavin Ewart. FaBoCo
Two thousand years are far enough! It Isn't Far to Bethlehem. Arthur R. Macdougall, Jr. PGD
Two Tile Beaks. Maria Amalia Fonte Boa, *tr. fr. Portuguese by* Willis Barnstone *and* Nelson Cerqueira. BoWoP
Two Times Two Is Four. H. Leivick, *tr. fr. Yiddish by* Ruth Whitman. VWA
Two Tramps in Mud Time. Robert Frost. AP; BLPL; CMoP; CoBMV; LiTA; LiTM; MasP; MoAB; MoAmPo; NePA; NoAM; PrIm; TrGrPo
Two Trees, The. W. B. Yeats. BrPo; OAEL-2; VLP
Two Trinities. Kenneth Mackenzie. CBAP
Two Triolets. Harrison Robertson. HBV-1
What He Said.
What She Thought.
Two Variations. Denise Levertov. NaP; PPoe
2 Variations: All About Love. Philip Whalen. NeAP
Two vases stood on the Shelf of Life. Vases. Nan Terrell Reed. BLPA
Two Vast Enjoyments Commemorated. John Danforth. SCAP
Two Veterans. Walt Whitman. *See* Dirge for Two Veterans.
Two Views of a Cadaver Room. Sylvia Plath. CMoP; GoYe; NMP
Two Views of Two Ghost Towns. Charles Tomlinson. NoAM
Two Villages. Rose Terry Cooke. HBV-2
Two virtues ride, by stallion, by nag. The Death of Myth-making. Sylvia Plath. PoA
Two Voices. Edmund Blunden. OBWP
Two Voices. Alice Corbin. HBMV
Two Voices, The. Tennyson. MasP

Two voices are there: one is of the deep. A Sonnet [*or* A Sonnet on Wordsworth *or* Wordsworth]. James Kenneth Stephen. BXAP; CenHV; DBV; FaBoCo; FaBoPa; FiBHP; HBV-1; NOBL; Par; SpRo; WhC
Two voices are there; one is of the Sea. Thought of a Briton on the Subjugation of Switzerland [*or* Sonnet: Thought of a Briton on the Subjugation of Switzerland *or* England and Switzerland 1802]. Wordsworth. ChER; EnRP; GTBS; GTBS-P; OBRV; SeCeV; SpRo
Two Voices in a Meadow. Richard Wilbur. NePoAm-2; PAI; UnPo
Two-Volume Novel. Dorothy Parker. InMe
Two Voyages. Maurice James Craig. NeIP
Two Ways. John V. A. Weaver. HBMV
Two Weeks after an April Frost. Steven Helmling. AMV-80
Two Went Up to [*or* into] the Temple to Pray. Richard Crashaw. HAP; TRV
Two were silent in a sunless church, The. Her Dilemma. Thomas Hardy. BrPo
Two white ducks waddle past my door. Ducks. Robert Bly. PV
Two White Horses, *with music. Unknown.* AS
Two White Horses in a Line. *Unknown.* BluL
Two wild duck of the upland spaces. Duck. John Lyle Donaghy. BIrV; OxBI
Two winding rails. The Transandean Railway. Thomas Kretz. AMV-80
Two Windows by Magritte. Ruth Roston. PoDr
Two Wise Generals. Ted Hughes. MoBS
Two Witches. Robert Frost. CMoP
Witch of Coös, The, *sel.* AP; CoBMV; LiTM; MoAB; NoAM; NePA; NOBA; SeCeV; ViBoPo
Two Witches, The. Robert Graves. SO
Two Witches. Alexander Resnikoff. RHPC
Two Wives, The. Daniel Henderson. ShM
Two Wives, The. William Dean Howells. AA
Two Women. Naomi Replansky. NMM
Two Women. Tania Van Zyl. PeSA
Two Women. Nathaniel Parker Willis. BeLS; OBVV
(Unseen Spirits.) AA; HBV-1
Two women had these words engraved. Epitaphs: For a Fickle Man. Mark Van Doren. ViBoPo
Two women, here in April, prayed alone. Miss Packard and Miss Giles. Owen Dodson. GLGT
Two women on the lone wet strand. The Watchers. William Stanley Braithwaite. PoNe
Two Women with Mangoes. Steven Cramer. AMV-80
Two Words; a Wedding. B. P. Nichol. NOBC
Two worlds in one. The Children of the State. James Lewisohn. LFAC
Two Wrestlers. Robert Francis. LiSp
Two X. E. E. Cummings. FaBoMo
Two-Year-Old Has Had a Motherless Week, The. Karl Shapiro. WeW
Two Years Later. John Wieners. CoPo; PoM
Two years the blank walls stared at him. A History. John Williams. NePoAm-2
Two years thus spent in gathering knowledge. Tom Brainless as Student and Preacher. John Trumbull. *Fr.* The Progress of Dulness. AmPP
Two young maids in a beauty fair. *Malay Oral Tradition, tr. by* R. O. Winstedt. WTO
Two Young Men, 23 to 24 Years Old. C. P. Cavafy, *tr. fr. Greek by* Edmund Keeley *and* Philip Sherrard. PeHV
Twoborn. Rokwaho. STE
'Twould ring the bells of Heaven. The Bells of Heaven. Ralph Hodgson. BrPo; EaLo; GoJo; LiTM; MoAB; MoBrPo; NOBE; OBEV; PPON; SiSoSe; TreFT
Ty Cobb Story, The. Tom Clark. LiSp
Tyburn and Westminster. John Heywood. ACP
Tyger, The. Blake. *See* Tiger, The.
Tyin' a Knot in the Devil's Tail. Gail Gardner. FSW
Tying her bonnet under her chin. The Love-Knot. Nora Perry. AA; HBV-1
Tyl it was noon, they stoden for to se. At the Gate. Chaucer. *Fr.* Troilus and Criseyde. SeCePo
Tymes Goe by Turnes. Robert Southwell. *See* Times Go by Turns.
Tyndarus attempting too kis a fayre lasse with a long nose. Of Tyndarus, That Frumped a Gentlewoman. *Unknown, tr. by* Richard Stanyhurst. BIrV
Tyne Dock. Francis Scarfe. NeBP
Type of the antique Rome! Rich reliquary. The Coliseum. Poe. AmPP; AP; NOBA
Typewriter Revolution, The. D. J. Enright. NoP
Typical 6:00 P.M. in the Fun House, A. Daniel Berrigan. LFAC
Tyrannic [*or* Tyrannick] Love, *sels.* Dryden.
Ah, How Sweet It Is to Love! *fr.* IV, i. HBV-1; HoPM; ViBoPo
(Song: "Ah how sweet it is to love.") CavP; FaBoEn
Epilogue to "Tyrannick Love." SeCV-2
(Epilogue: "Hold! are you mad? you damned, confounded dog!") OAEP; ViBoPo
Prologue: "Self-love (which never rightly understood)." OAEP; ViBoPo
Tyranny of Moths. Gerald Vizenor. VoR
Tyrant Apple Is Eaten, The. Norman McCaig. NeBP
Tyrant, why swel'st thou thus. Bible, *O.T.* Psalms, LII, *paraphrased by* Countess of Pembroke. OBVE
Tyr'd with all these for restfull death I cry. *See* Tired with all these . . .
Tyre brought me up, who born in thee had been. Of Himself. Meleager, *tr. by* Richard Garnett. AWP
Tyre of the West, and glorying in the name. England. Cardinal Newman. ACP; GoBC
Tyson's Corner. Primus St. John. PoBA
Tywater. Richard Wilbur. CMoP; ConAP; LiTA; LiTM; MiAP; MoAB; NePA
Tzu Yeh Songs, *sels. Tr. fr. Chinese by* Arthur Waley. BoWoP
"All night I could not sleep."
"At the time when blossoms."
"I heard my love was going to Yang-chou."
"I will carry my coat and not put on my belt."

U

U bet u wer. To a Poet I Knew. Jewel C. Latimore. PoBA
U feel that way sometimes. Mixed Sketches. Don L. Lee. BPo; TAP
U is for Umbrellas. Phyllis McGinley. *Fr.* All Around the Town. TiPo
U Name This One. Carolyn M. Rodgers. BlSi; NMM; PoBA
U.S. Coast and Geodetic Survey Ship *Pioneer*, The. Robert Hershon. NeAC
U.S. 1946 King's X. Robert Frost. NIP
U.S. Sailor with the Japanese Skull, The. Winfield Townley Scott. LiTM; MiAP; NMP; WaP
U-S-U Range, The. *Unknown.* CoSo
Ubi Sunt Qui ante Nos Fuerunt? *Unknown.* HAP; NoP; PrIm *in Middle English and tr. into mod. English by* George Perkins; SeCeV; WeW, *abr.*
(Contempt of the World.) MeEL
(Ubi Sount Qui ante Nos Fuerount?) OAEP
(Ubi Sunt, *longer version.*) OxBM
(Where Are the Ones Who Lived Before? *mod. English.*) HAP
("Were beeth they biforen us weren.") EBEV; OAEP
Ubique. *At. to* Joshua Sylvester. *See* Were I as Base as Is the Lowly Plain.
Uccello. Gregory Corso. FF; NeAP; PoM
Uccello on the Heath. Geoffrey Grigson. WaP
Uffia. Harriet R. White. NA
Ug was a hairy but painstaking artist. The Story of Ug. Edwin Meade Robinson. HBMV; YaD
Ugliest little boy. The Life of Lincoln West. Gwendolyn Brooks. FB
Ugly Chile. Clarence Williams. TW
Ugly old man, An. No Great Matter. David Lawson. VGW
Ugstabuggle, The. Peter Wesley-Smith. AmMo
Uh—go down, go down, you little red. Go Down, You Little Red Rising Sun. *Unknown.* OuSiCo
Uhuru. Mari Evans. CNA
Ula Masondo's Dream. William Plomer. MoBS
Ulalume—a Ballad. Poe. AA; AmPP; AP; AWP; BLPL; LiTA; NePA; NOBA; OxBA; TAP; TreF; ViBoPo; WHA
Ulcerated tooth keeps me awake, there is. Letters from a Father. Mona Van Duyn. FYAP
Ulezalka, Ulezalka. The Tailor. Patricia Garfinkel. AMV-80
Ulf in Ireland. Charles De Kay. AA
Ulinda. David Campbell. CBAP
Ulric Dahlgren. Kate Brownlee Sherwood. PAH
Ulster. Hans Adler. AMV-81
Ulsterman, An. "Lynn Doyle." OnYI
Ultima Ratio Regum. Stephen Spender. CMoP; FaFP; LiTB; LiTM; OAEL-2; OBWP; SeCePo; WaaP; WaP
Ultima Thule. Longfellow. MOS; ViBoPo
Ultimate Anthology. Martin Bell. POL
Ultimate Antientropy, The. Theodore Weiss. NoAM
Ultimate Equality. Ray Durem. *See* You Know, Joe.
Ultimate Exile IV. Ralph Nixon Currey. PeSA
Ultimate Poem Is Abstract, The. Wallace Stevens. PoA
Ultimate Problems. William Stafford. NU
Ultimate Reality. Ogden Nash. *See* Limerick: "There was an old man in a trunk."
Ultimatum. Peggy Pond Church. TRV
Ultra-Germano-Criticasterism. Leigh Hunt. PP
Ulysses. Robert Graves. ChMP; CMoP; FaBoTw; NoAM; OxBI; PrIm

Ulysses, *sel.* James Joyce.
Yes. FF
Ulysses. Tennyson. AWP; CABA; EBEV; FaPoR; FF; FiP; FPL; HAP; HBV-2; HeIP; HoPM; InPK; InPS; LiTB; LoBV; MOS; NIP; NOBE; NoP; OAEL-2; OAEP; PAI; PoPle; PoRA; PPoe; PPP; PrIm; SCV; SeCePo; SeCeV; SoSe; TEP; TreF; TrGrPo; UnPo; ViBoPo; VLP; WeW; WHA
Sels.
"Come, my friends." TRV
"I am a part of all that I have met." TRV
"There lies the port; the vessel puffs her sail." EtS
Ulysses Advises Achilles. Shakespeare. *Fr.* Troilus and Cressida, III, iii. LiTB
Ulysses and His Dog. Homer, *tr. fr. Greek by* Pope. *Fr.* The Odyssey, XVII. FiP; OBEC
Ulysses and the Siren. Samuel Daniel. CABA; ElL; EnRePo; HAP; LoBV; NOBE; NoP; OBEV; OBSC; PoEL-2; TEP; ViBoPo
Ulysses has come back to me again! Ulysses Returns, I. Roselle Mercier Montgomery. HBMV
Ulysses Hears the Prophecies of Tiresias. Homer, *tr. fr. Greek by* George Chapman. *Fr.* The Odyssey, XI. LoBV
Ulysses in the Waves. Homer, *tr. fr. Greek by* George Chapman. *Fr.* The Odyssey, V. OBS
Ulysses Leaves the Nymph Calypso. Homer, *tr. fr. Greek by* George Chapman. *Fr.* Odyssey, V. JCP
Ulysses' Library. David Daiches. PoA
Ulysses Returns, *sels.* Roselle Mercier Montgomery.
"Oh, the hearts of men, they are rovers, all," IV. HBMV
"So swift to bloom, so soon to pass, Love's flower," II. HBMV
"Ulysses has come back to me again!," I. HBMV
"Was it I, was it I who dallied there," III. HBMV
Umber dowagers of Henry Street, The. September. Marilyn Hacker. NYP
Umber slant lands under the Apennines, The. To the South. Brewster Ghiselin. LiTA; NePA
Umber was painting of a lion fierce. Upon Umber: Epigram. Robert Herrick. CaPo
Umbilical. Eve Merriam. CTBA; RHPC
Umbrella, The. Ann Stanford. NYBP
Umbrella, An/ And a raincoat. Conversation. Buson. NTCP
Umbrella Brigade, The. Laura E. Richards. SoPo; SUS; TiPo
Umbrella, the Cane, and the Broom, The. Eliezer Steinbarg, *tr. fr. Yiddish by* Curt Leviant. VWA
Umbrellas. Rowena Bennett. TiPo
Ummmmh oh ain't got no mama now. That Black Snake Moan. *Unknown.* BluL
Umpire, The. Walker Gibson. NePoAm
Un Canadien Errant (An Exiled Canadien). *Tr. fr. French.* FSW
Unable to breathe, I inhaled the classic Aegean. Small Perfect Manhattan. Peter Viereck. MiAP
Unaccompanied. Harvey Andrews. OBET
Unaccustomed ripeness in the wood, An. Elizabeth. Robert Lowell. *Fr.* Harriet. CAPP
Unalterables. Arthur Gregor. NYBP
Un-American Investigators. Langston Hughes. BPo
Unanswered. Martha Dickinson Bianchi. AA
Unanswered Prayers. Ella Wheeler Wilcox. WGRP
Unanswered yet the prayer your lips have pleaded. Pray without Ceasing [*or* Sometime, Somewhere]. Ophelia Guyon Browning. BLPA; BLPL; BLRP; STF
Unarmed Combat. Henry Reed. Lessons of the War, III. HeIP; LiTB
Unawares. Emma A. Lent. PoLF
Unawkward Singers, The. David Ferry. NePoAm-2
Unbeliever, The. Elizabeth Bishop. LiTA; NoAM
Unbeliever, An. Anna Hempstead Branch. WGRP
Unbeliever. Dorothy Dow. HBMV
Unbeseechable, The. Frances Cornford. MoBrPo
Unblinding, The. Laurence Lieberman. NYBP
Unborn, The. Thomas Hardy. CMoP
Unborn. Irene Rutherford McLeod. HBMV
Unborn children are rowing out to the far edge of the sky, The. Cloud River. Charles Wright. GeTw
Unbounded is thy range; with varied style. The Stormy Hebrides. William Collins. *Fr.* An Ode on the Popular Superstitions of the Highlands of Scotland. NOBE
Unbridled Now. Laura Lourene LeGear. GoYe
Uncautiously, unheeding, thinking. The Thieves of Love. R. A. D. Ford. PeCV
Uncertain State of a Lover, The. *Unknown.* ElL
Uncertain What to Wear. William Jay Smith. TDH
Uncessant minutes, whil'st you move you tell. To His Watch, When He Could Not Sleep. Lord Herbert of Cherbury. JCP; MePo; NOBE; PoEL-2
Unchangeable, The. Shakespeare. *See* Sonnets, CIX.
Unchanging Jesus. Karl Johann Philipp Spitta, *tr. fr. German by* R. Massie. BLRP
Unclaimed. Florida Watts Smyth. PH
Uncle. Harry Graham. RHPC
Uncle. Philip Levine. NNaP
Uncle Ambrose. James Still. AmFN
Uncle Ananias. E. A. Robinson. MoAmPo; NePA; NIP
Uncle Bull-Boy. June Jordan. PoBA
Uncle Charlie lived alone. All Up and Down the Lines. Robert Cooperman. AMV-80
Uncle Claude. David Allan Evans. Str
Uncle Death. Walter Clark. NCSH
Uncle Dog: the Poet at 9. Robert Sward. CoAP; CoPo; PrIm; VGW
Uncle Eddie told him how it was. Forget about It. Robert Currie. Str
Uncle Eph's Banjo Song. James Edwin Campbell. BANP
Uncle Gabe's White Folks. Thomas Nelson Page. AA
Uncle Henry. W. H. Auden. NOBL; PeHV
Uncle Iv Surveys His Domain from His Rocker. Jonathan Williams. OBAL
Uncle Jack. David Kherdian. FAZ
Uncle Jim. Countee Cullen. BANP
Uncle Joe. *Unknown.* FSW
(Hop Up, My Ladies.) OuSiCo, *with music*
Uncle Mells and the Witches' Tree. Elizabeth Madox Roberts. WSC
Uncle Remus and His Friends, *sels.* Joel Chandler Harris.
My Honey, My Love. AA; FaBoBe
Plough-Hands' Song, The. AA
Revival Hymn. HBV-2
Uncle Reuben. *Unknown.* FSW
Uncle Robert. Robert Morgan. GeTw
Uncle sent for O. T. told him we have to fight. O. T.'s Blues. Waring Cuney. MAT
Uncle Simon and Uncle Jim. "Artemus Ward." NA
Uncle tries his best, An. Rhapsodies. Cyril Dabydeen. BrSi
Uncle, whose inventive brains. Uncle. Harry Graham. RHPC
Unclench Yourself. Marge Piercy. NeAC
Uncomly in cloistre I cowre ful of care. Choristers Training. *Unknown.* OxBM
Unconcerned, The. Thomas Flatman. FaBoCh
Unconquerably, men venture on the quest. The Polar Quest. Richard Burton. AA
Unconquer'd captive!—close thine eye. Virginia Capta. Margaret Junkin Preston. PAH
Unconscious of amused and tolerant eyes. Portrait of a Child. Louis Untermeyer. HBMV
Unconstant Lover, The, *with music. Unknown.* TrAS
Unconsumable material is everywhere. The Square at Dawn. James Tate. NoAM
Uncontrollable night, An. Fist Fight. Doug Cockrell. Psk
Uncouth Knight, The. Hugh McCrae. PoAu-1
Uncultivated Accent. *Unknown.* DBV
Undead, The. Richard Wilbur. CAPP; CoAP; ConAP; OxBC
Undefined Tenderness, An. Joel Oppenheimer. PPJ; VGW
Under. George Bowering. NeAC
Under. J. C. Squire. FaBoTw
Under a bent when the night was deep. William Morris. *Fr.* The Earthly Paradise. PChr
Under a budding hedge I hid. While April Rain Went By. Shaemas O'Sheel. HBMV
Under a dung-cake. Fable. D. J. Opperman, *tr. by* Jack Cope. PeSA
Under a Hill. *Unknown.* OxNR
Under a Lady's Picture. Edmund Waller. EnLoPo
Under a lawne, than skyes more cleare. Upon Roses. Robert Herrick. SeCP
Under a lonely sky a lonely tree. On a Lonely Spray. James Stephens. OnYI
Under a sky studded with asterisks. On the Night in Question. Patricia Goedicke. TAP
Under a southern wind. Song. Theodore Roethke. CrMA
Under a splintered mast. A Talisman. Marianne Moore. GoJo; MoAB; MoAmPo; NCSH; ViBoPo
Under a spreading chestnut-tree. The Village Blacksmith. Longfellow. AA; BLPL; FaBoBe; FaFP; FaPON; FaPoR; HBV-2; HBVY; OBAL; OBCA; PaPo; PoPl; TreF; WBLP
Under a spreading gooseberry bush the village burglar lies. The Village Blacksmith. *Unknown.* FiBHP
Under a Stagnant Sky. W. E. Henley. SyP
Under a sultry, yellow sky. Mercedes. Elizabeth Stoddard. AA
Under a swaying. El Dorado. Richard Ryan. BIrV
Under a toadstool. The Elf and the Dormouse. Oliver Herford. AA; FaBoBe; FaPON; HBV-1; HBVY; OnMSP; RHPC; SoPo; TiPo
Under a tree. Mary Is with Child. *Unknown.* MeEL

Under a white coverlet of snow. January. John Heath-Stubbs. OBCP
Under a Wiltshire Apple Tree. Anna de Bary. CH
Under All This Slate. James Hayford. NePoAm-2
Under an elm tree where the river reaches. Captured. Archibald MacLeish. HBMV
Under Ben Bulben. W. B. Yeats. CMoP; HAP; NoAM; OxBTC
Sels.
"Cast a cold eye." FaBoEE
"Under bare Ben Bulben's head." FaBoRV; WeW
Under broad banners and barbarian. Against the Age. Louis Simpson. NePoEA-2
Under Cancer. John Hollander. CoAP
Under clouds, at the tag end of August. Lighting the Night Sky. Kenneth O. Hanson. FYAP
Under cool trees the City tombs. Bunhill's Fields. Anne Ridler. NeBP
Under cracking pieces of the moon, eelpout. Spawning in Northern Minnesota. David McElroy. AmPA
Under Creag Mhor. Stewart Conn. PoSH
Under dusky laurel leaf. A Cyprian Woman. Margaret Widdemer. HBV-2
Under enormous and cemented cliffs. The Second Iron Age. Michael Harrington. CaP
Under every cathedral. The Invention of Fire. Andrew Taylor. CBAP
Under 500 kings three kingdoms groan. The Parliament Dissolved at Oxford. *Unknown.* APAS
Under glass, glass dishes which changed. The Fundamental Project of Technology. Galway Kinnell. SUW; SV
Under great yellow flags and banners of the ancient cold. The Shadow of Cain. Edith Sitwell. CoBMV; OxBTC
Under green apple boughs. Madonna Mia. Swinburne. HBV-1
Under hawk-watch. Fisherman. Philip Booth. LiSp; WOLT
Under her/ exaggerated hair. Pregnant Image of "Exaggerating the Village." Nora Dauenhauer. TWSS
Under her deep plush roof. "Vierge Ouvrante." Miriam Palmer. NMM
Under his careful crown he keeps. King Midas Has Asses' Ears. Donald Finkel. NePoEA-2
Under his helmet, up against his pack. Asleep. Wilfred Owen. MMA
Under his view the wind. The View. Howard Nemerov. NYBP
Under its brown fur. Rookery. Nora Dauenhauer. TWSS
Under Leafy Bowers. Judah al-Harizi, *tr. fr. Hebrew.* TrJP
Under light soft as seawater, sounds. The Obscure Pleasure of the Indistinct. Bin Ramke. MAYP
Under Milk Wood, *sel.* Dylan Thomas.
Johnnie Crack and Flossie Snail. FaPON; FiBHP; GoJo; PDV; RHPC
Under Monadnock. A New Hampshire Boy. Morris Bishop. HBMV
Under my hood I have a hat. Winter Clothes. Karla Kuskin. RHPC
Under my keel another boat. A Shadow Boat. Arlo Bates. HBV-1
Under my thoughts may I God-thoughts find. Thoughts of God. *Tr. from Gaelic by* Douglas Hyde. WTO
Under My Window. Thomas Westwood. HBV-1; HBVY
Under my window. Letter in Winter. Raymond R. Patterson. PoBA
Under my window Dolores sings. Spanish Song. Charles Divine. HBMV
Under my window-ledge the waters race. Coole Park and Ballylee, 1931. W. B. Yeats. CMoP; GTBS-P; NoAM; OBMV; PPP
Under Our Own Wings. Nellie Wong. BrSi
Under pared moons. The Horse. José María Eguren, *tr. by* Cheli Durán. WSC
Under Restless Clouds. Hanny Michaelis, *tr. fr. Dutch by* Marjolijn de Jager. VWA
Under Sirius. W. H. Auden. FaBoMo; NePA
Under Sorrow's Sign. Gofraidh Fionn O'Dalaigh, *tr. fr. Irish by* John Montague. BIrV
Under Stars. Tess Gallagher. GeTw; MAYP
Under Stone. Elaine Feinstein. VWA
Under the African lintel, Table Mountain. David Wright. *Fr.* South African Broadsheets. PeSA
Under the after-sunset sky. Two Pewits. Edward Thomas. CH; FM
Under the almond tree. In Kensington Gardens. Arthur Symons. EnLoPo
Under the Anheuser Bush. Andrew B. Sterling. OBAL
Under the apple bough. Remembrance. George Parsons Lathrop. AA
Under the Arc de Triomphe: October 17. Marilyn Hacker. PoA
Under the arch of life, where love and death. Soul's Beauty. Dante Gabriel Rossetti. The House of Life, LXXVII. OAEP; OBEV; OBVV; VLP
Under the azure where the noon sun totters. Antony and Cleopatra. Henri Coulette. NePoEA
Under the bamboo. T. S. Eliot. *Fr.* Sweeney Agonistes. UnPo
Under the Bamboo Tree, *with music.* Bob Cole. BLSo; FSN
Under the big 500-watted lamps, in the huge sawdusted government inspected slaughter-house. The Slaughter-House. Alfred Hayes. LiTA
Under the Blue. Francis Fisher Browne. AA
Under the Boathouse. David Bottoms. MAYP
Under the Boughs. Gene Baro. BoNaP
Under the bronze crown. A Baroque Wall-Fountain in the Villa Sciarra. Richard Wilbur. AmPP; BiP; CAPP; MP; NePoEA; NoP; NYBP; PoCh;TwCP
Under the bronze leaves a colt was foaled. Came such an one who laid. Song: Under the Bronze Leaves. "St.-J. Perse," *tr. by* T. S. Eliot. *Fr.* Anabasis. PoPl
Under the Casuarina. Elizabeth Riddell. PoAu-2
Under the Catalpa Trees. Gary Young. AMV-81
Under the Cliff. Geoffrey Grigson. WaP
Under the concrete benches. Weed Puller. Theodore Roethke. AmPP
Under the cover of night. Cities and Seas. Norman Jordan. PoNe
Under the crosses white on a foreign meadow. Silent Testimony. Catherine Parmenter. PGD
Under the dining room light. Business as Usual. Mark Vinz. Str
Under the Drooping Willow Tree. *Unknown.* OxBoLi
Under the dying sun. The Reaper. L. H. Allen. PoAu-1
Under the Earth. Abraham Sutskever, *tr. fr. Yiddish by* Ruth Whitman. VWA
Under the eaves, out of the wet. To a Phoebe-Bird. Witter Bynner. HBMV
Under the Edge of February. Jayne Cortez. BlSi
Under the Eildon Tree. Sydney Goodsir Smith. OxBS
Elegy XIII: "I got her in the Black Bull," *sel.* BSV
Under the El on Sunday afternoon. Aside. Alan Dugan. PoA
Under the financier's. The Jersey Marsh. David Galler. NYBP
Under the fire escape, crouched, one knee in cinders. The Desk. David Bottoms. MAYP
Under the forest, where the day is dark. The Manzanita. Yvor Winters. VGW
Under the Frontier Post. Wang Chang-ling, *tr. fr. Chinese by* Rewi Alley. ChTr
Under the great down-curving lilac branches. Lisa. Constance Carrier. SoSe
Under the great hill sloping bare. The King's Missive. Whittier. PAH
Under the green lamp-light her letter there. Letter of a Mother. Robert Penn Warren. MoAmPo
Under the Greenwood Tree ("A sodger laddie's socht a hoose"). "Hugh MacDiarmid," *after the Cretan.* OBVE
Under the Greenwood Tree. Shakespeare. *Fr.* As You Like It, II, v. AWP; BoNaP; CH; EIL; ELP; EnRePo; FaBoBe; FaFP; FaPON; GN; GTBS; GTBS-P; HBV-1; HeIP; HoPM; InPS; LiTB; NoP; OAEL-1; OAEP; OBEV; OHIP; SeCeV; TiPo; TrFS; UnPo; ViBoPo; WHA; WiR
(Amiens's Song.) OBSC
(Song: "Under the greenwood tree.") CTC; FiP
(Songs of the Greenwood.) TrGrPo
Under the Greenwood Tree ("In summer time when leaves grow green"). *Unknown.* GBP
Under the ground? Versions. Robert Kelly. The Book of Persephone, 12. PoM
Under the Hill. Richard Eberhart. PoA
Under the Hill. Daryl Hine. MoCV
Under the hills and veins of water. Last Letter to Pablo. Pat Lowther. NOBC
Under the hive-like dome the stooping haunted readers. The British Museum Reading Room. Louis MacNeice. LiTM; MoAB; MoBrPo; NOBE; SeCePo; WaP
Under the house, between the road the sea-cliff. Grass on the Cliff. Robinson Jeffers. *Fr.* The Trumpet. PoA
Under the ice with its bouldery death's faces. The Bread Hot from the Oven. John Thompson. NOBC
Under the Ladder to Heaven. Elizabeth Fenton. NMM
Under the Leaves. Albert Laighton. HBV-1; OHIP
Under the Leaves Green. *Unknown. See* My Fair Lady.
Under the light, yet under. Emily Dickinson. AP
Under the lightly leaved. On the House of a Friend. John Logan. DFF
Under the Lime Tree. Walther von der Vogelweide. *See* Under the Lindens.
Under the Lindens. Walter Savage Landor. HBV-1
Under the Lindens. Walther von der Vogelweide, *tr. fr. German by* Ford Madox Ford. CTC
(Tandaradei, *tr. by* Ford Madox Ford.) AWP
(Under the Lime Tree, *tr. by* Thomas Lovell Beddoes.) ErPo; GBL; UnTE
("Under the lime-tree, on the daisied ground," *tr. by* Thomas Lovell Beddoes.) OBVE
Under the Locust Blossoms. Frederick Goddard Tuckerman. NOBA
Under the long dark boughs, like jewels red. Cherry Robbers. D. H. Lawrence. MoAB; MoBrPo
Under the longleaf pines. A Quilled Quilt, a Needle Bed. Brad Leithauser. MAYP
Under the lucent glass. In the Egyptian Museum. Janet Lewis. NYBP; QFR

Under the Maud Moon. Galway Kinnell. NNaP
Under the Mirabeau Bridge the Seine/ Flows and our love. The Mirabeau Bridge. Guillaume Apollinaire, *tr. by* W. S. Merwin. OBVE
Under the Mirabeau bridge the Seine/ Flows with our loves. The Mirabeau Bridge. Guillaume Apollinaire, *tr. by* Quentin Stevenson. BoLoP
Under the Mistletoe. Countee Cullen. PChr
Under the mock-oranges the children spy. The People in the Park. Léonie Adams. MoVE
Under the most ideal remedy. A Poem on Inter-uterine Device. A. Rasheed Ghazi. PeD
Under the mountain, as when first I knew. Elegy in Six Sonnets. Frederick Goddard Tuckerman. *Fr.* Sonnets. AP; HAP; QFR; TAP
Under the night shade. Clickstone. Rokwaho. STE
Under the oak tree, oak tree. *Unknown, tr. fr. Spanish by* Willis Barnstone. BoWoP
Under the Old Elm, *sels.* James Russell Lowell.
Great Virginian, The, *fr.* VII. PGD
Imperial Man, *fr.* VIII. PGD
"Never to see a nation born," *fr.* VII. GOA
New-come Chief, The, *fr.* III. PAH
Ours, and All Men's, *fr.* V. PAL; PGD
(Washington.) GN; OHIP
"That lifted blade transformed our jangling clans," *fr.* VII. GOA
Whom We Revere, *fr.* III. PGD
Under the olive trees, from the ground. The Coward. Stephen Spender. NoAM
Under the opening fingers of the dawn. Homer, *tr. by* Robert Fitzgerald. The Odyssey, VIII-XI. NAWM-1
Under the orchards, under. Rogation Days. Kenneth Rexroth. NaP
Under the orchid, blooming as it bloomed. The Subway from New Britain to the Bronx. Randall Jarrell. NYP
Under the parabola of a ball. How to Kill. Keith Douglas. ChMP; FaBoMo; NOBE
Under the pent-house branches the eight swans have come. A Dark World. E. J. Scovell. MoVE
Under the Pines. Arthur S. Bourinot. OBCV
Under the pines and hemlocks. The Deer. Mary Austin. FaPON
Under the pink quilted covers. The Fortress. Anne Sexton. LiTM
Under the plum-blossoms are nightingales. Desolation. Amy Lowell. PoA
Under the pond, among rocks. The Dragonfly. Howard Nemerov. PoA
Under the Pondweed. *Unknown, tr. fr. Chinese by* Helen Waddell. *Fr.* Shi King. AWP
Under the Portrait of [John] Milton. Dryden. *See* Lines Printed under the Engraved Portrait of Milton.
Under the Pot. Robert Graves. FaBoEE
Under the Pyrenees. Alfred Noyes. *Fr.* The Last Voyage, Dedication. GoBC
Under the quince tree. Bible, *O.T.* The Song of Solomon, VIII:5. PBWP
Under the Red Cross. Chauncey Hickox. AA
Under the roof and the roof's shadow turns. The Merry-go-round. Rainer Maria Rilke, *tr. by* C. F. MacIntyre. CAD; WeW
"Under the roots of the roses." Mors et Vita. Richard Henry Stoddard. AA
Under the Rose. *Unknown.* OBET
Under the Ruins of Poland. Itzik Manger, *tr. fr. Yiddish by* Miriam Waddington. VWA
Under the scarlet-licking leaves. My Many-Coated Man. Laurie Lee. NYBP
Under the Scrub Oak, a Red Shoe. Dave Smith. GeTw
Under the sea, which is their sky, they rise. Submarine Mountains. Cale Young Rice. EtS
Under the Shade of the Trees. Margaret Junkin Preston. PAH
Under the shadow of a stately pile. At Florence. Wordsworth. VLP
Under the shadows of a cliff. A Rise. Ernest McGaffey. AA
Under the shape of his sail, Ulysses. Presence of an External Master of Knowledge. Wallace Stevens. NePA
Under the Shawl. Rose Drachler. VWA
Under the sheet of transparent wool. Penumbra. Pierre Louys. *Fr.* Chansons de Bilitis. PeHV
Under the Sign of Moth. David Wagoner. AMV-81
Under the slanting light of the yellow sun of October. The Modern Romans. Charles Frederick Johnson. AA
Under the slumber and winter of a silent night. In Lord Carpenter's Country. Barry O. Higgs. PeSA
Under the Snow. Robert Collyer. AA
Under the sovereign crests of dead volcanoes. On a Bougainvillæa Vine at the Summer Palace [*or* in Haiti]. Barbara Howes. MoAmPo; NYBP
Under the Stars. Wallace Rice. AA; OHIP
Under the sun, groaned Solomon. Solomon. Hermann Hagedorn. GoBC
Under the sun is nothing new? To the Archdeacon. George Farewell. NOEC
Under the surface of flux and of fear there is an underground movement. Louis MacNeice. *Fr.* The Kingdom. LiTM
Under the tall black sky you look out of your body. Endless. Muriel Rukeyser. NYBP
Under the thick beams of that swirly smoking light. The Examination. W. D. Snodgrass. CABA; CAPP; ConAP
Under the too white marmoreal Lincoln Memorial. The March 1. Robert Lowell. NoP
Under the trees the leaves go down. Rondel: Autumn. Matt Field. AMV-80
Under the Umbrella of Blood. William Pitt Root. GeTw
Under the viaduct, by the hot canal. Plaque. Bruce Ruddick. CaP
Under the Violets. Oliver Wendell Holmes. *Fr.* The Professor at the Breakfast Table. AA
Under the Violets. Edward Young. AA
Under the walls of Monterey. Victor Galbraith. Longfellow. PAH
Under the waning moon. Starting at Dawn. Sun Yün-feng, *tr. by* Kenneth Rexroth *and* Ling Chung. PBWP
Under the water tower at the edge of town. To the Evening Star: Central Minnesota. James Wright. NaP
Under the Waterfall. Thomas Hardy. BoLoP; CTC; LiTB
Under the Wattle. Douglas Brook Wheelton Sladen. OBVV
Under the wide and starry sky. Requiem. Robert Louis Stevenson. BrPo; BSV; DL; EBVV; FaBV; FaPoR; FPL; GoTS; HBV-2; HBVY; MoBrPo; NOBE; OBEV; OBNC; OBVV; OHFP; PoLF; PoPl; PoRA; TreF; TrGrPo; ViBoPo; WGRP; WHA
Under the Williamsburg Bridge. Galway Kinnell. NYP
Under the Willow Shades. Sir William Davenant. BoLoP; ELP
(Willow, The.) UnTE
Under the willow the willow. Recruiting Drive. Charles Causley. NePoEA; OxBTC; PPON; PrIm
Under the Window: Ouro Preto. Elizabeth Bishop. NYBP
Under the winter, dear. Song. Eugene Lee-Hamilton. OBVV
Under the Wood. *Unknown. See* Now Goeth Sonne under Wode.
Under the Woods. Edward Thomas. CH; LoBV
Under the yellow moon, when the young men and. The Last Fairy. Rosamund Marriott Watson. OBVV
Under the yellow sun. A White Tree in Bloom. John Richard Moreland. PGD
Under the yew-tree's heavy weight. Les Hiboux. Baudelaire, *tr. by* Arthur Symons. AWP
Under these historic skies. From Jerusalem: A First Poem. Gabriel Preil, *tr. by* Robert Friend. VWA
Under this crust. *Unknown.* WhC
Under this marble, or under this sill. Epitaph on Himself. Pope. FaBoEE
Under this real estate—squared street on street. Asphodel. David Malouf. CBAP
Under this sod and beneath these trees. On Samuel Pease [*or* An Epitaph]. *Unknown.* ShM
Under this sod lies a great bucking hoss. To Midnight [an Epitaph]. *Unknown.* BPAW; CoSo
Under this stone/ Lies a Reverend Drone. An Epitaph upon That Profound and Learned Casuist, the Late Ordinary of Newgate. Thomas Brown. OBSV
Under this stone, reader, survey. On [*or* Epitaph on] Sir John Vanbrugh [Architect]. Abel Evans. FaBoCo; FaBoEE; FiBHP; OBEC; PV; TreFT; ViBoPo
Under this stone there lieth at rest. An Epitaph of Sir Thomas Gravener [Knight]. Sir Thomas Wyatt. EnRePo; OBSC; SiPS
Under this town's ashes. On Learning That Certain Peat Bogs Contain Perfectly Preserved Bodies. Susan Ludvigson. MAYP
Under thy shadow may I lurk awhile. St. Peter's Shadow. Richard Crashaw. ACP
Under Which Lyre [a Reactionary Tract for the Times]. W.H. Auden. MoAB; MoBrPo; NOBL
Under white eyelids. The Sleeper. Isobel Hume. HBMV
Under yonder beech-tree single [*or* standing] on the green-sward. Love in the Valley. George Meredith. AWP; EBVV; ErPo; HBV-1; LiTB; NOBE; OAEL-2; OBEV; OBVV; TreFT; TrGrPo; UnTE; ViBoPo; VLP; WHA
Under your Milky Way. Return of the Goddess Artemis. Robert Graves. PoA
Under Your Voice, among Legends. Phyllis Beauvais. NMM
Underdeveloped Country, An. D. J. Enright. NOBL
Underfoot on the hill the water spurts. Sunday on Hampstead Heath. George Woodcock. NeBP
Underfoot rotten boards, forest rubble, bones. Remains of an Indian Village. Al Purdy. NOBC
Undergraduate. Merrill Moore. ErPo
Underground, The. Guy Boas. CenHV
Underground Gardens, The. Robert Mezey. NaP
Underground grower, blind and a common brown, An. Potato. Richard Wilbur. CAPP; CrMA; LiTA; MoAB; TrGrPo; TwAmPo

Underground Poetry. Pedro Pietri. NYP
Underground space, like water, is running out. Apartments on First Avenue. Cynthia Macdonald. NYP
Underground Stream, The. James Dickey. NOBA
Underground System. Edna St. Vincent Millay. SBG
Underneath a cypress shade, the Queen of Love sat mourning. *Unknown.* GBL
Underneath an old oak tree. The Raven. Samuel Taylor Coleridge. WiR
Underneath my belt. When I Was Lost. Dorothy Aldis. RHPC; SoPo
Underneath my lids another eye has opened. From the Prison House. Adrienne Rich. NNaP
Underneath My Window. Sir Philip Sidney. *See* Astrophel and Stella: Eleventh Song.
Underneath the boardwalk, way, way back. The Secret Cavern. Margaret Widdemer. FaPON
Underneath the growing grass. The Bourne. Christina Rossetti. ELP; FaBoEn; HBV-2; LoBV; OBNC
Underneath the tree on some. Like They Say. Robert Creeley. ELU
Underneath their eider-robe. The Poetry of a Root Crop. Charles Kingsley. LoBV
Underneath this ancient pew. *Unknown.* WhC
Underneath this greedy stone. Epitaph on Erotion. Leigh Hunt. OBRV
Underneath this marble hearse. *See* Underneath this sable hearse.
Underneath this marble stone/ Lie two beauties join'd in one. Epitaph [of Pyramus and Thisbe]. Abraham Cowley. EnLoPo; FaBoEE
Underneath this myrtle shade. The Epicure [*or* Another]. Abraham Cowley, *after the Greek of* Anacreon. *Fr.* Anacreontics. AWP; OBEV; SeCP
Underneath this pretty cover. With a Copy of Swift's Works. J. V. Cunningham. QFR
Underneath this sable [*or* marble] hearse [*or* herse]. On the Countess Dowager of Pembroke [*or* Epitaph on . . .]. William Browne, *wr. at. to* Ben Jonson. AWP; CABA; CavP; FaBoEE; HAP; HBV-2; InvP; JCP; LoBV; NIP; NOBE; NoP; OAEL-1; OBEV; OBS; PoEL-2; PoPle; PoRA; SeCeV; TreFS; ViBoPo; WeW; WHA
Underneath this wooden cross there lies. Epitaph. Karl Shapiro. *Fr.* Elegy for a Dead Soldier. OFD
Undersea Fever. William Cole. FiBHP
Underside of Trees, The. Charlotte DeClue. TWSS
Undersong, The. Emerson. *Fr.* Woodnotes, II. AA
Undersong. Mark Van Doren. PoCh
Understand, he is naked in the sea. The Loved One. Joseph Hansen. NYBP
Understand me: I am a mediocre being. Words to My Friend. Renée Vivien, *tr. by* Sandia Belgrade. PeHV
Understanding. Pauline E. Soroka. PoLF
Understanding of a medical man, The. Sonnet. Rex Warner. ChMP
Undertaker asks for clothes, The. Grave Clothes. Karen Swenson. AMV-80
Undertakers. Ambrose Bierce. DBV
Undertaker's Advertisement, An. Ernest G. Moll. WhC
Undertakers' Club, The. *Unknown.* GBP
Undertaker's Horse, The. Kipling. FaBoNo; FM
Undertaking, The. John Donne. MePo; NOBE
Undertaking, The. Gerrit Lansing. CoPo
Undertone. William Bedell Stanford. NeIP; OnYI
Undertow. Langston Hughes. LiTM
Underwater eyes, an eel's. An Otter. Ted Hughes. CMoP; NePoEA-2; NMP; NoAM
Underwear. Lawrence Ferlinghetti. CoPo; OBAL
Underwood. Howard Moss. MP; NePA; NePoEA-2; PP; TwCP
Undesirable you may have been, untouchable. September Song. Geoffrey Hill. NoP; OBWP
Undine. Irving Layton. ErPo
Undiscovered Country, The. Thomas Bailey Aldrich. AA
Undiscovered Planet, The. Norman Nicholson. ChMP
Undo! *Unknown.* NOCV; OxBM
Undo Your Heart. *Unknown.* MeEL
Undone, undone the lawyers are. The Downfall of Charing Cross. *Unknown.* FaBoCo
Undoubtedly the kangaroos. Nature Note. Arthur Guiterman. SUS
Undreamed, The. Elaine V. Emans. AMV-81
Undressing her hair. The Voyeur. Deanna Louise Pickard. AMV-80
Undue significance a starving man attaches. Emily Dickinson. LiTA; LiTM
Undulating currents of his mind, The. Graham Bell and the Photophone. G. F. Montgomery. SUW
Undulating golden waves of ripened. High Plains Harvest. Bruce Morton. AMV-81
Undulation, An/ on too many legs. Codes. Diana Chang. BrSi
Undulations of precision harass the mind. Kochia. Thomas Hornsby Ferril. NePoAm-2
Unduly elected body of our elders, An. Elegy for Yards, Pounds, and Gallons. David Wagoner. PoA
Undying Thirst. Antipater, *tr. fr. Greek by* Robert Bland. AWP
Une Idole Du Nord. Francis Stuart. NeIP
Une petite pêche dans un orchard fleurit. The Little Peach. *Unknown.* NA
Une Vie. Pentti Saarikoski, *tr. fr. Finnish by* Anselm Hollo. ELU
Unearned Increment. Christopher Morley. WhC
Unearth. Alfred Barrett. GoBC
Unearthing. Betsy Rosenberg. VWA
Uneasiness of the night surrounds me, The. In a Night. Ann Marie Savage. AMV-81
Uneasy Peace. Edmund Blunden. BrPo
Uneasy Rider. Diane Wakoski. NIP
Unemployed, The. LeVan Roberts. PGD
Unemployment. William Mills. HoPM
Unemployment in our bones, The. Derry. Seamus Deane. CIP
Unemployment/Monologue. June Jordan. WPOW
Unequal Distribution. Samuel Hoffenstein. TrJP
Unerring Guide, The. Anna Shipton. BLRP
Unexpected Pleasure, An. *Unknown.* FaBoCo
Unexplorer, The. Edna St. Vincent Millay. MoShBr; PoA; SUS
Unexpress'd, The. Walt Whitman. NePA; PP
Unfading, The. "Marie Madelaine," *tr. fr. German by* Ferdinand E. Kappey. PeHV
Unfading Beauty, The. Thomas Carew. *See* Disdain Returned.
Unfailing Friend, The. Joseph Scriven. *See* What a Friend We Have in Jesus.
Unfailing One, The. Phillips Brooks. *See* Our Burden Bearer.
Unfaithful Shepherdess, The. *Unknown.* GTBS; GTBS-P
(Adieu Love, Untrue Love.) ElL
(Faithless Shepherdess, The.) OBEV
(Philon.) OBSC
(Philon the Shepherd.) NOBE
Unfamiliar Quartet. Stephen Vincent Benét. WhC
Unfathomable Sea! Shelley. *See* Time.
Unfathomable sea, and time, and tears, The. To N. V. de G. S. Robert Louis Stevenson. BrPo
Unfathomable Sea! whose waves are years. Time. Shelley. EtS; FaBoRV; FPL; MOS; Par; PoLF
Unfinished History, An. Archibald MacLeish. NYBP; VGW
Unfinished Race, The. Norman Cameron. OxBS
"Unfit die, The—the fit both live and thrive." The Survival of the Fittest. Sarah N. Cleghorn. HBMV
Unflinching Dante of a later day. To an Imperilled Traveller. Nathan Haskell Dole. AA
Unflinching foot 'gainst foot was set. Bannockburn. Sir Walter Scott. *Fr.* The Lord of the Isles. BSV
Unfold, unfold! take in his light. The Revival. Henry Vaughan. ELP; NOCV; OBS; OxBoCh; PoEL-2; PoPle; TrGrPo
Unforgiven, The. E. A. Robinson. CMoP
Unfortunate admiral! Your poor America. To Columbus. Rubén Darío, *tr. by* Lysander Kemp. TTY
Unfortunate Coincidence. Dorothy Parker. BXAP; FaBoUs; NoP; PoPl; SBG; TreF; WhC
Unfortunate Lover, An. *Unknown.* OxBM
Unfortunate Lovers, The, *sel.* Sir William Davenant.
Song: "Roses and pinks will be strewn where you go." ViBoPo
Unfortunate Male, The. Kalonymos ben Kalonymos, *tr. fr. Hebrew by* J. Chotzner. *Fr.* The Touchstone. TrJP
Unfortunate Miller, The. A. E. Coppard. FaBoTw
Unfortunate Miller, The; or, The Country Lasses Witty Invention. *Unknown.* CoMu; OxBB
Unfortunate Miss Bailey. George Colman the Younger. DTC; FiBHP; FSW; GBP; ViBoFo
(Miss Bailey's Ghost.) FaBoBa; OxBoLi
Unfortunate Mole, The. Mary Kennedy. GoYe
Unfortunate Reminder, The. William Pattison. UnTE
Unfriendly Fortune. John Skelton. MeEL
(Go, Piteous Heart.) NCEP
Unfriendly friendly universe. The Child Dying. Edwin Muir. ChMP; FaBoTw; GTBS-P
Unfrocked Priest, The. Joseph Campbell. AnIL; OnYI
Unfulfillment. Frances Louisa Bushnell. AA
Unfurled gull on the tide, and over the skerry, The. December Day, Hoy Sound. George Mackay Brown. OxBS
Unfurls in rain. The Newest Banana Plant Leaf. Ingrid Wendt. NMM
Ungar and Rolfe. Herman Melville. *Fr.* Clarel. OxBA
Ungathered Apples, The. James Wright. ErPo
Ungathered Love. Philip Bourke Marston. OBNC
Ungrateful Garden, The. Carolyn Kizer. NePoEA-2
Unguarded. Ada Foster Murray. HBV-1
Unguarded Gates. Thomas Bailey Aldrich. AA; PAH
Unhand me nurse! thou saucy quean! Maternal Despotism; or, The Rights of Infants. Richard Graves. NOEC

Unhappie Light. Madrigal. William Drummond of Hawthornden. OBS
Unhappie Verse, the witnesse of my unhappie state. *See* Unhappy Verse, the witness of. . .
Unhappy about some far off things. The Stars Go over the Lonely Ocean. Robinson Jeffers. LiTA; LiTM; NePA; WaP
Unhappy Bella. *Unknown.* ErPo
Unhappy Boston. Paul Revere. PAH
Unhappy country what wings you have. Even here. Eagle Valor, Chicken Mind. Robinson Jeffers. ELU; LiTA; OxBA; WaP
Unhappy Diary Days. Gerald Vizenor. VoR
Unhappy dreamer, who outwinged in flight. On the Death of a Metaphysician. George Santayana. ViBoPo
Unhappy East (not in that awe). Reply. Sidney Godolphin. OBS
Unhappy Erin, what a lot was thine! National Presage. John Kells Ingram. OnYI
Unhappy, I observe the Ass. A Rondeau of Remorse. Burges Johnson. HBMV
Unhappy Lover, The. Judah al-Harizi, *tr. fr. Hebrew by* J. Chotzner. TrJP
Unhappy people in a happy world, An. Wallace Stevens. *Fr.* The Auroras of Autumn. CMoP
Unhappy Schoolboy, The. *Unknown.* OxBChV
Unhappy summer you. This Summer and Last. Thomas Hardy. OxBTC
Unhappy [*or* Unhappie] Verse, the witness[e] of my unhappy state. Iambicum Trimetrum [*or* Iambica]. Spenser. BoLoP; EBEV; EIL; OBEV; OxBoLi; PoEL-1
Unhappy youth betrayd by fate. Against the Love of Great Ones. Sir John Denham. AnAnS-2
Unharvested. Robert Frost. BoNaP
Unhatch you April butterflies. Ode to a Fat Cat. Annabel Farjeon. PCat
Unholy Missions. Bob Kaufman. CNA; TTY
Unhumans walk around. But, Still, He. Henry N. Lucas. AMV-81
Unhurried as a snake I saw Time glide. On Time. Richard Hughes. MoBrPo
Unhurt, untoucht did I complain. The Dissembler. Abraham Cowley. AnAnS-2
Unicorn, The. George Darley. *Fr.* Nepenthe. ChTr; FaBoEn; NBM; OBNC; PoEL-4
("Lo! in the mute mid wilderness.") OBRV
Unicorn, The. Ruth Pitter. MoBrPo; MoVE
Unicorn, The. E. V. Rieu. AmMo
Unicorn. William Jay Smith. RHPC; SO
Unicorn, The. Ella Young. FaPON; SoPo; TiPo
Unicorn and the Lady, The. Jean Garrigue. NYBP
Unicorn stood, like a king in a dream, The. The Unicorn. E. V. Rieu. AmMo
Unicorn to hand, A. Haste to the Wedding. Alex Comfort. ErPo
Unicorn with the long white horn, The. Unicorn. William Jay Smith. RHPC; SO
Unicorn's hoofs, The! Dance Song. *Unknown, tr. by* Arthur Waley. FaBoCh
Unicorns move furtively among. Lemon Sherbet. Marvin Solomon. NePoAm
Unidentified Flying Object. Robert Hayden. NCSH
Unifying Principle, The. A. R. Ammons. NOBA
Unillumined Verge, The. Robert Bridges (1858-1941). AA
Uninfected, The. E. L. Mayo. MiAP
Uninscribed Monument on One of the Battle-Fields of the Wilderness, An. Herman Melville. AA
Unintelligible Terms. Charles Simic. NoP
Uninvited, The. Dorothy Livesay. NOBC
Uninvited, The. William D. Mundell. NYBP
Union and Liberty. Oliver Wendell Holmes. OHIP
Union Barge on Staten Island, The. Louis Simpson. NYP
Union Maid. Woody Guthrie. FSW
Union Man. Albert Morgan. AmFP
Union Pier Michigan. We called it Shapiro. That Was Then. Isabella Gardner. FAZ; GP
Union Train. Lee Hays, Millard Lampell, *and* Pete Seeger. FSW
Unique among Girls. *Malay Oral Tradition, tr. by* R. J. Wilkinson *and* R. O. Winstedt. WTO
Unison, A. William Carlos Williams. NOBA; SeCeV
Unitarian Easter. Sandra McPherson. MAYP
Unite, unite, let us all unite. The Padstow Night Song. *Unknown.* ChTr; GBP
United. Paulus Silentiarius, *tr. fr. Greek by* W. H. D. Rouse. AWP
United Front. Bertolt Brecht *and* Hans Eisler. FSW
United States and *Macedonian,* The. *Unknown.* PAH
United States Prepare for the Permanent Revolution, The. George Hitchcock. EAS
Unity. Jakov de Haan, *tr. fr. Dutch by* David Soetendorp. VWA
Unity. Alfred Noyes. HBV-1
Unity of God, The. Panatattu, *tr. fr. Sanskrit.* WGRP
Unity of Mankind. *Fr.* Psalms. Bible, *O.T.* *See* To Dwell Together in Unity.
Univac to Univac. Louis B. Salomon. FF; QQQ
Universal Favorite, The. Carolyn Wells. InMe
Universal Passion, The. Edward Young. *See* Love of Fame, the Universal Passion.
Universal Prayer, The. Pope. BLPA; FaBoBe; FPL; GoBC; HBV-2; ILwL; NoP; OAEP; TreFT; WGRP
Universal Republic, The. Victor Hugo, *tr. fr. French.* PGD
Universality of things, The. The Eyeglasses. William Carlos Williams. NoAM
Universe, The. Mary Britton Miller. RHPC
Universe, The. May Swenson. SUW
Universe, The:/ We'd like to understand. The Observatory Ode. John Frederick Nims. SUW
Universe Is Closed and Has REMs, The. George Starbuck. SUW
University. Karl Shapiro. LiTA; OxBA
University Curriculum. William Price Turner. OxBS; POL
University Examinations in Egypt. D. J. Enright. MP; OxBTC; TwCP
Unkindness. George Herbert. HBV-2
Unkindness Has Killed Me. *Unknown.* MeEL
Unknown, The. John Davidson. MoBrPo
Unknown, The. E. O. Laughlin. BLPA
Unknown, The. Edward Thomas. GBL
Unknown Beloved, The. John Hall Wheelock. HBMV
Unknown Bird, The. Edward Thomas. DTC; FaBoEn
Unknown Child, The. Elizabeth Jennings. PBWP
Unknown Citizen, The. W. H. Auden. BiP; CABA; ChMP; FF; HeIP; InPK; LiTA; LiTM; MoAB; NePA; NIP; NOBL; NYBP; OBSV; PAI; PoRA; PPON; SoSe; TreFT; UnPo
Unknown City, The. Sir Charles G. D. Roberts. CaP
Unknown Color, The. Countee Cullen. FaPON; OBCA
Unknown Dead, The. Henry Timrod. AP
Unknown Eros, The. Coventry Patmore. *Poems indexed separately by titles and first lines.*
Unknown faces in the street. The Turning. Philip Levine. VGW
Unknown Girl in the Maternity Ward. Anne Sexton. CoPo; NAs; NoAM
Unknown God, The. "Æ." MoBrPo; WGRP
Unknown God, The. Henry Francis Lyte. TRV
Unknown God, The. Sir William Watson. WGRP
Unknown Grave, The. Letitia Elizabeth Landon. VLP
Unknown in history or in time they stand. Speakers, Columbus Circle. Raymond Souster. CaP
Unknown love/ Is as bitter a thing. Lady Otomo of Sakanoe, *tr. fr. Japanese by* Arthur Waley. *Fr.* Manyo Shu. AWP; PBWP
("Unknown love/ is bitter," *tr. by* Willis Barnstone.) BoWoP; LLLT
Unknown Man in the Morgue. Merrill Moore. MoAmPo
Unknown Master of Moulins, The. The Cardinal's Dog. John Glassco. MoCV
Unknown Shepherd's Complaint, The. Richard Barnfield. EIL
Unknown Soldier, The. Conrad Aiken. *Fr.* The Soldier. WaaP; WaP
Unknown Soldier. Alta Booth Dunn. PGD
Unknown Soldier, The. Alun Lewis. MoBrPo
Unknown Soldier, The. Billy Rose. BLPA; FPL; PAL
Unknown Soldiers. Edgar Lee Masters. *Fr.* The New Spoon River. NoAM; TAP
Unknown to all except a few. A Parable. George L. Kress. STF
Unknown Warrior. Elizabeth Daryush. SUMH
Unlawful Assembly. D. J. Enright. OxBTC
Unleashed dog walks back and forth, The. The Madman's Wife. Stephen Orlen. MAYP
Unless. Ella Dietz Glynes. AA
Unless the febrile brow be cool. Open Letter for John Doe. Edward Doro. TwAmPo
Unless We Guard Them Well. Jane Merchant. QQQ
Unless you can dance through a common bar. Mahsati, *tr. fr. Farsi by* Deirdre Lashgari. WPOW
Unless you knew just where to look. The Cobbler in Willow Street. George O'Neil. HBMV
Unless you remind me. Pavlov. Naomi Long Madgett. BPo
Unlike are we, unlike, O princely Heart! Sonnets from the Portuguese, III. Elizabeth Barrett Browning. HBV-1; OAEP; OBEV; OBVV; TrGrPo
Unlike my subject now shall be my song. Earl of Chesterfield. FaBoEE
Unlike Virgil's verse on the *Troiae bella.* The Bachelor's Ballade. David Fisher Parry. InMe
Unlikely angels, although by and large well met. Pacelli and the Ethiop. Turner Cassity. GP
Unloading Rails. *Unknown.* AmFP
Unloosed, unharnessed, turned back to the wild by love. The School of Desire. May Swenson. TwAmPo
Unloved to His Beloved, The. William Alexander Percy. HBMV
Unlucky Boat. George Mackay Brown. NePoEA-2

Unmanifest Destiny. Richard Hovey. AA; HBV-2; HBVY; PAL; TRV; WGRP
Unmasked, our friend confesses. Drained of hope. Murder Mystery. Timothy Steele. AMV-81
Unmindful of my low desert. The Quiet Nights. Katharine Tynan. HBV-2
"Unmitigated England." Great Central Railway, Sheffield Victoria to Banbury. John Betjeman. NYBP
Unmoored, unmanned, unheeded on the deep. The Derelict. Lucius Harwood Foote. AA
Unmoved by what the wind does. Sleeping with One Eye Open. Mark Strand. NYBP
Unmuzzle the broad joke. Catullus, *tr. fr. Latin by* James Michie. *Fr.* Hymeneal. PeHV
Unnamed Lake, The. Frederick George Scott. CaP; NOBC
Unnoted as the setting of a star. Mulford. Whittier. AA
Unnumbered suppliants crowd preferment's gate. Samuel Johnson. *Fr.* The Vanity of Human Wishes. OBSV
Unpacking our summer house, I found. An Untitled Poem, about an Uncompleted Sonnet. Sanford Pinsker. AMV-81
Unpardonable Sin, The. Vachel Lindsay. BiP; CMoP; NePA
Unplait the braided dark. To the Spring Sun. Freda Laughton. NeIP
Unplanned Design. Neal Bowers. AMV-80
Unpossessed, The. Adèle Naudé. PeSA
Unposted Birthday Card. Norman MacCaig. NAs
Unpraised Picture, An. Richard Burton. AA
Unpredictable but Providential. W. H. Auden. SUW
Unpredicted, The. John Heath-Stubbs. BoLoP; OxBC
Unprofitablenes. Henry Vaughan. AnAnS-1; SeCV-1
Unpurged images of day recede, The. Byzantium. W. B. Yeats. CABA; CMoP; CoBMV; EBEV; FaBoEn; FaBoMo; HAP; InPS; LiTM; LoBV; MoAB; MoBrPo; MoPo; NIP; NoAM; NOBE; NoP; OAEL-2; OAEP; OnYI; OxBTC; PPP; SeCePo; SeCeV; TEP
Unquiet Grave, The. *Unknown.* AmFP, *shorter version*; CH; DTC; ELP; EnSB; ESPB; FaBoBa; FSW; GBP; HAP; HeIP; InPK; LO; LoBV; NoP (A *vers.*); OAEL-1, *with music*; OBET; PoEL-1; PoPle; ViBoFo, *with music*; ViBoPo; WeW
(Unquiet Grave, The, *with music.*) OxBB
Unraveled Thought, An. Shlomit Cohen, *tr. fr. Hebrew by* Myra Glazer Schotz. VWA
Unreal silence, An. Swallows over the Camp. Uys Krige, *tr. by* Uys Krige *and* Jack Cope. PeSA
Unreal Song of the Old, The. James Koller. PoM
Unreal tall as a myth. The Bear on the Delhi Road. Earle Birney. BoAnP; HeIP; MoCV; NOBC; NoP; NYBP; PoCh; PrIm
Unreal the Buffalo Is Standing. *Unknown.* GOA
Unrealities, The. Schiller, *tr. fr. German by* James Clarence Mangan. AWP
Unrecorded Speech. Anna Adams. BrRo
Unregenerate. Jacqueline Embry. HBMV
Unrelenting Flood. William Matthews. GeTw
Unremarkable Year, The. Roy Fuller. OxBC
Unrest. Richard Watson Dixon. OBNC
Unrest. Don Marquis. HBMV
Unreturning, The. Wilfred Owen. MoBrPo
Unreturning, The. Clinton Scollard. PAH
Unreturning. Elizabeth Stoddard. AA
Unriddle me my riddle. Winter Rune. Elizabeth J. Coatsworth. SUS
Unrighteous Lord of love, what law is this. Amoretti, X. Spenser. NoP
Unromantic Song. Anthony Brode. DBV; FiBHP
Unsaid. A. R. Ammons. NOBA
Unsaid Word, An. Adrienne Rich. NMM
Unsatisfied Yearning. Richard Kendall Munkittrick. GDP; InMe
Unscarred Fighter Remembers France, The. Kenneth Slade Alling. HBMV
Unseasonable/ as bees in April. Vermont: Indian Summer. Philip Booth. NePoEA
Unseemly as a marvellous and astral renegade. Queen Anne's Lace. June Jordan. TAP
Unseen. Fanny Crosby. TrPWD
Unseen Bridge, The. Gilbert Thomas. HBMV
Unseen Deer, An. John Tagliabue. Psk
Unseen Fire, An. Michael G. Cooke. AMV-81
Unseen Fire. R. N. Currey. OBWP
"This is a damned inhuman sort of war," *sel.* OxBTC
Unseen Flight. Markos Georgeou. AMV-80
Unseen Horses. Joan Byers Grayston. PH
Unseen, snow slides from over-laden boughs. Fire-Queen. Ruth Fainlight. PoA
Unseen Spirits. Nathaniel Parker Willis. *See* Two Women.
Unsent Message to My Brother in His Pain. Leon Stokesbury. MAYP
Unsettled again and hearing Russian spoken. Hearing Russian Spoken. Donald Davie. GTBS-P; NePoEA-2
Unsettled Motorcyclist's Vision of His Death, The. Thom Gunn. NePoEA-2; PoA
Unsexed by the cold sea, prone out of it on the beach. Watch Hill. Winfield Townley Scott. ErPo
Unshrinking Faith. W. H. Balhurst. BLRP
Unshunnable is grief; we should not fear. Grief and God. Stephen Phillips. WGRP
Unsleeping City. Federico García Lorca, *tr. fr. Spanish by* Ben Belitt. NYP
Unsolicited Letters to Five Artists. Clive James. FaBoPa
Unsolved Mystery. George Ryan. WhC
Unspeakable. Margaret Avison. NOBC
Unstable dream[e], accordyng [*or* according] to the place. The Lover Having Dreamed of [*or* Enjoying of] His Love, Complaineth That the Dream[e] Is Not either Longer or Truer. Sir Thomas Wyatt. AAS; OAEP; WHA
Unsung Heroes, The. Paul Laurence Dunbar. BPo
Unsuspected Fact, An. Edward Cannon. NA
Unteaching, The. Carol Oles. SOTS
Unter der Linde. George Ellenbogen. AMV-81
Unthrift. Coventry Patmore. The Angel in the House, I, iii, 3. HBV-1 (Preludes, I). GoBC
Until a man should/ come. Man as He Shall Be. Rochelle Owens. CoPo
Until Death. Elizabeth Akers Allen. HBV-1
Until fall, a grasshopper/ Chose to chirr. The Grasshopper and the Ant. La Fontaine, *tr. by* Marianne Moore. NAWM-2
Until I learned to trust. Progress. *Unknown.* STF
Until I lose my soul and lie. A Prayer. Sara Teasdale. HBMV; TrPWD
Until I Reach-a Ma Home, *with music. Unknown.* BoAN-1
Until I Saw the Sea. Lilian Moore. NTCP; RHPC
Until I was a roustabout. Animal Fair. Philip Booth. NePoAm-2
Until my lamp and I. Discovery. Hildegarde Flanner. HBMV
Until Tatum passed. Standing on the Corner. Philip Levine. NNaP
Until that sun, which keeps. Trains Made of Stone. Ray A. Young Bear. CDW
Until the desert knows. Emily Dickinson. MoPo; NOBA
Until the Shadows Lengthen. Cardinal Newman. TRV
Until They Have Stopped. Sarah E. Wright. PoBA
Until thine hands clasp girdlewise the waist of the Belov'd. Ode. Sadi, *tr. by* R. A. Nicholson. AWP
Until this poem is over, I shall not leave. Windfall. F. R. Scott. CaP
Until We Built a Cabin. Aileen Fisher. TiPo
Until yesterday I was polite and peaceful. Opinions of the New Student. Regino Pedroso, *tr. by* Langston Hughes. TTY
Until your laughter. Tumult. Charles Enoch Wheeler. PoNe
Untitled. Daryl Hine. NoAM; TwCP
Untitled. James A. Randall, Jr. BPo
Untitled. Mah-do-ge Tohee. STE
Untitled I. Ishmael Reed. CNA
Untitled Poem, about an Uncompleted Sonnet, An. Sanford Pinsker. AMV-81
Untitled Requiem for Tomorrow. Conyus. PoBA
Unto a Child in Bethlehem-town. Eugene Field. *Fr.* Bethlehem Town. PGD
Unto a heavenly course decreed. Star Morals. Friedrich Nietzsche, *tr. by* Ludwig Lewisohn. AWP
Unto God let praise be brought. And It Came to Pass at Midnight. Yannai. TrJP
Unto Jehovah Sing Will I, *with music.* Henry Ainsworth. AH
Unto my faith as to a spar, I bind. Adrift. Elizabeth Dickinson Dowden. WGRP
Unto my thinking, thou beheld'st all worth. To Dante Alighieri. Guido Cavalcanti, *tr. by* Dante Gabriel Rossetti. AWP
Unto no body my woman saith she had rather a wife be. Catullus, *tr. fr. Latin by* Sir Philip Sidney. OBVE
Unto Our God Most High We Sing, *with music.* John Vance Cheney. AH
Unto the blithe and lordly Fellowship. Sonnets of the Months: Dedication. Folgore da San Geminiano, *tr. by* Dante Gabriel Rossetti. AWP
Unto the boundless ocean of thy beauty. To Delia. Samuel Daniel. LoBV; OAEP; OBSC
Unto the Breach. Andrea Poliziano, *tr. fr. Latin by* John Addington Symonds. PeHV
Unto the deep the deep heart goes. The Place of Rest. "Æ." WGRP
Unto the prison house of pain none willingly repair. The House of Pain. Florence Earle Coates. HBV-2
Unto the silver night. Revelation. Edmund Gosse. OBVV
Unto the temple of thy beauty. *Unknown.* OBSC
Unto the Upright Praise, *sel.* Moses Hayyim Luzzatto, *tr. fr. Hebrew by* Nina Davis Salaman.
Chorus: "All ye that handle harp and viol." TrJP
Unto this place when as the Elfin Knight. The Hill of the Graces. Spenser. *Fr.* The Faerie Queene, VI, 10. NOBE
Unto Us a Son Is Given. Alice Meynell. EBCP

Unto you a Child. Vision of the Shepherds. W. H. Auden. *Fr.* For the Time Being; a Christmas Oratorio. SBVL
Unto you, most froward, this letter I write. A Grotesque Love-Letter. *Unknown.* MeEL
Untold Want, The. Walt Whitman. MoAmPo
Untouched by Adam's curse—our Mary's soul! Hymn for Second Vespers; Feast of the Apparition of Our Lady of Lourdes. *Unknown, tr. by* Raymond F. Roseliep. ISi
Untouched grandeur in the hinterlands. Life in the Boondocks. A. R. Ammons. HAP
Untrammelled giant of the West. The Parting of the Ways. Joseph B. Gilder. HBV-2; PAH
Untrodden Ways. Agnes Maule Machar. CaP
Untutored Giraffe, The, *sel.* Oliver Herford.
"Once on a time a young giraffe." ShM
Untwine those ringlets! Ev'ry dainty clasp. Frangipanni. *Unknown.* NA
Unusual thing called a Troupial, An. A Troupial. Milton Bracker. TDH
Unusual Things. Tom Hennen. FAZ
Unutterable Beauty, The. G. A. Studdert-Kennedy. TrPWD
Unutterable void of Hell is stirred, The. The Lesbian Hell. Aleister Crowley. PeHV
Unveiling, The. Suzanne Bernhardt. VWA
Unwanted, The. C. Day Lewis. PoPl
Unwanted. Edward Field. CoPo; PPON; Psk
Unwanted, The. Mary Gordon. IHMS
Unwarmed by any sunset light. The World Transformed. Whittier. *Fr.* Snow-bound. AA
Unwatch'd, the garden bough shall sway. In Memoriam A. H. H., CI. Tennyson. ELP; FaBoPP; GTBS-P; OBNC; PoEL-5; PoPle; SCV; SeCeV
Unweary'd watch their list'ning leaders keep, Th'. Homer, *tr. by* Pope. *Fr.* The Iliad, X. OBVE
Unwelcome. Mary Elizabeth Coleridge. CH; OBEV; OBNC; OBVV; PoPle; WPE
Unwelcome. Irma Dovey. AMV-80
Unwelcome child. The Child Compassion. Margot Ruddock. OBMV
Unwilling Guest, The; an Urban Dialogue. Horace Gregory. CrMA
Unwilling Gypsy, The. Josephine Johnson. HBMV
Unwillingly Miranda wakes. A Lady Thinks She Is Thirty. Ogden Nash. PoPl
Unwinding the spool of the morning. Invocation. Vassar Miller. NCSH
Unwinking frog of malachite, The. Museum-Piece. Audrey Alexandra Brown. CaP
Unwritten Poems. William Winter. AA
Unyielding in the pride of his defiance. The Flying Dutchman. E. A. Robinson. MOS
Up a ladder weightless as bird legs, thinner. The Fifth Season. Reg Saner. FYAP
Up above, a passing breeze. Fir Forest. Ethel Romig Fuller. PGD
Up against the Wall. D. C. Berry. BXAP
Up against the Wall. Cleve Phillips. AMV-81
Up against the wall. To Fez Cobra. Ted Joans. GP
Up all night. The Wakening. Sam Hamill. AMV-80
Up aloft amid the rigging. Rolling Home. Charles Mackay. AmSS; FSW
Up and betimes across the asphalt water. Pepys Bar, West Forty-eighth Street, 8 a.m. L. E. Sissman. NYP
Up and Down. Shakespeare. *Fr.* A Midsummer Night's Dream, III, ii. CTC
Up and down, o'er hill and valley. Triumph. L. D. Stearns. BLRP
Up and down the beach. The Skin Divers. George Starbuck. NYBP
Up and down the City Road. Pop Goes the Weasel! *At. to* W. R. Mardale. EvOK; FaBoNo; OxNR; PoPle
Up and down. The Rose. Robert Creeley. AP
Up & Out. Nila NorthSun. STE
Up and up soars the Evening Star, hanging there in the sky. The Evening Star. *Aborigine Oral Tradition, tr. by* R. M. Berndt. *Fr.* The Moon-Bone Cycle. WTO
Up at a Villa—Down in the City. Robert Browning. FaBoPP; GTBS-P; HBV-1; NOBE; PoRA; PPP; SeCeV
Up at Piccadilly oh! Mother Goose. OxNR
Up, black, striped and damasked like the chasuble. The Skunk. Seamus Heaney. OxBC
Up, boy! arise, and saddle quick. The Message. Heine, *tr. by* Kate Freiligrath Kroeker. AWP
Up early while everyone sleeps. Sunday. Vern Rutsala. DFF
Up, Fairy! quit the chick-weed bower. The Second Quest. Joseph Rodman Drake. *Fr.* The Culprit Fay. AA
Up from my belly, up from my back. Chopping Fire-Wood. Robert Pack. NePoEA-2
Up from the Bed of the River. James Weldon Johnson. *Fr.* The Creation. EaLo
Up from the bottom. Flag. Reg Saner. GP
Up from the bronze, I saw. Roman Fountain. Louise Bogan. NoP; SBG; WPOW
Up from the darkness on the laughing stage. Villiers de l'Isle-Adam. Aldous Huxley. HBMV
Up from the desert desolate and bleak. The Organ Cactus. Dorothy Scarborough. BPAW
Up from the Egg: The Confessions of a Nuthatch Avoider. Ogden Nash. BoAnP; FiBHP; PoRA
Up from the log cabin to the Capitol. Edwin Markham. *Fr.* Lincoln, the Man of the People. OFD
Up from the low-roofed dockyard warehouses. Grain Elevator. A. M. Klein. CaP
Up from the meadows rich with corn. Barbara Frietchie. Whittier. AP; BeLS; CTC; FaBoBe; FaBV; FaFP; FaPo; FaPON; FaPoR; FPL; GN; HBV-2; HBVY; NOBA: OBAL; OBCA; PAH; PAL; PaPo; PoLF; PoSC; TreF; TrGrPo; WBLP; YaD
Up from the south, at break of day. Sheridan's Ride. Thomas Buchanan Read. BeLS; FaBoBe; FaBV; FaFP; GN; HBV-2; HBVY; OHFP; OHIP; PAH; TreF; WBLP; YaD
Up from the Wheelbarrow. Ogden Nash. FaBoBe
Up from West 86 St., banging, against all hope. The Fabulous Teamsters. Judith Johnson Sherwin. NYP
Up-front ones are marvelous, The. My Teeth. Ed Ochester. DFF; GP
Up, Helsum Hairt. Alexander Scott. OxBS
Up here at the wharepuni. He Waiata mo Te Kare. James K. Baxter. OCNZ
Up here I can see the/ glimmering lights. At Mexican Springs. Laura Tohe. STE
Up-Hill. *See* Uphill
Up I Arose in Verno Tempore. *Unknown.* GBP
Up in a dirty window in a dark room is a star. The Pilot. Russell Edson. LCAP
Up in Jackson County they have. Jutaculla Rock. Robert Morgan. SUW
Up in the Air. Allan Ramsay. BSV; NOEC
Up in the Air. James S. Tippett. SoPo; SUS; TiPo
Up in the attic, down in the cellar, and under. A Treasure. Reed Whittemore. NePoEA
Up in the heavenly saloon. Arizona Nature Myth. James Michie. NOBL
Up in the lift go we. *Unknown.* PBBP
Up in the Morning Early. Burns. PoSC
Up in the mountains, it's lonesome all the time. The Mountain Whippoorwill. Stephen Vincent Benét. TrGrPo; YaD
Up in the North, a long way off. Out Goes She. *Unknown.* OxBoLi; PoPle
Up in the Pine. Nancy Dingman Watson. RHPC
Up in this quiet room here, reading your letter. Fidelities. Jean Valentine. NYP
Up into the cherry tree. Foreign Lands. Robert Louis Stevenson. HBV-1; HBVY; SUS
Up Johnie raise in a May morning. Johnie Cock. *Unknown.* ESPB
Up leaps the lark. Delightful Spring once more. Edmund St. Gascoigne Mackie. *Fr.* Charmides. PeHV
Up-line platform bridges a metal road, The. Ravenglass Railway Station, Cumberland. Norman Nicholson. NYBP
Up on de Mountain, *with music.* *Unknown.* BoAN-1
Up on the Downs. John Masefield. FaBoEn; NOBE
("Up on the downs the red-eyed kestrels hover.") BrPo
Up on the mountain my Lord spoke. Every Time I Feel the Spirit. *Unknown.* FSW
Up on their brooms the witches stream. The Ride-by-Nights. Walter de la Mare. DuDa; FaPON; SiSoSe; TiPo; WSC
Up out of the African. Ted Joans. GP
Up! quit thy bower! late wears the hour. Wake, Lady! Joanna Baillie. HBV-1
Up Rising. Robert Duncan. *Fr.* Passages. NNaP
Up rose the sun; the mists were curl'd. Byron. *Fr.* Mazeppa. OBRV
Up-Set, The. Corey Ford. WhC
Up Silver Stairsteps. Jesse Stuart. AmFN
Up street and down street. *Unknown.* OxNR
Up, sun and mery wether! Sometime I Loved. *Unknown.* OxBM
Up-Tails All. *Unknown.* UnTE
Up tails all! Down and under! Undersea Fever. William Cole. FiBHP
Up the Airy Mountain. William Allingham. *See* Fairies, The.
Up the ash tree climbs the ivy. Upper Lambourne. John Betjeman. FaBoTw
Up the Barley Rows. Sora, *tr. fr. Japanese by* Harold G. Henderson. SoPo
Up the Country. Henry Lawson. CBAP
Up the crag. Weapons. Anna Wickham. MoBrPo
Up the dark-valleyed river stroke by stroke. The Dawn on the Lievre. Archibald Lampman. CaP
Up the dusty way from Frisco town. Walk, Damn You, Walk! William de Vere. PoLF

Up the hill/ Hurry me not. *Unknown.* PH
Up the Hill, down the Hill. Eleanor Farjeon. PoSC
Up the hillside, down the glen. Texas. Whittier. PAH
Up the Noran Water. Shy Geordie. Helen B. Cruickshank. BSV; GoTS; OxBS
Up the old hill to the old house again. The Long Race. E. A. Robinson. CrMA
Up the reputable walks of old established trees. The Campus on the Hill. W. D. Snodgrass. AP; LiTM; MP; NIP; NoAM; TAP; TwCP
Up the river, where it thins out. Leaving Here. Stephen Philbrick. AMV-81
Up the wooden hill. *Unknown.* OxNR
Up then, Melpomene, thou mournfulst Muse of nine. Dido My Dear, Alas, Is Dead. Spenser. *Fr.* The Shepheardes Calender: November. ChTr
Up There. W. H. Auden. OxBTC
Up there/ an imitation. Catwalk. Daniel L. Klauck. LFAC
Up there on the mountain road, the fireworks. Blue Ridge. Ellen Bryant Voigt. MAYP
Up through a cloudy sky, the sun. The Battle of Bennington. Thomas P. Rodman. PAH
Up through five green. And This Is My Father. Marcus J. Grapes. AMV-80
"Up, Timothy, up with your staff and away!" The Childless Father. Wordsworth. CH
Up to Date. "Hugh MacDiarmid." FaBoCo
Up to her chamber window. Nocturne. Thomas Bailey Aldrich. HBV-1
Up to my lips and over my gums. Toast. *Unknown.* CoSo
Up to the bed by the window, where I be lyin'. Old Shepherd's Prayer. Charlotte Mew. EaLo; MoAB; MoBrPo; OxBTC; WPE
Up to the ranch rides cowboy Freddy. From the Ballad of Two-Gun Freddy. Walter R. Brooks. SoPo
Up to the top of the haunted turf. Walter de la Mare Tells the Listener about Jack and Jill. Louis Untermeyer. *Fr.* Mother Goose Up-to-Date. MoAmPo
Up to thy summit, Lewesdon, to the brow. William Crowe. *Fr.* Lewesdon Hill. NOEC
Up! up! let us a voyage take. The Northern Seas. William Howitt. GN
Up, up, my drowsie Soule, where thy new eare. Our Companie in the Next World. John Donne. *Fr.* Of the Progresse of the Soul; the Second Anniversarie. OBS
Up! Up! my friend, and quit your books. The Tables Turned. Wordsworth. EnRP; HBV-1; OAEL-2; OAEP; OBRV
Up! Up! The sky's afloat. Song for a Camper. John Farrar. YeAr
Up! Up! the time for sleep is past! The Expensive Wife. Judah ibn Sabbatai. *Fr.* The Gift of Judah the Woman-Hater. TrJP
Up! Up! You brothers, now be strong. Song of the Cape of Good Hope. Christian Schubart, *ad. by* Robert Bly. NU
Up where the white bluffs fringe the plain. Prairie Wolves. Robert V. Carr. BPAW; PoOW
Up where the world grows cold. A North Pole Story. Menella Bute Smedley. OxBChV
Up with me! up with me into the clouds! To a Skylark. Wordsworth. FPL; HBV-1
Up with you, lazybones! Getting Out of Bed. Eleanor Farjeon. SiSoSe
Up yonder on the mountain. The Shepherd's Lament. Goethe, *tr. by* Bayard Taylor. AWP
Upanishads, *sels. Tr. fr. Sanskrit by* Raimundo Panikkar. ILwL
"He said to Patancala Kapya and to the students."
"One alone is God; there cannot be a second."
"Revealed and yet dwelling hidden in the cave."
Upended, it crouches on broken limbs. Poem. Charles Tomlinson. CMoP
Upgrade, past snow-tangled bramble, past. Sila. Robert Penn Warren. NoP
Up-Hill [*or* Uphill]. Christina Rossetti. BLPA; CH; EBVV; FaBoBe; FaBoRV; FPL; HAP; HBV-2; LoBV; NOBE; NoP; OAEL-2; OAEP; OBEV; OBNC; OBVV; PoRA; PPP; TrCP; TreFS; TrGrPo; ViBoPo; VLP; WeW; WGRP; WHA; WiR; WPE
Up hill and down dale. *Unknown.* OxNR
Upland. A. R. Ammons. NOBA
Upland flocks grew starved and thinned, The. The Lambs of Grasmere, 1860. Christina Rossetti. FM
Uplift a thousand voices full and sweet. Ode Sung at the Opening of the International Exhibition. Tennyson. VLP
Upon a Black Twist, Rounding the Arm of the Countess of Carlisle. Robert Herrick. CaPo
Upon a Braid of Hair in a Heart. Henry King. EnLoPo
Upon a Child. Robert Herrick. LoBV; OBS; SeCV-1; TrGrPo
("Here a pretty baby lies.") OBEV
Upon a Child That Died ("Here she lies, a pretty bud"). Robert Herrick. CaPo; CavP; CH; InPK; NoP; PAI; SeCV-1
(Epitaph upon a Child That Died.) OBEV
Upon a Christmas Morning. *Unknown.* AmFP
Upon a cloud among the stars we stood. The Flight. Lloyd Mifflin. AA; HBV-2
Upon a cock-horse to market I'll trot. *Unknown.* OxNR
Upon a dainty hill sometime. Nicholas Breton. PBBP
Upon a dark ball spun in time. Giraffe and Tree. W. J. Turner. CH; GrPl
Upon a dark, light, gloomy, sunshine day. A Messe of Nonsense. *Unknown.* OBS
Upon a darksome night. St. John of the Cross, *tr. fr. Spanish by* E. Allison Peers. ErPo
Upon a Day. Spenser. OAEP
Upon a day, came sorrow in to me. Sonnet: On the 9th of June 1290. Dante, *tr. by* Dante Gabriel Rossetti. AWP
Upon a Dead Man's Head. John Skelton. EnRePo; HAP; SeCePo
(Gift of a Skull, The.) ACP
(Uppon a Deedmans Hed.) AAS
Upon a Delaying Lady. Robert Herrick. PoPle
Upon a Diamond Cut in Form[e] of a Heart . . . Sent in a New-Yeares [*or* Year's] Gift. Sir Robert Ayton. ElL; OBS
(Crowned Heart, The, *shorter sel.*) PoPle
Upon a Dying Lady. W. B. Yeats. LiTB; UnPo
Upon a fibry fern-tree bough. Mid-Noon in January. "Fiona Macleod." *Fr.* Australian Transcripts. FM
Upon a Flie. Robert Herrick. FM
Upon a Fool. John Hoskyns. FaBoEE
Upon a Funeral. Sir John Beaumont. FaBoRV
Upon a Gloomy Night. St. John of the Cross. *See* Dark Night, The.
Upon a Great Shower of Snow That Fell on May-Day, 1654. Thomas Washbourne. NOCV
Upon a House Shaken by the Land Agitation. W. B. Yeats. CMoP
Upon a jolting wagonseat she rode. The Pioneer Mother. Ethel Romig Fuller. PGD
Upon A. M. Sir John Suckling. CavP; ErPo
Upon a Maid ("Gone she is a long, long way"). Robert Herrick. CaPo
Upon a Maid ("Here she lies in bed of spice"). Robert Herrick. CaPo; ChTr; FaBoCh; FaBoEE; OxBoLi
Upon a Maid That Died [*or* Dyed] the Day She Was Married [*or* Marryed]. Meleager, *tr. fr. Greek by* Robert Herrick. AWP; OBVE
("That morn which saw me made a bride.") NIP
Upon a Mole in Celia's Bosom[e]. Thomas Carew. AnAnS-2; CaPo
Upon a mountain['s] height, far from the sea. The Wanderer. Eugene Field. BPAW; PoOW; PoPl
Upon a night an aungell bright. Now the Most High Is Born. James Ryman. MeEL
Upon a Notorious Shrew. *Unknown.* FaBoEE
Upon a Passing Bell. Thomas Washbourne. FaBoRV
Upon a Ribband. Thomas Carew. AnAnS-2; CaPo; OAEL-1
Upon a Rich Country Gentleman. *Unknown.* FaBoEE
Upon a Ring of Bells. Bunyan. CH
Upon a Row of Old Books and Shoes in a Pawnbroker's Window. "Furnley Maurice." CBAP
Upon a Sabbath-day it fell. The Eve of Saint Mark. Keats. CH; EnRP; OBRV; WHA
Upon a Second Marriage. James Merrill. *See* For a Second Marriage.
Upon a showery night and still. The Dandelions. Helen Gray Cone. HBV-1
Upon a simmer Sunday morn. The Holy Fair. Burns. EnRP; LAuP; OAEP; OBSV
Upon a Snail. Bunyan. *See* Upon the Snail.
Upon a Spider Catching a Fly. Edward Taylor. AmPP; AP; NePA; NOBA; NoP; OxBA; PoEL-3; SCAP; TAP
Upon a sudden, as I gazing stood. Rachel Speght. *Fr.* A Dream. WPE
Upon a summer Sunday: sweet the sound. The Runaways. Mark Van Doren. PoRA
Upon a summer's time. A Pleasant New Court Song. *Unknown.* CoMu
Upon a time a neighing steed. The Council of Horses. John Gay. GN
Upon a time, before the faery broods. Lamia. Keats. EnRP; OAEP
Upon a tree there mounted guard. The Cock and the Fox. La Fontaine, *tr. by* Elizur Wright. AWP
Upon a tuffet of most soft and verdant moss. Little Miss Muffet, *parody. Unknown.* BXAP; FaBoPa
Upon a Virgin Kissing a Rose. Robert Herrick. SeCP; SeCV-1
Upon a Wasp Chilled [*or* Child] with Cold. Edward Taylor. FaBoEn; NOBA; NOCV; PoEL-3
Upon a Wife That Dyed Mad with Jealousie. Robert Herrick. CavP
Upon a Young Mother of Many Children. Robert Herrick. CaPo
Upon Absence. Katherine Philips. PBWP
Upon an Easter Morning. Eleanor Farjeon. PoSC
Upon an everlasting tide. The Epicurean. Sir Francis Hastings Doyle. OBVV
Upon an Hermaphrodite. John Cleveland. AnAnS-2
Upon an obscure night. The Obscure Night of the Soul. St John of the Cross, *tr. by* Arthur Symons. AWP; ILwL; OBMV

Upon an old estate from ancient sires descended. The Portraits. Anna Maria Lenngren, *tr. by* C. W. Stork. WPOW
Upon ane stormy Sunday. The Plaidie. Charles Sibley. HBV-1
Upon Apennine Slope. Arthur Hugh Clough. *See* Ah, That I Were Far Away.
Upon Appleton House, to My Lord Fairfax. Andrew Marvell. SeCP; SeCV-1
Sels.
After Floods on the Wharfe. FaBoPP
"And now to the abyss I pass." OAEL-1
Carrying Their Coracles. ChTr
"From that blest bed the hero came." JCP
Garden at Appleton House, The ("See how the flowers as at parade"). PoPle
(Garden, A.) HBV-1; OBEV
("See how the flowers, as at parade.") TrGrPo
Garden of Appleton House, The ("When in the east the morning ray"). NOBE
Hewel, or Woodpecker, The. ChTr
Kingfisher, The. ChTr; PB
"Oh thou, that dear and happy isle." OxBoLi
So when the shadows laid asleep. FaBoEn
"When first the eye this forest sees." PBBP
Upon Batt. Robert Herrick. AnAnS-2; FaBoEE
Upon Being Awakened at Night by My Four Year Old Daughter. Dachine Rainer. NePoAm-2
Upon Ben Jonson. Robert Herrick. CaPo; NoP; OAEP; OBS; SeCV-1
(Upon Master Ben Jonson: Epigram.) CaPo; OAEP
Upon Ben Jonson. Edmund Waller. SeCV-1
Upon Bishop Andrewes His Picture before His Sermons. Richard Crashaw. OBS
Upon Boys Diverting Themselves in the River. Thomas Foxton. OxBChV
Upon Bunce: Epigram. Robert Herrick. CaPo
Upon Castara's Absence. William Habington. AnAnS-2
Upon Christ His Birth. Sir John Suckling. NCEP
Upon Christmas Eve. Sir John Suckling. NCEP
Upon de Mountain, *with music. Unknown.* TrAS
Upon Drinking in a Bowl. Earl of Rochester. OBS; OxBoLi; SeCV-2
(Upon His Drinking Bowl.) CavP
Upon Eckington Bridge, River Avon. Sir Arthur Quiller-Couch. OBVV
Upon Fairford Windows. Richard Corbett. EyDe
(Upon Faireford Windowes.) AnAnS-2
Upon Fone a School-Master, Epigram. Robert Herrick. AnAnS-2
Upon Ford's Two Tragedies, "Loves Sacrifice" and "The Broken Heart." Richard Crashaw. OBS
Upon Glass: Epigram. Robert Herrick. JCP
Upon Groins: Epigram. Robert Herrick. CaPo
Upon Gryll. Robert Herrick. AnAnS-2
Upon Hearing His High Sweet Tenor Again. Joseph Langland. AMV-81
Upon Her Feet. Robert Herrick. CaPo; ViBoPo
Upon her head she weares a crowne of starres. An Angel Describes Truth. Ben Jonson. *Fr.* Hymenaei. OBS
Upon Her Soothing Breast. Emily Brontë. BoWoP
Upon Her Voice. Robert Herrick. CaPo
Upon himself a miracle he wrought. Eugenio Pacelli. Francis Neilson. GoYe
Upon His Departure Hence. Robert Herrick. FaBoRV; QFR
Upon His Drinking Bowl. Earl of Rochester. *See* Upon Drinking in a Bowl.
Upon his dull ear fell the stern command. The Black Draftee from Dixie. Carrie Williams Clifford. BlSi
Upon His Julia. Robert Herrick. SpRo
Upon His Leaving His Mistress. Earl of Rochester. EnLoPo; GBL; TEP; ViBoPo
(Upon Leaving His Mistress.) TrGrPo; UnTE
Upon His Majesty's Being Made Free of the City. Andrew Marvell. *See* On the Lord Mayor and Court of Aldermen, Presenting the Late King and Duke of York Each with a Copy of Their Freedoms.
Upon His Picture. Thomas Randolph. MePo; NOBE
Upon His Sister-in-Law, Mistress Elizabeth Herrick. Robert Herrick. CaPo
Upon His Spaniell Tracie. Robert Herrick. FM
Upon Jack and Jill: Epigram. Robert Herrick. AnAnS-2; CaPo
Upon Jone and Jane. Robert Herrick. AnAnS-2
Upon Julia. Ernest Radford. BXAP
Upon Julia Washing Herself in the River. Robert Herrick. CaPo
Upon Julia's Arctics. Bert Leston Taylor. OBAL
Upon Julia's Breasts. Robert Herrick. CaPo; NoP
Upon Julia's Clothes. Robert Herrick. AnAnS-2; AWP; CABA; CaPo; ChTr; EBEV; EnLoPo; FaBV; FaFP; FF; GBL; HAP; HBV-1; HeIP; HoPM; InPS; JCP; LiTB; LoBV; NIP; NOBE; NoP; OAEL-1; OAEP; OBEV; OBS; PAI; PoEL-3; PoPle; PPP; SeCeV; SeCP; SeCV-1; SpRo; TreF; TrGrPo; ViBoPo; WeW
(Whenas in Silks My Julia Goes.) BLPA: FPL; GTBS; GTBS-P; TEP
Upon Julia's Clothes. E. V. Knox. BXAP
Upon Julia's Fall. Robert Herrick. UnTE
Upon Julia's Petticoat. Robert Herrick. *See* Julia's Petticoat.
Upon Julia's Ribband. Robert Herrick. CaPo
Upon Julia's Voice. Robert Herrick. CABA; InPK; JCP; NOBE; SeCePo; SeCP; SoSe
Upon Kinde and True Love. Aurelian Townshend. CavP; MeLP; MePo; OBS
Upon Lazarus His Teares. Richard Crashaw. SeCV-1
Upon learning that the mother wrote verses. Soirée. Ezra Pound. DTC
Upon Leaving His Mistress. Earl of Rochester. *See* Upon His Leaving His Mistress.
Upon Leaving the Parole Board Hearing. Conyus. PoBA
Upon Lesbia—Arguing. Alfred Cochrane. HBV-1
Upon Looking at a Book of Astrology. David McFadden. NeAC
Upon Love ("Love brought me to a silent grove"). Robert Herrick. TrGrPo
Upon Love ("Love scorch'd my finger, but did not spare"). SeCV-1
Upon Love, by Way of Question and Answer. Robert Herrick. CaPo
Upon Love Fondly Refused for Conscience's Sake. Thomas Randolph. AnAnS-2; OAEL-1
Upon Lulls. Robert Herrick. CaPo
Upon Master Ben Jonson: Epigram. Robert Herrick. *See* Upon Ben Jonson.
Upon Master Edmund Spenser. Francis Beaumont. FaBoEE
Upon Master Fletcher's Incomparable Playes. Robert Herrick. OBS
Upon Master Walter Montagu's Return from Travel. Thomas Carew. CaPo
Upon Mrs. Anne Bradstreet Her Poems. John Rogers. SCAP
Upon Mistress Elizabeth Wheeler under the Name of Amarillis. Robert Herrick. CaPo; PBBP
Upon Moon. Robert Herrick. MOON
Upon my bier no garlands lay. Now. Mary Barker Dodge. AA
Upon my darling's beaming eyes. Auf meiner Herzliebsten Äugelein. Heine, *tr. by* Richard Garnett. AWP
Upon My Lady Carlisle's Walking in Hampton Court Garden. Sir John Suckling. AnAnS-2; CaPo; NoP
Upon my lap my sovereign sits. Lullaby [*or* Our Lady's Lullaby]. Richard Verstegan. ACP; CH; EIL; GoBC; HBV-1; ISi; LoBV; OBEV; ViBoPo
Upon My Lord Brohall's Wedding. Sir John Suckling. CaPo
Upon My Lord Chief Justice's Election of My Lady Anne Wentworth for His Mistress. Thomas Carew. CaPo
Upon my mantel-piece they stand. A Moral in Sèvres. Mildred Howells. HBV-1
Upon my right side I me lay. Prayer for Good Dreams. *Unknown.* OxBM
Upon New Year's Eve. Sir Arthur Quiller-Couch. OBVV
Upon Nirwána's brink the ráhat stood. The Ráhat. John Jerome Rooney. AA
Upon Nothing. Earl of Rochester. MePo; OBS; OBSV; PoEL-3; TrGrPo; ViBoPo
Upon One of the Maids of Honour to Queen Elizabeth. John Hoskyns. FaBoEE
Upon our eyelids, dear, the dew will lie. Before Dawn in the Woods. Marguerite Wilkinson. HBMV
Upon Our Saviour's Tomb Wherein Never Man Was Laid. Richard Crashaw. *See* To Our Blessed Lord upon the Choice of His Sepulchre.
Upon Pagget. Robert Herrick. CaPo; FaBoCh
Upon Parson Beanes. Robert Herrick. AnAnS-2
Upon Paul's steeple stands a tree. *Unknown.* OxNR
Upon Phillis Walking in a Morning before Sun-Rising. John Cleveland. AnAnS-2; MeLP
Upon Prew His Maid. Robert Herrick. *See* Upon Prue, His Maid.
Upon Prudence Baldwin Her Sickness[e]. Robert Herrick. JCP; OAEP; SeCV-1
Upon Prue, His Maid. Robert Herrick. JCP; NoP; OAEP; PAI
(Upon Prew, His Maid.) CaPo; CavP; InPK; SeCV-1
Upon Rook: Epigram. Robert Herrick. CaPo
Upon Roses. Robert Herrick. SeCP
Upon St. David's Day. *Unknown.* FaBoUs
Upon Scarlet and Blush-coloured Ribbands, Given by Two Ladies. James Shirley. GoBC
Upon Scobble. Robert Herrick. NoP; TW
(Upon Scobble: Epigram.) AnAnS-2; CaPo; FaBoEE
Upon Showbread: Epigram. Robert Herrick. CaPo
Upon Sibilla. Robert Herrick. *See* Upon Sybilla.
Upon Sir Francis Drake's Return from His Voyage about the World, and the Queen's Meeting Him. *Unknown.* CoMu; EIL; FaBoCh
Upon Sir John Lawrence's Bringing Water over the Hills to My Lord Middlesex's House at Wiston. Sir John Suckling. CaPo
Upon Some Alterations in My Mistress, after My Departure into France. Thomas Carew. CaPo
Upon Some Women. Robert Herrick. AnAnS-2; CaPo; DBV
Upon Sudds a Laundress[e]. Robert Herrick. AnAnS-2; DBV

Upon Sybilla. Robert Herrick. CaPo
(Upon Sibilla.) SeCePo
Upon that night, when fairies light. Halloween, *abr.* Burns. OBEC
Upon the Anonymous Author of Legion's Humble Address to the Lords. Thomas Brown. APAS
Upon the Author; by a Known Friend. Benjamin Woodbridge. SCAP
Upon the Author of a Play Called *Sodom.* John Oldham. TW
Upon the Author of the "Satire against Wit." Sir Charles Sedley. APAS
Upon the Author's First Seven Years' Service. Thomas Tusser. ElL
Upon the Bankruptcy of a Physician. Henricus Selyns. SCAP
Upon the barren sand. Pocahontas. George Pope Morris. PAH
Upon the beach are thousands of crabs. Crustaceans. Roy Fuller. NeBP; NoAM
Upon the black horse of midnight I ride. Night Musick for Thérèse. Dachine Rainer. NePoAm-2
Upon the Bleeding Crucifix. Richard Crashaw. *See* On the Bleeding Wounds of Our Crucified Lord.
Upon the Body of Our Blesséd Lord, Naked and Bloody. Richard Crashaw. *See* On Our Crucified Lord, Naked and Bloody.
Upon the Book and Picture of the Seraphical Saint Teresa. Richard Crashaw. *See* Flaming Heart, The.
Upon the boughs and tops of trees. Patrick Hannay. *Fr.* Philomela, the Nightingale. PBBP
Upon the branches of our silence hang our words. The Tree of Silence. Vassar Miller. NePoEA-2
Upon the branches of those trees. *Unknown. Fr.* An Elegy, or Friend's Passion, for His Astrophel. PBBP
Upon the Burning of Our House, July 10th, 1666. Anne Bradstreet. *See* Some Verses upon the Burning of Our House . . .
Upon the Crucifix. William Alabaster. PoEL-2
("Now I have found thee, I will ever more.") AnAnS-1
Upon the Curtain of Lucasta's Picture It Was Thus Wrought. Richard Lovelace. CaPo
Upon the Death of a Gentleman. Richard Crashaw. CavP
Upon the Death of G. B. John Cotton. SCAP
Upon the Death of George Santayana. Anthony Hecht. CoPo; NePA
Upon the Death of His Late Highness the Lord Protector. Andrew Marvell. *See* Poem upon the Death of Oliver Cromwell.
Upon the Death of His Much Esteemed Friend Mr. Jno Saffin Junr. Grindall Rawson. SCAP
Upon the Death of His Sparrow; an Elegie. Robert Herrick. FM
Upon the Death of Mr. King Drowned in the Irish Seas. John Cleveland. *See* On the Memory of Mr. Edward King. . .
Upon the Death of My Ever Desired Friend Doctor Donne Dean of Pauls. Henry King. AnAnS-2; SeCP
Upon the Death of Sir Albert[us] Morton's Wife. Sir Henry Wotton. AnAnS-2; BoLoP; EnLoPo; FaBoEE; NIP; NoP; OBEV; OBS; PoPle; SeCP; TreFT; ViBoPo; WeW
(On the Death of Sir Albert Morton's Wife.) TrGrPo
Upon the Death of the Earl of Dundee. Dryden. *See* Upon the Death of the Viscount of Dundee.
Upon the Death of the Lord Hastings. Dryden. SeCV-2
"Blisters with pride swelled, *sel.*" PeD
Upon the Death of the Viscount of Dundee. Dryden. OBS
(Upon the Death of the Earl of Dundee.) ACP
Upon the Decease of Mrs. Anne Griffin. John Fiske. SCAP
Upon the decks they take beef tea. Passage Steamer. Louis MacNeice. MOS
Upon the Double Murther of King Charles I. Katherine Philips. SBG
Upon the Downs. Sir George Etherege. ViBoPo
Upon the Dramatick Poems of Mr. John Fletcher. William Cartwright. OBS
Upon the earth there are so many treasures. Earth Felicities, Heavens Allowances. Richard Steere. SCAP
Upon the Eastern Shore of Windermere. On Windermere; Bowness Bay and Belle Isle. Wordsworth. *Fr.* The Prelude, I. FaBoPP
Upon the eighteenth day of June. Bonny John Seton. *Unknown.* ESPB
Upon the Ensignes of Christes Crucifyinge. William Alabaster. MePo
("O Sweete and bitter monuments of paine.") AnAnS-1
Upon the eyes, the lips, the feet. Extreme Unction. Ernest Dowson. ACP; MoBrPo; OAEL-2; OBMV; VLP
Upon the fifth day of November. On Mr. Pricke. *Unknown.* FaBoEE
Upon the First Sight of New England. Thomas Tillam. *See* Uppon the First Sight of New England, June 29, 1638.
Upon the flowery forefront of the year. Thalassius. Swinburne. VLP
Upon the Heavenly Scarp. A. M. Klein. *See* Psalm VI.
Upon the highest hill of all. The Apple Tree. Beatrice Curtis Brown. SiSoSe
Upon the Hill before Centreville. George Henry Boker. PAH
Upon the hill my lover stands. The House o' the Mirror. Helen Adam. MAT; NMM
Upon the hills new grass is seen. Twist-Rime on Spring. Arthur Guiterman. PoSC
Upon the hills of Phrygie near a teyle there stands a tree. Philemon and Baucis. Ovid, *tr. by* Arthur Golding. *Fr.* Metamorphoses, VIII. OBSC
Upon the Holy Sepulchre. Richard Crashaw. FaBoEE
Upon the Horse and His Rider. Bunyan. OxBChV
Upon the Image of Death. Robert Southwell. CH; ElL; NOBE; OBSC
(Before My Face the Picture Hangs.) OxBoCh
Upon the Infant Martyrs ("To see both blended in one flood"). Richard Crashaw. NoP; OAEL-1; PAI
Upon the King. Shakespeare. King Henry V, *fr.* IV, i. PPON
Upon the King's Return from Flanders. Henry Hall. APAS
Upon the King's Voyage to Chatham to Make Bulwarks against the Dutch. *Unknown.* APAS
Upon the Lake. Hayim Lenski, *tr. fr. Hebrew by* Robert Friend. VWA
Upon the lake. The Gramophone. James Reaney. CaP
Upon the Lark and the Fowler. Bunyan. CH; PBBP
Upon the level field behold. Baseball. Frank Dempster Sherman. OBCA
Upon the Loss[e] of His Mistresses. Robert Herrick. AnAnS-2; CaPo; OAEP; SeCV-1
Upon the Losse of His Little Finger. Thomas Randolph. AnAnS-2
Upon the man who's buried here. J. E. Thorold Rogers. FaBoEE
Upon the midsummer even, merriest of nichtis. *See* Apon the midsummer evin, mirriest of nichtis.
Upon the Most Useful Knowledge, Craft or Cunning, Which Is More Wisdom, as 'Tis Less Wit. William Wycherley. SeCV-2
Upon the Much-to Be Lamented Desease of the Reverend Mr. John Cotton. John Fiske. SCAP
Upon the Nipples of Julia's Breast. Robert Herrick. CaPo; ErPo; UnTE; ViBoPo
Upon the patch of earth that clings. Public Aid for Niagara Falls. Morris Bishop. InMe
Upon the poop the captain stands. The Shipwreck. E. H. Palmer. NA
Upon the Priory Grove, His Usual Retirement. Henry Vaughan. FaBoPP
Upon the rivers of Babylon, there we sat and wept. Bible, *O.T. (Douay-Rheims Version).* Psalms, CXXXVII. OAEL-1
Upon the road to Romany. From Romany to Rome. Wallace Irwin. HBV-1
Upon the Same [Detractor] ("I asked thee oft what poets thou hast read"). Robert Herrick. CaPo
Upon the Saying That My Verses Were Made by Another. Anne Killigrew. WPE
Upon the Shore. Robert Bridges. *See* Who Has Not Walked upon the Shore.
Upon the skyline i' the dark. The Universal Republic. Victor Hugo. PGD
Upon the slippery tops of humane state. Seneca, *tr. by* Abraham Cowley. *Fr.* Thyestes, II. OBVE
Upon the slow descending air. Rapunzel Song. Gerard Previn Meyer. DFT
Upon the Snail. Bunyan. ChTr
(Upon a Snail.) OxBChV
Upon the soft brown pillow of thy shore. Apostrophe to the Parret. E. H. Burrington. FaBoPP
Upon the Springs Issuing out from the Foot of Plimouth Beach. Samuel Sewall. SCAP
Upon the street they lie. The Children. William Soutar. BSV
Upon the Sudden Restraint of the Earl[e] of Somerset, [Then] Falling from Favo[u]r. Sir Henry Wotton. AnAnS-2; ELP; JCP; MePo; NOBE: NoP; OBS; SeCP
Upon the Swallow. Bunyan. OxBChV
Upon the threshold of the year we stand. The New Year. Homera Homer-Dixon. BLRP
Upon the Tomb of the Most Reverend Mr. John Cotton. Benjamin Woodbridge. SCAP
Upon the topmost branches dies. Doubt. Fernand Gregh, *tr. by* Ludwig Lewisohn. WGRP
Upon the tree of time. A Harvest to Seduce. Melville Cane. NYBP
Upon the Troublesome Times. Robert Herrick. CaPo
Upon the utmost corners of the warld. In Orknay. William Fowler. GoTS; OxBS
Upon the Weathercock. Bunyan. OxBChV
Upon the work of Walter Landor. Walter Savage Landor. Dorothy Parker. DBV
Upon the Works of Ben Jonson, *sel.* John Oldham.
"Let dull and ignorant pretenders art condemn." PP
Upon this cake of ice is perched. The Puffin. Robert Williams Wood. RHPC
Upon this greying page you wrote. On Looking at a Copy of Alice Meynell's Poems. Amy Lowell. SBG
Upon this happy New Year night. Eugene Field. *Fr.* A New Year Idyl. PoSC

Upon this leafy bush. The Linnet. Walter de la Mare. HBMV; LiTB; LoBV
Upon this marble bust that is not I. To Inez Milholland. Edna St. Vincent Millay. WPE
Upon this place the great Gustavus died. On Gustavus Adolphus, King of Sweden. Sir Thomas Roe. FaBoEE
Upon this primrose hill. The Primrose, Being at Montgomery Castle, upon the Hill, on Which It Is Situate. John Donne. FaBoPP; GBL
Upon This Rock. Ruthven Todd. PoA
Upon Thought Castara May Die. William Habington. ACP
Upon thy bended knees, thank God for work. Gratitude for Work. John Oxenham. PGD
Upon Time. Robert Herrick. OBS
Upon Umber: Epigram. Robert Herrick. CaPo
Upon Venus Putting on Mars His Armes. Richard Crashaw. SeCP
Upon Visiting His Lady by Moonlight. "A. W." CTC; MOON; OBSC
Upon Wedlock and Death of Children. Edward Taylor. AmPP; AP; NoP
Upon Westminster Bridge. Wordsworth. *See* Composed upon Westminster Bridge, September 3, 1802.
Upon Your Leaving. Etheridge Knight. NeAC; NNaP
Upon your snow-white shoulder. Your Snow-white Shoulder. Heine, *tr. by* Louis Untermeyer. UnTE
Upon your sunken cheek a hectic stain! Moriturus. "Marie Madelaine," *tr. by* Ferdinand E. Kappey. PeHV
Upone Tabacco. Sir Robert Aytoun. OxBS
Upper Canadian, The. James Reaney. NOBC
Upper Chamber, An. Frances Bannerman. HBV-2; OBEV
Upper chamber in a darkened house, An. Frederick Goddard Tuckerman. Sonnets, I, x. NOBA; NoP; TAP
Upper Family. Maxwell Bodenheim. OBAL
Upper Lake, The. Francis Stuart. NeIP
Upper Lambourne. John Betjeman. FaBoTw
Upper Room, An. Daniel Lawrence Kelleher. NeIP
Upper skies are palest blue, The. Robert Bridges. VLP
Upper slopes are busy with the cricket, The. Elegy on the Dust. Thom Gunn. NoAM
Uppon a Deedmans Hed. John Skelton. *See* Upon a Dead Man's Head.
Uppon the First Sight of New England, June 29, 1638. Thomas Tillam. GOA; SCAP
(Hail, Holy Land, *with music.*) AH
Upright and shrewd, more woo'd of fame. Henry Charles Beeching. *Fr.* The Masque of Balliol. CenHV
Uprising See the Fitful Lark. *Unknown.* NA
Uproar, An/ a spruce-green sky, bound in iron. The Butterfly. Margaret Avison. OBCV
Uprose the King of Men with speed. The Descent of Odin; an Ode from the Norse Tongue. Thomas Gray. LAuP
Upshore from the cloud. By a Lake in Minnesota. James Wright. AmFN
Upstairs a young man plays. Inside and Out. Robert Phillips. GeTw
Upstairs Downstairs. Hervey Allen. HBMV; PoA; PoNe
Upstairs on the third floor. Bottled [New York]. Helene Johnson. BlSi; CDC; PoBA
Upstood upstaffed passing sinuously away over an airy arch. Christophe. Russell Atkins. PoNe
Upstream. Carl Sandburg. HBMV; MoAB; MoAmPo
Uptown. Allen Ginsberg. FF; TW; TwCP
Uptown. Paul Zweig. NYP
Uptown on Lenox Avenue. Prime. Langston Hughes. PoBA
Uptown there's not a lot of living matter. Courthouse Square. Herbert Merrill. AmFN
Upward through crystal in a kümmel bottle. Dreamscape in Kümmel. Harold Witt. NYBP
Ur Burial. Richard Eberhart. NePoAm
Ur ol' Hyar lib in ur house on de hill. Ol' Doc' Hyar. James Edwin Campbell. BANP
Urania. Robert Andrews. NOEC
Urania. Matthew Arnold. HBV-1
Urania. Ruth Pitter. MoVE
Urania, Mary Sidney Wroth, Countess of Montgomery. WPE
Duke's Song, The.
Lindamira's Complaint.
Morea's Sonnet.
Pamphilia to Amphilanthus.
Pamphilia's Sonnet.
Verses of the Talkative Knight, The
Urania takes her morning flight. The Adventurous Muse. Isaac Watts. NOEC
Urban Convalescence, An. James Merrill. CoAP; NOBA; NYP
Urban Dream. Victor Hernandez Cruz. NBP
Urban Experience, The: Part One. Lew Blockcolski. VoR
Urban Experience, The: Part Two. Lew Blockcolski. VoR
Urban halfbreed, burro-faced. Poet Woman's Mitosis; Dividing All the Cells Apart. Wendy Rose. TWSS
Urban History. Chester Kallman. CrMA
Urban Ode. Sandra McPherson. MAYP
Urban Pollution. John Armstrong. *Fr.* The Art of Preserving Health. NOEC
Urban Roses. Ted Isaac. PoPl
Urceus Exit. Austin Dobson. *Fr.* Rose-Leaves. HBV-1; OBEV
(Triolet: "I intended an ode.") PoPle
Urge to stroke the dead, The. Rabbits. Dennis Schmitz. FiCP
Urgency. Betsy Sholl. AMV-80
Urgency. Sarah E. Wright. PoNe
Urging Her of a Promise. Ben Jonson. *Fr.* A Celebration of Charis. AnAnS-2; SeCP
Uriel. Emerson. AP; LiTA; NePA; NOBA; OxBA
Uriel, *sels.* William Force Stead.
"I thought the night without a sound was falling." TrPWD
(How Infinite Are Thy Ways.) OBMV
"Praise, then, to Uriel, who in unlikely places," IV, 3. OxBoCh
"Reach forth Thy hand!" V, 1. OxBoCh
Uriel to his charge/ Returned on that bright beam. Now Came Still Evening On. Milton. *Fr.* Paradise Lost, IV. FaBoRV
Urizen's Curse upon His Children. Blake. *Fr.* Vala; or, The Four Zoas. TW
Urn, The. Malcolm Cowley. MoVE
Urn Burial. Ted Hughes. EBEV
Urn I: Silent for Twenty-five Years, the Father of My Mother Advises Me, *sel.* Walter Lew.
"Careless/ but not fearless." BrSi
Urns and Odours Bring Away! Fletcher *and* Shakespeare. *See* Funeral Song.
Ursa Major. James Kirkup. ImOP
Ursula. Robert Underwood Johnson. HBV-1
Ursula. David Ray. VGW
Urumbula Song, The. *Unknown, tr. fr. Aranda by* T. G. H. Strehlow. CBAP
Uru-tu-sendo's Song. *Tr. fr. Tewa Indian by* H. J. Spinden. WTO
Us. David Ignatow. PPJ
Us. Julius Lester. PoBA
Us. Anne Sexton. CAPP
Us. Jiri Wyatt. LTB
Us Idle Wenches. *Unknown.* PoPle
Us Potes. Franklin P. Adams. PoPl; WhC
Us Two. A. A. Milne. OxBChV; TiPo
Us two was pals, the Kid and me. The Kid's Last Fight. *Unknown.* TreF
Us two wuz boys when we fell out. Our Two Opinions. Eugene Field. AA
Use all your hidden forces. Do not miss. Attainment. Ella Wheeler Wilcox. WGRP
Use force and chisel, be lapidary, not. Collages and Compositions. Richmond Lattimore. PP
Use maketh maistry [*or* mast'ry], this hath been said alway. Of Use. John Heywood. FaBoEE; PBBP
Use me, God, in Thy great harvest field. Send Me. Christina Rossetti. TRV
Use of Fiction, The. Naomi Shihab Nye. MAYP
Use, then, my lust for whisky and for thee. The Light of Life. "Hugh MacDiarmid." CMoP
Use three physicians still [*or* physicians' skill]: first Doctor Quiet. Health Counsel. Sir John Harington. FaBoUs, 2 *l.*; TreFT, 4 *ll.*
Use your money while you're living. Your Money and Mine. *Unknown.* STF
Used to have a gal, she was little and low. Step It Up and Go. *Unknown.* FSW
Used years. In Passing. J. Barrie Shepherd. AMV-81
Useful for Avoiding Collisions at Sea. *Unknown.* FaBoUs
Useful Plow, The. *Unknown.* HBV-1
Useless Day. Rosario Castellanos, *tr. fr. Spanish by* Maureen Ahern. WPOW
Useless to ask what this was. Bark. Don Welch. GP
Uselessness. Ella Wheeler Wilcox. TrPWD
Uses of Adversity, The. Shakespeare. *Fr.* As You Like It, II, i. LiTB; TreFS; TrGrPo
Uses of Light, The. Gary Snyder. PAI
Uses of Ocean, The. Sir Owen Seaman. FiBHP
Uses of Poetry. Winfield Townley Scott. DFF; PoA
Usk. T. S. Eliot. Landscapes, III. BiP; FaBoCh; NOCV
Usk, The. C. H. Sisson. NOCV
Usual exquisite boredom of patrols, The. Hugh Popham. OxBTC
Usually an Old Female Is the Leader. Tom Hennen. FAZ
Usually hateful crow, The. Beauty. Basho, *tr. by* Harold G. Henderson. SoPo
Usufruct. Austin Clarke. IPY
Usurpers, The. Edwin Muir. CMoP

Ut, re, mi, fa, sol, la. *Unknown.* FaBoNo
Utah. Anne Stevenson. NCSH
Utah Carroll. *Unknown.* CoSo, *with music*; FSW
Utah Iron Horse, The. *Unknown.* AmFP
Ute Lover, The. Hamlin Garland. AA
Ute Pass. Ernest Whitney. PoOW
Utilitarian View of the *Monitor's* Fight, A. Herman Melville. AmPP; AP; UnPo
Utmost in Friendship, The. John E. McCann. TreFT
Utmost island of Europe, loveliest land. Ireland Weeping. William Livingston. GoTS
"Utopia," The. Lee Harwood. EAS
Utopia. Jewel C. Latimore. BPo
Utopia of Lord Mayor Howard, The. Randolph Stow. PoAu-2
Utrillo's World. John Glassco. PeCV
Utter Passion Uttered Utterly, An. John Todhunter. BXAP
Utterance. Emily Dickinson. *See* I found the phrase to every thought.

V

V.A.D. Scullery-Maid's Song, The. M. Winifred Wedgwood. SUMH
V. B. Nimble, V. B. Quick ("V. B. Wigglesworth wakes at noon"). John Updike. CTBA; NYBP
V.D. Clinic. Adrien Stoutenburg. GP
V. D. F. *Unknown.* HBV-2
V. Innocentia Veritas Viat Fides Circumdederunt Me Inimici Mei. Sir Thomas Wyatt. AAS
V-J Day. John Ciardi. MiAP; PoPl
V-Letter. Karl Shapiro. AP; CoBMV; MiAP; NoAM; TrJP; WaP
(Love Letter.) NYBP
V-Letter to Karl Shapiro in Australia. Selden Rodman. WaP
Vacancy in the Park. Wallace Stevens. LCAP
Vacant Cage, The. Charles Tennyson Turner. FM
Vacant Chair, The. Henry Stevenson Washburn. FSW; TreFS
Vacant Lot, The. Gwendolyn Brooks. NoAM; NOBA
Vacation. Nixon Waterman. *See* Far from the Madding Crowd.
Vacation. William Stafford. AmFN; POL; Psk
"Vacation is coming, where shall we go?" Compromise. Laurence McKinney. InMe
Vacation is over. Leavetaking. Eve Merriam. PDV
Vacation Song. Edna St. Vincent Millay. YeAr
Vacation Time. Rowena Bennett. SiSoSe
Vacation Trip. William Stafford. CTBA; PV
Vacation? Well, our children took our love apart. Any Time. William Stafford. LCAP
Vachel, the stars are out. To Lindsay. Allen Ginsberg. ConAP
Vacillation. W. B. Yeats. MoVE; NoAM
"Must we part, Von Hügel, though much alike," *sel.* OBMV
Vacuum. Josephine Miles. MOON
Vacuum, The. Howard Nemerov. NePoEA; NIP
Vacuum cleaner held over my head, A. In a Dream. David Ignatow. PoA
Vagabond, The. Robert Louis Stevenson. BrPo; HBV-1; HBVY; TreFT; ViBoPo
Vagabond House. Don Blanding. BLPA
Vagabond Song, A. Bliss Carman. FaPON; GN; HBV-1; HBVY; PoSC
Vagabonds. Langston Hughes. SaC
Vagabonds. "Marie Madelaine," *tr. fr. German by* Ferdinand E. Kappey. PeHV
Vagabonds, The. John Townsend Trowbridge. AA; BeLS; BLPA; TreFS
Vagrant, A. Erik Axel Karlfeldt, *tr. fr. Swedish by* Charles Wharton Stork. PoPl
Vagrant, The. Pauline Slender. HBMV
Vague in plot but clear in style. Review of a Cook Book. Louise Dyer Harris. WhC
Vague Lyric by G. M. Max Beerbohm. FaBoEE
Vague sea thuds against the marble cliffs, The. Time. Robert Graves. LiTM
Vague winds of sorrow blow. Wandering. Hortense Flexner. HBMV
Vaguely I hear the purple roar of the torn-down 3rd Avenue El. You Are Gorgeous and I'm Coming. Frank O'Hara. NeAP
Vaile cobwebs from the white-ned floore. Upon Christmas Eve. Sir John Suckling. NCEP
Vain Advice at the Year's End. James Wright. NYBP
Vain and not to trust. Woman. Irving Layton. ErPo
Vain Britons, boast no longer with proud indignity. War and Washington. Jonathan Mitchell Sewall. PAH
Vain excess of flattering fortune's gifts, The. Gascoigne's Memories, II. George Gascoigne. EnRePo
Vain Finding. Walter de la Mare. BrPo
Vain, frail, short liv'd, and miserable Man. A Song of Emptiness to Fill up the Empty Pages Following. Michael Wigglesworth. SCAP
Vain Gratuities. E. A. Robinson. NePA
Vain Hope, Adieu. *Unknown.* EnRePo
Vain is the chiming of forgotten bells. Poets. Joyce Kilmer. WGRP
Vain is the fleeting wealth. On the Vanity of Man's Life. *Unknown.* OBSC
Vain man, born to no happiness. Chorus. Sidney Godolphin. LoBV
Vain Men, Whose Follies. Thomas Campion. NCEP
Vain Questioning. Walter de la Mare. MoVE
Vain, very vain, my weary search to find. Happiness Dependent on Ourselves. Goldsmith. *Fr.* The Traveller. OBEC
Vain Virtues. Dante Gabriel Rossetti. The House of Life, LXXXV. HBV-2; VLP
Vain World Adieu. *Unknown.* AmFP
Vain worldly yearnings in my breast. At Parting. Heine, *tr. by* Dwight Durling. NAWM-2
Vaine men, whose follies make a God of Love. Vain Men, Whose Follies. Thomas Campion. NCEP
Vainly ("Vainly/the epistles burn"). Nelly Sachs, *tr. fr. German by* Michael Roloff. NYBP
Vainly were the words of parting spoken. Hermotimus. William Edmondstoune Aytoun. OBVV
Vala; or, The Four Zoas, *sels.* Blake.
"Cities, The, send to one another saying 'My sons are mad.' " ViBoPo
Enion Replies from the Caverns of the Grave. OBNC
Enitharmon Revives with Los. OBNC
(Enitharmon's Song, 6*LL.*) ChTr
"I am made to sow the thistle for wheat." Prf
It Is Not So with Me. SeCePo
Lamentation of Enion, The. OBNC
"Night passed and Enitharmon eer the dawn returned in bliss." OAEL-2
"O Lord, wilt thou not look upon our sore afflictions." ViBoPo
Price of Experience, The. EnRP
Urizen's Curse upon His Children. TW
Vala, Night the Ninth Being the Last Judgment. OAEL-2
Vale. John Ciardi. MiAP
Vale! Roden Noel. OBVV
Vale from Carthage. Peter Viereck. LiTM; MiAP; MoAmPo
Vale of the waterfalls! The Call of the Morning. George Darley. OnYI
Vale of twilight filled with silver-gray, The. Experience. Hugo von Hofmannsthal, *tr. by* John N. Miller. AMV-81
Valediction, A: "Bid me not go where neither suns nor show'rs." William Cartwright. OBS
Valediction, A: "Crow's harsh dissyllables, A." Melvin Walker La Follette. CoPo
Valediction, A: Forbidding Mourning. John Donne. AnAnS-1; BLPL; CABA; EnRePo; FaBoEn; FF; HAP; HeIP; HoPM; InPK; InPS; JCP; LiTB; MasP; MeLP; MePo; NIP; NOBE; NoP; OAEL-1; OAEP; OBS; PAI; PoEL-2; PoPle; PPoe; PPP; PrIm; SeCeV; SeCP; SeCV-1; SoSe; TEP; TreFT; UnPo; WeW
Valediction: "Glory of soundless heaven, wheel of stars." John Hall Wheelock. NePoAm
Valediction, A: "God be with thee, my belovèd,—God be with thee!" Elizabeth Barrett Browning. HBV-1
Valediction, A: "If we must part." Ernest Dowson. BoLoP
Valediction: "Lady with the frilled blouse." Seamus Heaney. PPJ
Valediction, A: Of My Name in the Window. John Donne. EnRePo; QFR
Valediction, A: Of Weeping. John Donne. AnAnS-1; CABA; EnRePo; HAP; HeIP; MeLP; MePo; NoP; OAEL-1; OBS; SeCP; WeW
Valediction: "Sometimes I can believe." Lawrence Raab. AMV-81
Valediction: "Their verdure dare not show." Louis MacNeice. AnIL; MoVE
Valediction Forbidding Mourning, A. Adrienne Rich. NoAM; NoP
Valediction, A (Liverpool Docks). John Masefield. OBMV
Valediction to My Contemporaries. Horace Gregory. MoAmPo
Valediction to the River Duddon. Wordsworth. *See* After-Thought.
Valedictory. Tennyson. *See* In Memoriam—W. G. Ward *and* In the Garden at Swainston.
Valedictory Sonnet to the River Duddon. Wordsworth. *See* After-Thought.
Valedictory to Standard Oil of Indiana, A. David Wagoner. NYBP
Valentine, A. Matilda Betham-Edwards. OBVV; PeHV
Valentine. Len Gasparini. NeAC
Valentine. Donald Hall. GrPl; LLLT; NTCP; PCP
Valentine, A. Eleanor Hammond. TiPo; YeAr
Valentine. Ernest Hemingway. OBAL; TW
Valentine, A. Laura E. Richards. AA; YeAr
Valentine. Shel Silverstein. PoSC; RHPC
Valentine, A. Hal Summers. ChMP
Valentine. Hollis Summers. GoYe
Valentine. "C. W. T." YeAr
Valentine for a Lady, A. Lucilius, *tr. fr. Greek by* Dudley Fitts. OFD
Valentine for Earth. Frances Frost. QQQ

Valentine Promise. *Unknown.* PoSC
Valentine to a Little Girl. Cardinal Newman. GoBC
Valentine to My Mother, A, 1882. Christina Rossetti. OHIP
Valentine's Day. Aileen Fisher. YeAr
Valentines to My Mother, 1880. Christina Rossetti. OFD
Valentinian. John Fletcher. *See* Tragedy of Valentinian, The.
Valerius on Women. Thomas Heywood. *See* She That Denies Me.
Vales of the Medway, The, *sel.* A. J. Munby.
 Above the Medway. FaBoPP
Valiant Love. Richard Lovelace. SeCP
Valiant Seaman's Happy Return to His Love, The. *Unknown.* *See* Seaman's Happy Return, The.
Valley, The. Stanley Moss. NYBP; PCP
Valley and Villa of Horace, The. Arthur Hugh Clough. *See* So Not Seeing I Sung.
Valley floors. A Collage for Richard Davis—Two Short Forms. De Leon Harrison. PoBA
Valley Forge, *sel.* Maxwell Anderson.
 Lafayette to Washington. PAL
Valley Forge. Thomas Buchanan Read. *Fr.* The Wagoner of the Alleghanies. PAH
Valley lay smiling before me, The. The Song of O'Ruark, Prince of Breffni. Thomas Moore. OnYI
Valley of ancient life, how many visions died. The Other Journey. Katherine Garrison Chapin. MoVE
Valley of Decision, The. John Oxenham. PGD
Valley of Men, The. Uri Zvi Greenberg, *tr. fr. Hebrew by* Robert Mezey *and* Ben Zion Gold. VWA
Valley of the Black Pig, The. W. B. Yeats. ChTr
Valley of the Shadow. John Galsworthy. OHIP; TrPWD
Valley of Unrest, The. Poe. AmPP; AP; PoEL-4; ViBoPo
Valley of Vain Verses, The. Henry van Dyke. HBV-2
Valley Where I Don't Belong, A. Marge Piercy. IHMS
Valley with a silver-grayish mist, The. A Vision. Hugo von Hofmannsthal, *tr. by* Charles Wharton Stork. TrJP
Valor of Ben Milam, The. Clinton Scollard. HBV-2; PAH
Valse Jeune. Louise Imogen Guiney. AA
Valse Oubliée. John Heath-Stubbs. OxBTC
Valuable. Stevie Smith. OxBTC
Value of pi, The. *Unknown.* FaBoUs
Value of Dentistry, The. Solyman Brown. *Fr.* Dentologia; a Poem on the Diseases of the Teeth and Their Proper Remedies. FaBoUs
Values in Use. Marianne Moore. NePoAm-2
Vamp Passes, The. James J. Montague. HBMV
Vampire, The. Conrad Aiken. HBMV
Vampire, The. Kipling. BLPA; BLPL; HBV-1
Van Amburgh's Menagerie ("Van Amburgh is the man that goes with all the shows"). *Unknown.* BLPA
Van Dieman's Land. *Unknown.* BaBo; CoMu; FaBoBa; FSW; OBET (A *and* B *vers.*)
Van Elsen. Frederick George Scott. HBV-2
Van Gogh Influence, The. Shel Silverstein. ELU
Van Winkle. Hart Crane. *Fr.* The Bridge. AmPP; CrMA; FaBV; MoAB; MoAmPo
Vanbrug's House. Swift. PP
Vance Song, The, *with music.* *Unknown.* OuSiCo
Vancouver Island. Joan Swift. DFT
Vancouver Lights. Earle Birney. CaP
Vandals, The. Jenny Mastoraki, *tr. fr. Modern Greek by* Nikos Germanakos. BoWoP
Vane on Hughley steeple, The. Hughley Steeple. A. E. Housman. A Shropshire Lad, LXI. FaBoPP
Vane, young in yeares, but in sage counsell old. To Sir Henry Vane the Younger. Milton. OBS
Vanessa Vanessa. Ewart Milne. BIrV; NeIP
Vanguard of liberty, ye Men of Kent. To the Men of Kent. Wordsworth. OBWP
Vanguardia. Sandra Maria Esteves. LTB
Vanished. Emily Dickinson. AA
Vanished. Steve Eng. AMV-81
Vanished house that for an hour I knew, A. Souvenir. E. A. Robinson. NoAM
Vanished Night, The. Niall MacMurray, *tr. fr. Irish by* Frank O'Connor. KiLC
Vanishers, The. Whittier. AA
Vanishing Point. Peter Cooley. AmPA
Vanitas Vanitatum. John Webster. *See* All the Flowers of the Spring.
Vanitas Vanitatum. Israel Zangwill. TrJP
Vanity. Robert Graves. GTBS-P
Vanity. James Thomson ("B. V."). *See* Once in a Saintly Passion.
Vanity. Anna Wickham. FaBoTw
Vanity ("The fleet astronomer can bore"). George Herbert. MePo; NoP; SeCV-1
Vanity of All Worldly Things, The. Anne Bradstreet. NoP; SCAP
Vanity of Existence, The. Philip Freneau. AmPP; AP
Vanity of Human Wishes, The: The Tenth Satire of Juvenal Imitated. Samuel Johnson. CABA; EBEV; HeIP; LaA; LAuP; LoBV, *abr.;* MasP; NOEC; NoP; OAEL-1; PoEL-3; PrIm; TEP
 Sels.
 Charles XII of Sweden. NOBE; OBEC
 ("On what foundation stands the warrior's pride?") OBWP; ViBoPo
 Life's Last Scene. OBEC; SeCePo
 Power of Prayer, The. NOBE; OBWP; ViBoPo
 (Prayer: "Where then shall hope and fear their object find?") OBEC
 "Unnumbered suppliants crowd preferment's gate." OBSV
 "When first the college rolls receive his name." OBSV
 (Scholar's Life, The.) FaBoEn; NOBE; OBEC; SeCePo
Vanity of Spirit. Henry Vaughan. AnAnS-1
Vanity of the World, The. Francis Quarles. *See* False World, Thou Liest.
Vanity of Vanities. Bible, *O.T.* *Fr.* Ecclesiastes, I:2-11. NAWM-1; TrJP (2-9)
 (Words of the Preacher, The.) TreFS
Vanity of Vanities. Palladas, *tr. fr. Greek by* William M. Hardinge. AWP; TRV
Vanity of vanities, the Preacher saith. The One Certainty. Christina Rossetti. OBNC
Vanity, saith the preacher, vanity! The Bishop Orders His Tomb at Saint Praxed's Church. Robert Browning. AWP; CABA; EBVV; FiP; HAP; HBV-1; HeIP; NoP; OAEL-2; OAEP; PPoe; PPP; PrIm; SeCeV; TEP; ViBoPo
Vanity, vanity, all is vanity. Ha! Original Sin. Ogden Nash. FaBoCo
Vanquished. Francis Fisher Browne. AA; HBV-2
Vanquished, The. Charles Eglington. PeSA
Vanquished and weary was my soul in me. Sonnet: A Trance of Love. Cino da Pistoia, *tr. by* Dante Gabriel Rossetti. AWP
Vantage Point, The. Robert Frost. CoBMV; OxBA
Vanzetti. Charles Buckmaster. CBAP
Vapor Trail Reflected in the Frog Pond. Galway Kinnell. NoP; OBWP; VGW
Vapor Trails. Gary Snyder. CAPP
Vaporish closeness of this two-month fog, The. 1930's. Robert Lowell. NoP
Vaporish Maiden, A. Morris Bishop. TDH
 (Limerick.) WhC
Vapour and Blue. Wilfred Campbell. CaP
Vaquero. Edward Dorn. NeAP; PoM
Vaquero. Joaquin Miller. AA; BPAW
Variables of Green. Robert Graves. FaBoEE
Variation, A. Robert Creeley. DiL
Variation. Peter Wild. GP
Variation on a Line by Emerson. W. S. Merwin. NePA
Variation on a Sentence. Louise Bogan. FM; ImOP
Variation on a Theme by John Lyly. Sacheverell Sitwell. ViBoPo
Variation on Heraclitus. Louis MacNeice. NoAM
Variation on Ronsard. T. Sturge Moore. OBMV
Variation on the Gothic Spiral. W. S. Merwin. PoA
Variation on the Word *Sleep.* Margaret Atwood. NOBC
Variations, *sel.* Conrad Aiken.
 Queen Cleopatra, X. HBMV
Variations. Randall Jarrell. MiAP; VGW
Variations, Calypso and Fugue on a Theme of Ella Wheeler Wilcox. John Ashbery. LCAP
Variations Done for Gerald Van de Wiele. Charles Olson. NeAP; NoAM; NOBA; NoP
Variations for Two Pianos. Donald Justice. NYBP
Variations of an Air. G. K. Chesterton. *See* Variations on an Air . . .
Variations on a Late October Day. George Mosby, Jr. LFAC
Variations on a Line from Shakespeare's Fifty-sixth Sonnet. E. L. Mayo. PoCh
Variations on a Medieval Theme. Geoffrey Dutton. PoAu-2
Variations on a Still Morning. Thomas Cole. NePoAm
Variations on a Theme. John Hay. NePoAm
Variations on a Theme. Mark Vinz. Psk
Variations on a Theme. Anne Wilkinson. MoCV
Variations on a Theme by George Herbert. Marya Zaturenska. TrPWD
Variations on a theme by morning. Cocoa Morning. Bob Kaufman. AmNP
Variations on a Theme by Sidney Keyes. Eithne Wilkins. NeBP
Variations on a Theme by William Carlos Williams. Kenneth Koch. BXAP; CAPP; FF; NIP; NoP; PoM; PV; SpRo
Variations on a Theme. Oscar Williams. LiTA; NePA
Variations on a Time Theme, Edwin Muir.
 "At the dead centre of the boundless plain." MoVE; NoAM

"Child in Adam's field I dreamed away, A." NoAM
"Now at the road's quick turn." NoAM
"Ransomed from darkness and released in Time." NoAM
Variations on an Air Composed on Having to Appear in a Pageant as Old King Cole. G. K. Chesterton. FaBoPa; NOBL
(Variations of an Air.) Par
Sels.
Old King Cole ("Me clairvoyant"). BXAP
Old King Cole ("Of an old king in a story"). BXAP
Old King Cole ("Who smoke-snorts toasts o' My Lady Nicotine"). BXAP
Variations on an Old Nursery Rhyme. Edith Sitwell. *See* King of China's Daughter, The.
Variations on Sappho, *sels.* "Michael Field."
"Come, Gorgo, put the rug in place." PeHV
"Maids, not to you my mind doth change." PeHV
Variations on Southern Themes. Donald Justice. SV
Variations: The Air Is Sweetest That a Thistle Guards. James Merrill. NePoEA
Varick Street. Elizabeth Bishop. NYP
Variety, The. John Dancer. CavP
Variety. *Yoruba Oral Tradition, tr. by* E. Lasebikan. WTO
Various devices great mechanics gave. Means of Propulsion for Steam-Ships. Thomas Baker. *Fr.* The Steam Engine; or, The Power of Flame. FaBoUs
Various Ends. Ruthven Todd. NeBP; SeCePo
Various members of the hierarchy move, The. A Morning Letter. Robert Duncan. PoA
Various the Roads of Life. Walter Savage Landor. EnRP; NIP
("Various the roads of life; in one.") FaBoEE
Various Wakings. Vincent Buckley. PoAu-2
Varitalk. Weare Holbrook. NYBP
Varium et Mutabile. Sir Thomas Wyatt. *See* Is It Possible.
Varuna, The. George Henry Boker. PAH
Varuna. *Tr. fr. Sanskrit by* Raimundo Panikkar. *Fr.* Vedic Hymns. ILwL
Varus, whom I chanced to meet. A Fib Detected. Catullus, *tr. fr. Latin by* John Hookham Frere. AWP; OBVE
V-A-S-E, The. James Jeffrey Roche. HBV-1
Vase, The. Terence Tiller. ChMP
Vase of Flowers, A. John Ashbery. ConAP
Vase of Life, The. Dante Gabriel Rossetti. The House of Life, XCV. SyP
Vase was made of clay, The. Elegy to the Sioux. Norman Dubie. MAYP
Vases. Nan Terrell Reed. BLPA
Vashti. Frances E. W. Harper. BlSi
Vashti, *sel.* Lascelles Abercrombie. *Fr.* Emblems of Love.
Woman's Beauty. MoBrPo
Vast and immaculate; no pilgrim bands. The Sea Cathedral. E. J. Pratt. CaP
Vast Bodies of Philosophy [*or* Philosophie]. To Mr. Hobbes. Abraham Cowley. LoBV; SeCV
Vast Chaos, of eld, was God's dominion. He Made the Night. Lloyd Mifflin. HBV-1
Vast corridor through Nature's roofless halls. Ute Pass. Ernest Whitney. PoOW
Vast Light. Richard Eberhart. CMoP; NMP
Vast mild melancholy splendid. Canberra in April. J. R. Rowland. PoAu-2
Vast oceanic movements, the flux and reflux of immeasurable. Currents. Emma Lazarus. *Fr.* By the Waters of Babylon. WPE
Vast Pre-Cambrian microbial mats, The. The Supremacy of Bacteria. Robert Frazier. SUW
Vast superstition! Glorious stile of weaknesse! Chorus Quintus: Tartarorum. Fulke Greville. *Fr.* Mustapha. OBS
Vastness. Tennyson. VLP
Vaticide. Myron O'Higgins. IDB; PoBA
Vaudeville. Lincoln Kirstein. NoAM
Vaudracour and Julia, *sel.* Wordsworth.
"To a lodge that stood." EvOK
Vaulting Ambition. Shakespeare. *Fr.* Macbeth, I, vii. FiP
(Murder Pact, The.) WHA
Vaunting Oak. John Crowe Ransom. OxBA; VGW
Veäiry ring so round's the zun, A. Rings. William Barnes. NBM
Vedic Hymns, *sels. Unknown, tr. fr. Sanskrit.*
Brahma, the World Idea, *tr. by* Romesh Dutt. *Fr.* Rig Veda. WGRP
(Song of Creation, The, *tr. by* Raimundo Panikkar.) ILwL
Forgive, Lord, Have Mercy! *tr. by* Raimundo Panikkar. ILwL
Indra, the Supreme God, *tr. by* Romesh Dutt. *Fr.* Rig Veda. AWP
Pushan, God of Pasture, *tr. by* Romesh Dutt. *Fr.* Rig Veda. AWP
To the One God, *tr. by* Raimundo Panikkar. ILwL
Varuna, *tr. by* Raimundo Panikkar. ILwL
Veery, The. Henry van Dyke. AA
Veery-Thrush, The. Joseph Russell Taylor. *See* Blow Softly, Thrush.
Vegas. Charles Bukowski. NoP
Vegas. J. V. Cunningham. DBV
("I was in Vegas. Celibate and able.") PV
Vegetable Destiny. Nina Cassian, *tr. fr. Rumanian by* Michael Impey *and* Brian Swann. PBWP
Vegetable Loves. Erasmus Darwin. *Fr.* The Botanic Garden: The Loves of the Plants. OBEC; SeCePo
Vegetables. Eleanor Farjeon. FaPON; TiPo
Vegetables. Rachel Field. SoPo
Vegetables/ and jewelry, right displayed. For Instance. Robert McAlmon. PoA
Vegetarian Sings, A. Audrey Conard. AMV-81
Vegetation in the watershed. Family Chronicle. Anselm Parlatore. SUW
Vehicle gives a lurch but seems, The. Foetal Song. Joyce Carol Oates. IHMS; NAs
Veil not thy mirror, sweet Amine. To Amine. James Clarence Mangan. OBEV; OBVV
Veil of haze protects this, A. City Afternoon. John Ashbery. HeIP
Veil thine eyes, O belovèd, my spouse. The Bridegroom of Cana. Majorie Pickthall. CaP
Veil upon veil. Natura Naturans. Kathleen Raine. NYBP
Veiled are the heavens, veiled the throne. Dawn on Mid-Ocean. John Hall Wheelock. EtS
Veiled in that light amazing. The Dispraise of Absalom. *Unknown, tr. by* Robin Flower. BlrV; OxBI
Velasquez took a pliant knife. Castilian. Elinor Wylie. HBMV
Veld Eclogue, A: The Pioneers. Roy Campbell. OBSV
Velocity with which they write, The. Movie Actors Scribbling Letters Very Fast in Crucial Scenes. Jean Garrigue. TAP
Velvet beautiful and dark, A. Peace by Night. Sister Mary Madeleva. GoBC
Velvet Hand, The. Phyllis McGinley. TreFT
Velvet Shoes. Elinor Wylie. CH; FaPON; FPL; GoJo; MoAB; MoAmPo; PAI; PoPl; SiSoSe; SoPo; TreFS; TrGrPo; WHA
Velvet Sonneteers, The. Tom MacInnes. CaP
Vendors croon their welcoming harangues. Cedar Needles. Chase Twichell. MAYP
Vendor's Song. Adelaide Crapsey. HBV-2
Venerable Bee, The. A. M. Klein. TrJP
Venerable Mother Toothache. A Charm against the Toothache. John Heath-Stubbs. InPK; NePoEA; MP; TwCP
Veneris Venefica Agrestis. Charles Tomlinson, *after the Italian of Lucio Piccolo.* OBVE
Venetian Night, A. Hugo von Hofmannsthal, *tr. fr. German by* Ludwig Lewisohn. AWP
Venetian Scene. Anne Ridler. NMP
Venetian Serenade, The. Richard Monckton Milnes. OBRV
Venezuela. *Unknown.* FSW
Vengeance of Finn, The, *sel.* Austin Clarke.
Awakening of Dermuid, The. AnIV
Vengeance was once her nation's lore and law. Watkwenies. Duncan Campbell Scott. PeCV
Vengeful across the cold November moors. The Pity of the Leaves. E. A. Robinson. AA; MoAmPo
Veni Coronaberis. Geoffrey Hill. NoP
Veni Creator. Bliss Carman. *See* Overlord.
Veni Creator. Alice Meynell. ILwL; WPE
Veni, Creator Spiritus. *Unknown, at. to* Charlemagne, *to* Hrabanus Maurus, *and to* St. Gregory the Great, *tr. in paraphrase fr. Latin by* Dryden. AWP; FaPoR; GoBC; HBV-2; ILwL; SeCV-2; WGRP
Veni, Sancte Spiritus. *Unknown, at. to* Robert II, King of France, *tr. fr. Latin by* Catharine Winkworth. HBV-2
Venice. Byron. *Fr.* Childe Harold's Pilgrimage, IV. HBV-2, 4 *sts.*
("I stood in Venice, on the Bridge of Sighs.") EnRP, *abr.*; OAEP, *abr.*; OBRV, 9 *sts.*; ViBoPo, 3 *sts.*
(On the Bridge of Sighs, 4 *sts.*) FaBoPP
Venice. Longfellow. EyDe
Venice. Howard Moss. MoAB
Venice. John Addington Symonds. HBV-2
Venice. James Wright. AMV-81
Venice Recalled. Bruce Boyd. NeAP
Venice, thou Siren of sea-cities, wrought. Venice. John Addington Symonds. HBV-2
Venite Adoremus. Margery Cannon. GoBC
Venom. James Dickey. PoA
'Vention did in Boston meet, The. Convention Song. *Unknown.* PAH
Ventriloquist, The. Robert Huff. GP
Venus Abandoned. Shakespeare. *Fr.* Venus and Adonis. OBSC
Venus Accoutered as Mars. *Unknown, tr. fr. Greek by* Louis Untermeyer. UnTE
Venus again[e] thou mov'st a war[re]. To Venus. Horace, *tr. by* Ben Jonson. Odes, IV, 1. AWP; OBVE
Venus and Adonis. William Browne. ElL

Venus and Adonis. Shakespeare. BeLS
Sels.
"At this Adonis smiles as in disdain." EBEV
Courser and Jennet. NOBE
("But lo, from forth a copse that neighbours by.") FM; PH; PoPle
(Courser, The.) OBSC
(Courser and the Jennet, The.) LoBV
" 'Fondling,' she saith, 'since I have hemmed thee here.' " OAEL-1
"Imperiously he leaps, he neighs, he bounds." BoAnP
Lo! Here the Gentle Lark. ChTr
(Death of Adonis, The.) WHA
"O, what a war of looks was then between them!" UnTE
Poor Wat. OBSC
" 'Sweet boy,' she says, 'this night I'll waste in sorrow.' " ErPo
Venus Abandoned. OBSC
Venus and Cupid. Mark Alexander Boyd. *See* Fra Bank to Bank, Fra Wood to Wood I Rin.
Venus and Cupide. Sir Thomas More. EnRePo
Venus, by Adonis' side. Venus and Adonis. William Browne. EIL
Venus Fly Trap, The. Readymade. John Perreault. EAS
Venus glows in the east. Work to Do toward Town. Gary Snyder. VGW
Venus has lit her silver lamp. The Lamp in the West. Ella Higginson. AA; HBV-2
Venus of Bolsover Castle, The. Sacheverell Sitwell. HBMV
Venus of the Louvre. Emma Lazarus. AA; SBG
Venus of the Salty Shell. Denis Devlin. BIrV
Venus Pudica stands bent. The Lady of the Castle. John Hollander. GP
Venus' Runaway. Ben Jonson. *See* Beauties, Have Ye Seen This Toy.
Venus, take my votive glass. The Lady Who Offers Her Looking Glass [*or* A Farewell]. Plato, *tr. by* Matthew Prior. AWP; FaBoEE; NOEC; OBEV; ViBoPo
Venus Transiens. Amy Lowell. PoA
Venus Vigils. *Unknown. See* Vigil of Venus, The.
Venus, what mood inspires you to don. Venus Accoutered as Mars. *Unknown, tr. by* Louis Untermeyer. UnTE
Venus, with Young Adonis Sitting by Her. Bartholomew Griffin. *Fr.* The Passionate Pilgrim. ViBoPo
Ver and Hiems. Shakespeare. *See* When Icicles Hang by the Wall.
Vera, from My Childhood. Judy Grahn. The Common Woman, VII. GP
Veracruz. Robert Hayden. AmNP
Verandahs. R. F. Brissenden. CBAP
Veranius, my dear friend, the friend worth. Catullus, *tr. fr. Latin by* James Michie. PeHV
Verazzano. Hezekiah. Butterworth. PAH
Verb "To Think," The. D. J. Enright. OxBC
Verbal Critics. Pope. *Fr.* Epistle to Dr. Arbuthnot. OBEC
("Pains, reading, study, are their just pretense.") PP
Verbatim from Boileau. Pope. DBV
Verbum Caro Factum Est. *Unknown.* SBVL
Verdancy. *Unknown.* ShM
Verdant branch was swinging here, A. So Long Ago. Morris Rosenfeld, *tr. by* Elbert Aidline. TrJP
Verdict, The. Norman Cameron. SeCePo
Vergier. *Unknown, tr. fr. Provençal by* Ezra Pound. GBL
Vergissmeinnicht. Keith Douglas. ChMP; FaBoMo; GTBS-P; InPS; NePoEA; OBWP; OxBTC; SoSe
Verifying the Dead. James Welch. CDW
Verigin, Moving in Alone. John Newlove. NeAC
Verigin 3. John Newlove. NeAC
Verily/ The sky clears. The Sky Clears. *Tr. by* Frances Densmore. OBVE
Veritas. Oliver Wendell Holmes. *Fr.* Two Sonnets: Harvard. AP
Vermin only tease and pinch, The. On Fleas. Swift. TreFS
Vermont. Sarah N. Cleghorn. HBMV
Vermont Conversation. Patricia Hubbell. CTBA
Vermont: Indian Summer. Philip Booth. NePoEA
Vern. Gwendolyn Brooks. TiPo
Vernal Equinox. Martin Johnston. CBAP
Vernal Equinox. Ruth Stone. MoAmPo
Vernal Paradox. Kim Kurt. NePoAm-2
Vernal Sentiment. Theodore Roethke. ELU; MiAP
Vernon Castle. Harriet Monroe. HBMV
Verona. James Wright. NNaP
Vers de Société. H. D. Traill. Par
Vers la Vie. Arthur Upson. HBV-2
Vers Nonsensiques. George Du Maurier. HBV-2; NA
Versailles. Adrienne Rich. NePoEA
Versailles!—Up the chestnut alley. The Pompadour. George Walter Thornbury. BeLS
Verse. Richmond Lattimore. PP
Verse: "Past ruin'd Ilion Helen lives." Walter Savage Landor. *See* Past Ruined Ilion.
Verse: "What should we know." Oliver St. John Gogarty. AnIL; FaBoCh; OBMV; PoRA
Verse, a breeze 'mid blossoms straying. Youth and Age. Samuel Taylor Coleridge. BLPL; EnRP; FiP; GTBS; GTBS-P; HBV-1; OBEV; OBNC; OBRV; PoLF
Verse and Fame. John Donne. *Fr.* An Anatomy of the World. FaBoRV
Verse for a Certain Dog. Dorothy Parker. GDP
Verse for Vestigials. Elizabeth Allen. AMV-80
Verse hath a middle nature: heaven keepes Soules. Verse and Fame. John Donne. *Fr.* An Anatomy of the World. FaBoRV
Verse makes heroic[k] virtue live. To Mr. Henry Lawes, Who Had Then Newly Set a Song of Mine in the Year 1635. Edmund Waller. AnAnS-2; CTC; PP; SeCP; SeCV-1
Verse may find him who a sermon flies, A. On the Following Work and Its Author. Jonathan Mitchell. SCAP
Verse Written in the Album of Mademoiselle. Pierre Dalcour, *tr. fr. French by* Langston Hughes. PoNe; TTY
Verses: "I am confirm'd a woman can." Sir John Suckling. CavP
Verses: "I am monarch of all I survey." William Cowper. *See* Verses Supposed to be Written by Alexander Selkirk. . .
Verses: "Who strives to mount Parnassus hill." Richard Bentley. *See* Reply to an Imitation of the Second Ode in the Third Book of Horace.
Verses Addressed to a Friend, Just Leaving a Favourite Retirement. Samuel Henley. NOEC
Verses at Night. Dannie Abse. MP
Verses Composed on the Eve of His Execution. James Graham, Marquis of Montrose. *See* On Himself, upon Hearing What Was His Sentence.
Verses Copied from the Window of an Obscure Lodging-House, in the Neighbourhood of London. *Unknown.* ViBoPo
Verses for a First Birthday. George Barker. MoAB; MoBrPo
Verses for Fruitwomen, *sels.* Swift.
Apples. AnYI; OnYI
(Verses Made for Women Who Cry Apples.) NCEP
Herrings. AnIV; OnYI
Onions. AnIV; OnYI
(Onyons.) BIrV; FaBoUs
Verses for the 60th Birthday of T. S. Eliot. George Barker. ChMP
Verses Found in His Bible. Sir Walter Ralegh. *See* Even Such Is Time.
Verses Found in Thomas Dudley's Pocket after His Death. Thomas Dudley. SCAP
Verses from a Letter. Keats. *See* Song about Myself.
Verses from the Shepherd's Hymn. Richard Crashaw. *See* Shepherd's Hymn, The.
Verses Intended to Be Written below a Noble Earl's Picture. Burns. HoPM
Verses Intended to Go with a Posset Dish to My Dear Little Goddaughter, 1882. James Russell Lowell. AP
Verses Made for Women Who Cry Apples. Swift. *See* Apples.
Verses Made Sometime Since upon . . . the Indian Squa. John Josselyn. SCAP
Verses Made the Night before He Died. Michael Drayton. NOBE
(Last Verses.) FaBoEn
(So Well I Love Thee.) EnRePo
("So well I love thee, as without thee I.") GBL
Verses Made the Night before He Dyed. Sir Walter Ralegh. *See* Even Such Is Time.
Verses Occasioned by the Death of Dr. Aikman. James Thomson. *See* Finis.
Verses Occasioned by the Sudden Drying Up of St. Patrick's Well, *sel.* Swift.
"Wretched Ierne! with what grief I see." OBSV
Verses of Mans Mortalitie, with an Other of the Hope of His Resurrection. *Unknown. See* Man's Mortality.
Verses of the Talkative Knight, The. Mary Sidney Wroth, Countess of Montgomery. *Fr.* Urania. WPE
Verses on a Cat. Charles Daubeny. HBV-1
Verses on Accepting the World. Joseph Brodsky, *tr. fr. Russian by* Dimitry Pospielovsky *and* Keith Bosley. VWA
Verses on Blenheim. Martial, *tr. fr. Latin by* Swift. AWP
Verses on Daniel Good. *Unknown.* CoMu; OxBB
Verses on Sir Joshua Reynolds's Painted Window at New College, Oxford. Thomas Warton, the Younger. NOEC; OBEC; PoEL-3
Verses on the Death of Doctor [*or* Dean] Swift [D.S.P.D., Occasioned by Reading a Maxim in Rochefoucauld]. Swift. LoBV; NOEC; OxBoLi, *abr.;* PoEL-3; TEP
(On the Death of Doctor Swift.) ViBoPo
Sels.
"Behold the fatal day arrive!" SCV; ViBoPo
"Dean, if we believe Report, The." FaBoEn
"Doctors tender of their fame, The." NOBL
"From Dublin soon to London spread." ViBoPo; WHA
"Had he but spar'd his Tongue and Pen." FaBoEn
"He gave the little wealth he had." ViBoPo
"My female friends, whose tender hearts." NOBL; SeCePo; ViBoPo

"Perhaps I may allow, the Dean." FaBoEn; NOBE; OnYI
"Suppose me dead; and then suppose." NOBE
"Time is not remote when I, The." EBEV; NOBE; NOBL; OBEC; ViBoPo
Verses on the Prospect of Planting Arts and Learning in America. George Berkeley. *See* On the Prospect of Planting . . .
Verses Placed over the Door at the Entrance into the Apollo Room at the Devil Tavern. Ben Jonson. HBV-2
Verses Said to Be Written on the Union. Swift. APAS
Verses Supposed to Be Written by Alexander Selkirk, during His Solitary Abode on the Island of Juan Fernandez. William Cowper. HBV-2; NOEC; PoEL-3; PoLF
(Alexander Selkirk.) FiP
(Monarch, The.) TreFS
(Solitude of Alexander Selkirk, The.) GTBS; GTBS-P; LiTB; RoGo
(Verses.) FPL
Verses to Be Repeated by an Attorney Leaving His Lodging to Wait upon Judges Riding the Circuits from One County to Another, Least He Forget Some Necessary Thing. John Willis. FaBoUs
Verses to Miss ———. J. Wilde. NOEC
Verses under a Peacock Portrayed in Her Left Hand. Robert Greene. PBBP
Verses upon the Burning of Our House. Anne Bradstreet. *See* Some Verses upon the Burning of Our House, July 10th, 1666.
Verses Written during a Sleepless Night. Pushkin, *tr. fr. Russian by* Babette Deutsch. PoPl
Verses Written during the War, 1756-1763. Thomas Osbert Mordaunt, *formerly at. to* Sir Walter Scott. OBEC
Sound, Sound the Clarion, *sel.* FaPoR; NOBE
("Sound, sound the clarion, fill the fife!") FaBoEE
Verses Written in a Lady's Sherlock "Upon Death." Earl of Chesterfield. EBEV; OBEC
(To a Lady on Reading Sherlock "Upon Death.") NOEC
Verses Written in 1872. Robert Louis Stevenson. BLPA; BLPL
Verses Written in His Bible. Sir Walter Ralegh. *See* Even Such Is Time.
Verses Written on Sand. Melech Ravitch, *tr. fr. Yiddish by* Seymour Mayne *and* Rivka Augenfeld. VWA
Verses Written upon Windows. Swift. DBV
Verses Wrote in a Lady's Ivory Table-Book. Swift. NCEP
Version of a Song of Failure, A. Larry Eigner. FAZ
Versions. Robert Kelly. The Book of Persephone, 12. PoM
Versions of Love. Roy Fuller. LiTM
Versos de Montalgo, *with music.* *Unknown, pr. tr. fr. Spanish by* Frank J. Dobie. AS
Vertigo is my territory. Eagle. Robin Skelton. NOBC
Vertigos or Contemplation of Something That Is Over. Alejandra Pizarnik, *tr. fr. Spanish by* Yishai Tobin. VWA
Vertue. George Herbert. *See* Virtue.
Very acme of my woe, The. Little Son. Georgia Douglas Johnson. CDC
Very bitter weeping that ye made, The. Dante, *tr. by* Dante Gabriel Rossetti. La Vita Nuova, XXV. AWP
Very dark the autumn sky. A Belated Violet. Oliver Herford. AA
Very Early. Karla Kuskin. PDV; SoPo
Very Fair My Lot. Jacob David Kamzon, *tr. fr. Hebrew by* Sholom J. Kahn. TrJP
Very first blessing that Mary had, The. The Seven Blessings of Mary. *Unknown.* FSW
Very first joy that Mary had, The. The Joys of Mary. *Unknown.* AmFP
Very friendly, A/ prison. Tripart. Gayl Jones. BlSi
Very grandiloquent goat, A. The Grandiloquent Goat. Carolyn Wells. MoShBr
Very handsome gentleman, A. *Tr. fr. Chinese by* Arthur Waley. *Fr.* Shih Ching. BoWoP
Very Heroical Epistle in Answer to Ephelia, A. Earl of Rochester. APAS
Very like a Whale. Ogden Nash. BLPL; DTC; HAP; InPK; PoLF; TrGrPo; WeW
Very Little Sphinx, A, *sel.* Edna St. Vincent Millay.
Wonder Where This Horseshoe Went. SUS
Very Lovely. Rose Fyleman. SoPo; TiPo
Very Minor Poet Speaks, A. Isabel Valle. BLPA
Very Model of a Modern College President, The, *parody.* Harold A. Larrabee. WhC
Very Nearly. Queenie Scott-Hopper. FaPON; SoPo
Very Odd Fish, A. D'Arcy Wentworth Thompson. OxBChV
Very Old, The. Thomas Galloway. AMV-80
Very old are the woods. All That's Past. Walter de la Mare. GoJo; MoAB; NOBE; OAEL-2; OAEP; OBMV; OxBTC; SeCeV; TreFT; TrGrPo; ViBoPo; WHA
Very Old Song, A. "William Laird." HBV-1
Very Old Woman, A. Clayton Eshleman. MAT
Very pitiful lady, very young, A. Dante, *tr. by* Dante Gabriel Rossetti. *Fr.* La Vita Nuova, II. AWP; CTC
Very Polite Man, A. *Unknown.* TDH
Very portly crow, A. A Note on Master Crow. Jean Garrigue. BoAnP
Very Pretty Maid of this Town, and the Amorous 'Squire not One Hundred Miles from the Place, The. *Unknown.* CoMu
Very pulse of ocean now was still, The. Evening in Gloucester Harbor. Epes Sargent. EtS
Very small chickens in tattered feathers. The. A Study in Aesthetics. Robert Peters. BXAP
Very small children in patched clothing, The. The Study in Aesthetics. Ezra Pound. CMoP; InPS; NOBA; NoP
Very soon the Yankee teachers. Learning to Read. Frances E. W. Harper. BlSi
Very True, the Linnets Sing. Walter Savage Landor. TrGrPo
(Autumnal Song.) OAEL-2
"Very, very queer things have been happening to me." Queer Things. James Reeves. WSC
Vesi, the black one, the leaper who sprang. Praises of the King Dingana (Vesi). *Unknown.* PeSA
Vesica Piscis. Coventry Patmore. VLP
Vesperal. Ernest Dowson. OBMV
Vespers. W. H. Auden. *Fr.* Horae Canonicae. FaBoMo
Vespers. A. A. Milne. OxBChV; SpRo
Vespers. S. Weir Mitchell. WGRP
Vespers. Odell Shepard. TrPWD
Vessel that rests here at last, The. The Yacht. Walter Savage Landor. OBVV
Vessels. Howard Schwartz. VWA
Vesta. Whittier. TrPWD; WHA
Vestal, The. Nathalia Crane. TrJP
Vestal, The. Pope. *See* Eloïsa ("How happy is the blameless vestal's lot?").
Vestal in the Forum, The. James Wright. AMV-81
Vestal Lady on Brattle, The. Gregory Corso. NoAM
Vestal Virgin, The, *sel.* John Plummer Derwent Llwyd.
"Night is soft with summer, The; yon faint arch." CaP
Vestigia. Bliss Carman. CaP; WGRP
Vet, The. Guy Boas. BoAnP
Veteran, The. Edmund Blunden. BrPo
Veteran, The. Margaret Postgate Cole. SUMH
Veteran, The. Louis O. Coxe. MoVE
Veteran. Lola Ridge. WPE
Veteran Cowboy's Ruminations, A. John M. Kuykendall. PoOW
Veteran Greeks came home, The. The Return [*or* The Return of the Greeks]. Edwin Muir. CMoP; NoP
Veteran of Heaven, The. Francis Thompson. HBV-2
Veteran of the Great War, A. John Bensko. MAYP
Veteran Sirens. E. A. Robinson. NoAM; NOBA; QFR; SoSe
Veterans. George Johnston. NOBC
Veterans, The. Donagh MacDonagh. CIP; OnYI
Vet's Rehabilitation. Ray Durem. PoBA
Vetus Flamma. Robert Mezey. PoA
Vex no man's secret soul—if that can be. Help. Sadi, *tr. by* Sir Edwin Arnold. *Fr.* The Gulistan. AWP
Via Dolorosa. Phoebe Smith. PGD
Via Longa. Patrick McDonough. HBMV
Via, Veritas, et Vita. Alice Meynell. WGRP
Viable. A. R. Ammons. TAP
Viaticum. Ethna MacCarthy. NeIP
Vibrant mutants of the future. Anselm Hollo. FAZ
Vicar, The. George Crabbe. *Fr.* The Borough, Letter III. OBNC; OBSV
Vicar, The. Winthrop Mackworth Praed. *Fr.* Every-Day Characters. EnRP; HBV-1; InMe; NBM; OBEV; OBNC; OBRV; OBVV; PoEL-4
Vicar of Bray, The. *Unknown.* DBV; FSW; GBP; HBV-1; NOBE; NOBL; OBSV; OxBoLi; ViBoPo
(In Good King Charles's Golden Days.) InvP; OBEC
Vicar of Wakefield, The, *sels.* Goldsmith.
Elegy on the Death of a Mad Dog, An, *fr. ch.* 17. BeLS; BLPA; FaBoBe; FaBoCh; FaBoCo; FaFP; FPL; GDP; GN; HBV-2; HBVY; LAuP; NA; NOBE; NOEC; OAEP; OBEC; OBNV; PoPle; RoGo; ShM; TEP; TreF
Song: "When lovely woman stoops to folly," *fr. ch.* 24. AWP; BoLoP; LAuP; NOBE; NOEC; OBEC; PoPl; SeCePo; TrGrPo; ViBoPo
(Stanzas on Woman.) ELP; OnYI; OxBI
(When Lovely Woman Stoops to Folly.) GTBS; GTBS-P; HAP; HBV-1; HeIP; NoP; PAI; PrIm; SeCeV; TreF; UnPo
(Woman.) FPL; LiTB; OBEV
Vicarious Atonement. Richard Aldington. MoBrPo; WGRP
Vice. Anthony Hecht. OBAL
Vice ("Vice is a monster of so frightful mien"). Pope. *Fr.* Essay on Man, Epistle II. ELU; PoPl
Vice most obscene and unsavoury, A. Limerick. *Unknown.* NOBL
Vice now may lift aloft her speckled head. Spoken Extempore on the Death of Mr. Pope. *Unknown.* NOEC

Vicious winter finally yields, The. W. D. Snodgrass. Heart's Needle. NePoEA
Vicissitudes of the Creator. Archibald MacLeish. NePA
Vicissitudes of the world, O Olaad, are like the clouds of the seasons, The. To a Dictatorial Sultan. *Somali Oral Tradition, tr. by* B. W. Andrzejewski. WTO
Vickery's Mountain. E. A. Robinson. MoAmPo
Vicksburg. Paul Hamilton Hayne. AA; PAH
Vicomte is wearing a brow of gloom, The. Chez Brébant. Francis Alexander Durivage. AA
Victim, The. Ellen Bryant Voigt. MAYP
Victim not of an accident. A Proposal for Recycling Wastes. Marge Piercy. GP
Victim of Aulis, The. Dannie Abse. NoAM
Victor, The. William Young. HBMV
Victor Dog, The. James Merrill. NoP
Victor Galbraith. Longfellow. PAH
Victor of Antietam, The. Herman Melville. PAH
Victoria. Henry van Dyke. TRV
Victoria Markets Recollected in Tranquillity, The, *sel.* "Furnley Maurice."
"Winds are bleak, stars are bright." PoAu-2
Victorian Grandmother. Margo Lockwood. Psk
Victorian Song. John Farrar. GoYe
Victories of Love, The, *sels.* Coventry Patmore.
Lonely Cloud of Care, The, *fr.* II, vii. FaBoRV
Music of Forefended Spheres, The, *fr.* II, ii. FaBoRV
(Fragment: "He that but once too nearly hears.") NBM
Rain That Fell upon the Height, The, *fr.* II, v. FaBoRV
("Your love lacks joy, your letter says.") GBL
Victorious beauty, though your eyes. To the Countesse of Salisbury [*or* Loves Victory]. Aurelian Townshend. AnAnS-2; MeLP; MePo; OBS; SeCP
Victorious knights without reproach or fear. To the Returning Brave. Robert Underwood Johnson. PAH
Victorious Men of Earth. James Shirley. *Fr.* Cupid and Death. OBS; TrGrPo
(Death, the Conqueror.) GoBC
(Death's Emissaries.) LoBV
(Death's Subtle Ways.) HBV-2
(Last Conqueror, The.) GTBS; GTBS-P
(Song.) FaBoEn
Victors, The. Denise Levertov. NoP
Victory. Roger Axford. PGD
Victory. *Unknown.* CoMu; STF; WGRP
Victory Bells. Grace Hazard Conkling. HBV-2; PAH
Victory comes. The New Victory. Margaret Widdemer. WGRP
Victory comes late. Emily Dickinson. InPK
Victory Dance, A. Alfred Noyes. PoLF
Victory in Defeat. Edwin Markham. BLPL; PoLF; PoPl; TreFT
Victory in the Cabarets. Louis Untermeyer. HBMV
Victory of the Battle of Wounded Knee, The. Tom Parson. SOTS
Victory on the Last Green. Thomas Mathison. *Fr.* The Goff; an Heroi-comical Poem. NOEC
Victory Parade. George Edward Hoffman. PGD
Victory! Victory!—Yes! Yes! ah, yes, thou republican Zion. Arthur Hugh Clough. *Fr.* Amours de Voyage, Canto II, vi. EBVV
Victory-Wreck, The. Will Carleton. PAH
"Vierge Ouvrante." Miriam Palmer. NMM
Viet Cong Sapper Dies, A. Stephen Sossaman. AMV-81
Vietnam. Clarence Major. PoBA
Vietnam #4. Clarence Major. BOLo; FF; PoBA
Vietnamese Girl in the Madhouse, The. David Fisher. NPGG
Vieux Carré. Walter Adolphe Roberts. PoNe
View. Robin Munro. PoSH
View, The. Howard Nemerov. NYBP
View, A. Beverly Quint. NYBP
View. Christian J. Van Geel, *tr. fr. Dutch by* Emilie Peech *and* W. S. Di Piero. AMV-81
View, all ye eyes above, this sight which flings. Edward Taylor. Preparatory Meditations, XX. AP
View by Color Photography on a Commercial Calendar. William Carlos Williams. LCAP
View from a Window. Eldon Grier. PeCV
View from an Attic Window, The. Howard Nemerov. CoAP; ConAP
View from an Institution. Franz Wright. AMV-81
View from Father's Porch, The. Celeste Turner Wright. Str
View from Heights. Arthur Davison Ficke. Sonnets of a Portrait Painter, XIII. HBMV
View from Here, The. William Stafford. ELU; RFM
View from My Window. Alasdair MacLean. PoSH
View from the dungeon's barred slit is, The/ A tree. Pleasures. Albert Goldbarth. GeTw
View from the Gorge. Ben Belitt. NYBP
View from the Planetarium. David Barker. GP
View from the Window. Jane McCoy. AMV-80
View me [*or* mee], Lord, a work of Thine. Thomas Campion. OxBoCh; TrPWD
View now the winter storm! Above—one cloud. The Winter Storm at Sea. George Crabbe. *Fr.* The Borough, Letter I. EtS
View of a Pig. Ted Hughes. BoAnP; CABA; LiTM; MP; OxBTC; TwCP
View of Jersey, A. Edward Field. NeAP
View of Louisiana. Cleopatra Mathis. TAT
(Aerial View of Louisiana.) MAYP
View of the Brooklyn Bridge, A. William Meredith. MoVE
View of the Burning, A. James Merrill. NePoEA-2
View of the Capitol from the Library of Congress. Elizabeth Bishop. AmFN
View of the Cathedral, *sels.* Raymond Henri.
Chartres. EyDe
Duomo, Milan. EyDe
View of the Present State of Ireland, A. Edmund Blunden. BrPo
View of the Town, A. In an Epistle to a Friend, *sel.* Thomas Gilbert.
Against Homosexuality. NOEC
Viewing Russian Peasants from a Leningrad-bound Train. Roger Gaess. LTB
Viewless thing is the wind, A. Love Is Strong. Richard Burton. AA; HBV-1
Viewpoint. George Scarbrough. AMV-81
Views. Harriet Susskind. AMV-80
Views from the High Camp. W. S. Merwin. ConAP
Views of Boston Common and Nearby. R. P. Blackmur. MoVE
Views of Our Sphere. Ernest Sandeen. MOON
Views of the Favorite Colleges. John Malcolm Brinnin. GLGT; LiTA; MoAB
Views of the Oxford Colleges. Barbara Howes. GLGT
Views of the Oxford Colleges. Paris Leary. CoPo
Vigil. Marjorie Freeman Campbell. CaP
Vigil. Richard Dehmel, *tr. fr. German by* Ludwig Lewisohn. AWP
Vigil. W. E. Henley. In Hospital, VII. BrPo; LoBV
Vigil. Michael Knoll. LFAC
Vigil, The. Denise Levertov. NePoEA-2
Vigil, The. Shlomo Reich, *tr. fr. French by* Mira Reich. VWA
Vigil of the Assumption. Gertrude von Le Fort, *tr. fr. German by* Margaret Chanler. ISi
Vigil of the Wounded. Phillip Yellowhawk Minthorn. STE
Vigil of Venus, The. *Unknown, tr. fr. Latin by* Allen Tate. AWP; GBL; UnTE
Sels.
"Goddesse bade the nymphs remove, The," *tr. by* Thomas Stanley. OBVE
"Love he to morrow, who lov'd never," *tr. by* Thomas Stanley. OBVE
Vigil Strange I Kept on the Field One Night. Walt Whitman. LoBV; MoAmPo; NOBA; NoP; OBWP; PeHV; TAP; WaaP; WHA
Vigilantius, or a Servant of the Lord Found Ready. Cotton Mather. SCAP
Vigils. Siegfried Sassoon. CMoP
Down the Glimmering Staircase, *sel.* PoLF
Vigndig A Fremd Kind (Babysitter's Song). *Unknown, tr. fr. Yiddish.* FSW
Vignette: 1922. Lawrence P. Spingarn. AMV-81
Vigor, vitality, vim and punch. Pep. Grace G. Bostwick. WBLP
Vigorous matron of Baxter, A. Hog-calling. Roy Blount, Jr. TDH
Vihio Images ("Coyote/ pineneedles"). Judith Mountain Leaf Volborth. TWSS
Vihio Images ("In the buffalo's skull"). Judith Mountain Leaf Volborth. TWSS
Viking, The. Whitley Stokes. OnYI
Viking Dublin; Trial Pieces. Seamus Heaney. IPY
Viking 1 on Mars—July 20, 1976. Anne S. Perlman. SUW
Viking Terror, The. *Unknown, tr. fr. Old Irish.* AnIL, *tr. by* F. N. Robinson; OnYI, *tr. by* F. N. Robinson; KiLC, *tr. by* Frank O'Connor
(Vikings, The, *tr. by* John Montague.) BIrV
(Vikings, The, *tr. unknown.*) ChTr
Vile Stanhope, demons blush to tell. On Lord Chesterfield and His Son. *Unknown.* FaBoCo
Vilikins and His Dinah. *At. to* Edward Laman Blanchard. *See* Villikins and His Dinah.
Villa Sciarra: Rome. Christine Turner Curtis. GoYe
Villa Thermidor. George Hitchcock. GP
Village, The. George Crabbe. LAuP
Sels.
"No shepherds now, in smooth alternate verse." PP
Parish Poor-House, The. OBEC
Pauper's Funeral, The. FaBoEn; OBNC
Rural Life. NOBE
Truth in Poetry. OBEC; SeCePo

Village Life. PoEL-4
("Village life, and every care that reigns.") EnRP; NOEC; OAEL-1
Village, The. Marina Gashe. PBA
Village, The. Goldsmith. *See* Auburn.
Village. Juan Ramón Jiménez. *See* Lamb Was Bleating Softly, The.
Village, The. Meridel Le Sueur. GP
Village and Factory. Alexander Bezymensky, *tr. fr. Russian by* Babette Deutsch. TrJP
Village Atheist, The. Edgar Lee Masters. *Fr.* Spoon River Anthology. EaLo; LiTA
Village before Sunset. Frances Cornford. BoNaP
Village Blacksmith, The. Longfellow. AA; BLPL; FaBoBe; FaFP; FaPON; FaPoR; HBV-2; HBVY; OBAL; OBCA; PaPo; PoPl; TreF; WBLP
Village Blacksmith, The. *Unknown.* FiBHP
Village-born Beauty. *Unknown.* PaPo
Village Choir, The. *Unknown.* FaBoPa
Village, happy once, is splendid now, The. The Bailiff. Ebenezer Elliott. *Fr.* The Splendid Village. NBM
Village has always lain in the path of the conqueror, The. The Village. Meridel Le Sueur. GP
Village in Snowstorm. Norbert Krapf. FAZ
Village is submerged, houses and creatures, The. Ashokan. Dachine Rainer. NePoAm
Village Life. George Crabbe. The Village, I. PoEL-4
("Village life, and every care that reigns.") EnRP; LAuP; NOEC; OAEL-1
Village maid was leaving home, with tears her eyes were wet, A. Heaven Will Protect the Working Girl. Edgar Smith. FaFP; TreF
Village Noon; Mid-Day Bells. Merrill Moore. MoAmPo
Village of Balmaquhapple, The. James Hogg. BSV; FaBoCo; FaBoPP
Village of Erith, The. *Unknown. See* Erith, on the Thames.
Village of Reason, The. Michael Palmer. NPGG
Village of the Presents, The. James McMichael. AmPA
Village of Winter Carols. Laurie Lee. ChMP
Village Parson, The. Goldsmith. *Fr.* The Deserted Village. OBEC; WGRP
("Near yonder copse, where once the garden smiled.") TRV
Village Preacher, The. Goldsmith. *Fr.* The Deserted Village. TrGrPo
Village Schoolmaster, The. Goldsmith. *Fr.* The Deserted Village. GLGT; OBEC; TrGrPo
Village sleeps, a name unknown, till men, The. Distinction. Mark A. De Wolfe Howe. AA
Village Tale, A. May Sarton. BoAnP; GDP
Village! thy butcher's son, the steward now. The Steward. Ebenezer Elliott. *Fr.* The Splendid Village. NBM; OBSV
Village Tudda, The. Kenneth Patchen. VGW
Villagers all, this frosty tide. Christmas Carol [*or* Carol]. Kenneth Grahame. *Fr.* The Wind in the Willows. FaPON; OHIP; PChr
Villagers and Death, The. Robert Graves. HeIP
Villagers who gather round. Spiel of the Three Mountebanks. John Crowe Ransom. MoAB; MoAmPo
Villages Démolis ("The villages are strewn"). Sir Herbert Read. BrPo
Villages not half as wide. Anasazi at Mesa Verde. Reg Saner. NPAW
Villain, The. W. H. Davies. MoBrPo; OxBTC; SoSe; WHA
Villain shows his indiscretion. Curtain! Paul Laurence Dunbar. CenHV
Villancico. *Unknown, tr. fr. Spanish by* Thomas Walsh. AWP
Villanelle: "Every day our bodies separate." Marilyn Hacker. AmPA
Villanelle: "It is the pain, it is the pain, endures." William Empson. ChMP; CMoP; EnLoPo; NoAM; OAEL-2
Villanelle: "It's all a trick, quite easy when you know it." W. W. Skeat. FaBoCo; FiBHP
Villanelle: "Like twilight bleeding on a winter day." John Nist. AMV-81
Villanelle: "O winter wind, lat grievin be." Margaret Winefride Simpson. OxBS
Villanelle: "Proud inclination of the flesh." Dilys Laing. ErPo; NMP
Villanelle: The Psychological Hour. Ezra Pound. CTC
Villanelle, The: "Regard the motion of the villanelle." Donald Harington. AMV-81; FAZ
Villanelle: "Time can say nothing but I told you so." W. H. Auden. MoAB; MoBrPo
(If I Could Tell You.) PAI
(Time Will Say Nothing but I Told You So.) LiTA
Villanelle: "Woods we're lost in aren't real, The." Walter H. Kerr. NePoAm-2
Villanelle of a Villaness. Edwin Meade Robinson. HBMV
Villanelle of Acheron. Ernest Dowson. VLP
Villanelle of His Lady's Treasures. Ernest Dowson. HBV-1
Villanelle of Marguerites. Ernest Dowson. MoBrPo
Villanelle of Sunset. Ernest Dowson. BrPo
Villanelle of the Poet's Road. Ernest Dowson. OBMV; TrGrPo; UnPo
Villanelle of Washington Square. Walter Adolphe Roberts. PoNe
Villanelle with a Line by Yeats. Bruce Bennett. AMV-80
Villiers de l'Isle-Adam. Aldous Huxley. HBMV
Villikins [*or* Vilikins] and His Dinah. *At. to* Edward Laman Blanchard; *also at. to* Sam Cowell BaBo (A *and* B vers.); FSW; VLP
Villon's Ballade. Andrew Lang, *after* Villon. HBV-1
Villon's Good-Night. W. E. Henley, *after* Villon. CenHV
Villon's Straight Tip to All Cross Coves. W. E. Henley, *after* Villon. AWP; CenHV; FaBoCo; HBV-1; InMe; InvP; NA; SeCePo
Vilna. Moishe Kulbak, *tr. fr. Yiddish by* Joachim Neugroschel. VWA
Vilna Puzzle, A. Sasha Chorny, *tr. fr. Russian by* Daniel Weissbort. VWA
Vincent Corbet, farther knowne. An Elegie upon the Death of His Owne Father. Richard Corbett. AnAnS-2
Vincent Van Gogh. William Jay Smith. EyDe
Vindication. Daniil Kharms, *tr. fr. Russian by* George Gibian. FaBoNo
Vine, The. Robert Herrick. CaPo; CavP; ErPo; NoP; UnTE
Vine, The. James Thomson ("B. V."). Sunday up the River, XVIII. HBV-1; OBEV; OBVV
Vine and Fig Tree. Shalom Altman. FSW
Vine and the Goat, The. Aesop, *tr. fr. Greek by* William Ellery Leonard. AWP
Vine I see, and though 'tis time to glean, A. Overripe Fruit. Kasmuneh. TrJP
Vinegaroon. Witter Bynner. BPAW
Vines branching stilly. Carol. Louise Imogen Guiney. Five Carols for Christmastide, II. ISi; OBVV
Vineyard, The. W. S. Merwin. NNaP
Vineyard, The. *Unknown.* STF
Vingtaine. Alice Learned Bunner.
Immutabilis, II.
Separation, I.
Vintage, The. Belle Cooper. GoBC
Vintage to the Dungeon, The. Richard Lovelace. CaPo; SeCV-1
Violence on Television. Louis Jenkins. NU
Violent order is disorder, A. Connoisseur of Chaos. Wallace Stevens. LiTM; MoPo; SUW
Violent praise the destructive rites of the hawk, The. The Beaver's Story. Vernon Watkins. NYBP
Violent Space, The. Etheridge Knight. BPo
Violent Storm. Mark Strand. NYBP
Violet. John Hollander. FYAP
Violet, The. Sir Walter Scott. EnRP
Violet, The. William Wetmore Story. HBV-1
Violet, *sel.* Arthur Symons.
Declaration. BrPo; ViBoPo
Violet, The. Jane Taylor. HBV-1; HBVY; TreF
Violet and the Rose, The. Joseph Skipsey. OBVV
Violet and the Rose, The. Augusta Webster. HBV-1
Violet Bank, A. Shakespeare. *Fr.* A Midsummer Night's Dream, II, i. FaPON
("I know a bank where the wild thyme blows.") PoPle
(Where the Wild Thyme Blows.) TrGrPo
Violet in her greenwood bower, The. The Violet. Sir Walter Scott. EnRP
Violet in her lovely hair, A. Song. Charles Swain. HBV-1
Violet in the wood, that's sweet to-day, The. The Violet and the Rose. Augusta Webster. HBV-1
Violet invited my kiss, The. The Violet and the Rose. Joseph Skipsey. OBVV
Violet is much too shy, The. A Song the Grass Sings. Charles G. Blanden. HBV-1
Violet Twilights. Edith Södergran, *tr. fr. Swedish by* Stina Katchadourian. WPOW
Violet wash is streaked across the clouds, A. Dinosaur Spring. Marilyn Waniek. MAYP
Violets and Roses. *Unknown. See* Sweet Violets.
Violets blue of the eyes divine, The. Die blauen Veilchen der Äugelein. Heine, *tr. by* James Thomson. AWP
Violets, daffodils. Nosegay. Elizabeth J. Coatsworth. OBCA; TiPo
Violets for Mother. Lonny Kaneko. BrSi
Violets in Thaumantia's Bosome. Sir Edward Sherburne. OBS
Violin Calls, The. Florence Randal Livesay. CaP
Violin Tree, The. Joel Rosenberg. VWA
Violinist, A. Francis William Bourdillon. OBVV
Violinist, The. Archibald Lampman. CaP
Violinist's shadow vanishes, The. Cadenza. Ted Hughes. CMoP; NYBP
Violin's Complaint, The. William Roscoe Thayer. AA
Violins in Repose. Jorge Plescoff, *tr. fr. Spanish by* Yishai Tobin. VWA
Viper, The. Hilaire Belloc. FaBoNo
Viper, The. Ruth Pitter. FaBoTw
Viper stung a Cappadocian's hide, A. The Snake It Was That Died. Demodocus, *tr. by* J. H. Merivale. DBV
Vipers Bugloss beckons me, The. Song to My Love. Laurence McKinney. InMe
Virgidemiarum, *sels.* Joseph Hall.
"Great is the folly of a feeble brain," Bk. I, Satire VII. EBEV

"I first adventure, with foolhardy might," Prologue, Bk. I. ViBoPo
"Sturdy ploughman doth the soldier see, The," Bk. IV, *fr.* Satire VI. OBSV
"Time was, and that was termed the time of Gold," Bk. III, Satire I. OBSV
(Olden Days, The.) OBSC
"Who doubts? The laws fell down from heaven's height," Bk. II, Satire III. OBSV
Virgil: Georgics, Book IV. Dennis Schmitz. NPGG
Virgilia, *sel.* Edwin Markham.
"What was I back in the world's first wonder?" EtS
Virgil's Farewell to Dante. Dante, *tr. fr. Italian by* Laurence Binyon. *Fr.* Divina Commedia: Purgatorio, XXVII. FaBoTw
Virgil's Tomb. Robert Cameron Rogers. AA
Virgin. Padraic Fallon. OnYI
Virgin, The. *Unknown. See* Spring under a Thorn, The.
Virgin, The. Wordsworth. GoBC
(Sonnet to the Virgin.) ISi
Virgin and Unicorn. John Heath-Stubbs. NeBP
Virgin Country. Roy McFadden. NeIP
Virgin Declares Her Beauties, A. Francesco da Barberini, *tr. fr. Italian by* Dante Gabriel Rossetti AWP; ErPo
Virgin is thinking of a child, The. Leonardo's Secret. Robert Bly. NNaP
Virgin Martyrs. John Heath-Stubbs. OxBC
Virgin Mary, The. Edgar Bowers. NePoEA; QFR
Virgin Mary cannot enter into, The. And in Her Morning. Jessica Agnes Powers. ISi
Virgin Mary Had One Son. *Unknown.* FSW
Virgin Mary to Christ on the Cross, The. Robert Southwell. ViBoPo
Virgin Mary to the Child Jesus, The, *abr.* Elizabeth Barrett Browning. ISi
Virgin Mother, The, *sel.* D. H. Lawrence.
"I kiss you good-bye, my darling." ViBoPo
Virgin Mother walked barefoot, The. Begotten of the Spleen. Charles Simic. LCAP
Virgin Pictured in Profile. Rosanna Warren. AMV-81; MAYP
Virgin Sturgeon, The. *Unknown.* FSW
Virgin truly full of wonder. St. Ephrem, *tr. fr. Syriac by* W. H. Kent. *Fr.* Christmas Hymn. ISi
Virgin Unspotted, The. *Unknown.* OBET
Virginal, A. Ezra Pound. AP; CMoP; CoBMV; MoAB; MoAmPo; NePA; NIP; NoAM; NOBA; OxBA; TAP; TwAmPo
Virginia. T. S. Eliot. Landscapes, II. BiP
Virginia. Elouise Loftin. PoBA
Virginia Beach. Stanley Plumly. AMV-81
Virginia Britannia. Marianne Moore. MoVE
Virginia Capta. Margaret Junkin Preston. PAH
Virginia gave us this imperial man. Imperial Man. James Russell Lowell. *Fr.* Under the Old Elm. PGD
Virginia Song, The. *Unknown.* PAH
Virginian Voyage, The. Michael Drayton. *See* To the Virginian Voyage.
Virginiana. Mary Johnston. HBMV
Virginians of the Valley, The. Francis Orrery Ticknor. AA; HBV-2; PAH
Virginia's Bloody Soil. *Unknown.* AmFP
Virgins. Francis Carlin. HBMV
Virgins, The. Derek Walcott. OxBC; SoSe
Virgins are like the fair flower in its lustre. What Shall I Do to Show How Much I Love Her? John Gay. *Fr.* The Beggar's Opera. TEP
Virgins promis'd when I died [*or* dy'd]. An Epitaph upon a Child. Robert Herrick. FaBoEE; SeCV-1
Virgins, sing the virgin huntress. To Apollo and Diana. Horace, *tr. by* Branwell Brontë. Odes, I, 21. OBVE
Virgin's Slumber Song, The. Francis Carlin. ISi; YeAr
Virgin's Song, The. *Unknown.* NOBE; OxBM
(Cradle Song of the Virgin.) ISi
(Our Lady's Song.) OBEV
Virgins terrify too many men. Sonnet XII. Winfield Townley Scott. ErPo
Virgo Descending. Charles Wright. LCAP
Virile Christ, A. Rex Boundy. TRV; WGRP
Virtue. Walter de la Mare. MMA
Virtue. Nicholas Grimald. OBSC
Virtue. George Herbert. AWP; CABA; CH; ELP; HAP; HBV-2; HeIP; InvP; JCP; LoBV; NOBE; NOCV; NoP; OAEL-1; OBEV; PAI; PoRA; PPP; SeCeV; SoSe; TEP; TreFT; TrGrPo; ViBoPo; WGRP; WHA
(Vertue.) AnAnS-1; FaBoEn; FaBoRV; MeLP; MePo; OBS; PoPle; SeCP; SeCV-1
Virtue. Immanuel di Roma, *tr. fr. Hebrew by* J. Chotzner. *Fr.* Machberoth. TrJP
Virtue, alas, now let me take some rest. Astrophel and Stella, IV. Sir Philip Sidney. SiPS
Virtue conceal'd within our breast. Swift, *after the Latin of* Horace. OBVE
Virtue, dear friend, needs no defence. Horace, *tr. by* Earl of Roscommon. Odes, I, 22. OBVE
Virtue dwells rarely in the bright eyed and fair. Virtue. Immanuel di Roma, *tr. by* J. Chotzner. *Fr.* Machberoth. TrJP
Virtue may choose the high or low degree. The Triumph of Vice. Pope. *Fr.* Epilogue to the Satires. NOBE; OBSV
Virtue of Shape, A. Thom Swiss. AMV-80
Virtue's branches wither, virtue pines. Song [*or* A Priest's Song]. Thomas Dekker. *Fr.* Old Fortunatus. EIL; OBSC; WHA
Virtues of Carnation Milk, The. David Ogilvy. OBAL
Virtues of Sid Hamet, the Magician's Rod, The. Swift. APAS
Virtuosa. Mary Ashley Townsend. AA
Virtuous Fox and the Self-righteous Cat, The. John Cunningham. OnMSP
Virtuous Wife, The, *sel.* Thomas D'Urfey.
Sawney was Tall. OAEP
Virtuous Wife, The. Süsskind von Trimberg, *tr. fr. Middle High German.* TrJP
Virtuous, witty, proud and gay. The Romantic. Colin Ellis. POL
Virtuous Woman, The. Bible, *O.T.* Proverbs, XXXI: 10-31. TrJP; TRV
Virus, The. Christian Morgenstern, *tr. fr. German by* W. D. Snodgrass *and* Lore Segal. PV
Visage becomes armed, The: within. Armed Vision. N. P. Van Wyk Louw, *tr. by* Jack Cope *and* Uys Krige. PeSA
Viscous air, wheres' ere she fly, The. The Kingfisher. Andrew Marvell. *Fr.* Upon Appleton House. ChTr
Visibility stretches for miles, bringing the sea. Soup on a Cold Day. Nellie Hill. AMV-81
Visible Baby, The. Peter Redgrove. NAs
Visible, invisible. A Jellyfish. Marianne Moore. PCP
Visibly here the tide. Wellfleet Harbor. Paul Goodman. CoAP
Vision. Delmira Augustini, *tr. fr. Spanish by* Marti Moody. WPOW
Vision, The. Burns. BSV; OxBS
Vision, A. John Clare. ChTr; EBVV; FaBoRV; GTBS-P; NCEP; OAEL-2; OBNC; PPP
(I Lost the Love of Heaven.) ELP; LoBV
Vision, A, *sel.* "Barry Cornwall."
"First, I saw a landscape fair." OBRV
Vision. Harry Crosby. EAS
Vision, A. Geoffrey Dearmer. HBMV
Vision, The. Daniel Defoe. APAS
Vision. Richard Eberhart. NYBP
Vision, A. "Michael Field." SyP
Vision, A. Lord Herbert of Cherbury. AnAnS-2; SeCP
Vision, The ("I dreamed we both were in bed"). Robert Herrick. UnTE
(Vision to Electra, The.) SeCP
Vision, The ("Methought I saw as I did dream in bed"). Robert Herrick. CaPo
Vision, The ("Sitting alone as one forsook"). Robert Herrick. AnAnS-2; CaPo; ErPo; JCP; SeCP
(Sitting Alone.) UnTE
Vision, A. Hugo von Hofmannsthal, *tr. fr. German by* Charles Wharton Stork. TrJP
Vision. William Dean Howells. AA
Vision, A. Maria Konopnicka, *tr. fr. Polish by* Jerzy Peterkiewicz *and* Burns Singer. WPOW
Vision. W. S. Merwin. GP
Vision. Francis Reginald. MoCV
Vision. Frank Sidgwick. MMA
Vision, The. William Taylor. NOEC
Vision, The. Thomas Traherne. ILwL
Vision, A. Henry Vaughan. *See* World, The.
Vision, A. Yvor Winters. MoVE
Vision, A, *sel.* W. B. Yeats.
All Souls' Night. MoVE
Vision. Israel Zangwill. TrJP
Vision and breath. Outside White Earth. Gordon Henry. STE
Vision and Prayer. Dylan Thomas. LiTM; MoPo
Vision as of crowded city streets, A. Shakespeare. Longfellow. AWP
Vision by Sweetwater. John Crowe Ransom. AP; CMoP; CoBMV; CrMA; FaBoMo; MoAB; NOBA; OxBA
Vision Concerning Piers Plowman, The. William Langland. *See* Vision of Piers Plowman, The.
Vision floats/ over the death camps. 1976. Harvey Shapiro. FAZ
Vision in long filaments flows. Vision. Francis Reginald. MoCV
Vision of a Queen of Fairyland, A. Tadhg Dall O'Huiginn, *tr. by* the Earl of Longford. *Fr.* The First Vision. AnIL; BIrV
Vision of Belshazzar, The. Byron. FaPo; GN; HBV-2; OnMSP; RoGo
Vision of Beulah, The. Blake. *Fr.* Milton, II. NOBE; OAEL-2, *longer sel.*
(Birds, The.) PB
(Birdsong.) FaBoEn
(Choir of Day, The.) EnRP
(Lark's Song, The.) WiR
(Nightingale and Flowers.) LoBV

("Thou hearest the nightingale begin the song of spring.") OBRV; PBBP
(Vision of the Lamentation of Beulah over Ololon, A.) OBNC
Vision of Children, A. Thomas Ashe. EBVV
Vision of Christ that thou dost see, The. Blake. *Fr.* The Everlasting Gospel. OBRV
Vision of Connaught in the Thirteenth Century, A. James Clarence Mangan. *See* King Cahal Mor of the Wine-red Hand.
Vision of Delight Presented at Court in Chistmas, 1617, The. Ben Jonson. SeCV-1
Vision of Delight, The. Ben Jonson. PoEL-2
Vision of 400 Sunrises. Ruth Lisa Schechter. SOTS
Vision of Ita, The. *Unknown. See* Jesukin.
Vision of Jesus, The. William Langland. *Fr.* The Vision of Piers Plowman. ACP
Vision of Judgement, A, *sels.* Southey.
Absolvers, The. EnRP
Southey Looks out of the Window at Greta Hill. FaBoPP
Vision of Judgment, The. Byron. EnRP; MasP; OAEL-2; TEP
(At the Gate of Heaven, *abr.*) OBRV
Sels.
Archangel, The. LoBV
"At length with jostling, elbowing, and the aid." OBSV
George the Third. FiP
(George III.) TW, *abr.*
"Saint Peter sat by the celestial gate." OBSV; OxBoLi
Vision of Lazarus, The, *sel.* Fenton Johnson.
"Another sate near him, whose harp of gold." BANP
Vision of MacConglinne, The. MacConglinne, *tr. fr. Middle Irish.* BIrV, *tr. by* John Montague; CH, *tr. by* Kuno Meyer; FaBoNo, *longer sel., tr. by* Kuno Meyer; OBVE, *tr. by* John Montague
(Vision That Appeared to Me, *tr. by* Kuno Meyer.) OnYI
Vision of Nature, A. William Langland. *Fr.* The Vision of Piers Plowman. PoEL-1
("And I bowed my body and beheld all about.") CTC
Vision of Oxford, A, *sel.* William Alexander.
"Methought I met a lady yester even." OBVV
Vision of Piers Plowman, The, *sels.* William Langland.
Age of Reason, The, *mod. by* Donald Attwater. NOCV
"And I bowed my body and beheld all about." CTC
(Vision of Nature, A.) PoEL-1
"As for the birds and the beasts, the men in bygone times," *fr.* Passus XII. PBBP
Belling the Cat (C *text*). OxBM
"Birds I beheld building nests in the bushes," *fr.* Passus XI. PBBP
Civil Service, The, *mod. by* Donald Attwater. NOCV
Descent into Hell, The. PoEL-1
Entertainment Industry, The, *mod. by* Donald Attwater. NOCV
Et Incarnatus Est, *fr.* Passus II (C *text*). NOBE
"For trewthe telleth that loue is triacle of hevene." OBEV
(Incarnation, The.) PoEL-1
Friars. PPON
Glutton in the Tavern (C *text*). OxBM
(Glutton, The.) ACP
God's Mercy, *mod. by* Donald Attwater. NOCV
Good Works, *mod. by* Donald Attwater. NOCV
Grace for Theology. GoBC
Long Will in London (C *text*). OxBM
Our Needy Neighbours (C *text*). OxBM
(Poor, The.) PoEL-1
Palace of Truth, The. ACP
Palmer, The. ACP
Prologue: "In a summer season, when soft was the sun." OAEL-1, *mod. by* J. B. Trapp (B *text*)
(Field Full of Folk, The, A *text.*) OxBM
(Field of Folk, The.) PoEL-1
("In a somer seson, whan softe was the sonne.") EBEV
(On Malverne Hilles, the Place of Piers Plowman's Vision.) FaBoPP
Saint Called "Truth," A, *mod. by* Donald Attwater. NOCV
Trinity, The (C *text*). OxBM
Vision of Jesus, The. ACP
"What for feere of this ferly and of the false Jewes," *fr.* Passus XVIII. EBEV
"What this mountain means, and the murky dale," *fr.* Passus I (B *text*), *mod. by* J. B. Trapp. OAEL-1
"Yet I courbed on my knees and cried hire of grace," *fr.* Passus II. EBEV
Vision of Poets, A, *sel.* Elizabeth Barrett Browning.
"Fiery throb in every star, A." PeD
Vision of Rotterdam. Gregory Corso. NoAM
Vision of St. Bernard, The. M. Whitcomb Hess. ISi
Vision of Sin, The. Tennyson. OAEL-2; VLP
Song at the Ruin'd Inn, *sel.* PoEL-5
Vision of Sir Launfal, The. James Russell Lowell. OnMSP
Sels.
Brook in Winter, The, Prelude to Pt. II. GN
("Down swept the chill wind from mountain peak.") TreF
Day in June, A ("And what is so rare as a day in June?"), Prelude to Pt. I. FaPON
"Earth gets its price for what Earth gives us," *fr.* Prelude to Pt. I. TreF
"For a cap and bells our lives we pay," *fr.* Prelude to Pt. I. AA
"For Christ's sweet sake, I beg an alms," *fr.* Pt. II. WGRP
"Holy supper is kept, indeed, The," *fr.* Pt. II. TRV
June ("Over his keys the musing organist"), *fr.* Prelude to Pt. I. HBV-1; HBVY; OHFP; PoLF
June ("What is so rare as a day in June?"), Prelude to Pt. I. FaBV
June Weather, *fr.* Prelude to Pt. I. GN
"Lo, it is I, be not afraid!" *fr.* Pt. II, *st.* 8. TreF
Not Only around Our Infancy, *fr.* Prelude to Pt. I. FaFP; NePA
Now Is the High-Tide of the Year, *fr.* Prelude to Pt. I. TreFS
"Over his keys the musing organist," Prelude to Pt. I. LiTA
Sir Launfal and the Leper, *fr.* Pt. I. GN
What Is So Rare as a Day in June, *fr.* Prelude to Pt. I. BLPL; FaBoBe; FaFP; NePA
Winter Morning, A, *fr.* Pt. II. GN
Vision of Sorrow. Thomas Sackville. *Fr.* Induction to "A Mirror for Magistrates." LoBV
Vision of the Day of Judgment. Bible, *O.T., Moulton, Modern Reader's Bible.* Isaiah, LXIII. WGRP
Vision of the Lamentation of Beulah over Ololon, A. Blake. *See* Vision of Beulah, The.
Vision of the Mermaids, A, *sel.* Gerard Manley Hopkins.
"Rowing, I reach'd a rock—the sea was low." ChTr
Vision of the Sea, A. Shelley. MOS
Vision of the Shepherds. W. H. Auden. *Fr.* For the Time Being; a Christmas Oratorio. SBVL
Vision of the Snow, The. Margaret Junkin Preston. AA
Vision of the World's Instability, A. Richard Verstegan. EIL
Vision of Truth, A. J. C. Squire. NOBL
Vision of War, A. Thomas Sackville. *Fr.* Induction to "A Mirror for Magistrates." FaBoEn
(Shield of War, The.) NOBE
Vision Song (Cheyenne). Lance Henson. STE
Vision That Appeared to Me, A. MacConglinne. *See* Vision of MacConglinne, The.
Vision to Electra, The. Robert Herrick. *See* Vision, The ("I dreamed we both were in bed").
Vision upon This Conceit of the Faerie Queene, A. Sir Walter Ralegh. OBSC
(Faery Queen, The.) ViBoPo
(Of Spenser's Faery Queen.) SiPS
Visionary, The. Emily Brontë. BLPL; LiTB; LO; LoBV; NOBE; OAEP; OBNC; PBWP; SCV
(Silent Is the House.) CH; ELP
("Silent is the house—all are laid asleep," *longer vers.*) BrRo
Visions, *sel.* Blake.
"Moment of desire, The! the moment of desire! the virgin." ErPo
Visions, *sel.* William Browne.
"Rose, as fair as ever saw the north, A." ViBoPo
(Rose, The.) CH; HBV-1; OBEV
Visions, *sel.* Joachim du Bellay, *tr. fr. French by* Spenser.
"It was the time, when rest, soft sliding downe." AWP
Visions. Kathleen Spivack. AmPA
Visions of Mexico While at a Writing Symposium in Port Townsend, Washington. Lorna Dee Cervantes. FIA
Visions [of Petrarch], The. Petrarch, *tr. fr. Italian by* Spenser. *Fr.* Sonnets to Laura: To Laura in Death, Canzone III. AWP
I Saw a Phoenix in the Wood Alone, *sel.* ChTr
Visions of the Daughters of Albion. Blake. OAEL-2
Sels.
" 'Father of Jealousy, be thou accursed from the earth!' " ViBoPo
Take Thy Bliss, O Man. EnRP
Visions of the World's Vanity, *sel.* Spenser.
Huge Leviathan, The. ChTr
Visions you never saw, The. Grandfather. Lance Henson. CDW
Visit. A. R. Ammons. CoAP; GrPl; TwCP
Visit, A. Sherwood Anderson. PoA
Visit. Vic Coccimiglio. Str
Visit, The. Emerson. NOBA
Visit, The. Jim Gauer. AMV-81
Visit, The. Phillip William George. VoR
Visit, The. Ogden Nash. FiBHP
Visit. Randolph Outlaw. LFAC
Visit, The. William J. Rewak. AMV-80
Visit. James Welch. AmPA

Visit by Water. Floris Clark McLaren. OBCV
Visit from St. Nicholas, A. Clement Clarke Moore. AA; BeLS; BLPA; FaBoBe; FaBV; FaFP; FaPo; FaPON; FPL; HBV-1; HBVY; NTCP; OBAL; OBCA; OBCP; OnMSP; OxBChV; PaPo; PChr; PoPl; RHCP; SiSoSe; TiPo; TreF; YaD
Visit from the Sea, A. Robert Louis Stevenson. FM; GN; MOS
Visit Home, A. Joseph Glazer. VWA
Visit of Hope to Sydney Cove, near Botany-Bay. Erasmus Darwin. NOEC
Visit of the Gods, The. Schiller, *tr. fr. German by* Samuel Taylor Coleridge. OBVE
Visit to a Hospital. Jean Valentine Chace. GoYe
Visit to Bridge House, A. Richard Weber. BIrV
Visit to the Art Gallery, A, *sels.* Carlos Baker.
Chinese Mural, A. EyDe
On a Landscape of Sestos. EyDe
Visit to the Asylum, A. Edna St. Vincent Millay. SO
Visit to the Author's Paternal Seat, A. Richard Polwhele. *Fr.* The Influence of Local Attachment. NOEC
Visit to the Farm, A. Robert Siegel. GeTw
Visit to the Hermitage. Jack L. Anderson. LFAC
Visit to Van Gogh, A. Charles Causley. PoCh
Visitant, The. Theodore Roethke. CMoP; NMP; PPoe; UnPo
Visitant to our dumbly human home. The Great Moth. Robert Gittings. OxBTC
Visitation, The. Elizabeth Jennings. MoBS
Visitation, The. Calvin Le Compte. ISi
Visitations. Jennifer Crewe. AMV-80
Visitations. Lawrence Durrell. *Fr.* Eight Aspects of Melissa. MoBrPo; NeBP
Visitations: VII, *sel.* Louis MacNeice.
And the Lord Was Not in the Whirlwind. EaLo
Visiting Day. Al Young. NPGG
Visiting Emily Dickinson's Grave with Robert Francis. Robert Bly. LCAP
Visiting Father. Genny Lim. BrSi
Visiting Grandpa years ago, I. Foreign Soil. Dianne Hai-Jew. BrSi
Visiting Home, *sel.* Edward Field.
"*Yiskidor,* when he dies I won't know the Hebrew words to say." DiL
Visiting home to tell my people. A Long Overdue Thankyou Note to the Girl Who Taught Me Loving. Tom Schmidt. NeAC
Visiting Hour. Stewart Conn. BSV
Visiting Hour, The. David Wagoner. HoPM
Visiting Poet. John Frederick Nims. DBV; InPK; PV
Visiting the Dead. Ciaran Carson. CIP
Visiting the Oracle. Lawrence Raab. AmPA
Visiting you, we slept in the arms of. Pennsylvania Academy of Fine Arts. Ernest Kroll. AMV-80
Visitor, The. George Bogin. FAZ
Visitor, A. "Lewis Carroll." FaBoNo
Visitor, The. Patrick R. Chalmers. HBV-1; HBVY
Visitor, The. W. H. Davies. GBL
Visitor, The. Carolyn Forché. FYAP
Visitor. W. E. Henley. In Hospital, XX. BrPo
Visitor, The. Gregory Orr. MAYP
Visitor, The. Jack Prelutsky. AmMo
Visitor, The. Katherine Pyle. OnUR
Visitor to Warsaw. Portrait of a Jew Old Country Style. Jerome Rothenberg. NNaP
Visitors. Harry Behn. SoPo
Visitor's Parking. Anne Szumigalski. NOBC
Visits. Daniel L. Klauck. LFAC
Visits to St. Elizabeths. Elizabeth Bishop. CoAP; VGW
Vistas. Odell Shepard. HBMV
Vita Benefica. Alice Wellington Rollins. AA
Vita Brevis. *Unknown, tr. fr. German by* Louis Untermeyer. UnTE
Vita Nuova, La, *sels.* Dante, *tr. fr. Italian by* Dante Gabriel Rossetti.
"All my thoughts always speak to me of Love," VI. AWP
"All ye that pass along Love's trodden way," II. AWP
"At whiles (yea oftentimes) I muse over," IX. AWP
"Beyond the sphere which spreads to widest space," XXIX. AWP; CTC
"Canst thou indeed be he that still would sing," *fr.* XIII, b. AWP
"Day agone, as I rode sullenly, A," IV. AWP
"Death, always cruel, Pity's foe in chief," *fr.* III, b. AWP
"Even as the others mock, thou mockest me," VII. AWP
"Eyes that weep for pity of the heart, The," XIX. AWP; WGRP; *sl. diff. vers.*
"For certain he hath seen all perfectness," XVII. AWP
"Gentle thought there is will often start, A," XXVI. AWP
"I felt a spirit of love begin to stir," XV. AWP
"Ladies that have intelligence in love," X. AWP
"Love and the gentle heart are one same thing," XI. AWP
"Love hath so long possessed me for his own," XVIII. AWP
"Love's pallor and the semblance of deep ruth," XXIV. AWP
"Mine eyes beheld the blessed pity spring," XXIII. AWP
(Sonnet). PoPl
"My lady carries love within her eyes," XII. AWP
"My lady looks so gentle and so pure," XVI. AWP
"Song, 'tis my will that thou do seek out Love," V. AWP
Sonnet: "Beatrice is gone up into high Heaven," *fr.* XIX. GoBC
Sonnet: "With sighs my bosom always laboureth," *fr.* XIX. GoBC
Sonnet: "Wonderfully out of the beautiful form," *fr.* XIX. GoBC
"Stay now with me, and listen to my sighs," XX. AWP
"That lady of all gentle memories," XXII. AWP
"That she hath gone to Heaven suddenly," *fr.* III. CTC
"Thoughts are broken in my memory, The," VIII. AWP
"To every heart which the sweet pain doth move," I. AWP
"Very bitter weeping that ye made, The," XXV. AWP
"Very pitiful lady, very young, A," XIV. AWP; CTC, *shorter sel.*
"Weep, Lovers, with Love's very self doth weep," *fr.* III, a. AWP
"Whatever while the thought comes over me," XXI. AWP
"Woe's me! by dint of all these sighs that come," XXVII. AWP
"Ye pilgrim-folk, advancing pensively," XXVIII. AWP; CTC
"You that thus wear a modest countenance," *fr.* XIII, a. AWP
Vita Nuova. Stanley Kunitz. VGW
Vita Nuova. Sir William Watson. OBVV
Vitae Summa Brevis Spem Nos Vetat Incohare Longam. Ernest Dowson. AWP; BrPo; ChTr; EBVV; FaBoRV; HAP; HBV-2; LoBV; NOBE; NoP; OBEV; TrGrPo; ViBoPo; VLP; WGRP; WHA
(Envoy: "They are not long, the weeping and the laughter.") MoBrPo; PCP
(They Are Not Long.) PoRA; TreFT
Vitaï Lampada. Sir Henry Newbolt. BLPA; FaPoR; OBWP; PaPo; TreF
Vital Message. Robert Phillips. GeTw
Vital Spark of Heavenly Flame. Pope. *See* Dying Christian to His Soul, The.
Vitality. Maria Amália Fonte Boa, *tr. fr. Portuguese by* Willis Barnstone *and* Nelson Cerqueira. BoWoP
Vitamins and Roughage. Kenneth Rexroth. NoAM
Vitelli rides west toward Fano, the morning sun. The Death of Vitellozzo Vitelli. Irving Feldman. MP; TwCP
Vitrines of pearly gowns, bright porcelains. Fifth Avenue Parade. Anthony Hecht. NYP
Vittoria Colonna. Roy Marz. PoA
Vivaldi. Delmore Schwartz. NYBP
Vivaldi on the Far Side of the Bars. Michael Knoll. LFAC
Vivamus, Mea Lesbia, atque Amemus. Thomas Campion, *after* Catullus. *See* My Sweetest Lesbia, Let Us Live and Love.
Vive la Canadienne. *Tr. fr. French.* FSW
Vive la Compagnie. *Unknown.* FSW; PSoN, *with music*
Vive Noir! Mari Evans. BOLo; IHMS; PoBA
Vivérols. David Starr Jordan. AA
Vivid, alone, against the wide expanse. Pedro. Phoebe W. Hoffman. GoYe
Vivid and heavy, he strolls through dark brick kitchens. The Composer's Winter Dream. Norman Dubie. LCAP
Vivid hardened ocean, A. New Mexican Desert. Witter Bynner. BPAW
Vivien's Song. Tennyson. *See* In Love, if Love Be Love.
Vivien's Song ("But now the wholesome music of the wood"). Tennyson. *Fr.* Idylls of the King: Balin and Balan. OAEL-2
Vivisection, *abr.* Gene Fowler. LFAC
Vixen, The. John Clare. BoAnP
Vixen woman, The. Harold Monro. *Fr.* Natural History. OBMV
Vixi. *At. to* Charles Mackay. HBV-2
Vixi Puellis Nuper Idoneus. Sir Thomas Wyatt. *See* Lover Showeth How He Is Forsaken . . .
Vlamertinghe; Passing the Château, July 1917. Edmund Blunden. MMA; OBWP
Vobiscum Est Iope. Thomas Campion. *See* When Thou Must Home.
Vocation. Judith Herzberg, *tr. fr. Dutch by* Manfred Wolf. WPOW
Vocation. Rabindranath Tagore. FaPON
Voice, The. Walter de la Mare. WSC
Voice, The. Norman Gale. HBV-1; OHIP
Voice, The. Thomas Hardy. BoLoP; CMoP; EnLoPo; FaBoEn; GBL; GTBS-P; HAP; MoVE; NoAM; NoP; OAEL-2; OAEP; OBNC; PAI; PoEL-5; PoPle
Voice, The. Judith Herzberg, *tr. fr. Dutch by* Shirley Kaufman. VWA
Voice, The. Sister Maris Stella. GoBC
Voice. W. S. Merwin. NNaP
Voice. Stanley Moss. AMV-80
Voice, The. Theodore Roethke. VGW
Voice. Harriet Prescott Spofford. AA
Voice, The. Edmund Wilson. NYBP
Voice and Address. Michael Palmer. NPGG
Voice by the Cedar Tree, A. Tennyson. HBV-1
Voice from Danang. Thomas Dillon Redshaw. MAT

Voice from Galilee, The. Horatius Bonar. HBV-2
Voice from heaven was heard on earth, A. St. Andrew's Voyage to Mermedonia. *Unknown, tr. by* Charles W. Kennedy. *Fr.* Andreas. AnOE
Voice from Out of the Night, A. Lisel Mueller. GP
Voice from the dark is calling me, A. Divorce. Anna Wickham. MoBrPo
Voice from the heroic dead, A. What Is That Music High in the Air? A. J. M. Smith. NMP
Voice from the Invisible World, A. Goethe, *tr. fr. German by* James Clarence Mangan. AWP
Voice from the Roses, A. Maxine W. Kumin. NMM
Voice from the sea to the mountain. The Great Voices. Charles Timothy Brooks. HBV-2
Voice from the Waters, A. Thomas Lovell Beddoes. *See* Dirge: "Swallow leaves her nest, The."
Voice from the Well of Life Speaks to the Maiden, The. George Peele. *See* Song at the Well, The.
Voice from under the Table, A. Richard Wilbur. AmPP; HAP; NePoEA; NOBA; SeCeV
Voice in Darkness. Richard Dehmel, *tr. fr. German by* Margarete Münsterberg. AWP
Voice in the Blood. Barney Bush. STE
Voice in the Crowd. Ted Joans. *See* Truth, The.
Voice in the Dark. A. L. Strauss, *tr. fr. Hebrew by* Robert Friend. VWA
Voice of a Dissipated Woman inside a Tomb. Sor Violante do Céu, *tr. fr. Portuguese by* Willis Barnstone. BoWoP
Voice of America, 1961, The. James Liddy. CIP
Voice of Christmas, The. Harry Kemp. HBV-2
Voice of England is a trumpet tone, The. England. George Edgar Montgomery. AA
Voice of Experience, The. Goethe, *tr. fr. German by* Walter Kaufman. ErPo; PV
Voice of God, The. Katherine R. Barnard. BLRP; WBLP
Voice of God, The. Louis I. Newman. TreF
Voice of God, The. James Stephens. WGRP
Voice of God Is Calling, The, *with music.* John Haynes Holmes. AH
Voice of King Solomon's nightingale, The. A Snow in Jerusalem. Hayim Naggid, *tr. by* Shlomo Vinner *and* Howard Schwartz. VWA
Voice of magic melody, The. My Singing Aunt. James Reeves. ShM
Voice of my beloved, The! behold he. Bible, *O.T. Fr.* The Song of Solomon. PoPl
Voice of my darling, The. Bible, *O.T. Fr.* The Song of Solomon, *ad. by* Willis Barnstone. BoWoP
Voice of summer, keen and shrill. To a Cricket. William Cox Bennett. GN; HBV-1
Voice of the city is sleepless, The. Salute to Life. Dmitri Shostakovitch. FSW
Voice of the Crocus. Mildred N. Hoyer. AMV-80
Voice of the Derwent, The. Wordsworth. FaBoPP
Voice of the Devil, The. Blake. *Fr.* The Marriage of Heaven and Hell. NU
Voice of the Dove, The. Joaquin Miller. AA
Voice of the glutton I heard with disdain, The. The Glutton. John Oakman. OxBChV
Voice of the Grass, The. Sarah Roberts Boyle. AA; HBV-1; HBVY
Voice of the last cricket, The. Splinter. Carl Sandburg. FaPON; OBCA; SoSe; SUS; TiPo
Voice of the Lobster, The. "Lewis Carroll." *See* Alice's Recitation.
Voice of the Power of This World, The. Gregory Hall. NU
Voice of the river running through Chamonix. Chamonix. George Hookham. OBVV
Voice of the Studio Announcer. Archibald MacLeish. *Fr.* The Fall of the City. HoPM
Voice of the Void, The. George Parsons Lathrop. AA
Voice of the Western Wind. Edmund Clarence Stedman. HBV-1
Voice of Toil, The. William Morris. HBV-2
Voice of Webster, The, *sel.* Robert Underwood Johnson.
"Silence was envious of the only voice." AA
Voice of Wisdom, The. Bible, *O.T.* Proverbs, VIII: 22-31. TreFT
Voice on the winds, A. To Morfydd. Lionel Johnson. AnIV; MoBrPo; OAEL-2; OBMV
Voice out of the Tabernacle, A. Louis Zukofsky. VWA
Voice peals in this end of night, A. A Thrush before Dawn. Alice Meynell. HBMV; MoBrPo; WPE
Voice resounds like thunder-peal, A. Watch on the Rhine, The. Max Schneckenburger. HBV-2
Voice, A, said, "Follow, follow"; and I rose. Two Pursuits. Christina Rossetti. WPE
Voice, The, said, "Hurl her down!" The Lovely Shall Be Choosers. Robert Frost. CoBMV; MoAB; MoAmPo; NOBA; OxBA
Voice Sings, A. Samuel Taylor Coleridge. *Fr.* Remorse. CH
("Hear, sweet spirit, hear the spell.") ViBoPo
(Invocation, An.) OAEP
Voice Speaks from the Well, A. George Peele. *See* Song at the Well, The.
Voice That Beautifies the Land, The. *Unknown, tr. fr. Navaho Indian by* Washington Matthews. AWP
Voice that breathed o'er Eden, The. Holy Matrimony [*or* Epithalamium]. John Keble. HBV-1; NOCV; VLP
Voice went over the waters, A. Cuba to Columbia. Will Carleton. PAH
Voiceless, The. Oliver Wendell Holmes. *Fr.* The Autocrat of the Breakfast Table. AA; ViBoPo
Voices. Nora Dauenhauer. TWSS
Voices. Walter de la Mare. UnPo
Voices Answering Back: The Vampires. Lawrence Raab. AmPA
Voices at the Window. Sir Philip Sidney. *See* Astrophel and Stella: Eleventh Song.
Voices begin to flutter. Love for Instance. Dan Gerber. FAZ
Voices from the Other World. James Merrill. GP; MP; TwCP
Voices from Things Growing in a Churchyard. Thomas Hardy. OxBTC
Voices in the Winter. Ken McCullough. LTB
Voices Inescapable, The. Ann Stanford. IHMS
Voices lifted high in singing. Music. Malay Oral Tradition, *tr. by* R. O. Winstedt. WTO
Voices moving about in the quiet house. Falling Asleep. Siegfried Sassoon. MoBrPo; MoVE; OxBTC
Voices of Heroes. Horace Gregory. OFD
Voices of Nature, The. Thomas Edward Brown. PeD
Voices of the Air. Katherine Mansfield. HBMV
Voices of vegetables. Mother and Sister of the Artist. Olga Cabral. PoDr
Voices That Have Filled My Day. Fay Chiang. BrSi
Void, The. Gwendolyn MacEwen. *Fr.* The T. E. Lawrence Poems. NOBC
Void Between, The. John Lancaster Spalding. *Fr.* God and the Soul. AA
Void, damned weed! that hell's dry sweetmeats art. On Tobacco. Thomas Pestel. ElL
Void only. "Ping Hsin," *tr. by* Kenneth Rexroth *and* Ling Chung. *Fr.* Multitudinous Stars. PBWP
Void that's highly embraceable, The. Chorus. Jack Kerouac. *Fr.* Mexico City Blues. NeAP
Vois loude in that light to Lucifer seide, A. The Descent into Hell. William Langland. *Fr.* The Vision of Piers Plowman. PoEL-1
Vo'k a-Comen into Church. William Barnes. OxBoCh
Volatile Kerryman, The. Owen Roe O'Sullivan, *tr. fr. Irish by* Sean O'Riada. BIrV
Volcanic Venus. D. H. Lawrence. InPS; POL
Volcano. Derek Walcott. OxBC
Volcanoes. Bella Akhmadulina, *tr. fr. Russian by* W. H. Auden. PBWP
Vole, The. Marvin Solomon. NePoAm-2
Volleyball Teacher Ends the Game. José Y. Terán Jr. LFAC
Volpone, *sels.* Ben Jonson.
"Come, my Celia, let us prove," *fr.* III, vii. ElL; OBVE; TEP; WHA
(Come, My Celia.) CABA; FaBV; FF; HeIP; NIP; NoP; TrGrPo
(Song to Celia.) AnAnS-2; BiP; EnRePo; ErPo; JCP; OAEL-1, *with music*; OBS; SeCeV; SeCP; SeCV-1
(To Celia.) FaBoEn; LoBV; OAEP; UnTE
Fools, They Are the Only Nation, *fr.* I, ii. InvP
(Fools.) ElL
(Nano's Song.) LoBV; TrGrPo
(Song: "Fooles, they are the onely nation.") AnAnS-2
"If thou hast wisdom, hear me, Celia," *fr.* III, vii. ViBoPo
Voltaire and Gibbon. Byron. *Fr.* Childe Harold's Pilgrimage, III. OBRV
Voltaire at Ferney. W. H. Auden. LiTA; LiTM; NePA; PoA
Volubilis, North Africa. Ralph Nixon Currey. PeSA
Volume of Chopin, A. James Picot. PoAu-2
Voluntaries, *sels.* Emerson.
Duty ("So nigh is grandeur"), *last* 4 *ll. of* III. FaFP; GN; HBV-1; TreF; YaD
("So nigh is grandeur to our dust.") TRV
In an Age of Fops and Toys, III. FPL; LiTA; PoLF
(So Nigh Is Grandeur.) HBVY; TreFS
Voluntarily walled themselves up inside the stone. The Old Age Home. Daniel Hoffman. CoPo
Volunteer, The. Herbert Asquith. MMA; OBWP; OxBTC
Volunteer, The. Elbridge Jefferson Cutler. AA
Volunteer, A. Helen Parry Eden. SUMH
Volunteer, The. *Unknown.* NOEC
Volunteers, The. William Haines Lytle. PAH
Volunteer's Grave, A. William Alexander Percy. HBMV
Volunteer's Reply to the Poet, The. Roy Campbell. *Fr.* Talking Bronco. ViBoPo
Volunteer's Thanksgiving, The. Lucy Larcom. OBCA
Voluptuaries and Others. Margaret Avison. MoCV
Voluspo. *Unknown, tr. fr. Old Norse by* Henry Adams Bellows. *Fr.* The Elder Edda. AWP
Voodoo on the Un-Assing of Janis Joplin. Carolyn M. Rodgers. JB

Voortrekker, The. Kipling. HBV-1
Vor a Gauguin Picture zu Singen. Kurt M. Stein. FiBHP
Vorthy cit, von Vitsunday, A. Mr. and Mrs. Vite's Journey. *Unknown.* NOBL
Votaries know. A Poem for Integration. Alvin Saxon. PoBA
Vote, A, *sel.* Abraham Cowley.
This Only Grant Me. TreFT
(Of Myself.) OAEP; OBS
Voting Machine. Norman Nathan. AMV-80
Votive Ode. Erasmus, *tr. fr. Greek by* J. T. Walford. ISi
Votive Song. Edward Coate Pinkney. AA
Vow, A. Allen Ginsberg. OBWP
Vow, The. Anthony Hecht. ConAP; NePoEA; PoCh; Prf
Vow, The. Carl Rakosi. FAZ
Vow. John Updike. NYBP
Vow-Breaker, The. Henry King. OBS
Vow of Washington, The. Whittier. PAH
Vow to Heavenly Venus, A. Joachim du Bellay, *tr. fr. French by* Andrew Lang. AWP
Vow to Love Faithfully [Howsoever He Be Rewarded], A. Petrarch, *tr. fr. Italian by* the Earl of Surrey. Sonnets to Laura: To Laura in Life, CXIII. EIL; TrGrPo; ViBoPo
(Love's Fidelity.) AWP
("Set me wheras the sonne dothe perche the grene.") AAS
("Set me whereas the sun doth parch the green.") HAP; SiPS; TEP
(To His Lady.) OBSC
Vowel Movements. Daryl Hine. PoA
Vowels. Arthur Rimbaud, *tr. fr. French by* Kenneth Koch. SOTW
Vowels of Another Language, The. Tom Disch. PoA
Vowels plowed into other: opened ground. Seamus Heaney. Glanmore Sonnets, I. NoP
Vows, The. Andrew Marvell. TW
Vox Clero. *Unknown.* APAS
Vox Humana. Thom Gunn. NePoEA-2
Vox Oppressi, To the Lady Phipps. Richard Henchman. SCAP
Vox Populi. Dryden. *Fr.* The Medal[l]. NOBE; OBS
Vox Ultima Crucis. John Lydgate. OBEV; OxBoCh
"Voy wawm" said the dustman. Hymn to the Sun. Michael Roberts. FaBoCh; OxBTC
Voyage. John Lyle Donaghy. OxBI
Voyage, The. Heine, *tr. fr. German by* John Todhunter. AWP
Voyage. Josephine Miles. LiTM
Voyage, The. Edwin Muir. LiTM
Voyage. Donald G. H. Schramm. AMV-81
Voyage. Stanislaw Wygodski, *tr. fr. Polish by* Isaac Komem. VWA
Voyage of Bran, The, *sel. Unknown, tr. fr. Old Irish by* Kuno Meyer.
"Branch of the apple-tree from Emain, A." AnIL
Voyage of Discovery: 1935. Richmond Lattimore. TwAmPo
Voyage of Jimmy Poo, The. James A. Emanuel. AmNP; NNP
Voyage of Life, The. Cynewulf, *tr. fr. Anglo-Saxon by* Charles W. Kennedy. *Fr.* Christ 2. AnOE; MOS
Voyage of Maeldune, The. Tennyson. PoEL-5
Voyage of the soul is simply, The. The Helmsman; an Ode. J. V. Cunningham. MoVE
Voyage on the Thames, The. Pope. *Fr.* The Rape of the Lock, II. NOBE
("Not with more glories, in th' ethereal plain.") EBEV; FaBoEn, *shorter sel.*; NOEC; ViBoPo, *shorter sel.*; WHA
Voyage to Cythera. Baudelaire, *tr. fr. French by* John Gray. SyP
Voyage to the Island of Love, A, *sel.* Aphra Behn.
Dream, The. PBWP
Voyage to the Moon. William Dickey. MOON
Voyage to the Moon. Archibald MacLeish. MOON
Voyage to Tintern Abbey, A, *sel.* Sneyd Davies.
"Crooked bank still winds to something new, The." NOEC
Voyage West. Archibald MacLeish. VGW
Voyager upon life's sea. Paddle Your Own Canoe. Sarah K. Bolton. FaFP
Voyagers. Henry van Dyke. TRV
Voyager's Prayer, A. *Unknown, tr. fr. Chippewa Indian by* Tanner. TRV; WGRP
Voyager's Song. Clement Wood. HBMV
Voyages (I-VI). Hart Crane. AP; CMoP; NoAM; NOBA; NoP; TAP
Sels.
"Above the fresh ruffles of the surf," I. AmPP; CABA; MOS; OxBA; VGW
(Sea, The.) CrMA
"And yet this great wink of eternity," II. AmPP; CoBMV; DTC; HAP; LiTM; MoAB; MoAmPo; MoPo; MOS; MoVE; NePA; OxBA; PPoe; PPP; TwAmPo; UnPo; VGW
(Voyages, II.) FaBoEn; ViBoPo
"Infinite consanguinity it bears," III. MoPo; MoVE; OxBA
"Meticulous, past midnight in clear rime," V. MoPo; MoVE
"Where icy and bright dungeons lift," VI. CABA; HAP; MoAB; MoAmPo; MoVE; SeCeV; TwAmPo; UnPo
Voyages of Captain Cock, The. William Jay Smith. ErPo; UnTE
Voyageur. R. E. Rashley. CaP
Voyeur. John Edward Hardy. ErPo
Voyeur, The. Deanna Louise Pickard. AMV-80
Vuillard: "The Mother and Sister of the Artist." W. D. Snodgrass. CoAP
Vulcan contrive me such a cup. Upon Drinking in a Bowl. Earl of Rochester. CavP; OBS; OxBoLi; SeCV-2
Vulcan's Song. John Lyly. *See* Song in Making of the Arrows, A.
Vulgar Error, A. J. E. Thorold Rogers. FaBoEE
Vulgar of manner, overfed. Owed to New York. Byron Rufus Newton. BLPA; TreFS
Vulnerary, A. Jonathan Williams. PoM
Vulture, The. Hilaire Belloc. HBVY; OxBChV; RHPC
Vulture. Robinson Jeffers. BoAnP; NOBA; NoP
Vulture. X. J. Kennedy. GrPl
(Ecology.) BoAnP
Vulture. Kenneth Rexroth. *Fr.* A Bestiary. NNaP
Vulture and the Husbandman, The. Arthur Clement Hilton. CenHV; FaBoCo
Vulture eats between his meals, The. The Vulture. Hilaire Belloc. HBVY; OxBChV; RHPC
Vulture of the Plains, The. Hamlin Garland. BPAW
Vultures, The. David Diop, *tr. fr. French by* Ulli Beier. PBA; TTY
Vultures are being spring-cleaned, The. Building Society Blues. Roger Roughton. EAS
Vulture's very like a sack, The. Vulture [*or* Ecology]. X. J. Kennedy. BoAnP; GrPl
Vultures waft circles. Remnant Ghosts at Dawn. Oliver La Grone. FB
Vusumzi's Song. L. T. Manyase, *tr. fr. Xhosa by* C. M. Mcanyangwa *and* Jack Cope. PeSA

W

W. James Reeves. ChTr; NTCP
W. C. W. David Ray. POL
W. H. Auden & Mantan Moreland. Al Young. NPGG
W. H. Davies Simplifies the Simplicities He Loves. Louis Untermeyer. WhC
W. H. *Eheu!* Samuel Taylor Coleridge. FaBoEE
W. L. M. K. F. R. Scott. NOBC
W. resteth here, that quick could never rest. Of the Death of Sir T[homas]. W[yatt]. Earl of Surrey. FaBoEn
W/ round black eyes. The Caterpillar. Anselm Hollo. FAZ
W. S. Landor. Marianne Moore. OBAL
W. W. Amiri Baraka. HeIP; NBP; NOBA; PAI; PoBA
W was a wild worm. A Wild Worm. Carolyn Wells. TDH
Waäit till our Sally cooms in, fur thou mun a' sights to tell. The Northern Cobbler. Tennyson. EBEV
Waal, yass, stranger, them's fine cows. The Branding Iron Herd. Ralph Rigby. PoOW
Wabash Cannonball, *Unknown.* BLSo, *with music;* FSW; TreFT
Waddles after/ her mistress. Old Dog. Raymond Souster. GDP
Wade/ through black jade. The Fish. Marianne Moore. AmPP; MoAB; MoAmPo; MOS; MoVE; NoAM; OxBA; TwAmPo
Wade in the Water. *Unknown. See* God's a-Gwinter Trouble de Water.
Waders and Swimmers. Stanley Plumly. GeTw
Wading out was best. Low Tide. Warren Woessner. WOLT
Waement the deid. Coronach. Alexander Scott. OxBS
Wae's me, wae's me. The Cauld Lad's Song [*or* Song of the Cauld Lad of Hylton *or* The Cauld Lad of Hilton *or* The Ghost's Song *or* The Wandering Spectre]. *Unknown.* CH; ChTr; FaBoCh; GBP; OxBoLi
Waes-hael for [the] knight and [the] dame! King Arthur's Waes-Hael. Robert Stephen Hawker. ISi; OBEV; OBVV; OxBoCh
Wag a leg, wag a leg. *Unknown.* OxNR
Wages. Tennyson. OAEP
Waggon-Maker, The. John Masefield. EBEV
Waggoner, The. *Unknown.* GBP
Wagner. Rupert Brooke. FaBoTw; NOBL
Wagon Full of Thunder. Louis (LittleCoon) Oliver. STE
Wagon Train. E. L. Mayo. MiAP
Wagon Train, The. Sam L. Simpson. BPAW
"Wagon Wheel Gap is a place I never saw." Localities. Carl Sandburg. AmFN
Wagon Wheels. S. E. LaMoure. AMV-81
Wagoner of the Alleghanies, The, *sels.* Thomas Buchanan Read.
Brave at Home, The. HBV-2
Rising, The. PAH; TreFS

Valley Forge. PAH
Wagoner's Lad, The. *Unknown.* AmFP; BaBo (A *and* B *vers.*); FSW
Wagtail and Baby. Thomas Hardy. HBMV
Waif, The. Walter de la Mare. FaBoNo
Wail of a waking wind in a wide-flung wheat field, The. Sea Hunger. John Hanlon Mitchell. EtS
Wail of Archy, The, *sel.* Don Marquis. *Fr.* Archy and Mehitabel.
"Gods i am pent in a cockroach." FiBHP
Wail, wail, Ah for Adonis! Lament for Adonis. Bion, *tr. by* John Addington Symonds. AWP
Wail! wail ye o'er the dead! Dirge. George Darley. *Fr.* Sylvia; or, The May Queen. OBRV
Waile whit ase [*or* Wale whyt as] whalles bon, A. The White Beauty. *Unknown.* MeEL; OxBM
Wailful sweetness of the violin, The. Ode to the Setting Sun. Francis Thompson. GoBC
Wailing diminutive of me, be still. Diminutivus Ululans. Francis MacNamara. OxBI
Wailing, wailing, wailing, the wind over land and sea. Rizpah. Tennyson. PoEL-5; VLP
Wailing wind doth not enough despair, The. Awake. Mary Elizabeth Coleridge. OBNC
Wailings of a maiden I recite, The. Wednesday; or, The Dumps. John Gay. *Fr.* The Shepherd's Week. OAEL-1
Waillie. *Unknown. See* Waly, Waly ("When cockle shells turn silver bells").
Wain upon the northern steep, The. Astronomy. A. E. Housman. OBWP
Waistcoat, The. Padraic Fallon. OxBI
Wait, The. Phyllis Janowitz. AMV-80
Wait. Timothy Steele. PoA
Wait a Little. *Unknown.* NOCV; OxBM
Wait but a little while. Song. Norman Gale. HBV-1
Wait for Me. Robert Creeley. NOBA; PPP
Wait for the Hour. William Soutar. NeBP
Wait for the Wagon. *Unknown, at. to* R. Bishop Buckley. BLSo, *with music;* FSW; PAH; PSoN, *with music*
Wait here, and I'll be back, though the hours divide. Three Star Final. Conrad Aiken. OxBA
Wait! It would be insane to call. Do What You Will. Dorothy Hobson. GoBC
Wait, Kate! You skate at such a rate. To Kate, Skating Better than Her Date. David Daiches. CTBA; FiBHP; NYBP
"Wait. Let me think a minute," you said. The Wit. Elizabeth Bishop. NePoAm-2
Wait On! *Unknown.* STF
Wait . . . that tastes good . . . already it is on the wing. Rainer Maria Rilke, *tr. by* Christopher Hawthorne. *Fr.* Sonnets to Orpheus. SOTW
Wait; the great horned owls. Owls. W. D. Snodgrass. BoAnP; Psk
Wait till the darkness is deep. Wallada, *tr. fr. Arabic by* James Monroe *and* Deirdre Lashgari. WPOW
Wait 'till the Sun Shines, Nellie. Andrew B. Sterling. BLSo, *with music;* FSN, *with music;* FSW; TreFS
Wait till Then. Mark Van Doren. SO
Waiters. Mary Ann Hoberman. RHPC
Waiting. Harry Behn. SiSoSe; TiPo
Waiting. John Burroughs. AA; BLPA; FaBoBe; HBV-2; OHFP; TreF; TRV; WGRP
Waiting. Jane Cooper. TAP
Waiting. Hilary Corke. ErPo
Waiting. Robert Creeley. VGW
Waiting. John Davidson. ViBoPo
Waiting. John Freeman. CH
Waiting. W. E. Henley. *Fr.* In Hospital. BrPo; NBM; VLP
Waiting. Robert Pack. PPJ
Waiting. Judith Skillman. SUW
Waiting. Liz Stout. AMV-81
Waiting, The. Whittier. WGRP
Waiting. Yevgeny Yevtushenko, *tr. fr. Russian by* Robin Milner-Gulland *and* Peter Levi. LLLT
Waiting and Peeking. V. R. Lang. NePA
Waiting at the Church; or, My Wife Won't Let Me, *with music.* Fred W. Leigh. FSN
Waiting Both. Thomas Hardy. MoAB; MoBrPo; OxBoLi; WHA
Waiting Carefully. Nancy P. Kamm. AMV-80
Waiting Chords, The. Stephen Henry Thayer. AA
Waiting for a Second Time. Tauhindauli. STE
Waiting for breakfast, while she brushed her hair. Philip Larkin. NoAM
Waiting for Death. Mordecai Gebirtig, *tr. fr. Yiddish by* Joseph Leftwich. TrJP
Waiting for E. Gularis. Linda Pastan. SUW
Waiting for God. Harry Roskolenko. *Fr.* Baguio Poems. FAZ
Waiting for Her. Alden Nowlan. NeAC
Waiting for Icarus. Muriel Rukeyser. NNaP
Waiting for It. May Swenson. BoAnP
Waiting for Lilith. Jascha Kessler. VWA
Waiting for News. Richard Church. ChMP
Waiting for Nighthawks in Illinois. Roger Pfingston. FAZ
Waiting for the Bus. D. J. Enright. OxBTC
Waiting for the Dawning. *Unknown.* BLRP
Waiting for the Doctor. Colette Inez. IHMS
Waiting for the Emperor Tenji. Princess Nukada, *tr. fr. Japanese by* Cid Corman *and* Susumu Kamaike. PBWP
Waiting for the end, boys, waiting for the end. Just a Smack at Auden. William Empson. FaBoCo; LiTM; MoBrPo; UnPo
Waiting for the Fire. Philip Appleman. SOTS
Waiting for the Morning. *Unknown.* STF
Waiting for the Post. Dorothy Auchterlonie. CBAP
Waiting for these dry sticks in a vase. Aspects of Some Forsythia Branches. Ralph Gustafson. PeCV
Waiting for when the sun an hour or less. In Santa Maria del Popolo. Thom Gunn. CMoP; FaBoMo; GTBS-P; NePoEA-2; NMP; OxBC; QFR
Waiting for Winter. George Keithley. NPGG
Waiting for You to Come By. Simon J. Ortiz. CDW
Waiting in Faith. Michelangelo, *tr. fr. Italian.* ILwL
Waiting in Front of the Columnar High School. Karl Shapiro. HAP
Waiting is the poem of waiting. On Arrival. Richard Howard. TAP
Waiting like a trap-door spider for a rookie sell-out. Baseball or the name game? Four Poems for *The St. Louis Sporting News.* Jack Spicer. PoM
Waiting-Room, The. Robin Fulton. PoA
Waiting Rooms. Howard Nemerov. PoA
Waiting rooms are full of "characters," The. Pretending Not to Sleep. Ian Hamilton. NoAM
Waiting, the Hallways under Her Skin Thick with Dreamchildren. Lyn Lifshin. NeAC
Waiting to Be Fed. Ray A. Young Bear. CDW
Waiting to be served we look from the veranda. From the Other Shore. William Pitt Root. MAYP
Waiting today while planes roar over the seacoast. 1944—On the Invasion Coast. Jack Beeching. WaP
Waiting Watchers, The. Henry Treece. NeBP
Waitress. Karl Shapiro. TwAmPo
Waitress, The/ takes our order. Somewhere Else. Paula Rankin. MAYP
Waitress, with eyes so marvellous black. Salad: After Browning. Mortimer Collins. *Fr.* Salad. Par
Waits, The. Madeleine Nightingale. SUS
Waits are whining in the cold, The. From "A Vigo-Street Eclogue." Sir Owen Seaman. WhC
Wake. Langston Hughes. OBAL; ShM
Wake, The. Wyatt Prunty. AMV-80
Wake. Elizabeth Spires. AMV-80
Wake All the Dead. Sir William Davenant. *Fr.* The Law against Lovers. ELP; FaBoCh; HAP; SeCePo
(Song: "Wake all the Dead!") LoBV
Wake. And my eyes stun. I Wake, My Friend, I. Faye Kicknosway. IHMS
Wake as you will, but wake in me. To Song. Olga Berggolts, *tr. by* Daniel Weissbort. BoWoP
Wake at the Well, The. *Unknown.* GBP
Wake, child with the flute. Mirabai, *tr. fr. Hindi by* Willis Barnstone *and* Usha Nilsson. BoWoP
Wake Cry. Waring Cuney. BANP
Wake! for the sun has driven in equal flight. The Golfer's Rubaiyat. H. W. Boynton. BXAP
Wake! For the Sun who scattered into flight. Omar Khayyám, *tr. fr. Persian by* Edward Fitzgerald. *Fr.* The Rubáiyát of Omar Khayyám. AWP; BiP; FaBoBe; FaFP; FaPON; FF; HBV-2; LiTB: MasP; NoP; OBNC; PoEL-5; SeCeV; TrGrPo; ViBoPo; VLP. *See also* Awake! for morning in the bowl of night.
Wake, friend, from forth thy lethargy! The drum. An Epistle to a Friend, to Persuade Him to the Wars. Ben Jonson. TEP
Wake, Isles of the South, *with music.* William B. Tappan. AH
Wake, Israel, wake! Recall today. The Banner of the Jew. Emma Lazarus. AA; TrJP
Wake, Lady! Joanna Baillie. HBV-1
Wake me up at five-thirty please. Hotel. Adam Wazyk, *tr. by* Isaac Komem. VWA
Wake Nicodemus. Henry Clay Work. FSW
"Wake not, but hear me, love!" Song. Lew Wallace. *Fr.* Ben Hur. AA
Wake Not for the World-heard Thunder. A. E. Housman. CMoP; NoAM
Wake, now my love, awake; for it is time. Spenser. *Fr.* Epithalamion. GBL
Wake of William Orr, The. William Drennan. OnYI; OxBI
Wake, shake, day's a-breakin'. Green Corn. *Unknown.* FSW

Wake, Sleepy Thyrsis. *Unknown.* EnRePo
Wake stand on your feet. Moon Blast. Michelle Roberts. LFAC
Wake: the silver dusk returning. Reveille. A. E. Housman. A Shropshire Lad, IV. CMoP; FaFP; FPL; LiTB; LiTM; MasP; MoAB; MoBrPo; OAEP; PoLF; SoSe; TreF
Wake the Song of Jubilee, *with music.* Leonard Bacon. AH
Wake up, dear boy that holds the flute! Mirabai, *tr. fr. Hindi by* Usha Nilsson. WPOW
Wake up high up. Things to Do in New York (City). Ted Berrigan. NoAM
Wake Up, Jacob. *Unknown.* FSW
(Cowboy's Gettin'-up Holler.) CoSo; TrAS
Wake up mama turn your lamp down lo-ow. Statesboro Blues. *Unknown.* BluL
Wake-up Niggers. Don L. Lee. PoBA
Wake Up! Wake Up! Basho, *tr. fr. Japanese by* Harold G. Henderson. SoPo
Wake up, wake up, darlin' Cory [*or* Corey]. Darling Cory [*or* Darlin' Corey]. *Unknown.* AmFP; FSW; OuSiCo
"Wake up! Wake up! you bloomin' lot." Song of the Leadville Mine Boss. Don Cameron. PoOW
"Wake up, wake up, you drowsy sleeper." The Drowsy Sleeper. *Unknown.* BaBo
Waked by the Gospel's Powerful Sound, *with music.* Samson Occom. AH
Wakefield Second Shepherd's Play, The. *Unknown. See* Second Shepherd's Play, The.
Wakeful I lay all night [*or* all night I lay] and thought of God. Renunciation. Wathen Mark Wilks Call. OBVV; WGRP
Wakeful in the Township. Elizabeth Riddell. PoAu-2
Wakeful, vagrant, restless thing. The Power of Fancy. Philip Freneau. AmPP; AP
"Waken from your sleep." The Summons. W. W. E. Ross. CaP
Waken, lords and ladies gay. Hunting Song. Sir Walter Scott. *Fr.* The Lay of the Last Minstrel. EnRP; EvOK; GN; GTBS; GTBS-P; OAEP; TrGrPo; WiR
Wakening, The. Sam Hamill. AMV-80
Wakening, The. *Unknown. See* On a Time the Amorous Silvy.
Wakepick I. Kristjana Gunnars. NOBC
Wakers, The. John Freeman. HBMV
Waking. Annie Higgins. ELU
Waking. Patrick MacDonogh. NeIP
Waking. Hugh Maxton. BIrV; CIP
Waking. Lilian Moore. RHPC
Waking. Katherine Pyle. OBCA
Waking, The ("I strolled across/ An open field"). Theodore Roethke. RFM
Waking, The ("I wake to sleep, and take my waking slow"). Theodore Roethke. AmPP; AP; BiP; CoAP; CoBMV; CrMA; HAP; HeIP; InPS; LiTM; MoAmPo; MP; NIP; NoAM; NOBA; NoP; PoPl; PPP; PrIm; SeCeV; SoSe; TAP; TwCP; WeW
Waking Alone. *Unknown.* MeEL
Waking [*or* Walking] alone in a multitude of loves when morning's light. On the Marriage of a Virgin. Dylan Thomas. EnLoPo; ErPo
Waking an Angel. Philip Levine. NaP
Waking, Child, While You Slept. Ethel Anderson. *Fr.* Bucolic Eclogues. PoAu-2; WPE
Waking Early. R. L. Barth. AMV-81
Waking Early Sunday Morning. Robert Lowell. FaBoMo; NOBA; OxBC
Waking from a Nap on the Beach. May Swenson. NTCP; PCP; RFM
Waking from Sleep. Robert Bly. CAPP; EAS; InPS; NoAM; NOBA; NoP
Waking in New York, *sel.* Allen Ginsberg.
"On the roof cloudy sky fading sun rays," II. NYP
Waking in Nice. Patricia Traxler. AMV-81
Waking in the Blue. Robert Lowell. CoAP; MoAmPo; PPP; UnPo
Waking in the Dark. Dorothy Livesay. NOBC
Waking Jed. C. K. Williams. DiL
Waking Jesus sudden riding a scream like a/ train. I Scream You Scream. Don McKay. NOBC
Waking on a Greyhound. Gordon Henry. STE
Waking this morning. This Morning. Muriel Rukeyser. BoWoP; NMM
Waking Time. Ivy O. Eastwick. SiSoSe; TiPo
Waking to darkness; early silence broken. Drafts. Nora Bomford. SUMH
Waking Up. Edward Lense. AMV-80
Waking Up. Tom Schmidt. GP
Waking up late this morning, in full sunlight. 9:00. Patricia Hooper. AMV-81; HoAn
Waking with morning, I note the empty. The Landscape of Love. Thomas Cole. NePoAm
Waking Year, The. Emily Dickinson. *See* Lady red upon the hill, A.
Wakonda! Talako! deathonic turkey gobbling in the soft-footpatch night! Spontaneous Requiem for the American Indian. Gregory Corso. MAT; PoM
Wal, no! I can't tell whar he lives. *See* Wall, no! . . .
Walam [*or* Wallum] Olum; or, Red Score, *sels. Tr. fr. Delaware (Lenape) Indian.*
"After the Seizer there were ten chiefs, and there was much warfare south and east," *tr. by* Daniel G. Brinton. OBVE
Deluge, The, *tr. by* C. S. Rafinesque. LiTA
On the Creation and Ontogony, *tr. by* C. S. Rafinesque. LiTA
Wald my gude lady luve me best. The Garmont of Gude Ladies. Robert Henryson. GoTS
Waldeinsamkeit. Emerson. AP; HBV-1; NOBA; WGRP
Walden, *sel.* Henry David Thoreau.
Smoke, *fr. ch.* 13. AA; AWP; HeIP; NoP; OxBA
(Light-winged Smoke.) ViBoPo
(Light-winged Smoke, Icarian Bird.) AP; NOBA; TAP
Walden in July. Donald Junkins. NYBP
Walden Pond/ All those noxious gases rising from it. Jack Spicer. *Fr.* "Graphemics." VGW
Waldere 1: ". . . heard him gladly." *Unknown, tr. fr. Anglo-Saxon by* Charles W. Kennedy. AnOE
Waldere 2: "Waldere addressed him, the warrior brave." *Unknown, tr. fr. Anglo-Saxon by* Charles W. Kennedy. AnOE
Wale whyt as whalles bon, A. *See* Waile whit ase whalles bon, A.
Wales. Norman Nicholson. ChMP
Wales England wed; so I was bred. An Autobiography. Ernest Rhys. OBEV; OBVV
Wales Visitation. Allen Ginsberg. CAPP; NNaP; NOBA; NYBP; Prf
Wales, which I have never seen. For My Ancestors. Rolfe Humphries. PoRA
Walk, The. Thomas Hardy. CMoP; PoEL-5; PrIm
Walk. Frank Horne. BPo
Walk, A. Hedwig Lachmann, *tr. fr. German by* Jethro Bithell. TrJP
Walk. Brian Merriman, *tr. fr. Modern Irish by* Brendan Behan. *Fr.* The Midnight Court. BIrV
Walk, The. W. W. E. Ross. PeCV
Walk, A. Gary Snyder. NoAM; NOBA
Walk about the Subway Station. Charles Reznikoff. CAD; NYP
Walk by the Charles, A. Adrienne Rich. NePoEA; NYBP
Walk, Damn You, Walk! William de Vere. PoLF
Walk down the hall. Telephoning It. Murray Edmond. OCNZ
Walk east. Dawn polishes the sky. Direction. Roberta Hill. CDW
Walk fast in snow. A Devonshire Rhyme. *Unknown.* SiSoSe
Walk Home, The. Reed Whittemore. ConAP
Walk in Early March, A. Paul Mariani. DiL
Walk in Jerusalem Jus' like John, *with music. Unknown.* BoAN-2; FSW
Walk in Kyoto, A. Earle Birney. GoYe
Walk in March, A. Tim Reynolds. MAT
Walk in the Country, A. Galway Kinnell. NePoAm
Walk in the Garden, The. Conrad Aiken. PoCh
Walk in the half light of rain. Monsoon. Kenneth Slade Alling. NePoAm
Walk in the light! So shalt thou know. Walking in the Light. Bernard Barton. VLP
Walk in the Precepts. Moses ibn Ezra, *tr. fr. Hebrew by* Solomon Solis-Cohen. TrJP
Walk in Würzburg, A. William Plomer. NYBP
Walk in your sleep beyond Yeppoon. Assignation with a Somnambulist. John Manifold. CBAP
Walk into the prison, that domed citadel. My Lessons in the Jail. Miriam Waddington. MoCV
Walk, Jaw-Bone, *with music.* S. S. Steele. TrAS
Walk, Mary, down de Lane, *with music. Unknown.* BoAN-2
Walk on a Winter Day. Sara Van Alystyne Allen. YeAr
Walk on Snow, A. Peter Viereck. MiAP
Walk out into your country. Who Shall Die. James A. Randall, Jr. BPo
"Walk right in, Brother Wilson—how you feelin' today?" The Rain Song. Alex Rogers. BANP
Walk Slowly. Adelaide Love. BLPA
Walk this mile in silence. Pastourelle. Donald Jeffrey Hayes. AmNP
Walk Together Children. *Unknown.* BoAn-2, *with music*; BPo
Walk-up. W. S. Merwin. CoPo
Walk with de Mayor of Harlem. David Henderson. PoBA
Walk with the sun. Dream Song. Lewis Alexander. PoBA; PoNe
Walk with thy fellow-creatures: note the hush. Fragment. Henry Vaughan. TRV; WGRP
Walker of the Snow, The. Charles Dawson Shanly. OnYI
Walker River Night, The. Adrian C. Louis. STE
Walking. Grace Ellen Glaubitz. SoPo; TiPo
Walking. Frank O'Hara. TAT
Walking. Thomas Traherne. *See* To Walk Abroad.
Walking. H. L. Van Brunt. LTB
Walking against the Wind. Jon Stallworthy. OxBC
Walking all the day. Song for Ireland. Phil *and* June Colclough. OBET
Walking alone in a multitude of loves when morning's light. *See* Waking alone in a multitude of loves when morning's light.

Walking along beside the beach/ where the Mediterranean turns in sleep. The Sea Bird. Keith Douglas. ChMP
Walking along the Hudson. Donald Petersen. CoAP
Walking along the Sea of Galilee. Dovid Knut, *tr. fr. Russian by* John Glad. VWA
Walking among sceptre-headed. Walking-Sticks and Paperweights and Watermarks. Marianne Moore. PoA
Walking Around. David Galler. AMV-81
Walking Around. Pablo Neruda, *tr. fr. Spanish by* Robert Bly. EAS
Walking around in the park. Toads Revisited. Philip Larkin. CMoP; NOBL; SaC
Walking at last by the tame little edge of the sea. Evening before Rain. L. A. G. Strong. OxBTC
Walking at Night. Amory Hare. PoLF
Walking at Night. Henry Treece. WaP
Walking at night along the meadow way. *Unknown, tr. fr. Czech.* FSW
Walking at night in a hat fitted with twelve candles. Vincent Van Gogh. William Jay Smith. EyDe
Walking at night on asphalt campus. Death News. Allen Ginsberg. NoAM
Walking between the ruined walls. Walking in London. Wrey Gardiner. NeBP
Walking Blues. *Unknown.* BluL
Walking by map, I chose unwonted ground. On the Hall at Stowey. Charles Tomlinson. CMoP; NoAM
Walking cool. For Mulatto. Raymond Ringo Fernandez. LFAC
Walking docile as you do down the empty street. Abasis. Christopher Middleton. *Fr.* Herman Moon's Hourbook. NePoEA-2
Walking down Jalan Thamrin. R. F. Brissenden. CBAP
Walking down the alley. Alley-Walker. Joan Smith. AMV-80
Walking downhill from Suilven (a fine day, for once). No Accident. Norman MacCaig. PoSH
Walking eight hundred. Removal: Last Part. Carroll Arnett. VoR
Walking for That Cake, *with music.* Ed Harrigan. BLSo
Walking from the killing place. Death and the Arkansas River. Frank Stanford. FiCP
Walking Home at Night. Daniel Weissbort. VWA
Walking, I heard the water dripping, running in the gutter. Partly to My Cat. Ellen Bass. NMM
Walking in a Meadowe Greene. *Unknown.* BoLoP; ErPo
Walking in a Swamp. David Wagoner. HAP; NPAW
Walking in a valley green. The Shepherd's Ode. Robert Greene. *Fr.* Tullie's Love. OBSC
Walking in Beech Leaves. Andrew Young. MoVE
Walking in bright Phoebus' blaze. Dispraise of a Courtly Life. Sir Philip Sidney. LoBV; OAEP
Walking in London. Wrey Gardiner. NeBP
Walking in the Light. Bernard Barton. VLP
Walking in the Rain. Dan Saxon. DFF
Walking into the shadows, walking alone. Lee in the Mountains. Donald Davidson. MoVE
Walking Late. John Montague. CIP
Walking Milwaukee. Harold Witt. HoAn; TAT
Walking next day upon the fatal shore. Cyril Tourneur. *Fr.* The Atheist's Tragedy. ViBoPo; WaaP
Walking north toward the point, I come on a dead seal. The Dead Seal near McClure's Beach. Robert Bly. NNaP; NU
Walking on Sunday. Richard Murphy. IPY
Walking on the Green Grass. *Unknown.* AmFP
Walking on the Prayerstick. Wendy Rose. TWSS
Walking on the step of the shingle, here. Wales. Norman Nicholson. ChMP
Walking on Water. James Dickey. NePoEA-2
Walking on Water. Mario Petaccia. LFAC
Walking out, I flushed some meadowlarks. The Duck Pond at Mini's Pasture, a Dozen Years Later. Philip Dow. AmPA; NPGG
Walking out in the late March midnight. Thorn Leaves in March. W. S. Merwin. MP; TwCP
Walking out of the "big E." Before the Stuff Comes Down. Gary Snyder. HeIP
Walking Parker Home. Bob Kaufman. PoBA
Walking Past Paul Blackburn's Apt. on 7th St. Diane Wakoski. TAP
Walking Road, The. Richard Hughes. OBMV
Walking Song. William E. Hickson. OxBChV
Walking-Sticks and Paperweights and Watermarks. Marianne Moore. PoA
Walking the Beach. Sarah Youngblood. IHMS
Walking the small oval of Gibbs Pond. I Move to Random Consolations. William Heyen. AmPA
Walking the suburbs in the afternoon. Suburban Dreams. Edwin Muir. OxBTC
Walking the town as if I owned it all. In and Out [Severence of Connections, 1946]. L. E. Sissman. NYBP; TwCP
Walking the Wilderness. William Stafford. NaP
Walking through a Cornfield in the Middle of Winter I Stumble over a Cow Pie and Think of the Sixties Press. Barbara Harr. BXAP
Walking through a field. Cornfield Myth. Mary Goose. STE
Walking through the Upper East Side. Erica Jong. NYP
Walking through trees to cool my heat and pain. Not Dead. Robert Graves. HBMV
Walking through twisted hollow pathways. Peter Blue Cloud. VoR
Walking through usual flannels and faces. Aunt Cora. Kenneth Pitchford. CoPo
Walking to Bellrock. Michael Ondaatje. NOBC
Walking to Dedham. David Wright. NeBP
Walking to Sleep. Richard Wilbur. LCAP; NYBP
Walking to the Mail. Tennyson. VLP
Walking to the Museum. Bone Thoughts on a Dry Day: Chicago. George Starbuck. GoYe; MP; NYBP; TwCP
Walking to-day by a cottage I shed tears. Scazons. C. S. Lewis. EBEV
Walking to-day in your garden, O gracious lady. The Moss-Rose. Sir Henry Newbolt. HBV-2
Walking Tour, The. W. H. Auden. *See* Chorus: "To throw away the key and walk away."
Walking towards the house, the terraces. Sestina in Time of Winter. Patrick Anderson. PoA
Walking under the Tour. James I, King of Scotland. *Fr.* The Kingis Quair. SeCePo
Walking up sands, offal is gaped from a tunnel seaward. Reclaimed Area. Jon Silkin. NoAM
Walking, we talk about the test tube baby. Into the Future. Harold Witt. SOTS
Walking Westward, *sel.* C. K. Stead.
"Art has nothing to do with perfect circles." OCNZ
Walking with God. William Cowper. EnRP; NOCV; NOEC; OAEP; OBEC; PoEL-3; TEP; TRV
(O [*or* Oh] for a Closer Walk with God.) EBCP; FiP; OxBoCh
Walking with God. *Unknown.* BLRP
Walking with Lulu in the Wood. Naomi Lazard. NYBP
Walking with you. Friend. Gwendolyn Brooks. CNA
Walking with you and another lady. A Dream of Jealousy. Seamus Heaney. CIP
Walking Wounded. Vernon Scannell. OBWP
Walks in a Forest, *sel.* Thomas Gisborne.
Spring. PBBP
Walky-talky Jenny, *with music.* *Unknown.* AS
Wall, The. Ludvik Askenazy, *tr. fr. Czech.* VWA
Wall, The. Gwendolyn Brooks. *Fr.* Two Dedications. PoBA; PoNe
Wall, The. William Hawkins. MoCV
Wall, The. David Jones. PoA
Wall, The. Eve Merriam. TrJP
Wall, The. Arthur L. Phelps. CaP
Wall, The. Henry Reed. LiTB
Wall, Cave, and Pillar Statements, after Asôka. Alan Dugan. CoAP
Wall continues, The. Before the Actual Cold. Ray A. Young Bear. VoR
Wall [*or* Wal], no! I can't tell whar he lives. Jim Bludso [of the Prairie Belle]. John Hay. AA; BeLS; FaBoBe; FaFP; HBV-2; PaPo; TreFS; YaD
Wall of China, The. Padraic Colum. GrPl; RoGo
Wall of his environment, The. Walls. Hervey Allen. HBMV
Wall of Weeping, The, *sels.* Edmond Fleg, *tr. fr. French by* Humbert Wolfe.
End of Sorrow, The. TrJP
Wandering Jew Comes to the Wall, The. TrJP
Wall Shadows. Carl Sandburg. WSC
Wall should be low, as to say, The. The Wall. Arthur L. Phelps. CaP
Wall Test, The. Louis Simpson. GP
Wallabout Martyrs, The. Walt Whitman. GOA
Wallace, The, *sels.* Henry the Minstrel.
Description of Wallace, A, *fr.* IX. GoTS
(Schir William Wallace.) OxBS
Wallace's Lament for the Graham, *fr.* X. GoTS
(Lament for the Graham) OxBS
Wallace stature of greatness [*or* gretnes], and of hicht [*or* hycht]. A Description of Wallace [*or* Schir William Wallace]. Henry the Minstrel. *Fr.* The Wallace, IX. GoTS; OxBS
Wallace Stevens Gives a Reading. Harriet Zinnes. AMV-81
Wallace Stevens, what's he done? The Rouse for Stevens. Theodore Roethke. OBAL
Wallace's Lament for the Graham. Henry the Minstrel. *Fr.* The Wallace, X. GoTS
(Lament for the Graham.) OxBS
Walleye. Allen Hoey. WOLT
Wall-Flower, The. Walter Savage Landor. OBVV
(Widcombe Churchyard.) FaBoPP
Wall-Flower, The. Henrik Arnold Thaulov Wergeland, *tr. fr. Norwegian by* Sir Edmund Gosse. AWP

Wallflower to a Moonbeam. Louis Untermeyer. BXAP
Walloping Window-Blind, The. Charles Edward Carryl. *Fr.* Davy and the Goblin. InMe; MoShBr; NA; OBCA; TreFS; WhC
(Capital Ship, A.) FSW
(Nautical Ballad, A.) FaPON; HBV-2; OBAL
Wallowing in this bloody sty. The Drunken Fisherman. Robert Lowell. AmPP; AP; CMoP; CrMA; LiTA; LiTM; MoPo; MoVE; NOBA; OxBA; TwAmPo; VGW
Walls. Hervey Allen. HBMV
Walls. C. P. Cavafy, *tr. fr. Modern Greek by* Rae Dalven. TrJP
Walls. Robert Francis. CrMA
Walls are down to window height, The. At a Ruined Croft. John Manson. PoSH
Walls Breathe. Paul Mariah. LFAC
Walls Do Not Fall, The, *sels.* Hilda Doolittle ("H. D.").
"In me (the worm) clearly." NoAM
"Incident here and there, An." CrMA; NoAM; OBWP
"O heart, small urn." LLLT
"Sirius/ what mystery is this?" PBWP
"So we reveal our status." NoAM
"There is a spell, for instance." MoPo; NoAM
"We have seen how the most amiable." BoWoP; PBWP
"When in the company of the gods." NoAM
Walls have been shaded for so many years, The. The Soldier Walks under the Trees of the University. Randall Jarrell. OxBA; PoPl; WaP
Walls . . . iridescent with eyes. The Fifth-Floor Window. Lola Ridge. WPE
Walls of Ice. Janet Campbell Hale. STE
Walls of Jericho, The. Blanche Taylor Dickinson. CDC
Walls of the house are paper thin, The. Domestic Quarrel. Sally McInerney. GrPl
Walls of the maelstrom are painted with trees, The. Poem. Charles Madge. EAS
Walls of this town, The. Verses Written upon Windows. Swift. DBV
Wallum Olum, The. *See* Walam Olum.
Walnut. Jorge Carrera Andrade, *tr. fr. Spanish by* Philip Silver. ELU
Walnut bark, walnut sap. Dogget Gap. *Unknown.* AmFP
Walnut Tree, The. David McCord. OBCA
Walrus, The. Michael Flanders. RHPC
Walrus and the Carpenter, The. "Lewis Carroll." *Fr.* Through the Looking-Glass, *ch.* 4. BeLS: BLPA; FaBoBe; FaBoCo; FaBoNo; FaBV; FaPON; FPL; GN; HBV-2; HBVY; InMe; LiTB; NA; NOBL; OxBChV; PoRA; SoPo; TEP; TreF
" 'Time has come, The,' the Walrus said," *sel.* TiPo
Walrus Hunting. Aua, *tr. fr. Eskimo.* WTO
Walrus lives on icy floes, The. The Walrus. Michael Flanders. RHPC
Walsingham[e]. *Unknown, sometimes at. to* Sir Walter Ralegh. *See* As You Came from the Holy Land.
Walsinghame's Song. James Hogg. BXAP
Walt Whitman. Emanuel Carnevali. PoA
Walt Whitman. Edwin Honig. NePA; TAP
Walt Whitman. Harrison Smith Morris. AA
Walt Whitman. E. A. Robinson. NePA; OxBA
Walt Whitman. Francis Howard Williams. AA
Walt Whitman, a kosmos, of Manhattan the son. Walt Whitman. *Fr.* Song of Myself. NoP; SCV
Walt Whitman at Bear Mountain. Louis Simpson. ConAP; LiTM; NePoEA-2; PoCH; PP
Walt Whitman at the Reburial of Poe. Nicholas Christopher. MAYP
Walt Whitman wasn't much of a fisherman. Fishing with Buddies. Gary Eddy. WOLT
Walter de la Mare Tells the Listener about Jack and Jill. Louis Untermeyer. *Fr.* Mother Goose Up-to-Date. MoAmPo
Walter Jenks' Bath. William Meredith. HoPM
Walter Lesly. *Unknown.* BaBo; ESPB
Walter Rawely of the Middle Temple, in Commendation of the Steele Glasse. Sir Walter Ralegh. *See* In Commendation of George Gascoigne's Steel Glass.
Walter Savage Landor. Dorothy Parker. DBV
Walthena. Elisabeth Peck. AmFN
Waltz, The, *sel.* Byron.
"Muse of the many-twinkling feet! whose charms." OBSV
Waltz, The. Hilary Corke. NYBP
Waltz. Heather Tosteson Reich. AMV-80
Waltz. Edith Sitwell. *Fr.* Façade. OAEP
Waltz against the Mountains. Thomas Hornsby Ferril. VGW
Waltz Me Around Again Willie; or, 'Round, 'Round, 'Round. Will D. Cobb. FSN, *with music*; TreFT
Waltzer in the House, The. Stanley Kunitz. ErPo; NYBP; RHPC
Waltzing Matilda. A. B. Paterson. CBAP; ChTr; FSW; GBP; PoAu-1; WhC
Waly, Waly ("O Waly, Waly up the bank"). *Unknown.* BSV; EnSB; HAP; OBEV; OxBS; ViBoPo
(Forsaken.) HBV-1
(Forsaken Bride, The.) GTBS; GTBS-P
(Jamie Douglas.) ESPB; ViBoFo (A *and* B *vers.*); WHA
(Lament of Barbara Douglas.) PoPle
(Lord Douglas.) OxBB
(O Waly, Waly.) ELP; GoTS; OBS
("O Waly, Waly up the bank.") EnLoPo; FaBoBa; GBP
(Waly, Waly, Love Be Bonny.) PrIm
Waly, Waly ("When cockle shells turn silver bells"). *Unknown.* AmFP
(Waillie.) FSW
Waly, waly! bairns are bonny. A Scottish Proverb. *Unknown.* FaBoUs
Wan/ Swan. The Bereaved Swan. Stevie Smith. FaBoNo; FaBoTw
Wan, fragile faces of joy! Home-Thoughts from France. Isaac Rosenberg. MMA
Wander-Lovers, The. Richard Hovey. AA; HBV-1
Wander, oh, wander, maiden sweet. Goethe and Frederika. Henry Sidgwick. HBV-1
Wander-Thirst. Gerald Gould. HBV-1; TiPo
Wanderer, The. Zoë Akins. HBMV
Wanderer, The. W. H. Auden. CMoP; NoAM; SOTW; WeW
(Chorus: "Doom is dark and deeper than any sea-dingle.") GTBS-P
(Chorus from a Play.) MoAB; MoBrPo
(Doom Is Dark.) LiTB
(Something Is Bound to Happen.) CoBMV; OAEP; PoRA
Wanderer, The, *sels.* Christopher Brennan.
Come Out, Come Out, Ye Souls That Serve. PoAu-1
How Old Is My Heart. PoAu-1
I Cry to You as I Pass Your Windows. PoAu-1
Land I Came Thro' Last. PoAu-1
O Desolate Eves. PoAu-1
"When window-lamps had dwindled, then I rose." CBAP
Wanderer, The. Austin Dobson. HBV-1
Wanderer, The. Eugene Field. BPAW; PoOW; PoPl
Wanderer, The. Amanda Benjamin Hall. HBMV
Wanderer, The. Seamus Heaney. CIP
Wanderer, The. John Masefield. BrPo
Wanderer. Jessica Powers. AMV-80
Wanderer, The, *sel.* Roland Robinson.
"I reached that waterhole, its mud designed." CBAP
Wanderer, The. *Unknown, tr. fr. Anglo-Saxon.* AnOE, *tr by* Charles W. Kennedy; OAEL-1, *tr. by* Charles W. Kennedy; TEP *tr. by* Mark Caldwell
Wanderer, The. Claude Vigée, *tr. fr. French by* Anthony Rudolf. VWA
Wanderer, The. William Carlos Williams. TwAmPo
Wanderer, The, *abr.* Wordsworth. The Excursion, I. EnRP
(Ruined Cottage, The, *diff. version.*) NoP; OAEL-2
Sels.
"I see around me here." OBRV
(Wanderer Recalls the Past, The.) OBNC
"Such was the boy." OBRV
Wanderer, The. "Yehoash," *tr. fr. Yiddish by* Isidore Goldstick. TrJP
Wanderer is man from his birth, A. The Future. Matthew Arnold. OAEP
Wanderer Recalls the Past, The. Wordsworth. *See* Wanderer, The.
Wanderers, The. Robert Browning. *Fr.* Paracelsus. OBEV; OBVV
(Song: "Over the sea our galleys went.") OBRV
Wanderers. Charles Stuart Calverley. CenHV
Wanderers. Thomas Curtis Clark. TrPWD
Wanderers, chosen of God. Chosen of God. Stefan Zweig, *tr. by* Eden *and* Cedar Paul. *Fr.* Jeremiah. TrJP
Wanderer's Grave, The. Rufus B. Sage. BPAW; PoOW
Wanderer's Litany, A. Arthur Stringer. WGRP
Wanderer's Night-Songs, *sels.* Goethe, *tr. fr. German by* Longfellow.
"O'er all the hill-tops," II. AWP
(Second Poem the Night-Walker Wrote, The, *tr. by* Robert Bly.) NU
(Wanderer's Night Song.) PoPl
"Thou that from the heavens art," I. AWP
Wanderers outside the gates, in hollow. The Urn. Malcolm Cowley. MoVE
Wanderer's Song, A. John Masefield. MoAB; MoBrPo
Wanderer's Song. Arthur Symons. ViBoPo
Wanderers, wanderers we are. Emigrant Song. "S. Ansky," *tr. by* Joseph Leftwich. TrJP
Wanderin'. *Unknown.* AS (A *and* B *vers., with music*)
Wandering. Hortense Flexner. HBMV
Wandering. *Unknown.* FSW
Wandering by the heave of the town park, wondering. On the Closing of Millom Ironworks. Norman Nicholson. FaBoTw
Wandering Chorus. B. Alquit, *tr. fr. Yiddish by* Howard Schwartz. VWA
Wandering Cowboy, The. *Unknown.* CoSo
Wandering Jew, The. Robert Bridges. QFR

Wandering Jew, The. Benjamin Fondane, *tr. fr. French by* Edouard Roditi. VWA
Wandering Jew, The. Robert Mezey. NePoEA-2; VWA
Wandering Jew Comes to the Wall, The. Edmond Fleg, *tr. fr. French by* Humbert Wolfe. *Fr.* The Wall of Weeping. TrJP
Wandering Jew once met a man, A. The Eternal Jew. Jacob Cohen, *tr. by* I. M. Lask. TrJP
Wandering Jews. Nancy Keesing. VWA
Wandering Knight's Song, The. John Gibson Lockhart. ChTr; HBV-1
Wandering Lunatic Mind, The. Edward Carpenter. WGRP
Wandering Maiden, The; or, True Love at Length United. *Unknown.* CoMu
Wandering Outlaw, The. Byron. *Fr.* Childe Harold's Pilgrimage. FiP
Wandering oversea dreamer. Prayer after World War. Carl Sandburg. VGW
Wandering Shepherdess, The. *Unknown.* OBET
Wandering Spectre, The. *Unknown. See* Cauld Lad of Hilton, The.
Wandering through cold streets tangled like old string. Brussels in Winter. W. H. Auden. OxBTC
Wandering tribe called the Siouxs, A. Prevalent Poetry. Charles Follen Adams. CenHV
Wanderings of Oisin, The. W. B. Yeats. BrPo
"We galloped over the glossy sea," *sel.* SeCePo
Wand'ring in this place as a wilderness. *Unknown.* GBL
Wand'ring Minstrel, A. W. S. Gilbert. *Fr.* The Mikado. TreFS
Wandsworth Common. David Bromwich. PoA
Wang Peng's Recommendation for Improving the People. Paul Eldridge. ShM
Waning Moon, The. Shelley. CH; ChER; MOON; PoPle; TrGrPo
(Moon, The.) FaBoCh; OBEV
Waning moon looks upward, this grey night, The. Nostalgia. D. H. Lawrence. PoA
Waning of Love, The. "Arthur Lyon Raile." PeHV
Waning of the Harvest Moon, The. John Wieners. CoPo
Waning Summer. Thomas Nashe. *See* Fair Summer Droops.
Wanne mine eyhnen misten. How Death Comes. *Unknown.* MeEL
Want of You, The. Ivan Leonard Wright. BLPA; FaBoBe
Want quickens wit: Want's pupils needs must work. The Fishermen. Theocritus, *tr. by* Charles Stuart Calverley. *Fr.* Idylls. AWP; OBVE
Want to go to heab'n when I die. To See God's Bleedin' Lam'. *Unknown.* BoAN-2
Wanted. Josiah Gilbert Holland. *See* God, Give Us Men!
Wanted. Shel Silverstein. PV
Wanted/ to give away pride. A Defeat. Denise Levertov. PBWP
Wanted—a Man. Edmund Clarence Stedman. PAH
Wanted, a Minister's Wife. *Unknown.* BLPA; TreFS
Wanted—a Witch's Cat. Shelagh McGee. RHPC
Wanted: One Cave Man with Club. Margaret Fishback. WhC
Wanting a Child. Jorie Graham. MAYP
Wanting a Mummy. Sandra McPherson. AmPA; LCAP
Wanting for their young limbs praise. To the Girls of My Graduating Class. Irving Layton. ErPo
Wanting Out. Gavin Ewart. EAS
Wanting to Die. Anne Sexton. ConAP; IHMS; NoAM; TAP
Wanting to lie down on a bed. One of the Boys. Philip Dacey. Str
Wanting to say things. My Father's Song. Simon J. Ortiz. MAYP; STE
Wanton, *sel.* Silabhattarika, *tr. fr. Sanskrit*
"My husband is the same who took my maidenhead," *tr. by* Daniel H. H. Ingalls. PBWP
("My husband is the same man who first pierced me," *tr. by* Willis Barnstone.) BoWoP
Wanton, The, *sel.* Vidya, *tr. fr. Sanskrit by* Daniel H. H. Ingalls.
"Say, friend, if all is still well with the bowers." PBWP
Wanton herd of rakes protest, The. To Lydia. Horace, *tr. by* Philip Francis. Odes, I, 25. OBVE
Wanton Seed, The. *Unknown.* OBET
Wanton Trick, The. *Unknown.* CoMu
('Tis but a Wanton Trick.) UnTE
Wanton troopers riding by, The. The Nymph Complaining for the Death of Her Faun. Andrew Marvell. AnAnS-1; CH; FM; GoTL; HBV-1; HEIP; LoBV; MePo; OAEL-1; OBS, *abr.*; PoEL-2; SeCP; SeCV-1
Wanton with long delay the gay spring leaping cometh. April, 1885. Robert Bridges. NBM; OxBTC
Wants. Philip Larkin. GTBS-P; NoP
Wants of Man, The. John Quincy Adams. OBAL, *abr.*; PoLF
Wants to be admired. The Horse in the Drugstore. Tess Gallagher. AmPA
Wapentake. Longfellow. AA
Wapiti, The. Ogden Nash. MoShBr
War. Guillaume Apollinaire, *tr. fr. French by* Jessie Degen *and* Richard Eberhart. WaaP
War. Dryden. *Fr.* Alexander's Feast. TreFS
War. Georg Heym, *tr. fr. German by* Peter Viereck. AMV-80
War. Sulamith Ish-Kishor. GoYe
War, A. Randall Jarrell. DFF
War. Chief Joseph. PGD
War. Joseph Langland. FF; MP; NePoEA; PoCh
War! J. Gilchrist Lawson. WBLP
War. Li Po, *tr. fr. Chinese by* Rewi Alley. ChTr
War. William Alfred McLean, Jr. BOLo
War, The. W. S. Merwin. LCAP
War. Anthony Ostroff. FAZ
War. Richard Shelton. PPJ
War. Edgar Wallace. OBWP
War against the Trees, The. Stanley Kunitz. HAP; NoAM; PAI; PPON
War and Silence. Robert Bly. CAPP
War and Washington. Jonathan Mitchell Sewall. PAH
War-Baby. D. H. Lawrence. NAs
War Bird's Burlesque, A, *with music. Unknown.* AS
War Blinded. Douglas Dunn. BSV; OBWP
"War-bonnet" we'd say. A Second Molting. Ralph Salisbury. STE
War Bride. Douglas Worth. FF
War canoes were ready. Thirsty Island. Jim Tollerud. VoR
War Comes. Zalman Schneour, *tr. fr. Yiddish by* Joseph Leftwich. TrJP
War Cry: To Mary. Pope Leo XIII, *tr. fr. Latin by* Raymond F. Roseliep. ISi
War Dance, The. Robert V. Carr. PoOW
Wardance. Phillip William George. VoR
Wardance Soup. Phillip William George. VoR
War drum is beating, prepare for the fight, The. "We Conquer or Die." James Pierpont. PAH
War Film, A. Teresa Hooley. SUMH
War Girls. Jessie Pope. SUMH
War God wakened drowsily, The. The Awakened War God. Margaret Widdemer. WGRP
War God's Horse Song, The. *Unknown, tr. fr. Navajo by* Dane Coolidge *and* Mary Roberts Coolidge. LiTA
War, he sung, is toil and trouble. War. Dryden. *Fr.* Alexander's Feast. TreFS
War Horse, The. Bible, *O.T.* Job, XXXIX: 19-25. PH
War Horse, The. Eavan Boland. BIrV; CIP
War Horses. William Cole. PH
War in Chang-an City. Wang Tsan, *tr. fr. Chinese by* Rewi Alley. PPON
War Is Kind, *sels.* Stephen Crane.
Candid Man, The, IX. MoAmPo
Man Said to the Universe, A, XXI. AmPP; CrMA; FaBoEE; FF; ImOP; LiTM; NCEP; OBAL; OBSV; PrIm; TAP; TreFT; WeW; YaD
Newspaper Is a Collection of Half-Injustices, A, XII. AmPP; DBV; NCEP
(Newspaper Is, A.) ViBoPo
On the Desert, XI. LiTM
Peaks, The, XVIII. AA; HBV-1; WGRP
Slant of Sun on Dull Brown Walls, A, XIV. LiTM
There Was a Man with a Tongue of Wood, XVI. LiTA; NePA
(There Was a Man.) MoAmPo
Trees in the Garden Rained Flowers, The, XXVI. LiTM; PrIm
War Is Kind, I (title poem). HBV-2; LiTM; TAP; ViBoPo; WaaP
(Do Not Weep, Maiden, for War Is Kind.) AmPP; BiP; FPL; LiTA; NOBA; OBWP; PAL; PoLF
"Wayfarer, The,/ Perceiving the pathway to truth," XIII. AmPP
(Wayfarer, The.) LiTA; MoAmPo; NePA
War is no longer declared. Every Day. Ingeborg Bachmann, *tr. by* Michael Hamburger. PBWP
War is not declared any more. Every Day. Ingeborg Bachmann, *tr. by* Christopher Middleton. BoWoP
War Is the Statesman's Game. Shelley. *Fr.* Queen Mab, IV. FF; PPON
War of the Secret Agents, The, *sels.* Henri Coulette. NePoEA-2
Cinema at the Lighthouse, VI.
Denise: A Letter Never Sent, VIII.
Epilogue: Author to Reader, XII.
Phono, at the Boar's Head, IX.
War of the Worlds, The. Vern Rutsala. Psk
War of time O it seizes the soul tonight. Easter Eve, 1945. Muriel Rukeyser. MiAP
War on the Periphery. George Johnston. NOBC; PeCV
War-path is true and straight, The. Just One Signal. *Unknown.* PAH
War Poem. Ilya Ehrenburg, *tr. fr. Russian by* Leonard Opalov. AMV-81
War Poet. Roy Fuller. *See* January 1940.
War Poetry. John Philips. *Fr.* Blenheim. NOEC
War Requiem. Del Marie Rogers. LTB
War Ship of Peace, The. Samuel Lover. PAH
War shook the land where Levi dwelt. The Field of Glory. E. A. Robinson. HBV-2; MoAmPo

War Song, A. Bertrans de Born. *See* Well Pleaseth Me the Sweet Time of Easter.
War Song, A. Blake. *See* War Song to Englishmen, A.
War Song. John Davidson. NBM; OBNC
War Song. *Zulu Oral Tradition, tr. by* D. K. Rycroft. WTO
War Song of Dinas Vawr, The. Thomas Love Peacock. *Fr.* The Misfortunes of Elphin. AWP; CABA; EnRP; EvOK; FaBoCh; FaPoR; HAP; InvP; LoBV; NBM; OAEL-2; OBRV; OnMSP; PoPle; PrIm; ViBoPo, *4 ll.*; WaaP; WeW; WhC; WiR
War Song of O'Driscol. Gerald Griffin. OnYI
War Song of the Saracens, The. James Elroy Flecker. *Fr.* Hassan. FaBV; MoBrPo; OBVV; WHA
War Song to Englishmen, A. Blake. *Fr.* King Edward the Third. CH; WaaP
(War Song, A.) OHIP
War Story. Jon Stallworthy. DFF; ELU; OxBC
War Swaggers. Emanuel Litvinoff. WaP
War that we have carefully for years provoked, The. Black-out. Robinson Jeffers. LiTA; LiTM; NePA; WaP
War to save civilisation, A, you say? To Nearly Everybody in Europe To-Day. "Hugh MacDiarmid." DBV
War-Token, The. Longfellow. *Fr.* The Courtship of Miles Standish. PAH
War Walking Near. Ray A. Young Bear. CDW
War Year, The. Ts'ao Sung, *tr. fr. Chinese by* C. H. Kwock *and* Vincent McHugh. PPON
Waradgery Tribe, The. Mary Gilmore. PoAu-1
Waratah. Roland Robinson. PoAu-2
Ward, and still in bonds, one day, A. Regeneration. Henry Vaughan. AnAnS-1; CABA; JCP; LoBV; MeLP; MePo; NoP; OBS
Ward has no heart, they say, but I deny it. On J. W. Ward. Samuel Rogers. DBV; FaBoEE
Ward 130 in the passage on the right. 25 December 1960. Ingrid Jonker, *tr. by* Jack Cope *and* Uys Krige. PeSA
Ward Two. Francis Webb. CBAP
Ward X, *sel.* Lola Ridge.
"Salvation Army lass, The." WPE
Warden at ocean's gate. Liberty Enlightening the World. Edmund Clarence Stedman. PAH
Warden of the Cinque Ports, The. Longfellow. AA; HBV-2; WHA
Warden reads my mail and frowns, The. An Interview. Philip Brasfield. LFAC
Warden Said to Me the Other Day, The. Etheridge Knight. FF
Warden's Day. Carolyn Baxter. LFAC
Wardour Street. Humbert Wolfe. OxBTC
Wardrobe. Sister Mary Madeleva. GoBC
Waring. Robert Browning. PoEL-5; VLP
Waring of Sonora-Town. Henry Herbert Knibbs. BPAW
Warm Babies. Keith Preston. FiBHP; HBMV; WhC
Warm of heart shall never lack a fire, The. Elizabeth J. Coatsworth. TiPo
Warm rain, sunny wind start to break the chill. Li Ch'ing-chao, *tr. fr. Chinese by* Willis Barnstone *and* Sua Chu-chin. BoWoP
Warm rain whispers, but the earth knows best, A. Kenneth Leslie. *Fr.* By Stubborn Stars. PeCV
Warm shone the sun, the wind as warmly blew. Hay-Time; or, The Constant Lovers. A Pastoral. Josiah Relph. NOEC
Warm stones gather the rainfall. Looking for Buddha. Jaime Jacinto. BrSi
Warm summer sun. Epitaph Placed on His Daughter's Tomb. "Mark Twain," *ad. fr.* Robert Richardson. PoLF; TreF
Warm sun is failing, The; the bleak wind is wailing. Autumn; a Dirge. Shelley. CH; HBV-1
Warm walnut seats crisscross braces. Powwow remnants. Lew Blockcolski. VoR
Warm, wild, rainy wind, blowing fitfully. May Morning. Celia Thaxter. AA
Warm winds crossed from the eastern coast, The. The Boss's Wife. *Unknown.* CBAP
Warm wine, warm baths, warm women, onetime ladies. The Easiest Way. *Unknown, tr. by* Louis Untermeyer. UnTE
Warm Winter Day, A. Julian Cooper. BoNaP
Warming Up for the Real Thing. Lee Rudolph. TW
Warned, warned for years. Love Poem. Susan Irene Rea. AMV-80
Warning. John Ciardi. PDV
Warning, The. Adelaide Crapsey. WPE; WSC
(Cinquain: A Warning.) WeW
Warning, The. Robert Creeley. NeAP; TAP; VGW
Warning. Jesse Douglas. WhC
Warning. Langston Hughes. BPo
Warning. Jenny Joseph. OxBTC
Warning, A. Alexander Nicolson. PoSH
Warning, A. Coventry Patmore. EnLoPo
Warning, A. Mary A. Webber. TDH
Warning and Reply. Emily Brontë. OBVV; OxBI; WPE
Warning to a Guest. John Holloway. NePoEA
Warning to America, A. Philip Freneau. TAP
Warning to Beware, A. *Unknown.* OxBM
Warning to Children. Robert Graves. FaBoCh; FaFP; NoP; OAEL-2; SO
Warning to Conquerors, A. Donagh MacDonagh. CIP; OxBI
Warning to Cupid. *Unknown, tr. fr. Greek by* Louis Untermeyer. UnTE
Warning to My Love, A. David Wagoner. NePoEA-2
Warning to One. Merrill Moore. MoAmPo; TrGrPo; YaD
Warning to Those Who Serve Lords, A. *Unknown.* MeEL
Warning to Travailers Seeking Accomodations at Mr. Devills Inn. Sarah Kemble Knight. SCAP
Warning wind finds out my resting-place, A. The March Bee. Edmund Blunden. PoPle
Warnings, The. Alice Furlong. AnIV
Warp and Woof. Harry Halbisch. BLRP
Warren's Address [at Bunker Hill]. John Pierpont. FaBoBe; GN; GOA; HBV-2; HBVY; PAL; TreF
(General Joseph Warren's Address.) WBLP
(Warren's Address to the American Soldiers). AA; PAH
Warrior, A/ I have been. Song of Sitting Bull. *Unknown.* GOA
Warrior Maid, The. Anna Hempstead Branch. HBV-2
Warrior Nation Trilogy. Lance Henson. VoR
Warrior so bold and a virgin so bright, A. Alonzo the Brave and Fair Imogine. Matthew Gregory Lewis. *Fr.* The Monk. OBEC
Warrior to His Dead Bride, The. Adelaide Anne Procter. OBVV
Warrior with Shield. Michael Dennis Browne. PoDr
Warriors. Douglas Dunn. OxBC
Warriors. Michael Hogan. LFAC
Warrior's Lament, The. Sir Owen Seaman. FiBHP
Warriors Prancing, Women Dancing. Niema Rashidd. NBP
Warrior's Song. Mary Austin. BPAW
Warriors, tigers, flowers of Delacroix, The. Lightning for Atmosphere. Marya Zaturenska. TwAmPo
Warr'st thou 'gainst Athens? Shakespeare. Timon of Athens. *Fr.* IV, iii. EBEV
Wars, The. Conrad Aiken. *Fr.* The Soldier. WaaP
"Wars are to be," they say, they blindly say. The Lament of the Voiceless. Laura Bell Everett. PGD
War's Clown in the Proscenium. Gene Derwood. *See* In the Proscenium.
Wars of Santa Fe, The. *Unknown.* AmFP
Wars of the Roses, The. *Unknown.* GBP
War's wasted era is a desert shore. For a Survivor of the Mesopotamian Campaign. Elizabeth Daryush. SUMH
Wars we wage, The. Robert Gould Shaw. William Vaughn Moody. *Fr.* An Ode in Time of Hesitation. AA
Wartime Blues. *Unknown.* BluL
Wartime Dawn, A. David Gascoyne. LiTM; MoVE
Warty Bliggens, the Toad. Don Marquis. *Fr.* Archy and Mehitabel. FiBHP
Warum sind denn die Rosen so blass. Heine, *tr. fr. German by* Richard Garnett. AWP
Wary of time O it seizes the soul tonight. Easter Eve. Muriel Rukeyser. NePA; VGW
Was a Man. Philip Booth. NePoEA-2; NCSH; VGW
Was a Soule from farre away. Five Carols for Christmastide, IV. Louise Imogen Guiney. ISi
Was broken./ He bade a warrior abandon his horse. The Battle of Maldon. *Unknown, tr. by* Charles W. Kennedy. AnOE; OAEL-1
Was clenched on a fly's carcase like a golden. The Spider's Nest. George MacBeth. NMP
Was ever man of Nature's framing. Ode. Charles Cotton. CavP
Was he a mining on the flat. He Done His Level Best. "Mark Twain." BPAW
Was He Married? Stevie Smith. NoAM
Was I moving through the invisible glass. The Glass Door. Robert Watson. GP
Was I summoned. Eve's Birth. Kim Chernin. VWA
Was I surprised! Uncle Death. Walter Clark. NCSH
Was I too glib about eternal things. The Sequel. Theodore Roethke. NYBP
Was it a dream, or did I see it plain? Amoretti, LXXVII. Spenser. NIP
Was it a dream? The Books were men. The Wounded. Louise Louis. GoYe
Was it a dream? We sailed, I thought we sailed. A Dream. Matthew Arnold. GBL; GTBS-P; SeCePo
"Was it a little baby." A Tonversation with Baby. Morris Bishop. FiBHP; WhC
Was it a mirror then across a room. Mirrors. Elizabeth Jennings. NePoEA
Was It All Worth While? *Zulu Oral Tradition, tr. by* H. Tracey. WTO
Was it at Nazareth/ of the marvellous breath? Joy's Peak. Robert Farren. ISi

Was it fancy, sweet nurse. Don Marquis. *Fr.* Grotesques. FiBHP
Was it for this I braved a pathless, dark. A Mother before a Soldier's Monument. Winnie Lynch Rockett. PGD
Was it for this I uttered prayers. Grown-up. Edna St. Vincent Millay. NoAM; PAI
Was it his face that so unsettled him? Narcissus. Donald Petersen. NePoEA-2
Was it I, was it I who dallied there. Ulysses Returns, III. Roselle Mercier Montgomery. HBMV
Was It Not Curious? Stevie Smith. NoAM
Was it really you all the time? Dream Sequence, Part 9. Naomi Long Madgett. BPo
Was it the brown eagle feather that. Insight. Mary Goose. STE
Was it the proud full sail of his great verse. Sonnets, LXXXVI. Shakespeare. InvP; OAEL-1; OAEP; TEP
Was it wind off the dumps. Summer Home. Seamus Heaney. IPY
Was it worth while to paint so fair. The Morning-Glory. Florence Earle Coates. HBV-1
Was It You? Stewart I. Long. WBLP
Was Jesus chaste? or did He. Blake. *Fr.* The Everlasting Gospel. OBRV
Was my bones. What She Wanted. Ronald Koertge. GP
Was never aught by Nature's art. That All Things Are as They Are Used. George Turberville. EnRePo
Was never day came on my head. George Turberville. *Fr.* The Lover Abused Renounceth Love. ElL
Was never in Scotland hard nor sene. Christ's Kirk on the Green. *At. to* James V, King of Scotland. OxBS
Was never none other. Carol Naïve. John McClure. HBMV
Was She a Witch? Laura E. Richards. PDV; SoPo
Was she so chaste? She Rebukes Hippolyta. Hilda Doolittle ("H. D."). SBG
Was that a crystal butterfly's wing. Mistakable Identity. Elaine V. Emans. AMV-80
Was that the landmark? What,—the foolish well. The Landmark. Dante Gabriel Rossetti. The House of Life, LXVII. NBM
Was the arrangement made between the two couples legal? Some Litanies. Michael Benedikt. CoAP; TwCP
Was the love between them. His Lunch Bucket. Doug Cockrell. Psk
Was there ere sic a parish, a parish, a parish. Little Dunkeld. *Unknown.* GBP
Was there ever message sweeter. A Message. Elizabeth Stuart Phelps. PAH
Was there love once? I have forgotten her. Fulfilment. Robert Nichols. HBMV
Was this His coming! I had hoped to see. Ave Maria, Gratia Plena. Oscar Wilde. ISi
Was this his face, and these the finding eyes. On a Portrait of Columbus. George Edward Woodberry. AA
Was This the Face [That Launched a Thousand Ships]. Christopher Marlowe. *Fr.* Doctor Faustus. EBEV; GBL; HeIP; NIP; TreF; TrGrPo; ViBoPo
(Face of Helen, The.) FaBV
(Helen.) BLPL; FaFP; LiTB; WHA
(Helen of Troy.) FF
Was this world built for happiness, that man. Sydney Dobell. *Fr.* Balder. PeD
Was two sisters loved one man. The Two Sisters. *Unknown.* MAT
Was very kind. When she regained. The Raper from Passenack. William Carlos Williams. TW
Was Worm. May Swenson. BoAnP
Was you ever in Quebec? Hieland Laddie. *Unknown.* FSW
Wash. Eilean Ni Chuilleanain. BIrV; WPOW
Wash Day. Larry Mollin. NeAC
Wash-Day Wonder. Dorothy Faubion. QQQ
Wash is hanging on the line, The. Windy Wash Day. Dorothy Aldis. TiPo
Wash it well, and season it hot. To Stew a Rump-Steak. *Unknown.* FaBoUs
Wash man out of the earth, shear off. Wash. Eilean Ni Chuilleanain. BIrV; WPOW
Wash the dishes, wipe the dishes. Mother Goose. OxNR
Wash Well the Fresh Fish. *Unknown.* PoPle
Wash your hands, or else the fire. Another to the Maids. Robert Herrick. OHIP
Washback of the waters, swirl of time. Sea-Ruck. Richard Eberhart. MOS
Washed by the rain, dust and grime are laid. Starting Early from the Ch'u-ch'êng Inn. Po Chü-i, *tr. by* Arthur Waley. OBVE
Washed in Silver. James Stephens. ELU; MOON
Washed in the blood of the brave and the blooming. God Save the Flag. Oliver Wendell Holmes. FaFP; OHFP
Washed into the doorway. The Guest. Wendell Berry. AP
Washers of the Shroud, The. James Russell Lowell. AP; HBV-2; PAH
Washer-Woman, The. Otto Leland Bohanan. BANP
Washerwoman, The. Mary Collier. *Fr.* The Woman's Labour; an Epistle to Mr. Stephen Duck. NOEC
Washing. John Drinkwater. FaPON
Washing and Dressing. Ann Taylor. FaBoUs
Washing between the buildings. Larry Eigner. CoPo
Washing Day. *Unknown.* CoMu
Washing hanging from the lemon tree, The. The Five-Day Rain. Denise Levertov. NeAP
Washing hangs upon the line, A. Songs for a Colored Singer. Elizabeth Bishop. MiAP; PoNe
Washing Kai in the sauna. The Bath. Gary Snyder. DiL; GP; NNaP; TAP
Washing Machine, The. Jeffrey Davies. PCP
Washing My Son. Jonathan Holden. AMV-81
Washing the Dishes. Christopher Morley. PoLF
Washing up the dishes. The V.A.D. Scullery-Maid's Song. M. Winifred Wedgwood. SUMH
Washing Windows. Barry Spacks. NCSH
Washing Windows. Peter Wild. Str
Washington. Byron. *Fr.* Ode to Napoleon Buonaparte. OHIP; PAH; PAL
Washington. Mae Winkler Goodman. PGD
Washington. James Russell Lowell. *See* Ours, and All Men's.
Washington. Geraldine Meyrich. OHIP
Washington. Harriet Monroe. *Fr.* Commemoration Ode. AA; FaBoBe
Washington. Denis O'Crowley. OHIP
Washington. John A. Prentice. OHIP
Washington. James Jeffrey Roche. PAH
Washington. Nancy Byrd Turner. FaPON; RHPC; SoPo; TiPo; YeAr
Washington. *Unknown. See* Inscription at Mount Vernon.
Washington. B. Y. Williams. PGD
Washington. Mary Wingate. OHIP
(When Shall We See Thy Like Again?) PGD
Washington and Jefferson made many a joke. Presidents of the United States. *Unknown.* FaBoUs
Washington and Lincoln. Wendell Phillips Stafford. PGD
Washington Cathedral. Karl Shapiro. MiAP
Washington in Love. John Berryman. LCAP
Washington led armies. Footnote to History. Elizabeth J. Coatsworth. SiSoSe
Washington Monument by Night. Carl Sandburg. CMoP; FaPON; OFD; OHIP; PoSC
Washington Sequoia, The, *sel.* Milicent Washburn Shinn.
Yosemite. AA
Washington, the brave, the wise, the good. Inscription at Mount Vernon [*or* Washington]. *Unknown.* OFD; OHIP
Washington's Birthday. Arthur J. Burdick. OHIP
Washington's Monument. *Unknown.* OHIP; PAH
Washington's Monument, February 1885. Walt Whitman. OFD
Washington's Statue. Henry T. Tuckerman. AA
Washington's Tomb. Ruth Lawrence. OHIP
Washington's Vow. Whittier. OHIP
Washiri (Poet). Kattie M. Cumbo. BOLo
Washrags. Vern Rutsala. GP
Washyuma Motor Hotel. Simon J. Ortiz. GP
Wasn't it pleasant, O brother mine. Out to Old Aunt Mary's. James Whitcomb Riley. FaFP; OHFP
Wasn't popular in high school for. Harelip Mary. Ronald Koertge. GP
Wasn't That a Mighty Storm? *Unknown.* AmFP
Wasn't your mother a woman? Hennamma, *tr. fr. Kannada by* Willis Barnstone. BoWoP
Wasp, The. John Davidson. FM
Wasp, The. Daryl Hine. NYBP
Wasp, The. "Fiona Macleod." *Fr.* Transcripts from Nature. FM
Wasp. Alden Nowlan. BoAnP
Wasp, The. Joyce Carol Oates. GeTw
Wasp, The. William Sharp. FaPON
Wasp. William Welsh. SOTS
Wasp Bite Nobi on Her Conch-Eye, A, *with music. Unknown.* OuSiCo
Wasp, climbing the window pane. Epigrams, I-IX. Howard Nemerov. OBAL
Wasp Sex Myth (One). Anselm Hollo. PoM
Wasp Sex Myth (Two). Anselm Hollo. PoM
Waspish. Robert Frost. BoAnP
Wasps. Dorothy Aldis. RHPC
Wasp's Frolic, The. *Unknown.* PAH
Wasps' Nest, The. George MacBeth. OxBTC
Wasp's Song, The. "Lewis Carroll." FaBoNo
Wassail and wassail, all over the town. Somerset Wassail. *Unknown.* OBET
Wassail Song, The ("Here we come a-wassailing"). *Unknown.* FSW; OHIP; PoSC

(Here We Come a-Wassailing.) PChr
Wassail Song ("Wassail! wassail! all round the town"). *Unknown.*
Wassail Song ("We have been a walking"). *Unknown.* GBP
Wassail the trees, that they may bear. Robert Herrick. *Fr.* Ceremonies for Christmas. PChr
Wassail, Wassail. John Bale. ChTr
Wassail, wassail, all over the town! Gloucestershire Wassail. *Unknown.* OBET
Wassail, wassail, all over the town. Thames Head Wassailers' Song. *Unknown.* OBET
Wassail! Wassail! all over the town. Wassailer's Song. Robert Southwell. OHIP
Wassail! wassail! all round the town. Wassail Song. *Unknown.* OHIP
Wassail, wassail, out of the milk pail. Wassail, Wassail. John Bale. ChTr
Wassail, Wassail, Wassail, Sing We. *Unknown.* SBVL
Wassailer's Song. Robert Southwell. OHIP
Wassailing Song. *Unknown.* OBCP
Waste. Harry Graham. FaBoCo
(Aunt Maud.) MoShBr; ShM
Waste. G. A. Studdert-Kennedy. EBCP
Waste Land, The. T. S. Eliot. AmPP; AP; CABA; CMoP; CoBMV; FaBoMo; HAP; LiTA; LiTM; MasP; MoAB; MoAmPo; MoPo; MoVE; NePA; NoAM; NOBA; NOBE; NoP; OAEL-2; OAEP; OxBA; OxBTC; PPoe; TAP; UnPo
Sels.
Death by Water, IV. OBVE
Game of Chess, A, II. SCV
When Lil's Husband Got Demobbed, I Said. NAs
Waste of muscle, waste of brain. Waste. G. A. Studdert-Kennedy. EBCP
Waste of War, The. William L. Stidger. PGD
Waste Places, The. James Stephens. *See* In Waste Places.
Wasted Ammunition. Stoddard King. InMe
Wasted Day, A. Frances Cornford. HBMV; MoBrPo
Wasted Day, The. Robert F. Murray. EBVV
Wasted Land, The. Edward Pygge. FaBoPa
Wasted Night. *Unknown, tr. fr. Greek by* Louis Untermeyer. UnTE
Wasted Sympathy, A. Winifred Howells. AA
Wasted, wasted minutes that couldn't be worse. While Someone Telephones. Elizabeth Bishop. NMP
Wasted, Weary, Wherefore Stay. Sir Walter Scott. *Fr.* Guy Mannering, *ch.* 27. EnRP
Wasting thistle whitens on my crest, The. The Wild Knight. G. K. Chesterton. WGRP
Wastrel, The. Reginald Wright Kauffman. HBV-1
Watch, The. Frances Cornford. DTC; HBMV; HeIP; InPK; MoBrPo; OxBTC
Watch, The. Marge Piercy. GeTw
Watch, The. May Swenson. HAP
Watch a caterpillar. Biology Lesson. John D. Engle, Jr. AMV-80
Watch and Pray. Charlotte Elliott. STF
Watch Any Day. W. H. Auden. FaBoMo
(Free One, A.) CMoP
Watch Hill. Winfield Townley Scott. ErPo
Watch it. That's the body: what goes on. The Body. William Bronk. VGW
Watch Long Enough, and You Will See the Leaf. Conrad Aiken. Preludes for Memnon, XIX. CMoP; NePA; OxBA
Watch of a Swan, The. Sarah Morgan Bryan Piatt. AA
Watch on the Rhine, The. Max Schneckenburger, *tr. fr. German.* HBV-2
Watch out for the bus. Mercado. Greg Pape. AmPA
Watch out, my dear. Praxilla, *tr. fr. Greek by* John Dillon. PBWP
Watch, please, this painted ballet of the fed. Uccello on the Heath. Geoffrey Grigson. WaP
Watch Repair. Charles Simic. NoP
Watch that near my midriff ticks, The. Pocket and Steeple. M. A. DeWolfe Howe. WhC
Watch the Lights Fade. Robinson Jeffers. CMoP; NoAM; NOBA
Watch thou and fear; to-morrow thou shalt die. The Choice, 2. Dante Gabriel Rossetti. The House of Life, LXXII. HBV-2; OBVV
Watch upon my wrist, The. Parable. W. H. Auden. FaBoCo
Watch was up on the topsail-yard a-making fast the sail, The. One of Wally's Yarns. John Masefield. BrPo
Watch well the poor in this late hour. Temperance Note: and Weather Prophecy. James Agee. *Fr.* Two Songs on the Economy of Abundance. MoAmPo
Watch will tell the time of day, A. Mr. Coggs [Watchmaker]. E. V. Lucas. FaPON; HBV-1; HBVY
Watch Yourself Go By. Strickland Gillilan. BLPA
(Cure for Fault-finding, A, *abr.*) WBLP
Watched and well-known to the police, he walks. Variations on a Line from Shakespeare's Fifty-sixth Sonnet. E. L. Mayo. PoCh
Watcher, The. Sara Josepha Hale. AA
Watcher, The. John Peck. AmPA
Watcher, The. James Stephens. HBV-1; MoBrPo; OBEV; OBVV
Watcher, The. Ruth Stone. NYBP
Watcher, The. Margaret Widdemer. HBMV; OHIP
(Mother.) STF
Watcher of reedy places and cries. Theodore Roethke. Morton Paley. AMV-81
Watchers, The. Arlo Bates. AA
Watchers, The. Paul Blackburn. NMP; NYBP
Watchers, The. William Stanley Braithwaite. PoNe
Watchers. W. S. Merwin. NaP
Watchers, The. Muriel Rukeyser. NMP
Watching. "Fanny Forester." AA
Watching a Cloud. Dannie Abse. OxBC; TEP
Watching Clouds. John Farrar. SoPo
Watching Gymnasts. Robert Francis. LiSp
Watching Jim Shoulders. Leo Connellan. TAT
Watching My Daughter Sew. Katharine Privett. AMV-81
Watching oneself. Poem without a Main Verb. John Wain. NePoEA-2; NMP
Watching Salmon Jump. Simon J. Ortiz. CDW
Watching TV. To a Man in a Picture Window Watching Television. Mildred Weston. ELU
Watching Television. Robert Bly. BiP; CoAP
Watching the beautiful. This Day. Lawrence Raab. NoP
Watching the Dance. James Merrill. NIP
Watching the Jets Lose to Buffalo at Shea. May Swenson. LiSp
Watching the Moon. David McCord. YeAr
Watching the night contract the viridian fields. O Rose, O Rainbow. Nicholas Moore. NeBP
Watching the Old Man Die. Arthur James Marshall Smith. MoCV
Watching the Out-Door Movie Show. Ann Struthers. FAZ
Watching the shied core. As Bad as a Mile. Philip Larkin. ELU; InPK; OxBC
Watching the Sun Rise over Mount Zion. Ruth Whitman. VWA
Watching the White Image, electric moon. In a Moonlit Hermit's Cabin. Allen Ginsberg. MOON
Watching this dawn's mnemonic of old dawning. Sestina in a Cantina. Malcolm Lowry. MoCV
Watching you in the mirror I wonder. The Mirror. Louise Glück. GeTw; GP; MAYP
Watching You Walk. Ruthven Todd. NeBP
Watching Your Gray Eyes. Morton Marcus. GP
Watchman, The. Charles Kingsley. EBVV
Watchman, The. Abraham Reisen, *tr. fr. Yiddish by* Joseph Leftwich. TrJP
Watchman, Tell Me, *with music.* *Unknown.* AH
Watchman, Tell Us of the Night. John Bowring. TreFS
Watchman, watchman on your height. The Watchman. Abraham Reisen, *tr. by* Joseph Leftwich. TrJP
Watchman, What of the Night? Bible, *O.T.* Isaiah, XXI: 11-15. AWP
Watchman, What of the Night? Swinburne. WiR
"Watchman, what of the night?" The Watchman. Charles Kingsley. EBVV
Water. Hilda Conkling. PDV; TiPo
Water. Emerson. AmPP; PoEL-4
Water. Edmond Jabes, *tr. fr. French by* Anthony Rudolf. VWA
Water. Philip Larkin. FaBoMo
Water. Robert Lowell. CMoP; HeIP; LCAP; NOBA; NoP
Water. Judith McPheron. AMV-81
Water, *sel.* Kathleen Raine.
"There is a stream that flowed before the first beginning." ImOP
Water. Anne Sexton. CoPo
Water. Gary Snyder. LCAP
Water and Air. Robert Browning. *Fr.* Pauline. OBRV
("Night, and one single ridge of narrow path.") VLP
Water and Worship: An Open-Air Service on the Gatineau River. Margaret Avison. HAP
Water. As much in air as in the lake. Walleye. Allen Hoey. WOLT
Water astonishing and difficult altogether. Water Raining. Gertrude Stein. *Fr.* Tender Buttons. PBWP
Water Babies, The, *sels.* Charles Kingsley.
Lost Doll, The. FaPON; MoShBr; SoPo
("I once had a sweet little doll, dears.") TiPo
(Little Doll, The.) OxBChV
(Song: "I once had a sweet little doll, dears.") PaPo
Tide River, The. BoNaP; HBV-1; OxBChV
(Clear and Cool.) GN
Young and Old. BLPL; EBEV; FaBoBe; FaFP; FaPoR; HBV-1; OxBChV; PoLF; TreF
(Old Song, The.) OBVV
(When All the World.) ViBoPo
Water Below, The. Fleur Adcock. PAI

Water-Boy. *Unknown.* TrGrPo
Water bug is drawing the shadows, The. *Tr. fr. Yuman Indian by* Frances Densmore. OBVE
Water closing, The. Together. Maxine W. Kumin. BoWoP; NMM
Water Color. Stephen Mooney. NYBP
Water Color [*or* Watercolor] of Grantchester Meadows. Sylvia Plath. LCAP; NYBP; SBG
Water-Colour of Venice, A. Lawrence Durrell. MoBrPo
Water does not lie heavy and deep, The. Kinneret. Judith Herzberg, *tr. by* Shirley Kaufman. VWA
Water down the rocky wall, The. The Bunyip. Douglas Stewart. AmMo
Water-Drinker, The. Edward Jonson. BXAP; PeD
Water, first creature of the gods. Tea Poems. George Mackay Brown. OxBC
Water flooded everywhere. Rebirth. Catriona Stamp. BrRo
Water, for anguish of the solstice—nay. For "A Venetian Pastoral" by Giorgione. Dante Gabriel Rossetti. ViBoPo; VLP
Water-Girl. *Gond Oral Tradition, tr. by* V. Elwin *and* S. Hivale. WTO
Water gives, it gets us, The. Late Afternoon on a Good Lake. Dara Wier. MAYP
Water Glass of Whisky, A. X. J. Kennedy. CoPo
Water has to start, The. Coming Down to It. Malcolm Glass. BXAP
Water hen is hopping, A. May Evening. Eileen Brennan. NeIP
Water-Hole, The. Charles Erskine Scott Wood. BPAW
Water-Images. Mary Elizabeth Osborn. NePoAm-2
Water in my prison shatters in a prism, The. The Trout. Daryl Hine. CoAP
Water is cool, there is a faint smile, The. A Bather in a Painting. Ashton Greene. NePoAm
Water is practical. Mourning Pablo Neruda. Robert Bly. LCAP
Water Is Wide, The. *Unknown.* FSW; OBET
Water Island. Howard Moss. CoAP; MP; NePoEA-2; NYBP; Prf
Water Lady, The. Thomas Hood. CH; HBV-1; ViBoPo
Water like quartz, with the same kinds of strata, The. Nights Passed on Ward's Island, Toronto Harbour. Doug Fetherling. NeAC
Water-Lilies. Sara Teasdale. MoAmPo
Water-lilies in myriads rocked on the slight undulations. On the Atchafalaya. Longfellow. *Fr.* Evangeline. AA
Water-Lily, The. John Banister Tabb. AA; ACP; GoBC
Water Lily, The. David Wagoner. PoDr
Water-Lion is the God verray, The. King Arthur's Dream. *Unknown.* ACP
Water Mill, The. Sarah Doudney. *See* Lesson of the Water-Mill, The.
Water Music. Alun Lewis. ChMP
Water Music. "Hugh MacDiarmid." GoTS
Water Noises. Elizabeth Madox Roberts. BoNaP
Water-Nymph and the Boy, The. Roden Noel. OBVV
I Flung Me Round Him, *sel.* HBV-2
Water of Kane, The. *Tr. fr. Hawaiian by* N. B. Emerson. WTO
Water on the Highway. Nancy Simpson. AMV-80
Water-Ousel, The. Mary Webb. CH
Water Ouzel. William H. Matchett. CoAP; NePoEA; NYBP; PoCH
Water-Party, A. Robert Bridges. PoPle
Water Picture. May Swenson. BoNaP
Water plunges to devour us. Travel Song. Hugo von Hofmannsthal, *tr. by* Charles Wharton Stork. TrJP
Water pulls nervously whispering satin across cool roots, cold stones. Interval. Joseph Auslander. FYAP
Water Raining. Gertrude Stein. *Fr.* Tender Buttons. PBWP
Water rushes up. Open Hydrant. Marci Ridlon. RHPC
Water sings along our keel, The. Armistice. Sophie Jewett. AA
Water Song. Solomon ibn Gabirol, *tr. fr. Hebrew by* Israel Abrahams. TrJP
Water still flows. Illegitimate Things. William Carlos Williams. MoAB; MoAmPo
Water-still is the shade of old Coppelius. Dr. Coppelius. Wrey Gardiner. NeBP
Water strider skates upon the brook, A. Plane Geometer. David McCord. NYBP
Water Tap. Norman MacCaig. BSV
Water the ground with his tears. The Light. John Holloway. NePoEA
Water touches the boat. Sharks. Ron Overton. WOLT
Water Tower, The. James Paul. AMV-81
Water tower enclosures. Beyond Belief. Tom Luhrmann. AMV-81
Water-Truck, The. Patrick Lane. NeAC
Water under the Earth. Robert Bly. NNaP
Water understands, The. Water. Emerson. AmPP; PoEL-4
Water, water I desire. The Scare-Fire. Robert Herrick. HAP; NoP
Water-Wheel, The. Jack R. Clemo. ChMP
Water Whirligigs. D. J. Opperman, *tr. fr. Afrikaans by* Jack Cope *and* Uys Krige. PeSA
Water Witch, The, *sel.* James Fenimore Cooper.
My Brigantine, *fr. ch.* 15. AA; EtS; MOS
Water-Witch, The. Martha Eugenie Perry. CaP
Water, with lidless stare. Narcissus. Charles Gullans. NePoEA
Water without Sound. Malka Heifetz Tussman, *tr. fr. Yiddish by* Marcia Falk. VWA
Waterbird goes up, A. 5 Poems. Robert Gray. CBAP
Waterbirds sailing upon the darkness. Petron, the Desert Father. Lawrence Durrell. *Fr.* Eight Aspects of Melissa. NeBP
Waterchew! Gregory Corso. VGW
Watercolor of Grantchester Meadows. Sylvia Plath. *See* Water Color of Grantchester Meadows.
Watercress & Ice. Chase Twichell. MAYP
Watercress Seller, The. Thomas Miller. OxBChV
Watered Lilies, The. *Unknown. See* For the Master's Use.
Waterfall. Seamus Heaney. NoAM
Waterfall [*or* Water-Fall], The. Henry Vaughan. AnAnS-1; FaBoPP; MeLP; MePo; NOBE; NOCV; NoP; OAEP; OBS; PoEL-2; PrIm; SeCV-1; ViBoPo, *st.* 1; WiR
Waterfall. Anne Welsh. PeSA
Waterfalls. Vernon Watkins. NoAM
Water Fowl. Wordsworth. FM
Waterfront. Oliver Jenkins. EtS
Water-Front. Cecil French Salkeld. OnYI
Watergate. Ruth Herschberger. FAZ
Watergaw, The. "Hugh MacDiarmid." BSV; GoTS; NeBP; NoP
Watering the Horse. Robert Bly. NaP; NCSH
Waterloo. Byron. *Fr.* Childe Harold's Pilgrimage, III. FiP; OBRV; TrGrPo; WaaP; WHA
(Battle of Waterloo, The.) FaFP; TreF
(Eve of Waterloo, The.) BeLS; FaBoBe; FaBoCh; FaBoEn; FaBV; HBV-2; NOBE; OBNC
(Night before the Battle of Waterloo, The.) WBLP
(Night before Waterloo, The.) GN
("There was a sound of revelry by night.") EBEV; OBWP; ViBoPo
Waterloo. Sir Aubrey De Vere. HBV-2
Waterloo Bridge. Christopher Middleton. *Fr.* Herman Moon's Hourbook. NePoEA-2
Watermelon. Ted Joans. GP
Watermelons. Charles Simic. OBAL; PPJ
Waters above! eternal springs! The Shower. Henry Vaughan. BoNaP; ChTr; OBS
Waters chased him as he fled, The. Emily Dickinson. PoEL-5
Waters dance on the ocean crest, The. The Conger Eel. Patrick MacGill. OnYI
Water's Edge. Lillian Morrison. RHPC
Waters of earth come and go, The. Here and Now. Philip Levine. PoA; VWA
Waters of Life, The. Humbert Wolfe. MoBrPo
Waters of the Sea. Cecil Goldbeck. EtS
Waters of the well of life, The. The Well of Life. Sir Herbert Read. NoAM
Waters of Tyne, The. *Unknown.* GBP
Waters saw thee, O God, The. Bible, *O.T.* Psalms, LXXVII: 16-19. MOS
Water's shore-lapping signature, The. From a Rise of Land to the Sea. Roald Hoffmann. SUW
Watershed, The. W. H. Auden. OAEL-2
Watershed. Margaret Avison. OBCV
Watershed, The. Alice Meynell. SBG
Watershed. Robert Penn Warren. PoA
Waterspout. Luis de Camoes, *tr. fr.* Portuguese. EtS
Waterspout, The. William Hart-Smith. *Fr.* Christopher Columbus. PoAu-2
Watertower. Albert Bellg. FAZ
Waterwall Blues. Howard Moss. MoPo; NePA
Waterwitch, The. *Unknown.* PoAu-1
Watkwenies. Duncan Campbell Scott. PeCV
Watteau was slightly silly to equip. L'Embarquement pour Cythère. John Manifold. CBAP
Watts. Shirley Kaufman. NMM
Watts. Conrad Kent Rivers. BOLo; PoBA
Watts. Alvin Saxon. PoBA
Watt's Improvements to the Steam Engine. Thomas Baker. *Fr.* The Steam Engine; or, The Power of Flame. FaBoUs
Wave, The. Daryl Hine. Prf
Wave, The. David Phillips. NeAC
Wave, The. John Curtis Underwood. EtS
Wave approaching and the wave returning, The. Sequence. George Barker. PoA
Wave of coldness, A. Yosano Akiko, *tr. fr. Japanese by* Glenn Hughes *and* Yozan T. Iwasaki. WPOW
Wave swashes. Water's Edge. Lillian Morrison. RHPC
Wave Symphony, The. Arthur Davison Ficke. *Fr.* Four Japanese Paintings. PoA

Wave that is dark piles white and slips to its death, The. Fishing Season. Val Vallis. PoAu-2
Wave, wave your glorious battle-flags, brave soldiers of the North. Gettysburg. Edmund Clarence Stedman. PAH
Wave withdrawing, The. "Dover Beach"—a Note to That Poem. Archibald MacLeish. FF
Wavelength. David St. John. SUW
Wavering planet most unstable, The. *Unknown.* MOON
Waverley, *sels.* Sir Walter Scott.
"False love, and hast thou played me this," *fr. ch.* 9. ViBoPo
Hie Away [Hie Away], *fr. ch.* 12. EnRP; MoShBr; TiPo; ViBoPo
(Gellatley's Song to the Deerhounds.) OBRV
To an Oak Tree, *fr. ch.* 29. OBNC
Waverley Pen, The. *Unknown.* FaBoUs
Waves. Emerson. *See* Nahant.
Waves/ of/ Sahara sand. Brain Coral. Lois Bassen. SUW
Waves about Iona dirge, The. To William Sharp. Clinton Scollard. HBV-2
Waves bluster up the bay and through the throat. A Family Photograph 1939. James K. Baxter. OxBC
Waves come rolling, and the billowes rore, The. Sea-Monsters. Spenser. *Fr.* The Faerie Queene. FaBoEn
Waves forever move, The. The Sisters. John Banister Tabb. AA
Waves Gleam in the Sunshine, The. Heine, *tr. fr. German by* Emma Lazarus. *Fr.* Songs to Seraphine. TrJP
Waves rattling pebbles rocked me asleep. Recitative. Ronald McCuaig. PoAu-2
Waves surge higher still, The. Elegy: Ise Lamenting the Death of Empress Onshi. Lady Ise, *tr. by* Etsuko Terasaki *and* Irma Brandeis. BoWoP
Waves that were random. Ways of Seeing. William Stafford. SUW
Waves want/ to be wheels. Surf. Lillian Morrison. NTCP
Waving a Bough. Boris Pasternak, *tr. fr. Russian by* Babette Deutsch. TrJP
Waving Good-bye to My Father. Michael Blumenthal. DiL
Waving of a Hand, The. W. S. Merwin. DiL
Waving of the Corn, The. Sidney Lanier. AP
Wax. Winfield Townley Scott. ErPo
Waxen and the false grace of tulips, The. Elegy. G. S. Fraser. NeBP
Waxwings. Robert Francis. LCAP; NU
Way, The. Leslie Savage Clark. PGD
Way, The. Robert Creeley. AP; BoLoP; LiTM; NeAP; PPP
Way, The. Sidney Henry Morse. HBV-2
Way, The. Henry van Dyke. TRV
Way a child's hands stare through glass, The. The Sickness. Frederick Seidel. CoPo
Way a crow, The. Dust of Snow. Robert Frost. CMoP; MoShBr; OxBA; PAI; PDV; PrIm; RHPC; SoSe; TAP; TiPo; UnPo; WeW
Way a Ghost Dissolves, The. Richard Hugo. NoP
Way a tired Chippewa woman, The. Hush. David St. John. DiL; LCAP; MAYP
Way and the Way Things Are, The. Nila NorthSun. GP
Way at night these piping peepers, The. The Peepers in Our Meadow. Archibald MacLeish. NCSH
" 'Way back in eighty-two or three." The Dreadful Fate of Naughty Nate. John Kendrick Bangs. OBCA
Way Down, The. Philip Levine. NOBA
Way Down, The, *sel.* Jay MacPherson.
They Return. NOBC; PoA
Way down in Columbus, Georgia. Columbus Stockade Blues. Woody Guthrie. FSW
'Way Down in Cuba, *with music.* *Unknown.* AmSS
Way Down in Mexico. *Unknown.* CoSo
Way down in the bottom. Poor Little Johnny. *Unknown.* AmFP
Way down in the meadow where the lily first blows. Sweet Evelina. *Unknown.* FSW
Way down in yonders low valley, in some lonesome place. Pretty Saro. *Unknown.* AmFP
Way Down South. Daniel Webster Davis. *See* 'Weh Down Souf.
Way Down South. *Unknown.* EvOK; RHPC; SoPo
(Elephant and the Flea, The, *with music.*) TrAS
(Grasshopper and the Elephant, The.) OnUR
Way down South in Dixie. Song for a Dark Girl. Langston Hughes. AmPP; CDC; IDB; PoBA
Way down South in the land of cotton. Crazy Song to the Air of "Dixie." "Andy Lee." AS
Way down South where bananas grow. Way Down South [*or* The Elephant and the Flea *or* The Grasshopper and the Elephant]. *Unknown.* EvOK; OnUR; RHPC; SoPo; TrAS
Way down South where I was born. A Long Time Ago. *Unknown.* AmFP
Way down South where I was born. Roll the Cotton Down, *vers.* III. *Unknown.* ShS
Way Down the Ohio, *with music.* *Unknown.* TrAS
Way down upon the [*or* de] Swanee River [*or* ribber]. The Old Folks at Home. Stephen Collins Foster. AA; BLSo; FaBoBe; FaFP; FSW; HBV-2; PSoN; TreF; WBLP
Way down upon the Wabash. El-a-noy. *Unknown.* AS; FSW; TrAS
Way down yonder in the middle of the field. Let Me Fly. *Unknown.* FSW
Way enchased with glass and beads, A. The Temple. Robert Herrick. CaPo
Way feare with thy projectes, noe false fyre, A. William Alabaster. AnAnS-1
Way, hay, there she rises. Early in the Morning. *Unknown.* AmSS
Way her breasts meet is hidden from me, The. Old Fellow. Ernest Walsh. ErPo
Way high up in the Syree peaks. Tyin' a Knot in the Devil's Tail. Gail Gardner. FSW
'Way high up the Mogollons. The Glory Trail. Badger Clark. BPAW; PH
Way I gained my titles, The. Champagne Charlie. *At. to* George Leybourne. BLSo
Way I hear tell Aunt Jennie, The. Caledonia. Colleen J. McElroy. BlSi
Way I read a letter's—this, The. Emily Dickinson. InPS; WPE
Way I Was, The. Carol Lee Sanchez. TWSS
Way in which blackness appeals, The: it beckons, calls. Black. Nicholas Rinaldi. AMV-80
Way It Happens, The. Philip Dacey. LTB
Way It Is, The. Gloria C. Oden. CNA; IHMS
Way It Was, The. Lucille Clifton. WPE
Way My Ideas Think Me, The. José Garcia Villa. EaLo; TwAmPo
Way of Cape Race, The. E. J. Pratt. EtS; WHW
Way of It, The. John Vance Cheney. HBV-1
Way of Keeping, A. Nancy Willard. IHMS
Way of Life, A. Howard Nemerov. NIP
Way of Looking, A. Elizabeth Jennings. NePoEA; PP
Way of many ways, A: a god. Doctor Faustus. Geoffrey Hill. NePoEA-2; NMP
Way of Pain, The. Wendell Berry. AMV-80
Way of Perfect Love, The, *sel.* Georgiana Goddard King.
Song: "Something calls and whispers, along the city street." HBV-1
Way of Speaking, A. Gretel Ehrlich. MAYP
Way of the Air, The. Laura Riding. Three Sermons to the Dead, I. LiTA
Way of the World, The. Ella Wheeler Wilcox. *See* Solitude.
Way out in California. The Santa Barbara Earthquake. *Unknown.* AmFP
Way Out in Idaho ("Come all you jolly railroad men"). *Unknown.* AmFP; BPAW; OuSiCo, *with music*
Way Out in Idyho [*or* Idaho] ("Remember what I promised you"). *Unknown.* CoSo, *with music;* FSW
'Way out in Western Texas, where the Clear Fork's waters flow. The Cowboys' Christmas Ball. William Lawrence Chittenden. BPAW; CoSo
Way out upon the Platte, near Pike's Peak we were told. A Hit at the Times. A. O. McGrew. PoOW
Way Out West. Amiri Baraka. NeAP; NMP; PoBA
Way Out West. *Unknown.* CoSo
Way Over in the New Buryin' Groun', *with music.* *Unknown.* AS
Way Sun Keeps Falling Away from Every Window, The. Lyn Lifshin. NeAC
Way the Baby Slept, The. James Whitcomb Riley. AA
Way the Baby Woke, The. James Whitcomb Riley. AA
Way the ball, The. The Jump Shooter. Dennis Trudell. LiSp
Way the Bird Sat, The. Ray A. Young Bear. CDW; VoR
Way the buildings curve (as if a thought), The. Central Park South. Donald Revell. NYP
Way the cooked shoes sizzle, The. Amanda Is Shod. Maxine W. Kumin. PH
Way the earth stops at the wall, The. Honeysuckle. James Paul. HoAn
Way the hell-bent years consume my pleasure, The. Elegy. Pushkin, *tr. by* Robley Wilson, Jr. AMV-81
Way, the Truth, and the Life, The. Theodore Parker. HBV-2; TrPWD; TRV; WGRP
Way, The; the Truth; the Life. Samuel Judson Porter. BLRP
Way the word sinks into the deep snow of the page, The. Silence. Gregory Orr. GeTw
Way they do, The. Loo-wit. Wendy Rose. STE
Way Things Work, The. Jorie Graham. NPGG
Way Through, The. Denise Levertov. NeAP; PoM
Way through the Woods, The. Kipling. CH; FaBoCh; FaPON; MoVE; NOBE; OBEV; OBNC; OBVV; OxBChV; OxBTC; PoPle; RFM; SeCeV; VLP
Way to Arcady, The. H. C. Bunner. AA; InMe
Way to call up quick wishes. On Seeing a Torn Out Coin Telephone. Martin Robbins. MAT
Way to Heaven, The. Charles Goodrich Whiting. AA
Way to Hump a Cow [Is Not], The. E. E. Cummings. NoAM; NOBA; OxBA
Way to Live, The. *Unknown.* VLP

Way to Make a Living, A. James Wright. NNaP
Way to the River, The. W. S. Merwin. CoAP; NYBP
Way to the Sea, The. Laurence Lerner. NePoEA-2
Way Up on Clinch Mountain. *Unknown. See* Rye Whiskey.
Way up on de mountain, Lord! Up on de Mountain. *Unknown.* BoAN-1
Way Up on Old Smoky. *Unknown. See* On Top of Old Smoky.
Way up yonder in the sky. Buckeye Jim. *Unknown.* FSW
Way was long, the wind was cold, The. The Last Minstrel. Sir Walter Scott. *Fr.* The Lay of the Last Minstrel. TreFS
Way We Live Now, The. Robert Dana. AMV-80
Way We Wonder, The. Robert Pack. NePoEA
Wayah, we'll pay Paddy Doyle for his boots! Paddy Doyle. *Unknown.* ShS
Wayfarer, The. Stephen Crane. War Is Kind, XIII. LiTA; MoAmPo; NePA
("Wayfarer, The/ Perceiving the pathway to truth.") AmPP
Wayfarer, The. Padraic Pearse. OxBI
Wayfarers. Dana Burnet. EtS
Wayfarers in the Wilderness, *with music.* Alexander R. Thompson. AH
Wayfaring man though a fool, The. Though a Fool. Robert Francis. GP
Wayfaring Stranger. *Unknown. See* Poor Wayfaring Stranger.
Wayman in Love. Tom Wayman. NIP; NOBC
Wayne at Stony Point. Clinton Scollard. PAH
Ways, The. John Oxenham. HBMV; PoLF; TRV
Ways and Means. "Lewis Carroll." *See* White Knight's Song.
Ways and the Peoples, The. Randall Jarrell. PoA
Ways o' Men, The. Angelina Weld Grimké. CDC
Ways of Day. Robert Penn Warren. *Fr.* Notes on a Life to Be Lived. NoAM
Ways of God to Men, The. Milton. *Fr.* Samson Agonistes. OBS
("Many are the sayings of the wise.") SeCeV
Ways of Living Things, The. Jack Prelutsky. RHPC
Ways of Loving. Theodore Weiss. GP
Ways of Pronouncing "Ough." *Unknown.* FaBoUs
Ways of Seeing. William Stafford. SUW
Ways of Trains, The. Elizabeth J. Coatsworth. SoPo; TiPo
Ways of War. Lionel Johnson. AnIV
Wayside, The. James Herbert Morse. AA
Wayside Station, The. Edwin Muir. FaBoTw; MoVE
Wayside Virgin, The. Langdon Elwyn Mitchell. AA
Way-Side Well, The. Joseph S. Cotter, Sr. CDC; PoNe
Wayzgoose, The, *sel.* Roy Campbell.
"Attend my fable if your ears be clean." OBSV
Waz, adverse to thinking. No Bargains Today. Peggy Susberry Kenner. JB
Wazir Dandan for Prince Sharkan, The. *Unknown, tr. fr. Arabic by* E. Powys Mathers. *Fr.* The Thousand and One Nights. AWP
We/ little children in our shifts. Clap Your Hands for Herod. Josef Hanzlik, *tr. by* Ian Milner. OBCP
We all—/ stones, people, little shards of glass in the sun. Text. Aaron Zeitlin, *tr. by* Ruth Whitman. VWA
We all dazed—down by ocean, gold in jingles, inhalexhale all around. We Heart. Laura Chester. NPGG
We all go to the bones. Wenberi's Song. Wenberi, *tr. by* A. W. Howitt. CBAP
We all have/ A bench in the park to reach. George Jonas. NeAC
We all have our faults. Mine is trying to write poems. Singing Aloud. Carolyn Kizer. IHMS
We all heard the alarm. The planes were out. The Second Dream. Jean Valentine. LCAP
We all look on with anxious eyes. When Father Carves the Duck. Ernest Vincent Wright. BLPL; FaBV; FaFP; NTCP; PoLF; PoSC; TreF
We all must work with what we have. A Vegetarian Sings. Audrey Conard. AMV-81
We all scream, most of us inside. A Screamer Discusses Methods of Screaming. James Schevill. TAP
We all were watching the quiz on television. A Singular Metamorphosis. Howard Nemerov. ConAP
We always had to do our work at night. Before Action. Leon Gellert. CBAP
We always love the cradle. Rockingchair. Robert Morgan. PPJ
We always ran out when we heard it come. The Six-Horse Limited Mail. Ethel Romig Fuller. BPAW
We Am Clim'in' Jacob's Ladder, *with music.* *Unknown.* BoAN-1
(Jacob's Ladder.) FSW
We and the little cheerful goldfinch. Two Angels. Richard Monckton Milnes. OBRV
We are/ sorry to have to. You Understand the Requirements. Lyn Lifshin. NeAC
We are a band of brothers, and native to the soil. The Bonnie Blue Flag. Harry Macarthy. BLSo; PSoN
We are a garden wall'd around. The Church the Garden of Christ. Isaac Watts. NOCV
We are a little frightened of each other. An Afternoon in the Garden. Murray Edmond. OCNZ
We are a meadow where the bees hum. Bedtime. Denise Levertov. IHMS; NaP; TwCP
We are a part of this rough land. Our Heritage. Jesse Stuart. AmFN
We Are a People. Lance Henson. VoR
We are a people living in shells and moving. The British. A. S. J. Tessimond. ChMP
We Are Acrobats. Jozef Habib Gerez, *tr. fr. Turkish by* Musa Moris Farhi *and* Anthony Rudolf. VWA
We are all blind until we see. Man-making. Edwin Markham. PGD
We are all here. The Family Meeting. Charles Sprague. HBV-2
We are all in the dumps. *Unknown.* OxNR
We are all near to death. But in my friends. One Who Watches. Siegfried Sassoon. TrJP
We are all of us dreamers of dreams. Dreamer of Dreams. William Herbert Carruth. PoLF
We are all rushing nowhere. Who of Those Coming After. Darcy Gottlieb. AMV-81
We Are All Workmen. Rainer Maria Rilke, *tr. fr. German by* Babette Deutsch. EaLo
We are already on the moon. Vacuum. Josephine Miles. MOON
We are approaching sleep: the chestnut blossoms in the mind. Awakening. Robert Bly. ConAP; NaP
We are as clouds that veil the midnight moon. Mutability. Shelley. TEP
We are as mendicants who wait. The Mendicants. Bliss Carman. HBV-1
We are asleep under mirrors. What do I. Before the War. Marilyn Hacker. AmPA
We are at the hauling then hoping for it. W. S. Graham. *Fr.* The Nightfishing. BSV
We are being born again. For My Wife. Steven Lautermilch. AMV-80
We Are Brethren A'. Robert Nicoll. HBV-2
We are bringing back some canceled notes. Dividends. Hubert Creekmore. WaP
We Are Building a Strong Union. *Unknown.* FSW
We are building in sorrow or joy. Building for Eternity. N. B. Sargent. BLPA
We are burning/ in our heads. A Poet Recognizing the Echo of the Voice. Diane Wakoski. NIP
We are but a bleary blink. Recessional for the Class of 1959 of a School for Delinquent Negro Girls. Joseph R. Cowen. PoNe
"We are but clay," the preacher saith. Clay. E. V. Lucas. HBV-1
We are but two—the others sleep. The Brothers. Charles Sprague. AA
We are children of the sun. Children of the Sun. Fenton Johnson. BANP
We are climbing Jacob's ladder. *See* We Am Clim'in' Jacob's Ladder.
"We are closer than/ blood." Noni Daylight Remembers the Future. Joy Harjo. TWSS
We are come to dream, this reality. Open Dream Sequence. Carol Lee Sanchez. TWSS
We are coming, Cuba—coming; out starry banner shines. The Gathering. Herbert B. Swett. PAH
We are coming, Father Abraham, three hundred thousand more. Three Hundred Thousand More. James Sloan Gibbons. PAH
We are continually bored with the air. It's in the Egg. Joe Rosenblatt. NOBC
We are croaking as does the frog. We Object. *Tr. fr. Maori by* A. Armstrong. WTO
We are done with little thinking. The Bigger Day. G. E. Bishop. WBLP
We are drinking from one another. Drinking. Virginia R. Terris. FAZ
We are driving through South Dakota. Primer Lesson. Mark Vinz. TAT
We are far from what held us then. First Winter. Gail N. Harada. BrSi
We are festive weepers, etching names on every stone. In the Old City. Yehuda Amichai, *tr. by* Laya Firestone *and* Howard Schwartz. VWA
We are fishermen in a flat scene. Water. Anne Sexton. CoPo
We Are Four Bums, *with music.* *Unknown.* AS
We are ghost-ridden. The Dead Moon. Danske Bedinger Dandridge. AA
We are glad to have birds in our roof. Against Death. Peter Redgrove. NMP
We are God's chosen few. Swift. TRV
We Are Going. Kath Walker. CBAP
We are going down a long slide. Shirley Kaufman. BoWoP
We are hypnotized by the flash of sun. Sleeping at the Beach. Lucile Burt. AMV-81
We are in love's land to-day. Love at Sea. Swinburne, *after* Théophile Gautier. AWP; HBV-1
We are in Wieser, Idaho. Home Cooking Cafe. Greg Field. FAZ; PPJ
We are keeping an eye on the girls, so that the kvass. Marina Tsvetayeva, *tr. fr. Russian by* Elaine Feinstein *and* Angela Livingstone. PBWP
We are landless dream farmers. Dream Farmer. Jill Witherspoon Boyer. CNA

We are large with pity, slow and awkward. False Country of the Zoo. Jean Garrigue. LiTM; MP
We Are Leaning Away. Gayle Elen Harvey. AMV-80
We are led on. Juvenal, *tr. by* L. R. Lind. *Fr.* The Satires. PoPl
We are light. Laughter. Miriam Waddington. WHW
We are little airy creatures. On the Vowels—a Riddle. Swift. FaBoUs; GN; OnYI
We are living, we are dwelling. The Present Age. Arthur Cleveland Coxe. BLPA; TRV
We are lovely people. You Lovely People. Virginia Cerenio. BrSi
We are lovers/ after our fashion. The Dancer from the Dance. Suzanne Juhasz. IHMS
We are made of angle-iron and crossbrace. Homage to David Smith. John Haines. LCAP
We are na fou, we're nae that fou. Willie Brew'd a Peck o' Maut. Burns. EnRP
We are near, Lord. Tenebrae. Paul Celan, *tr. by* Joachim Neugroschel. VWA
We are never free of the voices. The Voices Inescapable. Ann Stanford. IHMS
We are not come to wage a strife. The Day-Breakers [*or* Daybreakers]. Arna Bontemps. AmNP; CDC; IDB; PoBA; PoNe
We are not going to steal the water tower. Stopping Near Highway 80. David Ray. TAT
We are not lovers. Man and Wife. Anne Sexton. CAPP
We are not the first. Shakespeare. *Fr.* King Lear, V, iii. PoPle
We are not wholly blest who use the earth. Charles Mair. *Fr.* Dreamland. CaP
We are nude beneath our costumes. The Metaphysical Paintings. John Perreault. EAS
We are old friends. Hunger. Charles Simic. NNaP
We Are on Our Journey Home, *with music.* *Unknown.* AH
We are our fathers' sons: let those who lead us know! No Hint of Stain. William Vaughan Moody. *Fr.* An Ode in Time of Hesitation. AA
We are our poems, their summation. Pushed to the Scroll. Winifred Hamrick Farrar. AMV-80
We are prepared: we build our houses squat. Storm on the Island. Seamus Heaney. NCSH
We are quite sure. He Will Give Them Back. "George Klingle." BLRP
We are resting here in the twilight. Compline. Duncan Campbell Scott. GoBC
We are rising, growing. Kneading. Barbara Crooker. SOTS
We Are Seven. Wordsworth. BLPA; BLPL; EnRP; GN; HBV-1; OxBChV; SpRo; TEP; TreF; WBLP
We are seven virgins. Seven lamps. There Is a Dream Dreaming Us. Norman Dubie. GeTw
We are sighing for you, far land. The Far Land. John Hall Wheelock. WGRP
We are singing for the face of cisco. Songs for the Cisco Kid; or, Singing for the Face. K. Curtis Lyle. PoBA
We are so tired; my heart and I. Rest. Mathilde Blind. SBG
We are sons of mighty Manitou. The Red Ghosts Chant. Lilian White Spencer. PoOW
We are sorry to inform you. In Answer to Your Query. Naomi Lazard. GP
We are sorry we cannot use the enclosed. Form Rejection Letter. Philip Dacey. AmPA
We are souls in hell, who hear no gradual music. A Prayer from 1936. Siegfried Sassoon. TrPWD
We are squared off in the snow. Brothers Together in Winter. Harley Elliott. NeAC
We Are Standing Facing Each Other. Margaret Atwood. NeAC; PAI
We Are Such Stuff as Dreams. Petronius Arbiter, *tr. fr. Latin by* Howard Mumford Jones. AWP
We are talking in bed. You show me snapshots. A Family Man. Maxine W. Kumin. IHMS; TAP
We are the Akhail. Our youth persists. Laila Boasting. Laila Akhyaliyya, *tr. by* Willis Barnstone. BoWoP
We are the Ancient People. The Song of the Ancient People. Edna Dean Proctor. AA
We are the birds always charmed by you. Postman Cheval. André Breton, *tr. by* David Gascoyne. EAS
We Are the Burden-Bearers! *abr.* William L. Stidger. PGD
"We are the dead," we shouted up in fun. Glen Lough. Goeffrey Grigson. FaBoPP
We are the desperate. Vagabonds. Langston Hughes. SaC
We are the fallen, who, with helpless faces. The Prayer of Beaten Men. William Hervey Woods. *Fr.* The House of Broken Swords. HBV-2
We are the frogs who will not turn to princes. Rebels from Fairy Tales. Hyacinthe Hill. DFT; SO
We are the hollow men. The Hollow Men. T. S. Eliot. AP; BiP; CoBMV; InPS; LiTA; LiTM; MoAB; MoAmPo; OAEL-2; OBMV; PoPl; TwAmPo
We are the lovers of Local 1. Theme Song for a Songwriters' Union. Al Graham. WhC
We are the music-makers. Ode [*or* The Music Makers]. Arthur O'Shaughnessy. FaBV; FaPoR; HBV-2; OBEV; OBVV; OnYI; OxBI; TreF; TrGrPo; ViBiPo; VLP; WHA
We are the only ones who will remember. Secret. Catherine Haydon Jacobs. GoYe
We are the poor children, come out to see the sights. The Carol of the Poor Children. Richard Middleton. OBCP
We are the precious chosen few. Predestination. *Unknown.* DBV
We are the roadside flowers. Roadside Flowers. Bliss Carman. HBMV
We are the same in our despair. Raymond R. Patterson. *Fr.* Riot Rhymes U.S.A. GP
We are the singing shadows beauty casts. Clement Wood. Eagle Sonnets, XX. HBMV
We are the toilers whom God hath barred. The Song of the Unsuccessful. Richard Burton. WGRP
We are the troop that ne'er will stoop. Pennsylvania Song. *Unknown.* PAH
We are the weavers. Macramé. Michael D. Riley. AMV-81
We are they who come faster than fate. War Song of the Saracens. James Elroy Flecker. *Fr.* Hassan. FaBV; MoBrPo; OBVV; WHA
We are thine, O Love, being in thee and made of thee. Hymn to Love. Lascelles Abercrombie. OBEV; OBVV
We are things of dry hours and the involuntary plan. Kitchenette Building. Gwendolyn Brooks. BALP; BPo; FF; NoP; PoNe; UnPo
We are those same children who amazed. Prelude XXIII. Stefan George, *tr. by* C. F. MacIntyre. WaaP
We Are Three Brethren Come from [*or* out of] Spain. *Unknown.* *See* Three Kinghts from Spain.
We are three women eating out. Crêpes Flambeau. Tess Gallagher. AMV-81; MAYP
We are tied to Mars' tail. The previous days. The Captain. Blanca Varela, *tr. by* Lynne Alvarez. WPOW
We are tired of your tiresome imitations of Mayakovsky. Answer to Voznesensky & Evtushenko. Frank O'Hara. HoAn; NNaP; PoM
We are told of a white flower. The Swarthmore Phi Beta Kappa Poem. Richmond Lattimore. GLGT
We are trained and quiet intellectuals. On Being Invited to a Testimonial Dinner. William Stafford. NePoAm-2
We Are Transmitters. D. H. Lawrence. OxBTC
We are travelling west of Alice Springs, and Sam is at the wheel. West of Alice. W. E. Harney. PoAu-1
We are trying to carry this timber to the building. Timber. *Unknown.* AS
We are turned to the sun. Evening Ceremony; Dream for G. V. Wendy Rose. TWSS
We are two countries girded for the war. Foreign Affairs. Stanley Kunitz. LiTM; NYBP; TwAmPo
We are two eagles. The Flight. Sara Teasdale. WHA
We are two travelers, Roger and I. The Vagabonds. John Townsend Trowbridge. AA; BeLS; BLPA; TreFS
We are unfair. We Own the Night. Amiri Baraka. BOLo; PoBA
We are used to the murmur. Engine Failure. Timothy Corsellis. WaP
We are very slightly changed. A General Summary. Kipling. HBV-1
We are waltzing now into the moonlit morning. Waltz against the Mountains. Thomas Hornsby Ferril. VGW
We are watching our old aunts. Indian Summer, 1927. Anne Hussey. AMV-81
We Are Watching, We Are Waiting, *with music.* William O. Cushing. AH
We are what suns and winds and waters make us. Walter Savage Landor. *Fr.* Regeneration. ViBoPo
We are what we hear. A well known singer died. Langaig. Richard Hugo. WOLT
We are with one another. No Smiles. Frank Lamont Phillips. AmNP
We are women of different origins. For Mariella, in Antrona. Tobey A. Simpson. AMV-80
We are your people. For the Queen Mother. John Betjeman. NAs
We artists have strange nerves! In a Hotel Writing-Room. John Cowper Powys. OxBTC
We ask for peace. We, at the bound. Surrender. Angelina Weld Grimké. CDC
We ask not that the slave should lie. Abolitionist Hymn. *Unknown.* TrAS
We Assume: On the Death of Our Son, Reuben Masai Harper. Michael S. Harper. AmPA; DiL; GeTw; LCAP
We ate our breakfast lying on our backs. Breakfast. W. W. Gibson. OBMV; OxBTC
We ate with steeps of sky about our shoulders. The Terrace. Richard Wilbur. MiAP
We Be Soldiers Three. *Unknown.* ChTr; GBP

We be the King's men, hale and hearty. Men Who March Away. Thomas Hardy. *Fr.* The Dynasts, Pt. I. CH
We Be Three Poor Mariners, *with music.* *Unknown.* AmSS
We Bear about No Cats' Skins. *Unknown.* NCEP
We bear sealed orders o'er life's weltered sea. Sealed Orders. Richard Burton. HBV-2
We Bear the Strain of Earthly Care. Ozora S. Davis. TRV
We Become New. Marge Piercy. TAP
We began this conversation in the spring. Becoming Real. Barry Goldensohn. AMV-81
We being so hidden from those who. The Children Look at the Parents. A. S. J. Tessimond. ChMP
We believe books and music. Words from the Window of a Railway Car. Anatoly Steiger, *tr. by* John Glad. VWA
We bern abowtyn non cattes skynnys. We Bear about No Cats' Skins. *Unknown.* NCEP
We bought him at auction, tranquillized to a drooping halt. Clancy. David Wagoner. PH
We break the glass, whose sacred wine. Song. Edward Coote Pinkney. AA; HBV-1
We Bring No Glittering Treasures, *with music.* Harriet C. Phillips. AH
We brush the other, invisible moon. Sleep. William Knott. EAS
We brushed our hair back and our. The Last Refuge. Augustus Young. BIrV
We built a palace for them, made of bedrooms. R-and-R Centre: An Incident from the Vietnam War. D. J. Enright. OxBC
We built a ship upon the stairs. A Good Play. Robert Louis Stevenson. FaPON; MoShBr; TiPo
We buried him darkly at dead of night. Paul Dehn. *Fr.* A Leaden Treasury of English Verse. DBV; PV
We buried of our dead the dearest one. Dulce et Decorum? Elinor Jenkins. SUMH
We but begin to hope to know, having known. Subject. Marie Ponsot. VGW
We call up the green to hide us. Summer Wish. Louise Bogan. TwAmPo
We call you Mother of our Lord and Savior. Hymn for Laudes; Feast of Our Lady, Help of Christians. *Unknown, tr. by* Sister Maura. ISi
We called him "Rags." He was just a cur. Rags. Edmund Vance Cooke. BLPA
We called you Grandma Lupton. To Shimá Sání. Laura Tohe. STE
We came by boat in the late arctic twilight. Visit by Water. Floris Clark McLaren. OBCV
We came for luck. The Last Resort. Robert Willson. FAZ
We came out through the high doors, our heads. A Prospect of Swans. Dorothy Donnelly. HoAn
We came to Tamichi in 1880. Song. Scott Judy *and* "Doc" Hammond. PoOW
We came to the edge. A Pretty Woman. Simon J. Ortiz. CDW
We came to the high cliffs of Bonaventure. Long-billed Gannets. Frances D. Emery. GoYe
We came to the islands. We came saying. The Quest. Harold Vinal. GoYe
We came to the outer light down a ramp in the dark. Westland Row. Thomas Kinsella. NoAM
We came to visit the cow. Freedom, New Hampshire. Galway Kinnell. LCAP; NaP
We came upon him sitting in the sun. The Veteran. Margaret Postgate Cole. SUMH
We can endure the eyes. At the Jewish Museum. Linda Pastan. VWA
We can go on a hundred years. The Pilot's Walk. Lee Gerlach. HoAn
We can no longer stay on shore. The Greenland Whale Fishery. *Unknown.* BaBo
We can only see a little of the ocean. God's Love. *Unknown.* BLRP
We can slide down the hill. Sliding. Myra Cohn. SiSoSe
We cannot go to the country. Raleigh Was Right. William Carlos Williams. NoAM; PP
We cannot kindle when we will. Morality. Matthew Arnold. HBV-2; TRV
We cannot rest, whose hearts are like the breakers. Architects of Dream. Lucia Trent. PGD
We cannot retrace our steps. Gertrude Stein. *Fr.* The Mother of Us All. CrMA
We cannot trap them in our zoos, oh, no! Dinosaurs. Carolyn Stoloff. NYBP
We cannot walk like Byron among Ayasoluk's ruined. The Pleasure of Ruins. J. D. McClatchy. PoA
We can't give them up, though. Avant Garde. Louis Dudek. *Fr.* Provincetown. MoCV
We can't tonight! We're overworked and busy. Tonight. Franklin P. Adams. FiBHP
We Cared for Each Other. Heine, *tr. fr. German by* John Todhunter. AWP
We caroused. I Met This Guy Who Died. Gregory Corso. NAs; Psk
We Carry Eggshells. Hanny Michaelis, *tr. fr. Dutch by* Marjolijn de Jager. VWA
We caught the tread of dancing feet. The Harlot's House. Oscar Wilde. EBVV; InPK; MoBrPo; SyP
We chanced in passing by that afternoon. The Black Cottage. Robert Frost. VGW
We climb'd the steep where headless Edwin lies. The Old Parish Church, Whitby. Hardwick Drummond Rawnsley. OBVV
We climbed the dark. We. The Island. George Woodcock. MoCV
We climbed to the very top that August day. Castle Rock. Frederick Morgan. AMV-81
We cobblers lead a merry life. The Cobbler's Song. *At. to* Charles Tilney. *Fr.* Locrine. OBSC
We come by a terrible gate. Eden: Or One View of It. Theodore Spencer. NePA
We come here tourist on a bad sky day. Cataldo Mission. Richard Hugo. FAZ
We come on the sloop *John B. John B.* Sails. *Unknown.* FSW
We come to another place. Mathematics. Joel Oppenheimer. CoPo
We come to uncrate the newness of this world. First Things. Lucienne Desnoues, *tr. by* Miller Williams. WPOW
We come together once more, we four, in the center. Head Couples. William H. Matchett. NYBP
We come! we come! to fill our graves. William B. Tappan. *Fr.* Song of the Three Hundred Thousand Drunkards in the United States. PeD
We Conquer or Die. James Pierpont. PAH
We Continue. W. S. Merwin. CAPP
We could be going home. The Second Angel. Philip Levine. NaP
We could get the whole town out on a Tuesday night. Summer Concert. Reed Whittemore. AmFN
We could have crossed the road but hesitated. The Interrogation. Edwin Muir. CMoP; LiTB; SeCePo
We could not ignore the sky in those days. Before the War. James Pendergast. AMV-81
We could not pause, while yet the noontide air. Obsequies of Stuart. John Randolph Thompson. PAH
We couldn't even keep the furnace lit! To Delmore Schwartz. Robert Lowell. NMP; NoAM
We count the broken lyres that rest. The Voiceless. Oliver Wendell Holmes. *Fr.* The Autocrat of the Breakfast Table. AA; ViBoPo
We crave your condescension. The Mulligan Guard. Ned Harrigan. BLSo
We crawled and cried and laughed. Autobiography. Mbella Sonne Dipoko. TTY
We crazed for you, aspired and fell for you. The Knights to Chrysola. Rachel Annand Taylor. OBVV
We cried: Good luck! and watched them go. The Last Ascent. John Lehmann. ChMP
We cross a stream and my horse. Under the Frontier Post. Wang Chang-ling, *tr. by* Rewi Alley. ChTr
We cross the prairie as of old. The Kansas Emigrants. Whittier. PAH
We crossed the broad Pecos, we forded the Nueces. The Brazos River. *Unknown.* PrIm
We curl into your eyes. The Female God. Isaac Rosenberg. FaBoTw
We cut into dead bodies for heat. Cutting Wood on Shell Creek. Gretel Ehrlich. MAYP
We Dance Like Ella Riffs. Carolyn M. Rodgers. CNA; PoBA
We dance round in a ring and suppose. The Secret Sits. Robert Frost. InPK; SoPo
We dance without passion but the movement. Waltz. Heather Tosteson Reich. AMV-80
We Delighted, My Friend. Léopold Sédar Senghor, *tr. fr. French by* Miriam Koshland. PBA; TTY
We descended the first night from Europe. Coming Back to America. James Dickey. NYBP; NYP
We deserved that earth-shot from the. Views of Our Sphere. Ernest Sandeen. MOON
We Did It. Yehuda Amichai, *tr. fr. Hebrew by* Harold Schimmel. BoLoP
We didn't think/ nuthin. Poems about Playmates. Ronda Davis. JB
We died in Zortman on a Sunday. The Renegade Wants Words. James Welch. CDW
We digged our trenches on the down. Song of the Dark Ages. Francis Brett Young. HBMV
We do accept thee, heavenly Peace! Acceptation. Margaret Junkin Preston. PAH
We do assemble that a funeral. An Elegy in Memory of the Worshipful Major Thomas Leonard Esq. Samuel Danforth, Jr. SCAP
We do lie beneath the grass. Dirge [*or* Sibilla's Dirge *or* Sybilla's Dirge]. Thomas Lovell Beddoes. *Fr.* Death's Jest Book. ELP; NBM; NOBE; OBNC; WiR
We do not know who made them. Negro Spirituals. Rosemary *and* Stephen Vincent Benét. AmFN; FaPON
We do not play on graves. Emily Dickinson. MoVE; NIP; PoEL-5

We do not see them come. Scala Coeli. Kathleen Raine. NYBP
We do not wish anything to happen. Chorus. T. S. Eliot. *Fr.* Murder in the Cathedral. OxBTC
We Don't Get No Justice Here in Atlanta, *with music. Unknown.* OuSiCo
We don't have much language for tragedy. Autumn. Thomas W. Shapcott. CBAP
We don't know. Land of the Free. Archibald MacLeish. AmFN
We don't know the ins and outs. The Wall. David Jones. PoA
We don't lack people here on the Northern coast. Amusing Our Daughters. Carolyn Kizer. VGW
We don't like that girl from Tooting Bec. *Unknown.* FaBoUs
We don't like your white cottage. Strangers. R. S. Thomas. NMP
We dream—it is good we are dreaming. Emily Dickinson. BoWoP
We dressed each other. Empress Eifuku, *tr. fr. Japanese by* Kenneth Rexroth. WPOW
We drive between lakes just turning green. Driving through Minnesota during the Hanoi Bombings. Robert Bly. NoP
We drive this Sunday south into the country. Baptism. Charles G. Bell. AmFN
We drove as far east as we could. Bar Harbor. Marita Garin. AMV-81
We drove far up into the canyon. Spring Catch. Greg Keeler. WOLT
We drove—our autoload gang—through the growing season. Rogue Pearunners. R. G. Everson. PeCV
We drove south from Burwash Landing. At White River. John Haines. FiCP
"We dwell in Him,"oh, everlasting Home. In Him. Annie Johnson Flint. BLRP; TRV
We ease Joe down and kick in. Skyhook. Gary Allan Kizer. LFAC
We eat and drink and laugh and energize. Death's Transfiguration. Israel Zangwill. TrJP
We edge the boat in tight among stumps. The Limits of Departure. Bruce Weigl. AMV-81
We enter the dismal wood where boughs black. The Wood of the Self-Destroyers. Samuel Yellen. NePoAm-2
We entered the city at noon! High bells. The radio on. One Night Stand. Amiri Baraka. NeAP
"We even had a swing band in our parade." The Late Show. Janet Sylvester. MAYP
We face the nations with one hand outstretched. Armistice. Eunice Mitchell Lehmer. PGD
We fear to judge a watermelon. A Comparison. *Unknown.* STF
We feed the birds in winter. Joe. David McCord. TiPo
We feel more than we see of the winter. An Unseen Fire. Michael G. Cooke. AMV-81
We fell in love at "Journey for Margaret." First Love. Judith Hemschemeyer. Psk
We few, we happy few, we band of brothers. Shakespeare. King Henry V, *fr.* IV, iii. UnPo
We fight. I am clubbed from behind. They pin me. Terminal Theater. Robert Sward. CoPo
We finished clearing the last. Above Pate Valley. Gary Snyder. CoAP; ConAP; LCAP; NaP; NoP
We fished close by the bank. No Idle Boast. Edward C. Lynskey. WOLT
We five owls were once alive. From a Printed Bill, Fixed in the Beak of One in a Group of Five Stuffed Owls in the Shop Window of a Bird Stuffer, at Richmond, Yorkshire. *Unknown.* FaBoUs
We fled from the sight inland and that night. Columbus Reaches Juana, 1492. Ralph Gustafson. NOBC
We flee away from cities, but we bring. Emerson. *Fr.* The Adirondacs. GLGT
We flung gravel out in arcs then cut. Before Breakup on the Chena outside Fairbanks. David McElroy. Psk
We fluttered from the ridge. Lochan. Roger Smith. PoSH
We follow where the Swamp Fox guides. The Swamp Fox. William Gilmore Simms. AA; BeLS; FaBoBe; PAH
We followed her unto the chamber-door. The Palace of Pleasant Regard. Lady of the Assembly. *Fr.* The Assembly of Ladies. WPE
We followed them into the west. The West. Edwin Muir. MoVE
We Fooled Ourselves. Jozef Habib Gerez, *tr. fr. Turkish by* Musa Moris Farhi *and* Anthony Rudolf. VWA
We found dead animals in our sagebrush hills. Dobbin. George Bowering. NOBC
We found him there on the desert. Bones in the Desert. Ned White. BPAW
We found some truth in the wet wood. Rain. John Haines. NPAW
We Free Singers Be. Etheridge Knight. FAZ
We from childhood play'd together. Comrades. Felix McGlennon. FSN
We galloped over the glossy sea. W. B. Yeats. *Fr.* The Wanderings of Oisin. SeCePo
We gather together to ask the Lord's blessing. Prayer of Thanksgiving. *Unknown, tr. by* Theodore Baker. BLSo
We gazed on Corryvrekin's whirl. Iona. Arthur Cleveland Coxe. AA
We get no good/ By being ungenerous. Reading. Elizabeth Barrett Browning. *Fr.* Aurora Leigh. GN
We Give Thee but Thine Own. William Walsham How. STF
We give Thee thanks, O Lord! Thanksgiving Day. Robert Bridges. OHIP
We Go. Karl Wolfskehl, *tr. fr. German.* TrJP, *tr. by* Carol North Valhope *and* Ernst Morwitz; VWA, *tr. by* Harry Zohn
We go back. Proclamation/ From Sleep, Arise. Carolyn M. Rodgers. JB
We go into it at night. The Orchard. Gretel Ehrlich. MAYP
We go no more to Calverly's. Calverly's. E. A. Robinson. NoAM
We go out in the stony midnight. Thomas McGrath. Letter to an Imaginary Friend, Part One, VIII, 4. NNaP
We Go Out Together. Kenneth Patchen. MoAmPo
We got away—for just two nights. To Be a Pilgrim. Robert Conquest. OxBC
We got sunlight on the sand. There Is Nothin' like a Dame. Oscar Hammerstein II. OBAL
We got this idea. Our Hands in the Garden. Anne Hébert, *tr. by* A. Poulin, Jr. BoWoP
"We grasp our battle spears: we don our breast-plates of hide." See "We hold our flat shields, we wear our jerkins of hide."
We Greet Each Other in the Side, *abr. Unknown.* BXAP; PeD
We grow to the sound of the wind. Dates. *Unknown, tr. by* E. Powys Mathers. *Fr.* The Thousand and One Nights. AWP; FaPON
We had a parade for the lady near Livorno. Snapshot: Ambassadress. George Garrett. NePoAm-2
We had a picnic. A Picnic. Aileen Fisher. SoPo
We had been in the tall grass for hours. At Midsummer. Norman Dubie. MAYP
We had been long in mountain snow. The Greeting of the Roses. Hamlin Garland. AA
We had better conserve our water. Inadequate Aqua Extremis. Ruth M. Walsh. QQQ
We had expected everything but revolt. Nightmare Number Three. Stephen Vincent Benét. MoAmPo; SaC
We had forgotten You, or very nearly. Christ in Flanders. Lucy Whitmell. SUMH
We had more than/ we could use. Words. Vern Rutsala. GP
We had red earth once to smear on our cheeks. Arrowy Dreams. Witter Bynner. GOA
We had the notion it was dawn. Five. Weldon Kees. PPP
We had to make catalogues. Patience. Bartola Cattafi, *tr. by* Rina Ferrarelli. AMV-81
We had to take the world as it was given. Ideal Landscape. Adrienne Rich. NoAM
We had to wait for the heat to pass. August Night. Elizabeth Madox Roberts. YeAr
We had waffles-with-syrup for breakfast. Birthdays. Marchette Chute. SiSoSe
We hang the holly up once more. Christmas Singing. Elsie Williams Chandler. SiSoSe
We have/ a map of the universe. Wings. Miroslav Holub, *tr. by* Ian Milner *and* George Theiner. SUW
We have a bed, and a baby too. The Laborer. Richard Dehmel, *tr. by* Jethro Bithell. AWP
We have a dear old daddy. Father's Whiskers. *Unknown.* FSW
We have a dog named "Here." Birthday. William Stafford. NAs
We have a lawn of moss. For Doreen. Donald Davie. NMP
We have a mountain at the end of our street. In a Desert Town. Lionel Stevenson. AmFN
We have a pretty witty King. Impromptu on Charles II. Earl of Rochester. ChTr
We have a secret, just we three. The Secret. *Unknown.* SoPo; TiPo
We have all been in rooms. Adultery. James Dickey. CAPP; TAP
We have all, one time or another, met a famous figure. Back Room Joys. Justin Richardson. FiBHP
We have an old mother that peevish is grown. The Mother Country. Benjamin Franklin. PAH
We have ascended to this paradise. The Attic. Henri Coulette. NePoEA-2; PoPl; PoRA
We have bathed, where none have seen us. Bridal Song to Amala [*or* Epithalamia *or* Song *or* Songs at Amala's Wedding]. Thomas Lovell Beddoes. *Fr.* Death's Jest Book. ChER; FaBoEn; GBL; LoBV; OBNC; OBVV; PoEL-4
We have been a walking. Wassail Song. *Unknown.* GBP
We Have Been Believers. Margaret Walker. PoBA; PoNe
We have been helping with the cake. Day before Christmas. Marchette Chute. NTCP
We Have Been Here Before. Morris Bishop. EvOK; FiBHP; InMe; NYBP; WhC
We have been on trial for our life for so many years. On the Jewish Day of Judgment in the Year 1942 (5703). Jozef Wittlin, *tr. by* Isaac Komem. VWA

We have been sailing in a certain small fountain. About This Course. David Shapiro. PoA
We have been shown. Six Variations. Denise Levertov. AmPP; ConAP; CoPo; LCAP
We have borne good sons to broken men. Miners' Wives. Joe Corrie. OxBS
We have climbed the mountain. Here in Katmandu. Donald Justice. CoAP; ConAP; HeIP; LiSp; NIP; RFM
We have come in the winter. Song for a Country Wedding. William Jay Smith. GrPl
We have come to the edge of the woods. Jacklight. Louise Erdrich. TWSS
We have come to the jungle. Jungle. Phyllis Haring. PeSA
We have come to your shrine to worship. A Plea for Mercy. Kwesi Brew. PBA
We have cried in our despair. When Helen Lived. W. B. Yeats. CMoP; ViBoPo
We have done with dogma and divinity. After Trinity. John Meade Falkner. OxBTC
We have faith in old proverbs full surely. Where There's a Will There's a Way. Eliza Cook. BLPA; FaFP; TreF
We have fed you all for a thousand years. Labor. *Unknown.* PGD
We have forgot, who safe in cities dwell. Sea-Sonnet. V. Sackville-West. SBG
We have forgotten Paris, and his fate. Helen Grown Old. Janet Lewis. QFR
We have found you out. Arson and Cold Lace. Worth Long. NBP
We have gone out in boats upon the sea at night. Passage over Water. Robert Duncan. NoAM; NOBA
We have heard no nightingales singing. Working Class. Bertram Warr. NOBC; OBCV; WaP
We have heard the trumpets calling Youth. Youth. Katharine Lee Bates. PGD
We have kept faith, ye Flanders' dead. In Flanders Now. Edna Jaques. CaP
We have little animals here. Robinson Jeffers. *Fr.* Skunks. BoAnP
We Have Lived and Loved Together. Charles Jefferys. BLPA; FaBoBe; TreFT
We have loitered and laughed in the flowery croft. A Garden Lyric. Frederick Locker-Lampson. HBV-1; PeD
We Have Lost Our Little Hanner. Max Adeler. FiBHP
We have loved each other in this time twenty years. An Unfinished History. Archibald MacLeish. NYBP; VGW
"We have made them fools and weak!" said the Strong Ones. God and the Strong Ones. Margaret Widdemer. HBMV
We have met. To a Butterfly. W. H. Davies. FM
We have met late—it is too late to meet. A Denial. Elizabeth Barrett Browning. GBL; OBNC
We have minted her beauty in multiple golden medallions. Ox-Bone Madonna. John Duffy. ISi
We have moving over us, over head and spire. Sunday. Josephine Miles. PoA
We have no heart for the fishing, we have no hand for the oar. The Dykes. Kipling. OBWP; VLP
We have no idea what his fantastic head. Archaic Torso of Apollo. Rainer Maria Rilke, *tr. by* Robert Bly. NU
We have no prairies. Bogland. Seamus Heaney. IPY; NoP
"We have no quarrel with the German nation." "No Quarrel." A. P. Herbert. DBV
We have no time for bridges. Seagulls. Patricia Hubbell. PDV
We have not been happy, my Lord, we have not been too happy. Chorus. T. S. Eliot. *Fr.* Murder in the Cathedral. OxBTC
We have once more caught. The Bear. Ann Stanford. WSC
We have opened the door. The Dead Feast of the Kol-Folk. Whittier. PoEL-4
We Have Paid Enough Long Since in Our Own Blood. Virgil, *tr. fr. Latin by* Richmond Lattimore. *Fr.* Georgics. WaaP
We have reached the end of pastime, for always. End of Play. Robert Graves. EBEV
We have sailed many months, we have sailed many weeks. "Lewis Carroll." *Fr.* The Hunting of the Snark. NA
We have scarcely time to tell thee. Shelly. James McIntyre. FiBHP
We have seen her/ the world over. Hilda Doolittle ("H. D."). *Fr.* Tribute to the Angels. VGW
We Have Seen His Star in the East. Molly Anderson Haley. PGD
We have seen how the most amiable. Hilda Doolittle ("H. D."). *Fr.* The Walls Do Not Fall. BoWoP; PBWP
We have seen thee, queen of cheese. Queen of Cheese. James McIntyre. FiBHP; PeD
We have sent him seeds of the melon's core. Ku Klux. Madison Cawein. AA; PAH
We have shared beauty and have shared grief, too. A Prayer for a Marriage. Mary Carolyn Davies. TrPWD
We have shot the last whiskey cup from the trapper's head. The Last Whiskey Cup. Paul Engle. YaD
We have states of things you never. The Undreamed. Elaine V. Emans. AMV-81
We have struck the regions wherein we are keel or reef. Zone. Louise Bogan. PoCh; WPE
We have sweat our share. Stable-Talk. Raymond Knister. CaP
We have tangled together. Growing Together. Joyce Carol Oates. IHMS
"We have the mauve or the cerise." Shop Talk. Roy Fuller. OxBC
We have the road here, the gate the key. Moved towards a Future. Laura Chester. NPGG
We have the statue for it—Liberty. Address to the Refugees. John Malcolm Brinnin. GOA
We have these drums. Percussions. Ron Welburn. CNA
We have to bury the urns. Leaving Seoul; 1953. Walter Lew. BrSi
We have tomorrow. Youth. Langston Hughes. AmFN
We have traveled. A Time of Turquoise. Judith Mountain Leaf Volborth. TWSS
We have tried words before—always in vain. The Knife. Milton Kaplan. TrJP
We have walked, looking at the actual trees. Leaves before the Wind. May Sarton. NePoAm
We have watched again. Among Hawks. Lance Henson. VoR
We heard her speaking of Chinese musicians. The Woman Who Disapproved of Music at the Bar. Horace Gregory. MoPo
We heard it calling, clear and low. The Cuckoo. Frederick Locker-Lampson. HBV-1
We heard the corncrake's call from close at hand. First Corncrake. John Hewitt. NeIP
We heard the thrushes by the shore and sea. In Kerry. J. M. Synge. FaBoPP; GBL; MoBrPo
We heard thunder. Nothing great—on high. Mouse Night: One of Our Games. William Stafford. NCSH
We Heart. Laura Chester. NPGG
We, Hermia. Helena and Hermia. Shakespeare. *Fr.* A Midsummer Night's Dream. GN
We hesitate along. A Graveyard in Queens. John Montague. IPY
"We hold our flat shields, we wear our jerkins of hide." Hymn to the Fallen [*or* The Battle]. *Unknown, at. to* Chu Yuan, *tr. by* Arthur Waley. OBWP; WaaP
We hold these truth to be self-evident. Decoy. John Ashbery. PoM
We hunted and we halloed. Cape Ann. *Unknown.* BLSo; FSW
We hurry on, nor passing note. Digby Mackworth Dolben. OBNC
We in our wandering. A Song of the Open Road. *Unknown, tr. by* John Addington Symonds. AWP
We Interrupt This Broadcast. Judith Hemschemeyer. Str
We invoke holy Patrick, Ireland's chief apostle. Prayer to St. Patrick. Ninine, *tr. by* Whitley Stokes *and* John Strachan. OnYI
We Irish pride ourselves as patriots. Ireland. John Hewitt. CIP; FaBoPP
We is gathahed hyeah, my brothahs. An Ante-Bellum Sermon. Paul Laurence Dunbar. BALP; BPo
We issue from the meat of Pineapple Street. On the Island. L. E. Sissman. NYBP
We jeer/ and we sneer. Tee-Vee Enigma. Selma Raskin. QQQ
We jest went out to git him, and we did. The Sheriff's Report. Arthur Chapman. BPAW
We journeyed through broad woodland ways. A Spring Journey. Alice Freeman Palmer. HBV-1
We keep going, we keep going. Parting. Michael Hogan. GP
We kept him an hour in the/ bottom. A Cocker of Snooks. Phyllis Gotlieb. NOBC
We kissed at the barrier; and passing through. On the Departure Platform. Thomas Hardy. NOBE; OBNC; OxBTC
We knew it would rain, for all the morn. Before the Rain. Thomas Bailey Aldrich. GN
We knew so much; when her beautiful eyes could lighten. Sagacity. William Rose Benét. MoAmPo
We knew the sand they must come to. Trinidad, 1958. Bob Mondy. WOLT
We know/ the winter earth. November Twenty-sixth Nineteen Hundred and Sixty-three. Wendell Berry. LiTM
We know he liked chockbeer and watermelon. A Choctaw Chief Helps Plan a Festival. Jim Barnes. TAT
We know it doesn't rhyme much anymore. What Is Poetry. James Scully. FYAP
We know not what it is, dear, this sleep so deep and still. The Two Mysteries. Mary Mapes Dodge. AA; HBV-2; TrCP; WGRP
We know not yet what life shall be. Mors et Vita. Samuel Waddington. HBV-2
We know she lives upon that thorny hill. Jezebel. Scudder Middleton. HBMV
We know that skin is the border of life. Skin. Philip K. Jason. AMV-81

We know the winter earth upon the body of the young President. November 26, 1963. Wendell Berry. AP
We ladies sense it is the cuckoo builds no nest. Liberation. Ruth Stone. BoWoP
We laugh and we are troubled. The Beating Heart. Heine, *tr. by* Louis Untermeyer. UnTE
We lay and ate sweet hurt-berries. Picnic. Rose Macaulay. SUMH
We lay in the trenches we'd dug in the ground. The Ballad of Bunker Hill. Edward Everett Hale. PAH
We lay red roses on his grave. Paul Laurence Dunbar. Robert Hayden. NoP
We lay, the air-conditioner on. Then. John Morgan. AMV-81
We lay together in the sultry night. Summer Storm. Louis Untermeyer. UnTE
We lay upon the southern slope, and saw. Coruisk. W. C. Smith. PoSH
We Lay Us Down to Sleep. Louise Chandler Moulton. AA
We learned that you don't shoot. Statement on Our Higher Education. W. M. Ransom. CDW
We learned to laugh. Although the flying bombs. Rackheath. Coman Leavenworth. Norfolk Memorials, II. LiTA
We leave the farmland for the formless coast. Summer Island. William Logan. MAYP
We leave the well-belovèd place. In Memoriam A. H. H., CII. Tennyson. EBVV; PoEL-5
We left/ The silent forest. Charles Mair. *Fr.* Tecumseh. OBCV
We left our rented farmhouse for three weeks. End of August. Gregory Orr. MAYP
We left the city when the summer day. Indolence. Robert Bridges. BrPo; VLP
We Let It Go That He Was a Perfect Man. Nicanor Parra, *tr. fr. Spanish by* Miller Williams. POL
We lie by towering hollyhocks. August Night, 1953. Elizabeth B. Harrod. NePoEA
We lie in that other darkness, ourselves. Now That My Father Lies Down beside Me. Stanley Plumly. DiL; GeTw
We lift our glad hearts, Lord, in thankfulness. Youth's Thankfulness. Edgar Daniel Kramer. PGD
We like March—his shoes are purple. Emily Dickinson. SOTW
We, like shades that were first conjured up. And through the Caribbean Sea. Margaret Danner. BPo
We listen, wind from where. The Runner with the Lots. Léonie Adams. MoPo; NePA
We Live in a Cage. William J. Harris. PoBA
We Live in a Rickety House. Alexander McLachlan. NOBC; OBCV
We live in fragments. Tight Rope. Amiri Baraka. CNA
We live, while we see the sun. Pedro Calderon de la Barca, *tr. by* Arthur Symons. *Fr.* Life Is a Dream. AWP
We lived in language all our black selves. When the Wine Was Gone. Alvin Aubert. CNA
We lived one and twenty year. Upon a Notorious Shrew. *Unknown.* FaBoEE
We look through these walls. A Poem of Broken Pieces. Andrew McCord Jones. LFAC
We looked over the white sea. Hill Love. James Macmillan. PoSH
We looked the part. Crossing the Border into Canada. Joy Harjo. STE
We looked, we loved, and therewith instantly. Pure Death. Robert Graves. CoBMV; GTBS-P; MoAB; MoPo
We Love the Venerable House, *with music.* Emerson. AH
We love thee, Ann Maria Smith. The Editor's Wooing. "Orpheus C. Kerr." OBAL
We love with great difficulty. Sing with Your Body. Janice Mirikitani. WPOW
We Love You the Way You Are. David McFadden. NeAC
We loved: we vowed our love should never die. Memoir. R. G. Howarth. PV
We loved the wild clamor of battle. The Song of the Flags. S. Weir Mitchell. PAH
We loved thee, Swordy Well, and love thee still. Swordy Well. John Clare. WHA
We loved them, so we only crushed the skulls. Cinco de Mayo, 1862. A. A. Rios. GP
We Lying by Seasand. Dylan Thomas. BiP; PoA; SyP
We made castles of grass, green halls, enormous stem-lined rooms. The Riders. Ann Stanford. WPE
We made our little girl. The Gingerbread House. John Ower. AMV-80; DFT
We make a home so as not to stay at home. Customs. Juan Gelman, *tr. by* Yishai Tobin. VWA
We make our meek adjustments. Chaplinesque. Hart Crane. AP; CMoP; CrMA; LiTM; NoAM; NOBA; OxBA; VGW
We make that lovely sighing sound. The Name. Eileen Duggan. ISi
We Manage Most When We Manage Small. Linda Gregg. AmPA; NPGG
We march into the suburbs led by a six-year-old kid. Some of Us Are Exiles from No Land. Diana O Hehir. NPGG
We marched, and saw a company of Canadians. Canadians. Ivor Gurney. FaBoTw
We marry our grandfathers. Extensions of Linear Mobility. Jeanine Hathaway. IHMS
We may go through the world, but it will be slow. People Will Talk. *Unknown.* TreFS
We may live without poetry, music and art. What We May Live Without. "Owen Meredith." *Fr.* Lucile. TreF
We may no longer stay on shore. The Greenland Whale Fishery. *Unknown.* OBET
We may not climb the heavenly steeps. Our Master. Whittier. BLRP; WBLP
We May Not Know. Cecil F. Alexander. TRV
We may not work a miracle. The Higher Calling. W. M. Czamanske. STF
We may well wonder at those froward hermits. The Eremites. Robert Graves. LiTB
We meet. And meeting repairs attention. Casual Meeting. Sam Bradley. AMV-81
We Meet in the Lives of Animals. Peter Everwine. NNaP
We meet 'neath the sounding rafter. The Revel [*or* Our Last Toast *or* Revelry for the Dying *or* Stand to Your Glasses]. Bartholomew Dowling. AnIV; BLPA; HBV-2; OnYI; TreF; YaD
We meet today in Freedom's cause. Hold the Fort. *Unknown.* FSW
We meet tonight to pass the point of blame. The Reckoning. Alice Friman. AMV-81
We meet upon the Level and we part upon the Square. The Level and the Square. Robert Morris. BLPA
We Men Are of Two Worlds. Mary Elizabeth Colman. CaP
We men of earth have here the stuff. Earth Is Enough. Edwin Markham. TreFS; TRV
We met, a hundred of us met. The Vision. William Taylor. NOEC
We met but in one giddy dance. To ———. Winthrop Mackworth Praed. HBV-1
We met for supper in your flat-bottomed boat. Dream Barker. Jean Valentine. PrIm; VGW
We Met on Roads of Laughter. Charles Divine. FaBoBe; HBMV
We might have known it always: music. An die Musik. David Malouf. CBAP
We mind not now the merits of our kind. Marriage and Money. Sir Charles Sedley. *Fr.* The Happy Pair. OBSV
We more than others have the perfect right. Song of the Moderns. John Gould Fletcher. AWP
We mourn the loss. Epitaph. Ambrose Bierce. DBV
We move from one. The River. Sam Cornish. PoBA
We move very fast and smoothly. Good Times and No Bread. Reginald Lockett. CNA
We moved like fingers. San Francisco Poem. John Logan. NNaP
We must admire her perfect aim. The Colder the Air. Elizabeth Bishop. MiAP
We Must Be Free or Die. Wordsworth. *See* It Is Not to Be Thought Of.
We must be nobler for our dead, be sure. The Watchers. Arlo Bates. AA
We must burn up. Vicente Rodríguez Nietzche, *tr. by* Julio Marzán. *Fr.* Mural. InW
We must kill our gods before they kill us. Black Trumpeter. Henry Dumas. PoBA
We must leave the handrails and the Ariadne-threads. À l'Ange Avantgardien. Francis Reginald. MoCV
We Must Make a Kingdom of It. Gregory Orr. MAYP
We must not, in our hurried lives. His Life Is Ours. Dorothy Conant Stroud. STF
We must not sever, you and I. Brotherhood. "J. J. W." PeHV
We must pass like smoke or live within the spirit's fire. Immortality. "Æ." AnIV; AWP; OBMV; WGRP
We must sit down. Councils. Marge Piercy. NeAC
We must stay away from our fathers. Little Father Poem. Marvin Bell. LCAP
We mustered at midnight, in darkness we formed. Bethel. A. J. H. Duganne. PAH
We mustn't get discouraged at the things which people say. Discouraged. Lucille Stanaback. STF
We Need a King. Arthur R. Macdougall, Jr. PGD
We need a new patriotism. A New Patriotism. Chauncey R. Piety. PGD
We Need a Whole Lot More of Jesus. *Unknown.* FSW
We need him now—his rugged faith that held. Abraham Lincoln, the Master. Thomas Curtis Clark. OHIP
We need no runners here. Booze is law. Harlem, Montana: Just Off the Reservation. James Welch. CDW; GP; STE
We Need Not Bid, for Cloistered Cell. John Keble. HBV-2
We need you now, strong guardians of our hearts. The Poets. Scudder Middleton. HBMV

We Needs Must Be Divided. George Santayana. ViBoPo
We never half believed the stuff. James Wetherell. E. A. Robinson. MoAmPo
We never knew the touch of fur and feather. Timber Line Trees. Jamie Sexton Holme. PoOW
We never know how high we are. Emily Dickinson. AP; TRV
We never know what to expect. Our Annual Return to the Lake. Robert D. Hoeft. AMV-81
We never meet, yet we meet day by day. Thoughts in Separation. Alice Meynell. ACP; GoBC
We Never Said Farewell. Mary Elizabeth Coleridge. WPE
We Never Speak as We Pass By. *Unknown.* TreFS
We never spent time in the mountains. Interlude. Welton Smith. PoBA
We, not content with naming distant views. Country Walk. Geoffrey Taylor. OxBI
We now mid hope vor better cheer. Jeäne. William Barnes. LO
We Object. *Tr. fr. Maori by* A. Armstrong. WTO
We only ask for sunshine. Song. Helen Hay Whitney. HBV-2
We only know that in the sultry weather. England and America, 1863. Richard Monckton Milnes. EBVV
We open here our treasures and our gifts. A Christmas Prayer. Herbert H. Hines. PGD
We outgrow love, like other things. Emily Dickinson. NOBA
We owe the ancients something. You have read. Fitz-Greene Halleck. *Fr.* Fanny. OBAL
We Own the Night. Amiri Baraka. BOLo; PoBA
We park and stare. A full sky of the stars. The Death of the Sheriff [*or* Noli Me Tangere]. Robert Lowell. LCAP; MoAB; MoAmPo
We pass a stranger. He glances. The Stranger Not Ourselves. William Stafford. NNaP
We Passed by Green Closes. John Clare. VLP
We passed each other, turned and stopped for half an hour, then went our way. On the Road to the Sea. Charlotte Mew. BrRo; PeHV
We passed the ice of pain. The Moment. Theodore Roethke. NYBP
We passed their graves. Peace. Langston Hughes. BPo
We pick/ the bittersweet grapes. Napa, California. Ana Castillo. WPOW
We Pity Our Bosses Five. *Unknown.* FSW
We pity; we should dread. The Terrible Dread. Mary Carolyn Davies. HBMV
We place Thy sacred name upon our brows. Still Thou Art Question. *Unknown.* PGD
We planned to shake the world together, you and I. Lamplight. May Wedderburn Cannan. SUMH
We planted a garden/ Of all kinds of flowers. Flowers. Harry Behn. FaPON
We play now very lightly, on the strings. Rondel for Middle Age. Louise Townsend Nicholl. NePoAm
We pledge ourselves to follow through the coming year. Facing the New Year. *Unknown.* PGD
We pledged our hearts, my love and I. The Exchange. Samuel Taylor Coleridge. FiBHP; HBV-1; OAEP; WhC
We plough and sow—we're so very, very low. The Song of the Lower Classes. Ernest Charles Jones. CoMu; OBVV; VLP
We Plough the Fields. Jane M. Campbell. FaPoR
We Poets in Our Youth. Wordsworth. *Fr.* Resolution and Independence. FaBoRV
We poets pride ourselves on what. On Hearing Mrs. Woodhouse Play the Harpsichord. W. H. Davies. BrPo
We Poets Speak. Francis Thompson. *Fr.* Sister Songs. FaBV
We pointed it out to his bed-ridden eyes. Hospital. G. C. Millard. PeSA
We poor Agawams. Mr. Ward of Anagrams Thus. Nathaniel Ward. SCAP
We Praise Thee, God, for Harvests Earned, *with music.* John Coleman Adams. AH
We Praise Thee, If One Rescued Soul, *with music.* Lydia H. Sigourney. AH
We praise Thee O God! Revive Us Again. William Paton Mackay. FSW
We praise thee, O God; we acknowledge thee to be the Lord. Te Deum Laudamus. *Unknown.* WGRP
We pray Thee, have mercy on Zion! Prayer for Redemption. *Unknown.* TrJP
We prayed for miracles: the prairie dry. Epilogue to the Outrider. Dorothy Livesay. CaP
We preside, brothers, over the twilight of freedom. Twilight of Freedom. Osip Mandelstam, *tr. by* Andrew Glaze. VWA
We pressed our faces. The Train Stops at Healy Fork. John Haines. TAT
We pulled for you when the wind was against us and the sails were low. Song of the Galley-slaves. Kipling. ChTr; GTBS-P; HAP; PoEL-5
We put Blake to sleep between us. Homosexual Sonnets. Kenneth Pitchford. GP
We put more coal on the big red fire. Father's Story. Elizabeth Madox Roberts. FaPON; PoSC
We put our heads into the window of a car which was passing. Leslie Scalapino. *Fr.* Hmmmm. NPGG
We put out our hands on the window—cold. In Time of Need. William Stafford. UnPo
We put the urn aboard ship. Sappho, *tr. fr. Greek by* Mary Barnard. PBWP
We quarreled that morning. Julia Miller. Edgar Lee Masters. *Fr.* Spoon River Anthology. MoVE
We Rainclouds. Marvin Wyche, Jr. AmNP
We Raise de Wheat. *Unknown. See* Song: "We raise de wheat."
We ran across the meadow scabbed with cow-dung. Geoffrey Hill. Mercian Hymns, XXII. HAP
We Reached Out Far. Peretz Markish, *tr. fr. Yiddish by* Jacob Sonntag. TrJP
We read and hear about you every day. To the Rulers. Howard Nemerov. OxBC
We Read of a People, *with music. Unknown.* AH
We Real Cool. Gwendolyn Brooks. CAPP; FF; HAP; HeIP; HoPM; IDB; InPK; NoP; PAI; PoA; PoBA; PrIm; SoSe; TAP; TTY; WeW
We Reason of These Things. Wallace Stevens. *Fr.* Notes toward a Supreme Fiction. CrMA
We reden ofte and finde y-write. Sir Orfeo. *Unknown.* OxBM
We remember now. The Survivors. Robert Slater. FAZ
We remember, we do not forget, O Trail Breakers. Trail Breakers. James Daugherty. AmFN
We remember well. Gravel. Paul Mariah. LFAC
We remember you/ calling America. Poetry Concert. Michael S. Harper. TAP
We ride down the coast hwy through the rain. The Great Santa Barbara Oil Disaster OR. Conyus. AmPA
We rise from the snow where we've. Selective Service. Carolyn Forché. MAYP
We road the hiways. The Ballgame. Amiri Baraka. DiL
We rode at a trot. Grenada. Mikhail Arkadyevich Svetlov, *tr. by* Alexander Kaun. WaaP
We run the dangercourse. We Walk the Way of the New World. Don L. Lee. BPo; NeAC; PoBA
We said *We understand,* and for a while. Urban History. Chester Kallman. CrMA
We sail out of season into an oyster-gray wind. Crossing the Atlantic. Anne Sexton. MOS; NoAM
We sail toward evening's lonely star. Song. Celia Thaxter. AA
We sailed and sailed upon the desert sea. Hope. William Dean Howells. AA; MOS
We sailed by the old world's tideways, down through the long sea-lanes. The Secret of the Deeps. Sidney Royse Lysaght. EtS
We sailed in sunshine; but then was black. The Peak. W. W. Gibson. PoSH
We sailed into the harbor. Island of Giglio. Harold Norse. GP
We sailed to and fro in Erie's broad lake. Perry's Victory. *Unknown.* PAH
We sat across the table. The Friend. Marge Piercy. NMM
We sat and talked. It was June, and the summer light. Horse in a Field. Walter de la Mare. HBMV
We sat at the hut of the fisher. Twilight. Heine, *tr. by* Louis Untermeyer. AWP
We sat in an old, crumbling house. Untitled. Mah-do-ge Tohee. STE
We sat in the Cambridge orchard drinking tea. In the Orchard. Robert Friend. GP
We sat together at one summer's end. Adam's Curse. W. B. Yeats. BIrV; CMoP; CoBMV; NoAM; NoP; OAEL-2; PP; SOTW; TEP; VLP
We sat, two children, warm against the wall. The Gate. Edwin Muir. CMoP; LiTM
We sat within the farm-house old. The Fire of Drift-wood. Longfellow. AmPP; AP; BLPL; HBV-2; NOBA; NoP; OxBA; TAP
We saw a bloody sunset over Courtland. Remembering Nat Turner. Sterling A. Brown. PoBA; PoNe
We saw a town by the track in Colorado. Holding the Sky. William Stafford. RFM
We saw and woo'd each other's eyes. To Castara [*or* The Reward of Innocent Love]. William Habington. *Fr.* Castara. ACP; CavP; LoBV
We saw, but surely, in the motley crowd. Cave of Staffa, I. Wordsworth. VLP
We saw him sleeping in his manger bed. Carol. Gerald Bullett. HBVY
We saw it all. We saw the souvenir shops, and sitting. Niagara Falls. Alan Dugan. PoA
We saw one first and thought it was the only one. Bloody Cranesbill on the Dunes. E. J. Scovell. ChMP
"We saw reindeer." Rigorists. Marianne Moore. NU; SBG
We saw the Brochan spectre from. Poem, 1972. Syd Scroggle. PoSH
We saw the light shine out a-far. The Golden Carol. *Unknown.* OHIP
We Saw the Swallows. George Meredith. Modern Love, XLVII. ELP; EnLoPo; FaBoEn; GTBS-P; NOBE; OAEL-2; OBNC; SeCeV; ViBoPo; WHA

We saw thee come in, a wee naked babe. Farewell to the Old Year. Eleanor Farjeon. SiSoSe
We saw Thee in Thy balmy nest. The Shepherd's Hymn [*or* A Hymn Sung as by the Shepherds *or* Verses from the Shepherd's Hymn]. Richard Crashaw. *Fr.* In the Holy Nativity of Our Lord. ACP; GoBC; OBEV; TrGrPo
We saw three boys. Dorothy Wordsworth. GLGT
We saw truth shining through the shabby compromise. Rededication. Emanuel Litvinoff. WaP
We say the sea is lonely; better say. The Open Sea. William Meredith. CoAP; GrPl; MOS; NePoEA; TAP; UnPo
We scatter seeds with careless hand. The Effect of Example. John Keble. HBV-2; HBVY
We search the world for truth; we cull. The Bible [*or* The Book Our Mothers Read.] Whittier. *Fr.* Miriam. BLRP; TreFT; TRV
We see each living thing finally die. Sonnet VII. Louise Labé, *tr. by* Willis Barnstone. BoWoP
We See Jesus. Annie Johnson Flint. BLRP
We see only his back. Two Windows by Magritte. Ruth Roston. PoDr
We see them not—we cannot hear. Are They Not All Ministering Spirits? Robert Stephen Hawker. GoBC; HBV-1
We seek to know, and knowing seek. In Immemoriam. "Cuthbert Bede." NA
We seem to tread the self-same street. Florence MacCarthy's Farewell to His English Lover. Aubrey Thomas de Vere. NBM
We send you word of the Mother. Two Presentations. Robert Duncan. InPS
We Separate the Days. Henrik Nordbrandt, *tr. fr Danish by* Nadia Christensen. AMV-81
We set out yesterday upon a winter drive. Alexandre Dumas, *tr. by* Gerard Manley Hopkins. *Fr.* The Lady of the Pearls. TTY
We Settled by the Lake. F. D. Reeve. NYBP
We shall be called harsh names by men unborn. Contemporary. Hortense Flexner. PoA
"We shall cede with a brotherly embrace." The Rise of Shivaji. Zulfikar Ghose. MoBS
We shall come to-morrow morning, who were not to have her love. Emily Hardcastle, Spinster. John Crowe Ransom. CMoP
We shall do much in the years to come. What Have We Done Today? Nixon Waterman. WBLP
We shall have everything we want and there'll be no more dying. Ode to Joy. Frank O'Hara. NeAP; PPP
We Shall Have Far to Go. James Wreford Watson. CaP
We shall have music. Love in Age. Charles G. Bell. NePoAm-2
We shall meet, but we shall miss him. The Vacant Chair. Harry Stevenson Washburn. FSW; TreFS
We shall not always plant while others reap. From the Dark Tower. Countee Cullen. BALP; BANP; BPo; CDC; IDB; LiTM; PoBA; PoNe
We Shall Not Be Moved. *Unknown.* FSW
We shall not cease from exploration. T. S. Eliot. *Fr.* Four Quartets: Little Gidding, V. ImOP
We Shall Not Escape Hell. Marina Tsvetayeva, *tr. fr. Russian by* Elaine Feinstein. BoWoP
We shall not ever meet them bearded in heaven. On the Death of Friends in Childhood. Donald Justice. ConAP; LCAP; NCSH
We shall not go up against you. This Be Our Revenge. Saul Tchernichowsky, *tr. by* Shalom Spiegel. TrJP
We Shall Overcome. *Unknown.* AH, *with music*; BLSo, *with music*; EaLo; FSW
We shall remember him. John Butler Yeats. Jeanne Robert Foster. GoYe
We Shall Say. Miriam Allen deFord. GoYe
We shall see her no more. The Rejected Member's Wife. Thomas Hardy. VLP
We Shall Walk through the Valley. *Unknown.* FSW
We shan't see Willy any more, Mamie. To a Bull-Dog. J. C. Squire. FM
We shared not one idea in thirty years. A Reformer to His Father. James Simmons. BIrV
We shift and bedeck and bedrape us. Swinburne. *Fr.* Dolores. UnTE
We should stay longer if we durst. Francis Beaumont. *See* Ye Should Stay Longer.
We shouldered like pigs along the rail to try. Returned to Frisco, 1946. W. D. Snodgrass. AP
We shut them out, the houses. Time Out. Oliver Jenkins. GoYe
We sigh above historic pages. The True Knight. Ella Wheeler Wilcox. PeD
We, sighing, said, "Our Pan is dead." Thoreau's Flute. Louisa May Alcott. AA; HBV-2
We sit and talk over lunch of the inevitable blow-out. Late Lunch, San Antonio. OCNZ
We sit by the old tent. What Are You Thinking About? James Macmillan. PoSH
We sit, crookbacked, at the bar. At the Telephone Club. Henri Coulette. CoAP
We sit in the basement kitchen, arranging. A Card Game; Kinjiro Sawada. Patricia Y. Ikeda. BrSi
We sit indoors and talk of the cold outside. There Are Roughly Zones. Robert Frost. CMoP; PPP
We sit late, watching the dark slowly unfold. September. Ted Hughes. BoLoP; OLR
We sit outside. Death of Dr. King. Sam Cornish. CNA; OFD; PoBA
We Sit Solitary. *Unknown.* TrJP
We sit watching the afternoon summer smell ripely. James Powell on Imagination. Larry Neal. BPo
We six pile in, the engine churning ink. Nigger Song: An Odyssey. Rita Dove. AmPA
We smile at astrological hopes. For the Conjunction of Two Planets. Adrienne Rich. ImOP
We smile at each other. Conversation. Ai. LTB
We sound like crying bullheads. Voices. Nora Dauenhauer. TWSS
We sow the fertile seed and then we reap it. Evening Hymn in the Hovels. Francis Lauderdale Adams. OxBS
We sow the glebe, we reap the corn. Mystery. Elizabeth Barrett Browning. OBVV
We spend our morning. The Memory of Elena. Carolyn Forché. MAYP
We spoke tonight/ of the departure from Egypt. The Departure. Jeremy Robson. VWA
We spurred our parents to the kiss. Children of Darkness. Robert Graves. NoAM
We stand in line all morning long to see it. The Most Expensive Picture in the World. Howard Nemerov. EyDe
We stand naked behind the line. On the Death of Sylvia Plath. Judith Herzberg. VWA, *tr. by* Shirley Kaufman; WPOW, *tr. by* Manfred Wolf
We stand on the edge of wounds, hugging canned meat. Dream of Rebirth. Roberta Hill Whiteman. CDW; TWSS
We stand talking in the cave whose walls are. On Meeting a Stranger in a Bookshop. Oscar Williams. NePA
We stayed the night in the pathless gorge. Oh, Lovely Rock. Robinson Jeffers. NoAM; NU
We steamed into New York harbor the other day. The Statue of Liberty. Sheila Jane Crooke. YaD
We Still Must Follow. E. L. Mayo. AMV-81
We stood at first before the mast. Gastric. "C. T." PeD
We stood beside an opening grave. "I Am the Resurrection and the Life," Saith the Lord! Robert Stephen Hawkes. GoBC
We stood by a pond that winter day. Neutral Tones. Thomas Hardy. BrPo; CABA; CMoP; CoBMV; EBVV; HAP; HeIP; InPK; MoBrPo; NoAM; OAEL-2; PPP; SyP; TEP; UnPo; VLP
We stood on the haunted island. The Phantom Ship. J. W. de Forest. EtS
We stood up before day. In the Dordogne. John Peale Bishop. OBWP; VGW
We stopped at her hut. The Ballad of Ballymote. Tess Gallagher. GP
We stopped the truck in the heat. Rumors of War in Wyoming. Tom Rea. SOTS
We strain toward Heaven and lay hold on Hell. Battle-Song of Failure. Amelia Josephine Burr. HBMV
We stumble down the pocked and cratered road. Madonna of the Exiles. James Edward Tobin. ISi
We summoned not the Silent Guest. The Skeleton at the Feast. James Jeffrey Roche. AA
We Survive! Hirsch Glick, *tr. fr. Yiddish by* Ruth Rubin. TrJP
We swing ungirded hips. The Song of the Ungirt Runners. Charles Hamilton Sorley. HBMV; MoBrPo; OBEV; TreFT
We take it with us, the cry. Departure. Carolyn Forché. AMV-80
We take place in what we believe. Elephant Rock. Primus St. John. PoBA
We talk of old men who have forgotten their/ thoughts. Errore. Pier Giorgio Di Cicco. NOBC
We talked all morning, she said. A Walk in the Country. Galway Kinnell. NePoAm
We talked of things but all the time we wanted each other. And What with the Blunders. Kenneth Patchen. NaP
We talked together in the Yung-shou Temple. The Letter. Po Chü-i, *tr. by* Arthur Waley. LoBV
We talked [*or* talk'd] with open heart, and tongue. The Fountain. Wordsworth. EnRP; GTBS; GTBS-P; OBRV; SeCePo
We Thank Thee! ("For glowing autumn's brimming yield"). Thomas Curtis Clark. PGD
We Thank Thee! ("Not for our lands, our wide-flung prairie wealth"). Thomas Curtis Clark. PGD, *abr.*
We Thank Thee ("For all life's beauties . . ."). John Oxenham. *See* For Beauty, We Thank Thee.
We Thank Thee ("For all Thy ministries"). John Oxenham. *Fr.* A Little Te Deum of the Commonplace. PGD; TRV
(We Thank Thee, Lord.) WBLP

We Thank Thee ("For mother-love and father-care"). *Unknown.* FaPON
We thank Thee for the joy of common things. A Prayer for Thanksgiving. Joseph Auslander. TrPWD
We thank Thee for the morning light. *Unknown.* BLRP
We Thank Thee, Lord, *with music.* Calvin W. Laufer. AH
We Thank Thee, Lord. John Oxenham. *See* We Thank Thee ("For all Thy ministries").
We thank Thee, Lord, for this our food. *Unknown.* BLRP
We thank Thee, now, O Father. The Most Acceptable Gift. Matthius Claudius, *tr. by* J. M. Campbell. BLRP
We, that did nothing study but the way. A Renunciation. Henry King. OBEV
We that with like hearts love, we lovers twain. A Vow to Heavenly Venus. Joachim du Bellay, *tr. by* Andrew Lang. AWP
We, the boys of Sanpete County, in obedience to the cause. The Boys of Sanpete County. *Unknown.* AmFP
We, the captives of a thousand skies. Farewell to Europe. William Pillen. VWA
We, the Fairies, blithe and antic. Song of Fairies Robbing an Orchard [*or* Fairy Song]. Thomas Randolph, *tr. by* Leigh Hunt. *Fr.* Amyntas. HBV-1; OBRV
We the People. The Question, Is It? Alfred G. Bailey. AMV-81
We, the rescued. Chorus of the Rescued. Nelly Sachs. VWA, *tr. by* Harry Zohn; WPOW, *tr. by* Ruth *and* Matthew Mead
We, the symmetrians, seek justice here. N. B., Symmetrians. Gene Derwood. LiTA; NePA
We, the unborn. Chorus of the Unborn. Nelly Sachs, *tr. by* Ruth Mead *and* Matthew Mead. NYBP
We the White Witches are, that free. Masque of the Virtues against Love. Mary Monck, *after the Italian of* Guarini. NOEC
We think to create festivals. Poems. Antonio Machado, *tr. by* John Dos Passos. AWP
We thirst at first—'tis nature's act. Emily Dickinson. NOCV; WGRP
(Thirst.) WGRP
We thought at first, this man is a king for sure. Blue Blood. James Stephens, *after the Irish of* David O'Bruaidar. MoAB; MoBrPo; OBMV; OxBI
We thought the grass. Photographs: A Vision of Massacre. Michael S. Harper. PoBA
We three are on the cedar-shadowed lawn. George Meredith. Modern Love, XXI. OAEP
We Three Kings of Orient Are. John Henry Hopkins, Jr. AH, *with music*; PChr
(We Three Kings.) OHIP
We thumbwrestle and I. All Thumbs. David Giber. AMV-81
We too (one cried), we too. To the Mother of Christ, the Son of Man. Alice Meynell. ISi
We too, we too, descending once again. The Too-late Born [*or* The Silent Slain]. Archibald MacLeish. CABA; CMoP; CoBMV; GoJo; LiTM; MoAB; MoAmPo; MoVE; NePA; OxBA; POL; SeCeV; TwAmPo; WaP
We too were created from clay. Vessels. Howard Schwartz. VWA
We took it to the woods, we two. Emerson. Mary Mapes Dodge. AA
We took no notes of contemplated light. To My Friends. Peter Levi. NePoEA-2
We took our turn at the guard that night, just Sourdough Charlie and I. The Stampede. Freeman E. Miller. BPAW
We took our work, and went, you see. Recreation. Jane Taylor. NBM; OBRV; OxBoLi
We tore the green tree down. Verifying the Dead. James Welch. CDW
We total it up for. Up & Out. Nila NorthSun. STE
We touched land. Not That Far. May Miller. BlSi
We trees were chopping down the monsters in the street to count their rings. The Slacker Apologizes. Peter Viereck. MiAP
We trekked into a far country. Translation. Anne Spencer. BANP
We turn out the light to undress by. Turn the Key Deftly. Edwin Brock. POL
We two are last in hell: what may we fear. Barley-Break; or, Last in Hell. Robert Herrick. CaPo
We Two Boys Together Clinging. Walt Whitman. PeHV
We two lying on sand. Child with Shell. R. G. Everson. PeCV
We two stood simply friend-like side by side. Inapprehensiveness. Robert Browning. VLP
We used to float the paper boats in spring. Poem. Donald D. Olsen. PoPl
We used to gather at the high window. When Mahalia Sings. Quandra Prettyman. IDB; PoBA
We used to picnic where the thrift. Trebetherick. John Betjeman. CMoP; EvOK
We Used to Play. Don Welch. Psk
We used to shadow-box on the shining grass. Dimidium Animae Meae. Charles A. Brady. GoYe
We used to spend the spring together. The Most Beautiful Girl in the World. Lorenz Hart. OBAL
We waged a war within a war. Karl Shapiro. Recapitulations, XI. PoNe
We wait our turn, as still as mice. The Hospital Waiting-Room. W. H. Davies. BrPo
We waited for an omnibus. Walking Song. William E. Hickson. OxBChV
We waited in the desert encircled. Sukkot. Sol Lachman. VWA
We waited out the lion weeks. Vernal Paradox. Kim Kurt. NePoAm-2
We wake to economical. Reconcilable Differences. Roger Sauls. AMV-81
We wake to hear the storm come down. The Storm. Edward Shanks. BoNaP
We walk alone on our roots. Prayer for Kafka and Ourselves. Anthony Rudolf. VWA
We walk, as all around walks on creation. In the Shadow of the Valley of Death. Abu al-Qasim al-Shabbi. DL
We walk back from the movies. Frightened Flower. William J. Harris. BOLo
We walk past the Han stallion. Museum with Chinese Landscapes. Walter Cybulski. AMV-81
We Walk the Way of the New World. Don L. Lee. BPo; NeAC; PoBA
We walk together, breathing different air. Chilled by Different Winds. Alice Mackenzie Swaim. AMV-80
We walked a mile from the road and with every step. Daisies. Alden Nowlan. NeAC
We walked [*or* walk'd] along, while bright and red. The Two April Mornings. Wordsworth. EBEV; EnRP; GTBS; GTBS-P; HBV-2
We Walked among the Whispering Pines. John Henry Boner. AA
We walked that night between the piled houses. The Window. Iain Crichton Smith. NePoEA-2
We wander now who marched before. Old Soldier. Padraic Colum. OBMV
We wandered to the pine forest. Shelley. *Fr.* The Recollection. CH
We wanted Li Wing. Lapsus Linguae. Keith Preston. OBAL; WhC
We was camped on the plains at the head of the Cimarron. Zebra Dun. *Unknown.* ViBoFo
We watch the only eagles in the world. At a Parade. F. T. Prince. NeBP; WaP
We watch'd her breathing thro' the night. The Death-Bed. Thomas Hood. ELP; EnRP; GTBS; GTBS-P; HBV-2; NOBE; OBEV; OBNC; OBRV; OBVV; TreFS
We watched/ a red rooster. Calypso. William Carlos Williams. NePoAm-2
We watched her breathing through the night. *See* We watch'd . . .
We watched our love burn with the lumberyard. The Lumberyard. Ruth Herschberger. LiTA; WPE
We watched the condors winging towards the moon. Condors. Padraic Colum. GoJo
We watched thy spirit flickering in the dark. In Memoriam: John Davidson. Ronald Campbell Macfie. GoTS
We Wear the Mask. Paul Laurence Dunbar. AmNP; CABA; CDC; FF; IDB; NIP; NoP; PoBA; TTY; UnPo
We went down to the river's brink. Explanation, on Coming Home Late. Richard Hughes. ELU
We went north/ to escape winter. Indian Song: Survival. Leslie Silko. CDW; VoR
We went off to the wake of the "whelpish youngster." Harvest of the Sea. Máire Mhac an tSaoi. PBWP
We went on a motorcycle on a straight road with people watching us. Areas. Leslie Scalapino. NPGG
We went out, early one morning. Out Fishing. Barbara Howes. LiSp; WPE
We went there on the train. Protocols. Randall Jarrell. LCAP; OxBC; VGW
We went there to confer. Detroit Conference of Unity and Art. Nikki Giovanni. HoPM
We went up the pass, she and I. San Ysidro, Cabezon. Paula Gunn Allen. TWSS
We were a multitude, until the hunters. Angels. Richard Burns. VWA
We were a tribe, a family, a people. Scotland 1941. Edwin Muir. BSV; OxBS
We were all passengers in that motorcade. Channel U.S.A.—Live. Adrien Stoutenburg. AmFN
We were all sitting round the table. Christmas Dinner. Michael Rosen. OBCP
We were all under God. God. Boris Slutsky, *tr. by* Dimitry Pospielovsky *and* Keith Bosley. VWA
We were alone and did your life. To Children. Lawrence McGaugh. PoBA
We were antagonists; we knew that. Reflections on Water. Kenneth Pitchford. CoPo
We were apart; yet, day by day. Isolation: To Marguerite [*or* Isolation]. Matthew Arnold. Switzerland, IV. EBVV; OAEP; TEP; TreFT; VLP
We were as tough as our glasses. Tyson's Corner. Primus St. John. PoBA

We were born grooms, in stable-straw we sleep still. A Dream of Horses. Ted Hughes. NePoEA-2
We Were Boys Together. George Pope Morris. AA
We were camped on the plains [*or* bend]. The Zebra Dun. *Unknown.* CoSo; FSW; PH
We were challenged by The Dingoes—they're the pride of Squatter's Gap. A Friendly Game of Football. Edward Dyson. CBAP
We were closed, each to each, yet dear. Each to Each. Melville Cane. GoYe
We were crowded in the cabin. Ballad of the Tempest [*or* The Captain's Daughter *or* The Tempest]. James Thomas Fields. BeLS; BLPL; EtS; FaBoBe; FaFP; HBV-1; HBVY; PoLF; TreF; YaD
We were driving the down express. The Engine Driver's Story. William Wilkins. BeLS
We were forty miles from Albany. The E-ri-e. *Unknown.* AS; FSW
We were glad together in gladsome meads. Adam Lindsay Gordon. *Fr.* The Rhyme of Joyous Garde. PoAu-1
We were hangin' "Rustler" Murphy for the stealin' of a horse. The Salvation of Texas Peters. J. W. Foley. ShM
We Were in the 8th Grade. John Berryman. GLGT
We were lying on a prairie on Slaughter's ranch one night. Home, Sweet Home. *Unknown.* CoSo
We were not even out of sight of land. Sea Monster. W. S. Merwin. WSC
We were not many, we who stood. Monterey. Charles Fenno Hoffman. AA; FaBoBe; HBV-2; PAH
We were not wrong, believing that it cared. The Empty House. Harold Monro. BrPo
We were ordered to Samoa from the coast of Panama. An International Episode. Caroline Duer. AA; PAH
We were out in Arizona, on the Painted Desert ground. Arizona. *Unknown.* AmFP
We Were Permitted to Meet Together in Prison to Prepare for Trial. Daniel Berrigan. LFAC
We were playing on the green together. "Is It Nothing to You?" May Probyn. GoBC; OBEV; OBVV
We were schooner-rigged and rakish, with a long and lissome hull. A Ballad of John Silver. John Masefield. EvOK
We were sure to interrupt the traveller's siesta. Nausicaa with Some Attendants. Tom Lowenstein. VWA
We were talking about poems he had written. Rhymes. Frank Steele. PPJ
We were talking about tent revivals. Sects. Jack Gilbert. NPGG
We were three women, three men. The Sorrow of Kodio. *Unknown, tr. by* Miriam Koshland. PBA
We were twin brothers, tall and hale. A Flight Shot. Maurice Thompson. AA
We were two daughters of one race. The Sisters. Tennyson. InvP; PAI
We were two pretty babes, the youngest she. Childhood Fled. Charles Lamb. EnRP
We were up before anyone. Liard Hot Springs. Gordon Massman. CTBA
We were very tired, we were very merry. Recuerdo. Edna St. Vincent Millay. AmFN; CTBA; EvOK; FaFP; FPL; LiTA; LiTM; NoAM; OxBA; PoA; TAP
We were walking and talking on the roof of the world. End of the Seers' Convention. Kenneth Fearing. LiTA
We were wrong to think. Form. Heather McHugh. GeTw
We were young, we were merry, we were very very wise. Unwelcome. Mary Elizabeth Coleridge. CH; OBEV; OBNC; OBVV; PoPle; WPE
We who also linger near the border of insanities. Near the Border of Insanities. Dannie Abse. PoA
We Who Are about to Die. Harold E. Fey. PGD
We Who Are Dead. Paul L. Benjamin. PGD
We Who Are Left. George Whalley. CaP
We who are left, how shall we look again. A Lament. W. W. Gibson. MMA; OxBTC
We who are old, old and gay. A Faery Song. W. B. Yeats. ViBoPo
We Who Build Visions. Stanton A. Coblentz. PGD
We who carry the endless seasons. Virginia Cerenio. BrSi
We who devour our unclean dead are now arisen. Letter to Robert. Mary Fabilli. IHMS
We who have come all ways into the city. The Trail. Edward Weismiller. WaP
We who have no perfection but to die. And Only Our Shadow Walks with Us. Eithne Wilkins. NeBP
We who must act as handmaidens. A Muse of Water. Carolyn Kizer. NMM
We, who play under the pines. The Rabbits' Song outside the Tavern [*or* Song of the Rabbits outside the Tavern]. Elizabeth J. Coatsworth. OBCA; SUS; TiPo
We Who Were Born. Eiluned Lewis. FaPON; TiPo
We who with songs beguile your pilgrimage. Prologue. James Elroy Flecker. *Fr.* The Golden Journey to Samarkand. BrPo; FaBoRV; FaPoR; GoJo; HBMV; OBMV; OxBTC
We Whom the Dead Have Not Forgiven. Sara Bard Field. PGD
We will deal in apples, plums and pears. The Way to Live. *Unknown.* VLP
We will go no more to Shaemus, at the Nip. Shaemus. Conrad Aiken. OxBA
We will go to the wood, says Robin to Bobbin. *Unknown.* OxNR
"We will kill." After the Killing. Dudley Randall. CNA; SoSe
We Will Not Fear, *with music.* David Diamond. AH
We will not whisper, we have found the place. Sonnet. Hilaire Belloc. MoBrPo
We will pull, we will haul, hearty, healthy, and gay. Blow the Man Down. *Unknown.* AmFP
We will remember, surely, how we stood. Last Rite. John V. Hicks. AMV-81
We will return to life. Comanche Ghost Dance: An Impression. Lance Henson. VoR
We Will Speak Out. James Russell Lowell. TreFT
We will take it seriously as we open our morning paper. Sonnet to Be Written from Prison. Robert Adamson. CBAP
We will wait by the chestnut and the ilex tree. Orion Seeks the Goddess Diana. Sacheverell Sitwell. *Fr.* Landscape with the Giant Orion. MoVE
We will watch the Northern Lights. *Unknown, tr. fr. Abanaki.* RFM
We wish to declare how the birds of the air. The Trail of the Bird. William John Courthope. HBVY
We wish to the new child. For C. K. at His Christening. Daniel Lawrence Kelleher. NeIP
We Wish You a Merry Christmas. *Unknown.* FSW
We with our Fair pitched among the feathery clover. The Individualist Speaks. Louis MacNeice. MoVE; OBMV
We woke early. Names in Monterchi: To Rachel. James Wright. NNaP
We Women. Edith Södergran, *tr. fr. Swedish by* Samuel Charters. WPOW
We wonder whether the dream of American liberty. Archibald MacLeish. *Fr.* Land of the Free. MoAB
We wondered what our walk should mean. Peace Walk. William Stafford. Psk
We wondered why he always turned aside. Inheritance. Mary Thacher Higginson. AA
We Won't Go Home till Morning, *with music.* *Unknown.* PSoN
We worked in the kitchen. The Function Room. Patrice Phillips. MAT
We would be building; temples still undone. Builders. Purd E. Deitz. TRV
We would climb the highest dune. With Kit, Age 7, at the Beach. William Stafford. RFM
We Would See Jesus. *Unknown.* STF
We Would See Jesus, *with music.* Anna B. Warner. AH
We wreathed about our darling's head. The Morning-Glory. Maria White Lowell. AA; HBV-1
We zealots, made up of stiff clay. Let Us All Be Unhappy on Sunday. Lord Neaves. FaBoCo
Weak and irresolute is man. Human Frailty. William Cowper. HBV-2
Weak is the assurance that weak flesh reposeth. By Her That Is Most Assured to Her Self. Spenser. Amoretti, LVIII. EnRePo
Weak Is the Will of Man, His Judgment Blind. Wordsworth. EnRP
Weak Monk, The. Stevie Smith. BoWoP; FaBoTw
Weak-winged is song. Ode Recited at the Harvard Commemoration. James Russell Lowell. AA; AP; HBV-2; NOBA; OBWP; PAH
Weakest Thing, The. Elizabeth Barrett Browning. HBV-2
Weakness of Nature. Richard Hurrell Froude. OBRV
Wealth. Emerson. ImOP
Wealth. Sadi, *tr. fr. Persian by* Sir Edwin Arnold. *Fr.* The Gulistan. AWP
Wealth and Wisdom. *At. to* Alfred, King of England. *Fr.* The Proverbs of Alfred. OxBM
Wealth covers sin—the poor. Epigram. Kassia, *tr. by* Patrick Diehl. WPOW
Wealth, my lad, was made to wander. Samuel Johnson. *Fr.* On the Coming of Age of a Rich Extravagant Young Man. ViBoPo
Wealth unto every man, I see. Worldly Wealth. Rowland Watkyns. FaBoEE
Wealthy Cit, grown old in trade, The. The Cit's Country Box. Robert Lloyd. NOEC
Wealthy dromedar, A. The Boar and the Dromedar. Henry Beissel. WHW
Weapon shapely, naked, wan. The Broad-Ax. Walt Whitman. *Fr.* Song of the Broad-Ax. MoAmPo
Weapon that comes down as still, A. The Ballot. John Pierpont. AA
Weapon that you fought with was a word, The. "He Knoweth Not That the Dead Are Thine." Mary Elizabeth Coleridge. ELU; OBNC
Weapons. Anna Wickham. MoBrPo
Wear it/ Like a banner. Color. Langston Hughes. BOLo
Wear it as a bangle on your arm. Fame. Eleanor Hollister Cantus. GoYe

Wear your tweed coat and checked hat. How to Find Your Way Home. Mario Petaccia. LFAC
Wearied arm and broken sword. Pocahontas. Thackeray. AmFN; FaPON; GN; OnMSP; PAH; PAL
Wearily, drearily. In Prison. William Morris. NBM
Wearily, still in her dressing gown. Eliza Telefair. Jocelyn Macy Sloan. GoYe
Wearin' o' the Green, The. *Unknown.* *See* Wearing of the Green, The.
Weariness of life that has no will, The. Everyman. Siegfried Sassoon. MoBrPo
Weariness of this dirt and labour, The. Fatigues. Richard Aldington. BrPo
Wearing/ a red, white/blue—paul revere hat. Warden's Day. Carolyn Baxter. LFAC
Wearing his equality like a too-small shoe. The Citizen. Vilma Howard. NNP
Wearing of the Green. Aileen Fisher. RHPC; YeAr
Wearing of the Green, The. *Unknown, add. words by* Dion Boucicault. AnIL; AnIV; AWP; FaFP; FaPoR; FSW; GBP; HBV-2; OnYI; OxBoLi; PoSC; TreF; WTO
Wearing the familiar Yankee pinstripes. And You Are There. Tom Clark. LiSp
Wearing worry about money like a hair shirt. Worry about Money. Kathleen Raine. FaBoTw
Wearisome Sonnetteer, feeble and querulous. The Soldier's Wife. George Canning *and* John Hookham Frere. Par
Weary already, weary miles to-night. A Match with the Moon. Dante Gabriel Rossetti. NCEP; VLP
Weary are the hours of a sailor boy. The Sailor Boy. *Unknown.* BaBo
Weary at heart with winter yesterday. April. Obadiah Cyrus Auringer. AA
Weary Blues, The. Langston Hughes. BALP; FaBV; InPK; NoAM; NOBA; NoP; PoNe
Weary day rins down and dies, The. A Jacobite's Exile. Swinburne. OBVV
Weary, I open wide the antique pane. Poetry and the Poet. H. C. Bunner. OBAL
Weary I was, and thought to sit at rest. Elizabeth Melvill, Lady Culross. *Fr.* A Godly Dream. WPE
Weary in Well-doing. Christina Rossetti. SeCePo; TrPWD
Weary is he, and sick of the sorrow of war. The Soldier Is Home. Shaw Neilson. CBAP
Weary Lot Is Thine, A. Sir Walter Scott. *See* Song: "Weary Lot is thine fair maid, A."
Weary men, what reap ye?—"Golden corn for the stranger." The Famine Year. Lady Wilde. OnYI
Weary of erring in this Desert Life. To Our Ladies of Death. James Thomson. GoTS
Weary of myself, and sick of asking. Self-Dependence. Matthew Arnold. HBV-2; OAEP; TreFS; VLP; WGRP
Weary of the day, of small-/ mindedness. At the Trough. Arthur Gregor. FAZ
Weary on ye, sad waves! On an Island. "Ethna Carbery." WPE
Weary one had rest, the sad had joy that day, The. Because We Do Not See. *Unknown.* BLRP
Weary Song to a Slow Sad Tune, A. Li Ch'ing-chao, *tr. fr. Chinese by* Kenneth Rexroth. BoWoP
Weary teacher sat alone, The. The Teacher's Dream. William Henry Venable. BeLS
Weary the cry of the wind is, weary the sea. Sorrow of Mydath. John Masefield. MoBrPo
Weary Traveler. *Unknown.* *See* Let Us Cheer the Weary Traveler.
Weary was when coming on a stream. Aswelay. Norman Henry Pritchard II. PoBA
Weary way-wanderer, languid and sick at heart. The Soldier's Wife. Robert Southey. OBEC
Weary, weary, desolate. Yuma. Charles Henry Phelps. AA
Weary weed, tossed to and fro, A. Gulf-Weed. Cornelius George Fenner. EtS
Weary Will. A. B. Paterson. BoAnP
Weary wind is slumbering on the wing, The. Sunset. Arthur Bayldon. PoAu-1
Weary with toil, I haste me to my bed. Sonnets, XXVII. Shakespeare. OBSC
Weary year his race now having run, The. Amoretti, LXII. Spenser. OBSC
Wearyin' fer You. Frank L. Stanton. HBV-1
Weasel, The. Robert Pack. CoPo
Weasel, The. *Unknown.* ChTr
Weasel (or a stoat), A. The Aesthete Weasel. Christian Morgenstern, *tr. by* Geoffrey Grigson. FaBoNo
Weasel and the wren consort, The. Mole Talk. Leo Kennedy. PeCV
Weasel, by a person caught, A. The Man and the Weasel. Phaedrus, *tr. by* Christopher Smart. AWP
Weather. Hilda Conkling. TiPo
Weather. Thomas Hardy. *See* Weathers.
Weather. Archibald MacLeish. *See* Cook County.
Weather. William Meredith. NYBP
Weather. *Unknown.* RHPC
Weather came down from Nevis, The. Eagle. Tom Bowker. PoSH
Weather Factory, The. Nancy Byrd Turner. SUS
Weather here is raw, The. At Torrey Pines State Park. Jerome Mazzaro. FiCP
Weather in London and Stratford-on-Avon was so, The. Shakespeare, Possibly, in California. Reed Whittemore. MoVE
Weather is the answer. Weather. Hilda Conkling. TiPo
Weather-leech of the topsail shivers, The. Tacking Ship Off Shore. Walter Mitchell. AA; EtS; FaBoBe; GN; HBV-1
Weather made no difference. Charter Boat. Norman Hindley. WOLT
Weather of Olympus, The. Robert Graves. FaBoEE
Weather of Six Mornings, The. Jane Cooper. IHMS; NYBP
Weather of the World, The. Howard Nemerov. SUW
Weather of this winter night, my mistress, The. Childlessness. James Merrill. ConAP
Weather Rhymes. Hamish Brown. PoSH
Weather Vanes. Frances Frost. SiSoSe
Weather was fine, The. They took away his teeth. John Berryman. *Fr.* Dream Songs. CAPP
Weather wept, and all the trees bent down, The. "The Shimmer of Evil." Theodore Roethke. NePoAm-2
Weather Wisdom [*or* Weather Wise *or* Observation *or* Rhymes about the Weather], *sels.* *Unknown.*
"Evening red and morning gray." FaBoBe; FaBoUs; HBV-1; HBVY; OxNR; TreF
"If bees stay at home." HBVY; OxNR; TreF
"If the oak is out before the ash." OxNR
"Mackerel sky." FaBoUs; OxNR
"March winds and April showers." FaBoBe; HBV-1; HBVY; OxNR; TreF
"Rain before seven." FaBoBe; HBV-1; HBVY; OxNR; TreF
"Rainbow at night." FaBoBe; HBV-1; HBVY; TreF
"Red sky at night." OxNR
"South wind brings wet weather, The." FaBoUs; HBV-1; HBVY; TreF
"Sunshiny shower, A." FaBoBe; HBV-1; HBVY; TreF
"When clouds appear like rocks and towers." FaBoUs; HBVY; OxNR; TreF
"When the clouds are upon the hills." OxNR
"When the wind is in the east." FaBoUs; OxNR
Weather Words. David McCord. ImOP
Weathercock. Elizabeth Jennings. NePoEA
Weathercock once again heading south, The. This Morning. Jon Stallworthy. NoP
Weathergrams are poems of about ten words. Lloyd J. Reynolds. FAZ
Weathering the Depths. Al Lee. AmPA
Weatherman has shown us everything, The. The Letters of Summer. Christopher Buckely. AMV-80
Weathers. Thomas Hardy. CH; EvOK; FaBoCh; FaBV; MoAB; MoBrPo; OBMV; PoPle; SeCePo
(Weather.) WHA
Weather's cleared, The. We're filming at Versailles. Clive James. *Fr.* To Pete Atkin: A Letter from Paris. OBSV
Weave no more silks, ye Lyons looms. Our Orders. Julia Ward Howe. AA
Weave Room Blues. *Unknown.* FSW
Weave the warp, and weave the woof. The Curse upon Edward. Thomas Gray. OBEV
Weaver, The. William H. Burleigh. BLPA
Weaver, The. Fanny Forrester. BLPA
Weaver, The. Lisel Mueller. AMV-81
Weaver, The ("I sat at my loom in silence"). *Unknown.* BLRP
Weaver, The ("I was a bachelor, I lived by myself"). *Unknown.* *See* Foggy, Foggy Dew.
Weaver and the Factory Maid, The. *Unknown.* OBET
Weaver sat by the side of his loom, A. The Weaver. Fanny Forrester. BLPA
Weavers. Heine, *tr. fr. German.* TrJP
Weaver's Life. *Unknown.* FSW
Weaving at the Window. Wang Chien, *tr. fr. Chinese by* William H. Nienhauser. SaC
Weaving Love-Knots. Hsüch T'ao, *tr. fr. Chinese by* Carolyn Kizer. BoWoP
Weaving Love-Knots 2. Hsüch T'ao, *tr. fr. Chinese by* Carolyn Kizer. BoWoP
Weaving of the Wing, The. Ralph Hodgson. BrPo
Web, The. Gregory O'Donoghue. BIrV

Web, The. Theodore Weiss. CoAP; NoAM
Web of Eros, The. Edith Sitwell. HBMV
Webern. Thomas W. Shapcott. *Fr.* Piano Pieces. CBAP
Webster; an Ode, *sel.* William Cleaver Wilkinson.
At Marshfield. AA
Webster Ross. Naomi Mitchison. PoSH
Webster was much possessed by death. Whispers of Immortality. T. S. Eliot. CMoP; CTC; LiTA; NePA; NoAM; NOBA; NoP; OBMV; TwAmPo
We'd face, I'm sure, with more aplomb. Unsolved Mystery. George Ryan. WhC
We'd found an old Boche dug-out, and he knew. The Sentry. Wilfred Owen. MMA
We'd gained our first objective hours before. Counter-Attack. Siegfried Sassoon. BrPo; MoBrPo; WaP
We'd have to love the nape of the neck more than the thigh. Conditions. José Luis Vega, *tr. by* Julio Marzán. InW
We'd rather have the iceberg than the ship. The Imaginary Iceberg. Elizabeth Bishop. LiTM; MoAB; MoAmPo; MoVE
Weddãsê Mãryãm. *Unknown, tr. fr. Ethiopian MS. by* Sir E. A. Wallis Budge. ISi
Wedded. Isaac Rosenberg. FaBoEn; PoPle
Wedded Bliss. Charlotte Perkins Gilman. HBV-1
Wedded light and heat, The. Wind and Wave. Coventry Patmore. NBM
Wedded Love. Milton. *See* Their Wedded Love.
Wedded Memories. Phillip Bourke Marston. VLP
Wedding, The. Conrad Aiken. CMoP; TAP
Wedding. George Mackay Brown. BSV
Wedding, The. Tom Hood. InMe
Wedding, The. Sandra Kohler. AMV-80
Wedding. Ewa Lipska, *tr. fr. Polish by* Peter Jay *and* Geri Lipshultz. VWA
Wedding. Dorothy Livesay. PeCV
Wedding, The. Coventry Patmore. *Fr.* The Angel in the House, II, xi. VLP
Wedding and Funeral. *Unknown.* GBP
Wedding bells were ringing on a moonlight winter's night, The. The Fatal Wedding. W. H. Windom. TreFS
Wedding Coat, The. Harriet Rose. BrRo
Wedding cortège, A. Wedding. Ewa Lipska, *tr. by* Peter Jay *and* Geri Lipshultz. VWA
Wedding Day at Nagasaki. Rodney Hall. CBAP
Wedding Feast, The. Luis de Góngora, *tr. fr. Spanish by* Edward Meryon Wilson. *Fr.* The First Solitude. OBVE
Wedding Gift, The. Minna Irving. BLPA
Wedding-Hymn. Sidney Lanier. TrPWD
Wedding is great Juno's crown. Shakespeare. *Fr.* As You Like It, V, iv. ViBoPo
Wedding Morn. D. H. Lawrence. MoAB; MoBrPo
Wedding Night, The. Johannes Secundus, *tr. by* George Ogle. *Fr.* Epithalamium. UnTE
Wedding Night, The. Anne Sexton. PoA
Wedding of Alcmane and Mya, The. George Chapman. *Fr.* Hero and Leander, Fifth Sestiad. OBSC
Wedding of the Clans, The. Aubrey Thomas De Vere. AnIL
Wedding Party. Donald Hall. LCAP
Wedding Poem, The, *sel.* Lawrence Russ.
"Night before you left, as you lay, The." AMV-80
Wedding Procession. James A. Emanuel. NNP
Wedding Signs. *Unknown.* TreFT
Wedding Song, A. John White Chadwick. AA
Wedding Song. *Unknown.* OBET
Wedding Song in honor of R. Solomon ben Matir, *sel.* Moses ibn Ezra, *tr. fr. Hebrew by* Solomon Solis-Cohen.
"Rejoice, O youth, in the lovely hind." TrJP
Wedding-Wind. Philip Larkin. MAT
Wedged into a hard huddle. The Edge. Ann Chandonnet. AMV-81
Wedgewood Bowl, A. Frances Beatrice Taylor. CaP
Wedlock. Bink Noll. GP
Wedlock; a Satire. Hetty Wright. NOEC
Wednesbury Cocking. *Unknown.* EnSB; FaBoBa
Wednesday. "Elspeth." WhC
Wednesday at North Hatley. Ralph Gustafson. NOBC
Wednesday in Holy Week. Christina Rossetti. PGD; TrCP
Wednesday, January 1, 1701. Samuel Sewall. *See* Once More, Our God, Vouchsafe to Shine!
Wednesday Night Prayer Meeting. Jay Wright. PoBA
Wednesday; or, The Dumps. John Gay. *Fr.* The Shepherd's Week. OAEL-1
Wednesdays at the bone orchard deliveries. Memo. Charles Lynch. PoBA
Wee Cooper of Fife, The. *See* Wife Wrapt in Wether's Skin, The.
Wee Davie Daylicht. Robert Tennant. OxBChV
Wee folk will be tripping, The. When a Ring's Around the Moon. Mary Jane Carr. TiPo
Wee Hughie. Elizabeth Shane. HBMV
Wee leave Creete Country; and our sayls unwrapped uphoysing. Virgil, *tr. by* Richard Stanyhurst. *Fr.* The Aeneid, III. OBVE
Wee Little Worm, A. James Whitcomb Riley. PDV; RHPC
Wee man o' leather. *Unknown.* ChTr; GBP
Wee, modest, crimson-tippèd flow'r [*or* flower]. To a Mountain Daisy [*or* The Daisy]. Burns. BoNaP; EnRP; GN; HBV-1; OAEP; PoLF; WBLP
Wee read of Kings and Gods that kindly tooke. A Cruell Mistris. Thomas Carew. AnAnS-2
Wee, sleeket [*or* sleekit], cow'rin' [*or* cowran], tim'rous beastie. To a Mouse on Turning Her Up in Her Nest with the Plough, November, 1785 [*or* To a Mouse *or* To a Field Mouse]. Burns. BiP; BSV; EnRP; FaFP; FF; FM; GoTS; GTBS; GTBS-P; HAP; HBV-1; HBVY; HeIP; InPS; LAuP; LoBV; NOEC; NoP; OAEL-1; OAEP; OBEC; OxBS; PoLF; PPP; PrIM; SeCeV; TEP; TreFS; TrGrPo; WHA
Wee strippit irritating beastie. To a Midge. Eilidh Nisbet. PoSH
Wee Tammy Tyrie. *Unknown.* OxNR
Wee Wee Man, The. *Unknown.* CH; EBEV; ELP; ESPB; FaBoCh; GBP; OAEL-1, *with music;* OxBB, *with music*
Wee, wee tailor. The Oviparous Tailor [*or* The Tailor]. Thomas Lovell Beddoes. NBM; WiR
Wee Willie Gray. Burns. OxBChV
Wee Willie Winkie rins [*or* runs] through the town. Willie Winkie [*or* Wee Willie Winkie]. William Miller. FaFP; HBV-1; HBVY; OxBChV; OxNR; SiSoSe; SoPo; TiPo
Weed, The. Elizabeth Bishop. MoPo
Weed. Robert Hass. MAYP
Weed and herb and foxy flower. Song for a Lost Art. Virginia Brasier. AMV-81
Weed Puller. Theodore Roethke. AmPP
Weeding in January. Louis Daniel Brodsky. AMV-80
Weeds. Ann Stanford. GrPl
Weeds grow shamelessly/ on my tongue. Self-Portrait. Cecil Bodker, *tr. by* Nadia Christensen. BoWoP
Weedy creek, A. Making a Door. Dennis Schmitz. LCAP
Weedy light through the uncurtained glass, The. Hiatus. Margaret Avison. HAP
Week ago to-day, when red-haired Sally, A. Done For. Rose Terry Cooke. AA
Week at Whinwood next to Christmas week, The. January: Cover Shooting. Wilfrid Scawen Blunt. *Fr.* An Idler's Calendar. VLP
Week is dealt out like a hand, The. Hope. Randall Jarrell. MoAB; MoAmPo
Week of Che Guevara, hunted, hurt. October and November. Robert Lowell. MAT
Week of Doodle, A. Reed Whittemore. NePoEA
Week on the Concord and Merrimack Rivers, A, *sels.* Henry David Thoreau.
All Things Are Current Found. ViBoPo
Atlantides, The. ViBoPo
Conscience. HBV-2
Haze. HeIP; NoP; PoPl
(Woof of the Sun [Ethereal Gauze].) AP; TAP; ViBoPo
Mist. AA; AmPP; AWP; OxBA
(Low-anchored Cloud.) ImOP; NoP; ViBoPo
Week-Seek. Jim Tollerud. VoR
Weekday, A. Larry Eigner. CoPo
Week-End. Harold Monro. SeCePo
"Train, The! The twelve o'clock for paradise," I. BSV; MoBrPo
Week-End by the Sea. Edgar Lee Masters. MoAmPo
Week-End Indian, The. Anita Endrezze Probst. VoR
Week-End Naturalist, The. Tom Buchan. BSV
Weekend Sonnets. Cilla McQueen. OCNZ
Weekend Stroll. Frances Cornford. BoNaP
Weekly at the start. The Face. Lucien Stryk. GP
Weeksville Women. Elouise Loftin. PoBA
Weel, gin ye speir, I'm no inclined. The Poets at Tea, IX. Barry Pain. Par
Weep, ah weep love's losing. Ode. Imr el Kais, *tr. by* Lady Anne Blunt *and* Wilfrid Scawen Blunt. *Fr.* The Mu'allaqát. AWP
Weep balm and myrrh, you sweet Arabian trees. Stanzas from Saint Peter's Complaint. Robert Southwell. *Fr.* Saint Peter's Complaint. ACP
Weep eyes, break heart! Parting. Thomas Middleton. *Fr.* A Chaste Maid in Cheapside. ElL
Weep for me, friends, for now that I am hence. Tears of the World. Mu'tamid, King of Seville, *tr. by* Dulcie L. Smith. AWP
Weep for the dead, for they have lost this light. On Himself. Robert Herrick. FaBoEE
Weep for the one so strong to slay, whom One has taken at last! Saul. George Sterling. HBMV

Weep him dead and mourn as you may. Keen. Edna St. Vincent Millay. HBMV
Weep, Israel! your tardy meed outpour. Bar Kochba. Emma Lazarus. TrJP
Weep, Lovers, sith Love's very self doth weep. Dante, *tr. by* Dante Gabriel Rossetti. La Vita Nuova, III, b. AWP
Weep No More. *At. to* John Fletcher. *Fr.* The Queen of Corinth, III, ii. CH; ElL; OBEV; ViBoPo
(Mourn No More.) TrGrPo
Weep no more for what is past. What Is Past. Sir William Davenant. TrGrPo
Weep no more, nor sigh nor groan. Weep No More [*or* Mourn No More]. *At. to* John Fletcher *Fr.* The Queen of Corinth, III, ii. CH; ElL; OBEV; TrGrPo; ViBoPo
Weep no more, woful Shepherds weep no more. Milton. *Fr.* Lycidas. FaBoRV
Weep not,/ You who loved her. Burial of the Young Love. Waring Cuney. BANP
Weep not because this child hath died so young. On the Death of Mistress Mary Prideaux. William Strode. JCP
Weep not, beloved friends! nor let the air. Epitaphs, I. Gabriello Chiabrera, *tr. by* Wordsworth. AWP
Weep not beside his tomb. Easter Day. Arthur Hugh Clough. PGD
Weep not for me, Loved Woman. Warrior's Song. Mary Austin. BPAW
Weep [*or* Weepe] not, my wanton, smile upon my knee. Sephestia's Song to Her Child [*or* Sephestia's Lullaby *or* Sephestia's Song]. Robert Greene. *Fr.* Menaphon. ElL; ELP; EnRePo; HBV-1; LoBV; NOBE; OBEV; OBSC; PoEL-2; SeCePo; TrGrPo; ViBoPo
Weep not, nor backward turn your beams. A Lover [upon an Accident Necessitating His Departure] Consults with Reason. Thomas Carew. CaPo; TrGrPo
Weep not the Brave Dead! Cean-Salla. James Clarence Mangan. OnYI
Weep Not To-Day. Robert Bridges. OBMV; OBVV
Weep not, weep not. Go Down Death. James Weldon Johnson. AmNP; DL; PoBA; TRV
Weep o'er the mis'ries of a wretched maid. The Dying Prostitute; an Elegy. Thomas Holcroft. NOEC
Weep! Weep! Weep! Tumadir Al-Khansa for Her Brother [*or* For Her Brother]. *Unknown, tr. by* E. Powys Mathers. *Fr.* The Thousand and One Nights. AWP; PBWP
Weep, weep, ye woodmen! wail. Robin Hood's Funeral [*or* Dirge *or* Song]. Anthony Munday. *Fr.* The Death of Robert, Earl of Huntingdon. CH; CTC; ElL; OBSC; WiR
Weep [*or* Weepe] with me, all you that read. Epitaph on S. P. [Salomon *or* Salathiel Pavy], a Child of Queen Elizabeth's Chapel. Ben Jonson. AnAnS-2; CABA; ElL; EnRePo; FaBoEn; GoBC; HBV-2; HeIP; HoPM; JCP; LoBV; MePo; NOBE; NoP; OAEL-1; OAEP; OBEV; OBS; PoEL-2; PoPle; PPP; SeCP; SeCV-1; TrGrPo; UnPo; ViBoPo
Weep [*or* Weepe] You No More [Sad Fountains]. *Unknown.* CH; EBEV; ElL; ELP; EnLoPo; GBL; HAP; LoBV; NoP; OAEP; OBSC; PoEL-2; PoPle; SoSe; TrGrPo; ViBoPo
(Sleep Is a Reconciling.) ChTr
(Tears.) NOBE; OBEV
Weepe not my wanton! smile upon my knee! *See* Weep not . . .
Weepe O mine eyes. *Unknown.* PoEL-2
Weepe with me all you that read. *See* Weep with me all you that read.
Weepe you no more, sad fountaines. *Unknown.* *See* Weep You No More.
Weeper, The. Richard Crashaw. *See* Saint Mary Magdalene.
Weepers Tower in Amsterdam, The. Paul Goodman. VGW
Weeping and wakeful all the night I lie. Rhodanthe. Agathias, *tr. by* Andrew Lang. AWP
Weeping Melpomene assist my lays. The Fatal Dream; or, The Unhappy Favourite. Emanuel Collins. NOEC
Weeping o'er the sacred urn. Ambrose Philips. *Fr.* To the Memory of Lord Halifax. FaBoCo
Weeping rose in her dark night of leaves, The. A Song at Morning. Edith Sitwell. CMoP
Weeping, Sad and Lonely. Charles C. Sawyer. FSW; TrAS, *with music*
(When This Cruel War Is Over.) AmFP
Weeping Sinner, Dry Your Tears, *with music.* Oliver Holden. AH
Weeping sorely as he journeyed. The Canadian Exile. Antoine Gerin-Lajoie, *tr. by* John Boyd. CaP
Weeping tree, A. What Am I? Abo Stoltzenberg, *tr. by* Gabriel Preil *and* Howard Schwartz. VWA
Weeping Willow. Richard Aldridge. NePoAm-2
Weeping Willow, The. *Unknown.* AmFP
Weeps out of western country something new. The Birth in a Narrow Room. Gwendolyn Brooks. BlSi; NAs; PoNe
Weet forenicht i' the yow-trummle, Ae. The Watergaw. "Hugh MacDiarmid." BSV
Weevily Wheat. *Unknown.* AmFP; AS, *with music;* FSW; TrAS, *with music*
'Weh Down Souf. Daniel Webster Davis. BANP
Wei Wind, *sel.* Confucius, *tr. fr. Chinese by* Ezra Pound. Pedlar. CTC; OBVE
Weigh me the fire; or canst thou find. To Finde God. Robert Herrick. WGRP
Weighing the Baby. Ethel Lynn Beers. HBV-1
Weighing the stedfastness and state. Man. Henry Vaughan. AnAnS-1; FaBoEn; HBV-1; MeLP; MePo; NOBE; NOCV; OBEV; OBS; PoEL-2; SeCV-1
Weight, The. William Aberg. LFAC
Weight distributed. One Down. Richard Armour. WhC
Weight of myself, The. The weight of my mother. Things Not of This Union. Linda Gregg. NPGG
Weight Room, The. Thomas Rabbitt. MAYP
Weightless Element, A. Gottfried Benn, *tr. fr. German by* Christopher Middleton. PoPl
Weir Bridge. Padraic Fallon. CIP
Weird Sister. In Salem. Lucille Clifton. AmPA; PAI
Wel/come back, brother. Huey. Etheridge Knight. NNaP
Wel mended tinker! sans dispute. Of John Bunyans Life. John James. SCAP
Weland knew fully affliction and woe. Deor's Lament. *Unknown, tr. by* Charles W. Kennedy. AnOE; OAEL-1
Weland, that dauntless man, well learned to bear. Deor. *Unknown, tr. by* Walter Kendrick. TEP
Welcome, A. William Browne. HBV-1; OBEV
(Welcome, Welcome, Do I Sing.) CaVP; ViBoPo
Welcome, The. Abraham Cowley. *Fr.* The Mistress. BoLoP; SeCV-1
Welcome, The [*or* A]. Thomas O. Davis. HBV-1; TreFT
Welcome. Harvey Feinberg. POL
Welcome, The. Freda Laughton. NeIP
Welcome. R. S. Thomas. NMP
Welcome. Rose Waldo. SoPo
Welcome all who lead or follow. Verses Placed over the Door at the Entrance into the Apollo Room at the Devil Tavern. Ben Jonson. HBV-2
Welcome! all Wonders in one sight! The Coming Child. Richard Crashaw. TRV
Welcome, boy, to these green fields. Alma Mater. Mary Elizabeth Osborn. NePoAm
Welcome! but yet no entrance, till we bless. The Entertainment, or Porch-Verse, at the Marriage of Master Henry Northleigh and the Most Witty Mistress Lettice Yard. Robert Herrick. CaPo
Welcome Christmas! heel and toe. Stocking Song on Christmas Eve. Mary Mapes Dodge. OHIP
Welcome dear book, souls Joy, and food! The feast. H. Scriptures. Henry Vaughan. AnAnS-1
Welcome, dear dawn of summer's rising sway. May-Day. Aaron Hill. NOEC
Welcome Eild. *Unknown.* GoTS
Welcome Every Guest, *with music.* *Unknown.* TrAS
Welcome, fayre chylde, what is thy name? Dalyaunce. *Unknown.* CH
Welcome for Etheridge, A. James Cunningham. JB
Welcome, Fortune. *Unknown.* BSV
Welcome freshness over the garden lay, A. Suspended Moment. Mariana B. Davenport. GoYe
Welcome, friend. Newton to Einstein. Jeannette Chappell. GoYe
Welcome, good friend; as you have served your term. "Black Bart, PO8." Ambrose Bierce. BPAW
Welcome, Great Cesar, welcome now you are. To the King, upon His Welcome to Hampton-Court. Robert Herrick. AnAnS-2
Welcome, grinned Henry, welcome fifty-one! John Berryman. *Fr.* Dream Songs. TAP
Welcome home, driving downhill. Lament City. Thomas Lux. AmPA
Welcome home from the exhausting voyage. Sea Legs. Susan Feldman. AmPA
Welcome, kind Death: my long tired spirit bear. Algernon Sidney's Farewell. *Unknown.* APAS
Welcome, maids of honor. To Violets. Robert Herrick. CaPo; HBV-1; JCP; OBEV; OBS; SeCP; TrGrPo; ViBoPo
Welcome me, if you will. For James Dean. Frank O'Hara. NeAP; NNaP
Welcome Morning. Anne Sexton. PAI
Welcome, most welcome, to our vows and us. To the King, upon His Coming with His Army into the West. Robert Herrick. AnAns-2; CaPo
Welcome, my old friend. To an Old Danish Song-Book. Longfellow. OBVV
Welcome My World. Denis Devlin. AnIV
Welcome now, Victoria. Queen Victoria. *Unknown.* CoMu
Welcome, O Great Mary. Alice O'Gallagher, *tr. fr. Gaelic by* Douglas Hyde. WTO
Welcome, old friend! These many years. To Age. Walter Savage Landor. EnRP; HBV-1; TreFS

Welcome! Our Messiah. *Unknown.* MeEL
Welcome, precious stone of the night. Welcome to the Moon. *Unknown.* BoNaP; ChTr; MOON
Welcome, Queen Sabbath. Zalman Schneour, *tr. fr. Hebrew by* Harry H. Fein. TrJP
Welcome, red and roundy sun. The Wood-Cutter's Night Song. John Clare. EnRP; OBRV
Welcome, Summer. Chaucer. *See* Now Welcome, Somer.
Welcome sweet and sacred cheer. The Banquet. George Herbert. AnAnS-1
Welcome sweet, and sacred feast; welcome life! The Holy Communion. Henry Vaughan. AnAnS-1
Welcome, Sweet Rest, *with music.* Michael Wigglesworth. AH
Welcome the lord of light, and lamp of day. Welcome to the Sun. Virgil, *tr. by* Gavin Douglas. *Fr.* The Aeneid. ACP
Welcome the Wrath. Stanley Kunitz. VGW
Welcome thou of high estate. Welcome, O Great Mary. Alice O'Gallagher, *tr. by* Douglas Hyde. WTO
"Welcome, Thou Safe Retreat!" William Habington. OxBoCh
Welcome, thrice welcome to this shady green. The Forest's Queen. Philip Massinger. GoBC
Welcome, thrice welcome to thy native place! Mary Gulliver to Captain Lemuel Gulliver. John Gay *and* Alexander Pope. OAEL-1
Welcome to Dr. Benjamin Apthorp Gould, A. Oliver Wendell Holmes. ImOP
Welcome to Freedom's birth-place—and a den! Ode to the Cameleopard. Thomas Hood. FaBoNo
Welcome to Sack, The. Robert Herrick. AnAnS-2; CaPo; SeCP; SeCV-1
Welcome to Spring. John Lyly. *See* Trico's Song: "What bird so sings . . ."
Welcome to the Moon. *Unknown, tr. fr. Gaelic.* BoNaP; ChTr; MOON
Welcome to the Nations. Oliver Wendell Holmes. PAH
Welcome to the New Year. Eleanor Farjeon. YeAr
Welcome to the Sun. Virgil, *tr. fr. Latin by* Gavin Douglas. *Fr.* The Aeneid. ACP
Welcome to This House. Faye George. AMV-80
Welcome to this my college, and thought late. To His Kinsman, Master Thomas Herrick, Who Desired to Be in His Book. Robert Herrick. CaPo
Welcome to us Holy Child. Christmas Night. Hugh MacCawell, *tr. by* Frank O'Connor. KiLC
Welcome to Venice, gentle courteous Knight. A Dialogue between the Lovelorn Sir Hugh and Certain Ladies of Venice. Thomas Deloney. UnTE
Welcome to you rich Autumn days. Rich Days. W. H. Davies. BoNaP
Welcome, Welcome, Do I Sing. William Browne. *See* Welcome, A.
Welcome, welcome, ev'ry guest. Welcome Every Guest. *Unknown.* TrAS
Welcome, wild Northeaster! Ode to the Northeast Wind. Charles Kingsley. FaPoR; GN
Welcome, Ye Hopeful Heirs of Heaven, *with music.* Phoebe Hinsdale Brown. AH
Welcome Yule. *Unknown.* CH
Welcomed to islands over the long water. Islanders, Inlanders. Michael Mott. PoA
Welcoming Party, A. John Montague. IPY
Weldon Kees. Larry Levis. FAZ
Weldon Kees in Mexico, 1965. David Wojahn. MAYP
Wele, herying and worshipe be to Christ that dere ous boughte. A Palm-Sunday Hymn. William Herebert. MeEL
Welfare Store. *Unknown.* BluL
Well, The. Denise Levertov. AP
Well, The. Luis Pales Matos, *tr. fr. Spanish by* Donald Walsh. InW
Well/ black mama, what's the/ matter with you today. My Black Mama. *Unknown.* BluL
Well/ If I had my way. If I Had My Way. *Unknown.* BluL
Well/ I'm gonna run, I'm gonna run. I'm Gonna Run to the City of Refuge. *Unknown.* BluL
Well/ we were hauf-roads up Schiehallion. Hauf-Roads up Schiehallion. Donald Campbell. PoSH
Well-aimed Stare, The. Hugo Margenat, *tr. fr. Spanish by* Julio Marzán. InW
"We'll all be rooned," said Hanrahan. Said Hanrahan. P. J. Hartigan. PoAu-1
We'll All Feel Gay. Winfield Townley Scott. MiAP
We'll All Go a-Hunting Today. *Unknown.* OBET
Well all you ladies gather 'round. Candy Man Blues. *Unknown.* BluL; FSW
Well, *alter ego,* Time has trudged. Why Do We Live? Israel Zangwill. TrJP
Well, aye, last evenen, as I shook. Zummer Thoughts in Winter Time. William Barnes. VLP
We'll begin with a box, and the plural is boxes. Why English Is So Hard. *Unknown.* FaBoUs
Well boss did it/ ever strike you. The Hen and the Oriole. Don Marquis. *Fr.* Archy and Mehitabel. EvOK; FiBHP
Well boss I met. Cheerio My Deario. Don Marquis. *Fr.* Archy and Mehitabel. FaBoCo
Well boss Mehitabel the cat. Mehitabel Sings a Song. Don Marquis. *Fr.* Archy and Mehitabel. InMe
Well-bred young girl of Gomorrah, A. Limerick. *Unknown.* PeHV
Well-buggered boy named Delpasse, A. Limerick. *Unknown.* PeHV
Well, come along boys and listen to my tale. The Old Chisholm Trail [*or* The Chisholm Trail]. *Unknown.* FSW; TrAS
Well, David said—it was snowing outside and his voice contained many. Paschal Lamb. Robert Hass. NPGG
Well, dear Mr. Wright, I must send you a line. To Henry Wright of Mobberley, Esq. on Buying the Picture of Father Malebranche. John Byrom. NOEC
Well, Did You Evah? Cole Porter. OBAL
Well dost thou, Love, thy solemn feast to hold. Saint Valentine's Day. Coventry Patmore. The Unknown Eros, XLIII. FaBoEn; GoBC; OBNC
Well Dressed Man with a Beard, The. Wallace Stevens. BiP
Well, Emily Sparks, your prayers were not wasted. Reuben Pantier. Edgar Lee Masters. *Fr.* Spoon River Anthology. GLGT
Well, every Monday mornin'. John Henry. *Unknown.* OuSiCo
Well fare the nightingale. *Unknown.* PBBP
Well formed is the child, well formed now. The Dawn of Day. Keaulumoko, *tr. by* M. W. Beckwith. *Fr.* The Kumulipo; a Creation Chant. WTO
Well, Froggie went a-courting and he did ride. Froggie Went a-Courting. *Unknown.* AmFP
"Well, General Grant, have you heard the news?" Lee's Parole. Marion Manville. PAH
Well, gentlemen,/ You flag wavers. To Those Who Sing America. Frank Marshall Davis. FB
We'll Go No More a-Roving. Byron. *See* So We'll Go No More a-Roving.
We'll Go No More a-Roving. W. E. Henley. Echoes, VIII. MoBrPo
We'll Go to Sea No More. *Unknown.* ChTr; EtS; GBP
(Fisherman's Song.) PoPle
Well, God don't like it, no, no. God Don't Like It. *Unknown.* OuSiCo
Well, God is/ love. Puerto Rico Song. William Carlos Williams. NYBP
Well hath the powerful hand of majesty. To Sir Thomas Egerton. Samuel Daniel. OBSC
We'll Have Another Drink before the Boat Shoves Off, *with music. Unknown.* ShS
We'll heave him up from down below. Susiana. *Unknown.* ShS
Well, Heaven be thanked my first-love failed. The County Ball. Coventry Patmore. *Fr.* The Angel in the House. EBVV
Well, here we are; well, here we are! Yale Boola! A. M. Hirsh. FSN
Well, Honest John. John Clare. NCEP
Well, honour is the subject of my story. Cassius Poisons Brutus' Mind. Shakespeare. *Fr.* Julius Caesar, I, ii. TreFS
Well, how d'ye do, Private William McBride. No Man's Land. Eric Bogle. OBET
Well I ain't got no use for your red apple juice. Red Apple Juice. *Unknown.* FSW
Well, I am a rambling, gambling man. Rambling, Gambling Man. Gil Houston. FSW
Well, I am thinking this may be my last. Canoe. Keith Douglas. NeBP
Well, I don't care if it rains or freezes. Plastic Jesus. *Unknown.* FSW
Well, I dreamed a dream the other night. Prospecting Dream. *Unknown.* FSW
Well, I drink to you, David Campbell, but I drop a curse in the cup. A Letter to David Campbell on the Birthday of W. B. Yeats, 1965. A. D. Hope. NAs
Well I got up this morning. The Jinx Blues. *Unknown.* BluL
Well, I had an old dog and his name was Blue. *See* I had a dog and his name was Blue.
Well, I had an old hen and she had a wooden leg. Turkey in the Straw. *Unknown.* FSW
Well, I have thought on't, and I find. The Retirement. John Norris. CavP; OBS
Well, I may now receive, and die: my sin. Satires, IV. John Donne. OBSV
Well I never, did you ever. *Unknown.* FaBoCh
Well I poisoned my man. Blood Hound Blues. *Unknown.* BluL
Well I Remember [How You Smiled]. Walter Savage Landor. *Fr.* Ianthe. HAP; LoBV; OBNC; TrGrPo; ViBoPo
(Her Name.) OBVV
(Ianthe.) FaBoEn
Well I say I work in the Conoco station. Hottest Brand Goin'. *Unknown.* BluL
Well I want all you women folks to fall in line. The Dirty Dozens. *Unknown.* BluL

Well, I was camped out on the draw at the head of Cimarron. The Zebra Dun. *Unknown.* AmFP
Well, I went down in Hell-town/ To see the Devil chain down. Johnny, Won't You Ramble. *Unknown.* OuSiCo
Well, I went to California in the year of Seventy-six. Root Hog or Die. *Unknown.* AmFP
Well I woke up this mornin'/ Half past four. Stamp Blues. *Unknown.* BluL
Well, I woke up this morning/ I was feeling mighty bad. Evil-hearted Man. *Unknown.* FSW
Well, I would have it so. I should have known. Elegies, III. André Chénier, *tr. by* Arthur Symons. AWP
Well, if a King's a lion, at the least. Pope. *Fr.* The First Epistle of the First Book of Horace Imitated. OBSV
Well; if ever I saw such another Man since my Mother bound my Head. Mary the Cook-Maid's Letter to Dr. Sheridan. Swift. LoBV; OnYI; OxBoLi
Well! If the Bard was weather-wise, who made. Dejection; an Ode [*or* A Letter to Sara Hutchinson]. Samuel Taylor Coleridge. CABA; EnRP; FaBoEn; FiP; HBV-2; LiTB; LoBV; MasP; NCEP; NOBE; NoP; OAEL-2; OAEP; OBNC; OBRV; PoEL-4; PPP; SeCePo
Well, if the thing is over, better it is for me. Mary, Helper of Heartbreak. Margaret Widdemer. HBMV
Well, if you must know all the facts. A Visitor. "Lewis Carroll." FaBoNo
Well, I'm a wild cowboy, I've roved the West o'er. Wild Bronc Peeler. *Unknown.* CoSo
Well! I'm goin' home. Special Rider Blues. *Unknown.* AmFP
Well I'm going to Memphis, come to stop at Cincinnat'. On the Wall. *Unknown.* BluL
Well, I'm in love with a feller, a feller you have seen. Common Bill. *Unknown.* AmFP
Well! in my many walks I've rarely found. The Pettichap's Nest. John Clare. PBBP
Well-informed Wight, A. Oliver Herford. TDH
Well-intentioned Question, The. Wendy Rose. STE; TWSS
Well it rained five days and the sky was dark as night. Back Water Blues. *Unknown.* FSW
Well, it was never mine. This Day, under My Hand. David Malouf. CBAP
Well, it's Mamma, Mamma, O Lawd, you don't know. Mamma, Mamma. *Unknown.* OuSiCo
Well, it's partly the shape of the thing. Limerick. *Unknown.* SoSe; WhC
Well its P.M agin. A Reflection of Night. T. Walking Eagle Marietta. LFAC
Well, Jesus died to save me in all of my sin. The Rock Island Line. *Unknown.* AmFP
Well last Monday morning. The Gray Goose. *Unknown.* FSW
Well look a-here, honey. Depot Blues. *Unknown.* AmFP
Well, mates, I don't like stories. California Joe. Jack Crawford. CoSo
Well may I weene, faire ladies, all this while. Spenser. The Faerie Queene, III, 6. OAEL-1
Well may that kisse be sweet that's giv'n t' a sleek. Giovanni Battista Guarini, *tr. by* Sir Richard Fanshawe. *Fr.* Il Pastor Fido. OBVE
Well may they write, that sit in parlours fine. On His Writing Verses. John Hawthorn. NOEC
Well meaning readers! you that come as friends. The Flaming Heart. Richard Crashaw. AnAnS-1; GoBC; LiTB; LoBV; OAEL-1; OxBoCh; PoEL-2; SeCePo; SeCV-1; TEP
We'll Meet Again. J. Danson Smith. STF
We'll meet beside the dusky glen, on yon burn side. By Yon Burn Side. Robert Tannahill. HBV-1
Well met, pretty nymph, says a jolly young swain. The Country Wedding. *Unknown.* HBV-1
"Well met, well met, my friend, all on the highway riding." The Husbandman and Serving-Man. *Unknown.* OBET
"Well met, well met, my own true love." The Demon Lover [*or* James Harris *or* The House Carpenter *or* The Carpenter's Wife]. *Unknown.* AmFP; BaBo; FSW; OBET; ViBoFo
Well mightst thou scorn thy readers to allure. Andrew Marvell. *Fr.* On Mr. Milton's Paradise Lost. PP
We'll Never Know. A. Hoellein. STF
We'll not weep for summer over. After Summer. Philip Bourke Marston. HBV-1
Well now, who does not know Katy Cline. Katy Cline. *Unknown.* FSW
Well now you know my mama told me. Six Week Old Blues. *Unknown.* BluL
We'll o'er the water and o'er the sea. O'er the Water to Charlie. Burns. FaBoCh
Well, of course. Leda and the Swan. Alice R. Friman. PoDr
Well of freshness, A. Juxta. Grover Jacoby. GoYe
Well of Life, The. Sir Herbert Read. NoAM
Well of St. Keyne, The. Robert Southey. BeLS; FaBoBe; HBV-2
Well of Vertew and Flour of Womanheid, The. *Unknown.* OxBS
Well, Old Flame, the fire's out. Static. Barton Sutter. AMV-81
Well, old spy. Award. Ray Durem. BPo; CABA; IDB; NNP; PoBA; SoSe; TTY
Well, Paul, when you were nine. Poem for My Son. John Logan. DiL
Well Pleaseth Me the Sweet Time of Easter. Bertrans de Born, *tr. by* Ezra Pound. InvP
(Song of Battle.) AWP; WaaP
(War Song, A.) CTC
Well pleasing 'tis to me. Goat's-Leaf. Marie de France, *tr. by* Aline Allard. PBWP
Well Rising, The. William Stafford. NaP
We'll Roll the Golden Chariot Along, *with music. Unknown.* ShS
(Roll the Chariot: "We'll roll, we'll roll the chariot along," *diff. vers., with music.*) AS
We'll sail from hence to Greece, to lovely Greece. The Song of Ithamore. Christopher Marlowe. *Fr.* The Jew of Malta. WHA
"We'll see who can stick." Fr Anselm Williams and Br Leander Neville. Elizabeth Smither. OCNZ
Well-shadowed landscape, fare ye well! Farewell to Love. Sir John Suckling. CaPo
We'll sing a song, a soldier's song. The Soldier's Song. Peadar Kearney. OnYI
Well, Sir, 'tis granted, I said D[ryden's] rhimes [*or* rhymes]. An Allusion to Horace [the Tenth Satire of the First Book]. Earl of Rochester. APAS; OBS
Well, So That Is That. W. H. Auden. *Fr.* For the Time Being; a Christmas Oratorio. LiTA; OAEL-2; OBCP
(After Christmas.) MoAB; MoBrPo
(Flight into Egypt, The.) OAEP; OxBA; SBVL
Well, some may hate, and some may scorn. Stanzas to ———. Emily Brontë. LoBV; WPE
Well, son, I'll tell you. Mother to Son. Langston Hughes. AmNP; CABA; CDC; CTBA; NTCP; OBCA; PoNe; SO; TTY
Well, standing on the corner with a dollar in my hand. Hesitation Blues. *Unknown.* FSW
"We'll talk all night until we swoon away," you promised. Eden Revisited. Vassar Miller. FAZ; GP
Well, that was silly; too near the edge. On Catching a Dog-Daisy in the Mower. Peter Redgrove. NePoEA-2
Well the baby crying on up to his mama's knee. That Crawling Baby Blues. *Unknown.* BluL
Well, the night was dark and drizzly. There Ain't No Bugs on Me. *Unknown.* FSW
Well, the other night when I came home. The Intoxicated Rat. *Unknown.* FSW
Well the sunset rays are shining. The Wild Mushroom. Gary Snyder. NoP
Well the ugliest little thing. Killer Diller. *Unknown.* BluL
Well then! I now do plainly see. The Wish. Abraham Cowley. *Fr.* The Mistress. CavP; HBV-1; LiTB; NOBE; NoP; OAEP; OBEV; OBS; SeCV-1; TrGrPo; ViBoPo; WHA
Well, then, the last day the sharks appeared. The Sharks. Denise Levertov. NeAP
Well then, the promis'd [*or* promised] hour is come at last. To My Dear Friend Mr. Congreve [on His Comedy Called "The Double-Dealer"]. Dryden. EBEV; FiP; OAEL-1; OBS; PoEL-3; SeCV-2
Well then, tomorrow! the wood exalts under the mild. Finally. Vittoria Aganoor Pompili, *tr. by* Brenda Webster. PBWP
Well there is in the west country, A. The Well of St. Keyne. Robert Southey. BeLS; FaBoBe; HBV-2
Well, they are gone, and here must I remain. This Lime-Tree Bower My Prison. Samuel Taylor Coleridge. EnRP; FaBoPP; HeIP; LoBV; NIP; PoEL-4
Well, they gave him his orders at Monroe, Virginia. The Wreck of the Old 97. *Unknown.* FSW
Well they'd made up their minds to be everywhere because why not. The Last One. W. S. Merwin. LCAP; NoAM; VGW
Well, they're quite dead, Rambuncto; thoroughly dead. Rambuncto. Margaret Widdemer. BXAP
Well, this bird comes, and under his wing is a crutch. The Bird. Moishe Leib Halpern, *tr. by* John Hollander. PPP
"Well, this is where I go down to the river." Heat. Kenneth Mackenzie. CBAP; PoAu-2
"Well, though it seems." Liddell and Scott; on the Completion of Their Lexicon. Thomas Hardy. OxBoLi
We'll to the woods and gather may. Alons au bois le may cueillir. Charles d'Orléans, *tr. by* W. E. Henley. AWP
We'll to the Woods No More. A. E. Housman. OAEL-2; PoRA
Well, to-day Jeane is my set time vor to goo. Come an' Meet Me wi' the Children on the Road. William Barnes. VLP
Well tonight the damnfool sunset pitched. What Maisie Know She Don't Want No. Judith Johnson Sherwin. NoAM

Well, traveling to the ruins of ancient rivalries. The Temple at Segesta. Raymond Henri. GLGT
Well-travelled Roadway, The. John Newlove. NeAC
Well, The: Two Songs. *Gond Oral Tradition, tr. by* V. Elwin *and* S. Hivale. WTO
We'll wander to the woods no more. The Woods No More. Jay MacPherson. PeCV
Well, Wanton Eye. Charles d'Orléans. HAP
Well was dry beside the door, The. Going for Water. Robert Frost. HBMV
Well Water. Randall Jarrell. NOBA; NoP; VGW
Well water. Eight Sandbars on the Takano River. Gary Snyder. CoPo
Well we done told you. Jesus Is Coming Soon. *Unknown.* BluL
Well—we have reached the precipice at last. On the Masquerades. Christopher Pitt. NOEC
"Well," we say, "time to go." So then we pack. After Vacation. Katherine Hanley. AMV-81
Well, we will do that rigid thing. Parting with Lucasia; a Song. Katherine Philips. PeHV
Well, well, I know the wise ones talk and talk. Augusta Webster. *Fr.* A Castaway. BrRo
Well, well, 'tis true. Plain Dealing. Alexander Brome. OBS
Well well well. Motherless Children. *Unknown.* BluL
Well, when all is said and done. Epilogue. "Æ." MoBrPo
Well when you can't see the forest. Orange Juice Song. David Phillips. NeAC
Well, whilst we here, sonny, having fun. Kentucky Blues. *Unknown.* BluL
Well-wishing to a Place of Pleasure, A. *Unknown.* GBL
Well, world, you have kept faith with me. He Never Expected Much. Thomas Hardy. NAs; NoAM; OxBTC; SCV
Well worthy to be magnified are they. The Pilgrim Fathers. Wordsworth. PAH
Well, yes, I've lived in Texas since the spring of '61. A Spool of Thread. Sophie E. Eastman. PAH
Well, yes, sir, dat am a comical name. Ashcake. Thomas Nelson Page. AA
Well yonder stands little Maggie. Little Maggie. *Unknown.* FSW
Well, you go back then to the central question. On the Last Page of the Last Yellow Pad. Miller Williams. AMV-80
Well, you know the sun is going down. Lowdown Dirty Blues. *Unknown.* AmFP
Well you wake up in the morning. Midnight Special. Leadbelly (Huddie Ledbetter). FSW
Well-a, jumpin', Jumpin' Judy. Drive It On. *Unknown.* OuSiCo
Welladay, welladay, poor Colin, thou art going to the ground. Dirge [*or* The Shepherd's Dirge]. George Peele. *Fr.* The Arraignment of Paris. EIL; OBSC
"Wellcome, to the Caves of Artá!" Robert Graves. NOBL; NYBP
Wellfleet Harbor. Paul Goodman. CoAP
Wellington. Byron. *Fr.* Don Juan, IX. OBRV
("Oh, Wellington (or 'Villainton") for Fame.") OBSV; OxBoLi
(On Wellington.) FiP
Wellington. Benjamin Disraeli. OBVV
Wellington. Bill Manhire. OCNZ
Wellington Letter, *sel.* Lauris Edmond.
"There are fixed points," *fr.* XI. OCNZ
Wells. Donald Hall. NMP
Wells of air pour down, The. Pour Down. John Holmes. NePoAm
Wells of Jesus Wounds, The. *Unknown. See* Jesus' Wounds So Wide.
Welsh Incident. Robert Graves. CMoP; NOBE; OxBTC; WSC
Welsh Landscape. R. S. Thomas. FaBoMo
Welsh Marches, The. A. E. Housman. FaBoTw
Welsh Sea, The. James Elroy Flecker. BrPo
Welshman by the pit whose Sabbath voice, The. E. W. Mandel. *Fr.* Minotaur Poems. OBCV
Welshman to Any Tourist, A. R. S. Thomas. OxBC
Welshmen of Tirawley, The. Sir Samuel Ferguson. OBVV; OnYI
Welt. Georgia Douglas Johnson. BANP
Welt ist dumm, die Welt ist blind, Die. Heine, *tr. fr. German by* James Thomson. AWP
Welter upon the waters, mighty one. Sonnet to the Sea Serpent. John G. C. Brainard. EtS
Weltschmerz. Frank Yerby. AmNP
Wemen's Wather. T. S. Law. OxBS
Wen first thy Eies unveil, give thy Soul leave. Rules and Lessons. Henry Vaughan. AnAnS-1
W'en us fellers stomp around, makin' lots o' noise. When a Feller's Itchin' to be Spanked. Paul Laurence Dunbar. BALP
We'n you see a man in woe. "Hullo!" S. W. Foss. CenHV; PaPo
Wenberi's Song. Wenberi, *tr. fr Woiworung by* A. W. Howitt. CBAP
Wendell Phillips. Amos Bronson Alcott. AA
Wendell Phillips, *sel.* John Boyle O'Reilly.
"What shall we mourn? For the prostrate." AA
Wendigo, The. Ogden Nash. AmMo; RHPC
Wendling. Coman Leavenworth. Norfolk Memorials, III. LiTA
Wendy in Winter. Kaye Starbird. RHPC
Wenes King Edward with his longe shankes. The Scots in Berwick (1296). *Unknown.* OxBM
Wenest thou, usher, with thyn cointise. A Schoolboy's Lot. *Unknown.* OxBM
Wenlock Edge ("On Wenlock Edge the wood's in trouble"). A. E. Housman. *See* On Wenlock Edge.
Wenlock Edge (" 'Tis time, I think; by Wenlock town"). A. E. Housman. A Shropshire Lad, XXXIX. FaBoPP
(" 'Tis time, I think, by Wenlock town.") PoPle
(Wenlock.) SeCePo
Wenne, wenne, wenchichenne. Charm against Wens. *Unknown.* OxBM
Wenslaydale Lad, The. *Unknown.* FaBoPP
Went down on Johnson Street. Bob McKinney. *Unknown.* BluL
Went down to St. Joe's infirmary. Those Gambler's Blues. *Unknown.* AS
Went into a shoestore to buy a pair of shoes. Sale. Josephine Miles. POL; WPE
"Went to NCC for a year." Sheepherder Blues. Luci Tapahonso. STE
Went up a year this evening. Emily Dickinson. HAP; WeW
Went up on the hill, 'bout 12 o'clock. Fishing Blues. *Unknown.* BluL
Went up on the mountain. Bile Them Cabbage Down. *Unknown.* FSW
Went weeping, little bones. But where? I Cry, Love! Love! Theodore Roethke. LCAP; MoVE
Wenzel knelt to his tied ram. Ram Time. William Heyen. GeTw
We're A' Dry wi' the Drinkin' O't. *Unknown.* ErPo; ELU
(We're All Dry.) NOBL, *sl. diff. vers.*
("We're all dry with drinking on't.") OxNR, *sl. diff. vers.*
"We're all Americans, except the Doc." A Mad Negro Soldier Confined at Munich. Robert Lowell. FaBoMo; NMP; OxBC
We're all at home. Having Eaten Breakfast. D. C. Berry. BXAP
We're All Bound to Go. *Unknown.* AmSS
We're All Dry. *Unknown. See* We're A' Dry wi' the Drinking O't.
We're All in the Dumps. *Unknown. See* In the Dumps.
We're all inclined to bore our friends. Ballade of a Summer Hotel. "Junia." WhC
We're all met here together. We Won't Go Home till Morning. *Unknown.* PSoN
We're all met together here, to sit and to crack. The Work of the Weavers. *Unknown.* FSW
Were all our sins so empty of enjoyment. The Muted Screen of Graham Greene. Phyllis McGinley. FaBoEE
We're alone, Doney Gal, in the rain [*or* wind] and hail. Doney Gal. *Unknown.* CoSo; FSW; OuSiCo
We're an Africanpeople. Don L. Lee. *Fr.* African Poems. CNA
Were [*or* Where] beth [*or* beeth] they [that] biforen us weren. Ubi Sunt Qui ante Nos Fuerunt? [*or* Contempt of the World]. *Unknown.* EBEV; HAP; MeEL; NoP; OAEP; OxBM; PrIm; SeCeV; WeW
Were But My Spirit Loosed upon the Air. Louise Chandler Moulton. AA; HBV-1
Were but that sigh a penitential breath. Melancholy. William Habington. *Fr.* Castara, II. LoBV
We're coming, we're coming, our brave little band. Away with Rum. *Unknown.* FSW
We're connecting. Poems for the New. Kathleen Fraser. IHMS; NMM
We're crossing the bar of another year. "I Am with Thee." Ernest Bourner Allen. BLRP
We're 'er Majesty's bold troubleshooter; wherever they send us we goes. Bold Troubleshooters. Peter Veale. NOBL
We're flattered they come so close. Animal Song. Heather McHugh. MAYP
We're foot—slog—slog—slog—sloggin' over Africa. Boots. Kipling. BLPA; FaPoR; FPL; MoBrPo; WHA
We're going to the fair at Holstenwall. Holstenwall. Sidney Keyes. FaBoTw
We're Gonna Move When the Spirit Says Move! *Unknown.* FSW
We're gonna roll, we're gonna roll. Roll the Union On. Claude Williams *and* Lee Hays. FSW
Were half the power that fills the world with terror. A Message of Peace. Longfellow. *Fr.* The Arsenal at Springfield. PGD; WBLP
We're having a lovely time to-day! Fun in a Garret. Emma C. Dowd. SUS; TiPo
Were he and the singing two songs, or one? Questions for the Candidate. John Holmes. PP
Were he composer, he would surely write. Portrait of the Boy as Artist. Barbara Howes. DFF; MoAmPo
"We're homeward bound," I hear them say. Homeward Bound, *vers.* II. *Unknown.* ShS

"We're homeward bound," I heard our captain say. Homeward Bound, *vers.* III. *Unknown.* ShS
"We're homeward bound!" I've heard them say. Homeward Bound, *vers. I. Unknown.* ShS
We're hoping to be arrested. Street Demonstration. Margaret Walker. BPo; CNA
Were I a happy bird. Faith Trembling. "Madeline Bridges." AA
Were I a king, I could command content. A Choice [*or* A Doubtful Choice *or* Epigram]. Edward de Vere, Earl of Oxford. EIL; FaBoEE; OBSC
Were I a real Poet, I would sing. James Thomson. Sunday up the River, X. OAEP
Were I a rose, and did you dare. The Amorist. *Unknown, tr. by* Louis Untermeyer. UnTE
Were I as Base as Is the Lowly Plain. *At. to* Joshua Sylvester. HBV-1
(Love's Omnipresence.) GTBS; GTBS-P
(Sonnet: "Were I as base as is the lowly plain.") EIL; OBSC; ViBoPo
(Ubique.) OBEV
Were I invited to a nectar feast. Sylvia. Samuel Croxall. NOEC
Were I Laid on Greenland's Coast. John Gay. *See* Song: "Were I laid on Greenland's coast."
Were I the palm tree which your love returning. E Questo il Nido in Che la Mia Fenice? A. D. Hope. OxBC
Were I the red-brushed fox, I should go warier. November Fugitive. Henry Morton Robinson. GoYe
Were I to Choose. Gabriel Okara. PBA
Were I to leave no more than a good friend. The Departure; an Elegy. Henry King. SeCP
Were I to Mount beyond the Field. Sidney Keyes. The Foreign Gate, V. MoPo
Were I to name, out of the times gone by. The Dearest Poets. Leigh Hunt. HBV-2
Were I to take an iron gun. Facts. "Lewis Carroll." FaBoUs
Were I transported to some distant star. A Plain Man's Dream. Frederick Keppel. AA
Were I west in green Arran. The Cup of O'Hara [*or* When Kian O'Hara's Cup Was Passed to Turlough O'Carolan]. Turlough Carolan, *tr. by* Sir Samuel Ferguson. AnIV; OnYI
Were I, who to my cost already am. A Satire [*or* Satyr] against [Reason and] Mankind. Earl of Rochester. FaBoEn; LiTB; MasP; NOBE; NoP; OAEL-1; OBS; OBSV; PoEL-3; SCV; SeCV-2
Were it undo that is y-do. He Is Far [*or* A Forsaken Maiden's Lament]. *Unknown.* OAEL-1; SeCePo
We're marching 'round the levee. Marching 'round the Levee. *Unknown.* AmFP
"We're married," said Eddie. The Newlyweds. John Updike. PV
Were My Heart [*or* Hart] as Some Men's Are. Thomas Campion. AAS; HBV-1
Were Not the Gael Fallen. Peadar O'Mulconry, *tr. fr. Early Modern Irish by* Robin Flower. AnIL
We're OK. Gloria Fuertes, *tr. fr. Spanish by* Philip Levine. WPOW
We're queer folks here. Just Folks. Edgar A. Guest. FaFP; TreFS
We're Racing, Racing down the Walk. Phyllis McGinley. RHPC
We're rolling on the living room floor. Shaggy Dog Story. Frank Steele. Str
We're sailing down the river from Liverpool. Santy Anno. *Unknown.* FSW; OuSiCo
Were Shakespeare born a twin, his lunar twin. To the Authoress of "Aurora Leigh." Sydney Dobell. PeD
We're sinking into beds of lights that. Night: Landing at Newark. Jonathan Holden. PPJ
We're Tenting To-Night. Walter Kittredge. *See* Tenting on the Old Camp Ground.
Were thanks with every gift expressed. Thanksliving. Chauncey R. Piety. PGD
We're the D-Day Dodgers, out [*or* way off] in Italy. Ballad of the D-Day Dodgers. *Unknown.* FSW; WTO
We're the hardrock men. Dynamite Song. *Unknown.* AmFP
Were the whole world good as you—not an atom better. The Question. *Unknown.* WBLP
Were ther outher in this town. His Sweetheart Slain. *Unknown.* OxBM
Were there lovers in the lanes of Atlantis. Song at Santa Cruz. Francis Brett Young. HBMV
Were there no crowns on earth. The Dead President. Edward Rowland Sill. PAH
Were they ever there, whether you. Displacement. Horace Hamilton. AMV-80
Were this impossible, I know full well. A House and Grounds. Leigh Hunt. OBRV
We're up in a balloon. Survey. Paul Lawson. GP
We're up in the morning ere breaking of day. The Railroad Corral. *Unknown.* TrAS
Were we now to fall. The Mechanic. Robert Creeley. NaP
Were you a leper bathed in wounds. Proving. Georgia Douglas Johnson. CDC
Were you born of lioness in the Libyan Mountains. Catullus, *tr. fr. Latin by* Horace Gregory. NAWM-1
Were You Ever in Dumbarton? *with music.* *Unknown.* ShS
Were you ever in Quebec. Donkey Riding. *Unknown.* WHW
Were You on the Mountain. *Unknown, tr. fr. Irish by* Douglas Hyde. PV
Were You There When They Crucified My Lord? *Unknown.* AH, *with music;* BoAN-2, *with music*; BPo; FSW
Were yu normal today did yu screw society. Christ I Wudint Know Normal if I Saw It When. Bill Bissett. NOBC
Werena My Heart Licht Wad Dee. Lady Grisel Baillie. *See* There Ance Was a May.
Were-Wolf. Julian Hawthorne. AA
Werfel dead? Hark. The forest is empty. The Shooting of Werfel. Vernon Watkins. WaP
Wersh an drumlie are the lees. Sang: Recoll o Skaith. Sidney Goodsir Smith. NeBP
Werther had a love for Charlotte. The Sorrows of Werther. Thackeray. BLPA; CenHV; FaBoCo; FiBHP; FPL; HBV-1; InMe; NA; NBM; NOBL; PoPle; ShM; TreF; VLP
Wes Hardin: From a Photograph. Raymond Carver. GeTw
Wesley in Heaven. Thomas Edward Brown. *See* Organist in Heaven, The.
Wessex Heights. Thomas Hardy. CMoP; EBVV; FaBoEn; FaBoPP; OAEL-2; OBNC; PoEL-5
West, The. Edwin Muir. MoVE
West and away the wheels of darkness roll. Revolution. A. E. Housman. Last Poems, XXXVI. BrPo; ImOP; NoP
West-Country Damosel's Complaint, The. *Unknown.* ESPB
West-Country Lover, The. Alice Brown. HBV-1
West-Easterly Divan, *sels.* Goethe, *tr. fr. German by* John Weiss. PeHV
Cupbearer Speaks, The, *fr.* Bk. 9.
"Market square's admiring throngs, The," *fr.* Bk. 9.
West End Blues. John Hollander. NYP
West Fifty-seventh Street. Byron Vazakas. FAZ
West Forties, The: Morning, Noon, and Night. L. E. Sissman. CoAP; NYBP; NYP
West Helena Blues. *Unknown.* BluL
West Indies, The, *sels.* James Montgomery.
Inspiration, The. PAH
Lust of Gold, The. PAH
West Lake. Kenneth O. Hanson. CoAP
West London. Matthew Arnold. FF; OAEP
West of Alice. W. E. Harney. PoAu-1
West of Chicago. John Dimoff. RFM
West of the Sierras where. The California Phrasebook. Dennis Schmitz. AmPA; NPGG
West of Your City. William Stafford. LiTM
West of your door, Blue Mountain dreams of melting. Blue Mountain. Roberta Hill. VoR
West Palm Beach Storm, The. *Unknown.* AmFP
West Ridge Is Menthol-cool, The. D. L. Graham. PoBA
West-running Brook. Robert Frost. AP; BLPL; MoAB; MoAmPo; NOBA; NoP
West, so they say, is the home of the jay, The. Forty-five Minutes from Broadway. George M. Cohan. FSN
West Sussex Drinking Song. Hilaire Belloc. MoBrPo
West Texas. *At. to* Leona Mae Austin. CoSo
West Wind, The. John Masefield. FaFP; FPL; LiTB; LiTM; MoAB; MoBrPo; PoPl; TreF
West Wind ("West wind tae the bairn"). *Unknown.* PoPle
West wind, blow from your prairie nest. The Song My Paddle Sings. E. Pauline Johnson. BPAW; CaP; FaPON; HBV-1
West wind dances down the lane and sets the robins winging, The. Spring Wind. Nancy Byrd Turner. SiSoSe
Westering. Douglas V. Kane. GoYe
Western Approach, The. Howard Nemerov. TAP
Western Formula. *Unknown.* PoOW
Western Magic. Mary Austin. AmFN
Western Movies. Jeffry Jensen. AMV-80
Western Rebel, The. *Unknown.* APAS
Western Star, *sel.* Stephen Vincent Benét.
"Americans are always moving on." AmFN
Western Sun withdraws the shorten'd [*or* shortened] day, The. Moonlight in Autumn. James Thomson. *Fr.* The Seasons: Autumn. NOBE; OBEC
Western Town. David Wadsworth Cannon, Jr. PoNe
Western Town. Karl Shapiro. NYBP
Western Trail, The. Robert V. Carr. PoOW
Western Wagons. Rosemary *and* Stephen Vincent Benét. BPAW
Western Waves of Ebbing Day, The. Sir Walter Scott. *Fr.* The Lady of the Lake, I. PoEL-4
Western Ways. Richmond Lattimore. AMV-80

Western Wind. *Unknown.* BiP; CABA; CTC; FF; GBP; HAP; HeIP; InPK; MAT; MeEL; NIP; NOBE; NoP; OAEL-1; PPP; UnPo
(Absence.) OBSC
(Lover in Winter Plaineth for the Spring, The.) OBEV; SpRo
(O Western Wind.) HoPM; LiTB; PoPle; SpRo; TrGrPo; UnTE
(Song: "Westron wynde when wyll thou blow.") SeCePo
("Western wind, when will [*or* wilt] thou blow.") BoLoP; EBEV; EnLoPo; FaBoCh; LLLT; OLR; PrIM; SeCeV; TEP; ViBoPo
(Westron Winde, When Will Thou Blow.) InvP; MeEL; PoEL-1; PPoe
("Westron wynd, when will thou blow.") GBL
(Westron Wynde.) PAI
Western wind has blown but a few days, The. The Cranes. Po Chü-i, *tr. by* Arthur Waley. OBVE
Western wind is blowing fair, The. Serenade. Oscar Wilde. HBV-1
Western Wind, When Will Thou Blow. *Unknown. See* Western Wind.
Westgate-on-Sea. John Betjeman. OxBoLi
Westland Row. Thomas Kinsella. NoAM
Westland Row. James Stephens. HBMV
Westminster Bridge. Wordsworth. *See* Composed upon Westminster Bridge, September 3, 1802.
Westminster Drollery, 1671. Aphra Behn. SBG
(That Beauty I Ador'd Before.) UnTE
Westminster Wedding, A; or, Like unto Like, Quoth the Devil to the Collier. *Unknown.* CoMu
Westphalian Song. *Unknown, tr. fr. German by* Samuel Taylor Coleridge. AWP; OBVE
Westron Winde, When Will Thou Blow. *Unknown. See* Western Wind.
Westron Wynde. *Unknown. See* Western Wind.
West's Asleep, The. Thomas Osborne Davis. OnYI
Westward, hit a low note, for a roarer lost. A Strut for Roethke. John Berryman. NOBA
Westward Ho! Joaquin Miller. AA; FaBoBe
Westward Ho. *Unknown.* CoSo
Westward I watch the low green hills of Wales. Clevedon Church. Andrew Lang. BSV; GoTS
Westward the field of the cloth of gold. A Visit. Sherwood Anderson. PoA
Wet almond-trees, in the rain. Bare Almond-Trees. D. H. Lawrence. FaBoPP
Wet August, A. Thomas Hardy. PPP
Wet Casements. John Ashbery. PoM
Wet dawn inks are doing their blue dissolve, The. Winter Trees. Sylvia Plath. LCAP; NMM; SBG
Wet day on the road, A: the slim blades cutting. Windshield. Robert Fitzgerald. CrMA
Wet gray day, A—rain falling slowly. Morels. William Jay Smith. BoNaP; MAT; NYBP; RFM
Wet Hair: If Now His Mother Should Come. Robert Penn Warren. *Fr.* Penological Study: Southern Exposure. NoAM
Wet Night, A. Richard Ryan. CIP
Wet or Fine. Amory Hare. HBMV
Wet Sheet and a Flowing Sea, A. Allan Cunningham. BSV; EnRP; EtS; GoTS; GTBS; GTBS-P; HBV-1; HBVY; OBRV; PaPo; RoGo; TiPo; TreFS
(Sea-Song, A.) FaBoBe; FaPoR; GN
Wet streets are undisturbed by that chronic, The. Sirens in Bad Weather. Sherod Santos. MAYP
Wet streets. It has rained drops big as silver coins. Eighteen. Maria Banus, *tr. by* Willis Barnstone *and* Matei Calinescu. BoWoP; VWA
Wet Summer. May Williams Ward. GoYe
Wet Thursday. Weldon Kees. NaP; NYBP
Wet, wayward fingers of the west wind wave the wheat. Corn Cañon. Patric Stevenson. NeIP
Wet Weather. Patricia Low. VGW
Wet Weather at Cannes. Edward Lear. FaBoNo
Wet your feet, wet your feet. To an Irish Blackbird. James MacAlpine. HBMV; HBVY
We've billards, bowls an' tennis courts, we've teas an' motor-rides. The Convalescent. Cicily Fox Smith. SUMH
We've come intil a gey queer time. Epistle to John Guthrie. Sydney Goodsir Smith. OxBS
We've despatched, pour la guerre. Message to General Montgomery. H. F. Ellis. WhC
We've [*or* We're] formed our band and are well manned. The Californian [*or* Sacramento]. *Unknown.* AmFP; TrAS
We've fought with many men acrost the seas. Fuzzy-Wuzzy. Kipling. BrPo; HBV-2; MoBrPo; TrGrPo
We've found this Scott Fitzgerald chap. Effervescence and Evanescence. Keith Preston. OBAL
We've hung David's *La Vierge et Les Saintes*. The Living Room. Gjertrud Schnackenberg. FYAP
We've kept the faith. Our souls' high dreams. To Our Friends. Lucian B. Watkins. BANP
We've lived for forty years, dear wife. The Ideal Husband to his Wife. Sam Walter Foss. InMe
We've made a great mess of love. The Mess of Love. D. H. Lawrence. OAEL-2
"We've no heard frae God this while." In Absentia. Alastair Mackie. BSV
We've nothing vast to offer you, no deserts. A Welshman to Any Tourist. R. S. Thomas. OxBC
We've put a fine addition on the good old church at home. The Ladies' Aid. *Unknown.* PoLF
We've [*or* I've] reached the land of desert sweet. Dakota Land. *Unknown.* AS; BPAW; CoSo; FSW
We've tabled it all. Tables. Naomi Clark. AMV-80
We've taken our burlap sacks and entered. The Killigrew Wood. Norman Dubie. AmPA
We've taken the dog for his walk. To a Child. S. S. Gardons. NePoEA-2
We've traveled together through life's rugged way. My Bible and I. *Unknown.* STF
We've trod the maze of error round. Late Wisdom. George Crabbe. *Fr.* Reflections. HBV-1; OBEV; OBRV; TrGrPo
Wexford Girl, The ("It was in the town of Wexford [*or* Waterford]"). *Unknown.* ShS, *diff. vers., with music;* ViBoFO
Wexford Girl, The ("My tender parents brought me here"). *Unknown.* AmFP
Wha gangs wi' us owre the hill. Owre the Hill. William Soutar. PoSH
Wha Is Perfyte. Alexander Scott. GoTS
Wha Is That at My Bower-Door? Burns. ErPo; InvP; UnTE
Wha kens on whatna Bethlehems. The Innumerable Christ. "Hugh MacDiarmid." EaLo; EBEV; NoP; OxBS
Wha lies here? Johnny Dow [*or* Doo]. *Unknown.* FaBoCo; FaBoEE; FiBHP; PV; WhC
Wha wadna be in love. Maggie Lauder. *Unknown, at. to* Francis Sempill. OBS; OxBS
Whacha mean you only goes fo bass? Roosevelt Considers Catfish Stew. R. T. Smith. WOLT
Whack Fol the Diddle. Peadar Kearney. FiBHP; OnYI
Whaddaya Do for Action in This Place? George Starbuck. NePoEA-2
Whalan of Waitin' a While. J. W. Gordon. PoAu-1
Whale. William Rose Benét. EtS; MoAmPo
Whale, The. Buson, *tr. fr. Japanese by* Harold G. Henderson. SoPo
Whale, The. John Donne. *Fr.* The Progress of the Soul. ChTr
Whale, The. Herman Melville. *See* Father Mapple's Hymn.
Whale, The ("Cethegrande is a fis"). *Unknown.* OxBM
Whale, The ("Now I will fashion the tale of a fish"). *Unknown, tr. fr. Anglo-Saxon by* Charles W. Kennedy. *Fr.* Physiologus. AnOE; MOS
(Whale, The ["To explain the nature of fishes in craft of verse"], *shorter sel., tr. by* Gavin Bone.) EBEV
Whale, The ("'Tis a hundred years,' said the bosun bold"). *Unknown.* EtS
Whale, The ("Twas [*or* It was] in the year of . . ."). *Unknown. See* Greenland Whale Fishery, The.
Whale and the *Essex*, The. A. M. Sullivan. EtS
Whale at Twilight. Elizabeth J. Coatsworth. BoAnP
Whale butting through scarps of moving marble, The. Explorations. Louis MacNeice. ChMP; CoBMV
Whale got my friend, The. One Thousand Feet of Shadow. David Craig. PoSH
Whale, His Bulwark, The. Derek Walcott. OxBC; TTY
Whale, improbable as lust, The. A Tall Tale; or, A Moral Song. Phyllis Webb. OBCV
Whale is killed as follows, A. Killing a Whale. David Gill. BoAnP
Whale Song. Francis Maguire. BoAnP; POL
Whaleman's Song, The. *Unknown.* EtS
Whalen's Fate, *with music. Unknown.* ShS
Whales. Scott Bates. BoAnP
Whales, The. Marguerite Young. WPE
Whales off Wales, The. X. J. Kennedy. OBCA
Whales Weep Not! D. H. Lawrence. CMoP; MOS; NU; PPoe
Wha'll buy [my] caller herrin? Caller Herrin'. Lady Nairne. HBV-1; OBRV; OxBS
Whaloon's waters, thick with algal bloom. Hooking the Rainbow. Tama Baldwin. WOLT
Wham!/ Comes the wrecking ball. Construction. Virginia Schonborg. QQQ
Whan bells war rung, an mass was sung. Sweet William's Ghost. *Unknown.* ESPB
Whan gloamin' grey out-owre the welkin keeks. The Farmer's Ingle. Robert Fergusson. BSV
Whan my faither's faither was a bairn. The Star. William Soutar. NeBP
Whan netilles in winter bere roses rede. Impossible to Trust Women. *Unknown.* MeEL
Whan that April[le] with his shoures [*or* showres] soote [*or* sote]. Chaucer.

The Canterbury Tales: Prologue. ChTr; CTC; FiP; GoBC; InPS; NIP; NoP; OAEL-1; OAEP; PPP; PrIm; SCV; SeCeV; TrGrPo; ViBoPo
Whan that Aprille with hise shoures soote. Aprilly. Bert Leston Taylor. OBAL
Whan that the knight had thus his tale ytold. The Miller's Prologue. Chaucer. *Fr.* The Canterbury Tales. OAEL-1
Whan the Hert Is Laich. Sidney Goodsir Smith. NeBP
Whango Tree, The. *Unknown.* NA
Whanne I this Supplicacioun. The Parting of Venus and Old Age. John Gower. *Fr.* Confessio Amantis, VIII. PoEL-1
Whanne ic se on Rode. I Ought to Weep. *Unknown.* MeEL
"Whar hae ye been a' day, my boy Tammy?" My Boy Tammy. Hector MacNeill. CH
Whare the braid planes in dowy murmurs wave. The Ghaists; a Kirk-yard Eclogue. Robert Fergusson. OxBS
"Wharefore sou'd ye talk o' love." Willie and Helen. Hew Ainslie. HBV-1
Wharf, May 1978, The. Carolyn Foster Segal. WOLT
Wharf of Dreams, The. Edwin Markham. HBV-2
Wharton. Pope. *Fr.* Epistle to Sir Richard Temple. AWP
("Wharton! the scorn and wonder of our days.") DBV
What? Langston Hughes. OBAL
What/ has happened. Here. Robert Creeley. NOBA
What/ is it about. The Universe. May Swenson. SUW
What a beautiful day for a wedding in May! For Me and My Gal. Edgar Leslie *and* E. Ray Goetz. BLSo
What a beautiful thought I'm thinking. The Great Speckled Bird. *Unknown.* FSW
What a calamity! What dreadful loss! Honesty at a Fire. J. C. Squire. FiBHP
What a charming thing's a battle! Air. Isaac Bickerstaffe. *Fr.* The Recruiting Serjeant. NOEC
What a commanding power. Prayer. Thomas Washbourne. WGRP
What a Court Hath Old England, *with music. Unknown.* TrAS, *incl.* You Simple Bostonians
What a cruel way to learn. For an Old Friend. Norbert Krapf. AMV-81
What a curious sculptor is Moore! A "Twiner." J. A. Lindon. DBV
What a drag it must be for you! Suzie's Enzyme Poem. Paul Zimmer. PPJ
What a fine cow your predecessor was! To a Sacred Cow. *Unknown, tr. by* W. E. Mashiel. WGRP
What a fine hunting day, it's as balmy as May. We'll All Go a-Hunting Today. *Unknown.* OBET
What a fine tower the little boy is building with his blocks. Time. Avraham Huss, *tr. by* Mark Elliott Shapiro. VWA
What a Friend We Have in Cheeses! William Cole. OBAL
What a Friend We Have in Jesus. Joseph Scriven. FSW; TreFT
(Unfailing Friend, The.) BLRP
What a Friend We Have in Mother. Charles E. Roat. FSW
What a girl called "the dailiness of life." Well Water. Randall Jarrell. NOBA; NoP; VGW
What a Grand and Glorious Feeling. Bill Wolff. FSW
What a grudge I am bearing the earth. A Translation from Petrarch. Petrarch, *tr. by* J. M. Synge. Sonnets to Laura: To Laura in Death, XXXII. MoBrPo
What a host you are, Mancinus. Martial, *tr. fr. Latin by* Peter Porter. OBVE
What a hot day it is! A Terrestrial Cuckoo. Frank O'Hara. SOTW
What a liar/ Was the tinker woman. Outside Dunsandle. Sacheverell Sitwell. ChMP
What a malicious sense of humour. The Comedian. Irving Layton. AMV-81
What a man may do for love. All for Love. *Unknown, tr. by* Louis Untermeyer. UnTE
What a moment of strange dreaming! Mind Flying Afar. Edgar Lee Masters. PoA
What a moment, what a doubt! Sneezing. Leigh Hunt. HBV-2
What a morning! We haven't had a day. Good Weather. Giuseppe Gioachino Belli, *tr. by* Miller Williams. AMV-81
What a night! The wind howls, hisses, and but stops. Snowstorm. John Clare. BoNaP; WiR
What a piece of work is a man! Man. Shakespeare. *Fr.* Hamlet, II, ii. TreF
What a plague is this o' mine. Jenny wi' the Airn Teeth. Alexander Anderson. HBV-1
What a pox do you mean with your pride and ill-nature. A Solitary Canto to Chloris the Disdainful. John Smith. NOEC
What a Proud Dreamhorse. E. E. Cummings. InvP; VGW
What a relief, to find it in the *language.* Lapsus Linguae. Richard Howard. NoAM
What a sorrowful sunset we had tonight! Winter Sunset. Jules Laforgue, *tr. by* Kate Flores. SyP
What a thrill. Cut. Sylvia Plath. CABA; CAPP; InPK; TAP
What a trick. Ragout. William Zaranka. BXAP
"What a waste of a beautiful girl!" Last Letter to the Western Civilization. D. T. Ogilvie. NBP
What a wonderful bird the frog are. The Frog. *Unknown.* MoShBr; NTCP; TreFT; WhC; YaD
What a word and I thought it would be. Alone. Richard Shelton. NYBP
What a world that was you planned us. John o' Dreams. Theodosia Garrison. HBMV
What about each Great Canadian Lake? The Great Lakes of Canada. Gordon Perry. FaBoUs
What about measure, I learnt. Peri Poietikes. Louis Zukofsky. CoPo
What about that bad short you saw last week. Black People! Amiri Baraka. BPo
What about the people who came to my father's office. The Questions. Robert Pinsky. NPGG
What about You? Edward Pygge. BXAP; FaBoPa
What! After your six-month drowsing and indolent sleeping. At the Edge of the Bay. Thomas Caldecot Chubb. EtS
What ailes Pigmalion? Is it lunacy. The Poem. Thomas Morton. SCAP
What ails John Winter, that so oft. John Winter. Laurence Binyon. MOS
What! alive and so bold, O Earth? Lines Written on Hearing the News of the Death of Napoleon. Shelley. ChER
What Am I? Abo Stoltzenberg, *tr. fr. Yiddish by* Gabriel Preil *and* Howard Schwartz. VWA
What am I in the place of nourishment. A Curse on Uruk. Enheduanna, *tr. fr. Sumerian.* BoWoP
What Am I, Life? John Masefield. *Fr.* Sonnets ("Long long ago"). ImOP
What am I? Nosing here, turning leaves over. Wodwo. Ted Hughes. NoAM
What am I to do with my Sister? Prince Yuhara. *Fr.* Manyo Shu. AWP
What Am I Who Dare to Call Thee, God! William Habington. OxBoCh
(What Am I Who Dare.) TrPWD
What an elusive target. The Fights. Milton Acorn. MoCV; NOBC
What? an English sparrow sing? Did You Ever Hear an English Sparrow Sing? Bertha Johnston. BLPA
What answer could she give. Innocence. Norman MacCaig. NMP
What answer shall we make to them that seek. Lincoln. Florence Kiper Frank. PGD
What are all the hillmen wanting. The Keeper of the Midnight Gate. George Mackay Brown. OxBC
What are days for? Days. Philip Larkin. EBEV; FaBoMo; OxBC
What Are Heavy? Christina Rossetti. FaBoRV; OxBChV
(Sea-Sand and Sorrow.) ChTr
("What are heavy? sea-sand and sorrow.") FaBoEE
What are little boys made of, made of? Mother Goose. FaFP; OxNR; TreF, 5 *sts.*
What are our light afflictions here. Our Light Afflictions. *Unknown.* BLRP
What Are Outward Forms? Isaac Bickerstaffe. OnYI
What are poets? Are they only drums commanding? No Armistice in Love's War. Ralph Cheyney. PGD
"What are ruins to us." At Lindos. May Sarton. WPE
"What are the bugles blowin' for?" said Files-on-Parade. Danny Deever. Kipling. BrPo; EBVV; FaBoBa; FaPoR; FPL; GTBS-P; HBV-2; InPS; LiTB; MoBrPo; NOBE; OAEP; OxBoLi; OxBTC; PoLF; SCV; SeCePo; TEP; TreFS; TrGrPo; UnPo; VLP; WaaP
What are the five dreams of the elders? The Five Dreams. John Woods. FiCP
What are the islands to me. The Islands. Hilda Doolittle ("H. D."). MoAmPo
What are the lays of artful Addison. The Charms of Nature. Joseph Warton. SeCePo
What are the long waves singing so mournfully evermore? Olivia. Edward Pollock. AA
What are the thoughts that are stirring his breast? Under the Shade of the Trees. Margaret Junkin Preston. PAH
What are the voices that harass their dreaming? Last Cargo. Silence Buck Bellows. EtS
What Are They Thinking. Bryan Guinness. OxBI
What are they waiting for? Aren't they going to call me? Call Out My Number. Julia de Burgos, *tr. by* Julio Marzán. InW
What are those Golden Builders doing? Blake. *Fr.* Jerusalem, I. OBRV
What are thou, frost? and whence are thy keen stores. Winter. James Thomson. *Fr.* The Seasons. OxBS
What are we first? First, animals; and next. Modern Love, XXX. George Meredith. GBL; HAP; NBM; NoP; OAEP; PoEL-5; ViBoPo
What are we gonna do with the baby-o? Prettiest Little Baby in the County-O. *Unknown.* FSW
What Are We Playing At? Andrée Chedid, *tr. fr. French by* Samuel Hazo *and* Mirene Ghossem. BoWoP
What are we to do with a heaven. Three Songs from the Temple. Don Domanski. NOBC

What Are Years? Marianne Moore. AP; BLPL; CMoP; CoBMV; EaLo; LiTA; MoAB; MoAmPo; MoPo; NoAM; NOBA; OxBA; TrGrPo
What are you able to build with your blocks? Block City. Robert Louis Stevenson. EyDe; FaPON; NTCP; SoPo; TiPo
What are you [*or* were you] carrying, Pilgrims, Pilgrims? Atlantic Charter, A.D. 1620–1942 [*or* Atlantic Charter: 1942]. Francis Brett Young. AmFN; PAL
What are you doing here in this strange world that goes on and off. Traffic Lights. Lina Kasdaglis, *tr. by* Edmund Keeley *and* Mary Keeley. BoWoP
What are you doing, my lady, my lady. Mouse and Mouser. *Unknown.* OxNR
"What are you doing there, Robin a Bobbin." "Talents Differ." Laura E. Richards. TiPo
What, are you drop't? John Webster. *Fr.* The White Devil, V, vi. PoEL-2
What are you going to do with us, who have. The Pleaders. Peter Davison. NYBP
What, are you hurt, Sweet? So am I. To a Hurt Child. Grace Denio Litchfield. AA
What are you, Lady?—naught is here. Portrait of a Lady in the Exhibition of the Royal Academy. Winthrop Mackworth Praed. *Fr.* Every-Day Characters. NBM; NOBL; PoEL-4
What are you, rose?—lips that lean back to meet. The Rose and God. Charles Wharton Stork. HBMV
What are you, then, my love, my friend, my father. The Quarry. Vassar Miller. NePoEA-2; WPE
What are you . . .? they ask, in wonder. Cold Colloquy. Patrick Anderson. *Fr.* Poem on Canada. CaP; NOBC; PeCV
What Are You Thinking About? James Macmillan. PoSH
What are you waiting for, George, I pray? Tardy George. *Unknown.* PAH
What art thou, Life? The shadow of a dream. Sonnet on Life. Sir Brooke Boothby. ViBoPo
What art Thou saying, Lord, to me. Thanksgiving. Gene H. Osborne. PGD
What asks the Bard? He prays for naught. After Horace. A. D. Godley. NOBL
What authors lose, their booksellers have won. On Authors and Booksellers. Pope. FaBoEE
"What bait do you use," said a Saint to the Devil. The Lure. John Boyle O'Reilly. HBV-1
"What be you a-lookin' at, Emily Ann?" The Pear-Tree. Mary Gilmore. PoAu-1
What beasts and angels practice I ignore. Little Ode. Paul Goodman. PoA
What beauty would have lovely styled. An Epitaph: On Elizabeth Chute. Ben Jonson. EnRePo
What Became of Them? *Unknown. See* Two Rats, The.
What beckoning [*or* beck'ning] ghost, along the moonlight shade. Elegy to the Memory of an Unfortunate Lady. Pope. FiP; HBV-2; LO; NOBE; NOEC; OAEL-1; OBEC; OBEV; SeCeV; TEP
What becomes of the girl who lives always alone? The Sorceress. Eugène Marais, *tr. by* Jack Cope *and* Uys Krige. PeSA
What began that bustle in the village. The Birth of Moshesh. D. G. T. Bereng, *tr. by* Dan Kunene *and* Jack Cope. PeSA; TTY
What Bids Me Leave. Herbert Trench. HBMV
What binds the atom together. Song. Philip Dow. NPGG
What bird is that, with voice so sweet. A Creole Slave-Song. Maurice Thompson. AA
What bird so sings, yet so does wail? Trico's Song [*or* The Spring *or* Song *or* Spring's Welcome *or* Welcome to Spring]. John Lyly. *Fr.* Alexander and Campaspe. CH; EIL; NOBE; OBEV; OBSC; PBBP; TrGrPo; ViBoPo
What Birds Were There. William Everson. NoAM
What Black Elk Said. R. T. Smith. LTB
"What bluid's that on thy coat lap." Edward. *Unknown.* ESPB
What body can be ploughed? Chanson un Peu Naïve. Louise Bogan. HBMV
What Booker can prognosticate. The King Enjoys His Own Again. Martin Parker. FaBoCh; OBS; OxBoLi
What; breathles nimphs? bright virgins let me know. The Tenth Nimphall. Michael Drayton. *Fr.* The Muses Elizium. AnAnS-2
What Bright Pushbutton? Samuel Allen. PoNe
What bright soft thing is this? The Tear [*or* The Teare]. Richard Crashaw. LiTB; MasP; OAEP; SeCP
What bring[s] you, sailor, home from the sea. Luck. W. W. Gibson. EtS; MoShBr; OBMV
What bullet killed him? Dead Soldier. Nicolás Guillén, *tr. by* Langston Hughes. TTY
What business have I here. Autumn Burial; a Meditation. Charles Gullans. QFR
What business, or what hope brings thee to town. To Sextus. Martial, *tr. by* Sir Charles Sedley. FaBoEE
What Called Me to the Heights. Lawrence Pilkington. PoSH
What can a man do that a beast cannot. In Shame and Humiliation. James Wright. CAPP
What can be the matter. The Wind. Dorothy Graddon. OnUR
What can be wrong. Housewife. Susan Fromberg Schaeffer. IHMS
What can console for a dead world? Believe and Take Heart. John Lancaster Spalding. AA
What can forgive us for. Failure. Eithne Wilkins. NeBP
What can he want. The Panda. Harley Elliott. *Fr.* Animals That Stand in Dreams. NeAC
What Can I Do? Horace Traubel. *Fr.* Chants Communal. TrJP
What can I do in Poetry. The Departure of the Good Daemon. Robert Herrick. FaBoRV
What can I do to drive away. To ———. Keats. OAEL-2
What can I give Him. My Gift. Christina Rossetti. *Fr.* A Christmas Carol: "In the bleak mid-winter." FaPON; PChr; SiSoSe
What can I give my dear. Doubt. Elinor Chipp. HBMV
What can I give thee back, O liberal. Sonnets from the Portuguese, VIII. Elizabeth Barrett Browning. HBV-1; OBVV
What can I say? walking here, aware. The Chinese Graves in Beechworth Cemetery. Philip Mead. AMV-81
What can I send you under the earth. Traditional Funeral Songs. *Tr. fr. Modern Greek by* Willis Barnstone *and* Elene Kolb. BoWoP
What Can I Tell My Bones? Theodore Roethke. AmPP; NOBA
What can it mean? Is it aught to Him. God Cares [*or* He Careth]. "Marianne Farningham." BLRP; WBLP
What can little T.O. do? *See* What can Tommy Onslow do?
What can melt a traveler's grief? Rhyming a Friend's Poem. Yü Hsüan-chi, *tr. by* Geoffrey Waters. BoWoP
What can the spirit believe? The Young Girl. Theodore Roethke. NoAM
What, can these dead bones live, whose sap is dried. The New Ezekiel. Emma Lazarus. AA
What can they do. The Low Road. Marge Piercy. LTB
What can Tommy Onslow [*or* little T.O.] do? On Thomas, Second Earl of Onslow [*or* On Tom Onslow, Earl of Onslow]. *Unknown.* FaBoCo; FaBoEE
What can you do. Why Write Poetry? Pamela Oberon Davis. AMV-80
What can you do with a woman under thirty? Green Apples. Dudley Randall. FB
What can you expect. Maryam bint Abi Ya'qub al-Ansari, *tr. fr. Arabic by* Elene Margot Kolb. WPOW
What cannot be committed to memory, this can save. Photograph. Quandra Prettyman. PoBA
What can't be cured. *Unknown.* FaFP
What Care I. George Wither. *See* Shall I, Wasting in Despair.
What care I for the leagues o sand. The Mither's Lament. Sydney Goodsir Smith. OxBS
What care I how black I be? *Unknown.* OxNR
What care I if good God be. Egocentric. Stevie Smith. FaBoNo
What care I, so they stand the same. Merops. Emerson. FaBoEn; OxBA
What care I tho' beauty fading. Spiritual Love. William Caldwell Roscoe. OBVV
What care I though she be faire. The Choyce. Thomas Beedome. CavP
"What care I, what cares he." The Cowboy. John Antrobus. AA; FaBoBe; FaPON
What care I who gets the credit? Credit. *Unknown.* STF
What care if the day. The Good Inn. Herman Knickerbocker Vielé. *Fr.* The Inn of the Silver Moon. HBV-1
What celebration should there be? Holiday. Horace, *tr. by* Louis Untermeyer. Odes, III, 28. AWP
What ceremony else? Shakespeare. *Fr.* Hamlet, V, i. EBEV
What Changes, My Love. Edwin Honig. PPJ
What Cheer? *Unknown.* SBVL
(Cheerful Welcome, A.) MeEL
What Child Is This? William Chatterton Dix. FSW
What Christ Is to Us. *Unknown.* BLRP
What Christ Said. George Macdonald. *See* Obedience.
What college kids we've grown up. For Randie. Geof Hewitt. NeAC
What Color Is Lonely. Carolyn M. Rodgers. BPo
What comfort by Him do we win. By Him. Ben Jonson. TRV
What, comrade of a night. Life. Alice Brown. AA
What conscience has Venus drunk? Our inebriated beauties. Juvenal, *tr. by* Peter Green. *Fr.* The Satires, VI. PeHV
What conscience, say, is it in thee. To Aenone [*or* Oenone]. Robert Herrick. HBV-1; OBEV
What Constitutes a State? Sir William Jones. BLPA; PGD
(Ode in Intimation of Alcaeus, An.) HBV-2
What Could Be. John Gill. NeAC
What could be dafter. John Skelton. Robert Graves. BrPo
What could be done? The house was full of folks! The Inn That Missed Its Chance. Amos Russell Wells. TrCP
What Could Be Lovelier than to Hear. Elizabeth J. Coatsworth. SiSoSe

What could he know of sky and stars, or heaven's all-hidden life. The Sooth-Sayer. Sadi, *tr. by* Sir Edwin Arnold. *Fr.* The Gulistan. AWP
"What could I make," Socrates might have asked. The Makers. David Galler. NYBP
What Could It Be? William Cole. BoAnP
What could make me more morose. The Ovibos. Robert Hale. FiBHP
What could she say to the fantastic foolybear. Lawrence Ferlinghetti. *Fr.* A Coney Island of the Mind. CAPP
What could thus high thy rash ambition raise? Honest Fame. Pope. *Fr.* The Temple of Fame. OBEC
What Counsel Has the Hooded Moon. James Joyce. Chamber Music, XII. MOON; OnYI; OxBI
What crowds by envied power, the wish of all. Sejanus. Juvenal, *tr. by* William Gifford. *Fr.* Satires, X. OBVE
What cruel laws depress the female kind. Elizabeth Tollet. *Fr.* Hypatia. NOEC
What cry was that. Encounter. Geraldine Hammond. IHMS
What cunning can express. White and Red. Edward de Vere, Earl of Oxford. ElL; OBSC
What Curious Dresses All Men Wear. Delmore Schwartz. ELU
What curses should I choose? Lines on Being Refused a Guggenheim Fellowship. Reed Whittemore. TW
What-D'Ye-Call-It, The, *sel.* John Gay.
Ballad, A: " 'Twas when the seas were roaring." HBV-1; ViBoPo
What dainty world is yours, in which you sleep. A Sleeping Beauty. Evelyn M. Watson. DFT
What danger is the pilgrim in. Bunyan. *Fr.* The Pilgrim's Progress. EBEV
What dawn is it? Aubade. Karl Shapiro. GP; VGW
What day was it she slid. Birth of Venus. Constance Urdang. PoA
What death is worse than this. Sir Thomas Wyatt. SiPS
What death means is not this. Canticle. Wendell Berry. AP
What delightful hosts are they. A Parting Guest. James Whitcomb Riley. HBV-2; TreFT
What demented malice, my silly Ravidus. Catullus, *tr. fr. Latin by* Celia *and* Louis Zukofsky. OBVE
What demons moved thee, what malicious fiends. To That Most Senseless Scoundrel, the Author of Legion's Humble Address to the Lords. Thomas Brown. APAS
What desperate nightmare rapts me to this land. Legacy: My South. Dudley Randall. NNP; PoBA; PoNe
What did he have in his wagon? Little Black Man with a Rose in His Hat. Audrey Wurdemann. YaD
What did Hiamovi, the red man, Chief of the Cheyennes have? All One People. Carl Sandburg. AmFN
What did I do on my blooming vacation? The Jokesmith's Vacation. Don Marquis. FiBHP
What Did I Dream? I Do Not Know. Robert Graves. DuDa
What did I study in your School of Night? The School Of Night. A. D. Hope. PoA
What did the captain say to the cook. A Capstan Chantey. Edwin James Brady. HBMV
What did the day bring? Letter from a Coward to a Hero. Robert Penn Warren. MoAmPo
What did the Indians call you? To the Avon River above Stratford, Canada. James Reaney. MoCV
What did they feel, those twenty-odd. Temple of the Muses. Beth Bentley. EyDe
What did we say to each other. Simile. N. Scott Momaday. CDW
What did you hear? Advent; a Carol. Patric Dickinson. OBCP
What did you see out there, my lad. Face to Face with Reality. John Oxenham. WBLP
What did you think when first. The Triple Mirror. Gloria C. Oden. IHMS
What Different Dooms Our Birthdays Bring! Thomas Hood. *Fr.* Miss Kilmansegg and Her Precious Leg. NAs
(Miss Kilmansegg's Birth, *longer sel.*) OxBoLi
What Dim Arcadian Pastures. Alice Corbin. HBMV
What dire offense from amorous [*or* am'rous] causes springs. The Rape of the Lock. Pope. BiP; CABA; HAP; MasP; NOEC; NoP; OAEL-1; OAEP; OBNV; PoEL-3; SeCeV; TEP; TrGrPo
What distant thunders rend the skies. On the Death of Captain Nicholas Biddle. Philip Freneau. PAH
What do a few crimes. Adultery. Alan Dugan. CAPP
"What Do I Care." Sara Teasdale. VGW
What do I care. Pursuit. Hilda Doolittle ("H. D."). WPE
What Do I Care for Morning. Helene Johnson. CDC
What do I care for sorrow. Flail. Power Dalton. HBMV
What do I see and hear of an April morning? Shore Roads of April. Bill Adams. EtS
What do I stare at—not the colt. The White Horse. W. H. Davies. OxBTC
What Do the Birds Think? Alfred Purdy. MoCV
What do the people say, and what does the government do? Arthur Hugh Clough. Amours de Voyage, Canto II, i. EBVV; OBSV
What Do They Do? Christina Rossetti. *See* What Does the Bee Do?
What do they know of penitence. Praise. Edith Daley. TRV
What do they mean—the stripes of red? The Flag We Fly. Aileen Fisher. YeAr
What Do They Say. Gary Snyder. NNaP
What do they sing, the last birds. Last Songs. Galway Kinnell. PAI
What do we know of what is behind us? History. Arthur Gregor. TAP
What do we need for love—a midnight fire. Need. Babette Deutsch. PCP
What Do We Plant [When We Plant the Tree]. Henry Abbey. FaPON; HBV-1; HBVY; OHIP; PGD; TiPo; WBLP
What do we share with the past? Again for Hephaistos, the Last Time. Richard Howard. GP
What do you call it, bobsled champion. Twentieth-Century Blues. Kenneth Fearing. CMoP
What do you care for Caesar, who yourself. Peter at Fourteen. Constance Carrier. NePoAm
What Do You Do When It's Spring? John Woods. ConAP
"What do you have for breakfast?" A Little Bird. Aileen Fisher. SoPo
What do you look for, what do you seek? Wishes. Norman Ault. HBMV; HBVY
What do you mean, you "don't like poetry?" Can Zone; or, The Good Food Guide. Rika Lesser. MAYP
"What do you paint, when you paint on a wall?" I Paint What I See. E. B. White. NYBP
What do you remember thinking back. Ever Since. Archibald MacLeish. NePA
What do you say to your mother on. Poem for My Mother. Lowell Jaeger. AMV-80
What Do You Say When a Man Tells You, You Have the Softest Skin. Mary Mackey. FF
What do you seek within, O soul, my brother? Introversion. Evelyn Underhill. WGRP
What do you sell, O ye merchants? In the Bazaars of Hyderabad. Sarojini Naidu. FaPON
What, do you think, is the gypsy bible? The Gypsy Bible. Julian Tuwim, *tr. by* Isaac Komem. VWA
What do you think of us in fuzzy endeavor. A Catch of Shy Fish. Gwendolyn Brooks. CAPP
What Do You Want? John Newlove. NOBC
What do you want. The Parson's Job. Madeline Ida Bedford. SUMH
What does a bird in Cross's air. *Unknown.* *Fr.* A Collection of Hymns . . . of the Moravian Brethren. NOEC
What Does a Man Think About. John Holmes. CrMA
What Does Easter Mean to You? May Ricker Conrad. PGD
What does he plant who plants a tree? The Heart of the Tree. H. C. Bunner. OHFP; OHIP; PGD
What Does Little Birdie Say? Tennyson. *Fr.* Sea Dreams. HBV-1; HBVY (Cradle Song). OxBChV
What does love look like? The Shape of Death. May Swenson. TAP
What does not change/ is the will to change. The Kingfishers. Charles Olson. CMoP; NeAP; NOBA; PoM
What does not fade? The tower that long had stood. Transience. John Armstrong. *Fr.* The Art of Preserving Health. NOEC
What does she put four whistles beside heated rugs for? Random Generation of English Sentences; or, The Revenge of the Poets. William Jay Smith. OBAL
What Does the Bee Do? Christina Rossetti. *Fr.* Sing-Song. OxBChV; SUS; TiPo
(What Do They Do?) FaPON
What does the cracker. Self. Norman Henry Pritchard II. PoBA
What does the horse give you. Horse. Louise Glück. MAYP
What does the storm say? The Ways and the Peoples. Randall Jarrell. PoA
What does the train say? The Baby Goes to Boston. Laura E. Richards. TiPo
What Does This Mean? Sir Thomas Wyatt. MeEL
What domes and pinnacles of mist and fire. Evening in Tyringham Valley. Richard Watson Gilder. AA
What domination of what darkness dies this hour. The City. "Æ." WGRP
What dost thou here. Moth-Song. Ellen Mackay Hutchinson Cortissoz. AA
What dost thou here, thou shining, sinless thing. A Butterfly in Church. George McClellon. BANP
What! dost thou pray that the outgone tide be rolled back on the strand. A Far Cry to Heaven. Edith M. Thomas. AA; WGRP
What doth it serve to see sun's burning face. Sonnet. William Drummond of Hawthornden. ElL
What doth this noise of thoughts within my heart. The Familie. George Herbert. AnAnS-1

What ecstasies her bosom fire! To a Lady on Her Passion for Old China. John Gay. FaFP; LiTB; LoBV; OBEC
What else can we do. What Are We Playing At? Andrée Chedid, *tr. by* Samuel Hazo *and* Mirene Ghossem. BoWoP
What else could we do, for the doors were guarded. Curfew. Paul Eluard, *tr. by* Quentin Stevenson. BoLoP
What end the gods may have ordained for me. To Leuconöe. Horace, *tr. by* Eugene Field. *Fr.* Odes, I, 11. AA
What essences from Idumean palm. Eugene Lee-Hamilton. Mimma Bella, XX. HBV-1
What ever 'tis, whose beauty here below. The Starre. Henry Vaughan. AnAnS-1; MePo
What face, in the water. Lament. William Carlos Williams. VGW
What face she put on it, we will not discuss. Conrad Aiken. Time in the Rock, LXXXIV. VGW
What Faire Pompe. Thomas Campion. Prf
(Love's Pilgrims.) OBSC
(Pilgrimage towards Loves Holy Land, A.) FaBoEn
("What fair[e] pomp[e] have I spied [*or* spide] of glittering ladies.") GBL; PoEL-2
"What fairings will ye that I bring?" The Singing Leaves. James Russell Lowell. GN
What fall amounts to is really a cold infusion. The End of Fall. Francis Ponge, *tr. by* Robert Bly. NU
What falls before us like snow. Moth. Lance Henson. VoR
What Far Kingdom. Arthur S. Bourinot. CaP
What Fifty Said. Robert Frost. NAs
What Finer Hills? J. K. Annand. PoSH
"What Five Books Would You Pick to Be Marooned with on a Desert Island?" Paris Leary. CoPo
What flecks the outer gray beyond. The Dead Ship of Harpswell. Whittier. EtS
What flower is my lady like? Of His Lady. *Unknown.* ElL
What flower is this that greets the morn. The Flower of Liberty. Oliver Wendell Holmes. HBVY
What For. Garrett Kaoru Hongo. MAYP
What for feere of this ferly and of the false Jewes. William Langland. *Fr.* The Vision of Piers Plowman. EBEV
What form or shape to describe? Kabir, *tr. fr. Hindi by* Shukako Singh *and* Linda Hess. ILwL
What Form the World Has. William Bronk. AMV-80
What fragrant-footed comer. The Little Knight in Green. Katharine Lee Bates. AA
What friendship can'st thou boast? what honours claim? Bristol. Richard Savage. FaBoPP
What from the founder Aesop fell. The Purpose of Fable-writing. Phaedrus, *tr. by* Christopher Smart. AWP
What fullness in the life is this which possesses. Eating Lechon, with My Brothers and Sisters. Luis Cabalquinto. BrSi
What gentle Ghost, besprent with April deaw. An Elegie on the Lady Jane Pawlet, Marchion: of Winton. Ben Jonson. SeCP
What gives it power makes it change its mind. The Beautiful Lawn Sprinkler. Howard Nemerov. PCP
What gives us that fantastic fit. Natura Naturata. Sir John Denham. NCEP
What gives you the right. Old Man Hall. P. L. Jacobs. LFAC
What glories would we? Motions of the soul? The Renewal. Theodore Roethke. VGW
What Glorious Vision, *with music. At. to* Thomas Cradock. AH
What God gives, and what we take. A Grace for Children. Robert Herrick. EBCP; OxBChV; OxBoCh; PoPle
What God Has Promised. Annie Johnson Flint. *See* What God Hath Promised!
What God hath joined together man has put. Ode on a Plastic Stapes. Chad Walsh. HoAn
What God Hath Promised! Annie Johnson Flint. BLRP; STF; TRV
(What God Has Promised.) WBLP
What God never sees. *Unknown.* OxNR
What gods are these? Bright red, or white and green. The Fox-Hunters. Ebenezer Elliott. TW
What gods or heroes, whose brave deeds none can dispute. At the Ball Game. Roswell Martin Field. InMe
What golden gaine made Higginson remove. The Reverend Mr. Higginson. Edward Johnson. SCAP
What good is it to me if long ago. Sonnet XXIII. Louise Labé, *tr. by* Willis Barnstone. BoWoP
What good is there, ah me, what good in Love? Rispetto. Agnes Mary Frances Robinson. HBMV
What Good Poems Are For. Tom Wayman. NoP
What grandeur makes a man seem venerable? Sonnet XXI. Louise Labé, *tr. by* Willis Barnstone. BoWoP
What Grandma Knew. Edward Field. CoPo; Psk
What great genius invented the waiting room? Waiting Rooms. Howard Nemerov. PoA
What great relief to stand here in the street. Walking Around. David Galler. AMV-81
What great yoked brutes with briskets low. Crossing the Plains. Joaquin Miller. AA; BPAW; GN
What greater torment ever could have been. Lonely Beauty. Samuel Daniel. *Fr.* The Complaint of Rosamond. CTC; OBSC
What Greece, when learning flourished [*or* flourish'd], only [*or* onely] knew. Prologue to the University of Oxford, 1673. Dryden. OBS; PP
What guile [*or* guyle] is this, that those her golden tresses. Amoretti, XXXVII. Spenser. NoP; OBSC; PAI; TrGrPo
What Habacuck once spake, mine eyes. Roger Williams. SCAP
What had become of the young shark? The Birth of a Shark. David Wevill. TwCP
What had become very clear to him. Abraham. Stephen Mitchell. VWA
What had November done? The Beautiful Ruined Orchard. Daniel Berrigan. FYAP
What had you been thinking about. The Tennis Court Oath. John Ashbery. NoAM; TAP
What hand trimmed these strident feathers for flight. Night Flight. George Whalley. CaP
What hand, what skill can form the artful piece. Advice to a Painter. *Unknown.* APAS
What Happened? John Wieners. PoM
What Happened Here Before. Gary Snyder. NNaP; PoM
What happened to Cassandra? Burn Down the Icons. Grace Schulman. GP
What happened to Joey on our block. Of Kings and Things. Lillian Morrison. CAD; NCSH
What happened to the ten lost tribes. Exile. Chana Bloch. GP
What Happens. June Jordan. BPo
What happens to a dream deferred? Harlem [*or* Dream Deferred]. Langston Hughes. *Fr.* Lenox Avenue Mural. AmNP; AmPP; BiP; CABA; FF; HeIP; HoPM; InPK; InPS; LiTM; NIP; NoP; PoBA; PoNe; PPP; SoSe
What happens when the dog sits on a tiger. What Happens. June Jordan. BPo
What happier fortune can one find. Exile. *Unknown, tr. by* Frank O'Connor. *Fr.* Men and Women. KiLC
What Happiness Can Equal Mine, *with music.* John David. AH
What happiness you gave to me. The Yew-Tree. *Unknown, tr. by* Geoffrey Grigson. ChTr; GBL
What happy, secret fountain. The Dwelling-Place. Henry Vaughan. MeLP; OBS; OxBoCh; TrPWD; WGRP
What harm have I done to the stars? Without My Friends the Day Is Dark. Moses ibn Ezra, *tr. by* Solomon Solis-Cohen. TrJP
What Harvest Half So Sweet Is. Thomas Campion. UnTE
"Dove alone expresses, The," *sel.* PBBP
What has aged you so. Yehuda Amichai. Seymour Mayne. VWA
What has become of our astonishment. The Way We Wonder. Robert Pack. NePoEA
What has bent you. The Pine at Timber-Line. Harriet Monroe. PoA
What Has Happened. Charles Angoff. AMV-81
What has happened in the world? Volcanic Venus. D. H. Lawrence. InPS; POL
What has poor Woman done, that she must be. Aphra Behn. *Fr.* Sir Patient Fancy, Epilogue. WPOW
What has risen in the dark and is? Voice in the Dark. A. L. Strauss, *tr. by* Robert Friend. VWA
What has that woman done to you, my dear! Tea. Jacqueline Embry. HBMV; YaD
What Has This Bugbear Death. Lucretius. *See* Against the Fear of Death.
What has this bugbear Death that's worth our care? Sonnet on Death. William Walsh. ViBoPo
What has want to give. Envoi. Kathleen Raine. WPE
"What has your country done for you." A Recruit from the Slums. Emily Orr. SUMH
What, hast thou run thy race? Art going down? Of the Going Down of the Sun. Bunyan. CH
"What hath man done that man shall not undo." Mercy Pleads for Mankind. Giles Fletcher. *Fr.* Christ's Victory and Triumph, I. JCP
What Hath Man Wrought Exclamation Point. Morris Bishop. NYBP
What have I done for you. England, My England. W. E. Henley. BLPL; HBV-2; MoBrPo; OBEV; OBVV; PoLF; TreF
"What have I earned for all that work," I said. The People. W. B. Yeats. CMoP
What have I gained by the toil of the trail? The Toil of the Trail. Hamlin Garland. HBV-1
What have I made. The Children. Constance Urdang. CoAP; IHMS
What! Have I thus betrayed [*or* betray'd] my liberty [*or* libertie]? The Yoke

of Tyranny. Sir Philip Sidney. Astrophel and Stella, XLVII. GBL; NIP; NoP; PoEL-1; SiPS; TrGrPo
What have I to give? In the Far Years. Wilson MacDonald. CaP
What Have They Done to the Rain. Malvina Reynolds. FSW
What Have We Done Today? Nixon Waterman. WBLP
What have we done? What cruel passion moved thee. Dialogue after Enjoyment. Abraham Cowley. BoLoP
What, have ye kithèd you a knight, Sir Douglas the Doughty. John Skelton. *Fr.* Against Garnesche. ViBoPo
"What have you looked at, Moon." To the Moon. Thomas Hardy. BoNaP; ChTr
What have you more than I, who crave you so? Zora Cross. Love Sonnets, LIV. CBAP
"What have you there?" the great Panjandrum said. The Truant. E. J. Pratt. NoAM; NOBC; NoP; OBCV
What! Hayes acquitted! Armstrong's magazine! True and Joyful News. *Unknown.* APAS
What he never thought to consider was whether. Death on a Crossing. Evangeline Paterson. EBCP
What He Said. Harrison Robertson. *Fr.* Two Triolets. HBV-1
What He Saw. Robert Currie. Str
What He Suffered. Ben Jonson. *See* What Hee Suffered.
What He Took. *Unknown.* CoMu
What heart could have thought you? To a Snowflake. Francis Thompson. BoNaP; EBCP; FaBV; HBV-1; ImOP; LoBV; MoAB; MoBrPo; PoPl; SeCePo; TrGrPo
What heartache—ne'er a hill! From the Flats. Sidney Lanier. NePA; NOBA; OxBA
What heave of grapnels will resurrect the fabric. S.S.R., Lost at Sea—*The Times.* Ralph Gustafson. OBCV
What heaven-entreated [*or* heaven-besiegèd] heart is this. To the Noblest and Best of Ladies, the Countess of Denbigh [*or* Against Irresolution *or* A Letter to the Countess of Denbigh]. Richard Crashaw. JCP; MeLP; MePo; OxBoCh; SeCP
What heavy-hoofed coursers the wilderness roam. The Fall of Tecumseh. *Unknown.* PAH
What Hee Suffered. Ben Jonson. *Fr.* A Celebration of Charis. AnAnS-2; SeCP
What helps it if of love I sing. Hadewijch, *tr. fr. Dutch by* Frans van Rosevelt. PBWP
What helps it those. For [*or* To] a Musician. George Wither. *Fr.* Hallelujah. OBS; OxBoCh
What Her Girl-Friend[s] Said to Her. Okkur Macatti, *tr. fr. Tamil by* A. K. Ramanujan. BoWoP; PBWP
What heroes from the woodland sprung. Seventy-six. Bryant. HBV-2; PAH
What hideous noyse was that? John Webster. *Fr.* The Duchess of Malfi, IV, ii. PoEL-2
What hills are like the Ochil hills? The Ochil Hills. *Unknown.* PoSH
What ho! my shepherds, sweet it were. A Sylvan Revel. Edward Cracroft Lefroy. *Fr.* Echoes from Theocritus. AWP
What hope is here for modern rhyme. In Memoriam A. H. H., LXXVII. Tennyson. PP
What hope is that? Alexander Smith. *Fr.* A Life-Drama. VLP
What hope of safety for our realm. On Sympathisers with the American Revolution. Charles Wesley. NOCV
What Horace says is. Eheu Fugaces. "Thomas Ingoldsby." FaBoEE; NBM; OxBoLi
What horrid sin condemned the teeming Earth. On Tobacco. Charles Cotton. OBSV
What hours I spent of precious time. Poetical Economy. Harry Graham. CenHV; FaBoCo; TreFS
What How? How now? Hath How such hearing found. On How the Cobler. *Unknown.* SCAP
What humour can be so rare. Sister Juana Inés de la Cruz, *tr. by* Judith Thurman. *Fr.* A Satirical Romance. PBWP
"What hundred books are best, think you?" I said. John Kendrick Bangs. CenHV
What hurrying human tides, or day or night! Broadway. Walt Whitman. NYP
What I Did Last Summer. Ron Ikan. AMV-80
What I Do Is Me. Gerard Manley Hopkins. *See* As Kingfishers Catch Fire.
What I Expected [Was]. Stephen Spender. CoBMV; MoAB; MoBrPo; MoPo; NoAM; NOBE; OAEP
What I fancy, I approve. No Loathsomnesse in Love. Robert Herrick. AnAnS-2; GBL
What I Have. Susan North. AMV-81
What I Have Done. Gerard Malanga. FAZ
What I have written, I cannot unwrite. Ending. Norman Jordan. PoNe
What I like about Clive. Lord Clive. E. C. Bentley. *Fr.* Clerihews. CenHV; DBV; MoShBr; NOBL; OxBoLi; PoPle; WhC
What I like most is when. Crimes of Passion: The Slasher. Terry Stokes. AmPA
What I Live For. George Linnaeus Banks. BLPA; FaBoBe; TreFS (My Aim.) WBLP
What I love best in all the world. Italy of the South. Robert Browning. *Fr.* "De Gustibus." FaBoPP
What I need is lots of money. Take I, 4:11:58. Philip Whalen. NeAP
What I remember. Memory of a Porch. Donald Justice. NCSH
What I remember about that day. Eviction [*or* The 1st]. Lucille Clifton. InPS; NTCP
What I remember is fire, orange fire. The Janitor; Kindergarten, Corinth. Charles Wright. *Fr.* Tattoos. GP
What I Saw. Robert Duncan. NoAM; NOBA
What I Saw in October. Warren Carrier. PoDr
What I saw was just one eye. The Bird at Dawn. Harold Monro. MoBrPo
What I See in Me. *Unknown.* STF
What I shall leave thee none can tell. To His Son [*or* Sonne], Vincent Corbet[t]. Richard Corbet. AnAnS-2; FaBoCh; OBS; OxBChV; TrGrPo
What I Tell Him. Simon J. Ortiz. CDW
What I Think of Hiawatha. J. W. Morris. Par; SpRo
What I thought was love. The Liar. Amiri Baraka. AmPP; NOBA
What I took in my hand. Song. Robert Creeley. NoP; PoA
What I walked down to the highway. Another Sunday Morning. Carter Revard. VoR
What I want from God, feared to be. Breath. Heather McHugh. GeTw
What I wanted. In Weather. Robert Hass. AmPA; GeTw
What I was would not work. Encounter in the Cage Country. James Dickey. BiP; CAPP
What I will ask, if one free wish comes down. A Boon. William Meredith. NePoEA
What I will say today. Lo Que Digo. *Unknown.* AS
What I would be doing if I were out. Dreaming about Freedom. Jimmy Santiago Baca. AMV-80
What If a Day [or a Month or a Year]. Thomas Campion. AAS; BiP; EBEV; ElL; EnRePo; PrIm
What If a Much of a Which of a Wind. E. E. Cummings. AP; BLPL; FaFP; LiTA; LiTM; MasP; MoAmPo; MoPo; MoVE; NePA; NOBA; NoP; OxBA; PoA; PoRA; PPP; SoSe; ViBoPo; WaP
What if, every time you walked, things. Lullaby. Frederick Eckman. FAZ
What if I bade you leave. Those Images. W. B. Yeats. CMoP; PP
What if I coasted near the shore. Voyager's Song. Clement Wood. HBMV
What if it *was* a. For Tinkers Who Travel on Foot. Margaret Avison. NoAM
What if jealousy is just a bad dream? Miriam Palmer. NMM
What if Orpheus. Orpheus in Greenwich Village. Jack Gilbert. NPGG; POL; PP
What if outside the dying pine trees sing in the clearing gale. Inside the Cave. Geoffrey Grigson. FaBoPP
What if small birds are peppering the sky. It Is Winter, I Know. Merrill Moore. MoAmPo
What If Some Little Paine the Passage Have. Spenser. *Fr.* The Faerie Queene, I, ix. CH; PoPle (Porte after Stormie Seas.) EtS
What if the air has a nipping tooth! A Skater's Valentine. Arthur Guiterman. SiSoSe
What if the body goes the sense. Image-Nation 3. Robin Blaser. PoM
What If the Saint Must Die, *with music.* John Peck. AH
What if the soul her real life elsewhere holds. The Soul in the Body. Edith M. Thomas. AA
What if the sun comes out. Boy Remembers in the Field. Raymond Knister. CaP; NOBC
What if the ways be stone. City Songs. Mark Van Doren. NYBP
What if there wasn't a metaphor. Stigmata. Patrick Lane. NOBC
What if these long races go on repeating themselves. Written in Dejection near Rome. Robert Bly. NaP
What if this man with his rough head. The Celebration. Robert Mezey. FAZ
What if this present were the world's last night? Holy Sonnets, XIII. John Donne. AnAnS-1; EBEV; HeIP; InPS; JCP; LiTB; MasP; NOCV; OAEP; OBS; SeCeV; TEP
What I'm Doing Here. Leonard Cohen. PeCV
What in our lives is burnt. August 1914. Isaac Rosenberg. EBEV; NOBE; OBWP; OxBTC
What, in the Register of Doom, is writ. Bishop Orders His Tomb in St. Praxed's. Morris Bishop. OBAL
What in the World? Eve Merriam. RHPC
What infants suffer when they breed their teeth. Infant Diseases and Their Treatment. M. Saint-Marthe. *Fr.* Paedotrophiae; or, The Art of Bringing Up Children. FaBoUs
What inn is this. Emily Dickinson. MasP; NePA
What instinct forces man to journey on. The Poet. Amy Lowell. WGRP

What Invisible Rat. Jean-Joseph Rebéarivelo, *tr. fr. French by* Alan Ryder. TTY
What! Irving? thrice welcome, warm heart, and fine brain. Irving. James Russell Lowell. *Fr.* A Fable for Critics. TAP
What Is. E. E. Cummings. MOS
What is/ eternity? Home Alone These Last Hours of the Afternoon, Dusk Now, the Sabbath Setting In, I Sit Back, and These Words Start Welling Up in Me. Stephen Levy. VWA
"What is a Bongaloo, Daddy?" The Bongaloo. Spike Milligan. AmMo
What is a Communist? One who has yearnings. On Communists. Ebenezer Elliott. NOBL
What is a day, what is a year of vain delight and pleasure? *Unknown.* OBSC
What is a first love worth except to prepare for a second? John Milton Hay. FaBoEE
What Is a Jewish Poem? Myra Sklarew. VWA
What is a kiss? Why this, as some approve. A Kiss. Robert Herrick. CaPo
What is a [*or* the] modern Poet's fate? The Poet's Fate [*or* To the Reviewers]. Thomas Hood. ELU; FaBoEE; FiBHP; PV; TW
What is a poet's love? The Poet's Lot. Oliver Wendell Holmes. PoEL-5
What is a shaman? Coyote, Coyote, Please Tell Me. Peter Blue Cloud. STE
What Is a Sonnet? Edward Watkins. AMV-80
What is a sonnet? 'Tis the pearly shell. The Sonnet. Richard Watson Gilder. AA; HBV-2
What is a woman that you forsake her. Harp Song of the Dane Women. Kipling. *Fr.* Puck of Pook's Hill. FaBoEn; HAP; OAEP; OBNC; PoRA; SeCePo
What is a yielded life? The Yielded Life. "W. A. G." BLRP
What is Africa to me. Heritage. Countee Cullen. AmNP; BALP; BANP; BPo; FaBV; MoAmPo; NoAM; NoP; PoBA; TTY
What is all this washing about. Washing. John Drinkwater. FaPON
What is ambition? 'Tis a glorious cheat! Ambition. Nathaniel Parker Willis. OBCA
What Is an Epigram? Samuel Taylor Coleridge. *See* Epigram: "What is an epigram? a dwarfish whole."
What is beautiful alters, has undertow. Whole and without Blessing. Linda Gregg. MAYP; NPGG
What Is Being Forgotten. Eloise Klein Healy. GP
What Is Black? Mary O'Neill. NTCP
What is black. Canto 4: Gullfish. Tom Weatherly. PoBA
What is bright or rare here, is called oriental. Two Figures. Molly Peacock. AMV-81
What Is Charm? Louisa Carroll Thomas. BLPA
What is death? 'Tis to be free. The Genius of Death. George Croly. HBV-2
"What is funny?" you ask, my child. The Anatomy of Humor. Morris Bishop. InMe; WhC
What is gold worth, say. Child's Song. Swinburne. OBVV
What Is Good? John Boyle O'Reilly. HBV-2; HBVY; TreF; WBLP
What is green in me. Stepping Westward. Denise Levertov. CAPP; NMM; VGW
What is happening to me now that loved faces. Childhood in Jacksonville, Florida. Jane Cooper. TAP
What is he buzzing in my ears? Confessions. Robert Browning. ELP; GTBS-P; NOBE; PoPle; ViBoPo
What is he, this lordling, that cometh from the fight? The Knight Stained from Battle [*or* Who Is This That Cometh from Edom]. William Herebert. MeEl; OxBM
What is home without a Bible? A Home without a Bible, *abr.* Charles D. Meigs. WBLP
What is hope? A smiling rainbow. Cui Bono? Thomas Carlyle. HBV-2; OBRV; WGRP
What is house, and what is home. House and Home [*or* Home]. Joseph Beaumont. GoTL; OBS
What Is It? Marie Louise Allen. TiPo
What-Is-It, A. Ruth McEnery Stuart *and* Albert Bigelow Paine. TDH
What is it about homework. Homework. Jane Yolen. RHPC
What is it, children, sons of the ancient house of Cadmus? Oedipus Tyrannus. Sophocles, *tr. by* Luci Berkowitz *and* Theodore F. Brunner. NAWM-1
What is it, inside them and undeniable. The King's Men. William Heyen. PoA
What is it like to have just one shirt. The Likeness. Leonard Nathan. GP
What is it men in women do require? The Question Answer'd [*or* A Question Answered]. Blake. *Fr.* Several Questions Answered. ELU; ErPo; FaBoEE; GBL; NIP; NoP; OAEL-2; ViBoPo
What is it more eyes doth wear. *Unknown.* GBP
What is it now with me. Fear of Death. John Ashbery. FaBoMo; TAP
What is it our mammas bewitches. Written for My Son, and Spoken by Him at His First Putting on Breeches. Mary Barber. NOEC
What is it so transforms the boulevard? Another Spirit Advances. Jules Romains, *tr. by* Joseph T. Shipley. AWP
What is it that stirs the heart and mind. The Hillman Looks Back. Rennie McOwan. PoSH
"What is it to be dead?" O Life. A Child's Question. Emma Huntington Nason. AA
What is it to grow old? Growing Old. Matthew Arnold. FaFP; FiP; HBV-1; OAEL-2; PoEL-5; VLP
What is it to remember? Bliss Carman. Songs of the Sea-Children, LXVI. OBCV
What is it when a woman sleeps, her head bright. Where You Go When She Sleeps. T. R. Hummer. MAYP
What is it with these people-swallowing streets. All of a Sudden. Teresa de Jesús, *tr. by* Maria A. Proser, Arlene Scully, *and* James Scully. WPOW
What is it you remember?—the summer mornings. To Any Member of My Generation. George Barker. WaP
"What is it you're mumbling, old Father my Dad?" By the Exeter River. Donald Hall. MoBS
What Is Left? Assata Shakur. AMV-80
What Is Left? István Vas, *tr. fr. Hungarian by* Emery George. VWA
What is left in field. An Early Illinois Winter. Alex Kuo. BrSi
What Is Life? Samuel Taylor Coleridge. FiP
What Is Life ("What is life or worldly pleasure?"). *Unknown.* EnRePo
What Is Liquid. Margaret Cavendish, Duchess of Newcastle. FaBoUs
What Is Lived. Carmen Valle, *tr. fr. Spanish by* Julio Marzán. InW
What Is Love? John Clare. NCEP
What Is Love? John Fletcher. *See* Tell Me, Dearest, What Is Love?
What is Love but the desire. Batte's Song. Michael Drayton. *Fr.* The Shepherd's Garland, Eclogue VII. LoBV
What is love? 'tis not hereafter. Shakespeare. *Fr.* Twelfth Night, II, iii. TreFT
What is lovelier than the gold. Casual Gold. Maud E. Uschold. SoPo; YeAr
What Is Man? Bible, *O.T.* Psalms, VIII. TrGrPo
(How Glorious Is Thy Name.) TrJP
(O Lord, How Excellent Is Thy Name.) TreFS
("O Lord, our Lord, how excellent [*or* glorious] is thy name [in all the earth"].) AWP; NAWM-1
("O Lorde oure governoure, howe excellent is thy name.") OBVE
What is man, that mindful of him. These Men. Philip Booth. GLGT
What is Man's Body? *Gond Oral Tradition, tr. by* V. Elwin *and* S. Hivale. WTO
What is more gentle than a wind in summer? Sleep and Poetry. Keats. EnRP; PP
What Is Needed. Marcos Rodríguez Frese, *tr. fr. Spanish by* Julio Marzán. InW
What Is Orange? Mary O'Neill. RHPC
What is our innocence. What Are Years? Marianne Moore. AP; BLPL; CMoP; CoBMV; EaLo; LiTA; MoAB; MoAmPo; MoPo; NoAM; NOBA; OxBA; TrGrPo
What Is Our Life? A Play of Passion. Sir Walter Ralegh. EBEV; EnRePo; FaBoEE; InPK; MePo; NIP; PAI; SiPS
(All the World's a Stage.) NOBE; OBSC
(On the Life of Man.) AAS; OAEL-1; OAEP; QFR
What Is Past. Sir William Davenant. TrGrPo
What Is Pink? Christina Rossetti. *Fr.* Sing-Song. GoJo; OnUR; OxBChV; RHPC; SoPo; SUS; TiPo
What Is Poetry. John Ashbery. LCAP
What Is Poetry. James Scully. FYAP
What is poetry? Is it a mosaic. Fragment. Amy Lowell. WGRP
What is poetry? Who Knows? Poetry. Eleanor Farjeon. RHPC
What Is Prayer? James Montgomery, *also at. to* ——— Robertson. BLRP; STF; TRV; WGRP
What Is Red? Mary O'Neill. RHPC
What is she now? My dreams are bad. She may bring me a curse. Tennyson. *Fr.* Maud. SyP
What is so nice in the dining room. Eunice in the Evening. Gwendolyn Brooks. TiPo
What Is So Rare as a Day in June? James Russell Lowell. *Fr.* The Vision of Sir Launfal. BLPL; FaBoBe; FaFP; NePA, *longer sel.*
(June.) FaBV
What is so rare as a day in June? Question and Answer. Samuel Hoffenstein. DBV; FiBHP; PV
What is so strange about a tree alone in an open field? Hunting Pheasants in a Cornfield. Robert Bly. ConAP
What is song's eternity? Song's Eternity. John Clare. FaBoCh; NCEP
What Is Terrible. Roy Fuller. WaP
What is that a-billowing there. Firstfruits in 1812. Wallace Rice. PAH
What is that growling! Screeching! Barking! Spring Cleaning. Phillip William George. VoR
What Is That in Thine Hand? Eva Gray. STF
What Is That Music High in the Air? A. J. M. Smith. NMP

What is the boy now, who has lost his ball. The Ball Poem. John Berryman. CoAP; FF; LiSp; MoAmPo; NoAM; NOBA; NoP
What Is the Case in Point? Abraham Reisen, *tr. fr. Yiddish by* Richard J. Fein. VWA
What is the head. Some Last Questions. W. S. Merwin. CAPP
What is the heart of a girl? The Heart of a Girl Is a Wonderful Thing. *Unknown.* BLPA
What is the horn that the dawn holds. The Horn. James Reaney. OBCV; PeCV
What is the little one thinking about? Cradle Song [*or* Babyhood]. Josiah Gilbert Holland. *Fr.* Bitter-sweet. AA; HBV-1
"What is the matter, grandmother dear?" Grandma's Lost Balance. Sydney Dayre. OBCA
What is the matter with Grandpapa? Poor Dear Grandpapa. D'Arcy W. Thompson. NA
What is the meaning of this Ideal. W. J. Turner. *Fr.* The Seven Days of the Sun. OBMV
What is the measure then, the magpie in the field. The Measure. Patrick Lane. NOBC
What is the metre of the dictionary? Altarwise by Owl-Light, IV. Dylan Thomas. CMoP
What is the mirror saying with its O? A Room in the Villa. William Jay Smith. NYBP
What is the modern Poet's fate? *See* What is a modern Poet's fate?
What is the moral? Who rides may read. The Winners [*or* L'Envoi]. Kipling. *Fr.* The Story of the Gadsbys. BLPA; FaPoR; FPL; MoBrPo; TrGrPo
What is the name of King Ringang's daughter? Beauty Rohtraut. Eduard Möricke, *tr. by* George Meredith. AWP; OBVE
What is the Old Year? 'Tis a book. The Old Year. Clarence Urmy. PGD
What is the opposite of a prince? Richard Wilbur. WSC
What is the opposite of riot. Some Opposites. Richard Wilbur. OBCA
What is the opposite of two? The Opposite of Two. Richard Wilbur. RHPC
"What is the real good?" What Is Good? John Boyle O'Reilly. HBV-2; HBVY; TreF; WBLP
What is the rhyme for porringer? Mother Goose. OxNR
"What is the song I am singing?" The Founts of Song. "Fiona Macleod." WGRP
What is the sorriest thing that enters Hell? Vain Virtues. Dante Gabriel Rossetti. The House of Life, LXXXV. HBV-2; VLP
What is the sound of the earth spinning? The Natural History of Pliny. Vincent McHugh. NePoAm-2
What is the thing of greatest price. The Soul. *Unknown.* STF
"What is the thing your eyes hold loveliest." The Newlyweds. Cloyd Mann Criswell. PoLF
What Is the Use? *sel.* Erastus Wolcott Ellsworth.
"I saw a man, by some accounted wise." AA
What is the use of the rule insane. The Solution. Brian Merriman, *tr. by* Arland Ussher. *Fr.* The Midnight Court. BIrV
What is the voice I hear. To America [or Britannia to Columbia]. Alfred Austin. GN; HBV-2; PAH
What is the word for "death." Flowers for Luis Bunuel. Stuart Z. Perkoff. NeAP
What Is the World? Dryden. *Fr.* To My Honor'd Friend Sir Robert Howard. TRV
"What is the world, O soldiers?" Napoleon. Walter de la Mare. FaBoCh; FaBoTw; MoVE; NOBE
What is the world? tell, Worldling (if thou know it). Mundus Qualis. Joshua Sylvester. FaBoEE
What is the Ziz? The Ziz. John Hollander. VWA
What Is There. Marvin Bell. GP
What is there for us. Song of the Bride. Susan Mernit. VWA
What is there hid in the heart of a rose. Song. Alfred Noyes. CH
What is there in my heart that you should sue. Lachrimae Amantis. Geoffrey Hill. NOCV
What is there they will not do to you? The First Test. Susan Fromberg Schaeffer. IHMS
What is there wanting in the Spring. The Wistful Days. Robert Underwood Johnson. AA
What is this?/ The white and crumbling clouds. Rapture: an Ode. Richard Watson Dixon. OxBoCh
What is this flesh and blood compounded of. Allen Tate. *Fr.* Sonnets of the Blood. PoA
"What is this golden bowl, mother." Ballad of the Golden Bowl. Sara Henderson Hay. OnMSP
What is this huge box painted red and buff. Ballade of the Old-Time Engine. Eda H. Vines. QQQ
What is this image in the clouded mirror. Image in a Mirror. Mae Winkler Goodman. GoYe
What is this knowledge but the sky-stolen fire. Much Knowledge, Little Reason [*or* Knowledge and Reason]. Sir John Davies. *Fr.* Nosce Teipsum. ChTr; FaBoRV: OBSC
What is this life if, full of care. Leisure. W. H. Davies. AWP; BoNaP; CH; FaBoBe; FaFP; FaPON: HBV-2; LiTB; LiTM; MoBrPo; MoShBr; NOBE: OBEV; OBMV; OBVV; PoRA; SeCePo; TiPo; TrGrPo; WHA
What is this life, this active guest. A Solemn Meditation. William Shenstone. NOEC
What is this recompense you'd have from me? From a Woman to a Greedy Lover. Norman Cameron. Three Love Poems, I. ELU; FaBoEE; FaBoTw; GTBS-P
What is this reverence in extreme delight. Ecstasy. Arthur Symons. UnTE
What is this strange and uncouth thing? The Crosse. George Herbert. AnAnS-1
What is this tempest. W. J. Turner. *Fr.* The Seven Days of the Sun. OBMV
What is this that I can see. O Death [*or* Oh! Death]. *Unknown.* AmFP; TrAS
What is this that I have heard? Dawn Has Yet to Ripple In. Melville Cane. MoAmPo
What is this that roareth thus? Motor Bus. Alfred Denis Godley. FaBoCo; FaBoNo; NOBL
What is this whisper of homelessness, good my heart. If the Heart Be Homeless. Annemarie Ewing. NePoAm-2
What Is This Why? *Unknown.* OxBM
What is this wonderful thing? Brown and everywhere! Looking at a Dry Canadian Thistle Brought In from the Snow. Robert Bly. NNaP
What Is to Come. W. E. Henley. HBV-2; TreFT
What Is Truth, *sel.* James Harold Manning.
"I have been/ Three separate times, in war." CaP
What is unseen. Vision. W. S. Merwin. GP
What Is Veal? *Unknown.* FaBoUs
What is weaker than a god? It groans hungry. Rosario Castellanos, *tr. fr. Spanish by* Willis Barnstone. BoWoP
What Is Winter? Edmund Blunden. ChMP
What Is Young Passion. Hartley Coleridge. NCEP
What is your feeling about the revolutionary spirit. Firebrand. Harry Crosby. EAS
What is your substance, whereof are you made. Sonnets, LIII. Shakespeare. CTC; EBEV; EIL; EnRePo; FaFP; LiTB; MasP; OAEL-1; OAEP; OBEV; OBSC; PeHV; ViBoPo
What is—"Paradise." Emily Dickinson. CMoP
What is't, fine Grand, makes thee my friendship fly. To Fine Grand. Ben Jonson. JCP
What is't, good prying friend, you say? The Alarm. Hildebrand Jacob. NOEC
What Is't to Us? Charles Churchill. *Fr.* Night; an Epistle to Robert Lloyd. SeCePo
What It Means, Living in the City. William Dickey. POL
What it must be like to be an angel. Parents. William Meredith. FYAP
What it showed was always the same. The Night Mirror. John Hollander. NYBP; Prf
What It Was. Robert Sward. CoPo
What jailhouse bars are more black. The Coweta County Courthouse. James Miller Robinson. AMV-80
What Jenner Said on Hearing in Elysium That Complaints Had Been Made of His Having a Statue [in Trafalgar Square]. Shirley Brooks. EyDe; FaBoEE
What joy attends the fisher's life. *See* What joys attend . . .
What joy hath yon glad wreath of flowers that is. The Garland and the Girdle. Michelangelo, *tr. by* John Addington Symonds. AWP
What joys attend [*or* joy attends] the fisher's life! The Fisher's Life. *Unknown.* ChTr; EtS; GBP
What, Kaiser dead? The heavy news. Kaiser Dead. Matthew Arnold. FM
What! kill a partridge in the month of May! On Mr. Partridge. *Unknown.* WhC
What Kin' o' Pants Does the Gambler Wear, *with music.* *Unknown.* AS
What Kind of a Guy Was He? Howard Nemerov. PCP
What kind of lovers could they have been. Coosaponakeesa (Mary Mathews Musgrove Bosomsworth), Leader of the Creeks, 1700-1783. Rayna Green. TWSS
What Kind of Mistress He Would Have. Robert Herrick. CaPo; TrGrPo; UnTE
What Kind of War? Larry Rottman. POL
What know I. The Song of the Arrow. Isabella Valancy Crawford. *Fr.* Gisli, the Chieftain. OBCV; PeCV
What lack you, sir? What seek you? What will you buy? Thomas Newbery. *Fr.* The Great Merchant, Dives Pragmaticus, Cries His Wares. OxBChV
What large, dark hands are those at the window. Love on the Farm. D. H. Lawrence. CMoP; ErPo; FaBV; FF; MoAB; MoBrPo; TrGrPo
What Larkin bawled to hungry crowds. Inscription for a Headstone. Austin Clarke. BIrV; CIP

What lewd, naked and revolting shape is this? Shopping for Meat in Winter. Oscar Williams. LiTA; LiTM; NePA
What life can compare with the jolly town-rakes. The Town-Rakes. *At. to* P. A. Motteux. CoMu
What Life Have You. T. S. Eliot. *Fr.* The Rock. EBCP
What lifts the heron leaning on the air. Snowy Heron. John Ciardi. WeW
What lightning shall light it? What thunder shall tell it? Martin Luther at Potsdam. Barry Pain. NA
What links are ours with orbs that are. Meditation under Stars. George Meredith. OAEP
What Lips My Lips Have Kissed. Edna St. Vincent Millay. BoLoP; HoPM; LiTA; LLLT; MoAB; MoAmPo; NIP; PrIm; TwAmPo; ViBoPo (Sonnet: "What lips my lips have kissed, and where, and why.") HBMV; MasP
What Literature Needs. John A. Holmes. InMe
What little throat. The Blackbird by Belfast Lough. *Unknown, tr. by* Frank O'Connor. KiLC
What lively lad most pleasured me. A Last Confession. W. B. Yeats. BoLoP; CMoP; ELP; ErPo; HAP; OAEL-2; WeW
What Love Is This. Edward Taylor. *Fr.* Preparatory Meditations, First Series. AmPP; AP; NOCV; PoEL-3; SCAP
What lovely names for girls there are! Girls' Names. Eleanor Farjeon. SUS; TiPo
What lovely things. The Scribe. Walter de la Mare. CMoP; FaBoCh; OBMV; TrCP; TrPWD
What made the place a landscape of despair. Claus Von Stauffenberg. Thom Gunn. OBWP
What made the porter stare so hard? At Devlin's Siding. Barcroft Boake. CBAP
What magic halo rings thy head. Aucassin and Nicolete. Francis William Bourdillon. HBV-1
What Maisie Know She Don't Want No. Judith Johnson Sherwin. NoAM
What makes a city great? Huge piles of stone. The City's Crown. William Dudley Foulke. HBMV; WGRP
What makes a garden? The Garden. Caroline Giltinan. HBMV
What Makes a Happy Life. Martial, *tr. fr. Latin by* Goldwin Smith. AWP
What makes a knave a child of God. Samuel Butler. *Fr.* Hudibras, III, i. NOBL; OBSV
What Makes a Nation Great? Alexander Blackburn. WBLP
What makes a nation's pillars high. A Nation's Strength. Emerson. PAL; PGD; TRV
What makes a plenteous harvest. Prelude. Virgil, *tr. by* Dryden. *Fr.* The Georgics. AWP
What makes all subjects discontent. Samuel Butler. FaBoEE
What makes me disinclined. Pretences. Ibn Rashiq, *tr. by* A. J. Arberry. TTY
What makes my bed seem hard, seeing it is soft? A Captive of Love. Ovid, *tr. by* Christopher Marlowe. Elegies, I, 2. AWP
What makes permeable the ghost? The Ghost. Hilary Corke. NYBP
What makes that blood on the point of your knife? Edward. *Unknown.* FSW
What makes the ducks in the pond, I wonder, go. Regent's Park. Rose Fyleman. SoPo
What makes us rove that starlit corridor. Science Fiction. Kingsley Amis. NePoEA-2
What makes you look so black, so glum, so cross? Eclogue. Edward Lear. FaBoNo
What makes you write at this odd rate? Epigram on Miltonicks. Samuel Wesley. OBEC; POL
What makes your lip so strange? Thomas Middleton. *Fr.* The Changeling, III, iv. PoEL-2
What man dost thou dig it for? Shakespeare. *Fr.* Hamlet, V, i. DL
What man is he that yearneth. Chorus. Sophocles, *tr. by* A. E. Housman. *Fr.* Oedipus at Colonus. AWP
What man is there so bold that he should say. Liberty. John Hay. AA
What man of ignorance undefiled. Oh Come, Little Children. Phyllis McGinley. FaBV
What man of you, having an hundred sheep. The Lost Sheep. Bible, *N.T. Fr.* St. Luke. TreF
What? Mars his sword? faire Cytherea say. Upon Venus Putting on Mars His Armes. Richard Crashaw. SeCP
What Matisse could have done. The Red Room. Judith Berke. PoDr
What Matter? *Gond Oral Tradition, tr. by* V. Elwin *and* S. Hivale. WTO
What matter if my words will be. To My Mother. Louis Ginsberg. PoSC
What matter if the sun be lost? Daffodil's Return. Bliss Carman. CaP
What matter makes my spade for tears or mirth. Digging. Edward Thomas. BrPo
What matter where the apple grows? The Journey. Scudder Middleton. HBMV
What matters all his love for me? A Sailor's Wife. Clara Bernhardt. CaP
What may we take into the vast Forever? The Future. Edward Rowland Sill. HBV-2
What may words say, or what may words not say. Astrophel and Stella, XXXV. Sir Philip Sidney. CABA; SiPS
What mean these dreams, and hideous forms that rise. George the Third's Soliloquy. Philip Freneau. NOBA
What mean these loud aerial cracks I hear? *Unknown. Fr.* Bedlam; a Poem on His Majesty's Happy Escape from His German Dominions. NOEC
What mean these peals from every tower. The Fall of Richmond. Herman Melville. PAH
What mean these showy and these sounding signs. The Feast of Blood. Joseph Fawcett. *Fr.* The Art of War. NOEC
What meane these mortall children of mine owne. Chorus Tertius: Of Time; Eternitie. Fulke Greville. *Fr.* Mustapha. OBS
What meanes this silence of Harvardine quils. A Supplement. Benjamin Tompson. SCAP
What meanest thou, my fortune. *Unknown.* EnLoPo
What meaneth this, that Christ an hymne did singe. William Alabaster. AnAnS-1
What meaneth this? When I lie alone. Sir Thomas Wyatt. GBL; SiPS
What means at this unusual hour the light. Sonnet in the Mail Coach. Henry Taylor. TEP
"What means this glory round our feet." A Christmas Carol. James Russell Lowell. PGD
What means this new-born child of planets' motion? Eternity's Speech against Time. Fulke Greville. *Fr.* Mustapha. JCP
What means this stately tablature. To My Noble Kinsman, Thomas Stanley, Esquire, on His Lyric Poems Composed by Master John Gamble. Richard Lovelace. CaPo
What means this watery canop' 'bout thy bed. On King Richard the Third, Who Lies Buried under Leicester Bridge. Sir John Suckling. CaPo
What measure fate to him shall mete. Love Serviceable. Coventry Patmore. *Fr.* The Angel in the House. EnLoPo
What men are they who haunt these fatal glooms. James Thomson. The City of Dreadful Night, XI. EBVV
What menethe this? When I lye alone. What Does This Mean? Sir Thomas Wyatt. MeEL
What mist hath dimmed that glorious face! The Virgin Mary to Christ on the Cross. Robert Southwell. ViBoPo
What Mr. Robinson Thinks. James Russell Lowell. *Fr.* The Biglow Papers, 1st Series, III. AA; AmPP; HBV-1; InMe; PAH; YaD
What modern muse will aid my funeral song? Elegy for a Dead Confederate. Robert McGovern. SOTS
What more? Where is the third Calixt. Ballad of the Lords of Old Time. Villon, *tr. by* Swinburne. AWP
What mournful metamorphosis. Variation on a Theme by John Lyly. Sacheverell Sitwell. ViBoPo
What moved me, was the way your hand. Lament. Dorothy Livesay. CaP
What moves that lonely man is not the boom. The Hermit. W. H. Davies. BrPo; MoBrPo
What Music. Joy Harjo. TWSS
What musical numbers float over the breeze. Petrillo, *parody.* "Gilbertulus." WhC
What Must I Do to Be Saved? *Unknown.* STF
What, must my lord be gone? Lord Vyet. A. C. Benson. OBVV
What My Child Learns of the Sea. Audre Lorde. NBP; PoBA
What My Lover Said. Homer Greene. AA; HBV-1; TreFS
What nedeth these thretning wordes and wasted wynde? Sir Thomas Wyatt, *after the Italian of* Serafino. OBVE
What Need Have I for Memory? Georgia Douglas Johnson. CDC
What need you, being come to sense. September 1913. W. B. Yeats. BrPo; CMoP; CoBMV; GTBS-P; HAP; NoAM; PoRA; PPoe
What needest thou?—a few brief hours of rest. Vain Questioning. Walter de la Mare. MoVE
What Needeth All This Travail. *Unknown.* EIL
What needs complaints. Comfort to a Youth That Had Lost His Love. Robert Herrick. NOBE; OBEV
What needs my Shakespeare for his honored [*or* honor'd] bones. On Shakespeare [*or* An Epitaph on the Admirable Dramatic Poet, W. Shakespeare]. Milton. FaBoEE; HBV-2; InvP; LoBV; MeLP; MePo; NoP; OAEP; PoRA; SeCePo; TrGrPo; ViBoPo; WHA
What new responsibilities are we hatching now. Green Ice. Vivienne Finch. BrRo
What News. Walter Savage Landor. BoLoP
What Night Would It Be? John Ciardi. PDV
What! no more favours? Not a ribbon more. To a Lady That Forbade to Love before Company. Sir John Suckling. CaPo
What no, perdie [*or* perdy]! ye may be sure! Rondeau [*or* No! Indeed]. Sir Thomas Wyatt. AAS; LoBV; MeEL; OBSC; PoEL-1
What noble courage must their hearts have fired. The Lonely Settler. Oliver Goldsmith, the Younger. *Fr.* The Rising Village. NOBC; OBCV; PeCV
What noise of viols is so sweet. Beggars. Francis Davidson. CH
What noise up there? Music in the Air. George Johnston. PeCV

What! not know our Clean Clara? Clean Clara. William Brighty Rands. HBV-2; HBVY
What nothing earthly gives, or can destroy. The Soul's Calm Sunshine. Pope. *Fr.* An Essay on Man, IV. FaBoRV
What now. Another Poem for Me. Etheridge Knight. NNaP
What now avails the pageant verse. Camoens in the Hospital. Herman Melville. ViBoPo
What now avails to gain a woman's heart. The Mortified Genius. James Graeme. NOEC
What nudity is beautiful as this. Portrait of a Machine. Louis Untermeyer. MoAmPo
What numerous votaries 'neath thy shadowy wing. To the Evening. John Codrington Bampfylde. NOEC
What nymph should I admire or trust. The Question to Lisetta. Matthew Prior. OBEV
What of earls with whom you have supped [*or* supt]. The Toad-Eater. Burns. POL; TW
What of her glass without her? the blank grey [*or* gray]. Without Her. Dante Gabriel Rossetti. The House of Life, LIII. GBL; NCEP; OBNC; PoEL-5; ViBoPo; VLP
What of it, that the realms of this epoch. The Animal Howl. "M. J.," *tr. by* A. Glanz-Leyeless. TrJP
What of lords [and dukes] with whom you have [*or* you've] supped. Addressed to a Gentleman at Table, Who Kept Boasting of the Company He Kept. Burns. DBV; PV
What of the bow? The Song of the Bow. Sir Arthur Conan Doyle. *Fr.* The White Company. HBV-2
What of the Darkness? Richard Le Gallienne. HBV-2
What of the faith and fire within us. Men Who March Away. Thomas Hardy. MMA; OBWP
What of these verses that I write. Narcissus: To Himself. David Galler. PoA
What of this fabulous country. Canoe-Trip. Douglas Le Pan. CaP; OBCV; PeCV
"What of vile dust?" the preacher said. The Praise of Dust. G. K. Chesterton. MoBrPo
What on earth! I fear and tremble. Darkened in the Soul. Napa, *tr. fr. Eskimo.* WTO
What Once I Was. Sir Thomas Wyatt. MeEL
What one art thou, thus in torn weed yclad? Virtue. Nicholas Grimald. OBSC
What One May and May Not Call a Woman. *Unknown.* TreF
What other form were worthy of your praise. Muna Lee. Sonnets, *foreword.* HBMV
What our Dame bids us do. Ben Jonson. *Fr.* The Masque of Queens. OFD; WSC
What Pablo Picasso Did in "Les Demoiselles d'Avignon." John Robert Colombo. PeCV
What pain, to wake and miss you! Quite Forsaken. D. H. Lawrence. BrPo
What painter has not with a careless smutch. Accident in Art. Richard Hovey. HBV-2
What palace-temple of the mystic East. Turris Eburnea. *Unknown.* GoBC
What passing-bells for these who die as cattle? Anthem for Doomed Youth. Wilfred Owen. BiP; BrPo; ChTr; CMOP; CoBMV; EBEV; EvOK; FaBoMo; FaBoRV; FaFP; GTBS-P; HAP; HBMV; HeIP; HoPM; LiTM; MoAB; MoBrPo; MoVE; NoAM; NOBE; NoP; OAEL; OAEP; OBEV; OBWP; OxBTC; PPP; SCV; SeCePo; SoSe; TreFT; TrGrPo; ViBoPo; WaP; WeW; WHA
What pleasure can this gaudy world afford? Consideratus Considerandus. John Saffin. SCAP
What pleasure have great princes. The Quiet Life. *Unknown, at. to* William Byrd. *Unknown.* EIL; GoBC; HBV-1; NOBE; OBSC
What poet wrote these lovely lines? Intermission, Please! Irwin Edman. WhC
What poets feel not, when they make. A Caution to Poets. Matthew Arnold. FaBoUs; PV
What poets mean by what they mean. The Reader Writes. Carl Crane. PoPl; WhC
What poor astronomers are they. *Unknown.* OBSC
What portents, from what distant region, ride. On the Ice Islands Seen Floating in the German Ocean. William Cowper. OAEL-1; PrIm
What potions have I drunk of siren tears. Sonnets, CXIX. Shakespeare. WHA
What precious thing are you making fast. Art. James Thompson. OBVV
What Price. Lulu Minerva Schultz. GoYe
What Profit? Immanuel di Roma, *tr. fr. Hebrew by* J. Chotzner. TrJP
What rage is this? what furor [*or* furour] of what kind [*or* kynd]? Sir Thomas Wyatt. AAS; EnLoPo; SiPS
What ran under the rosebush? Could It Have Been a Shadow? Monica Shannon. FaPON; RHPC; SoPo; TiPo
What Remains but Only Dying? *Unknown. See* Shall I Look?
What remains of summer. The Cold. Lance Henson. CDW
What Reward? Winifred M. Letts. SUMH
What Riches Have You. George Santayana. Sonnets, XXIX. HBV-2; TrGrPo
What Riddle Asked the Sphinx. Archibald MacLeish. HoPM
What Rider Spurs Him from the Darkening East. Edna St. Vincent Millay. TrCP; WPE
"What? rise again with all one's bones." Epigram. Samuel Taylor Coleridge. HBV-1
What Robin Told. George Cooper. FaPON; TiPo
What! Roses growing in a meadow. Wild Roses. Mary Effie Lee Newsome. CDC
What! Roses on thy tomb! and was there then. Ave! Nero Imperator. Duffield Osborne. AA
What Rules the World. William Ross Wallace. OHIP
What rumour'd heavens are these. To the Unknown Eros. Coventry Patmore. LO; OxBoCh; PoEL-5
What ruse of vision. The Bear. N. Scott Momaday. CDW
What saintly features do abound in the Vatican Museum and Church. The Church of the Sacred Heart. Ashton Greene. NePoAm
What saith the river to the rushes grey. Aeolian Harp. William Allingham. OnYI
What Sanguine Beast? LeRoy Smith, Jr. NePoAm
What savage beast would willfully consent to ride jammed haunch to haunch. Bus Ride. Lenore Kandel. NMM
What say the Bells of San Blas. The Bells of San Blas. Longfellow. OxBA
What says my brother?/ Death is a fearful thing. On Death. Shakespeare. *Fr.* Measure for Measure, III, i. FiP
What scenes appear where-e'er I turn my view. Eloisa. Pope. *Fr.* Eloisa to Abelard. SeCePo
What Schoolmasters Say. Martin Seymour-Smith. OxBTC
What scope/ is there where. The Rope. Tania Van Zyl. PeSA
What seas did you see. A Conversation. Dylan Thomas. RFM
What seas what shores what grey rocks and what islands. Marina. T. S. Eliot. ChMP; CMoP; FaBoMo; GTBS-P; HeIP; LiTA; MOS; NOBE; NOCV; TwAmPo
What Secret Desires of the Blood. Nelly Sachs, *tr. fr. German by* Keith Bosley. VWA
What seek'st thou at this madman's pace? His Quest. Lewis Frank Tooker. AA
What seems to us for us is true. Perspective. Coventry Patmore. *Fr.* The Angel in the House. FaBoEE; GBL
What Semiramis Said. Vachel Lindsay. Poems about the Moon, IV. MOON; TwAmPo
What shakes the eye but the invisible? The Decision. Theodore Roethke. VGW
What shall be added to your praises? Lines for a Feast of Our Lady. Sister Maris Stella. ISi
What shall be said between us here. Félise. Swinburne. BeLS
What shall he have that kill'd [*or* killed] the deer? Song [*or* Amíens's Song]. Shakespeare. *Fr.* As You Like It, IV, ii. CTC; OBSC; ViBoPo
What shall her silence keep? Dirge. Madison Cawein. AA
What shall I do to be for ever known. The Motto. Abraham Cowley. AnAnS-2; SeCP
What shall I do to be just? The Cry of the Age. Hamlin Garland. WGRP
What Shall I Do to Show How Much I Love Her? John Gay. *Fr.* The Beggar's Opera. TEP
What shall I do with this absurdity. The Tower. W. B. Yeats. CMoP; CoBMV; LiTB; LiTM; MoPo; NoAM; OAEP; SeCeV
What Shall I Give? Edward Thomas. FaBoCh; OxBChV
What Shall I Give My Children? Gwendolyn Brooks. *Fr.* The Womanhood: The Children of the Poor. BPo
("What shall I give my children? who are poor.") BALP; PoCh
What shall I leave my son. Testament. Langston Hughes. NePoAm-2
"What shall I render thee, Father Supreme." The Mother's Sacrifice. Lydia Huntley Sigourney. PaPo
What shall I render to thy Name. In Thankfull Remembrance for My Dear Husband's Safe Arrivall Sept. 3, 1662. Anne Bradstreet. TrPWD
What shall I say, because talk I must? The Yellow Flower. William Carlos Williams. HAP
What shall I say but, having written for use. Answering a Letter from a Younger Poet. Brewster Ghiselin. PoCh
What shall I say, my Lord? With what begin? Edward Taylor. Preparatory Meditations: Second Series, XXIX. HAP
What shall I send my love [*or* sweet] today. A Valentine. Matilda Betham-Edwards. OBVV; PeHV
What shall I sing when all is sung. All Sung. Richard Le Gallienne. OBVV
What shall I teach in the vivid afternoon. Going to School. Karl Shapiro. TrJP
What shall I wish thee? New Year's Wishes. Frances Ridley Havergal. BLRP; STF

What shall I wish thee this New Year? A New Year Wish. *Unknown.* BLRP
What shall I your true-love tell. Messages. Francis Thompson. CH
What Shall It Profit? William Dean Howells. AA
(Faith.) WGRP
What shall it profit a man. Anastasis. Albert E. S. Smythe. CaP
What shall Presto do for pretty prattle. Swift. Delmore Schwartz. PoA
What! shall that sudden blade. Custer. Edmund Clarence Stedman. BPAW; PAH
What shall the world do with its children? Romans Angry about the Inner World. Robert Bly. NoAM; NOBA; PPoe
What shall we be like when. Seeds. John Oxenham. WGRP
What shall we do. Songs of the Priestess. Malka Heifetz Tussman, *tr. by* Marcia Falk. VWA
What shall we do for Love these days? Epilogue. Lascelles Abercrombie. *Fr.* Emblems of Love. HBV-1; MoBrPo; OBVV
What shall we do for timber? Kilcash. *Unknown, tr. by* Frank O'Connor. BIrV; KiLC; OBMV; OxBI
What shall we do now, Mary being dead. Mary Booth. Thomas William Parsons. AA
What shall we do—what shall we think—what shall we say? Prelude XXIX. Conrad Aiken. *Fr.* Preludes for Memnon. FaBoMo
What Shall We Do with a Drunken Sailor? *Unknown.* FSW
(Drunken Sailor, The; or, Early in the Morning, *with music.*) ShS
What shall we mourn? For the prostrate. John Boyle O'Reilly. *Fr.* Wendell Phillips. AA
What Shall We Render. *Unknown.* BLRP
What shall we say it is to be forgiven? Forgiveness. Elizabeth Sewell. EaLo
What Shame Forbids to Speak. Robert Herrick. *See* To Anthea.
What she collects is men. The Collector. Raymond Souster. ErPo; OBCV
What she made in her body is broken. Poem for J. Wendell Berry. GeTw
What she remembers. Mother of the Groom. Seamus Heaney. PAI
What She Said. Maturai Eruttalan Centamputan, *tr. fr. Tamil by* A. K. Ramanujan. BoLoP
What She Said to Her Girl-Friend. Venmanipputi, *tr. fr. Tamil by* A. K. Ramanujan. PBWP
What She Thought. Harrison Robertson. *Fr.* Two Triolets. HBV-1
What She Wanted. Ronald Koertge. GP
What She Wished. Marilyn Throne. AMV-81
What Shines in Winter Burns. T. R. Hummer. MAYP
What Ship Is This? *Unknown. See* Old Ship of Zion.
What sholde I saye? but, at the monthes ende. The Wife's Fifth Husband. Chaucer. *Fr.* The Canterbury Tales: The Wife of Bath's Prologue. OxBM
What should be said of him cannot be said. Dante. Michelangelo, *tr. by* Longfellow. AWP
What should I be but a prophet and a liar. The Singing-Woman from the Wood's Edge. Edna St. Vincent Millay. HBMV
What should I care at all from what my name I take. The Trent Again. Michael Drayton. *Fr.* Polyolbion, Sixth and Twentieth Song. FaBoPP
What should I say. Farewell [*or* A Revocation]. Sir Thomas Wyatt. EnRePo; GBL; GoBC; LoBV; NOBE; NoP; OBEV; OBSC; PoEL-1; SiPS
What should one. The Picture of J. T. in a Prospect of Stone. Charles Tomlinson. PoCh; PPP
What should we be without the sexual myth. Men Made out of Words. Wallace Stevens. MoAB; NOBA; TAP; VGW
What should we do without the sirens. Sirens. Elliott Coleman. FAZ
What should we have taken. Provisions. Margaret Atwood. IHMS
What should we know. Verse. Oliver St. John Gogarty. AnIL; FaBoCh; OBMV; PoRA
What shulde I saye. *See* What should I say.
What sin was mine, sweet, silent boy-god, Sleep. Sleep. Statius, *tr. by* W. H. Fyfe. AWP
What since August, when the sound. Natural History. Richard Howard. TAP
What siren zooming is sounding our coming. The Exiles. W. H. Auden. OxBTC
What slender youth bedew'd with liquid odours. To Pyrrha [*or* To a Girl *or* Fifth Ode of Horace, The]. Horace, *tr. by* Milton. Odes, I, 5. AWP; EBEV; EnLoPo; OBVE; PoEL-3; WiR
What Smouldering Senses. Dante Gabriel Rossetti. The House of Life, VI. UnTE
(Kiss, The.) VLP
What so beyond all madness is the elf. Cupid Far Gone. Richard Lovelace. CaPo
What! soar'd the old eagle to die at the sun! The Death of Harrison. Nathaniel Parker Willis. PAH
What soft, cherubic creatures. Emily Dickinson. AmPP; AP; CABA; HAP; MoAB; MoAmPo; PPON; SoSe; WPE
What solemn sound the ear invades. Mount Vernon. *Unknown.* AmFP; OFD
What Someone Said When He Was Spanked on the Day before His Birthday. John Ciardi. RHPC
What songs found voice upon those lips. Helen Hunt Jackson. Ina Coolbrith. AA
What sort of a church would our church be. Just like Me. P. W. Sinks. BLRP
What soul would bargain for a cure that brings. Modern Love, XIV. George Meredith. HBV-1
"What sound awakened me, I wonder." The Deserter. A. E. Housman. OBMV; SeCeV
What sound awoke me? Dragon Skate. Gladys Cardiff. CDW
What sounds are those, Helvellyn, which are heard. The Fair below Helvellyn. Wordsworth. *Fr.* The Prelude, VII. FaBoPP
What sower walked over earth. Sunflower. Rolf Jacobsen, *tr. by* Robert Bly. NU
What sphinx of cement and aluminum bashed open their skulls. Allen Ginsberg. Howl, II. PoCh
What spirit touched the faded lambrequin. The Ilex Tree. Agnes Lee. PoA
What splendid names for boys there are! Boys' Names. Eleanor Farjeon. SUS; TiPo
What Splendid Rays, *with music.* Christian Gregor, *tr. fr. German.* AH
What stands 'tween me and her that I adore? Echo Poem. M. Allan. FiBHP
What sticks with me is the pit. Moonwalk. John Engels. MAT
What, Still Alive. Hugh Kingsmill. BXAP
(Poem, after A. E. Housman.) FaBoPa
("What, still alive at twenty-two.") DBV; FaBoCo; InPK; NOBL; SpRo
What strength! what strife! what rude unrest! Westward Ho! Joaquin Miller. AA; FaBoBe
What stripling now thee discomposes. Horace, *tr. by* Sir Richard Fanshaw. Odes, I, 5. OBVE
What sudden bugle calls us in the night. Reveillé. Louis Untermeyer. HBV-2
What sugred termes, what all-perswading arte. Diella, IV. Richard Lynche. AAS
What sweet relief the showers to thirsty plants we see. A True Love. Nicholas Grimald. EIL; OBEV; OBSC
What sweeter music[k] can we bring. A Christmas Carol [Sung to the King in the Presence at Whitehall]. Robert Herrick. GoJo; PChr; SBVL
What swords and spears, what daggers bright. Frost. W. H. Davies. BoNaP
What the Animals Said. Peter Serchuk. HoAn
What the Birds Said. Whittier. NOBA
What the Bones Know. Carolyn Kizer. NePoAm-2
What the Bullet Sang. Bret Harte. AA; OBEV; OBVV; PeD
What the cats do. The Cats. Weldon Kees. NaP
What the Chairman Told Tom. Basil Bunting. OxBTC
What the child wants longs the man for. Ice Cream in Paradise. Robert Hollander. AMV-80
What the Choir Sang about the New Bonnet. M. T. Morrison. BLPA
What the Devil Said. James Stephens. CMoP
What the Donkey Saw. U. A. Fanthorpe. OBCP
What the Earth Asked Me. James Wright. NYBP
What the Emanation of Casey Jones Said to the Medium. Arthur James Marshall Smith. MoCV
What the Engines Said. Bret Harte. BPAW
What the eye sees is a dream of sight. To the Hand. W. S. Merwin. EAS
What the Gray Cat Sings. Arthur Guiterman. MoShBr
What the heart wants comes true. To the Young Rebels. E. L. Mayo. FAZ
What the Moon Saw. Vachel Lindsay. CrMA; FaBoEE
What the Motorcycle Said. Mona Van Duyn. NIP
What the Old Man Said. C. Fox Smith. EtS
What the Orderly Dog Saw. Ford Madox Ford. CTC
What the people learn out of lifting and hauling. Carl Sandburg. The People, Yes, Sec. 32. OBAL
What the Prince of I Dreamt. Henry Cholmondeley-Pennell. NA
What the Red-haired Bo'sun Said. Charles H. Souter. PoAu-1
What the Rooster Does before Mounting. Cyn Zarco. BrSi
What the Serpent Said to Adam. Archibald MacLeish. NePA
What the Sonnet Is. Eugene Lee-Hamilton. HoPM; OBVV
What the sun gives us. Cows Grazing at Sunrise. William Matthews. AMV-81; NPAW
What the Thrush Said. Keats. EBEV; NIP
What the Toys Are Thinking. ffrida Wolfe. TiPo
What the Violins Sing in Their Baconfat Bed. Jean Arp, *tr. fr. French by* John Frederick Nims. WeW
What the warbler must have seen. Glass. Brendan Galvin. LTB

What the wind harried, the fire worried. Deadfall. Martha Keller. GoYe
What Then? *Unknown.* STF
What Then? W. B. Yeats. CMoP
What Then, Dancer? Kay Smith. CaP
What Then Is Love but Mourning. Thomas Campion. EnRePo; FaBoEn
What then is Merlyn's message, his word to thee weary of pain. Wilfrid Scawen Blunt. *Fr.* The Wisdom of Merlyn. ViBoPo
What then is poetry. Poetry. Claude Vigée, *tr. by* Anthony Rudolf. VWA
"What then, what if my lips do burn." Ulf in Ireland. Charles De Kay. AA
What There Is. Kenneth Patchen. LLLT
What there is once may not be twice. No Laws. Brian Allwood. WaP
What they are doing is turning. Turn (a Poem in 4 Parts). Ken Belford. NOBC
What They Are For. Dorothy Aldis. SoPo
What They Do to You in Distant Places. Marvin Bell. Psk
What thing/ should I sing. Dove. Norma Farber. PChr
What thing did I love that walks the street. The Contemporary Muse. Edgell Rickword. OBSV
What Thing Is Love? George Peele. *Fr.* The Hunting of Cupid. ElL; ELP; EnRePo; NOBE; OAEP; SeCePo; UnTE
(Love.) OBSC
What thing shall be held up to woman's beauty? Woman's Beauty. Lascelles Abercrombie. *Fr.* Vashti. MoBrPo
What things are steadfast? Not the birds. We Manage Most When We Manage Small. Linda Gregg. AmPA; NPGG
What think you of this age now. Song. *Unknown.* APAS
What this mountain means, and the murky dale. William Langland, *mod. by* J. B. Trapp. *Fr.* The Vision of Piers Plowman, Passus I. OAEL-1
What tho' thy home. True Riches. Bessie June Martin. STF
What tho', Valclusa, the fond bard be fled. Sonnet: To Valclusa. Thomas Russell. OBEC
What Thomas [*or* Tomas] an Buile Said in a Pub. James Stephens. MoAB; MoBrPo; PoRA; TrGrPo; WGRP
(What Tomas Said in a Pub.) CMoP; NoAM; PAI
What thou hast done thou hast done; for the heavenly horses are swift. Irrevocable. Mary Wright Plummer. WGRP
What thou lovest well remains. Ezra Pound. *Fr.* Cantos, LXXXI. CMoP; FaBoTw; InPS; MoAB; NePA; NOBE; OxBA; SeCeV; ViBoPo
What Thou Lovest Well, Remains American. Richard Hugo. GP; NIP; NPAW
What though, for showing truth to flatter'd state. Sonnet: Written on the Day That Mr. Leigh Hunt Left Prison. Keats. ChER
What though my harp, and viol be. To God, on His Sickness. Robert Herrick. OxBoCh
What though my joys and comforts die? Robert Lowry. *Fr.* How Can I Keep from Singing? TRV
What though my penne wax faynt. To Maystres Jane Blenner-Haiset. John Skelton. *Fr.* The Garlande of Laurell. AAS
What Though the Field Be Lost? Milton. *Fr.* Paradise Lost, I. EaLo
(Satan's Adjuration.) FaBoEn
What Though the Green Leaf Grow? Maybury Fleming. AA
What though the vulgar and received praise. Elegy for Doctor Dunn. Lord Herbert of Cherbury. AnAnS-2
What thought ye to burn, when ye kindled the pyre. Epigram IV. *Unknown.* *Fr.* Duel with Verses over a Great Man. TrJP
What thoughts I have of you tonight, Walt Whitman. A Supermarket in California. Allen Ginsberg. AmPP; CoAP; ConAP; HAP; HeIP; LiTM; NaP; NeAP; NOBA; PoM; PrIm; SOTW; TAP; TwCP; UnPo
What thoughts I have of you tonight, Walt Whitman, for I work late. A Pizza Joint in Cranston. Craig Weeden. BXAP
What throws/ this shadow. Viking 1 on Mars—July 20, 1976. Anne S. Perlman. SUW
What Tidings? John Audelay. OxBM
What tidings of reverent gladness are voiced by the bells that ring. On Easter Morning. Eben E. Rexford. BLRP
What time I hear the storming sea. Thrustararorum. Henry Nehemiah Dodge. EtS
"What time I see you passing by." Popular Songs of Tuscany. *Unknown, tr. by* John Addington Symonds. AWP
What time soft night had silently begun. Fame and Fortune. Michael Drayton. *Fr.* The Legend of Robert, Duke of Normandy. OBSC
What time the earth takes on the garb of Spring. Incipit Vita Nova. William Morton Payne. AA
What time the gifted lady took. George Sand. Dorothy Parker. FiBHP
What time the Lord drew back the sea. Panama. Amanda T. Jones. PAH
What time the noble Lovewell came. Lovewell's Fight. *Unknown.* PAH
What time the poet hath hymned. Oh, Hollow! Hollow! Hollow! W. S. Gilbert. *Fr.* Patience. FaBoNo
What time the rose of dawn is laid across the lips of night. The Angler's Reveille. Henry van Dyke. *Fr.* The Toiling of Felix. GN
What time the weary weather-beaten sheep. The Tenth Eclogue. Michael Drayton. *Fr.* The Shepherd's Garland. JCP
What time this world's great workmaster did cast. Beauty [*or* Soul Is Form]. Spenser. *Fr.* An Hymne in Honour of Beautie. GoBC, *abr.*; OBSC
What to Do. William Wise. TiPo
What Tomas [an Buile] Said in a Pub. James Stephens. *See* What Thomas an Buile Said in a Pub.
What Tongue Can Her Perfections Tell? Sir Philip Sidney. *Fr.* Arcadia. EnRePo; SiPS
What travellers of matchlesse Venice say. An Elegie Made by Mr. Aurelian Townshend in Remembrance of the Ladie Venetia Digby. Aurelian Townshend. AnAnS-2; SeCP
What treasure greater than a friend. A Friend. Santob de Carrion. *Fr.* Proverbios Morales. TrJP
What trifling coil do we poor mortals keep. Human Life. Matthew Prior. FaBoEE
What Trinkets? Thomas Hornsby Ferril. NePoAm-2
What Ulysses Said to Circe on the Beach of Aeaea. Irving Layton. ErPo
What vaileth trouth? or by it to take payn? Sir Thomas Wyatt. AAS
What various hindrances we meet. Exhortation to Prayer. William Cowper. NOCV
What voice did on my spirit fall. Peschiera. Arthur Hugh Clough. HBV-2
"What voice, what harp, are those we hear." The Minstrel. Goethe, *tr. by* James Clarence Mangan. AWP
What! want to be buggered, and cry when it's done! Epigram: To Papilus. Martial. PeHV
What wants thee, that thou art in this sad taking? London Sad London. *Unknown.* OBS
What was he doing, the great god Pan. A Musical Instrument [*or* The Great God Pan]. Elizabeth Barrett Browning. EBVV; FaBoBe; FaPON; HBV-2; HBVY; NoP; OAEL-2; OAEP; OBEV; OBVV; OnMSP; WiR; WPE
What was he like, my God, what was he like? Fleeting Return. Juan Ramon Jimenez, *ad. by* William Moritz. AMV-80
What was her beauty in our first estate. She. Richard Wilbur. AmPP; ConAP; CoPo; NIP
What was his name? I do not know his name. The Nameless Saints. Edward Everett Hale. WGRP
What was I back in the world's first wonder? Edwin Markham. *Fr.* Virgilia. EtS
What was it? The Death of the First Man. Nancy Sullivan. NIP
What was it/ that caught in our throats that day. The Greek Room. James W. Thompson. BPo
What was it called. Custer Lives in Humbolt County. Janet Campbell Hale. STE; VoR
What was it Colin gave to thee? I Lay My Lute beside Thy Door. Clarence Urmy. HBMV
What was it I was saving for my old age? Whatever It Was I Was Saving for My Old Age. Ann Darr. SUW
What was it I wonder? The Knife. Richard Tillinghast. MAYP
What was it like, that country house? Country Villa. Jean Garrigue. TAP
What was it like to. Great Man. B. S. Johnson. ELU
What was it the engines said. What the Engines Said. Bret Harte. BPAW
What was it you remember—the summer mornings. To Any Member of My Generation. George Barker. LiTM; ViBoPo
What was most striking about them. Concerning the Dead Women: The Munitions Plant Explosion: June, 1918. Elizabeth Libbey. AmPA
What Was My Dream? Joseph O'Connor. AA
What was our trust, we trust not. $E=MC^2$. Morris Bishop. ImOP
What Was Solomon's Mind? Geoffrey Scott. OBMV
"What was that sound we heard." Why Must You Know? John Wheelwright. CrMA; VGW
What was the first prophetic word that rang. Peace. Edwin Markham. WBLP
What was the promise that smiled from the maples at evening? Promises, I. Robert Penn Warren. DiL
What Was Your Name in the States? *with music.* *Unknown.* AS
What waspish whim of Fate. To a Portrait of Whistler in the Brooklyn Art Museum. Eleanor Rogers Cox. HBMV
What watch, what woe, what want, what wrack. The Shipmen. William Hunnis. OBSC
What way does the Wind come? What way does he go? Address to a Child during a Boisterous Winter Evening. Dorothy Wordsworth. OxBChV
What We Can. Ray A. Young Bear. VoR
What we do best is breed. A Christening. Donald Davie. OxBC
What we know to be not possible. Nones. W. H. Auden. *Fr.* Horae Canonicae. CoBMV
What we looked for always remained. The Friendship. Robert Mezey. NaP
What We May Live Without. "Owen Meredith." *Fr.* Lucile. TreF
What! We of Spear-Danes in spent days. *Unknown.* *Fr.* Beowulf. ViBoPo
What We Said. W. D. Snodgrass. GP

What We See Is What We Think. Wallace Stevens. SyP
What we were doing then was making good company. A Short History of the Better Life. Tess Gallagher. LTB
What weight of ancient witness can prevail. Private Judgement Condemned [*or* Confessio Fidei *or* A Prayer]. Dryden. *Fr.* The Hind and the Panther, I. FiP; NOBE; OBS
What well-heeled knuckle-head, straight from the unisex. An Old Malediction. Anthony Hecht. TW
What Were They Like? Denise Levertov. HeIP; NIP; OBWP; PAI; PPON; VGW; WPE
What were we playing? Was it prisoner's base? Running. Richard Wilbur. CoAP; NCSH
What were you carrying, Pilgrims, Pilgrims? *See* What are you carrying . . .
What, what, is virtue, but repose of mind? A Witching Song. James Thomson. *Fr.* The Castle of Indolence. OBEC
What, what, what,/ What's the news from Swat? A Threnody [*or* The Ahkoond of Swat]. George Thomas Lanigan. AA; CaP; CenHV; FiBHP; HBV-2; InMe; NA; PeCV; TreFS; WHW
What Wild Dawns There Were. Denise Levertov. NOBA
What will become of Hawaii? The Leper. Ka-'ehu, *tr. by* M. K. Pukui *and* A. L. Korn. WTO
What, will he come for me. Microcosmos, XVI. Nigel Heseltine. NeBP
What will it be like, the day death comes? The Day Death Comes. Faiz Ahmed Faiz, *tr. by* Naomi Lazard. AMV-81
What Will Remain after Me? Mendel Naigreshel, *tr. fr. Yiddish by* Joachim Neugroschel. VWA
What will they give me, when journey's done? Journey's End. Humbert Wolfe. TrJP
What will we do. Poem for Nana. June Jordan. BlSi
What Will We Do for Linen? *Unknown.* GBP
("Och! what shall we do for linen?") WTO
What will you do. What Then, Dancer? Kay Smith. CaP
What Will You Do, God, When I Die? Rainer Maria Rilke, *tr. fr. German by* Babette Deutsch. EaLo
What Will You Do, Love? Samuel Lover. OnYI
What will you give to a barefoot lass. A Song of Riches. Katharine Lee Bates. AA
"What will you have for your birthday?" Birthday Gifts. Herbert Asquith. OFD; SiSoSe
What will you ride on? Hey! My Pony! Eleonor Farjeon. FaPON
What winter holiday is this? The Man of Peace, *abr.* Bliss Carman. OHIP
What wisdom have I that I surely know. Certainty. Evelyn Hardy. HBMV
What wisdom have we that by wisdom all. Relativities. Louis Untermeyer. BXAP
What! without feeling? Don't we make pretense. Two Vast Enjoyments Commemorated. John Danforth. SCAP
What without speech we knew and could not say. Preludes to Definition, IV. Conrad Aiken. TwAmPo
What Women Are Not. *Unknown.* MeEl
What wonder strikes the curious, while he views. The Ants. John Clare. BoAnP
What wonders now I have to pen, sir. The Female Husband, Who Had Been Married to Another Female for Twenty-one Years. *Unknown.* CoMu
What wondrous [*or* wond'rous] life is this I lead! Andrew Marvell. *Fr.* The Garden. BoNaP; CH; ChTr
What Wondrous Love Is This. *Unknown. See* Wondrous Love.
What wondrous pretty things I've seen. Young Master's Account of a Puppet Show. John Marchant. OxBChV
What word have you, interpreters, of men. Of Heaven Considered as a Tomb. Wallace Stevens. PoA; QFR
What words are these have fallen from me. In Memoriam A. H. H., XVI. Tennyson. EBEV
What Words Have Passed. Milton. *Fr.* Paradise Lost, IX. TrCP
What work of honour and eternal name. De Guiana, Carmen Epicum. George Chapman. OBSC
What worlds of wonder are our books! Books. Eleanor Farjeon. YeAr
What worth to me the seven treasures. An Elegy on the Death of Furuhi. Yamanoue Okura. DL
What would earth do without her blessed boobs. Yes, What? Robert Francis. LCAP
What Would I Do White? June Jordan. NMM
What would I do without this world faceless incurious. Samuel Beckett. NoAM
What would it be like. A Sacred Grove. Fran Winant. BrRo
What would it mean for you and me. The Miracle of the Dawn. Madison Cawein. HBV-1
What would it mean to lose this life. Now It Can Be Told. Philip Levine. VWA
What would our mother say? Distress. Susan Griffin. NPGG
What would this Man? Now upward will he soar. Pope. *Fr.* An Essay on Man, Epistle I. HeIP
What would we do without them. The Dead of the World. Jeanne Finlay. AMV-81
What would'st thou have for easement after grief. Comfort of the Fields. Archibald Lampman. CaP
What wourde is that that chaungeth not. Sir Thomas Wyatt. AAS
What Yo' Gwine to Do When Yo' Lamp Burn Down? *Unknown.* BoAn-1; BPo
"What, you are stepping westward?" Stepping Westward. Wordsworth. CH; EnRP; HBV-1; OBRV; PoEL-4; SeCeV
What you call me, man? Dopefiends Trip. Hector Angulo. FIA
What you desire not starlight nor tearose. In the Web. E. L. Mayo. MiAP
What You Goin' to Do When the Rent Comes 'Round? Andrew B. Sterling. OBAL
What you gonna do. Wartime Blues. *Unknown.* BluL
What you gonna do when the liquor gives out, sweet thing? Sweet Thing. *Unknown.* FSW; OuSiCo
What you gwain to do when the meat gives out, my Baby? What Kin' o' Pants Does the Gambler Wear. *Unknown.* AS
What you have heard is true. The Colonel. Carolyn Forché. OBWP
What You Need. Kathleen Fraser. AmPA
What you see here is a colorful illusion. She Attempts to Refute the Praises That Truth, Which She Calls Passion, Inscribed on a Portrait of the Poet. Sister Juana Ines de la Cruz, *tr. by* Willis Barnstone. BoWoP
"What You See Is Me." Barbara Gibbs. NYBP
What You Should Know to Be a Poet. Gary Snyder. NNaP; PoM
What You Will Learn about the Brobinyak. John Ciardi. EvOK
What Zimmer Would Be. Paul Zimmer. Psk
What'd you get, black boy. Mr. Roosevelt Regrets. Pauli Murray. PoBA
Whate'er I be, old England is my dam! The Old Chartist. George Meredith. NBM
Whate'er is born of mortal birth. To Tirzah. Blake. *Fr.* Songs of Experience. EnRP; LO; NOBE; OAEL-2; OxBoCh
Whate'er the passion—knowledge, fame, or pelf. Human Folly. Pope. *Fr.* An Essay on Man, Epistle II. FiP; TrGrPo
Whate'er thy Countrymen have done. Written in the Beginning of Mezeray's History of France. Matthew Prior. NOBE; OBEC; PoEL-3
Whate'er we leave to God, God does. Inspiration. Henry David Thoreau. AmPP; AP; EBCP; NOBA; OxBA
Whate'er You Dream with Doubt Possest. Arthur Hugh Clough. OAEP
(All Is Well.) PAI
Whatever brawls disturb the street. Love between Brothers and Sisters. Isaac Watts. FaBoUs
Whatever Comes. William Stafford. NPAW
Whatever constitutes. The Act of Love. Robert Creeley. GP; HAP
Whatever damn thing goes wrong. The Engine; a Manual. Michael Dobberstein. AMV-81
Whatever else be lost among the years. Let Us Keep Christmas. Grace Noll Crowell. TRV
Whatever else withheld, withhold not from us. Belief in Plan of Thee. Walt Whitman. TRV
Whatever good is naturally done. Sonnet: Of Love, in Honor of His Mistress Becchina. Cecco Angiolieri da Siena, *tr. by* Dante Gabriel Rossetti. AWP
Whatever he does, you have to do too. Follow the Leader. Kathleen Fraser. RHPC
Whatever I do, and whatever I say. Aunt Tabitha. Oliver Wendell Holmes. CenHV
Whatever I find if I search will be wrong. The Other. Ruth Fainlight. BrRo
"Whatever is here, it is." Confessions of the Life Artist. Thom Gunn. CMoP
Whatever Is—Is Best. Ella Wheeler Wilcox. BLPA; TreFS
Whatever Is, Is Right. Frank Gaik. AMV-81
Whatever Is, Is Right. Pope. *Fr.* An Essay on Man, Epistle I. OBEC
Whatever it is, it must have. American Poetry. Louis Simpson. ELU; NoAM; NOBA; PP; TAP
Whatever it is, it's a passion. Love in America. Marianne Moore. GOA
Whatever It Was I Was Saving for My Old Age. Ann Darr. SUW
Whatever it was she had so fiercely fought. The Recognition of Eve. Karl Shapiro. *Fr.* Adam and Eve. MoAB
Whatever its function. The Purist to Her Love. Margaret Fishback. WhC
Whatever law of yours, O God Varuna. Varuna. *Tr. fr. Sanskrit by* Raimundo Panikkar. *Fr.* Vedic Hymns. ILwL
Whatever one toucan can do. Toucannery. Jack Prelutsky. OnUR
Whatever the books may say, or the plausible. December: Of Aphrodite. W. S. Merwin. NePoEA
Whatever they wanted for their sons. Déjà Vu. Shirley Kaufman. LCAP
Whatever we do, whether we light. Dilemma. David Ignatow. VGW
Whatever we found in that room was not easy. A Last Word. May Sarton. GLGT
Whatever while the thought comes over me. Dante, *tr. by* Dante Gabriel Rossetti. La Vita Nuova, XXI. AWP

Whatever you call it. Elegy 3. Seamus Deane. CIP
Whatever You Say Say Nothing. Seamus Heaney. OBWP; OxBC
"Whatever you want is yours." The Lay of the Battle of Tombland. Dunstan Thompson. LiTA; NePA
Whatever your eye alights on this morning is yours. Years of Indiscretion. John Ashbery. NOBA
Whatever's lost, it first was won. Elizabeth Barrett Browning. *Fr.* De Profundis. TrPWD
What'll Be the Title? Justin Richardson. FiBHP
What'll We Do with the Baby-O. *Unknown.* FSW
What're you gonna do with the pretty Bessie Larkin. Callahan. *Unknown.* OuSiCo
What's a poem? A flat piece of paper. A Poem—Good or Bad—a Thing—with One Attribute—Flat. Melech Ravitch, *tr. by* Ruth Whitman. VWA
"What's all this rich land," said I to the Meath man. The Boyne Walk. F. R. Higgins. OxBI
What's become of Waring. Waring. Robert Browning. PoEL-5; VLP
What's Fame? a fancied life in others' breath. Pope. *Fr.* Essay on Man, Epistle IV. ViBoPo
What's filling up the mirror? O, it is not I. The Fat Man in the Mirror. Robert Lowell. PoA
What's going to be the end for both of us—God? Twelve Lines about the Burning Bush. Melech Ravitch, *tr. by* Ruth Whitman. VWA
What's hallowed ground? Has earth a clod. Hallowed Ground. Thomas Campbell. BLPA; HBV-2
What's Hard. Laurence Lerner. NePoEA-2
What's he that, in yon gilded coach elate. A Remonstrance. John Gerrard. NOEC
What's in a Name? Helen F. More. PAH
What's in a Name? R. K. Munkittrick. InMe
What's in the Cupboard? *Unknown.* CH; ChTr; GBP; OxNR
What's in there? *Unknown.* CH; OxNR
What's life but full of care and doubt. Domestic Didactics by an Old Servant. Thomas Hood. OBRV; VLP
What's Living? Linda Hogan. AMV-81
What's love, when the most is said? When the Most Is Said. "Madeline Bridges." AA; HBV-2
What's my sweetheart?—A laundress is she. Jeannette. Otto Julius Bierbaum, *tr. by* Jethro Bithell. AWP
What's My Thought Like? Thomas Moore. FaBoEE; OBRV
(Riddle, A: "Why is a pump like V-sc—nt C-stl-r—gh?") FaBoCo
"What's new?"—What's old? what's anything. S. T. Coleridge Dismisses a Caller from Porlock. Gerard Previn Meyer. GoYe
What's she, so late from Penshurst come. On Her Coming to London. Edmund Waller. HBV-1
What's sweeter than at the end of a summer's day. Thanksgiving. Kenneth Koch. VGW
What's That? Florence Parry Heide. RHPC
What's that?/ An Egg. Whoroscope. Samuel Beckett. NoAM
What's that approaching like dusk like poverty. Ballad. Charles Simic. LCAP
What's that red stuff? Blood? Gee. The Last Supper. Stan Rice. NPGG
"What's that that hirples at my side?" Heriot's Ford. Kipling. PoRA
What's that we see from far? the spring of Day. A Nuptial[l] Song, or Epithalamie [*or* Epithalamy], on Sir Clipseby Crew and His Lady. Robert Herrick. CaPO; JCP; PoEL-3; SeCP; SeCV-1
What's the balm. Poem. Alan Dugan. CAPP
What's the best thing in the world? The Best Thing in the World [*or* The Best]. Elizabeth Barrett Browning. EBVV; OBVV
What's the brightness of a brow? Evanescence. Harriet Prescott Spofford. AA
What's the good of a wagon. The Gold-tinted Dragon. Karla Kuskin. SoPo
What's the greeting for a rajah riding on an elephant? Some Questions to Be Asked of a Rajah, Perhaps by the Associated Press. Preston Newman. FiBHP
What's the gud of these Pazons? They're the most despard rubbage go'n'. The Parsons. Thomas Edward Brown. DBV
"What's the horriblest thing you've seen?" Horrible Things. Roy Fuller. OnUR
What's the Life of a Man? *Unknown.* OBET
What's the news of the day. Mother Goose. OxNR
What's the oldest thing that's living? Catechisms: Talking with a Four-year-old. George Ella Lyon. Str
What's the Plural? *Unknown.* FaBoUs
What's the Railroad to Me? Henry David Thoreau. ELU; PoEL-4; TAP
(Railroad, The.) FaBV
What's the Use. Ogden Nash. PoPl
What's this? A dish for fat lips. The Shape of the Fire. Theodore Roethke. CMoP; LCAP; LiTA; MiAP; MoAB
What's this dull town to me? Robin Adair. Caroline Keppel. FaBoBe; HBV-1
What's this morn's bright eye to me. Morning Hymn. Joseph Beaumont. OxBoCh; TrPWD
What's this vain world to me? Rest Is Not Here. Lady Nairne. HBV-2
What's up, today, with our lovers? The Lovers Go Fly a Kite. W. D. Snodgrass. NYBP
What's worse than this past century? "Anna Akhmatova," *tr. fr. Russian by* Barbara Einzig. BoWoP
What's Wrong, Little Blonde, *with music.* *Unknown.* OuSiCo
What's Your Fancy. *Unknown.* UnTE
What's your name? Pudden Tame. *Unknown.* ChTr; FaBoNo
Whatso men sayn. Men Only Pretend. *Unknown.* MeEL
"Whatsoe'er He bids you—do it!" Leave the Miracle to Him. Thomas H. Allan. BLRP
Whatsoever Hath Been Made, God Made. Dadu, *tr. fr. Sanskrit.* ILwL
Whatsoever I Do. Mary Louise Hector. GoBC
Whatsoever thing I see. Love Dislikes Nothing. Robert Herrick. AnAnS-2; CavP
Whaup o' the Reed, *sel.* Will H. Ogilvie.
Blades of Harden, The. GoTS
Whaur are ye gaun. John Hielandman. *Unknown.* GBP
Whaur green abune the banks the links stretch oot. The Planticru. Robert Rendall. OxBS
Whaur yon broken brig hings owre. Song. William Soutar. GoTS; OxBS
Wheat Metropolis. Alfred Starr Hamilton. FAZ
Wheatfields of chiffon. Best of Show. Barbara Howes. GDP
Wheatlet Son of Milklet. MacConglinne, *tr. fr. Middle Irish by* Kuno Meyer. OnYI
Whee hee lo, whee hee. Evening on Howth Head. Eileen Brennan. NeIP
Wheear 'as tha been sin' ah saw thee? Ilkla Moor. *Unknown.* FaBoPP
Wheel, The. Wendell Berry. GeTw
Wheel, The. James Cole. FAZ
Wheel, The. Robert Hayden. BPo
Wheel, The. Edwin Muir. NoAM
Wheel, The. Sully-Prudhomme, *tr. fr. French by* William Dock. ImOP
Wheel, The. W. B. Yeats. GTBS-P; MoVE
Wheel Change, The. Bertolt Brecht, *tr. fr. German by* Eric Bentley. ELU
Wheel of Fortune, The. Thom Gunn. OxBC
Wheel of Fortune. *Unknown.* FSW
Wheel of the quivering meat, The. Chorus. Jack Kerouac. *Fr.* Mexico City Blues. NeAP; PoM
Wheel, oh, wheel,/ Wheel in de middle of a wheel. 'Zekiel Saw de Wheel. *Unknown.* BoAN-2
Wheel Revolves, The. Kenneth Rexroth. NoAM
Wheel Turning on the Hub of the Sun. William Pitt Root. MAYP
Wheelbarrow, The. Russell Edson. LCAP
Wheelbarrow. Eleanor Farjeon. FiBHP
Wheelchair Butterfly, The. James Tate. NoAM
Wheeler at Santiago. James Lindsay Gordon. PAH
Wheeler's Brigade at Santiago. Wallace Rice. PAH
Wheels ("Wheels are works of wit: the Greek with their neat"). Dorothy Donnelly. HoAn
Wheels flee on silky steel. We are seated. To the Shore. May Swenson. NePoAm-2
Wheels hurry onward, onward, The. A Cartload of Shoes. Abraham Sutskever, *tr. by* David G. Roskies. VWA
Wheel's inventor, nameless demigod, The. The Wheel. Sully-Prudhomme, *tr. by* William Dock. ImOP
Wheer 'asta beän saw long and meä liggin' 'ere aloän? Northern Farmer [Old Style]. Tennyson. VLP
Wheesht, Wheesht. "Hugh MacDiarmid." BSV; ELU; ErPo; HAP; InPK
Whelp that nipped its mother's dug in turning from her breast, The. The Lion's Cub. Maurice Thompson. AA
When. "Æ." OnYI
When. Dorothy Aldis. RHPC; SiSoSe
When. Philip Appleman. BXAP
When. "Susan Coolidge." HBV-2
When/ Dr./ Edith (Hon. D. Litt. [Leeds], Hon. D. Litt. [Durham]). A Thin Façade for Edith Sitwell. John Malcolm Brinnin. FiBHP; NYBP
When,/ Halting in front of it, I look. Hitomaro, *tr. by* Arthur Waley. *Fr.* Shui Shu. AWP
When/ my/ grandmother/ died. When My Grandmother Died. Sam Cornish. Psk
When/ Sir/ Beelzebub. Sir Beelzebub. Edith Sitwell. *Fr.* Façade. BoWoP; CoBMV; FaBoMo; HoPM; MoAB; MoBrPo; OxBTC; PrIm
When a Beau Goes In. Gavin Ewart. OBWP; OxBTC; WaP
When a Body. Gene Dawson. AMV-80
When a brass sun staggers above the sky. Tramp. Richard Hughes. MoBrPo
When a brisk gale against the current blows. John Gay. *Fr.* Rural Sports. FM

When a certain great King, whose initial is G. An Ancient Prophecy. Philip Freneau. PAH
When a daffadill [*or* daffodil] I see. Divination by a Daffadill [*or* Daffodil]. Robert Herrick. CaPo; CavP; OBS; SeCV-1
When a daughter tries suicide. The Risk. Anne Sexton. BoWoP
When a deed is done for Freedom, through the broad earth's aching breast. The Present Crisis. James Russell Lowell. OHFP
When a doctor leans over a body. Surgery. Carol Burbank. SUW
When a dream is born in you. A Pinch of Salt. Robert Graves. HBMV; MoBrPo
When a feller hasn't got a cent. Fellowship. *Unknown.* BLPA
When a Feller's Itchin' to Be Spanked. Paul Laurence Dunbar. BALP
When a fellow loves a maiden. La Cucaracha. *Unknown.* AS; TrAS
When a felon's not engaged in his employment. A [*or* The] Policeman's Lot. W. S. Gilbert. *Fr.* The Pirates of Penzance. NOBL; SaC; TreFT; TrGrPo
When a friend calls to me from the road. A Time to Talk. Robert Frost. NCSH
When a friend starts on a journey of a thousand miles. The End of the Year. Su Tung-p'o, *tr. by* Kenneth Rexroth. PoPl
When a Girl Looks Down. Kay Smith. CaP; OBCV; PeCV
When a goose meets a moose. Zhenya Gay. TiPo
When a great tree falls. To Be Answered in Our Next Issue. *Unknown.* RHPC
When a green fox looks. Fox. David Campbell. CBAP
When a lad, I stood one day by a cottage far away. She Was Bred in Old Kentucky. Harry Braisted. FSN
When a maid is sweet and fair. If a Maid Be Fair. Laura Goodman Salverson. CaP
When a man becomes tired of his life. Song, *Hamlet.* John Poole. BXAP
When a man gets troubled in mind. Sleepy Man Blues. *Unknown.* BluL
When a Man Has Married a Wife. Blake. ErPo; FaBoEE; FF; OAEL-2 (Marriage.) OxBoLi
When a Man Hath No Freedom to Fight for at Home. Byron. EnRP; FaBoEE; NIP; PoLF; PPoe; TrGrPo
(Stanzas: "When a man hath no freedom to fight for at home.") NoP; PAI
When a man like Silvestre Revueltas. To Silvestre Revueltas of Mexico, in His Death. Pablo Neruda, *tr. by* Harry Thomas. AMV-81
When a man sweats. The Dog in Us. John Barnie. AMV-81
When a Man's Busy. Robert Browning. WhC
When a missile goes over the moon. Same Old Trick. William W. Pratt. QQQ
When a mounting skylark sings. Heaven Is Heaven. Christina Rossetti. YeAr
When a' other bairnies are hushed to their hame. The Mitherless Bairn. William Thom. HBV-1
When a Ring's around the Moon. Mary Jane Carr. TiPo
When a sighing begins. Chansons d'Automne. Paul Verlaine, *tr. by* Arthur Symons. AWP
When a statue turns its real gaze. After Plotinus. William Stafford. PoA
When a twister a-twisting will twist him a twist. Twister Twisting Twine. John Wallis. ChTr; FaBoNo; OxNR
When a Warlock Dies. Isabella Gardner. NePA
When a Woman Blue, *with music.* *Unknown.* AS
When a woman cannot open her heart. Inscape. Susan Litwack. VWA
When Abraham Lincoln was shoveled into the tombs. Cool Tombs. Carl Sandburg. AmPP; AP; BLPL; CMoP; HAP; HBMV; HeIP; MoAB; MoAmPo; MoVE; NoAM; NOBA; PAL; PoLF; TAP; TrGrPo; TwAmPo; ViBoPo; WHA
When Adam broke the stone. Were I to Choose. Gabriel Okara. PBA
When Adam dalf [*or* delf] and Eve span. With I and E [*or* The Pointless Pride of Man]. *Unknown.* MeEL; OxBM
When Adam Day by Day. A. E. Housman. ELU; FiBHP; PoPl; WhC (Occasional Poem.) DBV; NOBL
When Adam Delved. *Unknown.* SaC
When Adam found his rib was gone. The Lady's-Maid['s] Song. John Hollander. ErPo; LiTM; MP; NePoEA; TW; TwCP
When Adam named in days of old. The Burro. J. J. Gibbons. PoOW
When Adam Was First Created. *Unknown.* OBET
(When Adam Was Created, *with music, diff. vers.*) TrAS
When, after storms that woodlands rue. A Requiem for Soldiers Lost in Ocean Transports. Herman Melville. PoEL-5
When against earth a wooden heel. Winter Sleep. Elinor Wylie. NePA
When age hath made me what I am not now. Upon His Picture. Thomas Randolph. MePo; NOBE
When Alcuin taught the sons of Charlemagne. The Student's Tale. Longfellow. *Fr.* Tales of a Wayside Inn, III. AmPP
When Alexander our kynge was dede. *See* Quhen Alexander our kynge was dede.
When Alexander Pope. E. C. Bentley. FiBHP
When Alexander Pope strolled in the city. Mr. Pope. Allen Tate. AP; CABA; MoAB; MP; NoAM; NOBA; TwCP; VGW
When all besides a vigil keep. The West's Asleep. Thomas Osborne Davis. OnYI
When all birds else do of their music fail. Money Makes the Mirth. Robert Herrick. CaPo
When all has passed. Genesis. Lotte Kramer. VWA
When All Is Done. Paul Laurence Dunbar. TRV
When all is done and said, in the end thus shall you find. Of [*or* On] a Contented Mind [*or* Content]. Thomas, Lord Vaux. EIL; EnRePo; GoBC; HBV-2; OBSC; QFR
When all is over and you march for home. The Spoils [of Love]. Robert Graves. HAP; NYBP; WeW
When all is still within these walls. The Man's Prayer. T. A. Daly. TrPWD
When All My Five and Country Senses See. Dylan Thomas. MoAB; MoBrPo; NoAM; PoA; SeCePo
When all my words were said. Enough. Digby Mackworth Dolben. EBVV
When all night long a chap remains. The Contemplative Sentry. W. S. Gilbert. *Fr.* Iolanthe. FiBHP
When all of us wore smaller shoes. Ancient Lights. Austin Clarke. BIrV; CMoP; IPY; NMP; OxBI
When all our hopes are sown on stony ground. A Note of Humility. Arna Bontemps. PoNe
When all the days are hot and long. Swimming. Clinton Scollard. FaPON
When all the ground with snow is white. The Snow-Bird. Frank Dempster Sherman. SiSoSe; SoPo; TiPo
When all the leaves are off the boughs. Thanksgiving Time. *Unknown.* SoPo
When All the World Is Full of Snow. N. M. Bodecker. RHPC
When all the world is young, lad. Young and Old [*or* The Old Song]. Charles Kingsley. *Fr.* The Water Babies, *ch.* 2. BLPL; EBEV; FaBoBe; FaFP; FaPoR; HBV-1; OBVV; OxBChV; PoLF; TreF; ViBoPo
When all the world was sore depressed. Shirley Temple. Cyril R. Michael. PeD
When all the world would keep a matter hid. The Fabulists. Kipling. ChMP
When all this All doth pass from age to age. Fulke Greville. Caelica, LXIX. EBEV; EnRePo
"When all this is over," said the swineherd. Swineherd. Eilean Ni Chuilleanain. BIrV; CIP; WPOW
When All Thy Mercies. Joseph Addison. OxBoCh
(Hymn: "When all thy mercies, O my God.") OBEC
When all were dreaming but Pastheen Power. The Song of the Ghost. Alfred Perceval Graves. AnIV
When all within is dark. From Thee to Thee. Solomon ibn Gabirol, *tr. by* Israel Abrahams. EaLo; TrJP
When all works that have. The Fool by the Roadside. W. B. Yeats. MoVE
When Almonds Bloom. Milicent Washburn Shinn. AA
When along the light ripple the far serenade. The Venetian Serenade. Richard Monckton Milnes. OBRV
When Alysandyr our king was dede. *See* Quhen Alexander our kynge was dede.
When Americans say a man. Language Lesson, 1976. Heather McHugh. MAYP
When an all-American gd. An All-American Guard. *Unknown.* TDH
When an elf is as old as a year and a minute. The Seven Ages of Elf-hood. Rachel Field. RHPC
When and how shall I earliest meet her? My Queen. *Unknown.* HBV-1
When and where did you first. Sexual Privacy of Women on Welfare. Pinkie Gordon Lane. BlSi
When André rode to Pont-du-lac. André's Ride. Augustus Henry Beesly. HBV-2
When Any Mortal (Even the Most Odd). E. E. Cummings. FaBoEE; PoPl
When April rains make flowers bloom. The Shamrock. Maurice Francis Egan. AA; HBV-1
When April skies are bright with sun. The Spectre Ship. Thomas Stephens Collier. EtS
When April with Its Sweet Showers. Chaucer. *Fr.* The Canterbury Tales: Prologue. PrIm
When are we gonna get married. Buffalo Boy. *Unknown.* FSW
When arms and numbers both have failed. Aguinaldo. Bertrand Shadwell. PAH
When Art goes bounding, lean. Art and Life. Lola Ridge. HBMV
When Arthur was homeless and broke. Limerick. *Unknown.* PeHV
When as a Lad. Isabel Ecclestone Mackay. HBV-1
When as a young and budding pote. De Senectute. Franklin P. Adams. HBMV
When as I do record. *Unknown.* EBEV
When as in Silks My Julia Goes. Robert Herrick. *See* Upon Julia's Clothes.

When as man's life, the light of human lust. *See* Whenas man's life . . .
When as the chill sirocco [*or* Charokko] blows. *See* Whenas the chill sirocco blows.
When as the nightingale chanted her vespers. *See* Whenas the nightingale.
When as the nightingale sang Pluto's mattins. The Author's Mock-Song to Mark Anthony. John Cleveland. AnAnS-2
When as the Rye. George Peele. *See* Whenas the Rye.
When as the sheriff of Nottingham. Robin Hood and the Golden Arrow. *Unknown.* ESPB
When as we sat all sad and desolate. Bible, *O.T., paraphrased by* Francis Bacon. Psalms, CXXXVII. OAEL-1
When asked, I used to say. What Zimmer Would Be. Paul Zimmer. Psk
When at break of day at a riverside. Piano and Drums. Gabriel Okara. NIP; PBA; TTY
When at home alone I sit. The Little Land. Robert Louis Stevenson. SoPo
When at last after long despair, our hopes ring true again. Catullus, *tr. fr. Latin by* Horace Gregory. NAWM-1
When at last he was well enough to take the sun. A Leg in a Plaster Cast. Muriel Rukeyser. MoAmPo
When at Night. Mark Perlberg. AMV-80
When Aunt Selina comes to tea. Aunt Selina. Carol Haynes. HBMV; HBVY
When Aurelia First I Courted. *Unknown.* OBS
When Autumn smiles, all beauteous in decay. William Somerville. *Fr.* Field Sports. FM
When autumn wounds the bough. Autumnal Spring Song. Vassar Miller. NePoEA
When awful darkness and silence reign. The Dong with a Luminous Nose. Edward Lear. AmMo; CenHV; ChTr; EBVV; FaBoCo; FaBoNo; FaBV; NBM; PoEL-5; VLP; WiR
When baby woke in woolly spread. Where Is My Butterfly Net? David McCord. FiBHP
When baby's cries grew hard to bear. L'Enfant Glacé. Harry Graham. FaBoCo
When Banners Are Waving. *Unknown.* GN; HBV-2
When bears are seen. B Stands for Bear. Hilaire Belloc. *Fr.* A Moral Alphabet. ShM
When beauty breaks and falls asunder. Juan's Song. Louise Bogan. NYBP
When beechen buds begin to swell. The Yellow Violet. Bryant. AP; BLPL; PoLF; TAP
When before those eyes, my life and light. Gaspara Stampa, *tr. fr. Italian by* J. Vitiello. BoWoP
When Bethlehem's manger first cradled the King. The Cradle and the Cross. A. S. Reitz. STF
When Bibo thought fit from the world to retreat. Epigram. Matthew Prior. FaBoEE
When Bill was a lad he was terribly bad. Those Two Boys. Franklin P. Adams. FiBHP; TrJP
When Billy the Kid Rides Again. S. Omar Barker. BPAW
When birds break open the sky, a smell of snow. Winter Burn. Roberta Hill. VoR
When biting Boreas, fell and doure. Burns. *Fr.* A Winter Night. BSV
When Black People Are. A. B. Spellman. BPo; CNA; PoBA
When black snails cross your path. *Unknown.* FaBoUs
When blam! my father's gun began the dash. Birth Report. X. J. Kennedy. *Fr.* Snapshots. NAs
When blessed Marie wip'd her Saviours feet. Marie Magdalene. George Herbert. AnAnS-1
When bold Leander sought his distant fair. On Leander's Swimming over the Hellespont to Hero. Thomas Warton the Younger, *after* Martial. FaBoEE
When both hands of the town clock stood at twelve. Village Noon; Mid-Day Bells. Merrill Moore. MoAmPo
When both lights you see ahead. Useful for Avoiding Collisions at Sea. *Unknown.* FaBoUs
When Both My Fathers Die. Robert Gillespie. FAZ
When Boys Go a-Courting, *with music. Unknown.* TrAS
When brave Van Rensselaer cross'd the stream. The Battle of Queenstown. William Banker, Jr. PAH
When breezes are soft and skies are fair. Green River. Bryant. AP; NOBA; OxBA
When bright Orion glitters in the skies. The Washerwoman. Mary Collier. *Fr.* The Woman's Labour; an Epistle to Mr. Stephen Duck. NOEC
When Britain first, at heaven's command. Rule, Britannia! James Thomson. *Fr.* Alfred, a Masque (*by* Thomson *and* David Mallett). FaPoR; GTBS; GTBS-P; HBV-2; NOEC; OAEP; OBEC; OBWP; TreF; WBLP
When Britain *really* ruled the waves. The House of Lords [*or* of Peers]. W. S. Gilbert. *Fr.* Iolanthe. InMe; TrGrPo
When Britain, with envy and malice inflamed. Capture of Little York. *Unknown.* PAH
When British troops first landed here. Cornwallis's Surrender. *Unknown.* PAH
When Brother Francis, rich in birds, arose. Saint Stephen in San Francisco. Melvin Walker La Follette. CoPo
When brother takes me walking. The Ordinary Dog. Nancy Byrd Turner. TiPo
When brothers build a city. Malcolm, a Thousandth Poem. Conrad Kent Rivers. CNA
When Brothers Forget. Jill Witherspoon Boyer. CNA
When Bunyan swung his whopping axe. Folk Tune. Richard Wilbur. AmFN
When Burnet perceived that the beautiful dames. An Excellent New Ballad, Called the Brawny Bishop's Complaint. Arthur Mainwaring. APAS
When by me in the dusk my child sits down. John Berryman. *Fr.* Homage to Mistress Bradstreet. CrMA
When by the marbled lake I lie and listen. Hymn. Wathen Mark Wilks Call. OBVV
When by thy scorn, O murd'ress[e] [*or* murderess], I am dead. The Apparition. John Donne. AnAnS-1; CABA; EnLoPo; EnRePo; GBL; HeIP; LoBV; MePo; NOBE; OAEL-1; OBEV; OBS; SCV; SeCP; SeCV-1; ViBoPo
When by Zeus relenting the mandate was revoked. Phoebus with Admetus. George Meredith. NOBE; OBEV; OBVV
When C. J. G. Arden goes out in the garden. To His Godson Gerald C. A. Jackson. A. E. Housman. WhC
When Caesar Augustus had raised a taxation. No Room at the Inn. *Unknown.* FSW
When calm is the night, and the stars shine bright. Sleighing Song. John Shaw. AA
When Captain O'Bruadir shook a sword across the sea. The Ballad of O'Bruadir. F. R. Higgins. EtS
When Carolina's hope grew pale. Sumter's Band. J. W. Simmons. PAH
When cats run home and light is come. The Owl [*or* Song: The Owl]. Tennyson. CH; FaBoCh; FaPON; GoJo; HBV-1; HBVY; MoShBr; OBRV; PB; PBBP; PoPle; SUS
When, Celia [*or* Coelia], must my old day set. To Celia [*or* To Coelia]. Charles Cotton. HBV-1; OBEV
When chapman [*or* chapmen] billies leave the street. Tam o' Shanter. Burns. BeLS; BSV; EnRP; GoTL; GoTS; HBV-2; NoP; OAEL-1; OAEP; OBEC; OBNV; OxBS; SeCePo; TrGrPo, *sl. abr.*; ViBoPo; WHA
When Charlie Bowdre married Manuela, we carried them. Michael Ondaatje. POL
When children, blundering on their fathers' guns. Prayer for Light. Stanton A. Coblentz. TrPWD
When Christ was born in Bethlehem. A Christmas Carol. *Unknown, tr. by* Longfellow. OHIP
When Christ was born in Bethlehem. Ballad of the Epiphany. Charles Dalmon. HBMV; OnMSP
When Christ with care and pangs of death opprest. Christs Sleeping Friends. Robert Southwell. AnAnS-1
When civil fury [*or* dudgeon] first grew high. Presbyterian Knight. Samuel Butler. *Fr.* Hudibras, I, 1. EBEV; NOBE; OAEL-1; SeCV-2; ViBoPo
When Claudius was emperor and grandeur still was Roman. Rise and Fall of Valentines. Fairfax Downey. InMe
When clear October suns unfold. Mallee in October. Flexmore Hudson. PoAu-2
When Cleomira disbelieves. The Force of Love. Samuel Jones. NOEC
When clerks and navvies fondle. For X. Louis MacNeice. Trilogy for X, I. BoLoP; EnLoPo; ErPo
When clouds appear like rocks and towers. Weather Wisdom. *Unknown.* FaBoUs; HBVY; OxNR; TreF
When clouds inch. The Horizon Is Definitely Speaking. Diana Chang. BrSi
When cockle shells turn silver bells. Waly, Waly [*or* Waillie]. *Unknown.* AmFP; AS; FSW
When, Coelia, must my old day set. *See* When, Celia, must my old day set.
When cold, I huddle up, foetal, cross/ arms. Christmas Eve. A. R. Ammons. NAs
When coldness wraps this suffering clay. The Immortal Mind. Byron. WGRP
When coltsfoot withers and begins to wear. Cuckoos. Andrew Young. ChTr
When conquering love did first my heart assail. Idea, XXIX. Michael Drayton. OAEP
When consummate the day hangs before you. Three Variations. Boris Pasternak, *tr. by* Babette Deutsch. TrJP
When country hills are soft with snow. Les Chasse-Neige. Ralph A. Lewin. FiBHP
When crazy Frankenstein pulled down the switch. Frankenstein Gets His Man. Frank Carr. AmMo

When cripples throw their crutches into the air. Cripples. Nina Cassian, *tr. by* Herbert Kuhner. VWA
When, cruel fair one, I am slain. The Tombe. Thomas Stanley. OBS
When curdling mists disturb the sight's. Midnight. Weldon Kees. NoAM
When curfew-bells begin. The Two Loves. Laurence Housman. HBMV
When Daddy/ Walks. Walking. Grace Ellen Glaubitz. SoPo; TiPo
When Daddy Died. Duane Ackerson. POL
When Daddy shaves and lets me stand and look. Daddy. Rose Fyleman. SiSoSe
When Daffodils Begin to Peer. Shakespeare. *Fr.* The Winter's Tale, IV, ii. ChTr; ElL; FaBoBe; FaBoCh; HBV-1; LoBV; NoP; PrIm; UnTE; ViBoPo; WhC
(Autolycus's Song.) FaBoEn; NOBE; OAEL-1; OBSC; PoPle
(Pedlar's Song, The.) OxBoLi
(Song: "When daffodils begin to peer.") FiP; PoEL-2
When Daisies Pied and Violets Blue. Shakespeare. *Fr.* Love's Labour's Lost, V, ii. BiP; EnRePo; FF; InPK; NOBE; NoP; PoEL-2; PoRA; PrIm; SeCeV
(Cuckoo Sings, The.) PoPle
(Song: "When daisies pied and violets blue.") HBV-2; FiP; PBBP; PoEL-2
(Song: Spring and Winter.) LoBV
(Spring.) ElL; HAP; HeIP; NIP; OAEL-1; OBEV; PAI; PoEL-2; SeCePo; TEP; TrGoPo; UnPo; ViBoPo
(Spring Song.) TreFT
(Ver and Hiems.) OBSC
When Damon First Began to Love. Aphra Behn. UnTE
When Daniel Boone goes by, at night. Daniel Boone. Rosemary *and* Stephen Vincent Benét. AmFN; GOA
When Daphne's lover here first wore the bays. To the River Isca. Henry Vaughan. FaBoPP
When Darby saw the setting sun. Darby and Joan. St. John Honeywood. AA
When dark December glooms the day. Sir Walter Scott. *Fr.* Marmion, *introd. to* V. OBRV
When darkness crept and grew. Under the Hill. Richard Eberhart. PoA
When darkness prevail'd and aloud on the air. The Tomb of the Brave. Joseph Hutton. PAH
When day declining sheds a milder gleam. The Naturalist's Summer-Evening Walk. Gilbert White. NOEC; PBBP
When day follows inarticulate day. Wait for the Hour. William Soutar. NeBP
When daylight was yet sleeping under the billow. Ill Omens. Thomas Moore. PoEL-4
When de Co'n Pone's Hot. Paul Laurence Dunbar. BANP
When de fiddle gits to singin' out a ol' Vahginny reel. Angelina. Paul Laurence Dunbar. HBV-2
When de night walks in, as black as a sheep. Pop Goes de Weasel. *Unknown.* PSoN
When de Saints Go Ma'chin' Home. Sterling A. Brown. AmNP
When de Whale Get Strike, *with music. Unknown.* OuSiCo
When, Dearest, I but Think of Thee. *At. to* John Suckling *and to* Owen Felltham. CavP; HBV-1; JCP; OBEV; OBS
(Song: "When, dearest, I but think on thee.") MePo; SeCeV
When Death Came April Twelve 1945. Carl Sandburg. AP
When Death Comes. *Unknown.* MeEL
When Death comes near to grimly claim his toll. May God Give Strength. Peter Van Wynen. BLRP
When death dances in. Last Rites. David Citino. AMV-80
When death, shall part us from these kids. A Dialogue between Thyrsis and Dorinda. Andrew Marvell. SeCP
When Death to Either Shall Come. Robert Bridges. HBV-1; OBEV; PoPl
When Delia on the plain appears. Tell Me, My Heart, if This Be Love [*or* Song]. George Lyttelton. HBV-1; OBEC
When descends on the Atlantic. Seaweed [*or* The Equinox]. Longfellow. AP; EtS; HBV-2; MOS; OxBA; TAP
When despair for the world grows in me. The Peace of Wild Things. Wendell Berry. GeTw; HeIP; NU; PCP; VGW
When Dey 'Listed Colored Soldiers. Paul Laurence Dunbar. BPo
When Diamonds, Nibbling in My Ears. W. H. Davies. BrPo
When did my manhood wake to its dying! Watching Jim Shoulders. Leo Connellan. TAT
When did the garden with its banked flowers. Death's Blue-eyed Girl. Linda Pastan. PPJ
When Did the World. Robert Clairmont. *See* Answers, The.
When did these gray ones. Duel in the Park. Lisa Grenelle. GoYe
When did you start your tricks. The Mosquito. D. H. Lawrence. BoAnP; PoPle
When Dido found Aeneas would not come. A Note on the Latin Gerunds. Richard Porson. FaBoCo; FaBoEE; FaBoUs
When do I see thee most, beloved one? Lovesight [*or* Sonnet]. Dante Gabriel Rossetti. The House of Life, IV. EBVV; FaBoEn; GTBS-P; HBV-1; OAEP; OBNC; OBVV; TrGrPo; ViBoPo; VLP; WHA
When Dobbin and Robin, unharnessed from the plow. The Circus-postered Barn. Elizabeth J. Coatsworth. MoAmPo
When doctrines meet with general approbation. Epigram. David Garrick. HBV-1
When Doris Danced. Richard Eberhart. CMoP; ErPo
When Dorothy and I took tea, we sat upon the floor. Small and Early. Tudor Jenks. AA
When down the stair at morning. My April Lady. Henry van Dyke. HBV-1
When down the windy vistas of the years. Clement Wood. Eagle Sonnets, XI. HBMV
When dreaming kings, at odds with swift-paced time. Washington. Harriet Monroe. *Fr.* Commemoration Ode. AA; FaBoBe
When dreams like stars collide. Lesson for Dreamers. Paul B. Janeczko. PCP
When droning summer earth had slewed the shadows. Wood-cut. V. Sackville-West. ChMP
When Dublin is a mist the quays are lost. Working the Rain Shift at Flanagan's. Gibbons Ruark. MAYP
When Dutchy Plays the Mouth Harp. Robert V. Carr. PoOW
When Duty comes a-knocking at your gate. Duty. Edwin Markham. HBMV; HBVY
When Earth's Last Picture Is Painted. Kipling. *See* L'Envoi: "When Earth's last picture is painted."
When Eastern lovers feed the fun'ral fire. Three Epitaphs on John Hewet and Sarah Drew, II. Pope. NIP
When Eire first rose from the dark-swelling flood. Eire. William Drennan. OnYI
When England's multitudes observed with frowns. Bungaloid Growth. Colin Ellis. FaBoEE
When Eubolus the Greek learned. Dionysus. Irving Layton. ErPo
When Eve did with the snake dispute. The Woman's Wish. Matthew Prior. FaBoEE
When Eve first saw the glistering day. Song with Words. James Agee. MoAmPo
When Eve upon the first of men. A Reflection [*or* Epigram]. Thomas Hood. FaBoEE; HBV-1; PAI; PV
When Eve walked in her garden. First Rain. Zoë Akins. HBMV
When Even Cometh On. Lucy Evangeline Tilley. AA
When evening came and the warm glow grew deeper. The Buzzards. Martin Armstrong. HBMV
When evening comes. Yakamochi. *Fr.* Manyo Shu. AWP
When every lip invokes young loveliness. To L. C. Lucy Hawkins. HBMV
When every one to pleasing pastime hies. Pamphilia to Amphilanthus. Mary Sidney Wroth, Countess of Montgomery. *Fr.* Urania. WPE
When everyone comes together. At the Party. Patricia Goedicke. FAZ
When Fabre took his children locust hunting. The Locust Hunt. Philip Murray. NePoAm-2
When face to face we stand. Paradox. Angelina Weld Grimké. CDC
When Faces Called Flowers Float Out of the Ground. E. E. Cummings. BoNaP; PrIm
When Faction, in league with the treacherous Gaul. The Lords of the Main. Joseph Stansbury. PAH
When fair Columbia was a child. The Daughter's Rebellion. Francis Hopkinson. PAH
When faith and love which parted from thee never. Sonnet: On the Religious Memorie of Mrs. Catherine Thomason My Christian Freind Deceas'd Decem. 1646. Milton. OBS
When faith in God goes, man, the thinker, loses his greatest thought. Have You Lost Faith? *Unknown.* WBLP
When falls the soldier brave. Sentinel Songs. Abram J. Ryan. HBV-2
When far-spent Night persuades each mortal eye. Astrophel and Stella, XCIX. Sir Philip Sidney. CABA; OBSC; SiPS
When Father Came Home for Lunch. Jim Mitsui. BrSi
When Father Carves the Duck. Ernest Vincent Wright. BLPL; FaBV; FaFP; NTCP; PoLF; PoSC; TreF
When Father Slept. James Anderson. AMV-80
When fierce political debate. Jolly Jack. Thackeray. HBV-1
When First. Edward Thomas. NoAM
When first Apollo got my brain with childe. The Author to His Book. George Alsop. SCAP
When first, descending from the moorlands. An Extempore Effusion [upon the Death of James Hogg]. Wordsworth. EBEV; FaBoRV; FiP; NOBE; NoP; OAEL-2; OBRV; SCV
When first Diana leaves her bed. The Progress of Beauty. Swift. CABA; NCEP
When first, fair mistress, I did see your face. To B. C. Sir John Suckling. CaPo

When first from sea I landed I had a roving mind. The Pride of Kildare. *Unknown.* OBET
When first I came here I had hope. When First. Edward Thomas. NoAM
When first I came to Frisco, boys, I went upon a spree. Off to Sea Once More, *vers.* II. *Unknown.* ShS
When first I came to Louisville, some pleasure for to find. The Lily of the West. *Unknown.* AmFP; FSW
When first I ended, then I first began. Michael Drayton. Idea, LXII. TrGrPO
When first I looked into thy glorious eyes. Sarah Helen Whitman. Sonnets from the Series Relating to Edgar Allan Poe, II. AA
When first I made/ Once more the circuit of our little Lake. Wordsworth. *Fr.* The Prelude, IV. OBRV
When First I Saw Her. George Edward Woodberry. Wild Eden, V. AA; HBV-1
When first I saw our banner wave. Astraea at the Capitol. Whittier. PAH
When first I saw sweet Peggy. The Low-backed Car. Samuel Lover. HBV-1
When first I saw the love-light in your eye. When You Were Sweet Sixteen. James Thornton. FSN; FSW
When first I saw true beauty, and thy joys. Mount of Olives. Henry Vaughan. AnAnS-1
When first I started out cow-driving, I drove them on the square. The Rustler. *Unknown.* CoSo
When first I took to cutlass, blunderbuss and gun. The Ballad of O'Bruadir. F. R. Higgins. OBMV
When first I went a waggoner. The Jolly Waggoner. *Unknown.* OBET
When first in this country a stranger. The Green Mossy Banks of the Lee. *Unknown.* OBET
When first mine eyes did view and mark. Sir Thomas Wyatt. SiPS
When first mine infant-ear. Christendom. Thomas Traherne. PoEL-2
When first my lines [*or* verse] of heav'nly [*or* heavenly] joy[e]s made mention. Jordan. George Herbert. AnAnS-1; MePo; OAEL-1; OBS; PP; PPP; SeCP
When first my way to fair I took. A. E. Housman. OAEP; POL
When first our eyes engaged the startled Bird. Recollection. Marilyn R. Mumford. AMV-80
When first the bride and bridegroom wed. At Last. Richard Henry Stoddard. HBV-1
When first the busy, clumsy tongue is stilled. Supersensual. Evelyn Underhill. WGRP
When first the college rolls receive his name. The Scholar's Life. Samuel Johnson. *Fr.* The Vanity of Human Wishes. FaBoEn; NOBE; OBEC; OBSV; SeCePo
When first the eye this forest sees. Andrew Marvell. *Fr.* Upon Appleton House. PBBP
When first the fiery-mantled sun. Ode to Winter. Thomas Campbell. GTBS; GTBS-P
When first the magick of thine eye. The Vow-Breaker. Henry King. OBS
When first the peasant, long inclin'd to roam. The Young Author. Samuel Johnson. LAuP
When first the post arrived at my tent. King Henry to Rosamond. Michael Drayton. *Fr.* England's Heroical Epistles. AnAnS-2; OBSC
When first the year, I heard the cuckoo sing. John Gay. *Fr.* The Shepherd's Week: Thursday; or, The Spell. PBBP
When first thou didst entice to thee my heart. Affliction. George Herbert. AnAnS-1; CABA; JCP; LiTB; MeLP; MePo; NOBE; NoP; OBS; OxBoCh; SeCP
When first thou on me, Lord, wrought'st thy sweet print. The Ebb and Flow. Edward Taylor. AmPP; AP; SCAP
When first thy sweet and gracious eye. The Glance. George Herbert. AnAnS-1
When First to This Country a Stranger I Came, *with music.* *Unknown.* OuSiCo
(When First unto This Country, *sl. diff. vers.*) FSW
When first we hear the shy-come nightingales. Early Nightingale. John Clare. PBBP
When first we met we did not guess. Triolet. Robert Bridges. BrPo
When first you learn to read a clock. Clock. Harold Monro. BrPo
When first you sang a song to me. Your Songs. Gwendolyn B. Bennett. CDC
When first your glory shone upon my face. Commemoration. Claude McKay. BANP
When fishes flew and forests walked. The Donkey. G. K. Chesterton. ACP; EBCP; FaBV; FaPoR; FPL; GoBC; HBVY; MoBrPo; OBEV; PoLF; TreFT; WGRP
When fishes set umbrellas up. Christina Rossetti. *Fr.* Sing-Song. FM
When fivepence a solid meal cannot supply. The Volunteer. *Unknown.* NOEC
When flighting time is on, I go. The Birdcatcher. Ralph Hodgson. MoBrPo
When Flora Had Ourfret the Firth. *Unknown.* NoP
(Four May Poems, I.) OxBS
(Quhen Flora Had O'erfret the Firth.) OBEV
When flowers thrust their heads above the ground. Bloom. Alfred Kreymborg. HBMV
When foes insult, and prudent friends dispense. Night; an Epistle to Robert Lloyd. Charles Churchill. NCEP
When fog come creepin' over Beccles. Molly Fitton. BXAP
When foolish kings, at odds with swift-paced time. Two Heroes. Harriet Monroe. *Fr.* Commemoration Ode. OHIP
When, for days, heavy air. Summer Storm. Richard B. Kent. AMV-80
When for eternal worlds we steer. Vain World Adieu. *Unknown.* AmFP
When for school o'er Little Field with its brook and wooden brig. John Clare. *Fr.* Remembrances. SaC
When for the thorns with which I long, too long. The Coronet. Andrew Marvell. AnAnS-1; LoBV; MeLP; MePo; NCEP; NOCV; NoP; OBS; OxBoCh; PoPle; PP; SeCV-1
When forced to wait and wait for luncheon. Assorted Relishes. Richard Armour. WhC
When, forehead full of torments hot and red. Les Chercheuses de Poux. Arthur Rimbaud, *tr. by* T. Sturge Moore. *Fr.* The Lice-Finders. AWP; SyP
When formed our band, we are all well manned. California. *Unknown.* AS
When fortune's blind goddess had shied my abode. Dick Turpin and Black Bess [*or* Bonnie Black Bess]. *Unknown.* AmFP; BPAW; CoSo
When Fortune's shield protects thee, then beware. Fortune's Treachery. Judah Halevi, *tr. by* Solomon Solis-Cohen. TrJP
When forty winters shall besiege thy brow. Sonnets, II. Shakespeare. BLPL; FF; LiTB; OBSC; TEP
When foxes eat the last gold grape. Escape. Elinor Wylie. LiTA; MoAmPo
When Francus comes to solace with his whore. In Francum. Sir John Davies. FaBoEE
When Freedom, dressed in bloodstained vest. Ode to Liberty. Thomas Chatterton. *Fr.* Goddwyn. TrGrPo
When Freedom, fair Freedom, her banner display'd. Truxton's Victory. *Unknown.* PAH
When Freedom, from her mountain height. The American Flag. Joseph Rodman Drake. AA; FaBoBe; FaFP; GN; HBV-2; HBVY; PAH; PAL; PaPo; PGD; TreF; WBLP
When Freedom, on her natal day. The Moral Warfare. Whittier. PAL
When Friday nights are lucky, you. Irving Wexler. *Fr.* Elegy for My Father. DiL
When Friendship or Love our sympathies move. Hours of Idleness [*or* The Tear]. Byron. EvOK; Par
When from a world of tumult we retreat. Casting All Your Care upon Him. *Unknown.* STF
When from afar these mountain tops I view. The Sonnet of the Mountain. Mellin de Saint-Gelais, *tr. by* Austin Dobson. AWP
When from Eternity were separate. Ceremonial Ode Intended for a University. Lascelles Abercrombie. OBVV
When from her beauty long I've strove. Song: Wit and Beauty. Robert Gould. CavP
When from her winter-prison. Spring. *Unknown.* SUS
When from my fumbling hand the tired pen falls. The Scribe's Prayer. Robert W. Service. TrPWD
When from the blossoms of the noiseful day. To My Friend. Francis Thompson. PoA
When from the Calyx-Canopy of Night. Freda Laughton. NeIP
When from the chrysalis of the tomb. On John Grubb. *Unknown.* WhC
When from the gloom of earth we see the sky. The Void Between. John Lancaster Spalding. *Fr.* God and the Soul. AA
When from the hush of this cool wood. The Cell. George Rostrevor Hamilton. TrPWD
When from the pallid sky the sun descends. Winter. James Thomson. *Fr.* The Seasons. OAEL-1; OxBS
When, from the tower whence I derive love's heaven. Sonnet. *Unknown.* *Fr.* Zepheria. EIL
When from the vaulted wonder of the sky. Faith's Vista. Henry Abbey. AA
When from the world I shall be ta'en. *Unknown.* LO
When frost is shining on the trees. At Mrs. Appleby's. Elizabeth Upham McWebb. SiSoSe; TiPo
When, full of warm and eager love. Snowdrop. William Wetmore Story. HBV-1
When furrowed fields of shaded brown. The Canadian Rossignol. Edward William Thomson. CaP
When fury sings like nothing, like a war. Variations on a Theme. John Hay. NePoAm
When gadding snow makes hill-sides white. Winter. Charles Mair. OBCV; PeCV; PoSC, *abr.*

When Gaffer be dead for a month or more. Martin Fagg. BXAP
When gardens shone with flowery pride. On a Little Boy's Endeavouring to Catch a Snake. Thomas Foxton. OxBChV
When Gauguin was visiting Fiji. Limerick. Victor Gray. NOBL
When geometric diagrams and digits. " Novalis," *tr. by* Robert Bly. NU
When George the King would punish folk. How We Became a Nation. Harriet Prescott Spofford. PAH
When George the Third was reigning a hundred years ago. A Ballad for a Boy [*or* The Two Captains]. William Cory. FaPoR; OxBChV
When George's Grandmamma was told. George. Hilaire Belloc. FiBHP
When getting my nose in a book. A Study of Reading Habits. Philip Larkin. NOBL; PPP; SoSe; TW
When Gilbert's birthday came last spring. The Nut's Birthday. Jessie Pope. SUMH
When God at first made Man. The Pulley [*or* The Gifts of God]. George Herbert. AWP; EaLo; EBCP; FaBoEn; GTBS; GTBS-P; HAP; HBV-1; HeIP; InPK; InPS; LiTB; MePo; NOBE; NOCV; NoP; OAEL-1; OAEP; OBEV; OBS; OxBoCh; PAI; PPP; PrIm; SeCeV; SeCP; SeCV-1; TEP; TreFT; TrGrPo; TRV; ViBoPo; WHA
When God Descends with Men to Dwell, *with music.* Hosea Ballou I. AH
When God, disgusted with man. Crow Blacker than Ever. Ted Hughes. TEP
When God First Said. Natan Zach, *tr. fr. Hebrew by* Peter Everwine *and* Shula Starkman. VWA
When God had finished Master Messerin. Sonnet: Of the Making of Master Messerin. Rustico di Filippo, *tr. by* Dante Gabriel Rossetti. AWP
When God had finished the stars and whirl of coloured suns. Frederick William Harvey. *Fr.* Ducks. EBCP
When God in the Bible wants to promise. As Sand. Natan Zach, *tr. by* Jon Silkin. VWA
When God Lets My Body Be. E. E. Cummings. MoAB; MoAmPo; NOBA
When God makes a great Man he intends all others to crush him. Arthur Hugh Clough. *Fr.* Amours de Voyage. OBSV
When God of old came down from Heaven. Whitsunday. John Keble. OBRV
When God put man in a garden. King Alfred Answers the Danes. G. K. Chesterton. *Fr.* Ballad of the White Horse. OxBoCh
When God wants to drill a man. God Knows What He's About. *Unknown.* STF
When God was learning to draw the human face. Two Masks Unearthed in Bulgaria. William Meredith. EyDe
When God was making the world. The World in Making. Sir Gilbert Parker. CaP
When gods had framed the sweet of women's face. Love and Jealousy. Robert Greene. ElL
When God's holy law is read out. Unity. Jakov de Haan, *tr. by* David Soetendorp. VWA
When God's parachute failed. Religion Back Home. William Stafford. OBAL
When gold was first discovered at Coloma, near the hill. The National Miner. *Unknown.* AmFP
When gold was found in forty-nine the people thought 'twas gas. The Fools of Forty-nine. *Unknown.* CoSo
When good King Arthur ruled this land. Mother Goose. FaBoNo; HBV-1; HBVY; NA; OxNR
When good-nights have been prattled, and prayers have been said. The Dance. Rudolph Chambers Lehmann. HBMV
When Goody O'Grumpity baked a cake. Goody O'Grumpity. Carol Ryrie Brink. FaPON
When gooseberries grow on the stem of a daisy. To Mollidusta. James Robinson Planché. NA
When Grandmamma fell off the boat. Indifference. Harry Graham. DBV
When Graphicus sat by the baths. Epigram. Strato. PeHV
When Grasshopper, chirping late. Fall of the Year. Henry Ellison. OBVV
When gray threads mar life's pattern. The Master Weaver. *Unknown.* STF
When green as a river was the barley. Daphne. Edith Sitwell. HBMV
When griping grief the heart doth wound. Music's Silver Sound. Shakespeare. *Fr.* Romeo and Juliet. GN
When groping farms are lanterned up. A Country God. Edmund Blunden. MoBrPo
When, hardly moving, you decorate night's hush. The Waters of Life. Humbert Wolfe. MoBrPo
When harvest is done all thing placed and set. Thomas Tusser. *Fr.* A Hundreth Good Poyntes of Husbandry. FaBoUs
When have I last looked on. Lines Written in Dejection. W. B. Yeats. NAs
When, having watched for a long time the trees. Grove and Building. Edgar Bowers. NePoEA
When he brings home a whale. Naughty Boy. Robert Creeley. NoAM; NOBA
When he came home Mother said he looked. My Father's Martial Art. Stephen Shu Ning Liu. BrSi
When he comes home at night. Wasp Sex Myth (One). Anselm Hollo. PoM
When he cuts off the outboard. Running the Trotline. Jim Elledge. WOLT
When he gave up mountains he became. Climbing. Daniel Mark Epstein. AMV-80
When he got into bed. Damon and Pythias. Robert Creeley. LCAP
When he had tired of playing big. A Handful of Small Secret Stones. Chris Bursk. AMV-81
When he heard the owls at midnight. Longfellow. *Fr.* The Song of Hiawatha. FM
When he killed the Mudjokivis. *See* He killed the noble Mudjokivis.
When he lies in the night away from her. The Jealous Lovers. Donald Hall. NYBP
When he married her he said. Thalamos. Peter Kane Dufault. ErPo
When he pushed his bush of black hair off his brow. Sicilian Cyclamens. D. H. Lawrence. ChMP; MoVE
When he sailed into the harbor. Korinna, *tr. fr. Greek by* Willis Barnstone. BoWoP
When He Spoke to Me of Love. M. A. Mokhomo, *tr. fr. Sotho by* Dan Kunene *and* Jack Cope. PeSA
When he takes a bath, the Antelope. Antelope. William Jay Smith. TiPo
When He Thought Himself Contemned. Thomas Howell. ElL
When he was eight years old he had become. Words and Monsters. Vernon Scannell. OxBC
When he was four years old, he stood at the window during a thunderstorm. A Son with a Future. Charles Reznikoff. *Fr.* Five Groups of Verse. DiL
When he was my age and I was already a boy. The Harp. Bruce Weigl. MAYP
When he was shot he toppled to the ground. Shot Who? Jim Lane! Merrill Moore. MoAmPo
When he was young and beautiful and bold. Peer Gynt. Charles Hamilton Sorley. HBMV
When he was young, he broke horses. The Passion Drinker. Anita Endrezze Probst. VoR
When he went blundering back to God. Of One Self-slain. Charles Hanson Towne. WGRP
When he who adores thee has left but the name. Pro Patria Mori. Thomas Moore. GTBS; GTBS-P; HoPM; OBRV
When he, who is the unforgiven. The Unforgiven. E. A. Robinson. CMoP
When He Would Have His Verses Read. Robert Herrick. CaPo; NOBE; OAEP; OBS; SeCV-1
When Helen first saw wrinkles in her face. Walter Savage Landor. *Fr.* Ianthe. EnLoPo
When Helen Lived. W. B. Yeats. CMoP; ViBoPo
When her large, fair, reluctant eyelids fell. Living Marble. Arthur O'Shaughnessy. VLP
When his bones are as seaweed, when his sweet tongue is parched. The White Rainbow. Starr Nelson. GoYe
When His Excellency Prince Norodom Chantaraingsey. Dead Soldiers. James Fenton. OBWP
When his match, when his match kept missing. Shaving. Charles David Wright. AMV-81
When his son-in-law. Shakuhachi. Jim Mitsui. BrSi
When hit come ter de question er de female vote. Brother Baptis' on Woman Suffrage. Rosalie Jonas. BlSi
When Hitler was the devil. The Silent Generation. Louis Simpson. NePoAm-2
When Howitzers Began. Hayden Carruth. Psk
When I/ die/ I'm sure. The Rebel. Mari Evans. AmNP; IDB; IHMS; PoBA
When I/ see you/ climb the walls. Pressure. Anne Waldman. PoM
When I/ took my. The Watch. May Swenson. HAP
When I a verse shall make. His Prayer to Ben Jonson. Robert Herrick. AnAnS-2; CaPo; CavP; JCP; NoP; OAEP; OBS; OxBoLi; PP; SeCeV; SeCV-1; TrGrPo
When I Admire the Greatness, *with music.* Jacob Steendam, *tr. fr. Dutch.* AH
When I admire the rose. The Rose [*or* A Fancy]. Thomas Lodge. *Fr.* The Life and Death of William Longbeard. ElL; OBSC
When I am aching with a pain or ills. Couplets for WCW. Martha Christina. AMV-80
When I am alone. The Fisherman's Wife. Amy Lowell. BoWoP
When I am an old woman I shall wear purple. Warning. Jenny Joseph. OxBTC
When I Am Dead. Hugh Barrie. PoSH
When I Am Dead. Georgia Douglas Johnson. CDC
When I Am Dead. George MacBeth. OxBTC
When I Am Dead. John G. Neihardt. HBMV
When I Am Dead. Christina Rossetti. *See* Song: "When I am dead, my dearest."

When I Am Dead. Albert Stillman. InMe
When I Am Dead. *Unknown.* OxBoLi
When I Am Dead. James Edward Wilson. PoLF
When I am dead and deep in dust. Reconciliation. John U. Nicolson. HBMV
When I am dead, and Doctors know not why. The Dampe. John Donne. SeCP
When I am dead and gone to dust. When I Am Dead. Albert Stillman. InMe
When I am dead and nervous hands have thrust. When I Am Dead. John G. Neihardt. HBMV
When I am dead and over me bright April. I Shall Not Care. Sara Teasdale. HBV-1; MoAmPo; PoPl; TrGrPo; UnPo
When I Am Dead and Sister to the Dust. Elsa Barker. HBV-2
When I am dead, even then. Then. Muriel Rukeyser. LCAP
When I am dead, I hope it may be said. On His Books. Hilaire Belloc. ACP; FaBoCo; FaBoEE; MoBrPo; OxBoLi; PoPl; TreFT; WeW; WhC
When I am dead I want you to dress me. When I Am Dead. *Unknown.* OxBoLi
When I Am Dead, My Dearest. Christina Rossetti. *See* Song: "When I am dead, my dearest."
When I am dead, no pageant train. Dirge of Alaric the Visigoth. Edward Everett. BeLS
When I am dead, withhold, I pray, your blooming legacy. When I Am Dead. Georgia Douglas Johnson. CDC
When I am dead you'll find it hard. He and She. Eugene Fitch Ware. PoLF; YaD
When I am grown an *hombre*. Ambition. Edith Agnew. TiPo
When I am grown to man's estate. Looking Forward. Robert Louis Stevenson. BrPo; CenHV; OxBChV
When I am in a great city, I know that I despair. City Life. D. H. Lawrence. CAD; OAEP
When I am living in the Midlands. The South Country. Hilaire Belloc. ACP; GoBC; HBV-2; MoBrPo; OBVV
When I Am Old. Caroline Atherton Briggs Mason. BLPA
When I am old and long turned gray. 2001: The Tennyson/ Hardy Poem. Ewart Gavin. FaBoCo
When I am old, and think of the old days. The Last Memory. Arthur Symons. HBV-1
When I am playing by myself. Water Noises. Elizabeth Madox Roberts. BoNaP
When I am sad and weary. Celia Celia. Adrian Mitchell. FaBoEE
When I am standing on a mountain crest. Love in the Winds. Richard Hovey. AA; HBV-1
When I am the sky. Cancion. Denise Levertov. PoM
When I am walking down the street. New Shoes. Marjorie S. Watts. SoPo
When I am walking sadly or triumphantly. The Shadow. Arthur Symons. OBVV
When I am walking with the children, and a girl. The Father. Donald Finkel. CoPo; PAI
When I am weary, throng'd with the cares of the. Day's End. Laurence Binyon. OBVV
When I asked the very old man. Quotations. George Oppen. NNaP
When I awake and look at my feet. My Feet. Louis Jenkins. GP
When I Awake I Am Still with Thee. Harriet Beecher Stowe. *See* Still, Still with Thee.
When I awake in the early mist. Very Early. Karla Kuskin. PDV
When I Awoke. Raymond R. Patterson. NNP; PoBA
When I awoke this morning. The Blue Animals. Jon Anderson. AmPA
When I awoke with cold. Coffee. J. V. Cunningham. MoAmPo; PrIm; VGW
When I began my love to sow. Husbandry. William Hammond. JCP
When I beheld the poet blind, yet bold. On Mr. Milton's Paradise Lost. Andrew Marvell. JCP; OAEP
When I behold a forrest spread. Art above Nature, to Julia. Robert Herrick. AnAnS-2
When I behold Becchina in a rage. Sonnet: Of Becchina in a Rage. Cecco Angiolieri da Siena, *tr. by* Dante Gabriel Rossetti. AWP
When I behold how black, immortal ink. Silet. Ezra Pound. MoAB; MoAmPo
When I behold that beauty's wonderment. Amoretti, XXIV. Spenser. HBV-1
When I behold the heavens as in their prime. Anne Bradstreet. *Fr.* Contemplations. PBWP
When I behold thee, blameless Williamson. Sonnet: True Ambition. Benjamin Stillingfleet. OBEC
When I beneath the cold red earth am sleeping. Last Verses. William Motherwell. HBV-2
When I bethink me on that speech whilere. Mutability. Spenser. *Fr.* The Faerie Queene, VII, 8. OAEL-1; OxBoCh
When I bought bubble gum. Why We Bombed Haiphong. Jonathan Holden. MAYP
When I burned our leaves, a wind from the dark. Looking West. William Stafford. NYBP
When I but think upon the great dead days. Piere Vidal Old. Ezra Pound. MoAB
When I Buy Pictures. Marianne Moore. EyDe; OxBA
When I call to the dead to speak, the graves. Is There Life across the Street? Robert Watson. GP
When I came back, he was gone. My Father's Leaving. Ira Sadoff. AmPA; DiL
When I Came from Colchis. W. S. Merwin. AP; NePoEA; VGW
When I came last to Ludlow. Friends. A. E. Housman. SeCePo
When I came on from Santa Fe. Desert Song. John Galsworthy. BPAW
When I Came to Israel. Bert Myers. AMV-80; VWA
When I Came to London. Rachael Castelete, *tr. fr. Judezmo by* Stephen Levy. VWA
When I came to show you my summer cottage. Summer. Josephine Miles. WPE
When I can hold a stone within my hand. Rumination. Richard Eberhart. LiTA; LiTM
When I can read my title clear. Ninety-fifth [*or* The Saint's Delight]. Isaac Watts. AmFP, 3 *sts.*; TrAS
When I carefully consider the curious habits of dogs. Meditatio. Ezra Pound. FaBoCh; OBAL
When I catch sight of your fair head. Sonnet. Louise Labé, *tr. by* Joan Keefe *and* Richard Terdiman. PBWP
When I chanced to look over the wall in the glade. Bah! Walter de la Mare. BoAnP
When I climb up. Drinking Fountain. Marchette Chute. TiPo
When I come down to sleep death's endless night. My City. James Weldon Johnson. BANP; CDC; PoNe
When I come groping back through mists of sleep. Mortal Combat. Alice Fay di Castagnola. GoYe
When I conceived the child with star-green eyes. Sea-Monster. Gertrud Kolmar, *tr. by* Henry A. Smith VWA
When I Consider. Margaret Griffith. AMV-80
When I Consider. Milton. *See* On His Blindness.
When I consider every thing that grows. Sonnets, XV. Shakespeare. AWP; BLPL; MasP; OAEP; OBSC; TEP; TrGrPo
When I consider how my life is spent. Reminiscent Reflection. Ogden Nash. FaBoCo
When I Consider How My Light Is Spent. Milton. *See* On His Blindness.
When I Consider Life. Dryden. *Fr.* Aureng-Zebe, IV, i. FiP
When I consider Life and its few years. Tears. Lizette Woodworth Reese. AA; HBV-2; HBVY; MoAmPo; TreFS; WGRP; WHA
When I consider life, 'tis all a cheat. When I Consider Life. Dryden. *Fr.* Aureng-Zebe, IV, i. FiP
When I consider men of golden talents. So That's Who I Remind Me Of. Ogden Nash. BLPL; PoLF
When I consider, Thérèse. Upon Being Awakened at Night by My Four Year Old Daughter. Dachine Rainer. NePoAm-2
When I Consider Thy Heavens. Bible, *O.T.* Psalms, VIII: 3-5. FaPON; ImOP
When I consider wearing white. When I Consider. Margaret Griffith. AMV-80
When I contemplate o'er me. The Night Serene. Luís de León, *tr. by* Thomas Walsh. TrJP
When I couldn't he always discussed things. Action Would Kill It/A Gamble. Robert Adamson. CBAP
When I crept over the hill, broken with tears. The Comforters. Dora Sigerson Shorter. CH; HBMV
When I Cut My Hair. Rayna Green. TWSS
When I decide I shall assemble you. Identity. Elizabeth Jennings. NePoEA
When I did wake this morn from sleep. Early Morn. W. H. Davies. CH
When I Die. Fenton Johnson. CDC; PoNe
When I Die. Brenda G. Macrow. *Fr.* All Flesh Is Grass. PoSH
When I died, the circulating library. Seth Compton. Edgar Lee Masters. *Fr.* Spoon River Anthology. LiTA
When I do count the clock that tells the time. Sonnets, XII. Shakespeare. Awp; EIL; EnRePo; FaFP; InPS; MasP; NoP; OAEL-1; OBSC; TEP; ViBoPo
When I dragged the rotten log. Kenneth Rexroth. *Fr.* The Signature of All Things. BoNaP
When I drift out on the Silver Sea. The Great Divide. Lew Sarett. HBMV
When I drive cab. After Anacreon. Lew Welch. *Fr.* Taxi Suite. NeAP; PoM
When I drive, every bridge is. Together Again. William Stafford. LCAP
When I dyed last, and, Deare, I dye. *See* When last I died, and, dear, I die.
When I entered the room and turned on the lights. The Man Hidden behind the Drapes. Pattiann Rogers. MAYP
When I entreat, either thou wilt not hear. Sonnet. Henry King. AnAnS-2

When I face north a lost Cree. Returned to Say. William Stafford. ConAP; NaP
When I faced the bowling of Hirst. George Hirst. E. C. Bentley. *Fr.* Clerihews. PoPle
When I faded back to pass. Ties. Dabney Stuart. GrPl; LiSp
When I fall asleep, and even during sleep. Baudelaire. Delmore Schwartz. MP; TwCP; VGW
When I Fall on My Knees. *Unknown. See* Let Us Break Bread Together.
When I First Came to This Land. Oscar Brand. FSW
When I first came to town, they called me a roving jewel. Katy Cruel. *Unknown* FSW
When I first heard about America. Nobody Lives on Arthur Godfrey Boulevard. Gerald Costanzo. MAYP
When I first opened my eyes. Autobiography. Janet Dubé. BrRo
When I first went a-wagoning, a-wagoning did go. The Jolly Wagoner. *Unknown.* TrAS
When I forth fare beyond this narrow earth. After Death. Charles Francis Richardson. AA
When I found myself faced directly. To Emily. Arthur Gregor. AMV-80
"When I found where we had crashed, in the snow." He Said. Jean Valentine. TAP
When I gaze at the sun. A Moment Please. Samuel Allen. AmNP; IDB; PAI; PoBA
When I gaze upon the sky. Reflection from Sea and Sky. Walter Savage Landor. FaBoEE
When I get big. Basketball Star. Karama Fufuka. RHPC
When I Get Time. Thomas L. Masson. BLPA; FPL
When I get to be a composer. Daybreak in Alabama. Langston Hughes. AmFN; CNA
When I get to heaven. Happy Day (or Independence Day). James Cunningham. JB
When I go. After Grave Deliberation. Elizabeth Flynn. AMV-80
When I go away from you. The Taxi. Amy Lowell. BoWoP; MoAmPo; PBWP
When I go back to earth. The Answer. Sara Teasdale. PoA
When I go, Earth, I shall not succumb. A Burnt Offering to Your Greenstone Eyes, Tangaroa. Hone Tuwhare. OCNZ
When I go home to the South the river lakes. The Gar. Charles G. Bell. AmFN
When I go I will give you surely. Courtship. Alice Corbin. BPAW
When I go into the garden, there she is. There She Is. Linda Gregg. NPGG
When I goe musing all alone. The Authors Abstract of Melancholy. Robert Burton. *Fr.* The Anatomy of Melancholy. OBS
When I grow old I hope to be. Growing Old. Rose Henderson. RHPC
When I grow old, if I should live till then. The Contented Bachelor. John Kendall. InMe
When I grow up. Exigencies. Michael William Gilbert. AMV-80
When I had firmly answered "No." The Last Ride Together (from Her Point of View). James Kenneth Stephen. BXAP; CenHV; FaBoCo; Par; UnPo
When I had met my love the twentieth time. Her Merriment. W. H. Davies. EnLoPo
When I had money, money, O! Money. W. H. Davies. OBEV; OBMV; OBVV
When I Had Need of Him. S. E. Kiser. BLRP
When I had spread it all on linen cloth. The Wife's Tale. Seamus Heaney. IPY
When I had wings, my brother. To a Seamew. Swinburne. EtS; VLP
When I ha'e a saxpence under my thoom. Todlin' Hame. *Unknown.* HBV-2
When I hang up my blue-and-white scarf. Jerusalem. Rose Ausländer, *tr. by* Ewald Osers. VWA
When I have a house . . . as I sometime may. Vagabond House. Don Blanding. BLPA
When I have been dead for several years. Poet's Wish. Valery Larbaud, *tr. by* William Jay Smith. GrPl
When I Have Borne in Memory. Wordsworth. EnRP; GTBS; GTBS-P; OBRV
(England, 1802, V.) HBV-2; OBEV
When I have ended, then I see. Dedication. Laurence Housman. TrPWD
When I Have Fears [That I May Cease to Be]. Keats. AWP; BiP; BLPL; CABA; EBEV; EnRP; HAP; HBV-2; HeIP; HoPM; InPK; LiTB; NiP; NoP; OAEL-2; OAEP; OBEV; OBRV; PAI; PoRA; PPoe; PrIm; SeCeV; TEP; TreFS; TrGrPo; UnPo; WHA
(Sonnet: "When I have fears that I may cease to be.") FiP; OBNC
(Sonnet: Written in January, 1818.) ChER
(Terror of Death, The.) GTBS; GTBS-P
When I have finished with this episode. When I Have Gone Weird Ways. John G. Neihardt. HBV-2
When I have folded up this tent. The Last Word. Frederic Lawrence Knowles. HBV-1
When I have forgotten your lips. The Desolate Lover. Eileen Shanahan. NeIP
When I Have Gone Weird Ways. John G. Neihardt. HBV-2
When I have grown foolish. Peregrine's Sunday Song. Elinor Wylie. NYBP
When I have heard small talk about great men. Grandeur of Ghosts. Siegfried Sassoon. MoBrPo; OBMV
When I have lain an hour watching the skies. Clouds. John Jay Chapman. EtS
When I have lost the power to feel the pang. Strangeness of Heart. Siegfried Sassoon. TrJP
When I have seen by time's fell hand defaced. Sonnets, LXIV. Shakespeare. AWP; BLPL; CABA; EIL; EnLoPo; EnRePo; FaFP; GTBS; GTBS-P; HAP; HeIP; LiTB; LO; NOBE; NoP; OAEL-1; OBSC; PoRA; PPoe; SeCeV; ViBoPo
When I have seen the sun emerge. Emily Dickinson. AP
When I have talked for an hour I feel lousy. The Dancers Inherit the Party. Ian Hamilton Finlay. FF
When I hear laughter from a tavern door. Wilfrid Scawen Blunt. *Fr.* Esther. NBM; OBMV; TrGrPo; ViBoPo
When I hear the old men. A Song of Greatness. *Unknown, tr. by* Mary Austin. AmFN; FaPON; TiPo
When I Hear Your Name. Gloria Fuertes, *tr. fr. Spanish by* Ada Long *and* Philip Levine. AMV-81
When I Heard at the Close of the Day. Walt Whitman. AmPP; AP; GBL; NePA; OxBA
When I Heard Dat White Man Say. Zack Gilbert. PoBA
When I heard that thunder, I rose up like a happy animal. Returning to the World. Laura Chester. NPGG
When I Heard the Learn'd Astronomer. Walt Whitman. AmPP; CABA; FF; FPL; HAP; MoAmPo; NoP; OxBA; PAI; SoSe; SUW; TAP; TreFT; TrGrPo; TRV; WeW; WHA
When I Held You to My Chest, You Fit. Jack Myers. AmPA
When I hit her on the head, it was good. Herbert White. Frank Bidart. AmPA
When I hold you in the night. Turn to the Left. Deems Taylor. UnTE
When I in wild defiance fled. In Tribute. Vernal House. CaP
When I kiss Eve. Eden. D. M. Thomas. NCSH
When I last wrote. Letter to a Young Father in Exile. John Logan. CAPP
When I lay back in my chair last night. Eat 'Em Up Smith Tells All in South Africa. Judith Johnson Sherwin. NoAM
When I lay down to sleep dream the Wishing Well it rings. I Am a Victim of the Telephone. Allen Ginsberg. GP; NYP
When I lay in my mother's womb. Before. Ann Stanford. GP
When I lay me down to sleep. Insomnia the Gem of the Ocean. John Updike. DFF; QQQ
When I leaned over a pool of black water. The King o' Spain's Daughter. Jeanne Robert Foster. HBMV
When I left Wanganui. Notes from a Journey. Sam Hunt. OCNZ
When I lie burning in thine eye. Song. Thomas Stanley. CavP; ViBoPo
When I lie where shades of darkness. Fare Well. Walter de la Mare. CoBMV; GTBS-P; MoVE; NOBE; OBEV
When I lived down in Devonshire. Autobiographical Fragment. Kingsley Amis. NePoEA-2
When I lived in Singapore. In Foreign Parts. Laura E. Richards. HBV-2; HBVY
When I look back across the waste of years. The Poet. Anita Grannis. HBMV
When I look back and in myself behold. On the Instability of Youth. Thomas, Lord Vaux. EnRePo
When I look back upon my life nigh spent. A Prayer. George Macdonald. TrPWD
When I look forth at dawning, pool. Nature's Questioning. Thomas Hardy. CoBMV; MoPo; TEP; VLP
When I look in the mirror. Hysteria. Chu Shu-chen, *tr. by* Kenneth Rexroth. NaP
When I look into a glass. A Thought. W. H. Davies. MoShBr
When I look into the mountain air. Chiliasm. Richard Eberhart. EaLo
When I looked at my poverty. Poverty. Charles Simic. MAT
When I looked at the stubborn dark Buddha. Byzantium Burning. Jack Gilbert. NPGG
When I looked into your eyes. Chinoiseries. Amy Lowell. PoRA
When I Loved You. Thomas Moore. HBV-1
(To ———.) EnLoPo
When I Loved You. Charles A. Wagner. InMe
When I marched away to war. Colleen Oge Asthore. *Unknown.* OnYI
When I meet the morning beam. The Immortal Part. A. E. Housman. A Shropshire Lad, XLIII. MasP; MoBrPo; UnPo; VLP
When I meet the skier she is always. Transit. Adrienne Rich. NoP
When I must come to you, O my God, I pray. A Prayer to Go to Paradise with the Donkeys. Francis Jammes, *tr. by* Richard Wilbur. EaLo

When I need string I can't find it. The String of My Ancestors. Nina Nyhart. Str
When I offer the sack. The Gifts. Charles Levendosky. TAT
When I opened your letter. A Thought of Marigolds. Janice Farrar. GoYe
When I pass. Four Choctaw Songs. Jim Barnes. STE
When I perceive your blond and graceful head. Sonnet X. Louise Labé, *tr. by* Willis Barnstone. BoWoP
When I Peruse the Conquer'd Fame. Walt Whitman. ELU; PoEL-5
When I pictured you. Ollie, Answer Me. Stephen Berg. NaP
When I play on my fiddle in Dooney. The Fiddler of Dooney. W. B. Yeats. EBVV; FaBoCh; HBV-2; OBVV; PoPle; TiPo
When I, poor Lais, with my crown. Lais to Aphrodite. E. A. Robinson, *after* Plato. FaBoEE
When I pulled the cork. The Bottle of Chianti. Raymond Souster. ELU
When I put her out, once, by the garbage pail. The Geranium. Theodore Roethke. CoAP; UnPo; WeW
When I put myself out on a saucer. Cannibalism. Diana Chang. WPOW
When I ran to snatch the wires off our roof. The Powerline Incarnation. Les A. Murray. CBAP
When I reached his place. It Was All Very Tidy. Robert Graves. OxBTC
When I read a poem that I feel. For Zorro. Diana Bickston. LFAC
When I Read Shakespeare. D. H. Lawrence. NoAM
When I remark her golden hair. Jessie. Eugene Field. InMe
When I remember again. The Sparrow's Dirge. John Skelton. *Fr.* Phyllyp Sparowe. FaBoCh; PBBP; SeCePo
When I remember the work camps. Mother. José Montoya, *tr. by* Toni Empringham. FIA
When I return I search for myself. On Going Home. Marjorie L. Agnew. GoYe
When I returned at last from Paris hoofbeats pounded. Hobbes, 1651. John Hollander. NoAM
When I returned with drinks and nuts, my friend. The Friend of the Fourth Decade. James Merrill. NYBP
When I ride my bicycle. Different Bicycles. Dorothy W. Baruch. FaPON; SUS; TiPo
When I rode the zebra past your door. Apparitions Are Not Singular Occurrences. Diane Wakoski. CoPo
When I rolled three 7's. Situation. Langston Hughes. OBAL
When I said farewell. Return. M. L. Sussman. AMV-81
When I said "You have grown thin." Meeting after Separation. Marula, *tr. by* Tambimuttu *and* G. V. Vaidya. BoWoP
When I sailed out of Baltimore. A Child's Pet. W. H. Davies. CH
When I Saw Sweet Nelly Home. Francis Kyle. PSoN, *with music.* (Seeing Nellie Home.) FSW
When I saw that clumsy crow. Night Crow. Theodore Roethke. DFF; ELU; HoPM; InPK; MoVE; NCSH; VGW
When I saw the dark clouds, I wept. The Clouds. Mirabai. NU
When I saw the grapefruit drying, cherries in each center lying. Arrogance Repressed. John Betjeman. FiBHP
When I saw the woman's leg on the floor of the subway train. The Leg in the Subway. Oscar Williams. LiTM; NePA; TwAmPo
When I Saw You Last, Rose. Austin Dobson. HBV-1
When I saw your head bow, I knew I had beaten you. The Last Word. Peter Davison. InPK
When I say my name, I am telling you. Conversation with God. Jeanine Hathaway. AMV-80
When I see a couple of kids. High Windows. Philip Larkin. FaBoMo
When I see a prairie schooner. The Prairie Schooner. Edward Everett Dale. BPAW
When I See Another's Pain. Mani-Leib, *tr. fr. Yiddish by* Joseph Leftwich. TrJP
When I see birches bend to left and right. Birches. Robert Frost. AmPP; BiP; CMoP; FaBV; FPL; HBMV; HeIP; LiTA; LiTM; MoAB; MoAmPo; MoVE; NIP; NoAM; NoP; OxBA; PAI; PoLF; PoPl; PoRA; TAP; TreF; TrGrPo; TwAmPo
When I see blood pouring down the valleys. The Damage You Have Done. Ellis Ayitey Komey. PBA
When I see buildings in a town together. Mr. Frost Goes South to Boston. Firman Houghton. Par
When I see carved so clearly on your face. Two Solitudes. Evelyn Ames. GoYe
When I see her walk before me. Sidewalk Orgy. Richard O'Connell. PV
When I see how high it is. So Beautiful Is the Tree of Night. Pauline Hanson. TAP
When I see milk spilled on the table. Spilled Milk. John Haines. GP
When I See Old Men. Raymond Souster. CaP
When I see some kid from Norway. High Wonders. Naomi Marks. BXAP
When I see the earth ornate and lovely. Veronica Gambara, *tr. fr. Italian by* Brenda Webster. PBWP
When I see the falling bombs. Conflict. F. R. Scott. CaP; PeCV
When I see the lark a-moving. The Lark. Bernart de Ventadorn, *tr. by* Ezra Pound. CTC
When I see your picture in its frame. As If You Had Never Been. Richard Eberhart. EyDe
When I Set Out for Lyonnesse. Thomas Hardy. BrPo; EBVV; InPS; MoBrPo; SeCePo; VLP
When I shall be without regret. Epitaph. J. V. Cunningham. ELU; InPK; PoCh
When I sit by myself at the close of the day. Good Company. *Unknown.* OBET
When I solidly do ponder. Francis Daniel Pastorius. SCAP
When I some antique jar behold. To a Lady. John Gay. OBEV
When I stand at the judgment seat of Christ. His Plan for Me. Martha Snell Nicholson. STF
When I stand in the center of that man's madness. Reflection by a Mailbox. Stanley Kunitz. TrJP; WaP
When I stepped homeward to my hill. Home-coming. Léonie Adams. HBMV; MoAmPo
When I strip,/ stop walking/ and drop into sleep. Anne-Marie Kegels, *tr. fr. French by* Willis Barnstone. BoWoP
When I survey [*or* survay] the bright. Nox Nocti Indicat Scientiam. William Habington. *Fr.* Castara, III. ACP; AnAnS-2; GoBC; HBV-2; JCP; LoBV; MeLP; MePo; NOBE; OBEV; OBS; OxBoCh
When I Survey the Wondrous Cross. Isaac Watts. AmFP; FaPoR; WGRP (Crucifixion to the World by the Cross of Christ.) NOCV; NOEC; OBEC
When I take my girl to the swimming party. The One Girl at the Boys Party. Sharon Olds. MAYP
When I think of all you've got. A Father's Heart Is Touched. Samuel Hoffenstein. FiBHP
When I think of death. Bop Lyrics. Allen Ginsberg. OBAL
When I think of my fear. The Unblinding. Laurence Lieberman. NYBP
When I Think of the Hungry People. O-Shi-O, *tr. fr. Japanese.* TRV
When I think of the last great round-up. The Great Round-up. *Unknown.* BPAW; CoSo
When I through all my many poems look. To the Most Virtuous Mistress Pot, Who Many Times Entertained Him. Robert Herrick. CaPo
When I Thy Parts Run O'er. Robert Herrick. UnTE
When I thy singing next shall heare. Againe. Robert Herrick. SeCP
When I try to skate. Skating. Herbert Asquith. FaPON; SoPo; SUS; TiPo
When I visit Europe and America's zoos. Zoo You Too! Ted Joans. GP
When I visited America. He Comforts Himself. Christopher Morley. *Fr.* Translations from the Chinese. EvOK
When I visited Fort Robinson. Fort Robinson. Ted Kooser. GP
When I wake and stir, he thumps his tail. Wedlock. Bink Noll. GP
When I wake in the early mist. Very Early. Karla Kuskin. SoPo
When I wake up again, when I wake up. The Report. Jon Swan. NYBP
When I walk home through snow or slush. Winter Song. David Daiches. NYBP
When I Want to Speak. Rav Abraham Isaac Kook, *tr. fr. Hebrew by* Ben Zion Bokser. VWA
When I was/ thirteen I. Spring. Ruth Whitman. IHMS
When I was a bachelor/ I lived by myself. Mother Goose. HBV-1
When I was a bachelor bold [*or* brisk] and young. Bachelor Bold and Young [*or* Blue Bottle]. *Unknown.* AmFP; OuSiCo
When I was a bachelor [*or* batchelor] I lived all alone [*or* early and young *or* lively and young *or* by myself *or* young and gay]. The [Foggy,] Foggy Dew. *Unknown.* AS; CoMu; DTC; ELP; FSW; GBP; LiTB; OBET (A *vers.*); OxBoLi; UnTE, *vers.* I *and* II
When I was a beggarly boy. Aladdin. James Russell Lowell. HBV-1; RoGo; TreFT
When I was a boy. The Piper's Progress. Francis Sylvester Mahony. FiBHP
When I was a boy, a relative. A Way to Make a Living. James Wright. NNaP
When I was a boy, and saw bright rows of icicles. Conrad Aiken. *Fr.* Improvisations: Light and Snow. BoNaP
When I was a boy desiring the title of man. George. Dudley Randall. BPo; ConAP; NoAM
When I was a boy, I used to go to bed. The Remorse for Time. Howard Nemerov. NCSH
When I was a boy in the Ozarks. Freemon Hawthorne. Melvin B. Tolson. FAZ
When I was a boy my mother often said to me. I Want a Girl. Will Dillon *and* Harry Von Tilzer. TreFS
When I was a boy, perhaps. My Dog Jock. Hayden Carruth. FAZ
When I was a boy, the Milky Way. The Milky Way. Jon Anderson. MAYP
When I was a boy we always did it this way. Hunting with My Father. Tom Absher. AMV-80
When I Was a Brave Cowboy, *with music. Unknown.* CoSo

When I was a child. Autobiographia Literaria. Frank O'Hara. NNaP; NOBA
When I was a child. Moon, Son of Heaven. Miyazawa Kenji, *tr. by* Gary Snyder. MOON
When I was a child. My People. Margery Himel. IHMS
When I was a child. Sophistication. Vassar Miller. NCSH
When I was a child. The Message of the Rain. Norman H. Russell. STE
When I was a child. The Truth about My Sister and Me. Anita Endrezze Probst. CDW
When I was a child. Why Do You Write about Russia? Louis Simpson. AMV-81; LCAP
When I was a child and thought as a child, I put. The Wandering Jew. Robert Mezey. NePoEA-2; VWA
When I was a child I knew red miners. Childhood. Margaret Walker. BOLo; IHMS; PBWP; PoBA; WPOW
When I was a child I liked being with people. Song for a New Generation. Gertrude May Lutz. AMV-80
When I was a child of five winters. Poor Wolf Speaks. Poor Wolf. NU
When I was a chile we used to play. Children's Rhymes. Langston Hughes. InPS
When I was a cowboy I learned to throw the line. The Sporting Cowboy. *Unknown.* OuSiCo
When I was a cowboy way out on de western plains. Leadbelly's Chisholm Trail. *Unknown.* CoSo
When I was a girl. Two Gifts. *Unknown*, tr. by Willis Barnstone. BoWoP
When I was a girl I saw with the old men. You Call That a Ts'ing; a Letter. Jedediah Barrow. BXAP
When I was a good and quick little girl. *Tr. fr. Pampa Indian by* W. S. Merwin. BoWoP
When I was a greenhorn and young. Song. Charles Kingsley. *Fr.* The Saint's Tragedy. NBM
When I was a kid. The External Element. David McFadden. NeAC
When I Was a King in Babylon. W. E. Henley. *See* Or Ever the Knightly Years Were Gone.
When I was a lad and so was my dad. *Unknown.* OxNR
When I was a lad I served a term. The First Lord's Song [*or* Sir Joseph's Song]. W. S. Gilbert. *Fr.* H. M. S. Pinafore. LiTB; TreFS
When I was a lad of twenty. I Was a Bustle-Maker Once, Girls. Patrick Barrington. PoPle; WhC
When I was a lad there were hansoms in London. Hansom Cabbies. Wilfrid Thorley. HBMV
When I was a learner, I sought both night and day. Go Tell [It on the Mountain]. *Unknown.* EBCP; FSW
When I was a little boy. Hope. Gamaliel Bradford. HBMV
When I was a little boy. *Unknown.* OxNR
When I was a little boy/ I lived by myself. *Unknown.* OxNR
When I was a little boy/ I washed my mammy's dishes. *Unknown.* OxNR
When I was a little boy/ My mammy kept me in. *Unknown.* OxNR
When I was a little boy as fat as I could roll. Toll-a-Winker. *Unknown.* OuSiCo
When I Was a Little Girl. Alice Milligan. OnYI; OxBI
When I was a little girl,/ About seven years old. Mother Goose. OxNR
When I was a little lad. Duna. Marjorie Pickthall. HBV-2
When I was a little lad. Haul Away Joe. *Unknown.* FSW
When I was a little maid. The Little Maid. Anna Maria Wells. OBCA
When I was a maid. The Old Story Over Again. James Kenney. OnYI
When I was a passenger in the barque *Windrush.* The Sun's Over the Foreyard. Christopher Morley. EtS
When I was a serving maid, down in Drury Lane. Bell-Bottom Trousers. *Unknown.* AmSS
When I was a single girl, I went dressed very fine. Oh, I Wish I Were Single Again. *Unknown.* AmFP
When I was a teacher. The Teacher. David Fisher. NPGG
When I was a wee thing. The Kirk of the Birds, Beasts and Fishes. *Unknown.* GBP
When I was a windy boy and a bit. Lament. Dylan Thomas. ErPo; MasP; PPP
"When I was a young girl, I used to seek pleasure." One Morning in May; or, The Young Girl Cut Down in Her Prime. *Unknown.* AmFP
When I Was a Young Maid. *Unknown.* AmFP
When I was a young man I carried a pack. The Band Played Waltzing Matilda. Eric Bogle. OBET
When I was a young man I lived rarely. A Poor Man's Work Is Never Done. *Unknown.* OBET
When I was a young man I lived upon the square. The Bad Boy. *Unknown.* CoSo
When I was about eight, I once stabbed somebody, another kid, a little girl. Blades. C. K. Williams. GeTw
When I was apprenticed in London. Blow the Candles Out. *Unknown.* FSW
When I was as high as that. A Memory. L. A. G. Strong. FaBoCo; NOBL; PoPl; WhC
When I was a-stealin' 'cross the deep blue sea. Trench Blues. *Unknown.* OuSiCo
When I was at the funeral. Snapshot: Politician. George Garrett. NePoAm-2
"When I was at the party." Betty at the Party. *Unknown.* OnUR
When I was born a happy child. Epitaph for a Timid Lady. Frances Cornford. ELU
When I was born in a world of sin. G. K. Chesterton on His Birth. A. E. Housman. FaBoNo
When I was born in the great house on the bank of the sea. Poem of Distant Childhood. Noémia da Sousa, *tr. by* Allan Francovich *and* Kathleen Weaver. PBWP
When I was born, my mother and father. Riddle: Cuckoo. *Unknown.* PBBP
When I was born, my mother taped my ears. Youth's Progress. John Updike. FiBHP
When I was born on Amman Hill. The Collier. Vernon Watkins. DTC; FaBoTw; MoVE
When I was bound apprentice, in famous Lincolnshire. The [Lincolnshire] Poacher. *Unknown.* CH; FSW; GBP; OnMSP; OxBoLi; WiR
When I was bound for London a lady met me there. The Sheffield Apprentice. *Unknown.* OBET
When I was but thirteen or so. Romance. W. J. Turner. CH; GoJo; HBMV; HBVY; MoBrPo; NOBE; OBMV; PoRA; TrGrPo; WHA
When I was christened. Perambulator Poem, V. David McCord. OBCA; OFD; WhC
When I was coming down from the country. The Forgotten City. William Carlos Williams. LiTA; NePA; PoPl
When I Was Conceived. Michael Ryan. MAYP
When I was down beside the sea. At the Seaside. Robert Louis Stevenson. FaPON; NTCP; OxBChV; SUS; TiPo
When I was eighteen years of age. McCaffery. *Unknown.* OBET
When I was eleven and they. Twins. William Matthews. MAYP
When I Was Fair and Young. Elizabeth I, Queen of England. CTC; NIP; NoP; PoRA
(Importune Me No More.) EIL; UnTE
("When I was fair and young and favour graced me.") CTC
(Youth and Cupid.) OBSC
When I was forty the stocktaker came. On My Fortieth Birthday. John Tripp. NAs
When I was four my father went to Scotland. The Truth. Randall Jarrell. DiL; OxBC
When I Was Growing Up. David Vogel, *tr. fr. Hebrew by* A. C. Jacobs. VWA
When I was happy in my youth. I Stand Corrected. Margaret Fishback. PoPl; WhC
When I was home de/ Sunshine seemed like gold. Po' Boy Blues. Langston Hughes. BANP
When I was ill in the long ago. The Market Town. Francis Carlin. HBMV
When I was in a summer valley. *Unknown, tr. by* John William Hey Atkins. *Fr.* The Owl and the Nightingale. PBBP
When I was in Missouri, would not let me be. I Will Turn Your Money Green. *Unknown.* BluL
When I was just a little boy. The Ships of Yule. Bliss Carman. CaP; HBVY; WHW
"When I was just as far as I could walk." The Telephone. Robert Frost. HBV-1; SO; SoSe
When I was led again to the Akedah. The Akedah. Matti Megged, *tr. by* Howard Schwartz. VWA
When I was little, oh a very small boy. So Long Folks, Off to the War. Anthony Ostroff. NePoAm-2; PoPl
When I was little, when. The Poplar's Shadow. May Swenson. NYBP
When I was lonely, I thought of death. The Secret of Poetry. Jon Anderson. MAYP
When I Was Lost. Dorothy Aldis. RHPC; SoPo
When I was lying in jail with my back turned to the wall. The Jailhouse Blues. *Unknown.* BluL
When I was making myself a game. Little Rain. Elizabeth Madox Roberts. SoPo; SUS
When I was marked for suffering, Love forswore. Sonnet. Cervantes, *tr. by* Sir Edmund Gosse. AWP
When I Was Nine. Raymond Roseliep. FAZ
When I was on Night Line. Ego. Philip Booth. MP; TwCP
When I was once in Baltimore. Sheep. W. H. Davies. LiTM; MoBrPo
When I was one. Sophisticate. Barbara Young. SiSoSe
When I was one. The End. A. A. Milne. SiSoSe
When I Was One-and-twenty. A. E. Housman. A Shropshire Lad, XIII. CMoP; ELP; FaBV; FaFP; FPL; HBV-1; HeIP; LiTB; LiTM; MasP; MoAB; MoBrPo; NoAM; OAEP; PoLF; PoPl; PoPle; SoSe; TreF; TrGrPo; ViBoPo; WHA

When I was one and twenty. The Shropshire Lad's Cousin. Samuel Hoffenstein. BXAP
When I was only six years old. When I Was Six. Zora Cross. FaPON; HBVY
When I Was Otherwise Than Now I Am. *Unknown.* NCEP
When I was seven. Growing Up. Harry Behn. PDV; RHPC; SiSoSe; SoPo
When I was seventeen, a man in the Dakar Station. Objets d'Art. Cynthia Macdonald. NMM
When I was seventeen I heard. To Critics. Walter Learned. AA; HBV-1
When I was sick and lay a-bed. The Land of Counterpane. Robert Louis Stevenson. BrPo; EBEV; EvOK; FaBoBe; FaFP; FaPON; HBV-1; HBVY; NTCP; OxBChV; PoPl; SoPo; TreF
When I Was Single. *Unknown.* FSW
When I was single. I Wish I Was Single [Again] [*or* The Single Girl]. *Unknown.* AmFP, *diff. vers.*; AS; TrAS
When I Was Six. Zora Cross. FaPON; HBVY
When I Was Small. André de Chénier, *tr. fr. French by* Elizabeth Gerteiny. ErPo
When I was small, this continent was mine. Four Spacious Skies. Susan Astor. AMV-80
When I was ten and she fifteen. Time's Revenge. Walter Learned. HBV-1
When I was the sissy of the block who nobody wanted on their team. The Sleeper. Edward Field. LiSp
When I was twelve I was kidnapped and sold as a slave. A Psalm of Onan for Harp, Flute and Tambourine. Alden Nowlan. NeAC
When I was twelve in that far land. Only for Me. Mark Van Doren. NCSH
When I was very small indeed. Palm Leaves of Childhood. G. Adali-Mortti. PBA
When I was very very. Mama Knows. Sharon Scott. JB
When I Was Well into Being Savored. Joanne Kyger. PoM
When I was young. "Chew Mail Pouch." D. L. Klauck. AMV-81
When I was young. Due Date. Seymour Cain. AMV-80
When I Was Young and Foolish, *with music.* *Unknown.* AS
When I was young and full o' pride. Blow Me Eyes! Wallace Irwin. HBMV; InMe
When I was young and in my prime,/ I flourished like a vine. Thyme. *Unknown.* AmFP
When I was young and in my prime,/ I thought I never could marry. Devilish Mary. *Unknown.* AmFP
When I was young and in my prime/ To me way I thought I'd go. A Long Time Ago, *vers.* III. *Unknown.* ShS
When I was young and in my prime, my age twenty-two. The Lightning Flash. *Unknown.* AmFP
When I was young, and ower young. The Deil o' Bogie. Sir Alexander Gray. BSV
When I was young and slender, a spender, a lender. Song for a Cracked Voice. Wallace Irwin. InMe
When I was young, and the day. Poem to Help My Father. Norma Richman. Str
When I was young and used to wander. Hubert's Museum. Louis Simpson. OxBC
When I was young and wanted to see the sights. On His Queerness. Christopher Isherwood. OxBTC; PeHV
When I was young I had a care. Soliloquy. Francis Ledwidge. HoPM
When I was young, I put on rouge. The Onion Skin. Kenneth Pitchford. *Fr.* Good for Nothing Man. CoPo
When I was young, I said to Sorrow. Sorrow. Aubrey Thomas De Vere. WiR
When I was young I scribbled, boasting, on my wall. The Summing-up. Stanley Kunitz. ELU
When I Was Young I Tried to Sing. Donald Finkel. GP
When I was young I us'd to wait on Massa and hand him de plate. The Blue-Tail Fly [*or* Jim Crack Corn]. *Unknown.* BLSo; FaFP; FSW; GBP; PSoN; TreFT; ViBoFo
When I was young, I went to school. The One Furrow. R. S. Thomas. HoPM; OxBC
When I was young I woke gladly in the morning. Hoelderlin's Old Age. Stephen Spender. NoAM
When I was young, just starting at our game. To My Least Favorite Reviewer. Howard Nemerov. TW
When I was young, love, and in full blossom. Love It Is Pleasing. *Unknown.* OBET
When I was young my adult peers. Hickory Stick. Hierarchy. Len G. Selle. AMV-80
When I was young, my ringlets waved. The Wasp's Song. "Lewis Carroll." FaBoNo
When I was young my teachers were the old. What Fifty Said. Robert Frost. NAs
"When I was young," said Aunt to me. Other Fabrics, Other Mores! Anna Maria Lenngren, *tr. by* Nadia Christensen *and* Mariann Tiblin. PBWP
When I was young the days were long. The Flying Wheel. Katharine Tynan. WGRP
When I was young the twilight seemed too long. Twilight. Agnes Mary Frances Robinson. HBV-1
When I was young, with sharper sense. A Summer Commentary. Yvor Winters. LiTM; QFR
When I was younger. Pastoral. William Carlos Williams. AmPP; OxBA
When I Watch the Living Meet. A. E. Housman. A Shropshire Lad, XII. CMoP; MasP; MoBrPo; NoP; OAEP; TrGrPo; VLP; WHA
When I watch you. Miss Rosie. Lucille Clifton. AmPA; BlSi; CNA; NMM; PoBA; TwCP
When I went/ to Gaza and met. Samson Rends His Clothes. Anadad Eldan, *tr. by* Ruth Nevo. VWA
When I went down past Charing Cross. The Poet. W. H. Davies. DTC
When I went down to the river, poor boy. Poor Boy. *Unknown.* FSW
When I went into my garden, I found. Sister Bertken, *tr. fr. Dutch by* Willis Barnstone. BoWoP
When I went into my room, at mid-morning. Man and Bat. D. H. Lawrence. BoAnP
When I Went Off to Prospect. *Unknown.* AmFP
When I Went Out. Karla Kuskin. NTCP
When I went out to kill myself, I caught. Saint Judas. James Wright. ConAP; LCAP; NMP; NOBA; PAI
When I Went to the Circus. D. H. Lawrence. CMoP; LiTB; NoAM
When I went up the minster tower. At Lincoln. Oscar Fay Adams. AA
When I went up to Clova glen. Change and Immutability. Syd Scroggie. PoSH
When I were at home wi' my fayther an' mother, I niver had na fun. The Wensleydale Lad. *Unknown.* FaBoPP
When I Woke. Raymond Patterson. PAI
When I woke, the lake-lights were quivering on the wall. Coming Awake. D. H. Lawrence. BrPo
When icicles by silver eaves. Winter Fairyland in Vermont. Francis P. Osgood. WeW
When Icicles Hang by the Wall. Shakespeare. *Fr.* Love's Labour's Lost, V, ii. AWP; BiP; EnRePo; FaPON; FF; GN; GoJo; InPK; InPS; LiTB; NOBE; PoRA; PoSC; PrIm; RoGo; SeCeV
(Hiems.) FaBoCh
(Merry Note, A.) WiR
(Song: "When icicles hang by the wall.") FiP; HBV-2; PBBP; PoEL-2
(Tu-Whit To-Who.) CH
(Ver and Hiems.) OBSC
(Winter.) BoNaP; ChTr; ElL; GTBS; GTBS-P; HAP; HeIP; NIP; OAEL-1; OBEV; PAI; SeCePo; TEP; TreFS; TrGrPo; UnPo; ViBoPo; WeW; WHA
(Winter's Song.) FaBoEn
When I'm a little older. My Plan. Marchette Chute. FaPON
When I'm Alone. Siegfried Sassoon. OBMV
(Alone.) MoBrPo
("'When I'm alone'—the words tripped off his tongue.") OxBTC
When I'm dead and buried. Don't You Weep after Me. *Unknown.* FSW
When I'm discharged in Liverpool 'n' draws my bit o' pay. Hell's Pavement. John Masefield. BrPo
When I'm Going Well. R. G. Everson. PeCV
When in April the sweet showers fall. Chaucer, *mod. vers. by* Nevill Coghill. *Fr.* The Canterbury Tales: Prologue. TEP
When in danger or in doubt. Sound Advice. *Unknown.* FaBoUs
When in disgrace with fortune and men's eyes. Sonnets, XXIX. Shakespeare. AWP; CTC; EBEV; ElL; FaBoEn; FaBoRV; FaBV; GBL; GTBS; GTBS-P; HAP; HBV-1; HeIP; InvP; LiTB; LoBV; MasP; NOBE; NoP; OAEL-1; OAEP; OBEV; OBSC; PeHV; PoEL-2; PoPl; PoRA; PPoe; PPP; Prf; PrIm; SCV; SeCeV; TEP; TreF; TrGrPo; TRV; ViBoPo; WeW; WHA
When in her face mine eyes I fix. Madrigal. Earl of Stirling. *Fr.* Aurora. ElL
When in mid-air the golden trump shall sound. Poet's Resurrection. Dryden. *Fr.* An Ode to the Pious Memory of Mrs. Anne Killigrew. WHA
When in My Arms. Pushkin, *tr. fr. Russian by* Babette Deutsch. ErPo
When in my dreams thy lovely face. Dream Land. Frances Anne Kemble. OBVV
When, in my effervescent youth. Who'd Be a Hero (Fictional)? Morris Bishop. FiBHP; OBAL
When in my walks I meet some ruddy lad. A Proem. Samuel Ward. AA
When in my youth I travelled. The Migration of the Grey Squirrels. William Howitt. OxBChV
When in nineteen-thirty-seven, Etta Moten, sweetheart. The Convert. Margaret Danner. BPo
When in Rome. Mari Evans. AmNP; SoSe
When in some sudden hush of earth. The Retreat. Sir Herbert Read. BrPo
When in that gold. Listening to Foxhounds. James Dickey. InPS; LiSp

When in the bedded dark of night. Marriage. Donald Hall. NePoEA
When in the chronicle of wasted time. Sonnets, CVI. Shakespeare. AWP; BLPL; CTC; EIL; EnLoPo; EnRePo; FaBoCh; FaBoEn; FaBV; FiP; GTBS; GTBS-P; HBV-1; LiTB; LoBV; MasP; NOBE; NoP; OAEL-1; OAEP; OBEV; OBSC; PoRA; PPoe; SeCeV; TEP; TreFT; TrGrPo; ViBoPo; WHA
When in the company of the gods. Hilda Doolittle ("H. D."). *Fr.* The Walls Do Not Fall. NoAM
When, in the dawn of love and my desire. The Miracle. Allan Dowling. ErPo
When in the east the morning ray. The Garden of Appleton House. Andrew Marvell. *Fr.* Upon Appleton House. NOBE
When in the festival of August heat. Horas Tempestatis Quoque Enumero: The Sundial. John Hollander. NePoEA
When in the First Great Hour. Edith M. Thomas. *Fr.* The Inverted Torch. AA
When in the mask of night there shone that cut. Landing on the Moon. May Swenson. TAP
When in the mirror of a permanent tear. Elegy [on Gordon Barber]. Gene Derwood. FaFP; LiTA; LiTM; NePA; TwAmPo
When in the silent midnight grove. The Temper of Aristippus. John Gilbert Cooper. *Fr.* Epistles to His Friends in Town. PBBP
When in the spring the swallows all return. Bliss Carman. Sappho, XCIII. PeCV
When in the sun the hot red acres smoulder. The Zulu Girl. Roy Campbell. ChMP; MoVE; OBMV; PoPl
When in the Woods I Wander All Alone. Edward Hovell-Thurlow. HBV-1; HBVY
When in thy glass thou studiest thy face. Afternoon. Wendell Phillips Garrison. *Fr.* Post-Meridian. AA
When inclined to be discouraged. Have Faith in God. Joe Budzynski. STF
When Indians heare that some there are. Roger Williams. SCAP
When isicles hang by the wall. *See* When Icicles Hang by the Wall.
When Israel against Philistia. David and Goliath. Nathaniel Crouch. OxBChV
When Israel came forth out of Egypt. Bible, *O.T.* Psalms, CXIV. TrJP
When Israel came from Egypt's coast. Bible, *O.T., paraphrased by* Christopher Smart. Psalms, CXIV. OBVE
When Israel, of the Lord beloved. Rebecca's Hymn. Sir Walter Scott. *Fr.* Ivanhoe, *ch.* 39. EnRP; ViBoPo
When Israel out of Egypt Came. A. E. Housman. LiTB
When Israel Was in Egypt's Land. *Unknown. See* Go Down, Moses.
When Israel's daughters mourn'd their past offences. Epigram in a Maid of Honour's Prayer-Book. Pope. FaBoEE
When it burns before the harps and freezes behind the easels. Hans Arp, *tr. fr. French by* Harriet Watts. FaBoNo
When it comes to a question of trusting. The Average Man. Margaret Elizabeth Sangster. WBLP
When it comes to sex with other men. Homosexual Sonnets. Kenneth Pitchford. GP
When it is all over. Lost Moment. Hoyt W. Fuller. PoBA
When it is finally ours, this freedom. Frederick Douglass. Robert Hayden. AmNP; BiP; CNA; GOA; GP; HoAn; IDB; PoBA; PoNe; TTY
When it is not yet day. Looking for Mushrooms at Sunrise. W. S. Merwin. NaP; NOBA
When it is the winter time. Ice. Dorothy Aldis. SUS; TiPo
When it rained five days and the skies turned dark as night. Back Water Blues. *Unknown.* BluL
When It Rains. H. A. Maxson. AMV-80
When it snowed hard, cars failed. Bystanders. William Matthews. NPAW
When it was late/ the Baal Shem Tov. Wonders. Shirley Kaufman. VWA
When it was spring in Wisconsin, and the roosting crows. The Crows. John Engels. AMV-81
When it's hot. Summer. Frank Asch. NTCP; RHPC
When it's just past April. The Flower-Cart Man. Rachel Field. SiSoSe; SoPo
When it's time. Listening. Aileen Fisher. NTCP
When I've a saxpence under my thumb. Todlen Butt, and Todlen Ben. *Unknown.* OBS
When Jack the King's commander. The Fate of John Burgoyne. *Unknown.* PAH
When Jacky's a [very] good boy. Mother Goose. EvOK; OxNR
When Jacob from the land of Canaan down. The Exodus from Egypt. Ezekielos of Alexandria, *tr. by* E. H. Gifford. TrJP
When James, our great monarch, so wise and discreet. Upon the King's Voyage to Chatham to Make Bulwarks against the Dutch. *Unknown.* APAS
When Januar' wind war blawing cauld. The Lass That Made the Bed for Me. Burns. InvP; UnTe
When Jemmy the Second, not Jemmy the First. A New Song Entitled the Warming Pan. *Unknown.* CoMu
When Jessie comes with her soft breast. Jessie. Thomas Edward Brown. HBV-1
When Jesus came to Golgotha they hanged Him on a tree. Indifference. G. A. Studdert-Kennedy. EBCP; PGD; TrCP; TRV
When Jesus was a little Child. Mother and Child. Ivy O. Eastwick. SiSoSe
When Jesus was a little thing. His Mother in Her Hood of Blue. Lizette Woodworth Reese. ISi; OHIP
When Jesus Wept, *with music.* William Billings. TrAS
When Jill complain[e]s to Jack for want of meat[e]. Upon Jack and Jill: Epigram. Robert Herrick. AnAnS-2; CaPo
When John Henry was a little babe [*or* fellow]. John Henry. *Unknown.* AmFP; BPo; FSW
When John Henry was a little boy. John Henry. *Unknown.* BaBo
When John Henry was about three days old. John Henry. *Unknown.* AmFN; TiPo
When John Henry was nothin' but a baby. John Henry. *Unknown.* FaBoBe
When John the Baptist was so young. Apocrypha. Babette Deutsch. HBMV
When Johnny Comes Marching Home. Patrick Sarsfield Gilmore. BLSo, *with music*; FSW; PAH; PAL; PoSC; PSoN, *with music*; TrAS, *with music*; TreF
When Johnson sought (as Shakespear says) that bourn. Introduction and Anecdotes. "Peter Pindar." *Fr.* Bozzy and Piozzi. PoEL-3
When Johnson's Ale Was New, *with music. Unknown.* ShS
(When Jones's Ale Was New, *diff. vers.*) AmFP
When Joseph was an old man. The Cherry-Tree Carol. *Unknown.* AmFP; FSW
When Julius Caesar went to town. The Same Old Story. James J. Montague. HBMV
When Julius Fabricius, Sub-Prefect of the Weald. The Land. Kipling. MoBrPo; OnMSP
When Kian O'Hara's Cup Was Passed to Turlough O'Carolan. Turlough Carolan. *See* Cup of O'Hara, The.
When Klopstock England defied. Blake. OAEL-2
When lads have done with labor. A. E. Housman and a Few Friends. Humbert Wolfe. BXAP; FiBHP; Par; SpRo; WhC
When lads were home from labour. Fancy's Knell. A. E. Housman. FaBoCh; OAEP; PoPle; PoRA
When Lalement and de Brébeuf, brave souls. Brébeuf and His Brethren. F. R. Scott. NOBC
When land is gone and money spent. *Unknown.* OxNR
When last I died [*or* When I dyed last], and, dear[e], I die [*or* dye]. The Legacy [*or* The Legacie]. John Donne. SeCP; TrGrPo
When Last Seen. Hortense Flexner. QQQ
When late I attempted your pity to move. An Expostulation. Isaac Bickerstaffe. FaBoCo; FiBHP; NIP; PV
When late I heard the trembling cello play. The Cello. Richard Watson Gilder. AA
When late in summer the streams run yellow. A Song of Early Autumn. Richard Watson Gilder. HBV-1
When lately King James, whom our sovereign we call. The Clerical Cabal. *Unknown.* APAS
When Lazarus left his charnel-cave. Tennyson. In Memoriam A. H. H., XXXI. EBVV
When learning's triumph o'er her barb'rous [*or* barbarous] foes. Prologue Spoken [by Mr. Garrick] [at the Opening of the Theatre in Drury-Lane, 1747]. Samuel Johnson. EBEV; LAuP; NOEC; NoP; OBEC; SeCeV
When leaves of April glisten. The Concert. Phyllis McGinley. YeAr
When leaves turn outward to the light. Poet and Lark. "Madeleine Bridges." AA; HBV-2
When leaving the primrose, bayberry dunes, seaward. The Constant. A. R. Ammons. HAP; WeW
When leaving with your loving in my veins. Late Light. Barbara Bellow Watson. NYBP
When Letty had scarce passed [*or* pass'd] her third glad year. Letty's Globe. Charles Tennyson Turner. HBV-1; OBEV; OBVV; OnUR
When Levin mowed Mashkin Hill. Mashkin Hill. Louis Simpson. SaC
When liberty is headlong girl. Liberty. Archibald MacLeish. GOA
When Life has borne its harvest from my heart. A Prayer in Late Autumn. Violet Alleyn Storey. TrPWD
When life hath run its largest round. Daniel Webster. Oliver Wendell Holmes. PAH
When life is quite through with. E. E. Cummings. CrMA
When like a bud my Julia blows. To Julia under Lock and Key. Sir Owen Seaman. BXAP; FaBoPa
When, like a Running Grave. Dylan Thomas. OAEL-2
When like the early rose. Eileen [*or* Aileen] Aroon. Gerald Griffin. AnIV; GoBC; HBV-1; OnYI
When like the rising day. Gerald Griffin. *Fr.* Eileen Aroon. OBEV

When like wistaria against this wall. A Weightless Element. Gottfried Benn, *tr. by* Christopher Middleton. PoPl
When Lilacs Last in the Dooryard Bloom'd. Walt Whitman. *Fr.* Memories of President Lincoln. AmPP; AP; AWP; BiP; CABA; FaBoEn, *abr.*; FPL; HAP; HBV-2; LiTA; LoBV; MasP; MoAmPo; NIP; NOBA; NoP; OxBA; PAI; PAL; PoEL-5; PoRA; PPoe; PPP; SeCeV; TAP; TreF; TrGrPo; ViBoPo
Sels.
Carol of Death, The. DL
("Come lovely and soothing death.") SCV
(Death Carol.) WHA
"In the swamp in secluded recesses." RFM
"When lilacs last in the dooryard bloom'd," 24 *ll.* OFD
When Lil's Husband Got Demobbed, I Said. T. S. Eliot. *Fr.* The Waste Land. NAs
When Lion sends his roaring forth. The Lion. Mary Howitt. FaPON
When little boys grow [*or* grown] patient at last, weary. Death of Little Boys. Allen Tate. LiTA; MoAB; MP
When little boys with merry noise. Reinforcements. Thomas Toke Lynch. OBVV
When little Fred/ Was called to bed Mother Goose. HBV-1; HBVY
When little heads weary have gone to their bed. The Plumpuppets. Christopher Morley. FaPON; RHPC; TiPo
When little John Hardy was four years old. John Hardy. *Unknown.* ViBoFo
When little people go abroad, wherever they may roam. To Henrietta, on Her Departure for Calais. Thomas Hood. OxBChV
When little Snow White's mother died. Snow White and the Seven Dwarfs. Roald Dahl. DFT
When London Calls. Victor Daley. CBAP
When Londons fatal bills were blown abroad. Marlburyes Fate. Benjamin Tompson. SCAP
When, long sequester'd from his throne. William Cowper. *Fr.* On the Queen's Visit to London, the Night of the Seventeenth of March, 1789. PeD
When longer yet dank death had wormed. Thomas Hardy. *Fr.* The Abbey Mason. PeD
When, looking on the present face of things. October 1803. Wordsworth. EnRP
When, loosened from winter's bonds. Princess Nukada, *tr. fr. Japanese.* PBWP
When lordly Saturn in a sable robe. Eurymachus's Fancy. Robert Greene. *Fr.* Francesco's Fortunes. OBSC
When Louis came home to the flat. Meet Me in St. Louis, Louis. Andrew B. Sterling. FSN; FSW; OBAL; TreFT
When love/ Had strove. Love. Joseph Beaumont. OBS
When Love arose in heart and deed. The Flowers. William Brighty Rands. OBVV
When love at first did move. Song. Ben Jonson. *Fr.* The Masque of Beauty. GoBC
When Love Comes Knocking. William Henry Gardner. AA
When Love ensnares my mind unbidden. Composition in Late Spring. Irving Layton. PeCV
When love in the faint heart trembles. Song of Eros. George Edward Woodberry. *Fr.* Agathon. AA; HBV-1
When love is a shimmering curtain. On Diverse Deviations. Maya Angelou. BlSi
When Love Meets Love. Thomas Edward Brown. OBVV; PeD; UnPo
When love on time and measure makes his ground. False Love [*or* Song]. *At. to* John Lilliat. ElL; OBSC
When love, our great immortal. The Rose of Stars. George Edward Woodberry. Wild Eden, IX. AA; HBV-1
When love with unconfinèd wings. To Althea, from Prison. Richard Lovelace. AnAnS-2; AWP; BiP; BLPA; CABA; CaPo; CavP; FaBoBe; FaBoEn; FPL; GBL; GTBS; GTBS-P; HAP; HBV-1; HeIP; InPS; JCP; LiTB; LoBV; MeLP; MePo; NOBE; NoP; OAEP; OBEV; OBS; PoPle; PoRA; SeCeV; SeCP; SeCV-1; SoSe; TEP; TreF; TrGrPo; ViBoPo; WHA
When Lovely Woman ("When lovely woman wants a favor"). Phoebe Cary. FaBoBe; HBV-1; TreFS
When lovely woman, prone to folly. Song. *Unknown.* FaBoPa
"When Lovely Woman Stoops to Folly." Mary Demetriadis. FaBoPa
When Lovely Woman Stoops to Folly. Goldsmith. *See* Song: "When lovely woman stoops to folly."
When love's brief dream is done. Remember. Georgia Douglas Johnson. PoNe
When lyart leaves bestrow the yird. The Jolly Beggars; a Cantata [*or* Love and Liberty]. Burns. EnRP; LAuP; NOEC; OAEP; PoEL-4
When Magritte died. Homage to René Magritte. George Melly. EAS
When Mahalia Sings. Quandra Prettyman. IDB; PoBA
When maidens are young, and in their spring. Song. Aphra Behn. *Fr.* The Emperor of the Moon. FF
When maidens such as Hester die. Hester. Charles Lamb. EnRP; GTBS; GTBS-P; HBV-2; LoBV; OBEV; OBRV
When Malindy Sings. Paul Laurence Dunbar. PoBA; PoNe
When Mama lay dying. Earth Changes. Kent Shire. AMV-80
When man and woman die, as poets sung. The Difference. Benjamin Franklin. WhC
When man has conquered space. Earth's Bondman. Betty Page Dabney. GoYe
When Man rose up out of the red mountains. The Return of Eve. G. K. Chesterton. ISi
When man, the pathfinder. Helpmate. Henry Chapin. FAZ
When man walketh moon. T. Griffiths. BXAP
When many years we'd been apart. Reminiscence. Wallace Irwin. FiBHP; NOBL
When Mary came to Bethlehem. Mary of Bethlehem. Mary King. ISi
When Mary Goes Walking. Patrick R. Chalmers. HBVY
When May bedecks the naked trees. The Maryland Yellow-Throat. Henry van Dyke. HBV-1
When May has come, and all around. The Archer. Clinton Scollard. FaPON
When May is here, and every morn. Fairy Music. Francis Ledwidge. YeAr
When May is in his prime, then may each heart rejoice. May. Richard Edwards. OBSC
When memory's fabled daughter. Notes for a History of Poetry. David Daiches. PoA
When men a dangerous disease did 'scape. To Doctor Empiric[k]. Ben Jonson. DBV; FaBoEE; NoP; SeCP
When men are old, and their friends die. Praematuri. Margaret Postgate Cole. SUMH
When men beeth meriest at her mele. Think on Yesterday. *Unknown.* OxBM
When men discovered freedom first. The Ash and the Oak. Louis Simpson. ConAP; NePoAm
When men must labor that the wheels may grind. History of the Modern World. Stanton A. Coblentz. PGD
When men shall find thy flow'r [*or* flower], thy glory, pass. *Fr.* To Delia. Samuel Daniel. ElL; HBV-1; NOBE; NoP; OBEV; OBSC; TrGrPo
When men were all asleep the snow came flying. London Snow. Robert Bridges. BoNaP; BrPo; CH; ChTr; CMoP; CoBMV; EBEV; EBVV; FaBoPP; GTBS-P; LiTB; LiTM; LoBV; MoAB; MoBrPo; NBM; NoAM; NOBE; OAEL-2; OBNC; OxBTC; PoEL-5; SeCePo; SeCeV; TrGrPo; VLP; WiR
When midnight comes a host of dogs and men. Badger. John Clare. EnRP; HAP; LiSp; LiTB; NBM; NCEP; NoP; NU; OAEL-2; PAI; PoEL-4; PrIm; VLP; WeW; WiR
When mighty roast beef was the Englishman's food. A Song in Praise of Old English Roast Beef. Richard Leveridge. OBEC
When mighty rost beef was the Englishman's food. The Roast Beef of Old England. Henry Fielding. *Fr.* Don Quixote in England. OBEC
When mild Favonius breathes, with warbling throat. Hoc Cygno Vinces. Henry Hawkins. ACP
When milder autumn summer's heat succeeds. Field Sports. Pope. *Fr.* Windsor Forest. OBEC; PBBP; SeCePo
When milkweed blows in the pasture. Horse-Chestnut Time. Kaye Starbird. PDV
When mine eynen misteth. All Too Late. *Unknown.* OAEL-1
When mine hour is come. When. "Æ." OnYI
When Miriam Tazewell heard the tempest bursting. Miriam Tazewell. John Crowe Ransom. TW
When Mrs. Gorm (Aunt Eloise). Opportunity. Harry Graham. DTC; FaBoCo
When Mrs. Taflan Gruffyd Lewis left Dai's flat. What about You? Edward Pygge. BXAP; FaBoPa
When moiling seems at cease. "According to the Mighty Working." Thomas Hardy. CMoP
When Molly Smiles. *Unknown.* HBV-1
When 'mongst the youths you lately came. Epigram. *Unknown, tr. by* Sydney Oswald. PeHV
When Monk laid it down. Two Handfuls of *Waka* for Thelonious Sphere Monk (d. Feb. 1982). Walter Lew. BrSi
When Monmouth the chaste read those impudent lines. An Excellent New Ballad Giving a True Account of the Birth and Conception of a Late Famous Poem Called the Female Nine. Charles Sackville. APAS
"When moonlight/ Near midnight." The Fairies in New Ross. *Unknown.* OnYI
When Moonlike ore the Hazure Seas. Thackeray. InMe; NA; WhC
When Morgan crossed the Murray to Peechelba and doom. Morgan. Edward Harrington. PoAu-1
When morning came. The Brother. Peter Everwine. FYAP; NNaP
When Moses an' his soldiers, f'om Egypt's lan' did flee. He's Jus' de Same Today. *Unknown.* BoAN-1

When Moses and his people. Just the Same Today. *Unknown.* BLRP; WBLP
When Moses in Horeb struck the rock. On Certain Wits. Howard Nemerov. OxBC
When Moses, musing in the desert, found. The Burning Bush. Norman Nicholson. EaLo; EBCP; NeBP; SeCePo
When Moses was as old as God. Moses and Joshua. Else Lasker-Schüler, *tr. by* Joachim Neugroschel. VWA
When Mosquitoes Make a Meal. Else Holmelund Minarik. RHPC
When mother comes each morning. Mother. Rose Fyleman. SiSoSe
When Mother Reads Aloud. *Unknown.* FaPON
When Mother takes me calling. The Extraordinary Dog. Nancy Byrd Turner. TiPo
When Mother takes the Fairy Book. The Fairy Book. Abbie Farwell Brown. HBV-1; HBVY
When mothers weep and fathers richly proud. The Confirmation. Karl Shapiro. ErPo
When mountain rocks and leafy trees. Nature's Lineaments. Robert Graves. FaBoTw
When mountains crumble and rivers all run dry. The Line of Beauty. Edward Dowden. OnYI
When Mr. Apollinax visited the United States. Mr. Apollinax. T. S. Eliot. PoA
When music, heav'nly maid, was young. The Passions, an Ode for [*or* to] Music. William Collins. GoTL; GTBS; GTBS-P; HBV-2; LAuP; LoBV; OBEC
When my arms wrap you round I press. He [*or* Michael Robartes] Remembers Forgotten Beauty. W. B. Yeats. BrPo; CTC; LLLT
When my Aunt Leratiny now. Make Me Hear You. Reginald Gibbons. MAYP
When my Beloved appears. Ibn al-Arabi, *tr. fr. Arabic.* ILwL
When My Beloved Sleeping Lies. Irene Rutherford McLeod. HBV-1
When my birthday was coming. Little Brother's Secret. Katherine Mansfield. FaPON; NAs; TiPo
When my blood flows calm as a purling river. Communism. Ella Wheeler Wilcox. PeD
When my brother Tommy. Two in Bed. Abram Bunn Ross. FaPON; NTCP; SoPo; TiPo
When my devotions could not pierce. Denial [*or* Deniall]. George Herbert. AnAnS-1; FaBoEn; JCP; MePo; NOBE; NoP; OAEL-1; PoEL-2
When My Dog Died. Freya Littledale. NTCP
When my father died. Between Here and Illinois. Ralph Pomeroy. Psk
When my father had been dead a week. White Apples. Donald Hall. TAP
When my father spoke in his natural voice. Before the Breaking. Lee Pennington. AMV-81
When my gloomy hour comes to me. Alexander McLachlan. *Fr.* Woman. CaP
When My Grandmother Died. Sam Cornish. Psk
When my grandmother left the races with Mr. Hughes. Mr. Hughes. David Campbell. CBAP
When my grave is broke up again[e]. The Relic [*or* The Relique]. John Donne. AnAnS-1; CABA; EIL; EnRePo; GBL; HAP; HeIP; LiTB; LoBV; MeLP; MePo; NOBE; NoP; OAEL-1; OAEP; OBS; PoEL-2; PoPle; PPP; SeCeV; SeCP; SeCV-1; WHA
When my house is full of flowers the brightness. Ann's House. Dick Lourie. DFF
When my husband. Ten Years and More. Miriam Waddington. NOBC
When my Italian son. In Front of a Poster of Garibaldi. Stanley Moss. DiL
When my last song is sung and I am dead. Requiem. Theodore Maynard. GoBC
When my life has enough of love, and my spirit enough of mirth. A Wanderer's Litany. Arthur Stringer. WGRP
When my love becomes/ All-powerful. Ono no Komachi, *tr. fr. Japanese by* Geoffrey Bownas *and* Anthony Thwaite. PBWP
When my love swear[e]s that she is made of truth. Sonnets, CXXXVIII. Shakespeare. AWP; BiP; CABA; EBEV; NoP; OAEL-1; OAEP; PAI; PoEL-2; PPP; SoSe; TEP; TrGrPo; ViBoPo
When my love was away. Robert Bridges. BrPo
When my mother died I was very young. The Chimney Sweeper. Blake. *Fr.* Songs of Innocence. CH; EnRP; FF; HeIP; InPK; LAuP; NOEC; OAEL-2; OxBChV; PAI; PPoe; PPP; SaC; SoSe; TEP
When My Ship Comes In. Robert J. Burdett. FaFP
When my spring unbound comes o'er us like a flood. In April. Ethelwyn Wetherald. CaP
When My Uncle Willie Saw. Carole Freeman. NMM
When my young brother was killed. War. Joseph Langland. FF; MP; NePoEA; PoCh
When Narcissus died the pool of his pleasure changed. The Disciple. Oscar Wilde. OAEL-2
When Nature bids us leave to live, 'tis late. To William Roe. Ben Jonson. SeCV-1
When Nature dreamt of making bores. Epigram: On Sir Roger Phillimore. *Unknown.* FaBoCo
When Nature had made all her birds. The Bobolinks. Christopher Pearse Cranch. AA; GN
When Nature Hath Betrayed the Heart That Loved Her. Sophie Jewett. AA
When Nature heard men thought her old. The Mistress. Sir William Davenant. JCP
When nature made her chief work, Stella's eyes. Astrophel and Stella, VII. Sir Philip Sidney. CABA; NIP; SiPS
When nature once in lustful hot undress. Giantess. Baudelaire, *tr. by* Karl Shapiro. ErPo
When nature's God for our offenses died. A Stanza Put on Westminster Hall Gate. *Unknown.* APAS
When Neptune from his billows London spied. Of London Bridge, and the Stupendous Sight, and Structure Thereof. James Howell. ChTr; FaBoPP
When nettles in winter bring forth roses red. Trust in Women. *Unknown.* NA
When news came that your mother'd. Kin. Michael Harper. LCAP
When next we met, she bade me turn. Apostasy. Aus of Kuraiza, *tr. by* Hartwig Hirschfeld. TrJP
When night drifts along the streets of the city. Solitaire. Amy Lowell. MoAmPo
When night falls. Japan That Sank under the Sea. Satoru Sato. PoPl
When night first bids the twinkling stars appear. London at Night. John Gay. *Fr.* Trivia; or, The Art of Walking the Streets of London. FaBoPP
When night is almost done. Emily Dickinson. TRV
When night is come, and all around is still. Safe in His Keeping. Edgar Cooper Mason. BLRP
When night plows the meadows of darkness. Lonely Are the Fields of Sleep. Mary Newton Baldwin. GoYe
When night shadows slipped across the plain, I saw a man. A Nation Wrapped in Stone. Roberta Hill. BoWoP; CDW
When night stirred at sea. The Planter's Daughter. Austin Clarke. CIP; OxBI; OxBTC
When no one listens. Stranger. Thomas Merton. EaLo
When Noah, perceiving 'twas time to embark. The Dog's Cold Nose. Arthur Guiterman. GDP; TiPo
When Nobody Prays. Merl A. Clapper. STF
When None Shall Rail. David Lewis. OBEC
When noon is warm, old Pensioners. Out of Soundings. Padraic Fallon. NeIP
When North first began. Lord North's Recantation. *Unknown.* PAH
When nothing is happening. How Everything Happens. May Swenson. HAP; RFM
When nothing whereon to lean remains. The Time to Trust. *Unknown.* BLRP
When November's night comes down. Hearth Song. Robert Underwood Johnson. YeAr
When now the end of agony was come. Apostrophe to Death. Caelius Sedulius, *tr. by* George Sigerson. *Fr.* Carmen Paschale. OnYI
When Oats Were Reaped. Thomas Hardy. OxBTC
When ocean-clouds over inland hills. Misgivings. Herman Melville. AP; NePA; NOBA; OxBA
When October gets too chilly. In the Yellow Light of Brooklyn. Al Lee. NYP
When o'er the hill the eastern star. My Ain Kind Dearie, O [*or* The Lea Rig]. Burns. BSV; GoTS
When, o'er the silent seas alone. The Meeting of the Ships. Thomas Moore. EtS
When o'er the wold the heedless lamb. Song. Thomas Holcroft. NOEC
When Ogden his prosaic verse. On Dr. Samuel Ogden. R. P. Arden. FaBoCo
When Oisin came back to Ireland. Paul Muldoon. *Fr.* Armageddon, Armageddon. CIP
When Ol' Sis' Judy Pray. James Edwin Campbell. BANP
When old cars get retired, they go to Maine. Maine. Philip Booth. AmFN
When old corruption first begun. Quid the Cynic's Song. Blake. *Fr.* An Island in the Moon. FaBoNo
When old crones wandered in the woods. Child Naming Flowers. Robert Hass. MAYP; NPGG
When old heads felt to-day. On Hearing a Broadcast of Ceremonies in Connection with Conferring of Cardinals' Hats. Denis Wrafter. NeIP
When Old John Bax drove the mail to Coonabarabran. Old John Bax. Charles H. Souter. PoAu-1
When old philosophers wrote the world's birth. A Panegyric on the Author of "Absalom and Achitophel." *Unknown.* APAS
When 'Omer Smote 'Is Bloomin' Lyre. Kipling. Par
When, on a yellowing hill, a tree. Patterns. Ruth Setterberg. AMV-81

When on Euphrates' banks we sate. Bible, *O.T., paraphrased by* Sir John Denham. Psalms, CXXXVII. OAEL-1
When on my bed the moonlight falls. In Memoriam A. H. H., LXVII. Tennyson. LoBV; NoP; SeCePo; SeCeV
When on my day of life the night is falling. At Last [*or* To Paths Unknown]. Whittier. AP; TreFS; TrPWD; TRV; WGRP
When on my sick bed I languish. A Thought of Death. Thomas Flatman. OBS
When on my soul in nakedness. The Quiet Pilgrim. Edith M. Thomas. AA
When on my time of living I reflect. My Thirty Years. Juan Fransico Manzano, *tr. by* Oliver Cobarn *and* Ursula Lehrburger. TTY
When, on our casual way. The Shakespearean Bear. Arthur Guiterman. CenHV; EvOK
When, on Ramillies' bloody field. Clare's Dragoons. Thomas Osborne Davis. OnYI
When on some balmy-breathing night of spring. The Glow-Worm. Charlotte Smith. FM
When on the barn's thatch'd roof is seen. Signs of Christmas. Edwin Lees. OHIP
When, on the bearing mother, death's. Childbirth. Ted Hughes. NAs
When on the high bluff discovering. From the North Saskatchewan. Eli Mandel. NOBC
When once a chic busts through a egg. Gettin' Born. Anthony Euwer. PoPl; WhC
When once I knew the Lord. Hymn of Sivaite Puritans. *Unknown.* WGRP
When once I rose at morning. Lament for the Woodlands. *Unknown, tr. by* Frank O'Connor. KiLC
When once the scourging prophet, with his cry. The Disused Temple. Norman Cameron. ChMP; OxBS; OxBTC
When once the sun sinks in the west. Evening Primrose. John Clare. CH; TrGrPo
When one calls on the Quinks they always say. The Quinks. Don Marquis. *Fr.* Savage Portraits. DBV; HBMV; YaD
When one climber fell to his doom, I also fell. The Climbing Rope. Alice V. Stuart. PoSH
When One Loves Tensely. Don Marquis. FiBHP
When one of those lilies-to-be-considered was looked at. Consider the Lilies. Dorothy Donnelly. HoAn
When one or other rambles. Francis Daniel Pastorius. SCAP
When one's been drunk, the best relief I know. Hangover Cure. Amphis. FaBoUs
When other fair ones [*or* ladies] to the shades [*or* groves] go down. On Certain Ladies [*or* Epigram]. Pope. FaBoCo; FaBoEE; PoEL-3
When Other Lips and Other Hearts. Alfred Bunn. *Fr.* The Bohemian Girl. TreF
When others mustered out in '46, you soldiered. The Sergeant. Don Johnson. MAYP
When others run to windows or out of doors. Part for the Whole. Robert Francis. PoA
When our babe he goeth walking in his garden. Garden and Cradle. Eugene Field. AA
When our brother Fire was having his dog's day. Brother Fire. Louis MacNeice. MoAB; NoAM; NOBE; OAEP; WaaP
When our brothers. Postcard from London, 23. 10. 1972. Andrew Salkey. FAZ
When our children cried in the shadow of the gallows. Nathan Alterman, *tr. by* Simon Halkin. *Fr.* From All Peoples. TrJP
When our dean took a pious young spinster. Limerick. Victor Gray. NOBL
When our ducks waddle to the pond. The Ducks. Alice Wilkins. TiPo
When Our Earthly Sun Is Setting, *with music.* Edwin H. Nevin. AH
When Our Lady sings the heavens. Madonna's Lullaby. Saint Alphonsus Liguori, *tr. by* James J. Galvin. ISi
When our rude and unfashion'd words, that long. To a Lady Who Did Sing Excellently. Lord Herbert of Cherbury. AnAnS-2; OBS; SeCP
When our tears are dry on the shore. Rediscovery. George Awoonor-Williams. TTY
When our two souls stand up erect and strong. Sonnets from the Portuguese, XXII. Elizabeth Barrett Browning. BoWoP; HBV-1; NOBE; OAEP; OBEV; OBVV; SBG; TreFT; TrGrPo; ViBoPo; VLP; WHA; WPE
When out at Shellbrook, round by stile and tree. Shellbrook. William Barnes. OBNC; VLP
When, over-arched by gorgeous night. The Unknown God. Sir William Watson. WGRP
When over the flowery, sharp pasture's. Flowers by the Sea. William Carlos Williams. CMoP; GoJo; MoAB; MoAmPo; NoAM; SeCeV; TAP
When pails empty the last brightness. O You among Women. F. R. Higgins. BIrV
When paper bags wallow like demons. Deliver Me, O Lord, from My Daily Bread. Jeanne Murray Walker. AMV-80
When paper snaps in machines. The Boss Machine-Tender after Losing a Son. Paul Corrigan. AMV-81
When Parnell's Irish in the House. Wilfred Owen's Photographs. Ted Hughes. OxBC
When passion makes me discontent. Organ Solo. Knute Skinner. GP
When passion's trance is overpast. To ———. Shelley. EnRP
When pavements were blown up, exposing nerves. Epilogue to a Human Drama. Stephen Spender. CMoP
When pensive on that portraiture I gaze. Sonnet on a Family Picture. Thomas Edwards. NOEC; OBEC
When people call this beast to mind. The Elephant. Hilaire Belloc. SoPo; TiPo
When people come with big muddy feet. Go Throw Them Out. Moishe Leib Halpern, *tr. by* Ruth Whitman. VWA
When people's ill they come to I. On Dr. Isaac Letsome [*or* Self-composed Epitaph on a Doctor by the Name of I. Letsome *or* On Dr. Lettsom, by Himself *or* The Candid Physician]. *Unknown.* FaBoCo; PV; TreFT; WhC
When periwigs came first in wear. The Bald Cavalier. *Unknown.* OxBChV
When Pershing's men go marching into Picardy. Marching Song. Dana Burnet. PAH
When Phoebe form'd a wanton smile. Sonnet. William Collins. EnLoPo
When Phoebus had melted the sickles of ice. Robin Hood and the Ranger. *Unknown.* ESPB
When Phoebus in the rainy cloud. Welcome Eild. *Unknown.* GoTS
When Phoebus lifts his head out of the winter's wave. Michael Drayton. *Fr.* Polyolbion: The Thirteenth Song. OBS; PBBP
When Piecrust first began to reign. A Fancy. *Unknown.* FaBoNo
When pleasing heat, and fragrant blooms inspire. William Diaper, *after the Greek of* Oppian. *Fr.* Halieutica. BXAP; PeD
When poetry walked the live, spring wood. Kingcups. Sacheverell Sitwell. MoBrPo
When poets print their works, the scribbling crew. To My Ingenious and Worthy Friend William Lowndes, Esq. John Gay. OBSV
When poets wrote and painters drew. Protogenes and Apelles. Matthew Prior. GoTL
When Polly lived back in the old deep woods. Stranger. Elizabeth Madox Roberts. MoAmPo
When Pontius wished an edict might be passed. Epigram. Matthew Prior. DBV
When Poor Mary Came Wandering Home, *with music.* *Unknown.* AS
When poppies in the garden bleed. The End of Summer. Edna St. Vincent Millay. BoNaP
When President John Quincy. John Quincy Adams. Rosemary *and* Stephen Vincent Benét. OBCA
When priests are more in word than matter. Shakespeare. *Fr.* King Lear, III, ii. ViBoPo
When primroses are out in Spring. Days Too Short. W. H. Davies. MoBrPo
When Psyche's friend becomes her lover. Friend and Lover. "Madeline Bridges." AA; HBV-1
When quacks with pills political would dope us. Canopus. Bert Leston Taylor. FiBHP; HBMV; InMe; NOBL; WhC
When quiet in my room I sit. My Companion. Charles Wesley. STF
When raging [*or* ragyng] love with extreme pain [*or* payne]. Consolation. Earl of Surrey. AAS; EBEV; EnLoPo; EnRePo; NOBE; OBSC; SiPS; TEP
When Reason's ray shines over all. On the Triumph of Rationalism. Alfred Ainger. FaBoCo
When Reedisdale and Wise William. Redesdale and Wise William. *Unknown.* ESPB
When Reuben Pantier ran away and threw me. Dora Williams. Edgar Lee Masters. *Fr.* Spoon River Anthology. HAP
When rites and melodies begin. The Proof [*or* The Trial]. W. H. Auden. NePA; OAEL-2
When roaring gloom surged inward and you cried. To His Dead Body. Siegfried Sassoon. NoAM
When Robin Hood, and his merry men all. Robin Hood and the Valiant Knight. *Unknown.* ESPB
When Robin Hood and Little John. Robin Hood's Death. *Unknown.* ESPB; FaBoBa; OBET; TrGrPo; ViBoFo
When Robin Hood in the green-wood livd. Robin Hood Rescuing Will Stutly. *Unknown.* ESPB
When Robin Hood was about eighteen [*or* twenty] years old. Robin Hood and Little John. *Unknown.* AmFP; ESPB; ViBoFo
When rosy plumelets tuft the larch. In Memoriam A. H. H., XCI. Tennyson. FaBoEn; OBNC; ViBoPo
When Ruth was left half desolate. Ruth; or, The Influences of Nature. Wordsworth. ChER; EnRP; GTBS; GTBS-P; PoEL-4

When ruthful time the South's memorial places. The Stricken South to the North. Paul Hamilton Hayne. PAH
When Sadness Fills a Journey. John Waller. NeBP
When sailors snug in harbor sit. Home Is the Sailor. Phyllis McGinley. DBV
When Sam goes back in memory. Sam. Walter de la Mare. FaBV; MoAB; MoBrPo; OnMSP; TiPo
When sane men gather in to talk of Love. Irene Rutherford McLeod. *Fr.* Sonnets. HBMV
When Sarah Pierrepont let her spirit rage. Address to the Scholars of New England. John Crowe Ransom. GOA; LiTM; NePA
When school is out, we love to follow. Sniff. Frances Frost. SiSoSe; TiPo
When science starts to be interpretive. Self-Protection. D. H. Lawrence. NoP
When Senses Fled. John Woods. CoPo
When Serpents Bargain for the Right to Squirm. E. E. Cummings. InPK; MP; PrIm; SoSe; TwCP
When seven years were come and gane. Sweet William's Ghost. *Unknown.* ESPB
When seyd was al this miracle, every man. Prologue to Sir Thopas. Chaucer. *Fr.* The Canterbury Tales. Par
When Shakespeare, Jonson, Fletcher ruled the stage. In Defense of Satire. Sir Carr Scroope. APAS
When Shakespeare leads the mind a dance. The Critic's Rules. Robert Lloyd. *Fr.* Shakespeare; an Epistle to David Garrick, Esq. OBEC
When shall I master this anxiety. August, Graf von Platen. Sonnets to Karl Theodore German, I. PeHV
When shall I see the half-moon sink again. End of Another Home Holiday. D. H. Lawrence. DTC; EBEV; FaBoMo; MoVE
When Shall My Pilgrimage, Jesus My Saviour, Be Ended? *with music. At. to* Andrew Rudman, *tr. fr. Swedish by* Ernest Edwin Ryden. AH
When shall the Island Queen of Ocean lay. The Bower of Peace. Robert Southey. *Fr.* Ode Written during the War with America, 1814. PAH
When Shall We All Meet Again? *with music. Unknown.* AH
When shall we be married. *Unknown.* OxNR
When shall we learn, what should be clear as day. Canzone. W. H. Auden. LiTA; MoVE
When Shall We See Thy Like Again? Mary Wingate. *See* Washington.
When shaven crown, and hallow'd girdle's power. Satyr III. John Oldham. *Fr.* Satyrs upon the Jesuits. SeCV-2
When shawes beene sheene, and shrads [*or* shradds] fyll [*or* full] fayre. Robin Hood and Guy of Gisborne. *Unknown.* ESPB; OAEP
When She a Maiden Slim. Maurice Hewlett. OHIP
When she came suddenly in. The Door. Robert Graves. LiTB
When she cannot be sure. Woman Alone. Denise Levertov. WPOW
When she carries food to the table and stoops down. Part of Plenty. Bernard Spencer. ErPo; GBL; LiTB; LiTM
When She Comes Home. James Whitcomb Riley. AA; BLPL; FaBoBe; HBV-1
When she fed the/ child. The Feeding. Joel Oppenheimer. NeAP
When she gives a "psychic reading." Crepe de Chine. Tennessee Williams. NYBP
When she opened her eyes the fields were gone into houses. For the Field. Eric Chock. BrSi
When she opens her eye this morning. For the Fourth Birthday of My Daughter. George Barker. NAs
When She Plays upon the Harp or Lute. Moses ibn Ezra, *tr. fr. Hebrew by* Solomon Solis-Cohen. TrJP
When she put her hand on me. The First Time. John Newlove. NeAC
When she rises in the morning. Gloire de Dijon. D. H. Lawrence. BrPo; CMoP; ELP; EnLoPo; ErPo; GBL; NoAM; OAEP; PAI
When she sleeps, her soul, I know. Doubts. Rupert Brooke. CH
When she still used words, my mother told. My Mother's Childhood. Barry Spacks. GP
When she walks by—astonishing! The Girl in the Foreign Movie. Patricia Goedicke. FAZ
When she was found. Visiting the Dead. Ciaran Carson. CIP
When she was in her garden. Ann and the Fairy Song. Walter de la Mare. *Fr.* A Child's Day. FaBV
When she was little. Poem for Aretha. Nikki Giovanni. PoBA
When Silence Divests Me. Henry Birnbaum. GoYe
When silver Diane full of beames bright. A Starscape. John Bellenden. ACP
When silver snow decks Susan's clothes. Blind-Man's Buff. Blake. WiR
When, sin-stricken, burdened, and weary. "My Grace Is Sufficient for Thee." *Unknown.* BLRP
When singing songs of scariness. The Worst. Shel Silverstein. WSC
When Sir Beelzebub. Edith Sitwell. *See* Sir Beelzebub.
When Sir Joshua Reynolds died. Sir Joshua Reynolds. Blake. ELU; FaBoCo; FaBoEE; FiBHP; OxBoLi; TW
When Sisyphus was pushing the stone up the mountain. Sisyphus. Josephine Miles. NYBP
When ski-ing in the Engadine. Patience. Harry Graham. FiBHP; MoShBr; WhC
When Skylab fell. How the Sky Begins to Fall. Joan Colby. AMV-81
When Slavery Seems Sweet. Ed Bullins. NBP
When sleep over takes me. All Night! Leon Baker. LFAC
When Sleeping Beauty wakes up. The Archaeology of a Marriage. Maxine W. Kumin. DFT
When slumbering in my convict cell my childhood days I see. The Convict. *Unknown.* CoSo
When sly Jemmy Twitcher had smugged up his face. The Candidate. Thomas Gray. PPP
When smoke stood up from Ludlow. The Blackbird. A. E. Housman. A Shropshire Lad, VII. HBV-1; MoBrPo
When snow like sheep lay in the fold. In Memory of Jane Frazer [*or* Fraser]. Geoffrey Hill. NePoEA; NoAM; OxBTC
When snow melts, green mountains slope. Summit Lake. Mark Thalman. AMV-81
When snow-balls pack on the horses' hoofs. Sugar Weather. Peter McArthur. CaP
When soft September brings again. Pont-y-Wern. Arthur Hugh Clough. *Fr.* Ambarvalia. FaBoPP
When Sol did cast no light. The [Valiant] Seaman's Happy Return [to His Love]. *Unknown.* ChTr; GBP
When Sol had loosed his weary teams. Juggy's Christening. *Unknown.* NOEC
When Solomon was reigning in his glory. Solomon and the Bees. John Godfrey Saxe. GN
When some beloved voice that was to you. Substitution. Elizabeth Barrett Browning. WGRP
When some beloveds, 'neath whose eyelids lay. Bereavement. Elizabeth Barrett Browning. WPE
When some boys. Some Boys. Chuck Ortleb. PeHV
When some great sorrow, like a mighty river. This, Too, Shall [*or* Will] Pass Away. Lanta Wilson Smith. BLPA; STF
When some grim sorceress, whose skill. To Helen. Winthrop Mackworth Praed. LoBV
When some proud son of man returns to earth. Epitaph to a Dog [*or* Inscription on the Monument of a Newfoundland Dog]. Byron. GDP; TEP
When someone fell. At the Roadside. John Knoepfle. FAZ
When someone hangs up, having said. The Business Life. David Ignatow. NNaP; TW
When Something Happens. James A. Randall, Jr. BPo
When sommer toke in hand the winter to assail. *See* When summer took in hand the winter to assail.
When souls that have put off their mortal gear. Recognition. John White Chadwick. AA
When Spanky goes. Basketball. Nikki Giovanni. RHPC
When sparrows build, and the leaves break forth. Song of the Old Love. Jean Ingelow. Supper at the Mill. HBV-1
When sparrows build churches and steeples high. *Unknown. Fr.* Trust in Women.
When Spoon River became a ganglion. Marx the Sign Painter. Edgar Lee Masters. *Fr.* The New Spoon River. NoAM; TAP
When sporgles spanned the floreate mead. Uffia. Harriet R. White. NA
When spring begins, the maids in flocks. Spring. Edith Sitwell. OAEP
When spring came. *Unknown, tr. fr. Tlingit Indian.* RFM
When spring came tiptoe up the hill. The Dress of Spring. May Justus. YeAr
When spring comes back to England. The World's May-Queen. Alfred Noyes. HBV-1; OBVV
When spring comes laughing. A Song of the Four Seasons. Austin Dobson. HBV-1
When spring is in the fields that stained your wing. To a Linnet in a Cage. Francis Ledwidge. OnYI; RoGo
When stags do rut in the Plym. Alan Gibson. BXAP
When stars are in the quiet skies. Night and Love. Sir Edward Bulwer-Lytton. *Fr.* Ernest Maltravers. HBV-1
When Stars Are Shrouded. "I. T." EIL
When stars pursue their solemn flight. Music in the Night. Harriet Prescott Spofford. AA
When stars ride in on the wings of dusk. Refuge. Lew Sarett. HBMV
When Statesmen gravely say "We must be realistic." W. H. Auden. FaBoCo; PV
When, staunchly entering port. The Beauty of the Ship. Walt Whitman. MOS
When stealthy age creeps on me unaware. A Litany for Old Age. Una W. Harsen. TrPWD
When Stella strikes the tuneful string. To Miss ——: On Her Playing upon the Harpsichord. Samuel Johnson. CABA
When stone-hewn storms knock against our cottage. Third and Fourth. Keidrych Rhys. NeBP

When storms arise. Hymn. Paul Laurence Dunbar. TrPWD; TRV
When storms blow loud, 'tis sweet to watch at ease. Suave Mari Magno. Lucretius, *tr. by* W. H. Mallock. *Fr.* De Rerum Natura. AWP
When storms go growling off to lonely places. The Whale and the *Essex.* A. M. Sullivan. EtS
When Structure Fails Rhyme Attempts to Come to the Rescue. William Carlos Williams. PP
When stubble-lands were greening, you came among the stooks. The Green Autumn Stubble. *Unknown, tr. by* Patrick Browne. OxBI; WTO
When suddenly he took, whom I had sought. The Disconnections. John Engels. WOLT
When Sue Wears Red. Langston Hughes. CNA; TTY
When summer calls. A Comfort Stop. Tony Beyer. OCNZ
When summer came, we locked up our lives and fled. The Gentle Snorer. Mona Van Duyn. NePA
When summer [*or* sommer] took [*or* toke] in hand the winter to assail. Love's Rebel. Earl of Surrey. AAS; OBSC; SiPS
When summer was approaching. First Love. *Unknown, tr. by* George F. Whicher. OLR
When summer's end is nighing. A. E. Housman. MoVE
When summer's in the city. The Ice-Cream Man. Rachel Field. FaPON; SiSoSe; SoPo
When Sun Came to Riverwoman. Leslie Silko. VoR
When Sun Doth Rise, *with music.* Roger Williams. AH
When sun, light-handed, sows this Indian water. Aubade: Lake Erie. Thomas Merton. NYBP
When sun the earth least shadow spares. The River Lynher. Richard Carew. *Fr.* Survey of Cornwall. FaBoPP
When sunset falls upon your day. Measure of Success. *Unknown.* STF
When sunset flows into golden glows. Star Song. Robert Underwood Johnson. HBV-1
When sunshine met the wave. In the Beginning. Harriet Monroe. AA
When supper time is almost come. Milking Time. Elizabeth Madox Roberts. FaPON; GoJo; OBCA; SUS
When Susanna Jones wears red. When Sue Wears Red. Langston Hughes. CNA; TTY
When Susan's work was done, she'd [*or* she would] sit. Old Susan. Walter de la Mare. CMoP; MoBrPo; TreFS
When swallows lay their eggs in snow. Fool's Song. Thomas Holcroft. NOEC
When Tadlow walks the streets the paviours cry. Tadlow. Abel Evans. FaBoCo
When tempest winnowed grain from bran. The Victor of Antietam. Herman Melville. PAH
When that Abe Lincoln was a boy. Prairie. K. N. Llewellyn. YeAr
When that day comes, whose evening sayes I'm gone. His Sailing from Julia. Robert Herrick. PoEL-3
When That I Was and a Little Tiny Boy. Shakespeare. *Fr.* Twelfth Night, V, i. CH; EBEV; EIL; EnRePo; FaBoCh; HBV-1; HeIP; LiTB; LoBV; NOBE; NoP; OAEL-1; OAEP; PoRA; PPoe; ViBoPo
(Feste's Song.) OBSC; OxBoLi
(Song.) FiP; PoEL-2
(Wind and the Rain, The.) WiR
When that my days were fewer. Middle Age. Rudolph Chambers Lehmann. HBV-1
When that old joke was new. Old Fashioned Fun. Thackeray. InMe
When that our English tongue. "That Did In Luve So Lively Write." Georgine M. Adams. InMe
When that rich Soule which to her heaven is gone. An Anatomy of the World; the First Anniversary. John Donne. AnAnS-1; MasP; SeCV-1
When that Seint George hadde sleyne ye draggon. Limerick. *Unknown.* NA
When that the chill Charocco blows. *See* Whenas the chill sirocco blows.
When that the Eternal deigned to look. Ballade of Illegal Ornaments. Hilaire Belloc. ACP
When the/ sun. August 2. Norman Jordan. PoBA
When the African Arts. At Home in Dakar. Margaret Danner. BlSi; FB
When the air is wine and the wind is free. Song of the Queen Bee. E. B. White. NYBP
When the *Alabama's* keel was laid. The *Alabama, vers.* I. *Unknown.* ShS
When the alcoholic passed the crucial point. Point of No Return. Robert Graves. BIrV
When the allegorical man came calling. The Inflatable Globe. Theodore Spencer. LiTA; NePA; WaP
When the Ambulance Came. Robert Morgan. Str
When the anchor's weigh'd and the ship's unmoored. Jack the Guinea Pig. *Unknown.* AmSS
When the Angels Are Exhausted. Yona Wallach, *tr. fr. Hebrew by* Leonore Gordon. VWA
When the angry passion gathering in my mother's face I see. The Patter of the Shingle. *Unknown.* BLPA
When the anxious hearts say "Where?" Missing. *Unknown.* WGRP
When the *Ark* and *Dove* within the glassy wave. The *Ark* and the *Dove.* Daniel Sargent. EtS
When the ash is before the oak. *Unknown.* FaBoUs
When the Assault Was Intended to the City. Milton. GTBS; GTBS-P; NoP; RoGo
(Sonnet: "Captain or colonel or knight in arms.") OAEL-1
When the Atlantic upsloped itself. Winter Tryst. Mark Van Doren. LiTA
When the autumn winds go wailing. Ungathered Love. Philip Bourke Marston. OBNC
When the badger glimmered away. The Badgers. Seamus Heaney. CIP
When the bare branch responds to leaf and light. Spain. Dorothy Livesay. NOBC
When the bat's on the wing and the bird's in the tree. The Starlighter. Arthur Guiterman. SiSoSe
When the bird flew from the Columbus hull. Jeremiad. Oscar Williams. LiTA
When the birds sang. *Unknown, tr. fr. Spanish by* Willis Barnstone. BoWoP
When the black. The Hours of a Bridge. W. S. Merwin. LCAP
When the black car came thundering from its pale. Proserpine at Enna. Ronald Bottrall. SeCePo
When the black herds of the rain were grazing. The Lost Heifer. Austin Clarke. BIrV; OxBI
When the blackbird in the spring. *See* As the blackbird in the spring.
When the blessed Saviour calls you. You Will Find a Joy in Service. Dorothy Conant Stroud. STF
When the bloated sun stands upon Black Mesa. Black Mesa. Ron Rogers. STE
When the bones walk out of me. Never. George Reavey. BIrV
When the boughs of the garden hang heavy with rain. Thunder in the Garden. William Morris. VLP
When the boy undressed. The Skull. Ian Young. NeAC
When the breath of twilight blows to flame the misty skies. By the Margin of the Great Deep. "Æ." HBMV; OBEV; OBVV
When the breeze from the bluebottle's blustering blim. To Marie. *Unknown.* NA
When the breeze of a joyful dawn blew free. Recollections of the Arabian Nights. Tennyson. VLP
When the British warrior queen. Boadicea; an Ode. William Cowper. BeLS; FaPo; FaPoR; HBV-2
When the bubble moon is young. June. Harrison Smith Morris. HBV-1
When the buffalo are all slaughtered. Poem after a Speech by Chief Seattle, 1855. Charles Brasher. AMV-81
When the burnt flesh is finally at rest. Annotations of Auschwitz. Peter Porter. NMP
When the Century Dragged. Robert Penn Warren. MoAmPo
When the child's forehead full of red torments. The Lice Seekers [*or* The Seekers of Lice]. Arthur Rimbaud. *Fr.* Illuminations. NAWM-2, *tr. by* Wallace Fowlie; SOTW, *tr. by* Kenneth Koch *and* George Gugy
When the chill Charoko blows. In Praise of Ale. *Unknown.* ViBoPo
When the Christ Child Came. Frederick E. Weatherly. OHIP
When the church seeks a pastor. Some Bird. *Unknown.* STF
When the city cast out the best. Ibycus. John Heath-Stubbs. PoCh
When the clatter of reckless thought. Woman in an Abandoned House. Michael Bily-Hurd. AMV-81
When the clock strikes five but it's only four. Wrimples. Jack Prelutsky. RHPC
When the clouds are upon the hills. *Unknown.* OxNR
When the clouds' swoln bosoms echo back the shouts. In Tenebris, II. Thomas Hardy. BrPo; CMoP; LiTM; NoAM; OxBTC; VLP
When the cold comes. Where? When? Which? Langston Hughes. BPo; NePoAm-2
When the completely charming. Bernard. Raymond Souster. POL
When the Cows Come Down to Drink. Allen Hoey. WOLT
When the crop is fair in the olive-yard. The Cocooning. Frédéric Mistral, *tr. by* Harriet Waters Preston. *Fr.* Mirèio. AWP; PoPl
When the curtain of night, 'tween the dark and the light. Whistling Boy. Nixon Waterman. PoLF
When the Curtains of Night Are Pinned Back. *See* I'll Remember You, Love, in My Prayers.
When the dark dawn humped off to die. A Little Girl on Her Way to School. James Wright. GLGT
When the dark-eyed lad, Columbus. Dark-eyed Lad Columbus. Nancy Byrd Turner. SiSoSe
When the dawn comes. *Unknown, tr. by* Arthur Waley. *Fr.* Kokin Shu. AWP
When the dawn flames in the sky. At Dawning. Nelle Richmond Eberhart. BLSo
When the Day. Thomas Sessler, *tr. fr. German by* Herbert Kuhner. VWA
When the day and the night do meete. Cobbe's Prophecies. *Unknown.* NA
When the day is stormy, and no sun shines through. A Trust-Song. Eben E. Rexford. BLRP

When the Days Grow Long. Hayyim Nahman Bialik, *tr. fr. Hebrew by* A. C. Jacobs. VWA
(When the Days Shall Grow Long, *tr. by* A. M. Klein.) TrJP
When the days were still as deith. The Rowan. Violet Jacob. PoSH
When the Dead Men Die. Rose O'Neill. HBMV
When the dew is on the grass. *Unknown.* OxNR
When the Dews Are Earliest Falling. Arthur Hugh Clough. OAEP
When the Drive Goes Down. Douglas Malloch. AmFN
When the drums come to your door. The Lost, Dancing. Edward Field. GP
When the Druzes come together. Diaspora Jews. Rachel Boimwell, *tr. by* Gabriel Preil *and* Howard Schwartz. VWA
When the dull dire sky weighs a heavy cover. Spleen. Baudelaire, *tr. by* Arthur Symons. SyP
When the Dumb Speak. Robert Bly. CAPP; NoAM; NOBA
When the dying flame of day. Hymn of the Moravian Nuns of Bethlehem. Longfellow. PAH
When the eager squadrons of day are faint and disbanded. The Cult of the Celtic. Anthony C. Deane. BXAP; NOBL
When the earth is turned in spring. The Worm. Ralph Bergengren. FaPON; RHPC; SiSoSe
When the echo of the last footstep dies. Song. E. W. Mandel. MoCV; OBCV
When the Ecstatic Body Grips. Eric Robertson Dobbs. ViBoPo
When the elephant's-ear in the park. Tea. Wallace Stevens. CABA
When the enemy surrounds you. The Precious Blood. *Unknown.* STF
When the evening came my love said to me. Prothalamion. Francis Brett Young. HBMV
When the exposed spirit, busy in daytime. Time Exposures. Muriel Rukeyser. PoA
When the Eye of Day Is Shut. A. E. Housman. OAEL-2
When the fair year. The Jews. Henry Vaughan. OBS
When the Fairies. Edward Dorn. NeAP; TAT
When the far south glittered. Pilgrimage. Austin Clarke. CIP; IPY; OxBI
When the farmer comes to town. The Farmer [*or* The Farmer Is the Man *or* The Farmer Comes to Town]. *Unknown.* AS; FSW; TrAS
When the Farmer's day is done. The Barnyard. Maude Burnham. TiPo
When the fat Prince french-kissed Sleeping Beauty. Pantomime Diseases. Dannie Abse. DFT
When the fat woman's two brats. Beef. Leon Stokesbury. GP
When the fields catch flower. April. Vidame de Chartres, *tr. by* Swinburne. AWP
When the fierce north wind with his airy forces. The Day of Judgement [*or* Judgment]; an Ode. Isaac Watts. HAP; LoBV; NOBE; NOEC; NoP; OBEC; OBEV; SeCePo
When the fifth month comes. Lady Ise, *tr. fr. Japanese by* Etsuko Terasaki *and* Irma Brandeis. BoWoP
When the fight begins within himself. Robert Browning. *Fr.* Bishop Blougram's Apology. TRV
When the first bad news came, my mother. News of the World. Philip Levine. AMV-81
When the first sound of the/ Carabao. Manong Jacinto Santo Tomas. Al Robles. BrSi
When the Five Prominent Poets. Josephine Jacobsen. TAP
When the flaming lute-thronged angelic door is wide. The Travail of Passion. W. B. Yeats. TrCP
When the flesh of summer piecemeal mars the lawn. Sonnet in Autumn. Donald Petersen. NePoEA-2
When the flowers turn to husks. Cells Breathe in the Emptiness. Galway Kinnell. NaP; VGW
When the flush of a newborn sun fell first on Eden's green and gold. The Conundrum of the Workshops. Kipling. HBV-1; MoBrPo
When the Flyin' Scot. Uncle Henry. W. H. Auden. NOBL; PeHV
When the folk of my household. Lament. Edward Walsh. OBVV
When the forests have been destroyed their darkness remains. The Asians Dying. W. S. Merwin. CAPP; CoAP; NaP; NOBA; NYBP
When the four quarters shall. Ark Overwhelmed. Jay Macpherson. *Fr.* The Ark. NOBC
When the French fleet lay. Running the Blockade. Nora Perry. PAH
When the Frost Is on the Punkin. James Whitcomb Riley. BoNaP; FaBoBe; FaBV; FaFP; FPL; HBV-1; HBVY; OBAL; PoLF; TreF
When the full fields begin to smell of sunrise. The Trappist Abbey: Matins. Thomas Merton. PoPl
When the full moon rises. Song of Black Cubans. Federico García Lorca, *tr. by* William B. Logan. SOTW
When the game began between them for a jest. Stage Love. Swinburne. NIP; PoEL-5
When the gardener has gone this garden. In a Garden. Elizabeth Jennings. NOCV
When the glow of fading sunlight. The Man of the Open West. Arthur W. Monroe. PoOW
When the gnats dance at evening. Gnat-Psalm. Ted Hughes. NoAM
When the god, needing something, decided to become a swan. Leda. Rainer Maria Rilke, *tr. by* Robert Bly. NU
When the God Returns. Russell Edson. GP
When the gold fever raged I was doing very well. The Miner's Lament. *Unknown.* AmFP
When the golden sun he knelt. The Good Day. Henry Howarth Bashford. HBV-2
When the gong sounds ten in the morning/ and I walk to school by our lane. Vocation. Rabindranath Tagore. FaPON
When the Grass Shall Cover Me. Ina Coolbrith. AA; HBV-1
When the grass was closely mown. The Dumb Soldier. Robert Louis Stevenson. OxBChV
When the grass, wet and matted. What Is There. Marvin Bell. GP
When the great, busy plants of our cities. What Then? *Unknown.* STF
When the great golden eagle of the West. Salt Lake City. Hayden Carruth. AmFN
When the Great Gray Ships Come In. Guy Wetmore Carryl. EtS; FaBoBe; HBV-2; PAH
When the green grass rose in the spring. On the Bright Side. Carter Revard. VoR
When the Green Lies over the Earth. Angelina Weld Grimké. CDC; PoNe
When the Green Woods Laugh. Blake. *See* Laughing Song.
When the grey lake-water rushes. The Solitary Woodsman. Sir Charles G. D. Roberts. CaP; OBCV
When the grey nets of winter skies hang. Spring Rites. Martin Robbins. AMV-81
When the gunner spoke in his sleep the hut was still. The Gunner. Francis Webb. CBAP
When the half-body dies its frightful death. Resurrection of the Right Side. Muriel Rukeyser. LCAP
When the hare and the pig had some pleasure to plan. The Hare and the Pig. L. J. Bridgman. RHPC
When the heat of the summer. A Dragonfly. Eleanor Farjeon. FaPON; OnUR; PDV; RHPC
When the herds were watching. Carol [*or* Bethlehem]. William Canton. HBVY; OHIP; YeAr
When the heron's in the high wood and the last long furrow's sown. Mary Shepherdess. Marjorie Pickthall. ISi
When the Himalayan peasant meets the he-bear in his pride. The Female of the Species. Kipling. BLPA; FPL; HBV-1; TreFS
When the horse has been unharnessed and we've flushed the old machine. Cleaning Up. Edward Dyson. PoAu-1
When the horses were no longer found in dreams. Second Avenue Winter. Charles Simic. NYP
When the hot sun smiles on the endless miles. The Stampede. *Unknown.* CoSo
When the Hounds of Spring [Are on Winter's Traces]. Swinburne. *Fr.* Atalanta in Calydon. FaBoBe; HBV-1; HeIP; LiTB; MasP; NoP; PrIm; TEP; TreF; TrGrPo; WHA
(Chorus: "When the hounds of spring are on winter's traces.") AWP; CTC; EBVV; EvOK; FaBoEn; GTBS-P; HAP; NOBE; OAEL-2; OBEV; PoPle; SeCeV; ViBoPo; WeW
(Hounds of Spring, The.) FaBV
When the house is silent. Song for a Little Cuckoo Clock. Elizabeth J. Coatsworth. SiSoSe
When the humid shadows hover. Rain on the Roof. Coates Kinney. HBV-1
When the hunter-star Orion. Retrospection. Sir Arthur Quiller-Couch. CenHV
When the hurricane unfolds. The Hurricane. Luis Palés Matos, *tr. by* Alida Malkus. FaPON
When the Iceworms Nest Again. Robert W. Service. FSW
When the inmate stirs, the birds retire discreetly. A Bird-Scene at a Rural Dwelling. Thomas Hardy. FM
When the kid's forehead is full of red torments. Lice-Hunters. Arthur Rimbaud, *tr. by* Ezra Pound. NAWM-2
When the King Enjoys His Own Again. Martin Parker. FaBoCh; OxBoLi
When the King of Siam disliked a courtier. In Dispraise of Poetry. Jack Gilbert. PP
When the Kye Comes Hame. James Hogg. HBV-1; OxBS
When the Lad for Longing Sighs. A. E. Housman. A Shropshire Lad, VI. MoBrPo; OLR
When the Lamp Is Shattered. Shelley. CH; FiP; OBRV; PPP; TEP; TreFT; TrGrPo; ViBoPo; WHA
(Flight of Love, The.) FPL; GTBS; GTBS-P; HBV-1; PoLF
(Lines: "When the lamp is shattered.") EnRP; FF; LoBV; NoP; OAEP; OBEV; OBNC; PoEL-4
When the landfolk of Galway converse with a stranger. Undertone. William Bedell Stanford. NeIP; OnYI
When the landlord wants the rent. Pensées de Noël. A. D. Godley. DBV; InMe

When the last bus leaves, moths stream toward lights. Depot in Rapid City. Roberta Hill. BoWoP
When the last child left. October. Judith Goren. AMV-81
When the last Flavius, drunk with fury, tore. Juvenal, *tr. by* William Gifford. *Fr.* Satires, IV. OBVE
When the last H-bomb blast has done its stuff. Brave Old World. Elisabeth Lambert. FaFP
When the last of gloaming's gone. The Shadow. Walter de la Mare. OnUR
When the Last Riders. Natan Zach, *tr. fr. Hebrew by* Peter Everwine *and* Shula Starkman. VWA
When the last sea is sailed, when the last shallow['s] charted. D'Avalos' Prayer. John Masefield. MOS; TrPWD
When the last star breathes like a rose. Sailors. Louis Simpson. NYBP
When the last voyage is ended. Requiem. Joseph Lee. OHIP
When the leaf is tight and gray. Look to the Leaf. *Unknown, tr. by* Louis Untermeyer. UnTE
When the lean, gray grasses. Give Love To-Day. Ethel Talbot. HBV-1
When the least whistling wind begins to sing. Her Hair. Sir Robert Chester. *Fr.* Love's Martyr. ElL
When the leaves in autumn wither. Autumnus. Joshua Sylvester. ElL; OBS; SoSe
When the lessons and tasks are all ended. The Children. Charles Monroe Dickinson. AA; HBV-1
When the Light Falls. Stanley Kunitz. MoAmPo
When the little armadillo. Mexican Serenade. Arthur Guiterman. FiBHP
When the little blue-bird. Let's Do It. Cole Porter. OBAL
When the little children die. Notre Dame des Petits. Louis Mercier, *tr. by* Liam Brophy. ISi
When the little Grecian cities went a-warring each with each. Little Songs. Marjorie Pickthall. CaP
When the little spent winds are at rest in the tamarack tree. In the Night Watches. Sir Charles G. D. Roberts. PeCV
When the loneliness of the tomb went down into the marketplace. Mona Sa'udi, *tr. fr. Arabic by* Kamal Boullata. WPOW
When the Lord brought back those that returned to Zion. Like unto Them That Dream. Bible, *O.T.* Psalms CXXVI. TrJP
When the Lord fashioned man, the Lord his God. The Mother. Catulle Mendès, *tr. by* W. J. Robertson. TrJP
When the low heavy sky weighs like a lid. Spleen LXXVIII. Baudelaire, *tr. by* Sir John Squire. NAWM-2
When the man arrives tomorrow, bearing a token. The Husband. Donald Finkel. ELU
When the mare shows you. Mare. Judith Thurman. PH
When the master lived a king and I a starving hutted slave beneath the lash, and. On Listening to the Spirituals. Lance Jeffers. PoBA
When the master sits at ease. Friend Cato. Anna Wickham. MoBrPo
When the men leave me. Summer in a Small Town. Linda Gregg. MAYP
When the merry lark doth gild. A Song for the Seasons. "Barry Cornwall." HBV-1
When the mice awaken. The Vigil. Denise Levertov. NePoEA-2
When the mild weather came. Sunrise at Sea. Epes Sargent. EtS
When the Mint Is in the Liquor. Clarence Ousley. PoLF
When the Mississippi Flowed in Indiana. Vachel Lindsay. CMoP
When the monkey in his madness. The Monkey's Glue. Goldwin Goldsmith. NA
When the moon appears. My Mother on an Evening in Late Summer. Mark Strand. FYAP; GeTw
When the moon comes up. The Moon Rises. Federico García Lorca, *tr. by* William B. Logan. SOTW
When the moon is on the wave. An Incantation. Byron. *Fr.* Manfred, I. OBRV
When the moon shines o'er the corn. The Field Mouse. "Fiona Macleod." FaPON; MoShBr
When the moon was full they came to the water. Moon Fishing. Lisel Mueller. CoAP
When the moon's splendour shines in naked heaven. To His Friend in Absence. Walafrid Strabo, *tr. by* Helen Waddell. PeHV
When the morning hymn. The Wonder-Teacher. Cynthia Ozick. VWA
When the morning star bleeds and silver-cry the Pleiades. Dream. Joseph Eliyia, *tr. by* Rae Dalven. VWA
When the morning was waking over the war. Among Those Killed in the Dawn Raid Was a Man Aged One Hundred. Dylan Thomas. MoPo
When the Most Is Said. "Madeline Bridges." AA; HBV-2
When the mouse died at night. The Mouse. Jean Garrigue. MP; TwCP
When the mouse died, there was a sort of pity. Death of a Whale. John Blight. CBAP; PoAu-2
When the music, warm of a summer's gleaming. Solstice. Emery George. HoAn
When the neat white. Duck. Valerie Worth. NTCP
When the Night and Morning Meet. Dora Greenwell. EBVV
When the night begins to fall. Where Are You Now? Mary Britton Miller. RHPC
When the night falls silently, the night falls silently. Glow Worm. Lila Cayley Robinson. BLSo
When the night her visions is weaving. The Harp of David. Yehoash, *tr. by* Alter Brody. TrJP
When the night is cloudy. In the Hours of Darkness. James Flexner. FaPON
When the night is still and far. The Highway. William Channing Gannett. WGRP
When the night kneels down by your bed. Faith. Preston Clark. HBMV
When the night wind howls in the chimney cowls, and the bat in the moonlight flies. Sir Roderic's Song. W. S. Gilbert. *Fr.* Ruddigore. ShM
When the Nightingale Sings. *Unknown.* OxBM
(Fairest between Lincoln and Lindsey.) MeEL
When the nightingale to his mate. Alba. Ezra Pound. *Fr.* Langue d'Oc. OBVE; VGW; WeW
When the nights are long and the dust is deep. Thistledown. Lizette Woodworth Reese. YeAr
When the Norn Mother saw the whirlwind hour. Lincoln, the Man of the People [*or* Lincoln the Great Commoner]. Edwin Markham. GN; HBV-2; MoAmPo; OHFP; OHIP; PAH; PAL; TreFS; TrGrPo
When the north wind moans thro' the blind creek courses. A Gallop of Fire. Marie E. J. Pitt. PoAu-1
When the old Cove Creek Dam first was started. The Song of Cove Creek Dam. *Unknown.* AmFP
When the old flaming prophet climbed the sky. On a Virtuous Young Gentlewoman That Died Suddenly. William Cartwright. HAP
When the old, long-preserved wine stands at the repast. Five Arabic Verses in Praise of Wine. *Unknown, tr. by* Hartwig Hirschfeld. TrJP
When the old ones die. Elegy. Karoniaktatie. STE
When the orchard that clings to the terrace. Love in Particular. John Malcolm Brinnin. NYP
When the Orient is lit by the great light. Vittoria Colonna, *tr. fr. Italian by* Brenda Webster. WPOW
When the other children go. The Invisible Playmate. Margaret Widdemer. FaPON
When the outlook is dark, try the uplook. Try the Uplook. *Unknown.* BLRP
When the pale moon hides and the wild wind wails. The Wolf. Georgia Roberts Durston. RHPC
When the petals of the plum tree. Last Breath. Laura Chester. NPGG
When the photographer comes in. Henry Miller: A Writer. Carol Lem. AMV-80
When the picnic was over. Beach Fire. Frances M. Frost. TiPo
When the Pilgrims. The First Thanksgiving. Jack Prelutsky. NTCP
When the pine tosses its cones. Woodnotes, I. Emerson. AmPP; NePA; NOBA
When the pistol muzzle oozing blue vapour. That Moment. Ted Hughes. FF
When the place was green with the shaky grass. Where the Lilies Used to Spring. David Gray. OxBS
When the plate was at pawn and the fob at an ebb. The Vows. Andrew Marvell. TW
When the pods went pop on the broom, green broom. A Runnable Stag. John Davidson. BrPo; BSV; EvOK; FaPoR; FM; GoTS; HAP; HBV-1; OBEV; OBVV; OxBTC; PrIm; WiR
When the Present has latched its postern behind my tremulous stay. Afterwards. Thomas Hardy. BoNaP; CH; ChMP; ChTr; CMoP; EBEV; FaBoEn; FaBoRV; GTBS-P; InPS; LiTB; LiTM; MoAB; MoBrPo; MoVE; NOBE; NoP; OAEL-2; OAEP; OBNC; PoEL-5; PoPl; QFR; SeCeV; TreFT; TrGrPo; ViBoPo
When the prime mover of my many sighs. To Vittoria Colonna. Michelangelo, *tr. by* Longfellow. AWP
When the proud World does most my world despise. Robert Nichols. *Fr.* Sonnets to Aurelia. OBMV
"When the Pulitzers showered on some dope." Words for Hart Crane. Robert Lowell. AP; CABA; CMoP; NMP
When the rain comes tumbling down. The Story of Flying Robert. Heinrich Hoffmann, *tr. fr. German.* SpRo
When the rain drums loud on the leaf. Resemblance. *Tr. fr. Hawaiian by* N. B. Emerson. WTO
When the rain is raining. Umbrellas. Rowena Bennett. TiPo
When the Rain Raineth. *Unknown.* GBP
When the rains began. The Prophetess. Dorothy Livesay. MoCV
When the rattlesnake bit, I lay. The Poisoned Man. James Dickey. PAI
When the reaper's task was ended, and the summer wearing late. The Swan Song of Parson Avery. Whittier. AA
When the Regime ordered that books with dangerous teachings. The Burning of Books. Bertolt Brecht, *tr. by* H. R. Hays. PoPl

When the returning sun begins to smile. James Dance. *Fr.* Cricket; an Heroic Poem. NOEC
When the ring gleamed white and your chair hugged the edge of it. Change of Address. Kathleen Fraser. NYBP
When the Ripe Fruit Falls. D. H. Lawrence. CMoP
When the ripe pears droop heavily. The Wasp. "Fiona Macleod." FaPON
When the road forked. The Angel and the Anchorite. Richard Shelton. NPAW
When the robust and brass-bound man commissioned first for sea. Poseidon's Law. Kipling. MOS
When the Roll Is Called up Yonder. James M. Black. TreFT
When the rooster jumps up on the windowsill. Cuba, 1962. Ai. AmPA
When the rose is brightest. To Giulia Grisi. Nathaniel Parker Willis. AA
When the rose of morn through the dawn was breaking. The Dream of Aengus Og. Eleanor Rogers Cox. HBMV
When the runner's whistle lights the last miles of darkness. Soldier (T. P.). Randall Jarrell. WaP
When the Saints Go Marchin' In. *Unknown.* EaLo; FSW
(When the Saints Come Marching In, *with music.*) BLSo, *ad. by* Edward C. Redding.
When the Saviour has given you a blessing, by paper or a book. Pass It On! *Unknown.* STF
When the scarlet cardinal tells. It Is July. Susan Hartley Swett. GN; YeAr
When the sea comes in at Horsey Gap. Horsey Gap. *Unknown.* FaBoPP; GBP
When the sea is as grey as her eyes. Soft White. Lee Harwood. EAS
When the sea is everywhere. North Atlantic. Carl Sandburg. MOS
When the Seed of Thy Word Is Cast, *with music.* Cotton Mather. AH
When the sheen on tall summer grass is pale. The Gazelles. T. Sturge Moore. BrPo; OBMV
When the sheep are in the fauld, and the kye [*or* cows] at hame. Auld Robin Gray. Lady Anne Lindsay. BeLS; BSV; CH; GoTS; GTBS; GTBS-P; HBV-1; NOEC; OBEC; OBEV; ViBoPo; WPE
When the shoals of plankton. Shooting Whales. Mark Strand. LCAP
When the shy, slender thrush. Spring Doggerel. Rhoda Coghill. NeIP
When the sky starts in a-rainin'. Let Be. *Unknown.* WBLP
When the Sleepy Man Comes. Sir Charles G. D. Roberts. *Fr.* The Book of the Native. HBV-1; HBVY
When the snail crawls over the bare flag-stone. Omens. James H. Cousins. OnYI
When the snow has gone away. The Procession. Margaret Widdemer. YeAr
When the snow starts melting. The French Mood. Abo Stoltzenberg, *tr. by* Gabriel Preil *and* Howard Schwartz. VWA
When the Son of Man Shall Come in His Glory. Bible, *N.T.* St. Matthew, XXV: 31-46. TreF
When the soul sought refuge in the place of rest. Self-Discipline. "Æ." MoBrPo
When the Spent Day Begins to Frail. E. E. Cummings. ErPo
When the spent sun throws up its rays on cloud. Acceptance. Robert Frost. CMoP; OxBA
When the spider dropped down from the ceiling. The Grandmother Came Down to Visit Us. Joseph Bruchac. CDW
When the spinning-room was here. The Maids of Elfin-Mere. William Allingham. OnYI
When the spruce wood ends, I step. The Visitor. Gregory Orr. MAYP
When the storm/ gave me its dark clouds. For Michael. Karen L. Mitchell. AMV-80
When the storm hit, I was fording the river. My Marriage with Mrs. Johnson. Jack Gilbert. NPGG
When the storm was fiercely raging. "It Is I, Be Not Afraid." A. B. Simpson. STF
When the storm was in the sky. The Beloved. May Probyn. GoBC
"When the Students Resisted, a Minor Clash Ensued." David Knight. MoCV
When the Sultan Goes to Ispahan. Thomas Bailey Aldrich. AA; BeLS; FaBoBe; HBV-1
When the summer fields are mown. Aftermath. Longfellow. AP; NOBA; TAP
When the sun/ falls behind the sumac. Loss. A. R. Ammons. ConAP
When the sun begins to throw. Skimmers. Ted Walker. NYBP
When the sun comes up from the salt sea. *Unknown.* *Fr.* The Phoenix. PBBP
When the sun gets low, in winter. Human Things. Howard Nemerov. BoNaP
When the sun has slipped away. The Skunk. Robert P. Tristram Coffin. FaPON; TiPo
When the sun rises on another day. Litany. Charles Angoff. TrPWD
When the sun shone hot the girl's arm was detected. Temperature. Gerard Malanga. NYBP
When the sun shouts and people abound. Summer Holiday. Robinson Jeffers. CrMA; MoAmPo; MoVE; OxBA
When the sun whipped our skins. Cortes. A. A. Rios. GP
When the sun's perpendicular rays. Beginning of an Undergraduate Poem. *Unknown.* FaBoCo
When the sun's whiteness closes around us. The Map. Gary Soto. MAYP
When the swans turned my sister into a swan. The Black Swan. Randall Jarrell. CMoP; NMP
When the sweet showers of April follow March. Chaucer, *mod. vers. by* Louis Untermeyer. *Fr.* The Canterbury Tales: Prologue. TrGrPo
When the swift-rolling brook, swollen deep. The Storm-Wind. William Barnes. NOBE
When the Sword of Sixty Comes Nigh His Head. Firdausi, *tr. fr. Persian by* Basil Bunting. NAs; OBVE
When the tea is brought at five o'clock. Milk for the Cat. Harold Monro. FaBoBe; FaFP; HBVY; MoBrPo; OBMV; PCat
When the teacher asks you to bound Texas. Texas. James Daugherty. TiPo
When the tide was out. A Ship Burning and a Comet All in One Day. Richard Eberhart. NYBP
When the Tigers claw the Bulldogs. College Song. Ed Anthony. InMe
When the time comes for me to die. Night. Thomas William Rolleston. HBV-2
When the time has arrived. Trala Trala Trala Le-le-la. William Carlos Williams. OFD
When the timeless, daily, tedious affair. The Poet at Seven. Robert Lowell. NaP
When the torch is taken. Seneca. Thomas Merton. CoPo
When the toys are growing weary. The Dustman. Frederic Edward Weatherly. HBV-1
When the Tree Bares. Conrad Aiken. MoAmPo
When the trial's in Belzoni. High Sheriff Blues. *Unknown.* BluL
When the Troops Were Returning from Milan. Niccolò degli Albizzi, *tr. fr. Italian by* Dante Gabriel Rossetti. *See* Prolonged Sonnet: When the Troops Were Returning from Milan.
When the troubled sea swells and surrounds. Vittoria da Colonna, *tr. fr. Italian by* Brenda Webster. PBWP
When the trumpet of the Lord shall sound. When the Roll Is Called up Yonder. James M. Black. TreFT
When the turf is thy tower. The Grave. *Unknown.* ChTr
When the two-lane highway was widened. Dreaming America. Joyce Carol Oates. GeTw
When the union's inspiration through the workers' blood shall run. Solidarity Forever. Ralph Chaplin. FSW
When the Vacation Is Over for Good. Mark Strand. NYBP
When the veil from the eyes is lifted. Si Jeunesse Savait! Edmund Clarence Stedman. AA
When the vengeance wakes, when the battle breaks. Battle Song. Robert Burns Wilson. PAH
When the voices of children are heard on the green/ And laughing is heard on the hill. Nurse's Song [*or* Play Time]. Blake. *Fr.* Songs of Innocence. AWP; BLPL; CH; EnRP; FaBoBe; FaPON; HBV-1; HBVY; LAuP; OBEC; OxBChV
When the voices of children are heard on the green/ And whisprings are in the dale. Nurse's Song. Blake. *Fr.* Songs of Experience. CABA; EnRP; FF; LAuP
When the War Will End. Reginald Arkell. InMe
(Rumors.) TreFT
When the war-cry of liberty rang through the land. The Death of Warren. Epes Sargent. PAH
When the warl's couped roun' as a peerie. Munestruck. "Hugh MacDiarmid." NeBP
When the warm zummer breeze do blow over the hill. The Shep'erd Bwoy. William Barnes. EBVV
When the water fell. Flooded Mind. Norman MacCaig. OxBC
When the water fowl are found, the falconers hasten. *Unknown.* *Fr.* The Parliament of the Three Ages. PBBP
When the waves of trouble roll. Show Me Thyself. Margaret E. Sangster. TrPWD
When the wayside tangles blaze. Goldenrod. Elaine Goodale Eastman. HBV-1
When the weather is rough, said the anxious child. Contemporary Song. Theodore Spencer. LiTA
When the weather suits you not. Try Smiling. *Unknown.* BLPA; FaFP; WBLP
When the white feet of the baby beat across the grass. Baby Running Barefoot. D. H. Lawrence. NoP
When the white flame in us is gone. Dust. Rupert Brooke. HBV-1; MoBrPo; OBVV; OxBTC
When the white fog burns off. The Depths. Denise Levertov. NaP; NU
When the white wave of a glory that is hardly I. Sinfonia Domestica. Jean Starr Untermeyer. HBMV; MoAmPo

When the wind blows. *Unknown.* OxNR
When the wind blows loud and fearful. The Beggar Boy. Cecil Frances Alexander. OxBChV
When the wind blows, walk not abroad. To the Maids Not to Walk in the Wind. Oliver St. John Gogarty. AnIL; ErPo
When the wind is in the east. Mother Goose. FaBoUs; OxNR
When the wind is in the thrift. By the Saltings. Ted Walker. NYBP
When the wind works against us in the dark. Storm Fear. Robert Frost. CMoP; HBV-1; OxBA; ViBoPo
When the Wine Was Gone. Alvin Aubert. CNA
When the words rustle no more. Stillness. James Elroy Flecker. BrPo; CH; GoJo; MoBrPo; SyP
When the Work's All Done This Fall. *Unknown.* AS, *with music*; BPAW; CoSo, *with music*; FSW
When the World Ends. Mark Van Doren. GoYe
When the world goes voodoo. Creed. Walter Lowenfels. PoNe
When the world is all against you. The Optimist. *Unknown.* PV
When the World Is Burning. Ebenezer Jones. OBEV; OBVV; PoPle; VLP
When the world takes over for us. Lear. William Carlos Williams. NOBA; PoA
When the world turns completely upside down. Wild Peaches. Elinor Wylie. LiTA; LiTM; OxBA; SBG; WPE
"When the World Was in Building." Ford Madox Ford. CTC
When the wounded seaman heard the ocean daughters. Legend. Ridgely Torrence. EtS
When the yellow bird's note was almost stopped. Rejoicing at the Arrival of Chi'en Hsiung. Po Chü-i, *tr. by* Arthur Waley. AWP
When the young Augustus Edward. On the Beach. C. S. Calverley. FiBHP
When the young hand of Darnley locked in hers. Mary Queen of Scots. Charles Tennyson Turner. HBV-2
When Thee (O holy sacrificed Lamb). To the Blessed Sacrament. Henry Constable. ACP
When their eyes opened, it was more than morning. The Land behind the Wind. David Wagoner. NPAW
When their last hour shall rise. Ex-Voto. Swinburne. MOS
When Theo: Roos: unfurled his bann. The Conversational Reformer. Harry Graham. InMe; YaD
When there are animals about, who else. Talking to Animals. Barbara Howes. GrPl
When there are minds to heal, and you. Girl in a White Coat. John Malcolm Brinnin. SaC
When there are so many we shall have to mourn. In Memory of Sigmund Freud. W. H. Auden. CoBMV; HAP; LiTB; OAEL-2; OxBA
When There Is Music. David Morton. HBMV
"When There Is Peace." Austin Dobson. PAH
When there was heard no more the war's loud sound. The Death of Ailill. Francis Ledwidge. OnYI
When there was not one moment left to us. By Return Mail. Richard Aldridge. NePoAm-2
When There Were Trees. Nancy Willard. HoAn
When these graven lines you see. A Happy Man. Carphyllides, *tr. by* E. A. Robinson. AWP
When these inland gulls. Desert Gulls. Dan Gillespie. TAT
When These Old Barns Lost Their Inhabitants. David Kherdian. TAT
When these old woods were young. Under the Woods. Edward Thomas. CH; LoBV
When these were past, thus gan the Titanesse. Mutability. Spenser. *Fr.* The Faerie Queene, VII. PoEL-1
When they ask your name. Children. Russell Edson. AmPA
When they come, we begin to go. The Ancestors. Christopher Middleton. NMP
When they confess that they have lost the penial bone. God Bless America. John Fuller. OBSV
When they entered through the back door. The Morning They Shot Tony Lopez, Barber and Pusher Who Went Too Far, 1958. Gary Soto. MAYP
When they escaped. Exodus. Harvey Shapiro. VWA
When they found Giotto. Allan M. Laing. FiBHP
When they found her prostrate in the garden. Cinderella. Roger Mitchell. DFT
When they go out walking the Sioux. The Sioux. *Unknown.* TDH
When They Grow Old. Nathan Ralph. CaP
When they had pitched their smoked tepees. Indian Dance. Frederick Niven. CaP
When they had won the war. The Inner Part. Louis Simpson. InPS
When They Have Lost. C. Day Lewis. MoAB; MoBrPo
When they [*or* Quhen thai] him fand, and gude [*or* gud] Wallace him saw. Wallace's Lament for the Graham [*or* Lament for the Graham]. Henry the Minstrel. *Fr.* The Wallace, X. GoTS; OxBS
When they in throngs a safe retirement seek. William Diaper, *after the Greek of* Oppian. *Fr.* Halieutica. OBVE
When they killed my mother it made me nervous. The State. Randall Jarrell. LiTM; MiAP
When they pull my clock tower down. The Clock Tower. Colleen Thibaudeau. WHW
When they restored. Passive Resistance. Joseph Bruchac. SOTS
When they said Carrickfergus I could hear. The Singer's House. Seamus Heaney. CIP; EBEV
When they said the time to hide was mine. The Rabbit. Elizabeth Madox Roberts. OBCA; RHPC; SoPo; TiPo
When they saw off Dai Evan's da. Fforestfawr. Kingsley Amis. *Fr.* The Evans Country. NOBL
When they say "To the wall." The Wall Test. Louis Simpson. GP
When they sd to me this. When. Philip Appleman. BXAP
When they shook the box, and poured out its chances. For a Daughter Gone Away. William Stafford. NPAW; SV
When they shot Malcolm Little down. At That Moment. Raymond R. Patterson. CABA; PoBA
When they stop poems. Today Is a Day of Great Joy. Victor Hernandez Cruz. TTY
When they threw him overboard. Historical Incidents. Clarence Day. InMe
When they woke me. Coming Back. Joseph Bruchac. CDW
When they write an end to war, when they blot away the battle. If We Break Faith. Joseph Auslander. TRV
When Thickly Beat the Storms of Life, *with music.* Gurdon Robins. AH
When thin-strewn memory I look through. Miss Loo [*or* Miss Lou]. Walter de la Mare. CMoP; HBV-1; OxBTC
When Things Go Wrong. *Unknown.* STF
When things go wrong, as they sometimes will. Don't Quit. *Unknown.* BLPA; FPL; STF
When Things Go Wrong with You. *Unknown.* FSW
When, think you, comes the Wind. The Rose and the Wind. Philip Bourke Marston. OBVV
When This Cruel War Is Over. Charles C. Sawyer. *See* Weeping Sad and Lonely.
When this fly[e] lived [*or* liv'd], she used [*or* us'd] to play. A Fly [*or* Flye] That Flew into My Mistress's [*or* Mistris] Eye. Thomas Carew. AnAnS-2; CaPo
When this is the thing you put on. Armor. James Dickey. CoAP
When This Old Hat Was New. *Unknown.* OBET
When this, our rose, is faded. Amantium Irae. Ernest Dowson. HBV-1
When This Tide Ebbs. Verna Loveday Harden. CaP
When this troubled life is over, hide Thou me. Hide Thou Me. *Unknown.* AmFP
When this yokel comes maundering. The Plot against the Giant. Wallace Stevens. CMoP; FF; OxBA
When thistle-blows do lightly float. November. C. L. Cleaveland. HBV-1
When those renoumed noble peers of Greece. Amoretti, XLIV. Spenser. CABA
When those we love die. Death in the Home. T. Sturge Moore. BrPo
When thou and I are dead, my dear. Inseparable. Philip Bourke Marston. BoLoP
When Thou Did Thinke I Did Not Love. Sir Robert Ayton. OBS
(When Thou Didst Think I Did Not Love.) ElL
When thou hast spent the ling[e]ring day in pleasure and delight. Gascoigne's [*or* Gascoygnes] Good-Night. George Gascoigne. AAS; NOCV
When Thou Must Home [to Shades of Underground]. Thomas Campion, *after the Latin of* Propertius. AWP; ElL; EnLoPo; EnRePo; FaBoEn; LoBV; NoP; OBSC; PoEL-2; PoRA; SeCeV; ViBoPo
(Among the Shades.) AAS; BoLoP; CABA; EBEV; GBL; HAP; NOBE; OBVE; PoPle
(Tell, O Tell.) TrGrPo
(To Shades of Underground.) ChTr
(Vobiscum Est Iope.) HBV-1; OBEV
When Thou Passest through the Waters. Henry Crowell. BLRP
"When thou passest through the waters." Passing Through [*or* Through the Waters]. Annie Johnson Flint. BLRP; STF
When thou, poor[e] excommunicate. To My [*or* His] Inconstant Mistress [*or* Song.] Thomas Carew. AnAnS-2; CaPo; CavP; EnLoPo; GBL; HBV-1; JCP; LoBV; MeLP; MePo; NOBE; NoP; OBEV; OBS; SeCePo; SeCP; SeCV-1; TrGrPo
When thou to my true love com'st. Westphalian Song. *Unknown, tr. by* Samuel Taylor Coleridge. AWP; OBVE
When thou turn'st away from ill. Approaches. George Macdonald. TRV
When thou wakest in the morning. Tell Jesus. *Unknown.* STF
When through the Whirl of Wheels. G. A. Studdert-Kennedy. EBCP
When through the winding cobbled streets of time. The Noonday April Sun. George Love. IDB; NNP
When thy beauty appears. Song. Thomas Parnell. OBEC; OBEV; UnTE
When Thy Heart with Joy O'erflowing, *with music.* Theodore Chickering Williams. AH

When Thy King Is a Boy, *sel.* Ed Roberson.
"You black out the sun." PoBA
When time has rocked the present age to sleep. To William Stanley Braithwaite. Georgia Douglas Johnson. BALP
When to any saint I pray. Saint Peray. Thomas William Parsons. HBV-2
When to assure us on our way. A Rhemish Carol. Robert Finch. NAs
When to Her Lute Corinna [*or* Corrina] Sings. Thomas Campion. AAS; CABA; NoP; OAEL-1; OBSC; SeCeV
(Corinna.) ElL; TrGrPo
(Of Corinna's Singing.) HBV-1
(When to Her Lute.) EnRePo
When, to my deadly [*or* deadlie] pleasure. Sir Philip Sidney. EnLoPo; PoEL-1
When to my eyes. Midnight. Henry Vaughan. AnAnS-1; OAEP
When to my lone soft bed at eve returning. Povre Ame Amoureuse. Louise Labé, *tr. by* Robert Bridges. AWP
When to My Serene Body. Freda Laughton. NeIP
When to sleep, babe, last night in a snow-white feather bed. I'm Worried Now but I Won't Be Worried Long. *Unknown.* OuSiCo
When to soft sleep we give ourselves away. Sleep. Thomas Bailey Aldrich. AA
When to the garden of untroubled thought. The Child in the Garden. Henry van Dyke. HBV-1
When to the sessions of sweet silent thought. Sonnets, XXX. Shakespeare. AWP; BiP; CABA; CTC; EBEV; ElL; EnRePo; FaBoEn; FaBoRV; FaBV; FaFP; FF; FPL; GBL; GTBS; GTBS-P; HAP; HBV-1; InPS; LiTB; LoBV; MasP; NOBE; NoP; OAEL-1; OAEP; OBEV; OBSC; PAI; PoEL-2; PoPle; PoLF; PoRA; PrIm; PPP; SeCeV; TEP; TreFS; TrGrPo; TRV; ViBoPo; WHA
When Toroi Bandi was alive. Toroi Bandi. *Mongol Oral Tradition, tr. by* C. R. Bawden. WTO
When trees have lost remembrance of the leaves. Crocus. Alfred Kreymborg. HBMV
When trials press and foes increase. Trials. Grace E. Troy. STF
When trouble comes your soul to try. The Friend Who Just Stands By. B. Y. Williams. PoLF
When trouble haunts me, need I sigh? The Stranger. John Clare. OxBoCh
When trout swim down Great Ormond Street. Priapus and the Pool, III. Conrad Aiken. NoAM; NOBA
When tulips bloom in Union Square. An Angler's Wish. Henry van Dyke. AA
When tunes jigged nimbler than the blood. Song from a Country Fair. Léonie Adams. GoJo; GrPl
When twilight comes to Prairie Street. The Winning of the TV West. John T. Alexander. AmFN; RHPC
When twins came, their father, Dan Dunn. The Twins. Berton Braley. TDH
When Two Are Parted. Heine, *tr. fr. German by* Louis Untermeyer. AWP
When two elephants fight. Some Pieces. Calvin Forbes. MAYP
When two lovers love each other well. Young Bearwell. *Unknown.* ESPB
When two men meet for the first time in all. Law in the Country of the Cats. Ted Hughes. TW
When Two Suns Do Appear. Sir Philip Sidney. *Fr.* Arcadia. EnRePo; MOON; SiPS
When two who love are parted. When Two Are Parted. Heine, *tr. by* Louis Untermeyer. AWP
When tyranny's pampered and purple-clad minions. Extermination. Richard D'Alton Williams. OnYI
When under Edward or Henry the English armies. Now as Then. Anne Ridler. WaP
When vain desire at last and vain regret. The One Hope. Dante Gabriel Rossetti. The House of Life, CI. HBV-2; OAEL-2; VLP
When Venus her Adonis found. The Death of Adonis. Philip Ayres, *after the Greek of* Theocritus. OBVE
When Very was a celibate. Varitalk. Weare Holbrook. NYBP
When very young/ I learned to run. Easy Does It. Henry Chapin. FAZ
When Viera was buried we knew it had come to an end. Because One Is Always Forgotten. Carolyn Forché. MAYP
When walking in a tiny rain. Vern. Gwendolyn Brooks. TiPo
When Wallaby would come to call on me. The Critic on the Hearth. L. E. Sissman. TW
When warfare blusters at high Lucifer's command. War Cry: To Mary. Pope Leo XIII, *tr. by* Raymond F. Roseliep. ISi
When wars and ruined men shall cease. Prayer against Indifference. Joy Davidman. TrPWD
When war's red banner trailed along the sky. Robert G. Shaw. Henrietta Cordelia Ray. BlSi
When was it that the particles became. Wallace Stevens. PoA
When waves invade the yellowing wheat. Composed While under Arrest. Mikhail Yuryevich Lermontov, *tr. by* Max Eastman. AWP
When we are dead, some Hunting-boy will pass. The Statue. Hilaire Belloc. ACP; MoVE; POL
When we are going toward someone we say. Simple Song. Marge Piercy. CTBA; LLLT
When we are gone, love. Wood-Song. Eugene Lee-Hamilton. OBVV
When we are in love, we love the grass. Love Poem. Robert Bly. BiP; InPS
When we are like/ two drunken suns. *See* When we are two drunk suns.
When we are old and these rejoicing veins. Sonnet XXVIII. Edna St. Vincent Millay. ErPo; VGW
When we are older and the hidden fires. Vera Wainwright. LO
When We Are Parted. Hamilton Aidé. HBV-1
When we are [like] two drunk[en] suns. Yvonne Caroutch, *tr. fr. French.* BoWoP, *tr. by* Willis Barnstone *and* Elene Kolb; LLLT, *tr. by* Carl Hermey
When we behold. Dahlias. Padraic Colum. GoJo; NePoAm
When we came down from the country, we were strangers to the sea. Down from the Country. John Blight. CBAP
When we came up from water, our eyes. Lying Down with Men and Women. John Woods. GP
When we come to that dark house. Edith Sitwell. *Fr.* The Sleeping Beauty. MoVE; OBMV
When we count out our gold at the end of the day. Service. Georgia Douglas Johnson. CDC
When We Court and Kiss. Thomas Campion. *See* I Care Not for These Ladies.
When we fell apart in the Badlands and lay still. In the Badlands. David Wagoner. UnPo
When we first met we did not guess. Robert Bridges. POL
When we first rade down Ettrick. Ettrick. Lady John Scott. BSV; WPE
When we for age could [*or* cou'd] neither read nor write. Of the Last Verses in the Book [*or* Of His Divine Poems]. Edmund Waller. AnAnS-2; EBEV; FaBoEn; FaBoRV; HAP; HBV-1; LoBV; MePo; NoP; OAEP; OBS; SeCP; SeCV-1; ViBoPo
When we fought the Yankees and annihilation was near. Jubilation T. Cornpone. Johnny Mercer. OBAL
When we get a good day here. Young Couples Strolling By. Carl Rakosi. InPS
When we go to the fields. Walking on the Prayerstick. Wendy Rose. TWSS
When we got home, there was our Old Man. Pa. Leo Dangel. AMV-81; Str
When we have come this long way. Anniversary Poem for the Cheyennes Who Fell at Sand Creek. Lance Henson. VoR
When we have run our passion's heat. Andrew Marvell. *Fr.* The Garden. WHA
When we have thrown off this old suit. The Question Whither. George Meredith. HBV-2; WGRP
When We Hear the Eye Open. Bob Kaufman. CNA
When we heard it announced. The Ambassadors. Paul Lawson. GP
When we in kind embracements had agre'd. *Unknown. Fr.* Zepheria. AAS
When we lay where Budmouth Beach is. Budmouth Dears. Thomas Hardy. *Fr.* The Dynasts, Pt. III. CH; LO; MoVE; PoPle
When we learn. It Is the Season. Josephine Jacobsen. TAP
When we lived in a city. Until We Built a Cabin. Aileen Fisher. TiPo
When We Looked Back. William Stafford. NYBP
When we loved. Loving. Jane Stembridge. NMM
When we moved here, pulled. An Oregon Message. William Stafford. CoAP; MOON
When we, my love, are gone to dust. A Song of Dust. Lord De Tabley. EnLoPo
When we on simple rations sup. Washing the Dishes. Christopher Morley. PoLF
When we, our weary limbs to rest. Bible, *O.T., paraphrased by* Nahum Tate *and* Nicholas Brady. Psalms, CXXXVII. OAEL-1
When we played in the nursery till seven. Hello There. Brian S. Salome. BXAP
When we rolled up the three armored vehicles. One Morning We Brought Them Order. Al Lee. FF
When we shall finally be. The Fathers. John N. Morris. GP
When we shuddered and took into ourselves. The Whole Story. William Stafford. NNaP
When we slept. Signature. Larry Mollin. NeAC
When we spurt off. Moving. William Matthews. POL
When we start breaking up in the wet darkness. Consolations of Philosophy. Derek Mahon. BIrV; CIP
When we told you minus twenty. A Correction. Robert Frost. WhC
When We Two Parted. Byron. BoLoP; ChER; EnRP; FiP; FPL; GTBS; GTBS-P; HBV-1; HoPM; LoBV; NOBE; NoP; OAEP; OBEV; OBNC; OBRV; OLR; PoLF; TreFS; TrGrPo; ViBoPo; WHA
When we went to the zoo. Our Visit to the Zoo. Jessie Pope. PoPle
When we were a soft amoeba. Ere You Were Queen of Sheba. Sir Arthur Shipley. FaBoCo

When we were building Skua Light. The Dancing Seal. W. W. Gibson. HBMV; OnMSP
When we were charming *Backfisch.* Friendship. Katherine Mansfield. PeHV
When we were children, clasping hands. But You, My Darling, Should Have Married the Prince. Kathleen Spivack. AmPA; NMM
When we were children old Nurse used to say. The Quiet House. Charlotte Mew. BrRo; EBEV; SBG
When we were farm-boys, years ago. Recollections of "Lalla Rookh." John Townsend Trowbridge. OBAL
When we were girl and boy together. Ballad of Human Life. Thomas Lovell Beddoes. BeLS
When we were idlers with the loitering rills. To a Friend [*or* Friendship *or* Sonnet]. Hartley Coleridge. HBV-2; OBEV; OBNC; OBRV; PoLF
When we were married eight years. Tryst. Eve Merriam. NMM
When we were silly sisters seven. Fair Mary of Wallington. *Unknown.* ESPB
When We Were Very Silly, *sels.* J. B. Morton.
Now We Are Sick. FaBoPa; PV; SpRo
Someone Asked the Publisher. FaBoPa
Theobald James. FaBoPa
When we would reach the anguish of the dead. Near an Old Prison. Frances Cornford. OBMV
When weakness now do strive wi' might. Withstanders. William Barnes. OxBoCh
When weary with the long day's care. To Imagination. Emily Brontë. VLP
When weight of all the garnered years. Love's Lord. Edward Dowden. HBV-2
When we're playing tag. No Girls Allowed. Jack Prelutsky. RHPC
When wert thou born, Desire? Of the Birth and Bringing Up of Desire. Edward de Vere, Earl of Oxford. FaBoEE; OBSC
When Wesley died, the Angelic orders. The Organist in Heaven [*or* Wesley in Heaven]. Thomas Edward Brown. OBNC; OBVV
When West Comes East. Carey Ford. InMe
When Westwall Downes [*or* Westwell Downs] I gan to tread. On Westwall Downes [*or* On Westwell Downs]. William Strode. FaBoEn; FaBoPP; JCP; PoEL-2
When what has helped us has helped us enough. The Place of Backs. W. S. Merwin. HoPM
)when what hugs stopping earth than silent is. E. E. Cummings. PoA
When whelmed the altar, priest and creed. Epigram. Sir William Watson. WGRP
When, when and whenever death closes our eyelids. Ezra Pound. *Fr.* Homage to Sextus Propertius. MoAB; NoAM; OBMV; PoA
When whispering strains do softly steal. In Commendation of Music. William Strode. ELP; OBEV
When Whistler's Mother's picture['s] frame. Don Marquis. *Fr.* To a Lost Sweetheart. FiBHP; POL
When Whistler's strongest colors fade. The Durable Bon Mot. Keith Preston. HBMV
When white man git to worryin'. *Unknown.* OuSiCo
When white people speak of being uptight. The Dancer. Al Young. PoBA
When Wild Confusion Wrecks the Air, *with music.* Mather Byles. AH
When Will He Come? *Unknown.* STF
When Will Love Come? Pakenham Beatty. HBV-1
When will men again. The Leaping Laughers. George Barker. OBMV
When will the fountain of my tears be dry? Give Me Leave [*or* Petition to Have Her Leave to Die]. "A. W." OBSC; TrGrPo
When will violence shake, when break me. The House. Winfield Townley Scott. MiAP
When will you ever, Peace, wild wooddove, shy wings shut. Peace. Gerard Manley Hopkins. EBCP; ELP; GTBS-P; OAEP; TrCP
"When will you marry me, William." The West-Country Damosel's Complaint. *Unknown.* ESPB
When William went from home (a trader styled). The Ear-Maker and the Mould-Mender. La Fontaine. UnTE
When willing nymphs and swains unite. The Judgement of Tiresias. Hildebrand Jacob. NOEC
When wilt Thou save the people? God Save the People. Ebenezer Elliott. BLPA; EaLo; WBLP
When Wilt Thou Teach the People? D. H. Lawrence. OBSV
When Windesor walles sustain'd my wearied arme. *See* When Windsor walls sustain'd my wearied arm.
When window-lamps had dwindled, then I rose. Christopher Brennan. *Fr.* The Wanderer. CBAP
When winds are locked along the tropic shore. The *Flying Dutchman.* A. M. Sullivan. EtS
When Winds Are Raging, *with music.* Harriet Beecher Stowe. AH
When winds go organing through the pines. The Wind in the Pines. Madison Cawein. AA
When winds that move not its calm surface sweep. The Ocean. [*or* From the Greek of Moschus]. Moschus, *tr. by* Shelley. AWP; MOS; OBVE
When Windsor [*or* Windesor] walls [*or* walls] sustain'd my wearied arm[e]. Earl of Surrey. AAS; SiPS
When wine runs low, it is not worth the sparing. Joshua Sylvester, *after the French of* Pierre Mathieu. FaBoEE
When winking stars at dusk peep through. Makes the Little Ones Dizzy. Samuel Hoffenstein. BXAP
When winter hoar no longer holds. The Lover's Song. Alfred Austin. OBVV
When winter nights fall like eyelids closing. Montana Remembered from Albuquerque; 1982. Ron Rogers. STE
When winter scourged the meadow and the hill. Ice. Sir Charles G. D. Roberts. BoNaP; OBCV; RHPC; WHW
When Winter snows upon thy sable hairs. *Fr.* To Delia. Samuel Daniel. CTC; EnRePo; OBSC; TEP
When winter's cold tempests and snows are no more. The Blue-Bird. Alexander Wilson. AA
When Winter's royal robes of white. A Parting Hymn. Charlotte Forten. BlSi
When wintry days are dark and drear. The Light'ood Fire. John Henry Boner. AA
When wintry weather's all a-done. The Spring. William Barnes. BoNaP; HBV-1
When wise Minerva still was young. The Origin of Didactic Poetry. James Russell Lowell. PoEL-5
When, with a serious musing, I behold. The Marigold. George Wither. OBS
When with eyes closed as in an opium dream. Parfum Exotique. Baudelaire, *tr. by* Arthur Symons. AWP
When with May the air is sweet. Love, Whose Month Was Ever May. Ulrich von Liechtenstein, *tr. by* Jethro Bithell. AWP
When with much pains this boasted learning's got. Charles Churchill. *Fr.* The Author. OBSV
When, with my little daughter Blanche. Presence of Mind. Harry Graham. WhC
When with staid mothers' milk and sunshine warmed. Alfred Austin. *Fr.* The Human Tragedy. FaBoCo
When with the virgin morning thou dost rise. Matins, or Morning Prayer. Robert Herrick. CaPo
When within my arms I hold you. Aurelia. Robert Nichols. OBMV
When without tears I looke on Christ, I see. William Alabaster. AnAnS-1
When women first Dame Nature wrought. Of Women. Richard Edwards. ElL
When working blackguards come to blows. Song. Ebenezer Elliott. EBEV; NBM
When world is water and all is flood, God said. Noah's Ark. Marguerite Young. MoPo; WPE
When ye hunt at the roe, then shall ye see there. Julians Barnes. *Fr.* Book of Hunting. WPE
When yesterday I went to see my friends. The Hospital Visitor. Alys Fane Trotter. SUMH
When Yon Full Moon. W. H. Davies. MoBrPo; MOON
When you and I go down. Midnight Lamentation. Harold Monro. BrPo; ChMP; LO; OBMV; OxBTC; ViBoPo
When you and I have play'd the little hour. Reunited. Sir Gilbert Parker. OBEV; OBVV
When You and I Must Part. *Unknown.* AmFP
When you and I on the Palos Verdes cliff. Shane O'Neill's Cairn. Robinson Jeffers. NoAM; NOBA
When You and I Were Young, Maggie. George W. Johnson. BLSo, *with music*; FSW; PSoN, *with music*; TreF
When you and my true lover meet. The Lady's Third Song. W. B. Yeats. *Fr.* The Three Bushes. FaBoTw
"When you are/ ill at ease." Granma's Words. Ted D. Palmanteer. STE
When you are caught breathless in an empty station. This Is the Place to Wait. Horace Gregory. *Fr.* The Passion of M'Phail. MoAmPo
When you are discouraged. Try This Once. *Unknown.* WBLP
When You Are Gone. Nance Van Winckel. AMV-81
When you are gone, I lie upon your bed. Suburban Wife's Song. Robert Hutchinson. NYBP
When you are in love, we love the grass. Love Poem. Robert Bly. PCP
When you are late and have not let me know. Not Late Enough. Hazel Townson. PV
When You Are Old. W. B. Yeats. AWP; BoLoP; CMoP; CTC; EBVV; FaBV; FaFP; FPL; GBL; GoJo; HBV-1; HeIP; InvP; LiTM; MoAB; MoBrPo; NoAM; NoP; OBEV; OBVV; OxBTC; PCP; PoLF; PoPl; PP; PrIm; TEP; TreFS
When you are old and beautiful. At Majority. Adrienne Rich. NePoEA-2
When you are old and gray and full of sleep. Villanelle with a Line by Yeats. Bruce Bennett. AMV-80
When you are traveling. Ijajee's Story. Charlotte DeClue. STE; TWSS

When you are very old, at evening. Of His Lady's Old Age. Pierre de Ronsard, *tr. by* Andrew Lang. AWP; CTC
When you are walking by yourself. Kick a Little Stone. Dorothy Aldis. SoPo
When you ask God in the morning. Be Thankful. Mark Bullock. STF
When you awake. The Sleeper. Sydney Clouts. PeSA; VWA
When you break your heart it changes. End Song. Ruth Krauss. LLLT
When you broke from me. Izumi Shikibu, *tr. fr. Japanese by* Willis Barnstone. BoWoP
When you buy clothes on easy terms. Cotton-Mill Colic. *Unknown.* OuSiCo
When you call, your cheerfulness thick as armadillo hide. Best Friends. Judith Hemschemeyer. AMV-81
When you came and you talked and you read. To William Carlos Williams. Galway Kinnell. NePoAm
When you came out of your house. Remembering Althea. William Stafford. NYBP
When you came, you were like red wine and honey. A Decade. Amy Lowell. MoAmPo; PoPl
When you come, as you soon must, to the streets of our city. Advice to a Prophet. Richard Wilbur. AmPP; CAPP; CoPo; FYAP; MAT; MoAmPo; MP; NMP; NYBP; OBWP; OxBC; PPP; SUW; TwCP
When you come to the end of a perfect day. A Perfect Day. Carrie Jacobs Bond. BLSo; TreF; WBLP
When you come to the other side. The Other. Peter Cooley. AMV-80; MAYP
When you consider the radiance, that it does not withhold. The City Limits. A. R. Ammons. NoAM; NOBA; NoP; NYP
When you dance. Creole Girl. Leslie Morgan Collins. PoNe
When you destroy a blade of grass. To Iron-Founders and Others. Gordon Bottomley. OBEV; OBMV; OBVV
When you drive on the freeway, cars follow you. Paranoia. Michael Dennis Browne. AmPA
When you enter. Al Fitnah Muhajir. Nazzam Al Sudan. NBP
When you feel like saying something. The Most Vital Thing in Life. Grenville Kleiser. SoSe
When you first feel the ground under your feet. Walking in a Swamp. David Wagoner. HAP; NPAW
When you first rub up against God's own skin. Ars Poetica about Ultimates. Tram Combs. MP; TwCP
When you get down to it, earth. A Physics. Heather McHugh. MAYP; SUW
When you get hard knocks and buffets. Keep the Glad Flag Flying. *Unknown.* FaFP
When you get out there. Catching a Horse. Barbara Winder. PH
When you get to heaven. Surprises. *Unknown.* STF
When You Go Away. W. S. Merwin. LCAP
When you go away. The Departure. Frank Steele. PPJ
When you go to a store in Ascutney. Limerick. Richard H. Field. WhC
When you ground the lenses and the moons swam free. The Emancipators. Randall Jarrell. PoA; WaP
When you had left our pirate fold. A Most Ingenious Paradox. W. S. Gilbert. *Fr.* The Pirates of Penzance. NAs
When you hark to the voice of the knocker. The Quarrelsome Trio. "L. G." WBLP
When you have bathed in the river. Submission. *Unknown, tr. by* E. Powys Mathers. ErPo
When you have come, the house is emptied quite. Evening. Mary Matheson. CaP
When You Have Forgotten Sunday: The Love Story. Gwendolyn Brooks. BPo; FF; WPOW
When you have tidied all things for the night. Solitude. Harold Monro. BSV; MoBrPo; TrGrPo
When you have wearied of the valiant spires of this country town. Oxford Canal. James Elroy Flecker. OxBTC
When you hear me walking. Nappy Head Blues. *Unknown.* BluL
When you kneel below me. Celebration. Leonard Cohen. ErPo
When You Laugh. Ingrid Jonker, *tr. fr. Afrikaans by* Elizabeth Jones. WPOW
When You Leave. Kimiko Hahn. BrSi
When you lie with a woman, at least so girls say. Epigram: To Polycharmus. Martial. PeHV
When you look down from the airplane you see lines. Field and Forest. Randall Jarrell. LCAP; VGW
When you look on my grave. *Unknown.* FaBoEE
When you lose your money please don't lose your mind. Married Man Blues. *Unknown.* BluL
When you lost touch with lovers' bare skin. John Donne. James Simmons. CIP
When you love, or speak of it. Aphra Behn. BoWoP
When you perceive these stones are wet. Epitaph. Sir William Davenant. ACP
When you plunged. The Otter. Seamus Heaney. IPY
When you put on the feet be sure. Dr. Potatohead Talks to Mothers. Judith Johnson Sherwin. NoAM
When you put up your walls afresh. To You Building the New House. Nelly Sachs, *tr. by* Keith Bosley. VWA
When You Reach the Hilltop the Sky Is on Top of You. Etta Blum. GoYe
When you reach to touch the markings. Indian Rock, Bainbridge Island, Washington. Duane Niatum. CDW
When You Read This Poem. Pinkie Gordon Lane. BlSi
When you ride on a train, a passenger train. Passenger Train. Edith Newlin Chase. SoPo
When you scuttled the ship, the shore was still in sight. Meditation of a Mariner. Dorothy Auchterlonie. CBAP
When you see a guy reach for stars in the sky. Guys and Dolls. Frank Loesser. OBAL
When you see a pretty maiden who has just turn'd seventeen. You're Not the Only Pebble on the Beach. Harry Braisted. FSN
When You See Millions of the Mouthless Dead. Charles Sorley. MMA; OBWP
When you send out invitations, don't ask me. Palladas, *tr. fr. Greek by* Tony Harrison. OBVE
When you shall see me in the toils of Time. She, to Him. Thomas Hardy. OBVV; OxBTC
When you show me. Colors for Mama. Barbara Mahone. CNA; PoBA
When you speak of dauntless deeds. The Deed of Lieutenant Miles. Clinton Scollard. PAH
When You Speak to Me. Tess Gallagher. LTB
When you start for San Francisco. Humbug Steamship Companies. *Unknown.* BPAW
When you swim in the surf off Seal Rocks, and your family. Family. Josephine Miles. FYAP; GP; GrPl
When you take off your clothes. In Nakedness. Marnie Pomeroy. ErPo
When you the sunburnt pilgrim see. Good Counsel to a Young Maid. Thomas Carew. CaPo; ErPo
When you think of the distances. The Distances. W. S. Merwin. NOBA
When you think of the hosts without no. Cautionary Limerick. *Unknown.* FaBoUs
When you turn down your glass it's a sign. Table Manners. James Montgomery Flagg. TDH
When you visit the barber. Barbershop. Martin Gardner. RHPC
When You Walk. James Stephens. PDV
When you walked down the stairs [*or* downstairs]. In Praise of Beverly. Steve Orlen. GP; MAYP
When you walked here. The Dumbfounding. Margaret Avison. NOBC
When you wanted a piano. Music. Naomi Shihab Nye. Str
When you wardance, sometimes you must. Wardance. Phillip William George. VoR
When you was down sick down on your bed. She's Gone Blues. *Unknown.* BluL
When you watch for. Feather or Fur. John Becker. FaPON; RHPC; TiPo
When you were. For Angela. Zack Gilbert. PoBA
When you were/ a girl, you pricked. Woman. Umberto Saba, *tr. by* Christopher Millis. AMV-81
When you were a tadpole and I was a fish. Evolution. Langdon Smith. BeLS; BLPA; FaBoBe; FaFP; HBV-1; TreF; YaD
When you were alive, my Leukothea. Leukothea. Keith Douglas. NeBP
When you were here in wonderful Detroit. Goodbye David Tamunoemi West. Margaret Danner. BPo
When You Were Sweet Sixteen. James Thornton. FSN, *with music*; FSW
When you were there, and you, and you. Dining-Room Tea. Rupert Brooke. BrPo; MoBrPo
When you were weary, roaming the wide world over. The Betrayal. Alice Furlong. AnIV
When You Will Walk in the Field. Leah Goldberg, *tr. fr. Hebrew by* Simon Halkin. TrJP
When you withdrew the dagger of your grin. Sonnet to a Tyrant. Mary Anne Ellis. AMV-80
When you woke [up] among them. After Grief. Stanley Plumly. AmPA; DiL; LCAP
When You Write Again. Ingrid Jonker, *tr. fr. Afrikaans by* Jack Cope *and* William Plomer. PBWP
When young-ey'd Spring profusely throws. Invocation to Fancy. Joseph Warton. *Fr.* Ode to Fancy. OBEC
When Young Hearts Break. Heine, *tr. fr. German by* Louis Untermeyer. AWP
When young I scribbled, boasting, on my wall. The Summing-up. Stanley Kunitz. OBAL; PoPl
When Young Ladies Get Married. *Unknown.* AmFP
When Young Melissa Sweeps. Nancy Byrd Turner. FaPON; NTCP
When Younglings First. *Unknown.* EnRePo
When your belly. The Peaches Joel Oppenheimer. CoPo
When Your Cheap Divorce Is Granted. "Orpheus C. Kerr." OBAL

When your Christian duty calls you. God Is There. Walter E. Isenhour. STF
When your client's hopping mad. The Advertising Agency Song. *Unknown.* FaBoUs; PV
When your eyes gaze seaward. Golden Moonrise. William Stanley Braithwaite. PoBA
When your eyes shall be closing, your mouth be opening. *Tr. from Gaelic by* Douglas Hyde. WTO
When your face/ appeared over my crumpled life. Colors. Yevgeny Yevtushenko, *tr. by* Robin Milner-Gulland *and* Peter Levi. LLLT
When your feet are like lead. Consolatory! St. John Emile Clavering Hankin. CenHV
When your grapes formed, you swore to save them. Hoarded Grapes. *Unknown, tr. by* Louis Untermeyer. UnTE
When your hour was rung at last. Rendez-vous Manqué dans la Rue Racine. J. M. Synge. BIrV
When Your Parents Grow Old. Joanne Hart. AMV-80
When your sperm enters me, it is altered. Adrienne Rich. *Fr.* Ghazals. CABA
When your widow had left the graveside. The Ritual of Memories. Tess Gallagher. GeTw
When you're a duck like me it's impossible. The Duck. Richard Digance. RHPC
When You're Away. Samuel Hoffenstein. FiBHP; POL
When you're lying awake with a dismal headache. Nightmare [*or* Lord Chancellor's Song]. W. S. Gilbert. *Fr.* Iolanthe. FaBoNo; NBM; NOBL; NoP; OxBoLi; PoRA
When you're out in smart society. Well, Did You Evah? Cole Porter. OBAL
"When you're together with her, and you have a good excuse." Jean Ruiz, *tr. by* Hubert Creekmore. *Fr.* The Book of True Love. ErPo
When Youth and Beauty Meet Togither. *Unknown.* ElL
When Youth Had Led. Earl of Surrey. EnRePo; SiPS
When Youth observes with pitying smile. In Praise of Commonplace. Sir Owen Seaman. InMe
When youth was lord of my unchallenged fate. On a Boy's First Reading of "King Henry V." S. Weir Mitchell. AA
When youthful faith hath fled. Lines. John Gibson Lockhart. OBEV; OBVV
When You've Been Here Long Enough. Lawrence Joseph. HoAn
"When you've got a good hat." Between a Good Hat and Good Boots. Kell Robertson. TAT
When you've grown up, my dears, and are as old as I. Toyland. Glen MacDonough. BLSo; FSN
When you've just been jugged by an upright judge. They Can't Do That. *Unknown.* WTO
Whenas from cups my Julia sups. Peter Titheradge. Teatime Variations: After Robert Herrick. FaBoPa
Whenas galoshed my Julia goes. Upon Julia's Arctics. Bert Leston Taylor. OBAL
Whenas in furs my Julia goes. Upon Julia's Clothes. E. V. Knox. BXAP
Whenas in Jeans. Paul Dehn. FiBHP
Whenas in perfume Julia went. Herrick's Julia. Helen Bevington. BXAP; SpRo
Whenas in Silks My Julia Goes. Robert Herrick. *See* Upon Julia's clothes.
Whenas [*or* When as] man's life, the light of human[e] lust. Sonnet. Fulke Greville. *Fr.* Caelica. LiTB; MePo; OBS; OxBoCh; PoEL-1
Whenas—methinks that is a pretty way. They Answer Back [*or* To His Ever-worshipped Will from W. H.]. "Francis." ErPo; FiBHP
Whenas Queen Anne of great renown. A New Ballad. Arthur Mainwaring. APAS
Whenas [*or* When as *or* When that] the chill sirocco [*or* charokko *or* charocco] blow[e]s. In Praise of Ale [*or* Give Me Ale *or* Pipe and Can II]. *Unknown, at. to* Thomas Bonham. FaBoCh; HBV-2; OBEV; OBS; ViBoPo
Whenas the mildest month. The Rose. Thomas Howell. ElL; OBSC
Whenas the Nightingale. John Cleveland. *See* Mark Anthony.
Whenas [*or* When as] the Rye [Reach to the Chin]. George Peele. *Fr.* The Old Wives' Tale. ELP; EnLoPo; FaBoCh; GBL; InvP; NoP; SeCePo; TEP; ViBoPo
(Song.) ElL; FaBoEn; LoBV; OBSC; OxBoLi; PoEL-2
(Summer Song, A.) NOBE; OBEV
Whenas to shoot my Julia goes. To Julia in Shooting Togs. Sir Owen Seaman. BXAP
Whenas we sat in Babylon. Bible, *O.T., paraphrased by* Thomas Sternhold *and* John Hopkins. Psalms, CXXXVII. OAEL-1
Whence and Whither. Hayyim Nahman Bialik, *tr. fr. Hebrew by* Helena Frank. TrJP
"Whence are you, learning's son?" The End of Clonmacnois. *Unknown, tr. by* Frank O'Connor. CIP; KiLC
Whence art thou, thirsty wind. O Thirsty Wind. *Tr. fr. Hawaiian by* N. B. Emerson. WTO
Whence came his feet into my field, and why? He and I. Dante Gabriel Rossetti. The House of Life, XCVIII. NBM
Whence came this man? As if on the wings. Abraham Lincoln. Samuel Valentine Cole. OHIP
Whence come ye, Cherubs? from the moon? The Chanting Cherubs—A Group by Greenough. Richard Henry Dana. AA
Whence come you, all of you so sorrowful? Sonnet: To Certain Ladies; When Beatrice Was Lamenting Her Father's Death. Dante, *tr. by* Dante Gabriel Rossetti. AWP
Whence comes my love? O heart, disclose! A Sonnet Made on Isabella Markham. John Harington. ElL; OBSC
Whence comes solace?—Not from seeing. On a Fine Morning. Thomas Hardy. VLP
Whence comes this rush of wings afar. Carol of the Birds. *Unknown, tr. fr. French.* OHIP
Whence Had They Come? W. B. Yeats. BoLoP
Whence, hardworn, drum. Tambour. István Vas, *tr. by* Jascha Kessler. VWA
Whence hast thou then, thou witless puss. Tiger at Play. Joanna Baillie. PCat
Whence let us go to. "The Nicest Phantasies Are Shared." Brian Coffey. CIP
Whence, O fragrant form of light. The Water-Lily. John Banister Tabb. AA; ACP; GoBC
Whence the sudden stir that roars through my vitals? Epithalamium for Mary Stuart and the Dauphin of France, *abr.* George Buchanan. GoTS
Whence this impatience fluttering in my breast! Urania. Robert Andrews. NOEC
Whence thou returnst, and whither wentst, I know. Leave Taking. Milton. *Fr.* Paradise Lost, XII. FaBoEn
Whene'er across this sinful flesh of mine. The Sign of the Cross. Cardinal Newman. GoBC
Whene'er bitter foe attack thee. Advice to Hotheads. Samuel ben Elhanan Isaac, Archevolti of Padua, *tr. by* A. B. Rhine. TrJP
Whene'er I come where ladies are. Love at Large. Coventry Patmore. *Fr.* The Angel in the House. EBVV
Whene'er I look into your eyes. I Love But Thee. Heine, *tr. by* Louis Untermeyer. AWP
Whene'er I quote I seldom take. The Bards We Quote. Bert Leston Taylor. HBMV; WhC
Whene'er I see soft hazel eyes. The Lapful of Nuts. Sir Samuel Ferguson. VLP
Whene'er I take my walks abroad. Praise for Mercies Spiritual and Temporal. Isaac Watts. NOEC
Whene'er with haggard eyes I view. Song [*or* Rogero's Song *or* Song of One Eleven Years in Prison]. George Canning, George Ellis, *and* John Hookham Frere. *Fr.* The Rovers. FaBoNo; FiBHP; NOEC; OBEC
Whenever a fellow called Rex. Limerick. *Unknown.* NOBL
Whenever a Little Child Is Born. Agnes Carter Mason. AA
Whenever a snowflake leaves the sky. Snowflakes. Mary Mapes Dodge. AA; HBVY
Whenever, Chloe, I begin. Song. Earl of Chesterfield. NOEC
Whenever he observes me purchasing. Sextus the Usurer. Martial, *tr. by* Kirby Flower Smith. AWP
Whenever I come on kelp-stained nets. Beacon Light. Leslie Savage Clark. PGD
Whenever I Go There. W. S. Merwin. NaP
Whenever I pause. The Noise of the Village. *Tr. by* Frances Densmore. OBVE
"Whenever I plunge my arm, like this." Under the Waterfall. Thomas Hardy. BoLoP; CTC; LiTB
Whenever I ride on the Texas plains. Texas Trains and Trails. Mary Austin. SoPo; TiPo
Whenever I Say "America." Nancy Byrd Turner. YeAr
Whenever I see him. Waking in the Dark. Dorothy Livesay. NOBC
Whenever I walk to Suffern along the Erie track. The House with Nobody in It. Joyce Kilmer. BLPA; BLPL
Whenever, in that ceiling sky. Grace at the Atlanta Fox. Turner Cassity. NIP
Whenever Mr. Edwards spake. The Theology of Jonathan Edwards. Phyllis McGinley. MoAmPo
Whenever Richard Cory went down town. Richard Cory. E. A. Robinson. AmPP; CMoP; DL; DTC; FaFP; FF; FPL; HAP; InPK; LiTA; LiTM; MasP; MoAB; MoAmPo; MoVE; NePA; NIP; NOBA; OxBA; PAI; PoLF; PoRA; PrIm; SoSe; TAP; TreF; TrGrPo
Whenever the dark cloud horses galloped. And Jesus Don't Have Much Use for His Old Suitcase Anymore. Tom Kryss. NeAC
Whenever the days are cool and clear. The Sandhill Crane. Mary Austin. BPAW; TiPo
Whenever the magician snaps his fingers. The Magician. Joan Colby. PoDr

Whenever the moon and stars are set. Windy Nights. Robert Louis Stevenson. GoJo; OxBChV; PH; PoRA; RHPC; SiSoSe; TiPo
Whenever the Presbyterian bell. J. Milton Miles. Edgar Lee Masters. *Fr.* Spoon River Anthology. CrMA
Whenever the Snakes Come. Hedva Harkavi, *tr. fr. Hebrew by* Tova Weizman. VWA
Whenever the summer-singed plains. Caller of the Buffalo. Mary Austin. BPAW
Whenever there is music, it is you. When There Is Music. David Morton. HBMV
Whenever there is silence around me. There Is a Man on the Cross. Elizabeth Cheney. PGD; TRV
Whenever troublous hours I find. Happiness amidst Troubles. Immanuel di Roma, *tr. by* J. Chotzner. TrJP
Whenever war is spoken of. The Great War. Vernon Scannell. OBWP
Whenever we touched, I thought of the Lying-in Hospital. Elegy. Robert Layzer. NePoEA; PoPl
Whenever we would open, there he stood. Murgatroyd. Celeste Turner Wright. Str
Whenever you drink all night you make. Martial, *tr. fr. Latin by* James Michie. FaBoEE
Whenever you want to leave the clay, the deep. Southern Exposures. G. E. Murray. AMV-81
Whenne ich see on roode. On the Passion. *Unknown.* OxBM
Whenne mine eynen misteth. All Too Late. *Unknown.* EBEV; OxBM
Wher one would be. Sir Edward Dyer. PoEL-1
Where. Walter de la Mare. NYBP
Where? Kenneth Patchen. LiTM
Where a Roman judged a foreign people. Notre Dame. Osip Mandelstam, *tr. by* James Greene. OBVE
Where a Roman Villa Stood, above Freiburg. Mary Elizabeth Coleridge. OBNC
Where a safe hearth glows warm. Art and Civilization. Robert Conquest. NoAM
Where all the winds were tranquil. A Pine-Tree Buoy. Harrison Smith Morris. AA
Where all things grow according to their own design. The Meadow. John Wieners. CoPo
Where am I from? From the green hills of Erin. A Broken Song. "Moira O'Neill." OBVV
Where am I now? And what. A Song in Passing. Yvor Winters. VGW
Where am I, O awesome friend? Yitzhak Lamdan, *tr. by* Simon Halkin. *Fr.* For the Sun Declined. TrJP
Where ancient forests round us spread. Hymn for the Dedication of a Church. Andrews Norton. AA
Where angel trumpets hail a brighter sun. My Own Hereafter. Eugene Lee-Hamilton. WGRP
Where are all thy beauties now, all hearts enchaining? Thomas Campion. GBL; OBSC
Where are Elmer, Herman, Bert, Tom and Charley. The Hill. Edgar Lee Masters. *Fr.* Spoon River Anthology. CMoP; FYAP; LiTA; LiTM; NePA; NoAM; NOBA; OxBA; SeCeV; TAP; ViBoPo
Where are my friends? I am alone. Schoolfellows. Winthrop Mackworth Praed. *Fr.* School and Schoolfellows. NBM
Where are my people? To Egypt. Gloria Davis. NBP
Where are now, in coign or crack. Ballade of England. Louis MacNeice. NYBP
Where are now the Captains. A Ballad of the Captains. E. J. Brady. EtS
Where are the bay-leaves, Thestylis, and the charms? The Incantation. Theocritus, *tr. by* Charles Stuart Calverley. *Fr.* Idylls. AWP
Where are the braves, the faces like autumn fruit. Indian Reservation: Caughnawaga. A. M. Klein. LiTM; NOBC; NoP; OBCV
Where are the dear domestics, white and black. Familiar Faces, Long Departed. Robert Hillyer. NYBP
Where are the friends that I knew in my Maying. Comrades. George Edward Woodberry. HBV-2
Where are the great, whom thou wouldst wish to praise thee? Isolation. Arthur Hugh Clough. *Fr.* Dipsychus. OBVV
Where are the hands and feet. Give Me My Infant Now. Te-whaka-io-roa, *tr. by* John White. NAs; WTO
Where Are the Hebrew Children? *with music. At. to* Peter Cartwright. AH
Where are the heroes of yesteryear? Where, O Where? Milton Bracker. LiSp
Where are the loves that we loved before. L'Envoi. Willa Cather. HBV-2
Where are the lumberjacks who came from the woods for Christmas. River Song. Elizabeth Brewster. CaP
Where Are the Men Seized in This Wind of Madness? Aldo do Espirito Santo, *tr. fr. Portuguese by* Alan Ryder. TTY; WPOW
Where are the old side-wheelers now. The River Boats. Daniel Whitehead Hicky. AmFN
Where Are the Ones Who Lived Before? *Unknown. See* Ubi Sunt Qui ante Nos Fuerunt?
Where are the opium ships—gulls of the Indian seas? Opium Clippers. Daniel Henderson. EtS
Where are the passions they essayed. Ballade of Dead Actors. W. E. Henley. EBVV; OBMV
Where are the people. Question. Norma Craig. POL
Where are the people as beautiful as poems. The Black Angel. Henri Coulette. CoAP
Where are the ribbons I tie my hair with? Ballade of Lost Objects. Phyllis McGinley. PoCh; PoRA
Where are the ships I used to know. The Ships of Saint John. Bliss Carman. EtS
Where are the swallows fled? A Doubting Heart. Adelaide Anne Procter. HBV-2
Where Are the War Poets? C. Day Lewis. FaBoMo; OBWP; OxBTC
Where Are the Waters of Childhood? Mark Strand. LCAP; WeW
Where are they gone, and do you know. The Little Ghosts. Thomas S. Jones, Jr. HBV-1
Where are they gone, the old familiar faces? The Old Familiar Faces. Charles Lamb. EnRP; FaBoRV
Where are they now, the softly blooming flowers. Irises. Padraic Colum. BoNaP
Where are they that barred the way. At Masada. Ernest Neufeld. AMV-81
Where are those legs with which you run. Johnny, I Hardly Knew Ye: In Dublinese, *parody. Unknown.* OnYI
Where are those that were before us. Ubi Sunt Qui ante Nos Fuerunt? *Unknown, tr. by* George Perkins. PrIm
Where are we. Bahamas. George Oppen. NYBP
Where are we going? where are we going. Song of Slaves in the Desert. Whittier. OBVV; OxBA
Where are we to go when this is done? Sonnet. Alfred A. Duckett. AmNP; PoBA; PoNe
"Where are you coming from, Lomey Carter." Old Christmas Morning. Roy Helton. MoAmPo
Where Are You Going. Eliza Lee Follen. SoPo
(Little Kittens, The, *diff. arrangement.*) TiPo
Where are you going? asked Manny the Mayor. Jig Tune: Not for Love. Thomas McGrath. VGW
Where Are You Going, Greatheart? John Oxenham. BLPA; PAL; PGD
"Where are you going, little cat?" Where Are You Going. Eliza Lee Follen. SoPo
"Where are you going, Master mine?" Whither Away? Mary Elizabeth Coleridge. CH
Where Are You Going, My Good Old Man? *Unknown.* FSW
"Where are you going, my little kittens?" The Little Kittens. Eliza Lee Follen. TiPo
"Where are you going, my pretty little dear." Dabbling in the Dew. *Unknown.* UnTE
"Where are you going [to], my pretty maid?" Mother Goose. HBVY; OxNR
Where are you going, my spiv, my wide boy. Spiv Song. Royston Ellis. PeHV
"Where are you going?" said the knight in the road. The False Knight upon the Road. *Unknown.* AmFP
Where are you going? To Scarborough Fair? Scarborough Fair. *Unknown.* OxBoLi
"Where are you going to-night, to-night." John Evereldown. E. A. Robinson. CMoP; NePA; OxBA
Where are you going, you little pig? Little Piggy. Thomas Hood. SoPo
Where Are You Now? Mary Britton Miller. RHPC
Where Are You Now Superman? Brian Patten. FF
Where are your ancient waves, O river. Home-coming. Albert Ehrenstein, *tr. by* Babette Deutsch *and* Avram Yarmolinsky. TrJP
Where are your heroes, my little black ones. Poem for Black Boys. Nikki Giovanni. BPo
Where are your oranges? The Children's Bells. Eleanor Farjeon. CH
Where art thou? Flathead and Nez Perce Sin-ka-ha. William S. Lewis. BPAW
Where art thou gone, light-ankled youth? To Youth. Walter Savage Landor. EnRP; HBV-1
Where art thou, Muse, that thou forget'st so long. Sonnets, C. Shakespeare. OBSC
Where art thou, my beloved son. The Affliction of Margaret. Wordsworth. EnRP; GTBS; GTBS-P; OBRV; PoEL-4
Where Athanase once hankered for a star. Letter to Karl Shapiro. E. L. Mayo. MiAP
Where Avalanches Wail. *Unknown.* NA
Where Babylon Ends. Nathaniel Tarn. VWA
Where balsams droop their fragrant boughs. Little Ponds. Arthur Guiterman. HBMV
Where be those roses gone which sweetened so our eyes? Astrophel and Stella, CII. Sir Philip Sidney. SiPS

Where Be You Going, You Devon Maid? Keats. ErPo; HBV-1; UnTE
Where beeth [*or* beth] they biforen us weren. *See* Were beth they biforen us weren.
Where, behind Keighley, the road. Matthew Arnold. *Fr.* Haworth Churchyard. FaBoPP
Where broods the Absolute. Quest. Edmund Clarence Stedman. *Fr.* Corda Concordia. AA
Where Cadmus, old Agenor's son, did rest and plant his reign. The Fate of Narcissus. William Warner. *Fr.* Albion's England. OBSC
Where Cape Delgado strikes the sea. E. J. Pratt. *Fr.* The Cachalot. CaP; MoCV
Where Children Live. Naomi Shihab Nye. MAYP
Where Claribel low-lieth. Claribel. Tennyson. PeD
Where close the curving mountains drew. Untrodden Ways. Agnes Maule Machar. CaP
Where could I meet you. There Are Oceans. Joy Harjo. TWSS
Where cows did slowly seek the brink. The Bwoat. William Barnes. VLP
Where Cross the Crowded Ways of Life. Frank Mason North. AH, *with music*
(City, The.) WGRP
Where Cumbria's mountains in the north arise. James Plumptre. *Fr.* Prologue to "The Lakers; a Comic Opera." NOEC
Where Did He Run To? Mark Van Doren. SO
"Where did I come from, Mother, and why?" Christmas Lullaby for a New-born Child. Yvonne Gregory. AmNP
Where did I dwell? I dwelt in the shadow of death. Wanderer. Jessica Powers. AMV-80
Where did Momotara go. Momotara. Rose Fyleman. TiPo
"Where did the blood come from?" On a Line in Sandburg. R. S. Thomas. NAs
Where did the voice come from? I hunted through the rooms. Bedtime Story for My Son. Peter Redgrove. NePoEA-2
Where Did You Come From? George Macdonald. *See* Baby, The.
Where did you come from. Cotton Eye Joe. *Unknown.* OuSiCo
Where Did You Get That Hat? Joseph J. Sullivan. FSN, *with music*; TreF
Where dips the rocky highland. The Stolen Child. W. B. Yeats. CMoP; NoP; OnYI; OxBI; WSC
Where do all the failed fathers. Failed Fathers. Lewis Turco. AMV-81
Where Do I Love You, Lovely Maid? Raymond F. Roseliep. ISi
Where do people go when they go to sleep? Nightgown, Wife's Gown. Robert Sward. ELU
Where Do the Gipsies Come From? H. H. Bashford. CH
"Where do the stars grow, little Garaine? Little Garaine. Sir Gilbert Parker. FaPON
"Where do the waters go that go." ¿Quien Sabe? Madge Morris. BPAW
Where do these voices stray. The Eccho. Richard Leigh. MePo
Where do we go, my love, who have been led. The Bed. James Merrill. NePoEA
Where do you come from, Mr. Jay? Strange Lands. Laurence Alma-Tadema. HBVY
Where do you go with your fury. Fury's Field. Cecil Bodker, *tr. by* Nadia Christensen. PBWP
Where do you sing your hymns. Lament for Richard Rolston. Sir Osbert Sitwell. ChMP
Where do you think the Fairies go. The Fairies' Shopping. Margaret Deland. HBVY
Where do you walk this moment that I fall? Next of Kin. H. B. Mallalieu. WaP
Where does Pinafore Palace stand? Lilliput Levee. William Brighty Rands. CenHV
Where dost [*or* do'st] thou careless[e] lie. An Ode to Himself. Ben Jonson. AnAnS-1; EnRePo; FaBoEn; HAP; JCP; LiTB; NOBE; NoP; OAEP; OBS; PoEL-2; PrIm; QFR; SeCePo; SeCeV; SeCP; SeCV-1
Where Dunwich Used to Be. Swinburne. *Fr.* By the North Sea, VI. FaBoPP
Where dwell the lovely, wild white womenfolk. The White Women. Mary Elizabeth Coleridge. BrRo
Where ends our chancel in a vaulted space. The Vicar. George Crabbe. *Fr.* The Borough. OBSV
Where Englands Damon us'd to keep. The Pastoral on the King's Death; Written in 1648. Alexander Brome. OBS
Where every female delights to give her maiden to her husband. Male & Female Loves in Beulah. Blake. *Fr.* Jerusalem, III. OBNC
Where fair Sabrina's wand'ring currents flow. William Somervile. *Fr.* The Bowling-Green. NOEC
Where Fire Burns. Gladys Cardiff. TWSS
Where five old graves lay circled on a hill. The Graveyard. Jane Cooper. NePoEA-2
Where Fled. John Wieners. CoPo
Where folds the central lotus. William Yeats in Limbo. Sidney Keyes. MoBrPo
Where forlorn sunsets flare and fade. Over the Hills and Far Away [*or* Stanzas]. W. E. Henley. HBV-2; HBVY; TreF
Where Foyle his swelling waters rolls northward to the main. The Maiden City. Charlotte Elizabeth Tonna. HBV-2
Where from the watch towers. Bay Poem. Lance Henson. VoR
Where glows the Irish hearth with peat. Cois na Teineadh. T. W. Rolleston. AnIV
Where go the birds when the rain. Jane Heap. PoA
Where Go the Boats? Robert Louis Stevenson. FaBoBe; FaBoCh; GoJo; NTCP; OxBChV; SoPo; SUS; TiPo; TreFT
Where Goblins Dwell. Jack Prelutsky. RHPC
Where great Pike's Peak his summit rears. Old Balaam. *Unknown.* PoOW
Where had I heard this wind before. Bereft. Robert Frost. LiTM; MoAB; MoAmPo; OxBA; SoSe; TwAmPo
Where hae ye been a' the day. *Unknown.* OxNR
Where has he of race divine. Chorus of Satyrs, Driving Their Goats. Euripides, *tr. by* Shelley. *Fr.* Cyclops. AWP
Where has tenderness gone, he asked the mirror. Delirium in Vera Cruz. Malcolm Lowry. FaBoTw; OxBTC
Where has ti been, maw canny hinny? Captain Bover. *Unknown.* GBP
Where hast been toiling all day, sweetheart. The Child on the Judgment Seat. Elizabeth Rundle Charles. BLPA
Where hast 'te been, ma' canny hinny? Ma Canny Hinny. *Unknown.* FaBoPP; GBP
Where hast thou been since I saw thee. Ilkley Moor Baht *Unknown.* FSW
Where hast thou floated? in what seas pursued. To the Immortal Memory of the Halibut on Which I Dined This Day, Monday, April 26, 1784. William Cowper. MOS; SeCePo
Where Have All the Indians Gone? Janet Campbell Hale. STE
Where have these hands been. Musician. Louise Bogan. GoJo; NYBP
Where have they gone. The Saint John. George Frederick Clarke. CaP
Where have they led you, into what disguise. The Kingdom. Jon Swan. NYBP
"Where have you been all day, Henry my son,/ Where have you been all day, my beloved one?" Henry My Son. *Unknown.* OBET
"Where have you been all day, Henry my son,/ Where have you been all day, my pretty one?" Green and Yellow. *Unknown.* OBET
Where have you been all the day, Billy boy, Billy boy? *Unknown.* OxNR
Where Have You Been Dear? Karla Kuskin. NTCP
Where Have You Been, My Good Old Man? *with music. Unknown.* OuSiCo
"Where have you been this while away." The Widow's Party. Kipling. VLP
Where Have You Gone? Mari Evans. BPo; NNP; PoNe; TTY
Where Have You Gone, Little Boy. Patty L. Harjo. VoR
Where have you gone to, Yesterday. Yesterday. Hugh Chesterman. SiSoSe
"Where have you hidden them?" I asked the sea. Lost Ships. Thomas Hornsby Ferril. EtS
Where He Hangs His Hat. Deborah Lee. BrSi
Where he rows the dark. The Bear Who Came to Dinner. Adrien Stoutenburg. SO
Where he stood and where. Jew. James A. Randall, Jr. BPo
Where he stood in boots in water to his calves. The Fishvendor. William Meredith. SaC
Where He Takes Tea with Cromwell. *Unknown.* DBV
Where Helen Comes. John Jerome Rooney. AA
Where Helen Sits. Laura E. Richards. AA
Where hills are hard and bare. Abraham's Knife. George Garrett. PoPl
Where hints of racy sap and gum. Wild Honey. Maurice Thompson. HBV-1
Where His Lady Keeps His Heart. "A. W." CTC; ElL; OBSC
Where Hudson's Wave. George Pope Morris. AA
Where I Am Now. Harvey Shapiro. GP
Where I go are flowers blooming. Les Planches-en-Montagnes. Michael Roberts. OBMV
Where I Live in This Honorable House of the Laurel Tree. Anne Sexton. TwAmPo
Where I lived the river. Eclogues. Dennis Schmitz. NPGG
Where I Walk in Nebraska. Nancy G. Westerfield. AMV-80
Where I walk out. Song. Yvor Winters. BoAnP; POL
Where I was born, near Stepney Green. Stepney Green. John Singer. WaP
Where icy and bright dungeons lift. Voyages, VI. Hart Crane. CABA; HAP; MoAB; MoAmPo; MoVE; SeCeV; TwAmPo; UnPo
Where Ignorance Is Bliss. Thomas Gray. *Fr.* On a Distant Prospect of Eton College. TreF
Where in blind files. Song. Eavan Boland. CIP
Where in the attic the dust encumbers. Mournful Numbers. Morris Bishop. WhC
Where in the summer-warm woodlands with the sweet wind. Iphione. Thomas Caulfield Irwin. EnLoPo
Where in the valley the summer rain. Summer Rain. Laurie Lee. MoVE

Where, in what ever-blissfully [or whatever happily] watered gardens. Rainer Maria Rilke. *Fr.* Sonnets to Orpheus, Pt. II. OBVE, *tr. by* James Blair Leishman; SOTW, *tr. by* Christopher Hawthorne
Where is every piping lad. Dawn of Day. William Browne. *Fr.* The Shepherd's Pipe. EIL
Where is he, that giddy sprite. Wordsworth. *Fr.* The Kitten and Falling Leaves. PBBP
Where Is Heaven? Bliss Carman. TRV
Where is it now? Look, there it flies in merry sport. The Swallow's Flight. Louis Levy, *tr. by* Martin S. Alwood *and* Sanford Kaufman. TrJP
Where Is Justice? Eliezer Steinbarg, *tr. fr. Yiddish by* Seth L. Wolitz. VWA
Where is my boy, my boy. Emily Sparks. Edgar Lee Masters. *Fr.* Spoon River Anthology. GLGT
Where Is My Butterfly Net? David McCord. FiBHP
Where is my chief, my master, this bleak night, mavrone? O'Hussey's Ode to the Maguire [*or* Ode to the Maguire]. Eochadh O'Hussey, *tr. by* James Clarence Mangan. AnIV; BIrV; OnYI; OxBI; SeCePo
Where is my roof that kept out the rain? Roses Gone Wild. John Taylor. AMV-80; FAZ
Where is my ruined life, and where the fame. Hafiz, *tr. by* Gertrude Lowthian Bell. Odes, V. AWP
Where Is My Wandering Boy Tonight? *Unknown, at. to* Robert Lowry. FaFP; FSW; TreF
"Where is now Elijah's God?" A Martyr's Death. Menahem ben Jacob. TrJP
Where Is Our Holy Church? *with music.* Edwin H. Wilson. AH
Where Is Paris and Heleyne [*or* Helene]? Thomas of Hales. *Fr.* A Love-Song. ChTr; OxBM
Where is poor Jesus gone? Jesus. Francis Lauderdale Adams. OxBS
Where is she now? Where all must be. *Unknown.* LO
Where is that plain door? Insomnia. Marge Piercy. DFF
Where is that sugar, Hammond. Early Evening Quarrel. Langston Hughes. UnPo
Where Is the Black Community? Joyce Carol Thomas. CNA
Where is the duke my father with his power? Shakespeare. King Richard II, *fr.* III, ii. PoPle
Where is the gallant race that rose. Thomas Mercer. *Fr.* Arthur's Seat. OxBS
Where is the Grand Duke Ruffanuff, who stole the Czar's first wife? And When They Fall. James J. Montague. HBMV
Where is the grave of Sir Arthur O'Kellyn? The Knight's Tomb. Samuel Taylor Coleridge. EnRP; FaBoCh; GN
Where is the hand to trace. With a Coin from Syracuse. Oliver St. John Gogarty. OBMV
Where is the home for me? The Home of Aphrodite. Euripides, *tr. by* Gilbert Murray. *Fr.* Bacchae. AWP
Where is the Jim Crow section. Merry-go-round. Langston Hughes. CTBA; PAI; PoNe
Where is the man who has been tried and found strong and sound? A Degenerate Age. Solomon ibn Gabirol, *tr. by* Emma Lazarus. TrJP
Where is the nightingale. Hilda Doolittle ("H. D."). Songs from Cyprus, II. MoAmPo
Where is the nymph, whose azure eye. Song. Thomas Moore. EnLoPo
Where Is the Sea? Felicia Dorothea Hemans. EtS
Where is the star of Bethlehem? Christmas 1959 et Cetera. Gerald William Barrax. OFD; PChr
Where is the true man's fatherland? The Fatherland. James Russell Lowell. GN; HBV-2; HBVY; PGD; PoPl
Where is the woman who unmoored this morning. The Woman. George Keithley. NPGG
Where is the word of Your youth and beauty. To the Young Man Jesus. Annie Charlotte Dalton. CaP
Where is the world? not about. Merchant Marine. Josephine Miles. TAP; VGW
Where is the world we roved, Ned Bunn? To Ned. Herman Melville. MOS; NOBA; PoEL-5; ViBoPo
Where is this stupendous stranger? The Nativity of Our Lord and Saviour Jesus Christ. Christopher Smart. *Fr.* Hymns and Spiritual Songs. EBEV; HAP; LAuP; LoBV; NAs; NOBE; NOCV; NOEC; PoEL-3; SBVL
Where is thy lovely perilous abode? To the Leanán Shee. Thomas Boyd. OnYI
Where Is Your Boy Tonight? *Unknown.* PaPo
Where It Is Winter. George O'Neil. HBMV
Where it says snow. Errata. Charles Simic. NNaP
Where Knock Is Open Wide. Theodore Roethke. HAP; VGW
Where Lackawanna's tracks graze our backyards. 'Laine. Robert Bagg. TwAmPo
Where laurel hedges hide the coal and coke. Crematorium. John Betjeman. PoA
Where leap the long Atlantic swells. The Cod-Fisher. Joseph C. Lincoln. EtS
Where Lies the Land [to Which the Ship Would Go]? Arthur Hugh Clough. Songs in Absence, VII. AWP; ChTr; EtS; FaBoBe; FaBoCh; FaBoRV; MOS; NOBE; OBVV; TreFT; WGRP
Where Lies the Land [to Which Yon Ship Must Go]? Wordsworth. EnRP; EtS; MOS; OBNC; OBRV; PoEL-4
(Sonnet: Where Lies the Land.) ChER
Where Lies the Truth? Has Man in Wisdom's Creed. Wordsworth. TrCP
Where light is. To a Woman Who Wants Darkness and Time. Gerald W. Barrax. PoBA
Where, like a pillow on a bed. The Ecstasy [*or* Extasie]. John Donne. AnAnS-1; BoLoP; CABA; EnLoPo; EnRePo; FaBoEn; FPL; HAP; InPS; JCP; LiTB; LoBV; MasP; MeLP; MePo; NOBE; NoP; OAEL-1; OBEV; PoEL-2; PPoe; PrIm; SeCePo; SeCeV; SeCP; SeCV-1; TEP; TrGrPo; UnTE; ViBoPo
Where Liver Eatin' Johnson lies. Old Trail Town, Cody, Wyoming. John Garmon. TAT
Where lives the man that never yet did hear. Orchestra; or, A Poem of Dancing. Sir John Davies. OBSC; SiPS
Where long the shadows of the wind had rolled. The Sheaves. E. A. Robinson. AP; AWP; CMoP; CoBMV; FaBV; HAP; MoAB; MoAmPo; NePA; NoAM; NOBA; OxBA; TAP; WHA
Where Love Is. Amelia Josephine Burr. HBV-1
Where Love Is King. Hilda Doolittle ("H. D."). HBMV
"Where Love, There's Heaven." Mary Jacobs. STF
Where marble stood and fell. Reflection in a Green Arena. Gregory Corso. VGW
Where may the wearied eye repose. Washington. Byron. *Fr.* Ode to Napoleon Buonaparte. OHIP; PAH; PAL
Where metalled road invades light thinning air. Sándor Weöres, *tr. by* Edwin Morgan. *Fr.* The Lost Parasol. OBVE
Where might there be a refuge for me. Tell Me, Tell Me. Marianne Moore. LiTM; NYBP
Where Mountain Lion Lay Down with Deer February 1973. Leslie Marmon Silko. STE; VoR; WPOW
Where murdered Mumford lies. Mumford. Ina M. Porter. PAH
Where My Books Go. W. B. Yeats. OBEV; OBVV
Where my fathers stood. Devon to Me. John Galsworthy. HBMV
Where my grandfather is is in the ground. Mi Abuelo. Alberto Ríos. MAYP
Where my grandmother lived. Number Four. Doughtry Long. CNA; PoBA; SO
Where my kindred dwell, there I wander. Dawn Boy's Song. *Unknown, tr. by* Washington Matthews. FaBV
Where My Word is unspoken. T. S. Eliot. *Fr.* The Rock. TRV
Where neither King nor shepheard want comes neare. Homer, *tr. by* George Chapman. *Fr.* The Odyssey, IV. CTC
Where no one was was where my world was stilled. Isle of Arran. Alastair Reid. BSV
Where Nothing Dwelt but Beasts of Prey, *with music.* Isaac Watts. AH
Where now/ are time and space. Wind Gardens. Louis Untermeyer. BXAP
Where Now Are the Hebrew Children? *with music. Unknown.* AH
Where now he roves, by wood or swamp whatever. Proem. Conrad Aiken. *Fr.* The Kid. MoAB
Where now the high-rise-village highways. Out of the Past. Robert Wallace. POL
Where now these mingled ruins lie. Stanzas Occasioned by the Ruins of a Country Inn [*or* On the Ruins of a Country Inn]. Philip Freneau. AA; OxBA
Where nowadays the Battery lies. Peter Stuyvesant's New Year's Call. Edmund Clarence Stedman. PAH
Where, O Where? Milton Bracker. LiSp
Where O Where Is Old Elijah, *with music. Unknown.* AS
Where, Oh Where Are the Hebrew Children? *Unknown.* BLPA
Where oh where is little Susie? Paw-Paw Patch. *Unknown.* FSW
Where, on prairie elevations. Fires. William Heyen. MAYP
Where on the wrinkled stream the willows lean. The Water-Ousel. Mary Webb. CH
Where once that flying red horse. Working at a Service Station, I Think of Shinkichi Takahashi. Dennis Finnell. FAZ
Where once the grey scrub's finches cried with thin. The Tank. Roland Robinson. PoAu-2
Where once we danced, where once we sang. An Ancient to Ancients. Thomas Hardy. ChMP; CMoP; CoBMV; GTBS-P; LiTM; MoPo; MoVE; OxBTC
Where once we hunted, white men have built many long-houses. Speech of the Salish Chief. Earle Birney. *Fr.* Damnation of Vancouver. OBCV
Where once you stood alert, alive. Ode to a Vanished Operator in an Automatized Elevator. Loyd Rosenfield. QQQ
Where only flowers fret. Aegean. Louis Simpson. GrPl; NYBP
Where or When. Philip Whalen. PoM
Where oxen do low and apples do grow. Dialogue, between Crab and

Gillian. Thomas D'Urfey. *Fr.* The Bath; or, The Western Lass. NOEC
Where peace goes whispering by. The Farm. Vassar Miller. NCSH
Where pollen crusts the pine bough. David Martinson. *Fr.* Nineteen Sections from a Twenty Acre Poem. TAT
Where racial memories, like snakes. Landscape of Violence. Ralph Nixon Currey. PeSA
Where rose the moutains, there to him were friends. Childe Harold. Byron. *Fr.* Childe Harold's Pilgrimage, III. OBRV
Where Runs the River. Francis William Bourdillon. HBV-2; WGRP
Where sea breaks inland, claiming the Quinalt. Tahola. Richard Hugo. WOLT
Where Shall a Sorrow Great. *Unknown.* EnRePo
Where shall Celia fly for shelter. Song. Christopher Smart. EnLoPo
Where Shall I Be When de Firs' Trumpet Soun'? *with music. Unknown.* BoAN-1
"Where shall I gang, my ain true love?" The Duke of Athole's Nurse. *Unknown.* ESPB
Where shall I go then. R. P. Blackmur. *Fr.* Sea Island Miscellany. MoVE
Where shall I have at mine own will. Sir Thomas Wyatt. SiPS
Where shall I hide my head and my face? Breaking. J. Alex Allan. PoAu-2
Where shall I learn to get my peace again? Keats. *Fr.* Lines to Fanny. ChER
Where shall my troubled soul, at large. Echo in a Church. Lord Herbert of Cherbury. AnAnS-2
Where Shall the Baby's Dimple Be? Josiah G. Holland. BLPA
Where Shall the Lover Rest. Sir Walter Scott. *Fr.* Marmion, III. CH; EnRP; GTBS; GTBS-P
(Song: "Where shall the lover rest.") NBM; OBRV; PoEL-4; ViBoPo
Where shall we find Thee—where art Thou, O God? Search. Margaret Widdemer. TrPWD
Where shall we go? August Afternoon. Marion Edey. YeAr
Where shall we go? The Hounded Lovers. William Carlos Williams. NYBP; TrGrPo
Where shall we our great professor inter. A Serio-comic Elegy. Richard Whately. ShM
Where shall we seek for a hero, and where shall we find a story? Crispus Attucks. John Boyle O'Reilly. PAH
Where Shall Wisdom Be Found? Bible, *O.T.* Job, XXVIII:12-20, 28. TreFT
Where She Her Sacred Bower Adorns. Thomas Campion. LoBV
(Her Sacred Bower.) HBV-1
Where she lived the close remained the best. The Way a Ghost Dissolves. Richard Hugo. NoP
Where She Told Her Love. John Clare. VLP
Where She Was Not Born. Yvonne. CNA
Where should he seek, to go away. The Mark. Louise Bogan. MoPo; MoVE
Where skies are thunderous, by a cypress walk. Some Negatives: X. at the Chateau. James Merrill. NePoEA-2
Where Somnus' temple rises from a ground. Laudanum. *Unknown.* NOEC
Where sunless rivers weep. Dream Land. Christina Rossetti. BrRO; VLP
Where swallows and wheatfields are. Refuge. Archibald Lampman. PeCV
Where swell the songs thou shouldst have sung. A Soldier Poet. Rossiter Johnson. AA
Where Sydney Cove her lucid bosom swells. Visit of Hope to Sydney Cove, near Botany-Bay. Erasmus Darwin. NOEC
Where the acorn tumbles down. The Fieldmouse. Cecil Frances Alexander. OxBChV
Where the bee sucks, there suck I. Ariel's Song [*or* Fairy Songs *or* A Fairy's Life]. Shakespeare. *Fr.* The Tempest, V, i. AWP; CABA; CH; CTC; ElL; EnRePo; FaBV; GN; HBV-1; HBVY; HeIP; NOBE; NoP; OBEV; OBSC; PDV; PoPl; SeCeV; TiPo TreFT; ViBoPo; WHA
Where the Blessed Feet Have Trod. "Michael Field." OxBoCh
Where the Blue Horses. Raymond Souster. PeCV
Where the camshaft weeps. Resting Place. Jon Silkin. VWA
Where the Canyon spreads on either hand. Hangman's Tree. Lillian Zellhoefer White. AmFN
Where the cedar leaf divides the sky. Passage. Hart Crane. CMoP; MoVE; NoAM; NOBA
Where the Cedars. Jacob Glatstein, *tr. fr. Yiddish by* Joseph Leftwich. TrJP
Where the city's ceaseless crowd moves on the livelong day. Sparkles from the Wheel. Walt Whitman. AP; BiP; FaBoEn
Where the Corrib river chops through the Claddagh. The Last Galway Hooker. Richard Murphy. IPY
Where the cow-boys roost on the green rolling prairie. A Kansas Cowboy. *Unknown.* CoSo
Where the Dead Men Lie. Barcroft Boake. CBAP; PoAu-1
Where the decay begins, the sun. The Smell on the Landing. Peter Porter. NMP
Where the dews and the rains of heaven have their fountain. The Battle in the Clouds. William Dean Howells. PAH
Where the dropwort springs up lithe and tall. John Lyle Donaghy. NeIP
Where the dusty lane. Daisies. Valerie Worth. PCP
Where the elk stood, stand I, worldly wise. Tall Trees by Still Waters. James Tate. MAYP
Where the Fight Was. Alice Corbin, *after Chippewa Indian.* BPAW
Where the flowers lean to their shadows on the wall. Shadows of Chrysanthemums. E. J. Scovell. MoVE
Where the graves were many, we looked for one. In Clonmel Parish Churchyard. Sarah Morgan Bryan Piatt. AA
Where the Great Northern plunged in. The Wreck of the Great Northern. Robert Hedin. AMV-81
Where the Hayfields Were. Archibald MacLeish. DuDa
Where the lazy wall is down. Sierran Vigil. Ewart Milne. NeIP
Where the Lilies Used to Spring. David Gray. OxBS
Where the living with effort go. The White Ship. Geoffrey Hill. OxBC
Where the lizard ran to its little prey. The Range in the Desert. Randall Jarrell. NOBA
Where the lone wind on the hilltop. The Empty House. Russell Hoban. WSC
Where the mob gathers, swiftly shoot along. John Gay. *Fr.* Trivia; or, The Art of Walking the Streets of London. OAEL-1
Where the Moosatockmaguntic. The Ballad of Hiram Hover. Bayard Taylor. BXAP; FaBoCo; OBAL
Where the Northern Ocean in vast whirls. Sea-Birds. James Thomson. EtS
Where the orange-branches mingle on the sunny garden-side. The Demon of the Mirror. Bayard Taylor. BeLS
Where the Pelican Builds. Mary Hannay Foott. PoAu-1
Where the Picnic Was. Thomas Hardy. OxBTC
Where the plow turned back. Hidden Valley. E. G. Burrows. HoAn
Where the pools are bright and deep. A Boy's Song. James Hogg. CH; FaPON; FaPoR; HBV-1; HBVY; MoShBr; OBEV; OnUR; OxBChV; PoPle; WiR
Where the printing-works buttress a church. The Coldness. Jon Silkin. CABA; VWA
Where the quiet-coloured end of evening smiles. Love among the Ruins. Robert Browning. FaBV; HAP; HBV-1; NOBE; OAEL-2; OAEP; OBEV; OBVV; PoEL-5; PrIm; VLP
Where the Rainbow Ends. Robert Lowell. AP; CoBMV; MoAB; MoAmPo; NePoEA; TrGrPo
Where the Rainbow Ends. Richard Rive. PBA; TTY
Where the ramparts tower in flame or shadow. Epitaph in Anticipation. Leonard Bacon. WhC
Where the Red Lion flaring o'er the way. A Description of an Author's Bedchamber. Goldsmith. BIrV
Where the remote Bermudas ride. Bermudas [*or* Song of the Emigrants *or* Song of the Emigrants in Bermuda]. Andrew Marvell. AnAnS-1; AWP; CABA; CH; ChTr; FaBoCh; FaBoEn; GN; GTBS; GTBS-P; HBV-2; JCP; LoBV; MePo; MOS; NOBE; NOCV; NoP; OAEP; OBEV; OBS; OxBoCh; PAH; PAI; SeCeV; SeCP; SeCV-1; ViBoPo
Where the ripe pears droop heavily. The Wasp. "Fiona Macleod." *Fr.* Transcripts from Nature. FM
Where the River Shannon Flows, *with music.* James I. Russell. FSN
Where the sea gulls sleep or indeed where they fly. The Ballet of the Fifth Year. Delmore Schwartz. MoAB; MP; OxBA; TwCP
Where the shimmering sands of the desert beat. Two Bits. Sharlot M. Hall. BPAW
Where the short-legged Esquimaux. An Arctic Vision. Bret Harte. PAH
Where the Single Men Go in Summer. Nina Bourne. FiBHP
Where the slanting forest eves. To Nature Seekers. Robert W. Chambers. MoShBr
Where the Slow Fig's Purple Sloth. Robert Penn Warren. NoP
Where the slow river/ meets the tide. Leda. Hilda Doolittle ("H. D."). HBMV
Where the snowy peaks gleam in the moonlight. Land Where the Columbines Grow. Arthur J. Fynn. PoOW
Where the sun shines in the street. Feet. Mary Carolyn Davies. WGRP
Where the thistle lifts a purple crown. Daisy. Francis Thompson. AWP; BeLS; BrPo; FaBV; GoBC; HBV-1; MoAB; MoBrPo; OBEV; OBNC; OBVV; WHA
Where the waters gently flow. The Song of the Reed Sparrow. *Unknown.* OxBChV
Where the waves of burning cloud are rolled. Ballade of the Dreamland Rose. Brian Hooker. HBMV
Where the western zun, unclouded. Zun-zet. William Barnes. PoEL-4
Where the wheel of light is turned. Pole Star [for This Year]. Archibald MacLeish. AP; CoBMV; NePA; OxBA
Where the wife is scouring the frying pan. Land of Little Sticks, 1945. James Tate. MAYP
Where the Wild Thyme Blows. Shakespeare. *See* Violet Bank, A.

Where the wild wave, from ocean proudly swelling. Fort Bowyer. Charles L. S. Jones. PAH
Where the wind. Footprints on the Glacier. W. S. Merwin. NoAM
Where the wind attacks the downs. A Kodak; Tregantle. Horatio Brown. PeHV
Where the world is grey and lone. The Ice King. A. B. Demille. WHW
Where then shall hope and fear their objects find? An Additional Poem. John Ashbery. FaBoMo
Where then shall hope and fear their objects find? The Power of Prayer [*or* Prayer]. Samuel Johnson. *Fr.* The Vanity of Human Wishes. NOBE; OBEC
Where there is personal liking we go. The Hero. Marianne Moore. *Fr.* Part of a Novel, Part of a Poem, Part of a Play. CMoP; NOBA; OxBA; PoA;TwAmPo
Where There's a Will There's a Way. Eliza Cook. BLPA; FaFP; TreF
Where they once dug for money. The Old Marlborough Road. Henry David Thoreau. PoEL-4
Where They Were, *with music. Unknown.* AS
Where thou dwellest, in what grove. The Birds. Blake. CH; OBRV
Where, thy true treasure? Gold Says, "Not in me." Edward Young. *Fr.* The Complaint; or, Night Thoughts, VI. OAEL-1
Where to, Lady? Where do you want to go? Experiential Religion. Travis Du Priest. AMV-80
Where to Seek Love. Blake. *Fr.* William Bond. TRV
Where tomahawks flash in the powwow. Late Late. George Starbuck. PPON
Where tom-tom drummed. The Inheritors. Dorothy Livesay. CaP
Where troops of virgins follow the Lamb. O Glory of Virgins. Fortunatus, *tr. by* Sister Maura. ISi
Where Two o'Clock Came From. Kenneth Patchen. SO
Where two or three were flung together, or fifty. The March 2. Robert Lowell. NoP
Where Unimaginably Bright. Oliver Hale. GoYe
Where voices vanish into dream. Elected Silence. Siegfried Sassoon. MoBrPo
Where Wards Are Weak. Robert Southwell. NCEP
Where was I at the hour of sowing. Questions. Dagmar Hilarova, *tr. by* Ewald Osers. VWA
Where was the boundary between the bitter water. Salmon Cycle. Avner Treinin, *tr. by* Robert Friend. VWA
Where was you last winter, boys. The Horse Trader's Song. *Unknown.* AmFP
Where wast thou when I laid the foundations of the earth? Bible, *O.T. Fr.* Job. ImOP
Where we live, the teakettle whistles out. Now. William Stafford. NNaP
Where we made the fire. Where the Picnic Was. Thomas Hardy. OxBTC
Where We Must Look for Help. Robert Bly. ConAP; NePoEA
Where we walk to school each day. Indian Children. Annette Wynne. SoPo; SUS; TiPo
Where we went in the boat was a long bay. The Mediterranean. Allen Tate. AP; FaBoMo; GOA; HAP; LiTA; LiTM; MoAB; MoAmPo; MOS; MoVE; NePA; PoCh; SeCeV; TwAmPo; VGW; WeW
Where we were walking in the day's light, seeing. Time in the Rock, XXXVII. Conrad Aiken. VGW
Where were the greenhouses going. Big Wind. Theodore Roethke. AmPP; CMoP; GoJo; InvP; NCSH; NoP; PPoe; VGW; ViBoPo
Where were the pathways that your childhood. First Pathways. Sidney Royse Lysaght. OBVV
Where were we going that. The Drive. Janet Reed McFatter. GrPl
Where were we in that afternoon? And where. Anniversary. Richmond Lattimore. NYBP; PoCh
Where were ye, birds, that bless His name. John Banister Tabb. *Fr.* The Child. AA
Where were you then? A Story. Margaret Avison. MoCV
Where wert thou, Soul, ere yet my body born. Soul and Body. Samuel Waddington. OBVV
Where? When? Which? Langston Hughes. BPo; NePoAm-2
Where, where are now the great reports. Fuimus Fumus. Joshua Sylvester. FaBoEE
Where, where but here have Pride and Truth. On Hearing That the Students of Our New University Have Joined the Agitation against Immoral Literature. W. B. Yeats. NoAM
Where white, stares, smokes or breaks. Aegean Islands 1940-41. Bernard Spencer. NeBP
Where will they stop, those breathing powers. Devotional Incitements. Wordsworth. OxBoCh
Where will they take us to. These Crossings, These Words. Quincy Troupe. LTB
Where will your training lead. The Boy Washington. Dorothy Brown Thompson. SiSoSe
Where wit is over-ruled by will. Desire's Government. "A. W." ElL
Where, without bloodshed, can there be. Long Feud. Louis Untermeyer. MoAmPo
Where yonder ancient willow weeps. Alexander McLachlan. *Fr.* A Backwoods Hero. CaP
Where you can go farther and see less. West Texas. *At. to* Leona Mae Austin. CoSo
Where You Go When She Sleeps. T. R. Hummer. MAYP
Where You Passed. Amelia Josephine Burr. HBMV
Where you traveled the body couldn't go. The Traveler. David Bottoms. AMV-80
Where young restless convicts. Jackson State Prison. Leon Baker. LFAC
Whereas Aongus, the philosophic. On a Cock Which Was Stolen from a Good Priest. Egan O'Rahilly, *tr. by* P. S. Dinneen *and* T. O'Donoghue. OnYI
Whereas, on certain boughs and sprays. The Lawyer's Invocation to Spring. Henry Howard Brownell. PoLF
Whereas the rebels hereabout. Tom Gage's Proclamation. *Unknown.* PAH
Whereas we twain, who still are bound for life. A Separation Deed. Sir Lewis Morris. OBVV
Whereat Erewhile I Wept, I Laugh. Robert Greene. *Fr.* Arbasto. ElL
Where-e'er My Flatt'ring Passions Rove. Isaac Watts. NOCV; OxBoCh
Where'er there's a thistle to feed a linnet. Poets and Linnets. Tom Hood. CenHV; HBV-1
Wherefore Hidest Thou Thy Face, and Holdest Me for Thine Enemy? Francis Quarles. *See* Why Dost Thou Shade Thy Lovely Face.
Wherefore, Lucinda, dost aspire. To Miss L. F. on the Occasion of Her Departure for the Continent. J. C. Squire. BXAP
Wherefore peep'st thou, envious day? *Unknown.* GBL
"Wherefore starts my bosom's lord." Comfort in Affliction. William E. Aytoun. InMe
Wherefore these revels that my dull eyes greet? The Royal Mummy to Bohemia. Charles Warren Stoddard. AA
Wherefore this busy labor without rest? Tuskegee. Leslie Pinckney Hill. BANP; PoNe
Wherefore tonight so full of care. Dejection. Robert Bridges. QFR
Wherefore, Unlaurelled Boy. George Darley. *See* Solitary Lyre, The.
Wherefore was that cry? "She Should Have Died Hereafter." Shakespeare. *Fr.* Macbeth, V, v. FiP
Wherein Consists the High Estate, *with music.* Ebenezer Dayton. AH
Wherelings Whenlings. E. E. Cummings. HAP; WeW
Where's Babe Ruth, the King of Swat. The Ballad of Dead Yankees. Donald Petersen. HeIP; LiSP
Where's Commander All-a-Tanto? Herman Melville. *Fr.* Bridegroom Dick. PoEL-5
Where's he that died o' Wednesday? Falstaff's Song. Edmund Clarence Stedman. AA; HBV-2
Where's Mary? Ivy O. Eastwick. TiPo
Where's now the object of thy fears. Resolution. Henry More. OxBoCh
Where's Peace? I start, some clear-blown night. Mr. Hosea Biglow to the Editor of the Atlantic Monthly. James Russell Lowell. *Fr.* The Biglow Papers, 2nd Series, X. AA
Where's the meeting place for. Shir Ma'alot/ A Song of Degrees. Richard Flantz. VWA
"Where's the need of singing now?" Momus. E. A. Robinson. ViBoPo
Where's the poet? show him! show him. The Poet. Keats. PP
Where's the Queen of Sheba? Gone. Walter de la Mare. GoJo
Where's the winning without chocolate. The Chocolate Soldiers. Calvin Forbes. MAT; MAYP
Wheresoe'er I turn mine eyes. God Everywhere. Abraham ibn Ezra, *tr. by* D. E. de L. TrJP
Wheresoe'er I turn my view. Lines on Thomas Warton's Poems [*or* Lines in Ridicule of Certain Poems Published in 1777]. Samuel Johnson. FaBoCo; FaBoEE
Wheresoever ye fare by frith or by fell. Julians Barnes. *Fr.* Book of Hunting. WPE
Whereto should I express. To His Lady. Henry VIII, King of England. CTC; EBEV; OBSC
Whereupon I told,/ That once in the stillness of a summer's noon. Books. Wordsworth. *Fr.* The Prelude, V. PoEL-4
Wherever God erects a house of prayer. Daniel Defoe. *Fr.* The True-born Englishman, I. NOBL; OBSV; TreF
Wherever I am, there's always Pooh. Us Two. A. A. Milne. OxBChV; TiPo
Wherever I go to find. Pigeons. Bert Meyers. EAS
Wherever I walked I went green among young growing. Trinity Churchyard. Muriel Rukeyser. NYP
Wherever in this city, screens flicker. Adrienne Rich. Twenty-one Love Poems, I. PeHV
Wherever on Italian ground. Italian Poppies. Joel Elias Spingarn. HBMV
Wherever shadow falls wherever the drowning. Contra Mortem. Hayden Carruth. PoA
Wherever smoke wreaths. Home. Stephen Chalmers. HBMV

Wherever the wind's head walks. The Wind's Head. John L. Sweeney. TwAmPo
Wherever your voice moves. Love Song. Kosrof Chantikian. AMV-81
Wherewith Shall I Come before the Lord? Bible, *O.T.* Micah, VI: 6-8. TRV
Whet all your wits and antidote your eyes. The Tragi-Comedy of Titus Oates. *Unknown.* APAS
Whet up your axe and whistle up your dog. Groundhog. *Unknown.* FSW
Whether at doomsday (tell, ye reverend wise). Quaerè. George Farewell. NOEC
Whether day my spirit's yearning. The Thought Eternal. Goethe, *tr. by* Ludwig Lewisohn. AWP
Whether dinner was pleasant, with the windows lit by gunfire. No Credit. Kenneth Fearing. CMoP
Whether his loves were many or but two. Before Rereading Shakespeare's Sonnets. T. Sturge Moore. BrPo
Whether I find thee bright with fair. Changeful Beauty. *Unknown, tr. by* Andrew Lang. EnLoPo
Whether I sit or lie. Ukihashi, *tr. fr. Japanese by* Kenneth Rexroth *and* Ikuko Atsumi. WPOW
Whether it's sunny or not, it's sure. Poem about Morning. William Meredith. NYBP
Whether Men Do Laugh or Weep. *At. to* Thomas Campion. *and to* Philip Rosseter. EnRePo; NCEP; OBSC
(All Is Vanity.) HBV-2
Whether on Ida's shady brow. To the Muses. Blake. ChTr; EnRP; HAP; HBV-2; HeIP; LAuP; LiTB; LoBV; NOBE; NOEC; NoP; OAEL-2; OAEP; OBEC; OBEV; SeCeV; TrGrPo; ViBoPo; WHA
Whether one paints five Helens. The Ultimate Antientropy. Theodore Weiss. NoAM
Whether or Not. D. H. Lawrence. MoBrPo
Whether or not I watch. The Egg of Nothing. John Taylor. AMV-81
Whether the bees have thoughts we cannot say. The Long Waters. Theodore Roethke. NYBP
Whether the graver did by this intend. On the Late Metamorphosis of an Old Picture of Oliver Cromwell's. *Unknown.* APAS
Whether the moorings are invisible. Conversation. John Berryman. LiTA; LiTM; NePA; WaP
Whether the rivals for a wife and mother can. L. E. Sissman. *Fr.* Tras Os Montes. DiL
Whether the sensitive plant, or that. Shelley. *Fr.* The Sensitive Plant. OAEL-2
Whether the Turkish new moon minded be. Astrophel and Stella, XXX. Sir Philip Sidney. SiPS
Whether the weather be fine. Weather. *Unknown.* RHPC
Whether There Is Sorrow in the Demons. John Berryman. LiTM
Whether they delve in the buried coal, or plow the upland soil. The Glory of Toil. Edna Dean Proctor. PGD
Whether to Ceaser he was friend or foe? Upon the Death of G. B. John Cotton. SCAP
Whether to sally and see thee, girl of my dreams. To Meet, or Otherwise. Thomas Hardy. OBNC
Whether to vegetate, or write with heart? Yaddo. Ruth Herschberger. FAZ
Whether two-backed beast or many-splendoured-thing. Onan. Paris Leary. CoPo
Whether we flee or pursue, we are the same. Leviathan; a Poem in Four Movements. Kenneth Pitchford. CoPo
Whether what we sense of this world. William Bronk. VGW
Whether White or Black be best. Verses Made Sometime Since upon . . . the Indian Squa. John Josselyn. SCAP
Whether you live by hut or throne. Certainties. Margaret Widdemer. HBMV
Which are the living? We who stride unyielding earth in engine fumes. Three City Cantos. Charles A. Wagner. GoYe
Which Are You? *Unknown.* FPL; PoLF
"Which do you love best, enigmatical man." The Stranger. Baudelaire, *tr. by* Arthur Symons. SyP
Which I wish to remark. Plain Language from Truthful James [*or* The Heathen Chinee]. Bret Harte. BeLS; BLPA; BPAW; CenHV; CTC; FaBoBe; FaBoCo; HBV-2; InMe; NOBL; OBAL; TreF; WhC; YAD
Which I wish to remark. The Heathen Pass-ee. A. C. Hilton. CenHV; FaBoCo; NOBL
Which Is a Proud, and Yet a Wretched Thing. Sir John Davies. *See* Man.
Which is man who wot, and what. This World Fares as a Fantasy. *Unknown.* OxBM
Which is our star this night? This Night. William Heyen. MAYP
Which is real. The Indigo Glass in the Grass. Wallace Stevens. PoA
Which is the best to hit your taste. Epigram on Two Ladies. Sophia Burrell. ErPo; POL
Which Is the Bow? *Unknown.* GBP
Which is the cosiest voice. Gray Thrums. Clara Doty Bates. OBCA
Which is the German's fatherland? The German Fatherland. Ernst Moritz Arndt. HBV-2
"Which is the way to Baby-land?" Baby-Land. George Cooper. HBV-1; HBVY
"Which is the way to the nearest town." Conversation with an April Fool. Rowena Bennett. SiSoSe
Which is the weakest thing of all. The Weakest Thing. Elizabeth Barrett Browning. HBV-2
Which is you, old two-in-one? What the Serpent Said to Adam. Archibald MacLeish. NePA
Which Loved Best? "Joy Allison." WBLP
(Which Loved Her Best?) OHIP
Which of those rebell Spirits adjudg'd to Hell. Gabriel Meets Satan. Milton. *Fr.* Paradise Lost, IV. LoBV
Which road, which road did you take. Exaltation. Franz Werfel, *tr. by* Edith Abercrombie Snow. TrJP
Which Shall It Be? Ethel Lynn Beers. BLPA; TreF
Which Side Am I Supposed to Be On? W. H. Auden. *See* Ode: To My Pupils.
Which Side Are You On? Florence Reese. FSW
Which Sword? Jason Noble Pierce. PGD
Which Washington? Eve Merriam. NTCP
Which way, and whence the lightning flew. Apollo's Song. Ben Jonson. *Fr.* The Masque of Augurs. LoBV
Which will you have, a ball or a cake? Choosing. Eleanor Farjeon. TiPo
Which-a-way/ which-a-way. Bye Bye Baby Blues. *Unknown.* BluL
Whichever harbours poison between cotton, or goes from breathing to a common form. 29th Dance—Having an Instrument—22 March 1964. Jackson MacLow. CoPo
Whichever Way the Wind Doth Blow. Caroline A. Mason. TreFS
(En Voyage.) HBV-2
Whigmaleerie, A. William Soutar. OxBS
Whigs' Lamentation for the Death of Their Dear Brother College, The. *Unknown.* APAS
Whig's the first letter of his odious name. An Acrostic on Wharton. *Unknown.* OBSV
While a thousand fine projects are planned ev'ry day. A Song. *Unknown.* NOEC
While Adam slept, from him his Eve arose. *See* Whilst Adam slept, Eve from his side arose.
While an intrinsic ardor prompts to write. To the University of Cambridge, in New-England. Phillis Wheatley. AmPP; BALP; SBG; TAP
While Anna's peers and early playmates tread. Wordsworth. *Fr.* The Stuffed Owl. Par
While April Rain Went By. Shaemas O'Sheel. HBMV
While at her bedroom window once. The Keys of Morning. Walter de la Mare. MoVE; NoP
While back, my father got some letters, A. The Violin Tree. Joel Rosenberg. VWA
While breaking the big rock. Stone Giant. Joseph Bruchac. CDW
While briers an' woodbines budding green. Epistle to John Lapraik [an Old Scottish Bard]. Burns. EnRP; OAEP
While Butler, needy wretch! was yet alive. On the Setting Up [of] Mr. Butler's Monument in Westminster Abbey. Samuel Wesley. InvP; NOEC; OBEC; PPON; WhC
While cattle stupidly stare. Christmas Eve. Robert Siegel. GeTw
While Cecil Snores: Mom Drinks Cold Milk. James Cunningham. JB
While crabapple now is a windfall. The Wilding. Philip Booth. NePoEA
While drinking, all at once I saw. The Three Kingdoms of Nature. Gotthold Lessing, *tr. by* Alfred Baskerville, *ad. by* Robert Bly. NU
While far along the eastern sky. After the Fire. Oliver Wendell Holmes. PAH
While Fell was reposing himself on the hay. On Fell. Gotthold Lessing. ShM
While gentlefolks strut in their silver and satins. Bartleme Fair. George Alexander Stevens. ELP; NOEC
While going the road to sweet Athy. Johnny, I Hardly Knew Ye. *Unknown.* AnIV; BIrV; ELP; FaBoBa; GBP; InPK; OnYI; OxBoLi; WaaP
While he slept, I poured salt in his ears. Judith Recalls Holofernes. Maura Stanton. AmPA
While he talked the wireless man listened. The Refugee. Dabney Stuart. GP
While he to whom her vexing thoughts still clung. Seven Sad Sonnets, III. Mary Aldis. HBMV
While here on earth it may not be. Yes, I Have Been to Calvary. Avis B. Christiansen. STF
While I Am Young, *with music.* Silas Ballou. AH
While I Have Vision. Peter Quennell. ChMP
While I recline. The Cotton Boll. Henry Timrod. AA; AmPP
"While I sit at the door." Eve. Christina Rossetti. CH; FM; GTBS-P; NBM; NIP; OxBoCh; PoEL-5; SeCeV

While I stood here, in the open, lost in myself. Milkweed. James Wright. LCAP; NaP; NOBA; NU
While I touch the string. Common Sense and Genius. Thomas Moore. NBM
While I was building neat. It Is Dangerous to Read Newspapers. Margaret Atwood. HeIP; OBWP
While I watch the Christmas blaze. The Reminder. Thomas Hardy. CMoP; OBCP
While I'm gone, white mother, kill the fattened oxen. The White and the Black. N. M. Khaketla, *tr. by* Dan Kunene *and* Jack Cope. PeSA
While in the mask of night there shone that cut. Landing on the Moon. May Swenson. MOON
While in the park I sing, the listning deer. At Penshurst. Edmund Waller. AnAnS-2; OAEP
While in this cavernous place employed. A Civil Servant. Robert Graves. InPK
While it's still light out. How to Eat Alone. Daniel Halpern. MAYP
While joy gave clouds the light of stars. The Villain. W. H. Davies. MoBrPo; OxBTC; SoSe; WHA
While ladling butter from alternate tubs. On the Historians Freeman and Stubbs. J. E. Thorold Rogers. FaBoEE
While leanest beasts in pastures feed. Supreme Fortune Falls Soonest. Robert Herrick. CaPo
While, Lydia, I was lov'd of thee. A Dialogue between Horace and Lydia. Horace, *tr. by* Robert Herrick. Odes, III, 9. OBVE
While malice, Pope, denies thy page. When None Shall Rail. David Lewis. OBEC
While Morpheus thus does gently lay. Song. Henry Killigrew. CH
While my father walked through mud. 1905. David Ignatow. VWA
While my hair was still cut straight across my forehead. The River Merchant's Wife; a Letter. Li Po, *tr. by* Ezra Pound. AmPP; AWP; BoLoP; CABA; DTC; FYAP; HAP; HeIP; InPK; InPS; LiTA; MoAB; MoAmPo; MoPo; MP; NIP; NoAM; NOBA; NOBE; NoP; OBMV; OBVE; OxBA; PPoe; PPP; PrIm; SOTW; TAP; TwAmPo; TwCP; UnPo; WeW
While my lady sleepeth. Serenade. John Gibson Lockhart. OBRV
While neighbouring cities waste the fleeting hours. Anna Seward. *Fr.* Colebrook Dale. NOEC
While Northward the hot sun was sinking o'er the trees. The Psalm. Robert Bridges. FaBoTw; LiTB
While not a leaf seems faded, while the fields. Sonnet: September, 1815. Wordsworth. ChER
While now the Pole Star sinks from sight. Crossing the Tropics. Herman Melville. AA
While now the Rising Village claims a name. Oliver Goldsmith, the Younger. *Fr.* The Rising Village. CaP
While now upon the win' do zwell. The Bells ov Alderburnham. William Barnes. EBVV
While o'er Our Guilty Land, O Lord, *with music.* Samuel Davies. AH
While o'er the Deep Thy Servants Sail, *with music.* George Burgess. AH
While people hunt for what can satisfy their wants. Shelter. Gene Derwood. NePA
While perils imminent by slender thread. The Poet's Terror at the Bailiffs of Exeter. Andrew Brice. *Fr.* Freedom; a Poem, Written in Time of Recess from the Rapacious Claws of Bailiffs. NOEC
While pleasure reigns unrivalled on this shore. Boston in Distress. *Unknown.* NOEC
While rain, with eve in partnership. Beyond the Last Lamp [Near Tooting Common]. Thomas Hardy. MoVE; NOBE; OBNC
While riding down that greenwood road. John of Hazelgreen. *Unknown.* BaBo
While round the armèd bands. The Execution of King Charles. Andrew Marvell. PoRA
While sauntering through the crowded street. Pre-Existence. Paul Hamilton Hayne. HBV-2
While Shepherds Watched [Their Flocks by Night]. Margaret Deland. GN; HBVY
While Shepherds Watched [Their Flocks by Night]. Nahum Tate. AmFP (1 *st.*); GN; HBV-1; HBVY; NOCV; OnYI; OxBI; TreFS
(Christmas.) OHIP
While Sherman stood beneath the hottest fire. Before Vicksburg. George Henry Boker. PAH
While snows the window-panes bedim. December. John Clare. OBCP
While snowy nightwinds, blowing bleak. Burncombe Hollow. William Barnes. OBNC
While some affect the sun, and some the shade. Robert Blair. *Fr.* The Grave. EnRP
While some are being flies. 37th Dance—Banding—22 March 1964. Jackson Mac Low. CoPo
While some go dancing reels. Three Old Brothers. Frank O'Connor. OnYI
While some on rights and some on wrongs. Fair and Free Elections. *Unknown.* FSW
While some "rap" over this turmoil. The Rhetoric of Langston Hughes. Margaret Danner. BlSi; FB
While Someone Telephones. Elizabeth Bishop. NMP
While sorrows encompass me round. Death-Bed Song. *Unknown.* AmFP
While standing on the brink of woe. He Gave Himself for Me. *Unknown.* STF
While Stars of Christmas Shine. Emilie Poulsson. OHIP
While strolling along with the city's vast throng. She May Have Seen Better Days. James Thornton. FSN
While strolling down the street one eve upon mere pleasure bent. Just Tell Them That You Saw Me. Paul Dresser. FSN; TreFS
While strolling through the hills one day. Tannhauser. Newman Levy. OBAL
While Strolling through the Park One Day. Ed Haley. BLSo, *with music;* FSW
(Fountain in the Park, The.) FSN
While tenderly around me cast. Neaera's Kisses. Johannes Secundus, *tr. by* John Nott. *Fr.* Basia. UnTE
While that my soul repairs to her devotion. Church Monuments. George Herbert. AnAnS-1; CABA; HAP; JCP; NOCV; NoP; OAEL-1; QFR
While that the sun with his beams hot. The Unfaithful [*or* Faithless] Shepherdess [*or* Philon the Shepherd *or* Adieu Love, Untrue Love]. *Unknown.* ElL; GTBS; GTBS-P; NOBE; OBEV; OBSC
While the Bells Ring. Lora Dunetz. NePoAm
While the blue noon above us arches. Annihilation. Conrad Aiken. CrMA; GBL; MoAB; MoAmPo
While the cobbler mused, there passed his pane. The Great Guest Comes In. Edwin Markham. WBLP
While the Days Are Going By. George Cooper. BLRP; STF; WBLP
While the evening here is approaching the mountain paths. Overnight in the Apartment by the River. Tu Fu. ChTr
While the heel rears up in petty arrogance. Oration on the Toes. Edward Brynes. AMV-81
While the king and his ministers keep such a pother. A Wicked Treasonable Libel. Swift. UnTE
While the leaves of the bamboo rustle. *Unknown, tr. fr. Japanese by* Geoffrey Bownas *and* Anthony Thwaite. BoLoP
While the milder Fates consent. A Lyric to Mirth. Robert Herrick. CaPo
While the one rides over earth from land to land. Nixons at Calvary. Howard Nemerov. SOTS
While the shot and shell were screaming upon the battlefield. Break the News to Mother. Charles Kassel Harris. FSN; TreFS
While the sky above Manhattan flaps with a thousand Jasper Johns. The Tall Poets. William Jay Smith. SOTS
While the storm clouds gather far across the sea. God Bless America. Irving Berlin. BLSo; TreFT
While the Summer Trees Were Crying. Valentin Iremonger. AnIV
(Evening in Summer.) NeIP
(Time, the Faithless.) OxBI
While the sun is finishing. From Garvey's Farm: Seneca, Wisconsin. Ed Hoeppner. AMV-80
While the Tragedy's afoot. Colophon. Oliver St. John Gogarty. OBMV
While the two contraries of black and white. The Brown Beauty. Lord Herbert of Cherbury. AnAnS-2
While the unturned stone. Exaction. John Sweeney. TwAmPo
While the warden peeps through the venetian. On Youth, the Warden & Solitary! Leon Baker. LFAC
While the water-wagon's ringing showers. In the Isle of Dogs. John Davidson. OBNC; VLP
While the women sliced bread and cold meat. The Thief's Niece. George Keithley. NPGG
While thir hearts were jocund and sublime. Samson Hath Quit Himself. Milton. *Fr.* Samson Agonistes. LoBV
While thirteen moons saw smoothly run. Stanzas Subjoined to the Yearly Bill of Mortality of the Parish of All Saints, Northampton; for the Year 1787. William Cowper. NOCV
While this America settles in the mould of its vulgarity, heavily thickening to empire. Shine, Perishing Republic. Robinson Jeffers. CMoP; FF; LiTA; LiTM; MAT; MoAB; MoVE; NePA; NoAM; NOBA; NoP; OxBA; PAI; PrIm; TAP; UnPo; VGW; ViBoPo
While this night I read, I'm battleground. Invalid. Audrey McGaffin. NePoAm-2
While Thracians shal with arrowes war, Iaziges with bowe. Ovid, *tr. by* Thomas Underdowne. *Fr.* Invective against Ibis. OBVE
While thus he spake, th'Angelic Squadron bright. Milton. *Fr.* Paradise Lost, IV. SCV
While thus he thought, a monst'rous wave up-bore. Homer, *tr. by* Pope. *Fr.* The Odyssey, V. OBVE
While thus, of power and fancy'd empire vain. Crusty Critics. George Crabbe. *Fr.* The Library. OBEC

While thus the imprisoned leaves and waking flowers. Spring. Thomas Gisborne. *Fr.* Walks in a Forest. PBBP
While Titian was grinding rose madder. Limerick. *Unknown.* NOBL
While upon the journey of life. The Mask. Patty L. Harjo. VoR
While U.S. marshals. *Wili Woyi,* Shaman, Also Known as Billy Pigeon. Robert J. Conley. STE
While visiting Arundel Castle. Limerick. Victor Gray. NOBL
While Waiting for Kohoutek. Christopher Erb. SOTS
While walking at dusk in a strange city. Elegy. Pinhas Sadeh, *tr. by* Gabriel Preil *and* Howard Schwartz. VWA
While walking down a crowded. If I Only Was the Fellow. Will S. Adkin. BLPA
While we are at peace. Albatross. Lele-io-Hoku, *tr. by* S. H. Elbert *and* N. Mahoe. WTO
While We Lowly Bow before Thee, *with music.* Daniel C. Colesworthy. AH
While we sail and laugh, joke and fight, comes death. In Memoriam; Ingvald Bjorndal and His Comrade. Malcolm Lowry. OBCV
While We Slept. David Wolff. TrJP
While we unloaded the hay from the truck, building. The Barn. Wendell Berry. EyDe
While we were fearing it, it came. Emily Dickinson. NCEP; NIP; PPP
While we were together. A Painful Love Song. Yehuda Amichai, *tr. by the author.* LLLT
While we were visiting David's grave. Despair. Denise Levertov. NNaP
While we were walking under the top. Poem. John Ashbery. EAS
While winds frae aff Ben-Lomond blaw. Epistle to Davie, a Brother Poet. Burns. OBEC
While with a strong and yet a gentle hand. Edmund Waller. *Fr.* A Panegyric to My Lord Protector. JCP; OBS; SeCV-1
While words of learned strength and thundering sound. Still the Wonder Grew. Goldsmith. *Fr.* The Deserted Village. TreF
While yet the grapes were green, thou didst refuse me. Grapes. *Unknown, tr. by* Alma Strettell. AWP
While yet the Morning Star. The Unicorn. Ella Young. FaPON; SoPo; TiPo
While you, my lord, the rural shades admire. A Letter from Italy, to the Right Honourable Charles Lord Halifax. Joseph Addison. NOEC
While you read. The Cat. William Matthews. AmPA
While you that in your sorrow disavow. A Christmas Sonnet. E. A. Robinson. EaLo
While young John runs to greet. Lines on the Celebrated Picture by Leonardo da Vinci, Called the Virgin of the Rocks. Charles Lamb. ISi
While your great-grandmother and her sons. Separate Parties. Dabney Stuart. NYBP
While you're all so frisky I'll sing a little song. Top Hand. *Unknown.* CoSo
Whiles someone did chant this lovely lay, The. Song of Bliss [*or* Gather the Rose]. Spenser. *Fr.* The Faerie Queene, II. ElL; FF; OBVE
Whilom, as olde stories tellen us. The Knightes Tale. Chaucer. *Fr.* The Canterbury Tales. GoTL
Whilom in the winter's rage. The Penitent Palmer's Ode. Robert Greene. *Fr.* Francesco's Fortunes. LoBV; OBSC
Whilst [*or* While] Adam slept, Eve from his side [*or* from him his Eve] arose. Adam and Eve [*or* Epigram]. *Unknown.* FaBoEE; HBV-1; PoPle
Whilst Alexis Lay Pressed [*or* Prest]. Dryden. *Fr.* Marriage a-la-Mode. ErPo; FF; PrIm; UnTE
(Song: "Whilst Alexis lay pressed [*or* prest].") BoLoP; CavP
Whilst Echo cries [*or* eccho cryes], "What shall become of me[e]?" Henry Constable. *Fr.* Diana. AAS; OBSC
Whilst human kind/ Throughout the lands lay miserably crushed. Beyond Religion. Lucretius, *tr. by* William Ellery Leonard. AWP
Whilst I beheld the neck o' th' dove. Patrick Cary. JCP
Whilst in her prime and bloom of years. On a Female Rope-Dancer. *Unknown.* NOEC
Whilst in peaceful quarters lying. The Battle of Monmouth. "R. H." PAH
Whilst in this cold and blust'ring clime. To My Dear and Most Worthy Friend, Mr. Isaac Walton. Charles Cotton. FaBoEn
Whilst in This World I Stay, *with music.* Philip Pain. AH
Whilst my soul's eye beheld no light. A Dialogue betwixt God and the Soul. *At. to* Sir Henry Wotton. MeLP; OBS; OxBoCh
Whilst on Septimius' panting breast [*or* brest]. Acme and Septimius [*or* Ode: Acme and Septimius]. Catullus, *tr. by* Abraham Cowley. AWP; OBVE; UnTE
Whilst on thy head I lay my hand. A Spell of Invisibility. *At. to* Christopher Marlowe. ChTr
Whilst some affect the sun and some the shade. Robert Blair. *Fr.* The Grave. NOEC
Whilst the red spittle of the grape-shot sings. Evil. Arthur Rimbaud, *tr. by* Norman Cameron. WaaP
Whilst thirst of praise and vain desire of fame. The Lady's Resolve. Lady Mary Wortley Montagu. BoWoP
Whilst thus my pen strives to eternize thee. Michael Drayton. Idea, XLIV. AAS; OBSC; ViBoPo
Whil'st thy weigh'd judgements, Egerton, I heare. To Thomas Lord Chancellor. Ben Jonson. OBS
Whilst walking a crowded city street the other day. Just Try to Be the Fellow That Your Mother Thinks You Are. Will S. Adkin. WBLP
Whilst we sing the doleful knell. Ding Dong. *Unknown.* *Fr.* Swetnam, the Woman-Hater. ElL
Whilst what I write I do not see. Written in Juice of Lem[m]on. Abraham Cowley. *Fr.* The Mistress. AnAnS-2; CABA; SeCP; SeCV-1
Whilst with his falling wings, the courtly dove. Jealousie Is the Rage of a Man. Countess of Winchilsea. FM
Whil'st with hot scent, the Popish Tory crew. A Hue and Cry after Blood and Murder. *Unknown.* APAS
Whilst yet to prove. Farewell to Love. John Donne. OAEL-1
Whim of Time, A. Stephen Spender. MoAB; MoBrPo
Whins are blythesome on the knowe, The. A New Spring. A. D. Mackie. OxBS
Whip, The. Robert Creeley. NaP; NeAP; NoAM; PoM
Whiplash. William Matthews. MAYP
Whipped by sorrow now. Song. Miklós Radnóti, *tr. by* Steven Polgar *and* Stephen Berg *and* S. J. Marks. VWA
Whippet. Prudence Andrew. GDP
Whipping, The. Robert Hayden. GP; GrPl; IDB; NCSH; PAI; PoBA; TW
Whipping Cheare. *Unknown.* FaBoBa
Whipp'will's singin' to de moon. Go Sleep, Ma Honey. Edward D. Barker. AA
Whirl, snow, on the blackbird's chatter. Eager Spring. Gordon Bottomley. MoBrPo
Whirl up, sea. Oread. Hilda Doolittle ("H. D."). AP; AWP; CMoP; GoJo; MoAmPo; MoVE; NoAM; NOBA; OxBA; SBG; TAP
Whirl'd off at last, for speech I sought. Coventry Patmore. *Fr.* The Angel in the House, II, xi. GBL
Whirlwind Road, The. Edwin Markham. AA
Whirlwinds of Danger. *Unknown.* FSW
Whirring Wheels. John Oxenham. TRV
Whiskey Bill—a Fragment. *Unknown.* BPAW
Whiskey for My Johnny. *Unknown.* *See* Whiskey Johnny.
Whiskey here and whiskey there. Whiskey, Johnny, *vers.* I. *Unknown.* AmFP; ShS
Whiskey in the Jar. *Unknown.* FSW
Whiskey is the life of man. Whiskey, Johnny, *vers.* III. *Unknown.* FSW; ShS
Whiskey Johnny, *diff. versions.* *Unknown.* AmFP; AS, *with music*; FSW; ShS, 3 *vers., with music*
(Whiskey for My Johnny, *with music.*) AmSS
Whiskey on your breath, The. My Papa's Waltz. Theodore Roethke. CMoP; CrMA; CTBA; DiL; FF; HAP; HeIP; HoPM; InPK; InPS; LCAP; LiTM; MiAP; MoAB; NCSH; NIP; NoAM; NOBA; NoP; PAI; PPoe; PPP; PrIm; TAP; VGW; WeW
Whisky, Drink Divine. Joseph O'Leary. OnYI
Whisky, frisky,/ Hippity hop. The Squirrel. *Unknown.* FaPON; PDV; SoPo; SUS; TiPo
Whisky Johnny. *Unknown.* *See* Whiskey Johnny.
Whisky Song, A. *Unknown.* STF
Whisper of yellow globes. Her Lips Are Copper Wire. Jean Toomer. NoAM
Whisper woke the air, A. Calumny. Frances Sargent Osgood. AA; HBV-2
Whisperer, The. Arthur Bullen. HBMV
Whisperer, The. James Stephens. WGRP
Whisperer, The. Mark Van Doren. MoAmPo; UnTE
Whisperers, The. W. W. Gibson. HBV-2
Whisperin' Bill. Irving Bacheller. PoLF
Whispering Clouds. Mariquita Platov. AMV-80
Whispering ghosts of the west. *Tr. fr. Maori by* John White. WTO
Whispering Hope, *with music.* Septimus Winner. PSoN
Whisperings in Wattle-Boughs. Adam Lindsay Gordon. OBVV
Whispers. Roberta Hill. CDW
Whispers. Myra Cohn Livingston. PDV
Whispers of Heavenly Death. Walt Whitman. LiTA; NePA; NoAM
Whispers of Immortality. T. S. Eliot. CMoP; CTC; LiTA; NePA; NoAM; NOBA; NoP; OBMV; TwAmPo
Whist. Eugene Fitch Ware. PoLF
Whistle, The. Charles Murray. GoTS; OxBS
Whistle, The/ of the bright. Belfast Lough. *Unknown, tr. by* John Montague. BIrV
Whistle Aloud, Too Weedy Wren. Wallace Stevens. *Fr.* Notes toward a Supreme Fiction. LiTA
Whistle, and I'll Come to Ye [*or* You], My Lad. Burns. OxBoLi; UnTE; ViBoPo

(O Whistle, and I'll Come to You [*or* Ye], My Lad.) BSV; ErPo; GoTS; InPS; PoEL-4
(Song: "O whistle, and I'll come to ye, my lad.") BoLoP
Whistle, Daughter, Whistle. *Unknown.* AmFP; ErPo; FSW; OBET; OxNR, *shorter vers.*
Whistle, Laddie, whistle. To Laddie. Anna Robinson. SUS
Whistle o'er the Lave o't. Burns. BSV; OxBS
Whistle o'er the Lave o't. *Unknown.* GBP
Whistle shrilled, A; the farm hands left the stack. Jack and Jill. Charles Powell. BXAP
Whistle under the water. Amy Lowell. *Fr.* Flute-Priest Song for Rain. UnS
Whistles. Rachel Field. TiPo
Whistles like light in leaves, O light. The Heart Flies Up, Erratic as a Kite. Delmore Schwartz. PoA
Whistling Boy, The. George Crabbe. TrGrPo
Whistling Boy. Nixon Waterman. PoLF
Whistling postman swings along, The. The Postman. *Unknown.* FaPON
Whistling Willie. Kaye Starbird. QQQ
Whit Monday. Louis MacNeice. OAEL-2
Whit Sunday. Joseph Beaumont. OxBoCh
Whit was His nakede brest. White Was His Naked Breast. *Unknown.* OxBM
White. Marguerite Bouvard. AMV-81
White. Karl Krolow, *tr. fr. German by* Paul Morris. AMV-81
White. George Woodcock. NeBP
White, a shingled path. Icos. Charles Tomlinson. GTBS-P
White an' Blue. William Barnes. GBL; GTBS-P
White and crimson, cheek and breast. Cantiga. Gil Vicente, *tr. by* Thomas Walsh. ISi
White and Red. Edward de Vere, Earl of Oxford. OBSC
(What Cunning Can Express.) ElL
White and the Black, The. N. M. Khaketla, *tr. fr. Sotho by* Dan Kunene *and* Jack Cope. PeSA
White Anemone, The, *sel.* "Owen Meredith."
"Tis the white anemone, fashioned so." GN
White Apples. Donald Hall. TAP
White are the far-off plains, and white. Snow. Archibald Lampman. PeCV
White armies. Minnesota Camp Grounds. Gerald Vizenor. STE
White arms, Love, you have, and thin fingers with glittering nails. She-Devil. Douglas Goldring. HBMV
White as coal-ash pressed. Queen of Heaven Mausoleum. Dennis Schmitz. LCAP
White as her hand fair Julia threw. The Snow-Ball. Soame Jenyns, *after the Latin of* Petronius Afranius. OBVE
White as paper a-sail in the air. *Malay Oral Tradition, tr. by* R. O. Winstedt. WTO
White as snow and snow it isn't. *Unknown.* GBP
White as the great white dusk through which he moves. The Hunter. Eleanor Glenn Wallis. NePoAm-2
White Autumn. Robert Morgan. Str
White Azaleas. Harriet McEwen Kimball. HBV-1
White Bear. Susan Griffin. GP
White Beauty, The, *orig. and mod. English prose. Unknown.* MeEL; OxBM
White Bird, The. Roy McFadden. NeIP
White Bird. Matti Megged, *tr. fr. Hebrew by* Howard Schwartz. VWA
White Bird, The. Wilfred Watson. MoCV
White bird, A. Shira. Howard Schwartz. VWA
White bird featherless/ Flew from Paradise. Riddle of Snow and Sun. *Unknown.* ChTr; GBP; NCEP; OxNR
White bird [featherless] floats down through the air, A. Riddle. *Unknown.* ChTr; GBP
White bird of the tempest! oh, beautiful thing. Lines Addressed to a Seagull. Gerald Griffin. OnYI
White Blossom, A. D. H. Lawrence. MoBrPo
White blossom, white, white shell; the Nazarene. Music of Colours—White Blossom. Vernon Watkins. LiTM; WaP
White Blossoms. Robert Mezey. NaP; VWA
White buck come in. Anadarko John. Carroll Arnett. VoR
White Butterflies. Swinburne. FaPON; PDV
(Envoi: "Fly, white butterflies, out to sea.") GoJo; SUS; VLP
White butterfly, A. The Graceful Bastion. William Carlos Williams. NYBP
White Canoe, The. Alan Sullivan. CaP
White-capped Waves. James Freeman Clarke. EtS
White Captain of my soul, lead on. A Soldier's Prayer. Robert Freeman. TrPWD
White Cat. Raymond Knister. WHW
White cat, The. Cat Ballerina Assoluta. Emilie Glen. GoYe
White Cat of Trenarren, The. A. L. Rowse. OxBTC; PCat
White Center. Richard Hugo. NoP
White chocolate jar full of petals, The Chez Jane. Frank O'Hara. CoAP; NeAP; NoAM; NOBA; PoA
White Christmas. W. R. Rodgers. ChMP; LiTM; MoAB; MoBrPo; PPON; SeCePo
White church on the hill, The. A New England Church. Wilson Agnew Barrett. WGRP
"White City, The." Richard Watson Gilder. PAH
White City, The. Claude McKay. BPo; NoAM; TAP; TW
White Cliffs, The, *sels.* Alice Duer Miller.
English Are Frosty, The. PoLF
I Have Loved England. BLPL; PoLF
White cloud drifts to meet a sail at sea, A. The Old Sailor. Glenn Ward Dresbach. EtS
White cloud passed over the land, The. The Final Painting. Lee Harwood. EAS
White Cockade, The. *Unknown, tr. fr. Modern Irish by* James Joseph Callanan. OnYI
White cock's tail, The. Ploughing on Sunday. Wallace Stevens. FaPON; GoJo; NCSH; PoPl; SOTW
White columns of towering masonry. Monserrat. William Edwin Collin. CaP
White Company, The, *sel.* Sir Arthur Conan Doyle.
Song of the Bow, The. HBV-2
White Conduit House. William Woty. NOEC
White coral bells upon a slender stalk. *Unknown.* PDV
White cormorants shaped like houses stare down at you, The. Party at Hydra. Irving Layton. HeIP
White cups white. *Turkish Love Songs, tr. by* Reza Baraheni *and* Zahra-Soltan Shokoohtaezeh. BoWoP
White curtains blowing inward. This Song Shows Me Pictures; Morningside Drive, New York City 1950-1960. Richard Oyama. BrSi
White curtains of infinite fatigue. And the Seventh Dream Is the Dream of Isis. David Gascoyne. EAS
White daisies are down in the meadow. Alone. John Farrar. YeAr
White day, black river. The Predicter of Famine. William Carlos Williams. VGW
White delightful swan, The. The Dying Swan. *Unknown.* ChTr
White Devil, The, *sels.* John Webster.
Call for the Robin Redbreast [and the Wren], *fr.* V, iv. ChTr; EBEV; FaBoCh; HAP; HeIP; NoP; OAEP; PAI; PoEL-2; PoRA; PrIm; SeCePo; SeCeV; ViBoPo
(Cornelia's Song.) InPS; OBS; TrGrPo
(Dirge, A: "Call for the robin-redbreast and the wren.") ElL; FaBoEn; HBV-2; LiTB; NOBE; OBEV; WHA
(Land Dirge, A.) CH; GTBS; GTBS-P; LoBV
Execration against Whores, An, *fr.* III, ii. TW
"What, are you drop't?" *fr.* V, vi. PoEL-2
White Dou o Truth. The Ineffable Dou. Sydney Goodsir Smith. OxBS
White Dove of the Wild Dark Eyes. Joseph M. Plunkett. HBMV
White Drake, The. *Unknown, tr. fr. French by* John Glassco. WHW
White Dream, The. May Doney. HBMV
White Dress, The. Roberta Spear. MAYP
White Dress, The. Marya Zaturenska. MoAmPo; TwAmPo
White Dusk. Marion M. Boyd. HBMV
White dusk moved ahead of them. Image of City. Lance Henson. VoR
White Dust, The. W. W. Gibson. MoBrPo
White Eagle, The. Nan McDonald. PoAu-2
White Earth Reservation 1980. Gerald Vizenor. STE
White England, shouldering from the sea. Fair England. Helen Gray Cone. AA
White faces,/ Like helpless petals on the stream. London in War. Helen Dircks. SUMH
White faces are lit below the high bank, The. Elver Fishers. Ivor Gurney. FaBoPP
White Fear. Winifred Welles. HBMV
White Fields. James Stephens. BoNaP; FaPON; MoShBr; PoSC; SiSoSe; SoPo; SUS
White Fisher, The. *Unknown.* ESPB
White Flag, The. John Hay. HBV-1
White fog lifting and falling on mountain-brow. Wales Visitation. Allen Ginsberg. CAPP; NNaP; NOBA; NYBP; Prf
"White folks is white," says Uncle Jim. Uncle Jim. Countee Cullen. BANP
White founts falling in the courts of the sun. Lepanto. G. K. Chesterton. FaBV; FaPo; FaPoR; GoBC; GoTL; HBMV; HBVY; MoBrPo; MOS; OBMV; OBNV; TreFS; WHA
White Fox. Elizabeth Alsop Shepard. GoYe
White frost comes. October Night. Agnes Louise Dean. YeAr
White full moon like a great beautiful whore, The. Entry August 27. Walter Benton. *Fr.* This Is My Beloved. UnTE
White goat Amaryllis, The. The Visitor. Patrick R. Chalmers. HBV-1; HBVY

White Goat, White Ram. W. S. Merwin. NePoEA; TwAmPo
White Goddess, The. Robert Graves. MoBrPo; OAEL-2
White-gowned woman making offering, A. Virgin Pictured in Profile. Rosanna Warren. AMV-81; MAYP
White Guardians of the Universe of Sleep. E. E. Cummings. NYBP
White gulls that sit and float. The Echoing Cliff. Andrew Young. PoSH
White gum showing, The. Pine Gum. W. W. E. Ross. OBCV
White-habited, the mystic swan. The Swan. Jay MacPherson. PeCV
White-haired Lover, *sel.* Karl Shapiro.
"I swore to stab the sonnet with my pen." PoA
White hands of langourous grace. He Praises His Wife When She Has Left [*or* Had Gone from] Him. *Unknown, tr. by* Robin Flower. AnIL; OxBI
White hard rock. Silica Carbonate Rock. Fred Berry. NU
White Hare, The. Lilian Bowes-Lyon. OxBTC; PoPle
White Heliotrope. Arthur Symons. BoLoP; EBEV; InPS
White hen she cackles, The. *Unknown.* PBBP
White hill-side is prickled with antlers, The. Knole. C. H. Sisson. NOCV
White Horse, The. W. H. Davies. OxBTC
White Horse, The. D. H. Lawrence. SOTW
White Horse, The. Mary Mills. NePoAm
White Horse, The. Tu Fu, *tr. fr. Chinese by* Rewi Alley. ChTr
White horse came to our farm once, A. The White Stallion. Guy Owen. InPK
White horse nuzzles a violin and two pink roses, The. Equestrienne. Joan Colby. PoDr
White Horse of the Father, White Horse of the Son. William Pitt Root. MAYP
White Horse of Westbury, The. Charles Tennyson Turner. EBEV; VLP
White horse will not emerge from the lake, The. Evening in a Lab. Miroslav Holub, *tr. by* Stuart Friebert *and* Dana Hábová. SUW
White Horses. Eleanor Farjeon. PDV; PH
White Horses. Winifred Howard. SoPo; SUS
White horses, tails high, rise from the cedar. E Uni Que A The Hi A Tho, Father. Roberta Hill. VoR
White-hot midday in the Snake Park, A. In the Snake Park. William Plomer. NoAM; NYBP; OxBTC
White House, The. Claude McKay. AmNP; AmPP; NIP; PoBA
(White Houses.) PoNe
White House Blues. *Unknown.* FSW; OuSiCo, *with music*
White houses bank the hill. The Rooftop. Thom Gunn. NoP
White howl of March, The. In like a Lion. Geof Hewitt. PPJ
White hummocks here are rounded to a thigh. Early Summer Sea-Tryst. Frederick T. Macartney. CBAP
White in the moon the long road lies. A. E. Housman. A Shropshire Lad, XXXVI. AWP; CMoP; ELP; LiTB
White Iris, A. Pauline B. Barrington. PoLF
White is the evening nature of my thought. White. George Woodcock. NeBP
White is the sail and lonely. A Sail. Mikhail Yuryevich Lermontov, *tr. by* Max Eastman. AWP
White Island, The; or, Place of the Blest. Robert Herrick. AnAnS-2; ChTr; HBV-2; JCP; NoP; OAEL-1; OBS; OxBoCh; WiR
White Isle of Leuce, The. Sir Herbert Read. FaBoTw
White Jessamine, The. John Banister Tabb. HBV-2
White Knight's Song, The. "Lewis Carroll." *Fr.* Through the Looking-Glass, *ch.* 8. FaBoCh; FaBoCo; InPS; NA; NOBE; NOBL; NoP; OAEL-2
(Aged Aged Man, The.) BXAP; FaBoPa; OxBChV; SpRo
(A-Sitting on a Gate.) PoRA
("I'll tell thee everything I can.") InvP; Par
(Ways and Means.) FiBHP
(White Knight's Ballad, The.) FaBoNo; HAP; VLP
White Lady has asked me to dance, The. Fourth Dance Poem. Gerald W. Barrax. PoBA
White lambs leap. Through miles of snow. The Fire in the Snow. Vernon Watkins. LiTM; MoVE
White little hands! Mother-Song. Alfred Austin. *Fr.* Prince Lucifer. HBV-1
White Magic; an Ode. William Stanley Braithwaite. PoNe
White man drew a small circle in the sand, The. Circles. Carl Sandburg. AmFN
White man is, The. 12 Gates to the City. Nikki Giovanni. IHMS; PoBA
White man is a tiger at my throat, The. Tiger. Claude McKay. BPo
"White man, pause and gaze around, for we tread on haunted ground." The Legend of Grand Lake. Joseph L. Westcott. PoOW
White Man Pressed the Locks, The. James C. Kilgore. InPK
White-maned, wide-throated, the heavy-shouldered children of the wind. Granite and Cypress. Robinson Jeffers. AmPP
White mares lashed to the sulky carriages. In Ohio. James Wright. NNaP
White mares of the moon rush along the sky, The. Night Clouds. Amy Lowell. MoAmPo; PoPl; WHA
White men's children spread over the earth. The Riddle. Georgia Douglas Johnson. PoBA
White mist drifts across the shrouds, A. Impressions: La Mer. Oscar Wilde. SyP; VLP
White Monster, The. W. H. Davies. AmMo; LiTB
White moon, The, gleams through scudding/ Clouds. Sorrow. Chu Shu-chen, *tr. by* Kenneth Rexroth. BoWoP
White moons like midnight's in the morning sun. Autumn Mushrooms. Kenneth Mackenzie. CBAP
White moth to the closing vine [*or* bine], The. The Gipsy Trail. Kipling. HBV-1; PoRA
White notch as of bone, A. A Suite of Six Pieces for Siskind. John Logan. LCAP
White Notes. Donald Justice. LCAP
White nymph wandering in the woods by night, A. Elegies, II. André Chénier, *tr. by* Arthur Symons. AWP
White ocean birds that seek the land. Gulls and Dreams. Lionel Stevenson. CaP
White, orphaned camel kid, The. *Mongol Oral Tradition, tr. by* C. R. Bawden. WTO
White Owl, The. George Meredith. *Fr.* Love in a Valley. ChTr
White Pass Ski Patrol. John Logan. BiP; CAPP
White Paternoster, The. *Unknown. See* Before Sleeping.
White Peace, The. "Fiona Macleod." FaBoBe; HBV-2
White Peacock, The. Mary Mills. NePoAm
White peacock roosting, The. What I Saw. Robert Duncan. NoAM; NOBA
White People. David Henderson. PoBA
"White phosphorous, white phosphorous." Overheard over S. E. Asia. Denise Levertov. BoWoP
White pine, yellow pine. Southern Pines. John Peale Bishop. GOA
White Pines. Barry Silesky. AMV-80
White pinnace on lactic waves, The. Birth by Anesthesia. George Scarbrough. GoYe
White Primit Falls. *Unknown.* ChTr
White Queen. John Fuller. NePoEA-2
White Rainbow, The. Starr Nelson. GoYe
White Rat, The. Marguerite Young. MoPo
White-robed against the threefold white. At Glan-y-Wern. Arthur Symons. Intermezzo: Pastoral, IV. VLP
White Rose, A. John Boyle O'Reilly. AA; ACP; HBV-1; OBEV; OBVV; OnYI; PoPl; SoSe
White-rose garland at her feet, The. E. B. B. James Thomson. HBV-2
White rose had a sorrow, A. The Betrayal of the Rose. Edith M. Thomas. AA
White rose in red rose-garden. Before the Mirror. Swinburne. OBVV
White Rose is a quiet horse. The Four Horses. James Reeves. PH
White rose tree that spent its musk, The. Old Gardens. Arthur Upson. HBV-1
White Roses. John Ashbery. TAP
White sagebrush desert, The. Noon. O Pioneers! John Peale Bishop. VGW
White sail upon the ocean verge. Arthur. William Winter. AA
White Sand, The. Edmund Wilson. NePoAm
White sand and cedars; cedars, sand. Sandy Hook. George Houghton. AA
White Season. Frances Frost. FaPON; TiPo
White Serpent. Nelly Sachs, *tr. fr. German by* Michael Hamburger. BoWoP
White shape is Loch Fionn, The. Ascent. Donald G. Saunders. PoSH
White sheep, white sheep, on a blue hill. *Unknown.* GBP; SoPo; TiPo
White sheet on the tail-gate of a truck, A. Elegy for a Dead Soldier. Karl Shapiro. AP; CoBMV; HAP; LiTM; MiAP; OBWP; OxBA; WaaP; WaP
White shields they carry in their hands. The Hosts of Faery. *Unknown, tr. by* Kuno Meyer. OnYI
White Ship, The. Geoffrey Hill. OxBC
White Ship, The. Dante Gabriel Rossetti. OBNV; VLP
White Ships and the Red, The. Joyce Kilmer. PAH
White-sided flowers are thrusting up on the hillside. Hawaii Dantesca. Charles Wright. LCAP
White Skirt, The. Stephen Dobyns. MAYP
White sky, over the hemlocks bowed with snow. The Buck in the Snow. Edna St. Vincent Millay. BoAnP; CrMA
White Spider. Marita Garin. AMV-80
White Stallion, The. Guy Owen. InPK
White, stamen-shadowed petals of wild rose. Dogrose. Patric Stevenson. NeIP
White star! that travellest at old Maggie's pace. Maggie's Star. Charles Tennyson Turner. FM
White Steed of the Prairies, The. J. Barber. BPAW; CoSo
White Summer Flower. W. S. Merwin. DFF
White sun. Zebra. Judith Thurman. RHPC

White Swan. A. Glanz-Leyeles, *tr. fr. Yiddish by* Keith Bosley. VWA
White swan of cities, slumbering in thy nest. Venice. Longfellow. EyDe
White-tailed Hornet, The. Robert Frost. OxBA
White the October air, no snow, easy to breathe. How to Get There. Frank O'Hara. NoP
White though ye be, yet, li[l]lies, know. How Li[l]lies Came White. Robert Herrick. AnAnS-2; CaPo
White-Throat Sings, A. Walter Prichard Eaton. HBMV
White through the azure. The Swimmer of Nemi. "Fiona Macleod." SyP
White Tintoretto clouds beneath my naked feet. The Strand. Louis MacNeice. AnIV
White to the neck he glides and plunges. Fencing School. John Manifold. CBAP
White Tree in Bloom, A. John Richard Moreland. PGD
White velvet covers the town. Jerusalem in the Snow. Anath Bental, *tr. by* Howard Schwartz. VWA
White Venus limpid wandering in the sky. Sonnet V. Louise Labé, *tr. by* Aliki *and* Willis Barnstone. BoWoP
White Violet. Marian Osborne. CaP
White violet, The. Sea Violet. Hilda Doolittle ("H. D."). NoP
White Violets. Benjamin R. C. Low. HBMV
White walls of the Institution, The. Now and Then. Ian Hamilton. NoAM
White Was His Naked Breast. *Unknown.* OxBM
White way is the wind's way, A. The Wind's Way. Grace Hazard Conkling. HBV-2
White Weekend. Quincy Troupe. NBP
White Whales Specked Black. Randolph Outlaw. LFAC
White wind whispers of the woes, The. The Four Winds. Shane Leslie. OnYI
White Window, The. James Stephens. SUS; TiPo
White wings of commerce sailing far. In Memory of General Grant. Henry Abbey. AA
White Witch, The. James Weldon Johnson. BANP; CDC
White woman have you heard. Montgomery. Sam Cornish. CNA; PoBA; Psk
White Women, The. Mary Elizabeth Coleridge. BrRo
White World. Hilda Doolittle ("H. D."). LLLT
Whitebeard on Videotape. James Merrill. NoP
Whitehall Stairs. Aaron Hill. NOEC
Whiteness. Isobel Hume. HBMV
Whiteness. Yunna Moritz, *tr. fr. Russian by* Elaine Feinstein. VWA
Whiteness of the lily once was thine, The. The Maid. Katherine Brégy. GoBC
Whiteness, or Chastity. Joseph Beaumont. LoBV
Whiter/ than the crust. The Wind Sleepers. Hilda Doolittle ("H. D."). WPE
Whiter there is not nor rosier. Peggy. Blanaid Salkeld. OnYI
Whitewinged circus/ of kittiewaking. Spring, St. Stephen's Green. Leslie Daiken. OnYI
Whither. John Vance Cheney. AA
Whither? Wilhelm Müller, *tr. fr. German by* Longfellow. AWP
Whither Away? Mary Elizabeth Coleridge. CH
Whither away, O Sailor! say? Outward. John G. Neihardt. HBV-1
Whither away, Robin. The Flight of the Birds. Edmund Clarence Stedman. GN
Whither depart the souls of the brave that die in the battle. Arthur Hugh Clough. Amours de Voyage, Canto V, vi. OAEP
Whither dost thou hide from the magic of my flute-call? The Snake-Charmer. Sarojini Naidu. PBWP
Whither I kneel or stand or sit in prayer. At Communion. Madeleine L'Engle. TrCP
Whither Is Gone [the Wisdom and the Power]. Hartley Coleridge. HBV-2; OBRV
Whither leads this pathway, little one? Whither. John Vance Cheney. AA
Whither, mad maiden, wilt thou roame? To His Muse. Robert Herrick. OAEP
Whither, midst falling dew. To a Waterfowl. Bryant. AA; AmPP; AP; AWP; BLPL; CH; EBCP; FaBoBe; FaBoEn; FaFP; GN; HBV-1; HBVY; HoPM; LiTA; NePA; NOBA; NoP; OBRV; OHFP; OxBA; PB; PoEL-4; PoLF; PrIm; SeCeV; SoSe; TAP; TreF; TrGrPo; TRV; WBLP; WGRP
Whither, O splendid ship, thy white sails crowding. A Passer-by. Robert Bridges. BrPo; CMoP; CoBMV; EtS; HBV-1; LiTB; LiTM; MoAB; MoBrPo; MOS; NBM; OAEL-2; OAEP; OBEV; OBNC; OBVV; OxBTC; PoPle; SeCeV; WiR
Whither, O, whither art thou fled. The Search. George Herbert. AnAnS-1
Whither, O whither didst Thou fly? The Eclipse. Henry Vaughan. HBV-2
Whither, O whither wander I forlorn? Oceana and Britannia. John Ayloffe. APAS
Whither, say whither shall I fly. The Frozen Zone; or, Julia Disdainful. Robert Herrick. CaPo
Whither shall I go. *Unknown, at. to* John Webster *and* William Rowley. *Fr.* The Thracian Wonder. GBL
Whither shall I, the fair maiden, flee from Sorrow? Sorrow. *Unknown, tr. by* W. R. S. Ralston. AWP
Whither So Fast? *Unknown.* ElL
"Whither thus hastes my little book so fast?" The Writer to His Book. Thomas Campion. OAEP
Whiting and the Snail, The. "Lewis Carroll." *See* Lobster Quadrille, The.
Whitman. Larry Levis. MAYP
Whitman's Ride for Oregon. Hezekiah Butterworth. PAH
Whitmonday. Louis MacNeice. NYBP
Whitsun Weddings, The. Philip Larkin. FaBoMo; NePoEA-2; NoAM; NoP; OxBTC
Whitsunday. John Keble. OBRV
Whitsuntide an' Club Walken. William Barnes. VLP
Whittier. James Russell Lowell. *Fr.* A Fable for Critics. AmPP; AP; NOBA; OxBA
Whittier. Margaret E. Sangster. AA
Whittingham Fair. *Unknown. See* Scarborough Fair.
Whittling. John Pierpont. GN
Who. Moishe-Leib Halpern, *tr. fr. Yiddish by* Joseph Leftwich. TrJP
Who. Edwin Honig. TAP
Who? Dan Jaffe. FAZ
Who/ Are you/ Who is born. Vision and Prayer. Dylan Thomas. LiTM; MoPo
Who Am I? Felice Holman. RFM
Who am I? I am a lady faithful to the ways. Lady of the Ferry Inn. Gwerfyl Mechain, *tr. by* Willis Barnstone. BoWoP
Who am I worthless that You spent such pains. A Prayer for the Self. John Berryman. *Fr.* Eleven Addresses to the Lord. PPP
Who among You Knows the Essence of Garlic? Garrett Hongo. HoAn
Who Are My People? Rosa Zagnoni Marinoni. BLPA
Who are the nobles of the earth. The True Aristocrat. W. Stewart. WBLP
"Who are the winds? Who are the winds?" The Winds. "John Eglinton." OnYI
Who are these among you. The Decision. Owen Dodson. PoNe
Who are these from the strange, ineffable places. Arabia. John Meade Falkner. OxBTC
Who are these people at the bridge to meet me? The Bee Meeting. Sylvia Plath. InPS; PPP; WPE
Who are these? Why sit they here in twilight? Mental Cases. Wilfred Owen. BiP; BrPo; CMoP; FaBoMo; MMA; NoAM; WaP
Who Are They? *Unknown, tr. fr. Delaware Indian by* D. G. Brinton. NIP
Who are they. The Passengers. David Antin. NYBP
Who are they talking to in the big temple? The Temple. C. H. Sisson. OxBTC
Who are they to be in their skin. The Subway Witnesses. Lorenzo Thomas. PoBA
Who are we here? Intra-Political. Margaret Avison. MoCV
Who are we to love. A Footnote to a Gray Bird's Pause. James Cunningham. JB
"Who are we waiting for?" "Soup burnt?" The Feckless Dinner Party. Walter de la Mare. FaBoTw
Who are ye, spirits, that stand. The Blazing Heart. Alice Williams Brotherton. AA
Who are you. To Desi as Joe as Smoky the Lover of 115th Street. Audre Lorde. CNA
"Who are you and whence do you come?" A Vagrant. Erik Axel Karlfeldt, *tr. by* Charles Wharton Stork. PoPl
"Who are you?" asked the cat of the bear. Elizabeth J. Coatsworth. TiPo
Who are you dusky woman, so ancient hardly human. Ethiopia Saluting the Colors. Walt Whitman. PAH; PoNe
Who are you, listening to me, who are you. Poem for Half White College Students. Amiri Baraka. BPo; CAPP; TAP; UnPo
Who Are You, Little I. E. E. Cummings. NYBP
"Who are you, Sea Lady." Santorin. James Elroy Flecker. FaBoTw; GoJo; OBMV
"Who are you, slim hipped tussler?" The Wrestling. Abbie Huston Evans. GP
"Who are you that so strangely woke." The Princess of Scotland. Rachel Annand Taylor. BSV; GoTS
Who are you there that from your icy tower. The Astronomers of Mont Blanc. Edgar Bowers. PoA; QFR
Who Be Kind To. Allen Ginsberg. NNaP
Who beckons the green ivy up. The Miracle. Walter de la Mare. LiTB; UnPo
Who believes/ he is dead? Under Stone. Elaine Feinstein. VWA
Who Bids Us Sing? Rhys Carpenter. WGRP
Who borrows all your ready cash. A Friend. Marguerite Power. FaBoCo; FaFP
Who builds a church within his heart. The Church in the Heart. Morris Abel Beer. TRV

Who builds him a house of stone or brick. Builders. Hortense Flexner. HBMV
Who builds of stone a shrine to bear his name. The Glory of Lincoln. Thomas Curtis Clark. PGD
Who built the house. The House. T. Walking Eagle Marietta. LFAC
"Who burst the barriers of my peaceful grave?" The Lament of the Damned in Hell. Edward Young. OxBoCh
Who bury the dead. The Heavenly Tree Grows Downward. Gerrit Lansing. CoPo
Who but the Lord? Langston Hughes. BPo
Who by Searching Can Find Out God? Eliza Scudder. *See* Quest, The.
"Who called?" I said, and the words. Echo. Walter de la Mare. MoVE; OBMV; SeCeV
Who Calls. Frances Clark Sayers. SiSoSe
Who calls her two-faced? Faces, she has three. The Three-faced. Robert Graves. FaBoEE
Who calls? Who calls? Who? For a Mocking Voice. Eleanor Farjeon. CH; TiPo
Who came in the quiet night. The Little Fox. Marion Edey *and* Dorothy Grider. TiPo
Who Can Be Born Black. Mari Evans. CNA
Who can bear/ The wail of a young orphan? Rabbi Yussel Luksh of Chelm. Jacob Glatstein, *tr. by* Nathan Halper. TrJP
Who can believe with common sense. Epigram on Fasting. Swift. OBVE
Who can find a virtuous woman? for her price is far above rubies. A Virtuous Woman [*or* The Good Wife]. Bible, *O.T.* *Fr.* Proverbs. SaC; TrGrPo; TRV
Who can forbear, and tamely silent sit. A Satire against Wit. Sir Richard Blackmore. APAS
Who can forget that ne'er forgotten night. On the Nativity of Our Saviour. Thomas Philipott. JCP
Who can grasp for the first time. New Music. Gwen Harwood. CBAP
Who can grasp the gray hearts of shopkeepers? Shopkeepers. Mani Leib, *tr. by* Richard J. Fein. AMV-81
Who can live in heart so glad. Shepherd and Shepherdess [*or* The Happy Countryman *or* The Merry Country Lad *or* Pastoral]. Nicholas Breton. *Fr.* The Passionate Shepherd. CH; ElL; ELP; LoBV; OBSC; ViBoPo
Who can make a delicate adventure. Advice to a Blue-Bird. Maxwell Bodenheim. HBMV
Who can remember back to the first poets. The Makers. Howard Nemerov. FYAP
Who can retell the things that befell us. Mi Y'Malel (Who Can Retell?). *Tr. fr. Hebrew.* FSW
Who can review, without a precious loss. The Passion. Ralph Knevet. JCP
Who Can Say. Alastair Reid. NePoEA
Who can say. Song. Tennyson. FaBoCh
Who can say. In the Heartland. Mark Vinz. GP
Who can support the anguish of love? Ode. Ibn al-Arabi, *tr. by* R. A. Nicholson. AWP
Who Can Tell? *Gond Oral Tradition, tr. by* V. Elwin *and* S. Hivale. WTO
Who can tell a man's real pain. Then Sings My Soul. Paul Mariani. GeTw; MAYP
Who can tell how the lobster got. The Lobster Pot. John Arden. ELU
Who Can Tell When He Is Awake. James Tate. MAYP
Who can the various city frauds recite. John Gay. *Fr.* Trivia; or, The Art of Walking the Streets of London, III. OAEL-1
Who comes dancing over the snow. The New Year. Dinah Maria Mulock Craik. YeAr
Who comes from far away, what old gray man. The Horse. A. E. Coppard. BoAnP
Who comes here?/ A grenadier. The Grenadier. *Unknown.* GBP; OxNR
Who comes to us in our dark. Isaac and Esau. Rose Drachler. VWA
Who comes to-night? We ope the doors in vain. Henry James. Robert Louis Stevenson. OBNC
Who could be smaller than this child. The Green Horse. Bin Ramke. MAYP
Who could believe an ant in theory? Credibility. John Ciardi. InPK
Who could dispute his choice. The Net and the Sword. Douglas LePan. NOBC
Who could hate you? Your patched-together face. Apology to My Lady. Edward Falco. AMV-80
Who could have thought, but for eight days in space. Space. X. J. Kennedy. MOON
Who could have thought that men and women could feel. Old Paintings on Italian Walls. Kathleen Raine. NYBP
Who could remember cause? The Victim. Ellen Bryant Voigt. MAYP
Who cries that the days of daring are those that are faded far. Deeds of Valor at Santiago. Clinton Scollard. HBV-2; PAH
Who crieth: "Woe"? who: "Alas"? The Drunkard. Bible, *O.T.* *Fr.* Proverbs. TrJP
Who dare complain or be ashamed. Celebrations. Austin Clarke. IPY; OxBI
Who dares to drop the pin destruction of our silence. Can You Change a Shilling? Toni Del Renzio. EAS
Who Dat a-Comin' ovah Yondah, *with music.* *Unknown.* BoAN-1
Who dat a-knockin' at the door below. What You Goin' to Do When the Rent Comes 'Round? Andrew B. Sterling. OBAL
Who decided what is useful in its beauty. Looking at Quilts. Marge Piercy. SaC
Who Did Swallow Jonah? *Unknown.* FSW
Who died on the wires, and hung there, one of two. The Silent One. Ivor Gurney. MMA; OBWP
Who does God's work will get God's pay. God's Pay. *Unknown.* STF
Who does not love the juniper tree? Juniper. Eileen Duggan. PChr
Who does not love the spring deserves no lovers. Georgian Spring. Roy Campbell. OBSV
Who Does Not Love Wine, Women and Song. J. H. Voss. FaFP
Who doth behold my mistress' face. The Fairest of Her Days. *Unknown.* ElL
Who doth desire that chaste his wife should be. Truth Doth Truth Deserve [*or* Advice to the Same]. Sir Philip Sidney. *Fr.* Arcadia. HBV-1; SiPS
Who Doth Not See the Measure of the Moon? Sir John Davies. MOON
Who doubts has met defeat ere blows can fall. Columbus the World-Giver. Maurice Francis Egan. PGD
Who doubts? The laws fell down from heaven's height. Joseph Hall. *Fr.* Virgidemiarum. OBSV
Who Drags the Fiery Artist Down? Clarence Day. FaBoCo
Who dreamed [*or* dream'd] that beauty passes like a dream? The Rose of the World. W. B. Yeats. BrPo; CMoP; FaBoEn; HBV-1; MoAB; MoBrPo; OBVV
Who drives the horses of the sun. The Happiest Heart. John Vance Cheney. AA; HBV-2; HBVY; TreFS; WGRP
Who e'er. *See* Whoe'er.
Who ere shee bee. *See* Whoe'er she be.
Who even dead, yet hath his mind entire! Cantos, XLVII. Ezra Pound. CMoP; CrMA; MoPo; VGW
Who ever. *See* Whoever.
Who fears to speak of Easter Week. Easter Week. *Unknown.* OnYI
Who fears to speak of Ninety-eight? The Memory of the Dead. John Kells Ingram. AnIV; HBV-2; OnYI; OxBI
Who feasts tonight? The Fairies Feast. Charles M. Doughty. CH
Who fed me from her gentle breast. My Mother. Ann *or* Jane Taylor. BLPA; BLPL; OHIP; OxBChV; PaPo; TreF, *sl. abr.*
Who feels a growing hunger for fair eyes. To Liebig. August, Graf von Platen, *tr. by* Reginald Bancroft Cooke. PeHV
Who findeth comfort in the stars and flowers. L'Envoi. Thomas Lovell Beddoes. *Fr.* Death's Jest Book. OBNC
Who first reform'd our stage with justest law[e]s. An Elegy on Ben Jonson. John Cleveland. MeLP; OBS
Who folds a leafe downe. *Unknown.* FaBoUs
Who Follows in His Train? Reginald Heber. *See* Son of God Goes Forth to War, The.
Who forced the Muse to this alliance? On Professor Drennan's Verse. Roy Campbell. GTBS-P; WhC
Who gave thee, O Beauty. Ode to Beauty. Emerson. AmPP; AP; PoEL-4
Who goes? On the Bus. Mitsuye Yamada. *Fr.* Camp Notes. WPOW
Who Goes round My Pinfold Wall. *Unknown.* GBP
Who goes there? God knows. I'm nobody. How should I answer? Etosion achthos aroures. Robert Bridges. QFR
Who goes there? hankering, gross, mystical, nude. Song of Myself, XX. Walt Whitman. TrGrPo
Who goes there, in the night? Apparitions. Thomas Curtis Clark. PGD; TRV
Who Goes with Fergus? W. B. Yeats. CABA; CMoP; FaBoCh; GoJo; InPK; NoAM; NOBE; PoRA
Who Grace, for Zenith had, from which no shadowes grow. Despair. Fulke Greville. *Fr.* Caelica. OBSC; PoEL-1
Who grafted quince on Western may. The Avengers. Robert Graves. HBMV
Who Guessed Amiss the Riddle of the Sphinx. James Merrill. TwAmPo
Who half asleep, or waking, does not hear it. The Furnace of Colors. Vernon Watkins. NYBP
Who has a feeling she will come one day. White Queen. John Fuller. NePoEA-2
Who has but dighted his tricks in a bed. This Is What the Watchbird Sings, Who Perches in the Lovetree. Bruce Boyd. NeAP
Who has described the wave. Thoughts in the Gulf Stream. Christopher Morley. EtS
Who has ever stopped to think of the divinity of Lamont Cranston? In Memory of Radio. Amiri Baraka. NeAP; NIP; NoP; PoM
Who Has Known Heights. Mary Brent Whiteside. BLPA

Who has not found the heaven below. God's Residence. Emily Dickinson. TRV
Who has not heard of the dauntless *Varuna?* The *Varuna.* George Henry Boker. PAH
Who has not heard of the Vale of Cashmere. The Light of the Harem [*or* Haram]. Thomas Moore. *Fr.* Lalla Rookh. EnRP; TEP
Who has not thought, when scuffing shells. Lower Forms of Life. Mary Winter. GoYe
Who Has Not Walked upon the Shore. Robert Bridges. CMoP; MOS
(After the Gale.) LoBV
(Upon the Shore.) EtS
Who Has Our Redeemer Heard, *with music.* Stephen Collins Foster. AH
Who has robbed the ocean cave. Song. John Shaw. AA; HBV-1
Who Has Seen the Wind? Christina Rossetti. *Fr.* Sing-Song. FaPON; GoJo; HBV-1; HBVY; NTCP; PDV; PoPl; RHPC; SUS; TiPo; TreFT
(Wind, The.) BLPL; FaBoBe; OxBChV
Who has strangled the tired voice. Appeal. Noémia da Sousa. TTY, *tr. by* Dorothy Guedes *and* Phillippa Rumsey; WPOW, *tr. by* Alan Ryder
Who Hath a Book. Wilbur D. Nesbit. BLPA; SiSoSe; TiPo; TreFS
Who hath desired the Sea?—the sight of salt water unbounded. The Sea and the Hills. Kipling. FaBV; MOS
Who hath gathered the wind in his fists? The Words of Agur. Bible, *O.T. Fr.* Proverbs. TrGrPo
Who hath given man speech? or what hath set therein. Chorus. Swinburne. *Fr.* Atalanta in Calydon. OAEL-2; ViBoPo
Who hath he[a]rd of such[e] cruelty[e] before? Epigram. Sir Thomas Wyatt. AAS; SiPS
Who Hath His Fancy [*or* Fancie] Pleased. Sir Philip Sidney. EIL; EnRePo; OAEP; PoEL-1; QFR
(Immortality.) OBSC
(Song: "Who hath his fancy pleasèd.") OBEV; SiPS
Who hath restored my sense, given me new breath. John Fletcher. *Fr.* The Faithful Shepherdess. LO
Who have been lonely once. Careless Love. Stanley Kunitz. WaP
Who Here Can Cast His Eyes Abroad, *with music.* Abiel Holmes. AH
Who I am. Song from the Unfinished Man. Paul David Ashley. LFAC
Who, in the dark, has cast the harbor-chain? Putting to Sea. Louise Bogan. LiTM; PoA
Who, in the garden-pony carrying skeps. Horses. Dorothy Wellesley. ChMP; OBMV; OxBTC
Who, in the public library, one evening after rain. Public Library. Dannie Abse. OxBC
Who invited him in? What was he doing here. The Dirty Little Accuser. Norman Cameron. OxBS
Who Is at My Window? *Unknown.* TrGrPo
Who is it calling by the darkened river. Voices. Walter de la Mare. UnPo
"Who is it knocking in the night." The Ballad of the Angel. Theodosia Garrison. HBV-1
Who is it runs through the many-storied mansion of myth. Dwarf of Disintegration. Oscar Williams. LiTM; MoPo; NePA; PoCh
Who Is It Talks of Ebony? Manmohan Ghose. OBMV
Who Is It That This Dark Night. Sir Philip Sidney. *See* Astrophel and Stella: Eleventh Song.
Who is like unto thee who teachest knowledge. Hymn of Unity. *Unknown, tr. by* H. M. Adler. TrJP
Who is lord of lordly fate. Charles Heavysege. *Fr.* Count Filippo. PeCV
Who Is My Brother? Pinkie Gordon Lane. BlSi
Who is my father in this world, in this house. The Irish Cliffs of Moher. Wallace Stevens. DiL; LCAP; NOBA; VGW
Who is not a stranger still. Stephany Fuller. BPo
Who is she coming, whom all gaze upon. Sonnet: A Rapture Concerning His Lady. Guido Cavalcanti, *tr. by* Dante Gabriel Rossetti. AWP
Who is she here that now I see. To Little Renée on First Seeing Her Lying in Her Cradle. William Aspenwall Bradley. HBV-1
Who is she that ascends so high. The Assumption. Sir John Beaumont. ACP; GoBC
Who is she that comes, makyng turn every man's eye. Sonnet [*or* Sonetto] VII. Guido Cavalcanti, *tr. by* Ezra Pound. CTC; OBVE
Who Is Silvia [*or* Sylvia]? Shakespeare. *Fr.* The Two Gentlemen of Verona. BLPL; EIL; EnRePo; FaBoBe; FaFP; GN; LiTB; OAEL-1; SeCeV; TreF; TrGrPo; WHA
(Silvia) OBEV
(Song: "Who is Silvia? what is she.") ViBoPo
(Song to Silvia.) OBSC
(Sylvia) HBV-1
("Who is Silvia? What is she?") OAEP
Who is so proud. The Performing Seal. Rachel Field. *Fr.* A Circus Garland. OBCA; RHPC; SoPo; TiPo
Who Is Sylvia? Shakespeare. *See* Who Is Silvia?
Who Is Tapping at My Window. A. G. Deming. SoPo
Who Is That a-Walking in the Corn? Fenton Johnson. PoNe
Who is that in the tall grasses singing. Song for Naomi. Irving Layton. WHW
Who is that pretty fellow. Work and Play. Martial, *tr. by* Louis Untermeyer. UnTE
Who is that student pale and importunate. Student. Josephine Miles. NoP
Who is the happy warrior? Who is he? Character of the Happy Warrior [*or* The Happy Warrior]. Wordsworth. EnRP; FaBoBe; FaFP; HBV-2; HBVY; LiTB; LoBV; OBRV; OHFP; TreF
Who Is the Man? *with music. Unknown.* TrAS
Who is the mighty master that can trace. To Haydn. Thomas Holcroft. NOEC
Who is the noblest beast you can name? The Horse. Shel Silverstein. PH
Who is the runner in the skies. The Runner in the Skies. James Oppenheim. TrJP
Who Is the Same, Which at My Window Peepes? Spenser. *Fr.* Epithalamion. NAs
Who is the sleeping giant. Giant's Tomb in Georgian Bay. "Katherine Hale." CaP
Who is the ugly one slump-slopping down the street? Robert Penn Warren. *Fr.* Homage to Theodore Dreiser on the Centennial of His Birth. GP
Who is the we, who is. Revolutionary Letter #36. Diane DiPrima. GP
Who is this ancient one. The Ancient One. Charles Culhane. LFAC
Who is this I hear?—Lo, this is I, thine heart. The Dispute of the Heart and Body of François Villon. Villon, *tr. by* Swinburne. AWP; OBVE
Who is this man out walking. Sunday Stroll. Michael Pettit. MAYP
Who is this Moses? who made him, we say. A Soliloquy of One of the Spies Left in the Wilderness. Gerard Manley Hopkins. TrCP
Who is this that comes in splendour, coming from the blazing East? The Airy Christ. Stevie Smith. NOCV
Who Is This That Cometh from Edom? William Herebert. *See* Knight Stained from Battle, The.
Who is this that cometh from Edom. Vision of the Day of Judgment. Bible, *O.T., Moulton, Modern Reader's Bible. Fr.* Isaiah. WGRP
Who is this that cometh up not alone. Bride Song. Christina Rossetti. OBVV
Who is this that darkeneth counsel by words without knowledge? Then the Lord Answered [*or* God Replies]. Bible, *O.T. Fr.* Job. AWP; TrGrPo
Who Is This Who Howls and Mutters? Stevie Smith. OxBC
Who is this whose feet. The Swan's Feet. E. J. Scovell. OxBTC
Who is this ye say is slain? Ellsworth. *Unknown.* PAH
Who is waiting at the doorstep now? Threshold. Charles David Webb. NePoAm-2
Who is, who is the rider there. Who. Moishe-Leib Halpern, *tr. by* Joseph Leftwich. TrJP
Who is wise?/ He who learns from everyone. The Good Man. *Fr.* The Talmud. TrJP
Who journeying when the days grow shorter, stops. Historic Time. Robert Eyres Landor. *Fr.* The Impious Feast. OBRV
Who keeps the owl's breath? Whose eyes desire? Elegy. David St. John. LCAP
Who Kill'd John Keats? Byron. EnRP
(John Keats.) FaBoEE
Who Kill'd Kildare? Who Dar'd Kildare to Kill? Swift. *See* Who Killed Kildare. . .
Who killed Christ?—my favorite subject. Letting in Cold. Marvin Bell. DiL
Who killed Cock [*or* poor] Robin? [*or* Here lies Cock Robin]. Mother Goose. AmFP; HBV-1; HBVY; OxBoLi; OxNR; PBBP
Who killed John Keats? *See* Who Kill'd John Keats.
Who Killed Kildare? Who Dared Kildare to Kill? Swift. TreFS
(Epigram: "Who killed Kildare? Who dared Kildare to kill?") HBV-1
(On the Earl of Kildare.) FaBoEE
Who Killed Lawless Lean? Stevie Smith. TEP
Who killed poor Robin? *See* Who killed Cock Robin?
Who knew her. On the Fifth Anniversary of Bluma Sach's Death. Vinnie-Marie D'Ambrosio. IHMS
"Who knocks at my door, so late in the night?" Pilgrims in Mexico. *Unknown.* OBCP
Who knocks at the Geraldine's door to-night. Ballad of the Little Black Hound. Dora Sigerson Shorter. OnYI
"Who knocks?" "I, who was beautiful." The Ghost. Walter de la Mare. BrPo; ChMP; CMoP; ELP; EnLoPo; HBMV; LiTM; MoAB; MoBrPo; MoVE; NOBE; OAEL-2; OxBTC
Who Knows? A. L. Milner-Brown. PBA; TTY
Who Knows? Nora Perry. AA
Who knows his will? Meditation on a Memoir. J. V. Cunningham. QFR
Who Knows if the Moon's. E. E. Cummings. MOON; SO
Who knows it not, who loves it not. A Racing Eight. James L. Cuthbertson. PoAu-1
Who knows the thoughts of a child. Who Knows? Nora Perry. AA

Who knows? This Africa so richly blest. Who Knows? A. L. Milner-Brown. PBA; TTY
Who knows this or that? Limits. Emerson. FM; PoEL-4
Who knows through what mysterious tensions these. The Ivory Tower. Robert Hillyer. NYBP
Who knows what days I answer for to-day? The Young Neophyte. Alice Meynell. ACP; GoBC
Who Knows Where. Detlev von Liliencron, *tr. fr. German by* Ludwig Lewisohn. AWP
Who knows whether the sea heals or corrodes? Plague of Dead Sharks. Alan Dugan. AP; LiTM; NoAM
Who Likes the Rain? Clara Doty Bates. TiPo
Who lingers always when the dream has blanched? Who? Dan Jaffe. FAZ
Who list the Romane greatnes forth to figure. Joachim du Bellay, *tr. by* Spenser. *Fr.* Ruins of Rome. OBVE
Who lit the furnace of the mammoth's heart? The Sun. Francis Thompson. *Fr.* Ode to the Setting Sun. MoAB; MoBrPo
Who lived at the top end of our street. The Retired Colonel. Ted Hughes. NePoEA-2
Who lives in suit of armor pent. Chant Royal of High Virtue. Sir Arthur Quiller-Couch. HBV-2
Who locked me. A Night in the Royal Ontario Museum. Margaret Atwood. PBWP
Who, long before she left her teens. An Old Song Resung. Charles Larcom Graves. CenHV
Who Loves a Garden. Louise Seymour Jones. BLPA
Who Loves the Rain. Frances Shaw. HBMV; TreFT
Who loves the sea has found its waters blue. Chameleon. Gordon LeClaire. EtS
Who lyst his welthe and eas retayne. V. Innocentia Veritas Viat Fides Circumdederunt Me Inimici Mei. Sir Thomas Wyatt. AAS
Who Makes the Journey. Cathy Song. BrSi
Who Maketh the Grass to Grow. Bible, *O.T.* Psalms, CXLVII, *greatly abr.* FaPON
Who masquerades behind the winds? Moods. Leib Kwitko, *tr. by* Joseph Leftwich. TrJP
Who may this be? Narcissus in Camden. Helen Gray Cone. BXAP
Who, mid the grasses of the field. Dante. Bryant. ViBoPo
Who minds if the wind whistles and howls. Windy Morning. Harry Behn. TiPo
Who, minter of medallions. Reading a Medal. Terence Tiller. FaBoTw; GTBS-P
Who must be blamed for the young head. The Landscape of the Heart. Geoffrey Grigson. LiTB; WaP
Who nearer Nature's life would truly come. Thoreau. Amos Bronson Alcott. AA
Who Needs Charlie Manson? Raymond Thompson. LFAC
Who Never Ate with Tears His Bread. Goethe, *tr. fr. German by* Farnsworth Wright. WGRP
Who never knew to sow. Neanderthal. Michael Jackson. OCNZ
Who, now, can speak of gods. The Gods. Dennis Lee. NOBC
Who now dare longer trust thy mother hand? San Francisco. John Vance Cheney. PAH
Who now does follow the foule Blatant Beast. Spenser. *Fr.* The Faerie Queene, VI, 10. OAEL-1
Who now regards Chloris, her tears, and her whining. Advice to the Ladies. William Somervile. FaBoUs
Who now remembers Almack's balls. Reminiscences of a Dancing Man. Thomas Hardy. MoVE
Who, now, seeing Her so. Et in Arcadia Ego. W. H. Auden. CMoP
Who of Those Coming After. Darcy Gottlieb. AMV-81
Who often found their way to pleasant meadows. Elegy for Minor Poets. Louis MacNeice. PP
Who on your breast pillows his head now. The Lost Jewel. Robert Graves. EnLoPo; NYBP
Who or why, or which, or what. The A[h]kond of Swat. Edward Lear. CenHV; FaBoCh; FaBoCo; FaBoNo; FiBHP; NA
Who owns the land where musket-balls are buried. Now. Richard Murphy. The Battle of Aughrim, I. IPY
Who owns the moonlit skies, the purple dawn. Owning. Wilmot B. Lane. CaP
Who owns these cattle, Corydon? The Herdsmen. Theocritus, *tr. by* Charles Stuart Calverley. *Fr.* Idylls. AWP
"Who owns these lands?" the Pilgrim said. The Staff and Scrip. Dante Gabriel Rossetti. OAEP
Who owns these scrawny little feet? Death. Examination at the Womb-Door. Ted Hughes. NAs; OxBC
Who pads through the wood. The Cat! Joseph Payne Brennan. ShM
Who plays the hand that plays the instrument? Bard. Theodore Black. AMV-81
Who plays with fire. Primer of Consequences. Virginia Brasier. ShM
Who pleasure follows pleasure slays. Sensuality. Coventry Patmore. OBVV
Who praises God the most, what says he more than he. Richard Chenevix Trench. *Fr.* A Century of Couplets. OBRV
Who Prayed? *Unknown.* STF
Who prop, thou ask'st, in these bad days, my mind? To a Friend. Matthew Arnold. OAEP
Who puts back into place a fallen bar. The Father's Business. Edwin Markham. TRV
Who puts off shift. My Naked Aunt. Archibald MacLeish. NePA
Who questions if the punctual sun unbars. Love Redeemed, LXXXII. William Baylebridge. PoAu-1
Who raps at my window? Halloween. Marnie Pomeroy. PoSC
Who reach their threescore years and ten. Threescore and Ten. Richard Henry Stoddard. HBV-1
Who Reigns? Shelley. *Fr.* Prometheus Unbound. SeCePo
Who remains in London. Spring Song in the City. Robert Buchanan. HBV-1
Who rides at night, who rides so late? The Invisible King. Goethe, *tr. by* Robert Bly. NU
Who rideth so fast as a fleet Navajo? Song of the Navajo. Albert Pike. PoOW
Who rideth through the driving rain. The King's Son. Thomas Boyd. AnIV; OBMV; OxBI
Who rose up like a goddess from the sea. The Museum. William Abrahams. WaP
Who rules the world with iron rod? Tall Hat. Victor Daley. CBAP
Who said "Peacock Pie?" The Song of the Mad Prince. Walter de la Mare. EBEV; FaBoCh; GoJo; MoVE; NoAM; NOBE; OAEP; OxBChV
Who (said the Moon). Edith Sitwell Assumes the Role of Luna. Robert Francis. MOON
Who said to the trout. Pisces. R. S. Thomas. OxBC
Who saw the petals. The Secret Song. Margaret Wise Brown. OBCA; PDV; RHPC
Who Says. Musa Moris Farhi. VWA
Who says/ That it's by my desire. People Hide Their Love. Wu-ti, *tr. by* Arthur Waley. OLR
Who says/ the old man/ stayed his hand? Psalm of the Jealous God. Henry Abramovitch. VWA
Who say[e]s that fictions onl[e]y and false hair. Jordan. George Herbert. CABA; FaBoEn; HAP; JCP; LiTB; MeLP; MePo; NOCV; NoP; OAEL-1; OBS; PoEL-2; PoPle; PP; PPP; SeCP; TEP; TrCP
Who says that Giles and Joan at discord be? On Giles and Joan. Ben Jonson. NOBL; TEP
"Who says that the Irish are fighters be birth?" The Peaceable Race. T. A. Daly. HBV-2
Who seeks for heaven alone to save his soul. The Way. Henry van Dyke. TRV
Who seeks perfection in the art. Perfection. Francis Carlin. FaFP; HBMV
Who sees him walk the street, can scarce forbear. Marvellous Martin. Charles Harpur. CBAP
Who sees the cross at Christmas? To See the Cross at Christmas. Roger Cooper. TrCP
Who sees the first marsh marigold. A Charm for Spring Flowers. Rachel Field. TiPo
Who sees with equal eye, as God of all. Pope. *Fr.* An Essay on Man. FaBoEn
Who sees you, G, surprises two in one. To Grosphus. Godfrey the Satirist. PeHV
Who Shall Deliver Me? Christina Rossetti. *See* Battle Within, The.
Who Shall Die? James A. Randall, Jr. BPo
Who shall doubt, Donne, where [*or* whe'er] I a Poet be[e]. To John Donne. Ben Jonson. AnAnS-2; JCP; NoP; SeCP; SeCV-1
Who shall have my fair [*or* faire *or* fayre] lady? My Fair Lady [*or* Under the Leaves Green]. *Unknown.* EnLoPo; OxBoLi; PoEL-1; UnTE
Who shall invoke when we are gone. Tragic Love. W. J. Turner. LO; OBMV
Who Shall Speak for the People? Carl Sandburg. The People, Yes, Sec. 24. OxBA
Who shall tell the lady's grief. On the Death of a Cat. Christina Rossetti. PCat
Who shall tell what did befall. Wealth. Emerson. ImOP
Who shall thy gay buffoonery describe? To the Mocking Bird. Richard Henry Wilde. BoAnP
Who shall understand the mysteries of Thy creations? The Royal Crown, XXIV. Solomon ibn Gabirol, *tr. by* Israel Zangwill. AWP
Who shall welcome home. The Hosts. George M. Brady. NeIP
Who Shapes a Balustrade? Conrad Aiken. EyDe
Who Shined Shoes in Times Square. Lance Jeffers. CNA
Who shot the snake? beat it to death on the road? In Memoriam S. L. Akintola. David Knight. MoCV

Who showed me. To Flossie. William Carlos Williams. NePoAm-2
Who Sleeps by Day and Walks by Night. Henry David Thoreau. PoEL-4
Who smoke-snorts toasts o' My Lady Nicotine. Variations on an Air: After Robert Browning. G. K. Chesterton. BXAP; FaBoPa; NOBL; Par
Who so late/ at the garden gate. At the Garden Gate. David McCord. FaPON
Who So List to H[o]unt, I Know Where Is an Hind [*or* Hynde]. Sir Thomas Wyatt. *See* Whoso List to Hunt. . .
Who so valiant to decide? Young Woman at a Window. Mark Van Doren. LiTA; MoPo
Who sows the seas, or ploughs the easy shore? Woman's Inconstancy. Phineas Fletcher. *Fr.* Sicelides. EIL
Who spurs his horse against the mountain-side. Fond Youth. Samuel Rogers. OBRV
Who stands, the crux left of the watershed. The Watershed. W. H. Auden. OAEL-2
Who strives to mount Parnassus Hill. A Reply to an Imitation of the Second Ode in the Third Book of Horace [*or* Verses]. Richard Bentley. OBEC; ViBoPo
Who strolls so late, for mugs a bait. French Lisette; a Ballad of Maida Vale. William Plomer. ErPo
"Who stuffed that white owl?" No one spoke in the shop. The Owl-Critic. James Thomas Fields. BLPA; CenHV; EvOK; HBV-1; OBAL; TreFS; WBLP; YaD
Who tamed your lawless Tartar blood. To Russia. Joaquin Miller. AA
Who tames the lion now? Lord Alcohol [*or* Song]. Thomas Lovell Beddoes. ViBoPo; WiR
Who Taught Caddies to Count? or, A Burnt Golfer Fears the Child. Ogden Nash. LiSp
"Who Then Is Crazy?" Barry Spacks. GP
Who, then was Cestius. Rome. Thomas Hardy. MoAB
Who thinks of June's first rose today? June, 1915. Charlotte Mew. SUMH
Who Thou art I know not. God the Architect [*or* To God, the Architect]. Harry Kemp. HBMV; TrPWD; TRV; WGRP
Who thought of the lilac? The Lilac. Humbert Wolfe. FaPON; HBVY
Who Threw the Overalls in Mistress Murphey's Chowder? *with music.* George L. Geifer. FSN
Who to the North, or South, doth set. Observation. Robert Herrick. FaBoUs
Who Translates a Poet Badly. Gonzalez Prada, *tr. fr. Spanish by* William M. Davis. ELU
Who travels by the weary wandering way. Despair. Spenser. *Fr.* The Faerie Queene. SeCePo
Who Walks with Beauty. David Morton. BLPA; FaBoBe; HBMV; TreFT
Who wants my jellyfish? The Jellyfish. Ogden Nash. FaPON
Who Was It Came. Daniel Hoffman. CoAP
Who Was It, Tell Me. Heine, *tr. fr. German by* Richard Garnett. TrJP (Sag' Mir Wer Einst die Uhren Erfund.) AWP
Who was it that took away my voice. Silence. Bella Akhmadulina, *tr. by* Daniel Halpern. BoWoP
Who was it then that lately took me in the wood? Faun-taken. Rose O'Neill. HBMV
Who was responsible for the very first arms deal. Peace. Michael Longley. CIP
Who was there had seen us. The Dark Girl's Rhyme. Dorothy Parker. InMe
Who was this girl. Looking at Pictures to Be Put Away. Gary Snyder. FF; InPS; NNaP
Who wd. cope in this Quick. The Web. Gregory O'Donoghue. BIrV
Who weds a sot to get his cot. *Unknown.* FaBoUs
Who weeps now anywhere in the world. Solemn Hour. Rainer Maria Rilke, *tr. by* C. F. MacIntyre. PoPl; TrJP
Who Were before Me. John Drinkwater. OBMV
Who were the builders? Question not the silence. The Nameless Doon [*or* Dun *or* Ruin]. William Larminie. AnIL; BIrV; NBM; OnYI; OxBI
Who were they, what lonely men. Jodrell Bank. Patric Dickinson. SUW
"Who Wert and Art and Evermore Shalt Be." William Channing Gannett. TrPWD
Who? Who? *Unknown.* CH
Who, who and who? The Dark Lord of Savaiki, *abr.* Alistair Campbell. OCNZ
"Who—who—the bride will be?" Who? Who? *Unknown.* CH
Who, who will be the next man to entrust his girl to a friend? Homage to Sextus Propertius, XII. Ezra Pound. FaBoMo; NoAM
Who will believe my verse in time to come. Sonnets, XVII. Shakespeare. OBSC
Who Will Buy a Poem? Mahon O'Heffernan, *tr. fr. Early Modern Irish by* Kenneth Jackson. AnIL
Who will endure. No Change of Place. W. H. Auden. OxBTC
Who will find this when I am lost indeed. Inscription in a Book. Gilean Douglas. AMV-81
Who Will Give Cover? Anadad Eldan, *tr. fr. Hebrew by* Ruth Nevo. VWA
Who will go drive with Fergus now. Who Goes with Fergus? W. B. Yeats. CABA; CMoP; FaBoCh; GoJo; InPK; NoAM; NOBE; PoRA
Who will in fairest book of Nature know. Astrophel and Stella, LXXI. Sir Philip Sidney. CABA; NoP; OAEL-1; SiPS
"Who will pay for the milk I gave you?" Let Me Go. *Gond Oral Tradition, tr. by* V. Elwin *and* S. Hivale. WTO
Who will protect you from the thrust of wings. To My Friend, behind Walls. Carolyn Kizer. NePoAm-2
Who will remember, passing through this Gate. On Passing the New Menin Gate. Siegfried Sassoon. OBMV
Who will say a word for a country town of a sultry summer night. Not without Beauty. John A. B. McLeish. CaP
Who will shoe my pretty little foot? The Lass of Roch Royal. *Unknown.* FSW
Who Will Shoe Your Pretty Little Foot? *Unknown. See* Lass of Lochroyan, The.
Who will show us where. At the Doors. Der Nistor, *tr. by* Joseph Leftwich. TrJP
Who Will Stop His Hand from Giving Warmth. Alejandra Pizarnik, *tr. fr. Spanish by* Alina Rivero. VWA
Who will take away. Spell against Sorrow. Kathleen Raine. PBWP
Who winds the clumsy flower clock now, I wonder. Heavy Heavy Heavy. John Malcolm Brinnin. NYBP
Who wins his love shall lose her. Lost Love. Andrew Lang. BSV; HBV-1
Who with the soldiers was stanch danger-sharer. The Daughter of the Regiment. Clinton Scollard. PAH
Who with thy leaves shall wipe (at need). To His Book[e] [*or* Another]. Robert Herrick. AnAnS-2; FaBoUs; JCP
Who Wot Nowe That Ys Here. *Unknown.* InPS
Who would/ who could. Now Ain't That Love? Carolyn M. Rodgers. BPo
Who would be/ A mermaid fair. The Mermaid. Tennyson. FaPON; GN; WSC
Who would be/ A merman bold. The Merman. Tennyson. FaPON; GN; WSC
Who Would Have Thought [That Face of Thine]. Thomas Howell. *Fr.* The Lover Deceived Writes to His Lady. EIL; POL
Who would have thought my shrivelled heart. George Herbert. LO
Who would linger idle. The Swimmer. Roden Noel. OBVV
Who Would List. *Unknown, tr. fr. French by* Andrew Lang. *Fr.* Aucassin and Nicolette. CTC
Who would live in others' breath? Epitaph: Iohannis Sande. Thomas Bastard. FaBoEE
Who would not be. The Laureate. William Edmonstoune Aytoun. BXAP; Par
Who would true valo[u]r see [*or* He who would valiant be]. The Pilgrim [*or* The Pilgrim's Song *or* To Be a Pilgrim]. Bunyan. *Fr.* The Pilgrim's Progress. CoMu; EBCP; EBEV; ELP; EvOK; FaPoR, *sl. diff. vers.*; GN; HBV-2; NOCV; OBS; WiR
Who wouldn't want such a bed? Woman Asleep on a Banana Leaf. Katha Pollit. PoDr
Who wrote *Who wrote Icon Basilike?* On ["Who Wrote Icon Basilike" by Dr.] Christopher Wordsworth, Master of Trinity. Benjamin Hall Kennedy. FaBoCo; FaBoEE; PV
Whoa Back, Buck. Leadbelly (Huddie Ledbetter). FSW
Who'd Be a Hero (Fictional)? Morris Bishop. FiBHP; OBAL
Who'd believe me if. The Third Dimension. Denise Levertov. NeAP; NoAM
Who'd ever think that Utah would stir the world so much? Marching to Utah. *Unknown.* AmFP
Who'd love again on this old rambling star. Wisdom. Padraic Fallon. OnYI
Whoe'er he be that to a taste aspires. James Bramston. *Fr.* The Man of Taste. NOEC
Whoe'er [*or* Who e'er *or* Who ere] she[e] be[e]. Wishes to His [*or* for the] Supposed Mistress[e]. Richard Crashaw. BoLoP; EBEV;GoBC; GTBS; GTBS-P; HBV-1; MeLP; MePo; OAEP; OBEV; PoEL-2; SeCP; SeCV-1; TreFT; ViBoPo, *abr.*; WHA
Whoe'er this book, if lost, doth find. *Unknown.* FaBoUs
Whoe'er thou art whose path in summer lies. Inscription. Mark Akenside. NOEC
Whoever colored the moon tonight didn't stay. A Visit to the Farm. Robert Siegel. GeTw
Whoever [*or* Who ever] comes to shroud me, do not harm[e]. The Funeral[l]. John Donne. AnAnS-1; AWP; BiP; BoLoP; CABA; EBEV; EnLoPo; EnRePo; HeIP; LO; MeLP; NoP; OAEL-1; OBEV; OBS; PoEL-2; PoPle; PoRA; SeCP; SeCV-1
Whoever despises the clitoris despises the penis. The Speed of Darkness. Muriel Rukeyser. LCAP
Whoever [*or* Who ever] guesses, thinks, or dream[e]s he know[e]s. The Curse. John Donne. OAEP; TW

Who ever had/ Such a whale of a plan? The Wall of China. Padraic Colum. GrPL; RoGo
Whoever has a yod in his name. Bella and the Golem. Rossana Ombres, *tr. by* Edgar Pauk. VWA
"Whoever has courage/ And fighting spirit in his heart." The Funeral Games for Anchises; Entellus. Virgil, *tr. by* Rolfe Humphries. *Fr.* The Aeneid, V. LiSp
Whoever has heard of St. Gingo. The New Cecilia. Thomas Lovell Beddoes. OAEL-2
Whoever hath her wish, thou hast thy Will. Sonnets, CXXXV. Shakespeare. OAEL-1
Whoever hath washed his hands of living. Courage. Sadi, *tr. by* Sir Edwin Arnold. *Fr.* The Gulistan. AWP
Whoever I am. When I Was Young I Tried to Sing. Donald Finkel. GP
Whoever is washed ashore at that place. Legend. Ralph Gustafson. CaP; PeCV
Whoever it was who brought the first wood and coal. Banking Coal. Jean Toomer. PoNe
Who Ever Loved, That Loved Not at First Sight? Christopher Marlowe. *See* It Lies Not in Our Power to Love or Hate.
Whoever loves, if he do not propose. Love's Progress. John Donne. Elegies, XVIII. LiTB; OAEL-1; ViBoPo
Who ever sailes neere to Bermuda coast. Caelica, LIX. Fulke. Greville. NCEP
Who ever saw so fair a sight. Constancy. Samuel Daniel. *Fr.* Hymen's Triumph. OBSC
Whoever swings an ax. Ax. Charles Simic. GP
Whoever to finding fault inclines. The Cynic. St. George Tucker. OBAL
Whoever weeps somewhere out in the world. Silent Hour. Rainer Maria Rilke, *tr. by* Jessie Lemont. AWP
Whoever with the compasses of his eyes. Waitress. Karl Shapiro. TwAmPo
Whoever without money is in love. Sonnet: Of Why He Is Unhanged. Cecco Angiolieri da Siena, *tr. by* Dante Gabriel Rossetti. AWP
Whoever you are. Little Sis. David Kherdian. AMV-80
Whoever you are, go out into the evening. Initiation. Rainer Maria Rilke, *tr. by* C. F. MacIntyre. TrJP
Whoever You Are Holding Me Now in Hand. Walt Whitman. InvP; PoEL-5
Whole and without Blessing. Linda Gregg. MAYP; NPGG
Whole Armour of God, The. Charles Wesley. NOCV
Whole day have I followed in the rocks, The. Fergus and the Druid. W. B. Yeats. VLP
Whole day long, under the walking sun, The. The Sleeping Giant. Donald Hall. GrPl; MP; NCSH; NePoEA; NYBP; PAI; Psk; TwCP
Whole Duty of Berkshire Brooks, The. Grace Hazard Conkling. HBMV; HBVY
Whole Duty of Children. Robert Louis Stevenson. EvOK; FaBoUs; HBV-1; HBVY; OxBChV; TreFS
Whole field of poppies billowed, my beloved, The. A Farewell Ballad of Poppies. Eva Brudne. VWA
Whole health resides with peace. Description of Elysium. James Agee. CrMA
Whole heap of nickles and a whole heap of dimes, A. Shout, Little Lulu. *Unknown.* AmFP
Whole landscape drifted away to the north, The. A Window on the North. R. A. D. Ford. MoCV
Whole process is a lie, The. The Ivy Crown. William Carlos Williams. NoP; PrIm
Whole Story, The. William Stafford. NNaP
Whole towns shut down. The Late Snow and Lumber Strike of the Summer of Fifty-four. Gary Snyder. NaP; NMP
Whole tribe dies, A. Elegy. Duane Big Eagle. STE
Whole universe is full of God, The. Yunus Emre, *tr. fr. Turkish by* W. S. Merwin *and* Talat Sait Halman. LLLT
Whole week, A. Hurting. Vi Gale. GP
Whole weight of history bears down, The. The Awful Mother. Susan Griffin. NPGG
Whole weight of the ocean smashes on rock, The. An Address to the Vacationers at Cape Lookout. William Stafford. NYBP
Whole white world is ours, The. White World. Hilda Doolittle ("H. D."). LLLT
Whole, wide world, turned selfless for a day, The. Alchemy. Adelaide Love. PGD
Whole world dances, The. October. Steve Hahn. PPJ
Whole world here, leavened with madness, swells, The. Ben Jonson. *Fr.* An Epistle to a Friend, to Persuade Him to the Wars. JCP
Whole world now is but the minister, The. Robert Bridges. The Growth of Love, III. VLP
Whole Year Christmas, The. Angela Morgan. TRV
Wholesome. William Meredith. TAP
Who'll Be a Witness for My Lord? *with music.* *Unknown.* BoAN-1
Who'll have the crumpled pieces of a heart? Laurana's Song. Richard Hovey. AA
Who'll marry me? Cold Saturday. Will he leave me? Questions and Answers. Diana O Hehir. NPGG
"Who'll rage against all government." The Lion and O'Reilly. Richard Weber. PPON
Who'll walk the fields with us to town? Market Day. Mary Webb. CH
Whom Do We Count a Good Man. Milton. *Fr.* Tetrachordon. NCEP
Whom Do You Visualize as Your Reader? Linda Pastan. PPJ
Whom first we love, you know, we seldom wed. Changes. Robert Bulwer-Lytton. PoLF
Whom I lay down for dead rises up in blood. In All the Argosy of Your Bright Hair. Dunstan Thompson. WaP
"Whom I shall kiss," I heard a Sunbeam say. Betrayal. John Banister Tabb. ACP
Whom Jesus Love. John Barford. PeHV
Whom Shall One Teach. Bible, *O.T.* Isaiah, XXVIII: 9–13. TrJP
Whom the Gods Love. Margaret E. Bruner. PoLF
Whom the Gods Love. Mark A. De Wolfe Howe. AA
"Whom the gods love die young" was said of yore. Byron. *Fr.* Don Juan, IV. OAEP
Whom the untaught shepherds call. Song of the Pixies. Samuel Taylor Coleridge. OBEC
Whom thus answered the Arch Fiend now undisguised. Satan's Guile. Milton. *Fr.* Paradise Regained, I. LiTB; OBS
Whom We Revere. James Russell Lowell. *Fr.* Under the Old Elm. PGD
Whomsoever there are. Stout Affirmation. Kenneth Burke. TwAmPo
Whon men beth muriest at her mele. All Turns into Yesterday. *Unknown.* MeEL
Whoop! the Doodles have broken loose. "Call All." *Unknown.* PAH
Whoopee Blues. *Unknown.* BluL
Whoopee Ti Yi Yo, Git Along Little Dogies. *Unknown.* *See* Git Along Little Dogies.
Whoopin' up cattle. Clear Rock's Chisholm Trail. CoSo
Whoops! *Unknown.* RHPC
("Horse and a flea and three blind mice, A.") FaFP; NTCP
Whore. Linda King. GP
Whore that rides in us abides, The. *Unknown.* SCAP
Whores are afraid to cross the street, The. Eclogue. David Bergman. AMV-80
Whores of Times Square troop to their stations, The. Times Square Parade. Robert Watson. NYP
Whoroscope. Samuel Beckett. NoAM
Who's for the trench. The Call. Jessie Pope. SUMH
Who's Gonna Shoe Your Pretty Little Foot? *Unknown.* *See* Lass of Lochroyan, The.
Who's In. Elizabeth Fleming. RHPC
Who's in the Next Room? Thomas Hardy. PoEL-5; PoPle; QFR; WSC
Who's killed the leaves? Leaves. Ted Hughes. OxBC
Who's Most Afraid of Death? [Thou]. E. E. Cummings. CMoP; SeCeV; VGW
Who's Next? *Unknown.* TDH
Who's that a-knocking at my door? Rollicking Bill the Sailor. *Unknown.* AmSS
Who's That at My Bedroom Window? *with music.* *Unknown.* ShS (Drowsy Sleeper, The.) BaBo (A *and* B *vers.*)
Who's that knocking on the window. Innocent's Song. Charles Causley. GTBS-P; OBCP
Who's that mysterious rider. The Horseman on the Skyline. Henry Lawson. CBAP
Who's that ringing at my door bell? *Unknown.* FaBoCh; OxNR
Who's that ringing at our door-bell? That Little Black Cat. D'Arcy Wentworth Thompson. OxBChV
"Who's that tickling my back?" said the wall. The Tickle Rhyme. Ian Serraillier. NTCP; OnUR; RHPC; SoPo
Who's the Dover-based day tripper. A Trifle for Trafalgar Day. Ted Pauker. NOBL
Who's the most important man this country ever knew? Barney Google. Billy Rose. OBAL
Who's the Pretty Girl Milkin' the Cow, *with music.* *Unknown.* AS
Who's Who. W. H. Auden. CABA; CoBMV; MoAB; MoBrPo; NoAM
Whose anger was it. Girl to Woman. Nixeon Civille Handy. AMV-80
Whose broken window is a cry of art. Boy Breaking Glass. Gwendolyn Brooks. NoAM; NoP
Whose candles light the tulip tree? Tulip Tree. Sacheverell Sitwell. MoBrPo
Whose cherry tree did young George chop? Mingled Yarns. X. J. Kennedy. OBCA
Whose doorway was it, in the sordid street. The Rainbow. Vine Colby. HBMV
Whose eye has marked his gendering? On his throne. The Tornado. Charles de Kay. EtS

Whose freedom is by suff'rance, and at will. William Cowper. *Fr.* The Task: The Winter Morning Walk. EnRP
Whose furthest footstep never strayed. Envoy. Richard Hovey. *Fr.* More Songs from Vagabondia. AA; HBV-2
Whose Hand. *Unknown, tr. fr. Hebrew by* Arthur Davis. TrJP
Whose is that noble dauntless brow? Verses Intended to Be Written below a Noble Earl's Picture. Burns. HoPM
Whose is the river, Excellency, whose the fish. The Geographers. Karl Shapiro. OxBA
Whose is the speech. The Two Poets. Alice Meynell. OBVV
Whose is this horrifying face. Ecce Homo. David Gascoyne. ChMP; LiTM; NeBP; OBWP
Whose kite was this? Treehouse Ted Kooser. PPJ
Whose little beast? Donkey. Mark Van Doren. EaLo
Whose little pigs are these, these, these? *Unknown.* OxNR
Whose love is given over-well. Partial Comfort. Dorothy Parker. FaBoCo; OBAL
Whose minds like horse or ox. The Learned Men. Archibald MacLeish. MoAB
Whose Old Cow? *Unknown.* CoSo
Whose Scene? Ruth Stone. BoWoP
Whose Voice. Barney Bush. STE
Whose woods these are I think I know. Stopping by Woods on a Snowy Evening. Robert Frost. AmPP; AP; BiP; BoNaP; CABA; CMoP; CoBMV; FaBoCh; FaBV; FaFP; FaPON; FF; FPL; GoJo; GrPl; HAP; HBMV; HeIP; HoPM; InPK; InPS; LiTA; LiTM; MasP; MoAB; MoAmPo; MoShBr; MoVE; MP; NePA; NiP; NoAM; NOBA; NoP; NTCP; OBCA; OxBA; PAI; PDV; PoRA; PoSC; PrIm; RHPC; SCV; SiSoSe; SoSe; SUS; TAP; TiPo; TreFS; TrGrPo; TwAmPo; TwCP; UnPo; ViBoPo; WHA
Whoso answers my questions. All or Nothing. Bayard Taylor. BXAP
Whoso delighteth to proven and assay. Thomas More to Them That Seek Fortune. Sir Thomas More. EnRePo
Whoso Draws Nigh to God. *Unknown.* TRV
Whoso has felt the Spirit of the Highest. Frederic W. H. Myers. *Fr.* Saint Paul. TRV
Whoso in harvest mindeth to reap. To His Child. William Bullokar. OxBChV
Whoso in love would bear the bell. Ballad[e] of Ladies' Love, [Number Two]. Villon, *tr. by* John Payne. ErPo; UnTE
Whoso List to Hunt [I Know Where Is an Hind]. Sir Thomas Wyatt, *after the Italian of* Petrarch. AAS; BoLoP; CABA; EBEV; EnRePo; GBL; HAP; InPK; InvP; NoP; OAEL-1; OBVE; PoEL-1; PrIm
(Hind, The.) OBSC, SeCeV; TrGrPo
(Sonnet: "Whoso list to hunt, I know where is an hind.") SiPS
Whoso ne knoweth the strength, power, and might. Venus and Cupide. Sir Thomas More. EnRePo
Whoso the path of law would tread. The Inflamed Disciple. Arthur Kramer. InMe
Whoso thou art that passest by this place. An Epitaph of Maister Win Drowned in the Sea. George Turberville. FaBoEE
Whoso to marry a minion wife. A Minion Wife. Nicholas Udall. *Fr.* Ralph Roister Doister. EIL
Whoso walks in solitude. Emerson. *Fr.* Woodnotes, II. OBVV
Whoso Would See This Song of Heavenly Choice, *with music.* John Wilson. AH
"Who've ye got there?" "Only a dying brother." "The Brigade Must Not Know, Sir!" *Unknown.* PAH
Whsst, and away, and over the green. Nothing. Walter de la Mare. WSC
Whummil Bore, The. *Unknown.* CH; ESPB
"Whu's aw thae fflag-poles ffur in Princess Street?" Heard in the Cougate. Robert Garioch. OxBTC
Why? Melba Joyce Boyd. BlSi
Why. Bliss Carman. OBVV
Why? Stephen Crane. *See* Behold, the Grave of a Wicked Man.
Why? Walter de la Mare. FiBHP
Why. Robert Freeman. PGD
Why? *Fr.* The Talmud. TrJP
Why/ Is the sky? Questions at Night. Louis Untermeyer. FaPON
Why,/ you. Double-barreled Ding-Dong-Bat. Dennis Lee. RHPC
Why Adam Sinned. Alex Rogers. BANP
Why all the racket, you chattering birds? Epigram. *Unknown, tr. fr. Greek by* Thomas Meyer. PeHV
Why, all the Saints and Sages who discuss'd. Omar Khayyám, *tr. by* Edward Fitzgerald. *Fr.* The Rubáiyát of Omar Khayyám of Naishápúr. TRV
Why all these fears and feigned alarms. Catalogue. Louis Untermeyer. HBMV
Why and Wherefore set out one day. Metaphysics. Oliver Herford. NA
"Why are all our women sickly?" Doctor Blenn. Ambrose Bierce. DBV
Why are her eyes so bright, so bright. Any Lover, Any Lass. Richard Middleton. HBV-1; OBVV
Why are our ancestors. Ancestors. Dudley Randall. BPo; CNA
Why Are Our Summer Sports so Brittle? *Unknown.* NCEP
Why are the public buildings so high? W. H. Auden. FaBoCo
Why are the stamps adorned with kings. Power to the People. Howard Nemerov. POL
Why are the things that have no death. Irony. Louis Untermeyer. TrJP
Why are these pipples taking their hets off? ? E. E. Cummings. FiBHP
Why are those tears? Why droops your head? The Farmer's Wife and the Raven. John Gay. PBBP
Why are we[e] by all creatures waited on? Holy Sonnets, XII. John Donne. AnAnS-1; CABA; JCP; MasP; NOCV; OBS; PoEL-2; TrCP
Why are women so energetic? Energetic Women. D. H. Lawrence. InPS
Why are ye wandering aye 'twixt porch and porch. Arcades Ambo. Charles Stuart Calverley. BXAP
Why are you dragged to be stoned? Why? *Fr.* The Talmud. TrJP
Why are you leaving. Song of Farewell. Nellie Wong. BrSi
"Why are you sad, my darling daughter?" The Ripe Fruit. *Unknown, tr. by* Louis Untermeyer. UnTE
"Why are your eyes as big as saucers—big as saucers?" Man in the Street. Robert Penn Warren. OBAL
Why Art Thou Silent. Wordsworth. HBV-1; OBRV
(Speak!) OBEV
(To a Distant Friend.) GTBS; GTBS-P
Why art thou silent and invisible. To Nobodaddy. Blake. OAEL-2
Why art thou slow, thou rest of trouble, Death. Death Invoked [*or* A Sad Song]. Philip Massinger. *Fr.* The Emperor of the East. ACP; OBS; ViBoPo
Why, as to that, said the engineer. The Ghost That Jim Saw. Bret Harte. ShM
Why be afraid of death, as though your life were breath? Emancipation [*or* Death]. Maltbie D. Babcock. BLRP; WBLP; WGRP
Why blush, dear girl, pray tell me why? On Seeing a Lady's Garter. *Unknown.* ErPo
Why boast we, Glaucus! our extended reign. Homer, *tr. by* Pope. *Fr.* The Iliad, XII. OBVE
Why bowest thou, O soul of mine. Heredity. Lydia Avery Coonley Ward. HBV-2
Why call the miser miserable? Byron. *Fr.* Don Juan, XII. UnPo
Why came I so untimely forth. To a Very Young Lady [*or* To a Girl *or* To My Young Lady Lucy Sidney]. Edmund Waller. AnAnS-2; MePo; OAEP; OBS; SeCP; TrGrPo; ViBoPo; WiR
Why cannot the Ear be closed to its own destruction? Blake. *Fr.* The Book of Thel. FaBoEn
Why cannot we eat enough for a week. Envying the Pelican. Richard Weber. CIP
Why Canst Thou Not. *Unknown, at. to* Samuel Daniel. EIL
(Appeal, The.) OLR
Why Can't I Leave You? Ai. AmPA; GeTw; GP
Why, Chloe, thus squander your prime. A Logical Song. *Unknown.* ErPo
Why climb the mountains? I will tell you why. How Small Is Man. John Stuart Blackie. PoSH
Why come ye hither, Redcoats [*or* stranger], your mind what madness fills? Rifleman's [*or* Riflemen's] Song at Bennington. *Unknown.* FSW; PAH
Why Come Ye Not to Court, *sel.* John Skelton.
"Such a prelate, I trow." OBSV
Why, Damon, with the forward day. The Dying Man in His Garden. George Sewell. GTBS; GTBS-P
Why dear Cousin,/ why. Monks. Cardinal Newman. GoBC
Why, Death, what dost thou here. On One Who Died in May. Clarence Chatham Cook. AA
Why did all manly gifts in Webster fail? Emerson. GOA
Why did He choose a garden fair. Thy Will Be Done. Albert Simpson Reitz. STF
Why did I laugh tonight? No voice will tell. Keats. TEP
Why did I let things go this far? Stone Song (Zen Rock) the Seer & the Unbeliever. Karoniaktatie. STE
Why Did I Write? Pope. *Fr.* Epistle to Dr. Arbuthnot. ChTr; FiP; OBEC, *longer sel.*; ViBoPo
("Why do I write? what sin to me unknown.") EBEV
Why did my parents send me to the schools. Nosce Teipsum. Sir John Davies. SiPS (*complete*)
Why did the children/ put beans in their ears? Carl Sandburg. The People, Yes, Sec. 41. OBAL
Why did the woman want to kill one dog? A Village Tale. May Sarton. BoAnP; GDP
Why Did They Dig Ma's Grave So Deep? George Cooper. TreFS
Why did you give no hint that night. The Going. Thomas Hardy. EBEV; ELP; LiTB; NOBE; PAI; UnPo
Why Did You Go. E. E. Cummings. VGW
Why did you hate to be by yourself. As to Being Alone. James Oppenheim. TrJP
Why did you kiss the girl who cried. What the Earth Asked Me. James Wright. NYBP

Why did you lay there asleep. Fragment from "Clemo Uti—the Water Lilies." Ring Lardner. FiBHP
"Why did you melt your waxen man." Sister Helen. Dante Gabriel Rossetti. BeLS; OAEP; VLP
Why did your spirit. Ark Astonished. Jay Macpherson. *Fr.* The Ark. NOBC
Why didst thou promise such a beauteous day. Sonnets, XXXIV. Shakespeare. OBSC
"Why do/ You thus devise." Susanna and the Elders. Adelaide Crapsey. WPE
Why do bells for Christmas ring? *See* Why do the bells of Christmas ring?
Why do I batten down my doors. Storm Warning. Alice Bardsley. AMV-80
Why do I curse the jazz of this hotel? The Jazz of This Hotel. Vachel Lindsay. PoPl
Why do I deny manna to another? Sather Gate Illumination. Allen Ginsberg. NeAP
Why do I hate that lone green dell? Emily Brontë. VLP
Why do I languish thus, drooping and dull. Dulnesse. George Herbert. AnAnS-1
Why do I see my house as a second body? House Poem. Jane Cooper. AMV-81
Why do I sing in the morning. Secret of Song. Christine White. STF
Why do I sleep amid the snows. Roger Williams. Hezekiah Butterworth. PAH
Why Do I Write? Pope. *See* Why Did I Write?
Why do men smile when I speak. Is It Because I Am Black? Joseph Seamon Cotter, Jr. BANP
Why do poets/ Like to die. More Letters Found near a Suicide. Frank Horne. BANP
Why do the bells of [*or* Why do bells for] Christmas ring? Christmas Song. Eugene Field, *wr. at. to* Lydia Avery Coonley Ward. OHIP; SoPo; YeAr
Why do the Gentiles tumult. Bible, *O.T., paraphrased by* Milton. Psalms, II. OBVE
Why do the Graces now desert the Muse? Walter Savage Landor. FaBoEE
Why do the houses stand. Song. George Macdonald. OBVV
Why do the lilies goggle their tongues at me. Grotesque. Amy Lowell. BoWoP
Why do the wheels go whirring round. The Shadow-Child. Harriet Monroe. HBV-1
Why do they come? What do they seek. On a Replica of the Parthenon. Donald Davidson. MoVE
Why do we grumble because a tree is bent. Variety. *Yoruba Oral Tradition, tr. by* E. Lasebikan. WTO
Why do we labor at the poem. Reasons for Music. Archibald MacLeish. NePA
Why Do We Lie. B. S. Johnson. ELU
Why Do We Live? Israel Zangwill. TrJP
Why Do We Love. Sir Benjamin Rudyerd. ElL
Why Do We Mourn Departing Friends? *with music.* Isaac Watts. AH
Why do [*or* doe] ye weep, sweet babes? To Primroses [Filled with Morning Dew]. Robert Herrick. AnAnS-2; HBV-1; OBS; PoPl; SeCV-1; ViBoPo
Why do you always stand there shivering. The Poplar. Richard Aldington. HBMV
Why do you cry out, why do I like to hear you. Sound of Breaking. Conrad Aiken. AWP
Why do you hide, O dryads! when we seek. Chant for Reapers. Wilfrid Thorley. OBEV; OBVV
Why do you lean beside the window, Will? Schoolroom: 158-. James E. Warren, Jr. GoYe
Why do you lie with your legs ungainly huddled. The Dug-out. Siegfried Sassoon. CH; MoBrPo; MoVE; OHIP; WaaP; WaP
Why do you look so gloomy, Naevolus? Juvenal. *Fr.* The Satires, IX. PeHV
Why do you love her? Questions [1]. Donald Hall. FF
Why do you play such dreary music. Radio. Frank O'Hara. PoA
Why do you reward him. Complaint of the Fisherman's Wife. Sheila Nickerson. WOLT
Why do you rush through the field in trains. The Fat White Woman Speaks. G. K. Chesterton. SpRo
Why do you talk so much. For Robert Frost. Galway Kinnell. NOBA; VGW
Why do you tear from me my darling son. The Mothers' Lament at the Slaughter of the Innocents. *Unknown, tr. by* Kuno Meyer. OnYI
Why Do You Want to Suffer Less. David Fisher. NPGG
"Why do you wear your hair like a man?" After Dilettante Concetti. Henry Duff Traill. BXAP; CenHV; FaBoCo; HBV-1; Par
Why Do You Write about Russia? Louis Simpson. AMV-81; LCAP
Why do your warships sail on my waters? I've Got to Know. Woody Guthrie. FSW
Why doe not all fresh maids appeare. Upon the Death of His Sparrow; an Elegie. Robert Herrick. FM
Why doe ye weep. *See* Why do ye weep . . .
Why does he keep bruising against me my dead father why still. Sestina with Refrain. Thomas W. Shapcott. CBAP
Why Does It Snow? Laura E. Richards. OBCA; SiSoSe
Why does it tear so. Hopi Lament. Charles Beghtol. BPAW
Why does my husband beat me? Poor Me. *Unknown, tr. by* Richard Beaumont. ErPo
Why does the raven cry aloud and no eye pities her? The Lamentation of Enion. Blake. *Fr.* Vala; or, The Four Zoas. OBNC
Why does the sea burn? Why do the hills cry? Zaydee. Philip Levine. NNaP; VWA
Why does the sea moan evermore? By the Sea. Christina Rossetti. BoNaP; MOS
Why does the thin grey strand. Sorrow. D. H. Lawrence. CMoP; GTBS-P; OBMV
Why does the wind so want to be. The Wind. Elizabeth Rendall. HBVY
Why does this seedy lady look. The Jilted Funeral. Gelett Burgess. ShM
"Why [*or* Quhy] does [*or* dois] your brand sae [*or* so] drop wi' blude [*or* drap wi bluid]." Edward [*or* Edward, Edward]. *Unknown.* BiP; BSV; CABA; CH; EBEV; ELP; EnRP; ESPB; FaBoBa; FaPoR; GoTS; HAP; HBV-2; HoPM; InPK; InPS; LiTB; NOBE; NoP; OAEP; OBEV; OxBB; OxBS; PAI; PoEL-1; PoRA; PPoe; PrIm; SeCeV; SoSe; TreFS; TrGrPo; TW; ViBoFo; WeW; WHA
"Why doesn't somebody buy *me* false ears?" From the Joke Shop. Roy Fuller. OxBC
Why don't I write in the language of air? Mona Sa'udi, *tr. fr. Arabic by* Kamal Boullata. WPOW
Why don't it come to the top. Boy Trash Picker. Jim Howard. FAZ
Why don't people leave off being lovable. Elemental. D. H. Lawrence. NoP
Why don't we rock the casket here in the moonlight? The Pale Blue Casket. Oliver Pitcher. NNP; PoBA; TTY
Why don't you/ catch me a pony. The Pony Blues. *Unknown.* BluL
Why don't you go back to the sea, my dear? Light Lover. Aline Kilmer. HBMV
Why don't you go down Old Hannah. Ol' Hannah. *Unknown.* BluL
Why don't you work like other men do? *See* Oh, why don't you work like other men do.
Why don't you write you never. Dear Reader. Peter Meinke. Psk
Why dost thou hail with songful lips no more. Memnon. Clinton Scollard. AA
Why dost thou haste away. Madrigal. Sir Philip Sidney. *Fr.* Arcadia. OBSC; SiPS
Why Dost Thou Shade Thy Lovely Face? Francis Quarles. *Fr.* Emblems. MeLP; OxBoCh; TrPWD
(Wherefore Hidest Thou Thy Face, and Holdest Me for Thine Enemy.) MePo; OBS
Why dost thou shade thy lovely face? O why. To His Mistress. Earl of Rochester. OBEV
"Why dost thou so explore." Homer, *tr. by* George Chapman. *Fr.* The Iliad, VI. OBVE
Why dost thou sound, my deare Aurelian. In Answer of an Elegiacall Letter upon the Death of the King of Sweden. Thomas Carew. AnAnS-2
Why doth heaven bear a sun. An Ode. Barnabe Barnes. *Fr.* Parthenophil and Parthenophe. ElL; OBSC
Why doth the eare so tempt the voyce. To Castara, of True Delight. William Habington. AnAnS-2
Why Doubt God's Word? A. B. Simpson. BLRP
Why English Is So Hard. *Unknown.* FaBoUs
Why fadest thou in death. Song. R. W. Dixon. ChTr
Why Fear to Die? Sir Philip Sidney. *Fr.* Arcadia. SiPS
(Since Nature's Works Be Good.) OAEP
Why fear to-morrow, timid heart? To-Day. Lydia Avery Coonley Ward. HBV-2
Why fearest thou thy outward foe. That Each Thing Is Hurt of Itself. *Unknown.* ElL
Why Flowers Change Color. Robert Herrick. HAP
"Why for your spouse this pompous fuss?" On Seeing a Pompous Funeral for a Bad Husband. *Unknown.* ShM
Why from the danger did mine eyes not start. Sonnet: Of His Pain from a New Love. Guido Cavalcanti, *tr. by* Dante Gabriel Rossetti. AWP
Why from this her and him. E. E. Cummings. NoAM
Why from this window am I watching leaves? The Location of Things. Barbara Guest. NYP
Why has our poetry eschewed. Food and Drink. Louis Untermeyer. MoAmPo
Why Has This Ache. Gevorg Emin, *tr. fr. Armenian by* Diana Der Hovanessian. AMV-81
Why hast thou breathed, O God, upon my thoughts. The Poet. Angela Morgan. TrPWD; WGRP

Why Hast Thou Forsaken Me? Chad Walsh. *Fr.* The Psalm of Christ. TrCP
Why hast thou nothing in thy face? Eros. Robert Bridges. CMoP; LiTB; NBM; NOBE; PoEL-5; QFR; SeCeV
Why have such scores of lovely, gifted girls. A Slice of Wedding Cake. Robert Graves. BoLoP; NOBE; OxBTC
Why have the Mighty lived—why have they died? Waterloo. Sir Aubrey De Vere. HBV-2
Why have they stripped the grass from the sides of the road. The Interpreters. D. J. Enright. PP
Why have ye no reuthe on my child? Mary Suffers with Her Son. *Unknown.* MeEL
Why have you come to the shining cliffs. The Knight without a Name. *Unknown.* WiR
Why have you lit so bright a fire. The Last Guest. Frances Shaw. HBMV
Why have you risen, to stand with naked feet. With the Dawn. Thomas Caulfield Irwin. BIrV; EnLoPo
Why, having won her, do I woo? The Married Lover. Coventry Patmore. The Angel in the House, II, xii, 1. GoBC; HBV-1; OBEV; TreFT; TrGrPo; VLP
Why He Was There. E. A. Robinson. CMoP; NOBA
Why here, on this third planet from the sun. Tellus. William Reed Huntington. AA
Why how now, Cupid, grown so wild? Cupid Ungodded. James Shirley. GoBC
Why I Am Afraid to Have Children. Bin Ramke. MAYP
Why I Am Not a Painter. Frank O'Hara. ConAP; HoAn; NeAP; NoAM; NOBA; PoM
Why I Am Offended by Miracles. David Bergman. AMV-80
Why I Can't Write a Poem about Lares. Iván Silén, *tr. fr. Spanish by* Julio Marzán. InW
Why I Can't Write My Autobiography. Rodger Kamenetz. VWA
Why I Didn't Go to Delphi. James Welch. CDW
Why I Drink. Henry Aldrich. NIP
("If on my theme I rightly think.") WhC
Why I Like Movies. Patricia Jones. BlSi
Why I Love Her. Alexander Brome. HBV-1
Why I Never Went into Politics. Richard Shelton. Str
Why I Sing the Blues. B. B. King. MAT
Why I tie about thy wrist. The Bracelet: To Julia. Robert Herrick. HBV-1; OBEV; TrGrPo
Why I Voted the Socialist Ticket. Vachel Lindsay. MoAmPo
Why I would bring a wagon into battle. Willie B (2). Lucille Clifton. InPS
Why I Write Not of Love. Ben Jonson. OAEP
Why, if Becchina's heart were diamond. Sonnet: Of Becchina, the Shoemaker's Daughter. Cecco Angiolieri da Siena, *tr. by* Dante Gabriel Rossetti. AWP
Why, if 'tis dancing you would be. The Power of Malt. A. E. Housman. *Fr.* A Shropshire Lad, LXII. HBV-2; WHA
Why is a pump like Viscount Castlereagh? What's My Thought Like? [*or* A Riddle]. Thomas Moore. FaBoCo; FaBoEE; OBRV
Why is everything I do in my life like a boomerang? Boomerang. John Perreault. EAS
Why is it. Lover's Meeting. Ray Mathew. CBAP
"Why is it," Queen Edain said. W. B. Yeats. *Fr.* Deirdre. ViBoPo
Why is it, when I am in Rome. On Being a Woman. Dorothy Parker. FPL; PoLF
"Why is my district death-rate low?" Municipal. Kipling. BrPo; BXAP; WhC
Why is my verse so barren of new pride. Sonnets, LXXVI. Shakespeare. EBEV; InvP; PP
Why is the child so pale. Louise. Stevie Smith. SBG
Why is the hail so wild. Haiku. Richard Wright. FAZ
Why is the princess so depressed. Noblesse Oblige. Celeste Turner Wright. Psk
Why is the word pretty so underrated? Pretty. Stevie Smith. NoP; TEP
Why is the world beloved, that fals is and vein. Despise the World. *Unknown.* MeEL
Why is there always a secret singing. Carl Sandburg. *Fr.* The Lawyers Know Too Much. DBV
Why is there in the least touch of her hands. Quid Non Speremus, Amantes? Ernest Dowson. HBV-1
Why is your forehead deep-furrowed with care? Call Me Not Back from the Echoless Shore. *Unknown.* BLPA
Why It Was Cold in May. Henrietta Robins Eliot. AA
Why, Jack, how now? I hear strange stories. An Epistle to My Friend J. B. Robert Dodsley. NOEC
Why lean over the fire, and who is this. In the Secret House. Christopher Middleton. FaBoMo
Why, let it run! who bids it stay? Clepsydra. Charles Cotton. CavP
Why Linger Yet upon the Strand? *with music.* Louis F. Benson. AH
Why, Liquor of Life? Turlough Carolan, *tr. fr. Modern Irish by* John D'Alton. OnYI
Why listen, even the water is sobbing for something. The Maid's Thought. Robinson Jeffers. ErPo
Why Log Truck Drivers Rise Earlier than Students of Zen. Gary Snyder. NNaP; SOTW
Why, Lord ("Why Lord, must something in us"). Mark Van Doren. AH, *with music;* TrPWD
Why, Love, beneath the fields of asphodel. George Edward Woodberry. Ideal Passion, XXXIII. HBMV
Why, lovely charmer, tell me why. Song. Sir Richard Steele. HBV-1; ViBoPo
Why lovest thou so this brittle [*or* brotle] worlde's joy? The Peace of a Good Mind. Sir Thomas More. *Fr.* The Twelve Weapons of Spiritual Battle. EnRePo; FaBoRV
Why, man, he doth bestride the narrow world. Portrait of Caesar. Shakespeare. *Fr.* Julius Caesar, I, ii. TrGrPo
Why Mira Can't Go Back to Her Old House. Mirabai, *tr. fr. Medieval Hindi; English version by* Robert Bly. NU
Why mourns my beauteous friend, bereft? To Urania. Benjamin Colman. SCAP
Why muse wee thus to see the wheeles run cross. The Town Called Providence, Its Fate. Benjamin Tompson. SCAP
Why Must You Know? John Wheelwright. CrMA; VGW
Why, no, Sir! If a barren rascal cries. Doctor Major. Lionel Johnson. BrPo
Why Not? Linda Pastan. FAZ
Why Not? *Unknown.* WhC
Why not despair of this world. The Radiance of Extinct Stars. Allan Kolski Horvitz. VWA
Why not mark out the land. Hard Questions. Margaret Tsuda. RFM
Why not? The mouths of the ginger blooms slide open. Chinoiserie. Charles Wright. AmPA
Why not try again, although the past. Why Not? Linda Pastan. FAZ
Why now so melancholy, Ben? Leviathan; or, A Hymn to Poor Brother Ben. *Unknown.* APAS
Why now the word "Kalahari." Kalahari. Luis Palés Matos, *tr. by* Rachel Benson. InW
"Why of the sheep do you not learn peace?" An Answer to the Parson. Blake. FaBoEE; OxBoLi
Why pay more for your funeral when. An Undertaker's Advertisement. Ernest G. Moll. WhC
Why practise, love, this small economy. To One on Her Waste of Time. Wilfrid Scawen Blunt. *Fr.* The Love Sonnets of Proteus. ViBoPo
Why puts our Grandame Nature on. On the Unusual Cold and Rainie Weather in the Summer, 1648. Robert Heath. OBS
Why quails my heart? God riding with. Saul. Isaac Rosenberg. VWA
Why rejoice in beauty? What. Reflections. Antoinette Deshoulières, *tr. by* Yvor Winters. PBWP
Why repeat? I heard you the first time. Carl Sandburg. *Fr.* The People, Yes, Sec. 42. OBAL
Why Run? Norah Smaridge. RHPC
Why say "death"? Death is neither harsh nor kind. The Presence. Robert Graves. ChMP
Why say the idiot is not. The Locus. Cid Corman. VGW
Why seraphim like lutanists arranged. Evening without Angels. Wallace Stevens. MoPo; VGW
Why shall I keep the old name? Blacklisted. Carl Sandburg. SaC
Why She Moved House. Thomas Hardy. FM
Why shou'd I thus employ my time. An Ode on Miss Harriet Hanbury at Six Years Old. Sir Charles Hanbury Williams. OBEC
Why Should a Foolish Marriage Vow. Dryden. *Fr.* Marriage à la Mode, I, i. HeIP; NIP; OAEP; ViBoPo
(Song: "Why should a foolish marriage vow.") AWP; SeCV-2
Why should I be eaten by love. Untitled. James A. Randall, Jr. BPo
Why should I blame her that she filled my days. No Second Troy. W. B. Yeats. BrPo; CABA; CMoP; EnLoPo; GTBS-P; NoAM; NOBE; OAEL-2; OxBTC; PoEL-5; PPP; SeCePo; WeW
Why Should I Care for the Men of Thames? Blake. ChTr
Why should I find Him here. Christ in the Clay-Pit. Jack Clemo. EBCP; GTBS-P
Why Should I Grieve? Moses ibn Ezra, *tr. fr. Hebrew by* Solomon Solis-Cohen. TrJP
Why should I hate you, love, or why despise. In Answer to a Question. Wilfrid Scawen Blunt. *Fr.* The Love Sonnets of Proteus. ViBoPo
Why should I keep holiday. Compensation. Emerson. FPL; LiTA; TAP
Why should I let the toad work. Toads. Philip Larkin. CMoP; NePoEA; NMP; NoAM; NOBL; OxBTC; PAI; SoSe
Why should I longer long to live. Being Forsaken of His Friend He Complaineth. "E. S." EIL
Why should I seek for love or study it? Ribh Considers Christian Love Insufficient. W. B. Yeats. TW

Why should I seek to ease intense desire. To Tommaso de' Cavalieri. Michelangelo, *tr. by* John Addington Symonds. PeHV
Why should I sing of women. Song against Women. Willard Huntington Wright. HBV-1
Why should I stay? Nor seed nor fruit have I. The Bubble. John Banister Tabb. AA
Why Should I Wander Sadly. Süsskind von Trimberg, *tr. fr. Middle High German.* TrJP
Why should I wish to see God better than this day? Encountering God. Walt Whitman. *Fr.* Song of Myself, XLVIII. TreFT
Why should my anxious breast repine. Friendship Is Love without His Wings. Byron. TreFT
"Why should not Wattle do." Under the Wattle. Douglas Brook Wheelton Sladen. OBVV
Why should not we all be merry. *Unknown.* OBS
Why should [the] scribblers discompose. The Scribblers. Walter Savage Landor. FaBoEE; OBSV
Why should this a desert be? Orlando's Rhymes. Shakespeare. *Fr.* As You Like It, III, ii. CTC; OBSC
Why should this flower delay so long. The Last Chrysanthemum. Thomas Hardy. CMoP; LiTB
Why should this Negro insolently stride. August. Elinor Wylie. MoAB; MoAmPo
Why should thy look requite so ill. A Paradox. William Herbert, Earl of Pembroke. ElL
Why Should Vain Mortals Tremble. Nathaniel Niles. *See* Bunker Hill.
Why should we praise them, or revere. Against Seasons. Robert Mezey. NYBP
Why should we waste and weep? Fledglings. Thomas Lake Harris. AA
Why should you believe in magic. Consumed. James Tate. MAT
Why should you [*or* shouldst thou] swear I am forsworn. The Scrutiny [*or* Scrutinie]. Richard Lovelace. AnAnS-2; BoLoP; CaPo; CavP; ELP; EnLoPo; GBL; InMe; MeLP; MePo; NoP; OBS; SeCP; TrGrPo
Why should you wake, my darling, at this hour. A Fairy Tale. Kenneth MacKenzie. PoAu-2
Why should your fair eyes with such sovereign grace. Michael Drayton. Idea, XLIII. OBSC
Why shouldst thou cease thy plaintive song. To an Obscure Poet Who Lives on My Hearth. Charles Lotin Hildreth. AA
Why shouldst thou swear I am forsworn. *See* Why should you swear. . .
Why, silly Man! so much admirest thou. George Wither. *Fr.* A Collection of Emblemes, Ancient and Moderne. SeCV-1
Why Sit'st Thou by That Ruin'd Hall. Sir Walter Scott. *Fr.* The Antiquary, *ch.* 10. EnRP
(Aged Carle, The.) OAEP
Why So Many of Them Die. Susan Wallbank. BrRo
Why So Pale and Wan [Fond Lover]? Sir John Suckling. *Fr.* Aglaura, IV, ii. AWP; ELP; EvOK; FaBV; FPL; HAP; HoPM; NOBE; OBEV; OBS; PoRA; SeCePo; TEP; TreFS; TrGrPo; UnPo; WHA
(Encouragements to a Lover.) FaFP; GTBS; GTBS-P
(Song: "Why so pale and wan, fond lover?") AnAnS-2; EnLoPo; HBV-1; HeIP; JCP; LoBV; MePo; NIP; PAI; PoEL-3; PoPl; PrIm; SeCP; SeCV-1; ViBoPo
Why so valiant to decide? Young Woman at a Window. Mark Van Doren. MoVE
Why, Soldiers, Why? *Unknown, at. to* James Wolfe. OBET
(How Stands the Glass Around?) PAH
Why, Some of My Best Friends Are Women. Phyllis McGinley. NMM
Why speak of memory and death. Two Views of Two Ghost Towns. Charles Tomlinson. NoAM
Why speak of the use. Hayden Carruth. VGW
"Why stand you, gentle mother." Premonition. Laura Goodman Salverson. CaP
Why Stone Does Not Sing by Itself. Anita Endrezze-Danielson. STE
Why that alarming sigh? Dialogue. Agathias Scholasticus, *tr. by* Dudley Fitts. OLR
Why the British Girls Give In So Easily. Nicholas Moore. WaP
Why the Resurrection Was Revealed to Women. Catharina Regina von Greiffenberg, *tr. fr. German by* Michael Hamburger. PBWP
Why the Robin's Breast Was Red. James Ryder Randall. AA
Why the Soup Tastes like the Daily News. Marge Piercy. MAT
Why the unbroken spiral, Virtuoso. Apple Peeler. Robert Francis. CrMA; LCAP; NePoAm
Why They Waged War. John Peale Bishop. NYBP
Why think'st thou, fool, thy beautie's rayes. The Sun and Wind. Owen Felltham. CavP
Why this delay? Why waste the time in kissing? A Plea for Haste. Petronius, *tr. by* Louis Untermeyer. UnTE
Why this girl has no fear. Carmen. Victor Hernandez Cruz. CAD; PoBA
Why Thus Longing? Harriet Winslow Sewall. AA
Why Tomas Cam Was Grumpy. James Stephens. CMoP; WhC
Why wait we for the torches' lights? Let Us Drink. Alcaeus, *tr. by* John Hermann Merivale. AWP
Why was a radio sinful? Lord knows. But it was. The Radio under the Bed. Reed Whittemore. NYBP
"Why was she lost?" my darling said aloud. Anecdote of 2 A.M. John Wain. NMP
Why We Bombed Haiphong. Jonathan Holden. MAYP
Why we should hesitate is not quite clear. Temporary Problems. Larry Rubin. AMV-80
"Why weep ye by the tide, ladie?" Jock of [*or* o'] Hazeldean. Sir Walter Scott. BeLS; EnRP; GN; GTBS; GTBS-P; HBV-1; OAEP; OBRV; OxBS; TEP
"Why weep ye by the tide, ladye?" John of Hazelgreen [*or* Haselgreen]. *Unknown.* BaBo; ESPB
Why were you born when the snow was falling? A Dirge. Christina Rossetti. ChTr; EBVV; LoBV; SBG; VLP
Why, when Sunday closes the lid on this world. Sunday in South Carolina. Robert Parham. AMV-80
Why, when we were dressed for darker weather. Another Return. Winfield Townley Scott. ELU
Why, whenever she can spy me. To Chloe [*or* Time to Choose a Lover]. Horace, *tr. by* Branwell Brontë. Odes, I, 23. OBVE; UnTE
Why, who makes much of a miracle? Miracles. Walt Whitman. HBVY
Why, why repine, my pensive friend. Resignation. Walter Savage Landor. HBV-2; TreFT
Why, why, what is this why. What Is This Why? *Unknown.* OxBM
Why will Delia thus retire. A Receipt to Cure [*or* for] the Vapours. Lady Mary Wortley Montagu. NOEC; PBWP
Why will they never sleep. Ode. John Peale Bishop. LiTA; LiTM; MoPo; MoVE; NePA; TwAmPo
Why will they never speak. The Grandfathers [*or* After a Line by John Peale Bishop]. Donald Justice. NCSH; PoCH
"Why, William, on that old grey [*or* gray] stone." Expostulation and Reply. Wordsworth. EnRP; HBV-1; OAEL-2; OAEP; OBRV
"Why wilt thou cast the roses from thine hair?" Mary Magdalene at the Door of Simon the Pharisee. Dante Gabriel Rossetti. GoBC
Why without cease do I think of a bold youth. The Haunting. Irving Layton. NeAC
Why Would I Have Survived? Edith Bruck, *tr. by* Anita Barrows. VWA
Why Would I Want. William J. Harris. PoBA
Why Write Poetry? Pamela Oberon Davis. AMV-80
Why ye Blossome Cometh before ye Leafe. Oliver Herford. AA
Why, ye tenants of the lake. On Scaring Some Waterfowl in Loch Turit, a Wild Scene among the Hills of Oughtertyre. Burns. PBBP
Whylom ther was dwellinge at Oxenford. The Milleres Tale. Chaucer. *Fr.* The Canterbury Tales. OAEL-1; OxBoLi
Whym Chow. "Michael Field." FM
Why'n't you bring me. To Greet a Letter-Carrier. William Carlos Williams. OBAL
Why's my friend so melancholy? The Counsel. Alexander Brome. CavP
Wi da lentenin days ida first o da Voar. Tuslag. T. A. Robertson. OxBS
Wi' patchit brose and ilka pen. Lilt Your Johnnie. *Unknown.* BXAP
Wichita Vortex Sutra. Allen Ginsberg. CAPP
"Face the Nation," *sel.* NaP
Wicked barons laid the landscape waste, The. The Middle Ages: Two Views. Leah Bodine Drake. NePoAm-2
Wicked Hawthorn Tree, The. W. B. Yeats. WSC
Wicked Neighbor, The. Zelda, *tr. fr. Hebrew by* Hannah Hoffman. WPOW
Wicked Tongues. *Unknown.* OxBM
Wicked Treasonable Libel, A. Swift. UnTE
Wicked witch, A/ Is Mizzable Scratch. Poison Ivy! Katherine Gallagher. SiSoSe
Wickedest Man in Memphis, The. Alex J. Brown. BeLS
Wickedness of Peter Shannon, The. Alden Nowlan. MoCV
Wicker Basket, A. Robert Creeley. CAPP; HAP; NoAM; NoP
Widcombe Churchyard. Walter Savage Landor. *See* Wall-Flower, The.
Widdecombe [*or* Widdicombe] Fair. *Unknown.* CH; MoShBr; PH
Widdy-widdy-wurkey. The Family. *Unknown, tr. by* Rose Fyleman. TiPo
Wide and shallow, in the cowslip marshes. Vermont. Sarah N. Cleghorn. HBMV
Wide are the streets, and driven clean. Brussels, 1919. Carola Oman. SUMH
Wide as this night, old as this night is old and young as it is young. Lullaby. Kenneth Fearing. CMoP
Wide door into sorrow, The. The Narrow Doors. Fannie Stearns Gifford. HBMV
Wide green earth is mine in which to wander, The. The Unwilling Gypsy. Josephine Johnson. HBMV
Wide, ho? Ezra Pound, *after the Chinese.* OBVE
Wide is our mouth and. Need Is Our Name. Luci Shaw. TrCP
Wide Land, The. A. R. Ammons. TwCP
Wide Mizzoura, The. *Unknown.* *See* Shenandoah.

Wide o'er the valley the pennons are fluttering. The Siege of Chapultepec. William Haines Lytle. PAH
Wide open and unguarded stand our gates. Unguarded Gates. Thomas Bailey Aldrich. AA; PAH
Wide Open Are Thy [Loving] Hands. Bernard of Clairvaux, *tr. fr. Latin by* Charles P. Krauth. AH, *with music*; TRV
Wide Open Spaces, The. Oscar H. Lear. InMe
Wide sleeves sway. Dancing. Yang Kuei-fei, *tr. by* Florence Ayscough *and* Amy Lowell. FaPON
Wide was the land. The Coming of the White Man. Patrick Anderson. Poem on Canada. CaP
Wide waters in the waste; or, out of reach. "Rivers Unknown to Song." Alice Meynell. HBMV
Wide, white, wing-boned washboards of twenty, The. Of Oystermen, Workboats. Dave Smith. MAYP
Widely is flung, warning of slaughter. The Song of the Valkyries. *Unknown, tr. by* Lee M. Hollander. WaaP
Widely we are scattered. An Endless Chain. Abraham Reisen, *tr. by* Keith Bosley. VWA
Widow, The. Mariana B. Davenport. AMV-80
Widow, The. Susan Ludvigson. MAYP
Widow, The. W. S. Merwin. NYBP; UnPo; VGW
Widow. Felix Pollak. FAZ
Widow, The. Allan Ramsay. HBV-2
Widow, The. Robert Southey. NOEC; OBEC
Widow at Windsor, The. Kipling. BrPo; NoP; OAEP
Widow bird sate mourning for her love, A. A Song [*or* A Widow Bird]. Shelley. *Fr.* Charles the First. CH; ELP; FaBoEn; FaPON; GTBS; GTBS-P; LO; LoBV; NOBE; OBNC; OBRV; PoEL-4; PoPle; SeCeV
Widow Brown's Christmas. John Townsend Trowbridge. BeLS
Widow can bake, and the widow can brew, The. The Widow. Allan Ramsay. HBV-2
Widow in Wintertime, A. Carolyn Kizer. NMP
Widow Machree. Samuel Lover. *Fr.* Handy Andy. HBV-2
Widow Malone, The. Charles Lever. *Fr.* Charles O'Malley, the Irish Dragoon. HBV-2; TreFS
Widow of Drynam, The. Patrick MacDonogh. NeIP; OnYI; OxBI
Widow Perez, The. Gary Soto. MAYP
Widow refuses sleep, for sleep pretends, The. Exile. Ellen Bryant Voigt. MAYP
Widow, A—she had only one! The Widow's Mite. Frederick Locker-Lampson. HBV-2
Widow Speaks, The. William Dunbar. *Fr.* The Book of the Two Married Women and the Widow. PoEL-1
Widow That Keeps the Cock Inn, The. *Unknown.* CoMu
Widow to Her Son. R. T. Smith. Str
Widow, well met; whither go you today? A Contention betwixt a Wife, a Widow, and a Maid. Sir John Davies. OBSC; SiPS
Widowed Heart, The. Albert Pike. AA
Widower, The. Royall Tyler. OBAL
Widows. Edgar Lee Masters. MoAmPo
Widows be woeful whose husbands be taken, The. A Ballad of the Rising in the North. *Unknown.* ACP
Widow's Hymn, A. George Wither. LO; OBEV
Widow's Lament. *Tr. fr. Chinese by* Arthur Waley. *Fr.* Shih Ching. BoWoP
Widow's Lament in Springtime, The. William Carlos Williams. AP; CMoP; CoBMV; HAP; LiTM; NoAM; NOBA; TAP
Widow's Mite, The. Bible, *N.T.* St. Luke, XXI: 1-4. TreFT
Widow's Mite, The. Frederick Locker-Lampson. HBV-2
Widow's Mites, The. Richard Crashaw. OxBoCh
Widow's Old Broom, The. *Unknown.* AmFP
Widow's Party, The. Kipling. VLP
Widow's Plot, The; or, She Got What Was Coming to Her. William Plomer. NoAM
Widow's Walk. Elizabeth Spires. MAYP
Widow's Weeds, A. Walter de la Mare. FaBV
Widsith, *sel. Unknown, tr. fr. Anglo-Saxon by* Charles W. Kennedy.
Widsith, the Minstrel. AnOE
Wie langsam kriechet sie dahin. Heine, *tr. fr. German by* Richard Monckton Milnes. AWP
Wife, The. Robert Creeley. AP; VGW
Wife, The. Anna Peyre Dinnies. AA
Wife, The. Theodosia Garrison. HBV-1
Wife, The. Denise Levertov. ErPo
Wife, A. Matthew Gregory Lewis. DBV; PV
Wife a-Lost, The. William Barnes. BoLoP; EBVV; ELP; EnLoPo; HAP; OBEV; OBVV
Wife and servant are the same. To the Ladies. Mary Lee, Lady Chudleigh. NOEC; WPE; WPOW
Wife a-Prais'd, A. William Barnes. EBVV
Wife—at daybreak I shall be, A. Emily Dickinson. AmPP
Wife from Fairyland, The. Richard Le Gallienne. HBV-1
Wife-Hater, The. *Unknown.* CoMu
Wife in London, A. Thomas Hardy. OBWP
"Wife, land of the wave fire." *Tr. fr. Icelandic by* George Johnston. *Fr.* The Saga of Gisli. OBVE
Wife of Aed mac Ainmirech, King of Ireland, Laments Her Husband, The. *Unknown, tr. fr. Old Irish by* Myles Dillon. AnIL
Wife of Auchtermuchty, The. *Unknown.* BSV; GoTS
Wife of Bath, The. Chaucer. *Fr.* The Canterbury Tales: Prologue. OxBM
("Good Wif was ther of biside Bathe, A.") BiP; EBEV; InPS; PPoe; ViBoPo
("Good Wyf was ther of bisyde Bathe, A.") TrGrPo
("There was a Wife from Bath, a well-appearing," *mod. vers. by* Louis Untermeyer.) TrGrPo
("Worthy woman from beside Bath city, A," *mod. vers. by* Nevill Coghill.) BiP
Wife of Bath's Prologue, The. Chaucer. *Fr.* The Canterbury Tales. OAEL-1; OxBoLi, *abr.*
(Prologue to the Wife of Bath's Tale, The.) PoEL-1
Sels.
"If poor (you say) she drains her husband's purse," *mod. vers. by* Pope. OBSV
"My fifthe housbonde, god his soule blesse!" FiP
Wife's Fifth Husband, The. OxBM
Wife of Bath's Tale, The. Chaucer. *Fr.* The Canterbury Tales. OAEL-1
"In th'olde dayes of the King Arthour," *sel.* ViBoPo
Wife of Kelso, The, *with music. Unknown.* ShS
Wife of Kohelet. Shlomit Cohen, *tr. fr. Hebrew by* Yishai Tobin. VWA
Wife of Usher's Well, The. *Unknown.* AmFP; AWP; BSV; CH; ChTr; EBEV; EnRP; EnSB; ESPB (A, B, C, *and* D *vers.*); FaBoBa; GoTS; HBV-2; LiTB; LoBV; NOBE; NoP (A *vers.*); OAEL-1, *with music*; OAEP; OBEV; OnMSP; OxBB, *with music*; OxBS; PoEL-1; PrIm; SeCeV; TreF; TrGrPo; ViBoFo (A, B, *and* C *vers.*)
Wife Talks to Herself, A. Stephen Berg. NaP
Wife to Her Husband, The. *Unknown.* HBV-1
Wife was sitting at her reel ae night, A. The Strange Visitor. *Unknown.* ChTr; FaBoCh; GBP
Wife Who Would a Wanton Be, The. *Unknown.* FaBoCo
Wife-Woman, The. Anne Spencer. BANP; NoAM
Wife Wrapt [*or* Wrapped] in Wether's Skin, The. *Unknown.* AmFP; BaBo (A, B, *and* C *vers.*); ESPB (A, B, D, *and* F *vers.*); ViBoFo (A *and* B *vers.*)
(Wee Cooper of Fife, The.) FSW
Wife's Complaint, The. *Unknown. See* Wife's Lament, The.
Wife's Fifth Husband, The. Chaucer. *Fr.* The Canterbury Tales: The Wife of Bath's Prologue. OxBM
Wife's Lament, The. *Unknown, tr. fr. Anglo-Saxon.* AnOE, *tr. by* Charles W. Kennedy; BoWoP, *tr. by* Willis Barnstone *and* Elene Kolb; PBWP, *tr. by* Kemp Malone; WPE
(Wife's Complaint, The, *tr. by* Michael Alexander.) BoLoP
Wife's Song, A. William Cox Bennett. HBV-1
Wife's Tale, The. Seamus Heaney. IPY
Wiggly Giggles. Stacy Jo Crossen *and* Natalie Anne Covell. RHPC
Wight in the Broom. *Unknown. See* Say Me, Wiit in the Brom.
Wigs and Beards. Robert Graves. NOBL
Wil the Merry Weaver, and Charity the Chamber-Maid; or, A Brisk Encounter between a Youngman and His Love. *Unknown.* CoMu
Wild, The. Wendell Berry. VGW
Wild air, world-mothering air. The Blessed Virgin Compared to the Air We Breathe. Gerard Manley Hopkins. BrPo; ISi; MoPo; OxBoCh; VLP
Wild and plunging seas have smote our sides, The. Columbus. Percy Hutchison. EtS
Wild Ass. Padraic Colum. MoBrPo
Wild (at Our First) Beasts Uttered Human Words. E. E. Cummings. FaBoMo; NYBP
Wild Barbaree, The. *Unknown. See* High Barbaree, The.
Wild Beasts. Evaleen Stein. SoPo
Wild Bees. James K. Baxter. NoP
Wild Bill Jones. *Unknown.* AmFP
Wild bird filled the morning air, A. The Fowler. W. W. Gibson. HBMV
Wild bird singer, sing on. Sand Creek. Charles G. Ballard. UnPo; VoR
Wild bird, whose warble, liquid sweet. In Memoriam A. H. H., LXXXVIII. Tennyson. PBBP
Wild Boar and the Ram, The. John Gay. *Fr.* Fables. FM; NOEC; PAI; PPON
Wild Boarder, The. Kenyon Cox. TDH
Wild Bronc Peeler. *Unknown.* CoSo
Wild Carthage held her, Rome. A Puritan Lady. Lizette Woodworth Reese. MoAmPo
Wild Cherry. Louise Townsend Nicholl. NePoAm
Wild Cherry Tree. Edmund Blunden. BrPo
Wild Colonial [*or* Colloina] Boy, The *(diff. versions). Unknown.* AmFP; FaBoBa; FSW; OuSiCo, *with music;* PoAu-1; ViBoFo

(Wild Montana Boy.) CoSo
Wild Common, The. D. H. Lawrence. CoBMV
Wild Crab. Mary Ellen Solt. BoWoP
Wild Dog Rose, The. John Montague. BIrV; CIP; IPY
Wild Dreams of a New Beginning. Lawrence Ferlinghetti. GP
Wild Dreams of Summer What Is Your Grief. George Barker. OxBTC
Wild Duck, The. John Masefield. BrPo
Wild duck startles like a sudden thought, The. Autumn Birds. John Clare. PBBP
Wild ducks/ float with the north wind. Sun Children. Leslie Silko. VoR
Wild Duck's Nest, The. Wordsworth. FM
(Sonnet: Wild Duck's Nest, The.) ChER
Wild Eden, *sels.* George Edward Woodberry.
Child, The, XXX. AA
Divine Awe, XVI. AA
Homeward Bound, XXV. AA
O, Inexpressible as Sweet, VII. AA; HBV-1
(Song: "O, inexpressible as sweet.") InMe
O, Struck beneath the Laurel, XXXIII. AA
Rose of Stars, The, IX. AA; HBV-1
Seaward, XLI. AA
Secret, The, VI. AA; HBV-1
So Slow to Die, XXXVIII. AA
When First I Saw Her, V. AA; HBV-1
Wild Eden, III. HBV-2
Wild-eyed team with horned and swaying heads, The. The Team. "Furnley Maurice." CBAP
Wild Flower Man, The. Lu Yu, *tr. fr. Chinese by* Kenneth Rexroth. NaP
Wild Flowers. Peter Newell. NA; RHPC
Wild Garden, The. Pope. *Fr.* An Essay on Man. PrIm
("Awake, my St. John! leave all meaner things.") NoP; OAEP; PoEL-3
Wild Geese. Elinor Chipp. FaPON; HBMV; TiPo
Wild Geese. William Hart-Smith. BoAnP
Wild Geese, The. Violet Jacob. BSV
Wild Geese, The. John Masefield. NoAM
Wild Geese, The. James Herbert Morse. AA
Wild Geese. Frederick Peterson. HBV-1; HBVY
Wild geese, flying in the night, behold, The. The Wild Geese. James Herbert Morse. AA
Wild geese returning, The. Tsumori Kunimoto. PDV
Wild geese, wild geese, ganging to the sea. *Unknown.* PBBP
Wild Goat, The. Claude McKay. CDC
Wild Honey. Maurice Thompson. HBV-1
Wild Honeysuckle [*or* Honey Suckle], The. Philip Freneau. AA; AmPP; AP; BLPL; HBV-1; LiTA; NOBA; OxBA; PoEL-4; PoLF; TAP; TrGrPo
Wild Horse. Elder Olson. GrPl
Wild Horse Jerry's Story. Sarah Elizabeth Howard. PoOW
Wild horses graze under a full moon. The Problem of Wild Horses. Barbara Winder. PH
Wild is its nature, as it were a token. Song of the Palm. Tracy Robinson. AA
Wild Knight, The. G. K. Chesterton. WGRP
Wild March. Constance Fenimore Woolson. YeAr
Wild Montana Boy, The. *Unknown. See* Wild Colonial Boy, The.
Wild Mushroom, The. Gary Snyder. NoP
Wild Mustard River, The. *Unknown.* AmFP
Wild Nature. Charles Newton. *Fr.* Stanzas. NOEC
Wild Negro Bill. *Unknown.* BPo
Wild nights!—wild nights! Emily Dickinson. AmPP; AP; NIP; NOBA; NoP; OLR; OxBA; PBWP; SBG; TAP; UnTE; WPE
Wild Oats. Philip Larkin. InPS
Wild Oats. Norman MacCaig. OxBTC
Wild Old Wicked Man, The. W. B. Yeats. AnIL; CMoP
Wild Peaches. Elinor Wylie. LiTA; LiTM; OxBA; SBG; WPE
Puritan Sonnet, IV. FPL; MoAB; MoAmPo; TrGrPo
("Down to the Puritan marrow of my bones.") BoWoP
Wild pigeon of the leaves. Birds. *Unknown, tr. by* E. Powys Mathers. *Fr.* The Thousand and One Nights. AWP
Wild Pigs. Ted Kooser. TAT
Wild Plum. Orrick Johns. HBMV
Wild Rattling Cowboy, A. *Unknown.* CoSo
Wild red-wing black, The/ bird. The Red-Wing Blackbird. William Carlos Williams. DFF
Wild Ride, The. Louise Imogen Guiney. AA, *abr.*; HBV-2
Wild Rippling Water, The. *Unknown.* CoSo, *with music*; FaBoBa
Wild Romantic Dell, A. William Julius Mickle. *Fr.* The Concubine. OBEC
(Riddle: Mute Swan.) PBBP
Wild Rose, *abr.* William Allingham. GN
Wild Rose of Alloway! my thanks. Burns. Fitz-Greene Halleck. AA
Wild Roses. Edgar Fawcett. HBV-1
Wild Roses. Mary Effie Lee Newsome. CDC
Wild roved the Indians once. Grand Rapids. Julia A. Moore. OBAL
Wild Rover. *Unknown.* FSW
Wild Sports of the West. John Montague. CIP
Wild Strawberries. Robert Graves. FaBoCh
Wild strawberries, gooseberries, trampled. Ave Eva. John Wheelwright. MoPo
Wild Strawberry. Maurice Kenny. STE
Wild stream the clouds, and the fresh wind is singing. The Hunt. Harriet Prescott Spofford. AA
Wild Swan, The. D. S. Savage. NeBP
Wild Swan: "My attire is noiseless when I tread the earth." *Unknown, tr. fr. Anglo-Saxon by* Charles W. Kennedy. *Fr.* Riddles (Exeter Book). AnOE
Wild Swans. Edna St. Vincent Millay. CMoP; MoAmPo; PBWP; UnPo
Wild Swans at Coole, The. W. B. Yeats. BoAnP; CABA; ChTr; CMoP; FaBoPP; FaBoRV; FM; HeIP; MoAB; MoBrPo; MoVE; NoAM; NoP; OAEP; OnYI; PB; PBBP; PPP; SoSe; SOTW; TEP; UnPo; WHA
Wild, the Free, The. Byron. RHPC
Wild the sea clamors from its echoing caves. All Souls' Eve. Mary E. Mannix. GoBC
Wild Thyme, The. Blake. *Fr.* Milton. WiR
Wild Thyme. Eleanor Farjeon. SiSoSe
Wild was the day; the wintry sea. The Twenty-second of December. Bryant. GN
Wild Weather. Katharine Lee Bates. PGD
Wild West. Mark Vinz. Psk
Wild white camel, camel wild, what behind. Camel. Gene Derwood. NePA
Wild, wild the storm, and the sea high running. Patrolling Barnegat. Walt Whitman. LoBV; MOS; NePA; NoP
Wild winds weep, The. Mad Song. Blake. EnRP; NOEC; OAEL-2; PoEL-4; PrIm; TEP; TrGrPo
Wild Wishes. Ethel M. Hewitt. HBV-1
Wild Worm, A. Carolyn Wells. TDH
Wildebeest, The. June Daly. FaPON
Wilderness, The. Sidney Keyes. LiTB
"Red rock wilderness, The," *sel.* NeBP; OBWP
Wilderness, The. Kathleen Raine. BoWoP; PoSH; WPE
Wilderness. Carl Sandburg. AP
Wilderness, The. Maura Stanton. MAYP
Wilderness a secret keeps, The. Ecce in Deserto. Henry Augustin Beers. AA
Wilderness, The: but otherwise. Esther K. Comes to America: 1931. Jerome Rothenberg. NNaP
Wilderness Gothic. Al Purdy. MoCV; NOBC; NoP
Wilderness Is Tamed, The. Elizabeth J. Coatsworth. *See* Conquest.
Wilderness Rivers. Elizabeth J. Coatsworth. AmFN
Wilderness Theme. Ian Mudie. PoAu-2
Wildernesse and the solitarie place shall be glad for them, The. Bible, *O.T.* Isaiah, XXXV. OBVE
Wildfire. Judit Tóth, *tr. fr. Hungarian by* Emery George. VWA
Wildflower. Stanley Plumly. LCAP
Wilding, The. Philip Booth. NePoEA
Wildness. Blanche Shoemaker Wagstaff. HBMV
Wildness in the grass has closed, A. Invocation from a Lawn Chair. Mary Jane Irion. AMV-80
Wildness of haggard flights. Nocturne. Roussan Camille, *tr. by* Seth L. Wolitz. TTY
Wildness sleeps upon the mountain. The Fisher Cat. Richard Eberhart. GrPl
Wildtrack, *sel.* John Wain.
Lie Easy in Your Secret Cradle. NAs
Wildwood Flower. *Unknown.* BLSo, *with music*; FSW
Wilfred Owen's Photographs. Ted Hughes. OxBC
Wilful waste brings woeful want. *Unknown.* OxNR
Wilhelmj. Robert J. Burdette. TDH
Wili Woyi, Shaman, Also Known as Billy Pigeon. Robert J. Conley. STE
Wilkes Booth came to Washington, an actor great was he. Booth Killed Lincoln. *Unknown.* AmFP; OFD
Will, The. John Donne. EBEV; LiTB; MePo; OAEP
Will. Ella Wheeler Wilcox. BLPA; FPL
Will Beauty Come. Robert Nathan. HBMV
Will days, indeed, yet come in forgiveness and grace. When You Will Walk in the Field. Leah Goldberg, *tr. by* Simon Halkin. TrJP
Will dissolves, the heart becomes excited, The. Soliloquy in an Air-Raid. Roy Fuller. PoA
Will God, always cold, have a temperature? Moral Ode. David Rosenmann-Taub, *tr. by* Charles Guenther. VWA
Will God forever cast us off. Jesse Mercer. AmFP
Will God's Patience Hold Out for You? Edythe Johnson. STF

Will he always love me? Lady Horikawa, *tr. fr. Japanese by* Kenneth Rexroth. BoWoP; OLR
Will He No Come Back Again? *Unknown.* OBEC; OBEV
Will It Be So? Edith M. Thomas. *Fr.* The Inverted Torch. AA
Will it last? he says. The Snowflake Which Is Now and Hence Forever. Archibald MacLeish. NoP
Will lightning strike me if I take. Thoughts of Loved Ones. Margaret Fishback. FiBHP
Will Love again awake. Muse and Poet. Robert Bridges. OBMV
Will night already spread her wings and weave. Night-Thoughts. Solomon ibn Gabirol, *tr. by* Emma Lazarus. TrJP
Will of God be done by us, The. Blessed Be the Holy Will of God. *Unknown, tr. by* Douglas Hyde. OnYI
Will of God we must obey, The. The Death of King Edward VII. *Unknown.* OxBoLi
Will people accept them? Tenzone. Ezra Pound. *Fr.* Contemporania. PoA
Will seeing Concan make a dog a lion? Ritual Not Religious. *Unknown.* WGRP
Will sprawl, now that the heat of day is best. Caliban upon Setebos; or, Natural Theology in the Island. Robert Browning. AWP; EBEV; NoP; OAEL-2; OAEP; VLP; WGRP
Will Stewart and John. *Unknown.* ESPB
Will the lady with locker key 43. Will You Come Out Now? Valerie Sinason. BrRo
Will the man who gets clean love his neighbor? Soap (II). Jerome Rothenberg. NNaP
Will the Weaver. *Unknown.* AmFP
Will the wolves lie down with the lambs and feed them? The End of Sorrow. Edmond Fleg, *tr. by* Humbert Wolfe. *Fr.* The Wall of Weeping. TrJP
Will there never come a season. The Pedestrian's Plaint. Edward Verrall Lucas. CenHV
Will there never come a season. To R. K. [1891]. James Kenneth Stephen. BXAP; CenHV; FaBoCo; FaBoEE; FaBoPa; NBM; NOBL; Par; VLP; WhC
Will there really be a morning? Emily Dickinson. OBCA; SiSoSe
(Child's Question, The.) WGRP
(Morning.) AA; FaPON; SoPo
Will they never fade or pass! The Farmer Remembers the Somme. Vance Palmer. PoAu-1
Will they stop. Requiem. Kenneth Fearing. CMoP
Will to be tickled wants; has got the itch. *Unknown.* FaBoEE
Will to Change, The. Adrienne Rich. NMM
Will to Live, The. Mekeel McBride. MAYP
Will to Win. F. R. Scott. OBCV
Will Waterproof's Lyrical Monologue. Tennyson. VLP
Will., Will., Hen. Steph. Hen. Dick, John Hen., Eddy Ned, Edward. The Kings and Queens of England. *Unknown.* FaBoUs
Will winter never be over? February. Adeline D. T. Whitney. YeAr
Will ye gang o'er the lee-rigg. The Lee Rigg. Robert Fergusson. BSV
Will ye gang wi' me and fare. The Bush aboon Traquair. John Campbell Shairp. OBVV
Will ye heare, what I can say. Upon His Julia. Robert Herrick. SpRo
Will Ye No Come Back Again? Lady Nairne. BSV
Will ye see what wonders love hath wrought. Sir Thomas Wyatt. SiPS
Will ye that I should sing. A Lady of High Degree. *Unknown, tr. by* Andrew Lang. AWP
Will Yer Write It Down for Me? Henry Lawson. CBAP
Will You [Be My Little Wife]? Kate Greenaway. MoShBr; SiSoSe
Will you always catch me unaware. To My Mother at 73. Elizabeth Jennings. NAs
Will You Be as Hard? Douglas Hyde, *tr. fr. Irish by* Lady Gregory. OBMV
Will you buy any tape. Shakespeare. *Fr.* The Winter's Tale, IV, iii. OBSC; ViBoPo
Will You Come? Edward Thomas. CH; GoJo; GrPl; LoBV
Will you come a boating, my gay old hag. The Gay Old Hag. *Unknown.* BIrV
Will You Come Out Now? Valerie Sinason. BrRo
Will you come to the bower I have shaded for you? Walter Savage Landor. *Fr.* A Reply to Lines by Thomas Moore. ChTr
Will you come with me, my Phyllis dear. Wait for the Wagon. *Unknown, at. to* R. Bishop Buckley. BLSo; FSW; PSoN
"Will you gang wi' me, Leezie Lindsay." Leezie Lindsay. *Unknown.* FaBoCh
Will you glimmer on the sea? Moonrise. Hilda Doolittle ("H. D."). PoA
Will You Go, Lassie, Go? *Unknown.* FSW
Will you hear of a bloody battle. The Downfall of Piracy. Benjamin Franklin. PAH
Will you heare a tale of Robin Hood. Robin Hood and the Pedlars. *Unknown.* ESPB
Will you lend me your mare to ride but a mile? *Unknown.* OxNR
Will you lend your eyes to Christ. Operation—Souls. *Unknown.* STF
Will You Love Me in December as You Do in May? James J. Walker. FSN, *with music*; TreFT
Will You Love Me When I'm Old? *Unknown.* BLPA; BLPL; FaBoBe
Will You, One Day. Marian Ramié. HBMV
Will you perhaps consent to be. "Mentrechè il Vento, Come Fa, Si Tace." Delmore Schwartz. TwAmPo
Will you see the Infancy of this sublime. The Third Century. Thomas Traherne. AnAnS-1
Will you sleep forever? Korinna, *tr. fr. Greek.* BoWoP, *tr. by* Willis Barnstone; PBWP, *tr. by* John Dillon
Will you, sometime, who have sought so long, and seek. The Finder Found. Edwin Muir. PoA
Will you take a sprig of hornbeam? Forester's Song. A. E. Coppard. FaPON
"Will you take a walk with me." The Clocking Hen. *Unknown.* HBVY
"Will you walk a little faster?" said a [*or* the] whiting to a [*or* the] snail. The Lobster Quadrille [*or* The Mock Turtle's Song *or* The Whiting and the Snail]. "Lewis Carroll." *Fr.* Alice's Adventures in Wonderland, *ch.* 10. ChTr; FaBoNo; FaPON; HBV-1; HBVY; MoShBr; OxBChV; Par; PoPle; VLP
"Will you walk into my parlor?" said the Spider to the Fly. The Spider and the Fly. Mary Howitt. BeLS; FaFP; FaPON; HBV-1; HBVY; OHFP; OnUR; OxBChV; Par; TreFS; WBLP
Will you wear white, O my dear, O my dear? Jennie Jenkins [*or* Jinnie Jinkins]. *Unknown.* AmFP; OuSiCo
Will You, Won't You. Mark Van Doren. NCSH
Willets, The. May Swenson. WPE
William and Helen. Sir Walter Scott, *imitated fr.* Lenore (*by* Gottfried August Bürger). EnRP; OAEP
William and Margaret. David Mallet. NOEC; OBEC
William and Mary. *Unknown.* AmFP
William and Mary,/ George and Anne. *Unknown.* OxNR
William and Phyllis. *Unknown.* OBET
William asked how veal was made. What Is Veal? *Unknown.* FaBoUs
William Blake. James Thomson ("B. V."). HBV-2; OAEP; OBVV
William Blake Sees God. Roy McFadden. NeIP
William Bond. Blake. NCEP; OxBB
Where to Seek Love, *sel.* TRV
Wm. Brazier. Robert Graves. NoBL
William Brown. Joaquin Miller. BPAW
William Dewy, Tranter Reuben, Farmer Ledlow late at plough. Friends Beyond. Thomas Hardy. CoBMV; EBVV; FaBoRV; GTBS-P; OBEV; OBVV; VLP
William Gifford. Walter Savage Landor. GTBS-P
("Clap, clap the double nightcap on!") FaBoEE
William Glen. *Unknown.* BaBo
William Hall. *Unknown.* AmFP
William is away, and I am minding. Letter from Caroline Herschel (1750-1848). Siv Cedering. SUW
William Jake Hall/ Got a buck and a fall. Campfire and Bunkhouse. *Unknown.* CoSo
William Jones. Edgar Lee Masters. *Fr.* Spoon River Anthology. ImOP
William Lisle Bowles. Byron. *Fr.* English Bards and Scotch Reviewers. OBNC
William McTrimbletoe. *Unknown.* OxNR
William P. Frye, The. Jeanne Robert Foster. PAH
William Penn/ Was the most level-headed of men. William Jay Smith. PV
William Street. Kenneth Slessor. CBAP
William Taylor. *Unknown.* OBET
William the Bastard. "Lakon." FiBHP
William the Conqueror long did reign. England's Sovereigns in Verse. *Unknown.* BLPA
William the Conqueror, ten sixty-six. *Unknown.* FaBoUs; OxNR
William the Norman conquers England's state. Lines on Succession of the Kings of England. *Unknown.* FaBoUs
William, the wild round plums are falling. The Dressing Stations. Norman Dubie. AmPA
William Wallace. Francis Lauderdale Adams. OxBS
William Was a Royal Lover. *Unknown.* AmFP
William Wilson. Malcolm Cowley. MoVE
William Wordsworth. Sidney Keyes. ChMP; OxBTC; SeCePo
William Yeats in Limbo. Sidney Keyes. MoBrPo
Williams Avenue Zionist Church, The. Russia. William Carlos Williams. VGW
Willie. *Unknown.* AmFP
Willie and Earl Richard's Daughter. *Unknown. See* Birth of Robin Hood, The.
Willie and Helen. Hew Ainslie. HBV-1
Willie and Lady Maisry. *Unknown.* ESPB (A *and* B *vers.*)
Willie and Lady Margerie. *Unknown.* OxBB
Willie and Nellie, one evening sat. Willie's and Nellie's Wish. Julia A. Moore. FiBHP

Willie B (2). Lucille Clifton. InPS
Willie Brew'd a Peck o' Maut. Burns. AWP; EnRP; OxBS; ViBoPo
(Willie Brewed.) OAEP
Willie Fitzgibbons who used to sell ribbons. Waltz Me Around Again Willie; or, 'Round, 'Round, 'Round. Will D. Cobb. FSN; TreFT
Willie had a purple monkey climbing on a yellow stick. In Memoriam. Max Adeler. DTC; FaBoCo
Willie has taen him oer the fame. *See* Willie's taen him . . .
Willie in his roguish way. *Unknown.* WhC
"Willie is fair, an Willie's rair." *See* Willie's fair . . .
Willie Leonard; or, The Lake of Cold Finn. *Unknown.* AmFP; BaBo
Willie Macintosh. *Unknown.* ESPB (A *and* B *vers.*); OxBoLi; ViBoFo
(Burning of Auchindown.) OxBB
Willie o Douglas Dale. *Unknown.* ESPB
Willie o [*or* of] Winsbury. *Unknown.* AmFP; ESPB (A *and* D *vers.*)
Willie poisoned Auntie's tea. Willie the Poisoner. *Unknown.* NTCP
Willie pushed his Aunt Eliza. Aunt Eliza. *Unknown.* ShM
Willie Riley. *Unknown.* BaBo (A *and* B *vers.*)
Willie saw some dynamite. Little Willie. *Unknown.* FaPON
Willie stands in his stable-door. The Mother's Malison, or, Clyde's Water. *Unknown.* BaBo
Willie, take your little drum. Patapan. Bernard de la Monnoye, *tr. fr. French.* PChr
Willie the Poisoner. *Unknown.* NTCP
Willie the Weeper (*diff. versions*). *Unknown.* BeLS; BLPA; OBAL; TrAS, *with music*; YaD
(Willy the Weeper.) AS, *with music*; FSW; GBP
Willie was a widow's son. Willie and Lady Maisry. *Unknown.* ESPB
Willie Wastle dwalt on Tweed. Sic a Wife as Willie Had. Burns. GoTS
"Willie, Willie, I'll learn you a wile." Willie's Lyke-Wake. *Unknown.* ESPB
Willie Winkie. William Miller. FaFP; HBV-1; HBVY; OxBChV
(Wee Willie Winkie.) SiSoSe, *st.* 1
("Wee Willie Winkie runs through the town," *st.* 1.) OxNR; TiPo
Willie, with a thirst for gore. Careless Willie. *Unknown.* FaPON
Willie worked in the prison kitchen. How One-Thumb Willie Got His Name. John L. Sellers. LFAC
Willie's and Nellie's Wish. Julia A. Moore. FiBHP
"Willie's [*or* Willie is] fair, and Willie's rare." Rare Willie Drowned in Yarrow; or, The Water o Gamrie. *Unknown.* BaBo; ESPB
Willie's Fatal Visit. *Unknown.* BaBo; ESPB
Willie's Lady. *Unknown.* ESPB; ViBoFo
Willie's Lyke-Wake. *Unknown.* ESPB
Willie's pa and ma were kind. Silly Willy. "R. L. B." ShM
Willie's [*or* Willie has] taen him o'er the fame. Willie's Lady. *Unknown.* ESPB; ViBoFo
Willing Mistress, The. Aphra Behn. *Fr.* The Dutch Lover. SBG; UnTE; ViBoPo
(Amyntas Led Me to a Grove.) ErPo
Willing Suspension, A. John Holmes. PoCh
Willingly I'll say there's been a sweet marriage. These Past Years. Passages, 10. Robert Duncan. PoM
Willis, The. David Law Proudfit. AA
Willis Beggs. Edgar Lee Masters. *Fr.* The New Spoon River. SaC
Willobie His Avisa, *sel.* Henry Willoby.
To Avisa. ElL
Willoughby liked being Willoughby. The Contentment of Willoughby. Frances Alexander. GoYe
Willow, The. Sir William Davenant. *See* Under the Willow Shades.
Willow. Richard Watson Dixon. *See* Song: "Feathers of the willow, The."
Willow, The. Tu Fu, *tr. fr. Chinese by* Kenneth Rexroth. NaP
Willow Bend and Weep. Herbert Clark Johnson. PoNe
Willow Garland, The. Robert Herrick. OAEP
Willow herb, The. Rose Bay Willow Herb. Judy Ray. AMV-81; FAZ
Willow leaves dancing. Eveningsong. Ramona Wilson. VoR
Willow-Man, The. Juliana Horatia Ewing. OxBChV
Willow Poem. William Carlos Williams. NCSH
Willow shining, The. The Knowledge of Light. Henry Rago. PoCh; VGW
Willow-tassels grow in tremors of the spring wind. Lines to Do with Youth. Witter Bynner. PoA
Willow-Tree, A. Thackeray. CenHV; HBV-1; InMe
Willow Tree, The. *Unknown.* OBET
Willows, The. Walter Prichard Eaton. FaPON; HBMV; OHIP
Willows, The. Bret Harte. BXAP; InMe
Willows. Joseph Langland. NePoEA
Willows. Laura Schreiber. AMV-81
Willows are taking the old river road, The. Old River Road. Blanche Whiting Keysner. GoYe
Willows are trees of life. They ride. Willows. Joseph Langland. NePoEA
Willows are willows everywhere. Willows in Alma-Ata. Aleksander Wat, *tr. by* Isaac Komem. VWA
Willows by the Water Side, The. *Unknown.* *See* Lover's Lament, A.
Willows carried a slow sound, The. Repose of Rivers. Hart Crane. AP; AWP; CMoP; CoBMV; LiTM; MOAB; MoAmPo; NoAM; NOBA; OxBA; SeCeV
Willows in Alma-Ata. Aleksander Wat, *tr. fr. Polish by* Isaac Komem. VWA
Willows in the Snow. Tsuru, *tr. fr. Japanese.* SUS
Willowware Cup. James Merrill. NoP
Willowwood. Dante Gabriel Rossetti. The House of Life, XLIX-LII. OAEL-2; OAEP; VLP
"I sat with Love," XLIX. PoEL-5; WHA
Wills. John Godfrey Saxe. *See* Woman's Will.
Will's Love, The. Besmilr Brigham. IHMS
Willy ("Willy, enormous Saskatchewan grizzly"). Richard Moore. MAT
Willy and the Lady. Gelett Burgess. HBMV
Willy boy, Willy boy,/ Where are you going? Mother Goose. OxNR
Willy Drowned in Yarrow. *Unknown.* *See* Rare Willie Drowned in Yarrow.
Willy Lyons. William Stafford. NNaP
Willy Reilly. *Unknown.* HBV-2; OnYI; OuSiCo, *with music*
Willy the Weeper. *Unknown.* *See* Willie the Weeper.
Willy to Jinny. Joseph Skipsey. VLP
Willy Wet-Leg. D. H. Lawrence. CMoP; TW
Willy, Willy, Harry, Ste. The Kings and Queens of England. *Unknown.* FaBoUs
Willy, Willy Wilkin. Mother Goose. OxNR
Willy-nilly, he comes or goes, with the clown's logic. Come Away, Death. E. J. Pratt. PeCV
"Willy's rare, and Willy's fair." Rare Willy Drowned in Yarrow [*or* Willy Drowned in Yarrow]. *Unknown.* BSV; ESPB; GBP; GoTS; HBV-1; OxBB
Wilson and Pilcer and Snack stood before the zoo elephant. Elephants Are Different to Different People. Carl Sandburg. MoAmPo
Wil't please your grace to go along with us? A Quotation from Shakespeare with Slight Improvements. "Lewis Carroll." FaBoNo
Wilt thou be gone? it is not yet near day. Romeo and Juliet in the Orchard. Shakespeare. *Fr.* Romeo and Juliet, III, v. TreFT
Wilt thou forgive that sin where I begun. A Hymn to God the Father [*or* For Forgiveness *or* To Christ]. John Donne. AnAnS-1; AWP; BiP; EaLo; EBCP; EBEV; EnRePo; GoBC; HAP; HBV-2; InPk; JCP; LiTB; LoBV; MeLP; MePo; NOBE; OAEL-1; OBS; OxBoCh; PAI; PoEL-2; PoRA; PPoe; SCV; SeCeV; SeCP; SeCV-1; TreFT; TrGrPo; TrPWD; ViBoPo; WGRP
Wilt thou go with me, sweet maid. An Invite to Eternity. John Clare. OAEL-2; OBNC
Wilt thou hunt the prey for the lion? Bible, *O.T.* *Fr.* Job. FM
Wilt Thou Lend Me Thy Mare? *Unknown.* ELU
("Wilt thou lend me thy mare to ride a mile?") OBS
Wilt thou love God, as He thee? then digest. John Donne. Holy Sonnets, XV. AnAnS-1; JCP; MasP; OBS; TrCP
Wilt Thou not visit me? The Prayer. Jones Very. EBCP; OxBA; TrCP; TrPWD
Wilt Thou Set Thine Eyes upon That Which Is Not? Francis Quarles. *See* False World, Thou Liest.
Wilt thou then serve the Philistines with that gift. Milton. *Fr.* Samson Agonistes. EBEV
Wilt thou upon the high and giddy mast. Shakespeare. King Henry IV, Pt. II, *fr.* III, i. MOS
Wilth Thou steer my frail black bark. The Heavenly Pilot. Cormac, *tr. by* George Sigerson. *Fr.* Book of Leinster. OnYI
Wiltshire Downs. Andrew Young. ChMP; GTBS-P; OxBTC
Win at First and Lose at Last; or, A New Game at Cards. Laurence Price. OxBoLi
Winander Lake. Wordsworth. *See* There Was a Boy.
Winchester. Lionel Johnson. OBVV
Winchester Wedding, The. Thomas D'Urfey. CavP
Wind. Hamish Brown. PoSH
Wind, The. Alice Corbin, *after Chippewa Indian.* BPAW
Wind, The. Padraic Colum. *See* I Saw the Wind Today.
Wind, The. W. H. Davies. SeCePo
Wind, The. Emily Dickinson. *See* Of all the sounds despatched abroad.
Wind. Sydney Dobell. PeD
Wind, The. Dorothy Graddon. OnUR
Wind. Ted Hughes. SoSe
Wind. *Malay Oral Tradition, tr. by* R. O. Winstedt. WTO
Wind, The. Harold Monro. OBVV
Wind, The. William Morris. NBM
Wind, The. James Reeves. RHPC
Wind, The. Elizabeth Rendall. HBVY
Wind, The. Christina Rossetti. *See* Who Has Seen the Wind.
Wind, The. James Stephens. AnIL; BoNaP; ELU; HeIP; InPK; NoAM; PAI
Wind, The. Robert Louis Stevenson. GN; HBVY; SoPo; SUS; TiPo

Wind, The. *Unknown.* FaBoCh
("Arthur O'Bower has broken his bands [*or* band].") GBP; OxNR
(High Wind, The.) ChTr
Wind ("At times I resort, beyond man's discerning"). *Unknown, tr. fr. Anglo-Saxon by* Charles W. Kennedy. *Fr.* Riddles (Exeter Book). AnOE
Wind/ flattening its gaunt furious self against. Anne Marriott. *Fr.* The Wind Our Enemy. CaP
Wind, The/ only. Song of the Trees. *Tr. by* Frances Densmore. OBVE
Wind all night, A. July 1st, French Creek. Kevin Roberts. WOLT
Wind and Impulse. Duane Big Eagle. STE
Wind and Lyre. Edwin Markham. TRV
Wind and Mist. Edward Thomas. BrPo
Wind and pines. Listening. Nancy Passy. AMV-81
Wind and Silver. Amy Lowell. BoWoP; HeIP; MoAmPo; MOON; PAI
Wind and the beam loved the Rose, The. Nydia's Song. Sir Edward Bulwer-Lytton. OBVV
Wind and the Bird, The. *Unknown, tr. fr. Bushman by* W. H. I. Bleek. PeSA
Wind and the Moon, The. George Macdonald. GoJo; HBV-1; HBVY; MoShBr; OnMSP; SUS; TreFS
Wind and the Rain, The. Shakespeare. *See* When That I Was and a Little Tiny Boy.
Wind and the rain are beating down, The. In My Dreams I Searched for You. *Gond Oral Tradition, tr. by* V. Elwin *and* S. Hivale. WTO
Wind and Wave. Coventry Patmore. NBM
Wind and Wave. Charles Warren Stoddard. AA
Wind at Dog Lake whispered "stranger" "stranger," The. Turtle Lake. Richard Hugo. NPAW
Wind at Penistone, The. Donald Davie. LiTM; NePoEA-2; NMP
Wind at the Door, The. William Barnes. ELP; GBL; GTBS-P; LO; PoEL-4
Wind at Your Door, The. Robert D. Fitzgerald. PoAu-2
Wind begun [*or* began] to rock [*or* knead] the grass, The. Emily Dickinson. HAP, *sl. diff*; WeW
(Thunder-Storm, A.) BoNaP
Wind billowing out the seat of my britches, The. Child on Top of a Greenhouse. Theodore Roethke. ELU; LCAP; MiAP; NCSH; PoPl; VGW
Wind, bird, and tree. The Words. David Wagoner. PoA
Wind blew all my wedding-day, The. Wedding-Wind. Philip Larkin. MAT
Wind Blow East, The, *with music.* *Unknown.* OuSiCo
Wind Bloweth Where It Listeth, The. Susan L. Mitchell. AnIV
Wind Blows, The. Donagh MacDonagh. NeIP
Wind blows, and with a little broom, The. Cathleen Sweeping. George Johnston. NOBC
Wind blows east, The—the wind blows west. A Salem Witch. Ednah Proctor Clarke. PAH
Wind blows hot, The. English and foreign birds. Christmas Eve. Karl Shapiro. NYBP
Wind blows out of the gates of the day, The. Fairy Song. W. B. Yeats. *Fr.* The Land of Heart's Desire. MoBrPo; OnYI; ViBoPo
Wind blows up the tent like a balloon, The. Crimson Tent. John Dos Passos. PoA
Wind blows wild on Bos'n Hill. Bos'n Hill. John Albee. AA
Wind came in for several thousand miles all night, The. On an East Wind from the Wars. Alan Dugan. AP
Wind came up out of the sea, A. Daybreak. Longfellow. FPL; HBV-2; PoLF; TreFT
Wind Carries Me Free, The. Dennis Shady. LFAC
Wind-Clouds and Star-Drifts, *sel.* Oliver Wendell Holmes.
Manhood. AP
Wind comes from opposite poles, The. The Marriage. Mark Strand. EAS; NoAM
Wind comes from the north, The. Suspense. D. H. Lawrence. MoBrPo
Wind comes like the chief mourner. Funeral. Joanna Thompson. AMV-81
Wind comes, singing, The. Glad Earth. Ella C. Forbes. YeAr
"Wind doth blow today, my love, The." The Unquiet Grave. *Unknown.* CH; DTC; ELP; ESPB; GBP; HAP; HeIP; InPK; LO; LoBV; NoP; OAEL-1; OxBB; PoEL-1; PoPle; ViBoPo; WeW
Wind exultant swept, The. A Mood. Winifred Howells. AA
Wind flapped loose, the wind was still, The. The Woodspurge. Dante Gabriel Rossetti. EBEV; ELP; FaBoEn; GTBS-P; HAP; HeIP; InPK; LoBV; NBM; NOBE; NoP; OAEL-2; OAEP; OBEV; OBNC; PoEL-5; PrIm; TreFT; UnPo; VLP; WeW; WHA
Wind Flowers. Margo Lockwood. DFF
Wind from off the sea says nothing new, The. The Marrow. Theodore Roethke. NYBP
Wind from the east, oh lapwing of the day. Hafiz, *tr. by* Gertrude Lowthian Bell. Odes, VII. AWP
Wind from the north: the young spring day. The Song of the Four Winds. Thomas Love Peacock. *Fr.* The Misfortunes of Elphin. OBRV; WiR
Wind from the river warm on our backs. Crazy Dogholkoda. Mary TallMountain. TWSS
Wind from the West, A. Lauchlan MacLean Watt. PoSH
Wind gallop up Maiden Lane, The. Last Impression of New York. Mason Jordan Mason. PoNe
Wind Gardens. Louis Untermeyer. BXAP
Wind, hark, The! the wind in the angry woods. Summer Storm. Lionel Johnson. BrPo
Windharp. John Montague. CIP
Wind has at last got into the clock, The. The Wind, the Clock, the We. Laura Riding. LiTA
Wind has blown that searchlight out, The. Autumn Squall—Lake Erie. Lola Ingres Russo. AmFN
Wind has blown the rain away and blown, A. Sonnet. E. E. Cummings. MoAB; MoAmPo
Wind has changed, and all the signs turned right, The. The Omens. Ann Stanford. WSC
Wind has grained the snow. I Walk on the River at Dawn. Joanne Hart. PoDr
Wind has no language to be chipped. Solar Signals. L. Pearl Schuck. AMV-81
Wind has scattered my city to the sheep, The. Ruins of the City of Hay. Randolph Stow. CBAP; PoAu-2
Wind has such a rainy sound, The. The Sound of the Wind. Christina Rossetti. *Fr.* Sing-Song. OnUR; TiPo
Wind has twisted the roof from an old house, The. House-hunting. David Wagoner. DFF
Wind Has Wings, The. *Unknown, tr. fr. Eskimo by* Raymond De Coccola *and* Paul King. GrPl; WHW
Wind, heavy from the land, irons the surf, The. Offshore Breeze. Milton Acorn. NeAC
Wind hits and returns, it is easy to personify, The. Sophia Nichols. Robin Blaser. CoPo
Wind in a Frolic, The. William Howitt. MoShBr; OxBChV
Wind in the Alleys. Lola Ridge. OnYI
Wind in the Elms, The. J. Corson Miller. HBMV
Wind in the Grass. Mark Van Doren. FaBV
Wind in the Pine. Lew Sarett. TrPWD; TRV
Wind in the Pines, The. Madison Cawein. AA
Wind in the Willows, The, *sels.* Kenneth Grahame.
Duck's [*or* Ducks'] Ditty. FaPON; GoJo; MoShBr; NTCP; OxBChV; PDV; PoPle; RHPC; SoPo; SUS; TiPo
Song of Mr. Toad, The. FaPON; FiBHP; GoJo; NOBL
"Villagers all, this frosty tide." PChr
(Carol.) OHIP
(Christmas Carol.) FaPON
Wind is a Cat. Ether Romig Fuller. SoPo
Wind is a man and goes out from his hut, The. The Wind and the Bird. *Unknown, tr. by* W. H. I. Bleek. PeSA
Wind is always blowing, A. Proverbial. John Seller Anson. AMV-80
Wind is awake, pretty leaves, pretty leaves, The. The Way of It. John Vance Cheney. HBV-1
Wind Is Blind, The. Alice Meynell. MoBrPo; SeCePo
Wind is blowing, A. The book being written. The Novel. Denise Levertov. AP; NoAM
Wind is blowing harshly on the lake, The. St. Mary's Loch. Geoffrey Faber. PoSH
Wind is carrying me round the sky, The. The Wind. Alice Corbin, *after Chippewa Indian.* BPAW
Wind is cold, The. Winter. Princess Shikishi, *tr. by* Hiroaki Sato. PBWP
Wind is desolate in the fields, The. The Deserted Homestead. Loren Eiseley. PoA
Wind is east but the hot weather continues, The. American Letter. Archibald MacLeish. AmPP; OxBA
Wind is enough to stack the snow, The. November Snow. E. J. Carson. AMV-81
Wind Is Ill, The. John Malcolm Brinnin. LiTA
Wind is not nigh. Zone of Death. William Everson. VGW
Wind is piercing chill, The. Battlefield. Richard Aldington. MMA; OBWP
Wind is ruffling the tawny pelt, A. A Far Cry from Africa. Derek Walcott. HeIP; NoAM; TTY; UnPo
Wind is shaking this house, The. The Storm House. Elizabeth Jennings. WPE
Wind is thin. *Tr. fr. Latin by* Willis Barnstone. *Fr.* Cambridge Songs. BoWoP
Wind it blew, and the ship it flew, The. The Earl o' Quarterdeck. George Macdonald. BeLS; EtS
Wind it blew from east to west, The. Get Up and Bar the Door. *Unknown.* AmFP
Wind it blew from sou' sou'-east, it blew a pleasant breeze, The. The Light on Cape May. *Unknown.* ShS

Wind It Blew up the Railroad Track, The, *with music. Unknown.* AS
Wind it wailed, the wind it moaned, The. Alec Yeaton's Son. Thomas Bailey Aldrich. EtS; MOS
Wind licks hairs on shiny heads. Settling In. Floyd C. Stuart. TAT
Wind like an ocean, The. Larry Eigner. PoM
Wind like this tonight, A. Exile. Audrey Beecham. NeBP
Wind may blow the snow about, The. A Country Boy in Winter. Sarah Orne Jewett. OBCA
Wind Me a Summer Crown. Menella Bute Smedley. HBV-2; OBVV
Wind meets me at Penistone, The. The Wind at Penistone. Donald Davie. LiTM; NePoEA-2; NMP
Wind mutters thinly on the sagging wire. Prairie Graveyard. Anne Marriott. CaP; NOBC; OBCV
Wind o' the East dark with rain. The Efficient Wife's Complaint. Confucius, *tr. by* Ezra Pound. *Fr.* Airs of Pei. CTC
Wind of dawning riffles the young furze, The. Drafts for a Quatrain. Edmund Wilson. OBAL
Wind of Hampstead Heath still burns my cheek, The. Breath of Hampstead Heath. Edith M. Thomas. AA
Wind of January, The. Christina Rossetti. YeAr
Wind of sage in which the world dreams. Buffalo Marrow on Black. Lance Henson. STE
Wind of the City Streets. To a June Breeze. H. C. Bunner. AA
Wind of the Cliff Ka Hea, The. Phyllis Thompson. FAZ
Wind of the North. The Four Winds. Charles Henry Luders. AA; HBV-1
Wind of the Prairie. Grace Clementine Howes. GoYe
Wind of the prairie, sweeping adown from the hills. Wind Song. Zoe A. Tilghman. BPAW
Wind of the West, that fans with fragrant wing. To the Western Wind. Judah Halevi, *tr. by* Solomon Solis-Cohen. TrJP
Wind on the Corn. Charles Tennyson Turner. EBVV
Wind on the Downs, The. Marian Allen. SUMH
Wind on the Hills, The. Dora Sigerson Shorter. HBMV
Wind on the Lyre. George Meredith. NBM
Wind one morning sprang up from sleep, The. The Wind in a Frolic. William Howitt. MoShBr; OxBChV
Wind Our Enemy, The, *sel.* Anne Marriott.
"Wind/ flattening its gaunt furious self against." CaP
Wind picks at the clapboard. Noah in New England. Tom Lowenstein. VWA
Wind rattles the apples. Gone. Ralph Pomeroy. DFF
Wind rifles itself up, The. Words to the Wind. Pier Giorgio Di Cicco. AMV-80
Wind, rising in the alleys. Wind in the Alleys. Lola Ridge. OnYI
Wind roars and the river roars, The. The Sounding Portage. Annie Charlotte Dalton. CaP
Wind rocks the car. Like This Together. Adrienne Rich. CoPo; VGW
Wind Rose in the Night, A. Aline Kilmer. HBMV
Wind runs free across our plains, The. For Adolf Eichmann. Primo Levi, *tr. by* Ruth Feldman *and* Brian Swann. VWA
Wind searching as a sieve of brass. Storm at Sea. *Malay Oral Tradition, tr. by* R. O. Winstedt. WTO
Wind Secrets. Diane Wakoski. AmPA
Wind shall lull us yet, The. From the Antique. Christina Rossetti. EnLoPo
Wind shifts dust, or, The. The Leaf. William Carson Fagg. LFAC
Wind Sleepers, The. Hilda Doolittle ("H. D."). WPE
Wind Song. Carl Sandburg. MoAB; MoAmPo; MoShBr; TwAmPo
Wind Song. Zoe A. Tilghman. BPAW
Wind-Song. *Unknown, tr. fr. Pima Indian by* Natalie Curtis. SUS
Wind Sou'west, The. *Unknown.* AmFP
Wind Sprang Up at Four O'Clock, The. T. S. Eliot. LiTB; NePA
Wind sprays pale dirt into my mouth, The. The Elements of San Joaquin. Gary Soto. NPGG
Wind, stirring in the dark foliage, brings, The. God's Harp. Gustav Falke, *tr. by* Ludwig Lewisohn. AWP
Wind stirs the willows, The. Songs of the Ghost Dance. *Unknown.* WSC
Wind stood up, and gave a shout, The. The Wind. James Stephens. AnIL; BoNaP; ELU; HeIP; InPK; NoAM; PAI
Wind sways the pines, A. Dirge in [the] Woods. George Meredith. FF; LoBV; OAEP; OBEV; OBNC; OBVV; SeCeV; VLP; WHA; WiR
Wind takes colour from the trees, The. Winds. Hugh McCrae. CBAP
Wind tapped like a tired man, The. Emily Dickinson. MoAB; MoAmPo; NePA
Wind That Shakes the Rushes, The. John Clare. PoRA
Wind that speeds the bee and plucks the bee-line. Awake! W. R. Rodgers. LiTM; WaP
Wind, the Clock, the We, The. Laura Riding. LiTA
Wind the other evening overthrew, The. Love Fallen to Earth. Paul Verlaine, *tr. by* Arthur Symons. SyP
Wind through the box-elder trees, The. Poem against the British. Robert Bly. ConAP; InPS
Wind took up the northern things, The. Emily Dickinson. SOTW
Wind voice calls and calls you, The. The Summons. Elizabeth Roberts MacDonald. CaP
Wind was a torrent of darkness among the gusty trees, The. The Highwayman. Alfred Noyes. BeLS; FaBV; FaFP; FaPON; FPL; HBV-2; HBVY; OBNV; OHFP; PoLF; TreFS
Wind was blowing over the moors, The. Charlotte Brontë. "Susan Coolidge." OBCA
Wind was in another country, and, The. Mirage. R. P. Blackmur. *Fr.* Sea Island Miscellany. MoVE
Wind Was There, The. Bravig Imbs. EAS
Wind went wooing the rose, The. A Summer Wooing. Louise Chandler Moulton. HBV-1
Wind whines and whines the shingle. On the Beach at Fontana. James Joyce. MoBrPo; OBMV; PoA; SoSe
Wind-Wolves. William D. Sargent. RHPC; TiPo
Wind would tear a dead man's shroud. Wind. *Malay Oral Tradition, tr. by* R. O. Winstedt. WTO
Windfall. Joel Arsenault. AMV-81
Windfall. David Mitchell. OCNZ
Windfall. F. R. Scott. CaP
Windhover, The. Gerard Manley Hopkins. ACP; BiP; BrPo; CABA; CMoP; CoBMV; EaLo; EBCP; EBVV; FaBoEn; GTBS-P; HAP; InPK; InPS; InVP; LiTB; LiTM; LoBV; MoAB; MoBrPo; MoPo; MoVE; NIP; NoAM; NOBE; NoP; OAEL-2; OAEP; OBNC; PAI; PBBP; PoEL-5; PoPl; PoPle; PoRA; PPoe; PPP; PrIm; SCV; SeCeV; SyP; TEP; TreFT; UnPo; VLP; WeW
Windigo. Paulette Jiles. NOBC
Winding Banks of Erne, The. William Allingham. AnIV; NBM
(Adieu to Belashanny.) OxBI
Winding Down the War. Philip Appleman. SOTS
Winding road lies white and bare, The. The Footpath Way. Katharine Tynan. HBV-1
Winding way the serpent takes, The. Norembega. Whittier. PAH
Winding, winding. The Lost Valley. Gordon J. Gadsby. PoSH
Windlass Song. William Allingham. GN
Windle-Straws. Edward Dowden. HBV-1
Windless city built on decaying granite, loose ends. Thomas McGrath. Letter to an Imaginary Friend, Part Two, II, 2-5. NNaP
Windmill, The. Lord De Tabley. NBM
Windmill, The. Longfellow. MoShBr
Windmill in March. Katharine Privett. AMV-80
Windmill of Evening, The. Shlomo Reich, *tr. fr. French by* Mira Reich. VWA
Windmill on the Cape. William Vincent Sieller. GoYe
Windmills, The. John Gould Fletcher. Arizona Poems, IV. CrMA
Window, The. Conrad Aiken. CMoP
Window. Anne Cherner. AMV-80
Window, The. Robert Creeley. CAPP; NoAM; NOBA; TAP; VGW
Window, The. Stephen Dobyns. MAYP
Window, The. Edwin Muir. LiTM
Window, The. Francis Scarfe. NeBP
Window. Bruce Smith. DiL
Window, The. Iain Crichton Smith. NePoEA-2
Window Boxes. Eleanor Farjeon. FaPON
Window Frames the Moon, The. Laureen Mar. BrSi
Window-Glance, The. Heine, *tr. fr. German by* John Todhunter. AWP
Window has four little pains [*or* panes], The. The Window Pane [*or* Nonsense Verses]. Gelett Burgess. HBV-2; HBVY
Window insulates me from the street, The. Maternity Gown. David Holbrook. OxBTC
Window is broken, A. The Night Has Twenty-four Hours. Pedro Juan Pietri. InW
Window is wide and lo, beyond its bars, The. Interlude: The Casement. Christopher Brennan. PoAu-1
Window Ledge in the Atom Age. E. B. White. OBAL
Window of the Tobacco Shop, The. C. P. Cavafy, *tr. fr. Greek by* Edmund Keeley *and* Philip Sherrard. PeHV
Window on the North, A. R. A. D. Ford. MoCV
Window, The; or, The Song of the Wrens, *sel.* Tennyson.
Ay. PBBP
Window pales, and by its paltry light, The. Aubade: Donna Anna to Juan, Still Asleep. Richard Howard. PoA
Window Pane, The. Gelett Burgess. HBVY
(Nonsense Verse: "Window has four little panes, The.") HBV-2
Window screen, The. Sunday Rain. John Updike. DFF
Window-screen sifts the blue cumulus, The. Garden Puzzle. Gray Burr. CoPo
Window showed a willow in the west, The. Elegy in a Firelit Room. James Wright. TwAmPo
Window Sill, The. Robert Graves. EnLoPo
Window to the East. Virginia Moran Evans. AMV-80

Window was made of ice with bears lumbering across it. Bad Dream. Louis MacNeice. NoAM
Window was open all night long, The. All Night Long. Nina Cassian, *tr. by* Herbert Kuhner. VWA
Windowed Habitations. Charles G. Bell. NePoAm-2
Windows, The. George Herbert. AnAnS-1; CABA; MeLP; NOCV; NoP; OAEP; SeCP; SeCV-1; TrCP
(Church Windows, The.) OBS
Windows. Mordechai Husid, *tr. fr. Yiddish by* Seymor Mayne *and* Rivka Augenfeld. VWA
Windows, The. Ron Loewinsohn. GP
Windows, The. W. S. Merwin. DFF
Windows, The/ look back into themselves. The Way We Live Now. Robert Dana. AMV-80
Windows are deep blue, The. The Blue Church. Peter Balakian. AMV-80
Windows are tiny postcards opening, The. The Interrogations. Michael Knoll. LFAC
Windows in Providence. Aliki Barnstone. BoWoP
Window's length beyond the Pleiades, A. First Snow on an Airfield. John Ciardi. PoA
Windows of Heaven were open wide, The. A Ballad of the Conemaugh Flood. Hardwick Drummond Rawnsley. PAH
Windows of Waltham, The. John Wieners. CoPo
Windows vanish, The: we cannot afford to buy. A House All Pictures. Emery George. AMV-81
Windrush down the timber chutes. Mountain Wind. Barbara Kunz Loots. RHPC
Winds, The. Jack Clemo. EBCP
Winds, The. "John Eglinton." OnYI
Winds. Hugh McCrae. CBAP
Winds, The. Thomas Tusser. WiR
Winds are bleak, stars are bright. "Furnley Maurice." *Fr.* The Victorian Markets Recollected in Tranquillity. PoAu-2
Winds are high on Helle's wave, The. Byron. *Fr.* The Bride of Abydos. OBRV
Winds are roaring out of the West, The. Inisgallun. Darrell Figgis. OnYI
Wind's bride seized me, The. In the Open Fields. Hugo Sonnenschein, *tr. by* Edouard Roditi. VWA
Winds had hushed at last as by command, The. The Sower. Mathilde Blind. SBG; WPE
Winds have talked with him confidingly, The. Longfellow. James Whitcomb Riley. AA
Wind's Head, The. John L. Sweeney. TwAmPo
Wind's in the heart of me, a fire's in my heels, A. A Wanderer's Song. John Masefield. MoAB; MoBrPo
Winds of Africa. Dorothy S. Obi. WPOW
Winds of autumn, winters dipped in mud. Mists and Rain. Baudelaire, *tr. by* Arthur Symons. SyP
Winds of Change, The. Charles G. Ballard. VoR
Winds of doctrine blow both ways at once, The. Conrad Aiken. *Fr.* A Letter from Li Po. VGW
Winds of Eros. "Æ." HBMV
Winds of Fate, The. Ella Wheeler Wilcox. BLPA; FPL; TRV; WBLP
Winds of the world for a little season, The. The Wind's Way. Richard Le Gallienne. HBMV
Wind's on the wold, The. Inscription for an Old Bed [*or* For the Bed at Kelmscott *or* Lines for a Bed at Kelmscott Manor]. William Morris. CH; FaBoRV; NBM; OBEV; OBVV; PoEL-5; WiR
Wind's overbearing voices, The. The Storm. John Hay. AMV-81
Wind's Song, The. "Gabriel Setoun." HBV-1; HBVY
Wind's spine is broken, The. Storm Tide on Mejit. *Unknown, tr. by* Augustin Kramer *and* Willard Trask. RFM
Winds that drift over the desert. Winds of Africa. Dorothy S. Obi. WPOW
Winds that once the Argo bore, The. Heroes. Edna Dean Proctor. HBV-2
Winds that sweep the southern mountains. Allatoona. *Unknown.* PAH
Winds they did blow, The. *Unknown.* OxNR
Winds through [*or* thro'] the olive trees. Long, Long Ago. *Unknown.* FaPON; OHIP; PChr; PDV; PoSC
Wind's Way, The. Grace Hazard Conkling. HBV-2
Wind's Way, The. Richard Le Gallienne. HBMV
Winds were yelling, the waves were swelling, The. The Last Buccaneer. Macaulay. EtS; HBV-1
Winds, whisper gently whilst she sleeps. Laura Sleeping. Charles Cotton. CavP; ELP; FaBoEn; LoBV; OBS; ViBoPo
Wind's word, the Hebrew Hallelujah, A. Hallelujah; a Sestina. Robert Francis. PoCh
Wind's Work. T. Sturge Moore. BrPo; HBMV; HBVY
Windshield. Robert Fitzgerald. CrMA
Windshield wipers clear an arc, The. Girl in Front of the Bank. Robert Wallace. DFF
Windsor Forest, *sels.* Pope.
Field Sports. OBEC; SeCePo
("When milder autumn summer's heat succeeds.") PBBP
"Groves of Eden, vanished now so long, The." OAEL-1; OBEC
Hunt, The. NIP
"See! from the brake the whirring Pheasant springs." FaBoEn; FM; PoEL-3
(Shoot, The.) PB
"Thy forests, Windsor! and thy green retreats." NOEC
Wind-swept Wheat, The. "Madeline Bridges." AA
Windy Bill, *with music. Unknown.* CoSo
Windy Bishop, The. Wilfred Watson. OBCV
Windy Day, A. Winifred Howard. FaPON
Windy Morning. Harry Behn. TiPo
Windy Night, The. Thomas Buchanan Read. GN
Windy night was blowing on Rome, A. The Rider at The Gate. John Masefield. BrPo
Windy Nights. Robert Louis Stevenson. GoJo; OxBChV; PH; PoRA; RHPC; SiSoSe; TiPo
Windy Planet, The. Annie Dillard. SUW
Windy Trees. A. R. Ammons. PPJ
Windy Wash Day. Dorothy Aldis. TiPo
Wine. Micah Joseph Lebensohn, *tr. fr. Hebrew by* Abraham M. Klein. TrJP
Wine and cakes for gentlemen. *Unknown.* OxNR
Wine and Dew. Richard Henry Stoddard. AA
Wine and Grief. Solomon ibn Gabirol, *tr. fr. Hebrew by* Emma Lazarus. TrJP
Wine and Love and Lyre. *Unknown. See* There's No Lust like to Poetry.
Wine and oil gleaming within their heads. Double Ode. Muriel Rukeyser. LCAP
Wine and Water. G. K. Chesterton. *Fr.* The Flying Inn. ACP; CenHV; FaBoCo; FiBHP; GoBC; HBMV; InMe; MoBrPo; ViBoPo
Wine and woman and song. Villanelle of the Poet's Road. Ernest Dowson. OBMV; TrGrPo; UnPo
Wine Bowl. Hilda Doolittle ("H. D."). NoP
Wine comes in at the mouth. A Drinking Song. W. B. Yeats. BoLoP; OAEL-2; POL
Wine Cup, The. Meleager, *tr. fr. Greek by* Dudley Fitts. OLR
Wine, friend, and truth, the proverb says, agree. Theocritus, *tr. by* T. Creech. Idylls, XXVI. PeHV
Wine from the Cape. Turner Cassity. AMV-81
Wine Jelly. *Unknown.* WhC
Wine-maiden. Midnight Dancer. Langston Hughes. FF
Wine Menagerie, The. Hart Crane. AP; NoAM; NOBA; OxBA; VGW
Wine o Living. Matt Marshall. PoSH
Wine of love is music, The. The Vine. James Thomson. *Fr.* Sunday up the River. HBV-1; OBEV; OBVV; ViBoPo
Wine of the new vintage they brought us. The New Vintage. Douglas Le Pan. OBCV
Wine-Press of Los, The. Blake. *Fr.* Milton. EnRP
Wine taken with excess. Temperance. *Unknown.* ACP
Wine upon beer, I counsel thee. *Unknown.* FaBoUs
Winemaker's Beat-étude, The. Alfred Purdy. MoCV
Wine-Songs, *sels.* Moses ibn Ezra, *tr. fr. Hebrew by* Solomon Solis-Cohen. TrJP
Awake, My Soul.
Bring Me the Cup.
Drink, Friends.
Rosy Days Are Numbered, The.
Wing Factory, The. Dona Stein. AMV-80
Wing of Separation, The. Ibn Darraj al-Andalusi, *tr. fr. Arabic by* J. B. Trend. AWP
Winged bull trundles to the wired perimeter, The. C. Day Lewis. *Fr.* Flight to Italy. OxBTC
Winged fancies of the learned quill, The. In Praise of Country Life. Robert Chamberlain. CavP
Winged Heart, A. Henry Vaughan. *Fr.* Of Life and Death. FaBoRV
Winged horses descend to drink, The. On a Bas-Relief. Wesley Trimpi. NePoEA
Wingèd lion on top of that column, The. Notes Made in the Piazza San Marco. May Swenson. CoAP
Winged Man. Stephen Vincent Benét. MoAmPo
Winged Mariner. Grace Clementine Howes. EtS
Winged mimic of the woods! thou motley fool! To the Mocking-bird. Richard Henry Wilde. AA
Winged wonder of motion. The Dragonfly. Theodore Harding Rand. CaP
Winged Worshippers, The. Charles Sprague. AA; HBV-2
Wings. Bible, *O.T.* Psalms, LV: 6-7. FaPON
Wings. Miroslav Holub, *tr. fr. Czech by* Ian Milner *and* George Theiner. SUW
Wings. Victor Hugo, *tr. fr. French.* TRV
Wings, The. Denise Levertov. CAPP

Wings. Judith Wright. CBAP
Wings and Seeds. Sandra McPherson. GeTw
Wings and Wheels. Nancy Byrd Turner. SoPo; SUS; TiPo
Wings at Dawn. Joseph Auslander. HBMV
Wings filmed, the threads of knowledge thicken. The Jam Trap. Charles Tomlinson. MoBrPo
Wings like pistols flashing at his sides. The Sparrow Hawk. Russell Hoban. RHPC
Wings of a bird, The. Totem. Nissim Ezekiel. VWA
Wings of Love, The. James H. Cousins. AnIV
Wings of Time are black and white, The. Compensation. Emerson. AmPP; AP; NOBA
Wings outstretched, a horned owl. Signatures. Daniel Hoffman. VGW
Wingtip. Carl Sandburg. PCP
Wingwalking in Oregon. Robert Peterson. NeAC
Winifred Waters. William Brighty Rands. OxBChV
Winifreda. *Unknown.* HBV-1; OBEV
(Translation from the Ancient British.) OBEC
Winked too much and were afraid of snakes. The Monkeys. Marianne Moore. CMoP; LiTA; NoAM; NOBA; OxBA; SeCeV; TwAmPo
Winnah, The! pure as snow. The Aftermath. William Carlos Williams. FAZ
Winners, The. Kipling. *Fr.* The Story of the Gadsbys. BLPA; FaPoR; FPL
(L'Envoi: "What is the moral? Who rides may read.") MoBrPo; TrGrPo
Winnie Whiney, all things grieve her. Ten Kinds. Mary Mapes Dodge. RHPC
Winning of Cales, The. Thomas Deloney. CoMu
Winning of the TV West, The. John T. Alexander. AmFN; RHPC
Winning way, a pleasant smile, A. Little Annie Rooney. Michael Nolan. FSN; TreF
Winnowers, The. Robert Bridges. OAEP
Winnsboro Cotton Mill Blues. *Unknown.* FSW
Wino. Ted Hughes. NoAM
Wino was eating soup, The. Tornado Soup. A. K. Redwing. VoR
Winslow Homer, Prisoners from the Front. Roger Blakely. PoDr
Winsome Torment rose from slumber, rubbed his eyes, and went his way. The Hammam Name. James Elroy Flecker. BrPo; PeHV
Winter. Bella Akhmadulina, *tr. fr. Russian by* Barbara Einzig. BoWoP
Winter, *sel.* Charles Cotton.
Winter's Troops. ChTr
Winter. William Cowper. *Fr.* The Task, IV. OBEC
Winter. Maurice Craig. OnYI
Winter. Walter de la Mare. ChTr; MoVE; OAEL-2; OBMV; YeAr
Winter. John Lyle Donaghy. BIrV
Winter. Gavin Douglas. *Fr.* Prologues to the Aeneid. SeCePo
Winter. Richard Hughes. OBMV
Winter. James Hurnard. PoSC
Winter. Jean Jaszi. SoPo
Winter. Mani Leib, *tr. fr. Yiddish by* Keith Bosley. VWA
Winter. Charles Mair. OBCV; PeCV; PoSC, *abr.*
Winter. Samuel Menashe. GrPl
Winter. Coventry Patmore. The Unknown Eros, I, iii. FaBoRV; NOBE; OBNC
("I, singularly moved.") LO
Winter. Thomas Sackville. *Fr.* An Induction to "A Mirror for Magistrates." ElL; SeCePo
Winter. Shakespeare. *Fr.* Love's Labour's Lost. *See* When Icicles Hang by the Wall.
Winter. Princess Shikishi, *tr. fr. Japanese by* Hiroaki Sato. PBWP
Winter. Spenser. *Fr.* The Faerie Queene, VII, 7. GN
Winter. Ruth Stone. BoWoP
Winter. J. M. Synge. OBMV; OxBTC; POL
Winter. James Thomson. *Fr.* The Seasons. OAEP, *abr.*
Sels.
Approach of Winter. OBEC
"As thus the snows arise, and foul and fierce." SeCePo
"Clear frost succeeds, and thro' the blew Serene." FaBoEn
"Drooping, the labourer ox." FM
"Fowls of heaven, The." PBBP
Frost at Night. OBEC
"Keener tempests come, The; and, fuming dun." EnRP; NoP; ViBoPo, *shorter sel.*
"Late, in the louring sky, red, fiery streaks." FaBoEn
"Lo! from the livid East, or piercing North." FaBoEn
"Now, solitary, and in pensive guise." FaBoEn
"Now, when the cheerless empire of the sky." BSV; OxBS
"See Winter comes, to rule the varied year." TEP
"What art thou, frost? and whence are thy keen stores." OxBS
"When from the pallid sky the sun descends." OAEL-1; OxBS
Winter Night, A. NOBE
Winter Scene, A. OBEC
Winter. *Unknown, tr. fr. Irish by* Frank O'Connor. KiLC
Winter. William Carlos Williams. NCSH
Winter. Sheila Wingfield. EnLoPo
Winter,/ late afternoon. The River. Don Welch. Str
Winter; a Dirge. Burns. HBV-1; LAuP
Winter again and it is snowing. W. D. Snodgrass. Heart's Needle, V. AP
Winter and night, the white frost and the darkness. Urania. Ruth Pitter. MoVE
Winter and Red Berries. Nicholas Moore. NeBP
Winter and Summer. Stephen Spender. MoAB; MoBrPo; MoPo
Winter and summer, whatever the weather. The Floor and the Ceiling. William Jay Smith. GrPl; OBCA
Winter, and the sky is a land of gray fiords. Grisaille with a Spot of Red. Samuel Yellen. NePoAm-2
Winter at Tomi. Ovid, *tr. fr. Latin by* F. A. Wright. AWP
Winter begins. Poem on the End of Sensation. Ken Stange. AMV-80
Winter birds, The. Migration. Pinkie Gordon Lane. BlSi
Winter blows on my eaves. Solstitium Saeculare. Robert Fitzgerald. MoVE
Winter Burn. Roberta Hill. VoR
Winter Circus. Aileen Fisher. YeAr
Winter clenched its fist, The. The Redwing. Patric Dickinson. BoAnP
Winter Climb. Beinn Eunaich. PoSH
Winter Clothes. Karla Kuskin. RHPC
Winter Coming On. Martin Bell, *after the French of* Jules Laforgue. FaBoMo; OBVE; OxBTC
Winter Count of Sean Spotted Wolf. Earle Thompson. STE
Winter Cricket. John Heath-Stubbs. OBCP
Winter Dawn. D. H. Lawrence. BrPo
Winter Day. Susannah Fried, *tr. fr. Slovak by* Anthony Rudolf. VWA
Winter Day. Whittier. *See* Storm, The.
Winter Daybreak above Venice, A. James Wright. LCAP
Winter Days. Henry Abbey. AA
Winter Days. Gareth Owen. OBCP
Winter days are drawin' nigh, De. Winter Is Coming. Waverly Turner Carmichael. BANP
Winter deepening, the hay all in, The. Sonnet. Richard Wilbur. PoPl
Winter Developing. Nora Dauenhauer. TWSS
Winter Drive. James McAuley. PoA
Winter: East Anglia. Edmund Blunden. LiSp; OxBTC
Winter Encounters. Charles Tomlinson. LiTM
Winter Evening, The ("Hark! 'tis the twanging horn o'er yonder bridge"). William Cowper. The Task, IV. OAEP; SeCePo
(Evening.) OBEC
(Post-Boy, The.) FiP
Winter Evening ("Just when our drawing-rooms begin to blaze"). William Cowper. *Fr.* The Task. NOEC
Winter Evening. Walter de la Mare. FaBoRV
Winter Evening. Archibald Lampman. NOBC; OBCV; PeCV
Winter Evening Poem. Laura Jensen. LCAP
Winter evening settles down, The. Preludes. T. S. Eliot. HeIP; InPS; LiTA; MoShBr, *1 st.*; MoVE; MP; NoP; OBMV; PoPl; PPP; SeCePo; SOTW; TwCP; UnPo; VGW; WeW
Winter Fairyland in Vermont. Francis P. Osgood. WeW
Winter Feast. Frances Frost. YeAr
Winter fells. Deathward. John Lyle Donaghy. BIrV
Winter flood is out, dully glazing the weald, The. The Flood. Andrew Young. ChMP
Winter for a moment takes the mind. Conrad Aiken. Preludes for Memnon, or Preludes to Attitude, I (IV). LiTA; LiTM; MoPo; MoVE; OxBA; TwAmPo
Winter Galaxy, The. Charles Heavysege. *See* Stars Are Glittering in the Frosty Sky, The.
Winter Garden. David Gascoyne. ChMP; GTBS-P
Winter Glass, The. Charles Cotton. HBV-2
Winter has a pencil. Pencil and Paint. Eleanor Farjeon. PDV
Winter has at last come. Minamoto no Shigeyuki, *tr. by* Arthur Waley. *Fr.* Shui Shu. AWP
Winter Has Come. *Unknown, tr. fr. Old Irish by* Kenneth Jackson. AnIL
Winter has come to the old folks' home. Passing the Masonic Home for the Aged. Herbert Scott. PPJ
Winter has come with scarcity. Winter Has Come. *Unknown, tr. by* Kenneth Jackson. AnIL
Winter has reached thee once again at last. To Hampstead. Leigh Hunt. OBRV
Winter has wrecked the legend of your wings. To the Ghost of a Kite. James Wright. NePoEA
Winter Heavens. George Meredith. CABA; NoP
Winter Holding off the Coast of North America. N. Scott Momaday. CDW
Winter Homily on the Calton Hill. Douglas Young. OxBS
Winter Hymn, A—to the Snow. Ebenezer Jones. OBNC
Winter in Another Country. Ai. AMV-81

Winter in Durnover Field. Thomas Hardy. MoBrPo
Winter in Étienburgh. Stephen Parker. NYBP
Winter in Lower Canada. Standish O'Grady. *Fr.* The Emigrant. NOBC; OBCV
Winter in Strathearn, *sel.* John Davidson.
Twinkling Earn, The. PoSH
Winter in the Fens. John Clare. BoNaP
Winter in the Sierras. Mary Austin. BPAW
Winter in the Wood. Ivy O. Eastwick. YeAr
Winter is a dreary season. Winter. *Unknown, tr. by* Frank O'Connor. KiLC
Winter Is Another Country. Archibald MacLeish. NCSH
Winter is cold-hearted. Summer. Christina Rossetti. BoNaP; ELP; NBM; PoPle
Winter is Coming. Waverly Turner Carmichael. BANP
Winter is fallen early. The Children of Stare. Walter de la Mare. BrPo
Winter is gone, and spring is over. Alfred Austin. FaBoCo
Winter Is Here. "Katri Vala," *tr. fr. Finnish by* Jaakko A. Ahokas. PBWP
Winter Is Icumen In. Bradford Smith. PoSC
Winter is icumen [*or* icummen] in. Ancient Music. Ezra Pound. BXAP; DBV; FaBoCo; FaBoPa; FF; HeIP; LiTM; NePA; OBAL; OxBA; Par; PPON; SpRo; TW
Winter is icumen in. Elegy for Ezra. Raymond Roseliep. SOTS
Winter is long in this climate. March. William Carlos Williams. NCSH
Winter is passing, and the bells. Spring in the Students' Quarter. Henri Murger, *tr. by* Andrew Lang. AWP
Winter Is Past, The. Bible, *O.T.* *Fr.* The Song of Solomon. *See* For, Lo, the Winter Is Past.
Winter is past, The. My Love Is like the Sun. *Unknown.* AnIV
Winter Journey. Stanislaw Wygodski, *tr. fr. Polish by* Isaac Komem. VWA
Winter Juniper. Joseph Langland. NePoEA
Winter kept us in the valleys. April, Glengarry. Philip Coxon. PoSH
Winter Lakes, The. Wilfred Campbell. BoNaP; NOBC; OBCV
Winter Landscape. John Berryman. AP; LiTA; LiTM; MoAmPo; MP; PoPl; TwCP
Winter Landscape. Stephen Spender. MoAB; MoBrPo
Winter Lightning for Paul, The. Howard Nemerov. MoVE
Winter Love. Elizabeth Jennings. BoLoP; NePoEA; PPJ
Winter Madrigal, A. Morris Bishop. Inme
Winter Mask. Allen Tate. NePA; OxBA; Prf
Winter Memories. Henry David Thoreau. AmPP; NePA; OxBA
(Within the Circuit of This Plodding Life.) AP; NOBA
Winter Moon. Langston Hughes. DuDa; RHPC
Winter Moon, The. Tagaki Kyozo, *tr. fr. Japanese by* James Kirkup *and* Nakamo Michio. LLLT
Winter Moon. Maria Luisa Spaziani, *tr. fr. Italian by* Lynne Lawner. PBWP
Winter Morning, A. James Russell Lowell. *Fr.* The Vision of Sir Launfal. GN
Winter Morning. William Jay Smith. BoNaP; NCSH
Winter Morning Walk, The. William Cowper. The Task, V. LAuP
Sels.
" 'Tis morning; and the sun with ruddy orb." PoEL-3
(Frosty Morning, A, *shorter sel.*) NOEC
"Whose freedom is by suff'rance, and at will." EnRP
Winter mornings. Back Road. Bruce Guernsey. AMV-81
Winter must be here, The. What We Can. Ray A. Young Bear. VoR
Winter: My Secret. Christina Rossetti. BrRo; TEP
Winter my theme confines; whose nitry wind. John Gay. *Fr.* Trivia: or, the Art of Walking the Streets of London, II. NOEC
Winter, New Hampshire. David Kherdian. TAT
Winter News. John Haines. PPJ
Winter Night, A. William Barnes. ChTr; FaBoRV; NOBE; OBNC
Winter Night, A, *sel.* Burns.
"When biting Boreas, fell and doure." BSV
Winter Night. Louis O. Coxe. NYBP
Winter Night. C. Day Lewis. PoA
Winter Night. Robert Fitzgerald. PoPl
Winter Night. Roy Fuller. NeBP
Winter Night. Boris Pasternak, *tr. fr. Russian by* Eugene M. Kayden. PoPl
Winter Night, A. James Thomson. *Fr.* The Seasons: Winter. NOBE
Winter Night. Whittier. *Fr.* Snow-bound. TrGrPo
Winter Night, Cold Spell. Howard Nelson. AMV-81
Winter night is cold and drear, The. Across the Delaware. Will Carleton. PAH
Winter Nightfall. Robert Bridges. MoAB; MoBrPo; OBEV
Winter Nightfall. J. C. Squire. OxBTC
Winter Nights. Thomas Campion. *See* Now Winter Nights Enlarge.
Winter Nights. Lora Dunetz. AMV-80
Winter Noon. Sara Teasdale. YeAr
Winter Ocean. John Updike. ELU; InPK; MOS; PAI; SoSe
Winter of '73, The, *with music.* Larry Gorman. ShS
Winter Offering. D. S. Savage. LiTB; NeBP
Winter on Black Mingo, *sel.* *Unknown.*
"Cold, deserted and silent." FiBHP
Winter over Nothing. Elliot Coleman. FAZ
Winter owl banked just in time to pass, The. Questioning Faces. Robert Frost. ELU; GrPl; NCSH
Winter owl skirts hemlock tree. Winter Sketch. Arthur S. Bourinot. CaP
Winter Piece, A. Bryant. AmPP; AP; OxBA
Winter-Piece, A. Ambrose Philips. NOEC; OBEC; SeCePo
(To the Earl of Dorset.) LoBV
Winter-Piece to a Friend Away, A. John Berryman. NOBA
Winter Ploughing. William Everson. NU
Winter Poem. Nikki Giovanni. PAI
Winter Pond. Ben Belitt. NYBP
Winter Portrait. Robert Southey. BoNaP
Winter pulls the body inward. In the Van Gogh Room. Traise Yamamoto. BrSi
Winter Rain. Christina Rossetti. BoNaP; WiR
Winter rain at night. Haiku. Richard Wright. FAZ
Winter Rains: Cataluña. Philip Levine. NaP
Winter Remembered. John Crowe Ransom. AP; HAP; MoAB; NOBA; OxBA; PrIm; UnPo; VGW
Winter Report. Ben Howard. PoA
Winter Rune. Elizabeth J. Coatsworth. SUS
Winter Saint. A. R. Ammons. TW
Winter Scene. William Cowper. *Fr.* The Task, VI. *See* Winter Walk at Noon, A.
Winter Scene, A. James Thomson. *Fr.* The Seasons: Winter. OBEC
Winter Scene, A. Reed Whittemore. NCSH
Winter Scene. Marguerite Young. NU; WPE
Winter Shore, The. Thomas Wade. NBM; OAEL-2
Winter Sign. Loren Eiseley. SUW
Winter Sketch. Arthur S. Bourinot. CaP
Winter Sketches. Charles Reznikoff. PoA
Winter-sky began to frown, The. Stella at Wood-Park. Swift. BIrV
Winter Sleep. Edith M. Thomas. AA
Winter Sleep. Elinor Wylie. NePA
Winter-Solitude. Archibald Lampman. PeCV
Winter Solstice—for Frank. Asphodel. BrRo
Winter Solstice Poem. Diana Scott. BrRo
Winter Song. David Daiches. NYBP
Winter Song. Juan Ramón Jiménez, *tr. fr. Spanish by* H. R. Hays. WSC
Winter Song. Elizabeth Tollet. NOEC
Winter Stars. Larry Levis. DiL; MAYP
Winter Storm at Sea, The. George Crabbe. *Fr.* The Borough, Letter I. EtS
Winter Streams. Bliss Carman. YeAr
Winter sunlight in Assisi, and the birds tilting. Soaping Down for Saint Francis of Assisi: The Canticle of Sister Soap. Gibbons Ruark. MAYP
Winter Sunrise, *sel.* Laurence Binyon.
"It is early morning within this room; without." ChMP
Winter Sunset. Jules Laforgue, *tr. fr. French by* Kate Flores. SyP
Winter Talent, A. Donald Davie. NePoEA-2; OAEL-2
Winter Term. John Malcolm Brinnin. GLGT
Winter, that coils in the thickets now. Deciduous Branch. Stanley Kunitz. TwAmPo
Winter, thy cruelty extend. Song on a Young Lady who Sung Finely. Wentworth Dillon, Earl of Roscommon. CavP
Winter Time. *See* Wintertime.
Winter Trees. Conrad Diekmann. LiSp
Winter Trees. Sylvia Plath. LCAP; NMM; SBG
Winter Trout. James Dickey. LiSp
Winter Tryst. Mark Van Doren. LiTA
Winter Tuesday, the city pouring fire, A. Coming Home, Detroit, 1968. Philip Levine. TAT
Winter Twilight, A. Arlo Bates. AA
Winter Twilight. George Tracy Elliot. AA
Winter Twilight, A. Angelina Weld Grimké. CDC; PoBA; PoNe
Winter Twilight. Jeff Schiff. AMV-81
Winter Twilight, Glowing Black and Gold, The. Delmore Schwartz. NoAM
Winter uses all the blues there are. Blue Winter. Robert Francis. LCAP
Winter Verse for My [*or* His] Sister. William Meredith. NYBP; TAP
Winter Views Serene. George Crabbe. *Fr.* The Borough. OBNC
Winter [*or* Wynter] Wakeneth All [*or* Al] My Care. *Unknown.* HAP; SeCePo
(This World's Joy.) OBEV
(Winter Wakens All My Care.) HAP, *mod. English*; OxBM
(Wynter Wakeneth.) OxBoCh
Winter Walk at Noon, The. William Cowper. The Task, VI.
Sels.
"Night was winter in his roughest mood, The." EnRP; TEP
(Winter Scene.) OBEC
"No noise is here, or none that hinders thought." BoAnP; PBBP

Winter Warfare. Edgell Rickword. OBWP; OxBTC
Winter Watch. Jeff Daniel Marion. AMV-80
Winter will bar the swimmer soon. Swimming Chenango Lake. Charles Tomlinson. FaBoMo; NoAM
Winter will be feasts and fires in the shut houses. Fall in Corrales. Richard Wilbur. CoPo
Winter Will Follow. Richard Watson Dixon. *See* Heaving Roses of the Hedge Are Stirred, The.
Winter will not let go of earth. In Defense of Felons. Robert Mezey. NePoEA
Winter Winds Cold and Blea. John Clare. GBL
 ("Winter winds blow cold and blea.") OBNC
Winter winds howled and the great barn creaked. The Barn in Winter. Claire Harris MacIntosh. CaP
Winter Wish, A. Robert Hinckley Messinger. AA; ViBoPo
 (Give Me the Old.) HBV-2
Winter with the Gulf Stream. Gerard Manley Hopkins. CMoP; NoAM; SyP; VLP
Winter without Snow, A. J. D. McClatchy. FYAP
Wintered Sunflowers. Richard Snyder. PPJ
Winterfall. *Unknown. See* Merry It Is.
Wintering. Sylvia Plath. NMM
Wintering Moon, A. R. Wayne Hardy. LFAC
Winter's a finger under the wool, spreading. Weekend Sonnets. Cilla McQueen. OCNZ
Winters at home brought wind. Once in a Lifetime, Snow. Les A. Murray. CBAP
Winters close, Springs open, no child stirs, The. John Berryman. *Fr.* Homage to Mistress Bradstreet. NAs; NoAM
Winter's Cold. W. R. Rodgers. EnLoPo
Winter's coming on, The. Sanctuary. Dorothy Hewett. CBAP
Winter's Dregs. George Bowering. PeCV
Winter's Edge. P. R. Roberts. SOTS
Winter's End. Howard Moss. NePoEA
Winter's Frosty Pangs. Henry Vaughan. *Fr.* To His Retired Friend, an Invitation to Brecknock. FaBoRV
Winter's Onset from an Alienated Point of View. Alan Dugan. FF
Winter's Song: "When Isicles hang by the wall." Shakespeare. *See* When Icicles Hang by the Wall.
Winter's Tale, A. Robert Patrick Dana. NYBP
Winter's Tale, A. D. H. Lawrence. MoAB; MoBrPo
Winter's Tale, The, *sels.* Shakespeare.
 Flowers of Perdita, The, *fr.* IV, iii. FiP
  (Flowers of Middle Summer, *shorter sel.*) YeAr
  ("Here's flowers for you.") GBL
  Perdita's Garden. WHA
  Some Flowers o' the Spring. ChTr
   ("I would I had some flowers o' the spring that might.") PoPle
 "Jog on, jog on, the footpath way," *fr.* IV, ii. FaBoCh; GN; HBV-2; HBVY; ViBoPo
  (Autolycus's Song.) OBSC; SpRo; WhC
  (Merry Heart, A.) ElL; TrGrPo
 "Lawn as white as driven snow," *fr.* IV, iii. OAEP; ViBoPo
  (Autolycus as Peddler.) OAEL-1
  (Autolycus's Song.) LoBV; OBSC
  (Come Buy! Come Buy!) ElL
  (Pedlar, The.) WiR
  (Pedlar's Song, The.) CH
 "When daffodils begin to peer," *fr.* IV, ii. ChTr; ElL; FaBoBe; FaBoCh; HBV-1; LoBV; NoP; PoPle; PrIm; UnTE; ViBoPo; WhC
  (Autolycus Sings.) NOBE
  (Autolycus's Song.) FaBoEn; OAEL-1; OBSC
  (Pedlar's Song, The.) OxBoLi
  (Song: "When daffodils begin to peer.") FiP; PoEL-2
 "Will you buy any tape," *fr.* IV, iii. ViBoPo
  (Autolycus's Song.) OBSC
Winter's Tale, A. Dylan Thomas. CMoP; LiTB; SeCeV
Winter's Troops. Charles Cotton. *Fr.* Winter. ChTr
Winterscape. Jess Perlman. AMV-80
Winterset, *sel.* Maxwell Anderson.
 In All These Turning Lights I Find No Clue. TreFT
Winter Time [*or* Winter-Time]. Robert Louis Stevenson. EBVV; MoBrPo; OxBChV
Winter time is bleak, the wind. Caoilte. *Unknown, tr. by* Frank O'Connor. KiLC
Winter time is coming. Cold Wave Blues. *Unknown.* BluL
Wintertime nighs. In Tenebris, I. Thomas Hardy. FaBoEn; LiTB; NOBE; NoP; OAEL-2; OAEP; PrIm; SeCePo; TreFS
Wintry blast goes wailing by, A. Christmas Night of '62. William Gordon McCabe. AA
Wintry west extends his blast, The. Winter; a Dirge. Burns. HBV-1; LAuP
Wintry winds have ceased to blow, The. Resurrection. George Crabbe. OxBoCh
Winwick, Lancashire. *Unknown.* GBP
Wire Monkey. Paul D. Shiplett. LFAC
Wires. Lee Bassett. SOTS
Wires strung with diamonds. Snowfall. "I. V. S. W." InMe
Wisdom, *sel.* Bible, Apocrypha.
 "For she is a vapour," VII: 25-26, *Douay vers.* ISi
Wisdom. Padraic Fallon. OnYI
Wisdom. Ford Madox Ford. HBV-1
Wisdom. Phyllis Hanson. GoYe
Wisdom. Langston Hughes. TiPo
Wisdom. Scudder Middleton. HBMV
Wisdom. Linda Peavy. PH
Wisdom. Christina Rossetti. OBVV
Wisdom. Hy Sobiloff. VGW
Wisdom. Sara Teasdale. MoAmPo
Wisdom. W. B. Yeats. TrCP
Wisdom. Frank Yerby. AmNP
Wisdom and Spirit of the universe! Influence of Natural Objects [*or* Boyhood]. Wordsworth. *Fr.* The Prelude, I. AWP; LoBV; NOBE; OBRV; WHA
Wisdom found no place where she might dwell. Wisdom's Plight. Bible, Pseudepigrapha. *Fr.* Enoch. TrJP
Wisdom has nothing to do with age. Wisdom. Hy Sobiloff. VGW
Wisdom hath builded her house. The House of Wisdom. Bible, *O.T. Fr.* Proverbs. TrGrPo
Wisdom is better than bread. Nevertheless. Gustav Davidson. GoYe
Wisdom is the finest beauty of a person. *Yoruba Oral Tradition, tr. by* Ulli Beier. WTO
Wisdom of Folly, The. Ellen Thorneycroft Fowler. HBV-2
Wisdom of Insecurity, The. Richard Eberhart. NePA
Wisdom of Merlyn, The, *sels.* Wilfrid Scawen Blunt.
 "What then is Merlyn's message, his word to thee weary of pain." ViBoPo
 "Wouldst thou be wise, O Man? At the knees of a woman begin." OBMV
Wisdom of Old Jelly Roll, The. A. J. M. Smith. PeCV
Wisdom of the Gazelle. George P. Solomos. GoYe
Wisdom of the World, The. Siegfried Sassoon. MoBrPo
Wisdom of the world said unto me, The. Sapientia Lunae. Ernest Dowson. HBV-2
Wisdom, out of Anguish by Denial. Pedigree. Mary Mills. NePoAm
Wisdom with better thoughts prevailed; aloof. The Jew's Home. Robert Eyres Landor. *Fr.* The Impious Feast. OBRV
Wisdom's Plight. Bible, Pseudepigrapha. Enoch, XLII: 1-3. TrJP
Wise, The. Countee Cullen. PoNe
Wise. Lizette Woodworth Reese. HBV-2
Wise and Foolish Virgins, The. Bible, *N.T.* St. Matthew, XXV: 1-13. TreF
Wise emblem of our politic [*or* politick] world. The Snail [*or* Snayl]. Richard Lovelace. CaPo; OAEL-1; PoEL-3
Wise Empty Landscape with a Death in the Foreground. N. Scott Momaday. CDW
Wise fish digs his silver in, The. Night Catch. Heather McHugh. AmPA
Wise guys, The. Kid Stuff. Frank Horne. AmNP; PChr; PoBA; PoNe
Wise Johnny. Edwina Fallis. SiSoSe; SUS; TiPo
Wise king dowered with blessings on his throne, The. The Trophy. Edwin Muir. LiTM
Wise man holds himself in check, A. Wisdom. Scudder Middleton. HBMV
Wise Men, The. Edgar Bowers. NePoEA
Wise Men and Shepherds. Sidney Godolphin. *See* Hymn: "Lord, when the wise men came from far."
Wise Men Ask the Children the Way, The. Heine, *tr. fr. German by* Geoffrey Grigson. OBCP
 (Kings from the East, The.) ChTr; GoTS, *tr. into Scottish by* Alexander Gray
Wise men come here to shit. From a Lavatory Wall. *Unknown.* FaBoEE
Wise Men of Gotham, The. Thomas Love Peacock. *See* Three Men of Gotham.
Wisemen to glossators unknown. Apocryphal Apocalypse. John Wheelwright. MoVE
Wise old apple tree in spring, The. A Pastoral. Robert Hillyer. BoNaP
Wise Old Owl, A. Edward Hersey Richards. BLPA; FaBoBe; FaFP; OxNR; TreF; YaD
Wise Rochefoucault a maxim writ. Swift. *Fr.* The life and Genuine Character of Dean Swift. NOBL
Wise to have gone so early to reward. The Wazir Dandan for Prince Sharkan. *Unknown, tr. by* E. Powys Mathers. *Fr.* The Thousand and One Nights. AWP
Wise Woman, The. Louis Untermeyer. HBMV
Wisely and well was it said of him. Addition to Kipling's "The Dead King (Edward VII), 1910." Max Beerbohm. FaBoEE

Wisemen. *See* Wise men.
Wiser than the Children of Light. Monk Gibbon. NeIP
Wisest of sparrows that sparrow which sitteth alone. Wisdom. Christina Rossetti. OBVV
Wisest of the wise, The. The One White Hair. Walter Savage Landor. HBV-1
Wisest scholar of the wight most wise, The. Astrophel and Stella, XXV. Sir Philip Sidney. NoP; OAEL-1; SiPS
Wisga. Lew Blockcolski. VoR
Wish, A. Matthew Arnold. DBV; HBV-2
Wish, The. Abraham Cowley. *Fr.* The Mistress. CavP; HBV-1; LiTB; NOBE; NoP; OAEP; OBEV; OBS; SeCV-1; TrGrPo; ViBoPo; WHA
Wish, A. Hamlin Garland. AA
Wish. Lance Henson. CDW
Wish, A. Fanny Kemble. WPE
Wish, A. Laurence Lerner. FF; OxBTC
Wish, A. Samuel Rogers. FaPoR; GTBS; GTBS-P; HBV-1; NOBE; OBEC; OBEV; OBVV; TreFS
Wish, The. Thomas Stanley, *after the Greek of* Anacreon. AWP
Wish, A. J. M. Synge. FaBoEE
Wish, The. Rowland Watkyns. CavP
Wish for a Young Wife. Theodore Roethke. NoAM; NoP; TAP
Wish for the New Year, A. Phillips Brooks. STF
Wish for Waving Goodbye, A. Roberta Hill. AMV-80
Wish I was in Bowling Green sittin' in a chair. Bowling Green. *Unknown.* FSW
Wish I was in London. Handsome Molly. FSW
Wish I was in Tennessee. Tennessee. *Unknown.* AmFP
Wish of Manchin of Liath, The. *Unknown, tr. fr. Old Irish by* Kenneth Jackson. AnIL
(Hermit's Song, A [*or* The].) BIrV, *tr. by* James Simmons; KiLC, *tr. by* Frank O'Connor; OnYI, *tr. by* Kuno Meyer
Wish, that of the living whole, The. In Memoriam A. H. H., LV. Tennyson. EBVV; HAP; HBV-2; LoBV; OBNC; PAI; SeCeV
"Wish to Be Believed, The." Mona Van Duyn. PoA
Wished Sunday's come: mirth brightens ev'ry face. White Conduit House. William Woty. NOEC
Wished to have been milk. Story. Dennis Saleh. NeAC
Wishes. Norman Ault. HBMV; HBVY
Wishes. Patty L. Harjo. VoR
Wishes. Robert Louis Stevenson. *See* Envoy: "Go little book and wish to all."
Wishes for Her. Denis Devlin. CIP
Wishes for My Son. Thomas MacDonagh. AnIV; GoBC; HBMV
Wishes for William. Winifred M. Letts. OnYI
Wishes of an Elderly Man. Sir Walter Alexander Raleigh. DBV; FaBoCh; FaBoCo; FaBoEE; FiBHP; FPL; NOBL; PV; WhC
("I wish I loved the human race.") CenHV
Wishes to His (Supposed) Mistress [*or* Mistresse]. Richard Crashaw. BoLoP; EBEV; HBV-1; MeLP; MePo; OAEP; OBEV; OBS; PoEL-2; SeCP; SeCV-1; TreFT; WHA
(Wishes for the Supposed Mistress.) GoBC; GTBS; GTBS-P
"Whoe'er she be./ That not impossible she," *sel.* ViBoPo
Wishful to add to my mental power. Ballade of Schopenhauer's Philosophy. Franklin P. Adams. HBMV
Wishin' Well, The. Helen B. Cruickshank. BSV
Wishing. William Allingham. FaPON; HBV-1; HBVY; OHIP; OxBChV
Wishing Africa. Marilyn Bowering. NOBC
Wishing for roses, I walk through the garden. Summer Garden. "Anna Akhmatova," *tr. by* Stephen Stepanchev BoWoP
Wishing My Death. *Unknown.* MeEL
Wishing Poem. *Unknown.* *See* Star Wish.
Wishmakers' Town, *sels.* William Young.
Bells, The. AA
Bridal Pair, The. AA
Conscience-Keeper, The. AA
Flower-Seller, The. AA
Losers, The. HBMV
Pawns, The. AA
Wisp of slight sound, an echo of an echo, A. The Monkish Mind of the Speculative Physicist. Bin Ramke. SUW
Wispy cuttings lie in rows, The. July in Indiana. Robert Fitzgerald. NYBP
Wisselton, wasselton, who lives here? Wassailing Song. *Unknown.* OBCP
Wistful,/ they speak of. The People. Robert Creeley. VGW
Wistful Days, The. Robert Underwood Johnson. AA
Wit, The. Elizabeth Bishop. NePoAm-2
Wit, Whither Wilt Thou? *Unknown.* ElL
Wit Wonders. *Unknown.* *See* God and Yet a Man, A?
Witch, A. William Barnes. VLP
Witch. Patricia Beer. OxBC
Witch, The. Mary Elizabeth Coleridge. BrRo; NCEP; WPE
Witch, The. Lord Alfred Douglas. HBMV
Witch, The. W. W. Gibson. *Fr.* Skye. PoSH
Witch, The. Katharine Tynan. OnYI
Witch, The, *sel.* Thomas Middleton.
"Black spirits and white, red spirits and gray," V, i. WSC
Witch, The. Robert Southey. *See* Old Woman of Berkeley, The.
Witch. Jean Tepperman. NMM
Witch, The. W. B. Yeats. ELU
Witch Cat. Rowena Bennett. SiSoSe
Witch Doctor. Robert Hayden. AmNP; MAT; NoAM; PAI
Witch-elms that counterchange the floor. In Memoriam A. H. H., LXXXIX. Tennyson. EBVV; OBNC
Witch Going Down to Egypt, A. Raquel Chalfi, *tr. fr. Hebrew by* Alexandra Meiri *and* Myra Glazer Schotz. VWA
Witch Hazel. Theodore Enslin. CoPo
Witch in the Glass, The. Sarah Morgan Bryan Piatt. AA
Witch o' Fife, The. James Hogg. BSV
Witch of Atlas, The, *sel.* Shelley.
"And whilst the outer lake beneath the lash." PBBP
Witch of Coös, The. Robert Frost. *Fr.* Two Witches. AP; CoBMV; LiTM; MoAB; NePA; NoAM; NOBA; SeCeV; ViBoPo
Witch of East Seventy-second Street, The. Morris Bishop. NYBP; NYP
Witch that came, The (the withered hag). Provide, Provide. Robert Frost. AmPP; CABA; CMoP; HAP; InPK; MoAB; MP; NIP; NoAM; NOBA; NoP; PPP; TAP; TwCP; UnPo; WeW
Witch, The! The Witch! Eleanor Farjeon. RHPC
Witchcraft by a Picture. John Donne. EyDe
Witchcraft: New Style. Lascelles Abercrombie. MoBrPo
Witchcraft was hung, in history. Emily Dickinson. WSC
Witches. Ted Hughes. GoYe
Witches, The. *Unknown.* *See* Hey-How for Hallowe'en.
Witches and poets co-embrace like fate. Fatales Poetae. Henry Parrot. FaBoEE
Witches' Ballad, The. William Bell Scott. *See* Witch's Ballad, The.
Witches' Charms, The. Ben Jonson. *Fr.* The Masque of Queens. ElL
(Witches' Sabbath, The.) WSC
Sels.
Song: "Owl is abroad, The." PoPle
Witches' Charm. FaBoCh; LoBV; NOBE, *abr.*
(Charme.) FM
Witches' Menu. Sonja Nikolay. RHPC
Witches' Ride, The. Karla Kuskin. PDV
Witches' Sabbath, The. Ben Jonson. *See*Witches' Charms, The.
Witches' Song, The. Ben Jonson. CH
Witches' Spells. Madeleine Edmondson. NTCP
Witches' Wood, The. Mary Elizabeth Coleridge. PBWP
Witching Song, A. James Thomson. *Fr.* The Castle of Indolence. OBEC
Witching Time of Night, The. Shakespeare. *Fr.* Hamlet, III, ii. TreFT
Witch's [*or* Witches] Ballad, The. William Bell Scott. CH; EvOK; NBM; OBEV; OBVV; VLP
Witch's Broomstick Spell, The. *Unknown.* ChTr; GBP
Witch's Cat, The. Ian Serraillier. SO; WSC
Witch's Chant, A. James Hogg. BSV
Witch's Spell, A. *Unknown.* ChTr
(Witch's Milking Charm.) GBP
Witch's Whelp, The. Richard Henry Stoddard. AA
Witch's Work Song, The. T. H. White. FaBoNo
Witchwood. May Justus. SiSoSe
With/Tattered grey fishnet eyes. Just an Old Man. Mary Goose. STE
With a Book at Twilight. Jakov Steinberg, *tr. fr. Hebrew by* Mark Elliott Shapiro. VWA
With a Bottle of Blue Nun to All My Friends. Madeline DeFrees. GP
With a China Chamberpot, to the Countess of Hillsborough. Lord Holland. FaBoUs
With a Coin from Syracuse. Oliver St. John Gogarty. OBMV
With a conscience we're able to see. The Conscience. Anthony Euwer. *Fr.* The Limeratomy. HBMV
With a Copy of Swift's Works. J. V. Cunningham. QFR
With a crossbow, late, in hand ready bent. Of a Daw. John Heywood. PBBP
With a cry of fear. Hidden Bow. Mordecai Temkin, *tr. by* Jeremy Garber. VWA
With a Daisy. Emily Dickinson. *See* Science, A—so the savants say.
With a First Reader. Rupert Hughes. HBMV
With a flick of her small wrist. With Cindy at Vallecito. Walter McDonald. WOLT
With a fork drive Nature out. Marigolds. Robert Graves. BrPo
With a garland[e] of thornes kene. The Seven Sins [*or* Christ Complains to Sinners]. *Unknown.* MeEL; OxBM
With a Gift of Rings. Robert Graves. GBL
With a great working of elbows. Wedding. George Mackay Brown. BSV

With a Guitar, to Jane. Shelley. EnRP; HBV-2; OAEL-2
(To a Lady, with a Guitar.) GTBS; GTBS-P
With a gull's beak I cry. The Bright Hillside. Rhoda Coghill. NeIP; OxBI
With a handful of weeds I weep in the slanting sun. Boudoir Lament. Yü Hsüan-chi, *tr. by* Geoffrey Waters. BoWoP
With a lantern that wouldn't burn. The Draft Horse. Robert Frost. CMoP; HeIP; HoPM; PAI
With a Lifting of the Head. "Hugh MacDiarmid." MoBrPo
With a Little Bit of Luck. Alan Jay Lerner. FaFP
With a love a madness for Shelley. I Am 25. Gregory Corso. CoPo
With a Nantucket Shell. Charles Henry Webb. AA
With a pert moustache and a ready candid smile. The Mixer. Louis MacNeice. FaBoTw
With a pick and with a shovel, and with a hoe. Words for Army Bugle Calls: Fatigue Call. *Unknown.* TreF
With a Posthumous Medal. John Malcolm Brinnin. SaC
With a Rod No Man Alive. Walther von der Vogelweide, *tr. fr. German by* Jethro Bithell. AWP
With a Rose from Conway Castle. Julia Caroline Ripley Dorr. AA
With a sadnes curtained. The Maiden. Rochelle Ratner. PCP
With a Sliver of Marble from Carrara. James Wright. EyDe
With a spoon. The King of Harlem. Federico García Lorca, *tr. by* Ben Belitt. NYP
With a Spray of Apple Blossoms. Walter Learned. AA
With a stronger wind. True Night. René Char, *tr. by* Jackson Mathews. PoPl
With a wall and a ditch between us, I watched the gate-legged dromedary. The Fruit of the Tree. David Wagoner. NYBP
With a whirl of thought oppressed. The Day of Judgement [*or* On the World]. Swift. AnIV; BIrV; FaBoEn; FaBoRV; NOBE; NOEC; OAEL-1; OBSV; PPP. *See also* Once, with a whirl of thought oppressed.
With all a woman's virtues but the pox. Pope. *Fr.* The Second Satire of the First Book of Horace Imitated. OBSV
With All Deliberate Speed. Don L. Lee. JB
With all its sinful doings, I must say. Italy [*or* Italy versus England]. Byron. *Fr.* Beppo. NOBE; OBRV; SeCePo
With all my heart, in truth, and passion strong. The Pride of a Jew. Judah Halevi, *tr. by* Israel Cohen. TrJP
With All My Heart, Jehovah, I'll Confess, *with music.* Henry Ainsworth. AH
With all my will, but much against my heart. A Farewell. Coventry Patmore. *Fr.* The Unknown Eros. ACP; BoLoP; EnLoPo; FaBoEn; GTBS-P; HBV-2; NOBE; OBEV; OBNC; OBVV; PoEL;-5; TrGrPo
With all the drifting race of men. Léonie Adams. *Fr.* April Mortality. TrGrPo
With all the heart in my body. Now Jentil Belly Down. *Unknown.* GBP
With all the powres my poor heart hath. The Hymn of Saint Thomas in Adoration of the Blessed Sacrament [*or* Hymn in Adoration of the Blessed Sacrament]. Richard Crashaw. MeLP; OBS
With all these loads of injuries opprest. Dryden. *Fr.* Absalom and Achitophel, Pt. I. EBEV
With an effort Grant swung the great block. Blocking the Pass. Charles Madge. FaBoMo
With an honest old friend and a merry old song. Harry Carey's General Reply, to the Libelling Gentry, Who Are Angry at His Welfare. Henry Carey. HBV-2
With an insane. Learning. Earl Simpson. GrPl
With Annie gone. For Anne. Leonard Cohen. ELU; FF; PoCh
With banked fire to mark the occasion. Family Evening. Dan Huws. NYBP
With banners and our smiles. Christopher Street Liberation Day, June 28, 1970. Fran Winant. PeHV
With banners furled, the clarions mute. The Night-March. Herman Melville. LiTA
With bent back, world's curve on it. Tom on the Beach. George Bruce. BSV
With blackest moss the flower-plots [-pots, *wr.*]. Mariana. Tennyson. AWP; BiP; CH; ChER; HBV-1; InPS; NOBE; NoP; OAEL-2; OAEP; OBEV; OBNC; OBRV; OBVV; PoEL-5; PoPle; TEP; TrGrPo; UnPo; ViBoPo; VLP; WiR
With blameless carriage I lived here. An Epitaph upon a Sober Matron. Robert Herrick. CaPo
With breath of thyme and bees that hum. To a Greek Girl. Austin Dobson. HBV-1
With Buck still tied to the log, on comes the light. Double Feature. Theodore Roethke. DFF
With buds embalmed alive in ice. A Mile from Eden. Anne Ridler. MoPo
With burning fervour. The Crystal. George Barker. LiTM; OBMV
With camel's hair I clothed my skin. Dream. Richard Watson Dixon. EBEV; LoBV; VLP
With candour I confess my love. Ezra Pound *and* Noel Stock, *fr. Egyptian hieroglyphics.* BoWoP
With careful tread, through dim green-pillared halls. Beetle Bemused. R. P. Lister. PV
With cassock black, baret and book. Grace Fallow Norton. Little Gray Songs from St. Joseph's, XXX. HBV-2
With caverned bole and twisted limb they bide. Olive Trees. Padraic Colum. NePoAm
With Child. Genevieve Taggard. MoAmPo
With Christ and All His Shining Train, *with music.* Thomas Prince. AH
With cicada's nymphal skin. The Largess. Richard Eberhart. LiTA
With Cindy at Vallecito. Walter McDonald. WOLT
With coat like any mole's, as soft and black. Mole Catcher. Edmund Blunden. OBMV
With conscience cocked to listen for the thunder. Luther. W. H. Auden. PAI
With Corse at Allatoona. Samuel H. M. Byers. PAH
With Cortez in Mexico. W. W. Campbell. PAH
With courage seek the kingdom of the dead. The Last Journey. Leonidas of Tarentum, *tr. by* Charles Merivale. AWP
With crafty brooding life turned to Jack Rose. Jack Rose. Maxwell Bodenheim. HBMV
With crayons and pieces of paper, I entered the empty room. The Room. Gregory Orr. GeTw
With crowbars and drag chains. Wrestling Angels. David Bottoms. MAYP
With death doomed to grapple. Epitaph for William Pitt [*or* Epigram]. Byron. FaBoEE; HBV-1
With deathlace tickling my throat. Death-Lace. David Ray. MAT
With deep affection/ And recollection. The Shandon Bells [*or* The Bells of Shandon]. Francis Sylvester Mahony. ACP; AnIV; CH; ChTr; GoBC; HBV-2; OBEV; OBRV; OBVV; OnYI; RoGo; TreFS
With deep snow. Cardinal. Barbara Howes. DFF
With delicate, mad hands, behind his sordid bars. To One in Bedlam. Ernest Dowson. ACP; BrPo; MoBrPo; OBMV; VLP; WHA
With difficulty the ship was built. The Critics. Theodore Spencer. NYBP
With dirty collar and shoes unpolished. Anarchist. Anthony Cronin. CIP
With Donne, whose muse on dromedary trots. On Donne's Poetry. Samuel Taylor Coleridge. CABA; InvP; NoP; OAEL-2; OAEP; PAI; PP; SeCePo
With doubt and dismay you are smitten. Opportunity. Berton Braley. WBLP
With drooping sail and pennant. The White Ships and the Red. Joyce Kilmer. PAH
With Due Deference to Thomas Wolfe. Joanne Townsend. AMV-81
With earliest spring, while yet in mountain cleughs. James Grahame. *Fr.* The Birds of Scotland. PBBP
With echoing step[s] the worshippers. Give Me Thy Heart. Adelaide Anne Procter. ACP; GoBC
With elbow buried in the downy pillow. Clarimonde. Théophile Gautier, *tr. by* Lafcadio Hearn. AWP
With Esther. Wilfrid Scawen Blunt. OBEV; OBVV
("He who has once been happy is for aye.") OBMV; OBNC; TrGrPo; ViBoPo
With every blow of the wind. My Soul Hovers over Me. Joshua Tan Pai, *tr. by* Yishai Tobin. VWA
With every movement, the soft particles. The Dusting of the Books. Dorothy Hughes. GoYe
With every note/ of the mountain temple. *Unknown, tr. fr. Japanese by* Willis Barnstone. BoWoP
With Every Rising of the Sun. Ella Wheeler Wilcox. TreFT
With every rolling stone place me in the breach. Place Me in the Breach. Yehuda Karni, *tr. by* Sholom J. Kahn. TrJP
With every soft gush of my feet. After Picking Rosehips. Harley Elliott. NeAC
With eyes a dying candle. The Aunt. Daniel Berrigan. TwAmPo
With Eyes at the Back of Our Heads. Denise Levertov. AmPP
With eyes hand-arched he looks into. Comradery. Madison Cawein. AA
With eyes like embers of an extraterrestrial civilization. Newborn Baby. Miroslav Holub, *tr. by* Stuart Friebert *and* Dana Hábová. SUW
With fair Ceres, Queen of Grain. Praise of Ceres. Thomas Heywood. *Fr.* The Silver Age. EIL
With fairest flowers,/ Whilst summer lasts. Shakespeare. *Fr.* Cymbeline, IV, ii. EBEV
With faith I trust in Christ the Lord. Mrs. Saunder's Experience. *Unknown.* AmFP
With favoring winds, o'er sunlit seas. Ultima Thule. Longfellow. MOS; ViBoPo
With favour and fortune fastidiously blest. Swift. FaBoEE
With Fifteen-ninety or Sixteen-sixteen. On an Anniversary. J. M. Synge. FaBoEE; OBMV; POL
With fingers weary and worn. The Song of the Shirt. Thomas Hood.

EBVV; EnRP; FaPoR; HBV-2; OBVV; PaPo; PPON, *abr.*; SaC; TEP; TreF; VLP; WBLP
With fires and lights we ward the winter off. Autumn Poem. Anthony Cronin. CIP
With fish, which always is served first. Red Wine. Justin Richardson. PV
With flintlocked guns and polished stocks. In Hardin County, 1809. Lulu E. Thompson. PoSC
With floods and storms thus we be tossed. God Our Help. *Unknown.* OxBoCh
With Flowers. Emily Dickinson. *See* If recollecting were forgetting.
With flowing tail, and flying mane. The Wild, the Free. Byron. RHPC
With focus sharp as Flemish-painted face. The [*or* A] Dome of Sunday. Karl Shapiro. AP; CMoP; CoAP; CoBMV; LiTM; MoAB; MoAmPo; MoPo; NePA; NoAM; OxBA; WaP
With fore-cloth smoothed by careful hands. Allah's Tent. Arthur Colton. HBV-2
With Fragrant Flowers We Strew the Way. Thomas Watson. *Fr.* The Honourable Entertainment Given to the Queen's Majesty in Progress at Elvetham, 1591. ElL
(Ditty of the Six Virgins, The.) OBSC
With Francis Furini. Robert Browning. *Fr.* Parleyings with Certain People of Importance in Their Day. VLP
With Freedom's Seed. Pushkin, *tr. fr. Russian by* Babette Deutsch. TTY
With frost again the thought is clear and wise. Frost. John Hewitt. NeIP
With ganial foire. The Crystal Palace. Thackeray. InMe
With Garments Flowing. John Clare. GBL
With gentle step I came at last. Afterward. Mary Matheson. CaP
With gentleness/ his eyes filmed. Monument. Milton Acorn. NeAC
With God and His Mercy, *with music.* Carl Olof Rosenius. AH
With God Conversing. Gene Derwood. LiTA; LiTM; NePA
With great good cheer the bells ring out. Bells of the New Year. Arthur Gordon Field. PGD
With grief and mourning I sit and spin. The Girl's Lamentation, *sl. abr.* William Allingham. SeCePo
With hairs, which for the wind to play with, hung. On Lydia Distracted. Philip Ayres. EnLoPo
With half a heart I wander here. In the States. Robert Louis Stevenson. BrPo
With half a hundred sudden loops and coils. The Hurrying Brook. Edmund Blunden. BoNaP
With half the Western world at stake. Sea and Land Victories. *Unknown.* PAH
With hands and faces nicely washed. Clever Peter and the Ogress. Katherine Pyle. OBCA
With Hands Like Leaves. James Still. GrPl
With hands tight clenched through matted hair. The Three Voices. "Lewis Carroll." BXAP
With Happiness Stretch[e]d across the Hills. Blake. EnRP; NoP
With hay, with how, with hoy! My Twelve Oxen. *Unknown.* OxBM
With heart at rest I climbed the citadel's. Epilogue. Baudelaire, *tr. by* Arthur Symons. AWP
With hearts of poor men it is so. The Poor. Emile Verhaeren, *tr. by* Ludwig Lewisohn AWP
With hearts responsive. John Oxenham. *Fr.* A Little Te Deum of the Commonplace. TrPWD
With hearts revived in conceit, new land and trees they eye. *At. to* Edward Johnson. *Fr.* Good News from New England. GOA
With heavy groans did I approach my friends. Wine and Grief. Solomon ibn Gabirol, *tr. by* Emma Lazarus. TrJP
With her eyes closed. Sabbath. David Rosenmann-Taub, *tr. by* Charles Guenther. VWA
With her voice. Hanabi-ko (Koko). Wendy Rose. TWSS
With Him. Julia E. Martin. STF
With him ther was his sone, a young Squyer. Chaucer. *Fr.* The Canterbury Tales: Prologue. TrGrPo
With him there was his son, a youthful Squire. Chaucer, *mod. vers. by* Louis Untermeyer. *Fr.* The Canterbury Tales: Prologue. TrGrPo
With his hat on the table before him. In January, 1962. Ted Kooser. Psk
With his kinde mother who partakes thy woe. Temple. John Donne. AnAnS-1; OBS
With his tusk-like fierce moustaches and double-pointed beard. A Bully. *Malay Oral Tradition, tr. by* R. J. Wilkinson. WTO
With his two-fist sword, enscintillant, he cut an apple down. The Uncouth Knight. Hugh McCrae. PoAu-1
With his unspent youth. Bargain. Louise Driscoll. HBMV
With his work, as with a glove, a man feels the universe. Open and Closed Space. Tomas Tranströmer, *tr. by* Robert Bly. EAS
With honeysuckle, over-sweet, festoon'd [*or* festooned]. Arbor Vitae. Coventry Patmore. The Unknown Eros, II, iii. GoBC; LoBV; NBM; OBNC; SeCePo; VLP
With Hopeless Love. Moses ibn Ezra, *tr. fr. Hebrew by* Solomon Solis-Cohen. TrJP
With horns and [with] hounds, I waken the day. Diana's Hunting-Song. Dryden. *Fr.* The Secular Masque. NOBE; SeCePo
With how! fox, how! With hay! fox, hay! The False Fox. *Unknown.* OxBM
With How Sad Steps, O Moon, Thou Climb'st the Skies. Sir Philip Sidney. Astrophel and Stella, XXXI. AWP; BoLoP; CH; ChTr; ElL; EnLoPo; EnRePo; FaBoEn; GBL; HAP; HBV-1; HeIP; InPK; InPS; InvP; MAT; MOON; NoP; OAEP; OBSC; PoEL-1; PoRA; PPoe; PPP; SeCeV; SiPS; TEP; TrGrPo; ViBoPo; WeW; WHA
(His Lady's Cruelty.) OBEV
(Languishing Moon, The.) BoNaP
(Moon, The.) LoBV
(To the Sad Moon.) NOBE
With hym ther rood a gentil Pardoner. Chaucer. *Fr.* The Canterbury Tales: Prologue. BiP
With hyphens, clip off endings that don't fit. Sonneteering Made Easy. S. B. Botsford. NYBP
With I and E, *orig. and mod. English prose.* *Unknown.* OxBM
(Pointless Pride of Man, The.) MeEL
With innocent wide penguin eyes, three. bird-witted. Marianne Moore. CMoP; FM
With its baby rivers and little towns, each with its abbey or its cathedral. England. Marianne Moore. CrMA; LiTA; MoAB; MoAmPo; TwAmPo
With its cloud of skirmishers in advance. An Army Corps on the March. Walt Whitman. InPS; PAL; PoLF; PPoe
With its rat's tooth the clock. The Alarum. Sylvia Townsend Warner. MoBrPo
With joy all relics of the past I hail. Old Ruralities. Charles Tennyson Turner. EBVV
With joy Britannia sees her fav'rite goose. To the Marquis of Graham on His Marriage. *Unknown.* OBSV
With Joy erst while,(when knotty doubts arose). Upon the Much-to Be Lamented Desease of the Reverend Mr. John Cotton. John Fiske. SCAP
With Kathy at Wisdom. Richard Hugo. FAZ
With kisses my lips were wounded by you. Healing the Wound. Heine, *tr. by* Louis Untermeyer. UnTE
With Kit, Age 7, at the Beach. William Stafford. RFM
With languages dispersed, men were not able. Four Epigrams on the Naturalization Bill. John Byrom. NOBL
With leaden foot Time creeps along. Absence. Richard Jago. HBV-1; OBEV
With leering looks, bullfac'd, and freckled fair. On Jacob Tonson, His Publisher. Dryden. ChTr; FaBoEE; OBSV
With Life and Death I walked when Love appeared. Hymn to Colour. George Meredith. OBNC
With lifted feet, hands still. Going Down Hill on a Bicycle [*or* Bicycling Song]. Henry Charles Beeching. GN; HBV-1; HBVY; OBEV; OBVV
With lights for eyes, our city turns. Lullaby. Dom Moraes. NePoEA-2
With Lilacs. Charles Henry Crandall. AA
With Lilacs in My Eye. Lucile Coleman. GoYe
With little here to do or see. To the Daisy [*or* To the Same Flower]. Wordsworth. EnRP; GTBS; GTBS-P; HBV-1; HBVY
With loitering step and quiet eye. In November. Archibald Lampman. NOBC; OBCV
With Long Black Wings. Trumbull Stickney. NCEP
With longing I am lad. A Maid Mars Me. *Unknown.* OxBM
With Love among the haycocks. A Song. Ralph Hodgson. GoJo
With love exceeding a simple love of the things. Melampus. George Meredith. OBVV; PoEL-5; VLP
With Love I garnered mirth, and dreams, and shame. James Branch Cabell. Retractions, VI. HBMV
With lovers 'twas of old the fashion. To a Young Lady, with Some Lampreys. John Gay. FaBoUs; NOEC
With low thunder, with red bushes smooth. Red Rock Ceremonies. Anita Endrezze Probst. CDW
With Lullay, Lullay, like a Child. John Skelton. *See* My Darling Dear, My Daisy Flower.
With maidenly and modest sips. The Kiss and the Cup. *Unknown, tr. by* Louis Untermeyer. UnTE
With marjoram [*or* margerain] gentle. To Mistress Margery Wentworth. John Skelton. *Fr.* The Garlande of Laurell. EBEV; EnLoPo; EnRePo; LoBV; NOBE; OAEL-1; OBEV; OBSC; TrGrPo; ViBoPo
With Me My Lover Makes. C. Day Lewis. OBMV
With me while present, may thy lovely eyes. To Miss Lucy F——, with a New Watch. George Lyttelton. FaBoUs
With Mercy for the Greedy. Anne Sexton. CAPP
With merry lark this maiden rose. Old-Time Service. Thomas Churchyard. *Fr.* A Fayned Fancy betweene the Spider and the Gowte. OBSC
With Metaphor. Sarah Wingate Taylor. GoYe

With mighty hand the Holy Lord. The Temptation and Fall of Man. *Unknown, tr. by* Charles W. Kennedy. *Fr.* Genesis. AnOE
With Monmouth cap and cutlass by my side. A Long Prologue to a Short Play. Sir Henry Sheers. APAS
With much ado you fail to tell. A Critic. Walter Savage Landor. ChTr; DBV; FaBoEE
With music strong I come, with my cornets and my drums. Song of Myself, XVIII. Walt Whitman. TrGrPo
With my breath I cut my way through the six forests. Lalleswari, *tr. fr. Kashmiri by* George Grierson; *ad. by* Deirdre Lashgari. WPOW
With my cousin/ I practiced motherhood. Still Birth. Catherine Rutan. AMV-81
With My Crowbar Key. William Stafford. ConAP
With my frailty don't upbraid me. Song. Congreve. POL
With My God, the Smith. Uri Zvi Greenberg, *tr. fr. Hebrew by* Robert Mezey *and* Ben Zion Gold. VWA
With My Grandfather. Zelda, *tr. fr. Hebrew by* Marcia Falk. VWA
With my hat on backwards. One More Time. Richard Shelton. GP
With my looks I am bound to look simple or fast. Magna Est Veritas. Stevie Smith. OxBC
With nerves all shattered and worn. Song of the Sheet. *Unknown.* BXAP
With nets and kitchen sieves they raid the pond. The Pond. Anthony Thwaite. MAT; NYBP
With night full of spring and stars we stand. Young Girls. Raymond Souster. HeIP
With nought to hide or to betray. L'Amitié et l'Amour. John Swanwick Drennan. BIrV
With oaken staff and swinging lantern bright. The Andalusian Sereno. Francis Saltus Saltus. AA
With oh such peculiar branching and over-reaching of wire. St. Saviour's, Aberdeen Park, Highbury, London, N. John Betjeman. MoVE
With one black shadow at its feet. Mariana in the South. Tennyson. VLP
With one consuming roar along the shingle. Felixstowe; or, The Last of Her Order. John Betjeman. OxBTC
With one letter of your many names. Love the Ruins. Malka Heifetz Tussman, *tr. by* Marcia Falk. VWA
With one step. Panic. Lloyd Davis. WOLT
With only his feeble lantern. Charon's Cosmology. Charles Simic. GeTw; NoP
With other women I beheld my love. Ballata: Of His Lady among Other Ladies. Guido Cavalcanti, *tr. by* Dante Gabriel Rossetti. AWP
With paciens thou hast us fed. Farewell! Advent. James Ryman. MeEL
With pale green nails of polished jade. Impression Japonais. Oscar Wilde. SyP
With paste of almonds Syb her hands doth scour[e]. Upon Sybilla [*or* Sibilla]. Robert Herrick. CaPo; SeCePo
With Pegasus upon a day. To John Taylor. Robert Burns. WhC
With pensive eyes the little room I view. The Garret. Pierre Jean de Béranger, *tr. by* Thackeray. HBV-1
With people conformed. Dear Girl. Gregory Corso. NoAM
With Pipe and Flute. Austin Dobson. VLP
With Poems Already Begun. Rachel Korn, *tr. fr. Yiddish by* Seymour Mayne *and* Rivka Augenfeld. VWA
With poisoned apple, comb, ring, garment. How to Murder Your Best Friend. Diana O Hehir. NPGG
With porcupine locks. The Katzenjammer Kids. James Reaney. MoCV; OBCV; PeCV
With proud thanksgiving, a mother for her children. For the Fallen. Laurence Binyon. NOBE; OBEV; OBWP; OxBTC
With prune-dark eyes, thick lips, jostling each other. Refugees. Louis MacNeice. LiTB; WaP
With rakish eye and plenished crop. The Crow. William Canton. HBV-1
With reeds and bird-lime from the desert air. On a Fowler. Isidorus, *tr. by* William Cowper. AWP
With restless step of discontent. Balboa. Nora Perry. PAH
With rhythmic thud. The Green Corn Dance. Alice Corbin. BPAW
With Rue My Heart Is Laden, *parody.* Samuel Hoffenstein. UnPo
With Rue My Heart Is Laden. A. E. Housman. A Shropshire Lad, LIV. AWP; BLPL; CMoP; FaFP; HAP; HeIP; HoPM; InPK; LiTB; LiTM; MasP; MoAB; MoBrPo; NoAM; NoP; OAEP; PAI; PrIm; SoSe; TreFT; TrGrPo; UnPo
"With sacrifice before the rising morn." Laodamia. Wordsworth. EnRP; OAEP
With sails full set, the ship her anchor weighs. Emigravit. Helen Hunt Jackson. AA
With saintly grace and reverent tread. Presentiment. Ambrose Bierce. AA
With Schoolchildren. Willis Barnstone. GLGT
With Self Dissatisfied. Frederick L. Hosmer. TrPWD
With Serving Still. Sir Thomas Wyatt. EIL; InPK; LoBV; SiPS; WHA (His Reward.) OBSC
With seven matching calfskin cases for his new suits. Home Leave. Barbara Howes. MP; TwCP
With sharpened pen and wit, one tunes his lays. The Praise of New Netherland. Jacob Steendam. PAH
With Ships the Sea Was Sprinkled [Far and Nigh]. Wordsworth. EnRP; HBV-1; MOS
With shot and shell, like a loosened hell. The Charge at Santiago. William Hamilton Hayne. PAH
With sick and famisht eyes. Longing. George Herbert. AnAnS-1; SeCV-1
With sighs my bosom always laboureth. Sonnet. Dante, *tr. by* Dante Gabriel Rossetti. *Fr.* La Vita Nuova. GoBC
With six small diamonds for his eyes. The Spider. Robert P. Tristram Coffin. ImOP
With slower pen men used to write. On the Hurry of This Time. Austin Dobson. HBV-1
With snow-white veil and garments as of flame. Divina Commedia, IV. Longfellow. NePA; TreFT
With sober pace an heav'enly Maid walks in. Abraham Cowley. Davideis, II, *and* III. SeCV-1
With song and sun-burst comes the Easter morn. Easter. Robert Whitaker. PGD
With song I seek my fate to cheer. Love's Longing. *Unknown, tr. by* John Addington Symonds. UnTE
With songs and honors sounding loud. Isaac Watts. AmFP
With splendour of a silver day. Night of Frost in May. George Meredith. VLP
With spray-can paint. SM. Stanley Moss. AMV-81; NYP
With stammering lips and insufficient sound. The Soul's Expression. Elizabeth Barrett Browning. VLP
With steadfast heart and true. "Go Forward." "A. R. G." BLRP
With Strawberries. W. E. Henley. HBV-1
With such a throb does blood. Joy of Knowledge. Isidor Schneider. TrJP
With such compelling cause to grieve. In Memoriam A. H. H., XXIX. Tennyson. EBVV
With sweet surprise, as when one finds a flower. On Finding the Truth. Jones Very. TrCP
With sweetest milk and sugar first. The Girl and Her Fawn. Andrew Marvell. *Fr.* The Nymph Complaining for the Death of Her Fawn. FaBoCh
With tears thy grief thou dost bemoan. Stanzas. Solomon ibn Gabirol, *tr. by* Emma Lazarus. TrJP
With Tendrils of Poems. Michael McClure. PoM
With that a thundring noise seem'd shake the skie. The Overthrow of Lucifer. Phineas Fletcher. *Fr.* The Purple Island. OBS
With that delight the royal captive's brought. The Lady A. L., My Asylum in a Great Extremity. Richard Lovelace. CaPo
With that he stripped him to the ivory skin. Amorous Neptune. Christopher Marlowe. *Fr.* Hero and Leander. NOBE
With that I saw two swans of goodly hue. Spenser. *Fr.* Prothalamion. PBBP
With that low cunning, which in fools supplies. A Critical Fribble [*or* A Criticaster *or* Character of a Critic]. Charles Churchill. *Fr.* The Rosciad. FaBoEn; NOEC; OBEC
With that pathetic impudence of youth. The Family of Nations. Willard Wattles.
With the Bait of Bread. Helene Pilbosian. AMV-81
With the boys busy. Philomena Andronico. William Carlos Williams. FaBoMo
With the Dawn. Thomas Caulfield Irwin. BIrV; EnLoPo
With the Door Open. David Ignatow. CTBA
With the effect as of carving, almost, the hillside. For an Age of Plastics. Plymouth. Donald Davie. NePoEA-2
With the exact length and pace of his father's stride. For a Father. Anthony Cronin. FaBoTw
With the Face. Laura Riding. NoAM
With the fierce rage of winter deep suffus'd [*or* suffused]. Frost at Night [*or* A Winter Night]. James Thomson. *Fr.* The Seasons: Winter. NOBE; OBEC
With the forks of flowers I eat the meat of morning. Lyric by Nine. *Unknown.* EAS
With the green lamp of the spirit. Into the Glacier. John Haines. CoAP
With the heavy steps of slow oxen. Slow Oxen. Ilya Rubin, *tr. by* Linda Zisquit. VWA
With the Herring Fishers. "Hugh MacDiarmid." BSV; LiTM
With the hooves of a doe. Lenox Avenue. Sidney Alexander. PoNe
With the last whippoorwill call of evening. Birmingham. Margaret Walker. PoBA
With the leftovers and etcetera of the poor. Building a Person. Stephen Dunn. FAZ
With the Most Susceptible Element, the Mind, Already Turned under the Toxic Action. Walter Benton. WaP
With the motion of angels, out of. Skiers. Robert Penn Warren. *Fr.* In the Mountains. LiSp
With the Nuns at Cape May Point. David Earle Anderson. AMV-81

With the old kindness, the old distinguished grace. Upon a Dying Lady. W. B. Yeats. LiTB; UnPo
With the one and the two and the three. A Beginning and an End. Edouard Roditi. VWA
With the other geese within the goosehouse. January. James Reaney. *Fr.* A Suit of Nettles. OBCV
With the Shell of a Hermit Crab. James Wright. NoP
With the shrewd and upright man. Fool and False. *Unknown, tr. by* Arthur W. Ryder. *Fr.* The Panchatantra. AWP
With the small birds. There Isn't Enough Bread. Charles Culhane. LFAC
With the spring moon's first beams. Spring Night. "Rana Mukerji." UnTE
With the stars. For the Coming Year. Peter Everwine. OFD
With the stylish young brood bitch, the old dog showed. Old Dog, New Dog. Sydney Lea. MAYP
With the Sun's Fire. David Ignatow. FAZ
With the thinking of winter. The Cook. Ray A. Young Bear. CDW
With the years my woes increased. The Paths of Prayer. Edouard Roditi. VWA
With Thee. Cora M. Pinkham. STF
With Thee a moment! Then what dreams have play! Desire. "Æ." ILwL; OBMV; TrPWD
With thee conversing I forget all time. Eve Speaks to Adam [*or* Eve to Adam]. Milton. *Fr.* Paradise Lost, IV. ChTr; FaBoEn; GBL; TreFS; WiR
With their boxing-glove muzzles. Cattle. Peter Skrzynecki. CBAP
With their harsh leaves old rhododendrons fill. The Mountain Cemetery. Edgar Bowers. ConAP; NePoEA
With their lithe, long, strong legs. Bullfrog. Ted Hughes. NYBP; RFM
With these heaven-assailing spires. New York. "Æ." OBMV
With these missing pieces. A Tribe Searching. Shlomo Reich, *tr. by* Mira Reich. VWA
With this ambiguous earth. Christ in the Universe. Alice Meynell. ACP; GoBC; HBMV; MoBrPo; NOBE
With this charm I keep the boy at six. The Magician Suspends the Children. Carole Oles. SoSe
With this stone his foes honor Apis the fighter. Monument to a Boxer. Lucilius, *tr. by* Tom Dodge. LiSp
With three great snorts of strength. The Night Express. Cosmo Monkhouse. OBVV
With thy small stock, why art thou venturing still. To a Weak Gamester in Poetry. Ben Jonson. JCP
With tiger pace and swinging head. The Known World. Brewster Ghiselin. MoVE
With Timbrels. Bible, Apocrypha. *Fr.* Judith. TrJP
With torches I have wandered the dark poppy world. The Double Axe. Anne Hazlewood-Brady. IHMS
With treble vivas and limp hedgerow flags. The Vanquished. Charles Eglington. PeSA
With trees backing them. A Photo of Miners. Brendan Galvin. LTB
With trembling eyes. Charm. Miklos Radnoti, *tr. by* Steven Polgar, Stephen Berg, *and* S. J. Marks. LLLT
With trembling fingers did we weave. In Memoriam A. H. H., XXX. Tennyson. EBVV
With troubled heart and trembling hand I write. In Memory of My Dear Grandchild [Anne Bradstreet]. Anne Bradstreet. BoWoP; TrCP
With twilight I gather you here. Conjuration. Agnes Gergely, *tr. by* Emery George. VWA
With Two Fair Girls. *Unknown, tr. fr. Greek by* Robert C. MacGregor. ErPo
With two 60's stuck on the scoreboard. Foul Shot. Edwin A. Hoey. RHPC
With two strange fires of equal heat possest. Love and Jealousy. Sir Philip Sidney. *Fr.* Arcadia. SiPS
With two white roses on her breasts. A Brown Girl Dead. Countee Cullen. TAP
With Usura. Cantos, XLV. Ezra Pound. CMoP; LiTM; MoPo; NePA; NOBA; TW
With visionary care. Summer Noon: 1941. Ivor Winters. CrMA
With walloping tails, the whales off Wales. The Whales off Wales. X. J. Kennedy. OBCA
With what anguish of mind I remember my childhood. The Old Oaken Bucket, *parody*. *Unknown.* BLPA; FaFP; WBLP
With what attentive courtesy he bent. The Guitarist Tunes Up. Frances Cornford. ELU; SoSe
With what attractive charms this goodly frame. Mark Akenside. *Fr.* The Pleasures of Imagination. EnRP
With what conviction the young man spoke. W. H. Auden. PV
With what deep murmurs through time's silent stealth. The Waterfall. Henry Vaughan. AnAnS-1; FaBoPP; MeLP; MePo; NOBE; NOCV; NoP; OAEP; OBS; PoEL-2; PrIm; SeCeV-1; ViBoPo; WiR
With what, O Codrus! is thy fancy smit? Edward Young *Fr.* Love of Fame, the Univeral Passion. OBSV
With what sharp checks I in my self am shent. Astrophel and Stella, XVIII. Sir Philip Sidney. SiPS
With what thou gavest me, O Master. Equipment. Paul Laurence Dunbar. TrPWD
"With Whom Is No Variableness, neither Shadow of Turning." Arthur Hugh Clough. TreFS; TRV; WGRP
(It Fortifies My Soul to Know.) OAEP; TrCP; VLP
With whomsoever I share the spring. Song. Jan Burroway. NePoAm-2
With wild surprise/ Four great eyes. The Christmas Tree in the Nursery. Richard Watson Gilder. HBVY; OHIP
With willing arms I row and row. The Barcarole of James Smith. Herbert S. Gorman. HBMV
With wine and words of love and every [*or* fervid] vow. Seduced Girl [*or* To Venus]. Hedylos, *tr. by* Louis Untermeyer. BoLoP; ErPo; UnTE
With wings held close and slim neck bent. Swans. Leonora Speyer. FYAP
With Wordsworth at Rydal. James Thomas Fields. AA
With wrath-flushed cheeks, and eyelids red. Ahmed. James Berry Bensel. AA
With wrinkled hide and great frayed ears. The Elephant [*or* Gunga]. Rachel Field. *Fr.* A Circus Garland. OBCA; SoPo
With yellow pears leans over. Half of Life. Friedrich Hölderlin. ChTr; OBVE, *tr.* by James Blair Leishman
With you a part of me hath passed away. George Santayana. *Fr.* To W. P. TrGrPo
With you first shown to me. William Barnes. EnLoPo
With you for mast and sail and flag. The Narrow Sea. Robert Graves. FaBoEE; FaBoMo; MOS
With you here at Mertu. Ezra Pound *and* Noel Stock, *fr. Egyptian hieroglyphics.* PBWP
With you, I know, my offering will find grace. Ben Jonson. *Fr.* Epistle to Elizabeth, Countess of Rutland. JCP
With your assistance, departed citizens. Certain Dead. John Haines. LCAP
With your fair eyes a charming light I see. Love, the Light-Giver [*or* To Tommaso de' Cavalieri]. Michelangelo, *tr. by* John Addington Symonds. AWP; PeHV
With your guns and drums and drums and guns. Johnny I Hardly Knew You. *Unknown.* FSW
With your kind attention a song I will trill. Down, Down, Down, *with music. Unknown.* OuSiCo
With your mercury mouth in the missionary times. Sad-eyed Lady of the Lowlands. Bob Dylan. BiP
With youth, is deade the hopes of loves returne. Sir Walter Ralegh. *Fr.* The Last Book of the Ocean to Scinthia. FaBoEn
With Zeus let our song begin! Praise of Zeus. Aratus of Soli, *tr. fr. Greek.* ILwL
Withal a meagre man was Aaron Stark. Aaron Stark. E. A. Robinson. MoAB; MoAmPo
Withdraw thee, soul, from strife. Sleep. Alice Brown. AA
Withdrawal, The. Robert Lowell. NoP
Withdrawn from layers of upper air, ice-blue and clear. Suburb Hilltop. Richard Moore. NYBP
Withdrawn on this warm ledge I lie. Summer Afternoon. Elizabeth B. Harrod. NePoEA
Withered leaves that drift in Russell Square, The. Drilling in Russell Square. Edward Shanks. OBMV
Withered Rose, A. "Yehoash," *tr. fr. Yiddish by* Isidore Goldstick. TrJP
Withering grass knows not its needs. After the Rain. Edward A. Collier. BLRP
Within a budding grove. Spring: The Lover and the Birds [*or* The Lover and the Birds]. William Allingham. OBNC; OBVV
Within a chamber of a tower. Quia Amore Langueo. *Unknown, tr. by* Em M. Clerke. ISi
Within a copse, I met a shepherd-maid. Ballata: Concerning a Shepherd-Maid. Guido Cavalcanti, *tr. by* Dante Gabriel Rossetti. AWP
Within a delicate grey ruin. The Vestal Lady on Brattle. Gregory Corso. NoAM
Within a 'dobe wall. In Old Tucson. Charles Beghtol. BPAW
Within a gloomy dimble she doth dwell. Mother Maudlin the Witch. Ben Jonson. *Fr.* The Sad Shepherd. ChTr
Within a greenwood sweet of myrtle savour. *Unknown, tr. fr. Italian.* GBL
Within a native hut, ere stirred the dawn. Nativity. Aquah Laluah. CDC; PBA; TTY
Within a poor man's squalid home I stood. Vision. William Dean Howells. AA
Within a thick and spreading hawthorn bush. The Thrush's Nest. John Clare. BoAnP; GoJo; PB
Within an English village yesterday. Nora. Dora Sigerson Shorter. HBMV
Within an open curled Sea of Gold. A Vision. Lord Herbert of Cherbury. AnAnS-2; SeCP

Within and Without, *sels.* George Macdonald.
Little White Lily. HBV-1; HBVY
"Lord of Thyself and me, through the sore grief." TRV
Within Heaven's circle I had not guessed at this. The Flight into Egypt. Peter Quennell. LiTB; LiTM
Within her gilded cage confined. The Contrast; the Parrot and the Wren. Wordsworth. FM
Within her hair Venus and Cupid sport them. Emaricdulfe. "E. C." ElL
Within his sober realm of leafless trees. The Closing Scene. Thomas Buchanan Read. AA; HBV-2
Within King's College Chapel, Cambridge. Wordsworth. *See* Inside of King's College Chapel, Cambridge.
Within mankind's duration, so they say. The Birds. J. C. Squire. HBMV
Within me are two souls that pity each. Duality. Arthur Sherburne Hardy. AA
Within My Breast. Sir Thomas Wyatt. EnRePo
Within my casement came one night. The Dawn of Love. Henrietta Cordelia Ray. BlSi
Within my garden, rides a bird. Emily Dickinson. AmPP
Within my head, aches the perpetual winter. Winter and Summer. Stephen Spender. MoAB; MoBrPo; MoPo
Within My Heart. Judah al-Harizi, *tr. fr. Hebrew.* TrJP
Within my heart a stab I felt. En las Internas Entrañas. St. Theresa of Ávila, *tr. by* Father Benedict Zimmerman. WPOW
Within my heart I long have kept. Blondel. Clarence Urmy. AA; HBMV
Within my house of patterned horn. The Tortoise in Eternity. Elinor Wylie. FaPON; ImOP
Within my twenty yer of age. The Dream of the Romaunt of the Rose. Guillaume de Lorris, *tr. by* Chaucer. *Fr.* The Romance of the Rose. LoBV
Within our happy castle there dwelt one. Stanzas Written in My Pocket Copy of Thomson's "Castle of Indolence." Wordsworth. EnRP
Within that awful volume lies. *See* Within this ample volume lies.
Within that porch, across the way. The Cat. W. H. Davies. NOBE; PCat
Within the Casket of thy Coelick Breast. An Acrostick on Mrs. Winifret Griffin. John Saffin. SCAP
Within the cave, it is dark. safe. Gimel. Stuart Z. Perkoff. VWA
Within the Circuit of This Plodding Life. Henry David Thoreau. *See* Winter Memories.
Within the cloister blissful of thy sides. Two Invocations of the Virgin, I. Chaucer. *Fr.* The Canterbury Tales: The Second Nun's Tale. ACP
Within the covert of a shady grove. Love Sleeping. Plato, *tr. by* Thomas Stanley. AWP; FaBoEE
Within the damp wind. Naming the Rain. Annette Arkeketa West. TWSS
Within the deep and luminous subsistence of the High Light. Dante, *tr. fr. Italian. Fr.* Divina Commedia: Paradiso. ILwL
Within the Dream You Said. Philip Larkin. InPS
Within the dungeon's noxious gloom. Sonnet: The Cell. John Thelwall. NOEC
Within the flower there lies a seed. Spell of Creation. Kathleen Raine. FaBoCh; OxBS
Within the garden of Beaucaire. Provençal Lovers. Edmund Clarence Stedman. HBV-1
Within the gentle heart Love shelters him. Canzone: Of the Gentle Heart. Guido Guinicelli, *tr. by* Dante Gabriel Rossetti. AWP; CTC; GoBC; OBVE
Within the Gorges there is no lack of men. Invitation to Hsiao Ch'u-shih. Po Chü-i, *tr. by* Arthur Waley. OBVE
Within the great grey flapping tent. The Auction Sale. Henry Reed. MoBrPo
Within the great wall's perfect round. The Window. Edwin Muir. LiTM
Within the introspection of my dying. Parable. Robert Pack. NePoEA-2
Within the iron cities. The Garden of God. "Æ." WGRP
Within the letter's rustling fold. Spring Flowers from Ireland. Denis Florence MacCarthy. ACP; GoBC
Within the mind strong fancies work. The Pass of Kirkstone. Wordsworth. HBV-2
Within the night, above the dark. Mary Gilmore. *Fr.* Swans at Night. PoAu-1
Within the oak a throb of pigeon wings. A Twilight in Middle March. Francis Ledwidge. BIrV; OnYI; OxBI; WHA
Within the pale blue haze above. The Storm. Coventry Patmore. EnLoPo
Within the purple graph of the Hokonuis, the dark. The Foxes. Janet Frame. WPE
Within the sand of what far river lies. Shadows of His Lady. Jacques Tahureau, *tr. by* Andrew Lang. AWP
Within the Shelter of Our Walls, *with music.* Elinor Lennen. AH
Within the soul a faculty abides. Wordsworth. *Fr.* The Excursion, IV. OBRV
Within the still, white room that gave me birth. Alien. Helen Frazee-Bower. HBMV
Within the thin. The Madman. S. J. Pretorius, *tr. by* Uys Krige *and* Jack Cope. PeSA
Within the Veil. Margaret E. Sangster. BLRP
Within the wires of the post, unloading the cans of garbage. Prisoners. Randall Jarrell. OxBA; WaP
Within the wood behind the hill. The Satyrs and the Moon. Herbert S. Gorman. HBV-1
Within These Doors Assembled Now, *with music.* Oliver Holden. AH
Within these walls, Pity will war with Death. A Hospital. Alfred Noyes. PoPl
Within this [*or* that] ample [*or* awful] volume lies. The Book of Books [*or* The Bible *or* Sir Walter Scott's Tribute]. Sir Walter Scott. *Fr.* The Monastery, *ch.* 12. BLRP; TreFT; TRV; WBLP
Within this black hive to-night. Beehive. Jean Toomer. IDB; PoBA; TTY
Within This Grave Do Lie. *Unknown.* ShM; WhC
(Epitaph: "Within this grave do lie.") TreFT
Within this lowly grave a Conqueror lies. The Conqueror's Grave. Bryant. AA
Within this mindless vault. Epigram. J. V. Cunningham. VGW
Within this place. Over Case's Door. John Case. FaBoUs
Within this restless, hurried, modern world. My Voice. Oscar Wilde. BrPo; EBVV
Within this silent palace of the Night. Moonrise. Frank Dempster Sherman. AA
Within this sober frame expect. Upon Appleton House, to My Lord Fairfax. Andrew Marvell. SeCP; SeCV-1
Within those walls where student zeal. The College Cat. Alfred Denis Godley. CenHV
Within unfriendly walls. Waiting. John Davidson. ViBoPo
Within Us, Too. R. H. Grenville. AMV-80
Within what weeks the melilot. Sweet Clover. Wallace Rice. HBV-1
Within your heart. Hold Fast Your Dreams. Louise Driscoll. TiPo
Within your magic web of hair lies furled. The Web of Eros. Edith Sitwell. HBMV
Without a door, through the smooth wall. At Night. Rachel Boimwell, *tr. by* Gabriel Preil *and* Howard Schwartz. VWA
Without a winter coat. Raising the Flag. Gerald Vizenor. VoR
Without and Within. James Russell Lowell. HBV-1
Without Benefit of Declaration. Langston Hughes. AmNP; TTY
Without Benefit of Tape. Dorothy Livesay. NOBC
Without Ceremony. Vassar Miller. CoPo; MoAmPo
Without dressmakers to connect. Because of Clothes. Laura Riding. LiTA; NoAM
Without excess (no galaxies). Civilities of Lamplight. Charles Tomlinson. OxBC
Without expectation. Summer Oracle. Audre Lorde. BlSi; PoBA
Without flocks or cattle or the curved horns. A Time of Change. Egan O'Rahilly, *tr. by* Eavan Boland. BIrV
Without Her. Dante Gabriel Rossetti. The House of Life, LIII. GBL; NCEP; OBNC; PoEL-5; ViBoPo; VLP
Without him still this whirling earth. Egotism. Edward Sanford Martin. AA
Without invention nothing is well spaced. William Carlos Williams. *Fr.* Paterson. PP
Without it, nothing exists. The Invention of Zero. Constance Urdang. VWA
Without Me You Won't be Able to See Yourself. Chaim Grade, *tr. fr. Yiddish by* Ruth Whitman. VWA
Without More Weight. Giuseppe Ungaretti, *tr. fr. Italian by* Allen Mandelbaum. PoPl
Without My Friends the Day Is Dark. Moses ibn Ezra, *tr. fr. Hebrew by* Solomon Solis-Cohen. TrJP
Without Name. Pauli Murray. AmNP; PoBA; PoNe
Without Names. Jeff Tagami. BrSi
Without Regret. Lilith Lorraine. PGD
Without so much/ as trying to look. You. Carroll Arnett. VoR
Without surprise, on that not distant shore. Delusions VI. Charles Madge. NeBP
Without tears. Words at Farewell. Vahan Derian, *tr. by* Diana Der Hovanessian. AMV-81
Without that once clear aim, the path of flight. Stephen Spender. CMoP
Without the evening dew and showers. Ode. Charles Cotton. ViBoPo
Without the hall, and close upon the gate. The Gardens of Alcinous. Homer, *tr. by* George Chapman. *Fr.* The Odyssey, VII. OAEL-1; OBVE
Without the Herdsman. Diotimus, *tr. fr. Greek by* John William Burgon. AWP
Without, the lonely night is sweet with stars. Martyrdom. Rufus Learsi. TrJP
Without the slightest basis/ for hypochondriasis. How Jack Found That Beans May Go Back on a Chap. Guy Wetmore Carryl. HoPM

Without the Way, there can be no going. The Way; the Truth; the Life. Samuel Judson Porter. BLRP
Without their helmets. Losers. Jonathan Holden. MAYP
Without this/ what is/ worth doing. Land. Carroll Arnett. VoR
Without thought, without remorse, without shame. Walls. C. P. Cavafy, *tr. by* Rae Dalven. TrJP
Without warning their nest. A Call to Action. Ch'iu Chin, *tr. by* Kenneth Rexroth *and* Ling Chung. PBWP
Without You. Cid Corman. GP
Without your knowledge they are turning your wounds into words. A Latter Purification. Haim Guri, *tr. by* Mark Elliott Shapiro. VWA
"Withouten Time is no erthely thinge." Time and Eternity. Stephen Hawes. *Fr.* The Pastime of Pleasure. PoEL-1
Withstanders. William Barnes. OxBoCh
Witlesse gallant, a young wench that woo'd, A. Michael Drayton. *Fr.* Idea. AAS
Witness. Jon Anderson. MAYP
Witness. Josephine Miles. GP
Witness how it comes to pass. Epitaph in Sirmio. David Morton. PoLF
Witness to Death. Richmond Lattimore. VGW
Witnesses, The. X. J. Kennedy. PChr
Witnesses, The. Longfellow. GOA
Witnesses. W. S. Merwin. LCAP
Witnesses, The, *sel.* Clive Sansom.
"It was a night in winter." PChr
Wits, The. Sir John Suckling. *See* Session[s] of the Poets, A.
Wit's a feather and a chief a rod, A. An Honest Man. Pope. Essay on Man, 2 *ll. fr.* Epistle IV. TreF
Wit's End Corner. Antoinette Wilson. BLRP; STF
Wit's perfection, Beauty's wonder. Epitaph. Francis Davison. OBSC
Witty as Horatius Flaccus. On Seeing Francis Jeffrey Riding on a Donkey. *At. to* Sydney Smith. FaBoEE
Wives, The. Donald Hall. CoAP
Wives in the Sere. Thomas Hardy. BrPo; NOBE; VLP
Wives of Mafiosi, The. Erica Jong. AmPA
Wives of Spittal, The. *Unknown.* GBP
Wizard Frost. Frank Dempster Sherman. YeAr
Wizard of Alderley Edge, The. Peter Coe. OBET
Wizard Oil, *with music. Unknown.* AS
Wizard's Funeral, The. Richard Watson Dixon. ELP; LoBV; VLP
Wmffre the Sweep. Rolfe Humphries. EaLo
Wo, his purple an' linen, too. Dives and Laz'us. *Unknown.* TTY
Wo worth the days! The days I spent. A Few Lines to Fill up a Vacant Page. John Danforth. SCAP
Wobbly Rock. Lew Welch. PoM
Wodwo. Ted Hughes. NoAM
Woe for the brave ship *Orient!* The Brave Old Ship, the *Orient.* Robert Traill Spence Lowell. AA; FaBoBe
Woe having made, with many fights, his own. Astrophel and Stella, LVII. Sir Philip Sidney. SiPS
Woe Is Me! ("Woe is me! for I am as the last of the summer fruits"). Bible, *O.T.* Micah VII: 1-6. TrJP
Woe is me, my soul says, how bitter is my fate. Rahel Morpurgo, *tr. fr. Hebrew by* Robert Alter. PBWP
Woe worth thee, woe worth thee, false Scottlande! Earl Bothwell. *Unknown.* ESPB
Woefully Arrayed. *Unknown, at. to* John Skelton. CABA; ChTr; EnRePo; LoBV; OxBoCh
(Wofully Araide.) MeEL
Woe's me! by dint of all these sighs that come. Dante, *tr. by* Dante Gabriel Rossetti. La Vita Nuova, XXVII. AWP
Wofully Araide. *Unknown. See* Woefully Arrayed.
Woggly bird sat on the whango tree, The. The Whango Tree. *Unknown.* NA
Woke up this morning. That Lonesome Train Took My Baby Away. *Unknown.* BluL
Woke up this morning, gal 'twixt mid night and day. Barbecue Blues. *Unknown.* BluL
Woke Up This Morning with My Mind on Freedom. *Unknown.* FSW
Woken, I lay in the arms of my own warmth and listened. First Things First. W. H. Auden. NePoAm-2; NYBP
Wol ze here a wonder thynge. Riddles Wisely Expounded. *Unknown.* ESPB
Wolcum be thu, hevene kyng. Welcome Yule. *Unknown.* CH
Wolde God that it were so. Love Undeclared. *Unknown.* OxBM
Wolf. Peter Blue Cloud. VoR
Wolf, The. Georgia Roberts Durston. RHPC
Wolf. Kenneth Rexroth. *Fr.* A Bestiary. NNaP
Wolf, A. *Unknown, tr. fr. Osage Indian.* RHPC
Wolf, A/ in thought. A Version of a Song of Failure. Larry Eigner. FAZ
Wolf also shall dwell with the lamb, The. The Peaceable Kingdom [*or* God's Rule]. Bible, *O.T. Fr.* Isaiah. FaPON; FM; PDV
Wolf and the Dog, The. La Fontaine, *tr. fr. French by* Elizur Wright. OBVE
Wolf and the Lamb, The. La Fontaine, *tr. fr. French by* Marianne Moore. NAWM-2
Wolf and the Stork, The. La Fontaine, *tr. fr. French by* Marianne Moore. FM; OBVE
Wolf-Boy. David Malouf. CBAP
Wolf Cry, The. Lew Sarett. FaPON; RHPC
Wolf Dream. Edward Lense. AMV-81
Wolf Hunting near Nashoba. Jim Barnes. STE
Wolfman, The. Greg Kuzma. GP
Wolfram's Dirge. Thomas Lovell Beddoes. *See* Dirge: If Thou Wilt Ease Thine Heart.
Wolfram's Song. Thomas Lovell Beddoes. *See* Song: "Old Adam, the carrion crow."
Wolf's profile hangs, The. From the Window of the Beverly Wilshire Hotel. Michael McClure. EAS
Wolsey. Shakespeare *and probably* John Fletcher. King Henry VIII, *fr.* III, ii. FaBoRV
(Wolsey's Regrets.) TreFS
Wolsey, or possibly my John of Gaunt. Santa Claus. Christopher Hassall. OxBTC
Wolsey's Farewell to His Greatness. Shakespeare *and probably* John Fletcher. *See* Cardinal Wolsey's Farewell.
Wolsey's Regrets. Shakespeare *and probably* John Fletcher. *See* Wolsey.
Wolves. John Haines. BoAnP; LCAP
Wolves, The. Galway Kinnell. NePoEA-2
Wolves. Louis MacNeice. NoAM; OxBTC
Wolves, The. Allen Tate. LiTA; LiTM; NoAM; NOBA; OxBA; PoA
Wolves can outeat anyone. The Wolf and the Stork. La Fontaine, *tr. by* Marianne Moore. FM; OBVE
Wolves for Company. *Unknown, tr. fr. Irish.* BIrV
Wolves of evening will be much abroad, The. Runes for an Old Believer. Rolfe Humphries. NYBP
Wolves say to the dogs, The. J. Michael Yates. *Fr.* The Great Bear Lake Meditations. HoPM
Woman. Ai. GP
Woman. Eaton Stannard Barrett. HBV-1; OnYI; OxBI
Woman. Jane Chambers. IHMS
Woman. Goldsmith. *See* Song: "When lovely woman stoops to folly."
Woman. Randall Jarrell. NoAM; NOBA
Woman, A. Denis Johnson. MAYP
Woman. Kalidasa. *Tr. fr. Sanskrit.* HBV-1
Woman, The. George Keithley. NPGG
Woman. Irving Layton. ErPo
Woman. Elouise Loftin. PoBA
Woman. Valente Goenha Malangatana, *tr. fr. Portuguese by* Dorothy Guedes *and* Philippa Rumsey. PBA; TTY
Woman, *sel.* Alexander McLachlan.
"When my gloomy hour comes to me." CaP
Woman. Milton. *Fr.* Samson Agonistes. OBS
Woman. Coventry Patmore. *See* Foreign Land, The.
Woman. Magda Portal, *tr. fr. Spanish by* Irene Vegas-Garcia *and* Kathleen Weaver. WPOW
Woman. Carl Rakosi. TAP
Woman. Umberto Saba, *tr. fr. Italian by* Christopher Millis. AMV-81
Woman, A. Mary Dixon Thayer. HBMV
Woman, The. R. S. Thomas. OxBC
Woman. ("A clever man builds a city"). *Unknown, tr. fr. Chinese by* H. A. Giles. *Fr.* Shi King. AWP
Woman. ("A comfort but a queer companion"). *Unknown, tr. fr. German by* Louis Untermeyer. UnTE
Woman, A/ sleeps next to me on the earth. Night in the Forest. Galway Kinnell. TAP
Woman, A/ who loves a woman. Rapunzel. Anne Sexton. DFT
Woman, a dog and a walnut tree, A. *Unknown.* FaBoUs
Woman, a pleasing but a short-lived flow'r. An Essay on Woman. Mary Leapor. NOEC
Woman Alone. Denise Levertov. WPOW
Woman and Nature, *sels.* Susan Griffin. NPGG
Acoustics.
Garden, The.
Prologue: "He says that woman speaks with nature."
Silence.
Woman and the Aloe, The. Perseus Adams. PeSA
Woman and Tree. Robert Graves. ErPo
Woman Asleep on a Banana Leaf. Katha Pollit. PoDr
Woman at the Piano. Marya Zaturenska. MoAmPo
Woman at the Washington Zoo, The. Randall Jarrell. AP; CoAP; HAP; LiTM; MP; NMP; OxBC; TAP; TwCP; UnPo
Woman, bathe this head of mine. The Bathing of Oisin's Head. *Unknown, tr. by* Eoin MacNeill. AnIL

Woman came to me, A. Michael Silverton. POL
Woman can't survive, A. Fire. Joy Harjo. TWSS
Woman-Captain, The, *sel.* Thomas Shadwell.
Let Some Great Joys Pretend to Find. OAEP
Woman coming down the snowy road, A. Grey Woman. Gladys Cardiff. CDW; TWSS
Woman Defending Herself Examines Her Own Character Witness, A. Susan Griffin. NPGG
Woman, Don't Be Troublesome. Augustus Young, *tr. fr. Irish.* CIP
Woman Driving the Country Squire, The. David Dayton. AMV-81
Woman! experience might have told me. To Woman. Byron. HBV-1; ViBoPo
Woman fears for man, he goes. Abel's Bride. Denise Levertov. VGW
Woman Free, *sel.* Elizabeth Wolstenholme-Elmy.
"Marriage, which might have been a mateship sweet." BrRo
Woman from the Book of Genesis, A. Dovid Knut, *tr. fr. Russian by* John Glad. VWA
Woman full of wile. Growing Old [*or* Autumn]. *Unknown, tr. by* Frank O'Connor. ErPo; KiLC; OBMV
Woman, Gallup, N. M. Karen Swenson. NYBP
Woman gave me butter now, A. A Present of Butter. Tadhg Dall O'Huiginn, *tr. by* the Earl of Longford. BIrV
Woman grew, with waiting, over-quiet, A. Narrative. Elisabeth Eybers. PeSA
Woman grows hard and skinny, A. Ride the Turtle's Back. Beth Brant. STE
Woman grows old secretly, A. For Jeanette Piccard Ordained at 79. Renny Golden. AMV-80
Woman Grows Soon Old, A. Larin Paraske, *tr. fr. Finnish by* Jaakko A. Ahokas. PBWP
Woman Guard. Pancho Aguila. LFAC
Woman had I seen, as I rode by, A. Bogac Bán. Darrell Figgis. AnIV
Woman Hanging from the 13th Floor Window, The. Joy Harjo. TWSS
Woman-Hater, The, *sel.* Beaumont *and* Fletcher.
Lullaby: "Come sleep, and with the sweet deceiving." FaBoEn
(Come, Sleep.) EIL; ELP
(Sleep.) HBV-2
Woman I Am, The. Glen Allen. BLPA
Woman I have never seen before, A. Transit. Richard Wilbur. LCAP
Woman I want, The. No More than Five. Fred Levinson. AmPA
Woman: If you weren't you who would you rather be? Flood. Roger McGough. FF
Woman in an Abandoned House. Michael Bily-Hurd. AMV-81
Woman in childbirth, fainting with cruel pain, A. To a Faithless Friend. Salaan Arrabey, *tr. by* M. Laurence. WTO
Woman in her room is standing at the mirror, The. The Importance of Mirrors. Helga Sandburg. IHMS
Woman in My Notebook, The. Lorna Dee Cervantes. WPOW
Woman in Oklahoma makes tobacco, A. Nanye'hi (Nancy Ward), the Last Beloved Woman of the Cherokees, 1738-1822. Rayna Green. TWSS
Woman in Sunshine, The. Wallace Stevens. BiP; MoVE
Woman in the, The. Marge Piercy. NMM
Woman in the garden. Duo. Olive Tilford Dargan. HBMV
Woman in the shape of a monster, A. Planetarium. Adrienne Rich. NIP; NoAM; NOBA
Woman in the Wagon, The. Clyde Robertson. PoOW
Woman Is a Branchy Tree, A. James Stephens. ErPo
Woman is a foreign land, A. The Foreign Land [*or* Woman]. Coventry Patmore. The Angel in the House, VI. HBV-1; OBVV
Woman Is a Worthy Thing, A. *Unknown.* FaBoCo; GBP; OxBM
(I Am as Light as Any Roe.) ViBoPo
(Women Are Worthy.) MeEL
Woman is perfected, The. Edge. Sylvia Plath. TAP
Woman is planting asters on the south wind side, A. And the Silver Turns into Night. Nathan Yonathan, *tr. by* Richard Flantz. VWA
Woman let her hand trail, The. A Virtue of Shape. Thom Swiss. AMV-80
Woman Looking at a Vase of Flowers. Wallace Stevens. CrMA
Woman Made of Stars. Earle Thompson. STE
Woman making advances publicly, A. Judith Kazantzis. BrRo
Woman may talk to a woman, A. On the Train. Rachel McAlpine. OCNZ
Woman Me. Maya Angelou. BlSi
Woman Mourned by Daughters, A. Adrienne Rich. IHMS; NCSH
Woman much missed, how you call to me, call to me. The Voice. Thomas Hardy. BoLoP; CMoP; EnLoPo; FaBoEn; GBL; GTBS-P; HAP; MoVE; NoAM; NoP; OAEL-2; OAEP; OBNC; PAI; PoEL-5; PoPle
Woman named Tomorrow, The. Four Preludes on Playthings of the Wind. Carl Sandburg. AP; CMoP; MoAB; MoAmPo; NePA; NOBA
Woman neither young or old, she moves, A. My Mother's Life. William Meredith. AMV-81
Woman of Beare, The. *Unknown. See* Hag of Beare, The.
Woman of the House, The. Richard Murphy. IPY
Woman of Three Cows, The. *Unknown, tr. fr. Late Middle Irish by* James Clarence Mangan. AnIL; OnYI; OxBI
Woman of Words, A. Amanda Benjamin Hall. HBMV
Woman on the other side, The. Kimono. Jorie Graham. MAYP
Woman one wonderful morning, A. Europa. William Plomer. MoBS
Woman Painter of Mithila. Erika Mumford. PoDr
Woman par Excellence. Rochelle Owens. CoPo
Woman Poem. Nikki Giovanni. BlSi; NMM; NoAM
Woman Poet, The. Gertrud Kolmar, *tr. fr. German by* Henry A. Smith. VWA
Woman, rest on my brow your balsam hands. Night of Sine. Léopold Sédar-Senghor, *tr. by* Ulli Beier. PBA
Woman sails, man must row. Sail and Oar. Robert Graves. MOS
Woman Sat Weeping, A. *Unknown.* OxBM
(Suddenly Afraid.) NCEP
Woman Seed Player. Roberta Hill Whiteman. STE
Woman Shaman's Song, A. Uvavnuk, *tr. fr. Eskimo into Danish by* Knud Rasmussen; *tr. into English by* Tom Lowenstein. WPOW
Woman singing in the house, The. Another Coast. David Wojahn. MAYP
Woman Sings of Her Love, A. *Somali Oral Tradition, tr. by* B. W. Andrzejewski *and* I. M. Lewis. WTO
Woman sits on her porch. Song. Earle Thompson. STE
Woman Skating. Margaret Atwood. IHMS
Woman speaks, A. The Hour of Feeling. Louis Simpson. FiCP
Woman supremely blest. Mulier Amicta Sole. Fray Angelico Chavez. ISi
"Woman, take away my tunic." Goll's Parting with His Wife. *Unknown, tr. by* Eoin MacNeill. AnIL
Woman Taken in Adultery, The. Bible, *N.T.* St. John, VIII: 2-11. TreFT
Woman That Had More Babies than That, The. Wallace Stevens. LiTA
Woman: that is to say. Of Women. *Unknown, tr. by* E. Powys Mathers. *Fr.* The Thousand and One Nights. DBV; ErPo; PV
Woman Thing, The. Audre Lorde. BlSi; NMM
Woman, though undependable. Experts on Woman. Arthur Guiterman. InMe
Woman! thoughtless, giddy creature. The Declaimer. Henry Baker. NOEC
Woman through the Window. Marcia Falk. VWA
Woman to Child. Judith Wright. PBWP; WPE
Woman to Her Lover, A. Christina Walsh. BrRo
Woman to Man. Ai. GP
Woman to Man. Judith Wright. CBAP; PoAu-2; WPE
Woman to man, they lie. In Bloemfontein. Alan Ross. BoLoP
Woman Waits for Me, A. Walt Whitman. ErPo; NOBA
Woman was cooking a mouse for her husband's dinner, A. The Mouse Dinners. Russell Edson. SoSe
Woman was heavy with child, The. The Flower Vendor. Luis Cabalquinto. BrSi
Woman was old and ragged and gray, The. Somebody's Mother. Mary Dow Brine. BeLS; BLPA; FaFP; TreF; WBLP
Woman watches her husband rubbing his nose, The. Twenty Below. R. A. D. Ford. CaP; NOBC
Woman weak and woman mortal, through the spirit's open portal. Streets of Baltimore. *Unknown.* BLPA
Woman Who Combed, The. Rush Rankin. FAZ
Woman Who Could Read the Minds of Dogs, The. Leslie Scalapino. NPGG
Woman Who Disapproved of Music at the Bar, The. Horace Gregory. MoPo
Woman who had been dressed by someone, in the same way that, A. Leslie Scalapino. *Fr.* Hmmmm. NPGG
Woman who has grown old, The. The Crows. Louise Bogan. SBG
Woman who is waiting for the evening draws, The. The Window. Stephen Dobyns. MAYP
Woman who lived, A. The Moon. Donald Hall. NCSH
Woman who lived in Holland, of old, A. Going Too Far. Mildred Howells. OnMSP; TiPo
Woman Who Loved to Cook, The. Erica Jong. TAP
Woman Who Loved Worms, The. Colette Inez. NMM
Woman Who Thought She Was More than a Samba, The. Jessica Hagedorn. BrSi
Woman Who Understands, The. Everard Jack Appleton. PoLF
Woman who walked home on the arm of John. Chant of Departure [a Missionary's Prayer]. Alfred Barrett. GoBC; ISi
Woman who writes feels too much, A. The Black Art. Anne Sexton. PoA
Woman whose face/ is a blurred map of roots. To Vera Thompson. John Haines. LCAP
Woman with a burning flame, A. Smothered Fires. Georgia Douglas Johnson. BlSi
Woman with broad, rough hands. Woman. Magda Portal, *tr. by* Irene Vegas-Garcia *and* Kathleen Weaver. WPOW
Woman with Child, The. Freda Laughton. OnYI
Woman with Flower. Naomi Long Madgett. AmNP; FB

Woman with Girdle. Anne Sexton. ErPo; NCSH; NoAM
Woman with no face walked into the light, A. Homage to Hieronymus Bosch. Thomas MacGreevy. BIrV; EAS; OnYI
Woman with the caught fox. Plea for a Captive. W. S. Merwin. NePoEA-2; NoAM; NYBP
Woman with the Serpent's Tongue, The. Sir William Watson. HBV-1
Woman, woman, let us say these things to each other. Prelude. Conrad Aiken. NYBP
Woman, women/ 1. An adult female person. The Dictionary Is an *His*torian: A Found Political Poem. Judith McCombs. IHMS
Woman Work. Maya Angelou. SaC
Woman working hard and wisely, A. Epigram. Kassia, *tr. by* Patrick Diehl. WPOW
Woman Wrapped in Silence, A, *sel.* John W. Lynch.
"Little girl, A/ Had wandered in the night," V. ISi
Woman, you are afraid of the forest. Maria Wine, *tr. fr. Swedish by* Nadia Christensen. PBWP
Woman, you'll never credit what. The Shepherd's Tale. James Kirkup. OBCP
Womanhood, The, *sels.* Gwendolyn Brooks.
Children of the Poor, The, I. PoA
"People who have no children can be hard," 1 *and* 2. PoA; WPE
"What shall I give my children? who are poor," 2. BALP; PoCh
(What Shall I Give My Children?) BPo
"Men of careful turns, haters of forks in the road." BALP
"One wants a Teller in a time like this," XI. WPE
Rites for Cousin Vit, The, VI. BPo; HAP; WeW; WPE
Womanhood [*or* Womanhod], wanton, ye want. John Skelton. AAS; NCEP
Womanisers. John Press. BoLoP; ErPo; NIP
Woman's Answer, A. *At. to* Earl of Surrey. SiPS
Woman's Answer to the Vampire, A. Felicia Blake. BLPA
Woman's Arms. Anacreon, *tr. fr. Greek by* Abraham Cowley. UnTE
Woman's Beauty. Lascelles Abercrombie. *Fr.* Emblems of Love: Vashti. MoBrPo
Woman's beauty is like a white, A. Song. W. B. Yeats. *Fr.* The Only Jealousy of Emer. MoAB
Woman's Constancy. John Donne. AnAnS-1; NoP; SeCV-1
Woman's Constancy. Sir John Suckling. CaPo
("There never yet was woman made.") AnAnS-2
Woman's Dream, The. Frances Horovitz. BrRo
Woman's Execution, A. Edward King. AA
Woman's face is full of wiles, A. Song. Humfrey Gifford. ElL
Woman's face with nature's own hand painted, A. Sonnets, XX. Shakespeare. ErPo; InvP; MasP; OAEL-2; PeHV
Woman's faith, and woman's trust. Sir Walter Scott. *Fr.* The Betrothed. ViBoPo
Woman's Inconstancy. Phineas Fletcher. *Fr.* Sicelides. ElL
Woman's Labour, The; an Epistle to Mr. Stephen Duck, *sel.* Mary Collier.
Washerwoman, The. NOEC
Woman's Last Word, A. Robert Browning. BLPA; BLPL; FaBoBe; FaFP; HBV-1; OAEP; TreFS; TrGrPo; UnTE; ViBoPo
Woman's Liberation. Sister Maura. AMV-81
Woman's Looks, A. *Unknown.* OBSC; TrGrPo
Woman's Love, A. John Hay. HBV-1
Woman's Love. *Unknown.* WBLP
Woman's love, April weather. Constancies. *Unknown, tr. by* Louis Untermeyer. UnTE
Woman's pink body could be preserved, A. Little Yellow Leaf. James Tate. NoAM
Woman's Question, A. Elizabeth Barrett Browning. WBLP
Woman's Question, A. Lena Lathrop. BLPA
Woman's Question, A. Adelaide Anne Procter. HBV-1
Woman's Reason, A. Gelett Burgess. FaBoNo
Woman's Ruling Passions. Pope. *Fr.* Moral Essays, Epistle II. OBEC
Woman's Shortcomings, A. Elizabeth Barrett Browning. BLPA; HBV-1
Woman's Song, A. Colleen J. McElroy. BlSi
Woman's Song. Judith Wright. PAI
Woman's Sorrow, A, *sel.* Ho Nansorhon, *tr. fr. Korean by* Peter H. Lee.
"Yesterday I fancied I was young." PBWP
Woman's Thought, A. Richard Watson Gilder. HBV-1
Woman's white body is a song. The Song of Songs. Heine, *tr. by* Louis Untermeyer. UnTE
Woman's Will. John Godfrey Saxe. FaFP; HBV-1; TreFT
(Wills.) ShM
Woman's Will. *Unknown.* HBV-1
Woman's Wish, The. Matthew Prior. FaBoEE
Womanwork. Paula Gunn Allen. TWSS
Womb Song. Susan Fromberg Schaeffer. IHMS
Womb-stolen woman, round woman. Protecting the Burial Grounds. Wendy Rose. TWSS
Wombat, The. Ogden Nash. CenHV
Women. Louise Bogan. HBMV; LiTA; MoAB; MoAmPo; MP; SBG; TwCP; VGW; WHA; WPE
Women. William Cartwright. ELU; ErPo
Women. ——— Heath. CTC; OBSC
(These Women All.) FaBoCo
Women. Adrienne Rich. NMM
Women. May Swenson. BoWoP; NMM; Prf
Women. Alice Walker. GOA; WPOW
Women ("She truly needs good character"). *Yoruba Oral Tradition, tr. by* Ulli Beier. WTO
Women,/ What fools we are. Two Strange Worlds. Francesca Yetunde Pereira. PBA
Women All Tell Me, The, *with music. Unknown.* BLSo
Women and Men. Hassan Sheikh Mumin, *tr. fr. Somali.* WTO
Women and poets see the truth arrive. Letter to the Front. Muriel Rukeyser. WaP
Women and Roses. Robert Browning. ViBoPo
Women are dark and seem, The. Old Photographs. David Harsent. POL
Women are door-mats and have been. Door-Mats. Mary Carolyn Davies. HBMV; YaD
Women Are Grieving, The. Linda Hogan. TWSS
Women are timid, cower and shrink. Betty Zane. Thomas Dunn English. PAH
Women Are Worthy. *Unknown. See* Woman Is a Worthy Thing, A.
Women at Munition Making. Mary Gabrielle Collins. SUMH
Women at the Corners Stand, The. Louis Golding. TrJP
Women at the Market. Angela Figueroa Aymerich, *tr. fr. Spanish by* Hardie St. Martin. PBWP
Women before were strangers. Dispatch Number Nine. Doug Fetherling. NeAC
Women ben full of ragerie. Imitation of Chaucer. Pope. FaBoPa; Par
Women Called Bossy Cowboys. Beth Jankola. AMV-80
Women Damned. Baudelaire, *tr. fr. French by* Joanna Richardson. PeHV
(Condemned Women, *tr. by* John Gray.) SyP
Women don't travel in clubcars. George Jonas. NeAC
Women Folk, The. James Hogg. HBV-1
Women have loved before as I love now. Sonnet. Edna St. Vincent Millay. PoA
Women have no share in the encampments of this world. Women and Men. Hassan Sheikh Mumin, *tr. fr. Somali.* WTO
Women have no wilderness in them. Women. Louise Bogan. HBMV; LiTA; MoAB; MoAmPo; MP; SBG; TwCP; VGW; WHA; WPE
Women Hoping for Rain. David Tillinghast. AMV-81
Women, if we held the oxhide shield. Lament for a Warrior. *Unknown, tr. by* Dan Kunene *and* Jack Cope. PeSA
Women in black picked up their violins. The Call. Jules Supervielle, *tr. by* Geoffrey Gardner. NU
Women in Old Parkas, The. Mary TallMountain. STE
Women in uniform. Omen of Victory. Mina Loy. InPK
Women in Vietnam, The. Grace Paley. NMM
Women know how to wait here. Lines for Marking Time. Roberta Hill Whiteman. BoWoP; CDW; TWSS
Women loving each other. Bad Girl Blues. *Unknown.* BluL
Women Men's Shadows. Ben Jonson. *See* That Women Are but Men's Shadows.
Women of My Land. Frankie Armstrong. BrRo
Women of Rubens, The. Wislawa Szymborska, *tr. fr. Polish by* Celina Wieniewska. WPOW
Women of the Better Class, The. Oliver Herford. HBMV
Women of the West, The. G. Essex Evans. PoAu-1
Women of Trachis, *sels.* Sophocles, *tr. fr. Greek by* Ezra Pound.
"Kupris bears trophies away." CTC
"Torn between griefs, which grief shall I lament." OBVE
Women Open Cautiously. Deborah Lee. BrSi
Women Pleased, *sels.* John Fletcher.
Song: "Oh fair sweet face, oh eyes celestial bright," *fr.* III, iv. OBS; PoEL-2
Women's Longing, *fr.* V, i. HBV-1
Women Singing. Sir Henry Taylor. OBVV
Women Speak Out in Defense of Themselves, The. Aristophanes, *tr. fr. Greek by B. B. Rogers. Fr.* The Thesmophoriazusae. TreFT
Women Speaking, The. Linda Hogan. TWSS
Women tell me every day, The. Thomas Moore. Odes of Anacreon, VII. LoBV
Women that are loved are more than lovable. The Colours of Love. Denis Devlin. IPY; OxBI
Women there are on earth, most sweet and high. Of Those Who Walk Alone. Richard Burton. HBV-1
Women Transport Corps. *Unknown, tr. fr. Chinese by* Kai-yu Hsu. WPOW
Women who do not love are free. The Free Woman. Theodosia Garrison. HBMV

Women, whoever wishes to know my lord. Gaspara Stampa, *tr. fr. Italian by* J. Vitiello. BoWoP
Women with hats like the rear ends of pink ducks. To a Waterfowl. Donald Hall. OBAL
Women, women,/ women, women. A Fixture. May Swenson. NYBP
Women's Degrees. A. D. Godley. GLGT; NOBL
Women's Jail, The. Miriam Waddington. NOBC
Women's Locker Room. Marilyn Waniek. MAYP
Women's Longing. John Fletcher. *Fr.* Women Pleased. HBV-1
Women's Marseillaise, The. F. E. M. Macaulay. BrRo
Women's Tug of War at Lough Arrow. Tess Gallagher. MAYP
Won' you ring, old hammer? Hammer, Ring. *Unknown.* AmFP
Wonder. Bernard Raymund. GDP
Wonder. Thomas Traherne. AnAnS-1; CH; HAP; LiTB; LoBV; NoP; PPoe; SeCePo; SeCeV; SeCP; SeCV-2; TrGrPo; WHA
Wonder, The/ of the bees. Virgil: Georgics, Book IV. Dennis Schmitz. NPGG
Wonder and a Thousand Springs. William Alexander Percy. HBMV
Wonder Clock, The, *sels.* Katherine Pyle. OBCA
Nine o'Clock.
One o'Clock.
Two O'Clock.
Wonder is not precisely knowing. Emily Dickinson. MoPo
Wonder not if I stay not here. To Master Davenant for Absence. Sir John Suckling. CaPo
Wonder of the world is o'er, The. The Twilight of Earth. "Æ." AnIL
Wonder stranger ne'r was known, A. The Suffolk Miracle. *Unknown.* BaBo; ESPB
Wonder-Teacher, The. Cynthia Ozick. VWA
Wonder Where This Horseshoe Went. Edna St. Vincent Millay. *Fr.* A Very Little Sphinx. SUS
Wonder Woman. Genny Lim. BrSi
Wonderful are thy works, as my soul overwhelmingly knoweth. The Royal Crown, I. Solomon ibn Gabirol, *tr. by* Israel Zangwill. AWP
Wonderful bears that walked my room all night. Bears. Adrienne Rich. NCSH; NePoEA; NYBP; PAI
Wonderful bird is the pelican, A. Limerick. Dixon Lanier Merritt. CenHV; FaBoCo
Wonderful Man, A. Aileen Fisher. SiSoSe
Wonderful Mother, A. Pat O'Reilly. BLPA
Wonderful Old Man, The. *Unknown.* NA
Wonderful "One-Hoss Shay," The. Oliver Wendell Holmes. *See* Deacon's Masterpiece, The.
Wonderful way is the King's Highway, A. The King's Highway. John Masefield. BLRP; TRV
Wonderful weather! The Sea's Last Gift; 1961. Milton Kessler. DiL
Wonderful workings of the world, The: wonderful. Cut the Grass. A. R. Ammons. HAP; PPP; TAP; WeW
Wonderful World, The. William Brighty Rands. FaPON; HBV-1; HBVY; TiPo
(Child's World, The.) OHIP; TreFT
(World, The.) OxBChV
(World, The; a Child's Song.) OBVV
Wonderfully out of the beautiful form. Sonnet. Dante, *tr. by* Dante Gabriel Rossetti. *Fr.* La Vita Nuova. GoBC
Wondering I gaze upon each lineament. Sonnet: The Corpse. George Moore. SyP
Wonderland. Harry Thurston Peck. AA
Wonders. Shirley Kaufman. VWA
Wonders. *Unknown.* EIL
(Thule, the Period of Cosmography.) HAP; NCEP
"Andalusian merchant, that returns, The," *sel.* FaBoCh
Wonders are many and none is more wonderful than man. Glengormley. Derek Mahon. CIP
Wonders of the World. Richard Shelton. DFF
"Wondrous life!" cried Marvell at Appleton House. Round. Weldon Kees. CoAP; NaP; NoAM
Wondrous Love. *Unknown, at. to* Alex Means. AmFP; BLSo, *with music*; FSW; TrAS, *with music*
(What Wondrous Love Is This, 2 *vers., with music.*) AH
Wondrous Motherhood. *Unknown.* PGD
Wondrous Show, A. James Thomson. *Fr.* The Castle of Indolence. OBEC
Wondrous Son of God. Berniece Goertz. STF
Wondrous the gods, more wondrous are the men. A Compliment to the Ladies. Blake. BXAP
Wondrous things have come to pass. Wizard Frost. Frank Dempster Sherman. YeAr
Wondrous this masonry wasted by Fate! The Ruin. *Unknown, tr. by* Charles W. Kennedy. AnOE; PrIm
Wonga Vine. Judith Wright. PoAu-2
Won't be rushed; will take. Old Men Working Concrete. Phillip Hey. FiCP
Won't you be my chauffeur. Me and My Chauffeur Blues. *Unknown.* BluL
Won't you come home Bill Bailey. Bill Bailey. Hughie Cannon. FSW
Won't you go down, old Hannah? Old Hannah. *Unknown.* FSW
"Won't you look out of your window, Mrs. Gill?" The Mocking Fairy. Walter de la Mare. MoBrPo; MoShBr
Woo Not the World. Mu'tamid, King of Seville, *tr. fr. Arabic by* Dulcie L. Smith. AWP
Wood. Thomas Hornsby Ferril. PoRA
Wood Butcher. Norman Hindley. AMV-81
Wood-Dove's Note, The. Emily Huntington Miller. HBV-1
Wood Floor Dreams. Lance Henson. VoR
Wood Flower. Richard Le Gallienne. HBMV
Wood is a good place to find, The. Walking with Lulu in the Wood. Naomi Lazard. NYBP
Wood is bare, The: a river-mist is steeping. Elegy. Robert Bridges. EBVV; OAEP; PoPle
Wood is full of shining eyes, The. The Magic Wood. Henry Treece. DuDa; EAS
Wood is one blue flame of love, The. Derbyshire Bluebells. Sacheverell Sitwell. ChMP
Wood louse sits on a splinter, The. Archygrams. Don Marquis. WhC
Wood Music. Ethel King. GoYe
Wood of Flowers, The. James Stephens. PDV
Wood of the Self-Destroyers, The. Samuel Yellen. NePoAm-2
Wood-Pigeons. John Masefield. ChMP
Woodpigeons at Raheny. Donald Davie. PP
Wood shakes in the breeze, The. The Old Tree. Andrew Young. GoJo
Wood So Wild, The. *Unknown. See* I Must Go Walk the Wood So Wild.
Wood Song, A. Ralph Hodgson. GoJo; HBV-1
Wood-Song. Eugene Lee-Hamilton. OBVV
Wood-Swallows, The. "Fiona Macleod." *Fr.* Australian Transcripts. FM
Wood, swollen with mushrooms, The. The Circle. Jean Garrigue. LiTA; MoPo
Wood, the Weed, the Wag, The. Sir Walter Ralegh. SiPS; TrGrPo
(Sir Walter Ralegh to His Son.) EnRePo
(Three Thing[e]s There Be[e] That Prosper Up Apace.) NoP; PoEL-2
(To His Son.) InPS; PPoe
Wood-Thrush. John Hall Wheelock. NePoAm
Woodtick. Joy Kogawa. BrSi
Wood was rather old and dark, The. The Little Boy Lost. Stevie Smith. FaBoTw
Woodbines in October. Charlotte Fiske Bates. AA
Woodbird. Charles G. Bell. NePoAm
Woodchuck Who Lives on Top of Mt. Ritter. John Oliver Simon. NeAC
Woodchuck who'd chucked lots of wood, A. Double Entendre. J. F. Wilson. TDH
Woodchucks. Maxine W. Kumin. HoPM; NIP
Woodchuck's very very fat, The. The Jolly Woodchuck. Marion Edey *and* Dorothy Grider. FaPON; PDV; TiPo
Wood-cut. V. Sackville-West. ChMP
Woodcut. R. N. D. Wilson. OxBI
Wood-Cutter's Night Song, The. John Clare. EnRP; OBRV
Woodcutter's Wife, The. William Rose Benét. AWP
Wooden Chamber, The. Anne Hébert, *tr. fr. French by* Birgit Swenson. WPOW
Wooden Horse then said, The. Jenny Mastoraki, *tr. fr. Modern Greek by* Nikos Germanakos. BoWoP; PBWP
Wooden Ships. David Morton. EtS
Wooden shoes resounded and died down. The European Night. Stanislav Vinaver, *tr. by* Vasa D. Mihailovich. VWA
Wooden Tiger, The. Samuel Yellen. NePoAm
Woodland and Worship. Ethelwyn Wetherald. CaP
Woodland Revel, A. Clarence Urmy. HBMV
Woodland sprite of the rakish kind, A. A Scandal among the Flowers. Charles S. Taylor. BLPA
Woodlands, The. William Barnes. BoNaP; OBVV
Woodlands. Sir Herbert Read. BrPo
Woodlore. Kim Kurt. NePoAm-2
Woodman, Spare That Tree. George Pope Morris. AA; BLPA; BLSo, *with music*; FaBoBe; FaFP; FaPON; FPL; FSW; HBV-1; OHIP; PaPo; PSoN, *with music*; TreF; WBLP
Woodman's Dog, The. William Cowper. *Fr.* The Task, V. ELU; GDP
Woodnotes I ("When the pine tosses its cones"). Emerson. AmPP; NePA; NOBA
Sels.
Heart of All the Scene, The. AA
"In unplowed Maine he sought the lumberers' gang." TAP
Woodnotes II ("As sunbeams stream through liberal space"). Emerson. NOBA
Sels.
"All the forms are fugitive." WGRP

"As the sunbeams stream through liberal space." OHIP
Mighty Heart, The. AA
Undersong, The. AA
"Whoso walks in solitude." OBVV
Woodpecker, The. Elizabeth Madox Roberts. FaPON; OBCA; TiPo
Woodpecker goes beating a little drum, The. Sleep. Charles Simic. CoAP
Woodpecker pecked out a little round hole, The. The Woodpecker. Elizabeth Madox Roberts. FaPON; OBCA; TiPo
Woodpeckers here are redheaded, The. Ornithology in Florida. Arthur Guiterman. BoAnP; InMe
Wood-Pile, The. Robert Frost. CABA; CoBMV; LiTA; NoAM; NoP; SeCeV; TwAmPo; VGW
Woods. W. H. Auden. NePA; NePoAm
Woods and downs have caught the mid-December, The. Stanzas Written on Battersea Bridge during a Southwesterly Gale. Hilaire Belloc. GoBC
Woods and Kestrel. Julian Bell. ChMP
Woods are lovely, dark and deep, The. Robert Frost. *Fr.* Stopping by Woods on a Snowy Evening. TRV
Woods are overhead over everywhere, The. James Cunningham. *Fr.* The Narrator's Trance. JB
Woods are purple with the haze, The. Autumn Color. Tom Robinson. YeAr
Woods Are Still, The. "Michael Field." OBVV
Woods at Night, The. May Swenson. DuDa
Woods decay, the woods decay and fall, The. Tithonus. Tennyson. CABA; FaBoEn; HAP; LiTB; LoBV; NOBE; NoP; OAEL-2; OAEP; OBNC; PAI; PoEL-5; PoPle; PPP; TEP; VLP; WHA
Woods Gets Religion. John Woods. GP
Woods have a way of slanting light, The. The Enlightenment. Patricia Sheppard. AMV-81
Woods Night. Tom Hennen. GP
Woods No More, The. Jay MacPherson. PeCV
Woods of Arcady are dead, The. The Song of the Happy Shepherd. W. B. Yeats. NoAM; VLP
Woods of the horizon, The. Men in the City. Alfonsina Storni, *tr. by* Rachel Benson. PBWP
Woods shall not decry the murderous stroke. On Some Trees Needlessly Slain. Stanton A. Coblentz. TRV
Woods we're lost in aren't real, The. Villanelle. Walter H. Kerr. NePoAm-2
Woodspurge, The. Dante Gabriel Rossetti. EBEV; ELP; FaBoEn; GTBS-P; HAP; HeIP; InPK; LoBV; NBM; NOBE; NoP; OAEL-2; OAEP; OBEV; OBNC; PoEL-5; PrIm; TreFT; UnPo; VLP; WeW; WHA
Woodstock. Joni Mitchell. NIP
Woodtown Manor. John Montague. IPY
Woodworker's Ballad. Herbert Edward Palmer. OBEV
Woody says, "Let's make our soap." Social Studies. Mary Neville. POL
Woodyards in the Rain. Anne Marriott. CaP
Wooed and Married and A'. Alexander Ross. HBV-1; OxBS
Woof of the Sun, Ethereal Gauze. Henry David Thoreau. *See* Haze.
Wooing, The. *Unknown, tr. fr. Latin by* John Addington Symonds. UnTE
Wooing Frog, The. James Reeves. SO
Wooing in a Dream. Nicholas Breton. *See* Report Song.
Wooing Lady, The. William Jay Smith. NePoEA
Wooing Maid, The. Martin Parker. CoMu
Wooing of Criseide, The. Chaucer. *Fr.* Troilus and Criseide, III. PoEL-1
Wooing of Etain, The. *Unknown, tr. fr. Irish by* John Montague. BIrV
Wooing Rogue, The. *Unknown.* CoMu
Wooing Song. Giles Fletcher. *Fr.* Christ's Victory and Triumph: Christ's Victory on Earth. EIL; HBV-1; OBEV
("Love is the blossom where there blows.") LO; ViBoPo
Wool Trade, The. John Dyer. *Fr.* The Fleece, III. OBEC; SeCePo
Woolworth Philodendron, The. Stephen Sandy. CoPo
Woosel [*or* Ousel] cock so black of hue, The. Bottom's Song. Shakespeare. *Fr.* A Midsummer Night's Dream, III, i. CTC; PB; PBBP; ViBoPo
Wops came down to the port, The. The City of Beggars. Alfred Hayes. WaP
Word, The. Margaret Avison. MoCV
Word, The. Bible, *N.T.* *Fr.* St. John. *See* In the Beginning Was the Word.
Word, The. Basil Bunting. PoA
Word, The. Gustave Kahn, *tr. fr. French by* Edouard Roditi. VWA
Word, The. Richard Realf. AA; TRV; WGRP
Word. Stephen Spender. NYBP; PAI; PP
Word, The. Tennyson. In Memoriam A. H. H., XXXVI. GoBC
Word, The. Neil Weiss. NYBP
Word about Freedom and Identity in Tel Aviv, A. Jon Silkin. VWA
Word bites like a fish, The. Word. Stephen Spender. NYBP; PAI; PP
Word Fitly Spoken, A. Bible, *O.T.* Proverbs, XXV: 11. FaPON
Word goes round Repins, The. An Absolutely Ordinary Rainbow. Les A. Murray. CBAP
Word has been abroad, The; is back, with a tanned look. Annunciations. Geoffrey Hill. NePoEA-2
Word has come and Martha the ticket girl. Stumptown Attends the Picture Show. David Bottoms. GP
Word has come from the kitchen. *See* Word's gane to the kitchen.
Word has come to May Margerie. Jellon Grame. *Unknown.* ESPB
Word has gane thro a' this land. The Bonny Lass of Anglesey (B *vers.*). *Unknown.* ESPB
Word in Edgeways, A. Charles Tomlinson. NOBL
Word is dead, A. Emily Dickinson. RHPC
Word Made Flesh, The. W. J. Turner. OBMV
Word Man, The. Larry Moffi. AMV-80
Word of a snail on the plate of a leaf, The? The Couriers. Sylvia Plath. LCAP
"Word" of a Watch-Dog, The. Sandag, *tr. by* C. R. Bawden. WTO
"Word" of a Wolf Encircled by the Hunt, The. Sandag, *tr. by* C. R. Bawden. WTO
Word of advice about matters and things, A. Written at the White Sulphur Springs. Francis Scott Key. OBAL
"Word" of an Antelope Caught in a Trap, The. Sandag, *tr. by* C. R. Bawden. WTO
Word of Encouragement, A. J. R. Pope. ELU; FiBHP; FPL; NOBL; PV
Word of God, The. Annie Johnson Flint. BLRP
Word of God, The. J. Harold Gwynne. STF
Word of God, across the Ages, *with music.* Ferdinand Q. Blanchard. AH
Word of God came unto me, The. In the Garden of the Lord. Helen Keller. TRV; WGRP
Word of God to Leyden Came, The. Jeremiah Eames Rankin. AA; HBV-2; PAH; PAL
Word of mystery is told, A. A Rime of the Rood. Charles L. O'Donnell. GoBC
Word of the Lord by night, The. Boston Hymn. Emerson. PAH; PAL; TRV; WGRP
Word of the Lord came unto me, saying, The. Chorus from "The Rock"—III. T. S. Eliot. *Fr.* The Rock. LiTB; TRV
Word of the Lord from Havana, The. Richard Hovey. HBV-2: PAH
Word of Warning, A. *Unknown.* *See* Pilgrim at Rome, The.
Word of Water, The. E. L. Mayo. PoA
Word over All. C. Day Lewis. OAEP
Word over all, beautiful as the sky. Reconciliation. Walt Whitman. FaBoEn; HAP; MoAmPo; NoP; OBWP; OxBA; PAI; TrGrPo; WaaP; WeW
Word *Plum,* The. Helen Chasin. NIP
Word Poem (Perhaps Worth Considering). Nikki Giovanni. BOLo; PoBA
Word sticks in the wind's throat, A. Apology. Richard Wilbur. NePoAm; Psk
Word to Husbands, A. Ogden Nash. POL
Word to New England, A. William Bradford. SCAP
Word to the West End, A. Thomas Ashe. EBVV
Word to the Wise, A. Caroline Duer. AA
Word was brought to the Danish king. The King of Denmark's Ride. Caroline E. S. Norton. BeLS; GN; HBV-1
Word went forth, The. St. Thomas Aquinas, *tr. fr. Latin by* Helen Waddell. NAWM-1
Words. Helen Morgan Brooks. NNP; PoNe
Words. Jean Burden. AMV-81
Words. Richard Eberhart. NePA
Words. Robert Finch. PoA
Words. Ulálume González De Leon, *tr. fr. Spanish by* Sara Nelson. AMV-81
Words. Charles Harpur. PoAu-1
Words, The. Lee Harwood. EAS
Words. Philip Levine. VWA
Words. David Phillips. NeAC
Words. Sylvia Plath. ConAP; LCAP
Words. Ernest Rhys. HBMV
Words. Vern Rutsala. GP
Words. *Unknown.* PoLF
Words, The. David Wagoner. PoA
Words. Miller Williams. AMV-81
Words/ across. Persimmons and Plums. Elizabeth Hodges. GrPl
Words and Monsters. Vernon Scannell. OxBC
Words and Music, *sel.* Samuel Beckett.
"Age is when to a man." BIrV
Words are deeds. The words we hear. Words. Charles Harpur. PoAu-1
Words Are Never Enough. Charles Bruce. CaP; OBCV
Words are sardines packed. Bell Too Heavy to Ring. Tom Kryss. NeAC
Words are written/ on the Wailing Wall. Identity. Robert Friend. GP; VWA
Words at Farewell. Vahan Derian, *tr. fr. Armenian by* Diana Der Hovanessian. AMV-81

Words can be stuffy, as sticky as glue. Alphabet Stew. Jack Prelutsky. RHPC
Words do not grow on the landscape. Jean Malley. PoA
Words for a Resurrection. Leo Kennedy. OBCV; PeCV
Words, for alas my trade is words, a barren burst of rhyme. To M. E. W. G. K. Chesterton. HBV-2
Words for Army Bugle Calls. *Unknown.* TreF
Words for Hart Crane. Robert Lowell. AP; CABA; CMoP; NMP
Words for his ugly mug his. Ludwig's Death Mask. Ted Hughes. NoAM
Words for the Raker of Leaves. Léonie Adams. PoCh
Words for the Wind. Theodore Roethke. AP; CoAP; NoAM; NOBA; PoCh
Words from a Bottle. Deborah Lee. BrSi
Words from an Old Spanish Carol. *Unknown, tr. fr. Spanish by* Ruth Sawyer. PChr
(Christmas Morn.) OBCP
(On Christmas Morn.) FaPON; PDV
Words from Hell. David Helwig. NOBC
Words from the Window of a Railway Car. Anatoly Steiger, *tr. fr. Russian by* John Glad. VWA
Word's gane to [*or* Word has come from] the kitchen. Mary Hamilton. *Unknown.* AmFP; ESPB; FaBoBa; NoP; OAEP; ViBoFo
Word's gone out, and now they spread the main, The. Defoe. *Fr.* The Spanish Descent. OBWP
Words have all fled the country, they are not expected back, The. Emigration. Anita Barrows. NMM
Words have grown old inside men, The. The Words Will Resurrect. Jorge de Lima, *tr. by* John Nist. TTY
Words in the Mourning Time, *sel.* Robert Hayden.
"For King, for Robert Kennedy." CNA
Words in Time. Archibald MacLeish. CrMA; NePA; PoCh; PoRA
Words, like fine flowers, have their colors too. Words. Ernest Rhys. HBMV
Words like Freedom. Langston Hughes. *See* Refugee in America.
Words, like Spiders. P. Wolny. PCP
Words Made of Water. Burns Singer. NePoEA-2
Words move, music moves. T. S. Eliot. Four Quartets: Burnt Norton, V. UnS; ViBoPo
Words of a poem should be glass. Glass. Robert Francis. DFF; PP
Words of Agur, The. Bible, *O.T.* Proverbs, XXX: 4, 15-16, 18-19, 24-28. TrGrPo
Words of Finn, The. *Unknown, tr. fr. Old Irish.* ChTr
Words of hymns abruptly plod, The. Hymn. Louise Townsend Nicholl. EaLo
Words of Oblivion and Peace. Gabriel Preil, *tr. fr. Hebrew by* Robert Friend. VWA
Words of our day, The. The Same Side of the Canoe. Alda do Espírito Santo, *tr. by* Allan Francovich *and* Kathleen Weaver. PBWP
Words of the All-Wise, The, *sel.* *Tr. fr. Icelandic by* W. H. Auden *and* Paul B. Taylor.
"Say, dwarf, for it seems to me." OBVE
Words of the Preacher, The. Bible, *O.T.* *Fr.* Ecclesiastes. *See* Vanity of Vanities.
Words on the Windowpane. Dante Gabriel Rossetti. SyP
Words scored upon a bone. Meditation on a Bone. A. D. Hope. TW
Words Spoken Alone. Dannie Abse. NYBP
Words Spoken by Pasternak during a Bombing. Bella Akhmadulina, *tr. fr. Russian by* Jean Valentine *and* Olga Carlisle BoWoP
Words That Speak of Death. Anadad Eldan, *tr. fr. Hebrew by* Anthony Rudolf *and* Natan Zach. VWA
Words, the Words, the Words, The. William Carlos Williams. BiP
Words to a Song. Agnes Nemes Nagy, *tr. fr. Hungarian by* Bruce Berlind BoWoP
Words to My Friend. Renée Vivien, *tr. fr. French by* Sandia Belgrade. PeHV
Words to My Mother. Alfonsina Storni, *tr. fr. Spanish by* Marion Hodapp *and* Mary Crow. AMV-80
Words to Remind Me of Grandmother. Andrés Castro Ríos, *tr. fr. Spanish by* Julio Marzán. InW
Words to the Wind. Pier Giorgio Di Cicco. AMV-80
Words were meant. Poet's Protest. Doris Hedges. CaP
Words Wherein Stinging Bees Lurk. Judah Halevi, *tr. fr. Hebrew by* Nina Davis Salaman. TrJP
Words Will Resurrect, The. Jorge de Lima, *tr. fr. Portuguese by* John Nist. TTY
Words without Music. Irving Layton. CaP
Words without Music. *Unknown.* WhC
Words! Words! Jessie Fauset. CDC
Words Words Words. Marilyn Krysl. AMV-80
Wordspinning. Olga Kirsch, *tr. fr. Afrikaans by* Jack Cope. PeSA
Wordsworth. William Wilberforce Lord. *Fr.* Ode to England. AA
Wordsworth. James Kenneth Stephen *See* Sonnet, A: "Two voices are there: one is of the deep."
Wordsworth I love, his books are like the fields. To Wordsworth. John Clare. OAEL-2
Wordsworth Skates on Esthwaite Water. Wordsworth. *Fr.* The Prelude, I. FaBoPP
Wordsworth, thou form almost divine, cried Henry. John Berryman. *Fr.* Dream Songs. CAPP
Wordsworth Unvisited. Hartley Coleridge. *See* He Lived amidst the' Untrodden Ways.
Wordsworth upon Helvellyn! Let the cloud. On a Portrait of Wordsworth by B. R. Haydon. Elizabeth Barrett Browning. HeIP
Wordsworth's Grave. Matthew Arnold. *Fr.* Memorial Verses. FaBoPP
Wordsworth's Grave. Sir William Watson. GoTL; HBV-2; OBNC; VLP, *abr.*
Work. Louis James Block. AA
Work. Andrei Codrescu. EAS
Work. Kenyon Cox. PGD
Work. D. H. Lawrence. OBMV
Work. James Russell Lowell. PoSC
Work. Pushkin, *tr. fr. Russian by* Babette Deutsch *and* Avrahm Yarmolinsky. AWP
Work. G. A. Studdert-Kennedy. EBCP
Work. Henry van Dyke. TRV
Work. Robert Penn Warren. *Fr.* Boy's Will, Joyful Labor without Pay, and Harvest Home. SaC
Work?/ I don't have to work. Necessity. Langston Hughes. NOBA
Work; a Song of Triumph ("Work!/ Thank God for the might of it"). Angela Morgan. PoLF; YaD
Work all week an' don' make enough. It's Hard on We Po' Farmers. *Unknown.* OuSiCo
Work and Play. Martial, *tr. fr. Latin by* Louis Untermeyer. UnTE
Work-basket made of an old armadillo, A. The Caledonian Market. William Plomer. ChMP
Work, for the night is coming. Annie L. Walker. SaC
Work Gangs. Carl Sandburg. SaC
Work Horses. Edith Newlin Chase. SoPo
Work in a mine and become a mine. Mine. Andrew Hudgins. AMV-80
Work [*or* Worke] is done, The. Young men and maidens, set. On Himself. Robert Herrick. CaPo; SeCP
Work of Artifice, A. Marge Piercy. IHMS; Psk
Work of Love, The. Margaret Sangster. BLRP
Work of the Weavers, The. *Unknown.* FSW
Work on the railroad. Roll on the Ground. *Unknown.* AmFP
Work Song. Raymond Mazisi Kunene, *tr. fr. Zulu by* D. K. Rycroft. WTO
Work-table, litter, books and standing lamp. Night Sweat. Robert Lowell. TAP; VGW
Work thou for pleasure. Work. Kenyon Cox. PGD
Work to Do toward Town. Gary Snyder. VGW
Work without Hope. Samuel Taylor Coleridge. BiP; BoNaP; EnRP; FiP; HBV-2; LoBV; NOBE; NoP; OBEV; OBRV; PAI; SaC; TEP
Workaday Morning. Astrid Tollefsen, *tr. fr. Norwegian by* Nadia Christensen. PBWP
Workbox, The. Thomas Hardy. InPK; UnPo
Worke is done, The: young men, and maidens set. *See* Work is done, The . . .
Worker, The. Gerald Massey. EBVV
Worker, The. Richard W. Thomas. PoBA; PoNe
Workers earn it. Money. Richard Armour. FaFP; PoPl; TreFS; WhC
Workers' flag is deepest red, The. *See* People's flag is deepest red, The.
Workers of Ireland, why crouch ye like cravens. New Words to the Tune of "O'Donnel Abu." Jim Connell. OnYI
Workers on the S.P. Line to strike sent out a call, The. Casey Jones (Union). Joe Hill. FSW
Workers Rose on May Day or Postscript to Karl Marx, The. Audre Lorde. GP
Workhouse Boy, The. *Unknown.* GBP; VLP
Working against Time. David Wagoner. MAT
Working at a Service Station, I Think of Shinkichi Takahashi Dennis Finnell. FAZ
Working Class. Bertram Warr. NOBC; OBCV; WaP
Working Girls. Carl Sandburg. SaC
Working in a weave-room, fighting for my life. Weave Room Blues. *Unknown.* FSW
Working is another way of praying. Song for Dov Shamir [*or* Song of a Hebrew]. Dannie Abse. VWA; WTO
Working Late. Louis Simpson. DiL
Working Man, The. Gregory Donovan. AMV-81
Working Man Blues. *Unknown.* BluL
Working near Lake Traverse. Tom Hennen. FAZ
Working Party, A. Siegfried Sassoon. CMoP; MMA
Working people long ago, The. Labor Day. Marnie Pomeroy. PoSC
Working Song. Buluguru, *tr. fr. Yaoro by* E. A. Worms. CBAP

Working the Rain Shift at Flanagan's. Gibbons Ruark. MAYP
Working the Skeet House. Jon Eastman. AMV-80
Working with God. "George Eliot." *Fr.* Stradivarius. TRV
Working with Tools. A. R. Ammons. NoAM
Workman plied his clumsy spade, A. Two Surprises. R. W. McAlpine. PoLF
"Workman, what will you make on the bench today?" Carpenter. George Mackay Brown. OxBC
Workmen. Herbert Morris. NePoAm-2
Work-out, The. Geoffrey Movius. MAT
Works and Days, *sel.* Hesiod, *tr. fr. Greek.*
"Next to my counsels an attention pay," *tr. by* Thomas Cooke. FaBoUs
Works of God, The. Moses ibn Ezra, *tr. fr. Hebrew by* Solomon Solis-Cohen. TrJP
Workshop, The. Aileen Fisher. SoPo
World, The. Francis Bacon. *See* Life of Man, The.
World, The. Robert Creeley. NaP; NoAM; NoP
World, The. William Drummond of Hawthornden. *See* Book of the World, The.
World, The. George Herbert. OBS; SeCV-1
World, The. Thomas Love Peacock. PV
World, The. Kathleen Raine. OxBTC
World, The. William Brighty Rands. *See* Wonderful World, The.
World, The. Christina Rossetti. BoWoP; VLP
World, The. Vern Rutsala. Psk
World, The. Henry Vaughan. AnAnS-1; AWP; CABA; EBEV; FaBoEn; FaBV; GoTL; HAP; HBV-2; HeIP; ILwL; JCP; LiTB; LoBV; MasP; MePo; NOBE; NOCV; OAEL-1; OAEP; OBS; OxBoCh; PoEL-2; PPoe; PPP; SeCeV; SeCP; SeCV-1; TEP; TrCP; TreFS; TrGrPo; ViBoPo; WGRP
(Eternity, *abr.*) OBEV
(Vision, A, *1 st.*) ImOP
World, The. Wordsworth. *See* World Is Too Much with Us, The.
World,/ world you are wonderful. A Round Song. Rhyll McMaster. CBAP
World, The; a Child's Song. William Brighty Rands. *See* Wonderful World, The.
World, The; a Ghazel. James Clarence Mangan. OBVV
World a Hunt, The. William Drummond of Hawthornden. NOBE; OBS
(World a Hunting Is, The.) FaBoEn
World an Illusion, The. *Unknown.* MeEL
World as Meditation, The. Wallace Stevens. AP; CABA; HeIP; LCAP; MoAB; NIP; PPP
World as Wave and Idea, The. Louis Coxe. SOTS
World Beautiful, The. Milton. *Fr.* Paradise Lost, IV. GN
World below the Brine, The. Walt Whitman. BiP; BoNaP; FM; InPS; MAT; NePA; NoP
World Beyond, A. Nathaniel Ingersoll Bowditch. AA
World can end any time, The. A Reliable Service. Allen Curnow. OCNZ
World did say to me, The. The Crazy World. William Gay. PoAu-1
World doesn't crumble apart, The. Watershed. Margaret Avison. OBCV
World Enough. Jeanine Hathaway. AMV-80
World feels dusty, The. Emily Dickinson. MoAmPo
World goes up and the world goes down, The. Dolcino to Margaret [*or* Hey Nonny!]. Charles Kingsley. HBV-1; OBVV
World has a glass center, The. Magnificat in Transit from the Toledo Airport. George Starbuck. SUW
World has held great Heroes, The. The Song of Mr. Toad. Kenneth Grahame. *Fr.* The Wind in the Willows. FaPON; FiBHP; GoJo; NOBL
World has room for the manly man, with the spirit of manly cheer, The. The Manly Man. *Unknown.* BLPA; WBLP
World hath conquered, the wind hath scattered like dust, The. Tara Is Grass. *Unknown, tr. by* Padraic Pearse. AnIL; AnIV; POL
World hath its own dead, The; great motions start. Edith Cavell. George Edward Woodberry. HBMV
World Hymn, The. J. Gilchrist Lawson. WBLP
World I Am Passing Through, The. Lydia Maria Child. AA; HBV-1
World I did not wish to enter, A. A Necessitarian's Epitaph. Thomas Hardy. FaBoEE
World in gloom and splendour passes by, The. To a Millionaire. Archibald Lampman. NOBC
World in Making, The. Sir Gilbert Parker. CaP
World is, The/ not with us enough. O Taste and See. Denise Levertov. NoP; PBWP; PPP; TAP
World Is a Beautiful Place, The. Lawrence Ferlinghetti. CAPP
World Is a Bundle of Hay, The. Byron. EnRP; FF
(Epigram on John Bull.) FaBoCo
World is a gift again, The. Spring Workman. Alan Creighton. CaP
World Is a Mighty Ogre, The. Fenton Johnson. AmNP
World Is a Musician's Cliff House, The. Rodney Hall. *Fr.* Black Bagatelles. CBAP
World is a well-furnished table, The. The World. Thomas Love Peacock. PV
World is all orange-round, The. The Walking Road. Richard Hughes. OBMV
World is charged with the grandeur of God, The. God's Grandeur. Gerard Manley Hopkins. AWP; BiP; BLPL; BrPo; CABA; CMoP; EBCP; EBVV; FaFP; FF; HAP; ILwL; InPK; InvP; LiTB; LiTM; LoBV; MoAB; MoBrPo; MoPo; MoVE; NoAM; NOBE; NoP; OAEL-2; OBNC; OxBoCh; PAI; PPP; PrIm; SeCeV; SoSe; SOTW; TEP; TrCP; TreFT; TrGrPo; UnPo; VLP; WeW
World is composed, The. The Grass Is a Reasonable Colour. John Newlove. NeAC
World is dull, the world is blind, The. Die Welt ist dumm, die Welt ist blind. Heine, *tr. by* James Thomson. AWP
World is full of care, much like unto a bubble, The. Epigram. Nathaniel Ward. POL
World is full of gladness, The. Lemon Pie. Edgar A. Guest. OBAL
World is full of loss, The; bring, wind, my love. Song. Muriel Rukeyser. MiAP
World is full of mostly invisible things, The. To David, about His Education. Howard Nemerov. DiL
World is full of wistful ones who hoard their souvenirs, The. Ballad of Culinary Frustration. Phyllis McGinley. FiBHP
World is great, The: the birds all fly from me. I Am Lonely. "George Eliot." *Fr.* The Spanish Gypsy. GN; HBV-1
World is heated seven times, The. A Night in June. Duncan Campbell Scott. OBCV
World is hollow like a pumpkin-shell, The. Truth. Jessica Nelson North. HBVY
World is in a mess today, The. Song about Whiskers. P. G. Wodehouse. FiBHP
World is in the Valley of Decision, The. The Valley of Decision. John Oxenham. PGD
World Is like a Woman of Folly, The. Moses ibn Ezra, *tr. fr. Hebrew by* Solomon Solis-Cohen. *Fr.* The World's Illusion. TrJP
World Is Mine, The. Florence Earle Coates. AA
(Song: "For me the jasmine buds unfold.") HBV-1
World is no longer good, The. Chorus from a Tragedy. Leonard Bacon. ViBoPo
World Is Not a Fenced-off Garden, The. Jakov Steinberg, *tr. fr. Hebrew by* Mark Elliott Shapiro. VWA
World Is Not a Pleasant Place to Be, The. Nikki Giovanni. PCP
World Is Really a Sugarplum House in the Forest, The. Aram Boyajian. NeAC
World is Rome, The; Carnuntum, on the Danube. Marcus Antoninus Cui Cognomen Erat Aurelius. Burns Singer. OxBS
World is several billion years of age, The. Winter Report. Ben Howard. PoA
World is so full of a number of things, The. Happy Thought. Robert Louis Stevenson. FaBoBe; HBV-1; HBVY; OxBChV; RHPC; TiPo; TreFS
World is something I must try, The. Tragedy. Mark Van Doren. NePoAm-2
"World is such a funny place, The." Relatively. Kathleen Millay. QQQ
World Is Too Much with Us, The. Wordsworth. AWP; BiP; CABA; ChTr; EnRP; FaBoEn; FaFP; FaPoR; FiP; FPL; GTBS; GTBS-P; HAP; HBV-1; HBVY; HeIP; HoPM; InPK; LiTB; MAT; NOBE; NoP; OAEL-2; OAEP; OBNC; OBRV; PAI; PoEL-4; PoLF; PoRA; PPoe; PPP; PrIm; SeCeV; SoSe; TEP; TreF; TrGrPo; WeW; WGRP; WHA
(Sonnet.) ChER; LoBV; OHFP; ViBoPo
(World, The.) OBEV; PPON
World is very evil, The. The Celestial Country. Bernard of Cluny, *tr. by* John Mason Neale. *Fr.* De Contemptu Mundi. GoBC
World is very flat, The. Night Thought of a Tortoise Suffering from Insomnia on a Lawn. E. V. Rieu. FiBHP
World is weaned from this one dead by the thread of a shawl, The. The Spoils of War. Vernon Watkins. WaP
World is white with cherry-trees, The. June. Wilson MacDonald. CaP
World is young to-day, The. Song. Digby Mackworth Dolben. LoBV; OBNC
World Looks On, The. Louis Newman. PoNe
World Morose, The. Frederick William Faber. *See* Mundus Morosus.
World Music. Frances Louisa Bushnell. AA
World of Bacteria. Sakutaro Hagiwara, *tr. fr. Japanese by* Graeme McD. Wilson. AMV-80
World of Darkness. Robert Chatain. PoA
World of fools has such a store, The. *Unknown.* DBV
World of Light, A. Elizabeth Jennings. NePoEA-2
World of Light, The. Henry Vaughan. *See* They Are All Gone into the World of Light.
World of mightie kings and princes I could name, A. Michael Drayton. *Fr.* Polyolbion, Twentieth Song. OBS

World of stars and space being His bauble, The. Receiving Communion. Vassar Miller. NePoEA-2
World Outside, The. Denise Levertov. ConAP
World Planners. Arvel Steech. PGD
World says No, The. No. E. M. Schorb. AMV-80
World-Secret. Hugo von Hofmannsthal, *tr. fr. German by* Charles Wharton Stork. TrJP
World sits at the feet of Christ, The. Whittier. *Fr.* The Over-Heart. TRV
World So Wide, The. *Unknown.* OxBM
World State, The. G. K. Chesterton. DBV
World, that all contains, is ever moving, The. Change. Fulke Greville. *Fr.* Caelica. EnRePo; NIP; OBSC
World, the Devil, and Tom Paine, The, *with music. Unknown.* AH
World Transformed, The. Whittier. *Fr.* Snow-bound. AA
World Turned Upside Down, The. *Unknown.* PAH
World turns and its turning wheels, The. The Epistemological Rag. Gray Burr. CoPo
World turns and the world changes, The. T. S. Eliot. *Fr.* The Rock. TiPo
World turns mild, The; democracy, they say. Tempora Mutantur. James Russell Lowell. HAP
World turns round and leaves the sun, The. Eve in My Legend. Denis Devlin. IPY
World turns softly, The. Water. Hilda Conkling. PDV; TiPo
World under the sky, The. A Gone. Larry Eigner. NeAP
World uprose as a man to find Him, The. At the End of Things. Arthur Edward Waite. WGRP
World War. Richard Eberhart. WaP
World War[s]. *Unknown.* FaFP; TreFT
World was first a private park, The. The Fisherman. Jay Macpherson. CABA; NOBC; PeCV
World was made when a man was born, The. Experience. John Boyle O'Reilly. ACP; OBVV
World Was Never Real to Me, The. George Randall Griffin. AMV-81
World was wide when I was young, The. Troia Fuit. Reginald Wright Kauffman. HBV-1
World Well Lost, The. Edmund Clarence Stedman. AA
World will burst like an intestine in the sun, The. Passengers. Denis Johnson. MAYP
World will not be understood, The. Comedy. Mark Van Doren. NePoAm-2
World Winter. Earle Birney. GrPl
World within a War, A. Sir Herbert Read. MoPo
World within a World. Debra Woolard Bender. AMV-80
"World without Objects Is a Sensible Emptiness, A." Richard Wilbur. ConAP; LiTM; MoAmPo; NoAM; NOBA; PoA
World world world world. Enueg II. Samuel Beckett. NoAM
World Youth Song. *Unknown.* FSW
Worlde So wide, th'air so remuable, The. The World So Wide. *Unknown.* OxBM
Worldly possessions? 'twas easy to find them. Tora's Song. Knut Hamsun, *tr. by* Charles Wharton Stork. PoPl
Worldly skinflints! We have your home-/ stead. Coralville, in Iowa. Marvin Bell. FAZ
Worldly Vanity. Dryden. *See* Conversion.
Worldly Wealth. Rowland Watkyns. FaBoEE
World's a bubble, and the life of man, The. The Life of Man [*or* The World *or* The World's a Bubble]. Francis Bacon. EIL; GTBS; GTBS-P; HBV-1; OBSC; TreFT; WHA
World's a floore, whose swelling heapes retaine, The. Francis Quarles. Emblems, II, 7. AnAnS-1
World's a Sea, The. Francis Quarles. ChTr
World's a sorry wench, akin, The. The Jester's Plea. Frederick Locker-Lampson. CenHV
World's a stage, The. The light is in one's eyes. Sonnet. Hilaire Belloc. DBV
World's a stage, The. The trifling entrance fee. Hilaire Belloc. OxBTC
World's a theater, the earth a stage, The. The Author to His Booke. Thomas Heywood. *Fr.* An Apology for Actors. OBS
World's a very happy place, The. The World's Music. "Gabriel Setoun." FaBoBe; HBV-1; HBVY
World's a weary place, The. All thro' the Year. *Unknown.* BLRP
World's a well strung fidle, mans tongue the quill, The. Nathaniel Ward. SCAP
World's an inn, The; and I her guest. On the World. Francis Quarles. HAP
Worlds are breaking in my head, The. Yves Tanguy. David Gascoyne. EAS
World's Bible, The. Annie Johnson Flint. STF; TRV
World's Bliss, Have Good Day! *Unknown.* OxBM
World's Bright Comforter, The. Barnabe Barnes. *Fr.* A Divine Century of Spiritual Sonnets. OxBoCh
(God's Virtue.) NOCV; OBSC
(Sonnet.) EIL
World's Desire, The. William Rose Benét. TrPWD
World's End, The. William Empson. CoBMV; MoVE
World's Fare. Charles Stetler. GP
World's gone forward to its latest fair, The. The Moor. Ralph Hodgson. MoBrPo
World's Great Age Begins Anew, The. Shelley. *See* Chorus: "World's great age begins anew, The."
World's great heart, whence all things strange and rare, The. The Death of Richard Wagner. Swinburne. LoBV
World's Greatest Tricycle Rider, The. C. K. Williams. NYBP
World's Illusion, The, *sels.* Moses ibn Ezra, *tr. fr. Hebrew by* Solomon Solis-Cohen. TrJP
All Ye That Go Astray.
He That Regards the Precious Things of Earth.
In Vain Earth Decks Herself.
Promises of the World, The.
World Is like a Woman of Folly, The.
Ye Anger Earth.
World's Justice, The. Emma Lazarus. HBV-2
World's Last Unnamed Poem, The. A. K. Redwing. VoR
World's love runs thin, The. To the Tune "The Phoenix Hairpin." T'ang Wan, *tr. by* Kenneth Rexroth *and* Ling Chung. WPOW
World's May-Queen, The. Alfred Noyes. OBVV
(When Spring Comes Back to England.) HBV-1
World's Music, The. "Gabriel Setoun." FaBoBe; HBV-1; HBVY
Worlds on Worlds. Shelley. *Fr.* Hellas.
(Chorus.) OAEP
(Choruses from "Hellas," 2.) EnRP
("Worlds on worlds are rolling ever.") NoP; TEP
World's So Big, The. Aileen Fisher. SoPo
World's so wide I cannot cross it, The. Fond Affection. *Unknown.* AS
World's Wanderers, The. Shelley. ViBoPo
World's Way, The. Thomas Bailey Aldrich. HBV-1
World's Way, The. Shakespeare. *See* Sonnets, LXVI.
World's Wonders, The. Robinson Jeffers. NePA
World's Worth. Dante Gabriel Rossetti. GoBC; VLP
Worlds, you must tell me. Round. Louis Untermeyer. WhC
Worm, The. Willis Barnstone. FAZ; VWA
Worm, The. Ralph Bergengren. FaPON; RHPC; SiSoSe
Worm, The. Raymond Souster. WHW
Worm artist, The. The Earth Worm. Denise Levertov. NOBA
Worm cries not against the storm, The. Microcosmos, XVII. Nigel Heseltine. NeBP
Worm Fed on the Heart of Corinth, A. Isaac Rosenberg. BrPo; MoPo; OAEL-2
Worm in the Whirling Cross, The. John Malcolm Brinnin. MoPo
Worm unto his love, The: lo, here's fresh store. The Coffin-Worm. Ruth Pitter. MoBrPo
Worms of History, The. Robert Graves. MoPo
Wormwood. Thomas Kinsella. CIP
Wormy apples at the grocery. Eco Right. Walt Gavenda. QQQ
Worn and torn by many fingers. A Family Album. Alter Brody. VWA
Worn-out voice of the clock breaks on the hour, The. Prize for Good Conduct. Kenneth Allott. OBWP
Worn with the battle of Stamford town. Saxon Grit. Robert Collyer. HBV-2
Worried Life Blues. *Unknown.* AmFP
Worried Man Blues. *Unknown.* FSW
Worried Skipper, The. Wallace Irwin. BLPA
Worry. George W. Swarberg. STF
Worry about Money. Kathleen Raine. FaBoTw
Worschippe ye that loveris bene this May. Spring Song of the Birds. James I, King of Scotland. OBEV
Worsening Situation. John Ashbery. NOBA
Worship, *sel.* William Wilberforce Lord.
"For them, O God, who only worship Thee." AA
Worship. Robert Whitaker. TrPWD
Worship. Whittier. NOCV
Worship of virtu is the mede. A Carol of St. George. *Unknown.* MeEL
Worship the Lord, the God of wild cold kind. The Lord in the Wind. James Picot. PoAu-2
Worshiper, The. Vassar Miller. NePoEA-2
Worst, The. Shel Silverstein. WSC
Worst Horror, The. Euripides, *tr. fr. Greek by* John Addington Symonds. DBV
Worst of all diseases, The. Sin and Its Cure. *Unknown.* STF
Worst side of it all, The. White Roses. John Ashbery. TAP
Worthless Heart, The. Immanuel di Roma, *tr. fr. Hebrew.* TrJP
Worth While. Ella Wheeler Wilcox. BLPA; FPL; TreF
Worthy art Thou,/ O Lord, of praise. Deliverance from a Fit of Fainting. Anne Bradstreet. TAP

Worthy Fool, A. Shakespeare. *See* Motley's the Only Wear.
Worthy kyng, quhen he has seyn, The. Before Bannockburn. John Barbour. *Fr.* The Bruce. OxBS
Worthy London Prentice, A. The London Prentice. *Unknown.* CoMu; UnTE
Worthy woman from beside Bath city, A. Chaucer, *mod. version by* Nevill Coghill. *Fr.* The Canterbury Tales: Prologue. BiP
Wot a marf 'e'd got. Epitaph on a Marf. *Unknown.* PV
"Wot's in a name?" she sez. . .An' then she sighs. The Play. C. J. Dennis. *Fr.* The Sentimental Bloke. PoAu-1
Wotton, my little Bere dwells on a hill. Ad Henricum Wottonem. Thomas Bastard. FaBoEE; FaBoPP
Woud ye hear of William Wallace. Gude Wallace. *Unknown.* ESPB
Wou'd you in love succeed, be brisk, be gay. The Advice. Charles Sackville. FaBoUs
Would a circling surface vulture. Mahadevi, *tr. fr. Kannada by* A. K. Ramanujan. BoWoP
"Would a man 'scape the rod?" Ben Karshook's Wisdom. Robert Browning. OAEP
Would Edison get the blues if he blew a fuse? Electricity Is Funny! John Currier. GrPl
Would God that I and my darling. *Tr. fr. Gaelic by* Frank O'Connor. *Fr.* A Beggarman's Song. WTO
Would God That It Were Holiday! Thomas Deloney. *Fr.* The Gentle Craft. ElL
Would I again were with you!—O ye dales. That Delightful Time. Mark Akenside. *Fr.* The Pleasures of Imagination. SeCePo
Would I Be Called a Christian? Mrs. J. F. Moser. STF
Would I Be Shrived? John D. Swain. BLPA
Would I could cast a sail on the water. The Collar-Bone of a Hare. W. B. Yeats. OxBTC
Would I describe a preacher, such as Paul. William Cowper. *Fr.* The Task. TRV
Would I Might Go Far over Sea. Marie de France, *tr. fr. French by* Arthur O'Shaughnessy. AWP; PoRA
Would I might lie like this, without the pain. In Hospital. James Elroy Flecker. OxBTC
Would I might mend the fabric of my youth. Welt. Georgia Douglas Johnson. BANP
Would I Might Rouse the Lincoln in You All. Vachel Lindsay. *Fr.* Litany of the Heroes. PoSC
(Lincoln.) OHIP
Would I were a king of children. The Child-King. Morris Wintchevsky, *tr. by* Alter Brody. TrJP
Would I were air that thou with heat oppress t. Thomas Stanley. FaBoEE
Would I were chang'd into that golden shower. Sir Arthur Gorges. GBL
Would I were on the sea-lands. The Sea-Lands. Orrick Johns. HBV-1
Would it please you if I strung my tears. The Race Question. Naomi Long Madgett. BPo
Would that I streamed like water. Like Water down a Slope. Zalman Schneour, *tr. by* Harry H. Fein. TrJP
Would That I Were. Arthur Hugh Clough. TrPWD
Would that the structure brave, the manifold music I build. Abt Vogler. Robert Browning. GoTL; HBV-2; OAEL-2; OAEP; VLP; WGRP
Would the lark sing the sweeter if he knew. An Open Secret. Caroline Atherton Briggs Mason. AA
Would the world know how Godfrey lost his breath? Truth Brought to Light, or Murder Will Out. Stephen College. APAS
Would we could coin for thee new words of praise. Washington's Tomb. Ruth Lawrence. OHIP
Would Wisdom for herself be wooed. The Joyful Wisdom. Coventry Patmore. *Fr.* The Angel in the House. HBV-2
Would write a letter with/ my scissors mouth. Young Woman's Neo-Aramaic Jewish Persian Blues. Jerome Rothenberg, *after Persian folk poem.* BoWoP
Would ye have fresh cheese and cream? Fresh Cheese and Cream. Robert Herrick. UnTE
Would you be famous and renowned in story. The Advice. *Unknown.* APAS
Would you be preserved from ruin? The Impartial Inspection. *Unknown.* APAS
Would you be young again? Heavenward. Lady Nairne. HBV-2
Would you believe some-/ one who said he. Dance and Eye Me (Wicked)ly My Breath a Fixed Sphere. Rochelle Owens. NMM
Would you believe, when you this monsieur see. On English Monsieur. Ben Jonson. NoP
Would you come back if I said the earth. Nadia Tueni, *tr. fr. French by* Willis Barnstone. BoWoP
Would You Have a Young Virgin? John Gay. *See* If the Heart of a Man.
Would you have a young virgin of fifteen years. What's Your Fancy. *Unknown.* UnTe
Would you have freedom from wage slavery? There Is Power. Joe Hill. FSW
Would you have me brand it, scars. The Secret Irish. Allen Hoey. AMV-81
Would you hear of an old-time sea-fight? Battle of the *Bonhomme Richard* and the *Serapis* [*or* John Paul Jones *or* An Old-Time Sea-Fight]. Walt Whitman. Song of Myself, XXXV-XXXVI. MOS; OnMSP; PAL; SeCeV; TrGrPo; UnPo
Would you hear of the River-Fight? Henry Howard Brownell. *Fr.* The River-Fight. AA; EtS
Would You in Venus' Wars Succeed. *Unknown.* ErPo
Would you like to sin. *Unknown.* PV
Would you make blazes. Ultra-Germano-Criticasterism. Leigh Hunt. PP
Would you, my friend, in little room express. Martial, *tr. fr. Latin by* Elijah Fenton. OBVE
Would you your son should be a sot or dunce. William Cowper. *Fr.* Tirocinium; or, A Review of Schools. OBSV
Wouldn't it be lovely if the rain came down. Very Lovely. Rose Fyleman. SoPo; TiPo
Wouldn't it be wonderful to come across in cabaret. Unromantic Song. Anthony Brode. DBV; FiBHP
Wouldnt think/t look at m. Panther Man. James A. Emanuel. BPo
Wouldn't this old world be better. I Know Something Good about You. Louis C. Shimon. BLPA
Wouldn't You Like to Know. John Godfrey Saxe. HBV-1
Wouldn't you like to know. Elementary. Jim Tollerud. VoR
Wouldn't you love. Lasagna. X. J. Kennedy. PPJ
Wouldn't you say,/ Wouldn't you say: one day. One Almost Might. A. S. J. Tessimond. ChMP
Would'st be happy, little child. To Theodora. *Unknown.* OxBChV
Wouldst know the artist? Then go seek. Art. Lilla Cabot Perry. AA
Wouldst know the lark? A Listener's Guide to the Birds. E. B. White. NYBP
Wouldst thou be wise, O Man? At the knees of a woman begin. Wilfrid Scawen Blunt. *Fr.* The Wisdom of Merlyn. OBMV
Would'st thou hear [*or* heare] what man can say. Epitaph on Elizabeth, L. H. [*or* Elizabeth L.H.]. Ben Jonson. AnAnS-2; BiP; CABA; ElL; ELP; EnRePo; FaBoEE; HAP; HBV-2; HeIP; NIP; NoP; OBEV; OBS; SeCP; SeCV-1; TreFT; ViBoPo; WHA
Wouldst thou live long? The only means are these. He Lives Long Who Lives Well. Thomas Randolph. WBLP
Wound, The. Thom Gunn. NePoEA
Wound-Dresser, The. Walt Whitman. AmPP; AP; NOBA; OBWP; PrIm; TAP; ViBoPo
Wound which the dragon had dealt him began, The. Beowulf's Death. *Unknown, tr. by* Charles W. Kennedy. *Fr.* Beowulf. AnOE
Wounded, The. Louise Louis. GoYe
Wounded American Indian. Indians at the Guthrie. Gerald Vizenor. STE
Wounded Breakfast, The. Russell Edson. LCAP
Wounded Cupid, The. Robert Herrick, *after the Greek of* Anacreon. AWP; OBVE; OFD
Wounded deer leaps highest, A. Emily Dickinson. AP; AWP; TAP
Wounded hare looks out, The. Hare in Winter. Marge Piercy. NeAC
Wounded Hawk, The. Herbert Palmer. FaBoTw
Wounded Man and the Swarm of Flies, The. William Somerville. FM
Wounded Person, The. Walt Whitman. *Fr.* Song of Myself. PoNe
Wounded wilderness of Morris Graves, The. Lawrence Ferlinghetti. *Fr.* A Coney Island of the Mind. NeAP
Wounds. Judith Minty. GeTw
Wow, but your letter made me vauntie! Epistle to Dr. Blacklock, *abr.* Burns. OBEC
Woyi, The. Lew Blockcolski. VoR
Wrack was dark an' shiny where it floated in the sea, The. Sea Wrack. "Moira O'Neill." OnYI
Wraggle Taggle Gipsies, The. *Unknown.* CH; EvOK; FSW
(Black Jack Davey [*or* Davy].) MAT; OuSiCo, *with music*
(Gipsy [*or* Gypsy] Laddie, The.) BSV; ESPB (A *and* B *vers.*); FaBoBa; FaBoCh; HAP; OxBoLi; ViBoFo (A *and* B *vers.*)
(Raggle, Taggle Gypsies, The.) FaPON; TiPo
(Wraggle Taggle Gipsies, O, The.) WiR
Wraith. Edna St. Vincent Millay. WSC
Wraith-Friend, The. George Barker. OBMV
Wrangler Kid, The. *Unknown.* BPAW
Wrap Me in Blankets of Momentary Winds. Harold Littlebird. VoR
Wrap Me Up in My Tarpaulin Jacket, *with music. Unknown.* AS
(Sailors.) OuSiCo
Wrap up in a blanket in cold weather and just read. Things to Do around a Lookout. Gary Snyder. CAPP; NaP; TAP
Wrapped Hair Bundles. Tauhindauli. STE
Wrapped in a twisted brown stocking, strangled in the rolled. Under the Scrub Oak, a Red Shoe. Dave Smith. GeTw
Wrapped in a yielding air, beside. As He Is. W. H. Auden. MoPo

Wrapped up, O Lord, in man's degeneration. Fulke Greville. *Fr.* Caelica. EnRePo; OxBoCh; QFR
Wrapt in my careless cloak, as I walk to and fro. Earl of Surrey. SiPS
Wrath. John Hollander. PV
Wrath of Peleus son, O muse, resound, The. Homer, *tr. by* Dryden. *Fr.* The Iliad, Invocation. OBVE
Wrathful [*or* Wrathfull] winter, 'proaching [*or* proching *or* prochinge] on apace, The. The Induction to "The Mirror for Magistrates" [*or* The Complaint of Henrie Duke of Buckinghame *or* Winter]. Thomas Sackville. AAS; EIL; OBSC; PoEL-1; SeCePo
Wreath, The. Robert Graves. BoLoP
Wreath, A. George Herbert. JCP; OAEL-1; SeCP
Wreath of flowers as cold as snow, A. The Birth. Rosemary Dobson. PoAu-2
Wreath that star-crowned Shelley gave, The. After a Lecture on Keats. Oliver Wendell Holmes. AA; ViBoPo
Wreathe no more lilies in my hair. The Summer Is Ended. Christina Rossetti. HBV-2
Wreathe the Bowl. Thomas Moore. HBV-2
Wreathed garland of deserved praise, A. A Wreath. George Herbert. JCP; OAEL-1; SeCP
Wreathmakertraining. Karl Patten. FAZ
Wreaths. Geoffrey Hill. PoA
Wreck, The. Walter de la Mare. MOS
Wreck. Noel Polk. AMV-81
Wreck of the Deutschland, The, *parody.* David Annett. BXAP
Wreck of the *Deutschland,* The. Gerard Manley Hopkins. BrPo; CMoP; CoBMV; FaBoMo; LiTB; LiTM; MasP; MoVE; NoAM; NOBE; OAEP; OBNC; PoEL-5; SeCeV; TEP; VLP
Sels.
"On Saturday sailed from Bremen." SeCePo
"Thou mastering me," Pt. 1. OxBoCh
Wreck of the Great Northern, The. Robert Hedin. AMV-81
Wreck of the *Hesperus,* The. Longfellow. BeLS; BLPA; EtS; FaBoBe; FaFP; FaPoN; FaPoR; FPL; GN; HBV-2; HBVY; MOS: OBCA; OBNV; PAH; PaPo; TreF; WBLP
Wreck of the *Julie Plante,* The. William Henry Drummond. CaP; FaPON; HBV-2; InMe; NA; OBCV; PeCV: TreFS; WhC
(*Julie Plante,* The.) BeLS: BLPA; FaBoBe
Wreck of the Old 97, The. *Unknown.* FSW; ViBoFo
Wreck of the Royal Palm, The. *Unknown.* AmFP
Wreck of Walsingham, The. *Unknown. See* Lament for the Priory of Walsingham, A.
Wreck on the Somerset Road, The, *with music. Unknown.* OuSiCo
Wrecker Driver Foresees Your Death, The. David Baker. MAYP
Wreckers' Prayer, The. Theodore Goodridge Roberts. OBCV; PeCV
Wrecks dissolve above us, The; their dust drops down from afar. The Deep-Sea Cables. Kipling. VLP
Wren, The. Issa, *tr. fr. Japanese by* R.H. Blyth. NTCP
Wren, The. *Unknown.* OxBChV
Wren she lies in care's bed, The. *Unknown.* PBBP
Wrens, The. Kenneth Burke. TwAmPo
Wrens and robins in the hedge. Christina Rossetti. *Fr.* Sing-Song. SUS; TiPo
Wrens are back, The! The Wrens. Kenneth Burke. TwAmPo
Wrestling, The. Abbie Huston Evans. GP
Wrestling. Kathleen Fraser. RHPC
Wrestling Angels. David Bottoms. MAYP
Wrestling Jacob. Charles Wesley. NOBE; NOCV; NOEC; OBEC; OBEV; PoEL-3; SeCePo
(Come, O Thou Traveller Unknown.) OxBoCh
Wretched Amintor with a flame. The Greater Trial. Countess of Winchilsea. TrGrPo
Wretched Catullus, play the fool no more. To Himself. Catullus, *tr. by* William Ellery Leonard. AWP
Wretched Flavia, on her couch reclined, The. Saturday: The Small-Pox. Lady Mary Wortley Montagu. *Fr.* Six Town Eclogues. NOEC; WPE
Wretched Ierne! with what grief I see. Swift. *Fr.* Verses Occasioned by the Sudden Drying Up of St. Patrick's Well. OBSV
Wretched Man. Earl of Rochester. *Fr.* A Satire against Mankind. SeCePo
Wretched thing it were, to have our heart, A. Retirement. Richard Chenevix Trench. OBVV
Wretchedness of my former years I have no need to brag, The. After Passing the Examination. Meng Chiao, *tr. by* Irving Y. Lo. GLGT
Wrights' Biplane, The. Robert Frost. WeW
Wrimples. Jack Prelutsky. RHPC
Wrinkled, but not inured by years. Spring; a Formal Ode. Fyodor Tyuchev, *tr. by* Charles Tomlinson. FaBoRV
Wrinkled, crabbed man they picture thee, A. Winter Portrait. Robert Southey. BoNaP
"Wrinkled ostler, grim and thin!" Song at the Ruin'd Inn. Tennyson. *Fr.* The Vision of Sin. PoEL-5
Wrinkling with laughter that made no sound. At a Country Fair. John Holmes. MoShBr
Writ on the Eve of My 32nd Birthday. Gregory Corso. NAs
Write as you will. Young Poets. Nicanor Parra, *tr. by* Miller Williams. POL
Write, Do Write. Marilyn Chin. BrSi
Write it down. Write it. In ordinary ink. Starvation Camp near Jaslo. Wislawa Szymborska, *tr. by* Jan Darowski. WPOW
Write it in gold—a spirit of the sun. Lines Written in a Blank Leaf of the Prometheus Unbound. Thomas Lovell Beddoes. OAEL-2
Write on my grave when I am dead. The Epitaph. Katharine Tynan. WGRP
Writer, The. Hildebrand Jacob. FaBoCo
Writer, The. Richard Wilbur. OxBC; Str
Writer, attend no schools. The Teacher. Virginia Brady Young. GoYe
Writer tenebrously moles away, The. Literary Zodiac. R. A. Piddington. PV
Writer to His Book, The. Thomas Campion. OAEP
Writing. Howard Nemerov. NYBP
Writing a letter he said. Buffalo-Isle of Wight Power Cable. Anselm Hollo. PoM
Writing for Money. Edward Field. PPJ
Writing, I crushed an insect with my nail. Interlude. Karl Shapiro. DFF
Writing in England Now. Philip O'Connor. OxBTC
Writing on Napkins at the Sunshine Club, Macon, Georgia 1971. David Bottoms. TAT
Writing on the Wall. Padraic Fallon. NeIP
Writing to Aaron. Denise Levertov. FAZ
Writing while My Father Dies. Linda Pastan. PCP
Writing you this, I can feel a dewclaw. Growing Wild. Jim Wayne Miller. GP
Written. Mary Ruelfe. AMV-81
Written after Swimming from Sestos to Abydos. Byron. InMe; LiSp; MOS; NoP; OBRV
Written [*or* in] at an Inn at Henley. William Shenstone. AWP; HBV-2; LoBV; NOBE; NOEC; OBEC; OBEV; ViBoPo
Written at Cambridge. Charles Lamb. EnRP; OBRV
Written at Florence. Wilfrid Scawen Blunt. OBVV
Written at the End of a Book. Langdon Elwyn Mitchell. AA
Written at the White Sulphur Springs. Francis Scott Key. OBAL
Written for My Son, and Spoken by Him at His First Putting on Breeches. Mary Barber. NOEC
Written Forty Miles South of a Spreading City. Robert Bly. NNaP
Written in a Copy of Swift's Poems, for Wayne Burns. James Wright. NOBA
Written in a Copy of "The Earthly Paradise," Dec. 25, 1870. William Morris. *Fr.* The Earthly Paradise. VLP
Written in a Lady's Prayer Book. Earl of Rochester. BoLoP
Written in a Little Lady's Little Album. Frederick William Faber. HBV-1; HBVY
Written in a Thunder Storm July 15th 1841. John Clare. VLP
Written in a Time of Crisis. Stephen Vincent Benét. PAL
Written in an Inn at Henley. William Shenstone. *See* Written at an Inn . . .
Written in an Ovid. Matthew Prior. FaBoEE; FaBoUs
Written in Butler's Sermons. Matthew Arnold. VLP
Written in Dejection near Rome. Robert Bly. NaP
Written in Early Spring. Wordsworth. *See* Lines Written in Early Spring.
Written in Exile. Kathleen Raine. TrCP; WPE
Written in Her French Psalter. Elizabeth I, Queen of England. PBWP; WPE
Written in Ireland. Mary Alcock. NOEC
Written in Juice of Lemmon [*or* Lemon]. Abraham Cowley. *Fr.* The Mistress. AnAnS-2; CABA; SeCP; SeCV-1
Written in July, 1824. Mary Russell Mitford. OBRV
Written in London, September, 1802. Wordsworth. TrGrPo
(England, 1802, I.) HBV-2; OBEV; PPON
(In London, September 1802.) EnRP
(London, 1802.) OBNC
(London, MDCCCII.) GTBS; GTBS-P
(Sonnet: Written in London, September, 1802.) ChER
Written in March. Wordsworth. BoNaP; EnRP; FaPON; GoJo; HBV-1; HBVY; NTCP; SUS; TiPo; UnPo; YeAr
(Merry Month of March, The.) EvOK; MoShBr; SoPo
Written in My Lady Speke's Singing-Book. Edmund Waller. CavP
Written in Northampton County Asylum. John Clare. *See* I Am.
Written in Prison. John Clare. OAEL-2
Written in the Album of a Child. Wordsworth. *See* To a Child.
Written in the Beginning of Mezeray's History of France. Matthew Prior. NOBE; OBEC; PoEL-3
Written in the Euganean Hills, North Italy. Shelley. *See* Lines Written among the Euganean Hills.

Written in the Visitors' Book at the Birthplace of Robert Burns. George Washington Cable. AA
Written in Unbridled Repugnance near Sioux Falls, Alabama—April 30, 1974. A. K. Redwing. VoR
Written in Very Early Youth. Wordsworth. EnRP
Written on a Blank Page in Shakespeare's Poems. Keats. *See* Bright Star! Would I Were Steadfast as Thou Art.
Written on a Fly-Leaf of Theocritus. Maurice Thompson. AA
Written on a Leaf. *Unknown, tr. fr. Chinese by* Geoffrey Waters. BoWoP
Written on a Looking-Glass. *Unknown.* FaBoEE
(Epigram: "I change, and so do women too.") HBV-1
Written on a Paper Napkin. Len Gasparini. NeAC
Written on a Sunday Morning. Robert Southey. OBEC
Written on a Wall at Woodstock. Elizabeth I, Queen of England. PBWP; WPE
Written on an Island off the Breton Coast. Venantius Fortunatus, *tr. fr Latin by* Helen Waddell. PeHV
Written on Seeing the Flowers, and Remembering My Daughter. Kao Ch'i, *tr. fr. Chinese.* DL
Written on the Banks of Wastwater during a Calm. "Christopher North." OBRV
Written on the Eve of Execution. Chidiock Tichborne. *See* Elegy: "My prime of youth is but a frost of cares."
Written on the Sense of Isolation in Contemporary Ireland. Robert Greacen. NeIP
Written on the Stub of the First Paycheck. William Stafford. *Fr.* The Move to California. InPK
Written on the Wall at Chang's Hermitage. Tu Fu, *tr. fr. Chinese by* Kenneth Rexroth. HoPM; NaP
Written on the Walls of His Dungeon. Luís de León, *tr. fr. Spanish by* Thomas Walsh. TrJP
Written over a Gate. John Sheffield, Duke of Buckingham and Normandy. NIP
Written the Night before His Execution. Chidiock Tichbourne. *See* Elegy: "My prime of youth is but a frost of cares."
Written under Capricorn, a land. Love Poem. Chris Wallace-Crabbe. PoAu-2
Written upon the Top of Ben Nevis. Keats. PoSH
Written with a Diamond on Her Window at Woodstock. Elizabeth I, Queen of England. PBWP; WPE
Wrong about birds. I cannot call. Paradox: The Birds. Karl Shapiro. CrMA
Wrong is made and measured by, The. Shame. Coventry Patmore. OBVV
Wrong Kind of Insurance, The. John Ashbery. NYP
Wrong me no more. Chang'd, yet Constant. Thomas Stanley. AnAnS-2
Wrong Not, Sweet[e] Empress of My Heart. Sir Walter Ralegh. HBV-1; LiTB; OBEV; OBS
(Merit of True Passion, The.) LiTB
(Silent Lover, II, The.) OBEV
Wrong Start, The. Marchette Chute. RHPC
Wronged Lover, The. Sir Philip Sidney. *Fr.* Arcadia. SiPS
Wrote the clergy: "Our Dear Madame Prynne." A Hawthorne Garland. Richard Harter Fogle. NIP; OBAL
Wry Rowan, The. *Unknown, tr. fr. Late Middle Irish by* Eoin MacNeill. OnYI
Wry Smile, A. Roy Fuller. WaaP; WaP
W's a well-informed wight. A Well-informed Wight. Oliver Herford. TDH
W's for Windows. Phyllis McGinley. *Fr.* All around the Town. TiPo
Wulf. Bill Manhire. OCNZ
Wulf and Eadwacer. *Unknown. See* Eadwacer.
Wull ye come in early Spring. Come! William Barnes. CH
Wundrfulness uv th Mountees Our Secret Police, Th. Bill Bissett. NOBC
Wunst I Had an Old Gray Mare, *with music. Unknown.* OuSiCo
W'y, one time wuz a little-weenty dirl. Maymie's Story of Red Riding-Hood. James Whitcomb Riley. DFT
Wyatt Resteth Here. Earl of Surrey. NCEP; NoP
(On the Death of Sir Thomas Wyatt.) GoTL
(Tribute to Wyatt.) SiPS
("Wyat resteth here, that quicke coulde never rest.") AAS
Wykehamist's Address to Learning, A. P. N. Shuttleworth. FaBoCo
Wykhamist, The. Nora Griffiths. SUMH
Wynken, Blynken, and Nod. Eugene Field. AA; BeLS; FaBoBe; FaFP; FaPON; HBV-1; HBVY; MOON; NTCP; OBAL; OBCA; OxBChV; PoRA; SoPo
(Dutch Lullaby, A.) BLPA; FPL; PoPl; TreF
Wynken de Worde. Frederick Von Ende. POL
Wynter Wakeneth Al My Care. *Unknown. See* Winter Wakeneth . . .
Wynyard Sailor. Ray Mathew. CBAP
Wyoming Massacre, The. Uriah Terry. PAH
Wyse men alwaye. A Mery Gest How a Sergeaunt Wolde Lerne to Be A Frere. Sir Thomas More. AAS
Wythin a garth, under a reid rosere. The Praise of Age. Robert Henryson. BSV
Wyvern. Charles Connell. AmMo
X of the Unknown, The. Tom Clark. LiSp
X-Ray. David Ray. NePoEA-2
X-Ray. Leonora Speyer. ImOP
X shall stand for playmates Ten. Roman Numerals. *Unknown.* FaBoUs; OxNR
Xantippe. Amy Levy. BrRo
Xenophanes. Emerson. NOBA
Xerox. Ben Belitt. NYP
Xkoagu, give me your heart. Prayer to the Hunting Star, Canopus. *Unknown, tr. by* W. H. I. Bleek *and* Jack Cope. PeSA
Xmas for the Boys. Gavin Ewart. OBSV
Xmas Time. Walta Karsner. ELU
Xochitepec. Malcolm Lowry. *See* Lupus in Fabula.
Xylographer started to cross the sea, A. The Zealless Xylographer. Mary Mapes Dodge. OBAL

Y

Y M & V Blues. *Unknown.* BluL
Y.M.C.A. "C. A. L. T." SUMH
Ya Se Van Los Pastores. Dudley Fitts. FYAP
Yacht, The. Catullus, *tr. fr. Latin by* John Hookham Frere. AWP; OBVE
("This racer of the watry plain," *tr. unknown.*) OBVE
Yacht, The. Walter Savage Landor. OBVV
Yachting in Arkansas. Craig Weeden. AMV-80
Yachts, The. William Carlos Williams. AmPP; AP; BiP; CMoP; CoBMV; HeIP; LiSp; LiTA; LiTM; MasP; MoAB; MoAmPo; MoPo; MOS; MoVE; NePA; NoAM; NOBA; NoP; OxBA; PPP; SeCeV; TwAmPo; ViBoPo
Yachts on the Nile. Bernard Spencer. ChMP
Yaddo. Ruth Herschberger. FAZ
Yahrzeit. Dan Jaffe. VWA
Yahrzeit. Susan Fromberg Schaeffer. VWA
Yahrzeit Candle. Jean Nordhaus. AMV-81
Yai—yai—yai. Musk Oxen. Igjugarjuk, *tr. fr. Eskimo.* WTO
Yak, The. Hilaire Belloc. FaBV; FaPON; HBVY; InMe; MoBrPo; NA; NOBL; OxBChV; TreFS
Yak, The. Oliver Herford. *Fr.* Child's Natural History. HBV-2; HBVY
Yak, The. Jack Prelutsky. RHPC
Yak, The. Virna Sheard. CaP; PeCV; WHW
Yak. William Jay Smith. TiPo
Yale Boola! *3 versions, with music.* H. S. Durand *and others.* FSN
Yall/ out there. A Chant for Young/Brothas and Sistuhs. Sonia Sanchez. BPo
Yamaha yamaha. Mysterious East. William Cole. OBAL
Yan, tan, tethera, tethera, pethera, pimp. A Lincolnshire Shepherd. *Unknown.* OBET
Yang-se-fu. "Yehoash," *tr. fr. Yiddish by* Isidore Goldstick. TrJP
Yankee boy, before he's sent to school, The. Whittling. John Pierpont. GN
Yankee country churchyard holds, A. He Laughed Last. Francis Whiting Hatch. WhC
Yankee Cradle. Robert P. Tristram Coffin. EvOK
Yankee Doodle (*diff. versions*). *Unknown, at. to* Richard Shuckburg *and to* Edward Bangs. AmFP; BLSo, *with music*; ChTr; FaFP; FaPON; FSW; GBP; HBV-2; OBAL; OxNR, 4 *ll.*; PAL; TrAS, *incl.* Cornwallis's Country Dance; TreF; YaD
(Yankeys' Return from Camp, The.) OxBoLi; PAH
Yankee Doodle Boy, The, *with music.* George M. Cohan. BLSo; FSN
Yankee Doodle sent to town. The Last Appendix to "Yankee Doodle." *Unknown.* PAH
Yankee Doodle went to war. The Run from Manassas Junction. *Unknown.* PAH
Yankee Doodle's Expedition to Rhode Island. *Unknown.* PAH
Yankee Man-of-War, The. *Unknown.* AA; AmSS, *with music*; EtS; FaBoBe; PAH; PaPo
(*Stately Southerner,* The.) AmFP; ShS, *with music*
Yankee Poet. Robley Wilson, Jr. AMV-81
Yankee Privateer, The. Arthur Hale. PAH
Yankee ship and a Yankee crew, A. The *Constitution's* Last Fight. James Jeffrey Roche. PAH
Yankee ship came [*or* comes] down the river, A. Blow, Boys, Blow [*or* Blow, Bullies, Blow]. *Unknown.* AmSS; TrAS
Yankee Thunders. *Unknown.* PAH
Yankeys' Return from Camp, The. *Unknown. See* Yankee Doodle.
Yaqui Women: Three Generations. Rick Casillas. GP

Yard by yard I let you. Sapper. Andrew Greig. BSV
Yardbird's Skull. Owen Dodson. AmNP; CNA; IDB; PoBA; VGW
Yardley Oak. William Cowper. LaA; NCEP; NOEC
Yarn of the *Loch Achray,* The. John Masefield. SeCeV
Yarn of the *Nancy Bell,* The. W. S. Gilbert. BeLS; BLPA; CenHV; EtS; EvOK; FaBoBe; FaBoCh; FaBoCo; FaBV; FaFP; HBV-2; HoPM; InMe; MOS; MoShBr; NOBL; OnMSP; TreFS; TrGrPo; VLP
Yarrow counted eight of them. July the First. Robert Currie. Psk
Yarrow had to learn it but he loved Young Jacob. Brothers. Robert Currie. Psk
Yarrow hears the scream. What He Saw. Robert Currie. Str
Yarrow Revisited. Wordsworth. EnRP; VLP
Yarrow Unvisited. Wordsworth. EnRP; GTBS; GTBS-P; HBV-2; PoRA
Yarrow Visited. Wordsworth. EnRP; GTBS; GTBS-P; HBV-2
Yattendon. Sir Henry Newbolt. HBMV
Yaw, Dot Is So! Charles Follen Adams. HBV-2
Yawcob Strauss. Charles F. Adams. PaPo
Yawn, The. Paul Blackburn. CTBA; ELU
Yawning. Eleanor Farjeon. RHPC
Ye Alps audacious, thro' the heavens that rise. The Hasty-Pudding, I. Joel Barlow. AmPP; AP; NOBA; OBAL; OxBA; TAP
Ye Ancient Divine Ones. Arthur Hugh Clough. *Fr.* Amours de Voyage. OBNC
Ye Angells bright, pluck from your Wings a Quill. Edward Taylor. *Fr.* Sacramental Meditations. PoEL-3
Ye Anger Earth. Moses ibn Ezra, *tr. fr. Hebrew by* Solomon Solis-Cohen. *Fr.* The World's Illusion. TrJP
"Ye are the Duke of Athol's nurse." The Duke of Athole's Nurse. *Unknown.* ESPB
Ye Are the Temple of God. Bible, *N.T.* First Corinthians, III: 16-17. TreFT
Ye are the temples of the Lord. The Exhortation of a Father to His Children. Robert Smith. OxBChV
Ye are young, ye are young. An Old Man's Song. Richard Le Gallienne. HBV-1
Ye ayres and windes, ye elves of hilles. Ovid, *tr. by* Arthur Golding. *Fr.* Metamorphoses, VII. OBVE
Ye Banks and Braes. Burns. *See* Banks o' Doon, The.
Ye banks and braes and streams around. Highland Mary. Burns. AWP; EnRP; GTBS; GTBS-P; HBV-1; OAEP; OBEC; OBEV; TreFS; TrGrPo; ViBoPo; WBLP
Ye Banks and Braes o' Bonnie Doon. Burns. *See* Banks o' Doon, The.
Ye Beauties, Beaux, ye Pleaders at the Bar. *Unknown. Fr.* London Evening Post. FaBoUs
Ye beauties! O how great the sun. On a Bed of Guernsey Lilies. Christopher Smart. NOEC; OBEC
Ye [*or* Yee] blushing virgins happy are. To Roses in the Bosom of Castara. William Habington. *Fr.* Castara, Pt. I. AnAnS-2; CavP; EnLoPo; GoBC; HBV-1; LoBV; MeLP; NIP; OBEV; SeCP; UnTE; ViBoPo
Ye brave bold men of 'Cotia. Robens' Promised Land. George Purdom. WTO
Ye brave Columbian bands! a long farewell! On Disbanding the Army. David Humphreys. PAH
Ye brave sons of Freedom, come join in the chorus. The Times. *Unknown.* PAH
Ye brood of Conscience—Spectres! that frequent. Wordsworth. *Fr.* Sonnets upon the Punishment of Death. PeD
Ye bubbling springs that gentle music makes. Love's Limit. *Unknown.* TrGrPo
Ye buds of Brutus' land, courageous youths, now play your parts! For Soldiers. Humphrey Gifford. CH; ElL
Ye call Me Master and obey Me not. Thus Speaketh Christ Our Lord. *Unknown.* PGD
Ye cannot shut the trees in. They All Belong to Me. Eliza Cook. PGD
Ye cats that at midnight spit love at each other. An Appeal to Cats in the Business of Love. Thomas Flatman. EnLoPo; GBL; HAP; PCat
Ye Clerke of ye Wethere. *Unknown.* BXAP
Ye clerks that on your shoulders bear the shield. Preachment for Preachers. Alexander Barclay. *Fr.* The Ship of Fools. ACP
Ye Clouds! that far above me float and pause. France; an Ode. Samuel Taylor Coleridge. EnRP; OAEP
Ye Columbians so bold, attend while I sing. Hull's Surrender. *Unknown.* PAH
Ye Commons and Peers. Jack Frenchman's Defeat [*or* Jack Frenchman's Lamentation]. Congreve. APAS; CoMu
Ye coop us up, and tax our bread. Caged Rats. Ebenezer Elliott. EBEV; VLP
Ye coopers and hoopers, attend to my ditty. The Cooper o' Dundee. *Unknown.* CoMu
Ye dainty [*or* dayntye] nymphs, that in this blessed brook. Elisa [*or* The Lay to Eliza]. Spenser. *Fr.* The Shepheardes Calender: April. NOBE; OBSC
Ye distant spires, ye antique towers. Ode on a Distant Prospect of Eton College. Thomas Gray. BLPL; CABA; GTBS; GTBS-P; HBV-2; HeIP; LAuP; LiTB; NOBE; NOEC; NoP; OAEL-1; OAEP; OBEC; PoEL-3; PrIm; SeCeV; ViBoPo
Ye dreary plains, that round me lie. Summer on the Great American Desert. Rufus B. Sage. BPAW; PoOW
Ye elms that wave on Malvern Hill. Malvern Hill. Herman Melville. AmPP; AP; FPL; PAH; TAP
Ye elves of hills, brooks, standing lakes, and groves. Magic. Shakespeare. *Fr.* The Tempest, V, i. AWP; EBEV; SCV
Ye famed physicians of this place. A Lamentable Case. Charles Hanbury-Williams. ErPo; UnTE
Ye flippering soule. An Address to the Soul Occasioned by a Rain [*or* Let by Rain]. Edward Taylor. AP; NOBA; OxBA; PoEL-3
Ye Flowery Banks o' Bonnie Doon. Burns. *See* Banks o' Doon, The.
Ye fog that creeps there in the uplands. Invocation for a Storm. *Tr. fr. Hawaiian.* WTO
Ye gallants of Newgate, whose fingers are nice. Newgate's Garland. John Gay. FaBoBa
Ye gentlemen and ladies fair. The Hunters of Kentucky; or, Half Horse and Half Alligator. Samuel Woodworth. AS; BLSo, *with music*; FSW; PAH; TrAS
"Ye gie corn to my horse." Clyde's Water [*or* The Mother's Malison]. *Unknown.* BSV; ESPB (A *and* B *vers.*)
Ye glowing seraphs, that now breathe above. Friendship in Perfection. Andrew Michael Ramsay. NOEC
Ye Goatherd Gods. Sir Philip Sidney. *Fr.* Arcadia. NoP
(Double Sestine.) LiTB; PoEL-1
("Ye goat-herd gods that love the grassy mountains.") HAP; NOBE; OAEL-1
Ye gods of love, look from above on a broken hearted maid. Young Billy Crane. Larry Gorman. ShS
Ye Gods! the raptures of that night! The Enjoyment. *Unknown.* ErPo
"Ye Golden Lamps of Heaven." Philip Doddridge. OxBoCh
(Hymn.) OBEC
"Ye graceful peasant-girls and mountain-maids." Ballata: His Talk with Certain Peasant Girls. Franco Sacchetti, *tr. by* Dante Gabriel Rossetti. AWP
Ye green-rob'd Dryads, oft' at dusky eve. The Enthusiast: or, The Lover of Nature. Joseph Warton. EnRP; FaBoEn; LAuP; NOEC; OBEC
Ye groves (the statesman at his desk exclaims). The Statesman in Retirement. William Cowper. *Fr.* Retirement. OBEC
Ye happy swains, whose hearts are free. A Song. Sir George Etherege. HBV-1; ViBoPo
Ye have been fresh and green. To Meadows [*or* Meddowes]. Robert Herrick. AWP; CaPo; CH; FaBoEn; HBV-1; JCP; LoBV; NOBE; OBEV; OBS; PoEL-3; QFR; SeCP; SeCV-1; ViBoPo
"Ye have robbed," said he, "ye have slaughtered and made an end." He Fell among Thieves. Sir Henry Newbolt. EBVV; FaPoR; HBV-2; HBVY; OBEV; OBVV; OBWP; OnMSP; OxBTC
Ye have seen a marvel in this town. The Lament for Yellow-haired Donough. *Unknown, tr. by* Frank O'Connor. KiLC
Ye have sung me your songs, ye have chanted your rimes. The Song of the Derelict. John McCrae. EtS
Ye Heavens, Uplift Your Voice. *Unknown.* OHIP
Ye Highlands [*or* hielands] and ye Lawlands [*or* lowlands]. The Bonny [*or* Bonnie] Earl of [*or* o'] Murray [*or* Moray]. *Unknown.* BSV; ELP; ESPB; FaBoBa; FaBoCh; FSW; GoTS; HBV-2; OBEV; OBS; OxBB; OxBS; PoPle; PrIm; ViBoFo
Ye holy Angels bright. Richard Baxter. *Fr.* A Psalm of Praise. NOCV
Ye humble souls that seek the Lord. Christ's Resurrection and Ascension. Philip Doddridge. NOCV
Ye jolly Yankee gentlemen, who live at home in ease. The C.S.A. Commissioners. *Unknown.* PAH
Ye jovial throng, come join the song. The Battle of Muskingum; or, The Defeat of the Burrites. William Harrison Safford. PAH
Ye Know My Heart. Sir Thomas Wyatt. LoBV
("Ye know, my heart, my lady dear.") SiPS
Ye ladies, walking past me piteous-eyed. Sonnet: To the Same Ladies; With Their Answer. Dante, *tr. by* Dante Gabriel Rossetti. AWP
Ye Laye of ye Woodpeckore. Henry A. Beers. NA
Ye learned sisters which have oftentimes. Epithalamion. Spenser. AAS; BoLoP; CABA; ElL; EnRePo; HBV-1; InPS; MaSP; NOBE; NoP; OAEL-1; OAEP; OBEV; OBSC; PoEL-1; SeCeV; TEP; ViBoPo
Ye lie, friend Pindar! and friend Thales! On a Quaker's Tankard. Walter Savage Landor. FaBoEE
Ye Little Birds That Sit and Sing. *At. to* Thomas Heywood. *Fr.* The Fair Maid of the Exchange. ElL; ViBoPo
(Message, The.) HBV-1
Ye living lamps, by whose dear light. The Mower to the Glow worms. Andrew Marvell. AnAnS-1; AWP;ELP; EnLoPo; InvP; MePo; NOBE; NoP; OAEL-1; OBS; OxBoLi; PoEL-2; PoPle; PPP; SeCP; TrGrPo

Ye lords of creation, men you are called. The Lords of Creation. *Unknown.* PoLF
Ye loyal Britons, I pray draw near. The Battle of Shiloh. *Unknown.* AmFP
Ye maggots, feed on Willie's brains. Burns. FaBoEE
Ye Mariners of England. Thomas Campbell. BLPA; EnRP; EtS; FaPoR; GN; GTBS; GTBS-P; HBV-2; NOBE; OBEV; OBRV; OBWP; TreF
Ye mariners of Spain. The Song of the Galley. *Unknown, tr. by* John Gibson Lockhart. AWP
Ye marshes, how candid and simple and nothing-withholding and free. Sidney Lanier. *Fr.* The Marshes of Glynn. TRV
Ye martial pow'rs, and all ye tuneful nine. Goliath of Gath. Phillis Wheatley. BALP
"Ye maun gang to your father, Janet." Fair Janet. *Unknown.* ESPB; OxBB
Ye may simper, blush, and smile. To Cherry-Blossomes. Robert Herrick. SeCV-1
Ye members of Parliament all. The Shash. *Unknown.* APAS
Ye merry hearts that love to play. Win at First and Lose at Last; or, A New Game at Cards. Laurence Price. OxBoLi
Ye mitered fathers of the land. The Sentiments. *Unknown.* APAS
Ye Mongers Aye Need Masks for Cheatrie. Sydney Goodsir Smith. OxBS
Ye morning glories, ring in the gale your bells. The New God. James Oppenheim. WGRP
Ye motions of delight, that though the fields. Imagination, How Impaired and Restored. Wordsworth. *Fr.* The Prelude, XII *and* XIII. OBNC
Ye mountain valleys, pitifully groan! Lament for Bion. Moschus, *tr. by* George Chapman. AWP
Ye muses, pour the pitying tear. A Great Man. Goldsmith. NA
Ye nymphs and ye swains that trip over the plains. Black Thing. *Unknown.* CoMu
Ye Nymphs forlorn, who pine away in Shades! From a Marriage Broker's Card, 1776. *Unknown.* FaBoUs
Ye nymphs! if e'er your eyes were red. On the [Lamented] Death of Mrs. Throckmorton's Bullfinch. William Cowper. HBV-1; LAuP; NOEC; PBBP; PPP
Ye Nymphs of Solyma! begin the song. Messiah. Pope. OxBoCh
Ye old mule, that thinck your self so fayre. Sir Thomas Wyatt. AAS
Ye Parliament of England. *Unknown.* AmSS, *with music*; AmFP; PAH
Ye paultry underlings of state. On the Irish Club. Swift. OBSV
Ye people of great Murrough['s Band]. On the Defeat of Ragnall by Murrough King of Leinster A.D. 994 [*or* Murrough Defeats the Danes, 994]. *Unknown.* KiLC, *tr. by* Frank O'Connor; OnYI, *tr. by* Kuno Meyer
Ye people of Ireland, both country and city. A New Song of Wood's Halfpence. *At. to* Swift. OxBoLi
Ye people that labour the world to measure. Geographers. Alexander Barclay. *Fr.* The Ship of Fools. ACP
Ye people who delight in sin. The Hanging of Sam Archer. *Unknown.* AmFP
Ye pilgrim-folk, advancing pensively. Dante, *tr. by* Dante Gabriel Rossetti. La Vita Nuova, XXVIII. AWP; CTC
Ye poor little sheep, ah well may ye stray. The Enquiry. John Dyer. OBEC
Ye powers above and heavenly poles. On Button the Grave-Maker. *Unknown.* FaBoEE
Ye powers unseen, to whom the bards of Greece. Inscription. Mark Akenside. OBEC
Ye Protestants of Ulster, I pray you join with me. Lisnagade. *Unknown.* WTO
Ye rascals of ringers, ye merciless foes. On Bell-Ringers. Voltaire. ShM
Ye Realms below the Skies, *with music.* Hosea Ballou II. AH
Ye saints who dwell on Europe's shore. The Handcart Song. *Unknown.* AmFP
Ye saw't floueran in my breist. The Mandrake Hert. Sydney Goodsir Smith. OxBS
Ye say they all have passed away. Indian Names. Lydia Huntley Sigourney. AmFN; FaPON; GOA; HBV-2; OBCA; PAH; PoLF
Ye Scattered Nations, *with music. Unknown, tr. fr. Latin by* Thomas Cradock. AH
Ye shadowy beings, that have rights and claims. Cave of Staffa, II. Wordsworth. VLP
Ye shepherds so chearful and gay. Pastoral Ballad. William Shenstone. OBEC
Ye Should Stay Longer. Francis Beaumont. *Fr.* The Masque of the Inner Temple. ViBoPo
(Songs from a Masque ["Ye should stay longer if we durst"].) TrGrPo
(Three Songs, II.) GoBC
("You should stay longer if we durst.") OBS
Ye silent shades, whose each tree here. To Groves. Robert Herrick. CaPo
Ye Simple Men. John Stuart Blackie. PoSH
Ye Sons of Columbia. Thomas Green Fessenden. PAH
Ye sons of Columbia, who bravely have fought. Adams and Liberty. Robert Treat Paine. PAH
Ye sons of Columbia, your attention I do crave [*or* attention now I pray]. Fuller and Warren. *At. to* Moses Whitecotton. AmFP; BeLS; CoSo; ViBoFo
Ye sons of earth prepare the plough. The Sower. William Cowper. SaC
Ye sons of freedom [*or* of toil], wake to glory! The Marseillaise. Claude Joseph Rouget de Lisle, *tr. by* Charles H. Kerr. HBV-2; TreFS; WBLP
Ye sons of Massachusetts, all who love that honored name. The Sudbury Fight. Wallace Rice. PAH
Ye sons of Sedition, how comes it to pass. On the Snake. *Unknown.* PAH
Ye sons of toil awake to glory! *See* Ye sons of freedom, wake to glory!
Ye Sorrowers. Franz Werfel, *tr. fr. German by* Ludwig Lewisohn. *Fr.* The Eternal Road. TrJP
Ye sorrowing people! who from bondage fly. The Fugitive Slaves. Jones Very. AP; TAP
Ye Spier Me. Sydney Goodsir Smith. BSV
Ye storm-winds of Autumn! Parting. Matthew Arnold. Switzerland, II. OAEP; VLP
Ye Swains who roam from fair to fair. Would You in Venus' Wars Succeed. *Unknown.* ErPo
Ye Sylphs and Sylphids, to your chief give ear! Pope. *Fr.* The Rape of the Lock. ViBoPo
Ye sylvan Muses, loftier strains recite. The Birth of the Squire; an Eclogue. John Gay. NOEC; PoEL-3
Ye tender-hearted people, I pray you lend an ear. Samuel Allen. *Unknown.* AmFP
Ye that have faith to look with fearless eyes. Victory. *Unknown.* WGRP
Ye that in love delight. On Clarastella Singing. Robert Heath. OBS
Ye that pasen by the weiye. Jesus to Those Who Pass By. *Unknown.* MeEL
Ye, too, marvellous twain, that erect on the Monte Cavallo. Ye Ancient Divine Ones. Arthur Hugh Clough. *Fr.* Amours de Voyage. OBNC
Ye traced me on the desert wide. Apache Kid. Ned White. BPAW
Ye tradeful [*or* tradefull] merchants, that with weary toil [*or* toyle]. Amoretti, XV. Spenser. HeIP; LiTB; NIP; OAEL-1; TrGrPo
Ye true lovers bold, come listen unto me. The True Lovers Bold. *Unknown.* AmFP
Ye vig'rous swains! while youth ferments your blood. The Hunt. Pope. *Fr.* Windsor Forest. NIP
Ye walls! sole witnesses of happy sighs. Walter Savage Landor. *Fr.* Ianthe. EnLoPo
Ye Wearie Wayfarer, *sel.* Adam Lindsay Gordon.
Sun and Rain and Dew from Heaven. PoLF
Ye weary, heavy laden souls. The Lonesome Dove. *Unknown.* AmFP
Ye wha are fain to hae your name. Braid Claith. Robert Fergusson. BSV; GoTS; NOEC; OBEC; OxBS
Ye who amid this feverish world would wear. Urban Pollution. John Armstrong. *Fr.* The Art of Preserving Health. NOEC
Ye who have scorn'd each other. The Holly Bough. Charles MacKay. OBVV
Ye who intelligent the third heaven move. The First Canzone of the Convito. Dante, *tr. by* Shelley. OBVE
Ye who pass by and would raise your hand. To the Wayfarer. *Unknown.* SiSoSe
Ye wild-eyed Muses, sing the Twins of Jove. Hymn to Castor and Pollux. *Unknown, tr. by* Shelley. *Fr.* Homeric Hymns. AWP
Ye winds that sweep the grove's green tops. The Mariner. Allan Cunningham. EtS
Ye worthy patriots go on. An Encomium upon a Parliament. Daniel DeFoe. APAS
Ye young debaters over the doctrine. The Village Atheist. Edgar Lee Masters. *Fr.* Spoon River Anthology. EaLo; LiTA
Yea, Dear, lay bare thy lovely soul, nor fear. Confession. Elsa Barker. *Fr.* The Spirit and the Bride. HBMV
Yea, gold is son of Zeus: no rust. Gold Is the Son of Zeus: Neither Moth nor Worm May Gnaw It. "Michael Field." OBMV
Yea, let me praise my lady whom I love. Sonnet: He Will Praise His Lady. Guido Guinicelli, *tr. by* Dante Gabriel Rossetti. AWP
"Yea, my King,"/ I began. Robert Browning. Saul, XIII–XIX, *sl. abr.* WGRP
Yea, she hath passed hereby, and blessed the sheaves. Kore. Frederic Manning, *wr. at. to* Ezra Pound. HBV-1; LoBV
Yea, the coneys are scared by the thud of hoofs. The Field of Waterloo [*or* Chorus *or* Chorus of the Years]. Thomas Hardy. *Fr.* The Dynasts. CMoP; FaBoCh; LoBV
Yea, we go down to sea in ships. At Sea. James Whitcomb Riley. MOS
Yeah./ they hang you up. To All Brothers. Sonia Sanchez. BPo
Yeah./ you can really. Rebolushinary X-mas. Carolyn M. Rodgers. JB
Yeah here am I. Two Jazz Poems. Carl Wendell Hines, Jr. AmNP
"Yeah" she said "my man's gone too." Conversation. Nikki Giovanni. CTBA

Yeah, you know Katie May's a good girl. Katie May. *Unknown.* BluL
Year, The. Coventry Patmore. EBVV
Year a bird flies against the drum, The. For Now. W. S. Merwin. CoPo; NaP
Year after year before my life began. The Tomb of Honey Snaps Its Marble Chains. Derek Stanford. NeBP
Year after year I have watched. Li Ch'ing-chao, *tr. fr. Chinese by* Kenneth Rexroth. BoWoP
Year after year the princess lies asleep. Parabola. A. D. Hope. PoA
Year ago December, Bob, we met, A. Fishing. Philip Dow. WOLT
Year ago how often did I meet, A. Samuel Hoar. Franklin Benjamin Sanborn. AA
Year ago I asked you for your soul, A. The Caged Bird. Arthur Symons. BrPo
Year ago I fell in love with the functional ward, A. The Hospital. Patrick Kavanagh. BIrV; CIP
Year ago you came, A. Pietà. James McAuley. CBAP; PoAu-2
Year Ahead, The. Horatio Nelson Powers. WBLP
"Year and I are dying out together, The." Lament in Autumn. Harold Stewart. PoAu-2
Year at its turn, The. The Last Day of the Year (New Year's Eve). Annette von Droste-Hülshoff, *tr. by* Willis Barnstone. BoWoP
Year dies fiercely, The: out of the north the beating storms. Year's End. William Everson. NoAM
Year 1812, The. Donald Davie, *after the Polish of* Adam Mickiewicz. OBVE; OBWP
Year grows darker, but each day more lamps, The. Autumnal Consummation. Patric Stevenson. NeIP
Year had all the days in charge, The. Why It Was Cold in May. Henrietta Robins Eliot. AA
Year has changed his mantle cold, The. Spring. Charles d'Orléans, *tr. by* Andrew Lang. AWP; CTC
Year has come to us as though out of hiding, A. Early January. W. S. Merwin. VGW
Year has run thin through the tuning room of my mind, The. A Spring Memorandum. Robert Duncan. PoA
Year in the life of a cat equates, A. How to Measure a Cat. Louis Johnson. OCNZ
Year is dead, for Death slays even time, The. Year's End. Nathaniel A. Benson. CaP
Year is done, the last act of the vaudeville, The. Midnight Show. Karl Shapiro. OxBA
Year is gone, beyond recall, The. The Opening Year. *Unknown, tr. by* F. Pott. BLRP
Year is round around me now, The. Green Song. Philip Booth. BoNaP
Year of Jubilee [*or* Jubilo], The. Henry Clay Work. *See* Kingdom Coming.
Year of Our Lord two thousand one hundred and seven, The. John Heath-Stubbs. *Fr.* An Ecclesiastical Chronicle. NOBL
Year of Sorrow, A, *sels.* Aubrey Thomas De Vere.
"Fall, snow, and cease not! Flake by flake." ACP
Spring. OBNC
Year of the Bird. Brian Swann. AmPA
Year of Winter, The. Tauhindauli. STE
Year opens with frozen pipes, The. Omens. Michael Hamburger. NMP
Year our neighbors' ancestors' Thor, The. Three Migrations. Ralph Salisbury. STE
Year Passes, A. Amy Lowell. MOON
Year stood at its equinox, The. The Milking-Maid. Christina Rossetti. 'BeLS
Year That Trembled and Reel'd beneath Me. Walt Whitman. PAI
Year That's Awa', The. John Dunlop. HBV-2
Year was the sixth of Constantine's sway, The. Constantine's Vision of the Cross. Cynewulf, *tr. by* Charles W. Kennedy. *Fr.* Elene. AnOE
Year well remembered! Happy who beheld thee! The Year 1812. Donald Davie, *after* Adam Mickiewicz. OBVE; OBWP
Year without Seasons, A. Mance Williams. NNP
Years. Jon Anderson. AmPA
Years. Walter Savage Landor. *See* Years, Many Parti-Coloured Years.
Years. Anna Margolin, *tr. fr. Yiddish by* Ruth Whitman. VWA
Years, The. John Hall Wheelock. CrMA
Years ago,/ he began dialing your number. The Obscene Caller. Philip Dacey. AmPA
Years ago, as dusk seeped from the blue. The Lost Children. Gregory Orr. GeTw
Years ago, at a private school. An Ever-fixed Mark. Kingsley Amis. ErPo; NoAM; PeHV
Years and years I have loved you. Gabriel Gillett. PeHV
Years are but half a score, The. On the Big Horn. Whittier. PAH
Years are flowers and bloom within, The. God's Garden. Richard Burton. TRV; WGRP
Year's at the Spring, The. Robert Browning. *Fr.* Pippa Passes. BLPA; FaBoBe; FaBV; InPK; PAI; WGRP; YeAr;
(Pippa's Song.) BLPL; EBCP; FaFP; FaPON; GoJo; LiTB; NTCP; OBEV; OBVV; OHIP; PDV; TEP; TrCP; TreF; TRV; UnPo
(Song: "Year's at the Spring, The.") HBV-1; HBVY; PoPl; SoSe; TrGrPo
Year's at the spring, and the birds do sing, The. Corinna Goes a-Singing. Frank Sidgwick. WhC
Year's Awakening, The. Thomas Hardy. CMoP; OxBTC
Year's Burden [1870], A. Swinburne. VLP
Years creep slowly by, Lorena. The. Lorena. H. D. L. Webster. BLPA; FSW; PSoN
Year's End. Nathaniel A. Benson. CaP
Year's End, The. Timothy Cole. HBV-1
Year's End. William Everson. NoAM
Year's End. Richard Wilbur. CAPP; CoAP; HeIP; LiTM; NePoEA
(At Year's End.) MiAP; NePA; NYBP
Year's Ending, The. St. J. Page Yako, *tr. fr. Xhosa by* C. M. Mcanyangwa *and* Jack Cope. PeSA
Years go by, and still both moor and mount. Grey Galloway. Thomas S. Cairncross. PoSH
Years had elapsed; the long room was the same. A Vision. Yvor Winters. MoVE
Years had rubbed out his youth, The. Sootie Joe. Melvin B. Tolson. FAZ
Years have flown since I knew thee first. Song. Richard Watson Gilder. *Fr.* The New Day. AA
Years have gone, The. It is spring. Andrée Rexroth. Kenneth Rexroth. PrIm; VGW
Years have made up my face, The. Toward Myself. Leah Goldberg, *tr. by* Robert Friend. VWA
Years Later. Laurence Lerner. NAs; PeSA
Years Later. Ruth Stone. BoWoP
Years, long years ago, I read of a death I envied. Schiehallion. Helen B. Cruickshank. PoSH
Years, Many Parti-coloured Years. Walter Savage Landor. ViBoPo
(Years.) HBV-1; OBEV
Years of Indiscretion. John Ashbery. NOBA
Years ride out from the world like couriers gone to a throne, The. Song of the Riders. Stephen Vincent Benét. *Fr.* John Brown's Body. MoAmPo
Years saw me still Acasto's mansion grace. An Old Cat's Dying Soliloquy. Anna Seward. NOEC
Years sped onward, The. He who forever sought. Seven Sad Sonnets, VI. Mary Aldis. HBMV
Years That Go to Make Me Man, The. Christopher Brennan. *Fr.* The Twilight of Disquietude. PoAu-1
Years they come and go, The. Ad Finem. Heine, *tr. by* Elizabeth Barrett Browning. AWP
Years they mistook me for you. Dodo. Henry Carlile. GP; Psk
Years, years ago, ere yet my dreams. The Belle of the Ball-Room. Winthrop Mackworth Praed. *Fr.* Every-Day Characters. EnRP; FaBoCo; HBV-1; InMe
Years, years she came to me to dress. The Hairdresser. David Hopes. AMV-81
Yeats in Dublin, *sel.* Vernon Watkins.
" 'The young poets,' he murmured." PP
Yeats' Tower. Vernon Watkins. NeBP
Yee blushing Virgins happie are. *See* Ye blushing virgins . . .
Yee Shall Not Misse of a Few Lines in Remembrance of Thomas Hooker. Edward Johnson. SCAP
Yeerd she hadde, enclosed al aboute, A. Chauntecleer. Chaucer. *Fr.* The Canterbury Tales: The Nun's Priest's Tale. PB
Yeh./ billie. if someone. For Our Lady. Sonia Sanchez. IHMS
Yehuda Amichai. Seymour Mayne. VWA
Yellow. De Leon Harrison. PoBA
Yellow. Josephine Jacobsen. GP
Yellow. Kenton Kilmer. GoYe
Yellow. David McCord. RHPC
Yellow. Charles Wright. AmPA
Yellow as flowers as dead fingers. Leave Train. Alan Ross. ChMP
Yellow becomes alive. Yellow. Josephine Jacobsen. GP
Yellow-belly, yellow-belly, come and take a swim. *Unknown.* OxBoLi
Yellow Bird, The. James W. Thompson. PoBA
Yellow Bird Sings, The. Rabindranath Tagore. *Fr.* The Gardener. OBMV
Yellow Bittern, The. Cathal Buidhe Mac Giolla Ghunna, *tr. fr. Irish.* BIrV, *tr. by* Thomas MacDonagh; CIP, *tr. by* Tom MacIntyre; OnYI, *tr. by* Thomas MacDonagh; OxBI, *tr. by* Thomas MacDonagh
Yellow blood on the dunes. Before the Pacific. Blanca Varela, *tr. by* Willis Barnstone. BoWoP
Yellow Budweiser signs over oaken bars. *See* Yellow-lit Budweiser signs . . .
Yellow butterflies. Korosta Katzina Song. *Unknown, at. to* Koianimptiwa, *tr. fr. Hopi Indian by* Natalie Curtis. AWP; WTO
Yellow canary trilled, A. Jealous Adam. Itzik Manger, *tr. by* Jacob Sonntag. TrJP

Yellow chrysanthemums, The. Sequence for a Young Widow Passing. Deborah Munro. IHMS
Yellow cloud rising up from that fighting. *Aborigine Oral Tradition.* WTO
Yellow dot on her forehead, A. Love Medicine. Eda Lou Walton. BPAW
Yellow dusk: messenger fails to appear. *Tr. fr. Chinese by* Arthur Waley. OBVE
Yellow Flower, The. William Carlos Williams. HAP
Yellow goldenrod is dressed, The. August. Helen Maria Winslow. YeAr
Yellow-haired Laddie, The. *Unknown.* GBP
Yellow is for regret, the distal, the second hand. Yellow. Charles Wright. AmPA
Yellow Jessamine. Constance Fenimore Woolson. AA; HBV-1
Yellow leaf, from the darkness, A. Brooding Grief. D. H. Lawrence. CMoP; LoBV
Yellow leaves do fly from the trees so high, The. The Lamenting Maid. *Unknown.* OBET
Yellow Light. Garrett Kaoru Hongo. HoAn; MAYP
Yellow-lit [*or* Yellow] Budweiser signs over oaken bars. Uptown. Allen Ginsberg. FF; TW; TwCP
Yellow Meal. *Unknown.* ShS
Yellow moon is a dancing phantom, The. On a Nightingale in April. "Fiona Macleod." HBV-1; OBVV
Yellow november/comes swaying. Rushing. Ray A. Young Bear. CDW
Yellow Pansy, A. Helen Gray Cone. HBMV
Yellow paper planes fly. Eagles. Elizabeth Woody. STE
Yellow Rose of Texas, The. *Unknown.* BLSo, *with music*; FSW; PSoN, *with music*; TreFT
Yellow Season, The. William Carlos Williams. MoAB; MoAmPo
Yellow Submarine. John Lennon *and* Paul McCartney. PPoe
Yellow sun yellow. The Ballad of Red Fox. Melvin Walker La Follette. BoAnP; NePoEA
Yellow Violet, The. Bryant. AP; BLPL; PoLF; TAP
Yellow Witch of Caribou, The. Clyde Robertson. BPAW; PoOW
Yellow Woman Speaks. Merle Woo. BrSi
Yellow's unstitching itself from the sun. Interior with Mme. Vuillard and Son. Kathleen Fraser. NPGG
Yen's sorry. A Magpie Rhyme, Northumberland. *Unknown.* GBP
Yeoman of the Guard, *sels.* W. S. Gilbert.
Family Fool, The. InMe
"Man who would woo a fair maid, A." FaBoUs
Yep, gold's where you find it. You betcha that's true. The Ol' Jinny Mine. Daisy L. Detrick. PoOW
Yere yernes ful yerne, and yeldes never like, A. The Passage of a Year. *Unknown. Fr.* Sir Gawain and the Green Knight. PoEL-1
Yes. Richard Doddridge Blackmore. HBV-1
Yes? H. C. Bunner. HBV-1
Yes. James Joyce. *Fr.* Ulysses. FF
Yes,/ And in that month when Proserpine comes back. That Sharp Knife. Thomas Wolfe. NCSH
Yes,/ You must crucify the worm. To a Little Boy Learning to Fish. Robert D. Hoeft. AMV-81
Yes, all the world must sure agree. Against Marriage to His Mistress. William Walsh. FaBoUs
Yes as alike as entirely. To My Father. W. S. Graham. FaBoTw
Yes, Atticus, take it from me. Ovid, *tr. by* Guy Lee. Amores, I, 9. NAWM-1
Yes! Beauty still rebels! Art, I. Alfred Noyes. OBEV
Yes, brother your word had come. Hearing James Brown at the Café des Nattes. Richard A. Long. AmNP
"Yes, But . . ." Theodore Weiss. TAP
Yes, contumelious fair, you scorn. The Author Apologizes to a Lady for His Being a Little Man. Christopher Smart. BoLoP
Yes, death is at the bottom of the cup. If. William Dean Howells. AA
Yes, do you remember an inn. Lament for Lost Lodgings. Phyllis McGinley. NYBP; SpRo
Yes, eight, when/ that was taken. The Photos from Summer Camp. Izora Corpman. FAZ
Yes, every poet is a fool. Epigram. Matthew Prior. FaBoCo; FaBoEE
Yes, faith is a goodly anchor. After the Burial. James Russell Lowell. AA; UnPo
Yes, farewell, farewell forever. Lady Byron's Reply to Lord Byron's "Fare Thee Well." *Unknown.* BLPA
Yes, fickle Cambridge, Perkin's found this true. On the University of Cambridge's Burning the Duke of Monmouth's Picture. George Stepney. APAS
Yes! from mine eyes the tears unbidden start. Distant View of England from the Sea. William Lisle Bowles. EnRP
Yes, from the ingrate heart, the street. The Fugitive. Alice Meynell. NOCV
Yes, he said, darling, yes, of course you tried. The Appointment. L. A. G. Strong. OxBTC
Yes, he was that, or that, as you prefer. T. A. H. Ambrose Bierce. AA; YaD
Yes, he's got her now. Blues. John Fuller. NOBL
Yes! hope may with my strong desire keep pace. To the Marchesana of Pescara [*or* Love's Justification]. Michelangelo, *tr. by* Wordsworth. AWP; CTC; OBVE
Yes, I admit that Proust is rather good. A Ballade of Diminishing Control. J. C. Squire. WhC
Yes, I am black! and radiant. Bible, *O.T.* The Song of Solomon, I:5-6. PBWP
"Yes," I answered you last night. The Lady's "Yes." Elizabeth Barrett Browning. HBV-1
Yes, I believe He loved them, too. The Young Workman. Mary Dillingham Frear. TrCP
Yes, I Could Love If I Could Find. *Unknown.* ErPo
Yes, I got another Johnny; but he was to Number One. My Other Chinee Cook. Brunton Stephens. PoAu-1
Yes, I Have Been to Calvary. Avis B. Christiansen. STF
Yes, I have heard the nightingale. Hast Thou Heard the Nightingale? Richard Watson Gilder. AA
Yes! I have seen the ancient oak. Felicia Dorothea Hemans. *Fr.* The Brereton Omen. CTC
Yes, I know what you say. Tempted. Edward Rowland Sill. AA
Yes, I only got here on my own. On My Own. Philip Levine. FYAP
Yes. I remember Adlestrop. Adlestrop. Edward Thomas. BrPo; CH; FaBoPP; GoJo; HAP; LiTB; NOBE; OBEV; OxBTC
Yes, I remember that pain precisely. The Blood. Nina Cassian, *tr. by* Laura Schiff. WPOW
Yes I rolled and I tumbled. Dough Roller Blues. *Unknown.* BluL
Yes, I said, go out there. Answers to the Snails. Arthur Solway. AMV-81
"Yes, I was only sidesman here when last." Bristol and Clifton. John Betjeman. CMoP
Yes, I was the head of our Halloween horse. To My Blood Sister. Christine E. Hemp. Str
Yes, I went down to the depot. Jesse James. *Unknown.* BaBo
Yes, I will love thee when the sun. A Love Song. W. F. Hawley. OBCV
Yes, I will love then, I will love. The Duel. Abraham Cowley. AnAnS-2
Yes, I will spend the livelong day. In May. W. H. Davies. OBVV
Yes: I Write Verses. Walter Savage Landor. *See* Time to Be Wise.
Yes, I'm in love, I feel it now. The "Je Ne Sais [*or* Sçay] Quoi." William Whitehead. OBEC; SoSe
Yes! in the sea of life enisled. To Marguerite—Continued [*or* Isolation]. Matthew Arnold. Switzerland, V. BoLoP; EBEV; EBVV; ELP; FaBoEn; FiP; GTBS-P; HBV-1; MOS; NOBE; NoP; OAEL-2; OAEP; OBEV; OBNC; OBVV; PoEL-5; PPP; PrIm; SeCeV; TEP; VLP
Yes, in the summer of 1773. Tom Wedgwood Tells. Brian W. Aldiss. NOBL
Yes, injured Woman! rise, assert thy right! The Rights of Woman. Anna Laetitia Barbauld. NOEC
Yes, it is beautiful ever, let foolish men rail at it never. Arthur Hugh Clough. *Fr.* Dipsychus. VLP
Yes, It Was the Mountain Echo. Wordsworth. EnRP
Yes, I've sev'ral kivers you can see. Kivers. Ann Cobb. AmFN
Yes, leave it with Him; the lilies all do. Leave It with Him. *Unknown.* BLRP
"Yes, let me go. Yon fields are green." Request of a Dying Child. Lydia Huntley Sigourney. OBCA
Yes! let the rich deride, the proud disdain. Goldsmith. *Fr.* The Deserted Village. OBSV
Yes, look at me; I am the mask it wears. The Mask the Wearer of the Mask Wears. William Bronk. GP
Yes Miss/ Put up your pretty little mouth for a kiss. Admonition to the Muse. Geoffrey Taylor. FaBoEE
Yes, muster them out, the valiant band. Muster Out the Rangers. *Unknown.* CoSo
Yes! my Lesbia! let us prove. Catullus, *tr. fr. Latin by* Walter Savage Landor. OBVE
Yes, my soul takes pleasure in shattering its chains. God. Alphonse de Lamartine. ILwL
Yes, Nancy Hanks. A Reply to Nancy Hanks. Julius Silberger. TiPo
Yes, our faces are ten blanks. The Hands. Daniel David Moses. AMV-80
Yes, so be it, though we already knew. The Sinking of the Mendi. S. E. K. Mqhayi, *tr. by* C. M. Mcanyangwa *and* Jack Cope. PeSA
Yes solid mountain mingle in my brain. Solid Mountain. George Bowering. NeAC
Yes, still I love thee! Time, who sets. Love Unchangeable. Rufus Dawes. AA
"Yes, stranger, them was red-hot times." Cow-Boy Fun. Wallace D. Coburn. PoOW
Yes, stranger! you well may say so. The Wickedest Man in Memphis. Alex J. Brown. BeLS

Yes, Tadeusz Rozewicz, I too. In Praise of Old Women. Marya Fiamengo. WPOW
Yes! that fair neck, too beautiful by half. Madame d'Albert's Laugh. Clement Marot, *tr. by* Leigh Hunt. AWP
Yes, the Agency Can Handle That. Kenneth Fearing. WeW
Yes, the candidate's a dodger. The Dodger. *Unknown.* AmFP; GBP; OuSiCo
Yes, the coneys are scared by the thud of hoofs. Before Waterloo. Thomas Hardy. *Fr.* The Dynasts. WaaP
Yes, the Secret Mind Whispers. Al Young. PoBA
"Yes, the Town Clerk will see you." In I went. The Town Clerk's Views. John Betjeman. CMoP
Yes, the year is growing old. Midnight Mass for the Dying Year. Longfellow. GoBC
Yes, there is holy pleasure in thine eye! Admonition to a Traveller. Wordsworth. GTBS; GTBS-P
Yes, these are the dog-days, Fortunatus. Under Sirius. W. H. Auden. FaBoMo; NePA
Yes, they are alive and can have those colors. A Blessing in Disguise. John Ashbery. PoM
Yes, theyll let you play. A Poem for Players. Al Young. GP
Yes, this is where I stood that day. Ballad of Hector in Hades. Edwin Muir. NoAM; NOBE
Yes, this is where she lived before she won. Interview. Sara Henderson Hay. DFT; OBCA
Yes, thou art gone! and never more. A Reminiscence. Anne Brontë. WPE
Yes: though the brine may from the desert deep. Frederick Goddard Tuckerman. Sonnets, II, iii. HAP
Yes! 'tis the time! I cried, impose the chain. On the Benefactions in the Late Frost. Pope. NOEC
Yes, true, children will take advantage of. The Little Girl. Nicholas Moore. ErPo; NeBP
Yes, we are fighting at last, it appears. Arthur Hugh Clough. *Fr.* Amours de Voyage, II. EBVV
Yes, we did a heap o' riggin'. Old Ship Riggers. H. A. Cody. EtS
Yes, we love this land together. Fatherland Song. Björnsterne Björnson, *tr. by* William Ellery Leonard. AWP
Yes, we were happy that Sunday, walking. Lisel Mueller. GP
Yes, we were looking at each other. Looking at Each Other. Muriel Rukeyser. NNaP
Yes, we'll rally round the flag, boys, we'll rally once again. Battle-Cry of Freedom. George Frederick Root. FaBoBe; PAH; PSoN; TreFS; YaD
Yes; we'll wed, my little fay. The Conformers. Thomas Hardy. ViBoPo
Yes, What? Robert Francis. LCAP
Yes when the dark withdrew I suffered light. A World of Light. Elizabeth Jennings. NePoEA-2
Yes; when the ways oppose. Ars Victrix. Austin Dobson. HBV-2; HBVY; SyP; VLP
Yes. Why do we all, seeing of a soldier, bless him? The Soldier. Gerard Manley Hopkins. WaaP
Yes, wonderful are dreams: and I have known. Charles Harpur. *Fr.* The Tower of the Dream. PoAu-1
Yes, write, if you want to, there's nothing like trying. A Familiar Letter to Several Correspondents. Oliver Wendell Holmes. FaBoUs; InMe
Yes, yes/ it's time. My Spring Thing. Everett Hoagland. BPo
Yes, yes, I grant the sons of earth. The Question. James Beattie. FaBoCo
Yes, yes, my boy, there's no mistake. McIlrath of Malate. John Jerome Rooney. PAH
Yes you have said enough for the time being. The End Is Near the Beginning. David Gascoyne. EAS
Yes you never miss your water water water. You Never Miss the Water. *Unknown.* BluL
Yes, yours, my love, is the right human face. The Confirmation. Edwin Muir. OxBS
Yesterday. Hugh Chesterman. SiSoSe
Yesterday. W. S. Merwin. DiL; FYAP
Yesterday. Carol Lee Sanchez. TWSS
Yesterday a Euclid took trees. Bright green. Breaking Green. Michael Ondaatje. NOBC
Yesterday a shark was reported cruising. With the Nuns at Cape May Point. David Earle Anderson. AMV-81
Yesterday all the past. The language of size. Spain 1937. W. H. Auden. LiTB; OBWP; WaP
Yesterday, at the Sessions held in Buckingham. A Case at Sessions. Walter Savage Landor. OBSV
Yesterday evening I saw your corpse. Joyce Mansour, *tr. fr. French by* Albert Herzing. WPOW
Yesterday, I discovered my wife. Living with Others. Al Zolynas. LTB
Yesterday I fancied I was young. Ho Nansorhon, *tr. by* Peter H. Lee. *Fr.* A Woman's Sorrow. PBWP
Yesterday I found one left. The Survivor. R. S. Thomas. FaBoTw
Yesterday I knew no lullaby. Child of Our Time. Eavan Boland. CIP
Yesterday I planted garlic. James K. Baxter. Jerusalem Sonnets, 18. OCNZ
Yesterday I skipped all day. Tiptoe. Karla Kuskin. PDV
Yesterday I stood on the balcony. Not Often. Ray Fraser. NeAC
Yesterday I wanted to. For Love. Robert Creeley. ConAP; NOBA
Yesterday I was/ given flowers. Anthology Poem. Petra von Morstein, *tr. by* Rosemarie Waldrop. BoWoP
Yesterday I was told. Byron vs. DiMaggio. Peter Meinke. LiSp
Yesterday in drizzling rain. A Tailor Called Sorrow. Betti Alver, *tr. by* Willis Barnstone *and* Felix Oinas. BoWoP
Yesterday in Oxford Street. Rose Fyleman. PDV; TiPo
Yesterday it blew alway. To Petronilla Who Has Put Up Her Hair. Henry Howarth Bashford. HBV-1
Yesterday it seems you were acting on a stage. Legend. John Waller. NeBP
Yesterday my children left for college. Missing the Children. Paul Zimmer. Str
Yesterday my gun exploded. The Perils of Obesity. Harry Graham. FiBHP
Yesterday rain fell in torrents. You Could Say. Robert Mezey. NaP
Yesterday, Rebecca Mason. Rebecca's After-Thought [*or* Truth the Best]. Elizabeth Turner. HBV-1; HBVY; OxBChV
Yesterday, Robin spoke to me. Charlotte DeClue. STE
Yesterday, sitting. Just. Judith Johnson Sherwin. TAP
Yesterday, the/ Valleys of Fires, today. Postcards. Mark Vinz. FAZ
Yesterday the fields were only gray with scattered snow. A Winter's Tale. D. H. Lawrence. MoAB; MoBrPo
Yesterday the gentle. St. Stephen's Day. Patric Dickinson. OBCP
Yesterday the twig was brown and bare. Miracle. Liberty Hyde Bailey. OHIP; YeAr
Yesterday, the usual stiff-necked shakedown. We Were Permitted to Meet Together in Prison to Prepare for Trial. Daniel Berrigan. LFAC
Yesterday three deer stood at the roadside. Deer at the Roadside. Iain Crichton Smith. *Fr.* Deer on the High Hills—a Meditation. PoSH
Yestreen I had a pint o' wine. Anna. Burns. TrGrPo; UnTE
Yestreen I stood on Ben Dorain, and paced its dark-/grey path. On Ben Dorain. Duncan Ban MacIntyre, *tr. by* Robert Buchanan. *Fr.* Last Farewell to the Hills. PoSH
Yestre'en the queen had four Maries. Mary Hamilton's Last Goodnight. *Unknown.* ViBoFo
Yet/ Ere the season died a-cold. Ezra Pound. *Fr.* Canto LXXXI. MoVE
Yet ah, that spring should vanish with the rose. Omar Khayyám, *tr. by* Edward Fitzgerald. *Fr.* The Rubáiyát of Omar Khayyám of Naishápúr. SeCeV
Yet another great truth I record in my verse. The Viper. Hilaire Belloc. FaBoNo
Yet but Three? Shakespeare. *Fr.* A Midsummer Night's Dream, III, ii. CTC
"Yet Chloe [*or* Cloe] sure was formed without a spot." Chloe. Pope. *Fr.* Moral Essays. AWP; ErPo; NOBE; OBSV
Yet Dish. Gertrude Stein. SOTW
Yet Do I Marvel. Countee Cullen. AmNP; BANP; BPo; CDC; FF; IDB; NoAM; PoBA; PoNe; TAP; TTY
Yet Each Man Kills the Thing He Loves. Oscar Wilde. *Fr.* The Ballad of Reading Gaol. TEP; TrGrPo; WHA
Yet Gentle Will the Griffin Be. Vachel Lindsay. Poems about the Moon, II. MOON; TwAmPo
Yet had his sun not risen; from his lips. The Final Struggle. Louis James Block. *Fr.* The New World. PAH
Yet I could think, indeed, the perfect call. Arthur Hugh Clough. *Fr.* Dipsychus. OBNC
Yet I courbed on my knees and cried hire of grace. William Langland. *Fr.* The Vision of Piers Plowman, II. EBEV
Yet If His Majesty, Our Sovereign Lord. *Unknown.* *See* Guest, The.
Yet if some voice that man could trust. In Memoriam A. H. H., XXXV. Tennyson. ViBoPo
Yet in spite/ Of pleasure won, and knowledge not withheld. Summer Vacation. Wordsworth. *Fr.* The Prelude, IV. PoEL-4
Yet is God a curteis lord. A Warning to Beware. *Unknown.* OxBM
Yet it is not all immaculate death. Not All Immaculate. Laura Riding. Three Sermons to the Dead, II. LiTA
Yet it was plain she struggled, and that salt. George Meredith. Modern Love, VIII. OAEP
Yet Listen Now. Amy Carmichael. TRV
Yet London, empress of the northern clime. Dryden. *Fr.* Annus Mirabilis. ViBoPo
Yet, love, mere love, is beautiful indeed. Sonnets from the Portuguese, X. Elizabeth Barrett Browning. CTC; HBV-1; VLP
Yet Love will dream and Faith will trust. Life and Love. Whittier. BLRP; TRV
Yet much may be performed, to check the force. Bedford Level. John Dyer. *Fr.* The Fleece, II. FaBoPP

Yet, O my friend—pale conjurer, I call. Bring Them Not Back. James Benjamin Kenyon. AA
Yet, O stricken heart, remember, O remember. In Memoriam F. A. S. Robert Louis Stevenson. BrPo
Yet often I think the king of that country. The Gospel of Labor. Henry van Dyke. TRV
Yet on the other side, faine would he start. Giovanni Battista Marino, *tr. by* Richard Crashaw. *Fr.* The Massacre of the Innocents. OBVE
Yet once again do I behold the forms. The Voice of the Derwent. Wordsworth. FaBoPP
Yet once more, O ye laurels, and once more. Lycidas. Milton. AWP; BiP; CABA; ChTr; EBEV; FaBoEn; FiP; GTBS; GTBS-P; HAP; HBV-2; InPK; InPS; JCP; LiTB; LoBV; MasP; NIP; NOBE; NoP; OAEL-1; OAEP; OBEV; OBS; PAI; PoEL-3; PPoe; PPP; PrIm; SeCeV; TrGrPo; UnPo; ViBoPo; WeW; WGRP; WHA
Yet one more hour, then comes the night. My Drinking Song. Richard Dehmel, *tr. by* Ludwig Lewisohn. AWP
Yet Ostia boasts of her regeneration. Daniel Defoe. *Fr.* Reformation of Manners. OBSV
Yet, planter, let humanity prevail. Slaves. James Grainger. *Fr.* The Sugar Cane. NOEC
Yet shall my soule in silence still. Bible, *O.T., paraphrased by* Countess of Pembroke. Psalms, LXII. PBWP
Yet sighs, dear sighs, indeed true friends you are. Astrophel and Stella, XCV. Sir Philip Sidney. SiPS
Yet there is no great problem in the world today. "Hugh MacDiarmid." *Fr.* Lament for the Great Music. OxBTC
"Yet there's one scruple with which I am much." Philip Massinger. *Fr.* The Renegado. ACP
Yet thou, they say, for marriage dost provide. Against Women: Satire VI. Juvenal, *tr. by* Dryden. UnTE
Yet to the wondrous St. Peter's, and yet to the solemn Rotonda. Ah, That I Were Far Away [*or* Upon Apennine Slope]. Arthur Hugh Clough. *Fr.* Amours de Voyage. FaBoPP; OBNC
Yet what are all such gaieties to me. "Lewis Carroll." VLP
Yet, when I muse on what life is, I seem. To a Republican Friend: Continued. Matthew Arnold. VLP
Yet while my Hector still survives, I see. Hector and Andromache. Homer, *tr. by* Pope. *Fr.* The Iliad, VI. OBEC
Yet wulde I nat the causer fared amisse. Subject to All Pain. *Unknown.* MeEl
Yet, yet a moment, one dim ray of light. Pope. The Dunciad, IV. OAEL-1; PoEL-3
Yetzer ha Ra. Edward Codish. VWA
Yeux Glauques. Erza Pound. *Fr.* Hugh Selwyn Mauberley. MoAmPo
Yevtushenko, Voznesensky and I. A Dream. Charles Tomlinson. OxBC
Yew-Tree, The. *Unknown, tr. fr. Welsh by* Geoffrey Grigson. ChTr; GBL
Yew-Tree, The. Vernon Watkins. EaLo; LiTB
Yew-Trees. Wordsworth. CABA; EnRP; UnPo
Y'heave ho! my lads, the wind blows free. Sailing Sailing [*or* Sailing]. Godfrey Marks. FSW; TreFS
Yickity-yackity, yickity-yak. The Yak. Jack Prelutsky. RHPC
Yiddish. Judith Herzberg, *tr. fr. Dutch by* Shirley Kaufman. VWA
Yiddish. Abraham Sutskever, *tr. fr. Yiddish by* Seymour Levitan. VWA
Yiddish Poet. A. C. Jacobs. VWA
Yiddish poet. Move On, Yiddish Poet. Jacob Glatstein, *tr. by* Ruth Whitman. VWA
Yield. Ronald Gross. InPK
Yield all, my love; but be withal as coy. Upon A. M. Sir John Suckling. CavP; ErPo
Yielded Life, The. "W. A. G." BLRP
Yielding. Shellie Keir Robbins. AMV-80
Yillow, yellow, yillow. Metamorphosis. Wallace Stevens. InPK; VGW
Yip-yap Rattletrap. Clyde Watson. RHPC
Yip! Yip! Yip! Yip! tunin' up the fiddle. The Cowboy's Ball. Henry Herbert Knibbs. PoOW
Yippee! she is shooting in the harbor! he is jumping. Blocks. Frank O'Hara. EAS
Yiskidor, when he dies I won't know the Hebrew words to say. Edward Field. *Fr.* Visiting Home. DiL
Yiya wo!/ This land of the Baca. Was It All Worth While? *Zulu Oral Tradition, tr. by* H. Tracey. WTO
Ylen's Song. Richard Hovey. *Fr.* The Birth of Galahad. AA
Yo ho, ma hahties, da's a hurricane a-brewin'. Black Sailor's Chanty. Charles Keeler. EtS
Yo Soy de la Tierra, *with music.* *Unknown.* OuSiCo
Yo soy india. Tribal Chant. Carol Lee Sanchez. TWSS
Yogi, don't go away. Mirabai, *tr. fr. Hindi by* Willis Barnstone *and* Usha Nilsson. BoWoP
Yoke, The. Kalonymos ben Kalonymos, *tr. fr. Hebrew by* J. Chotzner. *Fr.* The Touchstone. TrJP
Yoke of Tyranny, The. Sir Philip Sidney. *See* Astrophel and Stella, XLVII.
Yoke Soft and Dear, *with music.* John C. Kunze. AH
Yoke uneasy on the ox doth sit, The. Philip Ayres. FaBoEE
Yolp, Yolp, Yolp, Yolp. *Unknown.* ElL
Yom Kippur. Chana Bloch. VWA
Yom Kippur. Eric Chaet. VWA
Yom Kippur. Lucille Day. VWA
Yom Kippur. Linda Pastan. VWA
Yom Kippur. Israel Zangwill. TrJP
Yom Kippur: Fasting. Ruth Whitman. OFD
Yomi, Yomi. *Tr. fr. Yiddish.* FSW
Yon clouds that roam the deserts of the air. The Bedouins of the Skies. James Benjamin Kenyon. AA
Yon cottager who weaves at her own door. Simple Faith. William Cowper. *Fr.* Truth. OBEC
Yon Far Country. A. E. Housman. *See* Into My Heart an Air That Kills.
Yon is the laddie lo'ed to daunder far. Lintie in a Cage. Alice V. Stuart. OxBS
Yon laddie wi' the gowdan pow. A Riddle. William Soutar. OxBS
Yon silvery billows breaking on the beach. The Sonnet's Voice. Theodore Watts-Dunton. EtS; HBV-2
Yon spark's a poet, by my troth! The Difference. Tadhg Dall O'Huiginn, *tr. by* Robin Flower. BIrV
Yonder. Richard Eberhart. GOA
Yonder come Roberta! Tell me how do you know? Midnight Special. *Unknown.* AS
Yonder comes a courteous Knight. The Baffled [*or* Courteous] Knight. *Unknown.* ESPB; OxBB
Yonder comes dat ole Joe Brown. Walky-talky Jenny. *Unknown.* AS
Yonder comes my baby all dressed in blue. Cocaine Blues. *Unknown.* FSW
Yonder Comes My Pretty Little Girl, *with music.* *Unknown.* AS
Yonder comes the dawn. Uru-tu-sendo's Song. *Tr. fr. Tewa Indian by* H. J. Spinden. WTO
Yonder Comes the High Sheriff, *with music.* *Unknown.* AS
Yonder great shadow—that blot on the passionate glare of the desert. The Dead of the Wilderness. Hayyim Nahman Bialik, *tr. by* Maurice Samuel. AWP
Yonder in the heather there's a bed for sleeping. In City Streets. Ada Smith. HBV-1
Yonder See the Morning Blink. A. E. Housman. CMoP; MoShBr
Yonder stands a pretty fair maiden. No, Sir, No. *Unknown.* AmFP
Yonder, that swarm of things insectual. A Sequelula to "The Dynasts." Max Beerbohm. Par
Yonder they are coming. It Is Mine, This Country Wide. *Unknown.* GOA
Yonder, yonder see the fair rainbow. The Rainbow [*or* Corn-grinding Song]. *Tr. fr. Hopi Indian by* Natalie Curtis. SUS; WTO
Yonder you weep. Jamila. Nazik al-Mala'ika, *tr. by* Kamal Boullata. WPOW
Yond's the Cardinall's window: This fortification. John Webster. *Fr.* The Duchess of Malfi, V, iii. PoEL-2
Yonghy-Bonghy-Bo, The. Edward Lear. *See* The Courtship of the Yonghy-Bonghy-Bo.
Yonosa House. R. T. Smith. STE; Str
Yorkshire Bite, The. *Unknown.* BaBo
Yorktown Centennial Lyric. Paul Hamilton Hayne. PAH
Yorunomado sat in. The Black Hat. Clayton Eshleman. VGW
Yosemite. Milicent Washburn Shinn. *Fr.* The Washington Sequoia. AA
You. Carroll Arnett. VoR
You, *sels.* Tom Clark. EAS
"Chords knotted together like insane nouns," IV
"Door behind me was you, The," I.
"Today I get this letter from you and the sun," III.
"You are bright, tremendous, wow," II.
You. Kenneth Rexroth. *Fr.* A. Bestiary. HoPM
You. John Tagliabue. GP
You/ are the One who put. Stars in Apple Cores. Luci Shaw. TrCP
You/ my bell-clapper. Christmas Mass for a Little Atheist Jesus. Claude Maillard, *tr. by* Maxine *and* Judith Kumin. BoWoP
You/ Over there/ Beyond the hill. Echo. Mildred Weston. BoNaP
You/ Refuse to see. Out. Riots and Rituals. Richard W. Thomas. PoBA
You a man, man, man, who knows the other word. Compozishun—to James Herndon and Others. Ronald J. Goba. NCSH
You abandon me, woman, because I am very poor. El Abandonado. *Unknown, tr. by* Frank J. Dobie. AS
You accompanied me so far. A Last Address to My Ghosts. Gregory Orr. GeTw
You, after all, were good. Afterthoughts of Donna Elvira. Carolyn Kizer. NePoAm-2
You again. The ecstatic posture. The victory symbol. Memoir. Roger Weingarten. AMV-80
You agree/ With me. A Question. William Cole. BoAnP
You ain't part Indian. Wake-up Niggers. Don L. Lee. PoBA

You All Are Static; I Alone Am Moving. Peter Viereck. LiTA
You All Know the Story of the Other Woman. Anne Sexton. InPK
You Also, Gaius Valerius Catullus. Archibald MacLeish. NoAM; TAP
You also, laughing one. A Girl. Babette Deutsch. HBMV
You also, our first great. To Whistler, American. Ezra Pound. PoA
You always know what to expect. The Country House. Louis Simpson. NOBA
You an' me, bister, been giraffes. To and on Other Intellectual Poets on Reading That the U.S.A.F. Had Sent a Team of Scientists to Africa. Ramon Guthrie. NMP
You and I. Henry Alford. BLPA; FaBoBe
You and I and Amyas. Desire [or Latet Anguis]. William Cornish. OBEV; OBSC
You and I are like an old married couple. Lifesaving. Sandra McPherson. MAYP
You and I by this lamp with these. Together. Ludwig Lewisohn. HBMV; TrJP
You and I have found the secret way. The Secret Love. "Æ." HBV-1
You and I—we agitate. Minutes. Denis Johnson. MAYP
You and It. Mark Strand. NYBP
You, Andrew Marvell. Archibald MacLeish. AP; AWP; CMoP; CoBMV; FaBV; FYAP; HAP; HeIP; HoPM; LiTA; LiTM; MoAB; MoAmPo; MoVE; MP; NoAM; NOBA; NoP; OxBA; PoRA; PPP; PrIm; SoSe; TreFT; TrGrPo; TwAmPo; TwCP; ViBoPo; WeW
You approach me carrying a book. Superballs. Tom Clark. EAS
You are a beggar. Bonner's Ferry Beggar. Duane Clark. AMV-81
You are a [or the] friend then, as I make it out. Ben Jonson Entertains a Man from Stratford. E. A. Robinson. AmPP; MoAB; MoAmPo; MoPo; TwAmPo
You are a hard-boiled egg. Me? Lump. Robert Phillips. AMV-80
You Are a Jew! Delmore Schwartz. *Fr.* Genesis. TrJP
You are a landscape in the Tale of Terror. For Cora Lightbody, R.N. John Glassco. PoA
You Are a Part of Me. Frank Yerby. AmNP
You are a stool pigeon and. Kenneth Rexroth, *after the Latin of* Martial. NNaP
You are a sunrise. To a Golden-haired Girl in a Louisiana Town. Vachel Lindsay. MoAmPo
You are a tried and loyal friend. To My Setter, Scout. Frank H. Seldon. BLPA
You are a tulip seen today. A Meditation for His Mistress[e]. Robert Herrick. CaPo; JCP; NOBE; OBEV; OBS; SeCP
You are a woman. Another. Ellen Marie Bissert. PeHV
You are all these people. To a Single Shadow without Pity. Sam Cornish. NBP; PoBA
You Are Alms. James W. Thompson. PoBA
You are already/ asleep. Touch. Thom Gunn. CMoP
You are already flying away. Business Trips. Laurie Taylor. AMV-80
You are as gold. Song. Hilda Doolittle ("H. D."). LiTA; LiTM; MoAmPo; TwAmPo
You are beautiful. What Ulysses Said to Circe on the Beach of Aeaea. Irving Layton. ErPo
You are beautiful and faded. A Lady. Amy Lowell. MoAmPo
You are blind like us. Your hurt no man designed. To Germany. Charles Hamilton Sorley. MoBrPo
"You are brave," I told the Sleeping Beauty. The Sleeping Beauty. Leonard Cohen. DFT
You are bright, tremendous, wow. You, II. Tom Clark. EAS
You are but these to me: a freckled face. Sonnet Sequence. Darwin T. Turner. BALP
You are carried in a basket. Operation. W. E. Henley. In Hospital, V. BrPo
You are carrying me, full consciousness, god that has desires. Full Consciousness. Juan Ramón Jiménez, *tr. by* Robert Bly. NU
You are clear. The Garden. Hilda Doolittle ("H. D."). LiTA; TwAmPo
You are coming to woo me, but not as of yore. Lips That Touch Liquor. George W. Young. TreFT
You are coming toward us. Aunt Laura Moves toward the Open Grave of Her Father. Joseph de Roche. HeIP
You are coming very slowly, why do you delay. My Cobra Girl. *Gond Oral Tradition, tr. by* V. Elwin *and* S. Hivale. WTO
You are confronted with yourself. Each year. Rembrandt's Late Self-Portraits. Elizabeth Jennings. EyDe
You are disdainful and magnificent. Sonnet to a Negro in Harlem. Helene Johnson. AmNP; BANP; CDC; NIP
You are elect and young. The Phi Beta Kappa Poem. Richmond Lattimore. GLGT
You are falling asleep and I sit looking at you. After Dark. Adrienne Rich. LCAP; LiTM; VGW
You are famous in my mind. Before the Big Storm. William Stafford. NaP
You are fortunate, dear friends, that you can tell. Vidya, *tr. fr. Sanskrit by* Daniel Ingalls. WPOW
You are gazing now on old Tom Moore. *See* You are looking now on old Tom Moore.
You are going far away, far away from poor Jeannette. Jeannette and Jeannot. Charles Jeffries. BLPA
You Are Gorgeous and I'm Coming. Frank O'Hara. NeAP
You Are Growing into My Life. Louise Harris. AMV-81
You are here now. The Sleeping Fury. Louise Bogan. IHMS; LiTM
You are horizontal. Footpaths Cross in the Rice Field. "Lin Ling," *tr. by* Kenneth Rexroth *and* Ling Chung. PBWP
You are ill and so I lead you away. Poem. Al Purdy. NOBC
You are leaving soon. Already I Feel the Emptiness. Edgar Jackson. Three Songs, III. LFAC
You are less than one-half. The Speaker. Charles Ballard. VoR
You are like a sun of the tropics. Luxury. Donald Justice. HeIP
You are like a whispering branch. Metaphors. Miklós Radnóti, *tr. by* Steven Polgar *and* Stephen Berg *and* S. J. Marks. VWA
You are looking [or gazing] now on old Tom Moore. The Days of 'Forty-nine. *Unknown.* BPAW; CoSo; PAH
You are loveliness and all desire. Living and Dying. "Michael Lewis." *Fr.* Cherry Blossoms. UnTE
You are lying, O missionary! Raymond Mazisi Kunene. , *tr. fr. Zulu by* D. K. Rycroft. WTO
You are made of almost nothing. The Dragonfly. Louise Bogan. HeIP; NIP
You Are More than I Need. Rebbekka Kaplan. AMV-80
You are my friend. Lorine Niedecker. VGW
You are, my green island. Neither This nor That. Luis Palés Matos, *tr. by* Julio Marzán. InW
You are my shadow in the picture. Lines for Michael in the Picture. John Logan. CAPP
You are my song come true. Reparation. Helen Hoyt. HBMV
You are my stick, my prop. Houseplant. Felicity Napier. BrRo
You are naked and have no clothes. Your Presence. Mordecai Temkin, *tr. by* Jeremy Garber. VWA
You are no more, but sunken in a sea. Sea-Change. Genevieve Taggard. EtS
You are not alone on the mountain. Beinn A' Ghlo. Bill Tulloch. PoSH
You are not beautiful, exactly. To Dorothy. Marvin Bell. Psk
You are not here, I cannot touch you, or be still. Gemini Elegy. Margaret Gibson. MAYP
You are not here! the quaint witch Memory sees. To Maria Gisborne in England, from Italy. Shelley. *Fr.* Letter to Maria Gisborne. NOBE
You are not looked for through the smog. To the Moon. Babette Deutsch. MOON
You are not merry, brother. Why not laugh. The Prodigal Son. E. A. Robinson. MoAmPo
You are not nearer God than we. Annunciation. Rainer Maria Rilke, *tr. by* James Blair Leishman. OBVE
You are not wanted. Periphery. Ruth Stone. GP
You are now/ In London, that great sea. Shelley. *Fr.* Letter to Maria Gisborne. ChER; EBEV; OBRV
"You are old, Father William," the young man cried. The Old Man's Comforts [and How He Gained Them]. Robert Southey. HBV-1; HoPM; OxBChV; PaPo; Par; SpRo; UnPo
"You are old, Father William," the young man said. Father William. "Lewis Carroll." *Fr.* Alice's Adventure's in Wonderland. BiP; BXAP; FaBoCo; FaBoNo; FaBoPa; FaPON; FiBHP; FPL; GoJo; HBV-1; HoPM; InMe; LiTB; NOBL; OxBChV; Par; PDV; PoLF; PoRA; RHPC; SpRo; TiPo; TreF; TrGrPo; UnPo; WhC
"You are old, Father William," the young man said,/ "And your nose has a look of surprise." Father William. *Unknown.* NA
"You are old Munro bagger," the young man said. The Old Munro Bagger. *Unknown.* PoSH
You Are on U.S. 40 Headed West. Vera White. AmFN
You are only one of many. One of Many. Stevie Smith. OxBC
You are over there, Father Malloy. Father Malloy. Edgar Lee Masters. *Fr.* Spoon River Anthology. OxBA
You are perishing like the old men. Already your arms are gone. The Chorus Speaks Her Words as She Dances. Linda Gregg. NPGG
You are proof that it can happen. A Tardy Epithalamium for E. and N. Ralph Pomeroy. PeHV
You are right. In dreams I might well dance. Possession. Marie Ponsot. VGW
You are right. What we call Poetry is the boat. A New Poem. Robert Duncan. NNaP; PoM
You are rumpled like a sweater. Nothing More Will Happen [or Different Persuasions]. Marge Piercy. InPK; NeAC
You are small and intense. To a Child Running with Outstretched Arms in Canyon de Chelly. N. Scott Momaday. CDW

You are so beautifully thin and naive. Dear Patty, Dear Tania. Richard Mathews. GP
You are so small, I. Miss Cho Composes in the Cafeteria. James Tate. WeW
You are so witty, profligate, and thin. Epigram on Voltaire [*or* Extempore to Voltaire Criticising Milton]. Edward Young. FaBoCo; ViBoPo
You are speaking of Chile. Things That Are Worse than Death. Sharon Olds. MAYP
You are still the one with the stone and the sling. Man of My Time. Salvatore Quasimodo, *tr. by* Allen Mandelbaum. PoPl
You are such a well-rounded sponge. Sediment. David Ignatow. NYBP
You are "the best of cut-throats"—do not start. The Duke of Wellington. Byron. *Fr.* Don Juan. DBV
You Are the Brave. Raymond R. Patterson. NBP; NIP; PoBA (In Time of Crisis.) IDB
You are the cause of this destruction, Lesbia. Catullus, *tr. fr. Latin by* Horace Gregory. NAWM-1
You are the friend then, as I make it out. *See* You are a friend then, as I make out.
You are the grain. I Think of Housman Who Said the Poem Is a Morbid Secretion, like a Pearl. Judith Kroll. UnPo
You are the millions, we are multitude. The Scythians. Aleksandr Blok, *tr. by* Babette Deutsch *and* Avrahm Yarmolinsky. AWP; WaaP
You are the owner of one complete thought. Voice and Address. Michael Palmer. NPGG
You are the priest tonight. To Mary: At the Thirteenth Station. Raymond F. Roseliep. ISi
You are the problem I propose. The Metaphysical Amorist. J. V. Cunningham. TwAmPo; VGW
You are the town and we are the clock. Chorus. W. H. Auden. *Fr.* The Dog beneath the Skin. OxBTC
You are tired. The Midnight Tennis Match. Thomas Lux. AmPA
You are unspeakable in your mere death. On a Photo of a Baby Killed in the War. Mark DeFoe. SOTS
You are what you eat and I. Cheerios. Peter Meinke. GP
"You are wise, Mr. Dodgson," the young child said. Lewis Carroll. Eleanor Farjeon. OxBChV
You are with me this evening, all my friends. Evening in the Walls. Jean Wahl, *tr. by* Charles Guenther. VWA
You are writing a gospel. Your Own Version. Paul Gilbert. BLRP
You are wrong about the crocus. Crocus. Joan Murray. AMV-80
You arrive in Paradise feverish with anticipation, assuring. Home. Steve Kowit. AMV-81
You ask a sonnet?—well, it is your right. James Branch Cabell. Retractions, *introd. st.* HBMV
You ask a verse, to sing (ah, laughing face!). To a Lady. John James Piatt. AA
You ask how old am I. Twice Times Then Is Now. Ibn Hazm Al-Andalusi, *tr. by* Omar Pound. OBVE
You ask me. To Madame A. V. Pletneff. Karolina Pavlova, *tr. by* Paul Schmidt. PBWP
You ask me for a song, folks. Cousin Jack Song. *At. to* Charley Tregonning. AmFP
You ask me, Fresher, who it is. Ballade of Andrew Lang. Dugald Sutherland MacColl. CenHV
You ask me how Contempt who claims to sleep. Epigram. J. V. Cunningham. ELU; ErPo; NePoAm
You ask me, Lydia, "whether I." To "Lydia Languish." Austin Dobson. NBM; VLP
You ask me to sing, so I'll sing you a song. The Cranberry Song. Barney Reynolds. AmFP
You ask me, *What's love?*—Why, that virtue-fed vapour. Address to Lady ———, Who Asked What the Passion of Love Was? Charles Morris. NOEC
You ask me "why I like him." Nay. Friends. E. V. Lucas. HBV-2
You Ask Me, Why, though [*or* tho'] Ill at Ease. Tennyson. CABA; OAEP; VLP
You ask my love. What shall my love then be? On the Nature of Love. Wilfrid Scawen Blunt. *Fr.* The Love Sonnets of Proteus. ViBoPo
You ask what I have found, and far and wide I go. The Curse of Cromwell. W. B. Yeats. BIrV; SeCePo
You ask what it's like here. Prison Letter. Michael Knoll. LFAC
You ask what place I like the best. The Kinkaiders. *Unknown.* AS; CoSo
You ask why gold and velvet bind. On a New Duke. *Unknown.* FaBoEE
You ask why Mary was called contrary? Contrary Mary. Nancy Byrd Turner. HBMV; HBVY
You asked for green pepper. Coplas. *Tr. fr. Spanish.* FSW
You asked me to enter the holy cloister. Banishment from Ur. Enheduanna, *tr. fr. Sumerian.* BoWoP
You asked what. The Hosts. W. S. Merwin. GP
You at God's altar stand, His minister. Written on an Island off the Breton Coast. Venantius Fortunatus, *tr. by* Helen Waddell. PeHV
You, Atalanta, were so fleet. To Atalanta. Dorothy Dow. HBMV
You bad leetle boy, not moche you care. Leetle Bateese. William Henry Drummond. CaP
You balanced her within a cyclone. Woman Seed Player. Roberta Hill Whiteman. STE
You beat your pate, and fancy wit will come. Epigram. Pope. FaBoEE; HBV-1; PoPle; TreFT
You beautious ladies, great and small. The Famous Flower of Serving-Men; or, The Lady Turn'd Serving-Man. *Unknown.* ESPB; OBET; OxBB
You became/ In many acts and quiet observances. My Company. Sir Herbert Read. BrPo; MMA
You Begin. Margaret Atwood. NOBC; NoP
You, being less than either dew or frost. Love Song out of Nothing. Vassar Miller. NePoEA
You bells in the steeple, ring, ring out your changes. Seven Times Two—Romance. Jean Ingelow. *Fr.* Songs of Seven. GN
You better come on in my kitchen. Come On in My Kitchen. *Unknown.* BluL
You better learn how to treat everybody. You Got to Go Down. *Unknown.* BluL
You better sure shall live, not evermore. Horace, *tr. fr. Latin by* Sir Philip Sidney. Odes, II, 10. OBVE
You bible-sharps that thump on tubs. Villon's Good-Night. W. E. Henley. CenHV
You bid me to hold my peace. The Poet to the Birds. Alice Meynell. FM
You bid me try, Blue Eyes, to write. The Rondeau. Austin Dobson, *after the French of* Vincent Voiture. HBV-2
You Black Bright Stars. *Unknown.* EnRePo
You black out the sun. Ed Roberson. *Fr.* When Thy King Is a Boy. PoBA
You blame me that I do not write. Letter to a Friend. Jon Stallworthy. NoAM
You Blessed Bowers. *Unknown.* ElL
You boast about your ancient line. Family Trees. Douglas Malloch. OHIP
You brave heroic [*or* heroique] minds. To the Virginian Voyage. Michael Drayton. EnRePo; HAP; HBV-2; LOBV; NOBE; OAEP; OBEV; OBS; PAH; PoEL-2; SeCePo; TEP; ViBoPo
You breathe yellow smoke, you breathe lead. When You've Been Here Long Enough. Lawrence Joseph. HoAn
You bring me good news from the clinic. Face Lift. Sylvia Plath. InPK
You bring the Dardevle back fast. The Cedar River. Reginald Gibbons. MAYP
You bring the only changes to this season. For Nicholas, Born in September. Tod Perry. NYBP
You broke your teeth upon the question Why. The Resolution. Vassar Miller. CoPo
You brought me bdellium and onyx, stones. Your Light. Ann Lee. AMV-80
You build it where you will be heard only by chance. The Cabin North of It All. James McMichael. AmPA
You built the new Court House, Spoon River. Benjamin Franklin Hazard. Edgar Lee Masters. *Fr.* The New Spoon River. GOA
You burst into the world with smiles wide as April. Sleeping with Foxes. Roberta Hill. CDW
You buy some flowers for your table. Samuel Hoffenstein. *Fr.* Poems in Praise of Practically Nothing. DBV; FiBHP; InMe; TrJP
You buy yourself a new suit of clothes. Samuel Hoffenstein. *Fr.* Poems in Praise of Practically Nothing. DBV; InMe
You Call That a Ts'ing; a Letter. Jedediah Barrow. BXAP
You came/ nourished by/ seaweed and moss. Dinosaur. Bonnie Hearn. AMV-80
You came, and looked and loved the view. Green Sussex. Tennyson. *Fr.* Prologue to General Hamley. FaBoPP
You came. And you did well to come. Sappho, *tr fr. Greek by* Willis Barnstone. BoWoP
You came back to us in a dream and we were not here. Come Back. W. S. Merwin. NaP
You came like the dawn. On the Death of a Child. Edward Silvera. PoNe
You came to it through wild country, there the sea's voice. The House in the Green Well. John Hall Wheelock. MoAmPo
You came to me bearing bright roses. Crowned. Amy Lowell. HBV-1
You came with your sorrows drifting through your eyes. July. W. Ralph Johnson. AMV-81
You can be walking along the beach. American Landscape with Clouds & a Zoo. Jon Anderson. MAYP
You can call me Herbie Jr. or Ashamah. Unemployment/Monologue. June Jordan. WPOW
You can come in. Welcome. R. S. Thomas. NMP
You Can Dig My Grave. *Unknown.* FSW
You can find it only in attics or in ads. The Spinning Wheel. A. M. Klein. CaP

You can fool the hapless public. You Can't Fool God. Grenville Kleiser. STF
You Can Get Despondent. Maurice Careme, *tr. fr. French by* Norma Farber. AMV-81
You can go in the stall. Unclaimed. Florida Watts Smyth. PH
You can have daughters, sons. Inventing a Family. Dennis Saleh. *Fr.* A Guide to Familiar American Incest. NeAC
You can hear the quiet. Swimmers. Paul D. Shiplett. LFAC
You can hear the silence of it. David Jones. *Fr.* In Parenthesis. FaBoMo
You can look into my face. Poem. Mike Todachine. CTBA
You can make a tidy leaf-pot out of sarai leaves. A Man's Need. *Gond Oral Tradition, tr. by* V. Elwin *and* S. Hivale. WTO
You can never see him. The Figure in the Carpet. James Camp. TW
You can, of course. The Rock. Mary Fabilli. AMV-81
You can only have a lot of power. To Summer. Alan Nadel. AMV-80
You can read it in the morning paper. We Need a Whole Lot More of Jesus. *Unknown.* FSW
You can read my letter now sure don't know my mind. Ham Hound Crave. *Unknown.* BluL
You can see the beach and the waves, you can see the sky. Eight Miles South of Grand Haven. Dave Kelly. AMV-80
You can sigh o'er the sad-eyed Armenian. An Appeal to My Countrywomen. Frances E. W. Harper. BlSi
You can stop me. There's Somethin'. Adam Small. PeSA
You can take a tub with a rub and a scrub in a two-foot tank of tin. Pater's Bathe. Edward Abbott Parry. OxBChV
You can take away my mother. Umbilical. Eve Merriam. CTBA; RHPC
"You can talk about yer sheep dorgs." Daley's Dorg Wattle. W. T. Goodge. GDP; PoAu-1
You can talk about your farms and your Chinaman's charms. The Cowboy's Life Is a Very Dreary Life. *Unknown.* AmFP
You can tear a grey hair out of your head. Sacco-Vanzetti. Moishe Leib Halpern, *tr. by* David G. Roskies *and* Hillel Schwartz. VWA
You cannot build again what you have broken. The Witch. Lord Alfred Douglas. HBMV
You cannot cage a field. Lives. Henry Reed. BoNaP; LiTB
You cannot choose but love, lad. To an Old Tune. William Alexander Percy. HBMV
You cannot dream. Things Lovelier. Humbert Wolfe. TrJP
You cannot from the open window invade. The Crow. Rita Boumí-Pappás, *tr. by* Kimon Friar. PBWP
You Cannot Go Down to the Spring. Shaw Neilson. CBAP
You cannot hope. The British Journalist. Humbert Wolfe. DBV; FaBoEE; FiBHP; OxBTC; PV
You cannot justly of the Court complain. To a Witty Man of Wealth and Quality; Who, after His Dismissal from Court, Said, He Might Justly Complain of It. William Wycherley. SeCV-2
You cannot talk of violence. Revolutionary. James P. Friel. AMV-81
You cannot will to men your health. Some Things You Cannot Will to Men. Walter E. Isenhour. STF
You Can't Be Wise. Paul Engle. PoPl
You can't beat English lawns. Our final hope. Rolling the Lawn. William Empson. MoBrPo
You can't breathe, the hard earth wriggles with worms. Concert at the Station. Osip Mandelstam, *tr. by* Andrew Glaze. AMV-81; VWA
You can't escape. The Great Wave off Kanagwa. Constance Egemo. PoDr
You can't expect a cowboy to agitate his/ shanks. The Cowboy's Dance Song. *Unknown.* CoSo
You Can't Fool God. Grenville Kleiser. STF
You can't keep it, I say. Civilizing the Child. Lisel Mueller. CTBA
You Can't Keep No Brown. *Unknown.* BluL
You can't live in the city. Beggar. Nicanor Parra, *tr. by* Miller Williams. CAD
"You can't race me," said Johnny the Hare. The Hare and the Tortoise. Ian Serraillier. SO
You can't take three from two, two is less than three. New Maths. Tom Lehrer. FaBoUs
You can't tell me God would have Heaven. A Malemute Dog. Pat O'Cotter. BLPA
You captains brave and bold, hear our cries, hear our cries. Captain Kidd. *Unknown.* AmFP
You charm'd me not with that fair face. A Song. Dryden. *Fr.* An Evening's Love. CavP; SeCV-2
You child, how can you dare complain. Equals. Louis Untermeyer. UnTE
You close your book and put it down. Love. Louis Untermeyer. HBMV
You come/ in ancestral wisdom. On the Naming Day. Jewel C. Latimore. CNA
You come along . . . tearing your shirt . . . yelling about Jesus. To a Contemporary Bunkshooter. Carl Sandburg. WGRP
You come forth/ the color of a stone cliff. To Insure Survival. Simon J. Ortiz. CDW
You come not, as aforetime, to the headstone every day. Remember. William Johnson Cory. OBVV
You come to fetch me from my work tonight. Putting in the Seed. Robert Frost. ErPo; FaBoEn; NoAM; OxBA
You cotton this? Look Away/Look Away. Stephen Todd Booker. LFAC
You could be sitting now in a carrel. A Late Aubade. Richard Wilbur. PAI; SoSe
You could draw a straight line from the heels. Man Lying on a Wall. Michael Longley. CIP
You could not say, "What now?" you said, "Too late!" Letter to a Jealous Friend. James Simmons. CIP
You Could Say. Robert Mezey. NaP
You could smell the river. For E. C. J. Emmett Jarrett. NeAC
You couldn't bear to grow old, but we grow old. John Berryman. *Fr.* Dream Songs. TAP
You couldn't find it in the bird's weight. These Labdanum Hours. Kathleen Fraser. NPGG
You couldn't pack a Broadwood half a mile. The Song of the Banjo. Kipling. FaBoCh; PrIm; VLP
You courtiers scorn us country clowns. Court and Country Love. *Unknown.* UnTE
You crash over the trees. Storm. Hilda Doolittle ("H.D."). TiPo
You, Custer, you hated. Custer 1. Alison Baker. FAZ
You, Damon, covet to possess. The Lover's Choice. Thomas Bedingfield. HBV-1
You danced a magnetic dance. So Many Feathers. Jayne Cortez. BlSi
You dare not tell me. A Childless Witch. Raquel Chalfi, *tr. by* Alexandra Meiri *and* Myra Glazer Schotz. VWA
You dare to say with perjured lips. Mare Liberum. Henry van Dyke. PAH
You darling girls of Bagaduce, who live along the shore. The Schooner *Fred Dunbar.* Amos Hanson. AmFP
You, dead in '92 and '93. To the French of the Second Empire. Arthur Rimbaud, *tr. by* Robert Lowell. *Fr.* Eighteen-seventy. OBWP
You did it, Henry. Hammerin' Hank. D. Roger Martin. SOTS
You did late review my lays. To Christopher North. Tennyson. EvOK; FaBoEE; FiBHP
You did not come. A Broken Appointment. Thomas Hardy. BiP; DTC; GBL; NoAM; NoP; OAEP
You did not leave this fruited land. Evangeline. Norma E. Smith. CaP
You did not suck at my mother's breasts. Lament. Yonathan Ratosh, *tr. by* Howard Schwartz. VWA
You did not walk with me. The Walk. Thomas Hardy. CMoP; PoEL-5; PrIm
You did right, injured husband, to ruin the face. Insufficient Vengeance. Martial, *tr. by* Louis Untermeyer. UnTE
You didn't have to travel to become an airplane. Communication of His Thirtieth Birthday. Marvin Bell. CoAP
You died nine years ago today. February 11, 1977. Frederick Morgan. AMV-80
You died two thousand years ago, Catullus. To a Roman. J. C. Squire. HBMV
You dig instant revolution: against. Down Wind against the Highest Peaks. Clarence Major. NBP
You, Dinah! Come and set me whar de ribber-roads does meet. The Power of Prayer. Sidney *and* Clifford Lanier. HBV-2
You do look, my son, in a mov'd sort. Prospero. Shakespeare. *Fr.* The Tempest, IV, i. FiP
You do not do, you do not do. Daddy. Sylvia Plath. BiP; BoWoP; CAPP; CMoP; CoAP; InPK; InPS; LiTM; NaP; NIP; NMM; NMP; NoAM; NOBA; NoP; PAI; PrIm; TW; TwCP; UnPo
You Do Not Have to Love Me. Leonard Cohen. NoAM
You do not know how beautiful you are. Ode to a Beautiful Woman. Carl Clark. JB
You do not move about, but try. Getting Lost in Nazi Germany. Marvin Bell. VWA
You do not seem to realize that beauty is a liability. Roses Only. Marianne Moore. LiTM
You, Doctor Martin. Anne Sexton. MoAmPo
You don't/ know. Confession to Settle a Curse. Rosemarie Waldrop. TW
You don't have to tell how you live each day. It's in Your Face. *Unknown.* PoLF
You don't know I pretend my dumb. Plea to Those Who Matter. James Welch. AmPA
You Don't Know What Love Is. Raymond Carver. BXAP
You drag by the knees before. Jogging. Gary Stein. AMV-81
You dreamed it. From my ground. Ark Parting. Jay MacPherson. *Fr.* The Ark. NOBC
You dreamed up a bottomless lake down South. Love Is Loathing & Why. Dan Ford. AMV-81

You drive down Main Street. Tourist Guide: How You Can Tell for Sure When You're in South Dakota. Jim Heynen. GP
You Drive in a Circle. Ted Hughes. NYBP
You drop a pearl, 'twill keep its hue. *Malay Oral Tradition, tr. by* R. J. Wilkinson *and* R. O. Winstedt. WTO
You earthly Souls that court a wanton flame. La Belle Confidente. Thomas Stanley. FaBoEn; JCP; MeLP; MePo; OBS
You empress of the stars, the heavens' worthy crown. Spring-Joy Praising God; Praise of the Sun. Catharina Regina von Greiffenberg, *tr. by* George C. Schoolfield. WPOW
You Englishmen of each degree. The Labouring Man. *Unknown.* OBET
You enter the areas beyond veiled light. Sleep Watch. Lance Henson. VoR
You enter the garden and do not recognize it. Eden. Lev Mak, *tr. by* Daniel Weissbort. VWA
You entered my life in a casual way. To a Friend. Grace Stricker Dawson. BLPA
You, Farrell O'Reilly, I feared as a boy. Farrell O'Reilly. Oliver St. John Gogarty. OxBTC
You Fight On, *with music.* *Unknown.* AS
You find one drinking at the creek. Bees Awater. Robert Morgan. WeW
You fish for people. Aged Fisherman. Witter Bynner. GoYe
You Fit into Me. Margaret Atwood. NoP; POL; TW
You follow, dress held high above. Fishing with My Daughter in Miller's Meadow. Lucien Stryk. GP
You fool yourself and live a crazy day. Voice of a Dissipated Woman inside a Tomb. Sor Violante do Céu, *tr. by* Willis Barnstone. BoWoP
You found the green before the Spring was sweet. Ave atque Vale. Thomas S. Jones, Jr. HBV-2
You from Givenchy, since no years can harden. V. D. F. *Unknown.* HBV-2
You Gallants all, that love good Wine. A Ballad To the Tune of Bateman. Sir Charles Sedley. CoMu
You gave me roses, love, last night. The Mystery. Lilian Whiting. AA
"You gave me the key of your heart, my love." Constancy. John Boyle O'Reilly. OnYI
You gave your life, boy. What Reward? Winifred M. Letts. SUMH
You gaze at me teasingly through the window. Praxilla, *tr. fr. Greek by* Willis Barnstone. BoWoP
You generals all and champions bold. The Duke of Marlborough. *Unknown.* OBET
You, Genoese Mariner. W. S. Merwin. GOA
You gentleman and I up from the grime. December 24 and George McBride Is Dead. Richard Hugo. HoPM
You gentlemen of England far and near. The Wind Sou'west. *Unknown.* AmFP
You gentlemen of England who live at home at ease. The Bay of Biscay. *Unknown.* AmFP
You get a girl; and you say you love her. Samuel Hoffenstein. *Fr.* Poems in Praise of Practically Nothing. InMe
You get a line and I'll get a pole, honey. Crawdad. *Unknown.* FSW
You get to Gilead, let me know. Go Ahead; Goodbye; Good Luck; and Watch Out. William Bronk. GP
You girls who were seeking. Girls. Pablo Neruda, *tr. by* Donald D. Walsh. OLR
You give but little when you give of your possessions. On Giving. Kahlil Gibran. *Fr.* The Prophet. PoPl
You give your cheeks a rosy stain. Artificial Beauty. Lucianus, *tr. by* William Cowper. AWP
You go aboard a leaky boat and sail for San Francisco. A Ripping Trip. *Unknown.* CoSo
You Go, I'll Go wid You, *with music.* *Unknown.* BoAN-2
You go singing through my garden on little dancing feet. To Felicity Who Calls Me Mary. Frances Chesterton. HBMV
You go to your church, and I'll go to mine. Your Church and Mine. Phillips H. Lord. BLPA
You goat-herd Gods, that love the grassy mountains. *See* Ye Goatherd Gods.
You gods that have the power. Puerperium. Edmund Waller. JCP
You gods! to fold the charmer in my arms. The Rapture. Henry Baker. NOEC
You good folks of Nottingham I would have you draw near. The Red Wig. *Unknown.* CoMu
You Got a Right, *with music.* *Unknown.* BoAN-1
You Got to Cross It foh Yohself, *with music.* *Unknown.* AS
You Got to Go Down. *Unknown.* BluL
You Got to Love Her with a Feeling. *Unknown.* BluL
You got to walk that lonesome valley. Lonesome Valley. *Unknown.* FSW
You Gote-heard Gods, that love the grassie mountaines. *See* Ye Goatherd Gods.
You Gotta Go Down (and Join the Union). *Unknown.* FSW
You Gotta Have Your Tips on Fire. Víctor Hernández Cruz. InW
You grow up with music. The Second Violinist's Son. Debora Gregor. AMV-80
You Growing. Milton Acorn. NOBC
You had expected more. Now that I leave. The Departure. Robert Pack. NePoEA
You had no little maid, so I remember. A Nun Speaks to Mary. Sister Mary Madeleva. ISi
You had two girls—Baptiste. At the Cedars. Duncan Campbell Scott. CaP; NOBC
You hand me my key with a smile like a starched sheet. Registered at the Bordello Hotel (Vienna). Larry Rubin. FAZ
You happen to get well. Elegy and Kaddish. David Rosenmann-Taub, *tr. by* Charles Guenther. VWA
You have a most attractive pan. Poems of Passion, Carefully Restrained So as to Offend Nobody. Samuel Hoffenstein. InMe
You have anti-freeze in the car, yes. Christmas Card. Ted Hughes. OBCP
You have been good to me, I give you this. Idolatry. Arna Bontemps. AmNP; PoNe
You have beheld a smiling Rose. The Lilly [*or* Lily] in a Christal [*or* Crystal]. Robert Herrick. AnAnS-2; NoP; PoEL-3; SeCePo; SeCP
You have brought pearly beads. Pearly Beads. *Gond Oral Tradition, tr. by* V. Elwin *and* S. Hivale. WTO
You have coats and robes. You Will Die. *Unknown, tr. by* H. A. Giles. *Fr.* Shi King. AWP
You have come your way, I have come my way. Fronleichnam. D. H. Lawrence. GBL
You have consum'd my language, and my pen. Ovid, *tr. by* Henry Vaughan. De Ponto, Elegy III, 7. OBVE
You have granted me my full share of days. From the Crag. Mani Leib, *tr. by* David G. Roskies *and* Hillel Schwartz. VWA
You have heaped my hands with rubies. Odysseus' Song to Calypso. Peter Kane Dufault. ErPo
You have heard, I suppose, of the man in the moon. The Coolie Chinee. Septimus Winner. OBAL
You have just come in the door. The Confession. Peter Cooley. AmPA
You have loved forty women, but you have only one thumb. Personality. Carl Sandburg. CrMA
You have netted this dawn. The Archaeology of Love. Richard Murphy. EnLoPo
You have no mortal lineaments this day. Ordination. Sister Mary Immaculate. GoBC
You have not conquered me—it is the surge. Infidelity. Louis Untermeyer. TrJP
You have not heard my love's dark throat. A Song of Praise. Countee Cullen. BiP
You have not left me usurer's black blood. Lines to My Father. Leslie Daiken. NeIP; OxBI
You have put your two hands upon me, and your mouth. Betrothed. Louise Bogan. LLLT
You have red toenails, chestnut. Leda and Her Swan. Olga Broumas. PeHV
You have returned. You have returned, my joy. Edward James. *Fr.* Carmina Amico. PeHV
You have said, for certain. Confession. D. S. Savage. NeBP
You have so little. Martha Graham. Lyn Lifshin. LTB
You have spoken your holy command over the city. Inanna and the City of Uruk. Enheduanna, *tr. fr. Sumerian.* BoWoP
You have stopped short of love, your May is over. The Old Saint. Muriel Stuart. HBMV
You have taken back the promise. Fidelis. Adelaide Anne Procter. BLPA; FaBoBe
You have taught me laughter. The Masters. Margaret Widdemer. HBMV
You have the ingredients on hand. Recipe for an Ocean in the Absence of the Sea. Richard Howard. TAP
You Have the Lovers. Leonard Cohen. NOBC
You have to be brainy, not drippy. Spell It. *Unknown.* TDH
You have to be depraved to go at all. At the Spa. James H. Bowden. AMV-81
You Have What I Look For. Jaime Sabines, *tr. fr. Spanish by* W. S. Merwin. LLLT
You have your hat and coat on and she says she will be right down. The Evening Out. Ogden Nash. MoAmPo
You have your shadow. Your Shadow. Mark Strand. *Fr.* Elegy for My Father. Prf
You have your water and your grain. My Little Birds. *Unknown, tr. by* Henrietta Siksek-Su'ad. FaPON
You haven't got so very far. Spring. Orrick Johns. InMe
You headlong hippogriff who match the gale. Life Is a Dream. Pedro Calderón de la Barca, *tr. by* Roy Campbell. NAWM-1
You hear my step. To His Children in Darkness. James Dickey. DiL
You held my lotus blossom. To the Tune "Soaring Clouds." Huang O, *tr. by* Kenneth Rexroth *and* Ling Chung. BoWoP; PBWP; WPOW

You Hide ("You hide in the ostrich egg"). Edith Bruck, *tr. fr. Italian by* Ruth Feldman *and* Brian Swann. BoWoP
You hire a cook, but she can't cook yet. Samuel Hoffenstein. *Fr.* Poems in Praise of Practically Nothing. InMe; WhC
You hitched a thousand miles. August on Sourdough, a Visit from Dick Brewer. Gary Snyder. SOTW
You hold a silver ship/ Upon your arm. Our Lady of Good Voyage. Lucy A. K. Adee. ISi
You hold me now completely in your hands. The Woman Poet. Gertrud Kolmar, *tr. by* Henry A. Smith. VWA
You hold up your photograph. Photographs. William Peskett. AMV-81
You hollow-cheeked son. Baboon 2. *Unknown.* PeSA
You hug school books. Young Girl. Thomas Waltner. LFAC
You hungry birds, I bring my crumbs. Crumbs. Walter de la Mare. SoPo
You, husband, lying next to/ me. Prowling the Ridge. Judith Minty. GeTw
You husbandmen and ploughmen, of every degree. The Little Farm; or, The Weary Ploughman. *Unknown.* CoMu
You, I presume, could adroitly and gingerly. How the Women Will Stop War. Aristophanes, *tr. by* B. B. Rogers. *Fr.* Lysistrata. WaaP
You in Anger. James Reeves. OxBTC
"You inspire me," you said. Goat Dance. Ron Loewinsohn. GP
You intimidated me. I was thrown into hell without a trial. Denouement. Ruth Stone. BoWoP
You Jump First. Pedro Juan Pietri. InW
You jumped so long ago. Rooftop. Willis Barnstone. FAZ
You keep eating and raising a family. A Suite for Marriage. David Ignatow. NNaP
You keep me waiting in a truck. Twenty-Year Marriage. Ai. BoWoP; GP; MAYP
You Kicked and Stomped and Beat Me, *with music. Unknown.* OuSiCo
You Kissed Me. Josephine Slocum Hunt. BLPA; FaBoBe; FPL
You knew the odds on failure from the start. Archaeology. Katha Pollitt. MAYP
You knew—who knew not Astrophil? On Sir Philip Sidney. Matthew Royden. *Fr.* An Elegy, or Friend's Passion for His Astrophil. ElL
You Know. Jean Garrigue. NYBP; UnPo
You know. Eddie and Eve. Charles Bukowski. GP
You know, he didn't teach me any thing. Mark Van Doren. James Worley. AMV-81
You know her hustle. Asking for Ruthie. Judy Grahn. GP; NMM
You know I said to Mark that I'm furious at you. The Quarrel. Diane DiPrima. NMM
You know, I see, that four score years and ten. Exceptional. Thelma Lewis. AMV-80
You know it by the northern look of the shore. North Sea off Carnoustie. Anne Stevenson. HoAn
You know it's all bullshit. Coda: Revising History. Paul Mariani. MAYP
You know it's April by the falling-off. B Negative. X. J. Kennedy. ConAP; NePoEA-2
You Know It's Really Cold. Shirley Williams. PAI
You Know, Joe. Ray Durem. BOLo
(Ultimate Equality.) PoNe
"You know, my friends, with what a brave carouse." The Bride. Ambrose Bierce. AA
You know my secrets. Encounter. Dorothy Livesay. AMV-81
You know not how deep was the love your eyes did kindle. Ibn al-Abbar, *tr. fr. Arabic by* A. R. Nykl. PeHV
You know now mama. Alley Blues. *Unknown.* BluL
You know, or you don't know, that great Bacon saith. Byron. *Fr.* Don Juan. NOBL
"You know Orion always comes up sideways." The Star-Splitter. Robert Frost. ImOP
You know, she said, they made you. A Dress of Fire. Dahlia Ravikovitch, *tr. by* Chana Bloch. VWA
You know, sweetheart. A Letter. Rachel Korn, *tr. by* Ruth Whitman. VWA
You know that day at Peach Tree Creek. Logan at Peach Tree Creek. Hamlin Garland. PAH
You know that he is going to die. The Red Dog. Laura Jensen. LCAP
You know the answer to the last surmise. Sonnet for My Son. Melanie Gordon Barber. GoYe
You know the bloom, unearthly white. The Evening Primrose. Dorothy Parker. InMe
You know the fellow. A Public Nuisance. Reginald Arkell. LiSp
You know the old woman. The Old Woman. Beatrix Potter. GoJo; NTCP; PDV
You know the place: then. Sappho, *tr. fr. Greek by* Mary Barnard. PBWP
You know the way. *See* You that know the way.
You know there goes a tale. The Modern Jonas. *Unknown.* PAH
You know there is not much. To a Friend Concerning Several Ladies. William Carlos Williams. VGW
You know there were others before you. Friends. Mary Goose. STE
You know those rose sherbets. You Know. Jean Garrigue. NYBP; UnPo
You know those windless summer evenings, swollen to stasis. Cigales. Richard Wilbur. NePoEA; NoAM; NOBA
You know w'at for ees school keep out. Leetla Giorgio Washeenton. T. A. Daly. FaPON; PoSC
You know we French stormed [*or* storm'd] Ratisbon. Incident of the French Camp. Robert Browning. BeLS; FaPo; FaPoR; GN; HBV-2; HBVY; OBWP; RoGo; TreF; TrGrPo
You know we must be lonely, you and I. Souls. Paul Wertheimer, *tr. by* Jethro Bithell. TrJP
You know what it is to be born alone. Baby Tortoise. D. H. Lawrence. BoAnP; CMoP
You ladies all that are in fashion. A New Song called The Curling of the Hair. *Unknown.* CoMu
You landsmen and you seamen bold. The Loss of the *Due Dispatch. Unknown.* AmFP
You Laughed and Laughed and Laughed. Gabriel Okara. PBA
You lay a wreath on murdered Lincoln's bier. Abraham Lincoln. Tom Taylor. HBV-2; PAH
You lay across my childhood like a stone. Pedagogue Arraigned. John Wain. GLGT
You lay in wait. Sappho, *tr. fr. Greek by* Willis Barnstone. BoWoP
You leap out of bed; you start to get ready. Samuel Hoffenstein. *Fr.* Poems in Praise of Practically Nothing. InMe
You leaped from the white horses. The Distaff. Erinna, *tr. by* Marylin Arthur. WPOW
You learned Lear's *Nonsense Rhymes* by heart, not rote. A Plea to Boys and Girls. Robert Graves. GTBS-P
You leave the skyline. Descent to Bohannon Lake. Jim Barnes. FAZ
You led me to the hills. To Alan. Douglas Fraser. PoSH
You, Letting the Trees Stand as My Betrayer. Diane Wakoski. NoAM
You lie in my arms. Apocrypha. Stanley Moss. VWA
You lie now in many coffins. For Malcolm: After Mecca. Gerald W. Barrax. CNA; PoBA
You lie there, with your line of stiff red griffins. Museum Piece No. 16228. Elaine Watson. AMV-81
You like it under the trees in autumn. The Motive for Metaphor. Wallace Stevens. AP; MoAB; MoAmPo
You like the country better than the town. To a Friend in the Country. Oliver St. John Gogarty. OnYI
You like them in pigment. Mountains and Other Outdoor Things. Ruth Good. PoDr
You lit a firebrand. The Floating Candles. Sydney Lea. MAYP
You little, eager, peeping thing. The Awakening. Angela Morgan. OHIP
You little know the heart that you advise. In [*or* An] Answer to a Lady Who Advised Retirement. Lady Mary Wortley Montagu. OBEC
You Little Stars [*or* Starres] That Live in Skies. *Fr.* Caelica. Fulke Greville. ElL; NCEP; NoP
(His Lady's Eyes.) OBSC
You live here because there's no other place. So Long Solon. Jack Myers. AmPA
You live where the sounds of trucks. Tapwater. Laura Jensen. LCAP
You lived and moved among the best society. W. H. Auden. *Fr.* Letter to Lord Byron. OBSV
You look as though/ You know me. The Moon Ground. James Dickey. MOON
You look at me. A Drop of Dew. Shmuel Halkin, *tr. by* Jacob Sonntag. TrJP
You look at me, a hut or cage contains. Hilda Doolittle ("H. D."). *Fr.* Sagesse. NOCV
You look at yourself in the mirror, nothing. Primary Numbers. Edvard Kocbek, *tr. by* Herbert Kuhner *and* Peter Kersche. AMV-81
You looked at me with eyes grown bright with pain. Parting after a Quarrel. Eunice Tietjens. HBMV
You, love, and I. Counting the Beats. Robert Graves. DTC; ELP; GBL; GTBS-P; HAP; OxBTC; ViBoPo; WeW
You love? That's high as you shall go. The Attainment. Coventry Patmore. *Fr.* The Angel in the House. FaBoEE; GoBC; OBVV
You love us when we're heroes, home on leave. Glory of Women. Siegfried Sassoon. MMA; OBWP
You love us yet? Then really, what a One! Good Friday. John Frederick Nims. TW
You loved me for a little. Midsummer. Sydney King Russell. BLPA; FaBoBe
You loved me not at all, but let it go. Edna St. Vincent Millay. VGW
You loved the hay in the meadow. Her Way. William Rose Benét. HBMV
You Lovely People. Virginia Cerenio. BrSi
You made healing as you wanted us to make bread and poems. Mendings. Muriel Rukeyser. SaC
You Made It Rain. Ruby C. Saunders. BlSi

You made me feel so young again. Copper-Beech and Butter-Fingers. Pearse Hutchinson. CIP
You made your little lover kind. Little Lover. Leonora Speyer. HBMV
You making small talk to hide reality. Conversation. K. Malley. AMV-80
You marched off southward with the fire of twenty. Danny. Malcolm Cowley. PoA
You married men, whom Fate hath assign'd. The Merry Cuckold. *Unknown.* CoMu
You Masks of the Masquerade. Gustave Kahn, *tr. fr. French by* Jethro Bithell. TrJP
You, master of delays. Killing No Murder. Sylvia Townsend Warner. MoBrPo
You may brag about your breakfast foods you eat at break of day. Sausage. Edgar A. Guest. OBAL
You May Bury Me in de Eas', *with music. Unknown.* BoAN-1
You may call a woman a kitten. What One May and May Not Call a Woman. *Unknown.* TreF
You may call the cowboy horned and think him hard to tame. The Cowboy at Work. *Unknown.* CoSo
You may call, you may call. The Bad Kittens. Elizabeth J. Coatsworth. FaPON; OBCA
You may drink to your leman in gold. Wine and Dew. Richard Henry Stoddard. AA
You may get through the world, but 'twill be very slow. People Will Talk. Samuel Dodge. WBLP
You may give over plow, boys. Tommy's Dead. Sydney Dobell. HBV-2
You may have heard (she said) about a girl. Atalanta. Ovid, *tr. by* Rolfe Humphries. *Fr.* Metamorphoses. LiSp
You may hear a pygmy talking. No Doubt. Helen Baker Adams. STF
You may lift me up in your arms, lad, and turn my face to the sun. The Famous Ballad of the Jubilee Cup. Sir Arthur Quiller-Couch. InMe; NA; WhC
You may never see rain, unless you see. A Dance for Rain. Witter Bynner. BPAW
You may not believe it, for hardly could I. The Pumpkin. Robert Graves. PDV; RHPC; WSC
You may not stand in the halls of fame. Be Friendly. Walter E. Isenhour. STF
You may rock us, you may shock us. Frisco's Defi. A. S. Hooper. BPAW
You may search/ the ocean. Searching for the Desert Blues. *Unknown.* BluL
You may smile if you're a mind to, but perhaps you'll lend an ear. The Ghostly Crew, 2 *vers. Unknown.* ShS
You may talk about me just as much as you please. Hold the Wind. *Unknown.* GBP
You may talk o' gin and [*or* an'] beer. Gunga Din. Kipling. BrPo; EBVV; FaFP; FPL; LiTB; MoBrPo; OnMSP; PoPl; TreF; VLP
You may talk of Columbus's sailing. "Are Ye Right There, Michael?" (A Lay of the Wild West Clare.) Percy French. WTO
You may tempt the upper classes. Edgar Smith. *Fr.* Heaven Will Protect the Working-Girl. FiBHP
You may think it quite an easy task. The Preacher's Wife. *Unknown.* STF
You may write me down in history. Still I Rise. Maya Angelou. BlSi
You meaner beauties of the night. On [*or* To] His Mistress, the Queen of Bohemia [*or* Elizabeth of Bohemia]. Sir Henry Wotton. AnAnS-2; BoLoP; ElL; ELP; EnLoPo; FaBoCh; GBL; GTBS; GTBS-P; HAP; HBV-1; JCP; LoBV; MeLP; MePo; NOBE; NoP; OBEV; OBS; PoPle; SeCP; TrGrPo; ViBoPo
You meet a girl and you surrender. Samuel Hoffenstein. *Fr.* Poems in Praise of Practically Nothing. InMe
You meet your father after nine years. December 18, 1975. Michael Hogan. FAZ
You meet your friend, your face. Selected Epigrams. Kassia, *tr. by* Patrick Diehl. PBWP
You—Mermaid! Your sea-green hair and sin-sweet singing. Fisherman's Blunder off New Bedford, Massachusetts. Annemarie Ewing. NePoAm-2
You messenger that comes from Rome. To an Anti-poetical Priest. Giolla Brighde MacNamee, *tr. by* the Earl of Longford. AnIV
You might come here Sunday on a whim. Degrees of Gray in Philipsburg. Richard Hugo. CoAP; NoP; NPAW
You might suppose it easy. The Boatman. Jay MacPherson. MoCV; OBCV
You, Morningtide Star, now are steady-eyed, over the east. Lying Awake. Thomas Hardy. FaBoRV
You Move Forward. Thomas Sessler, *tr. fr. German by* Herbert Kuhner. VWA
You Mus' Hab Dat True Religion, *with music. Unknown.* BoAN-2
You must agree that Rubens was a fool. To English Connoisseurs. Blake. OxBoLi
"You must be very old, Sir Giles." Old Love. William Morris. PeD; VLP
You must do as they do at Hoo. Hoo, Suffolk. *Unknown.* GBP
"You must give back," her mother said. The Gifts Return'd. Walter Savage Landor. OBVV
You Must Have Been a Sensational Baby, *sel.* Harold Norse.
"Pair of muscular calves, A." GP
You must have been still sleeping, your wife there. The Sacred Hearth. David Gascoyne. FaBoTw
You must know that my uncle is a farmer. Down by the Old Mill Stream. John Read. TreFS
You must live through the time when everything hurts. The Double Shame. Stephen Spender. LiTB; LiTM
You Must Never Bath in an Irish Stew. Spike Milligan. RHPC
You must never take your eyes off it. Commanding a Telephone to Ring. Jack Anderson. AMV-81
You must not wonder, though you think it strange. For That He Looked Not upon Her. George Gascoigne. ElL; NoP
You must remain very much alone. Presences. Zoé Karélli, *tr. by* Kimon Friar. PBWP
You must remember. Circuit Breaker. Sid Gary. QQQ
You must remember structures beyond cotton plains. If Blood Is Black Then Spirit Neglects My Unborn Son. Conrad Kent Rivers. PoBA
You must remember this, the cold turning year. Note from an Intimate Diary. Emanuel Litvinov. NeBP
You must take the speckled stone, the dead-tired stone. Stonetalk. Jacques Hamelin, *tr. by* Ria Leigh-Louhuizen. AMV-80
You, my branch, my lopped limb! Tree to Flute. Anna Hajnal, *tr. by* Jascha Kessler. VWA
You, my son. The Open Door. Grace Coolidge. TRV
You Naughty, Naughty Men, *with music.* T. Kennick. BLSo
You, Nebuchadnezzah, whoa, sah! Nebuchadnezzar. Irwin Russell. HBV-2
You need lightning. To the Man Who Sidled Up to Me and Asked: "How Long You In Fer, Buddy?" Etheridge Knight. NeAC
You need not see what someone is doing. Sext. W. H. Auden. *Fr.* Horae Canonicae. SaC
You need the untranslatable ice to watch. Appendix to the Anniad. Gwendolyn Brooks. BlSi
"You never attained to Him." "If to attain." Via, Veritas, et Vita. Alice Meynell. WGRP
You never bade me hope, 'tis true. Maiden Eyes. Gerald Griffin. HBV-1
You Never Can Tell. Ella Wheeler Wilcox. BLPA; BLPL; TreFS; TreFT
You never frightened me. December 1970. John Tagliabue. GP
You never know what life means till you die. Robert Browning. *Fr.* The Ring and the Book, XI. OAEP
You never know who has your memory. You Gotta Have Your Tips on Fire. Víctor Hernández Cruz. InW
You never know with a doorbell. Doorbells. Rachel Field. FaPON; TiPo
You Never Miss the Water. *Unknown.* BluL
You never touch. Yosano Akiko, *tr. fr. Japanese by* Geoffrey Bownas *and* Anthony Thwaite. BoWoP; PBWP
You Northern Girl. Charles G. Ballard. VoR
You not alone, when You are still alone. Michael Drayton. Idea, XI. PoEL-2
You now solicit a few enemy thrusts. D. B. Wyndham Lewis. *Fr.* If So the Man You Are. OBSV
You now, you in the next century, and the next. Poem Touching the Gestapo. William Heyen. GeTw
You nymphs, call'd Naiads, of the windring brooks. Shakespeare. *Fr.* The Tempest, IV, i. ViBoPo
You, O Tsui-Xgoa. Hymn to Tsui-Xgoa. *Unknown.* PeSA
You of the covered breasts, the lovely head. Epitaph of a Faithful Man. Robert Mezey. ELU
You of the painted wagons, folk of the shimmering eye. Beggars. Rhys Carpenter. HBMV
You often went to breathe a timeless air. The Scholar. Frances Cornford. BrRo
You on the Tower. Thomas Hardy. SaC
You, once a belle in Shreveport. Snapshots of a Daughter-in-Law. Adrienne Rich. NCSH; NIP; NMM; NoP
You opened my eyes. Malcolm. Kattie M. Cumbo. BOLo
You ought to see my blue-eyed Sally. Stay All Night, Stay a Little Longer. *Unknown.* AmFP
You ought to see my Cindy. Cindy. *Unknown.* BLSo; FSW
You over there, young man with the guide book red-bound. Home Sweet Home with Variations. H. C. Bunner. BXAP; CenHV; InMe; OBAL
You Owe Them Everything. John Allman. SaC
You plant like Paul, you water like Apollos. The Rev. Nicholas Noyes to the Rev. Cotton Mather. Nicholas Noyes. SCAP
You play the flute. Longing. *Gond Oral Tradition, tr. by* V. Elwin *and* S. Hivale. WTO
You possess the sturdy elegance of a cannon. For Natalya Correia. Irving Layton. NeAC

You practice every possible virtue. Samuel Hoffenstein. *Fr.* Poems in Praise of Practically Nothing. InMe
You praise the firm restraint with which they write. On Some South African Novelists. Roy Campbell. ChMP; FaBoCo; FaBoEE; GTBS-P; InPK; MoBrPo; NOBL; OxBTC; PoPl; WhC
You prayer—, you blasphemy, you. Plashes the Fountain. Paul Celan, *tr. by* Michael Hamburger. OBVE
You Preach to Me of Laws. Iris Tree. HBMV
You prefer a buffoon to a scholar. Cynical Ode to an Ultra-cynical Public. Charles MacKay. DBV
You pried the oval jade. Lapis. Shawn Wong. BrSi
You probably could put their names to them. "As When Emotion Too Far Exceeds Its Cause." Gloria C. Oden. AmNP
You promise heavens free from strife. Mimnermus in Church. William Johnson Cory. HBV-1; LO; NOBE; OBEV; TreFT; VLP
You promised to meet me down by the spring. Deep Water. *Unknown.* FSW
You, proud curve-lipped youth, with brown sensitive face. Through the Long Night. Edward Carpenter. *Fr.* Towards Democracy. PeHV
You put your hand on my shoulder. Abdelfatteh. E. A. Lacey. PeHV
You raise the ax. The Anniversary. Ai. GP
You rambling boys of Liverpool, I'd have you to beware. The Banks of Newfoundland. *Unknown.* ShS
You read the New York Times. Alfred Corning Clark. Robert Lowell. NoAM
You read us your verse with your throat wrapped in wool. Martial, *tr. fr. Latin.* DBV
You recline that magnificent pair of buttocks. To Kyris. Strato, *tr. by* Teddy Hogge. PeHV
You recommend that the motive, in Chapter 8, should be changed. Yes, the Agency Can Handle That. Kenneth Fearing. WeW
You refuse to own. Margaret Atwood. NeAC
You remember that whitefaced actor. Mime. Dick Allen. AMV-81
You remember the big Gaston, for whom everyone predicted a bad end? Monsieur Gaston. A. M. Klein. MoCV
You remember the name was Jensen. She seemed old. What Thou Lovest Well, Remains American. Richard Hugo. GP; NIP; NPAW
You replaced the Douglas firs. You, Letting the Trees Stand as My Betrayer. Diane Wakoski. NoAM
You ride dat horse. Jesus, Won't You Come B'm-By? *Unknown.* AS
You Rise Up. Paul Eluard, *tr. fr. French by* Wallace Fowlie. PoPl
You roar over the meadow and roar. Last Days. Richard Hugo. PoA
You round a curve. Out in the Country, Back Home. Jeff Daniel Marion. PPJ
You ruthless flea, who desecrate my couch. Song of the Flea. Judah al-Harizi. TrJP
You, sad Captain, big-knobbed staff of life. The Voyages of Captain Cock. William Jay Smith. ErPo; UnTE
You said./ don't write me/ a love poem. Poem. Pearl Cleage Lomax. CNA
You said it went all the way. Last Words, 1968. Lance Henson. CDW
You said: My father didn't cry. Ancestral Weight. Alfonsina Storni, *tr. by* Marti Moody. WPOW
You said that your people. To Richard Wright. Conrad Kent Rivers. AmNP; CABA; IDB; PoBA
You said to me:/ I shall [*or* would] become your comrade. Nudities. André Spire, *tr. by* Stanley Burnshaw. TrJP; VWA
You said to me: But I will be your comrade. Nudities. André Spire, *tr. by* Jethro Bithell. AWP; ErPo
You sail and you seek for the Fortunate Isles. The Fortunate Isles. Joaquin Miller. WGRP
You sang round-dance songs. Farewell. Liz Sohappy Bahe. CDW
You sat with a bottle of beer. After the Death of an Elder Klallam. Duane Niatum. CDW
You say, as I have often given tongue. To a Poet, Who Would Have Me Praise Certain Bad Poets, Imitators of His and Mine. W. B. Yeats. CTC; DBV; FaBoEE; PV
You say, but with no touch of scorn. In Memoriam A. H. H., XCVI. Tennyson. NOCV; WGRP
You say I love not, 'cause I do not play. To His Mistress Objecting to Him neither Toying or Talking. Robert Herrick. FaBV
You say I touch the barberries. Barberries. Mary Aldis. HBMV
You say, "I will come." Lady Otomo of Sakanoe, *tr. fr. Japanese by* Kenneth Rexroth. OLR
You say it will cost much to follow. The Cost. Flora L. Osgood. STF
You say that I take a good deal upon myself. Monumentum Aere, Etc. Ezra Pound. NOBA
"You say that you believe in Democracy for everybody." Everybody but Me. Margaret Burroughs. BlSi; FB
You say the king commands that I appear. Diptych. Velma West Sykes. IHMS
You say, to me-wards your affection's strong. Love Me Little, Love Me Long. Robert Herrick. CaPo
You say, "Where goest Thou?" I cannot tell. The Poet's Simple Faith. Victor Hugo, *tr. by* Edward Dowden. TRV; WGRP
You say yes and I say yes. Point of No Return. Mari Evans. NNP
You say you love me, nay, can swear it too. Robert Heath. POL
You say your fine, flatchested stepmother. Snow White. Robert M. Chute. DFT
You scream, waking from a nightmare. Little Sleep's-Head Sprouting Hair in the Moonlight. Galway Kinnell. LCAP
You search out Bull Slough Road to slake your thirst. County Roads. Thomas Rabbitt. MAYP
You secret vales, you solitary fields. Henry Constable. *Fr.* Diana. OBSC
You see before you an icing of skin. The Root Canal. Marge Piercy. DFF; HoAn
You see me here, you gods, a poor old man. King Lear Pledges Revenge. Shakespeare. *Fr.* King Lear, II, iv. TreFT
You see, my darling. Map Reading. David Citino. AMV-81
You see, my whole life. Woman Poem. Nikki Giovanni. BlSi; NMM; NoAM
You see, the problem is. Blue like Death. James Welch. CDW
You see the sky now. How to Write a Poem about the Sky. Leslie Marmon Silko. NoP
You see the ways the fisherman doth take. Neither Hook nor Line. Bunyan. LiSp
You see the worst of love, but not the best. Walter Savage Landor. GBL
You see them vanish in their speeding cars. Fugue. Howard Nemerov. TAP
You see these little scars? Iambic Feet Considered as Honorable Scars. William Meredith. PoA
You see this Christmas tree all silver gold? Come Christmas. David McCord. PChr
You see this dog. It was but yesterday. Flush or Faunus. Elizabeth Barrett Browning. FM; NBM
You see this pebble-stone? It's a thing I bought. The Cock and the Bull. Charles Stuart Calverley. BXAP; FaBoCo; FaBoNo; FaBoPa; InMe; NA; Par; VLP, *abr.*
You send me your poems. The Conspiracy. Robert Creeley. PPJ
You Serve the Best Wines Always, My Dear Sir. Martial *tr. fr. Latin by* J. V. Cunningham. InPK
You Shall. *Unknown.* BluL
You Shall above All Things Be Glad and Young. E. E. Cummings. NePA; NoAM; NOBA; OxBA
You shall not vanish into dust today. Funeral. Murray Bennett. GoYe
You should be done with blossoming by now. To a Vine-clad Telegraph Pole. Louis Untermeyer. MoAmPo
You should have, Jean, stopped them. One More Time. Alvin Aubert. GP
You should never squeeze a weasel. Don't Ever Seize a Weasel by the Tail. Jack Prelutsky. RHPC
You should see these musical mice. New Strain. George Starbuck. MP; TwCP
You should try to hear the name. The Name. Jalal ed-Din Rumi, *ad. by* Robert Bly. NU
You should understand that I use my body now. At Bickford's. Gerald Stern. NYP
You shouldn't be afraid of the dark. Lullaby for My Dead Child. Denise Jallais, *tr. by* Maxine *and* Judith Kumin. BoWoP
You shout to me. Views. Harriet Susskind. AMV-80
You show me the poems of some woman. Translations. Adrienne Rich. WPOW
You shun me, Chloe, wild and shy. To Chloe. Horace, *tr. by* Austin Dobson. Odes, I, 23. AWP
You signed yourself into the loony bin so often. Mourningsong for Anne. David Posner. FAZ
You Simple Bostonians. *Unknown. See* What a Court Hath Old England.
You sing, you. The Songs of Maximus, VI. Charles Olson. *Fr.* The Maximus Poems. PAI
You sit at your high windows, old men. The Old Men. Alexander Javitz. TrJP
You sit behind your coffee. The Quarrel. Karen Swenson. GrPl
You sit in the middle of the bed. To a Friend's Child. Aliki Barnstone. BoWoP
You sit with hands folded. Girl Sitting Alone at Party. Donald Justice. DFF
You slapped me. For My Torturer, Lieutenant D——. Leila Djabali, *tr. by* Anita Barrows. WPOW
You sleep at the top of streets. To Waken a Small Person. Donald Justice. NYBP
You sleep upon your mother's breast. A Rhyme of One. Frederick Locker-Lampson. HBV-1
You sleeping child asleep, away. To Ping-ku, Asleep. Lawrence Durrell. ChMP; NeBP

You Smiled, You Spoke, and I Believed. Walter Savage Landor. BoLoP; GBL; OAEP
(To Ianthe.) PV
You sons of England, now listen to my rhymes. Pity Poor Labourers. *Unknown.* OBET
You Spaniards. You evil ones. Punto Final. Shirley Hill Witt. TWSS
You speak about immortality. Portraits. William Carson Fagg. LFAC
You speak. You say: Today's character is not. As You Leave the Room. Wallace Stevens. AP
You speed by with your camera and your spear. Interview with a Tourist. Margaret Atwood. IHMS
You spent all summer in cool Kabul. *Unknown, tr. fr. Pashto by* Saduddin Shpoon. PBWP
You spent fifty-five years. Father. Ted Kooser. Str
You spoke keys and looked. The Tyrant Apple Is Eaten. Norman McCaig. NeBP
You spoke me. The Long Word. Deirdre Ballantyne. AMV-80
You spot me in the rain journey. Rain Trip. Diane Wakoski. CABA
You Spotted Snakes [with Double Tongue]. Shakespeare. *Fr.* A Midsummer Night's Dream, II, ii. InvP; LiTB; NOBE; OBEV; PoRA; ViBoPo; WSC
(Fairies' Lullaby, The.) ElL; WHA
(Fairies' Song, The.) LoBV
(Fairy Lullaby.) FaPON
(Fairy Songs: "You spotted snakes with double tongue.") HBV-1; OBSC; TrGrPo
(Lullaby for Titania.) GN
(Song: "You spotted snakes with double tongue.") FiP
You stand and hold the post of my small house. Auvaiyar, *tr. fr. Tamil by* George Hart. WPOW
You stand atop your hill. New Hampshire Farm Woman. Rachel Graham. GoYe
You stand behind the old black mare. Why Can't I Leave You? Ai. AmPA; GeTw; GP
You stand near the window as lights wink. Twenty-third Street Runs into Heaven. Kenneth Patchen. ErPo
You stared out of the window on the emptiness. To a Spanish Poet. Stephen Spender. OAEP
You start it all. You are lovely. To Women. Richard Hugo. NIP
You still carry. Brother. Richard Shelton. Str
You still sometimes sleep. Heron. Stanley Plumly. AmPA
You strange, astonished-looking, angle-faced. To a Fish. Leigh Hunt. *Fr.* The Fish, the Man, and the Spirit. ChTr; EnRP; FiBHP; FM; HAP; MOS; NBM; NOBL; OBEV; PoEL-4; RoGo; SeCePo; ViBoPo
You strange old ghouls. The Ghouls. Helen Hamilton. SUMH
You strike everything down in battle. Inanna and Ishkur. Enheduanna, *tr. fr. Sumerian.* BoWoP
You strop my anger, especially. To the Pay Toilet. Marge Piercy. GP
You stump your way through the tangled/ brush. Song of the Fisherman's Lover. Roseann Lloyd. WOLT
You swear you are as healthy as the next person. At the Center of Everything Which Is Dying. Patricia Goedicke. FAZ
You swear you'll come, you name the time and place. Epigram: To Lygdus. Martial. PeHV
You take a bath, and sit there bathing. Samuel Hoffenstein. *Fr.* Poems in Praise of Practically Nothing. EvOK; InMe
You take a town you cannot keep. Love's Spite. Aubrey Thomas De Vere. HBV-1
You take any junkyard. Junkyards. Julian Lee Rayford. FAZ; PPJ
You take my hand and. Margaret Atwood. HAP
You take the dollar. For One Moment. David Ignatow. NNaP
You Take the Pilgrims, Just Give Me the Progress. Loyd Rosenfield. QQQ
You take what it gives you, what a spinster. A Place by the River. William Keens. TAT
You talk about the Soo Locks. Going Up and Down. Jim Daniels. AMV-81
You talk about your business. Speak Out for Jesus. *Unknown.* STF
You talk about your harbor girls. Haul Away, My Rosy. *Unknown.* OuSiCo
You talk fences. Safety or Something. P. L. Jacobs. LFAC
You talk of Gayety and Innocence. Sir Walter Scott. *Fr.* The Talisman, Chapter 13. NBM
You talk peaks and golden eagles. Llanberis Summer. Marianne Loyd. AMV-81
You taught me ways of gracefulness and fashions of address. To a Little Girl. Helen Parry Eden. HBV-1
You tell me/ you will be leaving. In the Mountains. Edgar Jackson. Three Songs, I. LFAC
You tell me over the telephone about your world. The Fish Upstairs. William Dickey. Psk
You tell me that silence. Gift. Leonard Cohen. NoAM; SoSe
You tell me that the day is fine. To My Hairdresser. Warham St. Leger. CenHV
You Tell Me to Sit Quiet. A. C. Jordan. PBA
You Tell Me Your Dream, I'll Tell You Mine, *with music.* Seymour Rice *and* Albert H. Brown. FSN
You tell me you're promised a lover. A Letter of Advice. Winthrop Mackworth Praed. HBV-1; NOBL; OBRV; OxBoLi; WhC
You tender hearted Christians, I pray you lend an ear. The Millman Song. *Unknown.* ShS
You tender virgins, fairer than the snow with which you play. Edward May, *after the Latin of* John Parkhurst. FaBoEE
You that a stranger in mid-Rome seek Rome. Rome. J. V. Cunningham, *after the Latin of* Janus Vitalis Panormitanus. OBVE
You that are sprung of northern stock. To a Calvinist in Bali. Edna St. Vincent Millay. NoAM
You that are weather-wise and pretend to know. Upon a Great Shower of Snow That Fell on May-Day, 1654. Thomas Washbourne. NOCV
You that crossed the ocean old. Ponce de Leon. Edith M. Thomas. PAH
You, that decipher out the fate. Mourning. Andrew Marvell. CABA; SeCP
You that do search for every purling spring. Astrophel and Stella, XV. Sir Philip Sidney. OAEL-1; OBSC; SiPS
You That Have Been Often Invited, *with music. Unknown.* AH
You that have spent the silent night. Gascoigne's Good-Morrow. George Gascoigne. AAS; EnRePo; NOCV
You that in love find[e] luck[e] and abundaunce [*or* habundance]. Sonnet [*or* May Time]. Sir Thomas Wyatt. AAS; OBSC; SiPS
You that know [*or* You know] the way. Lemuel's Blessing. W. S. Merwin. CAPP; CoPo; NYBP
You That Love England. C. Day Lewis. FaBoMo
You that prophane our windows with a tongue. Beauty in Worship. *Unknown. Fr.* A Poem, in Defence of the Decent Ornaments of Christ-Church, Oxon, Occasioned by a Banbury Brother, Who Called Them Idolatries. OBS
You that seek what life is in death. Time and Eternity. Fulke Greville. *Fr.* Caelica. EnRePo; OBSC
You That Sing in the Blackthorn. Alfred Noyes. *Fr.* The Last Voyage, II. GoBC
You that thus wear a modest countenance. Dante, *tr. by* Dante Gabriel Rossetti. La Vita Nuova, XIII, a. AWP
You that uphold the world. Pagan Prayer. Alice Brown. WGRP
You that with allegory's curious frame. Astrophel and Stella, XXVIII. Sir Philip Sidney. InPK; OAEL-1; SiPS
You, the woman; I, the man; this, the world. The Character of Love Seen as a Search for the Lost. Kenneth Patchen. NaP; VGW
You, the Young Rainbow. Edith Sitwell. MoVE
You there, and you, and you. Bacchanal. Irving Layton. OBCV
You think Fuseli is not a Great Painter. I'm glad. To Hunt. Blake. OxBoLi
"You think I am dead." Talking in Their Sleep. Edith M. Thomas. BoNaP; OHIP
You think it horrible that lust and rage. The Spur. W. B. Yeats. ELU; WeW
You think of him as one who fails. I Think of Him as One Who Fights. Anna Hempstead Branch. HBMV
You think that when a woman yields. In Your Arrogance. Lynne Lawner. ErPo
You think the ridge hills flowing, breaking. Rivulose. A. R. Ammons. SUW
You think they might come. Riding Double. Peter Wild. AmPA
You think you/ need me. Masquerade. Carolyn M. Rodgers. BlSi
You think you know what's in my heart. The Captive. William Franklin. LFAC
You thought I had the strength of men. A Clever Woman. Mary Elizabeth Coleridge. BrRo
You thought it was a falling leaf we heard. Rondel for September. Karle Wilson Baker. HBMV
You thunder at my side. The Snoring Bedmate. *Unknown, tr. by* John V. Kelleher. BIrV
You tickle the sophisticates. On Reading Mr. Ytche Bashes' Stories in Yiddish. Lester Ehrlichman. AMV-80
You tied Dick Randall to a tree. Bunny. Christopher Fahy. TAT
You to the left and I to the right. At the Crossroads. Richard Hovey. HBV-2
You to whom the earth's. Advice. E. di Pasquale. AMV-81
You told me Age was a black wolf that lay. Comfort. Margaret Widdemer. GoYe
You told me, early last fall, you never had no man at all. Fare Thee Well Blues. *Unknown.* BluL
You told me: "I am not worthy of you." Marguerite Burnat-Provins, *tr. fr. French by* Cassia Berman. BoWoP

You told me it was/ because of me. Izumi Shikibu, *tr. fr. Japanese by* Willis Barnstone. BoWoP
You told me, Maro, whilst you live. A Hinted Wish. Martial, *tr. by* Francis Lewis. AWP
You too if you work hard enough. Ponce de León: A Morning Walk. Al Young. HoPM; NPGG
You too listless to examine. Lines to Our Elders. Countee Cullen. CDC
You Too? Me Too—Why Not? Soda Pop. Robert Hollander. NIP
You took the world and embraced. Pedro. Luis Omar Salinas. FF
You touched my sleeve, and quickly spoke my name. At Swindon. Reginald Brett. PeHV
You tug at words. Modern Kabbalist. Marcia Falk. VWA
You Turn for Sugar an' Tea, *with music. Unknown.* OuSiCo
You turn the TV on. Soaps. Harold Witt. SOTS
You turn your back on me cleaning the smelt. The Smell of Fish. William Meissner. WOLT
You understand it? How they returned from Culloden. Culloden and After. Iain Crichton Smith. OxBS
You understand now/ what it means. On the Edge at Santorini. Michael C. Blumenthal. AMV-80
You Understand the Requirements. Lyn Lifshin. NeAC
You unseen lightning flash, you darkly radiant light. On the Ineffable Inspiration of the Holy Spirit. Catharina Regina von Greiffenberg, *tr. by* Michael Hamburger. PBWP
You used to ask me once what was wrong. In Memoriam I. Franco Fortini, *tr. by* Ruth Feldman. VWA
You used to be my sugar, but. Tooten Out Blues. *Unknown.* BluL
You vilify me, but I rise above grief. Lament after Her Husband Bishr's Murder. Al-Khirniq, *tr. by* Willis Barnstone. BoWoP
You Virgins. James Shirley. *See* Piping Peace.
You, Voyager, with exile-heart that yearns. Speak to the Sun. Dedie Huffman Wilson. GoYe
You wake, shuddering, and as I kiss your back. The Contagiousness of Dreams. Diane Middlebrook. AMV-81
You waken slowly. In your dream you're straying. Sonnet. William Bell. NePoEA
You walk down the road. Letting Go. Richard Shelton. AMV-81
You walk into a room of voices. Teaching Poetry. Cyn Zarco. BrSi
You walk on. A Door. W. S. Merwin. EAS
You walk the floor of autumn where her corpse. Autmnall. Joseph Bennett. NePA
You want clear spectacles: your eyes are dim. The Accusation of the Inward Man. Edward Taylor. LiTA
You want coins? Roman? Greek? Nice vase? Head of god, goddess. Ali Ben Shufti. Anthony Thwaite. OxBTC
You want the summer lightning, throw the knives. Ingeborg Bachmann, *tr. fr. German by* Daniel Huws. BoWoP
You want to go back. Margaret Atwood. NeAC
You want to integrate me into your anonymity. Black Narcissus. Gerald W. Barrax. PoBA
You want to know what's the matter with me, do yer? Reaping. Amy Lowell. SBG
You want to make some honey? Bee. X. J. Kennedy. OBCA
You want to sit here and write a poem. Poem to the Sun. Morty Sklar. FAZ
You wanted the perfect setting. For Anna. Irving Layton. NeAC
You watched out for him or. Travis, the Kid Was All Heart. Terry Stokes. AmPA
You wear the face. Izumi Shikibu, *tr. fr. Japanese by* Willis Barnstone. BoWoP
You wear the morning like your dress. Song [*or* Song: Inviting the Influence of a Young Lady upon the Opening Year]. Hilaire Belloc. OBEV; OBVV
You, weeping wide at war, weep with me now. The Coward. Eve Merriam. TrJP
You well-compacted groves, whose light and shade. Sonnet Made upon the Groves near Merlou Castle. Lord Herbert of Cherbury. JCP
You went away. Butch Is Back. Earl Gene Box. LFAC
You Went to the Verge, You Say, and Came Back Safely? Conrad Aiken. *Fr.* Preludes to Memnon. FaBoMo; LiTA; TwAmPo; TwCP
You were a girl of satin and gauze. The Wheel Revolves. Kenneth Rexroth. NoAM
You were a pretty boy once, Archestratus, and. Epigram. Philip of Thessalonica, *tr. by* Edith Morgan. PeHV
You were a sophist. Advice. Gwendolyn B. Bennett. BlSi; CDC
You were a witness, lamp, you saw him kneel. All-knowing Lamp. *Unknown, tr. by* Louis Untermeyer. UnTE
You were always a dreamer, Rose—red Rose. A Rose Will Fade. Dora Sigerson Shorter. HBV-1
You were amused to find you too could fear. Letter I. William Empson. ChMP; LiTB
You were at the door with the news. The Announcement. George Ellenbogen. AMV-80
You were born; must die; were loved; must love. Sonnet. Stephen Spender. MoAB; MoBrPo
You were born on the Esplanade des Invalides. On the Esplanade des Invalides. David Fisher. NPGG
You were brought up. Coming Up and Falling Down. Stephen Vincent. NeAC
You were dawn on the Cuillin and benign day on the Clarach. Sorley Maclean. Dain do Eimhir, LIV. NeBP
You were meticulous as a sculptor. Pentimento. Lori Fisher. PoDr
You were no more to me than many others. The Masquerader. Aline Kilmer. HBMV
You were praised, my books. Salutation the Second. Ezra Pound. NOBA; OxBA
You were tall and beautiful. First Love. Mary Dorcey. BrRo
You were that time's resemblance, whole and one. For Peter. Lee Gerlach. HoAn
You were the fence standing between our land and the descendants of Ali. Lament for a Dead Lover. Siraad Haad, *tr. by* B. W. Andrzejewski *and* I. M. Lewis. WTO
You were the morning star among the living. Aster. Plato, *tr. by* Peter Jay. PeHV
You Were Wearing. Kenneth Koch. CABA; CoAP; EAS; NiP; NNaP; NoAM; NoP
You were with me and it wasn't flying, exactly. A Dream as Reported. Virginia Earle. GoYe
You were writing a long poem, yes. Residue of Song. Marvin Bell. AmPA
You were young—but that was scarcely to your credit. Gerald Gould. *Fr.* Monogamy. OxBTC
You weren't even a. To L. Julianne Perry. PoBA
"You! What d'you mean by this?" I rapped. Inspection. Wilfred Owen. WaP
You who/ fail. Femina. Daphne Marlatt. NOBC
You who are earth, and cannot rise. To the World; the Perfection of Love. William Habington. AnAnS-2; JCP
You who are still and white. Slain. T. W. H. Crosland. OBWP
You who ask where I find the courage. A Return to the Tree of Time. Vesna Parun, *tr. by* Vasa D. Mihailovich *and* Ronald Morgan. WPOW
You who can grant, or can refuse, the pow'r. A Sea-Chaplain's Petition to the Lieutenants in the Ward-Room, for the Use of the Quarter-Gallery. "J. T." NOEC
You who descend river by river. Giraffe. *Unknown.* PeSA
You who desired so much—in vain to ask. To Emily Dickinson. Hart Crane. CMoP; NoAM; NOBA; NoP; TAP
You Who Dog My Footsteps. Leib Kwitko, *tr. fr. Yiddish by* Joseph Leftwich. TrJP
You who dread the cares and labors. The Last Landlord. Elizabeth Akers Allen. AA
You who dump the beer cans in the lake. Malediction. Barry Spacks. InPK; TW
You who give sustenance to your creatures, O God. Prayer for Rain. Sheikh Aqib Abdullahi Jama, *tr. by* B. W. Andrzejewski. WTO
You who go out on schedule. Two Variations. Denise Levertov. NaP; PPoe
You who have grown so intimate with stars. To an Aviator. Daniel Whitehead Hicky. RHPC
You who have listened to the heart of the night. Nocturne II. Ruben Dario, *tr. by* Jan Pallister. AMV-81
You who hunger and thirst. Back to the Angels. William Walter De Bolt. AMV-81
You, who in April laughed, a green god in the sun. Poem. Brenda Chamberlain. NeBP
You, who in Cupid's rolls inscribe your name. Ovid, *tr. fr. Latin by* Dryden. *Fr.* The Art of Love. FaBoUs
You, who in sultry weather. A Plea for a Plural. Rudolf Chambers Lehmann. CenHV
You who know unrequited love. Daphne and Apollo. George Macy. InMe
You who like a boulder stand. The Wildebeest. June Daly. FaPON
You who live secure. Shema. Primo Levi, *tr. by* Ruth Feldman *and* Brian Swann. VWA
You who make your escape from the tumult. Hyena. *Unknown.* PeSA
You Who Occupy Our Land. Manuela Margarido, *tr. fr. Portuguese by* Allan Francovich. WPOW
You who practise the four elegant occupations. Scroll-Section. Robert Finch. PeCV
You who sat safe at home. Transport of Wounded in Mesopotamia, 1917. Margery Lawrence. SUMH
You who snore with your sleeping wife so near. Tristan Corbière, *tr. by* Christopher Pilling. *Fr.* Litany of Sleep. OBVE

You who were darkness warmed my flesh. Woman to Child. Judith Wright. PBWP; WPE
You Who Were Made for This Music. Louis Zukofsky. CoPo
You who with birch or laurel. To the Harpies. Arthur Davison Ficke. HBV-2
You who would sorrow even for a token. Reciprocity. Vassar Miller. IHMS; NePoEA
You, Whoever You Are. Walt Whitman. AmFN
You whom I never knew. "The Sad Years." Eva Gore-Booth. HBMV
You whom the kings saluted; who refused not. To the Unknown Warrior. G. K. Chesterton. MMA
You whom the waters make fierce and the moon quiets. A Sestina for Cynthia. David Lougée. NePA
You, Whose Mother's Lover Was Grass. Gregory Corso. NoAM
You will ask how I came to be eavesdropping, in the first place. Confession Overheard in a Subway. Kenneth Fearing. LiTA; LiTM; WaP
You will come, my bird, Bonita? Juanita. Joaquin Miller. AA
You will come, your eyes full of night and of yesterday. Toward Lesbos. Renée Vivien, *tr. by* Sandia Belgrade. PeHV
You Will Die. *Unknown, tr. fr. Chinese by* H. A. Giles. *Fr.* Shi King. AWP
You Will Find a Joy in Service. Dorothy Conant Stroud. STF
You will find me drinking rum. The Logical Vegetarian. G. K. Chesterton. CenHV
You will have the road gate open, the front door ajar. In Memory of My Mother. Patrick Kavanagh. BIrV
You will know. Story from Bear Country. Leslie Silko. STE
You Will Know When You Get There. Allen Curnow. OCNZ
You will not be like those who turn their faces away. The Pipes. Lou Lipsitz. LTB
You will not see the sorrow of no time. No Time. Terence Tiller. NeBP
You will probably have three children. Love Poem Investigation for A.T. Frank Frate. AMV-80
You will remember that the Twelfth was always dry. The Glorious Twelfth. Robert Greacen. NeIP
You will remember the kisses, real or imagined. Resurrection. Kenneth Fearing. CMoP
You Will See Your Lord a-Coming, *with music. Unknown.* AH
You with that creeping, twining thing can play. To a Fine Young Woman. William Wycherley. TW
You within Love. Norman McCaig. NeBP
You Wi'yum, come 'ere, suh, dis minute. Wut dat you got under dat box? Kentucky Philosophy. Harrison Robertson. HBV-2
You wonder why Drab sells her love for gold? Epigram. J. V. Cunningham. NePoAm
You Work and Work. Samuel Hoffenstein. WhC
You worry me whoever you are. Badman of the Guest Professor. Ishmael Reed. BPo
You would give your red lips to press. A Woman. Mary Dixon Thayer. HBMV
You would have scoffed if we had told you yesterday. To a Child in Death. Charlotte Mew. MoAB; MoBrPo
You Would Have Understood Me. Paul Verlaine, *tr. fr. French by* Ernest Dowson. BoLoP; MoBrPo
(Lyric: "You would have understood me.") HBV-1
You would know, dear one. Byron in Greece. Norman Rosten. HoAn
You would not bend. For Kinte. Oliver La Grone. FB
You would not recognize me. The Tourist from Syracuse. Donald Justice. TwCP
You would sleep with the moon. Alternatives. Peter Cooley. AmPA
You would think I'd be a specialist in contemporary. The Put-Down Come On. A. R. Ammons. NoP
You would think the fury of aerial bombardment. The Fury of Aerial Bombardment. Richard Eberhart. BiP; CMoP; FaBoMo; FF; FYAP; HeIP; HoPM; InPK; LiTA; LiTM; MiAP; MP; NIP; NMP; NoAM; NoP; OBWP; PAI; PrIm; TAP; TwCP; UnPo; VGW; WaP
You wouldn't listen to my wordless temperance lecture. To the Fly in My Drink. David Wagoner. DFF
You write with ease, to shew your breeding. Clio's Protest. Sheridan. FaBoEE
You wrong me, Strephon, when you say. Song. "Ephelia." CavP
You wrote a line too much, my sage. Cynicus to W. Shakspere. James Kenneth Stephen. *Fr.* Two Epigrams. CenHV; WhC
You X-ari bush. Zebra. *Unknown.* PeSA
You, you are all unloving, loveless, you. The Sea. D. H. Lawrence. BoNaP; MOS
You. You running across the field. Orpheus and Eurydice. Jean Valentine. LCAP
You young friskies who to-day. The Next War. Robert Graves. BrPo
You'd always come across him, often as not. It's Not Bad Once the Water Goes Down. Thomas Reiter. WOLT
You'd be surprised how short the roads. Windy Trees. A. R. Ammons. PPJ
You'd be surprised, I'm sure, to know. A Little Word. *Unknown.* STF
You'd better be. The Skunk. Dorothy Baruch. SoPo
You'd have men's hearts up from the dust. Near Perigord. Ezra Pound. FaBoMo; LiTA; LiTM
Youd make capital of. Elegy. Alan Loney. OCNZ
You'd Say It Was a Funeral. James Reeves. ShM
You'd scarce expect one of my age. Tall Oaks from Little Acorns Grow [*or* The Boy Reciter]. David Everett. BLPA; FaFP; TreF
You'd think that at 3:00 A.M. L'Elisir d'Amore. Dallas E. Wiebe. MAT
Youghall Harbor. *Unknown, tr. fr. Modern Irish by* Sir Samuel Ferguson. OnYI
You'l marvel when I tell ye o. Loudon Hill; or, Drumclog. *Unknown.* ESPB
You'll [*or* You'le] ask, perhaps, wherefore I stay. An Excuse of Absence. Thomas Carew. CaPo; SeCP
You'll be my little seven stone missionary! T. S. Eliot. *Fr.* Sweeney Agonistes. UnPo
You'll come to our ball;—since we parted. Our Ball. Winthrop Mackworth Praed. *Fr.* Letters from Teignmouth. EnRP
You'll find me in the Laundromat. Laundromat. David McCord. QQQ
You'll find that I'm the sort. Abner Silver's "Pu-leeze! Mr. Hemingway!" Ring Lardner. OBAL
You'll find the road is long and rough, with soft spots far apart. Grantland Rice. *Fr.* Alumnus Football. TreFS
You'll go to the plaza. Camoes and the Debt. Sophia de Mello Breyner Andresen, *tr. by* Willis Barnstone *and* Nelson Cerqueira. BoWoP
You'll lose your measter soon, then, I do vind. Eclogue: Two Farms in Woone. William Barnes. NBM
You'll Love Me Yet! Robert Browning. *Fr.* Pippa Passes, sc. iii. OLR
(Song: "You'll love me yet! and I can tarry.") HBV-1
You'll make tea. Living Together. Tomioka Taeko, *tr. by* Sato Hiroaki. WPOW
You'll Never Miss Your Jelly. *Unknown.* BluL
You'll see sometime—half. Memorandum. William Stafford. NYBP
You'll wait a long, long time for anything much. On Looking Up by Chance at the Constellations. Robert Frost. CMoP; NePA
Young. Anne Sexton. NCSH
Young Acacia, The. Hayyim Nahman Bialik, *tr. fr. Hebrew by* Helena Frank. TrJP
Young Allan. *Unknown.* BaBo; ESPB
Young American, The. Alexander H. Everett. PaPo
Young and Old. Charles Kingsley. *Fr.* The Water Babies, *ch.* 2. BLPL; EBEV; FaBoBe; FaFP; FaPoR; HBV-1; OxBChV; PoLF; TreF
(Old Song, The.) OBVV
(When All the World.) ViBoPo
Young and Radiant, He Is Standing, *with music.* Allen Eastman Cross. AH
Young and Simple though I Am. Thomas Campion. FaBoEn; SeCeV
Young and trusting, blithe and fair. Surrender. Ruth Guthrie Harding. HBMV
Young Andrew. *Unknown.* ESPB
(Younge Andrew.) OxBB
Young Apollo, golden-haired, A. Youth [*or* Quatrain]. Frances Cornford. ELU; PCP
Young are quick of speech, The. On Teaching the Young. Yvor Winters. NoAM; NOBA
Young at his father's fire. Fathers and Sons. *Unknown, tr. by* Frank O'Connor. KiLC
Young Author, The. Samuel Johnson. LAuP
Young Barnswell. *Unknown.* OBET
Young Bather, The. *Unknown, tr. fr. Greek by* Louis Untermeyer. UnTE
Young Bearwell. *Unknown.* ESPB
Young bee falls between my window, A. Vincent O'Sullivan. Brother Jonathan, Brother Kafka, 32. OCNZ
Young Beichan (*diff. versions*). *Unknown.* EnSB; ESPB (A *and* C *vers.*); FaBoBa; ViBoFo
(Lord Bateman.) AmFP; FSW; OBET
(Lord Beichan and Susie Pye.) GN
(Loving Ballad of Lord Bateman, The.) BeLS; BLPA
(Young Beichan and Susie Pye.) HBV-2; OnMSP
(Young Bekie.) FaBoCh; OxBB, *with music*
Young Ben he was a nice young man. Faithless Sally Brown. Thomas Hood. FaBoCo; HBV-2; NOBL; OBNV; TreFS
Young Benjie. *Unknown.* ESPB; OxBB, *with music*
Young Billy Crane, *with music.* Larry Gorman. ShS
Young Birch, A. Robert Frost. BoNaP; LiTA
Young Blondes. Gavin Ewart. ErPo
Young bloods come round less often now, The. Horace, *tr. by* James Michie. Odes, I, 25. BoLoP
Young Bride's Dream, The. Rhoda Coghill. OxBI

Young Buck's Sunday Blues. Kenneth Pitchford. *Fr.* Good for Nothing Man. CoPo
Young Calves, The. Robert P. Tristram Coffin. TiPo
Young Charlottie [or, The Frozen Girl]. *Unknown.* AmFP; BeLS; BLPA; CoSo, *with music*
(Frozen Girl, The, *with music.*) AS
(Young Charlotte.) BaBo; FSW
Young cherry trees, The. April. Linda Pastan. Psk
Young child, Christ, is straight and wise, The. Child. Carl Sandburg. TRV
Young Colin Clout, a lad of peerless meed. Tuesday; or, The Ditty. John Gay. *Fr.* The Shepherd's Week. LoBV; NOEC
Young Companions, *with music. Unknown.* CoSo
Young composer, working that summer at an artist's colony, The. A Story about the Body. Robert Hass. GeTw; NPGG
Young Conquistador, The. Robert Peterson. GP
Young Cordwainer, The. Robert Graves. MoBS
Young Corydon [*or* Coridon] and Phyllis [*or* Phillis]. On the Happy Corydon and Phyllis. *At. to* Sir Charles Sedley. BoLoP; CoMu; ErPo
Young Corydon, th'unhappy shepherd swain. The Second Pastoral; or, Alexis. Virgil, *tr. by* Dryden. PeHV
Young Couples Strolling By. Carl Rakosi. InPS
Young Curate of Kidderminster, A. *Unknown.* TDH
Young David, A: Birmingham. Helen Morgan Brooks. PoNe
Young Dead Soldiers, The. Archibald MacLeish. OFD; WaP
Young Deer/Dust, A. Hemda Roth, *tr. fr. Hebrew by* Myra Glazer Schotz. VWA
Young Democracy, *sel.* Bernard O'Dowd.
"Hark! Young Democracy from sleep." PoAu-1
Young Dove, The. Moses ibn Ezra, *tr. fr. Hebrew by* Solomon Solis-Cohen. TrJP
Young Earl of Essex's Victory over the Emperor of Germany, The. *Unknown.* ESPB; OBET
Young Edward came to Emily his gold all for to show. Edwin in the Lowlands Low. *Unknown.* AmFP
Young Edwin in the Lowlands Low. *Unknown.* BaBo (A *and* B *vers.*); OBET
(Edwin in the Lowlands Low, *diff. vers.*) AmFP
Young Endymion sleeps Endymion's sleep, The. Keats. Longfellow. AP; TAP
Young engine-driver called Hunt, A. Limerick. Victor Gray. NOBL
Young eyes leave the volume and stray out, The. History Lesson. Mark Van Doren. NYBP
Young fairy with habits perverse, A. Limerick. *Unknown.* PeHV
Young Fellow from Boise, A. John Straley. TDH
Young Fellow Named Shear, A. John Ciardi. TDH
Young fellow walks about, The Charles Reznikoff. CTBA
Young Fenians, The. Padraic Fallon. BIrV
Young Fir-Wood, A. Dante Gabriel Rossetti. GN
Young fisherboys sing like the endless sea. That's Our Lot. Moishe Leib Halpern, *tr. by* Kathryn Hellerstein. VWA
Young flowers were whispering in melody. Song. Poe. *Fr.* Al Aaraaf. NOBA
Young flute player, The. Flute Player. *Gond Oral Tradition, tr. by* V. Elwin *and* S. Hivale. WTO
Young Forbest, *with music. Unknown.* ShS
Young Frederick the Great was a beaut. Limerick. *Unknown.* PeHV
"Young friend," 'e sez . . . Young friend! Well, spare/ me days! Pilot Cove C. J. Dennis. WhC
Young Girl. Ricarda Huch, *tr. fr. German by* Janine Canan *and* Deirdre Lashgari. WPOW
Young Girl, The. Theodore Roethke. NoAM
Young Girl. Thomas Waltner. LFAC
Young Girl and the Beach, The. Sophia de Mello Breyner Andresen, *tr. fr. Portuguese by* Alexis Levitin. WPOW
Young girl dancing lifts her face, The. The Dancer. W. J. Turner. OBMV
Young girl holds her left ankle, A. In the Sitting Room of the Opera. Criss E. Cannady. PoDr
Young girl moves like an ear of grain, A. The Young Girl and the Beach. Sophia de Mello Breyner Andresen, *tr. by* Alexis Levitin. WPOW
Young Girl of Asturias, A. *Unknown.* TDH
Young girl of thirteen, A. The Cloak. Violet Anderson. CaP
Young girl questions, The: "Whether were it better." Wisdom. Ford Madox Ford. HBV-1
Young girl stood beside me, The. The Orange Tree. Shaw Neilson. CBAP; PoAu-1
Young Girls. Raymond Souster. HeIP
Young girls, if you'll listen. Pearl Bryan. *Unknown.* ViBoFo
Young Girl's Song, A. Paul Heyse, *tr. fr. German by* E. H. Mueller. PoPl
Young Girl's Song. *Unknown. See* Maidens Came, The.
Young Glass-Stainer, The. Thomas Hardy. CTC; EyDe; SaC
Young Gray Head, The. Caroline Bowles Southey. BeLS
Young Harvard man, sweet and tender, A. Limerick. *Unknown.* PeHV
Young, having risen early, had gone, The. The Guardians. Geoffrey Hill. NePoEA-2; NoP
Young head in sunlight! Not a woman born. No Woman Born. Robert Farren. OxBI
Young Heroes. Gwendolyn Brooks. BPo
Young Highland Girl Studying Poetry, A. Iain Crichton Smith. NePoEA-2; PP
Young Hodge met Mog the miller's maid. Don't Be Foolish Pray. *Unknown.* CoMu
Young homosexuals and hot girls, The. Lone Gentleman. Pablo Neruda, *tr. by* Clayton Eshleman ErPo
Young hound howls, A. Unemployment. William Mills. HoPM
Young Housewife, The. William Carlos Williams. HeIP; NoAM; NoP; TAP
Young Hunting (*diff. versions*). *Unknown.* AmFP; BaBo; ESPB (A, C, *and* G *vers.*); OxBB; OxBoLi; ViBoFo
(Loving Henry.) BaBo
Young Hyllus, why refuse today. Epigram: A Riddle. Martial, *tr. by* Brian Hill. PeHV
Young I am, and yet unskill'd. Song for a Girl [*or* Sung by a Young Girl]. Dryden. ELP; ErPo; UnTE
Young I was who now am old. On Himself. Robert Herrick. UnTE
Young in Fall I said: the birds. Lorine Niedecker. VGW
Young is she, and slight to view. Dorothea. Sarah N. Cleghorn. HBMV
Young Janie was a strappin' lass. The Thocht. William Soutar. NeBP
Young Japanese son was in love with a servant boy, The. Dream Data. Robert Duncan. NeAP
Young Jemmy is a lad. England's Darling; or, Great Britain's Joy and Hope on That Noble Prince James, Duke of Monmouth. *Unknown.* CoMu
Young Jockey he courted sweet Mog the Brunette. Mog the Brunette. *Unknown.* CoMu
Young Johnnie Steele has an Oldsmobile. In My Merry Oldsmobile. Vincent Bryan. FSN
Young Johnny sails the sea, young Johnny sails the shore. The Green Bed. *Unknown.* AmFP
Young Johnny the miller he courted of late. The Gray Mare. *Unknown.* AmFP
Young Johnstone. *Unknown.* ESPB (A *and* B *vers.*); OxBB, *with music*
Young kangaroo, Miss Hocket, A. Miss Hocket. *Unknown.* TDH
Young Lady from Cork, A. Ogden Nash. TDH
Young Lady from Delaware, A. *Unknown.* TDH
Young Lady Named Bright, A. *See* Relativity.
Young Lady Named Sue, A. *Unknown.* TDH
Young Lady of Crete, A. *Unknown. See* There Was a Young Lady of Crete.
Young Lady of Ealing, A. *Unknown. See* Limerick: "There was a young lady of Ealing."
Young lady of fair Mytilene, A. Limerick. *Unknown.* CenHV
Young Lady of Lynn, A. *Unknown. See* Limerick: "There was a young lady of Lynn."
Young Lady of Munich, A. *Unknown.* TDH
Young Lady of Norway, A. Edward Lear. *See* There Was a Young Lady of Norway.
Young Lady of Oakham, A. *Unknown.* TDH
Young Lady of Tyre, The. Edward Lear. TDH
Young Lady of Wilts, A. *Unknown. See* Limerick: "There was a young lady of Wilts."
Young Lambs. John Clare. TrGrPo
Young Lincoln. Edwin Markham. OHIP
Young Lochinvar. Sir Walter Scott. *See* Lochinvar.
Young Lochinvar. *Unknown.* FiBHP; InMe
Young Lochinvar came in from the West. At Cheyenne. Eugene Field. BPAW
Young lords o' the north country, The. Lady Maisry. *Unknown.* ESPB; OxBB; ViBoFo
Young Love. Gerald Massey. OBVV
Young Love lies sleeping. Dream-Love. Christina Rossetti. CH; HAP; NBM; PoEL-5
Young man, alone, on the high bridge over the Tagus, A. The High Bridge above the Tagus River at Toledo. William Carlos Williams. CTC
Young man and maid, pray lend attention. *See* Young men and maids, pray lend attention.
Young Man and the Young Nun, The. A. D. Mackie. OxBS
Young man at the plate, bat bristling, The. A Post Card out of Panama. William D. Barney. LiSp
Young Man Cut Down in His Prime (St. James Hospital). *Unknown.* FSW
Young man, his face dark, A. Apollo. James Wright. LCAP
Young man in a carriage, driving like he's mad. Putting on the Style. *Unknown.* FSW
Young man is spaced out on the lawn, A. Maxims of a Park Vagrant. Nicholas Swift. AMV-80

Young man lately in our Town, A. The Maids Conjuring Book. *Unknown.* CoMu
Young man left his native shores, A. Look Out Below! Charles R. Thatcher. PoAu-1
Young Man Loves a Maiden, A. Heine, *tr. fr. German by* Ernest Feise. NAWM-2
Young man of twenty, A. Lost Picture. Ray Fraser. NeAC
Young Man on a Journey, A. *Unknown.* TDH
Young Man to an Old Woman Courting Him, A. John Cleveland. AnAnS-2
Young man, wearing a loose jacket of light brown, A. Puerto Ricans in New York, II. Charles Reznikoff. CTBA
Young Man Who Loved Rain, A. William Jay Smith. TDH
Young Man Who Loved the Girl Who Took Care of Her Aging Father, The. Greg Kuzma. AmPA
Young Man Who Wouldn't Hoe Corn. *Unknown.* FSW
Young Man's Epigram on Existence, A. Thomas Hardy. BrPo; NoAM
Young Man's Song, A. William Bell. FaBoTw; NePoEA
Young Martins, The. Andrew Young. FM
Young Mary, loitering once her garden way. Mary and Gabriel. Rupert Brooke. ISi
Young Master's Account of a Puppet Show. John Marchant. OxBChV
Young May Moon, The. Thomas Moore. ELP; EnRP; HBV-1; MOON; OAEP; OBEV
Young men and maids [*or* man and maid], pray lend attention. The Silver Dagger. *Unknown.* AmFP; BaBo
Young men and maids, pray tell your age. Locks and Bolts. *Unknown.* TrAS
Young Men Come Less Often, The—Isn't It So? Horace, *tr. fr. Latin by* Robert Fitzgerald. ErPo
Young men dancing, and the old. Youthful Age. Thomas Stanley. AWP; OBVE
Young men die in battle, The. Scapegoats. Eleanor D. Breed. PGD
Young men give ear to me a while. The Maid's Complaint for Want of a Dil Doul. *Unknown.* CoMu
Young men leave the country for the town, The. The Way to the Sea. Laurence Lerner. NePoEA-2
Young men on the roof watching the stars. Young Men You Are So Beautiful Up There. Patricia Goedicke. GP
Young men, they say, are bold and free. Beware, Oh, Take Care. *Unknown.* FSW
Young men walking the open streets. Remember Your Lovers. Sidney Keyes. WaP
Young Men You Are So Beautiful Up There. Patricia Goedicke. GP
Young Mrs. Snooks was sick of sex. Nursery Rhyme. Kenneth Burke. OBAL
Young Molly Ban [*or* Bawn]. *Unknown.* FaBoBa; OnYI
(Molly Bawn.) BaBo; ViBoFo
(Polly Vaughn.) AmFP
(Shooting of His Dear.) OxBoLi
Young Monroe at Gerry's Rock. *Unknown. See* Jam on Gerry's Rock, The.
Young moon is white, The. A Japanese Love-Song. Alfred Noyes. OBVV
Young moon, take my face up yonder. Re-birth. *Unknown, tr. by* W. H. I. Bleek *and* Jack Cope. PeSA
Young Negro Poet. Calvin C. Hernton. AmNP
Young Neophyte, The. Alice Meynell. ACP; GoBC
Young niggers/ die old. Dedication to the Final Confrontation. Lloyd M. Corbin, Jr. PoBA
Young Ones, The. Elizabeth Jennings. OxBTC
Young Ones, Flip Side, The. James A. Emanuel. PCP
Young Palmus was a ferryman. Shackley-Hay. *Unknown.* GBP
Young Paris was the shepherd's pride. George Crabbe. Posthumous Tales, XIX. OBRV
Young Peggy. *Unknown.* BaBo; ESPB
Young people all, attention give. Liverpool. *Unknown.* AmFP
Young people, all attention give. Mission. *Unknown.* AmFP
Young People Who Delight in Sin. *Unknown.* AmFP
Young Philander woo'd me long. Song. *Unknown.* ErPo
Young Pilgrim Finds Refuge with the Goatherds, The. Luis de Góngora, *tr fr. Spanish by* Edward Meryon Wilson. *Fr.* The First Solitude. OBVE
Young pinoy, A. Pick-up at Chef Rizal Restaurant. Virginia Cerenio. BrSi
Young Pithy, from your Djetis bed. Lines to Homo Somejerktensis. Earnest A. Hooton. WhC .
Young Poet. Myron O'Higgins. PoBA; PoNe
Young Poets. Nicanor Parra, *tr. fr. Spanish by* Miller Williams. POL
"Young poets, The," he murmured. Vernon Watkins. *Fr.* Yeats in Dublin. PP
Young poets swim in schools like minnows. Poets Observed. F. C. Rosenberger. AMV-80
Young Prince, The. Horatio Colony. TwAmPo
Young Prince and the Young Princess, The. John Ashbery. ConAP
Young prince violent in wrath, The. Young Prince, The. Horatio Colony. TwAmPo
Young Puppy, The. A. A. Milne. GDP
(Howard.) TDH
Young Recruit, The. Arthur Davison Ficke. ELU
Young Reynard. George Meredith. HoPM
Young Rhymer Snubbed, The. William Barnes. VLP
Young Roger came tapping at Dolly's window. Roger and Dolly. Henry Carey. CoMu; NOEC; OxNR, *st.* 1
Young Ronald. *Unknown.* ESPB
Young Rory O'More courted Kathleen bawn. Rory O'More; or, Good Omens. Samuel Lover. HBV-1
Young School Mistress, A. *Unknown.* TDH
Young Sea. Carl Sandburg. MOS
Young Shepherd Bathing His Feet. Peter Clarke. PBA
Young skull which the wind scrapes, which the sand. On the Relative Merit of Friend and Foe, Being Dead. Donald Thompson. WaP
Young Soul. Amiri Baraka. BPo; CNA
Young Stock. V. Sackville-West. OxBTC
Young Strephon and Phillis. *Unknown.* UnTE
Young Sycamore. William Carlos Williams. TAP
Young things who frequent picture-palaces, The. Limerick. *Unknown.* NOBL
Young to the end through sympathy with youth. James McCosh. Robert Bridges (1858-1941). AA
Young Training. Lawrence McGaugh. PoBA
Young Traveller Is Presented to the Goddess Dulness, A. Pope. *Fr.* The Dunciad, IV. NOEC
Young Una, you were a rose in a garden. Tomas Costello, *tr. by* Frank O'Connor. *Fr.* A Lament for Una. WTO
Young unmarried man, with a good name, A. Byron. *Fr.* Don Juan. NOBL
Young viper grows as it sits, The. *Zulu Oral Tradition, tr. by* T. Cope. *Fr.* Shaka. WTO
Young Virgins Plucked Suddenly. Berl Pomerantz, *tr. fr. Hebrew by* Harold Schimmel. VWA
Young was the woman. A Maiden Ring-adorned. Cynewulf, *tr. by* Mother Margaret Williams. *Fr.* Christ 2 . ISi
Young Washington. Arthur Guiterman. FaPON; OHIP; PoSC
Young Waters. *Unknown.* ESPB; OxBB, *with music*
Young Wife, A. D. H. Lawrence. BrPo; ChMP; ELP; MoBrPo
Young Wife, The. C. K. Stead. OCNZ
Young Willie stands in his stable door. Clyde's Waters. *Unknown.* OxBB
Young Windebank. Margaret L. Woods. HBV-2; HBVY
Young Woman. Howard Nemerov. ErPo
Young woman, A/ lies gathered to her breast. Portrait of My Mother on Her Wedding Day. Celia Gilbert. AMV-81; DFF
Young Woman at a Window. Mark Van Doren. LiTA; MoPo; MoVE
Young Woman from Aenos, The. *Unknown.* OBAL
Young Woman of Beare, The. Austin Clarke. NoAM
Young Woman's Neo-Aramaic Jewish Persian Blues. Jerome Rothenberg, *after Persian folk poem.* BoWoP
Young women are obsessed with beauty, The. The Clothes Pit. Douglas Dunn. OxBTC
Young women in their April moodiness. The True Weather for Women. Louis Simpson. NePoAm
Young women, they [*or* they'll] run like hares on the mountain. Hares on the Mountain. *Unknown.* ErPo; UnTE
Young Wordsworth's London, The. Wordsworth. *Fr.* The Prelude, VII. FaBoPP
Young Workman, The. Mary Dillingham Frear. TrCP
Younge Andrew. *Unknown. See* Young Andrew.
Younger Poet, A. Peter Schjeldahl. PoA
Younger Van Eyck, The. E. C. Bentley. FiBHP
Youngest Daughter, The. Cathy Song. MAYP
Your absence has gone through me. Separation. W. S. Merwin. HAP; NoP; PCP
Your Absence Has Not Taught Me. Doug Fetherling. NeAC
Your absent name at rollcall was more present. Anthony. Jane Shore. DFF
Your Air of My Air. Hugo Margenat, *tr. fr. Spanish by* Julio Marzán. InW
Your American mother. Halfbreed Chronicles; Isamu. Wendy Rose. TWSS
Your angel weighs heavier than your mortal. Of Angels. E. L. Mayo. FAZ
Your Animal. Gerald Stern. AMV-81
Your archival voice. The Music. Everett Hoagland. CNA
Your are/ Getting free. Thoughts for You (When She Came Back from the Mountains). Ranice Henderson Crosby. NMM
Your arms will clasp the gathered grain. The Island. Edwin Muir. OAEL-2

Your ashes will not stir, even on this high ground. In Carrowdore Churchyard. Derek Mahon. CIP
Your Attention Please. Peter Porter. OBWP; OxBTC
Your back is rough all. Margaret Atwood. NeAC
Your bare white legs. The Beach at Veracruz. George Bowering. NeAC
Your battle-wounds are scars upon my heart. To My Brother. Vera Brittain. SUMH
Your Beauty and My Reason. *Unknown.* TrGrPo
("Like two proud armies marching in the field.") OBSC
Your beauty is as timeless as the earth. Her Pedigree. Arthur Davison Ficke. Sonnets of a Portrait Painter, IX. HBMV
Your beauty, ripe and calm, and fresh. The Philosopher and the Lover: To a Mistress Dying [*or* Lover and Philosopher]. Sir William Davenant. ACP; FaBoEn; GoBC; LO; MePo; NOBE; OBEV; Prf
Your best friend is gone. Tomorrow. Mark Strand. PPJ
Your Birds Build Sun-Castles with Song. Daniel Sloate. AMV-81
Your Birthday Comes to Tell Me This. E. E. Cummings. NAs
Your Birthday in Wisconsin You Are 140. John Berryman. NAs
Your blond hair and autumn sweater. Janna. King D. Kuka. VoR
Your blood does not flow, not even a little. A Poem for Diane Wakoski. Ray A. Young Bear. CDW
Your blood reappears on my hands. For a Friend. David Steingass. TW
Your body derns. Scunner. "Hugh MacDiarmid." BSV; FaBoTw
Your body gleams like copper on the veld. The Fallen Zulu Commander. C. M. van Den Heever, *tr. by* Uys Krige *and* Jack Cope. PeSA
Your body has moved to unstaunchable distance. N. Hugh Seidman. PoA
Your body is a pipeline. Air. Tomaz Salamun, *tr. by* Aleksandar Nejgebauer. VWA
Your Body Is Stars. Stephen Spender. FaBoTw
Your body might have come from the loins of a prince. Moon of the Earth. *Gond Oral Tradition, tr. by* V. Elwin *and* S. Hivale. WTO
Your body to hold, your perfect breasts. Undine. Irving Layton. ErPo
Your bottoms are not purple. Horror Comic. Robert Conquest. OxBTC
Your boy's-ambition was to be a Horseman. Stud Groom. John Glassco. OBCV
Your brother brings you home from hunting. One Man Down. Ai. GeTw
Your brother is dead. Dreaming with a Friend. Stephen Berg. NaP
Your Burnt-out Body. Peretz Markish, *tr. fr. Yiddish by* Keith Bosley. VWA
Your buttonholes for eyes, your solemn face. The Statue. John Fuller. NePoEA-2
Your Catullus is depressed, Cornificus. Catullus, *tr. fr. Latin.* PeHV
Your celebrated hand. The Candidate. Allamae Ezell. AMV-80
Your Chase Had a Beast in View. John Peale Bishop. LiTA
Your cheeks flat on the sand. Venus Khoury-Gata, *tr. fr. French by* Willis Barnstone. BoWoP
Your children are not your children. On Children. Kahlil Gibran. *Fr.* The Prophet. PoPl
Your Church and Mine. Phillips H. Lord. BLPA
Your clear eye is the one absolutely beautiful thing. Child. Sylvia Plath. PBWP
Your closed eyes bulge like mushrooms. Letter to Kafka. Maura Stanton. AmPA
Your clothes of snow and satin and pure blood. The Bed. Karl Shapiro. NYBP
Your correspondent must be kidding when he says. Americana IX. Carl Rakosi. InPS
Your courtiers scorn we country clowns. A Ballad of the Courtier and the Country Clown. *Unknown.* CoMu
Your cousin tells you it's like fruit juice. Grape Daiquiri. Tina Koyama. BrSi
Your crops, old man, are in. Laying By. Randall Williams. AMV-80
Your death, she said, is covered. The Indian Women Are Listening; to the Nuke Devils. Wendy Rose. TWSS
Your desert land is. Navajo. William Haskel Simpson. BPAW
Your doctor, Lord. For Dr. and Mrs. Dresser. Margaret Avison. MoCV; PeCV
Your Dog Dies. Raymond Carver. GeTw
Your dog? What dog? You mean it?—that! Suzie's New Dog. John Ciardi. GDP
Your door is shut against my tightened face. The White House[s]. Claude McKay. AmNP; AmPP; NIP; PoBA; PoNe
Your downcast, harlequin, defenceless face. Lynched Negro. Maxwell Bodenheim. PoNe
Your dream had left me numb and cold. Salutation. "Æ." OnYI
Your dressing, dancing, gadding, where's the good in? On Ladies' Accomplishments. *Unknown.* FaBoUs
Your dusky shadow at the window lingers. Morning and Evening. Antoni Slonimski, *tr. by* Watson Kirkconnell. TrJP
Your elephant adolescence in sandlots Brooklyn. 16/53. Marge Piercy. NeAC
Your eyen [*or* Youre yen] two will slay me suddenly [*or* wol slee me sodenly]. Merciless Beauty [*or* A Rondel of Merciles Beaute *or* Three Roundels of Love Unreturned]. Chaucer. ACP; BoLoP; CTC; EBEV; EnLoPo; HAP; MeEL; NoP; OxBM; TrGrPo
Your Eyes. Kosrof Chantikian. AMV-81
Your eyes are as black as twin pools at night. Little Papoose. Arthur Chapman. BPAW
Your eyes are in khaki. Three Poems for Your Eyes. Rachel McAlpine. OCNZ
Your eyes are just. Four-Word Lines. May Swenson. WPE
Your eyes are open. Carious Exposure. Gladys Cardiff. CDW
Your eyes drink of me. The Mystery. Sara Teasdale. HBMV
Your Eyes Have Their Silence. Gerald W. Barrax. CNA; PoBA
Your eyes I can see in the dark. The Beacon. Arthur Gregor. GP
"Your eyes that once were never weary of mine." Ephemera. W. B. Yeats. BrPo
Your eyes were made for laughter. Don't. James Jeffrey Roche. HBV-1
Your eyes, your flowing hair. Auburn. Paul Verlaine, *tr. by* Lawrence M. Bensky. ErPo
Your face,/ so pale now it is blue. Poem. David St. John. AmPA
Your face broods from my table, Suicide. John Berryman. *Fr.* Dream Songs. CAPP; TAP
Your face did not rot. The Lost Pilot. James Tate. CoAP; DiL; NoP; OBWP; TwCP; UnPo
Your face has almost disappeared—a leaf. The End of a Meaningful Relationship. Kurt J. Fickert. AMV-81
Your face is an Eastern garden of response and gladness. Summa contra Gentiles. Paris Leary. CoPo
Your face is the face of all the others. The Face of Love. Ingrid Jonker, *tr. by* Jack Cope. PeSA
Your face reveals a down so light. Epigram: To Dindymus. Martial, *tr. by* Brian Hill. PeHV
Your face scrapes my sleep tonight. Letter to Be Disguised as a Gas Bill. Marge Piercy. WPE
Your face was lifted to the golden sky. Rupert Brooke. W. W. Gibson. HBMV
Your Fair Looks Inflame My Desire. Thomas Campion. UnTE
Your fair looks urge my desire. Be Wise and Fly Not. Thomas Campion. UnTE
Your faith is in what you hold. Chicago. Lola Ridge. PoA
Your father had gangrene. Moenkopi. Arthur Sze. BrSi
Your Father Knoweth. *Unknown. See* God Knoweth Best.
Your father's farm was lovely that October. The black barn. Persimmon Trees, She Remembers, Not Far Away. David Baker. AMV-81
"Your father's gone," my bald headmaster said. The Lesson. Edward Lucie-Smith. NCSH; OxBTC; TwCP
Your Flag and My Flag. Wilbur D. Nesbit. FaFP; WBLP
Your flute/ you carved from the shinbone of a mighty bull. Flute Players. Jean-Joseph Rabéarivelo, *tr. by* Langston Hughes. PBA
Your foe in war to overrate. Porson on His Majesty's Government. Richard Porson. FaBoCo
Your Friend. *Unknown.* TreFT
Your friends come fondly to your living room. Birthday Card for a Psychiatrist. Mona Van Duyn. IHMS
Your friends shall be the tall wind. For a Child. Fannie Stearns Davis. FaPON
Your friendship oft has made my heart to ache. *See* Thy friendship . . .
Your ghost steps are already gone. Cycle. Frank Lonergan. AMV-81
Your ghost will walk, you lover of trees. "De Gustibus." Robert Browning. HBV-2; InPS; OAEP
Your Glory, Lincoln. Mae Winkler Goodman. PGD
Your golden loins slake my lust for treasures. Prayer. Mike Newell. AMV-80
Your great sin. New Jersey White-tailed Deer. Joyce Carol Oates. GeTw
Your hair all wrinkled and you full of sweat, your. I Can Tell by the Way You Smell. *Unknown.* BluL
Your hair is growing long, Uncle Ambrose. Uncle Ambrose. James Still. AmFN
Your hand/ brushes my hair. Love Letters, Unmailed. Eve Merriam. DFF
Your Hand Full of Hours. Paul Celan, *tr. fr. German by* Michael Hamburger. OBVE
Your hand in mine, we walk out. A Sword in a Cloud of Light. Kenneth Rexroth. NMP
Your hand in your grandfather's. Michael's Room. Reginald Gibbons. AMV-81
Your hand trailed over the hammock's side. Ode to Joy. Daniel Hoffman. AMV-81
Your handkerchief should be blue. *Turkish Love Songs, tr. by* Reza Baraheni *and* Zahra-Soltan Shokoohtaezeh. BoWoP
Your Hands. Ernest Dowson. UnTE
Your Hands. Angelina Weld Grimké. CDC; PoBA
Your hands lie open in the long fresh grass. Silent Noon. Dante Gabriel

Rossetti. The House of Life, XIX. ELP; HAP; HBV-1; NoP; OAEP; OBNC; PoEL-5; TrGrPo; VLP; WHA
Your hands, my dear, adorable. The Chilterns. Rupert Brooke. MoBrPo
Your hands, strewn on the sheets, were my dead leaves. To a Sleeping Friend. Jean Cocteau, *tr. fr. French.* PeHV
Your hay it is mowed, and your corn is reaped. Harvest Home [*or* Song]. Dryden. *Fr.* King Arthur. PrIm; SeCV-2
Your health, Master Willow. Contrive me a bat. Tree Party. Louis MacNeice. OxBTC
Your heart is a music-box, dearest. Song. Frances Sargent Osgood. AA
Your heifer's pretty neck is not yet broke. Too Young for Love. Horace, *tr. by* Louis Untermeyer. UnTE
Your hooves have stamped at the black margin of the wood. On a Picture of a Black Centaur by Edmund Dulac. W. B. Yeats. SyP
Your hour approaching, to Latona cry. Labour. M. Saint-Marthe. *Fr.* Paedotrophiae; or, The Art of Bringing Up Children. FaBoUs
Your houseplant is a delicate thing. Why So Many of Them Die. Susan Wallbank. BrRo
Your hulk is like some. Cow. Janet Reed McFatter. GrPl
Your husband? Going to the same dinner as us? Ovid, *tr. by* Guy Lee. Amores, I, 4. NAWM-1
Your husband was a farmer. Grandmother. John Paul Minarik. LFAC
Your husband will be with us at the treat. To His Mistress. Ovid, *tr. by* Dryden. Amores, I, 4. BoLoP; ErPo
Your innocence snuffed out. Candle. Jacob Isaac Segal, *tr. by* Seymour Mayne. VWA
Your kind of night, David, your kind of night. Night Thoughts. Henri Coulette. FYAP
Your kindness is no kindness now. Kindness. Catherine Davis. NYBP
Your kindness, sir, to me, is really kind. Horace, *tr. fr. Latin by* Francis Howes. OBVE
Your kisses, and the way you curl. Leves Amores. Arthur Symons. UnTE
Your Lad, and My Lad. Randall Parrish. PAH
Your Last Drive. Thomas Hardy. OBNC
Your last name's the one I remember. Director. Lindeman. Mary Jane White. AMV-81
Your laughter is like a burst pomegranate. When You Laugh. Ingrid Jonker, *tr. by* Elizabeth Jones. WPOW
Your leaves bound up compact and fair. To an Author. Philip Freneau. AmPP; NOBA; OxBA
Your letter came.—Glutted the earth and cold. A Winter-Piece to a Friend Away. John Berryman. NOBA
Your life's a wreck; you're tired of living. Samuel Hoffenstein. *Fr.* Poems in Praise of Practically Nothing. DBV
Your Light. Ann Lee. AMV-80
Your lips were so laughing. Langston Blues. Dudley Randall. CNA; FB
Your Little Hands. Samuel Hoffenstein. FiBHP; TrJP
Your little voice/ Over the wires came leaping. E. E. Cummings. LLLT; OLR
Your looks so often cast. Sir Thomas Wyatt. EnRePo; SiPS
Your love is dead, lady, your love is dead. Madrigal. R. S. Thomas. BoLoP; ELU; EnLoPo
Your love lacks joy, your letter says. The Rain That Fell upon the Height. Coventry Patmore. *Fr.* The Victories of Love, I, v. FaBoRV; GBL
Your love, love. The Lover to Himself. David Phillips. NeAC
Your love turned my body into water. Empress Nur Jahan, *tr. fr. Persian by* Willis Barnstone. BoWoP
Your loveliness, I don't deny, needs lovers. Ovid, *tr. by* Guy Lee. Amores, III, 14. NAWM-1
Your lynx-eyes, Asia. "Anna Akhmatova," *tr. fr. Russian by* Stanley Kunitz *and* Max Hayward. BoWoP
Your men of the land, from the king to Jack Ketch. Epistle to a Desponding Sea-Man. Philip Freneau. MOS
Your midnight ambulances, the first knife-saw. Robert Sheridan Lowell. Robert Lowell. *Fr.* Marriage. NAs
Your midriff sags toward your knees. Woman with Girdle. Anne Sexton. ErPo; NCSH; NoAM
Your milk was already poisoned. Childhood. Edith Bruck, *tr. by* Anita Barrows. VWA
Your mind and you are our Sargasso Sea. Portrait d'une Femme. Ezra Pound. AP; CABA; CMoP; FF; HBMV; MoAB; MoAmPo; MoVE; MP; NoAM; NOBA; NoP; PAI; PPP; TAP; TwAmPo; TwCP
Your mind lies open like the map of rivers. Five Birds Rise. William Hayward. NYBP
Your Mission. Ellen M. Huntington Gates. BLPA; BLRP; TreFT
Your mistress, that you follow whores, still taxeth you. A Self Accuser. John Donne. FaBoEE
Your Money and Mine. *Unknown.* STF
Your Mother. Sam Cornish. CNA
Your mother poses on black rocks. Black Rocks. Laureen Mar. BrSi
Your Musgraves, Clarges, Harleys, Foleys, Lowthers. On Squire Neale's Projects. *Unknown.* APAS
Your name grows across. Calumet Early Evening. Annette Arkeketa West. TWSS
"Your name is Achilles Deatheridge?" Achilles Deatheridge. Edgar Lee Masters. AmFN
Your Need Is Greater than Mine. Theodore Enslin. CoPo
Your nurse could only speak Italian. Sailing Home from Rapallo. Robert Lowell. NoAM; TAP
Your obit. RIP. Jean Balderston. SOTS
Your old hat hurts me, and those black. Dad. Elaine Feinstein. VWA
Your Own Version. Paul Gilbert. BLRP
Your parents don't like me. Farewell, Sweet Mary. *Unknown.* AmFP
Your Passing, Fleet Passing. Joseph Eliyia, *tr. fr. Modern Greek by* Rae Dalven. VWA
Your peevish voice remarked "Oh, rats." To an Unknown Neighbor at the Circus. Rosemary Benét. DBV; InMe
Your petals open wet. Lesbian. Paula Jennings. PeHV
Your Phone Call at Eight A.M. Joy Harjo. TWSS
Your pinks, your tulips live an hour. To the Gardener at Nuneham. Horace Walpole. FaBoEE
Your Place. John Oxenham. BLRP; TRV
Your Presence. David Diop, *tr. fr. French by* Ulli Beier. PBA
Your Presence. Mordecai Temkin, *tr. fr. Hebrew by* Jeremy Garber. VWA
Your sculptured lips are sealed. To J.F.K. 14 Years After. Roger Weaver. AMV-80
Your Shadow. Mark Strand. *Fr.* Elegy for My Father. Prf
Your shadow I have seen you play with often. The Child and the Shadow. Elizabeth Jennings. NePoEA-2
Your shrunken head was bent. The Murder Trial. Perseus Adams. PeSA
Your sky is a hard and a dazzling blue. In Spain. Emily Lawless. AnIV
Your smile/ with the spectacular softness. After the Rain. Paul B. Janeczko. PCP
Your smile, delicate. Woman Me. Maya Angelou. BlSi
Your smiles are not, as other womens be. To the Lady May. Aurelian Townshend. GBL; MePo
Your smiling, or the hope, the thought of it. A Simile for Her Smile. Richard Wilbur. HoPM; InPK; MiAP; OLR
Your Snow-white Shoulder. Heine, *tr. fr. German by* Louis Untermeyer. UnTE
Your Songs. Gwendolyn B. Bennett. CDC
Your soul is a sealed garden. Clair de Lune. Paul Verlaine, *tr. by* Arthur Symons. AWP; MOON
Your soul is like a landscape choice and fair. A Pastel. Paul Verlaine, *tr. by* Arthur O'Shaughnessy. SyP
Your subjects hope, dread Sire. To the King's Most Excellent Majesty. Phillis Wheatley. TAP
Your tall French legs, my V for victory. Will to Win. F. R. Scott. OBCV
Your Tears. Edwin Markham. HBMV
Your tears, Niobe. Hayden Carruth. VGW
Your thighs are appletrees. Portrait of a Lady. William Carlos Williams. AmPP; CMoP; NoAM; NOBA; OxBA; TwAmPo
Your thighs your belly. Sea Flower. Mary Dorcey. BrRo
Your thoughts/ dreaming in a softened brain. A Cloud in Trousers, *abr.* Vladimir Mayakovsky, *tr. by* Peter Bogdanoff. SOTW
Your threats how vain, Corregidor. A Ballad of Manila Bay. Sir Charles G. D. Roberts. PAH
Your turn came, and you chose to take it. Winter Solstice—for Frank. Asphodel. BrRo
Your turn will come—time upon time your bones. Lucy Answers. Helen Ehrlich. SUW
Your two great eyes will slay me suddenly. A Rondel of Merciless Beauty. Chaucer, *mod. vers. by* Louis Untermeyer. TrGrPo
Your[e] ugly token [*or* tokyn]. Upon a Dead Man's Head [*or* The Gift of a Skull]. John Skelton. AAS; ACP; EnRePo; HAP; SeCePo
Your uncle, totem and curator bends. Christopher at Birth. Michael Longley. CIP
Your voice always whacked me right on the funny bone. Burying Blues for Janis. Marge Piercy. GeTw; NeAC
Your voice at times a fist. To a Husband. Maya Angelou. IHMS
Your voice is the color of a robin's breast. To O. E. A. Claude McKay. BANP; BPo
Your voice on the telephone. Donald Hall. FF
Your voice sister. Mississippi Born. Pearl Cleage Lomax. CNA
Your voice speaks:/ Great God of my life, I will praise Thee. Te Deum. Gertrude von Le Fort. ILwL
Your voice speaks:/ Little child out of eternity. Christmas. Gertrude von Le Fort, *tr. by* Margaret Chanler. ISi
Your voice speaks:/ The angel of the Lord came in unto Mary. Vigil of the Assumption. Gertrude von Le Fort, *tr. by* Margaret Chanler. ISi
Your walk sacerdotal and slow, undulant. A Black Girl Goes By. Emile Roumer, *tr. by* Edna Worthley Underwood. TTY
Your will is done. Its promise, that I fled. Oedipus to the Oracle. Wesley Trimpi. NePoEA

Your wistful eyes searched each one as he passed. Stray Dog. Charlotte Mish. PoLF
Your Woods. Margaret Holley. AMV-80
Your words dropped into my heart like pebbles into a pool. Absence. Claude McKay. CDC
Your words, my friend, (right healthful caustics), blame. Astrophel and Stella, XXI. Sir Philip Sidney. CABA; SiPS; TEP
Your World ("Your world is as big as you make it"). Georgia Douglas Johnson. AmNP
Your yen two wol slee me sodenly. *See* Your eyen two will slay me suddenly.
Your youth is like a water-wetted stone. Susan to Diana. Frances Cornford. MoVE
You're. Sylvia Plath. FaBoTw; NAs; NCSH
You're a good girl; you're gray with virtue. Samuel Hoffenstein. *Fr.* Poems in Praise of Practically Nothing. InMe
You're a Grand Old Flag, *with music.* George M. Cohan. FSN
"You're a hell of a temple" he said. The Gold Factory. William Hathaway. *Fr.* Rumplestiltskin Poems. DFT
You're a poet. *Unknown.* FaFP
You're a traitor convicted, you know very well! Jefferson D. H. S. Cornwell. PAH
"You're fired, Lane." The Water-Truck. Patrick Lane. NeAC
You're going into play? An instant more. To a Baseball. *Unknown.* LiSp
You're Going to Reap Just What You Sow. *Unknown.* AmFP
You're in my mind. To My Wife. James Forsyth. WaP
You're in the Army Now, *with music. Unknown.* BLSo
You're kind to women, children, worms. Samuel Hoffenstein. *Fr.* Poems in Praise of Practically Nothing. InMe
You're my friend/ I was the man the Duke spoke to. The Flight of the Duchess. Robert Browning. VLP
You're not alone when you are still alone. Idea, XI. Michael Drayton. TrGrPo
You're not supposed to roast a ghost. The Haunted Oven. X. J. Kennedy. WSC
You're Not the Only Pebble on the Beach, *with music.* Harry Braisted. FSN
You're Nothing but a Spanish Colored Kid. Felipe Luciano. PoBA
You're ravishing and, plain to see. To His Girl. Martial, *tr. by* Louis Untermeyer. UnTE
You're right. In the Library. Michael Patrick Hearn. NTCP
You're sickly pale—a crooked root. The Measuring. Jared Carter. AMV-80
You're Sorry, Your Mother Is Crazy, & I'm a Chinese Shiksa. Deborah Lee. BrSi
You're starting, my boy, on life's journey. *See* You've started today on life's journey.
You're sweating it out, no wonder you freeze. The Puritan Hacking Away at Oak. Todd Gitlin. AMV-80
You're the Flower of My Heart. Richard H. Gerard. *See* Sweet Adeline.
You're the Top. Cole Porter. OBAL; UnPo
You're through—now walking up and down. The Aging Athlete. Neil Weiss. LiSp
You're tired of this old world at last. Zone. Guillaume Apollinaire, *tr. by* Ron Padgett. SOTW
Youre ugly tokyn. *See* Your ugly token.
You're wondering if I'm lonely. Song. Adrienne Rich. PBWP
Youre yën two wol slee me sodeinly. *See* Your eyen two will slay me suddenly.
Your're a mean mistreating mama. Mean Mistreater Mama. *Unknown.* BluL
Yours is the face that the earth turns to me. Love Poem. Kathleen Raine. LiTB; MoAB; MoBrPo; MoPo; NeBP
Yours is the sullen sorrow. Last Words to Miriam. D. H. Lawrence. CoBMV
Yours Truly. Leonard Nathan. AMV-80
Yourself. Jones Very. AA; NePA; NOBA; OxBA; PoEL-4
Youth. Katharine Lee Bates. PGD
Youth. Preston Clark. HBMV
Youth. Virginia Woodward Cloud. AA
Youth. Frances Cornford. ELU; PCP
(Quatrain: "Young Apollo, golden-haired, A.") WhC
Youth, A. Stephen Crane. *See* Youth in Apparel That Glittered, A.
Youth. Bartholomew Griffin. *See* Sonnet: "I have not spent the April of my time."
Youth. "Laurence Hope." WeW
Youth. Langston Hughes. AmFN
Youth. Georgia Douglas Johnson. BANP; PoNe
Youth. Jessie B. Rittenhouse. HBMV
Youth. Blanaid Salkeld. OxBI
Youth. Richard Shelton. DFF
Youth. Barend Toerien, *tr. fr. Afrikaans by author.* PeSA
Youth. *Unknown.* OBSC
Youth. Robert Wever. *See* In Youth Is Pleasure.
Youth. James Wright. DiL; NaP; NoP
Youth and Age. George Arnold. HBV-1
Youth and Age. Bible, *O.T. Fr.* Ecclesiastes. *See* Remember Now Thy Creator.
Youth and Age. Byron. *See* Stanzas for Music.
Youth and Age. Samuel Taylor Coleridge. BLPL; EnRP; FiP; GTBS; GTBS-P; HBV-1; OBEV; OBNC; OBRV; PoLF
Youth and Age. Mimnermus, *tr. fr. Greek by* John Addington Symonds. AWP
Youth and Age. Shakespeare. *See* Crabbed Age and Youth.
Youth and Age. Earl of Surrey. *See* Laid in My Quiet Bed.
Youth and Age. W. B. Yeats. ELU; FaBoEE
Youth and Age on Beaulieu River, Hants. John Betjeman. ChMP; FaBoTw; MP; TwCP
Youth and Art. Robert Browning. CTC; HBV-1; ViBoPo
Youth and Beauty. Aurelian Townshend. AnAnS-2; GBL; MePo; SeCP
Youth and Cupid. Elizabeth I, Queen of England. *See* When I Was Fair and Young.
Youth and Love. John Gay. *Fr.* The Beggar's Opera, II, i. NOBE
(Song: "Youth's the season made for joys.") OBEC
(Youth's the Season.) WiR
Youth and Maidenhood. Sarah Williams. OBVV
Youth and Maturity. Fulke Greville. *Fr.* Caelica. OBSC
("Nurse-life wheat, within his green[e] husk[e] growing, The.") AAS; EnRePo; NCEP
(Sonnet: "Nurse-life wheat within his green husk growing, The.") JCP
Youth Dreams, The. Rainer Maria Rilke, *tr. fr. German by* Ludwig Lewisohn. AWP; TrJP
Youth gone, and beauty gone if ever there. Christina Rossetti. *Fr.* Monna Innominata. GBL; OBNC; ViBoPo
Youth hath many charms. Youth and Age. George Arnold. HBV-1
Youth in Apparel That Glittered, A. Stephen Crane. The Black Riders, XXVII. LiTA; NePA
(Youth, A.) MoAmPo
Youth in Arms, *sel.* Harold Monro.
Carrion, IV. MMA
Youth is conservative. A Human Instinct. Christopher Morley. *Fr.* Translations from the Chinese. EvOK
Youth Mowing, A. D. H. Lawrence. MoAB; MoBrPo; NoAM; TrGrPo
Youth of a Poet, The. James Beattie. *Fr.* The Minstrel; or, The Progress of Genius, I. NOEC
Youth of my heart, my beloved one. Love Song to King Shu-Suen. Kubatum, *tr. by* Thorkild Jacobsen. WPOW
Youth of Nature, The: Wordsworth's Country, *sel.* Matthew Arnold.
"Raised are the dripping oars." FaBoPP
Youth one day in a garden fair, A. The Story of the Rose. "Alice." FSN
Youth rambles on life's arid mount. The Progress of Poesy. Matthew Arnold. PP; VLP
Youth Sings a Song of Rosebuds. Countee Cullen. BANP; PoLF; PoNe
Youth there was, Elpenor was he nam'd, A. Homer, *tr. by* Pope. *Fr.* The Odyssey, X. OBVE
Youth walks up to the white horse, The. The White Horse. D. H. Lawrence. SOTW
Youth with the Red-gold Hair, The. Edith Sitwell. FaBoTw; MoVE
Youth worries all night long about whether he can, A. Tumbalalaika. *Tr. fr. Yiddish.* FSW
Youthful Age. Thomas Stanley, *after the Greek of* Anacreon. AWP
(Young Men Dancing.) OBVE
Youthful passion seeps through my mind. Tomb. David Semah, *tr. by* Yoffee Berkovitz. VWA
Youth's Antiphony. Dante Gabriel Rossetti. The House of Life, XIII. VLP
Youth's bright palace. Lament. Denis Florence MacCarthy. OBVV
Youth's Progress. John Updike. FiBHP
Youth's Spring-Tribute. Dante Gabriel Rossetti. The House of Life, XIV. VLP
Youth's Thankfulness. Edgar Daniel Kramer. PGD
Youth's the season made for joys. Youth and Love [*or* Song]. John Gay. *Fr.* The Beggar's Opera, II, i. NOBE; OBEC; WiR
You've already learned heels down. The Limits of Equitation. Barbara Winder. AMV-81
You've asked me what the lobster is weaving there. Enigmas. Pablo Neruda, *tr. by* Robert Bly. NU
You've Been a Good Old Wagon, but You've Done Broke Down. Ben Harney. OBAL
You've been a wanderer, you! The Quest. Gladys Cromwell. HBMV
You've come into my life like frost heaves. Frost Heaves. Michael Dorris. AMV-80
You've got halfway, and found it rather hard. Three Girls on a Buttress. Eilidh Nisbet. PoSH
You've got nice knees. Love Song. Gavin Ewart. OxBTC

You've Got to Be Taught. Oscar Hammerstein II. AmFN
You've got to speculate. Financial Wisdom. *Unknown.* FaBoUs
You've gotten in through the transom. To a Child Trapped in a Barber Shop. Philip Levine. InPK; NoAM; NOBA; PAI; TAP; VGW
"You've had your operation, Mrs. Brown." The Other Side. Roy Fuller. OxBC
You've had your problems. To Bert Campaneris. Tom Clark. LiSp
You've heard how a green thumb. My Aunt. Ted Hughes. WSC
You've heard of Slattery's light dragoons. O'Duffy's Ironsides. "Tom Moore, Jr." OnYI
You've heard of the Gresford disaster. The Gresford Disaster. *Unknown.* GBP; OBET
You've heard of the Turks and the Greeks. The Battle of Navarino. *Unknown.* CoMu
You've lost your religion, the Rabbi said. Debate with the Rabbi. Howard Nemerov. PoPl
You've made yourself in clay. Poem for a Son. Heather Cadsby. AMV-80
You've never heard the voice of God? The Voice of God. Katherine R. Barnard. BLRP; WBLP
You've plucked a curlew, drawn a hen. On an Island. J. M. Synge. BIrV; MoBrPo; OBVV
You've read of several kinds of cat. The Ad-dressing of Cats. T. S. Eliot. FM
You've seen a pair of faithful lovers die. Epilogue to "Mithridates, King of Pontus." Dryden. OAEP
You've seen a strawberry. Nevertheless. Marianne Moore. CMoP; MoAB; OxBA; SeCeV; SoSe
You've seen those old movies. The Late Show. William Heyen. GLGT
You've started today [*or* You're starting, my boy] on life's journey. Have Courage, My Boy, to Say No! L. M. Hilton. STF; WTO
You've told me, Maro, whilst you live. Martial, *tr. fr. Latin by* F. Lewis. NIP
You've toughed it out pretty well, old Body, done. Remarks of Soul to Body. Robert Penn Warren. NAs
Ypres. Laurence Binyon. MMA
Ys yt possyble. *See* Is it possible.
Yt fell abowght the Lamasse tyde. The Battle of Otterburn [*or* Oterborne]. *Unknown.* ESPB; OxBS
Yucca clump, The/ is blooming. The Yucca Moth. A. R. Ammons. NOBA
Yucca in the Moonlight. Glen Ward Dresbach. BPAW
Yucca Is Yellowing. William Haskel Simpson. BPAW
Yucca Moth, The. A. R. Ammons. NOBA
Yugoslav Cemetery. Celeste Turner Wright. DFF; WPE
Yuh Lookin Good. Carolyn M. Rodgers. BPo
Yule Days, The. *Unknown.* ChTr; GBP
Yule Log, The. William Hamilton Hayne. AA
Yule Log. Robert Herrick. *See* Ceremonies for Christmas.
Yule-log sparkled keen with frost, The. Tennyson. *Fr.* In Memoriam A. H. H., LXXVIII. TRV
Yule's Come, and Yule's Gane. *Unknown.* GBP
Yuma. Charles Henry Phelps. AA
Yung Wind, *sels.* Confucius, *tr. fr. Chinese by* Ezra Pound. CTC
  Baroness Mu Impeded in Her Wish to Help Famine Victims in Wei.
  Sans Equity and sans Poise.
Yussouf. James Russell Lowell. BeLS; BLPA; BLPL; FaBoBe
Yves Tanguy. David Gascoyne. EAS

Z

Z Is for Zoroaster. Eleanor Farjeon. WSC
Z, Y, X, and W, V. *Unknown.* OxNR
Zachary Zed. James Reeves. QQQ
Zack Bumstead uster flosserfize. A Philosopher. Sam Walter Foss. OBAL
Zack's eyes can't. Washing My Son. Jonathan Holden. AMV-81
Zagonyi. George Henry Boker. PAH
Zalinka. Tom MacInnes. PeCV
Zalka Peetruza. Ray Garfield Dandridge. BANP; PoBA
Zambra Dance, The. Dryden. *See* Beneath a Myrtle Shade.
Zapata & the Landlord. Alfred B. Spellman. NNP; PoBA
Zaph Describes the Haunts of Malzah. Charles Heavysege. *Fr.* Saul. OBCV
Zapolya, *sel.* Samuel Taylor Coleridge.
  Glycine's Song. CH; OBEV; PoPl
  (Song: "Sunny shaft did I behold, A.") PoSC; PBBP
Zarian was saying: Florence is youth. A Water-Colour of Venice. Lawrence Durrell. MoBrPo
Zayde, I drove all night to get here. A Place to Live. Martin Grossman. AMV-80
Zaydee. Philip Levine. NNaP; VWA
Zeal and Love. Cardinal Newman. TW
Zeal of Jehu, The. Cardinal Newman. OBRV
Zealless Xylographer, The. Mary Mapes Dodge. OBAL
Zealot without a Face. Charles Dobzynski, *tr. fr. French by* Anita Barrows. VWA
Zealots of Yearning. David Rokeah, *tr. fr. Hebrew by* I. M. Lask. TrJP
Zealous lock-smith dyed [*or* died] of late, A. On a Puritanicall Lock-Smith. William Camden. FaBoEE; ShM; WhC
Zealous Puritan, The. *Unknown.* OBS
Zebaoth. Else Lasker-Schüler, *tr. fr. German by* Jethro Bithell. TrJP
Zebra. "Isak Dinesen." GoJo; RFM
Zebra. William Jay Smith. TiPo
Zebra. Judith Thurman. RHPC
Zebra. *Unknown, tr. fr. Hottentot.* PeSA
Zebra, born both black and white, The. The Miscegenous Zebra. Roland Young. BoAnP
Zebra Dun, The, *diff. versions.* *Unknown.* AmFP; CoSo, *with music*; FSW; PH; ViBoFo
Zebra Stallion. *Unknown, tr. fr. Hottentot.* PeSA
Zebras, The. Roy Campbell. LiTB; MoBrPo; PoPle; PrIm; ViBoPo
Zechariah, *sels.* Bible, *O.T.*
  I Return unto Zion, VIII: 3-5. TrJP
  Open Thy Doors, O Lebanon, XI: 1-14. AWP
Zeenty, peenty, heathery, mithery. Counting-out Rhyme. *Unknown.* ChTr; GBP
Zeimbekiko. Robin Magowan. EAS
Zeke. L. A. G. Strong. MoBrPo
'Zekiel Saw de Wheel. *Unknown.* *See* Ezekiel Saw the Wheel.
Zek'l Weep, *with music.* *Unknown.* AS
Zelanto, the Fountain of Fame, *sel.* Anthony Munday.
  Love. OBSC
Zen Archer, The. James Kirkup. EaLo
Zen Buddhism and Psychoanalysis/ Psychoanalysis and Zen Buddhism. Jackson MacLow. PoM
Zen of Housework, The. Al Zolynas. LTB
Zen Poems, after Shinkichi Takahashi. Lucien Stryk. FAZ
  Afternoon.
  Downy Hair.
Zennor. Anne Ridler. MoVE
Zenocrate, lovelier than the love of Jove. Tamburlaine to Zenocrate. Christopher Marlowe. *Fr.* Tamburlaine the Great. WHA
Zepheria, *sel.* *Unknown.*
  "When we in kind embracements had agre'd." AAS
Zephyr. *Unknown.* TDH
Zephyr. Eugene Fitch Ware. PoLF
Zeppelin. Andrew Glaze. WeW
Zeppelins. Nancy Cunard. SUMH
Zermatt: To the Matterhorn. Thomas Hardy. OBNC
Zero/ zero/ zero/ the museum of modern art. The Story of the Zeros. Victor Hernandez Cruz. PoBA
Zest of Life, The. Henry van Dyke. *See* Let Me But Live from Year to Year.
Zeus,/ Brazen-thunder-hurler. The Faun Sees Snow for the First Time. Richard Aldington. MoBrPo
Zeus,—by what name soe'er. Hymn to Zeus. Aeschylus, *tr. by* Gilbert Murray. *Fr.* Agamemnon. WGRP
Zeus lies in Ceres' bosom. Cantos, LXXXI. Ezra Pound. FaBoMo; NoAM; NOBA; VGW
Zeus was once overheard to shout at Hera. The Weather of Olympus. Robert Graves. FaBoEE
Zeyde. Roberta Metz. AMV-81
Zig-zag bee, *zzz* and *zzz*-ing, came, A. The Bee. John Fandel. GoYe
Zillebeke Brook. Edmund Blunden. MMA
Zimbabwe. F. D. Sinclair. PeSA
Zimmer and His Turtle Sink the House. Paul Zimmer. Psk
Zimmer Drunk and Alone, Dreaming of Old Football Games. Paul Zimmer. MAT
Zimmer Envying Elephants. Paul Zimmer. GP
Zimmer in Fall. Paul Zimmer. PPJ
Zimmer in Grade School. Paul Zimmer. GP
Zimmer's Hard Dream. Paul Zimmer. GP
Zimmer's Head Thudding against the Blackboard. Paul Zimmer. PCP
Zimmer's Last Gig. Paul Zimmer. AMV-80
Zimri ("In the first rank of these did Zimri stand"). Dryden. *Fr.* Absalom and Achitophel, Pt. I. SeCePo
  ("In the first rank of these did Zimri stand.") HAP; ViBoPo
Zimri ("Some of their chiefs were princes of the land"). Dryden. *Fr.* Absalom and Achitophel, Pt. I. AWP
  ("Some of their chiefs were princes of the land.") EBEV; SCV

Zimri: The Duke of Buckingham ("A numerous host of dreaming saints succeed"). Dryden. *Fr.* Absalom and Achitophel, Pt. I. NOBE; OBSV
(Duke of Buckingham, The.) FaBoEn
Zinnias. Valerie Worth. NTCP
Zinnias, ochre, orange, chrome and amber, The. Transition. May Sarton. NePoAm
Zinnias, stout and stiff. Zinnias. Valerie Worth. NTCP
Zion, or the City of God. John Newton. *See* Glorious Things of Thee Are Spoken.
Zion, wilt thou not ask if peace's wing. Ode to Zion. Judah Halevi, *tr. by* Nina Davis Salaman. TrJP
Zionist Marching Song. Naphtali Herz Imber, *tr. fr. Hebrew by* Israel Zangwill. TrJP
Zion's Sons and Daughters. *Unknown.* AmFP
Zip Coon. *Unknown.* PSoN, *with music*; YaD
(Old Zip Coon, *with music, at. to* Bob Farrell.) TrAS
Zippora Returns to Moses at Rephidim. Rose Drachler. VWA
Zito the Magician. Miroslav Holub, *tr. fr. Czech by* Ian Milner *and* George Theiner. SUW
Ziz, The. John Hollander. VWA
Zizi's Lament. Gregory Corso. NeAP; VGW
Zlotchev, My Home. Moishe Leib Halpern, *tr. fr. Yiddish by* Richard J. Fein. VWA
Zobo Bird, The. Frank A. Collymore. AmMo; GoJo
Zodiac, The, *sel.* James Dickey.
"Tenderness, ache on me, and lay your neck." TAP
Zodiac Rhyme, The. *Unknown.* GBP
Zoe and the Ghosts. Dieter Weslowski. PPJ
Zog Nit Keynmol (Tell Us No More). *Unknown, tr. fr. Yiddish.* FSW
Zohara. Jack Hirschman. VWA
Zola. E. A. Robinson. MoVE; NePA; OxBA
Zolgotz. *Unknown.* AmFP
Zollicoffer. Henry Lynden Flash. PAH
Zollverein was hardly neutral, The. One recalls. Philatelic Lessons: The German Collection. Lawrence P. Spingarn. NYBP
Zone. Guillaume Apollinaire, *tr. fr. French by* Ron Padgett. SOTW
Zone. Louise Bogan. PoCh; WPE
Zone of Death. William Everson. VGW
Zong, A: "O Jenny, don't sobby! vor I shall be true." William Barnes. BoLoP
Zong Belegt Baatar. *Mongol Oral Tradition, tr. by* C. R. Bawden. WTO
Zonnebeke Road, The. Edmund Blunden. MMA; OBWP
Zoo, The. John Logan. LCAP
Zoo, The. Gilbert Sorrentino. NeAP
Zoo, The. Humbert Wolfe. MoShBr
Zoo Dream. David Barker. GP
Zoo in the City, The. Sara Van Alystyne Allen. GoYe
Zoo of You, The. Arthur Freeman. ErPo
Zoo You Too! Ted Joans. GP
Zooming across the sky. Up in the Air. James S. Tippett. SoPo; SUS; TiPo
Zophiël, *sels.* Maria Gowen Brooks. AA
Palace of the Gnomes.
Respite, The.
Zoroaster Devoutly Questions Ormazd. *At. to* Zoroaster. *See* Sacred Book, The.
Zounds, gramercy, and rootity-toot! Robin Hood. Phyllis McGinley. *Fr.* Speaking of Television. OBSV
Zounds! how the price went flashing through. Israel Freyer's Bid for Gold. Edmund Clarence Stedman. PAH
Zu fragmentarisch ist Welt und Leben. Heine. *See* This World and This Life Are So Scattered, They Try Me.
Zulu Girl, The. Roy Campbell. ChMP; MoVE; OBMV; PoPl
Zummer Stream. William Barnes. BoNaP
Zummer Thoughts in Winter Time. William Barnes. VLP
Zun a-Lighten Eyes a-Shut, The. William Barnes. VLP
Zun-zet. William Barnes. PoEL-4
Zürich, zum Storchem. Paul Celan, *tr. fr. German by* Joachim Neugroschel. VWA

AUTHOR INDEX

"A., F.P." *See* **Adams, Franklin Pierce**
"A.K." *See* **"K., A."**
"A.P." *See* **"P., A."**
"A.R.G." *See* **"G., A.R."**
"A.W." *See* **"W., A."**
Aal, Katharyn Machan
Ants.
He says he wrote by moonlight.
Aaronson, Leonard [*or* Lazarus]
Homeward Journey, The.
Pesci Misti.
Abba Arika. *See* **Rab.**
Abbe, George
Horizon Thong.
New York City.
Passer, The.
Abbey, Henry
Donald.
Faith's Vista.
In Memory of General Grant.
What Do We Plant [When We Plant the Tree].
Winter Days.
Abbott, Anthony S.
Out of Mourning.
Abbott, Clifton
Just Keep On.
Abbott, Steve
Reading Today's Newspaper.
Abbott, Wenonah Stevens
Soul's Soliloquy, A.
Abd-ar-Rahman I
Palm Tree, The.
À Beckett, Gilbert Abbott
Holiday Task, A.
Abeita, Louise. *See* **"E-Yeh-Shure'"**
Abelard, Peter
David's Lament for Jonathan.
Hymn for the Close of the Week.
Abenatar Melo, David
Thanksgiving.
Abercrombie, Lascelles
All Last Night.
Balkis.
Ceremonial Ode Intended for a University.
Emblems of Love, *sels.*
Epilogue: "What shall we do for Love these days?"
Epitaph: "Sir, you should [*or* shall] notice me: I am the Man."
Fear, The.
Fools' Adventure, The, *sel.*
Hope and Despair.
Hymn to Love.
Judith, *sel.*
Mary and the Bramble.
Seeker, The.
Small Fountains.
Song: "Balkis was in her marble town."
Stream's Song, The.
Vashti, *sel.*
Witchcraft: New Style.
Woman's Beauty.
Aberg, William
Dividing the Field.
Harvest, The.
Poem for John My Brother.
Sleepers, The.
Weight, The.
Abhau, Elliot
Indecision Means Flexibility.
Abrahams, Peter
Lonely Road.
Me, Colored.
Tell Freedom, *sel.*
Abrahams, William
In the Henry James Country.
Museum, The.
Poem in Time of War.
Séance.
Abramovitch, Henry
Psalm of the Jealous God.
Abrams, Robert J.
Two Poems.
Abse, Dannie
After the Release of Ezra Pound.
Angels.
Down the M4.
Duality.
Florida.
Inscription on the Flyleaf of a Bible.
Letter to Alex Comfort.
Mountaineers, The.
Near the Border of Insanities.
Pantomime Diseases.
Peachstone.
Poem and Message.
Portrait of a Marriage.
Public Library.
Second Coming, The.
Song for Dov Shamir.
Stethoscope, The.
Tales of Shatz.
Verses at Night.
Victim of Aulis, The.
Watching a Cloud.
Words Spoken Alone.
Absher, Tom
Hunting with My Father.
Abu al-Qasim al-Shabbi
In the Shadow of the Valley of Death.
Abu Bakr (of Marrakesh)
Sword, The.
Abu Dharr
Oranges, The.
Abu Dolama
Humorous Verse.
Abu Khalid, Fawziyya
Mother's Inheritance.
Abu-l-Ala al-Maarri
Aweary Am I.
Abu Nuwas
Escape, An.
Abutsu the Nun
Diary of the Waning Moon, The, *sel.*
Abu Zakariya
Bubbling Wine.
Acharya, Ananda
My Faith.
Realization.
Ackerley, Joe Randolph
After the Blitz, 1941.
Ackerman, Diane
Fine, a Private Place, A.
Ice Dragons.
In the Silks.
Ode to the Alien.
Patrick Ewing Takes a Foul Shot.
St. Augustine Contemplating the Bust of Einstein.
Space Shuttle.
Spiders.
Ackerson, Duane
Rip the Apple Seller Awakes; or, After 50 Years, the Great Depression (1929–79) Reawakens.
When Daddy Died.
Acorn, Milton
Blackfish Poem.
Fights, The.
Ghostly Story.
I'd Like to Mark Myself.
I've Gone and Stained with the Color of Love.
I've Tasted My Blood.
Knowing I Live in a Dark Age.
Lover That I Hope You Are.
Monument.
Offshore Breeze.
On Saint-Urbain Street.
Poem for a Singer.
Poem in June.
Saint-Henri Spring.
You Growing.
Acton, Ellen M. V.
Exodus from a Renaissance Gallery.
"Ada."
Lines: "From fair Jamaica's fertile plains."
Lines, Suggested on Reading "An Appeal to Christian Women of the South."
Oh, when this earthly tenement.
To the Memory of J. Horace Kimball.
Adaios
Epigram: "If you see someone beautiful."
Adair, Ivan
Real Presence: "Not on an Altar shall mine eyes behold Thee."
Adali-Mortti, G.
Palm Leaves of Childhood.
Adam, Helen
House o' the Mirror, The.
I Love My Love.
Adame, Leonard
Black and White.
Song for My Little Friends.
Adam of St. Victor
Hail, Mother of the Savior.
Adams, Anna
Her Dancing Days.
Unrecorded Speech.
Adams, Arthur Henry
Australian, The.
Adams, Bill (Bertram Martin Adams)
Homeward Bound, The.
Peg-Leg's Fiddle.
Shore Roads of April.
Stowaway.
Adams, Bob, David Lewis *and* **Paul Schindler.** *See* **Lewis, David, Paul Schindler** *and* Bob Adams
Adams, Charles Follen ("Yawcob Strauss")
John Barley-Corn, My Foe.
Misplaced Sympathy.
My Infundibuliform Hat.
Prevalent Poetry.
Repartée.
To Bary Jade.
Yaw, Dot Is So!
Yawcob Strauss.
Adams, Elijah
Ashland Tragedy, The, 2 *versions.*
Adams, Francis Lauderdale
Evening Hymn in the Hovels.
Hagar.

Jesus.
To the Christians.
William Wallace.
Adams, Franklin Pierce ("F.P.A.")
Ad Persephonen.
Ballade of Schopenhauer's Philosophy.
Baseball's Sad Lexicon.
Christopher Columbus.
Composed in the Composing Room.
De Senectute.
Double Standard, The.
February 14, 22 B.C.
Garland of Recital Programs, A.
Georgie Porgie.
Happy Lifetime to You.
If.
Life.
Lines Where Beauty Lingers.
Maud Muller Mutatur.
Poetry and Thoughts on Same.
Rarae Aves.
Regarding (1) the U. S. and (2) New York.
Rich Man, The.
Song: "Don't Tell Me What You Dreamt Last Night."
Such Stuff as Dreams.
Those Two Boys.
Thoughts on the Cosmos.
To a Lady.
To a Lady Troubled by Insomnia.
To a Thesaurus.
To the Polyandrous Lydia.
Tonight.
Translated Way, The.
Us Potes.
Adams, Georgia B.
Family Altar, The.
Helping Hand, A.
Hour of Prayer, The.
Secret Place of Prayer, The.
Thank Thee, Lord.
Adams, Georgine M.
"That Did in Luve So Lively Write."
Adams, Helen Baker
No Doubt.
Adams, Henry
Prayer to the Virgin of Chartres.
Adams, James Barton
At a Cowboy Dance.
Billy, He's in Trouble.
Cowboy's Life, The, *at.*
Dust of the Overland Trail, The.
Ruin of Bobtail Bend, The.
Tough Cuss from Bitter Creek, A.
Adams, Jean
Dream, or the Type of the Rising Sun, A.
Adams, John Coleman
We Praise Thee, God, for Harvests Earned, *with music.*
Adams, John G.
Heaven Is Here, *with music.*
Adams, John Quincy
Lip and the Heart, The.
Send Forth, O God, Thy Light and Truth, *with music.*
Wants of Man, The.
Adams, Léonie
Alas, Kind Element.
April Mortality.
Bell Tower.
Caryatid.
Counsel to Unreason.
Country Summer.
Death and the Lady.
Early Waking.
Figurehead, The.
Font in the Forest, The.
Ghostly Tree.
Grapes Making.
Gull Goes Up, A.
Home-coming.
Horn, The.
Kingdom of Heaven.
Light at Equinox.
Lullaby: "Hush, lullay."
Mount, The.
Night-Piece.
People in the Park, The.
Reminder, The.
River in the Meadows, The.
Runner with the Lots, The.
Song from a Country Fair.
Sundown.
This Measure.
Those Not Elect.
Thought's End.
Twilit Revelation.
With all the drifting race of men.
Words for the Raker of Leaves.
Adams, Marguerite Janvrin
They Who Possess the Sea.
Adams, Mary Mathews
Dead Love.
Adams, Nehemiah
Saints in Glory, We Together, *with music.*
Adams, Oscar Fay
At Lincoln.
On a Grave in Christchurch, Hants.
Adams, Perseus
Murder Trial, The.
My Grandmother.
Woman and the Aloe, The.
Adams, Samuel Hopkins
Centipede, The.
Adams, Sarah Flower
Mourners Came at Break of Day, The.
Nearer, My God, to Thee.
Adams, William Henry Davenport
Last Voyage of the Fairies, The.
Adamson, Robert
Action Would Kill It/A Gamble.
My House.
Ribbon-Fish, The.
Sail Away.
Sonnet to Be Written from Prison.
Things Going out of My Life.
Adcock, Arthur St. John
By Deputy.
Sam.
Adcock, Betty
Poetry Workshop in a Reform School.
Sixth Day, The.
Adcock, Fleur
Note on Propertius 1.5.
Water Below, The.
Addiego, John
Berkeley Pier, The.
Addison, Joseph
Blenheim.
Campaign, The, *sel.*
Cato, *sel.*
Cato's Soliloquy.
How Are Thy Servants Blest.
Hymn: "Spacious firmament on high, The."
Hymn: "When all thy mercies, O my God."
Hymn to the Creation.
Italy and Britain.
Letter from Italy [to the Right Honourable Charles Lord Halifax], A.
Ode: "How are thy servants blest, O Lord!"
Pastoral Hymn.
Play-House, The.
Poem to His Grace the Duke of Marlborough, A.
Song: "Oh the charming month of May!"
Spacious Firmament on High, The.
To a Rogue.
When All Thy Mercies.
Addison, Medora C. (Mrs. Charles Read Nutter)
Mountain Creed.
Some Day.
Spell, The.
Addison, William
Shadows among the Ettrick Hills.
Addleshaw, Percy ("Percy Hemingway")
Happy Wanderer, The.
Ade, George
Il Janitoro.
Microbe's Serenade, The.
R-E-M-O-R-S-E.
Adeane, Louis
Four Poems for April.
Night Loves Us, The.
Poem on Hampstead Heath.
Adee, Lucy A. K.
Our Lady of Good Voyage.
Adeler," , "Max (Charles Heber Clark)
In Memoriam.
Mr. Slimmer's Funeral Verses for the *Morning Argus.*
Obituary.
Out of the Hurly-Burly.
Sacred to the Memory of Maria (to Say Nothing of Jane and Martha) Sparks.
We Have Lost Our Little Hanner.
Adkin, Will S.
If I Only Was the Fellow.
Just Try to Be the Fellow That Your Mother Thinks You Are.
Adler, Felix
Hail! the Glorious Golden City.
Adler, Friedrich
By the Waterfall.
Adler, Hans
Protect Me.
Ulster.
Adler, Lucile
Travel[l]ing Out, The.
Adler, Mortimer J.
Fearless, The.
Adnan, Etel
Beirut-Hell Express, The, *sel.*
Adoff, Arnold
Chocolate Chocolate.
Dry July.
My Mouth.
Today Is Sun.
"Æ" (George William Russell)
Ancient.
Babylon.
By the Margin of the Great Deep.
Carrowmore.
Chivalry.
Cities, The.
City, The.
Continuity.
Dark Rapture.
Desire.
Dust.
Epilogue: "Well, when all is said and done."
Exiles.
Farewell, A: "I go down from the hill in gladness."
Frolic.
Garden of God, The.
Gates of Dreamland, The.
Gay, The.
Germinal.
Gift, The.
Great Breath, The.
Holy Hill, A.
Immortality.
Leader, A.
Lonely, The.
Man to the Angel, The.
Memory of Earth, A.
Mountain Wind, A.
New York.
On Behalf of Some Irishmen Not Followers of Tradition.
Outcast, The.
Pain.
Place of Rest, The.
Prisoner, A.
Reconciliation.
Refuge.

Salutation.
Secret, The.
Secret Love, The.
Self-Discipline.
Terence MacSwiney.
Tragedy.
Truth.
Twilight of Earth, The.
Unknown God, The.
When.
Winds of Eros.

Aeschylus
Chorus: "Great Fortune is an hungry thing."
God of War, The.
Hymn to Zeus.
Lament for the Two Brothers Slain by Each Other's Hand.
Persians, The, *sel.*
Prometheus Bound.
Salamis.
Seven against Thebes, The, *sel.*
Signal Fire, The.

Aesop (6th century B.C.
Ass in the Lion's Skin, The ("An ass put on a lion's skin and went").
Mountain in Labor, The.
Shepherd-Boy and the Wolf, The.
Swan and the Goose, The.
Vine and the Goat, The.

Agate, James
Eumenides at Home, The.

Agathias Scholasticus
Dialogue.
Not Such Your Burden.
Plutarch.
Rhodanthe.

Agee, James
Description of Elysium.
Happy Hen, The.
In Heavy Mind.
In Memory of My Father.
Lyric: "From now on kill America out of your mind."
Lyrics, *sels.*
Millions Are Learning How.
Permit Me Voyage.
Rapid Transit.
Red Sea.
Song with Words.
Sonnets, *sels.*
Sunday: Outskirts of Knoxville, Tennessee.
Temperance Note: and Weather Prophecy.
Two Songs on the Economy of Abundance.

Agnew, Edith
Ambition.
Let me tell to you the story.
Progress.
Summer Comes.

Agnew, Marjorie L.
On Going Home.

"Agricola"
Daventry Wonder, The.

Aguila, Pancho
Birthing: 2000.
Nuclear Racial Lockdowns.
St. Valentine.
Turnaround for Higherground, The.
Woman Guard.

Agustini, Delmira
Blindness.
From Far Away.

Aharoni, Ada
To a Captain in Sinai.

Ahmed-ud-Din, Feroz
Cinderella.

Ai (Florence Anthony)
Abortion.
Almost Grown.
Anniversary, The.
Child Beater.
Conversation.
Cuba, 1962.
Everything: Eloy, Arizona, 1956.
Expectant Father, The.
Guadalajara Hospital.
Hangman.
Hitchhiker, The.
I Have Got to Stop Loving You.
Ice.
Immortality.
Kid, The.
Mortician's Twelve-year-old Son, The.
One Man Down.
Pentecost.
She Didn't Even Wave.
Sweet, The.
29 (A Dream in Two Parts).
Twenty-Year Marriage.
Why Can't I Leave You?
Winter in Another Country.
Woman.
Woman to Man.

Aidé, Hamilton
Remember or Forget.
When We Are Parted.

Aidoo, Ama Ata
Cornfields in Accra.

Aig-Imoukhuede, Frank
One Wife for One Man.

Aiken, Conrad
A Is for Alpha: Alpha Is for A.
Accomplices, The.
All Lovely Things.
And in the Hanging Gardens.
Annihilation.
At a Concert of Music.
Awakening, The.
Beloved, Let Us Once More Praise the Rain.
Bend as the bow bends, and let fly the shaft.
Blind Date.
Bread and Music.
But How It Came from Earth.
Calyx of the Oboe Breaks, The.
Carver, The.
Cloister.
Crab, The.
Dear Uncle Stranger.
Discordants, *sels.*
Doctors' Row.
Elder Tree.
Evening Song of Senlin.
Evensong.
Farewell Voyaging World!
First note, simple, The; the second note, distinct.
Habeas Corpus Blues, The.
Hatteras Calling.
Herman Melville.
House of Dust, The, *sel.*
If Man, That Angel of Bright Conciousness.
Improvisations: Light and Snow, *sel.*
Keep in the Heart the Journal Nature Keeps.
Kid, The, *sels.*
Letter from Li Po, A, *sel.*
Limberick.
Limerick: "Animula vagula blandula."
Limerick: "It's time to make love: douse the glim."
Limerick: "On the deck of a ship called the Masm."
Limerick: "There once was a wonderful wizard."
Lovers, The.
Mandrill, The.
Mayflower.
Miracles.
Morning Dialogue.
Morning Song.
Morning Song of [*or* from] Senlin.
Multitudes Turn in Darkness.
Music.
Music I Heard [with You].
Nameless Ones, The.
Nocturne of Remembered Spring.
North Infinity Street.
Nothing to Say, You Say?
Nuit Blanche: North End.
Obituary in Bitcherel.
One Star Fell and Another.
Portrait of a Girl.
Portrait of One Dead.
Prelude: "Rimbaud and Verlaine, precious pair of poets."
Prelude: "This is not you? These phrases are not you?"
Prelude XXIX: "What shall we do—what shall we think—what shall we say?"
Prelude: "Woman, Woman, let us say these things to each other."
Prelude: "You went to the verge, you say, and come back safely?"
Preludes for Memnon; or, Preludes to Attitude, *sels.*
Priapus and the Pool, *sels.*
Proem to "The Kid."
Punch, the Immortal Liar, *sel.*
Puppet Dreams, The.
Quarrel, The.
Queen Cleopatra.
Return, The.
Rimbaud and Verlaine, Precious Pair of Poets.
Road, The.
Room, The.
Sea Holly.
Senlin, a Biography, *sels.*
Shaemus.
Sighed a dear little shipboard divinity.
Snowflake on asphodel, clear ice on rose.
Soldier, The, *sels.*
Sound of Breaking.
Sounding, The.
South End.
Stepping Stones, The.
Stone Too Can Pray.
Stood, at the closed door.
Summer.
Systole and Diastole.
Tetélestai.
There once was a wicked young minister.
Things, The.
This Is the Shape of the Leaf.
Three Star Final.
Time Has Come, the Clock Says Time Has Come, The.
Time in the Rock [or, Preludes to Definition], *sels.*
Unknown Soldier, The.
Vampire, The.
Variations, *sel.*
Walk in the Garden, The.
Wars, The.
Watch Long Enough, and You Will See the Leaf.
Wedding, The.
When the Tree Bares.
Who Shapes a Balustrade?
Window, The.
Winter for a moment takes the mind.
You Went to the Verge, You Say, and Came Back Safely?

Aiken, Joan
Down Below.
Fable: "Pity the girl with crystal hair."
Fisherman Writes a Letter to the Mermaid, The.
In the Old House.
John's Song.
Night Landscape.
Rhyme for Night.

Aikin, John
Picturesque; a Fragment.
Tit for Tat; a Tale.

Aikin, Lucy
Beggar Man, The.
Swallow, The.

Ainger, Alfred
On the Triumph of Rationalism.

Ainger, Arthur Campbell
God Is Working His Purpose Out.
Ainslie, Douglas
Stirrup Cup, The.
Ainslie, Hew
Ingle-Side, The.
Willie and Helen.
Ainsworth, Henry
Except the Lord, That He for Us Had Been, *with music.*
Fire in My Meditation Burned, *with music.*
Give Ear, O Heavens, to That Which I Declare, *with music.*
How Long, Jehovah? *with music.*
I Minded God, *with music.*
I Spread Out unto Thee My Hands, *with music.*
In the Distress upon Me, *with music.*
To God Our Strength Shout Joyfully, *with music.*
Unto Jehovah Sing Will I, *with music.*
With All My Heart, Jehovah, I'll Confess, *with music.*
'Aisha bint Ahmad al-Qurtubiyya
I am a lioness.
Ai Shih-te
Human Mind, The.
Aitchison, James
Landscape with Lapwings.
Ajukutooq
Song of Sukkaartik, the Assistant Spirit.
Akahito (Yamabe no Akahito)
I passed by the beach.
I wish I were close.
Mists rise over, The.
Akazome Emon
I, who cut off my sorrows.
In my heart's depth.
Akenside, Mark
Against Suspicion, *sel.*
Amoret.
Benevolence.
Complaint, The.
Created Universe, The.
Creative Process, The.
Early Influences.
England, Unprepared for War.
For a Grotto.
For a Statue of Chaucer at Woodstock.
Hymn to Science.
Inscription: "Whoe'er thou art whose path in summer lies."
Inscription: "Ye powers unseen, to whom the bards of Greece."
Inscription for a Grotto.
Invocation to the Genius of Greece.
Love of Nature.
Nature.
Nature's Influence on Man.
Nightingale, The.
Ode: To the Evening Star.
Ode to the Country Gentlemen of England, An, *sel.*
Ode to the Evening Star.
Pleasures of Imagination, The, *sels.*
Poet, The; a Rhapsody.
Poetic Genius.
Poets.
Song: "Shape alone let others prize, The."
That Delightful Time.
To the Evening Star.
Akerman, John Yonge
Harnet and the Bittle, a Wiltshire Tale, The ("A harnet zet in a hollur tree").
Akers, Elizabeth. *See* **Allen, Elizabeth Akers**
Akesson, Sonja
Autobiography.
Ears.
Evening Walk.
Akhenaton (Amenhotep IV)
Hymn to the Sun, The.
Thy Rising Is Beautiful.
Akhmadulina, Bella
At Night.
Autumn.
Bride, The.
Dream, A.
Fifteen Boys, or Perhaps Even More.
Goodbye.
In the Emptied Rest Home.
Names of Georgian Women, The.
Silence.
Sleepwalkers.
Small Aircraft.
Sound of Rain, The.
Volcanoes.
Winter.
Words Spoken by Pasternak during a Bombing.
Akhmatova, "Anna (Anna Andreyevna Gorenko)
Alone.
Each Day Is Anxious.
Everything Is Plundered.
Grey-eyed King, The.
Hands clenched under my shawl.
He loved three things in life.
How can you look at the Neva.
I taught myself to live simply and wisely.
I wrung my hands under my dark veil.
Land not mine, still, A.
Lot's Wife.
Requiem: "No, not far beneath some foreign sky then."
Summer Garden.
Tashkent Breaks into Bloom.
There is in human closeness a sacred boundary.
What's worse than this past century?
Your lynx-eyes, Asia.
Akhnaton. *See* **Akhenaton**
Akhyaliyya, Laila
Camel.
Laila Boasting.
Lamenting Tauba.
Akiko, Yosano. *See* **Yosano Akiko**
Akin, Gülten
Ellas and the Statues.
Akins, Zoë
Conquered.
First Rain.
I Am the Wind.
Norah.
Rain, Rain.
This Is My Hour.
Wanderer, The.
Akjartoq
Old Woman's Song, An.
Remembering.
Al-Aswad, Son of Ya'fur
Old Age.
Alabaster, William
Beehould a cluster to itt selfe a vine.
Haile gracefull morning of eternall Daye.
Incarnatio Est Maximum Donum Dei.
Jesu, thie love within mee is soe maine.
My soule a world is by Contraccion.
Night, the starlesse night of passion, The.
Now that the midd day heate doth scorch my shame.
O starry temple of unvalted space.
On the Reed of Our Lord's Passion.
Sonnet: "By what glass of resemblance may we see."
Sonnet: "God and man, though in this amphitheatre."
Sonnet: "Jesus is born. Peace, such high words forbear."
Sonnet: "Like as the fountain of all light created."
Sunne begins uppon my heart to shine, The.
Upon the Crucifix.
Upon the Ensignes of Christes Crucifyinge.
Way feare with thy projectes, noe false fyre, A.
What meaneth this, that Christ an hymne did singe.
When without tears I looke on Christ, I see.
Alasdair, Alisdair MacMhaighstir. *See* **MacDonald, Alexander**
Alba, Nanina
Be Daedalus.
For Malcolm X.
Albee, John
At the Grave of Champernowne.
Bos'n Hill.
Dandelions.
Landor.
Music and Memory.
Soldier's Grave, A.
Albert, Samuel L.
After a Game of Squash.
All of Her.
Honeymoon.
Near the Base Line.
One, Two, Three.
Rebuff.
Street-Walker in March.
Albiach, Anne-Marie
État, *sel.*
He accepts the circle, speech and so.
Albizzi, Niccolò degli
Prolonged Sonnet: When the Troops Were Returning from Milan.
When the Troops Were Returning from Milan.
Albright, Mary E.
Let Me Go Back.
Alcaeus [*or* Alkaios]
Armoury, An.
Epigram: "Nicander, ooh, your leg's got hairs!"
Let Us Drink.
Storm, The.
Alcman
Fragment: "Mountain summits sleep, glens, cliffs, and caves, The."
Sleep upon the World.
Alcock, Mary
Chimney-Sweeper's Complaint, The.
Written in Ireland.
Alcosser, Sandra
Fish to Feed All Hunger, A.
Alcott, Amos Bronson
Bartol.
Channing.
Emerson.
Garrison.
Hawthorne.
Margaret Fuller.
Thoreau.
Wendell Phillips.
Alcott, Louisa May
Little Kingdom I Possess, A.
Our Little Ghost.
Thoreau's Flute.
Alcuin
Lament for the Cuckoo.
Aldan, Daisy
Stones: Avesbury.
Aldana, Francesco de
Image of God, The.
Alden, Henry Mills
Magic Mirror, The.
Aldington, Richard
After Two Years.
At the British Museum.
Barrage.
Battlefield.
Bombardment.
Choricos.
Epilogue: "Have I spoken too much or not enough of love?"
Evening.
Fatigues.
Faun Sees Snow for the First Time, The.
Her Mouth.
Images.
In the Trenches.
Lesbia.
Loss.
On the March.

Poplar, The.
Possession.
Prelude: "How could I love you more?"
Reserve.
Ruined House, A.
Soliloquy I.
Soliloquy II.
Three Little Girls.
Vicarious Atonement.
Aldis, Dorothy
Balloon Man, The.
Blum.
Brooms.
Clouds.
Clown, The.
Everybody Says.
First Winter's Day.
Fourth of July Night.
Hands.
Hiding.
I Have to Have It.
Ice.
Kick a Little Stone.
Little.
My Brother.
My Nose.
Names.
Night and Morning.
On a Snowy Day.
Our Little Calf.
Our Silly Little Sister.
Radiator Lions.
Riddle: What Am I?
Setting the Table.
Snow.
Somersault.
Story of the Baby Squirrel, The.
Wasps.
What They Are For.
When.
When I Was Lost.
Windy Wash Day.
Aldis, Mary
Barberries.
Seven Sad Sonnets.
Aldiss, Brian W.
Progression of the Species.
Tom Wedgewood Tells.
Aldrich, Anne Reeve
April and Dying.
Crowned Poet, A.
Death at Daybreak.
Eternal Justice, The.
Fanny.
Fraternity.
In November.
Little Parable, A.
Love's Change.
Music of Hungary.
Recollection.
Song about Singing, A.
Suppose.
Aldrich, Henry
Catch, A.
Five Reasons [for Drinking].
Reasons for Drinking.
Why I Drink.
Aldrich, James
Death-Bed, A.
Aldrich, Thomas Bailey
Alec Yeaton's Son.
Andromeda.
Appreciation.
At a Reading.
Baby Bell.
Before the Rain.
Bells at Midnight, The.
By the Potomac.
Circumstance.
Enamored [*or* Enamoured] Architect of Airy Rhyme.
Face against the Pane, The.
Fannie ("Fannie has the sweetest foot").
Flight of the Goddess, The.
Forever and a Day.
Fredericksburg.
Guilielmus Rex.
Heredity.
Hint from Herrick, A.
Identity.
Kriss Kringle.
Lady of Castlenoire.
L'Eau Dormante.
Maple Leaves.
Marjorie's Almanac.
Masks.
Memories.
Memory.
Menu, The.
Nocturne: "Up to her chamber window."
October.
Ode, on the Unveiling of the Shaw Memorial on Boston Common [May 31st, 1897], An.
On an Intaglio Head of Minerva.
On Reading.
Outward Bound.
Palabras Cariñosas.
Petition, A.
Prescience.
Quits.
Reminiscence.
Sargent's Portrait of Edwin Booth at "The Players."
Shadow of the Night, A.
Sleep.
Tennyson.
Thalia.
Tiger-Lilies.
To Hafiz.
Turkish Legend, A.
Undiscovered Country, The.
Unguarded Gates.
When the Sultan Goes to Ispahan.
World's Way, The.
Aldridge, Richard
By Return Mail.
Matter of Life and Death, A.
Pine Bough, The.
Serendipity of Love, A.
Spring Night.
To Himself.
Weeping Willow.
Alegria, Claribel
Disillusionment.
Loneliness and July Ninth.
Search.
Small Country.
Aleichem, Sholom
Epitaph: "Here lies a simple Jew."
Sleep, My Child.
Aleixandre, Vincente
After Love.
Aleqaajik
Great grief came over me.
Alexander, Bonnie L.
Lapidary.
Alexander, Cecil Frances
Adoration of the Wise Men, The.
All Things Bright and Beautiful.
Beggar Boy, The.
Burial of Moses, The.
Christmas Hymn, A.
Creation, The.
Dreams.
Evening Song.
Fieldmouse, The.
His Are the Thousand Sparkling Rills.
Once in Royal David's City.
There Is a Green Hill [Far Away].
We May Not Know.
Alexander, Frances
Contentment of Willoughby, The.
Alexander, John T.
Winning of the TV West, The.
Alexander, Joseph Addison
Doomed Man, The.
Hidden Line, The.
Alexander, Lewis
Africa.
Dark Brother, The.
Day and Night.
Dream Song.
Enchantment.
Japanese Hokku.
Negro Woman.
Nocturne Varial.
Tanka (I–VIII).
Transformation.
Alexander, Lilla M.
Consolation, *at.*
There Is Never a Day So Dreary, *at.*
Alexander, S. J.
To San Francisco.
Alexander, Sidney
Castle, The.
Lenox Avenue.
Alexander, Sir William. *See* **Stirling, William Alexander, Earl of**
Alexander, William, Archbishop of Armagh
Birthday Crown, The.
Robert Burns.
Vision of Oxford, A, *sel.*
Alfieri, Vittorio
To Dante.
Al-Fituri, Muhammad
I Am a Negro.
Knell, The.
Alford, Henry
Gypsy Girl, The.
Harvest Home.
Ten thousand times ten thousand.
You and I.
Alford, Janie
Mother Love.
Thanks Be to God.
Alford, John
Glory, Glory to the Sun.
Alfred, King of England
Proverbs of Alfred, *sel., at.*
Wealth and Wisdom, *at.*
Alfred, William
Mary Lifted from the Dead, *with music.*
Alger, Horatio, Jr.
John Maynard.
Al-Hallaj
Ecstasy, The.
There is a selfhood in my nothingness.
Al-Harizi, Judah
Heavy-hearted.
Love Song: "Long closed door, oh open it again, The."
Song of the Flea.
Song of the Pen, The.
Under Leafy Bowers.
Unhappy Lover, The.
Within My Heart.
"Alice"
Story of the Rose, The, *with music.*
Aliesan, Jody
Arachne.
On a Wednesday.
Radiation Leak.
Sutra Blues; or, This Pain Is Bliss.
This Fall ("This fall the japanese maple turned coral red").
Aliger, Margarita
House in Meudon.
To a Portrait of Lermontov.
Two.
Alkaios. *See* **Alcaeus**
Al-Khansa
Elegy for Her Brother Sakhr.
For Her Brother.
In Death's Field.
Night, The.
On Her Brother.

On Her Brother Sakhr.
Rain to the Tribe.
Sleepless.
Al-Khirniq
Lament after Her Husband Bishr's Murder.
Allah, Fareedah. *See* **Saunders, Ruby C.**
Allan, Edwin
Ass, The ("The ass/ is decidedly middlecrass").
Allan, James Alexander
Breaking.
Allan, M.
Echo Poem.
Allan, Thomas H.
Leave the Miracle to Him.
Allen, Alice E.
Life's Common Things.
My Mother's Garden.
Allen, Dick
Green Pastures.
Mime.
Allen, Edward
Best Line Yet, The.
Allen, Elizabeth
Verse for Vestigials.
Allen, Elizabeth Akers
Bringing Our Sheaves.
Endurance.
In a Garret.
Last Landlord, The.
Left Behind.
Little Feet.
Lost Light.
My Dearling.
Rock Me to Sleep.
Sea-Birds.
Snow.
Toad, A.
Until Death.
Allen, Ernest Bourner
"I Am with Thee."
Allen, George Leonard
Portrait.
To Melody.
Allen, Glen
Woman I Am, The.
Allen, Grace Elisabeth
Pinkletinks.
Allen, Grant
Ballade of Evolution, A.
Allen, Hervey
Carolina Spring Song.
Moments.
Refuge.
Saga of Leif the Lucky, *sel.*
Shadow to Shadow.
Southward Sidonian Hanno.
Upstairs Downstairs.
Walls.
Allen, John Alexander
Admiral.
Allen, Jonathan
Sinners, Will You Scorn the Message? *with music.*
Allen, Leslie Holdsworth
Reaper, The.
Allen, Lyman Whitney
Coming of His Feet, The.
People's King, The.
Star of Sangamon, The.
Allen, Marian
Raiders, The.
Wind on the Downs, The.
Allen, Marie Louise
First Snow.
Mitten Song, The.
My Zipper Suit.
Sneezing.
What Is It?
Allen, Paula Gunn
Beautiful Woman Who Sings, The ("The beautiful woman at Laguna").
Catching One Clear Thought Alive.
Coyote's Daylight Trip.
Donna.
Grandmother.
Kopis'taya.
Madonna of the Hills.
Pocahontas to Her English Husband, John Rolfe.
Poem for Pat.
Powwow 79, Durango.
Rain for Ka-waik.
Recuerdo.
Robin.
San Ysidro, Cabezon.
Snowgoose.
Star Child Suite.
Suicid/ing(ed) Indian Women.
Trick Is Consciousness, The.
Womanwork.
Allen, Richard
God of Bethel Heard Her Cries, The, *with music.*
Allen, Samuel ("Paul Vesey")
Dylan, Who Is Dead.
If the Stars Should Fall.
Love Song: "Arrow rides upon the sky, An."
Moment Please, A.
My Friend.
Nat Turner.
Ski Trail.
Staircase, The.
To Satch.
What Bright Pushbutton?
Allen, Sara Van Alstyne
Marble Statuette Harpist.
Walk on a Winter Day.
Zoo in the City, The.
Allen, William J.
Erie Canal, The ("I've got a mule, her name is Sal").
Allen, Willis Boyd
Thalatta.
Allerton, Ellen Palmer
Beautiful Things.
Alline, Henry
Amazing Sight! The Saviour Stands.
Christ Inviting Sinners to His Grace, *sel.*
Hard Heart of Mine, *with music.*
Turn, Turn, Unhappy Souls, Return, *with music.*
Alling, Kenneth Slade
Beauty.
Dead Wasp.
Dr. Donne.
First World War.
Monsoon.
On the Park Bench.
Onion Skin in Barn.
Rain.
Unscarred Fighter Remembers France, The.
Allingham, William
Abbey Asaroe.
Abbot of Inisfalen, The.
Aeolian Harp.
At Ballyshannon, Co. Donegal.
Blowing Bubbles.
Bubble, The.
Death Deposed.
Dream, A [*or* The].
Earth's Night.
Evening, An.
Eviction, The.
Fairies, The.
Fairy Folk, The.
Four Ducks on a Pond.
Girl's Lamentation, The, *sl. abr.*
Homeward Bound.
Laurence Bloomfield in Ireland, *sel.*
Lion and the Wave, The.
Lovely Mary Donnelly.
Lover and Birds, The.
Lupracaun, or Fairy Shoemaker, The.
Maids of Elfin-Mere, The.
Meadowsweet.
Memory, A.
Mill, A.
Riding.
Robin Redbreast.
Sailor, The.
Song: "I walk'd in the lonesome evening."
Spring: The Lover and the Birds.
Swing Song, A.
Wild Rose, *abr.*
Winding Banks of Erne, The.
Windlass Song.
Wishing.
Allison, Drummond
Brass Horse, The.
Dedication: "Had there been peace there never had been riven."
No Remedy.
Allison, John
Okeechobee.
Reflection: After Visiting Old Friends.
"Allison, Joy" (Mary A. Cragin)
Which Loved Best?
Allison, William Talbot
O Amber Day, amid the Autumn Gloom.
Allison, Young Ewing
Derelict.
Allman, John
You Owe Them Everything.
Allott, Kenneth
Cheshire Cat.
Departure Platform.
Lament for a Cricket Eleven.
Prize for Good Conduct.
Statue, The.
Allston, Washington
America to Great Britain.
On the Late S. T. Coleridge.
Rosalie.
Allwood, Brian
No Laws.
Al-Mahdi
Preacher, The.
Al-Mala'ika, Nazik
Jamila.
Alma-Tadema, Laurence
If No One Ever Marries Me.
Playgrounds.
Strange Lands.
Alohikea, Alfred
Glory of Hanalei is its heavy rain, The.
Alonso, Ricardo
Tiempo Muerto.
Alpaugh, Ern *and* **Dewey G. Pell**
Swinging Chick.
Alphonsus Liguori, Saint
Madonna's Lullaby.
Alqamah
His Camel.
Alquit, B.
Light of the World, The.
Wandering Chorus.
Alsop, George
Author to His Book, The.
Be just (domestick monarchs) unto them.
Could'st thou (O Earth) live thus obscure, and now.
Heavens bright lamp, shine forth some of thy light.
Lines on a Purple Cap Received as a Present from My Brother.
Poor vaunting earth, gloss'd with uncertain pride.
'Tis said the Gods lower down that chain above.
To My Cosen Mrs. Eilinor Evins.
Trafique is earth's great Atlas, that supports.
Alston, Joseph Blynth
"Stack Arms!"
Alta
After Reading Sylvia Plath.
Art of Enforced Deprivation, The.
Bitter Herbs.
Daily Courage Doesn't Count.

Euch, are you having your period?
First Pregnancy.
He Said, Lying There.
Hunger for Me
I Don't Have No Bunny Tail on My Behind.
I Never Saw a Man in a Negligee.
Penus envy, they call it.
Altenburg, Michael
Battle Hymn.
Alterman, Nathan
From All Peoples, *sel.*
Poem about Your Face.
Saul.
Spinning Girl, The.
Tammuz.
This Night.
To the Elephants.
Altgood, Laurence
Song of the Brave.
Altman, Shalom
Vine and Fig Tree.
Altrocchi, Julia Cooley
Pigeon-Feeders in Battery Park, The.
Altrocchi, Rudolph
Insect Wives.
Alurista
Address.
Get Stuffed.
In the Barrio.
Must Be the Season of the Witch.
Our Barrio.
Alvarez, Alfred
Cemetery in New Mexico, A.
Dying.
Fortunate Fall, The.
Lost.
Mourning and Melancholia.
Operation.
Alver, Betti
Iron Heaven.
Painter in the Lion Cage, The.
Tailor Called Sorrow, A.
Titans, The.
Alyea, Dorothy
Keepsake from Quinault.
Ama Ata Aidoo, Christine
Prelude: "I am the bird of the wayside."
Amabile, George
Snowfall: Four Variations.
Twink Drives Back, in a Bad Mood, from a Party in Massachusetts.
Amarou
Drunken Rose, The.
Ambapali
Black and glossy as a bee and curled was my hair.
Ambrose, Saint
Hymn: "Framer of the earth and sky."
Amen, Grover
Cot, The.
Amenhotep IV. *See* **Akhenaton**
Amergin.
Aimirgin's Invocation, *at.*
Incantation, The, *at.*
Invocation to Ireland, *at.*
Mystery, The, *at.*
Ames, A. S.
Abraham Lincoln.
Ames, Bernice
Country of Water.
Ames, Evelyn
Because I Live.
Two Solitudes.
Ames, Jay
On Corwen Road.
Amichai, Yehuda
Advice.
God Has Pity on Kindergarten Children.
I Am a Leaf.
I Am Sitting Here.
I Think of Oblivion.
In the Old City.
Jerusalem, Port City.
Lament: "Diameter of the bomb was thirty centimeters, The."
Lay Your Head on My Shoulder.
My Mother Once Told Me.
Not like a Cypress.
Of Three or Four in a Room.
On the Day of Atonement.
On the Wide Stairs.
Painful Love Song, A.
Pity, A; We Were Such a Good Invention.
Quick and Bitter.
Shadow of the Old City.
Since Then.
Sodom's Sister City.
Song of Resignation.
To Carry on Living.
Town I Was Born In, The.
We Did It.
Amini, Johari. *See* **Latimore, Jewel C.**
Amir, Aharon
Cock.
Nothingness.
Amiri, Akhtar
I Am a Woman, *sel.*
Amis, Kingsley
Aberdarcy: The Chaucer Road.
Aberdarcy: The Main Square.
After Goliath.
Against Romanticism.
Aldport (Mystery Tour).
Alternatives.
Autobiographical Fragment.
Beowulf.
Bookshop Idyll, A.
Brynbwrla.
Departure.
Dream of Fair Women, A.
Evans Country, The, *sels.*
Ever-fixed Mark, An.
Fforestfawr.
Helbatrawss, The.
Langwell.
Last War, The.
Masters.
New Approach Needed.
Note on Wyatt, A.
Nothing to Fear.
Ode to Me.
On a Portrait of Mme. Rimsky-Korsakov.
Pendydd.
Poet's Epitaph, A.
Reborn.
St. Asaph's.
Science Fiction.
Shitty.
Sight Unseen.
Silent Room, The.
Terrible Beauty.
Tribute to the Founder, A.
Amis, Lewis R.
Jehovah, God, Who Dwelt of Old, *with music.*
Ammianus
Epitaph of Nearchos.
Amittai ben Shefatiah
Hymn of Weeping.
Ammons, Archie Randolph
Apologia pro Vita Sua.
Arc Inside and Out, The.
Auto Mobile.
Ballad: "I want to know the unity in all things."
Bay Bank.
Bridge.
Cascadilla Falls.
Chasm.
Choice.
Christmas Eve.
City Limits, The.
Clarity.
Classic.
Cleavage.
Close-up.
Confirmers, The.
Conserving the Magnitude of Uselessness.
Constant, The.
Coon Song.
Corsons Inlet.
Coward.
Cut the Grass.
Dark Song.
Dinah.
Diner.
Easter Morning.
80-Proof
Eternal City, The.
First Carolina Said-Song.
Gravelly Run.
Hardweed Path Going.
He Held Radical Light.
Hymn: "I know if I find you I will have to leave the earth."
Imperialist.
Kind.
Laser.
Life in the Boondocks.
Loss.
Mechanism.
Mirrorment.
Model.
My Father Used to Tell of An.
Needs.
Periphery.
Pet Panther.
Play.
Plunder.
Poetics.
Prospecting.
Put-Down Come On, The.
Rivulose.
Rocking.
Runoff.
Satisfaction.
Second Carolina Said-Song.
Self-Projection.
Silver.
Small Song.
So I Said I Am Ezra.
Spring Coming.
Terrain.
Time's Times Again.
Transaction.
Triphammer Bridge.
Unifying Principle, The.
Unsaid.
Upland.
Viable.
Visit.
Wide Land, The.
Windy Trees.
Winter Saint.
Working with Tools.
Yucca Moth, The.
Amon-Re
Hymn of Victory: Thutmose III.
Amorosi, Ray
Note in a Sanitorium.
Nothing Inside and Nothing Out.
Amoss, Harry
Pedagogical Principles.
Riding.
Amphis
Hangover Cure.
Amprimoz, Alexandre L.
Final Fall, The.
"An Pilibín" (John Hackett Pollock)
Retrospect.
Anacreon
Design for a Bowl.
Heat.
Picture, The.
To His Young Mistress.
Woman's Arms.
Andal
Cuckoo, noisy among the Shenbaka flowers.

O people who live in the world.
"Ande" (Angela Milne)
Coconut, The.
Andersen, Astrid Hjertenaes
Before the sun goes down.
Anderson, Alexander ("Surfaceman")
Cuddle Doon.
Jenny wi' the Airn Teeth.
Langsyne, When Life Was Bonnie.
Anderson, Bill
Letter from a Black Soldier.
Outbreak.
Anderson, David Earle
With the Nuns at Cape May Point.
Anderson, Don
Have You Thanked a Green Plant Today.
Anderson, Ethel Louisa Mason
Bucolic Eclogues, *sel.*
Kunai-mai-pa Mo.
Waking, Child, While You Slept.
Anderson, Forrest
Beach Homos, The.
Anderson, Gordon
First Hunt, The.
Anderson, Jack
Aesthetics of the Moon.
Commanding a Telephone to Ring.
Garden of Situations, A.
Going to Norway.
Invention of New Jersey, The.
Ode to Pornography.
Anderson, Jack L.
Another Letter to Joseph Bruchac.
Face in a Mirror.
Faces.
Reading Sign.
Visit to the Hermitage.
Anderson, James
When Father Slept.
Anderson, John
Clipper Ships.
Shadows of Sails.
Anderson, Jon
American Landscape with Clouds & a Zoo.
Blue Animals, The.
Falling in Love.
Homage to Robert Bresson.
In Autumn.
In Sepia.
John Clare.
Lives of the Saints.
Milky Way, The.
Parachutist, The.
Photograph of Myself, The.
Refusals.
Rosebud.
Secret of Poetry, The.
Witness.
Years.
Anderson, Kenneth L.
Hope.
Anderson, Lilian M.
Leave in 1917.
Anderson, Margaret Steele
Breaking, The.
Anderson, Maxwell
In All These Turning Lights I Find No Clue.
Judith of Minnewaulken, *sel.*
Lafayette to Washington.
Parallax.
Toll the Bell for Damon.
Valley Forge, *sel.*
Winterset, *sel.*
Anderson, Patrick
Camp.
Capital Square.
Cold Colloquy.
Coming of the White Man, The.
Drinker.
Houses Burning; Quebec.
My Bird-wrung Youth.
Poem on Canada, *sels.*
Sestina in Time of Winter.
Sleighride.
Anderson, Persis Greely
Lengthy Symphony.
Melodie Grotesque.
Anderson, S. E.
Junglegrave.
New Dance, A.
Sound of Afroamerican History Chapt I, The ("The history of blacklife is put down in the motions").
Sound of Afroamerican History Chapt II, The ("Smith at the organ is like an anvil being").
Anderson, Sherwood
Visit, A.
Anderson, Teresa
Delphine.
Our People.
Anderson, Violet
Cloak, The.
Through the Barber Shop Window.
Andrade, Mário de
Aspiration.
Rondeau for You.
André, John
Cow-Chace, The.
Andresen, Sophia de Mello Breyner
Camoes and the Debt.
Dead Men, The.
Dionysius.
Mirrors, The.
Small Square, The.
Young Girl and the Beach, The.
Andrew, Prudence
Whippet.
Andrew of Wyntoun
Macbeth.
Andrewes, Francis
Shepherdess' Valentine, *sel.*
Andrews, Albert Charlton
Our Modest Doughboys.
Andrews, Harvey
Unaccompanied.
Andrews, John
Anatomy of Baseness, The, *sel.*
To the Detracted.
Andrews, John Williams
La Madonna di Lorenzetti.
Andrews, Mary Raymond Shipman
Call to Arms, A.
Andrews, Robert
Mercury; on Losing My Pocket Milton at Luss near Ben Lomond, and Other Mountains.
Urania.
Andriello, Amelia
Autumn Eve.
Aneirin
Gododdin, The, *sels.*
Angelita, Sister Mary
Signum Cui Contradicetur.
To a Poet.
Angell, Walter Foster
To New Haven and Boston.
Angelou, Maya
Africa.
Chicken-Licken.
My Arkansas.
On Diverse Deviations.
Remembering.
Sepia Fashion Show.
Song for the Old Ones.
Southeast Arkanasia.
Still I Rise.
They Went Home.
To a Husband.
Woman Me.
Woman Work.
"Angelus Silesius" (Johannes Scheffler)
Cherubic Pilgrim, The.
In Thine Own Heart.
Angermayer, Frances
Conversion.
Last Thoughts of a Fighting Man.
Anghelaki-Rooke, Katerina
Before they ripen into diffused spririts.
Body Is the Victory and the Defeat of Dreams, The.
Notes on My Father, *sel.*
Angiolieri, Cecco, da Siena
Sonnet: He Argues His Case with Death.
Sonnet: He Is Past All Help.
Sonnet: He Rails against Dante, Who Had Censured His Homage to Becchina.
Sonnet: He Will Not Be Too Deeply in Love.
Sonnet: In Absence from Becchina.
Sonnet: Of All He Would Do.
Sonnet: Of Becchina, the Shoemaker's Daughter.
Sonnet: Of Becchina in a Rage.
Sonnet: Of Love, in Honor of His Mistress Becchina.
Sonnet: Of Love in Men and Devils.
Sonnet: Of the 20th of June 1291.
Sonnet: Of Why He Is Unhanged.
Sonnet: Of Why He Would Be a Scullion.
Sonnet: To Dante Alighieri (He Writes to Dante, Then in Exile at Verona, Defying Him as No Better Than Himself).
Sonnet: To Dante Alighieri (On the Last Sonnet of the Vita Nuova).
Anglund, Joan Walsh
Ladybug.
Angoff, Charles
God Is Here Again.
Litany: "When the sun rises on another day."
Little Girl, A.
What Has Happened.
Angulo, Hector
Dopefiends Trip.
Angus, Marion
Alas! Poor Queen.
Foxgloves and Snow.
Mary's Song.
Annan, Annie Rankin
Dandelion.
Annand, James King
Arctic Convoy.
O Aa the Manly Sports.
On the Croun o Bidean.
What Finer Hills?
Annett, David
Wreck of the Deutschland, The, *parody.*
Ansen, Alan
Fatness.
Fit of Something against Something, A.
Tennyson.
Ansky, "S. (Solomon Rappoport)
Emigrant Song.
Tailor, The.
Anson, John Seller
Lighthouse, The.
Proverbial.
Anstadt, Henry
Little Rhyme and a Little Reason, A.
Anster, John
If I Might Choose.
Prologue of Faust, *sel.*
Anstey, Christopher
Letter Containing a Panegyric on Bath.
New Bath Guide, The, *sels.*
"Anstey, F." (Thomas Anstey Guthrie)
Burglar Bill.
Conscience-Curst, The!
Limerick: "There was an old man of Bengal."
Ordinary valour only works, The.
Ant, Howard
Bucket of Sea-Serpents.
Antara
Abla.
Antella, Simone dall'
Prolonged Sonnet: In the Last Days of the Emperor Henry VII.
Anthony, Ed
College Song.

Anthony, Edward ("A. C. Gate")
Advice to Small Children.
Bloodhound, The.
Collies, The.
Dachshund, The.
I know a barber.
Let Others Share.
Oddity Land, *sel.*
Anthony, Florence. *See* **Ai**
Anthony, George
Autumn Evening.
Antin, David
Passengers, The.
Antipater of Sidon
Aristeides.
Erinna.
Never again, Orpheus.
Pindar.
Undying Thirst.
Antokolsky, Pavel Grigoryevich
Hate!
Antoninus, Brother. *See* **Everson, William**
Antrobus, John
Cowboy, The.
Anyte [*or* Anytes]
Alive, this man was Manes, a common slave.
I, Hermes, have been set up.
I am Hermes. I stand in the crossroads by a windy.
Lounge in the shade of the luxuriant laurel's.
Shepherd's Gift, A.
Aphek, Edna
Sarah.
Story of Abraham and Hagar, The.
Apolebieji, Odeniyi
Salute to the Elephant.
Apollinaire, Guillaume
Calligram, 15 May 1915.
It's Raining.
Little Car, The.
Mirabeau Bridge, The.
Moonlight.
Shadow.
War.
Zone.
Apollinaris Sidonius
Invitation to the Dance.
Appel, Benjamin
Talker, The.
Appleman, Philip
Amurrika!
East Hampton: The Structure of Sound.
In the Gazebo.
Is There a Voice.
It Is Enough.
La Misère.
Maples.
Memo to the 21st Century.
More.
My Friend.
On a Morning Full of Sun.
Peace with Honor.
So What.
Try.
Waiting for the Fire.
When.
Winding Down the War.
Appleton, Everard John [*or* Jack]
Fighting Failure, The.
Woman Who Understands, The.
Applewhite, James
Bordering Manuscript.
My Grandfather's Funeral.
Ravine, The.
Red Wing Hawk.
To Earth.
Aragon, Louis
Dirge; for the Barrel-Organ of the New Barbarism.
Lilacs and the Roses, The.
Aratus of Soli
Praise of Zeus.
Arbuthnot, John
Epitaph on Colonel Francis Chartres.
Archer, Kate Rennie
Lairdless Place, The.
Archer, Nuala
Flies Love Me.
Archestratus
Gastrology, *sel.*
Recipe: Hare.
Archevolti, Samuel ben Elhanan Isaac, of Padua
Advice to Hotheads.
Archias of Byzantium
Sea Dirge.
Archibald, Esther
In My Place.
Archilochus
Decks awash,/ Mast-top dipping.
Like Odysseus under the ram.
May he lose his way on the cold sea.
This island, garlanded with wild woods.
Tossed on a Sea of Trouble.
"Archpoet, The"
His Confession.
Arden, John
Lobster Pot, The.
Arden, Richard Pepper, Baron Alvanley
On Dr. Samuel Ogden.
Ardinger, Richard
At 85.
Arensberg, Walter Conrad
To Hasekawa.
Aretino, Pietro
Brother Alberto, one hot summer day.
Brother Astolfo sated appetite.
Stragglers.
Argentarius, Marcus
Epigram: "Hetero-sex is best for the man of a serious turn of mind."
Old Story, The.
Rumoresque Senum Severiorum.
Argüelles, Iván
Spanish Girls, The.
Aridjis, Umberto
Sun Set.
Ariosto, Ludovico
Angelica and the Ork.
Blessed angell not a word replies, The.
Aristaenetus
Pleasing Constraint, The.
Aristophanes
Birds, The, *sel.*
Chorus of Birds.
Clouds, The, *sel.*
Grand Chorus of Birds.
How the Women Will Stop War.
Lysistrata.
Song of the Clouds.
Thesmophoriazusae, The, *sel.*
Women Speak Out in Defense of Themselves, The.
Arkell, Reginald
Public Nuisance, A.
When the War Will End.
Arkwright, John Stanhope
Supreme Sacrifice, The.
"Arkwright, Peleg." *See* **Proudfit, David Law.**
Armand, Octavio
Possible Love Poem to the Usurer.
Armitage, Jennifer
To Our Daughter.
Armknecht, Richard F.
Crow's Nest.
Armour, Richard
Assorted Relishes.
Deus ex Machina.
Epitaph: "Insured for every accident."
Fish Story.
Good Sportsmanship.
Hiding Place.
Horses.
Money.
Not a Cloud in the Sky.
One Down.
Pillow Cases.
To a Human Skeleton.
Transportation Problem.
Travelling Companions.
Armstrong, Frankie
Collier Lass, The.
Month of January.
Out of the Darkness.
Women of My Land.
Armstrong, Hamilton Fish
Lines for the Hour.
Armstrong, J. A.
Another Reply to "In Flanders Fields."
Armstrong, John
Advantages of Washing, The.
Advice to Lovers.
Art of Preserving Health, The, *sels.*
Blest Winter Nights.
Dangers of Sexual Excess, The.
Home of the Naiads, The.
Madness.
Oeconomy of Love, The; a Poetical Essay, *sel.*
Transience.
Urban Pollution.
Armstrong, Margaret D.
Invocation for the New Year.
Armstrong, Martin
Buzzards, The.
On a Little Bird.
To a Jilt.
Armstrong, Peter
Butterfly.
Armstrong, Thomas [or Tommy]
Oakey Street Evictions, The.
Row between the Cages, The.
Trimdon Grange Explosion, The.
"Armytage, R." *See* **Watson, Rosamund Marriott**
Arnatkoak
Personal Song.
Arndt, Ernst Moritz
German Fatherland, The.
Arnett, Carroll (Gogisgi)
Anadarko John.
Ayohu Kanogisdi.
Bio-poetic Statement.
Drunk.
Land.
Last May.
Look Back.
Old Man Said, The.
Removal: Last Part.
Rock Painting.
Something for Supper.
Song of the Breed.
Story of My Life, The.
You.
Arnold, Sir Edwin
After Death in Arabia.
Almond Blossom.
Darien.
Destiny.
End Which Comes, The.
He and She.
Light of Asia, The, *sels.*
She and He.
To a Pair of Egyptian Slippers.
Arnold, George
Alone by the Hearth.
Beer.
Farewell to Summer.
Golden Fish, The.
In the Dark.
Jolly Old Pedagogue, The.
Jubilate.
September.
Sweet September.
Youth and Age.
Arnold, Gertrude Thomas
Desert Bloom.
Arnold, Irene (Mrs. Major Arnold)
Pray!

Thank God for the Country!
Arnold, Lila
Paisley Ceiling, The.
Arnold, Matthew
Absence.
Austerity of Poetry.
Bacchanalia; or, The New Age, *sels.*
Balder Dead, *sel.*
Buried Life, The.
Cadmus and Harmonia.
Calais Sands.
Callicles' Song.
Calm Soul of All Things.
Caution to Poets, A.
Courage.
Cruel, but composed and bland.
Death of Sohrab, The.
Desire.
Dover Beach.
Dream, A.
East London.
Empedocles on Etna.
Epilogue to Lessing's Laocoön.
Farewell, A: "My horse's feet beside the lake."
First-born Star, The.
Forsaken Merman, The.
Future, The.
Geist's Grave.
Growing Old.
Haworth Churchyard, *sel.*
Hayeswater Boat, The, *sel.*
If Birth Persists.
Immortality.
In Harmony with Nature.
In Utrumque Paratus.
Isolation ("We were apart; yet, day by day").
Isolation ("Yes! in the sea of life enisled").
Isolation: To Marguerite.
Jacopone da Todi.
Kaiser Dead.
Last Word, The.
Life and Thought.
Lines Written in Kensington Gardens.
Longing.
Matthias, *sels.*
Meeting.
Memorial Verses.
Memory-Picture, A.
Morality.
Nameless Epitaph, A.
Not Here, O Apollo.
Obermann Once More.
Palladium.
Parting.
Persistency of Poetry.
Philomela.
Poor Matthias.
Progress of Poesy, The.
Quiet Work.
Requiescat.
Resignation.
Rugby Chapel.
Scenes from Carnac.
Scholar-Gipsy, The.
Second Asgard, The.
Self-Dependence.
Separation.
Shakespeare.
So, some tempestuous morn in early June.
Sohrab and Rustum.
Song for Apollo.
Song of Callicles, The ("Far, far from here").
Song of Callicles, The ("Through the black, rushing smoke-burst").
Song of the Muses, The.
Stanzas from the Grande Chartreuse.
Stanzas in Memory of the Author of "Obermann."
Strayed Reveller, The.
Summer Night, A.
Switzerland.
Terrace at Berne, The.
Thyrsis.
To a Friend.
To a Republican Friend, 1848.
To a Republican Friend: Continued.
To Marguerite ("Yes! in the sea of life enisled").
Urania.
West London.
Wish, A.
Wordsworth's Grave.
Written in Butler's Sermons.
Youth of Nature, The: Wordsworth's Country, *sel.*
Arnstein, Flora J.
Timers.
Arowa, Omobayode
Dirge for Fajuyi, *sel.*
Arp, Hans
Domestic Stones, The (fragment).
I Am a Horse.
Two little arabs adult and arabesque.
When it burns before the harps and freezes behind the easels.
Arp, Jean
What the Violins Sing in Their Baconfat Bed.
Arrabey, Salaan
To a Faithless Friend.
Arriví, Francisco
Song for a Day, *sel.*
Song for a Transformation, *sel.*
Arrowsmith, Pat
Christmas Story (1980).
Political Activist Living Alone.
Arsenault, Joel
Windfall.
Arudra
Poeti-c Art ("The poetic cart").
Arundel, Philip Howard, 1st Earl of. *See* **Howard, Philip, 1st Earl of Arundel**
Arundel, Anne Howard, Duchess of. *See* **Howard, Anne, Duchess of Arundel**
Arvey, Michael
Concert.
Follower.
Arvey, Verna
All That I Am, *with music.*
Asbaje, Juana de. *See* **Juana Inés de la Cruz, Sister**
Asch, Frank
Alley Cat School.
Leaves.
Sugar Lady, The.
Summer.
Sunflakes.
Sunrise.
Asclepiades
Eumares.
Asgrímsson, Eysteinn
Author's Entreaty for His Lay.
Lilya, *sel.*
Ash, Sarah Leeds
Changeless Shore.
Ashbery, John
Additional Poem, An.
As One Put into the Packet-Boat.
Blessing in Disguise, A.
Boy, A.
Bungalows, The.
City Afternoon.
Civilization and Its Discontents.
De Imagine Mundi.
Decoy.
Dido.
Europe.
Everyman's Library.
Farm Implements and Rutabagas in a Landscape.
Faust.
Fear of Death.
For John Clare.
Friends.
Glazunoviana.
Grand Abacus.
He.
How Much Longer Will I Be Able to Inhabit the Divine Sepulcher.
Ice-Cream Wars, The.
Idiot, The.
If the Birds Knew.
Instruction Manual, The.
Last Month.
Last World, A.
Le Livre Est sur la Table.
Leaving the Atocha Station.
Man of Words, A.
Märchenbilder.
Melodic Trains.
Mixed Feelings.
My Erotic Double.
On Autumn Lake.
One Thing That Can Save America, The.
Our Youth.
Painter, The.
Paradoxes and Oxymorons.
Picture of Little J. A. in a Prospect of Flowers, The.
Poem: "While we were walking under the top."
Pyrography.
Rivers and Mountains.
Some Trees.
Soonest Mended.
Spring Day.
Tennis Court Oath, The.
Tenth Symphony.
These Lacustrine Cities.
They Dream Only of America.
Thoughts of a Young Girl.
To Redouté.
Two Sonnets.
Variations, Calypso and Fugue on a Theme of Ella Wheeler Wilcox.
Vase of Flowers, A.
Wet Casements.
What Is Poetry.
White Roses.
Worsening Situation.
Wrong Kind of Insurance, The.
Years of Indiscretion.
Young Prince and the Young Princess, The.
Ashburton, Robert Offley
Harrow Grave in Flanders, A.
Ashby, Cliff
Latter Day Psalms.
Stranger in This Land, A.
Ashby-Sterry, Joseph
Kindness to Animals.
King of the Cradle, The.
Portrait, A.
Spring's Delights.
Ashe, Thomas
City Clerk, The.
Corpse-bearing.
Machine Hand, A.
Meet We No Angels, Pansie?
No and Yes.
Vision of Children, A.
Word to the West End, A.
Ashley, Nova Trimble
Humiliation Revisited.
Ashley, Paul David
Beauty.
Prison.
Ritual, The.
Song from the Unfinished Man.
Sounds.
Askenazy, Ludvik
Wall, The.
Askew, Anne
Ballad Which Anne Askew Made and Sang When She Was in Newgate, The.
Asphodel (Pauline Long)
Full Moon in Malta.
On the Pilgrim's Way in Kent, as It Leads to the Coldrum Stones.

Winter Solstice—for Frank.
Asquith, Herbert
Birthday Gifts.
Elephant, The.
Hairy Dog, The.
Mare, The.
Skating.
Volunteer, The.
Astley, Thea
Droving Man.
Astor, Susan
Dame.
Four Spacious Skies.
Road the Crows Own, The.
Astra
Bloody Pause.
Daughters.
Now or Never.
Asturias, Miguel Angel
Indians Come Down from Mixco, The.
Asya (Asya Gay)
Celan.
Deer, The.
Grain of Moonlight, A.
My Strawlike Hair.
My True Memory.
Pause a Moment.
Atchity, Kenneth John
Delicate Impasse, A.
Atherstone, Edwin
Sunrise at Sea.
Atherton, John
Tank Town.
Atimantiyar
Nowhere, not among the warriors at their festival.
Atkins, Russell
At War.
Christophe.
"Dangerous Condition": Sign on Inner-City House.
Dark Area.
Editorial Poem on an Incident of Effects Far-reaching.
Inner-City Lullaby.
Irritable Song.
It's Here in The.
Narrative.
New Storefront.
Night and a Distant Church.
On the Fine Arts Garden, Cleveland.
Probability and Birds in the Yard.
At Taliq
I took leave of my beloved one evening: how I wish.
Attar
Return of the Dead, The, *sel.*
Sun of My Perfection Is a Glass, The.
Atwell, Roy
Some Little Bug.
Atwood, Margaret
Accident Has Occurred, The.
After the agony in the guest/ bedroom.
Against Still Life.
Animals in That Country, The.
At first I was given centuries.
At the Tourist Center in Boston.
Circle Game, The, *sels.*
Daguerreotype Taken in Old Age.
Death of a Young Son by Drowning.
Dream 2: Brian the Still-Hunter.
Dufferin, Simcoe, Grey.
Eden Is a Zoo.
Elegy for the Giant Tortoises.
Eventual Proteus.
Explorers, The.
Five Poems for Dolls.
Habitation.
I can change my-/ self more easily.
Interview with a Tourist.
It Is Dangerous to Read Newspapers.
Landcrab.
Lying here, everything in me.
Marrying the Hangman.
Night in the Royal Ontario Museum, A.
Notes towards a Poem That Can Never Be Written.
November.
Pig Song.
Provisions.
Settlers, The.
Siren Song.
Songs of the Transformed, *sel.*
Spelling.
There Is Only One of Everything.
They Eat Out.
This Is a Photograph of Me.
Variation on the Word *Sleep.*
We Are Standing Facing Each Other.
Woman Skating.
You Begin.
You Fit into Me.
You refuse to own.
You take my hand and.
You want to go back.
Your back is rough all.
Aua
Bear Hunting.
Morning Prayer.
Walrus Hunting.
Aubert, Alvin
Blood to Blood.
Levitation.
One More Time.
There Were Fierce Animals in Africa.
When the Wine Was Gone.
Aubert, Rosemary
Love Poem: "I want/ to make a myth of you."
Aubigné, Théodore Agrippa d'
Portrait of Henri III, A.
Tragiques, Les, *sel.*
Auchterlonie, Dorothy
Apopemptic Hymn.
Meditation of a Mariner.
Waiting for the Post.
Audelay, John
Be True to Your Condition in Life.
Fairest Flower, The.
In His Utter Wretchedness.
Love of God, The.
What Tidings?
Auden, Wystan Hugh
Advent.
Aesthetic Point of View, The.
After Christmas.
After Reading a Child's Guide to Modern Physics.
Alonso to Ferdinand.
Always the Following Wind.
Amor Loci.
Another Time.
Anthem: "Let us praise our Maker, with true passion extol Him."
As He Is.
As I Walked Out One Evening.
At Last the Secret Is Out.
At lucky moments we seem on the brink.
At the Grave of Henry James.
At the Manger Mary Sings.
Atlantis.
August for the People.
Autumn 1940.
Ballad: "O What Is That Sound."
Ballad of Barnaby, The.
Base words are uttered only by the base.
Birthday Poem.
Brussels in Winter.
Canzone: "When shall we learn, what should be clear as day."
Carry Her over the Water.
Casino.
Chorus: "Doom is dark and deeper than any sea-dingle."
Chorus: "Summer holds, The: upon its glittering lake."
Chorus: "To throw away the key and walk away."
Chorus: "You are the town and we are the clock."
Chorus from a Play.
City without Walls.
Commentary, *sel.*
Consider This and in Our Time.
Cultural Presupposition, The.
Dear, Though the Night Is Gone.
Decoys, The.
Dialogue between Mary and Gabriel.
Diaspora, The.
Dog beneath the Skin, The, *sels.*
Doggerel by a Senior Citizen.
Doom Is Dark.
Edward Lear.
Epilogue: " 'O where are you going?' said reader to rider."
Epitaph for the Unknown Soldier.
Epitaph on a Tyrant.
Et in Arcadia Ego.
Exiles, The.
Fairground.
Fall of Rome, The.
Far from the Heart of Culture.
First Things First.
Fish in the Unruffled Lakes.
Flight into Egypt, The.
For the Time Being; a Christmas Oratorio, *sels.*
For What as Easy.
Free One, A.
Fugal-Chorus ("Great is Caesar").
Good-bye to the Mezzogiorno.
Happy New Year, A, *sels.*
He Is the Way.
Hearing of Harvests Rotting in the Valleys.
Henry Adams.
Herman Melville.
History of Truth, The.
Horae Canonicae, *sel.*
Horatians, The.
Hunting Season.
I Am Not a Camera.
If, on Account of the Political Situation.
If I Could Tell You.
I'm beginning to lose patience.
In Due Season.
In Memoriam: Ernst Toller.
In Memory of Sigmund Freud.
In Memory of W. B. Yeats.
In Praise of Limestone.
In Time of War, *sel.*
Island Cemetery, The.
It's No Use Raising a Shout.
James Honeyman.
James Watt.
Jew Wrecked in the German Cell, The.
Journey to Iceland.
Jumbled in the Common Box.
Labyrinth, The.
Lady, Weeping at the Crossroads.
Lakes.
Lauds.
Law like Love.
Let the Florid Music Praise.
Letter, The.
Letter to Lord Byron, *sels.*
Look, Stranger, on This Island Now.
Lost on a fogbound spit of sand.
Love Feast, The.
Lullaby: "Din of work is subdued, The."
Lullaby: "Lay your sleeping head, my love."
Luther.
Many Happy Returns.
Marginalia, *sel.*
May with its light behaving.
Miss Gee.
Missing.
Moon Landing.

More Loving One, The.
Mundus et Infans.
Musée des Beaux Arts.
New Year Letter, *sels.*
Night Falls on China.
Night Mail, The.
1929.
No Change of Place.
Nones.
Note on Intellectuals.
Now the Leaves Are Falling Fast.
Now through Night's Caressing Grip.
Numbers and Faces, *sel.*
O for Doors to Be Open and an Invite with Gilded Edges.
O What Is That Sound [Which So Thrills the Ear].
O Where Are You Going?
Objects.
Ode: To My Pupils.
Ode to Terminus.
Ode to the Medieval Poets.
On Installing an American Kitchen in Lower Austria.
On the Circuit.
On This Island.
Once for candy cook had stolen.
Orators, The, *sel.*
Our Bias.
Our Hunting Fathers.
Paid on Both Sides, *sel.*
Parable.
Paysage Moralisé.
Perhaps.
Petition.
Pick a quarrel, go to war.
Plains.
Poem: "He watched with all his organs of concern."
Poem: "O who can ever praise enough."
Preface: "Aged catch their breath, The."
Prime.
Private faces in public places.
Progress?
Prologue: "By landscape reminded once of his mother's figure."
Prologue: "O love, the interest itself in thoughtless heaven."
Proof, The.
Question, The.
Refugee Blues.
Rimbaud.
Roman Wall Blues.
Sea and the Mirror, The, *sels.*
Seascape.
September 1, 1939.
Sext.
Shield of Achilles, The.
Silly Fool, The.
Since.
Sir Rider Haggard.
Sob, Heavy World.
Soldier Loves His Rifle, The.
Some thirty inches from my nose.
Something Is Bound to Happen.
Song: "Deftly, admiral, cast your fly."
Song: "Fish in the unruffled lakes."
Song: "Make this night loveable."
Song: "Say this city has ten million souls."
Song: "So large a morning, so itself, to lean."
Song: Stop all the Clocks.
Song for St. Cecilia's Day.
Song of the Master and Boatswain.
Song of the Ogres.
Song XI: "Lay your sleeping head, my love."
Sonnets from China, *sels.*
Spain.
Spain 1937.
Spring 1940.
Starling and a Willow-Wren, A.
Strings' Excitement, The.
Summer Night, A.
T. S. Eliot.
Taller to-day, we remember similar evenings.
Thanksgiving for a Habitat.
That Night When Joy Began.
Their Lonely Betters.
There Will Be No Peace.
This Lunar Beauty.
Traveller, The.
Trial, The.
Truest Poetry Is the Most Feigning, The; or, Ars Poetica for Hard Times.
Uncle Henry.
Under Sirius.
Under Which Lyre [a Reactionary Tract for the Times].
Unknown Citizen, The.
Unpredictable but Providential.
Up There.
Vespers.
Villanelle: "Time can say nothing but I told you so."
Vision of the Shepherds.
Voltaire at Ferney.
Walking Tour, The.
Wanderer, The.
Watch Any Day.
Watershed, The.
Well, So That Is That.
When Statesmen gravely say "We must be realistic."
Which Side Am I Supposed to Be On?
Who's Who.
Why are the public buildings so high?
With what conviction the young man spoke.
Woods.
Auerbach, Ephraim
Seismograph.
Augustine, Saint
Take My Heart.
Thou Hast Made Us for Thyself.
Augustini, Delmira
Vision.
Ault, Norman
Clouds.
Father Time.
Wishes.
"Aunt Effie." *See* **Browne, Jane Euphemia**
"Aunt Mary." *See* **Lathbury, Mary Artemisia**
Auringer, Obadiah Cyrus
April.
Ballad of Oriskany, The.
Flight of the War-Eagle, The.
Aus of Kuraiza
Apostasy.
Auslander, Joseph
Abraham Lincoln.
Blackbird Suddenly, A.
César Franck.
Elegy: "Fled is the swiftness of all the white-footed ones."
If We Break Faith.
Interval.
Near Dusk.
Prayer for Thanksgiving, A.
Sunrise Trumpets.
Three Things.
Wings at Dawn.
Ausländer, Rose
Father.
Hasidic Jew from Sadagora.
In Chagall's Village.
Jerusalem.
Lamed-Vov, The.
My Nightingale.
Passover.
Phoenix.
Ausonius, Decimus Magnus
Epigram: "Glad youth had come thy sixteenth year to crown."
Epigram: "Reincarnating Pythagoras, say."
I am that Dido which thou here do'st see.
Idyll of the Rose.
On the sicilian strand a hare well wrought.
To His Wife.
Auster, Paul
Convenant.
Hieroglyph.
Scribe.
Song of Degrees.
Austin, Albert Gordon
Chez-Nous.
Austin, Alfred
Agatha.
Britannia to Columbia.
Human Tragedy, The, *sel.*
Is Life Worth Living?
Last Redoubt, The.
Lover's Song, The.
Love's Trinity.
Maiden of the Smile, The.
Mother-Song.
Primroses.
Prince Lucifer, *sel.*
Thrush, The.
To America.
To Beatrice Stuart Wortley: Aetat 2.
Winter is gone, and spring is over.
Austin, John
Fain Would My Thoughts.
Hark, My Soul.
Austin, Leona Mae
West Texas, *at.*
Austin, Mary
At Carmel.
Beggar Wind, The.
Brown Bear, The.
Caller of the Buffalo.
Deer, The.
Eagle's Song, The.
Elf Owl.
Feller I Know, A.
Grizzly Bear.
Heart's Friend, The.
Little Song of Spring, A.
Prairie-Dog Town.
Prayer to the Mountain Spirit.
Rathers.
Rhyming Riddles, *sels.*
San Francisco.
Sandhill Crane, The.
Snow.
Texas Trains and Trails.
Warrior's Song.
Western Magic.
Winter in the Sierras.
Austin, Regina M.
Still Life.
Austin, William
Chanticleer.
Automedon
Epigram: "I dined with Demetrius last night."
Auvaiyar
Shall I charge like a bull.
You stand and hold the post of my small house.
Auxier, Sylvia
Breaking Point.
Ava, Frau
I am yours, you are mine.
Avane
Ageing Hunter, The.
Avery, Richard K.
And the Cock Begins to Crow, *with music.*
Avison, Margaret
Butterfly, The.
Butterfly Bones; or, Sonnet against Sonnets.
Civility a Bogey.
Dumbfounding, The.
For Dr. and Mrs. Dresser.
For Tinkers Who Travel on Foot.
Hiatus.
In a Season of Unemployment.
Intra-Political.
Janitor Working on Threshold.
Knowledge of Age.

Lament, A: "Gizzard and some ruby inner parts, A."
Meeting Together of Poles & Latitudes: In Prospect.
Nameless One, A.
New Year's Poem.
Party, The.
Person, or A Hymn on and to the Holy Ghost.
Perspective.
Rigor Viris.
Snow.
Story, A.
Stray Dog, near Écully, Valley of the Rhône.
Swimmer's Moment, The.
Tennis.
Thaw.
Two Selves, The.
Unspeakable.
Voluptuaries and Others.
Water and Worship: An Open-Air Service on the Gatineau River.
Watershed.
Word, The.

Avrett, Robert
Renaissance.

Awad, Joseph
Generations.
In a World of Change.

Awoonor, Kofi (George Williams)
Rediscovery.
Sea Eats the Land at Home, The.

Axelrod, David G.
Smell My Fingers.

Axelrod, Susan
Home, The.

Axford, Roger
Victory.

Axionicus
Recipe: Sausage.

Ayer, Ethan
Like a Whisper.

Ayer, Frederick Fanning
Indictment, The, *abr.*

Ayer, William Ward
Be Still.

Ayers, Vivian
Instantaneous ("Instantaneously!").

Ayloffe, John
Britannia and Raleigh.
Marvell's Ghost.
Oceana and Britannia.

Ayre, Anna Chandler
Jack o'Lantern.

Ayres, Philip
Cynthia on Horseback.
Death of Adonis, The.
Describes the Place Where Cynthia Is Sporting Herself.
Epigram on Woman, An.
Fly, The.
Invites His Nymph to His Cottage.
On a Fair Beggar.
On Lydia Distracted.
Yoke uneasy on the ox doth sit, The.

Ayton [*or* Aytoun], Sir Robert
Exercise of Affection, The.
I Loved [*or* **Lov'd**] **Thee Once.**
Inconstancy Reproved.
On a Woman's Inconstancy.
To an Inconstant [Mistress *or* One].
To His Forsaken Mistress.
Upon a Diamond Cut in Form[e] of a Heart . . . Sent in a New-Yeares [*or* Year's] Gift.
Upone Tabacco.
When Thou Did Thinke I Did Not Love.

Aytoun, William Edmonstoune [*or* Edmondstoune]
Biter Bit, The.
Broken Pitcher, The.
Comfort in Affliction.
Edinburgh after Flodden, *sel.*
Execution of Montrose, The.
Hermotimus.
Island of the Scots, The, *abr.*
La Mort d'Arthur.
Laureate, The.
Lay of the Levite, The.
Massacre of the Macpherson, The.
Old Scottish Cavalier, The.
Sonnet to Britain.

Aytoun, William Edmonstoune *and* Sir Theodore Martin
Cry of the Lovelorn, The.
Eastern Serenade.
Lay of the Lovelorn, The.

B

"B., C. B."
Because You Prayed.

"B., M."
Deportation.

"B., R."
This story's strange, but altogether true.

"B, R. L."
Silly Willy.

"B. H." *See* **"H., B."**

"B. L. T." *See* **Taylor, Bert Leston**

"B. V." ("Bysshe Vanolis"). *See* **Thomson, James (1834–82)**

Babcock, Donald Campbell
Adios.
America.
Anthill, The ("The anthill lay unsheltered in the sun").
". . .Discourse Heard One Day. . ."
In a Garden.
Meditation by Mascoma Lake.
Migrant, The.
Neoplatonic Soliloquy.
O God, in Whom the Flow of Days, *with music.*
Two Things.

Babcock, Maltbie Davenport
Be Strong.
Companionship.
Death.
Emancipation.
"Give Us This Day Our Daily Bread."
My Father's World.
Not to Be Ministered To.
This Is My Father's World.

Babcock, William Henry
Bennington.

Baca, Jimmy Santiago
Ancestor.
County Jail, The.
Dreaming about Freedom.
I Am Sure of It.
It Started.
New Warden, The.

Bacchylides
Peace on Earth.

Bachar, Eli
Dawn of Jaffa Pigeons, A.
Houses, Past and Present.
Room Poems.

Bacheller, Irving
Whisperin' Bill.

Bachmann, Ingeborg
Curriculum Vitae.
Days in White.
Every Day.
Firstborn Land, The.
Great Freight, The.
Instructed in love.
Out of the corpse-warm vestibule of heaven steps the sun.
Respite, The.
Songs in Flight, *sel.*
To the Sun.
You want the summer lightning, throw the knives.

Backus, Bertha Adams
Then Laugh.

Bacmeister, Rhoda Warner
Bridges.
Galoshes.

Bacon, Barbara
In Between the Curve.

Bacon, Francis
Life.
Life of Man, The.
World, The.

Bacon, Josephine Dodge Daskam
Brother, Lift Your Flag with Mine.
Motherhood.
Omar for Ladies, An.
Sleepy Dog, The.

Bacon, Leonard (1802–81)
Hail, Tranquil Hour of Closing Day, *with music.*
Pilgrim Fathers, The.
Wake the Song of Jubilee, *with music.*

Bacon, Leonard (1887–1954)
Archaeologist of the Future, The.
Chorus from a Tragedy.
Epitaph in Anticipation.
Fly-fisherman in Wartime.
Horatian Variation.
Reason, The.
Richard Tolman's Universe.
Tower of Ivory.

Bacon, Peggy
Hearth.
Token.

Baden-Powell, Sir Robert
Man, matron, maiden.

Baer, William
Books.

Bagg, Robert
Ballad in Blonde Hair Foretold.
For Her on the First Day Out.
'Laine.
Oracle at Delphi.
Ronald Wyn.
See That One?
Soft Answers.
Speak This Kindly to Her.

Baggesen, Jens
Childhood.

"Bagritsky, Eduard" (Eduard Dzyubin)
He Tries out the Concords Gently.
My Honeyed Languor.
Piece of Black Bread, A.

Baha Ad-din Zuhayr
On a Blind Girl.

Bahe, Liz Sohappy
And What of Me?
Farewell: "You sang round-dance songs."
Grandmother Sleeps.
Once Again.
Printed Words.
Ration Card, The.
Talking Designs.

Bailey, Alfred Goldsworthy
Algonkian Burial.
Border River.
Colonial Set.
Miramichi Lightning.
Question, Is It, The?
Shrouds and Away.
Tâo.

Bailey, Alice Morrey
Defiant One, The.

Bailey, Anthony
Green and the Black, The.

Bailey, H. Sewall
Sailor Man.

Bailey, Lansing C.
Eight Volunteers.

Bailey, Liberty Hyde
Farmer.
Miracle.

Bailey, Margaret
Prayer, A: "God, give me sympathy and sense."

Bailey, Philip James
Festus, *sel.*
My Lady.
Proem: "Poetry is itself a thing of God."
Baillie, Lady Grizel [Grisel *or* Grisell]
There Ance Was a May.
Werena My Heart Licht Wad Dee.
Baillie, Joanna
Blackcock, The.
Child to His Sick Grandfather, A.
Country Inn, The, *sel.*
Disappointment, A.
Horse and His Rider, The.
Mother to Her Waking Infant, A.
Outlaw's Song, The.
Song: "Though richer swains thy love pursue."
Song of the Outlaws.
Tiger at Play.
Trysting Bush, The.
Wake, Lady!
Bainbrigge, Philip
Achilles in Scyros, *sel.*
Chorus of Scyrian Maidens.
Baird, Martha
Effortlessly Democratic Santa Fe Trail.
Baker, Alison
Custer 1 ("You, Custer, you hated").
Custer 2 ("In this picture/ Custer is wearing").
Baker, Carlos
Chinese Mural, A.
Men of Sudbury, The.
On a Landscape of Sestos.
Visit to the Art Gallery, A, *sels.*
Baker, David
Caves.
8-Ball at the Twilight.
Hermit.
Persimmon Trees, She Remembers, Not Far Away.
Running the River Lines.
Wrecker Driver Foresees Your Death, The.
Baker, Donald W.
Formal Application
Baker, George Augustus
Thoughts on the Commandments.
Baker, Henry
Declaimer, The.
Love.
Rapture, The.
Baker, Howard
Letter from the Country, A.
Ode to the Sea.
Baker, J. G.
My Trundle Bed.
Baker, Julia Aldrich
Mizpah.
Baker, Karle Wilson ("Charlotte Wilson")
Beauty's Hands Are Cool.
Burning Bush.
Creeds.
Days.
Good Company.
I Shall Be Loved as Quiet Things.
Let Me Grow Lovely.
Morning Song.
Ploughman, The.
Poet Songs.
Pronouns.
Rondel for September.
Silver Lantern, A.
Baker, Leon
All Night!
Cap'n & Me.
Getting Back to Work.
Jackson State Prison.
On Youth, the Warden & Solitary!
Baker, Olaf
Little Saling.
Baker, Thomas
Electric Telegraph, The.
Means of Propulsion for Steam-Ships.
Steam Engine, The; or, The Power of Flame, *sels.*
Watt's Improvements to the Steam Engine.
Balaban, John
After Our War.
"Faith and Practice."
Guard at the Binh Thuy Bridge, The.
Balakian, Peter
Blue Church, The.
Father Fisheye.
Homage to Hart Crane.
In the Turkish Ward.
Jersey Bait Shack.
Balazs, Mary
Incident at Mossel Bay.
Pregnant Teenager on the Beach.
Balch, Emily Greene
Flag Speaks, The.
Baldenegro, Salomón R., Jr.
Man, I Felt Like Running All Night.
Balderston, Jean
RIP.
Baldwin, Mary Newton
Lonely Are the Fields of Sleep.
Baldwin, Michael
Death on a Live Wire.
Baldwin, Tama
Hooking the Rainbow.
Baldwin, Thomas
From Whence Doth This Union Arise? *with music.*
Baldwin, William
Beloved to the Spouse, The.
Christ, My Beloved.
Christ to His Spouse.
How Collingbourne Was Cruelly Executed for Making a Foolish Rhyme.
Spouse to the Beloved, The.
Bale, John
Wassail, Wassail.
Bales, C. O.
Discipleship.
Balhurst, W. H.
Unshrinking Faith.
Ball, Arthur
Above Ben Loyal.
Tall Sky, The.
Ballantine, James
Castles in the Air.
Creep afore Ye Gang.
Its Ain Drap o' Dew.
Ballantyne, Deirdre
Long Word, The.
Ballard, Charles G.
During the Pageant at Medicine Lodge.
Grandma Fire.
Memo.
Now the People Have the Light.
Sand Creek.
Speaker, The.
Spirit Craft, The.
Their Cone-like Cabins.
Winds of Change, The.
You Northern Girl.
Ballard, Colin Robert
Pacific Railway, The.
Ballard, Harlan Hoge
In the Catacombs.
Ballard, Rae
Father of the Victim.
Ballou, Hosea, I
Dear Lord, Behold Thy Servants, *with music.*
In God's Eternity, *with music.*
When God Descends with Men to Dwell, *with music.*
Ballou, Hosea, II
Ye Realms below the Skies, *with music.*
Ballou, Silas
Almighty God in Being Was, *with music.*
While I Am Young, *with music.*
Balsdon, Dacre
Endurance Test.
Bamberger, Augustus Wright
Each a Part of All.
Out of the Vast.
Bampfylde, John Codrington
On a Frightful Dream.
On a Wet Summer.
Sonnet: "As when, to one who long hath watched, the morn."
To the Evening.
Bancks, John
Description of London, A.
Fragment, A: "In Cloe's chamber, she and I."
Bancroft, Charles
Tadoussac.
Bancroft, James Henry
Brother, Though from Yonder Sky, *with music.*
Bangham, Mary Dickerson
Come, Holy Babe!
Bangs, Janet Norris
Design for Peace.
Bangs, John Kendrick
"Don't Care" and "Never Mind" (" 'Don't care' is no friend of mine").
Dreadful Fate of Naughty Nate, The.
Hired Man's Way, The.
If.
Lincoln's Birthday.
Little Elf, The.
May 30, 1893.
My Dog.
On File.
Philosopher, A.
Thanksgiving Day.
To a Withered Rose.
"What hundred books are best, think you?" I said.
Banim, John
He Said That He Was Not Our Brother.
Irish Mother in the Penal Days, The.
Soggarth Aroon.
Banker, William, Jr.
Battle of Queenstown, The.
Banks, George Linnaeus
My Aim.
What I Live For.
Bannerman, Frances
Upper Chamber, An.
Banning, Kendall
Once on a Time.
Banning, Lex
Captain Arthur Phillip and the Birds.
Bantock, Gavin
Bard.
Dirge: "Body lies under the ground."
Joy.
Banus, Maria
Eighteen.
Gift Hour.
New Notebook, The.
Baraka, Imamu Amiri (LeRoi Jones)
Agony, An. As Now.
Air.
At the National Black Assembly.
Audubon, Drafted.
Babylon Revisited.
Balboa, the Entertainer.
Ballad of the Morning Streets.
Ballgame, The.
Beautiful Black Women.
Biography.
Black Art.
Black Bourgeoisie.
Black Dada Nihilismus.
Black People!
Black People: This Is Our Destiny.
Bumi.
Clearing, The.
Cold Term.
Crow Jane.
Dance, The.
Das Kapital.
Dead Lady Canonized, The.

Death of Nick Charles, The.
Duncan Spoke of a Process.
Each Morning.
End of Man Is His Beauty, The.
Epistrophe.
Evil Nigger Waits for Lightnin'.
For Hettie.
Funeral Poem.
Guerrilla Handbook, A.
Hegel.
Horatio Alger Uses Scag.
Hymn for Lanie Poo, *sel.*
I Substitute for the Dead Lecturer.
In Memory of Radio.
In One Battle.
Incident.
Insidious Dr. Fu Man Chu, The.
Invention of Comics, The.
It's Nation Time.
Ka 'Ba.
Leadbelly Gives an Autograph.
Leroy.
Letter to E. Franklin Frazier.
Liar, The.
Like Rousseau.
Lines to Garcia Lorca.
New World, The.
Notes for a Speech.
Numbers, Letters.
One Night Stand.
Ostriches and Grandmothers!
People's Choice, The: The Dream Poems II.
Poem for Black Hearts, A.
Poem for Democrats, A.
Poem for Half White College Students.
Poem for Speculative Hipsters, A.
Poem for Willie Best, A.
Poem Some People Will Have to Understand, A.
Political Poem.
Politics of Rich Painters, The.
Preface to a Twenty Volume Suicide Note.
Pressures, The.
Red Light.
Return of the Native.
SOS.
Snake Eyes.
Song Form.
Study Peace.
Three Modes of History and Culture.
Tight Rope.
To a Publisher. . .Cut-out.
Turncoat, The.
W. W.
Way Out West.
We Own the Night.
Young Soul.

Barba, Sharon
Dykes in the Garden.

Barbauld, Anna Laetitia
Life.
Mouse's Petition, The.
Rights of Woman, The.
To Mr. S. T. Coleridge.

Barber, Frances
Play-acting.

Barber, J.
White Steed of the Prairies, The.

Barber, Mary
On Seeing an Officer's Widow Distracted.
Written for My Son, and Spoken by Him at His First Putting on Breeches.

Barber, Melanie Gordon
Sonnet for My Son.

Barber, William
Explanation.

Barberini, Francesco da
Of Caution.
Virgin Declares Her Beauties, A.

Barbour, George Hurlbut
Decoration Day.

Barbour, John
Battle of Bannockburn, The.
Before Bannockburn.
Bruce, The, *sels.*
Bruce Consults His Men.
Buik of Alexander, The, *sel.*
Freedom.
Prologue to the Avowis of Alexander.

Barclay, Alexander
Ballade to Our Lady.
Geographers.
Preachment for Preachers.
Ship of Fools, The, *sels.*
Star of the Sea.
Tudor Rose, The.

Barclay, Edwin
Human Greatness.

Barclay, Robert
Hic liber ad me pertinet.

Bardeen, Charles William
Birds' Ball, The.

Bardsley, Alice
Storm Warning.

Barford, John
Eric.
Serve Her Right.
Sundered.
Toleration.
Whom Jesus Love.

Barham, Richard Harris. *See* **"Ingoldsby, Thomas"**

Baring, Maurice
Ballad: "Roses in my garden, The."
Diffugere Nives, 1917.
Dying Reservist, The.
I Dare Not Pray to Thee.
I. M. H.
Julian Grenfell.
Leirioessa Kalyx.
Moan in the Form of a Ballade.

Baring-Gould, Sabine
Child's Evening Hymn.
For Evening.
Hymn: "Now the day is over."
Now the Day Is Over.
Olive Tree, The.
Onward, Christian Soldiers.
Through the Night of Doubt and Sorrow.

Barker, David
Lispy Bails Out.
Matisse Tits.
Packard.
View from the Planetarium.
Zoo Dream.

Barker, Edna L. S.
Child of the World.

Barker, Edward D.
Go Sleep, Ma Honey.

Barker, Elsa
Caresses.
Confession.
Consummation.
Fulfilment.
I Know.
Inscription, The: "Sealed with the seal of Life, thy soul and mine."
Love's Immortality.
Spirit and the Bride, The, *sels.*
When I Am Dead and Sister to the Dust.

Barker, George
Allegory of the Adolescent and the Adult.
And now there is nothing left to celebrate.
At midday they looked up and saw their death.
Calamiterror, *sel.*
Channel Crossing.
Crystal, The.
Death of Yeats, The.
Dog, Dog in My Manger.
Elegy V: Separation of Man from God.
Elegy: "These errors loved no less than the saint loves arrows."
Elegy on the Eve.
Evening Star.
Everywhere is our wilderness everywhere.
First Cycle of Love Poems (I–V).
For the Fourth Birthday of My Daughter.
From thorax of storms the voices of verbs.
He Comes Among.
Holy Poems (I–III).
House I Go to in My Dream, The.
In Memory of a Friend.
In Memory of David Archer, *sel.*
Keelhauled across the star-wrecked death of God.
Leaping Laughers, The.
Letter to a Young Poet.
Love Poem: "Less the dog begged to die in the sky."
Love Poem: "My joy, my jockey, my Gabriel."
Love Poem: "O tender under her right breast."
Memorial Couplets for the Dying Ego.
Munich Elegy No. 1.
My Joy, My Jockey, My Gabriel.
News of the World I ("Cold shuttered loveless star, skulker in clouds").
News of the World II ("In the first year of the last disgrace").
News of the World III ("Let her lie naked here, my hand resting").
O Golden Fleece.
O Tender under Her Right Breast.
Oak and the Olive, The.
Ode against St. Cecilia's Day.
Pacific Sonnets, *sels.*
Resolution of Dependence.
Sacred Elegy V.
Satan Is on Your Tongue.
Second Cycle of Love Poems, *sel.*
Secular Elegies, *sel.*
Sequence.
Shut the Seven Seas against Us.
So in a one man Europe I sit here.
Sonnet of Fishes.
Sonnet to My Mother.
Sonnets of the Triple-headed Manichee, *sel.*
Sparrow's Feather, A.
Summer Idyll.
Summer Song I.
Third Cycle of Love Poems, *sel.*
This is that month, Elizabeth.
Three Dead and the Three Living, The.
Three Memorial Sonnets.
To Any Member of My Generation.
To My Son, *sel.*
Today, the Twenty-sixth of February.
Triumphal Ode MCMXXXIX.
True Confession of George Barker, The, *sels.*
Turn on Your Side and Bear the Day to Me.
Verses for a First Birthday.
Wild Dreams of Summer What Is Your Grief.
Wraith-Friend, The.

Barker, Jane
Epitaph on the Secretary to the Muses.

Barker, Squire Omar
Code of the Cow Country.
Fine!
Hot Ir'n!
Jackrabbits.
Law West of the Pecos, The.
Rodeo Days.
Sheep Beezness, The.
Tall Men Riding.
To a Jack Rabbit.
When Billy the Kid Rides Again.

Barker, Thomas
Art of Angling, The, *sels.*
Baits for Various Fish.
How to Catch Trout.
Methods of Cooking Trout.

Barks, Coleman
Adam's Apple.
Brain.
Bruises.
Downy Hair in the Shape of a Flame.

Finger of Necessity.
Goosepimples.
Mule, The.
Semen.
Barlow, George
Dead Child, The.
Mellowness and Flight.
Soul, The.
Spiritual Passion.
Sweet Diane.
Barlow, Jane
Christmas Rede.
Out of Hearing.
Barlow, Joel
Advice to a Raven in Russia.
Along the Banks, *with music.*
Columbiad, The, *sel.*
First American Congress, The.
Freedom.
Hasty Pudding, The.
Judge Me, O God, *with music.*
O God of My Salvation, Hear, *with music.*
On the Discoveries of Captain Lewis.
One Centred System.
Song, A: "Fame let thy trumpet sound."
Barnard, Lady Anne. *See* **Lindsay, Lady Anne**
Barnard, Charlotte Alington ("Claribel")
Come Back to Erin.
I Cannot Sing the Old Songs.
Take Back the Heart.
Barnard, John
Nations That Long in Darkness Walked, *with music.*
Thrice Blest the Man, *with music.*
Barnard, Katherine R.
Voice of God, The.
Barnard, Mary
Pleiades, The.
Shoreline.
Solitary, The.
Barnefield, Richard. *See* **Barnfield, Richard**
Barnes, Barnabe
Content.
Divine Century of Spiritual Sonnets, A, *sels.*
God's Virtue.
Life of Man, The.
Ode: "Why doth heaven bear a sun."
Parthenophil and Parthenophe, *sels.*
Sonnet: "Ah, sweet Content! where is thy mild abode?"
Sonnet: "World's bright comforter, whose beamsome light, The."
To the Most Beautiful Lady, the Lady Bridget Manners.
World's Bright Comforter, The.
Barnes, Djuna
Transfiguration.
Barnes, Jeannette
Absence.
Barnes, Jim
Accident at Three Mile Island.
Autobiography, Chapter XII: Hearing Montana.
Autobiography, Chapter XVII: Floating the Big Piney.
Autobiography: Last Chapter.
Bone Yard.
Camping Out on Rainy Mountain.
Captive Stone, The.
Choctaw Chief Helps Plan a Festival, A.
Comcomly's Skull.
Descent to Bohannon Lake.
Four Choctaw Songs.
Four Things Choctaw.
Halcyon Days.
Last Look at La Plata, Missouri.
Lying in a Yuma Saloon.
Old Soldiers Home at Marshalltown, Iowa.
Paiute Ponies.
Sweating It Out on Winding Stair Mountain.
These Damned Trees Crouch.
Tracking Rabbits: Night.
Wolf Hunting near Nashoba.
Barnes, Jo
Clinic Day.
Barnes, Julians
Book of Hunting, *sels.*
Barnes, Kate
Hector the Dog.
Mare, A.
Barnes, William
Air an' Light.
Bean Vield, The.
Bells ov Alderburnham, The.
Be'mi'ster.
Black an' White.
Blackbird, The.
Blackmwore Maidens.
Burncombe Hollow.
Bwoat, The.
Child an' the Mowers, The.
Clote, The (Water-Lily).
Come!
Come an' Meet Me wi' the Children on the Road.
Day's Work a-Done.
Dobbin Dead.
Dock-Leaves.
Easter Zunday.
Eclogue: Common a-Took In, The.
Eclogue: Two Farms in Woone.
Evenen in the Village.
Evening, and Maidens.
Fall, The.
Girt Woak Tree That's in the Dell, The.
Grammer's Shoes.
Green.
Head-Stone, The.
Heedless o' My Love.
In the Spring.
Jeane.
Jenny's Ribbons.
Leady-Day, an' Ridden House.
Leane, The.
Leaves.
Liady-Day an' Ridden House.
Lost Little Sister, The.
Lowshot Light.
Lullaby: "Rook's nest do rock on the tree-top, The."
Mater Dolorosa.
May.
May Tree, The.
Melhill Feast.
Mother's Dream, The.
Musings.
My Love's Guardian Angel.
My Orcha'd in Linden Lea.
Oak-Tree, The.
Old House, The.
Readen ov a Head-Stwone.
Rings.
Round Things.
Rustic Childhood.
Sheep in the Sheade.
Shellbrook
Shep'erd Bwoy, The.
Slow to Come, Quick a-Gone.
Sonnet: "In every dream thy lovely features rise."
Sonnet: Leaves.
Spring, The.
Storm-Wind, The.
Times o' Year.
To Me.
Tokens.
Troubles of the Day.
Turnstile, The.
Vo'k a-Comen into Church.
White an' Blue.
Whitsuntide an' Club Walken.
Wife a-Lost, The.
Wife a-Prais'd, A.
Wind at the Door, The.
Winter Night, A.
Witch, A.
With you first shown to me.
Withstanders.
Woodlands, The.
Young Rhymer Snubbed, The.
Zong, A: "O Jenny, don't sobby! vor I shall be true."
Zummer Stream.
Zummer Thoughts in Winter Time.
Zun a-Lighten Eyes a-Shut, The.
Zun-zet.
Barnett, Anthony
Book of Mysteries, The.
Celan.
Cloisters.
Crossing.
Marriage, A.
Barnett, Ratcliffe
For Summer's Here.
Barnett, Stella
Evening in the Suburbs.
Barney, William D.
Caught in the Pocket.
Nearly Everybody Loves Harvey Martin.
Post Card out of Panama, A.
Rasslers, The.
Barnfield [*or* Barnefield], Richard
Affectionate Shepherd, The, *sels.*
As It Fell upon a Day.
Comparison of the Life of Man, A.
Daphnis to Ganymede.
If Music [*or* Musique] and Sweet Poetry [*or* Poetrie] Agree.
Nightingale, The.
Ode, An: "As it fell upon a day."
Olden Days, The.
Shepherd's Complaint, A.
Sonnet: "Ah no; nor I myselfe: though my pure love."
Sonnet: "But now my Muse toyled with continuall care."
Sonnet: "Cherry-lipt Adonis in his snowie shape."
Sonnet: "Here hold this glove (this milk-white cheveril glove)."
Sonnet: "Sighing, and sadly sitting by my Love."
Sonnet: "Some talk of Ganymede th' Idalian boy."
Sonnet: "Sometimes I wish that I his pillow were."
Sonnet: "Sporting at fancie, setting light by love."
Sonnet: "Sweet corrall lips, where Nature's treasure lies."
Sonnet: "Sweet Thames I honour thee, not for thou art."
Sonnet: "Thus was my love, thus was my Ganymed."
Sonnet: "Two stars there are in one faire firmament."
Sonnets, *sels.*
To His Friend Master R. L., in Praise of Music and Poetry.
Unknown Shepherd's Complaint, The.
Barnie, John
Dog in Us, The.
Barnstone, Aliki
Letter from the Hotel, A.
Mating the Goats.
To a Friend's Child.
Windows in Providence.
Barnstone, Andal
To Krishna Haunting the Hills.
Barnstone, Willis
Borges.
Changsha Shoe Factory.
Eyes of Cantonese Schoolmasters Remembered in Hong Kong, The.
Gas Lamp.
Good Breasts, The.
Grandfather.

I wish to paint my eyes.
Miklos Radnoti.
Paradise.
Rooftop.
Stained Glass.
With Schoolchildren.
Worm, The.

Baro, Gene
Cherry.
Ferns, The.
For Hani, Aged Five, That She Be Better Able to Distinguish a Villain.
Horsemen, The.
Judges, Judges.
Ladder, The.
Lament for Better or Worse.
Northern Spring, A.
Northwind.
Street, The.
Travelling Backward.
Under the Boughs.

Baron, Mary
For an Egyptian Boy, Died c. 700 B.C.
Letters for the New England Dead.

Barr, Alice M.
Guard Thy Tongue.

Barr, Isabel Harriss
Madaket Beach.

Barr, Matthias
Moon, So Round and Yellow.
Only a Baby Small.

Barratt, Ken
Burke and Wills.

Barrax, Gerald William
Black Narcissus.
Christmas 1959 et Cetera.
Efficiency Apartment.
For Malcolm: After Mecca.
Fourth Dance Poem.
If She Sang.
To a Woman Who Wants Darkness and Time.
Your Eyes Have Their Silence.

Barreno, Maria Isabel *and* **Maria Teresa Horta** *and* **Maria Velho da Costa.** *See* **Marias, The Three**

Barret, Pringle
Hint to the Wise, A.

Barrett, Alfred Joseph
Chant of Departure; a Missionary's Prayer.
Martyr's Mass, A.
Mary's Assumption.
Rosebush and the Trinity, The.
Unearth.

Barrett, Eaton Stannard
Woman.

Barrett, Wilson Agnew
New England Church, A.

Barrie, Hugh
When I Am Dead.

Barrington, Patrick
Air Sentry, The.
Here a Nit-Wit Lies.
I Had a Duck-billed Platypus.
I Had a Hippopotamus.
I Was a Bustlemaker Once, Girls.
Take Me in Your Arms, Miss Moneypenny-Wilson.

Barrington, Pauline B.
Education.
White Iris, A.

Barrios, Gregorio
Crazy Movie.

Barrios, Miguel de
Epitaph: "Daniel and Abigail."

Barrow, Jedediah
You Call That a Ts'ing; a Letter.

Barrows, Anita
Ancestors, The.
Avenue Y.
Emigration.
Letter to a Friend in an Unknown Place.
Reflections.

Barrows, Marjorie
Bug, The.

Barson, Alfred
On the Death of Parents.

Barstow, Henry H.
If Easter Be Not True.

Barth, John
Minstrel's Last Lay, The.

Barth, R. L.
Waking Early.

Barthgate, Dave
Rock Leader.

Bartlett, Elizabeth
After the Storm.
Behold This Dreamer.
Cage, The.
Dark Angel.
In Days of New.
Question Is Proof, The.

Bartlett, I. J.
Town of Don't-You-Worry, The.

Bartlett, Ruth Fitch
Belief.

Bartole, Genevieve
Canadian Farmer.

Barton, Bernard
Bruce and the Spider.
Not Ours the Vows.
Walking in the Light.

Barton, David
Solutions.

Barton, Fred
Death of the Sailor's Wife, The.

Barton, Joan
Mistress, The.

Baruch, Dorothy Walter
Automobile Mechanics.
Barber's Clippers.
Cat.
Different Bicycles.
Funny the Way Different Cars Start.
Lawn-Mower.
Merry-go-round.
On a Steamer.
Rabbits.
Riding in a Motor Boat.
Riding in an Airplane.
Skunk, The.
Stop—Go.

Baruch of Worms
Elegy: "Those reckless hosts rush to the wells."

Bashford, Sir Henry Howarth
Good Day, The.
Lullaby in Bethlehem.
To Petronilla Who Has Put Up Her Hair.
Where Do the Gipsies Come From?

Bashford, Herbert
Alice.
Song of the Forest Ranger, The.

Basho (Matsuo Basho)
All That Is Left.
As Firmly Cemented Clam-Shells.
Beauty.
Cicada-Shell.
Friend sparrow, do not eat, I pray.
Haiku: "Fish shop."
Haiku: "Lightning gleam, A."
Haiku: "Moor:/ point my horse."
Harbingers.
In My New Clothing.
Lightning in the clouds!
Lonely pond in age-old stillness sleeps, A.
Monkey's Raincoat, The.
O cricket, from your cheery cry.
Old men, white-haired, beside the ancestral graves.
Old Pond, The.
On à withered branch.
Only for Morning Glories.
Play About, Do.
Plum Blossoms ("Far across hill and dale").
Quick-falling dew.
Roadside thistle, eager, The.
Wake Up! Wake Up!

Bass, Ellen
Celia.
I am the sorrow in the wheat fields.
In Celebration.
Partly to My Cat.
September 7.

Bass, Tom
Spring Sunday on Quaker Street.

Basse, William
Anglers Song, The (*in* Izaak Walton's The Compleat Angler).
Elegy on Shakespeare.
Momento for Mortality, A.
On Mr. Wm. Shakespeare.
On the Tombs in Westminster Abbey, *at.*

Bassen, Lois
Brain Coral.

Bassett, A. A.
Twice Fed.

Bassett, Lee
Wires.

Bastard, Thomas
Ad Henricum Wottonem.
De Naevo in Facie Faustinae.
Epitaph: Iohannis Sande.
In Gaetam.
Methinks 'Tis Pretty Sport [to Hear a Child].

Bate, John
Cologne.

Bates, Arlo
America.
Conceits, *sels.*
Cyclamen, The.
In Paradise.
Kitty's Laugh.
Kitty's "No."
Like to a Coin.
On the Road to Chorrera.
Rose, A.
Shadow Boat, A.
Torch-Bearers, The, *sel.*
Watchers, The.
Winter Twilight, A.

Bates, Brainard L. *See* **Bates, Esther Willard** *and* **Brainard L. Bates**

Bates, Charlotte Fiske
André.
Character, A.
Clue, The.
Delay.
Living Book, The.
Woodbines in October.

Bates, Clara Doty
At Grandfather's.
Gray Thrums.
Thistle-Down.
Who Likes the Rain?

Bates, David
Speak Gently.

Bates, Esther Willard *and* **Brainard L. Bates**
Ipswich Bar.

Bates, G. E.
Pentagonia.

Bates, Herbert
Heavens Are Our Riddle, The.
Prairie.

Bates, Katharine Lee
America the Beautiful.
Changing Road, The.
Christmas Island.
Despised and Rejected.
Earth Listens.
For Deeper Life.
Gypsy-Heart.
In His Steps.
Kings of the East, The.
Little Knight in Green, The.
Robin's Secret.
Sarah Threeneedles.
Song of Riches, A.

Song of Waking, A.
Thou Knowest.
Wild Weather.
Youth.
Bates, Scott
Fable of the Talented Mockingbird.
Whales.
Bathgate, Dave
For Tony, Dougal, Mick, Bugs, Nick, *et al.*
Bat-Miriam, Yocheved
Distance Spills Itself.
Monasteries Lift Gold Domes, The.
Batterham, Eric N.
Once.
Baudelaire, Charles
Abyss, The.
Albatross, The.
Anywhere Out of the World.
At One o'Clock in the Morning.
Balcon, Le.
Be Drunken.
Beauté, La.
Beauty.
Blind, The.
Carrion, A.
Cat, The.
Condemned Women.
Correspondences.
Crowds.
Damned Women.
De Profundis Clamavi.
Don Juan in Hell.
Élévation.
Epilogue: "With heart at rest I climbed the citadel's."
Evening Twilight.
Flowers of Evil, The, *sel.*
Former Life.
Giantess.
Harmonie du Soir.
Heautontimoroumenos.
Her Hair.
Hiboux, Les.
I adore you as much as the vault of night.
Ideal, The.
Ill Luck.
Injured Moon, The.
Intimate Associations.
Invitation to the Voyage.
Inward Conversation.
Jewels, The.
Litany to Satan.
Lovers' Death, The.
Meditation.
Metamorphoses of the Vampire.
Mists and Rain.
Music, The.
Parfum Exotique.
Peace, Be at Peace, O Thou My Heaviness.
Sadness of the Moon, The.
Seven Old Men, The.
Sois sage o ma douleur.
Song of Autumn I.
Spleen LXXV ("Old Pluvius, month of rains, in peevish mood").
Spleen LXXVI ("I have more memories than if I had lived a thousand years").
Spleen LXXVII ("I'm like the king of a rain-country, rich").
Spleen LXXVIII ("When the low heavy sky weighs like a lid").
Stranger, The.
Swan, The.
To a Passer-by.
To Azrael.
To the Reader.
Voyage to Cythera.
Women Damned.
Bauer, Grace
Spring and All.
Bauer, Steven
Stopped in Memphis.
Baugh, Sue
Seal Rock.
Baum, Peter
Horror.
Psalms of Love.
Bax, Sir Arnold. *See* **"O'Byrne, Dermot"**
Bax, Clifford
Turn Back, O Man.
Baxter, Carolyn
Houston Street, N. Y.
Lower Court.
Masochistic Tendencies.
Toilet Bowl Congregation.
Warden's Day.
Baxter, James Keir
Apple Tree, The.
Autumn Testament, *sels.*
Buried Stream, The.
Dentist's Window, A.
East Coast Journey.
Evidence at the Witch Trials.
Family Photograph 1939, A.
He Waiata mo Te Kare.
How to Fly by Standing Still, *sel.*
Ikons, The.
Inflammable Woman, The.
Jerusalem Sonnets, *sels.*
Lament for Barney Flanagan.
Mandrakes for Supper.
New Zealand.
News from a Pacified Area.
Rope for Harry Fat, A.
To a Print of Queen Victoria.
Wild Bees.
Baxter, Richard
Lord, It Belongs Not to My Care.
Love Breathing Thanks and Praise, *sel.*
Psalm of Praise, A, *sel.*
Ye holy Angels bright.
Bayldon, Arthur
Marlowe.
Sunset.
Baylebridge, William (*originally* **Charles William Blocksidge)**
Life's Testament, *sels.*
Love Redeemed, *sels.*
Bayles, James C.
In the Gloaming.
Bayliss, John Clifford
Apocalypse and Resurrection.
October.
Seven Dreams.
Baylor, Byrd
Desert Tortoise.
Bayly, Thomas Haynes
Do You Remember.
Gaily the Troubadour, *with music.*
I'd Be a Butterfly.
Long, Long Ago.
Mistletoe Bough, The.
Oh, No! We Never Mention Her.
Oh! Where Do Fairies Hide Their Heads?
She Wore a Wreath of Roses.
Beach, Joseph Warren
Dropping Your Aitches.
Horatian Ode.
Beach, Seth Curtis
Mysterious Presence! Source of All, *with music.*
Thou One in All, Thou All in One, *with music.*
"Beachcomber." *See* **Morton, John Bingham**
Beaconsfield, Benjamin Disraeli, 1st Earl of. *See* **Disraeli, Benjamin, 1st Earl of Beaconsfield**
Beard, Cathy
Any April.
Beardsley, Aubrey
Ballad of a Barber, The.
Three Musicians, The.
Beatrice de Die
Handsome friend, charming and kind.
My true love makes me happy.
Beattie, James
Epitaph, An: "Escaped the gloom of mortal life, a soul."
Epitaph, An: "Like thee I once have stemm'd the sea of life."
Epitaph Intended for Himself, An.
Minstrel, The, *sels.*
Nature and the Poets.
Nature's Charms.
Question, The.
Retirement, *sel.*
Solitude.
To Mr. Alexander Ross.
Youth of a Poet, The.
Beattie, James Hay
On the Author of the *Treatise of Human Nature.*
Beatty, Pakenham
When Will Love Come?
Beaumont, Francis
Examination of His Mistress' Perfections, The.
Fit Only for Apollo.
Francis Beaumont's Letter from the Country to Jonson.
Indifferent, The.
Letter to Ben Jonson, A.
Masque of the Inner Temple and Gray's Inne, The, *sels.*
Mr. Francis Beaumont's Letter to Ben Johnson.
On the Marriage of a Beauteous Young Gentlewoman with an Ancient Man.
On the Tombs in Westminster Abbey, *at.*
Pining for Love.
Shake Off Your Heavy Trance.
Song for a Dance.
Songs from a Masque.
Songs from the Masque of the Gentlemen of Gray's-Inne and the Inner-Temple.
True Beauty.
Upon Master Edmund Spenser.
Ye Should Stay Longer.
Beaumont, Francis *and* **John Fletcher**
Another Song ("For Jillian of Berry, she dwells on a hill").
Aspatia's Song.
Away, Delights.
Bridal Song ("Cynthia, to thy power").
Captain, The, *sels.*
Come, Sleep.
Come, You Whose Loves Are Dead.
Cupid's Revenge, *sel.*
Hold Back Thy Hours.
I Died True.
Jillian of Berry.
Knight of the Burning Pestle, The, *sels.*
Laugh and Sing.
Lay a Garland on My Hearse.
Lovers Rejoyce [*or* Rejoice].
Love's Cure, *sel.*
Lullaby: "Come sleep, and with the sweet deceiving."
Maid's Tragedy, The, *sels.*
Merrythought's Song.
Mirth.
Month of May, The.
Sleep.
Song: "Heare ye ladies that despise."
Song: "Hence all you vaine delights."
Song: "Turn, turn thy beauteous face away."
To Bed, to Bed.
Woman-Hater, The, *sel.*
Beaumont, Sir John
Assumption, The.
Bosworth Field, *sel.*
Epitaph upon My Dear Brother, Francis Beaumont, An.
O Thou Who Art Our Author and Our End.
Of His Dear Son, Gervase.
Of My Dear Son, Gervase Beaumont.
Of Sir Philip Sidney.
Of True Liberty.
Relish of the Muse, The.
Richard III's Speech.

To His Late Majesty Concerning the True Form of English Poetry.
Upon a Funeral.
Beaumont, Joseph
Ascension, The.
Biothanatos.
Garden, The.
Gentle Check, The.
Gnat, The.
Home.
House and Home.
Love.
Morning Hymn.
Purification of the Blessed Virgin.
Whit Sunday.
Whiteness, or Chastity.
Beauvais, Phyllis (Phyllis Harris)
Furniture.
Outside.
Under Your Voice, among Legends.
Beaver, Bruce
Cow Dance.
Letters to Live Poets, *sels.*
Beccadelli, Antonio. *See* **"Panormitanus"**
Bechtel, Louise Seaman
Grandfather Frog.
Beck, Victor Emanuel
Sifting.
Becker, Edna
Beside the Line of Elephants.
Reflections.
Becker, John
Feather or Fur.
Beckett, Gilbert Abbott à. *See* **À Beckett, Gilbert Abbott**
Beckett, Samuel
Age is when to a man.
Alba.
Enueg I ("Exeo in a spasm").
Enueg II ("World world world world/ And the face grave").
Gnome.
I would like my love to die.
Malacoda.
What would I do without this world faceless incurious.
Whoroscope.
Words and Music, *sel.*
Bécquer, Gustavo Adolfo
They Closed Her Eyes.
Beddo, Frank
Jeff Buckner.
Beddoes, Thomas Lovell
Alpine Spirit's Song.
Ballad of Human Life.
Beautiful Night, A.
"Bona de Mortuis."
Bridal Song to Amala.
Bride's Tragedy, The, *sels.*
Bury Him Deep.
Carrion Crow, The.
Death's Jest Book; or, The Fool's Tragedy, *sels.*
Dirge: "If thou wilt ease thine heart."
Dirge: "Swallow leaves her nest, The."
Dirge: "We do lie beneath the grass."
Dirge Written for a Drama.
Dream-Pedlary.
Epithalamia.
Fragment: "Bury him deep. So damned a work should lie."
Fragments Intended for the Dramas, *sel.*
How Many Times Do I Love Thee, Dear?
If Thou Wilt Ease Thine Heart.
Ivory Gate, The, *sel.*
Last Man, The, *sel.*
L'Envoi: "Who findeth comfort in the stars and flowers."
Lines: "How lovely is the heaven of this night."
Lines: "I followed once a fleet and mighty serpent."
Lines Written in a Blank Leaf of the Prometheus Unbound.
Lord Alcohol.
Love-in-Idleness.
Mandrake's Song.
Man's Anxious, but Ineffectual Guard against Death.
Mariners' Song.
Mighty Thoughts of an Old World, The.
New Cecilia, The.
Old Adam.
Old Adam, the Carrion Crow.
Old Ghost, The.
Oviparous Tailor, The.
Phantom-Wooer, The.
Poor Old Pilgrim Misery.
Reason Why, The.
Resurrection Song.
Sailor's Song.
Sibilla's Dirge.
Silenus in Proteus.
Song: "A ho! A ho!/ Love's horn doth blow."
Song: "How many times do I love thee, dear?"
Song: "Old Adam, the carrion crow."
Song: "Strew not earth with empty stars."
Song: "We have bathed, where none have seen us."
Song: "Who tames the lion now?"
Song by Isbrand.
Song from the Ship.
Song from the Waters.
Song of Thanatos.
Song of the Stygian Naiades.
Song on the Water.
Songs at Amala's Wedding.
Sonnet: To Tartar, a Terrier Beauty.
Stanzas: "Mighty thought of an old world, The."
Stanzas from the Ivory Gate.
Sybilla's Dirge.
Tailor, The.
Threnody: "No sunny ray, no silver night."
To Night.
To Sea, to Sea!
Torrismond, *sel.*
Voice from the Waters, A.
Wolfram's Dirge.
Wolfram's Song.
"Bede, Cuthbert" (Edward Bradley)
Entrance Exams.
In Immemoriam.
Limerick: "There was a queer fellow named Woodin."
Queer Fellow Named Woodin, A.
Bede, The Venerable
Hymn, A: "Hymn of glory let us sing, A."
Bedford, Madeline Ida
Munition Wages.
Parson's Job, The.
Bedingfield, Thomas
Lover's Choice, The.
Beebe, Lucius
Quid Restat, *abr.*
Beecham, Audrey
Exile.
Beecham, Sir Thomas
Hark the herald angels sing/ Beecham's pills are just the thing.
Beecher, John
Aztec Figurine.
Desert Holy Man.
To Alexander Meiklejohn, *sel.*
To Live and Die in Dixie, *sels.*
Beeching, Henry Charles
Accidia.
Bicycling Song.
Blackbird, The.
Boy's Prayer, A.
Going Down Hill on a Bicycle.
Knowledge after Death.
Prayers.
Beeching, Jack
1944—On the Invasion Coast.
Beedome, Thomas
Broken Heart, The.
Choyce, The.
To His Mistresse on Her Scorne.
Beeler, Janet
Photographer's Wife, The.
Beenen, Jennivien-Diana
Morning Poem.
Be'er, Hayim
Love Song: "In the light of the moon."
Sequence of Generations, The.
Tabernacle of Peace.
Beer, Morris Abel
Church in the Heart, The.
Manhattan.
Beer, Patricia
Birthday Poem from Venice.
Christmas Carols.
Christmas Eve.
Christmas Tree, The.
Creed of Mr. Nicholas Culpeper.
Dilemma.
Fifth Sense, The.
Gallery Shepherds.
In the Cathedral.
Leaping into the Gulf.
Letter, The.
Lion Hunts.
Postilion Has Been Struck by Lightning, The.
Witch.
Beerbohm, Max
Addition to Kipling's "The Dead King (Edward VII), 1910."
Ballade Tragique à Double Refrain.
Brave Rover.
Elegy on Any Lady by George Moore.
Epitaph for G. B. Shaw.
Lines on a Certain Friend's Remarkable Faculty for Swift Generalization.
Luncheon, A.
On the Imprint of the First English Edition of "The Works of Max Beerbohm."
Police Station Ditties.
Road to Zoagli, The.
Savonarola ("Savonarola looks more grim today").
Sequelula to "The Dynasts," A.
Vague Lyric by G. M.
Beerbohm, Max *and* **William Rothenstein**
Eli the Thatcher.
Beer-Hofmann, Richard
"Evil Man, An!"
Jacob's Dream, *sel.*
Lullaby for Miriam.
Beers, Ethel Lynn
All Quiet along [*or* on] the Potomac.
Picket-Guard, The.
Weighing the Baby.
Which Shall It Be?
Beers, Henry Augustin
Biftek aux Champignons.
Ecce in Deserto.
On a Miniature.
Posthumous.
Singer of One Song, The.
Ye Laye of ye Woodpeckore.
Beesly, Augustus Henry
André's Ride.
Beeton, Douglas Ridley
Autumn.
Beevers, John
Atameros.
Beghtol, Charles
Hopi Lament.
Hopi Prayer.
In Old Tucson.
Behan, Dominic
Patriot Game, The.
Behm, Richard
Cleaning Fish.
Collector, The.
Hunt of the Poem, The.

Return to Lake Emily Chequamegon National Forest.
Trout Fishing; a Sign.

Behn, Aphra
Abdelazer, *sel.*
Amyntas Led Me to a Grove.
And Forgive Us Our Trespasses.
Beneath a Cool Shade.
Coquette, The.
Defiance, The.
Disappointment, The, *at.*
Dream, The.
Dutch Lover, The, *sels.*
Emperor of the Moon, *sels.*
Love's Witness.
Lucky Chance, The, *sel.*
Not to sigh and to be tender.
O What Pleasure 'Tis to Find.
On Her Loving Two Equally.
Sir Patient Fancy, *sel.*
Song: "Ah false Amyntas, can that hour."
Song: "All joy to mortals, joy and mirth."
Song: "Curse upon that faithless maid, A."
Song: Love Arm'd.
Song: "Love in fantastic [*or* fantastique] triumph sate [*or* sat]."
Song: "Oh! Love, that stronger art than wine."
Song: "When maidens are young, and in their spring."
Song by the Wavering Nymph.
Thousand Martyrs I Have Made, A.
To the Fair Clarinda, Who Made Love to Me, Imagin'd More than Woman.
Voyage to the Island of Love, A, *sel.*
Westminster Drollery, 1671.
When Damon First Began to Love.
When you love, or speak of it.
Willing Mistress, The.

Behn, Harry
Adventure.
Christmas Carol, A: "Angel told Mary, An."
Christmas Morning.
Curiosity.
Easter Snowfall.
Evening.
Flowers.
Follow the Leader ("Follow the leader away in a row").
Ghosts.
Gnome, The.
Growing Up.
Hallowe'en.
Invitation.
Kite, The.
Lesson.
Mr. Pyme.
Others.
Spring.
Spring Rain.
Surprise.
This Happy Day.
Trees.
Visitors.
Waiting.
Windy Morning.

Behrend, Alice
Snowflakes.

Beidler, Martha
Mohammed Ibrahim Speaks.

Beissel, Henry
Boar and the Dromedar, The.
In the one-two domestic goose one-two one-two step.
New Wings for Icarus, *sel.*

Beissel, Johann Conrad
Sun Now Risen, The, *with music.*

Beker, Ruth
Don't Show Me.

"Belasco, F. *See* **Rosenfeld, Monroe F.**

Belford, Ken
Blueline.
Branches Back Into.
Carrier Indians.
Dusk.
For Kelley.
Glove Glue.
Hunchbacked and corrected.
In spots/ it is warm enough.
New Potatoes.
Peanuts.
Stove.
Turn (a Poem in 4 Parts).

Belfrage, Sally
Progress.

Belisle, Eugene L.
At 21.

Belitt, Ben
Battery Park, High Noon.
Charwoman.
Karamazov.
Late Dandelions.
Papermill Graveyard.
Sand Painters, The.
View from the Gorge.
Winter Pond.
Xerox.

Belknap, Jeremy
Far from Our Friends, *with music.*
Thus Spake the Saviour, *with music.*

"Bell, Acton." *See* **Brontë, Anne**

Bell, Arthur W.
Case History.
Streamlined Stream-Knowledge.

Bell, Birdie
I Have Always Found It So.

Bell, Charles Dent
Solemn Rondeau.

Bell, Charles G.
Banana.
Baptism.
Blue-Hole, The.
Diretro al Sol.
Flood, The.
From Le Havre.
Gar, The.
Girl Walking.
Heraclitus in the West.
Island Dogs ("The island crawls with dogs").
Love in Age.
On a Baltimore Bus.
Termites.
This Little Vigil.
Two Families.
Windowed Habitations.
Woodbird.

"Bell, Currer." *See* **Brontë, Charlotte**

"Bell, Ellis." *See* **Brontë, Emily**

Bell, Henry Glassford
Mary, Queen of Scots.

Bell, J. J.
Boa, The.
Hedgehog, The.
Shark, The.

Bell, John Joy
On the Quay.

Bell, Juanita
Indian Children Speak.

Bell, Julian
Pluviose.
Redshanks, The.
Woods and Kestrel.

Bell, Martin
Footnote to Enright's "Apocalypse."
Songs, The.
Ultimate Anthology.
Winter Coming On.

Bell, Marvin
Acceptance Speech.
Cabin in Minnesota, A.
Communication of His Thirtieth Birthday.
Coralville, in Iowa.
Extermination of the Jews, The.
Fresh News from the Past.
Garlic.
Gemwood.
Getting Lost in Nazi Germany.
Here.
Hole in the Sea, The.
Home Front, The.
Impotence.
Iowa Land.
Israeli Navy, The.
Letting in Cold.
Little Father Poem.
Memory, A.
Music of the Spheres, The.
Mystery of Emily Dickinson, The.
New Formalists, The.
New Students.
Obsessive.
Origin of Dreams.
Parents of Psychotic Children, The.
Perfection of Dentistry, The.
Reflexes.
Residue of Song.
Stars Which See, Stars Which Do Not See.
These Green-going-to-Yellow.
Things We Dreamt We Died For.
3 Stanzas about a Tree.
To an Adolescent Weeping Willow.
To Dorothy.
Treetops.
True Story, A.
Two Pictures of a Leaf.
What Is There.
What They Do to You in Distant Places.

Bell, Maud Anna
From a Trench.

Bell, Maurice
Alabama, The.

Bell, Robert Mowry
Second Volume, The.
Tutelage, The.

Bell, Walker Meriwether
Jefferson Davis.

Bell, William
Coolin Ridge, The.
Elegy IX: "My dear, observe the rose! though she desire it."
Elegy X: "Now Christendom bids her cathedrals call."
Elegy: "Tonight the moon is high, to summon all."
On a Dying Boy.
On a Ledge.
Sonnet: "You waken slowly. In your dream you're straying."
To a Lady on Her Marriage.
Young Man's Song, A.

Bellamann, Henry
Charleston Garden, A.
Cups of Illusion.
Deeper Seas, The.
Gulf Stream, The.

Bellamy, Peter
Sweet Loving Friendship.

Belle, John Cross
Secret Prayer.

Belleau, Remy
April.

Bellenden, John
Starscape, A.

Bellerby, Frances
Bereft Child's First Night.
Inconclusive Evening, An.
It Is Not Likely Now.

Bellg, Albert
Raincoats for the Dead.
Watertower.

Belli, Giuseppe Gioacchino
Confessor, The.
Death with a Coda.
Good Weather.

Bellman, Carl Michael
Cradle Song: "Lullaby, my little one."

Belloc, Hilaire
Almighty God, Whose Justice Like a Sun.
B Stands for Bear.
Ballade of Hell and of Mrs. Roebeck.
Ballade of Illegal Ornaments.
Ballade of the Heresiarchs.
Ballade to Our Lady of Czestochowa.
Because My Faltering Feet.
Big Baboon, The.
Birds in their little nests agree.
Bison, The.
Camelopard, The.
Chamois, The.
Courtesy.
Crusade.
Cuckoo!
Dedication on the Gift of a Book to a Child.
Dedicatory Ode, *sel.*
Discovery.
Dodo, The ("Dodo used to walk around").
Dromedary, The.
Duncton Hill.
Early Morning, The.
Elephant, The.
Epitaph on the Favourite Dog of a Politician.
Epitaph on the Politician Himself.
False Heart, The.
Fatigue.
First in his pride the orient sun's display.
For False Heart.
Fragment, The: "Towards the evening of her splendid day."
Franklin Hyde.
Frog, The.
G.
Game of Cricket, The.
Garden Party, The.
George.
Gnu, The.
Godolphin Horne.
Grandmamma's Birthday.
Habitations.
Ha'nacker Mill.
Henry King [Who Chewed Bits of String].
Her Faith.
Heretics All.
Hippopotamus, The.
I am a sundial, turned the wrong way round.
I am a sundial. Ordinary words.
In a Boat.
Jack and His Pony, Tom.
Jim.
Jim, Who Ran Away from His Nurse, and Was Eaten by a Lion.
Juliet.
Justice of the Peace, The.
Leader, The.
Lines for a Christmas Card.
Lines to a Don.
Lion, The.
Llama, The.
Lord Abbott.
Lord Epsom.
Lord Finchley.
Lord Heygate.
Lord High-Bo.
Lord Lundy.
Matilda.
Moral Alphabet, A, *sels.*
Night, The.
Noël.
On a Dead Hostess.
On a General Election.
On a Great Election.
On a Hand.
On a Politician.
On a Puritan.
On a Sundial ("I am a sundial, and I make a botch").
On a Sundial ("Save on the rare occasion when the sun").
On a Sundial ("Stealthy the silent hours advance, and still").
On His Books.
On Hygiene.
On Lady Poltagrue, a Public Peril.
On Mundane Acquaintances.
On Noman, a Guest.
On Paunch, a Parasite.
On Two Ministers of State.
On Vital Statistics.
Our Lord and Our Lady.
Pacifist, The.
Prophet Lost in the Hills at Evening, The.
Python, The.
Rebecca, Who Slammed Doors for Fun and Perished Miserably.
Rhinoceros, The.
Sarah Byng [Who Could Not Read and Was Tossed into a Thorny Hedge by a Bull].
Scorpion, The.
Season's Greetings.
Song: Inviting the Influence of a Young Lady upon the Opening Year.
Song: "You wear the morning like your dress."
Song Called "His Hide Is Covered with Hair," The.
Song of Duke William.
Sonnet: "We will not whisper, we have found the place."
Sonnet: "World's a stage, The. The light is in one's eyes."
Sonnets, *sel.*
South Country, The.
Stanzas Written on Battersea Bridge during a Southwesterly Gale.
Statesman, The.
Statue, The.
Tarantella.
Telephone, The.
They Say That in the Unchanging Place.
This, the last ornament among the peers.
Tiger, The.
To Dives.
Viper, The.
Vulture, The.
West Sussex Drinking Song.
World's a stage, The. The trifling entrance fee.
Yak, The.
Bellows, Isabel Frances
Curious Charlie.
G Is for Gustave.
Ignorant Ida.
Naughty Young Nat.
Operatic Olivia.
Bellows, Silence Buck
Last Cargo.
Belsham, R. A.
Christ for Everything.
Belting, Natalia M.
Dark gray clouds, The.
Some say the sun is a golden earring.
Belvin, William
Palermo, Mother's Day, 1943.
Beman, Nathan S. S.
Jesus, I Come to Thee, *with music.*
Benbow, Margaret
Old Biograph Girl, The.
Bender, Debra Woolard
World within a World.
"Bendo, Brian"
Dream, The.
Benedict, Hester A.
Good-Night.
Benedikt, Michael
Clement Attlee.
Divine Love.
European Shoe, The.
Eye, The.
Fate in Incognito.
Fraudulent Days.
Future, The.
Grand Guignols of Love, The.
Life of Particles, The.
Meat Epitaph, The.
Of How Scientists Are Often Ahead of Others in Thinking, While the Average Man Lags Behind; and How the Economist (Who Can Only Follow in the Footsteps of the Average Man Looking for Clues to the Future), Remains Thoroughly Out of It.
Some Feelings.
Some Litanies.
Thoughts.
Benét, Laura
Adventure.
Mountain Convent.
Peter.
Rowers, The.
"She Wandered after Strange Gods."
Thrush, The.
Benet, Mayster
Alphabet of Aristotle, The, *at.*
Benét, Rosemary
Johnny Appleseed, *with music.*
To an Unknown Neighbor at the Circus.
Benét, Rosemary *and* Stephen Vincent Benét
Abraham Lincoln.
Benjamin Franklin 1706–1790.
George Washington.
John Adams.
Lewis and Clark.
Nancy Hanks.
Negro Spirituals.
Peregrine White and Virginia Dare.
Southern Ships and Settlers.
Thomas Jefferson [1743–1826].
Western Wagons.
Benét, Stephen Vincent
Aaron Burr.
American Names.
Andrew Jackson.
Ballad of William Sycamore, The.
Battle of Gettysburg, The.
Daniel Boone.
For All Blasphemers.
For City Spring.
General Public, The.
Hymn in Columbus Circle.
Innovator, The.
Invocation: "American muse, whose strong and diverse heart."
Jack Ellyat Heard the Guns.
John Brown's Body, *sels.*
John Quincy Adams.
King David.
Listen to the People: Independence Day, 1941, *sel.*
Litany for Dictatorships.
Love Came By from the Riversmoke.
Metropolitan Nightmare.
Mountain Whippoorwill, The.
Nightmare at Noon.
Nightmare Number Three.
Nightmare, with Angels.
1935.
Nonsense Song, A.
Out of John Brown's Strong Sinews.
Portrait of a Boy.
Rain after a Vaudeville Show.
Retort Discourteous, The.
Robert E. Lee.
Song of Breath, A.
Song of the Riders.
Thirteen Sisters, The.
Three Elements.
Unfamiliar Quartet.
Western Star, *sel.*
Winged Man.
Written in a Time of Crisis.
Benét, William Rose
Bast.
Brazen Tongue.
Debutantrum.
Eternal Masculine.

Falconer of God, The.
Fawn in the Snow, The.
Gaspara Stampa.
Her Way.
Horse Thief, The.
How to Catch Unicorns.
Inscription for a Mirror in a Deserted Dwelling.
Jesse James.
Lullaby of the Catfish and the Crab.
Mad Blake.
Merchants from Cathay.
Night.
Old Adam, The.
Old Bill's Memory Book.
On Sunday in the Sunlight.
Sagacity.
Strong Swimmer, The.
There Lived a Lady in Milan.
Third Row, Centre.
Tricksters.
Whale.
Woodcutter's Wife, The.
World's Desire, The.

Beneyto, Maria
Nocturne in the Women's Prison.

Benford, Lawrence
Beginning of a Long Poem on Why I Burned the City, The.

Benjacob, Isaac
Epitaph, An: "Here lies Nachshon, a man of great renown."

Benjamin, Park
Old Sexton, The.
To Arms.

Benjamin, Paul L.
We Who Are Dead.

Benjamin, Saul Hillel
At Summer's End.

Ben Kalir, Eleazar
O Hark to the Herald.
Palms and Myrtles.
Prayer for Dew.
Prophet Jeremiah and the Personification of Israel, The, *at.*
Terrible Sons, The.
To Him Who Is Feared.

Benlowes, Edward
Cynthia.
Evening Prayer.
Life and Death.
Theophila; or, Love's Sacrifice, *sels.*

Benn, Gottfried
Beautiful Youth.
Poplar.
Weightless Element, A.

Bennard, George
Old Rugged Cross, The, *with music.*

Bennett, Alan
Place-Names of China.

Bennett, Anna Elizabeth
Candle Song.
Hush Thee, Princeling, *with music.*

Bennett, Arnold
It Pays.
Limerick: "There was a young man of Montrose."
Love Affair, A.
There Was a Young Man of Montrose.

Bennett, Benjamin K.
Paradox.

Bennett, Bruce
Bad Apple, The.
Early.
Poetry Is.
Stick, The.
Success Story.
Villanelle with a Line by Yeats.

Bennett, Gertrude Ryder
Diary of a Raccoon.

Bennett, Gwendolyn B.
Advice.
Fantasy.
Hatred.
Heritage.
Lines Written at the Grave of Alexander [*or* Alexandre] Dumas.
Nocturne: "This cool night is strange."
Quatrains.
Secret.
Song: "I am weaving a song of waters."
Sonnet: "He came in silvern armor, trimmed with black."
Sonnet II: "Some things are very dear to me."
To a Dark Girl.
To Usward.
Your Songs.

Bennett, Henry
Saint Patrick.
St. Patrick Was a Gentleman.

Bennett, Henry Holcomb
Flag Goes By, The.

Bennett, John
Abbot of Derry, The.
God Bless You, Dear, To-Day!
Her Answer.
In a Rose Garden.
Ingenious Little Old Man, The.
Master Sky-Lark, *sels.*
Pentecost.
Sky-Lark's Song, The.
Song of the Hunt, The.
Song of the Spanish Main, The.
Tiger Tale, A.
Tiger's Tale, A.

Bennett, Joseph Deericks
Autumnall.
Complaint.
Earthly Love.
Headsong.
On the Nativity of Christ Our Lord.
Quatrina.
To Eliza, Duchess of Dorset.

Bennett, Lerone, Jr.
And Was Not Improved.
Blues and Bitterness.

Bennett, Murray
Funeral.

Bennett, Paula
To a Young Poet.

Bennett, Peggy
Mother Is a Sun, A.
Parable.
Shut Up, I Said.
Snap Judgement on the Llama, A.

Bennett, Rowena Bastin
Airplane, The ("An airplane has gigantic wings").
April Puddle.
Boats.
Come, Ride with Me to Toyland.
Conversation between Mr. and Mrs. Santa Claus.
Conversation with an April Fool.
End-of-Summer-Poem.
Four Seasons.
Freight Train, The.
If I Were a Pilgrim Child.
Meeting the Easter Bunny.
Modern Dragon, A.
Motor Cars.
Picture People.
Remembering the Winter.
Smoke Animals.
Sunrise.
Thanksgiving Magic.
Umbrellas.
Vacation Time.
Witch Cat.

Bennett, Sanford Fillmore
In the Sweet Bye-and-Bye [*or* In the Sweet By and By].

Bennett, William Cox
Baby May.
Invocation to Rain in Summer.
Lullaby, O Lullaby.
Summer Invocation.
To a Cricket.
Wife's Song, A.

Bensel, James Berry
Ahmed.

Bensko, John
Mail Call.
Mowing the Lawn.
Night-blooming Cactus, The.
Veteran of the Great War, A.

Benson, Arthur Christopher
Amen.
Ant-Heap, The.
Knapweed.
Land of Hope and Glory.
Lord Vyet.
Phoenix, The.
Prelude: "Hush'd is each busy shout."

Benson, Gerard
Horse.
Leavings.
Probatioun Officeres Tale, The.

Benson, Louis FitzGerald
Far Trumpets Blowing.
O Love That Lights the Eastern Sky, *with music.*
O Risen Lord upon the Throne, *with music.*
O Thou Whose Feet Have Climbed Life's Hill, *with music.*
O Thou Whose Gracious Presence Blest.
Why Linger Yet upon the Strand? *with music.*

Benson, Margaret
Once on a Time.

Benson, Mary Josephine
Smoking Flax.

Benson, Nathaniel Anketell
Holy Night.
Year's End.

Benson, Robert Hugh
Priest's Lament, The.
Teresian Contemplative, The.

Benson, Stella
Frost.
Now I Have Nothing.

Bental, Anath
Angel Michael, The.
Jerusalem in the Snow.

Bentley, Beth
Bridges and Tunnels.
Gnomes, The.
Lesson, The.
Temple of the Muses.
Therapeutist, The.

Bentley, Edmund Clerihew
Adam Smith.
Ballade of Liquid Refreshment.
Cervantes.
Clerihews, *sels.*
"Dear me!" exclaimed Homer.
Geoffrey Chaucer.
George Hirst.
"I quite realized," said Columbus.
John Stuart Mill.
Lord Clive.
Professor James Dewar, F.R.S.
Savonarola ("Savonarola/ Declined to wear a bowler").
Sir Christopher Wren.
Sir Humphry Davy.
When Alexander Pope.
Younger Van Eyck, The.

Bentley, Nicolas
On Mrs. W——.

Bentley, Richard
Reply to an Imitation of the Second Ode in the Third Book of Horace, A.
Verses: "Who strives to mount Parnassus hill."

Benton, Frank
Old Buck's Ghost.

Benton, Joel
At Chappaqua.
Grover Cleveland.

Poet, The.
Scarlet Tanager, The.
Benton, Myron B.
Mowers, The.
Benton, Patricia
Desert River.
Benton, Walter
Summary of the Distance between the Bomber and the Objective.
This Is My Beloved, *sels.*
With the Most Susceptible Element, the Mind, Already Turned under the Toxic Action.
Benveniste, Asa
Alchemical Cupboard, The.
Ben Yeshaq, Yosef Damana
Rusted Chain, The.
Ben-Yitzhak, Avraham
Blessed Are Those Who Sow and Do Not Reap.
I Didn't Know My Soul.
Psalm: "There are a very few moments when you."
Béranger, Pierre Jean de
Garret, The.
King of Yvetot, The.
Berchan
Fort of Rathangan, The, *at.*
Berenberg, David Paul
Two Sonnets.
Bereng,, David Granmer T.
Birth of Moshesh, The.
Berenguer, Amanda
Housework.
Berg, Sharon
Tongues.
Berg, Stephen
Animals, The.
Between Us.
Desnos Reading the Palms of Men on Their Way to the Gas Chambers.
Don't Forget.
Dreaming with a Friend.
Entering the Body, *sel.*
For My Father.
Glimpse of the Body Shop, A.
Gooseberries.
Holes, The.
Ollie, Answer Me.
People Trying to Love.
Survivor, The.
To My Friends.
Wife Talks to Herself, A.
Bergé, Carole
Chiaroscuro.
Bergengren, Ralph Wilhelm
Dirigible, The.
Worm, The.
Berger, Bruce
False Cadence.
Berggolts, Olga
Infidelity.
To My Sister.
To Song.
Bergman, Alexander
Chronicler, The.
Letter.
Bergman, David
Eclogue: "Whores are afraid to cross the street, The."
Why I Am Offended by Miracles.
Bergner, Zekharye Khone. *See* **Ravich, Melech**
Bergquist, Beatrice
Song of the Robin, The.
Bering, Betsy
Still Life.
Berke, Judith
Red Room, The.
Berkeley, George
On the Prospect of Planting Arts and Learning in America.
Berkson, Lee L.
Bogey.
Berlin, Irving
God Bless America.
Berlind, Bruce
Fragment: "No use/ being angry at the dead."
Period Piece.
Berman, Ruth
Blessing, The.
Snow Queen's Portrait.
Bernadine
It Begins Softly ("It begins inside first").
Letter from When, A.
Open Letter-Poem-Note to Vincent van G, An.
Bernard, Artis
Snowfall.
Bernard [*or* Bernart] de Ventadour [*or* Ventadorn]
Lark, The.
No Marvel Is It.
Bernard of Clairvaux, Saint
Jesus, Thou Joy of Loving Hearts.
Wide Open Are Thy [Loving] Hands.
Bernard of Cluny [*or* of Morlaix]
Celestial Country, The.
Contempt for the World.
De Contemptu Mundi, *sels.*
Jerusalem.
Jerusalem the Golden.
Bernhardt, Clara
Sailor's Wife, A.
Bernhardt, Suzanne
In a Dream Ship's Hold.
Unveiling, The.
Bernstein, Harriet
Gladioli for My Mother.
Berrigan, Daniel
Almost Everybody Is Dying Here: Only a Few Actually Make It.
Aunt, The.
Beautiful Ruined Orchard, The.
Everything That Is.
Great God Paused among Men.
Handicapped.
Haydn; the Horn.
Here the Stem Rises.
News Stand, The.
On the Birth of Dan Goldman.
Patience, Hard Virtue.
Rehabilitative Report: We Can Still Laugh.
Somewhere the Equation Breaks Down.
Typical 6:00 P.M. in the Fun House, A.
We Were Permitted to Meet Together in Prison to Prepare for Trial.
Berrigan, Ted
Bean Spasms.
Living with Chris.
Orange Jews.
Real Life.
Resolution.
Sonnet: "My dream a drink with Lonnie Johnson."
Stronger than alcohol, more great than song.
Things to Do in New York (City).
Berry, David Chapman
Alluding to the One-armed Bandit.
Cosmogony.
Dog.
Faces.
Forehead Dead-Ends Half-Way through the Poem.
Godiva.
Having Eaten Breakfast.
If Love's a Yoke.
In Blue.
Leaps over the Aisle of Syllogism.
On Reading Poems to a Senior Class at South High.
Robert Creeley Also Watches.
Robert Creeley Listens, Too.
Theodore Roethke Foots It.
Up against the Wall.
Berry, Eleanor
Multiplicity.
Berry, Fred
Silica Carbonate Rock.
Berry, H. W.
To an Egyptian Boy.
Berry, Martyn
Cairngorm, November 1971.
Berry, Wendell
Ascent.
Barn, The.
Buildings, The.
Canticle.
Earth and Fire.
For the Rebuilding of a House.
Gift of Gravity, The.
Grandmother, The.
Grief.
Guest, The.
In Rain.
Independence Day.
Inland Passages, *sel.*
Lilies, The.
Long Hunter, The.
Man Walking and Singing, A.
May Song.
Music, A.
My Great-Grandfather's Slaves.
9 Verses of the Same Song, *sel.*
November Twenty-sixth Nineteen Hundred and Sixty-three.
Peace of Wild Things, The.
Poem for J.
Reverdure, *sel.*
September 2.
Slip, The.
Snake, The.
Springs, The.
Stones, The.
To Know the Dark.
To My Children, Fearing for Them.
Way of Pain, The.
Wheel, The.
Wild, The.
Berryman, John
Again, his friend's death made the man sit still.
Alcoholic.
American Lights Seen from Off Abroad.
Apollo 8.
April Fool's Day, or, St. Mary of Egypt.
At Henry's bier let some thing fall out well.
Ball Poem, The.
Black Book, The, *sel.*
Cage, The.
Canto Amor.
Certainty before Lunch.
Cloud and Flame.
College of flunkeys, and a few gentlemen.
Conversation.
Deprived of his enemy, shrugged to a standstill.
Desires of Men and Women.
Dinch me, dark God, having smoked me out.
Dispossessed, The.
Elegy for W. C. W., the Lovely Man, An.
Eleven Addresses to the Lord, *abr.*
Filling her compact and delicious body.
Gislebertus' Eve.
Go, ill-sped book, and whisper to her or.
God bless Henry. He lived like a rat.
Governor your husband lived so long, The.
Grandfather, sleepless in a room upstairs.
He lay in the middle of the world, and twitcht.
He Resigns.
He stared at ruin. Ruin stared straight back.
Hello.
Henry's Confession.
Henry's mind grew blacker the more he thought.
Henry's pelt was put on sundry walls.
Henry's Understanding.
His Helplessness.
Homage to Mistress Bradstreet.
How this woman came by the courage, how she got.

Huffy Henry hid the day.
I am the little man who smokes & smokes.
I can't read any more of this Rich Critical Prose.
I have moved to Dublin to have it out with you.
Ill lay he long, upon this last return.
Irish have the thickest ankles in the world, The.
Keep your eyes open when you kiss: do: when.
King David Dances.
Lauds.
Lay of Ike, The.
Let us suppose, valleys and such ago.
Life, friends, is boring. We must not say so.
Marker slants, flowerless, day's almost done, The.
Minnesota Thanksgiving.
Moon and the Night and the Men, The.
New Year's Eve.
Noises from underground made gibber some.
Note to Wang Wei.
Of Suicide.
1 September 1939.
Our Sunday morning when dawn-priests were applying.
Parting as Descent.
Peter's not friendly. He gives me sideways looks.
Poet's Final Instructions, The.
Prayer for the Self, A.
Professor's Song, A.
Sabbath.
Sigh as It Ends.
Snow Line.
So Long? Stevens.
Song of the Demented Priest, The.
Song of the Tortured Girl, The.
Sonnet: "All we were going strong last night this time."
Sonnet: "Sometimes the night echoes to prideless wailing."
Sonnet: "They may suppose, because I would not cloy your ear."
Statue, The.
Strut for Roethke, A.
Sympathy, a Welcome, A.
There are voices, voices. Light's dying. Birds have quit.
There sat down, once, a thing on Henry's heart.
These massacres of the superior peoples.
Three around the Old Gentleman.
Thurn, A.
Traveller, The.
Washington in Love.
We Were in the 8th Grade.
Weather was fine, The. They took away his teeth.
Welcome, grinned Henry, welcome fifty-one!
Whether There Is Sorrow in the Demons.
Winter Landscape.
Winter-Piece to a Friend Away, A.
Winters close, Springs open, no child stirs, The.
Wordsworth, thou form almost divine, cried Henry.
You couldn't bear to grow old, but we grow old.
Your Birthday in Wisconsin You Are 140.
Your face broods from my table, Suicide.

Bersohn, Robert
Dignity of Labor, The.

Berssenbrugge, Mei-Mei
Book of the Dead, Prayer 14.
Chronicles: Number Three.
Farolita.
Membrane, The.
Sleep.
Spring Street Bar.
Translation of Verver, The.

Bertken [*or* Bertke], Sister (Bertha Jacobs)
Ditty, A: "I went into my garden to gather some herbs."
Love wears roses' elegance.
When I went into my garden, I found.

Bertolino, James
Night Was Smooth, The.

Bertrand, Sister Mary
Our Lady of Mercy.

Bertrans [*or* Bertrand] de Born.
Song of Battle.
War Song, A.
Well Pleaseth Me the Sweet Time of Easter.

Berwick, Thurso
Idleset: "Ill's the airt o the Word the day."

Besant, Sir Walter
Day Is Coming, The, *parody.*
To Daphne.

Best, Charles
Looke How the Pale Queene.
Moon, The.
Sonnet of the Moon, A.

Best, Susie Montgomery
Thanksgiving.

Betham-Edwards, Matilda Barbara
Pansy and the Prayer-Book, The.
Valentine, A.

Bethell, Mary Ursula. *See* **"Hayes, Evelyn"**

Bethune, George Washington
Blessed Name, The.
Jesus, Shepherd of Thy Sheep, *with music.*
O for the Happy Hour, *with music.*
There Is No Name So Sweet on Earth, *with music.*

Bethune, Lebert
Blue Tanganyika.
Bwagamoyo.
Harlem Freeze Frame.
Juju of My Own, A.
To Strike for Night.

Betjeman, Sir John
Advent 1955.
Archaeological Picnic, The.
Arrest of Oscar Wilde at the Cadogan Hotel, The.
Arrogance Repressed.
Back Again for the Holidays.
Before Invasion, 1940.
Before the Anaesthetic; or, A Real Fright.
Beside the Seaside, *sel.*
Bristol and Clifton.
Child Ill, A.
Christmas.
City, The.
Cottage Hospital, The.
Crematorium.
Death in Leamington.
Death of King George V.
Diary of a Church Mouse.
East Anglian Bathe.
Executive.
False Security.
Felixstowe; or, The Last of Her Order.
For Patrick, Aetat: LXX.
For the Queen Mother.
Great Central Railway, Sheffield Victoria to Banbury.
Heart of Thomas Hardy, The.
How to Get On in Society.
Hunter Trials.
Huxley Hall.
Hymn: "Church's Restoration, The."
In a Bath Teashop.
In Memoriam: A. C., R. J. O., K. S.
In Memory of Basil, Marquess of Dufferin and Ava.
In Memory of George Whitby, Architect.
In the Public Gardens.
In Westminster Abbey.
Incident in the Early Life of Ebenezer Jones, Poet, 1828, An.
Indoor Games near Newbury.
Inevitable.
Invasion Exercise on the Poultry Farm.
Ireland with Emily.
Late-flowering Lust.
Licorice Fields at Pontefract, The.
Longfellow's Visit to Venice.
Lord Cozens Hardy.
Matlock Bath.
Metropolitan Railway, The.
Middlesex.
Myfanwy.
NW5 and N6.
"New King Arrives in His Capital by Air. . ."—Daily Newspaper.
Norfolk.
Old Liberals, The.
On a Portrait of a Deaf Man.
Parliament Hill Fields.
Planster's Vision, The.
Potpourri [*or* Pot-Pourri] from a Surrey Garden.
Remorse.
St. Saviour's, Aberdeen Park, Highbury, London, N.
Seaside Golf.
Senex.
Shropshire Lad, A.
Slough.
Subaltern's Love-Song, A.
Summoned by Bells, *sels.*
Sunday Afternoon Service in St. Enodoc Church, Cornwall.
Sunday Morning, King's Cambridge.
Town Clerk's Views, The.
Trebetherick.
Tregardock.
Upper Lambourne.
Westgate-on-Sea.
Youth and Age on Beaulieu River, Hants.

Betts, Craven Langstroth
Don Quixote.
Hollyhocks, The.
To the Moonflower.

Betts, Frank
Pawns, The.

Betts, Mary Frances
Million Little Diamonds, A.

Bevington, Helen Smith
Academic Moon.
Cataract at Lodore, The.
Company of Scholars, The.
Herrick's Julia.
Man from Porlock, The.
Mr. Rockefeller's Hat.
Mrs. Trollope in America.
Nature Study, after Dufy.
Penguins in the Home.
Report from the Carolinas, *sel.*
Talk with a Poet.
Teacher, The.
Turner's Sunrise.

Beyer, Evelyn
Jump or Jiggle.

Beyer, Richard
Second Reading.

Beyer, Tony
Comfort Stop, A.
Cornwallis.
Cut Lilac.
Seventies, The.

Bezymensky, Alexander Ilyich
Village and Factory.

Bhartrihari
In former days we'd both agree.
Peace.
She who is always in my thoughts prefers.
Time.

Bhavabhūti
Deep in love.

Bialik, Hayyim Nahman [*or* Chaim Nachman]
After My Death.
Alone.
Beneath Thy Wing.
Blessing over Food.
City of Slaughter, The.
Dance of Despair, The.
Dead of the Wilderness, The.
Death of David, The.

Footsteps of Spring.
Grasshopper's Song, The.
Graveyard, The.
I Didn't Find Light by Accident.
I Scattered My Sighs to the Wind.
If Thou Wouldst Know.
Mathmid, The.
Midnight Prayer.
My Song.
Night.
Place Me under Your Wing.
Queen Sabbath.
Sea of Silence Exhales Secrets, The.
Should I Be a Rabbi?
Songs of the People, *sels.*
Stars Are Lit, The.
Summer Night.
Sunset.
Talmud Student, The.
Throbs the Night with Mystic Silence.
When the Days Grow Long.
Whence and Whither.
Young Acacia, The.

Bianchi, Martha Gilbert Dickinson
Heaven.
Her Music.
Priest's Prayer, A.
Reality.
Separation.
Unanswered.

Biasotti, Raymond
City.

Bibbs, Hart Leroi
Six Sunday.

Bible, Apocrypha
Baruch, *sel.*
Ecclesiasticus, *sels.*
First Maccabees, *sels.*
Judith, *sel.*
Tobit, *sel.*
Wisdom, *sel.*

Bible, New Testament
Acts, *sel.*
First Corinthians, *sels.*
First John, *sel.*
Hebrews, *sel.*
Philippians, *sel.*
Revelation, *sels.*
Romans, *sels.*
St. John, *sels.*
St. Luke, *sels.*
St. Mark, *sels.*
St. Matthew, *sels.*
Second Corinthians, *sel.*

Bible, Old Testament
Amos, *sel.*
Daniel, *sel.*
Deuteronomy, *sels.*
Ecclesiastes, *sels.*
Exodus, *sels.*
Ezekiel, *sels.*
First Kings, *sels.*
First Samuel, *sels.*
Genesis, *sels.*
Isaiah, *sels.*
Jeremiah, *sels.*
Job, *sels.*
Jonah, *sels.*
Judges, *sel.*
Lamentations, *sels.*
Micah, *sels.*
Numbers, *sels.*
Proverbs, *sels.*
Psalms, *sels.*
Ruth, *sels.*
Second Samuel, *sel.*
Song of Solomon, The, *sels.*
Zechariah, *sels.*

Bible, Pseudepigrapha.
Enoch, *sels.*

Bickerstaffe, Isaac
Air: "What a charming thing's a battle!"
Expostulation, An.
Love in a Village, *sels.*
Recruiting Serjeant, The, *sel.*
Song: "How happy were my days, till now."
Song: "There was a jolly miller once."
There Was a Jolly Miller.
What Are Outward Forms?

Bickersteth, Edward Henry, Bishop of Exeter
O God, the Rock of Ages.
Peace, Perfect Peace.

Bickford, Gerald
96 Vandam.

Bickston, Diana
As All Things Pass.
Collect Calls.
For Chicle & Justina.
For Zorro.
Pipe Dreams.

Bidart, Frank
Golden State.
Herbert White.

Bieiris de Romans
Lady Maria, in you merit and distinction.

Bierbaum, Otto Julius
Blacksmith Pain.
Jeannette.
Kindly Vision.
Oft in the Silent Night.

Bierce, Ambrose
Advice.
Another Way.
Art.
Attorney General, An.
Beneath this mound Charles Crocker now reposes.
"Black Bart, P08."
Bride, The.
By plain analogy we're told.
Commonwealth.
Compliance.
Condone.
Convicts' Ball, The.
Corporal.
Covet.
Creation.
Death of Grant, The.
Devil's Dictionary, The, *sels.*
Doctor Blenn.
Don't Steal.
Epitaph: "Here lies the remains of great Senator Vrooman."
Epitaph: "We mourn the loss."
Here Huntington's ashes long have lain.
Montefiore.
My country 'tis of thee./ Sweet land of felony.
Presentiment.
Sheriff.
Sir Francis Bacon.
T. A. H.
Undertakers.

Bierds, Linda
Elegy for 41 Whales Beached in Florence, Ore., June, 1979.
Mid-Plains Tornado.

Big Eagle, Duane
Birthplace.
Elegy: "Whole tribe dies, A."
My Grandfather Was a Quantum Physicist.
Recollection.
Wind and Impulse.

Bigelow, J. S.
Bat and the Scientist, The.

Bigger, Duff
Comedian Said It, The.
It Is When the Tribe Is Gone.

Biggs, Maurice
Spring Offensive, 1941.

Bilal
Muhammedan Call to Prayer.

Bilhana
Black Marigolds.

"Billings, Josh" (Henry Wheeler Shaw)
Explanation.

Billings, Robert
Beast Enough.

Billings, William
David's Lamentation.
Heavenly Vision.
Let Tyrants Shake Their Iron Rod, *with music.*
When Jesus Wept, *with music.*

Bily-Hurd, Michael
Woman in an Abandoned House.

Bingham, G. Clifton
Love's Old Sweet Song.

Binney, Thomas
Eternal Light!

Binns, Elsie
Christmas Is Remembering.

Binyon, Laurence
Amasis.
August.
Bab-Lock-Hythe.
Beauty.
Belfry, The.
Burning of the Leaves, The.
Day's End.
Dray, The.
Eleonora Duse as Magda.
Ezekiel.
Ferry Hinksey.
Fetching the Wounded.
Fog.
For the Fallen.
House That Was, The.
Hunger.
In Misty Blue.
Invocation to Youth.
John Winter.
Lament: "Fall now, my cold thoughts, frozen fall."
Little Dancers, The.
Little Hands.
Magnets.
Nothing Is Enough.
November.
O World, Be Nobler.
Sirens, The, *sel.*
Song, A: "For Mercy, Courage, Kindness, Mirth."
Sower, The.
Statues, The.
Tristram's End.
Winter Sunrise, *sel.*
Ypres.

Bion
Dream of Venus, A.
Lament for Adonis.

Biran, Paddy
Paddy Biran's Song.

Birch, Harry
Reuben and Rachel, *with music.*

Birche, William
Songe betwene the Quenes majestie and Englande, A.

Bird, Bessie Calhoun
Proof.

Bird, Dolly
Can I Say.

Bird, Edward
To His Coy Mistress, *parody.*

Bird, Harold. *See* **Littlebird, Harold**

Bird, Robert Montgomery
Fairy Folk, The.

Bird, Stephen Moylan
May.
Silent Ranges, The.

Birdseye, George
Paradise.
Paradise; a Hindoo Legend.

Birkenhead, Sir John
Four-legg'd Elder, The; or, A Horrible Relation of a Dog and an Elder's Maid.

Birnbaum, Henry
Room I Once Knew, A.
When Silence Divests Me.
Birney, Earle
Anglosaxon Street.
Bear on the Delhi Road, The.
Birthday.
Bushed.
Can. Hist.
Can. Lit.
Cartagena de Indias.
Charité Espérance et Foi.
Christchurch, N. Z.
Damnation of Vancouver, *sel.*
David.
El Greco: Espolio.
Ellesmereland I ("Explorers say that harebells rise").
Ellesmereland II ("And now in Ellesmereland there sits").
For Steve.
From the Hazel Bough.
Hot Springs.
Irapuato.
Mappemounde.
Monody on a Century.
Museum of Man.
My Love Is Young.
On Going to the Wars.
Pacific Door.
Poet-Tree.
Québec May.
Road to Nijmegen, The.
Sinalóa.
Slug in Woods.
Small Faculty Stag for the Visiting Poet, A.
Speech of the Salish Chief.
There Are Delicacies.
This Page My Pigeon ("This page is my pigeon sailing").
Twenty-third Flight.
Vancouver Lights.
Walk in Kyoto, A.
World Winter.
Birnie, Patrick
Auld Man's Mear's Dead, The.
Bishop, Elissa
At Nine o'Clock in the Spring.
Bishop, Elizabeth
Armadillo, The [—Brazil].
Arrival at Santos.
At the Fishhouses.
Bight, The.
Brazil, January 1, 1502.
Burglar of Babylon, The.
Cirque d'Hiver.
Cold Spring, A.
Colder the Air, The.
Cootchie.
Faustina, or Rock Roses.
Filling Station.
First Death in Nova Scotia.
Fish, The.
Florida.
From the Country to the City.
From Trollope's Journal.
House Guest.
Imaginary Iceberg, The.
In the Waiting Room.
Insomnia.
Invitation to Miss Marianne Moore.
Jeronimo's House.
Large Bad Picture.
Late Air.
Letter to N.Y.
Little Exercise [at 4. A.M.].
Love Lies Sleeping.
Man-Moth, The.
Manners [for a Child of 1918].
Manuelzinho.
Map, The.
Miracle for Breakfast, A.
Monument, The.
North Haven.
One Art.
Over 2000 Illustrations and a Complete Concordance.
Poem: "About the size of an old-style dollar bill."
Prodigal, The.
Questions of Travel.
Riverman, The.
Roosters.
Sandpiper.
Seascape.
Sestina: "September rain falls on the house."
Shampoo, The.
Sleeping on the Ceiling.
Some Dreams They Forgot.
Songs for a Colored Singer.
Squatter's Children.
Summer's Dream, A.
12 O'Clock News.
Two Mornings and Two Evenings.
Unbeliever, The.
Under the Window: Ouro Preto.
Varick Street.
View of the Capitol from the Library of Congress.
Visits to St. Elizabeths.
Weed, The.
While Someone Telephones.
Wit, The.
Bishop, G. E.
Bigger Day, The.
Bishop, John Peale
Admonition.
Always, from My First Boyhood.
Ancestors, The.
Apparition.
Birds of Paradise, The.
Boys, by Girls Held in Their Thighs.
Colloquy with a King-Crab.
Dream, The.
Fiametta.
Four Years Were Mine at Princeton.
Frieze, A.
Green and Pleasant Land, A.
Hours, The.
Hunchback, The.
In the Dordogne.
Interlude, An.
John Donne's Statue.
Metamorphoses of M.
O, Pioneers!
Ode: "Why will they never sleep."
Percy Shelley.
Perspectives Are Precipices.
Recollection, A.
Return, The.
Saint Francis.
Southern Pines.
Spare Quilt, The.
Speaking of Poetry.
Statue of Shadow, The.
Submarine Bed, The.
This Dim and Ptolemaic Man.
To a Swallow.
Triumph of Doubt, The.
Why They Waged War.
Your Chase Had a Beast in View.
Bishop, Morris
Ambition.
Anatomy of Humor, The.
At a Modernist School.
Car's in the Hall, The.
Complete Misanthropist, The.
Dementia Praecox.
Early Morning.
Ecclesiastes.
Englishman with an Atlas, An; or, America the Unpronounceable.
Epitaph for a Funny Fellow.
Eschatology.
For the Opening of the Hunting Season.
Gas and Hot Air.
Ghoulish Old Fellow in Kent, A.
Hog-calling Competition.
How to Treat Elves.
I Hear America Griping.
Immoral Arctic, The.
It Rolls On.
Limerick: "Clergyman out in Dumont, A."
Limerick: "Said old Peeping Tom of Fort Lee."
Limerick: "There's a vaporish maiden in Harrison."
Lines Written in a Moment of Vibrant Ill-Health.
Merry Old Souls.
Mournful Numbers.
Naughty Preposition, The.
New Hampshire Boy, A.
Opportunity's Knock.
Ozymandias Revisited.
Perforated Spirit, The.
Public Aid for Niagara Falls.
Salute to the Modern Language Association, Convening in the Hotel Pennsylvania, December 28th–30th, A.
Sensitive Man, A.
Settling Some Old Football Scores.
Sick Shark, The.
Sing a Song of the Cities.
Song of the Pop-Bottlers.
Sonnet and Limerick.
Strong-minded Lady, A.
There's a Lady in Washington Heights.
There's Money in Mother and Father.
Tonversation with Baby, A.
Vaporish Maiden, A.
We Have Been Here Before.
What Hath Man Wrought Exclamation Point.
Who'd Be a Hero (Fictional)?
Winter Madrigal, A.
Witch of East Seventy-second Street, The.
Bishop, Roy
Inefficacious Egg, The.
Bishop, Samuel
At Newmarket.
Epigram: "Need from excess—excess from folly growing."
Epigram: " " 'Twas not so in my time,' surly Grumio exclaims."
To His Wife on the Fourteenth Anniversary of Her Wedding-Day, with a Ring.
To Mary.
Touch-Stone, The.
Bishop, Verna
Choose.
Bishop, Wendy
Family History.
Bissert, Ellen Marie
Another.
Most Beautiful Woman at My Highschool Reunion, The.
Bisset, James
Ramble of the Gods through Birmingham, *sel.*
Bissett, Bill
Christ I Wudint Know Normal if I Saw It When.
Dont Worry Yr Hair.
Wundrfulness uv th Mountees Our Secret Police, Th.
Biton, Erez
Beginnings.
Bird's Nest, A.
Buying a Shop on Dizengoff.
Bitton, W. Nelson
Resurgam.
Bixler, William Allen
Beautiful.
Björnson, Björnstjerne
Boy and the Flute, The.
Fatherland Song.
Synnöve's Song.
Tree, The.

Bjornvig, Thorkild
Owl, The.
Black, Austin
Soul.
Black, Charles
All Too Little on Pictures.
Reach of Silence, The.
Black, Isaac J.
Roll Call: A Land of Old Folk and Children.
Talking to the Townsfolk in Ideal, Georgia.
Black, Jack
Awake!
Black, James M.
When the Roll Is Called up Yonder.
Black, MacKnight
Rock, Be My Dream.
Black, Theodore
Bard.
"Black Bart"
I've labored long and hard for bread.
Blackburn, Alexander
What Makes a Nation Great?
Blackburn, Paul
Assassination of President McKinley, The.
Assistance, The.
Bañalbufar, a Brazier, Relativity, Cloud Formations & the Kindness & Relentlessness of Time.
Clickety-Clack.
Continuity, The.
Crossing, The.
El Camino Verde.
Encounter, The.
Getting a Job.
Good Morning Love!
Hot Afternoons Have Been in West 15th Street.
In Winter.
Invitation Standing.
Letter, The.
Meditation on the BMT.
Mother, in the 45¢ Bottle.
Night Song for Two Mystics.
Once-over, The.
One-Night Stand, The: An Approach to the Bridge.
Park Poem.
Phone Call to Rutherford.
Plaza Reáal with Palmtrees.
Problem, The.
Proposition, The.
Purse-Seine, The.
Routine, The.
17. IV. 71.
Sign, The.
Sirventes.
Slogan, The.
Song of the Hesitations.
Stone, The.
Sunflower Rock.
Three Part Invention.
Tides, The.
Watchers, The.
Yawn, The.
Blackburn, Thomas
Aftermath, An.
Felo de Se.
Ganga.
Hospital for Defectives.
Lucky Marriage, The.
Oedipus.
Song for the Infant Judas.
Blackie, John Stuart
How Small Is Man.
My Loves.
Ye Simple Men.
Blackmore, Sir Richard
Circulation of the Blood, The.
Creation, *sel.*
Satire against Wit, A.
Blackmore, Richard Doddridge
Dominus Illuminatio Mea.
Yes.
Blackmur, Richard Palmer
All Things Are a Flowing.
Before Sentence Is Passed.
Dead Ride Fast, The.
Half-Tide Ledge.
In the Wind's Eye.
Mirage.
On Common Ground.
One grey and foaming day.
Rape of Europa, The.
Resurrection.
Scarabs for the Living.
Sea Island Miscellany, *sels.*
Sonnet: "Three silences made him a single word."
Too Much for One: Not Enough to Go Round.
Views of Boston Common and Nearby.
Where shall I go then.
Blackstock, Walter
Old Voyager.
Blackwell, Harriet Gray
Forest.
Hill People.
Blackwell, Will H.
Tides.
Bladen, Peter
Coronation Day at Melrose.
Blair, Eric. *See* **Orwell, George**
Blair, Lee
Apple a Day, An.
Raisin Bread.
Stop!
Blair, Robert
Church and Church-Yard at Night.
Friendship.
Grave, The, *sels.*
Blake, Felicia
Woman's Answer to the Vampire, A.
Blake, Howard
Argent Solipsism.
Blake, James Vila
In Him.
Blake, James W.
Sidewalks of New York, The.
Blake, Marie
Barter.
Blake, Mary Elizabeth McGrath
Dawning o' the Year, The.
Blake, William
Abstinence sows sand all over.
Ah! Sun-Flower [Weary of Time].
America; a Prophecy.
And Did Those Feet in Ancient Time.
Angel, The ("I asked a thief. . .").
Angel, The ("I dreamt a dream!").
Angel That Presided o'er My Birth, The.
Answer to the Parson, An.
Auguries of Innocence.
Bard, The.
Birds, The ("Where thou dwellest, in what grave").
Birdsong.
Blind-Man's Buff.
Blossom, The.
Book of Los, The, *sel.*
Book of Thel, The.
Caverns of the Grave I've Seen, The.
Character, A.
Chimney Sweeper, The ("A little black thing among the snow").
Chimney Sweeper, The ("When my mother died I was very young").
Choir of Day, The.
Clod and the Pebble, The.
Compliment to the Ladies, A.
Cradle Song: "Sleep, sleep, beauty bright."
Cradle Song, A: "Sweet dreams, form a shade."
Cromek.
Crystal Cabinet, The.
Dedication of the Illustrations to Blair's "Grave," *sel.*
Divine Image, A ("Cruelty has a Human heart").
Divine Image, The ("To mercy pity peace and love").
Door of Death, The.
Dream, A.
Earth's Answer.
Echoing [*or* Ecchoing] Green, The.
Empire Is No More.
Enion Replies from the Caverns of the Grave.
Enitharmon Revives with Los.
Epigraph: "I give you the end of a golden string."
Epilogue: "I am sure this Jesus will not do."
Epilogue: To the Accuser Who Is the God of This World.
Epilogue: "Truly, my Satan, thou art but a dunce."
Epitaph, An: "Come knock your heads against this stone."
Eternity ("He who binds [*or* bends] to himself a joy").
Ethinthus, Queen of Waters.
Europe, *sel.*
Everlasting Gospel, The, *sels.*
Fields from Islington to Marybone, The.
Fly, The.
For the Sexes: The Gates of Paradise.
French Revolution, The, *sel.*
Garden of Love, The.
Gates of Paradise, The, *sel.*
Give pensions to the learned pig.
Gnomic Verses.
Good English Hospitality.
Great Things.
Grown old in love from seven till seven times seven.
He has observed the golden rule.
Hear the Voice of the Bard (*Introd. to* Songs of Experience).
Hebrew nation did not write it, The.
Her Whole Life Is an Epigram.
Here lies John Trot, the friend of all mankind.
Holy Thursday ("Is this a holy thing to see").
Holy Thursday (" 'Twas on a Holy Thursday").
How Sweet I Roamed from Field to Field.
Human Abstract, The.
Human Image, The, *sel.*
I Asked a Thief.
I laid me down upon a bank.
I Saw a Chapel All of Gold.
I was buried near this dyke.
Immortal, The.
In Deadly Fear.
In Obtuse Angle's Study.
Infant Joy.
Infant Sorrow.
Island in the Moon, An, *sels.*
It Is Not So with Me.
Jerusalem,
King Edward the Third, *sel.*
Lamentation of Enion, The.
Land of Dreams, The.
Lark's Song, The.
Laughing Song.
Little Black Boy, The.
Little Boy Found, The.
Little Boy Lost, A ("Nought loves another as itself").
Little Boy Lost, The ("Father, father, where are you going").
Little Vagabond, The.
London ("I wander through each chartered [*or* dirty] street").
London ("There souls of men are bought and sold").
Long John Brown and Little Mary Bell.
Louis XVI.
Love's Secret.
Mad Song.
Male & Female Loves in Beulah.
Marriage.

Marriage of Heaven and Hell, The.
Mayors, The.
Memorable Fancy, A ("An Angel came to me and said").
Memorable Fancy, A ("As I was walking among the fires of hell").
Mental Traveller, The.
Milton, *sels.*
Mr. Cromek.
Mr. Cromek to Mr. Stothard.
Mock On, Mock On, Voltaire, Rousseau.
Mockery.
Monk, The.
Morning.
My Pretty Rose Tree.
My Spectre around Me Night and Day.
Nakedness of women, The.
Never pain to tell thy love.
Never Seek to Tell Thy Love.
Night.
Night passd and Enitharmon eer the dawn returnd in bliss.
Nightingale and Flowers.
Nurse's Song ("When the voices of children are heard on the green/ And laughing is heard on the hill").
Nurse's Song ("When the voices of children are heard on the green/ And whisprings are in the dale").
O Lapwing!
O why was I born with a different face?
On Another's Sorrow.
On Cromek.
Only man that e'er I knew, The.
Orator Prigg.
Piping Down the Valleys Wild (*Introd. to* Songs of Innocence).
Play Time.
Poems from MSS.
Poet's Voice, The.
Poison Tree, A.
Prelude: "And did those feet in ancient time."
Prelude: "England! awake! awake! awake!"
Prelude: "Fields from Islington to Marybone, The."
Price of Experience, The.
Pride of the peacock is the glory of God, The.
Question Answer'd, The.
Quid the Cynic's Song.
Reason and Imagination.
Reeds of Innocence.
Riches.
Robin Redbreast, A, *much abr.*
Schoolboy, The.
Secrets of the Earth, The.
Several Questions Answered, *sels.*
Shepherd, The.
Sick Rose, The.
Since all the riches of this world.
Sipsop's Song.
Sir Joshua Reynolds.
Smile, The.
Soft Snow.
Some people admire the work of a fool.
Song: "Fresh from the dewy hill, the merry year."
Song: "How sweet I roam'd from field to field."
Song: "Love and harmony combine."
Song: "Memory, hither come."
Song: "My silks and fine array."
Song of Liberty, A.
Songs of Experience, *sels.*
Songs of Innocence, *sels.*
Spring.
Suction's Anthem.
Sunflower, The.
Sword and the Sickle, The.
Take Thy Bliss, O Man.
Thel's Motto.
They said this mystery shall never cease.
Tiger, The.
To Autumn.
To English Connoiseurs.
To Flaxman.
To forgive enemies Hayley does pretend.
To God.
To Hunt.
To Morning.
To Mrs. Ann Flaxman.
To My Friend Butts I Write.
To Nobodaddy.
To Spring.
To Summer.
To the Christians.
To the Evening Star.
To the Muses.
To the Queen.
To Tirzah.
To William Hayley.
To Winter.
Urizen's Curse upon His Children.
Vala; or, The Four Zoas, *sels.*
Vision of Beulah, The.
Vision of the Lamentation of Beulah over Ololon, A.
Visions, *sel.*
Visions of the Daughters of Albion.
Voice of the Devil, The.
War Song, A.
War Song to Englishmen, A.
When a Man Has Married a Wife.
When Klopstock England defied.
Where to Seek Love.
Why Should I Care for the Men of Thames?
Wild Thyme, The.
William Bond.
Wine-Press of Los, The.
With Happiness Stretch[e]d across the Hills.

Blakely, Henry
H. Rap Brown.
Morning Song.

Blakely, Roger
Winslow Homer, Prisoners from the Front.

Blakeney, Lena Whittaker
Covered Wagon, The.

Blamire, Susanna
Siller Croun, The.
Stoklewath; or, The Cumbrian Village, *sel.*

Blanchard, Ferdinand Q.
O Child of Lowly Manger Birth, *with music.*
Word of God, across the Ages, *with music.*

Blanchard, Laman
Nell Gwynne's Looking-Glass.
Ode to the Human Heart.

Bland, Edith Nesbit. *See* **Nesbit, Edith.**

Bland, James A.
Carry Me Back to Old Virginny.
In the Evening by the Moonlight.
Oh, Dem Golden Slippers!
Old Virginny.

Blanden, Charles Granger
Quatrain: "Christ bears a thousand crosses now."
Rose Is a Royal Lady, The.
Song the Grass Sings, A.
Songs I Sing, The.

Blandiana, Ana
Couple, The.
I need only fall asleep/ to return.

Blanding, Don
Hollywood.
Vagabond House.

Blankner, Frederika
Remainder.

Blaser, Robin
Faerie Queene, The, *sel.*
4 Part Geometry Lesson, A.
Herons.
Image-Nation (the Poēsis).
Image-Nation 3.
Image-Nation 13 (the Telephone).
Park, The.
Poem: "And when I pay death's duty."
Poem: "For years I have heard."
Poem by the Charles River.
Sophia Nichols.
Suddenly.

Blasing, Randy
Horse.

Blauner, Laurie
Billiards.

Blazek, Douglas
Eichmann.
Greed.
My Definition of Poetry.

Blenkhorn, Ada
Heavenly Stranger, The.

Blessing, Richard
Eagle, The.

Blewett, Jean
At Quebec.

Blight, John
Becalmed.
Cormorants.
Death of a Whale.
Down from the Country.
Evolution.
Gate's Open, The.
Letter, The.
Morgan.
Pearl Perch.
Tenant at Number 9.

Blind, Mathilde
After-Glow, The.
April Rain.
Dare Quam Accipere.
Dead, The.
Hymn to Horus.
Internal Firesides.
Lassitude.
Love in Exile, *sels.*
Manchester by Night.
Mourning Women.
On a Forsaken Lark's Nest.
Reapers.
Rest.
Sakiyeh, The.
Soul-Drift.
Sower, The.

Blind Blake (Blake Alphonso Higgs)
Delia's Gone.
Run Come See.

"Blind Harry." *See* **Henry the Minstrel**

Blishen, Edward
Abroad Thoughts.

Bliss, Philip Paul
Almost Persuaded, *with music.*
Hold the Fort.

Blitzstein, Marc
Art for Art's Sake.
Cradle Will Rock, The, *sel.*

Bliven, Bruce
Not Lost in the Stars.

Blixen, Karen. *See* **"Dinesen, Isak"**

Bloch, Alice
Six Years.

Bloch, Chana
Converts, The.
Death of the Bronx, The.
Deer in the Bush.
Exile.
Furniture.
Goodbye.
Life, A.
Noah.
Paradise.
Sacrifice, The.
Yom Kippur.

Bloch, Jean-Richard
Idea of a Swimmer.

Block, Allan
Causeway.

Block, Louis James
Fate.
Final Struggle, The.
Garden Where There Is No Winter, The.

New World, The, *sel.*
Tuberose.
Work.
Blockcolski, Lew
After the First Frost.
Flicker, The.
Flint Hills, The.
49 Stomp, The
Indian Love Song.
Langston Hughes.
My Dream.
Peyote Vision.
Playing Pocahontas.
Powwow Remnants.
Reservation Special.
Urban Experience, The: Part One.
Urban Experience, The: Part Two.
Wisga.
Woyi, The.
Blocklyn, Paul
Days, The.
Blocksidge, Charles William. *See* **Baylebridge, William**
Blodgett, E. D.
Fossil.
Snails.
Bloede, Gertrude. *See* **"Sterne, Stuart"**
Blok, Aleksandr [*or* Alexander] Aleksandrovich
Black night./ White snow.
Dances of Death, *sel.*
Little Catkins.
Red Glow in the Sky, A.
Russia.
Scythians, The.
She Came Out of the Frost.
Twelve, The, *sel.*
Blood, Henry Ames
Comrades.
Shakespeare.
Bloom, Barbara
From the Ice Age.
Bloomfield, Robert
Banks of Wye, The, *sels.*
Coracle Fishers, The.
Farmer's Boy, The, *sels.*
Live, trifling incidents, and grace my song.
Meandering Wye.
Moonlight . . . Scattered Clouds.
Shooter's Hill, *sel.*
Summer.
Bloomgarden [*or* Blumgarten], Solomon. *See* **"Yehoash"**
Blossom, Henry
Because You're You, *with music.*
Kiss Me Again.
Streets of New York, The, *with music.*
Blount, Charles
Dialogue between King William and the Late King James on the Banks of the Boyne, A.
Blount, Roy, Jr.
Against Broccoli.
For the Record.
Gryll's State.
Hearty Cook, A.
Hog-calling.
Lady Track Star, A.
Song against Broccoli.
Strong Feeling for Poultry, A.
Blue Cloud, Peter
Composition.
Coyote, Coyote, Please Tell Me.
Death Chant.
Dogwood Blossoms.
Elderberry Flute Song.
Hawk Nailed to a Barn Door.
Sweat Song.
To-ta Ti-om.
Walking through twisted hollow pathways.
Wolf.
Blue-Swartz, Janice
Return to Prinsengracht.
Blum, Etta
When You Reach the Hilltop the Sky Is on Top of You.
Blumenthal, Michael C.
Flirtation, The.
In Assisi.
Mushroom Hunting in Late August, Peterborough, N.H.
On the Edge at Santorini.
Squid.
Today I Am Envying the Glorious Mexicans.
Waving Good-bye to My Father.
Blumenthal, Walter Hart
Da Silva Gives the Cue.
Blumenthal-Weiss, Ilse
Jewish Child Prays to Jesus, A.
Blumgarten, Solomon. *See* **"Yehoash"**
Blumstein, Rachel. *See* **Rachel**
Blundell of Crosby, William
England's Prayer.
Blunden, Edmund
Almswomen.
At the Great Wall of China.
Barn, The.
Behind the Line.
Bleue Maison.
Country God, A.
Eastern Tempest.
Festubert: The Old German Line.
Forefathers.
Giant Puffball, The.
Gods of the Earth Beneath, The.
Hurrying Brook, The.
Idlers, The.
In Festubert.
Infantryman, An.
Into the Salient.
Late Light.
Les Halles d'Ypres.
Lonely Love.
March Bee, The.
May Day Garland, The.
Memory of Kent, The.
Midnight Skaters, The.
Mole Catcher.
New Moon, The.
1916 Seen from 1921.
Old Homes.
Pike, The.
Poor Man's Pig, The.
Psalm, A: "O God, in whom my deepest being dwells."
Recovery, The.
Reliques, *sel.*
Report on Experience.
Sheepbells.
Shepherd.
Sighing Time, The.
Silver Bird of Herndyke Mill, The.
Sunlit Vale, The.
Survival, The.
Thiepval Wood.
Thoughts of Thomas Hardy.
Threshold.
Trees on the Calais Road.
Two Voices.
Uneasy Peace.
Veteran, The.
View of the Present State of Ireland, A.
Vlamertinghe; Passing the Château, July 1917.
What Is Winter?
Wild Cherry Tree.
Winter: East Anglia.
Zillebeke Brook.
Zonnebeke Road, The.
Blunt, Wilfrid Scawen
And then fate strikes us. First our joys decay.
As to His Choice of Her.
Deeds That Might Have Been, The.
Depreciating Her Beauty.
Esther, *sels.*
Falcon, The.
Farewell: "Juliet, farewell. I would not be forgiven."
Farewell to Juliet ("I see you, Juliet, still, with your straw hat").
Farewell to Juliet ("Lame, impotent conclusion to youth's dreams").
Gibraltar.
He Has Fallen from the Height of His Love.
Honour Dishonoured.
Idler's Calender, An, *sel.*
In Answer to a Question.
In Vinculis, *sel.*
January: Cover Shooting.
Joy's Treachery.
Love Sonnets of Proteus, The, *sels.*
Mockery of Life, The.
Nocturne, A: "Moon has gone to her rest, The."
Old Squire, The.
On the Nature of Love.
Pleasures of Love, The.
St. Valentine's Day.
Sinner-Saint, The.
Song: "Oh [*or* O] fly not, Pleasure, pleasant-hearted Pleasure."
Storm in Summer, A.
To Manon, as to His Choice of Her.
To Manon, Comparing Her to a Falcon.
To Manon, on Her Lightheartedness.
To One on Her Waste of Time.
To One Who Would Make a Confession.
When I hear laughter from a tavern door.
Wisdom of Merlyn, The, *sels.*
With Esther.
Written at Florence.
Bly, Robert
After Drinking All Night with a Friend, We Go Out in a Boat at Dawn to See Who Can Write the Best Poem.
After Long Busyness.
After the Industrial Revolution, All Things Happen at Once.
After Working.
Afternoon Sleep.
Andrew Jackson's Speech.
Asian Peace Offers Rejected without Publication.
At a March against the Vietnam War.
At Mid-Ocean.
At the Funeral of Great-Aunt Mary.
August Rain.
Awakening.
Barnfire during Church.
Black Pony Eating Grass.
Busy Man Speaks, A.
Christmas Eve Service at Midnight at St. Michael's.
Clear Air of October, The.
Come with Me.
Counting Small-Boned Bodies.
Dead Seal near McClure's Beach, The.
Depression.
Dream of Suffocation, A.
Driving through Minnesota during the Hanoi Bombings.
Driving to Town Late to Mail a Letter.
Driving toward the Lac Qui Parle River.
Ducks.
Evolution from the Fish.
Executive's Death, The.
Extra Joyful Chorus for Those Who Have Read This Far, An.
Finding the Father.
Fishing on a Lake at Night.
For My Son, Noah, Ten Years Old.
Great Society, The.
Hatred of Men with Black Hair.
Hearing Men Shout at Night on MacDougal Street.
Hollow Tree, A.
Hunting Pheasants in a Cornfield.
Hurrying Away from the Earth.
In a Mountain Cabin in Norway.

In a Train.
In Danger from the Outer World.
Johnson's Cabinet Watched by Ants.
Late Spring Day in My Life, A.
Laziness and Silence.
Leonardo's Secret.
Long Walk before the Snows Began, A.
Looking at a Dead Wren in My Hand.
Looking at a Dry Canadian Thistle Brought In from the Snow.
Looking at New-fallen Snow from a Train.
Looking at Some Flowers.
Looking into a Face.
Looking into a Tide Pool.
Love Poem: "When we are in love, we love the grass."
Man Whom the Sea Kept Awake, The.
Melancholia.
Missouri Traveller Writes Home, A: 1830.
Mourning Pablo Neruda.
My Father's Wedding.
Night.
November Day at McClure's.
Old Boards.
Origin of the Praise of God, The.
Poem against the British.
Poem against the Rich.
Poem in Three Parts.
Possibility of New Poetry, The.
Puritan on His Honeymoon, The.
Reading in Fall Rain.
Romans Angry about the Inner World.
Silence.
Six Winter Privacy Poems.
Sleet Storm on the Merritt Parkway.
Small Bird's Nest Made of White Reed Fiber, A.
Snowbanks North of the House.
Snowfall in the Afternoon.
Solitude Late at Night in the Woods.
Summer, 1960, Minnesota.
Sunday in Glastonbury.
Surprised by Evening.
Teeth Mother Naked at Last, The.
Thinking of "The Autumn Fields."
Those Being Eaten by America.
Three Presidents.
Turning Away from Lies.
Visiting Emily Dickinson's Grave with Robert Francis.
Waking from Sleep.
War and Silence.
Watching Television.
Water under the Earth.
Watering the Horse.
When the Dumb Speak.
Where We Must Look for Help.
Written Forty Miles South of a Spreading City.
Written in Dejection near Rome.

Blyton, Carey
Manatee, The.

Boake, Barcroft Henry
Allegory, An.
At Devlin's Siding.
Where the Dead Men Lie.

Boas, Guy
Underground, The.
Vet, The.

Bobango, Gerald
Educational Administration Professor's Prayer, The.

Boccaccio, Giovanni
Fiammetta.
Inscription for a Portrait of Dante.
Of Fiammetta Singing.
Of His Last Sight of Fiammetta.
Of Three Girls and of Their Talk.
Queen of the Angels, The.
Sonnets, *sels.*
To Dante in Paradise, after Fiammetta's Death.
To One Who Had Censured His Public Exposition of Dante.
Tribute to Dante, A.

Bock, Frederick
Aubade: The Desert.
Big, Fat Summer—and the Lean and Hard.
Return from the Wars, A.

Bode, John E.
To the End.

Bodecker, N. M.
Good-by My Winter Suit.
Island of Yorrick, The.
John.
Miss Bitter.
Mr. 'Gator.
Sing Me a Song of Teapots and Trumpets.
When All the World Is Full of Snow.

Bodenheim, Maxwell
Advice to a Blue-Bird.
Advice to a Forest.
City Girl.
Death.
Jack Rose.
Lynched Negro.
Negroes.
New York City.
Poem: "O men, walk on the hills."
Poem to Negro and Whites.
Poet to His Love.
To an Enemy.
Upper Family.

Bodker, Cecil
Calendar.
Fury's Field.
Self-Portrait.

Boethius (Anicius Manlius Severinus Boethius)
Consolation of Philosophy, The, *sels.*
Happy That First White Age When We.
Happy Too Much.
Metrum V.
O Thou Whose Power.

Bogan, Jim
Discriminations, The; Virtuous Amusements and Wicked Demons.

Bogan, Louise
After the Persian.
Alchemist, The.
Animal, Vegetable and Mineral.
Baroque Comment.
Betrothed.
Cartography.
Cassandra.
Changed Woman, The.
Chanson un Peu Naïve.
Come, Break with Time.
Crossed Apple, The.
Crows, The.
Daemon, The.
Decoration.
Dragonfly, The.
Dream, The.
Evening in the Sanitarium.
Exhortation.
Fiend's Weather.
Frightened Man, The.
Henceforth, from the Mind.
Hypocrite Swift.
I Saw Eternity.
Juan's Song.
July Dawn.
Knowledge.
Late.
M., Singing.
Man Alone.
March Twilight.
Mark, The.
Medusa.
Meeting, The.
Men Loved Wholly beyond Wisdom.
Musician.
Night.
Old Countryside.
Packet of Letters.
Portrait.
Putting to Sea.
Question in a Field.
Roman Fountain.
Several Voices out of a Cloud.
Simple Autumnal.
Sleeping Fury, The.
Song for a Lyre.
Song for the Last Act.
Spirit's Song.
Statue and Birds.
Summer Wish.
To an Artist, to Take Heart.
To Be Sung on the Water.
To My Brother.
Train Tune.
Variation on a Sentence.
Women.
Zone.

Bogardus, Edgar
Eastward to Eden.

Bogart, Elizabeth ("Estelle")
He Came Too Late.

Bogin, George
Alone in the House.
Troopship for France, War II.
Visitor, The.

Bogle, Eric
Band Played Waltzing Matilda, The.
No Man's Land.
Now I'm Easy.

Bohanan, Otto Leland
Dawn's Awake, The!
Washer-Woman, The.

Boiarski, Phil
Still Wrestling.

Boilleau, Joan
I Saw a Ghost.

Boimwall, Rachel
At Night.
Diaspora Jews.
Lifelong.
Round: "Everything is round."

Boker, George Henry
Ballad of New Orleans, The.
Ballad of Sir John Franklin, A.
Battle of Lookout Mountain, The.
Before Vicksburg.
Black Regiment, The.
Countess Laura.
Crossing at Fredericksburg, The.
Cruise of the *Monitor,* The.
Dirge for a Soldier.
Ferry, The.
God to Thee We Humbly Bow, *with music.*
Hooker's Across!
Lincoln.
On Board the *Cumberland.*
Sonnets, *sel.*
To England.
To My Lady.
Upon the Hill before Centreville.
Varuna, The.
Zagonyi.

Boland, Eavan
Athene's Song.
Child of Our Time.
New Territory.
Song: "Where in blind files."
War Horse, The.

Bold, Alan
I drink to forget, but whenever I think.
Malfeasance, The.
Realm of Touching, The.
Space for Colour.
That's Life?

Bold, Henry
Song: "Chloris, forbear a while."
Song: "Fire, fire."

Boleyn, Anne
O Death, Rock Me Asleep, *at.*

Boleyn, George
O Death, Rock Me Asleep, *at.*

Bolles, Matthew
Here, Lord, Retired, I Bow in Prayer, *with music.*
Bolton, Edmund
Carol, A: "Sweet music, sweeter far."
Palinode, A.
To Favonius.
Bolton, Sarah Knowles
Inevitable, The.
Paddle Your Own Canoe.
Bolz, Judy
Migration as a Passage in Time.
Bomford, Nora
Drafts.
Bomze, Nahum
City of Light.
Pshytik.
Bonar, Horatius
Be True.
Beyond the Smiling and the Weeping.
Blessing, and Honor.
He Liveth Long Who Liveth Well.
Honesty.
How We Learn.
Little While, A.
Lost but Found.
Love Is of God.
Master's Touch, The.
More of Thee.
My Prayer.
This Do in Remembrance of Me.
Thy Way, Not Mine.
Voice from Galilee, The.
Bonaventure, Saint
Psalter of the Blessed Virgin Mary.
Bond, Carrie Jacobs
I Love You Truly.
Perfect Day, A.
Bond, Harold
Glove, The.
Letter from Birmingham.
Swallowing.
Bond, Julian
Bishop of Atlanta, The: Ray Charles.
Habana.
Look at That Gal.
Rotation.
Bone, Edith
On Myself.
Bone, Florence
Prayer for a Little Home, A.
Boner, John Henry
Light'ood Fire, The.
Poe's Cottage at Fordham.
Remembrance.
We Walked among the Whispering Pines.
Bonifacius, Balthasar
All those I love die young: Zoilus, I'll try.
Bonn, John Louis
Madonna: 1936.
Bontemps, Arna
Black Man Talks of Reaping, A.
Blight.
Close Your Eyes!
Day-Breakers, The.
Gethsemane.
God Give to Men ("God give the yellow man").
Golgotha Is a Mountain.
Homing.
Idolatry.
Lancelot.
Length of Moon.
Miracles.
Nocturne at Bethesda.
Nocturne of the Wharves.
Note of Humility, A.
Reconnaissance.
Return, The.
Southern Mansion.
To a Young Girl Leaving the Hill Country.
Tree Design, A.
Boodson, Alison
Carol: "Fire is what's precious now."
Night Alert.
Poem: "He lying spilt like water from a bowl."
Poem: "I do not want to be your weeping woman."
Booker, Betty
David in April.
Booker, Stephen Todd
Flash.
Look Away/Look Away.
Lynched.
No Fig.
Paperweight Escape.
Booth, Barton
Song: "Sweet are the charms of her I love."
Booth, Eva Gore-. *See* **Gore-Booth, Eva**
Booth, Philip
Animal Fair.
Barred Islands.
Big Dog.
Catwise.
Cold Water Flat.
Countershadow, The.
Crossing.
Crows.
Day the Tide, The.
Deer Isle.
Dreamscape.
Ego.
Elegy for a Diver.
First Lesson.
Fisherman.
Great Farm.
Green Song.
Hard Country.
Heron.
How to See Deer.
If It Comes.
Incredible Yachts, The.
Jake's Wharf.
Late Spring, A: Eastport.
Lines from an Orchard Once Surveyed by Thoreau.
Maine.
Marin.
Misery of Mechanics, The.
North.
Old Man.
One Man's Wife.
Photographer.
Round, The: "Skunk cabbage, bloodroot."
Rout.
Seeing Auden Off.
Siasconset Song.
Stove.
Thanksgiving.
These Men.
Tower, The.
Turning, The.
Twelfth Night.
Vermont: Indian Summer.
Was a Man.
Wilding, The.
Boothby, Sir Brooke
Sonnet on Life.
Boothroyd, John Basil
"And Now. "
Best of Two Worlds.
Holy Order.
Please Excuse Typing.
Sanctuary.
Borawski, Walta
Normal as Two Ships in the Night.
Borenstein, Emily
Grandfather Yoneh.
Life of the Letters.
Borges, Jorge Luis
Afterglow.
Dagger, The ("A dagger rests in a drawer").
Hengest Cyning.
Ode Written in 1966.
Plainness.
Things That Might Have Been.
Borgese, Giuseppe Antonio
Dream of a Decent Death.
Easter Sunday, 1945.
Borie, Lysbeth Boyd
Five Years Old.
Boring, Mollie
September Butterfly.
Borregaard, Ebbe
Each Found Himself at the End Of. . .
Some Stories of the Beauty Wapiti.
Borrell, D. E.
Another Death.
Borson, Roo
Flowers.
Gray Glove.
In the Cafe.
Jacaranda.
Now and Again.
Talk.
Transparence of November, The.
Borthwick, Jane
Light Shining out of Darkness.
Bosman, Herman Charles
Learning Destiny.
Old I Am.
Seed.
Bossert, Shirley
At Arm's Length.
Bossidy, John Collins
Boston ("And this is good old Boston").
Boston Toast, A.
On the Aristocracy of Harvard.
To Boston.
Bost, Marcia Inzer
Mountain Born.
Bostwick, Grace G.
Pep.
Bostwick, Helen Louise Barron
Little Dandelion.
Boswell, Arthur
Roughchin, the Pirate.
Boswell, Margie B.
Texas Ranger, The.
Bosworth, Martha
Angle of Vision.
Botsford, S. B.
Sonneteering Made Easy.
Bottomley, Gordon
Blanid's Song.
Crier by Night, The, *sel.*
Dawn.
Eager Spring.
Eagle Song.
End of the World, The.
Hymn of Form, A.
Hymn of Touch, A.
"L'Apparition" of Gustave Moreau.
L'Oiseau Bleu.
Louse crept out of my lady's shift, A.
Maid of Arc, The.
Suilven and the Eagle, *sel.*
To Iron-Founders and Others.
Bottoms, David
Coasting toward Midnight at the Southeastern Fair.
Copperhead, The.
Desk, The.
Faith Healer Come to Rabun County.
In a U-Haul North of Damascus.
Sign for My Father, Who Stressed the Bunt.
Stumptown Attends the Picture Show.
Traveler, The.
Under the Boathouse.
Wrestling Angels.
Writing on Napkins at the Sunshine Club, Macon, Georgia 1971.
Botton, Isaac de
Desire.
Bottrall, Ronald
Darkened Windows.

Icarus.
Mating Answer.
Proserpine at Enna.
Rondeau: "Homage to change that scatters the poppy seed."
Botwood, Edward
Hot Stuff.
Boufflers, Marie-Francoise-Catherine de Beauveau, Marquise de
Air: Sentir avec Ardeur.
Boufflers, Stanislas Jean, Marquis de
A B C for Grown Gentlemen, An.
Boumí-Pappás, Rita
Crow, The.
Boundy, Rex
Virile Christ, A.
Boundzekei-Dongala, Emmanuel
Fantasy under the Moon.
Bourdillon, Francis William
Aucassin and Nicolete.
Eurydice.
Light.
Lost God, A, *sel.*
Night Has a Thousand Eyes, The.
Violinist, A.
Where Runs the River.
Bourinot, Arthur Stanley
Dark Flows the River.
Johnny Appleseed.
Legend of Paul Bunyan, A.
Nicolas Gatineau.
Only Silence.
Paul Bunyan ("He came,/ striding").
Snow Anthology.
Sonnets to My Mother.
Tom Thomson.
Under the Pines.
What Far Kingdom.
Winter Sketch.
Bourke, Sharon
Sopranosound, Memory of John.
Bourne, David
Parachute Descent.
Bourne, Nina
Where the Single Men Go in Summer.
Bourne, Vincent
Cricket, The.
Housekeeper, The.
Jackdaw, The.
Snail, The ("The frugal snail with forecast of repose").
Snail, The ("To grass, or leaf, or fruit, or wall").
Bouvard, Marguerite
White.
Bouvé, Thomas Tracy
Shannon and the *Chesapeake,* The.
Bovshover, Joseph
To the Laggards.
Bowden, James H.
At the Spa.
Bowden, Samuel
Paper Kite, The, *sel.*
Bowditch, Nathaniel Ingersoll
World Beyond, A.
Bowen, Charles Synge Christopher Bowen, Baron
Just and Unjust.
Rain, The.
Rain It Raineth, The.
Bowen, Donna
Little Searcher, The.
Bowen, Edward Ernest
Forty Years On.
Bowen, James K.
Edge, The.
Bowen, John Eliot
Man Who Rode to Conemaugh, The.
Bowen, Robert Adger
Gloaming.
Bower, Helen Frazee-. *See* **Frazee-Bower, Helen**
Bowering, George
Beach at Veracruz, The.
Circus Maximus.
Dobbin.
Egg, The.
Envies, The.
Está Muy Caliente.
Grandfather.
Grass, The.
Grass, Grass.
House, The.
In the Forest.
Inside the Tulip.
Moon Shadow.
My Atlas Poet.
Smoking Drugs with Strangers.
Solid Mountain.
Summer Solstice, *sel.*
Under.
Winter's Dregs.
Bowering, Marilyn
Russian Asylum.
Seeing Oloalok.
Wishing Africa.
Bowers, Edgar
Adam's Song to Heaven.
Aix-la-Chappelle, 1945.
Astronomers of Mont Blanc, The.
Centaur Overheard, The.
Dark Earth and Summer.
From William Tyndale to John Frith.
Grove and Building.
Mirror, The.
Mountain Cemetery, The.
Prince, The.
Stoic, The: For Laura von Courten.
To the Contemporary Muse.
Two Poems on the Catholic Bavarians.
Virgin Mary, The.
Wise Men, The.
Bowers, Neal
Archetypes.
Unplanned Design.
Bowes-Lyon, Lilian
Feather, The.
Shepherd's Coat, A.
Stars Go By, The.
White Hare, The.
Bowie, Beverly
To My New Mistress.
Bowie, Walter Russell
God of the Nations.
O Holy City Seen of John, *with music.*
Bowie, William C.
Before the Statue of a Laughing Man.
Bowker, Richard Rogers
Thomas à Kempis.
Bowker, Tom
Eagle.
Bowles, Caroline Anne (Caroline Anne Bowles Southey)
Young Gray Head, The.
Bowles, Paul
Extract.
Bowles, William Lisle
At Dover Cliffs [July 20, 1787].
Bells of Ostend, The.
Butterfly and the Bee, The.
Distant View of England from the Sea.
Dover Cliffs.
Hope.
Influence of Time on Grief.
Sonnet: At Dover Cliffs.
Sonnet: At Ostend.
Sonnet: "Evening, as slow thy placid shades descend."
Sonnet: "O time! who knows't a lenient hand to lay."
Sonnet July 18th 1787.
Time and Grief.
To the River Itchin, near Winton.
Bowman, Gladys M.
Only One Life.
Bowman, Louise Hollingsworth
Quiet Hour, The.
Bowman, Louise Morey
Sea Lavender.
She Plans Her Funeral.
Bowman, P. C.
Homing.
Route 95 North: New Jersey.
Bowndheri, Ilmi
As Camels Who Have Become Thirsty.
Bowring, Sir John
God Is Love.
In the Cross of Christ I Glory.
Watchman, Tell Us of the Night.
Bowsher, Kathryn T.
My Hiding Place.
Thy Nail-pierced Hands.
Box, Earl Gene
Aunt Beulah's Wisdom.
Butch Is Back.
Midwife.
Old Man Con.
Trash.
Boyajian, Aram
American Commencement.
Blok: Let Me Learn the Poem.
Death of the Epileptic Poet Yesenin, The.
George Washington Goes to a Girlie Movie.
Hairs in My Nose, The.
Poetry Is in the Darkness.
World Is Really a Sugarplum House in the Forest, The.
Boyars, Arthur
Initial.
Boyd, Bruce
Sanctuary.
This Is What the Watchbird Sings, Who Perches in the Lovetree.
Venice Recalled.
Boyd, Marion Margaret
To One Older.
White Dusk.
Boyd, Mark Alexander
Fra Bank to Bank, Fra Wood to Wood I Rin.
Boyd, Melba Joyce
Beer Drops.
Sunflowers and Saturdays.
Why?
"Boyd, Nancy." *See* **Millay, Edna St. Vincent**
Boyd, Thomas
Heath, The.
King's Son, The.
Love on the Mountain.
To the Leanán Shee.
Boyden, Polly Chase
Mud ("Mud is very nice to feel").
New Mexico.
Boye, Karin
Dedication, A, *sel.*
Sword, A.
Boyer, Jill Witherspoon
Detroit City.
Dream Farmer.
King Lives.
When Brothers Forget.
Boyesen, Hjalmar Hjorth
Thoralf and Synnöv.
Boyle, Kay
Communication to Nancy Cunard, A.
For James Baldwin.
Monody to the Sound of Zithers.
New Emigration, The.
Thunderstorm in South Dakota.
To a Seaman Dead on Land.
Boyle, Sarah Roberts
Voice of the Grass, The.
Boyle, Virginia Fraser
Tennessee.
Boynton, H. W.
Golfer's Rubaiyat, The.
Bozanic, Nick
Crane's Ascent, The.
Brabant, Suzanne
Morgans in October.

Two at Showtime.
Bracken, Thomas
Not Understood.
Bracker, Milton
P Is for Paleontology.
Troupial, A.
Where, O Where?
Brackett, Anna Callender
Benedicite.
In Hades.
Bradbury, Bianca
Nor'easter.
Bradby, Godfrey Fox
In Hoc Signo.
Bradford, Gamaliel
Ardor.
Exit God.
God.
Hope.
My Delight.
Bradford, William
And Truly It Is a Most Glorious Thing, *with music.*
Epitaphium Meum.
New England's Growth.
Of Boston in New England.
Word to New England, A.
Bradley, Edward. *See* **"Bede, Cuthbert"**
Bradley, George
In Bed with a River.
Swing One, Swing All.
Bradley, Katherine *and* **Edith Cooper.** *See* **"Field, Michael"**
Bradley, Mary Emily Neely
Beyond Recall.
Chrysalis, A.
In Death.
Spray of Honeysuckle, A.
Bradley, Sam
Casual Meeting.
Bradley, William Aspenwall
To Little Renée on First Seeing Her Lying in Her Cradle.
Bradstreet, Anne
Another ("As loving hind that, hartless, wants her deer").
Another Letter to Her Husband, Absent upon Publick Employment.
As Spring the Winter.
As Weary Pilgrim, Now at Rest.
Author to Her Book, The.
Before the Birth of One of Her Children.
Childhood.
Contemplations.
Deliverance from a Fit of Fainting.
Flesh and the Spirit, The.
Four Seasons of the Year, The.
In Honour of That High and Mighty Princess Queen Elizabeth of Happy Memory.
In Memory of My Dear Grandchild [Anne Bradstreet].
In Memory of My Dear Grandchild Elizabeth Bradstreet, [Who Deceased August, 1665, Being a Year and a Half Old].
In Reference to Her Children, 23 June, 1656.
In Thankfull Remembrance for My Dear Husband's Safe Arrivall Sept. 3, 1662.
Letter to Her Husband, A ("Phoebus, make haste").
Letter to Her Husband, Absent upon Public Employment, A ("As loving hind. . .").
Letter to Her Husband, Absent upon Publick Employment, A ("My head, my heart, mine eyes . . .").
Longing for Heaven.
Mariner that on smooth waves doth glide, The.
Of the Four Ages of Man, *sel.*
On My Dear Grand-Child Simon Bradstreet.
Prologue, The: "To sing of wars, of captain[e]s, and of kings."
Silent alone, where none or saw, or heard.
So he that saileth in this world of pleasure.
Some Verses upon the Burning of Our House, July 10th, 1666.
To My Dear and Loving Husband.
Upon the Burning of Our House, July 10th, 1666.
Vanity of All Worldly Things, The.
Bradstreet, Samuel
Almanack for the Year of Our Lord, 1657, An.
Brady, Charles A.
Dimidium Animae Meae.
Brady, Edwin James
Ballad of the Captains, A.
Capstan Chantey, A.
Coachman's Yarn, The.
Lost and Given Over.
Brady, George M.
Autumn House, The.
Day, The.
Garden, The.
Generations, The.
Hosts, The.
Land-Fall.
Old Michael.
Settled Men, The.
Brady, June
Far Trek.
Brady, Nicholas *and* **Nahum Tate.** *See* **Tate, Nahum** *and* **Nicholas Brady**
Bragdon, Claude
Beautiful Necessity, The, *sel.*
Point, the Line, the Surface and Sphere, The.
Bragg, Linda Brown
Our Blackness Did Not Come to Us Whole.
Poem about Beauty, Blackness, Poetry, A.
Brainard, John Gardiner Calkins
Captain, The, *abr.*
Deep, The.
Epithalamium: "I saw two clouds at morning."
I Saw Two Clouds at Morning.
Mr. Merry's Lament for "Long Tom."
On the Death of Commodore Oliver H. Perry.
Sonnet to the Sea Serpent.
To Thee, O God, the Shepherd Kings, *with music.*
Brainard, Mary Gardiner
Not Knowing, *sel.*
Braiser, Virginia
Time of the Mad Atom.
Braisted, Harry
She Was Bred in Old Kentucky, *with music.*
You're Not the Only Pebble on the Beach, *with music.*
Braithwaite, William Stanley
Del Cascar.
Golden Moonrise.
House of Falling Leaves, The.
Hymn for the Slain in Battle.
If I Could Touch.
In a Grave-Yard.
Ironic: LL.D.
October XXIX, 1795.
Rhapsody.
Rye Bread.
Sandy Star and Willie Gee (*Complete,* I–V).
Scintilla.
Sic Vita.
To
Turn Me to My Yellow Leaves.
Twenty Stars to Match His Face.
Two Questions.
Watchers, The.
White Magic; an Ode.
Braley, Berton
Business Is Business.
Church Bells.
Do It Now.
Loyalty.
Opportunity.
Prayer, A: "Lord, let me live like a Regular Man."
Success!
Thinker, The.
Twins, The.
Bramston, James
Art of Politics [*or* Politicks], The, *sel.*
Man of Taste, The, *sels.*
Time's Changes.
Branch, Anna Hempstead
Grieve Not, Ladies.
Her Words.
I Think of Him as One Who Fights.
Mathematics or the Gift of Tongues.
Monk in the Kitchen, The.
Song for My Mother, A: Her Hands.
Song for My Mother, A: Her Stories.
Song for My Mother, A: Her Words.
Songs for My Mother, *sels.*
To a New York Shop-Girl Dressed for Sunday.
Unbeliever, An.
Warrior Maid, The.
Branch, M. W.
Schmaltztenor!
Branch, Mary Lydia Bolles
Petrified Fern, The.
Brand, Millen
All One.
Clausa Germanis Gallia.
Last Families in the Cabins, The.
Longing for the Persimmon Tree.
Lost.
Thirty Childbirths.
Brand, Oscar
When I First Came to This Land.
Brandi, John
How to Get to New Mexico.
Brant, Beth
For All My Grandmothers.
Native Origin.
Ride the Turtle's Back.
Brant, LeRoy V.
Green Plumes of Royal Palms, *with music.*
Oh, Day of Days, *with music.*
Brantingham, Philip
Sarentino-South Tyrol.
Brasch, Charles
Night Cries, Wakari Hospital.
Brasfield, James
Stringer, The.
Brasfield, Philip
Censorship.
Inebriates.
Interview, An.
Rune.
Trouble.
Brasher, Charles
Poem after a Speech by Chief Seattle, 1855.
Brasier, Virginia
Primer of Consequences.
Song for a Lost Art.
Brass, Perry
I Think the New Teacher's a Queer.
Brathwaite, Edward
Cherries, *sel.*
So When the Hammers of the Witnesses of Heaven Are Raised All Together.
Brathwaite, Richard
Nature's Embassy, *sel.*
Nightingale, The.
Of Maids' Inconstancy.
Strappado for the Devil, A, *sel.*
Braude, Michael
Curtain Speech.
Braun, Richard Emil
Domestic Duties.
Goose.
Niagara.
Brautigan, Richard
All Watched Over by Machines of Loving Grace.
Day They Busted the Grateful Dead, The.
Haiku Ambulance.
Have You Ever Had a Witch Bloom like a Highway.
In a Cafe.

Late Starting Dawn.
Brawley, Benjamin
Chaucer.
My Hero.
Braxton, Jodi
Sometimes I Think of Maryland.
Brazelton, Ethel M. C.
Poor Lil' Brack Sheep.
Brecht, Bertolt
Burning of Books, The.
Children's Crusade 1939.
Difficult Times.
First Psalm, The.
Time's Mutability.
Brecht, Bertolt *and* **Hans Eisler**
United Front.
Breck, Mrs. Frank A.
They Two.
Breed, Eleanor D.
Scapegoats.
Brégy, Katherine Marie Cornelia
Maid, The.
"Breitman, Hans." *See* **Leland, Charles Godfrey**
Bremser, Ray
Blood.
Poem of Holy Madness, *sel.*
Brenan, Joseph
Come to Me, Dearest.
Brennan, Christopher John
Adam to Lilith.
Anguish'd Doubt Broods over Eden, The.
Because She Would Ask Me Why I Loved Her.
Come Out, Come Out, Ye Souls That Serve.
How Old Is My Heart.
I Cry to You as I Pass Your Windows.
I Said, This Misery Must End.
I Saw My Life as Whitest Flame.
Interlude: The Casement.
Land I Came Thro' Last, The.
Let Us Go Down, the Long Dead Night Is Done.
Lilith, *sels.*
Lilith on the Fate of Man.
My Heart Was Wandering in the Sands.
O Desolate Eves.
Pauca Mea, *sel.*
Quest of Silence, The, *sel.*
Towards the Source, *sels.*
Twilight of Disquietude, The, *sels.*
Wanderer, The, *sels.*
Years That Go to Make Me Man, The.
Brennan, Eileen
Evening on Howth Head.
May Evening.
One Kingfisher and One Yellow Rose.
Thoughts at the Museum.
Brennan, Gerald
Mornin's Mornin', The.
Brennan, J. Keirn
Let the Rest of the World Go By.
Brennan, John Michael
Air Is.
Brennan, Joseph Payne
Cat, The!
Raccoon on the Road.
Brennan, Matthew
Noon Glare.
Seeing in the Dark.
Brent, Hally Carrington
I Think I Know No Finer Things than Dogs.
Brereton, Jane
On Mr. Nash's Picture at Full Length.
Brereton, John Le Gay
Buffalo Creek.
Cling to Me.
Bretherton, C. H.
In Winter.
Breton, André
Dreams.
Freedom of Love.
Postman Cheval.
Spectral Attitudes, The.
Breton, Nicholas
Aglaia.
Assurance, An.
Country Song.
Cradle Song, A: "Come, little babe, come, silly soul."
Happy Countryman, The.
His Wisdom.
Honourable Entertainment Given to the Queen's Majesty in Progress at Elvetham, 1591, The, *sels.*
I Would Thou Wert Not Fair [*or* I Were Wise].
Invective against the Wicked of the World, An, *sel.*
Ipsa Quae.
Merry Country Lad, The.
Odd Conceit, An.
Olden Love-making.
Passionate Shepherd, The, *sels.*
Pastoral, A: "In the merry month of May."
Pastoral, A: "On a hill there grows a flower."
Pastoral, A: "Sweet birds! that sit and sing amid the shady valleys."
Pastoral: "Who can live in heart so glad."
Phyllida and Corydon ("In the merry month of May").
Phyllida and Corydon ("On a hill there grows a flower").
Phyllis.
Ploughman's Song, The.
Pretty Twinkling Starry Eyes.
Rare News.
Report Song, A.
Shepherd and Shepherdess.
Strange Fortunes of Two Excellent Princes, The, *sel.*
Supplication, A.
Sweet Lullaby, A.
To His Muse.
Upon a dainty hill sometime.
Brett, Peter
Night Teeth.
Pickers.
Brett, Reginald Baliol, 2d Viscount Esher
At Swindon.
Brew, Kwesi
Ancestral Faces.
Lonely Traveller, The.
Plea for Mercy, A.
Search, The.
Brewer, Ebenezer Cobham
Signs of the Zodiac, The.
Brewster, Elizabeth
Anti-Love Poems.
Death by Drowning.
East Coast—Canada.
Egoist Dead, The.
Eviction.
Great-Aunt Rebecca.
If I Could Walk Out into the Cold Country.
In the Library.
Playing the Bones.
Princess Addresses the Frog Prince, The.
River Song.
Brewster, Martha
Stately Structure of This Earth, The, *with music.*
Brice, Andrew
Freedom; a Poem, Written in Time of Recess from the Rapacious Claws of Bailiffs, *sel.*
Poet's Terror at the Bailiffs of Exeter, The.
Brick, Norman
Of Snow.
"Bridges, Madeline" (Mary Ainge De Vere)
Breath, A.
Faith Trembling.
Farewell, A: "I put thy hand aside, and turn away."
Friend and Lover.
God Keep You.
Life's Mirror.
Poet and Lark.
Spinner, The.
When the Most Is Said.
Wind-swept Wheat, The.
Bridges, Robert (1844–1930)
Affliction of Richard, The.
After the Gale.
Angel Spirits of Sleep.
April, 1885.
Awake, My Heart, to Be Loved.
Cheddar Pinks.
Cliff-Top, The.
Clouds Have Left the Sky, The.
Dejection.
Elegy: "Clear and gentle stream!"
Elegy: Summer-House on the Mound, The.
Elegy: "Wood is bare, The: a river-mist is steeping."
Elegy on a Lady, Whom Grief for the Death of Her Betrothed Killed.
Epistle II: To a Socialist in London, *sel.*
Eros.
Ethick.
Etosion achthos aroures ("Who goes there? God knows. I'm nobody. How should I answer?").
Evening Darkens Over, The.
First Spring Morning, The.
Flycatchers.
Fortunatus Nimium.
Founder's Day.
Garden in September, The.
Gheluvelt.
Growth of Love, The, *sels.*
Hill Pines Were Sighing, The.
Hymn of Nature, A.
I Have Loved Flowers.
I Love All Beauteous Things.
I Heard a Linnet Courting.
I Never Shall Love the Snow Again.
I Will Not Let Thee Go.
Idle Flowers, The.
Idle Life I Lead, The.
Indolence.
Introduction: " 'Twas late in my long journey, when I had clomb to where."
Johannes Milton, Senex.
Laus Deo.
Linnet, The.
London Snow.
Low Barometer.
Melancholia.
Muse and Poet.
My Delight and Thy Delight.
Nightingales.
Nimium Fortunatus.
Noel; Christmas Eve, 1913.
North Wind Came Up Yesternight, The.
North Wind in October.
November.
O Weary Pilgrims.
On a Dead Child.
Our Lady.
Palm Willow, The.
Passer-by, A.
Pater Filio.
Philosopher to His Mistress, The.
Poor Poll.
Psalm, The: "While Northward the hot sun was sinking o'er the trees."
Riding adown the country lanes.
Say who is this with silvered hair.
Since We Loved.
Snow Lies Sprinkled on the Beach, The.
So Sweet Love Seemed.
Song: "I have loved flowers that fade."
Song: "I love my lady's eyes."
South Wind, The.
Spirits.
Spring Goeth All in White.
Storm Is Over, The.
Testament of Beauty, The, *sels.*
Thanksgiving Day.
There Is a Hill.
Thou Didst Delight My Eyes.

To L. B. C. L. M.
To the United States of America.
Triolet: "All women born are so perverse."
Triolet: "When first we met we did not guess."
Upon the Shore.
Upper skies are palest blue, The.
Water-Party, A.
Weep Not To-Day.
When Death to Either Shall Come.
When my love was away.
When we first met we did not guess.
Who Has Not Walked upon the Shore.
Winnowers, The.
Winter Nightfall.
Bridges, Robert (1858–1941)
James McCosh.
Toast to Our Native Land, A.
Unillumined Verge, The.
Bridges-Adams, W.
Fragment from the Elizabethans.
Bridget, Saint
Feast of Saint Brigid of Kildare, The,*At.*
Heavenly Banquet, The,*at.*
I Should Like to Have a Great Pool of Ale, *at.*
Bridgman, L. J.
Hare and the Pig, The.
Brierre, Jean
Harlem.
Briggs, C.
Framework-Knitters Petition, The.
Briggs, Olga Hampel
Brief History.
Brigham, Besmilr
Tell Our Daughters.
Will's Love, The.
Bright, Verne
Revelation.
Brine, Mary Dow
Hearts and Flowers, *with music.*
Somebody's Mother.
Bringhurst, Robert
Deuteronomy.
Notes to the Reader.
These Poems, She Said ("These poems, these poems").
Brininstool, Earl Alonzo
Back to Arizona.
Range Rider's Soliloquy, The.
Stampede, The.
Brink, Carol Ryrie
Goody O'Grumpity.
Brinnin, John Malcolm
Address to the Refugees.
American Plan.
Angel Eye of Memory.
Ascension, The: 1925.
At the Airport.
At the Band Concert.
At the Museum.
Cape Ann; a View.
Carmarthen Bar.
Dachau.
End of My Sister's Guggenheim, The.
Every Earthly Creature.
Fêtes, Fates.
Flight 539.
Girl in a White Coat.
Heavy Heavy Heavy.
Hotel Paradiso e Commerciale.
John without Heaven.
Letter from an Island.
Letter to Statues.
Love in Particular.
My Father, My Son.
New England Sampler, A.
Nuns at Eve.
Roethke Plain.
Saul, Afterward, Riding East.
Skin Diving in the Virgins.
Thin Façade for Edith Sitwell, A.
Views of the Favorite Colleges.
Wind Is Ill, The.
Winter Term.
With a Posthumous Medal.
Worm in the Whirling Cross, The.
Brisby, Stewart
Artist, The.
Attica Is.
Cyclone, The.
Poem for Edie Sedgwick Who Slept in a Swimming Pool.
Public School 168.
Brissenden, Robert Francis
Verandahs.
Walking down Jalan Thamrin.
Bristol, Augusta Cooper
Pyxidanthera, The.
Bristowe, Sybil
Over the Top.
Britt, Alan
After Spending All Day at the National Museum of Art.
Serenade: "Frog will serenade, The."
Brittain, Vera
Lament of the Demobilised, The.
Perhaps.
To My Brother.
Bro, Marguerite Harmon
Prayer: "God, listen through my words to the beating of my heart."
Broaddus, Andrew
Help Thy Servant, *with music.*
Brock, Edwin
Catastrophe.
Curtain Poem, The.
Five Ways to Kill a Man.
To His Love in Middle-Age.
To My Mother.
Turn the Key Deftly.
Brock, Van K.
Sea Birds, The.
Brockerhoff, Hans
Pygmalion.
Brockman, Zoe Kincaid
Grapevine, The.
Brod, Max
Goldfish on the Writing Desk.
Hebrew Lesson.
Brode, Anthony
Breakfast with Gerard Manley Hopkins.
Calypsomania.
Obituary.
Unromantic Song.
Brodie, Hugh R.
Sergeant's Prayer, A.
Brodsky, Joseph
Etude.
Jewish Cemetery near Leningrad, A.
Monument to Pushkin.
Odysseus to Telemachus.
Pilgrims.
Six Years Later.
Soho.
To a Tyrant.
Verses on Accepting the World.
Brodsky, Louis Daniel
Ancestry.
Buffalo.
Death Comes to the Salesman.
My Flying Machine.
Sitting in Bib Overalls, Workshirt, Boots on the Monument to Liberty in the Center of the Square, Jacksonville, Illinois.
Weeding in January.
Brody, Alter
Cry of the Peoples, The.
Family Album, A.
Ghetto Twilight.
Lamentations.
Brome, Alexander
Anti-Politician, The.
Contrary, The.
Counsel, The.
Courtship.
Drinking Song.
Love's without Reason.
Pastoral on the King's Death, The; Written in 1648.
Plain Dealing.
Resolve, The.
Riddle, The: "No more, no more,/ We are already pin'd."
Royalist, The.
To a Painted Lady.
To His Friend J. H.
Why I Love Her.
Bromley, Isaac H.
Passenjare, The.
Bromwich, David
From the Righteous Man Even the Wild Beasts Run Away.
Oedipus, Pentheus.
Wandsworth Common.
Bronk, William
After the Spanish Chroniclers.
Aspects of the World like Coral Reefs.
Body, The.
Continuance, The.
Feeling, The.
Go Ahead; Goodbye; Good Luck; and Watch Out.
March, Upstate.
Mask the Wearer of the Mask Wears, The.
Metonymy as an Approach to a Real World.
Postcard to Send to Sumer, A.
What Form the World Has.
Whether what we sense of this world.
Bronson, Daniel Ross
Cleaning Up, Clearing Out.
Brontë, Anne ("Acton Bell")
Arbour, The.
Captive Dove, The.
Doubter's Prayer, The.
He Doeth All Things Well.
If This Be All.
Lines Composed in a Wood on a Windy Day.
Memory.
Prayer, A: "My God (oh, let me call Thee mine)."
Reminiscence, A.
Brontë, Charlotte ("Currer Bell")
Home-Sickness.
Mementos, *sel.*
On the Death of Anne Brontë.
Stanzas: "Often rebuked, yet always back returning," *at.*
Brontë, Emily ("Ellis Bell")
A. E.
Ah! Why, because the Dazzling Sun.
All Hushed and Still within the House.
And when thy heart is resting.
Anticipation.
Appeal, The.
At Castle Wood.
At such a time, in such a spot.
Ay—There It Is!
D. G. C. to J. A.
Day Dream, A.
Death.
Dream, A.
Enough of Thought, Philosopher.
Evening Sun, The.
Fall, Leaves, Fall.
God of Visions.
Holyday.
Hope.
How still, how happy! These [*or* Those] are words.
I Am the Only Being Whose Doom.
I die; but when the grave shall press.
I gazed upon the cloudless moon.
I Gazed Within.
I saw thee, child, one summer's day.
I'll come when thou art saddest.
I'm Happiest When Most Away.
Ladybird! Ladybird!

Last Lines.
Last Words.
Lines: "Shall earth no more inspire thee."
Linnet in the Rocky Dells, The.
Little While, a Little While, A.
Long Neglect Has Worn Away.
Love and Friendship.
Morning Star, The.
My Lady's Grave.
Night Is Darkening round Me.
Night Wind, The.
No Coward Soul [Is Mine].
Old Stoic, The.
Plead for Me.
Prisoner, The.
R. Alcona to J. Brenzaida.
Redbreast, Early in the Morning.
Remembrance.
Shall Earth No More Inspire Thee?
Sleep Brings No Joy.
Sleep Not, Dream Not.
Song: "Fall, leaves, fall; die, flowers, away."
Song: "Linnet in the rocky dells, The."
Song: "Night is darkening round me, The."
Stanzas: "I'll not weep that thou art going to leave me."
Stanzas: "Often rebuked, yet always back returning," *at.*
Stanzas to ——— ("Well, some may hate").
Sun Has Set, The.
Sympathy.
Tell Me, Tell Me, Smiling Child.
That Wind.
There Let Thy Bleeding Branch Atone.
To Imagination ("O [*or* Oh] thy bright eyes must answer now").
To Imagination ("When weary with long day's care").
'Twas one of those dark, cloudy days.
Two Children, The.
Upon Her Soothing Breast.
Visionary, The.
Warning and Reply.
Why do I hate that lone green dell?
Brooke, Fulke Greville, 1st Baron. *See* **Greville, Fulke, 1st Baron Brooke**
Brooke, Henry
Air: "Arise, arise, arise!"
Air: "For often my mammy has told."
Jack the Giant Queller; an Antique History, *sels.*
Brooke, Jocelyn
Three Barrows Down.
Brooke, Rupert
Busy Heart, The.
Channel Passage, A.
Chilterns, The.
Clouds.
Colloquial.
Day That I Have Loved.
Dead, The ("Blow out, you bugles, over the rich dead!").
Dead, The ("These hearts were woven of human joys and cares").
Dear, They Have Poached the Eyes You Loved So Well.
Dining-Room Tea.
Doubts.
Dust.
Failure.
Fish, The.
Fragment: "I strayed about the deck, an hour, to-night."
Great Lover, The.
Heaven.
Hill, The.
Letter to a Live Poet, A.
Mary and Gabriel.
Memory, A.
Menelaus and Helen.
Mummia.
Mutability.
Night Journey, The.
1914, *sels.*
Oh! Death Will Find Me.
Old Vicarage, Grantchester, The.
One before the Last, The.
Peace.
Safety.
Second Best.
Soldier, The.
Song: " 'Oh! Love,' they said, 'is King of Kings.' "
Song of the Pilgrims, The, *sel.*
Sonnet: "Not with vain tears, when we're beyond the sun."
Sonnet: "Oh! Death will find me, long before I tire."
Sonnet Reversed.
Success.
There's Wisdom in Women.
Thoughts on the Shape of the Human Body.
Tiare Tahiti.
Wagner.
Brooke, Stopford Augustus
Courage.
Earth and Man, The.
Brookhouse, Christopher
For Stephen.
Man in the Ocelot Suit, The.
Brooks, Charles Timothy
Great Voices, The.
Plea for Flood Ireson, A.
Brooks, Edwin
Tulips from Their Blood.
Brooks, Francis
Down the Little Big Horn.
Brooks, Fred Emerson
Barnyard Melodies.
Foreigners at the Fair.
Kissing, *sel.*
Pat's Opinion of Flags.
Brooks, Gwendolyn
Andre.
Anniad, The.
Appendix to the Anniad.
Aspect of Love, Alive in the Ice and Fire, An.
Ballad of Chocolate Mabbie, The.
Bean Eaters, The.
Beverly Hills, Chicago.
Big Bessie Throws Her Son into the Street.
Birth in a Narrow Room, The.
Black Wedding Song. A.
Blackstone Rangers, The.
Boy Breaking Glass.
Boys. Black.
Bronzeville Man with a Belt in the Back.
Catch of Shy Fish, A.
Chicago *Defender* Sends a Man to Little Rock, The.
Chicago Picasso, The.
Children of the Poor, The.
Cynthia in the Snow.
Egg Boiler, The.
Empty Woman, The.
Estimable Mable.
Eunice in the Evening.
First Fight. Then Fiddle. [Ply the Slipping String].
Five Men against the Theme "My Name Is Red Hot. Yo Name Ain Doodley Squat."
Flags.
Friend.
Horses Graze.
Jessie Mitchell's Mother.
Keziah.
Kitchenette Building.
Last Quatrain of the Ballad of Emmet Till, The.
Life of Lincoln West, The.
Lovely Love, A.
Lovers of the Poor, The.
Malcolm X.
Martin Luther King, Jr.
Medgar Evers.
Mother, The.
Murder, The.
My Dreams, My Works, Must Wait Till after Hell.
Narcissa.
Negro Hero.
Of De Witt Williams on His Way to Lincoln Cemetery.
Of Robert Frost.
Old People Working (Garden, Car).
Old-Marrieds, The.
Old Tennis Player.
Otto.
Paul Robeson.
Penitent Considers Another Coming of Mary, A.
Pete at the Zoo.
Piano after War.
"Pygmies Are Pygmies Still, Though Percht on Alps."
Riot.
Rites for Cousin Vit, The.
Rudolph Is Tired of the City.
Sadie and Maud.
Second Sermon on the Warpland, The.
Sermon on the Warpland, The.
Song in the Front Yard, A.
Steam Song.
"Still Do I Keep My Look, My Identity . . ."
Street in Bronzeville, A: Southeast Corner.
Strong Men, Riding Horses.
Sunset of the City, A.
Third Sermon on the Warpland, The.
To Be in Love.
Two Dedications.
Vacant Lot, The.
Vern.
Wall, The.
We Real Cool.
When You Have Forgotten Sunday: The Love Story.
Womanhood, The, *sels.*
Young Heroes.
Brooks, Helen Morgan
Plans.
Words.
Young David, A: Birmingham.
Brooks, Jonathan Henderson
And One Shall Live in Two.
Last Quarter Moon of the Dying Year, The.
Muse in Late November.
My Angel.
Paean.
Resurrection, The.
She Said . . .
Brooks, Maria Gowen
Farewell to Cuba.
Palace of the Gnomes.
Respite, The.
Song of Egla.
Zophiël, *sels.*
Brooks, Phillips
Christmas Everywhere.
O Little Town of Bethlehem.
Our Burden Bearer.
Unfailing One, The.
Wish for the New Year, A.
Brooks, Shirley
For A' That and A' That, *parody.*
I paints and paints.
More Luck to Honest Poverty.
New Proverb.
Philosopher and Her Father, The.
"Prize" Poem, A.
To Disraeli.
What Jenner Said on Hearing in Elysium That Complaints Had Been Made of His Having a Statue [in Trafalgar Square].
Brooks, Walter Rollin
Ants, Although Admirable, Are Awfully Aggravating.
From the Ballad of Two-Gun Freddy.

Ode to Spring.
Ode to the Pig: His Tail.
Thoughts on Talkers.

Brooks, William E.
Inasmuch!
Memorial Day.
Three Wise Kings.

Broome, William
Rose-Bud, The.

Broomell, Myron Henry
Prayer for the Age.

Brophy, Liam
Assumpta Est Maria.

Brosman, Catharine Savage
Route 29.

Brotherton, Alice Williams
Blazing Heart, The.
First Thanksgiving Day, The.
My Enemy.
Thanksgiving.

Brough, Robert Barnabas
Early Christian, An.
Marquis of Carabas, The.
My Lord Tomnoddy.
Sir Menenius Agrippa, the Friend of the People.

Broughton, James Richard
Afterword: Song of Song.
Birds of America, The.
Feathers or Lead?
Genesis of Vowels.
It Was the Worm.
Lighthouse Keeper's Offspring, The.
Psalm of St. Priapus, The.
Psyche to Cupid: Her Ditty.
Those Old Zen Blues.

Broughton, T. Alan
My Father Dragged by Horses.
Thaw.

Broumas, Olga
Backgammon, *sel.*
Cinderella.
Elegy: "Somebody left the world last night, I felt it."
Epithalamion: "Our mound of earth dug up."
Landscape with Leaves and Figure.
Landscape with Next of Kin.
Leda and Her Swan.
Little Red Riding Hood.
Rapunzel.
Snow White.

Brown, Abbie Farwell
Fairy Book, The.
Fisherman, The.
Friends.
Grandser.
Lost Playmate, The.
On Opening a New Book.
Peach, The.
Pirate Treasure.

Brown, Alex J.
Wickedest Man in Memphis, The.

Brown, Alice
Artisan, The.
Benedictine Garden, A.
Candlemas.
Cloistered.
Edwin Booth.
Farewell, A: "Thou wilt not look on me?"
Hora Christi.
Life.
Pagan Prayer.
Revelation.
Road to Castaly, The, *sel.*
Seaward Bound.
Sensitive Cat, The.
Sleep.
Sunrise on Mansfield Mountain.
Trilby.
West-Country Lover, The.

Brown, Allan
Girl in a Black Bikini.

Brown, Audrey Alexandra
Amber Beads.
Dark Cat, The.
Goldfish, The.
Museum-Piece.
Night Boat.
Reveillé.
Strangers, The.

Brown, Beatrice Curtis
Apple Tree, The.
Jonathan Bing.
Jonathan Bing Dances for Spring.
New Song to Sing about Jonathan Bing, A.

Brown, Bruce Bennett
Return, The.

Brown, Catherine Bernard
Prayer for Pentecost, A.

Brown, Charles O.
History of Arizona, The: How It Was Made and Who Made It.

Brown, Edward Ernest
Shemuel.

Brown, Frank London
Jazz.

Brown, George Mackay
Beachcomber.
Carpenter.
Death of Peter Esson, The.
December Day, Hoy Sound.
Desertion of the Women and Seals, The.
Dream of Winter.
Five Voyages of Arnor, The.
Harald, the Agnostic Ale-loving Old Shepherd Enemy of the Whisky-drinking Ploughmen and Harvesters, Walks over the Sabbath Hill to the Shearing.
Keeper of the Midnight Gate, The.
Lodging, The.
Old Fisherman with Guitar.
Old Women, The.
Our Lady of the Waves.
Roads.
Seven Houses, The.
Stars.
Tea Poems.
Trout Fisher.
Unlucky Boat.
Wedding.

Brown, Hamish
Aye, There's Hills.
Beyond Feith Buidhe.
Footprints.
Harlot, The.
In the Rut.
Pitch Seven.
Ronas Hill.
Weather Rhymes.
Wind.

Brown, Harry
Drill, The.
Incident on a Front Not Far from Castel di Sangro.

Brown, Horatio
Bored.
Kodak, A; Tregantle.

Brown, Irene Fowler
Rear Guard, The.

Brown, Isabella Maria
Another Day.
Prayer: "I had thought of putting an/ altar."

Brown, John
Night.
Rhapsody, Written at the Lakes in Westmorland, A: "Now sunk the sun, now twilight sunk, and Night."

Brown, Joseph Brownlee
Thalatta! Thalatta!

Brown, Kate Louise
Christmas Candle, The.

Brown, Margaret Wise
Bumble Bee.
Dear Father/ hear and bless.
Fish with the Deep Smile, The.
Green Stems.
Little Black Bug.
Little Donkey Close Your Eyes ("Little donkey on the hill.")
Secret Song, The.

Brown, Melvin Douglass
Boxer Shorts Named Champion.
Dirt Doctor, The.
Message from Reverend Fat Back Made Possible by the International Society of Social Suckers, A.
Nuclear Family, The.
Steelworker, The.

Brown, Oliver Madox
Laura's Song.

Brown, Palmer
Spangled Pandemonium, The.

Brown, Phoebe Hinsdale
I Love to Steal Awhile Away, *with music.*
Private Devotion.
Welcome, Ye Hopeful Heirs of Heaven, *with music.*

Brown, Rita Mae
Aristophanes' Symposium.
Canto Cantare Cantavi Cantatum.
Dancing the Shout to the True Gospel; or, The Song Movement Sisters Don't Want Me to Sing.
Disconnection, The.
Fire Island.
New Litany, The.
Sappho's Reply.

Brown, Solyman
Artificial Teeth.
Caries.
Dentologia; a Poem on the Diseases of the Teeth and Their Proper Remedies, *sels.*
Tartar.
Value of Dentistry, The.

Brown, Spencer
In an Old House.

Brown, Sterling Allen
After Winter.
Challenge.
Crispus Attucks McCoy.
Effie.
Foreclosure.
Long Gone.
Maumee Ruth.
Memphis Blues.
Odyssey of Big Boy.
Old Lem.
Old Woman Remembers, An.
Remembering Nat Turner.
Return.
Salutamus.
Sister Lou.
Slim Greer ("Listen to the tale").
Slim in Hell ("Slim Greer went to heaven").
Southern Cop.
Southern Road.
Strange Legacies.
Strong Men.
To a Certain Lady, in Her Garden.
When de Saints Go Ma'chin' Home.

Brown, Sydney
Maple Leaf Rag, *with music.*

Brown, Theron
His Majesty.

Brown, Thomas (Tom)
Colonels here in solemn manner meet, The.
Doctor Fell.
Epitaph upon That Profound and Learned Casuist, the Late Ordinary of Newgate, An.
Non Amo Te.
Our fathers took oaths as of old they took wives.
Reader, beneath this turf I lie.
Satire upon the French King, A.
To That Most Senseless Scoundrel, the Author of Legion's Humble Address to the Lords.

Upon the Anonymous Author of Legion's Humble Address to the Lords.
Brown, Thomas Edward
Between Our Folding Lips.
Braddan Vicarage.
Catherine Kinrade.
Conjergal Rights.
Disguises.
I Bended unto Me.
Ibant Obscuræ.
In the Coach, *sel.*
Jessie.
Lynton Verses, *sel.*
My Garden.
Opifex.
Organist in Heaven, The.
Pain, *sel.*
Parsons, The.
Preparation.
Roman Women, *sel.*
Salve!
"Social Science."
To E. M. O.
To K. H.
Voices of Nature, The.
Wesley in Heaven.
When Love Meets Love.
Brown, William Goldsmith
Mother, Home, Heaven.
Brown, William Laird. *See* **"Laird, William"**
Browne, Cecil
But not so odd.
Browne, Charles Farrar. *See* **"Ward, Artemus"**
Browne, Francis Fisher
Santa Barbara.
Under the Blue.
Vanquished.
Browne, Irving
At Shakespeare's Grave.
Man's Pillow.
My New World.
Browne, Isaac Hawkins
Boy! Bring an Ounce.
Fire Side, The; a Pastoral Soliloquy.
Foundling Hospital for Wit, The, *sel.*
In Imitation of Pope.
In Imitation of Young.
Pipe of Tobacco, A, *sels.*
Browne, Jane Euphemia ("Aunt Effie")
Great Brown Owl, The.
Little Raindrops.
Pleasant Changes.
Rooks, The.
"Browne, Matthew." *See* **Rand, William Brighty**
Browne, Michael Dennis
Delta, The.
Hallowe'en 1971.
Iowa.
Iowa, June.
King in May, The.
Lamb.
Man, The.
News from the House.
Paranoia.
Peter.
Plants, The.
Power Failure.
Roof of the World, The.
Warrior with Shield.
Browne, Moses
Shrimp, The, *sel.*
Survey of the Amphitheatre, A.
Browne, Sir Thomas
Colloquy with God, A.
Evening Hymn.
In yellow meadows I take no delight.
O for a toe, such as the funeral pyre.
Religio Medici, *sel.*
Browne, William (1591–1643)
Britannia's Pastorals, *sels.*
Celadyne's Song.
Complete Lover, The.
Course of the Tavy, The.
Dawn of Day.
Devonshire Walk, A.
Epitaph in Obitum M.S., X° Maij, 1614.
Frolic Mariners of Devon, The.
Gentle Nymphs, Be Not Refusing.
Glide Soft, Ye Silver Floods.
In Obitum M. S., X° Maij [*or* Maii], 1614.
Love Who Will, for I'll Love None.
Lydford Journey.
Memory ("Marina's gone, and now sit I").
Memory ("So shuts the marigold her leaves").
Mounting lark, day's herald, got on wing, The.
Ode, An: "Awake, faire Muse; for I intend."
On a Rope Maker Hanged.
On the Countess Dowager of Pembroke.
On the Dowager Countess of Pembroke.
Praise of Poets.
Rose, The.
Round, A: "Now that the spring hath filled our veins."
Shall I Love Again.
Shall I Tell You Whom I Love?
Shepherd's Pipe, The, *sel.*
Sirens' Song, The.
So Shuts the Marigold Her Leaves ("Marina's gone, and now sit I").
Song: "Choose now among this fairest number."
Song: "For her gait, if she be walking."
Song: "Shall I tell you whom I love?"
Song of the Sirens.
Song of the Syrens.
Venus and Adonis.
Visions, *sel.*
Welcome, A.
Welcome, Welcome, Do I Sing.
Browne, Sir William (1692–1774)
Epigram: "King to Oxford sent a troop of horse, The."
Oxford and Cambridge.
Browne, William (twentieth century)
Harlem Sounds: Hallelujah Corner.
Brownell, Florence Kerr
Coin in the Fist.
Brownell, Henry Howard
Abraham Lincoln.
Battle of Charlestown, The.
Bay Fight, The.
Burial of the Dane, The.
Bury Them.
Eagle of Corinth, The.
Lawyer's Invocation to Spring, The.
Night Quarters.
Old Cove, The.
River Fight, The.
Sphinx, The.
Sumter.
Would you hear of the River-Fight?
Browning, Elizabeth Barrett
Adequacy.
Aurora Leigh, *sels.*
Bereavement.
Best, The.
Best Thing in the World, The.
Bianca among the Nightingales.
Child's Thought of God, A.
Comfort.
Confessions.
Convinced by Sorrow.
Court Lady, A.
Cowper's Grave.
Cry of the Children, The.
Cry of the Human, The, *sel.*
Curse, The.
Curse for a Nation, A.
De Profundis, *sel.*
Dead Pan, The.
Denial, A.
Deserted Garden, The.
Face of all the world is changed, I think, The.
Farewells from Paradise.
Fiery throb in every star, A.
First Time He Kissed Me.
Florence.
Flush or Faunus.
Go from Me [Yet I Feel That I Shall Stand].
Great God Pan, The.
Grief.
Hiram Powers' "Greek Slave."
Hugh Stuart Boyd.
Hymn: "Since without Thee we do no good."
Inclusions.
Lady Geraldine's Courtship.
Lady's "Yes," The.
Lessons from the Gorse.
Look, The.
Lord Walter's Wife.
Mask, The.
Meaning of the Look, The.
Mediator, The.
Mother and Poet.
Musical Instrument, A.
My Doves.
My Heart and I.
My Kate.
Mystery.
North and the South, The.
Olives and Mountains.
On a Portrait of Wordsworth by B. R. Haydon.
Out in the Fields with God, *at.*
Patience Taught by Nature.
Pet Name, The.
Poet, The.
Poet's Vow, The, *sel.*
Portrait, A.
Praise of Earth.
Prologue: "I heard an angel speak last night."
Reading.
Reward of Service.
Romance of the Swan's Nest.
Rosalind's Scroll.
Round Our Restlessness.
Runaway Slave at Pilgrim's Point, The.
Sea-Mew, The.
Sleep, The.
Song for the Ragged Schools of London, A.
Sonnet: "Go from me. Yet I feel that I shall stand."
Sonnet: "How do I love thee? Let me count the ways."
Sonnet: "If thou must love me, let it be for naught."
Sonnet: "Unlike are we, unlike, O princely Heart!"
Sonnet: "When our two souls stand up erect and strong."
Sonnets from the Portuguese, *sels.*
Soul's Expression, The.
Soul's Travelling, the, *sel.*
Substitution.
Summing Up in Italy.
Tears.
To George Sand: A Desire.
To George Sand: A Recognition.
Tuscan Life.
Valediction, A: "God be with thee, my belovèd,—God be with thee!"
Virgin Mary to the Child Jesus, The, *abr.*
Vision of Poets, A, *sel.*
Weakest Thing, The.
Woman's Question, A.
Woman's Shortcomings, A.
Browning, Frederick G.
Amen.
Browning, Ophelia Guyon
Pray without Ceasing.
Sometime, Somewhere.
Browning, Robert
Abt Vogler.
Adam, Lilith, and Eve.
After.
All Service Ranks the Same with God.
Ancient Doctrine, The.
Andrea del Sarto.

Andromeda.
Any Wife to Any Husband.
Apparent Failure.
April in England.
Artemis Prologizes.
Asolando, *sels.*
Awakening of Man, The.
Bad Dreams, *sels.*
Belief and Unbelief.
Ben Karshook's Wisdom.
Bishop Blougram's Apology.
Bishop Orders His Tomb at Saint Praxed's Church, The.
Blot in the 'Scutcheon, A, *sel.*
Boot and Saddle ("Boot, saddle, to horse, and away!").
By the Fire-Side.
Caliban upon Setebos; or, Natural Theology in the Island.
Cardinal and the Dog, The.
Cavalier Tunes, *sels.*
"Childe Roland to the Dark Tower Came."
Christmas-Eve and Easter-Day, *sel.*
Cleon.
Confessional, The.
Confessions.
Count Gismond.
Cristina.
"De Gustibus."
Death in the Desert, A.
Development.
Dis Aliter Visum; or, Le Byron de Nos Jours.
Dramatis Personae, *sel.*
Earl Mertoun's Song.
Earth Breaks Up.
Englishman in Italy, The.
Epilogue: "At the midnight in the silence of the [*or* at] sleep-time."
Epilogue: "On the first of the Feast of Feasts."
Epilogue: " 'Poets pour us wine, The.' "
Epilogue to "Asolando."
Epistle, An: "Karshish, the picker-up of learning's crumbs."
Epistle Containing the Strange Medical Experience of Karshish, the Arab Physician, An.
Evelyn Hope.
Face, A.
Faith.
Fame.
Fifine at the Fair, *sel.*
Flight of the Duchess, The.
Flower's Name, The.
Fra Lippo Lippi.
Garden Fancies.
Give a Rouse.
Grammarian's Funeral, A.
Guardian Angel, The.
Heretic's Tragedy, The.
Hervé Riel.
Holy-Cross Day.
Home Thoughts from Abroad.
Home Thoughts, from the Sea.
House.
Householder, The.
How It Strikes a Contemporary.
How They Brought the Good News from Ghent to Aix.
In a Gondola.
In the Doorway.
Inapprehensiveness.
Incident of the French Camp.
Instans Tyrannus.
Italian in England, The.
Italy of the South.
James Lee's Wife, *sel.*
Johannes Agricola in Meditation.
Karshish, the Arab Physician ("Karshish, the picker-up of learning's crumbs").
Karshish and Lazarus.
Laboratory, The; Ancien Régime.
Last Ride Together, The.
Life in a Love.
Light Woman, A.
Likeness, A.
Lost Leader, The.
Lost Mistress, The.
Love.
Love among the Ruins.
Love in a Life.
Love's Pursuit.
Lyric Love.
Magical Nature.
Marching Along.
Master Hugues of Saxe-Gotha.
May and Death.
Meeting at Night.
Memorabilia.
Misconceptions.
Moment Eternal, The.
Moth's Kiss, First, The!
Muckle-Mouth Meg.
My Last Duchess.
My Star.
Natural Magic.
Ned Bratts.
Never the Time and the Place.
Now.
O Lyric Love.
O Never Star Was Lost.
Oh, the Wild Joy[s] of Living.
Old Pictures in Florence.
One Way of Love.
One Word More.
Orpheus and Eurydice.
Pan and Luna.
Paracelsus, *sels.*
Parleyings with Certain People of Importance in Their Day, *sel.*
Parting at Morning.
Patriot, The.
Pauline, *sels.*
Phases of the Moon.
Piano di Sorrento.
Pictor Ignotus.
Pied Piper of Hamelin, The.
Pippa Passes, *sels.*
Popularity.
Porphyria's Lover.
Prologue: " 'Poet's age is sad, The: for why?' "
Prospice.
Rabbi Ben Ezra.
Respectability.
Ring and the Book, The, *sels.*
Rudel to the Lady of Tripoli.
Saul.
Service.
Shelley.
Shop.
Sibrandus Schafnaburgensis.
Soliloquy of the Spanish Cloister.
Song: "All service ranks the same with God."
Song: "Give her but a least excuse to love me!"
Song: "Heap cassia, sandal-buds and stripes."
Song: "Moth's kiss, first, The!"
Song: "Nay but you, who do not love her."
Song: "Over the sea our galleys went."
Song: "You'll love me yet! and I can tarry."
Statue and the Bust, The.
Summum Bonum.
Thamuris Marching.
Through the Metidja to Abd-el-Kadr.
Thus the Mayne Glideth.
To Edward Fitzgerald.
Toccata of Galuppi's, A.
Transcendentalism; a Poem in Twelve Books.
Tray.
Two in the Campagna.
Up at a Villa—Down in the City.
Wanderers, The.
Waring.
Water and Air.
When a Man's Busy.
With Francis Furini.
Woman's Last Word, A.
Women and Roses.
Year's at the Spring, The.
You'll Love Me Yet!
Youth and Art.

Brownjohn, Alan
Camel.
Class Incident from Graves.
Elephant.
In This City.
Of Dancing.
Train, The.

"Brownjohn, John" (Charles Remington Talbot)
School-Master and the Truants, The.

Brownlie, W. S.
On First Looking into Chapman's Homer, *parody.*

Bruce, Charles
Attic, The.
Back Road Farm.
Biography.
Dreaming Trout, The.
Fisherman's Son.
Flowing Summer, The, *sels.*
Hayfield, The.
Words Are Never Enough.

Bruce, George
Fisherman, The.
Gateway to the Sea, A—St. Andrews.
Kinnaird Head.
My House.
Singers, The.
Sumburgh Heid.
Tom on the Beach.

Bruce, John
Pike, The.

Bruce, Lennart
Poem: "I meet Mother on the street."

Bruce, Michael
Elegy: In Spring, *sel.*
Ode: To the Cuckoo.
To the Cuckoo.

Bruce, Richard
Cavalier.
Shadow.

Bruce, Wallace
Our Nation Forever.
Parson Allen's Ride.
Two Argosies.

Bruchac, Joseph
City.
Coming Back.
Coots.
Elegy for Jack Bowman.
For a Winnebago Brave.
Frozen Hands.
Grandmother Came Down to Visit Us, The.
Hiking.
Migration.
Narrows, The.
Open.
Passive Resistance.
Poem for Jan.
Second Skins—a Peyote Song.
Stone Giant.
Sunlight.
There is a stream which rises.
Three Poems for the Indian Steelworkers.

Bruck, Edith
Birth.
Childhood.
Equality, Father!
Go, Then.
Let's Talk, Mother.
Sister Zahava.
Why Would I Have Survived?
You Hide ("You hide in the ostrich egg").

Brucker, H. P.
Praise Now Your God, *with music.*

Brudne, Eva
Farewell Ballad of Poppies, A.
Memento Vivendi.

Brummels, J. V.
Jeans.
Bruner, Margaret E.
Epitaph for a Cat.
Whom the Gods Love.
Brunini, John Gilland
Assumption, The.
Repeated Pilgrimage.
To Mary at Christmas.
Bruno, Giordano
Philosophic Flight, The.
Bruns, John Dickson
Foe at the Gates, The.
Brush, Thomas
Happy Poem, The.
Letter from the Street.
Bryan, Elizabeth Mabel
Father of the Man.
Bryan, Sharon
Big Sheep Knocks You About.
Corner Lot.
Hollandaise.
Lunch with Girl Scouts.
Bryan, Vincent
In My Merry Oldsmobile, *with music.*
Bryant, Frederick, Jr.
Cathexis.
Languages We Are, The.
Patience of a People.
Bryant, Helen
Lost Companions.
Bryant, John Frederick
On a Piece of Unwrought Pipeclay.
Bryant, John H.
At the Lincoln Tomb.
Bryant, William Cullen
Abraham Lincoln.
African Chief, The.
America.
Antiquity of Freedom, The.
As Shadows Cast by Cloud and Sun, *with music.*
Battle-Field, The.
Centennial Hymn.
Conqueror's Grave, The.
Dante.
Death of Lincoln, The.
Death of Slavery, The.
Death of the Flowers, The.
Dedication: "Thou, whose unmeasured temple stands."
Earth.
Evening Revery, An, *sel.*
Evening Wind, The.
Flood of Years, The.
Forest Hymn, A.
Forest Maid, The.
Gladness of Nature, The.
Green Mountain Boys, The.
Green River.
How Amiable Are Thy Tabernacles!
Hunter of the Prairies, The.
Hymn of the Sea, A.
In Memory of John Lothrop Motley.
Indian at the Burial-Place of His Fathers, An.
Inscription for the Entrance to a Wood.
June.
March.
May Sun Sheds an Amber Light, The.
Meditation on the Rhode Island Coal, A.
Mighty One, before Whose Face, *with music.*
Monument Mountain.
Mother's Hymn, The.
My Autumn Walk.
O thou great movement of the universe.
O Thou Whose Own Vast Temple Stands, *with music.*
Oh Fairest of the Rural Maids!
Oh Mother of a Mighty Race.
Other Sheep I Have, Which Are Not of This Fold.
Our Country's Call.
Past, The.
Planting of the Apple-Tree, The.
Poet, The.
Prairies, The.
Robert of Lincoln.
Seventy-six.
Snow-Shower, The.
Song of Marion's Men.
Summer Wind.
Thanatopsis.
Tides, The.
To a Waterfowl.
To Cole, the Painter, Departing for Europe.
To the Fringed Gentian.
To the Memory of Abraham Lincoln.
Truth, the Invincible.
Twenty-second of December, The.
Winter Piece, A.
Yellow Violet, The.
Brydges, Sir Samuel Egerton
Lines Written Immediately after Parting from a Lady.
Bryher, Winifred
Blue Sleep.
Thessalian.
Brynes, Edward
Oration on the Toes.
Bryusov, Valery Yakovlevich
Radiant Ranks of Seraphim.
Buber, Martin
Fiddler, The.
I Consider the Tree.
Buchan, John, 1st Baron Tweedsmuir
From the Pentlands, *sel.*
Leap in the Smoke.
Buchan, Tom
Everlasting Astronauts, The.
Week-End Naturalist, The.
Buchanan, Dugald
Day of Judgment, The.
Omnia Vanitas.
Buchanan, George
Epithalamium for Mary Stuart and the Dauphin of France, *abr.*
Of the Sad Lot of the Humanists in Paris.
Buchanan, Robert Williams
Ballad of Judas Iscariot, The.
Blind Linnet, The.
Churchyard, The.
Faëry Reaper, The.
Judas Iscariot.
Langley Lane.
Little Milliner, The.
Pilgrim and the Herdboy, The.
Spring Song in the City.
Starling, The.
Tom Dunstan; or, The Politician.
Buchwald, Emilie
Still Lives.
Buck, Byron
Song from a Two-Desk Office.
Buck, Chief John
Memorial Ode.
Buck, Richard Henry
Dear Old Girl, *with music.*
Kentucky Babe.
Buckaway, C. M.
Saskatchewan Dusk.
Buckham, James
Child of To-Day, A.
Heart's Proof, The.
Buckham, John Wright
Hills of God, Break Forth in Singing, *with music.*
O God, above the Drifting Years, *with music.*
Buckingham, George Villiers, 2d Duke of
Prayer: "Lord God of the oak and the elm."
To His Mistress.
Buckingham and Normanby, Duke of. *See* **Sheffield, John, Duke of Buckingham and Normanby**
Buckley, Christopher
Letters of Summer, The.
Light Rain.
Buckley, Vincent
Good Friday and the Present Crucifixion.
Late Tutorial.
No New Thing.
Parents.
Return of a Popular Statesman.
Various Wakings.
Buckmaster, Charles
Vanzetti.
Buckner, Samuel O.
Do It Right.
Budbill, David
Antoine and I Go Fishing.
New York in the Spring.
Budenz, Julia
Crockery.
Budzynski, Joe
Have Faith in God.
Buist, A. A.
Hills of God, The.
Bukowski, Charles
Another Academy.
Eddie and Eve.
For Jane.
Hell Hath No Fury.
Letters.
My Style.
Short Order.
Style.
Sun Wields Mercy, The.
3:16 and One Half.
Tragedy of the Leaves, The.
Trash Men, The.
Vegas.
Bulcke, Karl
There Is an Old City.
Bulfinch, Stephen Greenleaf
Hail to the Sabbath Day, *with music.*
Bulkeley, Peter, the Younger
Like to the Grass That's Green Today, *with music.*
Bull, Arthur J.
Eve.
Bullen, Arthur Henry
Whisperer, The.
Bullett, Gerald
Carol: "We saw him sleeping in his manger bed."
Church Mouse, The.
Footnote to Tennyson.
Bullins, Ed
When Slavery Seems Sweet.
Bullis, Jerald
Revelation.
Bullock, J.
Fear Not.
Bullock, Mark
Be Thankful.
Bullock, Mary
Blessed Nearness.
Bullokar, William
To His Child.
Bullwinkle, Marcia
There's a Feeling.
Buluguru
Working Song.
Bulwer-Lytton, Edward George Earle Lytton, 1st Baron Lytton
Absent yet Present.
Ernest Maltravers, *sel.*
Last Days of Pompeii, The, *sel.*
Night and Love.
Nydia's Song.
Bulwer-Lytton, Eward Robert, 1st Earl of Lytton. *See* **"Meredith, Owen"**
Bunin, Ivan Alekseyevich
Flax.
Bunn, Alfred
Bohemian Girl, The, *sels.*
I Dreamt I Dwelt in Marble Halls.
Light of Other Days, The.

When Other Lips and Other Hearts.
Bunner, Alice Learned
Immutabilis.
Separation.
Vingtaine.
Bunner, Freda Newton
Country Cemetery.
Bunner, Henry Cuyler
Appeal to Harold, The.
Behold the Deeds!
Candor.
Chaperon, The.
Da Capo.
Deaf.
Feminine.
Grandfather Watt's Private Fourth ("Grandfather Watts used to tell us boys").
Heart of the Tree, The.
Home, Sweet Home, with Variations, *parody*.
J. B.
Les Morts Vont Vite.
Old Flag, The.
On Reading a Poet's First Book.
One, Two, Three.
Pitcher of Mignonette, A.
Poetry and the Poet.
Shake, Mulleary, and Go-ethe.
She Was a Beauty.
Strong as Death.
To a June Breeze.
Way to Arcady, The.
Yes?
Bunting, Basil
Briggflatts,
Chomei at Toyama.
Coda.
Complaint of the Morpethshire Farmer, The.
Fearful Symmetry.
Fishermen.
Gin the Goodwife Stint.
On the Fly-Leaf of Pound's Cantos.
Orotava Road, The.
To Violet [with Prewar Poems].
What the Chairman Told Tom.
Word, The.
Bunyan, John
Enough!
My Little Bird.
Neither Hook nor Line.
Of the Boy and Butterfly.
Of the Child with the Bird on the Bush.
Of the Cuckoo.
Of the Going Down of the Sun.
Pilgrim, The.
Pilgrim's Progress, The, *sels.*
Pilgrim's Song, The.
Shepherd Boy Sings [in the Valley of Humiliation], The.
Shepherd's Song, The.
Song of Low Degree, A.
Song of the Shepherd in the Valley of Humiliation, The.
Time and Eternity.
Upon a Ring of Bells.
Upon the Horse and His Rider.
Upon the Lark and the Fowler.
Upon the Snail.
Upon the Swallow.
Upon the Weathercock.
Buonarroti. *See* **Michelangelo Buonarroti**
Burbank, Carol
Call to Order.
Surgery.
Burbidge, Thomas
She Bewitched Me.
Burden, Jean
Lost Word.
Poem before Departure.
Sabbath.
Words.
Burdette, Robert Jones
Limerick: "There was a young man of Cohoes."
Orphan Born.
Russian and Turk.
"Soldier, Rest!"
When My Ship Comes In.
Wilhelmj.
Burdick, Arthur J.
Washington's Birthday.
Burford, William
Christmas Tree, A.
Fire, The.
On the Apparition of Oneself.
Tomboy, The.
Burge, Maureen
Diet, The.
Disillusion.
Burgess, Anthony
Lines: Inspired by the Controversy on the Value or Otherwise of Old English Studies.
Burgess, Charles
Albatross.
Five Serpents.
Lady and Crocodile.
Two Garden Scenes.
Burgess, Gelett
Abstemia.
Abstrosophy.
Ah, Yes, I Wrote the "Purple Cow."
Ballad of the Hyde Street Grip.
Ego Sum.
Felicia Ropps.
I Wish That My Room Had a Floor.
Invisible Bridge, The.
Jilted Funeral, The.
Lament: "Ban of Time there is no disobeying, The."
Lazy Roof, The.
Limerick: "I wish that my room had a floor."
Limerick: "I'd rather have habits than clothes."
Low Trick, A.
My Feet.
Nonsense Quatrains: "Ah, yes! I wrote the 'Purple Cow.' "
Nonsense Quatrains: "I never saw a purple cow."
Nonsense Quatrains: "I sent my Collie to the wash."
Nonsense Quatrains: "Many people seem to think."
Nonsense Quatrains: "Proper way to leave a room, The."
Nonsense Verses: "I wish that my room had a floor."
Nonsense Verses: "I'd rather have fingers than toes."
Nonsense Verses: "My feet they haul me 'round the house."
Nonsense Verses: "Remarkable truly, is art!"
Nonsense Verses: "Window has four little panes, The."
On Digital Extremities.
On Drawing-Room Amenities.
Over the Hills with Nancy.
Parisian Nectar.
Protest of the Illiterate, The, *sel.*
Psycholophon.
Purple Cow, The.
Radical Creed, A.
Remarkable Art.
Roof, The.
Sequel to the Purple Cow.
Sunset, The.
Table Manners.
Trapping fairies in West Virginia.
Willy and the Lady.
Window Pane, The.
Woman's Reason, A.
Burgess, George
Harvest Dawn Is Near, The, *with music.*
While o'er the Deep Thy Servants Sail, *with music.*
Burghley, William Cecil, 1st Baron
To Mistress Anne Cecil, upon Making Her a New Year's Gift.
Burgin, Richard
Concertmaster.
Burgon, John William
Pedra.
Burgos, Julia de
Call Out My Number.
Nothing.
Pentachromatic.
Poem of the Intimate Agony.
Poem to My Death.
Poem with the Final Tune.
Río Grande de Loíza.
To Julia de Burgos.
Burgoyne, Arthur G.
"Everybody Works but Father" as W. S. Gilbert Would Have Written It.
Burgunder, Rose
Boy's Place, A.
Joyful.
Burke, Daniel
Ash Wednesday.
Teacher to Heloise, The (After Waddell).
Burke, Francis
Mediatrix of Grace, The.
Burke, Henry
Schooner *Blizzard*, The, *with music, at.*
Burke, Kenneth
Civil Defense.
Conspirators, The.
Enigma.
Frigate Jones, the Pussyfooter.
Heavy, Heavy—What Hangs Over?
If All the Thermo-nuclear Warheads.
Know Thyself.
Mercy Killing.
Nursery Rhyme.
Stout Affirmation.
Wrens, The.
Burke, Thomas
Piccadilly.
Burket, Gail Brook
Columbus Never Knew.
February 12, 1809.
From Countless Hearts, *with music.*
House in Springfield.
Noel.
So Touch Our Hearts with Loveliness, *with music.*
Thought for a New Year.
Burkholder, Clarence M.
Easter Beatitudes.
Burleigh, William Henry
Abide Not in the Realm of Dreams, *with music.*
Lead Us, O Father, in the Paths of Peace, *with music.*
Weaver, The.
Burnand, Sir Francis Cowley
Fishing for sticklebacks, with rod and line.
His Heart Was True to Poll.
Oh, My Geraldine.
Tubby or not tubby—there's the rub.
Burnat-Provins, Marguerite
Fruits you give me are more savory than others, The.
Sylvius, your hands near my mouth are heady flowers.
You told me: "I am not worthy of you."
Burnet, Dana
Marching Song.
Road to Vagabondia, The.
Song: "Love's on the highroad."
Wayfarers.
Burnett, Olive H.
Best for Us, The.
Burnham, Maud
Barnyard, The.
Five Little Fairies, The.
Burns, Carol
Long-Distance.

Burns, Diane
Big Fun.
DOA in Dulse.
For Carole.
Gadoshkibos.
Houston and Bowery, 1981.
Our People.
Sure You Can Ask Me a Personal Question.
Burns, Jim
End Bit, The.
Burns, Ralph
Only One.
Burns, Richard
Angels.
Mandelstam.
Burns, Robert
Address to a Haggis.
Address to the Deil.
Address to the Unco Guid, or the Rigidly Righteous.
Addressed to a Gentleman at Table, Who Kept Boasting of the Company He Kept.
Ae Fond Kiss.
Afton Water.
Anna.
As I Came O'er Cairney Mount.
Auld Lang Syne.
Ay Waukin O.
Banks o' Doon, The.
Before Bannockburn.
Bess and Her Spinning-Wheel.
Birks of Aberfeldy, The.
Blooming Nelly.
Bonnie Doon.
Bonnie Lesley.
Bonnie Wee Thing.
Bookworms, The.
Bruce's March to Bannockburn.
Ca' the Yowes.
Charlie, He's My Darling.
Child's Grace, A.
Chloe.
Comin' thro' [*or* through] the Rye (*diff. versions*).
Contented wi' Little.
Cotter's Saturday Night, The.
Could You Do That?
Daisy, The.
Day Returns, The.
Death and Doctor Hornbook.
Dedication to G**** H******* Esq., A, *sel.*
De'il's Awa' wi' the Exciseman, The.
Dream, A, *sel.*
Drinking Song.
Duncan Gray.
Elegy on Captain Matthew Henderson, *sel.*
Epigram on Elphinstone's Translation of Martial's Epigrams.
Epistle to a Young Friend.
Epistle to Davie, a Brother Poet.
Epistle to Dr. Blacklock, *abr.*
Epistle to James Smith.
Epistle to John Lapraik, an Old Scottish Bard.
Epistle to William Simpson, Ochiltree.
Epitaph for James Smith.
Epitaph on a Schoolmaster.
Epitaph on James Grieve, Laird of Boghead.
Epitaph on John Dove.
Exciseman, The.
Farewell, The: "It was a' for our rightfu' king."
Farewell to Nancy.
For A' That an' A' That ("The bonniest lass that ye meet neist"), *at.*
For A' That and A' That ("Is there, for honest poverty").
Gie the Lass her Fairin'.
Godly Girzie.
Grace after Dinner.
Green Grow the Rashes.
Guid-Mornin to Your Majesty!
Halloween, *abr.*
Hark! the Mavis.
Head pure, sinless quite of brain or soul, A.
Here cursing swearing Burton lies.
Here's a Health to Them That's Awa'.
Highland Mary.
Holy Fair, The.
Holy Willie's Prayer.
How Can I Keep My Maidenhead.
Humble Petition of Bruar Water to the Noble Duke of Athole, The, *sel.*
Hunting Song.
I Hae a Wife o' My Ain.
I Love My Jean.
I Murder Hate by Field or Flood.
I Once Was a Maid.
I'll Aye Ca' in by Yon Town.
I'm O'er [*or* Owre] Young to Marry Yet.
Inventory, in Answer to the Usual Mandate Sent by a Surveyor of the Taxes, Requiring a Return of the Number of Horses, Servants, Carriages, etc., Kept, The.
Is There for Honest Poverty.
It Was A' for Our Rightfu' King.
Jean.
John Anderson My Jo ("John Anderson my jo, John,/ I wonder what you mean", *at.*
John Anderson, My Jo ("John Anderson my jo, John,/ When we were first acquent").
Jolly Beggars, The.
Kirk's Alarm, The.
Lament for Culloden.
Lass and the Friar, The.
Lass That Made the Bed for Me, The.
Lea Rig, The.
Letter to a Young Friend.
Lines on the Author's Death.
Lo worms enjoy the seat of bliss.
Lord Galloway.
Love and Liberty; a Cantata.
Lovely Lass to the Friar Came, A, *at.*
Luath.
Macpherson's Farewell.
Man's Inhumanity to Man.
Mary Morison.
Mother's Lament for the Death of Her Son, A.
Muirland Meg.
My Ain Kind Dearie, O.
My Bonie Mary.
My Bonnie Highland Laddie.
My Heart's in the Highlands.
My Love, She's But a Lassie Yet.
My Luve's like a Red, Red Rose.
My Nannie's Awa'.
My Tocher's the Jewel.
My Wife's a Winsome Wee Thing.
Nine Inch Will Please a Lady.
No more of your titled acquaintances boast.
Nut-gathering Lass, The.
O, for Ane-and-twenty.
O, Saw Ye Bonny Lesley.
O Mally's Meek, Mally's Sweet.
O Merry Hae I Been Teethin' a Heckle.
O Were My Love Yon Lilac Fair.
O [*or* Oh], Wert Thou in the Cauld Blast.
O Whistle, and I'll Come to You, My Lad.
O'er the Water to Charlie.
Of A' the Airts [the Wind Can Blaw].
On a Noisy Polemic.
On a Wag in Mauchline.
On Andrew Turner.
On Elphinston's Translation of Martial.
On James Grieve, Laird of Boghead, Tarbolton.
On Lord Galloway.
On Mr. Pitt's Hair-Powder Tax.
On Scaring Some Waterfowl in Loch Turit, a Wild Scene among the Hills of Oughtertyre.
On Seeing the Royal Palace at Stirling in Ruins.
On the Birth of a Posthumous Child, Born in Peculiar Circumstances of Family Distress.
On William Graham, Esq., of Mossknowe.
Open the Door to Me, Oh!
Parson's Looks, The.
Patriach, The.
Plowman, The.
Poet's Grace, A.
Poet's Welcome to His Love-begotten Daughter, A.
Poor Mailie's Elegy.
Prayer in the Prospect of Death, A.
Prayer under the Pressure of Violent Anguish.
Rantin, Rovin Robin.
Rantin' Dog, the Daddie o't, The.
Red, Red Rose, A.
Rigs o' Barley, The.
Robin.
Saw Ye Bonie Lesley.
Scots Wha Hae [wi' Wallace Bled].
Second Epistle to Robert Graham.
She'll Do It.
Sic a Wife as Willie Had.
Silver Tassie, The.
So vile was poor Wat, such a miscreant slave.
Somebody.
Song: "Again rejoicing Nature sees."
Song: For A' That and A' That.
Song: Green Grow the Rashes.
Song: Mary Morison.
Song: "My luve is like a red, red rose."
Such a Parcel of Rogues in a Nation.
Supper Is Na Ready.
Suppertime.
Tam Glen.
Tam o' Shanter.
Tam Samson's Elegy.
Thou Lingering [*or* Ling'ring] Star.
Thrusting of It, The.
To a Field Mouse.
To a Louse [on Seeing One on a Lady's Bonnet at Church].
To a Mountain Daisy [on Turning One Down with the Plough, in April 1786].
To a Mouse [on Turning Her Up in Her Nest, with the Plough, November 1785].
To an Artist.
To John Taylor.
To Mary in Heaven.
To Terraughty, on His Birth-Day.
To William Simpson, Ochiltree.
Toad-Eater, The.
Tommie Makes My Tail Toddle.
Up in the Morning Early.
Vision, The.
Wee Willie Gray.
Wha Is That at My Bower-Door?
Whistle, and I'll Come to Ye.
Whistle o'er the Lave o't.
Willie Brew'd a Peck o' Maut.
Winter; a Dirge.
Winter Night, A, *sel.*
Ye Banks and Braes.
Ye Flowery Banks o' Bonnie Doon.
Ye maggots, feed on Willie's brains.
Burnshaw, Stanley
Bread.
End of the Flower World (A.D. 2300).
House in St. Petersburg.
Isaac.
Strange.
Talmudist.
Burr, Amelia Josephine
Battle-Song of Failure.
Certainty Enough.
Gorgio Lad.
Joyce Kilmer.
My Mother.
New Life.
Nocturne: "All the earth a hush of white."
Pershing at the Tomb of Lafayette.
Perugia.
Rain in the Night.
Romany Gold.
Song of Living, A.
Surrender.
To Her—Unspoken.
Where Love Is.

Where You Passed.
Burr, Gray
Butterfly, The.
Epistemological Rag, The.
Garden Puzzle.
Glance at the Album, A.
Indian Summer.
Play of Opposites, A.
Robin Hood.
Sailing, Sailing.
Skater's Waltz, A.
Burrell, Sophia
Epigram on Two Ladies.
Burrington, E. H.
Apostrophe to the Parret.
Burroughs, Alethea S.
Savannah.
"Burroughs, Ellen." *See* **Jewett, Sophie**
Burroughs, John
Song of the Toad, The.
Waiting.
Burroughs, Margaret Goss
Black Pride.
Everybody but Me.
Only in This Way.
To Soulfolk.
Burroway, Janet
Owed to Dickens, 1956.
Scientist, The.
Song: "With whomsoever I share the spring."
Burrowes, Elizabeth
O God, Send Men, *with music.*
Burrows, Edwin Gladding
Admiral's Daughter, The.
Dear Country Cousin.
Hidden Valley.
Bursk, Chris
Handful of Small Secret Stones, A.
Burstein, Abraham
Love of Hell, The.
Burt, Bates G.
O God of Youth, *with music.*
Burt, Dan
Poolhall, The.
Burt, Della
Little Girl's Dream World, A.
On the Death of Lisa Lyman.
Spirit Flowers.
Burt, J. F. A.
Southward Bound.
Burt, Lucile
Sleeping at the Beach.
Burt, Struthers
Fifty Years Spent.
I Know a Lovely Lady Who Is Dead.
Land, The, *sels.*
Resurgam.
Burton, Henry
Jesus Himself.
Pass It On.
There's a Light upon the Mountains.
Burton, John
Do I Really Pray?
Holy Bible, Book Divine.
Burton, Richard
Across the Field to Anne.
Black Sheep.
City of the Dead, The.
Extras.
First Song, The.
Forefather, The.
Glorious Game, The.
God's Garden.
Idols.
In Sleep.
Love Is Strong.
Of Those Who Walk Alone.
Old Santa Fe Trail, The.
On a Ferry Boat.
Polar Quest, The.
Rhyme for Remembrance of May.
Sealed Orders.
Song of the Sea.
Song of the Unsuccessful, The.
Unpraised Picture, An.
Burton, Sir Richard Francis
Do What Thy Manhood Bids Thee Do.
How then shall man so order life that when his tale of years is told.
In these drear wastes of sea-born land, these wilds where none may dwell but He.
Kasidah, The, *sels.*
Burton, Robert
Anatomy of Melancholy, The, *sel.*
Author's Abstract of Melancholy, The.
Burwell, Rex
Depression.
Busch, Ernst
Hans Beimler.
Bush, Barney
Another Old Song.
Blood.
It Is Finished.
Voice in the Blood.
Whose Voice.
Bush, Jocelyn
Little Red Sled, The.
Bushby, D. Maitland
Drifting.
Bushnell, Amy
Retreat.
Bushnell, Frances Louisa
In the Dark.
Unfulfillment.
World Music.
Bushnell, Samuel C.
Boston ("I come from the city of Boston"), *at.*
Buson (Taniguchi Buson)
Conversation.
Deep in the windless/ wood.
Haiku: "Halo of the moon, The."
Haiku: "Plum-viewing."
Piercing Chill I Feel, The.
Short Night, The.
Spring Scene.
Whale, The.
Busse, Carl
In the Night of the Full Moon.
Quiet Kingdom, The.
Buster, Marjorie Lorene
My Friend.
Butler, Alpheus
Death of a Fair Girl.
Butler, Arthur Gray
Edith and Harold.
Two Long Vacations: Grasmere.
Butler, Derek
Man's World Dissolving.
Parole Board.
Pigeons in Prison.
School Days/Rule Days.
Tryst.
Butler, Guy
Cape Coloured Batman.
Common Dawn.
Giotto's Campanile.
Myths.
Surveyor.
Butler, Lynne
Man in the Dream Is Death, The.
Butler, Palladas
Naked I reached the world at birth.
Butler, Samuel (1612–80)
Art of Love, The.
Ass will with his long ears fray, An.
Authority is a disease, and cure.
Convert's but a fly, that turns about, A.
Devil was more generous than Adam, The.
Far greater numbers have been lost by hopes.
Godly Casuistry.
Great philosopher did choke, A.
Greatest saints and sinners have been made, The.
Hudibras, *sels.*
Hypocrisy will serve as well.
Independent Squire.
Inventions.
Love, *sel.*
Married man comes nearest to the dead, A.
Méllonta taûta.
Metaphysical Sectarian, The ("He was in logick a great critic").
On William Prynne.
Portrait of Hudibras.
Portrait of Sidrophel.
Presbyterian Church Government.
Presbyterian Knight.
Presbyterian Knight and Independent Squire.
Religion.
Religion of Hudibras, The.
Satire upon the Licentious Age of Charles II, *sel.*
Sidrophel, the Rosicrucian Conjurer.
Sir Hudibras, His Passing Worth.
Sir Hudibras, His Passing Worth ("He was in logick a great critic").
Sir Hudibras's Religion.
Sir Sidrophel, the Conjuror.
What makes all subjects discontent.
Butler, Samuel (1835–1902)
O God! O Montreal!
Prayer, A: "Searcher of souls, you who in heaven abide."
Righteous Man, The.
Butler, William Allen
All's Well!
Incognita of Raphael.
Nothing to Wear.
Butler, William T.
Gathering on the Plains, The.
Butler-Andrews, C.
That Little Hatchet.
Butterfield, Frances Westgate
Time Out.
Butterworth, Hezekiah
Bird with a Broken Wing, The.
Church of the Revolution, The.
Death of Jefferson, The.
First Voyage of John Cabot, The.
Five Kernels of Corn.
Fountain of Youth, The.
Garfield's Ride at Chickamauga.
Legend of Waukulla, The.
Ortiz.
Roger Williams.
Thanksgiving for America, The.
Thanksgiving in Boston Harbor, The.
Verazzano.
Whitman's Ride for Oregon.
"Buttle, Myra" (Victor William Williams Saunders Purcell)
Sweeney in Articulo.
Sweeniad, The, *sel.*
Butts, Antony
Massenet/ Never wrote a Mass in A.
Butts, Mary Frances
Christmas Trees, The.
In Galilee.
That's July.
That's June.
Today.
Trot, Trot!
Buzea, Constanta
I'm Not Here / Never Was.
Byatt, Howard
Death.
Byers, Samuel H. M.
Sherman's March to the Sea.
Song of Sherman's March to the Sea.
With Corse at Allatoona.
Byfield, Bruce
Stood-up.
Byles, Mather
Great God, How Frail a Thing Is Man, *with music.*
Great God, Thy Works, *with music.*

To Thee the Tuneful Anthem Soars, *with music.*
When Wild Confusion Wrecks the Air, *with music.*

Bynner, Witter("Emanuel Morgan")
Adobe House, An.
Aged Fisherman.
Arrowy Dreams.
Autumn Walk, An.
Beforehand.
Chariots.
Dance for Rain, A.
Day, The.
Defeat.
Driftwood.
During a Chorale by César Franck.
Ecce Homo.
Fortune-Teller, A.
Golden Heart, The.
Grieve Not for Beauty ("Grieve not for the invisible, transported brow").
Haskell.
I Change.
I Need No Sky.
Jeremiah.
Lines to Do with Youth.
Mystic, The.
New God, The.
New Mexican Desert.
New World, The, *sel.*
Pittsburgh.
Poet, The.
Prayer: "Let us not look upon."
Prepare.
Republic to Republic.
Sandpiper, The.
Sentence.
Shasta.
Songs Ascending.
Spectra, *sel.*
To a Phoebe-Bird.
To a President.
Vinegaroon.

Byrd, William
Carol for Christmas Day, A.
Lulla La, Lulla Lulla Lullaby.
Song: "Let not the sluggish sleep."

Byrne, William A.
Bog Lands, The.

Byrom, John
Careless Content.
Contentment; or, The Happy Workman's Song.
Desponding Soul's Wish, The.
Epigram: "God bless the King—I mean the faith's defender!"
Epigram on Handel and Bononcini.
Epigram on the Feuds between Handel and Bononcini.
Extempore Verses upon a Trial of Skill between the Two Great Masters of the Noble Science of Defence, Messrs. Figg and Sutton.
Four Epigrams on the Naturalization Bill.
Full and True Account of a Horrid and Barbarous Robbery, A. *sel.*
Hymn for Christmas Day, A.
Hymn on the Omnipresence, An.
Jacobite Toast, A.
My Dog Tray.
My Spirit Longeth for Thee.
On Clergymen Preaching Politics.
On the Origin of Evil.
On Trinity Sunday, *sel.*
On Two Monopolists.
Pastoral, A: "My time, O ye muses, was happily spent."
Salutation of the Blessed Virgin, The.
To Henry Wright of Mobberley, Esq. on Buying the Picture of Father Malebranche.
Toast, A.
Tom the Porter.

Byron, George Gordon Noel Byron, 6th Baron
Address to the Ocean.
Age of Bronze, The, *sel.*
All for Love.
All Is Vanity, Saith the Preacher.
And I Have Loved Thee, Ocean!
And Thou Art Dead.
Apostrophe to the Ocean ("Roll on, thou deep and dark blue ocean").
Apostrophe to the Ocean ("There is a pleasure in the pathless woods").
Archangel, The.
At the Gate of Heaven.
At Thirty Years.
Ave Maria.
Battle of Waterloo, The.
Beppo; a Venetian Story.
Bride of Abydos, The.
Bright Be the Place of Thy Soul!
Bull Fight, The.
By the Deep Sea.
Castle of Chillon, The, *sel.*
Childe Harold ("Where rose the mountains, there to him were friends").
Childe Harold's Farewell to England.
Contemporary Poets.
Cornelian, The.
Corsair, The, *sel.*
Darkness.
Death of Haidée, The.
Dedication: "Bob Southey! You're a poet—poet-laureate."
Dedication: To Ianthe.
Dedication to the Poet Laureate.
Deep and Dark Blue Ocean.
Destruction of Sennacherib, The.
Don Juan, *sels.*
Don Juan's Education.
Donna Julia.
Dream, The.
Duke of Wellington, The.
Dying Gladiator, The.
Elegy: "O snatch'd away in beauty's bloom!"
Elegy on Thyrza.
English Bards, and Scotch Reviewers, *sels.*
Epigram: "With death doomed to grapple."
Epigram on John Bull.
Epilogue: "There's something in a stupid ass."
Epistle to Augusta.
Epistle to Mr. Murray.
Epitaph, An: Inscription on a Monument at Newstead Abbey.
Epitaph for Castlereagh, An.
Epitaph for William Pitt.
Epitaph to a Dog.
Evening.
Fame.
Fare Thee Well.
Farewell: "Farewell! if ever fondest prayer."
Farewell! If Ever Fondest Prayer.
Fatal Spell, The.
First Kiss of Love, The.
First Love.
For me, I know nought; nothing I deny.
Fragment: "I would to Heaven that I were so much clay."
Friendship Is Love without His Wings.
From the Turkish.
George the Fourth in Ireland.
George the Third.
Greece.
Growing Old.
Gulbeyaz.
Haidee ("It was the cooling hour, just when the rounded").
Haidee ("One of the two, according to your choice").
Hesperus the Bringer.
Highlands' swelling blue, The.
Hours of Idleness.
Immortal Mind, The.
Incantation, An.
Inscription on the Monument of a Newfoundland Dog.
Invocation: "Bob Southey! You're a poet—Poet-Laureate."
Island, The, *sel.*
Isles of Greece, The.
Isolation of Genius, The.
It Is the Hush of Night.
Italy.
John Keats.
Juan in England.
Lachin y Gair.
Lady Adeline Amundeville.
Lake Leman ("Clear, placid Leman! thy contrasted lake").
Lake Leman ("Lake Leman woos me with its crystal face").
Lambro's Return.
Lara, *sels.*
Lines Inscribed upon a Cup Formed from a Skull.
Lines on Hearing That Lady Byron Was Ill.
Love and Death.
Maid of Athens [Ere We Part].
Manfred: A Dramatic Poem.
Mazeppa.
My Days of Love are Over.
Napoleon.
Newstead Abbey.
Night.
Night before the Battle of Waterloo, The.
Night before Waterloo, The
Norman Abbey.
Nurse's Dole in the Medea, The.
Ocean, The ("Oh! that the desert were my dwelling-place").
Ocean, The ("There is a pleasure in the pathless woods").
Ocean ("Roll on, thou deep and dark blue ocean—roll!").
Ode to Napoleon Buonaparte, *sel.*
Ode to the Framers of the Frame Bill, An.
On John Adams, of Southwell.
On Jordan's Bank.
On My Thirty-third Birthday.
On the Bridge of Sighs.
On the Bust of Helen by Canova.
On the Castle of Chillon.
On This Day I Complete My Thirty-sixth Year.
On Wellington.
Poet and the World, The.
Poetical Commandments.
Poet's Credo.
Prisoner of Chillon, The.
Prometheus.
Remember Thee! Remember Thee!
Roll On, Thou Dark Blue Ocean.
Roll On, Thou Deep and Dark Blue Ocean.
Romantic to Burlesque.
Rome, by Metella's Tomb.
Sea, The.
Sennacherib.
She Walks in Beauty.
Shipwreck, The.
Siege of Corinth, The.
Sketch, A.
Sketch from Private Life, A.
Sky, Mountains, River!
So Late into the Night.
So We'll Go No More a-Roving.
Song: "So, we'll go no more a-roving."
Song of the Corsairs.
Sonnet on Chillon.
Southey and Wordsworth.
Stanzas: "Could love for ever."
Stanzas: "When a man hath no freedom to fight for at home."
Stanzas, for Music ("There be none of Beauty's daughters").
Stanzas for Music ("There's not a joy the world can give like that it takes away").
Stanzas to a Lady, with the Poems of Camoëns.
Stanzas to Augusta.
Stanzas to the Po.

Stanzas Written on the Road between Florence and Pisa.
Summer.
Sun of the Sleepless!
Sun Set, and Up Rose the Yellow Moon, The.
Sunset over the Ægean.
Swimming.
Tear, The.
That Idiot, Wordsworth.
There Is Pleasure in the Pathless Woods.
This day of all our days has done.
To Eddleston.
To England.
To Ianthe.
To Mr. Murray.
To My Son.
To our theme—The man who has stood on the Acropolis.
To the Ocean.
To Thomas Moore.
To Woman.
Two Foscari, The, *sel.*
Venice.
Vision of Belshazzar, The.
Vision of Judgment, The.
Voltaire and Gibbon.
Waltz, The, *sel.*
Wandering Outlaw, The.
Washington.
Waterloo.
Wellington.
When a Man Hath No Freedom to Fight for at Home.
When We Two Parted.
Who Kill'd John Keats?
Wild, the Free, The.
William Lisle Bowles.
World Is a Bundle of Hay, The.
Written after Swimming from Sestos to Abydos.
Youth and Age.

Byron, Henry James
Adage, An: "Gardener's rule applies to youth and age, The."
Rural Simplicity.

Byron, May Clarissa Gillington
Adventurers, The.
Fairy Thrall, The.
Pageant of Seamen, The.
Storm-Child, The.

C

"C.,, E."
Emaricdulfe.

"C.,, J."
Alcilia, *sel.*
Frailty of Beauty, The. "

"C. , R."
Persuasive Go-Gebtor.

"C. A. L. T". *See* T. C. A. L.
"C. A. W." *See* "W. C. A."
"C.B.B." *See* **"B.C.B."**
"C. G. H." *See* **"H., C. G.**
"C. N. S." *See* **"S., C. N."**
"C. T." *See* **"T., C."**
"C. W. T." *See* **"T., C. W."**

Cabalquinto, Luis
Blue Tropic.
Eating Lechon, with My Brothers and Sisters.
Flower Vendor, The.
Hometown.

Cabell, James Branch
Alone in April.
Easter Eve.
Garden-Song.
Retractions, *sels.*
Story of the Flowery Kingdom.

Cable, Franklin
Tree-building.

Cable, George Washington
New Arrival, The.
Written in the Visitors' Book at the Birthplace of Robert Burns.

Cabral, Olga
Another Late Edition, *sel.*
At the Jewish Museum.
Factory, The.
Hokusai's Wave.
Lillian's Chair ("Lillian had just arisen from her chair").
Mother and Sister of the Artist.
On the Death of Neruda.
Picasso's Women.
This Morning the Sun.

Cader, Teresa D.
On the Edge of a Safe Sleep.

Cadnum, Michael
Skull of a Neandertal.

Cadsby, Heather
Poem for a Son.
Reunion.

Caedmon
Approach of Pharaoh, The.
Caedmon's Hymn.
Far and Wide She Went.
Genesis, *sel.*
Hymn: "Now we must praise heaven-kingdom's Guardian."
Noah's Flood.
Son of Lamech let a black raven, The.
Temptation and Fall of Man, The.

Caesar, Irving
Tea for Two, *with music.*

Cain, John
At the Nursing Home.

Cain, Seymour
Due Date.
My Son, My Son.

Cairncross, Thomas S.
Grey Galloway.

Calder, Dave
At Kirk Yetholm.

Calderón de la Barca, Pedro
Dream Called Life, The.
Life Is a Dream.
Thou Art of All Created Things.

Caldwell, Arthur I.
Stampede, The.

Caldwell, John
Mule-Skinners, The, *at.*

Caldwell, William Warner
Robin's Come.

Calhoun, George
McKinley Brook, *with music.*
Perigoo's Horse, *at.*
Rufus's Mare, *with music.*

Calhoun, John
Messenger Song, The, *at.*
Peter Emberley, *vers.* I-III, *with music.*

Calisch,, Edward N. *and* **Penina Moise.** *See* **Moise, Penina** *and* **Edward N. Calisch**

Call, Frank Oliver
Blue Homespun.
Old Habitant, An.

Call, Wathen Mark Wilks
Hymn: "When by the marbled lake I lie and listen."
People's Petition, The.
Renunciation.
Summer Days.

Callanan, Jeremiah [*or* James]
Lines to the Blessed Sacrament.
Serenade: "Blue waves are sleeping, The."
Song: "Awake thee, my Bessy, the morning is fair."

Callimachus
Crethis.
Elegy on Herakleitos.
His Son.
One Who Runs Away, The.
Saon of Acanthus.
Sopolis.
To Archinus.

Callinus
Call to Action, A.

Calverley, Charles Stuart
Alphabet, The.
Arcades Ambo.
Ballad: "Auld wife sat at her ivied door, The."
Beer.
Cat, The.
Changed.
Cock and the Bull, The.
Companions.
Dover to Munich, *sels.*
Disaster.
First Love.
"Forever."
Gemini and Virgo.
"Hic Vir, Hic Est."
In the Gloaming ("In the gloaming to be roaming"), *parody*
Lines on Hearing the Organ.
Lines Suggested by the Fourteenth of February.
Love.
Lovers, and a Reflection.
Morning.
Motherhood.
Ode to Tobacco.
On the Beach.
Palace, The.
Peace.
Precious Stones.
Proverbial Philosophy: Of Reading.
Sad Memories.
Schoolmaster Abroad with His Son, The.
Striking.
Wanderers.

Calvert, George Henry
Bunker Hill.

Calvin, John
Salutation to Jesus Christ.

Cambridge, Ada
Faith.
On Australian Hills, *sel.*

Camden, William
On a Puritanicall Lock-Smith.

Camerino, Aldo
Calm.
Fear.
For a Voice That Is Singing.
Mother.
Night.
Recluse.

Cameron, Don
Drilling Missed Holes.
Song of the Leadville Mine Boss.

Cameron, George Frederick
Ah Me! the Mighty Love.
Future, The.
In After Days.
My Political Faith.
Relics.
Standing on Tiptoe.

Cameron, Norman
Bear in Mind, O Ye Recording Angels.
Compassionate Fool, The.
Dirty Little Accuser, The.
Disused Temple, The.
Firm of Happiness, Limited, The.
For the Fly-Leaf of a School-Book.
Forgive Me, Sire.
From a Woman to a Greedy Lover.
Green, Green Is El Aghir.
Hook for Leviathan, A.
In the Queen's Room.
Shepherdess.
Thespians at Thermopylae, The.
Three Love Poems.
Unfinished Race, The.
Verdict, The.

Camille, Roussan
Nocturne: "Wildness of haggard flights."

Camões [*or* Camoens], Luì de
Babylon and Sion (Goa and Lisbon).
Dear gentle soul, who went so soon away.
Lusiads, The, *sels.*
On Revisiting Cintra after the Death of Catarina.
On the Death of Catarina de Attayda.
Sonnet: "Leave me, all sweet refrains my lip hath made."
Sonnet: "Time and the mortal will stand never fast."
Waterspout.
Camp, James
Bruckner.
Figure in the Carpet, The.
Campana, Dino
Night Character.
Campanella, Tomasso
People, The.
Campbell, Alastair
Images.
Campbell, Alice B.
Sally and Manda.
Campbell, Alistair
Dark Lord of Savaiki, The, *abr.*
Campbell, Archibald Y.
Animula Vagula.
Dromedary, The.
Murie Sing.
Campbell, Calder
Burman Lover, The.
Ossian's Serenade.
Campbell, David
Ariel.
Australian Dream, The.
End of Exploring, The.
Fox.
Harry Pearce.
Men in Green.
Mr. Hughes.
Mothers and Daughters.
Night Sowing.
On Frosty Days.
Pallid Cuckoo.
Speak with the Sun.
Ulinda.
Campbell, Donald
Hauf-Roads up Schiehallion.
Campbell, James Edwin
Compensation.
Cunjah Man, De.
Negro Serenade.
Ol' Doc' Hyar.
Uncle Eph's Banjo Song.
When Ol' Sis' Judy Pray.
Campbell, Jane M.
We Plough the Fields.
Campbell, Joseph (Seosamh MacCathmhaoil)
Ad Limina.
Antiquary, The.
As I Came Over the Grey, Grey Hills.
Besom-Man, The.
Blanaid's Song ("Blanaid loves roses").
Blind Man at the Fair, The.
Butterfly in the Fields.
Chesspieces.
Dancer, The.
Darkness.
Fighting-Man, A.
Go, Ploughman, Plough.
Gombeen, The.
Harvest Song.
Herb-Leech, The.
Hills of Cualann, The.
I Am the Gilly of Christ.
I Am the Mountainy Singer.
I Will Go with My Father a-Ploughing.
Ideal and Reality.
Ninepenny Fidil, The.
O Glorious Childbearer.
Old Age Pensioner, The.
Old Woman, The.
On Waking.
Poet Loosed a Wingèd Song, The.
Three Colts Exercising in a Six-Acre.
Tinkers, The.
Unfrocked Priest, The.
Campbell, Marion
Levavi Oculos.
Campbell, Marjorie Freeman
Only the Heart.
Vigil.
Campbell, Nancy
Apple-Tree, The.
Campbell, Robert Bhain
Final Poem.
Task, The.
Campbell, Roy
Autumn.
Ballad of Don Juan Tenorio and the Statue of the Comendador.
Buffel's Kop.
Choosing a Mast.
Death of Polybius Jubb, The.
Driving Cattle to Casas Buenas.
Fishing Boats in Martigues.
Flaming Terrapin, The, *sel.*
Georgiad, The, *sels.*
Georgian Spring.
Golden Shower, The, *sel.*
Good Resolution, A.
Heartbreak Camp.
Horses on the Camargue.
Luis de Camões.
Mass at Dawn.
Mithraic Emblems, *sel.*
On Professor Drennan's Verse.
On Some South African Novelists.
On the Same [Some South African Novelists].
Palm, The.
Rounding the Cape.
Secret Muse, The.
Serf, The.
Sisters, The.
Talking Bronco, *sel.*
Theology of Bongwi, the Baboon, The.
To the Sun.
Toledo.
Tristan da Cunha.
Veld Eclogue, A: The Pioneers.
Volunteer's Reply to the Poet, The.
Wayzgoose, The, *sel.*
Zebras, The.
Zulu Girl, The.
Campbell, Thomas
Battle of the Baltic, The.
Beatific Sea, The.
Beech Tree's Petition, The.
Caroline, II: To The Evening Star.
Dead Eagle, The.
Exile of Erin.
Florine.
Freedom and Love.
Glenara.
Hallowed Ground.
Harper, The.
Hohenlinden.
Irish Harper and His Dog, The.
Jilted Nymph, The.
Last Man, The.
Lines on Leaving a Scene in Bavaria.
Lochiel's Warning ("Lochiel, Lochiel! beware of the day").
Lord Ullin's Daughter.
Maid of Neidpath, The.
Margaret and Dora.
Mighty Sea! Cameleon-like Thou Changest.
Napoleon and the British Sailor.
Ode to Winter.
Parrot, The.
Pilgrim of a Day, The.
Pleasures of Hope, The, *sel.*
River of Life, The.
Soldier's Dream, The.
Song: "Earl March looked on his dying child."
Song: "How delicious is the winning."
Song to the Evening Star.
Thought Suggested by the New Year, A.
To the Evening Star ("Gem of the crimson-colour'd even").
To the Evening Star ("Star that bringest home the bee").
To the Rainbow.
Ye Mariners of England.
Campbell, Walter Stanley. *See* **"Vestal, Stanley."**
Campbell, Wilfred (William Wilfred Campbell)
Bereavement of the Fields.
Hills and the Sea, The.
How One Winter Came in the Lake Region.
Indian Summer.
Morning on the Shore.
Vapour and Blue.
Winter Lakes, The.
With Cortez in Mexico.
Campion, Thomas
Advice to a Girl.
Amaryllis [*or* Amarillis].
Among the Shades.
And Would You See My Mistress' Face? *at.*
Are you what your faire lookes expresse?
Author of light, revive my dying spright.
Awake, Awake!
Bar Not the Door.
Be thou then my beauty named.
Be Wise and Fly Not.
Beauty Is but a Painted Hell.
Beauty Is Not Bound.
Beauty, Since You So Much Desire.
Blame not my cheeks, though pale with love they be.
Breake now my heart and dye! Oh no, she may relent.
Cherry-ripe.
Come, Cheerful Day!
Come, Follow Me.
Come, You Pretty False-eyed Wanton.
Content.
Corinna.
Cypress Curtain of the Night, The.
Dance, The, *at.*
Dear If I with Guile.
Devotion ("Follow thy fair sun").
Devotion ("Follow your saint").
Dismissal.
Dove alone expresses, The.
Elegye, An: "Constant to none, but ever false to me."
Fain Would I Wed a Fair Young Man.
First Love.
Follow.
Follow, follow.
Follow Thy Fair Sun [Unhappy Shadow].
Follow Your Saint [Follow with Accents Sweet].
Give Beauty All Her Right.
Harden Now Thy Tired Heart.
Hark, All You Ladies.
Her Sacred Bower.
Hours of Sleepy Night, The.
I Care Not for These Ladies.
I must complain, yet doe enjoy my love.
In Praise of Neptune.
In the Dark What the Day Doth Forbid.
Integer Vitae.
It Fell on a Summer's Day.
Jack and Joan.
Kind Are Her Answers.
Kisses, *at.*
Lamentation, A.
Laura.
Life Upright, The.
Lord Hay's Mask, *sel.*
Lord's Mask[e], The, *sel.*
Love Me or Not.
Lover's Plea, A.
Love's Pilgrims.
Maid's Complaint, A.

Man of Life Upright, The.
Mistress, Since You So Much Desire.
Mountebank's Mask, The, *sel.*
My Life's Delight.
My Sweetest Lesbia [Let Us Live and Love].
Neptune.
Never Love [Unless You Can].
Never Weather-beaten Sail[e].
Now Winter Nights Enlarge.
O Come Quickly!
Of Corinna's Singing.
Oft have I sigh'd for him that heares me not.
Out of My Soul's Depth.
Peaceful Western Mind, The.
Pilgrimage towards Loves Holy Land, A.
Place of Cupid's Fire, The.
Proserpina.
Raving warre, begot.
Rose-cheeked [*or* cheekt] Laura, Come.
Roses.
Secret Love or Two I Must Confess[e], A.
Seek the Lord.
Shall I come, if I swim? wide are the waves, you see.
Shall I Come, Sweet Love, to Thee?
Shall I then hope when faith is fled?
Sleep, Angry Beauty.
So Quick, So Hot.
So Tir'd Are All My Thoughts.
Song: To the Masquers Representing Stars.
Stars Dance, The.
Tell, O Tell.
There Is a Garden in Her Face.
There Is None, O None but You.
Think'st Thou to Seduce Me Then.
Thou Art Not Fair.
Thou Joy'st, Fond Boy.
Though You Are Young.
Thrice Toss [*or* Tosse] These Oaken Ashes in the Air [*or* Ayre].
To Lesbia.
To Music [*or* Musicke] Bent Is My Retired Mind.
To Shades of Underground.
Turn All Thy Thoughts.
Turn Back, You Wanton Flyer.
Vain Men, Whose Follies.
View me [*or* mee], Lord, a work of Thine.
Were My Heart [*or* Hart] as Some Men's Are.
What Faire Pompe.
What Harvest Half So Sweet Is.
What If a Day [or a Month or a Year].
What Then Is Love but Mourning.
When Thou Must Home [to Shades of Underground].
When to Her Lute Corinna [*or* Corrina] Sings.
When We Court and Kiss.
Where are all thy beauties now, all hearts enchaining?
Where She Her Sacred Bower Adorns.
Whether Men Do Laugh or Weep, *at.*
Winter Nights.
Writer to His Book, The.
Young and Simple though I Am.
Your Fair Looks Inflame My Desire.
Cane, Melville
After Reading the Reviews of "Finnegans Wake."
Alpine View.
Dawn Has Yet to Ripple In.
Each to Each.
Harvest to Seduce, A.
Hymn to Night.
Park Pigeons.
Presence of Snow.
Rural Dumpheap.
Snow toward Evening.
Sun and Cloud.
Tree in December.
Canfield, Harry Clifford
On the Loss of U.S. Submarine S4, *sel.*
Cannady, Criss E.
In the Sitting Room of the Opera.
Sunlight in a Cafeteria.
Cannan, May Wedderburn
Lamplight.
Love, 1916.
Rouen.
Since They Have Died.
Canning, Effie I.
Rock-a-Bye Baby, *with music.*
Canning, George
Ballynahinch.
Candid Friend, The.
Cat and the Bird, The.
Dutch, The.
Elderly Gentleman, The.
Epigram: Dutch, The.
Ipecacuanha.
Political Despatch, A.
Progress of Man, The, *sel.*
Canning, George, George Ellis, *and* John Hookham Frere
Rogero's Song.
Rovers, The, *sel.*
Song: "Whene'er with haggard eyes I view."
Song by Rogero [the Captive].
Song of One Eleven Years in Prison.
Canning, George *and* John Hookham Frere
Friend of Humanity and the Knife-Grinder, The.
Inscription: "For one long term, or e'er her trial came."
Inscription for the Door of the Cell in Newgate Where Mrs. Brownrigg, the 'Prentice-cide, Was Confined Previous to Her Execution.
Knife-Grinder, The.
New Morality, *sel.*
Sapphics: The Friend of Humanity and the Knife-Grinder.
Soldiers' Friend, The.
Soldier's Wife, The.
Cannon, David Wadsworth, Jr
Freedom in Mah Soul.
Western Town.
Cannon, Edward
Unsuspected Fact, An.
Cannon, Hughie
Bill Bailey Won't You Pleases Come Home.
Cannon, Margery
Venite Adoremus.
Cannon, Melissa
Crippled Child at the Window.
Canterbury, George
New Mexico and Arizona.
Canton, William
Bethlehem.
Carol: "When the herds were watching."
Crow, The.
Laus Infantium.
New Poet, A.
Cantus, Eleanor Hollister
Fame.
Canzoneri, Robert
Two.
Capetanakis, Demetrios
Abel.
Isles of Greece, The.
Capp, Joseph
Generalization.
Man Is a Fool.
Caragher, Mary E.
Tree Tag.
Carb, Alison B.
Israeli Soldier's Nightmare, An.
Carbell, E. T.
Frogs' Singing-School, The.
"Carbery, Ethna" (Anna Johnston MacManus)
Hills o' My Heart.
King of Ireland's Cairn, The, *abr.*
Love-Talker, The.
Mea Culpa.
On an Island, *abr.*
Shadow House of Lugh, The.
Cardenal, Ernesto
Epitaph for the Tomb of Adolfo Baez Bone.
Cárdenas, Reyes
Lowriders #2 ("Lowriders/ cruising the barrio").
Cardiff, Gladys
Carious Exposure.
Combing.
Dragon Skate.
Grey Woman.
Leaves like Fish.
Long Person.
Outer Space, Inner Space.
Owl and Rooster.
Simples.
Swimmer.
Tlanusi' Yi, the Leech Place.
To Frighten a Storm.
Tsa'lagi Council Tree.
Where Fire Burns.
Cardona-Hine, Alvaro
Geo-Politics.
Carducci, Giosuè
Petrarch.
Primo Vere.
Snowfall.
Careme, Maurice
You Can Get Despondent.
Carenza *and* Iselda
Tenson.
Carew, Richard
River Lynher, The.
Survey of Cornwall, *sel.*
Carew, Thomas
Another [Epitaph on the Lady Mary Villiers] ("Purest soul that e'er was sent, The").
Ask Me No More Where Jove Bestows.
Beautifull Mistress, A.
Boldness[e] in Love.
Celia Bleeding, to the Surgeon.
Celia Singing.
Comparison, The.
Complement, The.
Cruell Mistris, A.
Deposition from Love, A.
Disdain [*or* Disdaine] Returned.
Divine Mistris, A.
Elegy upon the Death of the Dean of Paul's, Dr. John Donne, An.
Epitaph, An: "This little vault, this narrow room."
Epitaph on Maria Wentworth.
Epitaph on the Lady Mary Villiers ("The Lady Mary Villiers lies").
Epitaph on the Lady Mary Villiers, An ("This little vault, this narrow room").
Eternity of Love Protested.
Excuse of Absence, An.
Fear Not, Dear Love.
Fly [*or* Flye] That Flew into My Mistress's [*or* Mistris Her] Eye, A.
For a Picture Where a Queen Laments over the Tomb of a Slain Knight.
Give Me More Love.
Good Counsel to a Young Maid.
Hymeneal Song on the Nuptials of the Lady Anne Wentworth and the Lord Lovelace, An.
Hymeneall Dialogue, An.
I Will Enjoy Thee Now.
In Answer of an Elegiacall Letter upon the Death of the King of Sweden.
Ingrateful[l] Beauty Threatened.
Inscription on the Tombe of the Lady Mary Wentworth, The.
Lady's Prayer to Cupid, A.
Looking-Glass, A.
Lover, upon an Accident Necessitating His Departure, Consults with Reason, A.
Love's Courtship.
Love's Force.
Maria Wentworth [Thomæ Comitis Cleveland,

Filia Præmortuæ Prima Virgineam Animam Exhalauit].
Mediocrity [*or* Mediocritie] in Love Rejected.
More Love or More Disdain.
Murdering Beauty.
New Year's Sacrifice, A: To Lucinda.
Now That the Winter's Gone.
Obsequies to the Lady Anne Hay.
On a Damaske Rose Sticking upon a Ladies Breast.
On His Mistress Looking in a Glass.
On Sight of a Gentlewoman's Face in the Water.
On the Death of Donne.
On the Marriage of T. K. and C. C., the Morning Stormy.
Other, An ("The purest soule that e're was sent").
Other, An ("This little vault, this narrow roome").
Pastorall Dialogue, A ("As Celia rested in the shade").
Pastorall [*or* Pastoral] Dialogue, A ("This mossie [*or* mossy] bank they prest").
Persuasions [*or* Perswasions] to Enjoy.
Persuasions to Love, *sel.*
Prayer to the Wind, A.
Protestation, The.
Rapture, A.
Red, and White Roses.
Second Rapture, The.
Secrecy Protested [*or* Secresie Protested].
Song, A: "Ask me no more where Jove bestows."
Song: "Give me more love or more disdain."
Song: Good Counsel to a Young Maid.
Song, A: "In her fair cheeks two pits do lie."
Song: Mediocrity in Love Rejected.
Song: Murdring Beautie.
Song: To Her Againe, She Burning in a Feaver.
Song: To My Mistris, I Burning in Love.
Song: To One That Desired to Know My Mistris.
Song: Willing Prisoner to His Mistress, The.
Spring, The.
Tinder, The.
To A. L.: Perswasions [*or* Persuasions] to Love.
To a Lady That Desired I Would Love Her.
To Ben Jonson [*or* Johnson].
To Celia, upon Love's Ubiquity.
To Her in Absence; a Ship.
To His Inconstant Mistress.
To My Cousin (C. R.) Marrying My Lady (A.).
To My Friend G. N. from Wrest.
To My Inconstant Mistress [*or* Mistris].
To My Mistress [*or* Mistris] Sitting by a River's Side; an Eddy.
To My Mistress[e] in Absence.
To My Mistris, I Burning in Love.
To My Worthy Friend Master Geo. [*or* George] Sands [on His Translation of the Psalmes].
To Saxham.
To T. H., a Lady Resembling My Mistress[e].
To the King, at His Entrance into Saxham: By Master John Crofts.
To the New Year.
To the Reader of Master William Davenant's Play "The Wits."
True Beauty, The.
Unfading Beauty, The.
Upon a Mole in Celia's Bosom[e].
Upon a Ribband.
Upon Master Walter Montagu's Return from Travel.
Upon My Lord Chief Justice's Election of My Lady Anne Wentworth for His Mistress.
Upon Some Alterations in My Mistress, after My Departure into France.

Carey, Lady Elizabeth
Mariam, *sels.*

Carey, Henry
Ballad of Sally in Our Alley, The.
Contrivances, The, *sel.*
Drinking-Song, A.
Happy Myrtillo.
Harry Carey's General Reply, to the Libelling Gentry, Who Are Angry at His Welfare.
Huntsman's Rouse, The.
Lilliputian Ode on Their Majesties' Accession, A.
Maiden's Ideal of a Husband, A.
Namby-Pamby; or, A Panegyric on the New Versification.
Roger and Dolly.
Sally in Our Alley.
Sally Sweetbread.

Carey [*or* Cary], Patrick
And now a fig for the lower house.
Hymn: Crucifixus pro Nobis.
Whilst I beheld the neck o' th' dove.

Carleton, Sara King
Late October.

Carleton, Will M.
Across the Delaware.
Betsey and I Are Out.
Country Doctor, The.
Cuba to Columbia.
Death-doomed.
Doctor's Story, The.
Johnny Rich, *sel.*
Little Black-eyed Rebel, The.
New Church Organ, The.
Out of the Old House, Nancy.
Over the Hill to the Poor-House.
Prize of the Margaretta, The.
Victory-Wreck, The.

Carlile, Henry
Dodo.
Flying.
Grandmother.
Grief of Our Genitals, The.
Listening to Beethoven on the Oregon Coast.
Spider Reeves.

Carlin, Francis (James Francis Carlin MacDonnell)
Ballad of Douglas Bridge.
Before I Stumbled.
Beyond Rathkelly.
Gray Plume, The.
Hope's Song.
Mac Diarmod's Daughter.
Market Town, The.
Perfection.
Plea for Hope.
Virgins.
Virgin's Slumber Song, The.

Carlson, Randolph
Rapture.

Carlyle, Jane Welsh (Mrs. Thomas Carlyle)
To a Swallow Building under Our Eaves.

Carlyle, Thomas
Adieu.
Cui Bono?
Sower's Song, The.
To-Day.

Carman, Bliss
April Morning, An.
Arnold, Master of the *Scud.*
Autumn Garden, An.
Christmas Eve Choral, A.
Christmas Song.
Daffodil's Return.
Daisies, The.
Daphne.
Deserted Pasture, The.
Envoy: "Have little care that life is brief."
Grave-Tree, The.
Gravedigger, The.
Hack and Hew.
Hem and Haw.
Heretic, The.
I Loved Thee, Atthis, in the Long Ago.
In a Copy of Browning.
In October.
In the House of Idiedaily.
Joys of the Road, The.
Lord of My Heart's Elation.
Lord of the Far Horizons.
Low Tide on Grand Pré.
Man of Peace, The, *abr.*
Marian Drury.
Mendicants, The.
Mr. Moon.
Moment Musicale.
More Ancient Mariner, A.
Morning in the Hills.
Northern Vigil, A.
Old Grey Wall, The.
Over the Wintry Threshold.
Overlord.
Roadside Flowers.
Sappho, *sel.*
Sea Child, A.
Seamark, A.
Ships of Saint John, The.
Ships of Yule, The.
Son of the Sea, A.
Song: "Love, by that loosened hair."
Songs of the Sea-Children, *sels.*
Spring Song.
Threnody for a Poet.
Trees.
Triumphalis.
Vagabond Song, A.
Veni Creator.
Vestigia.
Where Is Heaven?
Why.
Winter Streams.

Carmer, Carl
Antique Shop.

Carmi, T.
Author's Apology, The.
Condition, The.

Carmichael, Amy
Comforted.
Deliver Me.
Do We Not Hear Thy Footfall?
Evening Star, The.
Flame of God.
For All in Pain.
Have We Not Seen Thy Shining Garment's Hem.
Hope.
Last Defile, The.
Lord, Thou Hast Suffered.
Yet Listen Now.

Carmichael, Waverly Turner
Keep Me, Jesus, Keep Me.
Winter Is Coming.

Carnegie, James, Earl of Southesk
Flitch of Dunmow, The.

Carnevali, Emanuel
Queer Things.
Walt Whitman.

Carney, Julia A. Fletcher
Little Things.

Carolan [*or* O'Carolan], Turlough
Cup of O'Hara, The.
Mabel Kelly.
Peggy Browne.
When Kian O'Hara's Cup Was Passed to Turlough O'Carolan.
Why, Liquor of Life?

Caroutch, Yvonne
Child of silence and shadow.
I come to you with the vertigoes of the source.
Limb of forests rises up, The.
Night opens like an almond.
When we are [like] two drunk[en] suns.

Carpenter, Amelia Walstien Jolls
Old Flemish Lace.
Recollection.
Ride to Cherokee, The.

Carpenter, Edward
Among the Ferns.
Have Faith.

Love's Vision.
Mightier than Mammon, A, *sel.*
Over the Great City.
Songs of the Birds, The.
Stupid Old Body, The.
Through the Long Night.
Towards Democracy, *sel.*
Wandering Lunatic Mind, The.
Carpenter, Henry Bernard
Reed, The.
Carpenter, Joseph Edward
Do They Think of Me at Home.
Carpenter, Margaret Haley
September Afternoon.
Carpenter, Maurice
To S. T. C. on His 179th Birthday, October 12, 1951.
Carpenter, Rhys
Beggars.
Master Singers, The.
Who Bids Us Sing?
Carpenter, William
Autumn.
Fire.
Keeper, The.
Carpenter, William Boyd
Before Thy Throne.
Carphyllides
Happy Man, A.
Carr, Alan J.
Old Man.
Carr, Frank
Frankenstein Gets His Man.
Carr, John
Derwent; an Ode, *sel.*
Memories of Childhood.
Carr, Mary Jane
Big Swing-Tree Is Green Again, The.
Pirate Wind.
When a Ring's around the Moon.
Carr, Robert Van
Bill Haller's Dance.
Comin' to Town.
Cowboy and the Stork, The.
Cowboy's Salvation Song.
Enlightenment.
Good-by, Steer.
Home.
Old Cowboy's Lament, The.
Prairie Wolves.
Rattlesnake, The.
Remember the Promise, Dakotah.
Romance of the Range.
Roundup Cook, The.
Silhouette in Sepia.
War Dance, The.
Western Trail, The.
When Dutchy Plays the Mouth Harp.
Carrera Andrade, Jorge
Walnut.
Carrier, Constance
At Tripolis.
Colonel B.
Commencement.
Fugue.
Lisa.
Party.
Peter at Fourteen.
Pro Patria.
Seminary.
Transformation Scene.
Carrier, Warren
What I Saw in October.
Carrington, N. T.
On Seeing a Fine Frigate at Anchor in a Bay off Mount Edgecumbe, *sel.*
Carroll, Jim
Distances, The.
"Carroll, Lewis" (Charles Lutwidge Dodgson)
Aged Aged Man, The.
Alice's Adventures in Wonderland, *sels.*
Alice's Recitation.
A-Sitting on a Gate.
Atalanta in Camden-Town.
Baker's Tale, The.
Brother and Sister.
Disillusioned.
Doll Song.
Duchess's Lullaby, The.
Evidence Read at the Trial of the Knave of Hearts.
Facts.
Father William.
Fragment of a Song.
Fury Said to a Mouse.
Hiawatha's Photographing.
His sister named Lucy O'Finner.
How Doth the Little Crocodile.
Humpty Dumpty's Song [*or* Recitation].
Hunting of the Snark, The.
Jabberwocky.
King-Fisher Song, The.
Landing, The.
Limerick: "There was a young lady of station."
Little Birds.
Little Man That Had a Little Gun, The.
Lobster Quadrille, The.
Lullaby, A: "Speak roughly to your little boy."
Mad Gardener's Song, The.
Mad Hatter's Song.
Manlet, The.
Melancholetta, *sel.*
Melancholy Pig, The.
Mouse's Tale, The.
My Fairy.
My Fancy.
Palace of humbug, The.
Pig-Tale, A.
Poeta Fit, Non Nascitur.
Quotation from Shakespeare with Slight Improvements, A.
Rules and Regulations.
Sea Dirge, A.
She's All My Fancy Painted Him.
Song of Love, A.
Speak Roughly to Your Little Boy.
Sylvie and Bruno, *sels.*
Sylvie and Bruno Concluded, *sels.*
Tèma con Variazioni.
There was once a young man of Oporta.
Third Voice, The.
Three Badgers, The.
Three Voices, The.
Through the Looking-Glass, *sels.*
Turtle Soup.
Visitor, A.
Voice of the Lobster, The.
Walrus and the Carpenter, The.
Wasp's Song, The.
White Knight's Song, The.
Whiting and the Snail, The.
Yet what are all such gaieties to me.
Carroll, Paul
Father.
Carruth, Hayden
Ah, you beast of love.
Bouquet in Dog Time.
Contra Mortem, *sel.*
Cows at Night, The.
Dornröschen (The Sleeping Beauty).
Emergency Haying.
Fear and Anger in the Mindless Universe.
Hard Journey, A. Yes.
Insomniac Sleeps Well for Once and, The.
Keraunograph.
Little Fire in the Woods, The.
Loneliness.
Mending the Adobe.
My Dog Jock.
My Father's Face.
New Orleans.
On a Certain Engagement South of Seoul.
Once more by the brook the alder leaves.
Our Tense and Wintry Minds, *with music.*
Paragraph, A.
Privation.
Rimrock, Where It Is.
Salt Lake City.
Smallish Son, The.
So be it. I am.
Sonnet: "Cry, crow."
Speaking for Them.
Summer's Early End at Hudson Bay.
This Decoration.
Twilight Comes.
When Howitzers Began.
Why speak of the use.
Your tears, Niobe.
Carruth, William Herbert
Dreamer of Dreams.
Each in His Own Tongue.
Carryl, Charles Edward
Admiral's Caravan, The, *sel.*
Camel's Complaint, The.
Davy and the Goblin, *sels.*
My Recollectest Thoughts.
Nautical Ballad, A.
Plaint of the Camel, The.
Robinson Crusoe.
Sleepy Giant, The.
Song in the Dell, The.
Walloping Window-Blind, The.
Carryl, Guy Wetmore
Ballad, A: "As I was walkin' the jungle round, a-killin' of tigers an' time."
Domineering Eagle and the Inventive Bratling, The.
Embarrassing Episode of Little Miss Muffet, The.
Harmonious Heedlessness of Little Boy Blue, The.
How a Girl Was Too Reckless of Grammar [by Far].
How Jack Found That Beans May Go Back on a Chap.
How the Helpmate of Blue-Beard Made Free with a Door.
Little Red Riding Hood.
Microscopic Trout and the Machiavellian Fisherman, The.
Red Riding Hood.
Singular Sangfroid of Baby Bunting, The.
Sycophantic Fox and the Gullible Raven, The.
When the Great Gray Ships Come In.
Carsley, Sara E.
Little Boats of Britain, The.
Portrait of a Very Old Man.
Carson, Ciaran
Bomb Disposal, The.
Car Cemetery, The.
Insular Celts, The.
St. Ciaran and the Birds.
Visiting the Dead.
Carson, E. J.
November Snow.
Carson, Joseph
As I Grow Older and Fatten on Myself.
Carson, Mary Newland
My "Patch of Blue."
Carter, Aline Badger
Give Our Conscience Light.
Carter, Charlotte Osgood
Elephant and the Giraffe, The.
Carter, Elizabeth
Ode to Wisdom.
Carter, Hodding
In the Jury Room.
Slave Story.
Carter, Jared
At the Sign-Painter's.
For Jack Chatham.
Measuring, The.
Carter, John Marshall
Turn on the Footlights: The Perils of Pedagogy.
Carter, Sydney
Faith Came First, The.

First of My Lovers, The.
Lord of the Dance.

Cartwright, William
Dead Sparrow, The.
Falsehood.
House Blessing, A.
Lesbia on Her Sparrow.
New-Years-Gift to Brian Lord Bishop of Sarum, A.
No Platonic Love.
On a Virtuous Young Gentlewoman That Died Suddenly.
On the Queen's Return from the Low Countries.
Ordinary, The, *sel.*
Saint Francis and Saint Benedight.
Song of Dalliance, A.
To Chloe, Who Wished Herself Young Enough for Me.
Upon the Dramatick Poems of Mr. John Fletcher.
Valediction, A: "Bid me not go where neither suns nor show'rs."
Women.

Carver, Mabel MacDonald
Codicil.

Carver, Raymond
Bobber.
Forever.
Looking for Work.
Marriage.
Photograph of My Father in His Twenty-second Year.
Poem for Hemingway & W. C. Williams.
Prosser.
Wes Hardin: From a Photograph.
You Don't Know What Love Is.
Your Dog Dies.

Cary, Alice
Among the Beautiful Pictures.
Balder's Wife.
Dying Hymn.
Elihu.
Gray Swan, The.
Her Mother.
Make Believe.
My Creed.
Nobility.
November.
Order for a Picture, An.
To Mother Fairie.

Cary, Patrick. *See* **Carey, Patrick**

Cary, Phoebe
Day Is Done, The, *parody.*
Jacob.
Keep a Stiff Upper Lip.
Leak in the Dike, The.
Legend of the Northland, A.
Lovers, The.
Nearer Home.
One Sweetly Solemn Thought.
Our Heroes.
Peace.
Ready.
Samuel Brown.
Suppose.
Thaddeus Stevens.
When Lovely Woman ("When lovely woman wants a favor").

Cary, Thomas
On His Mistresse Going to Sea.

Caryll, John
Hypocrite, The.
Naboth's Vineyard.

Casa, Giovanni della
To Sleep.

Case, Elizabeth York
Faith.
There Is No Unbelief.

Case, John
From One of Case's Pill-Boxes.
Over Case's Door.
To Saffold's Customers, *at.*

Case, Mose
Arkansas Traveller, The ("How do you do?"), *with music.*

Case, Phila H.
Nobody's Child.

Casement, Roger
In the Streets of Catania.

Casewit, Curtis W.
End of the Affair.

Casey, John Keegan
Maire My Girl.
Rising of the Moon A.D. 1798, The.

Casey, Peter
Merry Jovial Beggar, The.

Casey, Thomas F.
Drill, Ye Tarriers, Drill! *at.*

Casillas, Rick
Yaqui Women: Three Generations.

Caskey, Noelle
Ripening.

Cassel, Irwin M.
I Love Life, *with music.*

Cassian, Nina
All Night Long.
Blood, The.
Cripples.
Hills picking up the/ moonlight like.
Knowledge.
Lady of Miracles.
Like Gulliver.
Ordeal.
Self-Portrait.
Vegetable Destiny.

Cassity, Turner
Calvin in the Casino.
Chronology.
Gardens of Proserpine, The.
Grace at the Atlanta Fox.
L'Aigle à Deux Jambes.
Pacelli and the Ethiop.
Technique on the Firing Line.
Wine from the Cape.

Castelete, Rachael
When I Came to London.

Castellanos, Rosario
Foreign Woman.
Great fish's eyes never shut, The.
O cloud that wants to be the sky's arrow.
Silence Concerning an Ancient Stone.
Useless Day.
What is weaker than a god? It groans hungry.

Casterline, Helen Annis
God Cares.

Castillejo, Cristóbal de
Some Day, Some Day.

Castillo, Ana
Napa, California.

Casto, Robert Clayton
Classical Autumn.
Salt Pork, The.

Castro, Michael
Grandfathers.
Percolating Highway.

Castro, Rosalía de
Crickets and locusts, cicadas.
How placidly shine/ The river, the spring, and the sun.
In the sky, clearest blue.
Long May.
Now all that sound of laughter, sound of singing.
Plants don't talk, people say.

Castro Ríos, Andrés
For Nothing.
Words to Remind Me of Grandmother.

Catacalos, Rosemary
Homecoming Celebration.

Cater, Catherine
Here and Now.

Cather, Willa Sibert
Dedicatory: "Somewhere, sometime, in an April twilight."
Grandmither, Think Not I Forget.
Hawthorn Tree, The.
L'Envoi: "Where are the loves that we loved before."
Likeness, A.
Palatine, The.
Spanish Johnny.

Catlin, Ellen Weston
Childlike Heart.

Cato, Nancy
Independence.

Cattafi, Bartola
Patience.

Catton, Bruce
Names from the War.

Catullus, Caius [*or* Gaius] Valerius
Acme and Septimius.
Ad Lesbiam.
Attis.
Caelius, my Lesbia, that one, that only Lesbia.
Catullus Talks to Himself.
Come, Lesbia, let us live and love.
Cominius, you reprobate old goat.
Death of Lesbia's Bird, The.
Death of the Starling, The.
Dialogue with a Door.
Dianae Sumus in Fide.
Each moment of the long-liv'd day.
Egnatius, because his teeth are white.
Egnatius has fine teeth, and those.
Expect no thanks ever from anyone.
Fabullus I will treat you handsomely.
Fib Detected, A.
Flavius, If Your Girl Friend.
Furius, Aurelius, bound to Catullus.
Gellius, what reason can you give why those ruddy lips of yours.
Hendecasyllables, help! Come to my call.
Hymeneal, *sel.*
Hymn to Diana.
I entrust my all to you, Aurelius.
I hate and love, wouldst thou the reason know?
I hate and love./ And if you ask me why.
I have something for you to laugh at, Cato.
I love and hate. Ah! never ask why so!
If a man can find rich consolation, remembering his good deeds.
If I could go on kissing your honeyed eyes.
I'll have you by the short and curly hair.
Invitation to an Invitation, An.
Juventius, could you not find in this great crowd of men.
Juventius, my honey, while you played.
Lesbia.
Lesbia Forever on Me Rails.
Lesbia loads me night and day with her curses.
Lesbia Railing.
Lesbia speaks evil of me with her husband near.
Love and Death.
Miserable Catullus, stop being foolish.
Miss her, Catullus? don't be so inept to rail.
My Lesbia let us love and live.
My life, my love, you say our love will last forever.
My mistress sayes she'll marry none but me.
My Woman.
My woman says that she would rather wear the wedding-veil for me.
Naso, you're all men's man, yet few.
No woman, if she is honest, can say that she's/ been blessed with greater love, my Lesbia.
Ode: Acme and Septimius.
Odi et Amo.
Of all our bath-house thieves the cleverest one.
Of you, if anyone, it can be said.
On the Burial of His Brother.
On the Inconstancy of Women.
Out of Catullus.
Phyllis Corydon clutched to him.

Poor damned Catullus, here's no time for nonsense.
Sappho.
Sirmio.
Sirmio, thou dearest dear of strands.
So help me God, I couldn't choose between.
Spring.
Suffenus whom you know, the witty.
That me alone you lov'd, you once did say.
That no fair woman will, wonder not why.
There are many who think of Quintia in terms of beauty.
There was a time, O Lesbia, when you said Catullus was the only man.
They make a pretty pair of debauchees.
To Himself.
To Lesbia ("Thy kisses dost thou bid me count").
To Naso.
To Varus.
True or False.
Unmuzzle the broad joke.
Unto no body my woman saith she had rather a wife be.
Veranius, my dear friend, the friend worth.
Were you born of lioness in the Libyan Mountains.
What demented malice, my silly Ravidus.
When at last after long despair, our hopes ring true again.
Yacht, The.
Yes! my Lesbia! let us prove.
You are the cause of this destruction, Lesbia.
Your Catullus is depressed, Cornificus.
"Caudwell, Christopher" (Christopher St. John Sprigg)
Classic Encounter.
Progress of Poetry, The.
Causley, Charles
Angel's Song.
Animals' Carol, The.
Armistice Day.
At Candlemas.
At the British War Cemetery, Bayeux.
Autobiography.
Ballad for Katharine of Aragon, A.
Betjeman, 1984.
Chief Petty Officer.
Colonel Fazackerley.
Cowboy Song.
Death of a Poet.
Death of an Aircraft.
Envoi: "I am the Prince."
For an Ex-Far East Prisoner of War.
I Saw a Jolly Hunter.
Infant Song.
Innocent's Song.
Loss of an Oil Tanker.
Mary's Song.
Nursery Rhyme of Innocence and Experience.
On Seeing a Poet of the First World War on the Station at Abbeville.
On the Thirteenth Day of Christmas.
Ou Phrontis.
Recruiting Drive.
Riley.
Sailor's Carol.
Song of Samuel Sweet, The.
Ten Types of Hospital Visitor.
Visit to Van Gogh, A.
Cavafy, Constantine P.
Alexander Jannai.
Days of 1896.
He Asked about the Quality.
In Despair.
Mirror in the Front Hall, The.
Next Table, The.
On the Street.
One of the Jews.
Return.
Their Beginning.
To Remain.
Twenty-fifth Year of His Life, The.
Two Young Men, 23 to 24 Years Old.
Walls.
Window of the Tobacco Shop, The.
Cavalcanti, Guido
Ballata: Concerning a Shepherd-Maid.
Ballata: He Reveals, in a Dialogue, His Increasing Love for Mandetta.
Ballata: In Exile at Sarzana.
Ballata V: "Light do I see within my Lady's eyes."
Ballata: Of a Continual Death in Love.
Ballata: Of His Lady among Other Ladies.
Canzone: Donna Mi Priegha.
Sonetto XXXV: To Guido Orlando.
Sonetto VII: "Who is she that comes, making turn every man's eye."
Sonnet: Guido Cavalcanti to Dante.
Sonnet: He Compares All Things with His Lady, and Finds Them Wanting.
Sonnet: He Speaks of a Third Love of His.
Sonnet: Of an Ill-Favored Lady.
Sonnet: Of His Pain from a New Love.
Sonnet: Of the Eyes of a Certain Mandetta.
Sonnet: On the Detection of a False Friend.
Sonnet: Rapture Concerning His Lady, A.
Sonnet: To a Friend Who Does Not Pity His Love.
Sonnet: To His Lady Joan, of Florence.
To Dante.
To Dante Alighieri.
To Dante Alighieri: He Mistrusts the Love of Lapo Gianni.
To Dante Alighieri: He Reports, in a Feigned Vision, the Successful Issue of Lapo Gianni's Love.
Cavanass, J. M.
By the Waters of Minnetonka, *with music.*
Cavendish, Margaret Duchess of Newcastle. *See* **Newcastle, Margaret Cavendish Duchess of**
Cavendish, William, Duke of Newcastle. *See* **Newcastle, William Cavendish, Duke of**
Cawein, Madison
Attainment.
Ballad of Low-lie-down.
Comradery.
Creek-Road, The.
Death.
Dirge: "What shall her silence keep?"
Enchantment.
Flight.
Here Is the Place Where Loveliness Keeps House.
Ku Klux.
"Mene, Mene, Tekel, Upharsin."
Miracle of the Dawn, The.
Morning Serenade.
Mosby at Hamilton.
Old Home, The.
Old Man Rain.
Opportunity.
Proem: "There is no rhyme that is half so sweet."
Rain-Crow, The.
Soul, The.
To a Wind-Flower.
Wind in the Pines, The.
Cawthorn, James
Of Taste; an Essay, *sel.*
Cayley, George John
Epitaph, An: "Lovely young lady I mourn in my rhymes, A."
Cecco, Angiolieri da Siena. *See* **Angiolieri, Cecco, da Siena**
Cedering, Siv. *See* **Fox, Siv Cedering**
Celan, Paul
Ash-Glory.
Cello Entry.
Corona.
Etched Away From.
Fugue of Death.
Hut Window.
In Egypt.
In Prague.
Irish.
Jugs, The.
Just Think.
Leap-Centuries.
Over Three Nipple-Stones.
Plashes the Fountain.
Psalm: "No one kneads [*or* moulds] us again [out] of earth and clay."
Speck of Sand, A.
Tenebrae.
Thread Suns.
Turn Blind.
Your Hand Full of Hours.
Zürich, zum Storchem.
Cennick, John
Be Present at Our Table, Lord, *at.*
Children of the Heavenly King.
Centamputan, Maturai Eruttalan
What She Said.
Cerenio, Virginia
Manong Benny.
Pick-up at Chef Rizal Restaurant.
Pinay.
You Lovely People.
Cernuda, Luis
Birds in the Night.
Cervantes, Lorna Dee
Beneath the Shadow of the Freeway.
Poem for the Young White Man Who Asked Me How I, an Intelligent, Well-read Person, Could Believe in the War between Races.
Visions of Mexico While at a Writing Symposium in Port Townsend, Washington.
Woman in My Notebook, The.
Cervantes Saavedra, Miguel de
Sonnet: "When I was marked for suffering, Love forswore."
Césaire, Aimé
Return to My Native Land, *sel.*
Céu, Sor Violante do
Voice of a Dissipated Woman inside a Tomb.
Chace, Jean Valentine
Visit to a Hospital.
Chadwick, Jerah
Runner, The.
Chadwick, John White
Abiding Love, The.
Auld Lang Syne.
Full Cycle.
Golden-Robin's Nest, The.
His Mother's Joy.
Hymn: "Eternal Ruler of the ceaseless round."
Hymn: "Father, we come not as of old."
Making of Man, The.
Mugford's Victory.
O Love, That Dost with Goodness Crown.
Recognition.
Rise of Man, The.
Starlight.
Wedding Song, A.
Chaet, Eric
Letter Catches Up with Me, A.
Yom Kippur.
Chaffee, Eleanor Alletta
Cobbler, The.
Chaffin, Lillie D.
Haiku, for Cinnamon.
Tourism.
Chaikin, Miriam
I Hate Harry.
Light Another Candle.
Ms. Whatchamacallit Thingamajig.
One-Upmanship.
Chalfi, Abraham
My Father.
One Who Is Missing, The.
Chalfi, Raquel
Childless Witch, A.
Like a Field Waiting.
Witch Going Down to Egypt, A.

Chalkhill, John
Angler, The.
Coridon's Song.
Rhotus on Arcadia.
Thealma and Clearchus, *sel.*
Chalmers, Patrick Reginald
Cuckoo, The.
Gardener's Cat, The.
"Hold."
In an Old Nursery.
Lavender's for Ladies.
My Woodcock.
Pan-Pipes.
Puk-Wudjies.
Road, The.
Tortoiseshell Cat, The.
Visitor, The.
When Mary Goes Walking.
Chalmers, Stephen
Home.
New Physician, The.
Chalpin, Lila
Curse of a Fisherman's Wife.
Chamberlain, Brenda
Dead Ponies.
First Woman's Lament.
Give No White Flower.
Lament: "My man is a bone ringed with weed."
Poem: "You, who in April laughed, a green god in the sun."
Second Woman's Lament.
Song: "Bone-aged is my white horse."
Song: "Heron is harsh with despair."
Song—Talysarn.
Chamberlain, Enola
After the Dark.
Chamberlain, Richard
To the Much Honoured R. F. Esq.
Chamberlain, Robert
In Praise of Country Life.
Chamberlayne, Sir James
Dedication: "This little book, my God and King."
Chambers, Jane
Woman.
Chambers, Robert William
"Grey Horse Troop," The.
Officer Brady.
Recruit, The.
To Nature Seekers.
Chamisso, Adelbert von
Tragic Story, A.
Chandler, Ellen Louise. *See* **Moulton, Louise Chandler**
Chandler, Elsie Williams
Christmas Singing.
Chandler, Janet Carncross
Leave the Top Plums.
To Drift Down.
Chandler, Len
I Would Be a Painter Most of All.
Chandonnet, Ann
Edge, The.
Chandra, G. Sharat
In Praise of Blur.
Chan Fang-sheng
Sailing Homeward.
Chang, Diana
Artists East and West.
Cannibalism.
Codes.
Horizon Is Definitely Speaking, The.
Once and Future.
Second Nature.
Trying to Stay.
Chang Heng
Bones of Chuang Tzu, The.
Chanler, Isaac
Awake My Soul, Betimes Awake, *with music.*
Thrice Welcome First and Best of Days, *with music.*
Channing, William Ellery
Barren Moors, The.
Edith.
Hymn of the Earth.
Lady, there is a hope that all men have.
Poet's Hope, A, *sel.*
Prayer, A: "To Thy continual Presence, in me wrought."
Tears in Spring.
Chantikian, Kosrof
Love Song: "Wherever your voice moves."
Your Eyes.
Chao Li-hua
Farewell: "My boat goes west, yours east."
Chao Luan-luan
Slender Fingers ("Slender, delicate, soft jade").
Chao, Ying-tou
Decrees of God, The.
Chapin, Carol Earle
Highway Construction.
Chapin, Edwin Hubbell
Hark! Hark! with Harps of Gold, *with music.*
O Thou, Who Didst Ordain the Word, *with music.*
Ocean Burial, The.
Chapin, Henry
Easy Does It.
Helpmate.
Quality of Air, A.
Threes.
Chapin, Katherine Garrison
On a Sea-Grape Leaf.
Other Journey, The.
Plain-Chant for America.
Portrait in Winter.
Chaplin, Ralph
Commonwealth of Toil, The.
Mourn Not the Dead.
Solidarity Forever.
To France.
Chapman, Arthur
Beecher Island.
Blanket Injun, The.
Dead Prospector, The.
Last Drift.
Little Papoose.
Out Where the West Begins.
Pete's Error.
Santa Fe Trail, The.
Sheep-Herder's Lament, The.
Sheriff's Report, The.
Chapman, George (1559?–1634)
Bridal Song ("Now, Sleep, bind fast the flood of air").
Bridal Song ("O! Come, soft rest of cares, come Night").
Bussy D'Ambois, *sels.*
Caesar and Pompey, *sel.*
Conspiracy of Charles, Duke of Byron, The, *sels.*
Corinna Bathes.
Coronet for His Mistress Philosophy, A, *sel.*
De Guiana, Carmen Epicum.
Descend, Fair Sun!
Epistle Dedicatory to Chapman's Translation of the Iliad, The, *sel.*
Epithalamion Teratos.
Eugenia, *sel.*
Euthymiae Raptus; or, The Teares of Peace, *sels.*
Hymne to Our Saviour on the Crosse, A.
Hymnus in Noctem.
Learning.
Love and Philosophy.
Masque of the Middle Temple and Lincoln's Inn, The, *sel.*
Masque of the Twelve Months, The, *sels, at.*
Master Spirit, The.
Natures Naked Jem.
Night.
Ovid's Banquet of Sense, *sel.*
Pilot, The.
Poet Questions Peace, The.
Poetry and Learning.
Praise of Homer.
Presage of Storme.
Repentance.
Rich Mine of Knowledge.
Shadow of Night, The.
Shine Out, Fair Sun [with All Your Heat], *at.*
Song: "O come, soft rest of cares! come, Night!"
Sonnet: "Muses that sing Love's sensual empery [emperie]."
Wedding of Alcmane and Mya, The.
Chapman, John Alexander
Gipsy Queen.
Chapman, John Jay
Clouds.
Lines on the Death of Bismarck.
Song: "Old Farmer Oats and his son Ned."
Toil Away.
Chapone, Hester
To Stella.
Chappell, Fred
Northwest Airlines (My Emergency Instructions Were in Chinese).
Spitballer.
Chappell, George S.
Innocence.
Chappell, Jeannette
Newton to Einstein.
Char, René
True Night.
Charasson, Henriette
Ave Maria.
Charles I, King of England
On a Quiet Conscience.
Charles, Dorthi
Concrete Cat.
Charles, Elizabeth Rundle
Child on the Judgment Seat, The.
Charles, Mary Grant
Flood.
Charles, Robert E.
Roundabout Turn, A.
Charles d'Orléans. *See* **Orléans, Charles, Duc d'**
Chartier, Alain
I turn you out of doors.
Chartres, Vidame de April.
Chase, Edith Newlin
New Baby Calf, The.
Passenger Train.
Tiger-Cat Tim.
Work Horses.
Chase, Frank
Tale of the Dixie-Belle, The.
Chasin, Helen
City Pigeons.
Falling Out.
Joy Sonnet in a Random Universe.
Looking Out.
Mythics.
Photograph at the Cloisters: April 1972.
Poetess Kō Ōgimi, The.
Recovery Room, The: Lying-in.
Word *Plum,* The.
Chatain, Robert
World of Darkness.
Chatt, George
At Elsdon.
Chatterton, Thomas
Aella; a Tragycal Enterlude, *sels.*
African Song, An.
Bristowe Tragedie; or, The Dethe [*or* Death] of Syr Charles Bawdin.
Copernican System, The.
Elinoure and Juga.
Excelente [*or* Excellent] Balade of Charitie, An.
Goddwyn, *sel.*
Last Verses.
Minstrel's Song.
My Love Is Dead.

Mynstrelles Songe: "Angelles bee wrogte to bee of neidher kynde."
Mynstrelles Songe: "Boddynge flourettes bloshes atte the lyghte, The."
Mynstrelles Songe: "O! synge untoe mie roundelaie".
Ode to Liberty.
Ode to Miss Hoyland.
Resignation.
Sentiment.
Song: "O sing unto my roundelay."
Song of the Three Minstrels.
Chaucer, Geoffrey
Against Women Unconstant.
At the Gate.
Balade: "Hide [*or* Hyd], Absalon, thy gilte tresses clear."
Balade de [*or* of] Bon Conseyl [*or* Conseil *or* Conseill].
Ballad of Good Counsel.
Ballade against Woman Inconstant, A.
Ballade of Good Counsel.
Ballade to Rosamund.
Birds' Rondel, The.
Book of the Duchess[e], The, *sels.*
But, sires, o word forgat I in my tale.
Canterbury Tales, The, *sels.*
Chaucer's Complaint to His Empty Purse.
Chauntecleer.
Clerk of Oxford, The.
Cock and the Hen, The.
Complaint of Chaucer to His Purse, The.
Complaint of Troilus, The.
Controlling the Tongue.
Cook's Tale, The.
Criseyde Sees Troilus Return from Battle.
Death and the Three Revellers.
Despair of Troilus, The.
Dream, The.
Eagle Converses with Chaucer, The.
Envoy, The: "Go, litel book, go litel myn tregedie."
Former Age, The.
Foules Rondel.
Franklin's Prologue, The.
Franklin's Tale, The.
Gentilesse.
Go, Little Book.
Good Parson, The.
House of Fame, The, *sels.*
Introduction to the Man of Law's Prologue.
Invocatio ad Mariam.
Invocation: "O mother-maid! O maiden mother free!"
Jove's Eagle Carries Chaucer into Space.
Knightes Tale, The.
La Prière de Nostre Dame.
Lady without Paragon, A.
Lak of Stedfastnesse.
Lat Take a Cat.
Legend of Good Women, The: Prologue.
Love Unfeigned, The.
Manciple's Tale, The, *sels.*
May Morning, *mod. vers.*
Merchant's Tale, The, *abr.*
Merciles[s] Beaute [*or* Beautée *or* Beauty].
Mice before Milk.
Mill at Trumpington, The.
Miller's Prologue, The.
Miller's Tale, The.
Nonne Preestes Tale, The.
Now Welcom[e], Somer [*or* Summer].
Nun's Priest's Prologue, The.
Nun's Priest's Tale, The.
Old Books.
Pardoner's Prologue and Tale, The.
Parlement of Foules, The, *sels.*
Parliament of Fowls, The.
Patient Griselda.
Poor Parson, The.
Prioress, The.
Prioress's Tale, The.
Proem to the Parlement of Foules.
Prologue of the Prioress's Tale, The.
Prologue to Sir Thopas.
Prologue to the Man of Law's Tale.
Prologue to the Second Nun's Tale, *sels.*
Prologue to the Wife of Bath's Tale, The.
Qui Bien Aime a Tard Oublie.
Reeve, The.
Reeve's Tale, The.
Rondel of Merciless Beauty, A.
Seven Pilgrims.
Seynt Valentynes Day.
Shipman, The ("A Schipman was ther, wonyng fer by weste").
Shipman, The ("The Parson him answered, 'Benedicte!' ").
Sir Thopas.
Song of Troylus, The.
Song to His Purse for the King, A.
Sorrow of Troilus, The.
Tale of Sir Thopas, The.
This Fresshe Flour.
Three Revellers Search for Death.
Three Roundels of Love Unreturned.
To Adam, His Scribe.
To Rosemond [*or* Rosamond].
Troilus and Criseyde [*or* Criseide], *sels.*
Truth.
Truth Shall Set You Free.
Two Invocations of the Virgin, I ("Within the cloister blissful of thy sides").
Two Invocations of the Virgin, II ("O mother maid, O maiden mother free!").
Welcome, Summer.
When April with Its Sweet Showers.
Wife of Bath, The.
Wife of Bath's Prologue, The.
Wife of Bath's Tale, The.
Wife's Fifth Husband, The.
Wooing of Criseide, The.
Chaudhari, Kirti
Inertia.
Chavez, Fray Angelico
Esther.
Lady of Lidice.
Lady of Peace.
Mary.
Mulier Amicta Sole.
Sea-Birds.
Chawner, George F.
Prayer, A: "Those who love Thee may they find."
Chayat, Juliet
Stone.
Chear, Abraham
To My Youngest Kinsman, R. L.
Chedid, Andrée
Future and the Ancestor, The.
What Are We Playing At?
Cheever, George Barrell
Blest Be the Wondrous Grace, *with music.*
Thy Loving Kindness, Lord, I Sing, *with music.*
Cheke, Henry
Of Perfect Friendship.
Cheney, Ednah Dow
Larger Prayer, The.
Prayer—Answer.
Cheney, Elizabeth
Overheard in an Orchard.
There Is a Man on the Cross.
Cheney, John Vance
Evenings Songs
Every One to His Own Way.
Happiest Heart, The.
Lincoln.
Man with the Hoe, The: A Reply.
On a Picture of Lincoln.
San Francisco.
Skilful Listener, The.
Strong, The.
Unto Our God Most High We Sing, *with music.*
Way of It, The.
Whither.
Cheney, Ralph *and* **Lucia Trent.** *See* **Trent, Lucia** *and* **Ralph Cheney**
Cheng Min
Student.
Chénier, André Marie de
Elegies.
When I Was Small.
Ch'en, Tzu-lung
Little Cart, The.
Cherbury, Edward Herbert, 1st Baron. *See* **Herbert of Cherbury**
Cherner, Anne
To Helen Frankenthaler.
To Mark Rothko.
To Morris Louis.
Window.
Chernick, Hank
Situation Normal.
Chernier, Anne
Everglade.
Chernin, Kim
Eve's Birth.
Cherry, Andrew
Green Little Shamrock of Ireland, The.
Cherwinski, Joseph
Forsythia Is the Color I Remember.
Manhattan Menagerie.
Chester, Anson G.
Tapestry Weavers, The.
Chester, Laura
Bees inside Me.
Go Round.
In a Motion.
Last Breath.
Moved towards a Future.
On the Wallowy.
Pavane for the Passing of a Child.
Returning to the World.
Simply.
Trellis.
28 VIII 69.
We Heart.
Chester, Sir Robert
Ditty: "O holy Love, religious saint!"
Her Hair.
Love's Martyr, *sels.*
Chesterfield, Philip Dormer Stanhope, 4th Earl of
Advice to a Lady in Autumn.
Advice to a Young Lady.
On Miss Eleanor Ambrose, a Celebrated Beauty in Dublin.
On Mr. Nash's Present of His Own Picture at Full Length.
Song: "Whenever, Chloe, I begin."
To a Lady on Reading Sherlock "Upon Death"
To Miss Eleanor Ambrose on the Occasion of Her Wearing an Orange Lily at a Ball in Dublin Castle on July the 12th.
Unlike my subject now shall be my song.
Verses Written in a Lady's Sherlock "Upon Death."
Chesterman, Hugh
Yesterday.
Chesterton, Frances
How Far Is It to Bethlehem?
To Felicity Who Calls Me Mary.
Chesterton, Gilbert Keith
Antichrist, or the Reunion of Christendom; an Ode.
Ballad of Abbreviations, A.
Ballad of the White Horse, The, *sels.*
Ballade d'une Grande Dame.
Ballade of Suicide, A.
Black Virgin, The.
By the Babe Unborn.
Christmas Carol, A: "Christ child lay on Mary's lap, The."
Citizenship; Form 8889512, Sub-Section Q.
Commercial Candour.
Convert, The.

Dedication, A: "He was, through boyhood's storm and shower."
Donkey, The.
Ecclesiastes.
Elegy in a Country Churchyard.
Englishman, The.
Fantasia.
Fat White Woman Speaks, The.
Feast of the Snow, The.
Flying Inn, The, *sel.*
For a War Memorial.
For the Crêche.
Geography.
Glencoe.
Gold Leaves.
Good Rich Man, The.
Happy Man, The.
Harp of Alfred, The.
History.
Holy of Holies, The.
Home at Last.
House of Christmas, The.
Hymn, A: "O God of earth and altar."
Hymn for the Church Militant.
King Alfred Answers the Danes.
Lepanto.
Logical Vegetarian, The.
Myth of Arthur, The.
Old King Cole ("Me clairvoyant").
Old King Cole ("Of an old king in a story").
Old King Cole ("Who smoke-snorts toasts o' My Lady Nicotine").
Old Song, The.
On a Prohibitionist Poem.
On the Dangers Attending Altruism on the High Seas.
Oneness of the Philosopher with Nature, The.
Praise of Dust, The.
Prayer: "O God of earth and altar."
Prayer in Darkness, A.
Regina Angelorum
Return of Eve, The.
Rolling English Road, The.
Secret People, The.
Skeleton, The.
Song against Grocers, The.
Song of Quoodle, The.
Song of the Strange Ascetic, The.
Songs of Education, *sels.*
Songs of Guthrum and Alfred, The.
Sword of Surprise, The.
To F. C. in Memoriam Palestine.
To M. E. W.
To the Unknown Warrior.
Variations of an Air.
Variations on an Air Composed on Having to Appear in a Pageant as Old King Cole.
Wild Knight, The.
Wine and Water.
World State, The.

Chettle, Henry
Aeliana's Ditty.
Of Cupid.
Piers Plainness' Seven Years' Prenticeship, *sel.*
To His Flocks, *at.*

Chevalier, Albert
My Old Dutch; a Cockney Song.

Chew, Beverly
Old Books Are Best.

Cheyney, Ralph
Comrade Jesus.
No Armistice in Love's War.

Chiabrera, Gabriello
Epitaphs (I–IX).

Chiang, Fay
Letter to Peter, A.
Snow.
Voices That Have Filled My Day.

Chicken, Edward
Collier's Wedding, The, *sel.*

Ch'ien Wen-ti, Emperor
Lo-yang.

Chikamatsu Monzaemon
Farewell to the world, and to the night farewell.
Love Suicides at Sonezaki, The, *sel.*

Child, Lydia Maria
Apple-Seed John.
New-England Boy's Song about Thanksgiving Day, The.
Thanksgiving Day.
World I Am Passing Through, The.

Child, Philip
Basilisk, The.
Dancing Partners.
Descent for the Lost.
Lyric: "I touched a shining mote of sand."
Macrocosm.
Oak.

Childe, Wilfred Rowland
Our Lady with Two Angels.
Shepherd of Meriador, The.

Childers, David C.
Another One for the Devil.

Childress, W. Lomax
Beautiful World, The.

Childress, William
Korea Bound, 1952.
Metamorphosis of Aunt Jemima, The.

Chimako, Tada
Mirror.

Chin, Marilyn
Chinaman's Chance, A.
Grandmother Poems.
Landlord's Wife, The.
Write, Do Write.

Ching, Laureen
Memorial Day.

Chipp, Elinor
Before Dawn.
Doubt.
Lullaby: "Sleep, little baby, sleep and rest."
Wild Geese.

Chisoku
Dragonfly, The.

Chittenden, William Lawrence
Cowboys' Christmas Ball, The.
Ode to the Norther.
Texas Types—"The Bad Man."

Chitty, Cordelia
Galloping.

Ch'iu Chin
Call to Action, A.
To the Tune "The River Is Red."

Chivers, Thomas Holley
Chinese Serenade for the Ut-Kam and Tong-Koo, *sel.*
Lily Adair.
Moon of Mobile, The.
Railroad Song, *sel.*
To Allegra Florence in Heaven, *sel.*

Chiyo
After a long winter, giving/ each other nothing.
Don't dress for it.
Hardly spring, with ice.
Once my parents were older.

Chock, Eric
For the Field.
Mango Tree, The.
Papio.
Pulling Weeds.
Termites.

Cholmondeley, Hester H.
Betrayal.
Still as of Old.

Cholmondeley-Pennell, Henry
Bloated Biggaboon, The.
I've Lost My———.
Lay of the Deserted Influenzaed.
Night Mail North, The.
Our Traveller.
What the Prince of I Dreamt.

Chorley, Henry Fothergill
Brave Old Oak, The.

Chorny, Sasha
Vilna Puzzle, A.

Cho Wen-chün
Song of Snow-white Heads.

Choyce, A. Newberry
Come Michaelmas.
Let Me Love Bright Things.
Oblation.

Christensen, Inger
Men's Voices.

Christgau, Ferdinand G.
Two Jays at St. Louis.

Christian, Marcus B.
Craftsman, The.
Dialect Quatrain.
McDonogh Day in New Orleans.

Christiansen, Avis B.
Yes, I Have Been to Calvary.

Christina, Martha
Couplets for WCW.

Christopher, Nicholas
Big City Glissando.
Driver in Italy, The.
John Garfield.
Track, The.
Walt Whitman at the Reburial of Poe.

Chuang Tzu
P'eng That Was a K'un, The.

Chubb, Ralph
Book of God's Madness, The, *sel.*
Song of My Soul.
Sun Spirit, The, *sel.*

Chubb, Thomas Caldecot
At the Edge of the Bay.
Praise of New England.

Chudleigh, Mary Lee, Lady
Offering, The: Part One.
Resolve, The.
To the Ladies.

Chu Hsi
Boats Are Afloat, The.

Chuilleanáin, Eiléan Ní. *See* **Ní Chuilleanáin, Eiléan**

Church, Peggy Pond
Sheep Country.
Ultimatum.

Church, Richard
Alchemist, The.
Be Frugal.
Cat, The.
Nocturne: "See how the dying west puts forth her song."
On Hearing the First Cuckoo.
Waiting for News.

Churchill, Charles
Against Education.
Apology Addressed to the Critical Reviewers, The.
Author, The, *sels.*
Character of a Critic.
Conference, The, *sel.*
Conscience.
Critical Fribble, A.
Criticaster, A.
Dedication, The: "Health to great Gloucester—from a man unknown."
Dedication to the Sermons, The.
Duellist, The, *sel.*
European Crimes.
Ghost, The, *sel.*
Gotham, *sels.*
Hogarth.
Night; an Epistle to Robert Lloyd.
Nut, a World, a Squirrel, and a King, A.
On Himself.
On His Own Poetry.
Pains of Education, The.
Poet as King of Gotham, The.
Prophecy of Famine, The, *sels.*
Rosciad, The, *sel.*
Times, The, *sels.*
What Is't to Us?

Churchyard, Thomas
Farewell to a Fondling, A.
Fayned Fancy betweene the Spider and the Gowte, A, *sel.*
Old-Time Service.
Chu Shu-chen
Alone.
Hysteria.
Lost.
Morning.
Old Anguish, The.
Plum Blossoms ("The snow dances and the frost flies").
Sorrow.
Stormy Night in Autumn.
Chute, Marchette
Birthdays.
Cats.
Christmas.
Day before Christmas.
Drinking Fountain.
Easter Parade.
Fourth of July.
Going to Bed.
My Dog.
My Plan.
Presents.
Sliding.
Snowflakes.
Spring.
Spring Rain.
Tracks in the Snow.
Wrong Start, The.
Chute, Robert M.
Snow White.
Ch'ü Yüan
Great Summons, The.
Chworowsky, Karl M.
Motherhood.
Ciardi, John
About the Teeth of Sharks.
After Sunday Dinner We Uncles Snooze.
Apology for a Lost Classicism, An.
Ballad of the Icondic.
Birthday.
Camptown.
Captain Spud and His First Mate, Spade.
Cat Heard the Cat-Bird, The.
Censorship.
Composition for a Nativity.
Counting on Flowers.
Credibility.
Dawn of the Space Age.
Death's the Classic Look.
Dollar Dog, The.
Elegy: "My father was born with a spade in his hand and traded it."
Elegy Just in Case.
Epitaph: "Here, time concurring (and it does)."
Evil Eye, The.
Exit Line.
Faces.
Falling Asleep.
First Snow on an Airfield.
For My Twenty-fifth Birthday in Nineteen Forty-one.
Gift, The.
Goodmorning with Light.
Goodnight.
Happy Family, The.
Home Revisited: Midnight.
Homecoming—Massachusetts.
How to Tell the Top of a Hill.
I Took a Bow and Arrow.
I Wish I Could Meet the Man That Knows.
In Place of a Curse.
In the Hole.
In the Year of Many Conversions and the Private Soul.
Journal.
Letter from a Death Bed.
Light-House Keeper's White-Mouse, The.
Magus, A.
Man from the Woods, The.
Man in the Onion Bed, The.
Man Who Sang the Sillies, The.
Minus One.
Morning in the Park.
Most Like an Arch This Marriage.
Mummy Slept Late and Daddy Fixed Breakfast.
My Father's Watch.
Myra Song, The ("Myra, Myra, sing-song").
Mystic River.
No White Bird Sings.
Ode for the Burial of a Citizen.
Old Miser Named Quince, An.
On a Photo of Sgt. Ciardi a Year Later.
On Evolution.
On Learning to Adjust to Things.
Pilot in the Jungle, The.
Pinwheel's Song, The.
Poem for My Thirty-second Birthday.
Polo Match.
Rain Sizes.
Read This with Gestures.
Reason for the Pelican, The.
River Is a Piece of Sky, The.
Romping.
Seven Sharp Propeller Blades.
Snowy Heron.
Some Cook.
Some Sound Advice from Singapore.
Song: "Bells of Sunday rang us down, The."
Song for an Allegorical Play.
Stranger in the Pumpkin, The.
Suzie's New Dog.
That Summer's Shore.
To a Reviewer Who Admired My Book.
To Judith Asleep.
Two Egrets.
V-J Day.
Vale.
Warning.
What Night Would It Be?
What Someone Said When He Was Spanked on the Day before His Birthday.
What You Will Learn about the Brobinyak.
Young Fellow Named Shear, A.
Cibber, Colley
Blind Boy, The.
Cino da Pistoia
Canzone: His Lament for Selvaggia.
Madrigal: To His Lady Selvaggia Vergiolesi; Likening His Love to a Search for Gold.
Sonnet: Death Is Not without but within Him.
Sonnet: Of the Grave of Selvaggia, on the Monte della Sambuca.
Sonnet: To Love, in Great Bitterness.
Sonnet: Trance of Love, A.
To Dante Alighieri: He Conceives of Some Compensation in Death.
To Dante Alighieri: He Interprets Dante's Dream.
Citèkù Ndaaya
Ndaaya's Kàsàlà, *sel.*
Citino, David
Last Rites.
Map Reading.
Ciullo d'Alcamo
Dialogue: Lover and Lady.
Clairmont, Robert
Answers, The.
Hero in the Land of Dough, A.
Clampitt, Amy
Amphibian.
Berceuse.
Camouflage.
Cormorant in Its Element, The.
Curfew, A: December 13, 1981.
Mysterious Britain.
On the Disadvantages of Central Heating.
Clamurro, William
Edge of Town, The.
Clancy, Liam P.
Christmas Eve.
Gaelic Christmas, A.
Clanvowe, Sir Thomas
Cuckoo and the Nightingale, The, *sel.*
Clapp, Ross B.
Mother's Love.
Clapper, Merl A.
When Nobody Prays.
Clar, Clarence E.
In His Service.
Clare, John
Address to Plenty, *sel.*
After Reading in a Letter Proposals for Building a Cottage.
Ants, The.
Autumn ("The thistledown's flying. . .").
Autumn Birds.
Autumn Change.
Autumn Wind, The.
Badger ("When midnight comes a host of dogs and men").
Ballad: "Blackbird has built in the pasture agen, The."
Beans in Blossom.
Birds' Lament.
Birds' Nests.
Bits of Straw.
Bonny Lassie O!
Child Harold, *sels.*
Clock-a-Clay.
Come Hither.
Come Hither, My Dear One.
Cottager, The, *sel.*
Country Letter.
Crow Sat on the Willow, The.
Crows in Spring.
Death.
December.
Deluge.
Dewdrops.
Dying Child, The.
Early Nightingale.
Emmonsail's Heath in Winter.
Enclosure.
Eternity of Nature, The.
Evening.
Evening Primrose, The.
Evening Schoolboys.
Evening Star, The.
Faithless Shepherd, A.
Farewell: "Farewell to the bushy clump close to the river."
Fear of Flowers, The.
February.
Firetail's Nest, The.
Firewood.
First Love.
Flitting, The, *sel.*
Fox, The.
Fragment: "Cataract, whirling to the precipice, The."
Fragment: "Language has not the power to speak what love indites."
Fragment: "Some pretty face remembered in our youth."
Frightened Ploughman, The.
Gipsies ("The gipsies seek wide sheltering woods again").
Gipsies ("The snow falls deep; the forest lies alone").
Gipsy Camp, The.
Graves of Infants.
Hailstorm in June 1831, The.
Happy Bird, The.
Hedgehog, The.
Hen's Nest.
Hesperus.
I Am.
I Feel I Am.
I Hid My Love.
I Lost the Love of Heaven.

I Ne'er Was Struck.
In Epping Forest.
Invitation to Eternity.
John Clare.
Landrail, The.
Lark's Nest, The.
Little Trotty Wagtail.
London versus Epping Forest.
Lord, Hear My Prayer.
Lout, The.
Love.
Love, Meet Me in the Green Glen.
Love Lives Beyond the Tomb.
Lover's Invitation, The.
Love's Emblem.
Maid o' the West, The.
Martin cat long shaged of courage good, The.
Mary.
Milking Shed, The.
Missel-Thrush's Nest, The.
Mole, The.
Mother's Lullaby, The.
Mouse's Nest.
My Early Home.
Nature's Hymn to the Deity.
Nightingale, The.
No single hour can stand for naught.
Noon.
Northamptonshire Fens.
Old Cottagers, The.
Old Year, The.
Pastoral Poesy.
Peasant Poet, The.
Peggy Said Good Morning.
Pettichap's Nest, The.
Ploughboy, The.
Poets Love Nature.
Ragwort, The.
Remember Dear Mary.
Remembrances.
Sand Martin, The.
Schoolboys in Winter.
Sea Boy on the Giddy Mast, A.
Secret, The.
Secret Love.
She Tied Up Her Few Things.
Sheep in Winter.
Shepherd's [*or* Shepheards] Calendar, The, *sels.*
Signs of Winter.
Silent Love.
Snowstorm.
Solitude.
Song: "Go with your tauntings, go."
Song: "I peeled bits of straw and I got switches too."
Song: "I would not feign a single sigh."
Song: Love Lives beyond the Tomb.
Song's Eternity.
Spring Morning, A.
Stanzas: "Black absence hides upon the past."
Stanzas from "Child Harold."
Stranger, The.
Sudden Shower.
Summer.
Summer Images.
Summer Morning.
Sunrise in Summer.
Swordy Well.
Thrush's Nest, The.
To an Infant Daughter.
To Mary: I Sleep with Thee, and Wake with Thee.
To Mary: It Is the Evening Hour.
To the Snipe.
To Wordsworth.
Vision, A.
Vixen, The.
We Passed by Green Closes.
Well, Honest John.
What Is Love?
Where She Told Her Love.
Wind That Shakes the Rushes, The.
Winter in the Fens.
Winter Winds Cold and Blea.
With Garments Flowing.
Wood-Cutter's Night Song, The.
Written in a Thunder Storm July 15th 1841.
Written in Prison.
Young Lambs.

Clare, Josephine
Fine Body.

"Claribel." *See* **Barnard, Charlotte Alington**

Clark, Badger. *See* **Clark, Charles Badger, Jr.**

Clark, Carl
Allegory in Black.
Conundrum.
No More.
Ode to a Beautiful Woman.
Second Coming, The.
Thoughts from a Bottle.

Clark, Charles Badger, Jr. (Badger Clark)
Cottonwood Leaves.
Glory Trail, The.
Legend of Boastful Bill, The.
Night Herder, The.
Pioneers.
Ridin'.
Sheep-Herder, The.
Smoke-blue Plains, The.

Clark, Charles Heber. *See* **"Adeler, Max"**

Clark, David R.
Asylum.

Clark, Duane
Bonner's Ferry Beggar.

Clark, G. Orr
Night Is a Big Black Cat, The.

Clark, John Pepper
Agbor Dancer.
Fulani Cattle.
Ibadan.

Clark, Kevin
Death Comes for the Old Cowboy.

Clark, Leonard
House. For Sale.
November the Fifth.

Clark, Leslie Savage
Beacon Light.
In the Time of Trouble.
Litany for Peace.
Way, The.

Clark, Lewis Gaylord
Flamingo, The.

Clark, Martha Haskell
Red Geraniums.

Clark, Naomi
Tables.

Clark, Preston
Faith.
Youth.

Clark, Robert
Generations.

Clark, Stephen
Summer Visitors.

Clark, Thomas Curtis
Abraham Lincoln, the Master.
Apparitions.
At Mount Vernon.
Blow, Bugle!
Bugle Song of Peace.
Call, The.
Challenge.
Common Blessings.
Farewell and Hail!
For Those Who Died.
Forgotten Star, The.
Glory of Lincoln, The.
He Shall Speak Peace.
Keep Love in Your Life.
Lincoln, Come Back.
Message of the Bells, The.
Mother.
My Country, Right!
On a World War Battlefield.
Poet's Call, The.
Search, The.
This Is America.
Trees.
Trust the Great Artist.
Wanderers.
We Thank Thee! ("For glowing autumn's brimming yield").
We Thank Thee! ("Not for our lands, our wide-flung prairie wealth").

Clark, Tom
And You Are There.
Baseball.
Baseball and Classicism.
Crows.
Daily News.
Difference, A.
Doors.
Eyeglasses.
Going to School in France or America.
Greeks, The.
Knot, The.
Lake, The: Coda.
Like Musical Instruments.
Poem: "Tiny new emotions, The."
Sonnet: "Orgasm completely, The."
Superballs.
To Bert Campaneris.
Ty Cobb Story, The.
X of the Unknown, The.
You, *sels.*

Clark, Walter
After Snow.
Free Will.
Morning After, The.
Uncle Death.

Clarke, Andrew Stuart Currie
Prayer: "Bless Thou this year, O Lord!"

Clarke, Austin
Aisling.
Ancient Lights.
Awakening of Dermuid, The.
Burial of an Irish President.
Celebrations.
Cypress Grove.
Dirge: "He lies in state."
Early Unfinished Sketch.
Envy of Poor Lovers, The.
Fair at Windgap, The.
Gracey Nugent.
Inscription for a Headstone.
Intercessors.
Irish-American Dignitary.
Japanese Print.
Jest, The.
Jewels, The.
Last Republicans, The.
Living in Sin.
Loss of Strength, The.
Lost Heifer, The.
Lucky Coin, The.
Marriage.
Martha Blake at Fifty-one.
Miss Marnell.
Mnemosyne Lay in Dust, *sels.*
My mother wept loudly.
Night and Morning.
Penal Law.
Pilgrimage.
Pill, The.
Planter's Daughter, The.
Respectable People.
Sermon on Swift, A.
Straying Student, The.
Strong Wind, A.
Tenebrae.
Three Poems about Children.
Tiresias, *sel.*
Usufruct.
Vengeance of Finn, The, *sel.*
Young Woman of Beare, The.

Clarke, C. R.
Song of the Mariner's Needle.

Clarke, Ednah Proctor
Mocking-Bird, The.
Salem Witch, A.
Clarke, F. W.
Rhyme of the Rain Machine, The.
Clarke, Frances (Frances Clarke Sayers)
Who Calls.
Clarke, George Frederick
Saint John, The.
Clarke, George Herbert
Fog-Horn.
Halt and Parley.
Over Salève.
Santa Maria del Fiore.
Clarke, Grant
Rag Time Cowboy Joe.
Clarke, Isabel C.
Anniversary of the Great Retreat.
Clarke, James Freeman
Brother, Hast Thou Wandered Far, *with music.*
Dear Friend, Whose Presence in the House, *with music.*
White-capped Waves.
Clarke, John Henrik
Determination.
Sing Me a New Song.
Clarke, Joseph I. C.
Fighting Race, The.
Pro Libra Mea.
Clarke, Pauline
My Name Is.
Clarke, Peter
In Air.
Play Song.
Young Shepherd Bathing His Feet.
Clarke, Willis Gaylord
Remembrance, A.
Claudel, Alice Moser
Southern Season.
Claudel, Paul
Fourth Station.
Our Lady, Help of Christians.
Claudian (Claudius Claudianus)
Epitaph: "Fate to beauty still must give."
Lonely Isle, The.
Old Man of Verona, The.
Claudius, Matthias
Most Acceptable Gift, The.
Clayre, Alasdair
Professor Drinking Wine.
Clayton, Arnold *and* **B. Woolf.** *See* **Woolf, B.** *and* **Arnold Clayton**
Claytor, Gertrude
Grant at Appomattox.
Cleanthes
God Leads the Way.
Hymn to Zeus.
Cleaveland, C. L.
November.
Cleaveland, Elizabeth Hannah Jocelyn
No Sects [*or* Sect] in Heaven.
Cleavland, Benjamin
O Could I Find from Day to Day, *with music.*
Cleghorn, Sarah Norcliffe
Come, Captain Age.
Comrade Jesus.
Contented at Forty.
Dorothea.
Emilia.
Golf Links, The.
Hemlock Mountain.
Incentive, The.
Quatrain: "Golf links lie so near the mill, The."
Saint R. L. S.
Survival of the Fittest, The.
Vermont.
Cleland, William
Hallo My Fancy.
Clemens, Samuel Langhorne. *See* **"Twain, Mark"**
Clement of Alexandria (Titus Flavius Clemens)
Earliest Christian Hymn.
Clementelli, Elena
Etruscan Notebook, *sels.*
Clements, John R.
God's Trails Lead Home.
Clemmons, Carole Gregory
Ghetto Lovesong—Migration.
I'm Just a Stranger Here, Heaven Is My Home.
Love from My Father.
Migration.
Spring.
Clemo, Jack R.
Burnt Bush, The.
Calvinist in Love, A.
Charlotte Nicholls.
Christ in the Clay-Pit.
Growing in Grace.
Mould of Castile.
Neither Shadow of Turning.
On the Death of Karl Barth.
Water-Wheel, The.
Winds, The.
Clephane, Elizabeth Cecilia
Lost Sheep, The.
Ninety and Nine, The.
Clerk, Sir John, of Penicuik
Fane Wald I Luve, *at.*
Miller, The.
O Merry May the Maid Be.
Clerke, William
So, So.
Cleveland, John
And why so coffined in this vile disguise.
Antiplatonick, The.
Author's Mock-Song to Mark Anthony, The.
Elegy on Ben Jonson [*or* Johnson], An.
Epitaph on the Earl of Strafford.
Fair Nymph Scorning a Black Boy Courting Her, A.
Fuscara; or, The Bee Errant.
General Eclipse, The.
Hecatomb to His Mistress, The.
King's Disguise, The, *sel.*
Mark Anthony [*or* Antony].
On Scotland.
On the Memory of Mr. Edward King, Drowned in the Irish Seas.
Rebel [*or* Rebell] Scot, The, *sels.*
Square-Cap.
To the State of Love; or, The Senses' Festival.
Upon an Hermaphrodite.
Upon Phillis Walking in a Morning before Sun-Rising.
Whenas the Nightingale.
Young Man to an Old Woman Courting Him, A.
Cleveland, Philip Jerome
By Night.
I Yield Thee Praise.
There Is a Love.
Clewell, David
After the Seance.
Clifford, Carrie Williams
Black Draftee from Dixie, The.
Clifford, Ethel
Dark Road, The.
Harp of Sorrow, The.
Last Hour, The.
Clifford, George, 3d Earl of Cumberland
My Thoughts Are Winged with Hopes, *at.*
To Cynthia, *at.*
Clifford, John
Anvil of God's Word, The.
God's Word.
Hammers and Anvil.
Clifton, Lucille
Admonitions.
Africa.
At Last We Killed the Roaches.
Confession.
Daddy.
Driving through New England.
Eviction.
Explanations.
1st, The.
For de Lawd.
Forgiving My Father.
Friends Come.
God Send Easter.
Good Times.
Her Love Poem.
Holy Night.
I Once Knew a Man.
I went to the valley.
If I Stand in My Window.
If Something Should Happen.
In Populated.
In Salem.
In the Inner City.
Incandescence.
Let There Be New Flowering.
Light That Came, The.
Listen Children.
Lost Baby Poem, The.
Love Rejected.
Malcolm.
Miss Rosie.
Mother, I Am.
My Mama Moved among the Days.
Perhaps.
Poet, The.
Raising of Lazarus, The.
Salt.
Still.
Testament.
Thirty eighth year, The.
This Morning.
Those Boys That Ran Together.
To Bobby Seale.
To Joan.
Way It Was, The.
Willie B (2).
Clive, Caroline
Conflict.
Clockadale, Jill
Change of Venue.
Close, John
In Respectful Memory of Mr. Yarker, *sel.*
Clothier, Cal
Soaring.
Cloud, Virginia Woodward
Ballad of Sweet P, The.
Care.
Mother's Song, The.
Old Street, An.
Youth.
Clough, Arthur Hugh
Actaeon.
Ah, That I Were Far Away.
All Is Well.
Ambarvalia, *sel.*
Amours de Voyage, *sels.*
As I Sat at the Café.
Bothie of Tober-na-Vuolich, The, *sels.*
Columbus.
Come Back.
Come Home, Come Home!
Currente Calamo.
Dipsychus, *sels.*
Duty.
Easter Day, Naples, 1849.
Easter Day II.
Engagement, The.
Grasses green of sweet content, The.
Green Fields of England.
Here Have I Been These One and Twenty Years.
Highland Glen near Loch Ericht, A.
Hope Evermore and Believe.
How Pleasant It Is to Have Money.
I Have Seen Higher, Holier Things than These.
Is it true, ye gods, who treat us.
Isolation.
It Fortifies My Soul to Know.
It is not sweet content, be sure.

Juxtaposition.
Keeping On.
Latest Decalogue, The.
Les Vaches.
Letter from Rome, A.
Look you, my simple friend, 'tis one of those.
Mari Magno, *sel.*
My Wind Is Turned to Bitter North.
Natura Naturans.
O Thou Whose Image.
Peschiera.
Philip returned to his books, but returned to his Highlands after.
Pont-y-Wern.
Put forth thy leaf, thou lofty plane.
Qua Cursum Ventus.
Qui Laborat, Orat.
Reply to Dipsychus.
Resignation—to Faustus.
Rome.
Say Not the Struggle [Nought Availeth].
Serve in Thy Post.
Sic Itur.
So Not Seeing I Sung.
So Pleasant It Is to Have Money.
Songs in Absence, *sel.*
Spectator ab Extra.
Spirit from Perfecter Ages, A.
Spirit's Song, The.
"There Is No God," the Wicked Saith.
To spend uncounted years of pain.
Upon Apennine Slope.
Valley and Villa of Horace, The.
Whate'er You Dream with Doubt Possest.
When the Dews Are Earliest Falling.
Where Lies the Land [to Which the Ship Would Go]?
"With Whom Is No Variableness, neither Shadow of Turning."
Would That I Were.
Ye Ancient Divine Ones.

Clouts, Sydney
Animal Kingdom.
Dawn Hippo.
Earth, Sky.
Firebowl.
Grave's Cherub, The.
Of Thomas Traherne and the Pebble Outside.
Poetry Is Death Cast Out.
Portrait of Prince Henry, The.
Prince Henry the Navigator.
Sea and the Eagle, The.
Sleeper, The.

Coan, Titus Munson
Crystal, The.
Dream of Flowers, A.
Nihil Humani Alienum.

Coates, Carol
Choral Symphony Conductor.
Circle, The.
Country Reverie.
Light.

Coates, Florence Earle
Angelus, The.
Be Thou My Guide.
Buffalo.
By the Conemaugh.
Death.
Dream the Great Dream.
Hero, A.
His Face.
House of Pain, The.
India.
Morning-Glory, The.
New Mars, The.
Per Aspera.
Perdita.
Pilgrim Song.
Requiem for a Young Soldier.
Seeker in the Night, A.
Song: "For me the jasmine buds unfold."
Song: "If love were but a little thing."
Suppliant.
Survival.
Tennyson.
Thanksgiving.
To-Morrow.
World Is Mine, The.

Coats, Adelbert Sumpter
Common Lot, The.
Pentecost.

Coatsworth, Elizabeth Jane
All Goats.
April Fool.
August Smiles.
Bad Kittens, The.
Barn, The.
Calling in the Cat.
Circus-Postered Barn, The.
Cold winter now is in the wood.
Columbus and the Mermaids.
Conquest.
Counters.
Country Barnyard.
Daniel Webster's Horses.
Down the Rain Falls.
Easter.
Ever Since.
Footnote to History.
He who has never known hunger.
Horse would tire, A.
How Gray the Rain.
January.
Labor of Fields.
Lady Comes to an Inn, A.
Lullaby: "Sleep, mouseling, sleep."
March.
Mountain Brook.
Mouse, The.
Navajo, The.
No Shop Does the Bird Use.
Nosegay.
November.
Old Mare, The.
On a Night of Snow.
Open Door, The.
Pirates.
Pleiades, The.
Rabbits' Song outside the Tavern, The.
Rhyme: "I like to see a thunder storm."
Roosters.
Sea Gull.
Sleigh Bells at Night.
Snow.
Song for a Little Cuckoo Clock.
Song for Midsummer Night.
Song of the Camels.
Song of the Rabbits outside the Tavern.
Storm, The.
Straws.
Sunday.
This Is the Hay That No Man Planted.
Warm of heart shall never lack a fire, The.
Ways of Trains, The.
Whale at Twilight.
What Could Be Lovelier than to Hear.
"Who are you?" asked the cat of the bear.
Wilderness Is Tamed, The.
Wilderness Rivers.
Winter Rune.

Cobb, Alice S.
Angela Davis.
Searching, The.

Cobb, Ann
Kivers.

Cobb, Charlie
"Containing Communism."
For Sammy Younge.
Nation.
To Vietnam.

Cobb, Will D.
School Days.
Somebody's Sweetheart I Want to Be, *with music.*
Waltz Me Around Again Willie; or, 'Round, 'Round, 'Round.

Coblentz, Catherine Cate
Housewife, The.
Our History.

Coblentz, Stanton Arthur
Calm.
History of the Modern World.
Land's End.
Last Trail, The.
On Some Trees Needlessly Slain.
Prayer for Light.
We Who Build Visions.

Coburn, Wallace D.
Cow-Boy Fun.
Cowboy's Fate, The.
Stampede, The.

Coccimiglio, Vic
Visit.

Cochrane, Alfred
Eight-Day Clock, The.
Omnia Vincit.
To Anthea, Who May Command Him Anything (New Style).
Upon Lesbia—Arguing.

Cochrane, Frances
Face to Face.

Cochrane, Shirley
Leaving Home.

"Cockatoo Jack"
Numerella Shore, The.

Cockburn, Alison Rutherford
Flowers of the Forest, The.

Cocke, Zitella
My Cross.

Cockrell, Doug
Field Work.
Fist Fight.
His Lunch Bucket.
Hunting at Dusk.

Cocteau, Jean
Plain Song, *sel.*
To a Sleeping Friend.

Codish, Edward
Juggle of Myrtle Twigs, A.
Yetzer ha Ra.

Codrescu, Andrei
Grammar, A.
Imagination of Necessity, The.
Poetry Paper.
Work.

Cody, Hiram Alfred
Old Figurehead Carver, The.
Old Ship Riggers.

Coe, Alice Rollit
Turn of the Road, The.

Coe, Peter
Wizard of Alderley Edge, The.

Coffey, Brian
Advent, *sel.*
Headrock.
Missouri Sequence, *sel.*
Muse, June, Related, *sel.*
"Nicest Phantasies Are Shared, The."
Odalisque.

Coffin, Robert Barry ("Barry Gray")
Ships at Sea.

Coffin, Robert Peter Tristram
Alexander Graham Bell Did Not Invent the Telephone.
America Was Schoolmasters.
Christening-Day Wishes for My God-Child.
Covered Bridge.
Cows Are Coming Home in Maine.
Fog, The.
Graveyard.
Hound on the Church Porch.
Little Boys of Texas.
Pheasant, The ("The pheasant cock sprang into view").
Secret Heart, The.
Skunk, The.

Spider, The.
Square-toed Princes.
Starfish, The.
Yankee Cradle.
Young Calves, The.
Coghill, Mary
Knowing.
Coghill, Rhoda
Bright Hillside, The.
Dead.
In Wicklow.
Plough-Horse, The.
Poem: "Is to love, this—to nurse a name."
Runaway.
Spring Doggerel.
Young Bride's Dream, The.
Cohan, George M.
Forty-five Minutes from Broadway, *with music.*
Give My Regards to Broadway, *with music.*
Life's a Funny Proposition after All.
Mary's a Grand Old Name.
Yankee Doodle Boy, The, *with music.*
You're a Grand Old Flag, *with music.*
Cohen, Jacob
Eternal Jew, The.
Harp of David, The.
Surely My Soul.
Cohen, Leonard
Another Night with Telescope.
As the Mist Leaves No Scar.
Ballad: "My lady was found mutilated."
Bus, The.
Celebration.
Credo.
Elegy: "Do not look for him."
For Anne.
For E. J. P.
Genius, The.
Gift.
Heirloom.
I Have Not Lingered in European Monasteries.
I Wonder How Many People in This City.
Killers That Run, The.
Kite Is a Victim, A.
Music Crept by Us, The.
Only Tourist in Havana Turns His Thoughts Homeward, The.
Out of the Land of Heaven.
Poem: "I heard of a man."
Poem for Marc Chagall.
Prayer for Messiah.
Queen Victoria and Me.
Sleeping Beauty, The.
Story of Isaac.
Suzanne Takes You Down.
What I'm Doing Here.
You Do Not Have to Love Me.
You Have the Lovers.
Cohen, Robert David
Bones of Incontention, The.
Day on Kind Continent.
Storm, The.
Street of Named Houses, The.
Cohen, Shlomit
Same Dream, The.
Unraveled Thought, An.
Wife of Kohelet.
Cohn, Myra
Sliding.
Coignard, Gabrielle de
Prayer: "Fear of death disturbs me constantly, The."
Cokayne, Sir Aston
Epitaph on a Great Sleeper.
Funeral Elegy on the Death of His Very Good Friend, Mr. Michael Drayton.
Of a Mistress.
To Plautia.
Colaizzi, Randall
Telemachus and the Bow.
Colby, Joan
Equestrienne.
How the Sky Begins to Fall.
Magician, The.
Old Nudists, The.
Rose Red to Snow White.
Colby, Vine
Rainbow, The.
Colclough, Phil *and* June Colclough
Blood on the Sails.
Song for Ireland.
Colcord, Lincoln
Fishing Fleet, The.
Cole, Barry
Men Are Coming Back, The.
Cole, Bob
Under the Bamboo Tree, *with music.*
Cole, Eugene Roger
Oh, You Wholly Rectangular.
Cole, George Douglas Howard
Civil Riot, *sel.*
Cole, Harriet
End of the Way, The.
Cole, James
Wheel, The.
Cole, Joanna
Driving to the Beach.
Happy New Year, Anyway.
Hippopotamus.
Cole, Margaret Postgate
Afterwards.
Falling Leaves, The.
Praematuri.
Veteran, The.
Cole, Samuel Valentine
Abraham Lincoln.
Hammer and Anvil.
Satisfied.
Trees, The.
Cole, Thomas
By the Beautiful Sea.
La Grande Jatte: Sunday Afternoon.
Landscape of Love, The.
Life of Hubert, The, *sels.*
Memories of a Dorset Childhood in the 1730's.
My Lady Takes the Sunlight for Her Gown.
Old Woman's Song.
Praise to Light.
Spider.
Tray, The.
Variations on a Still Morning.
Cole, Timothy
Year's End, The.
Cole, William
Alma Mater, Forget Me.
Back Yard, July Night.
Bananananananananana.
Did You?
Epitaph on a Career Woman.
Geeandess.
Have I Got Dogs!
Hypnopompic Poem.
Just Dropped In.
Lost Contact.
Marriage Couplet.
Mutual Problem.
Mysterious East.
Poor Kid.
Question, A.
Saturday Review, The.
Sneaky Bill.
Time Piece.
Undersea Fever.
War Horses.
What a Friend We Have in Cheeses!
What Could It Be?
Coleman, Elliott
Sirens.
Winter over Nothing.
Coleman, Emily Holmes
Liberator, The.
Coleman, Helena
As Day Begins to Wane.
More Lovely Grows the Earth.
Coleman, Herbert T. J.
Cockle-Shell and Sandal-Shoon.
Poet Confides, The.
Coleman, Horace
Black Soldier Remembers, A.
Poem for a "Divorced" Daughter.
Remembrance of Things Past.
Coleman, Lucile
With Lilacs in My Eye.
Coleman, Mary Joan
Grandfather.
Coleman, Victor
Day Twenty-three.
How the Death of a City Is Never More than the Sum of the Deaths of Those Who Inhabit Its Spaces.
Coleridge, Hartley
Address to Certain Gold Fishes.
Butter's Etymological Spelling Book ("Butter's books I ne'er have read").
Death-Bed Reflections of Michel-Angelo.
Dedicatory Sonnet to S. T. Coleridge.
Early Death.
Friendship.
From Country to Town.
Full Well I Know.
Hast Thou Not Seen an Aged Rifted Tower.
He Lived amidst th' Untrodden Ways.
How Shall a Man Fore-doomed.
If I Have Sinn'd in Act.
Lines
Long Time a Child.
May, 1840.
"Multum Dilexit."
Night.
November.
On the Death of Echo.
On Wordsworth.
Poietes Apoietes.
Prayer: "Be not afraid to pray—to pray is right."
Reply.
She Is Not Fair [to Outward View].
Solitary-Hearted, The.
Song: "She is not fair to outward view."
Song: " 'Tis sweet to hear the merry lark."
Sonnet: "Long time a child, and still a child, when years."
Sonnet: To a Friend.
Sonnets to the Seasons, *sel.*
Summer Rain.
There Lived among the Untrodden Ways.
Three Sonnets, *sel.*
'Tis Strange to Me.
To a Cat.
To a Deaf and Dumb Little Girl.
To a Friend.
To a Lofty Beauty, from Her Poor Kinsman.
What Is Young Passion.
Whither Is Gone [the Wisdom and the Power].
Coleridge, Mary Elizabeth
After Reading Certain Books.
After St. Augustine.
At a Friends' Meeting.
Awake.
Blue and White.
Change.
Clever Woman, A.
Companionship.
Cut It Down.
Death, *sel.*
Dedication, A: "Life of my learning, fire of all my Art."
Depart from Me.
Deserted House, The.
Egypt's Might Is Tumbled Down.
From My Window.
Gibberish.
Gifts.
Gone.
Good Friday in My Heart.
"He Knoweth Not That the Dead Are Thine."

Huguenot, A.
I Saw a Stable.
In Dispraise of the Moon.
Jealousy.
King, The.
L'Oiseau Bleu.
Lord of the Winds.
Marriage.
Mortal Combat.
"My True Love Hath My Heart and I Have His."
On Such a Day.
Other Side of a Mirror, The.
Our Lady.
Punctilio.
Street Lanterns.
There.
"There Was No Place Found."
Three Helpers in Battle.
Unwelcome.
We Never Said Farewell.
Where a Roman Villa Stood, above Freiburg.
White Women, The.
Whither Away?
Witch, The.
Witches' Wood, The.

Coleridge, Samuel Taylor
Aeolian Harp, The.
Answer to a Child's Question.
Apologia pro Vita Sua.
Ballad of the Dark Ladie, The.
Broken Friendship.
Charity in Thought.
Child's Evening Prayer, A.
Christabel.
Christmas Carol, A: "Shepherds went their hasty way."
Cologne.
Complaint.
Dejection; an Ode.
Desired Swan-Song, The.
Destiny of Nations, The, *sels.*
Eolian Harp, The.
Epigram: "What is an epigram? a dwarfish whole."
Epigram: " 'What? rise again with all one's bones.' "
Epitaph: "Stop, Christian passer-by!—Stop, child of God."
Epitaph on Himself ("Here sleeps at length poor Col, and without screaming").
Exchange, The.
Fears in Solitude.
Fragment, A: "Encinctured with a twine of leaves."
Fragment: "Spruce and limber yellow-hammer, The."
France; an Ode.
Frost at Midnight.
Fruit Plucker, The.
Glycine's Song.
Good Great Man, The.
He Prayeth Best.
Human Life; on the Denial of Immortality.
Hymn before Sunrise, in the Vale of Chamouni[x].
If I Had but Two Little Wings.
In a Moonlight Wilderness.
Inscription for a Fountain on a Heath.
Invocation, An: "Hear, sweet Spirit, hear the Spell."
Knight's Tomb, The.
Koskiusko.
Kubla Khan; or, A Vision in a Dream.
La Fayette.
Lewti.
Life.
Limbo.
Looking Down on Nether Stowey.
Love.
Love's Apparition and Evanishment.
Mathematical Problem, A.
Metrical Feet.
Modern Critics.
My Baptismal Birthday.
Ne Plus Ultra.
Nightingale, The.
O, Lift One Thought.
O My Mother Isle! ("Not yet enslaved, not wholly vile.")
O My Mother Isle! ("O native Britain! O my Mother Isle!")
Ode on the Departing Year, *sel.*
Ode to the Departing Year.
On a Bad Singer.
On a Discovery Made Too Late.
On a Lord.
On a Ruined House in a Romantic Country.
On Donne's Poem "To a Flea."
On Donne's Poetry.
On My Joyful Departure [from the City of Cologne].
Or wren or linnet.
Pains of Sleep, The.
Pantisocracy.
Phantom.
Phantom or Fact.
Raven, The.
Recollections of Love.
Reflections on Having Left a Place of Retirement.
Religious Musings.
Remorse, *sel.*
Rhymester, A.
Rime of the Ancient Mariner, The.
Scars Remaining, The.
Sea-ward, White Gleaming [through the Busy Scud].
Seen from the Quantocks.
Self-Knowledge.
Silent Icicles, The.
Something Childish, but Very Natural.
Song: "Sunny shaft did I behold, A."
Song of the Pixies.
Sonnet: Oft o'er My Brain.
Sonnet: To the River Otter.
Sonnet to a Friend Who Asked, How I Felt When the Nurse First Presented My Infant to Me.
Swans Sing [before They Die].
This Lime-Tree Bower My Prison.
Three Graves, The, *sel.*
Time, Real and Imaginary.
To a Young Ass.
To a Young Friend, *sel.*
To Nature.
To the Reverend W. L. Bowles.
To William Wordsworth.
Tombless Epitaph, A, *sel.*
Truth I pursued, as Fancy sketch'd the way.
Voice Sings, A.
W. H. *Eheu!*
What Is Life?
Work without Hope.
Youth and Age.
Zapolya, *sel.*

Coleridge, Sara
Garden Year, The.
He Came Unlook'd For.
I Was a Brook.
Months, The.
Mother, The.
Phantasmion, *sels.*
Song: "He came unlook'd for, undesir'd."
Trees.

Coles, Don
Natalya Nikolayevna Goncharov.
Photograph in a Stockholm Newspaper for March 13, 1910.

Colesworthy, Daniel C.
While We Lowly Bow before Thee, *with music.*

College, Stephen
Raree Show, A.
Truth Brought to Light, or Murder Will Out.

Collier, Edward A.
After the Rain.

Collier, John
Pluralist and Old Soldier, The.

Collier, Mary
Washerwoman, The.
Woman's Labour, The; an Epistle to Mr. Stephen Duck, *sel.*

Collier, Michael
Counting.

Collier, Thomas Stephens
Cleopatra Dying.
Compensation.
Disappointment.
Infallibility.
Power.
Spectre Ship, The.
Time.

Collin, Sepley
Schooner *Kandahar*, The, *with music, at.*

Collin, William Edwin
Monserrat.
Sancho.

Collins, Anne
Song: "My straying thoughts, reduced stay."

Collins, Emanuel
Fatal Dream, The; or, The Unhappy Favourite.

Collins, Helen Johnson
To an Avenue Sport.

Collins, John
Chapter of Kings, The.
Tomorrow.

Collins, Leslie Morgan
Creole Girl.
Stevedore.

Collins, Martha
Retreat.

Collins, Mary Gabrielle
Women at Munition Making.

Collins, Mortimer
Ad Chloen, M.A.
If.
Kate Temple's Song.
Martial in London.
My Thrush.
Positivists, The.
Queen and Slave.
Salad, *sels.*
To F. C.

Collins, Ruth
Song of a Factory Worker, The.

Collins, W. F.
Lincoln Statue, The.

Collins, William
Captain Molly.
Fidele.
How Sleep the Brave.
Lookout, The.
Ode Occasioned [*or* Occasion'd] by the Death of Mr. Thomson.
Ode on the Poetical Character.
Ode on the Popular Superstitions of the Highlands of Scotland, An [Considered as the Subject of Poetry].
Ode to Evening.
Ode to Fear.
Ode to Mercy.
Ode to Pity.
Ode to Simplicity.
Ode Written in 1746.
Passions, The; an Ode for [*or* to] Music.
St. Kilda.
Sleep of the Brave, The.
Sonnet: "When Phoebe form'd a wanton smile."
Stormy Hebrides, The.
To Evening.

Collinson, Laurence
Sea and the Tiger, The.

Collop, John
Leper Cleansed, The.
To the Soul.

Collyer, Robert
Saxon Grit.
Under the Snow.
Collymore, Frank A.
Zobo Bird, The.
Colman, Saint
Hymn against Pestilence, *sel, at.*
Colman, Benjamin
Another to Urania.
God of My Life!
Hymn of Praise on a Recovery from Sickness, A.
Poem on Elijahs Translation, A.
Quarrel with Fortune, A.
To Philomela.
To Urania.
Colman, George, the Younger
Gluggity Glug.
Maid of the Moor, The; or, The Water-Fiends, *sel.*
My Muse and I, Ere Youth and Spirits Fled.
Myrtle and the Vine, The, *sel.*
On Sir Nathaniel Wraxall the Historian.
Unfortunate Miss Bailey.
Colman, Mary Elizabeth
We Men Are of Two Worlds.
Colombo, John Robert
How They Made the Golem.
Ideal Angels.
Riverdale Lion.
What Pablo Picasso Did in "Les Demoiselles d'Avignon."
Colonna, Vittoria, marchesa di Pescara
As When Some Hungry Fledgling Hears and Sees.
I live on this depraved and lonely cliff.
Like a hungry fledgeling that watches and hears.
O what transparent waves, what a tranquil sea.
When the Orient is lit by the great light.
When the troubled sea swells and surrounds.
Colony, Horatio
Autumnal.
Ghost Pet.
Gold That Fell on Danae.
Summer Lightning.
Thunder over Earth.
Young Prince, The.
Colquitt, Betsy
Photographing the Facade—San Miguel de Allende.
Colton, Arthur Willis
Allah's Tent.
Faustine.
Harps Hung Up in Babylon.
Phillis and Corydon.
Song with a Discord, A.
Colton, Walter
Leap for Life, A.
Colum, Mary M.
Dirge of the Lone Woman.
Colum, Padraic
Across the Door.
After Speaking of One Dead a Long Time.
At Ferns Castle.
Ballad of Downal Baun, The.
Belfast: High Street.
Book of Kells, The.
Burial of Saint Brendan, The.
Catalpa Tree.
Condors.
Cradle Song, A: "O men from the fields."
Dahlias.
Drover, A.
Dublin: The Old Squares.
Fourth Station.
Fuchsia Hedges in Connacht.
Garadh.
Garland Sunday.
I Saw the Wind Today.
Interior.
Irises.
Knitters, The.
Lilies.
Lullaby: "O men from the fields."
Monkeys.
No Child.
Old Man Said, An.
Old Soldier.
Old Woman of the Roads, An.
Olive Trees.
On Not Hearing the Birds Sing in Ireland.
Peach Tree with Fruit.
Plougher, The.
Poor Scholar of the 'Forties, A.
Poplar Tree.
Puppet Play, The.
River-Mates.
Sea Bird to the Wave, The.
She Moved through the Fair.
Spider.
Stations of the Cross, The.
Terrible Robber Men, The.
Toy-Maker, The.
Tulips.
Wall of China, The.
Wild Ass.
Wind, The.
Columcille [*or* Columba], Saint
Clamour of the wind making music.
Columcille's Greeting to Ireland, *abr., at.*
Day of Wrath, The.
Farewell to Ireland, *at.*
On a Dead Scholar, *sel.*
On some island I long to be.
Combe, William
Dr. Syntax in Search of the Picturesque, *sels.*
In Search of the Picturesque.
Combs, Tram
Ars Poetica about Ultimates.
Aware Aware.
I Flung Up My Arm Half from Sleep.
Just after Noon with Fierce Shears.
Cometas
Country Gods.
Comfort, Alex
After Shakespeare.
After You, Madam.
Atoll in the Mind, The.
Epitaph: "One whom I knew, a student and a poet."
Fear of the Earth.
Haste to the Wedding.
Hoc Est Corpus.
I saw a woman in a green field.
In the stony night move the stars' white mouths.
Letter to an American Visitor.
Love Poem: "There is a white mare that my love keeps."
Lovers, The.
Moon fills up its hollow bowl of milk, The.
Notes for My Son.
Pick upon Pick.
Poem: "One whom I knew, a student and a poet."
Postures of Love, The, *sels.*
Song for the Heroes.
Song of Lazarus, The, *sel.*
Sublimation.
This was Briseis' way: she was a bridge.
Comfort, Florence Crocker
Make Way!
Compiuta Donzella
To leave the world and serve God.
Comyn, Michael
Oisin in the Land of Youth.
Conant, Isabel Fiske
Emergency.
Many Wings.
Conant-Bissell, Jane
Milton's Wife on Her Twenty-third Birthday.
Conard, Audrey
Clinic: Examination.
Vegetarian Sings, A.
Conder, Josiah
Bread of Heaven, on Thee We Feed.
Day by Day the Manna Fell.
Cone, Helen Gray ("Coroebus Green")
Arraignment.
Ballad of Cassandra Brown, The.
Common Street, The.
Contrast, The.
Dandelions, The.
Fair England.
Heartbreak Road.
Last Cup of Canary, The.
Narcissus in Camden.
Ride to the Lady, The.
Spring Beauties, The.
Thisbe.
Yellow Pansy, A.
Confucius
Airs of Pei, *sel.*
Alba ("Creeper grows over thorn").
Aliter.
Baroness Mu Impeded in Her Wish to Help Famine Victims in Wei.
Chou and the South.
Classic Anthology, The, *sel.*
Deer Sing, *sel.*
Efficient Wife's Complaint, The.
Fraternitas.
Pedlar.
Sans Equity and sans Poise.
Shao and the South, *sels.*
Songs of Ch'en, *sels.*
Songs of Cheng, *sels.*
Songs of T'ang, *sel.*
Wei Wind, *sel.*
Yung Wind, *sels.*
Congdon, Kirby
Daredevil.
Conger, Marion
Fall Days.
Congreve, William
Amoret.
Better Bargain, The.
Buxom Joan.
Doris.
False Though She Be.
Hue and Cry after Fair Amoret, A.
Jack Frenchman's Defeat.
Letter to Viscount Cobham.
Love for Love, *sel.*
Mourning Bride, The, *sels.*
Nil Admirari.
Nymph and a Swain, A.
Old Bachelor, The, *sel.*
Pious Selinda [*or* Celinda].
Soldier and a Sailor, A.
Song: "Ah stay! ah turn! ah whither would you fly."
Song: "False though she be to me and love."
Song: "Pious Selinda goes to prayers."
Song: "See, see, she wakes! Sabina wakes."
Souldier and a Sailor, A.
Conkling, Grace Hazard
After Sunset.
Goatherd, The.
I Have Cared for You, Moon.
Letter to Elsa, A.
Little Rose Is Dust, My Dear, The.
Nightingales.
Road to the Pool, The.
Snail, The.
Star, The.
Tampico.
To a New-born Baby Girl.
Victory Bells.
Whole Duty of Berkshire Brooks, The.
Wind's Way, The.
Conkling, Hilda
Butterfly.
Chickadee.
Dandelion.
Fairies.

I Am.
Little Papoose.
Little Snail.
Loveliness.
Moon Song.
Mouse.
Spring Song.
Water.
Weather.

Conley, Robert J.
Hills of *Tsa la gi,* The.
Ned Christie.
Rattlesnake Band, The.
Tom Starr.
Wili Woyi, Shaman, Also Known as Billy Pigeon.

Conn, Stewart
Marriage on a Mountain Ridge.
Todd.
Under Creag Mhor.
Visiting Hour.

Connell, Charles
Wyvern.

Connell, Hugh
Dream, A.
Erris Coast, 1943.
Mountain Tree, The.

Connell, Jim
New Words to the Tune of "O'Donnel Abu."
Red Flag, The.

Connellan, Leo
Watching Jim Shoulders.

Conniff, Richard
Dublin Doggerel.
Misogynist.

Connolly, Francis X.
No More Destructive Flame.

Connolly, Myles E.
Quo Vadis?
Said the Innkeeper.

Connor, Tony
Apologue.
Elegy for Alfred Hubbard.
Lancashire Winter.

Connor, Torrey
Old Casa, The.

Conolly, Luke Aylmer
Enchanted Island, The.

Conquest, Robert
Adriatic.
Agents, The.
Aids to Composition.
Appalachian Convalescence.
Art and Civilization.
By Rail through Istria.
Excerpt from a Report to the Galactic Council.
Generalities.
Guided Missiles Experimental Range.
Horror Comic.
Lake Success.
Man and Woman.
Motives of Rhythm, The.
Near the Death of Ovid.
On the Danube.
Rokeby Venus, The.
Seal Rocks: San Francisco.
Semantic.
747 (London–Chicago).
To Be a Pilgrim.

Conrad, May Ricker
What Does Easter Mean to You?

Conrard, Harrison
Dead on the Desert.
Hopi Prayer, A.
In Old Tucson.

Constable, Henry
Damelus' [*or* Damelias'] Song to [*or* of] His Diaphenia, *at.*
Diaphenia, *at.*
Love's Franciscan.
My Lady's Presence Makes the Roses Red.
Needs Must I Leave, and Yet Needs Must I Love.
O Gracious Shepherd.
Of the Nativity of the Lady Rich's Daughter.
On Sir Philip Sidney.
On the Death of Sir Philip Sidney.
Sonnet: "Dear to my soul! then leave me not forsaken!"
Sonnet: "If ever Sorrow spoke from soul that loves."
Sonnet: "My lady's presence makes the roses red."
Sonnets to Diana.
To God the Father.
To God the Son.
To His Flocks, *at.*
To Live in Hell, and Heaven to Behold.
To Our Blessed Lady.
To Saint Catherine.
To Saint Margaret.
To Saint Mary Magdalen.
To Sir Philip Sidney's Soul.
To the Blessed Sacrament.

Constable, Thomas
Old October.

Constantine of Rhodes
Before the Ikon of the Mother of God.

Contoski, Victor
Broken Treaties, *sel.*
Dream 1971.
Invitation.
Mailman, The.
Money.
Moonlit Night in Kansas.
Nocturne for the U.S. Congress.
Suicides of the Rich, The.
Those I Love.

Contractus, Hermanus
Alma Redemptoris Mater, *at.*
Salve Regina, *at.*

Converse, Florence
Rune of Riches.

Conway, Hugh
Falkland at Newbury, 1643.

Conway, Katherine Eleanor
Heaviest Cross of All, The.
Saturninus.

Conway, Margaret Devereaux
Annunciation, The.

Conyus
Great Santa Barbara Oil Disaster Or, The.
He's Doing Natural Life.
San Francisco County Jail Cell B-6.
Six Ten Sixty-nine.
Untitled Requiem for Tomorrow.
Upon Leaving the Parole Board Hearing.

Coogler, J. Gordon
Alas! Carolina!
Alas! for the South.
Byron.
In Memorial.
Mustacheless Bard, A.
Poor South! Her books get fewer and fewer.
Pretty Girl, A.
To Amy.

Cook,
So nigh is grandeur to man.

Cook, Clarence Chatham.
On One Who Died in May.

Cook, Eliza
Englishman, The.
Indian Hunter, The.
Mouse and the Cake, The.
My Old Straw Hat.
Old Arm-Chair, The.
Sailor's Grave, The.
Song of the Seaweed, *sel.*
They All Belong to Me.
Where There's a Will There's a Way.

Cook, Joseph
Rhyme for a Chemical Baby.
Rhyme for a Geological Baby.
Rhyme for Astronomical Baby.
Rhyme for Botanical Baby.

Cook, Mrs. M. A. W.
In Some Way or Other the Lord Will Provide, *with music.*

Cook, Mike
Bootie Black and the Seven Giants.

Cook, Paul H.
Driving through the Pima Indian Reservation.

Cook, R. L.
Tonight the City.

Cook, Russell Sturgis
Just as Thou Art, *with music.*

Cook, Stanley
Christmas Tree.

Cook, Warren F.
Revelation.

Cook, William W.
Hudson Hornet.

Cooke, Edmund Vance
Born without a Chance.
Fin de Siècle.
How Did You Die?
Moo-Cow-Moo, The.
"Off Manilly."
Perfect Gift, The.
Rags.

Cooke, John Esten
Band in the Pines, The.

Cooke, Michael G.
Unseen Fire, An.

Cooke, Philip Pendleton
Florence Vane.

Cooke, Rose Terry
Arachne.
Bluebeard's Closet.
Death of Goody Nurse, The.
Done For.
In Vain.
Lise.
Segovia and Madrid.
Snow-filled Nest, The.
Then.
Two Villages.

Coolbrith, Ina
From Russian Hill.
Fruitionless.
Helen Hunt Jackson.
Mariposa Lily, The.
When the Grass Shall Cover Me.

Cooley, Julia. *See* **Altrocchi, Julia Cooley**

Cooley, Peter
Alternatives.
Confession, The.
Frog Hunting.
Other, The.
Such Comfort as the Night Can Bring to Us.
To a Wasp Caught in the Storm Sash at the Advent of the Winter Solstice.
Vanishing Point.

Coolidge, Grace Goodhue (Mrs. Calvin Coolidge)
Open Door, The.

"Coolidge, Susan" (Sarah Chauncey Woolsey)
Bind-Weed.
Calvary and Easter.
Charlotte Brontë.
Child's Thought of Harvest, A.
Commonplace.
Easter Song, An.
Edenhall.
Gulf Stream.
Helen.
How the Leaves Came Down.
Measles in the Ark.
New Every Morning.
Time to Go.
When.

Coon, Jeanette Saxton
Mother's Prayer, A.

Cooper, Alice Cecilia
San Juan Capistrano.

Cooper, Belle
Street Melody, A.
Vintage, The.
Cooper, Charles
Dreams.
Honky.
Idle Chatter.
Rubin.
Cooper, Edith *and* **Katherine Bradley.** *See* **"Field, Michael"**
Cooper, George
Baby-Land.
Bob White.
Come, Little Leaves.
October's Party.
Only One Mother.
Our Mother.
Sweet Genevieve.
What Robin Told.
While the Days Are Going By.
Why Did They Dig Ma's Grave So Deep?
Cooper, James Fenimore (1789–1851)
My Brigantine.
Water Witch, The, *sel.*
Cooper, James Fenimore (1892–1918)
Fate.
To a Friend.
Cooper, Jane
Childhood in Jacksonville, Florida.
Circle, a Square, a Triangle and a Ripple of Water, A.
Faithful, The.
For a Very Old Man, on the Death of His Wife.
Graveyard, The.
House Poem.
Hunger Moon.
In the House of the Dying.
Knowledge That Comes through Experience, The.
Morning on the St. John's.
My Young Mother.
Obligations.
Praise.
Rent.
Rock Climbing.
Waiting.
Weather of Six Mornings, The.
Cooper, John Gilbert
Epistles to His Friends in Town, *sel.*
Temper of Aristippus, The.
Cooper, Julian
Warm Winter Day, A.
Cooper, Junius
Jabberwocky; as the Author of "The Faerie Queene" Might Have Written It.
Cooper, Leonard
Rhyming Prophecy for a New Year.
Cooper, Roger
To See the Cross at Christmas.
Cooperman, Hasye
Mists Are Rising Now, The.
Cooperman, Robert
All Up and Down the Lines.
Cooperman, Stanley
Redemption.
Cope, Jack
Flying Fish, The.
If You Come Back.
Rock Painting.
Sappho.
Sons.
Cope, Wendy
Budgie Finds His Voice.
Mr. Strugnell.
Copeland, Benjamin
Christ's Life Our Code, *with music.*
Our Fathers' God, *with music.*
Copenhaver, Laura S.
Heralds of Christ, *with music.*
Coppard, Alfred Edgar
Apostate, The.
Epitaph: "Like silver dew are the tears of love."
Forester's Song.
Horse, The.
Mendacity.
Unfortunate Miller, The.
Coppinger, Matthew
Song, A: "I will not tell her that she's fair."
To Clelia.
Corbet, Richard
Certain True Woords Spoken Concerning One Benet Corbett [after Her Death].
Distracted Puritan, The.
Elegie upon the Death of His Owne Father, An.
Epitaph on Doctor Donne, Deane of Pauls, An.
Faeryes Farewell, The; or, God-a-Mercy Will.
Fairies' Farewell, The.
Farewell, Rewards and Fairies.
Farewell to the Fairies.
Great Tom.
Like to the Thundering Tone.
Little lute, when I am gone.
Non Sequitor, A.
Nonsense.
On Mr. Francis Beaumont (Then Newly Dead).
Proper New Ballad, Intituled The Fairies [*or* Faeryes] Farewell, A; or, God-a-Mercy Will.
To His Son [*or* Sonne], Vincent Corbet[t] [on His Birth-Day, November 10, 1630].
Upon Fairford Windows.
Corbett, E. R.
Inventor's Wife, The.
Corbett, Elizabeth T.
Misspelled Tail, A.
Tail of the See, A.
Three Wise Couples, The.
Three Wise [Old] Women.
Corbière, Tristan (Edouard Joachim Corbière)
Epitaph: "Or many things adulterate."
Litany of Sleep, *sel.*
Paris at Night.
To My Mouse-colored Mare.
To the Eternal Feminine.
Toad, The.
Corbin, Alice (Alice Corbin Henderson)
Buffalo Dance.
Courtship.
Echoes of Childhood.
Fallen.
Green Corn Dance, The.
Indian Death.
Juan Quintana.
Listening.
Love Me at Last.
Parting.
Sand Paintings.
Two Voices.
What Dim Arcadian Pastures.
Where the Fight Was.
Wind, The.
Corbin, Lloyd M. Jr. (Djangatolum)
Ali.
Dedication to the Final Confrontation.
Corcos, Francine
I Suppose Her Mother Told Her.
Corder, W.
Murder of Maria Marten, The.
Coren, Alan
By the Klondike River.
Corey, Del
Hypodermic Release.
Corinna (fl. c.500? B.C.). *See* **Korinna**
"Corinna" (contemporary)
Sehnsucht; or, What You Will.
Corke, Hilary
Any Man to His Secretary.
Calm Winter Sleep.
Chair, Dog, and Clock.
Choice, The.
Destroying Angel.
Ghost, The.
November Poppies.
Poem at Equinox.
Snake, The.
Storm of Love, A.
Waiting.
Waltz, The.
Corkery, Daniel
Call, The.
No Miracle.
Cormac Mac Cuilenan
Book of Leinster, *sel.*
Heavenly Pilot, The.
Cormack, Barbara Villy
Reprieve.
Corman, Cid
Big Grave Creek.
Blessings Are.
Call it a louse—I'm.
Cincinnati.
Container, The.
Deceased.
Desk, The.
Detail, The.
I Promessi Sposi.
I'm a Baby.
It's Food.
La Selva.
Locus, The.
Old Men, The.
Old Pines, The.
Poppy, The.
So Little Wanted.
There are things to be said. No doubt.
This Is the Non-existent Beast.
Three Tiny Songs.
Tortoise, The.
Toy, The.
Without You.
Cormican, P. J.
True Son of God, Eternal Light, *with music.*
Corn, Alfred
Darkening Hotel Room.
Deception.
Documentary on Brazil, The.
Dreambooks.
Fifty-seventh Street and Fifth.
Fire: The People.
Grass.
Moving: New York—New Haven Line.
Tokyo West.
Cornelius, Maxwell N.
Some Time We'll Understand.
Cornelius, Peter
Christmas Tree, The.
Cornell, Annette Patton
Sailor's Woman.
Cornford, Frances (Darwin)
After the Party.
All Souls' Night.
At Night.
Autumn Morning at Cambridge.
Childhood.
Coast, The: Norfolk.
Corner of the Field, The.
Country Bedroom, The.
Daybreak.
Epitaph for a Timid Lady.
For M.S. Singing *Fruhlingsglaube* in 1945.
Glimpse, A.
Guitarist Tunes Up, The.
Herd, The.
Hills, The.
In France.
In the Backs.
Inscription for a Wayside Spring.
London Despair.
Near an Old Prison.
Night Song.
On the Beach.
Parting in Wartime.
Preëxistence.
Quatrain: "Young Apollo, golden-haired, A."
Recollection, A.
Scholar, The.
She Warns Him.

Single Woman, The.
Summer Beach.
Susan to Diana.
To a Fat Lady Seen from the Train.
Unbeseechable, The.
Village before Sunset.
Wasted Day, A.
Watch, The.
Weekend Stroll.
Youth.
Cornford, John
Full Moon at Tierz; before the Storming of Huesca.
Huesca.
Letter from Aragon, A.
Cornish, Sam
April 68.
Black Man, A.
Death of Dr. King.
Dory Miller.
Frederick Douglass.
Home.
Lenox Christmas Eve 68.
Montgomery.
One Eyed Black Man in Nebraska.
Panther.
Ray Charles.
River, The.
Sam's World ("Sam's mother has").
Sooner or Later.
To a Single Shadow without Pity.
When My Grandmother Died.
Your Mother.
Cornish, William
Desire.
Gratitude.
Knight and the Lady, The.
Latet Anguis.
Pleasure It Is.
Spring.
"Cornwall, Barry" (Bryan Waller Procter)
Blood Horse, The.
Fate of the Oak, The.
For a Fountain.
Hermione.
Hunter's Song, The.
Inscription for a Fountain.
Is My Lover On the Sea?
Poet's Song to His Wife, The.
Sea, The.
Sea, The—in Calm.
Sit Down, Sad Soul.
Softly Woo Away Her Breath.
Song for the Seasons, A.
Stormy Petrel, The.
Vision, A, *sel.*
Cornwallis, Kinahan
Battle of Murfreesboro, The.
Cornwell, Henry Sylvester
Jefferson D.
May.
Sunset City, The.
Corpi, Lucha
Dark Romance.
Corpman, Izora
Photos from Summer Camp, The.
Corretjer, Juan Antonio
Convoy, The.
In Jail.
Corrie, Joe
Image o' God, The.
Miners' Wives.
Corrigan, Paul
Boss Machine-Tender after Losing a Son, The.
Corrington, John William
Second Coming, The.
Corrothers, James David
At the Closed Gate of Justice.
Dream and the Song.
In the Matter of Two Men.
Indignation Dinner, An.
Negro Singer, The.
Paul Laurence Dunbar.
Road to the Bow, The.
Corsellis, Timothy
Engine Failure.
Repression.
They Have Taken It from Me.
Thrush, The.
To Stephen Spender.
Corso, Gregory
Birthplace Revisited.
Body Fished from the Seine.
But I Do Not Need Kindness.
Dear Girl.
Dialogue—2 Dollmakers.
Difference of Zoos, A.
Dream of a Baseball Star.
Dreamed Realization, A.
Eastside Incidents.
From Another Room.
God Is a Masturbator.
Hello.
I Am 25.
I Held a Shelley Manuscript.
I Met This Guy Who Died.
In the Fleeting Hand of Time.
Italian Extravaganza.
Last Warmth of Arnold, The.
Mad Yak, The.
Marriage.
New York City—1935.
Notes after Blacking Out.
Paranoia in Crete.
Paris.
Poets Hitchhiking on the Highway.
Reflection in a Green Arena.
Requiem for "Bird" Parker.
Seed Journey.
Spontaneous Requiem for the American Indian.
Uccello.
Vestal Lady on Brattle, The.
Vision of Rotterdam.
Waterchew!
Writ on the Eve of My 32nd Birthday.
You, Whose Mother's Lover Was Grass.
Zizi's Lament.
Cortez, Jayne
For Real.
Grinding Vibrato.
I Am New York City.
In the Morning.
Initiation.
Lead.
Orange Chiffon.
Orisha.
Phraseology.
So Long.
So Many Feathers.
Under the Edge of February.
Cortissoz, Ellen Mackay Hutchinson
April Fantasie.
Bride's Toilette, The.
Cry from the Shore, A.
Harvest.
Her Picture.
Moth-Song.
On Kingston Bridge.
Pamela in Town.
Praise-God Barebones.
Quaker Ladies.
Quest, The.
Sea-Way.
So Wags the World.
Corvo, Baron. *See* **Rolfe, Frederick William**
Corwin, Norman
Man unto His Fellow Man.
On a Note of Triumph, *sel.*
Corwin, Phillip
Achilles.
Cory, David
Miss You.
Cory, William Johnson
Amaturus.
Anteros.
Ballad for a Boy, A.
Dirge, A: "Naiad, hid beneath the bank."
Eton Boating Song.
Europa.
Heraclitus.
Invocation, An: "I never prayed for Dryads, to haunt the woods again."
Mimnermus in Church.
Mortem, Quae Violat Suavia, Pellit Amor.
Notes of an Interview.
Oh, Earlier Shall the Rosebuds Blow.
Poor French Sailor's Scottish Sweetheart, A.
Remember.
Separation, A.
Cosier, Tony
Not This Leaf Haunts Me.
Cosmas, Saint
Menaion, *sel.*
Purification, The.
Costanzo, Gerald
Braille.
Introduction of the Shopping Cart.
Jeane Dixon's America.
Man Who Invented Las Vegas, The.
Meeting, The.
Nobody Lives on Arthur Godfrey Boulevard.
Costello, Tomas
Lament for Una, A, *sel.*
Cothi, Lewis Glyn
On the Death of His Son.
Cottam, Samuel Elsworth
To G. R.
Cotter, Joseph Seamon Sr.
Tragedy of Pete, The.
Way-Side Well, The.
Cotter, Joseph Seamon Jr.
And What Shall You Say?
April Day, An.
Band of Gideon, The.
Deserter, The.
Is It Because I Am Black?
Prayer, A: "As I lie in bed."
Rain Music.
Sonnet to Negro Soldiers.
Supplication.
Cottle, Joseph
Industrial Evils.
Malvern Hills, *sel.*
Cotton, Charles
Alice.
Angler's Ballad, The.
Clepsydra.
Epitaph on M. H., An.
Epitaph on Mr. Robert Port.
Epitaph on Mistress Mary Draper.
Evening.
Joys of Marriage, The.
Laura Sleeping.
Les Amours.
Litany, The: "From a ruler that's a curse."
Madrigal: "To be a whore, despite of grace."
Margaret.
New Year, The.
Noon Quatrains.
Ode: "Come, let us drink away the time," *at.*
Ode: "Good night, my love, may gentle rest."
Ode: "Was ever man of Nature's framing."
Ode: "Without the evening dew and showers."
Ode to Chloris.
Ode to Cupid.
Old Tityrus to Eugenia, *sel.*
On My Pretty Marten.
On Tobacco.
Resolution in Four Sonnets, of a Poetical Question Put to Me by a Friend, Concerning Four Rural Sisters.
Retirement, The.
Song: "Join once again, my Celia, join."
Song: "See, how like twilight slumber falls."
Song of Sack, A, *at.*
Sonnet: "Chloris, whilst thou and I were free."

Summer Evening.
Tempest, The.
To Celia.
To Chloris.
To Mr. Izaak Walton, *sel.*
To My Dear and Most Worthy Friend, Mr. Isaac Walton.
Two Rural Sisters.
Winter, *sel.*
Winter Glass, The.
Winter's Troops.

Cotton, Elizabeth
Oh, Babe, It Ain't No Lie.

Cotton, John (1584–1652)
Fragments.
In Saram.
Old Movies.
Pigs.
Pumpkins.
Thankful Acknowledgment of God's Providence, A.
To My Reverend Dear Brother, M. Samuel Stone.
Toad.

Cotton, John (*fl.* 1676)
Bacon's Epitaph, Made by His Man, *at.*
Upon the Death of G. B.

Cotton, John (1925–)

Cotton, Nathaniel
Bee, the Ant, and the Sparrow, The.
Contentment.
Early Thoughts of Marriage.
Marriage.
To a Child Five Years Old.

Cottrau, Teodoro
Santa Lucia.

Coulette, Henri
Antony and Cleopatra.
At the Telephone Club.
Attic, The.
Black Angel, The.
Blue-eyed Precinct Worker, The.
Cinema at the Lighthouse.
Denise: A Letter Never Sent.
Emeritus, n.
Epilogue: Author to Reader.
Family Goldschmitt, The.
Intaglio.
Junk Shop, The.
Night Thoughts.
Phono, at the Boar's Head.
Sickness of Friends, The.
War of the Secret Agents, The, *sels.*

Coulter, John
Morning Bus.

Councilman, Emily Sargent
Between the Tides.

Counselman, Mary Elizabeth
Gift with the Wrappings Off.

Coupey, Pierre
Study No. X.

Coursen, H. R.
Fall Again.

Court, Wesli
Academic Curse; an Epitaph.

Courthope, William John
Trail of the Bird, The.

Cousens, Mildred
American Vineyard.

Cousins, James H.
Behind the Plough.
Corn Crake, The.
Curse on a Closed Gate, A.
High and Low.
Omens.
Starling's Spring Rondel, A.
Wings of Love, The.

Coutts, Francis Burdett Money-. *See* **Money-Coutts, Francis Burdett**

Covell,, Natalie Anne *and* **Stacy Jo Crossen.** *See Crossen, Stacy Jo and* **Natalie Anne Covell**

Coward, Noel
Boy Actor, The.
Mad Dogs and Englishmen.
Stately Homes of England, The.
There Are Bad Times Just around the Corner.
To Noël Coward.

Cowdery, Mae V.
I Sit and Wait for Beauty.

Cowen, Joseph R.
Recessional for the Class of 1959 of a School for Delinquent Negro Girls.

Cowing, Sheila
Hinge, The.

Cowley, Abraham
Against Hope.
Age.
Anacreontic on Drinking.
Anacreontics: The Epicure.
Anacreontics: The Swallow.
Anacreontiques: The Grashopper.
Annunciation, The.
Another.
Beauty.
Change, The.
Chronicle, The; a Ballad.
Clad All in White.
Country Mouse, The.
Creation, The.
David and Jonathan.
Davideis, *sels.*
Destinie.
Dialogue after Enjoyment.
Dissembler, The.
Drinking.
Duel, The.
Epicure, The ("Fill the bowl with rosy, wine").
Epitaph: "Underneath this marble stone."
Epitaph of Pyramus and Thisbe.
Essay on Solitude, *sel.*
Extasie, The.
Frailty, The.
Garden, The, *sel.*
Grasshopper, The.
Great Diocletian.
Hell.
Honour.
Hymn: To Light.
Hymn to Light.
Leaving Me, and Then Loving Many.
Love ("I'll sing of heroes, and of kings").
Mistress, The, *sels.*
Motto, The.
Ode: Of Wit.
Ode upon Doctor Harvey.
Of Myself.
Of Solitude.
Of Wit.
On the Death of Crashaw.
On the Death of Mr. Crashaw.
On the Death of Mr. William Hervey [*or* Harvey].
Platonic Love.
Power of Numbers, The.
Prophet, The.
Reason, the Use of It in Divine Matters.
Request, The.
Sleep.
Solitude and Reason, in the Village.
Soul, The.
Spring, The.
Supplication, A.
Swallow, The.
Thief, The.
This Only Grant Me.
Thraldome, The.
To Mr. Hobbes [*or* Hobs].
To Sir William Davenant: Upon His Two First Books of Gondibert.
To the Royal Society.
Today Is Ours.
Vote, A, *sel.*
Welcome, The.
Wish, The.
Written in Juice of Lemmon [*or* Lemon].

Cowley, Abraham *and* Richard Crashaw
On Hope by Way of Question and Answer between Abraham Cowley and Richard Crashaw.

Cowley., Malcolm
Blue Juniata, *sel.*
Danny.
Eight Melons.
Hill above the Mine, The.
Long Voyage, The.
Nocturnal Landscape.
Piney Woods.
Stone Horse Shoals.
Streets of Air, The.
Tumbling Mustard.
Urn, The.
William Wilson.

Cowper, William
Absence of Occupation.
Acquiescence of Pure Love, The.
Addressed to a Young Lady.
Against Slavery.
Alexander Selkirk.
Beau's Reply.
Boadicea [an Ode].
Capability Brown.
Castaway, The.
Contrite Heart, The.
Diverting History of John Gilpin, The.
Dog and the Water-Lily, The.
Ease.
England.
Epigram on the Refusal of the University of Oxford to Subscribe to His Translation of Homer.
Epistle to Robert Lloyd, Esq., An.
Epitaph: "Here Johnson lies—a sage by all allow'd."
Epitaph on a Free but Tame Redbreast.
Epitaph on a Hare.
Evening.
Exhortation to Prayer.
Faithful Friend, The.
Father, who designs his babe a priest, The.
Fragment: "Pity, Religion has so seldom found."
Frosty Morning, A.
Garden, The, *sel.*
God Made the Country.
God Moves in a Mysterious Way.
Hatred and Vengeance, My Eternal Portion.
Hope, *sel.*
How to Grow Cucumbers.
Human Frailty.
I Was a Stricken Deer, That Left the Herd.
Jehovah Our Righteousness.
John Gilpin.
Joy and Peace in Believing.
Light and Glory of the World, The.
Light Shining out of Darkness.
Lines on a Bill of Mortality, 1790.
Lines on Receiving His Mother's Picture.
Lines Written during a Period of Insanity.
Lines Written on [*or* upon] a Window Shutter at Weston.
London Suburbs.
Loss of the *Royal George.*
Love Constraining to Obedience.
Love of England.
Lovest Thou Me?
Monarch, The.
My Former Hopes Are Fled.
My Mary.
My Soul Thirsts for God.
Mysterious Way, The.
Nightingale and the Glowworm, The.
"O Lord, My Best Desire Fulfill."
Ode: Secundum Artem, An.
Oh! [*or* O!] for a Closer Walk with God.
Old-Testament Gospel.

On a Similar Occasion for the Year 1790.
On a Similar Occasion for the Year 1792.
On a Spaniel Called Beau Killing a Young Bird.
On Friendship, *sel.*
On His Portrait.
On the Death of Mrs. Throckmorton's Bullfinch.
On the Ice Islands Seen Floating in the German Ocean.
On the Loss of the *Royal George*.
On the Queen's Visit to London, the Night of the Seventeenth of March, 1789, *sel.*
On the Receipt of My Mother's Picture out of Norfolk [the Gift of My Cousin Ann Bodham].
Pernicious Weed.
Playthings.
Poetic Pains.
Poplar Field, The.
Post-Boy, The.
Prudent Simplicity.
Retired Cat, The.
Retirement.
Rural Sights and Sounds.
Self-Acquaintance.
Shrubbery, The.
Simple Faith.
Slaves Cannot Breathe in England.
Sofa, The.
Solitude of Alexander Selkirk, The.
Sonnet to Mrs. Unwin.
Sonnet to William Wilberforce, Esq.
Sower, The.
Spirit's Light, The.
Squirrel in Sunshine.
Stanzas Subjoined to the Yearly Bill of Mortality of the Parish of All Saints, Northampton; for the Year 1787.
Statesman in Retirement, The.
Stricken Deer, The.
Sweet Meat Has Sour Sauce; or, The Slave-Trader in the Dumps.
Table Talk, *sel.*
Task, The, *sels.*
Timepiece, The, *sel.*
Tirocinium; or, A Review of Schools, *sels.*
To a Young Lady.
To Mary.
To Mary Unwin.
To Mr. Newton on His Return from Ramsgate.
To the Immortal Memory of the Halibut on Which I Dined This Day [Monday, April 26, 1784].
To the Rev. Mr. Newton.
To the Same.
To the Swallow.
Town and Country.
Truth, *sels.*
Verses: "I am monarch of all I survey."
Verses Supposed to Be Written by Alexander Selkirk, during His Solitary Abode on the Island of Juan Fernandez.
Walking with God.
Winter.
Winter Evening, The ("Hark! 'tis the twanging horn o'er yonder bridge").
Winter Evening ("Just when our drawing-rooms begin to blaze").
Winter Morning Walk, The.
Winter Scene.
Winter Walk at Noon, The.
Woodman's Dog, The.
Yardley Oak.

Cox, Eleanor Rogers
Dream of Aengus Og, The.
Return, The.
Three White Birds of Angus.
To a Portrait of Whistler in the Brooklyn Art Museum.

Cox, Elizabeth
Mask.

Cox, Kenyon
Bumblebeaver, The.
Kangarooster, The.
Octopussycat, The.
Wild Boarder, The.
Work.

Cox, Leo
Bells of Ste. Anne des Monts, The.
Cornfield.
Easter Thought.

Cox, Palmer
Brownies' Celebration, The.
Lazy Pussy, The.
Mouse's Lullaby, The.

Cox, Samuel K.
Lord, Thou Hast Promised, *with music.*

Coxe, Arthur Cleveland
America.
Father, Who Mak'st Thy Suff'ring Sons, *with music.*
He Standeth at the Door.
In the Silent Midnight Watches.
Iona.
Present Age, The.
Saviour, Sprinkle Many Nations, *with music.*

Coxe, Louis O.
Autumnal.
Dead Marine.
From the Window Down.
Hannah Dustin.
Lake, The.
Nightsong.
Old Lecher, The.
Pin-up Girl.
Red Right Returning.
Squaring the Circle.
Veteran, The.
Winter Night.
April, Glengarry.
World as Wave and Idea, The.

Coxon, Philip

Crabbe, George
Ancient Mansion, The, *sels.*
Ancient Virgin, An.
Books.
Borough, The, *sels.*
Caroline, The.
Critics.
Crusty Critics.
Dean's Lady, The.
Dejected Lover, The.
Delay Has Danger.
East Anglian Fen.
Frank Courtship, The, *sels.*
Frenzy.
His Mother's Wedding Ring.
His Wife's Wedding Ring.
In Suffolk.
Inebriety.
Jonas Kindred's Household.
Lady of the Manor, The.
Late Wisdom.
Library, The, *sels.*
Life.
Marriage Ring, A.
Marriages.
Meeting.
Newspaper, The, *sel.*
Parish Poor-House, The.
Parish Register, The, *sels.*
Pauper's Funeral, The.
Peter Grimes.
Phoebe Dawson.
Poor of the Borough, The: Peter Grimes.
Posthumous Tales, *sel.*
Reflections, *sel.*
Resurrection.
Rural Life.
Sad Lover, The.
Sailing upon the River.
Schools.
Sir Eustace Grey, *sels.*
Slum Dwelling, A.
Spring to Winter.
Suffolk Shore, The.
Tales, *sels.*
Tales of the Hall, *sels.*
Truth in Poetry ("Fled are those times").
Vicar, The.
Village, The.
Village Life.
Whistling Boy, The.
Winter Storm at Sea, The.
Winter Views Serene.

Craddle, W.
Egoism.
Male and Female.
On a Certain Scholar.

Cragin, Mary A. *See* **"Allison, Joy"**

Craig, Alexander
Hillside.
Sonnet: "Go you, O winds that blow from north to south."

Craig, David
One Thousand Feet of Shadow.
One Way Down.

Craig, John
O Hear My Prayer, Lord, *with music.*
O Lord, That Art My God and King, *with music.*

Craig, Maurice

Craig, Maurice James
Ballad to a Traditional Refrain.
Fable: "Tale is every time the same, The."
From Burton the Anatomist.
Love Poem: "First line."
Poem: "High on a ridge of tiles."
Two Voyages.
Winter.

Craig, Norma
Question.

Craik, Dinah Maria Mulock
Autumn's Processional.
Douglas, Douglas, Tender and True.
Four Years.
Friendship.
God Rest Ye, Merry Gentlemen.
Green Things Growing.
Highland Cattle, *sel.*
In Our Boat.
Lettice.
New Year, The.
Now and Afterwards.
Philip, My King.
Plighted.
Too Late.

Cramer, Steven
Two Women with Mangoes.

Cranch, Christopher Pearse
After the Centennial.
Bear and the Squirrels, The.
Bobolinks, The.
Gnosis.
I in Thee, and Thou in Me.
Old Cat's Confessions, An.
Pines and the Sea, The.
So Far, So Near.
Stanza from an Early Poem.
Thought.

Crandall, Charles Henry
Human Plan, The.
Stella.
Three Trees.
With Lilacs.

Crane, Carl
Reader Writes, The.

Crane, Hart
Air Plant, The.
At Melville's Tomb.
Atlantis.
Ave Maria.
Bathers, The.
Black Tambourine.
Broken Tower, The.

Cape Hatteras, *sel.*
Carrier Letter.
Chaplinesque.
Cutty Sark.
Dance, The.
Emblems of Conduct.
Enrich My Resignation.
For the Marriage of Faustus and Helen.
Harbor Dawn, The.
Hurricane, The.
Imperator Victus.
In Shadow.
Indiana.
Infinite consanguinity it bears.
Island Quarry.
Key West.
Legend.
March.
Meticulous, past midnight in clear rime.
My Grandmother's Love Letters.
Name for All, A.
National Winter Garden.
North Labrador.
O Carib Isle!
Paraphrase.
Passage.
Phantom Bark, The.
Power.
Praise for an Urn.
Quaker Hill.
Recitative.
Reliquary.
Repose of Rivers.
River, The.
Royal Palm.
Sad Indian, The.
Sea, The.
Three Songs, *sel.*
To Brooklyn Bridge.
To Emily Dickinson.
Tunnel, The.
Van Winkle.
Voyages (I–VI).
Wine Menagerie, The.

Crane, Nathalia
Janitor's Boy, The.
Spooks.
Vestal, The.

Crane, Orin L.
Slow Me Down, Lord!

Crane, Stephen
Behold, the Grave of a Wicked Man.
Black Riders, The, *sels.*
Blades of Grass, The.
Book of Wisdom, The.
Candid Man, The.
God in Wrath, A.
Hymn: "Slant of sun on dull brown walls, A."
I Saw a Man Pursuing the Horizon.
I Stood upon a High Place.
In the Desert.
"It Was Wrong to Do This," Said the Angel.
Learned Man, A.
Man Adrift on a Slim Spar, A.
Man Saw a Ball of Gold in the Sky, A.
Many Workmen.
Newspaper Is a Collection of Half-Injustices, A.
Ocean said to me once, The.
On the Desert.
Once There Came a Man.
Peaks, The.
'Scaped.
Slant of Sun on Dull Brown Walls, A.
Tell me not in joyous numbers.
There is a grey thing that lives in the tree-tops.
There Was a Crimson Clash of War.
There Was a Man with a Tongue of Wood.
There Was One I Met upon the Road.
"Think as I Think."
Trees in the Garden Rained Flowers, The.
War Is Kind, *sels.*
Wayfarer, The.
Why?
Youth in Apparel That Glittered, A.

Crane, Walter
Crocus, The.
Seat for Three, A: Written on a Settle.

Cranston, Claudia
In the Name of Jesus Christ.

Crapsey, Adelaide
Amaze.
Cradle-Song: "Madonna, Madonna [*or* Madonnina]."
Dirge: "Never the nightingale."
For Lucas Cranach's Eve.
Guarded Wound, The.
Niagara.
Night Winds.
November Night.
Roma Aeterna.
Rose-Marie of the Angels.
Snow.
Song: "I make my shroud but no one knows."
Susanna and the Elders.
To Man Who Goes Seeking Immortality.
Triad.
Vendor's Song.
Warning, The.

Crase, Douglas
Heron Weather.
Summer.

Crashaw, Richard
Against Irresolution.
And He Answered Them Nothing.
Answer for Hope.
Apologie for the Precedent Hymnes on Teresa, An.
Apology for the Foregoing Hymn, An.
Charitas Nimia; or, The Dear[e] Bargain.
Christ Crucified.
Coming Child, The.
Death's Lecture at the Funeral of a Young Gentleman.
Epitaph upon Husband and Wife Who [*or* Which] Died and Were Buried Together, An.
Epitaph upon Mr. Ashton, a Conformable Citizen, An.
Epithalamium: "Come, virgin tapers of pure wax."
Flaming Heart, The.
For Hope.
Holy Nativity of Our Lord God, The.
Hymn in Adoration of the Blessed Sacrament.
Hymn of Saint Thomas in Adoration of the Blessed Sacrament, The.
Hymn of the Nativity.
Hymn Sung as by the Shepherds, A.
Hymn to the Name and Honour [*or* Honor] of the Admirable Saint[e] T[h]eresa, A.
Hymne for the Epiphanie, A.
Hymne of the Nativity, Sung as by the Shepheards, An.
Hymnes on Teresa.
I Am the Door.
In Memory of the Vertuous and Learned Lady Madre de Teresa.
In the Glorious Assumption of Our Blessed Lady.
In the Glorious Epiphanie of Our Lord God.
In the Holy Nativity of Our Lord God.
In the Nativity of Our Lord.
Love's Horoscope.
Love's Nightingale.
Luke XI: Blessed Be the Paps Which Thou Hast Sucked.
M. Crashaw's Answer for Hope.
Music's Duel.
Nativity, The.
New Year's Day.
O Heart! the equal poise of love's both parts.
Ode Which Was Prefixed to a Prayer Booke Given to a Young Gentlewoman, An.
On a Prayer Book Sent to Mrs. M.R., *sel.*
On Dives.
On Marriage.
On Mr. G[eorge] Herbert's Book[e] [Intituled the Temple of Sacred Poems, Sent to a Gentlewoman].
On Our Crucified Lord, Naked and Bloody.
On the Assumption.
On the Baptized Ethiopian.
On the Bleeding Wounds of Our Crucified Lord.
On the Blessed Virgin's Bashfulness.
On the Glorious Assumption of Our Blessed Lady.
On the Miracle of Loaves.
On the Name of Jesus.
Out of the Italian: A Song.
Prayer: "Lo, here a little volume, but great book!"
Quaerit Jesum Suum Maria.
Qui Perdiderit Animam Suam.
Saint[e] Mary Magdalene; or, The Weeper.
St. Peter's Shadow.
Samson to His Delilah.
Shepherds' Hymn, The ("Gloomy night embraced the place").
Shepherd's Hymn, The ("We saw Thee in Thy balmy nest").
Song, A: "Lord, when the sense of Thy sweet grace."
Song of Divine Love, A.
Tear [*or* Teare], The.
Temperance or the Cheap Physitian upon the Translation of Lessius.
To a Young Gentle-Woman, Councel Concerning Her Choice.
To Our Blessed Lord upon the Choice of His Sepulchre.
To Our Lord, upon the Water Made Wine.
To the Infant Martyrs ("Go, smiling souls, your new-built cages break").
To the Name above Every Name, the Name of Jesus, a Hymn.
To the Noblest and Best of Ladies [*or* Ladyes], the Countess [*or* Countesse] of Denbigh.
Two Went Up to [*or* into] the Temple to Pray.
Upon Bishop Andrewes His Picture before His Sermons.
Upon Ford's Two Tragedies, "Loves Sacrifice" and "The Broken Heart."
Upon Lazarus His Teares.
Upon Our Saviour's Tomb Wherein Never Man Was Laid.
Upon the Bleeding Crucifix.
Upon the Body of Our Blesséd Lord, Naked and Bloody.
Upon the Death of a Gentleman.
Upon the Holy Sepulchre.
Upon the Infant Martyrs ("To see both blended in one flood").
Upon Venus Putting on Mars His Armes.
Verses from the Shepherd's Hymn.
Widow's Mites, The.
Wishes to His (Supposed) Mistress [*or* Mistresse].

Crashaw, Richard *and* **Abraham Cowley.** *See* **Cowley, Abraham** *and* **Richard Crashaw**

Craster, Mrs. Edward
Centipede Was Happy Quite, A.
Puzzled Centipede, The.

Craveirinha, José
Poem of the Future Citizen.

"Crawford, Captain Jack" (John Wallace Crawford)
Broncho versus Bicycle.
California Joe.
Death of Custer, The.

Crawford, Dan
Jesus and I.

Crawford, Francis Marion
New National Hymn.

Crawford, Isabella Valancy
Axe of the Pioneer, The.
Battle, A.

Camp of Souls, The.
Canoe, The.
City Tree, The.
Dark Stag, The.
Gisli, the Chieftain, *sel.*
Laughter.
Lily Bed, The.
Love Me, Love My Dog.
Love's Land.
Malcolm's Katie, *sels.*
Said the Canoe.
Song of the Arrow, The.
True and False.

Crawford, John Wallace. *See* **Crawford, Captain Jack"**

Crawford, Louisa Macartney
Kathleen Mavourneen.

Crawford, Tom
Phone Call.

Crawford, Vesta Pierce
Pioneer Woman.

Creekmore, Hubert
Concert at Sea.
Dividends.
Music in the Rec Hut.
Pocket Guide for Service Men.

Creeley, Robert
Act of Love, The.
After Lorca.
Air: "Cat bird singing."
Air: "Love of a woman, The."
All That Is Lovely in Men.
America.
And.
Anger.
Awakening, The.
Ballad of the Despairing Husband.
Business, The.
City, The.
Conspiracy, The.
Counterpoint, A.
Cracks, The.
Crisis, The.
Crow, The.
Damon and Pythias.
Death of Venus, The.
Distance.
Door, The.
Fancy.
Figures, The.
Fire, The.
Flower, The.
For Fear.
For Love.
For My Mother: Genevieve Jules Creeley.
For No Clear Reason.
For the New Year.
Form of Women, A.
Gift, The.
Gift of Great Value, A.
Hart Crane.
Here.
Heroes.
Hill, The.
House, The.
I Keep to Myself Such Measures.
I Know a Man.
If You.
Immoral Proposition, The.
Innocence, The.
Invoice, The.
Joy.
Just Friends.
Kind of Act Of, The.
Kore.
Language, The.
Like They Say.
Love Comes Quietly.
Man, The.
Marriage, A.
Mechanic, The.
Memory, The.
Moon, The.
Mountains in the Desert, The.
Name, The.
Naughty Boy.
Oh No.
Operation, The.
People, The.
Pool, The.
Prayer to Hermes.
Quick-Step.
Rain, The.
Reason, A.
Rescue, The.
Rhythm, The.
Rose, The.
Saints, The.
She Went to Stay.
Sight, A.
Signboard, The.
Sing Song.
Snow, The.
Something.
Somewhere.
Song: "Those rivers run from that land."
Song: "What I took in my hand."
Sounds.
Statue, The.
Three Ladies, The.
Tiger, The.
Time.
Token, A.
Turn, The.
Variation, A.
Wait for Me.
Waiting.
Warning, The.
Way, The.
Whip, The.
Wicker Basket, A.
Wife, The.
Window, The.
World, The.

Creelman, Josephine Rice
My Mother.

Creighton, Alan
Pastoral: "Farmhouse skyline, draped with trees, The."
Return of a Reaper.
Spring Workman.

Cresson, Abigail
Market Day.

Crew, Helen Coale
In a Low Rocking-Chair.

Crewe, Jennifer
Visitations.

Crews, Jacquelyne
Auguries for Three Women.

Crews, Judson
Declaration at Forty.
Love Poem: "Oh your thighs."
Oh Beach Love Blossom.

Crichton, John
Bed of Campanula, A. "

Crinagoras
Epitaph on an Infant.

Cripps, Arthur Shearly
Les Belles Roses sans Mercie.

Criswell, Cloyd Mann
Newlyweds, The.

Crites, Lucile
Folks and Me.

"Critics, The"
Grey October.

Crocker, Henry
Evangelize!

Crocker, T. F. Dillon
To shave, or not to shave? that is the question.

Croffut, William Augustus
Dirge, A: "And so our royal relative is dead!"
Living Memory, A.

Croft, Roy
Love ("I love you,/ Not only for what you are"), *at.*

Croly, George
A Fauxbourg.
Death and Resurrection.
Death of Leonidas, The.
Genius of Death, The.
Leonidas.

Cromwell, Gladys
Crowning Gift, The.
Folded Power.
Quest, The.

Cronin, Anthony
Anarchist.
Apology.
Autumn Poem.
Baudelaire in Brussels.
Consolation.
Elephant to the Girl in Bertram Mills' Circus, The.
For a Father.
On the bog road the blackthorn flowers, the turf-stacks.
R.M.S. *Titanic, sel.*
Surprise.

Crooke, Sheila Jane
Statue of Liberty, The.

Crooker, Barbara
Kneading.
Moving.

Cros, Charles
Smoked Herring, The.

Crosby, Epes Sargent
Deeds of Kindness.

Crosby, Ernest
Choir Practice.
In the Garden.
"Rebels."
Search, The.
Soul of the World, The.
Tournament of Man, The.

Crosby, Fanny (Frances Jane Crosby)
All the Way My Saviour Leads Me.
Best of All, The.
Blessed Assurance, *with music.*
Blind but Happy.
Jesus, Keep Me Near the Cross, *with music.*
Keep Thou My Way, O Lord.
There's Music in the Air, *with music.*
Unseen.

Crosby, Harry
Firebrand.
Telephone Directory.
Vision.

Crosby, Ranice Henderson
Poem about a Seashell.
Thoughts for You (When She Came Back from the Mountains).

Crosland, T. W. H.
Slain.

Cross, Allen Eastman
Gray Hills Taught Me Patience, The, *with music.*
Though Fatherland Be Vast, *with music.*
Young and Radiant, He Is Standing, *with music.*

Cross, Zora
Elegy on an Australian Schoolboy, *sel.*
Love Sonnets, *sels.*
When I Was Six.

Crossen, Stacy Jo *and* Natalie Anne Covell
Wiggly Giggles.

Crossman, Samuel
I said sometimes with tears.
My Song Is Love Unknown.

Croswell, William
Clouds, The.
Lord! Lead the Way the Saviour Went, *with music.*

Crouch, Mary Blake French
Ella of the Cinders.

Crouch, Nathaniel
David and Goliath.
Tower of Babel, The.
Crouch, Pearl Riggs
Snowstorm, The.
Story in the Snow, A.
Crouch, Stanley
After the Rain.
Albert Ayler: Eulogy for a Decomposed Saxophone Player.
Blackie Thinks of His Brothers.
Chops Are Flyin.
No New Music.
Riding across John Lee's Finger.
Crow, Mary
Foreign Streets.
Rain-in-the-Face.
Crowe, Ronald
Guns.
Crowe, William
Lewesdon Hill, *sel.*
Crowell, Grace Noll
Because of Thy Great Bounty.
Let Us Keep Christmas.
Poet Prays, The.
Quiet Things.
Crowell, Henry
When Thou Passest through the Waters.
Crowell, Norman H.
My Candidate.
Crowley, Aleister
Lesbian Hell, The.
Crowne, John
Kind Lovers, Love On.
"Crowquill, Alfred." *See* **Forrester, Alfred A.**
Croxall, Samuel
Sylvia.
Cruceius, Annibal
Fair Ursly, in a merry mood.
Cruickshank, Helen B.
Caenlochan.
Comfort in Puirtith.
Schiehallion.
Shy Geordie.
Wishin' Well, The.
Crummy, Biddy
Poem to Be Said on Hearing the Birds Sing, A.
Cruz, Victor Hernandez
African Things.
Bring the Soul Blocks.
California #2.
Carmen.
Cities #8, *sel.*
Electric Cop, The.
Energy.
Going Uptown to Visit Miriam.
Man I Thought You Was Talking Another Language That Day.
Sometimes on My Way Back Down to the Block.
Spirits.
Story of the Zeros, The.
Today Is a Day of Great Joy.
224 Stoop.
Urban Dream.
You Gotta Have Your Tips on Fire.
Csoori, Sandor
It Must Be Summer.
Cubalquinto, Luis
Big One, The.
Cudahy, Sheila
Heroes of the Strip.
Cuelho, Art
My Own Brand.
Culhane, Charles
Ancient One, The.
Death Row.
Green Haven Halls.
Straw Men, The.
There Isn't Enough Bread.
Cullen, Cornelius C.
Battle of Somerset.
Cullen, Countee
Black Magdalens.
Black Majesty.
Brown Boy to Brown Girl.
Brown Girl Dead, A.
For a Lady I Know.
For a Mouthy Woman.
For a Pessimist.
For a Poet.
For a Virgin Lady.
For Amy Lowell.
For John Keats, Apostle of Beauty.
For My Grandmother.
For Paul Laurence Dunbar.
Four Epitaphs.
From the Dark Tower.
Fruit of the Flower.
Heritage.
I Have a Rendezvous with Life.
In Memory of Colonel Charles Young.
Incident.
Judas Iscariot.
Lady I Know, A.
Lines to Our Elders.
Litany of the Dark People, The.
Magnets.
Mary, Mother of Christ.
Only the Polished Skeleton.
Protest.
Saturday's Child.
Scottsboro, Too, Is Worth Its Song.
Simon the Cyrenian Speaks.
Song in Spite of Myself.
Song of Praise, A.
Tableau.
That Bright Chimeric Beast.
Thorn Forever in the Breast, A.
Three Epitaphs.
Timid Lover.
To Certain Critics.
To John Keats, Poet, at Springtime.
To Lovers of Earth: Fair Warning.
Uncle Jim.
Under the Mistletoe.
Unknown Color, The.
Wise, The.
Yet Do I Marvel.
Youth Sings a Song of Rosebuds.
Cullen, Paula B.
Cousins.
Cullum, J. W.
Roses, Revisited, in a Paradoxical Autumn.
Cumbo, Kattie M.
Black Sister.
Ceremony.
Dark People.
Domestics.
I'm a Dreamer.
Malcolm.
Morning after . . . Love, The.
Nocturnal Sounds.
Washiri (Poet).
Cummings, David
Emily's Haunted Housman.
From the Brothers Grimm to Sister Sexton to Mother Goose; One Transmogrification.
Sweeney, Old and Phthisic, among the Hippopotami.
Cummings, Edward Estlin
All Ignorance Toboggans into Know.
All in Green Went My Love Riding.
All Which Isn't Singing Is Mere Talking.
Always before Your Voice My Soul.
Annie Died the Other Day.
Anyone Lived in a Pretty How Town.
As Freedom Is a Breakfastfood.
As Is the Sea Marvelous.
As Joe Gould says in.
Being to Timelessness as It's to Time.
Buffalo Bill's.
But/ he" i/ staring.
Buy Me an Ounce and I'll Sell You a Pound.
Cambridge Ladies Who Live in Furnished Souls, The.
Chansons Innocentes, *sels.*
Come, Gaze with Me upon This Dome.
Darling! Because My Blood Can Sing.
Dive for dreams.
Doll's boy's asleep.
Dominic Has a Doll.
Enter No (Silence Is the Blood Whose Flesh).
Faithfully Tinying at Twilight Voice.
First of All My Dreams, The.
Flotsam and Jetsam.
For Prodigal Read Generous.
Four III.
Gee I Like to Think of Dead.
Goodby Betty, Don't Remember Me.
Great, A.
Greedy the People, The.
He as O, A.
Her Careful Distinct Sex Whose Sharp Lips Comb.
Hist Whist.
Hours Rise Up Putting Off Stars and It Is, The.
How many moments must (amazing each).
I.
I am a Little Church (No Great Cathedral).
I Am So Glad and Very.
I Carry Your Heart with Me (I Carry It In.
I Like My Body When It Is with Your Body.
I Sing of Olaf Glad and Big.
I Thank You God for Most This Amazing.
I was sitting in mcsorley's.
I Will Be.
If Everything Happens That Can't Be Done.
If I Have Made, My Lady, Intricate.
If I Should Sleep with a Lady Called Death.
If in Beginning Twilight.
If There Are Any Heavens.
If (touched by love's own secret) we, like homing.
If You Can't Eat You Got To.
(Im)C-A-T(mo).
Impression.
Impressions, Number III.
IN) all those who got.
In Heavenly Realms of Hellas Dwelt.
It Is at Moments after I Have Dreamed.
It Is So Long Since My Heart Has Been with Yours.
It May Not Always Be So [and I Say].
It Was a Goodly Co.
Item.
It's Over a (See Just).
Jake Hates All the Girls.
Jehovah Buried, Satan Dead.
L (a.
La Guerre.
Ladies and Gentlemen This Little Girl.
Life Is More True.
Listen.
Little joe gould has lost his teeth and doesn't know where.
Love is a place.
Maggie and Milly and Molly and May.
Man Who Had Fallen among Thieves, A.
May I Feel Said He.
Me Up at Does.
Might these be thrushes climbing through almost.
Mr. U Will Not Be Missed.
My Father Moved through Dooms of Love.
My Love.
My specialty is living said.
My Sweet Old Etcetera.
Next to of Course God America I.
Nine Birds.
No Man, if Men Are Gods.
Nobody Loses All the Time.
Noone and a Star Stand,Am to Am.
Noone" autumnal this great lady's gaze.
Notice the Convulsed Orange Inch of Moon.
Now Does Our World Descend.

O By the By.
O Sweet Spontaneous.
Of Nicolette.
Old Age Sticks.
One!
One Times One, *sel.*
One winter afternoon.
One X.
Paris; This April Sunset Completely Utters.
Pity This Busy Monster, Manunkind.
Plato Told [Him].
Poem: "Maggie and Milly and Molly and May."
Poem, or Beauty Hurts Mr. Vinal.
Politician, A.
Ponder, Darling, These Busted Statues.
Pretty a Day, A.
Purer than Purest Pure, *with music.*
Q:dwo.
R-P-O-P-H-E-S-S-A-G-R.
Raise the Shade.
Salesman Is an It That Stinks Excuse, A.
Season 'Tis, My Lovely Lambs, The.
Serene immediate silliest and whose.
She Being Brand.
Silence.
Since Feeling Is First.
Slightly before the middle of Congressman Pudd.
Somewhere I Have Never Travelled [Gladly Beyond].
Song: "Thy fingers make early flowers of all things."
Sonnet: "This is the garden: colours come and go."
Sonnet: "Wind has blown the rain away and blown, A."
Sonnet Entitled How to Run the World.
Sonnets—Actualities, *sel.*
Sonnets—Realities, *sels.*
Sonnets—Unrealities, *sel.*
Space Being (Don't Forget to Remember) Curved.
Spring is like a Perhaps Hand.
Spring Omnipotent Goddess.
Sunset.
"Sweet spring is your."
Than (By Yon Sunset's Wintry Glow).
This Is the Garden.
This Little Bride and Groom Are.
Twenty-seven Bums Give a Prostitute the Once.
2 little whos.
Two X.
Way to Hump a Cow [Is Not], The.
What a Proud Dreamhorse.
What If a Much of a Which of a Wind.
What Is.
When Any Mortal (Even the Most Odd).
When Faces Called Flowers Float Out of the Ground.
When God Lets My Body Be.
When life is quite through with.
When Serpents Bargain for the Right to Squirm.
When the Spent Day Begins to Frail.
)when what hugs stopping earth than silent is.
Wherelings Whenlings.
White Guardians of the Universe of Sleep.
Who Are You, Little I.
Who Knows if the Moon's.
Who's Most Afraid of Death? [Thou].
Why Did You Go.
Why from this her and him.
Wild (at Our First) Beasts Uttered Human Words.
You Shall above All Things Be Glad and Young.
Your Birthday Comes to Tell Me This.
Your little voice/ Over the wires came leaping.

Cummins, Evelyn Atwater
I Know Not Where the Road Will Lead, *with music.*

Cumpian, Carlos
Cuento.

Cunard, Nancy
Zeppelins.

Cuney, Waring
Burial of the Young Love.
Conception.
Crucifixion.
Death Bed, The.
Dust.
Finis.
I Think I See Him There.
My Lord, What a Morning.
No Images.
Radical, The.
Threnody: "Only quiet death."
Triviality, A.
Troubled Jesus.
True Love.
Wake Cry.

Cunningham, Allan
Gone Were But the Winter Cold.
Hame, Hame, Hame.
John Grumlie.
Loyalty.
Mariner, The.
Spring of the Year, The.
Sun Rises Bright in France, The.
Wet Sheet and a Flowing Sea, A.

Cunningham, James (Olumo)
City Rises, The.
Covenant, The.
Footnote to a Gray Bird's Pause, A.
For Cal.
From a Brother Dreaming in the Rye.
Happy Day (or Independence Day).
High-cool/ 2.
Incidental Pieces to a Walk.
Lee-ers of Hew.
Leg-acy of a Blue Capricorn.
Narrator's Trance, The, *sels.*
Plea to My Sister, A.
Portrait of Rudy, A.
Rapping Along with Ronda Davis.
St. Julien's Eve.
Slow Riff for Billy.
Solitary Visions of a Kaufmanoid.
Street in Kaufman-ville, A.
Tambourine.
Welcome for Etheridge, A.
While Cecil Snores: Mom Drinks Cold Milk.

Cunningham, James Vincent
Aged Lover Discourses in the Flat Style, The.
Agnosco Veteris Vestigia Flammae.
All in Due Time.
And Now You're Ready Who While She Was Here.
Ars Amoris.
Chase, The.
Choice.
Coffee.
Dear Child Whom I Begot.
Elegy for a Cricket.
Envoi: "Hear me, whom I betrayed."
Epigram: "After some years Bohemian came to this."
Epigram: "And now you're ready who while she was here."
Epigram: "And what is love? Misunderstanding, pain."
Epigram: "Arms and the man I sing, and sing for joy."
Epigram: "Dark thoughts are my companions. I have wined."
Epigram: "Dear, if unsocial privacies obsess me."
Epigram: "Dear, my familiar hand in love's own gesture."
Epigram: "Elders at their services begin, The."
Epigram: "Friend, on this scaffold Thomas More lies dead."
Epigram: "Good Fortune, when I hailed her recently."
Epigram: "Here lies my wife. Eternal peace."
Epigram: "Homer was poor. His scholars live at ease."
Epigram: "How we desire desire! Joy of surcease."
Epigram: "I had gone broke, and got set to come back."
Epigram: "I married in my youth a wife."
Epigram: "If wisdom, as it seems it is."
Epigram: "In whose will is our peace? Thou happiness."
Epigram: "Life flows to death as rivers to the sea."
Epigram: "Man who goes for Christian resignation, The."
Epigram: "This Humanist whom no beliefs constrained."
Epigram: "This is my curse, Pompous, I pray."
Epigram: "Time heals not: it extends a sorrow's scope."
Epigram: "Within this mindless vault."
Epigram: "You ask me how Contempt who claims to sleep."
Epigram: "You wonder why Drab sells her love for gold?"
Epigraph from *The Judge Is Fury.*
Epitaph: "When I shall be without regret."
Epitaph for Someone or Other.
Five Epigrams.
For a College Yearbook.
For My Contemporaries.
Hang up your weaponed wit.
Helmsman, The; an Ode.
History of Ideas.
Horoscope.
I Married in My Youth a Wife.
In the thirtieth year of life.
Interview with Doctor Drink.
It Was in Vegas.
Lady, of anonymous flesh and face.
Lector Aere Perennior.
Lip.
Meditation on a Memoir.
Meditation on Statistical Method.
Metaphysical Amorist, The.
Miramar Beach.
Modern Love.
Montana Fifty Years Ago.
Montana Pastoral.
Moral Poem, A.
Motto for a Sun Dial.
Neaera when I'm there is adamant.
Nescit Vox Missa Reverti.
On a cold night I came through the cold rain.
On the Calculus.
Periphrastic Insult, Not a Banal, A.
Phoenix, The.
Pick-up, The.
Pope from penance purgatorial, The.
Rome.
Some twenty years of marital agreement.
Sonnet on a Still Night.
Three Epigrams.
To a Friend, on Her Examination for the Doctorate in English.
To the Reader.
To What Strangers, What Welcome.
To Whom It May Concern.
Vegas.
With a Copy of Swift's Works.

Cunningham, John
Day; a Pastoral.
Epigram: "Member of the modern great, A."
Kate of Aberdeen.
Miller, The.
Morning.
On a Certain Alderman.
Sent to Miss Bell H   , with a Pair of Buckles.
Virtuous Fox and the Self-righteous Cat, The.

Cunningham, Julia
Hymn to Joy.
Cunninghame-Graham, Robert. *See* **Graham, Robert**
Curnow, Allen
Balanced Bait in Handy Pellet Form, A.
Bring Your Own Victim.
Canst Thou Draw Out Leviathan with an Hook.
Dichtung und Wahrheit.
Excellent Memory, An.
Framed Photograph, A.
Incorrigible Music, An.
Kitchen Cupboard, The.
Reliable Service, A.
This Beach Can Be Dangerous.
Trees, Effigies, Moving Objects, *sels.*
You Will Know When You Get There.
Curran, Edwin
Autumn.
Clod, The.
First Frost.
Painted Hills of Arizona, The.
Curran, John Philpot
Cushla Ma Chree.
Deserter, The.
Deserter's Lamentation, The.
Let Us Be Merry before We Go.
Curran, Mary Doyle
No Fear.
Currey, Ralph Nixon
Children Waking: Indian Hill Station.
Cock-Crow.
Halo.
In Memoriam: Roy Campbell.
Jersey Cattle.
Landscape of Violence.
Marrakech.
Remembering Snow.
Song: "There is no joy in water apart from the sun."
Ultimate Exile IV.
Unseen Fire.
Volubilis, North Africa.
Currie, Mary Montgomerie Currie, Baroness. *See* **"Fane, Violet"**
Currie, Robert
Brothers.
Forget about It.
Home Place, The.
July the First.
Musician at His Work, The.
Rope and Drum.
What He Saw.
Currier, John
Electricity Is Funny!
Curtis, Christine Turner
Villa Sciarra: Rome.
Curtis, George William
Ebb and Flow.
Egyptian Serenade.
Curtis, Simon
Satie, at the End of Term.
Curtis, Thelma
God's Will Is Best.
Curtis, Tony
To My Father.
Curtright [*or* Curtwright], Wesley
Close of Day, The.
Heart of the Woods.
Curzon, Colin
Not Tonight, Josephine.
Curzon, George Nathaniel, Marquis Curzon
On an Insignificant Fellow.
Cuscaden, R. R.
In Detroit, I walk out Woodward Avenue.
Cushing, William O.
We Are Watching, We Are Waiting, *with music.*
Cushman, Charlotte
God's Work.
Cushman, Ralph Spaulding
His Presence Came like Sunrise.
Secret, The.
Sheer Joy.
Cussons, Sheila
1945.
Cust, Henry
Non Nobis.
Custance, Olive (Lady Alfred Douglas)
Parting Hour, The.
Twilight.
Cuthbertson, David Cunninghame
Picture, A.
Cuthbertson, James Lister
Racing Eight, A.
Cutler, Bruce
Results of a Scientific Survey.
Cutler, Elbridge Jefferson
Volunteer, The.
Cutler, Julian S.
Through the Year.
Cutting, Edith E.
Against Gravity.
Cutting, Sewall Sylvester
God of the World, Thy Glories Shine, *with music.*
Gracious Saviour, We Adore Thee, *with music.*
Cutts, John, Baron Cutts
Innocent Gazer, The.
Song: "Only tell her that I love."
Cybulski, Walter
Museum with Chinese Landscapes.
Cynewulf
Christ 2, *sels.*
Constantine's Vision of the Cross.
Death of Saint Guthlac.
Elene, *sels.*
Fates of the Apostles, *sel.*
Guthlac, *sel.*
Helena Embarks for Palestine.
Juliana, *sel.*
Maiden Ring-Adorned, A.
Voyage of Life, The.
Czamanske, W. M.
Higher Calling, The.

D

"D., D."
Boston Boy Went out to Yuma, A.
"D., H." *See* **Doolittle, Hilda**
"D., J."
Essay on the Fleet Riding in the Downes, An.
"D. N. R." *See* **"R., D. N."**
Dabney, Betty Page
Earth's Bondman.
Dabydeen, Cyril
Folklore.
Lives.
Posterity.
Rehearsal.
Rhapsodies.
Dacey, Philip
Animals' Christmas, The.
Another Stone Poem.
Birthday, The.
Black Death, The.
Edward Weston in Mexico City.
Form Rejection Letter.
How I Escaped from the Labyrinth.
Obscene Caller, The.
One of the Boys.
Poem as Striptease, The.
Prisms.
Ring Poem, The: A Husband Loses His Wedding Band as He Gestures from a Bridge.
Small Dark Song.
Thumb.
Way It Happens, The.
Dacre, Harry
Daisy Bell; or, A Bicycle Built for Two, *with music.*
Dadié, Bernard
Dry Your Tears, Africa!
I Give You Thanks My God.
Dadu
Whatsoever Hath Been Made, God Made.
Dahl, Roald
Aunt Sponge and Aunt Spiker.
Little Red Riding Hood and the Wolf.
Snow White and the Seven Dwarfs.
Dahlberg, Edward
Kansas City West Bottoms.
Daiches, David
Notes for a History of Poetry.
To Kate, Skating Better than Her Date.
Ulysses' Library.
Winter Song.
Daigon, Ruth
Like an Ideal Tenant.
Night Flight.
Daiken, Leslie
Bohernabreena.
June Song of a Man Who Looks Two Ways.
Larch Hill.
Lines to My Father.
Lines Written in a Country Parson's Orchard.
Nostalgie d'Automne.
Spring, St. Stephen's Green.
Dakin, Laurence
Pyramus and Thisbe, *sel.*
Song: "Peasant sun went crushing grapes, The."
Tancred, *sels.*
Dalcour, Pierre
Verse Written in the Album of Mademoiselle.
Dale, Edward Everett
Prairie Schooner, The.
Dale, Peter
Fragments, The, *sel.*
Rite, The.
Daley, Edith
Praise.
Daley, Victor James
Ascetic, The.
Dreams.
Faith.
In a Wine Cellar.
Lachesis.
Narcissus and Some Tadpoles.
Night, *sel.*
Tall Hat.
Tamerlane.
When London Calls.
Dali, Salvador
Art of Picasso, The.
Dallas, Sir George
India Guide, The; or, Journal of a Voyage to the East Indies in 1780, *sel.*
Miss Emily Brittle Sails for India.
Dallas, Mary Kyle
He'd Nothing but His Violin.
Dallman, Elaine
From the Dust.
Dalmon, Charles
Ballad of the Epiphany.
Early Morning Meadow Song.
Legend of Cherries, A.
O What If the Fowler.
Dalton, Annie Charlotte
For an Eskimo.
Neighing North, The.
Robin's Egg, The.
Sounding Portage, The.
To the Young Man Jesus.
Dalton, Power (Harold Caleb Dalton)
Finite.
Flail.
Dalven, Rae
My Father.
Daly, James Jeremiah
Latin Tongue, The.
Daly, John
Toast to the Flag, A.

Daly, June
Wildebeest, The.
Daly, Thomas Augustin
Boy from Rome, Da.
Leetla Boy, Da.
Leetla Giorgio Washeenton.
Man's Prayer, The.
Mia Carlotta.
Peaceable Race, The.
Pennsylvania Places.
Sanctum, The.
Tides of Love, The.
Dalziel, Kathleen
He Could Have Found His Way.
Damagetus
Spartan Wrestler, The.
Damas, Léon
Put Down.
They Came This Evening.
Damascene, Saint John. *See* **John of Damascus, Saint**
D'Ambrosio, Vinnie-Marie
Grace of Cynthia's Maidenhood, The.
Moon as Medusa.
On the Fifth Anniversary of Bluma Sach's Death.
Dammers, Kim
MANICdepressant.
Dana, Mary Stanley Bunce
O Sing to Me of Heaven, *with music.*
Dana, Richard Henry
Chanting Cherubs, The—a Group by Greenough.
Immortality.
Little Beach-Bird, The.
Moss Supplicateth for the Poet, The.
Dana, Robert
Horses.
Mineral Point.
Way We Live Now, The.
Dana, Robert Patrick
Notes on a Child's Coloring Book.
Winter's Tale, A.
Dance, James
Cricket; an Heroic Poem, *sel.*
Dancer, John
Variety, The.
Dandridge, Danske Bedinger
Dead Moon, The.
On the Eve of War.
Spirit of the Fall, The.
Dandridge, Ray Garfield
Drum Majah, De.
'Ittle Touzle Head.
Sprin' Fevah.
Time to Die.
Zalka Peetruza.
Dane, Barbara *and* Irwin Silber.
Hallelujah I'm a Bum ("I read in the news, the President said").
Dane, Barbara *and* **Jack Warshaw.** *See* **Warshaw, Jack** *and* **Barbara Dane**
Dane, Barbara *and others*
Bring 'Em Home.
Danforth, John
Few Lines to Fill up a Vacant Page, A.
Mercies of the Year, The.
On My Lord Bacon.
Pindarick Elegy upon the Renowned Mr. Samuel Willard, *sel.*
Poem upon the Triumphant Translation of . . . Mrs. Anne Eliot, A.
Profit and Loss; an Elegy upon the Decease of Mrs. Mary Gerrish.
Two Vast Enjoyments Commemorated.
Danforth, Samuel (1626–74)
Almanac Verse.
Awake yee westerne nymphs, arise and sing.
Danforth, Samuel, Jr. (1666–1727)
Ad Librum.
Elegy in Memory of the Worshipful Major Thomas Leonard Esq., An.
Dangel, Leo
Pa.
Plowing at Full Moon.
Daniel, Arnaut
Autet e bas.
Bel m'es quan lo vens m'alena.
Daniel, George
Anti-Platonicke.
Ode: "Poor bird, I do not envy thee."
Pure Platonicke.
Robin, The.
Daniel, H. J.
My Epitaph.
Daniel, Marky
Crabbing.
Daniel, Peter *and* **Karl Ernst.** *See* **Ernst, Karl** *and* **Peter Daniel**
Daniel, Robert T.
Time Will Surely Come, The, *with music.*
Daniel, Samuel
Appeal, The.
Are They Shadows [That We See]?
Beauty, Time and Love.
Care-Charmer Sleep.
Chorus: "Behold what furies still."
Chorus: "How dost thou wear and weary out thy days."
Chorus: "Then thus we have beheld."
Civil Wars, The, *sel.*
Cleopatra, *sels.*
Complaint of Rosamond, The, *abr.*
Constancy.
Description of Beauty, A.
Early Love.
English Poetry.
Enjoy Thy April Now.
Epistle to Henry Wriothesley, Earl of Southampton.
Eyes, Hide My Love.
Fair Is My Love.
Had Sorrow Ever Fitter Place.
Half-blown Rose, The.
Heavenly Eloquence.
Henry's Lament.
Hymen's Triumph,
Lonely Beauty.
Love.
Love Is a Sickness[e].
Most Unloving One, The.
Musophilus; or, Defence of All Learning, *sels.*
None other fame mine unambitious muse.
O Blessed Letters.
Ode: "Now each creature joys the other."
Poet and Critic.
Rosamond's Appeal.
Secrecy.
Shadows.
Song: "Are they shadowes that we see?"
Song: "Love is a sickness full of woes."
Sonnet: "Beauty [*or* Beautie], sweet Love, is like the morning dew[e]."
Sonnet: "But love whilst that thou may'st be loved again."
Sonnet: "Care-charmer sleep[e], son[ne] of the sable night."
Sonnet: "Fair[e] is my love, and cruel[l] as she is fair[e]."
Sonnet: "I must not grieve my Love, whose eyes would read."
Sonnet: "Let others sing of knights and paladins."
Sonnet: "Look, Delia, how we esteem the half-blown rose."
Sonnet: "When men shall find thy flower, thy glory, pass."
Sorrow.
Tethys' Festival, *sel.*
To Delia, *sels.*
To His Reader.
To Sir Thomas Egerton.
To the Lady Lucy, Countess of Bedford.
To the Lady Margaret, Countess[e] of Cumberland.
To the Reader.
To the Right Worthy Knight Sir Fulke Greville.
Tragedie of Philotas, The, *sel.*
Ulysses and the Siren.
Daniel ben Judah
Living God, The.
Daniells, Roy
Buffalo.
Deeper into the Forest, *sel.*
Farewell to Winnipeg.
Journey.
Mole, The.
Noah.
Summer Days.
Daniels, Jim
Going Up and Down.
Danner, Margaret
And through the Caribbean Sea.
At Home in Dakar.
Best Loved of Africa.
Convert, The.
Dance of the Abakweta.
Elevator Man Adheres to Form, The.
Far from Africa: Four Poems.
Garnishing the Aviary.
Goodbye David Tamunoemi West.
Grandson Is a Hoticeberg, A.
Painted Lady, The.
Rhetoric of Langston Hughes, The.
Sadie's Playhouse.
Slave and the Iron Lace, The.
This Is an African Worm.
Dante Alighieri
And now we walked along the solid mire.
Ballata: He Will Gaze upon Beatrice.
Canzone: He Beseeches Death for the Life of Beatrice.
Celestial Pilot, The.
Divina Commedia, *sels.*
First Canzone of the Convito, The.
Francesca and Paolo.
Now hoisteth sail the pinnace of my wit.
Pier delle Vigne.
Saint Bernard's Prayer to Our Lady.
Saints in Glory, The.
Sestina; of the Lady Pietra degli Scrovigni.
Sonnet: "Beatrice is gone up into high heaven."
Sonnet: "Because mine eyes can never have their fill."
Sonnet: "Last All Saints' holy-day, even now gone by."
Sonnet: "Mine eyes beheld the blessed pity spring."
Sonnet: Of Beatrice de' Portinari, on All Saints' Day.
Sonnet: Of Beauty and Duty.
Sonnet: On the 9th of June 1290.
Sonnet: To Brunetto Latini.
Sonnet: To Certain Ladies; When Beatrice Was Lamenting Her Father's Death.
Sonnet: To Guido Cavalcanti.
Sonnet: To the Lady Pietra degli Scrovigni.
Sonnet: To the Same Ladies; with Their Answer.
Sonnet: "With sighs my bosom always laboureth."
Sonnet: "Wonderfully out of the beautiful form."
Virgil's Farewell to Dante.
Vita Nuova, La, *sels.*
Dante da Maiano *See* **Maiano, Dante da**
Da Ponte, Lorenzo
Capriccio Dramatico, Il, *sel.*
Don Giovanni, *sel.*
"Giovinette, Che Fate All'Amore."
To an Artful Theatre Manager.
D'Arcy, Hugh Antoine
Face upon [*or* on] the Floor, The.
D'Arcy, Jack
Conservative Shepherd to His Love, The.

Darcy, M. M.
Astronaut's Choice.
Dargan, Olive Tilford
Duo.
New Freedom, The.
Path Flower.
Rescue.
To William Blake.
Dargan, Vere
City Trees.
Darío, Rubén (Félix Rubén García Sarmiento)
Alleluya.
Nocturne II: "You who have listened to the heart of the night."
Three Kings, The.
To Columbus.
Darion, Joe
Impossible Dream, The, *with music*
Darley, George
Call of the Morning, The.
Chorus of Sirens.
Chorus of Spirits.
Deadman's Dirge.
Dirge: "Wail! wail ye o'er the dead!"
Dove's Loneliness, The.
Enchanted Lyre, The.
Enchanted Spring, The.
Errors of Ecstasie, *sel.*
Ethelstan, *sel.*
Fallen Star, The.
Flower of Beauty, The.
Hoopoe.
Hundred-gated Thebes.
Hundred-sunned Phenix.
Hurry Me Nymphs.
In Dreamy Swoon.
It Is Not Beauty I Demand.
Last Night.
Lay of the Forlorn.
Lilian's Song.
List no more the ominous din.
Loveliness of Love, The.
Love's Likeness.
Lyre, The.
Mermaidens' Vesper-Hymn, The.
Nepenthe, *sels.*
O Blest Unfabled Incense Tree.
O'er the Wild Gannet's Bath.
On the Death of a Recluse.
Onward to Far Ida.
Phoenix, The ("O blest unfabled incense tree").
Phoenix, The ("O fast her amber blood doth flow").
Robin's Cross.
Runilda's Chant.
Sea Ritual, The.
Serenade: "Awake thee, my lady-love."
Serenade of a Loyal Martyr.
Solitary Lyre, The.
Song, A: "It is not beauty I demand."
Song: "Down the dimpled green-sward dancing."
Song: "I've taught thee Love's sweet lesson o'er."
Song: "Streams that wind among the hills, The."
Song: "Sweet in her green cell the flower of beauty slumbers."
Song of the Mermaids.
Sylvia; or, The May Queen, *sels.*
Syren Songs, *sels.*
Thomas à Becket, a Dramatic Comedy, *sel.*
To the Moon.
Unicorn, The.
Wherefore, Unlaurelled Boy.
Darnley, Henry Stuart [*or* Stewart], Lord
Gife Langour.
To the Queen.
Darr, Ann
About Motion Pictures.
For Great Grandmother and Her Settlement House.
Gift, The.
Love Is.
Oblique Birth Poem.
Pot-bellied Anachronism, The.
Whatever It Was I Was Saving for My Old Age.
Darring, Walter
Surprised by Me.
Darwin, Erasmus
Action of Electricity, The.
Action of Invisible Ink, The.
Botanic Garden, The, *sels.*
Economy of Vegetation, The, *sels.*
Eliza.
Immortal Nature.
Loves of the Plants, The.
Nightmare.
Protection of Plants, The.
Reproduction of Life.
Steam Power.
Temple of Nature, The; or, The Origin of Society, *sels.*
Vegetable Loves.
Visit of Hope to Sydney Cove, near Botany-Bay.
Daryush, Elizabeth
Armistice.
Autumn, Dark Wanderer.
Eyes That Queenly Sit.
Farewell for a While.
Flanders Fields.
For a Survivor of the Mesopotamian Campaign.
Fresh Spring.
Frustration.
How on Solemn Fields of Space.
Look, The.
November.
November Sun.
O Strong to Bless.
Still-Life.
Subalterns.
Throw Away the Flowers.
Unknown Warrior.
Das, Kamala
House-Builders, The.
Introduction, An: "I don't know politics but I know the names."
Daubeny, Charles
Verses on a Cat.
Dauenhauer, Nora
Breech Birth.
Genocide.
Jessy.
Kelp.
Pregnant Image of "Exaggerating the Village."
Rookery.
Seal Pups.
Skiing on Russian Christmas.
Tlingit Concrete Poem.
Voices.
Winter Developing.
Daugherty, James Henry
Texas.
Trail Breakers.
Daugherty, Michael
Buzzard.
Daumal, Rene
Four Cardinal Times of Day, The.
Daunt, John
Daybreak on a Pennsylvania Highway.
Davenant [*or* D'Avenant], Sir William
Aubade: "Lark now leaves his watery [*or* wat'ry] nest, The."
Christians Reply to the Phylosopher, The.
Endimion Porter and Olivia.
Epitaph: "When you perceive these stones are wet."
For the Lady Olivia Porter; a Present upon a New Year's Day.
Gondibert, *sels.*
Law against Lovers, The, *sel.*
Life and Death.
Lover and Philosopher.
Mistress, The.
Morning.
Morning Song.
O Thou That Sleep'st like Pig in Straw.
Philosopher and the Lover, The: To a Mistress Dying.
Praise and Prayer.
Rivals, The, *sel.*
Soldier Going to the Field, The.
Song: "Before we shall again behold."
Song: Endimion Porter and Olivia.
Song: "Lark now leaves his wat'ry nest, The."
Song: "Roses and pinks will be strewn where you go."
Song: Souldier going to the Field, The.
Song: "Wake all the dead!"
Storm at Sea.
To a Mistress Dying.
To the Queen[e], Entertain'd at Night by the Countess[e] of Anglesey.
Under the Willow Shades.
Unfortunate Lovers, The, *sel.*
Wake All the Dead.
What Is Past.
Willow, The.
Davenport, Guy
Medusa, The.
Davenport, Mariana B.
Suspended Moment.
Widow, The.
Davenport, R. A.
Serious Danger, A.
Davey, Frank
Piano, The.
She'd Say.
David, John
What Happiness Can Equal Mine, *with music.*
David ap Gwilim
Cywdd to Morvydd, The.
David ben Meshullam
Be Not Silent.
Davidman, Joy
Prayer against Indifference.
Princess in the Ivory Tower, The.
Davidson, Donald
John Darrow.
Lee in the Mountains.
On a Replica of the Parthenon.
Davidson, Francis
Beggars.
Davidson, Gustav
Ambushed by Angels.
Nevertheless.
Somewhere I Chanced to Read.
Davidson, John
Ballad in Blank Verse of the Making of a Poet, A, *sel.*
Ballad of a Nun, A.
Ballad of Heaven, A.
Ballad of Hell, A.
Butterflies.
Christmas Eve.
Cinque Port, A.
Dedication to the Generation Knocking at the Door.
Eclogue: Queen Elizabeth's Day.
Frosty Morning, A.
Greenock.
Holiday.
Holiday at Hampton Court.
I Haunt the Hills That Overlook the Sea.
Imagination.
In a Music-Hall.
In Romney Marsh.
In the Isle of Dogs.
Labourer's Wife, A.
Last Journey, The.
London.
Merchantmen, The.
New Year's Eve, *sel.*
Northern Suburb, A.
Price, The.

Runnable Stag, A.
St. Michael's Mount.
Song: "Boat is chafing at our long delay, The."
Song: "Closes and courts and lanes."
Song of a Train.
Summer.
Testament of John Davidson, The, *sel.*
Thirty Bob a Week.
To the Street Piano, *sel.*
Twinkling Earn, The.
Two Dogs ("Two dogs on Bournemouth beach: a mongrel, one").
Unknown, The.
Waiting.
War Song.
Wasp, The.
Winter in Strathearn, *sel.*

Davidson, Thomas
And There Will I Be Buried.

Davie, Donald
At Knaresborough.
Autumn Imagined.
Barnsley and District.
Christening, A.
Corrib: An Emblem.
Evangelist, The.
For an Age of Plastics. Plymouth.
For Doreen.
Forests of Lithuania, The, *sel.*
Fountain, The.
G. M. B.
Garden Party, The.
Gardens No Emblems.
Having No Ear.
Hearing Russian Spoken.
Heigh-ho on a Winter Afternoon.
Homage to William Cowper.
Life of Service, The.
Meeting of Cultures, A.
Mushroom Gatherers, The.
New York in August.
On Bertrand Russell's "Portraits from Memory."
Orpheus.
Priory of St. Saviour, Glendalough, The.
Prose for Des Esseintes.
Remembering the 'Thirties.
Thanks to Industrial Essex.
Time Passing, Beloved ("Time passing, and the memories of love").
To a Teacher of French.
Wind at Penistone, The.
Winter Talent, A.
Woodpigeons at Raheny.
Year 1812, The.

Davieau, Robert Stiles
Arizona Village.

Davies, Hugh Sykes
Music in an Empty House.
Poem: "In the stump of the old tree, where the heart has rotted out."
Poem: "It doesn't look like a finger it looks like a feather of broken glass."

Davies, Idris
Gwalia Deserta, *sel.*
High Summer on the Mountains.
Lay Preacher Ponders, The.

Davies, J. R. S.
Cranes.

Davies, Jeffrey
Washing Machine, The.

Davies, John, of Hereford
Against Gaudy-Bragging-Undoughty Daccus.
Against Proud Poor Phryna.
Author Loving These Homely Meats, Specially, viz.: Cream, Pancakes, Buttered Pippin-Pies, The.
Of Kate's Baldness.
Scourge of Folly, The, *sel.*
Sonnet: "It is as true as strange, else trial feigns."
Sonnet: "So shoots a star as doth my mistress glide."

Davies, Sir John
Acclamation, An.
Affliction.
Contention between Four Maids Concerning That Which Addeth Most Perfection to That Sex.
Contention betwixt a Wife, a Widow, and a Maid, A.
Dance of Love, The.
Dancing Sea, The.
Dedication I: "To that clear majesty which in the north."
Dedication II: "Strongest and the noblest argument, The."
Gulling Sonnets, *sel.*
Hymns of Astraea, *sels.*
I Know Myself a Man.
If you would know the love which I you bear.
Immortality of the Soul, The, *sel.*
In Francum.
In Fuscum.
In Librum.
In What Manner the Soule Is United to the Body.
Kate Being Pleased.
Knowledge and Reason.
Man.
Mariner's Song, The.
Much Knowledge, Little Reason.
Muse Reviving, The.
Nosce Teipsum.
Of Astraea.
Oft did I hear our eyes the passage were.
On a Pair of Garters.
On the Deputy of Ireland's Child.
Once did my Philomel reflect on me.
Orchestra; or, A Poem[e] of Da[u]ncing.
Praise of Dancing, The.
Sea Danceth, The.
Sickness, intending my love to betray.
Sight.
Sonnets to Philomel, *sels.*
Soul and the Body, The.
To His Lady.
To Queen Elizabeth.
To the Nightingale.
To the Rose.
To the Spring.
Which Is a Proud, and Yet a Wretched Thing.
Who Doth Not See the Measure of the Moon?

Davies, Mary Carolyn
Be Different to Trees.
David.
Dead Make Rules, The.
Door, The.
Door-Mats.
Easter.
Feet.
Fishing Pole, The.
Gown, The.
If I Had Known.
I'll Wear a Shamrock.
June.
Man's Woman, A.
Men Are the Devil.
New Year, A.
Out of the Earth.
Prayer for a Marriage, A.
Prayer for a Sleeping Child, A.
Prayer for Every Day, A.
Rust.
Terrible Dread, The.
Traps.
Tree Birthdays.

Davies, Russell
Book Reviews.
Dear Father Christmas.

Davies, Samuel
Eternal Spirit, Source of Light, *with music.*
Lord, I Am Thine, *with music.*
While o'er Our Guilty Land, O Lord, *with music.*

Davies, Sneyd
Scene after Hunting at Swallowfield in Berkshire, A.
Voyage to Tintern Abbey, A, *sel.*

Davies, William Henry
Ambition.
Battle, The.
Beautiful, The.
Best Friend, The.
Bird of Paradise, The.
Cat, The.
Chase, The.
Child and the Mariner, The.
Child's Pet, A.
Christ, the Man.
Come, Let Us Find.
Days That Have Been.
Days Too Short.
Dog, The.
Dreams of the Sea.
Dumb World, The.
Early Morn.
Elements, The.
Epitaph, An: "Beneath this stone lies one good man; and when."
Example, The.
Eyes.
Facts.
Flirt, The.
Flying Blossoms.
Fog, The.
Frost.
Ghost, The.
Great Time, A.
Greeting, A.
Heap of Rags, The.
Her Merriment.
Hermit, The.
Hospital Waiting-Room, The.
Hour of Magic, The.
In May.
Inquest, The.
Jenny Wren.
Joy and Pleasure.
Kingfisher, The.
Lamorna Cove.
Last Years, The.
Leaves.
Leisure.
Love's Caution.
Loyalty.
Maiden and Her Hair, A.
Mind's Liberty, The.
Money.
Moon, The.
Muse, The.
My Garden.
Oh, Sweet Content.
On Hearing Mrs. Woodhouse Play the Harpsichord.
One Poet Visits Another.
One Token.
Poet, The.
Pond, The.
Poor Kings.
Power of Silence, The.
Rabbit, The.
Rain, The.
Rainbow, The.
Rat, The.
Rich Days.
Robin Redbreast.
Sailor to His Parrot, The.
School's Out.
Sea, The.
Sheep.
Sluggard, The.
Songs of Joy.
Sweet Stay-at-Home.
Thought, A.

Thunderstorms.
To a Butterfly.
To a Lady Friend.
To the Wind at Morn.
Trick, The.
Truly Great.
Truth, The.
Two Stars, The.
Villain, The.
Visitor, The.
When Diamonds, Nibbling in My Ears.
When Yon Full Moon.
White Horse, The.
White Monster, The.
Wind, The.

Davis, Abijah
Blest Is the Man Whose Tender Breast, *with music.*

Davis, Catherine
After a Time.
Insights.
Kindness.
Nausea.

Davis, Daniel Webster
Hog Meat.
'Weh Down Souf.

Davis, F. W.
Thankful Heart.

Davis, Fannie Stearns
For a Child.
Forbidden Lure, The.
Moods, The.
Narrow Doors, The.
Souls.
Turn of the Road, The.

Davis, Florence Boyce
This and That.
Three Wise Monkeys, The.

Davis, Francis
Nanny.

Davis, Frank Marshall
Arthur Ridgewood, M.D.
Dancing Gal.
Flowers of Darkness.
Four Glimpses of Night.
Giles Johnson, Ph.D.
I Sing No New Songs.
"Onward Christian Soldiers!"
Robert Whitmore.
Snapshots of the Cotton South.
To Those Who Sing America.

Davis, Gloria
To Egypt.

Davis, Gussie L.
In the Baggage Coach Ahead.

Davis, Harold Lenoir
Stalks of Wild Hay.

Davis, Helen Bayley
Jack Frost.
Song for a Child.

Davis, Jack
Day Flight.

Davis, John
Sun, The.

Davis, Julia Johnson
Loss.
She Sews Fine Linen.
To My Little Son.

Davis, Katherine
Act II.

Davis, Leasa
Old woman sits, The.

Davis, Leland
Ballad of Adam's First, The.

Davis, Lloyd
Armstrong Spring Creek.
Bad Day on the Boulder.
Last Day of the Trip.
Panic.

Davis, Mary Evelyn Moore
Battle-Flag, The.
Counsel.

Davis, Norma L.
Daydreamers.

Davis, Ossie
To a Brown Girl.

Davis, Ozora Stearns
At Length There Dawns the Glorious Day, *with music.*
We Bear the Strain of Earthly Care.

Davis, Pamela Oberon
Why Write Poetry?

Davis, Paul
Afternoon at Cannes.

Davis, Robert A.
Dust Bowl.

Davis, Ronda
Invitation (To the Night and All Other Things Dark).
Parasitosis.
Personality Sketch, A: Bill.
Poems about Playmates.
Spacin.

Davis, Roy
Retrospect.
Thoughts.

Davis, Thadious M.
Asante Sana, Te Te.
Double Take at Relais de L'Espadon.
"Honeysuckle Was the Saddest Odor of All, I Think."
It's All the Same.
Remembering Fannie Lou Hamer.

Davis, Thomas Osborne
Battle Eve of the [Irish] Brigade, The.
Clare's Dragoons.
Fate of King Dathi, The.
Fontenoy.
Irish Hurrah, The.
Lament for the Death of Eoghan Ruadh O'Neill.
My Grave.
My Land.
O, the Marriage!
Tone's Grave.
Welcome, The [*or* A].
West's Asleep, The.

Davis, William Virgil
Chandelier as Protagonist, The.
To My Son, Not Yet Born.

Davison, Edward
Enchanted Heart, The.
In This Dark House.
Nocturne: "Be thou at peace this night."
Novice, The.
Owl, The.
Snare, The.
Sonnet: "She is so young, and never never before."

Davison, Francis
Are Women Fair?,*at.*
Cupid's Pastime.
Epitaph: "Lovely boy, thou art not dead."
Epitaph: "Thou alive on earth, sweet boy."
Epitaph: "Wit's perfection, Beauty's wonder."
Her Commendation.
His Farewell to His Unkind and Unconstant Mistress.
I Muse Not.
Madrigal: "Some there are as fair to see to."
Madrigal: "Sound of thy sweet name, my dearest treasure, The."
My Only Star.
Song: "Lady, you are with beauties so enriched."
To Cupid.

Davison, Francis Douglas
Bought.

Davison, Peter
Artemis.
Bed Time.
Breaking of the Day, The.
Cost of Pretending, The.
Finale: Presto.
Housing Starts.
Last Word, The.
Lunch at the Coq d'Or.
Magpie.
Money Cry, The.
My Lady the Lake.
North Shore.
Peeper, The.
Pleaders, The.
Star Watcher, The.

Davison, Walter
At Her Fair Hands.
How Can the Heart Forget Her?
Ode: "At her fair hands how have I grace entreated."
To His Lady, Who Had Vowed Virginity.

Dawe, Bruce
Abandonment of Autos.
Americanized.
City, The: Midnight.
Drifters.
Homecoming.
Not-so-good Earth, The.
Only the Beards Are Different.
Perpetuum Immobile.

Dawe, Gerald
Lives.

Dawes, Rufus
Love Unchangeable.

Dawson, Daniel Lewis
Seeker in the Marshes, The.

Dawson, Gene
When a Body.

Dawson, Grace Stricker
To a Friend.

Dawson, William James
Deliverance.
Inspirations.

Day, Beth
Three Gates.

Day, Clarence
And/Or.
Historical Incidents.
Man Is but a Castaway.
Might and Right.
Parting injunctions, The.
Sad Story.
Who Drags the Fiery Artist Down?

Day, Dorothea
My Captain.

Day, George Edward
Master of Laborers, The.

Day, James William
Rowan County Crew, The, *at.*

Day, John
Ditty, A: "Peace, peace, peace, make no noise."
Humour Out of Breath, *sel.*
Parliament of Bees, The, *sel.*

Day, Lucille
Labor.
Neural Folds.
Reject Jell-o.
Self-Portrait with Hand Microscope.
Tumor.
Yom Kippur.

Day, Richard Edwin
England.
To Shakespeare.

Day, Thomas Fleming
Clipper, The.
Main-Sheet Song, The.
Making Land.

Day, William
Mount Vernon, the Home of Washington.

Day Lewis, Cecil
Album, The.
Almost Human.
As One Who Wanders into Old Workings.
Birthday Poem for Thomas Hardy.
Bombers.
But Two There Are.
Can the Mole Take.

Chiefly to Mind Appears.
Chorus: "Since you have come thus far."
Christmas Eve.
Chrysanthemum Show, The.
Circus Lion.
Come, Live with Me and Be My Love.
Come Up, Methuselah.
Committee, The.
Conflict, The.
Consider These, for We Have Condemned Them.
Dead, The.
Departure in the Dark.
Desire is a witch.
Do Not Expect Again a Phoenix Hour.
Double Vision, The.
Emily Brontë.
Failure, A.
Few Things Can More Inflame.
Flight, The.
Flight to Italy, *sel.*
Fox, The.
From Feathers to Iron, *sels.*
Great Magicians, The.
Happy View, A.
In Heaven, I Suppose, Lie Down Together.
In the Heart of Contemplation.
It Is Becoming Now to Declare My Allegiance.
I've Heard Them Lilting at Loom and Belting.
Jig.
"Let Us Now Praise Famous Men."
Love Was Once Light as Air.
Magnetic Mountain, The, *sels.*
Maple and Sumach.
Marriage of Two.
Meeting, A.
My Mother's Sister.
Nabara, The.
Nearing Again the Legendary Isle.
Newsreel.
Noah and the Waters, *sel.*
Now I have come to reason.
Now She Is like the White Tree-Rose.
O Dreams, O Destinations.
Oh Light Was My Head.
On Not Saying Everything.
On the Sea Wall.
One and One.
Overtures to Death, *sel.*
Pegasus.
Poet, The.
Reconciliation.
Rest from Loving [and Be Living].
Room, The.
Sheepdog Trials in Hyde Park.
Son and Father.
Sonnet: "To travel like a bird, lightly to view."
Stand-to, The.
Statuette: Late Minoan.
Sun Came Out in April, The.
Tempt Me No More.
Third Enemy Speaks.
Though Bodies Are Apart.
Time to Dance, A, *sel.*
Two Songs.
Two Songs [Written to Irish Airs].
Unwanted, The.
When They Have Lost.
Where Are the War Poets?
Winter Night.
With Me My Lover Makes.
Word over All.
You That Love England.

Dayre, Sydney
Grandma's Lost Balance.
Lesson for Mamma, A.
Morning Compliments.

Dayton, David
Woman Driving the Country Squire, The.

Dayton, Ebenezer
Wherein Consists the High Estate, *with music.*

Dayton, Irene
Ear Is Not Deaf.

Deagon, Ann
Certified Copy.
Man and Wife Is One Flesh.
There Is No Balm in Birmingham.

Deal, Susan Strayer
These Trees Are.

Deamer, Dulcie
Artemis.

Dean, Agnes Louise
October Night.

Dean, Elma
Old Men's Ward.

Dean, John
Schedules ("Schedules come in different forms, all crushing").
Seeing and Doing.

Deane, Anthony C.
Cult of the Celtic, The.
Here Is the Tale.
Jack and Jill—as Kipling Might Have Written It.
Mary, Mary.
Ode, An: "I sing a song of sixpence, and of rye."
Rural Bliss.
Rustic Song, A.

Deane, Seamus
Derry.
Fording the River.
Northern Ireland: Two Comments.
Return.
Scholar II.

Dearmer, Geoffrey
Turkish Trench Dog, The.
Vision, A.

De Baca, Marc
Lizards of La Brea, The.

De Bary, Anna Bunston
As Rivers of Water in a Dry Place.
Snowdrop, The.
Under a Wiltshire Apple Tree.

De Bevoise, Arlene
Good Friday.
Two Gardens.

De Bolt, William Walter
Back to the Angels.
Thesis.

De Boully, Monny
Beyond Memory.

De Brun, Padraig
In Memoriam.

DeBurgh, H. J.
Half Hours with the Classics.

Dec, Frederick
Bulldozers.
Class of 19—.

De Casseres, Benjamin
Moth-Terror.

DeClue, Charlotte
Diary.
Healing.
Ijajee's Story.
In Memory of the Moon (A Killing).
Morning Song.
Place-of-Many-Swans.
61.
To the Spirit of Monahsetah.
Underside of Trees, The.
Yesterday, Robin spoke to me.

Dederick, Robert
Karoo Town.
Robben Island.

Deems, Charles F.
I Shall Not Want: In Deserts Wild, *with music.*

Defoe, Daniel
Encomium upon a Parliament, An.
English Race, The.
Hymn to the Pillory, A, *sels.*
London.
More Reformation, *sel.*
Reformation of Manners, *sels.*
Spanish Descent, The.
True-born Englishman, The.
Vision, The.

DeFoe, Mark
Euphoria, Euphoria.
On a Photo of a Baby Killed in the War.
13 Ways of Eradicating Blackbirds.

DeFord, Miriam Allen
Ronsard.
Traveller's Ditty.
We Shall Say.

De Forest, John William
Miss Ravenel's Conversion, *sel.*
National Hymn, A.
Phantom Ship, The.
Sea-Maiden, The.

DeFrees, Madeline
In the Hellgate Wind.
Letter to an Absent Son.
Odd Woman, The.
With a Bottle of Blue Nun to All My Friends.

De Gasztold, Carmen Bernos
Noah's Prayer.
Prayer of the Cat, The.
Prayer of the Donkey, The.
Prayer of the Goldfish, The.
Prayer of the Little Ducks, The.
Prayer of the Mouse, The.
Prayer of the Old Horse, The.

DeGravelles, Charles
Astrologer Argues Your Death, The.
Night Out, Tom Cat.

Dehmel, Richard
Before the Storm.
Harvest Song.
Laborer, The.
My Drinking Song.
Silent Town, The.
To———?: "I have baptized thee Withy, because of thy slender limbs."
Trysting, A.
Vigil.
Voice in Darkness.

Dehn, Paul
Alternative Endings to an Unwritten Ballad.
Armistice.
At the Dark Hour.
Come unto these yellow sands.
Fern House at Kew.
Game of Consequences, A.
Geiger, geiger, ticking slow.
I wandered angry as a cloud.
Lament for a Sailor.
Leaden Treasury of English Verse, A, *sels.*
O nuclear [*or* Nuclear] wind, when wilt thou blow.
Quake, Quake, Quake: a Leaden Treasury of English Verse.
Reunion.
Rhymes for a Modern Nursery, *sels.*
Ring-a-ring o' neutrons.
St. Aubin d'Aubigne.
Twinkle, twinkle, little star.
Whenas in Jeans.

Dei-Anang, Michael
My Africa.

Deitz, Purd Eugene
Builders.

DeJong, David Cornel
On the Twenty-fifth of July.

De Kay, Charles
Arcana Sylvarum.
Draft Riot, The.
Tornado, The.
Ulf in Ireland.

Dekker, Thomas
Basket Maker's Song.
Bridal Song, A.
Cold's the Wind.
Country Glee.

Cradle Song, A: "Golden slumbers kiss your eyes."
Drinking Song.
Entertainment to James, *sel.*
Fortune.
Fortune and Virtue.
Golden Slumbers [Kiss Your Eyes].
Happy Heart, The.
Haymakers, Rakers.
Hey Derry Derry.
Honest Whore, The, *sel.*
King's Entertainment, The.
Lullaby: "Golden slumbers kiss your eyes."
May.
Maytime.
Oh, the Month of May!
Old Fortunatus, *sels.*
Pleasant Comedy of Patient Grissell [*or* Grissel *or* Grissill], The, *sels.*
Priest's Song, A.
Saint Hugh.
Shoemaker's Holiday, The, *sels.*
Song: "O the month of May, the merry month of May."
Song: "Virtue's branches wither, virtue pines."
Sun's Darling, The, *sels.*
Sweet Content.
Troll the Bowl!
Troynovant ("Troynovant is now no more a city").

Delafield, Harriet L.
No Escape.

De la Mare, Walter ("Walter Ramal")
Afraid.
Alas, Alack.
All but Blind.
All That's Past.
Alone.
Alulvan.
Ann and the Fairy Song.
Antiques.
Arabia.
Archery.
As Soon as Ever Twilight Comes.
At Ease.
At the Keyhole.
At the Zoo.
Autumn.
Away.
Bah!
Ballad of Christmas, A.
Bandog, The.
Barber's, The.
Bards, The.
Bees' Song, The.
Berries.
Bindweed, The.
Birthnight, The; to F.
Bishop Winterbourne.
Bones.
Bookworm, The.
Bottle, The.
Breughel's Winter.
Bunches of Grapes.
Buttons.
Chart, The.
Chicken.
Children of Stare, The.
Child's Day, A, *sels.*
Clear Eyes.
Comb, The.
Corner Stone, The.
Corporal Pym.
Crumbs.
Cupboard, The.
Dark Château, The.
Dream-Song.
Drugged.
Dunce, The.
Dust to Dust.
Echo.
Eel, The.
Empty House, The.
End, The.
Epitaph, An: "Here lies a most beautiful lady."
Estranged.
Eyes.
Faint Music.
False Dawn.
False Gods.
Fare Well.
Feckless Dinner Party, The.
Five Eyes.
Fly, The.
Full Moon.
Funeral, The.
Galliass, The.
Ghost, The.
Go Far; Come Near.
Gone.
Good-Bye.
Green.
Hare, A.
Hawthorn Hath a Deathly Smell, The.
Holly, The.
Horse in a Field.
Horseman, The.
Hunt, The.
Huntsmen, The.
I Met at Eve.
Immanent.
In Memory of G. K. Chesterton.
In the Dock.
In the Local Museum.
Iron.
It Might Be a Lump of Amber.
J. J.
Jim Jay.
John Mouldy.
Keys of Morning, The.
Kiph.
Last Chapter, The.
Last Coachload, The.
Linnet, The.
Listeners, The.
Little Bird, The.
Little Creature, The.
Little Green Orchard, The.
Lovelocks.
Lucy.
Maerchen.
Many a Mickle.
March Hares.
Marionettes, The.
Martha.
Me.
Mermaids, The.
Mima.
Miracle, The.
Miss Loo.
Miss Pheasant.
Miss T.
Mistletoe.
Mocking Fairy, The.
Moonlight.
Moonshine.
Moth, The.
Motley.
Mountains, The.
Napoleon.
Ned Vaughan.
Never More, Sailor.
Nicholas Nye.
Nod.
Nostalgia.
Nothing.
Old Angler, The.
Old Men, The.
Old Shellover.
Old Summerhouse, The.
Old Susan.
Peace.
Ponjoo.
Pooh!
Poor Henry.
Portrait, A.
Quack!
Quiet Enemy, The.
Railway Junction, The.
Rainbow, The.
Rats.
Reserved.
Revenant, The.
Ride-by-Nights, The.
Robin, A.
Sam.
Santa Claus.
Scarecrow, The.
Scholars.
Scribe, The.
Seeds.
Shadow, The.
She Said.
Ship of Rio, The.
Shubble, The.
Silver.
Silver Penny, The.
Sleeper, The.
Sleeping Beauty.
Sleepyhead.
Slim Cunning Hands.
Snow.
Snowflake, The.
Solitude.
Someone [*or* Some One].
Somewhere.
Song of Finis, The.
Song of Shadows, The.
Song of the Mad Prince, The.
Spectre, The.
Still Life.
Stranger, The.
Summer Evening.
Sunk Lyonesse.
Sunken Garden, The.
Supper.
Susannah Prout.
Tartary.
Tat for Tit.
Theologians.
There Blooms No Bud in May.
Things.
Thomas Hardy.
Thomas Logge.
Three Cherry Trees, The.
Three Sisters.
Thunder.
Tillie.
Tired Tim.
Titmouse.
To a Candle.
Tom's Little Dog.
Tomtit, The.
Trees.
Truants, The.
Vain Finding.
Vain Questioning.
Virtue.
Voice, The.
Voices.
Waif, The.
Where.
Why?
Widow's Weeds, A.
Winter.
Winter Evening.
Wreck, The.

Deland, Margaret
Affaire d'Amour.
Christmas Silence, The.
Clover, The.
Doubt.
Fairies' Shopping, The.
Love and Death.
Love's Wisdom.
Sent with a Rose to a Young Lady.

While Shepherds Watched [Their Flocks by Night].
Delaney, John
Golf Ball.
Delaney, W. W. *See* **"Lee, Andy"**
Delany, Clarissa Scott
Interim.
Joy.
Mask, The.
Solace.
De la Selva, Salomon
Tropical Town.
De León, Nephtalí
In the Plaza We Walk.
Delius, Anthony
Brief Farewell.
Deaf-and-Dumb School.
Distance.
Footnote.
Gamblers, The.
Intuition.
Lady Anne Bathing.
Shadow.
Thinker, The.
Deloney, Thomas
Dialogue between the Lovelorn Sir Hugh and Certain Ladies of Venice, A.
Gentle Craft, The, *sels.*
Joyful [*or* Joyfull] New Ballad, A.
Song: "Primrose in the green forest, The."
Winning of Cales, The.
Would God That It Were Holiday!
Del Medigo, Joseph Solomon
Epigram: "If men be judged wise."
Del Monte, Crescenzo
One Thing to Take, Another to Keep.
Roman Roman, A.
Those Zionists.
De Long, Juanita
My Hereafter.
De Longchamps, Joanne
Blind, I Speak to the Cigarette.
Tortoise.
Del Renzio, Toni
Can You Change a Shilling?
Demarest, Mary Lee
My Ain Countree.
Demetriadis, Mary
"When Lovely Woman Stoops to Folly."
Demetrio, Herrera S.
Training.
Demille, A. B.
Ice King, The.
De Mille, James
Gallant Highwayman, The.
Lines to Miss Florence Huntingdon, *at.*
Maiden of Passamaquoddy, The.
Deming, A. G.
Who Is Tapping at My Window.
Demodocus
Snake It Was That Died, The.
Demon, Andrew
Reflections of a Trout Fisherman.
De Morgan, Augustus
Great Fleas ("Great fleas have little fleas").
Dempster, Barry
Mother.
Dempster, Roland Tombekai
Africa's Plea.
Is This Africa.
DenBoer, James
Charming the Moon.
Spring in Washington.
Denby, Edwin
Air.
City without Smoke.
Dishonor.
Northern Boulevard.
Against the Love of Great Ones.
Cooper's Hill.
Elegie upon the Death of the Lord Hastings, An.
Grasse-Hopper, The.
Had Cowley ne'er spoke, Killigrew ne'er writ.
Love in the First Age: To Chloris.
Lucasta Weeping ("Lucasta wept, and still the bright").
Natura Naturata.
On Mr. Abraham Cowley [His Death and Burial amongst the Ancient Poets].
On the Earl of Strafford's Trial and Death.
Thames, The.
There Faunus and Sylvanus keep their courts.
To the Five Members of the Honourable House of Commons.
Denney, Reuel
Connecticut River, The.
Fixer of Midnight.
Laboratory Midnight, The.
McSorley's Bar.
March with All Drums Muffled, A.
Dennis, C. J.
Intro, The.
Martyred Democrat, The.
Pilot Cove.
Play, The.
Sentimental Bloke, The, *sel.*
Triantiwontigongolope, The.
Dennis, Carl
Band, The.
Chosen, The.
Dennis, Zelma S.
Irish Wind, An.
Denny, Sir Edward
Hope of Our Hearts.
Dennys, John
Angler's Song, The.
Secrets of Angling, The, *sel.*
Dent, Tom
Come Visit My Garden.
Love.
Denwood, Jonathan
Bleeberrying.
Denza, Luigi
Funiculi, Funicula.
De Regniers, Beatrice Schenk
I Looked in the Mirror.
Keep a Poem in Your Pocket.
Night Comes.
Der Hovanessian, Diana
Poultry.
Derian, Vahan
Words at Farewell.
Derleth, August
Planetary Arc-Light, The.
Dermody, Thomas
Decayed Monastery, A.
John Baynham's Epitaph.
Ode to Myself, An.
Petition of Tom Dermody to the Three Fates in Council Sitting, The.
Shepherd's Despair, The.
"Der Nistor" (Pinhas Kahanovitch)
At the Doors.
De Roche, Joseph
Aunt Laura Moves toward the Open Grave of Her Father.
Blond.
Derosier, Lola
Last Day, The.
Derwood, Gene
After Reading St. John the Divine.
Bird, Bird.
Camel.
Elegy: "When in the mirror of a permanent tear."
Elegy on Gordon Barber.
In Common.
In the Proscenium.
Innocent, The.
Mailed to G. B.
N. B., Symmetrians.
Rides.
Shelter.
Spring Air.
Third Madrigal.
To George Barker.
War's Clown in the Proscenium.
With God Conversing.
Derzhavin, Gavril Romanovich
O, Thou Eternal One!
Desbordes-Valmore, Marceline
Roses of Sa'adi, The.
Deshoulières, Antoinette
Reflections.
Desmond, Gerald Fitzgerald, 4th Earl of
Against Blame of Women.
Desnoues, Lucienne
First Things.
Desportes, Philippe
Conquest.
His Lady's Might.
Desprez, Frank
Lasca.
Dessner, Lawrence Jay
Tennis Pro.
Dessus, Ronald James
Difference between a Lie and the Truth, The.
Geronimo: Old Man Lives On.
Imagine a world of people whose motto is.
Surrounded by Walls Am I.
Ta wa nee ta wa nee—i softly call into the gentle night.
De Tabley, John Byrne Leicester Warren, 3d Baron
Anticipation.
Chorus: "Sweet are the ways of death to weary feet."
Chorus: "Throned are the gods, and in."
Churchyard on the Sands, The.
Circe.
Fortune's Wheel.
Frosty Day, A.
Knight in the Wood, The.
Lines to a Lady-Bird.
Medea, *sel.*
Nuptial Song.
Ode: "Sire of the rising day."
Philoctetes, *sel.*
Pilgrim Cranes, The.
Power of Interval, The.
Song of Dust, A.
Sonnet: "Record is nothing, and the hero great."
Study of a Spider, The.
Two Old Kings, The.
Windmill, The.
Detrick, Daisy L.
Little Johnny Mine, The.
Ol' Jinny Mine, The.
Dett, Robert Nathaniel
Rubinstein Staccato Etude, The.
Deutsch, Babette
Aged Woman to Her Sons, The.
Apocrypha.
Barges on the Hudson.
Bull, A.
Capriccio.
Dancers, The.
Destruction of Letters.
Earliness at the Cape.
Fireworks.
Girl, A.
Homage to the Philosopher.
Hound, The.
In a Museum.
Late Reflections.
Memory.
Morning Workout.
Need.
New Words for an Old Song.
New York—December, 1931.
No Moon, No Star.
Old Women.
Paradigm.
Piano Recital.

Pig Is Never Blamed, A.
Pity.
Poem, The: "Painter of Dante's awful ferry-ride, The."
Reflections in a Little Park.
Scene with Figure.
Small Colored Boy in the Subway.
Solitude.
Songs.
Stranger than the Worst.
Tak for Sidst.
They Came to the Wedding.
To the Moon.

Devaney, James
Evening Gleam, The.
Mortality.
Song of the Captured Woman.

Dever, Joseph
Queen of Horizons.

De Vere, Sir Aubrey
Children Band, The.
Opening of the Tomb of Charlemagne, The.
Reality.
Right Use of Prayer, The.
Rock of Cashel, The.
Waterloo.

De Vere, Aubrey Thomas
Autumnal Ode.
Ballad of Sarsfield, A.
Coleridge.
Divine Presence, The.
Epitaph: "He roamed half-round the world of woe."
Evening Melody.
Florence MacCarthy's Farewell to His English Lover.
Flowers I Would Bring.
Human Life.
Hymn for the Feast of the Annunciation.
Implicit Faith.
In Ruin Reconciled.
Little Black Rose, The.
Love's Spite.
Mater Amabilis.
May Carols, *sels.*
Religio Novissima.
Roisin Dubh.
Sacraments of Nature, The.
Scene in a Madhouse.
Serenade: "Softly, O midnight Hours!"
Song: "Seek not the tree of silkiest bark."
Song: "Sing the old song, amid the sound dispersing."
Sorrow.
Spring.
Sun God, The.
Three Woes, The.
Wedding of the Clans, The.
Year of Sorrow, A, *sels.*

De Vere, Edward, 17th Earl of Oxford
Choice, A.
Doubtful Choice, A.
Epigram: "Were I a king, I could command content."
If Women Could Be Fair.
Of the Birth and Bringing Up of Desire.
Pains and Gains.
Renunciation, A
White and Red.

De Vere, William

Devlin, Denis
Ank'hor Vat.
Anteroom: Geneva.
Ascension.
Ballad of Mistress Death.
Colours of Love, The.
Daphne Stillorgan.
Encounter.
Eve in My Legend.
Farewell and Good.
From Government Buildings.
Heavenly Foreigner, The, *sel.*
Jansenist Journey.
Lough Derg.
Memoirs of a Turcoman Diplomat.
Passion of Christ, The.
Renewal by Her Element.
Statue and the Perturbed Burghers, The.
Tomb of Michael Collins, The.
Venus of the Salty Shell.
Welcome My World.
Wishes for Her.

De Vries, Peter
Bacchanal.
Beth Appleyard's Verses.
Christmas Family Reunion.
Loveliest of Pies.
Mirror.
Psychiatrist.
Theme and Variation.
To My Friends.

De Vries, Rachel
Jealousy.

Dewar, A. W.
Life and the Weaver.

Dewdney, Christopher
Out of Control; the Quarry.
This Is of Two Worlds.

Dewey, Berenice C.
Conversation.

Dewey, George Washington
Blind Louise.

DeWitt, Samuel A.
Two Sonnets for a Lost Love.

Dexter, R. P.
Shadow Dirge.

Dey, Richard Morris
Fog 9/76.

De Young, Lily A.
I Have a Place.

Diamond, David
We Will Not Fear, *with music.*

Diaper, William
Brent; a Poem to Thomas Palmer Esq.
Eclogue: "Lycon begin—begin the mournful tale."
Eels and Tortoises.
Halieutica, *sels.*
Nereides; or, Sea-Eclogues, *sels.*
Sea Eclogue.

Dibben, Dennis
Some Modern Good Turns.

Dibdin, Charles
Anchorsmiths, The.
Blow High! Blow Low!
Captain Wattle and Miss Roe.
Heaving the Lead, *at.*
Jack's Fidelity.
Jolly Young Waterman, The.
Lady's Diary, The.
Leadsman's Song, The, *at.*
Nongtongpaw.
Poor Jack.
Poor Tom; or, The Sailor's Epitaph.
Popular Functionary, A.
Tom Bowling.

Dibdin, Thomas
Child That Has a Cold [We May Suppose], A.

Di Caprio, Isabelle
Jabber-Whacky.

Di Castagnola, Countess Alice Fay
Mortal Combat.

Di Cicco, Pier Giorgio
Errore.
Flying Deeper into the Century.
Friendship Game, The.
Head Is a Paltry Matter, The.
Male Rage Poem.
Words to the Wind.

Dickens, Charles
Cannibals' Grace before Meat, The.
Fine Old English Gentleman, The; New Version.
Ivy Green, The.
Pickwick Papers, The, *sel.*

Dickenson, John
Shepherd's Complaint, The, *sel.*
Tityrus to His Fair Phyllis.

Dickey, James
Adultery.
After the Night Hunt.
Armor.
At Darien Bridge.
Bee, The.
Beholders, The.
Being, The.
Between Two Prisoners.
Birth, A.
Birthday Dream, The.
Bread.
Buckdancer's Choice.
Bums, on Waking.
By Canoe through the Fir Forest.
Call, The.
Cancer Match, The.
Celebration, The.
Chenille.
Cherrylog Road.
Coming Back to America.
Common Grave, The.
Dog Sleeping on My Feet, A.
Driver, The.
Drowning with Others.
Dusk of Horses, The.
Encounter in the Cage Country.
Faces Seen Once.
Falling.
Fence Wire.
Fiend, The.
Firebombing, The.
Flash, The.
For the Death of Vince Lombardi.
For the Last Wolverine.
For the Nightly Ascent of the Hunter Orion over a Forest Clearing.
For the Running of the New York City Marathon.
Gamecock.
Goodbye to Serpents.
Heaven of Animals, The.
Hedge Life.
Hospital Window, The.
Hunting Civil War Relics at Nimblewill Creek.
Ice Skin, The.
In the Marble Quarry.
In the Mountain Tent.
In the Pocket.
In the Tree House at Night.
Inside the River.
Landfall, The.
Leap, The.
Lifeguard, The.
Listening to Foxhounds.
Looking for the Buckhead Boys.
Madness.
Magus, The.
Moon Ground, The.
Movement of Fish, The.
On the Hill below the Lighthouse.
Owl King, The.
Performance, The.
Poisoned Man, The.
Pursuit from Under.
Reincarnation [I] ("Still, passed through the spokes of an old wheel").
Reincarnation [II] ("One can do one begins to one can only").
Scratch, The.
Shark's Parlor, The.
Sheep Child, The.
Slave Quarters.
Springer Mountain.
Summons, The.
Sun.
To His Children in Darkness.
To Landrum Guy, Beginning to Write at Sixty.

Trees and Cattle.
Underground Stream, The.
Venom.
Walking on Water.
Winter Trout.
Zodiac, The, *sel.*
Dickey, Martha
Studies from Life.
Dickey, R. P.
Early June.
Santo Domingo Corn Dance.
Takes All Kinds.
Dickey, William
Another Given: The Last Day of the Year.
Canonical Hours.
Dolls Play at Hansel and Gretel, The.
Face-Paintings of the Caduveo Indians.
Fish Upstairs, The.
For Every Last Batch When the Next One Comes Along.
Happiness.
Hope.
Horn, Mouth, Pit, Fire.
Love among the Manichees.
Poet's Farewell to His Teeth, The.
Resolving Doubts.
Spectrum.
Teaching Swift to Young Ladies.
Things Kept.
Tutankhamen.
Voyage to the Moon.
What It Means, Living in the City.
Dickinson, Blanche Taylor
Four Walls.
Poem: "Ah, I know what happiness is!"
Revelation.
That Hill.
To an Icicle.
Walls of Jericho, The.
Dickinson, Charles Monroe
Children, The.
Dickinson, Emily
Afraid? Of whom am I afraid?
After a hundred years.
After great pain, a formal feeling comes.
Ah, necromancy sweet!
Ah, Teneriffe!
Alter! When the hills do.
Altered look about the hills, An.
Although I put away his life.
Ample make this bed.
Apparently with no surprise.
Arcturus is his other name.
As by the dead we love to sit.
As imperceptibly as grief.
At half-past three a single bird.
At least—to pray—is left—is left.
Auctioneer of parting, The.
Aurora.
Baffled for just a day or two.
Bat is dun, with wrinkled wings, The.
Battlefield, The.
Beauty—be not caused—it is.
Because I could not stop for death.
Because you are going.
Beclouded.
Bee his burnished carriage, A.
Bee! I'm expecting you!
Before I got my eye put out.
Behind me—dips eternity.
Besides the autumn poets sing.
Bible is an antique volume, The.
Bird, A.
Bird came down the walk, A.
Birthday of but a single pang.
Bloom is result. To Meet a flower.
Bone that has no marrow, The.
Book, A ("He ate and drank the precious words").
Book, A. ("There is no frigate like a book").
Brain, within its groove, The.
Brain is wider than the sky, The.
Bring me the sunset in a cup.
Bustle in a house, The.
By the Sea.
Called Back.
Cemetery, A.
Certain Slant of Light, A.
Chariot, The.
Chartless.
Child's Question, The.
Choice.
Clock stopped, A.
Color—caste—denomination.
Come slowly, Eden.
Constant.
Crumbling is not an instant's act.
Death.
Departed—to the judgment.
Did our best moment last.
Did the harebell loose her girdle.
Difference between despair, The.
Dost Thou Remember Me?
Doubt me, my dim companion!
Drama's vitallest expression is the common day.
Drowning is not so pitiful.
Drunkard cannot meet a cork, A.
Dying.
Dying tiger, A—moaned for drink.
Dying! To be afraid of thee.
Elysium is as far as to.
Essential oils—are wrung.
Eternity.
Evening.
Exclusion.
Exultation is the going.
Faded boy in sallow clothes, A.
Faith is a fine invention.
Faith—is the pierless bridge.
Fame is a fickle food.
Final Inch, The.
Finding is the first act.
First day's night had come, The.
Four trees upon a solitary acre.
Frigid and sweet her parting face.
Fringed Gentian.
From all the jails the boys and girls.
Further [*or* farther] in summer than the birds.
Fuzzy fellow without feet, A.
Gentian weaves her fringes, The.
Glass was the street.
Go not too near a house of rose.
God is a distant, stately lover.
God is indeed a jealous God.
God made a little gentian.
God's Residence.
Going—to—her!
Grass, The.
Grass so little has to do, The.
Great streets of silence led away.
Have you got a brook in your little heart.
He ate and drank the precious words.
He fumbles at your soul.
He preached upon "Breadth" till it argued him narrow.
He scanned it, staggered, dropped the loop.
He was weak, and I was strong—then.
Heart asks pleasure first, The.
Heart, we will forget him!
Heaven is what I cannot reach.
"Heavenly Father," take to thee.
Helping the Handicapped.
Her breast is fit for pearls.
Her face was in a bed of hair.
Her sweet weight on my heart a night.
Her—"last poems."
His mansion in the pool.
Hope is the thing with feathers.
How happy is the little stone.
How many times these low feet staggered.
How the waters closed above him.
Hummingbird, A.
I am alive—I guess.
I asked no other thing.
I breathed enough to take the trick.
I can wade grief.
I cannot live with you.
I could bring you jewels—had I a mind to.
I died for beauty—but was scarce.
I dreaded that first robin, so.
I dwell in Possibility.
I envy seas, whereon he rides.
I felt a cleavage [*or* cleaving] in my mind.
I felt a funeral, in my brain.
I gave myself to him.
I got so I could hear his name.
I had been hungry, all the years.
I had not minded walls.
I have a king who does not speak.
I have never seen volcanoes.
I have not told my garden yet.
I heard a fly buzz—when I died.
I held a jewel in my fingers.
I know a place where summer strives.
I know that He exists.
I like a look of agony.
I like to see it lap the miles.
I meant to have but modest needs.
I measure every grief I meet.
I never hear that one is dead.
I never hear the word "escape."
I never lost as much but twice.
I never saw a moor.
I read my sentence steadily.
I reason, earth is short.
I reckon—when I count at all.
I saw no way—the heavens were stitched.
I shall know why—when time is over.
I should have been too glad, I see.
I started early, took my dog.
I stepped from plank to plank.
I taste a liquor never brewed.
I took my power in my hand.
I watched the moon around the house.
I went to heaven.
I would not paint—a picture.
I years had been from home.
If I can stop one heart from breaking.
If I should die.
If I shouldn't be alive.
If my bark sink.
If recollecting were forgetting.
If you were coming in the Fall.
I'll tell you how the sun rose.
I'm ceded, I've stopped being theirs.
I'm nobody! Who are you?
I'm wife; I've finished that.
Immortal is an ample word.
Immortality.
In lands I never saw, they say.
In the Garden.
In winter in my room.
Indian Summer.
It dropped so low—in my regard.
It is an honorable thought.
It makes no difference abroad.
It sifts from leaden sieves.
It sounded as if the streets were running.
It struck me every day.
It was not Death, for I stood up.
It would have starved a gnat.
I've seen a dying eye.
Jesus! thy Crucifix.
Just lost, when I was saved!
Lad of Athens, faithful be.
Last night that she lived, The.
Lay this laurel on the one.
Lest any doubt that we are glad that they were born today.
Life.
Light exists in spring, A.
Lightly stepped a yellow star.
Lightning is a yellow fork, The.
Little madness in the spring, A.
Little Tippler, The.
Locomotive, The.

Lonely House, The.
Long, long sleep, a famous sleep, A.
Love is that later thing than death.
March.
Martyr poets, The—did not tell.
Me from myself—to banish.
Mine enemy is growing old.
Mine—by the right of the white election.
Missing all, prevented me, The.
Moon upon her fluent route, The.
Moon was but a chin of gold, The.
Morning.
Morning after Death, The.
Mountains grow unnoticed, The.
Mushroom is the elf of plants, The.
Musicians wrestle everywhere.
My country need not change her gown.
My friend must be a bird.
My life closed twice before its close.
My life had stood—a loaded gun.
My period had come for prayer.
My portion is defeat—today.
My triumph lasted till the drums.
Mysteries.
Name—of it—is "Autumn," The.
Narrow fellow in the grass, A.
No passenger was known to flee.
No rack can torture me.
No Time to Hate.
Not any sunny tone.
Now I knew I lost her.
Of all the souls that stand create.
Of bronze and blaze.
Of course I prayed.
Of God we ask one favor.
Once a Child.
One dignity delays for all.
One need not be a chamber—to be haunted.
Only ghost I ever saw, The.
Only news I know, The.
Our journey had advanced.
Our little kinsmen after rain.
Our lives are Swiss.
Our share of night to bear.
Ourselves we do inter with sweet derision.
Ourselves were wed one summer—dear.
Over the fence.
Pain has an element of blank.
Papa above!
Parting.
Pedigree.
Pedigree of honey, The.
Perception of an object costs.
Pink, small and punctual.
Pit, A—but heaven over it.
Poets Light But Lamps, The.
Precious to me—she still shall be.
Presentiment—is that long shadow—on the lawn.
Proud of my broken heart since thou didst break it.
Publication—is the auction.
Purple Clover.
Railway Train, The.
Read, sweet, how others strove.
Rearrange a wife's affection?
Remorse is memory awake.
Renunciation.
Reportless subjects, to the quick.
Resurgam.
Return, The.
Revolution is the pod.
Robin is the one, The.
Route of evanescence, A.
Safe despair it is that raves.
Safe in their alabaster chambers.
Said Death to Passion.
Satisfaction—is the agent.
Savior! I've no one else to tell.
Secret, The.
Shady friend for torrid days, A.
She dealt her pretty words like blades.
She rose to his requirement, dropped [*or* dropt].
She sweeps with many-colored brooms.
Show is not the show, The.
Sky is low, the clouds are mean, The.
Snake, A.
Snow, The.
So proud she was to die.
Softened by time's consummate plush.
Some keep the Sabbath [*or* Sunday] going to church.
Some things that fly there be.
Some we see no more, Tenements of Wonder.
Some wretched creature, savior take.
Sorrow.
Soul selects her own society, The.
Spider holds a silver ball, The.
Split the lark—and you'll find the music.
Spring is the period.
Stars are old, that stood for me, The.
Step lightly on this narrow spot!
Storm, The.
Success is counted sweetest.
Summer Shower.
Sunrise and Sunset.
Sunset and Sunrise.
Surgeons must be very careful.
Suspense.
Tell all the truth but tell it slant.
That after horror that was us.
That it will never come again.
That love is all there is.
That such have died enables us.
Their height in heaven comforts not.
There are two Mays.
There came a day at summer's full.
There came a wind like a bugle.
There is a languor of the life.
There is a morn by men unseen.
There is a pain—so utter.
There is a shame of nobleness.
There is a solitude of space.
There is no frigate like a book.
There is no silence in the earth—so silent.
There's a certain slant of light.
There's been a death in the opposite house.
These are the days when birds come back.
They called me to the window, for.
They might not need me, but they might.
They put us far apart.
They shut me up in prose.
Thirst.
This consciousness that is aware.
This dirty little heart.
This is my letter to the world.
This world is not conclusion.
Though the great waters sleep.
Thunder-Storm, A.
Tint I cannot take is best, The.
'Tis so much joy! 'tis so much joy!
'Tis true—they shut me in the cold.
Title divine—is mine!
To fight aloud is very brave.
To flee from memory.
To hear an oriole sing.
To know just how He suffered would be dear.
To learn the transport by the pain.
To make a prairie it takes a clover and one bee.
To my quick ear the leaves conferred.
To see her is a picture.
Too happy time dissolves itself.
Too Late.
Train, The.
Triumph may be of several kinds, A.
Truth is as old as God.
'Twas like a maelstrom, with a notch.
'Twas warm—at first—like us.
Two lengths has every day.
Under the light, yet under.
Undue significance a starving man attaches.
Until the desert knows.
Utterance.
Vanished.
Victory comes late.
Waking Year, The.
Waters chased him as he fled, The.
Way I read a letter's—this, The.
We do not play on graves.
We dream—it is good we are dreaming.
We like March—his shoes are purple.
We never know how high we are.
We outgrow love, like other things.
We thirst at first—'tis nature's act.
Went up a year this evening.
What inn is this.
What is—"Paradise."
What soft, cherubic creatures.
When I have seen the sun emerge.
When night is almost done.
While we were fearing it, it came.
Wife—at daybreak I shall be, A.
Wild nights!—wild nights!
Will there really be a morning?
Wind begun [*or* began] to rock [*or* knead] the grass, The.
Wind tapped like a tired man, The.
Witchcraft was hung, in history.
With a Daisy.
With Flowers.
Within my garden, rides a bird.
Wonder is not precisely knowing.
World feels dusty, The.
Wounded deer leaps highest, A.

Dickinson, Goldsworthy Lowes
I never asked for more than thou hast given.

Dickinson, John
Liberty Song, The, *with music.*

Dickinson, Patric
Advent; a Carol.
Hounds, The.
Jodrell Bank.
Lines for an Eminent Poet and Critic.
On a Female Snob, Surprised.
Redwing, The.
St. Stephen's Day.
Swallows, The.

Dickinson, Peter
By-Election Idyll.

Dickson, Aimor R.
Company One Keeps, The, *at.*

Dickson, John
Art Gallery.
Looking Down on West Virginia.

Die, Countess Beatritz de
Estat ai en greu cossirier.
I sing a song reluctantly.
Lately I've felt a grave concern.

Diego Padró, Jose I. de
Epistolary Briefs to Proclus, *sel.*

Diekmann, Conrad
Winter Trees.

Dienstag, Alan
Three Women.

Diespecker, Dick
Between Two Furious Oceans, *sel.*

Dietmar von Aist
Bird Was Singing, A.
Lady Stood, A.
Linden Tree, The.
Parting at Morning.

Digance, Richard
Ants at the Olympics, The.
Duck, The.

Digby, John
One Night Away from Day.
Sooner or Later.

Digby, Sir Kenelm
On His Late Espoused Saint.

Dillard, Annie
Arches and Shadows.
Light in the Open Air.
Windy Planet, The.

Dillard, Richard H. W.
Hats.
How Copernicus Stopped the Sun.

How Einstein Started It Up Again.
Meditation for a Pickle Suite.
Dillenback, John D.
Colorado.
Diller, John Irving
Lullaby Town.
Dillon, Dan
Testing, Testing.
Dillon, George
Hard Lovers, The.
Kind Inn, A.
Remember, Though the Telescope Extend.
Dillon, Will *and* Harry Von Tilzer
I Want a Girl.
Dillow, H. C.
Confrontations of March.
Di Michele, Mary
Moon and the Salt Flats, The.
Piccante.
Dimmette, Celia
Apology of the Young Scientists.
Dimoff, John
West of Chicago.
Dimond, William
Mariner's Dream, The.
"Dinesen, Isak" (Karen Blixen)
Zebra.
Dinnies, Anna Peyre
Wife, The.
Diogenes Laertius
Be gone ye blockheads, Heraclitus cries.
Diop, Birago
Breaths.
Diop, David
Africa.
He Who Has Lost All.
Suffer, Poor Negro!
Those Who Lost Everything.
Vultures, The.
Your Presence.
Diotimus
Without the Herdsman.
DiPasquale, Emanuel
Advice.
First Surf.
Incantation to Get Rid of a Sometime Friend.
Rain.
Di Piero, W. S.
Fat Tuesday.
Four Brothers.
Lines to a Friend in Trouble.
"Living, A."
On Christmas Eve.
Second Horn.
Dipoko, Mbella Sonne
Autobiography.
DiPrima, Diane
Goodbye Nkrumah.
In Memory of My First Chapatis.
Jungle, The.
Moon Mattress.
Practice of Magical Evocation, The.
Quarrel, The.
Revolutionary Letter # 4 ("Left to themselves people").
Revolutionary Letter # 19 ("If what you want is jobs").
Revolutionary Letter # 29 ("Beware of those/ who say").
Revolutionary Letter # 36 ("Who is the we, who is/ the they").
Revolutionary Letter # 40 ("If the power of the word is anything, America").
Dircks, Helen
After Bourlon Wood.
London in War.
Disch, Tom
Homage to Carracci.
Vowels of Another Language, The.
Dismond, Binga
At Early Morn.
Status Quo.
Disraeli, Benjamin, 1st Earl of Beaconsfield
Wellington.
Ditlevsen, Tove
Morning.
Old Folk, The.
Self Portrait 4.
Ditmars, Rembrandt William B.
Lincoln.
Ditsky, John
Chamber Music.
Epithalamium: "First a princess."
Mainline.
Ditta, J. M.
In the Surgery.
Divine, Charles
At the Lavender Lantern.
Look Not to Me for Wisdom.
Never Will You Hold Me.
Paris; the Seine at Night.
Spanish Song.
We Met on Roads of Laughter.
Divine, Jay
Coal Miner's Grace.
Dix, William Chatterton
As with Gladness Men of Old.
What Child Is This?
Dixon, Alan
Chops.
Dixon, Henry
Description of a Good Boy, The.
Dixon, Maynard
Laguna Perdida.
Navajo Song.
Plains, The.
Dixon, Melvin
Man Holding Boy.
Richard, Richard: American Fuel.
Tour Guide: La Maison des Esclaves.
Dixon, Richard Watson
Both Less and More.
By the Sea.
Dream.
Fallen Rain.
Heaving Roses of the Hedge Are Stirred, The.
Humanity.
Judgment of the May, The.
Love's Consolation, *sel.*
O Ubi? Nusquam.
Ode: Spirit Wooed, The.
Ode on Advancing Age.
Rapture; an Ode.
Song: "Feathers of the willow, The."
Song: "Oh, bid my tongue be still."
Song: "Why fadest thou in death."
Sonnet: "Give me the darkest corner of a cloud."
Unrest.
Willow.
Winter Will Follow.
Wizard's Funeral, The.
Dixon, Sarah
Lines Occasioned by the Burning of Some Letters.
Dixon, Stephen
Fable of the Water Merchants.
Djabali, Leila
For My Torturer, Lieutenant D
Djangatolum. *See***Corbin, Lloyd M., Jr.**
Djanikian, Gregory
Michelangelo: "The Creation of Adam."
Djellaladin Pasha, Mahmud
Song: "If you love God, take your mirror between your hands and look."
Djurberaui
All You Others, Eat.
Doak, Hugo Larmour
Beggar, The.
Scarecrow, The.
Doane, George Washington
Bishop Doane on His Dog.
Evening.
Evening Contemplation.
Fling Out the Banner! *with music.*
Life Sculpture.
Once More, O Lord, *with music.*
Robin Redbreast.
Thou Art the Way, *with music.*
"Doane, Jerry." *See* **Morse, Katharine Duncan**
Doane, William Croswell
Ancient of Days.
Modern Baby, The.
Preacher's Mistake, The.
Dobberstein, Michael
Engine, The; a Manual.
Dobbs, Eric Robertson
When the Ecstatic Body Grips.
Dobbs, Jeannine
Kitchen Song.
Dobbs, Kildare
Exequy: To Peter Allt.
Dobell, Bertram
Microcosm.
Dobell, Eva
Gramophone Tunes.
Night Duty.
Pluck.
Dobell, Sydney Thompson
America.
Balder, *sels.*
Ballad of Keith of Ravelston, The.
Botanist's Vision, The.
Chanted Calendar, A.
Daft Jean.
Desolate.
Eden-Gate.
Even-Song, An.
German Legion, The.
He Loves and He Rides Away.
How's My Boy?
Isabel.
Keith of Ravelston.
Nuptial Eve, A.
Orphan's Song, The.
Procession of the Flowers, The.
Return!
Sonnet: Army Surgeon, The.
Sonnet: Common Grave, The.
Sonnets on the War, *sel.*
To the Authoress of "Aurora Leigh."
Tommy's Dead.
Wind.
Dobson, A. M.
Bidean Nam Bian.
Dobson, Austin (Henry Austin Dobson)
Ars Victrix.
Ballad of Heroes, A.
Ballad of Imitation, The.
Ballad to Queen Elizabeth, A.
Ballade of the Armada, A.
Before Sedan.
Child-Musician, The.
City Flower, A.
Clean Hands.
Curé's Progress, The.
Dance of Death, The.
Dead Letter, A.
Dialogue from Plato, A.
Don Quixote.
Dora versus Rose.
Fame and Friendship.
Fame Is a Food That Dead Men Eat.
Fancy from Fontenelle, A.
For a Copy of Theocritus.
Garden Song, A.
Gentleman of the Old School, A.
Good Night, Babette!
Growing Gray.
Henry Wadsworth Longfellow.
In After Days.
Incognita.
Kiss, A.
Ladies of St. James's, The.
Maltworm's Madrigal, The.
Milkmaid, The.

On a Fan That Belonged to the Marquise de Pompadour.
On the Hurry of This Time.
Rondeau, The: "You bid me try, Blue Eyes, to write."
Rose-Leaves.
Song of Angiola in Heaven, A.
Song of the Four Seasons, A.
To a Greek Girl.
To "Lydia Languish."
Urceus Exit.
Wanderer, The.
When I Saw You Last, Rose.
"When There Is Peace."
With Pipe and Flute.
Dobson, John
Robin; a Pastoral Elegy.
Dobson, Rosemary
Across the Straits.
Being Called For.
Birth, The.
Bystander, The.
Child with a Cockatoo.
Detail from an Annunciation by Crivelli.
Devil and the Angel, The, *sel.*
In a Café.
Methuselah.
Raising of the Dead, The.
Three Fates, The.
Dobyns, Stephen
Cemetery Nights.
Counterparts.
Delicate, Plummeting Bodies, The.
Dream.
Fear.
Getting Up.
Girl in White.
Japanese Girl with Red Table.
Oatmeal Deluxe.
Triangular Field, The.
White Skirt, The.
Window, The.
Dobzynski, Charles
Fable Merchant, The.
Memory Air.
Never Again, The.
Zealot without a Face.
Dock, Christopher
O Children, Would You Cherish? *with music.*
"Doc Long." *See* **Long, Doughtry, Jr.**
Dodat, François
Dromedary.
Ladybug.
Dodd, Lee Wilson
Comrade, The.
Flower, The.
Dodd, Leonard
Compel Them to Come In.
Dodd, Wayne
Night Poem.
Doddridge, Philip
Awake, My Soul!
Christ's Resurrection and Ascension.
Dum Vivimus, Vivamus.
How Gentle God's Commands.
Hymn: "Ye golden Lamps of Heav'n, farewel."
Live While You Live.
Meditations on the Sepulchre in the Garden.
O God of Bethel.
"Ye Golden Lamps of Heaven."
Dodge, Anacreon
Thracian Filly, The.
Dodge, Henry Nehemiah
Spirit of Freedom, Thou Dost Love the Sea.
Thrustarararorum.
Dodge, Mary Barker
Now.
Dodge, Mary Mapes
Brave Knight, A.
Emerson.
In Trust.
Letters at School, The.
Mayor of Scuttleton, The.
Melons.
Minuet, The.
Now the Noisy Winds Are Still.
Once before, this self-same air.
One and One.
Poor Crow!
Shadow Evidence.
Snowflakes.
Stars, The.
Stocking Song on Christmas Eve.
Ten Kinds.
That's What We'd Do.
Two Mysteries, The.
Żealless Xylographer, The.
Dodge, Ossian E.
Ho! Westward Ho! *with music.*
Dodge, Samuel
People Will Talk.
Dodgson, Charles Lutwidge. *See* **"Carroll, Lewis"**
Dodington, George Bubb, Baron Melcombe
Ode: "Love thy country, wish it well."
Dodsley, Robert
Agriculture, *sel.*
Epistle to My Friend J. B., An.
Method of Preserving Hay from Being Mow-Burnt, or Taking Fire, A.
Dodson, Margery
Poem: "Entombed in my heart no blood flows to you."
Dodson, Owen
Ballad of Badmen.
Confession Stone, The.
Counterpoint.
Decision, The.
Drunken Lover.
Epitaph for a Negro Woman.
For Edwin R. Embree.
For My Brother.
Hymn Written after Jeremiah Preached to Me in a Dream.
I Break the Sky.
Job's Ancient Lament.
Mary Passed This Morning.
Miss Packard and Miss Giles.
Morning Duke Ellington Praised the Lord, The.
Open Letter.
Poems for My Brother Kenneth, *sel.*
Rag Doll and Summer Birds.
Sailors on Leave.
Sickle Pears.
Six o'Clock.
Sorrow Is the Only Faithful One.
Yardbird's Skull.
Döhl, Reinhold
Pattern Poem with an Elusive Intruder.
Dolben, Digby Mackworth
After Reading Homer.
April of the Ages, The.
Enough.
Flowers for the Altar.
Garden, The.
He Would Have His Lady Sing.
Homo Factus Est.
I Asked for Peace.
Prayer, A: "From falsehood and error."
Requests.
Sea Song, A.
Shrine, The.
Song, A: "World is young today, The."
Strange, All-absorbing Love.
We hurry on, nor passing note.
Dole, Nathan Haskell
Russia.
Russian Fantasy, A.
To an Imperilled Traveller.
Dolgorukov, Florence
Intersection.
Three Sunrises from Amtrak.
Dollard, James B.
Fairy Harpers, The.
Dolliver, Clara
No Baby in the House.
Domanski, Don
Deadsong.
Three Songs from the Temple.
Domett, Alfred
Christmas Hymn, A.
Christmas Hymn, 1837, A.
Glee for Winter, A.
Maori Girl's Song, A.
Domin, Hilde
Birthdays.
Catalogue.
Cologne.
Dreamwater.
Domino, Ruth
Sparrow in the Dust, A.
Donaghy, John Lyle
At My Whisper.
Duck.
Ebb.
Fossil, The.
Glenarm.
Grave, The.
Heron, The.
Leitrim Woman, A.
Linota Rufescens.
Portrait.
Seeing.
Voyage.
Where the dropwort springs up lithe and tall.
Winter.
Donaghy, William A.
Fourth Station.
Thirteenth Station.
Donahue, Jack
Brave Donahue, *at.*
Donaldson, Islay Murray
Skye Summer ("Skye rasps the mind").
Doney, May
Comfort.
White Dream, The.
Donian, Mitchell
If someone asks you.
Donne, John
Absence, *sometimes at.*
Air [*or* Aire] and Angels.
Anatomy [*or* Anatomie] of the World, An: The First Anniversary.
Anniversary [*or* Anniversarie], The.
Annunciation.
Antiquary.
Apparition, The.
Ascention.
Autumnal, The.
Bait [*or* Baite], The.
Blossom [*or* Blossome], The.
Blow Your Trumpets, Angels.
Break of Day ("Stay, O sweet, and do not rise").
Break [*or* Breake] of Day ("'Tis true, 'tis day; what through it be").
Broken Heart, The.
Burnt Ship, A.
Calm [*or* Calme], The.
Canonization, The.
Change.
Comparison, The.
Computation, The.
Contemplation of Our State in Our Deathbed.
Crucifying.
Curse, The.
Dampe, The.
Dark Churches.
Daybreak.
Death.
Devout Fits.
Dissolution, The.
Doth Not a Tenarif, or Higher Hill.
Dream [*or* Dreame], The ("Dear[e] love, for nothing less[e] than thee").
Ecstasy, The.

Elegie: His Parting from Her.
Elegie: On His Mistris.
Elegie VII: "Natures lay ideot, I taught thee to love."
Elegie XIX: To His Mistris Going to Bed.
Elegies, *sels.*
Elegy on Mistress Boulstred.
Elegy V: His Picture.
Elegy XIX: Going to Bed.
Epithalamion Made at Lincolnes Inne.
Epithalamion on the Lady Elizabeth and Count Palantine Being Married on St. Valentine's Day, An, *sel.*
Expiration, The.
Extasie, The.
Farewell to Love.
Fever, A.
Flea, The.
For Forgiveness.
Forget.
Funeral [*or* Funerall], The.
Go and Catch a Falling Star.
God grant thee thine own wish, and grant thee mine.
Going to Bed.
Good Friday [*or* Goodfriday], 1613. Riding Westward.
Good Morrow, The.
Hail, Bishop Valentine.
His Parting from Her.
His Picture.
Holy Sonnets.
Hymn [*or* Hymne] to Christ, at the Author's Last Going into Germany, A.
Hymn [*or* Hymne] to God My God, in My Sickness[e].
Hymn [*or* Hymne] to God the Father, A.
I am a little world made cunningly.
Indifferent, The.
Jealosie.
Jeat Ring Sent, A.
La Corona.
Lame Beggar, A.
Lecture upon the Shadow, A.
Legacy [*or* Legacie], The.
Letter to Sir H. Wotton at His Going Ambassador to Venice.
Litanie, The: "Father of heaven, and him, by whom."
Lovers Infiniteness[e].
Love's Alchemy [*or* Alchymie].
Love's Deity [*or* Deitie].
Love's Diet.
Love's Growth.
Love's Progress.
Message, The.
Nativitie [*or* Nativity].
Nocturnal upon St. Lucy's Day [Being the Shortest Day], A.
On Death.
On His Mistress [*or* Mistris].
Our Companie in the Next World.
Paradox, The.
Perfume, The.
Phryne.
Primrose, Being at Montgomery Castle, The.
Progress[e] of the Soul[e], The ("I sing the progress of a deathless soul").
Prohibition, The.
Relic, The.
Religion.
Resurrection.
Sacrament, The.
Satire: "Away, thou fondling motley humorist."
Satire: "Sir: though (I thank God for it) I do hate."
Satire: "Well, I may now receive, and die: my sin."
Satire V: "Thou shalt not laugh in this leaf, Muse, nor they."
Satyre: Of [*or* On] Religion.
Seek True Religion!
Self Accuser, A.
She, she is dead; she's dead: when thou knowest this.
Song: "Go and catch a falling star."
Song: "Sweetest love, I do not go[e]."
Sonnet: "As due by many titles I resigne."
Sonnet: "At the round earths imagin'd corners, blow."
Sonnet: "Death be not proud, though some have called thee."
Sonnet: "Father, part of his double interest."
Sonnet: "I am a little world made cunningly."
Sonnet: "If faithfull soules be alike glorifi'd."
Sonnet: "If poysonous mineralls, and if that tree."
Sonnet: "O might those sighs and tears returne again."
Sonnet: "O my black soule! now thou art summoned."
Sonnet: "Oh, to vex me, contraryes meet in one."
Sonnet: "Show me deare Christ, thy spouse, so bright and clear."
Sonnet: "Since she whom I lov'd hath payd her last debt."
Sonnet: "Spit in my face you Jewes, and pierce my side."
Sonnet: "This is my playes last scene, here heavens appoint."
Sonnet: "Thou hast made me. And shall thy worke decay?"
Sonnet: "What if this present were the worlds last night?"
Sonnet: "Why are wee by all creatures waited on?"
Sonnet: "Wilt thou love God, as he thee! then digest."
Soules Ignorance in This Life and Knowledge in the Next, The.
Storm, The.
Storm at Sea, A.
Sun [*or* Sunne] Rising, The.
Teach Me How to Repent.
Temple.
This Is My Play's [*or* Playes] Last Scene, Here Heavens Appoint.
To Christ.
To Mr. C. B. ("Thy friend, whom thy deserts to thee enchaine").
To Mr. George Herbert.
To Mr. I. L.
To Mr. R. W. ("Kindly I envy the songs perfection").
To Mr. Rowland Woodward.
To Mr. T. W.
To Mr. Tilman after He Had Taken Orders.
To Sir Edward Herbert at Julyers.
To Sir H. W. at His Going Ambassador to Venice.
To the Countesse of Bedford, on New-Yeares Day.
To the Countesse of Bedford ("Honour is so sublime perfection").
Triple Fool, The.
Truth.
Twicknam Garden.
Undertaking, The.
Valediction, A: Forbidding Mourning.
Valediction, A: Of My Name in the Window.
Valediction, A: Of Weeping.
Verse and Fame.
Whale, The.
Will, The.
Witchcraft by a Picture.
Woman's Constancy.

Donnell, David
Canadian Prairies View of Literature, The.
Hotels.
Open Roads.
Potatoes.
Stepfathers.

Donnelly, Charles
Flowering Bars, The.
Heroic Heart.
Last Poem.
Tolerance of Crows, The.

Donnelly, Dorothy
Blue Flag.
Chinese Baby Asleep.
Consider the Lilies.
Girandole.
Glass World.
Leaflight.
Prospect of Swans, A.
Recollection.
Serenade: "Tin-type tune the locusts make, The."
Three-toed Sloth.

Donnelly, Susan
Rilke Speaks of Angels.

Donnelly, Tom
Myself When Young.

Donohue, James J.
Last Antiphon: To Mary.

Donovan, Gregory
Working Man, The.

Donovan, Rhoda
No Signal for a Crossing.
Ten Week Wife.

Donzella, D. W.
Last Job I Held in Bridgeport, The.

Dooher, Muredach J.
Renascence.

Dooley, Ebon
Easter Bunny Blues, The, or All I Want for Xmas Is the Loop.
Prophet's Warning or Shoot to Kill, The.
Query.

Doolittle, Esther Hull
Secret.

Doolittle, Hilda ("H. D.")
Acon.
Adonis.
Ah (You Say), This Is Holy Wisdom.
At Baia.
At Ithaca.
Birds in Snow.
Callypso Speaks.
Centaur Song.
Circe.
Cities.
Egypt.
Epigram: "Golden one is gone from the banquets, The."
Erige Cor Tuum ad Me in Caelum.
Eurydice.
Evadne.
Evening.
Flowering of the Rod, The, *sels.*
Fragment Thirty-six: "I know not what to do."
Fragment 113: "Not honey,/ not the plunder of the bee."
From Citron-Bower.
Garden, The.
Good Frend, *sel.*
Halcyon, *sel.*
Heat.
Helen.
Helen in Egypt, *sels.*
Helmsman, The.
Hermes of the Ways.
Hippolytus Temporizes.
Holy Satyr.
Hymen, *sel.*
In Time of Gold.
Islands, The.
Lais.
Leda.
Let Zeus Record, *sel.*
Lethe.
Mid-Day.
Moon in Your Hands, The.
Moonrise.

Mysteries Remain, The.
Never More Will the Wind.
Not Honey.
Orchard.
Oread.
Pear Tree.
Phaedra.
Pool, The.
Pursuit.
Pygmalion, *sel.*
Sagesse, *sel.*
Sea Gods.
Sea Rose.
Sea Violet.
She Contrasts with Herself Hippolyta.
She Rebukes Hippolyta.
Sigil.
Sitalkas.
Socratic.
Song: "You are as gold."
Songs from Cyprus, *sels.*
Stars Wheel in Purple.
Storm.
There Is a Spell, for Instance.
Tribute to the Angels, *sels.*
Walls Do Not Fall, The, *sels.*
Where Love Is King.
White World.
Wind Sleepers, The.
Wine Bowl.

Dor, Moshe
Among the Pine Trees.
Dwelling, The.
Nightingales Are Not Singing.
Small Bones Ache.

Doran, Louise A.
Ship, The.

Dorcey, Mary
First Love.
Sea Flower.

Doreski, William
Amish, The.

Dorgan, John Aylmer
Beautiful, The.
Dead Solomon, The.

Doria, Prinzivalle
Canzone: Of His Love, with the Figure of a Sudden Storm.

Doriot, Jeanne
Indian.

Dorman, Sonya
Elegy for Bella, Sarah, Rosie, and All the Others.
N.Y. to L.A. by Jet Plane.
Teacher.

Dorn, Alfred
Challengers.
Symphony.

Dorn, Edward
Air of June Sings, The.
Are They Dancing.
Biggest Killing, The.
Chronicle.
Comforted by Limestone.
Eugene Delacroix Says.
For the New Union Dead in Alabama.
From Gloucester Out.
Gunslinger, *sels.*
Hide of My Mother, The.
Home on the Range, February 1962.
Idle Visitation, An.
La Máquina a Houston.
Los Mineros.
Morning to Remember, A; or, E Pluribus Unum.
Mourning Letter, March 29 1963.
On the Debt My Mother Owed to Sears Roebuck.
Oxford, *sel.*
Rick of Green Wood, The.
Song, The: "So light no one noticed."
Song, A: "There is a blue sky."

Sousa.
Thesis.
Vaquero.
When the Fairies.

Dorney, Elizabeth
Chemistry of Character, The.

Doro, Edward
Open Letter for John Doe.
To a Lad Who Would Wed Himself with Music.

Dorothy Ann, Sister Mary
Exchange.

Dorr, Henry R.
Comrades.

Dorr, Julia Caroline Ripley
Fallow Field, The.
Legend of the Organ-Builder, The.
No More the Thunder of Cannon.
O Earth! Art Thou Not Weary?
Outgrown.
Two Paths.
With a Rose from Conway Castle.

Dorrance, Dick
Cockpit in the Clouds.

Dorris, Michael
Frost Heaves.

Dorset, Catherine Ann
Peacock "At Home," The.

Dorset, Charles Sackville, 6th Earl of. *See* **Sackville, Charles, 6th Earl of Dorset**

Dorset, Thomas Sackville, 1st Earl of. *See* **Sackville, Thomas, 1st Earl of Dorset**

Dos Passos, John
Crimson Tent.

Doten, Elizabeth (Lizzie)
Farewell to Earth, *sel.*
In a Hundred Years, *at.*
Reconciliation, *sel.*

Doty, M. R.
Sleep

Doty, Walter G.
Best Firm, The.

Doudney, Sarah
Christian's "Good-Night," The.
Lesson of the Water-Mill, The.
Water Mill, The.

Doughty, Charles Montague
Bladyn's Song of Cloten.
Dawn in Britain, The, *sels.*
Fairies' Feast, The.
Gauls Sacrifice, The.
Hymn to the Sun.
Roman Officer Writes, A.

Douglas, Lord Alfred Bruce
City of the Soul, The.
Dead Poet, The.
Each New Hour's Passage Is the Acolyte.
Green River, The.
Hen, The.
Impression de Nuit; London.
Lighten Our Darkness.
Prayer, A: "Often the western wind has sung to me."
Shark, The.
To , with an Ivory Hand-Glass.
To Olive.
Two Loves.
Witch, The.

Douglas, Ernest
Out Where the West Begins: A Parody.

Douglas, Gawin [*or Gavin*]
Difficulties of Translation, The, *abr.*
Evening and Morning in June, An.
Evening and Morning in Winter, An.
Hart's Castle.
King Hart, *sel.*
Nightmare.
Palace of Honor, The, *sel.*
Prologue to Book VII, The.
Prologue to Book XIII, The.
Prologues to the Aeneid, *sels.*
Winter.

Douglas, Gilean
Inscription in a Book.

Douglas, Jesse
Warning.

Douglas, Keith
Aristocrats.
Behaviour of Fish in an Egyptian Tea Garden.
Cairo Jag.
Canoe.
Deceased, The.
Desert Flowers.
Gallantry.
How to Kill.
Landscape with Figures.
Leukothea.
Offensive, The.
On a Return from Egypt.
Oxford.
Poem: "These grasses, ancient enemies."
Remember Me.
Round Number, A.
Russians.
Sea Bird, The.
Simplify Me When I'm Dead.
Snakeskin and Stone.
Song: "Do I venture away too far."
Time Eating.
Vergissmeinnicht.

"Douglas, Marian" (Annie Douglas Green Robinson)
Ant-Hills.
Good Thanksgiving, A.
One Saturday.
Snow-Man, The.

Douglas, William
Annie Laurie.

Douglass, Suzanne
No Holes Marred.
Progress.

Douskey, Franz
Regressing.

Dove, Rita
Adolescence—II.
Champagne.
Dusting.
Nigger Song; an Odyssey.
Ö.
Planning the Perfect Evening.
This Life.

Dovey, Irma
Unwelcome.

Dow, Dorothy
Song: "I could make you songs."
Things.
To Atalanta.
Unbeliever.

Dow, Philip
Air.
Bottom's Dream.
Doe.
Dried Fruit.
Drunk Last Night with Friends, I Go to Work Anyway.
Duck Pond at Mini's Pasture, a Dozen Years Later, The.
Early Morning.
Elegy: "And if our lives spill."
Fishing.
Ghazal.
Goodbye "Hello."
It Comes during Sleep.
Letter.
Life, The.
Mother.
Skunk, The.
Snow Geese in the Wind.
Song: "What binds the atom together."
Suite for Celery and Blind Date.
Sussyissfriin, *sel.*
Twilight in California.

Dowd, Emma C.
Fun in a Garret.

Dowden, Edward
Autumn Song.
Communion.
In the Cathedral Close.
Line of Beauty, The.
Love's Lord.
Mona Lisa.
New Hymns for Solitude, *sel.*
Oasis.
Renunciants.
Seeking God.
Windle-Straws.
Dowden, Elizabeth Dickinson
Adrift.
Dower, E.
New River Head, a Fragment, The.
Dowland, John
Come Away, Come, Sweet Love, *at.*
Dowling, Allan
I Sought with Eager Hand.
Joy of Love, The.
Miracle, The.
Dowling, Bartholomew
Our Last Toast.
Revel, The.
Revelry for the Dying.
Stand To Your Glasses.
Dowling, Basil
Autumn Scene.
Downer, Ann
Koko.
Downey, Fairfax
Rise and Fall of Valentines.
Downie, Freda
Elsdon.
Downing, Ellen Mary Patrick
My Owen.
Dowson, Ernest Christopher
Ad Domnulam Suam.
Amantium Irae.
Autumnal.
Breton Afternoon.
Carthusians.
De Amore.
Dead Child, The.
Dregs.
Envoy: "They are not long, the weeping and the laughter."
Epigram: "Because I am idolatrous and have besought."
Exchanges.
Exile.
Extreme Unction.
Flos Lunae.
Garden of Shadow, The.
Impenitentia Ultima.
Jadis.
Last Word, A.
Non Sum Qualis Eram Bonae sub Regno Cynarae.
O Mors! Quam Amara Est Memoria Tua Homini Pacem Habenti in Substantiis Suis.
Princess of Dreams, The.
Quid Non Speremus, Amantes?
Saint Germain-en-Laye.
Sapientia Lunae.
Spleen ("I was not sorrowful").
To One in Bedlam.
Valediction, A: "If we must part."
Vesperal.
Villanelle of Acheron.
Villanelle of His Lady's Treasures.
Villanelle of Marguerites.
Villanelle of Sunset.
Villanelle of the Poet's Road.
Vitae Summa Brevis Spem Nos Vetat Incohare Longam.
Your Hands.
Doxey, W. S.
Cathedrals.
Doyle, Sir Arthur Conan
Cremona.
Song of the Bow, The.
White Company, The, *sel.*
Doyle, Sir Francis Hastings
Epicurean, The.
Loss of the *Birkenhead,* The.
Private of the Buffs, The; or, the British Soldier in China.
Doyle, Kirby
Strange.
"Doyle, Lynn" (Leslie Alexander Montgomery)
Ulsterman, An.
Doyle, Marion
Golden Month, The.
Month of the Thunder Moon, The.
Doyle, Susanne
November Walk.
Drachler, Rose
As I Am My Father's.
Dark Scent of Prayer, The.
Prelude: "You went to the verge, you say, and come back safely?"
Isaac and Esau.
Letters of the Book, The.
Under the Shawl.
Zippora Returns to Moses at Rephidim.
Drake, Francis
To the Memory of the Learned and Reverend, Mr. Jonathan Mitchell.
Drake, Joseph Rodman
American Flag, The.
Assembling of the Fays, The.
Culprit Fay, The, *sels.*
Elfin Song.
Fairy Dawn.
Fairy in Armor, A.
Fay's Crime, The.
Fay's Departure, The.
Fay's Sentence, The.
First Quest, The.
Second Quest, The.
Throne of the Lily-King, The ("The throne was reared upon the grass").
To the Defenders of New Orleans.
Drake, Joseph Rodman *and* **Fitz-Greene Halleck.** *See* **Halleck, Fitz-Greene** *and* **Joseph Rodman Drake**
Drake, Leah Bodine
Final Green, The.
Honey from the Lion.
Middle Ages, The: Two Views.
Precarious Ground.
Rider, The.
Drannan, William F.
Old Scout's Lament, The.
Dransfield, Michael
Bum's Rush.
Epiderm.
Geography, *sels.*
Loft.
Pas de Deux for Lovers.
Portrait of the Artist as an Old Man.
Rainpoem.
That Which We Call a Rose.
Draper, A. S.
Indian Summer.
Draper, George
Rink Keeper's Sestina.
Draper, Jane
I Look into the Stars.
Drayton, Michael
Agincourt.
Arming of Pigwiggen, The.
As love and I, late harbour'd in one inn.
Ballad of Agincourt, The.
Ballad of Dowsabell, The.
Baron's War, The, *sel.*
Batte's Song.
Battle of Agincourt, The.
Birds in the Fens.
Cassamen and Dowsabell.
Charnwood Forest.
Christopher Marlowe.
Cloris and Mertilla.
Come, Let Us Kiss and Part.
Crier, The.
Description of Elizium, The.
Dowsabel.
Dwindling Forest of Arden, The.
Earl of Surrey to Geraldine, The.
Eclogue: "Late 'twas in June, the fleece when fully grown."
Endimion and Phoebe, *sels.*
Endymion's Convoy.
England's Heroical Epistles, *sels.*
Epistle of Rosamond to King Henry the Second, The.
Fame and Fortune.
Farewell to Love.
Fen-Men of Lincolnshire's Holland, The.
Fine Day, A.
First Steps up Parnassus.
Fools Gaze at Painted Courts.
Gorbo and Batte.
Henry to Rosamond.
His Remedie for Love.
I hear some say, "This man is not in love!"
I Pray Thee Leave, Love Me No More.
Idea, *sels.*
Jovial Shepheard's Song, The.
King Henry to Rosamond.
Last Verses.
Legend of Robert, Duke of Normandy, The, *sel.*
Like an Adventurous Sea-Farer Am I.
Lincolnshire's Holland Speaks of Her Waterfowl.
Lines: "Clear had the day been from the dawn."
Love's Farewell.
Moone-Calfe, The, *sel.*
Muses' Elysium [*or* Elizium], *sels.*
Night and Day.
Nimphidia.
Ninth Eclogue, The.
Noah's Flood, *sels.*
Nymphidia, the Court of Fairy.
Ode Written in the Peak[e], An.
Owl, The.
Parting, The.
Phoebe on Latmus.
Piers Gaveston, *sel.*
Pigwiggin Arms Himself.
Poets' Paradise, The.
Polyolbion, *sels.*
Queen's Chariot, The.
Roundelay, A: "Tell me, thou skilful shepherd's swain."
Rowland's Rhyme.
Sacrifice to Apollo, The.
Second Nimphall, The.
Seventh Nimphall, The.
Severn, The.
Shepherd's Daffodil, The.
Shepherd's Garland, The, *sels.*
Shepherd's Sirena, The, *sel.*
Sirena.
Sixt Nimphall, The.
Skeltoniad, A.
Song to Beta.
Sonnet: "Black pitchy night, companion of my woe."
Sonnet: "Dear, why should you command me to my rest."
Sonnet: "Evil spirit, your beauty haunts me still, An."
Sonnet: "How many paltry, foolish, painted things."
Sonnet: "Since there's no help, come let us kiss and part."
Sonnet: To the Critic.
Stonehenge.
Tenth Eclogue, The.
Tenth Nimphall [*or* Nymphal], The.
Third Eclogue, The, *sel.*
To Cupid.
To Henry Reynolds, of Poets and Poesy, *sel.*

To Himselfe and the Harpe, *abr.*
To His Coy Love.
To His Valentine.
To My Most Dearly-loved Friend, Henry Reynolds, Esquire, of Poets and Poesy.
To the New Yeere.
To the Reader of These Sonnets.
To the Virginian Voyage.
Trent, The.
Trent Again, The.
Verses Made the Night before He Died.
Virginian Voyage, The.
When first I ended, then I first began.
Drennan, John Swanwick [*or* Swanick]
Epigram: "Golden casket I designed, A."
Epigram: "Love signed the contract blithe and leal."
L'Amitié et l'Amour.
On the Telescopic Moon.
Drennan, William
Eire.
Wake of William Orr, The.
Dresbach, Glenn Ward
Autumn Road, An.
Cave, The.
Desert Song ("There's no hiding here in the glare of the desert").
In Western Mountains, *sel.*
Last Corn Shock, The.
Life or Death.
Old Sailor, The.
Since Youth Is All for Gladness.
Yucca in the Moonlight.
Dresser, Paul
Just Tell Them That You Saw Me.
My Gal Sal.
On the Banks of the Wabash, Far Away, *with music.*
Drewry, Carleton
Evensong.
"Drinan, Adam." *See***Macleod, Joseph Gordon**
Drinkwater, John
Bird's Nest, The.
Birthright.
Bobby Blue.
Christmas Eve.
Crowning of Dreaming John, The.
Deer.
I Want to Know.
Invocation: "As pools beneath stone arches take."
May Garden.
Moonlit Apples.
My Estate.
Petition.
Prayer, A: "Lord, not for light in darkness do we pray."
Reciprocity.
Snail.
Sun, The.
Sunrise on Rydal Water.
Tiptoe Night.
Washing.
Who Were before Me.
Driscoll, Jack
Ice.
Middle of the Day.
Driscoll, Louise
Bargain.
Epitaph: "Here lies the flesh that tried."
God's Pity.
Good Hour, The.
Grace for Gardens.
Highway, The.
Hold Fast Your Dreams.
Idol, The.
July Meadow.
Mid-August.
My garden is a pleasant place.
November Garden.
Spring Market.
Thanksgiving.
Driver, C. J.
Birthdays.
In Solitary Confinement, Sea Point Police Cells.
To Jann, in Her Absence.
Dromgoole, Will Allen
Bridge Builder, The.
Building the Bridge for Him.
Old Ladies.
Dropkin, Celia
Circus Dancer, A.
Droste-Hülshoff, Annette von
In the Grass.
Last Day of the Year, The (New Year's Eve).
On the Tower.
Drummond, William, of Hawthornden
Angels, The.
Angels for the Nativity of Our Lord, The.
Baptist, The.
Book, The.
Book of the World, The.
Change Should Breed Change.
Doth then the world go thus, doth all thus move?
Flowers of Sion, *sel.*
For the Baptist[e].
For the Magdalene.
Her Passing.
Hymne of the Ascension, An.
I Know That All beneath the Moon Decays.
Inexorable.
Invocation: "Phoebus, arise!"
Iöas' Epitaph.
Ivory, Coral, Gold, The.
Kiss, A.
Kisses Desired.
Lament: "Chaste maids which haunt fair Aganippe's well."
Lessons of Nature, The.
Like the Idalian Queen.
Love which is here a care.
Madrigal: "Beauty [*or* Beautie], and the life, The."
Madrigal: "Ivory, coral, gold, The."
Madrigal: "Like the Idalian Queen[e]."
Madrigal: Love Vagabonding.
Madrigal: "My thoughts hold mortal[1] strife."
Madrigal: "Poor turtle, thou bemoans."
Madrigal: "This life, which seem[e]s so fair[e]."
Madrigal: "Unhappie Light."
Nativitie, The.
No Trust in Time.
Of Phyllis.
On Mary Magdalene.
On the Margin Wrought.
Phoebus, Arise.
Phyllis.
Regrat.
Saint John Baptist.
Sanquhar, whom this earth could scarce contain.
Sleep, Silence' Child [Sweet Father of Soft Rest].
Solitary Life, A.
Sonet to Sleepe.
Song: "It Autumnne was, and on our hemispheare."
Song: "Phoebus arise."
Sonnet: "Alexis, here she[e] stayed; among these pines."
Sonnet: "As in a duskie and tempestuous night."
Sonnet: Content and Resolute.
Sonnet: "Dear quirister, who from those shadows sends."
Sonnet: Death's Last Will.
Sonnet: "How that vast heaven intitled First is rolled."
Sonnet: "I fear to me such fortune be assign'd."
Sonnet: "I know that all beneath the moon decays."
Sonnet: "In minds pure glasse when I my selfe behold."
Sonnet: "Lamp of heaven's crystal hall that brings the hours."
Sonnet: "My lute, be as thou wast when thou didst grow."
Sonnet: "Passing glance, a lightning long the skies, A."
Sonnet: "Sleep, Silence' child, sweet father of soft rest."
Sonnet: "Sweet soul, which in the April of thy years."
Sonnet: "Sweet Spring, thou turn'st with all thy goodly [*or* goodlie] train[e]."
Sonnet: "That learned Graecian (who did so excell)."
Sonnet: "What doth it serve to see sun's burning face."
Spring Bereaved 1 ("That zephyr every year").
Spring Bereaved 2 ("Sweet Spring, thou turn'st with all thy goodly train").
Spring Bereaved 3 ("Alexis, here she stay'd; among these pines").
Statue of Medusa, The.
Stolen Pleasure.
Summons to Love.
Tears on the Death of Moeliades, *sel.*
Tell Me No More.
This Life.
Thrice Happy He.
Thy Sun Posts Westward.
To a Nightingale.
To His Lute.
To Sir William Alexander.
To the Nightingale.
Trojan Horse, The.
World, The.
World a Hunt, The.
Drummond, William Henry
Johnnie Courteau.
Julie Plante, The.
Leetle Bateese.
Log Jam, The.
Madeleine Verchères.
Two Hundred Years Ago.
Wreck of the *Julie Plante,* The.
Dryden, John
Absalom and Achitophel, Pt. I.
Achitophel: The Earl of Shaftesbury.
After the Pangs of a Desperate Lover.
Ah, Fading Joy.
Ah How Sweet It Is to Love.
Albion & Albanius, *sel.*
Alexander's Feast; or, The Power of Music [*or* Musique].
All, All of a Piece [Throughout].
All for Love, *sel.*
Amboyna; or, The Cruelties of the Dutch to the English Merchants, *sel.*
Amphitryon, *sels.*
Annus Mirabilis, *sels.*
Assignation, The, *sel.*
Astraea Redux, *sels.*
Aureng-Zebe, *sels.*
Ave atque Vale.
Beneath a Myrtle Shade.
Can Life Be a Blessing.
Catholic Church, The.
Character of a Good Parson, The.
Charm, A.
Chorus: "All, all of a piece throughout."
Church of England, The.
Churches of Rome and of England, The.
Church's Testimony, The.
Cleomenes, *sel.*
Cleopatra and Antony.
Conquest of Granada, The, *sels.*
Conversion.
Crown Prince of Dullness, The.
Cymon and Iphigenia.
Damon and Celimena.
Death the Consequence of the Fall.
Diana's Hunting-Song.
Duke of Buckingham, The.

Epigram: "Here lies my wife: here let her lie!"
Epigram on Milton.
Epilogue: "Hold! are you mad? you damned, confounded dog!"
Epilogue: "They who have best succeeded on the stage."
Epilogue Spoken by Mrs. Boutell.
Epilogue to "Mithridates, King of Pontus."
Epilogue to "Tyrannick Love."
Epitaph Intended for His Wife.
Epitaph on His Wife.
Evening's Love, An, *sels.*
Fair Iris and Her Swain.
False Achitophel, The.
Farewell, Ungrateful Traitor.
Fife and Drum.
Finite Reason.
Fire of London, The.
Fourth Day's Battle, The.
Great Fire, The.
Harvest Home.
Here Lies My Wife.
Heroique Stanzas, Consecrated to the Glorious Memory of His Most Serene and Renowned Highnesse, Oliver, Late Lord Protector of This Common-Wealth.
Hidden Flame.
Hind and the Panther, The, *sels.*
Horat. Ode 29. Book 3. Paraphras'd in Pindarique Verse.
Hourly I Die.
How Happy the Lover.
Human Happiness.
I Feed a Flame Within.
Imitation of Horace, *sel.*
Incantation to Oedipus.
Indian Emperor, The, *sels.*
Jacob Tonson, His Publisher.
Kind Keeper, The, *sel.*
King Arthur, *sels.*
King James II.
Kiss Me, Dear.
Lady's Song, The.
Lines Printed under the Engraved Portrait of Milton [in Tonson's Folio of the "Paradise Lost," 1688].
London.
London after the Great Fire, 1666.
Long Betwixt Love and Fear.
Lord Shaftesbury.
Love.
Love Triumphant, *sel.*
Love's Despair.
Love's Fancy.
MacFlecknoe; or, A Satire [*or* Satyr] upon the True-Blue [*or*-Blew] Protestant Poet T. S.
Maiden Queen, The, *sel.*
Malcontents, The.
Marriage à la Mode, *sels.*
Medal [*or* Medall], The, *sel.*
Mercury's Song to Phædra.
Midnight.
New London, The.
No, No, Poor Suffering Heart.
Oak, The.
Ode in Honor of St. Cecilia's Day, The.
Ode on the Death of Mr. Henry Purcell, An, *sel.*
Ode to the Pious Memory of the Accomplished Young Lady, Mrs. Anne Killigrew.
Oedipus, *sel.*
Og and Doeg.
On Jacob Tonson, His Publisher.
One Happy Moment.
Palamon and Arcite, *sel.*
Parts of the Whole Are We; but God the Whole.
Poet Shadwell, The.
Poet's Resurrection.
Popish Plot, The.
Portrait of Milton, The.
Power of Love, The.
Prayer, A: "What weight of ancient witness can prevail."
Predestination and Free Will.
Presbyterians, The.
Priestcraft and Private Judgement.
Primacy of Dullness, The.
Private Judgement Condemned.
Prologue: "If yet there be a few that take delight."
Prologue: "Our author by experience finds it true."
Prologue: "See my lov'd Britons, see your Shakespeare rise."
Prologue: "Self-love (which never rightly understood)."
Prologue to "Aureng-Zebe."
Prologue to "Love Triumphant."
Prologue to "Secret-Love; or, The Maiden-Queen."
Prologue to "The Tempest."
Prologue to the University of Oxford, 1673.
Reason and Revelation.
Religio Laici.
Rondelay: "Chloe found Amyntas lying."
Scriptures, The.
Sea Battle, The.
Secret Love; or, The Maiden Queen, *sel.*
Secular Masque, The.
Shaftesbury.
Sigismonda and Guiscardo, *sel.*
Song: "After the pangs of a desperate Lover."
Song: "Ah fading joy, how quickly art thou past?"
Song, A: "Ah how sweet it is to love."
Song: "All, all of a piece throughout."
Song, A: "Calm was the even, and cleer was the sky [*or* skie]."
Song: "Can Life be a blessing."
Song, A: "Celia, that I once was blest."
Song, A: "Celimena, of my heart."
Song: "Fair Iris I love, and hourly I die."
Song, A: "Fair, sweet and young, receive a prize."
Song, A: "Farewell ungratefull traytor [*or* traitor]."
Song, A: "Go tell Amynta gentle swain."
Song: "I feed a flame within, which so torments me."
Song: "No, no, poor suff'ring heart no change endeavour."
Song: "Sylvia the fair, in the bloom of fifteen."
Song, A: "Whil'st Alexis lay prest."
Song, A: "You charm'd me not with that fair face."
Song: "Your hay it is mow'd, and your corn is reap'd."
Song for a Girl.
Song for St. Cecilia's Day, 1687, A.
Song from the Italian, A.
Song of the River Thames, A.
Song of the Zambra Dance.
Song of Venus.
Song to a Fair Young Lady, Going Out of [the] Town in the Spring.
Spanish Friar [*or* Fryar], The, *sel.*
Spell, A.
State of Innocence, The, *sels.*
Sung by a Young Girl.
Sylvoe, *sel.*
To His Sacred Majesty, a Panegyrick on His Coronation, 1661, *sel.*
To My Dear Friend Mr. Congreve [on His Comedy Called "The Double-Dealer"].
To My Friend, Dr. Charleton, on His Learned and Useful Works; and More Particularly This of Stone-Heng, by Him Restored to the True Founders.
To My Honor'd Friend Sir Robert Howard, *sel.*
To My Honour'd Kinsman, John Driden, of Chesterton.
To the Memory of Mr. Oldham.
To the Pious Memory of the Accomplished [*or* Accomplisht] Young Lady, Mrs. Anne Killigrew.
To the University of Oxford, 1674: Epilogue.
Tradition.
Troilus and Cressida, *sels.*
Tyrannic [*or* Tyrannick] Love, *sels.*
Under the Portrait of [John] Milton.
Upon the Death of the Earl of Dundee.
Upon the Death of the Lord Hastings.
Upon the Death of the Viscount of Dundee.
Vox Populi.
War.
What Is the World?
When I Consider Life.
Whilst Alexis Lay Pressed [*or* Prest].
Why Should a Foolish Marriage Vow.
Worldly Vanity.
Zambra Dance, The.
Zimir.

Dryden, John *and* **Nahum Tate.** *See* **Tate, Nahum** *and* **John Dryden**

Dryden, Myrtle May
Just Forget.

Dubé, Janet
Autobiography.
So to Tell the Truth.

Du Bellay, Joachim
Antiquitez de Rome.
Heureux Qui, comme Ulysse, A Fait un Beau Voyage.
Hymn to the Winds.
Regrets, *sel.*
Rome.
Ruins of Rome, *sels.*
Sonnet to Heavenly Beauty, A.
To His Friend in Elysium.
Visions, *sel.*
Vow to Heavenly Venus, A.

Dubie, Norman
At Midsummer.
Balalaika.
Circus Ringmaster's Apology to God, The.
Coleridge Crossing the Plain of Jars; 1833.
Comes Winter, the Sea Hunting.
Composer's Winter Dream, The.
Dressing Stations, The.
Elegy to the Sioux.
Elizabeth's War with the Christmas Bear [1601].
Everlastings, The.
February; the Boy Breughel.
Fox Who Watched for the Midnight Sun, The.
Funeral, The.
Ganges, The.
Hours, The.
In the Dead of the Night.
Killigrew Wood, The.
Monologue of Two Moons, Nudes with Crests. 1938.
Norway.
Parish.
Pastoral: "It all happened so fast. Fenya was in the straight chair."
Sacrifice of a Virgin in the Mayan Ball Court.
There Is a Dream Dreaming Us.

DuBois, William Edward Burghardt
Litany of [*or* at] Atlanta, A.
Song of the Smoke, The.

Duché, Jacob
Chilled by the Blasts of Adverse Fate, *with music.*
Great Lord of All, Whose Work of Love, *with music.*

Duck, Stephen
On Mites; to a Lady.
Thresher's Labour, The, *sel.*

Duckett, Alfred A.
Portrait Philippines.
Sonnet: "Where are we to go when this is done?"

Dudek, Louis
Air by Sammartini, An.
Atlantis, *sel.*

Avant Garde.
Coming Suddenly to the Sea.
Dawn.
Dead, The.
Europe, *sels.*
Fishing Village.
García Lorca.
I Have Seen the Robins Fall.
Jungle, The.
Marine Aquarium, The.
Morning Light.
Mountains, The.
Mouths.
Narrative.
News.
Ocean, The.
Pomegranate, The.
Provincetown, *sels.*
Store-House, A.
Street in April, A.
Dudley, Dorothy
La Rue de la Montagne Sainte-Gèneviève.
Dudley, Thomas
Verses Found in Thomas Dudley's Pocket after His Death.
Dudley, William E.
City, Lord, Where Thy Dear Life, The, *with music.*
Duemer, Joseph
Curses.
Duer, Caroline
International Episode, An.
Portrait, A.
Word to the Wise, A.
Duerden, Richard
Dance with Banderillas.
Moon Is to Blood.
Musica No. 3.
Duewel, Wesley
On with the Message.
Dufault, Peter Kane
Black Jess.
Evensong.
In an Old Orchard.
Letter for Allhallows, A.
Notes on a Girl.
Odysseus' Song to Calypso.
On Aesthetics, More or Less.
Owl.
Possibilities.
Thalamos.
Tour de Force.
Duff, Esther Lilian
Black and White.
Lad's Love.
Not Three—but One.
Of a Certain Green-eyed Monster.
Duff, James L.
Cradle Song: "Sleep enfold thee,/ Jesukin."
Loan of a Stall, The.
Duffett, Thomas
To Francelia.
Duffield, George, Jr
Stand Up for Jesus.
Duffield, Samuel Willoughby
Two of a Trade.
Duffy, Charles Gavan
Irish Rapparees, The.
Duffy, John
Annunciation, The.
Our Lady's Labor.
Ox-Bone Madonna.
Duffy, Maureen
Evesong.
Sonnet: "Afterwards there are dogends in."
Duffy, Nona Keen
Spring Is in the Making.
Dugan, Alan
Actual Vision of Morning's Extrusion.
Adultery.
American against Solitude.
Aside.
Coat of Arms.
Dedication for a Building.
Elegy: "I know but will not tell."
Elegy for a Puritan Conscience.
Fabrication of Ancestors.
For an Obligate Parasite.
For Masturbation.
From Heraclitus.
From Rome, for More Public Fountains in New York City.
Funeral Oration for a Mouse.
How We Heard the Name.
I never saw any point.
Let Heroes Account to Love.
Love Song: I and Thou.
Memorial Service for the Invasion Beach Where the Vacation in the Flesh Is Over.
Mirror Perilous, The.
Morning Song.
Niagara Falls.
On a Professional Couple in a Side-Show.
On a Seven-Day Diary.
On Alexander and Aristotle, on a Black-on-Red Greek Plate.
On an East Wind from the Wars.
On Don Juan del Norte, Not Don Juan Tenorio del Sur.
On Hurricane Jackson.
On Rape Unattempted.
On Visiting Central Park Zoo.
On When McCarthy Was a Wolf amoung a Nation of Queer-Queers.
Plague of Dead Sharks.
Poem: "Person who can do, The."
Poem: "What's the balm."
Prison Song.
Stutterer.
Thesis, Antithesis and Nostalgia.
To a Red-headed Do-good Waitress.
Trial, A.
Tribute to Kafka for Someone Taken.
Two shots down and I'm exalted.
Wall, Cave, and Pillar Statements, after Asôka.
Winter's Onset from an Alienated Point of View.
Dugan, Mrs. D. H.
Christ Is Risen!
Dugan, Michael
Gumble.
Duganne, A. J. H.
Bethel.
Dugdale, Norman
Anarchist.
Duggan, Eileen
After the Annunciation.
Epiphany.
Juniper.
Name, The.
Du Guillet, Pernette
Epigram: "As the body denies the means to look."
Non Que Je Veuille Ôter la Liberté.
Duke, Richard
After the fiercest pangs of hot desire.
Epithalamium upon the Marriage of Captain William Bedloe, An.
Panegyric upon Oates, A.
Duke, William
Hail Our Incarnate God! *with music.*
Dumas, Alexandre
Lady of the Pearls, The, *sel.*
Dumas, Edmund
Our School Now Closes Out, *with music.*
Dumas, Henry
America.
Black Star Line.
Black Trumpeter.
Buffalo.
Image.
Knock on Wood.
Du Maurier, George
Legend of Camelot, A.
Little Work, A.
Lost Illusion, A.
Music.
Trilby, *sel.*
Vers Nonsensiques.
"Dum-Dum." *See* **Kendall, John Kaye**
Dunann, Louella
Hot Line.
Dunbar, Paul Laurence
Accountability.
After the Quarrel.
Angelina.
Ante-Bellum Sermon, An.
Boy's Summer Song, A.
Compensation.
Curtain!
Dawn.
Death Song, A.
Debt, The.
Differences.
Encouraged.
Equipment.
Ere Sleep Comes Down to Soothe the Weary Eyes.
Frederick Douglass.
Get Somebody Else.
Harriet Beecher Stowe.
Haunted Oak, The.
Howdy, Honey, Howdy!
Hymn, A: "Lead gently, Lord, and slow."
Hymn: "When storms arise."
Hymn, A, after Reading "Lead, Kindly Light."
In the Morning.
Life.
Little Black Sheep, The.
Little Brown Baby.
Lover's Lane.
Master-Player, The.
Misapprehension.
My Sort o' Man.
Negro Love Song, A.
Ode to Ethiopia.
Old Cabin, The.
Paradox, The.
Party, The.
Philosophy.
Poet, The.
Prayer, A: "O Lord, the hard-won miles."
Ships That Pass in the Night.
Soliloquy of a Turkey.
Song, A: "Thou art the soul of a summer's day."
Spiritual, A.
Sympathy.
Theology.
To a Captious Critic.
Too Busy.
Unsung Heroes, The.
We Wear the Mask.
When a Feller's Itchin' to Be Spanked.
When All Is Done.
When de Co'n Pone's Hot.
When Dey 'Listed Colored Soldiers.
When Malindy Sings.
Dunbar, William
Amendis to the Telyouris and Sowtaris for the Turnament Maid on Thame, The.
Amends to the Tailors and Soutars.
Ane Ballat of Our Lady.
Ballad of Kynd Kittok, The.
Ballad of Our Lady.
Book of the Two Married Women and the Widow, The, *sel.*
Dance of the Sevin Deidly Synnis [*or* Seven Deadly Sins], The.
Done Is a Battle.
Fear of Death Confounds Me, The.
Followis How Dumbar Wes Desyrd to Be ane Freir.
Golden [*or* Goldyn] Targe, The.
Hymn of the Resurrection, A.
Hymn to Mary, A.

In Honour of the City of London.
Lament for the Makaris [*or* Makars].
Lord Is Risen, The.
Man of Valour to His Fair Lady, The.
Meditation in Winter.
O Wretch, Beware.
Of the Resurrection of Christ.
On the Nativity of Christ.
On the Resurrection of Christ.
Petition of the Gray Horse, Auld Dunbar, The.
Poet's Dream, The.
Quod Dunbar to Kennedy.
Remonstrance to the King.
Rorate Coeli [*or* Celi] Desuper.
Testament of Mr. Andro Kennedy, The.
Timor Mortis Conturbat Me.
To a Lady [*or* Ladye].
To Aberdein.
To the City of London.
To the Merchantis of Edinburgh.
Tretis of the Tua Mariit Wemen and the Wedo, The.
Twa Mariit Wemen and the Wedo, The.
Widow Speaks, The.

Dunbar-Nelson, Alice
Music.

Duncan, Mary Lundie
Jesus Tender Shepherd.

Duncan, Rea Lubar
Juncture.

Duncan, Robert
African Elegy, An.
After a Passage in Baudelaire.
As in the Old Days, Passages 8.
At Christmas.
At the Loom.
Ballad of Mrs. Noah, The.
Coming Out Of.
Correspondences.
Dance, The.
Dante, *sel.*
Dream Data.
Envoy: "Good Night, at last."
Eyesight II.
Fire, The.
Food for Fire, Food for Thought.
Fourth Song the Night Nurse Sang.
Hero Song.
Homage and Lament for Ezra Pound in Captivity.
Ingmar Bergman's "Seventh Seal."
Interlude, An.
Lover, The.
Morning Letter, A.
My Mother Would Be a Falconress.
New Poem, A.
Night Scenes.
Often I Am Permitted to Return to a Meadow.
Owl Is an Only Bird of Poetry, An.
Part-Sequence for Change, A.
Passage over Water.
Passages, *sels.*
Persephone.
Poem Beginning with a Line by Pindar, A.
Poetry, a Natural Thing.
Question, The.
Reaper, The.
Returning to Roots of First Feeling.
Roots and Branches.
Set of Romantic Hymns, A, *sel.*
Shelley's "Arethusa" Set to New Measures.
Song of the Borderguard, The.
Sonnet I: "Now there is a love of which Dante does not speak unkindly."
Spring Memorandum, A.
Strains of Sight.
Temple of the Animals, The.
These Past Years, Passages 10.
This Place Rumord to Have Been Sodom.
Torso, The: Passages 18.
Tribal Memories.
Turning Into.
Two Presentations.
Up Rising.
What I Saw.

Dunetz, Lora
Ailing Parent, The.
All That Summer.
"And All the While the Sky Is Falling. . ."
Black Cat.
On the Night Express to Madrid.
Treason.
While the Bells Ring.
Winter Nights.

Dunkels, Marjorie
Faith.

Dunkin, William
Epistle to Robert Nugent, Esq. with a Picture of Doctor Swift in Old Age, An, *sel.*

Dunlop, John
Dinna Ask Me.
Year That's Awa', The.

Dunn, Alta Booth
Unknown Soldier.

Dunn, Douglas
After the War.
Clothes Pit, The.
Dream of Judgement, A.
Drying-Green, The.
Emblems.
Estuarial Republic, The.
Glasgow Schoolboys, Running Backwards.
Harp of Renfrewshire, The.
House Next Door, The.
Listening.
Musical Orchard, The.
On Roofs of Terry Street.
Patricians, The.
Remembering Lunch.
Removal from Terry Street, A.
Supreme Death.
War Blinded.
Warriors.

Dunn, Gwen
Journey Back to Christmas.

Dunn, Max
I Danced before I Had Two Feet.

Dunn, Stephen
Beached Whales off Margate.
Building a Person.
Building in Nova Scotia.
California, This Is Minnesota Speaking.
Day and Night Handball.
I Come Home Wanting to Touch Everywhere.
Looking for a Rest Area.
On Hearing the Airlines Will Use a Psychological Profile to Catch Potential Skyjackers.
Rapist, The.
Small Town: The Friendly.

Dunn, Stephen P.
Prayer of the Young Stoic.

Dunnam, Ouida Smith
Prayer of a Beginning Teacher.

Dunne, Carol
Nursing the Hide.

Dunning, Stephen
Player.

Dunsany, Edward John Moreton Drax Plunkett, 18th Baron
Bringing Him Up.
Call to the Wild, A.
Deserted Kingdom, The.
Great guns of England, they listen mile on mile, The.
Heterodoxy, A.
Memory, The.
On the Safe Side.

Dupree, Edgar
Light of Faith, The.

Du Priest, Travis
Experiential Religion.

Durack, Mary
Red Jack.

Durand, H.S., *and others*
Yale Boola! *3 versions, with music.*

Durand, Oswald
Black Man's Son, The.

Durbin, Harriet Whitney
Little Dutch Garden, A.

Durell, Ann
Cornish Magic.

Durem, Ray
Award.
Basic.
Friends.
I Know I'm Not Sufficiently Obscure.
Problem in Social Geometry—the Inverted Square!
Ultimate Equality.
Vet's Rehabilitation.
You Know, Joe.

D'Urfey [*or* Durfey], **Thomas**
Bath, The; or, The Western Lass, *sel.*
Born with the Vices.
Bright Was the Morning.
Brother Solon's Hunting Song.
Bully, The, *at.*
Chloe Divine.
Dialogue, between Crab and Gillian.
Fool's Preferment, A, *sel.*
I'll Sail upon the Dog-Star.
Marriage-Hater Match'd, The, *sel.*
Sawney was Tall.
Shepherd Kept Sheep on a Hill So High, A.
Song, A: "Boast no more fond Love, thy power."
Song, A: "Night her blackest sables wore, The."
Song: Noble Name of Spark, The, *at.*
To Cynthia; a Song.
Virtuous Wife, The, *sel.*
Winchester Wedding, The.

Durgnat, Raymond
Scrap Iron.

Durivage, Francis Alexander
Chez Brébant.

Durrell, Lawrence
Adepts, The.
Alexandria.
At Epidaurus.
Ballad of the Good Lord Nelson, A.
Ballad of the Oedipus Complex.
By the Lake.
Conon in Alexandria.
Coptic Poem.
Cradle Song: "Curled like a hoop in sleep."
Death of General Uncebunke, The; a Biography in Little, *sel.*
Delos.
Eight Aspects of Melissa, *sels.*
Encounter, The.
Epitaph: "Stavro's dead. A truant vine."
In Arcadia.
In Crisis.
In the Garden: Villa Cleobolus.
Lesbos.
Mythology.
Nemea.
Night, The.
On First Looking into Loeb's Horace.
On Seeming to Presume.
Paphos.
Petron, the Desert Father.
Poggio.
Prospect of Children, A.
Rising Sun, The.
Salamis.
Sarajevo.
Seferis.
Stoic.
Swans.
This Unimportant Morning.
To Argos.
To Ping-ku, Asleep.
Visitations.
Water-Colour of Venice, A.

Durston, Georgia Roberts
Hippopotamus, The.
Rabbit, The.
Wolf, The.
Duryee, Mary Ballard
Homestead—Winter Morning.
Du Toit, J.D. *See* **"Totius"**
Dutton, G. J. F.
February Thaw.
Hut.
Magma.
Of Only a Single Poem.
Dutton, Geoffrey
January.
Stranded Whales, The.
Time of Waiting.
Variations on a Medieval Theme.
Duval, Quinton
Absent Star.
I Point Out a Bird.
Morning Fog.
DuVall, Jack
Metroliner.
Dwight, Timothy
As Down a Lone Valley, *with music.*
Assault on the Fortress, The.
Columbia.
I Love Thy Kingdom, Lord, *with music.*
Love to the Church.
Shall Man, O God of Light, *with music.*
Sing to the Lord Most High, *with music.*
Smooth Divine, The.
Star of Columbia.
To the Federal Convention.
Triumph of Infidelity, The, *sel.*
Dwyer, Frank
On the Edge.
Dyer, Lady Catherine
Epitaph on the Monument of Sir William Dyer at Colmworth, 1641.
Sir William Dyer, Knight, *sel.*
Dyer, Sir Edward
Corydon to His Phyllis.
Cynthia.
Epitaph on Sir Philip Sidney, *at.*
Fancy, Farewell.
Kingdom.
Love Is Love.
Modest Love, A.
My Mind [*or* Minde *or* Mynde] to Me a Kingdom [*or* Kyngdome] Is.
Silent Love, A.
Wher one would be.
Dyer, John
Bedford Level.
British Commerce.
English Fog, The.
English Weather.
Enquiry, The.
Grongar Hill.
Happy Workhouse and the Good Effects of Industry, The.
How to Shear Sheep.
Looking Back, *sel.*
My Ox Duke.
Nation's Wealth, A.
O may I with myself agree.
Ruins of Rome, The, *sel.*
To Clio, from Rome.
Wool Trade, The.
Dylan, Bob
Dear Mister Congressman.
Desolation Row.
Mister Tambourine Man.
Sad-eyed Lady of the Lowlands.
Subterranean Homesick Blues.
Dyment, Clifford
As a boy with a richness of needs I wandered.
Children, The.
Man and Beast.
Pastoral: "In the old days the white gates swung."
Sanctuary.
Sea Shanty.
Snow, The.
Swans, The.
Switch Cut in April, A.
Temple, The.
Dyson, Edward
Cleaning Up.
Friendly Game of Football, A.
Old Whim Horse, The.
Dzyubin, Edward. *See* **"Bagritsky, Edward"**

E

"E." *See* **Fullerton, Mary Elizabeth**
"E. H. K. *See* **"K.,E.H."**
"E. O. G." *See* **"G., E.O."**
"Eagle, Solomon." *See* **Squire, Sir John Collings**
Eakman, Florence
Our Clock.
Earle, Virginia
Dream as Reported, A.
Earley, Tom
Jackdaw.
Moorhen Pond, The.
"Eastaway, Edward." *See* **Thomas, Edward**
Eastburn, James Wallis
O Holy, Holy, Holy, Lord, *with music.*
Easter, Marguerite Elizabeth
My Laddie's Hounds.
Eastman, Barrett
How We Burned the *Philadelphia.*
Joy Enough.
Richard Somers.
Eastman, Charles Gamage
Dirge: "Softly!/ She is lying/ With her lips apart."
Eastman, Elaine Goodale
Ashes of Roses.
Baby.
Countrywoman of Mine, A.
Goldenrod.
Eastman, Jon
Working the Skeet House.
Eastman, Max
Animal.
At the Aquarium.
Diogenes.
Hymn to God in Time of Stress, A.
Invocation: "Truth, be more precious to me than the eyes."
Rainy Song.
Eastman, Sophie E.
Spool of Thread, A.
Eastwick, Ivy O.
Dark Danny.
First Snow.
Jack-in-the-Pulpit.
Lucy Lavender.
May Mornings.
Midsummer Magic.
Mother and Child.
My True Love.
Robber, The.
Shadow Dance.
Sing a Song of Moonlight.
Sing a Song of Sunshine.
Snow in Spring.
Stay, Christmas!
Thanksgiving.
Timothy Boon.
Waking Time.
Where's Mary?
Winter in the Wood.
Eaton, Anthony
Dove Apologizes to His God for Being Caught by a Cat, The.
Eaton, Arthur Wentworth Hamilton
Egyptian Lotus, The.
Phantom Light of the Baie des Chaleurs, The.
Pray for the Dead.
Eaton, Burnham
Technique.
Eaton, Charles Edward
Cubistic Lovers, The.
Peony for Apollo, A.
Seascape with Bookends.
Eaton, Evelyn Sibyl Mary
Gardener, The.
Eaton, Walter Prichard
White-Throat Sings, A.
Willows, The.
Ebberts, Ruth N.
Kitchen Window.
Eberhart, Nelle Richmond
At Dawning, *with music.*
Eberhart, Richard
Advantage of the Outside, The.
Analogue of Unity in Multeity.
As If You Had Never Been.
At Lake Geneva.
At Night.
Attic, The ("The attic and the cedar closet—nostalgia!").
Ball Game.
Burr Oaks, *sel.*
Cancer Cells, The.
Chiliasm.
Dam Neck, Virginia.
Enigma, The.
Father and Son.
Fear Death by Water.
Fisher Cat, The.
Flux.
For a Lamb.
Forgotten Rock, The.
From Four Lakes' Days.
Fury of Aerial Bombardment, The.
Gnat on My Paper.
Go to the Shine That's on a Tree.
Goal of Intellectual Man, The.
Groundhog, The.
Half-bent Man.
Horse Chestnut Tree, The.
Human Being Is a Lonely Creature, The.
I Walked Out to the Graveyard to See the Dead.
I walked over the grave of Henry James.
I Went to See Irving Babbitt.
If I Could Only Live at the Pitch That Is near Madness.
Imagining How It Would Be to Be Dead.
In a Hard Intellectual Light.
In the Garden.
Inability to Depict an Eagle.
Kaire.
La Crosse at Ninety Miles an Hour.
Largess, The.
Legend of Viable Women, A.
Long Term Suffering.
"Loon Call, A."
Lost Children, The.
Man Is God's Nature.
Man of Sense, A.
Marrakech.
Matin Pandemoniums, The.
Meditation, A.
"Mysticism Has Not the Patience to Wait for God's Revelation."
New England Bachelor, A.
New Hampshire, February.
1934.
Ode to the Chinese Paper Snake.
On a Squirrel Crossing the Road in Autumn, in New England.
On Shooting Particles beyond the World.
Passage.
Plain Song Talk.
Preacher Sought to Find Out Acceptable Words, The.

Rainscapes, Hydrangeas, Roses, and Singing Birds.
Reading Room, the New York Public Library.
Roc, The.
Rumination.
Sainte Anne de Beaupre.
Sea Bells.
Sea Burial from the Cruiser "Reve."
Sea-Hawk.
Sea-Ruck.
Seals, Terns, Time.
Ship Burning and a Comet All in One Day, A.
Snowfall, A.
Soul Longs to Return Whence It Came, The.
Spider, The.
Spring Mountain Climb.
Stone, A.
Stone Words for Robert Lowell.
Storm and Quiet.
To Auden on His Fiftieth.
To Evan.
To the Field Mice.
Tobacconist of Eighth Street, The.
Two Loves.
Under the Hill.
Ur Burial.
Vast Light.
Vision.
When Doris Danced.
Wisdom of Insecurity, The.
Words.
World War.
Yonder.

Eberling, Georgia Moore
Centuries Are His, The.

Eberly, Ralph D.
Prodigal's Return.

Ebright, Frederick
Memorial to the Great Big Beautiful Self-sacrificing Advertisers.

Echeruo, Michael
Melting Pot.

Eckman, Frederick
Aka.
Lullaby: "What if, every time you walked, things."

Economou, George
Poem for a Suicide.
Seventh Georgic.

Eddy, Gary
Fishing with Buddies.
High Field—First Day of Winter.

Eddy, Mary Baker
O'er Waiting Harp-Strings of the Mind, *with music.*
Shepherd, Show Me How to Go, *with music.*

Eddy, Zachary
Floods Swell around Me, Angry, Appalling, *with music.*
Jesus, Enthroned and Glorified, *with music.*

Edelman, Elaine
How Beautiful You Are: 3.

Edelman, Katherine
Irish Grandmother.
Saturday Shopping.

Edelstein, Hyman
Indian Night Tableau.
Last Mathematician.
Palimpsest.

Eden, Helen Parry
Four-Paws.
Poet and the Wood-Louse, The.
To a Little Girl.
To Betsey-Jane, on Her Desiring to Go Incontinently to Heaven.
Volunteer, A.

Edey, Marion
August Afternoon.
Christmas Eve.
Midsummer Night.
Open the Door.
Our Birthday.

Edey, Marion *and* Dorothy Grider
Ant Village, The.
Jolly Woodchuck, The.
Little Fox, The.
So Many Monkeys.
Trot Along, Pony.

Edgar, Marriott
Lion and Albert, The.

Edgar, Mary S.
Camp Hymn, The.
Prayer-Poem, A.

Edman, Irwin
Advice to a Young Man (Of Letters) Who Doesn't Know How to Take Care of Himself.
Curse of Faint Praise, The.
Flower for a Professor's Garden of Verses.
Intermission, Please!
Kiss-Fest, The.
La Donna E Perpetuum Mobile.
Little Bow to Books on How To, A.
New Hellas, The.
Peace.
Prayer for All Poets at This Time.
To Harold Jacoby.
To Henry David Thoreau.

Edmeston, James
Prayer to the Trinity.

Edmond, Lauris
Commercial Traveller.
Difficult Adjustment, A.
Going to Moscow.
Love Poem: "Everything will happen. Your friend."
Names, The.
3 A.M.
Three Women.
Town Ghost.
Wellington Letter, *sel.*

Edmond, Murray
Afternoon in the Garden, An.
Cell Lay inside Her Body, The.
My Return to Czechoslovakia.
Patching Together, A, *sel.*
Stopping the Heart.
Telephoning It.

Edmondson, Madeleine
Witches' Spells.

Edmunds, William H.
To Be or Not to Be, *parody.*

Edson, C. L.
Ravin's of Piute Poet Poe.

Edson, Russell
Automobile, The.
Childhood of an Equestrian, The.
Children.
Cottage in the Wood, A.
Counting Sheep.
Death of an Angel, The.
Fall, The.
In All the Days of My Childhood.
In the Forest.
Journey through the Moonlight, A.
Little Lady, The.
Long Picnic, The.
Mouse Dinners, The.
Old Man's Son, An.
Out of Whack.
Performance at Hog Theater, A.
Pilot, The.
Prophylactic, The.
Retirement of the Elephant, The.
Wheelbarrow, The.
When the God Returns.
Wounded Breakfast, The.

Edwards, Amelia Blandford
Give Me Three Grains of Corn, Mother.

Edwards, Harry
How to Change the U.S.A.

Edwards, Jeannette Slocomb
Hester MacDonagh.

Edwards, Matilda Barbara Betham. *See* **Betham-Edwards, Matilda Barbara**

Edwards, Matilda C.
Church Walking with the World, The.

Edwards, Richard
Amantium Irae [Amoris Redintegratio].
May.
Of Women.

Edwards, Solomon
Brothers.
Dream.
Shoplifter.

Edwards, Thomas
On the Edition of Mr. Pope's Works with a Commentary and Notes.
Sonnet on a Family Picture.

Eedes, Richard
No Love, to Love of Man and Wife.
Of Man and Wife.

Egan, Maurice Francis
Columbus the World-Giver.
He Made Us Free.
Madonna of the Empty Arms.
Maurice de Guerin.
Old Violin, The.
Shamrock, The.

Egar, J. H.
Sing, Sing for Christmas.

Egemo, Constance
Great Wave off Kanagwa, The.

Egerton, Helen Merrill
Sandpipers.

Egerton, Sarah Fyge
Emulation, The.

Eggerth, Chuck
Much of Me.

Eglington, Charles
Arrival and Departure.
Buffalo.
Lourenço Marques.
Lowveld, The.
Vanquished, The.

"Eglinton, John" (William Kirkpatrick Magee)
Winds, The.

Eguren, José María
Horse, The.

Ehrenburg, Ilya Grigoryevich
Our Children's Children Will Marvel.
Sons of Our Sons, The.
Tree, The.
Trumpet, The.
War Poem.

Ehrenstein, Albert
Ares.
Home-Coming.
Homer.
Suffering.

Ehrhart, William Daniel
Money in the Bank.
To Maynard on the Long Road Home.
Turning Thirty.

Ehrlich, Gretel
Cutting Wood on Shell Creek.
Orchard, The.
Sheeprancher Named John, A.
Way of Speaking, A.

Ehrlich, Helen
Love Song to Lucy.
Lucy Answers.

Ehrlich, Shelley
On Linden Street.

Ehrlichman, Lester
On Reading Mr. Ytche Bashes' Stories in Yiddish.

Ehrmann, Max
Prayer, A: "Let me do my work each day."

Eibel, Deborah
Freethinkers.
Hagar to Ishmael.
Kabbalist, The.

Eichenrand, Lazer
From Life.
Mute City, The.
Prologue: "In your words."

Eifuku, Empress
We dressed each other.
Eigner, Larry
After Shiki.
All Intents.
B.
Bare trees, The/ alternate.
Closed System, The.
Do It Yrself.
Don't go.
Elysee.
Environs.
Fete, A.
Flake diamond of/ the sea.
Fleche.
From the sustaining air.
Gone, A.
I have felt it as they've said.
I will have an image.
Keep Me Still, for I Do Not Want to Dream.
Letter for Duncan.
Noise Grimaced.
Open.
Passages.
Remember Sabbath Days.
School Bus, The.
Shock, The.
Sleep, A.
That the neighborhood might be covered.
Version of a Song of Failure, A.
Washing between the buildings.
Weekday, A.
Eiseley, Loren C.
Deserted Homestead, The.
Spider, The.
Winter Sign.
Eisenberg, Susan
Grandpa Bear.
Eisler, Hans *and* **Bertolt Brecht.** *See* **Brecht, Bertolt** *and* **Hans Eisler**
Ejong, Yityangu
Love Song: "Tiny children."
Ela, David H.
Chosen Three, on Mountain Height, The, *with music.*
Elam, William C.
Mecklenburg Declaration, The.
Eldan, Anadad
Samson Rends His Clothes.
Who Will Give Cover?
Words That Speak of Death.
Elder, Anne
Carried Away.
Farmer Goes Beserk.
One Foot in the Door.
School Cadets.
Eldridge, Paul
To a Courtesan a Thousand Years Dead.
Wang Peng's Recommendation for Improving the People.
Eldridge, Richard Burdick
Soul Remembers, The.
Eleazar
Thy Faithful Sons.
Elijah ben Menahem Hazaken of Le Mans.
Precepts He Gave His Folk.
"Eliot, George" (Mary Ann [*or* Marian] Evans Lewes Cross)
At Set of Sun.
Brother and Sister, *abr.*
Choir Invisible, The.
Count That Day Lost.
I Am Lonely.
Spanish Gypsy, The, *sel.*
Stradivarius, *sel.*
Tide of Faith, The.
Two Lovers.
Working with God.
Eliot, Henrietta Robins
Why It Was Cold in May.
Eliot, Thomas Stearns
Ad-dressing of Cats, The.
Animula.
Ash Wednesday.
Aunt Helen.
Boston Evening Transcript, The.
Burbank with a Baedeker; Bleistein with a Cigar.
Burnt Norton.
Cape Ann.
Cat Morgan Introduces Himself.
Chorus: "We do not wish anything to happen."
Chorus: "We have not been happy, my Lord, we have not been too happy."
Chorus from "The Rock"—III.
Conversation Galante.
Coriolan, *sel.*
Cousin Nancy.
Cultivation of Christmas Trees, The.
Dedication to My Wife, A.
Dry Salvages, The.
East Coker.
Eyes That Last I Saw in Tears.
Forgive Us, O Lord.
Four Quartets, *sels.*
Fragment of an Agon.
Game of Chess, A.
Gerontion.
Growltiger's Last Stand.
Gus: The Theatre Cat.
Hippopotamus, The.
Hollow Men, The.
Journey of the Magi.
La Figlia Che Piange.
Landscapes, *sels.*
Last Temptation, The.
Lines for an Old Man.
Lines for Cuscuscaraway and Mirza Murad Ali Beg.
Lines to Ralph Hodgson, Esqre.
Little Gidding.
Love Song of J. Alfred Prufrock, The.
Macavity: The Mystery Cat.
Marina.
Morning at the Window.
Mr. Apollinax.
Murder in the Cathedral, *sels.*
New Hampshire.
Portrait of a Lady.
Prelude: "Winter evening settles down, The."
Preludes (I–IV).
Rannoch, by Glencoe.
Rhapsody on a Windy Night.
Rock, The, *sels.*
Rum Tum Tugger, The.
Skimbleshanks: The Railway Cat.
Song for Simeon, A.
Song of the Jellicles, The.
Sweeney Agonistes, *sels.*
Sweeney among the Nightingales.
Sweeney Erect.
There Shall Always Be the Church.
Triumphal March.
Usk.
Virginia.
Waste Land, The.
What Life Have You.
When Lil's Husband Got Demobbed, I Said.
Whispers of Immortality.
Wind Sprang Up at Four O'Clock, The.
Eliyia, Joseph
Dream.
Epilogue: "I too was a little child once."
Rebecca.
Slender Maid.
Your Passing, Fleet Passing.
Elizabeth I, Queen of England
Daughter of Debate, The.
Doubt of Future Foes, The.
Importune Me No More.
On Fortune.
On Monsieur's Departure.
When I Was Fair and Young.
Written in Her French Psalter.
Written on a Wall at Woodstock.
Written with a Diamond on Her Window at Woodstock.
Youth and Cupid.
Elizabeth of York, Queen
My Heart Is Set upon a Lusty Pin.
Elledge, Jim
Running the Trotline.
Ellenbogen, George
Announcement, The.
Unter der Linde.
Eller, David
To a God Unknown.
Ellerton, John (1826–1893)
Day Thou Gavest, Lord, Is Ended, The.
God of the Living, The.
Ellerton, John Lodge (1801–1873)
Now the Laborer's Task Is O'er.
Elliot, C. W. *and* **J. R. Thomas**
Bonny Eloise.
Elliot, Gabrielle
Pierrot Goes to War.
Elliot, George Tracy
Winter Twilight.
Elliot, Sir Gilbert
Amynta.
Elliot, Henry Rutherford
Laugh It Off.
Elliot, Jane
Flowers of the Forest, The; or, The Battle of Flodden.
Lament for Flodden, A.
Elliot, Jean
Exercise in a Meadow.
Elliott, Charlotte
Hour of Prayer, The.
Just as I Am.
Watch and Pray.
Elliott, Ebenezer
Bailiff, The.
Battle Song.
Beware of Dogmas.
Caged Rats.
Drone v. Worker.
Four Dears, The.
Fox-Hunters, The.
God Save the People.
Here lies the man who stripp'd Sin bare.
How Different!
Land Which No One Knows, The.
On a Rose in December.
On Communists.
Paddy, I have but stol'n your living.
Plaint.
Song: "Child, is thy father dead?"
Song: "When working blackguards come to blows."
Spirits and Men, *sel.*
Splendid Village, The, *sels.*
Steam, *sel.*
Steward, The.
Tree of Rivelin, The.
Elliott, George P.
Her Dwarf.
Sayer.
Elliott, Harley
After Picking Rosehips.
Animals That Stand in Dreams, *sel.*
Blessed and Resting Uncle.
Brothers Together in Winter.
Crazy Horse Returns to South Dakota.
For the Man Who Stole a Rose.
Landscape Workers.
Natural Order of Things, The.
Numbers.
On a Country Road.
Panda, The.
Planting, The.
Thinking Twice in the Laundromat.
Elliott, Mary
Think before You Act.

Ellis, Colin
Adder's Epigrams.
Bungaloid Growth.
Epitaph, An: "He worshipped at the altar of Romance."
International Conference.
Modern World, The.
New Vicar of Bray, The.
Old Ladies, The.
On a Gentleman Marrying His Cook.
Romantic, The.
Spaniel's Sermon.
Ellis, Edwin John
Himself, *sel.*
Ellis, George. *See* **Gander, Sir Gregory"**
Ellis, H. F.
Message to General Montgomery.
Ellis, John
Sarah Hazard's Love Letter.
Ellis, Mary Anne
Sonnet to a Tyrant.
Ellis, Royston
Cherry Boy, The, *sels.*
Spiv Song.
Ellis, Vivian Locke
At Common Dawn.
Ellison, Henry
Fall of the Year.
Ellison, Joan Wyrick
Mountain Heritage, A.
Ellsworth, Erastus Wolcott
I saw a man, by some accounted wise.
Mayflower, The.
What Is the Use? *sel.*
Ellwanger, William De Lancey
To Jessie's Dancing Feet.
Ellwood, Thomas
Prayer: "Oh! that mine eye might closed be."
Elmslie, W. G.
Hand That Held It, The.
Elson, Virginia
How Stars and Hearts Grow in Apples.
Not Being Wise.
"Elspeth" (Elspeth MacDuffie O'Halloran)
Sentimental Journey.
Wednesday.
Elton, Charles
Luriana, Lurilee.
Eluard, Paul
Curfew.
Lady Love.
You Rise Up.
Elys, Edmund
My Mind Keeps Out the Host of Sin.
Emans, Elaine V.
Mistakable Identity.
Undreamed, The.
Emanuel, James A.
Black Muslim Boy in a Hospital.
Church Burning: Mississippi.
Emmett Till.
For "Mr. Dudley," a Black Spy.
Get Up, Blues.
Negritude.
Negro, The.
Nightmare.
Old Black Men Say.
Panther Man.
Son.
Treehouse, The.
Voyage of Jimmy Poo, The.
Wedding Procession.
Young Ones, Flip Side, The.
Emanuel, Lynn
Berlin Interior with Jews, 1939.
Frying Trout while Drunk.
Of Your Father's Indiscretions and the Train to California.
Sleeping, The.
Embry, Jacqueline
Tea.
Unregenerate.
Embury, Emma Catherine
Love Unsought.
Pilgrim, The.
Emerson, Ida *and* **Joseph E. Howard.** *See* **Howard, Joseph E.** *and* **Ida Emerson**
Emerson, Ralph Waldo
Adirondacs, The, *sel.*
Alphonso of Castile.
And When I Am Entombèd.
Apology, The.
April.
April and May.
Atom from Atom.
Bacchus.
Beyond Winter.
Blight.
Bohemian Hymn, The.
Borrowing.
Boston Hymn.
Brahma.
Celestial Love, *sel.*
Character.
Chickadee, The.
Compensation.
Concord Hymn.
Days.
Duty.
Each and All.
Earth, The.
Eros.
Excelsior, *sel.*
Experience.
Fable: "Mountain and the squirrel, The."
Forbearance.
Forerunners.
Fragments on Nature and Life, *sel.*
Fragments on the Poet and the Poetic Gift, *sel.*
Gardener.
Give All to Love.
Good-bye.
Grace.
Guy.
Hamatreya.
Heart of All the Scene, The.
Heroism.
Humble-Bee, The.
Hymn Sung at the Completion of the Concord Monument April 19, 1836.
I have an arrow that will find its mark.
Informing Spirit, The.
Intellect.
Letter, A.
Limits.
Love's Nobility.
May-Day, *sel.*
Merlin.
Merops.
Mighty Heart, The.
Miracle, The.
Mithridates.
Music.
Musketaquid.
Nahant.
Nature.
Needless Worry.
Nemesis.
Ode: Inscribed to W. H. Channing.
Ode: "O tenderly the haughty day."
Ode Inscribed to W. H. Channing.
Ode to Beauty.
Orator.
Parks and Ponds.
Past, The.
Poet, The, *sel.*
Poet ("To clothe the fiery thought").
Problem, The.
Prudence.
Quatrains, *sels.*
Rhodora, The [On Being Asked Whence Is the Flower].
Saadi.
Sacrifice.
Seashore [*or* Sea-Shore].
Snow-Storm, The.
Solution.
Song of Nature.
Song of Seyd Nimetollah of Kuhistan.
Sphinx, The.
Stars, the stars everlasting are fugitives also, The.
Terminus.
Test, The.
Thine Eyes Still Shined.
Thought.
Threnody: "South-wind brings, The."
Two Rivers.
Undersong, The.
Uriel.
Visit, The.
Voluntaries, *sels.*
Waldeinsamkeit.
Water.
Waves.
We Love the Venerable House, *with music.*
Wealth.
Why did all manly gifts in Webster fail?
Woodnotes I ("When the pine tosses its cones").
Woodnotes II ("As sunbeams stream through liberal space").
Xenophanes.
Emeruwa, Leatrice W.
Personals.
Emery, Frances D.
Long-billed Gannets.
Emin, Gevorg
Doesn't It Seem to You.
Why Has This Ache.
Emmett, Daniel Decatur
Boatman's Dance.
Dixie ("I wish I was in the land of cotton").
Old Dan Tucker.
Emmons, Dick
Cold Fact.
Grass, Alas, The.
Empson, William
Arachne.
Aubade: "Hours before dawn we were woken by the quake."
Bacchus.
Beautiful Train, The.
Camping Out.
Courage Means Running.
Dissatisfaction with Metaphysics.
Earth Has Shrunk in the Wash.
Flighting for Duck.
Four Legs, Two Legs, Three Legs.
Homage to the British Museum.
Ignorance of Death.
Invitation to Juno.
Just a Smack at Auden.
Legal Fiction.
Let It Go.
Letter I ("You were amused to find you too could fear").
Letter IV ("Hatched in a rasping darkness of dry sand").
Manchouli.
Missing Dates.
Note on Local Flora.
Reflection from Rochester.
Rolling the Lawn.
Scales, The.
Sea Voyage.
Sonnet: "Not wrongly moved by this dismaying scene."
Success.
Teasers, The.
This Last Pain.
To an Old Lady.
Villanelle: "It is the pain, it is the pain, endures."
World's End, The.
Emre, Yunus
Whole universe is full of God, The.

Endrezze-Danielson, Anita
Blue Horses; West Winds.
Canto Llano.
Dream Feast, The (Three Poems).
Eclipse.
Exodus.
In the Flight of the Blue Heron: To Montezuma.
Learning the Spells; a Diptych.
Manifest Destiny.
Night Mare.
Notes from an Analyst's Couch.
Passion Drinker, The.
Raven/Moon.
Red Rock Ceremonies.
Song-Maker.
Stripper, The.
There Are Three Bones in the Human Ear.
Truth about My Sister and Me, The.
Week-End Indian, The.
Why Stone Does Not Sing by Itself.
Eng, Steve
Vanished.
Engel, Mary
Promised Land.
Engels, John
Angler's Vade Mecum, An.
Crows, The.
Disconnections, The.
Moonwalk.
Engels, Norbert
Ex Maria Vergine.
Engle, John D., Jr.
Biology Lesson.
Midway.
Sonnet Sonnet.
Engle, Paul
American Child.
Beasts.
Chameleon.
Dancer: Four Poems.
Ending, The.
In a Bar near Shibuya Station, Tokyo.
Last Whiskey Cup, The.
Lord of Each Soul, *with music.*
Modern Romance, A.
Moving In.
New World, The.
Together.
You Can't Be Wise.
Engler, Robert Klein
Dichterliebe.
English, Maurice
Form Was the World.
English, Thomas Dunn
Arnold at Stillwater.
Assunpink and Princeton.
Battle of Monmouth, The.
Battle of New Orleans, The.
Battle of the Cowpens, The.
Battle of the King's Mill.
Ben Bolt.
Betty Zane.
Burning of Jamestown, The.
Charge by the Ford, The.
Fall of Maubila, The.
Old Mill, The.
Sack of Deerfield, The.
Engman, John
Rainer Maria Rilke Returns from the Dead to Address the Junior Military School at Sankt Pölten.
Enheduanna
Antiphonal Hymn in Praise of Inanna.
Appeal to the Moongod Nanna-Suen to Throw Out Lugalanne.
Banishment from Ur.
Condemning the Moongod Nanna.
Crimes of Lugalanne.
Curse on Uruk, A.
Final Prayer.
Inanna and An.
Inanna and Ebih.
Inanna and Enlil.
Inanna and Ishkur.
Inanna and the Anunna.
Inanna and the City of Uruk.
Inanna and the Divine Essences.
Inanna Exalted, *sel.*
Restoration of Enheduanna to Her Former Station, The.
Ennius, Quintus
Annales, *sel.*
Ennodius, Saint (Magnus Felix Ennodius)
How of the Virgin Mother shall I sing?
Hymnus Sanctae Mariae, *sel.*
Enright, Dennis Joseph
Along the River.
Anecdote from William IV Street.
Apocalypse.
Buy One Now.
Guest.
History of World Languages.
In Cemeteries.
Interpreters, The.
Last Democrat, The.
Laughing Hyena, by Hokusai, The.
Midstream.
Names.
No Offence.
Noodle-Vendor's Flute, The.
Parliament of Cats.
Poet Wondering What He Is Up To.
R-and-R Centre: An Incident from the Vietnam War.
Royalties.
Since Then.
Typewriter Revolution, The.
Underdeveloped Country, An.
University Examinations in Egypt.
Unlawful Assembly.
Verb "To Think," The.
Waiting for the Bus.
Enriqueta, María
Thoughts of a Little Girl.
Enslin, Theodore
Belongings, The.
Forms, *sel.*
Landscape with Figures.
On Such a Windy Afternoon.
Stance.
Tangere.
Tansy for August.
Witch Hazel.
Your Need Is Greater than Mine.
"Ephelia" (Joan Philips)
Maidenhead.
Song: "Know, Celadon, in vain you use."
Song: "You wrong me, Strephon, when you say."
To Phylocles, Inviting Him to Friendship.
Ephrem, Saint
Christmas Hymn, *sel.*
Virgin truly full of wonder.
Epstein, Daniel Mark
At the Millinery Shop.
Cash Only, No Refund, No Return.
Climbing.
First Precinct Fourth Ward.
Follies, The.
Mannequins.
Miami.
Night Song from Backbone Mountain.
Epstein, Elaine
Luck.
Erasmus, Desiderius
Votive Ode.
Erb, Christopher
While Waiting for Kohoutek.
Erdrich, Louise
Balinda's Dance.
Dear John Wayne.
Jacklight.
Lady in the Pink Mustang, The.
Painting of a White Gate and Sky.
Snow Train.
Strange People, The.
Turtle Mountain Reservation.
Erinna
Baucis.
Distaff, The.
Eristi-Aya
Letter to Her Mother, A.
Ernst, John F.
O Jesus Christ, True Light of God, *with music.*
Ernst, Karl *and* **Peter Daniel**
Freiheit (Freedom).
Erskine, John
Apparition.
At the Front.
Dialogue.
Kings and Stars.
Modern Ode to the Modern School.
Shepherd Speaks, The.
Erskine, Thomas Erskine, 1st Baron
James Alan Park/ Came naked stark.
On Scott's [Poem] "The Field of Waterloo."
On Tom Moore's Translation of Anacreon.
Erskine, William
Epigram: "This house, where once a lawyer dwelt."
This House Where Once a Lawyer Dwelt.
Erskine, Francis Robert St. Clair, Earl of Rosslyn
Bedtime.
Esbensen, Barbara J.
Postcard from Zamboanga.
Esher, Reginald Baliol Brett, 2d Viscount. *See* **Brett, Reginald Baliol, 2d Viscount Esher**
Eshleman, Clayton
Black Hat, The.
Very Old Woman, A.
Espaillat, Rhina P.
From the Rain Down.
Espírito Santo, Alda do
Same Side of the Canoe, The.
Where Are the Men Seized in This Wind of Madness?
Espy, Willard R.
Gemini Jones.
Singular Singulars, Peculiar Plurals.
Essex, Edwin
Loneliness.
Essex, Robert Devereux, 2d Earl of
Change Thy Mind since She Doth Change.
Content.
Happy Were He.
Esson, Louis (Thomas Louis Buvelot Esson)
Shearer's Wife, The.
"Estelle." *See* **Bogart, Elizabeth**
Estes, Lawrence E.
Contentment.
Esteves, Sandra Maria
From the Commonwealth.
Vanguardia.
E'tesami, Parvin
To His Father on Praising the Honest Life of the Peasant.
Etherege, Sir George
Chloris, 'Tis Not in Your Power.
Comical Revenge, The, *sels.*
Ephelia to Bajazet.
Letter to Lord Middleton, A.
Rival, The, *at.*
She Would if She Could, *sel.*
Silvia.
Song: "If she be not as kind as fair."
Song, A: "Ye happy swains, whose hearts are free."
Song: "Ladies, though to your conquering eyes."
Song: "Tell me no more I am deceived."
To a Lady Asking Him How Long He Would Love Her.
To a Very Young Lady.
To Little or No Purpose.
Upon the Downs.

Etter, Dave
Chicken.
Fighter, The.
House by the Tracks, A.
Old Dubuque.
Romp.
Snow Country.
Eubulus
Benefits and Abuse of Alcohol, The.
Eugenius III, Pope
Dedication: "Eugenius, thy son, who guards the Rock."
Eunaich, Beinn
Winter Climb.
Euripides
Aftermath, The.
Alcestis, *sel.*
Andromache, *sel.*
Bacchae, *sel.*
Bellerophon.
Chorus: "And Pergamos,/ City of the Phrygians."
Chorus: Kings of Troy, The.
Chorus of Satyrs, Driving Their Goats.
Cyclops, *sels.*
Earth and Sky.
Greek Athlete, The.
Hippolytus.
Home of Aphrodite, The.
Iphigenia [*or* Iphigeneia] in Aulis, *sels.*
Love Song: "One with eyes the fairest."
Medea.
No More, O My Spirit.
O for the Wings of a Dove.
Prayer to Peace.
Strength of Fate, The.
There Are No Gods.
Worst Horror, The.
Euwer, Anthony
Ankle, The.
As a Beauty I Am Not a Star.
Conscience, The.
Ears, The.
Face, The.
Gettin' Born.
Hands, The.
Limeratomy, The.
Limerick: "As a beauty I'm not a great star."
Limerick: "No matter how grouchy you're feeling."
My Face.
Note.
Smile, The.
Sneeze, The.
True Facts of the Case, The.
Evald, Johannes. *See* **Ewald, Johannes**
Evans, Abbie Huston
By the Salt Margin.
Come to Birth.
Euroclydon.
Fundament Is Shifted, The.
In Space-Time Aware.
On the Curve-Edge.
Primary.
Return to Life.
Sun-up in March.
This World.
Wrestling, The.
Evans, Abel
Author's Epitaph, An. Written by Himself.
Epitaph on Sir John Vanbrugh [Architect].
For Sir John Vanbrugh, Architect.
Keep the commandments, Trapp, and go no further.
On Blenheim House.
On Sir John Vanbrugh [Architect].
Tadlow.
Evans, David Allan
Bullfrogs.
Ford Pickup.
Neighbors.
Retired Farmer.
Story of Lava, The.
Sunset.
Uncle Claude.
Evans, Donald
In the Vices.
Evans, Florence Wilkinson
At the Salon.
Students.
Evans, George Essex
Women of the West, The.
Evans, H. A. C.
Egotist, The.
If Not.
Liftman, The.
Montgomery.
Evans, Humphrey
And Again.
Evans, Mari E.
Alarm Clock, The.
And the Hotel Room Held Only Him.
And the Old Women Gathered.
Black Jam for Dr. Negro.
Daufuskie.
Emancipation of George-Hector (a Colored Turtle), The.
How Will You Call Me, Brother.
I Am a Black Woman.
If There Be Sorrow.
Into Blackness Softly.
Langston.
Marrow of My Bone.
Point of No Return.
Rebel, The.
Shrine to What Should Be.
Spectrum.
Status Symbol.
To Mother and Steve.
Uhuru.
Vive Noir!
When in Rome.
Where Have You Gone?
Who Can Be Born Black.
Evans, Mary Ann [*or* Marian]. *See* **"Eliot, George"**
Evans, Nathaniel
To Thee, Then, Let All Beings Bend, *with music.*
Evans, Patrick
At Morning an Iris.
Green Grass Growing.
Evans, Sebastian
Fifteen Days of Judgement, The.
Seven Fiddlers, The.
Evans, Virginia Moran
Window to the East.
Evarts, Prescott, Jr.
Hornpout.
Everard, Harrison
Holloe Menn, The.
Everett, Alexander Hill
Young American, The.
Everett, David
Boy Reciter, The.
Tall Oaks from Little Acorns Grow.
Everett, Edward
Dirge of Alaric the Visigoth.
Everett, Graham
Thirteen, Full of Life.
Everett, Laura Bell
Lament of the Voiceless, The.
Resurgence.
Everson, Ronald G.
Child with Shell.
Cold-Weather Love.
Injured Maple.
Laprairie Hunger Strike.
Letter from Underground.
Loaves, The.
Old Snapshot.
One-Night Expensive Hotel.
Pauper Woodland.
Rogue Pearunners.
Stranded in My Ontario.
When I'm Going Well.
Everson, William (Brother Antoninus)
Advent.
Canticle to the Waterbirds, A.
First Winter Storm.
Flight in the Desert, The.
Gash, The.
I Am Long Weaned.
In All These Acts.
Kingfisher Flat.
Making of the Cross, The.
March.
Narrows of Birth, The.
Poet Is Dead, The.
Presence, The.
Raid, The.
Song the Body Dreamed in the Spirit's Mad Behest, The.
South Coast, The.
Stranger, The.
What Birds Were There.
Winter Ploughing.
Year's End.
Zone of Death.
Everts, Lillian
Playmates.
Everwine, Peter
Brother, The.
Burden of Decision, The.
Clearing, The.
Distance.
Drinking Cold Water.
For the Coming Year.
Going.
In the End.
Learning to Speak.
Marsh, New Year's Day, The.
Night.
Perhaps It's as You Say.
Routes.
Someone Knocks.
We Meet in the Lives of Animals.
"Evoe." *See* **Knox, Edmund George Valpy**
Evtushenko, Evgeny. *See* **Yevtushsenko, Yevgeny**
Ewald [*or* Evald], Johannes
King Christian.
Ewart, Gavin
Bofors A.A. Gun, The.
Christmas Message, A.
Cigarette for the Bambino.
Deceptive Grin of the Gravel Porters, The.
Dell, The.
Exeter Riddle, An.
Fiction: A Message.
"For Whom the Bell Tolls."
From V. C. (a Gentleman of Verona).
Hymn to Proust.
John Betjeman's Brighton.
Lifelines.
Lines: "Other day I was loving a sweet little fruitpie-and-cream, The."
Love Song: "You've got nice knees."
Lovesleep, The.
Miss Twye.
New Poet Arrives, A.
Nymphs and Satyrs.
Officers' Mess.
On the Tercentenary of Milton's Death.
Pastoral: "Dominic Francis Xavier Brotherton-Chancery."
Poem: "To go, to leave the classics and the buildings."
Prayer: "Lord I am not entirely selfish."
Psychoanalysis.
Sonnet: Dolce Stil Novo.
Sonnet: "Point where beauty and intelligence meet, The."
2001: The Tennyson/Hardy Poem.
Wanting Out.
When a Beau Goes In.
Xmas for the Boys.
Young Blondes.

Ewer, W. N.
Chosen People, The.
Ewing, Annemarie
Ballad: "Mother mine, Mother mine, what do you see?"
Fisherman's Blunder off New Bedford, Massachusetts.
If the Heart Be Homeless.
Man Within, The.
Rhyme from Grandma Goose.
Sleep, Madame, Sleep.
Ewing, Juliana Horatia
Burial of the Linnet, The.
Dolls' Wash, The.
For Good Luck.
Friend in the Garden, A.
Garden Lore.
Willow-Man, The.
Eybers, Elisabeth
Hagar.
Narrative.
Röntgen Photograph.
Sleep-Walking Child.
Snail.
"E-Yeh-Shure'" (Louise Abeita)
Beauty.
Ezekiel, Nissim
How My Father Died.
Lamentation.
Totem.
Ezekielos of Alexandria
Exodus from Egypt, The.
Ezell, Allamae
Candidate, The.
Ezobi, Joseph
Barren Soul, A.
Silver Bowl, The, *sel.*

F

"F. L. H." *See* **"H., F. L."**
"F.P.A." *See* **Adams, Franklin Pierce**
Faber, Frederick William
All-embracing, The.
Cherwell Waterlily, The.
Come to Jesus.
Dog, The.
Expectation, The.
Faith of Our Fathers.
God Our Father.
Hymn: "There's a wideness in God's mercy."
Mundus Morosus.
My God, How Wonderful Thou Art.
Nearest Friend, The.
O Paradise! O Paradise!
Our Heavenly Father, *sel.*
Our Lady in the Middle Ages.
Our Lady's Expectation, *sel.*
Paradise.
Right Is Right.
Shadow of the Rock, The.
There's a Wideness in God's Mercy.
World Morose, The.
Written in a Little Lady's Little Album.
Faber, Geoffrey
St. Mary's Loch.
Faber, Norma
Hatch, The.
Fabilli, Mary
Letter to Robert.
Rock, The.
Fabio, Sarah Webster
All Day We've Longed for Night.
Back into the Garden.
Black Man's Feast.
Chromo.
Evil Is No Black Thing.
To Turn from Love.
Fabyan, Robert
Dedication of the Chronicles of England and France.
Fadiman, Clifton
Alimentary.
Jacobean.
Theological.
Fagg, Martin
Burialle of the Dede.
Elegy: "O spare a tear for poor Tom Hood."
Elegy on Thomas Hood.
When Gaffer be dead for a month or more.
Fagg, William Carson
Book, The.
Eclipse.
Leaf, The.
Portraits.
Reaching.
Fahy, Christopher
Bunny.
Miss Ada.
Fahy, Francis A.
Little Mary Cassidy.
Ould Plaid Shawl, The.
Fainlight, Harry
Bride, A.
Morning.
Fainlight, Ruth
Another Full Moon.
Fire-Queen.
God's Language.
Hebrew Sibyl, The.
Lilith.
Other, The.
Sibyl of the Waters.
Sleep-Learning.
"Fair, C. A."
Chinese Poems: Arthur Waley.
Fairbridge, Wolfe Seymour
Consecration of the House.
Fairchild, B. H.
Late Game.
Faiz, Faiz Ahmed
Day Death Comes, The.
Falckner, Justus
Rise, Ye Children, *with music.*
Falco, Edward
Apology to My Lady.
Falconer, Edmund (Edmund O'Rourke)
Killarney.
Falconer, Raymond
No Voice of Man.
Falconer, William
All Hands Unmoor!
Description of a Ninety Gun Ship.
High o'er the Poop the Audacious Seas Aspire.
Midshipman, The.
Shipwreck, The, *sels.*
Shortening Sail.
Faleti, Adebayo
Independence.
Falk, Marcia
Modern Kabbalist.
Shulamit in Her Dreams.
Woman through the Window.
Falke, Gustav
God's Harp.
Strand-Thistle.
Falkenbury, Francis E.
South Street.
Falkner, John Meade
After Trinity.
Arabia.
Christmas Day; the Family Sitting.
Epilogue: "Painted autumn overwhelms, The."
Fallis, Edwina
Prairie Spring.
September.
Wise Johnny.
Fallon, Padraic
Assumption.
Elegy for a Countryman.
Farmer.
For Paddy Mac.
Head, The.
Lady Day.
Long John.
Mary Hynes.
Mater Dei.
Odysseus.
Out of Soundings.
Pot Shot.
Raftery's Dialogue with the Whiskey.
River Walk, The.
Virgin.
Waistcoat, The.
Weir Bridge.
Wisdom.
Writing on the Wall.
Young Fenians, The.
"Falstaff, Jake" (Herman Fetzer)
Beautiful Sunday.
Dick Johnson Reel, The.
Fandel, John
Bee, The.
Indians.
Fane, Julian
Ad Matrem.
Fane, Mildmay, Earl of Westmorland. *See* **Westmorland, Mildmay Fane, 2d Earl of**
"Fane, Violet" (Mary Montgomerie Currie, Baroness Currie)
Afterwards.
In Green Old Gardens.
May Song, A.
Fanshawe, Catherine Maria
Fragment: "There is a river clear and fair."
Fragment in Imitation of Wordsworth.
Fragments.
Imitation of Wordsworth, An.
Riddle, A: "'Twas whispered in Heaven [*or* "'Twas in heaven pronounced, and], 'twas muttered in hell."
Fanshawe, Sir Richard
Fall, The.
Great Favorit Beheaded, A.
Hope.
Il Pastor Fido, *sels.*
Now War Is All the World About; or, An Ode, upon Occasion of His Majesties Proclamation in the Year 1630.
Ode, upon Occasion of His Majesties Proclamation in the Year[e] 1630, An.
Rose, A.
Rose of Life, The.
Fanthorpe, U. A.
BC:AD.
Reindeer Report.
What the Donkey Saw.
Farallon, Cerise
Pride and Hesitation.
Serpent of God, The.
Farber, Norma
Beyond the Tapestries.
Bow Down, Mountain, *with music.*
Crooked Carol.
Dove.
Hog at the Manger.
How They Brought the Good News by Sea.
Jubilate Herbis.
Judas, Joyous Little Son.
Ladybug's Christmas.
Nothing Gold Can Stay.
Oh the Toe-Test!
Spider.
Farbstein, W. E.
Double Duty.
Farewell, George
Adieu to My Landlady, An.
Country Man, The, *sel.*
Molly Moor.
Privy-Love for My Landlady.
Quaerè.
There's Life in a Mussel; a Meditation.

To the Archdeacon.
Fargas, Laura
Island of Geological Time, The.
Natural History.
Rorschach.
Farhi, Musa Moris
God and Nature.
Paths to God.
Smile at Me.
Thirst.
Who Says.
Faricy, Austin
Through Warmth and Light of Summer Skies, *with music.*
Farjeon, Annabel
Ode to a Fat Cat.
Farjeon, Eleanor
Alexander to His Horse.
Bedtime.
Blackfriars.
Bliss.
Blow the Stars Home.
Books.
Boys' Names.
C Is for Charms.
Cat.
Cats.
Children's Bells, The.
Children's Carol, The.
Choosing.
Circus.
City Streets and Country Roads.
Coach.
Down! Down!
Dragonfly, A.
Earth and Sky.
Easter Monday.
Farewell to the Old Year.
For a Dewdrop.
For a Mocking Voice.
For Snow.
Geography.
Getting Out of Bed.
Girls' Names.
Good Bishop Valentine.
Great Discovery, The.
Hey! My Pony!
Holly and Mistletoe.
In the Week When Christmas Comes.
Jenny White and Johnny Black.
Jill Came from the Fair.
Jim at the Corner.
Keeping Christmas.
Kitten, A.
Lewis Carroll.
Light the Lamps Up, Lamplighter!
Milk-cart Pony, The.
Mrs. Malone.
Mrs. Peck-Pigeon.
Moon-Come-Out.
Music.
News! News!
Night Will Never Stay, The.
Now Every Child.
Now That You Too.
October's Song.
On the Staircase.
Peace.
Pencil and Paint.
Poetry.
Quarrel, The.
Riding of the Kings, The.
School-Bell.
Shopman, The.
Sisters.
Sounds in the Morning, The.
Tailor.
There Are Big Waves.
There Isn't Time.
Three Little Puffins.
Tide in the river, The.
Up the Hill, down the Hill.
Upon an Easter Morning.
Vegetables.
Welcome to the New Year.
Wheelbarrow.
White Horses.
Wild Thyme.
Window Boxes.
Witch, The! The Witch!
Yawning.
Z Is for Zoroaster.
Farjeon, Herbert
Apologia.
Farley, Blanche
Sort of Elegy, A.
Farley, Henry
Bounty of Our Age, The.
Farley, Susan
How to Own Land.
Farmer, Edward
Little Jim.
Farnaby, Giles
Among the Daffadillies.
Farnham, Jessie
Garland for a Storyteller.
"Farningham, Marianne" (Mary Ann Hearn)
God Cares.
He Careth.
Last Hymn, The.
Farrar, Janice
Thought of Marigolds, A.
Farrar, John Chipman
Alone.
Brest Left Behind.
Bundles.
Chanticleer.
Choice.
Comparison, A.
Critic, The.
Hillside Farmer, A.
Parenthood.
Roller Skates.
Song for a Camper.
Threnody. "Red leaves fall upon the lake, The."
Time Is Today, The.
Victorian Song.
Watching Clouds.
Farrar, Winifred Hamrick
Pushed to the Scroll.
Farrell, J. R.
Bank Thief, The.
Farren, Robert (Roibéard O'Faracháin)
All That Is, and Can Delight.
Beset Wife, The.
Cool Gold Wines of Paradise, The.
Immolation.
Joy's Peak.
Mary.
Mason, The.
No Woman Born.
Pets, The.
To the Bell-Ringer.
Farrington, Harry Webb
I Know Not How That Bethlehem's Babe, *with music.*
Our Christ.
Farrokhzad, Forugh
Born Again.
I'm Sad.
In the land of dwarfs.
O Realm Bejewelled.
On Earth.
Once More.
Someone like No One Else.
Fatchen, Max
So Big!
Faubion, Dorothy
Wash-Day Wonder.
Faucher, Real
Archaeologists.
Faulkner, Margherita
Suppositions.
Fauset, Jessie Redmond
Christmas Eve in France.
Dead Fires.
Enigma.
Fragment: "Breath of life imbued those few dim days, The."
La Vie C'est la Vie.
Noblesse Oblige.
Oblivion.
Oriflamme.
Rencontre.
Return, The.
Touché.
Words! Words!
Fawcett, Brian
Hand, The.
Fawcett, Edgar
Fireflies.
January Is Here.
To an Oriole.
Wild Roses.
Fawcett, John
Blest Be the Tie That Binds.
Fawcett, Joseph
Art of War, The, *sel.*
Feast of Blood, The.
Fawcett, Susan
Fisherman, The.
Fawkes, Francis
Brown Jug, The.
Elegy on the Death of Dobbin, the Butterwoman's Horse, An.
Fazio degli Uberti
Canzone: His Portrait of His Lady, Angiola of Verona.
Of England, and of Its Marvels.
Fearing, Kenneth
American Rhapsody.
Any Man's Advice to His Son.
Aphrodite Metropolis.
C Stands for Civilization.
Confession Overheard in a Subway.
Cultural Notes.
Dirge: "1–2–3 was the number he played but today the number came 3–2–1."
Elegy in a Theatrical Warehouse.
End of the Seers' Convention.
Evening Song.
Green Light.
Love, 20¢ the First Quarter Mile.
Lullaby: "Wide as this night, old as this night is old and young as it is young."
Memo.
Minnie and Mrs. Hoyne.
No Credit.
Obituary.
Operative No. 174 Resigns.
Pact.
Pay-off.
People vs. the People, The.
Portrait.
Readings, Forecasts, Personal Guidance.
Requiem: "Will they stop."
Resurrection.
Tomorrow.
Twentieth-Century Blues.
Yes, the Agency Can Handle That.
Federman, Raymond
Lune Concrete.
Fedo, David
Camping at Thunder Bay.
Feeeman, Carol
Gift.
Feela, David J.
Cut.
Feeney, Leonard
Because of Her Who Flowered So Fair.
Family Portrait.
Song for a Listener, *sel.*
Feeney, Thomas Butler
Captain Kelly Lets His Daughter Go to Be a Nun.

Fein, Cheri
Obscene Caller, The.
Feinberg, Harvey
Welcome.
Feinman, Alvin
November Sunday Morning.
Feinstein, Elaine
Against Winter.
Calliope in the Labour Ward.
Coastline.
Dad.
June.
Magic Apple Tree, The.
Medium, The.
Our Vegetable Love Shall Grow.
Patience.
Survivors.
Under Stone.
Feinstein, Martin
Burning Bush.
Feirstein, Frederick
Boarder, The.
"Grandfather" in Winter.
Spring.
Feldman, Irving
Curse, A.
Death of Vitellozzo Vitelli, The.
Double, The.
Flood.
Handball Players at Brighton Beach, The.
Little Lullaby.
My Olson Elegy.
No-Night, The.
Old Men, The.
"Portrait de Femme."
Pripet Marshes, The.
Scene of a Summer Morning.
So It Happens.
Feldman, Ruth
Lilith.
Nocturne: Homage to Whistler.
Feldman, Susan
How the Invalids Make Love.
Intruder.
Lamentations of an Au Pair Girl.
Sea Legs.
Fell, Alison
Significant Fevers.
Felltham, Owen
Contentment.
On the Duke of Buckingham, Slain by Felton, the 23rd August, 1628.
Sun and Wind, The.
Fenderson, Mark
Smart Little Bear, The.
Fenner, Cornelius George
Gulf-Weed.
Fenollosa, Ernest Francisco
Golden Age, The.
Fenton, Elijah
To a Lady Sitting before Her Glass.
Fenton, Elizabeth
Masks.
Under the Ladder to Heaven.
Fenton, James
Dead Soldiers.
Pitt-Rivers Museum, Oxford, The.
Fenton, James *and* John Fuller
Poem against Catholics.
Ferber, Edna
To William Allen White.
Ferebe, George
Houseless Downs, The.
Shepherds' Song, Sung before Queen Anne, on the Wiltshire Downs, 11 June 1613, The, *sel.*
Ferguson, James
Auld Daddy Darkness.
Ferguson, John
Cock Crowing in a Poulterer's Shop, A.
Ferguson, Roy
Island of Rhum, The.
Ferguson, Sir Samuel
Abdication of Fergus Mac Roy, The.
Burial of King Cormac, The.
Fairy Thorn, The.
Forging of the Anchor, The.
Lament for the Death of Thomas Davis.
Lament for Thomas Davis.
Pretty Girl of Loch Dan, The.
Welshmen of Tirawley, The.
Fergusson, Robert
Braid Claith.
Daft Days, The.
Epigram on a Lawyer's Desiring One of the Tribe to Look with Respect to a Gibbet.
Farmer's Ingle, The.
Ghaists, The; a Kirk-Yard Eclogue.
Hallow-Fair.
Lee Rigg, The.
Leith Races, *sel.*
My Winsome Dear.
Rising of the Session, The.
Sow of Feeling, The.
Ferlinghetti, Lawrence
After the Cries of the Birds.
Assassination Raga.
Away above a Harborful.
Christ Climbed Down.
Coney Island of the Mind, A, *sels.*
Crazy/ to be alive in such a strange.
Dog.
Fortune.
Frightened/ by the sound of my own voice.
Funny Fantasies Are Never So Real as Oldstyle.
He.
I Am Waiting.
In a Surrealist Year.
In Golden Gate Park That Day.
In Goya's Greatest Scenes [We Seem to See].
Lost Parents.
New York—Albany.
One Thousand Fearful Words for Fidel Castro.
Oral Messages, *sel.*
Pennycandystore beyond the El, The.
Phoenix at Fifty, A.
Pictures of a Gone World, *sels.*
Pound at Spoleto.
Sea and Ourselves at Cape Ann, The.
Starting from San Francisco.
Tentative Description of a Dinner to Promote the Impeachment of President Eisenhower.
Terrible/ a horse at night.
This life is not a circus where.
True Confessional.
Underwear.
What could she say to the fantastic foolybear.
Wild Dreams of a New Beginning.
World Is a Beautiful Place, The.
Fernández, Abraham
If You Happy Would Be, *with music.*
Fernandez, Raymond Ringo
Cell-Rap #27.
For Mulatto.
Lies and Gossip.
Poem for the Conguero in D-Yard.
Real Deal Revelation.
Ferne, Doris
Nijinsky.
Sounding.
Ferre, Rosario
I Hear You've Let Go.
Ferril, Thomas Hornsby
Always Begin Where You Are.
Basic Communication.
House in Denver.
Kochia.
Lost Ships.
Man Who Thought He Was a Horse, The.
Morning Star.
Old Men on the Blue.
Swallows.
Train Butcher, The.
Waltz against the Mountains.
What Trinkets?
Wood.
Ferriter, Pierce
He Charges Her to Lay Aside Her Weapons.
Lay Your Arms Aside.
Ferry, David
Antagonist, The.
Johnson on Pope.
Lines for a Dead Poet.
On the Way to the Island.
Out of That Sea.
Poem about Waking.
Unawkward Singers, The.
Fertig, Nelle
I Have Come to the Conclusion.
Fessenden, Thomas Green
Ye Sons of Columbia.
Fet [*or* Foeth], Afanasi Afanasievich
Morning Song.
Fetherling, Doug
Bathing with Father.
Dialogue 4 1 Voice Only.
Diseases of the Moon.
Dispatch Number Nine.
Dispatch Number Sixteen.
Dispatch Number Sixty.
Elijah Speaking.
Explorers as Seen by the Natives.
Genius Loci of the Morning.
Nights Passed on Ward's Island, Toronto Harbour.
Sex Play in Four Acts.
Shacked Up at the Ritz.
She Employed the Familiar "Tu" Form.
Your Absence Has Not Taught Me.
Fetter, George Griffith
Name of Mother, The.
Fetzer, Herman. *See* **"Falstaff, Jake"**
Fewell, Richard
"Duke" and the "Count," The.
Fewster, Ernest
Cliff Rose, The.
Pearly Everlasting, The.
Fey, Harold E.
We Who Are about to Die.
Fey, Isabella
Bad Example.
ffrench Salkeld, Cecil
Water-Front.
Fiacc, Padraic
Boy and the Geese, The.
Brendan Gone.
Deranged.
Gloss.
Haemorrhage.
Poet, The.
Stolen Fifer, The.
Fialkowski, Barbara
To Sleep.
Fiamengo, Marya
In Praise of Old Women.
Fiawoo, F. K.
Soliloquy on Death.
Fichman, Jacob [*or* Jakov]
Abishag.
Eve.
In the Old City.
Ficke, Arthur Davison
Alcibiades to a Jealous Girl.
April Moment.
Don Quixote.
Epitaph for the Poet V., *sels.*
Father.
Four Japanese Paintings, *sel.*
Her Pedigree.
In That Dim Monument Where Tybalt Lies.
Oracle, The.
Perspective of Co-ordination.
Sonnets of a Portrait Painter, *sels.*
Spring Landscape.
Summons.
Three Sisters, The.

To the Harpies.
Troubadours.
View from Heights.
Wave Symphony, The.
Young Recruit, The.

Fickert, Kurt J.
End of a Meaningful Relationship, The.
Sleeping Alone.

Fiedler, Leslie A.
Dumb Dick.
No Ghost Is True.

Field, Arthur Gordon
America Prays.
Bells of the New Year.
Discoverer, The.
Name of Washington, The.
New Song, The.
Perpetual Christmas.

Field, Charles K.
Barriers Burned.

Field, Edward
Both My Grandmothers ("Both my grandmas came from far away").
Bride of Frankenstein, The.
Curse of the Cat Woman.
Dirty Floor, The.
Donkeys.
Event, An.
Floor Is Dirty, The.
For Arthur Gregor.
Frankenstein.
Graffiti.
Lost, Dancing, The.
Mae West.
My Polish Grandma.
New York.
Nightmare.
Notes from a Slave Ship.
Ode to Fidel Castro.
Reservoir, The.
Roaches.
Sentimentalist, The.
Sleeper, The.
Snowfish, The.
Statue of Liberty, The.
Telephone, The.
Tulips and Addresses.
Unwanted.
View of Jersey, A.
Visiting Home, *sel.*
What Grandma Knew.
Writing for Money.

Field, Eugene
At Cheyenne.
Bachelor Hall.
Bethlehem Town.
Bibliomaniac's Prayer, The.
Boy, The.
Casey's Table d'Hote.
Chipeta.
Christmas Eve.
Christmas Song.
Clink of the Ice, The.
Colorado Sand Storm, A.
Dibdin's Ghost.
Dinkey-Bird, The.
Duel, The.
Dutch Lullaby, A.
Garden and Cradle.
In the Firelight.
Jessie.
Jest 'fore Christmas.
Little Boy Blue.
Little Peach, The.
Lyttel Boy, The.
My Sabine Farm.
New Year Idyl, A, *sel.*
Night Wind, The.
Nightfall in Dordrecht.
Norse Lullaby.
Our Two Opinions.
Piazza Tragedy, A.
Pioneer, The.
Play on Words, A.
Rock-a-by Lady, The.
Seein' Things.
Sioux, The.
Star of the East.
Sugar-Plum Tree, The.
Three Kings, The.
'Tis Strange.
To Phyllis.
Truth about Horace, The.
Wanderer, The.
Wynken, Blynken, and Nod.

Field, Greg
Home Cooking Cafe.

Field, Matt
Farm Wife.
Rondel: Autumn.

"Field, Michael" (Katherine Bradley *and* Edith Cooper)
After Mass.
And on My Eyes Dark Sleep by Night.
Aridity.
Bury Her at Even.
Depression.
Descent from the Cross.
Dream, The.
Dying Viper, A.
Gold Is the Son of Zeus: Neither Moth nor Worm May Gnaw It.
If They Honoured Me, Giving Me Their Gifts.
Macrinus against Trees.
Renewal.
Sweeter Far than the Harp, More Gold than Gold.
To the Lord Love.
Tragic Mary Queen of Scots, The, I ("Ah me, if I grew sweet to man").
Tragic Mary Queen of Scots, The, II ("I could wish to be dead!").
Variations on Sappho, *sels.*
Vision, A.
Where the Blessed Feet Have Trod.
Whym Chow.
Woods Are Still, The.

Field, Mildred Fowler
Carpenter Christ.

Field, Nathaniel
Amends for Ladies, *sel.*
Matin Song.
Rise, Lady Mistress, Rise!
Song: "Rise Lady Mistresse, rise."

Field, Rachel Lyman
Acrobat.
Almost.
Animal Store, The.
At the Theater.
Barefoot Days.
Birthday, A.
Busy Body, The.
Charm for Spring Flowers, A.
Chestnut Stands.
Circus Garland, A, *sels.*
City Lights.
City Rain.
Dancing Bear, The.
Dog Day, A.
Doorbells.
Eighth Street West.
Elephant, The.
Elfin Town.
Epilogue: "Nothing now to mark the spot."
Equestrienne.
Flower-Cart Man, The.
For My Father.
Fourth of July.
General Store.
Girl on the Milk-white Horse, The.
Gunga.
Ice-Cream Man, The.
I'd Like to Be a Lighthouse.
If Once You Have Slept on an Island.
Little Rose Tree, The.
Manhattan Lullaby.
My Inside-Self.
New Year's Day.
Next Day.
Old Wharves, The.
Parade.
Performing Seal, The.
Picnic Day.
Playhouse Key, The.
Pointed People, The.
Pretzel Man, The.
Pushcart Row.
Roads.
Seven Ages of Elf-hood, The.
Skyscrapers.
Snow in the City.
Some People.
Something Told the Wild Geese.
Song for a Blue Roadster.
Spring Signs.
Summer Morning, A.
Taxis.
Ticking Clocks.
Vegetables.
Whistles.

Field, Richard H.
Limerick: "When you go to a store in Ascutney."

Field, Roswell Martin
At the Ball Game.

Field, Sara Bard (Mrs. Charles Erskine Scott Wood)
We Whom the Dead Have Not Forgiven.

Field, Thomas
Common Sense.

Fielding, Henry
A-Hunting We Will Go.
Don Quixote in England, *sels.*
Hunting Song.
Roast Beef of Old England, The.

Fields, Annie
Cedar Mountain.
Little Guinever.
On Waking from a Dreamless Sleep.
Return, The.
"Song to the Gods, Is Sweetest Sacrifice."
Theocritus.

Fields, Dorothy
I Can't Give You Anything but Love, *with music.*

Fields, James Thomas
Alarmed Skipper, The.
Ballad of the Tempest.
Captain's Daughter, The.
Jupiter and Ten.
Mabel, in New Hampshire.
Nantucket Skipper, The.
On a Watchman Asleep at Midnight.
Owl-Critic, The.
Song of the Turtle and Flamingo.
Tempest, The.
Turtle and the Flamingo, The.
With Wordsworth at Rydal.

Fields, Julia
Aardvark.
Alabama.
Birmingham.
Black Students.
Harlem in January.
High on the Hog.
I Heard a Young Man Saying.
Madness One Monday Evening.
Moths.
No Time for Poetry.
Poem for Heroes, A.
Poems: Birmingham 1962–1964.

Figgis, Darrell ("Micheal Ireland")
Bogac Bán.
Inisgallun.

Figueroa Aymerich, Angela
Women at the Market.

Filicaja, Vincenzo da
Italy.
Finch, Anne (1908–)
Essay on Marriage, *sel.*
Finch, Anne, Countess of Winchilsea. *See* **Winchilsea, Anne Finch, Countess of**
Finch, Francis Miles
Blue and the Gray, The.
Nathan Hale.
Finch, Robert
Alone.
Aria Senza da Capo.
Collective Portrait, The.
Crib, The.
Egg-and-Dart.
Jardin de la Chapelle Expiatoire.
Last Visit.
Lost Tribe, The.
Mountain, The.
Network, The.
Peacock and Nightingale.
Rhemish Carol, A.
Room.
Scroll-Section.
Silverthorn Bush.
Statue, The.
Time's Bright Sand.
Train Window.
Turning.
Words.
Finch, Vivienne
Green Ice.
Inertia.
Finefrock, Margaret
Demonstration.
Fineran, Mary C.
Night Train.
Finerty, John F.
May-Day at Sea.
Fink, William W.
Larrie O'Dee.
Finkel, Donald
Bush on Mount Venus, The.
Cain's Song.
Clothing's New Emperor, The.
Cocteau's Opium: 1 ("Still, no one has paid much tribute to the man").
Cocteau's Opium: 2 ("Picasso, who knows everything, will tell you").
Cross-eyed Lover, The.
Esthetic of Imitation, An.
Father, The.
Feeding the Fire.
Finders Keepers.
Flagpole Sitter, The.
Genealogy.
Gesture.
Give Way.
Great Wave, The: *Hokusai.*
Hands.
How Things Fall.
Hunting Song.
Husband, The.
Imbecile, The.
Joyful Noise, A.
Juan Belmonte, Torero.
King Midas Has Asses' Ears.
Lame Angel.
Letter to My Daughter at the End of Her Second Year.
Lilith.
Metaphysic of Snow.
Note in Lieu of a Suicide.
Oedipus at San Francisco.
Sirens, The.
Solo for Bent Spoon.
Spring Song.
Target Practice.
They.
Time Out.
When I Was Young I Tried to Sing.
Finlay, Ian Hamilton
Bedtime.
Dancers Inherit the Party, The.
Horizon of Holland, The.
Island Moment.
Orkney Interior.
Twice.
Finley, C. Stephen
October Dusk.
To One Far Away, Dancing.
Finley, Jeanne
Dead of the World, The.
Divorce Dress, The.
Finley, John
Bachelor's Hall.
Birthday Prayer, A.
Finne, Diderik
Apollo 113.
Finnell, Dennis
Working at a Service Station, I Think of Shinkichi Takahashi.
Finnigan, Joan
May Day Rounds: Renfrew County, *sel.*
I Closed My Shutters Fast Last Night.
Finnin, Olive Mary
Farm near Norman's Lane, The.
Firdausi (Abul Kasim Mansur)
Alas for Youth.
Dream of Dakiki, The.
When the Sword of Sixty Comes Nigh His Head.
Firestone, Laya
Crow, Straight Flier, but Dark.
For Gabriel.
Listen to the Bird.
Thoughts for My Grandmother.
Firkins, Chester
On a Subway Express.
Firsoff, Axel
Spirit of the Cairngorms, The.
"Firth"
Britannia Rules of Orthography.
Fischer, Helen Field
Mystic Borderland, The.
Fischer, Otakar
From the Depths.
Fishback, Margaret
Brooklynese Champion.
Christmas Pageant.
Complacent Cliff-Dweller, The.
Hallowe'en Indignation Meeting.
Hell's Bells.
I Stand Corrected.
I Take 'Em and Like 'Em.
In Extremis.
Kerchoo!
Midsummer Melancholy.
On Viewing a Florist's Whimsy at Fifty-ninth and Madison.
Poem for Mother's Day.
Purist to Her Love, The.
Sentimental Lines to a Young Man Who Favors Pink Wallpaper While I Personally Lean to the Blue.
Sitting Pretty.
Thoughts of Loved Ones.
Triolet on a Dark Day.
Triolet on a Downhill Road.
Wanted: One Cave Man with Club.
Fisher, A. G.
Day by Day.
Fisher, A. Hugh
Ceylon.
Fisher, Aileen
Away We Go.
Bells of Peace, The.
Birthday Cake.
But That Was Yesterday.
Cat in the Snow.
Christmas Tree.
Cinderella Grass.
Counting Sheep.
December.
Down in the Hollow.
Early, Early Easter Day.
Fall.
Fireflies.
Flag We Fly, The.
Halloween Concert.
Houses.
I Like It When It's Mizzly.
January Snow.
June.
Light in the Darkness.
Light the Festive Candles.
Listening.
Little Bird, A.
Little Talk.
Merry Christmas.
My Puppy.
Newspaper.
November.
On Mother's Day.
Otherwise.
Outdoor Christmas Tree, The.
Package, The.
Picnic, A.
Puppy.
Raccoons.
Seed, The.
Snoring.
Snowman's Resolution, The ("The snowman's hat was crooked").
Tummy Ache.
Until We Built a Cabin.
Valentine's Day.
Wearing of the Green.
Winter Circus.
Wonderful Man, A.
Workshop, The.
World's So Big, The.
Fisher, David
Analyst.
Birds of Arles, The.
Child's Christmas without Jean Cocteau, A.
Death of Rimbaud.
Emergency Room, The.
Harvest Poem.
Junkie with a Flute in the Rain, A.
Keepsake Corporation, The.
Lost.
Mutilated Soldier, The.
Mycenae.
Old Man, The.
On the Esplanade des Invalides.
Pastor Speaks Out, The.
Rehearsal.
Retarded Class at F. A. O. Schwarz's Celebrates Christmas, The.
Spassky at Reykjavik.
Teacher, The.
Vietnamese Girl in the Madhouse, The.
Why Do You Want to Suffer Less.
Fisher, Ed
Talk of the Town, The.
Fisher, I.H. *See* **"Hume, Isobel"**
Fisher, Lori
Pentimento.
Fisher, Mahlon Leonard
As an Old Mercer.
In Cool, Green Haunts.
November.
On a Sculptured Head of the Christ.
Fisher, Robert
Minotaur.
Monster Alphabet.
Phoenix, The.
Fisher, Roy
As He Came near Death.
Entertainment of War, The.
Fishman, Charles
August 12, 1952.
Fish Story, A.

Fishman, Rachel
Even If.
In the Beginning.
Fiske, John
Upon the Decease of Mrs. Anne Griffin.
Upon the Much-to Be Lamented Desease of the Reverend Mr. John Cotton.
Fitch, Eleazar Thompson
By Vows of Love Together Bound, *with music.*
Lord, at This Closing Hour, *with music.*
Fitger, Arthur
Evening Prayer.
Fitton, Molly
Linger longer, Olga.
When fog come creepin' over Beccles.
Fitts, Dudley
Southwest Passage.
Ya Se Van Los Pastores.
Fitz-Geffry [*or* Fitzgeffry], Charles
Bee, The.
Holy Transportations, *sel.*
Sir Francis Drake, *sel.*
Take Frankincense, O God.
Fitzgerald, Edward
Because.
Chivalry at a Discount.
Meadows in Spring, The.
Old Song.
Three Arrows, The.
Fitzgerald, F. Scott (Francis Scott Key Fitzgerald)
Epitaph from *The Great Gatsby.*
Obit on Parnassus.
There'd Be an Orchestra.
Thousand-and-First Ship, *sel.*
Fitzgerald, Robert
Before Harvest.
Celestine.
Cobb Would Have Caught It.
Colorado.
Errantry.
History.
Imprisoned, The.
Jesu, Joy of Man's Desiring.
July in Indiana.
Metaphysical.
Metaphysician.
Midsummer.
Mise en Scène.
Painter, The.
Park Avenue.
Patrum Propositum.
Queens, The.
Sea Pieces.
Shore of Life, The.
Solstitium Saeculare.
Song for September.
Souls Lake.
Windshield.
Winter Night.
Fitzgerald, Robert David
Back from the Paved Way.
Bog and Candle.
Edge.
Essay on Memory, *sel.*
Face of the Waters, The.
Favour.
Macquarie Place.
1918–1941.
Wind at Your Door, The.
Fitzherbert, Sir Anthony
Husbandry, *sel.*
Memorial Verses for Travellers.
Fitzpatrick, Susan
More Than.
Fitzsimon, Henry
Swearing.
Fixmer, Clyde
Canal Street, Chicago.
Flaccus (Statyllius Flaccus)
Epigram: "Just as he is growing a beard."
Flagg, James Montgomery
Table Manners.
Flagg, James Montgomery *and* **Julian Street.** *See* **Street, Julian** *and* **James Montgomery Flagg**
Flagg, Wilson
O'Lincon Family, The.
Flagg, Hannah. *See* **Gould, Hannah Flagg**
Flaischlen, Cäsar
Most Quietly at Times.
Flanders, Jane
Fairy Tales.
Stars Shine So Faithfully.
Flanders, Michael
First and Second Law.
Hummingbird, The.
Walrus, The.
Flanner, Hildegarde
Daphne.
Discovery.
Farewell, A: "My cat was a southerner and a lady."
Flowers of Apollo, The.
Hawk Is a Woman.
Let Us Believe.
Memo.
Moon Song.
Prayer for This Day.
Sonnets in Quaker Language, *sels.*
Swift Love, Sweet Motor.
This Day.
To One of Little Faith.
Flantz, Richard
Shir Ma'alot/ A Song of Degrees.
Flash, Henry Lynden
Gallant Fifty-one, The.
Stonewall Jackson.
Zollicoffer.
Flatman, Thomas
Advice, The.
Appeal to Cats in the Business of Love, An.
Bachelor's Song, The.
Defiance, The.
On Marriage.
Sad Day, The.
Thought of Death, A.
Unconcerned, The.
Flavell [*or* Lavelle], Thomas
County of Mayo, The, *at.*
Flax, Hjalmar
Art.
Littoral.
Flecker, James Elroy
Ballad of Camden Town, The.
Ballad of Hampstead Heath, The.
Ballad of the Londoner.
Brumana.
Dying Patriot, The.
Epilogue: "Away, for we are ready to a man!"
Epithalamion: "Smile then, children, hand in hand."
Gates of Damascus.
Golden Journey to Samarkand, The.
Hammam Name, The.
Hassan, *sels.*
In Hospital.
In Phæacia.
Inscription for Arthur Rackham's Rip Van Winkle.
November Eves ("November evenings! Damp and still").
Oak and Olive.
Old Ships, The.
Oxford Canal.
Painter's Mistress, The.
Parrot, The.
Prayer: "Let me not know how sins and sorrows glide."
Prologue: "We who with songs beguile your pilgrimage."
Queen's Song, The.
Rioupéroux.
Saadabad.
Santorin.
Ship, an Isle, a Sickle Moon, A.
Stillness.
Tenebris Interlucentem.
To a Poet a Thousand Years Hence.
Town without a Market, The.
War Song of the Saracens, The.
Welsh Sea, The.
Flecknoe, Richard
Noble Love.
Silence Invoked.
Fleg, Edmond
Dead Cities Speak to the Living Cities, The.
End of Sorrow, The.
Wall of Weeping, The, *sels.*
Wandering Jew Comes to the Wall, The.
Fleisher, Bernice
Perfectionist, The.
Fleming, Carrol B.
Boundaries.
Fleming, Elizabeth
In the Mirror.
Who's In.
Fleming, Gerald
Let Go: Once.
Fleming, Marjory
Melancholy Lay, A.
Six-Year-Old Marjory Fleming Pens a Poem.
Sonnet, A: "O lovely O most charming pug."
Sonnet on a Monkey, A.
Fleming, Maybury
To Demeter.
To Sleep.
What Though the Green Leaf Grow?
Fletcher, Bob
Love Dirge to the Whitehouse, A.
Fletcher, Curley W.
High-loping Cowboy, The.
Strawberry Roan, The.
Fletcher, Giles the Elder
Licia, *sels.*
Sonnet: "Like Memnon's rock, touched with the rising sun."
Time.
Fletcher, Giles, the Younger
Celestial City, The.
Easter Morn.
Excellency of Christ.
Halcyon's Nest, The.
He Is a Path.
Heavenly Jerusalem, The.
Mercy Pleads for Mankind.
On the Crucifixion.
Wooing Song.
Fletcher, John
Arm, Arm, Arm, Arm!
Beauty Clear and Fair.
Beggars' Bush, *sel.*
Care-charming Sleep, [Thou Easer of All Woes].
Cast Our Caps and Cares Away.
Chances, The, *sel.*
Come, Shepherds, Come!
Come Hither, You That Love.
Dead Host's Welcome, The.
Dearest, Do Not You Delay Me.
Elder Brother, The, *sel.*
Evening Knell, The.
Evening Song.
Faithful Shepherdess, The, *sels.*
Folding the Flocks.
God Lyaeus, Ever Young.
God of Sheep, The.
Hear [*or* Heare], Ye Ladies [That Despise].
Hence, All You Vain Delights.
Hymn to Pan.
Into Slumbers.
Invocation to Sleep.
Little French Lawyer, The, *sel.*
Love Song: "Now the lusty Spring is seen."
Lover's Progress, The, *sel.*
Love's Emblems.
Mad Lover, The, *sels.*
Melancholy.
Mighty Love.

Mourn No More.
Music, *at.*
Nice Valour, The, *sel.*
O Sweetest Melancholy.
Orpheus with His Lute, *at.*
Passionate Man's Song, The.
Power of Love, The.
Priest's Chant, The.
River God, The.
River-God's Song, The.
Satyr's Farewell, The ("Thou divinest, fairest, brightest").
Satyr's Song ("See the day begins to break").
Song: "Care charming sleep, thou easer of all woes."
Song: "Do not fear to put thy feet."
Song: "Oh fair [*or* O faire] sweet face, oh eyes celestial[l] bright."
Song for the Sick Emperor.
Song in the Wood.
Song to Sleep.
Spanish Curate, The, *sels.*
Sweet Music's Power, *at.*
Tell Me, Dearest, What Is Love?
Thou Easer of All Woes.
'Tis Late and Cold.
To Pan.
To Sleep.
Tragedy of Valentinian, The, *sels.*
Valentinian.
Weep No More, *at.*
What Is Love?
Women Pleased, *sels.*
Women's Longing.

Fletcher, John *and* William Rowley
Maid in the Mill, The, *sel.*

Fletcher, John *and* **William Shakespeare.** *See* **Shakespeare, William** *and* **John Fletcher**

Fletcher, John *and others*
Drink To-Day.
Drinking Song.
Hide, Oh, Hide Those Hills of Snow.
Queen of Corinth, The, *sel.*

Fletcher, John Gould
Arizona Poems, *sels.*
Before Olympus.
Blue Symphony.
Down the Mississippi.
Elegy on a Nordic White Protestant.
Green Symphony.
Irradiations, *sels.*
Last Judgment.
Lincoln.
London Nightfall.
Mexican Quarter.
Monadnock, The.
Rain in the Desert.
Rebel, A.
Road, The.
Skaters, The.
Song of the Moderns.
There Was a Darkness in This Man.
Windmills, The.

Fletcher, Louisa
Land of Beginning Again, The.

Fletcher, Phineas
All-seeing Intellect, The.
Apollyonists, The, *sel.*
Brittain's Ida, *sel.*
Cambridge and the Cam.
Chromis.
Desiderium.
Divine Wooer, The, *sel.*
Drop, Drop, Slow Tears.
Elisa, or an Elegy upon the Unripe Decease of Sir Antony Irby, *sel.*
Hymn: "Drop, drop, slow tears."
Lines Written at Cambridge, to W. R., Esquire.
Litany, A: "Drop, drop, slow tears."
Locusts, or Apollyonists, The, *sels.*
Overthrow of Lucifer, The.
Piscatorie Eclogues, *sels.*
Purple Island, The, *sels.*
Sicelides, *sel.*
Sin, Despair, and Lucifer.
Song: "Fond men! whose wretched care the life soon ending."
To My Ever-honoured Cousin W. R. Esquire, *sel.*
To My Soul.
Woman's Inconstancy.

Fletcher, Robert H.
Ballad of Pug-nosed Lil, The.
Bloody Brother, The, *sels.*

Flexner, Hortense
Builders.
Contemporary.
French Clock.
Poets.
Wandering.
When Last Seen.

Flexner, James
In the Hours of Darkness.

Flint, Annie Johnson
Answered Prayer, The.
At the Place of the Sea.
Blessings That Remain, The.
Cross and the Tomb, The.
Daily with You.
Everlasting Love, The.
He Giveth More [Grace].
His Will Be Done.
Hitherto and Henceforth.
In Him.
Mary and Martha.
Not I, but God.
Old Year and the New, The.
Our Father's Hand.
Passing Through.
Pray—Give—Go.
Red Sea Place in Your Life, The.
Sepulcher, The.
Sometimes.
This Moment.
Thou Remainest.
Through the Waters.
Thy Will Be Done.
We See Jesus.
What God Hath Promised!
Word of God, The.
World's Bible, The.

Flint, Francis Stewart
Eau-Forte.
Lilac.
Prayer: "As I walk through the streets."

Flint, James
In Pleasant Lands Have Fallen the Lines, *with music.*

Flint, Roland
August from My Desk.

Flohr, Natalie
Martyr, The.

Flood, John
To His Coy Mistress, *parody.*

Florencia del Pinar
Another Song of the Same Woman, to Some Partridges, Sent to Her Alive.

Florio, John
Of Books.

Flower, Robin
Say Not That Beauty.
Troy.

Flynn, Desirée (Sheila Desirée Savory Rodd)
Collector, The.
From the Rain Forest.

Flynn, Elizabeth
After Grave Deliberation.

Flynn, Joseph
Down Went McGinty.

Foerster, Richard
Archne.
Nantucket's Widows.
Those Guyana Nights.

Foeth, Afanasi. *See* **Fet, Afanasi Afanasievich**

Fogel, Ephim G.
Shipment to Maidanek.

Fogle, Richard Harter
Hawthorne Garland, A.

Folcachiero de' Folcachieri
Canzone: He Speaks of His Condition through Love.

Foley, James William
Drop a Pebble in the Water.
Salvation of Texas Peters, The.
Scientific Proof.

Folger, Peleg
Praise Ye the Lord. O Celebrate His Fame, *with music.*

Folgore da San Gemignano. *See* **San Geminiano, Folgore da**

Follansbee, Mitchell D.
I Like to Quote.

Follen, Eliza Lee (Cabot)
Good Moolly Cow, The.
Little Kittens, The.
Lord, Deliver, Thou Canst Save, *with music.*
Moon, The.
Where Are You Going.

Fondane, Benjamin
By the Waters of Babylon.
Hertza.
Lullaby for an Emigrant.
Plain Song.
Wandering Jew, The.

Fonte Boa, Maria Amalia
Two Tile Beaks.
Vitality.

Foote, Lucius Harwood
Derelict, The.
Don Juan.
El Vaquero.
On the Heights.
Poetry.
Sutter's Fort, Sacramento.

Foote, Samuel
Great Panjandrum, The [Himself].

Foott, Mary Hannay
Where the Pelican Builds.

Forbes, Calvin
Chocolate Soldiers, The.
Gabriel's Blues.
Lullaby for Ann-Lucian.
M. A. P.
Other Side of This World, The.
Reading Walt Whitman.
Some Pieces.

Forbes, Ella C.
Glad Earth.

Forbes, John
Four Heads & How to Do Them.
TV.

Forché, Carolyn
Because One Is Always Forgotten.
Burning the Tomato Worms.
City Walk-up, Winter 1969.
Colonel, The.
Departure.
Dulcimer Maker.
Endurance.
For the Stranger.
Kalaloch.
Memory of Elena, The.
Reunion.
Selective Service.
Taking Off My Clothes.
Visitor, The.

Ford, Charles Henri
"Baby's in jail; the animal day plays alone."
Bad Habit, The.
January wraps up the wound of his arm.
Overturned Lake, The.
Plaint.
Somebody's Gone.
There's No Place to Sleep in This Bed, Tanguy.

Ford, Corey
Up-Set, The.
When West Comes East.
Ford, Dan
Love Is Loathing & Why.
Ford, Ford Madox (*originally* Ford Madox Hueffer)
A Solis Ortus Cardine.
Cat of the House, The.
Children's Song.
Iron Music, The.
Old Houses of Flanders, The.
On Heaven.
Sanctuary, The.
What the Orderly Dog Saw.
"When the World Was in Building."
Wisdom.
Ford, Francis Alan
Song of the Gulf Stream.
Ford, Gena
Legacy.
Lines for a Hard Time.
Nude on the Bathroom Wall, The.
Ford, John
Broken Heart, The, *sels.*
Can You Paint a Thought?
Dawn.
Dirge: "Glories, pleasures, pomps, delights, and ease."
Fly Hence, Shadows.
Glories, Pleasures.
Lady's Trial, The, *sel.*
Lover's Melancholy, The, *sels.*
Love's Martyrs.
Pleasures, Beauty.
Song: "Fly hence, shadows, that do keep."
Song, A: "Glories, pleasures, pomps, delights, and ease."
Song: "O, no more, no more, too late."
Ford, Mary A.
Hundred Years from Now, A.
Ford, Michael C.
Mellow Groove Grave Elegy.
Ford, Robert
Bonniest Bairn in a' the Warl', The.
Ford, Robert Arthur Douglas
Back to Dublin.
Earthquake.
Lynx.
Revenge of the Hunted.
Roadside near Moscow.
Sakhara.
Sleeplessness of Our Time.
Thieves of Love, The.
Twenty Below.
Window on the North, A.
Ford, S. Gertrude
Fight to a Finish, A.
Nature in War-Time.
Tenth Armistice Day, The.
Ford, Sara de
Sleeping Beauty, The.
Ford, Thomas
There Is a Lady [Sweet and Kind], *at.*
Ford, Walter H.
Sunshine of Paradise Alley, The, *with music.*
Foresman, Rebecca
If.
"Forester, Fanny" (Emily Chubbuck Judson)
My Bird.
Watching.
Weaver, The.
Forker, Greg
And the Gas Chamber Drones in the Distance.
And the Winner Is.
Christ.
Reasons to Go Home.
Test of Competence, A.
Torch, The.
Forman, Elizabeth Chandler
Three Lads, The.
Forman, Nicole
Labour of the Brain, Ballad of the Body.
Forrest, Frederick
St. Anthony and His Pig; a Cantata.
Forrest, William
Marigold, The.
New Ballade of the Marigolde, A.
Forrester, Alfred A. ("Alfred Crowquill")
To My Nose.
Forster, Frederick J.
Lobsters and the Fiddler Crab, The ("The lobsters came ashore one night").
Forster, William
Devil and the Governor, The, *sel.*
Love Has Eyes.
Poor of London, The.
Sonnet on the Crimean War.
Forsyth, James
Artillery Shoot.
Soldier's Dove.
To My Wife.
Forsyth, Sarah
My Christmas; Mum's Christmas.
Fort, Paul
Ballade: "Pretty maid she died, she died, in love-bed as she lay, The."
Pan and the Cherries.
Sailor and the Shark, The.
Forten, Charlotte
Parting Hymn, A.
Poem: "In the earnest path of duty."
To W. L. G. on Reading His "Chosen Queen."
Fortini, Franco
For Our Soldiers Who Fell in Russia.
Gutter, The.
In Memoriam I ("You used to ask me once what was wrong").
In Memoriam II ("I do not understand").
Fortunatus. *See* **Venantius Fortunatus, Saint**
Fosdick, Harry Emerson
O God, in Restless Living.
Prince of Peace His Banner Spreads, The, *with music.*
Fosdick, W. W.
Aura Lea [*or* Lee], *with music.*
Foss, Sam Walter
Calf-Path, The.
Coming American, The, *sel.*
Higher Catechism, The.
House by the Side of the Road, The.
"Hullo!"
Husband and Heathen.
Ideal Husband to His Wife, The.
Man from the Crowd, The.
Philosopher, A.
Then Ag'in.
Foster, Donald
Triad.
Foster, Jeanne Robert
John Butler Yeats.
King o' Spain's Daughter, The.
Pair of Lovers, A.
William P. Frye, The.
Foster, Stephen Collins
Beautiful Dreamer.
Camptown Races, The [*or* De].
Come Where My Love Lies Dreaming.
Jeanie with the Light Brown Hair.
Massa's in de Cold Cold Ground.
My Old Kentucky Home.
Nelly Bly.
Oh! [*or* O] Susanna.
Old Black Joe.
Old Dog Tray.
Old Folks at Home.
Who Has Our Redeemer Heard, *with music.*
Foster, William Prescott
Icebergs.
Sea's Voice, The.
Foulke, William Dudley
Ad Patriam, *sel.*
City's Crown, The.
Land of My Heart.
Life's Evening.
Foulkes, William H.
Take Thou Our Minds, Dear Lord, *with music.*
Fowler, Andrew
Awake, My Soul! In Grateful Songs, *with music.*
O Gracious Jesus, Blessed Lord! *with music.*
Fowler, Ellen Thorneycroft
Wisdom of Folly, The.
Fowler, Elsie Melchert
If You've Never.
Fowler, Gene
Vivisection, *abr.*
Fowler, Hazel J.
Prayer: "Take from the earth its tragic hunger, Lord."
Fowler, Laurence
Gather Ye Rosebuds.
Fowler, Lona M.
Middle-Time, The.
Fowler, Mary B.
Promise, The.
Fowler, Russell T.
In Blanco County.
Fowler, William
If When I Die.
In Orknay.
Ship-broken Men Whom Stormy Seas Sore Toss.
Fowles, John
Barbarians.
Fox, Eldon Ray
Bumper Sticker, The, on His Pickup Said, "I'm a Lover, I'm a Fighter, I'm a Wild Bull Rider."
Fox, Gail
For Anne, Who Doesn't Know.
It Is Her Cousin's Death.
Portrait.
She Lay Wrapped.
Fox, Henry, 1st Baron Holland. *See* **Holland, Henry Fox, 1st Baron**
Fox, Lucia
Dream of the Forgotten Lover.
Fox, Moireen
Fairy Lover, The.
Fox, Ruth
Another Kind of Burning.
Fox, Siv Cedering
In the Planetarium.
In the Taxidermist's Shop.
Johannes Kepler (1571–1630).
Letter from Caroline Herschel (1750–1848).
Letters from the Astronomers, *sels.*
Nicholas Copernicus (1473–1543).
Nightmares.
Poem for My Mother.
To the Man Who Watches Spiders.
Fox-Smith, C.
Mules.
Fox-Smith, Cicely. *See* **Smith, Cicely, Fox**
"Foxton, E." (Sarah Hammond Palfrey)
Pilgrim, The.
Foxton, Thomas
On a Little Boy's Endeavouring to Catch a Snake.
Upon Boys Diverting Themselves in the River.
Fraire, Isabel
If night takes the form of a whale and.
Frame, Janet
Foxes, The.
Telephonist.
France, Judson
Aristocratic Trio, An.
Frances, Emmanuel ben David
Price of Begging, The.
Frances, Jacob ben David
Song of Hate.
Francesco da Barberino. *See* **Barberino, Francesco da**

"Francis."
They Answer Back: To His Ever-worshipped Will from W. H.
To His Ever-worshipped Will from W.H.
Francis, Colin
Tony O!
Francis, Joseph G.
Elephant Sat on Some Kegs, An.
Genial Grimalkin, The.
Francis, Marilyn
Neighbors.
Francis, Pat Therese
Poem for a Neighbor.
Telephone Operator, The.
Francis, Robert
Apple Peeler.
Base Stealer, The.
Beyond Biology.
Blue Jay [*or* Bluejay].
Blue Winter.
Bouquets.
Boy at a Certain Age.
Boy Riding Forward Backward.
Bulldozer, The.
Burial.
Buzz Plane, The.
By Night.
Catch.
Cats.
Cold.
Come Out into the Sun.
Cromwell.
Curse, The.
Cypresses.
Dandelion Gatherer, The.
December.
Delicate the Toad.
Diver.
Eagle Plain.
Edith Sitwell Assumes the Role of Luna.
Fair and Unfair.
Fall.
Farm Boy after Summer.
Fear, A.
Fisherman.
Glass.
Hallelujah; a Sestina.
High Diver.
History.
Hogwash.
Hound, The.
House Remembers, The.
Juniper.
Light Casualties.
Like Ghosts of Eagles.
Mr. Eliot's Day.
Night Train.
Now That Your Shoulders Reach My Shoulders.
Orb Weaver, The.
"Paper Men to Air Hopes and Fears."
Part for the Whole.
Picasso and Matisse.
Pitcher.
Play Ball!
Seagulls.
Seed-Eaters, The.
Sheep.
Silent Poem.
Sing a Song of Juniper.
Skier.
Spell.
Squash in Blossom.
Swimmer.
That Dark Other Mountain.
Though a Fool.
Three Darks Come Down Together.
Two Bums Walk Out of Eden.
Two Wrestlers.
Walls.
Watching Gymnasts.
Waxwings.
Yes, What?
Francis of Assisi, Saint
Cantica: Our Lord Christ: Of Order.
Canticle of the Sun.
Cantico del Sole.
Lord, Make Me an Instrument of Your Peace
Of Order in Our Lord Christ.
Praise of Created Things.
Prayer of St. Francis of Assisi for Peace.
St. Francis' Prayer.
Sermon to the Birds.
Song of the Creatures, The.
Francis Xavier, Saint
Hymn: "My God, I love thee, not because."
Francisco, Edward
Lilith's Child.
Francisco, Nia
Awéé'.
Men Tell and Talk.
Morning and Myself.
One Who Is Within, The.
Story Tellers Summer, 1980.
Franco, Veronica
No more words! To the field, to arms.
Frank, Florence Kiper
Baby.
Jew to Jesus, The.
Jewish Conscript, The.
Lincoln.
Now in the Bloom.
Frank, John Frederick
One No. 7.
Frankau, Gilbert
Gun Teams.
Frankel, Doris
Song of the Truck.
Frankenberg, Lloyd
Autumn Song on Perry Street.
Existentialism.
Hide in the Heart.
Sea, The.
Franklin, Benjamin
Difference, The.
Downfall of Piracy, The,*at.*
Enough Not One.
Epitaph: "Body, The/ of/ Benjamin Franklin."
Epitaph on a Talkative Old Maid.
Epitaph on a Worthy Clergyman.
Here Skugg lies snug.
Jack and Roger, *at.*
Mother Country, The.
Franklin, Michael
Scarecrow, The.
Franklin, William (Bob Grove)
Captive, The.
"Gotta' Smoke?"
Hunger Striker.
Lawn Order.
My Street Baby's Lament.
Paper Words.
Franzen, John
O God of Stars and Distant Space, *with music.*
Fraser, Alexander Louis
By Cobequid Bay.
Fraser, Barclay
Mountain Days.
Fraser, C. Lovat
Robin's Song, The.
Fraser, Douglas
Far in the West.
Freedom of the Hills.
Growing Old.
Lost Leader, The.
Mountain Vigil.
On Looking at an Old Climbing Photograph.
Quiet Glen, The.
Spell o' the Hills, The.
To Alan.
Fraser, George Sutherland
Bought Embrace, A.
Christmas Letter Home.
Crisis.
Elegy: "Waxen and the false grace of tulips, The."
Flemish Primitive.
Lean Street.
Letter to Anne Ridler.
Nilotic Elegy.
On a Memory of Beauty.
On the Persistence of Humanity.
Poem about Love, A.
Rostov.
S. S. *City of Benares.*
Song for Music.
Sonnet: "My simple heart, bred in provincial tenderness."
Time, The.
To a Scottish Poet.
Traveller Has Regrets, The.
Fraser, Hermia Harris
Copper Song, The.
Rousing Canoe Song, The.
Song of Welcome.
Fraser, John
Maiden and the Lily, The.
Fraser, Kath
Song: "I love you, Mrs. Acorn. Would your husband mind."
Fraser, Kathleen
Broom Balancing.
Casa de Pollos.
Change of Address.
Dresses.
Follow the Leader.
How Tuesday Began.
Interior with Mme. Vuillard and Son.
Joan Brown, about Her Painting.
Know, The.
La Reproduction Interdite/Not to Be Reproduced.
Les Jours Gigantesques/The Titanic Days.
Lily, Lois & Flaubert; the Site of Loss.
Locations.
Medusa's Hair Was Snakes. Was Thought, Split Inward.
1930.
Nuts and Bolts Poem for Mr. Mac Adams, Sr.
Poem in Which My Legs Are Accepted.
Poem Wondering If I'm Pregnant.
Poems for the New.
These Labdanum Hours.
What You Need.
Wrestling.
Fraser, Olive
Benighted to the Foothills of the Cairngorms.
Fraser, Ray
Cry of an Aged One, The.
Ecole St. Luc.
Flora.
Grotto, The.
In an Empty Window.
Lost Picture.
Not Often.
On Learning to Play the Guitar.
Policemen Laughing.
Souster.
Frate, Frank
Love Poem Investigation for A. T.
Frayn, Michael
Life of T. S. Eliot, A.
Frazee-Bower, Helen
Alien.
Certainties.
Courage.
Descent.
Flight.
Heights, The.
Song of Diligence, A.
Take Time to Talk with God.
Two Married (I-IV).
Frazier, Robert
Marie Curie Contemplating the Role of Women Scientists in the Glow of a Beaker.
Supremacy of Bacteria, The.

Telephone Ghosts.
Frear, Mary Dillingham
Young Workman, The.
Free, Spencer Michael
Human Touch, The.
Freebairn, A. L.
Ride 'Im Cowboy.
Freed, Ray
In an Hour the Sun.
Freedman, William
Benediction.
Formations.
Freeman, Anne Hobson
I'll Tell You What a Flapper Is.
Freeman, Arthur
Beauty, Sleeping.
Cat, Caged and Shrunken, The.
Cell of Himself, The.
Conversation Piece.
Naples Again.
On a Portrait by Copley.
Zoo of You, The.
Freeman, Carol [*or* Carole]
Christmas Morning I.
Do Not Think.
I Saw Them Lynch.
When My Uncle Willie Saw.
Freeman, Enoch W.
Hither We Come, Our Dearest Lord, *with music.*
Freeman, Hollis
Birds of the Air, The.
Freeman, James
Lord of the Worlds Below! *with music.*
Freeman, John
Armistice Day.
Asylum.
Black Poplar-Boughs.
Caterpillars.
Crowns, The.
Happy Death.
Hounds, The.
It Was the Lovely Moon.
Knocking at the Door.
Stone Trees.
To End Her Fear.
Waiting.
Wakers, The.
Freeman, Mary Eleanor Wilkins
Blue-eyed Mary.
Marm Grayson's Guests.
Ostrich is a silly bird, The.
Pretty Ambition, A.
Freeman, Robert
Braving the Wilds All Unexplored, *with music.*
Soldier's Prayer, A.
Why.
Freeman, William T.
Chekhov Comes to Mind at Harvard.
Freeth, John
Botany Bay.
Bunker's Hill, or the Soldier's Lamentation.
Colliers' March, The.
Cottager's Complaint, [on the Intended Bill for Enclosing Sutton-Coldfield], The.
New Navigation, The.
Freeze, Mary D.
Our Times Are in His Hands.
Freke, John
History of Insipids, The.
Frémont, John Charles
On Recrossing the Rocky Mountains after Many Years.
French, William Percy
"Are Ye Right There, Michael?" (A Lay of the Wild West Clare.)
Fighting McGuire.
Goosey Goosey Gander—by Various Authors.
Queen's Afterdinner Speech, The, *sel.*
Freneau, Philip
Adventures of Simon Swaugum, a Village Merchant, The.
Amanda's Complaint.
American Soldier, The.
Americans!
Ancient Prophecy, An.
Barney's Invitation.
Battle of Lake Champlain, The.
Battle of Stonington on the Seaboard of Connecticut, The.
Beauties of Santa Cruz, The, *sel.*
Bonhomme Richard and *Serapis,* The.
British Prison Ship, The, *sel.*
By Babel's Streams, *with music.*
Captain Jones' Invitation.
Columbus in Chains.
Columbus to Ferdinand.
Death.
Death's Epitaph.
Emancipation from British Dependence.
Epistle to a Desponding Sea-Man.
Epitaph: "Here—for they could not help but die."
Fading Rose, The, *sel.*
Female Frailty, *sel.*
George the Third's Soliloquy.
Hospital Prison Ship, The.
House of Night, The, *sels.*
Hurricane, The.
Indian Burying Ground, The.
Indian Convert, The.
Indian Student, The; or, Force of Nature.
Literary Importation.
Occasioned by General Washington's Arrival in Philadelphia, on His Way to His Residence in Virginia.
Ode: "God save the Rights of Man!"
On a Honey Bee.
On a Travelling Speculator.
On the British Invasion.
On the British King's Speech.
On the Capture of the *Guerrière.*
On the Death of Benjamin Franklin.
On the Death of Captain Nicholas Biddle.
On the Departure of the British from Charleston.
On the Emigration to America.
On the Religion of Nature.
On the Ruins of a Country Inn.
On the Uniformity and Perfection of Nature.
On the Universality and Other Attributes of the God of Nature.
Parting Glass, The.
Plato to Theon.
Power of Fancy, The.
Prophecy of King Tammany, The.
Reflections, *sel.*
Royal Adventurer, The.
Scurrilous Scribe, The.
Sir Henry Clinton's Invitation to the Refugees.
Song: "O'er the waste of waters cruising."
Song of Thyrsis.
Stanzas: "Princes and kings decay and die."
Stanzas Occasioned by the Ruins of a Country Inn, Unroofed and Blown Down in a Storm.
To a Caty-did.
To a Honey Bee.
To a Noisy Politician.
To a Republican.
To an Author.
To Sir Toby.
To the Memory of the Brave Americans.
Tobacco.
Vanity of Existence, The.
Warning to America, A.
Wild Honeysuckle [*or* Honey Suckle], The.
Frere, John Hookham
Bees and Monks.
Boy and the Parrot, The.
Boy and the Wolf, The.
Fable, A: "Dingy donkey, formal and unchanged, A."
Fable of the Piece of Glass and the Piece of Ice, The.
King Arthur and His Round Table, *sel.*
Loves of the Triangles, The, *sel.*
To a Lady, with a Present of a Walking-Stick.
Frere, John Hookham *and* **George Canning.** *See* **Canning, George** *and* **John Hookham Frere**
Frere, John Hookham, George Canning, *and* **George Ellis.** *See* **Canning, George, George Ellis,** *and* **John Hookham Frere**
Friar, Kimon
Greek Transfiguration.
Friebert, Stuart
Age of the Butcher, The.
Apron, The.
My Father's Heart.
Fried, Elliot
Amtrak.
Charlton Heston.
Daily I Fall in Love with Waitresses.
I Can't Figure You Out.
Mental Health.
Fried, Rivka
Sabbath.
Fried, Susannah
Scraps.
To My Father.
Winter Day.
Friedlaender, Violet Helen
Planting Trees.
Friedlander, Ginny
Here Be Dragons.
Friedmann, Pavel
Butterfly, The.
Friel, James P.
Revolutionary.
Friend, Robert
Doll, The.
Identity.
In the Orchard.
Letter to P.
Practice of Absence, The.
Riders, The.
Test, The.
Friman, Alice R.
Leda and the Swan.
Reckoning, The.
Fringell, Dieter
Hopes, The.
Frink, A. L.
Rose Still Grows beyond the Wall, The.
Frisch, Anthony
Convict, The.
Joan of Arc to the Tribunal.
Fritsch, H. S.
How Old Are You?
Frohlicher, John C.
Miners.
Froissart, Jean
Rondel: "Love, love, what wilt thou with this heart of mine?"
Frost, Frances Mary
Apple Season.
Apple Song.
Beach Fire.
Blue Smoke.
Christmas in the Wood.
Counting-out Rhyme for March.
Cover.
Dandelions.
Easter in the Woods.
Father.
First Departure.
Hallowe'en.
Hydrographic Report.
Kentucky Birthday; February 12, 1815.
Little Whistler, The.
Long Night Moon, The: December.
Maple Feast.
Night Heron.
Night of Wind.
Night Plane.
Nocturne: "Over New England now, the snow."
Sandpiper, The.
School Is Out.

Sea Town.
Sniff.
Song for December Thirty-first.
Spring in Hiding.
Trains at Night.
Valentine for Earth.
Weather Vanes.
White Season.
Winter Feast.

Frost, Richard
Last Bite, The.

Frost, Robert
Acceptance.
Acquainted with the Night.
After Apple-picking.
Aim Was Song, The.
All Revelation.
Armful, The.
At Woodward's Gardens.
August.
Away!
Axe-Helve, The.
Bear, The.
Bearer of Evil Tidings, The.
Bereft.
Beyond Words.
Birches.
Birthplace, The.
Black Cottage, The.
Blue Ribbon at Amesbury, A.
Blue-Butterfly Day.
Bonfire, The.
Brook in the City, A.
Brown's Descent; or, The Willy-Nilly Slide.
But God's Own Descent.
Canis Major.
Choose Something like a Star.
Christmas Trees (A Christmas Circular Letter).
Code, The.
Come In.
Considerable Speck, A.
Correction, A.
Cow in Apple Time, The.
Death of the Hired Man, The.
Demiurge's Laugh, The.
Departmental.
Desert Places.
Design.
Directive.
Draft Horse, The.
Drumlin Woodchuck, A.
Dust of Snow.
Early April.
Egg and the Machine, The.
Empty Threat, An.
Fear, The.
Fire and Ice.
Fireflies in the Garden.
Flower-Boat, The.
For Allan, Who Wanted to See How I Wrote a Poem.
For Once, Then, Something.
For Travelers Going Sidereal.
Forgive, O Lord, My Little Jokes on Thee.
Fountain, a Bottle, a Donkey's Ears and Some Books, A.
Freedom of the Moon, The.
From Plane to Plane.
Gathering Leaves.
Ghost House.
Gift Outright, The.
Going for Water.
Good-by and Keep Cold.
Happiness Makes Up in Height for What It Lacks in Length.
Hardship of Accounting, The.
Hill Wife, The.
Hillside Thaw, A.
Home.
Home Burial.
Home Defined.
House Fear.
Hundred Collars, A.
Hyla Brook.
Immigrants.
Importer, An.
Impulse, The.
In a Poem.
In Dives' Dive.
In Hardwood Groves.
In Neglect.
In Winter in the Woods Alone.
Innate Helium.
Investment, The.
John L. Sullivan Enters Heaven.
Kitchen Chimney, The.
Kitty Hawk, *sel.*
Last Word of a Bluebird, The.
Leaf-Treader, A.
Leaves Compared with Flowers.
Lesson for Today, The.
Lockless Door, The.
Lone Striker, A.
Loneliness.
Lost in Heaven.
Lovely Shall Be Choosers, The.
Lucretius versus the Lake Poets.
Meeting and Passing.
Mending Wall.
Middleness of the Road, The.
Minor Bird, A.
Moon Compasses.
Most of It, The.
Mountain, The.
Mowing.
My November Guest.
Need of Being Versed in Country Things, The.
Neither Out Far nor In Deep.
Never Again Would Birds' Song Be the Same.
New Hampshire, *sel.*
Not All There.
Not of School Age.
Not to Keep.
Nothing Gold Can Stay.
October.
Old Man's Winter Night, An.
On Looking Up by Chance at the Constellations.
On the Heart's Beginning to Cloud the Mind.
Once by the Pacific.
Onset, The.
"Out, Out."
Oven Bird, The.
Pan with Us.
Pasture, The.
Patch of Old Snow, A.
Pauper Witch of Grafton, The.
Peaceful Shepherd, The.
Peck of Gold, A.
Plowmen.
Pod of the Milkweed.
Prayer in Spring, A.
Pride of Ancestry.
Provide, Provide.
Putting in the Seed.
Questioning Faces.
Rabbit Hunter, The.
Range-finding.
Record Stride, A.
Reluctance.
Road Not Taken, The.
Rose Family, The.
Runaway, The.
Sand Dunes.
Secret Sits, The.
Semi-Revolution, A.
Servant to Servants, A.
Silken Tent, The.
Sky Pair, A.
Soldier, A.
Sound of the Trees [*or* of Trees], The.
Span of Life, The.
Spring Pools.
Star-Splitter, The.
Stopping by Woods on a Snowy Evening.
Storm Fear.
Strong Are Saying Nothing, The.
Subverted Flower, The.
Telephone, The.
There Are Roughly Zones.
Time to Talk, A.
To a Young Wretch.
To Earthward.
To the Right Person.
To the Thawing Wind.
Tree at My Window.
Trespass.
Tuft of Flowers, The.
Two Look at Two.
Two Tramps in Mud Time.
Two Witches.
Unharvested.
U.S. 1946 King's X.
Vantage Point, The.
Waspish.
West-running Brook.
What Fifty Said.
White-tailed Hornet, The.
Witch of Coös, The.
Wood-Pile, The.
Wrights' Biplane, The.
Young Birch, A.

Frost, Thomas
Death of Colman, The.
Guns in the Grass, The.

Frothingham, Nathaniel Langdon
Crossed Swords, The.
O God Whose Presence Glows in All, *with music.*

Frothingham, Octavius Brooks
Thou Lord of Hosts, Whose Guiding Hand, *with music.*

Froude, Richard Hurrell
Weakness of Nature.

Frug, Simeon Grigoryevich
Sail Peacefully Home.
Talmud, The.

Frumkin, Gene
Meeting Anais Nin's Elena.
Old Stories, The.

Fry, Herbert
As I'd Nothing Else to Do.

Fry, Nan
Apple.
Snow.

Fry, Susie
Fickle in the Arms of Spring.

Fuertes, Gloria
Autobiography.
Climbing.
Human Geography.
I Write Poems.
Interior Landscape.
Love Which Frees.
We're OK.
When I Hear Your Name.

Fuest, Milan
Moses' Account.

Fufuka, Karama
Basketball Star.
Lil' Bro'.

Fuguet, Dollett
Blithe Mask, The.

Fu Hsüan
Gentle Wind, A.

Fujiwara Ietaka
Old Scent of the Plum Tree.

Fuller, Ethel Romig
Diary, *sel.*
Fir Forest.
Mother—a Portrait.
Pioneer Mother, The.
Proof.
Six-Horse Limited Mail, The.
Wind is a Cat.

Fuller, Hoyt W.
Lost Moment.
Seravazza.
Fuller, Jean Overton
Not Marching Away to Be Killed.
Fuller, John
Band Music.
Blues.
God Bless America.
In a Railway Compartment.
Morvin.
Owls.
Snapshot.
Statue, The.
White Queen.
Fuller, John *and* **James Fenton.** *See* **Fenton, James** *and* **John Fuller**
Fuller, Margaret
Jesus a Child His Course Begun, *with music.*
Fuller, Margaret Witter
Dryad Song.
Passion-Flower, The.
Fuller, Roy
Autobiography of a Lungworm.
Ballad: "Father, through the dark that parts us."
Barber, The.
Be a Monster.
Bringing Up Babies.
Christmas Day.
Consolations of Art.
Crustaceans.
Dark, The.
Day, The.
Death.
Edmond Halley.
End of a Leave, The.
Epitaph on a Bombing Victim.
Family Cat, The.
Faust's Servant.
From the Joke Shop.
Giraffes, The.
Good-bye for a Long Time.
Green Hills of Africa, The.
Horrible Things.
Ides of March, The.
Image, The.
January 1940.
Last Sheet.
Letter to My Wife.
Meetings and Absences.
Metamorphoses.
Middle of a War, The.
Mythological Sonnets, *sels.*
Native Working on the Aerodrome.
Nino, the Wonder Dog.
November, 1941.
October 1942.
Other Side, The.
Outside the Supermarket.
Perturbations of Uranus, The.
Petty Officers' Mess, The.
Pigeon.
Plains, The.
Poem: "Pity, repulsion, love and anger."
Reading in the Night.
Sadness, Glass, Theory.
Shop Talk.
Shore Leave Lorry.
Soliloquy in an Air-Raid.
Sonnet: "Crumbled rock of London is dripping under, The."
Spring 1942.
Spring 1943.
Statue, The.
Those of Pure Origin.
Translation.
Tribes, The.
Unremarkable Year, The.
Versions of Love.
War Poet.
What Is Terrible.
Winter Night.
Wry Smile, A.
Fuller, Stephany
In the Silence.
Let Me Be Held When the Longing Comes.
My Love When This Is Past.
That We Head Towards.
Who is not a stranger still.
Fullerton, Mary Elizabeth ("E.")
Communal.
Cubes.
Emus.
Farmer, The.
Flesh.
Inspiration.
Lichen.
Lion.
Lovers.
Man's Sliding Mood, A.
Martyr.
Ninety.
Stupidity.
Fulton, Alice
Chain Letters.
Gone Years, The.
Great Aunts of My Childhood, The.
How to Swing Those Obbligatos Around.
Magistrate's Escape, The.
Fulton, Dorothy R.
Open Your Hand.
Softly, White and Pure.
Fulton, Robin
Cleared Land, A, *sel.*
More than People.
Stopping by Shadows.
Waiting-Room, The.
Funge, Robert
Arcady Revisited.
Funk, Wilfred John
Rest in Peace.
Funkhouser, Erica
Hammer.
Hand Saw.
Furlong, Alice
Betrayal, The.
My Share of the World.
Triad of Things Not Decreed, The.
Warnings, The.
Furness, William Henry
Evening Hymn.
In the Morning I Will Pray, *with music.*
Light of Stars, The.
Fyleman, Rose
Balloon Man, The.
Best Game the Fairies Play, The.
Bingo Has an Enemy ("Bingo is kind and friendly").
Birthday Child, The.
Child Next Door, The ("The child next door has a wreath on her hat").
Daddy.
Dentist, The.
Fairies.
Fairy Went a-Marketing, A.
Goblin, The.
Have You Watched the Fairies?
Husky Hi.
I Don't Like Beetles.
Jonathan.
Mary Middling.
Mice.
Mr. Minnitt.
Mrs. Brown.
Momotara.
Mother.
My Donkey.
My Policeman.
New Neighbor, The.
October.
Regent's Park.
Shop Windows.
Singing-Time.
Sometimes.
Spring, The.
Temper.
There Are No Wolves in England Now.
Very Lovely.
Fynn, Arthur J.
Land Where the Columbines Grow.

G

"G., A. R."
"Go Forward."
"G., E.O."
My Church ("My church has but one temple").
"G., G."
To W. J. M.
"G., L."
Quarrelsome Trio, The.
"G., W.A."
Yielded Life, The."
Gabriel, Charles H.
My Evening Prayer.
Gadbury, John
Ballad upon the Popish Plot, A.
Gadsby, Gordon J.
Lost Valley, The.
Gaess, Roger
Fall Lightly on Me.
Viewing Russian Peasants from a Leningrad-bound Train.
Gafford, Charlotte
Quills.
Gág, Wanda
A B C Bunny, The.
Gaik, Frank
Whatever Is, Is Right.
Galai, Benyamin
To My Generation.
Galbraith, Georgie Starbuck
No Mixed Green Salad for Me, Thanks.
Gale, Norman
Bartholomew.
Bobby's First Poem.
Child of Loneliness.
Content.
Country Faith, The.
Dawn and Dark.
Fairy Book, The.
Pastoral, A: "Along the lane beside the mead."
Prayer, A: "Tend me my birds, and bring again."
Question, The.
Second Coming, The.
Shaded Pool, The.
Song: "This peach is pink with such a pink."
Song: "Wait but a little while."
Voice, The.
Gale, Vi
After Illness.
Hurting.
Shore Birds.
Gale, Zona
Credo.
Gal'ed, Zerubavel
Chickory.
Gallagher, Dorothy Hamilton
Morning.
Gallagher, Joseph
John J. Curtis.
Gallagher, Katharine
Chant for Skippers.
Poison Ivy!
Gallagher, Tess
Ballad of Ballymote, The.
Black Money.
Black Silk.
Breasts.
Complicity.
Crêpes Flambeau.

Each Bird Walking.
Harmless Streets.
Horse in the Drugstore, The.
Keeping You Alive.
Kidnaper.
Meeting, The.
Ritual of Memories, The.
Shirts, The.
Short History of the Better Life, A.
Skylights.
Some Painful Butterflies Pass Through.
Stepping Outside.
Tableau Vivant.
To You on the Broken Iceberg.
Under Stars.
When You Speak to Me.
Women's Tug of War at Lough Arrow.
Gallagher, William Davis
Autumn in the West.
Cardinal Bird, The.
Mothers of the West, The.
Gallaudet, Thomas H.
Jesus, in Sickness and in Pain, *with music.*
Galler, David
Ballade of the Session after Camarillo.
Execrators, The.
Jersey Marsh, The.
Makers, The.
Narcissus: To Himself.
Walking Around.
Galloway, George
To the Memory of Gavin Wilson (Boot, Leg and Arm Maker).
Galloway, Thomas
Very Old, The.
Galsworthy, John
Desert Song ("When I came on from Santa Fe").
Devon to Me.
Limerick: "Angry young husband called Bicket, An."
Past.
Peace in the World.
So Might It Be.
Valley of the Shadow.
Gálvez, Javier
This Morning.
Galvin, Brendan
Glass.
Photo of Miners, A.
Galvin, James
Hematite Lake.
Galvin, James J.
Lady of O.
Morning Star.
Ox-Bone Madonna.
Galvin, Martin
Doorman.
Heron's Bay.
Hubert Horatio Humphrey (1911–1978).
Shooting Gallery.
Gambara, Veronica
When I see the earth ornate and lovely.
Gambold, John
Mystery of Life, The.
"Gander, Sir Gregory" (George Ellis)
Rondeau Humbly Inscribed to the Right Hon. William Eden, Minister Plenipotentiary of Commercial Affairs at the Court of Versailles, *at.*
Twelve Months, The.
Gannett, William Channing
Consider the Lilies.
From Heart to Heart, *with music.*
He Hides within the Lily, *with music.*
Highway, The.
Stream of Faith, The.
"Who Wert and Art and Evermore Shalt Be."
Ganse, Hervey Doddridge
Lord, I Know Thy Grace Is nigh Me, *with music.*
Garabrant, Nellie M.
Fairy Artist, The.
Garbutt, Vin
Mr. Gunman.
García Lorca, Federico
Ballad of Luna, Luna.
Blind Panorama of New York.
Casida of the Rose.
Dawn.
Faithless Wife, The.
Guitar.
Half Moon.
It Is True.
King of Harlem, The.
Lament for Ignacio Sánchez Mejías.
Landscape of the Vomiting Multitudes.
Little Viennese Waltz.
Madrigal de Verano.
Madrigal to the City of Santiago.
Moon Rises, The.
New York.
Ode to Walt Whitman.
Sleepwalkers' Ballad.
Song of Black Cubans.
Tree, Tree.
Unsleeping City.
Garcia Villa, José. *See* **Villa, José Garcia.**
Gard, Lillian
Her "Allowance!"
Gardiner, Wrey
Dr. Coppelius.
Our True Beginnings.
Poetry Is Happiness.
Walking in London.
Gardner, Alan
On Walking Back to the Bus.
Gardner, Carl
Dead Man Dragged from the Sea, The.
Reflections.
Gardner, Edmund
Sonnet Written in Tintern Abbey, Monmouthshire.
Gardner, Gail
Tyin' a Knot in the Devil's Tail.
Gardner, Isabella
At a Summer Hotel.
Cock-a-Hoop.
Gimboling.
In the Museum.
Letter from Slough Pond.
Masked Shrew, The.
Mathematics of Encounter.
Milkman, The.
Nightmare.
Part of the Darkness.
Sloth, The.
That "Craning of the Neck."
That Was Then.
When a Warlock Dies.
Gardner, John
Lizard, The.
Gardner, Martin
Barbershop.
Soap.
Gardner, Stephen
Another Cross.
Carpenter's Real Anguish, The.
Gardner, William Henry
When Love Comes Knocking.
Gardons, S. S.
Mother, The.
To a Child.
Garfinkel, Patricia
Tailor, The.
Garin, Marita
Bar Harbor.
White Spider.
Garioch, Robert (Robert Sutherland)
And They Were Richt.
At Robert Fergusson's Grave, October 1962.
Campidoglio.
Elegy: "They are lang deid, folk that I used to ken."
Embro to the Ploy.
Ghaisties.
Heard in the Cougate.
I Was Fair Beat.
Judgment Day.
Nemo Canem Impune Lacessit.
On Seein an Aik-Tree Sprent Wi Galls.
Sanct Christopher II ("Sanct Christopher's a muckle sanct and strang").
Sisyphus.
Garland, Hamlin
Color in the Wheat.
Cry of the Age, The.
Dakota Wheat-Field, A.
Do You Fear the Wind?
Gift of Water, The.
Goin' Back T'morrer.
Gold-Seekers, The.
Greeting of the Roses, The.
Herald Crane, The.
Horses Chawin' Hay.
In the Grass.
Logan at Peach Tree Creek.
Lost in a Norther.
Massasauga.
Meadow Lark, The.
Mountains Are a Lonely Folk, The.
My Prairies.
Passing of the Buffalo, The.
Pioneers.
Prairie Fires.
Toil of the Trail, The.
Tribute of Grasses, A.
Ute Lover, The.
Vulture of the Plains, The.
Wish, A.
Garland, Jim
I Don't Want Your Millions Mister.
Garlick, Phyllis L.
St. Patrick, *sel.*
Garmon, John
Light Morning Snow, We Wait for a Warmer Season.
Old Trail Town, Cody Wyoming.
Paths They Kept Barren.
Garnett, Jane
Paris.
Garnett, Louise Ayres
Hello!
Moon, The.
Song of Liberty, *sel.*
Garnett, Richard
Ballad of the Boat, The.
Epigram: "Amid all Triads let it be confest."
Epigram: " 'I hardly ever ope my lips,' one cries."
Epigram: "Philosopher, whom dost thou most affect."
Epigram: " 'Tis highly rational, we can't dispute."
Fading-Leaf and Fallen-Leaf.
Fair Circassian, The.
Marigold.
Nocturne: "Keen winds of cloud and vaporous drift."
Sonnet: Age.
Garrett, George
Abraham's Knife.
Caedmon.
On Reading the *Metamorphoses*.
Romantic.
Saints.
Snapshot: Ambassadress.
Snapshot of a Pedant.
Snapshot: Politician.
Tiresias.
Garrick, David
David Garrick, the Actor, to Sir John Hill.
Epigram: "When doctrines meet with general approbation."

Epitaph on Laurence Sterne.
Friend Col and I, both full of whim.
Heart of Oak.
On a Certain Lord Giving Some Thousand Pounds for a House.
On Oliver Goldsmith.
On Sir John Hill, M.D., Playwright.
To Mr. Gray on the Publication of His Odes.

Garrigue, Jean
Amsterdam.
Amsterdam Letter.
Apologia.
Beside a fall there is a round wood pipe.
Bleecker Street.
Catch What You Can.
Circle, The.
Clovers, The.
Cortege for Colette.
Country Villa.
Epitaph for My Cat.
False Country of the Zoo.
Forest.
From This There's No Returning.
From Venice Was That Afternoon.
Homage to Ghosts.
Lightly like music running, our blood.
Morality.
Mouse, The.
Movie Actors Scribbling Letters Very Fast in Crucial Scenes.
Note on Master Crow, A.
Now Snow Descends.
Of History More Like Myth.
Old Haven.
Primer of Plato.
Remember That Country.
Shore.
Song for "Buvez les Vins du Postillion"—Advt.
Stranger, The.
Unicorn and the Lady, The.
You Know.

Garrison, Theodosia Pickering
April.
Ballad of the Angel, The.
Ballad of the Cross, The.
Closed Door, The.
Cynic, The.
Days, The.
Dreamers, The.
Free Woman, The.
Green Inn, The.
Ilicet.
John o' Dreams.
Kerry Lads, The.
Memorial Day.
Monseigneur Plays.
Neighbors, The.
Poplars, The.
Prayer, A: "Let me work and be glad."
Road's End, The.
Shade.
Shepherd Who Stayed, The.
Stains.
Torch, The.
Wife, The.

Garrison, Wendell Phillips
Afternoon.
Evening.
Post-Meridian, *sels.*

Garrison, William Lloyd
Freedom for the Mind.
Liberty for All.

Garrison, Winfred Ernest
Book, The.
Thy Sea So Great.

Garrod, Heathcote William
Thou should'st be living at this hour.

Garstin, Crosbie
Figure-Head, The.
Nocturne: "Red flame flowers bloom and die, The."

Garth, Sir Samuel Dispensary, The.

Garthwaite, Jimmy (Wymond Bradbury Garthwaite)
Engineers.

Garvin, Amelia Beers Warnock. *See* **"Hale, Katherine"**

Garvin, Margaret Root
To Each His Own.

Gary, Sid
Circuit Breaker.
Pythagorean Razzle-Dazzle.

Gascoigne, George
Young, Gary
Adventures of Master F. I., The, *sel.*
All were to little for the merchauntes hande.
And every yeare a worlde my will did deeme.
And If I Did What Then?
Arraignment of a Lover, The.
Before mine eye to feede my greedy will.
Constancy of a Lover, The.
Councell Given to Master Bartholmew Withipoll.
Dan Bartholmew's Dolorous Discourses.
Divorce of a Lover, The ("Divorce me nowe good death").
Farewell, A: "And if I did, what then?"
Farewell with a Mischeife.
Fie, Pleasure, Fie!
For That He Looked Not upon Her.
For why? the gaines doth seldome quitte the charge.
Fruits of War, The, *sel.*
Gascoigne's Good Morrow.
Gascoigne's Lullaby [*or* Lullabie].
Gascoigne's Memories, *sels.*
Gascoigne's [*or* Gascoygnes] Good-Night.
Gascoigne's Passion.
Gascoigne's Praise of His Mistress.
Gascoigne's Woodmanship.
Gascoygnes Good Night.
Green Knight's Farewell to Fancy, The.
I Could Not though I Would.
In Praise of a Gentlewoman.
Inscription in a Garden.
Looks of a Lover Enamoured, The.
Lover's Lullaby, A.
Lullaby [*or* Lullabie] of a Lover, The.
Memories.
No haste but good, where wisdome makes the waye.
Of All the Birds That I Do Know.
Passion of a Lover, The.
Praise of Philip Sparrow, The.
Sonet Written in Prayse of the Browne Beautie, A.
Steele Glas, The.
Strange [*or* Straunge] Passion of a Lover, A.
To prinke me up and make me higher plaste.

Gascoyne, David
And the Seventh Dream Is the Dream of Isis.
Apologia.
Autumn Park, An.
Cage, The.
Cubical Domes, The.
De Profundis.
Ecce Homo.
Elegy, An: "Friend, whose unnatural early death."
End Is near the Beginning, The.
Eve.
Ex Nihilo.
Gravel-Pit Field, The.
In Defence of Humanism.
Jardin du Palais Royal.
Kyrie.
Lachrymae.
Landscape.
Miserere.
On the Grand Canal.
Orpheus in the Underworld.
Patmos.
Pieta.
Rex Mundi.
Sacred Hearth, The.
Salvador Dali.
Sanctus.
Spring MCMXL.
Tenebrae.
Tough Generation, A.
"Truth Is Blind, The."
Wartime Dawn, A.
Winter Garden.
Yves Tanguy.

Gaselee, Sir Stephen
On China Blue.

Gasetsu
Iris, The.

Gashe, Marina
Village, The.

Gaskin, Bob
Letter to My Kinder.

Gasparini, Len
Accident, The.
Greasy Spoon Blues.
Kafka's Other Metamorphosis.
Niagara Falls Nocturne.
Valentine.
Written on a Paper Napkin.

Gass, William H.
On Being Photographed.

"Gate, A.C." *See***Anthony, Edward**

Gates, D. Weston
Transformed.

Gates, Ellen M. Huntington
Home of the Soul.
I Shall Not Cry Return.
Sleep Sweet.
Your Mission.

Gatty, Sir Alfred Scott
Three Little Pigs, The.

Gauer, Jim
Visit, The.

Gauldin, Sara Saper
Old Argonaut.

Gautier, Théophile
Art.
Clarimonde.
Posthumous Coquetry.

Gavenda, Walt
Eco Right.

Gawsworth, John
Skye.

Gay, Asya. *See***Asya**

Gay, John
About in London.
Achilles, *sel.*
Acis and Galatea, *sels.*
Air: "Fox may steal your hens, sir, A."
Air XXXV: "How happy could I be with either."
Air: "O ruddier than the cherry."
Air: "Since laws were made for ev'ry degree."
Air XXIII: "Sleep, O sleep."
Air: "Sportsmen keep hawks, and their quarry they gain, The."
Ballad: "Of all the girls that e'er were seen."
Ballad: " 'Twas when the seas were roaring."
Before the Barn-Door Crowing.
Beggar's Opera, The
Birth of the Squire, The; an Eclogue.
Blouzelinda's Funeral.
Butterfly and the Snail, The.
Council of Horses, The.
Damon and Cupid.
Ditty, The: "Young Colin Clout."
Elegy on a Lap-Dog, An.
Elephant and the Bookseller, The.
Employments of Life, The.
Epigram: "Life is a jest, and all things show it."
Fables, *sels.*
Fan, The, *sel.*
Farmer's Wife and the Raven, The.
Fox at the Point of Death, The.
Great Frost, The.

Hare with Many Friends, The.
Highwaymen, The.
His Own Epitaph.
If the Heart of a Man.
I'm like a skiff on the ocean tost.
Lion and the Cub, The.
London at Night.
Love in Her Eyes [Sits Playing].
Macheath and Polly.
Mr. Pope's Welcome from Greece.
Modes of the Court, The.
Molly Mog; or, The Fair Maid of the Inn.
My Own Epitaph.
New Song, A.
New Song of New Similies, A.
Newgate's Garland.
O Ruddier than the Cherry.
Ode for the New Year, An, *at.*
Over the Hills and Far Away.
Painter Who Pleased Nobody and Everybody, The.
Poet and the Rose, The.
Polly; an Opera, *sels.*
Receipt for Stewing Veal, A.
Rural Sports, *sels.*
She who hath felt a real pain.
Shepherd's Week, The, *sels.*
Soldier and a Sailor, A.
Song: "Before the barn-door crowing."
Song: "Can love be controll'd by advice?"
Song: "If any wench Venus's girdle wear."
Song: "Love in her eyes sits playing."
Song: "O ruddier than the cherry!"
Song: "Sleep, O sleep."
Song: "Think of dress in ev'ry light."
Song: "Thus when the swallow, seeking prey."
Song: "Were I laid on Greenland's coast."
Song: "Youth's the season made for joys."
Sweet William's Farewell to Black-eyed Susan.
Think of Dress in Every Light.
Thursday; or, The Spell.
To a Lady.
To a Lady on Her Passion for Old China.
To a Young Lady, with Some Lampreys.
To My Ingenious and Worthy Friend William Lowndes, Esq.
Trivia; or, The Art of Walking the Streets of London, *sels.*
Tuesday; or, The Ditty.
Turkey and the Ant, The.
Turtle thus with plaintive crying, The.
Wednesday; or, The Dumps.
What Shall I Do to Show How Much I Love Her?
What-D'Ye-Call-It, The, *sel.*
Wild Boar and the Ram, The.
Would You Have a Young Virgin?
Youth and Love.

Gay, John *and* **Alexander Pope**
Mary Gulliver to Captain Lemuel Gulliver, *abr.*

Gay, William
Crazy World, The.

Gay, Zhenya
I was lying still in a field one day.
I'd like to be a worm.
When a goose meets a moose.

Gearhart, Gladys M.
He Is Coming.

Gebirtig, Mordecai
Waiting for Death.

Geddes, Alexander
Epistle to the President of the Scottish Society of Antiquaries: On Being Chosen a Correspondent Member.
Satire: "Satire, my friend ('twixt me and you)."

Geddes, Gary
Inheritors, The.
Transubstantiation.

Gegna, Suzanne
Relics.

Geifer, George L.
Who Threw the Overalls in Mistress Murphey's Chowder? *with music.*

Geisel, Theodor Seuss. *See* **"Seuss, Dr."**

Gellert, Christian Fürchtegott
Jesus Lives!

Gellert, Lawrence
Ah'm Broke an' Hungry, *with music.*
Ku Kluck Klan, *with music.*
Look over Yonder, *with music.*

Gellert, Leon
Anzac Cove.
Before Action.
House-Mates.
In the Trench.
Jester in the Trench, The.
These Men.

Gelman, Juan
Customs.
Knife, The.
Stranger, The.

Genestet, Petrus Augustus de
Such Is Holland!

Genet, Jean
Man Sentenced to Death, The, *sel.*

Genoveva, Sister Mary
Archers of the King.

Genser, Cynthia Kramer
Club 82: Lisa.

Geoghegan, Arthur Gerald
After Aughrim.

Geoghegan, J. B.
Down in a Coal Mine.

Georgakas, Dan
Acrobat from Xanadu disdained all nets, The.

George, Daniel
Ode to the Fourth of July, *with music.*

George, Emery E.
Homage to Edward Hopper.
House All Pictures, A.
Solstice.

George, Faye
Welcome to This House.

George, M. A.
Morning.

George, Marguerite
Prisoner.

George, Phillip William
America's Wounded Knee.
Battle Won Is Lost.
First Grade.
Moon of Huckleberries.
Morning Vigil.
Name Giveaway.
Old Man, the Sweat Lodge.
Prelude to Memorial Song: 100 Years Later.
Spokane Falls 1874.
Spring Cleaning.
Spruce.
Sunflower Moccasins.
Visit, The.
Wardance.
Wardance Soup.

George, Stefan
Homecoming.
Invocation and Prelude.
Jahr der Seele, Das, *sel.*
Lord of the Isle, The.
Lyre Player, The.
Prelude XXIII: "We are those same children who amazed."
Rapture.
Stanzas Concerning Love.
To a Young Leader of the First World War.

Georgeou, Markos
Unseen Flight.

Gerard, Edwin ("Trooper Gerardy")
Lofty Lane.

Gerard, Jim
Angora, The.

Gerard, Richard H.
Sweet Adeline.

Gerber, Dan
Love for Instance.

Gerez, Jozef Habib
Call from the Afterworld.
We Are Acrobats.
We Fooled Ourselves.

Gergely, Agnes
Birth of a Country.
Conjuration.
Crazed Man in Concentration Camp.
Desert.

Gerhardt, Paul
Courage.
Give to the Winds Thy Fears.

Gerin-Lajoie, Antoine
Canadian Exile, The.

Gerlach, Lee
For Peter.
Pilot's Day of Rest, The.
Pilot's Walk, The.

Gernes, Sonia
Practicing.

Gerondi, Abraham
Hymn for the Eve of the New Year.

Gerrard, John
Remonstrance, A.

Gershwin, Ira
Blah, Blah, Blah.
Embraceable You, *with music.*
It Ain't Neccessarily So.

Gessner, Muriel M.
For February Twelfth.

Gezelle, Guido
To the Sun from a Flower.

Ghai, Gail
Six Divine Circles.

Ghalib, Mirza
Ghazal XII.

Ghazi, A. Rasheed
Poem on Inter-uterine Device, A.

Ghigna, Charles
Child Bearing.

Ghiselin, Brewster
Answering a Letter from a Younger Poet.
Catch, The.
Credo.
Crotalus Rex.
Dana Point.
Headland.
Known World, The.
Meridian.
New World.
Of the New Prosody.
Rattler, Alert.
To the South.

Ghitelman, David
Grand Street and the Bowery.

Ghose, Manmohan
Who Is It Talks of Ebony?

Ghose, Zulfikar
Crows, The.
Rise of Shivaji, The.

Giandi, Paul
Midwestern Man.

Gibb, Robert
Minotaur, The.

Gibbon, Monk
Babe, The.
Bees, The.
Discovery, The.
Dispossessed Poet.
Forebears.
French Peasants.
From Disciple to Master.
Salt.
Shawls, The.
Song: "Singer within the little streets."
Wiser than the Children of Light.

Gibbons, J. J.
Burro, The.

Gibbons, James Sloan
Three Hundred Thousand More.

Gibbons, Reginald
Breath.
Cedar River, The.
Eating.
"Luckies."
Make Me Hear You.
Michael's Room.
Ruined Motel, The.
Gibbs, Barbara
"What You See Is Me."
Gibbs, Jessie Wiseman
If We Believed in God.
Giber, David
All Thumbs.
Gibran, Kahlil
Of Love.
On Children.
On Giving.
Prophet, The, *sels.*
Gibson, Barbara
After the Quarrel.
Gibson, Douglas
January.
Gibson, Evelyn K.
Heartsearch.
Gibson, George Herbert ("Ironbark")
Ballad of Queensland (Sam Holt), A.
My Mate Bill.
Gibson, Margaret
Burning the Root.
Catechism Elegy.
Gemini Elegy.
Long Walks in the Afternoon.
October Elegy.
To Speak of Chile.
Gibson, Morgan
Beyond the Presidency.
Gibson, Walker
Advice to Travelers.
Allergy.
Athletes.
Billiards.
Blues for an Old Blue.
Circus Ship *Euzkera,* The.
David.
Epistle to the Reader.
Essay in Defense of the Movies.
Essay on Lunch.
Game, The.
In Memory of the Circus Ship *Euzkera,* [Wrecked in the Caribbean Sea, 1 September 1948].
Killer Too, The.
Love.
Soliloquy in a Motel.
Thaw.
Umpire, The.
Gibson, Wilfrid Wilson
All Being Well.
Back.
Breakfast.
By the Weir.
Dancers, The.
Dancing Seal, The.
Drove-Road, The.
Eagles and Isles.
Fires, *sel.*
Fisherman's Luck.
Flannan Isle.
Fowler, The.
Henry Turnbull.
Home.
Ice, The.
Inspiration.
Lament: "We who are left, how shall we look again."
Long Tom.
Luck.
Mark Anderson.
Marriage.
Messages, The.
Old Skinflint.
On Hampstead Heath.
Parrot, The.
Parrots, The.
Peak, The.
Ponies, The.
Prelude: "As one, at midnight, wakened by the call."
Proem: "Snug in my easy chair."
Question, The.
Rupert Brooke.
Sight.
Skye, *sel.*
Song: "If once I could gather in song."
Stone, The.
Tenants.
Whisperers, The.
White Dust, The.
Witch, The.
Gibson, William
Circe.
Gidlow, Elsa
For the Goddess Too Well Known.
Invocation to Sappho.
Gifford, Fannie Stearns Davis. *See* **Davis, Fannie Stearns**
Gifford, Humphrey [*or* Humfrey]
For Soldiers.
Prayer, A: "O mighty God, Which for us men."
Song: "Woman's face is full of wiles, A."
Gifford, William
Baviad, The, *sel.*
Della Cruscans, The.
Gilbert, Celia
Portrait of My Mother on Her Wedding Day.
Gilbert, Chris
Philonous' Paradox.
Gilbert, Christopher
Beginning by Example, *sel.*
Blue.
Charge.
Now.
Saturday Morning at the Laundry.
Touching.
Gilbert, Ellen
Prodigal.
Gilbert, Fred
Man Who Broke the Bank at Monte Carlo, The.
Midnight March, The.
Gilbert, Jack
Abnormal Is Not Courage, The.
All the Way from There to Here.
Bird Sings to Establish Frontiers, A.
Burning and Fathering; Accounts of My Country.
Byzantium Burning.
Don Giovanni on His Way to Hell II ("How could they think women a recreation").
Don Giovanni on His Way to Hell ("The oxen have voices").
Fashionable Heart, The.
In Dispraise of Poetry.
Lives of Famous Men, The.
Lord Sits with Me Out in Front, The.
More than Fifty.
Movies, The.
My Marriage with Mrs. Johnson.
New York, Summer.
On Growing Old in San Francisco.
Orpheus in Greenwich Village.
Perspective He Would Mutter Going to Bed.
Pewter.
Playing House.
Prospero Dreams of Arnaud Daniel Inventing Love in the Twelfth Century.
Prospero on the Mountain Gathering Wood.
Prospero without His Magic.
Revolution, The.
Sects.
Susanna and the Elders.
Translation into the Original.
Gilbert, James Stanley
Beyond the Chagres.
Gilbert, Lady. *See* **Mulholland, Rosa**
Gilbert, Mercedes
Friendless Blues, *with music.*
Gilbert, Michael William
Exigencies.
Gilbert, Morris
Epitaph on a Madman's Grave.
Gilbert, Paul
Your Own Version.
Gilbert, Paul T.
Triolet: "I love you, my Lord!"
Gilbert, R. V.
Great Victory, The.
Gilbert, Sandra M.
Elegy: "Pages of history open, The."
Fog Dream, The.
Rissem.
Gilbert, Thomas
Against Homosexuality.
View of the Town, A. In an Epistle to a Friend, *sel.*
Gilbert, Virginia
Finding You.
Gilbert, Sir William Schwenck
Anglicized Utopia.
Arac's Song.
Ben Allah Achmet; or, The Fatal Tum.
Bishop of Rum-ti-Foo, The.
Bunthorne's Song.
Captain Reece.
Contemplative Sentry, The.
Darned Mounseer, The.
Disagreeable Man, The.
Duke of Plaza-Toro, The.
Ellen M'Jones Aberdeen.
Emily, John, James, and I ("Emily Jane was a nursery maid").
Englishman, The.
Etiquette.
Fable of the Magnet and the Churn, The.
Family Fool, The.
Ferdinando and Elvira; or, The Gentle Pieman.
First Lord's Song, The.
Flowers That Bloom in the Spring, The, *with music.*
Folly of Brown, The.
General John.
Gentle Alice Brown.
Gondoliers, The, *sels.*
Grand Inquisitor's Song, The.
H. M. S. Pinafore, *sels.*
House of Lords, The.
House of Peers, The.
I Am the Captain of the Pinafore.
I Am the Monarch of the Sea.
Iolanthe, *sels.*
King Goodheart.
King of Canoodle-Dum, The.
Ko-Ko's Song ("As some day it may happen that a victim must be found").
Ko-Ko's (Winning) Song ("On a tree by a river").
Little Buttercup.
Lord Chancellor's Song.
Lost Mr. Blake.
Major-General's Song.
Mikado, The, *sels.*
Modern Major-General, The.
Most Ingenious Paradox, A.
My Object All Sublime.
Nightmare.
Oh, Hollow! Hollow! Hollow!
Oh! my name is John Wellington Wells.
Patience, *sels.*
Philosophic Pill, The.
Pirates of Penzance, The, *sels.*
Policeman's Lot, A [*or* The].
Princess Ida, *sel.*
Professor Called Chesterton, A.
Rival Curates, The.
Ruddigore, *sels.*
Sing for the Garish Eye.

Sir Joseph's Song.
Sir Roderic's Song.
Sorcerer, Mr. Wells, The, *sel.*
Story of Prince Agib, The.
Suicide's Grave, The.
There Lived a King.
There Was an Old Man of St. Bees.
They'll None of 'Em Be Missed.
Thomas Winterbottom Hance.
Titwillow.
To Phoebe.
To Sit in Solemn Silence.
To the Terrestrial Globe.
Wand'ring Minstrel, A.
Yarn of the *Nancy Bell,* The.
Yeoman of the Guard, *sels.*

Gilbert, Zack
For Angela.
For Stephen Dixon.
In Spite of All This Much Needed Thunder.
My Own Hallelujahs.
"O.D."
When I Heard Dat White Man Say.

"Gilbertulus." *See* **Howe, Mark Antony De Wolfe**

Gilboa, Amir
Birth.
Isaac.
Joshua's Face.
Moses.
My Brother Was Silent.
Samson.
Saul.
Seeds of Lead.

Gilburt, S. Gale
Bequest.

Gilchrist, Alan
Assynt.

Gilchrist, Marie Emilie
Apples in New Hampshire.

Gilder, Jeanette Leonard
My Creed.

Gilder, Joseph B.
Parting of the Ways, The.

Gilder, Richard Watson
After-Song.
Ah, Be Not False.
At the President's Grave.
Birds of Bethlehem, The.
Call Me Not Dead.
Celestial Passion, The.
Cello, The.
Charleston.
Child, A.
Christmas Tree in the Nursery, The.
Comfort of the Trees, The.
Credo, *sel.*
Doubter, The.
Evening in Tyringham Valley.
God of the Strong, God of the Weak.
Great Nature Is an Army Gay.
Hast Thou Heard the Nightingale?
Heroic Age, The.
How to the Singer Comes the Song?
Hymn: "God of the strong, God of the weak," *abr.*
I Count My Time by Times That I Meet Thee.
Invisible, The.
Memorial Day.
Midsummer Song, A.
My Love for Thee.
New Day, The, *sels.*
Noel.
O, Love Is Not a Summer Mood.
Ode: "I am the spirit of the morning sea."
Of One Who neither Sees nor Hears.
On the Life-Mask of Abraham Lincoln.
Prelude: "Night was dark, though sometimes a faint star, The."
Sherman.
Song: "Because the rose must fade."
Song: "Not from the whole wide world I chose thee."
Song: "Years have flown since I knew thee first."
Song of a Heathen, The.
Song of Early Autumn, A.
Sonnet, The: "What is a sonnet? 'Tis the pearly shell."
Sonnets after the Italian, *sels.*
To Thee, Eternal Soul, Be Praise, *with music.*
"White City, The."
Woman's Thought, A.

Gildner, Gary
After an All-Night Cackle with Sloth and Co. I Enter Mansion and Greet the Dawn.
Around the Kitchen Table.
Comanche.
Digging for Indians.
First Practice.
Geisha.
House on Buder Street, The.
Johann Gaertner (1793–1887).
Letter to a Substitute Teacher.
Life of the Wolf, The.
Meeting the Reincarnation Analyst.
My Father after Work.
Nails.
Poems.
Porch, The.
Runner, The.
Then.
They Have Turned the Church Where I Ate God.
Tongue River Psalm.

Gilead, Zerubavel
Absalom.
Flying Letters.
Pomegranate Tree in Jerusalem ("The pomegranate tree in my garden adorns itself").**Gilfillan, Caroline**
Lesbian Play on T.V.

Gilfillan, Robert
Exile's Song, The.

Gilkey, James G.
O God, in Whose Great Purpose, *with music.*
Outside the Holy City, *with music.*

Gill, Brendan
Girls' Voices.

Gill, David
Killing a Whale.

Gill, John
As a Child Seeing a Cardinal.
Before the Thaw.
First Hymn.
"I Don't Hear Any Melody Breathing I Hear."
Late Spring: A Heaving, a Turning.
Poem: "Something broke the dream."
What Could Be.

Gill, Julia
Christ and the Little Ones.

Gilleland, Anna M.
Give My Heart a Song.

Gillespie, Dan
Abandoned Copper Refinery.
Desert Gulls.
Strip Mining Pit.

Gillespie, Robert
Snow White.
When Both My Fathers Die.

Gillies, Andrew
Two Prayers.

Gillies, Valerie
Clouds and Clay.

Gillilan, Strickland W.
Cure for Fault-finding, A.
Finnigin to Flannigan.
Folks Need a Lot of Loving.
Lines Written on the Antiquity of Microbes.
Need of Loving.
On the Antiquity of Microbes.
Other Fellow's Job, The.
Reading Mother, The.
Watch Yourself Go By.

Gillman, Frederick J.
God Send Us Men, *sel.*

Gillman, Richard
Bones of a French Lady in a Museum.
Moved by Her Music.
On a Very Young, Very Dead Soldier.
Snow Fell with a Will.

Gillom, Arthur L.
I Want You.

Gilman, Caroline
Anna Playing in a Graveyard.
Boat, The.
Dead Sister, The.

Gilman, Charlotte Perkins Stetson
Beds of Fleur-de-Lys, The.
Common Inference, A.
Conservative, A.
Give Way!
Living God, The.
Resolve.
Similar Cases.
To Labor.
Tree Feelings.
Two Prayers.
Wedded Bliss.

Gilman, Samuel
O God, Accept the Sacred Hour, *with music.*

Gilmore, Anna Neil
February, Tall and Trim.

Gilmore, Joseph Henry
He Leadeth Me.

Gilmore, Mary
Baying Hounds, The.
Disinherited, The, *sel.*
Eve-Song.
Fourteen Men.
Heritage.
Myall in Prison, The.
Nationality.
Never Admit the Pain.
Nurse No Long Grief.
Old Botany Bay.
Pear-Tree, The.
Shepherd, The.
Song of the Woman-Drawer, The.
Swans at Night, *sel.*
Tenancy, The.
Waradgery Tribe, The.

Gilmore, Patrick Sarsfield ("Louis Lambert")
When Johnny Comes Marching Home.

Gilpin, Laura
Two-headed Calf, The.

Giltinan, Caroline
Builder, The.
Garden, The.
Overnight, a Rose.
Spring.

Gingell, Dave
In Memoriam.
Older Now.

"Ginger." *See***Irwin, Wallace**

Ginsberg, Allen
Aether.
America.
Bayonne Turnpike to Tuscarora.
Bop Lyrics.
Cafe in Warsaw.
Death News.
Death to Van Gogh's Ear!
Don't Grow Old.
Dream Record: June 8, 1955.
End, The.
First Party at Ken Kesey's with Hell's Angels.
Footnote to "Howl."
Friday the Thirteenth.
Howl.
Hymmnn.
I Am a Victim of the Telephone.
Ignu.
In a Moonlit Hermit's Cabin.
In Back of the Real.
In the Baggage Room at Greyhound.

Kaddish.
Kral Majales.
Last Night in Calcutta.
Love Poem on Theme by Whitman.
Malest Cornifici Tuo Catullo.
Maybe Love.
Memory Gardens.
Message.
My Alba.
My Sad Self.
Night-Apple, The.
On Burroughs' Work.
On Neal's Ashes.
Please Master.
Poem Rocket.
Prophecy, A.
Psalm III: "To God: to illuminate all men. Beginning with Skid Row."
Sather Gate Illumination.
Shrouded Stranger, The.
Song: Fie My Fum.
Sunflower Sutra.
Supermarket in California, A.
This Form of Life Needs Sex.
Thus Crosslegged on Round Pillow Sat in Space.
To Aunt Rose.
To Lindsay.
Uptown.
Vow, A.
Waking in New York, *sel.*
Wales Visitation.
Who Be Kind To.
Wichita Vortex Sutra.

Ginsberg, Louis
Biography of an Agnostic.
Buttercups.
Clocks.
Hounds of the Soul, The.
Hymn to Evil.
Morning in Spring.
Old Ships.
Prices.
Roots.
Song: "I know that any weed can tell."
Song in Spring.
Soon at Last My Sighs and Moans.
To My Mother.

Gioia, Dana
Sunday Night in Santa Rosa.

Gioseffi, Daniela
Buildings.

Giovanni, Nikki
Adulthood.
Basketball.
Beautiful Black Men.
Certain Peace, A.
Concerning One Responsible Negro with Too Much Power.
Conversation.
Detroit Conference of Unity and Art.
Dreams.
Ego Tripping.
For Saundra.
Funeral of Martin Luther King, Jr., The.
Kidnap Poem.
Knoxville, Tennessee.
Legacies.
Master Charge Blues.
Mothers.
Mother's Habits.
My Poem.
Nikki-Rosa.
One ounce of truth benefits.
Poem for Aretha.
Poem for Black Boys.
Poem for Flora.
Poem for Unwed Mothers.
Poem (No Name No. 2).
Poem of Angela Yvonne Davis.
Poetry.
Reason I Like Chocolate, The.
Revolutionary Dreams.
Robin's Poem, A.
Scrapbooks.
Seduction.
They Clapped.
True Import of Present Dialogue, Black vs. Negro, The.
Twelve Gates to the City.
Winter Poem.
Woman Poem.
Word Poem (Perhaps Worth Considering).
World Is Not a Pleasant Place to Be, The.

Gippius, Zinaida Nikolayevna
She.

Gira, R. P.
Mouth of the Amazon.

Gisborne, Thomas
Spring.
Walks in a Forest, *sel.*

Gitlin, Todd
Puritan Hacking Away at Oak, The.

Gittings, Robert
Great Moth, The.

Gitzen, Julian
Pheasant Hunter and the Arrowhead, The.

Gjellerup, Karl
O, Let Me Kiss.
Pair, A.

Gladden, Washington
O Lord of Life, *with music.*
O Master, Let Me Walk with Thee.
Service.

Glaenzer, Richard Butler
Ballad of Redhead's Day, A.

Glancy, Diane
Looking for My Old Indian Grandmother in the Summer Heat of 1980.
Lunar Eclipse.
Mary Ackerman, 1938.
There Won't Be Another.
Two Animals, One Flood.

Glang, Gabriele
August Evenings in Hatteras.

Glanz-Leyeles, A.
Castles.
Madison Square.
White Swan.

Glaser, Elton
Figure and Ground.

Glaser, Michael S.
Initials.

Glasgow, Alex
Escalator, The.
Little Tommy Yesterday.

Glasgow, J. Scott
Pipes o' Gordon's Men, The.

Glass, Malcolm
Boy, The; or, Son of Rip-off.
Coming Down to It.
Mullet Snatching.
Staying Ahead.

Glassco, John
Brummell at Calais.
Burden of Junk, The.
Cardinal's Dog, The.
Day, The.
Deserted Buildings under Shefford Mountain.
Entailed Farm, The.
For Cora Lightbody, R.N.
One Last Word.
Quebec Farmhouse.
Rural Mail, The.
Stud Groom.
Utrillo's World.

Glatstein, Jacob
Back to the Ghetto.
Bratzlav Rabbi to His Scribe, The.
Evening Bread.
I'll Find My Self-Belief.
In a Ghetto.
Like Weary Trees.
Loyal Sins.
Memorial Poem.
Move On, Yiddish Poet.
Mozart.
Poet Lives, The.
Rabbi Yussel Luksh of Chelm.
Where the Cedars.

Glaubitz, Grace Ellen
Christmas Birthday.
Walking.

Glaukos
Epigram: "Time was when once upon a time, such toys."

Glaze, Andrew
Fantasy Street.
Outlanders, The.
Zeppelin.

Glazebrook, Harriet A.
Lips That Touch Liquor Shall Never Touch Mine, The.

Glazer, Joseph
Visit Home, A.

Gleason, Madeline
Once and Upon.

Glen, Duncan
Ane to Anither.
Stanes.

Glen, Emilie
Cat Ballerina Assoluta.

Glick, Hirsch [*or* Glik, Hirsh]
Shtil Di Nacht (Silent Is the Night).
We Survive!

Glickman, Susan
Night Song for an Old Lover.

Glik, Hirsh. *See* **Glick, Hirsch**

Gloag, John
Board Meets, The.

Glover, Guy
Lucifer, The.

Glover, Jean
Owre the Muir amang the Heather.

Glover, R. W.
It Isn't the Town, It's You.

Glover, Richard
Admiral Hosier's Ghost.

Glück, Louise
All Hallows.
Brooding Likeness.
Cottonmouth Country.
Dedication to Hunger.
Descending Figure.
For Jane Myers.
For My Mother.
Garden, The.
Gift, The.
Gratitude.
Gretel in Darkness.
Happiness.
Horse.
Jeanne d'Arc.
Lamentations.
Magi, The.
Mirror, The.
Mock Orange.
Night Song.
Palais des Arts.
Phenomenal Survivals of Death in Nantucket.
Portrait.
Racer's Widow, The.
School Children, The.

Glynes, Ella Dietz
Unless.

Goba, Ronald J.
Compozishun—to James Herndon and Others.

Godeschalk
Sequaire.

Godfrey the Satirist
To Grosphus.

Godin, Deborah
January.

Godley, Alfred Denis
After Horace.
College Cat, The.

Eureka!
Football and Rowing—an Eclogue.
Lines on a Mysterious Occurrence.
Motor Bus.
Pénsees de Noël.
Women's Degrees.
Godolphin, Sidney
Chorus: "Vain man, born to no happiness."
Constancye.
Hymn: "Lord, when the wise men came from far[r]."
Quatrains.
Reply.
Song: "Cloris, it is not thy disdaine."
Song: "Noe more unto my thoughts appeare."
Song: "Or love me less [*or* mee lesse], or love me more."
Song: " 'Tis affection but dissembled."
Sonnet: "Madam, 'tis true, your beauties move."
To the Tune of, In Fayth I Cannot Keepe My Father's Sheepe.
Godric, Saint
Cry to Mary, A.
Godsey, Edwin S.
I Hope I Don't Have You Next Semester, But.
Godwin, A.
Absent Lover, An.
Song for My Lady.
Song in His Lady's Absence, A.
Goedicke, Patricia
After the Second Operation.
At the Center of Everything Which Is Dying.
At the Party.
Daily the Ocean between Us.
Death Balloon, The.
Girl in the Foreign Movie, The.
Great Depression, The.
On the Night in Question.
One More Time.
Serious Merriment of Women, The.
Young Men You Are So Beautiful Up There.
Goertz, Berniece
Wondrous Son of God.
Goethe, Johann Wolfgang von
Chorus of the Archangels, The.
Christ Is Arisen.
Easter Chorus.
Entoptic Colours (1817).
Erl-King, The.
Faust, *sels.*
Holy Longing, The.
Irish Lamentation, An.
King of Thulé, The.
Lay of the Captive Count, The.
Lose This Day Loitering.
Mignon.
Minstrel, The.
O Child of Beauty Rare.
On Lavater's Song of a Christian to Christ.
Pariah's Prayer, The.
Permanence in Change.
Poet to the Sleeping Saki, The.
Prologue in Heaven.
Prometheus.
Rest.
Rose, The.
Second Poem the Night-Walker Wrote, The.
Shepherd's Lament, The.
Soldier's Song.
Thought Eternal, The.
To a Golden Heart, Worn round His Neck.
To the Moon.
To the Parted One.
True Enough: To the Physicist (1820).
True Rest.
Voice from the Invisible World, A.
Voice of Experience, The.
Wanderer's Night-Songs, *sels.*
West-Easterly Divan, *sels.*
Who Never Ate with Tears His Bread.
Goetz, E. Ray *and* **Edgar Leslie.** *See* **Leslie, Edgar** *and* **E. Ray Goetz**
Goffstein, M. B
On This Day.
Gogarty, Oliver St. John
After Galen.
Anachronism.
Between Brielle and Manasquan.
Colophon.
Conquest, The.
Crab Tree, The.
Death May Be Very Gentle.
Dedication: "Tall unpopular men."
Exorcism.
Farrell O'Reilly.
Forge, The.
Golden Stockings.
Hay Hotel, The.
Image-Maker, The.
Johnny, I Hardly Knew Ye: In Miltonese, *parody.*
Leda and the Swan.
Marcus Curtius.
Non Dolet.
O Boys! O Boys!
On the Use of Jayshus.
On Troy.
Palinode.
Parable for Poetasters, A.
Per Iter Tenebricosum.
Plum Tree by the House, The.
Portrait with Background.
Ringsend.
To a Boon Companion.
To a Friend in the Country.
To an Old Tenor.
To Death.
To Petronius Arbiter.
To the Liffey with the Swans.
To the Maids Not to Walk in the Wind.
To W. B. Yeats Who Says That His Castle of Ballylee Is His Monument.
Verse: "What should we know."
With a Coin from Syracuse.
Gogisgi. *See* **Arnett, Carroll**
Going, Charles Buxton
Armistice.
At the Top of the Road.
Spring in England.
They Who Wait.
To Arcady.
Gold, Artie
I Don't Have the Energy.
Life.
Gold, Jiri
In the Cellars.
Inhabited Emptiness, An.
Goldbarth, Albert
Accountings, The.
All-Nite Donuts.
"And Now Farley Is Going to Sing *While I Drink a Glass of Water!*"
Before.
Dime Call.
Distances.
Film, A.
Form and Function of the Novel, The.
Greed Song, The.
History of Civilization, A.
History of Photography, A.
Note from an Exhibition.
Orphan Boy, Fishing.
Pleasures.
Recipe.
Theory of Wind, A.
Goldbeck, Cecil
Waters of the Sea.
Goldberg, Israel. *See* **"Learsi, Rufus"**
Goldberg, Leah
Answer.
Blade of Grass Sings to the River, The.
God Once Commanded Us, A.
Heavenly Jerusalem, Jerusalem of the Earth.
My Mother's House, *sel.*
Nameless Journey, *sel.*
Observation of a Bee.
Of Myself.
On the Hazards of Smoking.
Our Backs Are to the Cypress.
Symposium, The, *sel.*
Toward Myself.
When You Will Walk in the Field.
Goldemberg, Isaac
Bar Mitzvah.
Jews in Hell, The.
Golden, Renny
For Jeanette Piccard Ordained at 79.
Goldensohn, Barry
Becoming Real.
Goldensohn, Lorrie
Ambulance Call.
Goldin, Judah
Reading Faust.
Golding, Louis
Broken Bodies.
Doom-devoted.
"I."
Is It Because of Some Dear Grace.
Jack.
Judaeus Errans.
O Bird, So Lovely.
Ploughman at the Plough.
Prophet and Fool.
Quarries in Syracuse.
Second Seeing.
Women at the Corners Stand, The.
Goldman, Michael
Crack, The.
Goldrick, O. J.
Grand Opening of the People's Theatre.
Goldring, Douglas
Newport Street, E.
She-Devil.
Streets.
Goldring, Maude
Drowned Seaman, The.
Goldsmith, Goldwin
Monkey's Glue, The.
Goldsmith, Oliver
Auburn.
Blest Retirement.
Britain.
Captivity, The; an Oratorio, *sels.*
Common Man, The.
David Garrick.
Description of an Author's Bedchamber, A.
Double Transformation, The.
Edmund Burke.
Elegy, An: "Good people all, with one accord."
Elegy on Mrs. Mary Blaize.
Elegy on That [*or* the] Glory of Her Sex, Mrs. Mary Blaize, An.
Elegy on the Death of a Mad Dog, An.
Emma.
Epilogue to "The Sister," *sel.*
Farewell to Poetry.
First, Best Country, The.
France.
Great Man, A.
Happiness Dependent on Ourselves.
Hope.
Memory.
New Simile in the Manner of Swift, A.
O luxury! Thou curst by Heaven's decree.
On a Beautiful Youth Struck Blind with Lightning.
On a Bookseller.
Parson Gray.
Real Happiness.
Retaliation.
She Stoops to Conquer, *sel.*
Sir Joshua Reynolds.
Song: "Let school-masters puzzle their brain."
Song: "O memory! thou fond deceiver."
Song: "When lovely woman stoops to folly."
Still the Wonder Grew.

Sweet, Smiling Village.
Three Jolly Pigeons, The.
Travel[l]er, The, *sels.*
Vicar of Wakefield, The, *sels.*
Village, The.
Village Parson, The.
Village Preacher, The.
Village Schoolmaster, The.
Woman.
Goldsmith, Oliver, the Younger
Lonely Settler, The.
Goldstein, Jonas
On Philosophy.
Goldstein, Roberta B.
Shattered Sabbath.
Golffing, Francis C.
Higher Empiricism, The.
Goll, Claire
Prayer: "In the bright bay of your morning, O God."
Goll, Iwan [*or* Yvan]
Clandestine Work.
John Landless Leads the Caravan.
Lilith.
Neïla.
Pear-Tree, The.
Raziel.
Song for a Jewess.
Gom, Leona
All.
Arrowheads.
Gomez, Antonio Enriquez
Elegy: "I die for Your holy word without regret."
Gomez de Avellaneda, Gertrudis
On Leaving.
On Leaving Cuba, Her Native Land.
Gonçalves Dias, Antônio
Song of Exile, *sel.*
Góngoray Argote, Luis de
First Solitude, The, *sels.*
Let Me Go Warm.
River Compared to an Oratorical Sentence, The.
Rosemary Spray, The.
Wedding Feast, The.
Young Pilgrim Finds Refuge with the Goatherds, The.
Gonick, Catherine
Boys Brushed By, The.
Gonsalves, Ricardo
And.
González, Angel
I Look at My Hand.
González De Leon, Ulálume
Words.
Good, Ruth
Mountains and Other Outdoor Things.
Goodale, Dora Read
Flight of the Heart, The.
Judgment, The.
Ripe Grain.
Soul of Man, The.
Goodchild, John Arthur
Firstborn, The.
Goodenough, J. B.
Orchard Snow.
Goodge, W. T.
Daley's Dorg Wattle.
How We Drove the Trotter.
Goodman, Mae Winkler
Image in a Mirror.
Memorial.
Washington.
Your Glory, Lincoln.
Goodman, Mitchell
Coming and Going.
Man and Wife.
Goodman, Paul
April 1962.
Classical Quatrain, A.
Don Larsen's Perfect Game.
"Dreams Are the Royal Road to the Unconscious."
Good Riddance to Bad Rubbish O at Last.
I planned to have a border of lavender.
Kent State, May 4, 1970.
Lines: "His cock is big and red when I am there."
Little Ode.
Little Prayer, A.
Long Lines.
Lordly Hudson, The.
March, 1941.
Messiah-Blower, The.
North Percy, *sel.*
Our Lucy (1956-1960).
Pagan Rites.
Poems of My Lambretta.
Saint Harmony my patroness.
Sonnet 21: "I start awake at night afraid of death."
Stanzas: "I thought I woke: the midnight sun."
Surfers at Santa Cruz.
Weepers Tower in Amsterdam, The.
Wellfleet Harbor.
Goodman, Ryah Tumarkin
Silence Spoke with Your Voice.
Goodreau, William
Longing, The.
Goodrich, Samuel Griswold ("Peter Parley")
Higglety, Pigglety, Pop!
Lake Superior.
Goodwill, E. S.
Here is a beetle as black as my hat.
Goodwin, Edward B.
English History in Rhyme, or a Rhyming Epitome of the History of England, from B.C. 55 to A.D. 1872, *sel.*
Principal British Writers.
Roman History in Rhyme, *sel.*
Goodwin, Sandra
Traveling on My Knees.
Googe, Barnabe
Coming Homeward out of Spain.
Epitaph of the Death of Nicholas Grimald, An.
Fly, The.
Going towards Spain.
Of Mistress D. S.
Of Money.
Once Musing as I Sat.
Out of Sight, Out of Mind.
Refusal, A.
To Alexander Neville.
To Doctor Bale.
To Master Edward Cobham.
To the Translation of Palingenius.
Goose, Mary
Cornfield Myth.
Friends.
Insight.
Just an Old Man.
Last Night in Sisseton, S. D.
Gorbanevskaya [*or* Gorbanyevskaya], Natalya Yevgenevna
And there is nothing at all—neither fear.
"Don't touch me!" I scream at passers-by.
Here, as in a painting, yellow noon burns [*or* noon burns yellow].
In my own twentieth century.
Love, love! What nonsense it is.
Not because of you, not because of me, just that.
This world/ is amazingly flat.
To I. Lavrentevaya.
Gordett, Marea
Marriage.
Gordon, A. C.
Kree.
Roses of Memory.
"Gordon, A.M.R." *See* **Rose, Alexander MacGregor**
Gordon, Adam Lindsay
After the Quarrel.
Dedication, A: "They are rhymes rudely strung with intent less."
Hippodromania; or, Whiffs from the Pipe, *sel.*
How We Beat the Favourite.
Rhyme of Joyous Garde, The, *sel.*
Sick Stockrider, The.
Sun and Rain and Dew from Heaven.
Whisperings in Wattle-Boughs.
Ye Wearie Wayfarer, *sel.*
Gordon, Charles F.
Long Night Home, The.
Gordon, Don
Free Fall.
Laocoon.
Sea.
Gordon, James Lindsay
Wheeler at Santiago.
Gordon, James William ("Jim Grahame")
Whalan of Waitin' a While.
Gordon, Judah Leib
Simhat Torah.
Gordon, Mary
Unwanted, The.
Gordon, Ruth McKee
Summer Sky.
Gordon, W. J. J.
IBM Hired Her.
Gore-Booth, Eva
Crucifixion.
Harvest.
Little Waves of Breffny, The.
"Sad Years, The."
Goren, Judith
October.
Gorenko, Anna Andreyevna. *See* **"Akhmatova, Anna"**
Gorey, Edward
Babe, with a cry brief and dismal, The.
From Number Nine, Penwiper Mews.
From the bathing machine came a din.
Lady who signs herself "Vexed," The.
Lord Cray.
Number Nine, Penwiper Mews.
Some Harvard men, stalwart and hairy.
There was a young woman named Plunnery.
Gorges, Sir Arthur
Henceforth I will not set my love.
She that holds me under the laws of love.
Would I were chang'd into that golden shower.
Goring, J. H.
Home.
Gorman, Herbert Sherman
Barcarole of James Smith, The.
Lèse-Majesté.
Satyrs and the Moon, The.
Gorman, Larry (Lawrence E. Gorman)
Beware of Larry Gorman, *with music.*
Boys of the Island, The, *with music.*
Byrontown, *with music.*
Gull Decoy, The, *with music.*
History of Prince Edward Island, The.
McCullam Camp.
Scow on Cowden Shore, The, 3 *vers. with music.*
Tomah Stream, *with music.*
Winter of '73, The, *with music.*
Young Billy Crane, *with music.*
Gormley, Queen of Ireland
Gormley's Laments, *sel.*
Gorton, Samuel
Serpent with a voyce, so slie and fine, The.
Gosse, Sir Edmund William
Charcoal-Burner, The.
Dream of November, A.
Epithalamium: "High in the organ loft with lilied hair."
Illusion.
Impression.
Labor and Love.
Lying in the Grass.
Missive, The.
On Yes Tor.
Revelation.

Swan, The.
Gotlieb, Phyllis
Cocker of Snooks, A.
Death's Head.
How and When and Where and Why.
Late Gothic.
Morning Prayers of the Hasid, Rabbi Levi Yitzhok, The.
This One's on Me.
Three-handed Fugue.
Gottfried von Strassburg
To Mary.
Gottheil, Gustav
Come, O Sabbath Day, *with music.*
Gottlieb, Ann
Lady Luck.
Gottlieb, Darcy
Who of Those Coming After.
Gottlieb, Frantisek
Between Life and Death.
Just a While.
Gottlieb, Lynn
Eve's Song in the Garden.
Goudge, Elizabeth
Thanksgiving for the Earth.
Gould, Dorothy
Armistice Day Vow.
Dreamer, The.
His Task—And Ours.
In the Name of Our Sons.
Reconsecration.
Gould, Gerald
Compensation.
Happy Tree, The.
Lancelot and Guinevere.
Monogamy, *sel.*
Sea-Captain, The.
This is the horror that, night after night.
Wander-Thirst.
Gould, Hannah Flagg
Day of God! Thou Blessed Day, *with music.*
Dying Child's Request, The.
Frost, The.
Name in the Sand, A.
Spider, The.
Gould, Mona
This Was My Brother.
Gould, Robert
Fair, and Soft, and Gay, and Young.
Song: Wit and Beauty.
Goulder, Dave
January Man.
Long and Lonely Winter, The.
Gourmont, Remy de
Hair.
Govan, Donald D.
Recollection.
Gower, Jean Milne
Big Thompson Can[y]on.
Curtain, The (Old Tabor Grand Opera House).
Gower, John
Adrian and Bardus.
Confessio Amantis, *sels.*
Jason and Medea.
Medea's Magic.
Parting of Venus and Old Age, The.
Gower, Mick
Christmas Thank You's.
Graddon, Dorothy
Wind, The.
Grade, Chaim
Miracle, The.
Refugees.
Sodom.
To Life I Said Yes.
Without Me You Won't be Able to See Yourself.
Graeme, James
Mortified Genius, The.
Grafflin, Margaret Johnston
Like Mother, like Son.
To My Son.
Grafton, Richard
Months of the Year, The.
Graham, Al
Casey's Daughter at the Bat.
Folks, I Give You Science!
Interplanetary Limericks.
Theme Song for a Songwriters' Union.
Graham, Charles
Picture That Is Turned toward the Wall, The.
Graham, D. L.
Soul.
Tony Get the Boys.
West Ridge Is Menthol-cool, The.
Graham, Harry ("Col. D. Streamer")
Appreciation.
Aunt Eliza.
Aunt Maud.
Bath, The.
Billy.
Cockney of the North, The.
Common Sense.
Conversational Reformer, The.
Gourmand, The.
Grandpapa ("Grandpapa fell down a drain").
Impetuous Samuel.
Indifference.
Late Last Night.
L'Enfant Glacé.
Lord Gorbals.
Misfortunes Never Come Singly.
Mr. Jones.
My First Love.
Necessity.
Opportunity.
Patience.
Perils of Obesity, The.
Poetical Economy.
Presence of Mind.
Quiet Fun.
Stern Parent, The.
Tender-heartedness.
Uncle.
Waste.
Graham, James, Marquess of Montrose
Epitaph on King Charles I.
His Metrical Prayer.
His Metrical Vow [on the Death of King Charles I].
I'll Never Love Thee More.
Lines on the Execution of King Charles I.
Montrose to His Mistress.
My Dear and Only Love.
On Himself, upon Hearing What Was His Sentence.
Graham, Jorie
Age of Reason, The.
Artichoke for Montesquieu, An.
At the Long Island Jewish Geriatric Home.
Drawing Wildflowers.
Erosion.
History.
How Morning Glories Could Bloom at Dusk.
In What Manner the Body Is United with the Soule.
Kimono.
Love.
My Garden, My Daylight.
Netting.
On Why I Would Betray You.
Reading Plato.
Salmon.
To Paul Eluard.
Two Paintings by Gustav Klimt.
Wanting a Child.
Way Things Work, The.
Graham, Joyce Anstruther Maxtone. *See* **"Struther, Jan."**
Graham, Muriel Elsie
Battle of the Swamps, The.
Lark above the Trenches, The.
Graham, Rachel
New Hampshire Farm Woman.
Graham, Robert (Robert Cunninghame-Graham)
Cavalier's Song.
If Doughty Deeds.
O Tell Me How to Woo Thee.
Graham, Rudy Bee
Memorandum.
Some Ruthless Rhymes, *sel.*
Graham, William Sydney
Baldy Bane.
Beast in the Space, The.
Children of Greenock, The.
Constructed Space, The.
Dark Dialogues, The, *sels.*
Definition of My Brother.
Gigha.
Hill of Intrusion, The.
Johann Joachim Quantz's Five Lessons.
Letter II.
Letter V ("Lie where you fell and longed").
Letter VI ("A day the wind was hardly").
Listen. Put on Morning.
Many without Elegy.
Nightfishing, The, *sel.*
Night's Fall.
Poem: "O gentle queen of the afternoon."
Thermal Stair, The.
To My Father.
Grahame, James
Birds of Scotland, The, *sel.*
Sunday Morning.
"Grahame, Jim." *See* **Gordon, James William**
Grahame, Kenneth
Carol: "Villagers all, this frosty tide."
Christmas Carol: "Villagers all, this frosty tide."
Duck's [*or* Ducks'] Ditty.
Song of Mr. Toad, The.
Wind in the Willows, The, *sels.*
Grahn, Judy
Asking for Ruthie.
Carol, in the Park, Chewing on Straws.
Common Woman, The, *sels.*
Edward the Dyke and Other Poems, *sel.*
Ella, in a Square Apron, along Highway 80.
History of Lesbianism, A.
In the place where.
Margaret, Seen through a Picture Window.
Vera, from My Childhood.
Grainger, James
Compost.
How to Exterminate Rats.
How to Fertilize Soil.
Ode to Solitude, *sel.*
Slaves.
Solitude, *abr.*
Sugar Cane, The, *sels.*
Granade, John A.
Come All Ye Mourning Pilgrims, *with music.*
Sweet Rivers of Redeeming Love, *with music.*
Grandsen, K. W.
Interview, An.
Grannis, Anita
Poet, The.
Grano, Paul Langton
"New Shirt, A!" Why?
Grant, Gordon
Last Gloucesterman, The.
Old Quartermaster, The.
Grant, Lillian
Lines Written in a Mausoleum.
Grant, Richard E.
Broken Heart, Broken Machine.
Grant, Sir Robert
Majesty and Mercy of God, The.
Granville, Charles
Traveller's Hope.
Granville [*or* Grenville], George, Baron Lansdowne
Cloe ("Bright as the day, and like the morning fair").
Cloe's the wonder of her sex. To Cloe.
Love.
To Cloe.

Grapes, Marcus J.
And This Is My Father.
Grass, Günter
Family Matters.
Gasco; or, The Toad.
How I Was Her Kitchen-Boy.
Grave, John
If Thou Wilt Hear, *with music.*
Graves, Alfred Perceval
Father O'Flynn.
Irish Lullaby, An.
Little Red Lark, The.
Song of the Ghost, The.
Graves, Charles Larcom
Horace, Book V, Ode III.
Old Song Resung, An.
Graves, John Woodcock
John Peel.
Graves, Richard
Maternal Despotism; or, The Rights of Infants.
Graves, Robert
Advice to Colonel Valentine.
Allie ("Allie, call the birds in").
Ambrosia of Dionysus and Semele, The.
At First Sight.
Avengers, The.
Babylon.
Bards, The.
Beauty in Trouble.
Bedpost, The.
Birth of a Great Man.
Blue-Fly, The.
Broken Girth, The.
Call It a Good Marriage
Carol of Patience.
Cat Goddesses.
Certain Mercies.
Change.
Children of Darkness.
Civil Servant, A.
Clearing, The.
Climate of Thought, The.
Confess, Marpessa.
Conversation Piece.
Cool Web, The.
Corner Knot, The.
Corporal Stare.
Counting the Beats.
Cry Faugh!
Damocles.
Dead Cow Farm.
Death Room, The.
Defeat of the Rebels.
Devil's Advice to Story-Tellers, The.
Door, The.
Down, Wanton, Down!
1805.
End of Play.
English Wood, An.
Epitaph on an Unfortunate Artist.
Eremites, The.
Escape.
Eugenist, The.
Face in the Mirror, The.
Fallen Tower of Siloam, The.
Finland.
Flying Crooked.
For the Rain It Raineth Every Day.
Forced Music, A.
Foreboding, The.
Frog and the Golden Ball, The.
From the Embassy.
Frosty Night, A.
Full Moon.
Galatea and Pygmalion.
General Elliott, The.
Gift of Sight.
Glutton, The.
Great-Grandmother, The.
Grotesque ("Dr. Newman with the crooked pince-nez").
Grotesque ("Sir John addressed the Snake-god in his temple").
Grotesques.
Hag-ridden.
Haunted House, The.
Hedges Freaked with Snow.
Henry and Mary.
Henry Was a Worthy King.
Hero, The.
Hide and Seek.
History of Peace, A.
Homage to Texas.
I Will Write.
I Wonder What It Feels Like to Be Drowned?
I'd Love to Be a Fairy's Child.
In Broken Images.
In Her Praise.
In Procession.
In the Beginning Was a Word.
In the Wilderness.
In Time.
Intercession in Late October.
Interruption.
It Was All Very Tidy.
It's a Queer Time.
Jealous Man, A.
John Skelton.
Kit Logan and Lady Helen.
Lament for Pasiphae.
Last Post, The.
Laureate, The.
Legion, The.
Legs, The.
Lollocks.
Lost Acres.
Lost Jewel, A [*or* The].
Lost Love.
Lost World, A.
Love and a Question.
Love Story, A.
Love without Hope.
Lovers in Winter.
Lust in Song.
Marigolds.
Mid-Winter Waking.
Mirror, Mirror.
My Name and I.
Naked and the Nude, The.
Narrow Sea, The.
Nature's Lineaments.
Neglectful Edward.
Never Such Love.
Next War, The.
Not Dead.
O Love in Me.
Ogres and Pygmies.
Oldest Soldier, The.
On Dwelling.
On Portents.
Persian Version, The.
Philatelist Royal.
Pier-Glass, The.
Pinch of Salt, A.
Plea to Boys and Girls, A.
Poet's Corner.
Point of No Return.
Portrait, The.
Pot and Kettle.
Presence, The.
Primrose Bed, The.
Pumpkin, The.
Pure Death.
Queen Mother to New Queen.
Quiet Glades of Eden, The.
Read Me, Please!
Recalling War.
Reproach to Julia.
Return of the Goddess Artemis.
Richard Roe and John Doe.
Rocky Acres.
Sail and Oar.
Saint.
Sea Horse, The.
Sea Side.
Second-fated, The.
Sergeant-Major Money.
Sharp Ridge, The.
She Tells Her Love while Half Asleep.
Sick Love.
Sirocco at Deyá.
Six Badgers, The.
Slice of Wedding Cake, A.
Song: How Can I Care?
Song: Lift Boy.
Song: One Hard Look.
Spoils.
Star-Talk.
Straw, The.
Succubus, The.
Surgical Ward: Men.
Survivor, The.
Symptoms of Love.
Theseus and Ariadne.
Thieves, The.
Three-faced, The.
Tilth.
Time.
To an Ungentle Critic.
To Bring the Dead to Life.
To Calliope.
To Juan at the Winter Solstice.
To Lucia at Birth.
To Sleep.
To Whom Else?
Travel[l]er's Curse after Misdirection.
Troll's Nosegay, The.
Trudge, Body.
Turn of the Moon.
Twins.
Two Fusiliers.
Two Witches, The.
Ulysses.
Under the Pot.
Vanity.
Variables of Green.
Villagers and Death, The.
Warning to Children.
Weather of Olympus, The.
"Wellcome, to the Caves of Artá!"
Welsh Incident.
What Did I Dream? I Do Not Know.
White Goddess, The.
Wigs and Beards.
Wild Strawberries.
Wm. Brazier.
Window Sill, The.
With a Gift of Rings.
Woman and Tree.
Worms of History, The.
Wreath, The.
Young Cordwainer, The.
Gray, Sir Alexander
Deil o' Bogie, The.
Epitaph on a Vagabond.
On a Cat, Ageing.
Scotland.
Sir Halewyn.
"Gray, Barry." *See* **Coffin, Robert Barry**
Gray, David
Cross of Gold, The.
Divided.
Envoy: "Sweet World, if you will hear me now."
Golden Wedding, The.
In the Shadows, *sel.*
My Epitaph.
On Lebanon.
Sonnet: "If it must be; if it must be, O God!"
Where the Lilies Used to Spring.
Gray, Eva
Christ, My Salvation.
It Was for Me.
Light and Love, Hope and Faith.
My Daily Prayer.

What Is That in Thine Hand?
Gray, John
Barber, The.
Flying Fish, The.
Gazelles and Unicorn.
Green.
Les Demoiselles de Sauve.
Long Road, The, *sel.*
Lord, If Thou Art Not Present.
Mishka.
Night Nurse Goes Her Round, The.
Odiham.
Poem: "Geranium, houseleek, laid in oblong beds."
To a Madonna.
Gray, Pat
Girl, The/The Girlie Magazine.
Gray, Patrick Worth
Beyond the Firehouse.
Bread Loaf to Omaha, Twenty-eight Hours.
Lines for My Father.
MACV Advisor.
Robert Lowell Is Dead.
Gray, Robert
5 Poems.
Gray, Stephen
Girl with Doves.
Girl with Long Dark Hair.
Gray, Thomas
Bard, The.
Candidate, The.
Cat and the Fish, The.
Curse upon Edward, The.
Death of Hoel, The.
Descent of Odin, The; an Ode from the Norse Tongue.
Elegy Written in a Country Churchyard.
Epitaph on Dr. Keene.
Epitaph on Dr. Keene's Wife.
Fatal Sisters, The.
Fragment: "There pipes the wood-lark, and the song thrush there."
Hymn to Adversity.
Impromptu.
Ode on a Distant Prospect of Eton College.
Ode on the Death of a Favourite [*or* Favorite] Cat, Drowned in a Tub [*or* Bowl] of Gold Fishes.
Ode on the Pleasure Arising from Vicissitude.
Ode on the Spring.
On a Distant Prospect of Eton College.
On Dr. Keene, Bishop of Chester.
On Lord Holland's Seat near Margate, Kent.
On the Death of a Favorite Cat, Drowned in a Tub of Gold Fishes.
On the Death of Mr. Richard West.
Pindaric Ode, A.
Progress of Poesy, The.
Satire upon the Heads.
Sketch of His Own Character.
Song: "Thyrsis, when we parted, swore."
Sonnet on the Death of [Mr.] Richard West.
Stanzas to Mr. Bentley.
Tophet.
Triumphs of Owen, The.
Where Ignorance Is Bliss.
Gray, Victor
Limerick: "Charlotte Brontë said, 'Wow, sister! *What* a man!' "
Limerick: "Old East End worker called Jock, An."
Limerick: "One morning old Wilfrid Scawen Blunt."
Limerick: "Taxi-cab whore out at Iver, A."
Limerick: "There was a young fellow called Crouch."
Limerick: "When Gauguin was visiting Fiji."
Limerick: "When our dean took a pious young spinster."
Limerick: "While visiting Arundel Castle."
Limerick: "Young engine-driver called Hunt, A."
Gray, William B.
She Is More to Be Pitied than Censured.
Grayson, Caroline
After.
Grayston, Joan Byers
Dexter.
Unseen Horses.
Graziano, Frank
Potato Eaters, The.
Greacen, Robert
Bird, The.
Curse.
Cycling to Dublin.
Far Country, The.
Glorious Twelfth, The.
Michael Walked in the Wood.
To a Faithless Lover.
Written on the Sense of Isolation in Contemporary Ireland.
Greeff, Adele
Sonnet XI: "Is God invisible? This very room."
Green, Brenda Heloise
New England Is New England Is New England.
"Green, Coroebus." *See* **Cone, Helen Gray**
Green, F. Pratt
Old Couple, The.
Green, Henry MacKenzie
Cicada, The.
Green, J. Charles
Day of Notes, A.
Departure.
Freedom.
Isolation Cell Poem.
Parole Denial.
Green, Jane
Songs of Divorce.
Green, Joseph
Permit Us, Lord, to Consecrate, *with music.*
Green, Judith
Bush-Fiddle, The.
Green, Mary McBride
Aeroplane.
Taking Off.
Green, Matthew
Cure for the Spleen, A.
Epistle, An: "And may my humble dwelling stand."
In Praise of Water-Gruel.
On Barclay's Apology for the Quakers.
On Even Keel.
Sparrow and Diamond, The.
Spleen, The, *sels.*
Green, Rayna
Another Dying Chieftain.
Coosaponakeesa (Mary Mathews Musgrove Bosomsworth), Leader of the Creeks, 1700–1783.
Mexico City Hand Game.
Nanye'hi (Nancy Ward), the Last Beloved Woman of the Cherokees, 1738–1822.
Old Indian Trick.
Palace Dancer, Dancing at Last.
Road Hazard.
When I Cut My Hair.
Green, Roger Lancelyn
On First Looking into the Dark Future.
Green, Stanley Roger
Death's-Head Moth.
Old Bing, The.
Greenaway, Kate
Alphabet, The.
Boat Sails Away, The.
Five Little Sisters Walking in a Row.
Higgledy, piggledy! see how they run!
In go-cart so tiny.
Little Blue Shoes.
Little Jumping Girls, The.
Little Wind.
Naughty Blackbird, The.
Oh, Susan Blue.
On the Bridge.
Ring-a-Ring.
School is over.
Tommy was a silly boy.
Will You [Be My Little Wife]?
Greenberg, Alvin
So?
Sungrazer.
Greenberg, Barbara L.
Judge Kroll.
Greenberg, Blu
Mikveh, The.
Greenberg, Eliezer
Dog and Tiger.
Greenberg, Samuel
Blank Book Letter, The.
Conduct.
Essence.
Essentials.
Glass Bubbles, The.
I Cannot Believe That I Am of Wind.
Immortality.
Killing.
Man.
Opponent Charm Sustained, The.
Peace.
Philosophic Apology, The.
Soul's Kiss.
Spirituality.
To Dear Daniel.
Tusks of Blood, The.
Greenberg, Uri Zvi
Great Sad One, The.
Hour, The.
How It Is.
Jerusalem, *sel.*
Jerusalem the Dismembered.
Like a Woman.
On the Pole.
Song at the Skirts of Heaven.
There Is a Box.
Valley of Men, The.
With My God, the Smith.
Greene, Albert Gorton
Baron's Last Banquet, The.
Old Grimes.
Greene, Ashton
Bather in a Painting, A.
Church of the Sacred Heart, The.
Lagoon, The.
Parade, The.
Greene, Homer
My Daughter Louise.
What My Lover Said.
Greene, Richard Leighton
Autolycus' Song (in Basic English).
Song to Imogen (in Basic English.)
Greene, Robert
Arbasto, *sels.*
Barmenissa's Song.
Coridon and Phillis.
Description of Sir Geoffrey Chaucer, The.
Doralicia's Song.
Doron's Description of Samela.
Doron's Jigge.
Eurymachus's Fancy.
Fair Is My Love for April's in Her Face.
Farewell to Follie [*or* Folly], *sel.*
Fawnia.
Fie, Fie on Blind Fancy!
Francesco's Fortunes, *sels.*
Greene's Farewell to Folly, *sel.*
Greene's Groatsworth of Wit, *sels.*
Greene's Mourning Garment, *sels.*
Greene's Vision, *sel.*
Hexametra Alexis in Laudem Rosamundi.
In Praise of His Loving and Best-beloved Fawnia.
Infida's Song.
Jig, A.
Lamilia's Song.
Love and Jealousy.
Madrigal, A: "Swans, whose pens as white as ivory, The," *sel.*

Maesia's Song.
Mars and Venus.
Menaphon, *sels.*
Mind Content, A.
Never Too Late, *sels.*
Of His Mistress.
Palinode, A.
Palmer's Ode, The.
Pandosto, *sel.*
Penitent Palmer's Ode, The.
Perimedes [*or* Perimedes, the Blacksmith], *sels.*
Phillis and Corydon.
Philomela, the Lady Fitzwater's Nightingale, *sels.*
Poor Estate, The.
Samela.
Sephestia's Song to Her Child[e].
Shepherd's Ode, The.
Shepherd's Wife's Song, The.
Sir Geoffrey Chaucer.
Song: "Sweet are the thoughts that savour of content."
Sonnet: "Fair is my love, for April is her face."
Sonnet or Dittie: "Mars in a fury gainst love's brightest Queen."
Tullie's Love, *sels.*
Verses under a Peacock Portrayed in Her Left Hand.
Whereat Erewhile I Wept, I Laugh.

Greene, Sarah Pratt McLean
Lamp, The.
Sheepfol', De.

Greenfield, Eloise
Moochie ("Moochie likes to keep on playing").

Greenleaf, Lawrence N.
Lodge Room over Simpkins' Store, The.
Pike's Peakers, The.

Greenwell, Bill
King Ethelred the Unready.

Greenwell, Dora
Battle-Flag of Sigurd, The.
Home.
Man with Three Friends, The.
Picture, A.
Saturday Review, The.
Sun-Flower, The.
When the Night and Morning Meet.

Greenwood,———,, Dr.
Epitaph—on the Wife of Dr. Greenwood.

"Greenwood, Grace" (Sara Jane Clarke Lippincott)
Illumination for Victories in Mexico.

Greenwood, Theresa
Here I sit in my infested cubicle.

Greger, Debora
Armorer's Daughter, The.
Compline.
Light Passages, The.
Man on the Bed, The.
Patches of Sky.

Gregg, Linda
Alma to Her Sister.
As When the Blowfish Perishing.
Beckett Kit, The.
Being with Men.
Children among the Hills.
Choosing the Devil.
Chorus Speaks Her Words as She Dances, The.
Color of Many Deer Running, The.
Coming Back.
Death Looks Down.
Euridice Saved.
Eurydice.
Girl I Call Alma, The.
Gnostics on Trial.
Gods Must Not Know Us, The.
Goethe's Death Mask.
Growing Up.
How the Joy of It Was Used Up Long Ago.
Lilith.
Marriage and Midsummer's Night.
Not Saying Much.
Not Wanting Myself.
River Again and Again, The.
Sigismundo.
Small Lizard, The.
Summer in a Small Town.
Sun Moon Kelp Flower or Goat.
There She Is.
Things Not of This Union.
Trying to Believe.
We Manage Most When We Manage Small.
Whole and without Blessing.

Gregh, Fernand
Doubt.

Gregor, Arthur
At the Trough.
Beacon, The.
Enough.
Guide, The
History.
Irreconcilables.
Late Last Night.
Likeness, The.
Lyric: "Embodiment of what, The."
Nameless Recognition, A.
Poem: "So many pigeons at Columbus."
Spirit-like before Light.
Spirits, Dancing.
To Emily.
Two Shapes.
Unalterables.

Gregor, Christian
What Splendid Rays, *with music.*

Gregor, Debora
Second Violinist's Son, The.

Gregory, Augusta Gregory,, Lady
Come ride and ride to the garden.
Old Woman Remembers, The.

Gregory, Carole C.
Freedom Song for the Black Woman, A.
Greater Friendship Baptist Church, The.
Love Letter.
Revelation.

Gregory, Horace
And of Columbus.
Ask No Return.
Beggar on the Beach, The.
Chorus for Survival, *sel.*
Death and Empedocles 444 B.C.
Elegy and Flame.
For You, My Son.
Foreigner Comes to Earth on Boston Common, A.
Fortune for Mirabel.
Haunted Odysseus: The Last Testament.
If It Offend Thee.
Longface Mahoney Discusses Heaven.
Lunchroom Bus Boy Who Looked like Orson Welles, The.
Night-Walker, The.
On a Celtic Mask by Henry Moore.
Passion of M'Phail, The, *sels.*
Poems for My Daughter.
Postman's Bell Is Answered Everywhere, The.
Prisoner's Song.
Rehearsal, The.
Siege at Stony Point.
Stanzas for My Daughter.
They Found Him Sitting in a Chair.
They Were All like Geniuses.
This Is the Place to Wait.
To the Last Wedding Guest.
Unwilling Guest, The; an Urban Dialogue.
Valediction to My Contemporaries.
Voices of Heroes.
Woman Who Disapproved of Music at the Bar, The.

Gregory the Great, Saint
Behold, the Shade of Night Is Now Receding, *with music.*
Morning Hymn.

Gregory, Leona
Silence, an Eloquent Applause.

Gregory, Padraic
Dream-Teller, The.

Gregory, Yvonne
Christmas Lullaby for a New-born Child.

Greiffenberg, Catharina Regina von
On the Ineffable Inspiration of the Holy Spirit.
Spring-Joy Praising God; Praise of the Sun.
Why the Resurrection Was Revealed to Women.

Greig, Andrew
Glove, The.
In Galloway.
Marry the Lass?
Men on Ice, *sel.*
On Falling.
Sapper.

Greig, Desmond A.
On a Scooter.
To a Flea in a Glass of Water.

Gréki, Anna
Before Your Waking.
Future is for tomorrow, The.

Grenelle, Lisa
Duel in the Park.

Grenfell, Julian
Hills, The.
Into Battle.

Grenville, R. H.
Pawnshop Window.
Within Us, Too.

Gresham, Walter S.
Crowded Ways of Life.

Greville, Fanny Macartney
Prayer for Indifference, A.

Greville, Fulke, 1st Baron Brooke
Absence and Presence.
Caelica, *sels.*
Caelica and Philocell.
Change.
Chorus: "O wearisome condition of humanity."
Chorus Primus: Wise Counsellors.
Chorus Quintus: Tartarorum.
Chorus Sacerdotum.
Chorus Tertius: Of Time; Eternitie.
Cynthia ("Away with these self-loving lads").
Despair.
Downe in the depth of mine iniquity.
Epitaph on Sir Philip Sidney, *at.*
Eternity's Speech against Time.
Farewell to Cupid.
His Lady's Eyes.
Love and Fortune.
Love and Honour.
Love's Glory.
More than Most Fair.
Mustapha, *sels.*
Myra.
Of His Cynthia.
Of Human Learning, *sel.*
Saving God, The.
Sion Lies Waste [and Thy Jerusalem].
Song to His Cynthia.
Sonnet: "Caelica, I overnight was finely used."
Sonnet: "Downe in the depth of mine iniquity."
Sonnet: "Earth with thunder torn, with fire blasted, The."
Sonnet: "Eternall Truth, almighty, infinite."
Sonnet: "Love is the peace, whereto all thoughts do strive."
Sonnet: "Man, dream[e] no more of curious mysteries."
Sonnet: "Men, that delight to multiply desire."
Sonnet: "Nurse-life wheat within his green husk growing, The."
Sonnet: "O false and treacherous Probability."
Sonnet: "Three things there be in Mans opinion deare."
Sonnet: "When as man's life, the light of human lust."
Three Things There Be [in Man's Opinion Dear].
Time and Eternity.
To His Lady.

To Myra.
Youth and Maturity.
Grew, Gwendolyn
Burning the Letters.
Grey of Fallodon, Pamela Grey, Viscountess
Echo.
Grier, Eldon
I Am Almost Asleep.
In Memory of García Lorca.
Kissing Natalia.
More Than Most People.
Mountain Town—Mexico.
My Winter Past.
On the Subject of Waves.
Quebec.
Sensible Is the Label.
View from a Window.
Grierson, Constantia
To Miss Laetitia Van Lewen.
Grieve, Christopher Murray. *See* **"MacDiarmid, Hugh"**
Griffin, Bartholomew
Fidessa, More Chaste than Kind, *sels.*
Her Heart.
My Love.
Sleep.
Sonnet: "Fair[e] is my love that feeds among the lilies."
Sonnet: "I have not spent the April of my time."
Venus, with Young Adonis Sitting by Her.
Youth.
Griffin, George Randall
World Was Never Real to Me, The.
Griffin, Gerald
Aileen Aroon.
Eileen Aroon ("When like the early rose").
Gone! Gone! Forever Gone.
Hy-Brasail—the Isle of the Blest.
I Love My Love in the Morning.
Know Ye Not That Lovely River.
Lines Addressed to a Seagull.
Maiden Eyes.
O Brazil, the Isle of the Blest.
Place in Thy Memory, A.
Sleep That Like the Couchéd Dove.
Song: "Place in thy memory, dearest, A."
To the Blessed Virgin Mary.
War Song of O'Driscol.
Griffin, Howard
Suppose in Perfect Reason.
Griffin, "Sin-Killer"
Man of Calvary, The.
Griffin, Susan
Acoustics.
Awful Mother, The.
Bad Mother, The.
Chance Meeting.
Chile.
Distress.
Dogs.
Field.
Garden, The.
I Like to Think of Harriet Tubman.
Letter to the Revolution.
Love Should Grow Up like a Wild Iris in the Fields.
My Child.
Nineteen Pieces for Love, *sel.*
Perfect Mother, The.
Perversity.
Pot of Tea.
Prologue: "He says that woman speaks with nature."
Silence.
Sitting.
Song My.
Teeth.
Three Poems for Women.
Three Shades of Light on the Windowsill.
Tissue.
White Bear.
Woman and Nature, *sels.*
Woman Defending Herself Examines Her Own Character Witness, A.
Griffith, Margaret
When I Consider.
Griffith, William
Aloha.
Canticle.
I, Who Fade with the Lilacs.
Pierrette in Memory ("Pierrette has gone, but it was not").
Griffiths, Nora
Wykhamist, The.
Griffiths, T.
La Belle Dame sans Merci, *parody.*
On First Looking into Chapman's Homer I, *parody.*
Grigson, Geoffrey
Above the High.
Administrator, An.
Before a Fall.
Bibliotheca Bodleiana.
Burials.
By the Road.
Critics and Poets.
End of the Affair.
Four, The.
Glen Lough.
Hardy's Plymouth.
Heart Burial.
His Swans.
Inside the Cave.
June in Wiltshire.
Landscape of the Heart, The.
Lecture Note: Elizabethan Period.
May Trees in a Storm.
Meeting by the Gjulika Meadow.
On a Birth.
On a Lover of Books.
On the Eve of a Birthday.
On the Relinquishment of a Title.
Professionals, The.
To Wystan Auden.
Tresco.
Two Are Together.
Uccello on the Heath.
Under the Cliff.
Grimald, Nicholas
Garden, The.
True Love, A.
Truelove, A.
Virtue.
Grimes, John
Queen of Crete, The.
Grimes, Willard M.
Piazza di Spagna.
Grimké, Angelina Weld
At April.
Black Finger, The.
Dusk.
Eyes of My Regret, The.
For the Candle Light.
Grass Fingers.
Greenness.
Hushed by the Hands of Sleep.
I Weep.
Mona Lisa, A.
Paradox.
Puppet Player, The.
Surrender.
Tenebris.
To Clarissa Scott Delany.
To Keep the Memory of Charlotte Forten Grimké.
Ways o' Men, The.
When the Green Lies over the Earth.
Winter Twilight, A.
Your Hands.
Grindal, Edmund
Give Peace in These Our Days, O Lord, *with music.*
Griswold, Alexander V.
Holy Father, Great Creator, *with music.*
Groesbeck, Amy
Momist.
Grosholz, Emily
Letter from Germany.
Rodin to Rilke.
Gross, June
Drivers of Boston, The.
Gross, Ronald
Yield.
Grossbardt, Andrew
At Pont-Aven, Gauguin's Last Home in France.
Jogging at Dusk.
River in Asia, A.
Grosseteste, Robert
Little Song, A.
Grossman, Allen
By the Pool.
Lilith.
Grossman, Florence
Riding.
Grossman, Martin
Bread of Our Affliction, The.
Into the Book.
Place to Live, A.
Grossman, Reuben
Therefore, We Thank Thee, God.
Grossman, Richard
Art of Love, The.
Group, Verda
I Know.
Grove, Bob. *See* **Franklin, William**
Grove, Matthew
In Praise of His Lady.
Pelops and Hippodamia, *sel.*
Gruber, Abraham L.
My Neighbor's Roses.
Gruber, Edmund L.
Caisson Song, The.
Gruber, Johann A.
Love That's Pure, Itself Disdaining, *with music.*
Grudin, Louis
Citizen.
Dust on Spring Street.
Grundtvig, Nicolai Frederik Severin
I Know a Flower So Fair and Fine, *with music.*
Grünewald, Alfred
Lamp Now Flickers, The.
Grutzmacher, Harold M.
Knowledge.
Grynberg, Henryk
Anti-Nostalgia.
Dead Sea, The.
Listening to Confucius.
Poplars.
Guarini, Giovanni Battista
Claim to Love.
Golden Age, The.
Of Beauty.
Spring.
Thus saith my Chloris bright.
Guérin, Charles
Partings.
Guernsey, Bruce
Apple, The.
Back Road.
June Twenty-first.
Guernsey, Wellington
Alice, Where Art Thou?
Guerzo di Montecanti
Sonnet: He Is Out of Heart with His Time.
Guest, Barbara
Direction.
Location of Things, The.
Luminous, The.
Parachutes, My Love, Could Carry Us Higher.
Parade's End.
Piazzas.
Red Lilies.
River Road Studio.
Santa Fe Trail.

Sunday Evening.
20.
Guest, Edgar Albert
Becoming a Dad.
Friend's Greeting, A.
Grace at Evening.
Home.
It Couldn't Be Done.
Just Folks.
Lemon Pie.
Lord, Make a Regular Man out of Me.
Myself.
Out Fishin'.
Prayer for the Home, *sel.*
Sausage.
Sittin' on the Porch.
Stick to It.
Success.
Things that Make a Soldier Great, The.
Guidacci, Margherita
All Saints' Day, *sel.*
At Night.
Guido delle Colonne
Canzone: To Love and to His Lady.
Guild, Marilla Merrimar
Ocotillo in Bloom, The.
Guillaume de Lorris
Dream of the Romaunt of the Rose, The.
Garden of Amour, The.
Guillaume de Lorris *and* Jean de Meun
Romance [*or* Romaunt] of the Rose, The, *sels.*
There is no place in paradise.
Guillaume de Poitiers
Behold, the Meads.
Count William's Escapade.
Guillén, Jorge
Metropolitan Night.
Guillén, Nicolás
Dead Soldier.
Guadalupe, W.I.
Proposition.
Sightseers in a Courtyard.
Guiney, Louise Imogen
Carol: "Vines branching stilly."
Deo Optimo Maximo.
Footnote to a Famous Lyric, A.
In Leinster.
John Brown; a Paradox.
Kings, The.
Martyr's Memorial.
Ode for a Master Mariner Ashore.
Of Joan's Youth.
On First Entering Westminster Abbey.
Out in the Fields with God, *at.*
Outdoor Litany, An.
Pax Paganica.
Sanctuary.
Song: "I try to knead and spin, but my life is low the while."
Tryste Noël.
Valse Jeune.
Wild Ride, The.
Guinicelli, Guido
Canzone: He Perceives His Rashness in Love, but Has No Choice.
Canzone: Of the Gentle Heart.
Of the Gentle Heart.
Sonnet: He Will Praise His Lady.
Sonnet: Of Moderation and Tolerance.
Guinness, Bryan
Summer Is Coming, The.
What Are They Thinking.
Guir, Haim
Rain.
Guiterman, Arthur
Ain't Nature Commonplace!
Alibi.
Ambiguous Dog, The.
Ancient History.
Anthologistics.
Anthony Wayne.
Bears.
Blessing on Little Boys.
Brief Essay on Man.
Call to the Colors, The.
Consolation.
Constitution for a League of Nations.
Coyote and the Star.
Dance of Gray Raccoon, The.
Daniel Boone.
Dog Parade, The.
Dog's Cold Nose, The.
Edinburgh.
Elegy: "Jackals prowl, the serpents hiss, The."
Ephraim the Grizzly.
Epilogue to a Book of Verse.
Everything in Its Place.
Experts on Woman.
For a Good Dog.
Haarlem Heights.
Habits of the Hippopotamus.
Harvest Home.
He Leads Us Still.
Heredity.
Hills.
House Blessing.
How Are You?
In Praise of Llamas.
In the Hospital.
Indian Pipe and Moccasin Flower.
Lament for the Alamo.
Legend of the First Cam-u-el, The.
Little Lost Pup.
Little Ponds.
March.
Mavrone.
Mexican Serenade.
Motto for a Dog House.
Nature Note.
Ode of Odium on Aquariums.
Ode to the Hayden Planetarium.
Of Certain Irish Fairies.
Of Courtesy.
Of Giving.
Of Quarrels.
Of Tact.
Offer, An.
On the Vanity of Earthly Greatness.
Oregon Trail, The.
Ornithology in Florida.
Pilgrims' Thanksgiving Feast, The.
Pioneer, The.
Polliwog, The.
Prairie Dog, The.
Quivira.
Reward of Virtue.
Routine.
Rush of the *Oregon,* The.
School Days in New Amsterdam.
Scribe's Prayer, The.
Sea-Chill.
Shakespearean Bear, The.
Skater's Valentine, A.
Song of Hate for Eels.
Starlighter, The.
Storming of Stony Point, The.
Strictly Germ-proof.
Superstitious Ghost, The.
Thanksgiving Wishes.
Tradition.
Twist-Rime on Spring.
What the Gray Cat Sings.
Young Washington.
Gulick, Alida Carey
On Waking.
Gullans, Charles
Autumn; an Ode.
Autumn Burial; a Meditation.
First Love.
Narcissus.
Poema Morale.
Satyr.
To a Friend.
Gumilev, Nikolai Stepanovich
Giraffe, The, *sel.*
How Could We, Beforehand, Live in Quiet.
Gummere, Francis Barton
John Bright.
Gunn, Louise D.
Conversation with Rain.
Gunn, Thom
Allegory of the Wolf Boy, The.
Annihilation of Nothing, The.
Apartment Cats.
Autumn Chapter in a Novel.
Baby Song.
Back to Life.
Before the Carnival.
Black Jackets.
Breakfast.
Byrnies, The.
Carnal Knowledge.
Cherry Tree, The.
Claus von Stauffenberg.
Confessions of the Life Artist.
Considering the Snail.
Corridor, The.
Das Liebesleben.
Discovery of the Pacific, The.
Elegy on the Dust.
Expression.
Faustus Triumphant.
Fever.
For several weeks I have been reading. Expression.
From the Highest Camp.
From the Wave.
Hampstead; the Horse Chestnut Trees.
High Fidelity.
Idea of Trust, The.
In Santa Maria del Popolo.
In the Tank.
Incident on a Journey.
Innocence.
Jesus and His Mother.
Lebensraum.
Loot.
Merlin in the Cave: He Speculates without a Book.
Messenger, The.
Mirror for Poets, A.
Misanthropos, *sel.*
Modes of Pleasure.
Moly.
My Sad Captains.
Nature of an Action, The.
New York.
No Speech from the Scaffold.
On the Move.
Painkillers.
Rooftop, The.
Slow Waker.
St. Martin and the Beggar.
Street Song.
Tamer and Hawk.
To Yvor Winters, 1955.
Touch.
Trucker, A.
Unsettled Motorcyclist's Vision of His Death, The.
Vox Humana.
Wheel of Fortune, The.
Wound, The.
Gunnars, Kristjana
Changeling VIII.
Wakepick I.
Gunning, Sara Ogan
Girl of Constant Sorrow.
Gurevitch, Zali
Not Going with It.
Short Eulogy.
Guri, Haim [*or* Chaim]
Anath.
And on My Return.
But We Shall Bloom.

Isaac.
Latter Purification, A.
My Samsons.
Nine Men out of a Minyan.
Piyyut for Rosh Hashana.
Prayer: "Thy blessing on the boys—for time has come."
Gurney, Diana
Fallen, The.
Gurney, Dorothy Frances
Lord God Planted a Garden, The.
Gurney, Ivor
Ballad of the Three Spectres.
Bohemians, The.
Canadians.
Dawns I Have Seen.
Elver Fishers.
Epitaph on a Young Child.
High Hills, The.
Larches.
Love Song, The: "Out of the blackthorn hedges."
Possessions.
Rainy Midnight.
Requiem: "Pour out your light, O stars."
Silent One, The.
Song: "Only the wanderer."
Strange Hells.
To His Love.
Gurney, Lawrence
Nevada.
Gustafson, Ralph
Armorial.
Aspects of Some Forsythia Branches.
At the Ocean's Verge.
Carta Canadensis.
Columbus Reaches Juana, 1492.
Dedication: " 'They shall not die in vain,' we said."
Fish, The.
In the Yukon.
Legend.
Meaning, The.
Mothy Monologue.
My Love Eats an Apple.
On the Road to Vicenza.
On the *Struma* Massacre.
On This Sea-Floor.
Ramble on What in the World Why.
S.S.R., Lost at Sea—*The Times.*
Swans of Vadstena, The.
Transfigured Night.
Wednesday at North Hatley.
Guthrie, Charles E.
God's Will.
Guthrie, James
Last Song.
Guthrie, Ramon
Clown, The: He Dances in the Clearing by Night.
Noël Tragique.
Postlude: For Goya.
To and on Other Intellectual Poets on Reading That the U.S.A.F. Had Sent a Team of Scientists to Africa.
Guthrie, Thomas Anstey. *See* **"Anstey, F."**
Guthrie, Woody
Columbus Stockade Blues.
Hard Traveling.
I've Got to Know.
Jesus Christ ("Jesus Christ was a man that travelled through the land").
Ludlow Massacre, The.
1913 Massacre, The.
Pastures of Plenty.
Plane Wreck at Los Gatos [Deportee].
Tom Joad, *with music.*
Union Maid.
Gutiérrez, José Angel
22 Miles.
Gutteridge, Bernard
Burma Hills.
Man into a Churchyard.
Namkwin Pul.
Patrol; Buonamary.
Guyon, Jeanne Marie Bouvier de la Motte
Adoration.
By Thy Life I Live.
Little Bird I Am, A.
Gwillim, Joy
Ritual, The.
Gwynn, Stephen Lucius
Ireland.
Gwynne, J. Harold
Word of God, The.
Gyles, Althea
Sympathy.

H

"H., B."
Anacreon to the Sophist.
"H., C.G."
Power of Innocence, The.
"H., F.L."
Father Knows, The.
"H., H." *See* **Jackson, Helen Hunt**
"H., M. G."
He Never Will Forget.
"H., R."
Battle of Monmouth, The.
"H.D." *See* **Doolittle, Hilda**
"H——, Captain"
Imitation of Martial, Book II Ep. 105, An.
Haad, Siraad
Lament for a Dead Lover.
Haag, Terri
Truck Drivers.
Haan, Jakov de
All Is God's.
God's Gifts.
Hanukah.
Sabbath.
Unity.
Habercom, David
Life Not Given, The.
Habib Gerez, Jozef. *See* **Gerez, Jozef Habib**
Habington, William
Against Them Who Lay Unchastity to the Sex of Women.
Castara.
Compliment, The.
Description of Castara, The.
Dialogue betweene Araphill and Castara, A.
Elegie: "Goe stop the swift-wing'd moments in their flight."
Fine Young Folly.
His Muse Speakes to Him.
Melancholy.
Nox Nocti Indicat Scientiam.
Pretty Sport.
Queen of Aragon, The, *sel.*
Quoniam Ego in Flagella Paratus Sum.
Reward of Innocent Love, The.
Song: "Fine young folly, though you were."
"Time! where didst thou those years inter."
To a Friend, Inviting Him to a Meeting upon Promise.
To a Wanton.
To Castara ("Doe not their prophane orgies heare").
To Castara ("Give me a heart where no impure").
To Castara ("We saw and woo'd each others eyes").
To Castara, of True Delight.
To Castara, upon an Embrace.
To Castara, upon Beautie.
To Castara, Ventring to Walke Too Farre in the Neighbouring Wood.
To Death, Castara Being Sicke.
To Roses in the Bosom[e] of Castara.
To the Right Honourable the Countesse of C.
To the World, the Perfection of Love.
Upon Castara's Absence.
Upon Thought Castara May Die.
"Welcome, Thou Safe Retreat!"
What Am I Who Dare to Call Thee, God!
Hacker, Marilyn
After the Revolution.
Alba: March.
Aube Provençale.
Before the War.
Elektra on Third Avenue.
Hang-Glider's Daughter, The.
La Fontaine de Vaucluse.
Lines Declining a Transatlantic Dinner Invitation.
Living in the Moment.
Ordinary Women I ("I am the woman you see in Bloomingdale's").
Ordinary Women II ("Mrs. Velez of the Tenants' Association").
Presentation Piece.
September.
Sonnet Ending with a Film Subtitle.
Under the Arc de Triomphe: October 17.
Villanelle: "Every day our bodies separate."
Hackett, Francis
Sea Dawn.
Hackett, J. W.
Haiku: "Bitter morning, A."
Hackleman, Kris
Not to March.
Hadden, Maude Miner
Creative Force.
Hadewijch
Ah yes, when love allows.
All Things Confine.
Had I been mindful of my high descent.
Love has seven names.
What helps it if of love I sing.
Hadley, Lydia
Four Calls, The.
Hadrian, Emperor (Publius Aelius Hadrianus)
Animula Vagula, Blandula.
Hadrian's Address to His Soul When Dying.
To His Soul.
Haenigsen, H. W.
Listen, Pigeon, Bend an Ear.
Hafen, Ann Woodbury
Mountain Liars.
Hafiz
Lips of the one I love are my perpetual pleasure, The.
Love is where the glory falls.
Odes, *sels.*
Persian Song of Hafiz, A.
Hafsa bint al-Hajj
Shall I come there, or you here?
Hagarty, Sir John H.
Funeral of Napoleon I.
Hagedorn, Hermann
Early Morning at Bargis.
Evening Prayer.
Eyes of God, The.
Mother in the House, The.
Prayer during Battle.
Solomon.
Song: "Song is so old."
Troop of the Guard, A.
Hagedorn, Jessica Tarahata
Listen.
Ming the Merciless.
Motown/Smokey Robinson.
Song for My Father.
Woman Who Thought She Was More than a Samba, The.
Hageman, Samuel Miller
Silence.
Hagen, John Milton
Cowboy and His Love, The, *with music.*

Hagerup, Inger
Emily Dickinson.
Hagg, Esther Lloyd
His Garments.
It Was Not Strange.
Hagiwara, Sakutaro
World of Bacteria.
Hahn, Kimiko
Dance Instructions for a Young Girl.
Daughter.
Girl Combs Her Hair, A.
When You Leave.
Hahn, Oscar
Adolph Hitler Meditates on the Jewish Problem.
Hahn, Steve
July Storm, A: Johnson, Nemaha County, Nebraska.
October.
Hai-Jew, Dianne
Days Ago.
Foreign Soil.
Thirst of the Dragon.
This Night.
Haines, John
And When the Green Man Comes.
At Slim's River.
At White River.
Awakening.
Cauliflower, The.
Certain Dead.
Child in the Rug, The.
Cicada.
Cloud Factory, The.
Color, The.
Dream of the Lynx.
Dusk of the Revolutionaries.
End of the Street, The.
Flight, The.
For Daphne at Lone Lake.
Foreboding.
Forest without Leaves, *sel.*
Goshawk, The.
Homage to David Smith.
If the Owl Calls Again.
Into the Glacier.
Invaders, The.
Lake in the Sky, The.
Legend of Paper Plates, The.
Little Cosmic Dust Poem.
Marigold.
Men against the Sky.
Middle Ages, The.
Mole, The.
Paul Klee.
Poem like a Grenade, A.
Prayer to the Snowy Owl.
Rain.
Ryder.
Snowbound City, The.
Snowy Night.
Spilled Milk.
To Turn Back.
To Vera Thompson.
Train Stops at Healy Fork, The.
Tundra, The.
Winter News.
Wolves.
Hajek, Louise
No Madam Butterfly.
Hajnal, Anna
Dead Girl.
Fear.
Felled Plane Tree, The.
Half Past Four, October.
That's All?
Tree to Flute.
Hake, Thomas Gordon
Snake-Charmer, The.
Halas, František
Again.
Halbisch, Harry
Warp and Woof.
Haldane, John Burdon Sanderson
Cancer's a Funny Thing.
Haldane, Sean
I Meant to Tell You.
Hale, Arthur
Manila Bay.
Yankee Privateer, The.
Hale, Edward Everett
Adrian Block's Song.
Alma Mater's Roll.
Anne Hutchinson's Exile.
Ballad of Bunker Hill, The.
Columbus.
From Potomac to Merrimac.
Lamentable Ballad of the Bloody Brook, The.
Lend a Hand.
Look Up.
Marching Song of Stark's Men, The.
Nameless Saints, The.
New England's Chevy Chase, April 19, 1775.
Omnipresence.
One Thousandth Psalm, The.
Put It Through.
Hale, Janet Campbell
Aaron Nicholas, Almost Ten.
Backyard Swing.
Cinque.
Custer Lives in Humbolt County.
Desmet, Idaho, March 1969.
On Death and Love.
Scene from a Dream.
Six Feet Under.
Walls of Ice.
Where Have All the Indians Gone?
"Hale, Katherine" (Amelia Beers Warnock Garvin)
Eternal Moment.
Giant's Tomb in Georgian Bay.
Lost Garden.
Portrait of a Cree.
Hale, Oliver
Where Unimaginably Bright.
Hale, Robert Beverly
Big Nasturtiums, The.
Denise.
Ovibos, The.
Hale, Sarah Josepha Buell
Alice Ray.
Mary's Lamb.
Mole and the Eagle, The.
Our Father in Heaven, *with music.*
Watcher, The.
Halevi, Judah
Awake, My Fair.
Dove, The.
Earth in Spring, The.
Fortune's Treachery.
God, Whom Shall I Compare to Thee?
Grey Hair, The.
He Cometh.
Hymn for Atonement Day.
Immortal Israel.
Israel's Duration.
Letter to His Friend Isaac, A.
Longing.
Longing for Jerusalem.
Lord, Where Shall I Find Thee?
Love Song A: "Let my sweet song be pleasing unto Thee."
Love Song: "See'st thou o'er my shoulders falling."
Marriage Song.
Meditation on Communion with God.
Mirror, The.
My Heart Is in the East.
My Sweetheart's Dainty Lips.
Ode to Zion.
On Parting with Moses ibn Ezra.
Ophra.
Parting.
Pride of a Jew, The.
Sabbath, My Love.
Song of Loneliness.
Time-Servers.
To the Western Wind.
To Zion.
Words Wherein Stinging Bees Lurk.
Haley, Ed
While Strolling through the Park One Day.
Haley, Molly Anderson
"And Lo, the Star!"
Christmas Prayer, A.
"He Is Our Peace."
We Have Seen His Star in the East.
Haley, Vanessa
At the Smithsonian.
"Haliburton, Hugh." *See* **Robertson, James Logie**
Halkin, Shimon
Do Not Accompany Me.
Halkin, Shmuel
Drop of Dew, A.
Hall, Agnes Maxwel-. *See* **Maxwell-Hall, Agnes**
Hall, Amanda Benjamin
Great Farewells, The.
I'll Build My House.
It Seems That God Bestowed Somehow, *with music.*
Joe Tinker.
Joy o' Living.
Too Soon the Lightest Feet.
Wanderer, The.
Woman of Words, A.
Hall, Caroline Breese
Chicken Soup Therapy: Its Mode of Action.
Hall, Carolyn
Fireflies.
Hall, Charles Sprague
Glory Hallelujah! or, John Brown's Body, *at.*
Hall, Donald
Abroad Thoughts from Home.
Afternoon.
Airstrip in Essex, 1960, An.
Alligator Bride, The.
Apples.
Beautiful Horses, The.
Black Faced Sheep, The.
Blue Wing, The.
Body Politic, The.
Brain Cells, The.
Breasts.
By the Exeter River.
Child, The.
Christ Church Meadows, Oxford.
Christmas Eve in Whitneyville [1955].
Clown, The.
Cold Water.
Crew-Cuts.
Detroit.
Exile.
Farm, The.
Five Epigrams.
For an Early Retirement.
Foundation of American Industry, The.
Gold.
Henyard Round, The.
In the Old House.
Je Suis une Table.
Jealous Lovers, The.
Kicking the Leaves, *sel.*
Laocoon.
Long River, The.
Marriage.
Mirror.
Moon, The.
Morning Porches, The.
Munch's Scream.
My Son, My Executioner.
Names of Horses.
New Hampshire.
1934.
Old Pilot, The.
On a Horse Carved in Wood.
Ox Cart Man.
Philander.
Poet at Twenty, A.

Professor Gratt.
Questions [1] ("Why do you love her").
Questions [2] ("How is it now").
Raisin, The.
Reclining Figure.
Second Stanza for Dr. Johnson, A.
Self-Portrait, as a Bear.
Sestina: "Hang it all, Ezra Pound, there is only the one sestina!"
Shudder, The.
Six Poets in Search of a Lawyer.
Sleeping Giant, The.
Snow, The.
Sudden Things.
Swan.
T. R.
Three Movements, The.
To a Waterfowl.
Town of Hill, The.
Valentine.
Wedding Party.
Wells.
White Apples.
Wives, The.
Your voice on the telephone.

Hall, Eugene J.
Engineer's Story, The.

Hall, Gertrude
Angels.
Dust, The.
Mrs. Golightly.
My Old Counselor.

Hall, Gregory
Voice of the Power of This World, The.

Hall, Hattie Vose
Two Temples.

Hall, Hazel
Footsteps.
Foreboding.
June Night.
Late Winter.
Maker of Songs.
My Song.
Twilight.

Hall, Henry
Ballad on the Times, A.
On Sir John Fenwick.
Upon the King's Return from Flanders.

Hall, J. C.
Montgomery.

Hall, James Baker
Mad Farmer Stands Up in Kentucky for What He Thinks Is Right, The.
Modern Chinese History Professor Plays Pool Every Tuesday and Thursday, The.
Old Athens of the West Is Now a Blue Grass Tour, The.
Song of the Mean Mary Jean Machine, The.
Stafford in Kansas.

Hall, James Norman
Eat and Walk.

Hall, Janet Campbell
On a Catholic Childhood.
Salad La Raza.

Hall, Joan Joffe
Graffiti for Lovers.
Homeless, The.

Hall, John (1627–56)
Call, The.
Epicurean Ode, An.
On an Houre-glasse.
Pastoral [*or* Pastorall] Hymn, A.

Hall, John (b. 1943)
Dark Shadows.

Hall, Joseph
Prologue: "I first adventure, with foolhardy might."
Satire XII: Love-Sicke Poet, The.
Virgidemiarum, *sels.*

Hall, Katie V.
Old, Filthy Beer Pail, The.

Hall, Kay DeBard
Deer in Aspens.

Hall, Margaret S.
Life Is So Short.

Hall, Mary Lee
Turn Again to Life.

Hall, Owen
Tell Me Pretty Maiden; or, English Girls and Clerks, *with music.*

Hall, R. W.
Last Longhorn, The, *at.*

Hall, Radclyffe
Forgotten Island, *sel.*

Hall, Rodney
After a Sultry Morning.
Black Bagatelles, *sels.*
Eyewitness.
Lips and Nose.
Mrs. Macintosh.
My Coffin Is a Deckchair.
October.
Owner of My Face, The, *sels.*
Some Magnetism in the Sea.
Text for These Distracted Times, A.
They're Dying Just the Same in Station Homesteads.
Wedding Day at Nagasaki.
World Is a Musician's Cliff House, The.

Hall, Sharlot Mabridth
Arizona.
Away Out West.
Cash In.
In Old Tucson.
Last Camp-Fire, The.
Road Runner.
Song of the Colorado, The.
Two Bits.

Hall, Walter
That Brings Us to the Woodstove in the Wilds, at Night.

Hall, William
Auctioneer's Handbill, An.

Hallack, Cecily
Divine Office of the Kitchen, The.

Hallam, Arthur Henry
On the Picture of the Three Fates in the Palazzo Pitti, at Florence.

Halleck, Fitz-Greene
Alnwick Castle.
Burns.
Field of the Grounded Arms, The.
Joseph Rodman Drake.
Marco Bozzaris.
On His Friend, Joseph Rodman Drake.
On the Death of Joseph Rodman Drake.
Red Jacket.
Song: "There's a barrel of porter at Tammany Hall."

Halleck, Fitz-Greene *and* Joseph Rodman Drake **("The Croakers")**
Croaker Papers, The, *sels.*
Man Who Frets at Worldly Strife, The.
National Paintings, The.
Ode to Fortune.

Hallet, Mary
Calvary.

Hall-Evans, Jo Ann
Cape Coast Castle Revisted.
Seduction.

Halley, Anne
Against Dark's Harm.
Autograph Book/ Prophecy.
Housewife's Letter: To Mary.
O Doctor Dear My Love.
Pride of Ladies, A.

Hallock, C. Wiles
Braggin' Bill's Fortytude, *at.*

Halloran, Laurence Hynes
Animal Magnetism; the Pseudo-Philosopher Baffled.

Halperin, Mark
Concerning the Dead.

Halpern, Daniel
Arriving.
Dance, The.
Direction from Zulu.
Dutch April.
Epithalamium: "In the streets the crowds go about their business."
Ethnic Life, The.
Fish.
Gossip, The.
Hermit, The.
How to Eat Alone.
Hunt, The.
Landing, The.
Late.
Nude.
Portoncini dei Morti.
Return, Starting Out.
Snapshot of Hue.
Street Fire.
Summer, 1970.
Summer Rentals, The.

, Halpern, Leivick. *See* **Leivick, H.**

Halpern, Moishe Leib
Bird, The.
Considering the Bleakness.
Gingilee.
Go Throw Them Out.
Isaac Leybush Peretz.
Just Because.
Memento Mori.
My Portrait.
Restless as a Wolf.
Sacco-Vanzetti.
That's Our Lot.
Who.
Zlotchev, My Home.

Halpine, Charles Graham
Baron Renfrew's Ball.
Irish Astronomy.
Janette's Hair.
Lecompton's Black Brigade.
"Mr. Johnson's Policy of Reconstruction."
Sambo's Right to Be Kilt.
Song of Sherman's Army, The.

Halsall, Martyn
Return to Ararat.

"Halsham, John" (G. Forrester Scott)
My Last Terrier.

Ham, Marion Franklin
As Tranquil Streams, *with music.*
O Thou Whose Gracious Presence Shone, *with music.*
Prayer, A: "I pray not for the joy that knows."
Touch Thou Mine Eyes, *with music.*

Hambleton, Ronald
Comrades as We Rest Within.
Sockeye Salmon.
That Strain Again.

Hamblin, Robert W.
On the Death of the Evansville University Basketball Team in a Plane Crash, December 13, 1977.

Hamburger, Michael
At Staufen.
Blind Man.
Child Accepts, A.
Death of an Old Man, The.
Dostoievsky's Daughters.
Dual Site, The.
Epitaph for a Horseman.
Homage to the Weather.
In October.
Instead of a Journey.
Lines on Brueghel's *Icarus.*
London Tom-Cat.
Man of the World.
Mathematics of Love.
Memory.
Note-Book of a European Tramp, The, *sel.*
Omens.
Poet's Progress, A.

Search, The.
Security.
Song about Great Men, A.
Squares.
Hamelin, Jacques
Stonetalk.
Hamill, Gerry
It was far in the night and the bairnies grat.
Song of the GPO, A.
To His Coy Mistress, *parody.*
Hamill, Sam
Gnostology.
Reno, 2 A.M.
Wakening, The.
Hamilton, Alfred Starr
Wheat Metropolis.
Hamilton, Ann
Chanson d'Or.
Inscription: "It is not hard to tell of a rose."
Pause.
Hamilton, Anna Elizabeth
Hem of His Garment, The.
Hamilton, Bobb
America.
Poem to a Nigger Cop.
Hamilton, Cicely
March of the Women, The.
Non-Combatant.
Hamilton, Clayton
Lines Written on November 15, 1933 by a Man Born November 14, 1881 to Another Born November 15, 1881.
Hamilton, Elizabeth
My Ain Fireside.
Hamilton, George Rostrevor ("George Rostrevor")
Bodily Beauty.
Cell, The.
Don's Holiday.
Exchange.
Exile.
Imperfect Artist, The.
No Occupation.
Old Ox, The.
On a Distant Prospect of an Absconding Bookmaker.
On a Statue of Sir Arthur Sullivan.
Schoolmaster.
To the Greek Anthologists.
Hamilton, Harold
School of Sorrow, The.
Hamilton, Helen
Ghouls, The.
Romancing Poet, The.
Hamilton, Horace
Before Dawn.
Displacement.
Hamilton, Ian
Complaint.
Now and Then.
Pretending Not to Sleep.
Recruits, The.
Hamilton, John
Cold Blows the Wind.
Hamilton, Marion Ethel
Bird at Night.
Hamilton, Robert Browning
Along the Road.
Hamilton, William
Braes of Yarrow, The.
Hamlet, Frances Crosby
Our Flag.
Hamm, Timothy
Finding a Friend Home.
Hammarskjöld, Dag
Lord—Thine the Day.
Hammerstein, Oscar, II
All the Things You Are, *with music.*
June Is Bustin' Out All Over, *with music.*
Kansas City.
Money Isn't Everything!
Ol' Man River, *with music.*
There Is Nothin' like a Dame.
You've Got to Be Taught.
Hammon, Jupiter
Address to Miss Phillis Wheatley, An, *sel.*
Evening Thought, An.
Hammond, "Doc" *and* **Scott Judy.** *See* **Judy, Scott** *and* **"Doc" Hammond**
Hammond, Eleanor
April Fool.
From a Street Corner.
Valentine, A.
Hammond, Geraldine
Encounter.
Hammond, Karla M.
Expectancies: The Eleventh Hour.
Testing Ground.
Hammond, Mac
In Memory of V.R. Lang.
Hammond, William
Husbandry.
Man's Life.
Mutual Love.
Rose, The.
To Her Questioning His Estate.
Hamod, Sam
Anthropology in Fort Morgan, Colorado.
Hampl, Patricia
Artist Draws a Peach, An.
Blue Bottle.
Hamsun, Knut
Tora's Song.
Hanaford, Phoebe A.
Cast Thy Bread upon the Waters, *with music.*
Hanby, Benjamin Russel
Darling Nelly Gray.
Handley, Helen
Deer Hunt, Salt Lake Valley.
Handy, Nixeon Civille
Girl to Woman.
Handy, Will
Didn't He Ramble.
Handy, William Christopher
St. Louis Blues.
Hanes, Leigh
Deserts.
Old Fence Post.
Hanim, Leylâ
Let's get going.
Hanim, Nigâr
Tell Me Again.
Hankey, Katherine
I Love to Tell the Story.
Hankin, St. John Emile Clavering
Consolatory!
De Gustibus.
Editor's Tragedy, The.
Elegy on the Late King of Patagonia, An.
Soul-Severance.
Hanley, Katherine
After Vacation.
Hann, Isaac
After Reading the Life of Mrs. Catherine Stubbs in Isaac Ambrose's "War with the Devils."
Hanna, Tom
Tree Poem on My Wife's Birthday.
Hannay, Patrick
Philomela, the Nightningale, *sel.*
Hannigan, Des
Ben Alder 1963–1977.
Hannigan, Paul
Carnation, The.
Hanrahan, Agnes I.
Rosies.
Hanscombe, Gillian Eve
Jezebel: Her Progress, *sel.*
Hansen, Chadwick
Creator of Infinities, *with music.*
Hansen, Joseph
Dakota: Five Times Six.
Loved One, The.
Hanson, Amos
Schooner *Fred Dunbar*, The.
Trip to the Grand Banks, A.
Hanson, Howard G.
As Rocks Rooted.
That Is Not Indifference.
Hanson, Joseph Mills
Laramie Trail.
Springfield Calibre Fifty, The.
Hanson, Kenneth O.
Before the Storm.
Bouzouki.
First of All.
Lighting the Night Sky.
Nikos Painting.
Take It from Me.
West Lake.
Hanson, Pauline
And I Am Old to Know.
From Creature to Ghost.
So Beautiful Is the Tree of Night.
Hanson, Phyllis
Wisdom.
Hanzlicek, C. G.
One Song, The.
Hanzlik, Josef
Clap Your Hands for Herod.
Harada, Gail N.
First Winter.
New Year.
Painted Passages.
Pomegranate.
Harbaugh, Henry
Aloe Plant, The.
Jesus, I Live to Thee, *with music.*
Harbaugh, Thomas Chalmers
Trouble in the "Amen Corner."
Harbord, A. M.
At Euston.
Harburg, E. Y. ("Yip" Harburg)
Atheist.
Brother, Can You Spare a Dime?
Saint . . . He Ain't, A.
Hard, Walter
Medical Aid.
Hardeman, Louise
In Search of a Short Poem for My Grandmother.
Harden, Verna Loveday
Post Mortem.
When This Tide Ebbs.
Hardenberg, Friedrich von. *See* **"Novalis"**
Hardin, Glenn
Fools.
Harding, George
Reply to a Creditor.
Harding, Mike
Christmas 1914.
Harding, Ruth Guthrie
Call to a Scot, The.
Daffodils.
From a Car-Window.
Returning.
Surrender.
Threnody: "There's a grass-grown road from the valley."
Hardt, Ernst
Specter, The.
Hardy, Arthur Sherburne
Duality.
Immortality.
Iter Supremum.
Hardy, Elizabeth Clark
Some Time at Eve.
Hardy, Elizabeth Stanton
Echo.
Hardy, Evelyn
Certainty.
Hardy, Jane L.
Lincoln.
Hardy, John Edward
Voyeur.
Hardy, R. Wayne
Lone Biker, The.

Meeting Halfway.
October Hill.
Poem Written before Mother's Day for Mrs. Lopez from the South.
Wintering Moon, A.
Hardy, Thomas
Abbey Mason, The,
"According to the Mighty Working."
After a Journey.
After Jena.
After the Club-Dance.
After the Fair.
After the Last Breath.
After the Visit.
Afterwards.
Agnosto Theo (To an Unknown God).
Ah, Are You Digging on My Grave?
Albuera.
Ancient to Ancients, An.
"And There Was a Great Calm."
Anniversary, An.
Architectural Masks.
At a Hasty Wedding.
At a Watering Place.
At Casterbridge Fair, *sels.*
At Castle Boterel.
At Lulworth Cove a Century Back.
At the Altar-Rail.
At the Draper's.
August Midnight, An.
Backward Spring, A.
Bags of Meat.
Ballad-Singer, The.
Beauty, The, *sel.*
Beeny Cliff.
Before Life and After.
Before Waterloo.
Bereft.
Beyond the Last Lamp.
Bird-Scene at a Rural Dwelling, A.
Birds at Winter Nightfall.
Blinded Bird, The.
Boatman's Song, The.
Broken Appointment, A.
Budmouth Dears.
Bullfinches, The.
By Her Aunt's Grave.
Cardinal Bembo's Epitaph on Raphael.
Channel Firing.
Children and Sir Nameless, The.
Choirmaster's Burial, The.
Chorus: "Yea, the coneys are scared by the thud of hoofs."
Chorus of the Years.
Christmas Ghost-Story, A.
Christmas: 1924.
Church Romance, A.
Colonel's Soliloquy, The.
Comet at Yell'ham, The.
Commonplace Day, A.
Compassion.
Conformers, The.
Contretemps, The.
Convergence of the Twain, The; Lines on the Loss of the *Titanic.*
Country Wedding, The (A Fiddler's Story).
Curate's Kindness, The.
Curtains Now Are Drawn, The.
Dark-eyed Gentleman, The.
Darkling Thrush, The.
Dead and the Living One, The.
Dead Quire, The.
Dead "Wessex" the Dog to the Household.
Domicilium.
Dream-Follower, The.
Drizzling Easter Morning, A.
Drummer Hodge.
During Wind and Rain.
Dynasts, The, *sels.*
Embarcation.
Enemy's Portrait, The.
Epitaph: "I never cared for Life: Life cared for me."
Epitaph for George Moore.
Epitaph on a Pessimist.
Eve of Waterloo, The.
Exeunt Omnes.
Faded Face, The.
Faintheart in a Railway Train.
Fallow Deer at the Lonely House, The.
Farm-Woman's Winter, The.
Field of Talavera, The.
Field of Waterloo, The.
First or Last.
First Sight of Her and After.
Five Students, The.
For Life I Had Never Cared Greatly.
Former Beauties.
Friends Beyond.
Garden Seat, The.
God's Funeral.
Going, The.
Going and Staying.
Great Things.
Green Slates.
Hap.
Haunter, The.
He Abjures Love.
He Never Expected Much.
He Resolves to Say No More.
Heiress and Architect.
Her Dilemma.
Heredity.
His Immortality.
Horses Aboard.
House of Hospitalities, The.
How Great My Grief.
I Am the One.
I Found Her Out There.
I Look into My Glass.
I Looked Up from My Writing.
I Need Not Go.
I Said to Love.
I Say I'll Seek Her.
I watched a blackbird on a budding sycamore.
If It's Ever Spring Again.
If You Had Known.
Impercipient, The.
In a Cathedral City.
In a Museum.
In a Wood.
In Childbed.
In Church.
In Death Divided.
In Front of the Landscape.
In Tenebris.
In the Days of Crinoline.
In the Evening.
In the Moonlight.
In the Restaurant.
In the Servants' Quarters.
In the Vaulted Way.
In Time of "The Breaking of Nations."
Ivy-Wife, The.
Jezreel.
Jog-Trot Pair, A, *sel.*
Julie-Jane.
Lacking Sense, The.
Last Chrysanthemum, The.
Last Words to a Dumb Friend.
Lausanne.
Let Me Enjoy [(Minor Key)].
Levelled Churchyard, The.
Liddell and Scott; on the Completion of Their Lexicon.
Lines: To a Movement in Mozart's E-Flat Symphony.
Looking at a Picture on an Anniversary.
Lying Awake.
Man He Killed, The.
Marble-streeted Town, The.
Men Who March Away ("We be the King's men").
Men Who March Away ("What of the faith and fire within us").
Midnight on the Great Western.
Minute before Meeting, The.
Moments of Vision.
Mound, The.
Mute Opinion.
My Spirit Will Not Haunt the Mound.
Nature's Questioning.
Near Lanivet, 1872.
Necessitarian's Epitaph, A.
Neutral Tones.
New Year's Eve.
Newcomer's Wife, The.
Night of the Dance, The.
Night of Trafalgar, The.
1967.
No Buyers; a Street Scene.
Nobody Comes.
Old Furniture.
On a Fine Morning.
On an Invitation to the United States.
On Sturminster Foot-Bridge.
On the Departure Platform.
On the Doorstep.
On the Portrait of a Woman about to Be Hanged.
Once at Swanage.
One We Knew.
Overlooking the River Stour.
Oxen, The.
Pedigree, The.
Phantom Horsewoman, The.
Pity of It, The.
Placid Man's Epitaph, A.
Poet, A.
Popular Personage at Home, A.
Practical Woman, A.
Proud Songsters.
Puzzled Game Birds, The.
Rain on a Grave.
Refusal, A.
Regret not me.
Rejected Member's Wife, The.
Reminder, The.
Reminiscences of a Dancing Man.
Respectable Burgher, The.
Roman Road, The.
Rome.
Ruined Maid, The.
Sacrilege, The.
Satin Shoes, The.
Satires of Circumstance, I-XV.
Schreckhorn, The.
Self-Unseeing, The.
Selfsame Song, The.
Seventy-four and Twenty.
Shadow on the Stone, The.
She: At His Funeral.
She, to Him.
Sheep Fair, A.
Shelley's Skylark.
Shut Out That Moon.
Singer Asleep, A.
Snow in the Suburbs.
Souls of the Slain, The.
Statue of Liberty, The.
Stranger's Song, The.
Subalterns, The.
Sunshade, The.
Surview.
Tess's Lament.
This Summer and Last.
Thoughts of Phena [at News of Her Death].
Thunderstorm in Town, A.
To an Unborn Pauper Child.
To C. F. H. on Her Christening-Day.
To Lizbie Browne.
To Meets or Otherwise.
To the Moon.
Trafalgar.
Trampwoman's Tragedy, A.

Transformations.
Tree and the Lady, The.
Two Lips.
Unborn, The.
Under the Waterfall.
Voice, The.
Voices from Things Growing in a Churchyard.
Wagtail and Baby.
Waiting Both.
Walk, The.
Weathers.
Wessex Heights.
Wet August, A.
When I Set Out for Lyonnesse.
When Oats Were Reaped.
Where the Picnic Was.
Who's in the Next Room?
Why She Moved House.
Wife in London, A.
Winter in Durnover Field.
Wives in the Sere.
Workbox, The.
Year's Awakening, The.
You on the Tower.
Young Glass-Stainer, The.
Young Man's Epigram on Existence, A.
Your Last Drive.
Zermatt: To the Matterhorn.

Hare, Amory
Life.
Walking at Night.
Wet or Fine.

Hare, Maurice Evan
Determinism.
Limerick: "There once was a man [*or* There was a young man] who said, 'Damn!' "

Haresnape, Geoffrey
African Tramp, The.

Harford, David K.
From the Batter's Box.

Harford, Lesbia
Beauty and Terror.
Day's End.
Experience.
He Had Served Eighty Masters.
Revolution.
This Way Only.

Haring, Phyllis
Earth Asks and Receives Rain, The.
Foetus.
Forbidden, The.
Jungle.
Overture to Strangers.
Twin.

Harington, Donald
Villanelle, The: "Regard the motion of the villanelle."

Harington, Henry
Abbey Church at Bath, The.

Harington, John (*fl.* 1550)
Elegy Wrote in the Tower, 1554, *shorter vers.*
I See My Plaint, *at.*
Sonnet Made on Isabella Markham, A.

Harington [*or* Harrington], Sir John (1561-1612)
Against an Old Lecher.
Author, of His Own Fortune, The.
Author to His Wife, of a Woman's Eloquence, The.
Epigram: "Treason doth never prosper; what's the reason?"
Fair, Rich, and Young.
Hate and Debate Rome through the World Hath Spread.
Health Counsel.
In Roman.
Of a Fair Shrew.
Of a Zealous Lady.
Of an Heroical Answer of a Great Roman Lady to Her Husband.
Of Treason.
To My Lady Rogers, the Authors Wives Mother, How Doctor Sherwood Commended Her House in Bathe.

Harington, Lucy, Countess of Bedford
Elegy: "Death be not proud, thy hand gave not this blow."

Harjo, Joy
Anchorage.
Blanket around Her, The.
Blood-letting, The.
Conversations between Here and Home.
Crossing the Border into Canada.
Cuchillo.
Early Morning Woman.
Fire.
For Alva Benson, and for All Those Who Have Learned to Speak.
He Told Me His Name Was Sitting Bull.
I Am a Dangerous Woman.
Ice Horses.
It's the Same at Four A.M.
Last Song, The.
Moonlight.
Morning Once More.
New Orleans.
Noni Daylight Remembers the Future.
Obscene Phone Call #2.
Origins.
Remember.
Scholder Indian Poem, A.
She Had Some Horses.
She Was a Pretty Horse.
Someone Talking.
Talking to the Moon.
Talking to the Moon #002.
There Are Oceans.
There Was a Dance, Sweetheart.
Two Horses.
What Music.
Woman Hanging from the 13th Floor Window, The.
Your Phone Call at Eight A.M.

Harjo, Patty L. ("Ya-Ka-Nes")
Death.
Mask, The.
Taos Winter.
To an Indian Poet.
Where Have You Gone, Little Boy.
Wishes.

Harkavi, Hedva
It Was Gentle.
Talk to Me, Talk to Me.
Whenever the Snakes Come.

Harlow, S. Ralph
O Young and Fearless Prophet.

Harmon, William
Bureaucratic Limerick ("The Bureau of Labor Statistics").
Dawn Horse, A.
There.

Harney, Ben
Mister Johnson.
You've Been a Good Old Wagon, but You've Done Broke Down.

Harney, W. E.
West of Alice.

Harney, William Wallace
Adonais.
Stab, The.

Harnick, Sheldon
Merry Minuet, The.

Harper, Frances Ellen Watkins
Appeal to My Countrywomen, An.
Bury Me in a Free Land.
Crocuses, The.
Deliverance.
Double Standard, A.
Learning to Read.
Let the Light Enter.
Mission of the Flowers, The.
She's Free!
Slave Auction, The.
Vashti.

Harper, Michael S.
American History.
Barricades.
"Bird Lives": Charles Parker in St. Louis.
Blue Ruth: America.
Br'er Sterling and the Rocker.
Cannon Arrested.
Come Back Blues.
Dance of the Elephants, The.
Dark Way Home, The: Survivors.
Dear John, Dear Coltrane.
Deathwatch.

"Hashimura Togo." *See* **Irwin, Wallace**
Debridement: Operation Harvest Moon: *On Repose.*
Effendi.
Elvin's Blues.
Grandfather.
Here Where Coltrane Is.
Homage to the New World.
Ice-fishing House, The: Long Lake, Minnesota.
Kin.
Landfill.
Last Affair: Bessie's Blues Song.
Love Medley: Patrice Cuchulain.
Mahalia.
Martin's Blues.
Mother Speaks, A: The Algiers Motel Incident, Detroit.
Newsletter from My Mother.
Nightmare Begins Responsibility.
Photographs: A Vision of Massacre.
Poetry Concert.
Reuben, Reuben.
We Assume: On the Death of Our Son, Reuben Masai Harper.

Harpur, Charles
Bush Justice.
Coast View, A, *sel.*
Creek of the Four Graves, The, *sels.*
Love Sonnets, VIII.
Marvellous Martin.
Midsummer Noon in the Australian Forest, A.
Temple of Infamy, The, *sel.*
Tower of the Dream, The, *sel.*
Words.

Harr, Barbara
Walking through a Cornfield in the Middle of Winter I Stumble over a Cow Pie and Think of the Sixties Press.

"Harriet Annie"
Death of Gaudentis

Harrigan, Ed [*or* Ned]
Mulligan Guard, The, *with music.*
Walking for That Cake, *with music.*

Harrigan, Edward
My Dad's Dinner Pail.

Harrigan, Stephen
Over to God.

Harriman, Dorothy
Cat on the Porch at Dusk.

Harrington, Edward
Bushrangers, The.
Morgan.
My Old Black Billy.

Harrington, John. *See* **Harington, John**
Harrington, Sir John. *See* **Harington, Sir John**

Harrington, Michael
Gazeteer of Newfoundland.
Second Iron Age, The.

Harris, Benjamin
Account of the Cruelty of the Papists, An.
God save the King, that King that sav'd the land.
Of the French Kings Nativity.

Harris, Charles Kassell
After the Ball Is Over, *with music.*
Break the News to Mother.

Harris, Hazel Harper
Sailor's Song, A.

Harris, Joel Chandler
My Honey, My Love.

Plough-Hands' Song, The.
Revival Hymn.
Uncle Remus and His Friends, *sels.*
Harris, Louise
You Are Growing into My Life.
Harris, Louise Dyer
Crossing Boston Common.
Review of a Cook Book.
Harris, Marguerite
My Sun-killed Tree.
Harris, Max
Martin Buber in the Pub.
Tantanoola Tiger, The.
Harris, Michael
Ice Castle, The.
Harris, Norman
Fable: "There is an inevitability."
Harris, Phyllis. *See* **Beauvais, Phyllis**
Harris, Sydney Justin
I Come to Bury Caesar.
Harris, Thomas Lake
Fledglings.
Sea-Sleep.
Harris, William J.
For Bill Hawkins, a Black Militant.
Frightened Flower.
Give Me Five.
Grandfather Poem, A.
Hey Fella Would You Mind Holding This Piano a Moment.
Historic Moment, An.
Modern Romance.
On Wearing Ears.
Practical Concerns.
Rib Sandwich.
They Live in Parallel Worlds.
Truth Is Quite Messy, The.
We Live in a Cage.
Why Would I Want.
Harrison, Ada M.
New Year, 1916.
Harrison, De Leon
Collage for Richard Davis, A—Two Short Forms.
Room, The.
Seed of Nimrod, The.
Some Days/ Out Walking Above.
Yellow.
Harrison, Eugene M.
Soul Winner's Prayer, The.
Harrison, Henry Sydnor
Osculation.
Harrison, James
Easier.
Eve's Version.
Harrison, Janet E.
Lament of a Last Letter.
Harrison, Jim
After the Anonymous Swedish.
After the "invitation" by the preacher she collapsed in the.
Drinking Song.
Fair/ Boy Christian Takes a Break.
Ghazals, *sels.*
Horse.
Locations.
Poem: "Form is the woods: the beast."
Returning at Night.
Sketch for a Job Application Blank.
Sound.
Suite to Fathers.
Trader.
Traverse City Zoo.
Harrison, Sam
After the Show.
Chez Madame.
Journey.
Meeting.
Poem: "This room is very old and very wise."
Rain.
Harrison, Sam G.
Fisherman, The.
Harrison, Susan Frances ("Seranus")
At St. Jerome.
Chateau Papineau.
Harrison, Tony
Bedbug, The.
Hands, The.
Schwiegermutterlieder.
Harrison, Virginia Bioren
Music of the Dawn.
One Gift I Ask.
Harrison, William
In Praise of Laudanum.
Harrod, Elizabeth B.
August Night, 1953.
Calvinist Autumnal.
Sonnet against the Too-Facile Mystic.
Summer Afternoon.
"Harry"
Feet.
Harsen, Una W.
Litany for Old Age, A.
Prayer before Meat.
Harsent, David
Old Photographs.
Hart, Elizabeth Anna
Mother Tabbyskins.
Sweeping the Skies.
Hart, James
Blemishes.
Hart, Joanne
I Walk on the River at Dawn.
When Your Parents Grow Old.
Hart, John
Confrontation.
Hart, Lorenz
Blue Room, The.
Lady Is a Tramp, The.
Manhattan.
Most Beautiful Girl in the World, The.
Mountain Greenery.
My Heart Stood Still, *with music.*
Harte, Bret (Francis Bret Harte)
Aged Stranger, The.
Arctic Vision, An.
At the Hacienda.
Caldwell of Springfield.
Chicago.
Chiquita.
Colenso Rhymes for Orthodox Children.
Coyote.
Crotalus.
Dickens in Camp.
Dow's Flat.
Further Language from Truthful James.
Ghost That Jim Saw, The.
Greyport Legend, A.
Grizzly.
Guild's Signal.
Heathen Chinee, The.
Her Letter.
Jessie ("Jessie is both young and fair").
Jim.
John Burns of Gettysburg.
Madroño.
Mission Bells of Monterey, The.
Mrs. Judge Jenkins [Being the Only Genuine Sequel to "Maud Muller"], *parody.*
Mountain Heart's-Ease, The.
Personified Sentimental, The.
Plain Language from Truthful James ("Which I wish to remark").
Ramon.
Relieving Guard.
Reveille, The.
San Francisco from the Sea.
Schemmelfennig.
Second Review of the Grand Army, A.
Society upon the Stanislaus, The.
Swiss Air.
Tale of a Pony, The.
That Heathen Chinee.
To a Sea-Bird.
Truthful James.
What the Bullet Sang.
What the Engines Said.
Willows, The.
Harte, Walter
Enchanted Region, The; or, Mistaken Pleasures.
Hartford, John
Poor Old Prurient Interest Blues, The.
Hartigan, Patrick Joseph ("John O'Brien")
Said Hanrahan.
Tangmalangaloo.
Hartman, Charles O.
Inflation.
Trading Chicago.
Hartmann von Aue
None Is Happy.
Hartnett, Michael
All the Death-Room Needs.
Death of an Irishwoman.
Domestic Scene.
Enamoured of the Miniscule.
Farewell to English, A, *sel.*
For My Grandmother, Bridgid [*or* Bridget] Halpin.
I Have Exhausted the Delighted Range.
I Think Sometimes.
Retreat of Ita Cagney, The.
Small Farm, A.
Sonnet: "I saw magic on a green country road."
Hart-Smith, William
Christopher Columbus, *sels.*
Cipangu.
Comes Fog and Mist.
Departure.
Otters.
Rhinoceros.
Space.
Waterspout, The.
Wild Geese.
Hartsough, Lewis
Come, Friends and Neighbors, Come, *with music.*
Let Me Go Where Saints Are Going, *with music.*
Harvey, Christopher
Comfort in Extremity.
Harvey, Frederick William
Ducks.
November.
Prisoners.
Sleepers, The.
Harvey, Gayle Elen
Tonight When You Leave.
We Are Leaning Away.
Harvey, J. E.
Forgetting God.
Harvey, Richard
Two Lovers, The.
Harwood, Gwen
At the Sea's Edge.
Carnal Knowledge.
Father and Child.
In the Park.
Last Meeting.
Lion's Bride, The.
New Music.
Night Thoughts: Baby & Demon.
Panther and Peacock.
Prize-giving.
Second Life of Lazarus, The.
Suburban Sonnet.
Harwood, Lee
Final Painting, The.
Rain Journal: London: June 65.
Soft White.
"Utopia," The.
Words, The.
Harwood, Ruth
Shoe Factory, The.
"Hashimura Togo." *See* **Irwin, Wallace**
Hashin
Loneliness.

No Sky at All.
Hashmi, Alamgir
"Banquet of the Century, The" in Persepolis.
Haskell, Jefferson
My Latest Sun Is Sinking Fast, *with music.*
Haskins, Minnie Louise
Gate of the Year, The, *sel.*
Hass, Robert
After the Gentle Poet Kobayashi Issa.
Against Botticelli.
Apple Trees at Olema, The.
Child Naming Flowers.
Churchyard.
Fall.
Feast, The.
Harbor at Seattle, The.
In Weather.
January.
Late Spring.
Maps.
Measure.
Meditation at Lagunitas.
Museum.
Old Dominion.
On the Coast near Sausalito.
Origin of Cities, The.
Palo Alto; the Marshes.
Paschal Lamb.
Return of Robinson Jeffers, The.
Rusia en 1931.
San Pedro Road.
Song: "Afternoon cooking in the fall sun."
Songs to Survive the Summer.
Spring Drawing II.
Story about the Body, A.
Tall Windows.
Weed.
Hassall, Christopher Vernon
Santa Claus.
Hassan, Mahammed Abdille
Denunciation, A.
To a Friend Going on a Journey.
Hassler, Donald M.
Fishing Lines.
Haste, Gwendolen
Montana Wives.
Tomorrow Is a Birthday.
Hastings, Fanny de Groot
Late Comer.
Hastings, Maria
Sing, Little Bird.
Hastings, Thomas
Exhortation.
Hail to the Brightness of Zion's Glad Morning, *with music.*
In Sorrow.
Jesus, Merciful and Mild! *with music.*
Latter Day, The.
Now Be the Gospel Banner, *with music.*
Now from Labor and from Care, *with music.*
Hatch, Francis Whiting
He Laughed Last.
So This Is Middle Age!
Hatfield, Edwin Francis
Hallelujah! Praise the Lord, *with music.*
Hathaway, Baxter
Again My Fond Circle of Doves.
Gorilla, The.
Hathaway, Jeanine
Conversation with God.
Extensions of Linear Mobility.
In Random Fields of Impulse and Repose.
Reflections on a Womb Which Is Called "Vacant."
World Enough.
Hathaway, William
Antistrophe.
Apology for E. H.
Coloring Margarine.
Gold Factory, The.
In Dead Air, under Furious Sun.
Liar Rumplestiltskin Loves.
Rumplestiltskin Poems, *sels.*
Hatshepsut
Now my heart turns to and fro.
Obelisk Inscriptions, *sel.*
Hatton, Joseph
Christmas Bills.
Hatun, Mihri. *See* **Mihri Hatun**
Haug, James
Long Season, The.
Hauk, Barbara
Getting Older Here.
Hauroa, Matangi
Lament: "I lie in darkness, as the dead shades gather."
Hausgen, Mattie Lee
Her Favorites.
Hausman, Gerald
Poem for Lorry.
Havens, Mrs.
Ask, and Ye Shall Receive.
Havergal, Frances Ridley
Afterwards.
Another Year.
Another Year Is Dawning.
At the Portal.
For Every Day.
God Is Faithful.
Happy Christmas, A.
Life-Mosaic.
New Year Wish, A.
New Year's Wishes.
Reality.
Take My Life and Let It Be.
Teacher's Prayer, A.
Thou Art Coming!
Haweis, Hugh Reginald
Homeland, The.
Hawes, Stephen
Dame Music.
Epitaph: "O mortal folk, you may behold and see."
Epitaph of [La] Grande Amoure, The.
His Epitaph.
Pair of Wings, A.
Palace of Pleasure, The.
Passetyme, The.
Pastime of Pleasure, The, *sels.*
Seven Deadly Sins, The.
Time and Eternity.
True Knight, The.
Hawker, Robert Stephen
Aishah Schechinah.
And Shall Trelawny Die?
Are They Not All Ministering Spirits?
Aunt Mary.
Butterfly, The.
Christ-Cross Rhyme, A.
Cornish Emigrant's Song, The.
Datur Hora Quieti.
Death Song.
Doom-Well of St. Madron, The.
Featherstone's Doom.
First Fathers, The.
"I Am the Resurrection and the Life," Saith the Lord!
King Arthur's Waes-hael.
Legend of the Hive, A.
Morwennæ Statio.
Mystic Magi, The.
Poor Man and His Parish Church, The.
Quest of the Sangraal, The, *sels.*
Silent Tower of Bottreaux, The.
Song of the Western Men, The.
Southern Cross, The.
Hawkes, Henry Warburton
Amid the Din of Earthly Strife.
Hawkins, Henry
Bee, The.
Hoc Cygno Vinces.
Hawkins, Lucy
To L. C.
Hawkins, Walter Everette
Death of Justice, The.
Spade Is Just a Spade, A.
Hawkins, William
New Light, A.
Spring Rain.
To a Worm Which the Author Accidentally Trode Upon.
Wall, The.
Hawkshaw, Ann
Little Raindrops, *at.*
Hawley, Charles B.
My Little Love.
Hawley, Richard A.
January.
Hawley, W. F.
Love Song, A: "Yes, I will love thee when the sun."
Hawling, Francis
Author Consults a Critic and Sells His Manuscript, The.
Signal, The; or, A Satire against Modesty, *sel.*
Hawthorn, John
Deathbed, A.
Journey and Observations of a Countryman, The, *sel.*
On His Writing Verses.
"Hawthorne, Alice." *See* **Winner, Septimus**
Hawthorne, Hildegarde
Song, A: "Sing me a sweet, low song of night."
Hawthorne, Julian
Were-Wolf.
Hawthorne, Nathaniel
Star of Calvary, The.
Hay, Clarence Leonard
Down and Out.
"Hay, Elijah." *See* **Seiffert, Marjorie Allen**
Hay, George Campbell
Flooer o the Gean.
Old Fisherman, The.
Song: "Day will rise and the sun from eastward."
Sonnet: "Beckie, my luve!—What is't, ye twa-faced tod?"
Still Gyte, Man?
Two Neighbours, The.
Hay, John (b. 1915)
Aboriginal Sin.
And Grow.
Bird Song.
Chickadees, The.
December Storm.
Defend Us, Lord, from Every Ill, *with music.*
Energy of Light, The.
Life Must Burn.
Music by the Waters.
Natural Architecture.
Old Man of Tennessee.
Railway Station.
Sent Ahead.
Silver Leaf, The.
Storm, The.
Town Meeting.
Variations on a Theme.
Hay, John Milton (1838–1905)
Christine.
Enchanted Shirt, The.
Good Luck and Bad ("Good luck is the gayest of all gay girls").
Jim Bludso [of the Prairie Belle].
Liberty.
Little Breeches.
Miles Keogh's Horse.
Not in Dumb Resignation.
Pledge at Spunky Point, The.
Religion and Doctrine.
Stirrup Cup, The.
Surrender of Spain, The.
Thy Will Be Done.
What is a first love worth except to prepare for a second?
White Flag, The.

Woman's Love, A.
Hay, Sara Henderson
Ballad of the Golden Bowl.
Benefactors, The.
"Bottle Should Be Plainly Labeled 'Poison.' "
Christmas, the Year One, A.D.
Daily Manna, The.
Daily Paradox.
Interview.
Juvenile Court.
Marriage, The.
Name, The.
On Being Told That One's Ideas Are Victorian.
One of the Seven Has Somewhat to Say.
Prayer in April.
Princess, The.
Rapunzel.
Sleeper, The.
Hayakawa, Samuel Ichiye
To One Elect.
Hayden, Joe
Hot Time in the Old Town, A.
Hayden, Robert Earl
Aunt Jemima of the Ocean Waves.
Baha'u'llah in the Garden of Ridwan.
Ballad for Sue Ellen Westerfield, The.
Ballad of Nat Turner, The.
Ballad of Remembrance, A.
Ballad of Sue Ellen Westerfield, The.
Beginnings, *sel.*
Crispus Attucks.
Diver, The.
El-Hajj Malik El-Shabazz.
Frederick Douglass.
Full Moon.
Homage to the Empress of the Blues.
In the Mourning Time.
Incense of the Lucky Virgin.
Kid.
Locus.
Middle Passage.
Mourning Poem for the Queen of Sunday.
" 'Mystery Boy' Looks for Kin in Nashville."
Night, Death, Mississippi.
Night-blooming Cereus, The.
O Daedalus, Fly Away Home.
Paul Laurence Dunbar.
Peacock Room, The.
Plague of Starlings, A.
Richard Hunt's Arachne.
Road in Kentucky, A.
Runagate Runagate.
Sojourner Truth.
Stars.
Sub Specie Aeternitatis.
"Summertime and the Living."
Those Winter Sundays.
Tour 5.
Unidentified Flying Object.
Veracruz.
Wheel, The.
Whipping, The.
Witch Doctor.
Words in the Mourning Time, *sel.*
Hayes, Alfred
Angel, The.
City of Beggars, The.
Death of the Craneman, The.
Epistle to the Gentiles.
Joe Hill.
Nice Part of Town, A.
Slaughter-House, The.
Hayes, Donald Jeffrey
After All.
Alien.
Appoggiatura.
Auf Wiedersehen.
Benediction.
Confession.
Haven.
Inscription: "He wrote upon his heart."
Night.
Nocturne: "Softly blow lightly."
Pastourelle.
Poet.
Prescience.
Threnody: "Let happy throats be mute."
"Hayes, Evelyn" (Mary Ursula Bethell)
Garden-Lion.
Hayes, J. Milton
Green Eye of the Yellow God, The.
Hayes, James M.
Our Lady of the Skies.
Hayes, John Russell
Old-fashioned Garden, The.
Hayes, Nancy M.
Shiny Little House, The.
Hayford, Gladys May Casely (Aquah Laluah)
Baby Cobina.
Nativity.
Rainy Season Love Song.
Serving Girl, The.
Shadow of Darkness.
Hayford, James
Horn.
In a Closed Universe.
Overseer of the Poor.
Resident Worm, The.
Under All This Slate.
Hayley, William
Card of Invitation to Mr. Gibbon, at Brighthelmstone, 1781, A.
Hayman, Jane
Murdered Girl Is Found on a Bridge, The.
Hayman, Robert
Mad Answer of a Madman, A.
Of the Great and Famous Ever to Be Honoured Knight, Sir Francis Drake [and of My Little-Little Selfe].
Pleasant Life in Newfoundland, The.
Hayne, Paul Hamilton
Aspects of the Pines.
Battle of Charleston Harbor, The.
Between the Sunken Sun and the New Moon.
Beyond the Potomac.
Butler's Proclamation.
Charleston.
In Harbor.
Little While I Fain Would Linger Yet, A.
Macdonald's Raid.
Pre-Existence.
Rose and the Thorn, The.
South Carolina to the States of the North.
Storm in the Distance, A.
Stricken South to the North, The.
True Heaven, The.
Vicksburg.
Yorktown Centennial Lyric.
Hayne, William Hamilton
Autumn Breeze, An.
Charge at Santiago, The.
Cyclone at Sea, A.
Exiles.
Moonlight Song of the Mocking-Bird.
Night Mists.
Sea Lyric, A.
Sleep and His Brother Death.
Southern Snow-Bird, The.
To a Cherokee Rose.
Yule Log, The.
Haynes, Albert E., Jr.
Law, The.
Haynes, Carol
Any Wife or Husband.
Aunt Selina.
Haynes, Renée
Ingenious Raconteur.
Hays, Hoffman Reynolds
Age?
Case, The.
For One Who Died Young.
January.
Manhattan.
Sacred Children, The.
Hays, Lee
Talking Union.
Hays, Lee *and* **Claude Williams.** *See* **Williams, Claude** *and* **Lee Hays**
Hays, Lee, Millard Lampell, *and* Pete Seeger. *See* **Seeger, Pete, Millard Lampell** *and* **Lee Hays**
Hays, Will S.
O'Grady's Goat.
Hayward, William
Five Birds Rise.
Hazard, Caroline
Great Swamp Fight, The.
In Shadow.
Hazard, James
To the Carp, and Those Who Hunt Her.
Hazlewood-Brady, Anne
Closer First to Earth.
Double Axe, The.
Hazo, Samuel
After the Hurricane.
God and Man.
Maps for a Son Are Drawn as You Go.
Next Time You Were There, The.
Skycoast.
Head, Gwen
Slug.
Stinging Nettle.
Healy, Eloise Klein
Dark.
Los Angeles.
My Love Wants to Park.
What Is Being Forgotten.
Healy, Ian
Advice from a Nightwatchman.
Air Shaft.
Poems from the Coalfields, *sels.*
Healy, Patrick
My Wishes.
Heaney, Seamus
Advancement of Learning, An.
At a Potato Digging.
Badgers, The.
Barn, The.
Blackberry-picking.
Bog Queen.
Bogland.
Cana Revisited.
Casualty.
Constable Calls, A.
Death of a Naturalist.
Digging.
Docker.
Dream of Jealousy, A.
Drink of Water, A.
Early Purges, The.
England's Difficulty.
Exposure.
Follower.
Gifts of Rain.
Given Note, The.
Glanmore Sonnets, *sels.*
Grauballe Man, The.
Gravities.
Guttural Muse, The.
In Small Townlands.
Kinship.
Limbo.
Linen Town.
Mid-Term Break.
Mossbawn: Two Poems in Dedication.
Mother.
Mother of the Groom.
New Song, A.
Northern Hoard, A, *sel.*
Otter, The.
Outlaw, The.
Personal Helicon.
Play Way, The.
Postcard from North Antrim, A.
Punishment.
Requiem for the Croppies.

Rite of Spring.
Singer's House, The.
Skunk, The.
Song: "Rowan like a lip-sticked girl, A."
Storm on the Island.
Strand at Lough Beg, The.
Summer Home.
Sunlight.
Thatcher.
Tollund Man, The.
Traditions.
Triptych.
Trout.
Twice Shy.
Valediction: "Lady with the frilled blouse."
Viking Dublin; Trial Pieces.
Wanderer, The.
Waterfall.
Whatever You Say Say Nothing.
Wife's Tale, The.

Heap, Jane
Where go the birds when the rain.

Heard, Lillian G.
Humble Service.

Hearn, Bonnie
Dinosaur.

Hearn, Mary Ann. *See* **"Farningham, Marianne"**

Hearn, Michael Patrick
In the Library.
Rhinos Purple, Hippos Green.

Hearst, James
Behind the Stove.
Dragon Lesson.
Hard Way to Learn.
New Calf, The.
Pause between Clock Ticks.

Heath, Ella
Poetry.

Heath, Gertrude E.
Merry Crocodile, The.

Heath, Robert
On Clarastella Singing.
On Clarastella Walking in Her Garden.
On the Unusual Cold and Rainie Weather in the Summer, 1648.
Seeing Her Dancing.
Song in a Siege.
To Clarastella on St. Valentines Day Morning.
You say you love me, nay, can swear it too.
These Women All.

Heath, William
Cold Feet in Columbus.
Women.

Heath-Stubbs, John
Address Not Known.
Artorius, *sels.*
Beggar's Serenade.
Carol for Advent.
Charm against the Toothache, A.
Churchyard of St. Mary Magdalene, Old Milton.
Dark Planet, The.
Death of Digenes Akritas, The.
December: Prayer to St. Nicholas.
Ecclesiastical Chronicle, An, *sel.*
Epitaph: "Mr. Heath-Stubbs as you must understand."
February.
Ghost in the Cellarage, The.
Gifts, The.
History of the Flood, The.
Ibycus.
January.
Lady's Complaint, The.
Mozart.
Not Being Oedipus.
Old King, The.
Poet of Bray, The.
Poetry Today.
Preliminary Poem.
Send for Lord Timothy.
Titus and Berenice.
To a Poet a Thousand Years Hence.
Two Men in Armour.
Unpredicted, The.
Valse Oubliée.
Virgin and Unicorn.
Virgin Martyrs.
Winter Cricket.

Heaton, John Langdon
Sea Irony.

Heavysege, Charles
Count Filippo, *sels.*
Dead, The.
How Great unto the Living Seem the Dead!
Jephthah's Daughter, *sel.*
Malzah's Song.
Night.
Saul, *sels.*
Stars Are Glittering in the Frosty Sky, The.
Winter Galaxy, The.
Zaph Describes the Haunts of Malzah.

Heber, Reginald
Brightest and Best of the Sons of the Morning.
By Cool Siloam's Shady Rill.
From Greenland's Icy Mountains.
Holy, Holy, Holy.
Hymn: "Brightest and best of the sons of the morning."
If Thou Wert by My Side, My Love.
Providence.
Son of God Goes Forth to War, The.
Sympathy.
Thrice Holy.
Who Follows in His Train?

Hebert, Albert J., Jr.
Heart for All Her Children.

Hébert, Annabelle
Dream about Sunsets.

Hébert, Anne
Alchemy of Day, The.
Bread Is Born.
Crown of Happiness.
Great Fountains, The.
Life in the Castle.
Offended, The.
Our Hands in the Garden.
Skinny Girl, The.
Someone Could Certainly Be Found.
Spring over the City.
Tomb of the Kings, The.
Wooden Chamber, The.

Hecht, Anthony
Adam.
Alceste in the Wilderness.
Application for a Grant.
Behold the Lilies of the Field.
Birdwatchers of America.
Clair de Lune.
Cost, The.
Dover Bitch, The.
Drinking Song.
End of the Weekend, The.
Epitaph: "Here lies a poet, briefly known as Hecht."
Feast of Stephen, The.
Fifth Avenue Parade.
Firmness.
From the Grove Press.
Ghost in the Martini, The.
Gift of Song, The.
Going the Rounds; a Sort of Love Poem.
Hill, A.
Improvisations on Aesop.
"It Out-Herods Herod. Pray You, Avoid It."
Japan.
Jason.
La Condition Botanique.
Letter, A.
Lizards and Snakes.
Lot of Night Music, A.
Man Who Married Magdalene, The: Variation on a Theme by Louis Simpson.
"More Light! More Light!"
Old Malediction, An.
Origin of Centaurs, The.
Ostia Antica.
Pig.
Place of Pain in the Universe, The.
Samuel Sewall.
Sestina d'Inverno.
Tarantula or the Dance of Death.
Third Avenue in Sunlight.
Transparent Man, The.
Upon the Death of George Santayana.
Vice.
Vow, The.

Hector, Mary Louise
Whatsoever I Do.

Hedge, Frederic Henry
Sovereign and Transforming Grace, *with music.*

Hedges, Doris
Onwardness.
Poet's Protest.
Prayer: "O God of goodness, forwardness, and fulness."

Hedin, Mary
On Rears.

Hedin, Robert
Wreck of the Great Northern, The.

Hedylos
Seduced Girl.
To Venus.

Heffernan, Michael
Daffodils.
Kennedy.
Naked War.
Putting On My Shoes I Hear the Floor Cry Out beneath Me.
Sunday Service.
Table, The.

Heginbothom, Ottiwell
Great God, let all my tuneful pow'rs.

Heguri, Lady
Parting.

Heide, Florence Parry
Rocks.
What's That?

Heidenstam, Verner von
Fellow-Citizens.
Home.
How Easily Men's Cheeks Are Hot.

Heikel, Karin Alice. *See* **"Vala, Katri"**

Heimler, Eugene
After an Eclipse of the Sun.
Psalm: "Oh Lord, I have been staring into a mirror."

Hein, Piet
Lilac Time.

Heine, Heinrich
Ad Finem.
And When I Lamented.
Anno 1829.
Asra, The.
At Parting.
Auf meiner Herzliebsten Äugelein.
Azra, The.
Babylonian Sorrows.
Beating Heart, The.
Best Religion, The.
By the Waters of Babylon.
Coffin, The.
Dear Maiden.
Dearest Friend, Thou Art in Love.
Du bist wie eine Blume.
Enfant perdu.
Epilog: "Like the ears of wheat in a wheat-field growing."
Epilogue: "Like the stalks of wheat in the fields."
Es fällt ein Stern herunter.
Es stehen unbeweglich.
Evening Twilight.
Farewell: "Linden blossomed, the nightingale sang, The."
Fichtenbaum Steht Einsam, Ein.

Fresco-Sonnets to Christian Sethe.
Good Fortune.
Healing the Wound.
Hebrew Melodies, *sel.*
Heimkehr, Die, *sels.*
Homeward Bound, *sels.*
How Slowly Time, the Loathsome Snail.
I, a Most Wretched Atlas.
I Close Her Eyes.
I Love But Thee.
I Met by Chance.
I Wept as I Lay Dreaming.
Ich Weiss Nicht Was Soll es Bedeuten.
If, Jerusalem, I Ever Should Forget Thee.
I'm Black and Blue.
Im Traum sah ich ein Männchen klein und putzig.
Katharine.
Kings from the East, The.
Lassie, What Mair Wad You Hae?
Lorelei.
Love's Résumé.
Mädchen mit dem rothen Mündchen.
Maiden Lies in Her Chamber, A.
Mein Herz, mein Herz ist traurig.
Mein Kind, Wir Waren Kinder.
Mein Liebchen, wir sassen zusammen.
Message, The.
Migratory Rats, The.
Mir träumte von einem Königskind.
Mir träumte wieder der alte Traum.
Mond ist aufgegangen, Der.
Morning After, The.
Morphine.
Mortal, Sneer Not at the Devil.
My Beauty, My Love, You Have Bound Me.
My Heart, My Heart Is Mournful.
My Songs Are Poisoned ("My songs, they say, are poisoned").
New Jewish Hospital at Hamburg, The.
Night by the Sea, A.
North Sea, The, *sels.*
Oh Lovely Fishermaiden.
Precaution.
Princess Sabbath.
Proem: "Out of my own great woe."
Rose, the Lily, the Sun and the Dove, The.
Sag' Mir Wer Einst die Uhren Erfund.
Sag', wo ist dein schönes Liebchen.
Sea Hath Its Pearls, The.
Shadow-Love.
Silesian Weavers, The.
Solomon.
Song: "There stands a lonely pine-tree."
Song of Songs, The.
Song of the Vivandière.
Songs to Seraphine, *sels.*
Sonnet to My Mother, A.
Spruce Is Standing Lonely, A.
Storm, The.
Tannhäuser, *sel.*
This White and Slender Body.
This World and This Life Are So Scattered, They Try Me.
Thou Hast Diamonds.
Three Holy Kings from Morgenland.
Three Sweethearts.
To Angélique, *sel.*
To Edom.
To My Mother.
Twilight.
Voyage, The.
Warum sind denn die Rosen so blass.
Waves Gleam in the Sunshine, The.
We Cared for Each Other.
Weavers.
When Two Are Parted.
When Young Hearts Break.
Who Was It, Tell Me.
Wie langsam kriechet sie dahin.
Window-Glance, The.
Wise Men Ask the Children the Way, The.
Young Man Loves a Maiden, A.
Your Snow-white Shoulder.
Zu fragmentarisch ist Welt und Leben.

Heinrich von Rugge
He That Loves a Rosy Cheek.

Helburn, Theresa
Mother.

"Helen"
Another Cynical Variation.

Helen, Sister Mary
Identity.

Heller, Binem
Pesach Has Come to the Ghetto Again.

Hellyer, Jill
Calculating Female.

Helmer, Charles D.
Battle of Oriskany, The.

Helmling, Steven
Two Weeks after an April Frost.

Helmore, Thomas
Christmas Carol: "Christ was born on Christmas day."

Helphingtine, Mary J.
Blessings of Surrender, The.

Helsley, Shel
Christ Alone.

Helton, Roy
Glimpses.
In Passing.
Lonesome Water.
Old Christmas Morning.

Helwig, David
Considerations.
Dead Weasel, A.
Drunken Poem.
For Edward Hicks.
Words from Hell.

Hemans, Felicia Dorothea
Agony in the Garden, The.
Brereton Omen, The, *sel.*
Casabianca.
Child's First Grief, The.
Cid's Rising, The.
Corinne at the Capitol.
Death-Hymn, A.
Dirge: "Calm on the bosom of thy God."
England's Dead.
Fairy Song.
First Grief, The.
Foliage.
Graves of a Household, The.
He Never Smiled Again.
Homes of England, The.
Hour of Death, The.
Hymn for Christmas.
Indian Woman's Death-Song.
Landing of the Pilgrim Fathers [in New England], The.
Memorial Pillar, The.
Orange Bough, The.
Prayer, A: "Father in Heaven! from whom the simplest flower."
Properzia Rossi.
Siege of Valencia, The, *sel.*
To the Poet Wordsworth.
Where Is the Sea?

Hemenway, Abby Maria ("Marie Josephine")
Annunciation Night.
Mary of Nazareth, *sel.*

Hemingway, Ernest
Champs d'Honneur.
Chapter Heading.
Earnest Liberal's Lament, The.
Neo-Thomist Poem.
Valentine.

"Hemingway, Percy. *See* **Addleshaw, Percy**

Hemminger, Graham Lee
This Smoking World.
Tobacco.

Hemp, Christine E.
To My Blood Sister.

Hemschemeyer, Judith
Best Friends.
Dirty-billed Freeze Footy, The.
First Love.
Flight.
Gift.
My Grandmother Had Bones.
My Mother's Death.
Painters, The.
Settlers, The.
Strawberries.
That Summer.
We Interrupt This Broadcast.

Hemsley, Stuart
S.P.C.A. Sermon.

Henchman, Richard
In Consort to Wednesday, Jan. 1st, 1701.
Vox Oppressi, to the Lady Phipps.

Henderson, Alice Corbin. *See* **Corbin, Alice**

Henderson, Daniel
Homing Heart, The.
Hymn for a Household.
Nantucket Whalers.
Opium Clippers.
Poet of Gardens, The.
Road to France, The.
St. Swithin.
Scarlet Thread, The.
Stranger, The.
Two Wives, The.

Henderson, David
Do Nothing till You Hear from Me.
Documentary on Airplane Glue, A.
Downtown-Boy Uptown.
It Is Not Enough.
Keep On Pushing.
Louisiana Weekly #4, The.
Number 5—December.
Psychedelic Firemen.
Sketches of Harlem.
They Are Killing All the Young Men.
Walk with de Mayor of Harlem.
White People.

Henderson, Florence L.
Garden That I Love, The.

Henderson, Hamish
Ding Dong Dollar.
First Elegy [for the Dead in Cyrenaica].
Flyting o' Life and Daith, The.

Henderson, Jock
Martyr and the Army, The.

Henderson, Mary H. J.
Incident, An.

Henderson, Peggy
Serpent Muses, The.

Henderson, Rose
Growing Old.

Hendrie, K. G. P.
Beckon Me, Ye Cuillins.

Hendry, J. F.
Constant North, The.
Inverberg.
Orpheus.
Ship, The.
Tir-Nan-Og.

Henley, Samuel
Verses Addressed to a Friend, Just Leaving a Favourite Retirement.

Henley, William Ernest
After.
All in a Garden Green.
Anterotics.
Apparition.
As Like the Woman as You Can.
At Queensferry.
Ave, Caesar!
Ballade Made in the Hot Weather.
Ballade of Dead Actors.
Ballade of Ladies' Names.
Ballade of Youth and Age.
Before.
Blackbird, The.

Bowl of Roses, A.
Casualty.
"Chief, The."
Children: Private Ward.
Clinical.
Collige Rosas.
Culture in the Slums.
Desolate Shore, A.
Discharged.
England, My England.
Enter Patient.
Envoy: "Do you remember."
Epilogue to Rhymes and Rhythms.
Etching.
Falmouth.
Fill a Glass with Golden Wine.
From a Window in Princes Street.
Full Sea Rolls and Thunders, The.
Gulls in an äery morrice.
Home.
House-Surgeon.
I am the Reaper.
I. M.—R. T. Hamilton Bruce.
I Took a Hansom on To-Day.
In Hospital.
In Memoriam: Margaritae Sorori.
In the Dials.
Inter Sodales.
Interior.
Interlude.
Invictus.
Lady-Probationer.
Largo e Mesto.
London Voluntaries, *sels.*
Madam Life's a Piece in Bloom.
Made in the Hot Weather.
Margaritae Sorori [I. M.].
Music.
Nocturn.
O Gather Me the Rose.
On the Way to Kew.
Operation.
Or Ever the Knightly Years Were Gone.
Orientale.
Out of Tune.
Over the Hills and Far Away.
Pastoral: "It's the Spring."
Prologue to "Rhymes and Rhythms."
Rain.
Romance.
Rondel: Beside the Idle Summer Sea.
Scherzando.
Scrubber.
Since Those We Love and Those We Hate.
So Be My Passing.
Some Late Lark Singing.
Space and Dread and the Dark.
Spirit of Wine, The.
Staff-Nurse: New Style.
Staff-Nurse: Old Style.
Stanzas: "Where forlorn sunsets flare and fade."
Suicide.
To A. D.
To Robert Louis Stevenson.
Two Days.
Under a Stagnant Sky.
Vigil.
Villon's Good-Night.
Villon's Straight Tip to All Cross Coves.
Visitor.
Waiting.
We'll Go No More a-Roving.
What Is to Come.
When I Was a King in Babylon.
With Strawberries.

Hennamma
Wasn't your mother a woman?

Hennell, Thomas
Mermaiden, A.
Queen Anne's Musicians.
Shepherd and Shepherdess.

Hennen, Tom
Job Hunting.
Unusual Things.
Usually an Old Female Is the Leader.
Woods Night.
Working near Lake Traverse.

Henniker-Heaton, Peter J.
Post Early for Space.
To His Lady.

Henry VIII, King of England
As the Holly Groweth Green.
Good Company.
Green Groweth the Holly.
Holly, The.
Love Ever Green.
Pastime.

Henri, Adrian
Mrs. Albion You've Got a Lovely Daughter.

Henri, Raymond
At the Woodpile.
Bridge from Brooklyn, The, *sel.*
Chartres.
Duomo, Milan.
Temple at Segesta, The.
View of the Cathedral, *sels.*

Henry VIII, King of England
As the Holly Groweth Green.
Good Company.
Green Groweth the Holly.
Holly, The.
Love Ever Green.
Pastime.
To His Lady.

Henry, Francis
Old Settler's Song, The.

Henry, Gordon
Freeze Tag.
Leaving Smoke's.
Outside White Earth.
Pine Point, You Are.
Waking on a Greyhound.

"Henry, O." (William Sidney Porter)
Last Fall of the Alamo.
Options.
Tamales.

Henry the Minstrel ("Blind Harry")
Description of Wallace, A.
Lament for the Graham.
Schir William Wallace.
Wallace, The, *sels.*
Wallace's Lament for the Graham.

Henryson, Robert
Abbey Walk, The.
Assembly of the Gods, The.
Bludy Serk, The.
Cresseid's Complaint against Fortune.
Cressida's Leprosy.
Garment of Good Ladies, The.
Praise of Age, The.
Preiching of the Swallow, The.
Robene and Makyne ("Robene [*or* Robin] sat on gude green hill").
Taill of the Foxe, That Begylit the Wolf, in the Schadow of the Mone, The.
Tale of the Upland Mouse and the Burgess Mouse, The, *abr.*
Testament of Cresseid, The
To Our Lady.

Hensley, Sophia Almon
Because of You.

Henson, Lance
Among Hawks.
Anniversary Poem for the Cheyennes Who Fell at Sand Creek.
At Chadwicks Bar and Grill.
Bay Poem.
Between Rivers and Seas.
Buffalo Marrow on Black.
Cold, The.
Comanche Ghost Dance: An Impression.
Crazy Horse: The Last Morning.
Curtain.
Dawn in January.
Epitaph: Snake River.
Flock.
Grandfather.
Image of City.
Last Words, 1968.
Moon at Three A.M.
Moth.
North.
Old Man Told Me.
Old Story.
Other.
Our Smoke Has Gone Four Ways.
Poem for Carroll, Descendant of Chiefs.
Poem near Midway Truck Stop.
Rain.
Scattered Leaves.
Sitting Alone in Tulsa Three A.M.
Sleep Watch.
Sundown at Darlington 1878.
Travels with the Band-Aid Army.
Vision Song (Cheyenne).
Warrior Nation Trilogy.
We Are a People.
Wish.
Wood Floor Dreams.

Henson, Pauline
On the Edge of the Copper Pit.

Henze, Helen Rowe
Etruscan Warrior's Head.

Hepburn, Thomas Nicoll. *See* **"Setoun, Gabriel"**

Heppenstall, Rayner
Actaeon.
Consolation in July.
Fleur de Lys.
Hagiograph.
St. Stephen's Word.
Spring Song.
Tammuz.

Herbert, Sir Alan Patrick
At the Theater.
Bacon and Eggs.
Beaucourt Revisited.
Bowline, The.
Centipede, The.
Chameleon, The.
Come to Britain; a Humble Contribution to the Movement.
Cupid's Darts.
Farmer, The.
Finale.
Green Estaminet, The.
Hattage.
"He Didn't Oughter."
I Can't Think What He Sees in Her.
Inst., Ult., and Prox.
I've Got the Giggles Today.
Less Nonsense.
Lines for a Worthy Person Who Has Drifted by Accident into a Chelsea Revel.
"No Quarrel."
Perseverance; or, Half a Coronet, *sel.*
Prodigy, The.
Racing-Man, The.
Recipe.
Snail, The.
Stop, Science—Stop!
To a Junior Waiter.
Tomato Juice.
'Twas at the Pictures, Child, We Met.
Two Gentlemen of Soho, *parody, sel.*

Herbert, Edward. *See* **Herbert of Cherbury, Edward Herbert, 1st Baron**

Herbert, George
Aaron.
Affliction ("Broken in pieces all asunder").
Affliction ("When first thou didst entice to thee my heart").
Agonie [*or* Agony], The.
Altar, The.
Ana(Mary-Army)gram.
Answer, The.

Artillerie [*or* Artillery].
Assurance.
Avarice.
Bag, The.
Banquet, The.
Be Useful.
Bitter-sweet.
British Church, The.
Bunch of Grapes, The.
Christmas.
Church Floor[e], The.
Church Lock and Key.
Church Militant, *sel.*
Church Monuments.
Church Musick.
Church Porch, The.
Church Windows, The.
Clasping of Hands.
Collar, The.
Confession.
Conscience.
Crosse, The.
Dawning, The.
Death.
Decay.
Dedication, The: "Lord, my first fruits present themselves to thee."
Denial.
Dialogue.
Discipline.
Dooms-Day.
Dulnesse.
Easter ("I got me flowers to straw thy way").
Easter Wings.
Elixir, The.
Employment ("He that is weary, let him sit").
Employment ("If as a flowre doth spread and die").
Even-Song.
Familie, The.
Flower, The.
Forerunners, The.
Frailty.
Gifts of God, The.
Glance, The.
Grace.
Grieve Not the Holy Spirit.
H. Baptisme ("Since, Lord, to thee/A narrow way and little gate").
H. Communion, The ("Not in rich furniture or fine aray").
H. Scriptures, The.
Heart to Praise Thee, A.
Heaven.
Holy Baptism[e].
Hope.
Iesu.
Invitation, The.
Jesu.
Jews, The.
Jordan ("When first my lines of heav'nly joyes made mention").
Jordan ("Who say[e]s that fictions on[e]ly and false hair").
Judgement.
L'Envoy: "King of glorie, King of peace."
Life.
Longing.
Love ("Immortal love, autho[u]r of this great frame").
Love ("Love bade me welcome; yet my soul drew back").
Love-Joy.
Love Unknown.
Man.
Man's Medley.
Marie Magdalene.
Mattens.
Miserie.
Mortification.
Nature.
Obedience.
Odour, The.
Our Life Is Hid with Christ in God.
Our Prayer.
Paradise.
Parodie, A: "Souls joy, when thou art gone."
Peace.
Pearl, The.
Pearl. Matth. 13, The.
Philosophers Have Measured Mountains.
Pilgrimage, The.
Praise.
Prayer: "Prayer the church's [*or* churches] banquet, angels' age."
Priesthood, The.
Pulley, The.
Quidditie, The.
Quip, The.
Redemption.
Repentance.
Reprisall, The.
Rose, The.
Sacrifice, The.
Search, The.
Second Thanksgiving, The; or, The Reprisal.
Sepulchre.
Shall I Be Silent?
Sighs and Grones.
Sin.
Sins' Round.
Sion.
Sonne, The.
Sonnet: "Sure Lord, there is enough in thee to dry."
Starre, The.
Storm, The.
Submission.
Sunday.
Superliminare.
Temper, The.
Thanksgiving, The.
Time.
To All Angels and Saints.
True Hymn, A.
Twenty-third Psalm, The.
Unkindness.
Vanity ("The fleet astronomer can bore").
Virtue.
Who would have thought my shrivelled heart.
Windows, The.
World, The.
Wreath, A.
Herbert, Henry William
Come Back.
Herbert, Mary Sidney, Countess of Pembroke. *See* **Pembroke, Mary Sidney Herbert, Countess of**
Herbert, Moss
Gentle Park, A.
Herbert, William, Earl of Pembroke. *See* **Pembroke, William Herbert, Earl of**
Herbert, Zbigniew
Elegy of Fortinbras.
Herbert of Cherbury, , Edward Herbert, 1st Baron
Brown Beauty, The.
Description, A.
Ditty in Imitation of the Spanish, A.
Echo in a Church.
Echo to a Rock.
Elegy for Doctor Dunn.
Elegy over a Tomb.
Epitaph. Cæcil. Boulstr.
Epitaph for Himself.
First Meeting, The.
Green-Sickness Beauty, The.
In a Glass-Window for Inconstancy.
Kissing.
Love Speaks at Last.
Loves End.
Madrigal: "Dear, when I did from you remove."
Madrigal: "How should I love my best?"
October 14, 1644.
Ode upon a Question Moved, Whether Love Should Continue for Ever, An?
Parted Souls.
Platonick Love.
Sinner's Lament, A.
Sonnet: "Innumerable Beauties, thou white haire."
Sonnet: "Thus ends my love, but this doth grieve me most."
Sonnet Made upon the Groves near Merlou Castle.
Sonnet of Black Beauty.
Tears, Flow No More.
Thought, The.
To a Lady Who Did Sing Excellently.
To Her Eyes.
To his Friend Ben. Johnson, of his Horace made English.
To His Mistress for Her True Picture.
To His Watch, When He Could Not Sleep.
To Mrs. Diana Cecyll.
Vision, A.
Herbertson, Agnes Grozier
Airman, R.F.C.
Seed-Merchant's Son, The.
Herbin, John Frederic
Diver, The.
Haying.
Herbkersman, Gretchen
Cosmetic.
Herder, Johann Gottfried von
Esthonian Bridal Song.
Sir Olaf.
Herea, Te Heuheu
Mourning-Song for Rangiaho, A.
Herebert, William
Devout Man Prays to His Relations, The.
Knight Stained from Battle, The.
My Folk, What Have I Done Thee?
Palm-Sunday Hymn, A.
Who Is This That Cometh from Edom?
Heredia, José-Maria de
Flute, The; a Pastoral.
Laborer, The.
Herford, Oliver
Autograph Bore, The.
Bashful Earthquake, The, *sel.*
Belated Violet, A.
Bunny Romance, A.
Cat, The.
Child's Natural History, *sels.*
Chimpanzee, The.
Conservative Owl, The.
Cow, The.
Crocodile, The.
Dog, The.
Elf and the Dormouse, The.
Eternal Feminine, The.
Eve.
Fall of J. W. Beane, The.
Fastidious Yak, The.
Feminine Seal, The.
Geese.
Grumbler Gruff, A.
Hen, The.
Here Lies Bill.
Hippopotamus, The.
Humorous Ant, The.
I Heard a Bird Sing.
If This Little World To-Night.
Inquisitive Leopard, The.
Japanesque.
Kind Armadillo, The.
Last Violet, The.
Laughing Willow, The.
Limerick: "There was a young lady of Twickenham."
Mendacious Mole, The.
Metaphysics.
Milk Jug, The.
Misapprehended Goose, The.
Missing Link, The.

Mrs. Seymour Fentolin.
Mock Miracle, A.
Mon-goos, The.
More Animals, *sel.*
Music of the Future, The.
Musical Lion, The.
My Sense of Sight.
Nature and Art.
Omnivorous Bookworm, The.
Oratorical Crab, The.
Ounce of Detention, The.
Penguin, A.
Platypus, The.
Proem: "If this little world to-night."
Quoter, A.
Seal, A.
Silver Question, The.
Smile of the Goat, The.
Smile of the Walrus, The.
Snail's Dream, The.
Sole-hungering Camel.
Some Geese.
Song: "Gather kittens while you may."
Stairs.
Tact.
Thoroughbred Horse, The.
Tra-La-Larceny.
Two Smiles.
Untutored Giraffe, The, *sel.*
Well-informed Wight, A.
Why ye Blossome Cometh before ye Leafe.
Women of the Better Class, The.
Yak, The.

Herman, Reinhold W.
Now I Set Me.

"Hermes, Paul." *See* **Thayer, William Roscoe**

Hernton, Calvin C.
D Blues.
Distant Drum, The.
Elements of Grammar.
Fall Down.
Jitterbugging in the Streets.
Madhouse.
Young Negro Poet.

Herrick, Robert
Againe.
All Things Decay and Die.
Amber Bead, The.
Ambition.
Anacreontic ("Born I was to be old").
Anacreontic ("I must/ Not trust").
Another.
Another on Her.
Another to the Maids.
Apparition of His Mistress Calling Him to Elysium [*or* Elizium], The.
Apron of Flowers, The.
Argument of His Book, The.
Art above Nature, to Julia.
Bad Season Makes the Poet Sad, The.
Bag of the Bee, The.
Barley-Break; or, Last in Hell.
Beggar to Mab, the Fairy [*or* Fairie] Queen, The.
Bellman, The.
Body, The.
Bracelet, The: To Julia.
Bubble, The; a Song.
Canticle to Apollo, A.
Captived Bee, The; or, The Little Filcher.
Cat, A/ I keep, that plays about my.
Ceremonies for Candlemas Day, The.
Ceremonies for Candlemas[se] Eve.
Ceremonies for Christmas[se].
Ceremony upon Candlemas Eve.
Changed to Corinna, The.
Charm, A.
Charm[e], or an Allay for Love, A.
Charmes.
Cheat of Cupid, The; [or, The Ungentle Guest].
Cherry-Pit.
Cherry-ripe.
Child's Grace, A.
Child's Present to His Child-Saviour, A.
Chop-Cherry.
Christmas Carol, A: "What sweeter music can we bring."
Christmas Caroll Sung to the King in the Presence at White-Hall, A.
Christmas Eve—Another Ceremony.
Clothes Do but Cheat and Cozen Us.
Cock-Crow.
Comfort to a Youth That Had Lost His Love.
Coming of Good Luck, The.
Conjuration, to Electra, A.
Corinna's Going a-Maying.
Country Life, A: To His Brother, Master Thomas Herrick.
Crosses.
Cruel Maid, The.
Crutches.
Curse, The; a Song.
Dean-bourn, a Rude River in Devon, by Which Sometimes He Lived ("Dean-bourn, farewell; I never look to see").
Definition of Beauty, The.
Delight in Disorder.
Departure of the Good Daemon, The.
Dew Sat on Julia's Hair.
Dirge upon the Death of the Right Valiant Lord, Bernard Stuart, A.
Discontents in Devon.
Distrust.
Divination by a Daffadill [*or* Daffodil].
Dreams.
End of His Work, The.
Entertainment, or Porch-Verse, at the Marriage of Master Henry Northleigh and the Most Witty Mistress Lettice Yard, The.
Epitaph on Sir Edward Giles and His Wife.
Epitaph on the Tomb of Sir Edward Giles and His Wife in the South Aisle of Dean Prior Church, Devon.
Epitaph upon a Child, An ("Virgins promis'd when I died").
Epitaph upon a Child That Died ("Here she lies, a pretty bud").
Epitaph upon a Sober Matron, An.
Epitaph upon a Virgin, An.
Epithalamy to Sir Thomas Southwell and His Lady, An.
Eternity.
Eye, The.
Fair Days; or, Dawns Deceitful.
Fairies, The.
Fairy Temple, The; or Oberon's Chapel.
Fame.
Fame Makes Us Forward.
Farewell Frost; or, Welcome the Spring.
Four Sweet Months, The.
Four Things Make Us Happy Here.
Fresh Cheese and Cream.
Frolic, A.
Frozen Heart, The.
Frozen Zone, The; or Julia Disdainful.
Funeral [*or* Funerall] Rites of the Rose, The.
God to Be First Served.
Going a-Maying.
Good Christians.
Good Men Afflicted Most.
Good-Night, or Blessing, The.
Grace before Meat.
Grace for a Child.
Grace for Children ("What God gives, and what we take").
Hag, The ("The hag is astride").
Hag, The ("The staff is now greased").
Her Legs.
His Age, Dedicated to His Peculiar Friend, Master John Wickes, under the Name of Posthumus.
His Cavalier.
His Charge to Julia at His Death.
His Content in the Country.
His Creed.
His Desire.
His Ejaculation to God.
His Fare-well to Sack.
His Grange, or Private Wealth.
His Hope or Sheet-Anchor.
His Lachrimae or Mirth, Turn'd to Mourning.
His Letanie, to the Holy Spirit.
His Litany to the Holy Spirit.
His Own Epitaph.
His Poetry His Pillar.
His Prayer for Absolution.
His Prayer to Ben Jonson [*or* Johnson].
His Request to Julia.
His Return[e] to London.
His Sailing from Julia.
His Saviour's Words, Going to the Cross.
His Tears to Thamasis [*or* Thamesis].
His Winding-Sheet.
His Wish to God.
Hock-Cart, or Harvest Home, The.
Hour-Glass, The.
How Lil[l]ies Came White.
How Marigolds Came Yellow.
How Roses Came Red.
How Violets Came Blue.
Hymn to Bacchus, A.
I Call and I Call.
I'll Come to Thee.
Impossibilities to His Friend.
In the Dark None Dainty.
Instead of Neat Inclosures.
Invitation, The.
Julia's Petticoat.
July: The Succession of the Four Sweet Months.
Kiss, A.
Kisse, The.
Kisses Loathesome.
Kissing and Bussing.
Lilly in a Christal, The.
Lips Tongueless.
Long and Lazy.
Love Dislikes Nothing.
Love Me Little, Love Me Long.
Love Perfumes All Parts.
Love What It Is.
Lovers How They Come and Part.
Lyric for Legacies.
Lyric to Mirth, A.
Lyrick for Legacies.
Mad Maid's Song, The.
Man's Dying-Place Uncertain.
Matins, or Morning Prayer.
Meddow Verse, The; or, Aniversary to Mistris Bridget Lowman.
Meditation for His Mistress[e], A.
Mercy and Love.
Mirth.
Moderation.
Money Gets the Mastery.
Money Makes the Mirth.
More White than Whitest Lilies.
Mount of the Muses, The.
Music.
Neutrality Loathsome.
New-Year's Gift Sent to Sir Simeon Steward, A.
New-Yeeres Gift, The; or, Circumcisions Song, Sung to the King in the Presence at White Hall.
Night-Piece, to Julia, The.
No Coming to God without Christ.
No Difference in the Dark.
No Fault in Women.
No Loathsom[e]nesse in Love.
No Lock against Lechery.
Not Every Day Fit for Verse.
Not to Love.
Nothing New.
Nuptial[l] Song, or Epithalamie [*or* Epithalamy], on Sir Clipseby Crew and His Lady, A.
Oberon's Feast.
Oberon's Palace.

Observation.
Ode for Ben Jonson, An.
Ode for Him, An.
Ode of the Birth of Our Saviour, An, *sel.*
Ode on the Birth of Our Saviour, An.
Ode to Master Endymion Porter, upon His Brother's Death, An.
Old Wives Prayer, The.
On Ben Jonson.
On Himself[e] ("Born[e] I was to meet with age").
On Himself ("Here down my wearied limbs I'll lay").
On Himself ("I fear no earthly powers").
On Himself ("I will no longer kiss").
On Himself ("I'll write no more of love, but now repent").
On Himself ("Let me not live, if I not love").
On Himself ("Weep for the dead, for they have lost this light").
On Himself[e] ("The work[e] is done. Young men and maidens, set").
On Himself ("Young I was who now am old").
Orpheus.
Panegyric to Sir Lewis Pemberton, A.
Parcae, The, or Three Dainty Destinies: The Armillet.
Parting Verse, the Feast There Ended, The.
Perfume, The.
Peter-Penny, The.
Pillar of Fame, The.
Plaudite, or End of Life, The.
Poet Loves a Mistress[e] But Not to Marry, The.
Poetry Perpetuates the Poet.
Power and Peace.
Power in the People, The.
Prayers Must Have Poise.
Primrose, The.
Rock of Rubies, The.
Rosarie, The.
Rubies and Pearls.
Sadness of Things for Sappho's Sickness, The.
Scare-Fire, The.
Science in God.
Second Vision, The.
Shoe-tying, The.
Short Hymne to Venus, A.
Sins Loathed, and Yet Loved.
So Look the Mornings.
Spell, The.
Star-Song, The; a Carol to the King; sung at White-Hall.
Steam in Sacrifice.
Succession of the Four Sweet Months, The.
Supreme Fortune Falls Soonest.
Suspition upon His Over-much Familiarity with a Gentlewoman, The.
Temple, The.
Temptation.
Ternarie of Littles, upon a Pipkin of Jelly [*or* Jellie] Sent to a Lady, A.
Thanksgiving.
Thanksgiving to God, for His House, A.
This Cross-Tree Here.
'Tis Hard to Find God.
Tithe, The: To the Bride.
To a Bed of Tulips.
To a Gentlewoman Objecting to Him His Grey Hairs.
To Aenone.
To Anthea ("Ah, my Anthea! must my heart still break?").
To Anthea ("If deare Anthea, my hard fate it be").
To Anthea ("Now is the time, when all the lights wax dim").
To Anthea Lying in Bed.
To Anthea, Who May Command Him [in] Anything.
To Blossoms.
To Cherry-Blossomes.
To Critics.
To Crown It.
To Daffodils [*or* Daffadills].
To Daisies, Not to Shut So Soon[e].
To Dean Bourn, a Rude River in Devon [by Which Sometimes He Lived].
To Dianeme ("Dear, though to part it be hell").
To Dianeme ("Give me one kiss").
To Dianeme ("Show me thy feet; show me thy legs, thy thighs").
To Dianeme ("Sweet, be not proud of those two eyes").
To Electra ("I dare not ask a kiss").
To Electra ("I'll come to thee in all those shapes").
To Finde God.
To Fortune.
To God.
To God, on His Sickness.
To Groves.
To His Book ("Go thou forth, my book, though late").
To His Book ("Have I not blessed thee? Then go forth; nor fear").
To His Booke ("Who with thy leaves shall wipe at need").
To his book's end this last line he'd have placed.
To His Conscience.
To His Dying Brother, Master William Herrick.
To His Ever-loving God.
To His Friend, on the Untunable Times.
To His Honoured and Most Ingenious Friend, Master Charles Cotton.
To His Kinsman, Master Thomas Herrick, Who Desired to Be in His Book.
To His Kinswoman, Mistress Penelope Wheeler.
To His Lovely Mistresses.
To His Maid Prew.
To His Mistress Objecting to Him neither Toying or Talking.
To His Mistress[e] ("Choose me your valentine").
To His Mistresses ("Help me! Help me! now I call").
To His Mistresses ("Put on your silks, and piece by piece").
To His Muse.
To His Saviour, a Child; a Present, by a Child.
To His Tomb-Maker.
To Julia ("How rich and pleasing thou, my Julia, art").
To Julia ("Julia, when thy Herrick dies").
To Julia, the Flaminica Dialis, or Queen-Priest.
To Keep a True Lent.
To Larr.
To Laurels.
To Live Merrily, and to Trust to Good Verses.
To Master Denham, on His Prospective Poem.
To Master Henry Lawes, the Excellent Composer of Lyrics.
To Meadows.
To Mistress Katherine Bradshaw the Lovely, That Crowned Him with Laurel.
To Music ("Begin to charm, and as thou strok'st mine ears").
To Music; a Song.
To Music, to Becalm a Sweet-sick Youth.
To Music, to Becalm His Fever.
To My Ill Reader.
To Oenone ("Thou saist Love's dart").
To Oenone ("What conscience, say, is it in thee").
To Perilla.
To Phillis [*or* Phyllis], to Love and Live with Him.
To Primroses Fill'd [*or* Filled] with Morning-Dew.
To Robin Redbreast.
To Sycamores.
To the Generous Reader.
To the King, upon His Com[m]ing with His Army into the West.
To the King, upon his Welcome to Hampton-Court.
To the Most Fair and Lovely Mistress Anne Soame, Now Lady Abdie [*or* Abdy].
To the Most Learned, Wise, and Arch-Antiquary, M. John Selden.
To the Most Virtuous Mistress Pot, Who Many Times Entertained Him.
To the Reverend Shade of His Religious Father.
To the Rose; a Song.
To the Sour[e] Reader.
To the Virgins, to Make Much of Time.
To the Water Nymphs, Drinking at the Fountain.
To the Western Wind.
To the Willow-Tree.
To the Yew and Cypress to Grace His Funeral.
To Violets.
To Virgins.
To Vulcan.
To Women, to Hide Their Teeth, if They Be Rotten or Rusty.
Transfiguration, The.
Trapped Fly, A.
Upon a Black Twist, Rounding the Arm of the Countess of Carlisle.
Upon a Child.
Upon a Child That Died ("Here she lies, a pretty bud").
Upon a Delaying Lady.
Upon a Flie.
Upon a Maid ("Gone she is a long, long way").
Upon a Maid ("Here she lies in bed of spice").
Upon a Virgin Kissing a Rose.
Upon a Wife That Dyed Mad with Jealousie.
Upon a Young Mother of Many Children.
Upon Batt.
Upon Ben Jonson.
Upon Bunce: Epigram.
Upon Fone a School-Master, Epigram.
Upon Glass: Epigram.
Upon Groins: Epigram.
Upon Gryll.
Upon Her Feet.
Upon Her Voice.
Upon His Departure Hence.
Upon His Julia.
Upon His Sister-in-Law, Mistress Elizabeth Herrick.
Upon His Spaniell Tracie.
Upon Jack and Jill: Epigram.
Upon Jone and Jane.
Upon Julia Washing Herself in the River.
Upon Julia's Breasts.
Upon Julia's Clothes.
Upon Julia's Fall.
Upon Julia's Petticoat.
Upon Julia's Ribband.
Upon Julia's Voice.
Upon Love ("Love brought me to a silent grove").
Upon Love, by Way of Question and Answer.
Upon Lulls.
Upon Master Fletcher's Incomparable Playes.
Upon Mistress Elizabeth Wheeler under the Name of Amarillis.
Upon Moon.
Upon Pagget.
Upon Parson Beanes.
Upon Prew His Maid.
Upon Prudence Baldwin Her Sickness[e].
Upon Prue, His Maid.
Upon Rook: Epigram.
Upon Roses.
Upon Scobble.
Upon Showbread: Epigram.
Upon Sibilla.
Upon Some Women.
Upon Sudds a Laundress[e].
Upon Sybilla.

Upon the Death of His Sparrow; an Elegie.
Upon the Loss[e] of His Mistresses.
Upon the Nipples of Julia's Breast.
Upon the Same [Detractor] ("I asked thee oft what poets thou hast read").
Upon the Troublesome Times.
Upon Time.
Upon Umber: Epigram.
Vine, The.
Vision, The ("I dreamed we both were in bed").
Vision, The ("Methought I saw as I did dream in bed").
Vision, The ("Sitting alone as one forsook").
Vision to Electra, The.
Welcome to Sack, The.
What Kind of Mistress He Would Have.
What Shame Forbids to Speak.
When He Would Have His Verses Read.
When I Thy Parts Run O'er.
Whenas in Silks My Julia Goes.
White Island, The; or, Place of the Blest.
Why Flowers Change Color.
Willow Garland, The.
Wounded Cupid, The.
Yule Log.

Herschberger, Ruth
Coup d'Etat.
Huron, The.
In Panelled Rooms.
Lumberyard, The.
Mulberry Street.
O Terry why is sex so quick.
Poem: "Love being what it is, full of betrayals."
Song: "Sergei's a flower."
Summer Mansions.
Watergate.
Yaddo.

Herschel-Clarke, May
For Valour.
Nothing to Report.

Herschell, William M.
Kid Has Gone to the Colors, The.

Hersey, Harold
Lavender Cowboy, The.
Lay of the Last Frontier.

Hershenson, Miriam
Husbands and Wives.
Love Poem—1940.

Hershon, Robert
Boy Who Smells like Cocoa, A.
Cooper & Bailey Great London Circus, The.
Four Translations from the English of Robert Hershon.
How to Walk in a Crowd.
Ireland Lake.
Kelly.
Responses.
Spitting on Ira Rosenblatt.
Swimming Lesson, The.
U.S. Coast and Geodetic Survey Ship *Pioneer*, The.

Hervey, Christopher
Confusion.

Herzberg, Judith
Commentaries on the Song of Songs.
Kinneret.
Nearer.
On the Death of Sylvia Plath.
Reunion.
Vocation.
Voice, The.
Yiddish.

Herzing, Albert
Small Boy, Dreaming, A.

Heseltine, Nigel
Microcosmos, *abr.*

Hesiod
Works and Days, *sel.*

Hesketh, Phoebe
Dipper, The.
Ducks.

Hess, M. Whitcomb
Vision of St. Bernard, The.

Hesse, Hermann
It's Just the Same to Me.
Night.
Sometimes.
Spring Song.

Hester, M. L., Jr.
International Motherhood Assoc.
Second Night, The.

Hetherington, George
Charles at the Siege.
Palm House, Botanic Gardens.
Sonnet: "Now keep that long revolver at your side."
Sonnet: "Since I keep only what I give away."

Hewett, Dorothy
Moon-Man.
Sanctuary.
This Version of Love.

Hewison, R. J. P.
Genius.

Hewitt, Ethel M.
Wild Wishes.

Hewitt, Geof
Behind That Wall My Roommate Fucks His Girl.
Ben Plays Hide and Seek in the Deep Woods.
Chickens.
Conversion.
Emergency at 8.
Explanation.
For Bill.
For Randie.
In like a Lion.
Rip-off # 1: Hippie Capitalism.

Hewitt, John
Because I Paced My Thought.
First Corncrake.
From a Museum Man's Album.
Frontier, The.
Frost.
Glens, The.
Ireland.
Irishman in Coventry, An.
Leaf.
Little Lough, The.
Load.
Lyric: "Let but a thrush begin."
Minor Victorian Painter, A.
Once Alien Here.
Poem in May.
Ram's Horn, The.
Spectacle of Truth, The.
Swathe Uncut, The.
Turf Carrier on Aranmore.

Hewlett, Maurice
Rosa Nascosa.
When She a Maiden Slim.

Hey, Phil
For Sue.
Old Men Working Concrete.
True Ballad of the Great Race to Gilmore City, The.

Heyen, William
Auction.
Berries, The.
Birds and Roses Are Birds and Roses.
Children, The.
Dark, The.
Dark in the Reich of the Blond.
Dog Sacrifice at Lake Ronkonkoma.
Driving at Dawn.
Elm's Home, The.
Existential.
Fires.
I Move to Random Consolations.
King's Men, The.
Late Show, The.
Mantle.
Mother and Son.
Poem Touching the Gestapo.
Ram Time.
Riddle: "From Belsen a crate of gold teeth."
Ryókan.
Snapper, The.
Spirit of Wrath, The.
Stadium, The.
This Night.
Trail beside the River Platte, The.

Heym, Georg
War.

Heynen, Jim
Tourist Guide: How You Can Tell for Sure When You're in South Dakota.

Heyrick, Thomas
Martial.
On a Peacock.
On a Sunbeam.
On an Indian Tomineois, the Least of Birds.
On the Crocodile.
On the Death of a Monkey.

Heyse, Paul
Rispetti: On the Death of a Child.
Young Girl's Song, A.

Heyward, DuBose
Dusk.
Equinox, The.
Gamesters All.
Porgy, Maria, and Bess.

Heyward, Janie Screven
Autumn Leaves.
Spirit's Grace, The.

Heywood, Jasper
Look or You Leap.
Lookers-on, The.

Heywood, John
All a green willow, willow, willow, *abr.*
Art Thou Heywood.
Cardinal Fisher.
Cock and the Hen, The.
English Schoolboy, The.
"Gloria Patri," The.
If Love, for Love of Long Time Had.
Of a Daw.
Of Birds and Birders.
Of Use.
On Botching.
On the Princess Mary.
Palmer, The.
Play of the Four P.P., The, *sel.*
Play of the Weather, The, *sel.*
Praise of His Lady, A, *at.*
Tyburn and Westminster.

Heywood, Thomas
Apology for Actors, An, *sel.*
Author to His Booke, The.
Golden Age, The, *sel.*
Good Morrow.
Hierarchie of the Blessed Angles, *sel.*
Hymn to Diana.
Jupiter and Ganimede.
Matin Song.
Message, The. *At. to*
Pack, Clouds, Away.
Passing Bell, The.
Praise of Ceres.
Rape of Lucrece, The, *sels.*
Search for God, The, *abr.*
She That Denies Me [I Would Have].
Silver Age, The, *sel.*
Valerius on Women.
Ye Little Birds That Sit and Sing. *At. to*

Hickey, Agnes MacCarthy
Old Essex Door.

Hickey, Emily Henrietta
Belovèd, It Is Morn.

Hickey, Mark
Road along the Thumb and Forefinger, The ("The road all the way up along the coast").

Hickock, Eliza M.
Prayer: "I know not by what methods rare."

Hickox, Chauncey
Under the Red Cross.

Hicks, Berryman
Time Is Swiftly Rolling On, The.
Hicks, George A.
Mormon Immigrant Song, A, *at.*
Hicks, John V.
Are You There, Mrs. Goose?
Last Rite.
Trumpet Shall Sound, The.
Hickson, William E.
Walking Song.
Hicky, Daniel Whitehead
Georgia Towns.
Nocturne: Georgia Coast.
Okefenokee Swamp.
River Boats, The.
Say That He Loved Old Ships.
To an Aviator.
Hiebert, Paul Gerhardt
Farmer and the Farmer's Wife, The.
Steeds.
Hiers, Lois Smith
On Laying Up Treasure.
Higgins, Annie
Waking.
Higgins, Brian
Analogy.
Baedeker for Metaphysicians.
Corrupt Man in the French Pub, The.
Genesis.
Higgins, Frederick Robert
Ballad of O'Bruadir, The.
Boyne Walk, The.
Chinese Winter.
Father and Son.
Gallows Tree, The.
Little Clan, The.
O You among Women.
Old Air, An.
Old Jockey, The.
Padraic O'Conaire, Gaelic Storyteller.
Higginson, Ella
Beggars.
Four-Leaf Clover.
Grand Ronde Valley, The.
Lamp in the West, The.
Month of Falling Stars, The.
Moonrise in the Rockies.
Higginson, Mary Potter Thacher
Changelings.
Ghost-Flowers.
In the Dark.
Inheritance.
Higginson, Thomas Wentworth
Decoration.
Ode to a Butterfly.
Past Is Dark with Sin and Shame, The, *with music.*
Since Cleopatra Died.
Snowing of the Pines, The.
Such Stuff as Dreams Are Made Of.
Things I Miss, The.
To Duty.
To Thine Eternal Arms, O God, *with music.*
Higgons, Bevil
Mourners, The.
Higgs, Barry O.
Deaf.
In Lord Carpenter's Country.
Night Shore.
Parson's Pleasure.
Reversion.
Higgs, Blake Alphonso. *See* **Blind Blake**
Higgs, Ted
From Mistra: A Prospect.
Higham, Charles
Barnacle Geese.
Highet, Gilbert
Homage to Ezra Pound.
Higo, Aig
Hidesong.
Hikmet, Nazim
I Come and Stand at Every Door.
Hilarova, Dagmar
Questions.
Hildegard von Bingen
Like the honeycomb dropping honey.
O crimson blood.
Hildreth, Charles Lotin
At the Mermaid Inn.
Implora Pace.
To an Obscure Poet Who Lives on My Hearth.
Hill, Aaron
Alone in an Inn at Southampton, April the 25th, 1737.
Lord's Prayer in Verse, The.
May-Day.
Strong Hand, A.
Whitehall Stairs.
Hill, Benjamin Dionysius
To St. Mary Magdalen.
Hill, Clyde Walton
Lincoln.
Hill, Donald L.
Buzzing Doubt, The.
Hill, Elton (Abu Ishak)
Theme Brown Girl.
Hill, Geoffrey
Annunciations.
Apology for the Revival of Christian Architecture in England, An, *sel.*
Asmodai [*or* Asmodeus].
Christmas Trees.
Dead Bride, The.
Distant Fury of Battle, The.
Doctor Faustus.
"Domaine Public."
Genesis
Gideon at the Well.
God's Little Mountain.
Guardians, The.
Imaginative Life, The.
In Memory of Jane Fraser [*or* Frazer].
In Piam Memoriam.
Lachrimae, *sel.*
Lachrimae Amantis.
Laurel Axe, The.
Mercian Hymns, *sels.*
Merlin.
Of Commerce and Society.
Orpheus and Eurydice.
Ovid in the Third Reich.
Pastoral, A: "Mobile, immaculate and austere."
Pentecost Castle, The, *abr.*
Picture of a Nativity.
Re-Birth of Venus, The.
Requiem for the Plantagenet Kings.
September Song.
Short History of British India, A.
Song from Armenia, A.
To the (Supposed) Patron.
Turtle Dove, The.
Two Chorale Preludes.
Veni Coronaberis.
White Ship, The.
Wreaths.
Hill, George
Song of the Elfin Steersman.
Hill, Hyacinthe
Old Emily.
Rebels from Fairy Tales.
Hill, Jeanne
Lines from a Misplaced Person.
Hill, Joe
Casey Jones (Union).
Preacher and the Slave, The, *at.*
Rebel Girl, The.
Tramp, The.
Hill, Leslie Pinckney
Christmas at Melrose.
So Quietly.
Summer Magic.
Teacher, The.
Tuskegee.
Hill, Nellie
Soup on a Cold Day.
Hill, Pati
On the beach/ a big dog lies.
Two lovers sitting on a tomb.
Hill, Quentin
Time Poem.
Hill, Roberta. *See* Whiteman, Roberta Hill
Hill, Rowland M.
Idiot Boy.
Hill, Thomas
Bobolink, The.
Hille, Peter
Beauty.
Maiden, The.
Hillert, Margaret
About Feet.
Just Me.
Hillhouse, Augustus Lucas
Forgiveness of Sins a Joy Unknown to Angels.
Trembling before Thine Awful Throne, *with music*
Hillhouse, James Abraham
Demon-Lover, The.
Hadad, *sel.*
Hillman, Brenda
Ballet.
Hills, Elijah Clarence
To Pikes Peak.
Hillyer, Robert Silliman
And When the Prince Came.
As One Who Bears beneath His Neighbor's Roof.
Assassination, The.
Bats, The.
Elegy on a Dead Mermaid Washed Ashore at Plymouth Rock.
Epigram: "Bring hemlock, black as Cretan cheese."
Eppur Si Muove?
Eternal Return, The.
Familiar Faces, Long Departed.
In the Shadowy Whatnot Corner.
Intermezzo.
Ivory Tower, The.
Letter to Charles Townsend Copeland, A: Le Baron Russell Briggs, *sel.*
Letter to Robert Frost, A.
Lullaby: "Long canoe, The."
Mentis Trist.
Moo!
Nocturne: "If the deep wood is haunted, it is I."
Over Bright Summer Seas.
Pastoral: "So soft in the hemlock wood."
Pastoral, A: "Wise old apple tree in spring, The."
Prothalamion, *sel.*
Relic, The.
Sonnets, *sels.*
Thought in Time, A.
To a Scarlatti Passepied.
Hilton, Arthur Clement
Ding Dong.
Heathen Pass-ee, The, *parody.*
Limerick: "There was a young critic of King's."
Limerick: "There was a young genius of Queens'."
Limerick: "There was a young gourmand of John's."
Limerick: "There was a young man of Sid. Sussex."
Limerick: "There was an old fellow of Trinity," *at.*
Octopus.
Vulture and the Husbandman, The.
Hilton, David
Poet Tries to Turn In His Jock, The.
Hilton, John
Madrigal: "My mistress frowns when she should play," *at.*

Hilton, L. M.
Have Courage, My Boy, to Say No!
Himel, Margery
My People.
Himmell, Sophie
In the Month of Green Fire.
Hind bint Utba
Fury against the Moslems at Uhud.
Tambourine Song for Soldiers Going into Battle.
Hind bint Uthatha
To a Hero Dead at al-Safra.
Hindley, Charles
Mother Shipton's Prophecies, *at.*
Hindley, Norman
Charter Boat.
Off Molokai.
Trout.
Wood Butcher.
Hinds, Samuel
Baby Sleeps.
Hine, Daryl
After the Agony in the Garden.
August 13, 1966.
Bewilderment at the Entrance of the Fat Boy into Eden, A.
Bluebeard's Wife.
Doppelganger, The.
English Elegy, An.
Fabulary Satire IV.
In Praise of Music in Time of Pestilence.
Lady Sara Bunbury Sacrificing to the Graces, by Reynolds.
Plain Fare.
Point Grey.
Survivors, The.
Trompe L'Œil.
Trout, The.
Under the Hill.
Untitled.
Vowel Movements.
Wasp, The.
Wave, The.
Hines, Carl Wendell, Jr.
Two Jazz Poems.
Hines, Herbert H.
Christmas Prayer, A.
Hines, J. A.
August Second Syndrome Poem, The.
Cancel My Subscription.
For Myself.
Hinkson, Katharine Tynan. *See* **Tynan, Katharine**
Hinshaw, Dawn
Not-Knowing.
Hippisley, John
Sweet Is the Budding Spring of Love, *with music.*
Hippius, Zinaida
Grey Frock, A.
L'Imprévisibilité.
Hipple, Ted
Traditional Grammarian as Poet, The.
Hirsch, Edward
Chinese Vase, A.
Dawn Walk.
Dino Campana and the Bear.
Factories.
For the Sleepwalkers.
In the Middle of August.
Little Political Poem.
Matisse.
Poor Angels.
Hirsch, Mannie
Cry for a Disused Synagogue in Booysens.
Hirschfield, Theodore H.
A. M.—P.M.
Hirschman, Jack
NHR.
Zohara.
Hirshbein, Peretz
Captive.
I Shall Weep.
Stars Fade.
Hirst, Henry Beck
Fringilla Melodia, The.
Funeral of Time, The.
Hitchcock, George
Chauffeur of Lilacs, The.
Departure.
Figures in a Ruined Ballroom.
May All Earth Be Clothed in Light.
One Whose Reproach I Cannot Evade, The.
Song of Expectancy.
Three Found Poems.
Three Portraits.
United States Prepare for the Permanent Revolution, The.
Villa Thermidor.
Hitchner, John T.
Remembering Apple Times.
Hitomaro (Kakinomoto no Hitomaro)
Gossip grows like weeds.
Hittan of Tayyi
Hamasah, *sel.*
His Children.
Hoagland, Everett
Anti-Semanticist, The.
It's a Terrible Thing!
Love Child—a Black Aesthetic.
Music, The.
My Spring Thing.
Night Interpreted.
Hoare, Prince
Arethusa, The.
Hoban, Russell
Boy with a Hammer.
Egg Thoughts.
Empty House, The.
Homework.
Jigsaw Puzzle.
Maine Sea Gulls.
Soft-boiled Egg.
Sparrow Hawk, The.
Stupid Old Myself.
Tin Frog, The.
Hobbs, Valine
Change of Heart, A.
One Day When We Went Walking.
Hoberman, Mary Ann
Bugs, *sels.*
Changing.
Clickbeetle.
Cockroach.
Combinations.
Folk Who Live in Backward Town, The.
It's fun to go out and buy new shoes to wear.
Meg's Egg.
Night.
Praying Mantis.
Slushy snow splashes and sploshes, The.
Waiters.
Hobsbaum, Philip
Lesson in Love, A.
Timon Speaks to a Dog.
Hobson, Archie
Base Chapel, Lejeune 4/79.
Hobson, Dorothy
Do What You Will.
Hobson, Geary
Barbara's Land Revisited—August 1978.
For My Brother and Sister Southwestern Indian Poets.
Going to the Water.
Lonnie Kramer.
Tiger People.
Hobson, Katherine Thayer
Duality.
Hobson, Rodney
Man about the Kitchen, A.
Hoccleve [*or* Occleve], Thomas
Anxious Thought.
De Regimine Principum, *sels.*
Description of His Ugly Lady, A.
Hoccleve's Humorous Praise of His Lady.
Lament for Chaucer.
Lament for Chaucer and Gower.
Prologue: "Musing upon the restless bisinesse."
To Chaucer.
Hoch, Edward Wallis
Charity, *at.*
Hochman, Sandra
Clay and Water.
Couple, The.
Elephant, The.
Eyes of Flesh, The.
Goldfish Wife, The.
I Want to Tell You.
Postscript.
Hoddis, Jakov van (Hans Davidsohn)
Air Vision, The.
End of the World.
Tohub.
Hodes, Aubrey
Jew Walks in Westminster Abbey, A.
Hodgdon, Florence B.
How Can I Smile?
Hodge, Arthur J.
Five Were Foolish, *with music.*
Hodge, Marion
True Child ("True Child of God, stand innocently awed").
Hodges, Elizabeth
Blue Ridge.
Persimmons and Plums.
Hodgson, Ralph
After.
Babylon.
Bells of Heaven, The.
Birdcatcher, The.
Bride, The.
Bull, The.
Eve.
Flying Scrolls, *sels.*
Gently, years, gently!
Ghoul Care.
Gipsy Girl, The.
Great Auk's Ghost, The.
Hammers, The.
House across the Way, The.
Hymn to Moloch.
I heard the hymn of being sound.
I Love a Hill.
Late, Last Rook, The.
Moor, The.
Mystery, The.
Past comes back, The.
Reason Has Moons.
Riddle, The: "He told himself and he told his wife."
Sedge-Warbler, The.
Silver Wedding.
Song, A: "With Love among the haycocks."
Song of Honor [*or* Honour], The.
Stupidity Street.
Thrown.
Time.
Time, You Old Gypsy Man.
Weaving of the Wing, The.
Wood Song, A.
Hodgson, William Noel
Before Action.
Hoeft, Robert D.
Forty Pounds of Blackberries Equals Thirteen Gallons of Wine.
Our Annual Return to the Lake.
To a Little Boy Learning to Fish.
Hoellein, Alma
There Is a Place.
We'll Never Know.
Hoeppner, Ed
From Garvey's Farm: Seneca, Wisconsin.
Hoey, Allen
Casting at Night.
Secret Irish, The.
Walleye.
When the Cows Come Down to Drink.

Hoey, Edwin A.
Foul Shot.
Hoey, George
Asleep at the Switch.
Hoffenstein, Samuel
As the Crow Flies, *sel.*
Bird, The.
Birdie McReynolds.
Breathes There a Man.
Calf, the Goat, the Little Lamb, The.
Cradle Song: "Fear not the atom in fission."
Dry.
Father's Heart Is Touched, A.
For Little Boys Destined for Big Business.
I Burned My Candle at Both Ends.
I'd rather listen to a flute.
If you love me, as I love you.
Invocation: "Come, lovely Muse, desert for me."
Love-Songs, at Once Tender and Informative.
Lullaby: "Sleep, my little baby, sleep."
Madrigal Macabre.
Makes the Little Ones Dizzy.
Mamma Sings.
Mr. Vachel Lindsay Discovers Radio.
Mr. Walter de la Mare Makes the Little Ones Dizzy.
Pansy, The.
Poem Intended to Incite the Utmost Depression, A.
Poems in Praise of Practically Nothing.
Poems of Passion, Carefully Restrained So as to Offend Nobody.
Question and Answer.
Says Something Too.
Sheep.
Shropshire Lad's Cousin, The.
Song, on Reading That the Cyclotron Has Produced Cosmic Rays, *sel.*
Unequal Distribution.
When You're Away.
With Rue My Heart Is Laden, *parody.*
You Work and Work.
Your Little Hands.
Hoffman, Balthasar
Be Glorified Eternally, *with music.*
Hoffman, Charles Fenno
Mint Julep, The.
Monterey.
Sparkling and Bright.
Hoffman, Daniel Gerard
Armada of Thirty Whales, An.
As I Was Going to Saint Ives.
Ballad of No Proper Man.
Buddha.
Center of Attention, The.
Christ.
City of Satisfactions, The.
Dysynni Valley, The.
È, the Feasting Florentines.
Exploration.
First Flight.
Flushing Meadows, 1939.
Halflives.
Himself.
In Humbleness.
In the Beginning.
In the Days of Rin-Tin-Tin.
Inviolable.
Letter to Wilbur Frohock, A.
Lines Written near Linton, on Exmoor.
Meeting, A.
1956.
Ode to Joy.
Old Age Home, The.
Outwit Song, The.
Princess Casamassima, The.
Seals in Penobscot Bay, The.
Signatures.
Slick.
Sonnet, The: "Sonnet, she told the crowd of bearded, The."
Three Jovial Gentlemen.
Two Hundred Girls in Tights & Halters.
Who Was It Came.
Hoffman, George Edward
December 26.
Victory Parade.
Hoffman, Jill
Evening Ride
Stable, The.
To a Horse.
Hoffman, Phoebe W.
Pedro.
Hoffmann, Heinrich
Cruel Frederick.
Story of Augustus, Who Would Not Have Any Soup, The.
Story of Fidgety Philip, The.
Story of Flying Robert, The.
Story of Johnny Head-in-Air, The.
Story of Little Suck-a-Thumb, The.
Story of the Wild Huntsman, The.
Hoffmann, Roald
Finnair Fragment.
From a Rise of Land to the Sea.
Hoffman, William M.
Screw Spring.
Hofmannsthal, Hugo von
Ballad of the Outer Life.
Experience.
Many Indeed Must Perish in the Keel.
Ship's Cook, a Captive Sings, The.
Stanzas on Mutability.
Travel Song.
Two.
Venetian Night, A.
Vision, A.
World-Secret.
Hofstein, David
My Thread.
Hogan, Linda
Black Hills Survival Gathering, 1980.
Blessing.
Calling Myself Home.
Cities behind Glass.
Diary of Amanda McFadden, The.
Going to Town.
Heritage.
Leaving.
Nativity.
Oil.
Red Clay.
Saint Coyote.
Song for My Name.
What's Living?
Women Are Grieving, The.
Women Speaking, The.
Hogan, Michael
Child of Blue.
Condor, The.
December 18, 1975.
Fish.
Food Strike.
Indulgences.
O'Neill's War Song.
Parting.
Prison Break.
Rust.
Scrimshaw.
Spring.
Survivors.
Warriors.
Hogg, James ("The Ettrick Shepherd")
Boy's Song, A.
Flying Tailor, The.
Isabelle.
James Rigg.
Kilmeny.
Lock the Door, Lariston.
Love Is like a Dizziness.
McLean's Welcome.
Moggy and Me.
My Love She's But a Lassie Yet.
Queen's Wake, The, *sel.*
Skylark, The.
There's Gowd in the Breast.
Village of Balmaquhapple, The.
Walsinghame's Song.
When the Kye Comes Hame.
Witch o' Fife, The.
Witch's Chant, A.
Women Folk, The.
Hogg, Robert
Little Falls.
Poem: "In its going down, the moon."
Song: "Sun in mine, The."
Holbrook, David
Delivering Children.
Drought.
Fingers in the Door.
Living? Our Supervisors Will Do That for Us!
Maternity Gown.
Poor Old Horse.
Holbrook, John
Fishing the Big Hole.
Holbrook, Weare
Varitalk.
Holcroft, Thomas
Dying Prostitute, The; an Elegy.
Fool's Song.
Gaffer Gray.
On Shakespeare and Voltaire.
Seasons, The.
Song: "When o'er the wold the heedless lamb."
To Haydn.
Holden, Jonathan
Alone.
American Boyhood, An.
Dancing School.
December Sunset.
Liberace.
Losers.
Night: Landing at Newark.
Poem for Ed "Whitey" Ford, A.
Remembering My Father.
Seventeen.
Swimming Pool, The.
Washing My Son.
Why We Bombed Haiphong.
Holden, Molly
Giant Decorative Dahlia.
Hare.
Photograph of Haymaker, 1890.
Holden, Oliver
How Sweet Is the Language of Love, *with music.*
Weeping Sinner, Dry Your Tears, *with music.*
Within These Doors Assembled Now, *with music.*
Holden, Stephen
In Praise of Antonioni.
Hölderlin, Friedrich
All the fruit is ripe, plunged in fire, cooked.
Bread and Wine, *sel.*
Half of Life.
Life Half Lived.
Ripe, Being Plunged into Fire.
Sanctimonious Poets, The.
Holland, Henry Fox, 1st Baron
With a China Chamberpot, to the Countess of Hillsborough.
Holland, Hugh
Epitaph on Prince Henry.
Shakespeare Dead.
Holland, Josiah Gilbert
Babyhood.
Bitter-sweet, *sels.*
Christmas Carol, A: "There's a song in the air!"
Cradle Song: "What is the little one thinking about?"
Daniel Gray.
God, Give Us Men!
Gradatim.
Hymn: "For Summer's bloom and Autumn's blight."
Lullaby: "Rockaby, lullaby, bees in the clover!"

Mistress of the Manse, The, *sel.*
Song of Doubt, A.
Song of Faith, A.
There's a Song in the Air.
To My Dog "Blanco."
Wanted.
Where Shall the Baby's Dimple Be?

Holland, Norah M.
Little Dog-Angel, A.
Sea Song.

Holland, Sir Richard
Buke of the Howlat, The, *sel.*

Holland, Robert
Eve in Old Age.
Fisherman Casts His Line into the Sea, The.

Hollander, Gad
Argument against Metaphor.
Axioms.
Fugato (Coda.)
In Memoriam Paul Celan.

Hollander, John
Adam's Task.
Altarpiece Finished, The.
Appearance and Reality.
Aristotle to Phyllis.
Breadth. Circle. Desert. Monarch. Month. Wisdom.
Curse, The.
Danish Wit.
Fear of Trembling, The.
Great Bear, The.
Hall of Ocean Life.
Helicon.
Heliogabalus.
Historical Reflections.
Hobbes, 1651.
Horas Tempestatis Quoque Enumero: The Sundial.
Jefferson Valley.
Lady of the Castle, The.
Lady's-Maid's Song, The.
Last Quarter.
Last Words.
Lion Named Passion, A.
Lower Criticism, The.
Movie-Going.
Night Mirror, The.
Ninth of July, The.
No Foundation.
Non Sum Qualis Eram in Bona Urbe Nordica Illa.
Paysage Moralisé.
Skeleton Key.
Slepynge Long in Greet Quiete Is Eek a Greet Norice to Leccherie.
Something about It, *sel.*
State of Nature, A.
Sunday Evenings.
Swan and Shadow.
Tales Told of the Fathers.
To the Lady Portrayed by Margaret Dumont.
Under Cancer.
Violet.
West End Blues.
Wrath.
Ziz, The.

Hollander, Robert
Audiences.
Ice Cream in Paradise.
You Too? Me Too—Why Not? Soda Pop.

Holley, Horace
Hill, The.

Holley, Margaret
Your Woods.

Holliday, Carl
Thus Speak the Slain.

Hollis, Jocelyn
Meeting, The.

Hollis, Mark
Careless Talk.
'Twixt Cup and Lip.

Hollo, Anselm
After Verlaine.
Amazing Grace.
Buffalo—Isle of Wight Power Cable.
Caterpillar, The.
Discovery of LSD a True Story, The.
Le Jazz Hot.
Out of the "Kalevala," *sel.*
Rain.
That Old Sauna High.
Troll Chanting.
Vibrant mutants of the future.
Wasp Sex Myth (One).
Wasp Sex Myth (Two).

Holloway, John
Brothers, The.
Elegy for an Estrangement.
Family Poem.
Journey through the Night.
Light, The.
Warning to a Guest.

Holloway, John Wesley
Black Mammies.
Calling the Doctor.
Corn Song, The.
Miss Melerlee.

Holloway, Lucy Ariel Williams
Northboun'.

"Holm, Saxe." *See* **Jackson, Helen Hunt**

Holman, Felice
City Dump, The.
Clock, The.
Halloween Witches.
I Can Fly.
Leave Me Alone.
Sulk.
Supermarket.
They're Calling.
Who Am I?

Holman, Jesse L.
Lord, in Thy Presence Here, *with music.*

Holman, M. Carl
And on This Shore.
Letter across Doubt and Distance.
Mr. Z.
Notes for a Movie Script.
Picnic: the Liberated.
Song: "Dressed up in my melancholy."
Three Brown Girls Singing.

Holme, Jamie Sexton
Mountain Evenings.
Timber Line Trees.

Holmes, Abiel
To Thee, O God, *with music.*
Who Here Can Cast His Eyes Abroad, *with music.*

"Holmes, Alec." *See* **Scott, Aimee Byng**

Holmes, Georgiana Klingle. *See* **"Klingle, George"**

Holmes, John
At a Country Fair.
Broken One, The.
Bucyrus.
But Choose.
Carry Me Back.
Chance, The.
Core, The.
Evening Meal in the Twentieth Century.
Fear of Dying, The.
Fortune Teller, The.
Grass.
Herself.
Letter, The.
Man at Work.
Map of My Country.
Metaphor for My Son.
Misery.
New View, The.
Overgrown Back Yard, The.
Peace Is the Mind's Old Wilderness, *with music.*
Poetry Defined.
Pour Down.
Questions for the Candidate.
Rhyme of Rain.
Somerset Dam for Supper, The.
Spiral, The.
Table for One.
Thrifty Elephant, The.
What Does a Man Think About.
What Literature Needs.
Willing Suspension, A.

Holmes, John Haynes
God of the Nations, Near and Far, *with music.*
Hymn: "Great Spirit of the speeding spheres."
Hymn: "Thou God of all, whose presence dwells."
O'er Continent and Ocean, *with music.*
Voice of God Is Calling, The, *with music.*

Holmes, Oliver Wendell
Additional Verses to Hail Columbia.
Aestivation [an Unpublished Poem by My Late Latin Tutor].
After a Lecture on Keats.
After the Fire.
Angel of Peace, Thou Hast Wandered Too Long, *with music.*
As on the gauzy wings of fancy flying.
Aunt Tabitha.
Autocrat of the Breakfast-Table, The, *sels.*
Ballad of the Boston Tea-Party, A.
Ballad of the Oysterman, The.
Bill and Joe.
Boys, The.
Broomstick Train, The, *sel.*
Brother Jonathan's Lament for Sister Caroline.
Cacoëthes Scribendi.
Chambered Nautilus, The.
"Christo et Ecclesiae" 1700.
Contentment.
Crooked Footpath, The.
Daily Trials.
Daniel Webster.
Deacon's Masterpiece, The; or, The Wonderful "One-Hoss Shay."
Dorchester Giant, The.
Dorothy Q.
Eggstravagance, An.
Epilogue to the Breakfast-Table Series.
Familiar Letter to Several Correspondents, A.
Farewell to Agassiz, A.
Flower of Liberty, The.
God Save the Flag.
Grandmother's Story of Bunker-Hill Battle.
Height of the Ridiculous, The.
Hymn of Trust.
In Thine Arms.
Iron Gate, The, *sel.*
La Grisette.
Last Leaf, The.
Lexington.
Limerick: "Reverend Henry Ward Beecher, The," *at.*
Living Temple, The.
Manhood.
Music Grinders, The.
My Aunt.
Ode for a Social Meeting.
Old Ironsides.
Old Man Dreams, The.
On Lending a Punch-Bowl.
On the Death of President Garfield.
One-Hoss Shay, The.
Our Father! While Our Hearts Unlearn, *with music.*
Peau de Chagrin of State Street, The.
Poem, A: "Father of all! in Death's relentless claim," *sel.*
Poem for the Meeting of the American Medical Association, A.
Poet at the Breakfast Table, The, *sel.*
Poet's Lot, The.
Professor at the Breakfast Table, The, *sels.*
Sea Dialogue, A.
September Gale, The, *sel.*

Sherman's in Savannah.
Strong Heroic Line, The.
Sun-Day Hymn, A.
Then as to Feasting.
To an Insect.
To the Portrait of "A Gentlemen."
Two Sonnets: Harvard.
Two Streams, The.
Under the Violets.
Union and Liberty.
Veritas.
Voiceless, The.
Welcome to Dr. Benjamin Apthorp Gould, A.
Welcome to the Nations.
Wind-Clouds and Star-Drifts, *sel.*

Holmes, W. K.
Old Mountaineer, The.
On the Heights.

Holshouser, W. L.
Turning Point.

Holt, Jessie
Dying.

Hölty, Ludwig Heinrich Christoph
Harvest Song.

Holtz, Barry
Isaac.

Holub, Miroslav
Brief Reflection on the Insect.
Dog in the Quarry, A, *sel.*
Evening in a Lab.
Hominization.
How to Paint a Perfect Christmas.
Newborn Baby.
Poem Technology.
Teaching about Arthropods.
Teeth.
Wings.
Zito the Magician.

Holyday, Barten
Bogs, purgatory, wolves and ease, by fame.
Clay, sand, and rock, seem of a diff'rent birth.
Pride cannot see itself by mid-day light.
Song: "O harmless feast."
Technogamia, *sel.*

Holz, Arno
Buddha.
Leave-Taking, A.
Phantasus.
Roses Red.

Holzapfel, Rudi
Employee, The.

"Home, Cecil." *See* **Webster, Augusta**

Homer
Achilles Shows Himself in the Battle by the Ships.
Achilles to Lycaon.
Ajax the swift swerv'd never from the side.
All grave old men, and souldiers they had bene, but for age.
And as in winter time when Jove his cold-sharpe javelines throwes.
And as when with the West-wind's flawes the sea thrusts up her waves.
And now Eurynome had bath'd the king.
And now his well-known bow the master bore.
And now the Queene of women had intent.
And now was Paris come/ From his high towres.
And when they came together in one place.
Andromache's Lamentation.
As when an architect some palace wall.
As when devouring flames some forest seize.
As when of frequent bees.
At her departure his disdain return'd.
At this th' impatient hero sowrly smil'd.
Big with great purposes and proud, they sat.
But now, no longer deaf to honour's call.
Death of Hector, The.
End of the Suitors, The.
Fierce they drove on, impatient to destroy.
Funeral Games for Patroclus, The: The Boastful Boxer.
Funeral Games for Patroclus, The: Wrestling to a Draw.
Gardens of Alcinous, The ("Close to the gates a spacious garden lies").
Gardens of Alcinous, The ("Without the hall and close upon the gate").
Ghost of Patroclus, The.
Hector and Andromache.
Hektor to Andromache.
Helen's Lamentation.
Iliad, The, *much abr.*
Like leaves on trees the race of man is found.
Nausicaa.
Nestor.
New Coasts and Poseidon's Son.
Night Encampment outside Troy.
Nor lingered Paris in the lofty house.
Nor long the trench or lofty walls oppose.
Now toils the heroe; trees on trees o'erthrown.
Odysseus and the Phaeacian Games.
Odyssey, The, *sels.*
Parting of Hector and Andromache, The.
Patroclus' Body Saved.
Priam and Achilles.
Pyre of Patroclus, The.
Sacrifice, The.
Sarpedon to Glaukos.
Scylla and Charybdis.
Trojans outside the Walls, The.
Ulysses and His Dog.
Ulysses Hears the Prophecies of Tiresias.
Ulysses in the Waves.
Ulysses Leaves the Nymph Calypso.
Youth there was, Elpenor was he nam'd, A.

Homer-Dixon, Homera
New Year, The.

Ho Nansorhon
Woman's Sorrow, A, *sel.*

Honestus
Requirements: "Not too old, and not too young."

Honeywood, St. John
Darby and Joan.
Radical Song of 1786, A.

Hongo, Garrett Kaoru
Hiking Up Hieizan with Alam Lau/Buddha's Birthday 1974.
Hongo Store 29 Miles Volcano Hilo, Hawaii, The.
Off from Swing Shift.
On the Road to Paradise.
What For.
Who among You Knows the Essence of Garlic?
Yellow Light.

Honig, Edwin
As a Great Prince.
Being Somebody.
Happening.
November through a Giant Copper Beech.
Now, My Usefulness Over.
Some Knots.
Tall Toms, The.
Tête-à-Tête.
Through You.
Walt Whitman.
What Changes, My Love.
Who.

Hood, E. P.
God, Who Hath Made the Daisies.

Hood, Thomas
Address to Mr. Cross, of Exeter 'Change, on the Death of the Elephant.
Athol Brose.
Autumn.
Black Job, A, *sel.*
Bridge of Sighs, The.
Carelesse Nurse Mayd, The.
Choosing Their Names.
Death.
Death-Bed, The.
Death of Leander, The.
Domestic Asides; or, Truth in Parentheses.
Domestic Didactics by an Old Servant.
Dream of Eugene Aram, The.
Dust to Dust.
Epigram: "After such years of dissension and strife."
Epigram: "When Eve upon the first of men."
Fair Ines.
Fairy's Reply to Saturn, The.
Faithless Nelly [*or* Nellie] Gray.
Faithless Sally Brown.
False Poets and True.
Farewell, Life.
Flowers.
Friendly Address, A.
Gold.
Good Night.
Green Dryad's Plea, The.
Haunted House, The.
Hero and Leander, *sels.*
I Remember, I Remember.
I'm Not a Single Man.
Irish Schoolmaster, The.
It Was the Time of Roses.
Last Man, The.
Lay of the Labourer, The.
Little Piggy.
Mary's Ghost.
Melodies of Time, The.
Miss Kilmansegg and Her Precious Leg, *sels.*
Natural Tears.
No!
Nocturnal Sketch, A.
November.
Ode: Autumn.
Ode on a Distant Prospect of Clapham Academy.
Ode to Autumn.
Ode to the Cameleopard.
Ode to the Moon.
On a Royal Demise.
On Mistress Nicely, a Pattern for Housekeepers.
On the Death of the Giraffe.
Our Village—by a Villager.
Parental Ode to My Son [Aged Three Years and Five Months], A.
Past and Present.
Peter's Tears.
Plea of the Midsummer Fairies, The, *sels.*
Please to Ring the Belle.
Poet's Fate, The.
Poor dear dead have been laid out in vain, The.
Quadrupedremian Song, A.
Queen Mab.
Reflection, A.
Ruth.
Sailor's Apology for Bow-Legs, A.
Sally Simpkin's Lament.
Scylla's Lament.
Sea of Death, The.
Serenade: "Ah, sweet, thou little knowest how."
Shakespeare.
Silence.
Song: "Lake and a fairy boat, A."
Song of the Shirt, The.
Sonnet: "It is not death, that sometime in a sigh."
Sonnet: Silence.
Sonnet to Vauxhall.
Stars Are with the Voyager, The.
Sun Was Slumbering in the West, The.
Tender Babes.
Tim Turpin.
Time of Roses.
Titania.
To Henrietta, on Her Departure for Calais.
To Minerva.
To My Son, Aged Three Years and Five Months.
To the Reviewers.
Tom Tatter's Birthday Ode.
Two Swans, The.
Water Lady, The.

What Different Dooms Our Birthdays Bring!
Hood, Tom (Thomas Hood, Jr.)
All in the Downs.
Cannibal Flea, The.
Catch, A.
Confounded Nonsense.
Few Muddled Metaphors by a Moore-ose Melodist, A.
How Singular.
Little tigers are at rest, The.
Muddled Metaphors.
Poets and Linnets.
Ravings.
Sunset in the Sea.
Wedding, The.
Hood-Adams, Rebecca
Family Portrait.
Hook, Theodore
Address to Children.
Cautionary Verses to Youth of Both Sexes.
Hooker, Brian
Ballade of the Dreamland Rose.
From Life.
Little Person, A.
Mother of Men.
Portrait, A.
Song: "Only a little while since first we met."
Hookham, George
Chamonix.
Hooley, Teresa
To-day I saw a butterfly.
War Film, A.
Hooper, Ellen Sturgis
Beauty and Duty.
Duty.
Hooper, H. S.
Frisco's Defi.
Hooper, Lucy Hamilton
Three Loves.
Hooper, Patricia
9:00.
Other Lives.
Psalm: "It's not the sun."
Hooton, Earnest Albert
Fat-buttocked Bushmen, The.
Lines to Homo Somejerktensis.
Ode to a Dental Hygienist.
To Chloe.
Hoover, Paul
Barnabooth Enters Russia.
Hope, Alec Derwent
Advice to Young Ladies.
As Well as They Can ("As well as it can, the hooked fish while it dies").
Australia.
Bed, The.
Brides, The.
Chorale: "Often had I found her fair."
Circe.
Coup de Grâce.
Death of the Bird, The.
Double Looking Glass, The.
Dunciad Minor, *sels.*
E Questo il Nido in Che la Mia Fenice?
Elegy, The: "Madam, no more! The time has come to eat."
Epistle, An: "First, last and always dearest, closest, best."
Female Principle, The.
Gateway, The.
House of God, The.
Imperial Adam.
Letter to David Campbell on the Birthday of W. B. Yeats, 1965, A.
Lingam and the Yoni, The.
Martyrdom of St. Teresa, The.
Meditation on a Bone.
Moschus Moschiferus.
Observation Car.
On an Engraving by Casserius.
On Shakespeare Critics.
Parabola.
Paradise Saved.
Prometheus Unbound.
Pronunciation of Erse, The.
Pyramis; or, The House of Ascent.
School of Night, The.
Tiger.
Hope, Francis
Peeping Tom.
Hope, James Barron
John Smith's Approach to Jamestown.
"Hope, Laurence" (Adela Florence Cory Nicolson)
Ashore.
Bride, The.
For This Is Wisdom.
Kashmiri Song ("Pale hands I love").
Khristna and His Flute.
Masters, The.
Teak Forest, The, *sel.*
Youth.
Hope, Margaret
Through the Ages.
Hope, T.
Death Again.
Hopegood, Peter
Dithyramb in Retrospect.
Protagonist, The.
Hopes, David
Hairdresser, The.
Hopkins, Gerard Manley
Alchemist in the City, The.
Andromeda.
As Kingfishers Catch Fire [Dragonflies Draw Flame].
Ashboughs.
At a Welsh Waterfall.
Barnfloor and Winepress.
Beginning of the End, The.
Binsey Poplars (Felled 1879).
Blessed Virgin Compared to the Air We Breathe, The.
Brothers.
Bugler's First Communion, The.
By Magdalen Bridge, Oxford.
Caged Skylark, The.
Candle Indoors, The.
Carrion Comfort.
"Child Is Father to the Man, The."
Cuckoo, The.
Duns Scotus's Oxford.
Easter Communion.
Epithalamion: "Hark, hearer, hear what I do."
Felix Randal.
Fragment: "Mark you how the peacock's eye."
Fragment: "Repeat that, repeat."
God's Character.
God's Grandeur.
Golden Echo, The.
Habit of Perfection, The.
Harry Ploughman.
Heaven-Haven.
Henry Purcell.
Hurrahing in Harvest.
I am like a slip of comet.
I Wake and Feel the Fell of Dark, Not Day.
In Honour of St. Alphonsus Rodriguez.
In the Valley of the Elwy.
Inversnaid.
Justus Quidem Tu Es, Domine.
Lantern out of Doors, The.
Leaden Echo and the Golden Echo, The.
Let me be to Thee as the circling bird.
Life Death Does End.
May Magnificat, The.
Mrs. Hopley, on Seeing Her Children Say Goodnight to Their Father.
Moonless Darkness Stands Between.
Moonrise.
My own heart let me more have pity on.
No Worst, There Is None.
O Deus, Ego Amo Te.
Of virtures I most warmly bless.
On a Poetess.
On St. Winefred.
Oxford Bells.
Patience, Hard Thing!
Peace.
Pied Beauty.
Rainbow, The.
Rosa Mystica.
Sea and the Skylark, The.
Six Epigrams, *sel.*
Soldier, The.
Soliloquy of One of the Spies Left in the Wilderness, A.
Sonnet: "Not, I'll not, carrion comfort, Despair, not feast on thee."
Sonnet: "Patience, hard thing! the hard thing but to pray."
Spelt from Sibyl's Leaves.
Spring.
Spring and Death.
Spring and Fall.
Starlight Night, The.
Summer Malison, The.
Terrible Sonnets, The.
That Nature Is a Heraclitean Fire and of the Comfort of the Resurrection.
Thee, God, I come from, to thee go.
Thou Art Indeed Just, Lord, If I Contend.
To His Watch.
To Oxford.
To R. B.
To Seem the Stranger Lies My Lot.
Tom's Garland: Upon the Unemployed.
Vision of the Mermaids, A, *sel.*
What I Do Is Me.
Windhover, The.
Winter with the Gulf Stream.
Wreck of the *Deutschland,* The.
Hopkins, John (c. **1520–70)**
Thou, Lord, Hast Been Our Sure Defense, *with music.*
Hopkins, John Henry, Jr. (1820–1891)
Alleluia! Christ Is Risen Today, *with music.*
God of Our Fathers, Bless This Our Land, *with music.*
We Three Kings of Orient Are.
Hopkins, Josiah
O Turn Ye, O Turn Ye, *with music.*
Hopkins, Lee Bennett
Girls Can, Too!
Hopkins, Tim
Do Not Go Gentle ("Do not go gentle into Death's esteemed vale").
Hopkinson, Francis
American Independence.
Arise and See the Glorious Sun, *with music.*
At Length the Busy Day Is Done, *with music.*
Battle of the Kegs, The.
British Valor Displayed.
Daughter's Rebellion, The.
Enraptured I Gaze, *with music.*
New Roof, The.
On the Late Successful Expedition against Louisbourg.
Hopkinson, Joseph
Hail, Columbia.
Hoppe, Anna
Precious Child, So Sweetly Sleeping, *with music.*
Hopper, Edward
Jesus Saviour, Pilot Me.
They Pray the Best Who Pray and Watch, *with music.*
Hopper, Nora
Dark Man, The.
Fairy Fiddler, The.
June.
King of Ireland's Son, The.
March.
Marriage Charm, A.
'Tis I Go Fiddling, Fiddling.
Hopper, Virginia Shearer
In the Canadian Rockies.

Horace (Quintus Horatius Flaccus)
Ad Leuconoen.
Ad Ministram.
Ad Xanthiam Phoceum.
Albi, Ne Doreas.
Another to the Same.
Ars Poetica.
Art of Poetry, The, *sels.*
Ask Not Ungainly.
Barine, the Incorrigible.
By the Flat Cup.
Country Life.
Dialogue between Horace and Lydia, A.
Diffugere Nives.
Epistles, *sel.*
Epodes, *sel.*
Extremum Tanain.
Fie on Eastern Luxury! ("Persicos odi").
Fifth Ode of Horace, The.
Golden Mean, The.
Good bailiff of my farm, that snug domain.
Happiness.
Happy the Man.
Holiday.
If, O Maecenas, versed in lore antique.
If you can lie, Torquatus, when you take.
Immortality of Verse, The.
Invocation: "Maidens young and virgins tender."
It Always Happens.
Lydia, in Heavens Name.
Odes, *sels.*
Passing of Lydia, The.
Persian Fopperies.
Philippus, for his pleadings famed afar.
Pine Tree for Diana, The.
Praise of Pindar, The.
Profane, The.
Revenge!
Ribald Romeos Less and Less Berattle.
Ship of State, The.
Teasing Lovers, The.
This Monument Will Outlast.
Time to Choose a Lover.
To a Girl.
To an Ambitious Friend.
To Apollo and Diana.
To Aristius Fuscus.
To Chloe ("Vitas hinnuleo").
To Fuscus Aristus.
To Leuconöe.
To Licinius.
To Lydia.
To Maecenas.
To Phidyle.
To Pyrrha ("Quis multa gracilis").
To Sally.
To Thaliarchus.
To the Fountain of Bandusia.
To the Ship on Which Virgil Sailed to Athens.
To Venus.
Too Young for Love.
Virtue, dear friend, needs no defence.
Young Men Come Less Often, The—Isn't It So?
Your kindness, sir, to me, is really kind.
Horan, Robert
By Hallucination Visited.
Emblems of Evening.
Farewell to Narcissus.
Little City.
Horder, John
Sick Image of My Father Fades, The.
Horgan, Paul
Now Evening Puts Amen to Day, *with music.*
Horikawa, Lady
How long will it last?
Will he always love me?
Horn, Edward Newman
Darling, If You Only Knew.
In the Tub We Soak Our Skin.
Pussycat Sits on a Chair.
Tiger stalking in the night, The.
Horn, Herschel
Landscape near a Steel Mill.
Horne, Frank
Immortality.
Kid Stuff.
Letters [*or* Notes] Found near a Suicide.
Mamma!
More Letters Found near a Suicide.
Nigger.
On Seeing Two Brown Boys in a Catholic Church.
Patience.
Resurrection.
Symphony.
To a Persistent Phantom.
To "Chick."
To James.
To Mother.
To You.
Toast.
Walk.
Horne, Herbert P.
If She Be Made of White and Red.
Nancy Dawson.
Horne, Lewis B.
Moving Day.
Muscae Volitantes.
Suppose.
Horne, Richard Henry [*or* Hengist]
Orion, *sels.*
Plough, The.
Solitude and the Lily.
Horner, Joyce
Public Holiday: Paris.
Horovitz, Frances
Messenger, The.
Moon.
Woman's Dream, The.
Horsburgh, Wilma
Train to Glasgow, The.
Horta, Maria Teresa
Saved.
Swimming Pool.
Horta, Maria Teresa *and* **Maria Isabel Barreno** *and* **Maria Velho da Costa.** *See* **Marias, The Three**
Horton, George
Night in Lesbos, A.
Horton, George Moses
Eye of Love, The.
New Fashions.
On Liberty and Slavery.
Powers of Love, The.
Setting Sun, The.
Snaps for Dinner, Snaps for Breakfast, and Snaps for Supper.
Swan, The—Vain Pleasures.
To a Departing Favorite.
Horvitz, Allan Kolski
King Saul.
Radiance of Extinct Stars, The.
Hosking, Arthur Nicholas
Land of the Free.
Hoskins, John. *See* **Hoskyns, John**
Hoskins, Katherine
Baucis and Philemon.
Bee and the Petunia, The.
Byfield Rabbit, The.
Côte d'Azur.
Not Lotte.
Nuit Blanche.
Hoskyns [*or* **Hoskins**], **John**
Absence.
Bellows Maker of Oxford, The.
Epitaph on Sir Walter Pye.
Epitaph on the Fart in the Parliament House.
Here lies the man that madly slain.
His Own Epitaph, When He Was Sick.
Ode: "Absence, hear thou my protestation."
Of the Loss of Time.
On a Contentious Companion.
On a Whore.
On One That Lived Ingloriously.
Present in Absence.
To His Little Son Benedict from the Tower of London.
To His Son Bennet.
Upon a Fool.
Upon One of the Maids of Honour to Queen Elizabeth.
Hosmer, Frederick Lucian
From Age to Age They Gather, *with music.*
Hear, Hear, O Ye Nations, *with music.*
My Dead.
O Beautiful, My Country.
O Day of Light and Gladness, *with music.*
Prophecy Sublime, The.
Through Unknown Paths.
Through Willing Heart and Helping Hand, *with music.*
Thy Kingdom Come, O Lord.
Thy Kingdom Come ("Thy kingdom come—on bended knee").
With Self Dissatisfied.
Hosmer, William Henry Cuyler
Song of Texas.
Hoss, E. Embree
O God, Great Father, Lord, and King, *with music.*
Houck, James A.
Children's Lenten Wisdom.
Hough, Graham
Age of Innocence.
Dark Corner.
Hough, Lindy
Portrait of the Father.
Houghton, Firman
Mr. Frost Goes South to Boston.
She Sees Another Door Opening.
Houghton, George Washington Wright
Handsel Ring, The.
Legend of Walbach Tower, The.
Manor Lord, The.
March Winds, The.
Sandy Hook.
Houghton, Richard Monckton Milnes, 1st Baron. *See* **Milnes, Richard Monckton, 1st Baron Houghton**
House, Vernal
In Tribute.
Houselander, Caryll
Litany to Our Lady.
Reed, The.
Housman, Alfred Edward
Along the Field as We Came By.
Alta Quies.
Amelia Mixed the Mustard.
As I Gird on for Fighting.
Astronomy.
Away with Bloodshed.
Be still, my soul, be still; the arms you bear are brittle.
Because I Liked You Better.
Blackbird, The.
Bredon Hill.
Carpenter's Son, The.
Chestnut Casts His Flambeaux, [and the Flowers,] The.
Could Man Be Drunk for Ever.
Crossing Alone the Nighted Ferry.
Day of Battle, The.
Deserter, The.
Easter Hymn.
Eight o'Clock.
1887.
Elephant, or the Force of Habit, The.
Epilogue: " 'Terence, this is stupid stuff.' "
Epitaph: "Here dead lie we because we did not choose."
Epitaph on an Army of Mercenaries.
Fairies break their dances, The.
Fancy's Knell.
Far in a Western Brookland.
Farewell to Barn and Stack and Tree.

For My Funeral.
Fragment of a Greek Tragedy.
Friends.
From Far, from Eve and Morning.
From the Wash the Laundress Sends.
G. K. Chesterton on His Birth.
Good Creatures, Do You Love Your Lives.
Grenadier.
Half-way, for One Commandment Broken.
Hallelujah!
He Would Not Stay for Me; and Who Can Wonder?
Hell Gate.
Her Strong Enchantments Failing.
Here Dead Lie We.
Ho, Everyone That Thirsteth.
Hughley Steeple.
I Did Not Lose My Heart in Summer's Even.
I Hoed and Trenched and Weeded.
I Knew a Cappadocian.
I Promise Nothing.
I to My Perils.
Immortal Part, The.
In my own shire, if I was sad.
In the Morning, in the Morning.
In valleys green and still.
Infant Innocence.
Inhuman Henry.
Into My Heart an Air That Kills.
Is My Team Ploughing [*or* Plowing]?
Isle of Portland, The.
Jar of Nations, The.
Lads in Their Hundreds, The.
Lancer.
Laws of God, the Laws of Man, The.
Lent Lily, The.
Look Not in My Eyes, for Fear.
Loveliest of Trees [the Cherry Now].
March.
Merry Guide, The.
Mill-stream, now that noises cease, The.
New Mistress, The.
New Year's Eve.
Night Is Freezing Fast, The.
Now Dreary Dawns the Eastern Light.
O Billows Bounding Far.
O Have You Caught the Tiger?
Occasional Poem.
Oh, See How Thick the Goldcup Flowers.
Oh, When I Was in Love with You.
Oh Who Is That Young Sinner [with the Handcuffs on His Wrists?]
Olive, The.
On Forelands High in Heaven.
On moonlit heath and lonesome bank.
On the idle hill of summer.
On Wenlock Edge [the Wood's in Trouble].
Oracles, The.
Others, I Am Not the First.
Parta Quies.
Power of Malt, The.
Profoundly True Reflections on the Sea.
Rain, it streams on stone and hillock, The.
Rainy Pleiads Wester, The.
Recruit, The.
Reveille.
Revolution.
Say, lad, have you things to do?
Shades of Night, The.
Shot? So Quick, So Clean an Ending?
Sigh that heaves the grasses, The.
Smooth between Sea and Land.
Soldier from the Wars Returning.
Some can gaze and not be sick.
Stars, I Have Seen Them Fall.
Stars Have Not Dealt Me, The.
Street Sounds to the Soldiers' Tread, The.
Tell Me Not Here [It Needs Not Saying].
Terence, This Is Stupid Stuff.
There Is Hallelujah Hannah.
They Say My Verse Is Sad: No Wonder.
Think no more, lad; laugh, be jolly.
To an Athlete Dying Young.
To His Godson Gerald C. A. Jackson.
To Stand Up Straight.
To Think That Two and Two Are Four.
Twice a Week the Winter Thorough.
Wake Not for the World-heard Thunder.
We'll to the Woods No More.
Welsh Marches, The.
Wenlock Edge ("On Wenlock Edge the wood's in trouble").
Wenlock Edge ("'Tis time, I think; by Wenlock town").
When first my way to fair I took.
When I Was One-and-twenty.
When I Watch the Living Meet.
When Israel out of Egypt Came.
When summer's end is nighing.
When the Eye of Day Is Shut.
When the Lad for Longing Sighs.
White in the moon the long road lies.
With Rue My Heart Is Laden.
Yon Far Country.
Yonder See the Morning Blink.

Housman, Laurence
All Fellows, *sel.*
Comrades.
Continuing City, The.
Dead Warrior, A.
Dedication: "When I have ended, then I see."
Deus Noster Ignis Consumens.
Farewell to Town.
Gardener, The.
God's Mother.
Settlers, The.
Spikenard.
Two Loves, The.

Houston, Gil
Rambling, Gambling Man.

Hovde, A. J.
I Shall Never Go.
Of Mouse and Men.
On Hearing a Beautiful Young Woman Describe Her Class in Physical Anthropology.

Hovell-Thurlow, Edward, 2d Baron Thurlow
Heron, The.
May.
When in the Woods I Wander All Alone.

Hover, Donald H.
Other Person's Place, The.

Hovey, Richard
Accident in Art.
At the Crossroads.
At the End of the Day.
Barney McGee.
Battle of Manila, The.
Birth of Galahad, The, *sel.*
Call of the Bugles, The.
Chanson de Rosemonde.
Dartmouth Winter-Song.
Eleazar Wheelock.
Envoy: "Whose furthest footstep never strayed."
Hunting-Song.
Immanence.
Kavanagh, The.
Laurana's Song.
Love in the Winds.
More Songs from Vagabondia, *sel.*
Sea Gypsy [*or* Gipsy], The.
Spring, *sel.*
Stein Song, A.
Taliesin, *sel.*
Transcendence.
Unmanifest Destiny.
Wander-Lovers, The.
Word of the Lord from Havana, The.
Ylen's Song.

How, William Walsham
O Word of God Incarnate.
We Give Thee But Thine Own.

Howard, Anne, Duchess of Arundel
Elegy on the Death of Her Husband.

Howard, Ben
Lynx.
Winter Report.

Howard, Dorothy S.
Birkett's Eagle.

Howard, Frances Minturn
Heron in Swamp.
Narcissus in a Cocktail Glass.
Prophecy in Flame.
Sampler from Haworth.

Howard, Henry. *See* **Surrey, Henry Howard, Earl of**

Howard, Jim
Boy Trash Picker.
Newspaper Hats.

Howard, Joseph E.
Good Bye, My Lady Love, *with music.*

Howard, Joseph E. *and* **Ida Emerson**
Hello, Ma [*or* My] Baby.

Howard, Leonard
Humours of the King's Bench Prison, a Ballad, The.

Howard, Philip, 1st Earl of Arundel
Hymn: "O Christ, the glorious Crown."

Howard, Quentin R.
In the Corn Land.

Howard, Richard
Again for Hephaistos, the Last Time.
Aubade: Donna Anna to Juan, Still Asleep.
Author of *Christine,* The.
Bonnard; a Novel.
Compulsive Qualifications, *sels.*
Crepuscular.
1864.
Far Cry after a Close Call, A.
Gaiety, *sel.*
Giovanni da Fiesole on the Sublime; or, Fra Angelico's "Last Judgment."
Landed: A Valentine.
Lapsus Linguae.
Natural History.
1915: A Pre Raphaelite Ending, London.
On Arrival.
Oystering.
Queer's Song.
Recipe for an Ocean in the Absence of the Sea.
Saturday Morning.
Secular Games.
209 Canal.

Howard, Sir Robert
To the Unconstant Cynthia.

Howard, Sir Robert *and* John Dryden
Indian Queen, The, *sel.*

Howard, Sarah Elizabeth
Round-up, The.
Wild Horse Jerry's Story.

Howard, Vilma
Citizen, The.

Howard, Winifred
Fairy Wings.
White Horses.
Windy Day, A.

Howard-Jones, Stuart
Hibernia.

Howarth, B. L.
Brown paper worn next to the skin.

Howarth, Ellen Clementine
'Tis but a Little Faded Flower.

Howarth, Robert Guy
Memoir.
On a Row of Nuns in a Cemetery.

Howe, Ed
Instead of loving your enemies, treat your friends a little better.

Howe, George
Sun-Witch to the Sun, The.

Howe, Joseph
Acadia, *sel.*
Song of the Micmac, The.

Howe, Julia Ward
Battle Hymn of the Republic, The.
Decoration Day.

J. A. G.
Message of Peace, The.
Our Country.
Our Orders.
Pardon.
Parricide.
Robert E. Lee.
Howe, Mark Antony De Wolfe ("Gilbertulus")
Distinction.
Petrillo, *parody.* "
Pocket and Steeple.
Travellers, The.
Whom the Gods Love.
Howe, Solomon
Our Kind Creator, *with music.*
Howe, William Walsham
Funeral Hymn.
Howell, Elizabeth Lloyd
Milton's Prayer for [*or* of] Patience.
Howell, James
Of London Bridge, and the Stupendous Sight, and Structure Thereof.
Howell, Thomas
Lover Deceived Writes to His Lady, The, *sels.*
Of Misery.
Rose, The.
When He Thought Himself Contemned.
Who Would Have Thought [That Face of Thine].
Howells, Mildred
God's Will.
Going Too Far.
Moral in Sevres, A.
Howells, William Dean
Battle in the Clouds, The.
Change.
Earliest Spring.
Faith.
From Generation to Generation.
Hope.
If.
In August.
In Earliest Spring.
Judgment Day.
Prayer, A: "Lord, for the erring thought."
Song the Oriole Sings, The.
Thanksgiving, A.
Two Wives, The.
Vision.
What Shall It Profit?
Howells, Winifred
Forthfaring.
Mood, A.
Past.
Poet and the Child, The.
Wasted Sympathy, A.
Howes, Barbara
At 79th and Park.
Best of Show.
Cardinal.
Cat on Couch.
Chimera.
City Afternoon.
Conversation, A.
Danaë.
Death of a Vermont Farm Woman.
Don, The.
Dressmaker's Dummy as Scarecrow, The.
Early Supper.
Flight.
Four Fawns.
Gulls.
Home Leave.
In Autumn.
Indian Summer.
Jim.
Landscape, Deer Season.
Letter from the Caribbean, A.
Light and Dark.
L'Ile du Levant: The Nudist Colony.
Looking Up at Leaves.
Mistral.
Monkey Difference.
On a Bougainvillæa Vine at the Summer Palace.
On Galveston Beach.
Out Fishing.
Portrait of an Artist.
Portrait of the Boy as Artist.
Returning to Store Bay.
Rune for C., A.
Sea School.
Talking to Animals.
Triumph of Chastity, The.
Triumph of Death, The.
Views of the Oxford Colleges.
Howes, Grace Clementine
Wind of the Prairie.
Winged Mariner.
Howitt, Mary
Broom Flower, The.
Buttercups and Daisies.
Fairies of the Caldon-Low, The.
Lion, The.
Monkey, The.
Old Christmas.
Rose of May, The.
Sale of the Pet Lamb, The.
Seagull, The.
Spider and the Fly, The.
Howitt, William
Migration of the Grey Squirrels, The.
Northern Seas, The.
Wind in a Frolic, The.
Howland, Edward
Condemned, The.
Howland, Mary Woolsey
In the Hospital.
Ho Xuan Huong
Buddhist Priest, A.
Carved on an Areca Nut.
Jackfruit, The.
Hoy, Albert L.
Hour of Prayer, The.
Hoyem, Andrew
Circumambulation of Mt. Tamalpais.
Hoyer, Mildred N.
Voice of the Crocus.
Hoyt, Charles Hale
Bowery, The.
Hoyt, Helen
Ellis Park.
Golden Bough.
In the Park.
Memory.
Reparation.
Sense of Death, The.
Hoyt, Henry Martyn
Land of Dreams, The.
1917–1919.
Spell, The.
Hoyt, Ralph
Old.
Hricz, Lucy
Modern American Nursing.
Hroswitha von Gandersheim
In Praise of Virginity.
Paphnutius, *sel.*
Hsiao Yen
Spring Song of Tzu-yeh, A.
Hsi-chün
Lament of Hsi-chün.
Hsieh Wang-ying. *See* **"Ping Hsin"**
Hsüch T'ao
Weaving Love-Knots.
Weaving Love-Knots 2.
Hsüeh T'ao
Spring-gazing Song.
Hsü Pên
Hermit, The.
Huang-fu Jan
Spring Thoughts.
Huang O
Every morning I get up/ Beautiful as the Goddess.
Farewell to a Southern Melody, A.
To the Tune "Red Embroidered Shoes."
To the Tune "Soaring Clouds."
To the Tune "The Fall of a Little Wild Goose."
Hubbard, Jake T. W.
Newton's Third.
Hubbard, P. M.
Subjectivity at Sestos.
To Cynthia, not to let him read the ladies' magazines.
Hubbell, Nelson
Monologue through Bars.
Hubbell, Patricia
Abandoned House, The.
Autumn.
Black Snake, The.
Christmas Present, The.
Concrete Mixers.
Fairies, The.
Message from a Mouse, Ascending in a Rocket.
Night.
Our Washing Machine.
Prayer for Reptiles.
Seagulls.
Vermont Conversation.
Huch, Ricarda
Arrival in Hell.
Death Seed.
Music stirs me, for you.
Young Girl.
Huckel, Oliver
O Mind of God, Broad as the Sky.
Huddle, David
Croquet.
Field, The.
History of the Pets, A.
Icicle.
In White Tie.
Janie Swecker and Me and Gone with the Wind.
Kitchen Tables.
Mrs. Green.
My Brother, Beautiful Shinault, That Goat.
My Grandaddy Mostly with His Knife.
Hudgins, Andrew
Cats and Egypt.
Mine.
Hudson, Deatt
Some Tips on Watching Birds.
Hudson, Flexmore
Mallee in October.
Hudson, Frederick B.
My Relatives for the Most Part.
Hueffer, Ford Madox. *See* **Ford, Ford Madox**
Huff, Barbara A.
Afternoon with Grandmother.
Library, The.
Huff, Robert
Course, The.
Getting Drunk with Daughter.
Rainbow.
Smoker, The.
Traditional Red.
Ventriloquist, The.
Huffstickler, Albert
Prospectus.
Huggins, Peter
Blackberry Winter.
Hughes, Dorothy
Age of Sheen, The.
Dusting of the Books, The.
Strawberries.
Hughes, Henry
Song: "I prithee send me back my heart," *at.*
Hughes, James D.
My Son.
Hughes, John
Court of Neptune, The.
Hughes, Langston
Acceptance.
African Dance.
Alabama Earth.

American Heartbreak.
Angola Question Mark.
April Rain Song.
As I Grew Older.
Aunt Sue's Stories.
Backlash Blues, The.
Bad Morning.
Ballad of the Landlord.
Beale Street.
Be-Bop Boys.
Birmingham Sunday.
Birth.
Black Man Speaks, The.
Black Pierrot, A.
Border Line.
Brass Spittoons.
Carol of the Brown King.
Catch.
Children's Rhymes.
Christ in Alabama.
City.
College Formal: Renaissance Casino.
Color.
Corner Meeting.
Cross.
Cultural Exchange.
Cycle.
Daybreak in Alabama.
Death in Yorkville.
Dinner Guest: Me.
Dive.
Dream Boogie.
Dream Variation [*or* Variations].
Dreams.
Drum.
Dust Bowl.
Early Evening Quarrel.
Ennui.
Esthete in Harlem.
Fantasy in Purple.
50-50.
Fire.
Florida Road Workers.
Frederick Douglass: 1817-1895.
Freedom.
Go Slow.
Gone Boy.
Hard Daddy.
Harlem ("Here on the edge of hell").
Harlem ("What happens to a dream deferred").
Harlem Sweeties.
Havana Dreams.
Heaven.
Homesick Blues.
Hope.
House in Taos, A.
I Dream a World.
I Thought It Was Tangiers I Wanted.
I, Too.
Impasse.
In Time of Silver Rain.
Jazz Band in a Parisian Cabaret.
Jazzonia.
Juke Box Love Song.
Junior Addict.
Justice.
Ku Klux.
Last Call.
Late Corner.
Late Last Night.
Lenox Avenue Mural.
Let America Be America Again.
Lincoln Monument: Washington.
Little Lyric (of Great Importance).
Long Trip.
Lord Has a Child, The, *with music.*
Lumumba's Grave.
Madam and Her Madam.
Madam and the Minister.
Madam's Past History.
Mama and Daughter.
Me and the Mule.
Merry-go-round.
Mexican Market Woman.
Midnight Dancer.
Militant.
Moonlight Night: Carmel.
Morning After.
Mother to Son.
Motto.
Necessity.
Negro Servant.
Negro Speaks of Rivers, The.
New Wind a-Blowin', A, *with music.*
Night Funeral in Harlem.
October 16: The Raid.
Old Walt.
Oppression.
Passing Love.
Peace.
Pennsylvania Station.
Personal.
Po' Boy Blues.
Poem: "I loved my friend."
Poem: "Night is beautiful, The."
Prayer: "I ask you this."
Preference.
Prime.
Question and Answer.
Refugee in America.
Request for Requiems.
Sailor.
Same in Blues.
Saturday Night.
Share-Croppers.
Shepherd's Song at Christmas.
Situation.
Slave.
Snail.
Song for a Dark Girl.
Song for a Suicide.
Special Bulletin.
Still Here.
Stony Lonesome.
Suicide's Note.
Sun Song.
Sylvester's Dying Bed.
Testament.
Theme for English B.
Third Degree.
This Little House Is Sugar.
Today.
Trip: San Francisco.
Troubled Woman.
Trumpet Player.
Two Somewhat Different Epigrams.
Un-American Investigators.
Undertow.
Vagabonds.
Wake.
Warning.
Weary Blues, The.
What?
When Sue Wears Red.
Where? When? Which?
Who but the Lord?
Winter Moon.
Wisdom.
Without Benefit of Declaration.
Youth.

Hughes, Richard
Burial of the Spirit of a Young Poet.
Explanation, on Coming Home Late.
Felo de Se.
Glaucopis.
Image, The.
Invocation to the Muse.
Lover's Reply to Good Advice.
Old Cat Care.
On Time.
Ruin, The.
Sermon, The.
Tramp.
Walking Road, The.
Winter.

Hughes, Rupert
Martyrs of the *Maine,* The.
With a First Reader.

Hughes, Ted
After Lorca.
Bear, The.
Birth of Rainbow.
Born to these gentle stones and grass. Urn Burial.
Bull Moses, The.
Bullfrog.
Cadenza.
Cat and Mouse.
Childbirth.
Childish Prank, A.
Christmas Card.
Cleopatra to the Asp.
Crag Jack's Apostasy.
Crow Blacker than Ever.
Crow's First Lesson.
Crow's Last Stand.
Deaf School.
Dove, A.
Dove-Breeder, The.
Dream of Horses, A.
Esther's Tomcat.
Examination at the Womb-Door.
Famous Poet.
Fern.
Full Moon and Little Frieda.
Gnat-Psalm.
Hawk Roosting.
Her Husband.
His Legs Ran About.
Horses, The.
Howling of Wolves, The.
In Laughter.
Jaguar, The.
Kreutzer Sonata.
Lake, The.
Law in the Country of the Cats.
Leaves.
Ludwig's Death Mask.
Lupercalia.
March Calf, A.
Minstrel's Song.
Moon-Witches.
My Aunt.
My Brother Bert.
My Sister Jane.
Nessie.
New Year's Song.
November.
Otter, An.
Owl's Song.
Pause for Breath, A.
Pennines in April.
Pibroch.
Pike.
Ravens.
Retired Colonel, The.
Reveille.
Revenge Fable.
River in March, The.
Roarers in a Ring.
Roger the Dog.
Salmon Eggs.
Second Glance at a Jaguar.
Secretary.
September.
Singing on the Moon.
Six Young Men.
Skylarks.
Snowdrop.
Song: "O lady, when the tipped cup of the moon blessed you."
Song of a Rat.
Stations.
Stealing Trout.
Still-Life.
That Moment.

Theology.
Thistles.
Thought-Fox, The.
Thrushes.
To Paint a Water Lily.
Trees.
Truth Kills Everybody.
Two Wise Generals.
Urn Burial.
View of a Pig.
Wilfred Owen's Photographs.
Wind.
Wino.
Witches.
Wodwo.
You Drive in a Circle.
Hughes, Thomas
Dolgelley Hotel, The.
Hugo, Richard
Cataldo Mission.
Church on Comiaken Hill, The.
December 24 and George McBride Is Dead.
Degrees of Gray in Philipsburg.
Dog Lake with Paula.
Drums in Scotland.
Freaks at Spurgin Road Field, The.
Graves at Elkhorn.
Graves in Queens.
Greystone Cottage.
Here, but Unable to Answer.
In Your Bad Dream.
Invasion North.
Lady in Kicking Horse Reservoir, The.
Landscapes.
Langaig.
Last Days.
Letter to Bell from Missoula.
Letter to Garber from Skye.
Letter to Levertov from Butte.
Letter to Logan from Milltown.
Letter to Reed from Lolo.
Letter to Scanlon from Whitehall.
Letter to Wagoner from Port Townsend.
Letter to Welch from Browning.
Map of Montana in Italy, A.
Maratea Porto: Saying Goodbye to the Vitolos.
Mill at Romesdal.
Museum of Cruel Days.
Napoli Again.
Night at the Napi in Browning, A.
Open Country.
Places and Ways to Live.
Plans for Altering the River.
Salt Water Story.
1614 Boren.
Skykomish River Running.
Snapshot of Uig in Montana, A.
Tahola.
To Women.
Turtle Lake.
Way a Ghost Dissolves, The.
What Thou Lovest Well, Remains American.
White Center.
With Kathy at Wisdom.
Hugo, Victor
After Six Thousand Years.
Age Is Great and Strong, The.
Be like the Bird.
Et Nox Facta Est.
Feuilles d'Automne, *sels.*
Genesis of Butterflies, The.
Good Night.
Grave and the Rose, The.
Heard on the Mountain.
House and Home.
Memory of the Night of the Fourth.
More Strong than Time.
Poet's Simple Faith, The.
Poor Children, The.
Reverie.
Russia 1812.
Sowing Season. Evening.
Sunset, A.
To Make the People Happy.
Tomorrow, at Daybreak.
Universal Republic, The.
Wings.
Hull, John Mervin
Gates of the Year, The.
Hulme, Thomas Ernest
Above the Dock.
Autumn.
Conversion.
Embankment, The.
Fantasia of a Fallen Gentleman on a Cold Bitter Night on the Embankment.
Image.
Mana Aboda.
Hultman, J. A.
Thanks to God.
Hume, Alexander
Midsummer Day in France.
Of Gods Omnipotencie.
Of the Day Estivall.
Summer Day, A.
Summer's Day, A.
"Hume, Isobel" (I. H. Fisher)
Home-coming.
Sleeper, The.
Whiteness.
Hume, Tobias
Fain Would I Change That Note. *Unknown, at. to*
Humes, Harry
Road of Birds, The.
Hummer, T. R.
Any Time, What May Hit You.
Beating, The.
Cruelty.
Lifelines.
Love Poem: Dispossessed, The.
What Shines in Winter Burns.
Where You Go When She Sleeps.
Hummer, Terry
Naming, The.
Humphrey, Frances
My Book of Life.
Humphrey, J. Lee
All Things Being Equal.
Humphreys, David
On Disbanding the Army.
Humphries, Rolfe
Aria.
Around Thanksgiving.
Cynneddf, The.
Dafydd ap Gwilym Resents the Winter.
For My Ancestors.
Frisbee.
Heresy for a Class-Room.
Offering of the Heart Tapestry from Arras, XV Century, The.
Polo Grounds.
Render unto Cæsar.
Runes for an Old Believer.
Seasons, The.
Summer Landscape, The; or, The Dragon's Teeth.
Wmffre the Sweep.
Hunnis, William
Nosegay Always Sweet, for Lovers to Send for Tokens of Love at New Year's Tide, or for Fairings, A.
Shipmen, The.
Hunt, Josephine Slocum
You Kissed Me.
Hunt, Leigh
Abou Ben Adhem.
Captain Sword.
Christmas.
Cupid Drowned.
Dearest Poets, The.
Epitaph on Erotion.
Fish and the Man, The.
Fish Answers, A.
Fish, the Man, and the Spirit, The.
Fish to Man.
Glove and the Lions, The.
House and Grounds, A.
Jaffar.
Jenny Kiss'd [*or* Kissed] Me.
Nile, The.
Nun, The.
Nymphs, The, *sel.*
On Seeing a Pigeon Make Love.
Places of Nestling Green.
Royal Line, The.
Sneezing.
Story of Rimini, The, *sels.*
Thought of the Nile, A.
Three Sonnets.
To a Fish.
To Hampstead.
To the Grasshopper and the Cricket.
To the Spirit Great and Good.
Two Heavens.
Ultra-Germano-Criticasterism.
Hunt, Sam
April Fool.
Notes from a Journey.
Stabat Mater.
Fish Replies, A.
Hunter, Anne
My Mother Bids Me Bind My Hair.
Hunter, John
Dear Master, in Whose Life I See.
Hunter, William
"Go Bring Me," Said the Dying Fair, *with music.*
Joyfully, Joyfully Onward I Move, *with music.*
Hunter-Duvar, John
De Roberval, *sels.*
Emigration of the Fairies, The, *sel.*
La Belle Sauvage.
Twilight Song.
Huntington, George
International Hymn.
Huntington, William Reed
Authority.
Tellus.
Huntley, Stanley
Annabel Lee, *parody.*
Hurd, Harry Elmore
Black and White Shuffle.
Hurdis, James
Favourite Village, The, *sel.*
Hurley, Mary Rita
Beach House.
Hurnard, James
Winter.
Husid, Mordechai
Cry of Generations, The.
On the Way.
Windows.
Huss, Avraham
Classic Idyll, A.
Green Refrain, A.
Nocturnal Thoughts.
Time.
Hussey, Anne
Cinderella Liberated.
Indian Summer, 1927.
Hutchinson, Abby
Kind Words Can Never Die, *with music.*
Hutchinson, Ellen Mackay. *See* **Cortissoz, Ellen Mackay Hutchinson**
Hutchinson, Jesse
Lincoln and Liberty, *at.*
Hutchinson, M. M.
Ten Little Indian Boys.
Hutchinson, Pearse
Copper-Beech and Butter-Fingers.
Distortions.
Gaeltacht.
Into Their True Gentleness.
Malaga.

Hutchinson, Robert
Suburban Wife's Song.
Hutchison, A. G.
A'Chuilionn.
Hutchison, Joseph
This Year.
Hutchison, Percy
Columbus.
Hutton, Joseph
Tomb of the Brave, The.
Hutton, Laurence
Doves of Venice, The.
Hutton, Mary
Sleeping Beauty, The.
Huws, Daniel
Family Evening.
Goodbye to Regal.
Huxley, Aldous
Canal, The.
Doors of the Temple.
First Philosopher's Song.
Frascati's.
Jonah.
Ninth Philosopher's Song.
September.
Soles Occidere et Redire Possunt, *sel.*
Villiers de l'Isle-Adam.
Huxley, Thomas Henry
Tennyson.
Hu Yun-shang. *See* **"Lin Ling"**
Hwang Chin-i
Blue hill is my desire, The.
I cut in two/ A long November night.
Mountains are steadfast but the mountain streams.
Hyde, Abby Bradley
And Canst Thou, Sinner, Slight, *with music.*
Dear Saviour, If These Lambs Should Stray, *with music.*
Hyde, Douglas
Cold, Sharp Lamentation.
Cooleen, The.
He Meditates on the Life of a Rich Man.
Will You Be as Hard?
Hyde, Lewis
Ants.
"Hyde, Robin" (Iris Guiver Wilkinson)
Deserted Village, The.
Pihsien Road.
Hyde, William deWitt
Creation's Lord, We Give Thee Thanks, *with music.*
Hyett, Barbara Helfgott
Last Flight of the Great Wallenda, The.
Hymes, Lucia M. *and* James L., Jr.
Oodles of Noodles.
Tombstone.

I

"I. T." *See* **"T., I."**
"I. V. S. W." *See* **"W., I. V. S."**
Ibarbourou, Juana de
Life-Hook.
Assignation, The.
Strong Bond, The.
Ibn Adiya, Al-Samau'al
Are We Not the People, *sel.*
Oh, Would That I Knew.
Oh, Ye Censurers.
Ibn al-Abbar
You know not how deep was the love your eyes did kindle.
Ibn al-Arabi
He praises me, and I praise Him.
My heart has become capable of every form.
Ode: "They journeyed,/ When the darkness of night."
Ode: "Who can support the anguish of love?"
When my Beloved appears.
Ibn Chasdai, Abraham
Advice to Bores.
Elusive Maid, The.
Meek and the Proud, The.
Poor Scholar, The.
Ibn Darraj al-Andalusi
Wing of Separation, The.
Ibn Ezra, Abraham
Ages of Man, The, *at.*
Far Sweeter than Honey.
Freedom.
God Everywhere.
Law, The.
Living God, The.
My Stars.
Out of Luck.
Song of Chess, The, *at.*
Ibn Ezra, Moses
All Ye That Go Astray.
Awake, My Soul.
Beautiful Is the Loved One.
Beauty of the Stars, The.
Book of Tarshish, The, *sel.*
Bring Me the Cup.
Drink, Friends.
Dying Wife to Her Husband, A.
Elegy: "In pain she bore the son who her embrace."
Elegy: "My thoughts impelled me to the resting-place."
End of Man Is Death, The.
God That Doest Wondrously.
He That Regards the Precious Things of Earth.
Hot Flame of My Grief, The.
I Went Out into the Garden.
In Vain Earth Decks Herself.
Joy of Life.
Man Is a Weaver.
Men Are Children of This World.
My Love is Like a Myrtle.
On My Sorrowful Life.
Promises of the World, The.
Rosy Days Are Numbered, The.
Splendor of Thine Eyes, The.
Strange Love.
Those Beauteous Maids.
To a Plagiarist.
Walk in the Precepts.
Wedding Song in honor of R. Solomon ben Matir, *sel.*
When She Plays upon the Harp or Lute.
Why Should I Grieve?
Wine-Songs, *sels.*
With Hopeless Love.
Without My Friends the Day Is Dark.
Works of God, The.
World Is like a Woman of Folly, The.
World's Illusion, The, *sels.*
Ye Anger Earth.
Young Dove, The.
Ibn Gabirol, Solomon
Almighty! What Is Man?
Defiance.
Degenerate Age, A.
From Thee to Thee.
In Praise of Wisdom.
Invitation.
Meditations.
Morning Song.
My God.
Night.
Night-Thoughts.
O Soul, with Storms Beset.
Royal Crown, The, *abr.*
Song of the Wind and the Rain.
Stanzas: "With tears thy grief thou dost bemoan."
Water Song.
Wine and Grief.
Ibn Hazm Al-Andalusi
Twice Times Then Is Now.
Ibn Kolthum
Pour Us Wine.
Ibn Rashiq
Pretences.
Ibn Sabbatai, Judah
Expensive Wife, The.
Gift of Judah the Woman-Hater, The, *sel.*
Ibn Tibbon, Judah
Father's Testament, A.
Ibn Zaydun
Cordova.
Ibsen, Henrik
Brand, *sel.*
In the Orchard.
"Idas." *See* **Wayland, John Elton**
Idley, Peter
Covetousness.
Sources of Good Counsel.
Igjugarjuk
Musk Oxen.
Ignatius, Sister Mary
Our Lady of the Libraries.
Ignatius of Loyola, Saint
Teach Us to Serve Thee, Lord.
Ignatow, David
Against the Evidence.
All Quiet.
Allegory, An.
And the Same Words.
Bagel, The.
Bowery.
Brightness as a Poignant Light.
Business Life, The.
City, The.
Dilemma.
Dream, The.
Each Day.
East Bronx.
Elegy: "I must wait for a stranger to knock on my door."
Escapade, The.
Europe and America.
Father and Son.
For One Moment.
Gardeners.
Get the Gasworks.
He Puts Me to Rest.
Heart, The.
How Come?
I'm Here.
In a Dream.
In No Way.
Journey, The.
Last Night.
My Own House.
News Report.
Night at an Airport.
1905.
No Theory.
Notes for a Lecture.
Oedipus.
Paper Cutter, The.
Park.
Professional, The.
Promenade.
Requiem, A: "My father listening to opera, that's me."
Rescue the Dead.
Ritual Three.
Sediment.
Self-Employed.
Signal, The.
Simultaneously.
Six Movements on a Theme.
Sky Is Blue, The.
Suite for Marriage, A.
Their Mouths Full.
Thoughts.
Threnody: "Mother, in my unwanted suffering, I turn to you."
Time of Night, A.
To Nowhere.

Us.
With the Door Open.
With the Sun's Fire.
Ikan, Ron
Madrid, Iowa.
Manitou.
Two Hopper.
What I Did Last Summer.
Ikeda, Patricia Y.
Card Game, A; Kinjiro Sawada.
Recovery.
Translations.
Ikhnaton. *See* **Akhenaton**
Ikinilik
Song of the Trout Fisher, The.
Ilce, Ana
Summer Street.
Image, Selwyn
Meditation for Christmas, A.
Iman, Yusef
Love Your Enemy.
Imber, Naphtali Herz
Hatikvah—a Song of Hope.
Zionist Marching Song.
Imbs, Bravig
Sleep.
Wind Was There, The.
Immanuel di Roma
Elegy: "Floods of tears well from my deepest heart, The."
Happiness amidst Troubles.
Love.
Machberoth, *sels.*
My Sweet Gazelle!
Oh, Let Thy Teachings.
On the Wall.
Paradise.
Virtue.
What Profit?
Worthless Heart, The.
Imr el Kais
Ode: "Weep, ah weep love's losing."
Inada, Lawson Fusao
Discovery of Tradition, The.
From Our Album.
Making Miso.
Plucking Out a Rhythm.
Since When As Ever More.
Inber, Vera
Leningrad: 1943.
Pulkovo Meridian, The, *sel.*
Inez, Colette
Better to Spit on the Whip than Stutter Your Love like a Worm.
Letters of a Name, The.
Crucial Stew.
Mercedes, Her Aloneness.
Qua Song.
Waiting for the Doctor.
Woman Who Loved Worms, The.
Ingalls, Jeremy
My Head on My Shoulders.
Ingalls, John James
Opportunity.
Tribute to Grass.
Ingamells, Rex
Golden Bird, The.
Great South Land, The, *sel.*
Memory of Hills, *sel.*
Ship from Thames.
Inge, Charles Cuthbert
Certain Young Gourmet, A.
Limerick: "Certain young gourmet of Crediton, A."
On Monsieur Coué.
Inge, William Ralph
Limerick: "There was a good Canon of Durham."
Limerick: "There was an old man of Khartoum," *at.*
Ingelow, Jean
Apprenticed.
Child and Boatman.
Divided.
Echo and the Ferry.
Feathers and Moss.
For Exmoor.
High Tide on the Coast of Lincolnshire, The (1571).
Like a Laverock in the Lift.
Long White Seam, The.
Longing for Home.
Maternity.
Noble Tuck-Man, The.
One Morning, Oh, So Early!
Sea-nurtured.
Seven Times One: Exultation.
Seven Times Three—Love.
Seven Times Two—Romance.
Singing-Lesson, The.
Song of the Old Love.
Songs of Seven.
Songs on the Voices of Birds, *sel.*
Sorrow Humanize Our Race.
Sweet Is Childhood.
Ingemann, Bernard Severin
Pilgrim's Song.
Ingham, John Hall
Genesis.
George Washington.
Summer Sanctuary, A.
"Ingoldsby, Thomas" (Richard Harris Barham)
As I Laye a-Thynkynge.
Confession, The.
Cynotaph, The.
Eheu Fugaces.
Hon. Mr. Sucklethumbkin's Story.
Ingoldsby Legends, The, *sels.*
Jackdaw of Rheims, The.
Last Lines.
Lay of St. Gengulphus A, *sel.*
Lines Left at Mr. Theodore Hook's House in June, 1834.
Misadventures at Margate.
Not a Sou Had He Got.
St. Cuthbert Intervenes.
Ingram, John Kells
Memory of the Dead, The.
National Presage.
Social Future, The.
Inib-sarri
Letter to Her Father, A.
Inman, Will
108 Tales of a Po'Buckra, *sel.*
Shaman.
Innes, Guy
It's Three No Trumps.
"Innsley, Owen" (Lucy White Jennison)
Bondage.
Burden of Love, The.
Dream of Death, A.
Ipcar, Dahlov
Fishes' Evening Song.
"Ireland, Michael." *See* **Figgis, Darrell**
Ireland, W. H.
To starve, or not to starve? that is the question.
Iremonger, Valentin
Descending.
Dog, The.
Elizabeth.
Evening in Summer.
Going Down the Mountain.
Hector.
Icarus.
In New Ross.
In This River.
Invocation: "Ten bloody years with this quill lying."
Recollection in Autumn.
Spring Stops Me Suddenly.
These Apple Trees.
This Houre Her Vigill.
Time, the Faithless.
While the Summer Trees Were Crying.
Irihapeti Rangi te Apakura
Reply to Marriage Proposal.
Irion, Mary Jane
Invocation from a Lawn Chair.
Iris, Scharmel
After the Martyrdom.
Irish, Jeff
Boy Thirteen, A.
"Ironbark." *See* **Gibson, George Herbert**
"Ironquill." *See* **Ware, Eugene Fitch**
Irvin, Eric
Christmas 1942.
Irvin, Margaret
Chanticleer.
Irving, Minna
Betsy's Battle Flag.
His Living Monument.
Lincoln Leads.
Old Year's Prayer, The.
Wedding Gift, The.
Irving, Washington
Certain Young Lady, A.
Irwin, Thomas Caulfield
December.
Faerie's Child, The.
Iphione.
Objects of the Summer Scene, The.
Swift, *sel.*
With the Dawn.
Irwin, Wallace ("Ginger"; "Hashimura Togo")
Aunt Nerissa's Muffin.
Blow Me Eyes!
Constant Cannibal Maiden, The.
Fate of the Cabbage Rose, The.
From Romany to Rome.
Grain of Salt, A.
Powerful Eyes o' Jeremy Tait, The.
Reminiscence.
Rhyme of the Chivalrous Shark, The.
Science for the Young.
Sea Serpant, The.
Sensitive Sydney.
Song for a Cracked Voice.
Such a Pleasant Familee.
Worried Skipper, The.
Isaac, Ted
Urban Roses.
Isaac ben Samuel of Dampière
His Hand Shall Cover Us.
Isaacs, Jorge
Nima, The.
Isaacson, Jose
Pre-Positions.
Isanos, Magda
Apricot Tree.
Isbell, Hugh O.
Crucifixion.
Ise, Lady
Because we suspected/ the pillow would say "I know."
Correspondence:/ when I have sad thoughts.
Elegy: Ise Lamenting the Death of Empress Onshi.
Eleven Tanka, *sel.*
Even in my dreams/ I must no longer meet you.
Flower of waves, A.
Hanging from the branches of a green/ willow tree.
If I consider/ My body like the fields.
If it is you, there/ in the light boat on the pond.
Like a ravaged sea/ this bed.
Near a Waterfall at Ryumon.
News of the palace.
Not even in dreams/ Can I meet him anymore.
On Seeing the Field Being Singed.
Rains of Spring, The.
Seeing the Plum Blossoms by the River.
Seeing the Returning Geese.
Since "the pillow knows all."
Sleeping with Someone Who Came in Secret.
They are rebuilding/ the old bridge, the Nagara.
When the fifth month comes.

Ise Tayu
Clear water of the imperial pond, The.
Farmer's clothes are soaked through and never dried, The.
Iselda. *See* **Carenza** *and* **Iselda**
Isenhour, Walter E.
Be Friendly.
Down-Pullers, The.
Give Us Sober Men.
God Is There.
Going Home with Jesus.
Happiness.
If You're the Man You Ought to Be.
It's Wonderful.
Jesus Never Fails.
Keeping Victory.
Some Things You Cannot Will to Men.
Ishak, Abu. *See* **Hill, Elton**
Isherwood, Christopher
Common Cormorant, The.
On His Queerness.
Ish-Kishor, Sulamith
War.
Ishigaki Rin
Clams.
Cocoon.
Isidorus
On a Fowler.
Island, E. H. L.
Penny Whistle Blues.
Issa (Kobayashi Issa)
Buddha's Birthday: April 8, 1819.
Buddha's Death Day: February 15, 1815.
Crawl, laugh.
New Moon, The.
Once upon a time.
Oraga Haru, *sels.*
Wren, The.
Issaia, Nana
Dream.
Sacrifice.
Ita, Saint
Jesukin, *at.*
Saint Ita's Fosterling.
Itzin, Charles
Malcom, Iowa.
Ivanov, Vyacheslav Ivanovich
Holy Rose, The.
Ivens, Michael
First Day at School
Ives, George
Message, A.
Once.
Ives, Rich
Memory, a Small Brown Bird.
Ivie, Kelly
Gull Lake Reunion.
Iwa no Hime, Empress
Longing for the Emperor.
Izard, Forrest
"Art of Our Necessities Is Strange, The."
Izembō
Shower, A.
Izumi Shikibu
After the Death of Her Daughter in Childbirth.
As the rains of spring.
Fifty-one Tanka, *sel.*
From darkness/ I go onto the road/ of darkness.
From that first night.
Here in this world/ I won't live.
I go out of darkness/ Onto a road of darkness.
I left my hills.
I wish you would come.
If you have no time.
If you love me.
In the dusk the path.
It is the time of rain and snow.
Love.
Never could I think/ Our love a worldly commonplace.
On nights when hail/ falls noisily.
On this winter night.
Orange leaves are gone.
Recklessly/ I cast myself away.
Since that night/ I cannot know myself.
Someone else/ looked at the sky.
When you broke from me.
You told me it was/ because of me.
You wear the face.

J

"J., M."
Animal Howl, The.
Funeral, The.
Song of a Jewish Boy.
"J., W."
City Eclogue, A.
"J. C." *See* **C., J."**
"J. D." *See* **"D., J."**
"J. H. S." *See* **"S., J. H."**
"J. J. W." *See* **"W., J. J."**
"J. T." *See* **"T., J."**
Jabès, Edmond
Book Rises Out of the Fire, The.
Circular Cry, A.
Condemned, The.
Pulverized Screen, The.
Song: "On the side of the road."
Song of the Last Jewish Child.
Song of the Trees of the Black Forest.
Water.
Jacinto, Antonio
Monangamba.
Jacinto, Jaime
Beads, The.
Fire Breather, Mexico City, The.
Looking for Buddha.
Reflections on the Death of a Parrot.
Jackett, Will
Extraordinary Will.
Jackowska, Nicki
Family Outing—A Celebration.
Insect Kitchen, The.
Meeting, The.
Sisters, The.
Jackson, Ada
I Have a Roof.
In Memoriam.
Jackson, Angela
Blackmen: Who Make Morning.
Jackson, Byron. *See* **Jackson, Kathryn** *and* **Byron Jackson**
Jackson, David
Grandmother Jackson.
Jackson, Edgar
Already I Feel the Emptiness.
Hunter Sees What Is There, The.
I'm Coming I'm Coming.
In the Mountains.
Magic Word.
Self-Portrait.
Sinew of Our Dreams, The.
Three Songs.
Jackson, Haywood
Children Grown, The.
On the Latest Crisis of Confidence.
Jackson, Helen Hunt ("H. H."; "Saxe Holm"
Ballad of the Gold Country, A.
Cheyenne Mountain.
Coronation.
Doubt.
Down to Sleep.
Emigravit.
Grab-Bag.
Habeas Corpus.
Last Prayer, A.
Morn.
My Legacy.
October's Bright Blue Weather.
Poppies in [*or* on] the Wheat.
September.
September Days Are Here.
Song of Clover, A.
Spinning.
That Things Are No Worse, Sire.
Jackson, Kathryn *and* **Byron Jackson**
Noonday Sun.
Open Range.
Jackson, Laura Riding. *See* **Riding, Laura**
Jackson, Leroy F.
Beela by the Sea.
Columbus.
Grandpa Dropped His Glasses.
Hero, The.
Hippity Hop to Bed.
I've Got a New Book from My Grandfather Hyde.
Old Father Annum.
Simple Sam.
Jackson, Mae
Blues Today, The.
For Some Poets.
I Remember.
I Used to Wrap My White Doll Up In.
January 3, 1970.
Reincarnation.
Jackson, Maud Frazer
New Years and Old.
Jackson, Michael
Australia.
Mask-Maker.
Neanderthal.
Red Flag, The.
Sudan.
Jackson, Richard
Holding On.
Jackson, William (Haywood)
Making an Impression.
Out of the Deepness.
Jacob, Hildebrand
Alarm, The.
Here Delia's buried at fourscore.
Judgement of Tiresias, The.
Swain, give o'er your fond pretension.
To Cloe.
To Geron.
Writer, The.
Jacob, Max
It May Be.
To Modigliani to Prove to Him That I Am a Poet.
Jacob, Violet
Gean Trees, The.
Last o' the Tinkler, The.
Pride.
Rowan, The.
Tam i' the Kirk.
Wild Geese, The.
Jacob, Zerea
Salutation.
Jacobs, A. C.
Isaac.
Painting.
Poem for My Grandfather.
Yiddish Poet.
Jacobs, Alex. *See* **Karoniaktatie**
Jacobs, Bertha. *See* **Bertken, Sister**
Jacobs, Catherine Haydon
Autumn Orchard.
Secret.
Jacobs, Elijah L.
High Wheat Country.
Saturday in the County Seat.
Jacobs, Frank
Bat, The.
Jacobs, Henry Eyster
Lord Jesus Christ, We Humbly Pray, *with music.*
Jacobs, Henry S.
How Goodly Is Thy House, *with music.*
Jacobs, Leland B.
Queenie ("Queenie's strong and Queenie's tall").

Taste of Purple.
That May Morning.
Jacobs, Maria
Embroidery.
Song of the Intruder.
Jacobs, Mary
"Where Love, There's Heaven."
Jacobs, P. L.
Abbreviated Rumination.
Electrocution Script.
Fish Story.
Obligatory Love Poem.
Old Man Hall.
Safety or Something.
Jacobsen, Josephine
Animals, The.
Class, The.
Destinations.
Eyes of Children at the Brink of the Sea's Grasp, The.
For Any Member of the Security Police.
For Murasaki.
49th and 5th, December 13.
Interrupted, The.
It Is the Season.
Matadors, The.
Mollesse.
Murmurers, The.
Planet, The.
Power Failure.
Rainy Night at the Writers' Colony.
Reindeer and Engine.
Sea Fog, The.
Shade-Seller, The.
Short Short Story.
There Is Good News.
Thief, The.
When the Five Prominent Poets.
Yellow.
Jacobsen, Rolf
Country Roads.
Road's End.
Sunflower.
Jacobson, Ethel
Atomic Courtesy.
Lines Scratched in Wet Cement.
Jacoby, Grover
Juxta.
Jacopo da Lentino
Canzonetta: He Will Neither Boast nor Lament to His Lady.
Canzonetta: Of His Lady, and of His Making Her Likeness.
Sonnet: Of His Lady in Heaven.
Sonnet: Of His Lady's Face.
Jacopone da Todi
Nativity Song.
Stabat Mater [*or* Stabat Mater Dolorosa], *at.*
Jaeger, Lowell
Poem for My Mother.
Jaffe, Dan
Owl in the Rabbi's Barn, The.
This One Is About the Others.
Who?
Yahrzeit.
Jaffray, Norman R.
Beatnik Limernik.
Sliding Scale.
Jäger, Maria
O World, Be Not So Fair.
Jagger, Mick *and* **Keith Richard**
Live with Me.
Jago, Richard
Absence.
Edge-Hill; or, The Rural Prospect Delineated and Moralised, *sel.*
Goldfinches, The.
Hamlet's Soliloquy Imitated.
Iron Industry in Birmingham, The.
Jahan, Nur, Empress
Moon of Id came, The.
Your love turned my body into water.
Jahin, Salah
Quatrains.
Jahns, T. R.
Song of the Farmworker.
Jalal ed-Din Rumi. *See* **Rumi, Jalal ed-Din**
Jallais, Denise
Lullaby for My Dead Child.
Jama, Sheikh Aquib Abdullahi
Prayer for Rain.
Jamal, Yasmeen (Cathleen McDonald)
All That Jazz.
Canteen Pimpin'.
Did Ya Hear?
Gate, The.
I bet God understands about givin up five.
James I, King of England
Admonition to Montgomerie.
Heaven and Earth.
Sonnet: "Azured vault, the crystal circles bright, The."
James I, King of Scotland
Coming of Love, The.
Good Counsel.
He Sees His Beloved.
Kingis Quair, The, *abr.*
Nightingale's Song, The.
Spring Song of the Birds.
Walking under the Tour.
James V, King of Scotland
Christ's Kirk on the Green, *at.*
Jolly Beggar, The, *at.*
James, Alice Archer Sewall
Butterfly, The.
Processionals.
Sinfonia Eroica.
James, Clive
Peregrine Prykke's Pilgrimage, *sel.*
To Pete Atkin: A Letter from Paris, *sel.*
Unsolicited Letters to Five Artists.
James, David
After Your Death.
Famous Outlaw Stops In for a Drink, The.
James, Edward
Carmina Amico, *sels.*
James, Elizabeth Ann
Artificial Death, II.
James, John
Of John Bunyans Life.
On the Decease of the Religious and Honourable Jno Haynes Esqr.
James, Nicholas
Complaints of Poverty, The, *sel.*
James, Sibyl
Patty Hearst Hoists the Carbine.
James, Thomas
Hunting for Blueberries.
Letter to a Mute.
Letters to a Stranger.
Mummy of a Lady Named Jemutesonekh XXI Dynasty.
Reasons.
Jamison, Roscoe Conkling
Negro Soldiers, The.
Jammes, Francis
Amsterdam.
Child Reads an Almanac, The ("The child reads on; her basket of eggs stands by").
Little Donkey, The.
Love.
Prayer to Go to Paradise with the Asses.
Robinson Crusoe Returns to Amsterdam.
Jana Bai
She was my staff and I am blind.
Janeczko, Paul B.
After the Rain.
Lesson for Dreamers.
Janik, Phyllis
In the Field.
Sleeping Peasants.
Story of Good, The.
Jankola, Beth
Women Called Bossy Cowboys.
Janosco, Beatrice
Garden Hose, The.
Janowitz, Phyllis
Case.
Wait, The.
Jansen, Annette
Prayer for Neighborhood Evangelism.
Janvier, Francis DeHaes
God Save Our President.
Janvier, Thomas A.
Santiago.
Jaques, Edna
In Flanders Now.
Jaques, Florence Page
Goblinade, A.
There Once Was a Puffin.
Janvier, Margaret Thomson. *See* **"Vandegrift, Margaret"**
Jarman, Mark
Desire of Water, The.
Jarrell, Randall
Aging.
Augsburg Adoration, The.
Author to the Reader, The.
Bats.
Bird of Night, The.
Black Swan, The.
Blind Sheep, The.
Breath of Night, The.
Burning the Letters.
Camp in the Prussian Forest, A.
Chipmunk's Day, The.
Chipmunk's Song, The.
Cinderella.
Come to the Stone.
Country Life, A.
Cow wandering in the bare field, The.
Dead in Melanesia, The.
Dead Wingman, The.
Death of the Ball Turret Gunner, The.
Eighth Air Force.
Elementary Scene, The.
Emancipators, The.
Field and Forest.
For an Emigrant.
Forsaken Girl, The.
Front, A.
Game at Salzburg, A.
Girl in a Library, A.
Gunner.
Hope.
House in the Wood, The.
Hunt in the Black Forest, A.
In Galleries.
In Montecito.
In Nature There Is neither Right nor Left nor Wrong.
Islands, The.
Jamestown.
Jerome.
Jews at Haifa.
Knight, Death, and the Devil, The.
Lady Bates.
Lines, The: "After the centres' naked files, the basic line."
Lonely Man, The.
Losses.
Lost Children, The.
Lullaby, A: "For wars his life and half a world away."
Märchen, The (Grimm's Tales).
Mockingbird, The.
Moving.
Nestus Gurley.
Next Day.
90 North.
Officers' Prison Camp Seen from a Troop Train, An.
Old and the New Masters, The.
Orient Express, The.
Pilot from the Carrier, A.
Pilots, Man Your Planes.

Port of Embarkation.
Prisoners.
Protocols.
Range in the Desert, The.
Refugees, The.
Say Goodbye to Big Daddy.
Second Air Force.
Seele im Raum.
Sick Child, A.
Sick Nought, The.
Siegfried.
Sleeping Beauty, The: Variation of the Prince.
Snow-Leopard, The.
Soldier (T. P.).
Soldier Walks under the Trees of the University, The.
Soul, A.
State, The.
Subway from New Britain to the Bronx, The.
Thinking of the Lost World.
Truth, The.
Variations.
War, A.
Ways and the Peoples, The.
Well Water.
Woman.
Woman at the Washington Zoo, The.

Jarrett, Emmett
Dear Mother.
For E. C. J.
"Hamlet."
Human Relations.
Song: "Help me now."
Trip, The.
Two of Cups, The.

Jason, Philip K.
Skin.

Jastrun, Mieczyslaw
Encirclement.
Jews, The.

Jaszi, Jean
Clock, The.
My Horses.
Winter.

Jauss, David
For My Son, Born during an Ice Storm.
Sounding.

Javitz, Alexander
Old Men, The.

Jayadeva
Gita Govinda, The, *sels.*
Hymn to Vishnu.

Jeck, Randolph
Ode of Lament.

Jeffers, Lance
Black Soul of the Land.
Breath in My Nostrils.
Grief Streams Down My Chest.
How High the Moon.
Love Pictures You as Black and Long-faced.
My Blackness Is the Beauty of This Land.
Nina Simone.
On Listening to the Spirituals.
Trellie.
Who Shined Shoes in Times Square.

Jeffers, Robinson
Age in Prospect.
Animals.
Answer, The.
Ante Mortem.
Antrim.
Apology for Bad Dreams.
Artist, An.
Ascent to the Sierras.
Ave Caesar.
Battle.
Beaks of Eagles, The.
Beauty of Things, The.
Birds.
Birds and Fishes.
Birth-Dues.
Black-out.
Bloody Sire, The.
Boats in a Fog.
But I Am Growing Old and Indolent.
Calm and Full the Ocean.
Carmel Point.
Cassandra.
Clouds of Evening.
Compensation.
Continent's End.
Credo.
Cremation.
Cruel Falcon, The.
Crumbs or the Loaf.
Divinely Superfluous Beauty.
Eagle Valor, Chicken Mind.
Evening Ebb.
Eye, The.
Fawn's Foster-Mother.
Fire on the Hills.
Fourth Act.
Gale in April.
Granite and Cypress.
Grass on the Cliff.
Gray Weather.
Hands.
Haunted Country.
House Dog's Grave, The.
Hurt Hawks.
I Shall Laugh Purely.
Inquisitors, The.
Iona; the Graves of the Kings.
Joy.
Let Them Alone.
Life from the Lifeless.
Little Scraping, A.
Love the Wild Swan.
Maid's Thought, The.
May–June, 1940.
My Burial Place.
New Mexican Mountain.
Night.
Noon.
Nova.
November Surf.
Ocean.
Oh, Lovely Rock.
Original Sin.
Pelicans.
Phenomena.
Post Mortem.
Prescription of Painful Ends.
Promise of Peace.
Purse-Seine, The.
Rearmament.
Reference to a Passage in Plutarch's Life of Sulla.
Return.
Roan Stallion.
Rock and Hawk.
Science.
Self-Criticism in February.
Shane O'Neill's Cairn.
Shine, Perishing Republic.
Shine, Republic.
Shiva.
Signpost.
Skunks, *sel.*
Stars Go over the Lonely Ocean, The.
Still the Mind Smiles.
Summer Holiday.
To His Father.
To the Stone-Cutters.
Tor House.
Trumpet, The, *sel.*
Vulture.
Watch the Lights Fade.
We have little animals here.
World's Wonders, The.

Jefferson, Joseph
Immortality.

Jefferys, Charles
Jeannette and Jeannot.
Jeannot's Answer.
We Have Lived and Loved Together.

Jeffrey, Francis, Lord Jeffrey
Epitaph: "Here lies the body of Richard Hind."
Epitaph in Christ Church, Bristol, on Thomas Turner, Twice Master of the Company of Bakers.
Epitaph on Peter Robinson.
On Peter Robinson.

Jeffrey, Mildred
Death.

Jeffrey, William
Carlyle on Burns.
Glen Rosa.
On Glaister's Hill, *sel.*
Stones.

Jeffries, Christie
Lone Huntsman.

Jeffries, Sir Charles
Floral Tribute.

Jeitteles, Alois
To My Distant Beloved.

Jeitteles, Benedict
Epitaph for a Judge.

Jekyll, Joseph
Two Heads Are Better than One.

Jellicoe, S. Charles
Advice to a Lover.

Jemmat, Catherine
Rural Lass, The.

Jenkins, Brooks
Loneliness.

Jenkins, Christina
Sunday Morning.

Jenkins, Elinor
Dulce et Decorum?

Jenkins, Louis
Library.
My Feet.
Violence on Television.

Jenkins, Oliver
Merry-go-round.
Ship Comes In, A.
Time Out.
Waterfront.

Jenks, Orville
Dying Mine Brakeman, The.

Jenks, Tudor
Accommodating Lion, An.
Hard to Bear.
On the Road.
Small and Early.
Spirit of the *Maine,* The.

Jenkyn, Patherické
Love and Respect.

Jenner, Charles
Eclogue IV: Poet, The, *sel.*
Soliloquy in the Suburbs, A.

Jenner, Edward
Sent to a Patient, with the Present of a Couple of Ducks.
Signs of Rain.

Jennett, Sean
And the Dead.
Barge Horse, The.
Cycle: Seven War Poems.
I Was a Labourer.
Island, The.
Mahoney.
Merchandise.
My Subtle and Proclamant Song.
Old Joyce.
Omphalos: The Well.
Quick, The.

Jennings, Elizabeth
Afterthought.
Animals' Arrival, The.
Answers.
Beyond Possession.
Birthday in Hospital, A.
Child and the Shadow, The.
Climbers, The.

Communication.
Counterpart, The.
Death, A.
Delay.
Disguises.
Escape and Return.
Fountain.
Ghosts.
Harvest and Consecration.
Identity.
Idler, The.
In a Garden.
In Praise of Creation.
In the Night.
Interrogator, The.
Meditation on the Nativity.
Mirrors.
Not in the Guide-Books.
Old Man.
One Flesh.
Parting, The.
Rembrandt's Late Self-Portraits.
Room, The.
Song at the Beginning of Autumn.
Song for a Birth or a Death.
Song for a Departure.
Storm, The.
Storm House, The.
Teresa of Avila.
To My Mother at 73.
Unknown Child, The.
Visitation, The.
Way of Looking, A.
Weathercock.
Winter Love.
World of Light, A.
Young Ones, The.
Jennings, Humphrey
Prose Poem.
Jennings, Kate
Divorce.
Jennings, Leslie Nelson
Belden Hollow.
Jennings, Paula
Lesbian.
Jennison, C. S.
I'm Leery of Firms with Easy Terms.
Jennison, Lucy White. *See* **"Innsley, Owen"**
Jensen, Jeffry
Western Movies.
Jensen, Johannes V.
Bathing Girl, A.
Jensen, Laura
After I Have Voted.
Age, An.
Ajax Samples, The.
As the Window Darkens.
Candles Draw Well after All, The.
Cloud Parade, The.
House Is an Enigma.
Household.
In the Hospital.
Indian.
Kite.
Red Dog, The.
Sleep in the Heat.
Starlings.
Talking to the Mule.
Tapwater.
Winter Evening Poem.
Jenyns, Soame
Art of Dancing, The, *sels.*
Doctor Johnson.
Epistle Written in the Country to the Right Honourable the Lord Lovelace, An, *sel.*
Epitaph on Dr. Johnson.
Modern Fine Gentleman, The, *sel.*
Modern Fine Lady, The.
Snow-Ball, The.
Temple of Venus, The.
Jephcott, Sydney
Thredbo River.
Jerome, Judson
Child's Game.
Deer Hunt.
Plexus and Nexus.
Psychology Today.
Jerome, William
Bedelia, *with music.*
Jesús, Teresa de
All of a Sudden.
They go by, go by, love, the days and the hours.
Jewett, Eleanore Myers
Down among the Wharves.
Jewett, Ellen A.
Sermon in a Stocking.
Jewett, John H.
Those Rebel Flags.
Jewett, Sarah Orne
Country Boy in Winter, A.
Jewett, Sophie ("Ellen Burroughs")
Armistice.
If Spirits Walk.
In the Dark.
Least of Carols, The.
Smiling Demon of Notre Dame, A.
Song: "Thy face I have seen as one seeth."
When Nature Hath Betrayed the Heart That Loved Her.
Jewsbury, Maria Jane
Partings.
To a Young Brother.
Jigmed, Chimedin
For the Cultural Campaign.
Satirical Poem about Drink, A, *sel.*
Jiles, Paulette
Paper Matches.
Time to Myself.
Tin Woodsman, The.
Windigo.
Jiménez, Juan Ramón
Conclusive Voyage, The.
Deep Night.
Fleeting Return.
Full Consciousness.
Galante Garden: I ("Spring morning").
Galante Garden: II ("There was no one. The water—no one?").
I recognized you because when I saw the print.
"In the Subway."
Lamb Was Bleating Softly, The.
New Leaves.
New Spring.
Oceans.
Winter Song.
Jito, Empress
Spring is passing and.
Jitrik, Noe
Addio a la Mamma.
Joachim, Paulin
Burial.
Joad, C. E. M.
Materialism.
Joans, Ted
Chickitten Gitten!
It Is Time.
Its Curtains.
Knee Deep.
Lester Young.
Love Tight.
Miles' Delight.
My Ace of Spades.
Protective Grigri, The.
Scenery.
.38, The.
To Fez Cobra.
Truth, The.
Up out of the African.
Voice in the Crowd.
Watermelon.
Zoo You Too!
Johannes Secundus (Jan Nicolai Everaerts)
Basia, *sels.*
Epithalamium: "Hour is come, with pleasure crowned," *sel.*
Insatiate, The.
Neaera's Kisses.
Wedding Night, The.
John, Gwen
Child's Winter Evening, A.
John Damascene, Saint. *See* **John of Damascus, Saint**
John Frederick, Sister Mary
Joculator Domini.
John of Damascus, Saint [*or* **St. John Damascene**
Day of Resurrection, The.
Resurrection.
John of the Cross, Saint
Coplas about the Soul Which Suffers with Impatience to See God, *sel.*
Dark Night, The.
O Flame of Living Love.
O Living Flame of Love.
Obscure Night of the Soul, The.
Romance VIII.
Songs of the Soul in Rapture at Having Arrived at the Height of Perfection, Which Is Union with God by the Road of Spiritual Negation.
John II of Castile
Cancion: "O love, I never, never thought."
Johns, Orrick
Home Fire, The.
Interpreter, The.
Mothers and Children.
Sea-Lands, The.
Shopping Day.
Spring.
Tree-Toad, The.
Wild Plum.
Johnson, Alicia Loy
Black Lotus.
Black Poetry Day, A.
Johnson, B. S.
All This Sunday Long.
Great Man.
Why Do We Lie.
Johnson, Burges
Anxious Farmer, The.
Contentment.
Gnu Wooing, The.
My Sore Thumb.
Remarks from the Pup.
Rondeau of Remorse, A.
Service, The.
Soap, the Oppressor.
Johnson, Charles
Sleeping Beauty.
Johnson, Charles Bertram
Little Cabin, A.
Negro Poets.
Johnson, Charles Frederick
Modern Romans, The.
Then and Now.
Johnson, Denis
Boarding, The.
Minutes.
Passengers.
Woman, A.
Johnson, Don Allen ("Mustafa")
Above the Falls at Waimea.
Brainwashing Dramatized.
Night Dive.
Night Flight.
O White Mistress.
Ripper Collins' Legacy.
Sergeant, The.
Tick Picking in the Quetico.
Johnson, Donald
Indian Summer Here, You in Honolulu.
Johnson, Dorothy Vena
Epitaph for a Bigot.
Green Valley.
Johnson, Emily Pauline ("Tekahionwake")
Cattle Thief, The.
Corn Husker, The.

Lost Lagoon, The.
Marshlands.
Ojistoh.
Shadow River.
Song My Paddle Sings, The.
Trail to Lillooet, The.
Train Dogs, The.

Johnson, Edward
Among These Troopes of Christs Souldiers, Came. . .Mr. Roger Harlackenden.
Good News from New-England, *at.*
Mr. Eliot Pastor of the Church of Christ at Roxbury.
Mr. Thomas Shepheard.
Oh King of Saints, how great's thy work, say we.
Onely the Reverend Grave and Godly Mr. Buckly Remaines.
Reverend Mr. Higginson, The.
Yee Shall Not Misse of a Few Lines in Remembrance of Thomas Hooker.

Johnson, Edythe
Will God's Patience Hold Out for You?

Johnson, Esther ("Stella")
To Dr. Swift on His Birthday, 30th November 1721.

Johnson, Fenton
Aunt Jane Allen.
Banjo Player, The.
Children of the Sun.
Counting.
Daily Grind, The.
Lonely Mother, The.
Marathon Runner, The.
Negro Peddler's Song, A.
New Day, The.
Old Repair Man, The.
Puck Goes to Court.
Rulers: Philadelphia.
Scarlet Woman, The.
Tired.
Vision of Lazarus, The, *sel.*
When I Die.
Who Is That a-Walking in the Corn?
World Is a Mighty Ogre, The.

Johnson, Fred
Arabesque.
Coda.
Fire, Hair, Meat and Bone.
Noises.

Johnson, George W.
When You and I Were Young, Maggie.

Johnson, Georgia Douglas
Black Woman.
Common Dust.
Conquest.
Credo.
Dreams of the Dreamer, The.
Escape.
Heart of a Woman, The.
Hope.
I Closed My Shutters Fast Last Night.
I Want to Die While You Love Me.
Interracial.
Lethe.
Little Son.
Lovelight.
My Little Dreams.
Old Black Men.
Poet Speaks, The.
Prejudice.
Proving.
Recessional.
Remember.
Service.
Smothered Fires.
Suppliant, The.
To William Stanley Braithwaite.
Trifle.
Welt.
What Need Have I for Memory?
When I Am Dead.
Your World ("Your world is as big as you make it").
Youth.

Johnson, H. B.
Stuff.

Johnson, Helen Armstead
Affirmation.
Philodendron.

Johnson, Helene
Bottled [*or* Bottled: New York].
Fulfillment.
Invocation: "Let me be buried in the rain."
Magalu.
Poem: "Little brown boy."
Remember Not.
Road, The.
Sonnet to a Negro in Harlem.
Summer Matures.
Trees at Night.
What Do I Care for Morning.

Johnson, Henry
Derelict.
Funeral Parlor, The.
Journey, The.
Mask of Stone.
Search for Love.

Johnson, Herbert Clark
Boy's Need, A.
Crossing a Creek.
On Calvary's Lonely Hill.
Willow Bend and Weep.

Johnson, Hilda
Ballade of Expansion.

Johnson, James Weldon
Brothers.
Creation, The.
Envoy: "If homely virtues draw from me a tune."
Fifty Years.
From the German of Uhland.
Glory of the Day Was in Her Face, The.
Go Down Death.
Lift Every Voice and Sing.
Listen, Lord [a Prayer].
My City.
O Black and Unknown Bards.
Sence You Went Away.
Up from the Bed of the River.
White Witch, The.

Johnson, Joe
Anna.
If I Ride This Train.
Judeebug's Country.
Samurai and Hustlers.
True Love.

Johnson, Josephine
Supplication.
Unwilling Gypsy, The.

Johnson, Josephine Winslow
Final Autumn.

Johnson, Lionel Pigot
Age of a Dream, The.
Bagley Wood.
Beyond.
By the Statue of King Charles at Charing Cross.
Cadgwith.
Church of a Dream, The.
Comrades.
Dark Angel, The.
Darkness, The.
Dead.
Doctor Major.
Friend, A.
Friends.
In Memory, *sel.*
Ireland.
Laleham: Matthew Arnold's Grave.
London Town.
Magic.
Mystic and Cavalier.
Our Lady of France.
Our Lady of the May.
Oxford.
Oxford Nights.
Plato in London.
Precept of Silence, The.
Roman Stage, The.
Sancta Silvarum.
Song: "Now in golden glory goes."
Stranger, A.
Summer Storm.
Te Martyrum Candidatus.
To a Traveler [*or* Traveller].
To Morfydd.
To the Dead of '98.
Troopship, The.
Ways of War.
Winchester.

Johnson, Louis
Coming and Going.
How to Measure a Cat.
This Particular Christian.

Johnson, Margaret
Day Dreams, or Ten Years Old.

Johnson, Michael L.
Nancy, You Dance.
On the Dates of Poets.

Johnson, Nick
Sleeping Gypsy, The.

Johnson, Paul
Because.

Johnson, Pauline. *See* **Johnson, Emily Pauline**

Johnson, Pyke, Jr.
Me and Samantha.
Toucan, The.

Johnson, Rita
Corner, The.

Johnson, Robert
Love in Vain.

Johnson, Robert Underwood
As a Bell in a Chime.
Blossom of the Soul, The.
Browning at Asolo.
Dewey at Manila.
English Mother, An.
Hearth Song.
In Tesla's Laboratory.
Irish Love-Song, An.
Italian Rhapsody.
Love Once Was like an April Dawn.
Silence was envious of the only voice.
Star Song.
To the Returning Brave.
Ursula.
Voice of Webster, The, *sel.*
Wistful Days, The.

Johnson, Ronald
Letters to Walt Whitman, *sels.*

Johnson, Rossiter
Evelyn.
Soldier Poet, A.

Johnson, Samuel (1709–84)
Anacreon's Dove.
Ballad: "I put my hat upon my head."
Burlesque of Lope De Vega.
Charles XII [of Sweden].
Comets and Princes.
Epitaph on Claudy Phillips, a Musician, An.
Epitaph on William Hogarth.
Epitaph upon the Celebrated Claudy Philips, Musician, Who Died Very Poor, An.
Good-natur'd Man, The, *sel.*
Hermit Hoar.
If the Man Who Turnips Cries.
Imitation of the Style of * * * *.
Life's Last Scene.
Lines on the Death of Mr. Levett.
London; a Poem in Imitation of the Third Satire of Juvenal.
On the Coming of Age of a Rich Extravagant Young Man, *sel.*
On the Death of Mr. [*or* Dr.] Robert Levet, a Practiser in Physic.
Poverty in London.

Power of Prayer, The.
Prologue: "Prest by the load of life, the weary mind."
Prologue Spoken [by Mr. Garrick] at the Opening of the Theatre [Royal] in Drury-Lane, 1747.
Prologue to "A Word to the Wise."
Scholar's Life, The.
Short Song of Congratulation, A.
To Miss : On Her Playing Upon the Harpsichord.
To Mrs. Thrale on Her Thirty-fifth Birthday.
To robbers furious, and to lovers tame.
Translation of Lines by Benserade.
Vanity of Human Wishes, The: The Tenth Satire of Juvenal Imitated.
Young Author, The.

Johnson, Samuel (1822–82)
City of God.
Father, in Thy Mysterious Presence Kneeling, *with music.*
I Bless Thee, Lord, for Sorrows Sent, *with music.*
Inspiration.
Life of Ages, Richly Poured.
Prayer for Strength.

Johnson, Siddie Joe
Midnight in Bonnie's Stall.

Johnson, Thomas
Best Dance Hall in Iuka, Mississippi, The.
Some Scribbles for a Lumpfish.

Johnson, Tom
Becoming Is Perfection.

Johnson, Victoria Saffelle
Dedication: "Holy Jesus, Thou art born."

Johnson, W. Ralph
July.

Johnson, Willard
Indian Song.

Johnson, William Martin
On Snow-Flakes Melting on His Lady's Breast.

Johnson, William Samuel
Chiffons! *with music.*

Johnston, Bertha
Did You Ever Hear an English Sparrow Sing?

Johnston, George
Bliss.
Bulge, The.
Cathleen Sweeping.
Eating Fish.
Flight.
Frost.
Huntress, The.
Indoors.
Music in the Air.
Music on the Water.
Noctambule.
O Earth, Turn!
Rest Hour.
Veterans.
War on the Periphery.

Johnston, Gordon
Hot Day and Human Nature, The.

Johnston, Martin
Airport.
Directions for Dreamfishing.
Quantum.
Vernal Equinox.

Johnston, Mary
Virginiana.

Johnstone, Henry, Lord Johnstone
Fastidious Serpent, The.

Johnstone, Sir Thomas
There is many a slipton.

Jonas, Ann Rae
Causes of Color, The.

Jonas, Anne Rae
Cat in the Box, The.

Jonas, George
Eight Lines for a Script Girl.
Exit Lines.
Five Stanzas on Perfection.
For the Record.
Four Stanzas Written in Anxiety.
Glass Eaters, The.
Let me put it this way.
Once More.
Peace.
Portrait; the Freedom Fighter.
Sleep only with strangers.
Temporal.
To Christian Montpelier, *sel.*
We all have/ A bench in the park to reach.
Women don't travel in clubcars.

Jonas, Gerald
Day the T.V. Broke, The.
In Passing.
Love.
Night Thought.

Jonas, Rosalie
Ballade des Belles Milatraisses.
Brother Baptis' on Woman Suffrage.

Jonas, Samuel Alroy
Lines on the Back of a Confederate Note.

Jonas, Steve
Poem: "It's a dull poem."

Jones, Amanda Theodosia
Panama.

Jones, Andrew McCord
Escape.
Morning Kiss, A.
Poem of Broken Pieces, A.
Snowman.
Somewhere West.

Jones, Charles L. S.
Fort Bowyer.
Hero of Bridgewater, The.

Jones, Cullen
Now That the Flowers.

Jones, David
A, a, a, Domine Deus.
Anathemata, The, *sels.*
Angle-Land.
But sweet sister Death has gone debauched today and stalks.
Five Unmistakable Marks, The.
In Parenthesis, *sels.*
King Pellam's Launde.
Wall, The.
You can hear the silence of it.

Jones, Douglas G.
Annunciation.
Beautiful Creatures Brief as These.
Boy in the Lamont Poetry Room, Harvard.
For Spring.
From Sex, This Sea.
I Thought There Were Limits.
Northern Water Thrush.
On a Picture of Your House.
Perishing Bird, The.
Poem for Good Friday.
River, The; North of Guelph.
Soliloquy to Absent Friends.
These Trees Are No Forest of Mourners.

Jones, Ebenezer
Development of Idiotcy, A.
Hand, The.
When the World Is Burning.
Winter Hymn, A—to the Snow.

Jones, Edward Smyth
Song of Thanks, A.

Jones, Elijah
How Big Was Alexander?

Jones, Emily B. C.
Jerked Heartstrings in Town.
Middle-Age.

Jones, Ernest Charles
Song of the Lower Classes, The.

Jones, Evan
Noah's Song.

Jones, Frederick Scheetz
On the Democracy of Yale.
To New Haven.

Jones, G. W.
Portrait of the Pornographer.

Jones, Gayl
Journal, *sel.*
Many Die Here.
Satori.
3-31-70.
Tripart.

Jones, Glyn
Esyllt.
Gold.
Night.
Song: "I kept neat my virginity."

Jones, H. Bedford
How Do You Do?

Jones, Herbert
True Romance, The.

Jones, Howard
Fall To.

Jones, John
To Lydia, with a Coloured Egg, on Easter Monday.

Jones, John P.
Silver Jack's Religion.

Jones, Joshua Henry
To a Skull.

Jones, L. E.
Epigram on the Unknown Inventor of Scissors.

Jones, Lawrence M.
I Am the Flag.

Jones, LeRoi. *See* **Baraka, Imamu Amiri**

Jones, Louise Seymour
Who Loves a Garden.

Jones, M. Keel
Election Reflection.

Jones, Mary Hoxie
Four Deer, The.

Jones, Nancy
Running Blind.

Jones, Patricia
14th St/New York, *abr.*
I Done Got So Thirsty That My Mouth Waters at the Thought of Rain.
Why I Like Movies.

Jones, Paul
Native African Revolutionaries.

Jones, Paul R.
Becoming a Frog.

Jones, Rae Desmond
Age.

Jones, Ralph M.
Bed-Time.

Jones, Richard
Three Car Poems.

Jones, Robert
Madrigal: "O I do love, then kiss me."
These Days.

Jones, Rodney
First Birth, The.
For the Eating of Swine.
Mosquito, The.
Remembering Fire.
Thoreau.

Jones, Samuel
Force of Love, The.
Ploughman, in Imitation of Milton, The.
Poverty, in Imitation of Milton.

Jones, Thomas
This is Thomas Jones's book.

Jones, Thomas Samuel, Jr.
As in a Rose-Jar.
Ave atque Vale.
Clonard.
Daphne.
In the Fall o' Year.
Little Ghosts, The.
Path of the Stars, The.
Sometimes.
To Song.

Jones, Sir William
Baby, The.

Epigram: "On parent knees, a naked new-born child."
Moral Tetrastich, A.
Ode in Imitation of Alcæus, An.
What Constitutes a State?
Jones-Quartey, K. B.
Stranger, Why Do You Wonder So?
Jong, Erica
Alcestis on the Poetry Circuit.
Becoming a Nun.
Buddha in the Womb, The.
Climbing You.
Dearest Man-in-the-Moon.
Divorce.
For a Marriage.
How You Get Born.
In Praise of Clothes.
In Sylvia Plath Country.
Jubilate Canis.
Man under the Bed, The.
Seventeen Warnings in Search of a Feminist Poem.
Sexual Soup.
Walking through the Upper East Side.
Wives of Mafiosi, The.
Woman Who Loved to Cook, The.
Jonker, Ingrid
Begin Summer.
Child Who Was Shot Dead by Soldiers at Nyanga, The.
Dog.
Don't Sleep.
Face of Love, The.
I Am with Those.
I Don't Want Any More Visitors.
I Drift in the Wind.
Journey round the World.
Lost City.
Pregnant Woman.
Time of Waiting in Amsterdam.
25 December 1960.
When You Laugh.
When You Write Again.
Jonson, Ben
Aeglamour's Lament.
Alchemist, The, *sels.*
All Your Fortunes We Can Tell Ye.
Angel Describes Truth, An.
Another Birthday.
Another. In Defence of Their Inconstancie.
Another Ladyes Exception Present at the Hearing.
Answer to Master Wither's Song, "Shall I, Wasting in Despair?"
Apollo's Song.
Ask Not to Know This Man.
Beauties, Have Ye Seen This Toy.
Begging Another, on Colour of Mending the Former.
Ben. Johnsons Sociable Rules for the Apollo.
Buz, Quoth the Blue Fly.
By Him.
Catch, A.
Celebration of Charis [in Ten Lyric Pieces (*or* Lyrick Peeces)], A.
Charme.
Chorus: "Spring all the Graces of the age."
Clayming a Second Kisse by Desert.
Come, My Celia [Let Us Prove].
Cupid.
Cynthia's Revels, *sels.*
Death and Love.
Dream [*or* Dreame], The.
Echo's Lament for Narcissus.
Echo's Song.
Elegie, An: "Let me be what I am, as Virgil cold."
Elegie, An: " 'Tis true, I'm broke! Vowes, oathes, and all I had."
Elegie on the Lady Jane Pawlet, Marchion. of Winton, An.
Elegy, An: "Since you must go, and I must bid farewell."
Elegy, An: "Though beauty be the mark of praise."
Elegy on the Lady Venetia Digby, Wife of Sir Kenelm Digby, *sel.*
Elizabeth L. H.
Epicoene; or, The Silent Woman, *sel.*
Epigram to King Charles for an Hundred Pounds He Sent Me in My Sickness, An.
Epigram to the Queen Then Lying In, An.
Epistle Answering to One That Asked to be Sealed of the Tribe of Ben, An.
Epistle to a Friend, to Persuade Him to the Wars, An.
Epistle to Elizabeth, Countess of Rutland, *sels.*
Epistle to Lady Rutland, An.
Epistle to Sir Edward Sackville, Now Earl of Dorset, An.
Epitaph, An: On Elizabeth Chute.
Epitaph on Elizabeth, L. H.
Epitaph on Master Philip Gray, An.
Epitaph on Master Vincent Corbett, An.
Epitaph on S. P. [Salomon *or* Salathiel Pavy], a Child of Queen Elizabeth's Chapel.
Epode.
Execration upon Vulcan, An.
Faery Beam upon You, The.
Fit of Rime [*or* Rhyme] against Rime [*or* Rhyme], A.
Fools.
Fools, They Are the Only Nation.
Ghyrlond of the Blessed Virgin Marie, The.
Gipsy Song.
Glove, The.
Gypsies Metamorphosed, *sels.*
Her Man Described by Her Owne Dictamen.
Hesperus' Hymn to Cynthia [*or* Hesperus' Song].
His Discourse with Cupid.
His Excuse for Loving.
Hour-Glass [*or* Hourglass], The.
How He Saw Her.
Hue and Cry after Cupid, The, *sel.*
Humble Petition of Poor Ben to the Best of Monarchs, Masters, Men, King Charles, The.
Hymenaei, *sel.*
Hymn: "Queen and huntress, chaste and fair."
Hymn [*or* Hymne] on the Nativity [*or* Nativitie] of My Saviour, A.
Hymn to Comus.
Hymn to Cynthia.
Hymn to Diana.
Hymn to God the Father, A.
Hymn to the Belly.
Hymne: "Queene and Huntresse, chaste, and faire."
Hymne on the Nativitie of My Saviour, A.
Hymne to God the Father, A.
In the Person of Woman Kind.
Inviting a Friend to Supper.
It Is Not Growing like a Tree.
It Was a Beauty That I Saw.
Karolin's Song.
Kiss, The.
Lady Venetia Digby, The.
Lincolnshire; from the Wolds to the Fens.
Little Shrub Growing By, A.
Love.
Lovel's Song.
Love's Triumph.
Mab the Mistress-Fairy.
Masque of Augurs, The, *sel.*
Masque of Beauty, The, *sel.*
Masque of Christmas, The.
Masque of Queens, The, *sels.*
Masque of the Gypsies, The.
Metamorphosed Gipsies, The.
Mother Maudlin the Witch.
My Picture Left in Scotland.
Nano's Song.
Neptune's Triumph, *sel.*
New Inn, The, *sel.*
New yeares, expect new gifts: Sister, your Harpe.
New-Yeares-Gift Sung to King Charles, 1635, A.
Noble Balm, The.
Noble Nature, The.
Nymph's Secret, A.
Oak and Lily.
Oberon, the Fairy Prince, *sel.*
Ode to Himself[e] ("Come leave the loathèd stage").
Ode to Himself[e], An ("Where do'st thou careless lie").
Ode to Sir Lucius Cary and Sir H. Morison, An, *sel.*
Ode to Sir William Sydney, on His Birth-Day.
On Court-Worme.
On Don Surly.
On English Monsieur.
On Giles and Joan.
On Gut.
On His First Sonne.
On Lieutenant Shift.
On Lucy Countess[e] of Bedford.
On Margaret Ratcliffe.
On My First Daughter.
On My First Son [*or* Sonne].
On Playwright.
On Something, That Walks [*or* Walkes] Somewhere.
On Spies.
On the Portrait of Shakespeare Prefixed to the First Folio Edition, 1623.
On the twenty-second of June, *at.*
Pans Anniversarie.
Part of an Ode, A.
Patrico's Song.
Penshurst.
Picture of Her Mind, The.
Pleasure Reconciled to Virtue [*or* Vertue].
Poetaster, The, *sels.*
Power of Poets, The.
Praises of a Countrie Life, The.
Proportion.
Queen and Huntress.
Queen Mab.
Queene and Huntresse.
Return of Astraea, The.
Sad Shepherd, The, *sels.*
Satyr, The, *sel.*
Satyres Catch.
Silent Woman, The.
Simplex Munditiis.
Slow, Slow, Fresh Fount.
So Sweet Is She.
So White, So Soft, So Sweet.
Song: "Come my Celia, let us prove."
Song: "Fooles, they are the onely nation."
Song: "If I freely may discover."
Song: "O, that joy so soon should waste!"
Song, A: "Oh[*or* O]do[e] not wanton with those eyes."
Song: "Slow, slow, fresh fount, keep time with my salt tears."
Song: "Still to be neat, still to be drest."
Song: That Women Are but Men's Shadows.
Song: "Though I am young, and cannot tell."
Song: To Celia ("Drink to me only with thine eyes").
Song: To Celia ("Kiss me, sweet; the wary lover").
Song: "When love at first did move."
Song of Echo.
Song of the Satyrs.
Song to Celia ("Come my Celia, let us prove").
Song to Celia ("Drink to me only with thine eyes").
Sonnet, to the Noble Lady, the Lady Mary Worth, A.
Still to Be Neat [Still to Be Drest (*or* Dressed)].
Sweet Swan of Avon! what a sight it were.

That Women Are but Men's Shadows.
To a Weak Gamester in Poetry.
To Celia ("Come my Celia, let us prove").
To Celia ("Drink[e] to me, on[e]ly, with thine eyes").
To Celia ("Kiss me, sweet; the wary lover").
To Dr. Delaney, *sel.*
To Doctor Empirick [*or* Empiric].
To Edward Allen.
To Elizabeth, Countess of Rutland.
To Fine Grand.
To Fine Lady Would-Be.
To Fool, or Knave.
To Francis Beaumont.
To Heaven.
To John Donne ("Donne, the delight of Phoebus, and each Muse").
To John Donne ("Who shall doubt, Donne, where I a poet bee").
To King James.
To Lucy, Countesse of Bedford, with Mr. Donnes Satyres.
To Mary Lady Wroth.
To My Book[e].
To Penshurst.
To Pertinax Cob.
To Sir Henrie Savile [upon His Translation of Tacitus].
To Sir Henry Cary.
To Sir Robert Wroth.
To the Ghost of Martial.
To the Immortal[l] Memory [*or* Memorie] and Friendship of That Noble Pair[e], Sir Lucius Cary and Sir Henry Morrison.
To the Learned Critic.
To the Memory of My Beloved Master William Shakespeare [and What He Hath Left Us].
To the Reader ("Pray thee, take care, that tak'st my book in hand").
To the Reader ("This figure, that thou here seest put").
To the Same.
To the World; a Farewell for a Gentlewoman, Virtuous and Noble.
To Thomas Lord Chancellor.
To William Camden.
To William Earle of Pembroke.
To William Roe.
Triumph, The.
Triumph of Charis, The.
Urging Her of a Promise.
Venus' Runaway.
Verses Placed over the Door at the Entrance into the Apollo Room at the Devil Tavern.
Vision of Delight, The.
Vision of Delight Presented at Court in Christmas, 1617, The.
Volpone, *sels.*
What Hee Suffered.
What our Dame bids us do.
Whole world here, leavened with madness, swells, The.
Why I Write Not of Love.
Witches' Charms, The.
Witches' Song, The.
With you, I know, my offering will find grace.
Women Men's Shadows.

Jonson, Edward
Water-Drinker, The.

Jordan, A. C.
You Tell Me to Sit Quiet.

Jordan, Barbara Leslie
Desert Shipwreck.

Jordan, Charlotte Brewster
To Borglum's Seated Statue of Abraham Lincoln.

Jordan, David Starr
Food for a Cat.
Men Told Me, Lord!
Vivérols.

Jordan, Ethel Blair
Disarm the Hearts.

Jordan, June
All the World Moved.
Cameo No. II.
For My Mother.
Getting Down to Get Over.
If You Saw a Negro Lady.
In Memoriam: Martin Luther King, Jr.
My Sadness Sits around Me.
Nobody Riding the Roads Today.
Okay "Negroes."
Poem about Intelligence for My Brothers and Sisters, A.
Poem for My Family.
Poem for Nana.
Poem from the Empire State.
Poem to My Sister, Ethel Ennis, Who Sang "The Star-spangled Banner" at the Second Inauguration of Richard Milhous Nixon.
Queen Anne's Lace.
Reception, The.
Towards a City That Sings.
Uncle Bull-Boy.
Unemployment/Monologue.
What Happens.
What Would I Do White?

Jordan, Norman
August 2.
Black Warrior.
Cities and Seas.
Ending.
Feeding the Lions.
July 31.

Jordan, Thomas
Coronemus Nos Rosis Antequam Marcescant.
Let Us Drink and Be Merry.
Pyms Anarchy, *at.*

Jordana, Elena
Tango.

Jōsa
Crocuses.

Joseph, Chief
War.

Joseph, Jenny
Back to Base.
Dog body and cat mind, The.
Lost Continent, The.
Rose in the Afternoon.
Warning.

Joseph, Lawrence
When You've Been Here Long Enough.

Joseph, Rosemary
Baking Day.

Joseph of the Studium, Saint
Finished Course, The.

Joslin, Dorothy
Sonnet for a Loved One.

Joso
Haiku: "No need to cling."
Haiku: "These branches."
Little Duck, The.
That duck, bobbing up.

Josselyn, John
And the bitter storm augments; the wild winds wage.
Description of a New England Spring
Verses Made Sometime Since upon . . . the Indian Squa.

Joyce, J.
Soil Searcher.

Joyce, James
All Day I Hear [the Noise of Waters].
Alone.
Bahnhofstrasse.
Ballad of Persse O'Reilly, The.
Because your voice was at my side.
Bid Adieu to Maidenhood.
Ecce Puer.
Finnegans Wake, *sels.*
Flood.
Flower Given to My Daughter, A.
Gas from a Burner.
Gentle lady, do not sing.
Goldenhair.
Holy Office, The.
I Hear an Army [Charging upon the Land].
Memory of the Players in a Mirror at Midnight, A.
Nightpiece.
Noise of Waters, The.
O Sweetheart, Hear You [*or* Thou].
On the Beach at Fontana.
Ondt and the Gracehoper, The.
She Weeps over Rahoon.
Simples.
Sleep now, O sleep now.
Song: "O, it was out by Donnycarney."
Strings in the Earth.
There was a kind Lady called Gregory.
This Heart That Flutters near My Heart.
Though I Thy Mithridates Were.
Tutto è Sciolto.
Ulysses, *sel.*
What Counsel Has the Hooded Moon.
Yes.

Joyce, Robert Dwyer
Leprahaun, The.

Joyce, William
Small Town.

Juan de la Cruz, San. *See* **John of the Cross, Saint**

Juana Inés de la Cruz, Sister (*originally* Juana de Asbaje)
First Dream, *sel.*
Green enravishment of human life.
I can't hold you and I can't leave you.
In Which She Satisfies a Fear with the Rhetoric of Tears.
Satirical Romance, A, *sels.*
She Attempts to Refute the Praises That Truth, Which She Calls Passion, Inscribed on a Portrait of the Poet.
She Proves the Inconsistency of the Desires and Criticism of Men Who Accuse Women of What They Themselves Cause.
Stay, shade of my shy treasure! Oh, remain.
This coloured counterfeit that thou beholdest.
This evening, my love, even as I spoke vainly.

Judkins, Charles Otis
Play, The.

Judson, Adoniram
Come Holy Spirit, Dove Divine, *with music.*
In Spite of Sorrow.
Our Father, God, *with music.*

Judson, Emily Chubbuck. *See* **"Forester, Fanny"**

Judson, Sarah
Proclaim the Lofty Praise, *with music.*

Judy, Scott *and* **"Doc" Hammond**
Song: "We came to Tamichi in 1880."

Juergensen, Hans
Anne Sexton.

Juhász, Ferenc
Birth of the Foal.

Juhasz, Suzanne
Dancer from the Dance, The.
Saying Goodbye.

Jumper, Will C.
California Quail in January.

Junge, Carl S.
Dinosaur, The.

"Junia"
Ballade of a Summer Hotel.

Junkins, Donald
Walden in July.

Justema, William
Song: "This is the song of those who live alone."

Justice, Donald
About My Poems.
After a Line by John Peale Bishop.
Anonymous Drawing.
Another Song ("Merry the green, the green hill shall be merry").
Beyond the Hunting Woods.
Birthday Candle, A.

Bus Stop.
But That Is Another Story.
Childhood.
Counting the Mad.
Crossing Kansas by Train.
Dancer's Life, A.
Dreams of Water.
Elegy Is Preparing Itself, An.
Elsewheres.
First Death.
Girl Sitting Alone at Party.
Grandfathers, The.
Here in Katmandu.
Houses.
In Bertram's Garden.
Incident in a Rose Garden.
Ladies by Their Windows.
Landscape with Little Figures.
Local Storm, A.
Love's Stratagems.
Luxury.
Man Closing Up, The.
Memo from the Desk of X.
Memory of a Porch.
Men at Forty.
Missing Person, The.
Ode to a Dressmaker's Dummy.
On a Painting by Patient B of the Independence State Hospital for the Insane.
On the Death of Friends in Childhood.
Party.
Poem: "Time and the weather wear away."
Poem to Be Read at 3 A.M.
Poet at Seven, The.
Sestina: "I woke by first light in a wood."
Snowfall, The.
Sonatina in Yellow.
Song: "Morning opened/ Like a rose."
Sonnet for My Father.
Sonnet to My Father.
Southern Gothic.
Tales from a Family Album.
To Waken a Small Person.
Tourist from Syracuse, The.
Tune for a Lonesome Fife.
Variations for Two Pianos.
Variations on Southern Themes.
White Notes.

Justus, May
Dress of Spring, The.
Footwear.
Jessica Jane ("Jessica Jane is the kind of cook").
Remember September.
Strawberry Jam.
Witchwood.

Juvenal (Decimus Junius Juvenalis)
Against Women.
But of all the plagues, the greatest is untold.
Celestial Wisdom.
Faggots in Ancient Rome.
Give store of days, good Jove, give length of years.
Hannibal.
Satires, *sels.*
Sejanus ("How many men are killed by power, by power").
Sejanus ("Some ask for envy'd pow'r; which publick hate").
Sejanus ("What crowds by envied power, the wish of all").

K

"K."
How Firm a Foundation.

"K., A"
La Donna E Mobile.

"K., E. H."
City Church, The.

Kaberry, C. J.
Indian Elephant, The.

Kabir
Clay Jug, The.
Radiance, The.
Simple Purification, The.
Songs of Kabir.
What form or shape to describe?

Kaccipettu Nannakaiyar
My lover capable of terrible lies.

Ka-'ehu
Leper, The.

Kaffka, Margit
Father.

Kaga no Chiyo
Haiku: "Autumn's bright moon."
Haiku: "Dew of the rouge-flower, The."
Haiku: "Spring rain."

Kagawa, Toyohiko
Love.
Meditation.

Kageyama, Yuri
Day in a Long Hot Summer, A.
Disco Chinatown.
Love Poem: "I like/ the feel of your pulsating fibers."
My Mother Takes a Bath.
Strings/Himo.

Kahanovitch, Pinhas. *See* **"Der Nistor"**

Kahn, Gustave
Homage.
Paris by Night.
Pilgrim from the East, The.
Song: "O lovely April, rich and bright."
Temple, The.
Word, The.
You Masks of the Masquerade.

Kahn, Hannah
Signature.
To Be Black, to Be Lost.

Kaiama
Song: "Misty and dim, a bush in the wilds of Kapa'a."

Kalidasa
Salutation of the Dawn, *at.*
Seasons, The.
Woman.

Kallman, Chester
Dead Center.
Little Epithalamium.
Night Music.
Nightmare of a Cook.
Romance, A.
Tellers of Tales.
Urban History.

Kalmar, Bert *and* **Harry Ruby**
"America, I Love You."

Kalola
Fathomless Is My Love.

Kalonymos ben Judah
Although Tormented.

Kalonymos ben Kalonymos
Hypocrite, The.
Touchstone, The, *sels.*
Unfortunate Male, The.
Yoke, The.

Kalonymos ben Moses of Lucca
Sovereignty, His.

Kamenetz, Rodger
Pilpul.
Why I Can't Write My Autobiography.

Kaminsky, Marc
Erev Shabbos.

Kamm, Nancy P.
Waiting Carefully.

Kammeyer, Virginia Maughan
Compensation.

Kamzon, Jacob David
Very Fair My Lot.

Kanalenstein, Ruben
Jerusalem.

Kandel, Lenore
Blues for Sister Sally.
Bus Ride.

Kane, Douglas V.
Westering.

Kane, Julie
Cornelia's Window.

Kaneko, Lonny
Coming Home from Camp.
Family Album.
Secret, The.
Violets for Mother.

Kanié, Anoma
All That You Have Given Me, Africa.

Kanik, Orban Veli
Being Sad.
People.

Kao Ch'i
Written on Seeing the Flowers, and Remembering My Daughter.

Kaplan, Allan
Marvelous.

Kaplan, Milton
Ballet.
Circus, The.
Knife, The.

Kaplan, Rebbekka
You Are More than I Need.

Karélli, Zoé
Presences.

Karibo, Minji
Superstition.

Karlen, Arno
Bury Me in America.

Karlfeldt, Erik Axel
Imagined Happiness.
Vagrant, A.

Karni, Yehuda
Chambers of Jerusalem.
Four of Them, The.
Place Me in the Breach.

Karoniaktatie (Alex Jacobs)
Dead Heroes.
Elegy: "When the old ones die."
Face, The.
Stone Song (Zen Rock) the Seer & the Unbeliever.

Karp, Vickie
Last Farmer in Queens, The.

Karsner, Walta
Xmas Time.

Kasa, Lady
I dreamed I held/ A sword against my flesh.
I love and fear him.
To love somebody/ Who doesn't love you.
To love someone/ Who does not return that love.

Kaschnitz, Marie Luise
Humility.
Resurrection.

Kasdaglis, Lina
Traffic Lights.

Kasmuneh
Overripe Fruit.
Timid Gazelle, The.

Kass, Jerry
Fidelity.

Kassia
Epigram: "Poverty? wealth? seek neither."
Epigram: "Wealth covers sin—the poor."
Epigram: "Woman working hard and wisely, A."
Mary Magdalene.
Sticheron for Matins, Wednesday of Holy Week.

Kästner, Erich
Anonymous Gravestone.
Moral Taxi Ride, The.
Ragoût Fin de Siècle (with Reference to Certain Cafés).

Katav, Shalom
Pleading Voices.

Kates, J.
Life Story.
Katz, Bobbi
Patience.
Runaway, The.
Samuel.
Spring Is.
Things to Do If You Are a Subway.
Katz, Menke
In the Year of Two Thousand.
Katzin, Olga. *See* **"Sagittarius"**
Kauffman, Reginald Wright
Call, The.
Troia Fuit.
Wastrel, The.
Kaufman, Bob
African Dream.
Afterwards, They Shall Dance.
Battle Report.
Benediction.
Blues Note.
Cincophrenicpoet.
Cocoa Morning.
Falling.
Forget Me Not.
I, Too, Know What I Am Not.
I Have Folded My Sorrows.
Mingus.
Patriotic Ode on the Fourteenth Anniversary of the Persecution of Charlie Chaplin.
Response.
To My Son Parker, Asleep in the Next Room.
Unholy Missions.
Walking Parker Home.
When We Hear the Eye Open.
Kaufman, George Simon
Lines to a Man Who Thinks That Apple Betty with Hard Sauce Is Food for a Human Being.
Kaufman, Shirley
Always She Moves from Me.
Apples.
Beetle on the Shasta Daylight.
Burning of the Birds, The.
Déjà Vu.
Dinosaur Tracks in Beit Zayit.
Her Going.
His Wife.
I see bodies in the morning kneel.
Leah.
Looking at Henry Moore's Elephant Skull Etchings in Jerusalem during the War.
Looking for Maimonides: Tiberias.
Loving.
Mothers, Daughters.
Nechama.
New Graveyard: Jerusalem.
Next Year, in Jerusalem.
Room.
Starting Over.
There are caverns/ under our feet.
Watts.
We are going down a long slide.
Wonders.
Kavanagh, P. J.
Birthday.
Temperance Billiards Rooms, The.
Kavanagh, Patrick
Ante-natal Dream.
Auditors In.
Bluebells for Love.
Canal Bank Walk.
Candida ("Candida is one today").
Christmas Childhood, A.
Come Dance with Kitty Stobling.
Dear Folks.
Epic.
Father Mat.
Glut on the Market, A.
Great Hunger, The, *sels.*
Hospital, The.
I Had a Future.
If Ever You Go to Dublin Town.
Important Statement.
In Memory of My Mother.
Inniskeen Road: July Evening.
Intimate Parnassus.
Is.
Lecture Hall.
Lines Written on a Seat on the Grand Canal, Dublin.
Long Garden, The.
Memory of Brother Michael.
Morning.
October.
One, The.
Pegasus.
Prelude: "Give us another poem, he said."
Question to Life.
Road to Hate, The.
Sanctity.
Self-Slaved, The.
Shancoduff.
Spraying the Potatoes.
Stony Grey Soil.
Tarry Flynn, *sel.*
"Through the Open Door."
Tinker's Wife.
To Hell with Commonsense.
To the Man after the Harrow.
Kawai Chigetsu-ni
Grasshoppers/ Chirping in the sleeves.
Kay, Ellen
Pathedy of Manners.
Kay, Ellen de Young
Cante Hondo.
Magnanimous, The.
Tiresias' Lament.
To a Blue Hippopotamus.
Kay, W. Lowrie
Lancaster County Tragedy.
Kaye-Smith, Sheila
Lady Day in Harvest.
Kazan, Molly
Thanksgiving, 1963.
"Kazanova, Kid." *See* **Stack, Philip**
Kazantzis, Judith
Arachne.
Frightened Flier Goes North, The.
In Memory, 1978.
Woman making advances publicly, A.
Keach, Benjamin
How Glorious Are the Morning Stars, *with music.*
Kearney, Lawrence
Cuba.
Cyclist, The.
Kearney, Peadar
Down by the Glenside.
Soldier's Song, The.
Tri-colored Ribbon, The.
Whack Fol the Diddle.
Kearns, Josie
Planets Line Up for a Demonstration, The.
Kearns, Lionel
Environment.
Foreign Aid.
In-Group.
Insight.
Stuntman.
Keate, George
Burlesque Ode, on the Author's Clearing a New House of Some Workmen, A, *sel.*
Keating, Geoffrey
Keen Thyself, Poor Wight.
Mourn for Yourself.
My Grief on Fál's Proud Plain, *sel.*
O Woman Full of Wile. *At. to*
Keating, Joseph
Charles Gustavus Anderson, *vers.* II, *at.*
Keating, Norma
Never, Never Can Nothingness Come.
Keating, William
Down, Down, Down, *with music.*
Keats, John
Addressed to Haydon.
After Dark Vapours.
Apollo then,/ With sudden scrutiny and gloomless eyes.
Are Then Regalities All Gilded Masks?
Banquet, The.
Bards of Passion and of Mirth.
Bright Star.
Bright Star, Would I Were Steadfast [*or* Stedfast] as Thou Art!
Bruised Titans, The.
Cancelled Stanza of the Ode on Melancholy.
Daisy's Song.
Dawlish Fair.
Day Is Gone, The.
December.
Dedication: To Leigh Hunt, Esq.
Den of the Titans, The.
Dove, The.
Dream, A.
Endymion [a Poetic Romance],
Epistle to John Hamilton Reynolds.
Eve of St. Agnes, The.
Eve of Saint Mark, The.
Fairy Song.
Fall of Hyperion, The, *sels.*
Fancy.
Fragment of an Ode to Maia [Written on May Day, 1818].
Goldfinches.
Happy Insensibility.
He Saw Far in the Concave Green of the Sea.
Here Is Wine.
His Last Sonnet.
How Many Bards Gild the Lapses of Time!
Human Seasons, The.
Hymn to Pan.
Hyperion; a Fragment.
I Had a Dove [and the Sweet Dove Died].
I Stood Tiptoe [upon a Little Hill].
If by Dull Rhymes Our English Must Be Chained.
Imitation of Spenser.
Isabella; or, The Pot of Basil.
Keen, Fitful Gusts [Are Whispering Here and There].
La Belle Dame sans Merci.
Lamia.
Life Again.
Lines on Seeing a Lock of Milton's Hair.
Lines on the Mermaid Tavern.
Lines Supposed to Have Been Addressed to Fanny Brawne.
Lines to Fanny, *sel.*
Love and Friendship.
Magic Casements.
Meg Merrilies [*or* Merrilees].
Mermaid Tavern, The.
Minnows.
Modern Love.
Morning.
O Sorrow!
Ode: "Bards of passion and of mirth."
Ode on a Grecian Urn.
Ode on Indolence.
Ode on [*or* to] Melancholy.
Ode on the Poets.
Ode to a Nightingale.
Ode to Fanny, *sel.*
Ode to Psyche.
On a Dream.
On a Grecian Urn.
On Death.
On Fame ("Fame, like a wayward girl, will still be coy").
On Fame ("How fever'd is that man").
On First Looking into Chapman's Homer.
On Melancholy.
On Mrs. Reynolds's Cat.
On Oxford.
On Seeing a Lock of Milton's Hair.

On Seeing the Elgin Marbles [for the First Time].
On Sitting Down to Read "King Lear" Once Again.
On the Grasshopper and [the] Cricket.
On the Sea.
On the Sonnet.
Poet, The.
Poetry of Earth, The.
Portrait, A.
Realm of Fancy, The.
Recollection of the Stone Circle near Keswick, A.
Robin Hood.
Saturn.
Sharing Eve's Apple.
Shell's Song, The.
Sigh of Silence, The.
Sleep and Poetry.
Sleeping Youth, A.
Solitude.
Song: "I had a dove and the sweet dove died."
Song: "O Sorrow,/ Why dost borrow."
Song about Myself.
Song of the Indian Maid, The ("Beneath my palm-trees, by the riverside").
Song of the Indian Maid ("O Sorrow,/ Why dost borrow").
Sonnet: "After dark vapours have oppress'd our plains."
Sonnet: "Bright star! would I were steadfast as thou art."
Sonnet: "Fresh morning gusts have blown away all fear."
Sonnet: "Keen, fitful gusts are whisp'ring here and there."
Sonnet: On a Picture of Leander.
Sonnet: On First Looking into Chapman's Homer.
Sonnet: On the Sea.
Sonnet: To Homer.
Sonnet: "To one who has been long in city pent."
Sonnet: "When I have fears that I may cease to be."
Sonnet: Written at the End of "The Floure and the Lefe."
Sonnet: Written in January, 1818.
Sonnet: Written on the Day That Mr. Leigh Hunt Left Prison.
Sonnet on the Sea.
Sonnet to Ailsa Rock.
Spenserian Stanzas on Charles Armitage Brown.
Stanzas: "In a drear-nighted December."
Sweet Peas.
Terror of Death, The.
There Was a Naughty Boy.
Thing of Beauty [Is Joy a Forever], A.
This Living Hand [Now Warm and Capable].
'Tis the witching hour of night.
To   : "Time's sea hath been five years at its slow ebb."
To   : "What can I do to drive away."
To a Cat.
To Ailsa Rock.
To Autumn.
To Charles Cowden Clarke.
To Fancy.
To Fanny.
To Homer.
To Leigh Hunt, Esq.
To My Brother George.
To My Brothers.
To One Who Has Been Long in City Pent.
To Psyche.
To Sleep.
To Sorrow,/ I bade good-morrow.
To the Nile.
To the Poets.
Two Sonnets on Fame.
What the Thrush Said.
When I Have Fears [That I May Cease to Be].
Where Be You Going, You Devon Maid?
Why did I laugh tonight? No voice will tell.
Written upon the Top of Ben Nevis.

Keaulumoku
Crawlers, The.
Dawn of Day, The.
Dog Child, The.
Kumulipo, The; a Creation Chant, *sels.*

Keble, John
Balaam.
Christian Year, The, *sels.*
Effect of Example, The.
Eleventh Sunday after Trinity.
Epithalamium: "Voice that breathed o'er Eden, The."
Evening.
Fill High the Bowl.
Forest Leaves in Autumn, *sel.*
Help Us to Live.
Holy Matrimony.
Hymn: "New every morning is thy love."
Morning.
Morning Hymn.
New Every Morning.
November.
Purity of Heart.
"Red o'er the Forest."
Third Sunday in Lent.
We Need Not Bid, for Cloistered Cell.
Whitsunday.

Keeler, Charles Augustus
Black Sailor's Chanty.
Cleaning Ship.
Ocean Lullaby, An.

Keeler, Greg
American Falls.
Nymphing through Car Windows (East Gallatin).
Salmon Fly Hatch on Yankee Jim Canyon of the Yellowstone.
Spring Catch.

Keeling, Mildred
God's World.

Keenan, Deborah
Folds of a White Dress/Shaft of Light.

Keens, William
Place by the River, A.

Kees, Weldon
Aspects of Robinson.
Back.
Beach in August, The.
Brief Introduction to the History of Culture, A.
Cats, The.
Colloquy.
Coming of the Plague, The.
Contours of Fixation, The.
Conversation in the Drawing Room, The.
Crime Club.
Distance from the Sea, A.
Early Winter.
Five.
For My Daughter.
Guide to the Symphony.
Heat in the Room, The.
Henry James at Newport.
Homage to Arthur Waley.
Hourglass, The, *sel.*
January.
La Vita Nuova.
Midnight.
1926.
Obituary.
Patient Is Rallying, The.
Problems of a Journalist.
Relating to Robinson.
Report of the Meeting.
River Song.
Robinson.
Robinson at Home.
Round: " 'Wondrous life!' cried Marvell at Appleton House."
Saratoga Ending.
Small Prayer.
Smiles of the Bathers, The.
Testimonies.
Wet Thursday.

Keesing, Nancy
Bread.
Revelation.
Reverie of a Mum.
Wandering Jews.

Kefala, Antigone
Saturday Night.

Kegels, Anne-Marie
I write to make you suffer.
Nocturnal Heart.
When I strip,/ stop walking/ and drop into sleep.

Keiter, Anna
Sunday Funnies.

Keith, Joseph Joel
Immaculate Palm.
In the First House.
She Walks.
Though She Slumbers.

Keithley, George
Black Hawk in Hiding.
Buster Keaton & the Cops.
Child, The.
Donner Party, The, *sel.*
Morning Star Man.
On Clark Street in Chicago.
Song for New Orleans, A.
Thief's Niece, The.
To Bring Spring.
Waiting for Winter.
Woman, The.

Keizer, Garret
Tourist, The.

Kell, Richard
Calypso.
Fishing Harbour towards Evening.
Makers, The.
Memorandum for Minos.
Pigeons.

Kelleher, Daniel Lawrence
For C. K. at His Christening.
Its Name Is Known.
Mother.
Upper Room, An.

Kelleher, John
Snow.

Keller, David
In the Dream of the Body.

Keller, Helen
In the Garden of the Lord.

Keller, Martha
Andrew Jackson.
Deadfall.
Mountain Meadows.

Kelley, Andrew J. *See* **"Mix, Parmenas"**

Kelley, Parham J.
Heir to Several Yesterdays.

Kelley, Reeve Spencer
Back Again from Yucca Flats.
Rain in the Southwest.
Sound of Morning in New Mexico, The.

Kelley, Shannon Keith
That Man in Manhattan.

Kellog, Arthur L.
Hayseed, The.

Kelly, Blanche Mary
Brother Juniper.
Housewife's Prayer, The.
Kingfisher, The.
Mirror, The.
Omniscience.

Kelly, Conor
Nocturne: Lake Huron.

Kelly, Dave
And Then What.
Day the Beatles Lost One to the Flesh-eating Horse, The.
Eight Miles South of Grand Haven.

Fall Letter.
Kelly, Dennis
Chicken.
Kelly, John W.
Slide, Kelly, Slide.
Throw Him Down M'Closkey.
Kelly, M.
Last Week I Took a Wife, *with music.*
Kelly, Robert
Alchemist, The.
Boar, The.
Boat, The.
Book of Persephone, The, *sels.*
Dance, The.
Exchanges II, The.
Fourth Ode to Persephone.
Glade, The.
Going.
Knee Lunes.
Last Light.
Moonshot.
Parallel Texts.
Poem for Easter.
Process, The.
Round Dance, and Canticle.
Second Ode to Persephone.
Sound, The.
Sun of the Center.
Third Ode to Persephone.
To Her Body, against Time.
Versions.
Kelly, Roy
Death, Don't Be Boring.
Ode to a Nightingale, *parody.*
Kelly, Thomas
Head That Once Was Crowned with Thorns, The.
Kelly, Walt
Boston Charlie.
How Low Is the Lowing Herd.
Kelso, Ian
Busy Old Fool.
Kemble, Frances Anne (Fanny)
Dream Land.
Faith.
Lament of a Mocking-Bird.
Wish, A.
Kemp, Harry Hibbard
Alienation.
Blind.
Conquerors, The.
Farewell: "Tell them, O Sky-born, when I die."
God the Architect.
He Did Not Know.
Humming Bird, The.
Joses, the Brother of Jesus.
Literary Love.
Love-Faith.
Passing Flower, The.
Phantasy of Heaven, A.
Prayer: "I kneel not now to pray that Thou."
Resurrection.
Seaman's Confession of Faith, A.
Tell All the World.
To God, the Architect.
Voice of Christmas, The.
Kempf, Elizabeth
Before the Dive.
Kempis, Thomas à. *See* **Thomas à Kempis**
Ken, Thomas
Anodyne, An.
Awake, My Soul.
Direct This Day.
Evening Hymn, An.
Glory to Thee, My God, This Night.
Morning Hymn.
Now.
Priest of Christ, The.
Kendall, Henry Clarence
Bell-Birds.
Beyond Kerguelen.
Christmas Creek.
Jim the Splitter.
Last of His Tribe, The.
Mooni.
Orara.
September in Australia.
Kendall, John Kaye ("Dum-Dum")
Cat That Followed His Nose, The.
Circumstance without Pomp.
Contented Bachelor, The.
Hug Me Tight.
My Last Illusion.
Ode to the Nightingale.
Pipes in the Sty.
Problem of the Poles, The.
Soldier of Weight, A.
Kendall, Laura E.
Evening Prayer, An.
Kendall, May
Ballad: "He said: 'The shadows darken down.' "
Lay of the Trilobite, The.
Seraph and the Snob, The.
Taking Long Views.
Kendrick, John F.
Christians at War.
Kennedy, Benjamin Hall
Memorial Lines on the Gender of Latin Substantives.
On Christopher Wordsworth, Master of Trinity.
On "Who Wrote Icon Basilike" by Dr. Christopher Wordsworth, Master of Trinity.
Roman Calendar, The.
Kennedy, Charles William
I've Worked for a Silver Shilling.
Kennedy, Edward D.
Strange, Is It Not.
Kennedy, Edwin O.
Prayer for Charity, A.
Kennedy, Geoffrey Anketell Studdert-. *See* **Studdert-Kennedy, Geoffrey Anketell**
Kennedy, Gerta
At the Nadir.
Chesapeake.
Christmas Songs.
Song of January.
Kennedy, Harry
Say "Au Revoir," but Not "Good-bye," *with music.*
Kennedy, James
Exile's Reveries, The, *sel.*
Kennedy, Leo
Epithalamium: "This body of my mother, pierced by me."
Mole Talk.
Rite of Spring.
Words for a Resurrection.
Kennedy, Mary
Indolent Gardener, The.
Newborn Colt, The.
Unfortunate Mole, The.
Kennedy, Sara Beaumont
Prayer Rug, The.
Kennedy, Terry
Easy Poem, An.
Kennedy, Walter
Honour with Age.
Kennedy, X. J.
Abominable Baseball Bat, The.
Aged Wino's Counsel to a Young Man on the Brink of Marriage, The.
Apocrypha.
Ars Poetica.
Artificer.
At a Low Mass for Two Hot-Rodders.
B Negative.
Bee.
Birth Report.
Consumer's Report.
Cross Ties.
Death of Professor Backwards, The.
Down in Dallas.
Driving Cross-Country.
Ecology.
Edgar's Story, *sel.*
Epitaph for a Postal Clerk.
Faces from a Bestiary.
Father and Mother.
First Confession.
For the ERA Crusaders.
Golgotha.
Great-great Grandma, Don't Sleep in Your Treehouse Tonight.
Haunted Oven, The.
Hearthside Story.
Help!
Hickenthrift and Hickenloop.
In a Prominent Bar in Secaucus [One Day].
In the Motel.
Japanese Beetles.
Keep a Hand on Your Dream.
Lasagna.
Last Lines.
Lilith.
Little Elegy.
Loose Woman.
Mingled Yarns.
Mother's Nerves.
Nature might chicken out, but "I love you."
Nude Descending a Staircase.
Old Men Pitching Horseshoes.
On a Boxer.
On a Child Who Lived One Minute.
One A.M.
One Winter Night in August.
Overheard in the Louvre.
Snapshots, *sel.*
Solitary Confinement.
Song to the Tune of "Somebody Stole My Gal."
Space.
To Dorothy on Her Exclusion from the *Guinness Book of World Records.*
To Mercury.
To Someone Who Insisted I Look Up Someone.
Vulture.
Water Glass of Whisky, A.
Whales off Wales, The.
Witnesses, The.
Kennelly, Brendan
Grip, The.
My Dark Fathers.
Proof.
Thatcher, The.
Kenner, Peggy Susberry
Black Taffy.
Comments.
Image in the Mirror.
No Bargains Today.
Round Table, The.
Kennet, Lord
Bird in the Bush, A.
Kenney, James
Old Story Over Again, The.
Kennick, T.
You Naughty, Naughty Men, *with music.*
Kenny, Maurice
Corn-Planter.
December.
Going Home.
They Tell Me I Am Lost.
Wild Strawberry.
Kenseth, Arnold
B-52's.
How They Came from the Blue Snows.
To the Ladies.
Kent, Margaret
Stammerers, The.
Kent, Richard B.
Summer Storm.
Kent, Rolly
Old Wife, The.
Kenyon, Bernice Lesbia
Homecoming in Storm.
Night of Rain.
Kenyon, James Benjamin
Bedouins of the Skies, The.

Bring Them Not Back.
Challenge, A.
Come Slowly, Paradise.
Death and Night.
Play, The.
Tacita.
Two Spirits, The.
Kenyon, John
Champagne Rosée.
Keohler, Thomas
Night's Ancient Cloud.
Keown, Anna Gordon
Reported Missing.
Keppel, Lady Caroline
Robin Adair.
Keppel, David
Trouble.
Keppel, Frederick
Plain Man's Dream, A.
Ker, L.
Death of the Gods, The; an Ode Written in Imitation of Pindar.
Ker, W. P.
Song of Degrees, A.
Theme and Variations.
There Is Snowdrift on the Mountain.
Kerehoma, Rarawa
Sentinel's Song, A.
Kernahan, Coulson
I ran for a catch.
Kerner, Justinus
Home-Sickness.
Kerouac, Jack (John Kerouac)
Chorus: "Big Engines, The."
Chorus: "Essence of Existence, The."
Chorus: "Glenn Miller and I were heroes."
Chorus: "Got up and dressed up."
Chorus: "Love's multitudinous boneyard."
Chorus: "Nobody knows the other side."
Chorus: "Old Man Mose."
Chorus: "Only awake to Universal Mind."
Chorus: "Praise be man, he is existing in milk."
Chorus: "Saints, I give myself up to thee."
Chorus: "Void that's highly embraceable, The."
Chorus: "Wheel of quivering meat, The."
How to Meditate.
In the ocean there's a very sad turtle.
Mexico City Blues, *sels.*
My Gang.
Pull My Daisy.
Sea Shroud, The.
Kerr, Alexander
Mary and Her Dead Canary.
Kerr, Hugh Thomson
Thy Will Be Done.
"Kerr, Orpheus C." (Robert Henry Newell)
American Traveller, The.
Columbia's Agony.
Dear Father, Look Up.
Editor's Wooing, The.
Neutral British Gentlemen, The.
O, Be Not Too Hasty, My Dearest.
Picciola.
Rejected "National Hymns," The.
Tuscaloosa Sam.
When Your Cheap Divorce Is Granted.
Kerr, Walter H.
Curtains for a Spinster.
Dignity of Man, The—Lesson #1.
Proud Trees, The.
Villanelle: "Woods we're lost in aren't real, The."
Kerr, Watson
Ancient Thought, The.
Kersch, Gerald
Soldier, A: His Prayer.
Kessler, Jascha
Looting.
Still Life, A.
Waiting for Lilith.
Kessler, Milton
Sea's Last Gift, The; 1961.
Ketchum, Annie Chambers
Bonnie Blue Flag, The.
Ketchum, Arthur
Candle-lighting Song.
Countersign.
Spirit of the Birch, The.
Thanksgiving.
Kethe, William
Old Hundredth.
Scotch Te Deum.
Such as in God the Lord Do Trust, *with music.*
Thy Mercies, Lord, to Heaven Reach, *with music.*
Kettle, Thomas Michael
Lady of Life, The.
Parnell.
To My Daughter Betty, the Gift of God.
Key, Francis Scott
Hymn: "Lord, with glowing heart I'd praise thee."
On a Young Lady's Going into a Shower Bath.
Our Rock.
Star-spangled Banner, The.
To My Cousin Mary, for Mending My Tobacco Pouch.
Written at the White Sulphur Springs.
Keyes, Sidney
Anti-Symbolist, The.
Death and the Plowman.
Early Spring.
Elegy: "April again and it is a year again."
Foreign Gate, The, *sels.*
Gardener, The.
Grail, The.
Greenwich Observatory.
Holstenwall.
Moon is a poor woman, The.
Moonlight Night on the Port.
Neutrality.
Plowman.
Remember Your Lovers.
Rome Remember.
Snow, The.
Time Will Not Grant.
Timoshenko.
Were I to Mount beyond the Field.
Wilderness, The.
William Wordsworth.
William Yeats in Limbo.
Keysner, Blanche Whiting
Old River Road.
Kgositsile, Keorapetse
For Eusi, Ayi Kwei and Gwen Brooks.
Ivory Masks in Orbit.
My Name Is Afrika.
Origins.
Spirits Unchained.
Khaketla, B. Makalo
Lesotho.
Khaketla, N. M.
White and the Black, The.
Khansa
Tears.
Kharms, Daniil
Connection, The.
Sonnet, A: "Amazing thing happened to me, An."
Vindication.
Khayyám, Omar. *See* **Omar Khayyám**
Kherdian, David
Dear Mrs. McKinney of the Sixth Grade.
For My Father: Two Poems.
Little Sis.
Melkon.
That Day.
Uncle Jack.
When These Old Barns Lost Their Inhabitants.
Winter, New Hampshire.
Khoury-Gata, Venus
Autumn made colors burn, The.
Your cheeks flat on the sand.
Kibkarjuk
Song of the Rejected Woman.
Kickham, Charles Joseph
Irish Peasant Girl, The.
Rory of the Hill.
Kicknosway, Faye
Cigarette Poem, The.
Crystal.
Gracie.
Horse, The.
I Wake, My Friend, I.
In Mysterious Ways.
Mr. Muscle-on.
There Is No.
"Kid Kazanova." *See* **Stack, Philip**
Kiefer, Rita Brady
Agent Orange.
Kieffaber, Alan
Easter Egg.
Kieran, John
Advice from an Expert.
Kii, Lady
I know the reputation/ of the idle ways.
Kikaku
Butterfly, The.
Cock Again, The.
Kikurio
Daffodils.
Kilgore, James C.
Gray Oak Twilight, The.
She Told Me.
White Man Pressed the Locks, The.
Killigrew, Anne
Farewel to Worldly Joyes, A ("Farewel to unsubstantial joyes").
On Death.
Upon the Saying That My Verses Were Made by Another.
Killigrew, Henry
Song: "While Morpheus thus doth gently lay."
Kilmer, Aline
Ambition.
Experience.
I Shall Not Be Afraid.
Light Lover.
Masquerader, The.
To Aphrodite; with a Mirror.
Wind Rose in the Night, A.
Kilmer, Joyce
Ballade of My Lady's Beauty.
Blue Valentine, A.
Easter.
Gates and Doors.
House with Nobody in It, The.
King's Ballad, The.
Mid-Ocean in War-time.
Poets.
Prayer of a Soldier in France.
Roofs.
Rouge Bouquet.
Servant Girl and Grocer's Boy.
Trees.
White Ships and the Red, The.
Kilmer, Kenton
Yellow.
Kilner, Dorothy
Henry's Secret.
Kimball, Hannah Parker
Beyond.
Soul and Sense.
Kimball, Harriet McEwen
All's Well.
Azaleas.
Guest, The.
White Azaleas.
Kimball, Jacob
Thy Praise, O God, in Zion Waits, *with music.*
Kim Nam-jo
My Baby Has No Name Yet.
Kim Yo-sop
Shooting at the Moon.

King, Alfred Castner
Miner, The.
Ruined Cabin, The.
King, Anna M.
Faith and Sight.
King, B. B.
Why I Sing the Blues.
King, Ben (Benjamin Franklin King)
Cultured Girl Again, The.
Hair-Tonic Bottle, The.
How Often.
If I Should Die Tonight.
Mermaid, The.
Pessimist, The.
Sum of Life, The.
That Cat.
King, E. L. M.
Robin's Song.
King, Edith
Duck, The.
Rabbit, The.
King, Edward
Tsigane's Canzonet, The.
Woman's Execution, A.
King, Eleanor Hamilton
Garden of the Holy Souls, The.
Hours of the Passion, *sel.*
King, Ethel
Wood Music.
King, Francis
Séance.
King, Georgiana Goddard
Man Called Dante, I Have Heard, A.
Song: "Something calls and whispers, along the city street."
Way of Perfect Love, The, *sel.*
King, Henry, Bishop of Chichester
Anniverse, The; an Elegy.
Contemplation upon Flowers, A.
Dear loss! since thy untimely fate.
Departure, The; an Elegy.
Elegy, An: "I will not weep, for 'twere as great a sin."
Elegy upon My Best Friend, An.
Elegy upon the Most Incomparable King Charles the First, An, *sel.*
Exequy on [*or* upon] His Wife.
Farwell, The ("Farwell, fond Love, under whose childish whipp").
Legacy, The.
Madam Gabrina, or the Ill-favour'd Choice.
My Midnight Meditation.
Of Human Life.
On the Life of Man.
Paradox: That Fruition Destroys Love, *sel.*
Renunciation, A.
Retreat, The.
Sic Vita.
Sonnet: Double Rock, The.
Sonnet: "Tell me[e] no more how fair[e] she[e] is."
Sonnet: "When I entreat, either thou wilt not hear."
Surrender, The.
That Distant Bliss.
To a Lady Who Sent Me a Copy of Verses at My Going to Bed.
To His Unconstant Friend.
To My Dead Friend Ben: Johnson.
To My Honoured Friend Mr. George Sandys.
Upon a Braid of Hair in a Heart.
Upon the Death of My Ever Desired Friend Doctor Donne Dean of Pauls.
Vow-Breaker, The.
King, Jenny
I Enter by the Darkened Door.
King, Jill
Grief Plucked Me Out of Sleep.
King, Linda
Great Poet, The.
Hooked on the Magic Muscle.
I Wasn't No Mary Ellen.
Whore.
King, Mary
Mary of Bethlehem.
King, Stoddard
Breakfast Song in Time of Diet.
Commissary Report.
Difference, The.
Étude Géographique.
Hearth and Home.
Song of Switzerland.
Wasted Ammunition.
King, William
Art of Cookery, The, *sel.*
Art of Making Puddings, The, *sel.*
Beggar Woman, The.
Mountown! Thou Sweet Retreat.
Mully of Mountown, *sels.*
Kingsley, Charles
Airly Beacon.
Alton Locke, *sel.*
Andromeda, *sel.*
Ballad: "It was Earl Haldan's daughter."
Dolcino to Margaret.
Drifting Away.
Easter Week.
Farewell, A: "My fairest child, I have no song to give you."
Hey, Nonny!
Instruction sore long time I bore.
Killarney.
Last Buccaneer, The.
Lost Doll, The.
Margaret to Dolcino.
Myth, A.
Nereids, The.
Ode to the North-east Wind.
Old Buccaneer, The.
Old Song, The.
Poetry of a Root Crop, The.
Saint's Tragedy, The, *sels.*
Sands of Dee, The.
Sing Heigh-Ho!
Song: "I once had a sweet little doll, dears."
Song: "Oh! that we two were Maying."
Song: "When I was a greenhorn and young."
Three Fishers, The.
Tide River, The.
Watchman, The.
Water Babies, The, *sels.*
Young and Old.
Kingsley, Henry
At Glastonbury.
Magdalen.
Kingsmill, Hugh
Poem, after A. E. Housman, A.
'Tis summer time on Bredon.
Two Poems (after A. E. Housman).
What, Still Alive.
Kingston, Jeremy
Distances.
Kinnell, Galway
After Making Love We Hear Footsteps.
Angling, a Day.
Another Night in the Ruins.
Avenue Bearing the Initial of Christ into the New World, The.
Bear, The.
Braemar.
Brother of My Heart.
Burning.
Call across the Valley of Not Knowing, The, *sel.*
Cells Breathe in the Emptiness.
Chicago.
Correspondence School Instructor Says Goodbye to His Poetry Students, The.
Crying.
Daybreak.
Dead Shall Be Raised Incorruptible, The.
Duck-chasing.
Fergus Falling.
First Song.
Flower Herding on Mount Monadnock.
For Robert Frost.
For the Lost Generation.
Fossils, The.
Freedom, New Hampshire.
Full Moon.
Fundamental Project of Technology, The.
Getting the Mail.
Goodbye.
Hen Flower, The.
Homecoming of Emma Lazarus, The.
How Many Nights.
In a Parlor Containing a Table.
In Fields of Summer.
In the Twentieth Century of My Trespass on Earth.
Island of Night.
Kissing the Toad.
La Bagarède.
Last Songs.
Leaping Falls.
Little Sleep's-Head Sprouting Hair in the Moonlight.
Looking at Your Face.
Middle of the Way.
Near Barbizon.
Night in the Forest.
On Hardscrabble Mountain.
Passion.
Path among the Stones, The.
Poem, The: "On this hill crossed."
Poems of Night.
Porcupine, The.
Promontory Moon.
Rain over a Continent.
Reply to the Provinces.
River That Is East, The.
Room of Return.
Ruins under the Stars.
Saint Francis and the Sow.
Spindrift.
Spring Oak.
Supper after the Last, The.
To Christ Our Lord.
To William Carlos Williams.
Told by Seafarers.
Under the Maud Moon.
Under the Williamsburg Bridge.
Vapor Trail Reflected in the Frog Pond.
Walk in the Country, A.
Wolves, The.
Kinney, Coates
Rain on the Roof.
Kinney, Elizabeth Clementine
Blind Psalmist, The.
Dream, A.
Quakeress Bride, The.
To the Boy.
Kinnick, B. Jo
Fish Story.
Kinsella, Thomas
Ancestor.
Another September.
Baggot Street Deserta.
Ballydavid Pier.
C. G. Jung's "First Years."
Chrysalides.
Clarence Mangan.
Country Walk, A.
Cover Her Face.
Crab Orchard Sanctuary; Late October.
Death Bed.
Dispossessed, The.
Fifth Sunday after Easter.
Finistére.
First Light.
Folk Wisdom.
Hen Woman.
In the Ringwood.
Je T'Adore.
King John's Castle.
Landscape and Figure.
Laundress, The.

Mask of Love.
Midsummer.
Mirror in February.
Nightwalker.
Old Atheist Pauses by the Sea, An.
Pause en Route.
Ritual of Departure.
Sacrifice.
Scylla and Charybdis.
Secret Garden, The.
Tear.
Technical Supplement, A, *sels.*
Westland Row.
Wormwood.

Kinwelmersh, Francis
Carol for Christmas Day, A.

Kipling, Rudyard
Arithmetic on the Frontier.
Astrologer's Song, An.
Ballad of East and West, The.
Ballad of Fisher's Boardinghouse, The.
Ballad of Minepit Shaw, The.
Batteries Out of Ammunition.
Beasts Are Very Wise, The.
Beginner, The.
Betrothed, The.
Big Steamers.
Boots.
Boy of Quebec, The, *at.*
Bridegroom, The.
Bridge-Guard in the Karroo.
Buddha at Kamakura, The.
By the Hoof of the Wild Goat.
Camel's Hump, The.
Certain Maxims of Hafiz.
Chant-Pagan.
Cities and Thrones and Powers.
Coastwise Lights, The.
Code of Morals, A.
Cold Iron.
Common Form.
Commonplaces.
Conundrum of the Workshops, The.
Coward, The.
Dane-Geld.
Danny Deever.
Dead Statesman, A.
Dedication, A: "My new-cut ashlar takes the light."
Deep-Sea Cables, The.
Delilah.
Derelict, The.
Dove of Dacca, The.
Drifter off Tarentum, A.
Dykes, The.
'Eathen, The.
Eddi's Service.
Edgehill Fight.
Epitaphs of the War, 1914-18.
Equality of Sacrifice.
Evarra and His Gods.
Explorer, The.
Fabulists, The.
Female of the Species, The.
Flight of the Bucket, The.
Flowers, The.
"Follow Me 'Ome."
For All We Have and Are.
For to Admire.
Ford o' Kabul River.
Frankie's Trade.
Fuzzy-Wuzzy.
Galley-Slave, The.
General Summary, A.
Gertrude's Prayer.
Gethsemane.
Giffen's Debt.
Gipsy Trail, The.
Glory of the Garden, The.
Gods of the Copybook Headings, The.
Great-Heart.
Gunga Din.
Harp Song of the Dane Women.
Heriot's Ford.
Horses.
Hump, The.
Hyaenas, The.
If.
In Springtime.
Jam-Pot, The.
Jane Smith.
Job That's Crying to Be Done, The.
Jungle Book, The, *sels.*
Just-so Stories, *sel.*
King, The.
La Nuit Blanche.
Ladies, The.
Land, The.
Last Chantey, The.
Last Lap, The.
Law of the Jungle, The.
Legends of Evil, The.
L'Envoi: "There's a whisper down the field where the year has shot her yield."
L'Envoi: "What is the moral? Who rides may read."
L'Envoi: "When Earth's last picture is painted, and the tubes are twisted and dried."
Lie, The.
Light That Failed, The, *sel.*
Long Trail, The.
Looking Glass, The.
Mandalay.
Mary Gloster, The.
McAndrew's Hymn.
Mesopotamia.
Mother o' Mine.
Municipal.
My Rival.
Nativity, A.
Non Nobis Domine.
O Mary Pierced with Sorrow.
Old Men, The.
Pagett, M. P.
Pan in Vermont.
Pink Dominoes.
Plain Tales from the Hills, *sels.*
Poseidon's Law.
Post That Fitted, The.
Power of the Dog, The.
Predestination.
Prelude to "Departmental Ditties."
Puck of Pook's Hill, *sels.*
Rebirth.
Recessional.
Refined Man, The.
Return, The.
Rhyme of the Three Captains, The.
Road-Song of the Bandar-Log.
Runes on Weland's Sword, The.
St. Helena Lullaby, A.
Salonikan Grave.
Screw-Guns.
Sea and the Hills, The.
Seal Lullaby.
Sergeant's Weddin', The.
Service Man, The.
Sestina of the Tramp-Royal.
Shillin' a Day.
Sing-Song of Old Man Kangaroo, The.
Smuggler's Song, A.
"Soldier an' Sailor Too."
Son, A.
Song before Action, *sel.*
Song of the Banjo, The.
Song of the Galley-Slaves.
Sons of Martha, The ("The sons of Mary seldom bother, for they have inherited that good part").
Storm Cone, The.
Story of the Gadsbys, The, *sel.*
Story of Uriah, The.
Study of an Elevation, in Indian Ink.
Supplication of the Black Aberdeen.
There was a strife 'twixt man and maid.
Tomlinson.
Tommy.
Twelve hundred million men are spread.
Undertaker's Horse, The.
Vampire, The.
Voortrekker, The.
Way through the Woods, The.
When Earth's Last Picture Is Painted.
When 'Omer Smote 'Is Bloomin' Lyre.
Widow at Windsor, The.
Widow's Party, The.
Winners, The.

Kipp, Allan F.
Cubist Blues in Poltergeist Major.

Kirby, Patrick F.
Compline.
Consecration.
Rain.
Riddles.
Sequel to Finality.
Song for These Days.

Kircher, Pamela
In the Small Boats of Their Hands.

Kirk, William F.
Sonnet on Stewed Prunes.

Kirkconnell, Watson
Crow and the Nighthawk, The.
Tide of Life, The, *sel.*

Kirkup, James
Baby's Drinking Song.
Correct Compassion, A.
Earth Tremor in Lugano.
Gay Boys.
Giving and Taking.
In a London Schoolroom.
Japanese Fan.
La Bête Humaine.
Lonely Scarecrow, The.
Love of Older Men, The.
Mortally.
Nature of Love, The.
Old Gramophone Records.
Poet, The.
Shepherd's Tale, The.
To My Children Unknown, Produced by Artificial Insemination.
Ursa Major.
Zen Archer, The.

Kirkwood, Judith
Last Born.

Kirsch, Olga
Blockhouse.
Wordspinning.

Kirsch, Sarah
Dandelions for Chains ("Dandelions meet me wherever I am").
Sad Day in Berlin.

Kirstein, Lincoln
Bath.
Das Schloss.
Fall In.
Foresight.
Rank.
Vaudeville.

Kiser, Samuel Ellsworth
Fighter, The.
When I Had Need of Him.

Kiss, Jozsef
New Ahasuerus, The.

Kitchel, Mary Eva
So Runs Our Song.

Kito
Haiku: "Seaweed/ between rocks."

Kittaararter
Take Your Accusation Back!

Kittner, Alfred
Blue Owl Song.
Old Jewish Cemetery in Worms.

Kittredge, Walter
Tenting on the Old Camp Ground.
We're Tenting To-Night.

Kitzman, Darlene Button
Doll House, The.
Kivkarjuk
I am but a little woman.
Kiwus, Karin
All Splendor on Earth.
Kiyowara Fukayabu
River-Fog.
Kizer, Carolyn
Afterthoughts of Donna Elvira.
Amusing Our Daughters.
Columns and Caryatids.
Copulating Gods, The.
For Jan, in Bar Maria.
Great Blue Heron, The.
Hera, Hung from the Sky.
Intruder, The.
Lines to Accompany Flowers for Eve.
Lovemusic.
Muse of Water, A.
One to Nothing.
Poet's Household, A.
Postcards from Rotterdam.
Pro Femina, *sels.*
Singing Aloud.
Skein, The.
Summer near the River.
Through a Glass Eye, Lightly.
To a Visiting Poet in a College Dormitory.
To Li Po from Tu Fu.
To My Friend, behind Walls.
Ungrateful Garden, The.
What the Bones Know.
Widow in Wintertime, A.
Kizer, Gary Allan
Boxer Turned Bartender, The.
Even the Best.
For Laurence Jones.
Oil and Blood.
One Year After.
Skyhook.
Klappert, Peter
Invention of the Telephone, The.
J'Accuse.
Lord's Chameleons, The.
O'Connor the Bad Traveler.
Poem for L. C.
Klauber, Edgar
On Buying a Dog.
Klauck, Daniel L.
Catwalk.
"Chew Mail Pouch."
Dirty Joke.
Einstein's Father.
Eulogy for a Tough Guy.
Inside a Prison Cell at Count Time.
Myths.
Visits.
Klein, Abraham Moses
And in That Drowning Instant.
Autobiographical.
Baal Shem Tov.
Ballad of the Days of the Messiah.
Bandit.
Bestiary.
Biography.
Bread.
Break-up, The.
Design for Mediæval Tapestry.
For the Sisters of the Hôtel Dieu.
Grain Elevator.
Haggadah.
Heirloom.
In re Solomon Warshawer.
Indian Reservation: Caughnawaga.
Monsieur Gaston.
Montreal.
Orders.
Political Meeting.
Portrait of the Poet as Landscape.
Psalm of the Fruitful Field.
Psalm VI: "And on that day, upon the heavenly scarp."
Psalm XII: "These were the ones who thanked their God."
Psalter of Avram Haktani, The, *sels.*
Quebec Liquor Commission Store.
Rabbi Yom-Tob of Mayence Petitions His God.
Rev Owl.
Rocking Chair, The.
Spinning Wheel, The.
Still Small Voice, The.
Sugaring, The.
Upon the Heavenly Scarp.
Venerable Bee, The.
Klein, Chris
Bright Winter Morning.
Kleiser, Grenville
Challenge, The.
Most Vital Thing in Life, The.
My Daily Prayer.
You Can't Fool God.
Kline, Betsy W.
Be Still.
"Klingle, George" (Georgiana Klingle Holmes)
As Thy Days So Shall Thy Strength Be.
At Dawn of the Year.
"He Will Give Them Back."
Kloefkorn, William
During the War.
Good Folks at the Camp Meeting, The.
I Love Old Women.
Loony, *sels.*
My Love for All Things Warm and Breathing.
Otoe County in Nebraska.
Knapp, Shepherd
Lord God of Hosts, *with music.*
Not Only Where God's Free Winds Blow, *with music.*
Knevet, Ralph
Passion, The.
Knibbs, Henry Herbert
Ballad of Billy the Kid, The.
Boomer Johnson.
Bosky Steer, The.
Cowboy's Ball, The.
Desert, The.
Indigo Pete's J. B.
Long Road West, The.
Lost Range, The.
Oro Stage, The.
Out There Somewhere.
Riders of the Stars.
Shallows of the Ford, The.
Waring of Sonora-Town.
Knickman, Lester
Could You Spare Some Time for Jesus?
Knies, Elizabeth
Circles.
Knight, Arthur Winfield
Impotence.
Knight, David
Chief of the West, Darkling, The.
In Memoriam S. L. Akintola.
Palms, The.
"When the Students Resisted, a Minor Clash Ensued."
Knight, Douglas
Sleeping Beauty: August.
Knight, Etheridge
Another Poem for Me.
Apology for Apostasy?
As You Leave Me.
Bones of My Father, The.
Cell Song.
Feeling Fucked Up.
For Black Poets Who Think of Suicide.
For Dan Berrigan.
For Freckle-faced Gerald.
Haiku: "Eastern guard tower."
Hard Rock Returns to Prison from the Hospital for the Criminal Insane.
He Sees Through Stone.
Huey.
I Sing of Shine.
Idea of Ancestry, The.
It Was a Funky Deal.
My Life, the Quality of Which.
Nickle Bet, A.
On the Birth of a Black/Baby/Boy.
On Watching Politicians Perform at Martin Luther King's Funeral.
Poem to Galway Kinnell, A.
Portrait of Malcolm X.
Prison Graveyard.
Sun Came, The.
To Dinah Washington.
To the Man Who Sidled Up to Me and Asked: "How Long You In Fer, Buddy?"
2 Poems for Black Relocation Centers.
Upon Your Leaving.
Violent Space, The.
Warden Said to Me the Other Day, The.
We Free Singers Be.
Knight, Henry Coggswell
Lunar Stanzas.
Knight, John
Father to the Man.
Knight, Sarah Kemble
Pleasent Delusion of a Sumpteous Citty.
Resentments Composed because of the Clamor of Town Topers Outside My Apartment.
Thoughts on Pausing at a Cottage near the Paukataug River.
Thoughts on the Sight of the Moon.
Warning to Travailers Seeking Accomodations at Mr. Devills Inn.
Knister, Raymond
Boy Remembers in the Field.
Change.
February's Forgotten Mitts.
Feed.
Hawk, The.
Lake Harvest.
Nell.
Plowman, The ("All day I follow").
Plowman's Song ("Turn under, plow").
Row of Stalls, A, *sel.*
Stable-Talk.
White Cat.
Knoepfle, John
At the Roadside.
Riverfront, St. Louis.
Ten-fifteen Community Poems, The, *sel.*
Those Who Come What Will They Say of Us.
Knoll, Michael
Dangerous Music, A.
Interrogations, The.
Overture, An.
Prison Letter.
To My Sister, from the Twenty-seventh Floor.
Vigil.
Vivaldi on the Far Side of the Bars.
Knott, William ("Saint Geraud")
Death.
(End) of Summer (1966).
Goodbye.
Hair Poem.
Poem: "After your death."
Poem: "At your light side trees shy."
Poem: "Only response, The."
(Poem) (Chicago) (The Were-Age).
Sleep.
Song: "She was lyin face down in her face."
Knowlan, Alden A.
Marian at the Pentecostal Meeting.
Knowles, Frederic Lawrence
If Love Were Jester at the Court of Death.
Last Word, The.
Laus Mortis.
L'Envoi: "O love triumphant over guilt and sin."
Love Triumphant.
Memory, A.
Nature: The Artist.

On a Fly-Leaf of Burns's Songs.
Out of the Depths.
Pasture, A.
Song of Desire, A.
To Jesus of Nazareth.
To Mother Nature.

Knowles, James D.
O God, though Countless Worlds of Light, *with music.*

Knox, Edmund George Valpy ("Evoe")
At the Water Zoo.
Inspiration.
Last Bus, The.
Limerick: "There was a young curate of Hants."
Mr. A. E. Housman on the Olympic Games.
Nimble Stag, The.
Stately Homes of England, The, *parody.*
To the God of Love.
Upon Julia's Clothes.

Knox, J. Mason
Co-operation.

Knox, Ronald Arbuthnott
Absolute and Abitofhell.
Anglican curate in want, An.
Idealism.
Limerick: "Clergyman in want, A."
Limerick: "Evangelical vicar in want."
Tryst, The.

Knox, Warren
Man of Letters.

Knox, William
Oh [*or* O]! Why Should the Spirit of Mortal Be Proud?

Knut, Dovid
Haifa.
Rosh Pina.
Safed.
Walking along the Sea of Galilee.
Woman from the Book of Genesis, A.

Kobbé, Gustav
From the Harbor Hill.
To a Little Girl.

Kober, Arthur
Evidence.

Kocan, Peter
Bill.
Sleepers, The.

Kocbek, Edvard
Primary Numbers.

Koch, Christopher
Half-heard.

Koch, James H.
To a Young Lady Swinging Upside Down on a Birch Limb over a Winter-swollen Creek.

Koch, Kenneth
Art of Love, The, *sels.*
Down at the Docks.
Fresh Air.
Geography.
In Love with You.
Locks.
Lunch.
Mending Sump.
Permanently.
Poem: "Thing, The/ To do/ Is organize."
Poem for My Twentieth Birthday.
Poem of the Forty-eight States, A.
Railway Stationery, The.
Schoolyard in April.
Sleeping with Women.
Taking a Walk with You.
Thank You.
Thanksgiving.
To You.
Variations on a Theme by William Carlos Williams.
You Were Wearing.

Koehler, G. Stanley
Ground Swell.
New Construction: Bath Iron Works.
Siciliana: The Landings at Gela.

Koehler, Ted
I've Got the World on a String, *with music.*

Koenig, Alma Johanna
Intimations.

Koenig, Robert L.
Isolation Ward.

Koeppel, Frederic
October.

Koertge, Ronald
For My Daughter.
Harelip Mary.
He.
Magic Words, The.
Please.
Refusing What Would Bind You to Me Irrevocably.
Tonto.
12 Photographs of Yellowstone.
What She Wanted.

Koethe, John
Mission Bay.
Picture of Little Letters.

Kogawa, Joy
Ancestors' Graves in Kurakawa.
Dream after Touring the Tokyo Tokei.
Hiroshima Exit.
On Meeting the Clergy of the Holy Catholic Church in Osaka.
Woodtick.

Kohler, Sandra
Wedding, The.

Koller, James
I Have Cut an Eagle.
O Dirty Bird Yr Gizzard's Too Big & Full of Sand.
Some Magic.
Unreal Song of the Old, The.

Kolmar, Gertrud
Jewish Woman, The.
Out of the Darkness.
Paris.
Sea-Monster.
Woman Poet, The.

Komey, Ellis Ayitey
Damage You Have Done, The.
Oblivion.

Komunyakaa, Yusef
April Fools' Day.
Copacetic Mingus.
Somewhere near Phu Bai.
Starlight Scope Myopia.
Stepfather: A Girl's Song.

Konek, Carol
Daring.

Konopnicka, Maria
Vision, A.

Kook, Rav Abraham Isaac
First One Drew Me, The.
Radiant Is the World Soul.
When I Want to Speak.

Koopman, Harry Lyman
Icarus.
John Brown.
Revealed.
Satirist, The.
Sea and Shore.

Kooser, Ted
Abandoned Farmhouse.
Camera.
Central.
Christmas Eve.
Country-Western Music.
Father.
First Snow.
Fort Robinson.
Gates.
History Lesson for My Son.
In a Country Cemetery in Iowa.
In January, 1962.
Late Lights in Minnesota.
My Grandfather Dying.
Phil.
Pocket Poem.
Poem: "Get your tongue."
Room in the Past, A.
Rooming House.
Snow Fence.
Themes for Country-Western Singers, *sel.*
Tom Ball's Barn.
Treehouse.
Wild Pigs.

Kopp, Karl
Judge, The.
Manly Diversion.

Korinna [*or* Corinna]
Although I was her pupil,/ even I reproach Myrtis.
I blame Myrtis.
I disapprove even of eloquent/ Myrtis.
I Korinna am here to sing the courage.
Kithairon sang of cunning Kronos.
Terpsichore looks kindly on me.
To the white-mantled maidens.
When he sailed into the harbor.

Korn, Rachel
From Here to There.
I'm Soaked Through with You.
Keep Hidden from Me ("Keep from me all that I might comprehend!").
Letter, A.
Longing.
My Body.
New Dress, A.
Put Your Word to My Lips.
Sometimes I Want to Go Up.
Thirty-one Camels, The.
Too Late.
With Poems Already Begun.

Körte, Sister Mary Norbert
Ghost Poem Five.

Korzhavin, Naum
Children of Auschwitz.

Kostelanetz, Richard
Concentric.
Tribute to Henry Ford.

Kovner, Abba
I Don't Know if Mount Zion.
Near.
Observation at Dawn.

Kowit, Steve
Home.

Koyama, Tina
Definitions of the Word *Gout.*
Grape Daiquiri.
Next.
Ojisan after the Stroke; Three Notes to Himself.

Kozer, José
Cleaning Day.
My Father, Who's Still Alive.
Store in Havana, The.

Koziol, Urszula
Alarum.

Kramer, Aaron
Kennedy Airport.
Now, before Shaving.
Portrait by Alice Neel.

Kramer, Arthur
Inflamed Disciple, The.

Kramer, Edgar Daniel
Sequence.
Youth's Thankfulness.

Kramer, Larry
Overcoats.

Kramer, Lotte
Genesis.

Krapf, Norbert
Dürer's Piece of Turf.
For an Old Friend.
Rural Lines after Breughel.
Village in Snowstorm.

Krasilovsky, Alexis
Sensational Relatives.

Kraus, Karl
Express Train.

On the Threshold.
Krauss, Ruth
End Song.
Song: "I'd much rather sit there in the sun."
Song: "Reading about the Wisconsin Weeping Willow."
Kredenser, Gail
Brontosaurus.
Polar Bear.
Kreps, Gretchen
Leopard.
Kresensky, Raymond
Comrade, Remember.
Kress, George L.
Parable, A.
Kretz, Thomas
Transandean Railway, The.
Kreymborg, Alfred
Arabs.
Ballad of the Common Man.
Ballad of the Lincoln Penny.
Bloom.
Crocus.
Festoons of Fishes.
Indian Sky.
Life.
Madonna di Campagna.
Man Whom Men Deplore, A.
Nun Snow.
Race Prejudice.
Ribbon Two Yards Wide, A.
To W. C. W. M. D.
Tree, The.
Kriebel, Casper
Now Sleep My Little Child So Dear, *with music.*
Kriel, Margot
Annunciation, The.
Krige, Uys
Distant View.
Encounter.
Farm Gate.
Soldier, The.
Swallows Over the Camp.
Kriloff, Ivan Andreevich
Peasant and the Sheep, The.
Krishnamurti, M.
Cloth of Gold, The, *sel.*
Spirit's Odyssey, The.
Krmpotic, Vesna
December Forest, A.
Kroetsch, Robert
Stone Hammer Poem.
Kroll, Ernest
Mockingbird in Winter.
Pennsylvania Academy of Fine Arts.
Telephone Lineman.
Kroll, Judith
Dick and Jane.
I Think of Housman Who Said the Poem Is a Morbid Secretion, like the Pearl.
Not Thinking of America.
Sestina: "Is this the object."
Kroll, Steven
McIntosh Apple.
Krolow, Karl
White.
Kronthal, Joseph
Be Careful What You Say.
Krows, Jane W.
Lesson, The.
Little Satellite.
Milkman, The.
My House.
Space Travel.
Kruger, Fania
Passover Eve.
Krysl, Marilyn
Words Words Words.
Kryss, Tom
And Jesus Don't Have Much Use for His Old Suitcase Anymore.
Ballad of an Empty Table.
Bell Too Heavy to Ring.
Breaking Ground in Me.
Nothing Strange.
Suicide, A.
This Wind.
Kshetrayya
Dancing-Girl's Song.
Kuapakaa
Ocean Is like a Wreath, The.
Kubatum
Love Song to King Shu-Suen.
Kudaka, Geraldine
Birthright.
Death Is a Second Cousin Dining with Us Tonight.
Giving Up Butterflies.
Okinawa Kanashii Monogatari.
On Writing Asian-American Poetry.
Kuder, Blanche Bane
Blue Bowl, The.
Kuka, King D.
Evening.
February Morning.
Gallery of My Heart.
Jackie.
Janna.
My Friend the Wind.
My Song.
Kulbak, Moishe
I Just Walk Around, Around, Around.
Spring.
Summer.
Two.
Vilna.
Kumin, Maxine W.
Absent Ones, The.
Accidentally.
After Love.
Amanda Dreams She Has Died and Gone to the Elysian Fields.
Amanda Is Shod.
Appointment, The.
Archaeology of a Marriage, The.
At a Private Showing in 1982.
At the End of the Affair.
Creatures.
Family Man, A.
For a Shetland Pony Brood Mare Who Died in Her Barren Year.
For My Son on the Highways of His Mind.
400-Meter Freestyle.
Fräulein Reads Instructive Rhymes.
Getting Through.
Halfway.
Hermit Picks Berries, The.
Hermit Wakes to Bird Sounds, The.
Horses, The.
How It Goes On.
Life's Work.
Lunar Probe, The.
Masochist, The.
May 10th.
Microscope, The.
Morning Swim.
Mummies, The.
Our Ground Time Here Will Be Brief.
Presence, The.
Prothalamion.
Retrieval System, The.
Riding in the Rain.
Song for Seven Parts of the Body, *sels.*
Sound of Night, The.
Together.
Voice from the Roses, A.
Woodchucks.
Kunene, Raymond Mazisi
Work Song.
You are lying, O missionary!
Kunimoto, Tsumori
Wild geese returning, The.
Kunitz, Stanley Jasspon
Abduction, The.
After the Last Dynasty.
Approach to Thebes, The.
Benediction.
Between the Acts.
Careless Love.
Choice of Weapons, A.
Dark and the Fair, The.
Daughters of the Horseleech, The.
Deciduous Branch.
End of Summer.
Father and Son.
Flight of Apollo, The.
For the Word Is Flesh.
Foreign Affairs.
Goose Pond.
He.
Hemorrhage, The.
Illumination, The.
Intimations of Mortality.
Knot, The.
Last Picnic, The.
Layers, The.
Lovers Relentlessly.
Mulch, The.
Old Cracked Tune, An.
Portrait, The.
Prophecy on Lethe.
Quinnapoxet.
Reflection by a Mailbox.
River Road.
Robin Redbreast.
Route Six.
Science of the Night, The.
Scourge, The.
She Wept, She Railed.
Snakes of September, The.
Spark of Laurel, A.
Summing-Up, The.
Testing-Tree, The.
Thief, The.
Vita Nuova.
Waltzer in the House, The.
War against the Trees, The.
Welcome the Wrath.
When the Light Falls.
Kunjufu, Johari M. *See* **Latimore, Jewel C.**
Kunze, John C.
Yoke Soft and Dear, *with music.*
Kuo, Alex
Did You Not See.
Early Illinois Winter, An.
Loss.
On a Clear Day I Can See Forever.
There Is Something I Want to Say.
Kuroda, Saburoh
Afternoon 3.
Kurt, Kim
Runaway.
Sun-Bather, The.
Vernal Paradox.
Woodlore.
Kurtz, Aaron
Behold the Sea, *sel.*
They Got You Last Night.
Kushner, Aleksander
To Boris Pasternak.
Kushniroff, Aaron
Die My Shriek.
Kuskin, Karla
Balloon, The.
Bug Sat in a Silver Flower, A.
Catherine.
Full of the Moon.
Gold-tinted Dragon, The.
Lewis Has a Trumpet.
Me.
Middle of the Night, The.
Question, The.
Rules.
Spring.
Tiptoe.
Very Early.

When I Went Out.
Where Have You Been Dear?
Winter Clothes.
Witches' Ride, The.
Kuykendall, John M.
Veteran Cowboy's Ruminations, A.
Kuykendall, Mabel M.
Baseball Pitcher.
Kuzma, Greg
After Sex.
Along South Inlet.
Among Friends.
Crossing Raquette Lake at Night.
Darkness.
Dump, The.
For My Father on His Birthday.
Hose and Iron.
In Love with the Bears.
Journal of the Storm.
Monster, The.
Night Fishing.
Peace, So That.
Pelican, The.
Poetry.
Sometimes.
South Inlet.
Wolfman, The.
Young Man Who Loved the Girl Who Took Care of Her Aging Father, The.
Kwitko, Leib
Esau.
Moods.
My Fiddle.
You Who Dog My Footsteps.
Kwon, Paula
Talking across Kansas.
Kyd, Thomas
Cornelia, *sel.*
Of Fortune, *abr.*
Kyei, Kojo Gyinaye
African in Louisiana.
Talking Drums, The.
Kyger, Joanne
August 18.
Don't Hope to Gain by What Has Preceded.
I Have No Strength for Mine.
My Father Died This Spring.
Of All Things for You to Go Away Mad.
Pigs for Circe in May, The.
When I Was Well into Being Savored.
Kyle, Francis
When I Saw Sweet Nelly Home.
Kynaston, Sir Francis
To Cynthia, on Concealment of Her Beauty.
To Cynthia, on Her Changing.
To Cynthia, on Her Embraces.
To Cynthia on Her Being an Incendiary.
Kyorai
Haiku: "Even in my village."
I called to the wind.
Kyozo, Tagaki
Winter Moon, The.

L

"L., C. G."
Master, The.
"L. E. L." *See* **Landon, Letitia Elizabeth**
Labé, Louise
Elegy XXIII: "How does it help me if, with flawless art."
Povre Ame Amoureuse.
Sonnet XVI: "After an age when thunderbolts and hail."
Sonnet XIX: "After having slain very many beasts."
Sonnet XIV: "Although I cry and though my eyes still shed."
Sonnet IX: "As soon as I lie down in my soft bed."
Sonnet VI: "Coming of that limpid star is twice, The."
Sonnet XXIV: "Don't blame me, ladies, if I've loved. No sneers."
Sonnet IV: "From that first flash when awful Love took flame."
Sonnet XVII: "I flee the city, temples, and each place."
Sonnet VIII: "I live, I die, I burn myself and drown."
Sonnet XX: "I was foretold that on a certain day."
Sonnet XIII: "If I could linger on his lovely chest."
Sonnet XVIII: "Kiss me again, re-kiss and kiss me whole."
Sonnet XII: "Lute, companion of my calamity."
Sonnet I: "Not Ulysses, no, nor any other man."
Sonnet XXII: "O blazing Sun, how happy you are there."
Sonnet XI: "O eyes clear with beauty, O tender gaze."
Sonnet II: "O handsome chestnut eyes, evasive gaze."
Sonnet III: "O interminable desires, O futile hope."
Sonnet XV: "To honor the return of sparkling sun."
Sonnet VII: "We see each living thing finally die."
Sonnet XXIII: "What good is it to me if long ago."
Sonnet XXI: "What grandeur makes a man seem venerable?"
Sonnet X: "When I perceive your blond and graceful head."
Sonnet V: "White Venus limpid wandering in the sky."
LaBombard, Joan
Heart.
Sibyl, The.
Labriola, Gina
Orgy (That Is, Vegetable Market, at Sarno).
Labrunie, Gérard. *See* **Nerval, Gérard de**
Lacaussade, Auguste
Salaziennes, Les, *sel.*
Lacey, E. A.
Abdelfatteh.
Guest.
Mesón Brujo.
Ramon.
Lachman, Sol
Sukkot.
Lachmann, Hedwig
Home-Sickness.
Walk, A.
Lady of the Arbour
Flower and the Leaf, The, *sel.*
Lady of the Assembly
Assembly of Ladies, The, *sel.*
Palace of Pleasant Regard, The.
Laederach, Monique
Penelope, *sels.*
La Farge, Christopher
Prayer for Living and Dying.
La Farge, Peter
Ballad of Ira Hayes.
La Follette, Melvin Walker
Arrivals and Departures.
Ballad of Red Fox, The.
Blue Horse, The.
Didactic Sonnet.
Hunt.
I Knew a Boy with Hair like Gold.
Love for a Hare.
Saynt Stephen in San Francisco.
Sleeping Saint, The.
Spring Landscape.
Summerhouse.
Valediction, A: "Crow's harsh dissyllables, A."
La Fontaine, Jean de
Aesop's Fable of the Frogs.
Cat into Lady.
Cock and the Fox, The.
Crow and the Fox, The.
Cudgelled but Contented Cuckold, The.
Dairymaid and Her Milk-Pot, The.
Donkey and the Lapdog, The.
Eagle and the Beetle, The.
Ear-Maker and the Mould-Mender, The.
Fair Exchange, A.
Fox and the Crow, The.
Fox and the Grapes, The.
Frog Who Would Be an Ox, The.
Gascon Punished, The ("A Gascon, being heard one day to swear").
Grasshopper and the Ant, The.
Hag and the Slavies, The.
Love and Folly.
Man and His Image, The.
Oak and the Reed, The.
Rat and the Elephant, The.
Superfluous Saddle, The.
To Promise Is One Thing, to Perform Is Another.
Town Rat and the Country Rat, The.
Wolf and the Dog, The.
Wolf and the Lamb, The.
Wolf and the Stork, The.
Laforgue, Jules
Asides from the Clowns, *sel.*
End of a Day in the Provinces, The.
For the Book of Love.
Legend.
Lightning of the Abyss.
Winter Sunset.
Lagerkvist, Pär
Beauty Is Most at Twilight's Close.
Purple Blemish, The.
Lagerlof, Selma
Child of Peace, The.
La Grone, Oliver
Africland.
Bathed Is My Blood.
For Kinte.
My America.
Remnant Ghosts at Dawn.
This Hour.
Lahpu
Butterfly maidens.
Laight, Frederick E.
Drought.
Soliloquy.
Laighton, Albert
Under the Leaves.
Laing, Alexander Kinnan
My Ain Wife.
Original Sin.
Laing, Allan M.
Family Life.
Instead of blushing cherry hue.
Jack the Ripper.
Samuel Pepys.
When they found Giotto.
Laing, Dilys Bennett
Aubade: "My bed rocks me gently."
Eros Out of the Sea.
Farm Hands, The.
Gentled Beast, The.
How Music's Made.
Lines on the Sea.
Villanelle: "Proud inclination of the flesh."
Laing, Ronald David
Finger Points to the Moon, A.
Jill.
Laing, V. R.
Suicide, The.
"Laird, William" (William Laird Brown)
Prayer, A: "Lord, make my childish soul stand straight."
Traümerei at Ostendorff's.

Very Old Song, A.
Lake, Paul
Old Folks Home, An.
Lake, Richard
Atavism.
"Lakon"
William the Bastard.
Lal Ded
I drag a boat over the ocean.
Impermanence.
Lalleswari
Good repute is water carried in a sieve.
I set forth hopeful—cotton-blossom Lal.
With my breath I cut my way through the six forests.
Laluah, Aquah. *See* **Hayford, Gladys May Casely**
Lamantia, Philip
Hermetic Bird.
Man Is in Pain.
Morning Light Song.
She Speaks the Morning's Filigree.
Still Poem 9.
Terror Conduction.
Lamar, Mirabeau Buonaparte
Daughter of Mendoza, The.
Lamarre, Hazel Washington
Time and Tide.
Lamartine, Alphonse Marie Louis de
Cedars of Lebanon, The.
God.
Lamb, Arthur J.
Asleep in the Deep.
Bird in a Gilded Cage, A.
Bird on Nellie's Hat, The, *with music.*
Lamb, Charles
Childhood Fled.
Farewell to Tobacco, A.
Free Thoughts on Several Eminent Composers.
Going or Gone.
Hester.
Hypochondriacus.
In My Own Album.
Lines on the Celebrated Picture by Leonardo Da Vinci, Called the Virgin of the Rocks.
Nonsense Verses.
Old Familiar Faces, The.
On an Infant Dying as Soon as Born.
Parental Recollections.
Triumph of the Whale, The.
Written at Cambridge.
Lamb, Charles *and* **Mary Lamb**
Anger ("Anger in its time and place").
Boy and the Snake, The.
Choosing a Name.
Cleanliness.
Envy.
Feigned Courage.
First Tooth, The.
Going into Breeches.
Lamb, Mary
Child, A.
Helen.
Maternal Lady with the Virgin Grace.
Two Boys, The.
Lambdin, Sylvia S.
January.
Lambert, Elisabeth
Brave Old World.
"Lambert, Louis." *See* **Gilmore, Patrick Sarsfield**
Lamdan, Yitzhak
For the Sun Declined, *sel.*
Massada, *sel.*
La Monnoye, Bernard de
Patapan.
Lamont, Colin
Rothiemurchus.
LaMoure, S. E.
Wagon Wheels.
Lampman, Archibald
After the Shower.
Among the Millet.
Among the Orchards.
City of the End of Things, The.
Comfort of the Fields.
Dawn on the Lievre, The.
Heat.
In November.
January Morning, A.
Largest Life, The.
Life and Nature.
Midnight.
Personality.
Prayer, A: "O Earth, O dewy mother, breathe on us."
Refuge.
September.
Snow.
Solitude.
Summer Evening, A.
Sunset at Les Éboulements, A.
Temagami.
Thunderstorm, A.
To a Millionaire.
Truth, The.
Violinist, The.
Winter Evening.
Winter-Solitude.
Lamport, Felicia
Capsule Philosophy.
Progress.
Lancaster, Osbert
Afternoons with Baedeker, *sels.*
Eireann.
English.
French.
Italian.
Manhattan.
Landau, Zishe
I Have a Big Favour to Ask You, Brothers.
Little Pig, The.
Of Course I Know.
Parts.
Tuesday.
Landeweer, Elizabeth
Dakota Badlands.
Landles, William
Border Forecast, A.
On Ellson Fell.
Landon, Letitia Elizabeth ("L. E. L.")
Child Screening a Dove from a Hawk, A.
Little Shroud, The.
Unknown Grave, The.
Landor, Robert Eyres
Babylon.
Festival, The.
Historic Time.
Impious Feast, The, *sels.*
Jew's Home, The.
Nineveh.
Sleep.
Landor, Walter Savage
Above all gifts we most should prize.
Absence.
Advice.
Age.
Alas, How Soon the Hours.
Alas! 'Tis Very Sad to Hear.
Alciphron and Leucippe.
Around the Child.
Art thou afraid the adorer's prayer.
Autumnal Song.
Before a Saint's Picture.
Behold, O Aspasia! I Send You Verses.
Bourbons.
Called Proud.
Case at Sessions, A.
Citation and Examination of William Shakespeare, The, *sel.*
Copy of Verses Sent by Cleone to Aspasia, A.
Corinna, from Athens, to Tanagra.
Corinna, to Tanagra, from Athens.
Corythos, *sel.*
Critic, A.
Daniel Defoe.
Dead Marten, The.
Death.
Death of Artemidora, The.
Death of the Day.
Death Stands above Me.
Defiance.
Dirce.
Distribution of Honours for Literature.
Do You Remember Me?
Dragon-Fly, The.
Duke of York's Statue, The.
Dull Is My Verse.
End, The.
Envoi: "I strove with none, for none was worth my strife."
Epigram: "Joy is the blossom, sorrow is the fruit."
Epigram: "No truer word, save God's, was ever spoken."
Epigrams must be curt, nor seem.
Examination of Shakespeare, The.
Exhausted now her sighs, and dry her tears.
Faesulan Idyl.
Fame.
Fate! I Have Asked.
Fault Is Not Mine, The.
Fiesolan Idyl, A.
Finis.
Florence.
For an Epitaph at Fiesole.
Foreign Ruler, A.
Gebir, *sels.*
Georges, The.
Gifts Return'd, The.
God Scatters Beauty.
Graceful Acacia.
Had we two met, blythe-hearted Burns.
Hamadryad, The.
Have I, this moment, led thee from the beach.
Heart's Abysses, The.
Hearts-Ease.
Helen and Corythos.
Hellenics, The, *sels.*
Her Name.
Here lies Landor.
His Epitaph.
How often, when life's summer day.
I Entreat You, Alfred Tennyson.
I Know Not Whether I Am Proud.
Ianthe, *sels.*
Idle Words.
In Clementina's Artless Mien.
Interlude.
Iphigeneia and Agamemnon ("Iphigeneia, when she heard her doom").
Ireland.
Ireland Never Was Contented.
Is it no dream that I am he.
Izaac Walton, Cotton, and William Oldways.
Joy Is the Blossom.
Kiss, The.
Last Fruit Off an Old Tree, *sels.*
Late Leaves.
Lately Our Poets.
Leaf after Leaf.
Lines to a Dragon-Fly.
Loves who many years held all my mind, The.
Maid's Lament, The.
Malvolio.
Masar.
Memory.
Mild Is the Parting Year.
Mimnermus Incert.
Mother, I Cannot Mind My Wheel.
Myrtis, *sel.*
Neither in idleness consume thy days.
Night Airs.
No, thou hast never griev'd but I griev'd too.
No charm can stay, no medicine can assuage.
No Truer Word.
O fond, but fickle and untrue.
O friends! who have accompanied thus far.

O Friendship! Friendship! the shell of Aphrodite.
Observing a Vulgar Name on the Plinth of an Ancient Statue.
Of Clementina.
On a Child.
On a Quaker's Tankard.
On Catullus.
On Death.
On Grey Cliffs.
On Himself.
On His Ninth Decade.
On His Own Agamemnon and Iphigeneia.
On His Own Death.
On His Seventy-fifth Birthday.
On Lucretia Borgia's Hair.
On Man.
On Music.
On Seeing a Hair of Lucretia Borgia.
On Ternissa's Death.
On the Dead.
On the Death of M. D'Ossoli and His Wife, Margaret Fuller.
On the Death of Southey.
On the Heights.
On the Hellenics.
On the smooth brow and clustering hair.
On Thomas Hood.
One White Hair, The.
Our youth was happy: why repine.
Parrot and Dove.
Past Ruined [*or* Ruin'd] Ilion Helen Lives.
Pericles and Aspasia, *sels.*
Plays.
Poem: "I cannot tell, not I, why she."
Poet! I like not mealy fruit; give me.
Portrait.
Proem to Hellenics.
Progress of Evening.
Quarrelsome Bishop, A.
Reflection from Sea and Sky.
Regeneration, *sel.*
Remain, Ah Not in Youth Alone.
Reply to Lines by Thomas Moore, A, *sel.*
Resignation.
Retired this hour from wondering crowds.
Rose Aylmer.
Scentless laurel a broad leaf displays, The.
Scribblers, The.
Sea-Nymph's Parting, The.
Sensible Girl's Reply to Moore's, A.
Shepherd and the Nymph, The.
Silent, you say, I'm grown of late.
So Late Removed from Him She Swore.
So Then, I Feel Not Deeply!
Some of Wordsworth.
Song: "Often I have heard it said."
Sweet Was the Song.
Tamar's Wrestling.
Ternissa! You Are Fled.
Test, The.
There Are Sweet Flowers.
There are two miseries in human life.
Time to Be Wise.
To a Spaniel.
To Age.
To Alfred Tennyson.
To an Old Poet.
To His Verse.
To Ianthe ("You smiled, you spoke, and I believed").
To Miss Arundell.
To My Child Carlino.
To My Ninth Decade [I Have Tottered On].
To One Who Quotes and Detracts.
To Our House-Dog Captain.
To Poets.
To Robert Browning.
To Shelley.
To the Poet T. J. Mathias.
To the Sister of Elia.
To Wordsworth.
To Youth.
Torch of love dispels the gloom, The.
Twenty Years Hence.
Under the Lindens.
Various the Roads of Life.
Verse: "Past ruin'd Ilion Helen lives."
Very True, the Linnets Sing.
Wall-Flower, The.
Well I Remember [How You Smiled].
What News.
Why do the Graces now desert the Muse?
Widcombe Churchyard.
William Gifford.
Yacht, The.
Years.
Years, Many Parti-coloured Years.
You see the worst of love, but not the best.
You Smiled, You Spoke, and I Believed.

Landy, Francis
Lament for Azazel.
Midrash on Hamlet.
Princess Who Fled to the Castle, The.
Selichos.

Lane, Franklin K.
I Am What You Make Me.

Lane, Joy M.
Road to School, The.

Lane, Patrick
At the Edge of the Jungle.
Beware the Months of Fire.
Elephants.
Gray Silk Twisting.
If.
Love.
Loving She Stood Apart.
Measure, The.
Mountain Oysters.
Passing into Storm.
Sleep on the Fraser.
Stigmata.
Surcease.
Treaty-Trip from Shulus Reservation.
Water-Truck, The.

Lane, Pinkie Gordon
Migration.
Nocturne: "Listening for the sound."
On Being Head of the English Department.
Sexual Privacy of Women on Welfare.
When You Read This Poem.
Who Is My Brother?

Lane, Randy
Song: "Sometimes in the fast food kitchen."

Lane, Wilmot B.
Owning.

Lang, Andrew
Almae Matres.
Ballade of Middle Age.
Ballade of the Primitive Jest.
Brahma.
But now the dentist cannot die.
Clevedon Church.
Heliodore.
Homeric Unity.
I'd Leave.
Jubilee before Revolution.
Limerick: "My name's Mister Benjamin Bunny."
Limerick: "There was a young lady of Limerick."
Limerick: "There was an auld birkie ca'ed Milton."
Lost Love.
Man and the Ascidian.
New Shakespeare, A.
Odyssey, The.
Psalm of Life, A, *parody.*
Remembered Melody.
Romance.
Scythe Song.
Tired of Towns.
Twilight on Tweed.
Villon's Ballade.

Lang, Andrew *and* **Edward Burnett Tylor**
Double Ballade of Primitive Man.

Lang, Jon
Someone Sits at the Harp.

Lang, V. R.
Waiting and Peeking.

Langer, Jiri Mordecai
On the Margins of a Poem.
Riddle of Night.

Langfield, Angela
Living with You.

Langfield, June Mercer
Full fathom five thy father lies.

Langhorne, John
Country Justice, The.
Evening Primrose, The.
Gypsies.
Owen of Carron, *sel.*
Poor, The.

Langland, Joseph
Aria for Flute and Oboe.
Crane.
Ecclesiastes.
Hunters in the Snow: Brueghel.
Pruners: Conca di Marini ("Pruners have come again among the vineyards").
Sacrifice of a Red Squirrel.
Sea-Change, A: For Harold.
Serpent, The.
Upon Hearing His High Sweet Tenor Again.
War.
Willows.
Winter Juniper.

Langland, William
Age of Reason, The.
Belling the Cat.
Civil Service, The.
Descent into Hell, The.
Entertainment Industry, The.
Et Incarnatus Est.
Field of Folk, The.
Friars.
Glutton, The.
Glutton in the Tavern.
God's Mercy.
Good Works.
Grace for Theology.
Incarnation, The.
Long Will in London.
On Malverne Hilles, the Place of Piers Plowman's Vision.
Our Needy Neighbours.
Palace of Truth, The.
Palmer, The.
Poor, The.
Saint Called "Truth," A.
Trinity, The.
Vision of Jesus, The.
Vision of Nature, A.
Vision of Piers Plowman, The, *sels.*

Langley, Eve
Native Born.

Langton, Daniel J.
Expecting.

Langton, Stephen
Hymn to the Holy Spirit.

Langworthy, Yolande
Drifting Sands and a Caravan.

Lanier, Clifford *and* **Sidney Lanier.** *See* **Lanier, Sidney** *and* **Clifford Lanier**

Lanier, Emilia
Eves Apologie.

Lanier, H. Glenn
O Christ of Bethlehem, *with music.*

Lanier, Sidney
Ballad of Trees and the Master, A.
Betrayal.
Centennial Meditation of Columbia, The.
Corn.
Crystal, The, *sels.*
Dear Land of All My Love.
Dying Words of Stonewall Jackson, The.

Evening Song.
From the Flats.
Harlequin of Dreams, The.
Hound, The.
Hymns of the Marshes, *sel.*
Into the Woods My Master Went.
Jaquerie, The, *sels.*
Land of the Wilful Gospel.
Lexington.
Marsh Song—At Sunset.
Marshes of Glynn, The.
Mocking Bird, The.
My Springs.
Night and Day.
Opposition.
Psalm of the West, *sels.*
Raven Days, The.
Resurrection.
Revenge of Hamish, The.
Ship of Earth, The.
Song of the Chattahoochee.
Stirrup-Cup, The.
Story of Vinland, The.
Struggle.
Sunrise.
Symphony, The.
Thar's More in the Man than Thar Is in the Land.
Triumph, The.
Waving of the Corn, The.
Wedding-Hymn.

Lanier, Sidney *and* **Clifford Lanier**
Power of Prayer, The.

Lanigan, George Thomas
Ahkoond of Swat, The.
Dirge of the Moolla of Kotal.
Quatrain: "Squeak's heard in the orchestra, A."
Threnody, A: "What, what, what/ What's the news from Swat?"

Lankford, Frances Stoakley
Required Course.

Lanning, Jane McKay
To Search Our Souls.

Lansing, Gerrit
Conventicle.
Ghazel of Absence, A.
Heavenly Tree Grows Downward, The.
Malefic Surgeon, The.
Tabernacles.
Undertaking, The.

Lanusse, Armand
Epigram: " 'Do you not wish to renounce the Devil?' "

Lao-tzŭ
Philosopher, The.

LaPage, Geoffrey
Mr. Giraffe.

Lape, Fred
Going to Town.
Horse Graveyard.
Lambs Frolicking Home.
Laughing Faces of Pigs, The.
Midsummer Pause.
Old Grey.
Puppy.

LaPena, Frank. *See* **Tauhindauli**

Lapidus, Jacqueline
Coming Out.

Laramore, Vivian Yeiser
Talk to Me Tenderly.

Larbaud, Valery
Poet's Wish.

Larcom, Lucy
Apple Blossoms.
Brown Thrush, The.
Dumpy Duck.
Giles Corey.
Hannah Binding Shoes.
Hymn Written for the Two Hundredth Anniversary of the Old South Church, Beverly, Massachusetts.
In the Tree-Top.
Mistress Hale of Beverly.
Mountains.
Nature's Easter Music.
Nineteenth of April, The.
Plant a Tree.
Sinking of the *Merrimac,* The.
Spring Whistles.
Strip of Blue, A.
Thanksgiving, A.
Tolling.
Trees, The.
Volunteer's Thanksgiving, The.

Lardner, Ring
Abner Silver's "Pu-leeze! Mr. Hemingway!"
Fragment from "Clemo Uti—the Water Lilies."
Hail to Thee, Blithe Owl.
Hardly a Man Is Now Alive.
Parodies of Cole Porter's "Night and Day."
Quiescent, a Person Sits Heart and Soul.

Larkin, Philip
Absences.
Age.
Ambulances.
Annus Mirabilis.
Arrivals, Departures.
Arundel Tomb, An.
As Bad as a Mile.
At Grass.
Aubade: "I work all day, and get half drunk at night."
Born Yesterday.
Card-Players, The.
Church Going.
Coming.
Cut Grass.
Days.
Deceptions.
Dedicated, The.
Dockery and Son (" 'Dockery was junior to you' ").
Dry-Point.
Dublinesque.
Explosion, The.
Faith Healing.
Fiction and the Reading Public.
First Sight.
Going.
Here.
High Windows.
Homage to a Government.
Home Is So Sad.
I Remember, I Remember.
If, My Darling.
Lines on a Young Lady's Photograph Album.
Love Songs in Age.
Maiden Name.
Mr. Bleaney.
Myxomatosis.
Next, Please.
Night-Music.
MCMXIV.
No Road.
Nothing to Be Said.
Places, Loved Ones.
Poetry of Departures.
Posterity.
Reasons for Attendance.
Sad Steps.
Self's the Man.
Send No Money.
So through that unripe day you bore your head.
Spring.
Study of Reading Habits, A.
Sunny Prestatyn.
Take One Home for the Kiddies.
Talking in Bed.
Toads.
Toads Revisited.
Waiting for breakfast, while she brushed her hair.
Wants.
Water.
Wedding-Wind.
Whitsun Weddings, The.
Wild Oats.
Within the Dream You Said.

Larminie, William
Killarney.
Moytura, *sel.*
Nameless Doon [or Dun], The.
Nameless Ruin, The.
Sword of Tethra, The.

Larrabee, Harold A.
Itch to Etch, The.
Professors.
Very Model of a Modern College President, The, *parody.*

Larremore, Wilbur
Madam Hickory.

Larsen, Carl
Plot to Assassinate the Chase Manhattan Bank, The.

Larsson, Raymond Ellsworth
To Our Lady, the Ark of the Covenants.

Lasker-Schüler, Else
Abel.
Abraham and Isaac.
Always in the Parting Year.
End of the World.
Hagar and Ishmael.
Homesick.
I Have a Blue Piano.
I Know That I Must Die Soon.
Jacob.
Jacob and Esau.
Lord, Listen.
Love Song, A: "Come to me in the night—we shall sleep closely together."
Love's Flight.
Moses and Joshua.
My Love-Song.
My People.
Pharaoh and Joseph ("Pharaoh rejects his blossoming wives").
Reconciliation.
Rock Crumbles, The.
Saul.
Zebaoth.

Lasnier, Rina
Serenade of Angels.

Lathbury, Mary Artemisia ("Aunt Mary")
Bread of Life, The.
Break Thou the Bread of Life.
Day Is Dying in the West, *at.*
Easter Song.
Song of Hope.
Summer Sunshine.

Lathrop, Adele
Because He Lives.

Lathrop, George Parsons
Child's Wish Granted, The.
Feather's Weight, A.
Flown Soul, The.
Keenan's Charge.
Marthy Virginia's Hand.
Remembrance.
South-Wind.
Sunshine of thine eyes, The.
Voice of the Void, The.

Lathrop, Lena
Woman's Question, A.

Lathrop, Rose Hawthorne
Clock's Song, The.
Dorothy.
Give Me Not Tears: Despaır.
Give Me Not Tears: Joy.
Song before Grief, A.

Lathrop, Walter
Here Is a Toast That I Want to Drink.

Latimer, Bette Darcie
For William Edward Burghardt Du Bois on His Eightieth Birthday.

Latimore, Jewel C. (Johari Amini; Johari M. Kunjufu)

Before/ and After.
Brother.
Ceremony.
Childhood.
On the Naming Day.
Positives.
Promise, The.
Return.
Saint Malcolm.
Signals.
Sun Heals, A.
To a Poet I Knew.
Utopia.

Lattimore, Richmond
Academic Overture, The.
Anniversary.
Bathtubs.
Collages and Compositions.
December Fragments.
Despair in Seascape.
Dislike of Tasks.
Dolphin Seen Alone.
Failure.
Father, The.
Game Resumed.
It.
Krankenhaus of Leutkirch, The.
Max Schmitt in a Single Scull.
Memory of a Scholar.
Monastery on Athos.
North Philadelphia, Trenton, and New York.
Phi Beta Kappa Poem, The.
Remorse.
Report from a Planet.
Reports of Midsummer Girls.
Rise and Shine.
Shadowgraphs, The.
Ship Bottom.
Siding near Chillicothe, A.
Sky Diving.
Spider.
Swarthmore Phi Beta Kappa Poem, The.
Tudor Portrait.
Verse.
Voyage of Discovery: 1935.
Western Ways.
Witness to Death.

Lau, Alan Chong
Crossing Portsmouth Bridge.
Day of the Parade.
Father Takes to the Road and Lets His Hair Down.
Letters from Kazuko (Kyoto, Japan—Summer 1980).
Living in the World.

Laube, Clifford James
At the Battery Sea-Wall.
Ave, Vita Nostra!

Laufer, Calvin W.
We Thank Thee, Lord, *with music.*

Laughlin, Elmer Osborn
Unknown, The.

Laughlin, James
Letter to Hitler, A.
Mountain Afterglow, The.
Step on His Head.
Summons, The.
Swarming Bees, The.

Laughton, Freda
At the Party.
Bull, The.
Rain on a Cottage Roof.
To the Spring Sun.
Welcome, The.
When from the Calyx-Canopy of Night.
When to My Serene Body.
Woman with Child, The.

Lauren, Joseph
Butterfly and the Caterpillar, The.

Laurence, Elsie
Alone.

Lautermilch, Steven
Christmas Morning.
For My Wife.

Lavant, Christine
Buy Us a Little Grain.
Do Not Ask.

Lavater, Louis
Faithless.
Mopoke.

Lavelle, Thomas. *See* **Flavell, Thomas**

Law, T. S.
Wemen's Wather.

Lawder, Douglas
Field, The.

Lawless, Emily
After Aughrim.
Clare Coast.
Dirge of the Munster Forest.
Fontenoy. 1745.
In Spain.
In Spain: Drinking Song.
Stranger's Grave, The.

Lawlor, Joanne
Gray Days.

Lawn, Beverly
No Difference.

Lawner, Lynne
In Your Arrogance.
Possession.
Rino's Song.

Lawrence, David Herbert
All I ask of a woman is that she.
All Souls.
Almond Blossom.
American Eagle, The.
Andraitx—Pomegranate Flowers.
Autumn Rain.
Aware.
Baby Running Barefoot.
Baby Tortoise.
Ballad of Another Ophelia.
Bare Almond-Trees.
Bat.
Bavarian Gentians.
Bei Hennef.
Birds.
Birthday.
Blue Jay, The.
Bombardment.
Bride, The.
Britannia's Baby.
Brooding Grief.
Butterfly.
Cherry Robbers.
City Life.
Collier's Wife, The.
Coming Awake.
Cypresses.
Deepest Sensuality, The.
Delicate Mother Kangaroo.
Desire Is Dead.
Discord in Childhood.
Doe at Evening, A.
Don Juan.
Don'ts.
Dreams Old and Nascent.
Elemental.
Elephant Is Slow to Mate, The.
Elephants in the Circus.
End of Another Home Holiday.
Energetic Women.
English Are So Nice, The!
Enkindled Spring, The.
Fate and the Younger Generation.
Figs.
Flowers and Men.
Food of the North.
Fronleichnam.
Gazelle Calf, The.
Giorno dei Morti.
Gloire de Dijon.
Gods, The! The Gods!
Green.
"Gross, Coarse, Hideous" (Police Description of My Pictures).
History.
How Beastly the Bourgeois Is.
Humming-Bird.
Hymn to Priapus.
In Trouble and Shame.
Intimates.
It's No Good!
Kangaroo.
Kisses in the Train.
Last Words to Miriam.
Lightning.
Little Fish.
Living, A.
Lizard.
Lord Tennyson and Lord Melchett.
Love on the Farm.
Lucifer.
Man and Bat.
Medlars and Sorb-Apples.
Mess of Love, The.
Middle of the World.
Moonrise.
Morning Work.
Mosquito, The.
Mountain Lion.
My Way Is Not Thy Way.
Mystic.
New Heaven and Earth.
New Moon.
New Year's Eve.
North Country, The.
Nostalgia.
Nothing to Save.
O! Start a Revolution.
On the Balcony
Passing Visit to Helen.
Pax.
Peace.
People.
Piano ("Softly, in the dusk, a woman is singing to me").
Piano, The ("Somewhere beneath that piano's superb sleek black").
Proper Pride.
Quite Forsaken.
Red Geranium and Godly Mignonette.
Red-Herring.
Release.
River Roses.
Roses on the Breakfast Table.
Salt of the Earth.
Sea, The.
Sea-Weed.
Self-Pity.
Self-Protection.
Shadows.
Ship of Death, The.
Sicilian Cyclamens.
Sinners.
Snake.
Snap-Dragon.
Song of a Man Who Has Come Through.
Sorrow.
Spray.
Spring Morning.
Stand Up!
Suburbs on a Hazy Day.
Sunday Afternoon in Italy.
Suspense.
Swan.
They Say the Sea Is Loveless.
Things Men Have Made.
To Women, as Far as I'm Concerned.
Tommies in the Train.
Tortoise Family Connections.
Tortoise Gallantry.
Tortoise Shell.
Tortoise Shout.
Trees in the Garden.

Twilight.
Virgin Mother, The, *sel.*
Volcanic Venus.
War-Baby.
We Are Transmitters.
Wedding Morn.
Whales Weep Not!
When I Read Shakespeare.
When I Went to the Circus.
When the Ripe Fruit Falls.
When Wilt Thou Teach the People?
Whether or Not.
White Blossom, A.
White Horse, The.
Wild Common, The.
Willy Wet-Leg.
Winter Dawn.
Winter's Tale, A.
Work.
Young Wife, A.
Youth Mowing, A.
Lawrence, J. B.
I Believe.
Lawrence, Margery
Lost Army, The.
Transport of Wounded in Mesopotamia, 1917.
Lawrence, Ruth
Washington's Tomb.
Lawrence, Terry
Harvester, The.
Lawrence, Thomas Edward
To S. A.
Lawson, David
No Great Matter.
Lawson, Henry
Andy's Gone with Cattle.
Ballad of the Drover.
Faces in the Street.
Grog-an'-Grumble Steeplechase.
Horseman on the Skyline, The.
Ned's Delicate Way.
Ripperty! Kye! Ahoo!
Sliprails and the Spur, The.
Talbragar.
Teams, The.
Up the Country.
Will Yer Write It Down for Me?
Lawson, James Gilchrist
All Nature Has a Voice to Tell.
O Lord, I Come Pleading.
War!
World Hymn, The.
Lawson, Marie A.
Halloween.
Lawson, Paul
Ambassadors, The.
Survey.
Lawson, Sylvia
Trader's Return.
Lawson, Will
Bill the Whaler.
Lawton, William Cranston
My Fatherland.
Song, Youth, and Sorrow.
Laxness, Halldór
She Was All That You Loved.
Lay, Norma
Sea Sonnet.
Layamon
Brut, The, *sel.*
Death of Arthur, The.
Layton, Irving
Aran Islands.
Bacchanal.
Berry Picking.
Birth of Tragedy, The.
Boys in October.
Bull Calf, The.
Butterfly on Rock.
Cain.
Cold Green Element, The.
Comedian, The.
Composition in Late Spring.
Day Aviva Came to Paris, The.
Dionysus.
El Gusano.
Fertile Muck, The.
For Anna.
For Mao Tse-tung; a Meditation on Flies and Kings.
For Musia's Grandchildren.
For My Brother Jesus.
For Natalya Correia.
From Colony to Nation.
Golfers.
Gothic Landscape.
Grand Finale.
Haunting, The.
Hostia.
Improved Binoculars, The.
Jewish Main Street.
Letter to a Librarian.
Misunderstanding.
Nausicäa.
Newsboy.
Ohms.
Osip Mandelshtam.
Overheard in a Barbershop.
Party at Hydra.
Song for Naomi.
Spider Danced a Cozy Jig, A.
Swimmer, The.
Tall Man Executes a Jig, A.
To the Girls of My Graduating Class.
Two Communist Poets.
Undine.
What Ulysses Said to Circe on the Beach of Aeaea.
Woman.
Words without Music.
Layzer, Robert
Elegy: "Whenever we touched, I thought of the Lying-in Hospital."
Insult, The.
Lawn Roller, The.
Saint's Parade.
Sleeping Beauty, The.
Lazar, David
Doctor Freud.
Lazard, Naomi
In Answer to Your Query.
Ordinance on Winning.
Walking with Lulu in the Wood.
Lazarus, Emma
Banner of the Jew, The.
Bar Kochba.
By the Waters of Babylon, *sels.*
Cranes of Ibycus, The.
Crowing of the Red Cock, The.
Currents.
Echoes.
Epochs.
Exodus, The (August 3, 1492).
1492.
Gifts.
In Exile.
In Memoriam: Rev. J. J. Lyons, *sel.*
Kindle the Taper, *with music.*
Lines on Carmen Sylva.
Magnetism.
Mater Amabilis.
New Colossus, The.
New Ezekiel, The.
On the Proposal to Erect a Monument in England to Lord Byron.
Success.
Venus of the Louvre.
World's Justice, The.
Lea, Fanny Heaslip
Dead Faith, The.
Lea, Sydney
Accident.
Bernie's Quick-Shave (1968).
Coon Hunt, Sixth Month (1955).
Floating Candles, The.
Night Trip across the Chesapeake and After.
Old Dog, New Dog.
Train Out, The.
Leach, Christopher
Blackbird.
Leadbelly (Huddie Ledbetter)
Bring Me a Little Water, Sylvie.
Ha Ha This-a-Way.
In the Pines (Where Did You Sleep Last Night?).
It's Almost Day.
Midnight Special.
Old Reilly (In Dem Long Hot Summer Days).
Poor Howard.
T. B. Blues.
Take a Whiff on Me.
Whoa Back, Buck.
Leaf, Walter
Better Way, The.
Leahy, Jack
How We Built a Church at Ashcroft.
Leamy, Edmund
Ticket Agent, The.
Leapor, Mary
Epistle to a Lady, An.
Essay on Woman, An.
Mira's Will.
Lear, Edward
After Tennyson.
Akond of Swat, The.
Alphabet ("A tumbled down, and hurt his Arm, against a bit of wood").
At Dingle Bank.
C was papa's gray cat.
Calico Pie.
Children of the Owl and the Pussy-Cat, The.
Cold Are the Crabs.
Courtship of the Yonghy-Bonghy-Bo, The.
Cummerbund, The.
Dingle Bank.
Dong with a Luminous Nose, The.
Duck and the Kangaroo, The.
Eclogue: "What makes you look so black, so glum, so cross?"
Fatal Mistake, A.
Floating Old Man, The.
How Pleasant to Know Mr. Lear.
Incidents in the Life of My Uncle Arly.
Jumblies, The.
Letter to Evelyn Baring, A.
Limerick: "There once was an old man of Lyme," *at.*
Limerick: "There was a young lady in white."
Limerick: "There was a young lady of Corsica."
Limerick: "There was a young lady of Hull."
Limerick: "There was a young lady of Russia."
Limerick: "There was a young lady of Ryde/ Whose shoe-strings were seldom untied."
Limerick: "There was a young lady whose eyes."
Limerick: "There was a young person of Crete."
Limerick: "There was a young person of Smyrna."
Limerick: "There was an old man in a boat."
Limerick: "There was an old man in a pew."
Limerick: "There was an old man in a tree."
Limerick: "There was an old man of Dumbree."
Limerick: "There was an old man of Dundee."
Limerick: "There was an old man of El Hums."
Limerick: "There was an old man of Girgenti."
Limerick: "There was an old man of Hong Kong."
Limerick: "There was an old man of Kamschatka."
Limerick: "There was an old man of Leghorn."
Limerick: "There was an old man of Madras."
Limerick: "There was an old man of Spithead."
Limerick: "There was an old man of the coast."
Limerick: "There was an old man of the Dargle."
Limerick: "There was an old man of the Dee."

Limerick: "There was an old man of The Hague."
Limerick: "There was an old man of Thermopylae."
Limerick: "There was an old man of Three Bridges."
Limerick: "There was an old man of Vesuvius."
Limerick: "There was an old man of Whitehaven."
Limerick: "There was an old man on the Border."
Limerick: "There was an old man who said: 'How.' "
Limerick: "There was an old man who said, 'Hush!' "
Limerick: "There was an old man who supposed."
Limerick: "There was an old man whose despair."
Limerick: "There was an old man with a beard."
Limerick: "There was an old man with a gong."
Limerick: "There was an old man with a poker."
Limerick: "There was an old man with a ribbon."
Limerick: "There was an old person of Anerley."
Limerick: "There was an old person of Bar."
Limerick: "There was an old person of Bromley."
Limerick: "There was an old person of Brussels."
Limerick: "There was an old person of Crowle."
Limerick: "There was an old person of Dean."
Limerick: "There was an old person of Diss."
Limerick: "There was an old person of Dover."
Limerick: "There was an old person of Grange."
Limerick: "There was an old person of Gretna."
Limerick: "There was an old person of Harrow."
Limerick: "There was an old person of Hove."
Limerick: "There was an old person of Ickley."
Limerick: "There was an old person of Lear."
Limerick: "There was an old person of Philae."
Limerick: "There was an old person of Shoreham."
Limerick: "There was an old person of Skye."
Limerick: "There was an old person of Twickenham."
Limerick: "There was an old person of Ware."
Limerick: "There was an old person of Wick."
Limerick: "There was an old person of Woking."
Limerick: "There was an old person whose habits."
Limerick: "There was once a man with a beard."
Lines to a Young Lady.
Love Song: "O lovely pussy, O pussy, my love."
M.
Menu.
Mr. and Mrs. Discobbolos.
Mr. and Mrs. Spikky Sparrow.
Mrs. Jaypher.
Mrs. Jaypher on Lemons.
New Vestments, The.
Nonsense Alphabet, A.
Nutcrackers and the Sugar-Tongs, The.
Old Man of the Hague, The.
Old Man of the Nile, An.
Old Man with a Beard.
Old Person of Cromer, An.
Owl and the Pussy-Cat, The.
Pelican Chorus, The.
Pobble Who Has No Toes, The.
Quangle Wangle's Hat, The.
Rice and Mice.
Says I to Myself.
Scraps of Lear.
Self-Portrait of the Laureate of Nonsense.
She sits upon her Bulbul.
Sonnet, A: "Cold are the crabs that crawl on yonder hills."
Table and the Chair, The.
Tea by the Sea.
Teapots and Quails.
There is a young lady, whose nose.
There Was a Young Lady of Norway.
There Was a Young Lady of Portugal.
There was a young lady of Sweden.
There was a young lady whose bonnet.
There was a young lady whose chin.
There Was a Young Lady Whose Nose.
There Was a Young Person of Smyrna.
There was an old lady of Chertsey.
There Was an Old Man, on Whose Nose.
There was an old man in a Barge.
There Was an Old Man in a Tree.
There was an old man of Bohemia.
There was an old man of Cape Horn.
There Was an Old Man of Dumbree.
There was an old man of Dunblane.
There Was an Old Man of Hong Kong.
There was an old man of Ibreem.
There was an old man of Peru/ Who never knew what he should do.
There was an old man of the East.
There was an old man of the West.
There was an old man of West Dumpet.
There was an old man who screamed out.
There Was an Old Party of Lyme, *at.*
There was an old person of Basing.
There was an old person of Blythe.
There was an old person of Bow.
There was an old person of Buda.
There was an old person of Burton.
There was an old person of Cassel.
There was an old person of Dutton.
There Was an Old Person of Gretna.
There was an old person of Prague.
There was an old person of Rhodes.
Two Old Bachelors, The.
Wet Weather at Cannes.
Yonghy-Bonghy-Bo, The.
Young Lady of Norway, A.
Young Lady of Tyre, The.

Lear, Oscar H.
Wide Open Spaces, The.

Learmont, John
Address to the Plebeians, An, *sel.*

Learned, Walter
Growing Old.
In Explanation.
Last Reservation, The.
On the Fly-Leaf of a Book of Old Plays.
On the Fly-Leaf of Manon Lescaut.
Prime of Life, The.
Time's Revenge.
To Critics.
With a Spray of Apple Blossoms.

"Learsi, Rufus" (Israel Goldberg)
Martyrdom.

Leary, Paris
Elegy for Helen Trent.
First Reader.
Love Lifted Me.
Manifesto.
Onan.
Oxford Commination.
September 1, 1965.
Summa contra Gentiles.
Views of the Oxford Colleges.
"What Five Books Would You Pick to Be Marooned with on a Desert Island?"

Leavenworth, Coman
Norfolk Memorials.
North Pickenham.
Rackheath.
Wendling.

Leax, John
Fire Burns Low, The.
Incarnation Poem.
That Day.

Lebensboim, Razel. *See* **Margolin, Anna**

Lebensohn, Micah Joseph
Wine.

Lechlitner, Ruth
Aubade: "Long ago when I shouted in red letters."
Kansas Boy.
Lizard, The.

Lecky, William Edward Hartpole
Early Thoughts.
Of an Old Song.
On an Old Song.

LeClaire, Gordon
Chameleon.
Love.
Miser.
Old Seawoman.

Le Clercq, J. G. Clemenceau. *See* **"Tanaquil, Paul"**

Le Compte, Calvin
Visitation, The.

Leconte de Lisle, Charles Marie René
Hialmar Speaks to the Raven.

LeCron, Helen Cowles
Little Charlie Chipmunk.

Ledoux, Louis V.
At Sunset.
Fulfilment.
Slumber Song.

Le Dressay, Anne
Roger and Me.
Song in White.

Ledward, Patricia
Evening in Camp.

Ledwidge, Francis
Ardan Mór.
August.
Death of Ailill, The.
Dream of Artemis, A, *sel.*
Fairy Music.
Had I a Golden Pound.
Herons, The.
Homecoming of the Sheep, The.
June.
Lament for the Poets: 1916.
Lament for Thomas MacDonagh.
Little Boy in the Morning, A.
Mother's Song, A.
My Mother.
Ships of Arcady, The.
Soliloquy.
Thomas MacDonagh.
To a Linnet in a Cage.
To a Sparrow.
Twilight in Middle March, A.

Lee, Agnes
Convention.
Ilex Tree, The.
Motherhood.
Old Lizette on Sleep.
Statue in a Garden, A.
Sweeper, The.

Lee, Al
Among Sharks.
Far Side of Introspection, The.
In the Yellow Light of Brooklyn.
Karl Marx.
Lie, The.
Maiden Lane.
One Morning We Brought Them Order.
Poem for the Year Twenty Twenty.
Weathering the Depths.

"Lee, Andy" (W. W. Delaney)
Crazy Song to the Air of "Dixie," *with music.*

Lee, Ann
Your Light.

Lee, Arthur
Prophecy, A.

Lee, B. J.
Eight Witches.

Lee, Deborah
Taking Care of It.
Where He Hangs His Hat.
Women Open Cautiously.
Words from a Bottle.
You're Sorry, Your Mother Is Crazy, & I'm a Chinese Shiksa.
Lee, Dennis
Alligator Pie.
Civil Elegies, *sel.*
Double-barreled Ding-Dong-Bat.
Freddy.
Gods, The.
Last Cry of the Damp Fly, The.
Muddy Puddle, The.
Tony Baloney ("Tony Baloney is fibbing again").
Lee, Don L. (Haki R. Madhubuti)
African Poems, *sel.*
Afterword, An: For Gwen Brooks.
Assassination.
Awareness.
Back Again, Home.
Big Momma.
Black Sketches.
But He Was Cool; or, He Even Stopped for Green Lights.
Change Is Not Always Progress.
Change-up.
Communication in Whi-te.
Cure All, The.
Education.
Gwendolyn Brooks.
Judy-One.
Man and Woman.
Man Thinking about Woman.
Mixed Sketches.
Mwilu/ or Poem for the Living.
New Integrationist, The.
Nigerian Unity/ or Little Niggers Killing Little Niggers.
One Sided Shoot-out.
Poem for a Poet, A.
Poem to Complement Other Poems, A.
Positives for Sterling Plumpp.
Primitive, The.
Re-act for Action ("Re-act to Animals").
Revolutionary Screw, The.
Self-Hatred of Don L. Lee, The.
Stereo.
Taxes.
To Be Quicker.
Wake-up Niggers.
We Walk the Way of the New World.
With All Deliberate Speed.
Lee, Harry
My Master Was So Very Poor.
Lee, J. B.
Clumsy.
Lee, Jack H.
Death Valley.
Lee, Joseph
Requiem: "When the last voyage is ended."
Lee, Laurie
Boy in Ice.
Christmas Landscape.
Day of These Days.
Edge of Day, The.
Field of Autumn.
First Love.
Juniper.
Larch Tree.
Long Summer.
Milkmaid.
Moment of War, A.
My Many-Coated Man.
Summer Rain.
Sunken Evening [in Trafalgar Square].
Town Owl.
Village of Winter Carols.
Lee, Muna
As Helen Once.
Sonnets, *sels.*
Lee, Nathaniel
Nathaniel Lee to Sir Roger L'Estrange.
Lee, Rena
Old Story, An.
Lee, Walter M.
Father, Teach Me.
Lee-Hamilton, Eugene
Death of Puck, The.
Elfin Skates.
Fairy Godmothers.
Idle Charon.
Lost Years.
Mimma Bella, *sels.*
My Own Hereafter.
Snail's Derby, A.
Song: "Under the winter, dear."
Sunken Gold.
To My Tortoise Ananke.
To My Tortoise Chronos.
What the Sonnet Is.
Wood-Song.
Lees, Edwin
Signs of Christmas.
Le Fanu, Joseph Sheridan
Drunkard to His Bottle, A.
Hymn: " 'Hush! oh ye billows.' "
Legend of the Glaive, The, *sel.*
Song of the Spirits, The.
Lefcowitz, Barbara F.
At the Western Wall.
Driftwood Dybbuk.
Mirrors of Jerusalem, The.
Le Fevre, Adam
Metal Fatigue.
Lefevre, H. T.
This I Can Do.
Le Fort, Gertrude von
Christmas.
Te Deum.
Vigil of the Assumption.
Lefroy, Edward Cracroft
Ageanax.
Cleonicos.
Cricket Bowler, A.
Echoes from Theocritus, *sels.*
Epitaph of Eusthenes, The.
Flute of Daphnis, The.
Football Player, A.
Grave of Hipponax, The.
Monument of Cleita, The.
On a Spring-Board.
Sacred Grove, A.
Summer Day in Old Sicily, A.
Sylvan Revel, A.
Thyrsis.
Leftwich, Joseph
Tailor, The.
Le Gallienne, Richard
After the War.
All Sung.
Ballad of London, A.
Ballade-Catalogue of Lovely Things, A.
Beatus Vir.
Brooklyn Bridge at Dawn.
Called Away.
Dream Tryst.
Easter Hymn, An.
Lady April.
May Is Building Her House.
Melton Mowbray Pork Pie, A.
Old Man's Song, An.
Passionate Reader to His Poet, The.
Prayer, A: "Out of the deeps I cry to thee, O God!"
Second Crucifixion, The.
Song: "She's somewhere in the sunlight strong."
Song: "Take it, love!"
Spirit of Sadness.
What of the Darkness?
Wife from Fairyland, The.
Wind's Way, The.
Wood Flower.
Legaré, James Matthew
Ahab Mohammed.
Amy.
To a Lily.
LeGear, Laura Lourene
Unbridled Now.
Léger, Alexis Saint-Léger. *See* **"Perse, St.-John"Legg, Bernice Hall**
Forest Meditation, A.
Le Guin, Ursula K.
Mind Is Still, The.
Lehman, David
For David Shapiro.
In Praise of Robert Penn Warren.
Ode: "People in the middle ages didn't think they were living."
Perpetual Motion.
Lehmann, Geoffrey
Auntie Bridge and Uncle Pat.
I Was Born at a Place of Pines.
Last Campaign, The.
Music Is Unevennesses.
My Father's a Still Day.
Pigs, The.
Ross's Poems, *sels.*
Saving the Harvest.
Some of Our Koorawatha Saints.
Song for Past Midnight.
There Are Some Lusty Voices Singing.
Lehmann, John
Ballad of Banners (1944), The.
Death in Hospital, A.
Last Ascent, The.
Sphere of Glass, The.
Summer Story, The.
This Excellent Machine.
Lehmann, Rudolph Chambers
Bath, The.
Bird in the Room, The.
Dance, The.
Middle Age.
Plea for a Plural, A.
Singing Water.
Lehmer, Eunice Mitchell
Armistice.
Lehrer, Tom
Elements, The.
New Maths.
Leib, Mani
Door and Window Bolted Fast.
From the Crag.
Hush, Hush.
In Little Hands.
Plum, A.
Psalmodist.
Pyre of My Indian Summer, The.
Shopkeepers.
They.
When I See Another's Pain.
Winter.
Leifer, Jay
Six-forty-two Farm Commune Struggle Poem.
Leigh, Amy E.
If I But Knew.
Leigh, Fred W.
Waiting at the Church; or, My Wife Won't Let Me, *with music.*
Leigh, Frederick *and* **Frederick Murray.** *See* **Murray, Frederick** *and* **Frederick Leigh**
Leigh, Henry Sambrooke
Cossimbazar.
Not Quite Fair.
Only Seven.
Rhymes (?).
Saragossa.
'Twas Ever Thus.
Twins, The.
Leigh, Richard
Eccho, The.
Her Window.
Sleeping on Her Couch.

Thus Lovely Sleep.
Leighton, Louise
Earthly Illusion.
Leighton, Robert
Bunch of Larks, The.
Leiper, Esther M.
Black Bottom Bootlegger, The.
Shaman.
Leipoldt, C. Louis
Banded Cobra, The.
On My Old Ramkiekie.
Leiser, Dorothy
Migrations of People, The.
Leiser, Joseph
Kol Nidra.
Leitch, Mary Sinton
From Bethlehem Blown.
Poet, The.
River, The.
Sea Words.
Leithauser, Brad
Angel.
Between Leaps.
Expanded Want Ad, An.
Ghost of a Ghost, The.
Quilled Quilt, a Needle Bed, A.
Leitner, Della Adams
Forbearance.
Tomorrow.
Leitner, S. N.
That's Faith.
Leivick, H. (Leivick Halpern)
How Did He Get Here?
I Hear a Voice.
Through the Whole Long Night.
Two Times Two Is Four.
Leland, Charles Godfrey ("Hans Breitman")
Ballad: "Noble Ritter Hugo, Der."
Ballad by Hans Breitmann.
Ballad of Charity, The.
Ballad of the Mermaid.
Breitmann in Politics, *sel.*
El Capitan-General.
Hans Breitmann's Party [*or* Barty].
Legend of Heinz von Stein, The.
Out and Fight.
Two Friends, The.
Leland, John
Evening Shade.
Now Behold the Saviour Pleading, *with music.*
Lele-io-Hoku
Albatross.
Lem, Carol
Henry Miller: A Writer.
L'Engle, Madeleine
At Communion.
From St. Luke's Hospital.
O Simplicitas.
Three Songs of Mary, *sel.*
Lengyel, Cornel
Fool Song.
Lennen, Elinor
His Last Week.
Nor House nor Heart.
On Entering a Forest.
Pilgrimage.
Praetorium Scene: Good Friday.
Prayer for a Play House.
Within the Shelter of Our Walls, *with music.*
Lenngren, Anna Maria
Other Fabrics, Other Mores!
Portraits, The.
Lennon, Florence Becker
Little White Schoolhouse Blues.
Lennon, John *and* **Paul McCartney**
Day in the Life, A.
Eleanor Rigby.
Fool on the Hill, The.
For No One.
I Am the Walrus.
Yellow Submarine.
"Lennox"
Neighbors.
Le Noir, Phil
Ol' Dynamite.
Lenowitz, Harris
Fringes, The.
Panegyric.
Lenox, Jean
I Don't Care, *with music.*
Lense, Edward
Waking Up.
Wolf Dream.
Lenski, Hayim
Language of Ancients.
Purity.
Upon the Lake.
Lenski, Lois
Fourth of July Song.
People.
Sing a Song of People.
Lent, Emma A.
Memorial Day.
Unawares.
Lentino, Jacopo da. *See* **Jacopo da Lentino**
Lento, Takako Uchino
Glass.
Leo XIII, Pope
War Cry: To Mary.
León, Luis Ponce de
About the Heavenly Life.
Life of the Blessed, The.
Love Song: "That haughty tyranny of thine."
Night Serene, The.
On Leaving Prison.
To Retirement.
Written on the Walls of His Dungeon.
Leonard, Eddie
Ida, Sweet as Apple Cider.
Leonard, Priscilla
Happiness.
Tide Will Win, The.
Leonard, William Ellery
Image of Delight, The.
Indian Summer.
Two Lives, *sel.*
Leone da Modena. *See* **Modena, Leone da**
Leong, George
Sometimes Love Poem, A.
This Is Our Music.
Leonidas of Alexandria
Menodotis.
Leonidas of Tarentum
Cleitagoras.
Fisherman, The.
Last Journey, The.
Philocles.
Spinning Woman, The.
Tomb of Crethon, The.
Leontius Scholasticus
To an Aging Charioteer.
Leopardi, Giacomo
A Sè Stesso.
Infinito, L'.
Saturday Night in the Village.
Setting of the Moon, The.
Terror by Night, The.
To Italy.
Le Pan, Douglas
Canoe-Trip.
Country without a Mythology, A.
Coureurs de Bois.
Incident, An.
Lion, Leopard, Lady.
Net and the Sword, The.
New Vintage, The.
Nimbus.
One of the Regiment.
Lepkowski, Frank J.
Two Poems Based on Fact.
Lepore, Dominick J.
Northward.
Lermontov, Mikhail Yuryevich
Composed While under Arrest.
Daemon, The, *sel.*
Dagger.
Mountain, The.
Reed, The.
Sail, A.
Thought, A.
Lerner, Alan Jay
With a Little Bit of Luck.
Lerner, Laurence David
All Day and All October.
14 July 1956.
In a Shoreham Garden.
Meditation upon the Toothache, A.
Poet at Fifty, The.
Raspberries.
St. Enda.
Way to the Sea, The.
What's Hard.
Wish, A.
Years Later.
Lesemann, Maurice
Cow-Ponies.
Ranchers.
Leslie, Cy
On Riots.
Leslie, Edgar *and* **E. Ray Goetz**
For Me and My Gal.
Leslie, Kenneth
By Stubborn Stars, *sels.*
Escapade.
From Soil Somehow the Poet's Word.
Halibut Cove Harvest.
Knife and Sap.
My Love Is Sleeping.
Silver Herring Throbbed Thick in My Seine, The.
Sonnet: "Silver herring throbbed thick in my seine, The."
Sudden Assertion.
Leslie, Shane
Fleet Street.
Four Winds, The.
Monaghan.
Muckish Mountain (The Pig's Back).
Prayer for Fine Weather.
Priest or Poet.
Two Mothers, The.
Lesoro, E. A. S.
Muscovy Drake, The.
Lesser, Rika
Can Zone; or, The Good Food Guide.
Canopic Jar.
Degli Sposi.
527 Cathedral Parkway.
La Banditaccia, 1979.
News & the Weather, The.
Translation.
Lessing, Gotthold Ephraim
I Asked My Fair, One Happy Day.
On Fell.
Three Kingdoms of Nature, The.
Lester, Julius
In the Time of Revolution, *sels.*
On the Birth of My Son, Malcolm Coltrane.
Us.
Lestey, George
Fire and Brimstone; or, The Destruction of Sodom, *sel.*
Lament of the Sodomites.
L'Estrange, Sir Roger
Loyalty Confin'd.
Le Sueur, Meridel
Dead in Bloody Snow.
I Light Your Streets.
Village, The.
Letts, Winifred
Letts, Winifred M.
Boys.
Casualty.
Children's Ghosts, The.

Connaught Rangers, The.
Deserter, The.
In Service.
My Blessing Be on Waterford.
Quantity and Quality.
Screens.
Soft Day, A.
Somehow, Somewhere, Sometime.
Spires of Oxford, The.
Synge's Grave.
Tim, an Irish Terrier.
To Scott.
What Reward?
Wishes for William.

Lettsom, John Coakley
Candid Physician, The.

Levendosky, Charles
Gifts, The.
Heart Mountain Japanese Relocation Camp, The: 30 Years Later.
Nova.

Levenson, Christopher
Prophecy, A.

Lever, Charles James
Bad Luck to This Marching.
Harry Lorrequer, *sel.*
It's Little for Glory I Care.
Larry M'Hale.
Man for Galway, The.
Pope He Leads a Happy Life, The.
Widow Malone, The.

Leverett, Ernest
S F.

Leveridge, Lilian
Cry from the Canadian Hills, A.
First Robin, The.

Leveridge, Richard
Song in Praise of Old English Roast Beef, A.

Levertin, Oscar
At the Jewish Cemetery in Prague.
Solomon and Morolph, Their Last Encounter.

Levertov, Denise
Abel's Bride.
About Marriage.
Absence, The.
Ache of Marriage, The.
Adam's Complaint.
Advent 1966.
Altars in the Street, The.
Anteroom, The.
Art.
Autumn Journey.
Barricades, The.
Bedtime.
Beyond the End.
Breathing, The.
By Rail through the Earthly Paradise, Perhaps Bedfordshire.
Cabdriver's Smile, The.
Cancion: "When I am the sky."
Cat as Cat, The.
Charge, The.
Christmas 1944.
Claritas.
Closed World, The.
Come into Animal Presence.
Common Ground, A.
Continuum.
Crystal Night.
Day Begins, A.
Dead Butterfly, The.
Defeat, A.
Depths, The.
Despair.
Dog of Art, The.
During the Eichmann Trial, *sels.*
Earliest Spring.
Earth Psalm.
Earth Worm, The.
"Else a Great Prince in Prison Lies."
Embroidery, An.
Epilogue: "I thought I had found a swan."
Everything That Acts Is Actual.
February Evening in New York.
Five-Day Rain, The.
Folding a Shirt.
From the Roof.
Gathered at the River.
Goddess, The.
Good Dream, The.
Grace-Note, The.
Gulf, The.
Hands, The.
Hypocrite Women.
Illustration, The—a Footnote.
Illustrious Ancestors.
In Mind.
Invocation: "Silent, about-to-be-parted-from house."
Jacob's Ladder, The.
Libation.
Life at War.
Living.
Losing Track.
Mad Song.
Malice of Innocence, The.
Map of the Western Part of the County of Essex in England, A.
Matins.
Merritt Parkway.
Moon Tiger.
Movement.
Mutes, The.
90th Year, The.
Note to Olga (1966), A.
Novel, The.
Novices, The.
O Taste and See.
Obsessions.
Offender, The.
Old Adam, The.
Olga Poems.
One A.M.
Our Bodies.
Overheard.
Overheard over S.E. Asia.
Overland to the Islands.
Partial Resemblance.
Peachtree, The.
Pleasures.
Poem: "Some are too much at home in the role of wanderer."
Poem Rising by Its Own Weight, The.
Postcards, The; a Triptych.
Presence, The.
Psalm Concerning the Castle.
Psalm—People Power at the Die-in.
Psalm Praising the Hair of Man's Body, A.
Pure Products.
Quarry Pool, The.
Rainwalkers, The.
Recognition, The.
Relearning the Alphabet.
Resolve, The.
Scenes from the Life of the Peppertrees.
Secret, The.
Seems Like We Must Be Somewhere Else.
Shalom.
Sharks, The.
Six Variations.
Solitude, A.
Song for Ishtar.
Springtime, The.
Stepping Westward.
Sunday Afternoon.
Tenebrae.
Third Dimension, The.
To the Reader.
To the Snake.
Triple Feature.
Two Variations.
Victors, The.
Vigil, The.
Way Through, The.
Well, The.
What Were They Like?
What Wild Dawns There Were.
Wife, The.
Wings, The.
With Eyes at the Back of Our Heads.
Woman Alone.
World Outside, The.
Writing to Aaron.

Levi, Adele
Death of Friends, The.

Levi, David
Bible, The, *sel.*

Levi, Peter
He Met Her at the Green Horse.
In a Corner of Eden.
In stone settlements when the moon is stone.
L'Aurore Grelottante.
Life Is a Platform, *sel.*
Ship-Building Emperors Commanded.
To My Friends.

Levi, Primo
For Adolf Eichmann.
Lilith.
Shema.

Levi ben Amittai
Kibbutz Sabbath.

Levi Yitzhok [*or* Isaac] of Berditshev
Invocation: "Good morning to you, Lord of the world!"
Kaddish.

Levien, Michael
In the Falling Deer's Mouth.

Levin, Gabriel
Adam's Death.
Etude for Voice and Hand.
Ishmael.

Levin, Phillis
Everything Has Its History.

Levine, Al
Bottle, The.

Levine, Ellen
One Morning.

Levine, Molly Myerowitz
Safed and I.

Levine, Norman
Crabbing.

Levine, Philip
Above It All.
After.
Animals Are Passing from Our Lives.
Any Night.
Ashes.
At the Fillmore.
Autumn.
Baby Villon.
Blasting from Heaven.
Businessman of Alicante, The.
Cemetery at Academy, California, The.
Children's Crusade, The.
Clouds.
Coming Home, Detroit, 1968.
Commanding Elephants.
Cutting Edge, The.
Distant Winter, The.
Drunkard, The.
Everything.
Face, The.
For Fran.
Gangrene.
Get Up.
He Faces the Second Winter.
Heaven.
Helmet, The.
Here and Now.
Horse, The.
How Much Earth.
In the New Sun.
Keep Talking.
Late Moon.
Lost Angel, The.
Mad Day in March.

Midget, The.
Milkweed.
My Angel.
My Life like Any Other.
My Son and I.
Negatives, The.
New Season.
News of the World.
Night Thoughts over a Sick Child.
1933.
Now It Can Be Told.
On a Drawing by Flavio.
On My Own.
On the Edge.
Poem Circling Hamtramck, Michigan All Night in Search of You, The.
Red Dust.
Reply, The.
Salami.
Second Angel, The.
Sierra Kid, *sel.*
Silent in America.
Something Has Fallen.
Spring in the Old World.
Standing on the Corner.
Sunday Afternoon.
They Feed They Lion.
To a Child Trapped in a Barber Shop.
To My God in His Sickness.
Turning, The.
Uncle.
Waking an Angel.
Way Down, The.
Winter Rains: Cataluña.
Words.
Zaydee.

Levinson, Fred
No More than Five.
Poem: "Country, The/ was back in the hands of the patriots."
Poem against Rats, A.
Sharks in Shallow Water.
Translation From, A.

Levis, Larry
Bat Angels.
Blue Stones.
Family Romance.
Fish.
For Zbigniew Herbert, Summer, 1971, Los Angeles.
Irish Music.
Linnets.
Ownership of the Night, The.
Picking Grapes in an Abandoned Vineyard ("Picking grapes alone in the late autumn sun").
Poem You Asked For, The.
Quilt, The.
Sensationalism.
To a Wall of Flame in a Steel Mill, Syracuse, New York, 1969.
Weldon Kees.
Whitman.
Winter Stars.

Levy, Amy
Birch-Tree at Loschwitz, The.
Epitaph: "This is the end of him."
London Plane-Tree, A.
London Poets.
New Love, New Life.
Xantippe.

Levy, Louis
Swallow's Flight, The.

Levy, Newman
Ballad of Sir Brian and the Three Wishes, The.
Belle of the Balkans, The.
Carmen.
I Wonder What Became of Rand, McNally.
Midsummer Fantasy.
Midsummer Jingle.
Reporters, The.
Revolving Door, The.
Rigoletto.
Scandalous Tale of Percival and Genevieve, The.
Tannhauser.
Thais.
Tristan and Isolda.

Levy, Robert J.
Give Us This Day Our Daily Day.

Levy, Stephen
Freely, from a Song Sung by Jewish Women of Yemen.
Friday Night after Bathing.
Home Alone These Last Hours of the Afternoon, Dusk Now, the Sabbath Setting In, I Sit Back, and These Words Start Welling Up in Me.
Judezmo Writer in Turkey Angry, A.

Lew, Walter
Fan.
Leaving Seoul; 1953.
Two Handfuls of *Waka* for Thelonious Sphere Monk (d. Feb. 1982).
Urn I: Silent for Twenty-five Years, the Father of My Mother Advises Me, *sel.*

Lewandowski, Stephen
Nantucket/Mussels/October.
Night Fishing.
Opening the Seams.

Lewin, Ralph A.
Les Chasse-Neige.

Lewis, Alonzo
Death Song.

Lewis, Alun
All Day It Has Rained.
Bivouac.
Dawn on the East Coast.
Goodbye.
In Hospital: Poona, I ("Last night I did not fight for sleep").
In Hospital: Poona, II ("The sun has sucked and beat the encircling hills").
Jungle, The.
Must/ All this aching.
Peasants, The.
Postscript for Gweno.
Sacco Writes to His Son.
Sentry, The.
Song: "First month of his absence, The."
To a Comrade in Arms.
To Edward Thomas.
Troopship in the Tropics.
Unknown Soldier, The.
Water Music.

Lewis, Angelo
America Bleeds.
Clear.

Lewis, Cecil Day. *See* **Day Lewis, Cecil**

Lewis, Claudia
Frightening.
How Strange It Is.

Lewis, Clive Staples
Apologist's Evening Prayer, The.
Awake, My Lute!
Eden's Courtesy.
Epigrams and Epitaphs, *sel.*
Evensong.
Evolutionary Hymn.
Late Passenger, The.
Naked Seed, The.
Nativity, The.
On a Vulgar Error.
Passing today by a cottage, I shed tears.
Pilgrim's Problem.
Prayer: "Master, they say that when I seem."
Scazons.
Sonnet: "Bible says Sennacherib's campaign was spoiled, The."

Lewis, David
When None Shall Rail.

Lewis, David, Paul Schindler *and* **Bob Adams**
Mother Pin a Rose on Me, *with music.*

Lewis, Dominic Bevan Wyndham ("Timothy Shy")
Envoi: "I warmed both hands before the fire of Life."
Having a Wonderful Time.
If So the Man You Are, *sels.*
Jig for Sackbuts.
Sapphics.
Seated one day at the organ/ I jumped as if I'd been shot.
Shot at Random, A.

Lewis, Eiluned
We Who Were Born.

Lewis, Gardner E.
How to Tell Juan Don from Another.
Poem, neither Hillâryous Norgay.

Lewis, J. Patrick
Pelicanaries ("Pelicanaries are homely birds").

Lewis, Janet
At Carmel Highlands.
Candle Flame, The.
For Elizabeth Madox Roberts.
Girl Help.
Helen Grown Old.
In the Egyptian Museum.
Lines with a Gift of Herbs.
Love Poem: "Instinctively, unwittingly."
Lullaby, A: "Lulee, lullay."
Remembered Morning.

Lewis, Matthew Gregory
Allan Water.
Alonzo the Brave and Fair Imogine.
Monk, The, *sel.*
Wife, A.

"Lewis, Michael" (Louis Untemeyer)
Broken Monologue.
Cherry Blossoms, *sels.*
Cursing and Blessing.
Leaving.
Living and Dying.
Longing.
Remembering.

Lewis, Percy Wyndham
One-Way Song, *sels.*
Song of the Militant Romance, The.

Lewis, Steven
Fort Wayne, Indiana 1964.

Lewis, Thelma
Exceptional.

Lewis, William S.
Blackfoot Sin-ka-ha.
Flathead and Nez Perce Sin-ka-ha.

Lewisohn, James
Basketball.
Blind Man, The.
Children of the State, The.
Guernica.
Minimum Security.
Poem: "Day when I can not, A."

Lewisohn, Ludwig
Heinrich Heine.
Together.

Leybourne, George
Champagne Charlie, *at.*

Leyden, John
Lay of the Ettercap, The.
Lords of the Wilderness.

L'Heureux, John
Discovering God Is Waking One Morning.

Liadan
Liadan Laments Cuirithir.

Liagarang
Snails.

Liasides, Pavlos
Fountain, The

Libbey, Elizabeth
Before the Mountain.
Concerning the Dead Women: The Munitions Plant Explosion: June, 1918.
Gesture, The.
Marceline, to Her Husband.
To Her Dead Mate: Montana, 1966.

Libera, Sharon Mayer
Mother.
Patty, 1949–1961.
Li Ch'ing-chao
After kicking on the swing.
Clear Bright.
How many evenings in the arbor by the river.
I let the incense grow cold.
Last night thin rain, gusty wind.
Light mist, then dense fog.
Melting in thin mist and heavy clouds.
Poem to the Tune of "Tsui hua yin."
Poem to the Tune of "Yi chian mei."
Rattan bed, paper netting. I wake from morning sleep.
Red lotus incense fades on/ the jewelled curtain.
Sky links cloud waves, links dawn fog.
Tune: Butterfly Woos the Blossoms, The.
Tune: Crimson Lips Adorned.
Tune: Endless Union.
Tune: Magnolia Blossom.
Two Springs.
Warm rain, sunny wind start to break the chill.
Weary Song to a Slow Sad Tune, A.
Year after year I have watched.
Lichtenstein, Alfred
Journey to the Insane Asylum, The.
Repose.
Li Chü
Harvesting Wheat for the Public Share.
Liddell, Catherine C.
Jesus the Carpenter.
Liddy, James
History.
Paean to Eve's Apple.
Republic 1939, The.
Thinking of Bookshops.
Voice of America, 1961, The.
Lieber, Francis
Ship Canal from the Atlantic to the Pacific, The.
Lieberman, Elias
Classroom in October.
Heart Specialist.
I Am an American.
Notation in Haste.
Sholom Aleichem.
Lieberman, Laurence
Coral Reef, The.
Interview.
Lamb and Bear; Jet Landing.
My Father Dreams of Baseball.
Orange County Plague: Scenes.
Osprey Suicides, The.
Unblinding, The.
Liessin, Abraham
Spring Nocturne.
Lietz, Robert
After the Deformed Woman Is Made Correct.
Lifshin, Lyn
Beryl.
Even There.
Family 8.
For a Friend.
In Spite of His Dangling Pronoun.
Marrakesh Women.
Martha Graham.
Not Quite Spring.
On the New Road.
Pulling Out.
Remember the Ladies.
To Poem.
Waiting, the Hallways under Her Skin Thick with Dreamchildren.
Way Sun Keeps Falling Away from Every Window, The.
You Understand the Requirements.
Lifson, Martha
Quiet by Hillsides in the Afternoon.
Liggett, Rosy
Obsession, The.
Lighthall, William Douw
Caughnawaga Beadwork Seller, The.
Lightman, Alan P.
First Rainfall.
Getting Under.
In Computers.
Lignell, Kathleen
Calamity Jane Greets Her Dreams.
Liliencron, Detlev, Freiherr von
After the Hunt.
Autumn.
Death in the Corn.
Who Knows Where.
Lillard, Charles
Bushed.
Lobo.
Lilliard, R. W.
America's Answer.
Lilliat, John
False Love, *at.*
Song: "When love on time and measure makes his ground," *at.*
Lillington, Kenneth
Ballade to My Psychoanalyst.
Lily, John. *See* **Lyly, John**
Lim, Genny
Departure.
Sweet 'n Sour.
Visiting Father.
Wonder Woman.
Lima, Frank
Memory of Boxer Benny (Kid) Paret, The.
Lima, Jorge de
Papa John.
Words Will Resurrect, The.
Lima, Robert
Peripatetic.
Lincoln, Abraham
Faith of Abraham Lincoln, The.
I Am Not Bound to Win.
Memory.
Lincoln, Joseph Crosby
Cod-Fisher, The.
Lincoln, Mary W.
Kings of France.
Lindberg, Gene
Home Winner, The.
Linden, Eddie
Sunday in Cambridge, A.
Lindh, Stewart
Settler.
Lindner, Carl
Mismatch.
Lindon, J. A.
Gilbertian Recipe for a Politician.
Learner.
London Sparrow's If, A.
More to It than Riding.
My Garden, *parody.*
"Twiner," A.
Lindquist, Ray
On the Land.
Lindsay, Lady Anne (Lady Anne Lindsay Barnard)
Auld Robin Gray.
East Coast Lullaby.
My Heart Is a Lute.
Lindsay, Sir David
After the Flood.
Ane Satire [*or* Satyre] of the Three [*or* Thrie] Estaitis, *sels.*
Ane Supplication in Contemptioun of Syde Taillis, *abr.*
Complaint of the Common Weill of Scotland.
Dreme, The, *sels.*
Historie of Squyer William Meldrum, The, *sel.*
Monarche, The, *sel.*
Of the Realme of Scotland.
Pardoner's Sermon, The.
So Young ane King.
Squire Meldrum at Carrickfergus.
Lindsay, Jack
Budding Spring.
Lindsay, Maurice
At Hans Christian Andersen's Birthplace, Odense, Denmark.
Exiled Heart, The.
Highland Shooting Lodge.
Hurlygush.
In the Cheviots.
Picking Apples.
Shetland Pony.
Lindsay, Olive E.
Despair.
Lindsay, T.
Theological Limerick.
Lindsay, Vachel
Abraham Lincoln Walks at Midnight.
Aladdin and the Jinn.
Apple-Barrel of Johnny Appleseed, The.
At Mass.
Booker Washington Trilogy, The, *sels.*
Broncho That Would Not Be Broken, The.
Bryan, Bryan, Bryan, Bryan.
Chinese Nightingale, The.
Congo, The.
Daniel.
Daniel Jazz, The.
Dirge for a Righteous Kitten.
Dove of New Snow, The.
Eagle That Is Forgotten, The.
Euclid.
Every Soul Is a Circus, *sel.*
Explanation of the Grasshopper, An.
Factory Windows Are Always Broken.
Flower-fed Buffaloes, The.
Flute of the Lonely, The.
General William Booth Enters into Heaven.
Ghosts of the Buffaloes, The.
Haughty Snail-King, The.
Horrid Voice of Science, The.
I Heard Immanuel Singing.
I Went Down into the Desert to Meet Elijah.
Indian Summer Day on the Prairie, An.
Jazz of This Hotel, The.
John Brown.
Johnny Appleseed.
King of Yellow Butterflies, The.
Knight in Disguise, The.
Leaden-eyed, The.
Lincoln.
Lion, The.
Litany of the Heroes, *sel.*
Little Turtle, The.
Moon's the North Wind's Cooky, The.
My Fathers Came from Kentucky.
Mysterious Cat, The.
Nancy Hanks, Mother of Abraham Lincoln.
Negro Sermon, A: Simon Legree.
Net to Snare the Moonlight, A.
On the Building of Springfield.
Oration, Entitled "Old, Old, Old, Old Andrew Jackson," An, *abr.*
Poems about the Moon.
Pontoon Bridge Miracle, The.
Potatoes' Dance, The.
Rain.
Scissors-Grinder, The.
Sea Serpent Chantey, The.
Sense of Humour, A.
Simon Legree—a Negro Sermon.
Sorceress, The!
Spider and the Ghost of the Fly, The.
To a Golden-haired Girl in a Louisiana Town.
Traveler, The.
Two Old Crows.
Unpardonable Sin, The.
What Semiramis Said.
What the Moon Saw.
When the Mississippi Flowed in Indiana.
Why I Voted the Socialist Ticket.
Would I Might Rouse the Lincoln in You All.
Yet Gentle Will the Griffin Be.
Lindsey, Jim
Blank Verse for a Fat Demanding Wife.

Lindsey, Therese Kayser
Man Christ, The.
Lindsey, William
En Garde, Messieurs.
Hundred-Yard Dash, The.
Lindskoog, Kathryn
Light Showers of Light.
Lingard, William Horace
Captain Jinks.
Link, Carolyn Wilson
Elements.
Link, Gordden
Artist and Ape.
Link, Lenore M.
Holding Hands.
"Lin Ling" [*or* "Li Chi"] (Hu Yun-shang)
Footpaths Cross in the Rice Field.
Linnell, Kathleen
Two Birds.
Linthicum, John
April.
Linton, William James
Epicurean.
Faint Heart.
Spring and Autumn.
Lipkin, Jean
Apocalypse.
Father.
Pre Domina.
Lipman, Ed
Because Our Past Lives Every Day.
Because San Quentin Killed Two More Today.
4 1/2 Point 5.
Matrix III.
Nights Primarily III.
Li Po
Clearing at Dawn.
Drinking Alone in the Moonlight.
Exile's Letter.
Girls on the Yueh River.
His Dream of the Sky-Land: A Farewell Poem, *sel.*
I Am a Peach Tree.
In the Mountains on a Summer Day.
Jewel Stairs' Grievance, The ("The jewelled steps are already quite white with dew").
Lament of the Frontier Guard.
Long War, The.
Moon at the Fortified Pass, The.
One set on the highway to sing.
Poem by the Bridge at Ten-shin.
River Merchant's Wife, The; a Letter.
Separation on the River Kiang.
Taking Leave of a Friend.
To Tan Ch'iu.
Two Letters from Chang-kan.
War.
Lippincott, Sara Jane Clarke. *See* **"Greenwood, Grace"**
Lippmann, Julie Mathilde
Love and Life.
Pines, The.
Stone Walls.
Lipshitz, Fay
Aleph Bet, The.
Encounter in Jerusalem.
Judean Summer.
Lipsitz, Lou
After Visiting a Home for Disturbed Children.
Bedtime Story.
Brooklyn Summer.
Conjugation of the Verb, "To Hope."
Pancho Villa.
Pipes, The.
Prospect Beach.
Radical in the Alligator Shirt, The.
Sirens, The.
Thaw in the City.
To a Fighter Killed in the Ring.
Tree Is Father to the Man, The.
Lipska, Ewa
Cock, The.
Flood, The.
If God Exists.
Wedding.
Lisboa, Henriqueta
Minor Elegy.
Lisle, Rouget de. *See* **Rouget de Lisle, Claude Joseph**
Lisle, Thomas
Power of Music, The.
Lissauer, Ernst
Chant of Hate against England, A.
Lister, Richard Percival
At the Ship.
Beetle Bemused.
Bone China.
Cuckoo.
Gemlike Flame, The.
Human Races, The.
I Thought I Saw Stars.
Lament of an Idle Demon.
On a Horse and a Goat.
On Becoming Man.
Postscript to Die Schöne Müllerin.
Revolutionaries, The.
Tale of Jorkyns and Gertie, The; or, Vice Rewarded.
Time Passes.
Listmann, Thomas
Sixties, The.
Litchfield, Grace Denio
My Letter.
My Other Me.
To a Hurt Child.
Little, Arthur J.
Christ Unconquered, *sel.*
Invocation: "Mother of God, mother of man reborn."
Little, Katharine Day
Hazlitt Sups.
Little, Philip Francis
Three Poplars, The.
Littlebird, Harold (Harold Bird)
After the Pow-Wow, *sel.*
Alone Is the Hunter.
Circle Begins, A.
Coming Home in March.
Could I Say I Touched You.
For Drum Hadley.
For the Girls 'cause They Know.
For Tom Numkena, Hopi/Spokane.
Gaa-a-Muna, a Mountain Flower.
Hummingbird.
Hunter's Morning.
If You Can Hear My Hooves.
In a Double Rainbow.
Mother/Deer/Lady.
Oh but It Was Good.
Old Moke.
Pennsylvania Winter Indian 1974.
Wrap Me in Blankets of Momentary Winds.
Littledale, Freya
When My Dog Died.
Littlefield, Hazel
Not for Its Own Sake.
Littlefield, Milton S.
Come, O Lord, Like Morning Sunlight.
O Son of Man, Thou Madest Known.
Littleton, Edward
Spider, The.
Littlewort, Dorothy
Prayer of a Teacher.
Litvinoff, Emanuel
All Ruin Is the Same.
Garrison Town.
If I Forget Thee.
Note from an Intimate Diary.
Poem for the Atomic Age.
Rededication.
To T. S. Eliot.
War Swaggers.
Litwack, Susan
Creation of the Child.
Havdolah.
Inscape.
Tonight Everyone in the World Is Dreaming the Same Dream.
Liu, Stephen Shu Ning
Adultery at a Las Vegas Bookstore.
I Lie on the Chilled Stones of the Great Wall.
My Father's Martial Art.
On Pali Lookout.
Pair of Fireflies, A.
Tours.
Livesay, Dorothy
Abracadabra.
Children's Letters, The.
Colour of God's Face, The, *sels.*
Contact.
Encounter.
Epilogue to the Outrider.
Fantasia.
Green Rain.
Improvisation on an Old Theme.
Inheritors, The.
Interval with Fire.
Lament: "What moved me, was the way your hand."
Land, The.
Leader, The.
On Looking into Henry Moore.
Pause.
People, The: Village.
Prophetess, The.
Serenade for Strings.
Signature.
Spain.
Uninvited, The.
Waking in the Dark.
Wedding.
Without Benefit of Tape.
Livesay, Florence Randal
Tim, the Fairy.
Violin Calls, The.
Livingston, Edna
Question, A.
Livingston, Myra Cohn
Car Wash.
Conversation with Washington.
Father.
German Shepherd.
Grunion.
Halloween.
History.
Lazy Witch.
Martin Luther King.
Mill Valley.
Mr. Pratt ("Mr. Pratt has never left").
Mrs. Spider.
Night, The.
October Magic.
Old People.
On Reading: Four Limericks.
Only a Little Litter.
Silly Dog.
74th Street.
Tape, The.
Time for Building, A.
12 October.
Whispers.
Livingston, William
Ireland Weeping.
Message to the Bard.
Livingstone, Douglas
Evasion, An.
King, The.
One Time.
Peace Delegate.
Sunstrike.
To a Dead Elephant.
Llewellyn, Karl Nickerson
Prairie.
Lloréns Torres, Luis
Love without Love.
Maceo.

Lloyd, Arthur
I'll Strike You with a Feather.
Lloyd, Cecil Francis
March Winds.
Truth.
Lloyd, Charles
Essay on the Genius of Pope, The, *sel.*
Lloyd, Donald J.
Bridal Couch.
Lloyd, Evan
Methodist, The, *sels.*
Religion and the Lower Classes.
Lloyd, Robert
Cit's Country Box, The.
Critic's Rules, The.
Familiar Epistle to J. B. Esq., A, *sels.*
Public Schools.
Sent to a Lady, with a Seal.
Shakespeare; an Epistle to David Garrick, Esq., *sels.*
True Genius.
Lloyd, Roseann
Song of the Fisherman's Lover.
Lluellyn, Martin
Cock-throwing.
Llwyd, John Plummer Derwent
Vestal Virgin, The, *sel.*
Llywarch the Aged
Hearth of Urien, The.
Lochhead, Liz
Tam Lin's Lady.
Lochhead, Marion
Nox Est Perpetua.
Lochore, Robert
Marriage and the Care o't.
Locke, Lawrence
Animal Pictures.
Leaving Mendota, 1956.
River.
Locker, Malka
Clocks.
Drunken Streets.
Locker-Lampson, Frederick
At Her Window.
Cuckoo, The.
Garden Lyric, A.
Jester's Plea, The.
Love, Time and Death.
Mrs. Smith.
My Mistress's Boots.
Nice Correspondent, A.
Old Buffer, An.
On an Old Muff.
Our Photographs.
Rhyme of One, A.
St. James's Street.
Skeleton in the Cupboard, The.
Terrible Infant, A.
To My Grandmother.
Widow's Mite, The.
Lockett, Reginald
Good Times and No Bread.
Lockhart, John Gibson
Lament for Captain Paton.
Lines: "When youthful faith hath fled."
Serenade: "While my lady sleepeth."
Wandering Knight's Song, The.
Locklin, Gerald
Bobbie's Cat.
Don't Answer the Phone for Me the Same.
Dwarf, The.
Gunfighter.
Pedagogy.
Poop.
Toad, The.
Lockman, John
Penitent Nun, The.
Lockwood, Margo
December Eclipse.
Victorian Grandmother.
Wind Flowers.
Lockyer, Milton
Dark Mountains.
Lodge, Edith
Song of the Hill.
Lodge, George Cabot
Song of the Wave, A.
Lodge, Thomas
Armistice.
Beauty, Alas, Where Wast Thou Born, *at.*
Carpe Diem.
Coridon's Song.
Earth, Late Choked with Showers, The.
Fancy, A ("First shall the heavens want starry light").
Fancy, A ("When I admire the rose").
Fidelity.
For Pity, Pretty Eyes, Surcease.
Her Rambling.
Life and Death of William Longbeard, The, *sels.*
Love Guards the Roses of Thy Lips.
Lover's Protestation, A.
Love's Protestation.
Love's Witchery.
Margarite of America, A, *sel.*
Melancholy.
Montanus' Sonnet.
My Mistress.
Ode: "Now I find thy looks were feigned."
Of Rosalind.
Old Damon's Pastoral.
Phillis.
Phoebe's Sonnet.
Phyllis, *sels.*
Pluck the Fruit and Taste the Pleasure.
Robert, Second Duke of Normandy, *sel.*
Rosader's Sonnet.
Rosalynde; or Euphues' Golden Legacy, *sels.*
Rose, The.
Scilla's Metamorphosis, *sel.*
Song: "Now I see thy looks were feigned."
Song: "Pluck the fruit and taste the pleasure."
Sonnet: "O shady vales, O fair enriched meads."
To Phyllis.
To Phyllis, the Fair Shepherdess.
Truth's Complaint over England.
Loesser, Frank
Guys and Dolls.
Once in Love with Amy, *with music.*
Praise the Lord and Pass the Ammunition!
Loewenthal, Tali
Hebrew Script.
Loewinsohn, Ron
Against the Silences to Come.
Goat Dance.
Insomniac Poem.
Leaves, The.
Mrs. Loewinsohn &c.
My Sons.
Pastoral: "Death./ The death of a million."
Stillness of the Poem, The.
Thing Made Real, The.
Windows, The.
Loftin, Elouise
Pigeon.
Virginia.
Weeksville Women.
Woman.
Lofting, Hugh
Mister Beers.
Picnic.
Lofton, Blanche De Good
Song of the Seasons.
Logan, George B., Jr.
Dawn.
Logan, John (1748–88)
Braes of Yarrow, The.
Logan, John Daniel
Heliodore.
Logan, John (b. 1923)
Believe It.
Century Piece for Poor Heine, A.
Coming of Age.
Concert Scene.
Experiment That Failed, The.
First Prelude. Dream in Ohio; the Father.
Letter to a Young Father in Exile.
Library, The.
Lines for a Friend Who Left.
Lines for a Young Wanderer in Mexico.
Lines for Michael in the Picture.
Lines on His Birthday.
Lines to His Son on Reaching Adolescence.
Love Poem: "Last night you would not come."
Monument and the Shrine, The.
Nude Kneeling in Sand.
On the Death of Keats.
On the House of a Friend.
Pass, The.
Picnic, The.
Poem for My Son.
Poem in Progress, *sel.*
Rescue, The.
San Francisco Poem.
Saturday Afternoon at the Movies.
Shore Scene.
Spring of the Thief.
Suite of Six Pieces for Siskind, A.
Three Moves.
Three Poems on Morris Graves' Paintings.
To a Young Poet Who Fled.
Trip to Four or Five Towns, A.
White Pass Ski Patrol.
Zoo, The.
Logan, Robert
On a Prize Crucifix by a Student Sculptor.
Logan, William
Debora Sleeping.
Green Island.
Protective Colors.
Summer Island.
Sutcliffe and Whitby.
Logau, Friedrich von
Retribution.
Logue, Christopher
Epitaph: "I am old."
Foreword to New Numbers.
Friday. Wet Dusk.
Letters from an Irishman to a Rat.
Loines, Russell Hillard
On a Magazine Sonnet.
Lom, Iain (John MacDonald)
Day of Inverlochy, The.
To Mackinnon of Strath.
Lomax, Alan *and* W. B. Richardson
Rocks and Gravel.
Lomax, Pearl Cleage
Glimpse.
Jesus Drum.
Mississippi Born.
Poem: "You said./ don't write me/ a love poem."
London, Jonathan
Batches of New Leaves.
Driving Home.
Lonergan, Frank
Cycle.
Loney, Alan
Elegy: " 'Crusher' never scared me, The. Tho that giant."
Elegy: "In my collection, the words are, we use."
Elegy: "Youd make capital of."
Eternal Return, The.
Of Flowers.
Long, Doughtry, Jr. ("Doc Long")
Ginger Bread Mama.
Negro Dreams.
Number Four.
One Time Henry Dreamed the Number.
Poem No. 21.
Long, Elizabeth-Ellen
Autumn Song.
Christmas Song.

Mountain Medicine.
Rain Clouds.
Long, Haniel
Butterflies.
Dead Men Tell No Tales.
Faun, The.
Girl Athletes.
Herd Boy, The.
Poet, The.
Song: "Poppies paramour the girls."
Long, Pauline. *See* **Asphodel**
Long, Peter
Remember Thy Creator Now, *with music.*
Long, Richard A.
Hearing James Brown at Café des Nattes (Sidi-bou-Saïd, Tunisia).
Juan de Pareja: Painted by Velázquez.
Long, Richard Hoopell
Poet and Peasant.
Skylark's Nest, The.
Long, Robert
Saying One Thing.
Long, Stewart I.
Was It You?
Long, Virginia
Mares of Night.
112 at Pesidio.
Long, William. *See* **"Yates, Peter"**
Long, Worth
Arson and Cold Lace.
Longfellow, Henry Wadsworth
Aftermath.
Arrow and the Song, The.
Arsenal at Springfield, The.
As Brothers Live Together.
Autumn.
Ballad of the French Fleet, A.
Battle of Lovell's Pond, The.
Belfry of Bruges, The.
Belisarius.
Bells of Lynn, The.
Bells of San Blas, The.
Birds of Killingworth, The.
Bridge, The.
Builders, The.
Building of the *Long Serpent,* The.
Building of the Ship, The.
Challenge, The.
Chamber over the Gate, The.
Charlemagne.
Chaucer.
Children's Hour, The.
Christmas Bells.
Christus; a Mystery, *sels.*
Church Scene, The.
Courtship of Miles Standish, The.
Cross of Snow, The.
Cumberland, The.
Curfew.
Dante ("Oft have I seen at some cathedral door").
Dante ("Tuscan, that wanderest through the realms of gloom").
Day Is Done, The.
Daybreak.
Death of Minnehaha, The.
Decoration Day.
Divina Commedia (*poems introductory to* Longfellow's *tr. of the* Divine Comedy, I-VI).
Drowned Mariner, The.
Dutch Picture, A.
Embarkation, The.
Endymion.
Equinox, The.
Evangeline.
Evangeline in Acadie.
Excelsior.
Expedition to Wessagusset, The.
Fate of the Prophets, The.
Fiftieth Birthday of Agassiz, The.
Finding of Gabriel, The.
Fire of Drift-Wood, The.
Flight into Egypt, The.
Flowers.
Follow Me.
From My Arm-Chair.
Galley of Count Arnaldos, The.
Ghosts, The.
Giles Corey of the Salem Farms, *sels.*
Giotto's Tower.
God's-Acre.
Golden Legend, The, *sel.*
Golden Mile-Stone, The.
Hanging of the Crane, The, *sel.*
Harvest Moon, The.
Hawthorne.
Heights, The.
Hiawatha's Canoe.
Hiawatha's Childhood.
Hiawatha's Wooing.
Him Evermore I Behold.
Home Song.
Hymn of the Moravian Nuns of Bethlehem.
Hymn to the Night.
I Heard the Bells on Christmas Day.
In the Churchyard at Cambridge.
Introduction: "Should you ask me, whence these stories?"
It Is Too Late ("It is too late! Ah, nothing is too late").
Jericho's Blind Beggar.
Jewish Cemetery at Newport, The.
John Endicott, *sels.*
Jugurtha.
Keats.
Kéramos, *sel.*
Killed at the Ford.
King Robert of Sicily.
Ladder of St. Augustine, The, *sel.*
Lakes of the Atchafalaya, The.
Let War's Tempests Cease.
Life.
Little Hiawatha, The.
Maidenhood.
Manuscripts of God, The.
Message for Peace, A.
Mezzo Cammin.
Midnight Mass for the Dying Year.
Midnight Ride of Paul Revere, The.
Milton.
Monk of Casal-Maggiore, The.
Moonlight.
Morituri Salutamus, *sel.*
My Books.
My Lost Youth.
Nature.
New Household, A.
Norman Baron, The, *sel.*
Nuremberg.
O Ship of State.
Ocean of Life, The.
Ode to the Inhabitants of Pennsylvania.
Oft Have I Seen At Some Cathedral Door.
Old Bridge at Florence, The.
Old Clock on the Stairs, The.
On the Atchafalaya.
Paul Revere's Ride.
Peace on Earth.
Phantom Ship, The.
Potter's Song, The.
Prelude: "This is the forest primeval."
President Garfield.
Primeval Forest, The.
Proclamation, The.
Prologue: "Delusions of the days that once have been."
Prologue: "To-night we strive to read, as we may best."
Psalm of Life, A.
Rain in Summer, *sl. abr.*
Rainy Day, The.
Reaper and the Flowers, The.
Republic, The.
Resignation.
Revenge of Rain-in-the-Face, The.
Ropewalk, The.
Saga of King Olaf, The, *sels.*
Sail On, O Ship of State!
Sea Memories.
Seaweed.
Secret of the Sea, The.
Serenade: "Stars of the summer night!"
Shakespeare.
Ship of State, The.
Ships That Pass in the Night.
Sicilian's Tale, The.
Sir Humphrey Gilbert.
Skeleton in Armor, The.
Slave Singing at Midnight, The.
Slave's Dream, The.
Snow-Flakes.
Song: "Stay, stay at home, my heart, and rest."
Song of Hiawatha, The, *sels.*
Sonnet: "Oft I have seen at some cathedral door."
Sonnets on the Divina Commedia.
Sound of the Sea, The.
Spanish Student, The, *sel.*
Spirit of Poetry, The.
Student's Tale, The.
Suspiria.
Tales of a Wayside Inn, *sels.*
This Is Indeed the Blessed Mary's Land.
Three Kings, The.
Three Sonnets on the Divina Commedia.
Tide Rises, the Tide Falls, The.
To a Child, *sel.*
To an Old Danish Song-Book.
To the Driving Cloud.
Too Late?
Trial, The.
Twilight.
Ultima Thule.
Venice.
Victor Galbraith.
Village Blacksmith, The.
Wapentake.
War-Token, The.
Warden of the Cinque Ports, The.
Windmill, The.
Witnesses, The.
Wreck of the *Hesperus,* The.
Longfellow, Samuel
Again as Evening's Shadow Falls, *with music.*
Christian Life, The.
Church Universal, The.
God, Through All and in You All.
God of the Earth, the Sky, the Sea.
Holy Spirit, Truth Divine, *with music.*
O Life That Maketh All Things New, *with music.*
Summer days are come again, The.
'Tis Winter Now, *with music.*
Longley, Michael
Christopher at Birth.
Desert Warfare.
Emily Dickinson.
Epithalamion: "These are the small hours when."
Fleadh.
Irish Poetry.
Kindertotenlieder.
Letter to Three Irish Poets, A.
Man Lying on a Wall.
Miscarriage.
Peace.
Small Hotel, The.
Longman, Doris
Flight 382.
Longstaff, W. D.
Take Time to Be Holy.
Lonzano, Menahem ben Judah
Gentleman, The.
Looke, John
Famous Sea-Fight, A.

Loomis, Charles Battell
Classic Ode, A.
Jack and Jill.
Propinquity Needed.
Timon of Archimedes.
Loots, Barbara Kunz
Mountain Wind.
Lope de Vega Carpio, Félix
At Dawn the Virgin Is Born.
Christmas Cradlesong, A.
Little Carol of the Virgin, A.
Song of the Virgin Mother, A.
To-Morrow.
Lopez-Penha, Abraham Z.
Dusk.
López Velarde, Ramón
Malefic Return, The.
My Cousin Agueda.
Lorca, Federico García. *See* **García Lorca, Federico**
Lord, Everett W.
Legend of the Admen, The.
Lord, May Carleton
Old Man with a Mowing Machine.
Prayer: "Keep me from fretting, Lord, today."
Lord, Phillips H.
Your Church and Mine.
Lord, William Wilberforce
Brook, The.
Keats.
Ode to England, *sels.*
On the Defeat of Henry Clay.
To Rosina Pico.
Wordsworth.
Worship, *sel.*
Lorde, Audre
And Fall Shall Sit in Judgment.
And What About the Children.
Between Ourselves.
Birthday Memorial to Seventh Street, A.
Chain.
Coal.
Eulogy for Alvin Frost.
Father, the Year Is Fallen.
Father Son and Holy Ghost.
For Each of You.
From the House of Yemanjá.
Hanging Fire.
Harriet.
If You Come Softly.
Movement Song.
Naturally.
Now That I Am Forever with Child.
One Year to Life on the Grand Central Shuttle.
Outside.
Oya.
Pirouette.
Poem for a Poet, A.
Recreation.
Rites of Passage.
Suffer the Children.
Summer Oracle.
To Desi as Joe as Smoky the Lover of 115th Street.
To My Daughter the Junkie on a Train.
Trip on the Staten Island Ferry, A.
What My Child Learns of the Sea.
Woman Thing, The.
Workers Rose on May Day or Postscript to Karl Marx, The.
Lorentz, Pare
River, The, *sels.*
Loring, Frederick Wadsworth
In the Old Churchyard at Fredericksburg.
Lorr, Katharine Auchincloss
Beekeeper's Dream, The.
Peking Man, Raining.
Lorraine, Lilith
If These Endure.
Let Dreamers Wake.
Without Regret.
"Lothrop, Amy." *See* **Warner, Anna Bartlett**
Lott, Clarinda Harriss
Living in the Present.
Lougée, David
Sestina for Cynthia, A.
Louis, Adrian C.
Captivity Narrative, September 1981.
Elegy for the Forgotten Oldsmobile.
Hemingway Syndrome, The.
Indian Education.
Walker River Night, The.
Louis, Louise
Wounded, The.
Lourie, Dick
Ann's House.
Dream about Junior High School in America, The.
Getting a Poem in the Rain.
Gift, The.
Pearl Harbor Day 1970.
September 30.
Sharks.
Stumbling.
Telegram.
Thinking of You.
Louthan, Robert
Elegy for My Father.
Louw, N. P. van Wyk
Armed Vision.
At Dawn the Light Will Come.
Ballad of the Drinker in His Pub.
From the Ballad of Evil.
Gods Are Mighty, The.
Little Chisel, The.
Oh the Inconstant.
Louÿs, Pierre
Absence.
Agonizing Memory, The.
Bilitis.
Breasts of Mnasidice, The.
Chansons de Bilitis, *sels.*
Complaisant Friend, The.
Desire.
Despairing Embrace, The.
Endearments.
Kiss, The.
Little House, The.
Love.
Meeting, The.
Penumbra.
Remorse.
Songs of Bilitis, The, *sels.*
Love, Adelaide
Alchemy.
No Sweeter Thing.
Poet's Prayer.
Walk Slowly.
Love, George
Noonday April Sun, The.
Love, John, Jr.
Barber, Spare Those Hairs.
Lovejoy, George Newell
Easter Carol: "O Earth! throughout thy borders."
Lovelace, Richard
A la Bourbon.
Advice to My Best Brother, Colonel Francis Lovelace.
Anniversary, An.
Anniversary on the Hymeneals of My Noble Kinsman, Thomas Stanley, Esquire, An.
Another ("As I behold a winters evening air").
Another ("The Centaur, Syren, I foregoe").
Ant, The.
Apostasy of One and But One Lady, The.
Black Patch on Lucasta's Face, A.
Calling Lucasta from Her Retirement.
Cupid Far Gone.
Duel, The.
Elinda's Glove.
Falcon, The.
Fly about a Glass of Burnt Claret, A.
Fly Caught in a Cobweb, A.
Fool much bit by fleas put out the light, A.
Grasshopper, The.
Gratiana Dancing [*or* Dauncing] and Singing.
In Allusion to the French Song.
La Bella Bona Roba.
Lady A. L., My Asylum in a Great Extremity, The.
Lady with a Falcon on Her Fist, A.
Loose Saraband, A.
Love Enthroned.
Love Made in the First Age: To Chloris.
Lucasta Laughing.
Lucasta's Fan, with a Looking-Glass in It.
Lucasta's World.
Mock Charon, A.
Mock Song, A.
Night.
Orpheus to Beasts.
Orpheus to Woods.
Painture.
Rose, The.
Scrutiny [*or* Scrutinie], The.
Snail, The.
Song: To Lucasta, Going to the Wars.
Song: "Why should you swear I am forsworn."
Strive Not, Vain Lover, to Be Fine.
To a Lady That Desired Me I Would Bear My Part with Her in a Song.
To Althea, from Prison.
To Amarantha, That She Would Dishevel[l] Her Hair[e].
To Dr. F. B. on His Book of Chess.
To Fletcher Reviv'd.
To Lucasta ("Ah, Lucasta, why so bright").
To Lucasta ("I laugh and I sing but cannot tell").
To Lucasta, from Prison.
To Lucasta: Her Reserved Looks.
To Lucasta, [on] Going beyond the Seas.
To Lucasta, [on] Going to the Wars [*or* Warres].
To Lucasta: The Rose.
To My Noble Kinsman, Thomas Stanley, Esquire, on His Lyric Poems Composed by Master John Gamble.
To My Truly Valiant, Learned Friend, Who in His Book Resolved the Art Gladiatory into the Mathematics.
To My Worthy Friend Master Peter Lely.
Upon the Curtain of Lucasta's Picture It Was Thus Wrought.
Valiant Love.
Vintage to the Dungeon, The.
Loveman, Robert
April Rain.
Hobson and His Men.
Rain Song.
Lover, Samuel
Angel's Whisper, The.
Ask and Have.
Barney O'Hea.
Birth of Saint Patrick, The.
Father Land and Mother Tongue.
Father Molloy.
Handy Andy, *sel.*
Low-backed Car, The.
Paddy O'Rafther.
Quaker's Meeting, The.
Rory O'More; or, Good Omens.
St. Kevin, *at.*
War Ship of Peace, The.
What Will You Do, Love?
Widow Machree.
Lovett, Robert
Forbidden Drink.
Loving, Pierre
Black Horse Rider, The.
Low, Benjamin Robbins Curtis
Due North.
Little Boy to the Locomotive, The.
Locomotive to the Little Boy, The.
To-Day.

White Violets.
Low, Patricia
First Day of the Hunting Moon, The.
Wet Weather.
Low, Samuel
To a Segar.
Lowbury, Edward
In the Old Jewish Cemetery, Prague, 1970.
Monster, The.
Roc, The.
Swan.
Tree of Knowledge.
Lowe, Robert, Viscount Sherbrooke
Songs of the Squatters.
Lowell, Amy
Carrefour.
Chinoiseries.
City of Falling Leaves, The.
Convalescence.
Crowned.
Cyclists, The.
Decade, A.
Desolation.
Dreams in War Time, *sel.*
Epitaph on a Young Poet Who Died before Having Achieved Success.
Fisherman's Wife, The.
Flute-Priest Song for Rain, *sel.*
Fragment: "What is poetry? Is it a mosaic."
Free Fantasia on Japanese Themes.
Fringed Gentians.
From One Who Stays.
Grievance.
Grotesque.
Katydids.
Lady, A.
Lilacs.
Little Ivory Figures Pulled with String.
Madonna of the Evening Flowers.
Meeting-House Hill.
Music.
Night Clouds.
On Looking at a Copy of Alice Meynell's Poems.
Painted Ceiling, The.
Patterns.
Poet, The.
Proportion.
Reaping.
Sea Shell.
Sisters, The.
Solitaire.
Sprig of Rosemary, A.
Streets.
Taxi, The.
Texas.
Thorn Piece.
To a Friend.
Venus Transiens.
Wind and Silver.
Year Passes, A.
Lowell, James Russell
After the Burial.
Aladdin.
America's Gospel.
Auf Wiedersehen.
Auspex.
Autograph, An.
Bibliolaters, *sel.*
Biglow Papers, The, *sels.*
Birthday Verses Written in a Child's Album.
Boss, The.
Brook in Winter, The.
Bryant.
Candidate's Letter, The.
Christmas Carol, A: " 'What means this glory round our feet.' "
Columbus, *sel.*
Commemoration Ode, The.
Commitment.
Cooper.
Courtin', The.
Day in June, A.
Debate in the Sennit, The.
Emerson.
Ez fer War.
Fable for Critics, A, *sels.*
Fatherland, The.
First Snowfall [*or* Snow-Fall], The.
Fitz Adam's Story.
Flawless His Heart.
Fountain, The.
God Is Not Dumb.
Great Virginian, The.
Hawthorne.
Hear now this fairy legend of old Greece.
Hebe.
Heritage, The.
His Throne Is with the Outcast.
Hob Gobbling's Song.
Holmes.
Imperial Man.
In a Copy of Omar Khayyám.
In an Album.
In the Twilight.
International Copyright.
Irving.
James Fenimore Cooper.
Jonathan to John.
June ("Over his keys the musing organist").
June ("What is so rare as a day in June?").
June Weather.
Letter, A ("That kind o'sogerin' ain't a mite like our October trainin' ").
Letter, A ("Thrash away, you'll hev to rattle").
Lincoln.
Lowell.
Misconception, A.
Mr. Hosea Biglow to the Editor of the Atlantic Monthly.
My Love.
Not Only around Our Infancy.
Now Is the High-Tide of the Year.
Ode Recited at the Harvard Commemoration, *sel.*
On Board the '76.
On Freedom.
On Himself.
On Receiving a Copy of Mr. Austin Dobson's "Old World Idylls."
Once to Every Man and Nation.
Oriental Apologue, An.
Origin of Didactic Poetry, The.
Our Fathers Fought for Liberty.
Our Martyr-Chief.
Ours, and All Men's.
Palinode.
Parable, A, *sel.*
Poe and Longfellow.
Present Crisis, The.
Recall, The.
Rev. Homer Wilbur's "Festina Lente."
Rhoecus.
Search, The.
She Came and Went.
Shepherd of King Admetus, The.
Singing Leaves, The.
Sir Launfal and the Leper.
Sixty-eighth Birthday.
Slaves.
Spring.
Stanza on Freedom, A.
Stanzas on Freedom.
Stealing.
Sunthin' in the Pastoral Line.
Tempora Mutantur.
'Tis Sorrow Builds the Shining Ladder Up.
To His Countrymen.
To the Dandelion.
Under the Old Elm, *sels.*
Verses Intended to Go with a Posset Dish to My Dear Little Goddaughter, 1882.
Vision of Sir Launfal, The.
Washers of the Shroud, The.
Washington.
We Will Speak Out.
What Is So Rare as a Day in June?
What Mr. Robinson Thinks.
Whittier.
Whom We Revere.
Winter Morning, A.
Without and Within.
Work.
Yussouf.
Lowell, Maria White
Morning-Glory, The.
Song: "O Bird, thou dartest to the sun."
Lowell, Robert (1917–77)
After the Surprising Conversions.
Alfred Corning Clark.
As a Plane Tree by the Water.
At the Altar.
At the Indian Killer's Grave.
Between the Porch and the Altar.
Beyond the Alps.
Black Spring.
Bomber, The ("Bomber climb out on the roof").
Caligula.
Central Park.
Charles the Fifth and the Peasant.
Children of Light.
Child's Song.
Christmas Eve under Hooker's Statue.
Coastguard House, The.
Colloquy in Black Rock.
Commander Lowell.
Dead in Europe, The.
Death from Cancer.
Death of the Sheriff, The.
Dolphin.
Drunken Fisherman, The.
Epilogue: "Those blessèd structures, plot and rhyme."
Exile's Return, The.
Eye and Tooth.
Ezra Pound.
Fall 1961.
Falling Asleep over the Aeneid.
Fat Man in the Mirror, The.
Father.
For George Santayana.
For John Berryman, I.
For Sale.
For the Union Dead.
Ford Madox Ford.
Fourth of July in Maine.
Ghost, The.
Grandparents.
Harriet.
Her Dead Brother.
History.
Holy Innocents, The.
Home after Three Months Away.
Identification in Belfast (I.R.A. Bombing).
In Memory of Arthur Winslow.
In the Cage.
July in Washington.
Katherine's Dream.
Last Things, Black Pines at 4 a.m.
Lesson, The.
Long Summer, *sel.*
Mad Negro Soldier Confined at Munich, A.
Magnolia's Shadow, The.
Man and Wife.
March 1, The.
March 2, The.
Marriage, *sels.*
Mary Winslow.
Memories of West Street and Lepke.
Mexico, *sel.*
Middle Age.
Mr. Edwards and the Spider.
Mother Marie Therese.
Mouth of the Hudson, The.
My Last Afternoon with Uncle Devereux Winslow.

Near the Ocean.
New Year's Day.
News from Mount Amiata.
Night Sweat.
1930's.
Ninth Month.
Noli Me Tangere.
North Sea Undertaker's Complaint, The.
October and November.
Old Flame, The.
On the Eve of the Feast of the Immaculate Conception: 1942.
Opposite House, The.
Overhanging Cloud.
Picture, The.
Poet at Seven, The.
Public Garden, The.
Quaker Graveyard in Nantucket, The.
Reading Myself.
Robert Frost.
Robert Sheridan Lowell.
Robespierre and Mozart as Stage.
Sailing Home from Rapallo.
Saint-Just 1767–93 ("Saint-Just: his name seems stolen from the Missal").
Salem.
September.
Sheridan.
Skunk Hour.
Slough of Despond, The.
Soft Wood.
Sparrow Hills.
Sylvia.
T. S. Eliot.
This Golden Summer.
Those before Us.
To Delmore Schwartz.
"To Speak of Woe That Is in Marriage."
Turtle.
Waking Early Sunday Morning.
Waking in the Blue.
Water.
Where the Rainbow Ends.
Withdrawal, The.
Words for Hart Crane.
Lowell, Robert Traill Spence (1816–91)
After-Comers, The.
Brave Old Ship, the *Orient,* The.
Relief of Lucknow, The.
Lowenfels, Walter
Creed.
Lowenstein, Robert
Peek-a-Boo.
Lowenstein, Tom
Horizon without Landscape.
Nausicaa with Some Attendants.
Noah in New England.
Lowery, Mike
Nam.
Smell of Old Newspapers Is Always Stronger after Sleeping in the Sun, The.
Stroke.
Lowey, Mark
On Living with Children for a Prolonged Time.
Lowry, Betty
Beasts of Boston, The.
Lowry, Henry Dawson
Holiday.
Spring Will Come, The.
Lowry, Malcolm
After Publication of Under the Volcano.
Cain Shall Not Slay Abel Today on Our Good Ground.
Christ Walks in This Infernal District Too.
Delirium in Vera Cruz.
Drunkards, The.
For *Under the Volcano.*
He Liked the Dead.
In Memoriam; Ingvald Bjorndal and His Comrade.
Lighthouse Invites the Storm, The.
Lupus in Fabula.
Salmon Drowns Eagle.
Sestina in a Cantina.
Xochitepec.
Lowry, Robert
Beautiful River, *with music.*
How Can I Keep from Singing?
Lowther, Pat
Last Letter to Pablo.
Stone Diary, A.
Loy, Mina
Apology of Genius.
Der Blinde Junge.
Love Songs.
Lunar Baedeker.
Omen of Victory
Loyd, Marianne
Llanberis Summer.
Lo Yin
Book-burning Pit, The.
Lubke, Bernice W.
All-sufficient Christ, The.
Lucan (Marcus Annaeus Lucanus)
Cato's Address to His Troops in Lybia.
Coracle, The.
Pharsalia, *sels.*
Pompey and Cornelia.
Portents, The.
Lucas, Alice
Prayer before Sleep.
Lucas, Daniel Bedinger
In the Land Where We Were Dreaming.
Lucas, Edward Verrall
Clay.
Friends.
Mr. Coggs.
Pedestrian's Plaint, The.
Lucas, Henry N.
But, Still, He.
Lucas, St. John
Curate Thinks You Have No Soul, The.
Pain.
Luce, Morton
Thysia, *sels.*
Luciano, Felipe
You're Nothing but a Spanish Colored Kid.
Lucianus
Artificial Beauty.
Lucie-Smith, Edward
At the Roman Baths, Bath.
Caravaggio Dying, Porto Ercole, July 1610, Aged 36, *sel.*
Dodo, The.
Fault, The.
Giant Tortoise, The.
Ladybirds, The.
Lesson, The.
Meeting Myself.
On Looking at Stubb's Anatomy of the Horse.
Parrot, The.
Poet in Winter.
Rabbit Cry.
Lucilius [*or* Lucillius]
Advice to a Prizefighter.
Boxer Loses Face and Fortune.
First in the Pentathlon.
Lean Gaius, who was thinner than a straw.
Monument to a Boxer.
On an Old Woman.
Retired Boxer, The.
Treasure.
Valentine for a Lady, A.
Lucina, Sister Mary
Rain.
Luckey, Eunice W.
Babies of the Pioneers.
Lucretius (Titus Lucretius Carus)
Address to Venus.
Against the Fear of Death.
Beyond Religion.
Child Is like a Sailor Cast Up by the Sea, The.
Concerning the Nature of Love.
De Rerum Natura (On the Nature of Things), *sels.*
Fear of Death, The.
Nature of Love, The.
No Single Thing Abides.
Suave Mari Magno.
What Has This Bugbear Death.
Lucus, Lawrence A.
Another Meeting.
Lucy, Sean
Longshore Intellectual.
Senior Members.
Supervising Examinations.
Lüders, Charles Henry
Corsage Bouquet, A.
Four Winds, The.
Haunts of the Halcyon, The.
Heart of Oak.
Mountebanks, The.
Old Thought, An.
Ludlow, Fitz Hugh
Socrates Snooks.
Too Late.
Ludlum, William
Business Man's Prayer, A.
Radio Religion, The.
Ludvigson, Susan Bartels
Child's Dream, The.
Man Arrested in Hacking Death Tells Police He Mistook Mother-in-Law for Raccoon.
Motherhood.
On Learning That Certain Peat Bogs Contain Perfectly Preserved Bodies.
Widow, The.
Luff, W.
I Buried the Year.
Luhrmann, Tom
Beyond Belief.
Lui Chi
Poet Thinks, A.
Lulham, Habberton
Nested.
Lum, Wing Tek
At a Chinaman's Grave.
Chinatown Games.
Poet Imagines His Grandfather's Thoughts on the Day He Died, The.
To the Old Masters.
Translations.
Lummis, Charles Fletcher
Cannibalee; a Po'em of Passion.
John Charles Frémont.
Poe-'em of Passion, A.
Sidewinder, The.
Lumumba, Patrice Emery
Dawn in the Heart of Africa.
Lunt, George
Requiem: "Breathe, trumpets, breathe."
Lu Yu
Herd Boy, The.
Wild Flower Man, The.
Luria, Isaac
Sabbath of Rest, A.
Lushington, Franklin
No More Words.
Luther, Martin
All Hail, Thou Noble Guest.
Ane Sang of the Birth of Christ, with the Tune of Baw Lula Low.
Away in a Manger, *at.*
Hymn: "Mighty fortress is our God, A."
Mighty Fortress Is Our God, A.
Paraphrase of Luther's Hymn.
Luton, Mildred
Hossolalia.
Pliny Jane.
Luttinger, Abigail
Palace for Teeth, The.
Luttrell, Henry
Advice to Julia, *sels.*
Dress.
Honeymoon, The.

Lovers and Friends.
O death, thy certainty is such.
On a Man Run Over by an Omnibus.
Peace, The.
Lutz, Gertrude May
Cat of Many Years.
Prisoner of War.
Song for a New Generation.
Lux, Thomas
Barn Fire.
Farmers.
Flying Noises.
Graveyard by the Sea.
History and Abstraction.
If You See This Man.
Lament City.
Man Asleep in the Desert.
Midnight Tennis Match, The.
My Grandmother's Funeral.
Solo Native.
There Were Some Summers.
This Is a Poem for the Fathers and for Michael Ryan.
Luzzatto, Isaac
Death, Thou Hast Seized Me.
Luzzatto, Moses Hayyim, of Padua
Chorus: "All ye that handle harp and viol."
Unto the Upright Praise, *sel.*
Lyall, Sir Alfred Comyn
Badminton.
Hindu Ascetic, The.
Meditations of a Hindu Prince.
Studies at Delhi, *sels.*
Lydgate, John
Against Women's Fashions.
Balade Simple.
Boy Serving at Table, The.
Child Jesus to Mary the Rose, The.
Court of Sapience, *sel.*
Dance, The.
Dance of Death, The, *sel.*
Devotions of the Fowls, *sel.*
Duplicity of Women, The.
Fall of Princes, The, *sel.*
Froward Maymond ("A froward knave plainly to descrive").
Henry before Agincourt: October 25, 1415.
Lament: "Farewell Mercy, farewell thy piteous grace."
Like a Midsummer Rose.
Lover's New Year's Gift, A.
To the Virgin.
Transient as a Rose.
Vox Ultima Crucis.
Lyle, K. Curtis
Lacrimas or There Is a Need to Scream.
Sometimes I Go to Camarillo and Sit in the Lounge.
Songs for the Cisco Kid; or, Singing: Song # 2.
Songs for the Cisco Kid; or, Singing for the Face.
Terra Cotta.
Lyly, John
Alexander and Campaspe,*sels.*
Apelles' Song.
Apollo's Song.
Campaspe.
Cards and Kisses.
Cupid and Campaspe.
Cupid's Indictment.
Daphne.
Endymion, *sel.*
Fairy Song, A.
Fools in Love's College.
Galathea, *sel.*
Midas, *sels.*
Mother Bombie, *sel.*
O Cupid! Monarch over Kings.
Oh, For a Bowl of Fat Canary.
Pan's Song.
Sapho and Phao, *sels.*
Serving Men's Song, A.
Song: "It is all one in Venus' wanton school."
Song: "What bird so sings, yet so does wail?"
Song by Fairies.
Song in Making of the Arrows, A.
Song of Accius and Silena.
Song of Apelles.
Song of Apollo.
Song of Daphne to the Lute, A.
Song of Diana's Nymphs, A.
Spring, The.
Spring's Welcome.
Syrinx.
Trico's Song: "What bird so sings, yet so does wail?"
Vulcan's Song.
Lynch, Annette
Bridgework.
Gratitude.
Lynch, Charles
If We Cannot Live as People.
Jam Fa Jamaica.
Memo.
Shade.
Simfunny of Thee Hold Whorl.
Lynch, John W.
Woman Wrapped in Silence, A, *sel.*
Lynch, Stanislaus
Blue Peter.
Lynch, Thomas Toke
Lift Up Your Heads, Rejoice!
Reinforcements.
Thousand Years Have Come, A.
Lynche, Richard
Diella, *sels.*
Love's Despair.
Lynde, Benjamin
Lines Descriptive of Thomson's Island.
Lynskey, Edward C.
No Idle Boast.
Lyon, George Ella
Birth.
Catechisms: Talking with a Four-year-old.
Cousin Ella Goes to Town.
Lyon, Lilian Bowes. *See* **Bowes-Lyon, Lilian**
Lyon, Roger H.
Keep On Praying.
Lyons, Richard
Sisseton Indian Reservation, The.
Lyons, Richard J.
"Titus, Son of Rembrandt: 1665."
Lysaght, Sidney Royse
Deserted Home, A.
First Pathways.
New Horizons.
Secret of the Deeps, The.
Lyte, Henry Francis
Abide with Me.
Hymn: "Abide with me; fast falls the eventide."
Unknown God, The.
Lytle, William Haines
Antony and Cleopatra.
Antony to Cleopatra.
Siege of Chapultepec, The.
Volunteers, The.
Lyttelton, George, Baron Lyttelton
Song: "When Delia on the plain appears."
Tell Me, My Heart, if This Be Love.
To Miss Lucy F
To the Memory of a Lady, *abr.*
Lyttleton, Lucy
Simon the Cyrenean.
Lytton, Edward Robert Bulwer-Lytton, 1st Earl of. *See* **"Meredith, Owen"**
"Lywelyn"
Birds.

M

"M."
On the Frequent Review of the Troops.
"M., B. Q."
Old and the New, The.
"M. B.". *See* **"B., M."**
"M. J.". *See* **"J., M."**
Maas, Willard
Letter to R.
On Reading Gene Derwood's "The Innocent."
Mabuza, Lindiwe
Summer 1970.
McAfee, Thomas
If There Is a Perchance.
Macainsh, Noel
Kangaroo by Nightfall ("The kangaroo by the roadside").
McAleavey, David
At the Scenic Drive-in.
Can-Opener.
Driving; Driven.
Gate.
Starship.
McAllister, Claire
Aeneid.
Daphne.
Dedication, A: "Lucilla, saved from shipwreck on the seas."
July in the Jardin des Plantes.
Mystery.
McAlmon, Robert
For Instance.
MacAlpine, James
To an Irish Blackbird.
McAlpine, R. W.
Two Surprises.
McAlpine, Rachel
On the Train.
Test, The.
Three Poems for Your Eyes.
McAnally, Mary
Our Mother's Body Is the Earth.
Mac an Bhaird, Laoiseach
Civil Irish and Wild Irish.
Man of Experience, A.
Macarthur, Bessie J. B.
Nocht o' Mortal Sicht.
MacArthur, Gloria
Phineas Pratt.
McArthur, Peter
Earthborn.
Sugar Weather.
Macarthy [*or* McCarthy], Harry
Bonnie Blue Flag, The, *with music.*
Macartney, Frederick Thomas Bennett
Desert Claypan.
Early Summer Sea-Tryst.
No Less than Prisoners.
Macaulay, F. E. M.
Women's Marseillaise, The.
Macaulay, Rose
Picnic.
Shadow, The.
Macaulay, Thomas Babington Macaulay, 1st Baron
Armada, The [a Fragment].
Battle of Ivry, The.
Battle of Naseby, The.
Country Clergyman's Trip to Cambridge, The.
Horatius [at the Bridge].
Ivry.
Jacobite's Epitaph, A.
Last Buccaneer, The.
Lays of Ancient Rome, *sels.*
Radical War Song, A.
Sermon in a Churchyard.
McAuley, James Philip
Art of Poetry, An.
At Bungendore.
Because.
Canticle.
Convalescence.
In the Huon Valley.
Jesus.
Late Winter.
Letter to John Dryden, A, *sel.*
Merry-go-round.
New Guinea.

Pietà.
Winter Drive.
McAuley, James Philip *and* **Harold Stewart.** *See* **"Malley, Ern"**
MacBeth [*or* Macbeth], George
Ash.
Bats.
Bedtime Story.
Compasses, The.
Drawer, The.
Five-Minute Orlando MacBeth, The.
Killing, The.
Land-Mine, The.
Marshall.
Miner's Helmet, The.
Mother Superior.
Orlando Commercial, The.
Political Orlando, The.
Red Herring, The.
Return, The.
Scissor-Man.
Snowdrops.
Spider's Nest, The.
Star, A.
Suicides, The.
Wasps' Nest, The.
When I Am Dead.
McBride, Mekeel
Aubade: "She wakes long before he does. A fierce shock."
Blessing, A.
Over the Phone.
Will to Live, The.
McBurney, William B. ("Carroll Malone")
Croppy Boy, The.
McCabe, Angela
Back.
Blind Adolphus.
Bloom Street.
From Lois in London.
Inside History.
McCabe, Victoria
Reply.
McCabe, William Gordon
Christmas Night of '62.
Dreaming in the Trenches.
MacCaig, Norman
Above Inverkirkaig.
Aspects.
Basking Shark.
Beach Talk.
Betweens.
Birds All Singing.
By Achmelvich Bridge.
Byre.
Celtic Cross.
Close-ups of Summer.
Cock before Dawn.
Drowned, The.
Edinburgh Spring.
Ego.
Family.
Feeding Ducks.
Fetching Cows.
Flooded Mind.
Frogs.
Golden Calf.
Gone Are the Days.
High Up on Suilven.
In My Mind.
Incident.
Innocence.
Milne's Bar.
Moment Musical in Assynt.
Moorings.
Movements.
No Accident.
November Night, Edinburgh.
Nude in a Fountain.
Old Maps and New.
One of the Many Days.
Orgy.
Poem: "There is a wailing baby under every stone."
Ringed Plover by a Water's Edge.
Sheep Dipping.
Sleet.
Space Fiction.
Spate in Winter Midnight.
Starlings.
Street Preacher.
Summer Farm.
Too Bright a Day.
Two Musics.
Tyrant Apple Is Eaten, The.
Unposted Birthday Card.
Water Tap.
Wild Oats.
You within Love.
McCall, James Edward
New Negro, The.
McCann, John E.
Utmost in Friendship, The.
McCann, Michael Joseph
O'Donnell Aboo.
McCann, Rebecca
Humane Thought.
McCann, Richard
Fat Boy's Dream, The.
McCarriston, Linda
Spring.
McCarroll, James
Grey Linnet, The.
McCarthy, Denis Aloysius
Ah, Sweet Is Tipperary.
Land Where Hate Should Die, The.
Tailor That Came from Mayo, The.
MacCarthy, Denis Florence
Dead Tribune, The.
Foray of Con O'Donnell A.D. 1495, The, *sel.*
Irish Wolf-Hound, The.
Lament: "Youth's bright palace."
Spring Flowers from Ireland.
Summer Longings.
MacCarthy, Donal, 1st Earl Clancarty
Body's Speech, The.
MacCarthy, Ethna
Ghosts.
Insomnia.
Viaticum.
McCarthy, Eugene
Dogs of Santiago.
Kilroy.
Tamarack.
M'Carthy, Justin Huntly
Ballad of Dead Ladies, A.
McCartney, Mabel E.
Refuge.
MacCathmhaoil, Seosamh. *See* **Campbell, Joseph**
MacCawell, Hugh
Christmas Night.
McClane, Kenneth A.
Judge, The.
McClatchy, J. D.
Late Autumn Walk.
Pleasure of Ruins, The.
Winter without Snow, A.
McClaurin, Irma
I, Woman.
Mask, The.
To a Gone Era.
McClellan, George Marion
Butterfly in Church, A.
Dogwood Blossoms.
Feet of Judas, The.
Hills of Sewanee, The.
McClintock, Charles W.
Everybody Works but Father.
McCloskey, Mark
Lights Go On, The.
Too Dark.
McClure, John
Carol: "Month can never forget the year, The."
Carol Naïve.
Chanson Naïve.
Man to Man.
McClure, Michael
Aelf-Scin, The.
Baja—Outside Mexicali.
Breech, The.
Canticle.
Flowers of Politics, The, I ("This is the huge dream of us that we are heroes").
Flowers of Politics, The, II ("Only what is heroic and courageous moves our blood").
For Artaud.
From the Window of the Beverly Wilshire Hotel.
Hymn to St. Geryon, *sel.*
List, The.
Mad Sonnet 1.
May Morn.
Moiré.
Ode for Soft Voice.
Ode to Joy.
Oh Bright Oh Black Singbeast Lovebeast Catkin Sleek.
Oh Ease Oh Body-Strain Oh Love Oh Ease Me Not! Wound-Bore.
Peyote Poem.
Rant Block.
Rug, The.
With Tendrils of Poems.
MacColl, Dugald Sutherland
Ballade of Andrew Lang.
MacColl, Ewan
Ballad of Ho Chi Minh.
Dove, The.
First Time Ever I Saw Your Face, The.
Freeborn Man.
Go Down You Murderers.
MacColl, Ewan *and* Peggy Seeger
Ballad of Springhill (The Springhill Mine Disaster).
MacColmain, Rumann
Song of the Sea, *at.*
McCombs, Judith
Dictionary Is an *His*torian, The: A Found Political Poem.
Packing In with a Man.
MacConglinne
Vision of MacConglinne, The.
Vision That Appeared to Me, A.
Wheatlet Son of Milklet.
McCord, David
Afreet ("*Afreet* I am afraid of").
Any Day Now.
Ascot Waistcoat.
At the Garden Gate.
Axolotl, The.
Baccalaureate.
Big Chief Wotapotami.
Blessed Lord, What It Is to Be Young.
Books Fall Open.
Christmas Package, A, *sels.*
Cities and Science.
Cocoon.
Come Christmas.
Convalescence, I-VIII.
Conversation.
Cow has a cud, The.
Crickets.
Crows.
Epitaph on a Waiter.
Euterpe; a Symmetric ("Euterpe, you must think us common queer").
Every Time I Climb a Tree.
Father and I in the Woods.
Fisherman, The.
Fred.
Gloss.
Go Fly a Saucer.
Grasshopper, The.
Hex on the Mexican X, A.
History of Education.
Joe.

Kite.
Lacquer Liquor Locker, The.
Laundromat.
Lessons in Limericks, *sels.*
Mantis.
Mr. Bidery's Spidery Garden.
Mr. Macklin's Jack O'Lantern ("Mr. Macklin takes his knife").
Monday morning back to school.
New Chitons for Old Gods, *sel.*
Newt, The.
Notice.
On a Waiter.
Our Mr. Toad.
Perambulator Poems, I-VII.
Pickety fence, The.
Plane Geometer.
Progress.
Rainbow, The.
Reservation.
Singular Indeed.
Song of the Train.
Sportif.
Sportsman, The.
Thin ice/ Free advice.
This is my rock.
Tiger Lily.
Tiggady Rue.
To a Certain Most Certainly Certain Critic.
To Walk in Warm Rain.
Walnut Tree, The.
Watching the Moon.
Weather Words.
Where Is My Butterfly Net?
Yellow.

McCord, Howard
Bear That Came to the Wedding, The.
In Iceland.
Longjaunes His Periplus, *sel.*
My Cow.

McCormick, Virginia Taylor
To One Who Died in Autumn.
Twilight.

McCormick, Washington Jay
In Montana.
Rigger, The.

McCoy, Jane
View from the Window.

McCoy, Samuel
Thompson Street.

McCracken, Kathleen
I Have Seen.

McCrae, George Gordon
Mamba the Bright-eyed, *sel.*

McCrae, Hugh Raymond
Ambuscade.
Camden Magpie.
Colombine.
Enigma.
Evening.
I Blow My Pipes.
Joan of Arc.
June Morning.
Mad Marjory.
Mouse, The.
Muse-haunted.
Song of the Rain.
Uncouth Knight, The.
Winds.

McCrae, John
Anxious Dead, The.
Harvest of the Sea, The.
In Flanders Fields.
Song of the Derelict, The.

McCreery, John Luckey
There Is No Death.

McCuaig, Ronald
Au Tombeau de Mon Père.
L'Après Midi d'une Fille aux Cheveux de Lin.
Love Me and Never Leave Me.
Music in the Air.
Recitative.

McCulloch, Margaret
Aftermath.

McCullough, Ken
Voices in the Winter.

McCully, Laura E.
Canoe Song at Twilight.

McCurdy, Harold
August, at an Upstairs Window.
Petition.

MacDermott, Martin
Girl of the Red Mouth.

"MacDiarmid, Hugh" (Christopher Murray Grieve)
After Two Thousand Years.
Another Epitaph on an Army of Mercenaries.
Antenora.
At My Father's Grave.
Bagpipe Music.
Bonnie Broukit Bairn, The.
Bracken Hills in Autumn.
British Leftish Poetry, 1930–40.
By Wauchopeside.
Cattle Show.
Cloudburst and Soaring Moon.
Cophetua.
Crowdieknowe.
Crystals like Blood.
Day of the Crucifixion, The.
De Profundis.
Dead Liebknecht, The.
Deep-Sea Fishing.
Drunk Man Looks at the Thistle, A, *sel.*
Eemis-Stane, The.
Empty Vessel.
Facing the Chair.
Fleggit Bride, The.
Glass of Pure Water, The, *sel.*
Glen of Silence, The.
Great Wheel, The.
Harry Semen.
I Heard Christ Sing.
In the Children's Hospital.
In the Fall, *sel.*
In the Hedgeback.
In the Pantry.
Innumerable Christ, The.
Kind of Poetry I Want, The, *sels.*
Lament for the Great Music, *sel.*
Light of Life, The.
Love.
Love-sick Lass, The.
Man in the Moon, The.
Milk-Wort and Bog-Cotton.
Moonlight among the Pines.
Munestruck.
O Ease My Spirit.
O Jesu Parvule ("His mither sings to the bairnie Christ").
O Wha's the Bride?
Octopus, The.
Old Wife in High Spirits.
On the Ocean Floor.
On the Oxford Book of Victorian Verse.
Parley of Beasts.
Parrot Cry, The.
Perfect.
Prayer for a Second Flood, A.
Reflections in a Slum.
Robber, The.
Royal Stag, The.
Sauchs in the Reuch Heuch Hauch, The.
Scotland Small?
Scunner.
Second Hymn to Lenin.
Sic Transit Gloria Scotia.
Skeleton of the Future, The.
Spanish War, The.
Storm-Cock's Song, The.
To a Sea Eagle.
To Nearly Everybody in Europe To-Day.
Two Parents, The.
Under the Greenwood Tree ("A sodger laddie's socht a hoose").
Up to Date.
Water Music.
Watergaw, The.
Wheesht, Wheesht.
With a Lifting of the Head.
With the Herring Fishers.

MacDonagh, Donagh
Charles Donnelly, *sel.*
Childhood.
Dublin Made Me.
Galway.
Going to Mass Last Sunday.
Hungry Grass, The.
Invitation, The.
Just an Old Sweet Song.
Love's Language.
On the Bridge of Athlone; a Prophecy.
Prothalamium.
Revel, A.
Veterans, The.
Warning to Conquerors, A.
Wind Blows, The.

MacDonagh, Thomas
In Paris.
John-John.
Man Upright, The.
Night Hunt, The.
Of a Poet Patriot.
On a Poet Patriot.
Song: "Love is cruel, Love is sweet."
Wishes for My Son.

Macdonald, Agnes Foley
Eternal.

MacDonald, Alexander (Alasdair MacMhaighstir Alasdair)
Birlinn Chlann-Raghnaill.

Macdonald, Andrew
Lover's Leap, The; a Tale.

McDonald, Barry
Ingestion.

MacDonald, Cynthia
Accomplishments.
Apartments on First Avenue.
Celebrating the Freak.
Dr. Dimity Is Forced to Complain.
Dr. Dimity Lectures on Unusual Cases.
Instruction from Bly.
Lady Pitcher, The.
Late Mother, The.
Objets d'Art.
Stained Glass Man, The.

MacDonald, Elizabeth Roberts
Summons, The.

Macdonald, George
Adela Cathcart, *sel.*
Approaches.
At the Back of the North Wind, *sel.*
Baby, The.
Baby-Sermon, A.
Be with Me, Lord.
Carpenter, The.
Christmas Prayer, A.
Come Down.
Diary of an Old Soul, *sels.*
Dorcas.
Earl o' Quarterdeck, The.
Epigram: "Here lie I, Martin Elginbrodde," *at.*
Epitaph: "Here lie I, Martin Elginbrodde," *at.*
Evening Hymn, *sel.*
Hurt of Love, The.
Little White Lily.
Lost and Found.
Mammon Marriage.
My Morning Song.
Obedience.
Paul Faber, Surgeon, *sel.*
Prayer, A: "When I look back upon my life nigh spent."
Preacher's Prayer, The.
Shadows, The.
Shall the Dead Praise Thee?
Sheep and the Goat, The.

Sir Lark and King Sun; a Parable.
Song: "Where did you come from, baby dear?"
Song: "Why do the houses stand."
Sonnet: "This infant world has taken long to make."
Sweet Peril.
That Holy Thing.
That Thou Art Nowhere to Be Found.
This Day Be with Me.
To My God.
What Christ Said.
Where Did You Come From?
Wind and the Moon, The.
Within and Without, *sels.*

MacDonald, Goodridge
Elegy, Montreal Morgue.
Sailor, The.

MacDonald, James Edward Hervey
Gallows and Cross.
Hanging, The.
Kitchen Window.

MacDonald, John. *See* **Lom, Iain**

McDonald, L. A.
It's You.

MacDonald, Marie Bruckman
'Skeeter and Peter, The.

Macdonald, Mary
Alligator, The.

McDonald, Nan
Hatters, The.
White Eagle, The.

Macdonald, Nina
Sing a Song of War-Time.

McDonald, Roger
Bachelor Farmer.
Components.
Flights.
Hollow Thesaurus, The.
Two Summers in Moravia.

MacDonald, Susan
Children, The.

McDonald, Walter
On Teaching David to Shoot.
With Cindy at Vallecito.

MacDonald, Wilson Pugsley
Armand Dussault.
Baby Show, De.
Exit.
In a Wood Clearing.
In the Far Years.
John Graydon.
June.
Moonlight on Lake Sydenham.
Pierre of Timagami in New York.
Song of the Ski, The.
Teemothy Hatch.
Toll-Gate Man, The.

MacDonnell, James Francis Carlin. *See* **Carlin, Francis**

MacDonogh, Patrick
Be Still as You Are Beautiful.
Dodona's Oaks Were Still.
Escape to Love, *sel.*
Flowering Currant.
No Mean City.
Now the Holy Lamp of Love.
River, The.
She Walked Unaware.
Snare, The.
Song: "She spoke to me gently with words of sweet meaning."
Song for a Proud Relation.
Soon with the Lilac Fades Another Spring.
This Morning I Wakened among Loud Cries of Seagulls.
Waking.
Widow of Drynam, The.

MacDonough, Glen
Toyland, *with music.*

MacDonough, Patrick
Bring Home the Poet.
Via Longa.

McDougal, Violet
Sea Wolf, The.

Macdougall, Arthur R., Jr.
Bitter Question.
Captain of the Years.
It Isn't Far to Bethlehem.
We Need a King.

McDougall, Jean
Quarrel.

McDougall, Joseph Easton
New House, The.

MacDuff, Edward
Ed and Sid and Bernard.

McDuffee, Franklin
Hakluyt Unpurchased.

Mace, Frances Laughton
Alcyone.
Only Waiting.
Succession, The.

McElhaney, Georgia Lee
Conquistador.
Dervish.
Effigy.

McElroy, Colleen J.
Caledonia.
Looking for a Country under Its Original Name.
Ruth.
Woman's Song, A.

McElroy, David
Before Breakup on the Chena outside Fairbanks.
Dragging in Winter.
Making It Simple December 8, 1969.
Nocturn at the Institute.
Ode to a Dead Dodge.
Report from the Correspondent They Fired.
Spawning in Northern Minnesota.

MacEwen, Gwendolyn
Arcanum One.
Breakfast for Barbarians, A.
Caravan, The.
Dark Pines under Water.
Discovery, The.
Manzini; Escape Artist.
T. E. Lawrence Poems, The, *sels.*
There Is No Place to Hide.
Thing Is Violent, The.
Void, The.

McFadden, David
Art's Variety.
Day of the Pancreas, The.
Elephant.
External Element, The.
Fiddlehead, The.
Form of Passion, A.
House Plants.
It's a Different Story When You're Going into the Wind.
Kicking from Centre Field.
Lennox Island.
Pop.
Upon Looking at a Book of Astrology.
We Love You the Way You Are.

McFadden, Roy
Address to an Absolute.
Aged Writer, An.
Elegy: "Out on the roads of sky the moon stands poised."
Epithalamium: "So you are married, girl. It makes me sad."
Independence.
Mihailovich.
Orator, The.
Saint Francis and the Birds.
Virgin Country.
White Bird, The.
William Blake Sees God.

McFarland, Ron
Frost Warning.

McFatter, Janet Reed
Cow.
Drive, The.
Go Home.
Indian Camp.
Moving.
Sinkholes.

MacFayden, H. R.
Lone Wild Fowl, The, *with music.*

McFee, Michael
Buster Keaton.
Easter Monday.

Macfie, Ronald Campbell
In Memoriam: John Davidson.

McGaffey, Ernest
As the Day Breaks.
California Idyl, A.
Geronimo.
I Fear No Power a Woman Wields.
Little Big Horn.
Mark.
Rise, A.

McGaffin, Audrey
At Cambridge.
Avalon.
Cemetery Is, The.
Inertia.
Invalid.
Poor Relation, A.

McGahey, Jeanne
Oregon Winter.

McGarvey, Margaret
D-Dawn.

McGaugh, Lawrence
Glimpses #xii, *sel.*
To Children.
Two Mornings.
Young Training.

McGavin, Stewart
Kythans.

McGee, Clyde
Gratitude.
Mary at the Cross.

McGee, Shelagh
Wanted—a Witch's Cat.

McGee, Thomas D'Arcy
Celtic Cross, The.
Celts, The.
Irish Wife, The.
Jacques Cartier.
Man of the North Countrie, The.

McGeorge, Alice Sutton
Autumn's Fete.

McGiffert, Gertrude Huntington
Maine Trail, A.

MacGill, Patrick
Conger Eel, The.
Death and the Fairies.
Dedication: "I speak with a proud tongue of the people who were."
It's a Far, Far Cry.
Slainthe!

MacGillivray, Arthur
Madonna of the Dons.

Macgillivray, Pittendrigh
Return, The.

McGinley, Phyllis
About Children.
Adversary, The.
All Around the Town, *sels.*
Ballad of Culinary Frustration.
Ballade of Lost Objects.
Ballroom Dancing Class.
B's the Bus.
C Is for the Circus.
Certain Age, A.
Concert, The.
Conquerors, The.
Conversation in Avila.
Country Club Sunday.
Daniel at Breakfast.
Day after Sunday, The.
Daylight Saving Time.
Demagogue, The.

Enigma for Christmas Shoppers.
Evening Musicale.
F Is the Fighting Firetruck.
5:32, The.
Fourteenth Birthday.
Giveaway, The.
Good Humor Man, The.
Home Is the Sailor.
Homework for Annabelle.
How to Start a War.
I Know a Village, *sels.*
Independent, The.
Journey toward Evening.
J's the Jumping Jay-Walker.
Lament for Lost Lodgings.
Last Year's Discussion: The Nobel Russian.
Literary Landscape with Dove and Poet.
Malediction.
Midcentury Love Letter.
Muted Screen of Graham Greene, The.
My Six Toothbrushes.
New Order, The.
Occupation: Housewife.
Office Party.
Oh Come, Little Children.
Old Beauty, The.
On the Farther Wall, Marc Chagall.
Portrait of a Girl with Comic Book.
Primary Education.
Publisher's Party.
R is for the Restaurant.
Recipe for an Evening Musicale.
Reflections at Dawn.
Robin Hood.
Saint Francis Borgia; or, A Refutation for Heredity.
Spanish Lions, The.
Speaking of Television, *sel.*
Spectator's Guide to Contemporary Art, *sels.*
Squeeze Play.
Text for Today.
Theology of John Edwards, The.
Thunderer, The.
Tirade on Tea.
To a Talkative Hairdresser.
Trinity Place.
Triolet against Sisters.
Velvet Hand, The.
We're Racing, Racing down the Walk.
Why, Some of My Best Friends Are Women.

Mac Giolla Ghunna, Cathal Buidhe
Yellow Bittern, The.

McGlennon, Felix
Comrades, *with music.*
Love, Sweet Love.

McGonagall, William
Address to the New Tay Bridge, An.
Albion Battleship Calamity, The.
Death of Prince Leopold, The.
Newport Railway, The.
Railway Bridge of the Silvery Tay, The.
Richard Pigott, the Forger, *sel.*
Tay Bridge Disaster, The.

McGough, Robert
Fight of the Year, The.

McGough, Roger
Flood.
40—Love.
Goodbat Nightman.
Gruesome.
If Life's a Lousy Picture, Why Not Leave before the End.
Mother the Wardrobe Is Full of Infantrymen.
My Cat and I.
Newly Pressed Suit, The.
P. C. Plod Versus the Dale St Dog Strangler.

McGovern, Margaret
Madeline at Jefferson Market Night Court.

McGovern, Robert
Christmas Myth, 1973.
Elegy for a Dead Confederate.
Mr. Kurtz.
Perdido, Duke?

MacGowan, Liam
Connolly.

MacGowran, Hugh
O'Rourke's Feast.

Macgoye, Marjorie Oludhe
For Miriam.

McGrath, Thomas
Against the False Magicians.
Coal Fire in Winter, A.
Death for the Dark Stranger.
Jig Tune: Not for Love.
John Carey's Second Song.
Letter for Marian, A.
Letter to an Imaginary Friend, Part One, *sels.*
Letter to an Imaginary Friend, Part Two, *sels.*
Long Way outside Yellowstone, A.
Ode for the American Dead in Korea.
Odor of Blood, The.
Remembering That Island.
Repeated Journey, The.
Something Is Dying Here.
Song: "Lovers in ladies' magazines."
Travelling Song.

MacGreevy [*or* McGreevy], Thomas
Aodh Ruadh O'Domhnaill.
De Civitate Hominum.
Gioconda.
Homage to Hieronymus Bosch.
Homage to Jack Yeats.
Homage to Marcel Proust.
Nocturne of the Self-evident Presence.
Recessional.
Red Hugh.

MacGregor, Malcolm
Rannoch Moor.

McGrew, A. O.
Hit at the Times, A.

McGroarty, John Steven
Blow, Bugles, Blow.
Just California.
King's Highway, The.
Port o' Heart's Desire, The.

Machado, Antonio
Autumn Dawn.
Lament of the Virtues and Verses on Account of the Death of Don Guido.
Poems.
Rebirth.
Spanish Folk Songs.

Machado de Assis, Joaquim Maria
Blue Fly.

Machar, Agnes Maule
Untrodden Ways.

Machiavelli, Niccolò
Opportunity.

McHugh, Heather
Animal Song.
Breath.
Brightness.
Capital.
Corps d'Esprit.
Down, Down, Down.
Fence, The.
Form.
Gig at Big Al's.
Having Read Books.
I Knew I'd Sing.
Impressionist.
Language Lesson, 1976.
Lines: "Some are waiting, some can't wait."
Meantime.
Message at Sunset for Bishop Berkeley.
Night Catch.
Note Delivered by a Female Impersonator.
Physics, A.
Squeal.

McHugh, Vincent
Amphimachos the Dandy.
Crawl Blues.
Deposition by John Wilmot, A.
Mantis Friend, The.
Mice at the Door, The.
Natural History of Pliny, The.
Suite from Catullus.
Talking to Myself, *sel.*

McInerney, Sally
Domestic Quarrel.

MacInnes, Tom
Ballade of Faith.
Chinatown Chant.
Modernists, The.
Tiger of Desire, The.
To Walt Whitman.
Velvet Sonneteers, The.
Zalinka.

McInnis, Edgar
Fire Burial.

MacIntosh, Claire Harris
Barn in Winter, The.
Spirit of the *Bluenose,* The.

McIntosh, Joan
Are the Sick in Their Beds as They Should Be?

MacIntyre, Carlyle Ferren
Monologue of the Rating Morgan in Rutherford County.

MacIntyre, Duncan Ban
Last Farewell to the Hills, *sel.*
Last Leave of the Hills.
On Ben Dorain.
Praise of Ben Dorain, The.

McIntyre, James
On the High Cost of Dairy Products.
Queen of Cheese.
Shelly.

MacIntyre, Tom
Child.
Corrs, The.
On Sweet Killen Hill.

"M'K., S. C." Quiet from Fear of Evil.

Mack, Alexander
I Am the Lord, *with music.*

Mack, Cecil
Teasing; or, I Was Only, Only Teasing You, *with music.*

Mack, L. V.
Biafra.
Death Songs.

Mackail, John William
Positivists ever talk in s-/ Uch an epic style as Dawkins.

McKain, David
Four Pictures by Juan, Age 5.

MacKay, Charles
Cynical Ode to an Ultra-cynical Public.
Good Time Coming, The.
Holly Bough, The.
If I Were a Voice.
Little and Great.
Louise on the Door-Step.
Mowers, The: An Anticipation of the Cholera, 1848.
Poor Man's Sunday Walk, The.
Rolling Home.
Ship, The.
Three Preachers, The.
True Freedom.
Tubal Cain.
Vixi, *at.*

McKay, Claude
Absence.
Africa.
After the Winter.
America.
Baptism.
Barrier, The.
Commemoration.
Desolate.
Enslaved.
Exhortation: Summer, 1919.
Flame-Heart.
Flower of Love.
Harlem Dancer, The.
Harlem Shadows.

I Know My Soul.
If We Must Die.
In Bondage.
Lynching, The.
My House.
Negro's Tragedy, The.
North and South.
Outcast.
Pagan Isms, The.
Russian Cathedral.
Song of the Moon, A.
Spring in New Hampshire.
St. Isaac's Church, Petrograd.
Tiger.
Tired Worker, The.
To O. E. A.
To the White Fiends.
Tropics in New York, The.
Truth.
Two-an'-Six.
White City, The.
White House, The.
Wild Goat, The.

McKay, Don
Barbed Wire Fence Meditates upon the Goldfinch, A.
I Scream You Scream.
March Snow.

MacKay, Isabel Ecclestone
Fires of Driftwood.
Helen—Old.
When as a Lad.

McKay, J. T.
Making Port.

McKay, James Thompson
Cenotaph of Lincoln.

McKay, Lois Weakley
Night.

MacKay, Louis Alexander ("John Smalacombe")
Admonition for Spring.
Battle Hymn of the Spanish Rebellion.
Erotica Antiqua, *sel.*
I Wish My Tongue Were a Quiver.
Ill-tempered Lover, The, *sel.*
Look, I Have Thrown All Right.
Now There Is Nothing Left.
Nunc Scio, Quid Sit Amor.
Propertian.

Mackay, Margaret Mackprang
Dog Wanted.

Mackay, William Paton
Revive Us Again.

MacKaye, Percy
After Tempest.
Prayer of the Peoples, A.
To Sleep.

McKee, Gladys
Spring Cellar.

MacKellar, Dorothea
Dusk in the Domain.
Fancy Dress.
My Country.

McKellar, John Alexander Ross
Football Field: Evening.
Fourth Napoleon, *sel.*
Love in a Cottage.

Mackellar, Thomas
At the door of Mercy Sighing, *with music.*

McKelway, St. Clair
Boogie-woogie Ballads.

McKent, Robert J., Jr.
Pre-History Repeats.

Mackenzie, Compton
Lilies of the Field, The.
Song of Parting, A.

Mackenzie, Kenneth
Autumn Mushrooms.
Caesura.
Earth Buried.
Fairy Tale, A.
God! How I Long for You.
Heat.
Hospital, The—Retrospections.
Legerdemain.
Old Inmate, An.
Pat Young.
Spider, The.
Table-Birds.
Two Trinities.

McKeown, Tom
Early Morning of Another World.
Graveyard Road, The.
Invitation of the Mirrors.
Lost in Yucatan.
Night Clouds.
1937 Ford Convertible.

Mackey, Charles
Baby Mine, *with music.*

Mackey, Mary
What Do You Say When a Man Tells You, You Have the Softest Skin.

Mackey, Nate
New and Old Gospel.

MacKie, Alastair
At the Heich Kirk-Yaird, *sel.*
In Absentia.
Mongol Quine.
Passin Ben Dorain.

Mackie, Albert D.
Molecatcher.
New Spring, A.
Young Man and the Young Nun, The.

Mackie, Edmund St. Gascoigne
Charmides, *sel.*

McKinney, Laurence
Compromise.
English Horn.
Hubbub in Hub.
Old School Tie-up, The.
Song to My Love.

McKinnon, Barry
Bushed.
North, The.

MacKinstry, Elizabeth
Man Who Hid His Own Front Door, The.

Mackintosh, Ewart Alan
In Memoriam, Private D. Sutherland.

Mackintosh, H. S.
"Il Est Cocule Chef de Gare!"

Mackintosh, Newton
Fin de Siècle.
Limerick: "Cleopatra, who thought they maligned her."
Lucy Lake.

Macklin, Elizabeth
Leaving One of the State Parks after a Family Outing.

McKuen, Rod
Spring Song.
Thoughts on Capital Punishment.

McLachlan, Alexander
Arrival, The.
Backwoods Hero, A, *sel.*
Emigrant, The, *sels.*
God, *sel.*
O! Come to the Greenwood Shade.
Song: "Old England is eaten by knaves."
To an Indian Skull, *sel.*
We Live in a Rickety House.

Maclagan, Sir Douglas
Battle of Glentilt (1847), The.

McLaren, Floris Clark
Frozen Fire.
No More the Slow Stream.
Visit by Water.

Maclaren, Hamish
Dolphins, The.
Harp in the Rigging.
Sailor and Inland Flower.

McLaughlin, Joe-Anne
Another Mother and Child.

McLaughlin, Kathy
Suicide Pond.

Maclaurin, John, Lord Dreghorn
Elegy: "Nor Hammond's love nor Shenstone's was sincere."

McLean, Alan
Lizard.

Maclean, Alasdair
Death of a Hind.
Envoy: "On Meall nan Con, the Peak of the Dogs."
Hen Dying.
View from My Window.

MacLean, Crystal
Good Woman, The.

MacLean, Sorley
Autumn Day, An.
Cuillin, The, *sel.*
Dain do Eimhir, *sels.*
Dain Eile, *sel.*
Kinloch Ainort.
Knightsbridge of Libya.
Nightmare, The.
Sgurr Nan Gillean.
To a Depraved Lying Woman.

McLean, Jr, William Alfred
War.

MacLeish, Archibald
Alien.
America Was Promises, *sels.*
American Letter.
Ars Poetica.
Black Humor.
Boy in the Roman Zoo.
Brave New World.
Burying Ground by the Ties.
Calypso's Island.
Captured.
Conquistador, *sel.*
Cook County.
Corporate Entity.
Critical Observations.
Crossing.
Curse God and Die, You Said to Me.
Discovery of This Time.
Dr. Sigmund Freud Discovers the Sea Shell.
"Dover Beach"—a Note to That Poem.
Dusk.
Einstein.
Eleven.
Empire Builders.
End of the World, The.
Epistle to Be Left in the Earth.
Epistle to the Rapalloan.
Ever Since.
Ezry.
Fall of the City, The, *sel.*
Final Chorus.
Frescoes for Mr. Rockefeller's City.
Grazing Locomotives.
Hurricane.
Hypocrite Auteur.
Immortal Autumn.
In My Thirtieth Year.
Invocation to the Social Muse.
J. B., *sel.*
L'An Trentiesme de Mon Eage.
Land of the Free.
Landscape as a Nude.
Late Abed.
Learned Men, The.
Liberty.
Lines for an Interment.
Memorial Rain.
Men.
Mother Goose's Garland.
My Naked Aunt.
National Security.
"Not Marble nor the Gilded Monuments."
Panic, *sels.*
Peepers in Our Meadow, The.
Poem in Prose.
Poet Speaks from the Visitors' Gallery, A.
Pole Star.

Prologue: "And the way goes on in the worn earth."
Prologue: "These alternate nights and days, these seasons."
Psyche with the Candle.
Reasons for Music.
Reconciliation, The.
Reed-Player, The.
Reply to Mr. Wordsworth, *sel.*
Seafarer.
Signature for Tempo.
Silence, The.
Silent Slain, The.
Snowflake Which Is Now and Hence Forever, The.
Speech to a Crowd.
Speech to Those Who Say Comrade.
Spring in These Hills.
Survivor.
Theory of Poetry.
Too-late Born, The.
Unfinished History, An.
Vicissitudes of the Creator.
Voice of the Studio Announcer.
Voyage to the Moon.
Voyage West.
Weather.
What Riddle Asked the Sphinx.
What the Serpent Said to Adam.
Where the Hayfields Were.
Winter Is Another Country.
Words in Time.
You, Andrew Marvell.
You Also, Gaius Valerius Catullus.
Young Dead Soldiers, The.

McLeish, John A. B.
Not without Beauty.

McLellan, Jr, Isaac
New England's Dead!

MacLellan, Robert
Sang: "There's a reid lowe in yer cheek."

"Macleod, Fiona" (William Sharp)
Australian Transcripts, *sels.*
Autumnal Evening, An.
Bell-Bird, The.
Dawn amid Scotch Firs.
Dead Calm and Mist, A.
Dream Fantasy.
Eagle, The.
Field Mouse, The.
Fireflies.
Founts of Song, The.
Loch Coruisk (Skye).
Madonna Natura.
Mid-Noon in January.
Moon-Child, The.
Mystic's Prayer, The.
On a Nightingale in April.
Paris Nocturne, A.
Redeemer, The.
Rookery at Sunrise, The.
Shule, Agrah!
Sonnet VII: "Dull day darkens to its close, The The sheen."
Swimmer of Nemi, The.
Transcripts from Nature, *sels.*
Wasp, The.
White Peace, The.
Wood-Swallows, The.

Macleod, Joseph Gordon ("Adam Drinan")
Ecliptic, The: Cancer; or, The Crab, *sel.*
Love Song: "Soft as the wind your hair."
Men of the Rocks, *sels.*

McLeod, Irene Rutherford (Mrs. Aubrey de Sélincourt)
Is Love, Then, So Simple?
Lone Dog.
Prayer, A: "O Love, give me a passionate heart."
Rebel.
So Beautiful You Are, Indeed.
Song: "How do I love you?"
Song from "April."
Sonnets, *sels.*
Unborn.
When My Beloved Sleeping Lies.

MacLeod, Mairi
Complaint about Exile, A.

Macleod, Norman
Creed, A.
Me.
Trust in God and Do the Right.

MacLow, Jackson
1st Dance—Making Things New—6 February 1964.
2nd Dance—Seeing Lines—6 February 1964.
2nd Light Poem: For Diane Wakoski.
10th Dance—Coming On as a Horn—20 February 1964.
3rd Dance—Making a Structure with a Roof or under a Roof—6-7 February 1964.
37th Dance—Banding—22 March 1964.
12th Dance—Getting Leather by Language—21 February 1964.
29th Dance—Having an Instrument—22 March 1964.
Zen Buddhism and Psychoanalysis/ Psychoanalysis and Zen Buddhism.

"McM"
Allegro.

MacMahon, Bryan
Corner Boys.

McMahon, Michael Beirne
Once upon a Nag.
Trout Fishing in Virginia.

MacManus, Anna Johnston. *See* **"Carbery, Ethna"**

MacManus, Francis
Pattern of Saint Brendan.

MacManus, Seumas
In Dark Hour.
Lullaby: "Softly now the burn is rushing."
Shane O'Neill.

MacManus, Theodore F.
Cave Sedem!

MacMarcuis, Aindrais
Flight of the Earls, The.
This Night Sees Ireland [*or* Eire] Desolate.

McMaster, Guy Humphreys
Carmen Bellicosum.

McMaster, Rhyll
Profiles of My Father.
Round Song, A.
Tanks.

McMichael, James
Cabin North of It All, The.
Great Garret, or 100 Wheels, The.
Inland Lighthouse, The.
Lutra, the Fisher.
Terce.
Village of the Presents, The.

Macmillan, James
Hill Love.
Nightmare on Rhum.
To This Hill Again.
What Are You Thinking About?

MacMore, Dallan
Carroll's Sword, *at.*
Song of Carroll's Sword, The, *at.*

MacMuireadach, Niall Mor
Soraidh Slan Don Oidhche Areir.

MacMurray, Niall
Vanished Night, The.

Macnab, Roy
El Alamein Revisited.
Majuba Hill.
River, The.
Road to Bologna, The.
Seven of the Clock.

McNabb, Vincent
Spotless Maid, The.

Macnaghten, Hugh
Idyll: "In Switzerland one idle day."

McNair, Wesley
Bald Spot, The.

McNall, Sally
Metaphors.

McNally, Leonard
Lass of Richmond Hill, The, *with music.*

MacNamara, Brinsley
On Seeing Swift in Laracor.

MacNamara, Francis
Diminutivus Ululans.

MacNamee, Giolla Brighde
Childless.
To an Anti-poetical Priest.

MacNeice, Louis
Alcohol.
Among These Turf-Stacks.
And I remember Spain.
And Love Hung Still.
And the Lord Was Not in the Whirlwind.
As in Their Time.
Aubade: "Having bitten on life like a sharp apple."
August.
Autumn Journal, *sels.*
Bad Dream.
Bagpipe Music.
Ballade of England.
Bar-Room Matins.
Birmingham.
British Museum Reading Room, The.
Brother Fire.
Carrickfergus.
Charon.
Christina.
Christmas Shopping.
Circe.
Conversation.
Corner Seat.
County Sligo.
Cradle Song: "Clock's untiring fingers wind the wool of darkness, The."
Cradle Song: "Sleep, my darling, sleep."
Cradle Song for Miriam.
Creditor, The.
Day of Renewal.
Death of a Cat, The, *sels.*
Didymus.
Dublin.
Eclogue for Christmas, An.
Elegy for Minor Poets.
Entered in the Minutes.
Entirely.
Explorations.
Fanfare for the Makers, A, *abr.*
For X.
Galway.
Grey Ones, The.
Holes in the Sky, *sel.*
Homage to Wren.
Horses.
In Lieu.
Individualist Speaks, The.
Invocation: "Dolphin plunge, fountain play."
Jehu.
June Thunder.
Kingdom, The, *sels.*
Leaving Barra.
Les Sylphides.
Libertine, The.
London Rain.
Mahabalipuram.
Meeting Point.
Mixer, The.
Morning Sun.
Museums.
National Gallery, The.
Nature Morte.
Neutrality.
Nostalgia.
Nuts in May.
Old Story, The.
Passage Steamer.

Perdita.
Perseus.
Pet Shop.
Poussin.
Prayer before Birth.
Prayer in Mid-Passage.
Prognosis.
Refugees.
Sense of Smell, The.
Sligo and Mayo.
Snow.
Soap Suds.
Springboard, The.
Star-Gazer.
Strand, The.
Streets of Laredo, The.
Stylite.
Suicide.
Sunday Morning.
Sunlight on the Garden, The.
Taxis, The.
Thalassa.
This Is the Life.
Tree Party.
Trilogy for X, *sels.*
Truisms, The.
Turf-Stacks.
Valediction: "Their verdure dare not show."
Variation on Heraclitus.
Visitations: VII, *sel.*
Whit Monday.
Whitmonday.
Wolves.

MacNeill, Hector
My Boy Tammy.

Macomber, W.
Christ Is Coming.

McOwan, Rennie
Highland Loves.
Hillman Looks Back, The.
Hooded Crow, The.
Mountaineering Bus.
Things of the North, The.

McPeake, Francis
Jug of Punch, The.

McPheron, Judith
Water.

Macpherson, James ("Ossian")
Carthon; a Poem.
Fragments of Ancient Poetry, Collected in the Highlands of Scotland, *sel.*
Oithona; a Poem.

Macpherson, Jay
Ark, The, *sels.*
Ark Anatomical.
Ark Apprehensive.
Ark Artefact.
Ark Articulate.
Ark Astonished.
Ark Overwhelmed.
Ark Parting.
Beauty of Job's Daughters, The.
Boatman, The.
Eurynome.
Eve in Reflection.
Fisherman, The.
Go Take the World.
Hail Wedded Love!
Ill Wind, The.
Innocents, The.
Leviathan.
Lost Soul, A.
Marriage of Earth and Heaven, The.
Martyrs, The.
Natural Mother, The.
Ordinary People in the Last Days.
Sun and Moon.
Swan, The.
They Return.
Third Eye, The.
Way Down, The, *sel.*
Woods No More, The.

McPherson, Sandra
Alleys.
Butchery.
Centerfold Reflected in a Jet Window.
Coconut for Katerina, A.
Collapsars.
Elegies for the Hot Season.
For Elizabeth Bishop.
Games.
Gnawing the Breast.
His Body.
Letter with a Black Border.
Lifesaving.
Loneliness.
Marlow and Nancy.
Michael.
Morning Glory Pool.
Museum of the Second Creation, The.
Open Casket.
Page.
Peter Rabbit.
Pisces Child.
Poppies.
Pornography, Nebraska.
Pregnancy.
Resigning from a Job in a Defense Industry.
Seaweeds.
Sentience.
Sisters.
To an Alcoholic.
Unitarian Easter.
Urban Ode.
Wanting a Mummy.
Wings and Seeds.

McQueen, Cilla
Matinal.
To Ben, at the Lake.
Weekend Sonnets.

McQuilkin, Rennie
New England Greenhouse.
Tree Man.

Macrow, Brenda G.
All Flesh Is Grass, *sel.*
At the Shelter-Stone.
Climb in Torridon.
In Praise of Ben Avon.
When I Die.

McTell, Ralph
First and Last Man.

Macuilxochitl
Battle Song.

MacVeagh, F. W.
Here Ananias lies because he lied.

McWebb, Elizabeth Upham
At Mrs. Appleby's.

Macy, Arthur
Peppery Man, The.
Rollicking Mastodon, The.

Macy, George
Daphne and Apollo.

Madden, David
Surfaces.

Madden, F. A. V.
I put my hat upon my head, *parody.*

Maddow, Ben
City, The.

Madeleva, Sister Mary
Apology for Youth.
Ballade on Eschatology.
Design for a Stream-lined Sunrise.
Gates.
Motif for Mary's Dolors.
New Things and Old.
November Afternoons.
Nun Speaks to Mary, A.
Of Wounds.
Peace by Night.
Snow Storm.
Wardrobe.

Madge, Charles
At War.
Birds of Tin, The.
Blocking the Pass.
Delusions VI.
Fortune.
In Conjunction.
Landscape I ("The character of a landscape stands always in a mysterious relation").
Loss.
Lusty Juventus.
Monument, A.
Nightly Deed, A.
On One Condition.
Poem: "Walls of the maelstrom are painted with trees, The."
Rumba of the Three Lost Souls.
Solar Creation.
Times, The.
To Make a Bridge.

Madgett, Naomi Long (Naomi Long Witherspoon)
Alabama Centennial.
Black Woman.
Deacon Morgan.
Dream Sequence, Part 9.
Exits and Entrances.
Her Story.
Midway.
Mortality.
New Day.
Nocturne: "See how dark the night settles on my face."
Nomen.
Offspring.
Pavlov.
Quest.
Race Question, The.
Refugee.
Simple.
Star Journey.
Woman with Flower.

Madhubuti, Haki R. *See* **Lee, Don L.**

Madison, Dolly
La Fayette.

Maeterlinck, Maurice
Last Words, The.
Song: "Three little maidens they have slain."

Magaret, Helene
Impiety, *sel.*

Magee, Michael
It Is the Stars That Govern Us.

Magee, John Gillespie, Jr
High Flight.

Magee, William Kirkpatrick. *See* **"Eglinton, John"**

"Maggie"
Passionate Encyclopedia Britannica Reader to his Love, The.

Magid, Margo
Night Watch.

Magil, A. B.
They Are Ours.

Maginn, William
I Give My Soldier Boy a Blade.
Irishman and the Lady, The.
Rime of the Auncient Waggonere, The.
St. Patrick of Ireland, My Dear!

Maglow, T. O.
Dylan Thomas.

Magogo, Princess
Teasing Song.

Magonan, Robin
Pastoral: "Mountain/ rises out of paper."

Magowan, Robin
Days of 1956.
Paros.
Susan.
Zeimbekiko.

Magrath, Andrew
Andrew Magrath's Reply to John O'Tuomy.
Boatman's Hymn, *at.*
Lament of the Mangaire Sugach.

Maguire, Francis
Whale Song.

Maguire, Tom
Bold Robert Emmet.
Mahadevi (Mahadeviyakka)
Like/ treasure hidden in the ground.
Like a silkworm weaving.
Like an elephant.
O brothers, why do you talk.
People,/ male and female.
Riding the blue sapphire mountains.
Till you've earned.
Would a circling surface vulture.
Mahapatra, Jayanta
Rain of Rites, A.
Mahlmann, Siegfried August
Allah ("Allah gives light in darkness").
Mahon, Derek
Afterlives.
Banished Gods, The.
Consolations of Philosophy.
Dark Country, A.
Departure, A.
Disused Shed in Co. Wexford, A.
Ecclesiastes.
Exit Molloy.
Girls in Their Seasons.
Glengormley.
Grandfather.
I Am Raftery ("I am Raftery, hesitant and confused").
Image from Beckett, An.
In Carrowdore Churchyard.
Matthew V. 29-30.
My Wicked Uncle.
Snow Party, The.
Mahone, Barbara
Colors for Mama.
Poem for Positive Thinkers, A.
Sugarfields.
Mahony, Francis Sylvester ("Father Prout")
Attractions of a Fashionable Irish Watering-Place, The.
Bells of Shandon, The.
In Mortem Venerabilis Andreae Prout Carmen.
L'Envoy to W. L. H. Ainsworth, Esq.
Panegyric on Geese, A.
Piper's Progress, The.
Red-Breast of Aquitania, The.
Sabine Farmer's Serenade, The.
Shandon Bells, The.
Mahony, Medb
Shells.
Mahsati
Better to live as a rogue and a bum.
Gone are the games we played all night.
Good-looking, I'll never stoop for you.
I knew like a song your vows weren't strong.
Unless you can dance through a common bar.
Maiano, Dante da
Sonnet: He Craves Interpreting of a Dream of His.
To Dante Alighieri: He Interprets Dante Alighieri's Dream.
Maiden, Jennifer
Climbing.
Dew.
Slides.
Mailer, Norman
Devils.
Dr. Hu/ speaks.
Eternities.
Maillard, Claude
Christmas Mass for a Little Atheist Jesus.
Maino, Jeannette
Harvest.
Sky Patterns.
Mainwaring, Arthur
Excellent New Ballad, Called the Brawny Bishop's Complaint, An.
Excellent New Song Called "Mat's Peace," An.
New Ballad, A.
Queen's Speech, The.
Tarquin and Tullia.
Mair, Alexander
Hesiod, 1908.
Mair, Charles
Dreamland, *sel.*
Fireflies, The, *sel.*
Last Bison, The, *sel.*
Tecumseh, *sels.*
Winter.
Maisel, Carolyn
Dream of Women, A.
Girl in the Willow Tree, The.
Letter from a Friend, A.
Maitland, Sir Richard
Against the Thieves of Liddesdale.
Solace in Age.
Major, Clarence
Blind Old Woman.
Celebrated Return.
Design, The.
Down Wind against the Highest Peaks.
New Pietà, The: For the Mothers and Children of Detroit.
Swallow the Lake.
Vietnam.
Vietnam #4.
Major, Joseph
Poem for Thel—The Very Tops of Trees.
Major, Nadine
Agatha.
Mak, Lev
Eden.
Flood, The.
Prayer: "From your high bridge wave & wail."
Makai, Emil
Comet, The.
Makere
Lament for Taramoana.
Makhfi (Zibu'n-Nisa)
Beauty of the Friend it was that taught me, The.
Maksimovic, Desanka
For All Mary Magdalenes.
Malam, Charles
Neighbors.
Steam Shovel.
Malancioiu, Ileana
Bear's Blood.
Malanga, Gerard
Temperature.
What I Have Done.
Malangatana, Valente Goenha
To the Anxious Mother.
Woman.
Malarkey, Susannah P.
Above the Wall.
Maleska, Eugene T.
Assembly: Harlem School.
Countee Cullen.
To a Negro Boy Graduating.
Malins, Joseph
Fence or an Ambulance, A.
Mallalieu, Herbert B.
Cozzo Grillo.
Empedocles on Etna.
Epilogue: "Phoenix on the hot sirocco's breath."
Look for Me on England.
New Year's Eve.
Next of Kin.
Platform Goodbye.
To Naples.
Mallarmé, Stéphane
Afternoon of a Faun, The.
Album Leaf.
All the soul indrawn.
Anguish.
Après-midi d'un Faune, L'.
Autumn Complaint.
Flowers.
Future Phenomenon, The.
Glazier, The.
Hérodiade.
Lace curtain stands effaced, A.
Little Air.
Old Saxony Clock, The.
Saint.
Sea Breeze.
Sea-Wind.
Sigh.
Sonnet: "This virgin, beautiful and lively day."
Swan, The.
Tomb of Edgar Poe, The.
Mallet, David
Birks of Endermay, The.
William and Margaret.
Mallet, David *and* **James Thomson.** *See* **Thomson, James** *and* **David Mallet**
"Malley, Ern" (James McAuley *and* **Harold Stewart)**
Dürer; Innsbruck, 1495.
Malley, Jean
Words do not grow on the landscape.
Malley, K.
Conversation.
Malloch, Douglas
Ain't It Fine Today!
Be the Best of Whatever You Are.
Comrade Rides Ahead, A.
Family Trees.
If Easter Eggs Would Hatch.
It's Fine Today.
June.
When the Drive Goes Down.
Mallock, William Hurrell
Brussels and Oxford.
Softly the Evening.
Mally, E. Louise
Moon Rock.
"Malone, Carroll." *See* **McBurney, William B.**
Malone, Walter
Agnostic's Creed, The.
He Who Hath Loved.
Masterpiece, The.
October in Tennessee.
Opportunity.
Maloney, J. J.
Beyond the Wall.
City Jail.
Getting Out.
Poems from Prison, 1 ("Day after day after day").
Poems from Prison, 2 ("They have built us a golf course").
Prison Guard, The.
Somewhere Down below Me Is a Street.
Malouf, David
An die Musik.
Asphodel.
At My Grandmother's.
Early Discoveries.
Snow.
This Day, under My Hand.
Wolf-Boy.
Mammone, Ken
Sun and I.
Man, Gill
Mist.
Mandel, Charlotte
I'm Lucky.
Mandel, Eli W.
David.
Envoi: "My country is not a country."
Fire Place, The.
Four Songs from the Book of Samuel.
From the North Saskatchewan.
Houdini.
Job.
Madwomen of the Plaza de Mayo, The.
Merits of Laughter and Lust.
Minotaur Poems, *sels.*
On the Death of Ho Chi Minh.
On the 25th Anniversary of the Liberation of Auschwitz.
Phaeton.
Rapunzel (Girl in a Tower).

Song: "When the echo of the last footstep dies."
Mandela, Zindzi
Lock the Place in Your Heart.
Mandelstam, Osip Emilyevich
Ariosto.
Arteries Juicy with Blood.
Batyushkov.
Bitter Bread.
Concert at the Station.
Like a Young Levite.
Lines Concerning the Unknown Soldier, *sel.*
Not yet dead, not yet alone.
Notre Dame.
Phaedra.
Reed, A.
This Night.
Twilight of Freedom.
Mandeville, Bernard
On Honour.
Manfred, Freya
For a Young South Dakota Man.
Grandma Shorba and the Pure in Heart.
Moon Light.
Mangan, James Clarence
Advice against Travel.
Cean-Salla.
Dawning of the Day, The.
Fair Hills of Eiré, O, The.
Gone in the Wind.
Irish Language, The.
Karamanian Exile, The.
King Cahal Mor of the Wine-red Hand.
Nameless One, The.
Rest Only in the Grave.
St. Patrick's Hymn before Tara[h].
Shapes and Signs.
Siberia.
Three Khalandeers, The.
Time of the Barmecides, The.
To Amine.
To My Native Land.
To the Ingleezee Khafir, Calling Himself Djann Bool Djenkinzun.
Twenty Golden Years Ago.
Vision of Connaught in the Thirteenth Century, A.
World, The; a Ghazel.
Mangan, Kathy
Absence.
Cold Snap.
Manger, Itzig [*or* Itzik]
Abishag Writes a Letter Home.
Abraham and Sarah.
Adam and Eve.
Alone.
Autumn.
Dark Hand, A.
Dying Thief.
Evening.
Fairy Tales.
I Am the Autumn.
Jealous Adam.
Mother Sarah's Lullaby ("Mother Sarah rocks the cradle").
On the Road There Stands a Tree.
Rachel Goes to the Well for Water ("Rachel stands by the mirror and plaits").
Strange Guest, The.
Under the Ruins of Poland.
Mangoaela, Z. D.
Boast of Masopha.
Manhire, Bill
Collection, The.
Elaboration, The.
Importance of Personal Relationships, The.
Last Things.
Party Going.
Poetry Reading, The.
Summer.
Wellington.
Wulf.
Manifold, John Streeter
Assignation with a Somnambulist.
Bunyip and the Whistling Kettle, The.
Camouflage.
Defensive Position.
Deserter, The.
Fencing School.
Fife Tune.
Garcia Lorca Murdered in Granada.
Griesly Wife, The.
"Heureux Qui comme Ulysse."
L'Embarquement pour Cythère.
Listening to a Broadcast.
Makhno's Philosophers.
Making Contact.
Night Piece.
Ration Party.
Sirens, The.
Song: "My dark-headed Käthchen, my spit-kitten darling."
Tomb of Lt. John Learmonth, A.I.F., The.
Manner, Eeva-Liisa
Cambrian, *sels.*
Lunar Games, The.
Mannes, Marya
Age.
Canticles to Men.
First, The.
Manning, Frederic
Kore.
Manning, James Harold
What Is Truth, *sel.*
Manning, Robert. *See* **Mannyng, Robert**
Manning-Sanders, Ruth
Come Wary One.
Old City, The.
Mannix, Mary E.
All Souls' Eve.
Mannyng [*or* Manning], Robert
Bishop's Harp, The.
Dancers of Colbek, The.
Handlyng Synne, *sels.*
Praise of Women.
Round Table, The.
Mansel, William Lort
Sun's Perpendicular Rays, The.
Mansfield, Katherine
Arabian Shawl, The.
Friendship.
Little Brother's Secret.
Sleeping Together.
To L. H. B.
Two Nocturnes.
Voices of the Air.
Mansfield, Margery Swett
Blessing Mrs. Larkin.
Mansfield, Richard
Eagle's Song, The.
Manson, John
At a Ruined Croft.
Mansour, Joyce
Auditory Hallucinations.
Embrace the Blade.
Last night I saw your corpse.
North Express.
Seated on her bed legs spread open.
Sun in Capricorn, The.
Yesterday evening I saw your corpse.
Manville, Marion
Lee's Parole.
Surrender of New Orleans, The.
Manyase, L. T.
Mother Crab and Her Family, The.
Vusumzi's Song.
Manzano, Juan Fransico
My Thirty Years.
Mao Tse-tung
Midstream.
Mapes, Edith L.
Oh, If They Only Knew!
Mar, Laureen
At Wonder Donut.
Black Rocks.
Immigration Act of 1924, The.
My Mother, Who Came from China, Where She Never Saw Snow.
Window Frames the Moon, The.
Marais, Eugène
Dance of the Rain, The.
Desert Lark, The.
Heart-of-the-Daybreak.
Sorceress, The.
Maran, René
Human Soul.
Marano, Russell
Now I Am a Man.
Spring Death.
Marcabrun
At the Fountain.
Marcela de Carpio de San Felix, Sister
Amor Mysticus.
Marchant, John
Little Miss and Her Parrot.
Young Master's Account of a Puppet Show.
Marcus, Mordecai
Book of Verses, A.
Bouquet for Jerry Ford, A.
Election, An.
Proud Resignation.
Survivors.
Two Refugees.
Marcus, Morton
Look Closely.
Watching Your Gray Eyes.
Marcus Argentarius. *See* **Argentarius, Marcus**
Margarido, Manuela
You Who Occupy Our Land.
Margenat, Hugo
Living Poetry.
Well-aimed Stare, The.
Your Air of My Air.
Margetson, George Reginald
Fledgling Bard and the Poetry Society, The, *much abr.*
Margolin, Anna (Razel Lebensboim)
Ancient Murderess Night.
Homecoming.
Mother Earth.
My Kin Talk.
Years.
Margolis, Gary
On the Eve of Our Anniversary.
Margolis, Silvia
Never Ask Me Why.
Marguerite de Navarre
Autant en Emporte le Vent.
Smell of death is so powerful, The.
Mariah, Paul
Always We Watch Them.
At Their Place.
Gravel.
Grey Him.
Quarry/Rock.
Walls Breathe.
Mariani, Paul
Coda: Revising History.
Girl Who Learned to Sing in Crow, The.
Golden Oldie.
Lesson, The.
Lines I Told Myself I Wouldn't Write.
News That Stays News.
Ring, The.
Then Sings My Soul.
Walk in Early March, A.
Marias, The Three (Maria Isabella Barreno *and* Maria Teresa Horta *and* Maria Velho da Costa)
Conversation between the Chevalier de Chamilly and Mariana Alcoforado in the Manner of a Song of Regret.
Saddle and Cell.
Marie de France
Chartivel, *sel.*
Goat's-Leaf.

Lay of the Honeysuckle, The.
Nightingale, The.
Sarrazine's Song to Her Dead Lover.
Song from Chartivel.
Two Lovers, The.
Would I Might Go Far over Sea.
"Marie Josephine" *See* **Hemenway, Abby Maria**
"Marie Madelaine" (Baroness von Puttkamer)
Crucifixion.
End Is Now, The.
Foiled Sleep.
Moriturus.
Unfading, The.
Vagabonds.
Marietta, T. Walking Eagle
Child of Hers, A.
House, The.
I watched them as thay raised their voices to the sky.
Reflection of Night, A.
Two Coyotes, The.
Marini, Giambattista. *See* **Marino, Giovanni Battista**
Marino, Giovanni Battista
Fading Beauty.
Lips and Eyes.
Madrigal: "Love now no fire hath left him."
Massacre of the Innocents, The, *sel.*
Sospetto d'Herode.
Strage degli innocenti, La, II, *sel.*
Marinoni, Rosa Zagnoni
Who Are My People?
Marion, David
Her Eyes Don't Shine like Diamonds, *with music.*
Marion, Jeff Daniel
Out in the Country, Back Home.
Winter Watch.
Maris Stella, Sister
Afternoon in a Tree.
Bay Violets.
Cause of Our Joy.
Grapes.
I Who Had Been Afraid.
It Is the Reed.
Lines for a Feast of Our Lady.
Love Is Not Solace.
Now That Can Never Be Done.
Oxford Bells.
Pelicans My Father Sees, The.
San Marco Museum, Florence.
This One Heart-shaken.
Voice, The.
Mark, Diane Mei Lin
And the Old Folks Said.
Kula . . . a Homecoming.
Liberation.
Rice and Rose Bowl Blues.
Susie Wong Doesn't Live Here.
"Mark Twain." *See* **"Twain, Mark"**
Markham, Edwin
At Little Virgil's Window.
Avengers, The.
Brotherhood.
Christ of the Andes, The, *sel.*
Conscripts of the Dream, *sel.*
Courage, All.
Creed, A.
Duty.
Earth Is Enough.
Errand Imperious, The.
Father's Business, The.
Forgotten Man, The.
Free Nation, A.
Great Guest Comes In, The.
Guard of the Sepulcher, A.
How Shall We Honor Them?
How the Great Guest Came.
How to Go and Forget.
Invisible Bride, The.
Joy of the Morning.
Last Furrow, The.
Lincoln, the Man of the People.
Lizard, The.
Look into the Gulf, A.
Man with the Hoe, The.
Man-Making.
My Comrade.
Need of the Hour, The.
New Trinity, The.
Night Moths, The.
Outwitted.
Peace.
Place of Peace, The.
Poet, The.
Poetry.
Prayer, A: "Teach me, Father, how to go."
Preparedness.
Revelation.
Right Kind of People, The.
Rules for the Road.
San Francisco Arising.
San Francisco Falling.
Shine on Me, Secret Splendor.
Song to a Tree.
Task That Is Given to You, The.
There Is a High Place, *with music.*
Third Wonder, The.
Toiler, The, *sel.*
Two at a Fireside.
Victory in Defeat.
Virgilia, *sel.*
Wharf of Dreams, The.
Whirlwind Road, The.
Wind and Lyre.
Young Lincoln.
Your Tears.
Markham, Gervase
Fragment: "I walk'd [*or* walked] along a stream for pureness rare."
Markham, Lucia Clark
Bluebells.
Markish, Peretz
In the Last Flicker of the Sinking Sun.
We Reached Out Far.
Your Burnt-out Body.
Markman, Stephanie
Rime of the Ancient Feminist, The, *sel.*
Marks, Edward B.
Little Lost Child, The.
My Mother Was a Lady; or, If Jack Were Only Here.
Marks, Godfrey
Sailing.
Sailing Sailing.
Marks, Naomi
Come Live with Me.
High Wonders.
Marks, S. J.
How.
Marks, Shirley
Early Warning.
Marlatt, Daphne
Femina.
Imagine: a Town.
Steveston, *sel.*
Marlatt, Earl Bowman
Spirit of Life, in This New Dawn, *with music.*
Through the Dark the Dreamers Came, *with music.*
Marlowe, Christopher
Amorous Neptune.
And now the sun that through the horizon peeps.
Bloody Conquests of Mighty Tamburlaine, The.
Divine Zenocrate.
Doctor Faustus.
Edward the Second, *sel.*
Emperor of the Threefold World.
End of Doctor Faustus, The.
End of Faustus, The.
Face of Helen, The.
Fair Is Too Foul an Epithet.
Faustus Faces His Doom.
Finale.
Helen.
Hero and Leander.
Hero Feels the Shaft of Love.
Hero the Fair[e].
If All the Pens That Ever Poets Held.
It Lies Not in Our Power to Love or Hate.
Jew of Malta, The, *sels.*
Love at First Sight ("It lies not in our power").
Mine Argosy from Alexandria.
Overreacher, The.
Passionate Shepherd to His Love, The.
Perfect Bliss and Sole Felicity.
Shepherd to His Love, The.
Shepherd's Plea, The.
Song of Ithamore, The.
Spell of Invisibility, A, *at.*
Tamburlaine the Great, *sels.*
To Entertain Divine Zenocrate.
Tragedy of Dido, The, *sel.*
Was This the Face [That Launched a Thousand Ships].
Who Ever Loved, That Loved Not at First Sight?
Marlowe, Christopher *and* Thomas Nashe
I Have an Orchard.
Marot, Clément
Ballade of a Friar.
Friar Lubin.
Love-Lesson, A.
Madame d'Albert's Laugh.
Marquess of Crewe
Posy Ring, The.
Seven Years.
Marquis, Don (Donald Robert Marquis)
Another Villon-ous Variation.
Archy, the Cockroach, Speaks.
Archy a Low Brow.
Archy and Mehitabel, *sels.*
Archy at the Zoo.
Archy Confesses.
Archy Does His Part, *sel.*
Archy Experiences a Seizure.
Archygrams.
Archys Autobiography.
Archys Last Name.
Archys Life of Mehitabel, *sels.*
Artists Shouldnt Have Offspring.
Awakening, The.
Ballade: "Outcast bones from a thousand biers."
Ballade of the Under Side.
Certain Maxims of Archy.
Chant Royal of the Dejected Dipsomanic.
Cheerio My Deario.
Confession of a Glutton.
Down in a Wine Vault.
Fate Is Unfair.
Froggles.
Gentleman of Fifty Soliloquizes, A.
Gilk.
God-Maker, Man, The.
Googs, The.
Grotesques, *sel.*
Heir and Serf.
Hen and the Oriole, The.
Honey Bee, The.
Hot-Weather Song, A.
In the Bayou.
Jokesmith's Vacation, The.
King Cophetua and the Beggar Maid.
Little While, A.
Mehitabel Sings a Song.
Melissa.
Name, The.
Noah an' Jonah an' Cap'n John Smith.
Old Trouper, The.
Only Thy Dust.
Pete at the Seashore.
Prohibition.
Quinks, The.
Reverie.

Savage Portraits.
Song of Mehitabel, The.
Time time said old King Tut.
To a Lost Sweetheart.
Tom-Cat, The.
Tristram and Isolt.
Trouble.
Unrest.
Wail of Archy, The, *sel.*
Warty Bliggens, the Toad.
When One Loves Tensely.

Marr, Barbara
Prayer: "Lord, make me sensitive to the sight."

Marriot, John
On John Donne's Book of Poems.

Marriott, Anne
As You Come In.
Beaver Pond.
Prairie Graveyard.
Sandstone.
Search.
Wind Our Enemy, The, *sel.*
Woodyards in the Rain.

Marron, Os
Nocturnal.

Marryat, Frederick
Captain Stood on the Carronade, The.
Old Navy, The.
Port Admiral.
Snarleyyow; or, The Dog Fiend, *sel.*

Mars, Ann (Annalita Marsigli)
Shadow.

Marsh, Daniel L.
Greatest Person in the Universe, The.

Marsh, E. L.
Magic Piper, The.

Marshak, Samuel
Little House in Lithuania, The.

Marshall, Austin John
Dancing at Whitsun.

Marshall, Edward
Leave the Word Alone.
Memory as Memorial in the Last.
Sept. 1957.
Two Poems.

Marshall, Jack
Hitchhiker.

Marshall, James
Oregon Trail: 1851.

Marshall, Lenore G.
Invented a Person.

Marshall, Matt
Wine o Living.

Marshall, Tom
Astrology.
Interior Monologue 666.
Politics.
Summer.

Marshall, William E.
Brookfield, *sel.*
To a Mayflower.

Marston, John
Antonio and Mellida, *sel.*
Antonio's Revenge, *sel.*
Delicious Beauty.
Malcontent, The, *sel.*
Metamorphosis of Pygmalion's Image, The, *sel.*
Nut-brown Ale, The.
Prologue: "Rawish dank of clumsy winter ramps, The."
Satire, *sel.*
Scourge of Villainy [*or* Villanie], The, *sel.*
Song: "Delicious beauty that doth lie."
Song: "O Love, how strangely sweet."
To Detraction [I Present My Poesie].
To Everlasting Oblivion.

Marston, Philip Bourke
After.
After Summer.
At the Last.
How My Songs of Her Began.
If You Were Here.
Inseparable.
Little time for laughter, A. After.
Not Thou but I.
Old Churchyard of Bonchurch, The.
Rose and the Wind, The.
Speechless [Upon the Marriage of Two Deaf and Dumb Persons].
Too Late.
Two Burdens, The.
Ungathered Love.
Wedded Memories.

Marti, Jose
Guantanamera.
Simple Verses, *sels.*
Two Countries.

Martial (Marcus Valerius Martialis)
Abnegation.
Advantages of Learning, The.
Bad Joke, A.
Believe me, sir, I'd like to spend whole days.
Bought Locks.
Country Pleasures.
Critics.
Dasius, chucker-out/ at the Turkish Baths.
De Coenatione Micae.
Either get out of my house or conform to my tastes, woman.
Epigram: "Charm of my life, my dearest care."
Epigram: "Give me a boy whose tender skin."
Epigram: Go, Happy Rose.
Epigram: "Insomuch, Bassa, as I never saw."
Epigram: Likeness, The.
Epigram: "Me Polytimus vexes and provokes."
Epigram: "Milo's from home; and, Milo being gone."
Epigram: "My better half, why turn a peevish scold."
Epigram: On a Slanderer.
Epigram: On Hedylus.
Epigram: Riddle, A.
Epigram: To Charinus, a Catamite.
Epigram: To Dindymus.
Epigram: To Labienus.
Epigram: To Lygdus.
Epigram: To Papilus.
Epigram: To Philaenis.
Epigram: To Phoebus.
Epigram: To Polycharmus.
Epigrams, *sels.*
Epitaph for Erotion.
Erotion.
Familiarity Breeds Indifference.
Garland of roses, whether you come.
Happy Life, The.
Hinted Wish, A.
I hear that Lycoris has buried.
In a cell I am bunked.
Incentive, The.
Insufficient Vengeance.
Laid with papyrus to catch fire.
Lentinus! thou dost nought but fume, and fret.
Lycoris darling, once I burned for you.
Martial's Quiet Life.
Mistaken Resolve, The.
Near Neighbors.
Near the Vipsanian columns where the aqueduct.
On the Death of a Young and Favorite Slave.
Post-Obits and the Poets.
Prithee die and set me free.
Procrastination.
Roman Presents.
Roman Thank-You Letter, A.
Sextus the Usurer.
Temperament.
Things That Cause a Quiet Life, The.
Though you serve richest wines.
To Cloe.
To His Book[e] ("To read my book, the virgin shy").
To His Girl.
To Sextus.
Too Literal Pupil, The.
Verses on Blenheim.
What a host you are, Mancinus.
What Makes a Happy Life.
Work and Play.
Would you, my friend, in little room express.
You read us your verse with your throat wrapped in wool.
You Serve the Best Wines Always, My Dear Sir.

Martin, Ada Louise
Sleep.

Martin, Bessie June
Let Me Look at Me.
True Riches.

Martin, C. D.
God's Goodness.

Martin, Charles
Leaving Buffalo.

Martin, Connie
Progress.

Martin, D. Roger
Hammerin' Hank.

Martin, D. S.
"O-U-G-H-"; or, The Cross Farmer.

Martin, David
Gordon Childe.
I Am a Jew.

Martin, Edward Sandford
Egotism.
Girl of Pompeii, A.
Little Brother of the Rich, A.
Sea Is His, The.

Martin, Herbert
Antigone I.
Antigone VI.
Lines: "Singularly and in pairs the decade has been ripped by bullets."
Negro Soldier's Viet Nam Diary, A.

Martin, John
God's Dark.

Martin, Julia E.
With Him.

Martin, Margaret Nickerson
Judas Iscariot.

Martin, Michael C.
Electric Storm.
Guard.

Martin, Philip
In March.

Martin, Richard
Sister Rose.

Martin, Sarah Catherine
Comic Adventures of Old Mother Hubbard and Her Dog, The.
Old Mother Hubbard.

Martin, Sir Theodore
Thieves' Anthology, The, *sel.*

Martin, Sir Theodore, *and* **William Edmonstoune Aytoun.** *See* **Aytoun, William Edmonstoune** *and* **Sir Theodore Martin**

Martin, William Wesley
Apple Orchard in the Spring, An.

Martinez, Lorri
Person, a Mexican, A.
Slow Death.
Twenty-two Minutes.

Martinez, Maurice
Suburbia.

Martinson, David
Nineteen Sections from a Twenty Acre Poem, *sels.*

Martinson, Harry
Sea Wind, The.

Marty, Sid
In the Dome Car of the "Canadian."

Marula
Meeting after Separation.

Marvell, Andrew
After Floods on the Wharfe.
Ametas and Thestylis Making Hay-Ropes.
Bermudas.
Carrying Their Coracles.

Charles II.
Clorinda and Damon.
Coronet, The.
Cromwell Dead.
Damon the Mower.
Definition of Love, The.
Dialogue between the Resolved Soul, and Created Pleasure, A.
Dialogue between the Soul and Body, A.
Dialogue between Thyrsis and Dorinda, A.
Dutch in the Medway, The.
Epitaph, An: "Enough; and leave the rest to fame."
Execution of King Charles, The.
Eyes and Tears.
Fair Singer, The.
From that blest bed the hero came.
Gallery, The.
Garden, The ("How vainly men themselves amaze").
Garden, A ("See how the flowers, as at parade").
Garden of Appleton House, The.
Hewel, or Woodpecker, The.
Horatian Ode upon Cromwel[l]'s Return from Ireland, An.
King Charles on [*or* upon] the Scaffold.
King Charles upon the Scaffold.
Kingfisher, The.
Last Instructions to a Painter, The.
Loyal Scot, The, *sel.*
Match, The.
Mourning.
Mower against Gardens, The.
Mower to the Glow-Worms [*or* Glowworms], The.
Mower's Song, The.
Nymph Complaining for the Death of Her Faun, The.
On a Drop of Dew.
On Mr. Milton's Paradise Lost.
On the Lord Mayor and Court of Aldermen, Presenting the Late King and Duke of York Each with a Copy of Their Freedoms.
Picture of Little T. C. in a Prospect of Flowers, The.
Poem upon the Death of Oliver Cromwell, A, *sel.*
Second Advice to a Painter, The.
Song of the Emigrants [in Bermuda].
Third Advice to a Painter, The.
Thoughts in a Garden.
To His Coy Mistress.
To His Noble Friend, Mr. Richard Lovelace, upon His Poems.
To His Worthy Friend Doctor Witty upon His Translation of the "Popular Errors."
Upon Appleton House, to My Lord Fairfax.
Upon the Death of His Late Highness the Lord Protector.
Vows, The.

Marx, Anne
Lacemaker (Vermeer), The.

Mary Benvenuta, Sister
Mater Incognita.

Mary Catherine, Sister
New Testament; Revised Edition.

Mary Honora, Sister
After Mardi Gras.
Eighteen.
Land of the Free.

Mary Immaculate, Sister
Ordination.

Mary Queen of Scots
Prayer before Execution.

Maryam bint Abi Ya'qub al-Ansari
What can you expect.

Marz, Roy
Vittoria Colonna.

Marzán, Julio
Epitaph: "Hours before my death."
Friday Evening.
Graduation Day, 1965.

Marzials, Théophile Julius Henry
May Margaret.
Pastoral, A: "Flower of the medlar."
Song: "There's one great bunch of stars in heaven."
Tragedy, A.
Twickenham Ferry.

Masahongva
Corn-blossom maidens.
Now from the east.

Masaoka Shiki
Haiku: "Things long forgotten."

Maschler, Fay
Little Bits of Soft-boiled Egg.

Masefield, John
All through the windless night the clipper rolled.
August, 1914.
Ballad of John Silver, A.
Biography, *sel.*
Book and Bookplate.
C. L. M.
Captain Stratton's Fancy.
Cargoes.
Choice, The.
Clipper Loitered South, The.
Consecration, A.
Creed, A.
Crowd, The.
Dauber, *sels.*
D'Avalos' Prayer.
Dawn.
Dead Knight, The.
Epilogue, An: "I have seen flowers come in stony places."
Everlasting Mercy, The, *sels.*
Flesh, I Have Knocked at Many a Dusty Door.
Fox Awakes, The.
Hell's Pavement.
How Many Ways.
I Could Not Sleep for Thinking of the Sky.
Is There a Great Green Commonwealth of Thought.
John Fitzgerald Kennedy.
June Twilight.
King's Highway, The.
Laugh and Be Merry.
Lemmings, The.
Lollingdon Downs, *sels.*
Midnight.
Night Is on the Downland, on the Lonely Moorland.
Night on the Downland.
Old Song Re-sung, An.
On Eastnor Knoll.
On Growing Old.
One of Wally's Yarns.
Partridges.
Passing Strange, The.
Port of Holy Peter.
Port of Many Ships.
Reynard the Fox, *sels.*
Rider at the Gate, The.
Rose of the World, The.
Rounding the Horn.
Sea Change.
Sea Fever.
Seekers, The.
Sonnet: "Flesh, I have knocked at many a dusty door."
Sonnet: "Here in the self is all that men can know."
Sonnet: "I never see the red rose crown the year."
Sonnet: "Is there a great green commonwealth of Thought."
Sonnet: "There, on the darkened deathbed, dies the brain."
Sonnets ("Long long ago"), *sels.*
Sorrow of Mydath.
Spanish Waters.
Tewkesbury Road.
To His Mother, C. L. M.
Tomorrow.
Trade Winds.
Tragedy of Pompey the Great, The, *sel.*
Truth.
Twilight.
Up on the Downs.
Valediction, A (Liverpool Docks).
Waggon-Maker, The.
Wanderer, The.
Wanderer's Song, A.
West Wind, The.
What Am I, Life?
Wild Duck, The.
Wild Geese, The.
Wood-Pigeons.
Yarn of the *Loch Achray,* The.

Mason, Agnes Louisa Carter
Whenever a Little Child Is Born.

Mason, Caroline Atherton Briggs
Do They Miss Me at Home?
Eventide.
Open Secret, An.
President Lincoln's Grave.
Reconciliation.
When I Am Old.
Whichever Way the Wind Doth Blow.

Mason, Caroline Atwater
En Voyage.

Mason, Edgar Cooper
Safe in His Keeping.
Satisfied.

Mason, Guy
Adventure.
Independence.

Mason, Madeline
Janus.

Mason, Mary Augusta
My Little Neighbor.
Scarlet Tanager, The.

Mason, Mason Jordan
Big Man.
In War.
Last Impression of New York.
Pen Hy Cane ("Pen Hyrogliphic Cane").
Pico della Mirandola.
Things of the Spirit.

Mason, Ronald
Self-Congratulatory Ode on Mr. Auden's Election to the Professorship of Poetry at Oxford.

Mason, W. L.
My Airedale Dog.

Mason, William
English Garden, The, *sels.*
How to Build a Ha-ha.
Landscape.
Ode to a Friend.
Sonnet: Anniversary, February 23, 1795.
Thomas Gray's View of Nature.

Massey, Gerald
All's Right with the World.
Desolate.
England.
His Banner over Me.
Little Willie.
Mother's Idol Broken, The, *sel.*
O, Lay Thy Hand in Mine, Dear!
Our Wee White Rose.
Parting.
Worker, The.
Young Love.

Massinger, Philip
Death Invoked.
Emperor of the East, The, *sel.*
Forest's Queen, The.
Maid of Honour, The, *sel.*
Men May Talk of Country-Christmasses.
Picture, The, *sel.*
Renegado, The, *sel.*
Sad Song, A.

Song: "Blushing rose and purple flower, The."
Song: "Why art thou slow, thou rest of trouble, Death."
Song of Pleasure, A.
Massman, Gordon
Liard Hot Springs.
Masson, Tom (Thomas Lansing Masson)
Enough.
He Took Her.
My Poker Girl.
Tragedy, A.
When I Get Time.
Master, Thomas
Cat and the Lute, The.
Masters, Edgar Lee
Aaron Hatfield.
Achilles Deatheridge.
Alfonso Churchill.
Amanda Barker.
Anne [*or* Ann] Rutledge.
Arlo Will.
Benjamin Franklin Hazard.
"Butch" Weldy.
Carl Hamblin.
Cassius Hueffer.
Catherine Ogg.
Circuit Judge, The.
Cooney Potter.
Daisy Fraser.
Davis Matlock.
Dora Williams.
Editor Whedon.
Edmund Pollard.
Elliott Hawkins.
Elsa Wertman.
Emily Sparks.
English Thornton.
Father Malloy.
Fiddler Jones.
Frank Drummer.
Hamilton Greene.
Harry Wilmans.
Henry C. Calhoun.
Herman Altman.
Hill, The.
Howard Lamson.
In Memory of Bryan Lathrop.
J. Milton Miles.
Jacob Godbey.
John Horace Burleson.
Jonathan Houghton.
Jonathan Swift Somers.
Judge Somers.
Julia Miller.
Keats to Fanny Brawne.
Knowlt Hoheimer.
Lost Orchard, The.
Lucinda Matlock.
Marx the Sign Painter.
Meredith Phyfe.
Mind Flying Afar.
My Dog Ponto.
New Spoon River, The, *sels.*
New World, The, *sel.*
Perry Zoll.
Petit, the Poet.
Reuben Pantier.
Rhoda Pitkin.
Rutherford McDowell.
Scholfield Huxley.
Seth Compton.
Sexsmith the Dentist.
Silence.
Spoon River Anthology, *sels.*
Supplication.
Thing Is Sex, Ben, The.
Thomas Trevelyan.
Tomorrow Is My Birthday, *sel.*
Unknown Soldiers.
Village Atheist, The.
Week-End by the Sea.
Widows.
William Jones.
Willis Beggs.
Masters, Marcia Lee
At My Mother's Bedside.
Country Ways.
Impressions of My Father, *sel.*
Mastin, Florence Ripley
At the Movies.
Return to Spring.
Mastoraki, Jenny
Bridal bed, The. Above it.
Crusaders knew the Holy Places, The.
Death of a Warrior, The.
Prometheus.
Then they paraded Pompey's urn.
Vandals, The.
Wooden Horse then said, The.
Mastrolia, Lilyan S.
Golden Gate: The Teacher.
Matchett, William H.
Aunt Alice in April.
Cedar Waxwing.
Head Couples.
Old Inn on the Eastern Shore.
Packing a Photograph from Firenze.
Return to Lane's Island.
Water Ouzel.
Mather, Cotton
Epitaph: "Dummer the shepherd sacrific'd."
Eternal God, How They're Increased, *with music.*
Go then, my dove, but now no longer mine.
I Lift My Eyes Up to the Hills, *with music.*
My Heart, How Very Hard It's Grown, *with music.*
O Glorious Christ of God; I live.
Vigilantius, or a Servant of the Lord Found Ready.
When the Seed of Thy Word Is Cast, *with music.*
Mather, Joseph
File-Hewer's Lamentation, The.
God Save Great Thomas Paine.
Matheson, Annie
Love's Cosmopolitan.
Song of Handicrafts, A.
Matheson, George
Christian Freedom.
Christ's Bondservant.
O Love That Wilt Not Let Me Go.
Matheson, Mary
Afterward.
Evening.
Matheus, John Frederick
Requiem: "She wears, my beloved, a rose upon her head."
Mathew, Ray
At a Time.
Good Thing, A.
Love and Marriage.
Lover's Meeting.
'Morning, Morning.
Wynyard Sailor.
Mathews, Albert
To an Autumn Leaf.
Mathews, Cornelius
Poet, The.
Mathews, Esther
Song: "I can't be talkin' of love, dear."
Mathews, Richard
Dear Patty, Dear Tania.
Mathis, Cleopatra
Aerial View of Louisiana.
Celebrating the Mass of Christian Burial.
For Maria.
Getting Out.
Mimosa.
Pine Barrens: Letter Home.
Ruston, Louisiana: 1952.
View of Louisiana.
Mathison, Thomas
Goff, The; an Heroi-comical Poem, *sel.*
Victory on the Last Green.
Mattam, Donald
In a Town Garden.
Table Talk.
Matthews, Alice Clear
Of the Mathematician.
Matthews, Brander
American Girl, An.
Matthews, Harley
Return of the Native, The.
Matthews, T. S.
Invisible Man, The.
Song for Mother's Day.
Matthews, William
Airline Breakfast, An.
Bring the War Home.
Bystanders.
Cat, The.
Charming.
Cows Grazing at Sunrise.
Directions.
Elegy for Bob Marley, An.
Hello, Hello.
Housework.
In Memory of the Utah Stars.
Invention of Astronomy, The.
Living among the Dead.
Loyal.
Lust.
Moving.
Moving Again.
Nurse Sharks.
Oh Yes.
On the Porch at the Frost Place, Franconia, NH.
Our Strange and Lovable Weather.
Praise.
Search Party, The.
Taking the Train Home.
Twins.
Unrelenting Flood.
Whiplash.
Matthias, John
Evening Song.
In Columbus, Ohio.
Matuzak, Joseph
Nystagmus.
To Sherrie.
Matveyeva, Novella
Eggplants Have Pins and Needles, The.
Maunders, Ruth O.
Eureka.
Maura, Sister
Annunciation.
Blessing of St. Francis, The.
Deirdre's Song at Sunrise.
Rosary, The, *abr.*
Short History of the Teaching Profession, A.
Woman's Liberation.
Maura, Sister Mary
Our Lady of the Refugees.
To the Queen of Dolors.
"Maurice, Furnley" (Frank Wilmot)
Agricultural Show, Flemington, Victoria, The.
On a Grey-haired Old Lady Knitting at an Orchestral Concert.
Supremer Sacrifice, The.
Team, The.
Upon a Row of Old Books and Shoes in a Pawnbroker's Window.
Victoria Markets Recollected in Tranquillity, The, *sel.*
Maurice, Thomas
Epistle to the Right Hon. Charles James Fox, An, *sel.*
Mauropus, John
Our Lady of the Passion.
Mavimbela
My money! O, my money!
Mavity, Nancy Barr
Prisoners.

Maxson, H. A.
When It Rains.
Maxton, Hugh
Cernunnos.
Dialectique.
Landscape with Minute Wildflowers.
Mastrim; a Meditation, *sel.*
Waking.
Maxtone Graham, Joyce Anstruther. *See* **"Struther, Jan"**
Maxwell, James Clerk
In Memory of Edward Wilson.
Rigid Body Sings.
Maxwell-Hall, Agnes
Jamaica Market.
May, Beulah
Captain of St. Kitts, The.
Deprecating Parrots.
May, Curtis
Tucking the Baby In.
May, Edward
Five Things White.
To a Covetous Churl.
To Barba.
To Her Love.
You tender virgins, fairer than the snow with which you play.
May, Julia Harris
Day by Day.
May, Thomas
Dear, Do Not Your Fair Beauty Wrong.
Mayakovsky, Vladimir Vladimirovich
Brooklyn Bridge.
Cloud in Trousers, A, *abr.*
Our March.
Spring.
Maybin, Patrick
April 1940.
Ballykinlar: May 1940.
Fallen Tree, The.
Monks at Ards, The.
Thoughts from Abroad.
Mayer, Conny Hannes
Of the Beloved Caravan.
Mayer, Frank H.
At Timber Line.
Mayer, Gerda
Dandelions.
Mayer, Hansjörg
Oil.
Mayhall, Jane
City Sparrow.
For the Market.
Human Animal, The.
Marshes, The.
Surfaces.
Maynard, Don
Athlete.
Maynard, Theodore
Desideravi.
Dwell with Me, Lovely Images.
Faith's Difficulty.
If I Had Ridden Horses.
Requiem: "When my last song is sung and I am dead."
Mayne, Jasper
Time.
To the Memory of Ben Johnson, *sel.*
Mayne, John
Glasgow, *sel.*
Hallowe'en.
Logan Braes ("By Logan's streams that rin sae deep").
Mayne, Seymour
Abraham Sutskever.
Afternoon's Angel.
Before Passover.
In the First Cave.
Locusts of Silence.
Roots.
Yehuda Amichai.
Mayo, Edward Leslie
Anglo-Saxon.
At the Louvre.
D Minor, The.
Diver, The.
Doomed City, The.
El Greco.
En Route.
Envoi: "Running out of town on a rail is too good for."
Failure.
Fair Warning, A.
I Saw My Father.
In the Web.
Letter to Karl Shapiro.
Nausea.
Note on Modern Journalism during the Last Campaign.
Of Angels.
On the Night Train from Oxford.
Oracle.
Pool, The.
Sleeping Beauty, The.
Stone.
Stones of Sleep, The.
To the Young Rebels.
Uninfected, The.
Variations on a Line from Shakespeare's Fifty-sixth Sonnet.
Wagon Train.
We Still Must Follow.
Word of Water, The.
Mayröcker, Friederike
Patron of Flawless Serpent Beauty.
Maze, Mack
If you see my mother, partner, tell her pray for me.
Mazzaro, Jerome
At Torrey Pines State Park.
Fall Colors.
M'Baye, Annette
Silhouette.
Mberi, Antar S. K.
Nuflo de Olano (Who Sailed with Balboa).
Meacham, Harry M.
To a Young Poet.
Mead, Margaret
Misericordia.
Mead, Philip
Chinese Graves in Beechworth Cemetery, The.
Mead, Stella
Merry Man of Paris, The.
Mearns, Hughes
Alibi.
Antigonish.
Crime Note.
Frustrated Male.
I Met a Man.
Lady with Technique, The.
Later Antigonishes, *sels.*
Little Man Who Wasn't There, The.
Perfect Reactionary, The.
Reveille.
Mechain, Gwerfyl
In the Snowfall.
Lady of the Ferry Inn.
Mechtild of Magdeburg [*or* Mechthild von Magdeburg]
Flowering Light of the Godhead, The, *sel.*
Love Flows from God.
Medici, Lorenzo de'
Carnival Songs, *sel.*
Triumph of Bacchus and Ariadne.
Two Lyrics.
Meehan, John James
Race of the *Oregon,* The.
Meeks, Dodie
There Goes a Girl Walking.
Megged, Matti
Akedah, The.
Phoenix, The.
White Bird.
Mehri (Mihru'n-Nisa of Herat)
Coming Across.
Meidhre, Brian MacGiolla. *See* **Merriman, Brian**
Meigs, Charles D.
Home without a Bible, A, *abr.*
Others.
Meigs, Mildred Plew
Abraham Lincoln.
Johnny Fife and Johnny's Wife.
Organ Grinders' Garden, The.
Pirate Don Durk of Dowdee, The.
Shepherd Left Behind, The.
Silver Ships.
To Chicago at Night.
Meiners, Roger K.
Marginal Music.
Meinke, Peter
Absence.
Advice to My Son.
Artist, The.
Byron vs. DiMaggio.
Cheerios.
Dear Reader.
Elegy for a Diver.
Happy at 40.
Hermann Ludwig Ferdinand Von Helmholtz ("Hermann Helmholtz said the/problem").
Mendel's Law.
Progress.
Surfaces.
This Is a Poem to My Son Peter.
To a Daughter with Artistic Talent.
To an Athlete Turned Poet.
Meireles, Cecilia
Away from You.
Ballad of the Ten Casino Dancers.
Dead Horse, The.
Motive.
Pyrargyrite Metal, 9.
Roosters Will Crow, The.
Song: "I placed my dream in a boat."
Meïr of Rothenburg
Burning of the Law, The.
Meissner, William
Coal Mine Disaster's Last Trapped Man Contemplates Salvation, The.
Fishermen at Dawn.
Photographer Whose Shutter Died, The.
Slaughterhouse Boys, The.
Smell of Fish, The.
Mei Yao Ch'en
Friend Advises Me to Stop Drinking, A.
On the Death of a New Born Child.
Melcombe, Baron. *See* **Dodington, George Bubb, Baron Melcombe**
Meleager
Busy with love, the bumble bee.
Epigram: "And now I, Meleager, am among them."
Epigram: "As honey in wine/wine, honey."
Epigram: "At 12 o'clock in the afternoon."
Epigram: "Boys of Tyre are beautiful, The."
Epigram: "Breath of my life, The—no less."
Epigram: "Diodorus is nice, isn't he, Philocles?"
Epigram: "Drink, unhappy lover, drink."
Epigram: "I was thirsty."
Epigram: "It is true that I held Thero fair."
Epigram: "Listen, you know the pains of love."
Epigram: "Lo! Beauty flashed forth sweetly; from his eyes."
Epigram: "Love brought me quietly in the dreaming night."
Epigram: "One boy alone in all the world for me."
Garland for Heliodora, A.
I'll twine white violets and the myrtle green.
In the Spring.
Little Love-God, The.
Lost Desire.
Love at the Door.
Love's night and a lamp.
O Gentle Ships.

Of Himself.
Of His Death.
Spring.
Wine Cup, The.
Meléndez, Jesús Papoleto
Open Poetry Reading.
Melinescu, Gabriela
Birth.
Fall.
Time of Fish Dying.
Mellen, Grenville
Lonely Bugle Grieves, The.
Ode on the Celebration of the Battle of Bunker Hill, June 17, 1825, *sel.*
Mellichamp, Leslie
Epitaph: "Here he lies moulding."
Mello Breyner Andresen, Sophia de. *See* **Andresen, Sophia de Mello Breyner**
Melly, George
Belle de Jour.
Homage to René Magritte.
Meltzer, David
Eyes, the Blood, The.
15th Raga: For Bela Lugosi.
Midrash, *sel.*
Prayerwheel: 2.
Ragas, *sels.*
Revelations.
Tell Them I'm Struggling to Sing with Angels.
12th Raga: For Jon Wieners.
Meltzer, Richard
Poem moves down a page, A.
Melvill, Elizabeth, Lady Culross
Godly Dream, A, *sels.*
Melville, Herman
Aeolian Harp, The.
After the Pleasure Party.
Apparition, The.
Art.
At the Cannon's Mouth.
Attic Landscape, The.
Ball's Bluff.
Bench of Boors, The.
Berg, The.
Billy Budd, Foretopman, *sel.*
Billy in the Darbies.
Blue-Bird, The.
Bridegroom Dick, *sel.*
Buddha.
Camoens.
Camoens in the Hospital.
Clarel, *sels.*
College Colonel, The.
Commemorative of a Naval Victory.
Conflict of Convictions, The.
Crossing the Tropics.
Cumberland, The.
Dirge for McPherson, A.
Eagle of the Blue, The.
Enviable Isles, The.
Epilogue: "If Luther's day expand to Darwin's year."
Fall of Richmond, The.
Falstaff's Lament over Prince Hal Become Henry V.
Father Mapple's Hymn.
"Formerly a Slave."
Fragments of a Lost Gnostic Poem of the Twelfth Century.
Greek Architecture.
Healed of My Hurt.
House-Top, The.
Immolated.
In a Garret.
In the Pauper's Turnip-Field.
In the Prison Pen.
Inscription for Marye's Heights, Fredericksburg.
John Marr, *sel.*
L'Envoi: Return of the Sire de Nesle, The.
Lone Founts.
Lover and the Syringa-Bush, The.
Lyon.
Maldive Shark, The.
Malvern Hill.
March into Virginia, The.
Martyr, The.
Meditation, A.
Memorial: On the Slain at Chickamauga.
Misgivings.
Moby Dick, *sel.*
Monody.
My Jacket Old.
New Ancient of Days, The.
Night-March, The.
Of Rama.
Of Rome.
Old Age in His Ailing.
Old Counsel.
On Mammon.
On the Grave of a Young Cavalry Officer Killed in the Valley of Virginia.
Pebbles.
Pontoosuce.
Portent, The.
Prelusive.
Ravaged Villa, The.
Requiem for Soldiers Lost in Ocean Transports, A.
Return of the Sire de Nesle A. D. 16—, The.
Ribs and Terrors, The.
Running the Batteries.
Sheridan at Cedar Creek.
Shiloh; a Requiem.
Sodom.
Southern Cross.
Stone Fleet, The.
Surrender at Appomattox, The.
Temeraire, The.
To Ned.
Tuft of Kelp, The.
Ungar and Rolfe.
Uninscribed Monument on One of the Battle-Fields of the Wilderness, An.
Utilitarian View of the *Monitor's* Fight, A.
Victor of Antietam, The.
Whale, The.
Melville, James
Black Bastill, The; or, A Lamentation of the Kirk of Scotland, *sel.*
Robin at My Window.
Menahem ben Jacob
Harvesting of the Roses, The.
Martyr's Death, A.
Menahem ben Makhir of Ratisbon
How Sweet Thy Precious Gift of Rest.
Menander
I Hold Him Happiest.
Menashe, Samuel
Winter.
Mendelssohn, Asher
Cordoba.
Mendelssohn, Moses
Love the Beautiful.
Self-Portrait.
Mendès, Catulle
I Go by Road.
Mother, The.
Mendes, Moses
Ass, The.
Chaplet, The, *sels.*
On the Death of a Lady's Owl.
Philanderer, The.
Menebroker, Ann
In the Half-Point Time of Night.
To the Man I Live With.
Meng Chiao
After Passing the Examination.
Failing the Examination.
Menth, Robert
Cry from the Battlefield.
Menzies, G. K.
Poaching *in Excelsis.*
Mercantini, Luigi
Garibaldi Hymn, The.
Mercer, Ernestine
Artist.
Mercer, Jesse
Will God forever cast us off.
Mercer, Johnny
Glow-Worm, The.
I'm an Old Cowhand.
Jubilation T. Cornpone.
Mercer, Margaret
Exhortation to Prayer.
Mercer, Thomas
Arthur's Seat, *sel.*
Merchant, Jane
Flight Plan.
Unless We Guard Them Well.
Mercier, Louis
Notre Dame des Petits.
Meredith, George
Appeasement of Demeter, The.
Appreciation.
At dinner, she is hostess, I am host.
Ballad of Past Meridian, A.
Dirge in Woods.
Dusty Answer, A.
Empedocles.
Faith on Trial, A, *sel.*
Here Jack and Tom Are Paired with Moll and Meg.
Hymn to Colour.
Islet the Dachs.
Juggling Jerry.
Jump-to-Glory Jane.
King Harald's Trance.
Lark Ascending, The.
Lines: "Love within the lover's breast."
Love Dies.
Love in the Valley.
Love's Grave.
Lucifer in Starlight.
Marian.
Meditation under Stars.
Melampus.
Modern Love.
Night of Frost in May.
Ode to the Spirit of Earth in Autumn.
Old Chartist, The.
On the Danger of War.
Orchard and the Heath, The.
Penetration and Trust.
Phoebus with Admetus.
Promise in Disturbance, The.
Question Whither, The.
Sense and Spirit.
Should Thy Love Die.
Sonnet X: "But where began the change; and what's my crime?"
Sonnet I: "By this he knew she wept with waking eyes."
Sonnet XVIII: "Here Jack and Tom are paired with Moll and Meg."
Sonnet XLV: "It is the season of the sweet wild rose."
Sonnet XLIII: "Mark where the pressing wind shoots javelin-like."
Sonnet L: "Thus piteously Love closed what he begat."
Sonnet XXX: "What are we first? First, animals; and next."
Sweet o' the Year, The.
Test of Manhood, The, *sel.*
Thrush in February, The.
We Saw the Swallows.
White Owl, The.
Wind on the Lyre.
Winter Heavens.
Young Reynard.
Meredith, Joseph
Midnight, Walking the Wakeful Daughter.
"Meredith, Owen" (Edward Robert Bulwer-Lytton, 1st Earl of Lytton)
Aux Italiens.
Changes.

Check to Song.
Chess-Board, The.
Glenaveril, *sel.*
Going Back Again.
Last Lines, *sel.*
Last Wish, The.
Lucile, *sel.*
One Thing.
Portrait, The.
Since We Parted.
Tears.
Tempora Acta.
Twins.
What We May Live Without.
White Anemone, The, *sel.*
Meredith, William
Accidents of Birth.
At the Natural History Museum.
Bachelor.
Battle Problem.
Boon, A.
Chinese Banyan, The.
Consequences.
Country Stars.
Couple Overhead, The.
Do Not Embrace Your Mind's New Negro Friend.
Earth Walk.
Effort at Speech.
Fishvendor, The.
Fledglings.
For Guillaume Apollinaire.
His Plans for Old Age.
Homage to Paul Mellon, I. M. Pei, Their Gallery, and Washington City.
Iambic Feet Considered as Honorable Scars.
Illiterate, The.
Korean Woman Seated by a Wall, A.
Last Things.
Love Letter from an Impossible Land.
My Mother's Life.
Old Field Mowed, An.
On Falling Asleep by Firelight.
On Falling Asleep to Birdsong.
Open Sea, The.
Parents.
Perhaps the Best Time.
Picture of a Castle.
Poem about Morning.
Rainy Season, The.
Rhode Island.
Starlight.
Thoughts on One's Head.
To a Western Bard Still a Whoop and a Holler Away from English Poetry.
To the Thoughtful Reader.
Transport.
Traveling Boy.
Two Masks Unearthed in Bulgaria.
View of the Brooklyn Bridge, A.
Walter Jenks' Bath.
Weather.
Wholesome.
Winter Verse for My [*or* His] Sister.
Meredith, William Tuckey
Farragut.
Meredyth, Mr.
To Miss on the Death of Her Goldfish.
Meriluoto, Aila
Still.
Merivale, Herman Charles
Aetate XIX.
Darwinity.
Ready, Ay, Ready.
Merkel, Andrew
Tallahassee, *sel.*
Mernit, Susan
Scholar's Wife, The.
Song of the Bride.
Merriam, Eve
Alligator on the Escalator.
Ballad of the Double Bed.
Bam, Bam, Bam.
Blue Alert.
Catch a Little Rhyme.
Charm for Our Time, A.
Cheers.
City Traffic.
Coward, The.
Direct Song.
Fertile Valley of the Nile, The.
Finding a Poem.
Grandmother, Rocking.
Leaning on a Limerick, *sel.*
Leavetaking.
Love Letters, Unmailed.
Love-making, The: His and Hers.
Misnomer.
Moment before Conception, The.
Monogamania.
Neuteronomy.
One, Two, Three—Gough!
Rainbow Writing.
Reply to the Question: "How Can You Become a Poet?"
Restricted.
Sing a Song of Subways.
Some Uses for Poetry.
Summer Rain.
Teevee.
Think Tank.
Tryst.
Two People.
Umbilical.
Wall, The.
What in the World?
Which Washington?
Merrick, James
Chameleon, The.
Ignorance of Man, The.
Merrill, Arthur Truman
Spring in the Desert.
Merrill, Boynton, Jr.
Stallion, The.
Merrill, Herbert
Courthouse Square.
Merrill, James
About the Phoenix.
After Greece.
Angel.
Bed, The.
Birthday.
Black Mesa, The.
Black Swan, The.
Broken Bowl, The.
Broken Home, The.
Childlessness.
Cloud Country.
Country of a Thousand Years of Peace, The.
Current, The.
Days of 1964.
Developers at Crystal River.
Drowning Poet, The.
18 West 11th.
Foliage of Vision.
For a Second Marriage.
Friend of the Fourth Decade, The.
Furnished Room, The.
Getting Through.
Grand Canyon, The.
Green Eye, The.
Greenhouse, The.
Hotel de l'Univers et Portugal.
Kite Poem.
Laboratory Poem.
Last Words.
Lost in Translation.
Mad Scene, The.
Manos Karastefanis.
Matinees.
Mirror.
Octopus, The.
Olive Grove.
Parrot Fish, The.
Part of the Vigil.
Power Station, The.
Preface to the Memoirs, A.
Renewal, A.
Scenes of Childhood.
16. ix. 65.
Some Negatives: X. at the Chateau.
Swimming by Night.
Thistledown.
Thousand and Second Night, The.
Timepiece, A.
Tomorrows.
Transfigured Bird.
Upon a Second Marriage.
Urban Convalescence, An.
Variations: The Air Is Sweetest That a Thistle Guards.
Victor Dog, The.
View of the Burning, A.
Voices from the Other World.
Watching the Dance.
Whitebeard on Videotape.
Who Guessed Amiss the Riddle of the Sphinx.
Willowware Cup.
Merrill, Lynn
Steady Rain.
Merrill, William Pierson
Call to the Strong, The.
Festal Song.
Not Alone for Mighty Empire.
Rise Up, O Men of God, *with music.*
Merriman, Brian [*or*Brian MacGiolla Meidhre]
Country's Crisis, The.
Husband's Lament, The.
Irish Marriage Night, An.
Lament of the Unmarried Girl, The.
Maiden's Plight, The.
Midnight Court, The.
Now God Stand Up for Bastards.
Old Man's Tale, The.
Solution, The.
Walk.
Merritt, Dixon Lanier
Limerick: "Wonderful bird is the pelican, A."
Merry, Robert
Sir Roland; a Fragment.
Merryman, Mildred Plew. *See* **Meigs, Mildred Plew**
Mersar
Allace! So Sobir Is the Micht.
Mertins, Louis
Rain Chant.
Merton, Thomas
Argument, An—of the Passion of Christ.
Aubade: Lake Erie.
Baroque Gravure, A.
Blessed Virgin Mary Compared to a Window, The.
Cana.
Dark Morning, The.
Duns Scotus.
Elegy for the Monastery Barn.
Evening of the Visitation, The.
Figure for an Apocalypse.
For My Brother.
In the Year 1945 an Original Child Was Born.
Lent in a Year of War.
Original Child Bomb, *sel.*
Practical Program for Monks, A.
Responsory, 1948, A.
St. Malachy.
Seneca.
Stranger.
There Has to Be a Jail for Ladies.
To a Severe Nun.
Trappist Abbey, The: Matins.
Merwin, William Stanley
Air: "Naturally it is night."
Annunciation, The.
Another Year Come.
Approaches, The.
Asians Dying, The.

Assembly.
Avoiding News by the River.
Backwater Pond: The Canoeists.
Ballad of John Cable and Three Gentlemen.
Ballade of Sayings.
Birds Waking.
Black Plateau, The.
Blind Girl.
Blue Cockerel.
Bones, The.
Bread.
Broken, The.
Bucolic.
Burning Mountain.
Burning the Cat.
Caesar.
Camel.
Carol of the Three Kings.
Chaff, The.
Child, The.
Colloquy at Peniel.
Come Back.
Dead Hand.
December: Of Aphrodite.
December among the Vanished.
December Night.
Departure's Girl-Friend.
Dictum: For a Masque of Deluge.
Diggers, The.
Distances, The.
Divinities.
Door, A.
Drunk in the Furnace, The.
Dusk in Winter.
Early January.
Exercise.
February.
Finding a Teacher.
Fly.
Fog-Horn.
Footprints on the Glacier.
For a Coming Extinction.
For Now.
For the Anniversary of My Death.
Glass.
Gods, The.
Grandfather in the Old Men's Home.
Grandmother and Grandson.
Grandmother Watching at Her Window.
Herds, The.
Highway, The.
Home for Thanksgiving.
Horse, The.
Hosts, The.
Hours of a Bridge, The.
I Live up Here.
In the Night Fields.
In the Winter of My Thirty-eighth Year.
Indigestion of the Vampire, The.
Initiate, The.
It Is March ("It is March and black dust falls out of the books").
John Otto.
Judgment of Paris, The.
Last One, The.
Lemuel's Blessing.
Letter.
Leviathan.
Looking for Mushrooms at Sunrise.
Low Fields and Light.
Mariners' Carol.
Master, The.
Moths, The.
Mountain, The.
Native, The.
Odysseus.
Old Boast, The.
Old Room, The.
On the Subject of Poetry.
Owl, The.
Peasant.
Place of Backs, The.
Plea for a Captive.
Poem, The: "Coming late, as always."
"Portland" Going Out, The.
Resolution.
River of Bees, The.
Road.
Rock, The.
Room, The.
St. Vincent's.
Sapphire, The.
Sea Monster.
Separation.
Sire.
Small Woman on Swallow Street.
Snowfall.
Some Last Questions.
Song of Three Smiles.
Spring.
Students of Justice, The.
Sunset after Rain.
Surf-casting.
Things.
Thorn Leaves in March.
To the Hand.
Toro.
Trail into Kansas, The.
Trees.
Two Horses.
Variation on a Line by Emerson.
Variation on the Gothic Spiral.
Views from the High Camp.
Vineyard, The.
Vision.
Voice.
Walk-up.
War, The.
Watchers.
Waving of a Hand, The.
Way to the River, The.
We Continue.
When I Came from Colchis.
When You Go Away.
Whenever I Go There.
White Goat, White Ram.
White Summer Flower.
Widow, The.
Windows, The.
Witnesses.
Yesterday.
You, Genoese Mariner.
Mesens, E. L. T.
Arid Husband, The.
Messenger, Bill
Carol Took Her Clothes Off.
Messinger, Robert Hinckley
Give Me the Old.
Winter Wish, A.
Metastasio, Pietro
Age of Gold.
Metcalf, Nelson C.
Kid in Upper 4, The.
Metz, Jerred
Angels in the House.
Divination.
Her True Body.
Speak like Rain.
Metz, Roberta
Zeyde.
Mew, Charlotte
A Quoi Bon Dire.
Absence.
Again.
Beside the Bed.
Call, The.
Cenotaph, The.
Changeling, The.
Domus Caedet Arborem.
Exspecto Resurrectionem.
Fame.
Farmer's Bride, The.
Here Lies a Prisoner.
I Have Been Through the Gates.
I So Liked Spring.
In the Fields.
June, 1915.
Madeleine in Church.
May, 1915.
Monsieur Qui Passe.
Moorland Night.
Narrow Door, The.
Not for That City.
Old Shepherd's Prayer.
On the Asylum Road.
On the Road to the Sea.
Pedlar, The.
Quiet House, The.
Rambling Sailor, The.
Rooms.
Saturday Market.
Sea Love.
Smile, Death.
Song: "Love, love today, my dear."
To a Child in Death.
Trees Are Down, The.
Meyer, Bertha
God's Eye Is on the Sparrow.
Meyer, Conny Hannes
Beast That Rode the Unicorn, The.
Meyer, Gerard Previn
Rapunzel Song.
S. T. Coleridge Dismisses a Caller from Porlock.
Meyer, Lucy R.
He Was Not Willing.
Meyers, Bert
Dark Birds, The.
Daybreak.
Funeral.
Garlic, The.
Picture Framing.
Pigeons.
Stars Climb Girders of Light.
Suburban Dusk.
Meyerstein, Edward Harry William
Ivy and Holly.
Meynell, Alice (Mrs. Wilfrid Meynell)
At Night.
Chimes.
Christ in the Universe.
Crucifixion, The.
Dead Harvest, A.
Easter Night.
Father of Women, A.
Fugitive, The.
General Communion, A.
"I Am the Way."
In Early Spring.
In Manchester Square.
In Portugal, 1912.
In Sleep.
Lady of the Lambs, The.
Lady Poverty, The.
Launch, The.
Letter from a Girl to Her Own Old Age, A.
"Lord, I Owe Thee a Death."
My Heart Shall Be Thy Garden.
November Blue.
October Redbreast, The.
One Wept Whose Only Child Was Dead.
Parentage.
Poet of One Mood, A.
Poet to the Birds, The.
Rainy Summer, The.
Renouncement.
"Rivers Unknown to Song."
Roaring Frost, The.
San Lorenzo Giustiniani's Mother.
Shepherdess, The.
Singers to Come.
Song of Derivations, A.
Song of the Night at Daybreak.
Summer in England, 1914.
Thoughts in Separation.
Threshing Machine, The.
Thrush before Dawn, A.

To a Daisy.
To the Body.
To the Mother of Christ, the Son of Man.
To W.M.
Two Poets, The.
Two Questions, The.
Unto Us a Son Is Given.
Veni Creator.
Via, Veritas, et Vita.
Watershed, The.
Wind Is Blind, The.
Young Neophyte, The.

Meynell, Sir Francis
Permanence.

Meynell, Viola
Frozen Ocean, The.
Jonah and the Whale.

Meynell, Wilfrid
Folded Flock, The.
Joseph Mary Plunkett.

Meyrich, Geraldine
Washington.

Mezey, Robert
After Hours.
Against Seasons.
April Fourth.
Back.
Bedtime Story, A.
Being a Giant.
Celebration, The.
Confession, A.
Couplets 20 [*or* XX].
Epitaph of a Faithful Man.
Evening, An.
Friendship, The.
Funeral Home, The.
How Much Longer?
I Am Here.
If I Should Die before I Wake.
In Defense of Felons.
In the Environs of the Funeral Home.
In the Soul Hour.
In This Life.
Lovemaker, The.
My Mother.
New Year's Eve in Solitude.
Night on Clinton.
No Country You Remember.
One Summer.
Reaching the Horizon.
Salesman, The.
Simpler Thing, a Chair, A.
Street Scene.
There.
Theresienstadt Poems, *sel.*
To Her.
Touch It.
Underground Gardens, The.
Vetus Flamma.
Wandering Jew, The.
White Blossoms.
You Could Say.

Mezquida, Anna Blake
Chinatown.
Hope.

Mhac an tSaoi, Máire
Harvest of the Sea.

Miccolis, Leila
I wanted to see you,/ thighs showing.
Till Death Do Us Part.

Michael, Cyril R.
Shirley Temple.

Michael Marie, Sister
Our Lady on Calvary.

Michael of Kildare, Friar
Sweet Jesus.

Michaelis, Hanny
Listening.
Under Restless Clouds.
We Carry Eggshells.

Michal, M. L.
From Skye, Early Autumn.

Michelangelo Buonarroti
Celestial Love.
Dante.
Doom of Beauty, The.
Eternal Lord! Eased of a Cumbrous Load.
For Inspiration.
From thy fair face I learn, O my loved lord.
Garland and the Girdle, The.
Joy May Kill.
Love, the Light-Giver.
Love's Entreaty.
Love's Justification.
On the Brink of Death.
Prayer for Faith, A.
Prayer for Purification, A.
Soul of Dante, The.
Three Poems.
To Luigi del Riccio, after the Death of Cecchino Bracci.
To the Marchesana of Pescara.
To the Supreme Being.
To Tommaso de' Cavalieri ("Why should I seek to ease intense desire").
To Tommaso de' Cavalieri ("With your fair eyes a charming light I see").
To Vittoria Colonna.
Transfiguration of Beauty, The.
Waiting in Faith.

Michelson, Max
Bird, The.
Hymn to Night, A.
O Brother Tree.

Michie, James
Arizona Nature Myth.
Closing Time.
Dooley Is a Traitor.
Ghost of an Education, The.
Three Dreams.

Michie, Martial
Whenever you drink all night you make.

Mickle, William Julius
Concubine, The, *sels.*
Cumnor Hall.
Mariner's Wife, The.
Sailor's Wife, The.
Sunset.
There's Nae Luck about the House.
Wild Romantic Dell, A.

Middlebrook, Diane
Contagiousness of Dreams, The.
For You, Falling Asleep after a Quarrel.

Middleton, Bill
Cops and Robbers.

Middleton, Christopher
Abasis.
Alba after Six Years.
Ancestors, The.
Ant Sun, The.
Dress, The.
Edward Lear in February.
Forenoon, The.
Herman Moon's Hourbook, *sels.*
In Some Seer's Cloud Car.
In the Secret House.
Male Torso.
News from Norwood.
Ode on Contemplating Clapham Junction.
Oystercatchers.
Pointed Boots.
Tanker.
Thinking of Hölderlin.
Thousand Things, The.
Waterloo Bridge.

Middleton, Jesse Edgar
Huron Carol, The.
Jesous Ahatonhia.

Middleton, Richard
Any Lover, Any Lass.
Carol of the Poor Children, The.
Dream Song.
For He Had Great Possessions.
Lass That Died of Love, The.
Love's Mortality.
On a Dead Child.
Pagan Epitaph.
Serenade: "By day my timid passions stand."
Song of the King's Minstrel, The.

Middleton, Scudder
Jezebel.
Journey, The.
Poets, The.
Wisdom.

Middleton, Thomas
Blurt, Master Constable, *sels.*
Changeling, The, *sels.*
Chaste Maid in Cheapside, A, *sel.*
Lips and Eyes.
Mad World, My Masters, A, *sel.*
Midnight.
Parting.
Song: "Love for such a cherry lip."
To Vesta.
True Love Ditty, A.
Witch, The, *sel.*

Middleton, Thomas *and* William Rowley
Spanish Gipsy [*or* Gypsy], The, *sel.*
Trip It Gipsies, Trip It Fine.

Midlane, Albert
Above the Bright Blue Sky, *sel.*

Mieko, Kanai
House of Madam Juju, The.

Mifflin, Lloyd
Battle-Field, The.
Doors, The.
Fiat Lux.
Flight, The.
Half-Mast.
Harvest Waits, The.
He Made the Night.
Milton.
Sesostris.
Ship, The.
Sovereign Poets.
Sovereigns, The.
Theseus and Ariadne.
To a Maple Seed.
To the Milkweed.

Mihri, Hatun
At one glance/ I loved you.

Miklitsch, Robert
As in the Land of Darkness.

Milbauer, Joseph
Interior.

Milburn, Ken
Motive for Mercy.

Miles, C. Austin
In the Garden.

Miles, George Henry
Said the Rose.

Miles, Josephine
As difference blends into identity.
Away.
Belief.
Bounty.
Campaign, The.
Care.
Civilian.
Conception.
Conservancies.
Doctor Who Sits at the Bedside of a Rat, The.
Dream.
Entrepreneur chicken shed his tail feathers, surplus, The.
Family.
Find.
Forecast.
Government Injunction.
Gypsy.
Halt, The.
Housewife.
If You Will.
I've been going around everywhere without any skin.
Made Shine.

Memorial Day.
Merchant Marine.
Midweek.
Monkey.
Moving In.
None.
Oedipus.
On Inhabiting an Orange.
Preliminary to Classroom Lecture.
Purchase of a Blue, Green, or Orange Ode.
Reason.
Sale.
Savages, The.
Sisyphus.
So Graven.
Student.
Summer.
Sunday.
Sympathizers, The.
Tally.
Vacuum.
Voyage.
Witness.

Miles, Ron
Lives of the Poet.

Miles, Sara
Portrait in Available Light.

Miles, Susan (Ursula Roberts)
Cenotaph, The.
He Sports by Himself.
Microcosmos.

Millard, Bob
Bury Our Faces.

Millard, Geoffrey C.
Hospital.

Millard, Gertrude
Nostalgia.

Millay, Edna St. Vincent ("Nancy Boyd")
Above These Cares.
Admetus, from my marrow's core I do.
Afternoon on a Hill.
And You as Well Must Die, Beloved Dust.
Apostrophe to Man.
Ashes of Life.
Ballad of the Harp-Weaver, The.
Bean-Stalk, The.
Buck in the Snow, The.
Cameo, The.
City Trees.
Conscientious Objector.
Counting-out Rhyme.
Departure.
Dirge without Music.
Elegy: "Let them bury your big eyes."
Elegy before Death.
End of Summer, The.
Epitaph for the Race of Man, *sels.*
Euclid Alone Has Looked on Beauty Bare.
Even in the moment of our earliest kiss.
Exiled.
Feast.
Figs from Thistles.
First Fig.
From a Very Little Sphinx.
Gazing upon him now, severe and dead.
God's World.
Grown-up.
Hearing your words, and not a word among them.
Huntsman, What Quarry?
I, Being Born a Woman and Distressed.
I Dreamed I Moved among the Elysian Fields.
I Like Americans.
I Shall Forget You Presently, My Dear.
I Shall Go Back.
In the Grave No Flower.
Intention to Escape from Him.
Journal, *sels.*
Justice Denied in Massachusetts.
Keen.
Lament: "Listen, children:/ Your father is dead."
Look, Edwin!
Love is not blind. I see with single eye.
Memorial to D. C., *sel.*
Men Working.
Moriturus.
My most distinguished guest and learnèd friend.
Never May the Fruit Be Plucked.
Night is my sister, and how deep in love.
Not in a silver casket cool with pearls.
Not with Libations.
O God, I Cried, No Dark Disguise, *with music.*
Oh, oh, you will be sorry for that word!
Oh, Sleep Forever in the Latmian Cave.
Oh, Think Not I Am Faithful to a Vow!
On Hearing a Symphony of Beethoven.
On the Wide Heath.
Passer Mortuus Est.
Pear Tree, The.
Penitent, The, *satire.*
Philosopher, The.
Pity Me Not.
Plum Gatherer, The.
Poet and His Book, The.
Portrait by a Neighbor.
Ragged Island.
Recuerdo.
Renascence.
Return, The.
Say That We Saw Spain Die.
Second Fig.
She Is Overheard Singing.
Since of no creature living the last breath.
Singing-Woman from the Wood's Edge, The.
Snow Storm, The.
Song of a Second April.
Sonnet: "And you as well must die, belovèd dust."
Sonnet: "Euclid alone has looked on Beauty bare."
Sonnet XLI: "I, being born a woman and distressed."
Sonnet: "I know I am but summer to your heart."
Sonnet: "Love is not all: it is not meat nor drink."
Sonnet: "Not with libations, but with shouts and laughter."
Sonnet: "Oh, my belovèd, have you thought of this."
Sonnet: "Oh, think not I am faithful to a vow!"
Sonnet: "Say what you will, and scratch my heart to find."
Sonnet: "What lips my lips have kissed, and where, and why."
Sonnet XXVIII: "When we are old and these rejoicing veins."
Sonnet: "Women have loved before as I love now."
Sonnet to Gath.
Spring.
Strawberry Shrub, The.
Theme and Variations.
Think not, nor for a moment let your mind.
This Beast That Rends Me.
Those Hours When Happy Hours Were My Estate.
Thursday.
Time Does Not Bring Relief.
To a Calvinist in Bali.
To a Young Poet.
To Inez Milholland.
To Jesus on His Birthday.
To the Wife of a Sick Friend.
Travel.
Underground System.
Unexplorer, The.
Vacation Song.
Very Little Sphinx, A, *sel.*
Visit to the Asylum, A.
What Lips My Lips Have Kissed.
What Rider Spurs Him from the Darkening East.
Wild Swans.
Wonder Where This Horseshoe Went.
Wraith.
You loved me not at all, but let it go.

Millay, Kathleen
Relativity.

Miller, Adam David
Crack in the Wall Holds Flowers.
Hungry Black Child, The.

Miller, Albert G.
Pygmalion.

Miller, Alice Duer
American to France, An.
English Are Frosty, The.
I Have Loved England.
Song: "Light of spring, The."
Sonnet, A: "Dear, if you love me, hold me most your friend."
White Cliffs, The, *sels.*

Miller, Carolyn
Nocturnal Visitor.

Miller, Chris
Blue Flag, The.

Miller, Cincinnatus Heine [*or* Hiner]. *See* **Miller, Joaquin**

Miller, Emily Huntington
Land of Heart's Desire, The.
Wood-Dove's Note, The.

Miller, Errol
Tough Ones, The.

Miller, Freeman E.
Stampede, The.

Miller, Grace Maddock
Poetic Tale.

Miller, Harry S.
Cat Came Back, The.

Miller, Heather Ross
Quail Walk.

Miller, J. Corson
Epicedium.
Flying Fish.
March of Humanity, The.
Wind in the Elms, The.

Miller, James
Italian Opera.
Life of a Beau, The.

Miller, Jane
May You Always Be the Darling of Fortune.

Miller, Jim Wayne
Aunt Gladys's Home Movie No. 31, Albert's Funeral.
Family Reunion.
Growing Wild.
House of Readers, A.
Nostalgia for 70.
On the Wings of a Dove.

Miller, Joaquin (Cincinnatus Heine [*or* Hiner] Miller)
Alaska.
At the Grave of Walker.
Bravest Battle, The.
By the Pacific Ocean.
Byron, *sel.*
Columbus.
Crossing the Plains.
Cuba Libre.
Dead in the Sierras.
Defence of the Alamo, The.
Exodus for Oregon.
Fortunate Isles, The.
Greatest Battle That Ever Was Fought, The.
In Men Whom Men Condemn as Ill.
Juanita.
Kit Carson's Ride.
Mothers of Men, The.
Peter Cooper.
Rejoice.
Resurge San Francisco.
San Francisco.
San Francisco Bay.
Song: "There is many a love in the land, my love."

To Russia.
Twilight at the Heights.
Vaquero.
Voice of the Dove, The.
Westward Ho!
William Brown.
Miller, John N.
Prince Charming.
Miller, Joseph Dana
Hymn of Hate, The.
Miller, Madeleine Sweeny
How Far to Bethlehem?
Miller, Mary Britton
Camel.
Cat.
Foal.
Here She Is.
Shore.
They've All Gone South.
Universe, The.
Where Are You Now?
Miller, May
Gift from Kenya.
Not That Far.
Miller, Merlin G.
Just to Be Glad.
Miller, Nellie Burget
Shack, The.
Sun Drops Red, The.
Miller, Olive Beaupré
Circus Parade, The.
Miller, Peter
Capture of Edwin Alonzo Boyd, The.
Prevention of Stacy Miller, The.
Miller, Ruth
Birds.
Cycle, *sels.*
It Is Better to Be Together.
Long Since Last.
Penguin on the Beach.
Plankton.
Sterkfontein.
Miller, Thomas
Evening.
Sea-Deeps, The.
Watercress Seller, The.
Miller, Vassar
Accepting.
Adam's Footprint.
Apology.
At a Child's Baptism.
Autumnal Spring Song.
Awkward Goodbyes.
Beat Poem by an Academic Poet.
Bout with Burning.
Ceremony.
Christmas Mourning.
Clash with Cliches, A.
Defense Rests.
Eden Revisited.
Encounter.
Epithalamium: "Crept side by side beyond the thresh."
Faintly and from Far Away.
Farm, The.
Final Hunger, The.
Fulfillment.
Homecoming Blues.
How Far?
Invocation: "Unwinding the spool of the morning."
Joyful Prophecy.
Judas.
Lesson in Detachment, A.
Love Song for the Future.
Love Song out of Nothing.
No Return.
On Approaching My Birthday.
One Morning.
One Thing Needful, The.
Paradox.
Quarry, The.
Receiving Communion.
Reciprocity.
Resolution, The.
Slump.
Sophistication.
Spinster's Lullaby.
Though He Slay Me.
Tree of Silence, The.
Trimming the Sails.
Without Ceremony.
Worshiper, The.
Miller, William
Spring, *sel.*
Willie Winkie.
Millett, William
I Am Ham Melanite.
Milligan, Alice
Dark Palace, The.
Fainne Gael an Lae.
Song of Freedom, A.
When I Was a Little Girl.
Milligan, Spike
Baby Sardine, A.
Bongaloo, The.
Christmas 1970.
Edser.
Gofongo, The.
Hipporhinostricow.
Little tiny puppy dog.
Look at All Those Monkeys.
My Sister Laura.
On the Ning Nang Nong.
Thousand Hairy Savages, A.
You Must Never Bath in an Irish Stew.
Millikin, Richard Alfred
Groves of Blarney, The.
Mills, Harry Edward
Convicted, *sel.*
Early Frogs, The.
On a Rainy Night, *sel.*
Punkin Pie.
Mills, Kerry
At a Georgia Camp Meeting, *with music.*
Mills, Mary
Apostasy.
Fable: "Bough will bend, the leaf will sometime fall, The."
Garden Party.
Library, The.
Pedigree.
Postscript.
White Horse, The.
White Peacock, The.
Mills, Ralph J., Jr.
Chelsea Churchyard.
For Years.
Grasses.
March Light.
Mills, William
Unemployment.
Mills, William G.
Arise, O Glorious Zion, *with music.*
Millward, Pamela
Just as the Small Waves Came Where No Waves Were.
Milman, Henry Hart
Beacons, The.
Holy Field, The.
Samor, *sel.*
Milne, Alan Alexander
At the Zoo.
Ballad of Private Chadd, The.
Binker ("Binker—What I call him—is a secret of my own").
Buckingham Palace.
Disobedience.
Dormouse and the Doctor, The.
End, The.
Forgiven
Four Friends, The.
From a Full Heart.
Furry Bear.
Halfway Down.
Happiness.
Hoppity.
If I Were King.
King's Breakfast, The.
Lines Written by a Bear of Very Little Brain.
Market Square.
Miss James.
Missing.
More It Snows, The.
Old Sailor, The.
Politeness.
Puppy and I.
Sand-between-the-Toes.
Teddy Bear.
Three Foxes, The.
Us Two.
Vespers.
Young Puppy, The.
Milne, Angela. *See* **"Ande"**
Milne, Ewart
Could I Believe.
Deirdre and the Poets.
Diamond Cut Diamond.
Dublin Bay.
Evergreen.
Hills of Pomeroy, The.
In a Valley of This Restless Mind.
Martyred Earth, The.
Sierran Vigil.
Tinker's Moon.
Vanessa Vanessa.
Milne, J. C.
Dolomites.
Faur Wid I Dee?
Feels.
Lairig, The.
Patriot, The.
Milner, E. V.
Open to Visitors.
Milner-Brown, A. L.
Who Knows?
Milnes, Richard Monckton, 1st Baron Houghton
Brookside, The.
Columbus and the Mayflower.
England and America, 1863.
Good Night and Good Morning.
In Memoriam.
Lady Moon.
Men of Old, The.
Our Mother Tongue.
Palm-Tree and the Pine, The.
Shadows.
Sir Walter Scott at the Tomb of the Stuarts in St. Peter's.
Two Angels.
Venetian Serenade, The.
Milns, William
Federal Constitution, The.
Milosz, Czeslaw
Elegy for N. N.
Poor Christian Looks at the Ghetto, A.
Milton, John
Adam and Eve.
Adam Fallen.
Adam Speaks ("Oh, why did God,/Creator wise").
Adam Unfallen.
Adam's Morning Hymn.
All Is Best.
Arcades, *sels.*
Ark, The.
At a Solemn Music [*or* Musick].
At a Vacation Exercise, *sel.*
Athens.
Atonement, The.
Banishment, The ("So spoke our Mother Eve, and Adam heard").
Banishment from Paradise ("Descended Adam to the bower where Eve").
Before the Fall.
Beneath him with new wonder now he views.

Blindness of Samson, The.
But see here comes thy reverend Sire.
But to His Mother Mary.
Chastity.
Comus; a Masque Presented at Ludlow Castle.
Council of Satan, The.
Creation of Birds, The.
Creation of the Animals.
Death of Samson.
Delilah.
Deliverer, The.
Echo.
Eden.
Epilogue: "All is best, though we oft doubt."
Epitaph on the Marchioness of Winchester, An.
Eternal Spring, The.
Eve.
Eve Penitent.
Eve Speaks to Adam ("With thee conversing I forget all time").
Evening in Paradise.
Exit from Eden, The.
Expulsion from Paradise.
Fall, The.
Fall of the Angels, The.
Fallen Angels, The.
Farewell of the Attendant Spirit.
Feast and noon grew high, and sacrifice, The.
First Day of Creation, The.
First Temptation, The.
Gabriel Meets Satan.
Great Creator from His Work Returned, The.
Hail, Holy Light.
Heaven.
Hell.
Heroic Vengeance.
Holy Light.
How Soon Hath Time [the Subtle Thief of Youth].
Hymn, The: "It was the winter wild."
Hymn on the Morning of Christ's Nativity.
Hymn to Light.
I, dark in light, exposed.
I Did But Prompt the Age.
If thou beest he; but O how fall'n! how chang'd.
Il Penseroso.
Immortal Hate.
Invocation: "Of mans first disobedience, and the fruit."
Invocation of Comus, The.
Invocation to the Heavenly Muse.
Invocation to Urania.
Katherine Milton: Died MDCLVIII.
Lady Sings, The.
Lady's Song.
L'Allegro.
Last Came, and Last Did Go.
Leave Taking.
Let Us with a Gladsome Mind.
Leviathan.
Light.
Lycidas.
Magi, The.
Mask, A.
May Morning.
Messiah, The.
Methought I Saw.
Mirth, with Thee I Mean to Live.
Moon and the Nightingale, The.
Morning Hymn of Adam [and Eve].
New Worlds.
Night Falls on Eden.
No Time for Lamentation Now.
Now Came Still Evening On ("Uriel to his charge . . .").
O Dark, Dark, Dark.
O Nightingale.
O Nightingale, That on Yon Bloomy Spray.
Ode: On the Morning of Christ's Nativity.
On His Blindness.
On His Deceased Wife.
On His Having Arrived at the Age of Twenty-Three.
On His Late Wife.
On His Twenty-third [*or* 24th] Birthday.
On Shakespeare.
On the Detraction Which Followed upon My Writing Certain Treatises.
On the Late Massacre in Piedmont [*or* Piemont].
On the Lord Gen. Fairfax at the Siege of Colchester.
On the Massacre in Piedmont.
On the New Forcers of Conscience under the Long Parliament.
On the Oxford Carrier.
On the Same.
On the University Carrier (Who Sickn'd in the Time of His Vacancy).
On Time.
Pandemonium and Its Architect.
Panorama, The.
Paradise.
Paradise Lost, *sels.*
Paradise Regained, *sels.*
Parthians, The.
Place of the Damned, The.
Plan of Salvation, The.
Praise the Lord.
Prospect of Eden, The.
Retreat from Paradise, The.
Rivers Arise; a Fragment.
Rome.
Sabrina Fair.
Samson Agonistes.
Satan and His Host.
Satan and the Fallen Angels.
Satan as Rebel-Liberator.
Satan Beholds Adam and Eve in Eden.
Satan Defiant.
Satan ("He ceased; and Satan stayed not . . .").
Satan ("He scarce had ceas't when . . .").
Satan ("His pride/ Had cast him out from Heaven").
Satan Journeys to the Garden of Eden.
Satan Looks upon Adam and Eve in Paradise.
Satan Ponders His Fallen State.
Satan Views the World.
Satan's Address to the Sun.
Satan's Adjuration.
Satan's Guile.
Satan's Legions and the Beech Leaves of the Casentino.
Satan's Soliloquy.
Scene in Paradise, A.
Sin and Death.
Song: "Nymphs and shepherds dance no more."
Song: "O'er [*or* O're] the smooth enameled green."
Song: "Star that bids the shepherd fold, The."
Song: "Sweet Echo, sweetest nymph, that liv'st unseen."
Song: "To the ocean now I fly."
Song on May Morning.
Sonnet: "Captain or colonel, or knight in arms."
Sonnet: "Cyriack, whose grandsire on the royal bench."
Sonnet: "Daughter to that good Earl, once President."
Sonnet: "Lawrence of vertuous father vertuous son."
Sonnet: On His Blindness.
Sonnet: On His Having Arrived at the Age of Twenty-three.
Sonnet: On the Religious Memorie of Mrs. Catherine Thomason My Christian Friend Deceas'd Decem. 1646.
Sonnet: To Mr. H. Lawes, on His Aires.
Sonnet on His Blindness.
Sonnet on His Deceased Wife.
Spirit Epiloguizes, The.
Standing on Earth.
Subject of Heroic Song, The.
Summons, The.
Sweet Echo, Sweetest Nymph.
Table Richly Spread, A.
Temperance and Virginity.
Tetrachordon, *sel.*
Their Banishment.
Their Wedded Love.
Then When I Am Thy Captive, Talk of Chains.
This having learnt, thou hast attaind the summe.
Thus Eve to Adam.
To Cyriack Skinner ("Cyriack, whose grandsire").
To Mr. Cyriack Skinner upon His Blindness.
To Mr. H. Lawes on His Airs.
To Mr. Lawrence.
To Sir Henry Vane the Younger.
To the Lady Margaret Ley.
To the Lord General[l] Cromwell, May 1652.
To the Nightingale.
To the Ocean Now I Fly.
Transcendence of God, The.
True and False Glory.
Ways of God to Men, The.
Wedded Love.
Weep no more, woful Shepherds weep no more.
What Though the Field Be Lost?
What Words Have Passed.
When I Consider How My Light Is Spent.
When the Assault Was Intended to the City.
Whom Do We Count a Good Man.
Woman.
World Beautiful, The.

Mimnermus
Youth and Age.

Minard, Michael D.
Musician Returning from a Cafe Audition, A.

Minarik, Else Holmelund
When Mosquitoes Make a Meal.

Minarik, John Paul
Basic Writing 702.
Grandmother.
Letter from Home, A.
There's Nothing Polite about a Tank.
To Be in Love while in Prison.

Minck, Peter
Pain Paint.

Minczeski, John
Another Sunset.
Old Ego Song ("Old ego climbing out of the trap door on the top of my head").
Renaissance/a Triptych.

Minde, Henry S.
Thou Who Taught the Thronging People.

Miner, Virginia Scott
Channel Water.
Elegy for Former Students.
Golden Spurs.
Nichols Fountain.

Minor, James
Feeling the Quiet Strike.
Lilies for Neal.

Minot, Laurence
Burgesses of Calais, The.
Halidon Hill.

"Minsky, Nicolai Maksimovich" (Nikolai Maksimovich Vilenkin)
Immortality.

Minthorn, Phillip Yellowhawk
Daybreak.
Earth Cycle Dream, The.
From Which War.
Vigil of the Wounded.

Minty, Judith
Burning against the Wind.
End of Summer, The.
Legacy, The.
Letters to My Daughters, 11.
Look to the Back of the Hand.
Making Music.
News from Detroit.

Orchids.
Prowling the Ridge.
Spring Sequence.
Wounds.

Mirabai [*or* Mira Bai]
At the Holi festival of color.
Clouds, The.
Friend, don't be angry.
Friend, how can I meet my lord?
Hari, look at me a while.
Hari helps his people.
I can't break with the Dark One.
I don't sleep. All night.
Keep me as your servant, O Girdhar.
Let me see you.
Mira is dancing with bells tied on her ankles.
My eyes are thirsty.
My love is in my house.
O King, I know you gave me poison.
Rana, I know you gave me poison.
Rana, why do you treat me as your enemy?
Wake, child with the flute.
Wake up, dear boy that holds the flute!
Why Mira Can't Go Back to Her Old House.
Yogi, don't go away.

Miranda, Gary
Field Trip.

Mirikitani, Janice
Breaking Silence.
Breaking Tradition.
Sing with Your Body.

Mish, Charlotte
Stray Dog.

"Miss X *and* Miss Y"
Merry Month, The.

Mistral, Frédéric
Cocooning, The.
Leaf-picking, The.
Mares of the Camargue, The.
Mirèio, *sels.*

Mistral, Gabriela (*originally* Lucila Godoy Alcayaga)
Ballad: "He passed by with another."
Bread.
Close to Me.
Death Sonnet I.
Drops of Gall.
Dusk.
Everything Is Round.
Little Girl That Lost a Finger, The.
Midnight.
Poem of the Son.
Sister.
Sleep Close to Me.
Slow Rain.
To Drink.
To Noel.
To See Him Again.

Mitchell, Adrian
Accountant in His Bath, The ("The accountant dried his imperfect back").
Another Prince Is Born.
Banana.
Beatrix Is Three.
Beggar, The.
Calypso's Song to Ulysses.
Celia Celia.
Fifteen Million Plastic Bags.
Lying in State.
Norman Morrison.
Private Transport.
Quite Apart from the Holy Ghost.
Remember Suez?
Riddle: "Their tongues are knives, their forks are hands and feet."
Telegram One.
To Whom It May Concern.

Mitchell, Archie
Hills of the Middle Distance.

Mitchell, Cyprus R.
Soul of Jesus Is Restless, The.

Mitchell, David
Celebrant.
Windfall.

Mitchell, James
Gay Epiphany.

Mitchell, John
Reply to "In Flanders Fields."

Mitchell, John Hanlon
City Song, A.
Farm Wife.
Sea Hunger.

Mitchell, Jonathan
On the Following Work and Its Author.

Mitchell, Joni
Woodstock.

Mitchell, Karen L.
For Michael.

Mitchell, Langdon Elwyn
Carol: "Mary, the mother, sits on the hill."
Fear.
Purpose.
Sweets That Die.
Technique.
To a Writer of the Day, *sels.*
To One Being Old.
Wayside Virgin, The.
Written at the End of a Book.

Mitchell, Lorna
Hermaphrodite's Song, The.

Mitchell, Lucy Sprague
Back and Forth.
House of the Mouse, The.
It Is Raining.
Lost Ball, The.
My Bed.

Mitchell, Matthew
Printing Jenny ("Printing Bibles is Jenny's daily chore").

Mitchell, Noah
K. K. K. Disco, The.
Momma's Not Gods Image.
Out of Question & Mind.
Those Not Confused Are Prisoners of War.
Truth, A.

Mitchell, Nora
Fisherman's Wife, The.

Mitchell, Roger
Cinderella.

Mitchell, Ruth Comfort
Bride, The.
He Went for a Soldier.
Night Court, The.
Travel Bureau, The.

Mitchell, Silas Weir
Decanter of Madeira, Aged 86, to George Bancroft, Aged 86, A.
Good-Night.
Herndon.
How the *Cumberland* Went Down.
Idleness.
Kearsarge.
Lincoln.
Of One Who Seemed to Have Failed.
On a Boy's First Reading of "King Henry V."
Quaker Graveyard, The.
Song of the Flags, The.
To a Magnolia Flower in the Garden of the Armenian Convent at Venice.
Vespers.

Mitchell, Stephen
Abraham.
Adam in Love.
Jacob and the Angel.

Mitchell, Susan
From the Journals of the Frog Prince.

Mitchell, Susan Langstaff
Heart's Low Door, The.
Immortality.
Irish Council Bill, 1907, The [*parody on the Shan Van Vocht*], *sel.*
Living Chalice, The.
Wind Bloweth Where It Listeth, The.

Mitchell, Thomas
Open Range.

Mitchell, Walter
Cheer of the *Trenton,* The.
Reefing Topsails.
Tacking Ship off Shore.

Mitchison, Naomi
Boar of Badenoch and the Sow of Atholl, The.
Buachaille Etive Mor and Buachaille Etive Beag.
Webster Ross.

Mitford, Mary Russell
Rienzi to the Romans.
Written in July, 1824.

Mitsuhashi Takajo
Hair ornament of the sun, The.

Mitsui, Jim
Graffiti in a University Restroom: "Killing People Is Easier than Writing Poetry."
Letter to Tina Koyama from Elliot Bay Park.
Mexico City, 150 Pesos to the Dollar.
Shakuhachi.
When Father Came Home for Lunch.

"Mix, Parmenas" (Andrew J. Kelley)
New Doctor, The.

Miyazawa, Kenji
Moon, Son of Heaven.
Snow on Saddle Mountain, The.

Mizer, Ray
To a Loudmouth Pontificator.

Mkalimoto, Ernie
Energy for a New Thang.

Mocarski, Timothy P.
City.

Modena, Leone da
Epitaph: "Implacable angel, The/ Has shot his dart."

Modisane, Bloke
Black Blues.
Blue Black.
Lonely.
One Thought for My Lady ("One thought into one word.")

Moffatt, Gertrude MacGregor
All Night I Heard.

Moffett, Judith
Diehard.
Dirge for Small Wilddeath.
Evensong.
Going to Press.
Twinings Orange Pekoe.

Moffi, Larry
February.
Good Start, A.
Word Man, The.

Moffitt, John
To Look at Any Thing.

Mohodahi
On the holy day of your going out to war.

Mohr, Joseph
Silent Night! [Holy Night!]

Moise, Penina *and* Edward N. Calisch.
God Supreme! To Thee We Pray, *with music.*

Mokhomo, M. A.
When He Spoke to Me of Love.

Molesworth, Charles
Horned Lizard.

Molière (Jean Baptiste Poquelin)
Tartuffe; or, The Impostor.
To Monsieur de la Mothe le Vayer.

Moll, Ernest G.
After Reading a Book on Abnormal Psychology.
At the Grave of a Land-Shark.
Eagles over the Lambing Paddock.
Fishing in the Australian Alps.
Gnarled Riverina Gum-Tree, A.
Undertaker's Advertisement, An.

Mollin, Larry
As the World Turns.
Bunky Boy Bunky Boy Who's My Little Bunky Boy.
My Elbow Ancestry.

Signature.
Tubes.
Wash Day.
Mollineux, Mary
Solitude.
Molloy, James Lyman
Bantry Bay.
Kerry Dance, The.
Molodovski [*or* Molodovsky *or* Molodwsky], Kadia [*or* Kadya]
And Yet.
God of Mercy.
In Life's Stable.
Jerusalem.
Night Visitors.
Song of the Sabbath.
Molofsky, Merle
Reflections.
Momaday, N. Scott
Angle of Geese.
Bear, The.
Before an Old Painting of the Crucifixion.
But Then and There the Sun Bore Down.
Carriers of the Dream Wheel.
Colors of Night, The.
Delight Song of Tsoai-Talee, The.
Eagle-Feather Fan, The.
Earth and I Gave You Turquoise.
Fear of Bo-talee, The.
Forms of the Earth at Abiquiu.
Gourd Dancer, The.
Pit Viper.
Plainview: 3.
Rainy Mountain Cemetery.
Simile.
Story of a Well-made Shield, The.
To a Child Running with Outstretched Arms in the Canyon de Chelly.
Trees and Evening Sky.
Winter Holding off the Coast of North America.
Wise Empty Landscape with a Death in the Foreground.
Mombert, Alfred
Along the Strand.
Chimera, The.
Idyl: "And my young sweetheart sat at board with me."
Sleeping They Bear Me.
Moment, John J.
Best Treasure, The.
Monaghan, Pat
Christmas at Vail: On Staying Indoors.
Monaghan, Patricia
One Who Grew to Be a Wolf, The.
Monat, Donald
Rhymed Mnemonic of the Forty Counties of England.
Monck, Mary
Masque of the Virtues against Love.
On a Romantic Lady.
Mondy, Bob
Canadice Lake.
Fishing Drunk.
Trinidad, 1958.
Monette, Paul
Bathing the Aged.
Degas.
Into the Dark.
Money-Coutts, Francis Burdett
Any Father to Any Son.
Dream, The.
Empires.
Little Sequence, A, *sels.*
Mors, Morituri Te Salutamus.
On a Fair Woman.
On a Wife.
Monkhouse, Cosmo
Dead March, A.
In Arcady.
Limerick: "Lady there was of Antigua, A."
Limerick: "Poor benighted Hindoo, The."
Limerick: "There once was a girl of New York."
Limerick: "There once was a person of Benin."
Limerick: "There was a young girl of Lahore."
Limerick: "There was a young lady of Niger,"*at.*
Limerick: "There were three young women of Birmingham."
Master of Arts.
Night Express, The.
Satisfied Tiger, The,*at.*
Song of the Seasons, A.
To a New-born Child.
Monkman, Robina
Sea Burial.
Monks, Arthur W.
Twilight's Last Gleaming.
Monod, Theodore
Christ Alone.
None of Self and All of Thee.
Monro, Harold
At a Country Dance in Provence.
Bird at Dawn, The.
Bitter Sanctuary.
Carrion.
Cat's Meat.
Children of Love.
City-Storm.
Clock.
Dawn of Womanhood.
Dog.
Empty House, The.
Every Thing.
Flower Is Looking, A.
Foundered Tram, The.
Fresh Air, The.
Goldfish.
Hearthstone.
Hurrier, The.
If Suddenly a Clod of Earth.
Living.
London Interior.
Man Carrying Bale.
Midnight Lamentation.
Milk for the Cat.
Natural History, *sel.*
Nightingale near the House, The.
Officers' Mess (1916).
Overheard on a Saltmarsh.
Real Property.
Rebellious Vine, The.
She Was Young and Blithe and Fair.
Silent Pool, The.
Solitude.
Strange Meetings, *sels.*
Street Fight.
Suburb.
Terrible Door, The.
Thistledown.
Week-End.
Wind, The.
Youth in Arms, *sel.*
Monroe, Arthur W.
Cliff Dwelling, The.
Forest Fire, The.
Lost in a Blizzard.
Man of the Open West, The.
Toll of the Desert, The.
Monroe, Harriet
Blue Ridge, The.
Commemoration Ode, *sels.*
Democracy.
Farewell, A: "Good-bye!—no [*or* nay], do not grieve that it is over."
Fortunate One, The.
I Love My Life, but Not Too Well.
In High Places.
In the Beginning.
Inner Silence, The.
Lincoln.
Mountain Song.
Nancy Hanks.
Now.
On the Porch.
Pine at Timber-Line, The.
Romney, The.
Shadow-Child, The.
Two Heroes.
Vernon Castle.
Washington.
Monsell, John Samuel Bewley
Light of the World.
Montagu, Charles
Story of the Pot and the Kettle, The.
Montagu, Lady Mary Wortley
Answer to a Lady Advising Me to Retirement, An.
Epistle from Mrs. Yonge to Her Husband.
Epitaph: "Here lies John Hughes and Sarah Drew."
Farewell to Bath.
Good Advice.
In Answer to a Lady Who Advised Retirement.
Lady's Resolve, The.
Lover, The; a Ballad.
On the Death of Mrs. Bowes.
Receipt for the Vapours.
Receipt to Cure the Vapours, A.
Saturday: The Small-Pox.
Six Town Eclogues, *sel.*
Montague, James Jackson
And When They Fall.
Same Old Story, The.
Sleepytown Express, The.
Vamp Passes, The.
Montague, John
All Legendary Obstacles.
Cage, The.
Cave of Night, The, *sel.*
Chosen Light, A.
Courtyard in Winter.
Dowager.
Edge.
Grafted Tongue, A.
Graveyard in Queens, A.
Herbert Street Revisited.
Lament for the O'Neills.
Leaping Fire, The.
Like Dolmens Round My Childhood, the Old People.
Murphy in Manchester.
New Siege, A; an Historical Meditation, *sel.*
Point, The.
Poisoned Lands.
Road's End, The.
Same Gesture, The.
Severed Head, A, *sel.*
Special Delivery.
Summer Storm.
That Room.
Time Out.
Trout, The.
Walking Late.
Welcoming Party, A.
Wild Dog Rose, The.
Wild Sports of the West.
Windharp.
Woodtown Manor.
Montale, Eugenio
Eel, The.
Life's Evil.
Montemayor, Carlos
Heth.
Montemayor, Jorge de
Diana, *sel.*
Song: "Shepherd, who can pass such wrong."
Montgomerie, Alexander
Adieu to His Mistress.
Admonition to Young Lassies, An.
Away Vane World.
Cherry and the Slae, The, *sel.*
Description of Tyme, A.
Nicht Is Neir Gane, The.
Night Is Near [*or* Neir] Gone, The.

Royal Palace of the Highest Heaven, The,*at.*
Solsequium, The.
Sweethairt, Rejoice in Mind.
To Henry Constable and Henry Keir.
To His Mistress [*or* Maistres].
To R. Hudson.

Montgomerie, William
Author Unknown.
Elegy: "Narrowing of knowledge to one window to a door, A."
Elegy for William Soutar.
Epitaph: "My brother is skull and skeleton now."
Estuary.
Glasgow Street.
Kinfauns Castle, *sel.*
Stags.

Montgomery, Carol Artman
Jimmy Bruder on Quincey Street.
Triangle Ladies, The.

Montgomery, Carrie Judd
Discerning the Lord's Body.

Montgomery, F.
Mother's Love ("A mother's love—how sweet the name!").

Montgomery, G. F.
Graham Bell and the Photophone.

Montgomery, George Edgar
At Night.
Dead Soldier, A.
England.
To a Child.

Montgomery, Jack
Addict.

Montgomery, James
Angels, from the Realms of Glory.
Arnold von Winkelried.
At Home in Heaven.
Christ Our Example in Suffering.
Field Flower, A.
Good Tidings of Great Joy to All People.
Indian Mother about to Destroy Her Child, An.
Inspiration, The.
Lift up your heads, ye gates of brass!
Lust of Gold, The.
Make Way for Liberty.
Nativity.
Night.
Patriot's Pass-Word, The.
There Is a Land.
West Indies, The, *sels.*
What Is Prayer?

Montgomery, James Stuart
Swashbuckler's Song, The.

Montgomery, Leslie Alexander. *See* **"Doyle, Lynn"**

Montgomery, Lucy Maud
Off to the Fishing Ground.

Montgomery, Mary Sidney Wroth, Countess of. *See* **Wroth, Mary Sidney, Countess of Montgomery**

Montgomery, Niall
Eyewash.

Montgomery, Robert
Omnipresence of the Deity, The, *sel.*

Montgomery, Roselle Mercier
Counsel.
Ulysses Returns, *sels.*

Montgomery, Whitney
Death Rode a Pinto Pony.

Montoro, Antonio de
El Ropero.

Montoya, José
Louie.
Mother.

Montrose, James Graham, 5th Earl and 1st Marquess of. *See* **Graham, James, Marquess of Montrose**

Montross, Lois Seyster
Codes.
Decent Burial.
I Wear a Crimson Cloak To-Night.

Moodie, Susanna-Strickland
Canadian Herd-Boy, The.
Indian Summer.

Moody, Minnie Hite
Say This of Horses.

Moody, William Vaughn
Bracelet of Grass, The.
Faded Pictures.
Fire-Bringer, The, *sels.*
Gloucester Moors.
I Stood within the Heart of God, *with music.*
Menagerie, The.
No Hint of Stain.
Ode in Time of Hesitation, An.
Of Wounds and Sore Defeat.
On a Soldier Fallen in the Philippines.
Pandora Speaks.
Robert Gould Shaw.
Serf's Secret, The.
Thammuz.

Moon, Sheila
Existence.

Mooney, Stephen
At the Airport in Dallas.
Water Color.

Moor, George
Eternale Footeman's Tale, The.

Moore, Bertha
Child's Thought, A.

Moore, Charles Leonard
Disenchantment.
Or Ever the Earth Was.
Soul unto Soul Glooms Darling.
Spring Returns, The.
Then Shall We See.
Thou Livest, O Soul!
To England.

Moore, Clement Clarke
Lord of Life, All Praise Excelling, *with music.*
Night before Christmas, The.
Visit from St. Nicholas, A.

Moore, Edward
Goose and the Swans, The, *sel.*
To the Right Hon. Henry Pelham.

Moore, George
Parisian Idyl, A, *sel.*
Rondo: "Did I love thee? I only did desire."
Sapphic Dream, A.
Sonnet: Corpse, The.
Sonnet: "Idly she yawned, and threw her heavy hair."

Moore, James
Rothko.

Moore, Janice Townley
Below Bald Mountain.
Out of Body.

Moore, Jim
Instead of Features.

Moore, John
Broken Gull, A.
Dingman's Marsh.
Gaggle of Geese, a Pride of Lions, A.
Squall.

Moore, Sir John Henry
Duke of Benevento, The.
Song: "Indeed, my Caelia, 'tis in vain."

Moore, John Travers
Going Up.
Last Flower, The.
Tree Frog, The.

Moore, Julia A.
And now, kind friends, what I have wrote.
Ashtabula Disaster, The.
Author's Early Life, The.
Departed Friend, A.
Grand Rapids.
Grand Rapids Cricket Club, *sel.*
Little Libbie.
Sketch of Lord Byron's Life.
Willie's and Nellie's Wish.

Moore, Lilian
Bedtime Stories.
Foghorns.
Ground Hog Day.
Hey, Bug!
Listen!
Pigeons.
Something Is There.
Until I Saw the Sea.
Waking.

Moore, Marianne
Apparition of Splendor.
Arctic Ox, The.
Armour's Undermining Modesty.
Arthur Mitchell.
At Rest in the Blast.
Baseball and Writing.
Bird-witted.
Black Earth.
Buffalo, The.
Carnegie Hall: Rescued.
Carriage from Sweden, A.
Charity Overcoming Envy.
Critics and Connoisseurs.
Dream.
Egyptian Pulled Glass Bottle in the Shape of a Fish, An.
England.
Enough.
Face, A.
Fish, The.
Four Quartz Crystal Clocks.
Frigate Pelican, The.
Glory.
Granite and Steel.
Grave, A.
He "Digesteth Harde Yron."
Hero, The.
His Shield.
Hometown Piece for Messrs. Alston and Reese.
I May, I Might, I Must.
Icosasphere, The.
In Distrust of Merits.
In the Public Garden.
Jellyfish, A.
Jerboa, The.
Keeping Their World Large.
Labors of Hercules, The.
Leonardo Da Vinci's.
Love in America.
Marriage.
Melancthon.
Melchior Vulpius.
Mind, Intractable Thing, The.
Mind is an Enchanting Thing, The.
Monkeys, The.
Nevertheless.
New York.
Nine Nectarines and Other Porcelain.
No Swan So Fine.
O to Be a Dragon.
Old Amusement Park.
Pangolin, The.
Paper Nautilus, The.
Part of a Novel, Part of a Poem, Part of a Play, *sels.*
Past Is the Present, The.
Peter.
Pigeons.
Poetry.
Rigorists.
Roses Only.
Saint Nicholas.
St. Valentine.
See in the Midst of Fair Leaves.
Silence.
Snakes, Mongooses, Snake-Charmers and the Like.
Sojourn in the Whale.
Spenser's Ireland.
Staff of Aesculapius, The.
Steeple-Jack, The.
Student, The.
Talisman, A.

Tell Me, Tell Me.
That Harp You Play So Well.
Then the Ermine.
Those Various Scalpels.
To a Chameleon.
To a Snail.
To a Steam Roller.
Tom Fool at Jamaica.
Values in Use.
Virginia Britannia.
W. S. Landor.
Walking-Sticks and Paperweights and Watermarks.
What Are Years?
When I Buy Pictures.

Moore, Maurice
Easter, Day of Christ Eternal.

Moore, Merrill
And to the Young Men.
Book of How, The.
Domestic: Climax.
He Said the Facts.
How She Resolved to Act.
It Is Winter, I Know.
Noise That Time Makes, The.
Old Men and Old Women Going Home on the Street Car.
Pandora and the Moon.
Shot Who? Jim Lane!
They Also Stand.
Transfusion.
Undergraduate.
Unknown Man in the Morgue.
Village Noon; Mid-Day Bells.
Warning to One.

Moore, Nicholas
Act of Love.
Alcestis in Ely.
Fivesucked the features of my girl by glory.
Fred Apollus at Fava's.
Hair's-Breadth, The.
Incidents in Playfair House.
Island and the Cattle, The.
Little Girl, The.
Love.
O Rose, O Rainbow.
Patient, The.
Phallic Symbol, The.
Song: "Little onion lay by the fireplace, A."
Why the British Girls Give In So Easily.
Winter and Red Berries.

Moore, Richard
Busby, Whose Verse No Piercing Beams, No Rays.
Suburb Hilltop.
Swarm, The.
Willy ("Willy, enormous Saskatchewan grizzly").

Moore, Rosalie
Catalogue, *sel.*

Moore, Thomas
All That's Bright Must Fade.
Argument, An.
Argument to Any Phillis or Cloë, An.
At the Mid Hour of Night.
Believe Me, If All Those Endearing Young Charms.
Bendemeer.
Bird, Let Loose in Eastern Skies, The.
By Bendemeer's Stream.
Canadian Boat Song, A.
Cherries, The; a Parable.
Child's Song.
Come, Rest in This Bosom.
Come, Ye Disconsolate.
Common Sense and Genius.
Copy of an Intercepted Despatch from His Excellency Don Strepitoso Diabolo.
Cupid Stung ("Cupid once upon a bed").
Dear Fanny.
Dear Harp of My Country.
Did Not.
Duke Is the Lad, The.
Echo.
Echoes.
Epigram: " 'Come, come,' said Tom's father, 'at your time of life.' "
Epistle of Condolence.
Epitaph on a Tuft-Hunter.
Epitaph on a Well-known Poet.
Epitaph on Robert Southey.
Evenings in Greece, *sel.*
Farewell! But Whenever [You Welcome the Hour].
Fill the Bumper Fair.
Fly to the desert, fly with me.
Fragment of a Character.
French Cookery.
Fudge Family in Paris, The, *sels.*
Fum and Hum, the Two Birds of Royalty.
Garden Song, A.
Glory of God in Creation, The.
Go Where Glory Waits Thee.
Golden Hour, The.
Hark! the Vesper Hymn Is Stealing.
Harp That Once through Tara's Halls, The.
Has Sorrow Thy Young Days Shaded?
How Oft Has the Banshee Cried.
"I never nursed a dear gazelle."
I Pray You.
I Saw from the Beach.
I Wish I Was [*or* Were] by That Dim Lake.
Ill Omens.
Irish Antiquities.
Irish Peasant to His Mistress, The.
Joke Versified, A.
Journey Onwards, The.
Kiss, The.
Lake of the Dismal Swamp, The.
Lalla Rookh,
Last Rose of Summer, The.
Let Erin Remember the Days of Old.
Light of the Harem [*or* Haram], The.
"Living Dog, The," and "The Dead Lion."
Long, Long Be My Heart with Such Memories Filled.
Love Is a Hunter Boy.
Love's Young Dream.
Lying.
Meeting of the Ships, The.
Meeting of the Waters, The.
Minstrel Boy, The.
Miss Biddy Fudge to Miss Dorothy.
My Birth-Day.
Nonsense.
Odes of Anacreon, *sel.*
Odes to Nea, *sels.*
Of All the Men.
Oft, in the Stilly Night.
Oh Blame Not the Bard.
Oh, Breathe Not His Name!
Oh, Come to Me When Daylight Sets.
Oh, Thou! Who Dry'st the Mourner's Tear.
On a Squinting Poetess.
On Taking a Wife.
Paddy's Metamorphosis.
Pastoral Ballad by John Bull, A.
Peace to the Slumberers!
Peri's Lament for Hinda, The.
Pro Patria Mori.
Quantum Est Quod Desit.
Recent Dialogue, A.
Rhymes on the Road, *sel.*
Row Gently Here.
Scene from a Play, Acted at Oxford, Called "Matriculation."
She Is Far from the Land.
Snake, The.
Song: "Where is the nymph, whose azure eye."
Song of Fionnuala, The.
Song of O'Ruark, Prince of Breffni, The.
Sound the Loud Timbrel.
Stricken Deer, The.
Sweet Innisfallen.
Take Back the Virgin Page.
Temple to Friendship, A.
Thee, Thee, Only Thee.
They May Rail at This Life.
This Life Is All Chequer'd with Pleasures and Woes.
This World Is All a Fleeting Show.
Thou Art, O God.
Thoughts on Editors.
Thro' Grief and Thro' Danger.
Time I've Lost in Wooing, The.
'Tis the Last Rose of Summer.
To : "When I loved you, I can't but allow."
To Cara, after an Interval of Absence.
To Fanny.
To Ladies' Eyes.
To My Mother.
To Sir Hudson Lowe.
Tory Pledges.
Two Streams, The.
What's My Thought Like?
When I Loved You.
Wreathe the Bowl.
Young May Moon, The.

Moore, Thomas Sturge
Before Rereading Shakespeare's Sonnets.
Daughter of Admetus, A.
Days and Nights.
Death in the Home.
Duet, A.
Dying Swan, The.
Event, The.
From Sappho's Death: Three Pictures by Gustave Moreau.
From Titian's "Bacchanal" in the Prado at Madrid.
Gazelles, The.
Kindness.
Lubber Breeze.
On Harting Down.
Response to Rimbaud's Later Manner.
Sent from Egypt with a Fair Robe of Tissue to a Sicilian Vinedresser.
Shells.
Silence.
Summer Lightning.
To Silence.
Tongues.
Variation on Ronsard.
Wind's Work.

Moore, Tom Inglis
Comrade in Arms.
Star Drill.

"Moore, Tom, Jr."
O'Duffy's Ironsides.

Moore, William H. A.
Dusk Song.
It Was Not Fate.

Moorman, Charles
Lois in Concert.

Moraes, Dom
Final Word, The.
Girl.
John Nobody.
Letter to My Mother.
Lullaby: "With lights for eyes, our city turns."
Queen.
Santa Claus.
Song: "Gross sun squats above, The."

Moraff, Barbara
Let us suppose the mind.

Moran, Michael ("Zozimus")
Pharao's Daughter.

Mordaunt, Thomas Osbert
Call, The.
Sound, Sound the Clarion.
Verses Written during the War, 1756–1763.

Mordaunt, Charles Earl of Peterborough
Chloe.
I Said to My Heart.

Mordecai ben Isaac
Fair Thou Art.
Rock of My Salvation.
Morden, Phyllis B.
Godmother.
More, Hannah
Bas Bleu, *sel.*
Book, A.
Conversation.
Riddle, A: "I'm a strange contradiction; I'm new, and I'm old."
Riot, The; or, Half a Loaf Is Better than No Bread.
Search after Happiness, The, *sel.*
Solitude.
More, Helen F.
What's in a Name?
More, Henry
Argument of Democritus Platonissans, or the Infinitie of Worlds, The.
Eternal Life.
Hymn to Charity and Humility.
Hymne in Honour of Those Two Despised Virtues, Charitie and Humilitie, An.
Resolution.
More, Sir Thomas (Saint Thomas More)
Age.
Childhood.
Consider Well.
Death.
Eleventh Property, The.
Eternal Reward, Eternal Pain.
Eternity.
Fame.
First Property, The.
Fortune.
I Am Called Childhood.
Lewis, the Lost Lover.
Manhood.
Mery Gest How a Sergeaunt Wolde Lerne to Be a Frere, A.
Pageant Verses.
Peace of a Good Mind, The.
Rueful Lamentation [on the Death of Queen Elizabeth], A.
Seventh Property, The.
This Life a Dream and Shadow.
Thomas More to Them That Seek Fortune.
Time.
To Fortune.
Twelve Properties or Conditions of a Lover, The, *sels.*
Twelve Weapons of Spiritual Battle, The, *sels.*
Venus and Cupide.
Moreh, Shmuel
Melody.
Return, The.
Tree of Hatred, The.
Morejón, Nancy
Central Park *Some People (3 P.M.).*
Reason for Poetry, The.
Moreland, Jane P.
Argument, The.
Pony Girl.
Moreland, John Richard
Birch Trees.
Christ Is Crucified Anew.
Faith.
Grave, A.
His Hands.
"If a Man Die."
If I Could Grasp a Wave from the Great Sea.
O Years Unborn.
Only One King.
Sand Dunes and Sea.
Song of Thanksgiving.
Splendid Lover, The.
Symbols.
White Tree in Bloom, A.
Moreland, Wayne
Sunday Morning.
Morgan, Albert
Union Man.
Morgan, Angela
Awakening, The.
Choice.
God, the Artist.
God Prays.
June Rapture.
Let Us Declare! *sel.*
Poet, The.
Reality.
Song of the New World.
Thanksgiving.
Three Green Trees.
Today.
Whole Year Christmas, The.
Work; a Song of Triumph ("Work!/ Thank God for the might of it").
Morgan, Bessie
'Spacially Jim.
Morgan, Edwin
Aberdeen Train.
Absence.
Canedolia.
Computer's First Christmas Card, The.
From the Domain of Arnheim.
In the Snack-Bar.
Instamatic.
King Billy.
Message Clear.
Second Life, The.
Siesta of a Hungarian Snake.
Strawberries.
To Hugh MacDiarmid.
Morgan, Elizabeth
Caravati's Junkyard.
"Morgan, Emanuel." *See* **Bynner, Witter**
Morgan, Evan
Christmas Dawn at Sea, A.
Morgan, Frederick
Alexander.
Bones.
Castle Rock.
Choice, The.
February 11, 1977.
From a Diary.
I Saw My Darling.
Orpheus to Eurydice.
Morgan, James Appleton
Malum Opus.
Morgan, Jean
Misogynist, The.
Morgan, John
Our "Civilization."
Then.
Morgan, John Hunt
Similia Similibus.
Morgan, Robert
Bees Awater.
Brevard Fault.
Bricking the Church.
Buffalo Trace.
Canning Time.
Cedar.
Cow Pissing.
Face.
Finding an Old Newspaper in the Woods.
Hay Scuttle.
Horace Kephart.
Jutaculla Rock.
Lightning Bug.
Man and Machine.
Mountain Bride.
Passenger Pigeons.
Pumpkin.
Reuben's Cabin.
Rockingchair.
Secret Pleasures.
Thermometer Wine.
Uncle Robert.
When the Ambulance Came.
White Autumn.
Morgan, Robin
Invisible Woman, The.
Lesbian Poem.
Two Gretels, The.
Morgan, Sydney, Lady Morgan
Kate Kearney.
Morgan-Browne, L. E.
Purple, White and Green, The.
Morgenstern, Christian
Aesthete Weasel, The.
Fish's Nightsong.
Funnels, The.
Ghost.
Klabauterwife's Letter.
Knee on Its Own, The.
Korf's Clock.
Korf's Enchantment.
Korf's Joke.
Moonsheep, The.
On the Planet of Flies.
Philosophy Is Born.
Picket Fence, The.
Salmon, The.
Snail's Monologue, The.
Twelve-Elf raises his left hand, The.
Virus, The.
Morgridge, Harriet S.
Jack and Jill.
Mother Goose Sonnets, *sel.*
Simple Simon.
Morhange, Pierre
Jew.
Lullaby in Auschwitz.
Moriarty, Daniel J.
That Pure Place.
Mörike [*or* Möricke], Eduard Friedrich
Beauty Rohtraut.
Prayer: "Lord, as thou wilt, bestow."
Morin, Edward
Big One, The.
Filling Station.
Forecasting the Economy.
Notes on the Post-Industrial Revolution.
Morison, Ted
Avis.
Moritake, Arakida
Haiku: "Falling flower, A."
Moritz, Yunna
In Memory of Francois Rabelais.
Snow-Girl.
Whiteness.
Morley, Christopher
Animal Crackers.
At the Dog Show.
Confession in Holy Week.
Deny Yourself.
Elegy Written in a Country Coal-Bin.
Epitaph for Any New Yorker.
Epitaph on the Proofreader of the Encyclopedia Britannica.
Forever Ambrosia.
Gospel of Mr. Pepys, The.
Grapes of Wrath, The.
Grub Street Recessional, A.
He Comforts Himself.
Human Instinct, A.
In Honour of Taffy Topaz.
Man with the Rake, The.
Nursery Rhymes for the Tender-hearted, *sels.*
Of an Ancient Spaniel in Her Fifteenth Year.
Old Swimmer, The.
Plumpuppets, The.
Pre-Raphaelite, A.
Psychoanalysts.
Quickening.
Secret Laughter.
Secret Thoughts.
Six Weeks Old.
Smells (Junior).
Song for a Little House.
"Sun's Over the Foreyard, The."
This is all we ever say.

Thoughts for St. Stephen.
Thoughts in the Gulf Stream.
Thoughts on Being Invited to Dinner.
To a Child.
To a Post-Office Inkwell.
To the Little House.
Translations from the Chinese, *sels.*
Trees, The.
Tryst, The.
Unearned Increment.
Washing the Dishes.

Morley, David J.
Climbing Zero Gully.

Morley, Hilda
Nike of Samothrace, The.
Shirt, The.

Morningstar, Margaret
Teacher Sees a Boy, The.

Moronelli da Fiorenza, Pier
Canzonetta: A Bitter Song to His Lady.

Morpurgo, Rachel [*or* Rahel]
Song: "Ah, vale of woe, of gloom and darkness moulded."
Sonnet: "My soul surcharged with grief now loud complains."
Woe is me, my soul says, how bitter is my fate.

Morris, Alice S.
Mrs. Santa Claus' Christmas Present.

Morris, Betty
Strath of Kildonan, The.

Morris, Charles
Address to Lady
Country and Town.
Reason Fair to Fill My Glass, A.

Morris, George Hornell
Sailor's Prayer, A.

Morris, George Pope
Jeannie Marsh.
Main-Truck, The; or, A Leap for Life.
My Mother's Bible.
Near the Lake.
Pocahontas.
Retort, The.
We Were Boys Together.
Where Hudson's Wave.
Woodman, Spare That Tree.

Morris, Harrison Smith
Destiny.
Fickle Hope.
June.
Lonely-Bird, The.
Mohammed and Seid.
Pine-Tree Buoy, A.
Walt Whitman.

Morris, Harry
Girod Street Cemetery: New Orleans.

Morris, Herbert
Brahms, The.
North of Wales, The.
Road, The.
Spanish Blue.
This Alice.
Workmen.

Morris, Hilda
November Wears a Paisley Shawl.

Morris, Ida Goldsmith
Give to the Living.

Morris, J. W.
Collusion between a Alegaiter and a Water-Snaik.
What I Think of Hiawatha.

Morris, John N.
Child's Nativity, A.
Fathers, The.
Hating Your Life.
In the Hamptons.
Letter from a Friend, A.
Mirror, The.
My Children's Book.
One Snowy Night in December.
Right to Life, The.
Running It Backward.
Thanksgiving.
Three.

Morris, Sir Lewis
Beginnings of Faith, The.
Brotherhood, *sel.*
Christmas 1898, *sel.*
Heathen Hymn, A, *sel.*
On a Thrush Singing in Autumn.
Separation Deed, A.
Song: "Love took my life and thrill'd it."
Surface and the Depths, The.
To a Child of Fancy.
Tolerance.

Morris, Madge
In the Yucca Land.
¿Quien Sabe?
To the Colorado Desert.

Morris, Robert
Level and the Square, The.

Morris, Thomas
Sapphics: At the Mohawk-Castle, Canada.

Morris, Thomas Lake
California.

Morris, William
All for the Cause.
Ancient Castle, An.
Apology, An.
Atalanta's Race.
Autumn on the Upper Thames.
Blue Closet, The.
Brooding of Sigurd, The.
Day Is Coming, The.
Day of Days, The.
Defence of Guenevere, The.
Earthly Paradise, The,
Eve of Crecy, The.
Fair Is the World.
For the Bed [*or* Beds] at Kelmscott.
From Far Away.
Garden by the Sea, A.
Gilliflower of Gold, The.
Golden Wings.
Haystack in the Floods, The.
Hollow Land, The, *sel.*
I Know a Little Garden-Close.
Iceland First Seen.
In Prison.
Inscription for an Old Bed.
Judgement of God, The.
Life and Death of Jason, The, *sels.*
Lines for a Bed at Kelmscott Manor.
Love Is Enough, *sels.*
March ("He ended; and midst those who heard were some").
March ("Slayer of winter, art thou here again?").
Masters, in This Hall.
May ("O love, this morn when the sweet nightingale").
Message of the March Wind, The.
Minstrels and Maids.
Near Avalon.
Nymph's Song to Hylas, The.
October, *sels.*
Ogier the Dane.
Old Love.
Outlanders, The.
Pilgrims of Hope, The, *sel.*
Pomona.
Praise of My Lady.
Prologue: Wanderers, The.
Riding Together.
Road of Life, The.
Sailing of the Sword, The.
Sending to the War.
Shameful Death.
Sigurd Rideth to the Glittering Heath.
Sigurd's Ride.
Singer's Prelude, The.
Song: "Christ keep the Hollow Land."
Song: "Fair is the night, and fair the day."
Song: "Gold wings across the sea!"
Song from "Ogier the Dane."
Song of Jehane du Castel Beau, The.
Song of the Argonauts.
Story of Sigurd the Volsung, *sels.*
Summer Dawn.
Tapestry Trees.
Thunder in the Garden.
Two Red Roses across the Moon.
Voice of Toil, The.
Wind, The.
Written in a Copy of "The Earthly Paradise," Dec. 25, 1870.

Morrison, Lillian
Air Traveler.
Just for One Day.
Knockout, The.
Lobster Cove Shindig.
Of Kings and Things.
Sidewalk Racer, The; or, On the Skateboard.
Surf.
Water's Edge.

Morrison, M. T.
What the Choir Sang about the New Bonnet.

Morrison, Margaret
I'm the Police Cop Man, I Am.

Morrison, Mary
Nobody Knows but Mother.

Morse, James Herbert
Brook Song.
His Statement of the Case.
Silence.
Wayside, The.
Wild Geese, The.

Morse, Katharine Duncan ("Jerry Doane")
To : "They could not shut you out of heaven."

Morse, Madeline
Christmas Prayer.

Morse, Samuel French
Song in the Cold Season.
Track into the Swamp, The.

Morse, Sidney Henry
Way, The.

Morstein, Petra von
Anthology Poem.
For one who says he feels.
In the Case of Lobsters.
Justice.
. . . 1968 . . .
Thing Poem.

Morton, Bruce
High Plains Harvest.

Morton, David
After Storm.
Beyond Wars.
Boke of Two Ladies, *sel.*
Dead, The.
Epitaph in Sirmio.
Fields at Evening.
Immortalis.
Lover to Lover.
Mariners.
Old Ships.
Petition for a Miracle.
Ships in Harbour.
Symbol.
Touring.
When There Is Music.
Who Walks with Beauty.
Wooden Ships.

Morton, John Bingham ("Beachcomber")
Another Canto.
Ballade of Charon and the River Girl.
Dancing Cabman, The.
Epitaph: "Glassblower lies here at rest, A."
Epitaph: "Tread softly; bid a solemn music sound."
Epitaph for a Lighthouse-Keeper's Horse.
Epitaph on a Warthog.
Health and Fitness.
Let poets praise the softer winds of spring.
Now We Are Sick.

On Sir Henry Ferrett, M.P.
Someone Asked the Publisher.
Song of the Ballet.
Theobald James.
To a Lady.
Tripe.
When We Were Very Silly, *sels.*

Morton, Sarah Wentworth
To Aaron Burr, under Trial for High Treason.

Morton, Thomas
Carmen Elegiacum.
Epitaph: "Time that bringes all things to light."
New Canaans Genius; Epilogus.
New English Canaan; Prologue.
Poem, The: "I sing th' adventures of mine worthy wights."
Poem, The: "Rise Oedipus, and if thou canst unfould."
Poem, The: "What ailes Pigmalion? Is it lunacy."
Song, The: "Drinke and be merry, merry, merry boyes."

Mosby, George, Jr.
And "I Know Why the Caged Bird Sings"; a Villanelle.
Birthday: Tara Regina.
Of an Old Con.
Old, The.
To Night; to Judith.
Variations on a Late October Day.

Moschus
Cupid a Plowman.
Cupid Turned Plowman.
From the Greek of Moschus.
Lament for Bion.
Ocean, The.
Pan loved his neighbour Echo—but that child.

Moser, Mrs. J. F.
Would I Be Called a Christian?

Moser, John W.
Room Service.
Sea Food Thought.

Moses, Daniel David
Fall Song.
Hands, The.

Moses, William Robert
American History.
Angina Pectoris.
Big Dam.
Boy at Target Practice; a Contemplation.
Impulse of October, The.
Little-League Baseball Fan.
Nature of Jungles, The.
Night Wind in Fall.
Sitting in the Woods: A Contemplation.

Moskowitz, Lynn
Nightmares: Part Three.

Mosley, Jr, Joseph M.
Black Church on Sunday.

Moss, Howard
Around the Fish: After Paul Klee.
Arsenic.
At the Algonquin.
Balcony with Birds, A.
Burning Love Letters.
Cats and Dogs.
Chalk from Eden.
Colloquy with Gregory on the Balcony, A.
Crossing the Park.
Dead Leaf, A.
Elegy for My Father.
Elizabethan Tragedy; a Footnote.
Finding Them Lost.
Front Street.
Game of Chance, A.
Geography; a Song.
Gift to Be Simple, The.
Going to Sleep in the Country.
Great Spaces.
Hand, The.
Hermit, The.
Horror Movie.
King Midas.
Lesson from Van Gogh, A.
Lie, The.
Local Places.
Long Island Springs.
Meeting, The.
Movies for the Home.
Piano Practice.
Problem in Morals, A.
Pruned Tree, The.
Rain.
Refrigerator, The.
Roof Garden, The.
Stars.
Still Pond, No More Moving.
Summer Gone, A.
Tourists.
Traction: November 22, 1963.
Tragedy.
Underwood.
Venice.
Water Island.
Waterwall Blues.
Winter's End.

Moss, Stanley
Apocrypha.
Branch, The.
Centaur Song.
Central Park West.
Clams.
Exchange of Hats, An.
Fishermen.
God Poem.
Hangman's Love Song, The.
In Front of a Poster of Garibaldi.
Prayer: "Give me a death like Buddha's, let me fall."
Return, The.
Sailing from the United States.
Scroll.
SM.
Squall.
Two Fishermen.
Valley, The.
Voice.

Moss, Thomas
Beggar, The.

Mossman, Bina
I'm going to California.

Mother Goose
A was an apple pie, B bit it, C cut it.
As I was going along, long, long.
As I was going o'er London Bridge.
As I was going to St. Ives.
As I was going up Pippen Hill.
As little Jenny Wren/ Was sitting by the shed.
As round as an apple, as deep as a cup.
As soft as silk, as white as milk.
As Tommy Snooks and Bessy Brooks.
Baa, baa, black sheep, have you any wool?
Baby, baby, naughty baby.
Baby's Dance, The, *at.*
Barber, barber, shave a pig.
Bell horses, bell horses, what time of day?
Black within, and red without.
Bless you, bless you, burnie-bee.
Blow, wind, blow! and go, mill, go!
Bobby Shaftoe's gone to sea.
Boys and girls come out to play.
Bye, baby bunting.
Carrion crow sat upon an oak, The.
Cobbler, cobbler, mend my shoe.
Cock a doodle doo! / My dame has lost her shoe.
Cock crows [*or* Cocks crow] in the morning [*or* morn] to tell us to rise.
Cock doth crow, the wind doth blow, The.
Cock doth crow, The/ To let you know.
Come, let's to bed.
Come dance a jig.
Come when you're called.
Cross Patch/ Draw the latch.
Curly Locks! Curly Locks! wilt thou be mine?
Cushy cow, bonny, let down thy milk.
Daffy-down-dilly is new come to town [*or* Daffadowndilly has come up to town].
Dance, Thumbkin, dance.
Dance a baby diddy.
Dance to your [*or* thee] daddy [*or* daddie], *diff. versions.*
Diddle, diddle, dumpling, my son John.
Dillar, a dollar, A,/ A ten o'clock scholar.
Ding, dong, bell,/ Pussy's in the well.
Dingty diddlety.
Doctor Faustus was a good man.
Dove says, Coo, coo, The.
Elizabeth, Lizzy [*or* Elspeth], Betsy, and Bess.
Farmer went trotting upon his gray mare, A.
Flour of England, fruit of Spain.
For every evil under the sun.
For want of a nail.
Formed long ago, yet made today.
Four and twenty tailors.
Friday night's dream on a Saturday told.
Georgie Porgie, pudding and pie.
Girl in the lane, The.
Girls and boys, come out to play.
God made the bees.
Goosey, goosey, gander, where [*or* whither] shall I wander?
Grand old Duke of York, The.
Great A, little a.
Hark, hark, the dogs do bark.
Hart he loves the high wood, The.
Hector Protector was dressed all in green.
Here am I, little jumping Joan.
Here sits the Lord Mayor.
Hey, my kitten, my kitten.
Hey diddle dinkety, poppety, pet.
Hey [*or* High *or* Sing hey], diddle, diddle,/ The cat and the fiddle.
Hick-a-more, Hack-a-more.
Hickory, dickory, dock.
Higgledy, piggledy [*or* Higgleby, Piggleby *or* Hickety, pickety], my black [*or* fat] hen.
Higher than a house,/ Higher than a tree.
Hill full, a hole full, A.
Hippety hop to the barber shop.
Hot cross buns! Hot-cross buns!/ One a penny, two a penny.
How many days has my baby to play?
How many miles to Babylon [*or* Barley-Bridge]?
Humpty Dumpty sat on a wall.
I had a little husband.
I had a little moppet.
I had a little nut-tree; nothing would it bear.
I had a little pony.
I have a little sister, they call her Peep-Peep.
I love sixpence, jolly little sixpence.
I saw a ship a-sailing.
I saw three ships come sailing by.
I won't be my father's Jack.
I would, if I could.
If all the seas were one sea.
If all the world were [*or* was] apple-pie.
If I had [*or* I'd] as much money as I could spend.
If wishes were horses.
I'll tell you a story/ About Jack a Nory.
In a cottage in Fife.
In marble walls [*or* halls] as white as milk.
Intery, mintery, cutery corn.
Is John Smith within?
Jack and Jill [*or* Gill] went up the hill.
Jack be nimble.
Jack Sprat could eat no fat.
Jacky, come give me thy fiddle.
Jenny come tie my.
Jenny Wren fell sick.
Jerry Hall,/ He is so small.
John Cook had a little grey mare.
Johnny shall have a new bonnet.
King of France, the king of France, The/ with forty thousand men.

Ladybird, Ladybird fly away home.
Leg over leg.
Lion and the unicorn, The.
Little Bo-Peep has lost her sheep.
Little Boy Blue, come blow up your horn.
Little cock sparrow sat on a green tree, A.
Little girl, little girl,/ Where have you been?
Little Jack Horner sat in the corner.
Little maid, pretty maid,/ Whither goest thou?
Little Miss Muffet/ Sat on a tuffet.
Little Polly Flinders.
Little Robin Redbreast sat upon a tree.
Little Sally Waters.
Little Tommy Tucker.
Lives in winter.
London Bridge is broken down.
Long legs, crooked thighs.
Long-tailed pig, A.
Lucky Lock lost her pocket.
Man in the moon, The/ As he sails in the sky.
Man in the wilderness asked [of] me [*or* said to me], The [*or* A].
Margery Mutton-pie.
Mary, Mary [*or* Mistress Mary], quite contrary.
Monday's child is fair of face.
North wind doth blow, The.
Old King Cole was a merry old soul.
Old Mother Goose/ When she wanted to wander.
Old Mother Twitchett had [*or* has] but one eye.
Old woman, old woman,/ Shall we go a-shearing?
On Saturday night shall be my care.
One, two,/ Buckle my shoe.
One, two, three, four,/ Mary at the cottage door.
1, 2, 3, 4, 5!/I caught a hare alive.
One, two, three, four, five/Once I caught a fish alive.
One misty, moisty morning.
Pat-a-cake, pat-a-cake, baker's man.
Pease porridge [*or* pudding] hot.
Peter, Peter, pumpkin eater.
Peter Piper picked a peck of pickled peppers.
Poor old Robinson Crusoe!
Pretty John Watts.
Pussy cat ate the dumplings.
Pussy sits beside the fire.
Pussy-cat, Pussy-cat, where have you been?
Queen of Hearts, The / She made some tarts.
Rain, rain, go away.
Rain, rain, go to Spain.
Riddle, a riddle, as I suppose, A.
Riddle me, riddle me ree.
Ride a cock-horse to Banbury Cross,/ To see a fine lady upon a white horse [*or* an old woman get up on her horse].
Ride away, ride away/ Johnny shall ride.
Ring-a-ring o' roses, A.
Robert Barnes, fellow fine.
Robert Rowley rolled a round roll round.
Robin Hood, Robin Hood,/ Is in the mickle wood.
Robin-a-bobin.
Rock-a-bye [*or* Hush-a-bye] baby, on [*or* in] the tree top.
Rock-a-bye, baby, thy cradle is green.
Roses are red.
Rub a dub dub,/ Three men in a tub.
Runs all day and never walks.
See, see, what shall I see?
See-saw, Margery Daw,/ Jack[y] shall have a new master.
See-saw, Margery Daw,/ The old hen flew over the malt house.
See-saw, sacradown.
Shoe the colt, shoe the colt.
Simple Simon met a pieman.
Sing, sing,/ What shall I sing?
Sing a song of sixpence.
Six little mice sat down to spin.
Smiling girls, rosy boys.
Sneeze on a Monday, you [*or* you'll] sneeze for danger.
Solomon Grundy.
Sow came in with the saddle, The.
Speak when you're spoken to,/ Come for one call.
Spring is showery, flowery, bowery.
Taffy was a Welshman, Taffy was a thief.
There was a crooked man, and he went [*or* walked] a crooked mile.
There was a little boy and a little girl.
There was a little man,/ And he had a little gun.
There was a man of our town.
There was an old woman, and what do you think?
There was an old woman lived under a hill.
There was an old woman tossed up in a basket [*or* blanket].
There was an old woman who lived in a shoe.
There were two blackbirds sitting on a hill.
They that wash on Monday.
Thirty white horses upon a red hill.
This is the house that Jack built.
This is the way the ladies ride.
This little pig went to market.
Three wise men of Gotham.
To make your candles last for aye.
To market, to market, to buy a fat pig.
To market, to market/ To buy a plum bun.
Tom, Tom, the piper's son.
Tommy's tears and Mary's fears.
Trip upon trenchers, and dance upon dishes.
Tweedle-Dum and Tweedle-Dee.
Twelve pears hanging high.
Two legs sat upon three legs.
Up at Piccadilly oh!
What are little boys made of, made of?
What is the rhyme for porringer?
What's the news of the day.
When good King Arthur ruled this land.
When I was a bachelor/ I lived by myself.
When I was a little girl,/ About seven years old.
When Jacky's a [very] good boy.
When little Fred/ Was called to bed
When the wind is in the east.
"Where are you going [to], my pretty maid?"
Willy, Willy Wilkin.
Willy boy, Willy boy,/ Where are you going?

Motherwell, William
Cavalier's Song, The.
Jeanie Morrison.
Last Verses.
Sing On, Blithe Bird.

Mott, Michael
Islanders, Inlanders.
Meadow Grass.

Mott, Randy
Ghazal: Japanese Paintbrush.

Motteux, Peter Anthony[*or* Pierre Antoine]
Love's a Jest, *sel.*
Man Is for Woman Made.
Slaves to London.
Town-Rakes, The,*at.*

Moul, Keith
Playing Catch.

Moulton, Louise Chandler [Ellen Louise Chandler]
Hic Jacet.
Last Good-by, The.
Laura Sleeping.
Laus Veneris.
Louisa May Alcott.
Love's Resurrection Day.
Painted Fan, A.
Shadow Dance, The.
Somebody's Child.
Spring Is Late, The.
Summer Wooing, A.
To-Night.
Tryst, A.
We Lay Us Down to Sleep.
Were But My Spirit Loosed upon the Air.

Moultrie, John
Fairy Maimounè, The.
Forget Thee?
Sir Launfal, *sel.*

Mounsey, Messenger
Here lie my old bones: my vexation now ends.

Mountain, George J.
Indian's Grave, The.

Mousley, James P.
Prayer: "God of light and blossom."

Movius, Geoffrey
Work-out, The.

Mowrer, Paul Scott
Mozart's Grave.

Moxon, Edward
Moonlight.
Nightingale, The.
Similes.

Moyles, Lois
Report from California.
Tale Told by a Head, A.
Thomas in the Fields.

Mozeen, Thomas
Bedlamite, The.
Kilruddery Hunt, The.

Mozeson, Isaac Elchanan
Masada.

Mphahlele, Ezekiel
Exile in Nigeria.

Mqhayi, S. E. K.
Black Army, The.
Sinking of the Mendi, The.

Mririda n'Ait Attik
Azouou.
God Hasn't Made Room.
Like Smoke.
Mririda.

Msham, Mwana Kupona
Daughter, take this amulet.
Poem to Her Daughter, *sel.*

Mtshali, Oswald Mbuyiseni
Shepherd and His Flock, The.

Mudie, Ian
They'll Tell You about Me.
Wilderness Theme.

Mueller, Lisel
Alive Together.
Apples.
Civilizing the Child.
Drawings by Children.
Farewell, a Welcome, A.
For a Nativity.
Historical Museum, Manitoulin Island.
Life of a Queen.
Lonesome Dream, The.
Merce Cunningham and the Birds.
Monet Refuses the Operation.
Moon Fishing.
Night Song.
Palindrome.
People at the Party, The.
Reading the Brothers Grimm to Jenny.
Sans Souci.
Small Poem about the Hounds and the Hares.
Voice from Out of the Night, A.
Weaver, The.
Yes, we were happy that Sunday, walking.

Muhlenberg, William Augustus
Fulfillment.
Heaven's Magnificence.
I Would Not Live Alway.
Like Noah's Weary Dove, *with music.*
Saviour, Who Thy Flock Art Feeding, *with music.*

Muhringer, Doris
Questions and Answers.

Muir, E. A.
Gulls.

Muir, Edwin
Abraham.
Absent, The.
Animals, The.

Annunciation, The.
Antichrist.
At the dead centre of the boundless plain.
Ballad of Hector in Hades.
Ballad of the Flood.
Birthday, A.
Brothers, The.
Castle, The.
Child Dying, The.
Childhood.
Combat, The.
Confirmation, The.
Enchanted Knight, The.
Escape, The.
Face, The.
Fathers, The.
Finder Found, The.
For Ann Scott-Moncrieff.
Gate, The.
Good Man in Hell, The.
Good Town, The.
Great House, The.
Grove, The.
Horses, The ("Barely a twelvemonth after").
Horses ("Those lumbering horses in the steady plough").
Human Fold, The.
In Love for Long.
Interrogation, The.
Island, The.
Journey, The.
Killing, The.
Labyrinth, The.
Little General, The.
Love's Remorse.
Merlin.
Myth, The.
Mythical Journey, The.
Oedipus.
Old Gods, The.
One Foot in Eden.
Reading in War Time.
Recurrence, The.
Refugees, The.
Return, The ("The doors flapped open in Ulysses' house").
Return, The ("The veteran Greeks came home").
Return of the Greeks, The.
Rider Victory, The.
Road, The.
Robert the Bruce.
Scotland 1941.
Scotland's Winter.
Suburban Dream.
Three Mirrors, The.
Too Much.
Town Betrayed, The.
Transfiguration, The.
Transmutation, The.
Trophy, The.
Troy.
Usurpers, The.
Variations on a Time Theme,
Voyage, The.
Wayside Station, The.
West, The.
Wheel, The.
Window, The.

Muir, Henry D.
Soldier's Grave, The.

Muir, John
From garden to garden, ridge to ridge.

"Mukerji, Rana"
Spring Night.

Mukta Bai
Although he has no form.
I live where darkness/ is not.

Mulchinock, William Pembroke
Rose of Tralee, The, *at.*

Muldoon, Paul
Armageddon, Armageddon, *sel.*
Clonfeacle.
Dancers at the Moy.
Field Hospital, The.
Hedgehog.
Indians on Alcatraz, The.
Mules.

Mulholland, Rosa (Lady Gilbert)
Love and Death.

Mullen, Harryette
Saturday Afternoon, When Chores Are Done.

Müller, Wilhelm
Whither?

Mulligan, J. B.
Deja Vu.

Mullins, Cecil J.
Enemy, Enemy.

Mumford, Erika
Shaman.
Woman Painter of Mithila.

Mumford, Lewis
Consolation in War.

Mumford, Marilyn R.
Recollection.

Mumin, Sheikh Hassan
Women and Men.

Munby, Arthur Joseph
Above the Medway.
Doris; a Pastoral.
Vales of the Medway, The, *sel.*

Munday, Anthony
Beauty Bathing.
Beauty Sat Bathing [by a Spring].
Colin.
Death of Robert, Earl of Huntingdon, *sel.*
Dirge: "Weep, weep, ye woodmen, wail."
Fedele and Fortunio, *sel.*
I Serve a Mistress.
Love.
Primaleon of Greece, *sel.*
Robin Hood's Funeral.
Song: "Weep, weep, ye woodmen, wail!"
To Colin Clout.
Zelanto, the Fountain of Fame, *sel.*

Mundell, William D.
Uninvited, The.

Mundorf, Frank
Letter from a State Hospital.
Remembering Lincoln.

Mundy, Anthony
Concrete Poem, A.

Mungin, Horace
Blues.
Of Man and Nature.

Munkittrick, Richard Kendall
At the Shrine.
Bulb, A.
Ghosts.
Molasses River.
Old King Cabbage.
Redingote and the Vamoose, The.
Song of the Owl, The.
To Miguel de Cervantes Saavadra.
Unsatisfied Yearning.
What's in a Name?

Munro, Bruce Weston
Grandmother's Apple Pies.

Munro, Deborah
Sequence for a Young Widow Passing.
Song of the Strange Young Duckling.

Munro, Neil
Heather, The.
Nettles.

Munro, Robin
Apprentices.
Hills.
Shetland, Hill Dawn.
View.

Munson, C. C.
Dead Past, A,*at.*

Munson, Ida Norton
Assurance.

Mura, David
Hibakusha's Letter (1955), The.
Lan Nguyen; the Uniform of Death, 1971.
Natives, The.
Nisei Picnic, A.
Relocation.

Murasaki Shikibu, Lady
Someone passes.
Tale of Genji, The, *sels.*

Muratori, Fred
Real Muse, The.

Murger, Henry
Old Loves.
Spring in the Students' Quarter.

Murguía, Alejandro
O California.
Small Towns.

Murphey, Joseph Colin
Silver Racer, The.

Murphy, Beatrice M.
Letter, The.

Murphy, George E., Jr.
Conestoga.

Murphy, R. D.
Back Lane.

Murphy, Richard
Archaeology of Love, The.
Battle of Aughrim, The, *sels.*
Care.
Coppersmith.
Enigma.
Epitaph on a Fir-Tree.
Girl at the Seaside.
High Island.
Last Galway Hooker, The.
Little Hunger.
Now.
Pat Cloherty's Version of *The Maisie.*
Philosopher and the Birds, The.
Planter.
Poet on the Island, The.
Rapparees.
Reading Lesson, The.
Sailing to an Island.
Seals at High Island.
Stormpetrel.
Trouvaille.
Walking on Sunday.
Woman of the House, The.

Murray, Ada Foster (Mrs. Henry Mills Alden)
Above Salerno.
Her Dwelling-Place.
Old-fashioned Poet, An.
Prevision.
Unguarded.

Murray, Anne B.
Drumochter.
Then and Now.

Murray, Bertram
I Caught a Fish.

Murray, Charles
Bennachie.
In Lythe Strathdon.
Whistle, The.

Murray, Sir David
Caelia, *sel.*
Sonnet: "Ponder thy cares, and sum them all in one."

Murray, Frederick*and* Frederick Leigh
Charlie Piecan.

Murray, G. E.
California Dead.
On the Upside.
Shelby County, Ohio. November 1974.
Shopping for Midnight.
Sketch for a Morning in Muncie, Indiana.
Southern Exposures.

Murray, Joan
After the Murder of Jimmy Walsh.
Crocus.
Irish Blessing, An.
Lovers, The.

Murray, John
Hark! 'Tis the Saviour of Mankind, *with music.*
Murray, Kenton Foster
Challenge.
Murray, Les A.
Absolutely Ordinary Rainbow, An.
Bagman O'Reilly's Curse.
Names of the Humble, The.
Once in a Lifetime, Snow.
Portrait of the Autist as a New World Driver.
Powerline Incarnation, The.
Telling the Cousins.
Murray, Paul
Rain.
Murray, Pauli
Dark Testament.
Death of a Friend.
For Mack C. Parker.
Harlem Riot, 1943.
Inquietude.
Mr. Roosevelt Regrets.
Ruth.
Song: "Because I know deep in my own heart."
Without Name.
Murray, Philip
Carrara.
Cloud of Unknowing, The.
Finches, The.
Heron, The.
In the Annals of Tacitus.
Little Litany to St. Francis, A.
Locust Hunt, The.
Turning, The.
Murray, Robert Fuller
Andrew M'Crie.
Critic and Poet.
End of April, The.
Wasted Day, The.
Murray, Rona
Lizard, The.
Murry, Ann
Familiar Epistle, A.
Murry, Calvin
Challenge, The.
Logic.
On a Summer Day, 1972.
Prisoner aboard the S.S. *Beagle.*
Sisyphus Angers the Gods of Condescension.
Murton, Jessie Wilmore
Song of the Builders.
Mus, David
Conserves.
Joy of Cooking, The, *sel.*
Musgrave, Susan
Judas Goat, The.
Returning to the Town Where We Used to Live.
Muske, Carol
Child with Six Fingers.
Found.
Hyena.
Rice.
Swansong.
Musser, Benjamin Francis
Der Heilige Mantel von Aachen.
Holy Land of Walsingham, The.
Musset, Alfred de
Juana.
Souvenir.
Mu'tamid, King of Seville
"Mustafa." *See* **Johnson, don Allen**
Fountain, The.
I Traveled with Them.
Tears of the World.
Thy Garden.
Woo Not the World.
Muth, Eleanor
Night Enchantment.
Mutis, Alvaro
Amen.
Lied in Crete.
Muuse, 'Abdillaahi
Elder's Reproof to his Wife, An.
Mycall, John
Our States, O Lord, *with music.*
Myers, Bert
When I Came to Israel.
Myers, Ernest
Achilles.
Fiorentina.
Myers, Frederic William Henry
Evanescence.
Harold at Two Years Old.
Inner Light, The.
O God, How Many Years Ago.
Prayer, A: "O for one minute hark what we are saying!"
Saint Paul, *abr.*
Surrender to Christ.
Teneriffe, *sel.*
Myers, Jack
Apprentice Painter, The.
Day of Atonement.
Minyan, The.
Mirror for the Barnyard.
Mockingbird, Copy This.
So Long Solon.
Too Many Miles of Sunlight between Us.
When I Held You to My Chest, You Fit.
Myles, Glenn
Percy/ 68.
Mylonas, Eva
Holidays.

N

"N., A. M."
God's Treasure.
Na Gopaleen, Myles
Literary Criticism.
Nabbes, Thomas
Love Sets Order in the Elements.
Microcosmus, *sel.*
Nabokov, Vladimir
Ballad of Longwood Glen, The.
Evening of Russian Poetry, An.
Lines Written in Oregon.
Literary Dinner, A.
Ode to a Model.
On Discovering a Butterfly.
Rain.
Room, The.
Nadaud, Gustave
Carcassonne.
Nadel, Alan
To Summer.
Nadir, Moishe (Yitzhok Reis)
Adjectives.
Nadson, Semion Yakovlevich
Brother, The.
Nagase Kiyoko
Mother.
Naggid, Hayim
After the War.
Like a Pearl.
My Mother.
Snow in Jerusalem, A.
Nagy, Agnes Nemes
Bird.
I Carried Statues.
Storm.
Words to a Song.
Nahman of Bratzlav, Rabbi
Annul Wars.
Heart of the World, The.
Nahum
Spring Song.
Naidu, Sarojini
Coromandel Fishers.
Cradle Song: "From groves of spice."
In the Bazaars of Hyderabad.
Snake-Charmer, The.
Naigreshel, Mendel
Nation.
What Will Remain after Me?
Nairne, Carolina Oliphant, Baroness
Auld House, The.
Caller Herrin'.
Heavenward.
Land o' the Leal, The.
Lass o' Gowrie, The.
Lullaby: "Baloo, loo, lammy, now baloo, my dear."
Rest Is Not Here.
Rowan Tree, The.
Will Ye No Come Back Again?
Najara, Israel
God of the World.
Loved of My Soul.
Nakasuk
Gull, it is said, The.
Invocation: "Land earth-root."
Namanworth, Elaine
Fishermen's Wives, The.
Nance, Berta Hart
Cattle.
Moonlight.
Road to Texas, The.
Naone, Dana
Girl with the Green Skirt.
I make all the poetic pauses.
Long Distance.
Presence, The.
Sleep.
Napa
Darkened in the Soul.
Napier, Felicity
Houseplant.
Napier, George
To a Lady, with a Compass.
Nash, Dorothy
Kinloch, *sel.*
Road Moves On, The.
Nash, Ogden
Admiral Byrd.
Adventures of Isabel.
Among the Anthropophagi.
Amorous Señor, The.
Anatomy of Happiness, The.
And Three Hundred and Sixty-six in Leap Year.
Ant, The.
Arthur.
Autres Bêtes, Autres Moeurs.
Bankers Are Just like Anybody Else, except Richer.
Bat, The.
Benjamin.
Between Birthdays.
Boy Who Laughed at Santa Claus, The.
Calling Spring VII–MMMC.
Camel, The.
Canary, The.
Carol for Children, A.
Caution to Everybody, A.
Celery.
Centipede, The.
Columbus.
Confessions of a Born Spectator.
Consider the Auk.
Cow, The.
Custard the Dragon.
Do You Plan to Speak Bantu?
Dog, The.
Dog's Best Friend Is His Illiteracy, A.
Drink with Something in It, A.
Duck, The.
Edouard.
Eel, The.
England Expects.
Evening Out, The.
Exit, Pursued by a Bear.
Family Court.
Firefly, The.

First Families Move Over!
Fly, The.
Funebrial Reflections.
Genealogical Reflection.
Germ, The.
Golly, How Truth Will Out.
Goodbye Now, or, Pardon My Gauntlet.
Grackle, The.
Grandpa Is Ashamed.
Ha! Original Sin.
Hippopotamus, The.
Hunter, The.
I Can't Have a Martini, Dear, but You Take One.
I Never Even Suggested It.
Ill Met by Zenith.
Introduction to Dogs, An.
Introspective Reflection.
Invocation: "Senator Smoot (Republican, Ut.)."
Japanese, The.
Jellyfish, The.
Kangaroo, The.
Kind of an Ode to Duty.
Kindly Unhitch That Star, Buddy.
Kitten, The.
Lady Thinks She Is Thirty, A.
Lama, The.
Limerick: "There was an old man in a trunk."
Lines to a World-famous Poet Who Failed to Complete a World-famous Poem; or, Come Clean, Mr. Guest!
Lines to Be Embroidered on a Bib; or, The Child Is Father of the Man, but Not for Quite a While.
Lion, The.
Lucy Lake.
Malice Domestic.
Max Schling, Max Schling, Lend Me Your Green Thumb.
Morning Prayer.
New Nutcracker Suite, The, *sel.*
Notes for the Chart in 306.
Octopus, The.
Oh, Please Don't Get Up!
Oh, Stop Being Thankful All over the Place.
Old Men.
Oyster, The.
Panther, The.
Parsnip, The.
Peekaboo, I Almost See You.
People upstairs, The.
Perfect Husband, The.
Phoenix, The.
Pig, The.
Pizza, The.
Portrait of the Artist as a Prematurely Old Man.
Poultries, The.
Praying Mantis, The.
Private Dining Room, The.
Purist, The.
Reflection on Babies.
Reflections on Ice-breaking.
Reminiscent Reflection.
Requiem: "There was a young belle of old Natchez."
Rhinoceros, The.
Sea-Gull, The.
Seven Spiritual Ages of Mrs. Marmaduke Moore, The.
Shrew, The.
So That's Who I Remind Me Of.
Song of the Open Road.
Song to Be Sung by the Father of Infant Female Children.
Spring Comes to Murray Hill.
Squirrel, The.
Sweet Dreams.
Tableau at Twilight.
Taboo to Boot.
Tale of Custard the Dragon, The.
Tallyho-Hum.
Termite, The.
Terrible People, The.
That Reminds Me.
There Was a Young Lady of Rome.
They Don't Speak English in Paris.
Third Limick.
Thrifty Soprano, A.
To a Small Boy Standing on My Shoes While I Am Wearing Them.
Traveler's Rest.
Turtle, The.
Two and One Are a Problem.
Two Dogs Have I.
Ultimate Reality.
Up from the Egg: The Confessions of a Nuthatch Avoider.
Up from the Wheelbarrow.
Very like a Whale.
Visit, The.
Wapiti, The.
Wendigo, The.
What's the Use.
Who Taught Caddies to Count? or, A Burnt Golfer Fears the Child.
Wombat, The.
Word to Husbands, A.
Young Lady from Cork, A.

Nashe [*or* Nash], **Thomas**
A-Maying, a-Playing.
Adieu, Farewell Earth's Bliss.
Autumn.
Clownish Song, A.
Death's Summons.
Dust Hath Closed Helen's Eye.
Fair Summer Droops.
Harvest.
In Time of Pestilence.
Lord, Have Mercy On Us.
Song in Time of Plague.
Spring.
Spring, the Sweet Spring.
Summer's Last Will and Testament, *sels.*
Waning Summer.

Nashe, Thomas *and* **Christopher Marlowe.** *See* **Marlowe, Christopher** *and* **Thomas Nashe**

Nason, Emma Huntington
Child's Question, A.
Cricket's Story, The.

Nathan, Leonard
Diver, The.
Ellora.
Fantasia.
Fourth Dimension, The.
Likeness, The.
Niño Leading an Old Man to Market.
To a Foreign Friend.
Trying.
Yours Truly.

Nathan, Norman
Modern Architecture.
Voting Machine.

Nathan, Robert
At the Symphony.
Beauty Is Ever to the Lonely Mind.
Bells in the Country.
Christian, Be Up, *with music.*
Comes Fall.
Daughter at Evening, The.
Mountaineer, The.
Now Blue October.
Poet Describes His Love, The.
Sonnet: "Because my grief seems quiet and apart."
These Are the Chosen People.
Will Beauty Come.

Naudé, Adèle
Africa.
From a Venetian Sequence.
Idiot, The.
Portrait.
Unpossessed, The.

Nayadu, Sarojini *See* **Naidu, Sarojini**

Naylor, James Ball
David and Solomon.

Neagle, Dennis
I Caught This Morning at Dawning.

Neal, John
Men of the North.
Music of the Night.

Neal, Larry
Harlem Gallery: From the Inside.
James Powell on Imagination.
Malcolm X—An Autobiography.
Orishas.

Neale, John Mason
Hymn for Easter Morn.
Light's Glittering Morn.
Oh, Give Us Back the Days of Old.

Neaves, Lord Charles
Let Us All Be Unhappy on Sunday.

Neeld, Judith
Thinning Out the Grove.

Neele, Henry
Moan, Moan, Ye Dying Gales.

Negri, Ada
Make Way!

Neidhart von Reuental
On the Mountain.

Neidus, Leib
I Love the Woods.
I Often Want to Let My Lines Go.
In an Alien Place.

Neihardt, John G.
Battle Cry.
Child's Heritage, The.
Death of Crazy Horse, The.
Easter.
Easter, 1923.
Envoi: "Oh, seek me not within a tomb."
Let Me Live Out My Years.
Outward.
Prayer for Pain.
Red Cloud.
Shooting of the Cup, The.
Song of Jed Smith, The, *sel.*
Song of Three Friends, The, *sel.*
When I Am Dead.
When I Have Gone Weird Ways.

Neilson, Francis
Eugenio Pacelli.

Neilson, John Shaw
Beauty Imposes.
Break of Day.
Cool, Cool, Country, The.
Crane Is My Neighbour, The.
Flowers in the Ward.
In the Street.
Love's Coming.
May.
Orange Tree, The.
Poor Can Feed the Birds, The.
Soldier Is Home, The.
Song Be Delicate.
Strawberries in November.
Sundowner, The.
Take Down the Fiddle, Karl!
'Tis the White Plum Tree.
To a Blue Flower.
To a School-Girl.
You Cannot Go Down to the Spring.

Nekrasov, Nikolai Alekseyevich
Capitals Are Rocked, The.

Nelms, Sheryl L.
Edwin A. Nelms.
How About.
Killing the Rooster.

Nelson, Alice Dunbar Moore
I Sit and Sew.
Snow in October.
Sonnet: "I had no thought of violets of late."

Nelson, David
My Days are Gliding Swiftly By, *with music.*

Nelson, Howard
Cows near the Graveyard, The.
Winter Night, Cold Spell.
Nelson, Paula
House, The.
Nelson, Rodney
Anabasis.
Nelson, Sharon
Pedlar.
Nelson, Stanley
Immigrants.
Nelson, Starr
White Rainbow, The.
Nemerov, Howard
Absent-minded Professor.
After Commencement.
Alexandrine Magazine, An.
Angel and Stone.
At a Country Hotel.
Author to His Body on Their Fifteenth Birthday, 29.ii.80, The.
Backward Look, The.
Beautiful Lawn Sprinkler, The.
Because You Asked about the Line between Prose and Poetry.
Blue Swallows, The.
Book of Kells, The.
Boom!
Brainstorm.
Brief Journey West, The.
Carol: "Now is the world withdrawn all."
Central Park.
Ceremony.
Companions, The.
Conversing with Paradise.
Dandelions.
Death of God, The.
Debate with the Rabbi.
Dial Tone, The.
Dialogue.
Distances They Keep, The.
Dragonfly, The.
Dream of Flying Comes of Age, The.
Dying Garden, The.
Easter.
Ecstasies of Dialectic, The.
Elegy: "My Thompson, least attractive character."
Elegy for a Nature Poet.
Epigrams [I–IX].
Extract from Memoirs.
Fable of the War, A.
Fall Again, The.
First Leaf, The.
Fugue.
Ginkgoes in Fall.
Glass Dialectic.
Going Away.
Goldfish.
"Good-bye," said the river, "I'm going downstream."
Goose Fish, The.
Grace to Be Said at the Supermarket.
Guide to the Ruins.
Historical Judas, The.
History of a Literary Movement.
Holding the Mirror Up to Nature.
Human Things.
I Only Am Escaped Alone to Tell Thee.
Icehouse in Summer, The.
Learning by Doing.
Life Cycle of Common Man.
Lion & Honeycomb.
Lives of Gulls and Children, The.
Lot Later.
Make Love Not War.
Makers, The.
Mapmaker on His Art, The.
Marriage of Heaven and Earth, The.
May Day Dancing, The.
Metamorphoses.
Money.
Most Expensive Picture in the World, The.
Mousemeal.
Mud Turtle, The.
Murder of William Remington, The.
New Year's, 1978.
Nixons at Calvary.
On Being Asked for a Peace Poem.
On Certain Wits.
Painter Dreaming in the Scholar's House, The.
Phoenix, The.
Picture, A.
Pockets.
Political Reflection.
Power to the People.
Praising the Poets of That Country.
Primer of the Daily Round, A.
Print-out, The.
Redeployment.
Remorse for Time, The.
Runes.
Salt Garden, The.
Sanctuary, The.
Santa Claus.
Scales of the Eyes, The.
September, the First Day of School.
Sestina on Her Portrait.
Sigmund Freud.
Singular Metamorphosis, A.
Sleeping Beauty.
Small Moon.
Snowflakes.
Sparrow in the Zoo, The.
Speculation.
Spell before Winter, A.
Statues in the Public Gardens, The.
Storm Windows.
Style.
Sunday at the End of Summer.
Tapestry, The.
Three Towns, The.
To D——, Dead by Her Own Hand.
To David, about His Education.
To My Least Favorite Reviewer.
To the Rulers.
Town Dump, The.
Trees.
Truth.
Vacuum, The.
View, The.
View from an Attic Window, The.
Waiting Rooms.
Way of Life, A.
Weather of the World, The.
Western Approach, The.
What Kind of a Guy Was He?
Winter Lightning for Paul, The.
Writing.
Young Woman.
Nerber, John
Castaway.
Nerses, Saint
Annunciation, The.
Neruda, Pablo (*originally* Neftalí Ricardo Reyes Basualto)
Almería.
Always.
Battle of the Jarama, The.
Drunk as drunk on turpentine.
Enigmas.
Fickle One, The.
Ghost of the Cargo Boat, The.
Girls.
International Brigade Arrives at Madrid, The.
Lone Gentleman.
Materia Nupcial.
Nothing but Death.
Ode to Salt.
Ode to the Watermelon.
Queen, The.
To Silvestre Revueltas of Mexico, in His Death.
Tonight I can write the saddest line.
Walking Around.
Nerval, Gérard de (Gérard Labrunie)
Delfica.
Golden Lines.
Old Tune, An.
Nesbit, Edith (Edith Nesbit Bland)
Baby Seed Song.
Child's Song in Spring.
Fields of Flanders, The.
Mr. Ody met a body.
Spring in War-Time.
Summer Song.
Things That Matter, The.
Tragedy, A.
Nesbit, Wilbur D.
All to Myself.
Friend of Two, A.
Hymn of Thanksgiving, A.
Let Us Smile.
Who Hath a Book.
Your Flag and My Flag.
Nesbit, Wilbur Dick
Nesmith, James Ernest
Statue of Lorenzo de' Medici, The.
Netser, Eli
My Best Clothes.
Neufeld, Ernest
At Masada.
Neugroschel, Joachim
Doves.
Eve's Advice to the Children of Israel.
Neumeyer, Peter F.
Rope's End.
Neville, Helen
Body's Freedom.
Neville, Mary
Social Studies.
Nevin, Alice
God's Will.
Nevin, Edwin H.
Happy, Saviour, Would I Be, *with music.*
When Our Earthly Sun Is Setting, *with music.*
Newbery, Thomas
Great Merchant, Dives Pragmaticus, Cries His Wares, The, *sel.*
Newbolt, Sir Henry
Admiral Death.
Admirals All.
Cities Drowned.
Clifton Chapel.
Commemoration.
Craven.
Drake's Drum.
Fighting *Téméraire,* The.
Final Mystery, The.
Finis.
From Generation to Generation.
He Fell among Thieves.
Imogen.
Ireland, Ireland.
Master and Man.
Messmates.
Moonset.
Moss-Rose, The.
Only Son, The.
Rilloby-Rill.
Sailing at Dawn.
Song: "Flowers that in thy garden rise, The."
To a River in the South.
Vitaï Lampada.
Yattendon.
Newcastle, Margaret Cavendish, Duchess of
Convent of Pleasure, The, *sel.*
Hunting of the Hare, The.
Love, how thou'rt tired out with rhyme!
Mirth and Melancholy.
My Cabinets Are Oyster-Shells.
Nature's Cook, *sel.*
O do not grieve, Dear Heart, nor shed a tear.
Song: "My cabinets are oyster-shells."
Soul's Garment, The.
What Is Liquid.

Newcastle, William Cavendish, Duke of
Love Play.
Love's Matrimony.
Newcomb, Bobby
Big Sunflower, The, *with music.*
Newcombe, Rosemarie
At last I bless the hours.
Newell, J. R.
Christmas Carol: "From the starry heav'ns descending."
Newell, Mike
Prayer: "Your golden loins slake my lust for treasures."
Newell, Peter
Educated Love Bird, The.
Her Dairy.
Her Polka Dots.
Timid Hortense.
Wild Flowers.
Newell, Robert Henry. *See* **"Kerr, Orpheus C."**
Newlin, Edith. *See* **Chase, Edith Newlin**
Newlove, John
America.
Double-headed Snake, The.
First Time, The.
Good Company, Fine Houses.
Grass Is a Reasonable Colour, The.
I Talk to You.
Pride, The.
Samuel Hearne in Wintertime.
Succubi.
Verigin, Moving in Alone.
Verigin 3.
Well-travelled Roadway, The.
What Do You Want?
Newman, John Henry, Cardinal
Angel of the Agony.
Angelic Guidance.
Chorus of Angels.
Chorus of the Elements.
Discovery, The.
Dream of Gerontius, The, *sels.*
Elements, The.
England.
Guardian Angel.
Guidance.
Judaism.
Light in the Darkness.
Matins—Friday.
Matins—Sunday.
Monks.
My Lady Nature and Her Daughters.
My work is done.
Patient Church, The.
Pillar of Cloud, The.
Progress of Unbelief.
Queen of Seasons, The.
Refrigerium.
Rest.
St. Philip in Himself.
Sensitiveness.
Sign of the Cross, The.
Snapdragon.
Softly and gently, dearly ransom'd soul.
Soul before God, The.
Substance and Shadow.
Thanksgiving, A.
Trance of Time, The.
Until the Shadows Lengthen.
Valentine to a Little Girl.
Zeal and Love.
Zeal of Jehu, The.
Newman, Joseph S.
Hero and Leander.
Miss Tillie McLush.
Serpentine Verse.
Newman, Louis I.
Voice of God, The.
World Looks On, The.
Newman, Michael
Negative Passage.
Newman, Paul Baker
Mr. Cherry.
Newman, Preston
Some Questions to Be Asked of a Rajah, Perhaps by the Associated Press.
Newsome, Mary Effie Lee
Arctic Tern in a Museum.
Baker's Boy, The.
Little Birches.
Morning Light.
Pansy.
Quilt, The.
Quoits.
Sassafras Tea.
Sky Pictures.
Wild Roses.
Newton, Byron Rufus
Owed to New York.
Newton, Charles
Stanzas, *sel.*
Wild Nature.
Newton, Douglas
Gaiety of Descendants.
Invasion Weather.
Newton, Eileen
Last Leave.
Revision.
Newton, John
Amazing Grace.
Glorious Things of Thee Are Spoken.
How Sweet the Name of Jesus Sounds.
"In Evil Long I Took Delight."
In Sweet Communion.
Name of Jesus, The.
Thou Art Coming to a King.
Zion, or the City of God.
Newton, Mary Leslie
Queen Anne's Lace.
Neyroud, Gerard
Skunk to the Gnu, The.
Nezalhualcoyotl
In vain was I born.
Ngani, A. Z.
Praises of King George VI.
Ngatho, Stella
Footpath.
NíChonaill, Eibhlín Dhubh. *See* **O'Connell, Eibhlin Dubh**
Ní Chuilleanáin, Eiléan
Dead Fly.
Lucina Schynning in Silence of the Night.
Old Roads.
Site of Ambush, *sel.*
Swineherd.
Wash.
Niatum, Duane
After the Death of an Elder Klallam.
Ascending Red Cedar Moon.
Chief Leschi of the Nisqually.
Crow's Way.
Digging Out the Roots.
Elegy for Chief Sealth.
Homage to Chagall.
Indian Rock, Bainbridge Island, Washington.
No One Remembers Abandoning the Village of White Fir.
Novelty Shop, The.
Old Woman Awaiting the Greyhound Bus.
On Hearing the Marsh Bird's Water Cry.
On Leaving Baltimore.
On Visiting My Son, Port Angeles, Washington.
Raven.
Slow Dancer That No One Hears but You.
Song from the Maker of Totems.
Street Kid.
To Your Question.
Nibbelink, Herman
Meyer and I, we drove.
Nicander
Recipe: Gourds.
Nicarchus [*or* Nicarchos]
Requirements: "Not for me a giantess."
Nichol, B. P.
Gorg, a Detective Story.
Two Words; a Wedding.
Nichol, John
Good Night.
Nicholas, Michael
Today: The Idea Market.
Nicholas, Virginia Real
South of the Border.
Nicholl, Louise Townsend
Architect.
Ark of the Covenant.
Celestial Body.
Cigar Smoke, Sunday, after Dinner.
Cleavage.
Color Alone Can Speak.
Creation.
Cruse, The.
Different Speech, A.
Different Winter.
Hymn: "Words of hymns abruptly plod, The."
Improvising.
Incense.
Made Lake, The.
Ornamental Water.
Physical Geography.
Rondel for Middle Age.
Shape of the Heart, The.
Time in the Sun.
Wild Cherry.
Nicholls, W. Leslie
Albert Dürer.
Nichols, Kevin
Feast of Stephen, The.
Nichols, Robert
Aurelia.
Battery Moving Up to a New Position from Rest Camp: Dawn.
Burial in Flanders, The.
By the Wood.
Casualty.
Day's March, The.
Don Juan's Address to the Sunset.
Fisbo, *sel.*
Flower of Flame, The, *sel.*
Fulfilment.
Full Heart, The.
Harlot's Catch.
I Love a Flower.
Moon behind High Tranquil Leaves, The.
Our Dead.
Secret Garden, The.
Sonnets to Aurelia, *sels.*
Sprig of Lime, The.
Thanksgiving.
To———: "Asleep within the deadest hour of the night."
To D'Annunzio: Lines from the Sea.
Nicholson, John
On a Calm Summer's Night.
Nicholson, John Gambril
Chaplet of Southernwood, A, *sel.*
Nicholson, Martha Snell
His Plan for Me.
Home.
Nicholson, Meredith
From Bethlehem to Calvary.
Nicholson, Norman
Blackberry, The.
Burning Bush, The.
Caedmon.
Carol: "Mary laid her Child among."
Carol for the Last Christmas Eve.
Cleator Moor.
Cockley Moor, Dockray, Penrith.
For All Sorts and Conditions.
For the Bicentenary of Isaac Watts.
For the New Year.
Michaelmas.
Millom Old Quarry.
Motion of the Earth, The.
Now in the Time of This Mortal Life.

On the Closing of Millom Ironworks.
Poem for Epiphany.
Preachers, The.
Ravenglass Railway Station, Cumberland.
Rockferns.
Shepherds' Carol.
Song at Night.
To a Child before Birth.
Undiscovered Planet, The.
Wales.
Nicias
Fountain at the Tomb, The.
Nickens, Thomas G.
Jis' Knowin'.
Pacified.
Radcliff, Kentucky.
State Prison 4:00 P.M. ("Groups of me").
State Prison 5:00 P.M. ("The count bell rings").
Nickerson, Sheila
Complaint of the Fisherman's Wife.
Enchanted Halibut, The.
In the Fishing Village.
Nicochares
Hangover Cure.
Nicoïdski, Clarisse
Eyes.
Mouth.
Open Earth.
Remembering.
Nicol, Abioseh
African Easter.
Meaning of Africa, The.
Nicoll, Robert
Hero, The.
We Are Brethren A'.
Nicolson, Adela Florence Cory. *See* **"Hope, Laurence"**
Nicolson, Alexander
Warning, A.
Nicolson, John Urban
Old Maid.
Reconciliation.
String Stars for Pearls.
Nicophon
Beware of Figs.
Niditch, B. Z.
Passover Dachau.
Return to Dachau.
Niebuhr, Reinhold
Prayer for Serenity.
Niedecker, Lorine
As praiseworthy/ the power of breathing.
For best work.
My mother saw the green tree toad.
Old man who seined.
Smile/ to see the lake.
You are my friend.
Young in Fall I said: the birds.
Nietzsche, Friedrich Wilhelm
Solitary, The.
Star Morals.
To the Unknown God.
Nightingale, Madeleine
Scissor-Man, The.
Waits, The.
Nihoniho, Tuta
Government!
Nikitin, Ivan Savvich
Night in a Village, A.
Nikolay, Sonja
Witches' Menu.
Niles, John Jacob
In All the Magic of Christmas-Tide, *with music.*
Niles, Nathaniel
American Hero, The.
Bunker Hill, *with music.*
Nims, Bonnie
How to Get There.
Nims, John Frederick
Apocalypse.
Clock Symphony.
Clock without Hands.
Conclusion: "If what began (look far and wide) will end."
Dollar Bill.
Elegy for a Bad Poet, Taken from Us Not Long Since.
Eminent Critic.
Fairy Tale.
For My Son.
Good Friday.
La Ci Darem la Mano.
Love and Death.
Love Poem: "My clumsiest dear, whose hands shipwreck vases."
Madrigal: "Beside the rivers of the midnight town."
Midwest.
Necromancers, The.
New Year's Eve, 1938.
Non-Euclidean Elegy.
Observatory Ode, The.
Parting: 1940.
Tide Turning.
Trainwrecked Soldiers.
Visiting Poet.
Ninine
Prayer to St. Patrick.
Nisbet, Eilidh
Three Girls on a Buttress.
To a Midge.
Nist, John
Made to See.
Sings a Bird.
Villanelle: "Like twilight bleeding on a winter day."
Nitschmann, Anna
This Flock So Small, *with music.*
Nitzche, Jane Chance
Shopping.
Niven, Frederick
Indian Dance.
Cricket.
Deer.
Noailles, Anna de
Image.
Poem on Azure.
Noble, Fay Lewis
Prayer for Song.
No Ch'ŏn-myŭng
Noel, Roden Berkeley Wriothesley
Casual Song, A.
I Flung Me Round Him.
Lady to a Lover, A.
Old, The.
Swimmer, The.
Vale!
Water-Nymph and the Boy, The.
Noel, Thomas
Old Winter.
Pauper's Drive, The.
"Nogar, Rui"
Poem of the Conscripted Warrior.
Noguchi, Yone
Poet, The.
Noguere, Suzanne
Pervigilium Veneris.
Nohomaiterangi
Lullaby: "O my son, born on a winter's morn."
Nolan, Bertha
My Mother.
Nolan, Edward
Oxford Is a Stage.
Nolan, James
Mardi Gras/ Grandmothers—Portrait in Red and Black Crayon.
Sum.
Nolan, Michael
Little Annie Rooney.
Noll, Bink
Divorce.
Moving between Beloit and Monroe.
Picador Bit, The.
Shutting the Curtains.
Wedlock.
Nomberg, David
Russian Cradle Song, A.
Nordan, Lewis
He Fishes with His Father's Ghost.
Nordbrandt, Henrik
We Separate the Days.
Nordhaus, Jean
Yahrzeit Candle.
Norman, Charles
Portrait of a Senator.
Norman, Rosemary
Cabbage.
My Son and I.
Norris, Alfred
Prayer for Faith, A.
Norris, Gordon W.
Mi Corazón.
Song of the Border.
Norris, John
Aspiration, The.
Choice, The.
Hymn to Darkness.
Retirement, The.
Norris, John W.
Give Peace, O God, the Nations Cry, *with music.*
Norris, Kathleen
Evaporation Poems.
Focus.
Her Application to Elysium.
Memorandum/ The Accountant's Notebook.
Middle of the World, The.
Running through Sleep.
Stomach.
Norris, Leslie
Ballad of Billy Rose, The.
Camels of the Kings.
In Black Chasms.
Man in Our Village, A.
Merlin and the Snake's Egg.
Mice in the Hay.
Park at Evening, The.
Quiet-eyed Cattle, The.
Shepherd's Dog, The.
Stable Cat, The.
Norse, Harold
Behind the Glass Wall.
Breathing the Strong Smell.
Colosseum.
Island of Giglio.
You Must Have Been a Sensational Baby, *sel.*
"North, Christopher" (John Wilson)
Calm as the Cloudless Heaven.
Come Forth, Come Forth!
Evening Cloud, The.
Rose and the Gauntlet, The.
Sacred Poetry.
Written on the Banks of Wastwater during a Calm.
North, Frank Mason
City, The.
Where Cross the Crowded Ways of Life.
North, Jessica Nelson
Balloon Man.
Truth.
North, Susan
What I Have.
NorthSun, Nila
Falling Down to Bed.
Future Generation.
Little Red Riding Hood.
Red Road, The.
Sweat, The.
Up & Out.
Way and the Way Things Are, The.
Norton, Andrews
Hymn for the Dedication of a Church.
My God, I Thank Thee, *with music.*
Norton, Caroline Elizabeth
Arab's Farewell to His Horse [*or* Steed], The.
Arab to His Favorite Steed, The.

Bingen on the Rhine.
I Do Not Love Thee.
Juanita.
King of Denmark's Ride, The.
Love Not.
Not Lost, but Gone Before.
Norton, Eleanour
Chopin Prelude.
In a Restaurant, 1917.
Norton, Grace Fallow
Adventure.
Deer on the Mountain.
Little Gray Songs from St. Joseph's, *sels.*
Love Is a Terrible Thing.
O Sleep.
This Is My Love for You.
Norton, John
Funeral Elogy, upon . . . Mrs. Anne Bradstreet, A.
Norton, Thomas
Against Women either Good or Bad.
Norvig, Gerda
Desert March.
Joining, The.
Tree of Life Is Also a Tree of Fire, The.
Norwood, Eille
Limerick: "Pretty young actress, a stammerer, A."
Norwood, Robert
Man of Kerioth, The, *sel.*
Norworth, Jack
Take Me Out to the Ball Game.
Nottage, May Hastings
My Father's Voice in Prayer.
Nott-Bower, E. E.
Haulage.
Patience.
"Novalis" (Friedrich von Hardenberg)
Aphorisms.
Hymns to the Night, *sel.*
Second Hymn to the Night, The.
When geometric diagrams and digits.
November, Sharyn
Night Driving.
Nowell, M. H.
Of Disdainful Daphne.
Nowlan, Alden
Anatomy of Angels, The.
Aunt Jane.
Baptism.
Beets.
Beginning.
Bull Moose, The.
Daisies.
Execution, The.
For Jean Vincent d'Abbadie, Baron St.-Castin.
God Sour the Milk of the Knacking Wench.
Grove beyond the Barley, The.
Gypsies.
Helen's Scar.
Hens.
I, Icarus.
In the Operating Room.
Kyran's Christening.
Loneliness of the Long Distance Runner, The.
Palomino Stallion, The.
Party at Bannon Brook.
Porch.
Psalm of Onan for Harp, Flute and Tambourine, A.
Rivalry.
Semi-Private Room.
Stars.
Stoney Ridge Dance Hall.
Subway Psalm.
Suppose This Moment Some Stupendous Question.
Therese.
Waiting for Her.
Wasp.
Wickedness of Peter Shannon, The.
Noyes, Alfred
Art.
Assisi.
Barrel-Organ, The.
Betsy Jane's Sixth Birthday.
Blinded Soldier to His Love, The.
Call of the Spring, The.
Creation.
Daddy Fell into the Pond.
Double Fortress, The.
Edinburgh.
Epilogue: "Carol, every violet has."
Flower of Old Japan, The, *sel.*
Forty Singing Seamen.
Highwayman, The.
Hospital, A.
In the Cool of the Evening.
Japanese Love-Song, A.
Last Voyage, The, *sels.*
Love's Rosary.
Messages.
Messenger, The.
New Duckling, The.
Old Man Mountain.
On the Death of Francis Thompson.
Our Lady of the Sea.
Prayer, A: "Angels, where you soar."
River of Stars, The.
Sea-Distances.
Seagulls on the Serpentine.
Song: "I came to the door of the House of Love."
Song: "What is there hid in the heart of a rose."
Song of Sherwood, A.
Spring, and the Blind Children.
Strong City, The.
Sunlight and Sea.
Under the Pyrenees.
Unity.
Victory Dance, A.
World's May-Queen, The.
You That Sing in the Blackthorn.
Noyes, Nicholas
Consolatory Poem Dedicated unto Mr. Cotton Mather, A.
Praefatory Poem to the Little Book, Entituled, Christianus per Ignem, A.
Prefatory Poem, on . . . Magnalia Christi Americana, A.
Rev. Nicholas Noyes to the Rev. Cotton Mather, The.
To My Worthy Friend, Mr. James Bayley.
Noyes, Stanley
Nevada.
Noyle, Ken
Sea, The.
Nugent, Gerald
Farewell to Fál, A.
Nugent, Maude
Sweet Rosie O'Grady, *with music.*
Nugent, Robert, Earl Nugent
Epigram: "I loved thee beautiful and kind."
Epigram: "My heart still hovering round about you."
Epigram: "Since first you knew my am'rous smart."
I Loved Thee.
Revenge.
To Clarissa.
Nukada, Princess
Waiting for the Emperor Tenji.
When, loosened from winter's bonds.
Nunan, Thomas
Dreamer, The.
Nunes, Cassiano
Episode.
Nunley, R. W.
Salmon Draught at Inveraray.
Nutter, C. D.
On Time with God.
Nutter, Medora Addison. *See* **Addison, Medora C.**
Nuur, Faarah
Limits of Submission, The.
Our Country Is Divided.
Nweke, Chuba
Moon Song.
Nye, Naomi Shihab
Catalogue Army.
Driving North from Kingsville, Texas.
Grandfather's Heaven.
Hugging the Jukebox.
Jefferson, Texas.
Hymn of Pan.
Little Brother Poem, The.
Making a Fist.
Music.
My Father and the Fig Tree.
New Skills.
Night Shift.
Sleeping in a Cave.
Use of Fiction, The.
Where Children Live.
Nyhart, Nina
String of My Ancestors, The.
Tennis.

O

"O. Henry." *See* **"Henry, O."**
Oakes, Urian
Elegie upon That Reverend . . . Mr. Thomas Shepard, An.
To the Reader.
Oakes-Smith, Elizabeth. *See* **Smith, Elizabeth Oakes**
Oakley, Ebenezer S.
Thoughts That Move the Heart of Man, The.
Oakman, John
Glutton, The.
Oandasan, William
Past, The.
Round Valley Reflections.
Song of Ancient Ways, The.
Oates, Joyce Carol
Acceleration near the Point of Impact.
Baby.
Back Country.
Child-Bride, The.
Children Not Kept at Home.
City Graveyard, A.
Dreaming America.
First Dark.
Foetal Song.
Growing Together.
Insomnia.
Lines for Those to Whom Tragedy Is Denied.
Moving Out.
New Jersey White-tailed Deer.
Night.
Present Tense, The.
Stone Orchard, The.
Suicide, The.
Wasp, The.
Obi, Dorothy S.
Winds of Africa.
O'Bolger, T. D.
Counsels of O'Riordan, the Rann Maker, The.
O'Brien, Edward Joseph
Her Fairness, Wedded to a Star.
Irish.
Shepherd Boy, The.
O'Brien, Fitz-James
Kane.
Legend of the Easter Eggs, The.
Minot's Ledge.
Second Mate, The.
Ghost, The.
"O'Brien, John." *See* **Hartigan, Patrick Joseph**
O'Brien, Katharine
Spring Song.

O'Brien, R. C.
Poor Grandpa.
O'Brien, Thomas
Always Battling.
International Brigade Dead.
Terror.
O'Bruadair, David
Change, The.
Eire.
New Style, The.
O'Bruadair.
"O'Byrne, Dermot" (Sir Arnold Bax)
Dublin Ballad, A: 1916.
Ocampo, Silvina
In Front of the Seine, Recalling the Río de la Plata.
Prisoner between the Panes of Glass.
O'Carolan, Turlough. *See* **Carolan, Turlough**
"Occidente, Maria del." *See* **Brooks, Maria Gowen**
Occleve, Thomas. *See* **Hoccleve, Thomas**
Occom, Samson
Waked by the Gospel's Powerful Sound, *with music.*
Ochester, Ed
Among His Effects We Found a Photograph.
Ed Shreckongost.
Farewell to the Moon, A.
For My Daughter.
For Refugio Talamante.
Gift, The.
In the Library.
Killing Rabbits.
My Penis.
My Teeth.
Penn Central Station at Beacon, N.Y., The.
Rowing.
Snow White.
Toward the Splendid City.
110 Year Old House.
O'Connell, Eibhlin Dubh (Eibhlín Dhubh Ní Chonaill)
Lament for Art O'Leary.
O'Connell, Richard
Robert Lowell.
Sidewalk Orgy.
O'Connor, Frank (*originally* Michael O'Donovan)
Angry Poet, The.
Hope.
Mary Hynes.
Three Old Brothers.
O'Connor, Joseph
General's Death, The.
What Was My Dream?
O'Connor, Martin T.
Requiem: "Farewell my friend."
O'Connor, Michael
Reveille.
O'Connor, Patrick
Mantle of Mary, The.
O'Connor, Philip
Fag-End.
Poems (I-XI).
Raspberry in the Pudding, The.
Writing in England Now.
O'Connor, Tony
Last of the Poet's Car.
O'Conor, Norreys Jephson
Beside the Blackwater.
In Memoriam: Francis Ledwidge.
In the Moonlight.
To a Child (With a Copy of the Author's "Hansel and Gretel").
O'Cotter, Pat
Malemute Dog, A.
O'Crowley, Denis
Washington.
O'Curnain, Diarmad
Love's Despair.
O'Dala, Donnchadh Mor
At Saint Patrick's Purgatory.
O'Dalaigh, Gofraidh Fionn
Under Sorrow's Sign.
O'Dalaigh, Muireadach
On the Death of His Wife.
O'Daly, Carrol
Eileen Aroon ("Fain would I ride with thee").
Lover and Echo.
Odell, Jonathan
On Our Thirty-ninth Wedding Day.
Oden, Gloria C.
"As When Emotion Too Far Exceeds Its Cause."
Carousel, The.
Man White, Brown Girl and All That Jazz.
Map, The.
Private Letter to Brazil, A.
Review from Staten Island.
Riven Quarry, The.
This Child Is the Mother.
Triple Mirror, The.
Way It Is, The.
O'Donnell, Charles L.
Address to the Crown.
Process.
Prodigals.
Resolution.
Rime of the Rood, A.
Road of Ireland, A.
Security.
Shed, The.
Spinner, The.
Trelawny Lies by Shelley.
O'Donnell, George Marion
Semmes in the Garden.
O'Donnell, John Francis
By the Turnstile.
In the Market-Place.
Limmerich Towne, *sel.*
O'Donoghue, Gregory
Web, The.
O'Donovan, Michael. *See* **O'Connor, Frank**
O'Dowd, Bernard
Alma Venus, *sel.*
Australia.
Bush, The, *sels.*
Cow, The.
Young Democracy, *sel.*
O'Dugan [*or* Dugan], Maurice
Coolun, The.
O'Egan, Gerry
1867: Last Sounds.
Oehlenschläger, Adam
There Is a Charming Land.
Oerke, Andrew
Serengeti Sunset.
Sun, The.
O'Faracháin, Roibéard. *See* **Farren, Robert**
Offaly, Gerald Fitzgerald, Baron of
Gambler's Repentance, The.
O'Flaherty, Charles
Humours of Donnybrook Fair, The.
O'Gallagher, Alice
Welcome, O Great Mary.
Ogarev, Nikolay Platonovich
Road, The.
Ogburn, Charlton
Nature in Couplets.
O'Gillan, Angus
Clonmacnoise.
Dead at Clonmacnois, The.
Ogilvie, D. T.
Last Letter to the Western Civilization.
Ogilvie, Will H.
Blades of Harden, The.
Death of Ben Hall, The.
From the Gulf.
How the Fire Queen Crossed the Swamp.
If I Were Old.
Kingship of the Hills, The.
Whaup o' the Reed, *sel.*
Ogilvy, David
Virtues of Carnation Milk, The.
Og MacWard, Fearghal
Flight of the Earls, The, 1607, *sel.*
O'Gnive, Fearflatha
Downfall of the Gael, The.
O'Gorman, Ned
Childhood.
Kiss, The.
L'Annunciazione.
Myth.
O'Grady, Desmond
Arrival: The Capital.
Day Concludes Burning, The.
Dying Gaul, The.
Father, The.
If I Went Away.
Mad male-hearted woman in a prouder age, A.
Page from a Diary.
Pitch Piles Up in Part, The.
Poet in Old Age Fishing at Evening, The.
Poet Loves from Afar, The.
Professor Kelleher and the Charles River.
O'Grady, Standish
Emigrant, The, *sels.*
Old Nick in Sorel.
Winter in Lower Canada.
O'Grady, Tom
Aubade after the Party.
O'Halloran, Elspeth MacDuffie. *See* **"Elspeth"**
O'Hara, Frank
Abortion, An.
Answer to Voznesensky and Evtushenko.
Autobiographia Literaria.
Ave Maria.
Biotherm.
Blocks.
Chez Jane.
Day Lady Died, The.
Easter.
For James Dean.
Homosexuality.
Hôtel Transylvanie.
How to Get There.
Hunter, The.
In Favor of One's Time.
In Memory of My Feelings.
John Button Birthday.
Les Etiquettes Jaunes.
Les Luths.
Life on Earth, *sel.*
Meditations in an Emergency.
Music.
Ode: "Idea of justice may be precious, An."
Ode: Salute to the French Negro Poets.
Ode to Joy.
Ode to Michael Goldberg's Birth and Other Births.
On Rachmaninoff's Birthday.
Personal Poem.
Poem: "At night Chinamen jump."
Poem: "Eager note, The, on my door said, 'Call me.' "
Poem: "Hate is only one of many responses."
Poem: "I watched an armory combing its bronze bricks."
Poem: "I will always love you."
Poem: "Khrushchev is coming on the right day!"
Poem: "Lana Turner has collapsed!"
Poem: "There I could never be a boy."
Princess Elizabeth of Bohemia, as Perdita.
Radio.
Rhapsody.
Should We Legalize Abortion?
Sleeping on the Wing.
Song: "Is it dirty."
Step Away from Them, A.
Steps.
Terrestrial Cuckoo, A.
To Hell with It.
To My Dead Father.
To the Film Industry in Crisis.
To the Harbormaster.

True Account of Talking to the Sun at Fire Island, A.
Walking.
Why I Am Not a Painter.
You Are Gorgeous and I'm Coming.
O'Hara, Theodore
Bivouac of the Dead, The.
O'Hare, Felix
Shoofly, The.
O'Heffernan, Mahon
My Son, Forsake Your Art.
Who Will Buy a Poem?
O Hehir, Diana
Alone by the Road's Edge.
Anima.
Courtship.
House.
How to Murder Your Best Friend.
Infant.
Learning to Type.
Lost Objects.
Old Lady under the Freeway, The.
Payments.
Plan to Live My Life Again, A.
Power to Change Geography, The.
Private Rooms.
Questions and Answers.
Retarded Children Find a World Built Just for Them, The.
Shore.
Sleeping Pill.
Some of Us Are Exiles from No Land.
Summoned.
Tarantula.
Terminal Vision.
They Grow Up Too Fast, She Said.
O'Higgins, Myron
Blues for Bessie.
Sunset Horn.
Two Lean Cats.
Vaticide.
Young Poet.
O'Higgins, Tomas
To Tomas Costello at the Wars, *at.*
O'Huiginn, Tadhg Dall
Difference, The.
First Vision, The.
Present of Butter, A.
Second Vision, The.
O'Huiginn, Tadhg O'g
On the Breaking-up of a School.
O'Hussey, Eochadh [*or* Eochy]
Hugh Maguire.
O'Hussey's Ode to the Maguire.
Ojenke. *See* **Saxon, Alvin**
O'Kane, T. C.
My Mother's Prayer.
Okara, Gabriel
Call of the River Nun, The.
Mystic Drum, The.
Once upon a Time.
Piano and Drums.
To Adhiambo.
Were I to Choose.
You Laughed and Laughed and Laughed.
O'Keefe [*or* O'Keeffe], John
Air: "Flaxen-headed cow-boy, as simple as may be, A."
Amo, Amas.
Friar of Orders Gray, The.
I Want a Tenant; a Satire.
O'Keeffe, Adelaide
Beasts and Birds.
Butterfly, The.
Kite, The.
Rather Too Good, Little Peggy!
To George Pulling Buds.
O'Kelly, Patrick
Blessings on Doneraile.
Curse of Doneraile, The.
Okigbo, Christopher
Distances, *sel.*
Lament of the Flutes.
Okita, Dwight
Art of Holding On, The.
Crossing with the Light.
In Response to Executive Order 9066: All Americans of Japanese Descent Must Report to Relocation Centers.
Parachute.
Okkur Macatti
Rains, already old, The.
What Her Girl-Friend[s] Said to Her.
Oku, Princess
How will you cross the autumn mountain alone?
Olcott, Chauncey
My Wild Irish Rose.
Oldenburg, E. W.
In Canterbury Cathedral.
Older, Julia
Georges Bank.
Oldham, G. Ashton
America First!
Oldham, John
Careless Good Fellow, The.
Cup, The.
Letter from the Country to a Friend in Town, A.
Prologue: "For who can longer hold? when every Press."
Quiet Soul, A.
Satire, A, *sels.*
Satire Addressed to a Friend, A.
Satires, *sel.*
Satires upon the Jesuits, *sels.*
Satyr Address'd to a Friend That Is About to Leave the University, and Come Abroad in the World, A, *sels.*
Satyr III: "When shaven Crown, and hallow'd Girdle's Power."
Satyrs upon the Jesuits.
Upon the Author of a Play Called *Sodom.*
Upon the Works of Ben Jonson, *sel.*
Oldknow, Antony
Nude with Green Chair.
Oldmixon, John
I Lately Vowed, but 'Twas in Haste.
Olds, N. S.
Rivets.
Olds, Sharon
Death of Marilyn Monroe, The.
End of World War One, The.
First Love.
Soul before God, The.
Hostage and His Takers, The.
Leningrad Cemetery, Winter of 1941.
One Girl at the Boys Party, The.
Race Riot, Tulsa, 1921.
Rite of Passage.
Sex without Love.
Solitary.
Things That Are Worse than Death.
Time-Travel.
Oldys, William
Anacreontick, An.
On a Fly Drinking out of [*or* from] His Cup.
On Himself.
O'Leary, Joseph
Whisky, Drink Divine.
Oles, Carole
Magician Suspends the Children, The.
Stonecarver.
Unteaching, The.
Oleson, Helmer O.
Ballad of Johnny Appleseed, A.
Oliphant, Carolina. *See* **Nairne, Carolina Oliphant, Baroness**
Oliphant, Dave
Little Something for William Whipple, A.
Mexican Scrapbook, A.
Olitski, Leib
My Song to the Jewish People.
Olivares Figueroa, R.
Sower, The.
Oliver, Louis (LittleCoon)
Empty Kettle.
Indian Macho.
Materialized into an Owl.
Sharpbreasted Snake, The.
Wagon Full of Thunder.
Oliver, Mary
Aunt Elsie's Night Music.
Diviners, The.
Grandmothers, The.
Letter from Home, A.
Mussels.
Poem for My Father's Ghost.
Sleeping in the Forest.
Stark County Holidays.
Through Ruddy Orchards.
Truro Bear, The.
Oliver, Robert S.
Toad, The.
Oliver, Wade
Ships with Your Silver Nets.
Oliver, William
I'll Have a Collier for My Sweetheart.
Olsen, Donald D.
Poem: "We used to float the paper boats in spring."
Olsen, William
Addressing His Deaf Wife, Kansas, 1916.
Olson, Charles
Across Space and Time.
As the Dead Prey upon Us.
Celestial Evening, October 1967.
Cole's Island.
Death of Europe, The.
Distances, The.
In Cold Hell, in Thicket.
Kingfishers, The.
La Chute.
La Préface.
Letter for Melville 1951.
Letter 27.
Librarian, The.
Lordly and Isolate Satyrs, The.
Maximus Poems, The, *sels.*
Merce of Egypt.
Moon Is the Number 18, The.
Newly Discovered "Homeric" Hymn, A.
Praises, The.
Ring Of, The.
River Map, The and We're Done.
Songs of Maximus, The.
Variations Done for Gerald Van de Wiele.
Olson, Elder
Childe Roland, etc.
Ice-Skaters.
In Defense of Superficiality.
In Despair He Orders a New Typewriter.
Jack-in-the-Box.
Knight, with Umbrella.
Merry Christmas!
Night There Was Dancing in the Streets, The.
Nightfall.
Plot Improbable, Character Unsympathetic.
Wild Horse.
Olson, Ernst W.
God of Peace, in Peace Preserve Us, *with music.*
Olson, Ted
Hawk's Way.
Starlings.
Things That Endure.
Olumo. *See* **Cunningham, James**
O'Malley, Emanuela
False Prophet.
Oman, Carola
Ambulance Train 30.
Brussels, 1919.
Omar b. Abi Rabi'a
Damsel, The.
Omar Khayyám
Myself When Young Did Eagerly Frequent.

Oh Thou, Who Man of Baser Earth Didst Make.
Quatrains.
Rubáiyát of Omar Khayyám of Naishápúr, The.
Wake! For the Sun who scattered into flight.

Ombres, Rossana
Bella and the Golem.
Flower Ensnarer of Psalms.

O'Meally, Bob
Make Music with Your Life.

O'Mulconry, Peadar
Were Not the Gael Fallen.

Onakatomi no Yoshinobu
Deer on Pine Mountain, The.

Ondaatje, Michael
Bearhug.
Breaking Green.
Burning Hills.
Buying the Dog.
Cinnamon Peeler, The.
Gold and Black.
House Divided, A.
Letters & Other Worlds.
Prometheus, with Wings.
Walking to Bellrock.
When Charlie Bowdre married Manuela, we carried them.

Onderdonk, Henry Ustic
On Zion and on Lebanon, *with music.*
Spirit in Our Hearts, The, *with music.*
Though I Should Seek, *with music.*

O'Neil, George
Cobbler in Willow Street, The.
Events.
Where It Is Winter.

Oneil, Henrietta
Ode to the Poppy.

O'Neill, Lawrence T.
Train to Reflection.

O'Neill, Mary
Feelings about Words.
Mark's Fingers.
Miss Norma Jean Pugh.
Sound of Water.
What Is Black?
What Is Orange?
What Is Red?

O'Neill, Mary Devenport
Dead in Wars and in Revolutions.
Galway.
Old Waterford Woman, An.
Scene-Shifter Death.
Tramp's Song, The.

"O'Neill, Moira" (Nesta Higginson Skrine)
Birds.
Broken Song, A.
Corrymeela.
Fairy Lough, The.
Forgettin'.
Grand Match, The.
Her Sister.
Sea Wrack.
Song of Glenann, A.

O'Neill, Rose
Faun-taken.
When the Dead Men Die.

Onitsura
Directions.

Ono no Komachi
Color of the flowers, The/ has faded.
Doesn't he realize/ that I am not/ like the swaying kelp.
If it were real/ Perhaps I'd understand it.
No moon, no chance to meet.
Since I've felt this pain.
So lonely am I.
Thing which fades, A.
This night of no moon.
When my love becomes/ All-powerful.

Opdyke, Oliver (John Baker Opdyke)
My Road.
Spring Lay, A.

Opengart, Bea
Speak.

Opie, Amelia
Orphan Boy's Tale, The.

Opoku, Andrew Amankwa
River Afram.

Oppen, George
Bahamas.
Birthplace; New Rochelle.
Book of Job and a Draft of a Poem to Praise the Paths of the Living, The.
Building of the Skyscraper, The.
Exodus.
Five Poems about Poetry, *sels.*
Forms of Love, The.
From Virgil.
Gesture, The.
If It All Went Up in Smoke.
It Is Difficult Now to Speak of Poetry.
Latitude, Longitude.
Of Being Numerous, *sels.*
People, the People, The.
Population.
Psalm: "In the small beauty of the forest."
Quotations.
Sara in Her Father's Arms.
Some San Francisco Poems.
Street.

Oppenheim, James
Action.
As to Being Alone.
Death.
Future, The.
Handful of Dust, A.
Hebrews.
Immoral.
Lincoln-Child, The.
New God, The.
Night, *sel.*
Reason, The.
Runner in the Skies, The.
Saturday Night.
Slave, The.

Oppenheimer, J. Robert
Crossing.

Oppenheimer, Joel
Bath, The.
Blue Funk.
Bus Trip, The.
Cartography.
Couple, The.
Father Poem.
Feeding, The.
For the Barbers.
Innocent Breasts, The.
Leave It to Me Blues.
Love Bit, The.
Mare Nostrum.
Mathematics.
Mother Poem.
Numbers, The.
Peaches, The.
Torn Nightgown, The.
Undefined Tenderness, An.

Opper, Frederick B.
Sir Bedivere Bors.

Opperman, D. J.
Christmas Carol: "Three outas from the bleak Karoo."
Fable: "Under a dung-cake."
Fable of the Speckled Cow.
Water Whirligigs.

O'Rahilly [*or* O'Reilly], Egan
Brightest of the Bright, The.
Brightness of Brightness.
Geraldine's Daughter, The.
Grey Eye Weeping, A.
Inis Fal.
Lament for Banba.
Last Lines.
More Power to Cromwell.
On a Cock Which Was Stolen from a Good Priest.
On a Pair of Shoes Presented to Him, *sel.*
Reverie, The.
Sleepless Night, A.
Storm, The, *sel.*
Time of Change, A.

Orban, Otto
Computer.
Hymn: "Some sort of fire leaped out of the dirty and poor and merciless city."
Ray.

Orde, Julian
Changing Wind, The.

O'Reilly, Dowell
Sea-Grief.

O'Reilly, Egan. *See* **O'Rahilly, Egan**

O'Reilly, John Boyle
Art Master, An.
At Best.
At Fredericksburg.
Boston.
Builder's Lesson, A.
Chicago.
Constancy.
Crispus Attucks.
Cry of a Dreamer, The.
Cry of the Dreamer, The.
Disappointment.
Experience.
Forever.
Infinite, The.
Lure, The.
Mayflower.
Message of Peace, A.
Midnight—September 19, 1881.
Ride of Collins Graves, The.
Savage, A.
Song: "Love was true to me."
To-Day.
Wendell Phillips, *sel.*
What Is Good?
What shall we mourn? For the prostrate.
White Rose, A.

O'Reilly, Pat
Wonderful Mother, A.

Orente, Rose J.
Master City, The.

Oresick, Peter
After the Movement.
Elmer Ruiz.
Family Portrait 1933.

"Orestes"
Sonnet to Opium, A; Celebrating Its Virtues.

Orford, Horace Walpole, 4th Earl of. *See* **Walpole, Horace, 4th Earl of Orford**

"Orinda." *See* **Philips, Katherine**

O'Riordan, Conal
Hymn to the Virgin Mary.
Requiem: "Hush your prayers, 'tis no saintly soul."

Orléans, Charles, Duc d'
Rumors.
Alons au bois le may cueillir.
Come, Death—My Lady Is Dead, *at.*
Confession.
Dieu Qu'Il la Fait.
Go, Sad Complaint.
Kiss, The.
Lost.
Mistress without Compare, A, *at.*
My Ghostly Father, I Me Confess.
Oft in My Thought.
Rondel: "Strengthen, my Love, this castle of my heart."
Smiling Mouth and Laughing Eyen Grey, The.
Spring.
Well, Wanton Eye.

Orlen, Steve [*or* Stephen]
Aga Khan, The.
Bar Mitzvah.
Big Friend of the Stones.

Common Light, A.
Drunken Man, The.
Family Cups.
In Praise of Beverly.
Life Study.
Madman's Wife, The.
My Grandmother and the Voice of Tolstoy.
Permission to Speak.
Orlock, Carol
Signature.
Orlovitz, Gil
Art of the Sonnet, *sels.*
Orlovsky, Peter
Second Poem.
Ormond, John
At His Father's Grave.
To a Nun.
Ormsby, Frank
Amelia Street.
Child, The.
Inferno: A New Circle.
Interim.
On Devenish Island.
Ornaments.
O'Rourke, David
For Your Inferiority Complex.
O'Rourke, May
Minority, The: 1917.
Stick, The.
Orozco, Olga
Sphinxes Inclined to Be.
Orpingalik
My Breath.
Orr, Christine
Road, The.
Orr, Emily
Recruit from the Slums, A.
Orr, Gregory
Abandoned, Overgrown Cemetery in the Pasture near Our House, An.
Adolescence.
After a Death.
Beggar's Song.
Dinner, The.
Doll, The.
Driving Home after a Funeral.
End of August.
Gathering the Bones Together.
Girl with 18 Nightgowns, The.
Haitian Suite.
In an Empty Field at Night.
Last Address to My Ghosts, A.
Like Any Other Man.
Lost Children, The.
Love Poem: "Black biplane crashes into [*or* through] the window, The."
Morning Song.
On the Lawn at Ira's.
Poem: "This life like no other."
Project, The.
Room, The.
Silence.
Song of the Invisible Corpse in the Field.
Spring Floods.
Sweater, The.
Two Lines from the Brothers Grimm.
Visitor, The.
We Must Make a Kingdom of It.
Orr, Patrick
Annie Shore and Johnnie Doon.
Orred, Meta
In the Gloaming.
Ort, Daniel
Tho We All Speak.
Orten, Jiri
Small Elegy, A.
Ortiz, Simon J.
At the Salvation Army.
Bony.
Creation, The: According to Coyote.
Crossing the Colorado River into Yuma.
Forming Child Poems.
From Sand Creek, *sel.*
Hunger in New York City.
Indian Guys at the Bar.
Juanita, Wife of Manuelito.
My Father's Song.
My Mother and My Sisters.
New Story, A.
Pretty Woman, A.
San Diego Poem, A.
Serenity in Stones, The.
Significance of a Veteran's Day, The.
Story of How a Wall Stands, A.
Survival This Way.
To Insure Survival.
Waiting for You to Come By.
Washyuma Motor Hotel.
Watching Salmon Jump.
What I Tell Him.
Ortleb, Chuck
Some Boys.
Ortmayer, Constance
Dawn.
Orwell, George (Eric Blair)
As One Non-Combatant to Another.
Dressed man and a naked man, A.
Italian soldier shook my hand, The.
O'Ryan, Edmond
Ah! What Woes Are Mine.
Osadebay, Dennis C.
African Trader's Complaint, The.
Osaki, Mark
Amnesiac.
Contentment.
For Avi Killed in Lebanon.
Icon.
Turista.
Osborn, Laughton
Death of General Pike, The.
Osborn, Margot
Always the Melting Moon Comes.
Osborn, Mary Elizabeth
Alma Mater.
Come Not Near.
Exquisite Lady.
Mid-Century.
Old Man in the Park.
Rural Legend.
Thought for the Winter Season.
Water-Images.
Osborn, Selleck
Modest Wit, A.
Osborne, Duffield
Ave! Nero Imperator.
Osborne, Edith D.
Path of the Padres, The.
Osborne, Gene H.
Thanksgiving.
Osborne, Louis Shreve
Riding Down from Bangor.
Osborne, Marian
Trinity, The.
White Violet.
Osgood, Flora L.
Come unto Me.
Cost, The.
Osgood, Frances Sargent
Calumny.
Dancing Girl, A.
On a Dead Poet.
On Sivori's Violin.
Song: "Your heart is a music-box, dearest!"
To Sleep.
Osgood, Francis P.
Winter Fairyland in Vermont.
Osgood, Kate Putnam
Driving Home the Cows.
O'Shaughnessy, Arthur William Edgar
Barcarolle.
Black Marble.
Chaitivel, *sel.*
Doom.
Enchainment.
Fair Maid and the Sun, The.
Fountain of Tears, The.
If She but Knew.
Living Marble.
Love Symphony, A.
Music Makers, The.
Ode: "We are the music-makers."
St. John Baptist.
Silences.
Song: "Has summer come without the rose."
Song: "I made another garden, yea."
Song: "I went to her who loveth me no more."
O'Shea, Diarmuid
Prayer at Dawn.
O'Sheel, Shaemas
He Whom a Dream Hath Possessed.
Lover Thinks of His Lady in the North, The.
Mary's Baby.
They Went Forth to Battle but They Always Fell.
While April Rain Went By.
O-Shi-O
When I Think of the Hungry People.
"Ossian." *See* **Macpherson, James**
"O. Henry." *See* **"Henry, O."**
Ostenso, Martha
Return, The.
Ostriker, Alicia
Anxiety about Dying.
Old Men.
Ostroff, Anthony
End of the War in Merida.
Love.
River Glideth in a Secret Tongue, The.
So Long Folks, Off to the War.
Sparrows at the Airport, The.
War.
O'Sullivan, Daniel James
Dawn in Inishtrahull.
Drinking Time.
Glaucous-Gull's Death, The.
January.
Lament for Seán.
Moschatel.
Nightfall in Inishtrahull.
O'Sullivan, Owen Roe
His Request.
Rodney's Glory.
To the Blacksmith with a Spade.
Volatile Kerryman, The.
"O'Sullivan, Seumas" (James Starkey)
Birds.
Blessing on the Cows, A.
Convent, The.
Credo.
Half Door, The.
In North Great George's Street.
Lament for Sean MacDermott.
Lamplighter, The.
Land War, The.
Lullaby: "Husheen, the herons are crying."
Milkman, The.
My Sorrow.
Nelson Street.
Others, The.
Piper, A.
Praise.
Rain.
Sedges, The.
Sheep, The.
Sketch.
Splendid and Terrible.
Starling Lake, The.
Twilight People, The.
O'Sullivan, Vincent
Brother Jonathan, Brother Kafka, *sels.*
Bus Stop.
Further Instructions.
Late Lunch, San Antonio.
Medusa.
Talking to Her.

Otey, Harold LaMont
Birthday on Deathrow.
Haywood.
Lamentation.
Red White & Another Ism.
Tree.
Otomo of [*or* no] Sakanoe [*or* Sakanone], Lady
My brother has on/ a thin robe.
My heart, thinking/ "How beautiful he is."
Sent from the Capital to Her Elder Daughter.
Unknown love/ Is as bitter a thing.
You say, "I will come."
Otsuji
Into a forest.
Otto, Heinrich
Lord, Dear God! to Thy Attending, *with music.*
O'Tuomy, John
O'Tuomy's Drinking Song.
Otway, Thomas
Come, All Ye Youths.
Enchantment, The.
Orphan, The; or, The Unhappy Marriage, *sel.*
Oumar Bar
Drought.
Ou-ty, Emperor. *See* **Wu Ti, Emperor**
Ousley, Clarence
When the Mint Is in the Liquor.
Ouston, Hugh
Climber Surveys His Mountain, The.
Outlaw, Randolph
Down Home.
Still Life.
Tennessee Crickets.
Visit.
White Whales Specked Black.
720 Gabriel St.
Outram, George
Annuity, The.
On Hearing a Lady Praise a Certain Rev. Doctor's Eyes.
Strictures on the Economy of Nature.
Ou-yang Hsiu
Cicada, The.
Green Jade Plum Trees in Spring.
Overstreet, Bonaro W.
First Day of Teaching.
Overton, A. M.
He Maketh No Mistake.
Overton, Ron
Sharks.
Ovid (Publius Ovidius Naso)
Acteon.
Advice to a Fair Wanton.
Amores, *sels.*
Apology for Loose Behavior.
Art of Love, The, *sels.*
Atalanta.
Baucis and Philemon.
Captive of Love, A.
Complaisant Swain, The.
Conclusion: "Now have I brought a woork too end which neither Joves fierce wrath."
Constant Penelope sends to thee, careless Ulysses.
Corinna, Having Tried, with Her Own Hand.
Corinnae Concubitus.
Cyclops.
Daedalus.
Daphne and Apollo.
De Ponto, *sels.*
Death of Eurydice and Orpheus' Journey to Hell, The.
Elegies, *sels.*
Elegy: "In summer's heat and mid-time of the day."
Elegy to His Mistress.
Flood, The.
Golden Age, The.
Heroides, *sel.*
I ask but right: let her that caught me late.
Impotent Lover, The.
In Summer's Heat.
Invective against Ibis, *sel*
King Midas.
Lente, Lente.
Medea Casts a Spell to Make Aeson Young Again.
Meleager.
Metamorphoses, *sels.*
Of the Pythagorean Philosophy.
Offered a sexless heaven I'd say "No thank you."
Philemon and Baucis.
Phoenix Self-born, The.
Possessive Lover, The.
Pygmalion's Statue Comes to Life.
Shameful Impotence.
To His Mistress.
To Verse Let Kings Give Place.
Tristium, *sels.*
Winter at Tomi.
Your loveliness, I don't deny, needs lovers.
Owen, Gareth
Winter Days.
Owen, Guy
Poem to a Mule, Dead Twenty Years.
White Stallion, The.
Owen, J. Elgar
Maturity.
Owen, Sue
Lullaby: "This is where/ the light sleeps."
Owl, The.
Owen, Wilfred
A Terre.
Antaeus; a Fragment.
Anthem for Doomed Youth.
Apologia pro Poemate Meo.
Arms and the Boy.
Asleep.
Chances, The.
Conscious.
Disabled.
Dulce et Decorum Est.
End, The.
Exposure.
Fragment: "I saw his round mouth's crimson deepen as it fell."
From My Diary, July 1914.
Futility.
Greater Love.
Insensibility.
Inspection.
Le Christianisme.
Mental Cases.
Miners.
Next War, The.
Parable of the Old Man and the Young, The.
Roads Also, The.
Send-off, The.
Sentry, The.
Shadwell Stair.
Show, The.
Sleeping Beauty, The.
Soldier's Dream.
Sonnet to My Friend, with an Identity Disc.
Spring Offensive.
Strange Meeting.
Unreturning, The.
Owens, Rochelle
Between the Karim Shahir.
Chugachimute I Love the Name.
Dance and Eye Me (Wicked)ly My Breath a Fixed Sphere.
Evolution.
Macrobius Mingling with Nature.
Man as He Shall Be.
Medieval Christ Speaks on a Spanish Sculpture of Himself.
Power of Love He Wants Shih (Everything), The.
Strawberries mit Cream.
Woman
Ower, John
Cudworth's Undergraduate Ode to a Bare Behind.
Gingerbread House, The.
Owl Woman (Juana Manwell)
Songs for the Four Parts of the Night.
Oxenham, John (*originally* William Arthur Dunkerley)
After Work.
All One in Christ.
Bide a Wee!
Christ, The.
Credo.
Day, The—the Way.
Everymaid.
Face to Face with Reality.
For Beauty, We Thank Thee.
Goal and the Way, The.
God's Sunshine.
Gratitude for Work.
Influence.
Judgment Day.
Life's Chequer-Board.
Little Poem of Life, The.
Little Te Deum of the Commonplace, A, *sels.*
Live Christ.
Love.
Love's Prerogative.
No East or West.
Paul.
Per Ardua ad Astra.
Prayer, A: "Through every minute of this day."
Prince of Life, The.
Props.
Sacrament of Sleep, The.
Seeds.
So Little and So Much.
Some Blesseds.
Te Deum of the Commonplace, A, *sel.*
Thanksgiving.
To Whom Shall the World Henceforth Belong?
Valley of Decision, The.
Ways, The.
We Thank Thee, Lord.
We Thank Thee ("For all life's beauties . . .").
We Thank Thee ("For all Thy ministries").
Where Are You Going, Greatheart?
Whirring Wheels.
Your Place.
Oxford, Earl of. *See* **De Vere, Edward, 17th Earl of Oxford**
Oyama, Richard
Day after Trinity, The.
Dreams in Progress.
Obon by the Hudson.
This Song Shows Me Pictures; Morningside Drive, New York City 1950–1960.
Ozerov, Lev
Babi Yar.
Ozick, Cynthia
Riddle, A: "I walk on two legs."
Wonder-Teacher, The.

P

"P., A. B."
Scholastic Mouse, The.
Pace, Charles Nelson
Cross, The.
Pacernick, Gary
Babel.
I Want to Write a Jewish Poem.
Labor Day.
Pacheco, Jose Emilio
Fire.
Pack, Richardson
Epistle from a Half-Pay Officer in the Country to His Friend in London, An.

Pack, Robert
Adam on His Way Home.
Anecdote of the Sparrow.
Bird in Search of a Cage, A.
Boat, The.
Chopping Fire-Wood.
Departure, The.
Descending.
Don't Sit under the Apple Tree with Anyone Else but Me!
Election, The.
Everything Is Possible.
Faithful Lover, The.
Father.
Frog Prince, The.
Idyl in Idleness, An.
In a Field.
Kiss, The.
Mugger, The.
On the Seventh Anniversary of the Death of My Father.
Pack Rat, The.
Parable.
Poem for You.
Raking Leaves.
Resurrection.
Ring, The.
Self-Portrait.
Shooting, The.
Waiting.
Way We Wonder, The.
Weasel, The.
Packard, Frederick
Balearic Idyll.
Packard, William
Haircut.
Packard, Winthrop
Shoogy-Shoo, The.
Paddock, Nancy
"That First Gulp of Air We All Took When First Born."
Padeshah Khatun
Sovereign Queen.
Padgett, Ron
After the Broken Arm.
December.
Sandwich Man, The.
Strawberries in Mexico.
Paff, Eric W.
On Sitting Up Late, Watching Kittens.
Pagan, Isobel
Ca' the Yowes to the Knowes.
Page, B. Sanford
All Songs.
Page, Geoff
Coloratura.
Country Nun.
Page, Patricia K.
Adolescence.
After Rain.
Arras.
Bands and the Beautiful Children, The.
Crow, The.
Cullen ("Cullen renounced his cradle at fifteen").
Element.
Evening Dance of the Grey Flies.
Images of Angels.
Landlady.
Man with One Small Hand.
Permanent Tourists, The.
Photos of a Salt Mine.
Puppets.
Schizophrenic.
Snowman, The.
Stenographers, The.
Stories of Snow.
Summer.
Summer Resort.
T-Bar.
Page, Thomas Nelson
Ashcake.
Dragon of the Seas, The.
Uncle Gabe's White Folks.
Page, William
Painlessly out of Ourselves.
Pagis, Dan
Autobiography.
Brothers.
Draft of a Reparations Agreement.
Grand Duke of New York, The.
Hide and Seek.
Instructions for Crossing the Border.
Last Ones, The.
Scrawled in Pencil in a Sealed Railway Car.
Tower, The.
Pagliarani, Elio
It's Already Autumn.
Pagnucci, Gianfranco
Death of an Elephant, The.
Pain, Barry
Macaulay at Tea.
Martin Luther at Potsdam.
Oh! Weary Mother.
Poets at Tea, The.
Ride a Cock Horse.
Pain, Philip
Meditation 8 ("Scarce do I pass a day but that I hear").
Meditation 9 ("Man's life is like a rose, that in the spring").
Meditation 10 ("Alas, what is the world? A sea of glass").
Meditation 29 ("How mutable is every thing that here").
Meditation 62 ("How is it that I am so careless here").
Meditations for August 1, 1666.
Meditations for July 19, 1666.
Meditations for July 25, 1666.
Meditations for July 26, 1666.
Porch, The.
Whilst in This World I Stay, *with music.*
Paine, Albert Bigelow
Cooky-Nut Trees, The.
Dancing Bear, The.
Hills of Rest, The.
In Louisiana.
Little Child, The.
Mis' Smith.
Paine, Carol
Color Blind.
Paine, Robert Treat
Adams and Liberty.
Paine, Theodora L.
Danger.
Paine, Thomas
Liberty Tree.
Painter, John R.
Bob-tailed Flush, A.
"Pai Ta-shun." *See* **Peterson, Frederick**
"Pai Wei"
Madrid.
Palagyi, Louis
Aimless.
Palea
Piano at Evening.
Palen, Jennie M.
Early Dutch.
To a Race Horse at Ascot.
Palen, John
Missouri Town.
Palés Matos, Luis
Doorway to Time in Three Voices.
Elegy for the Duke of Marmalade.
Hurricane, The.
Kalahari.
Neither This nor That.
Well, The.
Paley, Grace
One day when I was a child, long ago.
Women in Vietnam, The.
Paley, Morton
Theodore Roethke.
Paley Francescato, Martha
Parody.
Semen.
Palfrey, Sarah Hammond. *See* **"Foxton, E."**
Palgrave, Francis Turner
City of God, The.
Creçy.
Eutopia.
God Save Elizabeth!
Linnet in November, The.
Trafalgar.
Palladas [*or* Pallades]
Grammar commences with a 5-line curse.
Loving the rituals that keep men close.
Poor devil that I am, being so attacked.
Racing, reckoning fingers flick.
Vanity of Vanities.
When you send out invitations, don't ask me.
Pallottini, Renata
Message.
Palma Acosta, Teresa
My Mother Pieced Quilts.
Palmanteer, Ted D.
Granma's Words.
Pass It On Grandson.
Palmer, Alice Freeman
Butterfly, The.
Communion Hymn, A.
Hallowed Places.
On a Gloomy Easter.
Spring Journey, A.
Palmer, David
Plato Instructs a Midwest Farmer.
Palmer, E. Harriet
Parterre, The.
Shipwreck, The.
Palmer, Herbert Edward
Aunt Zillah Speaks.
Ishmael.
Rock Pilgrim.
Woodworker's Ballad.
Wounded Hawk, The.
Palmer, John F.
Band Played On, The.
Palmer, John Williamson
Fight at [the] San Jacinto, The.
For Charlie's Sake.
Maryland Battalion, The.
Ned Braddock.
Reid at Fayal.
Stonewall Jackson's Way.
Theodosia Burr: The Wrecker's Story.
Palmer, Michael
Changes around the Bay.
Classical Style, The.
Comet, The.
Dearest Reader.
Documentation.
Notes for Echo Lake 5.
On the Way to Language.
Song of the Round Man.
Symmetrical Poem.
Theory of the Flower, The.
Village of Reason, The.
Voice and Address.
Palmer, Miriam
Raccoon Poem.
"Vierge Ouvrante."
What if jealousy is just a bad dream?
Palmer, Nettie
Mother, The.
Palmer, Ray
Faith.
I Saw Thee.
Jesus, These Eyes Have Never Seen, *with music.*
Lord, My Weak Thought in Vain Would Climb, *with music.*
My Faith Looks Up to Thee.
Palmer, Samuel
Shoreham: Twilight Time.
Twilight Time.

Palmer, T. H.
Try, Try Again, *at.*
Palmer, Vance
Farmer Remembers the Somme, The.
Palmer, William Pitt
Smack in School, The.
Palmer, Winthrop
Arlington Cemetery Looking toward the Capitol.
Palquera, Shem-Tob ben Joseph
Adapt Thyself.
Mouth and the Ears, The.
Paman, Clement
On Christmas Day.
On Christmas Day to My Heart.
Pan, Lady (Pan Chieh-yu)
Present from the Emperor's New Concubine, A.
Needle and Thread.
Panatattu
True Knowledge.
Unity of God, The.
Pan Chao
Pankey, Eric
Renaming the Evening.
"Panormitanus" (Antonio Beccadelli)
Epitaph on Pegasus, a Limping Gay.
Pape, Greg
For Rosa Yen, Who Lived Here.
In the City of Bogotá.
La Llorona.
Mercado.
My Happiness.
October.
Porpoise, The.
Sharks, Caloosahatchee River.
Papenhausen, Carol
Album.
Paramore, Edward E., Jr.
Ballad of Yukon Jake, The.
Paraone, Tiwai
Chant to Io.
Paraske, Larin
My Little Love Lies on the Ground.
Sad Is the Seagull.
Woman Grows Soon Old, A.
Parham, Robert
Sunday in South Carolina.
Parini, Jay
Amores (after Ovid).
Missionary Visits Our Church in Scranton, The.
Snake Hill.
Tanya.
To His Dear Friend, Bones.
Parish, Mitchell
Star Dust, *with music.*
Parisi, Philip
Niagara Falls.
Park, Frances
Sad Song about Greenwich Village, A.
Park, Roswell
Jesus Spreads His Banner o'er Us, *with music.*
Parke, Walter
His Mother-in-Law.
Limerick: "There was a princess of Bengal," *at.*
Limerick: "There was a young man who was bitten," *at.*
Limerick: "There was an old stupid who wrote," *at.*
Person of Note, A, *at.*
Parker, Dorothy
Autobiography.
Ballade of a Talked-off Ear.
Ballade of Big Plans.
Ballade of Unfortunate Mammals.
Bohemia.
Certain Lady, A.
Chant for Dark Hours.
Coda.
Comment.
Counselor, The.
Crusader, The.
Danger of Writing Defiant Verse, The.
Dark Girl's Rhyme, The.
De Profundis.
Dilemma.
Evening Primrose, The.
Experience.
Fair Weather.
Fighting Words.
Flaw in Paganism, The.
From a Letter from Lesbia.
Frustration.
Gentlest Lady, The.
George Sand.
Godmother.
Interior.
Interview.
Little Old Lady in Lavender Silk, The.
Love Song: "My own dear love, he is strong and bold."
Men.
News Item.
Observation.
Of a Woman, Dead Young.
On Being a Woman.
One Perfect Rose.
Partial Comfort.
Philosophy.
Portrait of the Artist.
Prologue to a Saga.
Résumé.
Social Note.
Some Beautiful Letters, *sels.*
Song of Perfect Propriety.
Sonnet for the End of a Sequence.
Story.
Symptom Recital.
Theory.
Threnody: "Lilacs blossom just as sweet."
Tombstones in the Starlight: The Fisherwoman.
Tombstones in the Starlight: The Very Rich Man.
Two-Volume Novel.
Unfortunate Coincidence.
Verse for a Certain Dog.
Walter Savage Landor.
Parker, Edgar
Contrary Waiter, The.
Parker, Edwin Pond
Master, No Offering, *with music.*
Parker, Sir Gilbert
Little Garaine.
Reunited.
World in Making, The.
Parker, Martin
Description of a Strange (and Miraculous) Fish, A.
Keep a Good Tongue in Your Head.
King Enjoys His Own Again, The.
Maunding Soldier, The; or, The Fruits of Warre Is Beggery.
Saylors for My Money.
When the King Enjoys His Own Again.
Wooing Maid, The.
Parker, Patricia
From the Cavities of Bones.
I Followed a Path.
There Is a Woman in This Town.
Parker, Stephen
Winter in Étienburgh.
Parker, Stewart
Chicago Allegory.
Health.
Three Fitts.
Parker, Theodore
Higher Good, The.
Jesus.
New Year Prayer, A.
Way, the Truth, and the Life, The.
Parkes, Francis Ernest Kobina
Apocalypse.
Blind Steersmen.
Three Phases of Africa.
Parkwood, Rose
Garden, The.
Parlatore, Anselm
Accommodation.
Although in a Crystal.
Cancer Research.
Family Chronicle.
Lovely Girls with Flounder on a Starry Night.
"Parley, Peter." *See* **Goodrich, Samuel Griswold**
Parmenter, Catherine
Christmas Eve.
Silent Testimony.
Parnell, Fanny
After Death.
Parnell, Thomas
Elegy, to an Old Beauty, An.
Hermit, The.
Hymn to Contentment, A.
Night Piece on Death.
Small Silver-coloured Bookworm, The.
Song: "When thy beauty appears."
Parnell, Thomas, *and* **Alexander Pope**
On Riding to See Dean Swift in the Mist of the Morning.
Parone, Edward
Morning Track, The.
Parra, Nicanor
Beggar.
I Move the Meeting Be Adjourned.
Manifesto, *sel.*
Seven.
We Let It Go That He Was a Perfect Man.
Young Poets.
Parrish, Elsie
Some Things That Easter Brings.
Parrish, John
Democratic Barber, The; or, Country Gentleman's Surprise.
Parrish, Lydia A.
Pay Me My Money Down.
Parrish, Randall
Your Lad, and My Lad.
Parrot, Henry
Fatales Poetae.
In Obitum Promi.
On a Poet.
Parrott, E. O.
Ode on a Grecian Urn, *parody.*
Parry, David Fisher
Bachelor's Ballade, The.
Miniver Cheevy, Jr., *parody.*
Parry, Edward Abbott
I Would Like You for a Comrade.
Jam Fish, The.
Pater's Bathe.
Parry, Joseph
New Friends and Old Friends.
Parry, Robert
Except I Love.
Mirror of Knighthood, The, *sels.*
Song: "Fond affection, hence, and leave me!"
Parson, Tom
Meeting at the Local.
Victory of the Battle of Wounded Knee, The.
Parsons, Clere
Different.
Introduction: "I bespeak words."
Parsons, Kitty
My Valentine.
Parsons, Thomas William
Andrew.
Dirge: "Room for a soldier! lay him in the clover."
Dirge for One Who Fell in Battle.
Her Epitaph.
Into the Noiseless Country.
Like as the Lark.
Mary Booth.
O Ye Sweet Heavens!
Obituary.
On a Bust of Dante.
Paradisi Gloria.

Saint Peray.
To a Lady.
To a Young Girl Dying.
Parsons, William
To a Friend in Love during the Riots.
Partridge, Sybil F.
Just for To-Day [*or* Today].
Partridge, William Ordway
Nathan Hale.
Parun, Vesna
Mother of Man.
Return to the Tree of Time, A.
Parvin, Betty
Edwardian Hat.
Pascal, Paul
Tact.
Pasolini, Pier Paolo
To a Pope.
Tuesday, 5 March (Morning) 1963.
Pass, John
Junction.
Theresa.
Passerat, Jean
Love in May.
Song: "Shephard loveth thow me vell?"
Passy, Nancy
Listening.
Pastan, Linda
After Reading Nelly Sachs.
After X-Ray.
April.
At the Jewish Museum.
City, The.
Death's Blue-eyed Girl.
Elsewhere.
Ethics.
Grammar Lesson.
In the Old Guerilla War.
Love Letter.
Marks.
Old Woman.
Pears.
Poet.
Real Story, A.
Secrets.
September.
Symposium, A: Apples.
Waiting for E. Gularis.
Whom Do You Visualize as Your Reader?
Why Not?
Writing while My Father Dies.
Yom Kippur.
Pasternak, Boris Leonidovich
Caucasus, The.
Definition of the Soul.
Fresh Paint.
Hops.
In the Breeze.
May It Be.
Poem: "So they begin. With two years gone."
Star of the Nativity.
Three Variations.
Waving a Bough.
Winter Night.
Pastorius, Francis Daniel
As often as some where before my feet.
Delight in books from evening.
Epigrams.
Extract the quint-essence.
Great God, Preserver of All Things, *with music.*
I have a pretty little flow'r.
If Any Be Pleased to Walk into My Poor Garden.
If thou wouldest roses scent.
Learn, lads and lasses, of my garden.
Most weeds, whilst young.
On His Garden Book.
Though My Thoughts, *with music.*
To God alone, the only donour.
When I solidly do ponder.
When one or other rambles.
Patchen, Kenneth
All the Roary Night.
And What with the Blunders.
Animal I wanted, The.
As We Are So Wonderfully Done with Each Other.
At the New Year.
Because Going Nowhere Takes a Long Time.
Because He Liked to Be at Home.
Because in This Sorrowing Statue of Flesh.
Because Sometimes You Can't Always Be So.
Because They Were Very Poor That Winter.
Behold, One of Several Little Christs.
Biography of Southern Rain.
Character of Love Seen as a Search for the Lost, The.
Constant Bridegrooms, The.
Deer and the Snake, The.
Do the Dead Know What Time It Is?
Easy Decision, An.
Elegy for the Silent Voices and the Joiners of Everything.
Empty Dwelling Places.
Everlasting Contenders, The.
Fog.
From My High Love.
Gautama in the Deer Park at Benares.
Hunted City, The, *sel.*
I Have Lighted the Candles, Mary.
I Went to the City.
I'd Want Her Eyes to Fill with Wonder.
In Judgment of the Leaf.
In Memory of Kathleen.
In Order To.
In the footsteps of the walking air.
Journal of Albion Moolight, The, *sels.*
Known Soldier, The.
Like a Mourningless Child.
Lions of fire, The.
Little Green Blackbird, The.
Magical Mouse, The.
Midnight Special.
Moon, Sun, Sleep, Birds, Live.
Naked Land, The.
Nice Day for a Lynching.
O All Down within the Pretty Meadow.
O Now the Drenched Land Wakes.
O terrible is the highest thing.
Orange Bears, The.
Origin of Baseball, The.
Pastoral: "Dove walks with slick feet, The."
Reason for Skylarks, The.
Saturday Night in the Parthenon.
Street Corner College.
Temple, A.
There Is Nothing False in Thee.
Trueblue Gentleman, A.
Twenty-third Street Runs into Heaven.
Village Tudda, The.
We Go Out Together.
What There Is.
Where?
Where Two o'Clock Came From.
Pater, Walter
Mona Lisa.
Paterson, Andrea
Because I Could Not Dump.
Paterson, Andrew Barton
Bush Christening, A.
Bushman's Song, A.
Clancy of the Overflow.
Man from Ironbark, The.
Man from Snowy River, The.
Old Man Platypus.
Road to Hogan's Gap, The.
Travelling Post Office, The.
Waltzing Matilda.
Weary Will.
Paterson, Evangeline
And That Will Be Heaven.
Armaments Race.
Death on a Crossing.
Parting from My Son.
Patey, Tom
Last of the Grand Old Masters, The.
Macinnes's Mountain Patrol.
Patmore, Coventry Kersey Dighton
Across the sky the daylight crept.
Angel in the House, The, *sels.*
Arbor Vitae.
Attainment, The.
Auras of Delight.
Azalea, The.
Barren Shore, The.
Cathedral Close, The.
Child's Purchase, The.
Constancy.
Constancy Rewarded.
County Ball, The.
Courtesy.
Dartmoor.
Dean, The.
Deliciae Sapientiae de Amore.
Demonstration, A.
Departure.
Devonshire Scenes.
Faint yet Pursuing.
Farewell, A: "With all my will, but much against my heart."
First Spousal, The.
Flesh-Fly and the Bee, The.
Foreign Land, The.
Fragment: "He that but once too nearly hears."
From the small life that loves with tooth and nail.
Going to Church.
Here, in This Little Bay.
Honor and Desert.
How fair a flower is sown.
If I Were Dead.
Impossibility, The.
In Love, at Stonehenge.
Joyful Wisdom, The.
King William's Dispatch to Queen Augusta.
Kiss, The.
Kites, The.
Legem Tuam Dilexi.
London Fête, A.
Lonely Cloud of Care, The.
Love at Large.
Love Serviceable.
Love's Reality.
Magna Est Veritas.
Married Lover, The.
Music of Forefended Spheres, The.
Nearest the Dearest.
Night and Sleep.
Perspective.
Platonic Love.
Poet's Confidence, The.
Rain That Fell upon the Height, The.
Rainbow, The.
Regina Coeli.
Remembered Grace.
Retrospect, A.
Revelation, The.
Rose of the World, The.
Rosy Bosom'd Hours, The.
Sahara.
Saint Valentine's Day.
Salisbury; the Cathedral Close.
Save by the Old Road none attain the new.
Science, the agile ape, may well.
Sensuality.
Shadow of Night, The.
Shame.
Spirit's Epochs, The.
Storm, The.
Tamerton Church-Tower; or, First Love, *sel.*
To the Body.
To the Unknown Eros.
Toys, The.
Tribute, The.
Truth.

Two Deserts, The.
Unthrift.
Vesica Piscis.
Victories of Love, The, *sels.*
Warning, A.
Wedding, The.
Whirl'd off at last, for speech I sought.
Wind and Wave.
Winter.
Woman.
Year, The.
Paton, Alan
I Have Approached.
Prison House, The.
Patrick, Johnstone G.
Closing Prayer.
Grace.
Prayer for Peace.
Patrick, Saint
Breastplate of St. Patrick, The, *at.*
Deer's Cry, The, *at.*
God's Blessing on Munster, *at.*
St. Patrick's Breastplate, *at.*
Patrick, Luther
Sleepin' at the Foot o' the Bed.
Patten, Brian
After Frost.
Beast, The.
Little Johnny's Confession.
Ode on Celestial Music.
Party Piece.
Portrait of a Young Girl Raped at a Suburban Party.
Small Dragon, A.
Through All Your Abstract Reasoning.
Where Are You Now Superman?
Patten, Karl
Mr. Secretary.
Wreathmakertraining.
Patterson, Charles
Listen.
Patterson, Lindsay
At Long Last.
When I Woke.
Patterson, Raymond R.
Accident, The.
At That Moment.
Birmingham 1963.
Black All Day.
In Time of Crisis.
I've Got a Home in That Rock.
Letter in Winter.
Love Song, A: "Do I love you?"
Night-Piece.
Riot Rhymes U.S.A., *sel.*
When I Awoke.
You Are the Brave.
Pattison, William
Unfortunate Reminder, The.
Patton, G. W.
Emigrant's Dying Child, The.
Patton, Margaret French
Needle Travel.
Patton, Patti
Birthday Party.
Pauker, Ted
Garland for a Propagandist.
Grouchy Good Night to the Academic Year, A.
Limeraiku.
Trifle for Trafalgar Day, A.
Paul, Dorothy
Captive Ships at Manila, The.
Figurehead.
Paul, James
Everything.
Feet, a Sermon.
Honeysuckle.
This Town.
Water Tower, The.
"Paul, John." *See* **Webb, Charles Henry**
Paul, Louis
Cynical Portraits.
Paul the Silentiary. *See* **Paulus Silentiarius.**
Paulding, James Kirke
Ode to Jamestown.
Old Man's Carousal, The.
Paulin, Tom
Evening Harbour.
Paulinaoq
Dead Man's Song, Dreamed by One Who Is Alive.
Paulinus of Nola
To Ausonius.
Pau-Llosa, Ricardo
Links.
Paulos
Epigram: "Kissing Hippomenes, I crave."
Paulus Silentiarius [*or* Paul the Silentiary]
Epitaph, An: "My name—my country—what are they to thee?"
In Peterborough Churchyard.
No Matter.
Tantalos.
United.
Pavlich, Walter
Revisiting the Field.
Pavlova, Karolina
To Madame A. V. Pletneff.
Paxton, Jean Grigsby
Preparedness.
Paxton, Tom
I Can't Help but Wonder Where I'm Bound.
My Ramblin' Boy.
Payn, James
I Never Had a Piece of Toast.
Payne, Anne Blackwell
Silver Sheep.
Payne, Gerrye
Claritas.
Payne, John
Kyrielle.
Of Three Damsels in a Meadow.
Rococo.
Rondeau Redoublé.
Payne, John Howard
Clari, the Maid of Milan, *sel.*
Payne, Nina
Bubble Gum.
Chocolate Cake.
Tag Along.
Payne, William Morton
"Ej Blot til Lyst."
Incipit Vita Nova.
Lohengrin.
Tannhäuser.
Paz, Octavio
Landscape.
Street, The.
Touch.
Peabody, Josephine Preston
Concerning Love.
Cradle Song: "Lord Gabriel, wilt thou not rejoice."
House and the Road, The.
Hymn: "Dear Lord, Whose serving-maiden."
Man's Bread, A.
Singing Man, The.
Song of a Shepherd Boy at Bethlehem.
Spinning in April.
To a Dog.
Peabody, William Bourne Oliver
Lament of Anastasius.
Peace, Angela
Indian Mounds.
Peach, Arthur Wallace
"Cap'n."
Mosaic Worker, The.
O Youth with Blossoms Laden.
Secret, The.
Peacham, Henry
Nuptial Hymn.
Period of Mourning, The, *sel.*
Peacock, Molly
Lull, The.
Now Look What Happened.
Old Roadside Resorts.
So, When I Swim to the Shore.
Two Figures.
Peacock, Thomas
Andonis, My Daughter.
Earth Song.
Fear.
For the Children.
In Respect of the Elderly.
Six Eagles.
Peacock, Thomas Love
Bacchus.
Beneath the Cypress Shade.
Border Ballad, A.
Castles in the Air.
Catch, A.
Chorus: "Hail to the Headlong! the Headlong Ap-Headlong!"
Chorus: "If I drink water while this doth last."
Crotchet Castle, *sels.*
For the Slender Beech and the Sapling Oak.
Glee—The Ghosts.
Grave of Love, The.
Gryll Grange, *sel.*
Headlong Hall, *sels.*
In His Last Binn Sir Peter Lies.
In the Days of Old.
Larissa.
Letter from School, A.
Lines from Crotchet Castle.
Love and Age.
Maid Marian, *sels.*
Margaret Love Peacock [for Her Tombstone, 1826].
Melincourt, *sels.*
Men of Gotham, The.
Merlin's Apple-Trees.
Misfortunes of Elphin, The, *sels.*
New Order of Chivalry, A.
Newark Abbey.
Nightmare Abbey, *sels.*
Priest and the Mulberry-Tree, The.
Rhododaphne, *sels.*
Rich and Poor; or, Saint and Sinner.
Seamen Three.
Song: "For the tender beech and the sapling oak."
Song: "In his last bin[n] Sir Peter lies."
Song: "It was a friar of orders free."
Song by Mr. Cypress.
Song of Gwythno.
Song of the Four Winds, The.
Sun-dial, The.
There Is a Fever of the Spirit.
Three Men of Gotham.
War Song of Dinas Vawr, The.
Wise Men of Gotham, The.
World, The.
Peake, Mervyn Laurence
My Uncle Paul of Pimlico.
Sensitive, Seldom and Sad.
Peale, Rembrandt
Don't Be Sorrowful, Darling.
Pearce, Ellen
Orange Tree, The.
Turtle's Belly, The.
Pearse, Mark Guy
Don't Trouble Trouble.
Facing the New Year.
Pearse, Padraic
Fool, The.
I Am Ireland.
Ideal.
Lullaby of the Woman of the Mountain.
Mother, The.
Rebel, The.
To Death.
Wayfarer, The.
Peavy, Linda
Riders.
Wisdom.

Peck, Elisabeth
Between the Walls of the Valley.
Walthena.
Peck, Harry Thurston
Heliotrope.
Other One, The.
Wonderland.
Peck, John
Cider and Vesalius.
Colophon for Lan-t'ing Hsiu-hsi.
Here Is a Song, *with music.*
Ringers, The.
Spring Festival on the River, The.
Watcher, The.
What If the Saint Must Die, *with music.*
Peck, Samuel Minturn
Autumn's Mirth.
Captain's Feather, The.
Kiss in the Rain, A.
My Little Girl.
Sassafras.
Southern Girl, A.
Pedroso, Regino
Opinions of the New Student.
Peele, George
And Who Has Seen a Fair Alluring Face.
Arraignment of Paris, The, *sels.*
Bethsabe's Song.
Celanta at the Well of Life.
Colin's Passion of Love.
David and Bethsabe, *sels.*
Dirge: "Welladay, welladay, poor Colin, thou art going to the ground."
Fair and Fair.
Fair Maiden.
Farewell to Arms.
Farewell to Sir John Norris and Sir Francis Drake, A.
Harvester's Song.
His Golden Locks Time Hath to Silver Turned.
Hunting of Cupid, The, *sels.*
Love.
Love of King David and Fair Bethsabe, The.
Not Iris in Her Pride.
O Gentle Love.
Oenone and Paris.
Oenone's Complaint.
Old Knight, The.
Old Wives' [*or* Wife's] Tale, The, *sels.*
Polyhymnia, *sel.*
Shepherd's Dirge, The.
Sonet, A: "His golden lockes, Time hath to silver turn'd."
Song: "Lo! here we come a-reaping, a-reaping."
Song: "When as the rye reach to the chin."
Song: "Whenas the rye reach to the chin."
Song at the Well, The.
Song of Coridon and Melampus.
Song of Oenone and Paris.
Spell, A.
Summer Song, A.
Voice from the Well of Life Speaks to the Maiden, The.
Voice Speaks from the Well, A.
What Thing Is Love?
When as the Rye.
Whenas [*or* When as] the Rye [Reach to the Chin].
Péguy, Charles
For the past three days she had been wandering, and following.
Happy Are Those Who Have Died.
Passion of Our Lady, The, *sel.*
Peifer, Mrs. Roy L.
Crucifixion.
Pell, Dewey G. *and* **Ern Alpaugh.** *See* **Alpaugh, Ern** *and* **Dewey G. Pell**
Pellew, George
Death.
On a Cast from an Antique.
Pellow, John Dynham Cornish
Temple of the Trees, The.
Peloubet, Maurice E.
Eternal Kinship, The.
Pembroke, Mary Sidney Herbert, Countess of
Antonius, *sel.*
If Ever Hapless Woman Had a Cause.
Of Death.
Pembroke, William Herbert, Earl of
Disdain Me Still.
Pence, Susan
Night Harvest.
Pendergast, James
Before the War.
Penfold, Gerda
La Pesadilla.
Lust for Murder, The.
Penkethman, John
Schoolmaster's Precepts, A.
Some Boys.
Pennant, Edmund
Hold My Hand.
Into & At.
Lost Explorer.
Pennecuik, Alexander
Marriage betwixt Scrape, Monarch of the Maunders, and Blobberlips, Queen of the Gypsies, A, *sel.*
Pennell, Henry Cholmondeley. *See* **Cholmondeley-Pennell, Henry**
Pennington, Lee
Before the Breaking.
Penny, Rob
And We Conquered.
Be Cool, Baby.
I Remember How She Sang.
Real People Loves One Another, The.
Penney, William Edward
Town of Nogood, The.
Penrose, Roland
Road Is Wider than Long, The, *sel.*
Penrose, Thomas
Helmets, The; a Fragment.
Percival, James Gates
Apostrophe to the Island of Cuba.
Coral Grove, The.
Elegiac.
It Is Great for Our Country to Die.
New England.
Percy, Thomas
O Nancy! Wilt Thou Go with Me.
Percy, William
Coelia, *sels.*
Sonnet: "It shall be said I died for Coelia!"
Sonnets to the Fairest Coelia.
Percy, William Alexander
Dirge: "Tuck the earth, fold the sod."
Epilogue: "Giver of bliss and pain, of song and prayer."
Farmers.
Hymn to the Sun.
In an Autumn Wood.
Little Shepherd's Song, The.
Overtones.
Page's Road Song, A.
They Cast Their Nets in Galilee, *with music.*
To an Old Tune.
To Butterfly.
Unloved to His Beloved, The.
Volunteer's Grave, A.
Wonder and a Thousand Springs.
Pereira, Francesca Yetunde
Burden, The.
Mother Dark.
Paradox, The.
Two Strange Worlds.
Péret, Benjamin
Little Song of the Maimed.
Making Feet and Hands.
Staircase with a Hundred Steps, The.
Peretz, Isaac [*or* Yitzchok] Leibush
All through the Stranger's Wood.
Believe Not.
Eternal Sabbath.
Hope and Faith.
In the Silent Night.
Little People.
Three Seamstresses, The.
Pérez de Ayala, Ramón
She Was a Pretty Little Girl.
Perez-Diotima, Leigh
Lake Walk at New Year's.
Perkins, David
Blue Gift, The.
Falling in Love.
"How Long Hast Thou Been a Gravemaker?"
Perkins, Emily Swan
Thou Art, O God, the God of Might, *with music.*
Perkins, James A.
Black Holes.
Perkins, Louis Saunders
Genius.
Perkins, Lucy Alice
"Laborers Together with God."
Perkins, Lucy Fitch
Honey Bee.
Perkins, Michael
Carpenter, The.
Perkins, Silas H.
Common Road, The.
Perkoff, Stuart Z.
Aleph.
Feasts of Death, Feasts of Love.
Flowers for Luis Bunuel.
Gimel.
Hai.
Recluses, The.
Perlberg, Mark
Hiroshige.
When at Night.
Perlin, Terry M.
Clarity of Apples, The.
Perlman, Anne S.
At Liberty.
Specialist, The.
Viking 1 on Mars—July 20, 1976.
Perlman, Jess
Winterscape.
Pernette du Guillet. *See* **Du Guillet, Pernette**
Perpetuo, Betty
Morning Prayer, A.
Perreault, Ellen
Those Trees That Line the Northway.
Perreault, John
Boomerang.
Metaphysical Paintings, The.
Readymade.
Shoe.
Perronet, Edward
All Hail the Power of Jesus' Name.
Coronation.
Perry, Georgette
Recognition.
Perry, Gordon
Aids for Latin.
Great Lakes of Canada, The.
Perry, Julianne
No Dawns.
To L.
Perry, Lilla Cabot
Art.
As It Was.
As She Feared It Would Be.
Life and Death.
Meeting after Long Absence, *sels.*
Perry, Martha Eugenie
Lonely Shell, The.
Mainspring, The.
Water-Witch, The.
Perry, Nora
Balboa.
Coming of Spring, The.
Coming of the Spring, The.
Cressid.
In June.

Love-Knot, The.
Riding Down.
Running the Blockade.
Some Day of Days.
Who Knows?

Perry, Ronald
Prologue for a Bestiary.
Shellpicker, The.
Still-Life.

Perry, Tod
For Nicholas, Born in September.

"Perse, St.-John" (Alexis Saint-Léger Léger)
Anabasis, *sel.*
Song: Under the Bronze Leaves.

Persius (Aulus Persius Flaccus)
Prologue to the First Satire.
Satires, *sel.*

Peseroff, Joyce
Hardness Scale, The.

Peskett, William
Photographs.

Pestel [*or* Pestell], Thomas
On Tobacco.
Psalm for Christmas Day.
Psalm for Sunday Night, A.
Relief on Easter Eve, The.
Song: "Silly boy, there is no cause."

Petaccia, Mario
Death in the Streets, A.
How to Find Your Way Home.
Leaving Raiford.
Six Days.
Walking on Water.

"Peter"
George III Visits Whitbread's Brewery.
Out of the Dark Wood.

Peters, Lenrie
After They Put Down Their Overalls.

Peters, Patricia
In Grandfather's Glasses.

Peters, Phillis Wheatley. *See* **Wheatley, Phillis**

Peters, Robert
Allen Ginsberg Blesses a Bride and Groom; a Wedding Night Poem.
Arrival, New York Harbor.
Beach, The.
Blessing a Bride and Groom; a Wedding Night Poem.
Buying a Record.
Claremont.
Crazy Bill to the Bishop.
Darkling Chicken, The.
Feathered Friends.
Final Soliloquy on a Randy Rooster (in a Key of Yellow).
I, Lessimus, of Salt Lake City.
Meeting Mick Jagger.
Melon-Slaughterer; or, A Sick Man's Praise for a Well Woman.
Reflecting on the Aging-Process.
Study in Aesthetics, A.

Petersen, Donald
Ballad of Dead Yankees, The.
Narcissus.
Sonnet in Autumn.
True to a Dream.
Walking along the Hudson.

Peterson, Arthur
Kelpius's Hymn.

Peterson, Elizabeth
Lesson, The.

Peterson, Frederick ("Pai Ta-shun")
Bridge, The.
Solitude.
Wild Geese.

Peterson, Henry
Death of Lyon, The.
Ode for Decoration Day.
Rinaldo.

Peterson, M.
Kitchen Prayer, A.

Peterson, Mattie J.
I Kissed Pa Twice after His Death.

Peterson, Peter
On First Looking into Chapman's Homer II, *parody.*

Peterson, Robert
At Veronica's.
Dear America.
For the Minority.
Groom's Lament, The.
Hands folded like napkins in my lap.
Highway Patrol Stops Me, Going Too Slow.
In the 2 A.M. Club, a working man's bar.
Robert's Rules of Order.
Swim in Ohuira Bay, A.
To Myself, Late, in a Myrtle Grove.
Wingwalking in Oregon.
Young Conquistador, The.

Peterson, Ruth Delong
Midwest Town.

Petrarch (Francesco Petrarca)
Bicause I have the still kept fro lyes and blame.
Description of the Contrarious Passions in a Lover.
Ever myn happe is slack and slo in commyng.
He Understands the Great Cruelty of Death.
Heart on the Hill, The.
If It Be Destined.
In Wintry Midnight, o'er a Stormy Main.
Last Trial, The.
Love That Doth Reign and Live within My Thought.
Lover Compareth His State to a Ship in Perilous Storm Tossed on the Sea, The.
Lover for Shamefastnesse Hideth His Desire within His Faithfull Hart, The.
Love's Fidelity.
Love's Inconsistency.
My Galley Charged with Forgetfulness.
Nightingale, The.
Ode to the Virgin.
Signs of Love.
Sonnet: "I find no peace, and all my war is done."
Sonnets to Laura, *sels.*
To His Lady.
Translation from Petrarch ("Mine old dear enemy, my froward master").
Translation from Petrarch ("What a grudge I am bearing").
Visions [of Petrarch], The.
Vow to Love Faithfully [Howsoever He Be Rewarded], A.

Petri, Paul
Dream, The.

Petrie, Paul
Church of San Antonio de la Florida, The.
Enigma Variations, The.
From the Point.
Murderer, The.
Not Seeing Is Believing.
Old Pro's Lament, The.
Phases of Darkness, The.
Story from Another World.

Petröczi, Kata Szidónia
Swift Floods.

Petronius Arbiter (Caius Petronius Arbiter)
Against Consummation.
Doing, a Filthy Pleasure Is, and Short.
Encouragement to Exile.
Fragmentum Petronius Arbiter, Translated.
Good God, What a Night That Was.
Malady of Love Is Nerves, The.
Plea for Haste, A.
Plea for Postponement, A.
We Are Such Stuff as Dreams.

Petroski, Henry
Chairs.
Horse-Girl.

Petrosky, Anthony
Jurgis Petrakas, the Workers' Angel, Organizes the First Miner's Strike in Exeter, Pennsylvania.

Petrova, Olga
To a Child Who Inquires.

Petrykewycz, Susan
Home Again.
Remembering Home.

Pett, Stephen
Trench.

Pettengill, Margaret Miller
There Will Be Peace.

Pettingell, Phoebe
Frog Prince.
Ode on Zero.

Pettit, Michael
A Cappella.
Day in My Union Suit, A.
Fire and Ice.
Herdsman.
Poker Poem.
Sunday Stroll.

Pevear, Richard
Ovid.

Pfeiffer, Edward Heyman
Soul Speaks, The.

Pfingston, Roger
About the Cows.
Entering the Room.
Photographer, The.
State Fair Pigs.
Waiting for Nighthawks in Illinois.

Pflum, Richard
Home in Indianapolis.

Phaedrus
Aesop at Play.
Dog in the River, The.
Man and the Weasel, The.
Purpose of Fable-writing, The.

Phair, George E.
Old-fashioned Pitcher, The.

Phelps, Arthur Leonard
Wall, The.

Phelps, Charles Henry
Henry Ward Beecher.
Rare Moments.
Yuma.

Phelps, Elizabeth Stuart. *See* **Ward, Elizabeth Stuart Phelps**

Phelps, Sylvanus D.
Saviour, Thy Dying Love, *with music.*
Something for Jesus.

Philbrick, Charles
New England Suite.

Philbrick, Stephen
Leaving Here.

Philemon
Recipe: Onions.

Philip, Sister Mary
Poet's Bread.
To-Day.

Philip of Thessalonica
Epigram: "You were a pretty boy once, Archestratus, and."

Philipott, Thomas
On the Death of a Prince; a Meditation.
On the Nativity of Our Saviour.

Philipps, Stephen
Poet's Prayer, The.

Philipps [*or* Phillipps], Thomas
I Love a Flower
Peace of the Roses, The.

Philips, Ambrose
Happy Swain, The.
Pastoral Landscape.
Pastorals, *sel.*
To Charlotte Pulteney.
To Miss Charlotte Pulteney in Her Mother's Arms.
To Signora Cuzzoni.
To the Earl of Dorset.
To the Memory of Lord Halifax, *sel.*
Winter-Piece, A.

Philips, Joan. *See* **"Ephelia"**
Philips, John
Blenheim, *sel.*
Cyder, *sels.*
How to Catch Wasps.
Pruning.
Splendid Shilling, The.
Thirsty Poet, The.
War Poetry.
Philips, Katherine ("Orinda")
Against Love.
Answer to Another Persuading a Lady to Marriage, An.
Friendship's Mystery [to My Dearest Lucasia].
Lucasia, Rosania and Orinda Parting at a Fountain, July 1663.
Orinda to Lucasia.
Orinda to Lucasia Parting, October, 1661, at London.
Parting with Lucasia; a Song.
Sea-Voyage from Tenby to Bristol, A.
To Antenor.
To Mr. Henry Lawes.
To My Excellent Lucasia, on Our Friendship.
To My Lucasia, in Defence of Declared Friendship.
To One Persuading a Lady to Marriage.
Upon Absence.
Upon the Double Murther of King Charles I.
Philips, Louis
78 Miners in Mannington, West Virginia.
Phillimore, John Swinnerton
In a Meadow.
Phillip, John
Lullaby: "Lullaby baby, lullaby baby."
Phillipps, Thomas. *See* **Philipps, Thomas**
Phillips, Cleve
Up against the Wall.
Phillips, David
Fighting Her.
Lover to Himself, The.
Notes on a Long Evening.
Old Storm.
Orange Juice Song.
Things of Late.
Wave, The.
Words.
Phillips, Frank Lamont
Daybreak.
Genealogy.
Maryuma.
No Smiles.
Special Moment, A.
Phillips, Harriet C.
We Bring No Glittering Treasures, *with music.*
Phillips, Homer
Handyman.
Phillips, J. A.
Factory Girl, The.
Phillips, Louis
Considering the Death of John Wayne.
Day at the Races, A.
Phillips, Marie Tello
Sorrow.
Phillips, Patrice
Function Room, The.
Phillips, Robert
Death of Janis Joplin, The.
Decks.
Inside and Out.
Letter to Auden, A.
Lump.
Married Man, The.
Miss Crustacean.
Persistence of Memory, the Failure of Poetry, The.
Six Haiku for Graham V. Phillips Who First Said the First One.
Vital Message.
Phillips, Rodney
Out of You.
Phillips, Stephen
Apparition, The.
Grief and God.
Phillips, Susan Kelly
Rose of Eden, The.
Phillpotts, Eden
Houses, The.
Man's Days.
Puddle, The.
Philodemos the Epicurean
Remonstrance.
Philpot, William
Maritae Suae.
Phocas, Nikos
Diver, The.
Piatt, John James
Child in the Street, The.
Dear President, The.
Farther.
Guerdon, The.
Ireland.
Leaves at My Window.
Lost Genius, The.
Mower in Ohio, The.
October Morning.
Purpose.
Rose and Root.
To a Lady.
To Abraham Lincoln.
Torch-Light in Autumn.
Piatt, Sarah Morgan Bryan
After Wings.
Call on Sir Walter Raleigh, A.
In Clonmel Parish Churchyard.
Into the World and Out ("Into the world he looked with sweet surprise").
Irish Wild-Flower, An.
My Babes in the Wood.
Term of Death, The.
Tradition of Conquest.
Transfigured.
Watch of a Swan, The.
Witch in the Glass, The.
Picano, Felice
Gilded Boys, The.
Heart Has Its Reasons, The.
Picasso, Pablo
Poem: "Hasten on your childhood to the hour when white."
Poem: "In secret."
Poem: "In the corner a violet jug the bells the folds of paper."
Piccione, Anthony
Raquette River, Potsdam, New York, The; Lying on a Rock Drinking Scotch while My Friends Fish Upstream.
Pichaske, David R.
H. S. Beeney Auction Sales.
Reflections.
Pickard, Cynthia
Cinderella.
Pickard, Deanna Louise
Old Polish Lesson, An.
Voyeur, The.
Pickard, Tom
Rape.
Pickering [*or* Pikeryng], John
Haltersick's Song.
Horestes, *sel.*
Song: "Farewell, adieu, that court-like life!"
Pickthall, Marjorie Lowry Christie
Bega.
Bridegroom of Cana, The.
Child's Song of Christmas, A.
Duna.
Ebb Tide.
I Sat among the Green Leaves.
Immortal, The.
Lamp of Poor Souls, The.
Little Sister of the Prophet, The.
Little Songs.
Lovers of Marchaid, The.
Mary Tired.
Mary Shepherdess.
Mother in Egypt, A.
On Amaryllis, a Tortoyse.
Père Lalemant.
Quiet.
Resurgam.
Swallow Song.
Two Souls.
Picot, James
Lord in the Wind, The.
Volume of Chopin, A.
Piddington, R. A.
Literary Zodiac.
Tudor Aspersions.
Pierce, Dorothy Mason
Good Night.
Sprinkling.
Pierce, Edith Lovejoy
Christmas Amnesty.
Great Powers Conference.
In the Wilderness.
Let Me Not Die.
O Christ, Thou Art within Me Like a Sea.
Prayer: "Bear with me, Master, when I turn from Thee."
Prayer for the Useless Days.
Song of the Wise Men.
Supplication.
Pierce, Jason Noble
Which Sword?
Piercy, Marge
Apron Strings.
Barbie Doll.
Beauty I Would Suffer For.
Burying Blues for Janis.
Common Living Dirt, The.
Councils.
For the Young Who Want To.
Friend, The.
Going In.
Gracious Goodness.
Hare in Winter.
Hummingbird.
I Awoke with the Room Cold.
Inside Chance, The.
Insomnia.
Kneeling Here, I Feel Good.
Learning Experience.
Let Us Gather at the River.
Letter to Be Disguised as a Gas Bill.
Looking at Quilts.
Low Road, The.
Market Economy, The.
Night Letter.
Noon of the Sunbather.
Nothing More Will Happen.
Peaceable Kingdom, The.
Proposal for Recycling Wastes, A.
Quiet Fog, The.
Rape Poem.
Root Canal, The.
Simple-Song.
16/53.
Snow, Snow.
Someplace Else.
Song of the Fucked Duck.
Spring Offensive of the Snail, The.
To Be of Use.
To the Pay Toilet.
Total Influence or Outcome of the Matter, The: The Sun.
Unclench Yourself.
Valley Where I Don't Belong, A.
Watch, The.
We Become New.
Why the Soup Tastes like the Daily News.
Woman in the, The.
Work of Artifice, A.
Pierpont, James S.
Jingle Bells.
We Conquer or Die.

Pierpont, John
Ballot, The.
Centennial Hymn.
Exile at Rest, The.
Fourth of July, The.
Fugitive Slave's Apostrophe to the North Star, The.
General Joseph Warren's Address.
Kidnapping of Sims, The.
My Child.
On Laying the Corner-Stone of the Bunker Hill Monument.
Pilgrim Fathers, The.
Warren's Address [at Bunker Hill].
Whittling.
Pierson, Philip
Technique.
Pietri, Pedro Juan
Night Has Twenty-four Hours, The.
Silent Movies.
Underground Poetry.
You Jump First.
Piety, Chauncey Roscoe
Come Back, Lincoln.
Gifts.
New Patriotism, A.
Soul of Lincoln, The.
Thanksliving.
Pigott, Mostyn T.
Hundred Best Books, The.
Pijewski, John
Labor Camp, The.
Pike, Albert
Buena Vista.
Dixie ("Southrons, hear your country call you").
Song of the Navajo.
To the Mocking-Bird.
Widowed Heart, The.
Pikeryng, John. *See* **Pickering, John**
Pilbosian, Helene
With the Bait of Bread.
Pilinszky, János
Desert of Love, The.
Fable: "Once upon a time/ there was a lonely wolf."
Pilkington, Francis
O Softly Singing Lute.
Pilkington, Laetitia
Song: "Lying is an occupation."
Pilkington, Lawrence
What Called Me to the Heights.
Pillen [*or* Pillin], William
Akriel's Consolation.
Farewell to Europe.
Night Poem in an Abandoned Music Room.
O, Beautiful They Move.
Ode on a Decision to Settle for Less.
Poem: "To be sad in the morning."
Poem for Anton Schmidt, A.
Pilling, Christopher
Adoration of the Magi, The.
Pilz, J. Michael
Renoir's Confidences.
Pincas, Israel
Mediterranean.
Pindar
Island of the Blest, The.
Life after Death.
Ode on Theoxenos.
Odes, *sel.*
"Pindar, Peter" (John Wolcott)
Apple Dumplings and a King, The.
Bozzy and Piozzi, *sel.*
Epigram: "Midas, they say, possessed the art of old."
George III and the Sailor.
Instructions to a Celebrated Laureat, *sel.*
Introduction and Anecdotes.
Ode: "That I have often been in love, deep love."
Ode to a Country Hoyden.
Razor-Seller, The.
Resignation; an Ode to the Journeyman Shoemakers, *sel.*
Royal Tour, and Weymouth Amusements, The, *abr.*
Sorrows of Sunday, The; an Elegy, *sel.*
To a Fly, Taken out of a Bowl of Punch.
To a Kiss.
Tray's Epitaph.
Piñero, Miguel
There Is Nothing New in New York.
"Ping Hsin" (Hsieh Wang-ying)
Falling star, The.
Multitudinous Stars, *sel.*
Orphan beat of my heart, The.
Spring Waters, *sels.*
Stars, The, *sels.*
Three Poems, *sel.*
"Pink"
Groaning Board, The.
Pinkerton, H. A.
Degrees of Shade.
Deprivation.
Error Pursued.
Prism, The.
Pinkerton, Helen
Indecision.
Pinkham, Cora M.
God's Ideal Mother.
With Thee.
Pinkney, Dorothy Cowles
Dame Liberty Reports from Travel.
Pinkney, Edward Coote [*or* Coate]
Health, A.
Serenade, A: "Look out upon the stars, my love."
Song: "We break the glass, whose sacred wine."
Votive Song.
Pinsker, Sanford
For Allen Ginsberg, Who Cut Off His Beard.
Untitled Poem, about an Uncompleted Sonnet, An.
Pinsky, Robert
Changes, The.
December Blues.
Discretions of Alcibiades.
Dying.
Essay on Psychiatrists, *sel.*
Explanation of America, An, *sel.*
Faeryland.
Figured Wheel, The.
History of My Heart.
Local Politics.
New Saddhus, The.
Poem about People.
Questions, The.
Ralegh's Prizes.
Serpent Knowledge.
Street, The.
Their Speech, Compared with Wisdom and Poetry.
Pinto, Vivian de Sola. *See* **Sola Pinto, Vivian de.**
Piper, Edwin Ford
Bindlestiff.
Church, The.
Gee-up Dar, Mules.
Piper, Linda
Missionaries in the Jungle.
Sweet Ethel.
Piron, Alexis
Here lies Piron—a man of no position.
Pisan, Christine de
Alone am I, and alone I wish to be.
Christine to Her Son.
Epistle of Othea to Hector, The (A Lytil Bibell of Knyghthod), *sel.*
Fountain of tears, river of grief.
I am a widow, robed in black, alone.
If Frequently to Mass.
I'll always dress in black and rave.
Marriage is a lovely thing.
Pise, Constantine
Let the Deep Organ Swell, *with music.*
Pistoia, Cino da *See* **Cino da Pistoia**
Pitcher, Oliver
Pale Blue Casket, The.
Raison d'Etre.
Salute.
Pitchford, Kenneth
Aunt Cora.
Blizzard Ape, The.
Blues Ballad.
Death Swoops.
Good for Nothing Man, *sels.*
Homosexual Sonnets.
Jacqueline Gray.
Leviathan; a Poem in Four Movements.
Lobotomy.
Off Viareggio.
104 Boulevard Saint-Germain.
Onion Skin, The.
Pickup in Tony's Hashhouse.
Queen, The.
Reflections on Water.
Young Buck's Sunday Blues.
Pitkin, Anne
Homes, The.
Pitt, Christopher
On the Masquerades.
Pitt, Marie Elizabeth Josephine
Gallop of Fire, A.
Pitt, William
Sailor's Consolation, The.
Pitter, Ruth
Bat, The.
Beautiful Negress, The.
But for Lust.
Coffin-Worm, The.
Dun-Colour.
Estuary, The.
Eternal Image, The.
For Sleep, or Death.
Help, Good Shepherd.
Hen under Bay-Tree.
Lost Tribe, The.
Military Harpist, The.
Old Woman Speaks of the Moon, An.
Rainy Summer.
Solemn Meditation, A.
Sparrow's Skull, The.
Stockdove, The.
Swan Bathing, The.
Task, The.
Three Cheers for the Black, White and Blue.
Time's Fool.
To J. S. Collis.
Unicorn, The.
Urania.
Viper, The.
Pittis, William
Battle Royal between Dr. Sherlock, Dr. South, and Dr. Burnet, The.
Pitts, William S.
Little Brown Church in the Vale.
Piuvkaq [*or* Pluvkag[
It Is Hard to Catch Trout.
Mocking Song against Qaqortingneq.
Pixner, Stef
Day in the Life, A.
Pizarnik, Alejandra
Apart from Oneself.
Dawn.
Fear.
Mask and the Poem, The.
Privilege.
Tree of Diana, The.
Vertigos or Contemplation of Something That Is Over.
Who Will Stop His Hand from Giving Warmth.
"Plácido" (Gabriel de la Concepción Valdés)
Farewell to My Mother.
Prayer to God.
Planché, James Robinson
Ching a Ring.
Literary Squabble, A.

Love, You've Been a Villain.
Sea-Serpent, The.
To Mollidusta.
Plantenga, Bart
Fire. 10/78.
Plantier, Therese
Doors.
Overdue Balance Sheet.
Planz, Allen
Handlining Tockers & Gizmos.
12 Oct.
Plarr, Victor
Che Sara Sara.
Epitaphium Citharistriae.
Stand Not Uttering Sedately.
Platen, August, Graf von (Karl August Georg Maximilian, Graf von Platen-Hallermünde)
Sonnets to Karl Theodore German, *sels.*
To Bülow.
To Liebig ("Longing for that true comrade of my need").
To Liebig ("Who feels a growing hunger for fair eyes").
To Rotenham.
To Schmidlein.
Plath, Sylvia
Aftermath.
All the Dead Dears.
Amnesiac.
Among the Narcissi.
Appearance, An.
Applicant, The.
Ariel.
Arrival of the Bee Box, The.
Babysitters, The.
Balloons.
Bed Book, The, *sel.*
Bee Meeting, The.
Beekeeper's Daughter, The.
Black Rook in Rainy Weather.
Blackberrying.
Blue Moles.
By Candlelight.
Candles.
Child.
Cinderella.
Colossus, The.
Couriers, The.
Cut.
Daddy.
Death and Co.
Death of Myth-making, The.
Disquieting Muses, The.
Edge.
Elm.
Elm Speaks, The.
Event.
Face Lift.
Fever 103°.
Flute Notes from a Reedy Pond.
Full Fathom Five.
Ghost's Leavetaking, The.
Gulliver.
Hardcastle Crags.
Lady Lazarus.
Last Words.
Life, A.
Love Letter.
Manor Garden, The.
Mary's Song.
Medallion.
Medusa.
Memoirs of a Spinach-Picker.
Metamorphosis.
Metaphors.
Mirror.
Moon and the Yew Tree, The.
Morning Song.
Munich Mannequins, The.
Mushrooms.
Mussel Hunter at Rock Harbor.
Mystic.
Nick and the Candlestick.
Night Dances, The.
Night Walk.
Point Shirley.
Poppies in July.
Poppies in October.
Rabbit Catcher, The.
Rival, The.
Sheep in Fog.
Sleep in the Mojave Desert.
Snakecharmer.
Stars over the Dordogne.
Stings.
Stones, The.
Suicide off Egg Rock.
Three Women.
Tulips.
Two Campers in Cloud Country.
Two Views of a Cadaver Room.
Water Color of Grantchester Meadows.
Winter Trees.
Wintering.
Words.
You're.
Plato
Apple, The, *at.*
Aster ("My star, star-gazing?—if only I could be").
Aster ("You were the morning star among the living").
Epigram: "All I said was—Alexis is gorgeous."
Epigram: "For Hekabê and the women of Ilion."
Farewell: "Far from the deep roar of the Aegean main."
Inner Man, The.
Kissing Helena.
Love Sleeping.
Morning and Evening Star.
On a Seal.
On Alexis.
On Archaeanassa.
On the Athenian Dead at Ecbatana.
Pan Piping.
To Stella.
Plato, Ann
Natives of America, The.
Reflections, Written on Visiting the Grave of a Venerated Friend.
To the First of August.
Platov, Mariquita
Whispering Clouds.
Playford, John
Jovial Marriner, The; or, The Sea-Man's Renown.
Plescoff, Jorge
Ladder Has No Steps, The.
Ourobouros.
Tongues of Fire.
Violins in Repose.
Plimpton, Florus B.
Fort Duquesne.
Plomer, William
Archaic Apollo.
Atheling Grange; or, The Apotheosis of Lotte Nussbaum.
Bamboo.
Blind Samson.
Caledonian Market, The.
Death of a Snake, The.
Devil-Dancers, The.
Europa.
Father and Son: 1939.
Flying Bum, The: 1944.
French Lisette; a Ballad of Maida Vale.
Ganymede.
Headline History.
In the Snake Park.
Levantine, A.
Mews Flat Mona.
Playboy of the Demi-World, The: 1938.
Positive, a Coxcomb.
Prisoner, The.
Right-of-Way, A: 1865.
Scorpion, The.
September Evening, 1938.
Seven Rainy Months.
Shot in the Park, A.
Tattooed.
To the Moon and Back.
Ula Masondo's Dream.
Walk in Würzburg, A.
Widow's Plot, The; or, She Got What Was Coming to Her.
Plowman, Max
Her Beauty.
Plumly, Stanley
After Grief.
American Ash.
Another November.
Blossom.
Early Meadow-Rue.
End of the Indian Poems, The.
Fifth and 94th.
For Esther.
Fungo.
Giraffe.
Heron.
Iron Lung, The.
My Mother's Feet.
Now That My Father Lies Down beside Me.
Out-of-the-Body Travel.
Peppergrass.
Posthumous Keats.
Virginia Beach.
Waders and Swimmers.
Wildflower.
Plummer, Mary Wright
Irrevocable.
Plumpp, Sterling
Beyond the Nigger ("Beyond the outstretched hands").
For Mattie and Eternity.
Half Black, Half Blacker.
I Told Jesus.
Living Truth, The.
Plumptre, Annabella
Ode to Moderation, *sel.*
Plumptre, James
Prologue to "The Lakers; a Comic Opera," *sel.*
Plunkett, Edward John Moreton Drax. *See* Dunsany
Plunkett, Joseph Mary
Claim That Has the Canker on the Rose, The.
I See His Blood upon the Rose.
My Lady Has the Grace of Death.
Our Heritage.
See the Crocus' Golden Cup.
Sic Transit.
Spark, The.
This Heritage to the Race of Kings.
To G. K. Chesterton.
White Dove of the Wild Dark Eyes.
Plutzik, Hyam
Airman Who Flew over Shakespeare's England, The.
Begetting of Cain, The.
Geese, The.
I Am Disquieted When I See Many Hills.
Importance of Poetry, or the Coming Forth from Eternity into Time, The.
Jim Desterland.
King of Ai, The.
Mythos of Samuel Huntsman, The.
Of Objects Considered as Fortresses in a Baleful Place.
On the Photograph of a Man I Never Saw.
To My Daughter.
Pluvkag. *See* **Piuvkaq.**
Po Chü-i
Cranes, The.
Eating Bamboo-Shoots.
Flower Market, The.
Invitation to Hsiao Ch'u-shih.

Lazy Man's Song.
Letter, The.
Lodging with the Old Man of the Stream.
Losing a Slave-Girl.
Old Charcoal Seller, An.
On Being Sixty.
People of Tao-chou, The.
Planting Flowers on the Eastern Embankment.
Red Cockatoo, The.
Rejoicing at the Arrival of Chi'en Hsiung.
Remembering Golden Bells.
Starting Early from the Ch'u-ch'êng Inn.
Temple, The.
To Li Chien.
Pocock, Isaac
Heir of Vironi, The, *sel.*
Song: "Oh! say not woman's love is bought."
Poe, Edgar Allan
Al Aaraaf.
Annabel Lee.
Assignation, The, *sel.*
Bells, The.
Coliseum, The.
Conqueror Worm, The.
Doomed City, The.
Dream within a Dream, A.
Dream-Land.
Dreams.
Eldorado.
Eulalie.
Evening Star.
Fall of the House of Usher, The, *sel.*
For Annie.
From Childhood's Hour.
Happiest Day, the Happiest Hour, The.
Haunted Palace, The.
Hymn: "At morn, at noon, at twilight dim."
Introduction: "Romance, who loves to nod and sing."
Israfel.
Lake, The.
Lenore.
Ligeia, *prose tale, sel.*
Raven, The.
Romance.
Sleeper, The.
Song: "Young flowers were whispering in melody."
Song from "Al Aaraaf."
Sonnet to Science.
Sonnet—Silence.
Tamerlane.
To Helen.
To My Mother.
To One in Paradise.
Ulalume—a Ballad.
Valley of Unrest, The.
Polite, Allen
Am Driven Mad.
Stopped.
Polite, Frank
Carmen Miranda.
Imitations Based on the American.
Lantern.
Mine.
Poliziano, Angelo [*or* Andrea] (Politian)
Three Ballate.
Unto the Breach.
Polk, Noel
Wreck.
Pollak, Felix
Dial Tone.
Speaking: The Hero.
Stone and the Obliging Pond.
Widow.
Pollard, Adelaide A.
Secret Place, The.
Pollard, Josephine
Price of a Drink.
Pollitt, Katha
Archaeology.
Composition in Black and White.
Discussion of the Vicissitudes of History under a Pine Tree, A.
In Memory.
Night Blooming Flowers.
Riverside Drive, November Fifth.
Seal Rock.
Turning Thirty.
Woman Asleep on a Banana Leaf.
Pollock, Edward
Olivia.
Pollock, John Hackett. *See* "An Pilibín"
Pollock, Walter Herries
Conquest, A.
Pollok, Robert
Ocean.
Polonsky, Yakov Petrovich
Cosmic Fabric, The.
Polson, Don
Sons.
Polwhele, Richard
Influence of Local Attachment, The, *sel.*
Visit to the Author's Paternal Seat, A.
Pomerantz, Berl
End of Summer.
Young Virgins Plucked Suddenly.
Pomerantz, Marsha
Adam and Eve at the Garden Gate.
How to Reach the Moon
Pomeroy, Marnie
April Fools' Day.
Ground Hog Day.
Halloween.
In Nakedness.
January 1.
Labor Day.
News.
Pomeroy, Ralph
Between Here and Illinois.
Confession.
Corner.
English Train, Summer.
Gone.
High Wind at the Battery.
In Hotels Public and Private.
In the Redwood Forest.
Islands.
Leather Bar, The.
Letter to Pasternak.
Looking at the Empire State Building.
Near Drowning.
Patrol.
Snow.
Tardy Epithalamium for E. and N., A.
To Janet.
To My Father.
To Words.
Trying to Sleep.
Pomfret, John
Choice, The.
Pomfret, Richard
July Wakes.
Pompili, Vittoria Aganoor
Fear.
Finally.
Ponciano, Angelo de
Empties Coming Back.
Ponge, Francis
Delights of the Door, The.
End of Fall, The.
Horse, The.
Oyster, The ("The oyster, about as large as a medium-sized stone").
Trees Lose Parts of Themselves inside a Circle of Fog.
Ponsot, Marie
Communion of Saints: The Poor Bastard under the Bridge.
Multipara: Gravida 5.
Possession.
Subject.
To the Age's Insanities.
Ponting, Herbert George
Sleeping-bag, The.
Poole, John
Song, *Hamlet.*
Poole, Tom
I/ wonder why/ some.
Poor Wolf
Poor Wolf Speaks.
Pope, Alexander
Alley, The; an Imitation of Spenser.
Alps on Alps.
Ambition.
Apologia pro Vita Sua.
As the Twig Is Bent.
At Timon's Villa.
Atticus.
Balance of Europe, The.
Bounce to Fop; an Heroick Epistle from a Dog at Twickenham to a Dog at Court.
Bufo.
Carnations and Butterflies.
Challenge, The.
Chaos.
Characters of Women: Flavia, Atossa, and Cloe.
Charity.
Chloe.
Contented Man, The.
Court of Charles II, The.
Coxcomb Bird, The.
Death of Buckingham, The.
Defence of Satire, The.
Descend, Ye Nine.
Dialogue, A.
Dire Dilemma, A.
Domicile of John, The.
Duke of Buckingham, The.
Dull, Sullen Prisoners.
Dying Christian to His Soul, The.
Elegy to the Memory of an Unfortunate Lady.
Eloïsa to Abelard.
Epigram: "Sir, I admit your general rule," *at.*
Epigram; "When other ladies to the shades go down."
Epigram: "You beat your pate, and fancy wit will come."
Epigram Engraved on the Collar of a Dog Given to His Royal Highness.
Epigram in a Maid of Honour's Prayer-Book.
Epigram on One Who Made Long Epitaphs.
Epilogue to the Satires [*or* 1738].
Epistle to a Lady: Of the Characters of Women.
Epistle to Miss [*or* Miss Teresa] Blount, on Her Leaving the Town after the Coronation.
Epistle to Richard Boyle, Earl of Burlington, An.
Epistle to Sir Richard Temple, *sel.*
Epitaph: "Nature and Nature's laws lay hid in night."
Epitaph for One Who Would Not Be Buried in Westminster Abbey.
Epitaph on Himself.
Epitaph on James Moore Smythe.
Epitaph on Sir Isaac Newton.
Essay on Criticism, An.
Essay on Man, An,
Faith.
Field Sports.
First Epistle of the First Book of Horace Imitated, The, *sel.*
First Epistle of the Second Book of Horace [Imitated], *sels.*
First Satire of the Second Book of Horace, The.
Gem and the Flower, The.
Hampton Court.
Happy Life of a Country Parson, The.
Heaven's Last Best Work.
Henry St. John, Viscount Bolingbroke.
Honest Fame.
Honest Man, An.
Hope ("Hope springs eternal in the human breast").
Hope humbly then; with trembling pinions soar.

Hope Springs Eternal ("Heav'n from all creatures hides the book of fate").
Human Folly.
Hunt, The.
Hymn Written in Windsor Forest, A.
Ideals of Satire, The.
Imitation of Chaucer.
In wit, as nature, what affects our hearts.
Intended for Sir Isaac Newton.
Know Then Thyself.
Life's Poor Play.
Lines by a Person of Quality, *at.*
Lines on Bounce.
Lines on Swift's Ancestors.
Lines Written in Windsor Forest.
Little Learning, A.
Lo, the Poor Indian!
Lock, The.
Lord Coningsby's Epitaph.
Messiah.
Moral Essays, *sels.*
Most Souls, 'Tis True, but Peep Out Once an Age.
Nature and Art.
Ode for Music on St. Cecilia's Day, *sel.*
Ode on [*or* to] Solitude.
Ode to Quinbus Flestrin.
Ode to Solitude.
Of the Characters of Women.
Of the Use of Riches.
Ombre at Hampton Court.
On a Certain Lady at Court.
On Authors and Booksellers.
On Certain Ladies.
On Dennis.
On J. M. S. Gent.
On Mr. Gay, in Westminster Abbey, 1732.
On Poets.
On Queen Caroline's Deathbed.
On the Benefactions in the Late Frost.
On the Candidates for the Laurel.
On the Erection of Shakespeare's Statue in Westminster Abbey.
One Thousand Seven Hundred and Thirty Eight.
Paragon of Animals, The.
Paraphrase on Thomas á Kempis, A.
Pastorals, *sel.*
Playing Cards, The.
Pleasure of Hope, The.
Poetical Numbers.
Poet's Use, The.
Power of Ridicule, The.
Prayer of St. Francis Xavier.
Pride, the Never-failing Vice of Fools.
Proper Study of Man [*or* Mankind], The.
Question of Libel, A.
Quiet Life, The.
Quoth Cibber to Pope, tho' in verse you foreclose.
Rape of the Lock, The.
Reign of Chaos, The.
Riddle of the World.
Rise, Crowned with Light.
Satire: "Ask you what provocation I have had?"
Second Epistle of the Essay on Man, The.
Second Satire of the First Book of Horace Imitated, The, *sel.*
Solitude.
Soul's Calm Sunshine, The.
Sound and Sense ("But most by numbers judge a poet's song").
Sound and Sense ("True ease in writing comes from art, not chance").
Sporus.
Sylvan Delights.
Temple of Fame, The, *sel.*
Three Epitaphs on John Hewet and Sarah Drew.
Timon's Villa.
To a Lady; of the Characters of Women.
To a Young Lady on Her Leaving the Town after the Coronation.
To Augustus, *sels.*
To Dr. Arbuthnot.
To Mr. Gay, Who Wrote Him a Congratulatory Letter on the Finishing of His House.
To Mr. Jervas, with Fresnoy's Art of Painting, Translated by Mr. Dryden.
To Mrs. M. B. on Her Birth-Day.
To Richard Boyle, Earl of Burlington: Of the Use of Riches.
To Robert Earl of Oxford and Earl Mortimer.
Toilet, The.
Tom Southerne's Birth-Day Dinner at Ld. Orrery's.
Triumph of Dullness [*or* Dulness], The.
Triumph of Vice, The.
Two or Three; a Recipe [*or* Receipt] to Make a Cuckold.
Universal Prayer, The.
Verbal Critics.
Verbatim from Boileau.
Vestal, The.
Vice ("Vice is a monster of so frightful mien").
Vital Spark of Heavenly Flame.
Voyage on the Thames, The.
Wharton.
Whatever Is, Is Right.
Why Did I Write?
Wild Garden, The.
Windsor Forest, *sels.*
Woman's Ruling Passions.
Young Traveller Is Presented to the Goddess Dulness, A.
1738.

Pope, Alexander, *and* **John Gay.** *See* **Gay, John,** *and* **Alexander Pope**

Pope, Alexander, *and* Thomas Parnell. *See* **Parnell, Thomas,** *and* **Alexander Pope**

Pope, Deborah
There Is Something.

Pope, J. R.
Word of Encouragement, A.

Pope, Jessie
Call, The.
Nut's Birthday, The.
Our Visit to the Zoo.
Socks.
War Girls.

Pope, Liston
Sea Turtle.

Pope, Walter
Old Man's Wish, The.

Popham, Hugh
Usual exquisite boredom of patrols, The.

Popham, Ivor
Child, The.

Poquelin, Jean Baptist *See* **Molière**

Pordage, Samuel
Corydon's Complaint.

Porson, Richard
Bathos, The.
Epigram on an Academic Visit to the Continent.
Mutual Congratulations of the Poets Anna Seward and Hayley, The.
Note on the Latin Gerunds, A.
On a Doctor of Divinity.
On a German Tour.
On an Imaginary Journey to the Continent.
On the Latin Gerunds.
Porson on German Scholarship.
Porson on His Majesty's Government.
Porson's Visit to the Continent.
To Dr. Kipling.

Portal, Magda
Film Vermouth: Six o'Clock Show.
Shores of anguish.
Woman.

Porter, Alan
Stallion, The.

Porter, Bruce
Limerick: "H was an indigent Hen."

Porter, Cole
Anything Goes.
Brush Up Your Shakespeare.
I Hate Men.
Let's Do It.
My Heart Belongs to Daddy.
Night and Day, *with music.*
So in Love, *with music.*
Well, Did You Evah?

Porter, Mrs. David
Thou Has Wounded the Spirit That Loved Thee.

Porter, Fairfield
Island in the Evening, The.

Porter, Hal
Lalique.
Sheep.

Porter, Ina M.
Mumford.

Porter, Jenny Lind
In the Beginning.

Porter, Katherine Anne
Requiescat.

Porter, Kenneth Wiggins
Beaver Sign.
Epitaph for a Man from Virginia City.
Old Thad Stevens.
Poem on a Slippery Sidewalk.
Street Scene—1946.
Thistle, Yarrow, Clover.

Porter, Peter
Annotations of Auschwitz.
Christenings.
Consumer's Report, A.
Exequy, An.
Gertrude Stein at Snails Bay.
London is full of chickens, on electric spits.
Made in Heaven.
May, 1945.
Metamorphosis.
Mort aux Chats.
Nine o'Clock Thoughts on the 73 Bus.
Non Piangere, Liù.
On This Day I Complete My Fortieth Year.
Phar Lap in the Melbourne Museum.
Smell on the Landing, The.
St. Cecilia's Day Epigram, A.
Your Attention Please.

Porter, Samuel Judson
Way, The; the Truth; the Life.

Porter, William Sidney. *See* **"Henry, O."**

Porumbacu, Veronica
Of Autumn.

Poseidippus
Doricha.

Posey, Alexander L.
On the Capture and Imprisonment of Crazy Snake, January, 1900.

Posner, David
Birds, The.
Campus, The.
Mourningsong for Anne.
On a Recent Protest against Social Conditions.

Post, Jonathan V.
Footnote to Feynman.

Poster, Carol
Robert Bly Finds Something in New Jersey.
Synthesizing Several Abstruse Concepts with an Experience.

Potamkin, Harry Alan
Cargoes of the Radanites.

Poteat, Edwin McNeill
Eternal God Whose Searching Eye Doth Scan.
Grace at Evening.
Prayer at Dawn.
Prayer for Contentment.

Potter, Beatrix
Old Woman, The.

Potter, Eugene, *and* Pierre Degeyter, Eugene
Internationale, The.

Potter, Reuben M.
Hymn of the Alamo.
Potts, Paul
For My Father.
Jean.
Muse to an Unknown Poet, The.
Poulin, A., Jr.
I Woke Up. Revenge.
Poulsson, Emilie
Baby's Breakfast.
Bed-Time Song.
Books Are Keys.
Breakfast Song, The.
First Christmas, The.
Lovable Child, The.
While Stars of Christmas Shine.
Pound, Ezra
Alba ("As cool as the pale wet leaves").
Alba ("When the nightingale to his mate").
Alchemist, The.
Ancient Music.
Ancient Wisdom, Rather Cosmic.
And the days are not full enough.
And Thus in Nineveh.
Apparuit.
April.
Ballad for Gloom.
Ballad of the Goodly Fere.
Ballatetta.
Bathtub [*or* Bath Tub], The.
Beautiful Toilet, The.
Brennbaum.
Cantos, *sels.*
Cino.
Clara.
Coda.
Coming of War, The: Actaeon.
Commission.
Contemporania, *sel.*
Dance Figure.
De Aegypto.
Doria.
E. P. Ode pour l'Election de Son Sepulchre.
Eleanor (she spoiled in a British climate).
Encounter, The.
Envoi: "Go, dumb-born book."
Envoi (1919).
Epilogue: "O chansons foregoing."
Fan-Piece, for Her Imperial Lord.
Faun, The.
Fine fish to net.
For an officer/ in the old Capital, fox fur.
For deep deer-copse beneath Mount Han.
For E. McC.
Fragmenti.
"From the colour the nature."
Full be the year, abundant be the grain.
Further Instructions.
Garden, The.
Garret, The.
Girl, A.
Greek Epigram.
Hang it all, Robert Browning.
Homage to Sextus Propertius, *sels.*
Hugh Selwyn Mauberley. (Life and Contacts).
I dreamt that I was God Himself.
Immorality, An.
Impressions of François-Marie Arouet (de Voltaire), *sel.*
In a Station of the Metro.
Ité.
Know then:/ Toward summer when the sun is in Hyades.
Koré.
Lake Isle, The.
Langue d'Oc, *sel.*
L'Art, 1910.
L'Homme Moyen Sensuel, *sels.*
Liu Ch'e.
Lustra, *sels.*
Medallion.
Meditatio.
Monumentum Aere, Etc.
Mr. Housman's Message.
Mr. Nixon.
Near Perigord.
N.Y.
O Atthis.
O flowers of Mekhmekh, give us peace!
Ortus.
Pact, A.
Phyllidula.
Pick a fern, pick a fern, ferns are high.
Piere Vidal Old.
Pine boat a-shift.
Portrait.
Portrait d'une Femme.
Pour l'Election de Son Sepulchre.
Provincia Deserta.
Reflection and Advice.
Rest, The.
Return, The.
Ritratto.
Said Jim X . . .
Salutation.
Salutation the Second.
Sestina: Altaforte.
"Siena Mi Fe'; Disfecemi Maremma."
Silet.
Soirée.
Song of the Bowmen of Shu.
South-Folk in Cold Country.
Study in Aesthetics, The.
Tame Cat.
Tea Shop, The.
Temperaments, The.
Tenzone.
There are flowers of Zait in the garden.
These fought in any case.
To Kalòn.
To Whistler, American.
Tomb of Akr Çaar, The.
Toujours la Politesse.
Translator to Translated.
Tree, The.
Ts'ai Chi'h.
Villanelle: The Psychological Hour.
Virginal, A.
What thou lovest well remains.
When, when and whenever death closes our eyelids.
Wide, ho?
Yeux Glauques.
Pound, Ezra *and* Noel Stock
I find my love fishing.
Pomegranate speaks, The.
So small are the flowers of Seamu.
Swallow sings "Dawn," The.
With candour I confess my love.
With you here at Mertu.
Pounds, Jessie B.
Beautiful Isle of Somewhere.
Pounds, Leonard
"Rake" Windermere.
Powell, Anthony
Caledonia.
Powell, Charles
Jack and Jill.
Power, John
Thy Name We Bless and Magnify.
Power, Marguerite (Countess of Blessington)
Friend, A.
Powers, Horatio Nelson
Chimney Swallows.
Our Sister.
Year Ahead, The.
Powers, Jessica Agnes
And in Her Morning.
Cancer Patient.
Cloud of Carmel, The.
Wanderer.
Powers, Star
Harvest Time.
Powys, John Cowper
In a Hotel Writing-Room.
Poyner, Ken
Therapy.
Pozzi, Antonia
To Trust.
Prada, Gonzalez
Who Translates a Poet Badly.
Praed, Winthrop Mackworth
Arrivals at a Watering-Place.
Belle of the Ball-Room, The.
Charade.
Chaunt of the Brazen Head, The, *sel.*
Convenanter's Lament for Bothwell Brigg, The.
County Ball, The, *sel.*
County Member, The.
Epitaph on the Late King of the Sandwich Isles.
Every-Day Characters, *sels.*
Fairy Song.
Goodnight to the Season!
Letter of Advice, A.
Letters from Teignmouth, *sel.*
Mater Desiderata.
Newly-wedded, The.
Ode to Popularity.
One More Quadrille.
Our Ball.
Portrait of a Lady in the Exhibition of the Royal Academy.
Royal Education.
School and Schoolfellows.
Schoolfellows.
Song: "Pints and the pistols, the pike-staves and pottles, The," *at.*
Song of Impossibilities, A.
Stanzas on Seeing the Speaker Asleep in His Chair.
Stanzas to the Speaker Asleep.
Talented Man, The.
Time's Song.
To———: "We met but in one giddy dance."
To Helen.
Vicar, The.
Prager, Marie-Francoise
I'll act out a weird dream.
Prather, W. H.
Indian Ghost Dance and War, The.
Pratt, Anna Maria
Early News.
Mortifying Mistake, A.
Pratt, Edwin John
Behind the Log, *sel.*
Brébeuf and His Brethren, *sels.*
Burial at Sea.
Cachalot, The, *sels.*
Come Not the Seasons Here.
Erosion.
Final Moments, The.
From Stone to Steel ("From stone to bronze, from bronze to steel").
Frost.
Gathering, The.
Ground-Swell, The.
Ice-Floes, The.
Invisible Trumpets Blowing.
Martyrdom of Brébeuf and Lalemant, 16 March 1649, The.
Precambrian Shield, The.
Prize Cat, The.
Ritual, The.
Roosevelt and the *Antinoe,* The, *sel.*
Sea Cathedral, The.
Sea Gulls.
Shark, The.
Silences.
There is a language in a naval log.
Titanic, The, *sels.*
Towards the Last Spike, *sels.*
Truant, The.
Way of Cape Race, The.
Pratt, Lenore
Midwinter Thaw.

Old Boat, The.
Pratt, William W.
Same Old Trick.
Praxilla
Adonis, Dying.
Lovely girl, you look at me through the window.
Most beautiful of things I leave is sunlight.
Watch out, my dear.
You gaze at me teasingly through the window.
Pray, Benjamin Sturgis
Motorcycle.
Preil, Gabriel
Arriving.
Autumn Music.
Biographical Note.
Fishermen.
From Jerusalem: A First Poem.
Giving Up on the Shore.
Late Manuscript at the Schocken Institute, A.
Lesson in Translation, A.
Letter Out of the Gray.
Like David.
Memory of Another Climate.
Parting.
Rains on the Island.
Summing Up, A.
Words of Oblivion and Peace.
Prelutsky, Jack
Alphabet Stew.
Bogeyman, The.
Children, Children Everywhere.
City, Oh, City!
Cow, The.
Creature in the Classroom, The.
Darkling Elves, The.
Dogs and Cats and Bears and Bats.
Don't Ever Seize a Weasel by the Tail.
First Thanksgiving, The.
Four Seasons, The.
Ghoul, The.
Harvey Always Wins.
Herbert Glerbett.
Hippopotamus, The.
Home! You're Where It's Warm Inside.
I'm Hungry!
It's Halloween.
Land of Potpourri, The.
Lion, The.
Long Gone.
Me I Am!
Nature Is.
No Girls Allowed.
Nonsense!
Pancake Collector, The.
Pumberly Pott's Unpredictable Niece.
Skeleton Parade.
Some People I Know.
Toucannery.
Troll, The.
Twickham Tweer.
Visitor, The.
Ways of Living Things, The.
Where Goblins Dwell.
Wrimples.
Yak, The.
Prentice, George Denison
Memories.
New England.
Ocean, The.
Prentice, John A.
Washington.
Prentiss, Elizabeth Payson
Kitty.
More Love to Thee, O Christ, *with music.*
Prescot, Kenrick
Balsham Bells.
Prescott, Mary Newmarch
In the Dark, in the Dew.
Press, John
African Christmas.
Farewell: "Smell of death was in the air, The."
Narcissus.
Womanisers.
Preston, Keith
Awful Responsibility, An.
Deep Stuff.
Durable Bon Mot, The.
Effervescence and Evanescence.
Good Reasons.
Humorist, The.
Lapsus Linguae.
Marital Tragedy.
Original Cuss, An.
Warm Babies.
Preston, Margaret Junkin
Acceptation.
Dirge for Ashby.
First Proclamation of Miles Standish, The.
First Thanksgiving Day, The.
Grave in Hollywood Cemetery, Richmond, A.
Hero of the Commune, The.
Last Meeting of Pocahontas and the Great Captain, The.
Mystery of Cro-a-tàn, The.
Under the Shade of the Trees.
Virginia Capta.
Vision of the Snow, The.
Pretorius, S. J.
Madman, The.
Prettyman, Quandra
Birth of the Poet, The.
Blues.
Crawl into Bed.
Lullaby: "Sleep, love, sleep."
Mood, The.
Photograph.
Still Life: Lady with Birds.
When Mahalia Sings.
Préavert, Jacques
Alicante.
Belle Saison, La.
Late Rising.
Message, The.
Price, Jonathan
Considered Reply to a Child, A.
Price, Laurence
Win at First and Lose at Last; or, A New Game at Cards.
Price, Nancy
Harbor.
Prideaux, Tom
Skip-Scoop-Anellie.
Priest, Nancy Woodbury (Nancy Amelia Woodbury Wafield)
Over the River.
Primrose, Lady Diana
Chain of Pearl, A, *sel.*
Fourth Pearl, The: Temperance.
"Primus"
Far from Somewhere.
Prince, Alison
Dog howled and howled, The.
Prince, Frank Templeton
At a Parade.
Babiaantje, The.
In a Province.
Old Age of Michelangelo, The.
Question, The.
Soldiers Bathing.
To a Friend on His Marriage.
Token, The.
Prince, Thomas
Give Ear, O God, to My Loud Cry, *with music.*
O Lord, Bow Down Thine Ear, *with music.*
With Christ and All His Shining Train, *with music.*
Pringle, Thomas
Afar in the Desert.
Hottentot, The.
Prior, Matthew
Advice to the Painter.
Against Modesty in Love.
Alma; or, The Progress of the Mind, *sel.*
Another True Maid.
Answer to Cloe [*or* Chloe] Jealous.
Better Answer (to Cloe Jealous), A.
Chameleon, The.
Chaste Florimel.
Cupid Mistaken.
Cupid's Mistaken.
Divine Blacksmith, The.
Dutch Proverb, A.
English Ballad, on the Taking of Namur by the King of Great Britain, 1695, An.
English Padlock, An.
Epigram: "Nobles and heralds, by your leave."
Epigram: "Thy nags (the leanest things alive)."
Epigram: "To John I ow'd great obligation."
Epigram: "Tom's sickness did his morals mend."
Epigram: "When Bibo thought fit from the world to retreat."
Epigram: "When Pontius wished an edict might be passed."
Epigram: "Yes, every poet is a fool."
Epitaph, An: "Interr'd beneath this marble stone."
Epitaph: "Meek Francis lies here, friend, without stop or stay."
Epitaph on Himself.
Epitaph on True, Her Majesty's Dog, An.
Fable, A: "In Aesop's tales an honest wretch we find."
Farewell, A: "Venus, take my votive glass."
Fatal Love.
Female Phaeton, The.
For My Own Monument.
Great Bacchus: From the Greek.
Human Life.
Jinny the Just.
Lady Who Offers Her Looking-Glass to Venus, The.
Letter, A.
Letter to the Honourable Lady Miss Margaret Cavendish Holles-Harley, A.
Love and Reason.
Lover's Anger, A.
Nonpareil.
Ode, An: "Merchant, to secure his treasure, The."
On Critics.
On Exodus 3: 14: "I am that I am."
On Himself.
On My Birthday, July 21.
Paraphrase from the French, A.
Phillis's Age.
Power.
Prior's Epitaph.
Protogenes and Apelles.
Question to Lisetta, The.
Quid Sit Futurum Cras Fuge Quaerere.
Quits.
Reasonable Affliction, A.
Remedy Worse than the Disease, The.
Simile, A.
Solomon on the Vanity of the World, *sels.*
Song, A: "If Wine and Musick have the Pow'r."
Song: "In vain you tell your parting lover."
To a Child of Quality [Five Years Old, the Author Supposed Forty].
To a Lady: She Refusing to Continue a Dispute with Me, and Leaving Me in the Argument.
To a Young Gentleman in Love; a Tale.
To Chloe Jealous.
To Cloe Jealous, a Better Answer.
Town Mouse and the Country Mouse, The.
True Maid, A.
Turtle and the Sparrow, The, *sel.*
Woman's Wish, The.
Written in an Ovid.
Written in the Beginning of Mezeray's History of France.
Pritam, Amrita
Annunciation, The.
Daily Wages.

Pritchard, N. H.
Metagnomy.
Pritchard, Sheila
Some Kind of Giant.
Pritchard, Norman Henry, II
Aswelay.
Gyre's Galax.
Self.
Pritzkow, Louis W.
Take Back Your Gold.
Privett, Katharine
Watching My Daughter Sew.
Windmill in March.
Probst, Anita Endrezze. *See* **Endrezze-Danielson, Anita**
Probyn, May
Bees of Middleton Manor, The.
Beloved, The.
Christmas Carol: "Lacking samite and sable."
"Is It Nothing to You?"
Procter, Adelaide Anne
Cleansing Fires.
Doubting Heart, A.
Fidelis.
Give Me Thy Heart.
Legend, A.
Lost Chord, A.
My Picture.
One by One.
Per Pacem ad Lucem.
Present, The.
Shadows of the Evening Hours, The.
Thankfulness.
Warrior to His Dead Bride, The.
Woman's Question, A.
Procter, Bryan Waller. *See* **"Cornwall, Barry"**
Proctor, Alan
At Night.
Proctor, Edna Dean
Brooklyn Bridge, The.
Captive's Hymn, The.
Columbia's Emblem.
Columbus Dying.
Forward.
Glory of Toil, The.
Heaven, O Lord, I Cannot Lose.
Heroes.
John Brown.
Lost War-Sloop, The.
Sa-cá-ga-we-a.
Song of the Ancient People, The.
Take Heart.
Respice Finem.
Prokosch, Frederic
Conspirators, The.
Eclogue: "No one dies cleanly now."
Fable: "O the vines were golden, the birds were loud."
Festival, The.
Gothic Dusk, The.
Propertius, Sextus
Ah Woe Is Me.
Elegies, *sels.*
Hylas.
Revenge to Come.
Turning Aside from Battles.
Proudfit, David Law ("Peleg Arkwright")
Willis, The.
"Prout, Father." *See* **Mahony, Francis Sylvester**
Provost, Sarah
These Magicians.
Prowse, William Jeffery
City of Prague, The.
Prudentius (Aurelius Clemens Prudentius)
Cathemerinon, *sel.*
O Noble Virgin.
Prudhomme, Sully-. *See* **Sully-Prudhomme**
Prunty, Wyatt
Repetition.
Wake, The.
"Prutkov, Kozma"
Junker Schmidt.
Pudney, John
After Bombardment.
For Johnny.
Map Reference T994724.
Missing.
On Seeing My Birthplace from a Jet Aircraft.
Stiles.
To You Who Wait.
Pugliesi, Giacomino
Canzone: Of His Dead Lady.
Canzonetta: Of His Lady in Absence.
Pulci, Luigi
Appeal for Illumination.
Morgante Maggiore, Il, *sel.*
Prophecy.
Pullen, Elisabeth Jones Cavazza
Alicia's Bonnet.
Derelict.
Her Shadow.
Love and Poverty.
Sea-Weed, The.
Pullen, Eugene Henry
"Now I Lay Me Down to Sleep."
Now I wake and see the light.
Pulsifer, Harold Trowbridge
Duel, The.
Harvest of Time, The.
I Accept.
Of Little Faith.
Thoughts upon a Walk with Natalie, My Niece, at Houghton Farm.
Pulsifer, Susan Nichols
Sounding Fog, The.
Purcell, Victor William Williams Saunders. *See* **"Buttle, Myra"**
Purdom, George
Robens' Promised Land.
Purdy, Alfred W.
Alive or Not.
At Roblin Lake.
Cariboo Horses, The.
Country North of Belleville, The.
Dead Poet, The.
Dead Seal.
Evergreen Cemetery.
Girl.
Lament for the Dorsets.
Landscape.
Love at Roblin Lake.
Night Song for a Woman.
Nine Bean-Rows on the Moon.
Poem: "You are ill and so I lead you away."
Rattlesnake, The.
Remains of an Indian Village.
Sculptors, The.
Spinning.
Trees at the Arctic Circle.
What Do the Birds Think?
Wilderness Gothic.
Winemaker's Beat-étude, The.
Purohit, Swami
I Know That I Am a Great Sinner.
Miracle Indeed, A.
Shall I Do This.
Pushkin, Aleksandr Sergeyevich
Autumn.
Elegy: "Way the hell-bent years consume my pleasure, The."
Eugene Onegin, *sel.*
I Loved You Once.
Message to Siberia.
No, Never Think.
Phantoms of the Steppe.
Prophet, The.
Verses Written during a Sleepless Night.
When in My Arms.
With Freedom's Seed.
Work.
Putnam, Howard Phelps (Phelps Putnam)
About Women.
Ballad of a Strange Thing.
Hasbrouck and the Rose.
Hymn to Chance.
Romeo and Juliet.
Puttenham, George
Cruel You Be.
Puttkamer, Baroness von. *See* **"Marie Madelaine"**
Puziss, Marla
Following Van Gogh (Avignon, 1982).
Pye, Henry James
Aerophorion, *sel.*
Air Balloon, The.
Pygge, Edward
Crow Resting.
Notes for a Revised Sonnet.
Notes for a Sonnet.
Occam's Razor Starts in Massachusetts.
Revised Notes for a Sonnet.
Shantih shantih shantih.
Wasted Land, The.
What about You?
Pyle, Katharine
August.
Circus Parade, The.
Clever Peter and the Ogress.
How the Little Kite Learned to Fly, *at.*
Nine o'Clock.
One o'Clock.
Sea Princess, The.
Toys Talk of the World, The.
Two o'Clock.
Visitor, The.
Waking.
Wonder Clock, The, *sels.*
Pyrlaeus, Johann C.
Jesu, Come on Board, *with music.*

Q

"Q." *See* **Quiller-Couch, Sir Arthur Thomas**
"Q. B. M." *See* **"M., B. Q."**
Qarshe, Cabdullaahi
Colonialism ("The colonialist governments").
Qorratu'l-Ayn (Umm-i Salma)
He the Beloved, *sel.*
Quagliano, Tony
Edward Hopper Retrospective, The.
Quarles, Francis
Are all such off'rings, as are crusht, and bruis'd.
Argalus and Parthenia, *sels.*
Authour's Dreame, The.
Be Sad, My Heart.
Canticle.
Divine Rapture, A.
Emblems, *sels.*
Epigram: "My soul, sit thou a patient looker-on."
Epigram: "Paul's midnight voice prevail'd; his music's thunder."
Epigram: Respice Finem.
False World, Thou Liest.
Forme of Prayer, A.
Good Night, A.
Hos Ego Versiculos.
I Am My Beloved's, and His Desire Is towards Me.
Like to the Arctic Needle.
My Beloved Is Mine, and I Am His; He Feedeth among the Lillies.
My Glass Is Half Unspent.
My soul, what's lighter than a feather? Wind.
O Whither Shall I Fly?
On the Cuckoo.
On the Infancy of Our Saviour.
On the Needle of a Sundial.
On the Plough-Man.
On the World.
On Those That Deserve It.
On Zacheus [*or* Zacchaeus].
Our God and soldiers we alike adore.

Respice Finem.
Some curse that traitor Judas life and limb.
Vanity of the World, The.
Wherefore Hidest Thou Thy Face, and Holdest Me for Thine Enemy?
Why Dost Thou Shade Thy Lovely Face?
Wilt Thou Set Thine Eyes upon That Which Is Not?
World's a Sea, The.

Quasimodo, Salvatore
Gentle Hill, The.
Going Back.
Man of My Time.
Rain's Already with Us, The.

Quennell, Peter
Divers, The.
Flight into Egypt, The.
Hero Entombed I.
Leviathan, *sel.*
Procne.
Small Birds.
While I Have Vision.

Queremel, Angel Miguel
Manifesto of the Soldier Who Went Back to War.

Quevedo y Villegas, Francisco Gómez de
Sonnet: Death Warnings.

Quick, Richard
Reagan, The.

Quick-To-See-Smith, Jaune
Ronan Robe Series, The.

Quickenden, Beatrice
Hail, Oh Hail to the King, *with music.*

Quigless, Helen G.
Concert.

Quiller-Couch, Sir Arthur Thomas ("Q")
Alma Mater.
Chant Royal of High Virtue.
De Tea Fabula.
Doom Ferry.
Famous Ballad of the Jubilee Cup, The.
Lady Jane (Sapphics).
Letter, A.
New Ballad of Sir Patrick Spens, The.
Planted Heel, The.
Retrospection.
Sage Counsel.
Splendid Spur, The.
Tim the Dragoon.
Upon Eckington Bridge, River Avon.
Upon New Year's Eve.

Quillet, Claude
Best Time for Conception, The.
Callipaedia; or, The Art of Getting Beautiful Children, *sels.*
How to Conceive Boys.
Process of Conception, The.

Quillinan, Edward
Hour Glass, The.

Quilter, Inez
Sall.

Quinn, John Robert
At Times I Feel like a Quince Tree.
Row of Houses.

Quinn, Roderic
Camp within the West, The.
Fisher, The.

Quint, Beverly
View, A.

Quintana, Leroy V.
Last Night There Was a Cricket in Our Closet.
Legacy II.
Nine Years after Viet Nam.

Quirino, Giovanni
Sonnet: To Dante Alighieri (He Commends the Work of Dante's Life).

Quirk, Cathleen
Another Night on the Porch Swing.

R

"R. B." *See* **"B., R."**
"R. C." *See* **"C., R."**
"R. L. B." *See* "B., R. L."

Raab, Esther
Folk Tune.
Serenade for Two Poplars, A.

Raab, Lawrence
Assassin's Fatal Error, The.
Attack of the Crab Monsters.
Pastoral: "Today in Peru, this first day of summer."
This Day.
Two Clouds.
Valediction: "Sometimes I can believe."
Visiting the Oracle.
Voices Answering Back: The Vampires.

Rab (Abba Arika)
Kingdom of God, The.

Raba, Gyorgy
Conversation.
Message.

Rabbitt, Thomas
Casino Beach.
County Roads.
Dancing Sunshine Lounge, The.
Gargoyle.
Rape.
Weight Room, The.

Rabéarivelo [*or* Rebéarivelo], Jean-Joseph
Flute Players.
Here She Stands.
What Invisible Rat.

Rabelais, François
Gargantua, *sel.*
Inscription above the Entrance to the Abbey of Theleme.
Shrovetide's Countenance.

Rabi'a of Balkh
My wish for you/ that God should make your love.

Rabi'a the Mystic. *See* **Rabi'a al-Adawiyya**

Rabi'a al-Adawiyya (Rabi'a the Mystic)
My Lord/ if I worship Thee from fear of Hell.
O my Lord, if I worship you from fear of Hell.
O my Lord, the stars glitter and eyes of men are closed.
Stars are shining/ the eyes of men are closed.

Rabi'a bint Isma'il of Syria
Sufi Quatrain.

Raboff, Paul
Jars.
Reb Hanina.

Rachel [*or* Rahel] (Rahel Blumstein *or* Rahel Blaustein)
Barren.
Dawn.
His Wife.
Jonathan.
Kinnereth.
My Dead.
My White Book of Poems.
Perhaps.
Rachel.
Revolt.
To My Country.

Rachow, George
Captured Bird.
Going Back.
Survival in a Stone Maze.
Textile Mills and Prison Reform.
Toward Tenses Two Moons.

Racine, Jean
Athalie, *sel.*
Phaedra (Phèdre).

Radcliffe, Anne
Night.
Sonnet: "Now the bat circles on the breeze of eve."
Stanzas: "How smooth that lake expands its ample breast!"

Radford, Ernest
Quiet.
Upon Julia.

Radford, Mrs. Ernest (Dollie Radford)
Plymouth Harbor.

Radnóti, Miklós
Charm.
Forced March.
Fragment: "I lived on this earth in an age."
Hesitating Ode.
I Hid You.
In Your Arms.
Letter to My Wife.
Metaphors.
Picture Postcards.
Ragged Robin Opens, The.
Rain Falls. It Dries.
Root.
Seventh Eclogue.
Song: "Whipped by sorrow now."

Rae, Hugh C.
Mountain Creed.

Raffel, Burton
Creation Myths.
Ecological Lecture.
On Watching the Construction of a Skyscraper.

Raftery, Anthony
County Mayo.
I Am Raftery.
Lass from Bally-na-Lee, The.

Raftery, Gerald
Apartment House.

Rago, Henry
Coming of Dusk upon a Village in Haiti, The.
Green Afternoon, The.
Knowledge of Light, The.
Monster, The.
Promise Your Hand.
Sky of Late Summer, A, *sel.*
Summer Countries, The.

Rahel. *See* **Rachel**

Rahschulte, Mark
See all the people getting off the bus.

"Raile, Arthur Lyon" (Edward Perry Warren)
Waning of Love, The.

"Raimar, Freimund." *See* **Rückert, Friedrich**

Raine, Craig
Anno Domini, *sel.*
Birth.
Martian Sends a Postcard Home, A.
Onion, Memory, The.

Raine, Kathleen Jessie
Air.
Ancient Speech, The.
Beinn Naomh, *sel.*
By the River Eden.
Crystal Skull, The.
Daisies of Florence.
Desire.
Easter Poem.
Eileann Chanaidh, *sel.*
Envoi: "Take of me what is not my own."
Envoi: "What has want to give."
Eudaimon.
Fall, The.
For Posterity.
Human Form Divine, The.
I used to watch you, sleeping.
Images.
In Time.
Instrument, The.
Invocation of Death.
Isis Wanderer.
Lachesis.
Last Things.
London Night.
Love Poem: "Yours is the face that the earth turns to me."
Message from Home.
My Mother's Birthday, *sel.*

Natura Naturans.
Night in Martindale.
Nocturne: "Night comes, an angel stands."
Old Paintings on Italian Walls.
On Leaving Ullswater.
Oreads.
Puer Aeternus.
Pythoness, The.
Question and Answer.
Requiem: "Past love, past sorrow, lies this darkness."
Rock, *sel.*
Rose.
Scala Coeli.
Seen in a Glass.
Seventh Day.
Shells.
Spell against Sorrow.
Spell of Creation.
Statues.
Still Life.
Still Pool, The.
Summit, The.
To My Mountain.
"Tu Non Se' in Terra, Si Come Tu Credi."
Two Invocations of Death.
Water, *sel.*
Wilderness, The.
World, The.
Worry about Money.
Written in Exile.

Rainer, Dachine
Ashokan.
At Eighty-seven.
Double Ritual.
Epithalamium for Cavorting Ghosts.
Night Musick for Thérèse.
Samis Idyll.
Upon Being Awakened at Night by My Four Year Old Daughter.

Rainsford, Christina
Shadbush.

Raisor, Philip
Demolition.

Rakosi, Carl
Americana IX: "Your correspondent must be kidding when he says."
Americana XIII: "Captain Patterson, the folks back home."
Americana XV: Simplicity.
Americana XVII: Reminder of William Carlos Williams, A.
Avocado Pit, The.
Being Natural.
China Policy, The.
Experiment with a Rat, The.
Florida.
In a Warm Bath.
Indomitable, The.
Lamentation, A.
Meditation ("How long will you remain a boy?").
Meditation ("Lord, what is a man?").
Meditation ("Men are children of this world").
Meditation ("Three things remind me of you").
Medium IV, The: Sights.
Memoirs, The.
No One Talks about This.
Poetry.
Tune.
Vow, The.
Woman.
Young Couples Strolling By.

Ralegh, Sir Walter
Advice, The.
Affection and Desire.
Another of the Same.
Author's Epitaph, Made by Himselfe, The.
Come to Me Soon, *at.*
Conceit Begotten by the Eyes.
Conclusion, The: "Even such is time, that takes in trust."
Description of Love, A.
Diana.
11th and Last Book of the Ocean to Cynthia, The.
Epitaph: "Even such is Time, which takes in trust."
Epitaph on Sir Philip Sidney, *at.*
Epitaph on the Earl of Leicester.
Even Such Is Time.
Excuse, The.
Faery Queen, The.
False Love.
Farewell to False Love, A.
Farewell to the Court.
Feed Still Thyself.
Give Me My Scallop-Shell of Quiet.
Heaven's Queene.
His Epitaph.
His Petition to Queen Anne of Denmark (1618).
Homage to Diana.
If Cynthia Be a Queen.
In Commendation of George Gascoigne's Steel Glass.
Last Book of the Ocean to Scinthia, The, *sels.*
Lie, The.
Like to a Hermit Poor, *at.*
Lines from Catullus.
Love and Time.
Merit of True Passion, The.
My Body in the Walls Captived.
My Pilgrimage.
My Thoughts Are Winged with Hopes, *at.*
My Woe Must Ever Last.
Nature, That Washed Her Hands in Milk[e].
Now What Is Love.
Nymph's Reply to the Shepherd, The.
Ocean to Cynthia, The.
Ocean's Love to Cynthia, The.
Ode to Himself.
Of Spenser's Faery Queen.
On Dulcina, *at.*
On the Cards and Dice.
On the Snuff of a Candle.
Passionate Man's Pilgrimage, The.
Pilgrimage, The.
Poem Entreating of Sorrow, A.
Poem of Sir Walter Rawleighs, A.
Poem Put into My Lady Laiton's Pocket, A.
Prognostication upon Cards and Dice, A.
Reply to Marlowe's "The Passionate Shepherd to His Love."
Shepherd's Description of Love, The.
Shepherd's Praise of Diana, The.
Silent Lover, The.
Sir Walter Ralegh to His Son.
Sir Walter Ralegh to the Queen.
Soul's Errand, The.
Sun May Set, The.
Sweet Unsure.
To His Mistress.
To His Son.
To the Queen.
To the Translator of Lucan's Pharsalia (1614).
Verses Written in His Bible.
Vision upon This Conceit of the Faerie Queene, A.
Walter Rawely of the Middle Temple, in Commendation of the Steele Glasse.
What Is Our Life? A Play of Passion.
Wood, the Weed, the Wag, The.
Wrong Not, Sweet Empress of My Heart.

Raleigh, Sir Walter Alexander (1861-1922)
Artist, The.

Alexis
Ballade of the Goth.
Eating Song.
Hangover Cure.
Stans Puer ad Mensam.
Wishes of an Elderly Man.

Ralph, Nathan
When They Grow Old.

"Ramal, Walter." *See* **De la Mare, Walter**

Ramanujan, A. K.
Hindoo, The: He Doesn't Hurt a Fly or a Spider Either.
Last of the Princes, The.
Small-scale Reflections on a Great House.
Some Indian Uses of History on a Rainy Day.

Ramanujan, Mahadevi
Other men are thorn.

Ramié, Marian
Will You, One Day.

Ramirez, Valentino
Fishin' Blues.

Ramke, Bin
Green Horse, The.
Magician, The.
Monkish Mind of the Speculative Physicist, The.
Obscure Pleasure of the Indistinct, The.
Sadness and Still Life.
Spring Poem.
Why I Am Afraid to Have Children.

Ramsaur, Hugh Wilgus
Epitaph, Found Somewhere in Space.

Ramsay, Allan
An Thou Were My Ain Thing, *sel.*
Carle He Came o'er the Croft, The.
Caterpillar and the Ant, The.
Dainty Sang, A.
Epigram: "Lasses, like nuts at bottom brown."
Gentle Shepherd, *sels.*
Lass o' Patie's Mill, The.
Lass with a Lump of Land.
Lochaber No More.
Look Up to Pentland's Tow'ring Tap.
My Peggy [Is a Young Thing].
Ode to Mr. F—— [*or* Forbes].
Peggy.
Poet's Wish, The; an Ode.
Polwart on the Green.
Sang: "My Peggy is a young thing."
Song: "At setting day and rising morn."
Twa Books, The.
Up in the Air.
Widow, The.

Ramsay, Allen Beville
No teacher I of boys or smaller fry.

Ramsay, Andrew Michael
Friendship in Perfection.

Ramsey, Jarold
Indian Painting, Probably Paiute, in a Cave near Madras, Oregon.
Lupine Dew.
Ontogeny.
Tally Stick, The.

Ramsey, Paul
On the Porch of the Antique Dealer.

Ranaivo, Flavien
Love Song: "Do not love me, my friend."

Ranasinghe, Anne
Auschwitz from Colombo.
Holocaust 1944.

Rand, Kenneth
Lonely Road, The.

Rand, Theodore Harding
Dragonfly, The.
June.
Loon, The.

Randall, Dudley
Abu.
After the Killing.
Analysands.
Ancestors.
Ballad of Birmingham.
Black Poet, White Critic.
Blackberry Sweet.
Booker T. and W. E. B.
Different Image, A.
George.
Green Apples.
Hail, Dionysos.
Idiot, The.

Intellectuals, The.
Langston Blues.
Legacy: My South.
Melting Pot, The.
Memorial Wreath.
Old Witherington.
On Getting a Natural.
Pacific Epitaphs.
Perspectives.
Primitives.
Profile on the Pillow, The.
Rite, The.
Roses and Revolutions.
Southern Road, The.
Souvenirs.
To the Mercy Killers.
Randall, James A, Jr.
Don't Ask Me Who I Am.
Execution.
Jew.
Untitled.
When Something Happens.
Who Shall Die?
Randall, James Ryder
John Pelham.
Maryland, My Maryland!
My Maryland.
Why the Robin's Breast Was Red.
Randall, Julia
For a Homecoming.
Rockland.
To William Wordsworth from Virginia.
Randall, Virginia D.
October Winds.
Randall-Mills, Elizabeth
Crossing the County Line.
Randolph, Anson Davies Fitz
Master's Invitation, The.
Randolph, Innes
Rebel, The.
Randolph, Thomas
Amyntas, *sel.*
Devout Lover, A.
Eclogue to Mr. Johnson, An, *sel.*
Elegie, An: "Love, give me leave to serve thee, and be wise."
Fairy Song.
Gratulatory to Mr. Ben Johnson for His Adopting of Him to Be His Son, A.
He Lives Long Who Lives Well.
Invocation: "Come from thy palace, beauteous Queen of Greece."
Maske for Lydia, A.
Milkmaid's Epithalamium, The.
Ode on Leaving the Great Town.
Ode to Mr. [*or* Master] Anthony Stafford to Hasten Him into the Country, An.
On a Maid[e] of Honour Seen[e] by a Schol[l]ar in Som[m]erset Garden.
On the Death of a Nightingale.
Parley with His Empty Purse, A.
Pastoral Courtship, A, *sel.*
Phyllis.
Poet, The.
Poetry and Philosophy.
Song of Fairies Robbing an Orchard.
This definition poetry doth fit.
To One Admiring Herself in a Looking Glass.
Upon His Picture.
Upon Love Fondly Refused for Conscience's Sake.
Upon the Losse of His Little Finger.
Rands, William Brighty ("Matthew Browne")
Cat of Cats, The.
Child's World, The.
Clean Clara.
Dream of a Boy Who Lived at Nine Elms, The.
Dream of a Girl Who Lived at Sevenoaks, The.
Drummer-Boy and the Shepherdess, The ("Drummer-boy, drummer-boy, where is your drum?").
First Tooth, The.
Fishing Song, A.
Flowers, The.
Gipsy Jane.
Godfrey Gordon Gustavus Gore.
Gypsy Jane.
I Saw a New World.
Kitty: What She Thinks of Herself.
Lilliput Levee.
Peddler's Caravan, The.
Praise and Love.
Reformation of Godfrey Gore, The.
Shooting Song, A.
Thought, The.
Topsy-turvy World.
Winifred Waters.
Wonderful World, The.
World, The.
World, The; a Child's Song.
Rangiaho
Song of Despair.
Rankin, Carroll Watson
Difficult Guest, A.
Rankin, Jeremiah Eames
Babie, The.
Fairest of Freedom's Daughters.
God Be with You till We Meet Again.
Laboring and Heavy Laden, *with music.*
Word of God to Leyden Came, The.
Rankin, Paula
Being Refused Local Credit.
For My Mother, Feeling Useless.
Love in Magnolia Cemetery.
Middle Age.
Somewhere Else.
Tending.
Rankin, Rush
Woman Who Combed, The.
Rankins, William
By this time long-gowned Lumen walked abroad.
Satire Septimus Contra Sollistam.
Satyrus Peregrinans, *sel.*
Ranko
Fall of the Plum Blossoms, The.
Plum Trees.
Ransford, R. W.
She Found Me Roots.
Ransom, John Crowe
Address to the Scholars of New England.
Agitato ma Non Troppo.
Amphibious Crocodile.
Antique Harvesters.
Armageddon.
Bells for John Whiteside's Daughter.
Blackberry Winter.
Blue Girls.
Captain Carpenter.
Conrad in Twilight.
Dead Boy.
Dog.
Emily Hardcastle, Spinster.
Equilibrists, The.
First Travels of Max.
Good Ships.
Her Eyes.
Here Lies a Lady.
Husband Betrayed.
Inland City.
Janet Waking.
Judith of Bethulia.
Lady Lost.
Little Boy Blue.
Man without Sense of Direction.
Master's in the Garden Again.
Miriam Tazewell.
Miss Euphemia.
Old Man Pondered.
Old Mansion.
Our Two Worthies.
Painted Head.
Painting: A Head.
Parting, without a Sequel.
Persistent Explorer.
Philomela.
Piazza Piece.
Prelude to an Evening.
Somewhere Is Such a Kingdom.
Spectral Lovers.
Spiel of the Three Mountebanks.
Survey of Literature.
Tom, Tom, the Piper's Son.
Triumph.
Two in August.
Vaunting Oak.
Vision by Sweetwater.
Winter Remembered.
Ransom, W. M.
Catechism, 1958.
Critter.
Grandpa's .45.
Indian Summer: Montana, 1956.
Message from Ohanapecosh Glacier.
On the Morning of the Third Night above Nisqually.
Statement on Our Higher Education.
Ransome, Basil
Travellers Turning Over Borders.
Raphael, Lennox
Infants of Summer.
Mike 65.
Rappoport, Solomon. *See* **"Ansky, S."**
Ras, Barbara
At the Beginnings of the Andes.
Rascas, Bernard
Love of God, The.
Rashidd, Amir
Eclipse.
Rashidd, Niema
Warriors Prancing, Women Dancing.
Rashley, R. E.
Caterpillar.
Portrait of an Indian.
Voyageur.
Raskin, Selma
Tee-Vee Enigma.
Rasof, Henry
Fourth Option, The.
Ratcliffe, Dorothy Una
Rake.
Remembrance Day in the Dales.
Song of Nidderdale, The.
Ratcliffe, Stephen
Postscript, on a Name.
Ratner, Rochelle
Davening.
Maiden, The.
Poor Shammes of Berditchev, The.
Ratosh, Yonathan
Lament: "You did not suck at my mother's breast."
Ratti, John
Division.
Inside, Outside, and Beyond.
Rauschenbusch, Walter
Postern Gate, The, *sel.*
Raven, John
Assailant.
Inconvenience, An.
Roach, The.
Ravenel, Beatrice
Alligator, The.
Intervals.
Ravenel de la Coste, Marie
Somebody's Darling.
Ravenscroft, Thomas
Hawking for the Partridge.
Madrigal: "My mistress is as fair as fine."
Ravikovich [*or* Ravikovitch], Dahlia
Blue West, The.
Dress of Fire, A.
Everlasting Forests, The.
Hills of Salt.
On the Road at Night There Stands the Man.
Poem of Explanations.

Requiem after Seventeen Years.
Surely You Remember.
Ravitch, Melech (Zekharye Khone Bergner)
Conscience.
Let Us Learn.
Poem, A—Good or Bad—a Thing—with One Attribute—Flat.
Twelve Lines about the Burning Bush.
Twilight Thoughts in Israel.
Verses Written on Sand.
Rawnsley, Hardwick Drummond
Ballad of the Conemaugh Flood, A.
Old Parish Church, Whitby, The.
Raworth, Tom
Collapsible.
Empty Pain-Killer Bottles, The.
Hot Day at the Races.
My Face Is My Own, I Thought.
Rawson, Grindall
To the Learned and Reverend Mr. Cotton Mather, on His Excellent Magnalia.
Upon the Death of His Much Esteemed Friend Mr. Jno Saffin Junr.
Ray, David
At Grand Canyon's Edge.
At the Washing of My Son.
Card-Players, The.
Carolinas, The.
Death-Lace.
Dragging the Main.
Extreme Unction in Pa.
Genitori.
Greens.
Hansel and Gretel Return.
Jogger, The: Denver to Kansas City.
Love Letter.
On a Fifteenth-Century Flemish Angel.
On the Poet's Leer.
Orphans.
Piece of Shrapnel, A.
Problems of a Writing Teacher, The.
Sonnet to Seabrook.
Stopping near Highway 80.
Ursula.
W. C. W.
X-Ray.
Ray, Henrietta Cordelia
Antigone and Oedipus.
Dawn of Love, The.
Idyl: Sunrise.
Idyl: Sunset.
Milton.
Robert G. Shaw.
To My Father.
Ray, Judy
Rose Bay Willow Herb.
Ray, Louise Crenshaw
Philippine Madonna.
Rayford, Julian Lee
Boom.
Junkyards.
Raymond, Grace (Annie Raymond Stillman)
Birth.
Raymond, Harry
Hallelujah, I'm a-Travelin'.
Raymond, Rossiter Worthington
Christus Consolator.
Concerning Them That Are Asleep.
Raymund, Bernard
Wonder.
Rea, Susan Irene
Love Poem: "Warned, warned for years."
Poem for Dorothy Holt.
Rea, Tom
Rumors of War in Wyoming.
Read, Elfreida
Return to the Valley.
Read, Sir Herbert
Beata l'Alma.
Bombing Casualties: Spain.
Champ de Manœuvres.
Childhood.
Cranach.
Crucifix, The.
End of a War, The.
Equation.
Execution of Cornelius Vane, The.
Falcon and the Dove, The.
Garden Party.
Happy Warrior, The.
Mutations of the Phoenix, *sel.*
My Company.
1945.
Northern Legion, A.
Refugees, The.
Retreat, The.
Seven Sleepers, The.
Sic et Non.
Song for the Spanish Anarchists, A.
Sorrow of Unicume, The.
Summer Rain.
To a Conscript of 1940.
Villages Démolis ("The villages are strewn").
Well of Life, The.
White Isle of Leuce, The.
Woodlands.
World within a War, A.
Read, John
Down by the Old Mill Stream.
Read, Sylvia
Owl.
Read, Thomas Buchanan
Attack, The.
Blennerhassett's Island.
Brave at Home, The.
Closing Scene, The.
Drifting.
Eagle and Vulture, The.
Flag of the *Constellation,* The.
Lines to a Blind Girl.
New Pastoral, The, *sel.*
Rising, The.
Sheridan's Ride.
Valley Forge.
Wagoner of the Alleghanies, The, *sels.*
Windy Night, The.
Read, Vail
This New Day, *with music.*
Realf, Richard
"De Mortuis Nil Nisi Bonum."
Defence of Lawrence, The.
Indirection.
Old Man's Idyl, An.
Word, The.
Reaney, James
Baby, The.
Branwell's Sestina.
Chough, The.
Clouds.
Drunken Preacher's Sermon, The.
Gramophone, The.
Granny Crack.
Great Lakes Suite, The.
Horn, The.
January.
June.
Katzenjammer Kids, The.
Le Tombeau de Pierre Falcon.
Lost Child, The.
November.
Oracular Portcullis, The.
Orange Lilies.
Plum Tree, The.
Red Heart, The.
School Globe, The.
Sequence in Four Keys, A, *sel.*
Suit of Nettles, A, *sels.*
To the Avon River above Stratford, Canada.
Upper Canadian, The.
Reape, Lisa
Leavetaking.
Reavey, George
Bridge of Heraclitus, The.
Dismissing Progress and Its Progenitors.
How many fires.
Never.
Rebéarivelo, Jean-Joseph. *See* **Rabéarivelo, Jean-Joseph**
Reccardi, Joe
Remembering Him.
Rechter, Judith
Fay Wray to the King.
Rector, Liam
My Grandfather Always Promised Us.
Redding
When the Saints Go Marchin' In.
Redfern, Roger A.
Night Expedition from Ben Alder Cottage.
Redgrove, Peter
Against Death.
Bedtime Story for My Son.
Christiana.
Corposant.
Curiosity-Shop, The.
Design.
Dismissal.
Dog Prospectus.
Eggs, The.
For No Good Reason.
Ghostly Father, The.
I Stroll.
Idea of Entropy at Maenporth Beach, The.
Intimate Supper.
Million, The.
Minerals of Cornwall, Stones of Cornwall.
New Forms.
On Catching a Dog-Daisy in the Mower.
Red Indian Corpse.
Required of You This Night.
Secretary, The.
Serious Readers.
Shearing Grass.
Story from Russian Author.
To the Postmaster General.
Visible Baby, The.
Redi, Francesco
Bacchus in Tuscany, *sel.*
Bacchus's Opinion of Wine, and Other Beverages.
Creation of My Lady, The.
Redl-Hlus, Carolyn D.
Melissa.
Redmond, Eugene B.
Definition of Nature.
Gods in Vietnam.
Love Necessitates.
Main Man Blues.
Midway in the Night: Blackman.
Redpath, Beatrice
But I Shall Weep.
Star, The.
Redshaw, Thomas Dillon
Voice from Danang.
Redwing, A. K.
Agent of Love.
Blue Jeaned Rock Queen in Search of Happiness on a Blind Thursday at 1/3 Speed and Crying, A.
Chrome Babies Eating Chocolate Snowmen in the Moonlight.
Cosmic Eye.
Hoofer, The.
Lost Mohican Visits Hell's Kitchen, A.
Sitting Bull's Will versus the Sioux Treaty of 1868 and Monty Hall.
Tornado Soup.
Two Hookers.
World's Last Unnamed Poem, The.
Written in Unbridled Repugnance near Sioux Falls, Alabama—April 30, 1974.
Reed, David, Jr.
Love Me, and the World Is Mine.
Reed, Edward Bliss
Despair.
Heritage, The.
Poplars.

Prayer: "She cannot tell my name."
September.
September Is Here.
Reed, Henry
Auction Sale, The.
Chard Whitlow.
Chrysothemis.
Door and the Window, The.
Judging Distances.
Lessons of the War.
Lives.
Map of Verona, A.
Morning.
Naming of Parts.
Sailor's Harbor.
Unarmed Combat.
Wall, The.
Reed, Ishmael
Al Capone in Alaska.
Badman of the Guest Professor.
Beware: Do Not Read This Poem.
Black Power Poem.
Feral Pioneers, The.
.05.
Gangster's Death, The.
I Am a Cowboy in the Boat of Ra.
Instructions to a Princess.
Rain Rain on the Splintered Girl.
Reactionary Poet, The.
Sermonette.
Skirt Dance.
Untitled I.
Reed, J. D.
Cripples.
Gorilla at Twenty Nine Years, The.
Lost Silvertip.
Organ Transplant.
Out from Lobster Cove.
Reports Come In, The.
Stony Brook Tavern.
Strange Kind (II).
Reed, John
Proud New York.
Reed, Joseph Samuel
Soldier's Plea for the Y.M.C.A., A.
Reed, Langford
Hail to the Town of Limerick.
Limerick: "Consider the lowering Lynx."
Patriot, A.
Reed, Nan Terrell
Life.
Vases.
Reed, Thomas
Indian, The.
Reedy, Arnold
Lament for Apirana Ngata.
Reedy, Carlyle
Have You Noted the White Areas.
Rees, Grover, III
Abelard at Cluny.
Reese, Florence
Which Side Are You On?
Reese, Lizette Woodworth
After.
Anne.
April Weather.
At Cockcrow.
Book, A.
Carol, A: "Mary the Mother/ Sang to her Son."
Christmas Folk-Song, A.
Compensation.
Daffodils.
Dust, The.
Flower of Mullein, A.
Ghost Night.
Girl's Mood, A.
Good Joan, The.
His Mother in Her Hood of Blue.
Holiday, A.
Immortality.
In Harbor.
In Time of Grief.
Keats.
Lark, The.
Little Song of Life, A.
Love Came Back at Fall o' Dew.
Lydia.
Lydia Is Gone This Many a Year.
Ownership.
Portrait of a Florentine Lady, The.
Possessions.
Prayer of an Unbeliever.
Puritan Lady, A.
Reserve.
Road of Remembrance, The.
Robert Louis Stevenson.
Spicewood.
Spring Ecstasy.
Street Scene, A.
Taps.
Tears.
Telling the Bees.
That Day You Came.
This Very Hour.
Thistledown.
Thomas à Kempis.
To a Town Poet.
Trust.
Wise.
Reese, S. Carolyn
Letter from a Wife.
Reeve, F. D.
Alcoholic.
Botany Lesson.
Falls, The.
Hope.
Plaque in the Reading Room for My Classmates Killed in Korea, The.
We Settled by the Lake.
Reeve, Paul Eaton
Succumbing.
Reeves, Goebel
Hobo's Lullaby.
Reeves, James
Bagatelle, A.
Beech Leaves.
Black Pebble, The.
Bogus-Boo, The.
Catullus to Lesbia.
Ceremonial Band, The.
Cows.
Doctor Emmanuel ("Doctor Emmanuel Harrison-Hyde").
Doze, The.
Fireworks.
Four Horses, The.
Giant Thunder.
Grey Horse, The.
Horn, The.
If Pigs Could Fly.
Intruder, The.
Little Brother, The.
Little Fan.
Mick.
Mr. Kartoffel ("Mr. Kartoffel's a whimsical man").
Mr. Tom Narrow.
My Singing Aunt.
Nonny, The.
Old Crabbed Men.
Old Mole.
Old Wife and the Ghost, The.
Pig Tale, A.
Queer Things.
Snitterjipe, The.
Stocking and Shirt.
Three Singing Birds, The.
Toadstool Wood, The.
Travelers, The.
Two Old Women of Mumbling Hill, The.
W.
Wind, The.
Wooing Frog, The.
You in Anger.
You'd Say It Was a Funeral.
Zachary Zed.
Regelson, Abraham
Moses on Mount Nebo.
Reginald, Francis
À l'Ange Avantgardien.
Cloth of Gold.
Lass in Wonderland, A.
Vision.
Regnier, Henri de
Je ne veux de personne aupres de ma tristesse.
Night.
Reich, Heather Tosteson
Waltz.
Reich, Max Isaac
For Every Man.
One Thing Needful, The.
Reich, Shlomo
Golem, The.
Tribe Searching, A.
Vigil, The.
Windmill of Evening, The.
Reid, Alastair
Calenture.
Casa d'Amunt.
Curiosity.
Daedalus.
Fall, The.
Figures on the Frieze, The.
For Her Sake.
Game of Glass, A.
Geneva.
Ghosts.
Ghosts' Stories.
Glass Town, The.
In Memory of My Uncle Timothy.
Instance, An.
Isle of Arran.
Lesson in Handwriting, A.
Me to You.
Outlook Uncertain.
Pigeons.
Small Sad Song.
Tale the Hermit Told, The.
To Lighten My House.
Who Can Say.
Reid, Christopher
Gladstone gave his name to the gladstone bag.
Letter to Myself.
Reid, Dorothy E.
Coach into Pumpkin.
Reid, Robert F., III
Shadow Life.
Reid of Stobo, John
Thre Prestis of Peblis, The, *sel., at.*
Reiner, Lois
Father.
Reingold, Paula
And This Is Love.
Reinmar von Hagenau
As on the Heather.
Childish Game, A.
Reinmar von Zweter
I Came a-Riding.
Reis, Yitzhok. *See* **Nadir, Moishe**
Reisen, Abraham
Burn Out Burn Quick.
Endless Chain, An.
Family of Eight, The.
Girls from Home.
Healing.
Newcomers.
Watchman, The.
What Is the Case in Point?
Reiss, James
Approaching Washington Heights.
Breathers, The.
Brothers (I).
Green Tree, The.
Habla Usted Español?
Macy's Poem, The.
On Hot Days.

Slight Confusion, A.
Sueños.
Reiter, Thomas
Bait Shop.
First Day Out, The.
First Lesson, The.
It's Not Bad Once the Water Goes Down.
Other Side, The.
Reitz, Albert Simpson
Cradle and the Cross, The.
Thy Will Be Done.
Relph, Josiah
Hay-Time; or, The Constant Lovers. A Pastoral.
Remaly, Nancy
August Afternoon.
Renaivo, Flavien
Song of a Common Lover.
Rendall, Elizabeth
And of Laughter That Was a Changeling.
Buttercup Cow.
Needs.
Wind, The.
Rendall, Robert
Angle of Vision.
Planticru, The.
Shore Tullye.
Rendleman, Danny
Toward a Theory of Instruction.
Renner-Tana, Patti
Hershey Kiss.
Replansky, Naomi
Brick not used in building, A.
Housing Shortage.
I Met My Solitude.
In the Sea of Tears.
Inheritance, An.
Mistress Addresses the Wife, The.
Two Women.
Repplier, Agnes
Le Repos en Egypte.
Resnikoff, Alexander
Bad and Good.
Josephine.
Two Witches.
Revard, Carter
Advice from Euterpe.
Another Sunday Morning.
"But Still in Israel's Paths They Shine."
Coming of Age in the County Jail.
Coyote, The.
Discovery of the New World.
Driving in Oklahoma.
Getting Across.
Home Movies.
January 15 as a National Holiday.
North of Santa Monica.
Not Just Yet.
On the Bright Side.
Support Your Local Police Dog.
Revell, Donald
Central Park South.
Revere, Paul
Unhappy Boston.
Rewak, William J.
"Quick Now, Here, Now, Always."
Visit, The.
Rewey, Marion Brimm
Love Song for a Tyrant.
Rexford, Eben Eugene
On Easter Morning.
Silver Threads among the Gold.
Trust-Song, A.
Rexroth, Kenneth
About the Cool Water.
Andrée Rexroth.
Antipater of Thessalonica.
Autumn Rain.
Bad Old Days, The.
Bestiary, A., *sels.*
City of the Moon, The, *sel.*
Deer.
Fact.
Fifty.
Fish Peddler and Cobbler.
For a Masseuse and Prostitute.
For Mary.
Fox.
Further Advantages of Learning.
Great Canzon, The.
Heart of Herakles, The.
Here is Klito's little shack.
Herring.
Horse.
I have sworn ten thousand times.
I Lais, once an arrow.
I used to tell you, "Frances, we grow old."
Kings River Canyon.
Letter to William Carlos Williams, A.
Lights in the Sky Are Stars, The, *sel.*
Lion.
Living Pearl, A.
Lute Music.
Lyell's Hypothesis Again.
Lysidike dedicates.
Marcus Argentarius.
Maximian Elegy V.
Mother Goose Rhyme.
Naked out of the dark we came.
Observations in a Cornish Teashop.
On Flower Wreath Hill, *sels.*
On the Eve of the Plebiscite.
Only Years.
Our Canoe Idles in the Idling Current.
Parity.
Proust's Madeleine.
Quietly.
Raccoon.
Rogation Days.
Signature of All Things, The.
Snow Storm.
Song for a Dancer.
Strength through Joy.
Sword in a Cloud of Light, A.
This Shall Be Sufficient.
Time Is the Mercy of Eternity.
Vitamins and Roughage.
Vulture.
Wheel Revolves, The.
Wolf.
You are a stool pigeon and.
You.
Reyes, Margarita Baldenegro
Old Man Who Is Gone Now, The.
Reyes Basualto, Neftali Ricardo. *See* **Neruda, Pablo**
Reynolds, Barney
Cranberry Song, The.
Reynolds, Elizabeth Gardner
Little Black Dog, The.
Reynolds, George Nugent
Mary Le More.
Reynolds, John
Death's Vision, *sel.*
Mysteries Revealed after Death.
Nosegay, A.
Reynolds, John Hamilton
Farewell to the Muses.
Peter Bell [a Lyrical Ballad].
Sonnet: "Sweet poets of the gentle antique line."
Sonnet to ———
Reynolds, Lloyd J.
Weathergrams are poems of about ten words.
Reynolds, Malvina
Little Boxes.
What Have They Done to the Rain.
Reynolds, Tim
To a Bad Heart.
Walk in March, A.
Reynolds, Tom
Corbitt's Barkentine, *with music, at.*
Rezmerski, John C.
Sonship.
Reznikoff, Charles
About an Excavation.
After I Had Worked All Day.
Autobiography: Hollywood.
Body Is like Roots Stretching, The.
Depression, *sel.*
Five Groups of Verse, *sels.*
Going To and Fro and Walking Up and Down, *sel.*
Hebrew of Your Poets, Zion, The.
How Shall We Mourn You Who Are Killed and Wasted.
I Will Go into the Ghetto.
I Will Write Songs against You.
Jacob.
Lament of the Jewish Women for Tammuz.
Lamps Are Burning, The.
Let Other People Come as Streams.
Letter, The.
Luzzato.
New Year's.
Old Men, The.
On a Sunday.
Out of the Strong, Sweetness.
Puerto Ricans in New York (I & II).
Raisins and Nuts.
Simple soul, who so early in the morning.
Son with a Future, A.
Te Deum.
These Days the Papers in the Street.
Two girls of twelve or so at a table.
Walk about the Subway Station.
Winter Sketches.
Young fellow walks about, The
Rhianus
Epigram: "Most inexplicable the wiles of boys I deem."
Rhinelander, Philip H.
Bathtub Gin.
Hangover.
It's Very Unwise to Kill the Goose.
Rhinow, Arthur B.
And Yet.
Rhodes, Eugene Manlove
Hired Man on Horseback, The.
Rhodes, Hugh
Rising in the Morning.
Rhodes, R.
Prize-winning Limerick, A.
Rhys, Ernest
Autobiography, An.
Dagonet's Canzonet.
Diana.
Words.
Rhys, Keidrych
Good Shepherd, The.
Letter to My Wife.
Third and Fourth.
Tragic Guilt.
Ribback, Alan
Ar(chibald')s Poetica.
Ribemont-Dessaignes, Georges
Sliding Trombone.
Ribera Chevremont, Evaristo
Boy and the Lantern, The, *abr.*
Rice, Albert
Black Madonna, The.
Rice, Cale Young
Chanson of the Bells of Oseney.
Kinchinjunga.
Litany for Latter-Day Mystics, A.
Mystic, The.
New Dreams for Old.
Nights on the Indian Ocean.
On the Moor.
Submarine Mountains.
To the Afternoon Moon, at Sea.
Rice, Grantland
Alumnus Football.
First Division Marches, The.
Two Sides of War.

Rice, Harvey
Cuba.
Rice, Les
Banks of Marble.
Rice, Stan
America the Beautiful.
Bicycle, The.
Cry-Bird Journey, The.
Dogchain Gang, The.
Flesh.
History: Madness.
Incanto.
Last Supper, The.
Metaphysical Shock while Watching a TV Cartoon.
Poem Following Discussion of Brain.
Round Trip.
Singing Death.
Skyjacker, The.
Some Lamb.
29th Month, The.
Rice, Thomas D.
Jim Crow.
Jump Jim Crow, *with music.*
Rice, Wallace
Armstrong at Fayal, The.
Battle-Song of the *Oregon.*
Blood Is Thicker than Water.
Brooklyn at Santiago, The.
Defeat and Victory.
Destroyer of Destroyers, The.
Dewey and His Men.
End, The.
First American Sailors, The.
Firstfruits in 1812.
Immortal Flowers.
Jackson at New Orleans.
Minute-Men of Northboro', The.
Spain's Last Armada.
Sudbury Fight, The.
Sweet Clover.
Under the Stars.
Wheeler's Brigade at Santiago.
Rice, Seymour *and* Albert H. Brown
You Tell Me Your Dream, I'll Tell You Mine, *with music.*
Rich, Adrienne
Abnegation.
After Dark.
Afterwake, The.
Annotation for an Epitaph.
Artificial Intelligence.
At a Bach Concert.
At Majority.
Attention.
August.
Aunt Jennifer's Tigers.
Autumn Sequence.
Bears.
Blood-Sister.
Breakfast in a Bowling Alley in Utica, New York.
Burning of Paper instead of Children, The.
Burning Oneself In.
Celebration in the Plaza, The.
Charleston in the 1860s.
Clock in the Square, A.
Coast to Coast.
Corpse-Plant, The.
Demon Lover, The.
Dialogue.
Diving into the Wreck.
Double Monologue.
Epilogue for a Masque of Purcell.
Face to Face.
For the Conjunction of Two Planets.
From a Survivor.
From an Old House in America.
From the Prison House.
Gabriel.
Ghazals: Homage to Ghalib, *sel.*
"I Am in Danger—Sir."
I Dream I'm the Death of Orpheus.
Ideal Landscape.
Insomniacs, The.
Insusceptibles, The.
Leaflets.
Like This Together.
Living in Sin.
Love in the Museum.
Lucifer in the Train.
Meditations for a Savage Child.
Merced.
Middle-aged, The.
Mirror in Which Two Are Seen as One, The.
Mourning Picture.
Moving in Winter.
Necessities of Life.
New Year's Eve in Troy.
Nightbreak.
Ninth Symphony of Beethoven Understood at Last as a Sexual Message, The.
Novella.
November 1968.
Orient Wheat.
Origins and History of Consciousness.
Orion.
Peeling Onions.
Phantasia for Elvira Shatayev.
Pictures by Vuillard.
Planetarium.
Power.
Primary Ground, A.
Prospective Immigrants Please Note.
Rape.
Raven, The.
Re-forming the Crystal.
Readings of History.
Recorders in Italy.
Revivalist in Boston, A.
Roofwalker, The.
Sisters.
Snapshots of a Daughter-in-Law.
Song: "You're wondering if I'm lonely."
Storm Warnings.
Stranger, The.
Survivors, The.
Tourist and the Town, The.
Toward the Solstice.
Transit.
Translations.
Trees, The.
Trying to Talk with a Man.
Tryst in Brobdingnag, A.
Twenty-one Love Poems, *sels.*
Two Songs.
Unsaid Word, An.
Valediction Forbidding Mourning, A.
Versailles.
Walk by the Charles, A.
Will to Change, The.
Woman Mourned by Daughters, A.
Women.
5:30 A.M.
33.
Rich, Hiram
Jerry an' Me.
Morgan Stanwood.
Skipper-Hermit, The.
Rich, Richard
Newes from Virginia.
Rich, Vera
Lion Gate.
Richard, Keith *and* **Mick Jagger.** *See* **Jagger, Mick** *and* **Keith Richard**
Richard of Caistre
Hymn to Jesus, A.
Richards, Edward Hersey
Wise Old Owl, A.
Richards, George
Almighty Spake, and Gabriel Sped, Th', *with music.*
Long as the Darkening Cloud Abode, *with music.*
Richards, Ivor Armstrong
Spendthrift.
Richards, Laura Elizabeth
Alibazan.
Antonio.
At Easter Time.
Baby Goes to Boston, The.
Bird Song.
Cave-Boy, The.
Difference, The.
Eletelephony.
Giraffe and the Woman, The.
Gregory Griggs.
High Barbaree, The.
In Foreign Parts.
Jippy and Jimmy.
Jumbo Jee.
Kindness to Animals.
King of the Hobbledygoblins, The.
Little John Bottlejohn.
Mermaidens, The.
Molly Pitcher.
Monkeys and the Crocodile, The.
Mrs. Snipkin and Mrs. Wobblechin.
My Uncle Jehoshaphat.
Nursery Song, A.
Owl and the Eel and the Warming-Pan, The.
Party, A.
Postman, The.
Prince Tatters.
Punkydoodle and Jollapin.
Some Fishy Nonsense.
Song of Two Angels, A.
"Talents Differ."
Umbrella Brigade, The.
Valentine, A.
Was She a Witch?
Where Helen Sits.
Why Does It Snow?
Richards, Michael
After Christmas.
Richardson, Charles Francis
After Death.
Conjecture, A.
Prayer: "If, when I kneel to pray."
Richardson, Dorothy Lee
Modern Grimm.
Richardson, Dorothy M.
Message.
Richardson, Dow
Cost-of-Living Mother Goose, The.
Richardson, James
Dividing the House.
Richardson, Jonathan
On My Late Dear Wife.
Self-Consciousness Makes All Changes Happy; Ode.
Richardson, Justin
Afterthought.
Back Room Joys.
Garlic.
High-Life Low-Down.
La Carte.
Oocuck, The.
Red Wine.
Rhyme for Remembering How Many Nights There Are in the Month.
Rhyme for Remembering the Date of Easter.
What'll Be the Title?
Richardson, Marion Muir
Gold Seekers, The.
Richardson, Robert
Epitaph: "Warm summer sun shine kindly here."
Epitaph Placed on His Daughter's Tomb.
Richardson, Thomas
Proper New Song, A, *sel.*
Take Heed of Gazing Overmuch.
Richardson, W. B. *and* **Alan Lomax.** *See* **Lomax, Alan** *and* **W. B. Richardson**
Richman, Norma
Poem to Help My Father.

Richter, C. F.
My Soul before Thee Prostrate Lies, *with music.*
Rickert, Wendy G.
Somedays now/ I can squash a cockroach.
Rickword, Edgell
Cascade, The.
Contemporary Muse, The.
Cosmogony.
Encounter, The.
Handmaid of Religion, The.
Rimbaud in Africa.
Trench Poets.
Winter Warfare.
Riddell, Elizabeth
Children March, The.
Soldier in the Park, The.
Suburban Song.
Under the Casuarina.
Wakeful in the Township.
Riddell, Henry Scott
Scotland Yet.
Ridge, Lola
Art and Life.
Bees, The.
Edge, The.
Electrocution.
Fifth-Floor Window, The.
Reveille.
Saint's Bridge.
Song, The: "That day, in the slipping of torsos and straining flanks."
Spring.
Veteran.
Ward X, *sel.*
Wind in the Alleys.
Ridhiana
Tricked Again.
Riding, Laura (Laura Riding Jackson)
Auspice of Jewels.
Because of Clothes.
Dear Possible.
Flowering Urn, The.
For-ever Morning.
Forgiven Past, The.
Head Itself.
Map of Places, The.
Nor Is It Written.
Not All Immaculate.
Opening of Eyes.
Respect for the Dead.
Three Sermons to the Dead.
Way of the Air, The.
Wind, the Clock, the We, The.
With the Face.
Ridings, J. Willard
Thesaurus Nightmare, A.
Ridland, John
Assassination Poems.
Light Year, The.
Ridler, Anne
Backgrounds to Italian Paintings: Fifteenth Century.
Bathing Song.
Beads from Blackpool.
Before Sleep.
Bunhill's Fields.
Choosing a Name.
Christmas and Common Birth.
Dream Observed, A.
Edlesborough.
For a Child Expected.
For a Christening.
Lumber of Spring.
Making Love, Killing Time.
Matter of Life and Death, A.
Mile from Eden, A.
Nothing Is Lost.
Now as Then.
Now Philippa Is Gone.
O Love, Answer.
On a Picture by Michele da Verona, of Arion as a Boy Riding upon a Dolphin.
Phoenix Answered, The.
Poem for a Christmas Broadcast.
River God's Song.
Speech of the Dead, The.
Spring Equinox, The.
Stone Angel.
Venetian Scene.
Zennor.
Ridley, George
Cushie Butterfield.
Ridlon, Marci
City, City.
Fernando ("Fernando has a basketball").
My Brother.
Open Hydrant.
That Was Summer.
Riedemann, Myra von
Horses.
Last Will of the Drunk.
There Are Places.
Rieu, Emile Victor
Flattered Flying Fish, The.
Green Train, The.
Lesser Lynx, The.
Meditations of a Tortoise Dozing under a Rosetree near a Beehive at Noon While a Dog Scampers about and a Cuckoo Calls from a Distant Wood.
Night Thought of a Tortoise Suffering from Insomnia on a Lawn.
Paint Box, The.
Sir Smasham Uppe.
Soliloquy of a Tortoise on Revisiting the Lettuce Beds after an Interval of One Hour While Supposed to Be Sleeping in a Clump of Blue Hollyhocks.
Tony the Turtle.
Two People ("Two people live in Rosamund").
Unicorn, The.
Rigby, Ralph
Branding Iron Herd, The.
Riggs, Dionis Coffin
Clamdigger, The.
Riggs, Lynn
Spring Morning—Santa Fe.
Rigsbee, David
Green Frogs.
Riley, C. L.
There Are Gods.
Riley, James Whitcomb
At Sea.
Away.
Back to Griggsby's Station.
Barefoot Boy, A.
Beetle, The, *sel.*
Bereaved.
Billy Could Ride.
Boy's Mother, A.
Craqueodoom.
Days Gone By, The.
Dear Lord! Kind Lord!
Diners in the Kitchen, The.
Dwainie.
Extremes.
Flying Islands of the Night, The, *sel.*
Good-by er Howdy-do.
He Is Not Dead.
Honey Dripping from the Comb.
Ike Walton's Prayer.
Just Be Glad.
Kentucky Thoroughbred, The.
Knee-deep in June.
Life-Lesson, A.
Lincoln.
Little Hunchback, The.
Little Orphant Annie.
Little Red Ribbon, The.
Longfellow.
Love's Prayer.
Lugubrious Whing-Whang, The.
Man by the Name of Bolus, A.
Man in the Moon, The.
Maymie's Story of Red Riding-Hood.
Name of Old Glory, The.
Nine Little Goblins, The.
Old Man and Jim, The.
Old Sweetheart of Mine, An.
Old Swimmin'-Hole, The.
Old Times Were the Best, The.
On the Death of Little Mahala Ashcraft.
Our Hired Girl.
Out of the Hitherwhere.
Out to Old Aunt Mary's.
Parting Guest, A.
Raggedy Man, The.
Rain.
Rose in October, A.
Sea-Song from the Shore, A.
Sleeping Beauty, A.
Spirk Troll-Derisive.
Way the Baby Slept, The.
Way the Baby Woke, The.
Wee Little Worm, A.
When She Comes Home.
When the Frost Is on the Punkin.
Riley, Michael D.
Macramé.
Rilke, Rainer Maria
Abishag.
Annunciation.
Annunciation over the Shepherds, *sel.*
Archaic Torso of Apollo.
Autumn.
Autumn Day.
Book of Pilgrimage, The.
Bridge of the Carousel.
Childhood.
Christ's Descent into Hell.
Closing Piece.
Do you know, I would quietly.
Duino Elegies, *sel.*
For, Lord, the Crowded Cities Be.
Foreboding.
From a Childhood.
Grief, The.
I live my life in growing orbits.
Initiation.
Joseph's Suspicion.
Kings of the world are growing old, The.
Knight, The.
Lament: "Oh, everything is far."
Last Evening.
Last Supper, The.
Leda.
Lovesong: "How shall I withhold my soul so that."
Man Watching, The.
Merry-go-round, The.
Moving Ahead.
On the Death of Mary.
Palm of the Hand.
Panther, The.
Pieta.
Praise.
Prayer of the Maidens to Mary.
Presaging.
Silent Hour.
Solemn Hour.
Solitary, The.
Solitude.
Song of Love, The.
Sonnets to Orpheus, *sels.*
We Are All Workmen.
What Will You Do, God, When I Die?
Youth Dreams, The.
Rimbaud, Arthur
After the Flood.
Charleville.
Chercheuses de Poux, Les.
Childhood, *sel.*
Dawn.
Drunken Boat, The.
Evil.
IV from Childhood.

Hunger.
Illuminations, *sels.*
Lice-Finders, The [*or* The Lice-Hunters *or* The Lice Seekers].
My mouth is often joined against his mouth.
Napoleon after Sedan.
Ophelia.
Poets Seven Years Old.
Poster of Our Dazzling Victory at Saarbrucken, A.
Royalty.
Sensation.
Shame.
Sleeper in the Valley, The.
Song of the Highest Tower.
Sonnet: "Dead men of 'ninety-two, also of 'ninety-three."
Strolling Player, The.
To the French of the Second Empire.
Tortured Heart, The.
Vowels.

Rimbaud, Arthur *and* Paul Verlaine
Sonnet: To the Asshole.

Rimmer, Christine
How Night Falls in the Courtyard.

Rimon, I. Z.
I Am a King.

Rimos, Moses, of Majorca
Elegy (for Himself).

Rinaldi, Nicholas
Black.
Teahouse.

Rinkart, Martin
Now Thank We All Our God.

Rioff, Suzanne Berger
Cycles, Cycles.
Seduction, The.

Ríos, Alberto
Belita.
Cinco de Mayo, 1862.
Cortes.
Lost on September Trail, 1967.
Man She Called Honey, and Married, The.
Man Who Named Children, The.
Mi Abuelo.
Morning.
Nani.
Purpose of Altar Boys, The.
Sleeping on Fists.
Sundays Visiting.

Ripley, Elizabeth
Jammy.

Ripley, G.
Poem for Vladimir.

Risley, Richard Vorhees
Dewey in Manila Bay.

Ritchey, Belle MacDiarmid
I Shall Not Weep.

Rittenhouse, Jessie Belle
Debts.
My Wage.
Seven Times the Moon Came.
Transformation.
Youth.

Ritter, Margaret Tod
Faith, I Wish I Were a Leprechaun.

Rive, Richard
Where the Rainbow Ends.

Rivera, Etnairis
I pull out of the depths of the earth.

Rivera, Marina
Man of O, The.

Rivera, Tomás
My Son Doesn't See a Thing.

Rivera-Avilés, Sotero
Good Memory.
Rainy Morning.

Rivero, Alina
In the Fall.

Rivers, Conrad Kent
Death of a Negro Poet, The.
For All Things Black and Beautiful.
Four Sheets to the Wind and a One-Way Ticket to France.
If Blood Is Black Then Spirit Neglects My Unborn Son.
In Defense of Black Poets.
Malcolm, a Thousandth Poem.
Mourning Letter from Paris, A.
On Passing Two Negroes on a Dark Country Road Somewhere in Georgia.
On the Death of William Edward Burghardt Du Bois
Prelude: "Night and the hood."
Still Voice of Harlem, The.
To Richard Wright.
Train Runs Late to Harlem, The.
Watts.

Rivers, James W.
Tonsilectomy.

Rives, Amélie
Before the Rain.
Mood, A.
My Laddie.
Sonnet, A: "Take all of me,—I am thine own, heart, soul."

Rixson, Denis
Glen Pean.
Ice Has Spoken, The.

Roat, Charles E.
What a Friend We Have in Mother.

Robbins, Howard Chandler
And Have the Bright Immensities, *with music.*
Put Forth, O God, Thy Spirit's Might, *with music.*
Sabbath Day Was By, The, *with music.*
Saviour, Whose Love Is Like the Sun.
Spirit from Whom Our Lives Proceed.

Robbins, Martin
Cantor's Dream before the High Holy Days, A.
On Seeing a Torn Out Coin Telephone.
Spring Rites.

Robbins, Richard
For My Grandfather.

Robbins, Shellie Keir
Yielding.

Roberson, Ed
Blue Horses.
Eclipse.
18,000 Feet.
If the Black Frog Will Not Ring.
Mayday.
Othello Jones Dresses for Dinner.
Poll.
Seventh Son.
When Thy King Is a Boy, *sel.*

Robert II, King of France
Strength, Love, Light.

Robert de Brunne. *See* **Mannyng, Robert**

Robert of Gloucester
Chronicle, *sel.*
Town against Gown at Oxford.

Roberts, Cecil
Charing Cross.
Prayer for a Pilot.
Springtime in Cookham Dean.

Roberts, Sir Charles G. D.
Afoot.
Aim, The.
April Adoration, An.
At Tide Water.
Autochthon.
Ballad of Manila Bay, A.
Book of the Native, The, *sel.*
Brook in February, The.
Brooklyn Bridge.
Canada.
Epitaph for a Sailor Buried Ashore.
Flight of the Geese, The.
Frosted Pane, The.
Hawkbit, The.
Herring Weir, The.
Ice.
Iceberg, The.
In Apia Bay.
In the Night Watches.
In the Wide Awe and Wisdom of the Night.
Kinship.
Marsyas.
Mowing, The.
O Earth, Sufficing All Our Needs.
O Solitary of the Austere Sky.
Pea-Fields, The.
Potato Harvest, The.
Recessional, The.
Salt Flats, The.
Skater, The.
Solitary Woodsman, The.
Songs of the Common Day, *sels.*
Sower, The.
Tantramar Revisited.
Unknown City, The.
When the Sleepy Man Comes.

Roberts, Daniel C.
God of Our Fathers, Whose Almighty Hand, *with music.*
National Hymn.

Roberts, Dick (Richard Edwin Roberts)
Duty to Death, LD.

Roberts, Dorothy
Cold.
Dazzle.
Goose Girl, The.
Sisters.

Roberts, Elizabeth Madox
August Night.
Autumn.
Big Brother.
Butterbean Tent, The.
Christmas Morning.
Cinderella's Song.
Circus, The.
Cold Fear.
Cornfield, The.
Crescent Moon.
Evening Hymn.
Father's Story.
Firefly.
Hens, The.
Horse.
In the Night.
Little Rain.
Milking Time.
Mr. Wells.
Mumps.
Orpheus.
People, The.
Rabbit, The.
Sky, The.
Strange Tree.
Stranger.
Twins, The.
Uncle Mells and the Witches' Tree.
Water Noises.
Woodpecker, The.

Roberts, Hortense Roberta
Farmers.

Roberts, Jean
I Never Saw the Train.

Roberts, Kevin
Fish Come In Dancing, The.
July 1st, French Creek.

Roberts, LeVan
Unemployed, The.

Roberts, Lloyd
Deep Dark River.
Fruit Rancher, The.
One Morning When the Rain-Birds Call.

Roberts, Lynette
Low Tide.
Poem from Llanybri.
Shadow Remains, The.
These Words I Write on Crinkled Tin.

Roberts, Mary M.
Little Pudding.

Roberts, Michael
Caves, The.
Green Lake, The.
H.M.S. *Hero*.
Hymn to the Sun.
In Our Time.
In the Flowering Season.
Les Planches-en-Montagnes.
Midnight.
St. Gervais.
St. Ursanne.
Roberts, Michele
Madwoman at Rodmell.
Magnificat.
Out of Chaos Out of Order Out.
Sibyl's Song, The.
Roberts, Michelle
Inconsistencies.
Last Generation.
Moon Blast.
No One Is Asleep Even while Dreaming.
Purple dry buds tight to gray branches.
Spell, The.
Roberts, P. R.
Winter's Edge.
Roberts, Richard Edwin.*See* **Roberts, Dick**
Roberts, Sheila
Poem for My Dead Husband.
Roberts, Theodore Goodridge
Blue Heron, The.
Fiddler's Green.
Gluskap's Hound.
Lost Shipmate, The.
Maid, The.
Reformed Pirate, The.
Wreckers' Prayer, The.
Roberts, Ursula. *See* **Miles, Susan**
Roberts, Walter Adolphe
On a Monument to Martí.
San Francisco.
Vieux Carré.
Villanelle of Washington Square.
Roberts, William H.
I Will Believe.
Robertson, Brian
Party at the Contessa's House, The.
Robertson, Clyde
Mistress of the Matchless Mine.
Woman in the Wagon, The.
Yellow Witch of Caribou, The.
Robertson, Edith Anne
Deean Tractorman, Clear, The.
Deean Tractorman, Deleerit, The.
Robertson, Harrison
Kentucky Philosophy.
Two Triolets.
What He Said.
What She Thought.
Robertson, James Logie ("Hugh Haliburton")
Spring on the Ochils.
Robertson, Kell
Between a Good Hat and Good Boots.
Crossing West Texas (1966).
Julio.
Landscape, New Mexico.
Robertson, Kirk
Clorox Kid, The.
Giant Squid of Tsurai, The.
Postcard to a Foetus.
Robertson, T. A.
Tuslag.
Robertson, W. Graham
Glad Day.
Robertson, Winifred
Perfect Garden, The.
Robey, George
Limerick: "Eeccentric old person of Slough, An."
Robins, Gurdon
There Is a Land Mine Eye Hath Seen, *with music.*
When Thickly Beat the Storms of Life, *with music.*
Robinson, Agnes Mary Frances
Ah Me, Do You Remember Still.
Ballad of Orleans, A.
Celia's Home-coming.
Cockayne Country.
Dawn-Angels.
Etruscan Tombs.
Le Roi Est Mort.
Let Us Forget.
Orchard at Avignon, An.
Red May.
Retrospect.
Rispetto.
Rosa Rosarum.
Sometimes When I Sit Musing All Alone.
Temple Garlands.
Twilight.
Robinson, Anne
April and May.
Conversation.
Drummer, The.
To Laddie.
Robinson, Annie Douglas Green. *See* **"Douglas, Marian"**
Robinson, Barbara B.
Foreign Student.
Robinson, Charles
Had I but strength enough, and time.
Robinson, Corinne Roosevelt
Belovèd, from the Hour That You Were Born.
Life, a Question.
Lincoln.
Path That Leads to Nowhere, The.
Sagamore.
Robinson, David
Awakening.
Robinson, Edwin Arlington
Aaron Stark.
As It Looked Then.
Ballade of Dead Friends.
Ben Jonson Entertains a Man from Stratford.
Bewick Finzer.
Calvary.
Calverly's.
Captain Craig, *sel.*
Cassandra.
Charles Carville's Eyes.
Children of the Night, The.
Christmas Sonnet, A.
Clavering.
Clerks, The.
Cliff Klingenhagen.
Companion, The.
Credo.
Dark Hills, The.
Demos.
Eros Turannos.
Eutychides.
Exit.
Field of Glory, The.
Firelight.
Flammonde.
Flying Dutchman, The.
For a Dead Lady.
George Crabbe.
Gift of God, The.
Hillcrest.
House on the Hill, The.
How Annandale Went Out.
Inscription by the Sea, An.
Isaac and Archibald.
James Wetherell.
John Evereldown.
John Gorham.
Karma.
Klondike, The.
Lais to Aphrodite.
L'Envoi: "Now in a thought, now in a shadowed word."
Leonora.
Llewellyn and the Tree.
Long Race, The.
Lost Anchors.
Luke Havergal.
Man against the Sky, The.
Many Are Called.
Master, The.
Mighty Runner, A (Variation of a Greek Theme.)
Mill, The.
Miniver Cheevy.
Momus.
Mr. Flood's Party.
New England.
New Tenants, The.
Nimmo.
Oh for a Poet—for a Beacon Bright.
Old King Cole.
Old Story, An.
Pasa Thalassa Thalassa.
Pity of the Leaves, The.
Prodigal Son, The.
Raven, The.
Reuben Bright.
Reunion.
Richard Cory.
Sheaves, The.
Sonnet: "Master and the slave go hand in hand, The."
Sonnet: "Oh for a poet—for a beacon bright."
Souvenir.
Supremacy.
Tact.
Thomas Hood.
Too Much Coffee.
Torrent, The.
Toussaint L'Ouverture.
Twilight Song.
Two Men.
Uncle Ananias.
Unforgiven, The.
Vain Gratuities.
Veteran Sirens.
Vickery's Mountain.
Walt Whitman.
Why He Was There.
Zola.
Robinson, Edwin Meade
Annual Solution, The.
David Jazz, The.
Disagreeable Feature, A.
How Homer Should Have Written the Iliad.
It Happens, Often.
Limericised Classics.
Ode to Eve.
Rubaiyat, The.
Shakespeare Might Have Boiled Othello.
Spoon River Anthology.
Story of Ug, The.
"To Lucasta, on Going to the Wars."
Villanelle of a Villaness.
Robinson, Eloise
To-Day I Saw Bright Ships.
Robinson, Elsie
Beauty as a Shield.
Robinson, Grant P.
I Fights Mit Sigel!
Robinson, Harriet H.
"Oh! isn't it a pity, such a pretty girl as I."
Robinson, Henry Morton
Chantey of Notorious Bibbers.
November Fugitive.
Second Wisdom.
Robinson, James Miller
Coweta County Courthouse, The.
Robinson, John
More Truth and Light.
Robinson, Kenneth Allan
American Laughter.
Lines to Dr. Ditmars.
Robinson, Lila Cayley
Glow Worm, *with music.*

Robinson, Lucy Catlin
Ballade of Islands, A.
Fire i' the Flint, The.
"Hic Me, Pater Optime, Fessam Deseris."
Robinson, Roland
Deep Well, *sel.*
Lyre-Bird, The.
Rock-Lily.
Tank, The.
Wanderer, The, *sel.*
Waratah.
Robinson, Selma
Bus Ride.
Ferry Ride, *sel.*
Gentle Name.
Harvesting.
Pendulum Rhyme.
Robinson, Tom
Autumn Color.
Little Lady Wren.
My Dog.
Rabbit.
Shoes.
Swallow Tails.
Robinson, Tracy
Song of the Palm.
Robinson, Wey
Horse & Rider.
Robles, Al
Boyang the Wandering Recluse.
Manong Federico Delos Reyes and His Golden Banjo.
Manong Jacinto Santo Tomas.
Mountain-Toilet Thief, A.
Sushi-Okashi and Green Tea with Mitsu Yashima.
Robson, Jeremy
Departure, The.
Robson, Joseph Philip
California.
Roche, James Jeffrey
"Albemarle" Cushing.
Andromeda.
Constitution's Last Fight, The.
Don't.
Fight of the *Armstrong* Privateer, The.
First Citizen.
Flag, The.
Gettysburg.
Gospel of Peace, The.
If.
Jack Creamer.
Kearsarge, The.
Men of the Alamo, The.
My Comrade.
Net of Law, The.
Panama.
Reuben James.
Sailor's Yarn, A.
Skeleton at the Feast, The.
V-a-s-e, The.
Washington.
Roche, Paul
Brick, The.
Courage for the Pusillanimous.
Rochester, John Wilmot, 2d Earl of
Against Constancy.
Allusion to Horace, An; the Tenth Satire of the First Book.
Bully, The, *at.*
Chaste Arabian Bird, The.
Commons' Petition to Charles II, The.
Constancy.
Description of Maidenhead, A.
Dialogue between Strephon and Daphne, A.
Disabled Debauchee, The.
Epigram: "Here lies a great and mighty king."
Epistolary Essay from M. G. to O. B. upon Their Mutual Poems, An.
Epitaph on Charles II.
Et Cetera.
Fall, The.
Farewell to the Court, *sel.*
Homo Sapiens.
Imperfect Enjoyment, The.
Impromptu on Charles II.
Insulting Beauty.
King Charles II.
King's Epitaph, The.
Letter from Artemisa in the Town, to Cloe, in the Country, A.
Love and Life.
Lycias.
Mistress, The; a Song.
Of a great heroine I mean to tell.
On Poet Ninny.
On the Supposed Author of a Late Poem "In Defense of Satire."
Panegyric on Nelly, A, *sel.*
Pastoral Courtship, A.
Platonic Lady, The.
Poet, whoe'er thou art, God damn thee.
Satire: "Some do for pimping, some for treach'ry rise."
Satire against [Reason and] Mankind, A.
Satire on Charles II, A, *sel.*
Sodom; or, The Quintessence of Debauchery, *sel. at.*
Song, A: "Absent from thee, I languish still."
Song, A: "As Chloris full of harmless thoughts."
Song: I Promised Sylvia.
Song, A: "My dear mistress has a heart."
Song: "Love a woman! y'are an ass."
Song: Noble Name of Spark, The, *at.*
Song: "Phillis, be gentler I advise."
Song: "Too late, alas! I must confess."
Song of a Young Lady to Her Ancient Lover, A.
Song to Cloris, A.
Spoken Extempore.
To Chuse a Friend, but Never Marry, *at.*
To His Mistress.
To Love and Nature all their rights restore, *at.*
Tunbridge Wells.
Upon Drinking in a Bowl.
Upon His Drinking Bowl.
Upon His Leaving His Mistress.
Upon Nothing.
Very Heroical Epistle in Answer to Ephelia, A.
Wretched Man.
Written in a Lady's Prayer Book.
Rock, Madeleine Caron
He Is the Lonely Greateness.
Rockett, Winnie Lynch
Mother before a Soldier's Monument, A.
Rockwell, Glen
Keys.
Rockwell, Levi
From a Connecticut Newspaper.
Rockwell, Margaret
Hiroshima.
Rodd, Sir James Rennell, 1st Baron Rennell
Roman Mirror, A.
Song of Autumn, A.
Rodger, Alex
Twilight at the Zoo.
Rodger, Alexander
Behave Yoursel' before Folk.
Rodgers, Carolyn
Mama's God.
Rodgers, Carolyn M.
And When the Revolution Came.
And While We Are Waiting.
Breakthrough.
Common Poem, A.
For H. W. Fuller.
For Muh' Dear.
For Sapphires.
How I Got Ovah.
"In This House, There Shall Be No Idols."
Jazz.
Jesus Was Crucified or: It Must Be Deep.
Look at My Face, a Collage.
Masquerade.
Me, in Kulu Se and Karma.
Missing Beat.
Newark, for Now (68).
Now Ain't That Love?
One.
Phoenix.
Poem for Some Black Women.
Poem/ Ditty-Bop.
Proclamation/ From Sleep, Arise.
Rebolushinary X-mas.
Remember Times for Sandy.
Setting/ Slow Drag.
Some Me of Beauty.
Somebody Call.
Testimony.
U Name This One.
Voodoo on the Un-Assing of Janis Joplin.,
We Dance Like Ella Riffs.
What Color Is Lonely.
Yuh Lookin Good.
Rodgers, William Robert
Airman, The.
Apollo and Daphne.
Armagh.
Autumn.
Awake!
Beagles.
Carol: "Deep in the fading leaves of night."
Christ Walking on the Water.
Directions to a Rebel.
Express.
Field Day.
Fountains, The.
Irish Lake, An.
Lent.
Life's Circumnavigators.
Lovers, The.
Nativity.
Neither Here nor There.
Net, The.
Paired Lives.
Pan and Syrinx.
Party, The.
Raider, The.
Scapegoat.
Sing, Brothers, Sing!
Snow.
Song for Peace.
Song for War.
Spring.
Stormy Day.
Stormy Night.
Summer Holidays.
Swan, The.
White Christmas.
Winter's Cold.
Roditi, Edouard
Aurora Borealis.
Beginning and an End, A.
Habakkuk.
Hand.
Kashrut.
Paths of Prayer, The.
Séance.
Shekhina and the Kiddushim.
Rodman, Frances
Lost Dog.
Spring Cricket.
Rodman, Selden
Daphne.
Harpers Ferry.
Man, Not His Arms.
Norris Dam.
On a Picture by Pippin, Called "The Den."
Time of Day.
V-Letter to Karl Shapiro in Australia.
Rodman, Thomas P.
Battle of Bennington, The.
Rodríguez, Aleida
Explorations/ Bronchitis: The Rosario Beach House.

Rodriguez, Judith
At the Nature-Strip.
Eskimo Occasion.
Rebeca in a Mirror.
Rodriguez, Magdalena de
June 10.
Rodríguez Frese, Marcos
Beginning.
Leit.
What Is Needed.
Rodríguez Nietzche, Vicente
As Yet.
Mural, *sel.*
Poem H.
Roe, Sir Thomas
On Gustavus Adolphus, King of Sweden.
Roethke, Theodore
Academic.
All Morning.
Another woman: a change of tears.
Bat, The.
Beast, The.
Big Wind.
Bound.
Ceiling, The.
Centaur, The.
Child on Top of a Greenhouse.
Chums, The.
Coming of the Cold, The.
Cow, The.
Cuttings ("Sticks-in-a-drowse droop over sugary loam").
Cuttings ("This urge, wrestle, resurrection of dry sticks").
Dance, The.
Decision.
Deep in their roots, all flowers keep the light.
Dinky.
Dolor.
Donkey, The.
Double Feature.
Dream, The.
Elegy: "Her face like a rain-beaten stone on the day she rolled off."
Elegy for Jane.
Epidermal Macabre.
Epigram: Mistake, The.
Exorcism, The.
Far Field, The.
Field of Light, A.
First Meditation.
Flight, The.
Four for Sir John Davies.
Frau Bauman, Frau Schmidt, and Frau Schwartze.
Geranium, The.
Give Way, Ye Gates.
Grandeurs of the crazy man alone, The.
Heard in a Violent Ward.
Her Longing.
Heron, The.
Hippo, The.
I Cry, Love! Love!
I Knew a Woman [Lovely in Her Bones].
I rasp like a sick dog.
I would be with the wind.
I'm Here.
I'm lost in my name.
In a Dark Time.
In Evening Air.
Infirmity.
Interlude.
Journey to the Interior.
Kitty-Cat Bird, The.
Lady and the Bear, The.
Light Breather, A.
Light Listened.
Lizard, The.
Long Live the Weeds.
Long Waters, The.
Lost Son, The.
Marrow, The.
Meadow Mouse, The.
Meditation at Oyster River.
Meditations of an Old Woman.
Mid-Country Blow.
Minimal, The.
Mistake, The.
Moment, The.
Moss-gathering
Motion, The.
My Dim-wit Cousin.
My Papa's Waltz.
Night Crow.
Night Journey.
North American Sequence.
Old Florist.
Open House.
Orchids.
Otto.
Partner, The.
Pipling.
Poem: "I knew a woman, lovely in her bones."
Prayer: "If I must of my senses lose."
Prayer before Study.
Reckoning, The.
Renewal, The.
Reply, The.
Return, The.
Root Cellar.
Rose, The.
Rouse for Stevens, A.
Second Shadow.
Sensualists, The.
Sequel, The.
Serpent, The.
Shape of the Fire, The.
She.
"Shimmer of Evil, The."
Siskins, The.
Sloth, The.
Slug.
Small, The.
Snake.
Song, The: "I met a ragged man."
Song: "From whence cometh song?"
Song: "Under a southern wind."
Song for the Squeeze-Box.
Specialist.
Storm, The.
Swan, The.
They Sing.
Thing, The.
Vernal Sentiment.
Visitant, The.
Voice, The.
Waking, The ("I strolled across/ An open field").
Waking, The ("I wake to sleep, and take my waking slow").
Weed Puller.
What Can I Tell My Bones?
Where Knock Is Open Wide.
Wish for a Young Wife.
Words for the Wind.
Young Girl, The.
Rogers, Alex
Rain Song, The.
Why Adam Sinned.
Rogers, D. H.
Homeward Bound.
Rogers, Del Marie
Sleep.
War Requiem.
Rogers, George
As Gentle Dews Distill, *with music.*
Rogers, J. E. Thorold. *See* **Thorold Rogers, J. E.**
Rogers, John
Upon Mrs. Anne Bradstreet Her Poems.
Rogers, Pattiann
Achieving Perspective.
Concepts and Their Bodies (The Boy in the Field Alone).
For Stephen Drawing Birds.
Man Hidden behind the Drapes, The.
This Evening, without Blinking.
Rogers, Robert Cameron
Dancing Faun, The.
Doubt.
Health at the Ford, A.
Rosary, The.
Shadow Rose, The.
Sleeping Priestess of Aphrodite, A.
Virgil's Tomb.
Rogers, Ron
Bear Dance.
Black Mesa.
Death of Old Joe Yazzie, The.
Elf Night.
Montana Remembered from Albuquerque; 1982.
Rogers, Samuel
Another and the Same.
Bologna, and Byron.
Byron Recollected at Bologna.
Captivity.
Epitaph on a Robin Redbreast, An.
Fond Youth.
Ginevra.
Human Life, *sels.*
Inscription on a Grot.
Interview near Florence, An.
Italy, *sels.*
Man's Going Hence.
On a Tear.
On J. W. Ward.
Pleasures of Memory, The, *sel.*
Sleeping Beauty, The.
Wish, A.
Rogers, Thomas
Spirit of Night, The.
Rokeah, David
Beginning.
I Am like a Book.
Zealots of Yearning.
Rokwaho
Amber the sky.
Clickstone.
Owl.
Prelude: "Lake loon paddles, A."
Twoborn.
Roland, Patrick
Spring Burning.
Roland-Holst, Henriëtte
Concerning the Awakening of My Soul.
I Looked for a Sounding-Board.
Mother of Fisherman.
Small Paths.
Throughout the day we are able to ban the voices.
Rolfe, Edwin
Elegy for Our Dead.
No Man Knows War.
Poem to Delight My Friends Who Laugh at Science-Fiction, A.
Song (2): "Keep the dream alive and growing always."
Rolfe, Frederick William (Baron Corvo)
Ballade of Boys Bathing.
Rolfe, Harvey E.
Resolutions?—New and Old.
Rolland, John
Seven Seages, The, *sel.*
Rolle of Hampole, Richard
Ghostly Gladness.
Love Is Life, *orig. and mod. English prose.*
Song of Love for Jesus, A.
Song of the Passion, A.
Rolleston, Thomas William Hazen
Cois na Teineadh.
Grave of Rury, The.
Night.
Song of Maelduin.
Rollins, Alice Wellington
Death of Azron, The.

Many Things Thou Hast Given Me, Dear Heart.
Vita Benefica.
Rolls, Eric
Little Sticks.
Sheaf-Tosser.
Rolnik, Joseph
At God's Command.
I'm Not Rich.
In Disguise.
Thank God.
Romaine, Harry
Ad Coelum.
Romains, Jules
Another Spirit Advances.
Church, The.
Romanelli, Samuele
From Battle Clamour.
Love.
Romanes, George John
Sloth, The.
Romanes, George John
Simple Nature.
Romano, Liboria E.
Lyric Barber.
Romilu, Myrtle
If to Die.
Ronan, John
Fat Cat.
Ronksley, William
To Cheer Our Minds.
Ronsard, Pierre de
And Lightly, like the Flowers.
Corinna in Vendome.
Deadly Kisses.
Fragment of a Sonnet.
His Lady's Death.
His Lady's Tomb.
Of His Lady's Old Age.
On His Lady's Waking.
Paradox of Time, The.
Revenge, The.
Rose, The.
Roses.
To His Young Mistress.
To the Moon.
Rooney, John Jerome
Beam of Light, A.
Homing, The.
Joined the Blues.
McIlrath of Malate.
Men behind the Guns, The.
Ráhat, The.
Where Helen Comes.
Root, Edward Merrill
Carpenter of Eternity.
Prayer for Dreadful Morning.
Root, George Frederick
Battle Cry of Freedom, The.
Just before the Battle, Mother.
Rosalie, the Prairie Flower, *with music.*
Tramp! Tramp! Tramp! or, The Prisoner's Hope.
Root, Judith C.
Gerbil Who Got Away, The.
Root, William Pitt
Answering Dance.
Circle of Struggle.
Exchanging Glances.
Fleshflower.
From the Other Shore.
Jellyfish, The.
Natural History of Dragons and Unicorns My Daughter and I Have Known, A.
Nightswim.
Sea-Grape Tree and the Miraculous.
Sometimes Heaven Is a Mean Machine.
Song of Returnings.
Under the Umbrella of Blood.
Wheel Turning on the Hub of the Sun.
White Horse of the Father, White Horse of the Son.
Rorie, David
Pawky Duke, The.
Rorty, James
Gray Shore.
Ros, Villeam. *See* **Ross, William**
Rosales, Luis
That Which You Call "Love Me."
Roscoe, William
Butterfly's Ball, The.
Roscoe, William Caldwell
For Ever.
Parting.
Poetic Land, The.
Spiritual Love.
Roscoe, William Stanley
To Spring: On the Banks of the Cam.
Roscommon, Wentworth Dillon, 4th Earl of
Essay on Translated Verse, An, *sel.*
On the Death of a Lady's Dog.
Song on a Young Lady Who Sung Finely.
Rose, Alexander Macgregor ("A. M. R. Gordon")
Kaiser and Co ("Der Kaiser auf der Vaterland").
Rose, Billy
Barney Google.
Does the Spearmint Lose Its Flavor on the Bedpost Overnight?
Unknown Soldier, The.
Rose, Sir George
Chancery Suit, A.
Rose, Greta Leora
Spring Is at Work with Beginnings of Things.
Rose, Harriet
Mellisandra.
Succubus, The.
Wedding Coat, The.
Rose, Mary Catherine
Clown, The.
Parade, A.
Rose, Wendy
America.
Builder Kachina; Home-going.
Calling Home the Scientists.
Celebration for My Mother.
Chasing the Paper-Shamans.
Detective Work.
Entering the Desert; Big Circles Running.
Epilog: "Drop a kernel of corn on a rock."
Epitaph: "Roots of mankind are tangled in my hair, The."
Evening Ceremony; Dream for G. V.
For Mabel: Pomo Basketmaker and Doctor.
For My People.
For Steph.
For Walter Lowenfels.
Grunion.
Halfbreed Chronicles; Isamu.
Hanabi-ko (Koko).
How I Came to Be a Graduate Student.
I Expected My Skin and My Blood to Ripen.
Indian Women Are Listening, The; to the Nuke Devils.
Julia.
Learning to Understand Darkness.
Long Division; a Tribal History.
Loo-wit.
Lost Copper, *sel.*
Man Who Dreamt He Was Turquoise, The.
Mount Saint Helens/ Loowit; an Indian Woman's Song.
Naming Power.
Oh Father.
Oh My People I Remember.
Parts of a Poet. The.
Poem to a Redskin.
Poet Haunted, The.
Poet Woman's Mitosis; Dividing All the Cells Apart.
Protecting the Burial Grounds.
Pueblo Women I Watched Get Down in Brooklyn, The.
Punk Party (They Told Me It Was Literary. . .).
Saint Patrick's Day, 1973.
Sarah: Cherokee Doctor.
Self Dirge.
They Sometimes Call Me.
Three Thousand Dollar Death Song.
To an Imaginary Father.
To Some Few Hopi Ancestors.
Walking on the Prayerstick.
Well-intentioned Question, The.
Roseliep, Raymond
Auden ("Auden is dead, and leaves").
Elegy for Ezra.
Marianne Moore (1887–1972).
When I Was Nine.
Roseliep, Raymond Francis
Lady of Letters.
Symphony in Blue.
To Mary: At the Thirteenth Station.
Where Do I Love You, Lovely Maid?
Rosemergy, Jim
Human Dilemma.
Rosen, Kenneth
Abstinence.
Act, An.
Confab.
Girls.
Rosen, Michael
Christmas Dinner.
Hidebehind, The.
I'm Alone in the Evening.
Rosenbaum, Benjamin
O Pity Our Small Size.
Rosenbaum, Nathan
Pictures at an Exhibition.
Rosenberg, Betsy
Bird Song.
Unearthing.
Rosenberg, David
Maps to Nowhere.
Rain Has Fallen on the History Books.
Rosenberg, Dorothy
Bim Bam.
Rosenberg, Harold
Epos.
Rosenberg, Isaac
August 1914.
Beauty.
Break of Day in the Trenches.
Burning of the Temple, The.
Chagrin.
Daughters of War.
Dead Heroes, The.
Dead Man's Dump.
Destruction of Jerusalem by the Babylonian Hordes, The.
Expression.
Female God, The.
Girl to Soldier on Leave.
God.
Home-Thoughts from France.
I Am the Blood.
If You Are Fire.
Immortals, The.
Jew, The.
Louse Hunting.
Love and Lust.
Marching.
Midsummer Frost.
My Soul Is Robbed.
On Receiving News of the War.
One Lost, The.
Returning, We Hear the Larks.
Saul.
Soldier: Twentieth Century.
Spiritual Isolation.
Spring.
Through These Pale Cold Days.
Wedded.
Worm Fed on the Heart of Corinth, A.
Rosenberg, Joel
First Wedding in the World, The.
Violin Tree, The.

Rosenberg, L. M.
For Leningrad, and My Jewish Ancestors.
Rosenberger, Francis Coleman
Are You Just Back for a Visit or Are You Going to Stay?
Poets Observed.
Rosenblatt, Joe
Ant Trap, The.
Cat.
Fish.
Ichthycide.
It's in the Egg.
Metamorpho I.
Of Dandelions & Tourists.
Saphire (Metamorpho's Chick).
Rosenfeld, Marjorie Stamm
David Homindae.
Rosenfeld, Monroe H. ("F. Belasco")
Johnny Get Your Gun, *with music.*
Those Wedding Bells Shall Not Ring Out! *with music.*
Rosenfeld, Morris Jacob
Another While.
Cry from the Ghetto, A.
Jewish May, The.
My Camping Ground.
Simchas Torah.
So Long Ago.
Rosenfeld, Rita
Stacking Up.
Rosenfield, Loyd
Ode to a Vanished Operator in an Automatized Elevator.
You Take the Pilgrims, Just Give Me the Progress.
Rosenhane, Gustav
Sonnet: "And then I sat me down, and gave the rein."
Sonnet: "Deep in a vale where rocks on every side."
Rosenius, Carl Olof
With God and His Mercy, *with music.*
Rosenmann-Taub, David
Elegy and Kaddish.
Moral Ode.
Prelude: "Afterwards, afterwards the wind between two mountains."
Reconciliation.
Sabbath.
To a Young Girl.
Rosensaft, Menachem Z.
Second Generation, The.
Rosenthal, Abby
June Song.
Rosenthal, John
Love's Fool.
Roskolenko, Harry
Baguio Poems, *sel.*
Come unto Us Who Are . . . Laden.
Nationalism.
Old World, New World.
Symbols.
Waiting for God.
Rosner, Martin C.
Listening-Post.
Rosner, Paul
Don't Say You Like Tchaikowsky.
Ross, Abram Bunn
Two in Bed.
Ross, Alan
Antwerp: Musée des Beaux-Arts.
At Only That Moment.
In Bloemfontein.
Koala.
Leave Train.
Mess Deck Casualty.
Off Brighton Pier.
Radar.
Stanley Matthews.
Ross, Alexander
Wooed and Married and A'.
Ross, Allison
Game out of Hand.
Ross, Charles Henry
Jack.
John, Tom, and James.
Old Woman, An.
Ross, Charles Sarsfield
Dear Old Mothers.
Ross, David
Briton Who Shot at His King, A.
I Am Your Loaf, Lord.
News Reel.
On Apples.
Ross, Gertrude Robison
I Was Made of This and This.
Ross, Sir Ronald
Lines Written after the Discovery by the Author of the Germ of Yellow Fever.
Ross, W. W. Eustace
Creek, The.
Diver, The.
Fish.
If Ice.
In the Ravine.
On Angels.
Pine Gum.
Saws Were Shrieking, The.
Snake Trying, The.
Summons, The.
Walk, The.
Ross, William [*or* Villeam Ros]
Another Song ("It is I that am under sorrow at this time").
Rosselson, Leon
Palaces of Gold.
Rossetti, Christina Georgina
Advent.
After Death.
All Things Wait upon Thee.
Aloof.
Amor Mundi.
Apple Gathering, An.
Ash Wednesday.
Autumn.
Battle Within, The.
Before the Beginning.
Before the Paling of the Stars.
Better Resurrection, A.
Birthday, A.
Bitter for Sweet.
Bourne, The.
Bride Song.
By the Sea.
Caterpillar.
Cherry Tree.
Child's Talk in April.
Christmas Carol, A: "In the bleak mid-winter."
Christmas Carol: "Thank God, thank God, we do believe."
City Mouse and the Garden Mouse, The.
Color.
Comparisons.
Consider.
Convent Threshold, The.
Crown of Windflowers, A.
December.
Dirge, A: "Why were you born when the snow was falling?"
Dream Land.
Dream-Love.
Easter Carol, An: "Spring bursts to-day."
Easter Monday.
Echo.
End, An.
Enrica, 1865.
Eve.
Ferry Me across the Water.
Ferryman, The.
First Day, The.
First Spring Day, The.
Flint.
Freaks of Fashion.
From Sunset to Star Rise.
From the Antique.
Goblin Market.
Golden Silence.
Good Friday.
Good Friday Evening.
Half Moon Shows a Face of Plaintive Sweetness, The.
Heaven Is Heaven.
"Heaven Is Not Far."
Heaven Overarches Earth and Sea.
Herself a Rose Who Bore the Rose.
Holy Innocents.
Hope and Joy.
How Many Seconds in a Minute?
Hurt No Living Thing.
I do not look for love that is a dream.
I dug and dug amongst the snow.
"I Will Accept."
If I Could Trust Mine Own Self.
If I Were a Queen.
If Only.
Immalee.
In an Artist's Studio.
In Progress.
Is the Moon Tired?
Italia, Io Ti Saluto.
Judge Not According to the Appearance.
Lady Moon.
Lambs of Grasmere, 1860, The.
Last Prayer.
Last Rites.
Laura and Lizzie Asleep.
Let's Be Merry.
Life's Parallels, A.
Long Barren.
Lord, Grant Us Calm.
Lord, Save Us, We Perish.
Love Is Stronger than Death.
Lowest Place, The.
Lullaby: "Love me—I love you."
Luscious and Sorrowful.
Marvel of Marvels.
Maude Clare.
May.
Meeting ("If we shall live, we live").
Meeting ("They made the chamber sweet with flowers and leaves").
Memory ("I have a room whereinto no one enters").
Memory ("I nursed it in my bosom while it lived").
Milking-Maid, The.
Minnie and Mattie.
Mirage.
Mix a Pancake.
Monna Innominata.
Months, The.
Mother Country.
My Dream.
My Gift.
Next of Kin.
"No, Thank You, John."
None Other Lamb [None Other Name].
November.
O Lady Moon.
O Lord, Seek Us.
Oh, Fair to See.
Oh Roses for the Flush of Youth.
Old and New Year Ditties, *sel.*
Old-World Thicket, An.
On the Death of a Cat.
On the Wing.
One Certainty, The.
Pancake, The.
Paradise.
Passing and Glassing.
Passing Away, Saith the World, Passing Away.
Pause of Thought, A.
Poor Ghost, The.
Prayer, A: "Clother of the lily, feeder of the sparrow."

Prince's Progress, The, *sel.*
Rainbow, The.
Remember.
Rest.
Riddle, A: "There is one that has a head without an eye."
Riddle: "First it was a pretty flower, dressed in pink and white."
Royal Princess, A.
Rushes in a watery place.
St. Peter.
Sea-Sand and Sorrow.
Seasons.
Send Me.
Shadows To-day.
Shepherds Had an Angel, The.
Shut Out.
Sketch, A.
Sleep at Sea.
Sleeping at Last.
Somewhere or Other.
Song: "Oh roses for the flush of youth."
Song: "She sat and sang alway."
Song: "When I am dead, my dearest."
Sonnet: "Remember me when I am gone away."
Soul, A.
Sound of the Wind, The.
Spring.
Spring Quiet.
Stay, June, Stay!
Summer.
Summer Is Ended, The.
Summer Wish, A.
Symbols.
They Toil Not neither Do They Spin.
Thread of Life, The, *sel.*
Three Enemies, The.
Three Seasons.
To My First Love, My Mother.
Triad, A.
Tune Me, O Lord, into One Harmony.
Twice.
Twilight Calm.
Two Pursuits.
Up-Hill.
Valentine to My Mother, A, 1882.
Valentines to My Mother, 1880.
Weary in Well-doing.
Wednesday in Holy Week.
What Are Heavy?
What Do They Do?
What Does the Bee Do?
What Is Pink?
When I Am Dead.
Who Has Seen the Wind?
Who Shall Deliver Me?
Wind, The.
Wind of January, The.
Winter: My Secret.
Winter Rain.
Wisdom.
World, The.

Rossetti, Dante Gabriel
Antwerp and Bruges.
Ardour and Memory.
Aspecta Medusa.
Autumn Idleness.
Autumn Song.
Ave.
Barren Spring.
Beauty and the Bird.
Birth-Bond, The.
Body's Beauty.
Bridal Birth.
Bride's Prelude, The.
Burden of Nineveh, The.
Card Dealer, The.
Chimes.
Choice, The.
Dark Glass, The.
Dawn on the Night-Journey.
Day-Dream, The.
Day of Love, A.
Death-in-Love.
Even So.
Fir-Tree of Bosnia, The.
For "A Venetian Pastoral" by Giorgione.
For "An Allegorical Dance of Women" by Andrea Mantegna.
For "Our Lady of the Rocks" by Leonardo da Vinci.
For "Ruggiero and Angelica" by Ingres.
For the Holy Family by Michelangelo.
For "The Wine of Circe" by Edward Burne-Jones.
Fragment: "At her step the water-hen."
Friar of Orders Grey, The.
Genius in Beauty.
He and I.
Heart's Compass.
Heart's Haven.
Heart's Hope.
Her Gifts.
Hill Summit, The.
Honeysuckle, The.
House of Life, The *sels.*
Inclusiveness.
Jenny.
Kiss, The.
Landmark, The.
Last Confession, A.
Life-in-Love.
Lilith.
Limerick: "There is an old he-wolf named Gambart."
Limerick: "There once was a painter named Scott."
Limerick: "There was a poor chap called Rossetti."
Limerick: "There's a combative artist named Whistler."
Limerick: "There's an Irishman, Arthur O'Shaughnessy."
Little While, A.
Lost Days.
Lost on Both Sides.
Love Enthroned.
Love Sight.
Love-Sweetness.
Lovers' Walk, The.
Love's Last Gift.
Lovesight.
Mary Magdalene at the Door of Simon the Pharisee.
Mary's Girlhood.
Match with the Moon, A.
Mid-Rapture.
Mirror, The.
My Sister's Sleep.
Not as These.
Nuptial Sleep.
Old Song Ended, An.
On Himself.
On Refusal of Aid between Nations.
On Robert Buchanan, Who Attacked Him under the Pseudonym of "Thomas Maitland."
On the Painter Val Prinsep.
On the Poet O'Shaughnessy.
On the Site of a Mulberry-Tree.
On the "Vita Nuova" of Dante.
One Hope, The.
Orchard-Pit, The.
"Our Lady of the Rocks."
Passover in the Holy Family, The.
Penumbra.
Portrait, The ("O Lord of all compassionate control").
Portrait, The ("This is her picture as she was").
Pride of Youth.
Saint Luke the Painter.
Sea Limits, The.
Sea-Spell [for a Picture], A.
Severed Selves.
Silent Noon.
Sister Helen.
Sleepless Dreams.
Song IV: Sudden Light.
Song of the Bower, The.
Song-Throe, The.
Sonnet, A: "Sonnet is a moment's monument, A."
Sonnet: Barren Spring.
Sonnet: Lovesight.
Sonnet: Nuptial Sleep.
Sonnet: Superscription, A.
Soul's Beauty.
Staff and Scrip, The.
Stratton Water.
Sudden Light.
Sunset Wings.
Superscription, A.
There is a big artist named Val.
There's combative artist named Whistler.
Three Shadows.
Through Death to Love.
To Art.
Tom Agnew, Bill Agnew.
Transfigured Life.
Vain Virtues.
Vase of Life, The.
What Smouldering Senses.
White Ship, The.
Willowwood.
Without Her.
Woodspurge, The.
Words on the Windowpane.
World's Worth.
Young Fir-Wood, A.
Youth's Antiphony.
Youth's Spring-Tribute.

Rossi, Azariah di
Epitaph: "From out the stormy sea unto the shore."

Rosslyn, Earl of. *See* **Erskine, Francis Robert St. Clair**

Rostand, Edmond
Cyrano de Bergerac, *sels.*

Rosten, Norman
Aesthetic.
Black Boy.
Byron in Greece.
Face on the Daguerreotype.
From the Provinces.
Out of Our Shame.
This Child ("This child, exile of hope").
To Ariake Kambara.

Roston, Ruth
Salesman.
Two Windows by Magritte.

"Rostrevor, George." *See* **Hamilton, George Rostrevor**

Rotella, Guy
High Summer.
Somewhere Farm.

Roth, Hemda
Song, The: "Song, The! the song!"
Treason of Sand.
Young Deer/Dust, A.

Roth, Joseph
Ahasuerus.

Rothenberg, Jerome
Alphabet Came to Me, The.
Beadle's Testimony, The.
Bodhisattva Undoes Hell, A.
Cokby, Part Two.
Dark bull quartered in my eye.
Esther K. Comes to America: 1931.
Fifth Hell, The.
Letter to Paul Celan in Memory, A.
"Little Boy Lost, A."
Others Hunters in the North the Cree, The.
Poem in Yellow after Tristan Tzara, A.
Poland/ 1931 "The Wedding."
Portrait of a Jew Old Country Style.
Seven Hells of Jigoku Zoshi, The, *sels.*
Seventh Hell, The.

Sightings I.
Sixth Hell, The.
Soap (II).
Stationmaster's Lament, The.
Structural Study of Myth, The.
Three Landscapes, *sel.*
Young Woman's Neo-Aramaic Jewish Persian Blues.
48 Words for a Woman's Dance Song.
Rothenstein, William *and* **Max Beerbohm.** *See* **Beerbohm, Max** *and* **William Rothenstein**
Rothfork, John
Deep Calling, The.
Rottman, Larry
What Kind of War?
Rouget de Lisle, Claude Joseph
Marseillaise, The [*or* La].
Roughton, Roger
Building Society Blues.
Soluble Noughts and Crosses; or, California, Here I Come.
Roumain, Jacques
Guinea.
Roumer, Emile
Black Girl Goes By, A.
Peasant Declares His Love, The.
Rounds, Emma
Johnny.
Plane Geometry.
Rous, Francis
Help, Lord, because the Godly Man, *with music.*
I to the Hills Will Lift Mine Eyes, *with music.*
Routhier, Adolphe
O Canada!
Rowbotham, David
Mullabinda.
Prey to Prey.
Town, The.
Rowe, Henry
Moon.
Sun.
Rowe, James Wilton
Lake Chemo.
Rowe, Nicholas
Colin's Complaint.
Fair Penitent, The, *sel.*
Rowell, Charles H.
Old Women Still Sing, The.
Rowland, J. R.
Canberra in April.
London.
Seven Days.
Traveller, A.
Rowlands, Samuel
Melancholy Knight, The, *sels.*
Poetaster, The.
Sir Eglamour.
Rowles, Catharine Bryant
New Snow.
Rowley, William *and* **Thomas Middleton.** *See* **Middleton, Thomas** *and* **William Rowley**
Rowse, Alfred Leslie
White Cat of Trenarren, The.
Rowswell, Albert K.
Should You Go First.
Royde-Smith, Naomi
Horse, The.
Royden, Matthew
Elegy, or Friend's Passion for His Astrophil, An, *sels.*
On Sir Philip Sidney.
Royle, Edwin Milton
Doan't You Be What You Ain't.
Rozewicz, Tadeusz
To the Heart.
Ruark, Gibbons
Finding the Pistol.
Goods She Can Carry, The: Canticle of Her Basket Made of Reeds.
Lost Letter to James Wright, with Thanks for a Map of Fano.
Nightmare Inspection Tour for American Generals.
Soaping Down for Saint Francis of Assisi: The Canticle of Sister Soap.
Talking Myself to Sleep in the Mountain.
Working the Rain Shift at Flanagan's.
Rubadiri, James D.
Stanley Meets Mutesa.
Rubenstein, Carol
Dayak Man Making Fishtrap.
Rubin, Ilya
Escape.
Handful of Ashes.
No Sense Grieving.
Poem from "The Revolution."
Slow Oxen.
Rubin, Larry
Addict, The.
Brother-in-Law, The.
Exile, The.
Lesson, The.
Manual, The.
Pact, The.
Registered at the Bordello Hotel (Vienna).
Son, Condemned, The.
Temporary Problems.
Ruby, Harry *and* **Bert Kalmar.** *See* **Kalmar, Bert** *and* **Harry Ruby**
Rückert, Friedrich ("Freimund Raimar")
And Then No More.
Barbarossa.
Ride round the Parapet, The.
Rudaki
Came to me.
Ruddick, Bruce
Freighter.
Plaque.
Ruddock, Margot
Autumn, Crystal Eye.
Child Compassion, The.
I Take Thee Life.
Love Song: "Though to think/ Rejoiceth me."
O Holy Water.
Spirit, Silken Thread.
Take Away.
Rudnik, Raphael
Amsterdam Street Scene, 1972.
Lady in the Barbershop, The.
Penny Trumpet.
Rudnitsky, Leah
Birds Are Drowsing on the Branches.
Rudolf, Anthony
Ancient of Days.
Ashkelon.
Dubrovnik Poem (Emilio Tolentino).
Evening of the Rose.
Hands Up.
Prayer for Kafka and Ourselves.
Rudolph, Lee
Warming Up for the Real Thing.
Rudyerd, Sir Benjamin
Why Do We Love.
Ruebner, Tuvia
Among Iron Fragments.
Document.
First Days.
I Left.
Ruelfe, Mary
Written.
Ruffin, Paul
Cleaning the Well.
Grandpa's Picture.
Hotel Fire: New Orleans.
Rufinus Domesticus
Andante, ma Non Assai.
Aut Neutrum . . . Vel Duos.
Complaint.
Epigram: "Boy-mad no longer."
Faint Heart.
Lover's Posy, The.
Requirements: "Not too chary, not too fast."
Requirements: "Not too lean, and not too fat."
Ruggles, Eugene
Deeper in the Tank—the Last Middle East Crisis, 1972.
Rugo, Mariève
In the Season of Wolves and Names.
Limbo.
Sundays.
Ruiz, Juan, Archpriest of Hita
Praise of Little Women.
Rukeyser, Muriel
Ajanta.
Akiba.
Along History.
Boy with His Hair Cut Short.
Boys of These Men Full Speed.
Ceiling Unlimited.
Children, the Sandbar, That Summer.
Children's Elegy.
Church of Galilee, The.
Columbus.
Crayon House.
Darkness Music.
Despisals.
Don Baty, the Draft Resister.
Double Ode.
Easter Eve.
Effort at Speech between Two People.
Eighth Elegy, *sel.*
Endless.
Even during War.
Eyes of Night-Time.
Fields Where We Slept.
Gates, The, *sel.*
Gauley Bridge.
George Robinson: Blues.
Gibbs, *sel.*
Holy Family.
Islands.
Käthe Kollwitz.
Leg in a Plaster Cast, A.
Letter to the Front.
Looking at Each Other.
Madboy's Song.
Meeting, The.
Mendings.
Mrs. Walpurga.
More Clues.
More of a Corpse than a Woman.
Motive.
Motive of All of It, The.
Myth.
Night Feeding.
No one ever walking this our only earth.
Nuns in the Wind.
Painters.
Place at Albert Bay, The.
Poem (I Lived in the First Century).
Poem out of Childhood.
Question, The.
Reading Time: 1 Minute 26 Seconds.
Resurrection of the Right Side.
Rondel: "Now that I am fifty-six."
Rotten Lake Elegy.
St. Roach.
Song: "World is full of loss, The; bring, wind, my love."
Soul and Body of John Brown, The.
Speaking Tree, The.
Speed of Darkness, The.
Tenth Elegy: Elegy in Joy.
Then.
This Morning.
This Place in the Ways.
Time Exposures.
To Be a Jew in the Twentieth Century.
Trial, The.
Trinity Churchyard.
Waiting for Icarus.
Watchers, The.
Rumaker, Michael
Fairies Are Dancing All Over the World, The.

Rumi, Jalal ed-Din [*or* al-Din]
Beauty That All Night Long, A.
Drunkards, The ("The drunkards are rolling in slowly").
Happy the moment when we are seated in the Palace.
I am your mother, your mother's mother.
Lo, for I to myself am unknown.
Name, The.
Not in India, where fire rivers are.
Rungren, Lawrence R.
Sunday.
Runyon, Damon (Alfred Damon Runyon)
Song of Panama, A.
Rushton, Edward
Human Debasement; a Fragment.
Ruskin, John
Awake! Awake!
My Dog Dash.
Needless Alarm, The.
Trust Thou Thy Love.
Russ, Lawrence
Price of Paper, The.
Wedding Poem, The, *sel.*
Russ, Lisa
Piano.
Russ, Virginia
Shape of Autumn, The.
Russell, Charles E.
Fleet at Santiago, The.
Russell, Ethel Green
Letter from the Vieux Carre.
Russell, George William. *See* **"Æ"**
Russell, Irwin
Christmas Night in the Quarters, *sel.*
Fust Banjo, De.
Nebuchadnezzar.
Russell, James I.
Where the River Shannon Flows, *with music.*
Russell, Norman H.
Appearance.
Cherokee Dean, The.
Indian School.
Message of the Rain, The.
Tornado, The.
Tree Sleeps in the Winter, The.
Russell, Sanders
Poem: "I keep feeling all space as my image."
Russell, Sydney King
Death Was a Woman.
Dust.
Midsummer.
Phyllis.
Russell, Thomas
Maniac, The.
Names and Order of the Books of the Old Testament.
New Testament, The.
Old Testament, The.
Philoctetes.
Sonnet: "Could then the babes from yon unshelter'd cot."
Sonnet: Suppos'd to Be Written at Lemnos.
Sonnet: To Oxford.
Sonnet: To Valclusa.
Sonnet Supposed to Be Written at Lemnos.
Russo, Lola Ingres
Autumn Squall—Lake Erie.
Rustico di Filippo
Sonnet: Of the Making of Master Messerin.
Rutan, Catherine
Still Birth.
Ruth, Fern Pankratz
Guyana.
Rutherford, Alison. *See* **Cockburn, Alison Rutherford**
Rutilius
Roma.
Rutledge, Archibald
O Mariners!
Oblique.
Rutsala, Vern
Bijou.
Eagle Squadron.
Fame.
Fat Man, The.
Final Cut, The.
Less Is More.
Marriage Contract.
Pursuit.
Sunday.
War of the Worlds, The.
Washrags.
Words.
World, The.
Ryan, Abram Joseph (Father Ryan)
Better than Gold ("Better than grandeur, better than gold").
Child's Wish, A.
Conquered Banner, The.
Rosary of My Tears, The.
Sentinel Songs.
Ryan, George
Unsolved Mystery.
Ryan, Margaret
Alexandrite Ring, The.
Ryan, Michael
After.
Barren Poem.
Consider a Move.
In Winter.
Letter from an Institution: III.
My Dreams by Henry James.
Prothalamion.
Speaking.
This Is a Poem for the Dead.
When I Was Conceived.
Ryan, Paddy
Man That Waters the Workers' Beer, The.
Ryan, Richard
Deafness.
El Dorado.
From My Lai the Thunder Went West.
Ireland.
Knockmany.
O, Saw Ye the Lass.
Wet Night, A.
Ryberg, Barbara Cornet
Step by Step.
Ryden, Ernest Edwin
Twilight Shadows round Me Fall, The, *with music.*
Ryerson, Alice
Death Watchers, The.
Ryman, James
Farewell Advent, *at.*
Now the Most High Is Born.
Ryojin Hisho
May the man who gained my trust yet did not come.
Ryota
Moon in the Water, The.
Ryskind, Morrie ("John P. Wintergreen")
Horace the Wise.
To Natalie.
Ryuho
Moon, The.
Ryvel
Pilgrimage to Testour, The.

S

"S, A. W."
Life That Counts, The.
"S., C. N."
Thenot Protests.
"S., E."
Being Forsaken of His Friend He Complaineth.
"S., J. H."
New Year's Wish, A.
"S. C. M'K." See **"M'K., S. C.**
Saadi, Rose
Factory Rainbow, A.
Saarikoski, Pentti
Guest, The.
Une Vie.
Saavedra, Guadalupe de
If You Hear That a Thousand People Love You.
Saba, Umberto
Goat, The.
Sleepless on a Summer Night.
Three Streets.
Woman.
Sabin, Edwin L.
Easter.
Sabina, Maria
Shaman.
Sabines, Jaime
Amen.
You Have What I Look For.
Saboly, Nicolas
Boots and Saddles.
Bring a Torch, Jeanette, Isabella.
Shepherd Boys, The.
Sacchetti, Franco
Ballata: His Talk with Certain Peasant-Girls.
Catch: On a Wet Day.
On a Wet Day.
Sach, Natan
No.
Sachs, Elizabeth Newton
Celebration.
Sachs, Nelly
Above the rocking heads of the mothers.
Awakening—/ Voices of birds
Burning Sand of Sinai.
But Perhaps.
Chorus of the Rescued.
Chorus of the Unborn.
Hasidim Dance.
In flight in escape.
In the blue distance.
Landscape of Screams.
Last one, The/ to die here.
Line Like.
O Night of the Crying Children.
O the Chimneys.
Oblivion! Skin.
One Chord.
Sleepwalker, The.
To You Building the New House.
Vainly ("Vainly/the epistles burn").
What Secret Desires of the Blood.
White Serpent.
Sackville, Charles, 6th Earl of Dorset
À Madame, Madame B, Beauté Sexagenaire.
Advice, The.
Dainty young heiress of Lincoln's Inn Fields, The.
Excellent New Ballad Giving a True Account of the Birth and Conception of a Late Famous Poem Called the Female Nine, An.
Fire of Love, The.
May the Ambitious Ever Find.
On Mr. Edward Howard, upon His British Princes.
On the Countess of Dorchester ("Dorinda's sparkling wit, and eyes").
On the Countess of Dorchester (Tell me, Dorinda, why so gay").
On the Young Statesmen.
Phillis for Shame Let Us Improve.
Song: "Dorinda's sparkling wit, and eyes."
Song: "Methinks the poor town has been troubled too long."
Song: "Phillis, for shame let us improve."
Song: "To all you ladies now at land."
Song: Written at Sea, in the First Dutch War (1665), the Night before an Engagement.
To Mr. Bays.

Sackville, Lady Margaret
Apple, The.
Epitaph, An: "As shining sand-drift."
Memory, A.
Resurrection.
Sacrament.
Sermon, A.
To One Who Denies the Possibility of a Permanent Peace.
Sackville, Thomas, 1st Earl of Dorset
Complaint of Henrie Duke of Buckinghame, The.
Induction to "A Mirror for Magistrates."
Midnight.
Mirror for Magistrates, A.
Shield of War, The.
Sleep.
Thomas Sackevyll in Commendation of the Worke to the Reader.
Troy.
Vision of Sorrow.
Vision of War, A.
Winter.
Sackville-West, Victoria Mary
Aquarium, San Francisco, The.
Black Tarn.
Bull, The.
Craftsmen.
Dream, A.
Full Moon.
Greater Cats, The.
Land, The, *sel.*
On the Lake.
Owl, The.
Persia.
Sea-Sonnet.
Sometimes When Night.
Song: "If I had only loved your flesh."
Song: "My spirit like a shepherd boy."
Spring.
To Any M. F. H.
Wood-cut.
Young Stock.
Sadeh, Pinhas
Elegy: "While walking at dusk in a strange city."
In the Forest.
In the Garden of the Turkish Consulate.
Raya Brenner.
Sadi [*or* Saadi] (Muslih-ud-Din)
Alas!
Bustan, The, *sels.*
Courage.
Dancer, The.
Friendship.
Gift of Speech, The.
Great Physician, The.
Gulistan, The, *sels.*
He Hath No Parallel.
Help.
Hyacinths to Feed Thy Soul.
Love's Last Resource.
Mesnevi.
Ode: "Until thine hands clasp girdlewise the waist of the Belov'd."
On the Deception of Appearances.
Sooth-Sayer, The.
Take the Crust.
Wealth.
Sadoff, Ira
Concise History of the World, A.
Fifties, The.
Hopper's "Nighthawks" (1942).
My Father's Leaving.
Poem after Apollinaire.
Seurat.
Sáez Burgos, Juan
That Poem.
This Afternoon.
Saffarzadeh, Tahereh
Birthplace.
Saffin, John
Acrostick on Mrs. Elizabeth Hull, An.
Acrostick on Mrs. Winifret Griffin, An.
Brief Elegie on My Dear Son John, A.
Consideratus Considerandus.
Elegie on the Deploreable Departure of the Honered and Truely Religious Chieftain John Hull, An.
Lamentation on My Dear Son Simon, A.
March 4th Anno 1698/9; a Charracteristicall Satyre.
One Presenting a Rare Book to Madame Hull.
Satyretericall Charracter of a Proud Upstart, A.
Sweetly (my Dearest) I left thee asleep.
To His Excellency Joseph Dudley.
Saffold, Thomas
Saffold's Cures, *At.*
Safford, William Harrison
Battle of Muskingum, The; or, The Defeat of the Burrites.
Safiya bint Musafir
At the Badr Trench.
Sagami, Lady
In the gathering dew.
Sage, Rufus B.
Night on the Prairie.
Summer on the Great American Desert.
Wanderer's Grave, The.
"Sagittarius" (Olga Katzin)
Nerves.
Sahl, Hans
Greeting from a Distance.
Memo.
Saidy, Fred
For a Little Lady.
Saigyo Hoshi
Although I do not know.
In my boat that goes.
Like those boats which are returning.
Mingling my prayer.
Since I am convinced.
Startled/ By a single scream.
Sail, Lawrence
Christmas Night.
Sainsbury, Ian
I put my hat upon my head, *parody.*
Loveliest of Counties, Shropshire Now.
Saint. *See* **undernames of individual saints**
Saint-Gelis, Mellin de
Sonnet of the Mountain, The.
"Saint Geraud." *See* **Knott, William**
St. Germain, Mark
Cannon Park.
St. John, David
Avenues, The.
Blue Waves.
Dolls.
Elegy: "Who keeps the owl's breath? Whose eyes desire?"
For Lerida.
Guitar.
Hotel Sierra.
Hush.
Iris.
Poem: "Your face,/so pale now it is blue."
Shore, The.
Slow Dance.
Two Sorrows.
Wavelength.
St. John, Peter
Descent on Middlesex, The.
St. John, Primus
Benign Neglect/ Mississippi, 1970.
Elephant Rock.
Lynching and Burning.
Morning Star, The.
Tyson's Corner.
St. Leger, Warham
False Gallop of Analogies, A.
To My Hairdresser.
Saint-Marthe, M.
Choosing a Wet-Nurse.
Cravings during Pregnancy.
Infant Diseases and Their Treatment.
Labour.
Paedotrophiae; or, The Art of Bringing Up Children, *sels.*
St. Martin, Laura
As I look out from the desk window.
Ocean is a strange, The.
St. Virginia, Sister Mary
Case of Thomas More, The.
Convent Cemetery, Mount Carmel.
Nun to Mary, Virgin, A.
Shrine in Nazareth.
Saiser, Marjorie
Morning.
Saito, Fumi
Palm of the hand, The,/ is not aware of dying.
Sakanoe [*or* **Sakanone], Lady Otomo of [***orno***].** *See* **Otomo of Sakanoe, Lady**
Sala, G. A.
Epitaph for John Camden Hotten.
Salamah, Son of Jandal
Gone Is Youth.
Salamun, Tomaz
Air.
Eclipse.
Salcman, Michael
Open Heart.
Saldaña, Diego de
Eyes So Tristful.
Saleh, Dennis
Bed, The.
Furniture of the Poem, The.
Guide to Familiar American Incest, A, *sel.*
Inventing a Family.
Nesting.
Return, The.
Story.
Thumb, The.
Salinas, Luis Omar
Pedro.
Salinas, Pedro
Razón de Amor, *sel.*
Salis-Seewis, Johann Gaudenz von
Song of the Silent Land.
Salisbury, Ralph
"Among the Savages. . ."
By Now.
Halo, A.
Second Molting, A.
This Is My Death-Dream.
Three Migrations.
Salkeld, Blanaid
Anchises.
Evasion.
Leave Us Religion.
Meditation.
Men Walked To and Fro.
No Uneasy Refuge.
Now Is Farewell.
Optimism.
Peggy.
Templeogue.
Terenure.
That Corner.
Youth.
Salkey, Andrew
Postcard from London, 23. 10. 1972.
Salome, Brian S.
Hello There.
Salomon, I. L.
Song for the Greenwood Fawn.
Salomon, Louis B.
Univac to Univac.
Salsbury, Nate
Apex.
Take Nothing for Granite.
Salsbury, Nate*and* Newman Levy
Ballade of the Ancient Wheeze.
Salsich, Albert
Staying Up on Jack's Fork near Eminence, Missouri.

Salter, Mary Jo
England.
Saltillo, José de
Rio Bravo—a Mexican Lament.
Saltman, Benjamin
Fathers, The.
Journey with Hands and Arms, The.
Saltus, Francis Saltus
Andalusian Sereno, The.
Bayadere, The.
Ideal, The.
Pastel.
Sphinx Speaks, The.
Salusbury, Sir John
Buen Matina.
Salverson, Laura Goodman
If a Maid Be Fair.
Premonition.
Salway, Owen C.
He Cares.
Salz, Helen
Late.
Sam, David A.
On the Pavement.
Samain, Albert
Pannyra of the Golden Heel.
Sammis, J. H.
All Needs Met.
Sampley, Arthur M.
Defender, The.
Sampter, Jessie E.
Kadia the Young Mother Speaks.
Promised Land, The.
Summer Sabbath.
Samuel ha-Nagid
Proverbs.
Sanborn, Franklin Benjamin
Ariana.
Samuel Hoar.
Sanchez, Carol Lee
Conversations from the Nightmare.
Open Dream Sequence.
Prologue: "Message-Bringer Woman."
Syl La Ble Speaks En Erg y/Sound, The.
Tribal Chant.
Way I Was, The.
Yesterday.
Sánchez, Ricardo
I Remember.
Sanchez, Sonia
Answer to Yo/ Question.
Black Magic.
Chant for Young/Brothas and Sistuhs, A.
Definition for Blk/ Children.
Don't Wanna Be.
For Our Lady.
Homecoming.
Hospital/ Poem.
Listenen to Big Black at S. F. State.
Memorial.
Nigger.
Now Poem. For Us.
Poem: "Look at me 8th."
Poem at Thirty.
Poem for Etheridge.
Poem for My Father, A.
Present.
Right On: White America.
Small Comment.
So This Is Our Revolution.
Summary.
Summer Words of a Sistuh Addict.
To All Brothers.
To All Sisters.
Sandag
"Word" of a Watch-Dog, The.
"Word" of a Wolf Encircled by the Hunt, The.
"Word" of an Antelope Caught in a Trap, The.
Sandburg, Carl
A. E. F.
Accomplished Facts.
Adelaide Crapsey.
Alice Corbin Is Gone.
All One People.
Aprons of Silence.
Arithmetic ("Arithmetic is where numbers fly like pigeons in and out of your head").
At a Window.
Auctioneer.
Baby Toes.
Balloon Faces.
Bas-Relief.
Bee Song.
Being Born Is Important.
Blacklisted.
Blue Island Intersection.
Bones.
Broken Sky.
Broken-Face Gargoyles.
Bronzes.
Buffalo Dusk.
Bundles.
Caboose Thoughts.
Chicago.
Chicago Boy Baby.
Child.
Circles.
Clinton South of Polk.
Clocks.
Cool Tombs.
Crapshooters.
Daybreak.
Death Snips Proud Men.
Early Copper.
Early Lynching.
Early Moon.
Electric Sign Goes Dark, An.
Elephants Are Different to Different People.
Falltime.
Fence, A.
Fish Crier.
Flash Crimson.
Fog ("The fog comes/ on little cat feet").
For You.
Four Preludes on Playthings of the Wind.
Fourth of July Night.
Gargoyle.
Gone.
Good Morning America, *sel.*
Grass.
Grassroots.
Handfuls.
Happiness.
Harbor, The.
Hazardous Occupations.
Horses and Men in the Rain.
I Am the People, the Mob.
Ice Handler.
Improved Farm Land.
In Tall Grass.
Jazz Fantasia.
Killers.
Laughing Child.
Lawyers Know Too Much, The.
Limited.
Little Candle.
Little Girl, Be Careful What You Say.
Localities.
Look at Six Eggs.
Losers.
Lost.
Love in Labrador.
Mammy Hums.
Man in the street is fed, The.
Manufactured Gods.
Milk-white Moon, Put the Cows to Sleep.
Mist Forms.
Mr. Attila.
Moist Moon People.
Muckers.
Mysterious Biography.
New Farm Tractor.
Nocturn Cabbage.
Nocturne in a Deserted Brickyard.
North Atlantic.
Old Flagman, The.
Old Timers.
On a Flimmering Floom You Shall Ride.
One Modern Poet.
Ossawatomie.
Our Prayer of Thanks, *sel.*
People Who Must.
People Will Live On, The.
People, Yes, The, *sels.*
Personality.
Pool.
Population Drifts.
Potomac Town in February.
Prairie, *sel.*
Prayer after World War.
Prayers of Steel.
Precious Moments.
Primer Lesson.
Psalm of Those Who Go Forth before Daylight.
Rat Riddles.
Repetitions.
River Roads.
Sandhill People.
Sea Hold, The.
Sea-Wash.
Shovel Man, The.
Sins of Kalamazoo, The.
Sketch.
Skyscraper.
Slippery.
Smoke and Steel, *sel.*
Soup.
Splinter.
Spring Grass.
Street Window.
Summer Stars.
Sunsets.
Ten Definitions of Poetry.
Theme in Yellow.
They All Want to Play Hamlet.
They Have Yarns.
Three Spring Notations on Bipeds.
Threes.
To a Contemporary Bunkshooter.
To Beachey, 1912.
To the Ghost of John Milton.
Trinity Place.
Upstream.
Wall Shadows.
Washington Monument by Night.
When Death Came April Twelve 1945.
Who Shall Speak for the People?
Why did the children/ put beans in their ears?
Wilderness.
Wind Song.
Wingtip.
Work Gangs.
Working Girls.
Young Sea.
Sandburg, Helga
Cantata for Two Lovers.
Importance of Mirrors, The.
Sandeen, Ernest
Nearing Winter.
Views of Our Sphere.
Sandell, Lina
Security.
Sanders, Edward
Fugs, The.
Holy Was Demeter Walking th' Corn Furrow.
Pindar's Revenge.
Sanders, Mark
Gone Fishing.
Happening In.
Stockton Lake; Stockton, Missouri.
Sanders, Thomas E.
Machine Out of the God.
Sanders, Velma
Old House Place.
Sandford, James
Of Love.

Sands, Robert Charles
Green Isle of Lovers, The.
Sandy, Stephen
Ballad of Mary Baldwin, The.
Declension.
Destruction of Bulfinch's House, The.
Et Quid Amabo Nisi Quod Aenigma Est.
Getting On.
Hiawatha.
Hunter's Moon.
Woolworth Philodendron, The.
Sandys, Edwin
In Pilgrim Life Our Rest, *with music.*
Sandys, George
Bounty of Jehovah Praise, The, *with music.*
Deo Opt. Max.
Judah in Exile Wanders, *with music.*
O Blest Estate, Blest from Above, *with music.*
Paraphrase on the Psalms of David, *sels.*
Saner, Reg
Anasazi at Mesa Verde.
Clear Night, Small Fire, No Wind.
Day the Air Was on Fire, The.
Fifth Season, The.
Flag.
Homing.
How the Laws of Physics Love Chocolate!
Orchestra.
Passing It On.
Space Eater Camps at Fifth Lake, The.
Sanfedele, Ann
Part of Fortune, The.
Sanfield, Steve
Dynamic Tension.
Sanford, Frank Elwood
Outcast, The.
San Geminiano, Folgore da
August.
Folk, Pat
On Knighthood.
Senile.
Sonnet: Of Virtue.
Sonnets of the Months.
Sangster, Charles
Evening.
Meadow-Field, The.
Pleasant Memories, *sel.*
Rapid, The.
Red Men, The.
St. Lawrence and the Saguenay, The, *sels.*
Sonnets Written in the Orillia Woods, *sels.*
Thousand Islands, The.
Sangster, Margaret Elizabeth (1984?-)
Mother's Prayer, A.
Security.
Work of Love, The.
Sangster, Margaret Elizabeth Munson (1898–1912)
Are the Children at Home?
Average Man, The.
Awakening.
Bit of the Book, A.
Building of the Nest, The.
Faith.
If Christ were here to-night, and saw me tired.
Midnight.
Now and Then.
Our Own.
Peace.
Show Me Thyself.
Sin of Omission, The.
Song for Our Flag, A.
Sunrise.
Thanksgiving.
They Never Quite Leave Us.
Thought, A.
Whittier.
Within the Veil.
Sannazaro, Jacopo (Actius Sincerus Sannazarius)
Celestial Queen.
De Partu Virginis, *sel.*
Like to these unmesurable montayns.
Sansom, Clive
Butterflies.
Innkeeper's Wife, The.
Ladybird.
Snowflakes.
Witnesses, The, *sel.*
Sant'Ana, Gloria de
African Day.
Sant' Angelo, Bartolomeo di
Sonnet: He Jests Concerning His Poverty.
Santayana, George
After Grey Vigils.
As in the Midst of Battle There Is Room.
Before a Statue of Achilles.
Faith.
I Would I Might Forget That I Am I.
Minuet on Reaching the Age of Fifty, A.
O Martyred Spirit.
O World.
O World, Thou Choosest Not the Better Part!
Ode: "My heart rebels against my generation."
Ode to the Mediterranean.
Odes, *sel.*
On the Death of a Metaphysician.
Prosit Neujahr.
Rustic at the Play, The.
Sonnet: "Deem not, because you see me in the press."
Sonnet: "O world, thou choosest not the better part!"
Sonnet: "What riches have you that you deem me poor?"
Sonnets, *sels.*
Sorrow.
To W. P., *sel.*
We Needs Must Be Divided.
What Riches Have You.
With you a part of me hath passed away.
Santob[*or* Shem-Tob] de Carrion
Consejos y Documentos al Rey Dom Pedro, *sel.*
Friend, A.
Jewish Poet Counsels a King, A.
Proverbios Morales, *sel.*
Resignation.
Self-Defense.
Santos, Sherod
Breakdown, The.
Childhood.
Country Landscape.
Enormous Aquarium, The.
Evening Refrain.
Goodbye.
Sirens in Bad Weather.
Sappho
About the cool water.
Achtung.
All the while, believe me, I prayed.
Alone.
Andromache's Wedding.
Andromeda/ forgot.
Be kind to me.
Beauty.
Come, holy tortoise shell.
Come out of Crete/ and find me here.
Come to me from Crete to this holy temple.
Don't ask me what to wear.
Dust of Timas, The.
Farewell to Anactoria.
Forever Dead.
Full Moon.
Glow and beauty of the stars, The.
He is more than a hero.
Here are fine gifts, children.
Hermes came to me in a dream. I said.
Hesperos, you bring home all the bright dawn disperses.
Honestly I wish I were dead!
I begin with words of air but delightful ones.
I could not hope/ to touch the sky.
I have had not one word from her.
I have no embroidered headband.
I hear that Andromeda.
If my nipples were to drip milk.
In gold sandals.
It would be wrong for us. It is not right.
Leave Krete and come to this holy temple.
Leaving Crete, come visit again our temple.
Life the very gods in my sight is he.
Like a mountain whirlwind.
Like a sweet apple reddening on the high.
Love.
Love—bittersweet, irrepressible.
Marriage of Hector and Andromache, The.
Moon Has Set, The.
Mother darling, I cannot work the loom.
My Atthis, although our dear Anaktoria.
My mother always said.
My muse, what ails this ardour?
Now in my/ heart I/ see clearly.
O dream from the blackness.
O Gongyla, my darling rose.
Ode to Anactoria.
Ode to Aphrodite.
On My Sweet Mother.
On your dazzling throne, Aphrodite.
One Girl.
Peer of the gods is that man, who.
People do gossip.
Round about Me.
"Sappho, if you do not come out."
Seizure.
Some say cavalry and others claim.
Some there are who say that the fairest thing seen.
Someone, I tell you,/ will remember us.
That labor/ a face to remember in wonder.
Then I said to the elegant ladies.
There's a man I really believe's in heaven.
To me he seems like a god.
Tonight I've watched.
We put the urn aboard ship.
You came. And you did well to come.
You know the place: then.
You lay in wait.
Sarett, Lew
Breakers of Broncos.
Four Little Foxes.
God Is at the Anvil.
Granite Mountain, The.
Great Divide, The.
Let Me Flower as I Will.
Let Me Go Down to Dust.
Loon, The.
Refuge.
Sheepherder, The.
Wind in the Pine.
Wolf Cry, The.
Sargent, Daniel
Ark and the *Dove,* The.
Preference.
Sargent, Elizabeth Nancy
Break, The.
Child.
Paradise.
Sailor at Midnight, A.
Sargent, Epes
Death of Warren, The.
Evening in Gloucester Harbor.
Heart's Summer, The.
Life on the Ocean Wave, A.
Summer Noon at Sea, A.
Sunrise at Sea.
Tropical Weather.
Sargent, John Osborne
Horace.
Sargent, N. B.
Building for Eternity.
Sargent, Nettie M.
Hymn of Trust, A.
Sargent, Robert
Concept of Force, The.
Epistemologist, over a Brandy, Opining, The.
Sargent, William D.
Wind-Wolves.

Sarmèd the Yahud
Quatrain: "Sarmèd, whom they intoxicated from the cup of love."
Quatrain: "This existence has, without the azure sphere, no reality."
Saroyan, Aram
Crickets.
Sarton, May
After All These Years.
After the palaces.
At Lindos.
Bears and Waterfalls.
Boulder Dam.
Burial.
Celebration, A.
Conversation in Black and White.
Fruit of Loneliness.
In Time like Air.
Last Word, A.
Leaves before the Wind.
Monticello.
Nativity.
Nobleman's House, A, *sel.*
Prayer before Work.
Prothalamium.
Sacred Order, The.
Santos: New Mexico.
Summer Music.
Three Things.
Transition.
Village Tale, A.
Sassoon, Siegfried
Absolution.
Aftermath.
Alone.
Arbor Vitae.
At Daybreak.
At Max Gate.
At the Grave of Henry Vaughan.
Attack.
Base Details.
Before Day.
"Blighters."
Brevities.
Case for the Miners, The.
Concert Party.
Conclusion: "Image dance of change, An."
Counter-Attack.
Dead Musicians.
Death-Bed, The.
December Stillness.
Does It Matter?
Down the Glimmering Staircase.
Dreamers.
Dug-out, The.
Early Chronology.
Elected Silence.
Everyman.
Everyone Sang ("Everyone suddenly burst out singing").
Falling Asleep.
Fancy Dress.
Fantasia on a Wittelsbach Atmosphere.
Fathers, The.
General, The.
Glory of Women.
Grandeur of Ghosts.
Haunted.
Hero, The.
I Stood with the Dead.
Imperfect Lover, The.
In Barracks.
In Me, Past, Present, Future Meet.
In the National Gallery.
"In the Pink."
Investiture, The.
Invocation: "Come down from heaven to meet me when my breath."
Kiss, The.
Lamentations.
Limitations.
Middle Ages.
Morning Glory.
Musical Critic Anticipates Eternity, A.
Mystic as Soldier, A.
Need, The.
On Passing the New Menin Gate.
One Who Watches.
One-legged Man, The.
Phoenix, The.
Picture-Show.
Post-Mortem, A.
Power and the Glory, The.
Prayer from 1936, A.
Prehistoric Burials.
Prelude: Troops, The.
Presences Perfected.
Rear-Guard, The.
Redeemer, The.
Repression of War Experience.
Sporting Acquaintances.
Stand-to: Good Friday Morning.
Storm on Fifth Avenue.
Strangeness of Heart.
Suicide in [the] Trenches.
"They."
To a Very Wise Man.
To an Old Lady Dead.
To His Dead Body.
Together.
Troops, The.
Two Old Ladies.
Vigils.
When I'm Alone.
Wisdom of the World, The.
Working Party, A.
Sato, Satoru
Japan That Sank under the Sea.
Satz, Mario
Coconut.
Fish.
Lemon.
Saucedo, María
About Women's Liberation.
Sa'udi, Mona
How do I enter the silence of stones.
When the loneliness of the tomb went down into the marketplace.
Why don't I write in the language of air?
Saul, George Brandon
By Winter Seas.
Elizabeth.
Spring Song.
Sauls, Roger
My Grandfather Burning Cornfields.
Reconcilable Differences.
Saunders, Donald G.
Ascent.
On Foinaven.
Saunders, Lesley
Mothers of Sons.
Saunders, Mary Wright
Remembering Day.
Saunders, R. Crombie
Empty Glen, The.
Ressaif My Saul.
Saunders, Ruby C. (Fareedah Allah)
Cinderella.
Funky Football.
Generation Gap, The.
Hush Honey.
Lawd, Dese Colored Chillum.
You Made It Rain.
Saunders, Thomas
End of Steel.
Horizontal World.
Savage, Ann Marie
In a Night.
Savage, Derek S.
Absent Creation.
Confession.
Fall of Leaves.
February.
Living.
Scenario.
Separation.
Wild Swan, The.
Winter Offering.
Savage, Frances Higginson
Duck in Central Park.
Savage, Minot Judson
Decorating the Soldiers' Graves.
Life's Common Duties.
My Birth.
Savage, Philip Henry
Infinity.
Morning.
Silkweed.
Solitude.
Savage, Richard
Animalcule, a Tale, The.
Authors of the Town, The, *sel.*
Bastard, The, *sel.*
Bristol.
Progress of a Divine, The, *sel.*
To a Young Lady.
Savant, John
In the Time of the Rose.
Savile, Jeremy
Health unto His Majesty, A.
Savoie, Terry
Far North, The.
Savonarola, Girolamo
O Star of Galilee.
Sawyer, C. P.
I Used to Love My Garden.
Sawyer, Charles Carroll
Weeping, Sad and Lonely.
When This Cruel War Is Over.
Sawyer, Frederick William
Recognition, The.
Sawyer, Mark
Kite Days.
Sawyer, Ruth
Feast o' Saint Stephen, The.
Sawyer, William
Turvey Top.
Saxe, John Godfrey
Blind Men and the Elephant, The.
Briefless Barrister, The.
Darling, Tell Me Yes.
Do I Love Thee?
Early Rising.
Game of Life, The.
How Cyrus Laid the Cable.
Justine, You Love Me Not!
My Familiar.
Puzzled Census Taker, The.
Pyramus and Thisbe.
Rhyme of the Rail[s].
Solomon and the Bees.
Sonnet to a Clam.
To Lesbia.
To My Love.
Too Candid by Half.
Wills.
Woman's Will.
Wouldn't You Like to Know.
Saxon, Alvin (Ojenke)
Black Power.
Poem for Integration, A.
Watts.
Saxon, Dan
Walking in the Rain.
Saxton, Andrew Bice
First Step, The.
Sayers, A. M.
It Always Seems.
Sayers, Dorothy Leigh
Choice of the Cross, The.
Devil to Pay, The, *sel.*
Sayers, Frances Clarke. *See* **Clarke, Frances**
Sayers, Henry J.
Ta-ra-ra Boom-der-é, *with music.*
Sayles, James M.
Star of the Evening.

Saylor, Mark
Hello, Sister.
Sayres, Cortlandt W.
Bankrupt.
Scalapino, Leslie
Areas.
Epilogue: Anemone.
Hmmmm, *sels.*
Seeing the Scenery.
Sequence, A.
Woman Who Could Read the Minds of Dogs, The.
Scannell, Vernon
Act of Love.
Any Complaints?
Autumn.
Dead Dog.
Discriminator, The.
Five Domestic Interiors.
Great War, The.
Incendiary.
Jailbird.
Jealous Wife, The.
Moods of Rain.
Moth, The.
Old Books, The.
Poetry Reading.
Reformed Drunkard.
Six Reasons for Drinking.
Spot-Check at Fifty.
Tightrope Walker.
Walking Wounded.
Words and Monsters.
Scantlebury, Elizabeth E.
Hymn of Dedication.
Scarborough, Dorothy
Organ Cactus, The.
Scarborough, George L.
To the Men Who Lose.
Scarbrough, George
Birth by Anesthesia.
Tenantry.
Viewpoint.
Scarbrough, Jessica
Birthsong.
Lunar Eclipse.
Professional prisoner.
There is no vacancy in this house.
Today, Prison Won.
Scarfe, Francis
Cats.
Cat's Eyes.
Clock, The.
Grotto, The.
Kitchen Poem.
Merry Window, The.
Ode in Honour.
Progression.
Tyne Dock.
Window, The.
Schaaf, Richard
Sparkling Water.
Schacht, Marshall
Not to Forget Miss Dickinson.
Schaechter-Gottesman, Beyle
Meditation.
Schaefer, Sister M. Cherubim
Rejoice, Let Alleluias Ring, *with music.*
Schaefer, Ted
Anxiety Pastorale.
Parents-Without-Partners Picnic, The.
Schaeffer, Susan Fromberg
First Test, The.
Housewife.
Truth.
Womb Song.
Yahrzeit.
Schauffler, Robert Haven
Nonsense.
Scum o' the Earth.
Schaukal, Richard
Images.
Schaumann, Ruth
Fourth Station.
Mary on Her Way to the Temple.
Schechter, Ruth Lisa
Vision of 400 Sunrises.
Schedler, Gilbert
Spring Day on Campus, A.
Scheele, Roy
August.
Fishing Blue Creek.
Gap in the Cedar, The.
Kitchen Memory, A.
Poppies.
Scheffauer, Ethel Talbot
Reply from the Akond of Swat, A.
Scheinert, David
Drunken Stones of Prague, The.
Stone and the Blade of Grass in the Warsaw Ghetto, The.
Scherzo, I. O.
Threnody: "Truth is a golden sunset far away."
Scheuer, Marjorie Somers
Fox, The.
Schevill, James
Crow-Marble Whores of Paris, The.
Death of a Cat.
Freud: Dying in London, He Recalls the Smoke of His Cigar Beginning to Sing.
Green Frog at Roadstead, Wisconsin.
Huck Finn at Ninety, Dying in a Chicago Boarding House Room.
Lesson in Hammocks, A.
London Pavement Artist.
Looking at Wealth in Newport.
Mixed Media.
Necessity of Rejection, The.
Old Peasant Woman at the Monastery of Zagorsk, The.
Screamer Discusses Methods of Screaming, A.
Story of Soutine, A.
Schierloh, Samuel
Bucko-Mate.
Schiff, Jeff
Winter Twilight.
Schiller, Johann Christoph Friedrich von
Columbus.
Maid of Orleans, The.
Piccolomini, The, *sel.*
Steer, Bold Mariner, On!
Thekla's Song.
To My Friends.
Unrealities, The.
Visit of the Gods, The.
Schimmel, Harold
Ancestors.
Schindler, Paul, Bob Adams *and* **David Lewis.** *See* **Lewis, David, Paul Schindler** *and* **Bob Adams**
Schjeldahl, Peter
Younger Poet, A.
Schlegel, Katharina von
Be Still, My Soul.
Schlesinger, John
South Shore Line.
Schlesinger,———
To the Parotid Gland.
Schlichter, Norman C.
Sledding Song, A.
Schlipf, Benjamin
Contentment.
Schloerb, Rolland W.
O Thou Eternal Source of Life.
Thou Light of Ages.
Schloss, David
Poem, The: "I had never heard of the whiteness."
Schmeltz, Susan Alton
Paper Dragons.
Schmid, Constance M.
Synekdechestai.
Schmidt, Lorenza
Heading for Eugene.
Schmidt, Tom
Black and White.
Broccoli.
Butcherboy.
Butter.
Civilization.
Creeper, The.
Drowning in Spanish.
In the Garden.
Long Overdue Thankyou Note to the Girl Who Taught Me Loving, A.
Seven Mexican Children.
Waking Up.
Schmitz, Dennis
Adolescence.
Arbeit Macht Frei.
California Phrasebook, The.
Chalk Angel, The.
Chicago: Near West-Side Renewal.
Coma.
Dressing Game.
Eclogues.
Gill Boy.
Goodwill, Inc.
If I Could Meet God.
Kindergarten.
Letter to Ron Silliman on the Back of a Map of the Solar System, A.
Making a Door.
Making Chicago.
Man Who Buys Hides, The.
Mile Hill.
Mole, The.
Name of Our Country, The.
News.
Picture of Okinawa, A.
Planting Trout in the Chicago River.
Poke-Pole Fishing.
Queen of Heaven Mausoleum.
Rabbits.
Skinning-the-Cat.
Star & Garter Theater.
String.
Virgil: Georgics, Book IV.
Schmolck, Benjamin
Consecration.
Schmuller, Aaron
Legend of His Lyre.
Schnackenberg, Gjertrud
Living Room, The.
Signs.
Schneckenburger, Max
Watch on the Rhine, The.
Schneider, Isidor
Insects.
Joy of Knowledge.
Schneider, Pat
In a Maple Wood.
Schneour, Zalman
Besieged.
Cherries.
Forsaken.
Last Words of Don Henriquez, The.
Like Water down a Slope.
Road, The.
Star There Fell, A.
War Comes.
Welcome, Queen Sabbath.
Schneurson, Zelda. *See* **Zelda**
Schoeck, Richard J.
Homage.
Scholem, Gershom
Trial, The.
Scholl, J. W.
Poet's Prothalamion, The, *sel.*
Scholten, Martin
Soliloquy by the Shore.
Schomberg, Ralph
Ay or Nay?
Courtier's a Riddle, A.
Judgment of Paris, The, *sels.*
Like Birds of a Feather.

Schonborg, Virginia
Construction.
Crowds.
Stickball.
Schorb, E. M.
Hush, Hush, New House in Charlotte.
No.
Schotz, Myra Glazer
First Love Poem, The.
Santa Caterina.
Thespian in Jerusalem.
Schramm, Donald G. H.
Voyage.
Schreiber, Laura
Delicate Balance, A.
Willows.
Schroeder, Peter
All Human Things.
Schubart, Christian
Song of the Cape of Good Hope.
Schubert, William H.
Educational Music or Erosion.
Schuck, L. Pearl
Solar Signals.
To a Butterfly.
Schuler, Ruth Wildes
Funeral of Rufino Contreras.
Schull, Joseph
Legend of Ghost Lagoon, The, *sel.*
Pirates' Fight, The.
Schulman, Grace
Burial of a Fisherman in Hydra.
Burn Down the Icons.
Epithalamion: "Look there! *The Lovers in the Flowers.*"
Law, The.
Schultz, Lulu Minerva
What Price.
Schultz, Philip
Apartment Hunter, The.
Balance.
For My Father.
Hemingway House in Key West, The.
Like Wings.
Mrs. Applebaum's Sunday Dance Class.
My Guardian Angel Stein.
Schulz, Dale
His Presence.
Schuyler, James
Buried at Springs.
"Can I Tempt You to a Pond Walk?"
Crocus Night.
Crystal Lithium, The.
December.
Dining Out with Doug and Frank.
"Elizabethans Called It Dying, The."
February.
Freely Espousing.
Greenwich Avenue.
Head, A.
Hudson Ferry.
Poem: "This beauty that I see."
Quick, Henry, the Flit!
Salute.
Self-Pity Is a Kind of Lying, Too.
Sorting, Wrapping, Packing, Stuffing.
Stun.
Schuyler, Montgomery
Carlyle and Emerson.
Schuyler-Lighthall, William Douw
Battle of La Prairie, The.
Schwabsky, Barry
Fragment of a Pastoral.
Schwager, Elaine
Tracks.
Schwartz, Delmore
Abraham.
All Clowns Are Masked.
All of us always turning away for solace.
America, America!
Aria.
At a Solemn Musick.
At This Moment of Time.
Ballad of the Children of the Czar, The.
Ballet of the Fifth Year, The.
Baudelaire.
Beautiful American Word, Sure, The.
Conclusion, The: "How slow time moves when torment stops the clock!"
Dark and Falling Summer, The.
Deceptive Present, the Phoenix Year, The.
Do They Whisper behind My Back?
Dog Named Ego, the Snowflakes as Kisses, A.
Dogs Are Shakespearean, Children Are Strangers.
During December's Death.
Far Rockaway.
Father and Son.
For Rhoda.
For the One Who Would Take Man's Life in His Hands.
Genesis, *sel.*
Heart Flies Up, Erratic as a Kite, The.
Heavy Bear Who Goes with Me, The.
I Am a Book I neither Wrote nor Read.
I Am Cherry Alive.
I Did Not Know the Truth of Growing Trees.
I Wakened to a Calling.
In the Naked Bed, in Plato's Cave.
Is It the Morning? Is It the Little Morning?
Jacob.
Let Us Consider Where the Great Men Are.
Little Morning Music, A.
Look, in the Labyrinth of Memory.
"Mentrechè il Vento, Come Fa, Si Tace."
Mind Is an Ancient and Famous Capital, The.
Passionate Shepherd to His Love, The.
Poem: "Old man in the crystal morning after snow."
Prothalamion.
Repetitive Heart, The, *sels.*
Sarah.
Self Unsatisfied Runs Everywhere, The.
Sequel, The.
Shenandoah, *sel.*
Socrates' Ghost Must Haunt Me Now.
Starlight like Intuition Pierced the Twelve.
Starlight's Intuitions Pierced the Twelve, The.
Swift.
Time Is the Fire.
Time's Dedication.
Tired and Unhappy, You Think of Houses.
Today Is Armistice, a Holiday.
True, the Good and the Beautiful, The.
Vivaldi.
What Curious Dresses All Men Wear.
Winter Twilight, Glowing Black and Gold, The.
You Are a Jew!
Schwartz, Hillel
Bedtime.
Schwartz, Howard
Abraham in Egypt.
Adam's Dream.
Blessing of the Firstborn.
Eve, The.
Gathering the Sparks
Iscah.
New Year for Trees, The.
Our Angels.
Prayers, The.
Psalm: "Father/ You are the trunk."
Shira.
Song, A: "Song, A/ That seemed so brief at first."
These Two.
Vessels.
Schwob, Marcel
Actions.
Moments.
Things Dead.
Scollard, Clinton
Ad Patriam.
Archer, The.
As I Came Down from Lebanon.
At the Tomb of Washington.
Ballad of Paco Town, The.
Battle of Plattsburg Bay, The.
Be Ye in Love with April-Tide.
Bell, A.
Boasting of Sir Peter Parker, The.
Cricket.
Daughter of the Regiment, The.
Deed of Lieutenant Miles, The.
Deeds of Valor at Santiago.
Eve of Bunker Hill, The.
First Thanksgiving, The.
First Three, The.
If Only the Dreams Abide.
Khamsin.
King of Dreams, The.
King Philip's Last Stand.
Man, A!
Memnon.
Men of the *Maine,* The.
Men of the *Merrimac,* The.
Montgomery at Quebec.
On a Bust of Lincoln.
Prayer, A: "Each day I walk with wonder."
Private Blair of the Regulars.
Rain Riders.
Riding with Kilpatrick.
Saint Leger.
Sidney Godolphin.
Sleeper, The.
Song for Memorial Day.
Sunflowers.
Swimming.
There Is a Pool on Garda.
To William Sharp.
Unreturning, The.
Valor of Ben Milam, The.
Wayne at Stony Point.
Scoloker, Anthony
Her Praises.
Scott, Aimee Byng ("Alec Holmes")
July 1st, 1916.
Scott, Alexander (1520?-1590?)
Bequest of His Heart, A.
Hence, Hairt, with Her That Must Depairt.
Lament, A; 1547.
Lament of the Master of Erskine.
Letter to Robert Fergusson.
My Heart Is High Above, *at.*
Of May.
Quha Is Perfyte.
Return Thee, Hairt.
Rondel of Love [*or* Luve], A.
To Luve Unluvit.
Up, Helsum Hairt.
Wha Is Perfyte.
Scott, Alexander (b. 1920)
Ballade of Beauties.
Calvinist Sang.
Coronach.
Haar in Princes Street.
Problems.
Recipe: To Mak a Ballant.
Scrievin.
Scott, Clement
Oh Promise Me.
Rus in Urbe.
Story of a Stowaway, The.
Scott, Diana
Lucy Taking Birth.
Prayer for the Little Daughter between Death and Burial.
Winter Solstice Poem.
Scott, Duncan Campbell
At Delos.
At Gull Lake: August, 1810.
At the Cedars.
Bells.
Compline.
Ecstasy.
En Route.
Fallen, The.

Forsaken, The.
Half-Breed Girl, The.
In the Selkirks.
Night and the Pines.
Night Hymns on Lake Nipigon.
Night in June, A.
Off Rivière du Loup.
On the Way to the Mission.
Onondaga Madonna, The.
Piper of Arll, The.
Prairie Water Colour, A.
Rapids at Night.
Sailor's Sweetheart, The.
Song, A: "In the air there are no coral-/ Reefs or ambergris."
Thoughts.
Watkwenies.

Scott, Elizabeth
Now Let Our Hearts Their Glory Wake, *with music.*
See How the Rising Sun, *with music.*

Scott, Francis Reginald
Bangkok.
Bonne Entente.
Calamity.
Canadian Authors Meet, The.
Caring ("Caring is loving, motionless").
Conflict.
Full Valleys.
Grain of Rice, A.
Lakeshore.
Laurentian Shield.
Night Club.
Old Song.
Recovery.
Saturday Sundae.
Tourist Time.
Trans Canada.
W. L. M. K.
Will to Win.
Windfall.

Scott, Fred Newton
Romeo and Juliet.

Scott, Frederick George
Dawn.
Easter Island.
In the Woods.
Requiescat.
Snowstorm, The.
Sting of Death, The.
"Te Judice."
Unnamed Lake, The.
Van Elsen.

Scott, G. Forrester. *See* **"Halsham, John"**

Scott, Geoffrey
All Our Joy Is Enough.
Frutta di Mare.
Skaian Gate, The, *sel.*
What Was Solomon's Mind?

Scott, Herbert
Butcher's Wife.
Help Is on the Way.
Letter from a Working Girl.
Passing the Masonic Home for the Aged.
That summer nothing would do.

Scott, Joe
Plain Golden Band, The, *at.*

Scott, John (1730–1783). *See* **Scott of Amwell, John**

Scott, Lady John
Comin' o' the Spring, The.
Ettrick.

Scott, Johnie
American Dream, The, *sel.*

Scott, Peter Dale
Argenteuil County.
Loon's Egg, The.

Scott, Robert Balgarnie Young
O Day of God, Draw Nigh, *with music.*

Scott, Sharon
Between Me and Anyone Who Can Understand.
Come On Home.
Discovering.
Fisk is/ a/ negroid/ institution.
For Both of Us at Fisk.
Just Taking Note.
Little More about the Brothers and Sisters, A.
Mama Knows.
Oh—-Yeah!
Okay.
On My Stand.
Our Lives.
Sharon Will Be No/Where on Nobody's Best-selling List.
Sometimes/ the poems.

Scott, Tom
Auld Sanct-Aundrians—Brand the Builder.
Real Muse, The.

Scott, Sir Walter
Abbess, The ("The abbess was of noble blood").
Aged Carle, The.
Alice Brand.
Allen-a-Dale.
And What though Winter Will Pinch Severe.
Annot Lyle's Song: "Birds of omen."
Antiquary, The, *sels.*
Ave Maria.
Bannockburn.
Battle, The ("But as they left the dark'ning heath").
Battle, The ("By this, though deep the evening fell").
Battle, The ("Not far advanced was morning day").
Betrothed, The, *sel.*
Bible, The.
Blue Bonnets over the Border.
Boat Song.
Bonnie Dundee.
Book of Books, The.
Border Ballad.
Border March.
Breathes There the [*or* a] Man [with Soul So Dead].
Bride of Lammermoor, The, *sel.*
Brignall Banks.
Chase, The.
Christmas in England.
Christmas in the Olden Time.
Claud Halcro's Invocation.
Coronach ("He is gone on the mountain").
County Guy.
Datur Hora Quieti.
Donald Caird.
Doom of Devorgoil, The, *sel.*
Dreary Change, The.
Edinburgh from the Pentland Hills.
Edmund's Song.
Ettrick Forest in November.
Eve of Saint John, The.
Farewell, Thou Minstrel Harp.
Farewell to the land where the clouds love to rest.
Father's Notes of Woe, A.
Fire, The.
Flodden.
Fortunes of Nigel, The, *sel.*
Gathering, The.
Gellatley's Song to the Deerhounds.
Gin by Pailfuls.
Glenfinlas; or, Lord Ronald's Coronach.
Guy Mannering, *sels.*
Hail to the Chief Who in Triumph Advances!
Harlaw.
Harold the Dauntless, *sel.*
Harold's Song: Rosabelle.
Heap On More Wood!
Heart of Midlothian, The, *sel.*
Hellvellyn.
Hie Away.
Hour with Thee, An.
Hunter's Song.
Hunting Song.
Hymn to the Virgin.
It's up Glenbarchan's braes I gaed.
Ivanhoe, *sels.*
Jock of Hazeldean.
Lady of the Lake, The, *sels.*
Last Minstrel, The.
Lay of the Last Minstrel, The, *sels.*
Legend of Montrose, The, *sel.*
Lochinvar.
Lord of the Isles, The, *sel.*
Love.
Love of Country.
Lucy Ashton's Song.
Lullaby of an Infant Chief.
MacGregor's Gathering.
Maid of Neidpath, The.
Man the Enemy of Man.
March, March, Ettrick and Teviotdale.
Marmion, *sels.*
Melrose Abbey.
Mermaids and Mermen.
Minstrel Responds to Flattery, The.
Monastery, The, *sels.*
My Native Land.
My Own, My Native Land!
Native Land.
Nativity Chant, The.
Nelson, Pitt, Fox.
November in Ettrick Forest.
O Caledonia!
O, Woman! ("O woman, in our hours of ease").
Old Christmastide.
Old Mortality, *sels.*
On a Day's Stint.
On Having Piles.
On Leaving Mrs. Brown's Lodgings.
One Crowded Hour.
Outlaw, The.
Patriotism [II] ("To mute and to material things").
Peveril of the Peak, *sel.*
Pibroch of Donuil [*or* Donald] Dhu.
Pirate, The, *sels.*
Pride of Youth, The.
Proud Maisie.
Quentin Durward, *sel.*
Rebecca's Hymn.
Red Harlaw.
Rob Roy, *sel.*
Roderick Dhu.
Rokeby, *sels.*
Rosabelle.
Rover, The.
Rover's Adieu, The.
Rover's Farewell, The.
St. Swithin's Chair.
Serenade, A: "Ah! County Guy, the hour is nigh."
Sir Walter Scott's Tribute.
Sir William of Deloraine at the Wizard's Tomb.
Soldier, Rest! [Thy Warfare O'er].
Soldier's Song.
Song: "Ah! County Guy, the hour is nigh."
Song: "O, Brignal banks are wild and fair."
Song: " 'Soldier, rest! thy warfare o'er.' "
Song: "Weary lot is thine, fair maid, A."
Song: "Where shall the lover rest."
Song of Albert Graeme.
Song of the Mermaids and Mermen.
Song of the Reim-Kennar, The.
Song of the White Lady of Avenel.
Talisman, The, *sel.*
'Tis Merry in Greenwood.
To a Lady with Flowers from the Roman Wall.
To a Lock of Hair.
To an Oak Tree.
To-Day I Leave Mrs. Brown's Lodgings.
Toils Are Pitched, The.
Twas when fleet Snowball's head was waxen gray.
Twist Ye, Twine Ye! Even So.
Violet, The.

Wasted, Weary, Wherefore Stay.
Waverley, *sels.*
Weary Lot Is Thine, A.
Western Waves of Ebbing Day, The.
When dark December glooms the day.
Where Shall the Lover Rest.
Why Sit'st Thou by That Ruin'd Hall.
William and Helen.
Young Lochinvar.

Scott, William Bell
Glenkindie.
Love's Calendar.
Robin, The.
Witch's [*or* Witches] Ballad, The.

Scott, Winfield Townley
Annual Legend.
Another Return.
Bermuda Suite.
Biography for Traman, *sel.*
Blue Sleigh.
Come Green Again.
Confidential.
Difference, The.
Double Tree, The.
First Reader, The.
Fish Sonata, The.
Five for the Grace of Man.
Grant Wood's American Landscape.
House, The.
Into the Wind.
Ivory Bed, The.
Landscape as Metal and Flowers.
May 1506 (Christopher Columbus Speaking).
Mr. Whittier.
Mrs. Severin.
O Lyric Love.
Sonnet: "I watched the sea for hours blind with sun."
Sonnet XIII: "Rise up, rise up, Jack Spratt. And you, his wife."
Sonnet XV: "This is the way we say it in our time."
Sonnet XII: "Virgins terrify too many men."
Swedish Angel.
Three American Women and a German Bayonet.
To L. B. S.
Two.
Two Lives and Others.
U.S. Sailor with the Japanese Skull, The.
Uses of Poetry.
Watch Hill.
Wax.
We'll All Feel Gay.

Scott of Amwell, John
Amoebaean Eclogues, *sel.*
How to Fertilize Soil.
I Hate That Drum's Discordant Sound.
Ode: "I hate that drum's discordant sound."
Retort on the Foregoing.

Scott-Hopper, Queenie
Very Nearly.

Scovell, Edith Jay
After Midsummer.
Alone.
Betrothal, A.
Bloody Cranesbill on the Dunes.
Dark World, A.
Elegy, An: "In early winter before the first snow."
In a Wood.
Love's Immaturity.
Open Air Performance of "As You Like It," An.
Shadows of Chrysanthemums.
Swan's Feet, The.

"Scrace, Richard" (Mrs. J. B. Williamson)
At the Place of the Roman Baths.
Gipsies, The.

Scriven, Joseph
Unfailing Friend, The.
What a Friend We Have in Jesus.

Scriven, R. C.
Marrog, The.

Scroggie, Syd
And Happy Am I.
Ante Mortem.
At Last.
Change and Immutability.
Drunken Dee, The.
Loch Ossian.
Long Ago.
Poem, 1972.
Space and Time.

Scroope, Sir Carr
Author's Reply, The.
In Defense of Satire.

Scudder, Eliza
Quest, The.
Thou Grace Divine, Encircling All, *with music.*
Thou Long Disowned, Reviled, Oppressed, *with music.*
To a Young Child.
Who by Searching Can Find Out God?

Scudder, Vida
Thy Kingdom, Lord, We Long For.

Scully, James
Crew Practice on Lake Bled, in Jugoslavia.
Day of the Night, The.
Enough!
Esperanza.
Fantasy of Little Waters, A.
Glass Blower, The.
Grandson, The.
Innocence.
Late Spring, A.
Midsummer.
What Is Poetry.

Scupham, Peter
To His Coy Mistress, *parody.*
Twelfth Night.

Seager, Francis
Prayer to Be Said When Thou Goest to Bed, A.

Seager, Ralph W.
Stump Is Not the Tombstone, The.
Taste of Prayer, The.

Seagrave, Artis
Let All Created Things, *with music.*

Seaman, E. William
Higgledy-piggledy/ Ludwig van Beethoven.

Seaman, Sir Owen
Ballad of a Bun, A.
Birthday Ode to Mr. Alfred Austin, A.
Bulbul, The ("The bulbul hummeth like a book").
England Expects?
From "A Vigo-Street Eclogue."
In Praise of Commonplace.
Ode to Spring in the Metropolis, An.
Of Baiting the Lion.
Of the Stalking of the Stag.
Old Songs, The.
Penalties of Baldness, The.
Plea for Trigamy, A.
Rhyme of the Kipperling, The.
Seamy Side of Motley, The.
Sitting Bard, The.
Song of Renunciation, A.
Time's Revenges.
To a Boy-Poet of the Decadence.
To Julia in Shooting Togs.
To Julia under Lock and Key.
Uses of Ocean, The.
Warrior's Lament, The.

Searing, Laura Redden
Disarmed.

Sears, Edmund Hamilton
Calm, on the Listening Ear of Night, *with music.*
Christmas Carols.
It Came upon the Midnight Clear.
Peace on Earth.

Sears, Peter
Rain.

Seaver, Edwin
To My People.

"Sec"
News, The.

Secundus, Johannes. *See* **Johannes Secundus**

Sedgwick, Henry Dwight
Leo to His Mistress.
To Julius.

Sedley, Sir Charles
Advice to the Old Beaux.
Ballad to the Tune of Bateman, A.
Child and Maiden.
Get You Gone.
Happy Pair, The, *sel.*
Hears Not My Phillis, How the Birds.
Indifference, The.
Marriage and Money.
On a Cock at Rochester.
On Fruition.
Out of French.
Phyllis Knotting.
Song: "Ah Chloris! that I now could sit."
Song: "Hears not my Phillis how the birds."
Song: "Love still has something of the sea."
Song: "Not, Celia, that I juster am."
Song: "Phillis is my only joy."
Song: "Phillis, let's shun the common fate."
Song: "Smooth was the water, calm the air."
Song to Celia.
To Celia.
To Chloris.
To Cloris ("Cloris, I cannot say your eyes").
To Nysus.
To Scilla.
To Sergius.
Upon the Author of the "Satire against Wit."

Sedulius, Caelius
Apostrophe to Death.
Carmen Paschale [*or* Easter Song], *sels.*
Christ Quiets the Tempest.
Hail, Maiden Root.
Invocation: "Eternal God omnipotent! The One."
Slaughter of the Innocents by Order of King Herod, The.

Sedulius Scottus
Apologia pro Vita Sua.
Easter Sunday.
Nunc Viridant Segetes.

Seeger, Alan
I Have a Rendezvous with Death.
Ode in Memory of the American Volunteers Fallen for France.
To———in Church.

Seeger, Peggy *and* **Ewan MacColl.** *See* **MacColl, Ewan** *and* **Peggy Seeger**

Seeger, Pete
Oleanna.

Seeger, Pete, Lee Hays *and* **Millard Lampell**
Get Thee behind Me, Satan.

Seelbinder, Emily
Spring Morning: Waking.
Union Train.

Segal, Carolyn Foster
Wharf, May 1978, The.

Segal, Jacob Isaac
Candle.
Rest.

Segal, Y. Y.
King Rufus.
Rhymes.

Segooa, Demetrius
Praises of the Train.

Seib, Kenneth
Fate of Birds, The.

Seidel, Frederick
Dayley Island.
Dimpled Cloud, A.
Negro Judge, A.
Sickness, The.
To Robert Lowell and Osip Mandelstam.

Seidman, Hugh
Drop the Wires.
Great Nebula in Andromeda, The.
Making of Color, The.
Modes of Vallejo Street, San Diego, Los Angeles, The, *sels.*
N.
Science as Art.
Tale of Genji.
Seifert, Jaroslav
Dance-Song.
Seiffert, Marjorie Allen ("Elijah Hay")
Ballad: "Follow, follow me into the South."
Cubist Portrait.
Dream House, The.
Italian Chest, An.
Seitz, Don C.
Night at Gettysburg.
Sekula, Irene
Mother Goose (circa 2054).
Seldon, Frank H.
To My Setter, Scout.
Seligman, Ulma
Truth Has Perished.
Selkirk, J. B.
Border Burn, A.
Epistle to Tammus, *sel.*
Sellar, Walter Carruthers *and* **Robert Julian Yeatman.** *See* **Yeatman, Robert Julian** *and* **Walter Carruthers Sellar**
Selle, Len G.
Hickory Stick Hierarchy.
Sellers, Bettie M.
If Justice Moved.
Morning of the Red-tailed Hawk, The.
Sellers, John L.
Catch-22 Test, A.
Hep-Cat.
How One-Thumb Willie Got His Name.
Mule-Train.
Tractor.
Seltzer, George R.
Come, All Ye People, *with music.*
Selyns, Henricus
Epitaph for Peter Stuyvesant.
Nuptial Song.
O Christmas Night.
Of Scolding Wives and the Third Day Ague.
On Maids and Cats.
On Mercenary and Unjust Bailiffs.
Reasons for and against Marrying Widows.
Upon the Bankruptcy of a Physician.
Semah, David
Prostration.
Tomb.
Sempill, Robert
Life and Death of Habbie Simson, the Piper of Kilbarchan, The.
Life and Death of the Piper of Kilbarchan, The.
Sendak, Maurice
October.
Seneca (Lucius Annaeus Seneca)
After death nothing is, and nothing death.
End of Being, The.
Hercules Furens, *sel.*
Hercules Oetaetus, *sel.*
Medea, *sels.*
Senec. Traged. ex Thyeste Chor. 2.
Thyestes, *sels.*
Troades, *sel.*
Senesh, Hannah
Blessed Match, The.
One—Two—Three.
Senghor, Léopold Sédar
Black Woman.
New York.
Night of Sine.
On the Appeal from the Race of Sheba: II.
Paris in the Snow.
Prayer for Peace: II.
Return of the Prodigal Son, *sel.*
Songs for a Three-String Guitar.
To New York.
We Delighted, My Friend.
Seng-ts'an.
On Trust in the Heart.
"Seranus." *See* **Harrison, Susan Frances**
Serchuk, Peter
Bent Tree.
What the Animals Said.
Sergeant, Howard
Inundation, The.
Man Meeting Himself.
Soft Landings.
Serraillier, Ian
After Ever Happily.
Andrew's Bedtime Story.
Death of the Cat.
Fox Rhyme, The.
Hare and the Tortoise, The.
Hen and the Carp, The.
Mouse in the Wainscot, The.
Old Sussex Road, The.
Suppose You Met a Witch, *sel.*
Tickle Rhyme, The.
Witch's Cat, The.
Service, Robert W.
Call of the Wild, The.
Carry On!
Cremation of Sam McGee, The.
Inspiration.
Law of the Yukon, The.
Men That Don't Fit In, The.
My Madonna.
Rhymes of a Rolling Stone, *sel.*
Scribe's Prayer, The.
Shooting of Dan McGrew, The.
Skeptic, The.
Spell of the Yukon, The.
When the Iceworms Nest Again.
Sessler, Thomas
Burnt Debris.
When the Day.
You Move Forward.
"Setoun, Gabriel" (Thomas Nicoll Hepburn)
Fairy Ship, The.
How the Flowers Grow.
Jack Frost.
Wind's Song, The.
World's Music, The.
Setterberg, Ruth
Mirage, A.
Patterns.
Settle, Elkanah
Medal Reversed, The.
"Seuss, Dr." (Theodor Seuss Geisel)
If We Didn't Have Birthdays.
Too Many Daves.
Sewall, Frank
Roll Out, O Song.
Sewall, Harriet Winslow
Why Thus Longing?
Sewall, Jonathan Mitchell
On Independence.
War and Washington.
Sewall, Samuel
Humble Springs of Stately Sandwich Beach, The.
Once More, Our God, Vouchsafe to Shine! *with music.*
This Morning Tom Child, the Painter, Died.
To Be Engraven on a Dial.
To the Rev'd Mr. Jno. Sparhawk on the Birth of His Son.
Upon the Springs Issuing out from the Foot of Plimouth Beach.
Wednesday, January 1, 1701.
Seward, Anna
Colebrook Dale, *sel.*
Elegy Written at the Sea-Side, and Addressed to Miss Honoria Sneyd.
Eyam, *sel.*
Favourite Cat's Dying Soliloquy, A.
Llangollen Vale, *sel.*
Old Cat's Dying Soliloquy, An.
Sonnet: "Ingratitude, how deadly is the smart."
Sonnet: To the Departing Spirit of an Alienated Friend: "Behold him now his genuine colours wear."
True Cat, A.
Sewell, Elizabeth
Epiphany: For the Artist.
Forgiveness.
Job.
Sewell, George
Dying Man in His Garden, The.
Sexton, Anne
Abortion, The.
Addict, The.
All My Pretty Ones.
Black Art, The.
Breast, The.
Child Bearers, The.
Consorting with Angels.
Crossing the Atlantic.
December 18th.
Division of Parts, The.
Eighteen Days without You, *sel.*
Farmer's Wife, The.
Flee on Your Donkey.
For Eleanor Boylan Talking with God.
For God While Sleeping.
For My Lover, Returning to His Wife.
Fortress, The.
Frog Prince, The.
Funnel.
Fury of Flowers and Worms, The.
Fury of Hating Eyes, The.
Her Kind.
Housewife.
In Celebration of My Uterus.
In the Beach House.
In the Deep Museum.
Kind Sir: These Woods.
Kiss, The.
Lament: "Someone is dead."
Letter Written on a Ferry Crossing Long Island Sound.
Little Girl, My Stringbean, My Lovely Woman.
Little Red-Riding Hood.
Lost Ingredient, The.
Love Song: "I was/ the girl of the chain letter."
Lullaby: "It is a summer evening."
Man and Wife.
Menstruation at Forty.
Moon Song, Woman Song.
Moss of His Skin, The.
Mothers.
Nude Swim, The.
Pain for a Daughter.
Rapunzel.
Riding the Elevator into the Sky.
Ringing the Bells.
Risk, The.
Road Back, The.
Rowing.
Rumpelstiltskin.
Said the Poet to the Analyst.
Snow White and the Seven Dwarfs.
Some Foreign Letters.
Starry Night, The.
Sun, The.
That Day.
Three Green Windows.
Truth the Dead Know, The.
Unknown Girl in the Maternity Ward.
Us.
Wanting to Die.
Water.
Wedding Night, The.
Welcome Morning.
Where I Live in This Honorable House of the Laurel Tree.
With Mercy for the Greedy.
Woman with Girdle.
You, Doctor Martin.

You All Know the Story of the Other Woman.
Young.
Seymour, William Kean
Caesar Remembers.
Foiled Reaper, The.
To Music.
Seymour-Smith, Martin
He Came to Visit Me.
What Schoolmasters Say.
Shackleford, Theodore Henry
Big Bell in Zion, The.
Shadwell, Bertrand
Aguinaldo.
Cervera.
Shadwell, Thomas
Expostulation, The.
Let Some Great Joys Pretend to Find.
Love and Wine.
Medal of John Bays, The; a Satire against Folly and Knavery.
Song: "Fringéd vallance of your eyes advance, The."
Squire of Alsatia, The, *sel.*
Woman-Captain, The, *sel.*
Shady, Dennis
Cell.
Grandfathers.
Moose Lake State Hospital.
Someone Gave Him Some Plastic Flowers Once.
Stories Relate Life.
Wind Carries Me Free, The.
Shairp, John Campbell
Bush aboon Traquair, The.
Shakely, Lauren
Definition.
Shakespeare, William
Absence.
Age and Youth.
All the World's a Stage.
All's Well That Ends Well, *sel.*
Ambition.
Amiens's Song: "Blow, blow, thou winter wind."
Amiens's Song: "Under the greenwood tree."
Amiens's Song: "What shall he have that killed the deer?"
And nothing can we call our own but death.
Angels and ministers of grace defend us!
Antony and Cleopatra, *sels.*
Antony's Oration.
Ariel's Song: "Come unto these yellow sands."
Ariel's Song: "Full fathom five thy father lies."
Ariel's Song: "Where the bee sucks, there suck I."
As You Like It, *sels.*
Asleep, my love?
At My Nativity.
At the Moated Grange.
Aubade: "Hark! Hark! the lark at heaven's gate sings."
Autolycus's Song ("Jog on, jog on . . .").
Autolycus's Song ("Lawn as white as driven snow").
Autolycus's Song ("When daffodils begin to peer").
Balthasar's Song.
Be Absolute for Death.
Beauty Is a Witch.
Before Agincourt ("Now entertain conjecture of a time").
Bird of Dawning, The.
Birdsong.
Blast of War.
Blind Love.
Blossom, The.
Blow, Blow, Thou Winter Wind.
Blow, Winds ("Blow, winds, and crack your cheeks!").
Bottom's Song.
Brave New World.
Brutus Explains Why He Murdered Caesar.
But, soft! What light through yonder window breaks.
But Man, Proud Man.
Caliban.
Cares of Majesty, The.
Carpe Diem.
Casket Song, A.
Cassius Poisons Brutus's Mind.
Charm, The.
Christmas.
Claudio's Lament.
Cleopatra.
Cleopatra and Her Barge.
Cleopatra's Barge.
Cleopatra's Death.
Cleopatra's Lament.
Clown's Song, The ("Come away, come away, death").
Clown's Song ("O mistris mine where are you roming?").
Come Away, Come Away, Death.
Come Buy! Come Buy!
Commonwealth of the Bees, The.
Consolation, A.
Country Song.
Course of True Love, The.
Courser and the Jennet, The.
Crabbed Age and Youth.
Cranmer's Prophecy of Queen Elizabeth.
Cymbeline, *sels.*
Death of Adonis, The.
Death of Antony.
Death of Cleopatra.
Death of Cowards, The.
Death of Death, The.
Death of Hamlet.
Death of Kings, The.
Death of Lear.
Death of Othello.
Desdemona's Song.
Did Not the Heavenly Rhetoric of Thine Eye.
Dirge of Love.
Divine Harmony, The.
Dover, the Samphire Cliff.
Dream of Wrecks, A.
Drinking Song, A.
Dumain's Rhymes.
Epilogue: "If we shadows have offended."
Epilogue: "Now my charms are all o'erthrown."
Epilogue: "Now the hungry lion roars."
Epilogue: "Thus far, with rough and all-unable pen."
Epitaph: "Done to death by slanderous tongues."
Everlasting Rest.
Evil Designs.
Fair Is My Love.
Fairies' Lullaby, The.
Fairy Blessing, The.
Fairy Lullaby ("You spotted snakes").
Fairy Song ("Come unto these yellow sands").
Fairy Song ("Now the hungry lion roars").
Fairy Song ("Now, until the break of day").
Fairy Song ("Over hill, over dale").
Fairy Song ("Where the bee sucks").
Fairy Song ("You spotted snákes with double tongue").
Fairy's Life, A.
Fairy's Wander-Song.
Fancy.
Farewell Content.
Farewell to Greatness.
Fear No More the Heat o' the Sun.
Fear of Death, The.
Feare No More.
Feste's Song ("Come away, come away, Death").
Feste's Song ("O mistress mine, where are you roaming?").
Feste's Song ("When that I was, and a little tiny boy").
Fidele.
Fidele's Dirge.
Flowers of Middle Summer.
Flowers of Perdita, The.
Food of Love, The.
For a Patriot.
Frailty, Thy Name Is Woman.
Friar Laurence's Cell.
Friar of Orders Grey, The.
Frost on the Flower.
Good Name, A.
Gracious Time, The.
Hamlet, *sels.*
Hark! Hark! the Lark.
Hate the Idle Pleasures.
He Jests at Scars [That Never Felt a Wound].
Helen of Troy.
Helena and Hermia.
Henry V at Harfleur.
Henry Fifth's Address to His Soldiers.
Here Lies Juliet.
Hiems.
Horse, The.
How Sweet the Moonlight Sleeps.
I Am Dead, Horatio.
I Come to Bury Caesar.
I Have Lived Long Enough.
I was a poor groom of thy stable, king.
Imagination.
Immortal Longings.
In Such a Night.
It Is the Cause, It Is the Cause, My Soul.
It Was a Lover, and His Lass.
Jog On, Jog On [the Foot-Path Way].
Juliet's Yearning.
Julius Caesar, *sels.*
King Henry IV, Pt. I, *sel.*
King Henry IV, Pt. II, *sels.*
King Henry V, *sels.*
King Henry VI, Pt. I, *sel.*
King Henry VI, Pt. III, *sels.*
King John, *sels.*
King Lear, *sels.*
King Richard II, *sels.*
King Richard III, *sels.*
Lament for Imogen.
Lament of Guiderius and Arviragus.
Lear and Cordelia.
Lear's Curse on Goneril.
Lear's Speech to the Storm.
Let Me Play the Fool.
Let's Talk of Graves.
Life without Passion, The.
Lion of Winter, The.
Living Juliet, The.
Lo! Here the Gentle Lark.
Love.
Love Concealed.
Love-in-Idleness.
Love Song: "Take, Oh take those lips away."
Lover's Complaint, A.
Lover's eyes will gaze an eagle blind, A.
Love's Despair.
Love's Labour's Lost, *sels.*
Love's Not Time's Fool.
Love's Perjuries.
Lullaby for Titania.
Lunatic, the Lover, and the Poet, The.
Macbeth, *sels.*
Madrigal, A: "Crabbed Age and Youth."
Madrigal: "Take, O take those lips away."
Madrigal: "Tell me where is Fancy bred."
Magic.
Man ("What a piece of work is a man!").
Man New Made.
Mark Antony Addresses the Mob.
Mark Antony's Lament.
Measure for Measure, *sels.*
Merchant of Venice, The, *sels.*
Mercutio's Queen Mab Speech.
Mercy ("The quality of mercy is not strained").
Merry Heart, A.
Merry Note, A.

Merry Wives of Windsor, The, *sel.*
Methought I Saw a Thousand Fearful Wrecks.
Midnight.
Midsummer Night's Dream, A, *sels.*
Mind Diseased, A.
Moonlight.
Morning Song, A ("Hark! hark! the lark").
Motley's the Only Wear.
Much Ado about Nothing, *sels.*
Murder Pact, The.
Murderers, The.
Muse of Fire, A.
Music.
Music's Silver Sound.
My Thoughts Do Harbour.
Noblest Roman, The.
Not Poppy, nor Mandragora.
Now, Until the Break of Day.
O! Full of Scorpions.
O Gentle Sleep.
O Mistress Mine, Where Are You Roaming?
O Romeo, Romeo! wherefore art thou Romeo?
Oberon and Titania to the Fairy Train.
Of the Death of Kings.
On a Day—Alack the Day!
On Death.
Once More unto the Breach.
Ophelia's Death.
Opportunity.
Orlando's Rhymes.
Orpheus with His Lute, *at.*
Othello, *sels.*
Othello's Farewell to His Career.
Our Revels Now Are Ended.
Out, Out, Brief Candle!
Outcry upon Opportunity, An.
Over Hill, over Dale.
Pages' Song, The.
Patience on a Monument.
Pedlar, The.
Pedlar's Song, The.
Perdita's Garden.
Perdition catch my soul.
Pericles, *sels.*
Perils of Darkness.
Petruchio Is Undaunted by Katharina.
Phoenix and [the] Turtle, The.
Polonius to Laertes.
Poor Naked Wretches.
Poor Wat.
Portia's Plea for Mercy.
Portrait of Brutus.
Portrait of Caesar.
Portrait of Cressida.
Portrait of Helen.
Post Mortem.
Power of Music, The.
Prospero.
Prospero Ends the Revels.
Puck and the Fairy.
Puck's Song.
Quality of Mercy [Is Not Strain'd], The.
Queen Mab.
Rape of Lucrece, The.
Remembrance.
Revolutions.
Richard II's Dejection.
Romeo and Juliet, *sels.*
Saint Valentine's Day.
Seals of Love.
Seven Ages of Man, The.
Shylock's Defense.
Sigh No More, Ladies [Sigh No More].
Silvia.
Sleep.
So Sweet a Kiss.
Soliloquy from "Hamlet."
Soliloquy on Sleep.
Some Flowers o' the Spring.
Song: "And will he not come again?"
Song: "Blow, blow, thou winter wind."
Song: "Come away, come away death."
Song: "Come unto these yellow sands."
Song: "Fear no more the heat o' the sun."
Song: "Full fadom five thy father lies."
Song: "Good morrow, 'tis St. Valentine's day."
Song: Hark, Hark ("Hark, hark!/ Bow-wow./ The watch-dogs bark").
Song: "Hark! hark! the lark at heaven's gate sings."
Song: "How should I your true love know."
Song: "If the scorn of your bright eyne."
Song: "It was a lover and his lass."
Song: "Master, the swabber, the boatswain, and I, The."
Song: "O mistress mine, where are you roaming?"
Song: "Over hill, over dale."
Song: "Pardon, goddess of the night."
Song: "Sigh no more, ladies, sigh no more."
Song: Spring and Winter.
Song: "Take, O take those lips away."
Song, A: "Tell me, where is fancy bred."
Song: "Tomorrow is Saint Valentine's day".
Song: "Under the greenwood tree."
Song: "What shall he have that kill'd the deer?"
Song: "When daffodils begin to peer."
Song: "When daisies pied, and violets blue."
Song: "When icicles hang by the wall."
Song: "When that I was and a little tiny boy."
Song: "Who is Silvia? what is she."
Song: "You spotted snakes with double tongue."
Song at the Moated Grange, A.
Song of the Witches.
Song to Imogen.
Song to Silvia.
Songs of the Greenwood.
Sonnet: "Against my Love shall be, as I am now."
Sonnet: "Ah wherefore with infection should he live."
Sonnet: "Alas, 'tis true I have gone here and there."
Sonnet: "As an unperfect actor on the stage."
Sonnet: "Being your slave, what should I do[e] but tend."
Sonnet: "Beshrew that heart that makes my heart to groan."
Sonnet: "But be contented: when that fell arrest."
Sonnet: "But wherefore do not you a mightier waie."
Sonnet: "Devouring Time, blunt thou the lion's paws."
Sonnet: "Did not the heavenly rhetoric of thine eye."
Sonnet: "Expense of spirit in a waste of shame, The."
Sonnet: "Farewell! thou art too dear for my possessing."
Sonnet: "For shame! deny that thou bear'st love to any."
Sonnet: "Forward violet thus did I chide, The."
Sonnet: "From fairest creatures we desire increase."
Sonnet: "From you have I been absent in the spring."
Sonnet: "Full many a glorious morning have I seen[e]."
Sonnet: "How can I then return in happy plight."
Sonnet: "How like a winter hath my absence been[e]."
Sonnet: "How oft, when thou, my music, music play'st."
Sonnet: "How sweet and lovely dost thou make the shame."
Sonnet: "If their bee nothing new, but that which is."
Sonnet: "If thou survive my well-contented day."
Sonnet: "In faith I do[e] not love thee with mine eyes."
Sonnet: "Is it for fear to wet a widow's eye."
Sonnet: "Is it thy wil, thy Image should keepe open."
Sonnet: "Let me confess that we two must be twain."
Sonnet: "Let me not to the marriage of true mind[e]s."
Sonnet: "Let those who are in favour with their stars."
Sonnet: "Like as the waves make towards the pebbled shore."
Sonnet: "Like as, to make our appetites more keen."
Sonnet: "Lo, as a careful housewife runs to catch."
Sonnet: "Look in thy glass, and tell the face thou viewest."
Sonnet: "Love is too young to know what conscience is."
Sonnet: "Music[k] to hear[e], why hear'st thou music[k] sadly?"
Sonnet: "My glass shall not persuade me I am old."
Sonnet: "My love is as a fever, longing still."
Sonnet: "My love is strengthen'd, though more weak in seeming."
Sonnet: "My mistress' eyes are nothing like the sun."
Sonnet: "No, Time, thou shalt not boast that I do change."
Sonnet: "No longer mourn for me when I am dead."
Sonnet: "No more be grieved at that which thou hast done."
Sonnet: "Not from the stars do I my judgement pluck."
Sonnet: "Not marble, nor the gilded monuments."
Sonnet: "Not mine own fears, nor the prophetic soul."
Sonnet: "O how much more doth beauty beauteous seem."
Sonnet: "O me! what eyes hath love put in my head."
Sonnet: "O, never say that I was false of heart."
Sonnet: "O! that you were yourself; but, love, you are."
Sonnet: "Or I shall live your epitaph to make."
Sonnet: "Poor soul, the center of my sinful earth."
Sonnet: "Say that thou didst forsake me for some fault."
Sonnet: "Shall I compare thee to a summer's day?"
Sonnet: "Sin of self-love possesseth all mine eye."
Sonnet: "Since brass, nor stone, nor earth, nor boundless sea."
Sonnet: "So am I as the rich, whose blessed key."
Sonnet: "So are you to my thoughts as food to life."
Sonnet: "So is it not with me as with that Muse."
Sonnet: "So now I have confessed that he is thine."
Sonnet: "So shall I live, supposing thou art true."
Sonnet: "Sweet love, renew thy force, be it not said."
Sonnet: "Take all my loves, my Love, yea, take them all."
Sonnet: "That thou hast her, it is not all my grief."
Sonnet: "That time of year mayst in me behold."
Sonnet: "That you were once unkind befriends me now."
Sonnet: "Then hate me when thou wilt; if ever, now."
Sonnet: "Then let not winter's ragged hand deface."

Sonnet: "They that have power to hurt, and will do none."
Sonnet: "Thine eyes I love, and they, as pitying me."
Sonnet: "Those hours, that with gentle work did frame."
Sonnet: "Those petty wrongs that liberty commits."
Sonnet: "Thus is his cheek the map of days outworn."
Sonnet: "Thy bosom is endeared with all hearts."
Sonnet: "Thy glass will show thee how thy beauties wear."
Sonnet: "Tired with all these, for restful death I cry."
Sonnet: "'Tis better to be vile than vile esteemed."
Sonnet: "To me, fair friend, you never can be old."
Sonnet: "Two loves I have of comfort and despair."
Sonnet: "Was it the proud full sail of his great verse."
Sonnet: "Weary with toil, I haste me to my bed."
Sonnet: "What is your substance, whereof are you made."
Sonnet: "What potions have I drunk of siren tears."
Sonnet: "When forty winters shall besiege thy brow."
Sonnet: "When I consider every thing that grows."
Sonnet: "When I do count the clock that tells the time."
Sonnet: "When I have seen by Time's fell hand defac'd."
Sonnet: "When in disgrace with fortune and men's eyes."
Sonnet: "When in the chronicle of wasted time."
Sonnet: "When my love swears that she is made of truth."
Sonnet: "When to the sessions of sweet silent thought."
Sonnet: "Where art thou, Muse, that thou forget'st so long."
Sonnet: "Who will believe my verse in time to come."
Sonnet: "Whoever hath her wish, thou hast thy Will."
Sonnet: "Why didst thou promise such a beauteous day."
Sonnet: "Why is my verse so barren of new pride."
Sonnet: "Woman's face with nature's own hand painted, A."
Sonnets, *sels.*
Soul and Body.
Spring.
Spring Song.
Stephano's Song.
Stuff of Dreams, The.
Such Stuff as Dreams Are Made On.
Sunrise on the Sea.
Sweet Rose, Fair Flower.
Take, O Take Those Lips Away.
Take Physic, Pomp.
Taming of the Shrew, The, *sel.*
Tell Me Where Is Fancy Bred.
Tempest, The, *sels.*
That Men Should Fear.
There Is a Tide [in the Affairs of Men].
This above All.
This Blessed Plot . . . This England.
This England ("This royal throne of kings, this sceptered isle").
This is the foul fiend Flibbertigibbet: he begins at.
This Royal Infant.
This Spring of Love.
Thou God of This Great Vast, Rebuke These Surges.
Thrice the Brinded Cat Hath Mewed.
Through the House.
Thus have I shunned the fire for fear of burning.
Thus with a Kiss I Die.
Time and Love ("Since brass, nor stone, nor earth, nor boundless sea").
Time and Love ("When I have seen by Time's fell hand defaced").
Time to Strike, The.
Time's Glory.
Timon Curses Athens and Mankind.
Timon of Athens, *sels.*
To Dream Again.
To Gild Refinèd Gold.
To His Love ("Shall I compare thee to a summer's day?").
To His Love ("When in the chronicle of wasted time").
To Thine Own Self Be True.
Tomorrow, and Tomorrow, and Tomorrow.
Tomorrow Is Saint Valentine's Day.
Tongues of Dying Men, The.
Tricks of Imagination, The.
Triumph of Death, The.
Troilus and Cressida, *sels.*
Troy Depicted.
True Love.
Tu-Whit To-Who.
Twelfth Night, *sels.*
Two Gentlemen of Verona, The, *sels.*
Ulysses Advises Achilles.
Unchangeable, The.
Under the Greenwood Tree.
Up and Down.
Upon the King.
Uses of Adversity, The.
Vaulting Ambition.
Venus Abandoned.
Venus and Adonis.
Ver and Hiems.
Violet Bank, A.
When Daffodils Begin to Peer.
When Daisies Pied and Violets Blue.
When Icicles Hang by the Wall.
When That I Was and a Little Tiny Boy.
Where the Wild Thyme Blows.
Who Is Silvia [*or* Sylvia]?
Wind and the Rain, The.
Winter.
Winter's Song: "When Isicles hang by the wall."
Winter's Tale, The, *sels.*
Witching Time of Night, The.
World's Way, The.
Yet but Three?
You Spotted Snakes [with Double Tongue].
Youth and Age.

Shakespeare, William *and* **John Fletcher**
Bridal Song, A.
Cardinal Wolsey's Farewell.
Dirge of the Three Queens.
Funeral Song.
King Henry VIII, *sels.*
Two Noble Kinsman, The, *sels.*
Wolsey.
Wolsey's Farewell to His Greatness.
Wolsey's Regrets.

Shakur, Assata
What Is Left?

Shalom, Shin
Spendor.

Shanahan, Eileen
Desolate Lover, The.
Epiphany.
Kilkenny Boy, The.
Shankill.
Three Children near Clonmel, The.

Shane, Elizabeth
Mountainy Childer, The.
Sheskinbeg.
Wee Hughie.

Shange, Ntozake
Dark Phrases.
For Colored Girls Who Have Considered Suicide When the Rainbow Is Enuf, *sel.*
Frank Albert and Viola Benzena Owens.
Nappy Edges (A Cross Country Sojourn).
No More Love Poems #1.
Somebody almost walked off wid alla my stuff.

Shanks, Edward
Boats at Night.
Drilling in Russell Square.
Glow-Worm, The.
Going In to Dinner.
High Germany.
Lady Godiva.
Night Piece, A.
Sleeping Heroes.
Storm, The.
To the Unknown Light.

Shanly, Charles Dawson
Civil War.
Walker of the Snow, The.

Shannon, Monica
Could It Have Been a Shadow?
Country Trucks.
Cow Time.
Gallop, Gallop to a Rhyme.
How to Tell Goblins from Elves.
Only My Opinion.
Our Hired Man (and His Daughter, Too).
Raking Walnuts in the Rain.
Tree Toad, The ("The tree Toad is a creature neat ").

Shapcott, Thomas William
Autumn.
Bicycle Rider, The.
Finches, The.
Flying Fox.
Litanies of Julia Pastrana (1832–1860), The.
Near the School for Handicapped Children.
Piano Pieces, *sels.*
Schoenberg Op. 11.
Sestina with Refrain.
Three Kings Came.
Webern.

Shapiro, Arnold L.
I Speak, I Say, I Talk.

Shapiro, David
Falling Upwards.

Shapiro, Harvey
Blue Max.
Exodus.
Father and Sons.
Feast of the Ram's Horn.
Glory.
Happiness of 6 A.M.
Heart, The.
Incident.
Jerusalem Notebook, A.
Like a Beach.
Lines for the Ancient Scribes.
Mountain, Fire, Thornbush.
Musical Shuttle.
National Cold Storage Company.
1976.
Past Time.
Provincetown, Mass.
Riding Westward.
Saul's Progress.
Six Hundred Thousand Letters, The.
Where I Am Now.

Shapiro, Karl
Adam and Eve, *sels.*
All Tropic Places Smell of Mold.
Alphabet, The.
Americans Are Afraid of Lizards.
Aubade: "What dawn is it?"
Auto Wreck.
Bed, The.
Bourgeois Poet, The, *sels.*
Boy-Man.

Buick.
Calder, A.
California Winter, *sel.*
Christmas Eve.
Confirmation, The.
Conscientious Objector, The.
Construction.
Cut Flower, A.
D. C.
Dirty Word, The.
Dome of Sunday, The.
Drug Store.
Elegy for a Dead Soldier.
Elegy for Two Banjos.
Elegy Written on a Frontporch.
Epitaph: "Underneath this wooden cross there lies."
Epitaph for John and Richard.
Essay on Rime, *sels.*
First Time, The.
Fly, The.
Full Moon; New Guinea.
Garage Sale.
Geographers, The.
Girls Working in Banks.
Glutton, The.
Going to School.
Haircut.
Hollywood.
Homecoming.
Hospital.
In India.
Intellectual, The.
Interlude.
Jew.
Jew at Christmas Eve, The.
Leg, The.
Love for a Hand.
Love Letter.
Lower the Standard: That's My Motto.
Man on Wheels.
Manhole Covers.
Midnight Show.
Minute, The.
Moving In.
Murder of Moses, The.
My Father's Funeral.
My Grandmother.
Necropolis.
Nigger.
Nostalgia.
October 1.
151st Psalm, The.
Paradox: The Birds.
Party in Winter.
Phenomenon, The.
Poet.
Poets of Hell, The.
Potomac, The.
Progress of Faust, The.
Puritan, The.
Quintana Lay in the Shallow Grave of Coral.
Recapitulations, *sel.*
Recognition of Eve, The.
Scyros.
Sickness of Adam, The.
Six Religious Lyrics, *sel.*
Southerner, The.
Sunday: New Guinea.
Travelogue for Exiles.
Troop Train.
Twins, The.
Two-Year-Old Has Had a Motherless Week, The.
University.
V-Letter.
Waiting in Front of the Columnar High School.
Waitress.
Washington Cathedral.
Western Town.
White-haired Lover, *sel.*

Shapiro, Mark Elliott
Dying under a Fall of Stars.
Shargel, Zvi
I Will Go Away.
Let Us Laugh.
Pictures on the Wall.
Sharman, Lyon (Abbie Mary Lyon Sharman)
Old Man Pot.
Sharp, Constance
I Show the Daffodils to the Retarded Kids.
Sharp, Saundra
Moon Poem.
Sharp, William. *See* **"Macleod, Fiona"**
Sharpe, Peter
Cold Front.
Sharpe, R. L.
Bag of Tools, A.
Sharpe, Richard Scrafton
Country Mouse and the City Mouse, The.
Dame Wiggins of Lee, *at.*
Sharpless, Stanley J.
Betjeman at the Post Office.
"Go to the Ant."
Hamlet.
In Praise of Cocoa, Cupid's Nightcap.
King Canute.
Paradise Lost.
Summonee's Tale, The.
To His Coy Mistress, *parody.*
Shatford, Sarah Taylor
Found.
Shauger, Carol
Preface: "Mother, don't read/ my poems."
Shaul, Anwar
Mother.
Prayers to Liberty.
To a Cactus Seller.
Shaver, Eva Gilbert
Dear Old Dad.
Shaw, Charles
Dissembler.
Shaw, Cuthbert
Time's Balm.
Shaw, David T.
Columbia, the Gem of the Ocean.
Red, White and Blue, The.
Shaw, Frances
Last Guest, The.
Little Pagan Rain Song.
Rain.
Who Loves the Rain.
Shaw, Henry Wheeler. *See* **"Billings, Josh"**
Shaw, Isabel
Christmas Chant.
Shaw, John
Sleighing Song.
Song: "Who has robbed the ocean cave."
Shaw, Knowles
Bringing in the Sheaves.
Handwriting on the Wall, The.
Shaw, Luci
Craftsman.
For They Shall See God.
Getting Inside the Miracle.
Groundhog, The.
Judas, Peter.
Man Cannot Name Himself.
May 20: Very Early Morning.
Need Is Our Name.
Small Song.
Stars in Apple Cores.
To a Christmas Two-Year-Old.
Shaw, Neufville
Drowned Sailor.
Shaw, Richard
Cat's Menu.
Shaw, Robert B.
Partial Draft.
Shaw, Winifred
Fine Clay.
Shea, John Augustus
Ocean, The.

Sheaks, Barclay
Friend's Passing, A.
Sheard, Virna
Exile.
Yak, The.
Sheck, Laurie
Deer, The.
Sleeping Beauty.
Shectman, Robin
Breakfast.
Telephone.
Sheehan, Timothy
At Camino.
Eclipse.
Sheers, Sir Henry
Long Prologue to a Short Play, A.
Sheffield, John, Duke of Buckingham and Normanby
Essay on Poetry, *sel.*
Essay upon Satire, An.
Happy Night, The.
Nine, The.
On Mr. Hobbs, and His Writings.
On One Who Died Discovering Her Kindness.
On Writing for the Stage.
Reconcilement, The.
Song: "Come, Celia, let's agree at last."
Written over a Gate.
Sheldon, Gilbert
St. Anthony's Township.
Shelley, Percy Bysshe
Adonais; an Elegy on the Death of John Keats.
Against Oblivion.
Alastor; or, The Spirit of Solitude.
Arethusa.
At Pompeii.
Autumn.
Autumn; a Dirge.
Aziola, The.
Beatrice's Last Words.
Bridal Song, A.
Cenci, The.
Charles the First, *sels.*
Child of Twelve, A.
Chorus: "Life of Life! thy lips enkindle."
Chorus: "World's great age begins anew, The."
Chorus: "Worlds on worlds are rolling ever."
Chorus from "Hellas."
Chorus of Spirits.
Cloud, The.
Daemon of the World, The, *sel.*
Daybreak.
Demogorgon's Speech.
Dirge, A: "Rough wind, that moanest loud."
Dirge for the Year.
Dream of the Unknown, A.
Elegy on the Death of John Keats, An.
England in 1819.
Epipsychidion.
Epistle to George Keats, *sel.*
Evening; Ponte al Mare, Pisa.
Ever as We Sailed.
Final Chorus, The.
Flight of Love, The.
Fragment: Rain.
Fragment: To the Moon.
From the Arabic; an Imitation.
Ginevra, *sel.*
Go Thou to Rome.
Good-Night.
Grave of Keats, The.
Hate-Song, A.
Hell is a city much like London.
Hellas, *sels.*
Hymn of Apollo.
Hymn to Intellectual Beauty.
Hymn to the Spirit of Nature.
I Fear Thy Kisses, Gentle Maiden.
I love snow and all the forms.
Indian Serenade, The.
Invitation, The.
Invitation, to Jane, The.

Invocation: "Earth, ocean, air, beloved brotherhood !"
Invocation: "Rarely, rarely, comest thou."
Isle, The.
Julian and Maddalo.
Lament, A: "O world! O life! O time!"
Letter to Maria Gisborne, *sels.*
Life of Life.
Lines: "Cold earth slept below, The."
Lines to an Indian Air.
Lines Written among the Euganean Hills.
Lines Written in the Bay of Lerici.
Lines Written on Hearing the News of the Death of Napoleon.
Love.
Love's Philosophy.
Lumen de Lumine.
Magic Car Moved On, The.
Mask [*or* Masque] of Anarchy, The.
Mont Blanc.
Moon, The.
Mourn Not for Adonais.
Music.
Music, When Soft Voices Die.
Mutability.
New World, A.
Night.
O Thou Immortal Deity.
Ode to Naples, *sel.*
Ode to the West Wind.
On a Painted Woman.
On a Poet's Lips I Slept.
On Fanny Godwin.
On Keats.
Orbed Maiden.
Ozymandias.
Peter Bell the Third, *sels.*
Poet's Dream, The.
Prometheus Unbound.
Queen Mab, *sels.*
Question, The ("I dream'd that, as I wander'd by the way").
Rain.
Recollection, The.
Remorse.
Revolt of Islam, The, *sels.*
St. Irvyne, *sel.*
Semichorus II: "There the voluptuous nightingales."
Sensitive Plant, The.
Seraph of Heaven.
Similes for Two Political Characters of 1819.
Song: "Rarely, rarely comest thou."
Song, A: "Widow bird sate mourning for her love, A."
Song to the Men of England.
Sonnet: "Lift not the painted veil which those who live."
Sonnet: Ozymandias.
Stand ye calm and resolute.
Stanzas: "Away! the moor is dark beneath the moon."
Stanzas—April, 1814.
Stanzas to Edward Williams.
Stanzas Written in Dejection near Naples.
Summer and Winter.
Time.
Time Long Past.
To ———: "I fear thy kisses, gentle maiden."
To ———: "Music, when soft voices die."
To ———: "One word is too often profaned."
To ———: "When passion's trance is overpast."
To a Lady, with a Guitar.
To a Skylark.
To Constantia Singing.
To Jane: The Invitation.
To Jane: The Keen Stars Were Twinkling.
To Jane: The Recollection.
To Maria Gisborne in England, from Italy.
To Mary.
To Night.
To the Lord Chancellor, *sels.*
To the Moon.
To the Night.
To the Nile.
To William Shelley.
To Wordsworth.
Trackless Deeps, The.
Tribute to America.
Triumph of Life, The.
True Love.
Two Spirits, The; an Allegory.
Unfathomable Sea!
Vision of the Sea, A.
Waning Moon, The.
War Is the Statesman's Game.
When the Lamp Is Shattered.
Who Reigns?
Witch of Atlas, The, *sel.*
With a Guitar, to Jane.
World's Great Age Begins Anew, The.
Worlds on Worlds.
World's Wanderers, The.
Written in the Euganean Hills, North Italy.

Shelton, Richard
Alone.
Angel and the Anchorite, The.
Brother.
Certain Choices.
Children of Night.
Connais-Tu le Pays?
Disintegration.
Excerpts from the Notebook of the Poet of Santo Tomas.
How to Amuse a Stone.
Letter to a Dead Father.
Letting Go.
On Lake Pend Oreille.
One More Time.
Prophets, The.
Requiem for Sonora.
Softly Softly.
Stone Garden, The.
War.
Why I Never Went into Politics.
Wonders of the World.
Youth.

Shembe, Isaiah
Come In.
Dance Hymn.
I Am the Beginning.
Let Zulu Be Heard.
Springtime of the earth has come, The.

Shen Ch'üan
Therefore We Preserve Life.

Shenhar, Aliza
Akedah, The.
Drunkenness of Pain, The.
Expectation.
Resurrection of the Dead.
Sea-Games.
Song of the Closing Service.
Trembling.

Shenstone, William
Elegy XI: "Ah me, my friend! it will not, will not last!"
Elegy: He Complains How Soon the Pleasing Novelty of Life Is Over.
Hint from Voiture.
Landscape, The.
O Sweet Anne Page.
On the Clerk of a Country Parish.
Pastoral Ballad.
Poet and the Dun, The.
Schoolmistress, The.
Shepherd's Home, The.
Solemn Meditation, A.
Song: Landskip, The.
Song: "O'er desert plains, and rushy meers."
Written at [*or* in] an Inn at Henley.

Shepard, Elizabeth Alsop
White Fox.

Shepard, Odell
Adventurer, The.
Elm, The.
Flock at Evening, The.
Hidden Weaver, The.
Home Thoughts.
In the Dawn.
Vespers.
Vistas.

Shepherd, Sir Fleetwood
Epitaph on the Duke of Grafton.

Shepherd, J. Barrie
In Passing.
Lent Tending.

Shepherd, Nan
Hill Burns, The.
Sgoran Dhu.

Shepherd, Nathaniel Graham
Calling the Roll.
Roll-Call.

Shepherd, Thomas
Alas, My God.
For Communion with God, *sel.*

Shepherd, William
Ode on Lord Macartney's Embassy to China.

Sheppard, Patricia
Enlightenment, The.

Sher, Steven
Groundhog Foreshadowed, The.
Pilgrimage to Hennessey's.

Sherburne, Sir Edward
And She Washed His Feet with Her Tears, and Wiped Them with the Hairs of Her Head.
Christus Mattaeum et Discipulos Alloquitur.
Conscience.
Ice and Fire.
Love's Arithmetic.
Magdalen, The.
Violets in Thaumantia's Bosome.

Sheridan, Helen Selina
Charming Woman, The.
Lament of the Irish Emigrant.
Love Hath a Language.
To My Son, *sel.*

Sheridan, Niall
Poem: "As rock to sun or storm."

Sheridan, Richard Brinsley
Air: "I ne'er could any lustre [*or* luster] see."
By Coelia's Arbor.
Clio's Protest.
Dry Be That Tear.
Duenna, The, *sels.*
Epigram: " 'I would,' says Fox, 'a tax devise.' "
Famous Toast, A.
Geranium, The.
Here's to the Maiden.
Let the Toast Pass.
Oh Yield, Fair Lids.
On Lady Anne Hamilton.
School for Scandal, The, *sel.*
Song: "Had I a heart for falsehood framed."
Song: "Here's to the maiden of bashful fifteen."

Sherman, Francis
Builder, The.
House of Colour, The.
In Memorabilia Mortis.
Let Us Rise Up and Live.

Sherman, Frank Dempster
At Midnight.
Baseball.
Blossoms.
Dawn.
February.
Golden Rod, The.
Hollyhock, A.
January.
Library, The.
Mary and the Lamb.
Moonrise.
On a Greek Vase.
On Some Buttercups.
Prayer, A: "It is my joy in life to find."

Quatrain, A: "Hark at the lips of this pink whorl of shell."
Rose's Cup, The.
Shadows, The.
Snow-Bird, The.
To a Rose.
Wizard Frost.
Sherman, Joseph
Sarai.
Sherman, Kenneth
My Father Kept His Cats Well Fed.
Sherman, Susan
Three Moments.
Sherry, Ruth Forbes
Promises.
Sherwin, Judith Johnson
Balance, The.
Construction #13.
Dr. Potatohead Talks to Mothers.
Eat 'Em Up Smith Tells All in South Africa.
Fabulous Teamsters, The.
Gentle Heart, A: Two.
Goddess.
Just.
Light Woman's Song, The.
Rhyme for the Child as a Wet Dog.
What Maisie Know She Don't Want No.
Sherwin, Richard
Jacob's Winning.
Sherwood, Grace Buchanan
After Laughter.
Sherwood, Kate Brownlee
Albert Sidney Johnston.
Molly Pitcher.
Thomas at Chickamauga.
Ulric Dahlgren.
Sherwood, Margaret
In Memoriam—Leo: A Yellow Cat.
Sherwood, Robert E.
Old Hokum Buncombe, The.
Sherwood, Rupe
Me and Prunes.
Shevin, David
Dawn.
Shechem.
Shields, Carol
Great-Grandma.
New Mothers, The.
Shields, Ren
In the Good Old Summertime.
Shiffert, Edith Marcombe
Manners.
Monkeys on Mt. Hiei.
Shadow of a Branch, The.
Shihab, Naomi. *See* **Nye, Naomi Shihab**
Shikishi, Princess
Autumn.
Blossoms have fallen, The.
Spring.
Winter.
Shiko
Lilies.
Maple Leaves.
Shillito, Edward
Prayer for a Preacher, A.
Prayer of a Modern Thomas.
Shimon, Louis C.
I Know Something Good about You.
Shinn, Milicent Washburn
Song and Science.
When Almonds Bloom.
Yosemite.
Shiplett, Paul D.
James Gerard.
Louie.
Rap Sheet.
State School.
Swimmers.
Wire Monkey.
Shipley, Sir Arthur
Ere You Were Queen of Sheba.
Shipley, Vivian
First Holes Are Fresh.
Shipman, Thomas
Resolute Courtier, The.
Shipp, E. Richard
Eighteen-ninety.
Shippen, William
Character of a Certain Whig, The.
Pasquin to the Queen's Statue at St. Paul's.
Shippey, Joseph
Columbia College, 1796.
Shipton, Anna
Unerring Guide, The.
Shiraishi Kazuko
Phallic Root.
Phallus.
Shire, Kent
Earth Changes.
Shirk, Ottis
Resolved.
Shirley, James
Bard, The.
Bard's Chant.
Commonwealth of Birds, The.
Contention of Ajax and Ulysses, The, *sel.*
Cupid and Death, *sels.*
Cupid Ungodded.
Cupids Call.
Death, the Conqueror.
Death's Emissaries.
Death's Final Conquest.
Death's Subtle Ways.
Epitaph Inscribed on a Small Piece of Marble.
Epitaph on the Duke of Buckingham.
Garden, The.
Glories of Our Blood and State, The.
Hymn, A: "O fly, my soul! What hangs upon."
Imposture, The, *sels.*
Io.
Last Conqueror, The.
Love's Victories.
O Fly My Soul.
Of Death.
On Her Dancing.
On the Duke of Buckingham.
Our Blood and State.
Passing Bell, The.
Piping Peace.
Saint Patrick for Ireland, *sel.*
Song: "Glories of our blood and state, The."
Song: "Victorious men of Earth, no more."
Song: "You virgins that did late despair."
Song of Nuns, A.
To His Mistris Confined.
To the Excellent Pattern of Beauty and Virtue, Lady Elizabeth, Countess of Ormond.
To the Painter Preparing to Draw M. M. H.
Triumph of Beautie Song, The, *sel.*
Upon Scarlet and Blush-coloured Ribbands, Given by Two Ladies.
Victorious Men of Earth.
You Virgins.
Shivell, Paul
In God's Eternal Studios.
Studios Photographic, The, *sel.*
Shlonsky, Avraham
Dress Me, Dear Mother.
Grape-gathering.
New Genesis, A.
Pledge.
Prayer: "Forgive me, you whom they cast in a name."
Stars on Shabbat, The.
Shockley, Martin Staples
Crossedroads.
Sholl, Betsy
Urgency.
Shorb, Michael
First Ice of Winter.
Shore, Jane
Anthony.
Astronomer's Journal, An.
Sleeping Beauty.
Shorey, George H.
Bubbles.
Short, Clarice
Old One and the Wind, The.
Short, John
Carol: "There was a boy bedded in bracken."
Shorter, Dora Sigerson
April.
Ballad of the Little Black Hound.
Bird from the West, A.
Comforters, The.
Gypsies' Road, The.
Ireland.
Kine of My Father, The.
Mother's Prayer, The.
New Year, A.
Nora.
Patchwork Quilt, The.
Piper on the Hill, The.
Rose Will Fade, A.
Sixteen Dead Men.
Wind on the Hills, The.
Shostakovitch, Dmitri
Salute to Life.
Shove, Fredegond
Dream in Early Spring, A.
Farmer, The.
Infant Spring.
New Ghost, The.
Song: "Spring lights her candles everywhere."
Sops of Light.
Showell, Samuel, Jr.
To the Borrower of This Book.
Shriver, Peggy
Spirit of 34th Street, The.
Shuford, Gene
Harvest.
Shuler, Chester E.
Faithful Few, The.
Shulman, David
Diary of the Sailors of the North, A.
Shulman, Max
Honest Abe Lincoln.
Shuraikh
Distich.
Shurmantine, Brad Lee
Tracks.
Shurtleff, Ernest W.
Lead On, O King Eternal, *with music.*
Shute, Evan V.
Luck.
Night Comes Apace.
Poor Fool.
Twenty Years After.
Shuttle, Penelope
Early Pregnancy.
Expectant Mother.
Gone Is the Sleepgiver.
Locale.
Maritimes.
Shuttleworth, P. N.
Wykehamist's Address to Learning, A.
Shuttleworth, Paul
Tornado Watch.
"Shy, Timothy." *See* **Lewis, Dominic Evan Wyndham**
Sibley, Charles
Plaidie, The.
Sickels, David Banks
It Cannot Be ("It cannot be that He who made").
Reincarnation.
Sidgwick, Frank
Aeronaut to His Lady, The.
Cheerful Chilterns, The.
Christmas Legend, A.
Corinna Goes a-Singing.
"Form Fours."
Glory of Early Rising, The.
His Hirsute Suit.
Imaginary Correspondence, *parody.*

Sing a Song of Sixpence, *parody.*
Vision.
Sidgwick, Henry
Goethe and Frederika.
Sidney, James A.
Irish Schoolmaster, The.
Sidney, Sir Philip
Absence.
Advice to the Same.
Arcadia, *sels.*
Arcadian Duologue.
Astrophel and Stella.
Complaint of Love.
Contentment.
Country Song, A.
Cupid.
Delight of Solitariness, The.
Desire.
Dispraise of a Courtly Life.
Ditty, A: "My true-love hath my heart, and I have his."
Dorus's Song.
Double Sestine.
Echo.
Eighth Song: "In a grove most rich of shade."
Eleventh Song: "Who is it that this dark[e] night."
Epithalamium: "Let mother Earth now deck herself in flowers."
Farewell, A: "Oft have I mused, but now at length I find."
Farewell World.
First Song: "Doubt you to whom my Muse these notes intendeth."
Fourth Song: "Only Joy! now here you are."
Geron and Histor.
Get Hence Foule Griefe.
Grammar-Rules.
Graven Thoughts.
He That Loves.
Heart Exchange.
His Being Was in Her Alone.
His Lady's Cruelty.
Immortality.
In Vain, Mine Eyes.
In wonted walks, since wonted fancies change.
Just Exchange.
Lady My Treasure.
Languishing Moon, The.
Leave Me, O Love.
Like as the Dove.
Litany, A: "Ring out your bells, let mourning shows be spread."
Love and Jealousy.
Love and Reason.
Love Me, O Love.
Lovers' Dialogue.
Madrigal: "Why dost thou haste away?"
Moon, The.
My Sheep Are Thoughts.
My True Love Hath My Heart [and I Have His.]
Night.
Nightingale, The.
Nightingale, as Soon as April Bringeth, The.
O Dear Life, When Shall It Be.
O You That Hear This Voice.
Oft Have I Mused.
Old Age.
Philomela.
Ring Out Your Bells.
Rural Poesy.
Sapphics.
Seven Wonders of England, The, *sel.*
Shepherd Song.
Shepherd's Tale, A.
Since So Mine Eyes.
Sixth Song: "O you that hear this voice."
Sleep ("Come, sleep, O sleep, the certain knot of peace").
Sleep ("Lock up, fair lids").
Sleep, baby mine, Desire, nurse Beauty singeth.
Solitariness (3 *sonnets*).
Song: "No, no, no, no, I cannot hate my foe."
Song: "O fair! O sweet! when I do look on thee."
Song: "Who hath his fancy pleasèd."
Sonnet: "Come, Sleep! O Sleep, the certain knot of peace."
Sonnet: "Highway, since you my chief Parnassus be."
Sonnet: "In truth, O Love, with what a boyish kind."
Sonnet: "Lock up, fair lids, the treasure of my heart."
Sonnet: "My true Love hath my heart, and I have his."
Sonnet: "With how sad steps, O Moon, thou climb'st the skies!"
Stella Sleeping.
Stonehenge.
Sweeter Saint I Serve, A.
Tale for Husbands, A.
Thou Blind Man's Mark.
To Sleep.
To Stella: "Doubt you to whom my Muse these notes intendeth."
To the Sad Moon.
True Love.
Underneath My Window.
Voices at the Window.
What Tongue Can Her Perfections Tell?
When, to my deadly [*or* deadlie] pleasure.
When Two Suns Do Appear.
Who Hath His Fancy [*or* Fancie] Pleased.
Who Is It That This Dark Night.
Why Fear to Die?
With How Sad Steps, O Moon, Thou Climb'st the Skies.
Wronged Lover, The.
Ye Goatherd Gods.
Yoke of Tyranny, The.
Siebert, Charles
City Butterfly.
Siebert, Diane
Train Song.
Siegel, Danny
Binni the Meshuggener.
Crippler, The.
Snow in the City.
Siegel, Eli
Alfred-Seeable Philadelphia Sky.
All the Smoke.
Disclaimer of Prejudice.
Duke of Parma's Ear.
Fare Thee Well.
Siegel, Robert
Air Field.
Center of America, The.
Christmas Eve.
Ego.
Mr. Brunt.
Revenant, The.
Rinsed with Gold, Endless, Walking the Fields.
Visit to the Farm, A.
Siegrist, Mary
League of Nations, The.
Sieller, William Vincent
Windmill on the Cape.
Sigerson, George
My Own Cáilin Donn.
Smith's Song.
Sigerson, Hester
Mad Song.
Sigourney, Lydia Huntley
Advertisement of a Lost Day.
Blessed Comforter Divine, *with music.*
California.
Columbus.
God Save the Plough.
Indian Names.
Indian's Welcome to the Pilgrim Fathers, The.
Laborers of Christ! Arise, *with music.*
Mother's Sacrifice, The.
On the Death of Mrs. Felicia Hemans, *sel.*
Onward, Onward, Men of Heaven, *with music.*
Request of a Dying Child.
Return of Napoleon from St. Helena, The.
We Praise Thee, If One Rescued Soul, *with music.*
Sikelianos, Anghelos
Doric.
Silabhattarika
He who stole my virginity/ is the same man.
Wanton, *sel.*
Silber, Irwin
I Just Wanna Stay Home.
Put My Name Down.
Silberger, Julius
Reply to Nancy Hanks, A.
Silberschlag, Eisig
Abraham.
Proust on Noah.
Silbert, Layle
Grand Hotel, Calcutta.
Silén, Iván
To Teresa.
Why I Can't Write a Poem about Lares.
Silentarius, Paulus. *See* **Paulus Silentarius**
Silesius, Angelus. *See* **"Angelus Silesius"**
Silesky, Barry
White Pines.
Silk, Dennis
Guide to Jerusalem.
Matronita.
Silkin, Jon
Coldness, The.
Death of a Bird.
Death of a Son.
Death to Us, A.
First It Was Singing.
Furnished Lives.
It Says.
Jerusalem.
Light.
Lilies of the Valley.
Reclaimed Area.
Respectabilities.
Resting Place.
Return, The.
Shirt, The.
Space in the Air, A.
Word about Freedom and Identity in Tel Aviv, A.
Silko, Leslie Marmon
Alaskan Mountain Poem #1.
Deer Song.
Four Mountain Wolves.
Hawk and Snake.
Horses at Valley Stores.
How to Write a Poem about the Sky.
In Cold Storm Light.
Indian Song: Survival.
Love Poem: "Rain smell comes with the wind."
Poem for Ben Barney.
Poem for Myself and Mei: Abortion.
Prayer to the Pacific.
Preparations.
Slim Man Canyon.
Story from Bear Country.
Sun Children.
Time We Climbed Snake Mountain, The.
Toe'osh; a Laguna Coyote Story.
When Sun Came to Riverwoman.
Where Mountain Lion Lay Down with Deer February 1973.
Sill, Edward Rowland
Baker's Duzzen uv Wize Sawz, A.
Before Sunrise in Winter.
Coup de Grace, The.
Dead President, The.
Fool's Prayer, The.
For the Gifts of the Spirit.
Force.
Future, The.
Home.

Life.
Lover's Song, The.
Opportunity.
Prayer, A: "O God, our Father, if we had but truth!"
Prayer for Peace, A.
Tempted.
Tropical Morning at Sea, A.

Sillè, Nicasius de
God Set Us Here, *with music.*

Sillery, Charles Doyne
She Died in Beauty.

Sillitoe, Alan
Picture of Loot.

Silvera, Edward S.
Forgotten Dreams.
Jungle Taste.
On the Death of a Child.
South Street.

Silverman, Maxine
Hair.

Silvers, Frances
Frankie Silvers.

Silverstein, David I.
There Are in Such Moments.

Silverstein, Shel (Shelley)
Beware, My Child.
Clarence ("Clarence Lee from Tennessee").
Dirtiest Man in the World, The.
Flag, The.
For Sale.
Friendship.
George Washington.
Hector the Collector.
Horse, The.
Hug o' War.
I must remember.
If I Had a Firecracker.
In That Dark Cave.
Jimmy Jet and His TV Set.
Lazy People, The.
Little Boy and the Old Man, The.
Magical Eraser.
My Invention.
Not Me.
Oh Did You Hear?
On Halloween.
One Inch Tall.
Peace and Joy.
Pie Problem.
Please Tell Me Just the Fabuli.
Sarah Cynthia Sylvia Stout Would Not Take the Garbage Out.
Slithergadee, The.
Smart.
Some Day.
There you sit.
Valentine.
Van Gogh Influence, The.
Wanted.
Worst, The.

Silverton, Michael
Adorable paratroopess alights, The.
Chasm, A.
Column A.
Food drops off a fork, The.
I am yours and you are mine so.
King of Sunshine, The.
Life in the Country.
Neckwear.
So long as Time & Space are the stars.
Woman came to me, A.

Simeon ben Isaac ben Abun of Mainz
All the Hosts of Heaven.
I Come to Supplicate.

Simic, Charles
Animal Acts.
Animals, The.
Ax.
Baby Pictures of Famous Dictators.
Ballad: "What's that approaching like dust like poverty."
Begotten of the Spleen.
Bestiary for the Fingers of My Right Hand.
Bird, The.
Breasts.
Brooms.
Butcher Shop.
Charon's Cosmology.
Classic Ballroom Dances.
Crows.
Elementary Cosmogony.
Empire of Dreams.
Errata.
Euclid Avenue.
Evening.
Fork.
Garden of Earthly Delights, The.
George Simic.
Harsh Climate.
Hunger.
Midpoint.
My Shoes.
Nothing.
Old Mountain Road.
Partial Explanation, The.
Pastoral: "I came to a field."
Poem: "Every morning I forget how it is."
Poem without a Title.
Poverty.
Prodigy.
Progress Report.
Psalm: "Old ones to the side."
Return to a Place Lit by a Glass of Milk.
Second Avenue Winter.
Sleep.
Solitude.
Spoon, The.
Starry Sky.
Stone.
Story, The.
Strictly for Posterity.
Tapestry.
Unintelligible Terms.
Watch Repair.
Watermelons.

Simison, Greg
My Family's under Contract to Cancer.

Simmerman, Jim
Cartoon.

Simmias of Thebes
To Prote.

Simmons, Gerald L., Jr.
Take Tools Our Strength.

Simmons, Herbert A.
Ascendancy.

Simmons, J. Edgar
Father in Tennessee, A.
Troubador.

Simmons, James
Art and Reality.
Cavalier Lyric.
Experience.
Fear Test: Integrity of Heroes.
First Goodbye Letter, The.
For Delphine.
Goodbye, Sally.
John Donne.
Letter to a Jealous Friend.
Reformer to His Father, A.
Summing Up, The.

Simmons, James Wright
Sumter's Band.

Simmons, Judy Dothard
Alabama.
Generations.
It's Comforting.
Survivor.

Simmons, Laura
At Christmastide.
Next Time.
Noel! Noel!

Simms, William Gilmore
Battle of Eutaw, The.
Decay of a People, The.
Grape-Vine Swing, The.
Lost Pleiad, The.
Night Storm.
Song in March.
Swamp Fox, The.

Simon, John
Ameinias.

Simon, John Oliver
Don't Tell Bad Dreams Says Tita's Mother.
For Alan Blanchard.
Living in the Boneyard.
Tryptych for Jan Bockelson, A.
Woodchuck Who Lives on Top of Mt. Ritter.

Simon, Paul
Richard Cory.

Simone, Nina
Four Women.

Simonides (of Ceos)
At Thermopylae.
Cleobulus' Epitaph.
Inscription to Spartans Dead at Thermopylae.
On the Army of Spartans, Who Died at Thermopylae.
On the Lacedaemonian Dead at Plataea.
On the Spartan Dead at Thermopylae.
On Two Brothers.
Thermopylae Ode, The.
Timocreon.

Simpson, Albert Benjamin
Abiding.
Believe the Bible.
His Best.
"It Is I, Be Not Afraid."
Keep Sweet.
Thanksgiving.
Why Doubt God's Word?

Simpson, Earl
Learning.

Simpson, F. A.
Lincoln and Liberty, *at.*

Simpson, George S.
Simpson's Rest.

Simpson, Henry
In February.

Simpson, Louis
Aegean.
After Midnight.
Against the Age.
American Dreams.
American Poetry.
As Birds Are Fitted to the Boughs.
Ash and the Oak, The.
Back in the States.
Battle, The.
Before the Poetry Reading.
Big Dream, Little Dream.
Birch.
Bird, The.
Boarder, The.
Carentan O Carentan.
Chocolates.
Climate of Paradise, The.
Constant Lover, The.
Country House, The.
Custom of the World, The.
Doubting.
Dream of Governors, A.
Dvonya.
Early in the Morning.
Friend of the Family, A.
Frogs.
Green Shepherd, The.
Heroes, The.
Hot Night on Water Street.
Hour of Feeling, The.
Hubert's Museum.
I Dreamed That in a City Dark as Paris.
In California.
In the Suburbs.
Inner Part, The.
Isidor.

It Was the Last of the Parades.
John the Baptist.
Laurel Tree, The.
Legend of Success, The Salesman's Story, The.
Lines Written near San Francisco.
Love and Poetry.
Man Who Married Magdalene, The.
Mashkin Hill.
Memories of a Lost War.
Middle-aged Man, The.
Morning Light, The.
Music in Venice.
My Father in the Night Commanding No.
New Lines for Cuscuscaraway and Mirza Murad Ali Beg.
Night in Odessa, A.
On the Lawn at the Villa.
Outward.
Photographer, The.
Quiet Desperation.
Redwoods, The.
Riders Held Back, The.
Rough Winds Do Shake.
Sailors.
Sensibility.
Silent Generation, The.
Simplicity.
Son of the Romanovs, A.
Song: "Let's sing a song together once."
Squeal.
Story about Chicken Soup, A.
Stumpfoot on 42nd Street.
Summer Storm.
Tailor's Wedding, The.
There Is.
Things.
To the Western World.
Tom Pringle.
Tonight the Famous Psychiatrist.
Troika, The.
True Weather for Women, The.
Union Barge on Staten Island, The.
Wall Test, The.
Walt Whitman at Bear Mountain.
Why Do You Write about Russia?
Working Late.

Simpson, Margaret Winefride
Villanelle: "O winter wind, lat grievin be."

Simpson, Nancy
On Certain Days of the Year.
Water on the Highway.

Simpson, Ronald Albert
Antarctica.
Diver.
Lake.
Night Out.

Simpson, Sam L.
Wagon Train, The.

Simpson, Tobey A.
For Mariella, in Antrona.

Simpson, William Haskel
Homesick Song.
Navajo.
Pity Not.
Saddle.
Taos Drums.
Yucca Is Yellowing.

Sims, George R.
Billy's Rose ("Billy's dead, and gone to glory").
Christmas Day in the Workhouse.
In the Workhouse: Christmas Day.
Lifeboat, The.
'Ostler Joe.

Sinason, Valerie
In the Beginning.
Renaming, The.
Will You Come Out Now?

Sinclair, Bennie Lee
Decoration Day.
Evangelist, The.

Sinclair, Donald
Path of the Old Spells, The.

Sinclair, F. D.
Zimbabwe.

Sinclair, John
Breakthrough.

Sinclair, May
Field Ambulance in Retreat.

Singer, Burns (James Burns Singer)
Birdsong.
Epilogue: "That death might not be casual."
I promise you by the harsh funeral.
Marcus Antoninus Cui Cognomen Erat Aurelius.
Nothing.
Old man dozed, The. The hospital quietened.
Peterhead in May.
Sonnets for a Dying Man, *sels.*
Still and All.
To see the petrel cropping in the farmyard.
Words Made of Water.

Singer, John
Stepney Green.

Singer, Sarah
Family Plot.

Sinks, P. W.
Just like Me.

Sipe, Muriel
Good Morning.

Sissman, Louis Edward
Critic on the Hearth, The.
Day in the City, A.
Disappearance in West Cedar Street, A.
Dying: An Introduction.
Elegy: E. W.
Going Home, 1945, *sel.*
Henley, July 4: 1914-1964.
In and Out.
Lüchow's and After.
New York Woman, The.
Nocturne, Central Park South.
On the Island.
Parents in Winter, *sel.*
Pepys Bar, West Forty-eighth Street, 8 a.m.
Safety at Forty; or, An Abecedarian Takes a Walk.
Sweeney to Mrs. Porter in the Spring.
Talking Union: 1964.
Tras Os Montes, *sel.*
West Forties, The: Morning, Noon, and Night.

Sisson, Charles Hubert
A and B.
Adam and Eve.
At First.
Carmen Saeculare.
Cato.
Cranmer.
Family Fortunes.
Human Relations.
Knole.
Letter to John Donne, A.
Marcus Aurelius.
Money.
Nature of Man, The.
Over the Wall: Berlin, May 1975.
Queen of Lydia, The.
Temple, The.
Usk, The.

Sitwell, Dame Edith
Ass-Face.
Aubade: "Jane, Jane,/ Tall as a crane."
Bat, The.
Canticle of the Rose, The.
Clowns' Houses.
Coat of Fire, The.
Colonel Fantock.
Country Dance.
Dancers, The.
Daphne.
Dark Song.
Dirge for the New Sunrise.
Drum, The: The Narrative of the Demon of Tedworth.
Elegy for Dylan Thomas.
Evening.
Façade, *sels.*
Fan, The.
Four in the Morning.
Gardener Janus Catches a Naiad.
Gold Coast Customs, *sel.*
Hambone and the Heart, The.
Harvest.
Heart and Mind.
Hornpipe.
How Many Heavens.
Innocent Spring, The.
Interlude.
King of China's Daughter, The.
Lament of Edward Blastock, The.
Lullaby: "Though the world has slipped and gone."
Madam Mouse Trots.
Mademoiselle Richarde.
Most Lovely Shade ("Most lovely dark, my Æthiopia born").
Neptune—Polka.
Old Woman, An.
Old Woman Laments in Spring-Time, An.
One fantee wave.
Panope.
Perpetuum Mobile.
Poet Laments the Coming of Old Age, The.
Sailor, What of the Isles?
Scotch Rhapsody.
Shadow of Cain, The.
Sir Beelzebub.
Sleeping Beauty, The, *sels.*
Solo for Ear-Trumpet.
Song: "Now that Fate is dead and gone."
Song: "Once my heart was a summer rose."
Song at Morning, A.
Spinning Song.
Spring.
Still Falls the Rain.
Street Song.
Swans, The.
Switchback.
Tears.
Three Poems of the Atomic Bomb, *sel.*
Trio for Two Cats and a Trombone.
Two Kitchen Songs.
Variations on an Old Nursery Rhyme.
Waltz.
Web of Eros, The.
When Sir Beelzebub.
When we come to that dark house.
You, the Young Rainbow.
Youth with the Red-gold Hair, The.

Sitwell, Sir Osbert
Elegy for Mr. Goodbeare.
England Reclaimed, *sel.*
English Beach Memory: Mr. Thuddock.
Fountains ("Proud fountains, wave your plumes").
Giardino Pubblico.
Lament for Richard Rolston.
Maxixe.
Mrs. Busk.
Mrs. Southern's Enemy.
Next War, The.
On the Coast of Coromandel.
Therefore Is the Name of It Called Babel.
To Charlotte Corday.

Sitwell, Sacheverell
Agamemnon's Tomb.
Derbyshire Bluebells.
Fountains ("This night is pure and clear as thrice refinèd silver").
Kingcups.
Landscape with the Giant Diana, *sel.*
Orion Seeks the Goddess Diana.
Outside Dunsandle.
"Psittachus Eois Imitatrix Ales ab Indis."
Red-gold Rain, The.
Rio Grande, The.
River God, The.

Tulip Tree.
Variation on a Theme by John Lyly.
Venus of Bolsover Castle, The.
Sivan, Arye
Children's Song.
Forty Years Peace.
In Jerusalem Are Women.
To Xanadu, Which Is Beth Shaul.
Sizemore, George
Drill Man Blues.
Sjolander, John P.
Last Longhorn's Farewell, The.
Pine of Whiting Wood, The.
Skeat, Walter William
Clerk Ther Was of Cauntebrigge Also, A.
Villanelle: "It's all a trick, quite easy when you know it."
Skeen, Anita
Instructions.
Letter to My Mother.
Modern Poetry.
Outside Every Window Is a Flowering Thing.
Sailing in Crosslight.
Skelton, John
Against Garnesche, *sel.*
Anathema of Cats.
Auncient Acquaintance, Madam, The.
Ballade of the Scottyshe Kynge, A.
Bowge of Courte, The.
Colin Clout, *sels.*
Commendations of Mistress Jane Scrope, The.
Curse on the Cat, A.
Funeral of Philip Sparrow, The, *abr.*
Garlande [*or* Garlands] of Laurell, The, *sels.*
Gift of a Skull, The.
Go, Piteous Heart.
Gup, Scot!
How the Doughty Duke of Albany like a Coward Knight Ran Away Shamefully, *sel.*
In Praise of Isabel Pennell.
Knowledge, Acquaintance.
L'Envoy: To His Book.
Lullay, Lullay.
Manerly Margery Mylk and Ale.
Mistress Margaret Hussey.
My Darling Dear, My Daisy Flower.
Parrot, The.
Parrot's Soliloquy.
Phyllyp Sparowe [*or* Philip Sparrow].
Prayer to the Father of [*or* in] Heaven, A.
Prelates, The.
Skelton Laureate, Defender, against Lusty Garnesche, Well-beseen Christopher, Challenger.
Sleeper Hood-winked, The.
Sparrow's Dirge, The ("Placebo, /Who is there? Who?").
Speak [*or* speke], Parrot, *sels.*
To Maystres Jane Blenner-Haiset.
To Mistress Anne.
To Mistress Gertrude Statham.
To Mistress Margaret Tilney.
To Mistress Margery Wentworth.
To Mistress [*or* Maystres] Isabell Pennell.
To Mistress [*or* Maystres] Margaret Hussey.
To My Lady Mirriel Howard.
Tunnyng [*or* Tunning] of Elynour [*or* Elinor] Rummyng [*or* Rumming], The, *sels.*
Unfriendly Fortune.
Upon a Dead Man's Head.
Why Come Ye Not to Court, *sel.*
With Lullay, Lullay, like a Child.
Womanhood [*or* Womanhod], wanton, ye want.
Skelton, Philip
"To God, Ye Choir Above."
Skelton, Robin
"Angel."
Ballad of a Mine, A.
Brigg, The.
Eagle.
Lakeside Incident.
Skene, Don
After Reading Twenty Years of Grantland Rice.
Skillman, Judith
Waiting.
Skinner, Constance Lindsay
Song of Basket-weaving.
Song of Cradle-making.
Song of the Full Catch.
Three Songs from the Haida.
Skinner, Cornelia Otis
To the Sistine Madonna.
Skinner, Jeffrey
His Side/ Her Side.
Skinner, John
Tullochgorum.
Skinner, Knute
Blackheads.
Brockton Murder, The; a Page out of William James.
Cold Irish Earth, The.
Imagine Grass.
Location.
Old Lady Watching TV, An.
Organ Solo.
Skipsey, Joseph
Dewdrop, Wind and Sun.
Get Up!
Golden Lot, A.
Hey Robin.
Merry Bee, A.
Mother Wept.
Time Hath Been, The.
Violet and the Rose, The.
Willy to Jinny.
Skirrow, Desmond
Ode on a Grecian Urn Summarized.
Skirving, Adam
Johnnie Cope.
Sklar, Morty
Poem to the Sun.
Sklarew, Myra
Benediction.
Hieroglyphic.
In Bed.
Instructions for the Messiah.
Origin of Species, The.
Poem of the Mother.
Red Riding Hood at the Acropolis.
What Is a Jewish Poem?
Skrine, Nesta Higginson. *See* **"O'Neill, Moira"**
Skrzynecki, Peter
Cattle.
Feliks Skrzynecki.
Skythinos
Epigram: "Great woe, fire & war come on me."
Sladen, Douglas Brook Wheelton
Summer Christmas in Australia, A.
Under the Wattle.
Slate, Ron
Accomplice, The.
Slater, Eleanor
Petition.
Sight and Insight.
Slater, Robert
Survival Kit.
Survivors, The.
Slavitt, David R.
Broads.
Dead Bird.
Eczema.
Griefs of Women, The.
In the Seraglio.
That Everything Moves Its Bowels.
Slemp, John Calvin
O Christ, Who Died.
Slender, Pauline
Vagrant, The.
Slesinger, Warren
Sandpaper, Sandpiper, Sandpit.
Slessor, Kenneth
Atlas, The, *sels.*
Beach Burial.
Bushranger, A.
Country Towns.
Dutch Seacoast.
Five Bells.
Five Visions of Captain Cook, *sel.*
King of Cuckooz, The.
Mermaids.
Metempsychosis.
North Country.
Out of Time, *sel.*
Polarities.
Post-Roads.
Serenade: "Thou moon, like a white Christus hanging."
South Country.
Two Chronometers.
William Street.
Slim, T-Bone
Popular Wobbly, The.
Sloan, Errol B.
And Yet.
Sloan, Jocelyn Macy
Eliza Telefair.
Sloate, Daniel
Your Birds Build Sun-Castles with Song.
Sloman, Joel
In a Remote Cloister Bordering the Empyrean.
Tree, The.
Slonimski, Antoni
All.
Conrad.
Conversation with a Countryman.
Elegy: "No more, no more Jewish townships in Poland."
He Is My Countryman.
Jerusalem.
London Spring.
Morning and Evening.
Remembrance.
Slowinsky, Stephanie
It's True I'm No Miss America.
Slutsky, Boris
Burnt.
Dreams of Auschwitz.
God.
How They Killed My Grandmother.
Sly, Muriel
Chimpanzee, The/ Is a most embarrassing animal to see.
"Smalacombe, John." *See* **MacKay, Louis Alexander**
Small, Adam
There's Somethin'.
Small, Floyd B.
Root Hog or Die, *parody.*
Smaridge, Norah
Why Run?
Smart, Christopher
Adoration.
All the Scenes of Nature Quicken.
Ascension of Our Lord Jesus Christ, The.
Author Apologizes to a Lady for His Being a Little Man, The.
Beauteous, Yea Beauteous More than These.
Catholic Amen, The.
Christmas Day.
Citizen and the Red Lion of Brentford, The.
Consideration for Others.
Elegance.
Epiphany.
For I Will Consider My Cat Jeoffry [*or* Jeoffrey].
For Saturday.
Gratitude.
Hop Garden, The, *sels.*
Hops along the Medway.
How to Cure Hops and Prepare Them for Sale.
Hymn: Nativity of Our Lord and Saviour Jesus Christ, The.
Hymn: St. Philip and St. James.
Hymn to the Supreme Being on Recovery from a Dangerous Fit of Illness, *sel.*

Hymns and Spiritual Songs, *sels.*
Hymns for the Amusement of Children, *sels.*
Instruments, The.
Jubilate Agno, *sels.*
Lark's Nest, A.
Long-Suffering of God.
Loveliness.
Man of Prayer, The.
Mirth.
Moderation.
Morning Hymn, A.
Morning-Piece, A; or, An Hymn for the Hay-Makers.
Mutual Subjection.
My Cat Jeoffry [*or* Jeoffrey].
Nativity of Our Lord and Saviour Jesus Christ, The.
Night-Piece, A; or, Modern Philosophy.
On a Bed of Guernsey Lilies.
On My Wife's Birth-Day.
Praise.
Pray Remember the Poor.
St. Mark.
St. Matthias.
St. Philip and St. James.
Song: "Where shall Celia fly for shelter."
Song of David, The.
Song to David, A.
Spring.
Stars, The, *sel.*.
Taste.

Smedley, Menella Bute
North Pole Story, A.
Wind Me a Summer Crown.

Smiley, Joseph Bert
St. Peter at the Gate.

Smith, Ada
In City Streets.

Smith, Alexander
Barbara.
Life-Drama, A, *sel.*
Scorned.

Smith, Arabella Eugenia
If I Should Die Tonight.

Smith, Alexander
Glasgow.

Smith, Arthur James Marshall
Archer, The.
Ballade un Peu Banale.
Brigadier.
Business as Usual 1946.
Common Man, The.
Dead, The.
Far West.
Fountain, The.
Good Friday.
Like an Old Proud King in a Parable.
Lonely Land, The.
My Death.
News of the Phoenix.
Ode: On the Death of William Butler Yeats.
On Knowing Nothing.
Plot against Proteus, The.
Political Intelligence.
Prothalamium.
Resurrection of Arp.
Sorcerer, The.
Taste of Space, The.
To Henry Vaughan.
Watching the Old Man Die.
What Is That Music High in the Air?
What the Emanation of Casey Jones Said to the Medium.
Wisdom of Old Jelly Roll, The.

Smith, Barbara
Next Door to Monica's Dance Studio.
Physical for My Son.

Smith, Bessie
Empty Bed Blues.

Smith, Bradford
Winter Is Icumen In.

Smith, Bruce
Pelvic Meditation.
Window.

Smith, Caroline Sprague
Tarry with Me, O My Saviour, *with music.*

Smith, Charlotte
Beachy Head, *sels.*
Elegiac Sonnet.
First Swallow, The.
Glow-Worm, The.
Gossamer, The.
He May Be Envied, Who with Tranquil Breast.
Invitation to the Bee.
Montalbert, *sel.*
Mute Is Thy Wild Harp, Now, O Bard Sublime!
Press'd [*or* Pressed] by the Moon, Mute Arbitress of Tides.
Sonnet Written at the Close of Spring.
Thirty-eight.
To Sleep.
To Spring.
To the Moon.

Smith, Cicely Fox
Hastings Mill.
Convalescent, The.
In Prize.
In the Trades.
Pictures.
What the Old Man Said.

Smith, Claude Clayton
Charlie Johnson in Kettletown.
Kiss, The.

Smith, Daniel
Donzella and the *Ceylon*, The, *with music, at.*

Smith, Dave
Antipastoral Memory of One Summer, An.
Blues for Benny Kid Paret.
Cumberland Station.
Dome Poem.
Elk Ghosts; a Birth Memory.
First Star.
Gramercy Park Hotel.
Hard Times, but Carrying On.
In the House of the Judge.
Leafless Trees, Chickahominy Swamp.
Mending Crab Pots.
Night Fishing for Blues.
Of Oystermen, Workboats.
On a Field at Fredericksburg.
Perspective and Limits of Snapshots, The.
Photographic Plate, Partly Spidered, Hampton Roads, Virginia, with Model T Ford Mid-Channel.
Pine Cones.
Pornography Box, The.
Purpose of the Chesapeake & Ohio Canal, The.
Roundhouse Voices, The.
Running Back.
Tide Pools.
Under the Scrub Oak, a Red Shoe.

Smith, Dexter
Our National Banner.

Smith, Dill Armor
Twenty Years Ago, *at.*

Smith, Douglas
Balcony Poems, The.

Smith, Edgar
Heaven Will Protect the Working Girl.

Smith, Elizabeth Oakes
Sinless Child, The, *sel.*

Smith, Eunice
Dear Brethren, Are Your Harps in Tune? *with music.*
Dear Happy Souls, *with music.*

Smith, Florence
Song: "How pleasant it is that always."

Smith, George
Country Lovers, The; or, Isaac and Marget Going to Town, on a Summer's Morning.

Smith, Harry Bache
Armorer's Song, The.
Gypsy Love Song, *with music.*
Idol's Eye, The, *sel.*
My Angeline.
Song of the Turnkey, The.
Tattooed Man, The.

Smith, Hilda Worthington
Carpenter of Galilee, The.

Smith, Horace [*or* Horatio]
Address to a Mummy.
Evening; an Elegy.
Gouty Merchant and the Stranger, The.
On a Stupendous Leg of Granite, Discovered Standing by Itself in the Deserts of Egypt, with the Inscription Inserted Below.
Tale of Drury Lane, A.

Smith, Horace *and* James Smith
Baby's Debut, The.
Loyal Effusion.
Macbeth.
Theatre, The.

Smith, Iain Crichton
At the Firth of Lorne.
Culloden and After.
Deer at the Roadside.
Deer on the High Hills—a Meditation, *sel.*
End of the Season on a Stormy Day—Oban.
For Angus MacLeod.
For My Mother.
John Knox.
Luss Village.
Old Woman.
Schoolgirl on Speech-Day in the Open Air.
Two Girls Singing.
Window, The.
Young Highland Girl Studying Poetry, A.

Smith, J. Danson
We'll Meet Again.

Smith, J. Moyr
Four and Twenty Merulae.
She Lost Her Sheep.

Smith, James
On the American Rivers.

Smith, James *and* Sir George Rose
Conversation in Craven Street, Strand.

Smith, Janet M.
Corries.

Smith, Jared
Something.

Smith, Joan
Alley-Walker.

Smith, John (1580-1631)
In the Due Honor of the Author Master Robert Norton.
John Smith of His Friend Master John Taylor.
Sea Marke, The.

Smith, John (1662-1717)
Solitary Canto to Chloris the Disdainful, A.
Strephon.

Smith, Kay
Eye of Humility, The.
Footnote to the Lord's Prayer, *sel.*
What Then, Dancer?
When a Girl Looks Down.

Smith, Ken
Possessions.
Train.

Smith, Langdon
Evolution.

Smith, Lanta Wilson
This, Too, Shall Pass Away.

Smith, Laurence
Christmas Tree.

Smith, LeRoy, Jr.
Salvation Prospect.
Sappho Rehung.
Spring Song.
What Sanguine Beast?

Smith, Lewis Worthington
News from Yorktown.

Smith, Lucy
Face of Poverty.

Smith, Margoret
Cataract.

Smith, Marion Couthouy
King of the Belgians.
Star, The.
Smith, Mary Brainerd
Poor for Our Sakes.
Smith, Mary Carter
Clubwoman.
Jungle.
Smith, May Riley
Departure.
God's Plans.
If We Knew.
My Life Is a Bowl.
My Uninvited Guest.
Scatter Seeds of Kindness.
Sometime.
Tired Mothers.
Tree-Top Road, The.
Smith, Mbembe Milton
Did They Help Me at the State Hospital for the Criminally Insane?
Smith, Michael
At the Appointed Hour They Came.
Blond Hair at the Edge of the Pavement.
Desolate Rhythm of Dying Recurs, The.
Here Is the Abattoir Where.
Smith, Ninna May
If Some Grim Tragedy.
Smith, Norma E.
Evangeline.
Smith, Oswald J.
Another Year.
God Is with Me.
God's Presence Makes My Heaven.
Heart That Weeps, A.
I Turn to Jesus.
Master's Call, The.
Smith, Phoebe
Via Dolorosa.
Smith, R. T.
Aunt Melissa.
Beneath the Mound.
Checking the Firing.
Long Joke, The.
Poem for David Janssen.
Red Anger.
Roosevelt Considers Catfish Stew.
Rural Route.
Saving the Fish.
Suppose a Man.
What Black Elk Said.
Widow to Her Son.
Yonosa House.
Smith, Ray
Apple, The.
Smith, Robert (d. 1555)
Exhortation of a Father to His Children, The.
Smith, Robert B.
Cafes.
Jailhouse Lawyers.
My Uncle Joe.
Razor.
Seabirds.
Smith, Robert Paul
Fielding Error.
Small Quiet Song.
Tie Your Tongue, Sir?
Smith, Roger
Lochan.
Smith, Samuel Francis
America.
As Flows the Rapid River, *with music.*
Daybreak.
Down to the Sacred Wave, *with music.*
Morning Light Is Breaking, The.
Softly Fades the Twilight Ray, *with music.*
Tree-planting.
Smith, Samuel J.
Arise, My Soul! With Rapture Rise! *with music.*
Smith, Seba
Mother in the Snow-Storm, The.
Smith, Sidney Goodsir. *See* **Smith, Sydney Goodsir**
Smith, Stephen E.
Death of Carmen Miranda, The.
Getting By on Honesty.
Smith, Stevie
Admire Cranmer!
Advice to Young Children.
After-Thought, The.
Airy Christ, The.
Anger's Freeing Power.
Autumn.
Away, Melancholy.
Be Off!
Bye Baby Brother.
Celtic Fringe, The.
Celts, The.
Childe Rolandine.
Cold as no love, and wild with all negation.
Correspondence between Mr. Harrison in Newcastle and Mr. Sholto Peach Harrison in Hull.
Dear Female Heart.
Death Sentence, The.
Dedicated Dancing Bull and the Water Maid, The, *sel.*
Distractions and the Human Crowd.
Edmonton, thy cemetery.
Egocentric.
Everything Is Swimming.
Exeat.
Frog Prince, The.
Galloping Cat, The.
Heavenly City, The.
Here Lies. . .
I Love.
I Remember.
I Rode with My Darling.
Little Boy Lost, The.
Lord Barrenstock.
Louise.
Magna Est Veritas.
Major Macroo.
Man Is a Spirit.
Miss Snooks, Poetess.
Monsieur Pussy-Cat, Blackmailer.
Mother, among the Dustbins.
Mr. Over.
Murderer, The.
My Cats.
My Hat.
No Categories!
Not Waving but Drowning.
Occasional Yarrow, The.
One of Many.
Our Bog is Dood.
Pad, Pad.
Papa Love Baby.
Parklands, The.
Pretty.
Private Means Is Dead.
Reversionary.
River God, The.
Satin-clad.
Scorpion.
Seymour and Chantelle; or, Un Peu de Vice.
Singing Cat, The.
Small Lady, The.
Some Are Born.
Sunt Leones.
Tenuous and Precarious.
This Englishwoman is so refined.
Thoughts about the Person from Porlock.
Thoughts on the Christian Doctrine of Eternal Hell.
To Carry the Child.
To School!
To the Tune of the Coventry Carol.
Valuable.
Was He Married?
Was It Not Curious?
Weak Monk, The.
Who Is This Who Howls and Mutters?
Who Killed Lawless Lean?
Smith, Sydney Goodsir
Bishop Blomfield's First Charge to His Clergy, *at.*
Can I Forget? ("Can I forget the sickle mune.")
Cokkils.
Deevil's Waltz, The.
Elegy XIII: "I got her in the Black Bull."
Epistle to John Guthrie.
Gangrel Rymour and the Pairdon of Sanct Anne, The, *sel.*
Hamewith.
Ineffable Dou, The.
Largo.
Leander Stormbound.
Loch Leven.
Mandrake Hert, The.
Mither's Lament, The.
Recipe for Salad.
Salad, A.
Sang: Recoll o Skaith.
Under the Eildon Tree.
Whan the Hert Is Laich.
Ye Mongers Aye Need Masks for Cheatrie.
Ye Spier Me.
Smith, Virginia E.
Daysleep.
Smith, Vivian
At an Exhibition of Historical Paintings, Hobart.
Bedlam Hills.
Fishermen, Drowned beyond the West Coast.
Last Summer, The.
Reflections.
Still Life.
Summer Band Concert.
Smith, W. Atmar, II
Piano Tuner, The.
Smith, Walter Chalmers
Coruisk.
Glenaradale.
Smith, Welton
Beast Section, The.
Folding and Unfolding, A.
Interlude.
Malcolm.
Nigga Section, The.
Strategies.
Smith, William
Chloris, *sels.*
My Love, I Cannot Thy Rare Beauties Place.
Sonnet: "My Love, I cannot thy rare beauties place."
To the Most Excellent and Learned Shepheard Collin Cloute.
Smith, William Jay
Abruptly All the Palm Trees.
American Primitive.
Antelope.
At the Tombs of the House of Savoy.
Autumn.
Beulah Louise.
Butterfly.
Closing of the Rodeo, The.
Convoy.
Crockett.
Crocodile.
Cupidon.
Dachshunds ("The dachshund leads a quiet life").
Dead Snake.
Death of a Jazz Musician.
Dog.
Dream.
Edmund Clerihew Bentley.
Elegy: "I stood between two mirrors when you died."
Epitaph of a Stripper.
Floor and the Ceiling, The.
Galileo Galilei.
Green Place, A.

Gull.
Hotel Continental.
Independence Day.
Jittery Jim.
Laughing Time.
Lion.
Love.
Lovebirds.
Lovers, The.
Massacre of the Innocents, The.
Miss Hartley.
Mr. Smith/ (With Nods to Mr. Lear and Mr. Eliot.)
Monkey.
Moon.
Morels.
Morning at Arnheim.
Neo-classical Poem.
Nightwood.
Oil Lamp, The.
Old Man by Salt Lake, An.
Old Man of Toulon, An.
Opossum.
Over and Under.
Owl, The.
Panda, The.
Park in Milan, The.
Pavane for the Nursery, A.
Persian Miniature.
Plain Talk.
Processional.
Quail in Autumn.
Queen of the Nile, The.
Random Generation of English Sentences; or, The Revenge of the Poets.
Rear Vision.
Rondeau: "Lord, I'm done for: now Margot."
Room in the Villa, A.
Seal.
Song for a Country Wedding.
Tall Poets, The.
Tempest, The.
There Was an Old Lady Named Crockett.
Things.
3 for 25.
Toaster, The.
Today I Have Touched the Earth.
Uncertain What to Wear.
Unicorn.
Vincent Van Gogh.
Voyages of Captain Cock, The.
William Penn/ Was the most level-headed of men.
Winter Morning.
Wooing Lady, The.
Yak.
Young Man Who Loved Rain, A.
Zebra.

Smither, Elizabeth
Beak, The.
Change of School.
Fr Anselm Williams and Br Leander Neville.
Feast of All Saints, The.
Song about My Father.
Sugar Daddy.

Smithyman, Kendrick
Friday Night.
Last Moriori, The.
Ordinary Day beyond Kaitaia, An.
Resort.

Smollett, Tobias George
Independence.
Ode to Leven-Water.
Tears of Scotland, The; Written in the Year 1746.
To Leven Water.

Smyth, Florida Watts
Eternal Contour.
Green Mountain Boy.
Unclaimed.

Smyth, John. *See* **Smith, John (1662–1717)**

Smythe, Albert Ernest Stafford
Anastasis.

Smythe, Daniel
Driftwood.
From My Thought.

Snaith, Stanley
Blue Ghosts.
Stack, The.

Snapp, Thomas
Actor, The.

Snodgrass, William DeWitt
After Experience Taught Me.
April Inventory.
Campus on the Hill, The.
Cardinal, A.
Dr. Joseph Goebbels.
Examination, The.
Flat One, A.
Friend, A.
Führer Bunker, The, *sel.*
Heart's Needle.
Here in the Scuffled Dust.
Lady, A.
Leaving the Motel.
Lobsters in the Window.
Lovers Go Fly a Kite, The.
Lying Awake.
Magic Flute, The.
Marsh, The.
Mementos, I ("Sorting out letters and piles of my old").
Mementos, II ("I found them there today").
Men's Room in the College Chapel, The.
Monet: "Les Nymphéas."
No Use.
Old Apple Trees.
Operation, The.
Owls.
Partial Eclipse.
Planting a Magnolia.
Powwow.
Returned to Frisco, 1946.
Setting Out.
Song: "Sweet beast, I have gone prowling."
Teen-Ager, A.
Ten Days Leave.
These Trees Stand.
Vuillard: "The Mother and Sister of the Artist."
What We Said.

Snow, Eliza R.
Think Not When You Gather to Zion, *with music.*

Snow, Karen
Dream Girl.
Gifts.

Snow, Laura A. Barter
God Is in Every Tomorrow.

Snow, Sophia P.
Annie and Willie's Prayer.

Snyder, Gary
Above Pate Valley.
After weeks of watching the roof leak.
After Work.
Again the ancient, meaningless.
All the Spirit Powers Went to Their Dancing Place.
All through the Rains.
August on Sourdough, a Visit from Dick Brewer.
August Was Foggy.
Autumn Morning in Shokoku-ji, An.
Bath, The.
Before the Stuff Comes Down.
Burning, *abr.*
Burning the Small Dead.
By Frazier Creek Falls.
Dead by the Side of the Road, The.
December.
Eight Sandbars on the Takano River.
Elwha River, The.
First Shaman Song.
For a Far-out Friend.
For John Chappell.
For Nothing.
For the Children.
For the West.
Four Poems for Robin.
Foxtail Pine.
Hay for the Horses.
Heifer Clambers Up, A.
Hitch Haiku.
Hop, Skip, and Jump.
How rare to be born a human being!
Hunting.
I Went into the Maverick Bar.
It.
It Pleases.
John Muir on Mt. Ritter.
Journeys.
Kyoto: March.
LMFBR.
Late Snow and Lumber Strike of the Summer of Fifty-four, The.
Logging, *sels.*
Long Hair.
Looking at Pictures to Be Put Away.
Manichaeans, The.
Marin-An.
Market, The.
Meeting the Mountains.
Mid-August at Sourdough Mountain Lookout.
Milton by Firelight.
Mother Earth; Her Whales.
Mountains and Rivers, *sels.*
Myths and Texts, *sels.*
Nansen.
Nature Green Shit.
Nooksack Valley.
Oil.
Once Only.
Out West.
Pine Tree Tops.
Piute Creek.
Praise for Sick Women.
Prayer for the Great Family.
Riprap.
Sappa Creek, The.
Second Shaman Song.
Some Good Things to Be Said for the Iron Age.
Song of the Taste.
Spring Night in Shokoku-ji, A.
Things to Do around a Lookout.
Things to Do around a Ship at Sea.
Things to Do around Kyoto.
This Poem Is for Bear.
This Poem Is for Deer.
This Tokyo.
Through the Smoke Hole.
To Hell with Your Fertility Cult.
Toward Climax.
Truth like the Belly of a Woman Turning, The.
Uses of Light, The.
Vapor Trails.
Walk, A.
Water.
What Do They Say.
What Happened Here Before.
What You Should Know to Be a Poet.
Why Log Truck Drivers Rise Earlier than Students of Zen.
Wild Mushroom, The.
Work to Do toward Town.

Snyder, Richard
Aging Poet, on a Reading Trip to Dayton, Visits the Air Force Museum and Discovers There a Plane He Once Flew, The.
Blue Sparks in Dark Closets.
Chicago, Summer Past.
Christmas at a Decade's End.
Homage to Marian Pyszko.
O Whose Are These Children.
Of Pardons, Presidents, and Whiskey Labels.
Small Elegy, A.

Sparrow in an Airport.
Wintered Sunflowers.
Snyder, Thurmond
Beale Street, Memphis.
Beast with Chrome Teeth, The.
Seeds.
Snyder, Zilpha Keatley
To Dark Eyes Dreaming.
Sobel, Lester A.
Transplantitis.
Sobiloff, Hy
Airship.
Child's Sight, The.
Family Screams.
Hans Christian Andersen in Central Park.
Little Girl Cat.
My Mother's Table.
Painting of a Lobster by Picasso.
Pittsburgh.
Wisdom.
Sobin, A. G.
Greeting Descendants.
Södergran, Edith
Decision, A.
Hope.
I saw a tree that was greater than all the others.
Pain.
Violet Twilights.
We Women.
Sola Pinto, Vivian de
At Piccadilly Circus.
Sologub, Fyodor
Amphora, The.
Austere the Music of My Songs.
Solomon, Marvin
Cages.
Cat and the Bird, The.
Garden, The.
Giraffe, The.
Lemon Sherbet.
Vole, The.
Solomon Ephraim ben Aaron of Lenczicz
These Things I Do Remember.
Solomos, George P.
Wisdom of the Gazelle.
Solon
Boys and Sport.
Solovyov-Sedoi, V. *and* **M. Matusovskii**
Moscow Nights.
Solt, Mary Ellen
Forsythia.
Marriage.
Moonshot Sonnet.
Rain Down.
Wild Crab.
Solway, Arthur
Answers to the Snails.
Solway, David
Powers of the Pawn, The.
Somervile [*or* Somerville], William
Address to His Elbow-Chair, New Cloath'd, An.
Advice to the Ladies.
Bowling-Green, The, *sel.*
Chace, The.
Chase, The, *sel.*
Field Sports, *sel.*
Hare-hunting.
Hudibras and Milton Reconciled.
On Presenting to a Lady a White Rose and a Red on the Tenth of June.
Wounded Man and the Swarm of Flies, The.
Somerville, Jane
Denials 1.
Sondheim, Stephen
Gee, Officer Krupke.
Soné
Blessed.
Song, Cathy
Beauty and Sadness.
Blue Lantern.
Day You Are Born, The.
Girl Powdering Her Neck.
Losing Track.
Lucky.
Who Makes the Journey.
Youngest Daughter, The.
Soniat, Katherine
Initial Response.
Resounding.
Sonnenschein, Hugo
In the Ghetto.
In the Open Fields.
Soodley, F. W.
I love this boy, not for his beauty only.
Sophocles
Ajax, *sel.*
Antigone.
Chorus: "Fair Salamis, the billow's roar."
Chorus: "Oh, may my constant feet not fail."
Chorus: "What man is he that yearneth."
Colonus' Praise.
Oedipus at Colonus, *sels.*
Oedipus Rex [*or* Oedipus Tyrannus].
Thebes of the Seven Gates.
Women of Trachis, *sels.*
Sora
Up the Barley Rows.
Sorell, Walter
All That Matters.
Sorley, Charles Hamilton
All the Hills and Vales Along.
Expectans Expectavi.
In Memoriam S. C. W., V. C.
Marlborough, *sel.*
Peer Gynt.
Rooks.
Seekers, The.
Song of the Ungirt Runners, The.
Sonnet: "Saints have adored the lofty soul of you."
Sonnet: "Such, such is Death: no triumph: no defeat."
To Germany.
Two Sonnets.
When You See Millions of the Mouthless Dead.
Soroka, Pauline E.
Understanding.
Sorrells, Helen
Amputation, The.
From a Correct Address in a Suburb of a Major City.
Mountain Corral.
To a Child Born in Time of Small War.
Town I Left.
Sorrentino, Gilbert
Anatomy.
Classic Case, A.
Handbook of Versification.
Zoo, The.
Soseki
Over the wintry.
Sossaman, Stephen
Viet Cong Sapper Dies, A.
Sostrom, Anne
Status Symbols.
Sotades
Banquet, A.
Sotheby, William
Netley Abbey; Midnight.
Soto, Gary
After Tonight.
Angel.
At the Cantina.
Black Hair.
Brown like Us.
Cruel Boys.
Elements of San Joaquin, The.
Evening of Ants, The.
Firstborn, The.
Getting Serious.
Heaven.
History.
In the Madness of Love.
Kearney Park.
Lantern.
Map, The.
Mission Tire Factory, 1969.
Morning They Shot Tony Lopez, Barber and Pusher Who Went Too Far, 1958, The.
Point, The.
Remedies.
Street, The.
Summer.
Widow Perez, The.
Soule, Jean Conder
Surprises: ("Surprises are round").
Sousa, John Philip
Feast of the Monkeys, The.
Have You Seen the Lady?
Sousa, Noémia da
Appeal.
Poem of Distant Childhood.
Souster, Raymond
All Animals Like Me.
Bed without a Woman, A.
Bernard.
Bottle of Chianti, The.
Choosing Coffins.
Collector, The.
Day before Christmas, The.
Dog in the Fountain.
Dog, Midwinter.
Falling of the Snow, The.
Flight of the Roller Coaster.
Hunter, The.
Ladybug.
Lagoons, Hanlan's Point.
Lift, The.
Man Who Finds That His Son Has Become a Thief, The.
May 15th.
Need of an Angel.
Not Wholly Lost.
Old Dog.
On the Rouge.
Reality.
Search.
Six-Quart Basket, The.
Speakers, Columbus Circle.
Summer Afternoon.
Sunday Night Walk.
This Poem Will Never Be Finished.
Ties.
When I See Old Men.
Where the Blue Horses.
Worm, The.
Young Girls.
Soutar, William
Among High Hills.
Auld House, The.
Auld Sang.
Ballad: "O! shairly ye hae seen my love."
Children, The.
Gowk, The.
Hint o' Snow, A.
Makar, The.
On the Hill.
Owre the Hill.
Permanence of the Young Men, The.
Riddle, A: "Yon laddie wi' the gowdan pow."
Room, The.
Scotland.
Song: "Whaur yon broken brig hings owre."
Star, The.
Supper.
Thocht, The.
Tryst, The.
Wait for the Hour.
Whigmaleerie, A.
Souter, Charles Henry
After Johnson's Dance.
Irish Lords.
Old John Bax.
What the Red-haired Bo'sun Said.
Southey, Caroline Anne Bowles. *See* **Bowles, Caroline Anne**

Southey, Robert
Absolvers, The.
After Blenheim.
Battle of Blenheim, The.
Bishop Hatto [and the Rats].
Bower of Peace, The.
Calm Sea, A.
Cataract of Lodore, The.
Curse of Kehama, The, *sels.*
Dancing Bear, The.
Ebb Tide, The.
Epitaph: "Time and the World, whose magnitude and weight."
Filbert, The.
God's Judgment [*or* Judgement] on a Wicked Bishop.
His Books.
Holly Tree, The.
Homeward Bound.
Imitated from the Persian.
Inchcape Rock, The.
Inscription for a Tablet on the Banks of a Stream.
Inscriptions for the Caledonian Canal.
Kehama's Curse.
Lord! Who Art Merciful as Well as Just.
Love Indestructible.
March to Moscow, The.
My Days among the Dead Are Passed [*or* Past].
Night.
O God! Have Mercy, in This Dreadful Hour.
Ode to a Pig while His Nose Was Being Bored.
Ode Written during the War with America, 1814, *sel.*
Old Man's Comforts [and How He Gained Them], The.
Old Woman of Berkeley, The.
On a Picture by J. M. Wright, Esq.
On the Death of a Favourite Old Spaniel.
Scholar, The.
She Comes Majestic with Her Swelling Sails.
Soldier's Wife, The.
Southey Looks out of the Window at Greta Hill.
Stream descends on Meru mountain, A.
Thalaba the Destroyer, *sels.*
To a Goose.
To a Spider.
Two forms inseparable in unity.
Vision of Judgement, A, *sels.*
Well of St. Keyne, The.
Widow, The.
Winter Portrait.
Witch, The.
Written on a Sunday Morning.
Southey, Robert *and* Samuel Taylor Coleridge
Devil's Thoughts, The.
Southgate, Margaret
Pale faced, tight laced.
Southwell, Robert
At Fotheringay.
At Home in Heaven.
Before My Face the Picture Hangs.
Burning Babe, The.
Child My Choice, A.
Christ's Sleeping Friends.
Content and Rich.
Decease, Release: Dum Morior Orior.
Ensamples of Our Savior.
Image of Death, The, *sel.*
Lewd Love Is Loss.
Look[e] Home.
Loss in Delay.
Love's Servile Lot.
Marie Magdalens Complaint at Christs Death.
Martyrdom of Mary, Queen of Scots, The.
Nativity of Christ, The.
New Heaven, New War[re].
New Prince, New Pomp[e].
Of the Blessed Sacrament of the Altar.
Our Lady's Salutation.
Saint Peter's Complaint, *sel.*
Seek Flowers of Heaven.
Sinnes Heavie Loade.
Stanzas from Saint Peter's Complaint.
Times Go [*or* Goe] by Turns.
Upon the Image of Death.
Virgin Mary to Christ on the Cross, The.
Wassailer's Song.
Where Wards Are Weak.
Southwick, Marcia
Burial, Green, A.
Dusk.
Marsh, The.
No Such Thing.
Owning a Dead Man.
Southwold, Stephen
Mother of Men.
Soyinka, Wole
Abiku.
Telephone Conversation.
Spacks, Barry
Emblem of Two Foxes, An.
Freshmen.
Last Fish, The.
Malediction.
Muse, The.
My Mother's Childhood.
October.
Teaching Penguins to Fly.
Washing Windows.
"Who Then Is Crazy?"
Spalding, Helen
Dream, The.
Spalding, John Lancaster
At the Ninth Hour.
Believe and Take Heart.
Et Mori Lucrum.
Forepledged.
God and the Soul, *sels.*
Nature and the Child.
Silence.
Starry Host, The.
Void Between, The.
Spalding, Susan Marr
Fate.
Sea's Spell, The.
Song's Worth, A.
Spargur, Jill
Tragedy.
Spark, Muriel
Canaan.
She Wolf, The.
Sparshott, Francis
Entanglement.
Improperia.
Naming of the Beasts, The.
Paysage Choisi.
Reply to the Committed Intellectual.
Three Seasons.
Spaziani, Maria Luisa
Journey in the Orient.
Winter Moon.
Speaking, Elijah
I expected this face but did not predict it.
Spear, Roberta
Anniversary, The.
August/ Fresno 1973.
Bat, The.
Boundaries.
Bringing Flowers.
Sale of Smoke, A.
White Dress, The.
Spears, Dorothea
Begetting.
Spears, Heather
My Love behind Walls.
Spears, Woodridge
Restoration.
Spector, Albert
Eastside Chick with Drive.
Speed, Samuel
Flower, The.
Peace.
Speer, Laurel
Mirror Images.
Speght, Rachel
Dream, A, *sels.*
Spellman, Alfred B.
For My Unborn and Wretched Children.
I Looked and Saw History Caught.
In Orangeburg My Brothers Did.
John Coltrane—an Impartial Review.
Tomorrow the Heroes.
When Black People Are.
Zapata & the Landlord.
Spence, Lewis
Prows o' Reekie, The.
Spence, Michael
DNA Lab.
Fish Will Swim as Before, The.
Orchard, The.
Spence, Skip
Motorcycle Irene.
Spencer, Anne
At the Carnival.
Before the Feast of Shushan.
Creed.
Dunbar.
For Jim, Easter Eve.
I Have a Friend.
Innocence.
Lady, Lady.
Letter to My Sister.
Life-long, Poor Browning.
Lines to a Nasturtium [a Lover Muses].
Neighbors.
Questing.
Substitution.
Translation.
Wife-Woman, The.
Spencer, Bernard
Aegean Islands 1940–41.
Behaviour of Money.
Boat Poem.
Castanets.
Cold Night, A.
Greek Excavations.
Hand, A.
Ill.
Letters.
On the "Sievering" Tram.
Part of Plenty.
Regent's Park Terrace.
Rendezvous, The.
Spring Wind, A.
Thousand Killed, A.
Yachts on the Nile.
Spencer, C. Mordaunt
Rose of Tralee, The, *at.*
Spencer, Caroline
Living Waters.
Spencer, Hiram Ladd
Hundred Years to Come, A.
Spencer, Lillian [*or* Lilian] White
Hopi Woman.
Red Ghosts Chant, The.
Spring Song of Aspens.
Spencer, Theodore
Californians, The.
Circle, A.
Contemporary Song.
Critics, The.
Eden: Or One View of It.
Entropy.
Epitaph: "She was a high-class bitch and a dandy."
Escapist's Song.
Inflatable Globe, The.
Invocation: "Empty my heart, Lord, of daily vices."
Narrative, A.
Phoenix, The.
Reason for Writing, A.
Return.
Song: "I who love you bring."

Spring Song.

Spencer, Thomas E.
How McDougal Topped the Score.

Spencer, William Robert
Beth Gêlert.

Spender, Stephen
Acts passed beyond the boundary of mere wishing.
After They Have Tired [of the Brilliance of Cities].
Auf dem Wasser zu Singen.
Awaking.
Barn, The.
Beethoven's Death Mask.
Central Heating System.
Childhood, A.
Coward, The.
Daybreak.
Discovered in Mid-Ocean.
Double Shame, The.
Drowned, The.
Elegy for Margaret, *sel.*
Elementary School Classroom [*or* Class Room] in a Slum, An.
Empty House, The.
Epilogue: "Time is a thing."
Express, The.
Farewell in a Dream.
From All These Events.
Funeral, The.
Generous Years, The.
Hoelderlin's Old Age.
How strangely this sun reminds me of my love!
"I" Can Never Be a Great Man, An.
I Think Continually of Those Who Were Truly Great.
Icarus.
Ice.
In Railway Halls.
Judas Iscariot.
Labourer in the Vineyard, The.
Landscape near an Aerodrome, The.
Marginal Field, The.
Marston.
Mask.
Missing My Daughter.
Moving through the Silent Crowd.
My Parents Kept Me from Children Who Were Rough.
New Year.
North, The.
Not Palaces [an Era's Crown].
O Night O Trembling Night.
On the Pilots Who Destroyed Germany in the Spring of 1945.
On the Third Day.
One More New Botched Beginning.
Perhaps.
Polar Exploration.
Port Bou.
Prisoners, The.
Pylons, The.
Rolled over on Europe: the sharp dew frozen to stars.
Room above the Square, The.
Seascape.
Shapes of Death, The.
Song: "Stranger, you who hide my love."
Sonnet: "You were born; must die; were loved; must love."
Statistics.
Stopwatch and an Ordnance Map, A.
Thoughts during an Air Raid.
To a Spanish Poet.
To My Daughter.
To Poets and Airmen.
To T. A. R. H.
Trance, The.
Two Armies.
Ultima Ratio Regum.
What I Expected [Was].
Whim of Time, A.
Winter and Summer.
Winter Landscape.
Without that once clear aim, the path of flight.
Word.
Your Body Is Stars.

Spenser, Edmund
Amoretti.
Aprill.
Artegall and Radigund.
Astrophel, *sel.*
At length nigh to the sea they drew.
August ("Tell me, Perigot").
August ("The sixth was August").
Autumn.
Balme.
Beauty.
Behold, O Man.
Bower of Bliss, The.
Bright Squadrons, The.
Britomart in the House of Busirane.
By Her That Is Most Assured to Her Self.
Cave of Despair, The.
Cave of Mammon, The.
Cease, Then, My Tongue!
Colin Clout's Come Home Again, *sels.*
Contempt of Poetry, The.
Cymochles and Phaedria.
Dame Nature.
Dance, The.
Dance of the Graces, The.
Daphnaida, *sel.*
Death of the Dragon, The.
Despair.
Dido My Dear, Alas, Is Dead.
Ditty, A: In Praise of Eliza, Queen of the Shepherds.
Ditty, A: "See where she sits upon the grassy green."
Dragon, The.
Easter.
Easter Morning.
Elegy, An: "She fell away in her first ages spring."
Elisa.
Envy.
Epithalamion: "Ye learned sisters which have oftentimes."
Faerie Queene, The, *sels.*
Fight of the Red Cross Knight and the Heathen Sansjoy, The.
Fresh Spring, the Herald of Love's Mighty King.
Garden of Adonis, The.
Garden of Proserpina, The.
Gather the Rose ("Eftsoones they heard a most melodious sound").
Gather the Rose ("The whiles some one did chant this lovely lay").
Guardian Angels.
Happy Isle, The.
Her Heards Be Thousand Fishes.
Hill of the Graces, The.
House of Ate, The.
House of Pride, The.
House of Richesse, The.
Huge Leviathan, The.
Hymn of Heavenly Beauty, An, *sel.*
Hymne in Honour of Beautie, An, *sel.*
I Saw a Phoenix in the Wood Alone.
Iambicum Trimetrum.
Invocation to the Faerie Queene.
January Eclogue.
Kinds of Trees to Plant.
Lament for Daphnaida.
Lay to Eliza, The.
Legend of the Knight of the Red Crosse, or of Holinesse, The.
Love.
Malbecco and Hellenore.
Mask of Cupid, The.
Mask of Mutability, The.
Masque of Cupid, The.
May.
Mermaids, The.
Mutability ("For, all that from her springs, and is ybredde").
Mutability ("When these were past, thus gan the Titanesse").
My Love Is like to Ice.
Nature's Reply to Mutability.
Next unto him was Neptune pictured.
Nought is on earth more sacred or divine.
November.
Oak and the Brere, The.
October.
October Eclogue.
Old January.
Pastoral, A: "From thence into the open fields he fled."
Perigot and Willye.
Port after Stormie Seas.
Prayer to Venus.
Prince Arthur.
Prothalamion.
Red-Cross Knight, The.
Rivers Come to the Hall of Proteus for the Marriage of the Thames and the Medway, The.
Roundelay, A: "It fell upon a holy eve."
Sea Monsters.
Seasons, The.
Shepheardes [*or* Shepeards *or* Shepherd's] Calender, The, *sels.*
Sleep after Toil.
Song of Bliss.
Sonnet: Lyke as a Ship.
Sonnet: "Men call you fair, and you do credit it."
Sonnet: "One day I wrote her name upon the strand."
Sonnet: "Weary year his race now having run, The."
Soul Is Form.
Summer.
Sweet and Sour.
Temple of Venus, The.
To Be or Not to Be.
Upon a Day.
Visions of the World's Vanity, *sel.*
What If Some Little Paine the Passage Have.
Who Is the Same, Which at My Window Peepes?
Winter.
With that I saw two swans of goodly hue.

Speyer, Leonora
A B C's in Green.
Duet.
I'll Be Your Epitaph.
Kleptomaniac, The.
Ladder, The.
Little Lover.
Mary Magdalene.
Measure Me, Sky.
Note from the Pipes, A.
Oberammergau.
Pain.
Protest in Passing.
Swans.
Tears for Sale.
X-Ray.

Spicer, Anne Higginson
Hail and Farewell.

Spicer, J. L.
Communion.

Spicer, Jack
Among the coffee cups and soup toureens walked Beauty.
Billy the Kid.
Book of Gawain, The.
Book of Merlin, The.
Book of Music, A.
Book of Percival, The.
Central Park West.

Five Words for Joe Dunn on His 22nd Birthday.
Four Poems for *The St. Louis Sporting News.*
"Graphemics," *sels.*
Holy Grail, The, *sel.*
Imaginary Elegies, I-IV.

Spilka, Arnold
Don't Tell Me That I Talk Too Much!
Flowers Are a Silly Bunch.
I Saw a Little Girl I Hate.
I'm Not Really Lazy.
Puzzle.

Spingarn, Joel Elias
Beauty.
Italian Poppies.
Spring Passion.

Spingarn, Lawrence P.
Museum Piece.
Philatelic Lessons: The German Collection.
Vignette: 1922.

Spire, André
Abishag.
Ancient Law, The.
Dust.
Hear, O Israel!
It Was Not You.
Lonely.
Now You're Content.
Nudities.
Poetics.
Pogroms.
Spring.

Spires, Elizabeth
Courtesan with Fan.
Skins.
Tequila.
Wake.
Widow's Walk.

Spitta, Karl Johann Philipp
O Blessèd House, That Cheerfully Receiveth.
Unchanging Jesus.

Spitteler, Carl
Theme.

Spivack, Kathleen
But You, My Darling, Should Have Married the Prince.
Child's Visit to the Biology Lab, A.
Dido: Swarming.
Drifting.
Dust.
Fugue.
Judgment, The.
Love u.s.a.
March 1st.
Meeting, The.
Mythmaking.
Private Pain in Time of Trouble.
Shining.
Visions.

Spofford, Harriet Prescott
Ballad: "In the summer even."
Can't.
Evanescence.
Every Day Thanksgiving Day.
Fossil Raindrops, The.
Godspeed.
Hereafter.
How We Became a Nation.
Hunt, The.
Music in the Night.
Only.
Phantoms All.
Pines, The.
Sigh, A.
Snowdrop, A, *abr.*
Voice.

Spooner, Lawrence
Looking-Glass for Smokers, A, *sel.*
On Giving Up Smoking.

Sprague, Charles
Brothers, The.
Curiosity, *sels.*
Family Meeting, The.
Fiction.
Indians.
News, The.
Winged Worshippers, The.

Spratt, Thomas
On His Mistress Drown'd.

Sprigg, Christopher St. John. *See* **"Caudwell, Christopher"**

Spriggs, Edward S.
For Brother Malcolm.

Spring-Rice, Cecil Arthur
In Memoriam, A. C. M. L., *sel.*

Sprod, G. N.
Request Number.

Sproull, Lyman H.
Emigrant's Child, The.
Stationed Scout, The.

Sprouse, Sarah Elizabeth
Little Song of Work, A.

Spurrier, Linda Westfall
Lines for the Planned Parenthood Clinic.

Squire, Sir John Collings ("Solomon Eagle")
Another Generation.
Approaching America.
Ballade of Any Father to Any Son, A.
Ballade of Diminishing Control, A.
Ballade of Soporific Absorption.
Ballade of the Poetic Life.
Birds, The.
"Break, Break, Break."
Celtic Lyric, The.
Country Wooing, *sel.*
Discovery, The.
Dog's Death, A.
Doris and Philemon, *sel.*
Elegy in the Cemetery of Spoon River instead of in That of Stoke Poges.
Epitaph, An: "Shiftless and shy, gentle and kind and frail."
Everlasting Mercy, The, *parody.*
Exquisite Sonnet, The.
Fresh Morning, A.
Hands-across-the-Sea Poem, The.
Happy Night, The.
Honesty at a Fire.
How They Do It.
If Gray Had Had to Write His Elegy in the Cemetery of Spoon River Instead of in That of Stoke Poges.
If Pope Had Written "Break, Break, Break."
It Did Not Last.
Lines: "Mine ears have heard your distant moan."
Little Commodore, The.
March, The.
My Father's Cot, *sel.*
Numerous Celts.
On Oculists.
Passing of Arthur, The.
Pipe, The.
Poor Old Man, The.
She Dwelt among the Untrodden Ways.
Ship, The.
Sonnet: "There was an Indian, who had known no change."
Stockyard, The.
Swallow, The, *sel.*
Three Hills, The.
To a Bull-Dog.
To a Roman.
To Miss L. F. on the Occasion of Her Departure for the Continent.
Under.
Vision of Truth, A.
Winter Nightfall.

Stack, Philip ("Kid Kazanova")
Admonition.

Stafford, Wendell Phillips
Invocation: "O Thou whose equal purpose runs."
Washington and Lincoln.

Stafford, William
Accountability.
Address to the Vacationers at Cape Lookout, An.
Adults Only.
After Plotinus.
Among Strangers.
Animal That Drank Up Sound, The.
Any Time.
Around You, Your House.
Ask Me.
At Cove on the Crooked River.
At the Bomb Testing Site.
At the Edge of Town.
At the Grave of My Brother.
At the Playground.
At the Un-National Monument along the Canadian Border.
Baby Ten Months Old Looks at the Public Domain, A.
Before the Big Storm.
Behind the Falls.
Berkeley, Madison, Ann Arbor, Kent.
Bess.
Bird inside a Box, A.
Birthday.
Bring the North.
Broken Home.
Ceremony.
Chickens the Weasel Killed.
Concealment, The: Ishi, the Last Wild Indian.
Day You Are Reading This, The.
Drummer Boy.
Ducks down in the Meadow.
Earth Dweller.
Epitaph Ending in And, The.
Escape, The.
Evening Walk, An.
Fall Journey.
Fall Wind.
Farm on the Great Plains, The.
Father and Son.
Father's voice.
Fifteen.
Fish Counter at Bonneville, The.
For a Daughter Gone Away.
For a Plaque on the Door of an Isolated House.
For the Grave of Daniel Boone.
Found in a Storm.
Friend Who Never Came.
Friends.
Help from History.
Holding the Sky.
Humanities Lecture.
In a Museum in the Capital.
In Dear Detail, by Ideal Light.
In Fur.
In the Deep Channel.
In the Morning All Over.
In the Oregon Country.
In Time of Need.
Lake Chelan.
Late at Night.
Letter from Oregon.
Lifting Illegal Nets by Flashlight.
Listening.
Long Distance.
Look.
Looking West.
Magic Lantern.
Maybe Alone on My Bike.
Memorandum.
Message from Space, A.
Moles.
Moment, The.
Monday.
Montana Eclogue.
Mountain That Got Little, The.
Mouse Night: One of Our Games.
Move to California, The, *sel.*
My Father; October 1942.
Near.

Notice What This Poem Is Not Doing.
Now.
Observation Car and Cigar.
Old Dog.
On Being Invited to a Testimonial Dinner.
One Home.
Oregon Message, An.
Our Kind.
Outside.
Parentage.
Passing Remark.
Peace Walk.
People of the South Wind.
People Who Went By in Winter.
Priest Lake.
Quiet Town.
Religion Back Home.
Remembering Althea.
Requiem: "Mother is gone. Bird songs wouldn't let her breathe."
Rescued Year, The.
Returned to Say.
Right Now.
Ritual to Read to Each Other, A.
Room 000.
Sayings from the Northern Ice.
School Days.
Shepherd.
So Long.
Sound from the Earth, A.
Stories from Kansas.
Story, A.
Story That Could Be True, A.
Stranger Not Ourselves, The.
Strangers.
Strokes.
Surviving a Poetry Circuit.
Swerve, The.
Testimony to an Inquisitor.
These Days.
These Leaves.
Things That Happen.
This Town: Winter Morning.
Together Again.
Tornado.
Traveling through the Dark.
Trip, The.
Trouble-shooting.
Ultimate Problems.
Vacation.
Vacation Trip.
View from Here, The.
Walking the Wilderness.
Ways of Seeing.
Well Rising, The.
West of Your City.
Whatever Comes.
When We Looked Back.
Whole Story, The.
Willy Lyons.
With Kit, Age 7, at the Beach.
With My Crowbar Key.
Written on the Stub of the First Paycheck.
Stager, Carol
In Its Place.
Stagnelius, Erik Johann
Memory.
Stalker, Philip A.
Talk.
Stallworthy, Jon
Again.
Almond Tree, The.
Beginning of the End, The.
Camel.
First Blood.
Here and There.
Letter from Berlin, A.
Letter to a Friend.
Miss Lavender.
Poem about Poems about Vietnam, A.
Question of Form and Content, A.
Sindhi Woman.
Source, The.
This Morning.
True Confession, A.
Walking against the Wind.
War Story.
Stam, Betty Scott
Open My Eyes.
Stamp, Catriona
Rebirth.
Stampa, Gaspara
At dawn of the day the Creator.
Deeply repentant of my sinful ways.
Holy angels, in envy I cast no sigh.
Hunger.
I am now so weary with waiting.
If I could believe that death.
Love made me such that I live in fire.
Often I compare my lord to heaven.
Often when alone I liken my lord/ to the cosmos.
Stars have given me a hard fate, The.
When before those eyes, my life and light.
Women, whoever wishes to know my lord.
Stanaback, Lucille
Discouraged.
Standing, Sue
Dead Neck.
Stanfield, Leontine
Little Cat Angel, The.
Stanford, Ann
Bear, The.
Beating, The.
Before.
Center of the Garden, The.
Deserted Garden. The.
Genia, The.
Gift, The.
Going Away.
Night of Souls.
Omens, The.
Rider, The.
Robert Fulton.
Umbrella, The.
Voices Inescapable, The.
Weeds.
Stanford, Derek
Carol for His Darling on Christmas Day.
Tomb of Honey Snaps Its Marble Chains, The.
Stanford, Frank
Death and the Arkansas River.
Stanford, William Bedell
Angelus-Time near Dublin.
Before Salamis.
To a Greek Ship in the Port of Dublin.
Undertone.
Stange, Ken
Poem on the End of Sensation.
Stanhope, Philip Dormer. *See* **Chesterfield, Philip Dormer Stanhope, 4th Earl of**
Stanhope, Rosamund
At Eighty.
Stanley, Robert M.
Not Blindly in the Dark.
Stanley, Thomas
All Things Drink.
Beauty.
Bracelet, The.
Celia Singing.
Chang'd, yet Constant.
Combat, The.
Deposition from Beauty, A.
Destiny.
Divorce, The.
Exequies, The.
Expectation.
Farewell, The: "Since fate commands me hence, and I."
Grasshopper, The.
La Belle Confidente.
La Belle Ennemie.
Leaves Come Again, The.
Loves Heretick.
Magnet, The.
Old I Am.
On a Violet in Her Breast.
Relapse, The.
Repulse, The.
Roses.
Self-Deceaver, The.
Snow-Ball, The.
Song: "Celinda, by what potent art."
Song: "Fool, take up thy shaft again."
Song: "I prithee [*or* prethee] let my heart alone."
Song: "When I lie burning in thine eye."
Spring.
Swallow, The.
Time Recover'd.
To Celia Pleading Want of Merit.
To One That Pleaded Her Own Want of Merit.
Tombe, The.
Wish, The.
Would I were air that thou with heat opprest.
Youthful Age.
Stansbury, Joseph
Lords of the Main, The.
New Song, A.
To Cordelia.
Stansbury, Mary Anna Phinney
How He Saved St. Michael's.
Surprise at Ticonderoga, The.
Stanton, Frank Lebby
Good Lawd Know My Name, De.
Graveyard Rabbit, The.
Just a Wearyin' for You.
Keep a-Goin'.
Little Way, A.
Mighty Lak' a Rose, *with music.*
Mocking-Bird, The.
Old Hymns, The.
One Country.
Our Flag Forever.
Plantation Ditty, A.
Sweetes' Li'l' Feller.
"Tollable Well!"
Wearyin' fer You.
Stanton, Henry T.
Moneyless Men, The.
Stanton, Maura
All-Night Waitress, The.
Biography.
Childhood.
Extracts: From the Journal of Elisa Lynch.
Judith Recalls Holofernes.
Letter to Kafka.
Little Ode for X.
Palinode.
Shoplifters.
Wilderness, The.
Stanway, Phil
Ten Sonnets for Today.
Stanyhurst, Richard
Nature in Her Working.
Prayer to the Holy Trinity, A.
Prayer to the Trinity, A.
Sometime Lively Gerald.
To the Trinity.
Staples, Barbara H.
Room for Jesus.
Stapylton, Sir Robert
Bard's Song, The.
Starbird, Kaye
Cockroaches.
Don't Ever Cross a Crocodile.
Eat-It-All Elaine.
Flying.
Horse-Chestnut Time.
Measles.
Minnie Morse.
Wendy in Winter.
Whistling Willie.
Starbuck, George
Albany schmalbany.
Aspects of Spring in Greater Boston.

Bone Thoughts on a Dry Day.
Chip.
Cold Fire.
Communication to the City Fathers of Boston.
Cora Punctuated with Strawberries.
High Renaissance.
Late Late.
Magnificat in Transit from the Toledo Airport.
Margaret Are You Drug.
Monarch of the Sea.
New Strain.
Of Late.
On First Looking in on Blodgett's Keats's "Chapman's Homer."
One Man's Goose; or, Poetry Redefined.
Out in the Cold.
Pit Viper.
Poems from a First Year in Boston.
Said ("Agatha Christie to").
Said ("J. Alfred Prufrock to").
Said ("President Johnson to").
Skin Divers, The.
Sonnet with a Different Letter at the End of Every Line.
Spell against Spelling, The.
Starry Night, The.
Technologies.
To His Chi Mistress.
Translations from the English.
Universe Is Closed and Has REMs, The.
Whaddaya Do for Action in This Place?

Starbuck, Victor
Moon-Madness.
Night for Adventures.
Seekers, The.

Stark, Bradford
Always Modern Times.

Stark, Lucien
Away.

Stark, Mary
Reign of Peace, The.

Starkey, James. *See* **"O'Sullivan, Seumas"**

Starkweather, Pauline
Two Mountains Men Have Climbed.

Starr, Hattie
Little Alabama Coon.

Statius, Publius Papinius
Sleep.
Sylvae, *sel.*

Staudt, David
Circa 1814.

Stauffer, Donald A.
Bulldozer, The.
Lemmings, The.
Time Zones for Forty-four.

Staughton, William
Tell Us, Ye Servants of the Lord, *with music.*

Stead, Christian Karlson
All Night It Bullied You.
Small Registry of Births and Deaths, A, *sel.*
Spring 1974.
This May Be Your Captain Speaking.
Twenty-one Sonnets, *sels.*
Walking Westward, *sel.*
Young Wife, The.

Stead, William Force
How Infinite Are Thy Ways.
I Closed My Eyes To-Day and Saw.
Sweet Wild April.
Uriel, *sels.*

Stearns, L. D.
Triumph.

Stebbins, Mary Elizabeth DeWitt
Harold the Valiant.
Sunflower to the Sun, The.

Stedman, Edmund Clarence
Aaron Burr's Wooing.
Abraham Lincoln.
Ballad of Lager Bier, The.
Corda Concordia, *sel.*
Cuba.
Custer.
Discoverer, The.
Doorstep, The.
Falstaff's Song.
Flight of the Birds, The.
Gettysburg.
Going a-Nutting.
Hand of Lincoln, The.
Helen Keller.
How Old Brown Took Harper's Ferry.
Hymn of the West.
Hymn to the West.
Invocation: "Thou,whose endearing hand once laid in sooth."
Israel Freyer's Bid for Gold.
Kearny at Seven Pines.
Liberty Enlightening the World.
Morgan.
Mors Benefica.
Mother's Picture, A.
On a Great Man Whose Mind Is Clouding.
Ordeal by Fire, The, *sel.*
Pan in Wall Street.
Peter Stuyvesant's New Year's Call.
Prelude: "I saw the constellated matin choir."
Provençal Lovers.
Quest.
Salem.
Si Jeunesse Savait!
Song from a Drama.
Sumter.
Toujours Amour.
Treason's Last Device.
Voice of the Western Wind.
Wanted—a Man.
World Well Lost, The.

Stedman, Jane W.
Geologist's Epitaph, A.

Steece, Arvel
There Is Yet Time.
World Planners.

Steegmuller, Francis
Le Hibou et la Poussiquette.

Steel, Laura A.
Exclusive Old Oyster, The.

Steele, Anne
O How Sweet Are Thy Words!

Steele, Frank
Country Greeting.
Departure, The.
Greener Grass.
Markings.
Rhymes.
Shaggy Dog Story.

Steele, Peggy
I Know a Man.

Steele, Sir Richard
Song: "Me Cupid made a happy slave."
Song: "Why, lovely charmer, tell me why."

Steele, Silas S.
Kiss Me Quick and Go, *with music.*
Walk, Jaw-Bone, *with music.*

Steele, Timothy
Epitaph: "Here lies Sir Tact, a diplomatic fellow."
Here Lies Sir Tact.
Murder Mystery.
Wait.

Steendam, Jacob
Complaint of New Amsterdam, The.
Oh, Sing to God, *with music.*
Praise of New Netherland, The.
When I Admire the Greatness, *with music.*

Steere, Richard
Earth Felicities, Heavens Allowances.
Monumental Memorial of Marine Mercy, A.
On a Sea-Storm nigh the Coast.
Poem upon the Caelestial Embassy, A.

Steese, Edward
Tenth Reunion.

Steiger, Anatoly
Ancient Custom, An.
Words from the Window of a Railway Car.

Steigman, Benjamin Morris
Opera in English?

Stein, Dona
Wing Factory, The.

Stein, Evaleen
Budding-Time Too Brief.
Flood-Time on the Marshes.
In Mexico.
In Youth.
November Morning.
Wild Beasts.

Stein, Gary
Jogging.

Stein, Gertrude
Before the Flowers of Friendship Faded Faded, *sel.*
Blue Coat, A.
Cézanne.
Four Saints in Three Acts, *sel.*
I Am Rose.
Ladies' Voices.
More.
Mother of Us All, The, *sel.*
Nothing Elegant.
Piano, A.
Sacred Emily.
Stanzas in Meditation, *sels.*
Susie Asado.
Tender Buttons, *sels.*
Water Raining.
Yet Dish.

Stein, Kurt M.
An Unserer Beach.
Mama's Advice.
Morning Song.
Reflection.
Vor a Gauguin Picture zu Singen.

Steinbarg, Eliezer
Bayonet and the Needle, The.
Horse and the Whip, The.
"Shatnes" or Uncleanliness.
Terrible Thought, A.
Umbrella, the Cane, and the Broom, The.
Where Is Justice?

Steinberg, David
Mason Jar.

Steinberg, Jakov [*or* Jacob]
Donkey Will Carry You, A.
Heart, The.
With a Book at Twilight.
World Is Not a Fenced-off Garden, The.

Steingart, Moishe
Generations.
Last Fire, The.

Steingass, David
For a Friend.

Steinman, David Barnard
Blueprint.

"Stella." *See* **Johnson, Esther**

Stellwagon, Russell
In Memory of Two Sons.

Stembridge, Jane
City.
Loving.
Mrs. Hamer.

Stencl, A. N.
Ezekiel.

Stennett, Samuel
Promised Land, The.

Stepanchev, Stephen
Autumn Song.
Inner Brother.
No Furlough.
Strength to War.

Stephanou, Lydia
"Case of Assault," A.

Stephen, Alexander Maitland
Bring Torches.
Capilano ("Capilano, in the canyon").

Stephen, James Kenneth
After the Golden Wedding, *sel.*

Ballade of the Incompetent Ballade-Monger, The.
Cynicus to W. Shakspere.
Drinking Song.
Election Address, An.
England and America.
Grievance, A.
Heaven and Hell.
Imitation of Robert Browning.
Imitation of Walt Whitman.
Last Ride Together, The (from Her Point of View).
My Education.
Of W. W. (Americanus).
Old School List, The.
On a Parisian Boulevard.
On a Rhine Steamer.
Senex to Matt. Prior.
Sincere Flattery of R. B.
Sincere Flattery of W. W. (Americanus).
Sonnet, A: "Two voices are there: one is of the deep."
Sonnet on Wordsworth, A.
Splinter, The.
Thought, A.
To R. K.
Triolets Ollendorfiens.
Two Epigrams.
Wordsworth.

Stephens, Alan
Prologue: Moments in a Glade

Stephens, Brunton
Dominion of Australia, The.
My Other Chinee Cook.

Stephens, Harry
Night-herding Song.

Stephens, James
April Showers.
Blue Blood.
Breakfast Time.
Cage, The.
Canal Bank, The.
Centaurs, The.
Check.
Chill of the Eve.
Christmas in Freelands.
College of Surgeons, The.
Crackling Twig, The.
Crest Jewel, The.
Daisies, The.
Danny Murphy.
Dark Wings.
Deirdre.
Devil's Bag, The.
Evening.
Evening Falls, An.
Fossils.
Glass of Beer, A.
Goat Paths, The.
Good and Bad.
Hate.
Hawks.
In the Night.
In the Orchard.
In the Poppy Field.
In Waste Places.
Lake, The.
Little Things.
Main-Deep, The.
Midnight.
Odell.
On a Lonely Spray.
Outcast, The.
Paedar Og Goes Courting.
Paps of Dana, The.
Psychometrist.
Red-haired Man's Wife, The.
Righteous Anger.
Rivals, The.
Road, The.
Sarasvati.
Satyr, The.
Secret, The.
Seumas Beg.
Shell, The.
Snare, The.
Sweet Apple.
Tanist.
To the Four Courts, Please.
Turn of the Road, The.
Voice of God, The.
Washed in Silver.
Waste Places, The.
Watcher, The.
Westland Row.
What the Devil Said.
What Thomas [*or* Tomas] an Buile Said in a Pub.
Whisperer, The.
White Fields.
White Window, The.
Why Tomas Cam Was Grumpy.
Wind, The.
Woman Is a Branchy Tree, A.
Wood of Flowers, The.

Stepney, George
On the University of Cambridge's Burning the Duke of Monmouth's Picture.

Sterling, Andrew B.
Coax Me, *with music.*
Meet Me in St. Louis, Louis.
On a Sunday Afternoon, *with music.*
Under the Anheuser Bush.
Wait 'till the Sun Shines, Nellie.
What You Goin' to Do When the Rent Comes 'Round?

Sterling, George
Abalone Song, The.
Black Vulture, The.
City by the Sea, The.
Cool, Grey City of Love, The.
Dust Dethroned, The.
Father Coyote.
Gardens of the Sea, The.
Guerdon of the Sun, The.
In Extremis.
Last Days, The.
Master Mariner, The.
Music at Twilight.
Night of Gods, The.
Oblivion.
Omnia Exeunt in Mysterium.
Pumas.
Sails.
Saul.
Sonnets on the Sea's Voice.
Three Sonnets on Oblivion.

Sterling, John
Alfred the Harper.
Louis XV.

Stern, Bert
Looking for a Home.

Stern, David E.
Old Man.

Stern, Gerald
At Bickford's.
Baja.
Dancing, The.
Days of 1978.
Hanging Scroll.
I Remember Galileo.
Immensity.
Modern Love.
One Foot in the River.
Power of Maples, The.
Sensitive Knife, The.
Straus Park.
Your Animal.

Stern, Noah
Grave at Cassino.
His Mother's Love.

Sternberg, Jacob
Little Birds.

"Sterne, Stuart" (Gertrude Bloede)
My Father's Child.
Night after Night.
Soul, Wherefore Fret Thee?

Sternhold, Thomas
I Lift My Heart to Thee, *with music.*
Majesty of God, The.
My Shepherd Is the Living Lord, *with music.*

Sterry, Joseph Ashby. *See* **Ashby-Sterry, Joseph**

Stetler, Charles
Arf, Said Sandy.
Free Enterprise.
Graduate, The.
Jeep.
Policy of the House.
To Ellen.
Toast, A.
World's Fare.

Stetson, Charlotte Perkins. *See* **Gilman, Charlotte Perkins Stetson**

Stevens, Alex
In Scorching Time.

Stevens, George Alexander
Bartleme Fair.
Pastoral, A: "By the side of a [*or* the] green stagnate pool."
Repentance.
Simple Pastoral, A.

Stevens, George W.
Organist, The.

Stevens, Maxine
How Can You?

Stevens, Wallace
Academic Discourse at Havana.
Anatomy of Monotony.
Anecdote of the Jar.
Anecdote of the Prince of Peacocks.
Angel Surrounded by Paysans.
Anglais Mort a Florence.
Annual Gaiety.
Another Weeping Woman.
Arrival at the Waldorf.
As You Leave the Room.
Asides on the Oboe.
Auroras of Autumn, The, *sels.*
Autumn Refrain.
Bantams in Pine-Woods.
Beginning, The.
Bethou Me, Said Sparrow.
Bouquet of Belle Scavoir.
Bowl.
Brave Man, The.
Candle, a Saint, The.
Comedian as the Letter C, The.
Connoisseur of Chaos.
Continual Conversation with a Silent Man.
Contrary Theses (I).
Conversation with Three Women of New England.
Cortège for Rosenbloom.
Course of a Particular, The.
Credences of Summer.
Crude Foyer.
Cuisine Bourgeoise.
Curtains in the House of the Metaphysician, The.
Dance of the Macabre Mice.
Death of a Soldier, The.
Depression before Spring.
Disillusionment of Ten o'Clock.
Domination of Black.
Dry Loaf.
Earthy Anecdote.
Emperor of Ice-cream, The.
Esthétique du Mal
Evening without Angels.
Extract from Addresses to the Academy of Fine Ideas, An.
Final Soliloquy of the Interior Paramour.
Flyer's Fall.
Gallant Château.
Girl in a Nightgown.

Glass of Water, The.
Great Statue of the General Du Puy, The.
Green is the night, green kindled and apparelled. The Candle, a Saint.
Gubbinal.
Hibiscus on the Sleeping Shores.
High poetry and low.
High-toned Old Christian Woman, A.
Holiday in Reality.
Homunculus et la Belle Étoile.
House Was Quiet and the World Was Calm, The.
How Red the Rose That Is the Soldier's Wound.
I feel an apparition.
Idea of Order at Key West, The.
Idiom of the Hero.
In the Carolinas.
Indigo Glass in the Grass, The.
Irish Cliffs of Moher, The.
Large Red Man Reading.
Le Monocle de Mon Oncle.
Less and Less Human, O Savage Spirit.
Life is a bitter aspic. We are not.
Lions in Sweden.
Lunar Paraphrase.
Man Carrying Thing.
Man on the Dump, The.
Man with the Blue Guitar, The.
Martial Cadenza.
Men Made Out of Words.
Metamorphosis.
Metaphor as Degeneration.
Metaphors of a Magnifico.
Motive for Metaphor, The.
Mrs. Alfred Uruguay.
New England Verses, *sel.*
No Possum, No Sop, No Taters.
Not Ideas about the Thing but the Thing Itself.
Notes toward a Supreme Fiction, *sels.*
Nuances of a Theme by Williams.
Of Heaven Considered as a Tomb.
Of Modern Poetry.
Of the Manner of Addressing Clouds.
Of the Surface of Things.
On an Old Horn.
On the Manner of Addressing Clouds.
On the Road Home.
Ordinary Women, The.
Our Stars Come from Ireland.
Owl in the Sarcophagus, The.
Parochial Theme.
Peter Quince at the Clavier.
Place of the Solitaires, The.
Plain Sense of Things, The.
Planet on the Table, The.
Pleasures of Merely Circulating, The.
Plot against the Giant, The.
Ploughing on Sunday.
Poem That Took the Place of a Mountain, The.
Poems of Our Climate, The.
Poetry Is a Destructive Force.
Postcard from the Volcano, A.
Prejudice against the Past.
Presence of an External Master of Knowledge.
President Ordains the Bee to Be, The.
Primitive like an Orb, A.
Prologues to What Is Possible.
Puella Parvula.
Quiet Normal Life, A.
Rabbit as King of the Ghosts, A.
Repetitions of a Young Captain.
River of Rivers in Connecticut, The.
Rock, The.
Room on a Garden, A.
Sad Strains of a Gay Waltz.
Sailing after Lunch.
Sea Surface Full of Clouds.
Sense of the Sleight-of-Hand Man, The.
Snow Man, The.
So-and-So Reclining on Her Couch.
Soldier, There Is a War between the Mind.
Soldier's Wound, The.
Song of Fixed Accord.
Souls of Women at Night, The.
Statue against a Clear Sky.
Study of Two Pears.
Sunday Morning.
Table Talk.
Tattoo.
Tea.
Tea at the Palaz of Hoon.
These locusts by day, these crickets by night.
Thirteen Ways of Looking at a Blackbird.
This Solitude of Cataracts.
To an Old Philosopher in Rome.
To the One of Fictive Music.
Two Figures in Dense Violet Light.
Two Illustrations That the World Is What You Make of It.
Ultimate Poem Is Abstract, The.
Vacancy in the Park.
We Reason of These Things.
Well Dressed Man with a Beard, The.
What We See Is What We Think.
When was it that the particles became.
Whistle Aloud, Too Weedy Wren.
Woman in Sunshine, The.
Woman Looking at a Vase of Flowers.
Woman That Had More Babies than That, The.
World as Meditation, The.

Stevenson, Alec Brock
Et Sa Pauvre Chair.

Stevenson, Anne
After Her Death.
Dear Ladies of Cincinnati, The.
From an Asylum; Kathy Chattle to Her Mother, Ruth Arbeiter.
Indian Summer: Vermont.
Love.
Mudtower, The.
North Sea off Carnoustie.
Stabilities.
Suburb, The.
Utah.

Stevenson, Burton Egbert
Henry Hudson's Quest.
Peace Message, The.

Stevenson, Candace Thurber
Public Library.
Signatures.

Stevenson, James
Gallant Fighting "Joe," The.

Stevenson, Lionel
Gulls and Dreams.
In a Desert Town.
Summer Interlude.

Stevenson, Matthew
Song: "Should I sigh out my dayes in griefe."

Stevenson, Patric
Anglo-Eire Vignette.
Autumnal Consummation.
Corn Cañon.
Dogrose.

Stevenson, Robert Louis
Alcaics; to H. F. B.
Armies in the Fire.
At the Seaside.
Autumn Fires.
Away with Funeral Music.
Bed in Summer.
Block City.
Blows the Wind Today.
Bright Is the Ring of Words.
Careful Angler, The.
Celestial Surgeon, The.
Christmas at Sea.
Christmas Prayer, A.
Christmas Sermon, A, *sel.*
Cow, The.
Day Returns, The.
Ditty: "Cock shall crow, The."
Dumb Soldier, The.
Envoy: "Go, little book, and wish to all."
Escape at Bedtime.
Evensong.
Farewell to the Farm.
Flowers, The.
Foreign Children.
Foreign Lands.
From a Railway Carriage.
Gardener, The.
Gather Ye Roses.
Go, Little Book.
Good and Bad Children.
Good Play, A.
Happy Thought.
He Hears with Gladdened Heart the Thunder.
Henry James.
Home No More Home to Me.
House Beautiful, The.
If This Were Faith.
Ille Terrarum.
In Memoriam F. A. S.
In the Highlands.
In the States.
Lad That Is Gone, A.
Lamplighter, The.
Land of Counterpane, The.
Land of Story-Books, The.
Last Sight, The.
Light-Keeper, The, *sel.*
Little Land, The.
Looking Forward.
Man Sails the Deep a While.
Marching Song.
Mile an' a Bittock, A.
My Bed Is a Boat ("My bed is like a little boat").
My Shadow.
My Ship and I.
My Wife.
Nest Eggs.
Not I.
O dull, cold northern sky.
O to Be Up and Doing.
Over the Sea to Skye.
Pirate Story.
Portrait, A.
Prayer: "I ask good things that I detest."
Prayer for the Household, A.
Rain.
Requiem: "Under the wide and starry sky."
Romance.
Say not of me that weakly I declined.
Sick Child, The.
Since Thou Hast Given Me This Good Hope, O God.
Singing.
Skerryvore.
Song of the Road, A.
Songs of Travel, *sels.*
Spaewife, The.
Stormy Nights.
Summer Sun.
Sun's Travels, The.
Swallows travel to and fro.
Swing, The.
System.
Ticonderoga; a Legend of the West Highlands.
Time to Rise.
To Be Honest, to Be Kind.
To K[atharine] de M[attos].
To My Wife.
To N. V. de G. S.
To S. R. Crockett.
To the Muse.
Travel.
Vagabond, The.
Verses Written in 1872.
Visit from the Sea, A.
Where Go the Boats?
Whole Duty of Children.
Wind, The.
Windy Nights.
Winter Time.

Wishes.
Stevenson, William
Back and Side Go Bare, Go Bare.
Gammer Gurton's Needle, *sel., at.*
Steward, Joseph
God from His Throne with Piercing Eye, *with music.*
My Soul Would Fain Indulge a Hope, *with music.*
Steward of Baldynneis, John. *See* **Stewart of Baldynnis, John**
Stewart, Anna Bird
Baby Talk.
Stewart, Arthur
Fossils.
Stewart, Douglas
At the Entrance.
Birdsville Track, The, *sel.*
Brindabella.
Bunyip, The.
Dosser in Springtime, The.
Garden of Ships, The.
Glencoe.
Lady Feeding the Cats, *sel.*
Mahony's Mountain.
Nesting Time.
Rock Carving.
Silkworms, The.
Snow-Gum, The.
Sunflowers, The.
Two Englishmen.
Stewart, Frank
Another Color.
Stewart, George Craig
As I Went Down to David's Town, *with music.*
Stewart, Gervase
I Burn for England with a Living Flame.
Landscape Lies within My Head, The.
Poem: "I burn for England with a living flame."
Poem: "I take four devils with me when I ride."
Red Cross Nurses.
Stewart, Harold
Lament in Autumn.
Leaf-Makers, The.
Stewart, Harold *and* **James Philip McAuley.** *See* **"Malley, Ern"**
Stewart, Pamela
Central Park, 1916.
Stewart, Phillips
Hope.
Stewart, Robert
Ballet under the Stars.
Plumber Arrives at Three Mile Island, The.
Stewart, W.
Aristocrats of Labor.
True Aristocrat, The.
Stewart, William
Thir Lenterne Dayis Ar Luvely Lang, *at.*
Stewart of Baldynnis [*or* Steward of Baldynneis], John
Medoro's Inscription for a Cave.
Roland Furious, *sel.*
To His Darrest Freind.
Stickney, Helen Frith
Habitue.
Stickney, Trumbull
Age in Youth.
At Sainte-Marguerite.
Athenian Garden, An.
Be Still. The Hanging Gardens Were a Dream.
Dramatic Fragment.
Driftwood, *abr.*
Eride, *sel.*
Fidelity.
He Said: "If in His Image I Was Made."
I Hear a River.
If I Have Wronged You.
If You Should Lightly.
In Ampezzo ("In days of summer let me go").
In Ampezzo ("Only once more and not again—the larches.")
In Summer.
In the Past.
Leave Him Now Quiet.
Like a Pearl Dropped.
Live Blindly.
Love, I Marvel What You Are.
Melancholy Year, The.
Mnemosyne.
Mount Lykaion.
Near Helikon.
Not That, If You Had Known.
Now in the Palace Gardens.
On Some Shells Found Inland.
Passions That We Fought With, The.
Six o'Clock.
Sonnets from Greece, *sel.*
Soul of Time, The.
This Is the Violin.
With Long Black Wings.
Stidger, William Leroy
Cross and the Tree, The.
I Saw God ("I saw God bare his soul one day").
I Saw God Wash the World.
Motherhood.
Waste of War, The.
We Are the Burden-Bearers! *abr.*
Still, James
Clabe Mott.
Dance on Pushback.
Rain on the Cumberlands.
Spring.
Trees in the Road, The.
Uncle Ambrose.
With Hands Like Leaves.
Still, John
Gammer Gurton's Needle, *sel., at.*
Stillingfleet, Benjamin
Sonnet: True Ambition.
Stillman, Albert
Ballad of the Faithful Clerk.
Truth about B. F., The.
When I Am Dead.
Stillman, Annie Raymond. *See* **"Raymond, Grace"**
Stilwell, Joseph W.
Lyric to Spring.
Stineford, Raymond
Breathe on the Glass.
Stinson, Sam S.
Such Foolish Old Dames.
Stirling, William Alexander, Earl of
Aurora, *sels.*
Madrigal: "When in her face mine eyes I fix."
Sonnet, XXV: "Cleare moving cristall, pure as the Sunne beames."
Sonnet, XXVI: "Ile give thee leave my love, in beauties field."
Sonnet: "I envy not Endymion now no more."
Sonnet: "Let others of the world's decaying tell."
Sonnet: "Oh, if thou knew'st how thou thyself dost harm."
Sonnet: "Then whilst that Latmos did contain her bliss."
To Aurora.
Stirling, Zan
I put my hat upon my head, *parody.*
Stirling-Maxwell, Sir William
To Anne.
Stites, Edgar P.
Beulah Land.
I've Reached the Land of Corn and Wine, *with music.*
Stock, Noel *and* **Ezra Pound.** *See* **Pound, Ezra** *and* **Noel Stock**
Stockard, Henry Jerome
As Some Mysterious Wanderer of the Skies.
Mocking-Bird, The.
Over Their Graves.
Stocking, Jay Thomas
O Master-Workman of the Race.
Stockton, John H.
Come, Every Soul, *with music.*
Stockwell, Brenda S.
Academic Affair.
Chances.
Easter Flood.
Stodart-Walker, Archibald
Counsel to Girls.
Early Bacon.
I had a duck and the young duck died.
Inflictis.
Moxford Book of English Verse, The, *sels.*
Stoddard, Charles Warren
Albatross.
Ave-Maria Bells.
Cocoa-Tree, The.
Rhyme of Life, A.
Royal Mummy to Bohemia, The.
Stigmata.
Wind and Wave.
Stoddard, Elizabeth
In the Still, Star-lit Night.
Last Days.
Mercedes.
November.
On the Campagna.
Poet's Secret, The.
Summer Night, A.
Unreturning.
Stoddard, Lavinia
Soul's Defiance, The.
Stoddard, Richard Henry
Abraham Lincoln.
Adsum.
Arab Song.
At Last.
Birds.
Catch, A.
Colonel Ellsworth.
Day and Night My Thoughts Incline.
Divan, The.
Dying Lover, The.
Falcon, The.
Flight of the Arrow, The.
Flight of Youth, The.
Gazelle, A.
Hymn to the Sea, A.
Jar, The.
Little Drummer, The.
Lover, The.
Men of the North and West.
Mors et Vita.
Old Song Reversed, An.
Sea, The.
Shadow, The.
Sky, The.
Songs ("How are songs begot and bred?").
Threescore and Ten.
Twilight on Sumter.
Two Anchors, The.
Wine and Dew.
Witch's Whelp, The.
Stoddart, Thomas Tod
Angler's Invitation, The.
Death-Wake or Lunacy, The, *sel.*
Her, a Statue.
Mirthful Lunacy.
Stokes, Francis G.
Blue Moonshine.
Stokes, Terry
All Morning.
Blood Supply in New York City Is Low, The.
Crimes of Passion: The Phone Caller.
Crimes of Passion: The Slasher.
Farmer, The.
Giving the Moon a New Chance.
Man All Grown Up Is Supposed To, A.
Travis, the Kid Was All Heart.
Stokes, Whitley
Viking, The.
Stokes, Will
Bugs.

Stokesbury, Leon
Beef.
Day Begins at Governor's Square Mall.
Funny Joke, A.
Gifts.
Morning Song.
To Laura Phelan: 1880-1906.
Unsent Message to My Brother in His Pain.
Stoloff, Carolyn
Dinosaurs.
Stoltzenberg, Abo
French Mood, The.
In Vistas of Stone.
What Am I?
Stone, Arlene
Germination.
Stone, John
Coming Home.
Double-Header.
Even Though.
Explaining about the Dachshund.
How I'd Have It.
Stone, John A.
Coming around the Horn.
Stone, Ruth
Advice.
Bargain.
Beginning to Live.
Burned Bridge, The.
Codicil.
Dark Conclusions.
Denouement.
I Have Three Daughters.
In a Liberal Arts Building.
In an Iridescent Time.
In the Interstices.
Liberation.
Magnet, The.
My Son.
On the Mountain.
Orchard.
Pear, The.
Periphery.
Private Pantomime.
Repetition of Words and Weather.
Room.
Salt.
Snow.
Talking Fish, The.
Vernal Equinox.
Watcher, The.
Whose Scene?
Winter.
Years Later.
Stone, Samuel John
Church's One Foundation, The.
Stone, Walter
Compelled to Love.
Couple.
Nature.
On the Welsh Marches.
Stoneback, H. R.
Toad Suck Ferry.
Stoner, Winifred Sackville
History of the U.S., The.
Stopes, Marie Carmichael
Night on the Shore.
Stopple, Libby
Calvary.
Storer, Thomas
Rivers.
Storey, Violet Alleyn
Dawn Song—St. Patrick's Day.
Neighborly.
Prayer after Illness, A.
Prayer for a Very New Angel.
Prayer for the New Year, A.
Prayer in Affliction.
Prayer in Late Autumn, A.
Rainy Day Song.
Stork, Charles Wharton
Bronze Statuette of Kwan-yin, A.
Flemish Madonna, A.
God, You Have Been Too Good to Me.
Painter in New England, A.
Rose and God, The.
Troubadour of God, The.
Storni, Alfonsina
Ancestral Weight.
Funeral Notices.
I Am Going to Sleep (Suicide Poem).
Lighthouse in the Night.
Men in the City.
My Sister.
Pain.
Sierra.
They've Come.
Words to My Mother.
Story, William Wetmore
Cleopatra.
English Language, The, *abr.*
Io Victis.
Praxiteles and Phryne.
Snowdrop.
Violet, The.
Stott, John G.
Scottish Mountaineering Club Song, The.
Stout, Liz
Waiting.
Stoutenburg, Adrien
Ants and Others.
Avalanche.
Bear Who Came to Dinner, The.
Brobdingnag.
Channel U.S.A.—Live.
Cicada.
Dogskin Rug.
Ivory Paper Weight.
Model T.
Night Train.
Rain.
Rhinoceros.
Sky Diver.
Traveller's Guide to Antarctica.
V.D. Clinic.
Stow, Randolph
As He Lay Dying.
Dust.
Jungle, The.
Ruins of the City of Hay.
Singing Bones, The.
Sleepers, The.
Strange Fruit.
Thailand Railway, *sels.*
Utopia of Lord Mayor Howard, The.
Stowe, Harriet Beecher
Abide in Me, O Lord, and I in Thee, *with music.*
Other World, The.
Still, Still, with Thee.
When I Awake I Am Still with Thee.
When Winds Are Raging, *with music.*
Stowman, Annette Burr
Fly, Ladybug.
Strabo, Walafrid. *See* **Walafrid Strabo**
Strachan, Ian
Silent Walls, The.
Silver in the Wind.
Strachey, Lytton
Cat.
Strahan, Bradley R.
Shabbat Morning.
Straley, John
Young Fellow from Boise, A.
Strand, Mark
Babies, The.
Black Maps.
Coming of Light, The.
Courtship.
Dance, The.
Dead, The.
Door, The.
"Dreadful Has Already Happened, The."
Dress, The.
Eating Poetry.
Elegy for My Father.
Empty Body, The.
From a Litany.
Garden, The.
Keeping Things Whole.
Kite, The.
Last Bus, The.
Letter.
Man in Black, The.
Man in the Mirror, The.
Man in the Tree, The.
Map, The.
Marriage, The.
Moontan.
Morning, A.
My Life by Somebody Else.
My Mother on an Evening in Late Summer.
New Year, The.
Night Piece.
Nights in Hackett's Cove.
Prediction, The.
Remains, The.
Shooting Whales.
Sleeping with One Eye Open.
Tomorrow.
Tunnel, The.
Violent Storm.
When the Vacation Is Over for Good.
Where Are the Waters of Childhood?
You and It.
Your Shadow.
Strato (Straton)
Epigram: "All through the night my eyes have streamed with rain."
Epigram: "At even, when the hour drew nigh at which we say farewell."
Epigram: "Boys' cocks, Diodore."
Epigram: "But yesterday, when from the bath he stept."
Epigram: "Even if I try not to ogle a boy in the street."
Epigram: "Gathering the bloom of all the fairest boys that be."
Epigram: "How shall I know if my love lose his youth."
Epigram: "I am provoked."
Epigram: "I delight in the prime of a boy of twelve."
Epigram: "I like them pale, fair or honey-skinned."
Epigram: "Like when the burning sun doth rise."
Epigram: "Long hair, endless curls trained by the devoted."
Epigram: "Now art thou fair, Diodorus."
Epigram: "Oh! trouble not Menèdemos by guile."
Epigram: "Passing the flower-stalls there did I perceive."
Epigram: "Perchance some coming after."
Epigram: "Stolen kisses, wary eyes."
Epigram: "There was this gym-teacher."
Epigram: "Those snooty boys in all their purple drag!"
Epigram: "Thy eyes are sparks, Lycines, god-like made."
Epigram: "When Graphicus sat by the baths."
To Kyris.
Strauss, A. L.
In Discreet Splendor.
Lament for the European Exile.
On the Path.
Voice in the Dark.
Strauss, Avner
Hollow Flute, The.
Portrait of a Widow.
"Strauss, Yawcob." *See* **Adams, Charles Follen**
Strawson, J. Adair
Token of Attachment, A.

"Streamer, Col. D." *See* **Graham, Harry**
Strebeck, George
Joyful Sound It Is, A, *with music.*
Street, Alfred Billings
Loon, The.
Settler, The.
Street, Julian *and* James Montgomery Flagg
Said Opie Read.
To Be Continued.
Streeter, Sebastian
King Shall Reign in Righteousness, A, *with music.*
Lo, What Enraptured Songs of Praise, *with music.*
Stricklin, Robert
Hoot Owl Shift.
Stringer, Arthur
At the Comedy.
Memories.
Morning in the North-west.
Sod-Breaker, The.
There Is Strength in the Soil.
Wanderer's Litany, A.
Stringer, R. E. C.
Sartorial Solecism.
Stripling, Kathryn
Lullabye! "Snow is lying on my roof."
Strobel, Marion
Captive.
Frightened Face.
Little Things.
Pastoral: "This is a place of ease."
Stroblas, Laurie
Circumstance.
Strode, William
Devonshire Song, A, *at.*
In Commendation of Music.
My love and I for kisses play'd.
Nightingale, The.
On a Gentlewoman Walking in the Snowe.
On Chloris Walking in the Snow.
On the Death of Mistress Mary Prideaux.
On Westwall Downes.
Strong, George
Epiphany, The.
Strong, George A.
Hiawatha Revisited.
Modern Hiawatha, The, *parody.*
Song of Milkanwatha, The, *parody, sel.*
Strong, Julia Hurd
Huckster's Horse, The.
Son and Surf.
Strong, Leonard Alfred George
Appointment, The.
Brewer's Man, The.
Coroner's Jury.
Door, The.
Evening before Rain.
From the Greek Anthology.
In Camus Fields.
Knowledgeable Child, The.
Lowery Cot.
Mad Woman of Punnet's Town, The.
Man's Way.
March Evening.
Memory, A.
Mother of Ten.
Old Dan'l.
Old Man at the Crossing, The.
Old Woman, outside the Abbey Theater, An.
Rufus Prays.
"Safe for Democracy."
Seals, The.
Sheepstor.
Sunday Morning.
Two Generations.
Zeke.
Strong, Nathan
Almighty Sovereign of the Skies! *with music.*
Summer Harvest Spreads the Fields, The, *with music.*
Swell the Anthem, Raise the Song, *with music.*
Strong, Phillips Burrows
Tongue, The.
Strongin, Lynn
Emily Dickinson Postage Stamp.
First Aspen, *sel.*
Miniatures IV.
Sayre.
Strongwolf, Chief Joseph
Indian Prayer.
Stroud, Dorothy Conant
Bible, The.
He Lives! He Lives to Bless!
His Life Is Ours.
No Room.
Not One Is Turned Away from God.
You Will Find a Joy in Service.
Stroud, Joseph
Above Machu Picchu, 129 Baker Street, San Francisco.
As for Me, I Delight in the Everyday Way.
Below Mount T'ui K'oy, Home of the Gods, Todos Santos Cuchumatán, Guatemalan Highlands.
City.
Documentary.
Dragon.
Exile.
Gold Country; Hotel Leger, Mokelumne Hill, Revisited, The.
Grandfather.
Lament: "Because the moon became my mother."
Machupuchare. What the Mountain Said.
Shaking the Dead Bones, Christmas Eve, 1974.
Memory.
Monte Albán.
Naming.
Poem on the Suicide of My Teacher.
Poem to Han-shan.
Poem to My Father.
Proportions.
Room above the White Rose, The.
Sibyl.
Signature II ("All morning he lay in the tight, dark room").
Signature III ("Tsangyang Gyatso was twelve years old").
To Christopher Smart.
Strunk, Jud
They're Tearing Down a Town.
"Struther, Jan" (Joyce Anstruther Maxtone Graham)
Biography.
R.I.P.
To Grow Older.
Traveling America.
Struthers, Ann
Tea.
Watching the Out-Door Movie Show.
Stryk, Lucien
Afternoon.
Awakening.
Downy Hair.
Face, The.
Farmer.
Fishing with My Daughter in Miller's Meadow.
Friendship.
Liberator, The.
Zen Poems, after Shinkichi Takahashi.
Stryker, Melancthon Woolsey
Almighty Lord, with One Accord, *with music.*
God of Our Fathers, *with music.*
Stuart, Alice V.
Climbing Rope, The.
Lintie in a Cage.
Stuart, Dabney
Begging on North Main.
Exchange.
Fisherman, The.
Lesson in Oblivion, A.
Refugee, The.
Rescue.
River, The.
Separate Parties.
Ties.
Stuart, Floyd C.
Gravestones.
Settling In.
Stuart, Francis
Coogan's Wood.
Ireland.
Southern Summer.
Une Idole Du Nord.
Upper Lake, The.
Stuart, James
Landlubber's Chantey, The.
Stuart, Jesse
By Sandy Waters.
Heart-summoned.
I Sing America Now!
My land is fair for any eyes to see.
Our Heritage.
Speaks the Whispering Grass.
Up Silver Stairsteps.
Stuart, John
Come unto Me (" 'Come unto Me,' said One below").
Stuart, Muriel
Forgotten Dead, I Salute You.
In the Orchard.
Old Saint, The.
Seed Shop, The.
Stuart, Ruth McEnery
Endless Song, The.
What-Is-It, A.
Stubbs, Charles William
Conscience.
'Twas Jolly, Jolly Wat.
Stubbs, Jane
Sim Ines.
Stubbs, John Heath-. *See* **Heath-Stubbs, John**
Stubbs, Marcia
In a Mirror.
Stubbs, William
Hymn on Froude and Kingsley, A.
Studdert-Kennedy, Geoffrey Anketell ("Woodbine Willie)
Awake, awake to love and work!
Christian Soldier, The, *sel.*
Great Wager, The.
Indifference.
Kiss of God, The.
Lord of the World, The.
My Peace I Give unto You.
Patience.
Rose, The.
Roses in December.
Unutterable Beauty, The.
Waste.
When through the Whirl of Wheels.
Work.
Stull, Richard
Dedication: "In my dreams we are always together."
Stults, Robert Morrison
Sweetest Story Ever Told, The.
Stump, Roger
Fear.
Stupp, John
First Cold Night of Autumn.
Sturgeon, Lorena W.
Love's Tribute.
Sturm, Frank Pearce
Still-Heart.
Style, Colin
100 Year Old Woman at Christmas Dinner.
Suasnavar, Constantino
I Have Lost My Shoes.
Succorsa, Janice Appleby
My Garden.
Suckling, Sir John
Actuality.
Against Absence.

Against Fruition.
Aglaura, *sels.*
Answer to Some Verses Made in His Praise, An.
Ballad [*or* Ballade] upon a Wedding, A.
Ballade upon a Wedding, A.
Barley-Break, A.
Besieged Heart, The.
Bride, The.
Candle, A.
Careless Lover, The.
Constancy.
Constant Lover, The.
Deformed Mistress, The.
Doubt of Martyrdom, A.
Farewell to Love.
Love and Debt Alike Troublesome, *at.*
Love's Clock.
Love's Offence.
Love's Siege.
Loves World.
Loving and Beloved.
Lutea Allison.
Metamorphosis, The.
Miracle, The.
My dearest Rival, least our Love.
On King Richard the Third, Who Lies Buried under Leicester Bridge.
On New-Year's Day 1640, to the King.
Pedlar of Small-Wares, A ("A pedlar I am, that take great care").
Poem, A: "Out upon it! I have loved."
Poem with the Answer, A.
Proffered Love Rejected.
Rejected Offer, The.
Session[s] of the Poets, A ("A session was held the other day").
Siege, The.
Sir J. S.
Sir Toby Matthews.
Soldier, A.
Song, A: "Hast thou seen the down in the air."
Song: "I prithee send me back my heart," *at.*
Song: "No, no, fair heretic[k], it needs must be."
Song: "Of thee, (kind boy), I ask no red and white."
Song to a Lute.
Sonnet: "Do'st see how unregarded now."
Sonnet: "Of thee (kind boy) I ask no red and white."
Sonnet: "Oh! for some honest lover's ghost."
'Tis Now, Since I Sat[e] Down Before.
To a Lady That Forbade to Love before Company.
To B. C.
To Master Davenant for Absence.
Upon A. M.
Upon Christ His Birth.
Upon Christmas Eve.
Upon My Lady Carlisle's Walking in Hampton Court Garden.
Upon My Lord Brohall's Wedding.
Upon Sir John Lawrence's Bringing Water over the Hills to My Lord Middlesex's House at Wiston.
Verses: "I am confirm'd a woman can."
Wits, The.
Woman's Constancy.

Suckow, Ruth
Grampa Schuler.

Sudan, Nazzam Al
Al Fitnah Muhajir.

Sugar, Maurice
Soup Song.

Suhl, Yuri
And the Earth Rebelled.
Permanent Delegate, The.

Sukenick, Lynn
Parting; a Game.

Suknaski, Andrew
Chinese Camp, Kamloops (circa 1883).
Snake, The.

Sullam, Sarah Copia
My Inmost Hope.

Sullivan, Aloysius Michael
Flying Dutchman, The.
Late Autumn.
Measurement.
Monument.
Psalm to the Holy Spirit.
Sextant, The.
Whale and the *Essex,* The.

Sullivan, Alan
Suppliant.
White Canoe, The.

Sullivan, James
As Sun, as Sea.

Sullivan, Jonny Kyoko
Sagimusume: The White Heron Maiden.

Sullivan, Joseph J.
Where Did You Get That Hat?

Sullivan, Nancy
Burial in the Sand.
Death of the First Man, The.
Eclipses.
His Necessary Darkness.
History of the World as Pictures, The.
Telling It.
To My Body.

Sullivan, Richard Webb
Star of the Sea.

Sullivan, Timothy Daniel
God Save Ireland.

Sully-Prudhomme, René François Armand
Appointment, The.
Naked World, The.
Struggle, The.
Wheel, The.

Sulpicia
At last love has come. I would be more ashamed.
Darling, I won't be your hot love.
Do you have a sweet thought, Cerinthus.
Drat my hateful birthday.
Have you heard? The troubles.
I'm grateful, really grateful.
It's nice that though you are casual about me.
Let your longing for me, my love.
My hated birthday is here, and I must go.

Summers, Hal
My Old Cat.
On the Cliff.
Valentine, A.

Summers, Hollis Spurgeon
Concerning Unnatural Nature: An Inverted Form.
Family Reunion.
Home.
Lost Pictures, The.
Valentine.

Summers, Thomas O.
Morning Bright, with Rosy Light, The, *with music.*

Summers, William C.
Pastor, The.
Soft Job.

Sumner, Jezaniah
Ode on Science, *with music.*

Sund, Robert
Afternoon,/ with just enough of a breeze for him to ride it.
Bunch Grass #37.
Dusty black beetle, A.

Sun-Ra
Nothing Is.
Plane, The: Earth.
Primary Lesson: The Second Class Citizens.

"Sunset Joe"
Lines on Mountain Villages.
Rivers of the West.

Sun Yün-feng
On the Road through Chang-te.
Starting at Dawn.
Trail up Wu Gorge, The.
Call, The.
Prophecy.

"Surfaceman." *See* **Anderson, Alexander**

Surrey, Henry Howard, Earl of
Although I had a check.
Another Tribute to Wyatt.
As oft as I behold and see.
Bonum Est Mihi Quod Humiliasti Me, *abr.*
Brittle Beauty.
Complaint by Night of the Lover Not Beloved, A.
Complaint of the Absence of Her Lover Being upon the Sea.
Complaint That His Ladie after She Knew of His Love Kept Her Face Alway Hidden
Consolation.
Cornet, The.
Death of Wyatt, The.
Description and Praise of His Love Geraldine.
Description of Spring [Wherein Each Thing Renews Save Only the Lover].
Divers Thy Death.
Epitaph on Thomas Clere.
Exhortation to Learn by Others' Trouble.
Frailty and Hurtfulness of Beauty, The.
Give Place, Ye Lovers.
Golden gift that nature did thee give, The.
Golden Mean, The.
His Incomparable Lady.
How No Age Is Content [with His Own Estate].
If care do cause men cry, why do not I complain.
If he that erst the form so lively drew.
In Cipres springes (wheras dame Venus dwelt).
In Praise of Wyatt's Psalms.
In the Rude Age.
In Windsor Castle.
In winter's just return, when Boreas gan his reign.
Lady Again Complains, The.
Lady Complains of Her Lover's Absence, A.
Laid in My Quiet Bed [in Study as I Were].
Lines to Ratclif.
Love's Rebel.
Night.
Of a Lady That Refused to Dance with Him.
Of the Death of Sir T[homas]. W[yatt].
Oh loathsome place! where I.
On the Death of Sir Thomas Wyatt.
Portrait of Henry VIII, The.
Praise of His Love, Wherein He Reproveth Them That Compare Their Ladies with His, A.
Prisoned in Windsor, He Recounteth His Pleasure There Passed.
Restless Heart, The.
Restless State of a Lover, The.
Sardanapalus.
Satire on London, A.
Since fortune's wrath envieth the wealth.
Soote Season, The.
Spring.
Such[e] wayward[e] ways [*or* wais] hath love, that most[e] part[e] in discord[e].
Summer Is Come.
Though I regarded not.
Too dearly had I bought my green and youthful years.
Tribute to Wyatt.
When Windsor [*or* Windesor] walls [*or* walls] sustain'd my wearied arm[e].
When Youth Had Led.
Woman's Answer, A, *at.*
Wrapt in my careless cloak, as I walk to and fro.
Wyatt Resteth Here.
Youth and Age.

Susskind, Harriet
Views.

Süsskind von Trimberg
O Thought!
Power of Thought, The.

Virtuous Wife, The.
Why Should I Wander Sadly.
Sussman, M. L.
Poet's Prayer.
Return.
Sutheim, Susan
For Witches.
Sutherland, Millicent
One Night.
Sutherland, Robert. *See* **Garioch, Robert**
Sutskever [*or* Sutzkever], Abraham
Banks of a River, The.
Cartload of Shoes, A.
Here I Am.
How?
Landscape.
Like Groping Fingers.
On My Wandering Flute.
Poetry.
Secret Town, The.
Song for a Dance.
Song of Praise for an Ox.
Songs to a Lady Moonwalker.
To My Child.
Toys.
Under the Earth.
Yiddish.
Sutter, Barton
Curse against the Owner, A.
Shoe Shop.
Static.
Sutton, Henry Septimus
Inward Light, The.
Sutu, S. D. R.
Night.
Thaba Bosio.
Su Tung-p'o
End of the Year, The.
Moon, Flowers, Man.
On the Birth of His Son.
Spring Night.
Terrace in the Snow, The.
To a Traveler.
Sutzkever, Abraham. *See* **Sutskever, Abraham**
Svetlov, Mikhail Arkadyevich
Grenada.
Swaim, Alice Mackenzie
Chilled by Different Winds.
Swain, Charles
Field-Path, The.
Home Is Where There Is One to Love Us.
Smile and Never Heed Me.
Song: "Violet in her lovely hair, A."
Tripping down the Field-Path.
Swain, John D.
Would I Be Shrived?
Swain, Leonard
My Soul, Weigh Not Thy Life, *with music.*
Swan, Emma
Connecticut Elm, The.
Swan, Jon
Among Commuters.
Father Father Son and Son.
In Her Song She Is Alone.
Kingdom, The.
March Weather.
Nebraska.
Report, The.
Their Party, Our House.
Swanger, David
Probity.
Swann, Brian
Desert in the Sea.
Lines: "There can be no power in a square."
Masks.
Paradigms of Fire.
Quiet.
Year of the Bird.
Swann, Thomas Burnett
Japanese Birthday Wish, A.
Swanton, John R.
Bear Song.
Swarberg, George W.
Mistakes.
Worry.
Sward, Robert
American Heritage.
Concert.
How totally unpredictable we are to one another.
Kissing the Dancer.
Mothers-in-Law.
Movies, Left to Right.
Nightgown, Wife's Gown.
Pet Shop.
Proposal.
Terminal Theater.
There Is No Reason Why Not to Look at Death.
Uncle Dog: the Poet at 9.
What It Was.
Swart, Edward Vincent
Casey Jones.
Tired of Eating Kisses.
Swarth, Hélène
Candles.
Ecstasy.
Swartz, Roberta Teale
Prayer by Moonlight.
Sweeney, Barbara
For We Are All Madwomen.
Sweeney, Francis
Boy Playing an Organ.
Sweeney, John L.
Exaction.
Separation.
Wind's Head, The.
Sweeney, Matthew
Alone with the Dawn.
Sweeney, Mildred Isabel McNeal
Chavez.
Sweetman, Elinor
Orchard by the Shore, The; a Pastoral.
Swenson, Karen
Come with Me into Winter's Disheveled Grass.
Grave Clothes.
Pro, The.
Quarrel, The.
Woman, Gallup, N. M.
Swenson, May
Above the Arno.
After the Dentist.
All That Time.
Almanac.
At the Museum of Modern Art.
Beginning to Squall.
Bronco Busting, Event #1.
Café Tableau.
Cardinal Ideograms.
Cat and the Weather.
Centaur, The.
Cloud-Mobile, The.
Cross Spider, The.
Death Invited.
Evolution.
Fashions in the 70's.
Feel like a Bird.
Feel Me.
Fire Island.
Five Horses.
Fixture, A.
Flying Home from Utah.
Four-Word Lines.
Frontispiece.
Garden at St. John's, The.
Green Red Brown and White.
Hearing the Wind at Night.
How Everything Happens.
How to Be Old.
In a Museum Cabinet.
July 4th.
Key to Everything, The.
Landing on the Moon.
Lion.
Living Tenderly.
Motherhood.
Naked in Borneo.
News from the Cabin.
Notes Made in the Piazza San Marco.
On Its Way.
Orbiter 5 Shows How Earth Looks from the Moon.
Out of the Sea, Early.
Painting the Gate.
Pair, A.
Poplar's Shadow, The.
Promontory Moment, The.
Question.
Rain at Wildwood.
Red Bird Tapestry, The.
Riding the "A."
School of Desire, The.
Scroppo's Dog.
Secret in the Cat, The.
Shape of Death, The.
Snow by Morning.
Snow in New York.
Some Small Shells from the Windward Islands.
Southbound on the Freeway.
Stone Gullets.
Sunday in the Country.
To the Shore.
To the Statue.
Universe, The.
Waiting for It.
Waking from a Nap on the Beach.
Was Worm.
Watch, The.
Watching the Jets Lose to Buffalo at Shea.
Water Picture.
Willets, The.
Women.
Woods at Night, The.
Swett, Herbert B.
Gathering, The.
Swett, John
In the Mines.
Swett, Susan Hartley
It Is July.
July.
Swift, Hildegarde Hoyt
I Came to the New World Empty-handed.
My Name Was Legion.
Swift, Joan
Line-up, The.
Oxygen.
Vancouver Island.
Swift, Jonathan
Abroad and at Home.
Apples.
Ballad to the Tune of "The Cut-Purse," A.
Baucis and Philemon.
Beautiful Young Nymph Going to Bed, A.
Behold the fatal day arrive!
Cadenus and Vanessa, *sels.*
Cassinus and Peter.
Cat and the Rain, The.
Church and clergy here, no doubt, The.
Clever Tom Clinch Going to Be Hanged.
Critics.
Daphne.
Day of Judgement [*or* Judgment], The.
Description of a City Shower, A.
Description of the Morning, A.
Dick, a Maggot.
Directions for Making a Birth-Day Song, *sel.*
Epigram: "As Thomas was cudgeled one day by his wife."
Epigram: "Lord Pam in the church (cou'd you think it) kneel'd down."
Epigram: "Who killed Kildare? Who dared Kildare to kill?"
Epigram on Fasting.
Epigram on Scolding.
Excellent New Song, Being the Intended Speech of a Famous Orator against Peace, An.

Excellent New Song on a Seditious Pamphlet, An.
Excellent New Song upon His Grace Our Good Lord Archbishop of Dublin, An.
Fable of Midas, The.
Flattery.
Fool, to put up four crosses at your door.
Furniture of a Woman's Mind, The.
Gentle Echo on Woman, A.
Herrings.
Holyhead, Sept. 25th, 1727.
In Sickness [Written Soon after the Author's Coming to Live in Ireland, upon the Queen's Death, October 1714].
Inscription for the Sign of *The Jolly Barber,* with a Razor in One Hand, and a Pot of Beer in the Other, *sel.*
Lady's Dressing Room, The.
Legion Club, The, *sel.*
Libel on Doctor Delaney and a Certain Great Lord, A.
Life and Genuine Character of Dean Swift, The, *sel.*
Market Women's Cries.
Mary the Cook-Maid's Letter to Dr. Sheridan.
Maypole, A.
Mrs. Frances Harris's Petition.
Mollis Abuti.
New Song of Wood's Halfpence, A, *at.*
On an Ill-managed House.
On an Upright Judge.
On Burning a Dull Poem.
On Dreams.
On Fleas.
On Himself.
On His Own Deafness
On Poetry; a Rhapsody.
On Stella's Birthday, 1719.
On the Astrologer and Almanac Maker, John Partridge.
On the Collar of Mrs. Dingley's Lap-Dog.
On the Death of Doctor Swift.
On the Irish Club.
On the Vowels—a Riddle.
On the World.
Onions.
Oysters.
Phyllis; or, The Progress of Love.
Place of the Damned, The.
Power of Time, The.
Progress of Beauty, The.
Progress of Poetry, The.
Riddle, A: "We are little airy creatures."
Riddle, A; the Vowels.
Satirical [*or* Satyrical] Elegy on the Death of a Late Famous General, A.
Shall I Repine.
Soldier and a Scholar, A, *sel.*
Stella at Wood-Park.
Stella's Birth-day, 1720 ("All travellers at first incline").
Stella's Birth-day; 1718/19 ("Stella this day is thirty-four").
Stella's Birthday, 1725 ("As when a beauteous nymph decays").
Stella's Birthday; March 13, 1726/27 ("This day, whate'er the fates decree").
To Form a Just and Finish'd Piece.
To Stella.
To the Earl of Oxford, Late Lord Treasurer.
To the Landlord.
To Their Excellencies the Lords Justices of Ireland, the Humble Petition of Frances Harris [Who Must Starve, and Die a Maid if It Miscarries].
True and Faithful Inventory of the Goods Belonging to Dr. Swift, Vicar of Laracor, A; upon Lending His House to the Bishop of Meath, till His Palace Was Rebuilt.
Twelve Articles.
Vanbrug's House.
Verses for Fruitwomen, *sels.*
Verses Made for Women Who Cry Apples.
Verses Occasioned by the Sudden Drying Up of St. Patrick's Well, *sel.*
Verses on the Death of Doctor [*or* Dean] Swift [D.S.P.D., Occasioned by Reading a Maxim in Rochefoucauld].
Verses Said to Be Written on the Union.
Verses Written upon Windows.
Verses Wrote in a Lady's Ivory Table-Book.
Virtue conceal'd within our breast.
Virtues of Sid Hamet, the Magician's Rod, The.
We are God's chosen few.
Who Killed Kildare? Who Dared Kildare to Kill?
Wicked Treasonable Libel, A.
With favour and fortune fastidiously blest.

Swift, Nicholas
Maxims of a Park Vagrant.

Swilky, Jody
Animation and Ego.
Nothing but Image.

Swinamer, George
Gale of August, '27, The, *with music.*

Swinburne, Algernon Charles
Anactoria, *sel.*
Apologia.
At a Month's End.
At Parting.
At the Piano.
Atalanta in Calydon, *sels.*
August.
Ave atque Vale.
Ballad of Dead Men's Bay, The.
Ballad of Dreamland, A.
Ballad of François Villon, A.
Ballad of Life, A.
Before Sunset.
Before the Beginning of Years.
Before the Mirror.
By the North Sea, *sels.*
Channel Passage, A.
Chastelard, *sel.*
Child's Laughter, A.
Child's Song.
Chorus: "Before the beginning of years."
Chorus: "When the hounds of spring are on winter's traces."
Chorus: "Who hath given man speech? or who hath set therein."
Christmas Antiphones, *sel.*
Christmas Carol, A: "Three damsels in the queen's chamber."
Christopher Marlowe.
Cleopatra.
Cliffside Path, The.
Come into the orchard, Anne.
Cor Cordium.
Dead King, A.
Death of Meleager, The.
Death of Richard Wagner, The.
Death of Urgan, The.
Dedication: "Sea gives her shells to the shingle, The."
Dedication: "Some nine years gone, as we dwelt together."
Dedication to "Songs of the Springtides."
Delphic Hymn to Apollo.
Dialogue, A.
Dolores.
Duriesdyke.
Envoi: "Fly, white butterflies, out to sea."
Erotion.
Étude Réaliste.
Evening by the Sea.
Evening on the Broads.
Ex-Voto.
Faustine.
Félise.
Forsaken Garden, A.
Fragoletta.
Garden of Cymodoce, The, *sel.*
Garden of Proserpine, The.
Hawthorn Dyke.
Hendecasyllabics.
Heptalogia, The, *sels.*
Hermaphroditus.
Hertha.
Hesperia.
Higher Pantheism in a Nutshell, The, *parody.*
Hope and Fear.
Hounds of Spring, The.
Hymn of Man.
Hymn to Proserpine.
In Guernsey.
In Harbour.
In Memory of "Barry Cornwall."
In Memory of Walter Savage Landor.
In the Orchard.
Interlude, An.
Interpreters, The.
Itylus.
Jacobite's Exile, A.
John Jones.
John Webster.
Lake of Gaube, The.
Laus Veneris.
Leave-taking, A.
Leper, The.
Love and Sleep.
Love at Sea.
Lyke-Wake Song, A.
Lyric, A: "There's nae lark loves the lift, my dear."
Madonna Mia.
Man.
Mary Beaton's Song.
Match, A.
May Janet.
Midsummer Holiday, A, *sel.*
Nephelidia.
Nympholept, A.
Oblation, The.
On Arthur Hugh Clough.
On the Cliffs.
On the Deaths of Thomas Carlyle and George Eliot.
Plus Ultra.
Poeta Loquitur.
Prelude to "Songs before Sunrise."
Proserpine.
Return, The.
Rococo.
Rondel: "Kissing her hair, I sat against her feet."
Rondel: "These many years since we began to be."
Sapphics.
Sark.
Sea, The.
Sestina: "I saw my soul at rest upon a day."
Seven Years Old.
Shakespeare.
Siena.
Singing Lesson, A.
Song: "Love laid his sleepless head."
Song in Time of Order 1852, A.
Song in Time of Revolution 1860, A.
Sonnet: "This is the golden book of spirit and sense."
Sonnet for a Picture.
Stage Love.
Stanzas: "I will go back to the great sweet mother."
Suffolk.
Sundew, The.
Sunrise at Sea.
Super Flumina Babylonis.
Swimming.
Thalassius.
To a Cat.
To a Seamew.
To Victor Hugo.
To Walt Whitman in America.
Tristram of Lyonesse, *sels.*

Triumph of Time, The.
Watchman, What of the Night?
When the Hounds of Spring [Are on Winter's Traces].
Where Dunwich Used to Be.
White Butterflies.
Year's Burden [1870], A.

Swingler, Randall
Letter I ("The midnight streets as I walk back").
Letter VIII ("On the first day of snow, my train)."
They Live.

Swiss, Thomas (Thom)
Letter from Des Moines.
Virtue of Shape, A.

Swope, Mary
Couple.

Sykes, Velma West
Diptych.

Sylvester, Janet
Arrowhead Christian Center and No-Smoking Luncheonette.
Hard Strain in a Delicate Place.
Late Show, The.
That Mulberry Wine.

Sylvester, Joshua
Autumnus.
Beware Fair Maide, *at.*
Contented Mind, A.
Du Bartas: His Divine Weeks and Works, *sels.*
Fuimus Fumus.
Go, Silly Worm.
I hate these phrases: Of power absolute.
Mundus Qualis.
Omnia Somnia.
Rome, Conqueror, Conquered.
Seventh Day of the First Week, The, *sel.*
Sonnet: "They say that shadow[e]s of deceased ghosts."
Sonnet: "Were I as base as is the lowly plain," *at.*
Sweet mouth, that send'st a musky-rosed breath.
Ubique, *at.*
Were I as Base as Is the Lowly Plain, *at.*
When wine runs low, it is not worth the sparing.

Sylvester, William
Hookerlumps in the Love Canal.

Symmons, Robert
Dam, Glen Garry, The.

Symonds, John Addington
Church Triumphant, The.
Farewell: "It is buried and done with."
Farewell: "Thou goest; to what distant place."
Human Outlook, The.
In February.
Invocation, An: "To God, the everlasting, who abides."
Ithocles, *sel.*
Koina ta ton Philon.
Le Jeune Homme Caressant Sa Chimère.
Love in Dreams.
Midnight at Baiae; a Dream Fragment of Imperial Rome.
Night.
On a Picture by Poussin Representing Shepherds in Arcadia.
Sonnet, The: "Sonnet is a fruit which long hath slept, The."
These Things Shall Be.
Venice.

Symons, Arthur
Abandoned, The.
Absinthe-Drinker, The.
Amends to Nature.
Amor Triumphans, *sel.*
Amoris Exsul, *sels.*
Andante of Snakes, The.
April Midnight.
At Carbis Bay.
At Dawn.
At Dieppe, *sels.*
At Glan-y-Wern.
At Toledo.
Bianca, *sel.*
By Loe Pool.
By the Pool at the Third Rosses.
Caged Bird, The.
City Nights: In Bohemia.
City Nights: In the Train.
Clair de Lune.
Credo.
Dance of the Daughters of Herodias, The.
Declaration.
Dream, The.
Dreams.
Ecstasy.
Emmy ("Emmy's exquisite youth and her virginal air").
Envoi: "All that remains for me."
Episode of a Night of May.
Escalade.
Fisher's Widow, The.
Gardener, The.
Grey Wolf, The.
Hallucination, I.
Impression.
In Bohemia.
In Ireland, *sel.*
In Kensington Gardens.
In the Bay.
In the Train.
In Winter.
Intermezzo: Pastoral, *sel.*
Javanese Dancers.
La Mélinite: Moulin-Rouge.
Last Memory, The.
Laus Virginitatis.
Leves Amores.
Loom of Dreams, The.
Magnificat.
Maquillage.
Modern Beauty.
Nerves.
Night and Wind.
Nun, The.
On an Air of Rameau.
On the Beach.
Palm Sunday: Naples.
Paris.
Pastel.
Prodigal Son, The.
Prologue: "My life is like a music-hall."
Prologue to "London Nights."
Rain on the Down.
Rat, The.
Return, The.
Roundel of Rest, A.
Scènes de la Vie de Bohème, *sel.*
Shadow, The.
Temptation of Saint Anthony, The.
Tune, A.
Violet, *sel.*
Wanderer's Song.
White Heliotrope.

Symons, Julian
And the World's Face.
For My Wife.
For the Depressed.
Gladstone.
Hart Crane.
Homage to Our Leaders.
Hospital Observation.
Mr. Symons at Richmond, Mr. Pope at Twickenham.
Pub.
Reflections in Bed.
Second Man, The.
Spring Poem.
Sunday, July 14th; a Fine Day at the Baths.

Synge, John Millington
At Dawn.
Beg-Innish.
Conviction, The.
Curse, The.
Dread.
Epitaph: "If fruits are fed on any beast."
Epitaph after Reading Ronsard's Lines from Rabelais.
I curse my bearing, childhood, youth.
I read about the Blaskets and Dunquin.
In a Dream.
In Dream.
In Glencullen.
In Kerry.
In May.
In Rebellion.
Is It a Month.
I've Thirty Months.
'Mergency Man, The.
Notre Dame des Champs.
On a Birthday.
On an Anniversary.
On an Island.
Passing of the Shee, The.
Patch-Shaneen.
Prelude: "Still south I went and west and south again."
Queens.
Question.
Rendez-vous Manqué dans la Rue Racine.
To the Oaks of Glencree.
Winter.
Wish, A.

"Syntax"
Soliloquy of the Returned Gold Adventurer.

Syquia, Luis
New Manong, The.
Pan-Asian Holiday Tour.

Sze, Arthur
Black Lightning.
Chance, The.
Cloud Chamber, The.
Dazzled.
Magnetized.
Moenkopi.
Moon Is a Diamond, The.

Szelki, Karl
Chestnut vendor, The.

Szumigalski, Anne
Angels.
Midwife's Story, A; Two.
Visitor's Parking.

Szymborska, Wislawa
Homecoming.
I am too near to be dreamt of by him.
In Praise of a Guilty Conscience.
Starvation Camp near Jaslo.
Women of Rubens, The.

T

"T., B. L." *See* **Taylor, Bert Leston**

"T., C."
Gastric.

"T., C. A. L."
Y.M.C.A.

"T., C. W."
Valentine.

"T., I."
When Stars Are Shrouded.

"T., J."
Sea-Chaplain's Petition to the Lieutenants in the Ward-Room, for the Use of the Quarter-Gallery, A.

Ta' Abbata Sharra
Ever Watchful.

Tabb, John Banister
Annunciation, The.
Anonymous.
Aspiration.
Assumption, The.
At Bethlehem.

Becalmed.
Betrayal.
Bicycles! Tricycles!
Bubble, The.
Bunch of Roses, A.
Child, The, *sels.*
Childhood.
Child's Prayer, A.
Christ and the Pagan.
Close Quarters.
Clover.
Communion.
Departed, The.
Druid, The.
Evolution.
Faith.
Fame.
Father Damien.
Foot Soldiers.
Fraternity.
God.
High and Low.
Immaculate Conception, The.
Indian Summer.
Insomnia.
Inspiration.
Missing.
Out of Bounds.
Overflow.
Reaper, The.
Rub, A.
Sisters, The.
Tax-Gatherer, The.
To a Wood-Violet.
To His Mother.
To Shelley.
To the Christ.
Tryst, The.
Water-Lily, The.
White Jessamine, The.

Tabrar, Joseph
Mary Ann.

Taeko, Tomioka
Living Together.

Taft, Margo
I have been my arm.

Tagami, Jeff
Foreman's Wife, The.
Horn Blow, The.
Now It Is Broccoli.
Stonehouse.
Without Names.

Taggard, Genevieve
American Farm, 1934.
Dilemma of the Elm.
Doomsday Morning.
Enamel Girl, The.
First Miracle.
Galatea Again.
Geraniums, The.
In the Tail of the Scorpion.
Little Girl with Bands on Her Teeth, The.
Millions of Strawberries.
Poem to Explain Everything about a Certain Day in Vermont, A.
Sea-Change.
Solar Myth.
Song for Unbound Hair.
Squirrel near Library.
To the Veterans of the Abraham Lincoln Brigade.
Train: Abstraction.
Try Topic.
With Child.

Taggert, George
Moth and the Flame, The.

Tagliabue, John
Archilochos.
Assuming the Name of Any Next Child.
Bare Arms of Trees, The.
By a Rich Fast Moving Stream.
Debussy and Proust.
December 1970.
I Sought All Over the World.
In the Palms of Ancient Bodhisattvas.
Just a Few Scenes from an Autobiography.
Pinta, the Nina and the Santa Maria, The.
Riding Stable in Winter, The.
Unseen Deer, An.
You.

Tagore, Rabindranath
Autumn.
Bird, The.
Day after Day.
Echo always mocks the sound, The.
Epigrams, *sel.*
Fairyland.
Gardener, The, *sels.*
Gitanjali, *sels.*
Home, The.
I Have Got My Leave.
If It Is Not My Portion.
In the Dusky Path of a Dream.
Journey Nears the Road-End, The.
My Song.
On the Slope of the Desolate River.
Paper Boats.
Thou Art the Sky.
Vocation.
Yellow Bird Sings, The.

Tahureau, Jacques
Moonlight.
Shadows of His Lady.

Tait, William J.
Gallow Hill.

Takahashi, Shinkichi
Fish.
Snail ("The snail crawls over blackness").
Sparrow in Winter.

Takvan, Marie
Deepest Bow, The.

Talbot, Charles Remington. *See* **"Brownjohn, John"**

Talbot, Ethel
Crab-Apple.
Give Love To-Day.

Taleb, Ali Ben Abu
Make Friends.

Taliessin
Song to the Wind, A.

Tall, Grace Cornell
Needle, The.

Tallet, José Zacarías
Rumba.

TallMountain, Mary
Crazy Dogholkoda.
Good Grease.
Indian Blood.
Ivory Dog for My Sister, The.
Last Wolf, The.
Matmiya.
Once the Striped Quagga.
There Is No Word for Goodbye.
Ts'eekkaayah.
Women in Old Parkas, The.

Tamekane, Kyōgoku
On Love.
Twenty-three Tanka, *sel.*

Tam'si, Tchicaya U
Debout, *sel.*

Tanaka, Ronald P.
Big Trimmer, The.
Snacks.

"Tanaquil, Paul" (J.G. Clemenceau Le Clercq)
History.

T'ang Wan
To the Tune "The Phoenix Hairpin."

Tangikuku, Hine
Song of Sickness, A.

Tankervil, George
Evensong.

Tannahill, Robert
Braes o' Gleniffer, The.
By Yon Burn Side.
Jessie, the Flower o' Dunblane.
Loudoun's Bonnie Woods and Braes.
Midges Dance aboon the Burn, The.
O! Are Ye Sleepin [*or* Sleeping], Maggie?

Tan Pai, Joshua
Life of Hard Times, The.
My Soul Hovers over Me.
Trees Once Walked and Stood.

Tan Ying
Drinking the Wind.

T'ao Ch'ien [*or* T'ao Yuan-ming]
I Built My Hut.
Long I Have Loved to Stroll.
Long time ago, A.
Once More Fields and Gardens.
Shady, Shady.
Two Drinking Songs.

Tapahonso, Luci
Belly of the Land, The.
Dust Will Settle, The.
Hills Brothers Coffee.
It Was a Special Treat.
Sheepherder Blues.

Tapp, Gary
Insect Shuffle Method, The.

Tappan, William Bingham
Gethsemane.
Hour of Peaceful Rest, The.
Ransomed Spirit to Her Home, The, *with music.*
Song of the Three Hundred Thousand Drunkards in the United States, *sel.*
'Tis Midnight and on Olive's Brow.
Wake, Isles of the South, *with music.*

Tapscott, Stephen
Parable: November.

Tarn, Nathaniel
Where Babylon Ends.

Tasso, Torquato
Aminta, *sel.*
Godfrey of Bulloigne; or, The Recoverie of Jerusalem, *sels.*
Golden Age, The.
Love.
Pastoral [*or* Pastorall], A: "Oh [*or* O] happy golden age."
Pastoral of Tasso, A.
Pluto's Council.
Prayer Brings Rain, A.
To His Mistress in Absence.

Tate, Allen
Aeneas at Washington.
Autumn.
Buried Lake, The.
Cross, The.
Death of Little Boys.
Emblems.
Eye, The.
Fire I praise was once perduring flame, The.
Horatian Epode to the Duchess of Malfi.
Idiot.
Jubilo.
Last Days of Alice.
Mediterranean, The.
Mr. Pope.
More Sonnets at Christmas.
Mother and Son.
Oath, The.
Ode: "Once more the country calls."
Ode to the Confederate Dead.
Paradigm, The.
Pastoral: "Enquiring fields, courtesies, The."
Pauper, A.
Robber Bridegroom, The.
Seasons of the Soul.
Shadow and Shade.
Sonnets at Christmas (I–II).
Sonnets of the Blood, *sels.*
Subway, The.
Swimmers, The.
Traveller, The.
What is this flesh and blood compounded of.
Winter Mask.

Wolves, The.
Tate, James
Blue Booby, The.
Box for Tom, A.
Coda.
Conjuring Roethke.
Constant Defender.
Consumed.
Dear Reader.
Distant Orgasm, The.
Flight.
If It Would All Please Hurry.
It's Not the Heat So Much as the Humidity.
Land of Little Sticks, 1945.
Little Yellow Leaf.
Lost Pilot, The.
Love Making.
Miss Cho Composes in the Cafeteria.
Motorcyclists, The.
My Great Great etc. Uncle Patrick Henry.
Pet Deer, The.
Pity Ascending with the Fog.
President Slumming, The.
Professor Waking, The.
Riven Doggeries.
Same Tits.
Sloops in the Bay.
Soup of Venus, The.
Square at Dawn, The.
Stray Animals.
Tall Trees by Still Waters.
Teaching the Ape to Write Poems.
Wheelchair Butterfly, The.
Who Can Tell When He Is Awake.
Tate, Nahum
Blessed Virgin's Expostulation, The.
Christmas.
Loyal General, The, *sel.*
Now if thou hast one dram of grace.
Old England.
Penance, The.
While Shepherds Watched [Their Flocks by Night].
Tate, Nahum *and* **John Dryden**
Absalom and Achitophel, Pt. II, *sels.*
Thomas Shadwell the Poet.
Tate, Nahum *and* **Nicholas Brady**
Lord, Who's the Happy Man, *with music.*
Tatersal, Robert
Bricklayer's Labours, The.
Tatham, John
Letter, The.
Reason.
Tauhindauli (Frank LaPena)
I Am Stone of Many Colors.
There was a time when the stars fell like rain.
Waiting for a Second Time.
Wrapped Hair Bundles.
Year of Winter, The.
Tawney, Cyril
Grey Funnel Line, The.
On a Monday Morning.
Reunion.
Sally Free and Easy.
Taylor, Allan
Ballad for the Unknown Soldier.
Still He Sings.
Time.
Taylor, Andrew
Developing a Wife.
Invention of Fire, The.
Taylor, Ann
Baby, The.
Jane and Eliza.
Meddlesome Matty.
My Mother.
Notorious Glutton, The.
Pin, The.
Plum-Cake, The.
Tumble, The.
Washing and Dressing.
Taylor, Ann *or* Jane Taylor
Cow, The.
Little Fish That Would Not Do as It Was Bid, The.
Sheep, The.
Taylor, Bayard
Ah, moment not to be purchased.
All or Nothing.
America.
Angelo Orders His Dinner.
Ariel in the Cloven Pine.
Ballad of Hiram Hover, The.
Bedouin Song.
Camerados.
Cimabuella.
Demon of the Mirror, The.
Deserter, The.
Fight of Paso del Mar, The.
Gettysburg Ode, The, *sel.*
Gwendoline.
Lincoln at Gettysburg.
National Ode, July 4, 1876, The.
Nauvoo.
Night with a Wolf, A.
Nubia.
Ode on [*or* to] a Jar of Pickles.
Palabras Grandiosas.
Poet's Journal, The, *sel.*
Promissory Note, The.
Quaker Widow, The.
Sir Eggnogg.
Song: "Daughter of Egypt, veil thine eyes!"
Song of the Camp, The.
Storm Song.
Story for a Child, A.
Sunshine of the Gods, The, *sel.*
Through Baltimore.
To M. T.
Taylor, Benjamin Franklin
Isle of the Long Ago, The.
Long Ago, The.
Taylor, Bert Leston ("B.L.T")
Aprilly.
Ataraxia.
Bards We Quote, The.
Bygones.
Canopus.
Dinosaur, The.
Doxology.
Hence These Rimes.
Old Stuff.
Post-Impressionism.
Road to Anywhere, The.
Those Flapjacks of Brown's.
To Lillian Russell.
To What Base Uses! *parody.*
Upon Julia's Arctics.
Taylor, Caleb J.
O Jesus, My Savior, I Know Thou Art Mine, *with music.*
Taylor, Charles S.
Scandal among the Flowers, A.
Taylor, Deems
Concerning Mme. Robert.
"Haec Olim Meminisse Iuvabit."
Hors d'Oeuvre.
Proof Positive.
Turn to the Left.
Taylor, Edward
Accusation of the Inward Man, The.
Address to the Soul Occasioned by a Rain, An.
Am I thy gold? Or purse, Lord, for thy wealth.
Angels Sung a Carol, The, *with music.*
Christ's Reply.
Ebb and Flow, The.
Elegy upon the Death of That Holy Man of God Mr. John Allen, An.
Experience, The.
Frowardness of the Elect in the Work of Conversion, The.
Glory of and Grace in the Church Set Out, The.
God's Determinations, *sels.*
God's Selecting Love in the Decree.
Huswifery.
Joy of Church Fellowship Rightly Attended, The.
Let by Rain.
Oh! Good, good, good, my Lord. What more love yet.
Oh! What a thing is man? Lord, who am I?
Our Insufficiency to Praise God Suitably for His Mercy.
Outward Man Accused, The.
Preface, The: "Infinity, when all things it beheld."
Preparatory Meditations before My Approach to the Lord's Supper, *sels.*
Prologue: "Lord, can a crumb of earth the earth outweigh."
Reflection, The.
Reflexion, The.
Souls Groan to Christ for Succour, The.
Thou Art the Tree of Life, *with music.*
Upon a Spider Catching a Fly.
Upon a Wasp Chilled [*or* Child] with Cold.
Upon Wedlock and Death of Children.
What Love Is This.
Taylor, Eleanor Ross
In the Churchyard.
Taylor, Emily
Mother.
Taylor, Frances Beatrice
Husbandman, The.
Wedgewood Bowl, A.
Taylor, Geoffrey
Admonition to the Muse.
Bluebell.
Boat-Haven, Co. Mayo.
Country Walk.
Cruel, Clever Cat.
English Liberal.
Epitaph: "Nor practising virtue nor committing crime."
From an Irish-Latin Macaronic.
Gentlemen.
Song: "Rousing to rein his pad's head back."
Taylor, Helen
Bless This House ("Bless this house, O Lord, we pray").
Taylor, Henry
Artichoke.
Breakings.
Campaign Promise.
Country Curate, The.
Depressed by the Death of the Horse That He Bought from Robert Bly.
Flying Change, The.
Getting at the Root of the Matter.
Horse Show at Midnight, The.
In Orbit.
J. V. Cunningham Gets Hung Up on a Dirty, of All Things, Joke.
Landscape with Tractor.
Miss Creighton.
Remembering Kevan MacKenzie.
Riding a One-eyed Horse.
Riding Lesson.
Robert Bly Says Something Too.
Shapes, Vanishings.
Sonnet in the Mail Coach.
Speech.
Taking to the Woods.
To Hear My Head Roar.
Taylor, Sir Henry
Elena's Song.
Philip van Artevelde, *sel.*
Song: "Bee to the heather, The."
Women Singing.
Taylor, Jane
Contented John.
Dirty Jim.
Disappointment, The.
Gleaner, The.
Good-Night.

Greedy Richard.
I Like Little Pussy.
I Love Little Pussy.
Morning.
Philosopher's Scales, The.
Pigs, The.
Pussy.
Recreation.
Star, The.
Violet, The.

Taylor, Jeffreys
Lion and the Mouse, The.

Taylor, Jeremy
My Soul Doth Pant towards Thee.
Penitent, The.

Taylor, John
Egg of Nothing, The.
End of the Line.
Mill, The.
Mockado, Fustian, and Motley.
Odcomb's Complaint, *sel.*
Roses Gone Wild.
Sonnet: "Sweet semi-circled Cynthia played at maw."
Trumpet of Liberty, The.

Taylor, John W.
Chipeta's Ride.

Taylor, Joseph Russell
Blow Softly, Thrush.
Breath on the Oat.
Dove's Nest.
Flute, The.
Veery-Thrush, The.

Taylor, Katherine Kelley
Flying Fish.

Taylor, Laurie
Business Trips.
Lake Harriet: Wind.

Taylor, Lucy
Leac A'Chlarsair.

Taylor, Rachel Annand
Ecstasy.
Joys of Art, The.
Knights to Chrysola, The.
May-Music.
Princess of Scotland, The.
Question, The.

Taylor, Rod
Dakota: October, 1822, Hunkpapa Warrior.

Taylor, Sarah Wingate
With Metaphor.

Taylor, Tom
Abraham Lincoln.

Taylor, Viola
Babylon.

Taylor, William
Vision, The.

Taylor, William Edward
Resurrection, The.

Tchaikovsky, Peter Ilich
Legend, A, *at.*

Tchernichowsky, Saul [*or* Tchernichovsky, Shaul]
Before the Statue of Apollo.
Dance of Saul with the Prophets, The.
Death of Tammuz, The.
Grave, The.
Grave in Ukraine, A.
I Believe.
Man Is Nothing But.
Saul's Song of Love.
This Be Our Revenge.
To Ashtaroth and Bel.

Teasdale, Sara
Answer, The.
Appraisal.
April.
August Night.
Barter.
Blue Squills.
Calm Morning at Sea.
Child, Child.
Coin, The.
Crystal Gazer, The.
December Day, A.
Epitaph: "Serene descent, as a red leaf's descending."
Falling Star, The.
February Twilight.
Flight, The.
Four Winds.
Full Moon; Santa Barbara.
Grace before Sleep.
"I Am Not Yours."
I Shall Not Care.
Immortal.
In the Carpenter's Shop.
Inn of Earth, The.
June Day, A.
Kiss, The.
Late October.
Leaves.
Let It Be Forgotten.
Like Barley Bending.
Long Hill, The.
Look, The.
Mastery.
May Day.
Moonlight.
Moon's Ending.
Morning Song.
Mystery, The.
New Moon, The.
Night.
Night Song at Amalfi.
On the South Downs.
Prayer, A: "Until I lose my soul and lie."
September Midnight.
Solitary, The.
Song: "Let it be forgotten, as a flower is forgotten."
Song Making.
Spring in War-Time.
Spring Night.
Stars.
There Will Come Soft Rains.
To Rose.
Water-Lilies.
"What Do I Care."
Winter Noon.
Wisdom.

Tegnér, Esaias
Frithiof's Saga, *sels.*

Teitoku
Both my child.

"Tekahionwake." *See* **Johnson, Emily Pauline**

Tekeyan, Vahan
Future, The.

Telemaque, Harold Milton
Adina.

Telesilla
O Artemis and your virgin girls.

Telfer, James
Goblin's Song, The.

Teller, Judah Leib
Lines to a Tree.
Minor Key.
To the Divine Neighbor.

Temkin, Mordecai
Foul Water.
Hidden Bow.
Seal of Fire.
Your Presence.

Templeton, J. D.
New Year, The.

Tennant, Edward Wyndham
Home Thoughts in Laventie.
I saw green banks of daffodil.

Tennant, Robert
Wee Davie Daylicht.

Tennant, William
Anster Fair, *sel.*
On the Road to Anster Fair.

Tennyson, Alfred Tennyson, 1st Baron
All in All.
Ancient Pistol, peacock Payne.
Ancient Sage, The.
Arthur's Disillusionment.
As Sometimes in a Dead Man's Face.
As thro' the Land at Eve We Went.
As When a Man.
Ask Me No More.
At Farringford.
Ay.
Aylmer's Field.
Ballad of the Fleet, A.
Balloon, The.
Becket,
Beggar Maid, The.
Black Bull of Aldgate.
Blackbird, The.
Break, Break, Break.
Brook, The; an Idyl, *sel.*
Brook's Song, The.
Bugle Song.
Captain, The.
Charge of the Light Brigade, The.
Choric Song: "There is sweet music here that softer falls."
City Child, The.
Claribel.
Columbus, *sel.*
Come into the Garden, Maud.
Come Not When I Am Dead.
Crossing the Bar.
Daisy, The.
Death of the Old Year, The.
Dedication: "These to His Memory—since he held them dear."
Deep Dark Night, The.
Defence of Lucknow, The.
Demeter and Persephone.
Despair.
Devil and the Lady, The, *sel.*
Doubt.
Dream of Fair Women, A, *sel.*
Duet.
Dying Swan, The.
Eagle, The.
Early Spring.
Edward Gray.
Elaine's Song.
England and America in 1782.
Enid's Song.
Enoch Arden.
Epic, The.
Farewell, A: "Flow down, cold rivulet, to the sea."
Fatima.
Flower, The.
Flower in the Crannied Wall.
Follow the Gleam.
For I Dipped [*or* Dipt] into the Future.
Fragment: "Flower in the crannied wall."
Frater Ave atque Vale.
Go By.
Godiva.
Green Sussex.
Guinevere, *sel.*
He Hears the Bugle at Killarney.
He Revisits Cambridge.
Hendecasyllabics.
Hesperides, The.
Higher Pantheism, The.
Home They Brought Her Warrior Dead.
Human Cry, The.
Hushing of the Wye, The.
I ran upon life unknowing, without or science or art.
Idyl, An: "Come down, O maid, from yonder mountain height."
Idylls of the King, *sels.*
Ilion, Ilion.
In Love, if Love Be Love.
In Memoriam A. H. H.
In Memoriam—W. G. Ward.
In my youth the growls.

In the Children's Hospital.
In the Garden at Swainston.
In the Valley of Cauteretz.
June Bracken and Heather.
Kraken, The.
Lady Clara Vere de Vere.
Lady Clare.
Lady of Shalott, The.
Lancelot and Elaine, *sel.*
Lancelot and the Grail.
Larger Hope, The.
Last Tournament, The, *sels.*
Leolin and Edith.
Letters, The.
Lilian.
Lincolnshire Shores ("A still salt pool locked in with bars of sand").
Lincolnshire Shores ("As the crest of some slow-arching wave").
Lincolnshire Wolds and Lincolnshire Sea.
Lines: "Here often, when a child, I lay reclined."
Lines on Cambridge of 1830.
Locksley Hall.
Locksley Hall, Sixty Years After.
Lost Love.
Lotos-Eaters, The.
Lucretius.
Lullaby: "Sweet and low, sweet and low."
Mariana.
Mariana in the South.
Marriage Morning.
Maud.
Mechanophilus, *sel.*
Merlin and the Gleam.
Merlin and Vivien.
Merlin's Riddling.
Mermaid, The.
Merman, The.
Midnight.
Miller's Daughter, The.
Milton.
Minnie and Winnie.
Morte d'Arthur.
My Lord and King.
Mystic, The.
Northern Cobbler, The.
Northern Farmer: New Style.
Northern Farmer: Old Style.
Not only with no sense of shame.
November in the Isle of Wight.
Now Sleeps the Crimson Petal.
O Swallow, Swallow, Flying South.
Oak, The.
Ode on the Death of the Duke of Wellington.
Ode Sung at the Opening of the International Exhibition.
Ode to Memory.
Oenone.
Of Old Sat Freedom on the Heights.
Of One Dead.
Olivia.
On a Mourner, *sel.*
On the Jubilee of Queen Victoria, *abr.*
Over the Dark World Flies the Wind.
Owl, The.
Palace of Art, The.
Pallid Thunderstricken Sigh for Gain, The.
Pelleas and Ettarre, *sel.*
Poet, The.
Poets and Their Bibliographies.
Poet's Song, The.
Popular.
Prayer: "More things are wrought by prayer."
Prayer, The: "O living will that share endure."
Prayer: "Pray for my soul. More things are wrought by prayer."
Prayer for the Dead.
Princess, The, *sels.*
Prologue: "Over! the sweet summer closes."
Prologue to General Hamley, *sel.*
Prophecy.
Pure Heart, The.
Recollections of the Arabian Nights.
Reconciliation, The.
Revenge, The.
Ring Out the Old, Ring In the New.
Rizpah.
Roses on the Terrace, The.
Sadness.
Sailor Boy, The.
St. Agnes' Eve.
St. Simeon Stylites.
Sea Dreams, *sel.*
Second Song.
See What a Lovely Shell.
Shell, The.
Shepherd's Song.
Sir Galahad.
Sisters, The.
Sleeping House, The.
Somebody.
Somersby, Lincolnshire; after Leaving the Rectory.
Song: "As thro' the land at eve we went."
Song: "Ask me no more: the moon may draw the sea."
Song: "Come down, O maid, from yonder mountain height."
Song: "Home they brought her warrior dead."
Song: "It is the miller's daughter."
Song: "O, let the solid ground."
Song: "Spirit haunts the year's last hours, A."
Song: "Splendor falls on castle walls, The."
Song: "Tears, idle tears, I know not what they mean."
Song: "Who can say."
Song at the Ruin'd Inn.
Song from "Maud."
Song of Love and Death, The.
Song of the Lotos-Eaters.
Song of the Milkmaid.
Song—the Owl.
Songs from the Princess.
Sonnet: "She took the dappled partridge flecked with blood."
Spirit Haunts the Year's Last Hours, A.
Splendor Falls, The.
Spring ("Dip down upon the northern shore").
Spring ("Now fades the last long streak of snow").
Summer Night.
Supposed Confessions of a Second-rate Sensitive Mind.
Sweet and Low.
Talking Oak, The, *sel.*
Tears, Idle Tears [I Know Not What They Mean].
There Is None like Her.
There Is Sweet Music Here.
Throstle, The.
Thy voice is heard through [*or* thro'] rolling drums.
Tiresias.
Tithonus.
To———: "All good things have not kept aloof."
To———: With the Following Poem.
To Christopher North.
To Edward Fitzgerald.
To E.L., on His Travels in Greece.
To Poesy.
To the Queen ("O loyal to the royal in thyself").
To the Rev. F. D. Maurice.
To Virgil.
Tristram's Song.
Two Voices, The.
Ulysses.
Valedictory.
Vastness.
Vision of Sin, The.
Vivien's Song.
Vivien's Song ("But now the wholesome music of the wood").
Voice by the Cedar Tree, A.
Voyage of Maeldune, The.
Wages.
Walking to the Mail.
What Does Little Birdie Say?
Will Waterproof's Lyrical Monologue.
Window, The; or, The Song of the Wrens, *sel.*
Word, The.
You Ask Me, Why, though [*or* tho'] Ill at Ease.

Tennyson, Charles. *See* **Turner, Charles Tennyson**

Tennyson, Frederick
Blackbird, The.
Glory of Nature, The.
Harvest Home.
Holy Tide, The.
Incident, An.
Iona.
Skylark, The.

Tepfer, Karen G.
Nets on the Andrea Doria, The.

Tepperman, Jean
Going through Changes.
Witch.

Terán, José Y., Jr.
Field's Retention, The.
Javier.
Rapist.
Tugs.
Volleyball Teacher Ends the Game.

Teresa, Saint, of Avila. *See* **Theresa, Saint, of Avila**

Terral, Rufus
Chant Royal from a Copydesk.

Terrell, Myra Burnham
Theodosia Burr.

Terrill, Richard
From.

Terris, Virginia R.
Drinking.

Terry, Ellen
No Funeral Gloom.

Terry, Lucy
Bars Fight, August 28, 1746.

Terry, Reba
Lineage.

Terry, Uriah
Wyoming Massacre, The.

Teschemacher, Edward
Because.

Tessimond, Arthur Seymour John
British, The.
Cats.
Children Look at the Parents, The.
Daydream.
Epitaph on Any Man.
Jamaican Bus Ride.
Middle-aged Conversation.
One Almost Might.

Te-whaka-io-roa
Give Me My Infant Now.

Thacker, Mary Afton
I Found God.

Thackeray, William Makepeace
Age of Wisdom, The.
At the Church Gate.
At the Zoo.
Ballad of Bouillabaisse, The.
Cane-bottomed Chair, The.
Chronicle of the Drum, The, *sel.*
Credo, A.
Crystal Palace, The.
Damages, Two Hundred Pounds.
Dr. Birch and His Young Friends, *sel.*
Due of the Dead, The.
End of the Play, The.
Foreign Literature.
Georges, The (I-IV).
Jeames of Buckley Square.
Jolly Jack.
King of Brentford, The.
King of Brentford's Testament, The, *abr.*

Little Billee.
Mahogany Tree, The.
Mr. Molony's Account of the Ball.
Old Fashioned Fun.
Pendennis, *sel.*
Pocahontas.
Rebecca and Rowena, *sel.*
Ronsard to His Mistress.
Sorrows of Werther.
Speculators, The.
Three Sailors, The.
When Moonlike ore the Hazure Seas.
Willow-Tree, A.

Thalman, Mark
Burial, The.
Summit Lake.

Thanet, Lesbia
In Time of War.

Thatcher, Charles Robert
Look Out Below!

Thatcher, Thomas
Love Letter to Elizabeth Thatcher, A.

Thaxter, Celia (Laighton)
As Happy Dwellers by the Seaside Hear.
August.
Compensation.
Cruise of the *Mystery*, The.
Flowers for the Brave.
Jack Frost.
Little Gustava.
May Morning.
Nikolina.
On Easter Day.
Sandpiper, The.
Seaward.
Song: "We sail toward evening's lonely star."

Thayer, Ernest Lawrence
Casey at the Bat.

Thayer, Louis E.
Hang to Your Grit!

Thayer, Mary Dixon
Prayer, A: "God, is it sinful if I feel."
To Our Lady.
Treasures.
Woman, A.

Thayer, Stephen Henry
Europa.
Poet of Earth.
Waiting Chords, The.

Thayer, William Roscoe ("Paul Hermes")
Last Hunt, The.
Man in Nature.
Violin's Complaint, The.

Thelwall, John
Lines Written at Bridgewater, 27 July 1797, *sel.*
Sonnet: Cell, The.

Theocritus
Countryman's Wooing, A.
Cyclops, The.
Death of Daphnis, The.
Enchantment, The.
Epitaph of Cleonicus.
Epitaph of Hipponax.
Eunica skornde me, when her I would have sweetly kist.
Fishermen, The.
Harvest-Home.
Herdsmen, The.
Idylls, *sels.*
Incantation, The.
Ortho's Epitaph.

Theognis
Enjoyment.
Hope.
Poverty.
To Kurnos.

Theresa [*or* Teresa], Saint, of Avila
Bookmark.
En las Internas Entrañas.
If, Lord, Thy Love for Me Is Strong.
Let Mine Eyes See Thee.
Life Above, the Life on High, The.
Lines Written in Her Breviary.
Poem: "Nothing move thee."
Santa Teresa's Book-Mark.
Shepherd, Shepherd, Hark.
To-Day a Shepherd.

Thérèse, Sister Mary
I Send Our Lady.

Thesen, Sharon
Kirk Lonegren's Home Movie Taking Place Just North of Prince George, with Sound.
Loose Woman Poem.
Mean Drunk Poem.

Thewlis, John
Song of a Happy Rising, The.

Thibaudeau, Colleen
Brown Family, The.
Clock Tower, The.
Green Family, The.
Poem: "I do not want only."

Thich Nhat Hanh
Condemnation.

Thiele, Colin
Bert Schultz.
Tom Farley.

Thiele, Ernest W.
Ludmilla; an Ode on the Occasion of Her Departure from These Shores ("Ludmilla, the Soviet lassie").

Thom, William
Blind Boy's Pranks, The.
Mitherless Bairn, The.
They Speak o' Wiles.

Thomas, Beatrice Llewellyn
To Puck.

Thomas, Charles F., Jr.
Cowboy Up to Date, The.

Thomas, Cordia
Lollypops, The.

Thomas, Donald Michael
Eden.
Smile.

Thomas, Dylan
After the Funeral.
Altarwise by Owl-Light.
Among Those Killed in the Dawn Raid Was a Man Aged One Hundred.
And Death Shall Have No Dominion.
Ballad of the Long-legged Bait.
Before I Knocked and Flesh Let Enter.
Ceremony after a Fire Raid.
Conversation, A.
Conversation of Prayer, The.
Countryman's Return, The.
Do Not Go Gentle into That Good Night.
Ears in the Turrets Hear.
Especially When the October Wind.
Fern Hill.
Force That through the Green Fuse Drives the Flower, The.
Ghost Story.
Hand That Signed the Paper Felled a City, The.
Holy Spring.
Hunchback in the Park, The.
I, in My Intricate Image.
I See the Boys of Summer.
If I Were Tickled by the Rub of Love.
If My Head Hurt a Hair's Foot.
In Country Sleep.
In Memory of Ann Jones.
In My Craft or Sullen Art.
In the White Giant's Thigh.
It is the sinners' dust-tongued bell claps me to churches.
January 1939.
Johnnie Crack and Flossie Snail.
Lament: "When I was a windy boy and a bit."
Light Breaks Where No Sun Shines.
Marriage of a Virgin, The.
Not from This Anger.
O make me a mask and a well to shut from your spies.
October.
On No Work of Words.
On the Marriage of a Virgin.
Out of a War of Wits.
Over Sir John's Hill.
Poem: "Especially when the October wind."
Poem: "Force that through the green fuse drives the flower, The."
Poem: "Process in the weather of the heart, A."
Poem in October.
Poem on His Birthday.
Process in the Weather of the Heart, A.
Refusal to Mourn the Death, by Fire, of a Child in London, A.
Song of the Mischievous Dog, The.
Sonnet: "Altarwise by owl-light in the halfway-house."
Sonnet: "Death is all metaphors, shape in one history."
Spire cranes, The. Its statue is an aviary.
This Bread I Break Was Once the Oat.
Tombstone told when she died, The.
Twenty-four Years.
Under Milk Wood, *sel.*
Vision and Prayer.
We Lying by Seasand.
When All My Five and Country Senses See.
When, like a Running Grave.
Winter's Tale, A.

Thomas, Edith Matilda
Autumn Fashions.
Babushka.
Betrayal of the Rose, The.
Breath of Hampstead Heath.
Christopher of the Shenandoah, A.
Cricket Kept the House, The.
Evoe!
Far Cry to Heaven, A.
Fir-Tree, The.
Frost.
If Still They Live.
In the Lilac-Rain.
Insomnia.
Inverted Torch, The, *sels.*
Little Boy's Vain Regret, A.
Mrs. Kriss Kringle.
Moly.
Mother England.
Mother Who Died Too, The.
Muses, The.
Music.
Patmos.
Ponce de Leon.
Quiet Pilgrim, The.
Reply of Socrates, The.
Soul in the Body, The.
Talking in Their Sleep.
Tears of the Poplars, The.
Tell Me.
Thefts of the Morning.
To Imagination.
To Spain—a Last Word.
Triumph of Forgotten Things, The.
When in the First Great Hour.
Will It Be So?
Winter Sleep.

Thomas, Edward ("Edward Eastaway")
Adlestrop.
After Rain.
And You, Helen.
As the Team's Head-Brass.
Aspens.
Barn, The.
Birds' Nests.
Bright Clouds.
Brook, The.
Cat, A.
Celandine.
Chalk-Pit, The.
Cherry Trees, The.
Clouds That Are So Light, The.
Cock-Crow.
Combe, The.

Cool Tombs.
Cuckoo, The.
Dark Forest, The.
Digging.
Early One Morning.
February Afternoon.
Fifty Faggots.
Gallows, The.
Glory, The.
Good-Night.
Green Roads, The.
Gypsy, The.
Haymaking.
Head and Bottle.
Health.
If I Should Ever by Chance.
In Memoriam (Easter, 1915).
It Rains ("It rains, and nothing stirs within the fence").
Liberty.
Lights Out.
Like the Touch of Rain.
Lob.
Long Small Room, The.
Man and Dog.
Manor Farm, The.
March the 3rd.
Melancholy.
New House, The.
No one cares less than I.
No One So Much as You.
October.
Old Man.
Out in the Dark.
Owl, The.
Path, The.
Penny Whistle, The.
Private, A.
Rain.
Sedge-Warblers.
Sheiling, The.
Sign-Post, The.
Snow.
Some Eyes Condemn.
Sowing.
Sun Used to Shine, The.
Swedes.
Tale, A.
Tall Nettles.
Tears.
Thaw.
There Was a Time.
There's Nothing like the Sun.
To-Night.
Trumpet, The.
Two Houses.
Two Pewits.
Under the Woods.
Unknown, The.
Unknown Bird, The.
What Shall I Give?
When First.
Will You Come?
Wind and Mist.

Thomas, Evan
To the Noble Woman of Llanarth Hall.

Thomas, Frederick William
Song: " 'Tis said that absence conquers love!"

Thomas, Gilbert
Cup of Happiness, The.
Invocation: "There is no balm on earth."
Ploughman, The.
Red Sky at Morning.
Unseen Bridge, The.

Thomas, J. R. *and* **C. N. Elliot.** *See* **Elliot, C. W.** *and* **J. R. Thomas**

Thomas, Jim
Dream Fishing.
Getting Loaded.
Spring Hawks.
Sunday Crappies.

Thomas, John
Last Frontier, The.

Thomas, Joyce Carol
Church Poem.
I Know a Lady.
MJQ, The.
Poem for Otis Redding.
Where Is the Black Community?

Thomas, Laurence W.
Etudes.

Thomas, Lorenzo
Onion Bucket.
Subway Witnesses, The.

Thomas, Louisa Carroll
What Is Charm?

Thomas, Richard W.
Amen.
Just Making It.
Life after Death.
Martyrdom.
Riots and Rituals.
To the New Annex to the Detroit County Jail.
Worker, The.

Thomas, Ronald Stuart
After Jericho.
Alpine.
Aside.
At It.
Blackbird Singing, A.
Country Clergy, The.
Day in Autumn, A.
Enigma.
Farm Child.
Hand, The.
Here.
Hill Farmer Speaks, The.
In a Country Church.
Invasion on the Farm.
January.
Lore.
Madrigal: "Your love is dead, lady, your love is dead."
Maker, The.
On a Line in Sandburg.
On the Farm.
One Furrow, The.
Over.
Petition.
Pisces.
Poetry for Supper.
Porch, The.
Postscript.
Selah.
Self-Portrait.
Son, The.
Strangers.
Survivor, The.
They.
Too Late.
Welcome.
Welsh Landscape.
Welshman to Any Tourist, A.
Woman, The.

Thomas, Rosemary
Between Two Worlds.
East River.

Thomas à Kempis
Imitation of Christ, *sels.*
Man Proposes.
Of Love of Silence and of Solitude.

Thomas Aquinas, Saint
Hymn: "Sing, my tongue, the Saviour's glory."
Word went forth, The.

Thomas More, Saint. *See* **More; Sir Thomas**

Thomas of Celano
Dies Irae.

Thomas of Erceldoune
Sir Tristrem, *sel., at.*
Tristrem and the Hunters., *at.*

Thomas of Hales
Love-Song, A, *sel.*
Where Is Paris and Heleyne [*or* Helene]?

Thompson, A. R.
Looking Down a Hill.

Thompson, Alexander R.
Wayfarers in the Wilderness, *with music.*

Thompson, Benjamin
On a Fortification at Boston Begun by Women.

Thompson, Clara Ann
His Answer.
Mrs. Johnson Objects.

Thompson, D'Arcy Wentworth
Crazy Arithmetic.
Funny Old Man and His Wife, The, *at.*
Poor Dear Grandpapa.
That Little Black Cat.
Two Magpies Sat on a Garden Rail.
Very Odd Fish, A.

Thompson, Donald
On the Relative Merit of Friend and Foe, Being Dead.

Thompson, Dorothy Brown
Arbor Day.
Autosonic Door.
Boy Washington, The.
Continental Crossing.
Fe-Fi-Fo-Fum, *sel.*
Getting Back.
Good Will to Men—Christmas Greetings in Six Languages.
I Like Housecleaning.
Lemonade Stand.
Maps.
Our House.
Pony Express, The.
This Is Halloween.

Thompson, Dunstan
Articles of War.
In All the Argosy of Your Bright Hair.
Knight of Ghosts and Shadows, A.
Largo.
Lay of the Battle of Tombland, The.
Moment of the Rose, The.
Nor Mars His Sword.
Ovid on the Dacian Coast.
This Loneliness for You Is like the Wound.

Thompson, Earle
Corral, The.
Mythology.
Song: "Woman sits on her porch."
Winter Count of Sean Spotted Wolf.
Woman Made of Stars.

Thompson, Edith Osborne
Monkeys, The.

Thompson, Edward
Humble Wish, An; off Porto-Sancto, March 29, 1779, *sel.*
Indian Maid, The; Demararie, Oct. 27, 1781.
To Emma, Extempore; Hyaena, off Gambia, June 4, 1779.

Thompson, Francis
After Woman, The.
All Flesh.
All's Vast.
Any Saint, *abr.*
Arab Love-Song, An.
Assumpta Maria.
At Lord's.
Child's Prayer, A.
Contemplation.
Correlated Greatness.
Counsel of Moderation, A.
Daisy.
Envoy: "Go, songs, for ended is our brief, sweet play."
Epilogue: "Heaven, which man's generations draws."
Ex Ore Infantium.
Fallen Yew, A.
From the Night of Forebeing.
Go, Songs.
Grace of the Way, *sel.*
Heart, The, *sels.*
Hound of Heaven, The.

Judgment in Heaven, A, *sel.*
Kingdom of God, The.
Lilium [*or* Lillium] Regis.
Lines for a Drawing of Our Lady of the Night.
May Burden, A.
Messages.
Mistress of Vision, The.
Ode to the Setting Sun.
Poppy, The.
Sister Songs, *sels.*
Sun, The.
To a Snowflake.
To Daisies.
To My Friend.
To Olivia.
Veteran of Heaven, The.
We Poets Speak.

Thompson, H. S.
Lilly Dale, *with music.*

Thompson, Irene
Rainy Nights.

Thompson, James W.
Constant Labor, A.
Greek Room, The.
Plight, The.
Spawn of Slums, The.
Yellow Bird, The.
You Are Alms.

Thompson, Joanna
Funeral.
Gone.

Thompson, John
Adventurers, The.
Bread Hot from the Oven, The.
Homecoming.
Letter to a Friend.
Now You Have Burned.
Onion, The.

Thompson, John, Jr.
Birthday Poem, November 4th.
Love for Patsy, A.

Thompson, John Randolph
Lee to the Rear.
Obsequies of Stuart.

Thompson, John Reuben
Ashby.
Burial of Latané, The.
Music in Camp.
On to Richmond.

Thompson, Larry
Black Is Best.

Thompson, Leslie
There Are So Many Ways of Going Places.

Thompson, Leslie P.
Song of Satisfaction on Completing an Overhauling of Fishing Tackle, A.

Thompson, Lulu E.
In Hardin County, 1809.

Thompson, Maurice
Ballad of Chickamauga, The.
Creole Slave-Song, A.
Early Bluebird, An.
Flight Shot, A.
Lincoln's Grave, *sel.*
Lion's Cub, The.
Prelude, A: "Spirit that moves the sap in spring."
Prophecy, A.
Wild Honey.
Written on a Fly-Leaf of Theocritus.

Thompson, Paul
Golden Stallion, The.

Thompson, Phyllis
Fairy Tale, A.
Wind of the Cliff Ka Hea, The.

Thompson, Raymond
Death may leap on a sunny day.
I Go to Whiskey Bars.
Journey.
North Clark Street.
Who Needs Charlie Manson?

Thompson, Samuel
April.
To a Hedgehog.

Thompson, Vance
Linen Bands.
Symbols.

Thompson, Will Henry
High Tide at Gettysburg, The.

Thompson, William
Happy Life, The, *sel.*

Thomson, Claire Aven
Tranquil Sea.

Thomson, Edward William
Aspiration.
Canadian Rossignol, The.

Thomson, James (1700–48)
Approach of Winter.
Autumn.
Autumnal Moon, The.
Birds in Spring.
Britannia, *sel.*
Britannia's Empire.
British Commerce.
Castle of Indolence, The, *sels.*
Enchanted Ground.
Finis.
For ever, Fortune, wilt thou prove. To Fortune.
Frost at Night.
Happy Britannia.
Hymn on Solitude.
Hymn on the Seasons, A.
Indifference to Fortune.
Land of Indolence, The.
Lavinia.
Liberty, *sel.*
Love of Nature.
Moonlight in Autumn.
Ode: "Tell me, thou soul of her I love."
On the Death of a Particular Friend.
On the Death of Mr. William Aikman the Painter, *sel.*
Praise of Industry, The.
Rule, Britannia!
Sea-Birds.
Seasons, The, *sels.*
Song: "One day the god of fond desire."
Sons of Indolence.
Spring.
Spring Flowers.
Storm, The.
Summer.
Summer Evening and Night.
Summer Morning.
To Amanda.
To Fortune.
To the Memory of Sir Isaac Newton, *sel.*
To the Reverend Mr. Murdoch.
Verses Occasioned by the Death of Dr. Aikman.
Winter.
Winter Night, A.
Winter Scene, A.
Witching Song, A.
Wondrous Show, A.

Thomson, James (1700–48) *and* **David Mallet**
Alfred, a Masque, *sel.*

Thomson, James (1834–82; "B.V." *or* **"Bysshe Vanolis")**
Art.
As I Came Through the Desert.
Bridge, The.
City, The.
City of Dreadful Night, The, *abr.*
City's Queen, The.
E. B. B.
Gifts.
In the Room.
In the Train.
Midsummer Courtship.
Once in a Saintly Passion.
Proem: "Lo, thus, as prostrate, 'In the dust I write.'l"
Requiem, A: "Thou hast lived in pain and woe."
Song: "Let my voice ring out and over the earth."
Song: "Like violets pale i' the Spring o' the year."
Song: "My love is the flaming sword."
Sunday at Hampstead, *sel.*
Sunday up the River, *sels.*
To Our Ladies of Death.
Vanity.
Vine, The.
William Blake.

Thomson, Mary A.
O King of Saints, We Give Thee Praise and Glory, *with music.*
O Sion, Haste, Thy Mission High Fulfilling, *with music.*

Thoreau, Henry David
All Things Are Current Found.
Among the Worst of Men That Ever Lived.
At Midnight's Hour I Raised My Head.
Atlantides, The.
Between the Traveller and the Setting Sun.
Conscience.
Epitaph on an Engraver.
Epitaph on the World.
Fall of the Leaf, The.
Fisher's Boy, The.
For Though the Caves Were Rabbited.
Forever in My Dream and in My Morning Thought.
Great Adventure, The.
Great Friend.
Great God, I Ask Thee for No Meaner Pelf.
Haze.
I Am a Parcel of Vain Strivings Tied.
I Am the Little Irish Boy.
I Was Born upon Thy Bank, River.
I Was Made Erect and Lone.
I'm Thankful That My Life Doth Not Deceive.
Indeed Indeed, I Cannot Tell.
Independence.
Inspiration.
Inward Morning, The.
Lately, Alas, I Knew a Gentle Boy.
Love.
Love Equals Swift and Slow.
Low-anchored Cloud.
Men Say They Know Many Things.
Mist.
Moon Now Rises [to Her Absolute Rule], The.
My Books I'd Fain Cast Off, I Cannot Read.
My Boots.
My Prayer.
Nature.
Old Marlborough Road, The.
On the Sun Coming Out in the Afternoon.
Our Country.
Pray to What Earth Does This Sweet Cold Belong.
Railroad, The.
River Swelleth More and More, The.
Smoke.
Tall Ambrosia.
This is my Carnac, whose unmeasured dome.
Though All the Fates Should Prove Unkind.
To a Marsh Hawk in Spring.
To the Maiden in the East.
To the Mountains.
Walden, *sel.*
Week on the Concord and Merrimack Rivers, A, *sels.*
What's the Railroad to Me?
Who Sleeps by Day and Walks by Night.
Winter Memories.

Thorley, Wilfrid
Buttercups.
Chant for Reapers.
Hansom Cabbies.
Happy Sheep, The.
Norse Sailor's Joy.

Of a Spider.
Thornbury, George Walter
Cavalier's Escape, The.
Court Historian, The.
Jester's Sermon, The.
La Tricoteuse.
Pompadour, The.
Sally from Coventry, The.
Three Troopers, The.
Thorne, Cyril Morton
To My Unborn Son.
Thornton, James
She May Have Seen Better Days, *with music.*
Streets of Cairo; or, The Poor Little Country Maid, *with music.*
When You Were Sweet Sixteen.
Thorold Rogers, J. E.
Here X. lies dead, but God's forgiving.
On a Distinguished Politician.
On the Historians Freeman and Stubbs.
Suggestion Made by the Posters of the *Globe,* A.
Upon the man who's buried here.
Vulgar Error, A.
Thorp, N. Howard
Billy the Kid or William H. Bonney.
Thorpe, Dwayne
Gathering, The.
Rooftop Winter.
Thorpe, Rose Hartwick
Curfew Must Not Ring Tonight.
Thrale, Hester Lynch
Three Warnings, The.
Throne, Marilyn
What She Wished.
Thurber, James
Further Fables for Our Time, *sel.*
Morals.
Thurlow, Edward, 2nd Baron. *See* **Hovell-Thurlow, Edward, 2nd Baron Thurlow**
Thurman, Judith
Lumps.
Mare.
Zebra.
Thurston, Harry
March Sound.
Thwaite, Anthony
Ali Ben Shufti.
At Birth.
At Dunwich.
Child Crying.
Looking On.
Manhood End.
Mr. Cooper.
Pond, The.
Rites for a Demagogue.
Sunday Afternoons.
Thwaites, Michael
Thermopylae.
Thynne, Francis
Ingratitude.
Tibble, Anne
Trials of a Tourist.
Tibullus, Albius
Dicamus Bona Verba.
Odes, *sels.*
Pastoral Elegy, A.
Tichborne [*or* Tichbourne], Chidiock
Elegy: "My prime of youth is but a frost of cares."
Lament the Night before His Execution, A.
Retrospect.
Written on the Eve of Execution.
Tichy, Susan
Hours, The.
Identity Card.
In an Arab Town.
Irrigation.
Tick, Edward
Kandinsky: "Improvisation No. 27."
To My Wife Asleep.
Tickell, Thomas
Colin and Lucy.
Fairies.
Kensington Garden, *sel.*
Ode Inscribed to the Earl of Sunderland at Windsor, An.
To the Earl of Warwick on the Death of Mr. Addison.
Ticknor, Francis Orrery [*or* Orray]
Albert Sidney Johnston.
Battle Ballad, A.
Little Giffen.
"Our Left."
Song for the Asking, A.
Virginians of the Valley, The.
Tieck, Johann Ludwig
Autumn Song.
Tiemer-Wille, Gertrude
Repast.
Tiempo, César (Israel Zierlin)
Harangue on the Death of Hayyim Nahman Bialik.
I Tell of Another Young Death.
Jewish Cemetery, The.
Tierney, Joseph Paul
Donne Redone.
Tietjens, Eunice
April.
Bacchante to Her Babe, The.
Completion.
Drug Clerk, The.
Fun with Fishing.
Great Man, The.
Imprisoned.
Most-Sacred Mountain, The.
Moving.
My Mother's House.
On the Height.
Parting after a Quarrel.
Pioneer Woman—in the North Country, The.
Psalm to My Beloved.
To My Friend, Grown Famous.
Tietz, Stephen
Pinball Queen of South Illinois St., The.
Tifft, Ellen
Nuclear Land.
Tilden, Stephen
Braddock's Fate, with an Incitement to Revenge.
British Lyon Roused, The.
O Heaven Indulge, *with music.*
Song of Braddock's Men, The.
Tilghman, Zoe A.
Alibi.
Wind Song.
Tillam, Thomas
Uppon the First Sight of New England, June 29, 1638.
Tiller, Terence
Bathers.
End of the Story, The.
Image in a Lilac Tree.
Killed in Action.
No Time.
Prothalamion.
Reading a Medal.
Street Performers, 1851.
Vase, The.
Tillett, Wilbur Fisk
Incarnate Love.
My Father Knows.
Tilley, Lucy Evangeline
When Even Cometh On.
Tillinghast, David
Women Hoping for Rain.
Tillinghast, Richard
Hearing of the End of the War.
Knife, The.
Our Flag Was Still There.
Return.
Shooting Ducks in South Louisiana.
Summer Rain.
Tillman, Charlie D.
Lost after All.
Tillyard, Aelfrida
Invitation au Festin.
Letter from Ealing Broadway Station, A.
Tilney, Charles
Cobbler's Song, The, *at.*
Locrine, *sel, at.*
Tilton, Theodore
Coeur de Lion to Berengaria.
Even This Shall Pass Away.
Flight from the Convent, The.
God Save the Nation.
Great Bell Roland, The.
King's Ring, The.
Sir Marmaduke's Musings.
Timrod, Henry
At Magnolia Cemetery.
Carolina.
Charleston.
Cotton Boll, The.
Cry to Arms, A.
Ethnogenesis.
Faint Falls the Gentle Voice, *with music.*
Most Men Know Love But as a Part of Life.
Ode: "Sleep sweetly in your humble graves."
Ode Sung on the Occasion of Decorating the Graves of the Confederate Dead.
Ode to the Confederate Dead [in Magnolia Cemetery].
Serenade: "Hide, happy damask, from the stars."
Sonnet: "Most men know love but as a part of life."
Spring.
Trifle, A.
Unknown Dead, The.
Ting, Walasse
Pepsi Generation.
Tio, Elsa
I am furious with myself.
Toplady, Thomas
Above the Hills of Time.
Grace, A.
Tippett, James Sterling
Autumn Woods.
Building a Skyscraper.
Busy Carpenters.
Ducks at Dawn.
Elevated Train, The.
Engine.
Familiar Friends.
Ferry-Boats.
Freight Boats.
George Washington.
Hang Out the Flags.
Hens, The.
Old Log House.
Park, The.
"Sh."
Sleet Storm.
Sunning.
Trains.
Trucks.
Tugs.
Up in the Air.
Tipple, E. H.
Hot Weather in the Plains—India.
Tisdale, Charles P. R.
My Childhood's Bedroom.
Origins of Escape, The.
Titheradge, Peter
New Improved Sonnet XVIII.
Titherington, Richard Handfield
Faithful unto Death.
Tobias, Ruby Weyburn
True Apostolate, The.
Tobin, James Edward
Madonna of the Exiles.
Tocqueville, Alexis de
America Is Great Because, *at.*
Todachine, Mike
Poem: "You can look into my face."

Todd, Ruthven
Joan Miró ("After that war, when death had gone away").
Joan Miró ("Once there were peasant pots and a dry brown hare").
Lonely Month, The.
Mantelpiece of Shells, A.
Paul Klee.
Personal History; for My Son.
Poem: "I walk at dawn across the hollow hills."
Six Winters.
To a Very Beautiful Lady.
Upon This Rock.
Various Ends.
Watching You Walk.
Todhunter, John
Aghadoe.
Banshee, The.
Black Knight, The.
Maureen.
O Mighty, Melancholy Wind.
Song: "Bring from the craggy haunts of birch and pine."
Utter Passion Uttered Utterly, An.
Toerien, Barend
Absent Daughter.
Campi Flegrei.
Firmament Displays on High, The.
Quatrain: "My bloodstream chokes on gall and spleen."
Youth.
Toffler, Alvin
League of Selves, The.
Tofte, Robert
Alba, *sel.*
Laura, *sel.*
Love's Labour Lost.
Tohe, Laura
At Mexican Springs.
Cat or Stomp.
Female Rain.
Male Rain.
Shooting, The.
To Shimá Sání.
Tohee, Mah-do-ge
Agnes.
Indian America.
Untitled.
Tolkien, John Ronald Renel
Dragon's Hoard, The.
Goblin Feet.
Hobbit, The, *sel.*
Mewlips, The.
Old Walking Song, The.
Oliphaunt.
Roads Go Ever Ever On.
Shadow-Bride.
Stone Troll, The.
Tollefsen, Astrid
Toulouse Lautrec.
Workaday Morning.
Toller, Ernst
Book I Held Grew Cold, The.
Corpses in the Wood.
O Heavy Step of Slow Monotony.
O Master Masons.
O My Swallows!
One Who Struggles, The.
To the Mothers.
Tollerud, Jim
Bird of Power.
Buzz.
Earth.
Elementary.
Eye of God.
Rainier.
Sunrise.
Thirsty Island.
Week-Seek.
Tollet, Elizabeth
Hypatia, *sel.*
Winter Song.
Tolnay, Thomas
Basement Watch, The.
Tolson, Melvin Beaunearus
African China.
Birth of John Henry, The.
Dark Symphony.
Do.
Freemon Hawthorne.
Harlem Gallery,
Lamda.
Legend of Versailles, A.
Libretto for the Republic of Liberia, *sel.*
On the Founding of Liberia.
PSI.
Peg Leg Snelson.
Satchmo.
Sea-Turtle and the Shark, The.
Sootie Joe.
Tomioka Taeko
Life Story.
Please Say Something.
Tomkis, Thomas
Gordion Knot, The.
Lingua, *sel.*
Tomlinson, Charles
At Barstow.
At Delft.
Cavern, The.
Chances of Rhyme, The.
Charlotte Corday.
Chestnut Avenue at Alton House, The.
Civilities of Lamplight.
Crane, The.
Death in the Desert, A.
Death of Will, The.
Descartes and the Stove.
Distinction.
Door, The.
Dream, A.
Farewell to Van Gogh.
Fiascherino.
Hand at Callow Hill Farm, The.
How Still the Hawk.
Icos.
In Arden.
In Defense of Metaphysics.
Jam Trap, The.
Las Trampas U. S. A.
Le Musée Imaginaire.
MacDuff.
Meditation on John Constable, A.
Mr. Brodsky.
More Foreign Cities.
Observation of Facts.
Ode to Arnold Schoenberg.
On the Hall at Stowey.
Oxen: Ploughing at Fiesole.
Paring the Apple.
Picture of J. T. in a Prospect of Stone, The.
Poem: "Upended, it crouches on broken limbs."
Return to Hinton.
Ruin, The.
Swimming Chenango Lake.
Through Binoculars.
Tramontana at Lerici.
Two Views of Two Ghost Towns.
Veneris Venefica Agrestis.
Winter Encounters.
Word in Edgeways, A.
Tompson, Benjamin
Chelmsfords Fate.
Edmund Davie 1682; Annagram.
Marlburyes Fate.
New-Englands Crisis.
Seaconk or Rehoboths Fate.
Seaconk Plain Engagement.
Supplement, A.
To My Honoured Patron Humphery Davie.
Town Called Providence, Its Fate, The.
Tomson, Graham R." *See* **Watson, Rosamund Marriott**
Tonks, Rosemary
Farewell to Kurdistan.
Story of a Hotel Room.
Tonna, Charlotte Elizabeth
Maiden City, The.
Tooker, Lewis Frank
"He Bringeth Them unto Their Desired Haven."
His Quest.
Homeward Bound.
Last Fight, The.
Old Conservative, The.
Sea-King, The.
Sleep.
Toomer, Jean
At Sea.
Banking Coal.
Beehive.
Blue Meridian, The.
Brown River, Smile.
Cotton Song.
Evening Song.
Face.
Five Vignettes.
Georgia Dusk.
Hair—/ silver-gray. Face.
Harvest Song.
Her Lips Are Copper Wire.
Lost Dancer, The.
November Cotton Flower.
Portrait in Georgia.
Reapers.
Song of the Son.
Toplady, Augustus Montague
Ah! Give Me, Lord, the Single Eye.
"Deathless Principle, Arise."
Happiness Found, *sel.*
Living and Dying Prayer for the Holiest Believer in the World, A.
Lord! It Is Not Life to Live.
Prayer, Living and Dying, A.
Rock of Ages.
Torain, Joseph
Tracks.
Torberg, Friedrich
Amalek.
Seder, 1944.
Törel, Ali Sedat Hilmi
My Indian Girl.
Nirvana.
Torgerson, Eric
One Year Later.
Torna
Lament for Corc and Niall of the Nine Hostages, *at.*
Tornai, József
Mr. T. S. Eliot Cooking Pasta.
Torrence, Ridgely
Adam's Dying.
Adam's Song of the Visible World.
Bird and the Tree, The.
Conclusion of the Whole Matter, The.
Evensong.
Eye-Witness.
House of a Hundred Lights, The, *sel.*
Legend.
Santa Barbara Beach.
Singers in a Cloud, The.
Son, The.
Tóth, Judit
Dead Embryos.
Remembering.
Southeast Ramparts of the Seine, The.
To the Newborn.
Wildfire.
"Totius" (J. D. Du Toit)
Forgive and Forget.
Touré, Askia Muhammad
Floodtide.
JuJu.
Tauhid.
Tourneur, Cyril
Atheist's Tragedy, The, *sels.*

Awake, oh Heaven, for (lo) the heavens conspire.
Epitaph on a Soldier.
Revenger's Tragedy, The, *sels.*
Soldier's Death, A.
Toussaint L'Ouverture, Isaac
Farewell: "Shores of my native land."
Towne, Anthony
Dead of Winter.
Towne, Charles Hanson
Around the Corner ("Around the corner I have a friend").
At Nightfall.
Best Road of All, The.
City Roofs.
Easter Canticle, An.
In Summer.
Messed Damozel, The.
Of One Self-slain.
Prayer for the Old Courage, A.
Quiet Singer, The.
Silence.
Song: "I saw the day's white rapture."
Song at Easter, A.
Time-Clock, The.
Townsend, Aurelian. *See* **Townshend, Aurelian**
Townsend, Charles
Lake Poets, The.
On the Lake Poets.
Townsend, Emily
Fish.
Townsend, F. H.
State the alternative preferred.
To the Cuckoo.
Townsend, George Alfred
Army Correspondent's Last Ride.
In Rama.
Townsend, Joanne
With Due Deference to Thomas Wolfe.
Townsend, Mary Ashley ("Xariffa")
At Set of Sun.
Creed.
Dead Singer, The.
Down the Bayou.
Embryo.
Georgia Volunteer, A.
Her Horoscope.
Reserve.
Virtuosa.
Townshend [*or* Townsend], Aurelian
Come Not to Me for Scarfs.
Constant Lover, The.
Dialogue betwixt Time and a Pilgrime [*or* Pilgrim], A.
Elegie Made by Mr. Aurelian Townshend in Remembrance of the Ladie Venetia Digby, An.
Let Not Thy Beauty.
Loves Victory.
Paradox, A.
Pure Simple Love.
Song: "Though regions farr devided."
Though Regions Far Divided.
To the Countesse of Salisbury.
To the Lady May.
Upon Kinde and True Love.
Youth and Beauty.
Townson, Hazel
Dirge: "Just at the blackest bit of my depression."
Not Late Enough.
Tracy, Neil
I Doubt a Lovely Thing Is Dead.
Traherne, Thomas
Amendment.
Approach, The.
Childhood.
Christendom.
Christian Ethics, *sels.*
Consummation.
Contentment.
Desire.
Eden.
For Man to Act.
Hosanna.
Innocence.
Insatiableness.
Life of Sabbaths here beneath, A!
Love.
Mankind Is Sick.
My Spirit.
News.
On Christmas Day.
On Leaping over the Moon.
Poverty.
Preparative, The.
Rapture, The.
Recovery, The.
Right Apprehension.
Salutation, The.
Serious and a Curious Night-Meditation, A.
Shadows in the Water.
Sin!/ O only fatal Woe.
Solitude.
Thanksgiving for the Body.
Thanksgivings for the Beauty of His Providence.
Third Century, The, *sels.*
To the Same Purpos[e].
To Walk Abroad.
Vision, The.
Walking.
Wonder.
Traill, Henry Duff
After Dilettante Concetti.
Drawing-Room Ballad, A.
Puss and the Boots, The, *sel.*
Vers de Société.
Tranströmer, Tomas
Allegro.
Man Awakened by a Song above His Roof, The.
Open and Closed Space.
Schubertiana.
Track.
Tranter, John
Crying in Early Infancy, *sels.*
Death Circus, The.
Trapnell, Edna Valentine
Fiddler, The.
Trapp, Joseph
Epigram: "King George, observing with judicious eyes."
Trask, Katrina (Kate Nichols Trask)
Aidenn.
At Last.
Love.
Sorrow.
Traubel, Horace Logo
Chants Communal, *sel.*
Epicedium.
How Are You, Dear World, This Morning?
I Served in a Great Cause.
If All the Voices of Men.
What Can I Do?
Trawick, Leonard
Feeling for Fish.
Traxler, Patricia
Waking in Nice.
Treasone, Grace
Life.
Tree, Iris
And afterwards, when honour has made good.
Of all who died in silence far away.
To My Father.
You Preach to Me of Laws.
Treece, Henry
Ballad: "Oh, come my joy, my soldier boy."
Birdwatcher.
Crimson Cherry Tree, The.
Dyke-Builder, The.
Haunted Garden, The.
Heart's Wild Geese, The.
Horror.
In the Beginning Was the Bird.
In the Third Year of War.
Magic Wood, The.
Poem: "Death walks through the mind's dark woods."
Poem: "In the dark caverns of the night."
Poem: "Through the dark aisles of the wood."
Prayer in Time of War.
That Summer.
Waiting Watchers, The.
Walking at Night.
Trefethen, Florence
Slipping Out of Intensive Care.
Tregonning, Charley
Cousin Jack Song.
Treinin, Avner
Cage, The.
Deserted Shrine.
Salmon Cycle.
Tremayne, Sydney
Discomfort in High Places.
Galloway Shore, The.
Moses.
North of Berwick.
Tremblay, Bill
Court We Live On, The.
Tremblay, Gail
Crow Voices.
Trench, Herbert
Charge, A.
Come, Let Us Make Love Deathless.
I Heard a Soldier.
I Seek Thee in the Heart Alone.
Jean Richepin's Song.
She Comes Not When Noon Is on the Roses.
To Arolilia, *sel.*
What Bids Me Leave.
Trench, Richard Chenevix
Century of Couplets, A, *sel.*
Gibraltar.
God Our Refuge.
If There Had Anywhere Appeared.
Kingdom of God, The.
Lord, Many Times.
Prayer: "Lord, what a change within us one short hour."
Prevailing Prayer.
Recollections of Burgos.
Retirement.
Some Murmur When Their Sky Is Clear.
Sonnet: "Lord, what a change within us one short hour."
Sonnet: "Open wound which has been healed anew, An."
Sonnet in a Pass of Bavaria.
Trent, Lucia (Mrs. Ralph Cheney)
Architects of Dream.
Armistice Day.
Bread of Brotherhood.
Dreamers Cry Their Dream, The.
From Beyond.
It Is Not Too Late.
Mary's Son.
Song for Tomorrow.
These Are My People.
Trent, Lucia *and* Ralph Cheyney
Toward a True Peace.
Trevathan, Charles E.
Bully Song, The, *with music.*
Trevisa, John
Prologue to a Translation.
Trías, Arturo
Act of Faith.
Ars Poetica.
This Shirt.
Triem, Eve
Bordello, Revisited.
Gardens Are All My Heart.
Gerda, My Husband's Wife.
Misdemeanor.
Trifilio, Jim
Hokkaido.

Trifonov, Gennady
For three swift days.
Triggs, Jeffery Alan
Man on Move Despite Failures.
Trimpi, Alison A.
Skull in the Desert, The.
Trimpi, W. Wesley
Lines for a Wedding Gift.
Oedipus to the Oracle.
On a Bas-Relief.
To Giotto.
Tripp, John
On My Fortieth Birthday.
Tropp, Stephen
My Wife Is My Shirt.
Trott, Harlan
Out from Gloucester.
Trott, Norman L.
No Time for God.
Trott, Perient
Negro Spiritual.
Trotter, Alys Fane
Hospital Visitor, The.
Trotter, Bernard Freeman
Poplars, The.
"Troubadour"
Law of Averages, The.
Reversible Metaphor, The.
Troubetzkoy, Ulrich
Christmas Lullaby.
Out of the Wilderness.
Troupe, Quincy
Day Duke Raised, The.
Dirge: "It is the endless dance of the dead."
For Malcolm Who Walks in the Eyes of Our Children.
In Texas Grass.
Old People Speak of Death, The.
Poem for Friends.
Sense of Coolness, A.
South African Bloodstone.
These Crossings, These Words.
Transformation.
White Weekend.
Trowbridge, John Townsend
At Sea.
Columbus at the Convent.
Cup, The.
Darius Green and His Flying-Machine.
Evening at the Farm.
Evening on the Farm.
Filling an Order.
Lincoln.
Midsummer.
Midwinter.
Pewee, The.
Recollections of "Lalla Rookh."
Vagabonds, The.
Widow Brown's Christmas.
Troy, Grace E.
I Would Not Ask.
Trials.
Truax, Hawley
Half.
Morning, Noon, And.
Trudell, Dennis
Hotel in Paris.
Jump Shooter, The.
Truesdale, C. W.
Amanda, Playing.
Little Roach Poem.
Trumbull, Annie Eliot
To O. S. C.
Trumbull, John
Amorous Temper, An.
Dick Hairbrain Learns the Social Graces.
Harriet Simper Has Her Day.
M'Fingal, *sels.*
Progress of Dulness, The, *sels.*
Prospect of the Future Glory of America.
Tom Brainless as Student and Preacher.
Truth, Sojourner
Ain't I a Woman?
Trypanis, Constantine A.
Four Lovely Sisters ("Four lovely spinsters, sisters to a king").
To Theon from His Son Theon.
Ts'ai Yen
Eighteen Verses Sung to a Tatar Reed Whistle, *sels.*
Tsaloumas, Dimitris
Rhapsody of Old Men, A, *sel.*
Ts'ao Sung
Protest in the Sixth Year of Ch'ien Fu, A.
War Year, The.
Tso Ssu
Scholar in the Narrow Street, The.
Tsuda, Kiyoko
To be a mistress.
Tsuda, Margaret
Commitment in a City.
Hard Questions.
Ts'uei T'u
On New Year's Eve.
Tsui, Kitty
Chinatown Talking Story.
It's in the Name.
Tsuru
Willows in the Snow.
Tsvetayeva, Marina
Ars.
Attempt at Jealousy, An.
I'd like to live with you.
Insomnia, *sel.*
Poem of the End, *sels.*
We are keeping an eye on the girls, so that the kvass.
We Shall Not Escape Hell.
Tucker, F. Bland
All Praise to Thee, *with music.*
Our Father, by Whose Name, *with music.*
Tucker, St. George
Cynic, The.
Days of My Youth.
Discontented Student, The.
Judge with the Sore Rump, The.
Tuckerman, Frederick Goddard
Cricket, The.
Elegy in Six Sonnets.
Hast thou seen reversed the prophet's miracle.
Here, where the red man swept the leaves away.
Not the round natural world, not the deep mind.
November.
Put off thy bark from shore, though near the night.
Question, The.
Refrigerium.
Roll On, Sad World!
Sonnet: "And change with hurried hand has swept these scenes."
Sonnet: "And faces, forms and phantoms, numbered not."
Sonnet: "And me my winter's task is drawing over."
Sonnet: "Breeze is sharp, the sky is hard and blue, The."
Sonnet: "But unto him came swift calamity."
Sonnet: "But we are set to strive to make our mark."
Sonnet: "By this low fire I often sit to woo."
Sonnet: "Companions were we in the grove and glen!"
Sonnet: "Even as a lover, dreaming, unaware."
Sonnet: "For Nature daily through her grand design."
Sonnet: "Gertrude and Gulielma, sister-twins."
Sonnet: "His heart was in his garden; but his brain."
Sonnet: "How most unworthy, echoing in mine ears."
Sonnet: Morning comes, The; not slow, with reddening gold."
Sonnet: "My Anna! though thine earthly steps are done."
Sonnet: "My Anna! When for her my head was bowed."
Sonnet: "O hard endeavor, to blend in with these."
Sonnet: "Oh for the face and footstep!—Woods and shores!"
Sonnet: "One still dark night, I sat alone and wrote."
Sonnet: "Perhaps a dream; yet surely truth has beamed."
Sonnet: "Roll on, sad world! Not Mercury or Mars."
Sonnet: "Still pressing through these weeping solitudes."
Sonnet: "Thy baby, too, the child that was to be."
Sonnet: "Under the mountain, as when first I knew."
Sonnets, *sels.*
Under the Locust Blossoms.
Upper chamber in a darkened house, An.
Yes: though the brine may from the desert deep.
Tuckerman, Henry Theodore
Washington's Statue.
Tuéni, Nadia
More distant than the dead sea.
Nothing but a man.
Would you come back if I said the earth.
Tu Fu
Clear after Rain.
Emperor, The.
Excursion, The.
Jade Flower Palace.
Little Rain, The.
Moon Festival.
Night in the House by the River.
Night Thoughts while Travelling.
Overnight in the Apartment by the River.
Road to Pengya, The.
White Horse, The.
Willow, The.
Written on the Wall at Chang's Hermitage.
Tu-kehu
Oh, how my love/ With a whirling power.
Tu-kehu *and* **Wetea**
O beautiful calm.
Tullar, Grant Colfax
As Thy Days.
Tulloch, Bill
Beinn A' Ghlo.
NN 616410.
Tunstall, Virginia Lyne
Evening on the Harbor.
Spinster Song.
Tupper, Helen Isabella
For Everything Give Thanks.
Give Thanks.
Thanks for Everything.
Tupper, Kathryn Munro
Fallen Leaves.
Tupper, Martin Farquhar
Anglo-Saxon Race, The; a Rhyme for Englishmen.
England's Heart.
Mercy to Animals: A Ballad of Humanity.
Of Curious Questions.
Of Invention, *sel.*
Train of Religion, The,
Tuquan, Fadwa
After Twenty Years.
From behind the Bars, *sel.*
From the Diary of———
Turberville, George
Epitaph of Maister Win Drowned in the Sea, An.
Lover Abused Renounceth Love, The, *sel.*
Lover Exhorteth His Lady to Take Time, While Time Is, The.
Lover to His Lady, The.

Lover to the Thames of London, to Favour [*or* Favor] His Lady Passing Thereon, The.
Of a Rich Miser.
Of Drunkenness.
Of One That Had a Great Nose.
Of the Clock and the Cock.
Pine to the Mariner, The, *abr.*
That All Things Are as They Are Used.
That He Findeth Others as Fair, but Not So Faithful as His Friend.
That No Man Should Write but Such as Do Excel.
To an Old Gentlewoman, Who Painted Her Face.
To His Friend.
To His Friend, Promising That Though Her Beauty Fade, Yet His Love Shall Last.
To His Love, That Sent Him a Ring Wherein Was Graved, "Let Reason Rule."
To His Ring, Given To His Lady, Wherein Was Graven This Verse, "My Heart Is Yours."
To One That Had Little Wit.
To the Roving Pirate.

Turbyfill, Mark
Benediction.

Turco, Lewis
Bell Weather.
Depot, The.
Failed Fathers.
House and Shutter.
Nightpiece.
Ordinary Evening in Cleveland, An.

Turei, Mohi
Ruaumoko—the Earthquake God.

Turner, Alberta
Choosing a Death.
Learning to Count.

Turner, Charles Tennyson
Artist on Penmaenmawr, The.
Bee-Wisp, The.
Buoy-Bell, The.
Cader Idris at Sunset.
Calvus to a Fly.
Country Dance, A.
Cowper's Three Hares.
Hydraulic Ram, The.
Julius Caesar and the Honey-Bee.
Lattice at Sunrise, The.
Letty's Globe.
Lion's Skeleton, The.
Maggie's Star.
Mary Queen of Scots.
Minnie and Her Dove.
Needles' Lighthouse from Keyhaven, Hampshire, The.
Old Ruralities.
Old Stephen.
On Finding a Small Fly Crushed in a Book.
On Shooting a Swallow in Early Youth.
On Some Humming-Birds in a Glass Cage.
On Startling Some Pigeons.
On the Eclipse of the Moon of October 1865.
Quiet Tide near Ardrossan, The.
Steam Threshing-Machine, The.
Summer Night in the Beehive, A.
Summer Twilight, A.
To a "Tenting" Boy.
Vacant Cage, The.
White Horse of Westbury, The.
Wind on the Corn.

Turner, Darwin T.
Death.
Guest Lecturer.
Love.
Night Slivers.
Sit-in, The.
Sonnet Sequence.
To Vanity.

Turner, Doris
Fragment Reflection I.
Reckoning A. M. Thursday.

Turner, Doug
Spirit, The.

Turner, Elizabeth
Bird's Nest, The.
Canary, The.
How to Write a Letter.
Politeness.
Rebecca's After-Thought.
Truth the Best.
Two Little Miss Lloyds, The.

Turner, Godfrey
Journal of Society, The.
Tattle.

Turner, Gordon
I Want To One Morning.

Turner, Nancy Byrd
Autumn!
Bagpipe Man, The.
Black and Gold.
Buccaneer, The.
Click o' the Latch.
Contrary Mary.
Dark-eyed Lad Columbus.
Death Is a Door.
Down a Sunny Easter Meadow.
Easter Joy.
Extraordinary Dog, The.
First Thanksgiving, The.
First Thanksgiving of All.
Going Up to London.
I Wish.
Immigrants.
Lincoln.
Little Road, The.
More than Flowers We Have Brought.
Old Quin Queeribus.
Ordinary Dog, The.
Planting a Tree.
Pop Corn Song, A.
Prayer on Fourth of July.
Rivers Remember, The.
Ships.
Spring Wind.
Sure Sign, A.
They Will Look for a Few Words.
Twenty Foolish Fairies.
Washington.
Weather Factory, The.
When Young Melissa Sweeps.
Whenever I Say "America."
Wings and Wheels.

Turner, Samuel S.
November.

Turner, Steve
Christmas Is Really for the Children.
How to Hide Jesus.

Turner, Walter James
Dancer, The.
Ecstasy.
Epithalamium: "Can the lover share his soul."
Giraffe and Tree.
Hunter, The.
Hymn to Her Unknown.
In the Caves of Auvergne.
In Time like Glass.
India.
Life and Death.
Lion, The.
Love-song, A.
Men Fade like Rocks.
Music of a Tree, The.
Navigators, The.
Poetry and Science.
Princess, The.
Reflection.
Robber, The.
Romance.
Seven Days of the Sun, The, *sels.*
Silence.
Song: "Lovely hill-torrents are."
Sun, The.
Talking with Soldiers.
Tragic Love.
Word Made Flesh, The.

Turner, William
Turners Dish of Lentten Stuffe; or, A Galymaufery.

Turner, William Price
Alien.
Coronary Thrombosis.
University Curriculum.

Tusiani, Joseph
Anticipation.
Rest O Sun I Cannot.

Tusser, Thomas
Hundreth Good Poyntes of Husbandry, A, *sel.*
Upon the Author's First Seven Years' Service.
Winds, The.

Tussman, Malka Heifetz
At the Well.
I Say.
Love the Ruins.
Mount Gilboa.
Songs of the Priestess.
Thou Shalt Not.
Water without Sound.

Tuttle, Stella Weston
Quickening, The.

Tuwhare, Hone
Burnt Offering to Your Greenstone Eyes, Tangaroa, A.
Ron Mason.
Snowfall.

Tuwim, Julian [*or* Juljan]
Gypsy Bible, The.
Jewboy.
Lodgers.
Mother.
Prayer, A: "I pray Thee O Lord."
Pursuit.
There Is No Country.

"Twain, Mark" (Sameul Langhorne Clemens)
Adventures of Huckleberry Finn, The, *sel.*
Aged Pilot Man, The.
Dirt Dumping.
Don't Copy Cat.
Emmeline Grangerford's "Ode to Stephen Dowling Bots, Dec'd."
He Done His Level Best.
Imitation of Julia A. Moore.
Missouri Maiden's Farewell to Alabama, A.
To be, or not to be; that is the bare bodkin.

Tweedsmuir, John Buchan, 1st Baron. *See* **Buchan, John**

Tweedy, Henry Hallam
Christmas at Babbitt's.
Eternal God, Whose Power Upholds, *with music.*
O Gracious Father of Mankind, *with music.*

Twichell, Chase
Abandoned House in Late Light.
Blurry Cow.
Cedar Needles.
Watercress & Ice.

Twig, John
Ballade of the Nurserie, A.

Twiss, Horace
Fashion.

Tyack, Jim
25 Spontaneous Lines Greeting the World.

Tylee, Edward Sydney
Outward Bound.

Tyler, Inez M.
Call to Pentecost, A.

Tyler, Parker
Anthology of Nouns.
Nijinsky.
To a Photograph.

Tyler, Royall
Anacreontic to Flip.
Gambling.
Hail to the Joyous Day, *with music.*
Independence Day.

Love Song, A: "By the fierce flames of love I'm in a sad taking."
Original Epitaph on a Drunkard.
Widower, The.
Tylor, Edward Burnett *and* **Andrew Lang.** *See* **Lang, Andrew** *and* **Edward Burnett Tylor**
Tymnes
Maltese Dog, A.
Tynan, Katharine (Katharine Tynan Hinkson)
Aux Carmélites.
Beloved, The.
Broken Soldier, The.
Chanticleer.
Cuckoo Song.
Dead Coach, The.
Desire, The.
Doves, The.
Epitaph, The: "Write on my grave when I am dead."
Farewell: "Not soon shall I forget—a sheet."
Flying Wheel, The.
Footpath Way, The.
Girl's Song, A.
In Time of Need.
Joining the Colours.
Larks.
Last Voyage, The.
Little Ghost, The.
Lux in Tenebris.
Making of Birds, The.
Mater Dei.
Memory, A.
Of an Orchard.
Old Love, The.
Passiontide Communion.
Prayer, A: "Now wilt me take for Jesus' sake."
Quiet Nights, The.
She Asks for New Earth.
Sheep and Lambs.
Turn o' the Year.
Witch, The.
Tyrrell, Henry
Masterful Man, The.
Tyrtaeus
How Can Man Die Better.
Tyutchev, Fyodor Ivanovich
As Ocean's Stream.
At Vshchizh.
Last Love.
Silentium.
Spring; a Formal Ode.
Tzara, Tristan
Evening.
Mothers.
Tzu Yeh
Bare branches tremble, The.
I had not fastened my sash over my gown.
It is night again.

U

Uba, George
Firefly.
Gary Gotow.
How Do You Spell "Missile"?: Preliminary Instructions in the Nuclear Age.
Old Photo, 1942.
Uceda, Julia
Time Reminded Me.
2976.
Udall [*or* Udal], Nicholas
I Mun Be Married a Sunday.
Minion Wife, A.
Ralph Roister Doister, *sels.*
Ufford, Edward Smith
Throw Out the Lifeline.
Ugaas, Raage
Poet's Lament on the Death of His Wife.
Uhland, Ludwig (Johann Ludwig Uhland)
Castle by the Sea, The.
Durand of Blonden.
Hostess' Daughter, The.
Ichabod! The Glory Has Departed.
In a Lovely Garden Walking.
King on the Tower, The.
Leaf, A.
Luck of Edenhall, The.
Spirits Everywhere.
Ukihashi
Whether I sit or lie.
Ulinover, Miriam
Havdolah Wine.
In the Courtyard.
Ullman, Leslie
Last Night They Heard the Woman Upstairs.
Proof.
Ulrich von Lichtenstein [*or* Liechtenstein]
Love, Whose Month Was Ever May.
Unamuno, Miguel de
Atheist's Prayer, The.
Castile.
Underhill, Evelyn
Introversion.
Lady Poverty, The.
Supersensual.
Theophany.
Underwood, John Curtis
Wave, The.
Underwood, Wilbur
Cattle of His Hand, The.
To the Brave Soul.
Ungaretti, Giuseppe
Quiet.
Without More Weight.
Unger, Barbara
Breasts.
Geological Faults.
Unik, Pierre
Manless Society, The.
Untermeyer, Jean Starr
Altar, The.
Autumn.
Clay Hills.
Country of No Lack.
Dew on a Dusty Heart.
False Enchantment.
From the Day-Book of a Forgotten Prince.
High Tide.
Lake Song.
Last Plea.
Little Dirge.
Passionate Sword, The.
Sinfonia Domestica.
Sung on a Sunny Morning.
Untermeyer, Louis
Appeal to the Phoenix.
Archibald MacLeish Suspends the Five Little Pigs.
At the Bottom of the Well.
Caliban in the Coal Mines.
Catalogue.
Cell-Mates.
Dance of Dust, The.
Dark Chamber, The.
Dream and the Blood, The.
Edgar A. Guest Considers "The Good Old Woman Who Lived in a Shoe" and the Good Old Truths Simultaneously.
Edna St. Vincent Millay Exhorts Little Boy Blue.
Einstein among the Coffee-Cups.
End of the Comedy.
Equals.
Feuerzauber.
Folk-Song: "Back she came through the trembling dusk."
Food and Drink.
Frustrate.
Glad Day.
Goliath and David.
Hair-dressing.
Infidelity.
Irony.
John Masefield Relates the Story of Tom, Tom, the Piper's Son.
Koheleth.
Landscapes.
Last Words before Winter.
Long Feud.
Love.
Mother Goose Up-to-Date, *parodies.*
On Hearing Prokofieff's Grotesque for Two Bassoons, Concertina and Snare-Drums.
Only of Thee and Me.
Portrait of a Child.
Portrait of a Machine.
Prayer: "God, though [*or* although] this life is but a wraith."
Prayer for a New House.
Prayer for This House.
Questions at Night.
Rapunzel.
Relativities.
Reveillé.
Round: "Worlds, you must tell me."
Sagging Bough, The.
Song Tournement [*or* Tournament]: New Style.
Spring Song of a Super-Blake.
Summer Storm.
Supplication.
To a Vine-clad Telegraph Pole.
Victory in the Cabarets.
W. H. Davies Simplifies the Simplicities He Loves.
Wallflower to a Moonbeam.
Walter de la Mare Tells the Listener about Jack and Jill.
Wind Gardens.
Wise Woman, The.
Updike, John
Amish, The.
August.
Bendix.
Child's Calendar, A, *sels.*
Commencement, Pingree School.
Deities and Beasts.
Die Neuen Heiligen, *sel.*
Dog's Death.
Ex-Basketball Player.
February 22.
From a Cheerful Alphabet.
Golfers.
Great Scarf of Birds, The.
Grief of Cafeterias, The.
Humanities Course.
I Like to Sing Also.
I Missed His Book, but I Read His Name.
Insomnia the Gem of the Ocean.
January.
May.
Minority Report.
Mosquito.
Newlyweds, The.
October.
Ode, An: "I'm going to write a novel, hey."
Ohio.
Party Knee.
Philological.
Player Piano.
Recital.
Scenic.
Seagulls.
Seven Stanzas at Easter.
Some Frenchmen.
Sonic Boom.
Sunday Rain.
Sunflower.
Superman.
Tao in the Yankee Stadium Bleachers.
Taste.
Telephone Poles.
Time's Fool.

V. B. Nimble, V. B. Quick ("V. B. Wigglesworth wakes at noon").
Vow.
Winter Ocean.
Youth's Progress.
Upham, Thomas Cogswell
Fear Not, Poor Weary One, *with music.*
Song of the Pilgrims.
Upson, Arthur W.
"Ex Libris."
Failures.
Old Gardens.
Song: "Flame at the core of the world."
Vers la Vie.
Upton, James
Lass of Richmond Hill, The.
Upton, Minnie Leona
No Talking Shop.
Urdang, Constance
Because the Three Moirai Have Become the Three Maries.
Birth.
Birth of Venus.
Bread.
Change of Life.
Children, The.
Day the Houses Sank, The.
Exercise for the Left Hand.
His Sleep.
Invention of Zero, The.
Leaving Mexico One More Time.
Madman, The.
Old Maid Factory, The.
One-eyed Bridegroom, The.
Roots of Revolution in the Vegetable Kingdom, The.
Safe Places.
Uribe, Armando
I love you and the rosebush.
Urmy, Clarence Thomas
Arrow, The.
As I came down Mount Tamalpais.
At the Edge of the Day.
Blondel.
I Lay My Lute beside Thy Door.
Old Year, The.
Woodland Revel, A.
Usborne, Richard
Casanova.
Epitaph on a Party Girl.
Uschold, Maud E.
Casual Gold.
March Wind.
November Rain.
Usher, John
Pipe of Tobacco, The, *at.*
Usher, Leila
I Am the Cat.
Utahania
Accusation.
U'Tamsi, Felix TchiKaya (Tchicaya U Tam'si)
Scorner, The.
Uvavnuk
Song of Joy.
Woman Shaman's Song, A.
Uvlunuaq
I Should Be Ashamed.

V

"V., B." *See* **Thomson, James (1834–82)**
Vakaló, Eléni
But there was/ once/ a time.
Genealogy.
My Father's Eye.
Song of the Hanged.
'Vala, Katri' (Karin Alice Heikel)
On the Meadow.
Winter Is Here.
Valdés, Gabriel de la Concepción. *See* **"Plácido"**
Valentine, Edward Abram Uffington
Helen.
Spirit of the Wheat, The.
Valentine, G. D.
Night up There.
Valentine, Jean
After Elegies.
Anaesthesia.
April.
December 21st.
Dream Barker.
Fidelities.
Field, The.
Forgiveness Dream, The; Man from the Warsaw Ghetto.
He Said.
Knife, The.
Messenger, The.
Moon Man.
Orpheus and Eurydice.
Pilgrims.
Sasha and the Poet.
Second Dream, The.
Silences; a Dream of Governments.
3 a.m. in New York.
Valéry, Paul
Caesar.
Helen.
Narcissus.
Valian, Maxine Kent
Blessing at Kellenberger Road.
Valis, Noel Maureen
Black Horse Running.
Vallana
After he stripped off my clothes.
Valle, Adriano del
Cradle Song of the Elephants.
Valle, Carmen
Glenn Miller's music is a trunk.
I'm going to break out.
What Is Lived.
Valle, Isabel
Very Minor Poet Speaks, A.
Valle, Victor M.
Food.
Vallejo, César
And don't bother telling me anything.
Anger that breaks a man down into boys, The.
I have a terrible fear of being an animal.
Poem to Be Read and Sung.
Valli, Maria
Crows, The.
Vallis, Val
Fishing Season.
Vanada, Lillian Schulz
Firefly.
Vanbrugh, Sir John
Aesop, *sel.*
In the Sprightly Month of May.
Van Brunt, H. L.
Cerberus.
In the Distance.
Lumière.
Motels, Hotels, Other People's Houses.
On the Death of Neruda.
Walking.
Vance, Thomas H.
Frozen Hero, The.
"Vandegrift, Margaret" (Margaret Thomson Janvier)
Clown's Baby, The.
Little Wild Baby.
Sandman, The.
Van Den Heever, C. M.
Fallen Zulu Commander, The.
Vanderlip, Brian
Encounter with Hunger.
Vander Molen, Robert
In the Bar.
Sunny.
Van de Water, Frederic F.
Last Tourney, The.
Van Doren, Mark
Ancient Couple on Lu Mountain, The.
And Did the Animals?
And Then It Rained.
Apple Hell.
April, 1942.
Autonomous.
Axle Song.
Burial.
Child at Winter Sunset, The.
City Songs.
Civil War.
Close Clan, The.
Comedy.
Distant Runners, The.
Donkey.
Down Dip the Branches.
Dunce Song 6.
End, The.
Envy the Old.
Epitaphs: For a Fickle Man.
Escape, The.
Eternity's Low Voice.
Family Prime.
First Snow of the Year, The.
Foreclosure.
Former Barn Lot.
Ghost Boy.
God of Galaxies, The.
Good Morning.
He's Coming.
History Lesson.
I Had to Be Secret.
If They Spoke.
Immortal.
Inconsistent.
It Should Be Easy.
King Wind.
Laly, Laly.
Merry-go-round.
Moments He Remembers, The.
Morning Worship.
Music God.
Nap.
Needles and Pins.
Old Ben Golliday.
Once the Wind.
Only for Me.
Our Lady Peace.
Praise Doubt.
Praise Him Who Makes Us Happy, *with music.*
Private Worship.
Proper Clay.
Pulse, The.
Return to Ritual.
Runaways, The.
Sad Child's Song, The.
Seven Sleepers, The.
Slowly, Slowly Wisdom Gathers.
Story-Teller, The.
Tall Tale God.
That Day.
This Amber Sunstream.
Tourist.
Tower, The.
Tragedy.
Undersong.
Wait till Then.
When the World Ends.
Where Did He Run To?
Whisperer, The.
Why, Lord ("Why Lord, must something in us").
Will You, Won't You.
Wind in the Grass.
Winter Tryst.
Young Woman at a Window.
Van Dusen, Ruth B.
Prayer in a Country Church.

Van Duyn, Mona
Billings and Cooings from "The Berkeley Barb."
Birthday Card for a Psychiatrist.
Fear of Flying, The.
Footnotes to "The Autobiography of Bertrand Russell," *sel.*
Gardener to His God, The.
Gentle Snorer, The.
Leda.
Leda Reconsidered.
Letters from a Father.
Open Letter from a Constant Reader.
Pieta, The, Rhenish, 14th C., The Cloisters.
Relationships.
Talker, The.
Twins, The.
What the Motorcycle Said.
"Wish to Be Believed, The."
Van Dyke, Henry
America for Me.
America's Prosperity.
Angler's Reveille, The.
Angler's Wish, An.
Builders, The, *sel.*
Burning Bush, The.
Child in the Garden, The.
Children in the Market-Place.
Envoy: "Legend of Felix is ended, the toiling of Felix is done, The."
Foundations.
Four Things.
Four Things to Do.
Gospel of Labor, The.
Great River, The.
Home.
Hymn of Joy.
Hymn of Labor.
If All the Skies [Were Sunshine].
Jesus, Thou Divine Companion.
Jesus Return.
Lily of Yorrow, The.
Lost Word of Jesus, A.
Lover's Envy, A.
Mare Liberum.
Maryland Yellow-Throat, The.
Mile with Me, A.
Mother's Birthday, A.
My April Lady.
One in Christ.
Peace Hymn of the Republic.
Prayer: "Lord, the newness of this day."
Prayer: "These are the gifts I ask of thee."
Reliance.
Roslin and Hawthornden.
Tennyson.
These Are the Gifts I Ask.
They Who Tread the Path of Labor.
Things I Prize, The.
Three Best Things, The, *sel.*
To the Child Jesus.
Toiling of Felix, The, *sels.*
Valley of Vain Verses, The.
Veery, The.
Victoria.
Voyagers.
Way, The.
Work.
Zest of Life, The.
Van Eck, Alice
Football Game, A.
Van Fossan, Josephine
Mourning.
Van Geel, Christian J.
View.
Van Noppen, Leonard Charles
Man of Men, A.
"Vanolis, Bysshe." *See* **Thomson, James (1834–1884)**
Van Rensselaer, James
Note on Lizard's Feet, A.
Van Rensselaer, Mariana Griswold
At Bedtime.
Love's Prisoner.
Manners.
Van Rensselaer, Peyton
At Twilight.
Van Slyke, Beren
Shepherds, The.
Van Spanckeren, Kathryn
Muse Poem.
Van Toorn, Peter
Mountain Study.
Shake'nbake Ballad.
Van Voorhis, Linda Lyon
Ad Matrem in Coelis.
"That Which Hath Wings Shall Tell."
To a Humble Bug.
Van Walleghen, Michael
Driving into Enid.
Van Winckel, Nance
When You are Gone.
Van Wyk Louw, N. P. *See*Louw, N P. van Wyk
Van Wynen, Peter
May God Give Strength.
Van Zyl, Tania
Horses of Marini, The.
House, The.
Man with the Hollow Breast, The.
Rope, The.
She Waited.
Two Women.
Vardhill, Anna Jane
To a Skeleton.
Varela, Blanca
Before the Pacific.
Captain, The.
Nobody will open the door for you.
Things I Say Are True, The.
Vas, István
Catacombs.
Just This.
Tambour.
What Is Left?
Vásquez, Ricardo
Maestro's Barber Shop, The.
Vaughan, Frances Downing
New Calf, The.
Vaughan, Henry
Admission.
As Time One Day by Me Did Pass.
Ascension-Day.
Ascension-Hymn ("Dust and clay").
Begging.
Bird, The.
Book, The.
Brecon Beacons and the Black Mountains, The.
Brittish Church, The.
Burial of an Infant, The.
Buriall.
Childhood.
Christ's Nativity.
Cock-crowing.
Come, come, what doe I here?
Constellation, The.
Corruption.
Dawning, The.
Dear, beauteous Death! the jewel of the just.
Death.
Dedication, The: "My God, thou that didst dye for me."
Distraction.
Dressing.
Dwelling-Place, The.
Easter Hymn.
Easter-Day.
Eclipse, The.
Eternity.
Evening-Watch, The.
Fragment: "Walk with thy fellow-creatures: note the hush."
From the Welsh of Aneirín.
God's Saints.
H. Scriptures.
Holy Communion, The.
I Walked [*or* Walkt] the Other Day [to Spend My Hour].
I Walkt the Other Day.
Idle Verse.
Incarnation and Passion, The.
Jews, The.
Joy of My Life! While Left Me Here.
Knot, The.
Lamp[e], The.
London in 1646.
Love and Discipline.
Man.
Mans Fall, and Recovery.
Midnight.
Morning-watch, The.
Mount of Olives.
Nativity, The.
Night, The.
Of Life and Death, *sel.*
Palm-Tree, The.
Passion, The.
Peace.
Pilgrimage, The.
Praise.
Pursuit[e], The.
Queer, The.
Quickness.
Regeneration.
Relapse, The.
Religion.
Resolve, The.
Resurrection and Immortality.
Retreat[e], The.
Revival, The.
Rom. Cap. 8 Ver. 19.
Rules and Lessons.
Sap, The.
Search, The.
Seed Growing Secretly, The.
Shall these early fragrant hours.
Shepheards, The.
Shepherds, The.
Shower, The.
Silence and Stealth of Days!
Son-Dayes.
Song to Amoret, A.
Starre, The.
Storm, The.
Sure, There's a Tie of Bodies!
Tempest, The.
They Are All Gone into the World of Light.
Timber, The.
To a Bird after a Storm.
To Amoret [Gone from Him].
To Etesia Looking from Her Casement at the Full Moon.
To His Books.
To His Friend
To His Retired Friend, an Invitation to Brecknock, *sels.*
To the River Isca.
True Christmas, The.
Unprofitablenes.
Upon the Priory Grove, His Usual Retirement.
Vanity of Spirit.
Vision, A.
Waterfall, The.
Winged Heart, A.
Winter's Frosty Pangs.
World, The.
Vaughan, Thomas
"So Have I Spent on the Banks of Ysca Many a Serious Hour."
Stone, The.
Vaughan-Thomas, Wynford
Farewell to New Zealand.
Hiraeth in N.W.3.
To His Not-so-coy Mistress.
Vaughan Williams, Ursula
Memorial Service.
Vaughn, F. E.
Ballad of Chicken Bill, The.

Vaughn, James P.
Four Questions Addressed to His Excellency, the Prime Minister.
Movie Queen.
So?
Three Kings.
Two Ladies Bidding Us "Good Morning."
Vaux, Thomas, 2d Baron Vaux of Harrowden
Aged Lover Renounceth Love, The.
Content.
Death in Life.
He Renounceth All the Effects of Love.
Image of Death, The.
No Pleasure without Some Pain.
Of a Contented Mind.
On a Contented Mind.
On the Instability of Youth.
Sins of Youth, The.
Vazakas, Byron
All the Farewells.
Enigmatic Traveler, The.
Midsummer Night's Dream.
Pavilion on the Pier, The.
Progress of Photography, The.
West Fifty-seventh Street.
Veale, Peter
Bold Troubleshooters.
I put my hat upon my head, *parody.*
Vega, José Luis
Brotherhood.
Conditions.
Erotic Suite, *sels.*
Vega Carpia, Lope de. *See* **Lope de Vega Carpio, Felix**
Velema
Tip-of-the-Single-Feather.
Veley, Margaret
Japanese Fan.
Velho de Costa, Maria, *and* **Maria Isabel Barreno** *and* **Maria Teresa Horta.** *See* **Marias, The Three**
Venable, William Henry
Battle Cry.
El Emplazado.
Founders of Ohio, The.
John Filson.
Johnny Appleseed.
My Catbird.
National Song.
School Girl, The.
Teacher's Dream, The.
Venantius Fortunatus, Saint
O Glory of Virgins.
Standards of the king go forth, The.
To the Lady Radegunde, with Violets.
Written on an Island off the Breton Coast.
Venmanipputi
What She Said to Her Girl-Friend.
Vere, Edward de, 17th Earl of Oxford. *See* **De Vere, Edward, 17th Earl of Oxford**
Vergil. *See* **Virgil.**
Verhaeren, Emile
Poor, The.
Verlaine, Paul
A Clymene.
A la Promenade.
Amour, *sels.*
Art of Poetry, The [*or* Art Poétique].
Auburn.
Avenue, The.
Bad Sleeper, A.
Chansons d'Automne.
Chevalier Malheur, Le.
Clair de Lune.
Colloque Sentimental.
Confession, A.
Cortège.
Crucifix, A.
Cythère.
Dans l'Allée.
En Bateau.
Fantoches.
Femme et Chatte.
God Has Spoken.
I Hate to See You Clad.
Il pleut doucement sur la ville.
Indolent, The.
Lassitude.
Lines in Order to Be Slandered.
Love Fallen to Earth.
Lyric: "You would have understood me, had you waited."
Mandoline.
Moonlight.
Mystical Dialogue.
Ode: To My Lovers.
Pantomime.
Parsifal.
Pastel, A.
Pensionnaires.
Puppets.
Retinue.
Sagesse, *sels.*
Sentimental Conversation [*or* Colloquy].
Sky Is Up above the Roof, The.
Spleen ("Around were all the roses red").
Spring.
Tears in my heart that weeps.
Thousands and Three.
You Would Have Understood Me.
Verne, Viviane
Kensington Gardens.
Vernon, William J.
Catching Soft Craws.
Verplanck, Gulian
"Prophecy."
Verry, Isabel Williams
Alcestis.
Verstegan [*or* Verstegen], Richard (Richardowlands)
Lullaby: "Upon my lap my sovereign sits."
Our Lady's Lullaby.
Vision of the World's Instability, A.
Very, Jones
Abdolonymus the Sidonian.
April Snow, The.
Barberry-Bush, The.
Broken Bowl, The.
Clouded Morning, The.
Columbine, The.
Cottage, The.
Created, The.
Day of Denial, The.
Dead, The.
Eagles, The.
Earth, The.
Enoch.
Fair Morning, The.
Fugitive Slaves, The.
Garden, The.
Gifts of God, The.
Grave-Yard, The.
Hand and Foot, The.
Health of Body Dependent on Soul.
I Was Sick and in Prison.
Idler, The.
In Him We Live.
Lament of the Flowers, The.
Latter Rain, The.
Life.
Light from Within, The.
Lost, The.
Love.
Man in Harmony with Nature.
Nature.
New Birth, The.
New Man, The.
New World, The.
Old Road, The.
On Finding the Truth.
On the Completion of the Pacific Telegraph.
On Visiting the Graves of Hawthorne and Thoreau.
Prayer, The: "Wilt Thou not visit me?"
Presence, The.
Psyche.
Slave, The.
Soul-Sickness.
Spirit Land, The.
Strangers, The.
Sumach Leaves, The.
Thy Beauty Fades.
Thy Brother's Blood.
To the Canary Bird.
Today.
Tree, The.
Trees of Life, The.
Yourself.
"Vesay, Paul." *See* **Allen, Samuel**
"Vestal, Stanley" (Walter Stanley Campbell)
Fandango.
Kit Carson's Last Smoke ("Kit Carson came to old Fort Lyons").
Oliver Wiggins.
Viau, Théophile de
Sleep.
Vicente, Gil
Cantiga.
Song: "If thou art sleeping, maiden."
Vickers, V. C.
Moon Bird, The.
Swank, The.
Vickridge, Alberta
In a V.A.D. Pantry.
Vidal, Peire
Song of Breath.
Vidame de Chartres. *See* **Chartres, Vidame de.**
Vidya (Vijjika)
Friends,/ you are lucky you can talk.
Hiding in the/ cucumber garden.
Please keep an eye on my house for a few moments.
Substantiations, *sel.*
Sun, The, *sel.*
Wanton, The, *sel.*
You are fortunate, dear friends, that you can tell.
Vielé, Herman Knickerbocker
Good Inn, The.
Inn of the Silver Moon, The, *sel.*
Viereck, George Sylvester
After the Battle.
Viereck, Peter
Affirmations (I-III).
Big Crash Out West.
Blindman's Buff.
Counter-Serenade: She Invokes the Autumn Instant.
Crass Times Redeemed by Dignity of Souls.
Don't Look Now but Mary Is Everybody.
Ennui.
For Two Girls Setting Out in Life.
From Ancient Fangs.
Graves Are Made to Waltz On.
Homecoming.
Kilroy.
Kilroy Was Here.
Love Song to Eohippus.
1912-1952, Full Cycle.
Now Kindness.
Planted Skull, The.
Poet.
Slacker Apologizes, The.
Small Perfect Manhattan.
Some Lines in Three Parts.
Some Refrains at the Charles River.
Space-Wanderer's Homecoming.
To Be Sung.
To Helen of Troy (N.Y.)
Vale from Carthage.
Walk on Snow, A.
You All Are Static; I Alone Am Moving.
Vigée, Claude
Destiny of the Poet.
Every Land Is Exile.
House of the Living.

Light of Judea.
Poetry.
Song of Occident.
Struggle with the Angel, The.
Tree of Death, The.
Wanderer, The.
Vigny, Alfred de
Nature.
Shepherd's House, The, *sel.*
Sound of the Horn, The.
Vilakazi, B. W.
Because.
I Heard the Old Song.
In the Gold Mines.
On the Gold Mines.
Then I'll Believe.
Vildrac, Charles
After Midnight.
Villa, José Garcia
Be Beautiful, Noble, like the Antique Ant.
Between God's Eyelashes.
God, Is, Like, Scissors.
God Said, "I Made a Man."
Manner of a Poet's Germination, The.
Mostly Are We Mostless.
My, Fellowship, with, God.
My Mouth Is Very Quiet.
Now, if You Will Look in My Brain.
Saw God Dead but Laughing.
There Came You Wishing Me.
229.
Way My Ideas Think Me, The.
Villanueva, Alma
I was always fascinated.
Villanueva, Salvador
I would go around biting my nails.
Maybe You Cannot Comprehend.
Temple is full of blood, The.
Villanueva, Tino
Aquellos Vatos.
Pachuco Remembered.
Villiers, George, 2nd Duke of Buckingham. *See* **Buckingham, George Villiers, 2nd Duke of**
Villon, François
Arbor Amoris.
Ballad against the Enemies of France.
Ballad of Dead Ladies, The.
Ballad of Ladies' Love, Number Two.
Ballad of the Gibbet.
Ballad of the Lords of Old Time.
Ballad of the Women of Paris.
Ballad of Villon and Fat Madge, The.
Ballad Written for a Bridegroom.
Ballade: "Brother humans who live on after us."
Ballade of Dead Ladies, The.
Ballade of Ladies' Love.
Ballade of the Fair Helm-Maker.
Ballade of the Women of Paris.
Ballade of Villon and Fat Margot.
Ballade to His Mistress.
Ballat o the Hingit.
Ballat o the Leddies o Langsyne.
Complaint of the Fair Armouress [*or* Armoress], The.
Dispute of the Heart and Body of François Villon, The.
Double Ballad of Good Counsel, A.
Epistle in Form of a Ballad to His Friends.
Epitaph in Form of a Ballad, The.
Fragment of Death.
Fragment on Death, A.
His Mother's Service to Our Lady.
Lament of the Lovely Helmet-Dealer.
No, I Am Not as Others Are.
Old Lady's Lament for Her Youth, The.
Old Woman's Lamentations, An.
Prayer of the Old Woman.
Rondel: "Good-by, the tears are in my eyes."
Snows of Yester-Year, The.
Testament, The, *abr.*
To Death, of His Lady.
Vinal, Harold
Enduring Music, The.
Flight.
Hymnal: "Bringer of sun, arrower of evening, star-begetter and moon-riser."
Lesbia Sewing.
Nights Remember, The.
Quest, The.
Sea Born.
Vinaver, Stanislav
Cathedral, A.
European Night, The.
Inscription, An: "Over the sheer rocks over the gorges."
Vincent, Stephen
Basketball.
Coming Up and Falling Down.
Elevator Landscapes, *sels.*
Floor: Five.
Floor: O.
Jealousy.
Mother.
Relationship, The.
Requiem: "I watch the roses float."
Song of This House, The.
Vines, Eda H.
Ballade of the Old-Time Engine.
Vinner, Shlomo
In the Cabinet.
Jerusalem.
Lullaby: "Sleep now."
Midnight and Ten Minutes.
Need to Love, The.
Parting.
Training on the Shore.
Vinograd, Julia
Investigation.
Vinz, Mark
Angler.
Business as Usual.
Children, The.
In the Heartland.
Mac.
Morning After.
November Song.
Old Doc.
Postcards.
Primer Lesson.
Variations on a Theme.
Wild West.
Violi, Paul
Concordance.
Viorst, Judith
Raising the Flag.
Mother Doesn't Want a Dog.
Since Hanna Moved Away.
Some Things Don't Make Any Sense at All.
Virgil [*or* Vergil] (Publius Vergilius Maro)
Aeneid, The, *abr.*
And oft the owle with rufull song complaind.
Arms, and the man I sing, who forc'd by fate.
As when a fragment, from a mountain torn.
Attentively he heard us, while we spoke.
Batalis and the Man, The.
Battle of Actium.
Care of Bees, The.
Corydon and Thyrsis.
Destruction of Troy, The.
Dido among the Shades.
Dido to Aeneas.
Dido's Hunting.
Eclogues, *sels.*
Entrance to Hell, The.
Funeral Games for Anchises, The: Entellus.
Georgics, *sels.*
Lycidas and Moeris.
Marcellus.
Messiah, The.
Onto the hallowit steid bryng in, thai cry.
Prelude: "What makes a plenteous harvest."
Second Pastoral, The; or, Alexis.
Shepherd's Gratitude, The.
Sibylline Prophecy, The.
Sicilian Muse, I Would Try Now a Somewhat Grander Theme.
Sixth Book of the Aeneis, The, *sel.*
We Have Paid Enough Long Since in Our Own Blood.
Welcome to the Sun.
Vittorelli, Jacopo
On a Nun.
Vivante, Arturo
To a Victim of Radiation.
Vivien, Renée
Pillory, The.
Toward Lesbos.
Words to My Friend.
Vizenor, Gerald
Anishinabe Grandmothers.
Auras on the Interstates.
Family Photograph.
February Park.
Haiku: "August heat."
Holiday Inn at Bemidji.
Indians at the Guthrie.
Minnesota Camp Grounds.
North to Milwaukee.
Seven Woodland Crows.
Thumbing Old Magazines.
Tribal Stumps ("Tribal mixed bloods").
Tropisms on John Berryman.
Tyranny of Moths.
Unhappy Diary Days.
White Earth Reservation 1980.
Vliet, R. G.
Girls on Saddleless Horses.
Love's own form.
Vogel, David
Black Flags Are Fluttering.
Days Were Great as Lakes.
How Can I See You, Love.
In Fine, Transparent Words.
Now I Have Forgotten All.
Our Childhood Spilled into Our Hearts.
Plain, Humble Letters.
When I Was Growing Up.
Vogelsang, Arthur
Americans in an Orange Grove.
Clouds, The.
Drive Imagining.
Feeling That Way Too.
Vogelweide, Walther von der. *See* **Walther von der Vogelweide**
Voigt, Ellen Bryant
Bat, The.
Blue Ridge.
Daughter.
Exile.
For My Husband.
January.
Jug Brook.
Lotus Flowers, The.
Pastoral: "Crouched in the yard."
Rescue.
Spring, The.
Victim, The.
Volborth, Judith Mountain Leaf
Corn-Woman Remembered.
Dusk Chant.
Goat-Woman Dares.
How Came She to Such Poppy-Breath?
Iron-Door-Woman.
Self-Portrait.
Three Songs to Mark the Night.
Time of Turquoise, A.
Vihio Images ("Coyote/ pineneedles").
Vihio Images ("In the buffalo's skull").
Volk, Joyce M.
Places I Have Been.
Vollmoeller, Karl Gustav
Nocturne in G Minor.
Voltaire (François Marie Arouet)
On Bell-Ringers.
On the Phrase, "To Kill Time."

Royal Love Scene, The.
Volwerk, Leen
Bog.
Staoineag.
Vondel, Joost van den
Adam's Hymn in Paradise.
Von Ende, Frederick
Wynken de Worde.
Von Hartmann, Max
Seed of Reality, The.
von Rugge, Heinrich. *See* **Heinrich von Rugge**
Von Tilzer, Harry *and* **Will Dillon.** *See* **Dillon, Will** *and* **Harry Von Tilzer**
Vories, William Merrell
Let There Be Light, *with music.*
Voronca, Ilarie
Quick and the Dead, The.
Seven-League Boots, The.
Vorpahl, Robert L.
Perspective.
Voss, J. H.
Who Does Not Love Wine, Women and Song.
Voznesensky, Andrei
Darkmotherscream.
Dead Still.
I Am Goya.
New York Bird.
Soccer.
Vrepont, Brian
Apple-Tree, The.
Net Menders, The.
Vriesland, Victor van
Ars Poetica.
Evening.
Vroman, Leo
Old Miniatures.
River, The.
Vulgarius, Eugenius
Metrum Parhemiacum Tragicum.

W

"W., A."
Desire's Government.
Dispraise of Love, and Lover's Follies.
Give Me Leave.
Hopeless Desire Soon Withers and Dies.
In Praise of a Beggar's Life.
In Praise of the Sun.
Ladies' Eyes Serve Cupid Both for Darts and Fire.
Petition to Have Her Leave to Die.
Play, Beggars, Play!
Song in Praise of a Beggar's Life, A.
To Time.
Upon Visiting His Lady by Moonlight.
Where His Lady Keeps His Heart.
"W., C. A."
To have it out or not? that is the question.
"W., J. J."
Brotherhood.
"W., I. V. S."
Snowfall.
"W. A. G." *See* **"G., W. A."**
"W. J." *See* **"J., W."**
Wabnitz, William S.
Hinds of Kerry, The.
Waddell, Jean Percival
Half-Light.
Rhythm.
Wadding, Luke
Christmas Day Is Come.
Waddington, Miriam
Advice to the Young.
Cadenza.
Catalpa Tree.
Desert Stone.
Field of Night, The.
Green World Two.
Icons.
Investigator.
Laughter.
Lullaby: "Hush dove the summer."
My Lessons in the Jail.
Old Women of Toronto.
Restricted.
Season's Lovers, The.
Survivors, The.
Ten Years and More.
Thou Didst Say Me.
Women's Jail, The.
Waddington, Samuel
Inn of Care, The.
Morning.
Mors et Vita.
Soul and Body.
Wade, Blanche Elizabeth
Song of the Christmas Tree, The.
Wade, John Stevens
May.
Wade, Thomas
True Martyr, The.
Winter Shore, The.
Wadsworth, Oliver A.
Over in the Meadow.
Wagner, Charles Abraham
Three City Cantos.
When I Loved You.
Wagner, Linda
Love Poem: "Isadora, your body charts a course."
Wagner, Mary Boyd
Lethal Thought, The.
Wagoner, David
After the Speech to the Librarians.
Being Herded Past the Prison's Honor Farm.
Calculation, The.
Clancy.
Closing Time.
Death of the Moon.
Diary.
Elegy for a Woman Who Remembered Everything.
Elegy for Yards, Pounds, and Gallons.
Elegy while Pruning Roses.
Emergency Maker, The.
Falling Asleep in a Garden.
Feast, The.
Fruit of the Tree, The.
Gift of a Mirror to a Lady.
House-hunting.
In Distress.
In the Badlands.
Labors of Thor, The.
Land behind the Wind, The.
Leaving Something Behind.
Looking for Mountain Beavers.
Lost.
Making Up for a Soul.
Man from the Top of the Mind, The.
Marsh Leaf.
Meeting a Bear.
Murder Mystery.
Muse.
My Father's Ghost.
My Physics Teacher.
Nesting Ground, The.
News from the Court.
Nine Charms against the Hunter.
Ode to the Muse on Behalf of a Young Poet.
Poets Agree to Be Quiet by the Swamp, The.
Relics.
Shooting of John Dillinger outside the Biograph Theater, July 22, 1934, The.
Snake Hunt.
Songs My Mother Taught Me.
Staying Alive.
Sudden Frost.
"Tan Ta Ra, Cries Mars. . ."
To My Friend Whose Parachute Did Not Open.
To the Fly in My Drink.
Trail Horse, The.
Travelling Light.
Tumbleweed.
Under the Sign of Moth.
Valedictory to Standard Oil of Indiana, A.
Visiting Hour, The.
Walking in a Swamp.
Warning to My Love, A.
Water Lily, The.
Words, The.
Working against Time.
Wagoner, Glenn E.
I Never Knew.
Wagstaff, Blanche Shoemaker
All Paths Lead to You.
Earth Trembles Waiting.
Quiet Waters.
Wildness.
Wah, Fred
Breathe Dust.
Wahl, Jean
Decayed Time.
Evening in the Walls.
Lean Day in a Convict's Suit, A.
Prayer of a Little Hope.
Wain, John
Anecdote of 2 A.M.
Anniversary.
Apology for Understatement.
Arrival.
Au Jardin des Plantes.
Boisterous Poem about Poetry, A, *sel.*
Brooklyn Heights.
Lie Easy in Your Secret Cradle.
New Sun, The.
Pedagogue Arraigned.
Poem: "Like a deaf man meshed in his endless silence."
Poem without a Main Verb.
Reason for Not Writing Orthodox Nature Poetry.
Short History of Twentieth-Century Scholarship.
Song about Major Eatherly, A.
This above All Is Precious and Remarkable.
Wildtrack, *sel.*
Wainwright, Vera
When we are older and the hidden fires.
Waite, Arthur Edward
At the End of Things.
Wakarpa
Golden Sea-Otter, The.
Kutune Shirka (The Ainu Epic), *sel.*
Wakefield, Samuel
Music of His Steps, The, *with music.*
Wakeman, John
Love in Brooklyn.
Wakoski, Diane
Aging.
Anticipation of Sharks.
Apology, An.
Apparitions Are Not Singular Occurrences.
Belly Dancer.
Coins and Coffins under My Bed.
Empress, The.
Father of My Country, The.
Fire Island Poem.
For a Man Who Learned to Swim When He Was Sixty.
For Whitman.
Greed, *sel.*
Having Replaced Love with Food and Drink.
Ice Eagle, The.
Inside Out.
Italian Woman.
Journey.
Justice Is Reason Enough.
Love Letter Postmarked Van Beethoven.
Mechanic, The.
Night a Sailor Came to Me in a Dream, The.
No More Soft Talk.
Ode to a Lebanese Crock of Olives.

Patriotic Poem.
Photos, The.
Placing a $2 Bet for a Man Who Will Never Go to the Horse Races Any More.
Poem to the Man on My Fire Escape.
Poet Recognizing the Echo of the Voice, A.
Rain Trip.
Ring, The.
Ringless.
Sestina from the Home Gardener.
Six of Cups.
Smudging.
Summer.
Thank You for the Valentine.
Turtle, The.
Uneasy Rider.
Walking Past Paul Blackburn's Apt. on 7th St.
Wind Secrets.
You, Letting the Trees Stand as My Betrayer.

Walafrid [*or* Walahfried] Strabo
To His Friend in Absence.

Walcott, Derek
Alba.
Bridge, The.
Chelsea, The.
Codicil.
Country Club Romance, A.
Crusoe's Island.
Europa.
Far Cry from Africa, A.
Fist, The ("The fist clenched round my heart").
For the Altarpiece of the Roseau Valley Church, Saint Lucia.
Force.
Gulf, The.
Letter from Brooklyn, A.
Man o' War Bird.
Moon.
Nearing La Guaira.
New World.
Nights in the Gardens of Port of Spain.
Piano Practice.
Pocomania.
Ruins of a Great House.
Sea Canes.
Sea-Chantey, A, *sel.*
Season of Phantasmal Peace, The.
Spring Street in '58.
Tales of the Islands.
Virgins, The.
Volcano.
Whale, His Bulwark, The.

Waldheim, Franklin
Help Wanted.

Waldman, Anne
Lady Tactics.
Memorial Day; a Collaboration, *sel.*
Pressure.

Waldo, Rose
Welcome.

Waldrop, Keith
Around the Block.
Before Bed.
Introducing a Madman.
Signals.
Song: Paper.

Waldrop, Rosemarie
Confession to Settle a Curse.
Morning Has No House.

Waley, Arthur
Censorship.

Walford, William W.
Sweet Hour of Prayer.

Walker, Alice
Black Mail.
Burial.
Chic Freedom's Reflection.
Early Losses; a Requiem.
Even as I Hold You.
Expect Nothing.
"Good Night, Willie Lee, I'll See You in the Morning."
In These Dissenting Times.
Light Baggage.
Love, *sel.*
Medicine.
On Stripping Bark from Myself.
Once.
Revolutionary Petunias.
So We've Come at Last to Freud.
Suicide.
Threatened ("Threatened by my rising need").
Women.

Walker, Annie L.
Work, for the night is coming.

Walker, Brad
Instructions for a Park.

Walker, Charlie
St. George.

Walker, David
Catching-up.
Passages.

Walker, Dee Lawrence
Et Cetera.

Walker, E. M.
Anno Domini.
To America, on Her First Sons Fallen in the Great War.

Walker, J.
Love Song of J. Alfred Prufrock, The, *parody.*

Walker, James
Safe.

Walker, James J.
Will You Love Me in December as You Do in May?

Walker, Jeanne Murray
Deliver Me, O Lord, from My Daily Bread.
Tracking the Sled, Christmas 1951.

Walker, Kath
Dawn Wail for the Dead.
Then and Now.
We Are Going.

Walker, Margaret Abigail
Ballad of the Hoppy-Toad.
Birmingham.
Childhood.
For Andy Goodman—Michael Schwerner—and James Chaney.
For Malcolm X.
For Mary McLeod Bethune.
For My People.
Girl Held without Bail.
Harriet Tubman.
Jackson, Mississippi.
Kissie Lee.
Lineage.
Molly Means.
October Journey.
Prophets for a New Day.
Street Demonstration.
Today.
We Have Been Believers.

Walker, Paul
Leaves.

Walker, Ted
Breakwaters.
By the Bridge.
By the Saltings.
Estuary.
Heron.
Homing Pigeons.
Lemons.
Mules.
On Scafell Pike.
Skimmers.

Walker, William
High o'er the Hills, *with music.*

Walker, William Sidney
Too solemn for day, too sweet for night.

Wallace, Bronwen
Generation Gap
Profile.

Wallace, Edgar
War.

Wallace, James Cowden
God the Omniscient, *at.*

Wallace, John Aikman
God the Omniscient, *at.*

Wallace, Jon
Linebacker at Forty, The.
Puberty.

Wallace, Lew
Ben Hur, *sel.*
Song: " 'Wake not, but hear me, love!' "

Wallace, Robert
After the Swimmer.
Among the Finger Lakes.
Aubade: N.Y.C.
Ballad of the Mouse.
Double Play, The.
Driving By.
Fly in December.
Girl in Front of the Bank.
Girl Writing Her English Paper, The.
Gold Nest, The.
In a Spring Still Not Written Of.
In One Place.
In the Field Forever.
In Winter.
On the College Archery Range.
Out of the Past.
Snapshot for Miss Bricka Who Lost in the Semifinal Round of the Pennsylvania Lawn Tennis Tournament at Haverford, July, 1960, A.
Star-nosed Mole, The.
Storm, The.
Swimmer in the Rain.
Tulip.
Two Old Gentlemen, The.

Wallace, Ronald
Art Work.
Bird Watcher.
Father and Son.
Prayer for Fish.
Real Thing, The.
Spring Again.

Wallace, William Ross
Hand That Rocks the Cradle Is the Hand That Rules the World, The.
What Rules the World.

Wallace-Crabbe, Chris
Ancient Historian.
Citizen.
Dirigible, The.
Love Poem: "Written under Capricorn, a land."
Rebel General, The.

Wallach, Yona
Cradle Song: "Imagine lamenting our longing, no."
Death; She Was Always Here.
When the Angels Are Exhausted.

Wallāda
I wonder: is there no way for us to meet again.
If you were just in keeping our pact of love.
To Ibn Zaidun.
Wait till the darkness is deep.

Wallbank, Susan
Why So Many of Them Die.

Waller, Edmund
Apology [*or* Apologie] for Having Loved Before, An.
At Penshurst ("Had Sacharissa lived when mortals made").
At Penshurt ("While in the park I sing, the listning deer").
Battel of the Summer-Islands, The.
Chloris and Hilas. Made to a Saraban.
Dancer, The.
Go [*or* Goe], Lovely Rose.
Instructions to a Painter.
Last Verses.
Of a Fair Lady Playing with a Snake.
Of English Verse.
Of His Divine Poems.

Of His Majesties Receiving the News of the Duke of Buckingham's Death.
Of Loving at First Sight.
Of My Lady Isabella Playing on the Lute.
Of the Last Verses in the Book.
Old Age.
On a Girdle.
On Her Coming to London.
On My Lady Isabella Playing on the Lute.
On St. James's Park, as Lately Improved by His Majesty.
On the Friendship betwixt Two Ladies.
Panegyric [*or* Panegyrick] to My Lord Protector, A.
Panegyrick upon O. Cromwell.
Plea for Promiscuity, A.
Poets Lose Half the Praise.
Puerperium.
Say, Lovely Dream.
Selfe Banished, The.
Song: "Chloris! farewell. I now must go."
Song: "Goe lovely Rose."
Song: "Say, lovely dream! where couldst thou find."
Song: "Stay Phoebus, stay."
Soul's Dark Cottage, The.
Story of Phoebus and Daphne Applied, Etc., The.
To a Fair Lady Playing with a Snake.
To a Girl.
To a Lady in a Garden.
To a Very Young Lady.
To Amoret.
To Flavia.
To Mr. Henry Lawes, Who Had Then Newly Set a Song of Mine in the Year 1635.
To My Young Lady, Lucy Sidney.
To One Married to an Old Man.
To Phillis.
To the Mutable Fair.
Under a Lady's Picture.
Upon Ben Jonson.
While with a strong and yet a gentle hand.
Written in My Lady Speke's Singing-Book.

Waller, Janet
Aviemore.

Waller, Sir John
Enemy, The.
Goldenhair.
Legend.
Limb and Mind.
When Sadness Fills a Journey.

Waller, John Francis
Kitty Neil.
Spinning Wheel, The.

Wallis, Eleanor Glenn
Deathless Ones, The.
Hunter, The.
In a City Square.
Iulus.
"Trade" Rat.

Wallis, George B.
Lovely Rivers and Lakes of Maine, The.

Wallis, John
Twister Twisting Twine.

Wally, Darryl
Tablerock.

Walpole, Henry
Martyrdom of Father Campion, The.
Song of Mary the Mother of Christ, The, *at.*

Walpole, Horace, 4th Earl of Orford
All praise your face, your verses none abuse.
Anne Grenville, Countess Temple, Appointed Poet Laureate to the King of the Fairies.
Epitaph on Lady Ossory's Bullfinch.
Epitaphs [*or* Epitaph] on Two Piping-Bullfinches of Lady Ossory's, Buried under a Rose-Bush in Her Garden.
Estate and an earldom at seventy-four, An!
On the Translation of Anacreon.
To Lady Anne Fitzpatrick, When about Five Years Old, with a Present of Shells, 1772.
To the Gardener at Nuneham.

Walsh, Chad
Invocation: "Great-hearted Christ, importunate and mild."
My God, My God, Look upon Me.
Ode on a Plastic Stapes.
Ode to the Finnish Dead.
Port Authority Terminal: 9 A.M. Monday.
Psalm of Christ, The, *sels.*
Quintina of Crosses, A.
There Is None to Help.
Why Hast Thou Forsaken Me?

Walsh, Christina
Prayer to Isis.
Woman to Her Lover, A.

Walsh, Edward
Fairy Nurse, The.
Kitty Bhan.
Lament: "When the folk of my household."

Walsh, Ernest
Doctor Bill Williams.
I Played on the Grass with Mary.
Old Fellow.
Serious Poem, A.
Sonnet: "My duchess was the werst she laffed she bitte."

Walsh, Sir George Etherege
Rivals, *at.*
Song: "Of all the torments, all the cares," *at.*

Walsh, Marnie
Thomas Iron-Eyes.

Walsh, Ruth M.
Inadequate Aqua Extremis.
Rift Tide.

Walsh, Thomas
La Preciosa.
Russian Spring Song with Minaiev, A.

Walsh, William
Abigail's Lamentation for the Loss of Mr. Harley.
Against Marriage to His Mistress.
Despairing Lover, The.
Epigram, An: "Epigram should be, An—if right."
Letter: The Japanese, to Her Husband at War.
Love and Jealousy.
Lyce.
Rivals, *at.*
Rival, The, *at.*
Song: "Of all the torments, all the cares," *at.*
Sonnet on Death.

Walter, Beatrice
Photograph the Cat Licks, The.

Walter, Howard Arnold
I Would Be True.
My Creed.

Walter, Nehemiah
Elegiack Verse on. . .Mr. Elijah Corlet.

Walter, Nina Willis
Candle and Book.

Walters, Anna
Hartico.
I Am of the Earth.
I Have Bowed before the Sun.
My Brothers.
Simplicity Aims Circularly.
Teacher Taught Me, A.

Walters, Dorothy
Cinéma Vérité.
Flannery O'Connor.
Two Roads, etc.

Walters, Lettice D'Oyly
Seville.

Walters, Lila V.
He Shall Speak Peace unto the Nations.

Walther von der Vogelweide
Awake!
When I Survey the Wondrous Cross.
Maria Bright.
Tandaradei.
There Is a Lady ("There is a lady conquering with glances").
Translation from Walter von der Vogelweide, A ("I never set my two eyes").
Under the Lime Tree.
Under the Lindens.
With a Rod No Man Alive.

Waltner, Thomas
Bell in the Orthodox Steeple, A.
March 23, 1982; Tuesday Night.
Raven at Lemon Creek Jail.
Young Girl.

Walton, Eda Lou
How Our Forefather Got His Wife.
Indian Death.
Love Medicine.
Marriage Dance, The.
Necessary Miracle, A.

Walton, Izaac
Angler's Wish, The.
Compleat Angler, The, *sel.*

Walton, John
God, the Port of Peace.

Walworth, Clarence A.
Holy God, We Praise Thy Name.

Wanek, Connie
Bucket in the Well.

Wangara, Malaika Ayo
From a Bus.

Wang Chang-ling
Under the Frontier Post.

Wang Chi
Tell Me Now.

Wang Chien
South, The.
Weaving at the Window.

Wang Ch'ing-hui
Now the lotuses in the imperial lake.

Wang Chung-ju
Complaint of a Young Girl

Wang I
Lychee, The.

Wang Tsan
War in Chang-an City.

Wang Wei
Seeking a Mooring.

Waniek, Marilyn Nelson
Dinosaur Spring.
Herbs in the Attic.
Light under the Door.
Old Bibles.
Other Women's Children.
Women's Locker Room.

Wanley, Nathaniel
Humaine Cares.
Resurrection, The.
Royal [*or* Royall] Presents.
Sigh, The.

"Ward, Artemus" (Charles Farrar Browne)
Uncle Simon and Uncle Jim.

Ward, Edward
Ballad on the Taxes, A.
Dialogue between a Squeamish Cotting Mechanic and His Sluttish Wife, in the Kitchen.
Extravagant Drunkard's Wish, The.
Journey to Hell, A; or, A Visit Paid to the Devil, *sel.*
Nuptial Dialogues, *sel.*
Parish Poor-Officers, The.

Ward, Elizabeth Stuart Phelps (Elizabeth Stuart Phelps)
Afterward.
Conemaugh.
Eternal Christmas.
Generous Creed, A.
Gloucester Harbor.
Lost Colors, The.
Message, A.
Room's Width, The.

Ward, Kenneth
Investor's Soliloquy.

Ward, Leo
Four Friends.

Last Communion, The.
Ward, Lydia Avery Coonley
Flag Song.
Heredity.
To-Day.
Ward, May Williams
Wet Summer.
Ward, Nathaniel
Epigram: "World is full of care, much like unto a bubble, The."
Mercury shew'd Apollo, Bartas Book.
Mr. Ward of Anagrams Thus.
Poetry's a gift wherein but few excell.
World's a well strung fidle, mans tongue the quill, The.
Ward, Robert
Tenant Farmer.
Ward, Samuel
Proem, A: "When in my walks I meet some ruddy lad."
Ward, Terence
Kevin Barry.
Ward, William Hayes
New Castalia, The.
To John Greenleaf Whittier.
Warden, Marine Robert
Ode to a Homemade Coffee Cup.
Ware, Eugene Fitch ("Ironquill")
Aztec City, The.
Ballad in "G," A.
He and She.
Manila.
Whist.
Zephyr.
Ware, Henry, Jr.
Great God, the Followers of Thy Son, *with music.*
Lift Your Glad Voices in Triumph on High, *with music.*
Warfield, Catherine Anne
Beauregard.
Manassas.
Waring, H. C.
Quite the Cheese.
Warman, Cy
Creede.
Doing Railroads for *The Rocky Mountain News.*
Old Red Hoss Mountain.
Rise and Fall of Creede, The.
Sweet Marie.
Warner, Anna Bartlett ("Amy Lothrop")
Jesus Loves Me, This I Know, *with music.*
One More Day's Work for Jesus, *with music.*
We Would See Jesus, *with music.*
Warner, Charles Dudley
Bookra.
Warner, Eva
Irony of God.
Warner, Rex
Chough.
Sonnet: "Understanding of a medical man, The."
Warner, Sylvia Townsend
Absence, The.
After He Had Gone.
Alarum, The.
Benicasim.
Building in Stone.
Country Thought.
Elizabeth.
Epitaph: "Her grieving parents cradled here."
Epitaph: "I, an unwedded wandering dame."
Epitaph: "I, Richard Kent, beneath these stones."
Epitaph: "John Bird, a laborer, lies here."
Green Valley, The.
Killing No Murder.
Modo and Alciphron.
Nelly Trim.
Rival, The.
Sad Green.
Sailor, The.
Song: "She has left me, my pretty."
Song from the Bride of Smithfield.
Triumph of Sensibility.
Warner, William
Albion's England, *sel.*
Fate of Narcissus, The.
My Mistress.
Warr, Bertram J.
Deviator, The.
Heart to Carry On, The.
On a Child with a Wooden Leg.
Poets in Time of War.
There Are Children in the Dusk.
Tress Who Are Distant.
Working Class.
Warren, Edward Perry. *See* **"Raile, Arthur Lyon"**
Warren, Eugene
Christographia 35.
Warren, Hamilton
Requiem: "Let the mountains stand forth."
Warren, James E., Jr.
Schoolroom: 158.
Seizure.
Warren, Joseph
Free America.
Warren, Mercy
Massachusetts Song of Liberty, *at.*
Warren, Robert Penn
After Night Flight.
American Portrait: Old Style.
Apology for Domitian.
Aubade for Hope.
Ballad of a Sweet Dream of Peace.
Ballad of Billie Potts, The.
Bearded Oaks.
Birth of Love.
Blow, West Wind.
Boy Wandering in Simms' Valley.
Boy's Will, Joyful Labor without Pay, and Harvest Home, *sel.*
Cardinal, The.
Colder Fire.
Commuter's Entry in a Connecticut Diary.
Country Burying (1919).
Debate: Question, Quarry, Dream.
Dragon Country: To Jacob Boehme.
Dream, Dump-Heap, and Civilization.
End of Season.
Fairy Story.
Fall Comes in Back-Country Vermont.
Flower, The.
Founding Fathers, Nineteenth-Century Style.
Garden, The.
He Was Formidable.
History.
History among the Rocks.
Homage to Theodore Dreiser on the Centennial of His Birth, *sel.*
Hunger and Thirst.
In the Mountains, *sel.*
Internal Injuries.
Kentucky Mountain Farm, *sels.*
Lessons in History.
Letter from a Coward to a Hero.
Letter of a Mother.
Letter to a Friend.
Limited, The.
Man in the Street.
Mango on the Mango Tree, The.
Mexico Is a Foreign Country: Four Studies in Naturalism, *sel.*
Mortmain.
Myth on Mediterranean Beach: Aphrodite as Logos.
Natural History.
Nightmare of Mouse.
Notes on a Life to Be Lived.
Original Sin: A Short Story.
Owl, The.
Patriotic Tour and Postulate of Joy.
Penological Study: Southern Exposure, *sel.*
Pondy Woods.
Pro Sua Vita.
Promises, *sels.*
Pursuit.
Real Question Calling for Solution, A.
Recollection Long Ago: Sad Music.
Remarks of Soul to Body.
Revelation.
Sila.
Skiers.
Small White House.
Swimming in the Pacific.
Terror.
There's a Grandfather's Clock in the Hall.
To a Little Girl, One Year Old, in a Ruined Fortress, *sel.*
Treasure Hunt.
Two Pieces after Suetonius.
Watershed.
Ways of Day.
Wet Hair: If Now His Mother Should Come.
When the Century Dragged.
Where the Slow Fig's Purple Sloth.
Work.
Warren, Rosanna
Alps.
Daylights.
Lily.
Omalos.
Virgin Pictured in Profile.
Warren, Sir Thomas Herbert
Lines for a Sundial.
May-Day on Magdalen Tower.
Warren, Valerie S.
I Was the Child.
Warren, William F.
I Worship Thee, O Holy Ghost, *with music.*
Warshaw, Jack *and* **Barbara Dane**
Kent State Massacre, The.
Warshawsky, Mark
Oyfn Pripetshuk (On the Hearth).
Warton, Joseph
Charms of Nature, The.
Dying Indian, The.
Enthusiast, The; or, The Lover of Nature.
Invocation to Fancy.
Ode: To the Nightingale.
Ode to Fancy, *sels.*
Warton, Thomas, the Elder
Retirement, an Ode, *sel.*
Warton, Thomas, the Younger
Come, gentle sleep, death's image though thou art.
Grave of King Arthur, The.
Inscription in a Hermitage.
Ode: First of April, The, *sel.*
On Leander's Swimming over the Hellespont to Hero.
Pleasures of Melancholy, The.
Solemn Noon of Night, The.
Sonnet: "Deem not, devoid of elegance, the sage."
Sonnet: To the River Lodon [*or* Loddon].
Sonnet: Written after Seeing Wilton-House.
Sonnet: Written in a Blank Leaf of Dugdale's "Monasticon."
Verses on Sir Joshua Reynolds's Painted Window at New College, Oxford.
Washbourne, Thomas
Casting All Your Care upon God, for He Careth for You.
Circulation, The.
Prayer: "What a commanding power."
Upon a Great Shower of Snow That Fell on May-Day, 1654.
Upon a Passing Bell.
Washburn, Henry Stevenson
Almighty God, Thy Constant Care, *with music.*
Song of the Harvest.
Vacant Chair, The.
Wason, Harriet L.
Slide at the Empire Mine, The.

Wassall, Irma
Singing in the Dark.
Stone from the Gods.
Wasson, David Atwood
Joy-Month.
Wastell, Simon,
Man's Mortality, *at.*
Microbiblion, *sel., at.*
Wat, Aleksander
There Is No Place.
Willows in Alma-Ata.
Waterbury, Jared Bell
I Have Fought the Good Fight, *with music.*
Sinner, Is Thy Heart at Rest? *with music.*
Waterhouse, Gilbert
This Is the Last.
Waterman, Cary
Death on the Farm.
Pig Poem.
Waterman, Charles
Neighbor.
New Cows, The.
Waterman, Nixon
Cheer for the Consumer.
Far from the Madding Crowd.
If We Didn't Have to Eat.
Johnny's Hist'ry Lesson.
Making a Man.
Recompense.
Rose to the Living, A.
To Know All Is to Forgive All.
Vacation.
What Have We Done Today?
Whistling Boy.
Watermeyer, G. A.
Harvest Time.
Waters, Michael
American Bandstand.
Among Blackberries.
Apples.
Catfish, The.
Frank Sinatra.
Mystery of the Caves, The.
Mythology.
Night Fishing.
Preserves.
Since Nothing Is Impossible.
Singles.
Stories in the Light, The.
Watkins, Edward
Acrobat.
Adam, Eve and the Big Apple.
Figures of Authority.
What Is a Sonnet?
Watkins, Grace V.
Greater Country, The.
Watkins, Lucian B.
Star of Ethiopia.
To Our Friends.
Two Points of View.
Watkins, Vernon
Ballad of the Three Coins.
Ballad of the Two Tapsters.
Beaver's Story, The.
Cave-Drawing, The.
Collier, The.
Compost Heap, The.
Cwmrhydyceirw Elegiacs.
Dead Words, The.
Demands of the Muse.
Discoveries.
Earth and Fire.
Feather, The.
Fingernail Sunrise.
Fire in the Snow, The.
First Joy.
Foal.
For a Wine Festival.
Furnace of Colors, The.
Gravestones.
Healing of the Leper, The.
Heron, The.
Hurdy-Gurdy Man in Winter.
Indolence.
Infant Noah.
Lady with the Unicorn, The.
Lover's Words, A.
Mother and Child, The.
Mummy, The.
Music of Colours: The Blossom Scattered.
Music of Colours—White Blossom.
Napkin and Stone.
Ophelia.
Peace in the Welsh Hills.
Poet and Goldsmith.
Prayer, A: "If I dare pray for one."
Returning from Harvest.
She That Is Memory's Daughter.
Shooting of Werfel, The.
Snow Curlew, The.
Song of the Good Samaritan, The.
Spoils of War, The.
Sunbather, The.
Swedenborg's Skull.
True Picture Restored, A.
Turning of the Leaves, The.
Two Decisions.
Waterfalls.
Yeats in Dublin, *sel.*
Yeats' Tower.
Yew-Tree, The.
Watkyns, Rowland
Antipathy.
Bad company is a disease.
Saul did much care and diligence express.
Strange Monsters.
Wish, The.
Worldly Wealth.
Watson, Albert Durrant
Breeze and Billow.
Hymn for Canada, A.
Priest and Pagan.
Soul Lifted.
Watson, Barbara Bellow
Late Light.
Watson, Clyde
Dilly Dilly Piccalilli.
Do the Baby Cake-Walk.
Huckleberry, Gooseberry, Raspberry Pie.
Phoebe in a Rosebush.
Rock, Rock, Sleep, My Baby.
Yip-yap Rattletrap.
Watson, Edward Willard
Absolution.
Watson, Elaine
Museum Piece No. 16228.
Watson, Evelyn M.
Sleeping Beauty, A.
Watson, J. Y.
Soldier, The.
Watson, James Wreford ("James Wreford")
Gatineaus, The.
Our Love Shall Be the Brightness.
Sic Transit Gloria Mundi.
Stay, Time.
We Shall Have Far to Go.
Watson, John Whittaker
Beautiful Snow.
Watson, Minor
Constancy.
Watson, Nancy Dingman
Up in the Pine.
Watson, Robert
Blue Whale, The.
Do You Love Me?
Glass Door, The.
Good Life, A.
Is There Life across the Street?
Times Square Parade.
Watson, Rosamund Marriott ("Graham R. Tomson"; "R. Armytage")
Ave atque Vale.
Farm on the Links, The.
Last Fairy, The.
Omnia Somnia.
Requiescat.
South Coast Idyll, A.
To My Cat.
Watson, Sara Ruth
Bouncing Ball.
Watson, Thomas
Come, Gentle Death!
Ditty of the Six Virgins, The.
Hecatompathia; or, Passionate Century of Love, *sels.*
Here Lieth Love.
Love's Grave.
My Love is Past.
Sonnet: "I saw the object of my pining thought."
Time.
With Fragrant Flowers We Strew the Way.
Watson, W. F. N.
Hicche-Hykeres Tale, The.
Watson, Wilfred
Canticle of Darkness.
Contempt for Dylan Thomas, A.
Emily Carr.
In the Cemetery of the Sun.
Invocation: "Appear, O Mother, was the perpetual cry."
Juniper Tree, The.
Lines: I Praise God's Mankind in an Old Woman.
O My Poor Darling.
White Bird, The.
Windy Bishop, The.
Watson, Sir William
April.
Autumn.
Church Today, The.
Dawn on the Headland.
Domine Quo Vadis?
Epigram: " 'Tis human fortune's happiest height, to be."
Epigram: "When whelmed the altar, priest and creed."
God-seeking.
Great Misgiving, The.
Hope of the World, The.
Hymn to the Sea.
Invention.
Key-Board, The.
Lacrimae Musarum.
Leavetaking.
Love.
Ode in May.
Poet, The.
Shakespeare.
Song: "April, April,/ Laugh thy girlish laughter."
Song: "O, like a queen's her happy tread."
Song to April.
Sonnets to Miranda, *sels.*
Sovereign Poet, The.
Things That Are More Excellent, The.
Two Epigrams.
Unknown God, The.
Vita Nuova.
Woman with the Serpent's Tongue, The.
Wordsworth's Grave.
Watt, Frederick B.
Inspection, The.
Watt, Lauchlan MacLean
I Bind My Heart.
Reapers, The.
Wind from the West, A.
Watt, T. S.
From My Rural Pen.
Watt, W. W.
So This Is Autumn.
Summer Song.
Watterman, Catharine H.
Come unto Me, When Shadows Darkly Gather, *with music.*

Wattles, Willard Austin
Builder, The.
Comrades of the Cross.
Creeds.
Family of Nations, The.
From the Parthenon I Learn.
Gabriel.
I Thought Joy Went by Me.
Jericho.
Pisgah.
Watts, Alaric Alexander
Austrian Army, An, *at.*
Watts, Isaac
Adventurous Muse, The.
Against Quarrelling and Fighting.
Broad Is the Road.
Church the Garden of Christ, The.
Comparison and Complaint, The.
Cradle Hymn, A.
Cradle Song, A: "Hush! my dear, lie still and slumber."
Crucifixion to the World by the Cross of Christ.
Day of Judgement [*or* Judgment], The.
Early, my God, without delay.
Felicity.
Few Happy Matches.
For the Lord's Day Evening.
From All That Dwell below the Skies.
God's Dominion and Decrees.
Great God, attend while Zion sings.
Heaven.
Heavens Declare Thy Glory, Lord!
Horace Paraphrased.
Hosanna to Christ.
How Doth the Little Busy Bee.
How long, dear Savior, O how long.
Hurry of the Spirits, in a Fever and Nervous Disorders, The.
I Sing the Mighty Power of God.
Incomprehensible, The.
Innocent Play.
Jesus Shall Reign Where'er the Sun.
Joy to the World.
King Triumphant.
Let Dogs Delight to Bark and Bite.
Little Busy Bee.
Look on Him Whom They Pierced, and Mourn.
Love between Brothers and Sisters.
Man Frail, and God Eternal.
Miracles at the Birth of Christ.
Ninetieth Psalm, The.
Ninety-fifth.
O God, Our Help in Ages Past.
O How I Love Thy Law.
Our God, Our Help in Ages Past.
Our Saviour's Golden Rule.
Passion and Exaltation of Christ, The.
Praise for Mercies Spiritual and Temporal.
Prospect of Heaven Makes Death Easy, A.
Quarrelling.
Recessional.
Saint's Delight, The.
Shortness and Misery of Life, The.
Sincere Praise, *sel.*
Sluggard, The.
Spare Us, O Lord, Aloud We Pray, *with music.*
Submission to Afflictive Providences.
"Sweet Muse."
Where Nothing Dwelt but Beasts of Prey, *with music.*
Where-e'er My Flatt'ring Passions Rove.
Why Do We Mourn Departing Friends? *with music.*
With songs and honors sounding loud.
Watts, Mabel
Maytime Magic.
Riveter, The.
Watts, Marjorie Seymour
New Shoes.
Policeman, The.
Watts-Dunton, Theodore
Coleridge.
First Kiss, The.
Mother Carey's Chicken.
Sonnet's Voice, The.
Waugh, Edwin
Dule's i' This Bonnet o' Mine, The.
Wayland, John Elton ("Idas")
Epilogue at Wallack's, An.
Wayman, Tom
Another Poem about the Madness of Women.
Chilean Elegies, The: 5. The Interior.
Picketing Supermarkets.
Poem Composed in Rogue River Park . . .
Wayman in Love.
What Good Poems Are For.
Wazyk, Adam
Ars Poetica.
Hotel.
Nike.
Weare, Meshech
Blasted Herb, The.
Weatherly, Frederic Edward
Carol, A: "Angels to the shepherds sang, The."
Cats' Tea-Party, The.
Dustman, The.
Holy City, The.
Tale of a Tart, The.
When the Christ Child Came.
Weatherly, Tom
Arroyo.
Cantos, *sels.*
First Monday Scottsboro Alabama.
Imperial Thumbprint.
Weaver, Edith
Lost Cinderella.
Weaver, John Van Alstyn
Drug Store.
Ghost.
Legend.
Nocturne: "Nothin' or everythin' it's got to be."
Two Ways.
Weaver, Roger
December 24, 1979.
To J.F.K. 14 Years After.
Weaving, Willoughby
Star, The.
Webb, Charles David
And Dust to Dust.
Jardin des Fleurs.
Monasteries.
Orestes Pursued.
Threshold.
Webb, Charles Henry ("John Paul")
At the Ball!
Autumn Leaves.
Dum Vivimus Vigilamus.
Gil, the Toreador.
March.
With a Nantucket Shell.
Webb, Francis
Airliner.
Drum for Ben Boyd, A, *sel.*
Five Days Old.
Gunner, The.
Idyll: "At noon the sun puffed up, outsize."
Leichhardt in Theatre, *sel.*
Papuan Shepherd, A.
Room, The.
Sea, The.
This Runner.
Ward Two.
Webb, Frederick G.
Dash for the Colors, The.
Webb, Mary
Autumn, 1914.
Green Rain.
Market Day.
Water-Ousel, The.
Webb, Phyllis
Days of the Unicorns, The.
Imperfect Sestina.
Kropotkin Poems, The, *sel.*
Making.
Marvell's Garden.
Poetics against the Angel of Death.
Propositions.
Rilke.
Spots of Blood.
Tall Tale, A; or, A Moral Song.
"Time of Man, The."
To Friends Who Have Also Considered Suicide.
Webb, Tessa Sweazy
Bright Abandon.
Webb, Thomas Harry Basil
Ancient Prayer, An.
Prayer, A: "Give us a good digestion, Lord."
Prayer Found in Chester Cathedral, A.
Webbe, Charles
Against Indifference.
Webber, Mary A.
Warning, A.
Weber, Helen
Lessons.
Weber, Nancy
Tidying Up.
Weber, Richard
Borderline Ballad.
Elizabeth in Italy.
Envying the Pelican.
In Memoriam I, Elizabeth at Twenty.
In Memoriam II, Elizabeth in Italy.
Lion and O'Reilly, The.
Observation.
On an Italian Hillside.
O'Reilly's Reply.
Poet's Day, The.
Primer for Schoolchildren, A.
Visit to Bridge House, A.
Weber, Tom
"I'm 92," Joe said.
Webster, A. W.
On the Wrong Side.
Webster, Augusta Davies ("Cecil Home")
Castaway, A, *sel.*
Medea in Athens, *sel.*
Pine, The.
Seeds.
Violet and the Rose, The.
Webster, Daniel
On the Death of My Son Charles.
Webster, Diane
Memory Movie.
Webster, H. D. L.
Lorena.
Webster, John
All the Flowers of the Spring.
Burial, The.
Call for the Robin Redbreast and the Wren.
Devil's Law Case, The, *sels.*
Dirge, A: "Call for the robin-redbreast and the wren."
Duchess of Malfi, The, *sels.*
Dutchesse of Malfy, The.
Execration against Whores, An.
Hark.
Hark [*or* Hearke], Now Everything Is Still.
I am come to make thy tomb.
Land Dirge, A.
Madman's Song, The.
Nets to Catch the Wind.
Song: "All the flowers of the spring."
Song: "Oh, let us howl some heavy note."
Summons to Execution.
Survey our progress from our birth.
Vanitas Vanitatum.
White Devil, The, *sels.*
Webster, M. M.
Marriage of Pocahontas, The.
Webster, Mary Morison
Grass.
I Set Aside.
Illi Morituri.
Ox, The.
Quiet of the Dead, The.
Secret, The.

Webster, W. J.
To His Coy Mistress, *parody.*
Wedde, Ian
Beautiful Poultry.
Cardrona Valley.
Dark Wood.
Earthly: Sonnets for Carlos, *sels.*
Hardon ("Get One Today").
It's Time.
Losing the Straight Way.
Wedderburn, James, John, *and* **Robert**
Balulalow.
Cradle Song: "O my deir hert, young Jesus sweit."
Wedderburn, John
Sang of the Birth of Christ, with the Tune of Baw Lula Low, Ane, *abr.*
Wedgefarth, W. Dayton
Bum.
Wedgwood, M. Winifred
Christmas, 1916.
V.A.D. Scullery-Maid's Song, The.
Weeden, Craig
Calvin in the Attic Cleans.
Pizza Joint in Cranston, A.
Yachting in Arkansas.
Weeden, Lula Lowe
Have You Seen It.
Little Dandelion, The.
Me Alone.
Robin Red Breast.
Stream, The.
Weekes, Charles
In Brittany.
Poppies.
Solstice.
Think.
Weeks, James Eyre
On the Great Fog in London, December 1762.
Weeks, Ramona
Indian Graveyard, The.
Weeks, Robert Kelley
Man and Nature.
Medusa.
Song for Lexington, A.
Weeks, Robert Lewis
Appalachian Front.
Weelkes, Thomas
Madrigal: "Ay me, alas, heigh ho, heigh ho!"
Weever, John
De Se.
Weever, Robert
In an Arbour Green.
Weigl, Bruce
Burning Shit at An Khe.
Harp, The.
Homage to Elvis, Homage to the Fathers.
Limits of Departure, The.
1955.
Snowy Egret.
Song of Napalm.
Weil, James L.
At a Loss.
Coney Island Life, A.
Weiman, Andrew
Andy-Diana DNA Letter.
Wein, Jules Alan
Genesis.
Weingarten, Roger
Blue Bog Children.
Ethan Boldt.
Her Apron through the Trees.
Memoir.
These Obituaries of Rattlesnakes Being Eaten by the Hogs.
Weiser, Conrad
Jehovah, Lord and Majesty, *with music.*
Weismiller, Edward
To the Woman in Bond Street Station.
Trail, The.
Weiss, Neil
Aging Athlete, The.
Word, The.
Weiss, Theodore
Art in America.
As You Like It.
Barracks Apt. 14.
Clothes Maketh the Man.
Dab of Color, A.
Dance Called David, The.
Death of Fathers, The.
Egyptian Passage, An.
Fire at Alexandria, The.
Greater Music, The.
Hayseed.
Homecoming.
House of Fire.
In the Round.
Last Day and the First, The.
Letter from the Pygmies, A.
Life of . . ., The.
Moral, The.
Off to Patagonia.
Out of Your Hands.
Preface: " 'Sonja Henie,' the young girl."
Reapings, The.
Sow's Ear, A.
This Narrow Stage.
To Forget Me.
Ultimate Antientropy, The.
Ways of Loving.
Web, The.
"Yes, But . . ."
Weissbort, Daniel
Anniversary.
Murder of a Community.
Walking Home at Night.
Weisslitz, E. F.
Baldpate Pond.
Welburn, Ron
Avoidances.
Cecil County.
Eulogy for Populations.
Percussions.
Regenesis.
Welby, Amelia B. Coppuck
Twilight at Sea.
Welch, Don
Armless, The.
Bark.
Blue Heron.
Carved by Obadiah Verity.
Dutchman, The.
Fishing, at Coot Shallows.
River, The.
Small, The.
Spade Scharnweber.
We Used to Play.
Welch, James
Across to the Peloponnese.
Arizona Highways.
Blue like Death.
Christmas Comes to Moccasin Flat.
D-Y Bar.
Directions to the Nomad.
Going to Remake This World.
Harlem, Montana; Just Off the Reservation.
In My First Hard Springtime.
In My Lifetime.
Lady in a Distant Face.
Magic Fox.
Man from Washington, The.
Only Bar in Dixon, The.
Plea to Those Who Matter.
Please Forward.
Renegade Wants Words, The.
Snow Country Weavers.
Surviving.
Thanksgiving at Snake Butte.
Verifying the Dead.
Visit.
Why I Didn't Go to Delphi.
Welch, Lew
After Anacreon.
Chicago Poem.
Song of the Turkey Buzzard.
Taxi Suite, *sel.*
Wobbly Rock.
Welch, Marie De L.
Mus Ridiculus Non.
Prelude to Commencement.
Welch, Myra Brooks
Touch of the Master's Hand, The.
Welch, Noel
Anne and the Peacock.
Welles, Winifred
Behind the Waterfall.
Child's Song to Her Mother, A.
Cruciform.
Curious Something.
Dogs and Weather.
Gesture.
"God's First Creature Was Light."
Green Grass and White Milk.
Green Moth.
Love Song from New England.
Man with a Little Pleated Piano, A.
Old Ellen Sullivan.
Silence.
Skipping Along Alone.
Starfish.
Stocking Fairy.
White Fear.
Wellesley, Dorothy, Duchess of Wellington
As Lambs into the Pen.
Asian Desert.
Buried Child, The.
Deserted House, *sel.*
Epilogue: "He is not dead nor liveth."
Fire.
Fishing.
Horses.
Lenin, *sel.*
Lighthouses.
Lost Lane.
Matrix, *sel.*
Morning After, The.
Wells, Amos Russel
Ambitious Ant, The.
Considerate Crocodile, The.
Inn That Missed Its Chance, The.
Mothers—and Others.
Pray!
Read the Bible Through.
Wells, Anna Maria
Cow-Boy's Song, The.
Little Maid, The.
Wells, Carolyn
Baker's Dozen of Wild Beasts, A, *sels.*
Bath-Bunny, The.
Beggarly Bear, A.
Careless Niece, The.
Corn-Pone-y, The.
Cream-Puffin, The.
Disobliging Bear, The.
Diversions of the Re-Echo Club.
Dragon, The.
Dresscessional, A.
Gnome Matter.
Grandiloquent Goat, The.
Happy Hyena, The.
How To Tell the Wild Animals.
Limerick: "Canner, exceedingly canny, A."
Limerick: "There was a young fellow [*or* person] named Tait [*or* Tate]," *at.*
Limerick: "Tutor who tooted a flute, A."
Marvel, A.
Mince-Python, The.
Old Lady from Dover, The.
Ossified Oyster, An.
Overworked Elocutionist, An.
Oyster-Crabs.
Policy.
Poster Girl, The.
Puzzled.
Swift Bullets, The.

Theater Hat, The.
Tidy Young Tapir, A.
To a Baked Fish.
Travelogue, A: Clovelly.
Tutor [Who Tooted a Flute], A.
Two Limericks.
Universal Favorite, The.
Wild Worm, A.
Wells, Faith
More than We Ask.
Wells, James
Golden Rule, The.
Wells, Marcus Morris
Holy Spirit, Faithful Guide, *with music.*
Wells, Rollin J.
Growing Old.
Growing Older.
Wells, Will
Fisherman, The.
Welsh, Anne
Between Seasons.
Many Birds.
Sharpeville Inquiry.
That Way.
Waterfall.
Welsh, Robert Gilbert
Azrael.
Welsh, William
8:00 A.M. Monday Morning.
Wasp.
Welsted, Leonard
Invitation, The.
Welte, Lou Ann
Those Last, Late Hours of Christmas Eve.
Welty, Eudora
Flock of Guinea Hens Seen from a Car, A.
Wenberi
Wenberi's Song.
Wendell, W. G.
Inscription in a Library.
Wendt, Ingrid
Newest Banana Plant Leaf, The.
Personal Poem.
Wenger, Renee
After Chagall.
Wentworth, William Charles
Australasia, *sel.*
Wen Yi-tuo
Confession, The.
Weöres, Sándor
Lost Parasol, The, *sel.*
Werfel, Franz
Eternal Road, The, *sel.*
Exaltation.
For I Have Done a Good and Kindly Deed.
Litany of the Rooms of the Dead.
Loneliness.
Song of Life, A.
Strangers Are We All upon the Earth.
Teach Us to Mark This, God.
To a Lark in War-Time.
Ye Sorrowers.
Wergeland, Henrik Arnold Thaulov
Wall-Flower, The.
Werner, Alice
Song of Fleet Street, A.
Werner, Martina
Monogram 4.
Monogram 29.
Monogram 23.
Wertheimer, Paul
Souls.
Wescott, Glenway
Poet at Night-Fall, The.
Summer Ending, The.
Wesley, Cecil Cobb
As Night Comes On.
Wesley, Charles
Ah! Lovely Appearance of Death! *with music.*
Charge to Keep I Have, A.
Christ, the Refuge of the Soul.
Come, O Thou Traveller Unknown.
Come, Thou Almighty King.
Divine Love.
Divine Lover, The.
During His Courtship.
Easter Hymn.
Ever-living Church, The.
Father, How Wide Thy Glories Shine.
For His Wife, on Her Birthday.
Free Grace.
Gentle Jesus [Meek and Mild].
Hark! the Herald Angels Sing.
Horrible Decree, The, *sel.*
Hymn: "O thou who camest from above."
I Know That My Redeemer Lives.
In Temptation.
Incarnation, The.
Inextinguishable Blaze.
Jesus [*or* Jesu], Lover of My Soul.
Love Divine, All Loves Excelling.
Morning Hymn, A.
My Companion.
Nativity, The.
O Thou Eternal Victim Slain.
O Thou Who Camest from Above.
On Sympathisers with the American Revolution.
On the Death of His Son.
Still, O Lord, for Thee I Tarry.
"Times without Number Have I Pray'd."
Whole Armour of God, The.
Wrestling Jacob.
Wesley, John
Hymn: "Thou hidden love of God, whose height."
John Wesley's Grace before Meals.
John Wesley's Rule.
Wesley, Samuel (1662-1735)
Pindaric on the Grunting of a Hog, A.
Wesley, Samuel (1691-1739)
Anacreontic, on Parting with a Little Child.
Epigram on Miltonicks.
Epitaph, An: "Here lie I, once a witty fair."
From a Hint in the Minor Poets.
Hymn to God the Father.
On the Setting Up [of] Mr. Butler's Monument in Westminister Abbey.
Wesley-Smith, Peter
Ugstabuggle, The.
Weslowski, Dieter
Zoe and the Ghosts.
West, Annette Arkeketa
Blackbird Winter.
Calumet Early Evening.
Child Poem.
Coyote Brother Song.
Glenpool.
Naming the Rain.
Poem for My Father.
Salt Man.
West, Arthur Graeme
God, How I Hate You.
West, Don
My South.
West, Jessamyn
Song of the Settlers.
West, John, 1st Earl de la Warr
Fair Hebe.
West, John Foster
Hill Hunger.
West, Kenyon
"Thou Shouldst Be Living at This Hour!"
West, Paul
Cumberbunce, The.
West, Robert A.
Come, Let Us Tune Our Loftiest Song, *with music.*
Westcott, Joseph L.
Legend of Grand Lake, The.
Westendorf, Thomas P.
I'll Take You Home Again, Kathleen.
Westerfield, Nancy G.
Carolers.
Where I Walk in Nebraska.
Westmorland, Mildmay Fane, Earl of
My Happy Life.
Weston, Mildred
Argument.
Bleat of Protest.
Central Park Tourney.
Cider Song.
Echo.
Episode of the Cherry Tree.
Father.
Hat Bar.
Hotel Lobby.
Query.
Song for Thrift Week.
To a Lady Holding the Floor.
To a Man in a Picture Window Watching Television.
Westrup, J. M.
Flying.
Westwood, Thomas
Little Bell.
Mine Host of "The Golden Apple."
Night of Spring.
Under My Window.
Wetherald, Ethelwyn
House of the Trees, The.
In April.
Woodland and Worship.
Wever, Robert
In Youth Is Pleasure.
Lusty Juventus, *sel.*
Of Youth He Singeth.
Youth.
Wevill, David
Birth of a Shark, The.
Body of a Rook.
In Love.
Irish Hotel.
Monsoon.
Poets, The.
Snow
Spiders.
Wexionius, Olof
On the Death of a Pious Lady.
Wexler, Irving
Elegy for My Father, *sel.*
Weyburn, Ruby T. [*or*]T. *See* **Tobias, Ruby Weyburn.**
Whalen, Philip
Denunciation; or, Unfrock'd Again.
For C.
For Kai Snyder.
For My Father.
Forty-five Years since the Fall of the Ch'ing Dynasty.
Further Notice.
How Was Your Trip to L.A.?
Life in the City: In Memoriam Edward Gibbon.
Literary Life in the Golden West.
Martyrdom of Two Pagans.
Same Old Jazz, The.
Sourdough Mountain Lookout.
Take I, 4:11:58.
Technicalities for Jack Spicer.
10:X:57, 45 Years Since the Fall of the Ch'ing Dynasty.
To the Muse.
25:I:68.
2 Variations: All About Love.
Where or When.
Whalley, George
Affair of Honour.
Night Flight.
We Who Are Left.
Wharton, Anne
How Hardly I Conceal'd My Tears.
Spite of Thy Godhead, Powerful Love.
Wharton, Thomas Wharton, 1st Marquess of
Lilliburlero.
Wharton, William H.
Ben Milam.

Whately, Richard, Archbishop
Serio-Comic Elegy, A.
Wheatcroft, John
Pisanello's Studies of Men Hanging on Gallows.
Wheatley, Phillis
Goliath of Gath.
His Excellency General Washington.
Hymn to the Evening, An.
Hymn to the Morning, An.
Liberty and Peace.
On Being Brought from Africa to America.
On Imagination.
On Virtue.
Should you, my lord, while you pursue my song.
To a Gentleman and Lady on the Death of the Lady's Brother and Sister, and a Child of the Name Avis, Aged One Year.
To a Lady on the Death of Her Husband.
To His Excellency George Washington.
To S. M. a Young African Painter, on Seeing His Work.
To the King's Most Excellent Majesty.
To the Right Honourable William, Earl of Dartmouth.
To the University of Cambridge, in New-England.
Wheeler, Charles Enoch
Adjuration.
Tumult.
Wheeler, Edward Jewett
Night's Mardi Gras.
Wheeler, Kathleen
New Leaf, A [*or* The].
Wheeler, Sylvia
Lost Contact.
Wheelock, John Hall
Afternoon: Amagansett Beach.
Amagansett Beach Revisited.
Beethoven.
Black Panther, The.
Bonac.
Dawn on Mid-Ocean.
Dear Men and Women.
Dialectics of Flight.
Divine Insect, The.
Earth ("Grasshopper, your fairy [*or* tiny] song").
Elegy: "Gnu up at the zoo, The."
Ernest Dowson.
Exile from God.
Far Land, The.
Fish-Hawk, The.
For Them All.
Gardener, The.
Hippopotamothalamion.
House in the Green Well, The.
I Do Not Love to See Your Beauty Fire.
Lion-House, The.
Love and Liberation.
New York.
Night Thoughts in Age.
Nirvana.
Prayer: "Have pity on us, Power just and severe."
Random Reflections on a Cloudless Sunday.
Random Reflections on a Summer Evening.
Reconciliation.
Sea-Voyage.
Silence.
Slow Summer Twilight.
Song on Reaching Seventy.
Sound of the Sea, The.
Sun Men Call It, The.
Sunday Evening in the Common.
Thanks from Earth to Heaven.
This Quiet Dust.
To the Modern Man.
Triumph of Love.
Two Societies, The.
Unknown Beloved, The.
Valediction: "Glory of soundless heaven, wheel of stars."
Wood-Thrush.
Years, The.
Wheelock, Lucy
Song of the Lilies, The.
Wheelwright, John
Apocryphal Apocalypse.
Ave Eva.
Canal Street.
Father.
Fish Food.
From Gestures to the Dead.
Huntsman, The.
Paul and Virginia.
There is No Opera like "Lohengrin."
Train Ride.
Why Must You Know?
Wheelwright, John Brooks
Forty Days, *sel.*
Second Ascension of Christ, The.
Whetham, Catherine Durning
Poet and the Butcher, The.
Whetstone, George
Give Me My Work.
Whicher, George Meason
Bacchylides.
To the Frivolous Muse.
Whinery, Verna
This Day is Thine.
Whipple, George
Three Cezannes.
Whisler, Robert F.
Collector, The.
Pigeons.
Whistler, Laurence
Form of Epitaph, A.
No Answer.
Portrait in the Guards, A.
Shape of a Bird, The.
Whitaker, Alexander
Leaving the Dance.
Whitaker, Robert
Easter.
My Country Is the World.
O Mothers of the Human Race.
Out-of-Doors.
Starred Mother, The.
Worship.
Whitbread, Thomas
CCC, The ("CCC campers near West Cummington").
Pool, A.
To My Fellow-Mariners, March, '53.
White, Christine
Secret of Song.
White, Christy
Running under Street Lights.
White, Claire Nicholas
Roses of Queens, The.
White, Cool
Lubly Fan, *with music.*
White, Edward Lucas
Genius.
Last Bowstrings, The.
White, Elwyn Brooks
Affidavit in Platitudes.
Apostrophe to a Pram Rider.
Circus, The.
Classic Waits for Me, A.
Commuter.
Dog around the Block.
Fashions in Dogs.
Father Does His Best, A.
I Marvel at the Ways of God.
I Paint What I See.
Listener's Guide to the Birds, A.
Marble-Top.
Red Cow Is Dead, The.
Song of the Queen Bee.
Sweet Reader.
To a Lady across the Way.
Window Ledge in the Atom Age.
White, Gail
Happy Endings.
Housecleaner, The.
Return to Astolat.
White, George
I Came to Jesus.
White, Gilbert
Naturalist's Summer Evening Walk, The.
On the Dark, Still, Dry, Warm Weather Occasionally Happening in the Winter Months.
White, Gleason
Primrose Dame, A.
White, Harriet R.
Uffia.
White, Henry Kirke
Clifton Grove, *sel.*
Description of a Summer's Eve.
Man's Littleness in Presence of the Stars.
On the Death of Dermody, the Poet.
Song from Fragment of an Eccentric Drama.
To an Early Primrose.
White, Hervey
I Saw the Clouds.
White, John
Clock Time by the Geyser.
White, Jon Manchip
Captain, The.
Count Orlo in England.
Orlo's Valediction.
Rout of San Romano, The.
White, Joseph Blanco
Black Is a Soul.
Night.
To Night.
White, Julie Herrick
Like Children of the Summertime Playing at Cards.
White, Lillian Zellhoefer
Hangman's Tree.
White, Mary Jane
Lindeman.
Of All Plants, the Tree.
White, Ned
Apache Kid.
Bones in the Desert.
White, Patrick
Lyre.
White, Richard Edward
Discovery of San Francisco Bay.
White, Terence Hanbury
To Myself, after Forty Years.
Witch's Work Song, The.
White, Vera
You Are on U.S. 40 Headed West.
White, William Allen
Intermezzo for the Fourth Act, An.
Rhyme of the Dream-Maker Man, A.
Whitebird, Joanie
Star.
Whitefield, George
Oh, Lovely Appearance of Death, *with music.*
Whitehead, Charles
Lamp, The.
Summer Storm, A.
Whitehead, James
About a Year after He Got Married He Would Sit Alone in an Abandoned Shack in a Cotton Field Enjoying Himself.
Delta Farmer in a Wet Summer.
He Records a Little Song for a Smoking Girl.
Local Man Remembers Betty Fuller, A.
Narrative Hooper and L.D.O. Sestina with a Long Last Line, The.
Poem Called Poem.
Whitehead, Paul
Apollo and Daphne, *sel.*
Gymnasiad, The, or Boxing Match, *sel.*
Hunting Song.
Whitehead, William
Charge to the Poets, A, *sel.*
Enthusiast, The; an Ode.
"Je Ne Sais [*or* Sçay] Quoi," The.
New Night Thoughts on Death; a Parody.

On Friendship.
Sweepers, The.
Whiteman, Roberta Hill
Beginning the Year at Rosebud, S.D.
Blue Mountain.
Depot in Rapid City.
Direction.
Dream of Rebirth.
E Uni Que A The Hi A Tho, Father.
Falling Moon.
In the Longhouse, Oneida Museum.
In the Madison Zoo.
Leap in the Dark.
Lines for Marking Time.
Long Parenthesis, The.
Midnight on Front Street.
Midwinter Stars.
Nation Wrapped in Stone, A.
Night along the Mackinac Bridge.
Notes for Albuquerque.
Seal at Stinson Beach.
Sleeping with Foxes.
Song for Healing.
Star Quilt.
Steps.
Swamp.
Whispers.
Winter Burn.
Wish for Waving Goodbye, A.
Woman Seed Player.
Whiteside, Mary Brent
Carpenter, The.
Who Has Known Heights.
Whitfield, James M.
From America.
Whiting, Charles Goodrich
Blue Hills beneath the Haze.
Eagle's Fall, The.
Way to Heaven, The.
Whiting, Lilian
Mystery, The.
Whiting, Nathaniel
Il Insonio Insonado, *sel.*
Office of Poetry, The.
Whiting, Seymour W.
Alamance.
Whiting, William
Eternal Father, Strong to Save.
Hymn: "Eternal Father, strong to save."
Whitman, Cedric
Dissonance.
Whitman, Ruth
Almost Ninety.
Bubba Esther, 1888.
Castoff Skin.
Dan, the Dust of Masada Is Still in My Nostrils.
Dead Center.
Flight.
Human Geography.
Listening to Grownups Quarreling.
Marriage Wig, The.
Mediterranean.
Sister Pharaoh.
Spring.
Translating.
Watching the Sun Rise over Mount Zion.
Yom Kippur: Fasting.
Whitman, Sarah Helen
Sonnets from the Series Relating to Edgar Allan Poe, *sels.*
Whitman, Walt
Aboard at a Ship's Helm.
After an Interval.
After the Dazzle of Day.
After the Sea-Ship.
After the Supper and Talk.
Ages and Ages Returning at Intervals.
All the Past We Leave Behind, *with music.*
America.
Are You the New Person Drawn toward Me?
Army Corps on the March, An.
As Adam Early in the Morning.
As I Ebb'd with the Ocean of Life.
As I Lay with My Head in Your Lap Camerado.
As I Pondered in Silence.
As If a Phantom Caress'd Me.
As Toilsome I Wander'd Virginia's Woods.
Base of All Metaphysics, The.
Battle of the *Bonhomme Richard* and the *Serapis.*
Beasts, The.
Beat! Beat! Drums!
Beautiful Swimmer, The.
Beauty.
Beauty of the Ship, The.
Beginners.
Beginning My Studies.
Belief in Plan of Thee.
Bivouac on a Mountain Side.
Boston Ballad, A.
Broad-Ax, The.
Broadway.
Broadway Pageant, A.
Brown Bird, The.
By Blue Ontario's Shore, *sels.*
By the Bivouac's Fitful Flame.
Carol of Death, The.
Cavalry Crossing a Ford.
Centenarian's Story, The.
City Dead-House, The.
City of Orgies.
Clear Midnight, A.
Come, Said My Soul.
Come Up from the Fields, Father.
Commonplace, The.
Crossing Brooklyn Ferry.
Dalliance of the Eagles, The.
Darest Thou Now O Soul.
Death Carol.
Dirge for Two Veterans.
Dismantled Ship, The.
Drayman, The.
Earth, My Likeness.
Encountering God.
Epigraph to "Drum-Taps."
Ethiopia Saluting the Colors.
Faces.
Facing West from California's Shore.
Farm Picture, A.
First Dandelion, The.
For You, O Democracy.
From Montauk Point.
From Paumanok Starting I Fly like a Bird.
From Pent-up Aching Rivers.
Give Me the Splendid Silent Sun.
Glimpse, A.
Good-bye My Fancy!
Grass.
Had I the Choice.
Halcyon Days.
Hand-Mirror, A.
Has Any One Supposed It Lucky to Be Born?
Here the Frailest Leaves of Me.
Heroes.
Hub for the Universe, A.
Hush'd Be the Camps To-Day.
I Am He That Aches with Love.
I Am He That Walks with the Tender and Growing Night.
I Dream'd in a Dream.
I Hear America Singing.
I Hear and See Not Strips of Cloth Alone.
I Hear It Was Charged against Me.
I Heard You Solemn-sweet Pipes of the Organ.
I Saw in Louisiana a Live-Oak Growing.
I Saw the Vision of Armies.
I Sing the Body Electric.
I Sit and Look Out.
I Think I Could Turn and Live with Animals.
Imprisoned Soul, The.
In Cabin'd Ships at Sea.
In Paths Untrodden.
Infinity.
John Paul Jones.
Joy, Shipmate, Joy!
Justified Mother of Men, The.
Last Invocation, The.
Long I Thought That Knowledge Alone Would Suffice.
Long, Too Long America.
Look Down Fair Moon.
Mannahatta.
March in the Ranks Hard-Prest, and the Road Unknown, A.
Me Imperturbe.
Memories.
Memories of President Lincoln.
Miracles.
Mocking-Bird, The.
Muse in the New World, The.
My Barbaric Yawp.
My 71st Year.
Myself.
Native Moments.
Night on the Prairies, *sel.*
No Labor-saving Machine.
Noiseless Patient Spider, A.
Not Heat Flames Up and Consumes.
Not Heaving from My Ribb'd Breast Only.
Now I will do nothing but listen.
Now Lift Me Close.
O Captain! My Captain!
O Hymen! O Hymenee!
O Living Always, Always Dying.
O Tan-faced Prairie-Boy.
Of the Terrible Doubt of Appearances.
Old Man's Thought of School, An.
Old-Time Sea-Fight, An.
On the Beach at Night.
On the Beach at Night Alone.
Once I Pass'd through a Populous City.
One's-Self I Sing.
Others May Praise What They Like.
Out of the Cradle Endlessly Rocking.
Out of the Rolling Ocean the Crowd.
Passage to India.
Patrol[l]ing Barnegat.
Pioneers! O Pioneers!
Poet, The.
Poets to Come.
Prayer of Columbus.
Reconciliation.
Recorders Ages Hence.
Respondez!
Roots and Leaves Themselves Alone.
Runaway Slave, The.
Runner, The.
Salut au Monde, *sel.*
Scented Herbage of My Breast.
Shut Not Your Doors.
Sight in Camp [in the Daybreak Gray and Dim], A.
Singer in the Prison, The.
Sleepers, The.
Sometimes with One I Love.
Song for All Seas, All Ships.
Song of Myself.
Song of the Answerer, *sel.*
Song of the Broad-Ax, *sel.*
Song of the Exposition, *sel.*
Song of the Open Road.
Song of the Redwood-Tree.
Song of the Universal.
Sparkles from the Wheel.
Spider, The.
Spontaneous Me.
Stallion, The.
Starting from Paumanok, *sels.*
Still Though the One I Sing.
Swiftly Arose.
Tears.
There Was a Child Went Forth.
This Compost.
Thou Mother with Thy Equal Brood, *sel.*

To a Common Prostitute.
To a Locomotive in Winter.
To a Stranger.
To Soar in Freedom and in Fullness of Power.
To the Garden the World.
To the Leaven'd Soil They Trod.
To the Man-of-War-Bird.
To the States.
To Think of Time.
To You.
To-Day and Thee.
Trickle Drops.
Trippers and askers surround me.
Two Veterans.
Unexpress'd, The.
Untold Want, The.
Vigil Strange I Kept on the Field One Night.
Wallabout Martyrs, The.
Walt Whitman, a kosmos, of Manhattan the son.
Washington's Monument, February 1885.
We Two Boys Together Clinging.
When I Heard at the Close of the Day.
When I Heard the Learn'd Astronomer.
When I Peruse the Conquer'd Fame.
When Lilacs Last in the Dooryard Bloom'd.
Whispers of Heavenly Death.
Whoever You Are Holding Me Now in Hand.
Woman Waits for Me, A.
World below the Brine, The.
Wound-Dresser, The.
Wounded Person, The.
Year That Trembled and Reel'd beneath Me.
You, Whoever You Are.

Whitmell, Lucy
Christ in Flanders.

Whitney, Adeline D. T.
Equinoctial.
February.
Humpty Dumpty.
Peace.

Whitney, Anna Temple
Kneeling Camel, The.
Submission and Rest.

Whitney, Ernest
Ute Pass.

Whitney, F. B.
God Knows the Answer.

Whitney, Geffrey
Content.
Song: "In crystal towns and turrets richly set."

Whitney, Helen Hay
Song: "We only ask for sunshine."
To Diane.

Whitney, Isabella
Sweet Nosegay, A, or Pleasant Posy,

Whitney, Joseph Ernest
Drop of Ink, A.

Whittaker, Frederick
Custer's Last Charge.

Whittemore, Reed
Abbreviated Interviews with a Few Disgruntled Literary Celebrities.
After Some Day of Decision.
Alfred Lord Tennyson.
American Takes a Walk, An.
Campus in Summer, A.
Clamming.
Day with the Foreign Legion, A.
Departure, The.
Fall of the House of Usher, The.
Floridian Museum of Art, A.
High School Band, The.
Learning Soul, The.
Line of an American Poet, The.
Lines on Being Refused a Guggenheim Fellowship.
Love Song: "I know not how to speak to thee, girl (damselle?)."
Notes on a Certain Terribly Critical Piece.
Ode to New York.
On First Knowing God.
On the Suicide of a Friend.
Only the Dead.
Out of My Study Window.
Party, The.
Projection, A.
Radio Under the Bed, The.
Recall.
Reflections upon a Recurrent Suggestion by Civil Defense Authorities That I Build a Bombshelter in My Backyard.
Science Fiction.
Self and the Weather, The.
Seven Days, The, *sel.*
Shakespeare, Possibly, in California.
Still Life.
Storm from the East, A.
Summer Concert.
Tarantula, The.
Teacher, A.
Thinking of Tents.
Treasure, A.
Walk Home, The.
Week of Doodle, A.
Winter Scene, A.

Whittier, John Greenleaf
Abraham Davenport.
Adjustment.
All's Well.
Among the Hills, *sel.*
Amy Wentworth.
Andrew Rykman's Prayer, *sels.*
Angel of Patience, The.
Angels of Buena Vista, The.
Astræa.
Astraea at the Capitol.
At Last.
At Port Royal.
Autograph, An.
Barbara Frietchie.
Barefoot Boy, The.
Bartholdi Statue, The.
Battle Autumn of 1862, The.
Bayard Taylor.
Bible, The.
Book Our Mothers Read, The.
Brewing of Soma, The.
Brown of Ossawatomie.
Burial of Barber.
Burning Drift-Wood.
Cable Hymn, The.
Call of the Christian, The.
Cassandra Southwick.
Centennial Hymn.
Chicago.
Clerical Oppressors.
Conductor Bradley.
Corn-Song, The.
Crisis, The.
Dead Feast of the Kol-Folk, The.
Dead Ship of Harpswell, The.
Dedication: "I would the gift I offer here."
Disarmament, *sel.*
Drop Thy Still Dews.
Emancipation Group, The, *sel.*
Eternal Goodness, The ("O friends! with whom my feet have trod").
Faith.
Farewell, The: "Gone, gone—sold and gone."
Firelight.
First-Day Thoughts.
Fishermen, The.
For a Little Girl Mourning Her Favorite Cat.
For an Autumn Festival, *sel.*
For Righteousness' Sake.
Forgiveness.
Friend's Burial, The.
From Our Master.
Frost Spirit, The.
Harvest Hymn.
Haschish, The.
Healer, The, *sel.*
Henchman, The.
Hymn from the French of Lamartine, *sel.*
I Call the Old Time Back.
Ichabod.
Immortal Love, Forever Full.
In Earthen Vessels.
In Memory of James T. Fields.
In School-Days.
In the "Old South."
Inscription: "Eagle, stooping from yon snow-blown peaks, The."
John Underhill.
July, *at.*
Kallundborg Church.
Kansas Emigrants, The.
King's Missive, The.
Laus Deo!
Le Marais du Cygne.
Lexington.
Life and Love.
Lost Occasion, The.
Maud Muller.
Memories.
Miriam, *sel.*
Moral Warfare, The.
Mother.
Mulford.
My Playmate.
My Triumph.
My Trust, *sel.*
Norembega.
Norsemen, The.
O Brother Man.
O Thou Who Bidst the Torrent Flow.
O Thou! Whose Presence Went Before, *with music.*
Old Burying-Ground, The.
On the Big Horn.
Our Master.
Over-Heart, The.
Palatine, The.
Palestine.
Pentucket.
Pipes at Lucknow, The.
Poor Voter on Election Day, The.
Prayer: "Dear Lord and Father of mankind."
Prelude: "Along the roadside, like the flowers of gold."
Proclamation, The.
Proem: "I love the old melodious lays."
Prophetess.
Pumpkin, The.
Riddle of the World, The.
Saddest Words, The.
St. John.
Shadow and the Light, The, *sel.*
Ship-Builders, The.
Sister.
Sisters, The.
Skipper Ireson's Ride.
Snow-Bound; a Winter Idyl.
Song of Slaves in the Desert.
Song of the Negro Boatman.
Songs of Labor, *sel.*
Storm, The.
Swan Song of Parson Avery, The.
Telling the Bees.
Texas.
Thou, Our Elder Brother.
Three Bells, The.
To John C. Frémont.
To My Old Schoolmaster.
To Paths Unknown.
To Pius IX.
To the Thirty-ninth Congress.
To William Lloyd Garrison.
Two Angels, The.
Vanishers, The.
Vesta.
Vow of Washington, The.
Waiting, The.
Washington's Vow.
What the Birds Said.

Winter Day.
Winter Night.
World Transformed, The.
Worship.
Whittingham, William
Now Israel May Say, and That Truly, *with music.*
Whittle, Daniel W.
Moment by Moment.
Whur, Cornelius
Female Friend, The.
Whyte-Melville, George John
Goodbye!
Whythorne, Thomas
Now That the Truth Is Tried.
Wickham, Anna
Affinity, The.
After Annunciation.
Cherry-Blossom Wand, The.
Conscience, The.
Contemplative Quarry, The.
Creatrix.
Dedication of the Cook.
Divorce.
Envoi: "God, thou great symmetry."
Fired Pot, The.
Fresh Start, The.
Friend Cato.
Gift to a Jade.
Last Round, The.
Meditation at Kew.
Nervous Prostration.
Sehnsucht.
Self-Analysis.
Ship near Shoals.
Singer, The.
Song: "I was so chill, and overworn, and sad."
Song-Maker, The.
Soul's Liberty.
Tired Man, The.
Tired Woman, The.
To a Crucifix.
To Men.
Vanity.
Weapons.
Widdemer, Margaret
As I Lay Quiet.
Awakened War God, The.
Barter.
Bear Hunt, The.
Certainties.
Comfort.
Cyprian Woman, A.
Dark Cavalier, The.
Factories, The.
God and the Strong Ones.
If You Should Tire of Loving Me.
Invisible Playmate, The.
Mary, Helper of Heartbreak.
Masters, The.
Modern Woman to Her Lover, The.
Mother.
Mother-Prayer.
New Victory, The.
Not unto the Forest.
Oiseaurie.
Old Road to Paradise, The.
Prescience.
Procession, The.
Rainuv; a Romantic Ballad from the Early Basque.
Rambuncto.
Search.
Secret Cavern, The.
Song: "Going down the old way."
Teresina's Face.
Watcher, The.
Widerberg, Siv
At Annika's Place.
Best?
Divorce.
Once.
Wiebe, Dallas E.
Epilogue: "My bibliography has grown."
L'Elisir d'Amore.
Wieber, Wendy
One, The Other, And.
Wieners, John
Acts of Youth, The.
Anniversary of Death, An.
For Jan.
In the Half Light of Holding and Giving.
Le Chariot.
Meadow, The.
Moon Poems.
Poem for Museum Goers, A.
Poem for Painters, A.
Poem for the Insane, A.
Poem for the Old Man, A.
Poem for Trapped Things, A.
Series 5.8, A.
Sol, Bronze Age came first Sol. The Windows of Waltham.
Two Years Later.
Waning of the Harvest Moon, The.
What Happened?
Where Fled.
Windows of Waltham, The.
Wier, Dara
Fear.
Keno.
Late Afternoon on a Good Lake.
This Cold Nothing Else.
Wigglesworth, Michael
Day of Doom, The.
For Just Men Light Is Sown, *with music.*
God's Controversy with New-England.
Prayer unto Christ the Judge of the World, A.
Song of Emptiness to Fill up the Empty Pages Following, A.
Welcome, Sweet Rest, *with music.*
Wightman, Richard
Pilgrim, The.
Servants, The.
Wilberforce, Robert
"Peace Is the Tranquillity of Order."
Wilberforce, Samuel
If I were a Cassowary.
Impromptu.
Wilbur, Richard
Advice to a Prophet.
After the Last Bulletins.
All These Birds.
Altitudes.
Apology.
April 5, 1974.
Aspen and the Stream, The.
At Year's-End.
Baroque Wall-Fountain in the Villa Sciarra, A.
Beasts.
Beautiful Changes, The.
Bell Speech.
Beowulf.
Black November Turkey, A.
Boy at the Window.
Ceremony.
Christmas Hymn, A.
Cigales.
Cottage Street, 1953.
Death of a Toad, The.
Digging for China.
Dubious Night, A.
Epistemology.
Event, An.
Exeunt.
Eye, The.
Fall in Corrales.
Fire-Truck, A.
First Snow in Alsace.
Folk Tune.
For K. R. on Her Sixtieth Birthday.
For the New Railway Station in Rome.
For the Student Strikers.
Grace.
Grasse: The Olive Trees.
Grasshopper, A.
He Was.
Hole in the Floor, A.
In a Churchyard.
In the Elegy Season.
In the Field.
In the Smoking-Car.
John Chapman.
Juggler.
Junk.
La Rose des Vents.
Lamarck Elaborated.
Late Aubade, A.
Looking into History.
Love Calls Us to the Things of This World.
Loves of the Puppets.
Lying.
Marginalia.
Merlin Enthralled.
Mill, The.
Miltonic Sonnet for Mr. Johnson on His Refusal of Peter Hurd's Official Portrait, A.
Mind.
Museum Piece.
My Father Paints the Summer.
O.
Objects.
October Maples, Portland.
On the Marginal Way.
Opposite of Two, The.
Pangloss' [*or* Pangloss's] Song.
Pardon, The.
Part of a Letter.
Piazza di Spagna, Early Morning.
Piccola Commedia.
Place Pigalle.
Playboy.
Potato.
Praise in Summer.
Proof, The.
Rillons, Rillettes.
Running.
Seed Leaves.
Shallot, A.
Shame.
She.
Simile for Her Smile, A.
Simplification, A.
Sleepless at Crown Point.
Some Opposites.
Sonnet: "Winter deepening, the hay all in, The."
Speech for the Repeal of the McCarran Act.
Statues.
Still, Citizen Sparrow.
Stop.
Storm in April, A.
Summer Morning, A.
Terrace, The.
Then When the Ample Season.
Thyme Flowering among Rocks.
To an American Poet Just Dead.
To the Etruscan Poets.
Transit.
Two Voices in a Meadow.
Tywater.
Undead, The.
Voice from under the Table, A.
Walking to Sleep.
What is the opposite of a prince?
"World without Objects Is a Sensible Emptiness, A."
Writer, The.
Year's End.
Wilbye, John
Risposta.
Wilcox, Ella Wheeler
Ad Finem.
Attainment.
Attraction.
Better, Wiser and Happier.

Christian's New-Year Prayer, The, *sel.*
Communism.
Faith.
Farewell of Clarimonde, The, *sel.*
Growing Old.
I Love You.
Illusion.
Inspiration, An.
Interlude.
Life's Scars.
Lifting and Leaning.
Midsummer.
My Ships.
Optimism.
Price He Paid, The.
Progress.
Queen's Last Ride, The.
Recrimination.
Solitude.
They Say.
To know thy bent and then pursue.
True Brotherhood.
True Knight, The.
Two Glasses, The.
Unanswered Prayers.
Uselessness.
Way of the World, The.
Whatever Is—Is Best.
Will.
Winds of Fate, The.
With Every Rising of the Sun.
Worth While.
You Never Can Tell.

Wild, Peter
Air Raid.
Dog Hospital.
For the El Paso Weather Bureau.
Gooseberries.
Ice Cream.
Riding Double.
Snakes.
Thomas and Charlie.
Variation.
Washing Windows.

Wild, Robert
Copy of the Last Verses Made by Dr. Wild, Author of "Iter Boreale," A, *sel.*
Epitaph for a Godly Man's Tomb.
Iter Boreale.
Poem upon the Imprisonment of Mr. Calamy in Newgate, A.

Wilde, Heather
Sister Bernardo.

Wilde, J.
Verses to Miss

Wilde, Lady Jane Francesca ("Speranza")
Famine Year, The.

Wilde, Oscar
Athanasia.
Ave Imperatrix!
Ave Maria, Gratia Plena.
Ballad of Reading Gaol, The.
By the Arno.
Disciple, The.
E Tenebris.
Endymion.
Fabien dei Franchi.
For Our Sakes.
Garden, The.
Harlot's House, The.
Hélas!
Impression de Paris.
Impression du Matin.
Impression Japonais.
Impressions, *sels.*
In Reading Gaol by Reading Town.
In the Forest.
In the Gold Room.
La Bella Donna Della Mia Mente.
La Fuite de la Lune.
La Mer.
Le Jardin ("The lily's withered chalice falls").
Les Ballons.
Les Silhouettes.
Magdalen Walks.
My Voice.
Portia.
Requiescat.
Serenade: "Western wind is blowing fair, The."
Sonnet on Hearing the *Dies Irae* Sung in the Sistine Chapel.
Sphinx, The, *sel.*
Symphony in Yellow.
Taedium Vitae.
Theocritus.
Theoretikos.
To Milton.
Yet Each Man Kills the Thing He Loves.

Wilde, Richard Henry
Farewell to America, A.
My Life Is like the Summer Rose.
Oh! dearer by far than the land of our birth.
Stanzas: "My life is like the summer rose."
To the Mocking-Bird.

Wilder, Amos Niven
De Profundis.
If I Have Lifted Up Mine Eyes to Admire.
Prayer: "Omnipotent confederate of all good."

Wilder, John Nichols
Stand by the Flag.

Wiljer, Robert
Moose.

Wilk, Melvin
Blessing.
Learning to Speak.

Wilkins, Alice
Ducks, The.
Elephant's Trunk, The.
New Shoes.
Snow.

Wilkins, Eithne
Anabasis.
And Only Our Shadow Walks with Us.
Barbed Wire.
Cockcrow.
Dreamers and the Sea, The.
Eye, The.
Failure.
High Place, A.
Parzival, *sel.*
Passage of an August.
Shark's Fin.
Spoken through Glass.
Variations on a Theme by Sidney Keyes.

Wilkins, Terri Meyette
Celebration 1982.
Child's Memory.
Prison Walls—Red Brick Crevices.

Wilkins, William
Engine Driver's Story, The.
Magazine Fort, Phoenix Park, Dublin, The.

Wilkinson, Anne
Adam and God.
Carol: "I was a lover of turkey and holly."
Cautionary Tale, A.
Daily the Drum.
Falconry.
In June and Gentle Oven.
Leda in Stratford, Ont.
Lens.
Nature Be Damned.
Once upon a Great Holiday.
Red and the Green, The.
Summer Acres.
Variations on a Theme.

Wilkinson, H. E.
Topsy-turvy Land.

Wilkinson, Iris Guiver. *See* **"Hyde, Robin"**

Wilkinson, Marguerite
Before Dawn in the Woods.
Chant Out of Doors, A.
End, The.
Guilty.
Pawnbrokers.
Proud Song, A.
Psalm to the Son, A.
Scatheless.
Song of Two Wanderers, A.
To the Lighted Lady Window.

Wilkinson, William Cleaver
At Marshfield.
Webster; an Ode, *sel.*

Will, Frederic
Fire a Simple Fire, A.
Long Lonely Lover of the Highway.

Will, James
Mountain Sculpture.

Willard, Emma Hart
Rocked in the Cradle of the Deep.

Willard, Nancy
Angels in Winter.
Blake Leads a Walk on the Milky Way.
Bone Poem.
Flea Circus at Tivoli, The.
Foxfire.
How the Hen Sold Her Eggs to the Stingy Priest.
In the Hospital of the Holy Physician.
Insects, The.
King of Cats Sends a Postcard to His Wife, The.
Lightness Remembered.
Moss.
Night Light.
No-Kings and the Calling of Spirits.
Original Strawberry.
Questions My Son Asked Me, Answers I Never Gave Him.
Saint Pumpkin.
Saints Lose Back.
Way of Keeping, A.
When There Were Trees.

Willems, J. Rutherford
Hebrew Letters in the Trees.

Willett, Florence White
Crowded Out.

Willette, Florence Hynes
For a Girl in Love.

William of Shoreham
Hours of the Passion, *sel.*
Song to Mary, A, *at.*

Williams, Bertye Young
Friend Who Just Stands By, The.
Trus' an' Smile.
Washington.

Williams, Beryle
Afterbirth.
Message to the Photographer Whose Prints I Purchased, A.

Williams, Charles
At the "Ye That Do Truly."
Dream, A.
Kings Came Riding.
Mount Badon.
Night Song for a Child.
Taliessin's Song of the Unicorn.

Williams, Sir Charles Hanbury
Come, Chloe, and Give Me Sweet Kisses.
Epigram of Martial, Imitated, An.
Isabella; or, The Morning, *sels.*
Lamentable Case, A.
Ode on Miss Harriet Hanbury at Six Years Old, An.
Old General, The.

Williams, Charles Kenneth
Blades.
Day for Anne Frank, A.
Downwards.
Floor.
From My Window.
Hood.
Rampage, The.
Spit.
Tar.
Waking Jed.
World's Greatest Tricycle Rider, The.

Williams, Clarence
Ugly Chile.
Williams, Claude *and* **Lee Hays**
Roll the Union On.
Williams, Emmett
Like Attracts Like.
Williams, Francis Howard
Electra.
Song: "Bird in my bower, A."
Walt Whitman.
Williams, George. *See* **Awoonor, Kofi**
Williams, Harry H.
In the Shade of the Old Apple Tree.
Williams, Helen Maria
To Hope.
Williams, Hugo
Butcher, The.
Couple Upstairs, The.
Some Kisses from "The Kama Sutra."
Williams, John (1664-1729)
Some Contemplations of the Poor, and Desolate State of the Church at Deerfield.
Williams, John (1761-1818)
Matrimony.
Williams, John (*b.* 1922)
Dead, The.
For My Students, Returning to College.
History, A.
Leaf, The.
Meaning of Violence, The.
On Reading Aloud My Early Poems.
Skaters, The.
Williams, John A.
Safari West.
Williams, John Lloyd
Naming of Private Parts.
Williams, Jonathan
Adhesive Autopsy of Walt Whitman, The.
Anthropophagites See a Sign on NC Highway 177 That Looks like Heaven, The.
Bitch-Kitty, The.
But pretty though as/ roses is. Three Sayings from Highlands, North Carolina.
Distances to the Friend, The.
Fast Ball.
Hermit Cackleberry Brown, on Human Vanity, The.
Honey Lamb, The.
In England's Green & (a Garland and a Clyster).
In Lucas, Kansas.
Little Tumescence, A.
Mahler, *sel.*
Mrs. Sadie Grindstaff, Weaver and Factotum.
Ovid, Meet a Metamorphodite.
Strung Out with Elgar on a Hill, *sel.*
Switch Blade, The; or, John's Other Wife.
Symphony No. 3, in D Minor.
Those Troublesome Disguises.
Three Sayings from Highlands, North Carolina.
Uncle Iv Surveys His Domain from His Rocker.
Vulnerary, A.
Williams, Kim
Requiem for a River.
Williams, Lucy Ariel. *See* **Holloway, Lucy Ariel Williams**
Williams, Mance
For Lover Man, and All the Other Young Men Who Failed to Return from World War II.
Year without Seasons, A.
Williams, Max
Empty House, The.
Williams, Miller
Alcide Pavageau.
Getting Experience.
Love Poem: "Six o'clock and/ the sun rises. . ."
Mardi Gras.
Neighbor, The.
Of Human Bondage.
On the Last Page of the Last Yellow Pad in Rome before Taking Off for Dacca on Air Bangladesh.
Plain.
Sale.
Words.
Williams, Oscar
Borrower of Salt, The.
By Fiat of Adoration.
Dinner Guest.
Dwarf of Disintegration.
Edgar Guest.
Golden Fleece, The.
I Sing an Old Song.
In Postures That Call.
Jeremiad.
Last Supper, The.
Leg in the Subway, The.
Little Steamboat.
Man Coming toward You, The.
Man in That Airplane, The.
Milk at the Bottom of the Sea.
Mirage, The.
On Meeting a Stranger in a Bookshop.
On the Couch.
On the Death of an Acquaintance.
One Morning the World Woke Up.
Praying Mantis Visits a Penthouse, The ("The praying mantis with its length of straw").
Seesaw, The.
Shopping for Meat in Winter.
Spring.
Spritely Dead, The.
Variations on a Theme.
Williams, Randall
Laying By.
Williams, Richard D'Alton
Dying Girl, The.
Extermination.
Williams, Roger
Adulteries, murthers, robberies, thefts.
Boast not proud English, of thy birth and blood.
Course bread and water's most their fare.
Courteous pagan shall condemne, The.
God gives them sleep on ground, on straw.
God Makes a Path.
How busie are the sonnes of men?
I have heard ingenuous Indians say.
If Birds That neither Sow nor Reap, *with music.*
Indians count of men as dogs, The.
Indians prize not English gold, The.
Mans restlesse soule hath restlesse eyes and ears.
One step twix't me and death, (twas Davids speech).
Our English gamesters scorne to stake.
Pagans wild confesse the bonds, The.
They see Gods wonders that are call'd.
Truth is a native, naked beauty; but.
What Habacuck once spake, mine eyes.
When Indians heare that some there are.
When Sun Doth Rise, *with music.*
Williams, Sarah
Deep Sea Soundings.
Is It True?
Old Astronomer to His Pupil, The.
Youth and Maidenhood.
Williams, Sherley Anne
Driving Wheel.
Empress Brand Trim, The: Ruby Reminisces.
House of Desire, The.
Say Hello to John.
Williams, Shirley
If He Let Us Go Now.
Killing of the Birds, The.
You Know It's Really Cold.
Williams, Tennessee
Carrousel Tune.
Crepe de Chine.
Gold Tooth Blues.
Heavenly Grass.
Kitchen Door Blues.
Life Story.
My Love Was Light.
Paper Lantern, The.
Recuerdo, *sel.*
Sugar in the Cane.
Williams, Theodore Chickering
Hast Thou Heard It, O My Brother, *with music.*
My Country, to Thy Shore, *with music.*
When Thy Heart with Joy O'erflowing, *with music.*
Williams, Trevor
Girl I Took to the Cocktail Party, The.
Williams, William
Christian Pilgrim's Hymn, The.
Divine Hand, The.
Williams, William Carlos
Abroad.
Act, The.
Address.
Aftermath, The.
All That Is Perfect in Woman.
Apology: Why Do I Write Today?
Approach to a City.
Après le Bain.
Artist, The.
Asphodel, That Greeny Flower, *sels.*
At Kenneth Burke's Place.
At the Ball Game.
Ballad of Faith.
Between Walls.
Botticellian Trees, The.
Bull, The.
Burning the Christmas Greens.
Calypso.
Catholic Bells, The.
Children, The.
Classic Scene.
Clouds, The.
Coda.
Cold Front, A.
Complaint.
Corn Harvest, The.
Daisy.
Dance, The.
Danse Russe.
Dawn.
Death.
Deceptrices, The.
Delineaments of the Giants, The.
Descent, The.
Descent of Winter, The (Section 10/30).
Drink.
Elegy for D. H. Lawrence, An.
End of the Parade, The.
Episode 17.
Eyeglasses, The.
Fine Work with Pitch and Copper.
First Praise.
Fish.
Flowers by the Sea.
Folded Skyscraper, A, *sel.*
For Eleanor and Bill Monahan.
Forgotten City, The.
4th of July.
Gift, The.
Goodnight, A.
Graceful Bastion, The.
Great Figure, The.
Gulls.
Hemmed-in Males.
High Bridge above the Tagus River at Toledo, The.
History of Love, A.
Horse Show, The.
Hounded Lovers, The.
House, The.
Hunters in the Snow, The.
Illegitimate Things.
Injury, The.
Intelligent Sheepman and the New Cars, The.
Iris.
Ivy Crown, The.
January.
January Morning.

Jungle, The.
Lament: "What face, in the water."
Landscape with the Fall of Icarus.
Last Turn, The.
Last Words of My English Grandmother, The.
Le Médecin Malgré Lui.
Lear.
Lighthearted William.
Locust Tree in Flower, The.
Lonely Street, The.
Love Song: "Sweep the house clean."
Manoeuvre, The.
March.
Marriage.
Mental Hospital Garden, The.
Metric Figure.
Monstrous Marriage, The.
Nantucket.
Ol' Bunk's Band.
On Gay Wallpaper.
Orchestra, The.
Pastoral: "Little sparrows, The."
Pastoral: "When I was younger."
Paterson, *sels.*
Peace on Earth.
Philomena Andronico.
Pictures from Brueghel, *sels.*
Pink Locust, The.
Place (Any Place) to Transcend All Places.
Poem: "As the cat."
Poem, The: "It's all in/the sound. A song."
Poem: "On getting a card."
Poem: "Rose fades, The."
Poor, The.
Porous.
Portrait of a Lady.
Pot of Flowers, The.
Predicter of Famine, The.
Preface: "To make a start."
Proletarian Portrait.
Puerto Rico Song.
Queen-Ann's Lace.
Rain.
Raleigh Was Right.
Raper from Passenack, The.
Red Wheelbarrow, The.
Red-Wing Blackbird, The.
Return to Work, The.
Right of Way, The.
Ritualists, The.
River Rhyme.
Rose, The.
Russia.
St. Francis Einstein of the Daffodils.
St. James' Grove.
Sappho, Be Comforted.
Savage Beast, The.
Sea-Elephant, The.
Self-Portrait, I.
Semblables, The.
Signs everywhere of birds nesting, while.
Slow Movement.
Smell.
Soothsay.
Sort of a Song, A.
Sparrow, The.
Sparrows among Dry Leaves ("The sparrows/ by the iron fence post").
Spring and All: ("By the road to the contagious hospital").
Spring and All ("So much depends").
Storm, The.
Sunday in the Park.
Term, The.
Testament of Perpetual Change, The.
These.
These Purists.
This Is Just to Say.
This Is Pioneer Weather.
To ("A child (a boy) bouncing").
To a Dead Journalist.
To a Dog Injured in the Street.
To a Friend Concerning Several Ladies.
To a Poor Old Woman.
To a Solitary Disciple.
To an Elder Poet.
To Be Recited to Flossie on Her Birthday.
To Daphne and Virginia.
To Elsie.
To Flossie.
To Ford Madox Ford in Heaven.
To Greet a Letter-Carrier.
To Mark Anthony in Heaven.
To Waken an Old Lady.
Tract.
Trala Trala Trala La-le-la.
Unison, A.
View by Color Photography on a Commercial Calendar.
Wanderer, The.
When Structure Fails Rhyme Attempts to Come to the Rescue.
Widow's Lament in Springtime, The.
Willow Poem.
Winter.
Words, the Words, the Words, The.
Yachts, The.
Yellow Flower, The.
Yellow Season, The.
Young Housewife, The.
Young Sycamore.

Williamson, Bruce
Afternoon in Anglo-Ireland.
For M.
Homage of War.
Thought for My Love, A.

Williamson, Mrs. J. B. *See* **"Scrace, Richard"**

Willis, Gary
Assignment: Descriptive Essay.

Willis, John
Verses to Be Repeated by an Attorney Leaving His Lodging to Wait upon Judges Riding the Circuits from One County to Another, Least He Forget Some Necessary Thing.

Willis, Love Maria
Father, Hear the Prayer We Offer, *with music.*

Willis, Nathaniel Parker
Ambition.
Chamber Scene.
Death of Harrison, The.
Declaration, The.
Lady Jane, The; a Humorous Novel in Rhyme, *sels.*
Leper, The.
Love in a Cottage.
On the Picture of a "Child Tired of Play."
Parrhasius.
To Giulia Grisi.
To Helen in a Huff.
To Laura W
To the Lady in the Chemisette with Black Buttons.
Torn Hat, The.
Two Women.
Unseen Spirits.

Willoby, Henry
To Avisa.
Willobie His Avisa, *sel.*

Willson, Dixie
Mist and All, The.
Tip-Toe Tail.

Willson, Forceythe
Boy Brittan.
In State, *sel.*
Old Sergeant, The.

Willson, Meredith
Seventy Six Trombones, *with music.*

Willson, Robert
Last Resort, The.

Wilmot, Frank. *See* **"Maurice, Furnley"**

Wilmot, John, 2d Earl of Rochester. *See* **Rochester, John Wilmot, 2d Earl of**

Wilson, Alexander
Blue-Bird, The.
Fisherman's Hymn, The.

Wilson, Antoinette
Wit's End Corner.

Wilson, August
Theme One: The Variations.

"Wilson, Charlotte." *See* **Baker, Karle Wilson**

Wilson, Dedie Huffman
Speak to the Sun.

Wilson, Edmund
Drafts for a Quatrain.
Lido, The.
Not Here.
Omelet of A. MacLeish, The.
On Editing Scott Fitzgerald's Papers.
Peterhof.
Something for My Russian Friends.
Voice, The.
White Sand, The.

Wilson, Edwin H.
Where Is Our Holy Church? *with music.*

Wilson, Elizabeth A.
Snow Crystals on Meall Glas.

Wilson, Ernest J., Jr.
Mae's Rent Party.
Paternal.

Wilson, Florence M.
Green Hunters, The.

Wilson, Gavin
From the *Caledonian Mercury.*

Wilson, Grace
Seaway.

Wilson, J. F.
Coloratura Named Luna, A.
Double Entendre.
Let X Equal Half.

Wilson, James
Casey's Revenge.

Wilson, James Edward
When I Am Dead.

Wilson, John (1588-1677)
Armada, 1588, The.

Wilson, John (1591-1667)
Confess We All, before the Lord, *with music.*
For Lo! My Jonah How He Slumped, *with music.*
Whoso Would See This Song of Heavenly Choice, *with music.*

Wilson, John (1627?-1696)
Claudius Gilbert.
Copy of Verses, A.

Wilson, John (1785-1854). *See* **"North, Christopher."**

Wilson, Keith
Arrival of My Mother, The.
Celt in Me, The.
Idiot, The.
Lake above Santos, The.
Lamb, The.
Old Women beside a Church.
On Drinking and a New Moon through the Window.
Rancher, The.
Twin Aces.

Wilson, Margaret Adelaide
Gervais.
Road to Babylon, The.

Wilson, Marjorie
To Tony (Aged 3).

Wilson, McLandburgh
Optimist and Pessimist. *At. to*

Wilson, Ramona
Bags Packed and We Expected This.
Eveningsong.
Keeping Hair.
Late in Fall.
Meeting, The.
Overnight Guest.
Reading Indian Poetry.
Spring at Fort Okanogan.
Spring in Virginia.
Summer.

Wilson, Raymond
Epigram: "Artic raven tracks the caribou, The."
Wilson, Robert
Conscience's Song.
New Brooms.
Simplicity's Song.
Three Ladies of London, The, *sels.*
Wilson, Robert Burns
Ballad of the Faded Field.
Battle Song.
Cut the Cables.
Dead Player, The.
It Is in Winter That We Dream of Spring.
Passing of March, The.
Such Is the Death the Soldier Dies.
Sunrise of the Poor, The.
To a Crow.
Wilson, Robert Noble Denison
Elegy in a Presbyterian Burying-Ground.
Woodcut.
Wilson, Robley,Jr.
Bridesmaid.
Porcupines.
Yankee Poet.
Wilson, T. P. Cameron ("Tipcuca")
Dulce et Decorum.
London.
Magpies in Picardy.
Wilson, V. B.
Ticonderoga.
Wilton, Richard
Hymn to the Holy Spirit.
Winans, A. D.
My Woman.
Winant, Fran
Christopher Street Liberation Day, June 28, 1970.
Sacred Grove, A.
To Begin.
Winchester, Caleb T.
Lord Our God Alone Is Strong, The, *with music.*
Winchester, Elhanan
Behold with Joy, *with music.*
Winchilsea, Anne Finch, Countess of
Appology, The.
Birthday of Catharine Tufton, The, *sel.*
Cautious Lovers, The, *sel.*
Clarinda's Indifference at Parting with Her Beauty.
Greater Trial, The.
Introduction, The: "Did I, my lines intend for publick view."
Jealousie Is the Rage of a Man.
Letter to Daphnis [*or* Dafnis], A.
Nocturnal Reverie, A.
On Myself[e].
Petition for an Absolute Retreat, The.
Portrait, The.
Song, A: "If for a woman I would die."
Song on the South Sea, A.
To Death.
To Melancholy.
To Silvia.
To the Nightingale.
To the Rt. Hon. the Lady C. Tufton.
Trail All Your Pikes.
Tree, The.
Winder, Barbara
Catching a Horse.
Cuban Refugees on Key Biscayne.
February.
Limits of Equitation, The.
On the Farm.
Problem of Wild Horses, The.
Windom, W. H.
Fatal Wedding, The.
Wine, Maria
Love Me.
Woman, you are afraid of the forest.
Wingate, Mary
Washington.
When Shall We See Thy Like Again?
Wingate, Philip
I Don't Want to Play in Your Yard.
Wingfield, Sheila
Lines for the Margin of an Old Gospel.
Odysseus Dying.
Winter.
Winkler, Manfred
I Love What Is Not.
If My Hands Were Mute.
One Goes with Me along the Shore.
She.
Somewhere You Exist.
Winn, Howard
Supreme Fiction.
Winner, Robert
Banjo, The.
Elegy: "I remember the feel of a hammer."
Miss Alderman.
Winner, Septimus ("Alice Hawthorne")
Abraham's Daughter, *with music.*
Coolie Chinee, The.
Der Deitcher's Dog, *with music.*
Lilliputian's Beer Song.
Listen to the Mocking Bird.
Ten Little Injuns.
Whispering Hope, *with music.*
Winslow, Anne Goodwin
Beaten Path, The.
Winslow, Helen Maria
August.
Winslow, Pete
Dream Motorcycle, The.
Geriatric Whore, The.
Mad Rapist of Calaveras County, The.
Winsor, Frederick
Limerick: "At the village emporium in Woodstock."
Little Bo-Peep.
Solomon Grundy.
Space Child's Mother Goose, The, *sels.*
This Little Pig Built a Spaceship.
Winstanley, John
Epigram on Florio.
Epigram on the First of April.
Fanny's Removal in 1714.
Inventory of the Furniture of a Collegian's Chamber, An.
Last Will and Testament, A.
Miss Betty's Singing-Bird.
On a Certain Effeminate Peer.
On a Stingy Beau.
To the Revd. Mr.
Wintchevsky, Morris
Child-King, The.
If I Felt Less.
Winter, Mary
Blessing the Hounds.
Lower Forms of Life.
Winter, William
Adelaide Neilson.
Age.
Arthur.
Asleep.
I. H. B.
My Queen.
Night Watch, The.
On the Verge.
Passing Bell at Stratford, The.
Queen, The.
Refuge.
Rubicon, The.
Unwritten Poems.
Winters, Bayla
Finisterra.
Janis Joplin and the Folding Company.
"Wintergreen, John P. *See* **Ryskind, Morrie"**
Winters, Yvor
April.
Aspen's Song, The.
At the San Francisco Airport.
Before Disaster.
By the Road to the Air-Base.
California Oaks, The.
Castle of Thorns, The.
Dedication for a Book of Criticism.
Elegy, An: "Noon is beautiful, The: the perfect wheel."
Fragment, A: "I cannot find my way to Nazareth."
Grave, The.
Hawk's Eyes.
Heracles.
Hymn to Dispel Hatred at Midnight.
John Sutter.
Journey, The.
Manzanita, The.
Marriage, The.
Night of Battle.
Nocturne for October 31st, A.
On a View of Pasadena from the Hills.
On Teaching the Young.
Orpheus.
Prayer for My Son, A.
Precision, The.
Quod Tegit Omnia.
Rows of Cold Trees, The.
Shadow's Song, The.
Sir Gawaine and the Green Knight.
Sleep.
Slow Pacific Swell, The.
Song: "Where I walk out."
Song in Passing, A.
Sonnet to the Moon.
Static Autumn.
Summer Commentary, A.
Summer Noon: 1941.
Theseus: A Trilogy.
Time and the Garden.
To a Military Rifle, 1942.
To My Infant Daughter.
To the Holy Spirit.
To the Moon.
Vision, A.
Winthrop, Theodore
But Once.
Wintle, Walter D.
Man Who Thinks He Can, The.
Thinking.
Winwar, Frances
Autumn.
Winward, Stephen F.
Day by Day.
"Wiolar"
Resolution.
Wise, Isaac M.
In Mercy, Lord, Incline Thine Ear, *with music.*
Wise, Joseph
Glory, *with music.*
Wise, William
After the Party.
Grownups.
Little Miss Pitt.
My Little Sister.
Telegram.
What to Do.
Wiseman, Christopher
Delaying Tactics.
Wissinger, Kay
In the Lake Country.
Wister, Owen
Pinto, The.
Said Aristotle unto Plato.
Sheep Ranching.
Smugglers, The.
Ten Thousand Cattle.
Wiswall, Ichabod
Judicious Observation of That Dreadful Comet, A.
Wither, George
Ah Me! Am I the Swaine.
Author's Resolution, The.
Brittan's Remembrancer, *sel.*
Choice, The.

Christmas Carol, A: "So now is come our joyful'st feast."
Collection of Emblemes, Ancient and Moderne, A, *sel.*
Divided Heart, The.
Fair Virtue, the Mistress of Philarete, *sels.*
Fidelia.
For a Musician.
For Scholars and Pupils.
Fourth Eglogue, The.
Hallelujah; or, Britain's Second Remembrancer, *sels.*
Hence, Away, You Sirens!
Hymn L: Rocking Hymn, A.
Hymne I: Generall Invitation to Praise God, A.
I Loved a Lass.
Kiss, The.
Lord, Many Times Thou Pleased Art, *with music.*
Lover's Resolution, A.
Lullaby, A: "Sweet baby, sleep! what ails my dear."
Manly Heart, The.
Marigold, The.
Our Joyful Feast.
Philarete Praises Poetry.
Philarete to His Mistress, *sel.*
Rocking Hymn, A.
Shall I, Wasting in Despair [*or* Dispaire].
Shepherd's Hunting, The, *sels.*
Sleep, Baby, Sleep.
Sonnet 4: "Shall I wasting in Dispaire."
Stolen Kiss, A.
Tired Petitioner, The, *sel.*
To a Musician.
What Care I.
Widow's Hymn, A.

Witherby, Diana
Casualty.

Withers, Carl
Charlie Chaplin Went to France, *at.*

Witherspoon, Naomi Long. *See* **Madgett, Naomi Long**

Witherup, William
Crows.

Withington, Leonard
O Saviour of a World Undone, *with music.*

Witt, Harold
Aerosol.
Conservative.
Dog Alive.
Dreamscape in Kümmel.
Her Birthday.
Into the Future.
Mrs. Asquith Tries to Save the Jacarandas.
More Nudes for Florence.
Notre Dame Perfected by Reflection.
Nude.
Rushmore ("Rushing to Rushmore, speeding as we read").
Soaps.
Superbull.
Surprise.
Walking Milwaukee.

Witt, Sandra
Fish.

Witt, Shirley Hill
Punto Final.
Seboyeta Chapel.

Wittenberg, Ernest
Sub-average *Time* Reader, The.

Wittlin, Jozef
Hymn about a Spoonful of Soup, A.
On the Jewish Day of Judgment in the Year 1942 (5703).
St. Francis of Assisi and the Miserable Jews.
To the Jews in Poland.

Woddis, Roger
Ethics for Everyman.
Final Curtain.
Hero, The.
Nothing Sacred.

Wodehouse, E. A.
Afforestation.

Wodehouse, Pelham Grenville
Gourmet's Love-Song, The.
Printer's Error.
Song about Whiskers.
Time like an Ever-rolling Stream.
To William (Whom We Have Missed.)

Woessner, Warren
Airwaves.
Chippewa Lake Park.
Driving to Sauk City.
Looking at Power.
Low Tide.

Wojahn, David
Another Coast.
Cold Glow: Icehouses.
Man Who Knew Too Much, The.
Weldon Kees in Mexico, 1965.

Wolcot, John. *See* **"Pindar, Peter"**

Wolcott, Roger
Heart Is Deep, The.
Matthew X. 28.

Wolcott, Samuel
Christ for the World! We Sing, *with music.*
Father! I Own Thy Voice, *with music.*

Wolf, Leonard
Peasant, The.
Sonnet: "Sits by a fireplace, the seducer talks."

Wolf, Phyllis
Akawense.
Lac Courte Orielles; 1936.
Manomin.
Midewiwan.
Rolling Thunder.

Wolf, Robert Leopold
Eve.
Man in the Dress Suit, The.
Pagan Reinvokes the Twenty-third Psalm, A.

Wolfe, Aaron R.
Complete in Thee, No Work of Mine, *with music.*
Parting Hymn We Sing, A, *with music.*

Wolfe, Charles
Burial of Sir John Moore after [*or* at] Corunna, The.
Go, Forget Me.
To Mary.

Wolfe, Edgar
Sparrows in College Ivy.

Wolfe, ffrida
Choosing Shoes.
Four and Eight.
What the Toys Are Thinking.

Wolfe, Humbert
A. E. Housman and a Few Friends.
Autumn.
Blackbird, The.
British Journalist, The.
D. H. Lawrence and James Joyce.
Dead Fiddle, The.
Dean Inge.
G. K. Chesterton.
Gray Squirrel, The.
Green Candles.
Hilaire Belloc.
Iliad.
Journey's End.
Lilac, The.
Love Is a Keeper of Swans.
Man.
On Dean Inge.
Things Lovelier.
This Is Not Death.
Tulip.
Wardour Street.
Waters of Life, The.
Zoo, The.

Wolfe, Thomas Clayton
Ben.
Burning in the Night.
Magic.
Observe the Whole of It.
Stone, a Leaf, a Door, A.
That Sharp Knife.

Wolfenstein, Alfred
Exodus 1940.

Wolfert, Adrienne
Golda.

Wolff, Bill
What a Grand and Glorious Feeling.

Wolff, David
While We Slept.

Wolfram von Eschenbach
His Own True Wife.

Wolfskehl, Karl
And Yet We Are Here!
From Mount Nebo.
Shekhina[h].
To Be Said at the Seder.
We Go.

Wolker, Jiří
Epitaph: "Here lies the poet Wolker, lover of the world."
On This My Sick-Bed Beats the World.

Wolny, P.
Before Good-bye.
From a Birch.
Harmonica Man.
Lightning rides.
Separation.
Words, like Spiders.

Wolstenholme-Elmy, Elizabeth
Woman Free, *sel.*

Wong, Nellie
Funeral Song for Mamie Eisenhower.
How a Girl Got Her Chinese Name.
New Romance.
Song of Farewell.
Under Our Own Wings.

Wong, Shawn
Island, An.
Lapis.
Periods of Adjustment.

Woo, Merle
Poem for the Creative Writing Class, Spring 1982.
Subversive, The.
Yellow Woman Speaks.

Wood, A. J.
Rolling John, *sel.*

Wood, Alfred E.
Fight at Dajo, The.

Wood, Charles Erskine Scott
Sagebrush.
Water-Hole, The.

Wood, Clement
Eagle Sonnets, *sels.*
Glory Road, De.
I Pass a Lighted Window.
Prayer in Time of Blindness, A.
Voyager's Song.

Wood, John A.
Morning from My Office Window.

Wood, Marnie *and* **Harnie Wood**
Corpulent Pig, A.

Wood, Mary
Flying Changes.

Wood, Peggy
My Aunt.

Wood, Robert W.
Parrot and the carrot we may easily confound, The.

Wood, Robert Williams
Puffin, The.

Wood, Stanley
Homes of the Cliff Dwellers.

Wood, Susan
Learning to Live without You.

Wood, William
A Deux.
Kinds of Shel-Fish.
King of waters, the sea shouldering whale, The.
Kingly lyon, and the strong arm'd beare, The.

Princely eagle, and the soaring hawke, The.
Trees both in hills and plaines, in plenty be.
Woodberry, George Edward
Agathon, *sel.*
America to England.
At Gibraltar (*Sonnets* I *and* II).
Child, The.
Comrades.
Divine Awe.
Edith Cavell.
Essex Regiment March.
Homeward Bound.
Ideal Passion, *sels.*
Islands of the Sea, The.
Life, A.
Love's Rosary.
My Country, *sels.*
O, Inexpressible as Sweet.
O, Struck beneath the Laurel.
O Land Beloved.
Old House, The.
On a Portrait of Columbus.
Our First Century.
Rose of Stars, The.
Seaward.
Secret, The.
So Slow to Die.
Song: "O, Inexpressible as sweet."
Song of Eros.
Sonnets Written in the Fall of 1914.
When First I Saw Her.
Wild Eden, *sels.*
"Woodbine Willie." *See* **Studdert-Kennedy, Geoffrey Anketell**
Woodbourne, Harry
Flute of May, The.
Woodbridge, Benjamin
Upon the Author; by a Known Friend.
Upon the Tomb of the Most Reverend Mr. John Cotton.
Woodcock, George
Green Grass and Sea.
Imagine the South.
Island, The.
Merthymawr.
Pacifists.
Paper Anarchist Addresses the Shade of Nancy Ling Perry.
Poem for Garcia Lorca.
Poem from London, 1941.
Sonnet: "Looking into the windows that doom has broken."
Sunday on Hampstead Heath.
Tree Felling.
White.
Woodford, Bruce P.
Going Through.
Woodhouse, James
Birmingham and Wolverhampton.
Life and Lucubrations of Crispinus Scriblerus, The, *sels.*
Tribulations of an Uneducated Poet in the 1760's, The.
Woodley, F. S.
Beautiful, The.
Woodrow, Constance Davies
To a Vagabond.
Woods, John
Deaths of Paragon, Indiana, The.
Five Dreams, The.
Girl Who Had Borne Too Much, The.
Guns.
Lie Closed, My Lately Loved.
Looking Both Ways before Crossing.
Lying Down with Men and Women.
Outburst from a Little Face.
Playwright.
Poem at Thirty.
Traveling North.
What Do You Do When It's Spring?
When Senses Fled.
Woods Gets Religion.
Woods, Margaret Louisa
Facing the Gulf.
Genius Loci.
March Thoughts from England.
Mariners, The.
Return, The, *sels.*
Young Windebank.
Woods, Nancy
I Read a Tight-fisted Poem Once.
Woods, William Hervey
House of Broken Swords, The, *sel.*
Prayer of Beaten Men, The.
Wood-Thompson, Susan
Territory.
Woodward, Charles
Midnight Ramble, The.
Woodworth, Samuel
Bucket, The.
Hunters of Kentucky, The.
Loves She Like Me?
Needle, The.
Old Oaken Bucket, The.
Woody, Elizabeth
Black Fear.
Custer Must Have Learned to Dance.
Eagles.
In Impressions of Hawk Feathers Willow Leaves Shadow.
Night Crackles.
Wooley, Celia Parker
Refracted Lights.
Woolf, B. *and* Arnold Clayton.
Pity the Down-trodden Landlord.
Woolf, Virginia
Let Us Go, Then, Exploring.
Woolner, Thomas
My Beautiful Lady.
Woolsey, Sarah Chauncey. *See* **"Coolidge, Susan"**
Woolsey, Theodore Dwight
Eclipse of Faith, The.
Woolson, Constance Fenimore
Kentucky Belle.
Wild March.
Yellow Jessamine.
"Worcester"
Pastoral, A; in the Modern Style.
Wordsworth, C. W. V.
Song in Praise of Paella.
Wordsworth, Christopher
All Saints' Day, Nov. 1.
O Day of Rest and Gladness.
Wordsworth, Dorothy
Address to a Child during a Boisterous Winter Evening.
Cottager to Her Infant, The.
He said he had been a soldier.
I gathered mosses in Easedale.
Loving and Liking.
We saw three boys.
Wordsworth, Elizabeth
Good and Clever.
Wordsworth, William
Address to My Infant Daughter, *sel.*
Admonition to a Traveller.
Affliction of Margaret, The.
After-Thought.
Airey-Force Valley.
Alice Fell; or, Poverty.
Alpine Descent.
Among all lovely things my love had been.
Anecdote for Fathers.
Apology.
At Florence.
At the Grave of Burns.
Blest statesman he, whose mind's unselfish will.
Books.
Boyhood.
By the Sea.
Calais, August 15, 1802.
Cambridge and the Alps.
Cave of Staffa, I ("We saw, but surely, in the motley crowd").
Cave of Staffa, II ("Ye shadowy beings, that have rights and claims").
Character of the Happy Warrior.
Characteristics of a Child Three Years Old.
Childhood and School-Time.
Childless Father, The.
Climb to Snowdon, The.
Complaint, A.
Composed at Neidpath Castle, the Property of Lord Queensberry, 1803.
Composed by the Sea-Side, near Calais, August 1802.
Composed upon an Evening of Extraordinary Splendour and Beauty.
Composed upon Westminster Bridge, September 3, 1802.
Conclusion: "It was a Summer's night, a close warm night."
Consummate Happiness.
Contrast, The; the Parrot and the Wren.
Daffodils.
Decay of Piety.
Dedicated Spirit, A.
Desideria.
Despondency Corrected.
Devotional Incitements.
Discourse of the Wanderer, and an Evening Visit to the Lake.
Dust as we are, the immortal spirit grows.
Earth Has Not Anything to Show More Fair.
Ecclesiastical Sonnets, *sels.*
Education of Nature, The.
Elegiac Stanzas, Suggested by a Picture of Peele Castle, in a Storm.
Ellen Irwin; or, The Braes of Kirtle.
England, 1802 ("Great Men have been among us . . .").
England, 1802 ("It is not to be thought that the flood").
England, 1802 ("Milton! thou should'st be living at this hour").
England, 1802 ("O Friend! I know not which way I must look").
England, 1802 ("When I have borne in memory what has tamed").
England and Switzerland 1802.
Evening on Calais Beach.
Evening Walk, An, *sels.*
Excursion, The, *sels.*
Expostulation and Reply.
Extempore Effusion Upon the Death of James Hogg.
Fair below Helvellyn, The.
Faith and Freedom.
Fidelity.
Fountain, The.
French and the Spanish Guerrillas, The.
French Revolution as It Appeared to Enthusiasts at Its Commencement, The.
Gladness of the May, The.
Goody Blake and Harry Gill, *sel.*
Great Men Have Been among Us.
Green Linnet, The.
Guilt and Sorrow, *sel.*
Happy Warrior, The.
Hart-Leap Well.
Her Eyes Are Wild.
Here Pause: The Poet Claims at Least This Praise.
I Grieved for Buonaparté.
I Traveled among Unknown Men.
I Wandered Lonely as a Cloud.
Idiot Boy, The.
If Thou Indeed Derive Thy Light from Heaven.
Imagination ("Imagination—here the Power so called").
Imagination and Taste, How Impaired and Restored.
In a Child's Album.
In London, September 1802.

In Patterdale.
Incident Characteristic of a Favourite Dog.
Influence of Natural Objects.
Inner Vision, The.
Inscribed upon a Rock.
Inside of King's College Chapel, Cambridge.
Intimations of Sublimity.
Introduction—Childhood and School-Time.
It Is a Beauteous Evening [Calm and Free].
It Is Not to Be Thought Of [That the Flood].
It Was an April Morning.
Kitten and [the] Falling Leaves, The, *sels.*
Laodamia.
Leaves that rustled on this oak-crowned hill, The.
Lesson, A.
Liberty, *sel.*
Lines: "Slumber did my spirit seal, A."
Lines Composed a Few Miles above Tintern Abbey [on Revisiting the Banks of the Wye during a Tour, July 13, 1798].
Lines Composed at Grasmere.
Lines Written in Early Spring.
Lines Written near Richmond, upon Thames, at Evening.
London, 1802 ("Milton! thou shouldst be living at this hour").
London, MDCCCII ("O friend! I know not which way I must look").
London, from Hampstead Heath.
Lost Love, The.
Louisa.
Lucy, *complete, in 5 parts.*
Lucy Gray; or, Solitude.
Lyre! though such power do in thy magic live.
Matron of Jedborough and Her Husband, The, *sel.*
Merry Month of March, The.
Methought I Saw the Footsteps of a Throne.
Michael.
Milton! Thou Shouldst Be Living at This Hour.
Most Sweet It Is with Unuplifted Eyes.
Mutability.
My Heart Leaps Up [When I Behold].
Nature and the Poet.
Near Dover, September 1802.
Newton.
Newton's Statue.
Night-Piece, A.
Noble, The.
November, 1806 ("Another year! another deadly blow").
Nuns Fret Not at Their Convent's Narrow Room.
Nutting.
O Nightingale! Thou Surely Art.
October 1803.
Ode: Intimations of Immortality from Recollections of Early Childhood.
Ode to Duty.
Oh! Mystery of Man.
Old Cumberland Beggar, The.
Old Man, An.
Old Man Travelling.
On the Beach at Calais.
On the Departure of Sir Walter Scott from Abbotsford, for Naples.
On the Extinction of the Venetian Republic.
On the Frozen Lake.
On the Power of Sound.
On the Solitary Fells around Hawkshead.
On Ullswater.
On Windermere; Bowness Bay and Belle Isle.
One Summer Evening.
Pass of Kirkstone, The.
Perfect Woman.
Personal Talk.
Pet Lamb, The.
Pilgrim Fathers, The.
Place of Burial in the South of Scotland, A.
Poet, A!—He Hath Put His Heart to School.
Poet's Epitaph, A.
Prefatory Sonnet: "Nuns fret not at their convent's narrow room."
Prelude, The [or, Growth of a Poet's Mind]
Prelude: "In desultory walk through orchard grounds."
Prospectus.
Quantocks, The.
Reaper, The.
Recluse, The, *sels.*
Redbreast, The, *sel.*
Residence at Cambridge.
Residence in France.
Residence in France (Continued).
Residence in London.
Resolution and Independence.
Return.
Reverie of Poor Susan, The.
Rise up, thou monstrous ant-hill on the plain.
River Duddon, The, *sels.*
Roaring in the Wind All Night.
Ruined Cottage, The.
Ruth.
Ruth; or, The Influences of Nature.
Sailor's Mother, The, *sel.*
Salisbury Plain and Stonehenge.
Same, The.
Scorn Not the Sonnet.
September, 1815.
September, 1802; near Dover.
She Dwelt among the Untrodden Ways.
She Was a Phantom of Delight.
Shepherd, The.
Simon Lee.
Simplon Pass, The.
Skaters, The.
Skating ("And in the frosty season, when the sun").
Skating ("So through the darkness and the cold we flew").
Slumber Did My Spirit Seal, A.
Small Celandine, The.
Snowdon Sunrise, The.
So Fair, So Sweet, Withal So Sensitive.
Solitary, The, *sel.*
Solitary Reaper, The.
Song at the Feast of Brougham Castle.
Song for the Spinning Wheel.
Sonnet: Composed after a Journey across the Hamilton Hills, Yorkshire.
Sonnet: Composed by the Side of Grasmere Lake.
Sonnet: Composed While the Author Was Engaged in Writing a Tract Occasioned by the Convention of Cintra.
Sonnet: "England! the time is come when thou shouldst wean."
Sonnet: French and the Spanish Guerillas, The.
Sonnet: It Is a Beauteous Evening [Calm and Free].
Sonnet: "It is not to be thought of that the Flood."
Sonnet: "Milton! thou shouldst be living at this hour."
Sonnet: "Nuns fret not at their convent's narrow room."
Sonnet: "Scorn not the sonnet; critic, you have frown'd."
Sonnet: September, 1815.
Sonnet: September, 1802.
Sonnet: September 1, 1802.
Sonnet: Surprised by Joy.
Sonnet: There Is a Bondage Worse.
Sonnet: Thought of a Briton on the Subjugation of Switzerland.
Sonnet: To ———
Sonnet: To the Lady Beaumont.
Sonnet: Where Lies the Land.
Sonnet: Wild Duck's Nest, The.
Sonnet: "World is too much with us, The; late and soon."
Sonnet: Written in London, September, 1802.
Sonnet Composed upon Westminster Bridge, September 3, 1802.
Sonnet to the Virgin.
Sonnets upon the Punishment of Death, *sels.*
Sparrow's Nest, The.
Speak!
Stanzas Written in My Pocket Copy of Thomson's "Castle of Indolence."
Steamboats, Viaducts, and Railways.
Stepping Westward.
Strange Fits of Passion Have I Known.
Stuffed Owl, The, *sel.*
Such was the Boy—but for the growing Youth.
Suggested by a Picture of the Bird of Paradise.
Summer Vacation.
Sun Has Long Been Set, The.
Sunbeam Said, Be Happy, The.
Surprised by Joy [Impatient as the Wind].
Swans.
Swiss Peasant, The.
Tables Turned, The.
There Was a Boy.
Thorn, The.
Thought [*or* Thoughts] of a Briton on the Subjugation of Switzerland.
Three Cottage Girls, The.
Three Years She Grew [in Sun and Shower].
Tintern Abbey.
'Tis Said That Some Have Died for Love.
To a Butterfly.
To a Child.
To a Distant Friend.
To a Highland Girl.
To a Skylark ("Ethereal minstrel! pilgrim of the sky!").
To a Skylark ("Up with me! up with me into the clouds!").
To a Young Lady.
To Catherine Wordsworth 1808–1812.
To Coleridge in Sicily.
To H. C.
To Hartley Coleridge.
To Lady Eleanor Butler and the Honourable Miss Ponsonby, Composed in the Grounds of Plas-Newydd, Llangollen.
To Milton.
To My Sister.
To Sleep.
To the Cuckoo.
To the Daisy ("Bright Flower! whose home is everywhere").
To the Daisy ("In youth from rock to rock I went").
To the Daisy ("With little here to do or see").
To the Highland Girl of Inversneyde.
To the Men of Kent.
To the River Duddon: After-Thought.
To the Same Flower.
To the Small Celandine.
To Toussaint L'Ouverture.
Tribute to the Memory of the Same Dog.
Trosachs, The.
Two April Mornings, The.
Valedictory Sonnet to the River Duddon.
Vaudracour and Julia, *sel.*
Virgin, The.
Voice of the Derwent, The.
Wanderer, The, *abr.*
Wanderer Recalls the Past, The.
Water Fowl.
We Are Seven.
We Must Be Free or Die.
We Poets in Our Youth.
Weak Is the Will of Man, His Judgment Blind.
Westminster Bridge.
When I Have Borne in Memory.
Where Lies the Land [to Which Yon Ship Must Go]?
Where Lies the Truth? Has Man in Wisdom's Creed.
Why Art Thou Silent.
Wild Duck's Nest, The.

Winander Lake.
With Ships the Sea Was Sprinkled [Far and Nigh].
Within King's College Chapel, Cambridge.
Wordsworth Skates on Esthwaite Water.
World, The.
World Is Too Much with Us, The.
Written in London, September, 1802.
Written in March.
Written in the Album of a Child.
Written in Very Early Youth.
Yarrow Revisited.
Yarrow Unvisited.
Yarrow Visited.
Yes, It Was the Mountain Echo.
Yew-Trees.
Young Wordsworth's London, The.

Work, Henry Clay
Come Home, Father.
Father, Dear Father, Come Home with Me Now.
Grandfather's Clock.
Kingdom Coming, *with music.*
Marching through Georgia.
Ship That Never Returned, The.
Wake Nicodemus.
Year of Jubilee [*or* Jubilo], The.

Worley, Mrs. J. B.
Mighty Hunter, The.

Worley, James
Mark Van Doren.
Touchstone.

Wormser, Baron
By-Products.
Mowing Crew, The.
Piano Lessons.
Poem to the Memory of H. L. Mencken.
Sunday Review Section.

Worsley, Alice F.
Has Been.

Worth, Douglas
Ghetto Summer School.
War Bride.

Worth, Kathryn
Smells.

Worth, Valerie
Body.
Chairs.
Christmas Lights.
Christmas Ornaments.
Crickets.
Daisies.
Dinosaurs.
Duck.
Fireworks.
Haunted House.
Zinnias.

Worthington, Kim
I Held a Lamb.

Wortman, Denis
God of the Prophets! Bless the Prophets' Sons, *with music.*
Today beneath Benignant Skies, *with music.*

Wotton, Sir Henry
Character of a Happy Life, The.
"D. O. M."
De Morte.
Dialogue betwixt God and the Soul, A, *at.*
Eternal[l] Mover.
Happy Life, The.
Hymn to My God in a Night of My Late Sicknesse, A.
May Day, A.
On a Bank [*or* Banck] as I Sat [*or* Sate] a-Fishing; a Description of the Spring.
On His Mistress [*or* Mistris], the Queen of Bohemia.
On the Death of Sir Albert Morton's Wife.
Poem Written by Sir Henry Wotton, in His Youth, A.
Tears at the Grave of Sir Albertus Morton.
To His Mistress, the Queen of Bohemia.
Upon the Death of Sir Albert[us] Morton's Wife.
Upon the Sudden Restraint of the Earl[e] of Somerset, [Then] Falling from Favo[u]r.

Wotton, Sir John
In Praise of His Daphnis.
In Praise of His Love.

Woty, William
Lines Written in the Dog-Days.
Mock Invocation to Genius, A, *sel.*
White Conduit House.

Wrafter, Denis
Braggart!
Old Man to His Scythe, The.
On Hearing a Broadcast of Ceremonies in Connection with Conferring of Cardinals' Hats.
Sabbath Reflection.

Wratislaw, Theodore
Eros D'Aute.
Orchids.
To a Sicilian Boy.

"Wreford, James." *See* **Watson, James Wreford**

Wreford, John R.
Lord, While for All Mankind.

Wright, Bruce McM.
African Affair, The.
Journey to a Parallel.

Wright, Carolyne
Early Fall: The Adirondacks.
Trestle Bridge, The.

Wright, Catharine Morris
Hillside Pause.

Wright, Celeste Turner
Daguerreotype of a Grandmother.
Kineo Mountain.
Murgatroyd.
Noblesse Oblige.
Thumbprint.
View from Father's Porch, The.
Yugoslav Cemetery.

Wright, Charles
Blackwater Mountain.
Chinoiserie.
Clear Night.
Cloud River.
Daughters of Blum, The.
Dead Color.
Death.
Delta Traveller.
Dog Creek Mainline ("Dog Creek: cat track and bind splay").
Dog Day Vespers.
Dog Yoga.
Fever Toy, The.
Firstborn.
Hawaii Dantesca.
Holy Thursday.
Invisible Landscape.
Janitor, The; Kindergarten, Corinth.
Laguna Blues.
Mount Caribou at Night.
Negatives.
New Poem, The.
Night letter.
Nightdream.
Photographs.
Portrait of the Artist with Hart Crane.
Self-Portrait in 2035.
Sitting at Night on the Front Porch.
Smoke.
Snake Handling Religious Service.
Snow.
Spider Crystal Ascension.
Stone Canyon Nocturne.
Tattoos, *sels.*
Two Stories.
Virgo Descending.
Yellow.

Wright, Charles David
Shaving.
Some Semblance of Order.

Wright, David
Anniversary Approaches, An; of the Birth of God.
Funeral Oration, A.
Grasmere Sonnets.
Invocation to the Goddess, An.
Kleomedes.
Monologue of a Deaf Man.
Moral Story II.
On the Death of an Emperor Penguin in Regent's Park, London.
On the Margin, *sel.*
Pastoral: "Afternoon wears on, The."
Rousecastle.
Seven South African Poems, *sels.*
South African Broadsheets, *sel.*
Walking to Dedham.

Wright, David McKee
Danny's Wooing.
Dark Rosaleen, *sels.*

Wright, Ernest Vincent
When Father Carves the Duck.

Wright, Franz
View from an Institution.

Wright, Frederick Adams
Letter to the City Clerk.

Wright, Fred W., Jr.
Couch, The.

Wright, George T.
Aquarium.

Wright, Helen M.
Golden Grain.

Wright, Hetty
To an Infant Expiring the Second Day of Its Birth.
Wedlock; a Satire.

Wright, Ivan Leonard
Want of You, The.

Wright, James
Against Surrealism.
American Twilights, 1957.
Apollo.
Arrangements with Earth for Three Dead Friends.
As I Step over a Puddle at the End of Winter, I Think of an Ancient Chinese Governor.
Assignation, The.
At the Slackening of the Tide.
At Thomas Hardy's Birthplace, 1953.
Autumn Begins in Martins Ferry, Ohio.
Avenger, The.
Before the [*or* a] Cashier's Window in a Department Store.
Blessing, A.
Breath of Air, A.
By a Lake in Minnesota.
Complaint.
Confession to J. Edgar Hoover.
Depressed by a Book of Bad Poetry, I Walk toward an Unused Pasture and Invite the Insects to Join Me.
Discoveries in Arizona.
Dream of Burial, A.
Eisenhower's Visit to Franco, 1959.
Elegy in a Firelit Room.
Evening.
For the Marsh's Birthday.
Gesture by a Lady with an Assumed Name, A.
Girl in a Window, A.
Having Lost My Sons, I Confront the Wreckage of the Moon: Christmas, 1960.
"I Am a Sioux Brave," He Said in Minneapolis.
I Try to Waken and Greet the World Once Again.
In Memory of Leopardi.
In Ohio.
In Response to a Rumor That the Oldest Whorehouse in Wheeling, West Virginia, Has Been Condemned.
In Shame and Humiliation.
In Terror of Hospital Bills.
Inscription for the Tank.

Jewel, The.
Lament for My Brother on a Hayrake.
Late November in a Field.
Life, The.
Lights in the Hallway, The.
Little Girl on Her Way to School, A.
Little Marble Boy.
Living by the Red River.
Love in a Warm Room in Winter.
Lying in a Hammock at William Duffy's Farm.
Mad Fight Song for William S. Carpenter, 1966, A.
Mantova.
Micromutations.
Milkweed.
Miners.
Minneapolis Poem, The.
Morality of Poetry, The.
Mutterings over the Crib of a Deaf Child.
Names in Monterchi: To Rachel.
Note Left in Jimmy Leonard's Shack, A.
Ohio Valley Swains.
Ohioan Pastoral.
Old Age Compensation.
Old Dog in the Ruins of the Graves at Arles, The.
On a Skeleton of a Hound.
On Minding One's Own Business.
On the Skeleton of a Hound.
Outside Fargo, North Dakota.
Paul.
Poem about Breasts, A.
Poems to a Brown Cricket.
Prayer to Escape from the Market Place, A.
Prayer to the Lord Ramakrishna, A.
Presentation of Two Birds to My Son, A.
Private Meeting Place, The.
Quest, The.
Rain.
Redwings.
Revelation, The.
Rip.
Saint Judas.
Sheep in the Rain.
Simon and the Tarantula.
Small Frogs Killed on the Highway.
Snowfall; a Poem about Spring.
Song for the Middle of the Night, A.
Speak.
Stages on a Journey Westward.
Three Sentences for a Dead Swan.
To a Blossoming Pear Tree.
To a Defeated Saviour.
To a Salesgirl, Weary of Artificial Holiday Trees.
To Flood Stage Again.
To the Evening Star: Central Minnesota.
To the Ghost of a Kite.
To the Muse.
Trouble.
Twilights.
Two Hangovers.
Two Poems about President Harding.
Two Postures beside a Fire.
Ungathered Apples, The.
Vain Advice at the Year's End.
Venice.
Verona.
Vestal in the Forum, The.
Way to Make a Living, A.
What the Earth Asked Me.
Winter Daybreak above Venice, A.
With a Sliver of Marble from Carrara.
With the Shell of a Hermit Crab.
Written in a Copy of Swift's Poems, for Wayne Burns.
Youth.

Wright, Jay
Altars and Sacrifice.
Charge, The.
Dead, The.
Death as History.
Homecoming Singer, The.
Invitation to Madison County, An.
This Morning.
Wednesday Night Prayer Meeting.

Wright, John
Poor Man's Province, The.

Wright, Judith
And Mr. Ferritt.
At Cooloolah.
Australia 1970.
Blind Man, The, *sel.*
Builders, The.
Bull, The.
Bullocky.
Country Dance.
Egrets.
Eli, Eli.
Extinct Birds.
Habitat, *sels.*
Hawthorn Hedge, The.
Legend.
Lyrebirds.
Night and the Child.
Old Prison, The.
Request to a Year.
Sanctuary.
South of My Days.
Sports Field.
Storm.
Surfer, The.
Tableau.
Train Journey.
Turning Fifty.
Twins, The.
Two Fires, The.
Wings.
Woman to Child.
Woman to Man.
Woman's Song.
Wonga Vine.

Wright, Kit
Dad and the Cat and the Tree.
I Don't Like You.

Wright, Richard
Between the World and Me.
Four Haiku.
Haiku: "Balmy spring wind, A."
Haiku: "Coming from the woods."
Haiku: "Crow flew so fast, The."
Haiku: "Dog's violent sneeze, The."
Haiku: "Empty sickbed, An."
Haiku: "Green cockleburs, The."
Haiku: "I would like a bell."
Haiku: "Just enough of rain."
Haiku: "Why is the hail so wild."
Haiku: "Winter rain at night."
Hokku: In the Falling Snow.
Hokku Poems.
I Have Seen Black Hands.

Wright, Sarah E.
To Some Millions Who Survive Joseph E. Mander, Sr.
Until They Have Stopped.
Urgency.

Wright, Willard Huntington
Song against Women.

Wright, William Bull
Brook, The, *sel.*

Wrighton, W. T.
Dearest Spot on Earth, The.

Wrigley, Robert
Binding Arbitration.
Pain.
Rattlesnake, The.

Wroth [*or* Wroath], Mary Sidney, Countess of Montgomery
Duke's Song, The.
Lindamira's Complaint.
Morea's Sonnet.
Pamphilia to Amphilanthus.
Pamphilia's Sonnet.
Urania.
Verses of the Talkative Knight, The.

Wurdemann, Audrey
Little Black Man with a Rose in His Hat.
Text.

Wu Ti, Emperor
Autumn Wind, The ("Autumn wind rises; white clouds fly").
People Hide Their Love.

Wu Tsao
Bitter rain in my courtyard.
For the Courtesan Ch'ing Lin.
In the Home of the Scholar Wu Su-chiang.

Wyatt, Edith Franklin
On the Great Plateau.

Wyatt, Jiri
Us.

Wyatt, Sir Thomas
Absence absenting causeth me to complain.
Accused though I be without desert.
After great storms the calm returns.
Ah, Robin,/ Jolly Robin.
Alas, poor man, what hap have I.
Alas! Madam, for Stealing of a Kiss.
Alas the grief, and deadly woful smart!
All heavy minds.
And if an eye may save or slay.
And Wilt Thou Leave Me Thus?
Answer that ye made to me, my dear, The.
Appeal, An [*or* The].
As power and wit will me assist.
At last withdraw your cruelty.
Behold, love, thy power how she despiseth!
Betrayal.
Blame Not My Lute for He Must Sound [*or* Sownde].
Comfort thyself, my woful heart.
Comparison of Love to a Streame Falling from the Alpes.
Constancy.
Courtier's Life, The.
Deem as ye list, upon good cause.
Deme as Ye List Uppon Goode Cause.
Disdain.
Disdain Me Not.
Divers Doth Use, as I Have Heard and Know.
Earnest Suit, An.
Eche man me telleth I chaunge moost my devise.
Epigram: "Enemy of life, decayer of all kind, The."
Epigram: "Face that should content me wonders well, A."
Epigram: "Fruit of all the service that I serve, The."
Epigram: "Lux my fair falcon, and your fellows all."
Epigram: "Sighs are my food, drink are my tears."
Epigram: "Who hath heard of such cruelty before?"
Epitaph of Sir Thomas Gravener, Knight, An.
Farewell, all my welfare.
Farewell, Unkist.
Farewell: "What should I say."
Farewell the reign of cruelty.
For want I will in woe I plain.
Forget Not Yet [the Tried Intent].
Fortune.
Full well it may be seen.
Galley, The.
Give place all ye that doth rejoice.
Hate Whom Ye List.
He is not ded that somtyme hath a fall.
Heart and service to you proffer'd, The.
Heart oppress'd with desperate thought.
Help Me to Seek.
Hind, The.
His Lady's Hand.
His Reward.
Honesty.
How Like You This?
How oft have I, my dere and cruell foe.

How Should I Be So Pleasant.
I am as I am and so will I be.
I have sought long with steadfastness.
I love, loved, and so doth she.
I see that chance hath chosen me.
If chance assign'd.
If ever man might him avaunt.
If fancy [*or* fansy] would favor.
If in the World There Be More Woe.
If Thou Wilt Mighty Be.
If waker care, if sodayne pale coulor.
If with complaint the pain might be express'd.
In Eternum.
In faith I wot not what to say.
In Spain.
Is It Possible ?
It May Be Good.
It Was My Choice.
Joy so short alas, the pain so near, The.
Knot which first my heart did strain, The.
Lament my losse, my labor, and my payne.
Liberty.
Like as the bird in the cage enclosed.
Like as the swan towards her death.
Lo, how I seek and sue to have.
Longer to muse.
Love doth again.
Lover Complaineth [*or* Complayneth] the Unkindness of His Love, The.
Lover Forsaken, The.
Lover Having Dreamed Enjoying of [*or* Enjoying of] His Love, Complaineth That the Dream Is Not either Longer or Truer, The.
Lover Like to a Ship Tossed on the Sea, The.
Lover Rejoiceth, The.
Lover Rejoiceth the Enjoying of His Love, The.
Lover Renounceth Love, The.
Lover Showeth How He Is Forsaken of Such as He Sometime Enjoyed, The.
Lover's Appeal, The.
Luckes, my faire falcon, and your fellowes all.
Lute Obeys, The.
Lux, My Fair Falcon.
Lyve thowe gladly, yff so thowe may.
Madame, withouten Many Wordes.
May Time.
Me list no more to sing.
Mistrustful minds be moved.
Most wretched heart, most miserable.
My hope, alas, hath me abused.
My Lute and I.
My Pen, Take Pain a Little Space.
Mye love toke skorne my servise to retaine.
No! Indeed.
Now all of change.
Now must I learn to live [*or* lerne to lyve] at rest.
O Goodly Hand.
O miserable sorrow, withouten cure.
Of His Returne from Spaine.
Of the Courtier's Life.
Pass forth, my wonted cries.
Patience.
Patience, for I have wrong.
Patience, Though I Have Not.
Patience for my device.
Patience of all my smart.
Piller pearisht is whearto I lent, The.
Process of time worketh such wonder.
Promise, A.
Protest, A.
Quondam was I in my lady's grace.
Renouncing of Love, A.
Resignation.
Resound my voyse [*or* voice], ye wodes [*or* woods] that here [*or* hear] me plain.
Restful place, reviver of my smart, The.
Revocation, A.
Robyn, A/ Joly Robyn.
Rondeau: "What no, perdie [*or* perdy]! ye may be sure!"
Satire 3: To Sir Francis Brian.
Satires, *sels.*
Say Nay.
Since love is such that as ye wot.
Since love will needs that I shall love.
Since so ye please to hear me plain.
Since ye delight to know.
Since you will needs that I shall sing.
So unwarely was never no man caught.
Some tyme I fled the fyre that me brent.
Sometime I sigh, sometime I sing.
Sonnet: "Divers doth use (as I have heard and know)."
Sonnet: "Each man me telleth I change most my devise."
Sonnet: "Farewell, love, and all thy laws for ever."
Sonnet: "I abide and abide and better abide."
Sonnet: "My galley charged with forgetfulness."
Sonnet: "My love took scorn my service to retain."
Sonnet: "To rail or jest, ye know I use it not."
Sonnet: "Whoso list to hunt, I know where is an hind."
Sonnet: "You that in love find luck and abundaunce."
Speak Thou and Speed.
Spite hath no power to make me sad.
Steadfastness.
Such hap as I am happed in.
Sufficed not, madame, that you did tear.
Supplication, A.
Tagus, Farewell.
Take heed betime, lest ye be spied.
That time that mirth did steer my ship.
There was never nothing more me pained [*or* payned].
They Flee [*or* Fle] from Me That Sometime Did Me Seek [*or* Seke].
Throughout the World [If It Were Sought].
To a Lady to Answer Directly with Yea or Nay.
To cause accord or to agree [*or* aggre].
To His Heart.
To His Lady.
To His Pen.
To seek each where where man doth live.
To wet your eye withouten tear.
To wish, and want, and not obtain.
Treizaine.
V. Innocentia Veritas Viat Fides Circumdederunt Me Inimici Mei.
Varium et Mutabile.
What death is worse than this.
What Does This Mean?
What meaneth this? When I lie alone.
What nedeth these thretning wordes and wasted wynde?
What Once I Was.
What rage is this? what furor [*or* furour] of what kind [*or* kynd]?
What vaileth trouth? or by it to take payn?
What wourde is that that chaungeth not.
When first mine eyes did view and mark.
Where shall I have at mine own will.
Whoso List to Hunt [I Know Where Is an Hind].
Will ye see what wonders love hath wrought.
With Serving Still.
Within My Breast.
Ye Know My Heart.
Ye old mule, that thinck your self so fayre.
Your looks so often cast.

Wyche, Marvin, Jr.
And She Was Bad.
Five Sense.
Leslie.
We Rainclouds.

Wycherley, William
Drinking-Song, against All Sorts of Disputes in Drinking, A.
Envious Critick, The.
Love in a Wood, *sel.*
Song, A: In the Name of a Lover, to His Mistress; Who Said, She Hated Him for His Grey Hairs, Which He Had at Thirty.
Spouse I Do Hate, A.
To a Fine Young Woman.
To a Good Physician.
To a Witty Man of Wealth and Quality; Who, after His Dismissal from Court, Said, He Might Justly Complain of It.
Upon the Most Useful Knowledge, Craft or Cunning, Which Is More Wisdom, as 'Tis Less Wit.

Wygodski, Stanislaw
Going to the North.
Those Betrayed at Dawn.
Voyage.
Winter Journey.

Wylie, Elinor
Address to My Soul.
Atavism.
August.
Beauty.
Birthday Sonnet.
Castilian.
Cold-blooded Creatures.
Confession of Faith.
Desolation Is a Delicate Thing.
Doomsday.
Eagle and the Mole, The.
Epitaph: "For this she starred her eyes with salt."
Escape.
Farewell, Sweet Dust.
Full Moon.
Golden Bough.
Hughie at the Inn.
Hymn to Earth.
I Hereby Swear That to Uphold Your House.
Innocent Landscape.
Knight Fallen on Evil Days, The.
Lament for Glasgerion.
Lavish Kindness.
Let No Charitable Hope.
Lodging for the Night, A.
Love Song: "Had I concealed my love."
Madman's Song.
Nebuchadnezzar.
O Virtuous Light.
One Person, *sels.*
Parting Gift.
Pebble, The.
Pegasus Lost.
Peregrine.
Peregrine's Sunday Song.
Peter and John.
Pretty Words.
Prophecy.
Proud Lady, A.
Puritan Sonnet.
Puritan's Ballad, The.
Sanctuary.
Sea Lullaby.
Shepherd's Holiday.
Simon Gerty.
Sleeping Beauty.
Sonnet: "I hereby swear that to uphold your house."
Sonnet: "Let us leave talking of angelic hosts."
Sonnet from "One Person."
This Corruptible.
To a Book.
Tortoise in Eternity, The.
True Vine.
Velvet Shoes.
Wild Peaches.
Winter Sleep.

Wynand, Derk
Observation.

Wyndham, Charles
Fair Thief, The.

Wyndham, Harald
Anarchist's Letter, An.

Wynne, Annette
Excuse Us, Animals in the Zoo.
Harebells in June.
Hearts Were Made to Give Away.
I Keep Three Wishes Ready.
Indian Children.
Leaves Do Not Mind at All, The.
Letter Is a Gypsy Elf, A.
Memorial Day.
Once When You Were Walking.
Outside the Door.
People Buy a Lot of Things.
Pilgrims Came, The.
Ring around the World.
Thanksgiving Day.
Tree Stands Very Straight and Still, The.
Wynne, John Huddlestone
Horse and the Mule, The.
Time.

X

"Xariffa." *See* **Townsend, Mary Ashley**
Xenos Palaestes
Requirements: "Not too pallid, as if bleacht."

Y

Yakamochi (Otomo no Yakamochi)
By way of pretext.
"Ya-Ka-Nes." *See* **Harjo, Patty L.**
Yako, St. J. Page
Year's Ending, The.
Yamada, Mitsuye
Camp Notes, *sels.*
In the Outhouse.
On the Bus.
Yamamoto, Traise
Biting Through.
Diving for Pearls.
In the Van Gogh Room.
Prelude: "Grace comes only after the long study of choice."
Yamamoue Okura
Elegy on the Death of Furuhi, An.
Yang Kuei-fei
Dancing.
Yannai
And It Came to Pass at Midnight.
Yates, David C.
Observer, The.
Yates, Edmund
All Saints'.
Yates, J. Michael
Great Bear Lake Meditations, The, *sels.*
Yates, Lynda
Disordering, The.
"Yates, Peter" (William Long)
Smelling the End of Green July.
Star of Eternal Possibles and Joy.
Thought and the Poet.
Ybarra, Thomas Russell
Christian Is a Man Who Feels, A.
Lay of Ancient Rome.
Ode to Work in Springtime.
Prose and Poesy; a Rural Misadventure.
Yearsley, Ann
To Mr. ———, an Unlettered Poet, on Genius Improved.
Yeatman, Jennette
Exile.
Yeatman, Robert Julian, *and* Walter Carruthers Sellar
How I Brought the Good News from Aix to Ghent (or Vice Versa).
Yeats, William Butler
Acre of Grass, An.
Adam's Curse.
Aedh Thinks of Those Who Have Spoken Evil of His Beloved.
Aedh Wishes for the Cloths of Heaven.
After Long Silence.
All Souls' Night.
All Things Can Tempt Me.
Among School Children.
Apologia Addressed to Ireland in the Coming Days.
Apparitions, The.
At Galway Races.
Ballad of Father Gilligan, The.
Ballad of Father O'Hart, The.
Balloon of the Mind, The.
Before the World Was Made.
Beggar to Beggar Cried.
Black Tower, The.
Bronze Head, A.
Brown Penny.
Byzantium.
Cap and Bells, The.
Cat and the Moon, The.
Chambermaid's Second Song, The.
Choice, The.
Chosen.
Church and State.
Circus Animals' Desertion, The.
Coat, A.
Cold Heaven, The.
Collar-Bone of a Hare, The.
Coming of Wisdom with Time, The.
Coole Park, 1929.
Coole Park and Ballylee, 1931.
Cradle Song, A: "Angels are stooping, The."
Crazed Girl, The.
Crazed Moon, The ("Crazed through much child-bearing").
Crazy Jane and Jack the Journeyman.
Crazy Jane and the Bishop.
Crazy Jane Grown Old Looks at the Dancers.
Crazy Jane on God.
Crazy Jane on the Day of Judgment.
Crazy Jane on the Mountain.
Crazy Jane Reproved.
Crazy Jane Talks with the Bishop.
Cuchulain's Fight with the Sea.
Curse of Cromwell, The.
Dawn, The.
Death.
Death of Cuchulain, The.
Deep-sworn Vow, A.
Deirdre, *sel.*
Dialogue of Self and Soul, A.
Dolls, The.
Down by the Salley Gardens.
Dream of Death, A.
Drinking Song, A.
Easter, 1916.
Ego Dominus Tuus.
Ephemera.
Everlasting Voices, The.
Faery Song, A.
Fairy Song.
Fallen Majesty.
Falling of the Leaves, The.
Fascination of What's Difficult, The.
Fergus and the Druid.
Fiddler of Dooney, The.
Fisherman, The.
Folly of Being Comforted, The.
Fool by the Roadside, The.
For Anne Gregory.
Four Ages of Man, The.
Fragment: "Locke sank into a swoon."
Fragments.
Friends.
Great Day, The.
Gyres, The.
Hawk, The.
He Hears the Cry of the Sedge.
He Remembers Forgotten Beauty.
He Thinks of His Past Greatness When a Part of the Constellations of Heaven.
Host of the Air, The.
Hosting of the Sidhe, The.
Hound Voice.
How shall I name you, immortal, mild, proud shadows?
"I Am of Ireland."
I See Phantoms of Hatred and of the Heart's Fullness and of the Coming Emptiness.
In Memory of Con and Eva Gore-Booth.
In Memory of Eva Gore-Booth and Con Markiewicz.
In Memory of Major Robert Gregory.
In the Seven Woods.
Indian Song, An.
Indian to His Love, The.
Indian upon God, The.
Into the Twilight.
Irish Airman Foresees His Death, An.
John Kinsella's Lament for Mrs. Mary Moore.
Lady's Third Song, The.
Lake Isle of Innisfree, The.
Lamentation of the Old Pensioner, The.
Land of Heart's Desire, The, *sel.*
Lapis Lazuli.
Last Confession, A.
Leaders of the Crowd, The.
Leda and the Swan.
Let All Things Pass Away.
Lines Written in Dejection.
Long-legged Fly.
Lover Mourns for the Loss of Love, The.
Lover Tells of the Rose in His Heart, The.
Lullaby: "Beloved, may your sleep be sound."
Mad as the Mist and Snow.
Magi, The.
Man Who Dreamed of Faeryland, The.
Meditations in Time of Civil War, *sels.*
Memory.
Meru.
Michael Robartes and the Dancer.
Michael Robartes Bids His Beloved Be at Peace.
Michael Robartes Remembers Forgotten Beauty.
Model for the Laureate, A.
Mohini Chatterjee.
Mongan Laments the Change That Has Come upon Him and His Beloved.
Moods, The.
Mother of God, The.
Municipal Gallery Revisited, The.
My Descendants.
My House.
My Table.
Never Give All the Heart.
New Faces, The.
News for the Delphic Oracle.
Nineteen Hundred and Nineteen.
Nineteenth Century and After, The.
No Second Troy.
Old Men Admiring Themselves in the Water, The.
Old Song Resung, An.
On a Picture of a Black Centaur by Edmund Dulac.
On a Political Prisoner.
On Being Asked for a War Poem.
On Hearing That the Students of Our New University Have Joined the Agitation against Immoral Literature.
On Woman.
Only Jealousy of Emer, The, *sel.*
Pardon, Old Fathers.
Parnell.
Parting.
Paudeen.
People, The.
Pity of Love, The.
Players Ask for a Blessing on the Psalteries and Themselves, The.
Poet to His Beloved, A.

Politics.
Prayer for My Daughter, A.
Prayer for My Son, A.
Priest of Coloony, The.
Purgatory.
Ragged Wood, The.
Red Hanrahan's Song about Ireland.
Renowned Generations, The.
Reprisals.
Responsibilities, *sel.*
Resurrection, The, *sel.*
Ribh Considers Christian Love Insufficient.
Road at My Door, The.
Rose of Peace, The.
Rose of the World, The.
Rose Tree, The.
Running to Paradise.
Sad Shepherd, The.
Sailing to Byzantium.
Scholars, The.
Second Coming, The.
September 1913.
Shadowy Horses, The.
Sixteen Dead Men.
Solomon and the Witch.
Solomon to Sheba.
Song: "Woman's beauty is like a white, A."
Song of the Happy Shepherd, The.
Song of the Old Mother, The.
Song of Wandering Aengus, The.
Sorrow of Love, The.
Spur, The.
Stare's Nest by My Window, The.
Statesman's Holiday, The.
Statues, The.
Stolen Child, The.
Swift's Epitaph.
Symbols.
That the Night Come.
Those Images.
Thought from Propertius, A.
Three Bushes, The.
Three Hermits, The.
Three Movements.
Three Things.
To a Friend Whose Work Has Come to Nothing.
To a Poet, Who Would Have Me Praise Certain Bad Poets, Imitators of His and Mine.
To a Shade.
To a Squirrel at Kyle-na-no.
To a Young Beauty.
To a Young Girl.
To an Isle in the Water.
To Be Carved on a Stone at Thoor Ballylee.
To Ireland in the Coming Times.
To the Rose upon the Rood of Time.
Tom O'Roughley.
Tom the Lunatic.
Tower, The.
Travail of Passion, The.
Two Songs from a Play.
Two Songs of a Fool.
Two Trees, The.
Under Ben Bulben.
Upon a Dying Lady.
Upon a House Shaken by the Land Agitation.
Vacillation.
Valley of the Black Pig, The.
Vision, A, *sel.*
Wanderings of Oisin, The.
What Then?
Wheel, The.
When Helen Lived.
When You Are Old.
Whence Had They Come?
Where My Books Go.
Who Goes with Fergus?
Wicked Hawthorn Tree, The.
Wild Old Wicked Man, The.
Wild Swans at Coole, The.
Wisdom.
Witch, The.
Youth and Age.

"Yehoash" (Solomon Bloomgarden [*or* Blumgarten]
At the Tomb of Rachel.
Harp of David, The.
Hunting.
Jephthah's Daughter.
Mystery.
Old Song, An.
Prayer, A: "Eternal God, our life is but."
Prophet, The.
Psalm: "Happy is the man whom Thou hast set apart."
Shadows.
Song, A: "Song of grass, A,/ A song of earth."
Song as Yet Unsung, A.
Strongest, The.
Terror.
Thanksgiving.
That Is All I Heard.
Tool of Fate, The.
Wanderer, The.
Withered Rose, A.
Yang-se-fu.

Yellen, Samuel
Cloisters, The.
Discourse on the Real.
Grisaille with a Spot of Red.
Personal.
Prognostic.
Time of Light, a Time of Shadow, A.
Wood of the Self-Destroyers, The.
Wooden Tiger, The.

Yerby, Frank
Calm after Storm.
Fishes and the Poet's Hands, The.
Weltschmerz.
Wisdom.
You Are a Part of Me.

Yeshurun, Avot
Poem on Our Mother, Our Mother Rachel, The.
Poem on the Guilt, The.
Poem on the Jews, The.

Yevtushenko, Yevgeny
Against Borders.
Birthday.
Colors.
People.
Waiting.

Yolen, Jane
Bluffalo, The.
Grandpa Bear's Lullaby.
Homework.

Yonathan, Nathan
And the Silver Turns into Night.
Another Poem on Absalom.
South Wind.

York, Eva Rose
I Shall Not Pass This Way Again.

York, Sarah E.
I Am Weary of Straying, *with music.*

Yosano Akiko
As I am unhappy.
Bird comes, A/ delicately as a little girl.
I can give myself to her.
No camellia.
Spring is short.
Wave of coldness, A.
You never touch.

Yoshihara, Sachiko
Madness.

Yots, Michael
On a Friend's Suicide.

Young, Al
Birthday Poem.
Blues Don't Change, The.
"Boogie with O. O. Gabugah."
Dance for Ma Rainey, A.
Dance for Militant Dilettantes, A.
Dance of the Infidels.
Dancer, The.
Dear Old Stockholm.
For Poets.
Ho.
Identities.
In a Mist.
Intimacy.
Kiss.
Lemons, Lemons.
Lester Leaps In.
Loneliness.
Lonesome in the Country.
Moon Watching by Lake Chapala.
Move Continuing, The.
Myself When I Am Real.
Not Her, She Aint No Gypsy.
Old O. O. Blues, The.
One West Coast.
Pachuta, Mississippi/ A Memoir.
Poem for Players, A.
Ponce de León: A Morning Walk.
Song Turning Back into Itself, The, *sel.*
Visiting Day.
W. H. Auden & Mantan Moreland.
Yes, the Secret Mind Whispers.

Young, Andrew
At Arley.
Beauty and Love.
Bee-Orchis, The.
Beech, The.
Black Rock of Kiltearn, The.
Christmas Day.
Climbing in Glencoe.
Cuckoo.
Cuckoos.
Culbin Sands.
Daisies.
Dead Bird, The.
Dead Crab, The.
Dead Mole, A.
Dead Sheep, The.
Dundonnel Mountains.
Eagle, The.
Echoing Cliff, The.
Elm Beetle, The.
Fairy Ring, The.
Fall of Glomach.
Fallen Tree, The.
Falls of Glomach, The.
Field-Glasses.
Flesh-Scraper, The.
Flood, The.
Go Now, My Song.
Hard Frost.
Haystack, The.
Hymn: "Lord, by whose breath all souls and seeds are living."
In December.
In Teesdale.
Last Snow.
Late Autumn.
Loch Luichart.
Man and Cows.
March Hares.
Mist.
Nightfall on Sedgemoor.
Old Tree, The.
On Middleton Edge.
On the Ridgeway.
Paps of Jura, The.
Passing the Graveyard.
Prospect of a Mountain.
Prospect of Death, A.
Round Barrow, The.
Scarecrow, The.
Sheaf, The.
Shepherd's Hut, The.
Snow Harvest.
Song for Autumn.
Stay, Spring.
Stockdoves, The.
Suilven.
Walking in Beech Leaves.
Wiltshire Downs.

Young Martins, The.
Young, Augustus
Advice of an Efficiency Expert, The.
After Five Years.
Elegy for a School-Friend.
Heritage.
Last Refuge, The.
She's My Love.
Woman, Don't Be Troublesome.
Young, Barbara
Being Gypsy.
"I Hear It Said."
Sophisticate.
Young, David
August at the Lake.
Boxcar Poem, The ("The boxcars drift by").
Death of the Novel, The.
"It's a Whole World, the Body. A Whole World!"—Swami Satchidandanda.
Mandelstam.
Occupational Hazards.
Thoughts of Chairman Mao.
Young, Douglas
Ballant o' the Laird's Bath, The.
Caller rain frae abune.
Deid sall ye ligg, and ne'er a memorie.
For a Wife in Jizzen.
Ice-Flumes Owregie Their Ladies.
Kirkyaird by the Sea, The, *sel.*
Last Lauch.
Minnie, I canna caa my wheel.
Winter Homily on the Calton Hill.
Young, Edith Lillian
Disappointment.
Young, Edward (1683-1765)
Art of Happiness, The.
Characters of Women.
Consolation, The.
Criminality of War, The.
Day of Judgement, The.
Epigram on Voltaire.
Epistles to Mr. Pope, *sel.*
Extempore to Voltaire Criticising Milton.
Happiness an Art.
Infidel Reclaimed, The.
Instalment, The, *sel.*
Lament of the Damned in Hell, The.
Love of Fame, the Universal Passion, *sels.*
Night.
Night Thoughts, *sels.*
Procrastination.
Satire III: "Long, Dodington, in debt, I long have sought."
Young, Edward (b. 1818)
Under the Violets.
Young, Edwin
Have I Done My Best for Jesus?
Young, Ella
Greeting.
Unicorn, The.
Young, Francis Brett
Atlantic Charter, A.D. 1620–1942.
Bête Humaine.
Dhows, The.
February.
Five Degrees South.
Island, The, *sel.*
Prothalamion.
Seascape.
Song at Santa Cruz.
Song of the Dark Ages.
Young, Gary
Doctor Rebuilds a Hand, The.
Equinox.
To an Estranged Wife.
Tornado Watch, Bloomington, Indiana.
Under the Catalpa Trees.
Young, George W.
Lips That Touch Liquor.
Young, Ian
At Rochdale.
Double Exposure.
Elephants from the Sea.
Honi Soit Qui Mal Y Pense.
It's no good/ being an actor.
Skull, The.
Sugar-Candy Bird, A.
Young, Jackman
Arkansas.
Young, Marguerite
Angels, The.
Death by Rarity.
Noah's Ark.
Speculative Evening.
Whales, The.
White Rat, The.
Winter Scene.
Young, Roland
Ape, The.
Flea, The.
Goat, The.
Miscegenous Zebra, The.
Pig, The.
Young, Virginia Brady
Taught to Be Polite.
Teacher, The.
Young, William
Bells, The.
Bridal Pair, The.
Conscience-Keeper, The.
Judith.
Losers, The.
Pawns, The.
Philomel to Corydon.
Victor, The.
Wishmakers' Town, *sels.*
Young Bear, Ray A.
Another Face.
Before the Actual Cold.
Black Dog.
Celebration.
Coming Back Home.
Cook, The.
Crow-Children Walk My Circles in the Snow, The.
Differences.
Grandmother.
In Dream: The Privacy of Sequence.
In Missing.
In the First Place of My Life.
Last Dream, The.
One Chip of Human Bone.
Place of O, The.
Place of V, The.
Poem for Diane Wakoski, A.
Poem for Viet Nam.
Remembrance of a Color inside a Forest, A.
Rushing.
Star Blanket.
These Horses Came.
This House.
Trains Made of Stone.
Waiting to Be Fed.
War Walking Near.
Way the Bird Sat, The.
What We Can.
Youngblood, Sarah
At the Western Shore.
Walking the Beach.
Yüan Chen
Pitcher, The.
Song of the Weaving Woman.
Yuan Mei
Only Be Willing to Search for Poetry.
Yud, Nachum
Like the Eyes of Wolves.
Yü Hsüan-chi
Advice to a Neighbor Girl.
Answering Li Ying Who Showed Me His Poems about Summer Fishing.
At the End of Spring.
Boudoir Lament.
Composed on the Theme "Willows by the Riverside."
Elegy for the Wife of a Friend.
For Hidden Mist Pavilion.
For Kuo Hsiang.
Letting My Feelings Out.
On a Visit to Ch'ung Chen Taoist Temple.
Poem to the Tune "Riverbank Willows."
Regretful Thoughts.
Rhyming a Friend's Poem.
Rhyming with a Friend.
Selling Ruined Peonies.
Sent to Wen T'ing-yün on a Winter Night.
Spring Thoughts Sent to Tzu-an.
Staying in the Mountains in Summer.
Telling My Feelings.
To the Minister Liu.
To Tzu-an.
Yungman, Moshe
Don't Say.
Encounter in Safed.
Melons.
Messiah, The.
Sacrifice, The.
Yvonne
Deborah Lee.
Emma.
Where She Was Not Born.

Z

"Z., Z."
Here lies a poet—where's the great surprise!
Zabel, Morton Dauwen
Journal to Stella.
Zach, Natan
Against Parting.
As Sand.
Foreign Country, A.
In This Deep Darkness ("In this deep heavy darkness").
Listening to Her.
Peaceful Song, A.
Perhaps It's Only Music.
Quiet Light of Flies, The.
Short Winter Tale, A.
To Be a Master in Your House.
When God First Said.
When the Last Riders.
Zaid, Gabriel
Late Again.
Zangwill, Israel
At the Worst.
At the Zoo.
Death's Transfiguration.
Despair and Hope.
Dreams.
Evolution.
In the City.
In the Morgue.
Inexhaustible.
Israel.
Jehovah.
"Might Is Right."
Moses and Jesus.
Seder-Night.
Sundered.
Tabernacle Thought, A.
Theodor Herzl.
To a Pretty Girl.
Vanitas Vanitatum.
Vision.
Why Do We Live?
Yom Kippur.
Zaranka, William
Conceit upon the Feet.
Continuation of *The Cook's Tale*, The.
Cropdusting, The.
Cry of the Child, The.
High-toned Old Fascist Gentleman, A.
In the Ladies' Room at the Bus Terminal.

Junk.
Lovers' Debouchment.
Memories of Aunt Maria-Martha.
Ode: "Mistah Berrybones, you daid?"
Parachuting Thoor Ballylee.
Peruke of Poets.
Quicksands.
Ragout.
Robert Frost's Left-leaning *Trespassers Will Be Shot* Sign.

Zarathustra. *See* **Zoroaster**

Zarco, Cyn
Lolo died yesterday.
Saxophonetyx.
Teaching Poetry.
What the Rooster Does before Mounting.

Zaturenska, Marya Alexandrovna (Mrs. Horace Gregory)
Bird and the Muse.
Daisy, The.
Descent of the Vulture, The.
False Summer, The.
Girl Takes Her Place among the Mothers, The.
Girl's Song.
Head of Medusa.
Hymn to Artemis, the Destroyer.
Intruder, The.
Lightning for Atmosphere.
Lovers, The.
Lunar Tides, The.
Once in an Ancient Book.
Ophelia's Song.
Song: "Life with her weary eyes."
Song of a Factory Girl.
Spinners at Willowsleigh.
Tempest, The.
Variations on a Theme by George Herbert.
White Dress, The.
Woman at the Piano.

Zavatsky, Bill
Being Adult.

Zawadiwsky, Christine
As Long as the Heart Beats.
Riddles and Lies.

Zeiger, L. L.
Snack, The.

Zeitlin, Aaron
Dream about an Aged Humorist, A.
Empty Apartment, The.
Ode to Freedom.
Text.

Zeitlin, Israel. *See* **Tiempo, César**

Zelda (Zelda Schneurson)
I Stood in Jerusalem.
In the Dry Riverbed.
Light a Candle.
Moon Is Teaching Bible, The.
Wicked Neighbor, The.
With My Grandfather.

Zeldis, Chayyim
Holy Ones, the Young Ones, The.

Zelvin, Elizabeth
Insomnia.

Zerbe, Evelyn Arcad
In Memory of My Arab Grandmother.

Zieroth, Dale
Baptism.
Beautiful Woman.
Hunters of the Deer, The.

Zimmer, Paul
Apple Blight.
Driving North from Savannah on My Birthday.
Lester Tells of Wanda and the Big Snow.
Lord Fluting Dreams of America on the Eve of His Departure from Liverpool.
Missing the Children.
One for the Ladies at the Troy Laundry Who Cooled Themselves for Zimmer.
Phineas Within and Without.
Poem Ending with an Old Cliché.
Suzie's Enzyme Poem.
Train Blues.
What Zimmer Would Be.
Zimmer and His Turtle Sink the House.
Zimmer Drunk and Alone, Dreaming of Old Football Games.
Zimmer Envying Elephants.
Zimmer in Fall.
Zimmer in Grade School.
Zimmer's Hard Dream.
Zimmer's Head Thudding against the Blackboard.
Zimmer's Last Gig.

Zimroth, Evan
Lilly's Song.

Zinnes, Harriet
Wallace Stevens Gives a Reading.

Zinzendorf, Nikolaus [*or* Nicolaus] Ludwig, Graf von
For Us No Night Can Be Happier, *with music.*
Jesu, to Thee My Heart I Bow, *with music.*
Lowly Bethlehem, *with music.*
On Earth There Is a Lamb So Small, *with music.*
Slain Lamb of God, *with music.*

Zisquit, Linda
Circumcision, The.
Rachel's Lament.
Sabbatical.

Zmuda, Bob
Love Song: "For love one must risk."

Zolotow, Charlotte
Dog, A.
Moment in Summer, A.
People.
Riddle, A: "Once when I was very scared."
River Winding.

Zolynas, Al
Incubation, The.
Living with Others.
Two Childhood Memories.
Zen of Housework, The.

Zoroaster [*or* Zarathrustra]
Sacred Book, The, *at.*
Zoroaster Devoutly Questions Ormazd, *at.*

"Zozimus." *See* **Moran, Michael**

Zu-Bolton, Ahmos, II
Beachhead Preachment.

Zuckmayer, Carl
My Death.

Zukofsky, Louis
"A" (1-12), *sels.*
"A 4."
"A 11."
Ask of the sun.
Cars once steel and green, now old.
Chloride of Lime and Charcoal.
1892-1941.
Expounding the Torah.
For you I have emptied the meaning.
From the Head.
Green Leaf, The.
Guests, The.
I walk in the old street.
In Arizona/ (how many years in the mountains).
It's hard to see but think of a sea.
Light, *sels.*
Lines of this new song are nothing, The.
"Mantis."
Non Ti Fidar.
Of Dying Beauty.
Peri Poietikes.
Poem Beginning "The."
Reading and Talking.
So That Even a Lover.
Tall and singularly dark you pass among the breakers.
This Is after All Vacation.
Voice out of the Tabernacle, A.
You Who Were Made for This Music.

Zupan, Vitomil
Fairy Tale, A.

Zussman, Ezra
At Dante's Grave.
Last, The.

Zweig, Paul
Father.
Uptown.

Zweig, Stefan
Chosen of God.
Flowering without End.
Jeremiah, *sels.*

Zwicker, Kenneth
Shantyboy's Song, The.

Zwicky, Fay
Chosen, The—Kalgoorlie, 1894.
Summer Pogrom.

Zychlinska, Rayzel
Clothes, The.
My Mother's Shoes.
Remembering Lutsky.

Zydek, Fredrick
Dark Room.
Pond.

SUBJECT INDEX

Entries in the Subject Index contain one or more of the following types of information: first, poems are listed that fall within the particular subject category; second, in many cases anthologies are listed that in whole or in part focus on the subject in question; third, there may be cross-references to related subjects.

The categories indexed here range from specific (for example, persons) to general (for example, abstractions such as **Separation***). Some categories, such as* **Love,** *are so broad that we have used them only to list anthologies.*

In this edition we have introduced some form and genre categories, for example, **Sestina (form).** *Poems in the form or genre in question may also be found by title of the form or genre in the Title and First Line Index. The emphasis here has been on including poems not identifiable by form in the Title and First Line Index, such as Dylan Thomas's villanelle "Do Not Go Gentle into That Good Night."*

For this edition we have increased the use of geographical subject headings. The user will recognize that listings under countries, states, and localities treat the concept of what a poem is "about" broadly.

Aachen, Germany
Aix-La-Chappelle, 1945. Bowers.
Aaron
Aaron. Herbert.
Aaron, Henry
Hammerin' Hank. Martin.
Abandonment
Airly Beacon. Kingsley.
Ballad of Camden Town, The. Flecker.
Banks o' Doon, The. Burns.
Butterflies. Davidson.
Cumnor Hall. Mickle.
Lady of Miracles. Cassian.
Abbey Theater, Dublin
Old Woman, Outside the Abbey Theater, An. Strong.
Abbeys. *See* **Monasteries.**
Abel. *See* **Cain and Abel.**
Abelard and Heloise
Eloisa to Abelard. Pope.
Sic et Non. Read.
Aberdeen, Scotland
On an Aberdeen Favourite. *Unknown.*
To Aberdein. Dunbar.
Abishag
Abishag. Spire.
Abolitionists
John Brown's Body. *Unknown.*
Lines, Suggested on Reading "An Appeal to Christian Women of the South," by A. E. Grimké. "Ada."
Runagate Runagate. Hayden.
To the Memory of J. Horace Kimball. "Ada."
To W. L. G. on Reading His "Chosen Queen." Forten.
Wake Nicodemus. Work.
Aborigines
We Are Going. Walker.
Abortion
Abortion. Ai.
Abortion, The. Sexton.
Cold Front, A. Williams.
Epitaph on a Child Killed by Procured Abortion. *Unknown.*
Inquest, The. Davies.
Lost Baby Poem, The. Clifton.
Mother, The. Brooks.
Nova. Levendosky.
Abraham
Abraham. Muir.
Abraham. Schwartz.
Abraham and Isaac. Lasker-Schüler.
Abraham and Sarah. Manger.
Abraham in Egypt. Schwartz.
Harlots' Catch. Nichols.
Parable of the Old Man and the Young, The. Owen.
Sacrifice, The. Bloch.
Story of Abraham and Hagar, The. Aphek.
Absalom
Another Poem on Absalom. Yonathan.
Dispraise of Absalom, The. *Unknown.*
Absence
Absence. Hoskins.
Absence. Jago.
Absence. Landor.
Absence. McKay.
Absence. Meinke.
Absence. Mew.
Absence. Morgan.
Absence, The. Warner.
Absence and Presence. *Fr.* Caelica. Greville.
Alone. De la Mare.
Appeal. Bronte.
Banks of Claudy, The. *Unknown.*
Celadyne's Song. *Fr.* Britannia's Pastorals. Browne.
Complaint of the Absence of Her Lover Being upon the Sea. Surrey.
Daisy, The. Tennyson.
Drinking Song. Harrison.
Elinda's Glove. Lovelace.
Ellen Taylor. *Unknown.*
For Anne. Cohen.
Forever and a Day. Aldrich.
Girl I Left behind Me, The. *Unknown.*
Glove, The. Greig.
Hello, Hello. Matthews.
Her Going. Kaufman.
Here Awa', There Awa'. *Unknown.*
How like a winter hath my absence been. Sonnets, XCVII. Shakespeare.

Hush. St. John.
I Live Not Where I Love. *Unknown.*
If I Had but Two Little Wings. Coleridge.
Lady Prayeth the Return of Her Lover Abiding on the Seas, The. *Unknown.*
Lamenting Maid, The. *Unknown.*
Late Light. Blunden.
Learning to Live without You. Wood.
Like as the culver on the bared bough. *Fr.* Amoretti. Spenser.
Love-Letter One. *Unknown.*
Love-Letter Two. *Unknown.*
Lying here alone. Izumi Shikibu.
Midwinter Stars. Whitman.
Never the Time and the Place. Browning.
Out of Sight, Out of Mind. Googe.
Queen of Hearts, The. *Unknown.*
Quite Forsaken. Lawrence.
Selfe Banished, The. Waller.
Separation. Merwin.
Since Hanna Moved Away. Viorst.
Small Moon. Nemerov.
Solitude. Monro.
Song, A: "Absent from thee I languish still." Rochester.
Song: "First month of his absence, The." Lewis.
Song: "I walk'd in the lonesome evening." Allingham.
Song: " 'Tis said that absence conquers love!" Thomas.
Song to a Fair Young Lady, Going Out of Town in the Spring, A. Dryden.
Spring, The. *Fr.* The Mistress. Cowley.
Sweethairt, Rejoice in Mind. Montgomerie.
To Amoret Gone from Him. Vaughan.
Voice, The. Hardy.
Western Wind. *Unknown.*
When, Dearest, I But Think on Thee. *At. to* Suckling *and to* Felltham.
Why Art Thou Silent. Wordsworth.
Winter Remembered. Ransom.
World Is Not a Pleasant Place to Be, The. Giovanni.
See also **Loneliness; Separation.**

Acacia
Whisperings in Wattle-Boughs. Gordon.
Young Acacia, The. Bialik.

Academia
To a Friend, on Her Examination for the Doctorate in English. Cunningham.

Acadia and Acadians
Evangeline. Longfellow.
Evangeline. Smith.
In ev'ry thought, in ev'ry wish I own. *Fr.* Acadia. Howe.

Accent
Uncultivated Accent. *Unknown.*

Accidents
Accident, The. Gasparini.
Accident, The. Patterson.
Ambulance Call. Goldensohn.
Another Kind of Burning. Fox.
At the Roadside. Knoepfle.
Ballad of Springhill (The Springhill Mine Disaster). MacColl *and* Seeger.
Blue-Tail Fly, The. *Unknown.*
Cut. Plath.
Down Went McGinty. Flynn.
Dying Mine Brakeman, The. Jenks.
Elegy for Jane. Roethke.
Falling. Dickey.
First Love. Olds.
Foundered Tram, The. Monro.
George Allen. *Unknown.*
Henry K. Sawyer. *Unknown.*
It's Here in The. Atkins.
Jack and Jill went up the hill. Mother Goose.
Lady Track Star, A. Blount.
Metal Fatigue. Le Fevre.
My Sore Thumb. Johnson.
New York City—1935. Corso.
Night Mare. Endrezze-Danielson.
Numbers. Elliott.
One Thousand Feet of Shadow. Craig.
"Out, Out." Frost.
Poems about Playmates. Davis.
Reflexes. Bell.
Ruth. McElroy.
Sir Smasham Uppe. Rieu.
Tay Bridge Disaster, The. McGonagall.
This Particular Christian. Johnson.
Tumble, The. Taylor.
White Dust, The. Gibson.
Worker, The. Thomas.
See also **Airplane Crashes; Automobile Accidents; Disasters; Railroad Wrecks; Shipwrecks.**

Accordions
Man with a Little Pleated Piano, A. Welles.

Accounting and Accountants
Hardship of Accounting, The. Frost.
Sum. Nolan.

Achilles
Achilles. Corwin.
Achilles Shows Himself in the Battle by the Ships. *Fr.* The Iliad. Homer.
Achilles with wild fury in his heart. *Fr.* The Iliad. Homer.
Before a Statue of Achilles. Santayana.
Shield of Achilles, The. Auden.

Acrobats
Acrobat from Xanadu disdained all nets, The. Georgakas.
See also **Circus; Gymnastics; Trapeze Artists.**

Actaeon
Actaeon. Clough.
Actaeon. Heppenstall.
Acteon. *Fr.* Metamorphoses. Ovid.
I Would I Were Actaeon. *Unknown.*

Acting and Actors
Author to His Booke, The. *Fr.* An Apology for Actors. Heywood.
Ballade of Dead Actors. Henley.
Boy Actor, The. Coward.
Charlton Heston. Fried.
David Garrick. *Fr.* Retaliation. Goldsmith.
"Ej Blot til Lyst." Payne.
Epitaph on S. P., a Child of Queen Elizabeth's Chapel. Jonson.
If I Were on the Stage. Blossom.
J. B. Bunner.
Movie Actors Scribbling Letters Very Fast in Crucial Scenes. Garrigue.
Old Trouper, The. *Fr.* Archy and Mehitabel. Marquis.
Santa Claus. Hassall.
Shirley Temple. Michael.
Strolling Player, The. Rimbaud.
These Men. Booth.
Thespians at Thermopylae, The. Cameron.
To the Film Industry in Crisis. O'Hara.

Adam and Eve
Adam and Eve. Bible, *O.T., Fr.* Genesis.
Adam and Eve. Manger.
Adam and Eve. Sisson.
Adam Driven from Eden. *Unknown.*
Adam in Love. Mitchell.
Adam in the Garden Pinning Leaves. *Unknown.*
Adam Lay Ibounden. *Unknown.*
Adam Unfallen. *Fr.* Paradise Lost. Milton.
Adam's Curse. Yeats.
Adam's Dream. Schwartz.
Adam's Footprint. Miller.
Adam's Task. Hollander.
Age of Innocence. Hough.
As Adam Early in the Morning. Whitman.
Begetting of Cain, The. Plutzik.
Circle, A. Spencer.
Epigram: "When Eve upon the first of men." Moore.
Epigram: "Whilst Adam slept, Eve from his side arose." *Unknown.*
Eve's Version. Harrison.
First Wedding in the World, The. Rosenberg.
Fortunate Fall, The. Alvarez.
Good Beasts, The. Barnstone.
Imperial Adam. Hope.
Jealous Adam. Manger.
Lady's-Maid Song, The. Hollander.
Lilith. Kennedy.
Naming of the Beasts, The. Sparshott.
Occasional Poem. Housman.
Old Adam, The. Benét.
Paradise. Bloch.
Poisoned Man, The. Dickey.
Reflection, A. Hood.
Reveille. Hughes.
Satan Beholds Adam and Eve in Eden. *Fr.* Paradise Lost. Milton.
Sickness of Adam, The. *Fr.* Adam and Eve. Shapiro.
Theology. Hughes.
229. Villa.
When Adam Was First Created. *Unknown.*

When Adam Day by Day. Housman.
See also **Eve.**
Adams, Henry
Henry Adams. Auden.
Adams, John
John Adams. Benét *and* Benét.
Twilight's Last Gleaming. Monks.
Adams, John Quincy
John Quincy Adams. Benét.
Adderley, Julian ("Cannonball")
Cannon Arrested. Harper.
Addison, Joseph
Atticus. *Fr.* Epistle to Dr. Arbuthnot. Pope.
To the Earl of Warwick, on the Death of Mr. Addison. Tickell.
Adobes
Mending the Adobe. Carruth.
Adolescence
Adolescence. Orr.
Adolescence. Schmitz.
Allegory of the Adolescent and the Adult. Barker.
Beautiful Creatures Brief as These. Jones.
Burning Hills. Ondaatje.
Certain Age, A. McGinley.
Child, The. Keithley.
Confirmation, The. Shapiro.
Cruel Boys. Soto.
Dimpled Cloud, A. Seidel.
Discovery. Flanner.
Epigram: "Most inexplicable the wiles of boys I deem." Rhianus.
Hanging Fire. Lorde.
Heaven. Soto.
Homework for Annabelle. McGinley.
I Remember How She Sang. Penny.
Initial Response. Soniat.
June Twenty-first. Guernsey.
Lines to His Son on Reaching Adolescence. Logan.
Little Girl, My Stringbean, My Lovely Woman. Sexton.
Mrs. Applebaum's Sunday Dance Class. Schultz.
Mrs. Green. Huddle.
Now That Your Shoulders Reach My Shoulders. Francis.
Overcoats. Kramer.
Pinay. Cerenio.
Portrait of a Girl with Comic Book. McGinley.
Puberty. Wallace.
Question, The. Rukeyser.
Romance. Turner.
September 7. Bass.
16/53. Piercy.
Spade Scharnweber. Welch.
Teen-ager, A. Snodgrass.
Two girls of twelve or so at a table. Reznikoff.
Waiting in Front of the Columnar High School. Shapiro.
Woman's Liberation. Sister Maura.
Young. Sexton.
Young Girls. Souster.
Young Ones, The. Jennings.
Adonis
Adonis. Doolittle ("H. D.").
Death of Adonis, The. Ayres.
Infida's Song. *Fr.* Never Too Late. Greene.
Venus and Adonis. Shakespeare.
Adoption and the Adopted
Gratulatory to Mr. Ben Johnson for His Adopting of Him to Be His Son, A. Randolph.
On Certain Days of the Year. Simpson.
Adultery
Adultery at a Las Vegas Bookstore. Liu.
Elsa Wertman. *Fr.* Spoon River Anthology. Masters.
Epigram: "Come, come, said Tom's father, at your time of life." Harington.
Epigram: The Mistake. Roethke.
For All Mary Magdalenes. Maksimovic.
In Memory, 1978. Kazantzis.
In the Restaurant. *Fr.* Satires of Circumstance. Hardy.
Marriage and Midsummer's Night. Gregg.
Modern Love. Cunningham.
Nothing to Fear. Amis.
Punishment. Heaney.
Queen Eleanor's Confession. *Unknown.*
Upon Scobble. Herrick.
Advent
Advent. Fletcher.
Christ's Coming. *Unknown.*
Farewell! Advent. Ryman.
Adventure and Adventurers
Adventure. Behn.
For Tony, Dougal, Mick, Bugs, Nick, *et al.* Bathgate.
Peregrine. Wylie.
Advertising
Advertisement. *Unknown.*
Advertising Agency Song, The. *Unknown.*
Clarence. Silverstein.
Double Standard, The. Adams.
Hymn in Columbus Circle. Benét.
Jabber-Whacky. Di Caprio.
Legend of the Admen, The. Lord.
Memorial to the Great Big Beautiful Self-sacrificing Advertisers. Ebright.
Poem, or Beauty Hurts Mr. Vinal. Cummings.
Song of the Open Road. Nash.
Summer Song. Watt.
Virtues of Carnation Milk, The. Ogilvy.
Faber Book of Useful Verse, The (FaBoUs), pp. 203–217. Simon Brett, ed.
See also **Billboards.**
Aegean Sea
Aegean. Simpson.
Santorin. Flecker.
Aeneas
Aeneas at Washington. Tate.
Aeneid, The, *sels.* Virgil.
Aeneid, The (Virgil)
Falling Asleep over the Aeneid. Lowell.
Aengus
Song of Wandering Aengus, The. Yeats.
Aesop
Improvisations on Aesop. Hecht.
Africa
Africa. Alexander.
Africa. Angelou.
Africa. Diop.
Africa. McKay.
Africa. Naudé.
African Affair, The. Wright.
African Dance. Hughes.
African Dream. Kaufman.
African Things. Cruz.
Africa's Plea. Dempster.
Africland. La Grone.
All That You Have Given Me, Africa. Kanié.
Blue Tanganyika. Bethune.
Bwagamoyo. Bethune.
Cape Coast Castle Revisited. Hall-Evans.
Ceremony. Cumbo.
Change Is Not Always Progress. Lee.
Colonialism. Qarshe.
Congo, The. Lindsay.
Coptic Poem. Durrell.
Dawn in the Heart of Africa. Lumumba.
Distance. Delius.
Driving through New England. Clifton.
Elephant of Moissel, hear my pious prayer. *Fr.* Return of the Prodigal Son. Senghor.
Far Cry from Africa, A. Walcott.
Far from Africa: Four Poems. Danner.
Hand, The. Fawcett.
Hearing James Brown at the Café des Nattes (Sidi-bou-Said, Tunisia). Long.
Heritage. Bennett.
Heritage. Cullen.
Heritage. Hughes.
Hottentot, The. Pringle.
Is This Africa? Dempster.
Meaning of Africa, The. Nicol.
My Africa. Dei-Anang.
Nubia. Taylor.
Ode to Ethiopia. Dunbar.
Song of the Cape of Good Hope. Schubart.
They Clapped. Giovanni.
Three Phases of Africa. Parkes.
Who Knows? Milner-Brown.
Wildebeest, The. Daly.
Penguin Book of South African Verse, The (PeSA). Jack Cope *and* Uys Krige, eds.
Poems from Black Africa (PBA). Langston Hughes, ed.

Afternoon
Daysleep. Smith.
Our Barrio. Alurista.
Post-Meridian. Garrison.
Afton River, Scotland
Afton Water. Burns.
Afzal Khan
Rise of Shivaji, The. Ghose.
Agamemnon
Agamemnon's Tomb. Sitwell.
Iphigeneia and Agamemnon. *Fr.* The Hellenics. Landor.
Agassiz, Louis
Farewell to Agassiz, A. Holmes.
Fiftieth Birthday of Agassiz, The. Longfellow.
Agincourt, Battle of (1415)
Agincourt. Drayton.
Agincourt Carol, The. *Unknown.*
Before Agincourt. *Fr.* King Henry V. Shakespeare.
Aging
Advice to Colonel Valentine. Graves.
Age. Mannes.
Aging. Jarrell.
All Souls' Night. Cornford.
Amen. Sabines.
Another Year Come. Merwin.
At Bickford's. Stern.
Author to His Body on Their Fifteenth Birthday, The. Nemerov.
But I Am Growing Old and Indolent. Jeffers.
Catching Up. Walker.
Change of Life. Urdang.
Chard Whitlow. Reed.
Collector, The. Flynn.
Coming of Wisdom with Time, The. Yeats.
Descending. Iremonger.
Descent, The. Williams.
Don't Grow Old. Ginsberg.
Due Date. Cain.
Echoing Green, The. Blake.
Edwin A. Nelms. Nelms.
Elegy XI: "Ah me, my friend! it will not, will not last!" Shenstone.
Father William. *Fr.* Alice's Adventures in Wonderland. "Carroll."
Fifty. Rexroth.
Folly of Being Comforted, The. Yeats.
Game Resumed. Lattimore.
Garden-Song. Cabell.
Growing Gray. Dobson.
Growing Old. Arnold.
Growing Old. Henderson.
Growing Old. *Unknown.*
His Golden Locks Time Hath to Silver Turned. *Fr.* Polyhymnia. Peele.
His Plans for Old Age. Meredith.
How Soon Hath Time. Milton.
I welcome the anonymity of the middle years. *Fr.* Letters to Live Poets. Beaver.
In a Prominent Bar in Secaucus One Day. Kennedy.
Journey toward Evening. McGinley.
Lamentation of the Old Pensioner, The. Yeats.
Let Me Grow Lovely. Baker.
Letter from a Girl to Her Own Old Age, A. Meynell.
Like as the waves make towards the pebbled shore. Sonnets, LX. Shakespeare.
Lines Written in Dejection. Yeats.
Little Dirge. Untermeyer.
Loveliest of Trees, the Cherry Now. Housman.
Magician Suspends the Children, The. Oles.
Minuet on Reaching the Age of Fifty, A. Santayana.
Mirror. Plath.
More Lovely Grows the Earth. Coleman.
More than Fifty. Gilbert.
Old Pro's Lament, The. Petrie.
Old Swimmer, The. Morley.
On a Cat, Ageing. Gray.
On My Fortieth Birthday. Tripp.
On Stella's Birthday, 1719. Swift.
Only Years. Rexroth.
Rabbi Ben Ezra. Browning.
Reports of Midsummer Girls. Lattimore.
Scene from a Dream. Hale.
Schiehallion. Cruickshank.
Spot-Check at Fifty. Scannell.
Stanzas for Music. Byron.
Stonecarver. Oles.
Strange, Is It Not. Kennedy.
Tea Shop, The. Pound.
Terminus. Emerson.
That time of year thou mayst in me behold. Sonnets, LXXIII. Shakespeare.
Thirty-eight. Smith.
To a Gentlewoman Objecting to Him His Grey Hairs. Herrick.
To Age. Landor.
To Earthward. Frost.
Tonight I've watched. Sappho.
Turning Thirty. Ehrhart.
Turning Thirty. Pollitt.
Veteran Sirens. Robinson.
What Lips My Lips Have Kissed, and Where, and Why. Millay.
When Aurelia First I Courted. *Unknown.*
When forty winters shall besiege thy brow. Sonnets, II. Shakespeare.
When Helen first saw wrinkles in her face. *Fr.* Ianthe. Landor.
When I consider every thing that grows. Sonnets, XV. Shakespeare.
Wild Swans at Coole, The. Yeats.
Will You Love Me in December as You Do in May? Walker.
Will You Love Me When I'm Old? *Unknown.*
Woman Making Advances Publicly, A. Kazantzis.
Writ on the Eve of My 32nd Birthday. Corso.
See also **Middle Age; Old Age.**
Agnew, Spiro Theodore
Proud Resignation. Marcus.
Agnosticism
Biography of an Agnostic. Ginsberg.
Harald, the Agnostic Ale-loving Old Shepherd Enemy of the Whisky-drinking Ploughmen and Harvesters, Walks over the Sabbath Hill to the Shearing. Brown.
Impercipient, The. Hardy.
See also **Doubt.**
Agoraphobia
Another Poem about the Madness of Women. Wayman.
Agriculture. *See* **Farming and Farmers; Farmworkers.**
Air
Air. Denby.
Air. Raine.
Blessed Virgin Compared to the Air We Breathe, The. Hopkins.
Fresh Air. Koch.
I Hear America Griping. Bishop.
Oxygen. Swift.
Quality of Air, A. Chapin.
Air Conditioning
I Hear America Griping. Bishop.
Air Plants
Air Plant, The. Crane.
Air Travel
At the San Francisco Airport. Winters.
Cockpit in the Clouds. Dorrance.
Day Flight. Davis.
Flight 539. Brinnin.
Flight Plan. Merchant.
Flight 382. Longman.
Flying Home from Utah. Swenson.
Mount Saint Helens/Loowit; an Indian Woman's Song. Rose.
N.Y. to L.A. by Jet Plane. Dorman.
Night: Landing at Newark. Holden.
Night Flight. Johnson.
On Seeing My Birthplace from a Jet Aircraft. Pudney.
Our Ground Time Here Will Be Brief. Kumin.
Sitting Down, Looking Up. Ammons.
Sparrows in an Airport. Snyder.
Twenty-third Flight. Birney.
Up Silver Stairsteps. Stuart.
See also **Airports.**
Air Warfare
Air Raid. Wild.
Airman, R. F. C. Herbertson.
Airstrip in Essex, 1960, An. Hall.
Americana XIII: "Captain Patterson, the folks back home." Rakosi.
Bombardment. Lawrence.
Bombers. Day Lewis.
Ceremony after a Fire Raid. Thomas.
De Civitate Hominum. MacGreevy.
Dead in Europe, The. Lowell.
Death of the Ball Turret Gunner, The. Jarrell.
Eighth Air Force. Jarrell.
Erige Cor Tuum ad Me in Caelum. Doolittle ("H. D.").
Firebombing, The. Dickey.
Front, A. Jarrell.

Fury of Aerial Bombardment, The. Eberhart.
Gods in Vietnam. Redmond.
Gunner, The. Webb.
Irish Airman Foresees His Death, An. Yeats.
Journal. Ciardi.
Losses. Jarrell.
Ops in a Wimpey. *Unknown.*
Pilots, Man Your Planes. Jarrell.
Radar. Ross.
Raider, The. Rodgers.
Raiders, The. Allen.
Refusal to Mourn the Death, by Fire, of a Child in London, A. Thomas.
Reprisals. Yeats.
Second Air Force. Jarrell.
Soliloquy in an Air-Raid. Fuller.
Still Falls the Rain. Sitwell.
Thoughts during an Air Raid. Spender.
Usual exquisite boredom of patrols, The. Popham.
When a Beau Goes In. Ewart.
Words Spoken by Pasternak during a Bombing. Akhmadulina.
Zeppelins. Cunard.

Airline Stewardesses
Falling. Dickey.

Airplane Crashes
Ceiling Unlimited. Rukeyser.
On the Death of the Evansville University Basketball Team in a Plane Crash, December 13, 1977. Hamblin.
Plan Wreck at Los Gatos. Guthrie.
When a Beau Goes In. Ewart.

Airplanes
Aeroplane. Green.
Airplane, The. Bennett.
Cockpit in the Clouds. Dorrance.
Heavenly Aeroplane, The. *Unknown.*
Night Plane. Frost.
Prayer for a Pilot. Roberts.
Riding in an Airplane. Baruch.
Silver Ships. Meigs.
Taking Off. Green.
Taking Off. *Unknown.*
Up in the Air. Tippett.
See also **Aviation and Aviators.**

Airports
At the Airport in Dallas. Monney.
At the San Francisco Airport. Winters.
Kennedy Airport. Kramer.
Night at an Airport. Ignatow.
Sparrow at the Airport. Ostroff.
Sparrows in an Airport. Snyder.
See also **Air Travel.**

Ajanta, India
Ajanta. Rukeyser.

Alabama (ship)
Alabama, The. *Unknown.*

Alabama (state)
Alabama. Fields.
Alabama. Simmons.
Alabama Bound. *Unknown.*
Alabama Bus. Hairston.
Alabama Earth. Hughes.
Ballad of Birmingham. Randall.
Birmingham. Fields.
Birmingham 1963. Patterson.
Birmingham Sunday. Hughes.
County Roads. Rabbit.
Craven. Newbolt.
Daybreak in Alabama. Hughes.
Laying By. Williams.
Letters from Birmingham. Bond.
Plain. Williams.
Young David, A: Birmingham. Brooks.

Alamo
Defense of the Alamo, The. Miller.
Hymn of the Alamo. Potter.
Lament for the Alamo. Guiterman.
Last Fall of the Alamo. "O. Henry."
Men of the Alamo, The. Roche.

Alaric I
Dirge of Alaric the Visigoth. Everett.

Alaska
Anchorage. Harjo.
Before Breakup on the Chena outside Fairbanks. McElroy.
Bell in the Orthodox Steeple, A. Waltner.
Edge, The. Chandonnet.
Funny Joke, A. Stokesbury.
Invaders, The. Haines.
Raven at Lemon Creek Jail. Waltner.
To Vera Thompson. Haines.
Train Stops at Healy Fork, The. Haines.

Albatrosses
Albatross, The. Baudelaire.
Albatross. Burgess.
Albatross. Stoddard.
Rime of the Ancient Mariner, The. Coleridge.

Albert, Prince
Dedication of Idylls of the King. Tennyson.

Alberta, Canada
In the Cemetery of the Sun. Watson.

Alcatraz, California
Indians on Alcatraz, The. Muldoon.

Alcestis
Alcestis. Verry.

Alchemy and Alchemists
Alchemist, The. Pound.

Alcoholism and Alcoholics
Benefits and Abuse of Alcohol, The. Eubulus.
Grand Street & the Bowery. Ghitelman.
Interview with Doctor Drink. Cunningham.
Lament for Barney Flanagan. Baxter.
Letters & Other Words. Ondaatje.
Reunion. Tawney.
See also **Drunkards.**

Alcott, Louisa May
Louisa May Alcott. Piatt.

Alder Trees
Victors, The. Levertov.

Ale
Back and Side Go Bare, Go Bare. *Fr.* Gammer Gurton's Needle. *At. to* Stevenson.
Bring Us In Good Ale. *Unknown.*
Doll Thy Ale. *Unknown.*
In Praise of Ale. *Unknown, at. to* Bonham.
Johnson's Ale. *Unknown.*
O mortal man, that lives by bread. *At. to* Ibbetson.
On a Quaker's Tankard. Landor.
Power of Malt, The. Housman.
When Jones's Ale Was New. *Unknown.*

Aleichem, Sholom
Sholom Aleichem. Lieberman.

Alexander, Sir William
To Sir William Alexander. Drummond of Hawthornden.

Alexander Jannaeus, King of Judah
Alexander Jannai. Cavafy.

Alexander the Great
Alexander. Morgan.
Alexander and the Gymnosophists. *Unknown.*
Alexander the Great. *Unknown.*
Alexander to His Horse. Farjeon.
Alexander's Feast; or, The Power of Music. Dryden.
How Big Was Alexander? Jones.
On Alexander and Aristotle, on a Black-on-Red Greek Plate. Dugan.
Santorin. Flecker.
Speaking Tree, The. Rukeyser.

Alfonso X, King of Castile and León
Alphonso of Castile. Emerson.

Alfred the Great
Alfred the Harper. Sterling.
Ballad of the White Horse, The, *Sels.* Chesterton.

Ali, Muhammad
Ali. Corbin.

Alienation
Advent. *Fr.* For the Time Being; a Christmas Oratorio. Auden.
Back Again, Home. Lee.
Between Me and Anyone Who Can Understand. Scott.
Blight. Emerson.
Chicken-Licken. Angelou.
Childhood. Stanton.
Chilled by Different Winds. Swaim.
Desolation Row. Dylan.
Dirge: "1-2-3 was the number he played but today the number came 3-2-1." Fearing.
Effort at Speech between Two People. Rukeyser.
Gerontion. Eliot.
Howl. Ginsberg.

I Am. Clare.
Invention of New Jersey, The. Anderson.
Love Song of J. Alfred Prufrock, The. Eliot.
Mr. Flood's Party. Robinson.
No Bargains Today. Kenner.
On the Apparition of Oneself. Burford.
Outcast. MacKay.
Personality Sketch, A: Bill. Davis.
Poem about People. Pinsky.
Refusals. Anderson.
Waste Land, The. Eliot.
Wave of coldness, A. Yosano Akiko.
Winter's Cold. Rodgers.
World Is Too Much with Us, The. Wordsworth.

All Souls' Night
All Souls' Night. Cornford.
All Souls' Night. *Fr.* A Vision. Yeats.
On Kingston Bridge. Cortissoz.

Allen, Ethan
Green Mountain Boy. Smyth.

Alligators
Alligator, The. Macdonald.
Alligator, The. Ravenel.
Alligator on the Escalator. Merriam.
Purist, The. Nash.
See also **Crocodiles.**

Almanacs
Child Reads an Almanac, The. Jammes.

Alphabet
Aleph Bet, The. Lipshitz.
Alphabet, The. Shapiro.
Alphabet Came to Me, The. Rothenberg.
Letters at School, The. Dodge.
Life of the Letters. Borenstein.

Alphabet Poems
ABC, An. *Unknown.*
A B C Bunny, The. Gág.
A B C for Grown Gentlemen, An. Boufflers.
A was an apple pie. Mother Goose.
A was an archer. *Unknown.*
Alphabet, The. Calverley.
Alphabet, The. Greenaway.
Alphabet ("A tumbled down . . .") Lear.
Alphabet of Aristotle, The. *At. to* Benet.
Austrian Army, An. Watts.
Curious Discourse That Passed between the Twenty-five Letters at Dinner-Time, A. *Unknown.*
From a Cheerful Alphabet. Updike.
He That Ne'er Learns His ABC. *Unknown.*
In Adam's fall/ We sinned all. *Fr.* The New England Primer. *Unknown.*
Letters of the Book, The. Drachler.
Lumberman's Alphabet, The. *Unknown.*
Monster Alphabet. Fisher.
Nonsense Alphabet, A. Lear.
Primer of the Daily Round, A. Nemerov.
Sailors' Alphabet, The. *Unknown.*
Single-Rhyme Alphabet, A. *Unknown.*
Tom Thumb's Alphabet. *Unknown.*

Alpheus
Alpheus and Arethusa. Daly.
Arethusa. Shelley.

Alphonsus Rodriguez, Saint
In Honour of St. Alphonsus Rodriguez. Hopkins.

Alps
Alpine Descent. *Fr.* The Prelude. Wordsworth.
Hymn before Sunrise, in the Vale of Chamouni. Coleridge.
Nocturne of the Self-evident Presence. MacGreevy.
Sarentino-South Tyrol. Brantingham.
Schreckhorn, The. Hardy.

Alsace, France
First Snow in Alsace. Wilbur.

Altar Boys
1955. Weigl.
Purpose of Altar Boys, The. Ríos.

Altars
Altar, The. Herbert.

Altgeld, John Peter
Eagle That Is Forgotten, The. Lindsay.

Altolaguirre, Manuel
To a Spanish Poet. Spender.

Alumni
Blues for an Old Blue. Gibson.
Tenth Reunion. Steese.

Amazons
White Women, The. Coleridge.

Ambition
Aim, The. Roberts.
Ambition. Davies.
Ambition. Herrick.
Chorus: "How dost thou wear and weary out thy days." *Fr.* The Tragedie of Philotas. Daniel.
Mills of the Gods, The. *Unknown.*

Ambulances
When the Ambulance Came. Morgan.

Amen Ra. *See* **Amon Ra.**

America
America. Dumas.
America. Hamilton.
America. McKay.
England. Moore.
God Bless America. Berlin.
Whenever I Say "America." Turner.
See also **United States.**

American Indians. *See* **Indians, American.**

American Revolution
Battle of the Kegs, The. Hopkinson.
Boston in Distress. *Unknown.*
Bunker Hill. Calvert.
Centenarian's Story, The. Whitman.
Chester. *Unknown.*
Concord Hymn. Emerson.
Dying Sergeant, The. *Unknown.*
Emily Geiger. *Unknown.*
Green Mountain Boys, The. Bryant.
Independence Bell—July 4, 1776. *Unknown.*
Lexington. Lanier.
Liberty and Peace, a Poem. Wheatley.
Little Britain. *Unknown.*
Molly Pitcher. Richards.
New England's Chevy Chase. Hale.
On Sympathisers with the American Revolution. Wesley.
Paul Revere's Ride. *Fr.* Tales of a Wayside Inn. Longfellow.
Prophecy in Flame. Howard.
Rise then, ere ruin swift surprize. *Fr.* M'Fingal. Trumbull.
Rising, The. Read.
Seventy-six. Bryant.
Song for Lexington, A. Weeks.
Song of Marion's Men. Bryant.
Swamp Fox, The. Simms.
To the Memory of the Brave Americans. Freneau.
Warren's Address at Bunker Hill. Pierpont.
What a Court Hath Old England. *Unknown.*
Yankee Doodle. *Unknown.*

Americans
American Laughter. Robinson.
American Primitive. Smith.
Ave Caesar. Jeffers.
Ballad of Abbreviations, A. Chesterton.
Boy-Man. Shapiro.
I Am an American. Lieberman.
I Hear America Singing. Whitman.
I Like Americans. Boyd.
I, Too, Sing America. Hughes.
In the Catacombs. Ballard.
On a Rhine Steamer. Stephen.
On the Circuit. Auden.
What Thou Lovest Well, Remains American. Hugo.
Young American, The. Everett.

Amish, The
Amish, The. Updike.

Amnesia
Amnesiac. Plath.

Amon Ra
Hymn to Amen Ra, the Sun God. *Unknown.*
I Am a Cowboy in the Boat of Ra. Reed.

Amputees
Amputation, The. Sorrells.
Black Soldier Remembers, A. Coleman.
Does It Matter? Sassoon.
Forget about It. Currie.
In the Children's Hospital. "MacDiarmid."
Leg, The. Shapiro.

Amsterdam, Netherlands
Amsterdam Letter. Garrigue.

Amsterdam Street Scene, 1972. Rudnik.
Return to Prinsengracht. Blue-Swartz.
Amusement Parks
Chippewa Lake Park. Woessner.
Coney Island Life, A. Weil.
Old Amusement Park. Moore.
Anarchism and Anarchists
Paper Anarchist Addresses the Shade of Nancy Ling Perry. Woodcock.
Ancestry and Ancestors
Ancestors. Randall.
Ancestors. Schimmel.
Ancestors' Graves in Kurakawa. Kogawa.
Ancestral Faces. Brew.
Ancestry. Brodsky.
And. Creeley.
Black Star Line. Dumas.
Dear Ladies of Cincinnati, The. Stevenson.
Fall of J. W. Beane, The. Herford.
Family Portrait 1933. Oresick.
Forebears. Gibbon.
Forefathers. Blunden.
Gadoshkibos. Burns.
Genealogy. Phillips.
Generations. Simmons.
Heirloom. Klein.
Heredity. Guiterman.
Heritage. Bennett.
Heritage. Cullen.
Idea of Ancestry, The. Knight.
Illustrious Ancestors. Levertov.
Lineage. Walker.
My Dark Fathers. Kennelly.
Planted Heel, The. Quiller-Couch.
Pride of Ancestry. Frost.
Song of Ancient Ways, The. Oandasan.
String of My Ancestors, The. Nyhart.
Then let us boast of ancestors no more. *Fr.* The True-born Englishman: Conclusion. Defoe.
Tour Guide: La Maison des Esclaves. Dixon.
Voice in the Blood. Bush.
Anchises
Anchises. Salkeld.
Anchorage, Alaska
Anchorage. Harjo.
Anchors
Anchor. *Fr.* Riddles (Exeter Book). *Unknown.*
Forging of the Anchor, The. Ferguson.
Andersen, Hans Christian
At Hans Christian Andersen's Birthplace, Odense, Denmark. Lindsay.
Hans Christian Andersen in Central Park. Sobiloff.
André, John
Brave Paulding and the Spy. *Unknown.*
Major André. *Unknown.*
Andrea Doria (ship)
Last Words. Hollander.
Nets on the *Andrea Doria,* The. Tepfer.
Andromache
Andromache's Lamentation. *Fr.* The Iliad. Homer.
Andromache's Wedding. Sappho.
Hector. Iremonger.
Andromeda
Andromeda. Aldrich.
Andromeda. *Fr.* Pauline. Browning.
Andromeda. Hopkins.
Anemones
To a Wind Flower. Cawein.
Wind Flowers. Lockwood.
Anesthesia
After the Dentist. Swenson.
Angels
Air and Angels. Donne.
Angel. Merrill.
Angel Describes Truth, An. *Fr.* Hymenaei. Jonson.
Angel Surrounded by Paysans. Stevens.
Angels. Abse.
Angels. Szumigalski.
Angels, The. Young.
Angels in the House. Metz.
Angels in Winter. Willard.
Angels' Song. Causley.
Apple-Tree, The. Campbell.
Fall. Melinescu.
Galloping Cat, The. Smith.
God's Language. Fainlight.
Guardian Angels. *Fr.* The Faerie Queene. Spenser.
How Grand and How Bright. *Unknown.*
Images of Angels. Page.
Israfel. Poe.
It Came upon the Midnight Clear. Sears.
Lame Angel. Finkel.
Michael. McPherson.
New Heaven, New War. Southwell.
No Categories! Smith.
Of Angels. Mayo.
On a Fifteenth-Century Flemish Angel. Ray.
On Angels. Ross.
Rilke Speaks of Angels. Donnelly.
Sonnet: "Bible says Sennacherib's campaign was spoiled, The." Lewis.
To an Artist. Burns.
Wrestling Jacob. Wesley.
Anger
Achilles. Corwin.
Anger. Creeley.
Anger ("Anger in its time and place"). Lamb.
Fragment: "No use/ being angry at the dead." Berlind.
He That Is Slow to Anger. Bible, *O.T., Fr.* Proverbs.
Let Dogs Delight to Bark and Bite. Watts.
Love Letter Postmarked Van Beethoven. Wakoski.
Peppery Man, The. Macy.
Poison Tree, A. *Fr.* Songs of Experience. Blake.
Red Anger. Smith.
Sulk. Holman.
Temper. Fyleman.
This Is a Poem to My Son Peter. Meinke.
Winter Moon, The. Kyozo.
Tygers of Wrath: Poems of Hate, Anger, and Invective (TN). X. J. Kennedy, ed.
See also **Quarrels.**
Angkor Wat, Cambodia
Ank'hor Vat. Devlin.
Animal Migration
Migration. Bruchac.
Migration as a Passage in Time. Bolz.
Something Told the Wild Geese. Field.
To a Waterfowl. Bryant.
Animals
Ad Limina. Campbell.
Age of Animals, The. *Unknown.*
Allie. Graves.
And Did the Animals? Van Doren.
Animal Fair. *Unknown.*
Animal Kingdom. Clouts.
Animal Pictures. Locke.
Animal Song. McHugh.
Animal Store, The. Field.
Animals, The. Jacobsen.
Animals, The. Muir.
Animals in That Country, The. Atwood.
At the Zoo. Milne.
At the Zoo. Thackeray.
Barnyard, The. *Unknown.*
Barnyard Melodies. Brooks.
Beasts. Wilbur.
Beasts and Birds. O'Keeffe.
Bestiary, A. Rexroth.
Burial of the Linnet, The. Ewing.
Butterfly's Ball, The. Roscoe.
Byre. MacCaig.
Cage, The. Stephens.
Christmas Folk Song, A. Reese.
Come into Animal Presence. Levertov.
Cow has a cud, The. McCord.
Creatures. Kumin.
Daydreamers. Davis.
Dog and Tiger. Greenberg.
Dogs and Cats and Bears and Bats. Prelutsky.
Dumb World, The. Davies.
Eau-Forte. Flint.
Eden's Courtesy. Lewis.
Excuse Us, Animals in the Zoo. Wynne.
Familiar Friends. Tippett.
Family, The. *Unknown.*
Farmyard Song, A. Hastings.
Feather or Fur. Becker.

Fiddle-I-Fee. *Unknown.*
Four Friends, The. Milne.
Friendly Beasts, The. *Unknown.*
Frog Went a-Courtin'. *Unknown.*
Good-Morning. Sipe.
Heaven of Animals, The. Dickey.
Hedge Life. Dickey.
History of the Pets, A. Huddle.
How to Tell the Wild Animals. Wells.
Hymn to Joy. Cunningham.
I Think I Could Turn and Live with Animals. *Fr.* Song of Myself. Whitman.
Jump or Jingle. Beyer.
Kindness to Animals. *Unknown.*
Kingly lyon and the strong arm'd beare, The. Wood.
Laughing Time. Smith.
Little Things. Stephens.
Menagerie, The. Moody.
Mercy to Animals: A Ballad of Humanity. Tupper.
Monkeys, The. Moore.
Mrs. Malone. Farjeon.
My Father Kept a Horse. *Unknown.*
Neighbors. Malam.
News from the Cabin. Swenson.
Over in the Meadow. *Unknown.*
Ovibos, The. Hale.
Pangolin, The. Moore.
Parley of Beasts. "MacDiarmid".
Peaceable Kingdom, The. Bible, *O.T., Fr.* Isaiah.
Peacock "At Home," The. Dorset.
Pet Shop. MacNeice.
Raccoon's Got a Bushy Tail. *Unknown.*
Sage Counsel. Quiller-Couch.
Self-Pity. Lawrence.
Snakes, Mongooses, Snake-Charmers and the Like. Moore.
Stockyard, The. Squire.
Take One Home for the Kiddies. Larkin.
Talking to Animals. Howes.
Tree in the Wood, The. *Unknown.*
Ways of Living Things, The. Prelutsky.
Why are we by all creatures waited on? *Fr.* Holy Sonnets. Donne.
Witnesses, The. Kennedy.
World of Darkness. Chatain.
Young Stock. Sackville-West.
Book of Animal Poems, A (BoAnP). William Cole, ed.
Fellow Mortals (FM). Roy Fuller, ed.
See also **Death of Animals.**

Animism
Golden Lines. Nerval.
Intimate Associations. Baudelaire.
Sometimes. Hesse.

Anne, Queen of England
Golden Age, The. *Unknown.*
New Ballad, A. Mainwaring.
Pasquin to the Queen's Statue at St. Paul's. Shippen.
Queen Anne. *Unknown.*
Queen's Speech, The. Mainwaring.

Anne of Denmark
His Petition to Queen Anne of Denmark. Ralegh.
On Queen Anne's Death. *Unknown.*

Anniversaries
Anniversary. Lattimore.
Golden Wedding, The. Gray.
Looking at a Picture on an Anniversary. Hardy.
On the Eve of Our Anniversary. Margolis.
To Mary. Bishop.

Annunciation of the Virgin
Annunciation. Donne.
Annunciation. Sister Maura.

Antaeus
Antaeus; a Fragment. Owen.

Antarctica
Traveller's Guide to Antarctica. Stoutenburg.

Anteaters
Pangolin, The. Moore.

Antelopes
Antelope. Smith.
Kob Antelope. Yoruba.
"Word" of an Antelope Caught in a Trap, The. Sandag.
See also Elands.

Anthony, Saint
Temptation of Saint Anthony, The. Symons.

Anthropologists
On Hearing a Beautiful Young Woman Describe Her Class in Physical Anthropology. Hovde.

Antietam Campaign (1862)
Battle of Antietam Creek, The. *Unknown.*

Antigone
Antigone and Oedipus. Ray.

Antiques
Antique Shop. Carmer.
Caledonian Market, The. Plomer.
Chair, Dog, and Clock. Corke.

Anti-Semitism
To T. S. Eliot. Litvinoff.

Antonioni, Michelangelo
In Praise of Antonioni. Holden.

Antony (Marc Antony)
Antony and Cleopatra. Coulette.
Antony to Cleopatra. Lytle.
Death of Antony. *Fr.* Antony and Cleopatra. Shakespeare.
Early in the Morning. Simpson.
Mark Anthony. Cleveland.
Tact. Pascal.

Antrim. *See* **County Antrim, Northern Ireland.**

Ants
Ant, The. Lovelace.
Ant, The. Nash.
Ant and the Cricket, The. *Unknown.*
Ant-Heap, The. Benson.
Ant-Hills. "Douglas."
Ant Trap, The. Rosenblatt.
Ant Village, The. Edey *and* Grider.
Ants. Aal.
Ants, The. Clare.
Ants. Hyde.
Ants, Although Admirable, Are Awfully Aggravating. Brooks.
Ants and Others. Stoutenberg.
Ants at the Olympics, The. Digance.
Country Roads. Jacobsen.
Departmental. Frost.
Four Things. Bible, *O.T., Fr.* Proverbs.
Go to the Ant. Bible, *O.T., Fr.* Proverbs.
Go to the Ant. Sharpless.
Grasshopper and the Ant, The. La Fontaine.
Immanent. De la Mare.
Ondt and the Gracehoper, The. *Fr.* Finnegans Wake. Joyce.
Turkey and the Ant, The. *Fr.* Fables. Gay.

Antwerp, Belgium
Antwerp: Musée des Beaux-Arts. Ross.

Anxiety
Humaine Cares. Wanley.
Overheard in an Orchard. Cheney.

Apartheid
Child Who Was Shot Dead by Soldiers at Nyanga, The. Jonker.
In Bloemfontein. Ross.
In the Gold Mines. Vilakazi.
Landscape of Violence. Currey.
Me, Colored. *Fr.* Tell Freedom. Abrahams.
Pass Office Song. *Unknown.*
Where the Rainbow Ends. Rive.
White and Black, The. Khaketla.

Apartments
Apartment-Hunter, The. Schultz.
Living in Sin. Rich.
Room of Return. Kinnell.

Apathy
Celestial Surgeon, The. Stevenson.
Elegy for N.N. Milosz.
Indifference. Studdert-Kennedy.
Musée des Beaux Arts. Auden.
Pooh! De la Mare.
Revelation, The. *Fr.* The Angel in the House. Patmore.
There Is None to Help. *Fr.* The Psalm of Christ. Walsh.
Written in a Thunder Storm July 15th 1841. Clare.

Apes
Ape, The. Young.
Ape, the Monkey and Baboon Did Meet, The. *Unknown.*
Artist and Ape. Link.
Best Loved of Africa. Danner.
First Philosopher's Song. Huxley.

Aphrodisiacs
In Praise of Cocoa, Cupid's Nightcap. Sharpless.
Virgin Sturgeon, The. *Unknown.*

Aphrodite
Aphrodite Pandemos. *Unknown.*
Blue Sleep. Bryher.
Myth on Mediterranean Beach; Aphrodite as Logos. Warren.
Ring Of, The. Olson.
See also **Venus (goddess).**
Apocalypse. *See* **End of the World.**
Apollinaire, Guillaume
I Am Almost Asleep. Grier.
Apollo
Before the Statue of Apollo. Tchernichowsky.
Canticle to Apollo, A. Herrick.
Delphic Hymn to Apollo. Swinburne.
Hymn of Apollo. Shelley.
Many Are Called. Robinson.
Phoebus, Arise. Drummond of Hawthornden.
Phoebus with Admetus. Meredith.
Sacrifice to Apollo, The. Drayton.
Song for Apollo. *Fr.* Empedocles on Etna. Arnold.
Song to Apollo. *Fr.* Midas. Lyly.
Story of Phoebus and Daphne Applied, Etc., The. Waller.
Translation into the Original. Gilbert.
Apostles
Ballad of the Goodly Fere. Pound.
Christus Matthaeum et Discipulos Alloquitur. Sherburne.
Last Supper, The. Williams.
Starlight like Intuition Pierced the Twelve. Schwartz.
Appalachia
Another Kind of Burning. Fox.
Appalachian Front. Weeks.
Apple Blossoms
Comparison, A. Farrar.
Apple Trees
After Apple-picking. Frost.
Afternoon in a Tree. Sister Maris Stella.
Apple Tree, The. Brown.
Mother. Dempster.
Old Apple Trees. Snodgrass.
Planting of the Apple-Tree, The. Bryant.
Tapestry Trees. Morris.
Apples
Adam Lay I bounden. *Unknown.*
After Apple-picking. Frost.
Apple. Fry.
Apple, The. Guernsey.
Apple Hell. Van Doren.
Apple Season. Frost.
Apple Song. Frost.
Apples. Kaufman.
Apples. Mueller.
Apples. *Fr.* Verses for Fruitwomen. Swift.
Apples. Waters.
Apples in New Hampshire. Gilchrist.
Cider Song. Weston.
Crossed Apple, The. Bogan.
How Stars and Hearts Grow in Apples. Elson.
Moonlit Apples. Drinkwater.
Mystic. Lawrence.
On Apples. Ross.
Paring the Apple. Tomlinson.
Pattern Poem with an Elusive Intruder. Döhl.
Picking Apples. Lindsay.
Sweet Apple. Stephens.
Symposium, A: Apples. Pastan.
Unharvested. Frost.
When It Rains. Maxson.
Appleseed, Johnny. *See* **Chapman, John.**
Apprentices
Sheffield Apprentice, The. *Unknown.*
Apricots
Apricot Tree. Isanos.
Vegetable Destiny. Cassian.
April
April. Garrison.
April. Loveman.
April. Pastan.
April. Shorter.
April. Teasdale.
April. Tietjens.
April and Dying. Aldrich.
April and May. Robinson.
April Day, An. Cotter.
April 1885. Bridges.
April Fantasie. Cortissoz.
April, Glengarry. Coxon.
April Inventory. Snodgrass.
April Midnight. Symons.
April Morning, An. Carman.
April of the Ages, The. Dolben.
April Rain. Blind.
April Rain. Loveman.
April Rain Song. Hughes.
April Snow, The. Very.
April Weather. Reese.
Aprilly. Taylor.
Be Ye in Love with April-Tide? Scollard.
Blue Squills. Teasdale.
Break-up, The. Klein.
Cherry Tree. Rossetti.
Concert, The. McGinley.
Day before April, The. Davies.
Dutch April. Halpern.
Early April. Frost.
Epigram on the First of April. Winstanley.
For City Spring. Benét.
Forsythia Is the Color I Remember. Cherwinski.
Great Farm. Booth.
Home-Thoughts, from Abroad. Browning.
In April. Wetherald.
Lady April. Le Gallienne.
Make Me Over, Mother April. *Fr.* Spring Song. Carman.
Now the Noisy Winds Are Still. Dodge.
Prayer in April. Hay.
Rain. Alling.
Shore Roads of April. Adams.
Song: "April, April,/ Laugh thy girlish laughter." Watson.
Song: "O Lovely April, rich and bright." Kahn.
Song from "April." McLeod.
Song of a Second April. Millay.
Spring. Millay.
Storm in April, A. Wilbur.
Street in April, A. Avison.
Sweet Wild April. Stead.
West Wind, The. Masefield.
Whan that Aprill with his shoures soote. *Fr.* The Canterbury Tales: Prologue. Chaucer.
While April Rain Went By. O'Sheel.
April Fools' Day
All Fools' Day. *Unknown.*
April Fool. Coatsworth.
April Fool. Hammond.
April Fools' Day. Pomeroy.
Oh Did You Hear? Silverstein.
Aquariums
Aquarium. Wright.
At the Aquarium. Eastman.
At the Water Zoo. Knox.
Ode of Odium on Aquariums. Guiterman.
Aquinas, St. Thomas. *See* **Thomas Aquinas, Saint.**
Arabia
Arabia. De la Mare.
Arabia. Falkner.
Arabs
Arab Love-Song, An. Thompson.
Arab to His Favorite Steed, The. Norton.
Arabs. Kreymborg.
Bedouin Song. Taylor.
In an Arab Town. Tichy.
Arachne
Arachne. Aliesan.
Arachne. Kazantzis.
Wedding, The. Aiken.
Aran Islands, Ireland
Aran Islands. Layton.
Arran. *Unknown.*
Arbor Day
Arbor Day. Thompson.
City Trees. Dargan.
Cross and the Tree, The. Stidger.
Fir Forest. Fuller.
Forest Meditation, A. Legg.
On Entering a Forest. Lennen.
Plant a Tree. Larcom.
Prayer, A. Markham.

Temple of the Trees, The. Pellow.
They All Belong to Me. Cook.
Tree-building. Cable.
Tree Feelings. Stetson.
Trees. Clark.
What Do We Plant? Abbey.
White Tree in Bloom, A. Moreland.
Woodman, Spare That Tree. Morris.

Arborvitae
Arabor Vitae. *Fr.* The Unknown Eros. Patmore.

Arbus, Diane
To D——, Dead by Her Own Hand. Nemerov.

Arbutus
Pink, small and punctual. Dickinson.
To a Mayflower. Marshall.

Arcadia
On a Picture by Poussin Representing Shepherds in Arcadia. Symonds.
Way to Arcady, The. Bunner.

Archaeology
Archaeological Picnic, The. Betjeman.
Archaeologists. Faucher.
Archaeology. Pollitt.
Archaeology of Love, The. Murphy.
Ashkelon. Rudolf.
Colossus, The. Plath.

Archery
Archer, The. Scollard.
On the College Archery Range. Wallace.

Architecture and Architects
Destruction of Bulfinch's House, The. Sandy.
Heiress and Architect. Hardy.
On Sir John Vanbrugh, Architect. Evans.
Eye's Delight: Poems of Art and Architecture (EyDe). Helen Plotz, ed.

Arctic
Ballad of Sir John Franklin, A. Boker.
Frozen Fire. McLaren.
Immoral Arctic, The. Bishop.
Song of the Rejected Woman. Kibkarjuk.
Wolf Cry, The. Sarett.

Arethusa
Arethusa. Shelley.

Argentina
For Refugio Talamante. Ochester.
Madwomen of the Plaza de Mayo, The. Mandel.

Arguments. *See* **Quarrels.**

Arion
On a Picture by Michele da Verona, of Arion as a Boy Riding upon a Dolphin. Ridler.

Aristotle
Humanities Lecture. Stafford.

Arithmetic
Arithmetic. Sandburg.
Seven Times One. Ingelow.

Arizona
Arizona Village. Davieau.
At Grand Canyon's Edge. Ray.
Back to Arizona. Brininstool.
Crossing the Colorado River into Yuma. Ortiz.
Discoveries in Arizona. Wright.
Driving through the Pima Indian Reservation. Cook.
Fair Warning, A. Mayo.
History of Arizona, The: How It Was Made and Who Made It. Brown.
Hitchhiker, The. Ai.
Mexican Quarter. *Fr.* Arizona Poems. Fletcher.
New Mexico and Arizona. Canterbury.
Painted Hills of Arizona, The. Curran.
Ragtime Cowboy Joe. Clarke, Muir, *and* Abrahms.
Yuma. Phelps.

Ark, The
Ark, The. *Fr.* Paradise Lost. Milton.
One More River. *Unknown.*
See also **Noah.**

Arkansas
Arkansas. Young.
Arkansas Traveler, The. *Unknown.*
Arkansaw Traveler, The. *Unknown.*
Getting Experience. Williams.
Little White Schoolhouse Blues. Lennon.
My Arkansas. Angelou.
Narrative Hooper and L.D.O. Sestina with a Long Last Line, The. Whitehead.
Sanford Barney. *Unknown.*
State of Arkansas, The. *Unknown.*
Toad Suck Ferry. Stoneback.
Yachting in Arkansas. Weeden.

Arlington National Cemetery, Virginia
Arlington Cemetery Looking toward the Capitol. Palmer.
Potomac, The. Shapiro.

Armada. *See* **Spanish Armada.**

Armenia
Out of the Deepness. Jackson.
Song from Armenia, A. Hill.
With the Bait of Bread. Pilbosian.

Armistice
"And There Was a Great Calm." Hardy.
Architects of Dream. Trent.
Armistice. Going.
Armistice. Lehmer.
Armistice Day. Causley.
Armistice Day. Trent.
Blow, Bugle! Clark.
Brotherhood. Markham.
Challenge. Clark.
Come, workers! Poets, artists, dreamers, more and more. *Fr.* Let Us Declare! Morgan.
Danger. Paine.
Day, The. Bynner.
Dreamers Cry Their Dream, The. Trent.
Everyone Sang. Sassoon.
Goal and the Way, The. Oxenham.
Great Powers Conference. Pierce.
Hymn of Hate, The. Miller.
Lessons. Weber.
Let Dreamers Wake. Lorraine.
Litany for Peace. Clark.
Make Way! Comfort.
Message of Peace, The. Howe.
New Song, The. Field.
Next Time. Simmons.
Peace. Markham.
Peace on Earth. Longfellow.
Prepare. Bynner.
Preparedness. Paxton.
"Put up the sword!" The voice of Christ once more. *Fr.* Disarmament. Whittier.
Song for Tomorrow. Trent.
Tenth Armistice Day, The. Ford.
This Is the Last. Waterhouse.
Today Is Armistice, a Holiday. Schwartz.
Tournament of Man, The. Crosby.
True Freedom. Mackay.
Valley of Decision, The. Oxenham.
Victory Bells. Conkling.
Victory Parade. Hoffman.
Waste of War, The. Stidger.
We Who Build Visions. Coblentz.
Were half the power, that fills the world with terror. *Fr.* The Arsenal at Springfield. Longfellow.
Where Are You Going, Great-Heart? Oxenham.
Which Sword? Pierce.
Wild Weather. Bates.
Without Regret. Lorraine.
World Planners. Steece.
See also **Peace.**

Armstrong, Johnie (Scots, *fl.* 1530)
Johnie Armstrong. *Unknown.*

Armstrong, Louis
Satchmo. Tolson.

Armstrong, William (Scots, *fl.* 1596)
Kinmont Willie. *Unknown.*

Army Life
Boots. Kipling.
Bus Stop. O'Sullivan.
By the Bivouac's Fitful Flame. Whitman.
Cavalry Crossing a Ford. Whitman.
Class Incident from Graves. Brownjohn.
Danny Deever. Kipling.
'Eathen, The. Kipling.
Going In to Dinner. Shanks.
Gunga Din. Kipling.
Lessons of the War. Reed.
Mandalay. Kipling.
Officers' Mess. Ewart.
Spring 1942. Fuller.

Stand-to: Good Friday Morning. Sassoon.
Tenting on the Old Camp Ground. Kettredge.
Words for Army Bugle Calls. *Unknown.*
Oxford Book of War Poetry, The (OBWP). Jon Stallworthy, ed.
See also **Soldiers.**

Arnold, Matthew
Dover Bitch, The. Hecht.
Laleham: Matthew Arnold's Grave. Johnson.
Pax Paganica. Guiney.

Arrows
Eulogy to the Bow and Arrow. Mongol.
I Wish My Tongue Were a Quiver. MacKay.
Song of the Arrow, The. *Fr.* Gisli, the Chieftain. Crawford.

Art and Artists
Accident in Art. Hovey.
Anecdote of the Jar. Stevens.
Anonymous Drawing. Justice.
Ars Victrix. Dobson.
Art. Flax.
Art. Levertov.
Art. Perry.
Art. *Unknown.*
Artist, An. Jeffers.
Art above Nature, to Julia. Herrick.
Artist, The. Raleigh.
Artist and Ape. Link.
Artists East and West. Chang.
At a Bach Concert. Rich.
At an Exhibition of Historical Paintings, Hobart. Smith.
Aunt Jennifer's Tiger. Rich.
Black Art. Baraka.
Chicago Picasso, The. Brooks.
Conundrum of the Workshops, The. Kipling.
Dab of Color, A. Weiss.
Drawing Wildflowers. Graham.
Epilogue to Lessing's Laocoön. Arnold.
Epitaph on an Unfortunate Artist. Graves.
Four Heads & How to Do Them. Forbes.
Gallery, The. Marvell.
Hand, The. Fawcett.
House All Pictures, A. George.
In Search of the Picturesque. Combe.
Italian Chest, An. Seiffert.
Japanese Print. Clarke.
Lapis Lazuli. Yeats.
L'Art, 1910. Pound.
Leaf-Makers, The. Stewart.
London Pavement Artist. Schevill.
Makers, The. Kell.
Man bent over his guitar, The. *Fr.* The Man with the Blue Guitar. Stevens.
Miltonic Sonnet for Mr. Johnson on His Refusal of Peter Hurd's Official Portrait, A. Wilbur.
Mosaic Worker, The. Peach.
Musée des Beaux Arts. Auden.
Museum Piece. Wilbur.
Ode on a Grecian Urn. Keats.
On Seeing the Elgin Marbles. Keats.
Paring the Apple. Tomlinson.
Play Way, The. Atwood.
Poem by a Perfectly Furious Academician. *Unknown.*
Primitives. Randall.
Protogenes and Apelles. Prior.
Ransom, The. Baudelaire.
Sovereigns, The. Mifflin.
Story of Ug, The. Robinson.
To My Son Parker, Asleep in the Next Room. Kaufman.
Upon Umber: Epigram. Herrick.
What Is Left? Vas.
When I Buy Pictures. Moore.
Why I Am Not a Painter. O'Hara.
Woodcut. Wilson.
Eye's Delight: Poems of Art and Architecture (EyDe). Helen Plotz, ed.
Poet Dreaming in the Artist's House, The; Contemporary Poems about the Visual Arts (PoDr). Emilie Buchwald *and* Ruth Roston, eds.
See also **Artists' Colonies.**

Artemis
Actaeon. Clough.
Artemis. Davison.
Artemis. Deamer.
Artemis Prologizes. Browning.
Hymn to Artemis, the Destroyer. Zaturenska.
Return of the Goddess Artemis. Graves.
See also **Diana.**

Arthurian Legend
Death of Arthur, The. *Fr.* The Brut. Layamon.
Defence of Guenevere, The. Morris.
Doom-Well of St. Madron, The. Hawker.
Grail, The. Keyes.
Grave of King Arthur, The. Warton.
King Arthur's Death. *Unknown.*
Lady of Shalott, The. Tennyson.
Lancelot. Bontemps.
Lancelot and the Grail. *Fr.* Idylls of the King. Tennyson.
Lancelot and Guinevere. Gould.
"Land is lonely now, The: Anathema." *Fr.* The Quest of the Sangraal. Hawker.
Legend of Camelot, A. Du Maurier.
Marriage of Sir Gawain, The. *Unknown.*
Merlin. Emerson.
Morte d'Arthur. *Fr.* Idylls of the King. Tennyson.
Myth of Arthur, The. Chesterton.
Near Avalon. Morris.
Passing of Arthur, The. Squire.
Passing of Arthur, The. *Fr.* Idylls of the King. Tennyson.
Percivale's Quest. *Fr.* Idylls of the King. Tennyson.
Round Table, The. Mannyng.
Salad—after Tennyson. Collins.
Sir Galahad. Tennyson.
Temptation of Sir Gawain, The. *Fr.* Sir Gawain and the Green Knight. *Unknown.*
Wizard of Alderley Edge, The. Coe.

Artichokes
Artichoke. Taylor.

Artifacts
Arrowheads. Gom.
Jutaculla Rock. Morgan.
Stone Hammer Poem. Kroetsch.

Artificial Insemination
To My Children Unknown, Produced by Artificial Insemination. Kirkup.

Artists' Colonies
Hillcrest. Robinson.
Yaddo. Herschberger.

Ascanius
Iulus. Wallis.

Ascension Day
Ascension-Day. Vaughan.
Ascention. Donne.
Holy Thursday (" 'Twas on a Holy Thursday, their innocent faces clean"). *Fr.* Songs of Innocence. Blake.
Hymne of the Ascension, An. Drummond of Hawthornden.
Second Ascension of Christ, The. *Fr.* Forty Days. Wheelwright.
They Are All Gone into the World of Light. Vaughan.

Ash Trees
Tapestry Trees. Morris.

Ash Wednesday
Ash Wednesday. Eliot.

Ashby, Turner
Ashby. Thompson.

Ashes
Ashes. Levine.
Burial, The. Thalman.
Children's Lenten Wisdom. Houck.

Asian-Americans
Discovery of Tradition, The. Inada.
Suzie Wong Doesn't Live Here. Mark.
Breaking Silence; an Anthology of Contemporary Asian American Poets (BrSi). Joseph Bruchac, ed.
See also **Chinese, The; Filipinos; Japanese, The.**

Aspen Trees
Aspen and the Stream, The. Wilbur.
Aspens. Thomas.
Spring Song of Aspens. Spencer.
See also **Poplar Trees.**

Asphodels
Of asphodel, that greeny flower. *Fr.* Asphodel, That Greeny Flower. Williams.
Snowflake on asphodel, clear ice on rose. Aiken.

Assassinations and Assassins
Assassination. Lee.
Assassination Poems. Ridland.
Assassination Raga. Ferlinghetti.
Booth Killed Lincoln. *Unknown.*
Channel U.S.A. Live. Stoutenburg.

Charles Guiteau. *Unknown.*
Claus Von Stauffenberg. Gunn.
Down in Dallas. Kennedy.
For Malcolm: After Mecca. Barrax.
League of Selves, The. Toffler.
Martyr, The. Melville.
On the Duke of Buckingham, Slain by Felton, the 23rd August, 1628. Felltham.
Traction: November 22, 1963. Moss.
White House Blues. *Unknown.*
Zolgotz. *Unknown.*

Asses. *See* **Donkeys.**

Assisi, Italy
Assisi. Noyes.

Assyrians
Destruction of Sennacherib, The. Byron.

Astarte
To Ashtaroth and Bel. Tchernichowsky.

Astrology
Astrologer's Song, An. Kipling.
Love's Horoscope. Crashaw.
Upon Looking at a Book of Astrology. McFadden.
Zodiac Rhyme, The. *Unknown.*

Astronauts
Astronaut's Choice. Darcy.
Everlasting Astronauts, The. Buchan.
From the Domain of Arnheim. Morgan.
Problems. Scott.

Astronomy and Astronomers
Astronomer's Journal, An. Shore.
Astronomers of Mont Blanc, The. Bowers.
Copernican System, The. Chatterton.
Footnote to Feynman. Post.
Gemini Jones. Espy.
Greenwich Observatory. Keyes.
Jodrell Bank. Dickinson.
Letter from Caroline Herschel (1750–1848). Cedering.
Letters from the Astronomers. Cedering.
Message from Space, A. Stafford.
Observatory Ode, The. Nims.
Old Astronomer to His Pupil, The. Williams.
Planetarium. Rich.
Planets Line Up for a Demonstration, The. Kearns.
Stargazer, The. *Unknown.*
When I Heard the Learn'd Astronomer. Whitman.

Astrophysics
Black Holes. Perkins.
Collapsars. McPherson.
Specialist, The. Perlman.

Atalanta
Atalanta in Calydon, *sels.* Swinburne.
Atalanta's Race. Morris.

Atheism
Atheist. Harburg.
Atheist's Prayer, The. Unamuno.
Death on a Crossing. Paterson.
Exit God. Bradford.
Impercipient, The. Hardy.
Old Atheist Pauses by the Sea, A. Kinsella.
Skeptic, The. Service.

Athena
Athene's Song. Boland.
See also **Minerva.**

Athens, Greece
Athens. *Fr.* Paradise Regained. Milton.
Spring Wind, A. Spencer.
Timon Curses Athens and Mankind. *Fr.* Timon of Athens. Shakespeare.

Athletes
Aging Athlete, The. Weiss.
Athletes. Gibson.
Confessions of a Born Spectator. Nash.
Ex-Basketball Player. Updike.
Girl Athletes. Long.
Greek Athlete, The. Euripides.
Of Kings and Things. Morrison.
Pole-Vaulter, The. *Unknown.*
Runner, The. Whitman.
To an Aging Charioteer. Leontius Scholasticus.
To an Athlete Dying Young. Housman.
To an Athlete Turned Poet. Meinke.

Atlanta, Georgia
Litany of Atlanta, A. Du Bois.

Atlantic Ocean
Castaway, The. Cowper.
Crossing the Atlantic. Sexton.
Georges Bank. Older.
How Cyrus Laid the Cable. Saxe.
Night Fishing for Blues. Smith.
Night Storm. Simms.
North Atlantic. Sandburg.
Seaweed. Longfellow.

Atlas, Charles
Dynamic Tension. Sanfield.

Atomic Bomb
Actual Vision of Morning's Extrusion. Dugan.
Any Day Now. McCord.
At the Bomb Testing Site. Stafford.
Atomic Courtesy. Jacobson.
Back Again from Yucca Flats. Kelley.
Celebration 1982. Wilkins.
Day after Trinity, The. Oyama.
Dirge for the New Sunrise. *Fr.* Three Poems of the Atomic Age. Sitwell.
Early Warning. Marks.
Earth. Wheelock.
Gathered at the River. Levertov.
Hark, the Herald Angels Sing. Dehn.
Hibakusha's Letter (1955), The. Mura.
Hiding Place. Armour.
Hydrogen Dog and the Cobalt Cat, The. *Fr.* The Space Child's Mother Goose. Winsor.
If All the Thermo-Nuclear Warheads. Burke.
In the Year 1945 an Original Child Was Born. *Fr.* Original Child Bomb. Merton.
Merry Minuet, The. Harnick.
Poem Ending with an Old Cliché. Zimmer.
Primer of Consequences. Brasier.
U.S. 1946 King's X. Frost.
See also **Hiroshima, Japan; Nuclear War.**

Atoms
Life of Particles, The. Benedikt.
Time of the Mad Atom. Braiser.

Atterbury, Francis, Bishop of Rochester
Epitaph: "Meek Francis lies here, friend, without stop or stay." Prior.

Attics
Attic, The. Coulette.
Calvin in the Attic Cleans. Weeden.
Herbs in the Attic. Waniek.
In a Garret. Allen.
Up There. Auden.

Attucks, Crispus
Crispus Attucks. Hayden.

Auctions
Auction Sale, The. Reed.
H. S. Beeney Auction Sales. Pichaske.
To Henry Wright of Mobberley, Esq. On Buying the Picture of Father Malebranche. Byrom.

Auden, Wystan Hugh
Auden. Roseliep.
Just a Smack at Auden. Empson.
Letter to Auden, A. Phillips.
Seeing Auden Off. Booth.
Self-congratulatory Ode on Mr. Auden's Election to the Professorship of Poetry at Oxford. Mason.
To Auden on His Fiftieth. Eberhart.
To Wystan Auden. Grigson.
W. H. Auden & Mantan Moreland. Young.

Aughrim, Battle of (1691)
After Aughrim. Geoghegan.
After Aughrim. Lawless.
Deep red bogs divided. *Fr.* The Battle of Aughrim. Murphy.

August
Angle of Vision. Bosworth.
August. Binyon.
August. Ledwidge.
August. *Fr.* Sonnets of the Months. Folgore da San Gemignano.
August. Swinburne.
August. Thaxter.
August. Updike.
August. Winslow.
August. Wylie.
August Afternoon. Edey.
August Midnight, An. Hardy.
August Night. Roberts.
August Smiles. Coatsworth.

Golden Month, The. Doyle.
Mid-August. Driscoll.
Mid-August at Sourdough Mountain Lookout. Snyder.
Month of Falling Stars, The. Higginson.
Augustine, Saint
St. Augustine Contemplating the Bust of Einstein. Ackerman.
Augustus. *See* **Caesar, Augustus.**
Auks
Great Auk's Ghost, The. Hodgson.
Aunt Jemima
Aunt Jemima of the Ocean Waves. Hayden.
Aunts
Aga Khan, The. Orlen.
Aunt Elsie's Night Music. Oliver.
Aunt Melissa. Smith.
Aunt Selina. Haynes.
Great Aunts of My Childhood, The. Fulton.
Mac. Vinz.
My Aunt. Holmes.
Pair of Fireflies, A. Liu.
To Aunt Rose. Ginsberg.
Aurora Borealis
Indian Night Tableau. Edelstein.
Auschwitz, Poland
Children of Auschwitz. Korzhavin.
Dreams of Auschwitz. Slutsky.
On the 25th Anniversary of the Liberation of Auschwitz. Mandel.
Your Attention Please. Porter.
Austin, Alfred
Birthday Ode to Mr. Alfred Austin, A. Seaman.
Australia
At Cooloolah. Wright.
Australia. Hope.
Australia. Jackson.
Botany Bay. Freeth.
Death of Morgan, The. *Unknown.*
Now I'm Easy. Bogle.
Staying Ahead. Glass.
Summer Christmas in Australia, A. Sladen.
Waltzing Matilda. Paterson.
Wild Colonial Boy, The. *Unknown.*
Collins Book of Australian Poetry, The (CBAP). Rodney Hall, ed.
Poetry in Australia (PoAu). T. Inglis Moore, ed.
Authorship and Authors
Absolute and Abitofhell. Knox.
After Dilettante Concetti. Traill.
Argument of His Book, The. Herrick.
August 12, 1952. Fishman.
Author to Her Book, The. Bradstreet.
Boatman, The. Macpherson.
Burning Hills. Ondaatje.
Cacoëthes Scribendi. Holmes.
Canadian Authors Meet, The. Scott.
For the Young Who Want To. Piercy.
Gas from a Burner. Joyce.
George Crabbe. Robinson.
Gods I am pent in a cockroach. *Fr.* The Wail of Archy. Marquis.
Hamlet's Soliloquy Imitated. Jago.
I Have Approached. Paton.
I Know That All beneath the Moon Decays. Drummond of Hawthornden.
Lake Isle, The. Pound.
Literary Zodiac. Piddington.
Novel, The. Levertov.
Obit on Parnassus. Fitzgerald.
On His Books. Belloc.
On Some South African Novelists. Campbell.
On the Same. Campbell.
Poet at Seven, The. Rimbaud.
Poetry Perpetuates the Poet. Herrick.
So That's Who I Remind Me Of. Nash.
Song of Perfect Propriety. Parker.
There Is No Opera Like "Lohengrin." Wheelwright.
To an Author. Freneau.
2001: The Tennyson/Hardy Poem. Ewart.
Upon the Saying That My Verses Were Made by Another. Killigrew.
Whom Do You Visualize as Your Reader? Pastan.
Words, like Spiders. Wolny.
Writing for Money. Field.
Young Author, The. Johnson.
"What hundred books are best, think you?" I said. Bangs.
Autism
Death of a Son. Silkin.
Private Rooms. O Hehir.
Automation
All Watched Over by Machines of Loving Grace. Brautigan.
Epitaph: "Here he lies moulding." Mellichamp.
Four Quartz Crystal Clocks. Moore.
Man about the Kitchen, A. Hobson.
Now I Set Me. Herman.
Valedictory to Standard Oil of Indiana, A. Wagoner.
You Take the Pilgrims, Just Give Me the Progress. Rosenfield.
Automobile Accidents
At 79th and Park. Howes.
Auto Wreck. Shapiro.
Big Crash Out West. Viereck.
Deaths at Paragon, Indiana, The. Woods.
Obituary. Fearing.
Whiplash. Matthews.
Wreck. Polk.
Wrecker Driver Forsees Your Death, The. Baker.
Automobile Racing
Racer's Widow, The. Glück.
Automobiles
Abandonment of Autos. Dawe.
Ambition. Bishop.
"As a Boy with a Richness of Needs I Wandered." Dyment.
At a Low Mass for Two Hot-Rodders. Kennedy.
Automobile, The. Edson.
Automobile Mechanics. Baruch.
Ballad of Faith. Williams.
Brides, The. Hope.
Buick. Shapiro.
Car Wash. Livingston.
Cherrylog Road. Dickey.
"Chew Mail Pouch." Klauck.
Dandy Horse, The. *Unknown.*
Deeper in the Tank—the Last Middle East Crisis, 1972. Ruggles.
Drive, The. McFatter.
Driver's Prayer, A. *Unknown.*
Driving Home. London.
Driving to the Beach. Cole.
Driving toward the Lac Qui Parle River. Bly.
Filling Station. Morin.
Fugue. Nemerov.
Funny the Way Different Cars Start. Baruch.
Gas and Hot Air. Bishop.
Heroes of the Strip. Cudahy.
In My Merry Oldsmobile. Bryan.
Johnson's Motor Car. *Unknown.*
Last of the Poet's Car. Connor.
Letter from Home, A. Minarik.
Little Car, The. Apollinaire.
Maine. Booth.
Man on Wheels. Shapiro.
Morning. Saiser.
Motor Cars. Bennett.
Moving between Beloit and Monroe. Noll.
1937 Ford Convertible. McKeown.
Nostalgia for 70. Miller.
Ode to a Dead Dodge. McElroy.
One, Two, Three. Albert.
Packard. Barker.
Pedestrian's Plaint, The. Lucas.
Plastic Jesus. *Unknown.*
Portrait of the Autist as a New World Driver. Murray.
Song for a Blue Roadster. Field.
Southbound on the Freeway. Swenson.
Spring Sunday on Quaker Street. Bass.
Stop—Go. Baruch.
Terraplane Blues. *Unknown.*
This Dim and Ptolemaic Man. Bishop.
Thoreau. Jones.
Three Car Poems. Jones.
Trip, The. Stafford.
True Ballad of the Great Race to Gilmore City, The. Hey.
Twink Drives Back, in a Bad Mood, from a Party in Massachusetts. Amabile.
Autumn
Adios. Babock.
Apple Song. Frost.
Autumn. Akhmadulina.
Autumn. Campbell.
Autumn. Clare.
Autumn. Curran.

Autumn. Hood.
Autumn. Hubbell.
Autumn. Hulme.
Autumn. Manger.
Autumn. *Fr.* Summer's Last Will and Testament. Nashe.
Autumn. Rodgers.
Autumn. Rossetti.
Autumn. Scannell.
Autumn. Shelley.
Autumn. Smith.
Autumn. Tagore.
Autumn. *Fr.* The Seasons. Thomson.
Autumn. *Unknown.*
Autumn. Untermeyer.
Autumn. Winwar.
Autumn; an Ode. Gullans.
Autumn Birds. Clare.
Autumn Change. Clare.
Autumn Color. Robinson.
Autumn, Dark Wanderer. Daryush.
Autumn Dawn. Machado.
Autumn Day. Rilke.
Autumn Eve. Andriello.
Autumn Fancies. *Unknown.*
Autumn Fashions. Thomas.
Autumn Fires. Stevenson.
Autumn Imagined. Davie.
Autumn in the West. Gallagher.
Autumn on the Upper Thames. Morris.
Autumn Poem. Cronin.
Autumn Song. Long.
Autumn Song. Stepanchev.
Autumn Wind, The. Clare.
Autumn Woods. Tippett.
Autumn's Fete. McGeorge.
Autumnal. Colony.
Autumnal. Dowson.
Autumnal Consummation. Stevenson.
Autumnal Ode. De Vere.
Autumnal Spring Song. Miller.
Autumnus. Sylvester.
Blue Smoke. Frost.
Burning of the Leaves, The. Binyon.
Calvinist Autumnal. Harrod.
Chant for Skippers. Gallagher.
Chestnut vendor, The. Szelki.
Child's Thought of Harvest, A. "Coolidge."
City of Falling Leaves, The. Lowell.
Clear after Rain. Tu Fu.
Counter-Serenade: She Invokes the Autumn Instant. Viereck.
Day in Autumn, A. Thomas.
Death of the Flowers, The. Bryant.
Difference, A. Clark.
Down! Down! Farjeon.
Dying Garden, The. Nemerov.
Early Fall: The Adirondacks. Wright.
Eggplants Have Pins and Needles, The. Matveyeva.
End of Fall, The. Ponge.
End of Summer. Kunitz.
End of Summer, The. Minty.
Epilogue: "Painted autumn overwhelms, The." Falkner.
Equinox. Young.
Fall, The. Barnes.
Fall. Francis.
Fall Again. Coursen.
Fall Colors. Mazzaro.
Fall Days. Conger.
Fall in Corrales. Wilbur.
Fall, Leaves, Fall. Brontë.
Fall Lightly on Me. Gaess.
Fall of Leaves. Savage.
Fall of the Leaf, The. Thoreau.
Fall Song. Moses.
Fall Wind. Stafford.
Falltime. Sandburg.
Farmer. Bailey.
Field of Autumn. Lee.
Final Fall, The. Amprimoz.
First Cold Night of Autumn. Stupp.
Frost Warning. McFarland.
God's World. Millay.
Gold Leaves. Chesterton.
Harvest Home. Guiterman.
Harvest Moon, The. Longfellow.
Heaving Roses of the Hedge Are Stirred, The. Dixon.
Hint o' Snaw, A. Soutar.
Hound, The. Deutsch.
How One Winter Came in the Lake Region. Campbell.
How the Leaves Came Down. "Coolidge."
Hurrahing in Harvest. Hopkins.
I Am the Autumn. Manger.
Immortal Autumn. MacLeish.
Indian Summer. Draper.
Indian Summer: Vermont. Stevenson.
Kitten and the Falling Leaves, The. Wordsworth.
Lament in Autumn. Stewart.
Last Flower, The. Moore.
Last Rite. Hicks.
Late Autumn. Sullivan.
Late Autumn. Young.
Late in Fall. Wilson.
Leaves Do Not Mind at All, The. Wynne.
Load. Hewitt.
Long and Lonely Winter, The. Goulder.
Maple and Sumach. Day Lewis.
Mist and All, The. Willson.
Mnemosyne. Stickney.
Monday morning back to school. McCord.
Morns are meeker than they were, The. Dickinson.
Mummies, The. Kumin.
Name of it is "Autumn," The. Dickinson.
New York—Albany. Ferlinghetti.
Night Wind in Fall. Moses.
North Wind in October. Bridges.
November. Fisher.
November Night. Crapsey.
O Amber Day, amid the Autumn Gloom. Allison.
October. Fyleman.
October. Koeppel.
October Maples, Portland. Wilbur.
Ode to Autumn. Keats.
Ode to the Spirit of Earth in Autumn. Meredith.
Ode to the West Wind. Shelley.
Of Autumn. Porumbacu.
On Lake Pend Oreille. Shelton.
Patterns. Setterberg.
Poem in October. Thomas.
Real Property. Monro.
Rich Days. Davies.
Ripe and Bearded Barley, The. *Unknown.*
Robin Redbreast. Allingham.
Rondel: Autumn. Field.
Scattered Leaves. Henson.
September. Fallis.
September. Jackson.
September. Lampman.
September Is Here. Reed.
September Midnight. Teasdale.
Shape of Autumn, The. Russ.
Sign, The. Blackburn.
So This Is Autumn. Watt.
Something Told the Wild Geese. Field.
Song: "Again rejoicing nature sees." Burns.
Song: "Feathers of the willow, The." Dixon.
Song: "Spirit haunts the year's last hours, A." Tennyson.
Song: "Why fadest thou in death." Dixon.
Song at the Beginning of Autumn. Jennings.
Song for Autumn. Young.
Song of Autumn I. Baudelaire.
Song of Early Autumn, A. Gilder.
Sonnet in Autumn. Petersen.
Spring and Fall. Hopkins.
Summer Is Gone. *Unknown.*
Survivor. MacLeish.
Tell Me Not Here, It Needs Not Saying. Housman.
This Fall. Aliesan.
Threnody: "Red leaves fell upon the lake, The." Farrar.
To Autumn. Blake.
To Autumn. Keats.
To the Fringed Gentian. Bryant.
Vagabond Song, A. Carman.
Watching the Moon. McCord.
When the Frost Is on the Punkin. Riley.
Wind and Silver. Lowell.

Winter Is Another Country. MacLeish.
Words for the Raker of Leaves. Adams.
Zimmer in Fall. Zimmer.

Auvergne, France
In the Caves of Auvergne. Turner.

Aviation and Aviators
Aging Poet, on a Reading Trip to Dayton, Visits the Air Force Museum and Discovers There a Plane He Once Flew, The. Snyder.
Air Field. Siegel.
Airman, R. F. C. Herbertson.
Airman Who Flew over Shakespeare's England, The. Plutzik.
Airstrip in Essex, 1960, An. Hall.
Buzz Plane, The. Francis.
Darius Greene and His Flying-Machine. Trowbridge.
Dream of Flying Comes of Age, The. Nemerov.
Ego. Booth.
Europe. Ashbery.
First Flight. Hoffman.
Flying. Carlile.
Frightened Flier Goes North, The. Kazantzis.
High Flight. Magee.
Icarus. Iremonger.
Icarus. Spender.
Landscape near an Aerodrome, The. Spender.
Leave in 1917. Anderson.
Losses. Jarrell.
Lost Pilot, The. Tate.
My Flying Machine. Brodsky.
Nocturne for October 31st, A. Winters.
Norfolk Memorials. Leavenworth.
Old Pilot, The. Hall.
San Diego Poem, A:/January–February 1973. Ortiz.
"Sing we the two lieutenants, Parer and M'Intosh." *Fr.* A Time to Dance: The Flight. Day Lewis.
Sonic Boom. Updike.
Sparrow at the Airport, The. Ostroff.
To an Aviator. Hicky.
To Beachey, 1912. Sandburg.
When a Beau Goes In. Ewart.
Winged bull trundles to the wired perimeter, The. *Fr.* Flight to Italy. Day Lewis.
Wrights' Biplane, The. Frost.
See also **Air Travel; Air Warfare; Airports.**

Avignon, France
Following Van Gogh (Avignon, 1982). Puziss.

Avoca, Ireland
Meeting of the Waters, The. Moore.

Avocados
Avocado Pit, The. Rakosi.

Avon River, Canada
To the Avon River above Stratford, Canada. Reaney.

Avon River, England
Ebb Tide, The. Southey.
Pastoral. Wright.
Upon Eckington Bridge, River Avon. Quiller-Couch.

Ayr, Scotland
Afton Water. Burns.
Quiet Tide near Ardrossan, The. Turner.

Azaleas
Azalea, The. *Fr.* The Unknown Eros. Patmore.
White Azaleas. Kimball.

Aztecs
Aztec City, The. Ware.
Song of Nezahualcoyotl. *Unknown.*

B

Baal
To Ashtaroth and Bel. Tchernichowsky.

Baal-Shem-Tov
Baal Shem Tov. Klein.

Babel, Isaac
Babel. Pacernick.

Babel, Tower of
From the four corners of the earth. *Fr.* The People, Yes. Sandburg.
Tower of Babel, The. Crouch.

Babies
At the Washing of My Son. Ray.
Babies, The. Strand.
Baby. Eastman.
Baby, The. *Fr.* At the Back of the North Wind. Macdonald.
Baby. Oates.
Baby at Play. *Unknown.*
Babyhood. *Fr.* Bitter-sweet. Holland.
Baby's Breakfast. Poulsson.
Baby's Dance, The. Taylor.
Baby's Drinking Song. Kirkup.
Baby's feet, like sea-shells pink, A. *Fr.* Étude Réaliste. Swinburne.
Bartholomew. Gale.
Breakfast Song, The. Poulsson.
Bringing Up Babies. Fuller.
Bunch of Roses, A. Tabb.
Candida. Kavanagh.
Chicago Boy Baby. Sandburg.
Child Crying. Thwaite.
Chinese Baby Asleep. Donnelly.
Clinic Day. Barnes.
Coming and Going. Johnson.
Cottager to Her Infant, The. Wordsworth.
Cradle Hymn. Watts.
Cradle Song: "Curled like a hoop in sleep." Durrell.
Cradle Song: "Sleep, sleep, beauty bright." Blake.
Cradle Song, A: "Sweet dreams form a shade." *Fr.* Songs of Innocence. Blake.
Dolls, The. Yeats.
Errantry. Fitzgerald.
First Step, The. Saxton.
First Tooth, The. Rands.
Five Days Old. Webb.
For My Son. Nims.
Frost at Midnight. Coleridge.
Ho! Ye Sun, Moon, Stars. *Unknown.*
I Found God. Thacker.
In Go-Cart So Tiny. Greenaway.
In the Forest. Bowering.
Infant. O Hehir.
Infant Joy. *Fr.* Songs of Innocence. Blake.
Infant Sorrow. *Fr.* Songs of Experience. Blake.
Kadia the Young Mother Speaks. Sampter.
Little. Aldis.
Little Brown Baby. Dunbar.
Little Person, A. Hooker.
Lucky. Song.
Magus, The. Dickey.
Mamma Sings. Hoffenstein.
Maternal Despotism; or, The Rights of Infants. Graves.
Methinks 'Tis Pretty Sport. Bastard.
Modern Baby, The. Doane.
Morning Song. Plath.
Mother to Her Waking Infant, A. Baillie.
Mundus et Infans. Auden.
My Little Lover. Sauvage.
Night Dances, The. Plath.
Night Feeding. Rukeyser.
Nursery Song, A. Richards.
O sleep, my babe, hear not the rippling wave. *Fr.* Phantasmion. Coleridge.
Only a Baby Small. Barr.
Perambulator Poem. McCord.
Prettiest Little Baby in the County-O. *Unknown.*
Rampage, The. Williams.
Rock-a-Bye Baby. Canning.
Rock-a-Bye, Baby. Mother Goose.
Sara in Her Father's Arms. Oppen.
Seeing and Doing. Dean.
Six Weeks Old. Morley.
Slippery. Sandburg.
Song for the Middle of the Night, A. Wright.
Song for the Newborn. *Unknown.*
Song My. Griffin.
Sonnet: Oft o'er My Brain. Coleridge.
Sonnet to a Friend Who Asked, How I Felt When the Nurse First Presented My Infant to Me. Coleridge.
Terrible Infant, A. Locker-Lampson.
To a Friend's Child. Barnstone.
To Miss Charlotte Pulteney in Her Mother's Arms. Philips.
To Our Daughter. Armitage.
To the Newborn. Tóth.
Tonversation with Baby, A. Bishop.
Trot, Trot! Butts.
Unknown Girl in the Maternity Ward. Sexton.

Untitled. Kuka.
Verses for a First Birthday. Barker.
Way the Baby Slept, The. Riley.
What'll We Do with the Baby-O? *Unknown.*
Where Is My Butterfly Net? McCord.
Young bee falls between my window, A. *Fr.* Brother Jonathan, Brother Kafka. O'Sullivan.
You're. Plath.
Home Book of Verse, The (HBV-1), pp. 3-29. Burton Egbert Stevenson, ed.
See also **Infant Death.**

Baboons
Ape, the Monkey and Baboon Did Meet, The. *Unknown.*
At the Zoo. De la Mare.
Baboon. *Unknown.*
Baboon. Zulu.
Baboon 2. *Unknown.*
Big Baboon, The. Belloc.
Theology of Bongwi, the Baboon, The. Campbell.

Babylon
Babylon. *Fr.* The Impious Feast. Landor.
Babylon. Hodgson.
Festival, The. *Fr.* The Impious Feast. Landor.

Baby-sitting
Babysitters, The. Plath.
Misnomer. Merriam.

Bacchus
Bacchus's Opinion of Wine, and Other Beverages. *Fr.* Bacchus in Tuscany. Redi.
Drinking Song, A. *Fr.* Antony and Cleopatra. Shakespeare.
Evoe! Thomas.
Great Bacchus: From the Greek. Prior.
Hymn to Bacchus, A. Herrick.

Bach, Johann Sebastian
Dream. Moore.
Jesu, Joy of Man's Desiring. Fitzgerald.
Living Room, The. Schnackenberg.
Theme and Variation. De Vries.

Bachelors
After the Ball Is Over. Harris.
Bachelor's Hall. Finley.
Bachelor's Life, A. *Unknown.*
Bachelor's Song, The. Flatman.
Burial of the Bachelor, The. *Unknown.*
I Don't Let the Girls Worry My Mind. *Unknown.*
Two Old Bachelors, The. Lear.
Where the Single Men Go in Summer. Bourne.

Backs
Saints Lose Back. Willard.

Bacon, Sir Francis
Sir Francis Bacon. Bierce.

Bacteria
Supremacy of Bacteria, The. Frazier.
World of Bacteria. Hagiwara.

Badgers
Badger. Clare.
Badgers, The. Heaney.
Catch, The. Ghiselin.
Grip, The. Kennelly.
Six Badgers, The. Graves.

Bagels
Bagel, The. Ignatow.

Baggage
In the Baggage Room at Greyhound. Ginsberg.

Bagpipes
Life and Death of the Piper of Kilbarchan, The. Carew.
Pipes at Lucknow, The. Whittier.

Bahamas
Bahamas. Oppen.

Baker, Josephine
So Many Feathers. Cortez.

Balaam
Balaam. Keble.

Balaclava, Crimea
Charge of the Light Brigade, The. Tennyson.

Baldness
Bald Cavalier, The. *Unknown.*
Of Kate's Baldness. Davies of Hereford.
Penalties of Baldness, The. Seaman.

Baldwin, James
For James Baldwin. Boyle.

Ballads and Folk Songs
American Folk Poetry; an Anthology (AmFP). Duncan Emrich, ed.
American Songbag, The (AS). Carl Sandburg, ed.
Ballad Book, The (BaBo). MacEdward Leach, ed.
Common Muse, The; an Anthology of Popular British Ballad Poetry, XVth-XXth Century (CoMu). Vivian de Sola Pinto *and* Allan Edwin Rodway, eds.
Cowboy Songs and Other Frontier Ballads (CoSo). John A. *and* Alan Lomax, eds.
English and Scottish Ballads (EnSB). Robert Graves, ed.
English and Scottish Popular Ballads (ESPB). Helen Child Sargent *and* George Lyman Kittredge, eds.
Faber Book of Ballads, The (FaBoBa). Matthew Hodgart, ed.
Folksinger's Wordbook (FSW). Irwin *and* Fred Silber, eds.
Home Book of Verse, The (HBV-2), pp. 2641-2834. Burton Egbert Stevenson, ed.
Our Singing Country (OuSiCo). John *and* Alan Lomax, eds.
Oxford Book of Ballads, The (OxBB). James Kinsley, ed.
Oxford Book of English Traditional Verse, The (OBET). Frederick Woods, ed.
Oxford Book of Scottish Verse, The (OxBS). John MacQueen *and* Tom Scott, comps.
Treasury of American Song, A (TrAS). Olin Downes *and* Elie Siegmeister, comps.
Viking Book of Folk Ballads of the English-speaking World, The (ViBoFo). Albert B. Friedman, ed.
See also **Blues (Music); Sea Chanteys.**

Ballet
Ballet. Kaplan.
For the Record. Blount.
I cannot dance upon my toes. Dickinson.
In the Sitting Room of the Opera. Cannady.
Pediment: Ballet. Nicholl.
Song of the Ballet. Morton.

Balloons
Air Balloon, The. *Fr.* Aerophorion. Pye.
Armadillo, The. Bishop.
Balloon, The. Kuskin.
Balloon Faces. Sandburg.
Balloon Man, The. Aldis.
Balloon Man, The. Fyleman.
Balloon Man. North.
Balloons. Plath.
Les Ballons. Wilde.
Pop. McFadden.
Tragedy. Spargur.

Ballrooms
Armadillo, The. Bishop.

Balls
Lost Ball, The. Mitchell.

Baltic Sea
Battle of the Baltic, The. Campbell.

Baltimore, Maryland
First Precinct Fourth Ward. Epstein.
Incident. Cullen.
Streets of Baltimore. *Unknown.*

Bamboo
Bamboo. Plomer.

Bananas
Banana. Bell.
Banana. Mitchell.

Bancroft, George
Decanter of Madeira, A. Mitchell

Bandits
Bandit. Klein.
See also **Crime and Criminals; Highwaymen.**

Bands
Band, The. Dennis.
Band Played On, The. Palmer.
High School Band, The. Whittemore.

Bangkok, Thailand
Bangkok. Scott.

Banjos
Banjo, The. Winner.
Banjo Player, The. Johnson.
Fust Banjo, De. Russell.
Mama Don't 'Low. *Unknown.*
Song of the Banjo, The. Kipling.

Banking and Bankers
Banks of Marble. Rice.
Girls Working in Banks. Shapiro.
Goody O'Grumpity. Brink.

Plot to Assassinate the Chase Manhattan Bank, The. Larsen.
See also **Financiers.**
Bannockburn, Battle of (1314)
Bannockburn. *Fr.* The Lord of the Isles. Scott.
Battle of Bannockburn, The. *Fr.* The Bruce. Barbour.
Scots Wha Hae. Burns.
Baptism
Baptism. Bell.
Baptism. Nowlan.
Holy Baptism. Herbert.
Jesus, Master, O Discover. *Unknown.*
My Baptismal Birthday. Coleridge.
On the Baptized Ethiopian. Crashaw.
Bar Kokba, Simon
Bar Kochba. Lazarus.
Bar Mitzvah
Bar Mitzvah. Goldemberg.
Bar Mitzvah. Orlen.
Barbecues. *See* **Picnics and Barbecues.**
Barberries
Barberry-Bush, The. Very.
Barbers
Ballad of a Barber, The. Beardsley.
Barber, barber, shave a pig. Mother Goose.
Barber's, The. De la Mare.
Barber's Clippers. Baruch.
Barbershop. Gardner.
For the Barbers. Oppenheimer.
Lyric Barber. Romano.
Maestro's Barber Shop, The. Vásquez.
To a Child Trapped in a Barber Shop. Levine.
To My Hairdresser. St. Leger.
Bards
Bard, The. *Fr.* Songs of Experience. Blake.
Bard, The. Gray.
Bard of Armagh, The. *Unknown.*
Bards, The. Graves.
Good Tradition, The. *Unknown.*
O Black and Unknown Bards. Johnson.
On the Breaking-up of a School. O'Huiginn.
Were Not the Gael Fallen. O'Mulconry.
Who Will Buy a Poem? O'Heffernan.
Barebone, Praise-God
Praise-God Barebones. Cortissoz.
Barley
Ripe and Bearded Barley, The. *Unknown.*
Barmaids
Glass of Beer, A. Stephens.
Barns
Barn, The. Berry.
Barn, The. Blunden.
Barn, The. Heaney.
Barn, The. Spender.
Barn, The. Thomas.
Barn in Winter, The. MacIntosh.
Byre. MacCaig.
Hay Scuttle. Morgan.
Human Things. Nemerov.
When These Old Barns Lost Their Inhabitants. Kherdian.
Barons' War (1263-1267)
Against the Barons' Enemies. *Unknown.*
Baroque
Baroque Comment. Bogan.
Barrel Organs. *See* **Hurdy-Gurdies.**
Barry, Kevin
Kevin Barry. Ward.
Bars
D-Y Bar. Welch.
Indian Guys at the Bar. Ortiz.
Indian Macho. Oliver.
Barters
Barter. Teasdale.
Barth, Karl
On the Death of Karl Barth. Clemo.
Baseball
Abominable Baseball Bat, The. Kennedy.
And You Are There. Clark.
At the Ball Game. Williams.
Ball Game. Eberhart.
Ballad of Dead Yankees, The. Petersen.
Ballgame, The. Baraka.
Base Stealer, The. Francis.
Baseball. Sherman.
Baseball and Classicism. Clark.
Baseball and Writing. Moore.
Baseball Pitcher. Kuykendall.
Baseball's Sad Lexicon. Adams.
Casey at the Bat. Thayer.
Casey's Revenge. Wilson.
Casey—Twenty Years Later. McDonald.
Catch. Francis.
Cobb Would Have Caught It. Fitzgerald.
Don Larsen's Perfect Game. Goodman.
Double Play, The. Wallace.
Double-Header. Stone.
Dream of a Baseball Star. Corso.
Fan. Lew.
From the Batter's Box. Harford.
Hometown Piece for Messrs. Alston and Reese. Moore.
July the First. Currie.
Lady Pitcher, The. Macdonald.
Little-League Baseball Fan. Moses.
Mantle. Heyen.
Mixed Media. Schevill.
My Father Dreams of Baseball. Lieberman.
Of Kings and Things. Morrison.
Old-fashioned Pitcher, The. Phair.
One to Nothing. Kizer.
Pitcher. Francis.
Poem for Ed "Whitey" Ford, A. Holden.
Polo Grounds. Humphries.
Post Card out of Panama, A. Barney.
Roundhouse Voices, The. Smith.
Sign for My Father, Who Stressed the Bunt. Bottoms.
Slide, Kelly, Slide. Kelly.
Spitballer. Chappell.
Take Me Out to the Ball Game. Norworth.
Tao in the Yankee Stadium Bleachers. Updike.
To a Baseball. *Unknown.*
To Bert Campaneris. Clark.
To Satch. Allen.
Two Hopper. Ikan.
Umpire, The. Gibson.
Where, O Where? Bracker.
Basketball
Basketball. Giovanni.
Basketball. Lewisohn.
Basketball. Vincent.
Basketball Star. Fufuka.
Charge. Gilbert.
Ex-Basketball Player. Updike.
Fernando ("Fernando has a basketball"). Ridlon.
Foul Shot. Hoey.
In Memory of the Utah Stars. Matthews.
Jump Shooter, The. Trudell.
Mismatch. Lindner.
Patrick Ewing Takes a Foul Shot. Ackerman.
Poet Tries to Turn In His Jock, The. Hilton.
Bass, Sam
Sam Bass. *Unknown.*
Bastille Day
14 July 1956. Lerner.
Bath, England
At the Roman Baths. Lucie-Smith.
If to the Pump Room in the morn we go. *Fr.* The Diseases of Bath; a Satire. *Unknown.*
Letter Containing a Panegyric on Bath. *Fr.* The New Bath Guide. Anstey.
Baths and Bathing
Ballant o' the Laird's Bath, The. Young.
Bath, The. Graham.
Bath, The. Snyder.
Bathtubs. Lattimore.
Delicate Impasse, A. Atchity.
Friday Night after Bathing. Levy.
Gloire de Dijon. Lawrence.
Hammam Name, The. Flecker.
I Wonder What It Feels Like to Be Drowned? Graves.
In a Warm Bath. Rakosi.
In the Tub We Soak Our Skin. Horn.
Miss Twye. Ewart.
My Mother Takes a Bath. Kageyama.
Old Man, the Sweat Lodge. George.
Pater's Bathe. Parry.

Soap, the Oppressor. Johnson.
Sweat, The. NorthSun.
That Old Sauna High. Hollo.
Voyage of Jimmy Poo, The. Emanuel.
Washing My Son. Holden.
Washing. Drinkwater.

Bathsheba
Bethsabe's Song. *Fr.* David and Bethsabe. Peele.

Bats
Bat, The. Jacobs.
Bat. Lawrence.
Bat, The. Nash.
Bat, The. Pitter.
Bat, The. Roethke.
Bat, The. Spear.
Bat and the Scientist, The. Bigelow.
Bat is dun, with wrinkled wings, The. Dickinson.
Bats, The. Hillyer.
Bats. Jarrell.
Intruder, The. Kizer.
Mad Hatter's Song, The. *Fr.* Alice's Adventures in Wonderland. "Carroll."
Man and Bat. Lawrence.
Mind. Wilbur.
Seven Mexican Children. Schmidt.

Battlefields
All That Is Left. Basho.
At Vshchizh. Tyutchev.
Battle of Blenheim, The. Southey.
Battlefield. Aldington.
Battle-Field, The. Bryant.
Concord Hymn. Emerson.
Grass. Sandburg.
Hunting Civil War Relics at Nimblewell Creek. Dickey.
In Flanders Fields. McCrae.
Inscription for Marye's Heights, Fredericksburg. Melville
No Man's Land. Bogle.
On a Field at Fredericksburg. Smith.
On a World War Battlefield. Clark.
On the Spartan Dead at Thermopylae. Simonides.
Remembering That Island. McGrath.
Shiloh; a Requiem. Melville.
Sleeper in the Valley, The. *Fr.* Eighteen-seventy. Rimbaud.
They Will Look for a Few Words. Turner.
Vergissmeinnicht. Douglas.

Battles. *See under name, e.g.,* **Bunker Hill, Battle of**

Baucis and Philemon
Philemon and Baucis. *Fr.* Metamorphoses. Ovid.
Then Lelex rose, an old experienc'd man. *Fr.* Metamorphoses. Ovid.

Baudelaire, Charles
Ave atque Vale. Swinburne.
Baudelaire. Schwartz.
Baudelaire in Brussels. Cronin.

Bavaria
Hohenlinden. Campbell.
Lines on Leaving a Scene in Bavaria. Campbell.
Munich Elegy No. 1. Barker.
Nuremburg. Longfellow.
Sonnet in a Pass of Bavaria. Trench.

Bay Trees. *See* **Laurels.**

Bayous
Down the Bayou. Townsend.
Shooting Ducks in South Louisiana. Tillinghast.

Beaches
Above the fresh ruffles of the surf. *Fr.* Voyages. Crane.
Afternoon: Amagansett Beach. Wheelock.
Afternoon at Cannes. Davis.
Amagansett Beach Revisited. Wheelock.
At Dieppe: On the Beach. Symons.
At the Slackening of the Tide. Wright.
Beach in August, The. Kees.
Beach Talk. MacCaig.
Burial in the Sand. Sullivan.
Children, the Sandbar, That Summer. Rukeyser.
Concerning Unnatural Nature: An Inverted Form. Summers.
Constant, The. Ammons.
Dover Beach. Arnold.
Driving to the Beach. Cole.
East Anglian Bathe. Betjeman.
German Shepherd. Livingston.
Hot Day and Human Nature, The. Johnston.
Littoral. Flax.
Miramar Beach. Cunningham.
Night on the Shore. Stopes.
On the beach/ a big dog lies. Hill.
On the Beach at Night. Whitman.
On the Beach at Night Alone. Whitman.
On the Marginal Way. Wilbur.
Point Shirley. Plath.
Prospect Beach. Lipsitz.
Rookery. Davenhaver.
Sandpiper, The. Thaxter.
Skin Divers, The. Starbuck.
Sleeping at the Beach. Burt.
Son and Surf. Strong.
Strand, The. MacNeice.
Summer Beach. Cornford.
Sunny. Vander Molen.
Waking from a Nap on the Beach. Swenson.
Watch Hill. Scott.
With Kit, Age 7, at the Beach. Stafford.

Beagles
Beagles. Rodgers.
On the Death of Echo. Coleridge.

Bean, Judge Roy
Fine! Barker.
Law West of the Pecos, The. Barker.
Roy Bean. *Unknown.*

Beards
Father's Whiskers. *Unknown.*
There Was an Old Man with a Beard. Lear.
To shave, or not to shave? that is the question. Croker.

Bears
Adventures of Isabel. Nash.
Bad Example. Fey.
Bear, The. Frost.
Bear, The. Hughes.
Bear, The. Kinnell.
Bear, The. Momaday.
Bear, The. Stanford.
Bear Hunting. Aua.
Bear on the Delhi Road, The. Birney.
Bear Who Came to Dinner, The. Stoutenburg.
Bears. Rich.
Brown Bear, The. Austin.
Dancing Bear, The. Field.
Dancing Bear, The. Southey.
Dino Campana and the Bear. Hirsch.
Elizabeth's War with the Christmas Bear. Dubie.
Ephraim the Grizzly. Guiterman.
Furry Bear. Milne.
Grandpa Bear's Lullaby. Yolen.
Grizzly. Harte.
Grizzly Bear. Austin.
Grizzly Bear. *Unknown.*
In Love with the Bears. Kuzma.
Infant Innocence. Housman.
Lady and the Bear, The. Roethke.
Lines Written by a Bear of Very Little Brain. Milne.
Lost Silvertip. Reed.
Meeting a Bear. Wagoner.
Part of the Darkness. Gardner.
Self-Portrait, as a Bear. Hall.
Squaring the Circle. Coxe.
Truro Bear, The. Oliver.
Willy. Moore.

Beatniks
Problem in Social Geometry—the Inverted Square! Durem.

Beatrice Portinari
Sonnet: "Last All Saints' holy-day, even now gone by." Dante.

Beaumont, Francis
Epitaph upon My Dear Brother, Francis Beaumont, An. Beaumont.
On Mr. Francis Beaumont (Then Newly Dead). Corbet.
To Francis Beaumont. Jonson.

Beaumont, Sir George
Elegiac Stanzas, Suggested by a Picture of Peele Castle, in a Storm. Wordsworth.

Beauty
Ah Cloris! That I Now Could Sit. *Fr.* The Mulberry Garden. Sedley.
Alabama. Fields.
Ask Me No More Where Jove Bestows. Carew.
Barbie Doll. Piercy.
Barter. Teasdale.
Beautiful. Bixler.

Beautiful Changes, The. Wilbur.
Beautiful Things. Allerton.
Beautiful Woman Who Sings, The. Allen.
Beautifull Mistress, A. Carew.
Beauty. Binyon.
Beauty. Cowley.
Beauty. E-Yeh-Shure'.
Beauty. Rosenberg.
Beauty. *Fr.* An Hymne in Honour of Beautie. Spenser.
Beauty. *Fr.* The Passionate Pilgrim. *Unknown.*
Beauty. Whitman.
Beauty and Terror. Harford.
Beauty as a Shield. Robinson.
Beauty Extoll'd. *Unknown.*
Beauty I Would Suffer For. Piercy.
Beauty Imposes. Neilson.
Beauty Is Ever to the Lonely Mind. Nathan.
Beauty of Things, The. Jeffers.
Beauty, sweet Love, is like the morning dew. *Fr.* To Delia. Daniel.
Beauty—what is it? A perfume without name. *Fr.* Epitaph for the Poet V. Ficke.
Beauty's Hands Are Cool. Baker.
Behold, O Aspasia! I Send You Verses. *Fr.* Pericles and Aspasia. Landor.
Believe Me, If All Those Endearing Young Charms. Moore.
Bonnie Lesley. Burns.
Brittle Beauty. Surrey.
Brown Beauty, The. Herbert of Cherbury.
Brown Is My Love. *Unknown.*
Changeful Beauty. *Unknown.*
Clarinda's Indifference at Parting with Her Beauty. Winchilsea.
Cold Term. Baraka.
Colours of Love, The. Devlin.
Commendations of Mistress Jane Scrope, The. *Fr.* Phyllup Sparrowe. Skelton.
Common Blessings. Clark.
Craftsman, The. Christian.
Dandelions. Nemerov.
Death's Warning to Beauty. *Unknown.*
Defiance, The. Flatman.
Definition of Beauty, The. Herrick.
Delight in Disorder. Herrick.
Description of Beauty, A. Daniel.
Divinely Superfluous Beauty. Jeffers.
Do Not, Oh, Do Not Prize. *Unknown.*
Each and All. Emerson.
Elegy, to an Old Beauty, An. Parnell.
Enjoy Thy April Now. *Fr.* A Description of Beauty. Daniel.
Epigram: "Beauty, a silver dew that falls in May." *Unknown.*
Euclid Alone Has Looked on Beauty Bare. Millay.
Fancy from Fontenelle, A. Dobson.
For Beauty kissed your lips when they were young. *Fr.* Epitaph for the Poet V. Ficke.
For Them All. Wheelock.
Frailty of Beauty, The. *Fr.* Alcilia. "J. C."
Give Beauty All Her Right. Campion.
Glory, The. Thomas.
Go, Lovely Rose! Waller.
Great Breath, The. "Æ."
Green-Sickness Beauty, The. Herbert of Cherbury.
Harvest of Time, The. Pulsifer.
Hen and the Oriole, The. Marquis.
Holy Poet, I have heard. *Fr.* Thanks from Earth to Heaven. Wheelock.
Hymn to Intellectual Beauty. Shelley.
I died for beauty—but was scarce. Dickinson.
I Love All Beauteous Things. Bridges.
Immortal, The. Pickthall.
Independence Day. Smith.
Ingratefull Beauty Threatened. Carew.
Inner Man, The. Plato.
It is ordained—or so Politian said. *Fr.* Epitaph for the Poet V. Ficke.
Judith of Bethulia. Ransom.
July 31. Jordan.
Lady's Dressing Room, The. Swift.
Lonely Beauty. *Fr.* The Complaint of Rosamond. Daniel.
Lord, I have not time to pray. *Fr.* Impiety. Magaret.
Lord of the Far Horizons. Carman.
Loveliness. *Fr.* Hymns for the Amusement of Children. Smart.
Madrigal: "Like the Idalian Queene." Drummond of Hawthornden.
Melissa. Marquis.
Merciles Beaute. Chaucer.
Minority, The: 1917. O'Rourke.
Modern Beauty. Symons.
Moment Musicale. Carman.
My mistress' eyes are nothing like the sun. Sonnets, CXXX. Shakespeare.
No Images. Cuney.
No Second Troy. Yeats.
Nonpareil. Prior.
O Love, That Dost with Goodness Crown. Chadwick.
Ode on a Grecian Urn. Keats.
Ode to Beauty. Emerson.
Of Beauty. Fanshawe.
Of Dying Beauty. Zukofsky.
Old Lady's Lament for Her Youth, The. Villon.
On Lucy Countesse of Bedford. Jonson.
Peculiar ghost!—great and immortal ghost! *Fr.* Epitaph for the Poet V. Fike.
Peter Quince at the Clavier. Stevens.
Pied Beauty. Hopkins.
Poem, or Beauty Hurts Mr. Vinal. Cummings.
Poet Recognizing the Echo of the Voice, A. Wakoski.
Prayer, A: "Each day I walk with wonder." Scollard.
Prayer: "Lord, make me sensitive to the sight." Marr.
Prelude: "This is not you? These phrases are not you?" Aiken.
Primer of Plato. Garrigue.
Progress of Beauty, The. Swift.
Quatrains: "Noe more unto my thoughts appeare." Godolphin.
Question in a Field. Bogan.
Rhodora, The. Emerson.
Saturday: The Small-Pox. *Fr.* Six Town Eclogues. Montagu.
Say Not That Beauty. Flower.
Scribe, The. De la Mare.
Shall I compare thee to a summer's day? Sonnets, XVIII. Shakespeare.
She Walks in Beauty. Byron.
Song, A: "In the air there are no coral/ Reefs or ambergris." Scott.
Song, A: "It is not Beauty I demand." Darley.
Song: "Oh fair sweet face, oh eyes celestial bright." *Fr.* Women Pleased. Fletcher.
Sonnet: "Of thee, kind boy, I ask no red and white." Suckling.
Sonnet: "Tell me no more how fair she is." King.
Sonnet of Black Beauty. Herbert of Cherbury.
Star, The. Weaving.
Stella's Birthday. Swift.
Stolen Pleasure. Drummond of Hawthornden.
Study in Aesthetics, The. Pound.
There are many who think of Quintia in terms of beauty. Catullus.
Thing of Beauty, A. *Fr.* Endymion. Keats.
Thou Art Not Fair. Campion.
Time stands still, with gazing on her face! *Unknown.*
Tinder, The. Carew.
To a Very Beautiful Lady. Todd.
To a Young Beauty. Yeats.
To Cynthia, on Concealment of Her Beauty. Kynaston.
To Dianeme ("Sweet, be not proud of those two eyes"). Herrick.
To Helen. Poe.
To His Friend, Promising That Though Her Beauty Fade, Yet His Love Shall Last. Turberville.
To me, fair friend, you never can be old. Sonnets, CIV. Shakespeare.
To the Most Beautiful Lady, the Lady Bridget Manners. Barnes.
To the Queen, Entertain'd at Night by the Countess of Anglesey. Davenant.
True Beauty. Beaumont.
True Beauty, The. Carew.
'Twas at that hour of beauty when the setting sun. *Fr.* The Testament of Beauty. Bridges.
Unusual Things. Hennen.
Unutterable Beauty, The. Studdert-Kennedy.
Upon Her Feet. Herrick.
Upon the Nipples of Julia's Breast. Herrick.
Valentine for a Lady, A. Lucilius.
Wayfarer, The. Pearse.
When in the chronicle of wasted time. Sonnets, CVI. Shakespeare.
Who Walks with Beauty. Morton.
Wishes to His Supposed Mistresse. Crashaw.
Woman's Beauty. *Fr.* Vashti. Abercrombie.

Beauty and the Beast
Mythics. Chasin.

Beauty Parlors
To a Talkative Hairdresser. McGinley.

Beavers
Beaver's Story, The. Watkins.
See also **Mountain Beaver.**

Bedrooms
Country Bedroom, The. Cornford.
Beds
Ah bed! the field where joy's peace some do see. *Fr.* Astrophel and Stella. Sidney.
Bed, The. Shapiro.
Bed Time. Davison.
Bed without a Woman, A. Souster.
Cot, The. Amen.
For the Bed at Kelmscott. Morris.
Formed long ago, yet made to-day. Mother Goose.
Insomnia the Gem of the Ocean. Updike.
Land of Counterpane, The. Stevenson.
My Bed Is a Boat. Stevenson.
Sleepin' at the Foot o' the Bed. Patrick.
These are the beds. *Fr.* The Bed Book. Plath.
Translation of Lines by Benserade. Johnson.
Beech Trees
Beech, The. Young.
Beech Tree's Petition, The. Campbell.
Beecher, Henry Ward
Henry Ward Beecher. Phelps.
Beef
"But hark! a sound is stealing on my ear." *Fr.* Beer. Calverley.
Roast Beef of Old England, The. *Fr.* Don Quixote in England. Fielding.
Song in Praise of Old English Roast Beef, A. Leveridge.
Beer
Ballad of Lager Bier, The. Stedman.
Beer. Arnold.
Beer. Calverley.
Glass of Beer, A. Stephens.
Hermit Hoar. Johnson.
Lilliputian's Beer Song. Winner.
Man That Waters the Workers' Beer, The. Ryan.
Quartermaster Store, The. *Unknown.*
Under the Anheuser Bush. Sterling.
Wine upon beer, I counsel thee. *Unknown.*
Bees
Against Idleness and Mischief. Watts.
Animal, Vegetable and Mineral. Bogan.
Arrival of the Bee Box, The. Plath.
As I went over Tipple Tyne. *Unknown.*
As I went owre the Hill o' Hoos. *Unknown.*
Bee, The. Dickey.
Bee, The. Fandel.
Bee, The. *Fr.* Sir Francis Drake. Fitzgeffry.
Bee. Kennedy.
Bee and the Petunia, The. Hoskins.
Bee Song. Sandburg.
Bee, the Ant, and the Sparrow, The. Cotton.
Bee Wassail. *Unknown.*
Bee-Wisp, The. Turner.
Beehive. Toomer.
Beekeeper's Dream, The. Lorr.
Bees, The. Gibbon.
Bees, The. Ridge.
Bees and Monks. *Fr.* King Arthur and His Round Table. Frere.
Bees Awater. Morgan.
Bees of Middleton Manor, The. Probyn.
Bumble Bee. Brown.
Butterfly and the Bee, The. Bowles.
Care of Bees, The. *Fr.* The Georgics. Virgil.
Cruelty. Hummer.
Daventry Wonder, The. "Agricola."
Dido: Swarming. Spivack.
Falling Asleep in a Garden. Wagoner.
Flesh-Fly and the Bee, The. Patmore.
Flowers. Behn.
Fuscara; or, The Bee Errant. Cleveland.
Honey Bee, The. Marquis.
Honey Bee. Perkins.
Humble-Bee, The. Emerson.
Invitation to the Bee. Smith.
Julius Caesar and the Honey-Bee. Turner.
Legend of the Hive, A. Hawker.
Like trains of cars on tracks of plush. Dickinson.
Little Busy Bee. Watts.
Mantova. Wright.
March Bee, The. Blunden.
More Ancient Mariner, A. Carman.
Near Dusk. Auslander.
Observation of a Bee. Goldberg.
On a Honey Bee. Freneau.
Opportunity. Graham.
Pedigree of honey, The. Dickinson.
Some Kind of Giant. Pritchard.
Song: "What binds the atom together." Dow.
Song of the Queen Bee. White.
Summer Night in the Beehive, A. Turner.
Swarm of bees in May, A. *Unknown.*
Swarming Bees, The. Laughlin.
Telling the Bees. Reese.
Telling the Bees. Whittier.
There Was an Old Man in a Tree. Lear.
To a Honey Bee. Freneau
Venerable Bee, The. Klein.
Virgil: Georgics, Book IV. Schmitz.
Wild Bees. Baxter.
Young bee falls between my window, A. *Fr.* Brother Jonathan, Brother Kafka. O'Sullivan.
Beethoven, Ludwig van
Beethoven. Wheelock.
Beethoven's Death Mask. Spender.
Composer's Winter Dream, The. Dubie.
Higgledy-piggledy/ Ludwig van Beethoven. Seaman.
Ninth Symphony of Beethoven Understood at Last as a Sexual Message, The. Rich.
On Hearing a Symphony of Beethoven. Millay.
Wrath. Hollander.
Beetles
Beetle Bemused. Lister.
Beetle on the Shasta Daylight. Kaufman.
Clickbeetle. Hoberman.
Dusty black beetle, A. Sund.
Eagle and the Beetle, The. La Fontaine.
I knew a black beetle, who lived down a drain. *Fr.* Nursery Rhymes for the Tender-hearted. Morley.
Shrilling locust slowly sheathes, The. *Fr.* The Beetle. Riley.
Wee man o' leather. *Unknown.*
Begging and Beggars
A-Begging Buttermilk I Will Go. *Unknown.*
Beggar, The. Moss.
Beggar. Parra.
Beggar, The. *Unknown.*
Beggar Boy, The. Alexander.
Beggar Man, The. Aikin.
Beggar Woman, The. King.
Beggars. Davidson.
Beggars Are Coming to Town. *Unknown.*
Beggar's Song. Orr.
Black Soldier Remembers, A. Coleman.
Blind Old Woman. Major.
Bonner's Ferry Beggar. Clark.
Cante Hondo. Kay.
Dives and Lazarus. *Unknown.*
Gaberlunzie Man, The. *Unknown.*
Glass of Beer, A. Stephens.
Grab-Bag. Jackson.
Happy Beggarman, The. *Unknown.*
Hark, hark! The dogs do bark. Mother Goose.
In Praise of a Beggar's Life. "A. W."
Jolly Beggar, The. *At. to* James V of Scotland.
Jolly Beggars, The. Burns.
Loving Mad Tom. *Unknown.*
Maunding Souldier, The; or, The Fruits of Warre Is Beggery. *Unknown.*
Merry Jovial Beggar, The. Casey.
Nothing but Image. Swilky.
Old Cumberland Beggar, The. Wordsworth.
On a Fair Beggar. Ayres.
Souling Song. *Unknown.*
See also **Homeless, the; Vagabonds.**
Beiderbecke, Bix
In a Mist. Young.
Belfast, Northern Ireland
Afterlives. Mahon.
Ballad to a Traditional Refrain. Craig.
Belgium
Antwerp: Musée des Beaux-Arts. Ross
Belfry of Bruges, The. Longfellow.
Bells of Ostend, The. Bowles.
Belgrade, Yugoslavia
Siege of Belgrade, The. *Unknown, at. to* Watts.

Belief. *See* **Faith.**
Belisarius
Belisarius. Longfellow.
Bell, Alexander Graham
Alexander Graham Bell Did Not Invent the Telephone. Coffin.
Graham Bell and the Photophone. Montgomery.
Bellbirds
Bell-Birds. Kendall.
Belloc, Hilaire
Hilaire Belloc. Wolfe.
Bells
Balsham Bells. Prescot.
Before the Anaesthetic. Betjeman.
Bega. Pickthall.
Belfry, The. Binyon.
Belfry of Bruges, The. Longfellow.
Bell Speech. Wilbur.
Bell Too Heavy to Ring. Kryss.
Bell Tower. Adams.
Bells, The. Poe.
Bells. Scott.
Bells of London, The. *Unknown.*
Bells of Ostend, The. Bowles.
Bells of Peace, The. Fisher.
Bells of Shandon, The. Mahony.
Bells of Alderburnham, The. Barnes.
Bredon Hill. *Fr.* A Shropshire Lad. Housman.
Broken Tower, The. Crane.
Catholic Bells, The. Williams.
Chanson of the Bells of Oseney. Rice.
Chimes. Meynell.
Christchurch Bells. *Unknown.*
Christmas Bells. Longfellow.
Church Bell in the Night, The. *Unknown.*
Jingle Bells. Pierpont.
Merry Are the Bells. *Unknown.*
Mission Bells of Monterey, The. Harte.
Oxford Bells. Sister Maris Stella.
Passing Bell, The. Shirley.
Ring Out, Wild Bells. *Fr.* In Memoriam A. H. H. Tennyson.
Ringing the Bells. Sexton.
School-Bell. Farjeon.
Sea Bells. Eberhart.
Sleigh Bells at Night. Coatsworth.
To My Father. Curtis.
Belshazzar
Belshazzar's Feast. Bible, *O.T., Fr.* Daniel.
Vision of Belshazzar, The. Byron.
Ben Bulben, Ireland
Deserted Mountain, The. *Unknown.*
Under Ben Bulben. Yeats.
Benbow, Admiral John
Death of Admiral Benbow, The. *Unknown.*
Bennington, Battle of
Riflemen at Bennington, The. *Unknown.*
Bentley, Edmund Clerihew
Edmund Clerihew Bentley. Smith.
Instead of blushing cherry hue. M. Laing.
Beowulf
Beowulf. Amis.
Beowulf. Wilbur.
Bergman, Ingmar
Ingmar Bergman's "Seventh Seal." Duncan.
Berkeley, George
Fountain, The. Davie.
Berkshire, England
Laleham: Matthew Arnold's Grave. Johnson.
Berkshire Hills, Massachusetts
Monument Mountain. Bryant.
Whole Duty of Berkshire Brooks, The. Conkling.
Bermuda
Battel of the Summer-Islands, The. Waller.
Bermuda Suite. Scott.
Bermudas. Marvell.
Berrigan, Daniel
For Dan Berrigan. Knight.
Berryman, John
For John Berryman, I. Lowell.
Ode: "Mistah Berrybones, you daid?" Zaranka.
Tropisms on John Berryman. Vizenor.
Winter's Edge. Roberts.
Bertrand de Born
Near Périgord. Pound.
Sestina: Altaforte. Pound.
Bethe, Hans
Concept of Force, The. Sargent.
Bethlehem
Bethlehem. Canton.
Christmas Morning. Roberts.
How Far Is It to Bethlehem? Chesterton.
Long, Long Ago. *Unknown.*
O Little Town of Bethlehem. Brooks.
Bethune, Mary McLeod
For Mary McLeod Bethune. Walker.
Betjeman, Sir John
Betjeman at the Post Office. Sharpless.
Betjeman, 1984. Causley.
Betrayal
Ballad of Hell, A. Davidson.
New Calf, The. Hearst.
Vow-Breaker, The. King.
Yet Each Man Kills the Thing He Loves. *Fr.* The Ballad of Reading Gaol. Wilde.
Biafra. *See* **Civil War, Nigerian.**
Bialik, Hayyim Nahman
Harangue on the Death of Hayyim Nahman Bialik. Tiempo.
Bible
Anvil of God's Word, The. Clifford.
Apocrypha. Kennedy.
Art of Poetry, An. McAuley.
Believe the Bible. Simpson.
Best of All, The. Crosby.
Bible is an antique volume, The. Dickinson.
Bible, The. Stroud.
Bible, The. Traherne.
Bit of the Book, A. Sangster.
Book of Books, The. *Fr.* The Monastery. Scott.
Book of Kells, The. Nemerov.
Book Our Mothers Read, The. Whittier.
Book, The. Garrison.
Colenso Rhymes for Orthodox Children. Harte.
From a London Bookshop. *Unknown.*
God's Precepts Perfect. Bible, *O.T., Fr.* Psalm XIX.
God's Treasure. "A. M. N."
Gospel According to You, The. *Unknown.*
H. Scriptures, The. Herbert.
H. Scriptures. Vaughan.
Holy Bible, Book Divine. Burton.
Home without a Bible, A. Meigs.
Inscription on the Flyleaf of a Bible. Abse.
Just One Book. *Unknown.*
Just the Same To-Day. *Unknown.*
Little Song of Work, A. Sprouse.
My Bible and I. *Unknown.*
My Companion. Wesley.
My Mother's Bible. Morris.
My Old Bible. *Unknown.*
Names and Order of the Books of the Old Testament. *Unknown.*
New Testament, The. Russell.
O How Sweet Are Thy Words! Steele.
Of the Incomparable Treasure of the Scriptures. *Unknown.*
Old Bibles. Waniek.
Old Testament Contents. *Unknown.*
Old-Testament Gospel. Cowper.
Read the Bible Through. Wells.
Scriptures, The. *Fr.* Religio Laici. Dryden.
Thou, Zion, old and suffering. *Fr.* The Bible. Levi.
Word of God, The. Flint.
Word of God, The. Gwynne.
Word of God, Across the Ages. Blanchard.
Bicentennial, U. S.
Children Grown, The. Jackson.
Tall Poets, The. Smith.
Bicycles and Bicycling
Bicycle, The. Rice.
Bicycle Rider, The. Shapcott.
Cyclists, The. Kearney.
Daisy Bell. Dacre.
Different Bicycles. Baruch.
Going down Hill on a Bicycle. Beeching.
Gol-darned Wheel, The. *Unknown.*
To a Bicycle. *Unknown.*

Big Thompson Canyon, Colorado
Big Thompson Canon. Gower.
Bigamy
Moth and the Flame, The. Taggart.
There Was an Old Party of Lyme. *Unknown*
Those Wedding Bells Shall Not Ring Out! Rosenfeld.
Billboards
"Chew Mail Pouch." Klauck.
Song of the Open Road. Nash.
Billiards
Billiards. Blauner.
Billy the Kid (William H. Bonney)
Ballad of Billy the Kid, The. Knibbs.
Billy the Kid ("Billy was a bad man"). *Unknown.*
Billy the Kid ("I'll sing you a true song of Billy the Kid"). *Unknown.*
Billy the Kid or William H. Bonney. Thorp.
Pizen Pete's Mistake. Honey.
When Billy the Kid Rides Again. Barker.
Bingen, Germany
Bingen on the Rhine. Norton.
Biochemistry
Supremacy of Bacteria, The. Frazier.
See also **Bacteria; Genetic Engineering.**
Biography
Art of Biography, The. *Fr.* Clerihews. Bentley.
But now the dentist cannot die. Lang.
Birch Trees
Birch-Tree at Loschwitz, The. Levy.
Birch Trees. Moreland.
Birches. Frost.
Little Birches. Newsome.
Young Birch, A. Frost.
Bird Migration. *See* **Animal Migration.**
Birds
Aesthetic. Rosten.
Afternoon in a Tree. Sister Maris Stella.
All These Birds. Wilbur.
And every bird shew'd in his proper kind. *Fr.* The Owle. Drayton.
Answer to a Child's Question. Coleridge.
"As When Emotion Too Far Exceeds its Cause." Oden.
Balcony with Birds, A. Moss.
Be like the Bird. Hugo.
Beat Poem by an Academic Poet. Miller.
Belfast Lough. *Unknown.*
Bird, The. Hoffenstein.
Bird, The. Michelson.
Bird, The. Tagore.
Bird, The. Vaughan.
Bird came down the walk, A. Dickinson.
Bird Song. Hay.
Bird Song. Richards.
Bird with a Broken Wing, The. Butterworth.
Bird-witted. Moore.
Birds, The. Blake.
Birds. Jeffers.
Birds. Lawrence.
Birds. "Llywelyn."
Birds. Miller.
Birds. "O'Neill."
Birds, The. Posner.
Birds, The. Squire.
Birds, The. *Unknown.*
Birds All Singing. MacCaig.
Birds and Fishes. Jeffers.
Birds' Ball, The. Bardeen.
Birds in Spring. *Fr.* The Seasons: Spring. Thomson.
Birds in the Fens. *Fr.* Polyolbion. Drayton.
Bird's Nest, The. Drinkwater.
Birds of America, The. Broughton.
Birds of Killingworth, The. *Fr.* Tales of a Wayside Inn. Longfellow.
Blind Linnet, The. Buchanan.
Blinded Bird, The. Hardy.
Blue Booby, The. Tate.
Blue Jay, The. Lawrence.
Camouflage. Clampitt.
Canticle. Griffith.
Canticle to the Waterbirds, A. Everson.
Cape Ann. *Fr.* Landscapes. Eliot.
Cat and the Bird, The. Solomon.
Cedar Waxwing. Matchett.
Chaste Arabian Bird, The. Rochester.
Choir of Day, The. *Fr.* Milton. Blake.
Chough. Warner.
Come Not Near. Osborn.
Come Wary One. Manning-Sanders.
Coppersmith. Murphy.
Dawn. Bottomley.
Dead Bird, The. Young.
Death of a Bird. Silkin.
Death of the Bird, The. Hope.
Decoys, The. Auden.
Dipper, The. Hesketh.
Dissonance. Whitman.
Distances They Keep, The. Nemerov.
Dream, The. *Fr.* The Book of the Duchesse. Chaucer.
Duck, and Mallard first, the falconers onely sport, The. *Fr.* Poly-olbion. Drayton.
Educated Love Bird, The. Newell.
End of the Suitors, The. *Fr.* The Odyssey. Homer.
Extinct Birds. Wright.
Faithful Friend, The. Cowper.
Fate of Birds, The. Seib.
Firetail's Nest, The. Clare.
Flying Fish, II, The. Gray.
For Stephen Drawing Birds. Rogers.
Fossil. Blodgett.
Four Birds. *Unknown.*
Freaks of Fashion. Rossetti.
Garnishing the Aviary. Danner.
Great Scarf of Birds, The. Updike.
Green Rain. Webb.
I Point Out a Bird. Duval.
In Glencullen. Synge.
In Her Song She Is Alone. Swan.
In the Morning All Over. Stafford.
Introduction. *Fr.* The Testament of Beauty. Bridges.
Invitation. Behn.
Jackdaw of Rheims, The. "Ingoldsby."
Joe. McCord.
Joy of the Morning. Markham.
Lady Lost. Ransom.
Letters from a Father. Van Duyn.
Linnet in November, The. Palgrave.
Listener's Guide to the Birds, A. White.
Little Bird, The. *Unknown.*
Little Birds. Sternberg.
Little Morning Music, A. Schwartz.
Little Trotty Wagtail. Clare.
L'Oiseau Bleu. Coleridge.
Lonely-Bird, The. Morris.
Making of Birds, The. Tynan.
Minor Bird, A. Frost.
Mirrorment. Ammons.
My Little Bird. Bunyan.
My Little Birds. *Unknown.*
Nest Eggs. Stevenson.
Nesting Time. Stewart.
Never Again Would Birds' Song Be the Same. Frost.
Nine Birds. Cummings.
No Shop Does the Bird Use. Coatsworth.
No White Bird Sings. Ciardi.
O Bird, So Lovely. Golding.
October Redbreast, The. Meynell.
Old Man in the Park. Osborn.
On a Little Bird. Armstrong.
On an Indian Tomineios, the Least of Birds. Heyrick.
On the Death of Mrs. Throckmorton's Bullfinch. Cowper.
Ornithology in Florida. Guiterman.
Oven Bird, The. Frost.
Overtones. Percy.
Oystercatchers. Middleton.
Paradox: The Birds. Shapiro.
Passenger Pigeons. Morgan.
People Buy a Lot of Things. Wynne.
Poet to the Birds, The. Meynell.
Presentation of Two Birds to My Son, A. Wright.
Pretty Wantons. *Unknown.*
Princely eagle, and the soaring hawke, The. Wood.
Reincarnation (II). Dickey.
Rivals, The. Stephens.
Roaring Frost, The. Meynell.
Robert of Lincoln. Bryant.
Robin, Wren, Martin, Swallow. *Unknown.*
Rooks, The. *Unknown.*

Rose, The. Roethke.
Sand Martin. Clare.
Sea Bird, The. Douglas.
Sea Birds, The. Brock.
Seabirds. Smith.
Sea-Change. Masefield.
Season of Phantasmal Peace, The. Walcott.
Seed-Eaters, The. Francis.
Selfsame Song, The. Hardy.
Shore Birds. Gale.
Siege at Stony Point. Gregory.
Silver Bird of Herndyke Mill, The. Blunden.
Sing Little Bird. Hastings.
Sing On, Blithe Bird. Motherwell.
Sky Patterns. Maino.
Small Birds. Quennell.
Snow-Bird, The. Sherman.
Snowgoose. Allen.
Snowy Heron. Ciardi.
Somewhere Is Such a Kingdom. Ransom.
Sparrow in an Airport. Snyder.
Spring: The Love and the Birds. Allingham.
Still Life: Lady with Birds. Prettyman.
Storm-Cock's Song, The. "MacDiarmid."
Suggested by a Picture of the Bird of Paradise. Wordsworth.
Sympathy. Dunbar.
That Is All I Heard. "Yehoash."
Three Poems on Morris Graves' Paintings. Logan.
Throstle, The. Tennyson.
Titmouse. De la Mare.
To a Waterfowl. Bryant.
To the Man-of-War-Bird. Whitman.
To Waken an Old Lady. Williams.
Tomtit, The. De la Mare.
Trail of the Bird, The. Courthope.
Trico's Song. *Fr.* Alexander and Campaspe. Lyly.
Trouble-shooting. Stafford.
Truth, The. Davies.
Two Birds. Linnell.
Two Pewits. Thomas.
Unknown Bird, The. Thomas.
Up from the Egg: The Confessions of a Nuthatch Avoider. Nash.
Vacant Cage, The. Turner.
Vision of the Lamentation of Beulah over Ololon. *Fr.* Milton. Blake.
Waders and Swimmers. Plumly.
Water Fowl. Wordsworth.
Water-Ousel, The. Webb.
Waxwings. Francis.
What Does Little Birdie Say. Tennyson.
Widow Bird, A. Shelley.
Wind and the Bird, The. *Unknown.*
Windhover, The. Hopkins.
Wings. Hugo.
Wingtip. Sandburg.
Winter Song. Jiménez.
You That Sing in the Blackthorn. *Fr.* The Last Voyage. Noyes.
Young Martins, The. Young.
Penguin Book of Bird Poetry, The (PBBP). Peggy Munsterberg, ed.
Poetry of Birds, The (PB). Samuel Carr, ed.
See also ***names of birds*** **(*e.g.*, Canaries).**

Birds' Nests
Bird's Nest, The. Drinkwater.
Birds' Nests. Thomas.
Brown Thrush, The. Larcom.
Building of the Nest, The. Sangster.
Discovery, The. Snaith.
For Saturday. Smart.
Hen's Nest. Clare.
Nesting Time. Stewart.
On a Forsaken Lark's Nest. Blind.
Pettichap's Nest, The. Clare.
Rule for Birds' Nesters, A. *Unknown.*

Birds of Paradise
Birds of Paradise, The. Bishop.
Bird of Paradise, The. Davies.

Bird-watching
Bird Watcher. Wallace.
Some Tips on Watching Birds. Hudson.
Up from the Egg: The Confessions of a Nuthatch Avoider. Nash.
Waiting for E. Gularis. Pastan.

Birmingham, Alabama
Ballad of Birmingham. Randall.
Birmingham. Fields.
Birmingham 1963. Patterson.
Birmingham Sunday. Hughes.
Letters from Birmingham. Bond.
Young David, A: Birmingham. Brooks.

Birmingham, England
Birmingham. MacNeice.
New Navigation, The. Freeth.

Birth
Almond Tree, The. Stallworthy.
Arrivals and Departures. La Follette.
At Birth. Thwaite.
Before the Birth of One of Her Children. Bradstreet.
Birth. Bruck.
Birth. Lyon.
Birth. Urdang.
Birth in a Narrow Room, The. Brooks.
Birth of a Great Man. Graves.
Birthdays. Domin.
Birthplace. Big Eagle.
Calliope in the Labour Ward. Feinstein.
Child Bearing. Ghigna.
Christmas and Common Birth. Ridler.
Christopher at Birth. Longley.
Crooked Carol. Farber.
Definition. Shakely.
Ecce Puer. Joyce.
First Birth, The. Jones.
For Alva Benson, and for All Those Who Have Learned to Speak. Harjo.
Gas Lamp. Barnstone.
It's Time. *Fr.* Earthly: Sonnets for Carlos. Wedde.
Labor. Day.
Labour. *Fr.* Paedotrophiae; or, The Art of Bringing Up Children. Saint-Marthe.
Love Medley: Patrice Cuchulain. Harper.
Mississippi Born. Lomax.
Nativity. Hayford.
Night Was Smooth, The. Bertolino.
On a Child Who Lived One Minute. Kennedy.
On the Birth of a Black/Baby/Boy. Knight.
One Morning. Levine.
Poem to Ease Birth. *Unknown.*
Queen Jane. *Unknown.*
Say Hello to John. Williams.
Squeal. McHugh.
Still Birth. Rutan.
Talking to the Moon. Harjo.
To a Child before Birth. Nicholson.
To Insure Survival. Ortiz.
Naked Astronaut, The: Poems on Birth and Birthdays (NAs). René Graziani, ed.

Birth Control
Lines for the Planned Parenthood Clinic. Spurrier.
See also **Abortion; Contraception.**

Birth Defects
Almond Tree, The. Stallworthy.
Metaphors. McNall.
Mongol Quine. Mackie.

Birthdays
Another Birthday. Jonson.
Betsy Jane's Sixth Birthday. Noyes.
Between Birthdays. Nash.
Birthday, A. Field.
Birthday, A. Muir.
Birthday, A. Rossetti.
Birthday Candle, A. Justice.
Birthday Child, The. Fyleman.
Birthday Gifts. Asquith.
Birthday of but a single pang. Dickinson.
Birthday Party. Patton.
Birthdays. Chute.
Birthdays. Driver.
Coming of Age. Logan.
Days of Birth. *Unknown.*
Driving North from Savannah on My Birthday. Zimmer.
For His Wife, on Her Birthday. Wesley.
For K. R. on Her Sixtieth Birthday. Wilbur.
Her Birthday. Witt.
If We Didn't Have Birthdays. Seuss.
Many Happy Returns. Auden.
Monday's child is fair of face. Mother Goose.
My Birth-Day. Moore.

Nut's Birthday, The. Pope.
On My Thirty-third Birthday. Byron.
On This Day I Complete My Fortieth Year. Porter.
Our Birthday. Edey.
Party, A. Richards.
Poem for My Twentieth Birthday. Koch.
Poem in October. Thomas.
Seven Times One. Ingelow.
Stella's Birthday. Swift.
To His Son, Vincent Corbet, on His Birth-Day, November 10, 1630, Being Then Three Years Old. Corbet.
To Mrs. M. B. on Her Birth-Day. Pope.
To Mrs. Thrale on Her Thirty-fifth Birthday. Johnson.
Trala Trala Trala La-Le-La. Williams.
Naked Astronaut, The: Poems on Birth and Birthdays (NAs). René Graziani, ed.

Birthplaces
Birthplace. Saffarzadeh.
Birthplace Revisited. Corso.
Domicilium. Hardy.

Bishop, Elizabeth
For Elizabeth Bishop. McPherson.

Bismarck, Otto von
Lines on the Death of Bismarck. Chapman.

Bison. *See* **Buffaloes.**

Black (color)
Sonnet of Black Beauty. Herbert of Cherbury.

"Black Bart"
Black Bart. *Unknown.*
"Black Bart, P08." Bierce.

Black Hawk
Black Hawk in Hiding. Keithley.

Black Hills (U. S.)
Dreary Black Hills, The. *Unknown.*
Rushmore. Witt.

Black Holes
Black Holes. Perkins.
Collapsars. McPherson.

Black Verse
American Negro Poetry (AmNP). Arna Bontemps, ed.
Black American Literature: Poetry (BALP). Darwin T. Turner, ed.
Black Out Loud; an Anthology of Modern Poems by Black Americans (BOLo). Arnold Adoff, ed.
Black Poets, The, (BPo). Dudley Randall, ed.
Black Sister (BlSi). Erlene Stetson, ed.
Book of American Negro Poetry, The (BANP). James Weldon Johnson, ed.
Book of American Negro Spirituals, The (BoAN). James Weldon Johnson, ed.
Caroling Dusk; an Anthology of Verse by Negro Poets (CDC). Countee Cullen, ed.
Celebrations; a New Anthology of Black American Poetry (CNA). Arnold Adoff, ed.
Forerunners, The: Black Poets in America (FB). Woodie King, Jr., ed.
Golden Slippers; an Anthology of Negro Poetry for Young Readers (GoSl). Arna Bontemps, comp.
I Am the Darker Brother (IDB). Arnold Adoff, ed.
Jump Bad; a New Chicago Anthology (JB). Gwendolyn Brooks, ed.
New Black Poetry, The (NBP). Clarence Major, ed.
New Negro Poets U.S.A. (NNP). Langston Hughes, ed.
Poems from Black Africa (PBA). Langston Hughes, ed.
Poetry of Black America, The (PoBA). Arnold Adoff, ed.
Poetry of the Negro 1746–1970, The (PoNe). Langston Hughes *and* Arna Bontemps, eds.
3000 Years of Black Poetry (TTY). Alan Lomax *and* Raoul Abdul, ed.

Blackberries
Blackberry, The. Nicholson.
Blackberry-picking. Heaney.
Blackberrying. Plath.
Forty Pounds of Blackberries Equals Thirteen Gallons of Wine. Hoeft.

Blackbirds
Bay Bank. Ammons.
Best of Two Worlds. Boothroyd.
Blackbird, The. Barnes.
Blackbird, The. Henley.
Blackbird. Leach.
Blackbird, The. Tennyson.
Blackbird, The. *Unknown.*
Blackbird, The. Wolfe.
Blackbird by Belfast Lough, The. *Unknown.*
Blackbird Singing, A. Thomas.
Blackbird startles from the homestead hedge, The. *Fr.* Child Harold. Clare.
Blackbird Winter. West.
I Watched a Blackbird. Hardy.
Naughty Blackbird, The. Greenaway.
O What If the Flower. Dalmon.
Red-Wing Blackbird, The. Williams.
Redwing, The. Dickinson.
Sing a song of sixpence. Mother Goose.
There were two blackbirds sitting on a hill. Mother Goose.
13 Ways of Eradicating Blackbirds. DeFoe.
Thirteen Ways of Looking at a Blackbird. Stevens.
To an Irish Blackbird. MacAlpine.
White Whales Specked Black. Outlaw.

Blackburn, Paul
Walking Past Paul Blackburn's Apt. on 7th St. Wakoski.

Blacks
Allegory in Black. Clark.
Assembly: Harlem School. Maleska.
At Home in Dakar. Danner.
Aunt Jemima of the Ocean Waves. Hayden.
Ballade des Belles Milatraisses. Jonas.
Beautiful Black Women. Baraka.
Beautiful Negress, The. Pitter.
Between Ourselves. Lorde.
Between the World and Me. Wright.
Birthday Poem. Young.
Black Art. Baraka.
Black Boy. Rosten.
Black Dada Nihilismus. Baraka.
Black Majesty. Cullen.
Black Marble. O'Shaughnessy.
Black Poetry Day. Johnson.
Black Pride. Burroughs.
Black Sister. Cumbo.
Black Sketches. Lee.
Black Tambourine. Crane.
Black Woman. Madgett.
Blackberry Sweet. Randall.
Blue-eyed Precinct Worker, The. Coulette.
Bones of My Father, The. Knight.
"Boogie with O. O. Gabugah." Young.
Bottled. Johnson.
Brother Baptis' on Woman Suffrage. Jonas.
Carol of the Brown King. Hughes.
Coal. Lorde.
Congo, The. Lindsay.
Cross. Hughes.
Dab of Color, A. Weiss.
Dark Phrases. Shange.
Dark Symphony. Tolson.
Dark Testament. Murray.
Different Image, A. Randall.
Dream Variation. Hughes.
"Duke" and the "Count," The. Fewell.
Ego Tripping. Giovanni.
For Black Poets Who Think of Suicide. Knight.
For Both of Us at Fisk. Scott.
For de Lawd. Clifton.
Freedom Song for the Black Woman, A. Gregory.
From the Dark Tower. Cullen.
Gee-up Dar, Mules. Piper.
Generation Gap, The. Saunders.
Good Times. Clifton.
Grandfather. Harper.
Grandson Is a Hoticeberg, A. Danner.
Heritage. Bennett.
Heritage. Cullen.
How Will You Call Me, Brother. Evans.
Hush, Honey. Saunders.
I Am a Black Woman. Evans.
I Am Ham Melanite. Millet.
I Came to the New World Empty-handed. Swift.
I, Too. Hughes.
I, Woman. McClaurin.
Identities. Young.
If We Must Die. McKay.
Image in the Mirror. Kenner.
In Defense of Black Poets. Rivers.
In Salem. Clifton.
Incident. Cullen.
It's Nation Time. Baraka.
Jesus Was Crucified or: It Must Be Deep. Rodgers.
Ka 'Ba. Baraka.

Lady I Know, A. Cullen.
Lawd, Dese Colored Chillum. Saunders.
Lift Every Voice and Sing. Johnson.
Litany of the Dark People, The. Cullen.
Little Black Boy, The. *Fr.* Songs of Innocence. Blake.
Mask, The. McClaurin.
Memorial. Sanchez.
Merry-go-round. Hughes.
Metamorphosis of Aunt Jemima, The. Childress.
Midway. Madgett.
Missing Beat. Rogers.
Moment Please, A. Allen.
Mr. Z. Holman.
Mrs. Johnson Objects. Thompson.
Nappy Edges (A Cross Country Sojourn). Shange.
Naturally. Lorde.
Negro Poets. Johnson.
Negro Servant. Hughes.
Negro Speaks of Rivers, The. Hughes.
Negro Spirituals. Benét.
New Negro, The. McCall.
Nigger. Shapiro.
Nikki-Rosa. Giovanni.
Notes for a Speech. Baraka.
Nuflo de Olano (Who Sailed with Balboa). Mberi.
O Daedalus, Fly Away Home. Hayden.
Ode in Time of Hesitation, An. Moody.
Of De Witt Williams on His Way to Lincoln Cemetery. Brooks.
Old Black Joe. Foster.
Old O. O. Blues, The. Young.
Old Thad Stevens. Porter.
On Being Brought from Africa to America. Wheatley.
Once. Walker.
Only in This Way. Burroughs.
Plaint. Ford.
Poem about Intelligence for My Brothers and Sisters, A. Jordan.
Poem for Black Hearts, A. Baraka.
Poem for Halfwhite College Students. Baraka.
Poem for Some Black Women. Rodgers.
Puzzled. Hughes.
Refugee in America. Hughes.
Remember Times for Sandy. Rogers.
Richard, Richard: American Fuel. Dixon.
Runaway Slave at Pilgrim's Point, The. Browning.
Sepia Fashion Show. Angelou.
Song: "I am weaving a song of waters." Bennett.
Song: "We raise de wheat." *Unknown.*
Sonnet: September 1, 1802. Wordsworth.
Sonnet to a Negro in Harlem. Johnson.
Sootie Joe. Tolson.
Southern Cop. Brown.
Stereo. Lee.
Strong Men. Brown.
Telephone Conversation. Soyinka.
Theme for English B. Hughes.
3-31-70. *Fr.* Journal. Jones.
Tired. Johnson.
To a Gone Era. McClaurin.
To Soulfolk. Burroughs.
To Usward. Bennett.
Touché. Fauset.
Tripart. Jones.
Upstairs Downstairs. Allen.
W. W. Baraka.
Way It Was, The. Clifton.
We Real Cool. Brooks.
Where my grandmother lived. Long.
Woman Poem. Giovanni.
Woman's Song, A. McElroy.
Women. Walker.
Golden Slippers (GoSl). Arna Bontemps, ed.
New Negro Poets U.S.A. (NNP). Langston Hughes, ed.
See also ***anthologies listed under*** **Black Verse.**

Blacksmiths
Anchorsmiths, The. Dibdin.
Blacksmith, The. *Unknown.*
Blacksmiths, The. *Unknown.*
Blacksmith's Song, The. *Unknown.*
Felix Randal. Hopkins.
Forge, The. Gogarty.
Forging of the Anchor, The. Ferguson.
Smith's Song. Sigerson.
Smoke-blackened Smiths. *Unknown.*
Village Blacksmith, The. Longfellow.

Blake, William
Mad Blake. Benét.
To William Blake. Dargan.
William Blake. Thomson.
William Blake Sees God. McFadden.

Blarney, Ireland
Groves of Blarney, The. Milliken.

Blasphemy
For All Blasphemers. Benét.

Blenheim, Battle of (1704)
Battle of Blenheim, The. Southey.
Blenheim. *Fr.* The Campaign. Addison.

Blessings
Blessing over Food. Bialik.
Here We Come a-Caroling. *Unknown.*

Blindness
All but Blind. De la Mare.
Blind Boy, The. Cibber.
Blind but Happy. Crosby.
Blind Fiddler, The. *Unknown.*
Blind Man. Hamburger.
Blind Man, The. Lewisohn.
Blind Man at the Fair, The. Campbell.
Blind Men and the Elephant, The. Saxe.
Blinded Bird, The. Hardy.
Blinded Soldier to His Love, The. Noyes.
Blindness of Samson, The. *Fr.* Samson Agonistes. Milton.
Braille. Costanzo.
Does It Matter? Sassoon.
Eggs and Marrowbone. *Unknown.*
Hugh Stuart Boyd. Browning.
In the Garden of the Lord. Keller.
Mock Medicine. *Unknown.*
On His Blindness. Milton.
Sight. Gibson.
Smoker, The. Huff.
Solitude, A. Levertov.
Spring, and the Blind Children. Noyes.
To Mr. Cyriack Skinner upon His Blindness. Milton.
Unblinding, The. Lieberman.
War Blinded. Dunn.

Blizzards
Lost in a Blizzard. Monroe.
Snowstorm, The. Crouch.

Blocks (toys)
Block City. Stevenson.

Blood
Circulation, The. Washbourne.
Circulation of the Blood, The. *Fr.* Creation. Blackmore.
On a Line in Sandburg. Thomas.
Poisoned Man, The. Dickey.
Temple is full of blood, The. Villanueva.

Bloodhounds
Bloodhound, the. Anthony.

Blue (color)
Australia. Jackson.
Blue Booby, The. Tate.
Blue Winter. Francis.
Variation on a Sentence. Bogan.

Blue Jays
Avis. Morison.
Blue Jay. Francis.
Invitation. Behn.

Bluebells
Bluebells. Markham.

Blueberries
Hermit Picks Berries, The. Kumin.

Bluebirds
Advice to a Blue-Bird. Bodenheim.
Blue-Bird, The. Melville.
Blue-Bird, The. Wilson.
Last Word of a Bluebird, The. Frost.

Bluefish
Night Fishing for Blues. Smith.

Blues (mood)
Blues. Mungin.
Blues. Prettyman.
Bound No'th Blues. Hughes.
Chromo. Fabio.
Death Sting Me Blues. *Unknown.*

Get Up, Blues. Emanuel.
Good Mornin', Blues. *Unknown.*
Habeas Corpus Blues. Aiken.
It was not death, for I stood up. Dickinson.
Kitchen Door Blues. Williams.
Sporting Life Blues. *Unknown.*
St. Louis Blues. Handy.
Weave Room Blues. *Unknown.*
Winnsboro Cotton Mill Blues. *Unknown.*

Blues (music)
Blues and Bitterness. Bennett.
Blues Don't Change, The. Young.
Blues Note. Kaufman.
Blues Today, The. Jackson.
Coal Loadin' Blues. *Unknown.*
D Blues. Hernton.
Depot Blues. *Unknown.*
East St. Louis Blues. *Unknown.*
Four o'Clock Flower Blues. *Unknown.*
Gonna Lay My Head Down on Some Railroad Line. *Unknown.*
Hard Daddy. Hughes.
Homage to the Empress of the Blues. Hayden.
I Remember How She Sang. Penny.
I Rode Southern, I Rode L. & N. *Unknown.*
Lowdown Dirty Blues. *Unknown.*
Mask, The. McClaurin.
Mississippi Blues. *Unknown.*
Music, The. Hoagland.
Po' Boy Blues. Hughes.
Poem for Otis Redding. Thomas.
Ragged and Dirty. *Unknown.*
Railroad Blues, The. *Unknown.*
Ray Charles. Cornish.
Special Rider Blues. *Unknown.*
To Dinah Washington. Knight.
Train Is off the Track, The. *Unknown.*
Weary Blues, The. Hughes.
Why I Sing the Blues. King.
Worried Life Blues. *Unknown.*
Worried Man Blues. *Unknown.*
Blues Line, The (BluL). Eric Sackheim, ed.

Boadicea
Boadicea. Cowper.

Boarding Houses
Mr. Bleaney. Larkin.
On Saint-Urbain Street. Acorn.
1614 Boren. Hugo.

Boasting
Primer Lesson. Sandburg.
Showing Off. *Unknown.*

Boats
Barges on the Hudson. Deutsch.
Beginning to Squall. Swenson.
Boat Poem. Spencer.
Boats. Bennett.
Boats at Night. Shanks.
Drunken Boat, The. Rimbaud.
Excursion, The. Tu Fu.
Fishing Boats in Martigues. Campbell.
Flower-Boat, The. Frost.
Freight Boats. Tippett.
Hayeswater. *Fr.* The Hayeswater Boat. Arnold.
In the Fishing Village. Nickerson.
Kayak, The. *Unknown.*
Last Galway Hooker, The. Murphy.
Little Steamboat. Williams.
Long River, The. Hall.
Lost. Sandburg.
My Plan. Chute.
Night Trip across the Chesapeake and After. Lea.
Old Boat, The. Pratt.
Old Ironsides. Holmes.
On a Steamer. Baruch.
Paper Boats. Tagore.
Reliable Service, A. Curnow.
Return, Starting Out. Halpern.
Riding in a Motor Boat. Baruch.
River Boats, The. Hicky.
Steamboat Bill. *Unknown.*
Where Go the Boats? Stevenson.
Whistles. Field.
Wreck of the *Hesperus,* The. Longfellow.
See also **Ferry Boats; Ships; Tugs; Yachts.**

Bobolinks
Bobolink, The. Hill.
Bobolinks, The. Cranch.
O'Lincoln Family, The. Flagg.
Robert of Lincoln. Bryant.

Bobwhites
Bob White. Cooper.

Bodies
Bath, The. Snyder.
Body, The. Herrick.
Body Is the Victory and the Defeat of Dreams, The. Anghelaki-Rooke.
Breasts. Unger.
Busts and Bosoms Have I Known. *Unknown.*
Case. Janowitz.
Chamber Music. Ditsky.
Dialogue between the Soul and Body, A. Marvell.
Ecstasy, The. Donne.
Epidermal Macabre. Roethke.
Fine Body. Clare.
Head Itself. Riding.
Heavy Bear, The. Schwartz.
Her True Body. Metz.
His Body. McPherson.
Human Geography. Fuertes.
I am the poet of the body. *Fr.* Song of Myself. Whitman.
I Like My Body When It Is with Your. Cummings.
I Sing the Body Electric. Whitman.
Innocent Breasts, The. Oppenheimer.
"It's a Whole World, the Body. A Whole World!"—Swami Satchidandanda. Young.
Map Reading. Citino.
Origin of the Praise of God, The. Bly.
Our Bodies. Levertov.
Question. Swenson.
Salutation, The. Traherne.
Soul's Garment, The. Newcastle.
Temple of Venus, The. Jenyns.
This Earthen Body. Gond.
Thoughts on the Shape of the Human Body. Brooke.
To My Body. Sullivan.
Waiting. Cooper.
What Do You Say When a Man Tells You, You Have the Softest Skin. Macey.
What Is Man's Body? Gond.
Zoo of You, The. Freeman.
See also **Nudity and Nudists.**

Bodybuilding
Dynamic Tension. Sanfield.

Boer War
Bridge-Guard in the Karroo. Kipling.
Christmas Ghost-Story, A. Hardy.
Colonel's Soliloquy, The. Hardy.
Drummer Hodge. Hardy.
Embarcation. Hardy.
Wife in London, A. Hardy.

Bogart, Humphrey
Bogey. Berkson.

Bogotá, Colombia
In the City of Bogotá. Pape.

Bogs
Bog. Volwerk.
Bog Queen. Heaney.
Bogland. Heaney.
Kinship. Heaney.
On Learning That Certain Peat Bogs Contain Perfectly Preserved Bodies. Ludvigson.
Tollund Man, The. Heaney.
Wester Ross. Mitchison.

Bohemian Life
City Nights: In Bohemia. Symons.
Lines for a Worthy Person Who Has Drifted by Accident into a Chelsea Revel. Herbert.
Problem in Social Geometry—The Inverted Square! Durem.
Spring Street in '58. Walcott.

Boleyn, Anne
My Dearling. Allen.
Whoso List to Hunt. Wyatt.

Boll Weevils
Ballit of de Boll Weevil, De. *Unknown.*

Bombs and Bombing
Ballad in Birmingham. Randall.

Entertainment of War, The. Fisher.
See also **Air Warfare.**
Bonaparte, Josephine
Appearance and Reality. Hollander.
Bonaparte, Louis Napoleon. *See* **Napoleon III.**
Bonaparte, Napoleon. *See* **Napoleon I.**
Bondone, Giotto di. *See* **Giotto.**
Bones
After X-Ray. Pastan.
Bone Thoughts on a Dry Day. Starbuck.
Bones. Morgan.
Epitaph on William Jones. *Unknown.*
Hollow Flute, The. Strauss.
Lady's-Maid's Song, The. Hollander.
Meditation on a Bone. Hope.
Ode on a Plastic Stapes. Walsh.
Postcard from the Volcano, A. Stevens.
See also **Skeletons.**
Bonhomme Richard (ship)
Battle of the *Bonhomme Richard* and the *Serapis*. *Fr.* Song of Myself. Whitman.
Bonhomme Richard and the *Serapis,* The. Freneau.
Paul Jones. *Unknown.*
Bonnivard, Francois de
Prisoner of Chillon, The. Byron.
Bononcini, Giovanni Battista
Epigram on Handel and Bononcini. Byrom.
Bonsai
Work of Artifice, A. Piercy.
Boobies
Blue Booby, The. Tate.
Book Clubs
Classic Waits for Me, A. White.
Book of Kells. *See* **Kells, Book of.**
Books
Against the Evidence. Ignatow.
Author to Her Book, The. Bradstreet.
Bibliomaniac's Prayer, The. Field.
Book, A. More.
Book, A. Reese.
Book, The. Vaughan.
Book of Verses, A. Marcus.
Books. Baer.
Books. Farjeon.
Books Are Keys. Poulsson.
Books Fall Open. McCord.
Bookworms, The. Burns.
Bookshop Idyll, A. Amis
Burning of Books, The. Brecht.
Classic Waits for Me, A. White.
Expostulation and Reply. Wordsworth.
Fiction and the Reading Public. Larkin.
Fire at Alexandria, The. Weiss.
First Reader. Leary.
Golden Spurs. Miner.
His Books. Southey.
House Was Quiet and the World Was Calm, The. Stevens.
If someone asks you. Donian.
Inscription in a Book. Douglas.
Insect Shuffle Method, The. Tapp.
I've Got a New Book from My Grandfather Hyde. Jackson.
Land of Story Books, The. Stevenson.
Letter to Hitler, A. Laughlin.
Library, The. Huff.
Library, The. Sherman.
O Blessed Letters. *Fr.* Musophilus. Daniel.
O for a Booke. *Unknown.*
Of Books. Florio.
Old Books Are Best. Chew.
On His Books. Belloc.
On Opening a New Book. Brown.
On the Detraction Which Followed upon My Writing Certain Treatises. Milton.
On the Fly-Leaf of a Book of Old Plays. Learned.
Reading in War Time. Muir.
Second Volume, The. Bell.
Shut Not Your Doors. Whitman.
Sibrandus Schafnaburgensis. *Fr.* Garden Fancies. Browning.
Study of Reading Habits, A. Larkin.
Tables Turned, The. Wordsworth.
There is no frigate like a book. Dickinson.
Thinking of Bookshops. Liddy.
To a Thesaurus. Adams.
To Fanny. Moore.
To His Books. Vaughan.
To My Booke. Jonson.
To the Lady with a Book. *Unknown.*
"What Five Books Would You Pick to Be Marooned with on a Desert Island?" Leary.
Who Hath a Book. Nesbit.
Bookworms
Bookworm, The. De la Mare.
Bookworms, The. Burns.
Boone, Daniel
Daniel Boone. Benét.
Daniel Boone. Guiterman.
For the Grave of Daniel Boone. Stafford.
Booth, Edwin
Edwin Booth. Brown.
Sargent's Portrait of Edwin Booth at "The Players." Aldrich.
Booth, John Wilkes
Booth Killed Lincoln. *Unknown.*
Pardon. Howe.
Booth, William
General William Booth Enters into Heaven. Lindsay.
Bootleggers
Black Bottom Bootlegger, The. Leiper.
Borden, Lizzie
Lizzie Borden. *Unknown.*
Borders (region), Scotland. *See* **Scottish Borders.**
Boredom
All in the Downs. Hood.
Life, friends, is boring. We must not say so. *Fr.* Dream Songs. Berryman.
Nervous Prostration. Wickham.
Bores
Arrogance Repressed. Betjeman.
Grandmamma's Birthday. Belloc.
In Extremis. Fishback.
La Donna E Perpetuum Mobile. Edman.
Pooh! De la Mare.
To a Lady Holding the Floor. Weston.
Borges, Jorge Luis
Borges. Barnstone.
Borgia, Lucretia
On Seeing a Hair of Lucretia Borgia. Landor.
Borgia, St. Francis
Saint Francis Borgia; or, A Refutation for Heredity. McGinley.
Borneo
Dayak Man Making Fishtray. Rubenstein.
Naked in Borneo. Swenson.
Bosch, Hieronymus
Homage to Hieronymus Bosch. MacGreevy.
Boston, Massachusetts
Beasts of Boston, The. Lowry.
Boston Burglar, The. *Unknown.*
Boston Toast, A. Bossidy.
Communication to the City Fathers of Boston. Starbuck.
Drivers of Boston, The. Gross.
For the Union Dead. Lowell.
New Order, The. McGinley.
On a Fortification of Boston Begun by Women. Tompson.
Poems from a First Year in Boston. Starbuck.
Public Garden, The. Lowell.
South End. Aiken.
Whaddaya Do for Action in This Place? Starbuck.
Where the Rainbow Ends. Lowell.
Boston Evening Transcript (newspaper)
Boston Evening Trascript, The. Eliot.
Boston Tea Party
Ballad of the Boston Tea-Party, A. Holmes.
New Song, A. *Unknown.*
Bosworth Field, Battle of (1485)
Richard III's Speech. *Fr.* Bosworth Field. Beaumont.
Botany Bay, Australia
Botany Bay. *Unknown.*
Bothwell, Scotland
Bothwell Bridge. *Unknown.*
Covenanter's Lament for Bothwell Brigg, The. Praed.
Bourgeoisie
How Beastly the Bourgeois Is. Lawrence.
Life Cycle of Common Man. Nemerov.
Marriage. Corso.
New-fashioned Farmer, The. *Unknown.*

Nut's Birthday, The. Pope.
Old Brown's Daughter. *Unknown.*
Street Preacher. MacCaig.
Tenebrae. Levertov.
Toads. Larkin.
Unknown Citizen, The. Auden.
Bowery, The (New York City)
Bowery, The. Hoyt.
Bowery. Ignatow.
Bowles, William Lisle
William Lisle Bowles. *Fr.* English Bards and Scotch Reviewers. Byron.
Bowls
Wedgwood Bowl, A. Taylor.
Boxing and Boxers
Advice to a Prizefighter. Lucilius.
As when two monarchs of the brindled breed. *Fr.* The Gymnasiad, or Boxing Match. Whitehead.
Blues for Benny Kid Paret. Smith.
Boxer Loses Face and Fortune. Lucilius.
Boxer Turned Bartender, The. Kizer.
Fights, The. Acorn.
Funeral Games for Anchises, The: Entellus. *Fr.* The Aeneid. Virgil.
Funeral Games for Patroclus, The: The Boastful Boxer. *Fr.* The Iliad. Homer.
Knockout, The. Morrison.
Monument to a Boxer. Lucilius.
My Lord, What a Morning. Cuney.
On a Boxer. Kennedy.
Retired Boxer, The. Lucilius.
Throw Him Down M'Closkey. Kelly.
To a Fighter Killed in the Ring. Lipsitz.
X of the Unknown, The. Clark.
Boy Scouts
Robert's Rules of Order. Peterson.
Some Modern Good Turns. Dibben.
Boyne, Battle of the (1690)
Boyne Water, The. *Unknown.*
Dialogue between King William and the Late King James on the Banks of the Boyne, A. Blount.
Boyne, Ireland
Boyne Walk, The. Higgins.
Father and Son. Higgins.
Boys
American Boyhood, An. Holden.
Barefoot Boy, The. Whittier.
Blessing on Little Boys. Guiterman.
Boy at a Certain Age. Francis.
Boy We Want, The. *Unknown.*
Boy's Song, A. Hogg.
Chicago, Summer Past. Snyder.
Dark Danny. Eastwick.
Extremes. Riley.
False Security. Betjeman.
First Song. Kinnell.
Fräulein Reads Instructive Rhymes. Kumin.
Fun with Fishing. Tietjens.
George. Belloc.
Godfrey Gordon Gustavus Gore. Rands.
Hiding. Aldis.
It chanced to be our washing day. *Fr.* The September Gale. Holmes.
My Lost Youth. Longfellow.
O Tan-faced Prairie-Boy. Whitman.
Portrait of the Boy as Artist. Howes.
There Was a Boy. *Fr.* The Prelude. Wordsworth.
Tired Tim. De la Mare.
To a Small Boy Standing on My Shoes While I Am Wearing Them. Nash.
See also **Childhood and Children; Youth.**
Bozzaris, Marco
Marco Bozzaris. Halleck.
Bracelets
Bracelet, The: To Julia. Herrick.
Bradstreet, Anne
Homage to Mistress Bradstreet. Berryman.
Upon Mrs. Anne Bradstreet. Norton.
Upon Mrs. Anne Bradstreet Her Poems. Rogers.
Upon the Author; by a Known Friend. Woodbridge.
Brahma
Brahma. Emerson.
Brahma, the World Idea. *Fr.* The Rig-Veda. *Unknown.*
Brahms, Johannes
Brahms, The. Morris.
Braithwaite, William Stanley
To William Stanley Braithwaite. Johnson.
Brandy
Brandy Leave Me Alone. *Unknown.*
Bread
Bread. Burnshaw.
Bread. Keesing.
Bread Is Born. Hébert.
Evening Bread. Glatstein.
Breakfast
Aubade after the Party. O'Grady.
Baby's Breakfast. Poulsson.
Breakfast in a Bowling Alley in Utica, New York. Rich.
Cowboy's Gettin'-up Holler. *Unknown.*
It's in the Egg. Rosenblatt.
Morning. *Unknown.*
Breasts
Breasts. Unger.
Busts and Bosoms Have I Known. *Unknown.*
I'll Tell You What a Flapper Is. Freeman.
Innocent Breasts, The. Oppenheimer.
Breath
Of you, if anyone, it can be said. Catullus.
Song of Breath, A. Benét.
Brébeuf, Jean de
Brébeuf and His Brethren, *sels.* Pratt.
Breeches
It chanced to be our washing day. *Fr.* The September Gale. Holmes.
Brendan, Saint
Burial of Saint Brendan, The. Colum.
Fish at Mass, The. *Unknown.*
Pattern of Saint Brendan. MacManus.
Breughel, Pieter. *See* **Brueghel, Pieter.**
Brian Boru
Lamentation of Mac Liag for Kincora. *Unknown.*
Bricklayers
Bricklayer's Labours, The. Tatersal.
Bricks
Brick, The. Roche.
Clay and Water. Hochman.
Brides
Bride, The. Akhmadulina.
Bride, The. Hodgson.
Brides, The. Hope.
False Bride, The. *Unknown.*
Rosy Apple, Lemon or Pear. *Unknown.*
See also **Weddings.**
Bridgeport, Connecticut
Last Job I Held in Bridgeport, The. Donzella.
Bridger, James
Mountain Liars. Hafen.
Bridges
Address to the New Tay Bridge, An. McGonagall.
At Darien Bridge. Dickey.
Bridges. Bacmeister.
Building the Bridge. Dromgoole.
Burned Bridge, The. Stone.
Covered Bridge. Coffin.
Hours of a Bridge, The. Merwin.
London Bridge. *Unknown.*
Of London Bridge, and the Stupendous Sight, and Structure Thereof. Howell.
Old Bridge at Florence, The. Longfellow.
Pass, The. Logan.
Railway Bridge of the Silver Tay, The. McGonagall.
Tay Bridge Disaster, The. McGonagall.
Bridges, Robert
To R. B. Hopkins.
Bridget, Saint
Feast of Saint Brigid of Kildare, The. *At. to* St. Brigid.
I Should Like to Have a Great Pool of Ale. *At. to* St. Bridget.
Bright, John
John Bright. Gummere.
Brighton, England
John Betjeman's Brighton. Ewart.
Bristol, England
Bristol. Savage.
Last Verses. Chatterton.
British Columbia, Canada
Breathe Dust. Wah.
Christ Walks in This Infernal District Too. Lowry.
Imagine: A Town. *Fr.* Steveston. Marlatt.

In the Dome Car of the "Canadian." Marty.
In the Selkirks. Scott.
July 1st, French Creek. Roberts.
Junction. Pass.
Trail to Lillooet, The. Johnson.

British Empire
Ballad of East and West, The. Kipling.
Boots. Kipling.
Britannia's Empire. *Fr.* Britannia. Thomson.
British Commerce. *Fr.* Liberty. Thomson.
Geography. *Fr.* Songs of Education. Chesterton.
Gunga Din. Kipling.
Hands-across-the-Sea Poem, The. Squire.
How cursed that country, how severe its doom. *Fr.* An Epistle to the Right Hon. Charles James Fox. Maurice.
Mandalay. Kipling.
Ode on Lord Macartney's Embassy to China. Shepherd.
On a Parisian Boulevard. Stephen.
Recessional. Kipling.
Song of the Banjo, The. Kipling.

British Museum, London
British Museum Reading Room, The. MacNeice.
Homage to the British Museum. Empson.

Brittany, France
Hervé Riel. Browning.
Scenes from Carnac. Arnold.

Broadway, New York City
Broadway. Whitman.
Broadway Pageant, A. Whitman.
Electric Sign Goes Dark, An. Sandburg.
Give My Regards to Broadway. Cohan.

Brock, Sir Isaac
Come All You Bold Canadians. *Unknown.*

Brontë, Anne
On the Death of Anne Brontë. Brontë.

Brontë, Charlotte
Charlotte Brontë. "Coolidge."
Charlotte Nicholls. Clemo.
Sampler from Haworth. Howard.
Where, behind Keighley, the road. *Fr.* Haworth Churchyard. Arnold.

Brontë, Emily
Emily Brontë. Day Lewis.

Bronx, New York City
After the Murder of Jimmy Walsh. Murray.
Death of the Bronx, The. Bloch.
East Bronx. Ignatow.
Inheritance. Replansky.
Tao in the Yankee Stadium Bleachers. Updike.

Brooke, Rupert
Rupert Brooke. Gibson.

Brooklyn Bridge
Blueprint. Steinman.
Brooklyn Bridge at Dawn. Le Gallienne.
Brooklyn Bridge. Mayakovsky.
Granite and Steel. Moore.
Roebling, his life and mind reprieved enough. *Fr.* The Bridge from Brooklyn. Henri.
To Brooklyn Bridge. *Fr.* The Bridge. Crane.
View of the Brooklyn Bridge, A. Meredith.

Brooklyn, New York City
Annunciation. Maura.
Brooklyn Heights. Wain.
Cage, The. Montague.
Centenarian's Story, The. Whitman.
Crossing Brooklyn Ferry. Whitman.
Meditation on the BMT. Blackburn.

Brooks, Gwendolyn
Afterword, An: For Gwen Brooks. Lee.
Gwendolyn Brooks. Lee.

Brooks, Van Wyck
Dear Men and Women. Wheelock.

Brooks and Streams
Ad Henricum Wottonem. Bastard.
As Rivers of Water in a Dry Place. De Bary.
Bendemeer's Stream. Moore.
Border Burn, A. *Fr.* Epistle to Tammus. Selkirk.
Brook, The. Thomas.
Brook, The. Tennyson.
Brook in February, The. Roberts.
Brook in the City, A. Frost.
Brook Song. Morse.
By the Bridge. Walker.
Can scenes like these withdraw thee from thy wood. *Fr.* The Borough. Crabbe.
Creek, The. Ross.
Crossing, The. Blackburn.
Dog Creek Mainline. Wright.
Dreaming Trout, The. *Fr.* The Flowing Summer. Bruce.
Elegy: "Clear and gentle stream!" Bridges.
Farewell, A: "Flow down, cold rivulet, to the sea." Tennyson.
Going for Water. Frost.
Highland Glen near Loch Ericht, A. *Fr.* The Bothie of Tober-na-Vuolich. Clough.
Hill Burns, The. Shepherd.
Hurrying Brook, The. Blunden.
Hyla Brook. Frost.
Inscription for a Tablet on the Banks of a Stream. Southey.
Inversnaid. Hopkins.
Ladder, The. Baro.
Mountain Brook. Coatsworth.
Ode to Leven-Water. Smollett.
On His Mistress Drown'd. Spratt.
Orara. Kendall.
Panic. Davis.
Resolve, The. Levertov.
Runoff. Ammons.
Singing Water. Lehmann.
Spring, The. Fyleman.
Stream, The. Weeden.
That Is All I Heard. "Yehoash."
There is a stream which rises. Bruchac.
Valley and Villa of Horace, The. *Fr.* Amours de Voyage. Clough.
Water. Snyder.
West-running Brook. Frost.
Whole Duty of Berkshire Brooks, The. Conkling.
See also **Rivers.**

Broom (plant)
Broom Flower, The. Howitt.

Brooms
Broom, Green Broom. *Unknown.*
Brooms. Simic.
Conscience's Song. *Fr.* Three Ladies of London. Wilson.

Brotherhood
Abou Ben Adhem. Hunt.
Ballad of East and West, The. Kipling.
Brother, The. Nadson.
Brotherhood. Markham.
Brotherhood. Vega.
Brothers, The. Muir.
Calamity. Scott.
Dance of Saul with the Prophets, The. Tchernichowsky.
Dark Testament. Murray.
Divine Image, The. *Fr.* Songs of Innocence. Blake.
Family. Miles.
Fellow-Citizens. Heidenstam.
For A' That and A' That. Burns.
Fraternitas. *Fr.* Deer Sing. Confucius.
Gentle Park, A. Herbert.
Goliath and David. Untermeyer.
He Is My Countryman. Slonimski.
Hymn for Nations. *Unknown.*
I Believe. Tchernichowsky.
I Dream a World. Hughes.
I Hear It Was Charged against Me. Whitman.
I Sought My Soul. *Unknown.*
In Distrust of Merits. Moore.
In the Mourning Time. Hayden.
Indian Prayer. Strongwolf.
Interracial. Johnson.
Like Water down a Slope. Schneour.
Little Black Boy, The. *Fr.* Songs of Innocence. Blake.
London Spring. Slonimski.
Love. Immanuel di Roma.
Man unto His Fellow Man. *Fr.* On a Note of Triumph. Corwin.
New Jewish Hospital at Hamburg, The. Heine.
New Patriotism, A. Piety.
No East or West. Oxenham.
O Blest Estate, Blest from Above. Sandys.
Out of Our Shame. Rosten.
Over the utmost hill at length I sped. *Fr.* The Revolt of Islam. Shelley.
Pebble, The. Wylie.
Poem of Distant Childhood. Sousa.
Round Table, The. Kenner.
Same Side of the Canoe, The. Do Espírito Santo.

Street Scene—1946. Porter.
These Things Shall Be. Symonds.
To Edom. Heine.
To Life I Said Yes. Grade.
To Some Millions Who Survive Joseph E. Mander, Senior. Wright.
Trouble. Brasfield.
True Brotherhood. Wilcox.
Tuft of Flowers, The. Frost.
Unity of Mankind. Bible, *O.T.*, *Fr.* Psalms.
We Are Brethren A'. Nicoll.
We Bear the Strain of Earthly Care. Davis.
When I See Another's Pain. Leib.
Where the Rainbow Ends. Rive.

Brothers
At the Grave of My Brother. Stafford.
Bank Thief, The. Farrell.
Bear Hunt, The. Widdemer.
Big Brother. Roberts.
Brother. Shelton.
Brothers. Currie.
Brothers, The. Muir.
Brothers (I). Reiss.
Family Cups. Orlen.
Flight Shot, A. Thompson.
Gathering the Bones Together. Orr.
Icicle. Huddle.
In the Tree House at Night. Dickey.
Lantern. Soto.
Lil' Bro'. Fufuka.
Little. Aldis.
Little Brother Poem, The. Nye.
Little Brother's Secret. Mansfield.
Memory. Stroud.
Murder, The. Brooks.
Poem for John My Brother. Aberg.
Postcard from London, 23.10.1972. Salkey.
Quarrel, The. Farjeon.
This Was My Brother. Gould.
Twa Brothers, The. *Unknown.*
Two in Bed. Ross.
Two-Year-Old Has Had a Motherless Week, The. Shapiro.
World, The. Creeley.

Brown, James
Hearing James Brown at the Café des Nattes (Sidi-bou-Said, Tunisia). Long.

Brown, John
Brown of Ossawatomie. Whittier.
Harper's Ferry. Rodman.
How Old Brown Took Harper's Ferry. Stedman.
John Brown. Koopman.
John Brown's Body. *Unknown.*
October 16: The Raid. Hughes.
Osawatomie. Sandburg.
Out of John Brown's Strong Sinews. *Fr.* John Brown's Body. Benét.
Portent, The. Melville.
Soul and Body of John Brown, The. Rukeyser.

Brown, Sterling A.
Br'er Sterling and the Rocker. Harper.

Brown (color)
Brown Beauty, The. Herbert of Cherbury.

Browning, Elizabeth Barrett
E. B. B. Thomson.
Her—"last poems." Dickinson.
Sisters, The. Lowell.
There they are, my fifty men and women. *Fr.* One Word More. Browning.
To Edward Fitzgerald. Browning.
To the Authoress of "Aurora Leigh." Dobell.

Browning, Robert
After Robert Browning. Chesterton.
Browning at Asolo. Johnson.
How I Brought the Good News from Aix to Ghent (or Vice Versa), parody. Yeatman *and* Sellar.
In a Copy of Browning. Carman.
Last Ride Together, The. Stephen.
Life-long, Poor Browning. Spencer.
Sincere Flattery. Stephen.
To Robert Browning. Landor.

Bruce, Robert
Bruce Addresses His Army. *Fr.* The Bruce. Barbour.
Bruce and the Spider. Barton.
Bruce Consults His Men. *Fr.* The Bruce. Barbour.
Bruce Meets Three Men with a Wether. *Fr.* The Bruce. Barbour.
Scots, Wha Hae wi' Wallace Bled. Burns.

Bruckner, Anton
Bruckner. Camp.

Brueghel, Pieter
Breughel's Winter. De la Mare.
Dance, The. Williams.
Et Quid Amabo Nisi Quod Aenigma Est. Sandy.
February; the Boy Breughel. Dubie.
Hunters in the Snow: Brueghel. Langland.
Lines on Brueghel's *Icarus.* Hamburger.
Musée des Beaux Arts. Auden.
Pictures from Brueghel, *sels.* Williams.
Proportions. Stroud.
Rural Lines after Breughel. Krapf.
Two Views of a Cadaver Room. Plath.

Brummell, Beau (George Bryan Brummell)
Brummell at Calais. Glassco.

Brunanburh, Battle of (937)
Battle of Brunanburh, The. *Unknown.*

Brussels, Belgium
Brussels in Winter. Auden.
Brussels, 1919. Oman.

Brutus (Marcus Junius Brutus)
Noblest Roman, The. *Fr.* Julius Caesar. Shakespeare.

Bryan, William Jennings
Bryan, Bryan, Bryan, Bryan. Lindsay.
Free Silver. *Unknown.*

Bryant, William Cullen
Bryant. *Fr.* A Fable for Critics. Lowell.

Bubbles
Lightness Remembered. Willard.
Madrigal: "This life which seemes so faire." Drummond of Hawthornden.

Buber, Martin
Martin Buber in the Pub. Harris.

Buckingham, George Villiers, 2d Duke of
Death of Buckingham, The. *Fr.* Moral Essays. Pope.
Duke of Buckingham, The. *Fr.* Absalom and Achitophel. Dryden.
Epitaph on the Duke of Buckingham. Shirley.
In the first rank of these did Zimri stand. *Fr.* Absalom and Achitophel. Dryden.
On the Duke of Buckingham, Slain by Felton, the 23rd August, 1628. Felltham.

Buckland, William
Serio-Comic Elegy, A. Whately.

Buddha
Buddha. Holmes.
Buddha. Melville.
Buddha at Kamakura, The. Kipling.
Buddha took some autumn leaves. *Fr.* The City of the Moon. Rexroth.
Buddha's Death Day: February 15, 1815. Issa.
Further Advantages of Learning. Rexroth.
Guatama in the Deer Park at Benares. Patchen.
Looking for Buddha. Jacinto.
Person after person. *Fr.* Oraga Haru. Issa.
Proofs of Buddha's Existence. *Unknown.*
So they rode/ Into a land of wells and gardens, where. *Fr.* The Light of Asia. Arnold.

Buffalo Bill (William Frederick Cody)
Buffalo Bill's. Cummings.
To William (Whom We Have Missed). Wodehouse.

Buffaloes
Bison, The. Belloc.
Bluffalo, The. Yolen.
Bone Yard. Barnes.
Buffalo. Daniells.
Buffalo. Eglington.
Buffalo, The. Moore.
Buffalo Dusk. Sandburg.
Buffalo Skinners, The. *Unknown.*
Caller of the Buffalo. Austin.
Death Chant. Blue Cloud.
Flower-fed Buffaloes, The. Lindsay.
Ghosts of the Buffaloes, The. Lindsay.
Passing of the Buffalo, The. Garland.
Song: "Hear me, ye smokeless skies and grass-green earth." *Fr.* The Last Bison. Mair.
Trail beside the River Platte, The. Heyen.

Bugles and Buglers
Danny Deever. Kipling.
No One Cares Less than I. Thomas.
Splendor Falls, The. *Fr.* The Princess. Tennyson.

Buildings and Builders
About an Excavation. Reznikoff.
Buildings. Gioseffi.
Construction. Shapiro.
Dome Poem. Smith.
Love Song: I and Thou. Dugan.
Midst the fair range of buildings which, new-reared. *Fr.* A Burlesque Ode, On the Author's Clearing a New House of Some Workmen. Keate.
On Watching the Construction of a Skyscraper. Raffel.
Bukhara, U. S. S. R.
Prayer Rug, The. Kennedy.
Bukowski, Charles
You Don't Know What Love Is. Carver.
Bulgaria
Two Masks Unearthed in Bulgaria. Meredith.
Bull Run, Battles of (1861, 1862)
Battle of Bull Run, The. *Unknown.*
Manassas. Warfield.
March into Virginia, The. Melville.
Our Left. Ticknor.
Run from Manassas Junction, The. *Unknown.*
Upon the Hill before Centreville. Boker.
Bullets
Like an Ideal Tenant. Daigon.
What the Bullet Sang. Harte.
Bullfights and Bullfighters
Bull Fight, The. *Fr.* Childe Harold's Pilgrimage. Byron.
Bullard's Song, The. *Unknown.*
Death Invited. Swenson.
Juan Belmonte, Torero. Finkel.
Lament for Ignacio Sánchez Mejías. García Lorca.
Matadors, The. Jacobsen.
Picador Bit, The. Noll.
Bullfinches
Bullfinches, The. Hardy.
Bulls
Bull, A. Deutsch.
Bull, The. Hodgson.
Bull, The. Sackville-West.
Bull, The. Williams.
Bull, The. Wright.
Bull Moses, The. Hughes.
Hoosen Johnny. *Unknown.*
Seventh Georgic. Economou.
Superbull. Witt.
Three Tall Men, The. *Unknown.*
Bundling
New Bundling Song, A. *Unknown.*
Bunker Hill, Battle of (1775)
Bunker Hill. Calvert.
Bunker Hill. *Unknown.*
Bunker's Hill, or the Soldier's Lamentation. Freeth.
Warren's Address at Bunker Hill. Pierpont.
Bunyan, John
For Tinkers Who Travel on Foot. Avison.
Of John Bunyan's Life. James.
Bunyan, Paul
Legend of Paul Bunyan, A. Bourinot.
Bureaucracy and Bureaucrats
Anteroom: Geneva. Devlin.
Committee, The. Day Lewis.
Constable Calls, A. Heaney.
Departmental Frost.
Frigate Jones, the Pussyfooter. Burke.
Pass Office Song. *Unknown.*
Unknown Citizen, The. Auden.
Burglars
Burglar Bill. "Anstey."
Burial
Call for the Robin Redbreast and the Wren. *Fr.* The White Devil. Webster.
Earth Buried. Mackenzie.
See also **Cemeteries; Funerals; Graves.**
Burke, Edmund
Edmund Burke. *Fr.* Retaliation. Goldsmith.
Burlesque. *See* **Striptease.**
Burma
Burma Hills. Gutteridge.
Mandalay. Kipling.
Burne-Jones, Edward
For "The Wine of Circe" by Edward Burne-Jones. Rossetti.
Burns, Robert
Address. Williams.
At the Grave of Burns. Wordsworth.
Burns. Halleck.
Had we two met, blythe-hearted Burns. Landor.
Mute Is Thy Wild Harp, Now, O Bard Sublime! Smith.
On a Fly-Leaf of Burns's Songs. Knowles.
Robert Burns. Alexander.
Written in the Visitors' Book at the Birthplace of Robert Burns. Cable.
Burr, Aaron
Aaron Burr. Benét.
Aaron Burr's Wooing. Stedman.
Colonel B. Carrier.
To Aaron Burr, under Trial for High Treason. Morton.
Burr, Theodosia
Theodosia Burr. Terrell.
Theodosia Burr; the Wrecker's Story. Palmer.
Burros. *See* **Donkeys.**
Burton, Sir Richard Francis (1821-1890)
Dedication: "Some nine years gone, as we dwelt together." Swinburne.
Bus Terminals
In the Baggage Room at Greyhound. Ginsberg.
Buses
Boarding, The. Johnson.
B's the Bus. *Fr.* All Around the Town. McGinley.
Bus, The. Cohen.
Bus Ride. Kandel.
Bus Ride. *Fr.* Ferry Ride. Robinson.
Interview. Lieberman.
Last Bus, The. Knox.
Motor Bus, The. Godley.
School Bus, The. Eigner.
Three Fitts. Parker.
Waking on a Greyhound. Henry.
Business and Businessmen
Accountant in His Bath, The. Mitchell.
Any Man to His Secretary. Corke.
Between a Contractor and His Wife. *Unknown.*
Business Is Business. Braley.
Dirge: "1-2-3 was the number he played but today the number came 3-2-1." Fearing.
Endurance Test. Balsdon.
Executive. Betjeman.
For Little Boys Destined for Big Business. Hoffenstein.
My Brother, Beautiful Shinault, That Goat. Huddle.
Salesman, A. Cummings.
Shopkeepers. Leib.
Wellington. Manhire.
See also **Accounting and Accountants; Advertising; Banking and Bankers; Capitalism; Commerce; Financiers; Insurance.**
Butchering and Butchers
Age of the Butcher, The. Friebert.
Butcher Shop. Simic.
Butcherboy. Schmidt.
Cock Crowing in a Poulterer's Shop, A. Ferguson.
Fifth Hell, The. *Fr.* The Seven Hells of the Jigoku Zoshi. Rothenberg.
Killing Rabbits. Ochester.
Leicester Chambermaid, The. *Unknown.*
My Father Owns the Butcher Shop. *Unknown.*
Reuben Bright. Robinson.
Same Old Story, The. Montague.
Songs from the Bride of Smithfield. Warner.
Stockyard, The. Squire.
Butler, Samuel (1612-1680)
English Liberal. Taylor.
On Butler who can think without just rage. *Fr.* A Satire. Oldham.
On the Setting up Mr. Butler's Monument in Westminster Abbey. Wesley.
Buttercups
Buttercups. Ginsberg.
Buttercups. Thorley.
Buttercups and Daisies. Howitt.
Butterflies
Blue-Butterfly Day. Frost.
Butterflies. Sansom.
Butterfly. Armstrong.
Butterfly, The. Burr.
Butterfly. Conkling.
Butterfly, The. Hawker.
Butterfly, The. James.
Butterfly, The. Kikaku.
Butterfly. Lawrence.
Butterfly, The. O'Keefe.

Butterfly, The. Palmer.
Butterfly. Smith.
Butterfly and the Bee, The. Bowles.
Butterfly and the Caterpillar, The. Lauren.
Butterfly and the Snail, The. *Fr.* Fables. Gay.
Butterfly in Church, A. McClellan.
Butterfly in the Fields. Campbell.
Butterfly on Rock. Layton.
City Butterfly. Siebert.
Corn-grinding Song. *Unknown.*
Dead Butterfly, The. Levertov.
Envoi: "Fly, white butterflies, out to sea." Swinburne.
Example, The. Davies.
Flying Blossoms. Davies.
Flying Crooked. Graves.
Fuzzy wuzzy, creepy crawly. Vanada.
Graceful Bastion, The. Williams.
Haiku: "Falling flower, A." Moritake.
Hoofer, The. Redwing.
I was round and small like a pearl. *Unknown.*
I'd Be a Butterfly. Bayly.
King of Yellow Butterflies, The. Lindsay.
Ode to a Butterfly. Higginson.
Of the Boy and Butterfly. Bunyan.
On Discovering a Butterfly. Nabokov.
Roots and Branches. Duncan.
September Butterfly. Boring.
To a Butterfly. Davies.
To a Butterfly. Schuck.
To a Butterfly. Wordsworth.
Was Worm. Swenson.
White Butterflies. Swinburne.
Wings. Wright.
"Yellow butterflies." Koianimptiwa.

Buzzards
Buzzard. Daugherty.
Buzzards, The. Armstrong.
Pondy Woods. Warren.
Song of the Turkey Buzzard. Welch.
See also **Vultures.**

Byrd, Richard Evelyn
Admiral Byrd. Nash.

Byron, George Gordon Noel Byron, 6th Baron
Bologna, and Byron. *Fr.* Italy. Rogers.
Byron. Coogler.
Byron in Greece. Rosten.
Byron Recollected at Bologna. *Fr.* Italy. Rogers.
Byron vs. DiMaggio. Meinke.
Memorial Verses. Arnold.
On the Proposal to Erect a Monument in England to Lord Byron. Lazarus.
On This Day I Complete My Thirty-sixth Year. Byron.
Sketch of Lord Byron's Life. Moore.
Very like a Whale. Nash.
You lived and moved among the best society. *Fr.* Letter to Lord Byron. Auden.

Byzantium
Byzantium. Yeats.
Sailing to Byzantium. Yeats.

C

Cabala
Modern Kabbalist. Falk.

Cabbages
Cabbage. Norman.

Cactus
Night-blooming Cereus, The. Hayden.
Organ Cactus, The. Scarborough.

Cadavers. *See* **Corpses.**

Cadiz, Spain, Battle of (1596)
Winning of Cales, The. Deloney.

Cads
Dinah. Ammons.
Rain It Raineth, The. Bowen.
Sidewalk Orgy. O'Connell.

Caedmon
Caedmon. Nicholson.

Caesar, Augustus
Fugal Chorus. *Fr.* For the Time Being. Auden.

Caesar, Julius
Antony's Oration. *Fr.* Julius Caesar. Shakespeare.
Brutus Explains Why He Murdered Caesar. *Fr.* Julius Caesar. Shakespeare.
Caesar Remembers. Seymour.
Julius Caesar. *Unknown.*
Palatine, The. Cather.
Pompey and Cornelia. *Fr.* Pharsalia. Lucan.
Rider at the Gate, The. Masefield.

Cafés
Grief of Cafeterias, The. Updike.
Home Cooking Cafe. Field.
In a Cafe. Brautigan.
In a Café. Dobson.

Cain and Abel
Abel. Capetanakis.
Abel. Lasker-Schüler.
Autobiography. Pagis.
Begetting of Cain, The. Plutzik.
Brothers. Pagis.

Cakes
After the Party. Wise.
Chocolate Cake. Payne.

Calais, France
Burgesses of Calais, The. Minot.

Calder, Alexander
Calder, A. Shapiro.

Calgary, Alberta
In the Cemetery of the Sun. Watson.

Caliban
Caliban upon Setebos; or, Natural Theology in the Island. Browning.

California
After the Cries of the Birds. Ferlinghetti.
As I Came Down Mount Tamalpais. Urmy.
At Carmel. Austin.
At Torrey Pines State Park. Mazzaro.
Banks of the Sacramento, The. *Unknown.*
Before the Stuff Comes Down. Snyder.
Berkeley Pier, The. Addiego.
Burning the Small Dead. Snyder.
Butter. Schmidt.
California. Harris.
California Dead. Murray.
California Oaks, The. Winters.
California Phrasebook, The. Schmitz.
California, This Is Minnesota Speaking. Dunn.
California 2. Cruz.
Californians, The. Spencer.
Changes around the Bay. Palmer.
Circumambulation of Mt. Tamalpais. Hoyem.
City: San Francisco. Hughes.
Clouds of Evening. Jeffers.
Death Looks Down. Gregg.
Elements of San Joaquin, The. Soto.
Grandfather. Stroud.
Hay for the Horses. Snyder.
Heading for Eugene. Schmidt.
Horse Named Bill, A. *Unknown.*
How Was Your Trip to L.A.? Whalen.
I met a Californian who would. *Fr.* New Hampshire. Frost.
In Montecito. Jarrell.
In the Redwood Forest. Pomeroy.
Just California. McGroarty.
Korea Bound, 1952. Childress.
Light Rain. Buckley.
Lizards of La Brea, The. De Baca.
Marin-An. Snyder.
Meridian. Ghiselin.
Mission Bay. Koethe.
Naming. Stroud.
Napa, California. Castillo.
Off from Swing Shift. Hongo.
Old Graves fell asleep. *Fr.* The Donner Party. Keithley.
On the Coast near Sausalito. Hass.
On the Road to Paradise. Hongo.
One West Coast. Young.
Open Casket. McPherson.
Orange County Plague: Scenes. Lieberman.
Palo Alto; the Marshes. Hass.
Report from California. Moyles.

Santa Barbara. Browne.
Seal Rock. Baugh.
Shore. O Hehir.
Sleep in the Mojave Desert. Plath.
Smudging. Wakoski.
Song of the Redwood-Tree. Whitman.
Street, The. Soto.
Trip: San Francisco. Hughes.
U.S. Coast and Geodetic Survey Ship *Pioneer,* The. Hershon.
View from an Institution. Wright.
Yosemite. Shinn.
Yugoslav Cemetery. Wright.

Caligula
Caligula. Lowell.

Calliope (muse)
To Calliope. Graves.

Calm
He That Is Slow to Anger. Bible, *O.T.* *Fr.* Proverbs.
Sonnet: "Blest Spirit of Calm that dwellest in these woods!" Sangster.

Calvary. *See* **Crucifixion, The.**

Calves
Bull Calf, The. Layton.
I Would Like You for a Comrade. Parry.
March Calf, A. Hughes.
New Baby Calf, The. Chase.
New Calf, The. Hearst.
New Calf, The. Vaughan.
Our Little Calf. Aldis.
Pastures, The. Frost.
Two-headed Calf, The. Gilpin.
What Is Veal? *Unknown.*
Young Calves, The. Coffin.

Calvin, John
Calvinist Autumnal. Harrod.

Calvinism
Calvin in the Casino. Cassity.
Calvinist in Love, A. Clemo.
Holy Willie's Prayer. Burns.
McAndrew's Hymn. Kipling.
Mr. Edwards and the Spider. Lowell.

Calypso (mythology)
Callypso Speaks. Doolittle ("H. D.").
Calypso. Kell.
Calypso's Island. MacLeish.
Forever Ambrosia. Morley.
Ulysses Leaves the Nymph Calypso. *Fr.* The Odyssey. Homer.

Calypso Music
Calypsomania. Brode.

Cambodia
Ank'hor Vat. Devlin.
Dead Soldiers. Fenton.

Cambridge, England
Autumn Morning at Cambridge. Cornford.
Cambridge and the Cam. *Fr.* The Apollyonists. Fletcher.
He Revisits Cambridge. *Fr.* In Memoriam. Tennyson.
Hic Vir, Hic Est. Calverley.
In the Backs. Cornford.
Inside of King's College Chapel, Cambridge. *Fr.* Ecclesiastical Sonnets. Wordsworth.
Residence at Cambridge. *Fr.* The Prelude. Wordsworth.
Water Color of Grantchester Meadows. Plath.
Written at Cambridge. Lamb.

Cambridge, Massachusetts
Cambridge Ladies, The. Cummings.
Professor Kelleher and the Charles River. O'Grady.
See also **Harvard University.**

Cambridge University
Autumn Morning at Cambridge. Cornford.
Inside of King's College Chapel, Cambridge. *Fr.* Ecclesiastical Sonnets. Wordsworth.
Lines on Cambridge of 1830. Tennyson.
On the University of Cambridge's Burning the Duke of Monmouth's Picture. Stepney.
Satire upon the Heads; or, Never a Barrel the Better Herring. Gray.
Winter Term. Brinnin.

Cambridgeshire, England
Bedford Level. *Fr.* The Fleece. Dyer.
Old Vicarage, Grantchester, The. Brooke.

Camden, William
To William Camden. Jonson.

Camden, New Jersey
Narcissus in Camden. Cone.

Camelot
Lady of Shalott, The. Tennyson.

Camels
Camel. Akhyaliyya.
Camel. Brownjohn.
Camel. Miller.
Camel, The. Nash.
Camel. Stallworthy.
Camel's Complaint, The. Carryl.
Camels, the Kings' Camels, The. Norris.
Dromedary, The. Campbell.
Dromedary. Dodat.
Exile. Sheard.
Fruit of the Tree, The. Wagoner.
Legend of the First Cam-u-el, The. Guiterman.
Plaint of the Camel, The. *Fr.* The Admiral's Caravan. Carryl.
Song of the Camels. Coatsworth.
Submission and Rest. *Unknown.*

Cameras. *See* **Photography and Photographers.**
Camera. Kooser.

Camões, Luis de
Camões and the Debt. Andresen.
Luis de Camões. Campbell.

Campaigns, Political
Autumn. Roberts.
What Mr. Robinson Thinks. Lowell.
See also **Voting and Voters.**

Campanula
Bed of Campanula, A. "Crichton."

Campbell, Roy
In Memoriam: Roy Campbell. Currey.

Camping
At the Shelter-Stone. Macrow.
August on Sourdough, a Visit from Dick Brewer. Snyder.
Discovery of the Pacific, The. Gunn.
Last Resort, The. Willson.
Lochan. Smith.
Minnesota Camp Grounds. Vizenor.
Morning in Camp. Bashford.
Night in Camp. Bashford.
Night in the Forest. Kinnell.
Oh, Lovely Rock. Jeffers.
Packing In with a Man. McCombs.
Staying Alive. Wagoner.
Talking Myself to Sleep in the Mountains. Ruark.
To Myself, Late, in a Myrtle Grove. Peterson.
Two Campers in Cloud Country. Plath.
What Are You Thinking About? Macmillan.

Campion, Edmund
Martyrdom of Father Campion, The. Walpole.

Campuses
Golgotha. Kennedy.
See also **Colleges and Universities.**

Canada
At the Tourist Center in Boston. Atwood.
Can. Lit. Birney.
Canada. Roberts.
Canada-I-O. *Unknown.*
Canadian Boat Song, A. Moore.
Canadian Boat Song, The. *Unknown.*
Carta Canadensis. Gustafson.
Crossing the Border into Canada. Harjo.
Deep Dark River. Roberts.
From Colony to Nation. Layton.
Let me put it this way. Jonas.
O Canada! Routhier.
Only Tourist in Havana Turns His Thoughts Homeward, The. Cohen.
Pierre of Timagami in New York. MacDonald.
Tadoussac. Bancroft.
Un Canadien Errant (An Exiled Canadian). *Unknown.*
Canadian Poetry in English (CaP). Bliss Carman, Lorne Pierce, *and* V. B. Rhodenizer, eds.
Modern Canadian Verse (MoCV). A. J. M. Smith, ed.
New American and Canadian Poetry (NeAC). John Gill, ed.
New Oxford Book of Canadian Verse, The (NOBC). Margaret Atwood, ed.
Oxford Book of Canadian Verse in English and French, The (OBCV). A. J. M. Smith, ed.
Penguin Book of Canadian Verse, The (PeCV). Ralph Gustafson, ed.
Wind Has Wings (WHW). Mary Alice Downie *and* Barbara Robertson, eds.
See also ***listings for Canadian provinces.***

Canals
Aged Pilot Man, The. "Twain."
Canal, The. Huxley.
Erie Canal, The. *Unknown.*
Lines Written on a Seat on the Grand Canal. Kavanagh.
Suez Crisis, The. *Unknown.*
Canaries
Canary, The. Nash.
Canary, The. Turner.
Poor Matthias. Arnold.
To the Canary Bird. Very.
Canberra, Australia
Canberra in April. Rowland.
Cancer (disease)
Bess. Stafford.
Cancer Cells, The. Eberhart.
Cancer Patient. Powers.
Cancer's a Funny Thing. Haldane.
Death from Cancer. *Fr.* In Memory of Arthur Winslow. Lowell.
Defiant One, The. Bailey.
Funeral, The. Dubie.
Mac. Vinz.
Miss Gee. Auden.
My Family's under Contract to Cancer. Simison.
Poem to Help My Father. Richman.
Tumor. Day.
Candlemas
Candlemas. Brown.
Ceremonies for Candlemas Day. Herrick.
Ceremonies for Candlemas Eve. Herrick.
Ceremony upon Candlemas Eve. Herrick.
Ground Hog Day. Pomeroy.
If Candlemas Day be dry and fair. *Unknown.*
If Candlemas Day be fair and bright. *Unknown.*
See also **Groundhogs.**
Candles
Candle, A. Suckling.
First Fig. Millay.
Little Nancy Etticoat *Unknown.*
Candy
Candy Man Blues. *Unknown.*
Chocolates. Simpson.
Dakota: Five Times Six. Hansen.
Girtonian Funeral, A. *Unknown.*
Pennycandystore beyond the El, The. *Fr.* A Coney Island of the Mind. Ferlinghetti.
Cannes, France
Afternoon at Cannes. Davis.
Cannibalism and Cannibals
Among the Anthropophagi. Nash.
Constant Cannibal Maiden, The. Irwin.
Donner Party, The. Keithley.
Juan embark'd—the ship got under way. *Fr.* Don Juan. Byron.
Little Billee. Thackeray.
Poe-'em of Passion, A. Lummis.
Snack, The. Zeiger.
Yarn of the *Nancy Bell*, The. Gilbert.
Canning
Canning Time. Morgan.
Canoes and Canoeing
Backwater Pond: The Canoeists. Merwin.
Canoe, The. Crawford.
Canoe-hauling Chant. Maori.
Canoe Song at Twilight. McCully.
Lullaby. Hillyer.
Paddling Song. *Unknown.*
Song My Paddle Sings, The. Johnson.
White Canoe, The. Sullivan.
Canonicus
Canonicus and Roger Williams. *Unknown.*
Canova, Antonio
On the Bust of Helen by Canova. Byron.
Cantors
Cantor's Dream before the High Holy Days, A. Robbins.
Caoilte
Caoilte. *Unknown.*
Cape Breton Island, Nova Scotia
In the Night Watches. Roberts.
Cape Cod, Massachusetts
Cape Cod Girls. *Unknown.*
Provincetown, *sels.* Dudek.
Provincetown, Mass. Shapiro.
Cape Horn
Round Cape Horn. *Unknown.*
Rounding the Horn. *Fr.* Dauber. Masefield.
Cape of Good Hope
Rounding the Cape. Campbell.
Cape Race
Way of Cape Race, The. Pratt.
Capital Punishment
But, Still, He. Lucas.
8:00 A.M. Monday Morning. Welsh.
Facing the Chair. "MacDiarmid."
Passive Resistance. Bruchac.
There is no chapel on the day. *Fr.* The Ballad of Reading Gaol. Wilde.
Ye brood of Conscience—Spectres! that frequent. *Fr.* Sonnets upon the Punishment of Death. Wordsworth.
See also **Executions.**
Capitalism
Aerosol. Witt.
After They Have Tired of the Brilliance of Cities. Spender.
Empire Builders. MacLeish.
Investor's Soliloquy. Ward.
Symphony, The. Lanier.
See also **Banking and Bankers; Business and Businessmen; Financiers.**
Cappadocia
I Knew a Cappadocian. Housman.
Caravaggio, Michelangelo Merisi da
In Santa Maria del Popolo. Gunn.
My own head. Seen in mirrors. Cleanly axed. *Fr.* Caravaggio Dying, Porto Ercole, July 1610, Aged 36. Lucie-Smith.
Carcassonne, France
Carcassonne. Nadaud.
Card Games
Game of Life, The. Saxe.
Ombre at Hampton Court. *Fr.* The Rape of the Lock. Pope.
To draw, or not to draw, that is the question. *Unknown.*
Cardinals (birds)
As a Child Seeing a Cardinal. Gill.
Cardinal. Howes.
Cardinal, The. *Fr.* Kentucky Mountain Farm. Warren.
Cardinal Bird, The. Gallagher.
Cargoes
Cargoes. Masefield.
See also **Freighters.**
aribbean Islands. *See* **West Indies.**
Caribbean Sea
For the Altarpiece of the Roseau Valley Church, Saint Lucia. Walcott.
See also **West Indies.**
Carlyle, Thomas
Carlyle and Emerson. Schuyler.
On the Deaths of Thomas Carlyle and George Eliot. Swinburne.
Thomas Carlyle. *Unknown.*
Carmel, California
Carmel Point. Jeffers.
Carnegie Hall, New York City
Carnegie Hall: Rescued. Moore.
Carnivals
Alone by the Road's Edge. O Hehir.
At the Carnival. Spencer.
Sunday Night in Santa Rosa. Gioia.
Caroline of Ansbach
On Queen Caroline's Deathbed. Pope.
Carousels. *See* **Merry-go-rounds.**
Carp
To the Carp, and Those Who Hunt Her. Hazard.
Carpe Diem
Advice, The. Flatman.
Advice to My Son. Meinke.
Age. Cowley.
Alarm, The. Jacob.
Apple, The. *At. to* Plato.
Argument, An. Moore.
Beauty. Guarini.
Birks of Endermay, The. Mallet.
Blue Girls. Ransom.
Bridal Couch. Lloyd.
But love whilst that thou mayst be loved again. *Fr.* To Delia. Daniel.
Choice, The. *Fr.* The House of Life. Rossetti.
Come Forth, Come Forth! "North."
Come, My Celia. *Fr.* Volpone. Jonson.
Come, Shepherds, Come! *Fr.* The Faithful Shepherdess. Fletcher.
Corinna in Vendome. Ronsard.
Corinna's Going a-Maying. Herrick.

Ditty in Imitation of the Spanish "Entre Tanto Que L'Avril." Herbert of Cherbury.
Enjoy Thy April Now. *Fr.* A Description of Beauty. Daniel.
Fading Beauty. *Unknown.*
From Far, from Eve and Morning. Housman.
Gather the Rose. *Fr.* The Faerie Queene. Spenser.
Gather Ye Roses. Stevenson.
Go, Lovely Rose. Waller.
Hope, like the hyaena, coming to be old. *Fr.* Diana. Constable.
In a Prominent Bar in Secaucus. Kennedy.
Is It Really Worth the While? *Unknown.*
Ladies, You See Time Flieth. *Unknown.*
Laugh and Be Merry. Masefield.
Lesbia. Catullus.
Let Us Drink and Be Merry. Jordan.
Logical Song, A. *Unknown.*
Look, Delia, how we 'steem the half-blown rose. *Fr.* To Delia. Daniel.
Look Up to Pentland's Tow'ring Tap. Ramsay.
Loveliest of Trees. Housman.
Love's Emblems. *Fr.* The Tragedy of Valentinian. Fletcher.
My Sweetest Lesbia, Let Us Live and Love. Campion.
Now Sleeps the Crimson Petal. *Fr.* The Princess. Tennyson.
Nymph's Reply to the Shepherd, The. Ralegh.
Of His Lady's Old Age. Ronsard.
Oh Mistress Mine. *Fr.* Twelfth Night. Shakespeare.
Passionate Shepherd to His Love, The. Marlowe.
Persuasions to Enjoy. Carew.
Pluck the Fruit and Taste the Pleasure. *Fr.* Robert, Second Duke of Normandy. Lodge.
Ponder, Darling, These Busted Statues. Cummings.
Quid Sit Futurum Cras Fuge Quaerere. Prior.
Rubáiyát of Omar Khayyám of Naishápúr, The. Omar Khayyám.
Sing We and Chant It. *Unknown.*
Sister, Awake. *Unknown.*
Song: "Young Philander woo'd me long." *Unknown.*
Song: "Youth's the season made for joys." *Fr.* The Beggar's Opera. Gay.
Song, on Reading That the Cyclotron Has Produced Cosmic Rays, Blasted the Atom into Twenty-two Particles, Solved the Mystery of the Transmutation of Elements and Devil Knows What. Hoffenstein.
Sonnet: "Fresh Spring, the herald of love's mighty king." *Fr.* Amoretti. Spenser.
Then Lose in Time Thy Maidenhead. *Unknown.*
Time. Taylor.
To A. L. Carew.
To Amarantha, That She Would Dishevel Her Hair. Lovelace.
To His Coy Mistress. Marvell.
To Phillis. Waller.
To the Virgins, to Make Much of Time. Herrick.
Villanelle of the Poet's Road. Dowson.
"Vive La Compagnie." *Unknown.*
Where Lies the Land. *Fr.* Songs in Absence. Clough.
Whole universe is full of God, The. Emre.
Young May Moon, The. Moore.
Young Men Come Less Often, The—Isn't It So? Horace.
See also **"Come Live with Me and Be My Love."**

Carpenters
At the Sign-Painter's. Carter.
Busy Carpenters. Tippett.
Craftsman. Shaw.
Work. Studdert-Kennedy.

Carpets. *See* **Rugs.**

Carriages
Carriage from Sweden, A. Moore.

"Carroll, Lewis"
Lewis Carroll. Farjeon.

Cars. *See* **Automobiles.**

Carson, Kit
Kit Carson's Last Smoke. "Vestal."
Kit Carson's Ride. Miller.
Oliver Wiggins. "Vestal."

Cartier, Jacques
Jacques Cartier. McGee.

Cary, Sir Lucius
To the Immortall Memorie, and Friendship of That Noble Paire, Sir Lucius Cary, and Sir H. Morison. Jonson.

Casabianca, Louis
Casabianca. Hemans.

Casanova, Giovanni
Casanova. Usborne.

Cassandra
Cassandra. Bogan.
Cassandra. Jeffers.
Cassandra. Robinson.

Castile, *See* Spain

Castle, Vernon
Vernon Castle. Monroe.

Castlereagh, Robert Stewart, 2d Viscount
Epitaph for Castlereagh, An. Byron.
Similes for Two Political Characters of 1819. Shelley.
What's My Thought Like? Moore.

Castro, Fidel
Ode to Fidel Castro. Field.
One Thousand Fearful Words for Fidel Castro. Ferlinghetti.

Catalpa Trees
Catalpa Tree. Colum.
Catalpa Tree. Waddington.

Catbirds
Air: "Cat bird singing." Creeley.
Cat Heard the Cat-Bird, The. Ciardi.
My Catbird. Venable.

Catechism
New Dial, The. *Unknown.*

Caterpillars
Biology Lesson. Engle.
Butterfly and the Caterpillar, The. Laruen.
Caterpillar, The. Hollo.
Caterpillar, The. *Fr.* Sing-Song. Rossetti.
Caterpillars. Freeman.
Cocoon. McCord.
Fuzzy wuzzy, creepy crawly. Vanada.
Only My Opinion. Shannon.
Psyche. Very.
Tickle Rhyme, The. Serraillier.

Catfish
Catfish, The. Waters.
Roosevelt Considers Catfish Stew. Smith.

Cather, Willa
Biography. Stanton.

Catherine of Siena, Saint
To Saint Catherine. Constable.

Catholicism
Catholic Bells, The. Williams.
Creek has to run muddy before it can run clear, The! *Fr.* Autumn Testament. Baxter.
First Confession. Kennedy.
Hind and the Panther, The, *sels.* Dryden.
Hippopotamus, The. Eliot.
Jansenist Journey. Devlin.
Lough Derg. Devlin.
On the Late Massacre in Piedmont. Milton.
Patient Church, The. Cardinal Newman.
Pill, The. Clarke.
Poem against Catholics. Fenton *and* Fuller.
To the Noblest and Best of Ladies, the Countess of Denbigh. Crashaw.
Anthology of Catholic Poets, An (ACP). Shane Leslie, ed.
Golden Book of Catholic Poetry, The (GoBC). Alfred Noyes, ed.

Cats
Ad-dressing of Cats, The. Eliot.
Alley Cat School. Asch.
Angora, The. Gerard.
Apartment Cats. Gunn.
Appeal to Cats in the Business of Love, An. Flatman.
Auld Seceder Cat, The. *Unknown.*
Bad Kittens, The. Coatsworth.
Belling the Cat. *Fr.* The Vision of Piers Plowman. Langland.
Black Cat. Dunetz.
Blessing, The. Berman.
Brothers. Edwards.
Burning the Cat. Merwin.
Bus Stop. O'Sullivan.
Calling in the Cat. Coatsworth.
Cat. Baruch.
Cat, The. Baudelaire.
Cat, The! Brennan.
Cat, The. *Fr.* Sad Memories. Calverley.
Cat, The. Church.
Cat! Farjeon.
Cat, The. Herford.
Cat. Miller.
Cat. Rosenblatt.
Cat, A. Thomas.
Cat and the Bird, The. Solomon.
Cat and the Moon, The. Yeats.
Cat & the Weather. Swenson.

Cat Ballerina Assoluta. Glen.
Cat, Caged and Shrunken, The. Freeman.
Cat Came Back, The. Miller.
Cat Goddesses. Graves.
Cat Heard the Cat-Bird, The. Ciardi.
Cat in the Snow. Fisher.
Cat Morgan Introduces Himself. Eliot.
Cat of Cats, The. *Fr.* The White Princess. Rands.
Cat of Many Years. Lutz.
Cat on Couch. Howes.
Cat on the Porch at Dusk. Harriman.
Cats. Chute.
Cats. Farjeon.
Cats. Francis.
Cats, The. Kees.
Cats. Scarfe.
Cats. Tessimond.
Cat's Conscience, A. *Unknown.*
Cat's Menu. Shaw.
Cats sleep fat and walk thin. *Fr.* Catalogue. Moore.
Cat's Song, The. *Unknown.*
Cheerio My Deario. *Fr.* Archy and Mehitabel. Marquis.
Chops. Dixon.
Civilization. Schmidt.
Country Barnyard. Coatsworth.
Cruel, but composed and bland. *Fr.* Matthias. Arnold.
Cruel Clever Cat. Taylor.
Curiosity. Reid.
Death of the Cat. Serraillier.
Diamond Cut Diamond. Milne.
Dirge for a Righteous Kitten. Lindsay.
Elegy: "My Thompson, least attractive character." Nemerov.
Epitaph for a Cat. Bruner.
Epitaph for My Cat. Garrigue.
Family Cat, The. Fuller.
Farewell, A. Flanner.
Fat Cat. Ronan.
Favourite Cat's Dying Soliloquy, A. Seward.
Femme et Chatte. Symons.
For a Little Girl Mourning Her Favorite Cat. Whittier.
For I Will Consider My Cat Jeoffrey. *Fr.* Jubilate Agno. Smart.
Four-Paws. Eden.
Freemon Hawthorne. Tolson.
Gaggle of Geese, Pride of Lions, A. Moore.
Galloping Cat, The. Smith.
Garden-Lion. Hayes.
Gardener's Cat, The. Chalmers.
Getting Up. Dobyns.
Growltiger's Last Stand. Eliot.
Gus: The Theatre Cat. Eliot.
Hearth. Bacon.
How to Measure a Cat. Johnson.
I Am the Cat. Usher.
I Like Little Pussy. Taylor.
In Honour of Taffy Topaz. Morley.
In Memoriam—Leo: A Yellow Cat. Sherwood.
Kilkenny Cats, The. *Unknown.*
Kitten, A. Farjeon.
Kitten, The. Nash.
Kitten and the Falling Leaves, The. Wordsworth.
Kitty. Prentiss.
Kitty: What She Thinks of Herself. Rands.
Last Words to a Dumb Friend. Hardy.
Lat Take a Cat. *Fr.* The Canterbury Tales: The Maunciple's Tale. Chaucer.
Lazy Pussy, The. Cox.
Leo to His Mistress. Sedgwick.
Listening. Fisher.
Little Cat Angel, The. Stanfield.
London Tom-Cat. Hamburger.
Love for a Hare. La Follette.
Macavity: The Mystery Cat. Eliot.
Man and Beast. Dyment.
Milk for the Cat. Monro.
Milk Jug, The. Herford.
Monk and His Pet Cat, The. *Unknown.*
Moon. Smith.
Mother Tabbyskins. Hart.
Music of the Future, The. Herford.
My Cats. Smith.
My Father Kept His Cats Well Fed. Sherman.
My Old Cat. Summers.
Mysterious Cat, The. Lindsay.
Nansen. Snyder.
Night. McKay.
O Cat of Carlish Kind. *Fr.* Philip Sparrow. Skelton.
Ode on the Death of a Favorite Cat, Drowned in a Tub of Goldfishes. Gray.
Old Cat's Confessions, An. Cranch.
Old Cat's Dying Soliloquy, An. Seward.
Old Trouper, The. *Fr.* Archy and Mehitabel. Marquis.
On a Cat, Ageing. Gray.
On a Night of Snow. Coatsworth.
On a Picture by J. M. Wright, Esq. Southey.
On Sitting Up Late, Watching Kittens. Paff.
Open Door, The. Coatsworth.
Owl and the Pussy-Cat, The. Lear.
Pangur Bán. *Unknown.*
Peter. Moore.
Poem: "As the cat." Williams.
Poem: "High on a ridge of tiles." Craig.
Prayer of the Cat, The. Gasztold.
Pussy-cat, pussy-cat, where have you been? Mother Goose.
Retired Cat, The. Cowper.
Rum Tum Tugger, The. Eliot.
Sad Memories. Calverley.
Secret in the Cat, The. Swenson.
Shadow. Delius.
Shuffling along in her broken shoes from the slums. *Fr.* Lady Feeding the Cats. Stewart.
Singing Cat, The. Smith.
Skimbleshanks: The Railway Cat. Eliot.
Song for a Child. Davis.
Song of Mehitabel, The. *Fr.* Archy and Mehitabel. Marquis.
Song of the Jellicles, The. Eliot.
Stable Cat, The. Norris.
Sunday. Coatsworth.
Teacher, The. Young.
That Cat. King.
Three Cheers for the Black, White and Blue. Pitter.
Three Little Kittens, The. *Unknown.*
Tiger-Cat Tim. Chase.
To a Cat. Coleridge.
To a Cat. Keats.
Tom-Cat, The. Marquis.
Tom Cat Blues. *Unknown.*
Tortoiseshell Cat, The. Chalmers.
Two Little Kittens. *Unknown.*
Two Songs of a Fool. Yeats.
Verses on a Cat. Daubeny.
Waiting for It. Swenson.
Wanted—a Witch's Cat. McGee.
Wet Thursday. Kees.
What Could It Be? Cole.
What the Gray Cat Sings. Guiterman.
White Cat. Knister.
"Who are you?" asked the cat of the bear. Coatsworth.
Why Did You Go. Cummings.
Witch Cat. Bennett.
Poetry of Cats, The (PCat). Samuel Carr, ed.

Cattle
Bags of Meat. Hardy.
Birth of Rainbow. Hughes.
Blond Hair at the Edge of the Pavement. Smith.
Branding Iron Herd, The. Rigby.
Cattle. Skrzynecki.
Driving Cattle to Casas Buenas. Campbell.
Drove-Road, The. Gibson.
Drover, A. Colum.
Eighteen-ninety. Shipp.
First Birth, The. Jones.
From the Gulf. Ogilvie.
Fulani Cattle. Clark.
Good-by, Steer. Carr.
Herdsman. Pettit.
Jersey Cattle. Currey.
Last Longhorn, The. Hall.
Macduff. Tomlinson.
March Calf, A. Hughes.
Names of the Humble, The. Murray.
Night-herding Song. Stephens.
Pastoral. Creighton.
Quiet-eyed Cattle, The. Norris.
Round-up, The. Howard.

Stampede, The. Brininstool.
Stampede, The. Coburn.
Stampede, The. Miller.
Ten Thousand Cattle. Wister.
See also **Bulls; Cowboys; Cows; Meat.**

Catullus
Ad Lesbiam. Catullus.
"Frater Ave atque Vale." Tennyson.
From a Letter from Lesbia. Parker.
On Catullus. Landor.
To a Roman. Squire.

Caucacus
Caucasus, The. Pasternak.

Cavalry
Cavalry Crossing a Ford. Whitman.
Charge of the Light Brigade, The. Tennyson.
Lancer. Housman.

Cavell, Edith
Edith Cavell. Woodberry.

Cavemen
Cave-Boy, The. Richards.
See also **Primitive Man.**

Caves
Ajanta. Rukeyser.
Cave of Staffa, I ("Ye shadowy beings, that have rights and claims"). Wordsworth.
Cave of Staffa, II ("We saw, but surely, in the motley crowd"). Wordsworth.
Cavern, The. Tomlinson.
Caves. Baker.
Secret Cavern, The. Widdemer.

Caviar
Virgin Sturgeon, The. *Unknown.*

Cayuga Lake, New York
Far above Cayuga's Waters. *Unknown.*

Cecilia, Saint
Alexander's Feast; or, The Power of Music. Dryden.
Ode against St. Cecilia's Day. Barker.
Song for St. Cecilia's Day. Auden.
Song for Saint Cecilia's Day, 1687. Dryden.

Celandine
Celandine. Thomas.
Small Celandine, The. Wordsworth.
To the Same Flower. Wordsworth.
To the Small Celandine. Wordsworth.

Celery
Celery. Nash.

Celibacy
Old Maid. Nicolson.
Old Saint, The. Stuart.
To Stella. Chapone.
See also **Bachelors; Spinsters; Virginity.**

Cellars
Root Cellar. Roethke.

Cellos
Cello, The. Gilder.

Celts
Celt in Me, The. Wilson.
Celts, The. McGee.
Celts, The. Smith.

Cemeteries
Air of June Sings, The. Dorn.
All Songs. Page.
Ancestors' Graves in Kurakawa. Kogawa.
Anniversary. Weissbort.
Apartments on First Avenue. Macdonald.
At the British War Cemetery, Bayeux. Causley.
At the Jewish Cemetery in Prague. Levertin.
Battlefield. Aldington.
Black Angel, The. Coulette.
Blows the Wind Today. Stevenson.
Cemetery at Academy, California, The. Levine.
Cemetery in New Mexico, A. Alvarez.
Cemetery Is, The. McGaffin.
Cemetery Nights. Dobyns.
Chelsea Churchyard. Mills.
Chinese Graves in Beechworth Cemetery, The. Mead.
Churchyard of St. Mary Magdalene, Old Milton. Heath-Stubbs.
Circa 1814. Staudt.
City Graveyard, A. Oates.
Cool Tombs. Sandburg.
Country Cemetery. Bunner.
Cows near the Graveyard, The. Nelson.
Crocus. Murray.
Dancing at Whitsun. Marshall.
Elegy in a Presbyterian Burying-Ground. Wilson.
Elegy Written in a Country Churchyard. Gray.
Etruscan Tombs. Robinson.
Family Plot. Singer.
Giorno dei Morti. Lawrence.
Graves at Elkhorn. Hugo.
Gravestones. Watkins.
Graveyard, The. Bialik.
Graveyard. Coffin.
Graveyard by the Sea. Lux.
Graveyard in Queens, A. Montague.
Hill, The. *Fr.* Spoon River Anthology. Masters.
In a Churchyard. Wilbur.
In a Country Cemetery in Iowa. Kooser.
In a Grave-Yard. Braithwaite.
In Flanders Field. McCrae.
In the Churchyard at Cambridge. Longfellow.
In the Old Jewish Cemetery, Prague, 1970. Lowbury.
Indian Burying Ground, The. Freneau.
Indian Graveyard, The. Weeks.
Island Cemetery, The. Auden.
Jewish Cemetery, The. Tiempo.
Jewish Cemetery at Newport, The. Longfellow.
Jewish Cemetery near Leningrad, A. Brodsky.
Leningrad Cemetery, Winter of 1941. Olds.
Levelled Churchyard, The. Hardy.
Lines Written at the Grave of Alexandre Dumas. Bennett.
Love in Magnolia Cemetery. Rankin.
Luss Village. Smith.
Memorial Day. Ching.
Mistress, The. Barton.
Mountain Cemetery, The. Bowers.
Mowing Crew, The. Wormser.
Ode to the Confederate Dead. Tate.
Old Burying-Ground, The. Whittier.
Old Churchyard of Bonchurch, The. Marston.
Old Jewish Cemetery in Worms. Kittner.
Papermill Graveyard. Belitt.
Passing the Graveyard. Young.
Place of Burial in the South of Scotland, A. Wordsworth.
Prairie Graveyard. Marriott.
Prison Graveyard. Knight.
Quaker Graveyard, The. Mitchell.
Soul Longs to Return Whence It Came, The. Eberhart.
This quiet dust was gentlemen and ladies. Dickinson.
To the Holy Spirit. Winters.
Town without a Market, The. Flecker.
Trinity Churchyard. Rukeyser.
Trinity Place. Sandburg.
Under bare Ben Bulben's head. *Fr.* Under Ben Bulben. Yeats.
Visiting Father. Lim.
Voices from Things Growing in the Churchyard. Hardy.
Widcombe Churchyard. Landor.
Wrestling Angels. Bottoms.
Yugoslav Cemetery. Wright.
See also **Burial; Graves.**

Censorship
Censorship. Waley.
Invocation: "Senator Smoot (Republican, Ut.)." Nash.
Lass in Wonderland, A. Scott.
Letter to a Librarian. Layton.
Penal Law. Clarke.

Centaurs
Ambuscade. McCrae.
Centaur, The. Roethke.
Centaurs, The. Stephens.

Centipedes
Centipede, The. Herbert.
Centipede, The. Nash.
Centipede Was Happy Quite, A. *Unknown.*

Central Park, New York City
Central Park. Lowell.
Central Park. Nemerov.
Central Park Tourney. Weston.
Central Park West. Moss.

Ceremonial Songs (genre)
Battle Song. Macuilxochitl.
Ho! Ye Sun, Moon, Stars. *Unknown.*
Hunting Song. *Unknown.*

Spell to Destroy Life, A. *Unknown.*
Moon-Bone Song, The. *Unknown.*
See also **Wedding Songs.**
Ceres. *See* **Demeter.**
Cereus, Night-blooming
Night-blooming Cereus, The. Hayden.
Cervantes Saavedra, Miguel de
Cervantes. Bentley.
To Miguel de Cervantes Saavedra. Munkitrick.
Ceylon. *See* **Sri Lanka.**
Cezanne, Paul
Oh, You Wholly Rectangular. Cole.
Three Cezannes. Whipple.
Chagall, Marc
After Chagall. Wenger.
Epithalamion: "Look there! *The Lovers/ in the Flowers.*" Schulman.
Homage to Chagall. Niatum.
On the Farther Wall, Marc Chagall. *Fr.* Spectator's Guide to Contemporary Art. McGinley.
Out of the Land of Heaven. Cohen.
Painting. Jacobs.
Poem for Marc Chagall. Cohen.
Chagres River, Panama
Beyond the Chagres. Gilbert.
Chairs
Address to His Elbow-Chair, New Cloath'd, An. Somervile.
Cane-bottomed Chair, The. Thackeray.
Chairs. Worth.
Grandmother's Old Armchair. *Unknown.*
Old Arm Chair, The. Cook.
Rocking Chair, The. Klein.
Rockingchair. Morgan.
White Autumn. Morgan.
Chaleur Bay, Canada
Phantom Light of the Baie des Chaleurs, The. Eaton.
Chameleons
Chameleon. Engle.
Chameleon, The. Herbert.
Lord's Chameleons, The. Klappert.
To a Chameleon. Moore.
Chamois
Chamois, The. Belloc.
Chamonix, France
Hymn before Sunrise in the Vale of Chamounix. Coleridge.
Chance. *See* **Fate; Fortune.**
Chancellorsville, Battle of (1863)
Keenan's Charge. Lathrop.
Change
Ancient to Ancients, An. Hardy.
Answering a Letter from a Younger Poet. Ghiselin.
Bricking the Church. Morgan.
Change. *Fr.* Caelica. Greville.
Change. Knister.
Change and Immutability. Scroggie.
Change-up. Lee.
Deserted Village, The. Goldsmith.
Disguises. Jennings.
Fault, The. Lucie-Smith.
Grandmother Watching at Her Window. Merwin.
In a World of Change. Awad.
In Drear-nighted December. Keats.
Lamentation of the Old Pensioner, The. Yeats.
Matter of Life and Death, A. Ridler.
Mutability. Shelley.
Mutability. *Fr.* Ecclesiastical Sonnets. Wordsworth.
New Sun, The. Wain.
Nothing Gold Can Stay. Frost.
Ö. Dove.
Other Fabrics, Other Mores! Lenngren.
Passin Ben Dorain. *Fr.* At the Heich Kirk-Yaird. Mackie.
Shall I compare thee to a summer's day? Sonnets, XVIII. Shakespeare.
Times Go by Turns. Southwell.
Van Winkle. *Fr.* The Bridge. Crane.
Varium et Mutabile. Wyatt.
Ways of God to Men, The. *Fr.* Samson Agonistes. Milton.
Wedding Party. Hall.
Western Approaches, The. Nemerov.
Where Dunwich Used to Be. *Fr.* By the North Sea. Swinburne.
Yardley-Oak. Cowper.
See also **Transcience.**
Channel Islands
Sark. *Fr.* The Garden of Cymodoce. Swinburne.
Channing, William Henry
Channing. Alcott.
Ode Inscribed to W. H. Channing. Emerson.
Chanteys. *See* **Sea Chanteys.**
Chanukah. *See* **Hanukkah.**
Chaos
Connoisseur of Chaos. Stevens.
Chaplin, Charlie
Chaplinesque. Crane.
Patriotic Ode on the Fourteenth Anniversary of the Persecution of Charlie Chaplin. Kaufman.
Chapman, George
On First Looking into Chapman's Homer. Keats.
Chapman, John (Johnny Appleseed)
Apple-Barrel of Johnny Appleseed, The. Lindsay.
Ballad of Johnny Appleseed, A. Oleson.
Johnny Appleseed. Benét.
Johnny Appleseed. Bourinot.
Johnny Appleseed. Lindsay.
Johnny Appleseed. Venable.
Chardin, Jean Baptiste
Still Life. De la Mare.
Charity
Charity. *Unknown.*
Charity Overcoming Envy. Moore.
Excelente Balade of Charitie, An. Chatterton.
"For Christ's sweet sake, I beg an alms." *Fr.* The Vision of Sir Launfal. Lowell.
Good King Wenceslas. Neale.
Good Works. *Fr.* The Vision of Piers Plowman. Langland.
How the Great Guest Came. Markham.
Husband and Heathen. Foss.
Hymne in Honour of Those Two Despised Virtues, Charitie and Humilitie, An. More.
I Shall Not Pass This Way Again. *Unknown.*
If I can stop one heart from breaking. Dickinson.
Karma. Robinson.
Offer, An. Guiterman.
Path Flower. Dargan.
Rather Too Good, Little Peggy! O'Keefe.
Tell Him So. *Unknown.*
See also Philanthropy and Philanthropists.
Charlemagne
Charlemagne. Longfellow.
Opening of the Tomb of Charlemagne, The. De Vere.
Charles I, King of England
And why so coffined in this vile disguise. *Fr.* The King's Disguise. Cleveland.
By the Statue of King Charles at Charing Cross. Johnson.
Fall, The. *Fr.* Il Pastor Fido. Fanshawe.
His Metrical View on the Death of King Charles I. Graham.
King Charles upon the Scaffold. *Fr.* An Horatian Ode upon Cromwell's Return from Ireland. Marvell.
Pastoral on the King's Death, The; Written in 1648. Brome.
Thou from th' enthroned martyrs blood-stain'd line. *Fr.* An Elegy upon the Most Incomparable King Charles the First. King.
To the King, upon His Comming with His Army into the West. Herrick.
To the King, upon His Welcome to Hampton-Court. Herrick.
Vows, The. Marvell.
Charles II, King of England
Ballad Called the Haymarket Hectors, A. *Unknown.*
Britannia and Raleigh. Ayloffe.
Charles II. *Fr.* Last Instructions to a Painter. Marvell.
Charles II. *Unknown.*
Commons' Petition to Charles II, The. Rochester.
Court of Charles II, The. *Fr.* To Augustus. Pope.
Dream of the Cabal, The; a Prophetical Satire. *Unknown.*
Epitaph on Charles II. Rochester.
Essay upon Satire, An. Sheffield.
History of Insipids, The. Freke.
Impromptu on Charles II. Rochester.
In pious times, ere priestcraft did begin. *Fr.* Absalom and Achitophel. Dryden.
Me thinks I see our mighty monarch stand. *Fr.* The Royal Angler. *Unknown.*
New Ballad, to an Old Tune, Called, I Am the Duke of Norfolk, etc., A. *Unknown.*
On the Lord Mayor and Court of Aldermen, Presenting the Late King and Duke of York Each with a Copy of Their Freedoms, Anno Dom. 1674. Marvell.
On the Prorogation. *Unknown.*
Parliament Dissolved at Oxford, The. *Unknown.*

Satire on Old Rowley. *Unknown.*
Song: Old Rowley the King. *Unknown.*
Tune to the Devonshire Cant, The. *Unknown.*
Upon His Majesty's Being Made Free of the City. Marvell.
Charles XII, King of Sweden
Charles XII. *Fr.* The Vanity of Human Wishes. Johnson.
Charles, Ray
Bishop of Atlanta, The: Ray Charles. Bond.
Blues Note. Kaufman.
Ray Charles. Cornish.
Charles River, Massachusetts
Professor Kelleher and the Charles River. O'Grady.
Some Refrains at the Charles River. Viereck.
Charleston, South Carolina
Charleston. Gilder.
Charleston. Hayne.
Charleston Garden, A. Bellamann.
Dusk. Heyward.
How He Saved St. Michael's. Stansbury.
Ode: "Sleep sweetly in your humble graves." Timrod.
Song about Charleston, A. *Unknown.*
Charm
What Is Charm? Thomas.
Charms (genre)
Charm, A. Dryden.
Charm for a Sudden Stitch. *Unknown.*
Charm for Unfruitful Land. *Unknown.*
Eastward I Stand, Mercies I Beg. *Unknown.*
Enchantment, The. *Fr.* Idylls. Theocritus.
House Blessing, A. Cartwright.
Hoping this night my true love to see. *Unknown.*
Marriage Charm, A. Hopper.
Nativity Chant, The. *Fr.* Guy Mannering. Scott.
New moon, new moon, I hail thee! *Unknown.*
St. Simon and Jude, on you I intrude. *Unknown.*
Spell of Invisibility, A. *At. to* Marlowe.
Twist Ye, Twine Ye! Even So. *Fr.* Guy Mannering. Scott.
Witches' Brew, The. *Fr.* Macbeth. Shakespeare.
Witches' Charms, The. *Fr.* The Masque of Queens. Jonson.
Witch's Broomstick Spell, The. *Unknown.*
Witch's Spell, A. *Unknown.*
Charon
Charon's Cosmology. Simic.
Dirce. *Fr.* Pericles and Aspasia. Landor.
Epigram: "When Bibo thought fit from the world to retreat." Prior.
Lost on a fogbound spit of sand. Auden.
There Charon stands, who rules the dreary Coast. *Fr.* The Aeneid. Virgil.
To Dives. Belloc.
Chartres, France
Chartres. *Fr.* View of the Cathedral. Henri.
Chattahoochee River, Georgia
Song of the Chattahoochee. Lanier.
Chatterton, Thomas
Last Verses. Chatterton.
We Poets in Our Youth. Wordsworth.
Chaucer, Geoffrey
Chaucer. Brawley.
Chaucer. Longfellow.
Continuation of *The Cook's Tale,* The. Zaranka.
Description of Sir Geoffrey Chaucer, The. *Fr.* Greene's Vision. Greene.
For a Statue of Chaucer at Woodstock. Akenside.
Lament for Chaucer. Hoccleve.
O reverend Chaucere, rose of rethoris all. *Fr.* The Goldyn Targe. Dunbar.
To Chaucer. *Fr.* De Regimine Principum. Hoccleve.
Cheese
Cheese it is a peevish elf. *Unknown.*
On Mites; to a Lady. Duck.
Queen of Cheese. McIntyre.
Quite the Cheese. Waring.
What a Friend We Have in Cheeses! Cole.
Chekhov, Anton
Chocolates. Simpson.
Chemical Warfare
Agent Orange. Kiefer.
Christmas 1924. Hardy.
Dulce et Decorum Est. Owen.
News That Stays News. Mariani.
Chemistry
Elements, The. Lehrer.
Sir Humphry Davy. *Fr.* Clerihews. Bentley.
Cherries
Adjectives. Nadir.
Cherries. Schneour.
Cherry-ripe. Herrick.
Cherry Trees
Cherry Tree, The. Gunn.
Cherry Trees, The. Thomas.
In a Town Garden. Mattam.
Loveliest of Trees. *Fr.* A Shropshire Lad. Housman.
Oh, Fair to See. Rossetti.
Orchard, The. Spence.
Under the Boughs. Baro.
Wild Cherry Tree. Blunden.
Chesapeake (ship)
Chesapeake and the *Shannon,* The. *Unknown.*
Shannon and the *Chesapeake,* The. Bouvé.
Chesapeake Bay
Chesapeake. Kennedy.
Night Trip across the Chesapeake and After. Lea.
Of Oystermen, Workboats. Smith.
Sea Hold, The. Sandburg.
Cheshire, England
Sands of Dee, The. Kingsley.
Chess
Duel in the Park. Grenelle.
Powers of the Pawn, The. Solway.
Prodigy. Simic.
Song of Chess, The. Ibn Ezra.
Spassky at Reykjavik. Fisher.
Chesterton, Gilbert Keith
G. K. Chesterton. Wolfe.
In Memory of G. K. Chesterton. De la Mare.
Lines to a Don. Belloc.
To G. K. Chesterton. Plunkett.
Chestnut Trees
Horse Chestnut Tree, The. Eberhart.
Chevy Chase. *See* **Otterburn, Battle of**
Chicago, Illinois
Bad Old Days, The. Rexroth.
Canal Street, Chicago. Fixmer.
Chicago. Kinnell.
Chicago. Ridge.
Chicago. Sandburg.
Chicago Allegory. Parker.
Chicago Poem. Welch.
Chicago, Summer Past. Snyder.
Dawn Patrol: Chicago. Durham.
Foreigners at the Fair. Brooks.
Journey. Thompson.
Making Chicago. Schmitz.
North Clark Street. Thompson.
On Clark Street in Chicago. Keithley.
On the Upside. Murray.
Stockyard, The. Squire.
Tenement Room: Chicago. Davis.
To Chicago at Night. Meigs.
To His Chi Mistress. Starbuck.
Tonight in Chicago. *Unknown.*
U Name This One. Rodgers.
Zoo, The. Logan.
Jump Bad; a New Chicago Anthology (JB). Gwendolyn Brooks, ed.
Chicanos
Black Hair. Soto.
Funeral of Rufino Contreras, The. Schuler.
Kearney Park. Soto.
Person, a Mexican, A. Martinez.
Fiesta in Aztlán (FIA). Toni Empringham, ed.
Chickadees
Chickadee. Conkling.
Chickadee, The. Emerson.
Chickadees, The. Hay.
Chickens
Beautiful Poultry. Wedde.
Blue Ribbon at Amesbury, A. Frost.
Chicken. De la Mare.
Chickens. Hewitt.
Chickens, The. *Unknown.*
Darkling Chicken, The. Peters.
Final Soliloquy on a Randy Rooster (in a Key of Yellow). Peters.
Gettin' Born. Euwer.
Hens, The. Roberts.
Henyard Round, The. Hall.

Orphan Born. Burdette.
Poultries, The. Nash.
See also **Hens; Roosters.**

Child Abuse
Child Beater. Ai.
Inquest, The. Davies.
Janitor, The; Kindergarten, Corinth. *Fr.* Tattoos. Wright.
Lilith's Child. Francisco.
Mary Arnold the Female Monster. *Unknown.*
Papa Love Baby. Smith.
Peter Grimes. *Fr.* The Borough. Crabbe.
Stepfather: A Girl's Song. Komunyakaa.
Whipping, The. Hayden.

Child Labor
Chimney Sweeper, The ("A little black thing among the snow"). *Fr.* Songs of Experience. Blake.
Chimney Sweeper, The. ("When my mother died I was very young"). *Fr.* Songs of Innocence. Blake.
Golf Links, The. Cleghorn.
Industrial Evils. *Fr.* Malvern Hills. Cottle.
Photo of Miners, A. Galvin.

Childhood and Children
Aaron Nicholas, Almost Ten. Hale.
About Children. McGinley.
After Visiting a Home for Disturbed Children. Lipsitz.
Age, An. Jensen.
Ajax Samples, The. Jensen.
Among School Children. Yeats.
Anecdote for Fathers. Wordsworth.
Another Grace for a Child. Herrick.
Baal-Shem Tov. Klein.
Baby Running Barefoot. Lawrence.
Babylon. Graves.
Back Road. Guernsey.
Ball Poem, The. Berryman.
Barefoot Boy, A. Riley.
Barefoot Boy, The. Whittier.
Barren. Rachel.
Bathers. Tiller.
Bearhug. Ondaatje.
Bears. Rich.
Beatrix Is Three. Mitchell.
Behold the child, by Nature's kindly law. *Fr.* An Essay on Man. Pope.
Birches. Frost.
Bitter Withy, The. *Unknown.*
Boy at the Window. Wilbur.
Boy Thirteen, A. Irish.
Boy with a Hammer. Hoban.
Boy with His Hair Cut Short. Rukeyser.
Boy's Song, A. Hogg.
Catechisms: Talking with a Four-year-old. Lyon.
Centaur, The. Swenson.
Certain Age, A. McGinley.
Characteristics of a Child Three Years Old. Wordsworth.
Child, The. Hall.
Child Ill, A. Betjeman.
Child Naming Flowers. Hass.
Child Next Door, The. Fyleman.
Child on Top of a Greenhouse. Roethke.
Childhood. Justice.
Childhood. More.
Childhood. Muir.
Childhood. O'Gorman.
Childhood. Read.
Childhood. Rilke.
Childhood and School-Time. *Fr.* The Prelude. Wordsworth.
Childhood Fled. Lamb.
Childless. MacConmidhe.
Children, The. Dickinson.
Children, The. Dyment.
Children, The. Soutar.
Children, The. Vinz.
Children and Sir Nameless, The. Hardy.
Children, Children Everywhere. Prelutsky.
Children Look at the Parents, The. Tessimond.
Children March, The. Riddell.
Children of Auschwitz. Korzhavin.
Children: Private Ward. *Fr.* In Hospital. Henley.
Children, the Sandbar, That Summer. Rukeyser.
Children's Elegy. *Fr.* Eighth Elegy. Rukeyser.
Children's Hour, The. Longfellow.
Child's First Grief, The. Hemans.
Child's Laughter, A. Swinburne.
Child's Sight, The. Sobiloff.
Chinatown Games. Lum.
Conversation. McCord.
Cradle Song, A. Blake.
Cry of the Children, The. Browning.
Cuddle Doon. Anderson.
David. Gibson.
Day You Are Born, The. Song.
Days Gone By, The. Riley.
Days of Birth. *Unknown.*
Deaf School. Hughes.
Deborah Lee. Yvonne.
Descending Figure. Glück.
Deserted Garden, The. Browning.
Digging for China. Wilbur.
Don't Forget. Berg.
Doorman. Galvin.
Drawings by Children. Mueller.
Earliest Spring. Levertov.
Early Supper. Howes.
Ecce Puer. Joyce.
Echo and the Ferry. Ingelow.
Efficiency Apartment. Barrax.
Elementary Scene, The. Jarrell.
Elementary School Classroom in a Slum, An. Spender.
Eleven. MacLeish.
Evening. Wright.
Ex Ore Infantium. Thompson.
Exigencies. Gilbert.
Experience. Kilmer.
False Security. Betjeman.
Family Reunions. Miller.
Farm Boy after Summer. Francis.
Farm Child. Thomas.
Father and Child. Harwood.
Fern Hill. Thomas.
Field Trip. Miranda.
First Song. Kinnell.
For a Child Expected. Ridler.
Four Pictures by Juan, Age 5. McKain.
Four Spacious Skies. Astor.
Freedom, New Hampshire. Kinnell.
Fresh News from the Past. Bell.
Frolic. "Æ."
Fruit Plucker, The. Coleridge.
Gardeners. Ignatow.
Germinal. "Æ."
Getting Experience. Williams.
Good and Bad Children. Stevenson.
Ha Ha This-a-Way. Leadbelly.
Harold at Two Years Old. Myers.
Hero, The. Graves.
Hiding. Aldis.
Holy Thursday ("Is this a holy thing to see"). *Fr.* Songs of Experience. Blake.
Holy Thursday (" 'Twas on a Holy Thursday, their innocent faces clean"). *Fr.* Songs of Innocence. Blake.
Holy Well, The. *Unknown.*
Horse Chestnut Tree, The. Eberhart.
House of Readers, A. Miller.
Humiliation Revisited. Ashley.
I Am Called Childhood. More.
I Don't Like Beetles. Fyleman.
I Don't Want to Play in Your Yard. Wingate.
I Have Seen a Curious Child. *Fr.* The Excursion. Wordsworth.
I Remember, I Remember. Hood.
I Remember, I Remember. Larkin.
"I remember my mother, the day that we met." *Fr.* Songs of Education. Chesterton.
I Would Like You for a Comrade. Parry.
If I Could Only Live at the Pitch That Is near Madness. Eberhart.
In just-/Spring when the world is mud. *Fr.* Chansons Innocentes. Cummings.
In Reference to Her Children, 23 June, 1656. Bradstreet.
In School-Days. Whittier.
In the Barrio. Alurista.
In the Waiting Room. Bishop.
Incident. Cullen.
Indian Children Speak. Bell.
Indoor Games near Newbury. Betjeman.
Infant Innocence. Housman.

It Was a Special Treat. Tapahonso.
Janet Waking. Ransom.
Jenny White and Johnny Black. Farjeon.
Jest 'fore Christmas. Field.
Jim, Who Ran Away from His Nurse, and Was Eaten by a Lion. Belloc.
Jo Jo, My Child. *Unknown.*
Judeebug's Country. Johnson.
Kicking the leaves today, as we walk home together. *Fr.* Kicking the Leaves. Hall.
Kindergarten. Schmitz.
Knock on Wood. Dumas.
Land of Counterpane, The. Stevenson.
Laughing Child. Sandburg.
Life-Lesson, A. Riley.
Lilliput Levee. Rands.
Lines: "Here often, when a child, I lay reclined." Tennyson.
Lisa. Carrier.
Little Boy Blue. Field.
Little Brother, The. Reeves.
Little Brother's Secret. Mansfield.
Little Dancers, The. Binyon.
Little Girl with Bands on Her Teeth, The. Taggard.
Little Orphant Annie. Riley.
Lives of Gulls and Children, The. Nemerov.
Lost Child, The. Reaney.
Lost Children, The. Jarrell.
Love. Lane.
Lullaby: "O! hush thee, my darling, sleep soundly my son." *Unknown.*
Lunch with Girl Scouts. Bryan.
Magician Suspends the Children, The. Oles.
Mamma! Horne.
Mein Kind, Wir Waren Kinder. Heine.
Memory. Lincoln.
Mighty Lak' a Rose. Stanton.
Minnie and Mattie. Rossetti.
Mrs. Johnson Objects. Thompson.
My Childhood's Bedroom. Tisdale.
My Father in the Night Commanding No. Simpson.
My Lost Youth. Longfellow.
My Parents Kept Me from Children Who Were Rough. Spender.
Names, The. Edmond.
Next War, The. Graves.
Nikki-Rosa. Giovanni.
Norfolk. Betjeman.
Nurse's Song ("When the voices of children are heard on the green/ And laughing is heard on the hill"). *Fr.* Songs of Innocence. Blake.
Nurse's Song ("When the voices of children, are heard on the green/ And whisprings are in the dale"). *Fr.* Songs of Experience. Blake.
O God, Great Father, Lord, and King. Hoss.
Ode: Intimations of Immortality from Recollections of Early Childhood. Wordsworth.
Ode on a Distant Prospect of Eton College. Gray.
Oft in the Stilly Night. Moore.
Oh Come, Little Children. McGinley.
Old Oaken Bucket, The. Woodworth.
On a Catholic Childhood. Hale.
On Children. *Fr.* The Prophet. Gibran.
On Living with Children for a Prolonged Time. Lowey.
On the Beach at Fontana. Joyce.
Ontogeny. Ramsey.
Palm Leaves of Childhood. Adali-Mortti.
Parental Recollections. Lamb.
Party. Carrier.
Party, The. Whittemore.
Party in Winter. Shapiro.
Past and Present. Hood.
Pet Name, The. Browning.
Piano. Lawrence.
Picnic, The. Logan.
Picture of Little T. C. in a Prospect of Flowers, The. Marvell.
Poem of Distant Childhood. Sousa.
Poet at Seven, The. Rimbaud.
Poop. Locklin.
Portrait. Glück.
Praise of a Child. Yoruba.
Prayer for My Daughter, A. Yeats.
Puer Aeternus. Raine.
Rebecca, Who Slammed Doors for Fun and Perished Miserably. Belloc.
Red Flag, The. Jackson.
Retreat, The. Vaughan.
Ring-a-Ring. Greenaway.
Rock Me to Sleep. Allen.
Romping. Ciardi.
Roundhouse Voices, The. Smith.
Rustic Childhood. Barnes.
School-Bell. Farjeon.
School Globe, The. Reaney.
Science for the Young. Irwin.
Sculpture. *Unknown.*
Settlers, The. Hemschemeyer.
Ships of Yule, The. Carman.
Shy Geordie. Cruickshank.
Sick Child, A. Jarrell.
Sick Child, The. Stevenson.
Sister Bernardo. Wilde.
Six of Cups. Wakoski.
Sleeping Giant, The. Hall.
Small, The. Welch.
Smell My Fingers. Axelrod.
So Long Folks, Off to the War. Ostroff.
Son and Surf. Strong.
Song about Myself, A. Keats.
Song for the Middle of the Night, A. Wright.
Spitting on Ira Rosenblatt. Hershon.
Spring and Fall. Hopkins.
Squatter's Children. Bishop.
Stern Parent, The. Graham.
Stevenson's Birthday. Miller.
Stove. Booth.
Suppose. Cary.
Tamerlane. Daley.
Testing-Tree, The. Kunitz.
There Was a Boy. *Fr.* The Prelude. Wordsworth.
There Was a Child Went Forth. Whitman.
There Was a Little Girl. Longfellow.
There Were Some Summers. Lux.
Thesis, Antithesis, and Nostalgia. Dugan.
They Grow Up Too Fast, She Said. O Hehir.
This Song Shows Me Pictures; Morningside Drive, New York City 1950–1960. Oyama.
Three Children near Clonmel, The. Shanahan.
Three Poems about Children. Clarke.
Three Years She Grew. Wordsworth.
Time of Light, a Time of Shadow, A. Yellen.
To a Child. Gardons.
To a Child. Montgomery.
To a Child. Morley.
To a Child Five Years Old. Cotton.
To a Child of Quality. Prior.
To a Child Trapped in a Barber Shop. Levine.
To a Small Boy Standing on My Shoes while I Am Wearing Them. Nash.
To H. C. Wordsworth.
To My Child Carlino. Landor.
To Myself, after Forty Years. White.
To One Older. Boyd.
Toyland. MacDonough.
Toys, The. Patmore.
Ts'eekkaayah. TallMountain.
Tumbling. *Unknown.*
Two Childhood Memories. Zolynas.
Two girls of twelve or so at a table. Reznikoff.
Ugly Chile. Williams.
Uncle Dog; the Poet at 9. Sward.
Verigin, Moving in Alone. Newlove.
Vision of Children, A. Ashe.
Waking in the Dark. Livesay.
War of the Worlds, The. Rutsala.
Warning to Children. Graves.
Washing My Son. Holden.
What I Did Last Summer. Ikan.
What Zimmer Would Be. Zimmer.
When a Feller's Itchin' to Be Spanked. Dunbar.
When I Was a Little Girl. Milligan.
When I Was Six. Cross.
When I Was Small. Chénier.
Where Are the Waters of Childhood? Strand.
Where Children Live. Nye.
Where Knock Is Open Wide. Roethke.
Whipping, The. Hayden.
Who Knows? Perry.
Whole Duty of Children. Stevenson.
Why? Boyd.
Windfall. Arsenault.
Windfall. Mitchell.

Wishes for My Son. MacDonagh.
With a First Reader. Hughes.
Woodman, Spare That Tree. Morris.
Young and Old. Kingsley.
Youth and Age. Coleridge.
Zimmer's Head Thudding against the Blackboard. Zimmer.
Home Book of Verse, The (HBV-1), pp. 250-326. Burton Egbert Stevenson, ed.
See also **Adolescence; Boys; Death in Childhood; Girls; Youth.**

Children's Verse
Faber Book of Children's Verse, The (FaBoCh). Janet Adam Smith, comp.
Faber Book of Useful Verse, The (FaBoUs), pp. 85-104. Simon Brett, ed.
Golden Numbers (GN). Kate Douglas Wiggin *and* Nora Archibald Smith, eds.
Home Book of Verse for Young Folks, The (HBVY). Burton Egbert Stevenson, ed.
New Treasury of Children's Poetry, A (NTCP). Joanna Cole, ed.
Once upon a Rhyme (OnUR). Sara *and* Stephen Corrin, eds.
Oxford Book of Children's Verse, The (OxBChV). Iona *and* Peter Opie, eds.
Oxford Book of Children's Verse in America, The (OBCA). Donald Hall, ed.
Oxford Nursery Rhyme Book, The (OxNR). Iona *and* Peter Opie, eds.
Piping Down the Valleys Wild (PDV). Nancy Larrick, ed.
Random House Book of Poetry for Children, The (RHPC). Jack Prelutsky, ed.
Sing a Song of Seasons (SiSoSe). Sara *and* John Brewton, eds.
Sound of Poetry, The (SoPo). Mary C. Austin *and* Queenie B. Mills, eds.
Sung Under the Silver Umbrella (SUS). Association for Childhood Education International.
Time for Poetry (TiPo). May Hill Arbuthnot, comp.
Wind Has Wings, The; Poems from Canada (WHW). Mary Alice Downie *and* Barbara Robertson, eds.
Year Around, The; Poems for Children (YeAr). Alice I. Hazeltine *and* Elva S. Smith, comps.

Chile
All of a Sudden. Jesús.
On the Death of Neruda. Cabral.
To Speak of Chile. Gibson.

Chillon Castle, Switzerland
Prisoner of Chillon, The. Byron.

Chimney Sweepers
Chimney Sweeper, The ("A little black thing among the snow"). *Fr.* Songs of Experience. Blake.
Chimney Sweeper, The ("When my mother died I was very young"). *Fr.* Songs of Innocence. Blake.
Chimney-Sweeper's Complaint, The. Alcock.
Sootie Joe. Tolson.
Wm. Brazier. Graves.
Wmffre the Sweep. Humphries.

Chimneys
Kitchen Chimney, The. Frost.

Chimpanzees
Chimpanzee, The. Herford.

China
At the Great Wall of China. Blunden.
Chee Lai! (Arise!). *Unknown.*
China Policy, The. Rakosi.
Chinese Nightingale, The. Lindsay.
Digging for China. Wilbur.
I Lie on the Chilled Stones of the Great Wall. Liu.
Merchants from Cathay. Benét.
Myths. Klauck.
Sea Gypsy, The. Hovey.
South, The. Wang Chien.
Wall of China, The. Colum.
Walls. Allen.

Chinatowns
Chinatown Games. Lum.
Day of the Parade. Lau.
Disco Chinatown. Kageyama.
My Son & I, between *Fu-Sang* and/ Cathay. *Fr.* Sussyissfriin. Dow.

Chinaware
Bone China. Lister.
In a China Shop. Hellman.
In a V. A. D. Pantry. Vickridge.
Moral in Sèvres, A. Howells.
No Swan So Fine. Moore.
To a Lady on Her Passion for Old China. Gay.
Willowware Cup. Merrill.

Chinese, The
At a Chinaman's Grave. Lum.
Chinaman's Chance, A. Chin.
Chinatown Talking Story. Tsui.
Grandmother Poems. Chin.
How a Girl Got Her Chinese Name. Wong.
Immigration Act of 1924, The. Mar.
Landlord's Wife, The. Chin.
Losing Track. Song.
My Father's Martial Art. Liu.
My Mother, Who Came from China, Where She Never Saw Snow. Mar.
Plain Language from Truthful James. Harte.
Second Nature. Chang.
Sweet 'n Sour. Lim.
We Are a Young Nation, Uncle. Chin.
Yellow Woman Speaks. Woo.

Chinoiseries
Chinoiseries: Reflections. Lowell.

Chipeta (Wife of Ute Chief Ouray)
Chipeta. Field.
Chipeta's Ride. Taylor.

Chipmunks
Chipmunk's Day, The. Jarrell.
Little Charlie Chipmunk. LeCron.

Chisholm Trail
Old Chisholm Trail, The. *Unknown.*

Choctaw Indians
Four Choctaw Songs. Barnes.
Four Things Choctaw. Barnes.

Cholera
Mowers, The; an Anticipation of the Cholera, 1848. Mackay.

Christenings
Kyran's Christening. Nowlan.
To C. F. H. on Her Christening-Day. Hardy.
See also **Baptism.**

Christianity and Christians
After Two Thousand Years. "MacDiarmid."
All One in Christ. Oxenham.
Call to the Strong, The. Merrill.
Challenge, The. Kleiser.
Christians at War. Kendrick.
Clarion-Call, The. *Unknown.*
Get Somebody Else. Dunbar.
God Wants a Man. *Unknown.*
In Earthern Vessels. Whittier.
In the Twentieth Century of My Trespass on Earth. *Fr.* The Dead Shall Be Raised Incorruptible. Kinnell.
Is This the Time to Sound Retreat? *Unknown.*
Kind pity chokes my spleen; brave scorn forbids. *Fr.* Satires. Donne.
Last Words of Don Henriquez, The. Schneour.
Light of Faith, The. Dupree.
Sunday Morning. Stevens.
Eerdmans Book of Christian Poetry (EBCP). Pat Alexander, comp.
New Oxford Book of Christian Verse, The (NOCV). Donald Davie, ed.
Oxford Book of Christian Verse, The (OxBoCh). Lord David Cecil, ed.
Treasury of Christian Poetry, The (TrCP). Lorraine Eitel, comp.

Christmas
Adoration of the Wise Men, The. Alexander.
Advent; a Carol. Dickinson.
Advent 1966. Levertov.
After Christmas. *Fr.* For the Time Being; a Christmas Oratorio. Auden.
Alchemy. Love.
Almighty Spake, and Gabriel Sped, Th'. Richards.
"And Lo, the Star!" Haley.
Ane Sang of the Birth of Christ, with the Tune of Baw Lula Low. Luther.
Angels, The. Drummond of Hawthornden.
Angels, from the Realms of Glory. Montgomery.
Apple Wassail. *Unknown.*
As I Sat on a Sunny Bank. *Unknown.*
As I Sat under a Sycamore Tree. *Unknown.*
As I Went Down to David's Town. Stewart.
As Joseph Was a-Walking. *Unknown.*
At Christmastide. Simmons.
BC:AD. Fanthorpe.
Babushka. Thomas.
Ballad of the Cross, The. Garrison.
Ballad of the Epiphany. Dalmon.
Barn, The. Coatsworth.
Before the Paling of the Stars. Rossetti.
Bethlehem Town. Field.
Bow Down, Mountain. Farber.
Brightest and Best of the Sons of the Morning. Heber.
Burning Babe, The. Southwell.
Burning the Christmas Greens. Williams.
Can I Not Sing. *Unknown.*

Carnal and the Crane, The. *Unknown.*
Carol, A: "Angels to the shepherds sang, The." Weatherly.
Carol, A: "He came all so still." *Unknown.*
Carol, A: "Mary the Mother." Reese.
Carol: "There was a Boy bedded in bracken." Short.
Carol: "We saw him sleeping in his manger bed." Bullett.
Carol: "When the herds were watching." Canton.
Carol for Children, A. Nash.
Carol for Christmas Day, A. Byrd.
Carol for Christmas Day, A. Kinwelmersh.
Carol for His Darling on Christmas Day. Stanford.
Carol of Patience. Graves.
Carol of the Poor Children, The. Middleton.
Carolers. Westerfield.
Cause for Wonder, A. *Unknown.*
Ceremonies for Christmas. Herrick.
Cherry-Tree Carol, The. *Unknown.*
Child Is Born, A. *Unknown.*
Childlike Heart. Catlin.
Child's Song of Christmas, A. Pickthall.
Christ Climbed Down. Ferlinghetti.
Christmas. Betjeman.
Christmas. Chute.
Christmas. Herbert.
Christmas Amnesty. Pierce.
Christmas at a Decade's End. Snyder.
Christmas at Babbitt's. Tweedy.
Christmas at Sea. Stevenson.
Christmas Bells. Longfellow.
Christmas Candle, The. Brown.
Christmas Carol, A: "Christ child lay on Mary's lap, The." Chesterton.
Christmas Carol, A: "Everywhere, everywhere, Christmas tonight." Brooks.
Christmas Carol: "From the starry hev'ns descending." Newell.
Christmas Carol, A: "In the bleak mid-winter." Rossetti.
Christmas Carol: "Lacking samite and sable." Probyn.
Christmas Carol, A: "Shepherds went their hasty way." Coleridge.
Christmas Carol, A: "So, now is come our joyful'st feast." Wither.
Christmas Carol, A: "There's a song in the air!" Holland.
Christmas Carol, A: "Three damsels in the queen's chamber." Swinburne.
Christmas Carol: "Three outas from the bleak Karoo." Opperman.
Christmas Carol: "Villagers all, this frosty tide." Grahame.
Christmas Carol, A: " 'What means this glory round our feet.' " Lowell.
Christmas Caroll Sung to the King in the Presence at White-Hall, A. Herrick.
Christmas Chant. Shaw.
Christmas Childhood, A. Kavanagh.
Christmas Cradlesong, A. Lope de Vega.
Christmas Dawn at Sea, A. Morgan.
Christmas Day. *Fr.* Hymns and Spiritual Songs. Smart.
Christmas Day. Young.
Christmas Day in the Workhouse. Sims.
Christmas Day Is Come. Wadding.
Christmas Day; the Family Sitting. Falkner.
Christmas Eve. Siegel.
Christmas Folk-Song, A. Reese.
Christmas Hymn, A. Domett.
Christmas Hymn, A. Wilbur.
Christmas in Freelands. Stephens.
Christmas in the Heart. *Unknown.*
Christmas in the Olden Time. *Fr.* Marmion. Scott.
Christmas in the Wood. Frost.
Christmas is coming/ The geese are getting fat. *Unknown.*
Christmas Is Really for the Children. Turner.
Christmas Is Remembering. Binns.
Christmas Island. Bates.
Christmas Lullaby. Troubetzkoy.
Christmas Morning. Roberts.
Christmas Morning I. Freeman.
Christmas Mourning. Miller.
Christmas Myth, 1973. McGovern.
Christmas Night. MacCawell.
Christmas 1959 et Cetera. Barrax.
Christmas 1914. Harding.
Christmas Now Is Drawing Near. *Unknown.*
Christmas Pageant. Fishback.
Christmas Prayer, A. Haley.
Christmas Prayer, A. Hines.
Christmas Prayer, A. Macdonald.
Christmas Prayer. Morse.
Christmas Prayer, A. Stevenson.
Christmas Singing. Chandler.
Christmas Song. Carman.
Christmas Song. Field.
Christmas Song. Long.
Christmas Songs. Kennedy.
Christmas Story (1980). Arrowsmith.
Christ's Nativity. Vaughan.
Come, Holy Babe! Bangham.
Come, Ride with Me to Toyland. Bennett.
Computer's First Christmas Card, The. Morgan.
Conversation between Mr. and Mrs. Santa Claus. Bennett.
Cradle and Throne. *Unknown.*
Cradle Hymn, A. Watts.
Crib, The. Finch.
Cultivation of Christmas Trees, The. Eliot.
Day before Christmas. Chute.
Day before Christmas, The. Souster.
Day Dawn of the Heart. *Unknown.*
Dear Son, Leave Thy Weeping. *Unknown.*
December Fragments. Lattimore.
December 24, 1979. Weaver.
December 26. Hoffman.
Earth and Sky. Farjeon.
Earth Listens. Bates.
Eighth Street West. Field.
End of the Play, The. *Fr.* Dr. Birch and His Young Friends. Thackeray.
Eternal Christmas. Phelps.
Ex Ore Infantium. Thompson.
Far Trumpets Blowing. Benson.
Farewell Advent. *At. to* Ryman.
First Christmas, The. *Fr.* St. Luke. Bible, *N.T.*
Flemish Primitive. Fraser.
Flight into Egypt, The. *Fr.* For the Time Being; a Christmas Oratorio. Auden.
For Us No Night Can Be Happier. Zinzendorf.
Forgotten Star, The. Clark.
Friendly Beasts, The. *Unknown.*
From Bethlehem Blown. Leitch.
Gates and Doors. Kilmer.
Gloucestershire Wassail. *Unknown.*
Groundhog, The. Shaw.
Guest, The. *Unknown.*
Hail, Comly and Clene. *Fr.* The Second Shepherds' Play. *Unknown.*
Happy Christmas, A. Havergal.
Hark! Hark! with Harps of Gold. Chapin.
Hay, Ay, Hay, Ay. *Unknown.*
"He Is Our Peace." Haley.
Heavenly Stranger, The. Blenkhorn.
Here we come a-caroling. *Unknown.*
His Name at the Top. *Unknown.*
Holy Night. Benson.
House of Christmas, The. Chesterton.
How Far Is It to Bethlehem? Chesterton.
How Far to Bethlehem? Miller.
Hymn: "Lord, when the wise men came from far." Godolphin.
Hymn for Christmas Day. Byrom.
Hymn on the Nativity of My Saviour, A. Jonson.
I Am Christmas. *Unknown.*
I Saw a Stable. Coleridge.
I Sing of a Maiden. *Unknown.*
In All the Magic of Christmas-Tide. Niles.
In Dulci Jubilo. *Unknown.*
In Honour of Christmas. *Unknown.*
In the Holy Nativity of Our Lord God. Crashaw.
In the Town. *Unknown.*
In the Week When Christmas Comes. Farjeon.
Incarnation, The. Wesley.
Inn That Missed Its Chance, The. Wells.
Innkeeper's Wife, The. Sansom.
Instead of Neat Inclosures. *Fr.* An Ode of the Birth of Our Saviour. Herrick.
It Came upon the Midnight Clear. Sears.
It is the day when he was born. *Fr.* In Memoriam A. H. H. Tennyson.
It Isn't Far to Bethlehem. MacDougall.
It Seems That God Bestowed Somehow. Hall.
It was a night in winter. *Fr.* The Witnesses. Sansom.
It Was Not Strange. Hagg.
It's Almost Day. Leadbelly.
Jesous Ahatonhia. Middleton.
Jest 'fore Christmas. Field.
Jew at Christmas Eve, The. Shapiro.
Journey Back to Christmas. Dunn.
Joy to the World. *Unknown.*

Karma. Robinson.
Kid Stuff. Horne.
Kings of the East, The. Bates.
Kriss Kringle. Aldrich.
Led by the light of an unusual star. *Fr.* For the Time Being; a Christmas Oratorio. Auden.
Let Christian Hearts Rejoice Today. *Unknown.*
Let me tell to you the story. Agnew.
Let Us Keep Christmas. Crowell.
Light Now Shineth, The. *Unknown.*
Little tree. *Fr.* Chansons Innocentes. Cummings.
Long, Long Ago. *Unknown.*
Lord of the World, The. Studdert-Kennedy.
Lullaby in Bethlehem. Bashford.
Lullaby of the Nativity, A. *Unknown.*
Mahogany Tree, The. Thackeray.
Man Exalted. *Unknown.*
Mary's Baby. O'Sheel.
Masters, in This Hall. Morris.
Medieval Poem of the Nativity, A. *Unknown.*
Meditation for Christmas, A. Image.
Mice in the Hay. Norris.
Miracles at the Birth of Christ. Watts.
Mrs. Santa Claus' Christmas Present. Morris.
More Sonnets at Christmas. Tate.
Nativitie. Donne.
Nativity. Hayford.
Nativity, The. Lewis.
Nativity, The. *Unknown.*
Nativity of Christ, The. Southwell.
Nativity of Our Lord and Saviour Jesus Christ, The. *Fr.* Hymns and Spiritual Songs. Smart.
New Heaven, New War. Southwell.
New Prince, New Pomp. Southwell.
New Things and Old. Sister Mary Madeleva.
1913 Massacre, The. Guthrie.
No Room at the Inn. *Unknown.*
No Sweeter Thing. Love.
Noël. Belloc.
Noel. Burket.
Noel. Gilder.
Noel; Christmas Eve, 1913. Bridges.
Noel! Noel! Simmons.
Nor House nor Heart. Lennen.
Now Every Child. Farjeon.
Now Is the Time of Christmas. *Unknown.*
Now the Most High Is Born. Ryman.
Nowell Sing We. *Unknown.*
O Christmas Night. Selyns.
O Years Unborn. Moreland.
Oh, Day of Days. Brant.
Old Christmas Greeting, An. *Unknown.*
On Christmas Day. Paman.
On Christmas Day. Traherne.
On Christmas Day. *Unknown.*
On Christmas Morn. Sawyer.
On the Morning of Christ's Nativity. Milton.
On the Nativity of Christ Our Lord. Bennett.
On the Nativity of Our Saviour. Philipott.
Outlanders, The. *Fr.* The Earthly Paradise. Morris.
Oxen, The. Hardy.
Pensées de Noël. Godley.
Perpetual Christmas. Field.
Pilgrimage. Lennen.
Precious Child, So Sweetly Sleeping. Hoppe.
Psalm for Christmas Day. Pestel.
Rejoice and Be Merry. *Unknown.*
Reminder, The. Hardy.
Riding of the Kings, The. Farjeon.
Rise Up, Shepherd, and Follow. *Unknown.*
Rorate Coeli Desuper. Dunbar.
Sailor's Carol. Causley.
Santa Claus. Nemerov.
Shepherds' Carol. Nicholson.
Shepherd's Dog, The. Norris.
Shepherd's Tale, The. Kirkup.
Simple Sam. Jackson.
Sing We Yule. *Unknown.*
Softly the Night. *Unknown.*
Somerset Wassail. *Unknown.*
Song of the Wise Men. Pierce.
Sonnets at Christmas. Tate.
Spirit, The. Turner.
Star of the East. Field.
Star of the Nativity. Pasternak.
Stars in Apple Cores. Shaw.
Stay, Christmas! Eastwick.
Sweet Was the Song. *Unknown.*
Thames Head Wassailers' Song. *Unknown.*
This Endris Night. *Unknown.*
Thou whose birth on earth. *Fr.* Christmas Antiphones. Swinburne.
Thoughts of Loved Ones. Fishback.
Three Kings, The. Longfellow.
Three Wise Kings. Brooks.
Through the Ages. Hope.
Through the Dark the Dreamers Came. Marlatt.
Time draws near the birth of Christ, The. *Fr.* In Memoriam A. H. H. Tennyson.
To a Young Wretch. Frost.
To Christ Our Lord. Kinnell.
To Jesus on His Birthday. Millay.
To See the Cross at Christmas. Cooper.
Tonight ungather'd let us leave. *Fr.* In Memoriam A. H. H. Tennyson.
True Christmas, The. Vaughan.
Twelve Days of Christmas, The. *Unknown.*
Upon a Christmas Morning. *Unknown.*
Upon Christ His Birth. Suckling.
Upon Christmas Eve. Suckling.
Virgin Unspotted, The. *Unknown.*
Visit from St. Nicholas, A. Moore.
Waits, The. Nightingale.
We Have Seen His Star in the East. Haley.
We Wish You a Merry Christmas. *Unknown.*
Welcome Yule. *Unknown.*
What the Donkey Saw. Fanthorpe.
What Tidings? Audelay.
While Shepherds Watched. Deland.
While Shepherds Watched. Tate.
White Christmas. Rodgers.
Whole Year Christmas, The. Morgan.
Widow Brown's Christmas. Trowbridge.
Wise Men Ask the Children the Way, The. Heine.
Words from an Old Spanish Carol. *Unknown.*
Yule Days, The. *Unknown.*
Yule Log, The. Hayne.
Home Book of Verse, The (HBV-1), pp. 201-230. Burton Egbert Stevenson, ed.
Home Book of Verse for Young Folks, The (HBVY), pp. 238-271. Burton Egbert Stevenson, ed.
Naked Astronaut, The: Poems on Birth and Birthdays (NAs), pp. 173-192. René Graziani, ed.
Oxford Book of Christmas Poems, The (OBCP). Michael Harrison *and* Christopher Stuart-Clark, eds.
Poems of Christmas (PChr). Myra Cohn Livingston, ed.
Shivering Babe, Victorious Lord; the Nativity in Poetry and Art (SBVL). Linda Ching Sledge, ed.

Christmas Cards
Lines for a Christmas Card. Belloc.

Christmas Carols
Angels We Have Heard on High. *Unknown.*
Away in a Manger. *Unknown.*
First Nowell, The. *Unknown.*
God Rest You Merry, Gentlemen. *Unknown.*
Good King Wenceslas. *Unknown.*
Hark! the Herald Angels Sing. Wesley.
Holly and the Ivy, The. *Unknown.*
I Saw Three Ships Come Sailing In. *Unknown.*
It Came upon the Midnight Clear. Sears.
Joy to the World. Watts.
O Little Town of Bethlehem. Brooks.
Oh Tannenbaum (Oh Christmas Tree). *Unknown.*
Silent Night. Mohr.
Twelve Days of Christmas, The. *Unknown.*
We Wish You a Merry Christmas. *Unknown.*
We Three Kings of Orient Are. Hopkins.

Christmas Eve
Christmas Eve. Day Lewis.
Christmas Eve. Edey.
Christmas Eve. Parmenter.
Christmas Eve. *Unknown.*
Visit from St. Nicholas, A. Moore.

Christmas Trees
Christmas Tree, A. Burford.
Christmas Tree. Cook.

Christmas Tree. Fisher.
Christmas Tree. Smith.
Christmas Tree in the Nursery, The. Gilder.
Little tree. *Fr.* Chansons Innocentes. Cummings.
Oh Tannenbaum (Oh Christmas Tree). *Unknown.*

Chrysanthemums
For Murasaki. Jacobsen.
Last Chrysanthemum, The. Hardy.
Shadows of Chrysanthemums. Scovell.

Chungking, China
Lyric to Spring. Stilwell.

Church of England
Battle Royal Between Dr. Sherlock, Dr. South, and Dr. Burnet, The. Pittis.
Bristol and Clifton. Betjeman.
British Church, The. Herbert.
Brittish Church, The. Vaughan.
Church of England, The. *Fr.* The Hind and the Panther. Dryden.
Church of England's Glory, The. *Unknown.*
Churches of Rome and England, The. *Fr.* The Hind and the Panther. Dryden.
New Catch in Praise of the Reverend Bishops, A. *Unknown.*
Paradox, The. *Unknown.*
Poem upon the Imprisonment of Mr. Calamy in Newgate, A. Wild.
Pulpit to Be Let, A. *Unknown.*
Sentiments, The. *Unknown.*
Vox Clero. *Unknown.*

Churches
All Saints'. Yates.
Angel Unawares, An. *Unknown.*
At Church Next Sunday. *Unknown.*
Base Chapel, Lejeune 4/79. Hobson.
Beauty in Worship. *Fr.* A Poem, in Defence of the Decent Ornaments of Christ-Church, Oxon, Occasioned by a Banbury Brother, Who Called Them Idolatries. *Unknown.*
Bricking the Church. Morgan.
Building in Stone. Warner.
Butterfly in Church, A. McClellan.
Cataldo Mission. Hugo.
Church, The. Piper.
Church and Church-Yard at Night. *Fr.* The Grave. Blair.
Church-Floore, The. Herbert.
Church Going. Larkin.
Church on Comiaken Hill, The. Hugo.
Church the Garden of Christ, The. Watts.
Church-Windows, The. *Fr.* A Poem, in Defence of the Decent Ornaments of Christ-Church, Oxon, Occasioned by a Banbury Brother, Who Called Them Idolatries. *Unknown.*
City Church, The. "E. H. K."
Country Thought. Warner.
Cowboy at Church, The. *Unknown.*
Dark Churches. *Fr.* A Hymn to Christ, at the Author's Last Going into Germany. Donne.
Dedication: "Thou, whose unmeasured temple stands." Bryant.
Diary of a Church Mouse. Betjeman.
Eighteen-forty-three. *Unknown.*
For the Altarpiece of the Roseau Valley Church, Saint Lucia. Walcott.
For the Lord's Day Evening. Watts.
Good Friday and the Present Crucifixion. Buckley.
Great Churches. *Unknown.*
Greater Friendship Baptist Church, The. Gregory.
How We Built a Church at Ashcroft. Leahy.
Hymn for the Dedication of a Church. Willard.
Hymn of Dedication. Scantlebury.
I Am a Little Church (No Great Cathedral). Cummings.
In a Country Church. Thomas.
In Memory of George Whitby, Architect. Betjeman.
In Santa Maria del Popolo. Gunn.
Inside of King's College Chapel, Cambridge. *Fr.* Ecclesiastical Sonnets. Wordsworth.
It Isn't the Church—It's You. *Unknown.*
Just Like Me. Sinks.
Knole. Sisson.
Ladies' Aid, The. *Unknown.*
Little Rhyme and a Little Reason, A. Anstadt.
London Bells. *Unknown.*
Manners. Shiffert.
Meeting-House Hill. Lowell.
Morwennae Statio. Hawker.
New England Church, A. Barrett.
Old Women beside a Church. Wilson.
On Seeing Two Brown Boys in a Catholic Church. Horne.
Pastor Speaks Out, The. Fisher.
Poor Man and His Parish Church, The. Hawker.
Prayer in a Country Church. Van Dusen.
Rugby Chapel. Arnold.
St. Isaac's Church, Petrograd. McKay.
St. Saviour's, Aberdeen Park, Highbury, London, N. Betjeman.
Seboyeta Chapel. Witt.
Show me deare Christ, thy spouse, so bright and clear. *Fr.* Holy Sonnets. Donne.
Some keep the Sabbath going to church. Dickinson.
Sunday Afternoon Service in St. Enodoc Church, Cornwall. Betjeman.
Sunday Morning, King's Cambridge. Betjeman.
Territory. Wood-Thompson.
Trouble in the "Amen Corner." Harbaugh.
Walking on Sunday. Murphy.
We Love the Venerable House. Emerson.
Wednesday Night Prayer Meeting. Wright.
What the Choir Sang about the New Bonnet. Morrison.

Churchill, John, Duke of Marlborough. *See* **Marlborough, John Churchill, 1st Duke of.**

Churchill, Winston Leonard Spencer
Homage to Our Leaders. Symons.

Churchyards
Churchyard, The. Buchanan.
Elegy Written in a Country Churchyard. Gray.

Cibber, Colley
Cibber! write all thy verses upon glasses. Pope.
Quoth Cibber to Pope, tho' in verse you foreclose. Pope.

Cicadas
Cicada, The. Green.
Cicada. Stoutenburg.
Cicada-Shell. Basho.
Cigales. Wilbur.
Invocation: "Unwinding the spool of the morning." Miller.

Cid *or* Cid Campeador
Cid's Rising, The. Keble.

Cigarettes
Blind, I Speak to the Cigarette. De Longchamps.
"Luckies." Gibbons.
See also **Smoking.**

Cigars
Betrothed, The. Kipling.
To a Segar. Low.

Cinderella
Cinderella. Jarrell.
Cinderella. Pickard.
Disenchantments; an Anthology of Modern Fairy Tale Poetry (DFT). Wolfgang Mieder, ed.

Cinque Ports, England
Cinque Port, A. Davidson.
Warden of the Cinque Ports, The. Longfellow.

Circe
Circe. De Tabley.
Circe. Doolittle ("H. D.").
Circe. Gibson.
Circe. Hope.
Circe. MacNeice.
Moly. Gunn.
Strayed Reveller, The. Arnold.
To a Lady. Morton.

Circumcision
Circumcision, The. Zisquit.

Circus
C is for the Circus. *Fr.* All Around the Town. McGinley.
Circus. Farjeon.
Circus, The. Kaplan.
Circus, The. Roberts.
Circus Garland, A. Field.
Circus Parade, The. Miller.
Circus Parade, The. Pyle.
Elephant to the Girl in Bertram Mills' Circus, The. Cronin.
Flying Trapeze, The. Leybourne.
Julia. Rose.
Last Flight of the Great Wallenda. Hyett.
Litanies of Julia Pastrana (1832-1860), The. Shapcott.
Tightrope Walker. Scannell.
To an Unknown Neighbor at the Circus. Benét.
What Happens. Jordan.
When I Went to the Circus. Lawrence.

Cities
Across the Straits. Dobson.

Air: "For often my mammy has told." *Fr.* Jack the Giant Queller; an Antique History. Brooke.
Always Modern Times. Stark.
America, America! Schwartz.
Approach to a City. Williams.
Assistance, The. Blackburn.
Aztec City, The. Ware.
Barrel-Organ, The. Noyes.
Beast Enough. Billings.
Change of Venue. Clockadale.
Christ Walks in This Infernal District Too. Lowry.
Cities and Science. McCord.
Cities behind Glass. Hogan.
City. Biasotti.
City. Hughes.
City, The. Ignatow.
City. Mocarski.
City. Stembridge.
City, City. Ridlon.
City Dump, The. Holman.
City in the Sea, The. Poe.
City is of Night, The; perchance of Death. *Fr.* The City of Dreadful Night. Thomson.
City-Life. Lawrence.
City, Oh, City! Prelutsky.
City Rises, The. Cunningham.
City Streets and Country Roads. Farjeon.
City without Smoke. Denby.
Commitment in a City. Tsuda.
Complacent Cliff-Dweller, The. Fishback.
Country Mouse, The. Cowley.
Countryman's Return, The. Thomas.
Dalesman's Litany, The. *Unknown.*
Disclaimer of Prejudice. Siegel.
Drat my hateful birthday. Sulpicia.
Faces in the Street. Lawson.
For, Lord, the Crowded Cities Be. Rilke.
From Country to Town. Coleridge.
From the Country to the City. Bishop.
Gorilla, The. Hathaway.
Grass, Alas, The. Emmons.
Greener Grass. Steele.
I Went to the City. Patchen.
Lion Named Passion, A. Hollander.
London; a Poem in Imitation of the Third Satire of Juvenal. Johnson.
London Town. Johnson.
Manchester by Night. Blind.
Master City, The. Orente.
More Foreign Cities. Tomlinson.
Nature of Jungles, The. Moses.
New York. Field.
Nocturnal Sounds. Cumbo.
Obedience. Macdonald.
Old World, New World. Roskolenko.
Poem for Democrats, A. Baraka.
Preludes. Eliot.
Roof Garden, The. Moss.
Rudolph Is Tired of the City. Brooks.
Sally in Our Alley. Carey.
Sing a Song of People. Lenski.
Thaw in the City. Lipsitz.
Tired of Towns. Lang.
To Nowshere. Ignatow.
To Sextus. Martial.
Unwilling Guest, The: An Urban Dialogue. Gregory.
Up at a Villa—Down in the City. Browning.
Upon Westminster Bridge. Wordsworth.
Urban History. Kallman.
What It Means, Living in the City. Dickey.
White City, The. McKay.
World Outside, The. Levertov.
City in All Directions; an Anthology of Modern Poems (CAD). Arnold Adoff, ed.
Civil Defense
Civil Defense. Burke.
Civil Rights. *See* **Protest, Social.**
Civil War, American
Abraham's Daughter. Winner.
All Quiet along the Potomac. Beers.
All Quiet on the Potomac. Fontaine.
Army Correspondent's Last Ride. Townsend.
Ball's Bluff. Melville.
Barbara Frietchie. Whittier.
Battle Cry of Freedom, The. Root.
Battle Hymn of the Republic. Howe.
Bivouac on a Mountainside. Whitman.
Blue and the Gray, The. Finch.
Bonnie Blue Flag, The. Macarthy.
Break the News to Mother. Harris.
Brother Green. *Unknown.*
Cannon Park. St. Germain.
Cavalry Crossing a Ford. Whitman.
Charleston. Timrod.
Civil War. Van Doren.
College Colonel, The. Melville.
Come Up from the Fields, Father. Whitman.
Craven. Newbolt.
Cripple for Life, The; or, The Poor Volunteer. *Unknown.*
Dan Ellis's Boys. *Unknown.*
Dirge for McPherson, A. Melville.
Dixie ("I wish I was in the land of cotton"). Emmett.
Dixie ("Southrons, hear your country call you!"). Pike.
Driving Home the Cows. Osgood.
Dying Ranger, The. *Unknown.*
Eagle's Song, The. Mansfield.
Epigraph to "Drum-Taps." Whitman.
Ethnogenesis. Timrod.
Fare You Well, My Darling. *Unknown.*
Farragut. Meredith.
For the Union Dead. Lowell.
From Trollope's Journal. Bishop.
Goin' 'cross the Mountain. *Unknown.*
Goober Peas. *Unknown.*
Grant at Appomattox. Claytor.
High Tide at Gettysburg, The. Thompson.
History among the Rocks. Warren.
Hunting Civil War Relics at Nimblewill Creek. Dickey.
I Fights mit Sigel! Robinson.
Joined the Blues. Rooney.
Just before the Battle, Mother. Root.
Kearny at Seven Pines. Stedman.
Keenan's Charge. Lathrop.
Kentucky Belle. Woolson.
Killed at the Ford. Longfellow.
Last Fierce Charge, The. *Unknown.*
Lee in the Mountains. Davidson.
Little Giffen. Ticknor.
Lost Occasion, The. Whittier.
Lyon. Melville.
Malvern Hill. Melville.
March in the Ranks Hard-prest, and the Road Unknown, A. Whitman.
March into Virginia, The. Melville.
Marching through Georgia. Work.
Meditation, A. Melville.
Memorial: On the Slain at Chickamauga. Melville.
Memorial Wreath. Randall.
Mower in Ohio, The. Piatt.
Music in Camp. Thompson.
My Maryland. Randall.
Negro Soldier's Civil War Chant. *Unknown.*
O Captain! My Captain! Whitman.
Ode: "Sleep sweetly in your humble graves." Timrod.
Ode to the Confederate Dead. Tate.
Portent, The. Melville.
Rebel, The. Randolph.
Red, White and Red, The. *Unknown.*
River Fight, The. Brownell.
Robert G. Shaw. Ray.
Roses of Memory. Gordon.
Sambo's Right to Be Kilt. Halpine.
Sheridan's Ride. Read.
Shiloh; a Requiem. Melville.
Sight in Camp in the Daybreak Gray and Dim, A. Whitman.
Stonewall Jackson's Way. Palmer.
Tenting on the Old Camp Ground. Kettredge.
Tramp! Tramp! Tramp! Root.
Uninscribed Monument on One of the Battle-Fields of the Wilderness, An. Melville.
Unknown Dead, The. Timrod.
Unsung Heroes, The. Dunbar.
Utilitarian View of the *Monitor's* Fight, A. Melville.
Vicksburg. Hayne.
Vigil Strange I Kept on the Field One Night. Whitman.
Volunteer's Thanksgiving, The. Larcom.

When Dey 'Listed Colored Soldiers. Dunbar.
When Johnny Comes Marching Home. Gilmore.
When This Cruel War Is Over. *Unknown.*
Whisperin' Bill. Bacheller.
Winslow Homer, Prisoners from the Front. Blakely.
Wound-Dresser, The. Whitman.
Home Book of Verse, The (HBV-2), pp. 2479–2531. Burton Egbert Stevenson, ed.

Civil War, Nigerian
Nigerian Unity/ or Little Niggers Killing Little Niggers. Lee.

Civil War, Spanish
And I remember Spain. *Fr.* Autumn Journal. MacNeice.
Battle Hymn of the Spanish Rebellion. MacKay.
Bombing Casualties in Spain. Read.
Freiheit (Freedom). Ernst *and* Daniel.
Full Moon at Tierz; before the Storming of Huesca. Cornford.
Hans Beimler. Busch.
Huesca. Cornford.
International Brigade Arrives at Madrid, The. Neruda.
Italian soldier shook my hand, The. Orwell.
Jarama Valley. *Unknown.*
Letter from Aragon, A. Cornford.
Los Cuatro Generales (The Four Insurgent Generals). *Unknown.*
Nabara, The. Day Lewis.
Of what a quality is courage made. *Fr.* Charles Donnelly. MacDonagh.
Port Bou. Spender.
Republic 1939, The. Liddy.
Say That We Saw Spain Die. Millay.
Si Me Quieres Escribir (If You Want to Write Me). *Unknown.*
Song for the Spanish Anarchists, A. Read.
Spain. Livesay.
Spain 1937. Auden.
Spanish War, The. "MacDiarmid."
To a Spanish Poet. Spender.
Toledo. Campbell.
Two Armies. Spender.
See also **Spain.**

Civil Wars, English
Boot and Saddle. Browning.
It was upon the twilight of that day. *Fr.* The Civil Wars. Daniel.
King Enjoys His Own Again, The. Parker.
O What's the Rhyme to Porringer. *Unknown.*
Parliament Soldiers, The. *Unknown.*
There Faunus and Sylvanus keep their courts. *Fr.* Cooper's Hill. Denham.

Civilization
Dream, Dump-Heap, and Civilization. Warren.
Invention of New Jersey, The. Anderson.
Long-legged Fly. Yeats.
Martian Sends a Postcard Home, A. Raine.
Meditations for a Savage Child. Rich.
Meru. Yeats.
Text for These Distracted Times, A. Hall.
That Which We Call a Rose. Dransfield.
Tired. Johnson.
Waste Land, The. Eliot.
Wilderness Is Tamed, The. Coatsworth.

Clams and Clamming
Acres of Clams. *Unknown.*
Clamdigger, The. Riggs.
Clamming. Whittemore.
Clams. Rin.
Mussels. Oliver.
Sonnet to a Clam. Saxe.

Clans
Massacre of the Macpherson, The. Aytoun.
See also **Culloden, Battle of; Scotland; Scottish Highlands.**

Clare. *See* **County Clare, Ireland.**

Clarke, Austin
Visit to Bridge House, A. Weber.

Class. *See* **Social Class.**

Classicism
Apology for a Lost Classicism, An. Ciardi.

Clay, Henry
On the Defeat of a Great Man. Lord.

Cleanliness
Advantages of Washing, The. *Fr.* The Art of Preserving Health. Armstrong.
Dirty Jim. Taylor.
Our fathers, who were wondrous wise. *Unknown.*
Racoon. Rexroth.

Clemens, Samuel Langhorne. *See* **"Twain, Mark."**

Cleopatra
Antony and Cleopatra. Coulette.
Antony to Cleopatra. Lytle.
Cleopatra. *Fr.* Antony and Cleopatra. Shakespeare.
Cleopatra. Story.
Cleopatra. Swinburne.
Cleopatra Dying. Collier.
Cleopatra to the Asp. Hughes.
Dead Cleopatra lies in a crystal casket. *Fr.* Discordants. Aiken.
Death of Cleopatra. *Fr.* Antony and Cleopatra. Shakespeare.
In Praise of a Gentlewoman. Gascoigne.
Queen Cleopatra. *Fr.* Variations. Aiken.
Tact. Pascal.

Clere, Thomas
Norfolk sprang thee, Lambeth holds thee dead. Surrey.

Clergy
Aaron. Herbert.
Abbot of Derry, The. Bennett.
Amorous Temper, An. *Fr.* The Progress of Dulness. Trumbull.
Auld Seceder Cat, The. *Unknown.*
Ballad of Father Gilligan, The. Yeats.
Baucis and Philemon; Imitated from the Eighth Book of Ovid. Swift.
Bishop and the Portmanteau, The. *Unknown.*
Bishop Orders His Tomb at Saint Praxed's Church, The. Browning.
Bishop's Last Directions, The. *Unknown.*
Buddhist Priest, A. Ho Xuan Huong.
Character of a Good Parson, The. Dryden.
Church of England's Glory, The. *Unknown.*
Confessional, The. *Unknown.*
Confessor, The. Belli.
Country Clergy, The. Thomas.
Country Curate, The. Taylor.
Curé's Progress, The. Dobson.
Eddi's Service. Kipling.
Epitaph on a Worthy Clergyman. Franklin.
Excellent New Ballad, Called the Brawny Bishop's Complaint, An. Mainwaring.
Father Mat. Kavanagh.
Father O'Flynn. Graves.
Fra Lippo Lippi. Browning.
Gentle Alice Brown. Gilbert.
God's Judgement on a Wicked Bishop. Southey.
Good Bishop, A. *Unknown.*
Grandfather. Bowering.
Habit of Perfection, The. Hopkins.
High Priest, The. *Unknown.*
I say the pulpit (in the sober use). *Fr.* The Task. Cowper.
If you for orders, and a gown design. *Fr.* A Satyr Address'd to a Friend That Is About to Leave the University, and Come Abroad in the World. Oldham.
In Church. *Fr.* Satires of Circumstance. Hardy.
Irish-American Dignitary. Clarke.
Jackdaw of Rheims, The. *Fr.* The Ingoldsby Legends. "Ingoldsby."
Let the bells ring, and let the boys sing. *Fr.* The Spanish Curate. Fletcher.
Lycidas. Milton.
Message from Reverend Fat Back Made Possible by the International Society of Social Suckers, A. Brown.
Model Sermon, A. *Unknown.*
My Record ends: But hark! e'en now I hear. *Fr.* The Parish Register. Crabbe.
On a Clergyman's Horse Biting Him. *Unknown.*
On Clergymen Preaching Politics. Byron.
On Hearing a Lady Praise a Certain Rev. Doctor's Eyes. Outram.
On Those That Deserve It. Quarles.
Paradox, The. *Unknown.*
Parsons, The. Brown.
Pastor, The. Summers.
Poor Parson, The. *Fr.* The Canterbury Tales: Prologue. Chaucer.
Preacher's Mistake, The. Doane.
Preacher's Prayer, The. Macdonald.
Preacher's Vacation, The. *Unknown.*
Preachment for Preachers. *Fr.* The Ship of Fools. Brant.
Priest of Christ, The. Ken.
Priestcraft and Private Judgement. *Fr.* Religio Laici. Dryden.
Priesthood, The. Herbert.
Priest's Lament, The. Benson.
Priest's Prayer, A. Bianchi.
Problem, The. Emerson.
Psalm LVIII: "Do ye indeed speak righteousness, O congregation?" Pembroke.

Rival Curates, The. Gilbert.
Sea-Chaplain's Petition to the Lieutenants in the Ward-Room, for the Use of the Quarter-Gallery, A. "J. T."
Sentiments, The. *Unknown.*
Smooth Divine, The. Dwight.
Soft Job. Summers.
Soliloquy of the Spanish Cloister. Browning.
Some Bird. *Unknown.*
Susan, the constant slave to mop and broom. *Fr.* The Sorrows of Sunday; an Elegy. "Pindar."
Thus spoke to my lady the knight full of care. *Fr.* A Soldier and a Scholar. Swift.
To an Anti-poetical Priest. MacNamee.
Tom Brainless as Student and Preacher. *Fr.* The Progress of Dulness. Trumbull.
Unfrocked Priest, The. Campbell.
Upon Bishop Andrewes His Picture before His Sermons. Crashaw.
Upon Glass: Epigram. Herrick.
Vicar, The. *Fr.* The Borough. Crabbe.
Vicar, The. *Fr.* Every-Day Characters. Praed.
Vicar of Bray, The. *Unknown.*
Village Parson, The. *Fr.* The Deserted Village. Goldsmith.
Wanted—a Minister's Wife. *Unknown.*
Windows, The. Herbert.
Witch Doctor. Hayden.
Would I describe a preacher, such as Paul. *Fr.* The Task. Cowper.
You Shall. *Unknown.*
See also **Rabbis.**

Clerks
Balance. Schultz.
Ballad of the Faithful Clerk. Stillman.
Clerks, The. Robinson.
Dolor. Roethke.
Report, The. Swan.
Song from a Two-Desk office. Buck.
Song of the GPO, A. Hamill.
Thirty Bob a Week. Davidson.
Ticket Agent, The. Leamy.
See also **Office Workers.**

Cleveland, Ohio
Ordinary Evening in Cleveland, An. Turco.

Clichés
Clash with Cliches, A. Miller.
On a Lover of Books. Grigson.

Cliff Dwellers
Cliff Dwelling, The. Monroe.
Homes of the Cliff Dwellers. Wood.
Testament of Perpetual Change, The. Williams.

Cliffs
Dover, the Samphire Cliff. *Fr.* King Lear. Shakespeare.
Wind of the Cliff Ka Hea, The. Thompson.

Clive, Robert
Lord Clive. *Fr.* Clerihews. Bentley.
Alarum, The. Warner.
Big Clock, The. *Unknown.*
Clock, The. Holman.
Clock, The. Jaszi.
Clock. Monro.
Clock in the Square, A. Rich.
Clock stopped, A. Dickinson.
Clock Tower, The. Thibaudeau.

Clocks
Clocks. Ginsberg.
Clocks. Locker.
Clocks. Sandburg.
Four Quartz Crystal Clocks. Moore.
French Clock. Flexner.
Gold Nest, The. Wallace.
Grandfather's Clock. Work.
Mr. Coggs. Lucas.
Old Clock on the Stairs, The. Longfellow.
Our Clock. Eakman.
Sad Tale of Mr. Mears, The. *Unknown.*
Song for a Little Cuckoo Clock. Coatsworth.
Sun-Dial, The. *Fr.* Melincourt. Peacock.
Ticking Clocks. Field.
Time Piece. Cole.
See also **Watches.**

Cloisters, The (New York City)
Cloisters, The. Yellen.

Clonmacnoise, Ireland
Dead at Clonmacnois, The. O'Gillan.
End of Clonmacnois, The. *Unknown.*

Clonmel, Ireland
Convict of Clonmala, The. *Unknown.*
In Clonmel Parish Churchyard. Piatt.

Clothing
Art above Nature, to Julia. Herrick.
Art of Dancing, The. Jenyns.
Box for Tom, A. Tate.
Braid Claith. Fergusson.
Clothes, The. Zychlinska.
Clothes Do but Cheat and Cozen Us. Herrick.
Cold Fact. Emmons.
Delight in Disorder. Herrick.
Dog in Us, The. Barnie.
Dress. *Fr.* Advice to Julia. Luttrell.
Dresses. Fraser.
Ellinda's Glove. Lovelace.
Her Favorites. Hausgen.
In Praise of Clothes. Jong.
Julia's Petticoat. Herrick.
Miss Nancy's Gown. Cocke.
My Best Clothes. Netser.
My Love in Her Attire. *Unknown.*
Nature and Art. Herford.
Nothing to Wear. Butler.
Old Cloak, The. *Unknown.*
Omar for Ladies, An. Bacon.
On a Girdle. Waller.
Pockets. Nemerov.
Relics. Gegna.
Sri Rama's Raiment. Malay.
Still to Be Neat. *Fr.* Epicoene; or, The Silent Woman. Jonson.
Think of Dress in Every Light. *Fr.* Achilles. Gay.
This Shirt. Trías.
Underwear. Ferlinghetti.
Upon Julia's Clothes. Herrick.
Upon Julia's Ribband. Herrick.
Winter Clothes. Kuskin.
Written for My Son, and Spoken by Him at His First Putting on Breeches. Barber.
See also **Jewelry.**

Clouds
Among the Millet. Lampman.
Bedouins of the Skies, The. Kenyon.
Broken Sky. Sandburg.
Cloud, The. Shelley.
Cloud Country. Merrill.
Cloud-Mobile, The. Swenson.
Cloud Parade, The. Jensen.
Clouded Morning, The. Very.
Clouds. Aldis.
Clouds. Ault.
Clouds. Brooke.
Clouds. Chapman.
Clouds. Levine.
Clouds. Reaney.
Clouds. *Unknown.*
Clouds, The. Williams.
Clouds and Clay. Gillies.
Clouds That Are So Light, The. Thomas.
Corn-grinding Song. *Unknown.*
For the Girls 'cause They Know. Littlebird.
Loaves, The. Everson.
Mist. *Fr.* A Week on the Concord and Merrimack Rivers. Thoreau.
Night Clouds. Lowell.
O cloud that wants to be the sky's arrow. Castellanos.
Sea Surface Full of Clouds. Stevens.
Sky Pictures. Newsome.
Song in White. Le Dressay.
Song of the Blue-Corn Dance. *Hopi.*
Summer Sky. Gordon.
Watching Clouds. Farrar.
Whispering Clouds. Platov.
Yellow cloud rising up from that fighting. *Aborigine.*

Clough, Arthur Hugh
On Arthur Hugh Clough. Swinburne.
Thyrsis. Arnold.
To a Republican Friend: Continued. Arnold.
To a Republican Friend, 1848. Arnold.

Clover
Clover. Tabb.
Four-Leaf Clover. Higginson.

Sweet Clover. Rice.
There is a flower that bees prefer. Dickinson.

Clowns
Clown, The. Aldis.
Clown, The. Hall.
Clown, The. Rose.
See also **Circus.**

Clumsiness
Love Poem: "My clumsiest dear, whose hands shipwreck vases." Nims.

Clyde, Firth of, Scotland
Clyde's Water. *Unknown.*

Coal Mining and Miners
Agape the sooty collier stands. *Fr.* A Descriptive Poem, Addressed to Two Ladies, at Their Return from Viewing the Mines, near Whitehaven. Dalton.
Avondale Mine Disaster, The. *Unknown.*
Blackleg Miner, The. *Unknown.*
Blantyre Explosion, The. *Unknown.*
Blue Monday. *Unknown.*
Brave Collier Lads. *Unknown.*
Caliban in the Coal Mines. Untermeyer.
Call the Horse, Marrow. *Unknown.*
Cleator Moor. Nicholson.
Coal Diggin' Blues. *Unknown.*
Coal Mine Disaster's Last Trapped Man Contemplates Salvation, The. Meissner.
Coal Miner's Goodbye, A. *Unknown.*
Coal Miner's Grace. Divine.
Collier, The. Watkins.
Collier Lad's Lament, The. *Unknown.*
Collier Lass, The. Armstrong.
Colliers' March, The. Freeth.
Collier's Rant, The. *Unknown.*
Collier's Wife, The. Lawrence.
Down in a Coal Mine. Geoghegan.
Dying Mine Brakeman, The. Jenks.
Explosion, The. Larkin.
Fourpence a Day. *Unknown.*
Gresford Disaster, The. *Unknown.*
Grey October. "The Critics."
Hill above the Mine, The. Cowley.
Hoot Owl Shift. Stricklin.
I'll Have a Collier for My Sweetheart. Oliver.
In Camus Fields. Strong.
John J. Curtis. *Unknown.*
Jowl, Jowl and Listen. *Unknown.*
Los Mineros. Dorn.
Meditation on Rhode Island Coal, A. Bryant.
Mine. Hudgins.
Miners. Owen.
Miner's Doom, The. *Unknown.*
Miner's Helmet, The. Macbeth.
Miner's Life, A. *Unknown.*
Numbers. Elliott.
Old Miner, The. *Unknown.*
Old Miner's Refrain, The. *Unknown.*
Recruited Collier, The. *Unknown.*
Robens' Promised Land. Purdom.
That Little Lump of Coal. *Unknown.*
Trimdon Grange Explosion, The. Armstrong.
Two-Cent Coal. *Unknown.*
Unseen Fire, An. Cooke.
Which Side Are You On? Reese.

Cobb, Tyrus Raymond (Ty)
Ty Cobb Story, The. Clark.

Cobblers. *See* **Shoemakers.**

Cockaigne, Land of
Land of Cockayne, The. *Unknown.*

Cockatoos
Red Cockatoo, The. Po Chü-i.

Cockfighting
Cock of the Game, The. *Unknown.*

Cockleburs
Haiku: "Green cockleburs, The." Wright.

Cockroaches
At Last We Killed the Roaches. Clifton.
Aubade: N.Y.C. Wallace.
Ballade of the Under Side. Marquis.
Cockroach. Hoberman.
Cockroaches. Starbird.
Fate Is Unfair. *Fr.* Archy Does His Part. Marquis.
Little Roach Poem. Truesdale.
Roach, The. Raven.
Roaches. Field.
Scuttle, scuttle, little roach. *Fr.* Nursery Rhymes for the Tender-hearted. Morley.
To a Humble Bug. Van Voorhis.
Whose Scene? Stone.

Cocks. *See* **Roosters.**

Cocktails.
R-e-m-o-r-s-e. Ade.

Cocoa
In Praise of Cocoa, Cupid's Nightcap. Sharpless.

Coconuts
Coconut, The. "Ande."
Coconut, The. Milne.

Cody, William. *See* **Buffalo Bill.**

Coffee
Hills Brothers Coffee. Tapahonso.

Coins
Money. Nemerov.

Cold
Cold. Francis.
Cold. Roberts.
Cold and Heat. *Hawaiian.*
Cremation of Sam McGee, The. Service.
On the Unusual Cold and Rainie Weather in the Summer, 1648. Heath.
Pray to What Earth Does This Sweet Cold Belong. Thoreau.
Prayer for Fish. Wallace.
Rooftop Winter. Thorpe.
Snow-Girl. Moritz.
There Are Roughly Zones. Frost.
Tramontana at Lerici. Tomlinson.
'Twas warm—at first—like us. Dickinson.
Twenty Below. Ford.
You Know It's Really Cold. Williams.
Young Charlottie. *Unknown.*

Colds (illness)
To Bary Jade. Adams.
Winter Scene, A. Whittemore.

Cole, Thomas
To Cole, the Painter, Departing for Europe. Bryant.

Coleridge, Hartley
To H.C. Wordsworth.

Coleridge, Samuel Taylor
Bards, The. De la Mare.
Coleridge. De Vere.
Coleridge. Hellman.
Coleridge. Watts-Dunton.
Coleridge Crossing the Plain of Jars; 1833. Dubie.
Dedicatory Sonnet to S. T. Coleridge. Coleridge.
Epitaph: "Stop, Christian passer-by!—Stop, child of God." Coleridge.
Man from Porlock, The. Bevington.
Next comes the dull disciple of thy school. *Fr.* English Bards and Scotch Reviewers. Byron.
On the Late S. T. Coleridge. Allston.
S. T. Coleridge Dismisses a Caller from Porlock. Meyer.
Thoughts about the Person from Porlock. Smith.
To Coleridge in Sicily. *Fr.* The Prelude. Wordsworth.
To S.T.C. on his 179th Birthday, October 12th, 1951. Carpenter.

Colette (Sidonie Gabrielle Colette)
Cortege for Colette. Garrigue.

Colleges and Universities
Almae Matres. Lang.
Campus in Summer, A. Whittemore.
Fisk is/ a negroid institution. Scott.
Late Show, The. Heyen.
Lucretius versus the Lake Poets. Frost.
Old College Song with Variant Lines to Suit. *Unknown.*
Song: "Whene'er with haggard eyes I view." *Fr.* The Rovers. Canning.
Student, The. Moore.
To a Visiting Poet in a College Dormitory. Kizer.
To the University of Cambridge, in New-England. Wheatley.
Town against Gown at Oxford. *Fr.* Chronicle. Robert of Gloucester.
Tuskegee. Hill.
University. Shapiro.
University Curriculum. Turner.
Verses on Sir Joshua Reynolds's Painted Window at New-College, Oxford. Warton.
Views of the Favorite Colleges. Brinnin.
Walk in Würzburg, A. Plomer.
Written at Cambridge. Lamb.
You Understand the Requirements. Lifshin.
See also **Students.**

Collies
Collies, The. Anthony.
Wonder. Raymund.
Collins, Michael
Tomb of Michael Collins, The. Devlin.
Cologne, West Germany
Cologne. Bate.
Cologne. Coleridge.
Cologne. Domin.
On My Joyful Departure. Coleridge.
Colonialism
Colonialism. Qarshe.
Environment. Kearns.
Foreign Aid. Kearns.
Hottentot, The. Pringle.
Verses on the Prospect of Planting Arts and Learning in America. Berkeley.
You Who Occupy Our Land. Margarido.
See also **British Empire; Imperialism.**
Colorado
Anasazi at Mesa Verde. Saner.
Anthropology in Fort Morgan, Colorado. Hamod.
Castle Rock. Morgan.
Christmas at Vail: On Staying Indoors. Monaghan.
Colorado. Dillenback.
Colorado Sand Storm, A. Field.
Creede. Warman.
Fifth Season, The. Saner.
Going to Press. Moffett.
House in Denver. Ferril.
Land Where the Columbines Grow. Fynn.
Ludlow Massacre, The. Guthrie.
New Story, A. Ortiz.
Rise and Fall of Creede, The. Warman.
Watching Jim Shoulders. Connellan.
Colorado River
Crossing the Colorado River into Yuma. Ortiz.
Rivers of the West. "Sunset Joe."
Song of the Colorado, The. Hall.
Colors
Artist, The. Meinke.
Causes of Color, The. Jonas.
Color. *Fr.* Sing-Song. Rossetti.
Distinctions. Tomlinson.
Dun-Colour. Pitter.
Furnace of Colors, The. Watkins.
Green and the Black, The. Bailey.
I Asked the Little Boy Who Cannot See. *Unknown.*
I planned to have a border of lavender. Goodman.
Light in the Open Air. Dillard.
Love Bit, The. Oppenheimer.
Paint Box, The. Rieu.
Rainbow Writing. Merriam.
Space for Colour. Bold.
To Mark Rothko. Cherner.
What Is Orange? O'Neill.
What Is Pink? *Fr.* Sing-Song. Rossetti.
What Is Red? O'Neill.
Yellow. Kilmer.
Yellow. McCord.
Colosseum, Rome
Coliseum, The. Poe.
Colosseum. Norse.
Death of Gaudentis. "Harriet Annie."
Survey of the Amphitheatre, A. Browne.
Coltrane, John
After the Rain. Crouch.
Dear John, Dear Coltrane. Harper.
Here Where Coltrane Is. Harper.
John Coltrane: An Impartial Review. Spellman.
JuJu. Touré.
Sopranosound, Memory of John. Bourke.
Colts
Broncho That Would Not Be Broken, The. Lindsay.
Newborn Colt, The. Kennedy.
Runaway, The. Frost.
Unclaimed. Smyth.
See also **Horses.**
Columba, Saint. *See* **Columcille, Saint.**
Columbia University
Columbia College, 1796. Shippey.
Columbines
Colombines. McCrae.
Columbus, Christopher
And of Columbus. Gregory.
Christofo Columbo. *Unknown.*
Columbus. Clough.
Columbus. Hutchison.
Columbus. Jackson.
Columbus. Miller.
Columbus. Nash.
Columbus. Schiller.
Columbus. Sigourney.
Columbus. Wynne.
Columbus and the Mermaids. Coatsworth.
Columbus Day. Gregory.
Columbus Never Knew. Burket.
Columbus Reaches Juana, 1492. Gustafson.
Columbus to Ferdinand. Freneau.
Dark-eyed Lad Columbus. Turner.
Discoverer, The. Field.
Discovery, The. Squire.
Great Discovery, The. Farjeon.
Light in the Darkness. Fisher.
May 1506 (Christopher Columbus Speaking). Scott.
Mysterious Biography. Sandburg.
On a Portrait of Columbus. Woodberry.
One day more. *Fr.* Columbus. Lowell.
Passage to India. Whitman.
Prayer of Columbus. Whitman.
There Was an Indian. Squire.
12 October. Livingston.
You, Genoese Mariner. Merwin.
Columbus, Ohio
Cold Feet in Columbus. Heath.
In Columbus, Ohio. Matthias.
Columcille, Saint
Colum-Cille's Farewell to Ireland. *At. to* St. Columcille.
St. Columcille the Scribe. *Unknown.*
St. Columcille's Island Hermitage. *Unknown.*
Combs
Comb, The. De la Mare.
"Come Live with Me and Be My Love"
Bacchanal. De Vries.
Bait, The. Donne.
Come, Live with Me and Be My Love. *Fr.* Two Songs. Day Lewis.
Daphnis to Ganymede. *Fr.* The Affectionate Shepherd. Barnfield.
Invitation au Festin. Tillyard.
Nymph's Reply to the Shepherd, The. Ralegh.
Passionate Shepherd to His Love, The. Marlowe.
Passionate Shepherd to His Love, The. Schwartz.
Comedians
Epitaph for a Funny Fellow. Bishop.
Comets
Comet, The. Makai.
Comet at Yell'ham, The. Hardy.
Comets and Princes. Johnson.
I am like a slip of comet. Hopkins.
Kohoutek. Ryan.
While Waiting for Kohoutek. Erb.
Comic Strips
Farm Implements and Rutabagas in a Landscape. Ashbery.
Katzenjammer Kids, The. Reaney.
Sunday Funnies. Keiter.
Commandments. *See* **Decalogue.**
Commencement Day
Academic Overture, The. Lattimore.
After Commencement. Nemerov.
Commencement. Carrier.
Commencement, Pingree School. Updike.
Commerce
British Commerce. *Fr.* The Fleece. Dyer.
British Commerce. *Fr.* Liberty. Thomson.
Wool Trade, The. *Fr.* The Fleece. Dyer.
See also **Barter; Business and Businessmen.**
Communes
Six-forty-two Farm Commune Struggle Poem. Leifer.
Communication
Medusa's Hair Was Snakes. Was Thought, Split Inward. Fraser.
There Was a Man. Crane.
Communion. *See* **Eucharist.**
Communism
Communism. Wilcox.

For the Cultural Campaign. Mongol.
Full Moon at Tierz; before the Storming of Huesca. Cornford.
Garland for a Propagandist. Pauker.
H——y P——tt. *Unknown.*
Kral Majales. Ginsberg.
Reveille. Ridge.

Commuters
Among Commuters. Swan.
Commuters. White.
Commuter's Entry in a Connecticut Diary. Warren.
See also **Suburbs.**

Companionship
Good Company. Baker.
Pasture, The. Frost.
See also **Friendship.**

Computers
All Watched Over by Machines of Loving Grace. Brautigan.
Artificial Intelligence. Rich.
Computer's First Christmas Card, The. Morgan.
Epitaph: "Here he lies moulding." Mellichamp.
In Computers. Lightman.
Man of Letters. Knox.
Neuteronomy. Merriam.
No Holes Marred. Douglass.
Perforated Spirit, The. Bishop.
Think Tank. Merriam.
Univac to Univac. Salomon.

Comraderie
Comrade in Arms. Moore.
Comrades. McGlennon.
See also **Friendship.**

Concentration Camps
Bird, The. Simpson.
Camp in the Prussian Forest, A. Jarrell.
Cradle Song: "Sleep, my child, my little daughter." *Unknown.*
Crazed Man in Concentration Camp. Gergely.
Dachau. Brinnin.
Day for Anne Frank, A. Williams.
Desnos Reading the Palms of Men on Their Way to the Gas Chambers. Berg.
From Tomorrow On. *Unknown.*
Funeral, The. M. J.
Gift, The. Ciardi.
Golda. Wolfert.
Labor Camp, The. Pijewski.
"More Light! More Light!" Hecht.
On the 25th Anniversary of the Liberation of Auschwitz. Mandel.
Passover Dachau. Niditch.
Peat Bog Soldiers. *Unknown.*
Protocols. Jarrell.
Return to Dachau. Niditch.
Shipment to Maidenek. Fogel.
Starvation Camp near Jasło. Szymborska.
Theresienstadt Poem. Mezey.
See also **Holocaust; Internment.**

Conception
Best Time for Conception, The. *Fr.* Callipaedia; or, The Art of Getting Beautiful Children. Quillet.
Catherine Ogg. *Fr.* The New Spoon River. Masters.
How to Conceive Boys. *Fr.* Callipaedia; or, The Art of Getting Beautiful Children. Quillet.
In the Planetarium. Fox.
Observation. Herrick.
Process of Conception, The. *Fr.* Callipaedia; or, The Art of Getting Beautiful Children. Quillet.

Concert Halls
Glory. Moore.

Concerts
Lois in Concert. Moorman.
Summer Band Concert. Smith.

Concord, Massachusetts
Concord Hymn. Emerson.

Concrete Poetry. *See* **Shaped Poetry.**

Condors
Condors. Colum.

Confederacy
Bonnie Blue Flag, The. Macarthy.
Conquered Banner, The. Ryan.
Dixie. Emmett.
Dixie. Pike.
Lines on the Back of a Confederate Note. Jonas.
My Maryland. Randall.
Ode: "Sleep sweetly in your humble graves." Timrod.
Ode to the Confederate Dead. Tate.
We Conquer or Die. Pierpont.
See also **Civil War, American.**

Confessions
Ancient Lights. Clarke.
Confession, The. Wen Yi-tuo.

Conformity
Among Friends. Kuzma.
Calf-Path, The. Foss.
Disillusionment of Ten o'Clock. Stevens.
I Never Even Suggested It. Nash.
Let Us Now Praise Famous Men. Day Lewis.
Little Boxes. Reynolds.
Love Poem Investigation for A. T. Frate.
Much madness is divinest sense. Dickinson.
Poetry of Departures. Larkin.
Radical in the Alligator Shirt, The. Lipsitz.
"Think as I Think." Black Riders, XLVII. Crane.
Unknown Citizen, The. Auden.

Congreve, William
To My Dear Friend Mr. Congreve, on His Comedy Called "The Double-Dealer." Dryden.

Connaught, Ireland
King of Connacht, The. *Unknown.*
Vision of Connaught in the Thirteenth Century, A. Mangan.

Connecticut
Christmas Eve in Whitneyville. Hall.
Commuter's Entry in a Connecticut Dairy. Warren.
Connecticut Elm, The. Swan.
Last Job I Held in Bridgeport, The. Donzella.
On the Democracy of Yale. Jones.
River of Rivers in Connecticut, The. Stevens.
Sleeping Giant, The. Hall.
Sparkling Water. Schaaf.
Vanished. Eng.
Winter without Snow, A. McClatchy.

Connecticut River
Connecticut River, The. Denney.
River of Rivers in Connecticut, The. Stevens.

Connolly, James
Connolly. MacGowan.

Conquistadors
Conquistador. McElhaney.
El Dorado. Ryan.

Conrad, Joseph
Conrad. Slonimski.
Mr. Kurtz. McGovern.

Conscience
Conscience. *Fr.* The Conference. Churchill.
Conscience. Herbert.
Conscience. Ravitch.
Conscience. Sherburne.
Conscience, The. Wickham.
In Praise of a Guilty Conscience. Szymborska.
Love is too young to know what conscience is. *Fr.* Sonnets. Shakespeare.
To His Conscience. Herrick.
With the Sun's Fire. Ignatow.

Conscientious Objectors
Conscientious Objector, The. Shapiro.
Supremer Sacrifice, The. "Maurice".
See also **Pacifism and Pacifists.**

Conscription, Military
Crippler, The. Siegel.
Drafts. Bomford.
Press-Gang, The. *Unknown.*

Conservation. *See* **Ecology.**

Consolation
Fish Upstairs, The. Dickey.
Life-Lesson, A. Riley.
Psalm of Life, A. Longfellow.
Rainy Day, The. Longfellow.

Constable, John
Meditation on John Constable, A. Tomlinson.

Constancy. *See* **Fidelity.**

Constantine I (Constantine the Great)
Constantine's Vision of the Cross. *Fr.* Elene. Cynewulf.

Constellations
Great Bear, The. Hollander.
Irish Astronomy. Halpine.
Jodrell Bank. Dickinson.
La Bagarède. Kinnell.

On Looking Up by Chance at the Constellations. Frost.
Orion. Rich.
Pleiades, The. Barnard.
Star-Talk. Graves.
See also **Sky; Stars.**

Constitution (ship)
Constitution and the *Guerrière,* The. *Unknown.*
Constitution's Last Fight, The. Roche.
Main-Truck, The; or, A Leap for Life. Morris.
Old Ironsides. Holmes.
Resurrection. Blackmur.

Construction Workers
Skyhook. Kizer.

Consumerism
Cheer for the Consumer. Waterman.
In Answer to Your Query. Lazard.
Life Cycle of Common Man. Nemerov.
Poem, or Beauty Hurts Mr. Vinal. Cummings.

Contentment
Careless Content. Byrom.
Character of a Happy Life, The. Wotton.
Choice, The. Pomfret.
Content. *Fr.* Parthenophil and Parthenophe. Barnes.
Content. Campion.
Content. Vaux.
Content. Whitney.
Contented John. Taylor.
Contentment. Cotton.
Contentment. Estes.
Contentment. *Fr.* The Autocrat of the Breakfast Table. Holmes.
Contentment. *Fr.* Christian Ethics. Traherne.
Contentment; or, The Happy Workman's Song. Byrom.
Cure for the Spleen, A. *Fr.* The Spleen. Green.
Garden, The. Marvell.
Gift, The. Ochester.
Good Company. *Unknown.*
Grongar Hill. Dyer.
Happy Life, The. Martial.
Happy Man, The. Chesterton.
Heart's Content. *Unknown.*
His Grange, or Private Wealth. Herrick.
Home. Beaumont.
How Happy the Man. *Unknown.*
How Pleasant Is This Flowery Plain. *Unknown.*
Hymn to Contentment, A. Parnell.
Jesu. Herbert.
Jolly Old Pedagogue, The. Arnold.
Lake Isle of Innisfree, The. Yeats.
Maesia's Song. *Fr.* Farewell to Folly. Greene.
My Mind to Me a Kingdom Is. Dyer.
Of a Contented Mind. Vaux.
Oh, Sweet Content. Davies.
Peace. Calverley.
Poet's Wish, The; an Ode. Ramsay.
Quiet Life, The. Byrd.
Quiet Mind, The. *Unknown.*
Resolve, The. Chudleigh.
Shepherd Boy Sings, The. *Fr.* The Pilgrim's Progress. Bunyan.
Squid. Blumenthal.
Sweet Content. *Fr.* The Pleasant Comedy of Patient Grissell. Dekker.
Truly Great. Davies.
Youth and Age. Arnold.
See also **Happiness.**

Continuity
Continuum. Levertov.
Milkweed. Levine.

Contraception
Pill, The. Clarke.
Poem on Inter-Uterine Device, A. Ghazi.
To Fine Lady Would-Be. Jonson.

Contrariness
I Want to Know. Drinkwater.

Convents
Convent, The. O'Sullivan.
Mountain Convent. Benét.
See also **Nuns.**

Conversation
Casual Meeting. Bradley.
Conversation. *Fr.* Bos Bleu. More.
La Donna È Perpetuum Mobile. Edman.
Little Talk. Fisher.
Recreation. Taylor.

Conversion
Call of the Christian, The. Whittier.
Compel Them to Come In. Dodd.
Grandmother. Carlile.
I Met the Master. *Unknown.*
Mr. Davis's Experience. *Unknown.*
Mrs. Saunder's Experience. *Unknown.*
Night, The. Vaughan.
On Being Brought from Africa to America. Wheatley.
Vicar of Bray, The. *Unknown.*

Cook, Captain James
Five Visions of Captain Cook, *sels.* Slessor.

Cooking and Cooks
Art of Cookery, The. King.
Baking Days. Joseph.
Banquet, A. Sotades.
French Cookery. *Fr.* The Fudge Family in Paris. Moore.
Grandmother's Apple Pies. Munro.
Haunted Oven, The. Kennedy.
Hollandaise. Bryan.
How to Eat Alone. Halpern.
Men May Talk of Country-Christmasses. Massinger.
Mummy Slept Late and Daddy Fixed Breakfast. Ciardi.
On a Gentleman Marrying His Cook. Ellis.
Roundup Cook, The. Carr.
Ship's Cook, a Captive Sings, The. Hofmannsthal.
Some Cook! Ciardi.
Squid. Blumenthal.
Sunlight. Heaney.
Thanksgiving Magic. Bennett.
Woman Who Loved to Cook, The. Jong.

Coole, Ireland
Coole Park and Ballylee, 1931. Yeats.
Coole Park, 1929. Yeats.
Wild Swans at Coole, The. Yeats.

Cooper, James Fenimore
Cooper. *Fr.* A Fable for Critics. Lowell.
James Fenimore Cooper. *Fr.* A Fable for Critics. Lowell.

Cooper, Peter
Peter Cooper. Miller.

Coots
Coots. Bruchac.

Copenhagen, Denmark
Non Sum Qualis Eram in Bona Urbe Nordica Illa. Hollander.

Copenhagen, Battle of (1801)
Battle of the Baltic, The. Campbell.

Copernicus, Nicholas
How Copernicus Stopped the Sun. Dillard.
Nicholas Copernicus. *Fr.* Letters from the Astronomers. Cedering.

Copley, John Singleton
On a Portrait by Copley. Freeman.

Coral
Brain Coral. Bassen.
Coral Grove, The. Percival.
Coralville, in Iowa. Bell.

Corinth, Greece
Siege of Corinth, The. Byron.

Cork. *See* County Cork, Ireland.

Cormac Mac Art
Burial of King Cormac, The. Ferguson.
Song of the Heads, The. *Unknown.*

Cormorants
Common Cormorant, The. Isherwood.
Cormorant in Its Element, The. Clampitt.
Cormorants. Blight.

Corn
Corn. Lanier.
Corn-grinding Song ("This way from the North"). *Unknown.*
Corn-Planter. Kenny.
Cornfield. Cox.
Cornfield, The. Roberts.
Cornfield Myth. Goose.
Korosta Katzina Song. *Unknown.*
Last Corn Shock, The. Dresbach.
Rainbow, The. *Unknown.*
Waving of the Corn, The. Lanier.

Corncrakes
Corncrake, The. Cousins.
First Corncrake. Hewitt.

Cornell University
Far above Cayuga's Waters. *Unknown.*

"Cornwall, Barry" (Bryan Waller Procter)
In Memory of "Barry Cornwall." Swinburne.
Cornwall, England
And Shall Trelawny Die? Hawker.
Back Again for the Holidays. *Fr.* Summoned by Bells. Betjeman.
Ballad of a Mine, A. Skelton.
In Memoriam: A.C., R.J.O., K.S. Betjeman.
Lamorna Cove. Davies.
March Evening. Strong.
Minerals of Cornwall, Stones of Cornwall. Redgrove.
St. Michael's Mount. Davidson.
Song of the Western Men, The. Hawker.
Trebetherick. Betjeman.
Tregardock. Betjeman.
Tresco. Grigson.
Cornwallis, Charles Cornwallis, 1st Marquis
Cornwallis's Surrender. *Unknown.*
Coronado, Francisco Vasquez de
Quivira. Guiterman.
Corpses
Two Views of a Cadaver Room. Plath.
Cortés, Hernán
Cortes. Rios.
With Cortez in Mexico. Campbell.
Coruña, La, Spain
Burial of Sir John Moore after Corunna, The. Wolfe.
Cosmetics
Government Injunction. Miles.
Maquillage. Symons.
Still to Be Neat. *Fr.* Epicoene; or, The Silent Woman. Jonson.
To a Painted Lady. Brome.
Valentine for a Lady, A. Lucilius.
Cosmology
Creation Myths. Raffel.
Eppur Si Muove? Hillyer.
Little Cosmic Dust Poem. Haines.
Universe, The. Swenson.
Universe Is Closed and Has REMs, The. Starbuck.
When Did the World Begin. Clairmont.
See also **Creation.**
Cotswold Hills, England
Adlestrop. Thomas.
Dawns I Have Seen. Gurney.
High Hills, The. Gurney.
On Westwell Downs. Strode.
Cotton
Cotton Boll, The. Timrod.
Cotton Song. Toomer.
Pick a Bale of Cotton. *Unknown.*
Poor Little Johnny. *Unknown.*
Roll the Cotton Down. *Unknown.*
Snapshots of the Cotton South. Davis.
Counterfeiting and Counterfeiters
Dark Girl Dressed in Blue, The. *Unknown.*
Counting
Counting-Out Rhymes. *Unknown.*
Country Dialects
Ech, Sic a Pairish. *Unknown.*
From My Rural Pen. Watt.
Irish Schoolmaster, The. Sidney.
Rustic Song, A. Deane.
Swell's Soliloquy. *Unknown.*
Country Life
At a Country Hotel. Nemerov.
Back to Griggsby's Station. Riley.
Before the Thaw. Gill.
Behold the Cot! where thrives th' industrious swain. *Fr.* The Parish Register. Crabbe.
Bess and Her Spinning-Wheel. Burns.
Boy's Song, A. Hogg.
Bright Abandon. Webb.
Bucket, The. Woodworth.
Bull, The. Sackville-West.
Childhood. Walker.
Cit's Country Box, The. Lloyd.
City Clerk, The. Ashe.
City Streets and Country Roads. Farjeon.
Cotter's Saturday Night, The. Burns.
Country Bedroom, The. Cornford.
Country Faith, The. Gale.
Country Life, A: To His Brother, Master Thomas Herrick. Herrick.
Country Lovers, The; or, Isaac and Marget Going to Town, on a Summer's Morning. Smith.
Country Mouse, The. Cowley.
Country North of Belleville, The. Purdy.
Country of No Lack. Untermeyer.
Country Reverie. Coates.
Country Summer. Adams.
Country Towns. Slessor.
Cranberry Song, The. Reynolds.
Crunking carne heard high amongst the clouds, The. *Fr.* The Country Man. Farewell.
Dance in the township hall is nearly over, The. *Fr.* The Blind Man. Wright.
Dance on Pushback. Still.
Darius Green and His Flying-Machine. Trowbridge.
Description of a Summer's Eve. White.
Deserted Village, The. Goldsmith.
Dialogue, between Crab and Gillian. *Fr.* The Bath; or, The Western Lass. D'Urfey.
Digging. Thomas.
Directive. Frost.
Disappointment, A. Baillie.
Early Morning at Bargis. Hagedorn.
Epic. Kavanagh.
Epistle to Miss Teresa Blount, on Her Leaving the Town after the Coronation. Pope.
Epode II. Horace.
Expanded Want Ad, An. Leithauser.
Far from the Madding Crowd. Waterman.
Farm, The. Miller.
Farm Picture, A. Whitman.
Farmer's Ingle, The. Fergusson.
Farrell O'Reilly. Gogarty.
Fire of Drift-Wood, The. Longfellow.
For E. G. J. Jarrett.
From where dark clouds of curling smoke arise. *Fr.* Stoklewath; or, The Cumbrian Village. Blamire.
Garden, The. Marvell.
Goin' Back T'morrer. Garland.
Grongar Hill. Dyer.
Happy Is the Country Life. *Unknown.*
Hardweed Path Going. Ammons.
Haymaking. Thomas.
He May Be Envied, Who with Tranquil Breast. Smith.
His Content in the Country. Herrick.
How Happy the Man. *Unknown.*
How It Goes On. Kumin.
How sweet it is, at first approach of morn. *Fr.* The Rising Village. Goldsmith.
I saw green banks of daffodil. Tennant.
In Praise of Country Life. Chamberlain.
In Time of "The Breaking of Nations." Hardy.
Johann Gaertner (1793–1887). Gildner.
Knoxville, Tennessee. Giovanni.
Lake Isle of Innisfree, The. Yeats.
Lonesome in the Country. Young.
Love on the Farm. Lawrence.
Maguire is not afraid of death, the Church will light him a candle. *Fr.* The Great Hunger. Kavanagh.
Mr. Francis Beaumont's Letter to Ben Johnson. Beaumont.
Montana Pastoral. Cunningham.
Mountain Born. Bost.
Mountain Greenery. Hart.
Muses' friend (grey-eyed Aurora) yet, The. *Fr.* Britannia's Pastoral. Browne.
My Happy Life. Fane.
My Own Brand. Cuelho.
Names of Horses. Hall.
Need of Being Versed in Country Things, The. Frost.
Noon. Clare.
North Country Maid, The. *Unknown.*
Not without Beauty. McLeish.
Ode on Leaving the Great Town. Randolph.
Ode to Leven Water. Smollett.
Ode to Mr. Anthony Stafford to Hasten Him into the Country, An. Randolph.
Ode, upon Occasion of His Majesties Proclamation in the Year 1630, An. *Fr.* Il Pastor Fido. Fanshawe.
Old Cottagers, The. Clare.
Old Love, The. Tynan.
Old Man of Verona, The. Claudian.
Old Squire, The. Blunt.

Out in the Country, Back Home. Marion.
Out in the Fields. *Unknown.*
Ox Cart Man. Hall.
Philemon and Baucis. *Fr.* Metamorphoses. Ovid.
Praises of a Countrie Life, The. Jonson.
Prelude: "Still south and I went west and south again." Synge.
Quiet Life, The. Byrd.
Reflections on Having Left a Place of Retirement. Coleridge.
Retirement, The. Cotton.
Rudolph Is Tired of the City. Brooks.
Rural Route. Smith.
Rural Simplicity. Byron.
Shelby County, Ohio. November 1974. Murray.
Shepherd and Shepherdess. *Fr.* The Passionate Shepherd. Breton.
Silent Poem. Francis.
Somewhere Farm. Rotella.
Spraying the Potatoes. Kavanagh.
Sweet Country Life, A. *Unknown.*
Thank God for the Country! Arnold.
There Is No God. *Fr.* Dipsychus. Clough.
There Were Some Summers. Lux.
Things of the North, The. McOwan.
Time allowed for sleep at length elapsed, The. *Fr.* The Life of Hubert. Cole.
To a Friend in the Country. Gogarty.
To Miss Laetitia Van Lewen. Grierson.
To My Honour'd Kinsman, John Driden, of Chesterton. Dryden.
To One Who Has Been Long in City Pent. Keats.
To Penshurst. Jonson.
Under the Greenwood Tree. *Fr.* As You Like It. Shakespeare.
Up at a Villa—Down in the City. Browning.
Upper Canadian, The. Reaney.
Vacation. Field.
Verses Addressed to a Friend, Just Leaving a Favourite Retirement. Henley.
Village, The. Crabbe.
Village, The. Gashe.
Visit to the Farm, A. Siegel.
When This Old Hat Was New. *Unknown.*
Wish, The. *Fr.* The Mistress. Cowley.
Wish, A. Rogers.
County Antrim, Northern Ireland
Carrickfergus. MacNeice.
County Clare, Ireland
Clare Coast. Lawless.
County Cork, Ireland
Attractions of a Fashionable Irish Watering-Place, The. Mahony.
Bells of Shandon, The. Mahony.
Castle Hyde. *Unknown.*
Curse of Doneraile, The. O'Kelly.
Groves of Blarney, The. Millikin.
County Donegal, Ireland
By the Pool at the Third Rosses. Symons.
Glen Lough. Grigson.
It's a Far, Far, Cry. Macgill.
Road of Ireland, A. O'Donnell.
Sheskinbeg. Shane.
County Galway, Ireland
Galway. MacNeice.
Galway. O'Neill.
High Island. Murphy.
Sailing to an Island. Murphy.
Wild Swans at Coole, The. Yeats.
County Kerry, Ireland
In Kerry. Synge.
County Kildare, Ireland
Lamenting Maid, The. *Unknown.*
County Mayo, Ireland
County Mayo. Raftery.
County of Mayo, The. *At. to* Flavell.
Sligo and Mayo. MacNeice.
Summer Is Coming, The. Guinness.
County Meath, Ireland
Boyne Walk, The. Higgins.
Father and Son. Higgins.
County Monaghan, Ireland
Shancoduff. Kavanagh.
Stony Grey Soil. Kavanagh.
County Sligo, Ireland
Lake Isle of Innisfree, The. Yeats.
Sligo and Mayo. MacNeice.
County Tyrone, Northern Ireland
Knockmany. Ryan.
County Waterford, Ireland
My Blessing Be on Waterford. Letts.
Courage
Abnormal Is Not Courage, The. Gilbert.
Any Complaints? Scannell.
Barbara Frietchie. Whittier.
Battle Cry. Neihardt.
Be Strong. Babcock.
Besieged. Schneour.
Captain Death. *Unknown.*
Charge of the Light Brigade, The. Tennyson.
Courage. Brooke.
Courage. Gerhardt.
Curfew Must Not Ring Tonight. Thorpe.
Defiance. Ibn Gabirol.
Feigned Courage. Lamb.
Gallantry. Douglas.
Harlaw. *Fr.* The Antiquary. Scott.
Hero, The. Sassoon.
How the Little Kite Learned to Fly. *Unknown.*
Husband with No Courage in Him, The. *Unknown.*
If We Must Die. McKay.
In an Age of Fops and Toys. *Fr.* Voluntaries. Emerson.
In White Tie. Huddle.
Inevitable, The. Bolton.
Invictus. *Fr.* Echoes. Henley.
Leak in the Dike, The. Cary.
Macpherson's farewell. Burns.
No Coward Soul Is Mine. Brontë.
Pilgrim's Song, The. *Fr.* The Pilgrim's Progress. Bunyan.
Road, The. Stephens.
Strong Men, Riding Horses. Brooks.
Thermopylae. Simonides.
Volunteer, A. Eden.
You Are the Brave. Patterson.
Coureurs de Bois
Coureurs de Bois. Le Pan.
Courtiers
Farwell to Arms. *Fr.* Polyhymnia. Peele.
Here Lies Sir Tact. Steele.
Little Shrub Growing By, A. Jonson.
Of the Courtier's Life. Wyatt.
Old and the New Courtier, The. *Unknown.*
Skelton Laureate, Defender, against Lusty Garnesche, Well-beseen Christopher, Challenger. Skelton.
Toad-Eater, The. Burns.
Upon the Sudden Restraint of the Earl of Somerset, Then Falling from Favour. Wotton.
Courtship
Advice, The. Sackville.
Advice to the Ladies of London in the Choice of Their Husbands. *Unknown.*
Arise, Arise. *Unknown.*
Bailiff's Daughter of Islington, The. *Unknown.*
Ballad of the Oysterman, The. Holmes.
Billy Boy. *Unknown.*
Call, The. Hall.
Candor. Bunner.
Change, The. *Fr.* The Mistress. Cowley.
Constancy; a Song. Rochester.
Courtin', The. *Fr.* The Biglow Papers. Lowell.
Courtship of the Yonghy-Bonghy-Bo, The. Lear.
Dialogue from Plato, A. Dobson.
Duncan Gray. Burns.
Fifteen Boys, or Perhaps Even More. Akhmadulina.
Grandma's Advice. *Unknown.*
Growing Old. Learned.
I Am No Subject unto Fate. *Unknown.*
Indian Macho. Oliver.
Kind Robin Lo'es Me. *Unknown.*
Laird o' Cockpen, The. Nairne.
Larrie O'Dee. Fink.
L'Eau Dormante. Aldrich.
Lord Thomas and Fair Ellinor. *Unknown.*
Love in Brooklyn. Wakeman.
Love Serviceable. *Fr.* The Angel in the House. Patmore.
Love's Siege. Suckling.
Luck. Shute.
Madame, withouten Many Words. Wyatt.
Man in the Dress Suit, The. Wolf.

Marriage. Corso.
Marriage and the Care o't. Lochore.
Mistress, The; a Song. Rochester.
My Man John. *Unknown.*
O Tell Me How to Woo Thee. Graham.
Oh, See How Thick the Goldcup Flowers. *Fr.* A Shropshire Lad. Housman.
Phillis for Shame Let Us Improve. Sackville.
Pleasant New Court Song, A. *Unknown.*
Polly Perkins. *Unknown.*
Pride of Kildare, The. *Unknown.*
Quoth John to Joan. *Unknown.*
Roger and Dolly. Carey.
Rory O'More; or, Good Omens. Lover.
Sagimusume: The White Heron Maiden. Sullivan.
Sally in Our Alley. Carey.
Song, A: "Fair, sweet and young, receive a prize." Dryden.
Song: "Love still has something of the sea." Sedley.
Song: "Or love me less, or love me more." Godolphin.
Subaltern's Love Song, A. Betjeman.
Tam Lin's Lady. Lochhead.
Think'st Thou to Seduce Me Then. Campion.
Three Knights from Spain. *Unknown.*
Time I've Lost in Wooing, The. Moore.
Time's Revenge. Learned.
To a Lady That Desired I Would Love Her. Carew.
To His Mistris Confined. Shirley.
Whistle, and I'll Come to Ye, My Lad. Burns.
Who shall have my fair lady? *Unknown.*
Why So Pale and Wan. *Fr.* Aglaura. Suckling.
With you first shown to me. Barnes.
Wooing Rogue, The. *Unknown.*
Yeomen of the Guard, The. Gilbert.
Yes? Bunner.
See also **Bundling.**

Cousins
Helen's Scar. Nowlan.
Slow Waker. Gunn.

Covenanters
Covenanter's Lament for Bothwell Brigg, The. Praed.

Coventry, England
I Remember, I Remember. Larkin.

Cowardice
Sonnet to Gath. Millay.

Cowboys
At a Cowboy Dance. Adams.
Bill Haller's Dance. Carr.
Branding Iron Herd, The. Rigby.
Breakers of Broncos. Sarett.
Bronko Busting, Event 1. Swenson.
Bucking Bronco. *Unknown.*
Buffalo Skinners, The. *Unknown.*
Bury Me Not on the Lone Prairie. *Unknown.*
Closing of the Rodeo, The. Smith.
Code of the Cow Country. Barker.
Cowboy, The. Antrobus.
Cow-Boy Fun. Coburn.
Cowboy Song. Causley.
Cowboy's Ball, The. Knibbs.
Cowboy's Dream, The. *At. to* Finger.
Cowboy's Fate, The. Coburn.
Cowboy's Lament, The. *Unknown.*
Cowboy's Life, The. *At. to* Adams.
Cowboy's Life Is a Very Dreary Life, The. *Unknown.*
Cowboy's Salvation Song. Carr.
Doney Gal. *Unknown.*
Eighteen-Ninety. Shipp.
El Vaquero. Foote.
From the Ballad of Two-Gun Freddy. Brooks.
Git Along Little Dogies. *Unknown.*
Gunfighter. Locklin.
High-Loping Cowboy, The. Fletcher.
Hired Man on Horseback, The. Rhodes.
Hot Ir'n! Barker.
I Am a Cowboy in the Boat of Ra. Reed.
I Ride an Old Paint. *Unknown.*
I Want to Be a Cowboy. *Unknown.*
I'm an Old Cowhand. Mercer.
Invasion Song. *Unknown.*
I've Got No Use for the Women. *Unknown.*
Lavender Cowboy, The. *Unknown.*
Little Joe the Wrangler. Thorp.
Man from Snowy River, The. Barton.
My Own Brand. Cuelho.
New-Chum's First Trip, The. *Unknown.*
Old Buck's Ghost. Benton.
Old Chisholm Trail, The. *Unknown.*
Old Cowboy's Lament, The. Carr.
Old Paint. *Unknown.*
Peeler's Lament, The. *Unknown.*
Poor Lonesome Cowboy. *Unknown.*
Rag Time Cowboy Joe. Clarke, Muir, *and* Abrahms.
Railroad Corral, The. *Unknown.*
Range Rider's Soliloquy, The. Brininstool.
Red Whiskey. *Unknown.*
Ride 'Im Cowboy. Freebairn.
Rodeo Days. Barker.
Romance of the Range. Carr.
Round-Up, The. Howard.
Roundup Cook, The. Carr.
Stampede, The. Brininstool.
Stampede, The. Coburn.
Tenderfoot, The. *Unknown.*
Texas Cowboy, The. *Unknown.*
Trail To Mexico. *Unknown.*
Utah Carroll. *Unknown.*
Vaquero. Dorn.
Vaquero. Miller.
Veteran Cowboy's Ruminations, A. Kuykendall.
Wake Up, Jacob. *Unknown.*
Watching Jim Shoulders. Connellan.
Way of Speaking, A. Ehrlich.
Western Formula. *Unknown.*
When Dutchy Plays the Mouth Harp. Carr.
When the Work's All Done This Fall. *Unknown.*
Wild Horse Jerry's Story. Howard.
Wild Rippling Water, The. *Unknown.*
Zebra Dun, The. *Unknown.*
Cowboy Songs and Other Frontier Ballads (CoSo). John A. Lomax *and* Alan Lomax, eds.
Poems of the Old West; a Rocky Mountain Anthology (PoOW). Levette J. Davidson, ed.

Cowley, Abraham
On Mr. Abraham Cowley. Denham.

Cowper, William
Cowper's Grave. Browning.
Homage to William Cowper. Davie.

Cows
About the Cows. Pfingston.
Ah, Yes, I Wrote the "Purple Cow." Burgess.
Being Herded Past the Prison's Honor Farm. Wagoner.
Blessing on the Cows, A. "O'Sullivan."
Blurry Cow. Twichell.
Buttercup Cow. Rendall.
Canadian Herd-Boy, The. Moodie.
Cattle. *Unknown.*
Colly, My Cow. *Unknown.*
Cow. McFatter.
Cow, The. Nash.
Cow, The. O'Dowd.
Cow, The. Prelutsky.
Cow, The. Roethke.
Cow, The. Stevenson.
Cow, The. Taylor.
Cow, The. *Unknown.*
Cow Dance. Beaver.
Cow in Apple Time, The. Frost.
Cow Pissing. Morgan.
Cow Time. Shannon.
Cow-Boy's Song, The. Wells.
Cows. Reeves.
Cows Are Coming Home in Maine. Coffin.
Cows at Night, The. Carruth.
Cows near the Graveyard, The. Nelson.
Cushy Cow, Bonny. *Unknown.*
Existence. Moon.
Fable of the Speckled Cow. Opperman.
Fetching Cows. MacCaig.
Four stiff-standers. *Unknown.*
Harmonious Heedlessness of Little Boy Blue, The. Carryl.
Herd, The. Cornford.
How fleet is air! how many things have breath. *Fr.* Mully of Mountown. King.
Man and Cows. Young.

Midsummer. Scully.
Milk-White Moon, Put the Cows to Sleep. Sandburg.
Milking Time. Roberts.
Moo! Hillyer.
Moo-Cow-Moo, The. Cooke.
Purple Cow, The. Burgess.
Red Cow Is Dead, The. White.
To a Sacred Cow. *Unknown.*
Trees and Cattle. Dickey.
See also **Cattle.**

Coyote (mythological)
Agnes. Tohee.
Coyote, Coyote, Please Tell Me. Blue Cloud.
Coyote's Daylight Trip. Allen.
Saint Coyote. Hogan.
Sweat Song. Blue Cloud.
Toe'osh; a Laguna Coyote Story. Silko.

Coyotes
Coyote. Harte.
Father Coyote. Sterling.
Prairie Wolves. Carr.
Sweat Song. Blue Cloud.
Toe'osh; a Laguna Coyote Story. Silko.

Crab Apple Trees
Crab Tree, The. Gogarty.

Crabbe, George
George Crabbe. Robinson.

Crabs and Crabbing
Crab, The. Aiken.
Crabbing. Daniel.
Crabbing. Levine.
Dead Crab, The. Young.
Landcrab. Atwood.
Lobsters and the Fiddler Crab, The. Forster.
With the Shell of a Hermit Crab. Wright.

Cracow. *See* **Krakow, Poland.**

Cradle Songs. *See* **Cradle Song** *and* **Lullaby** *in* **Title and First Line Index.**

Craftsmanship
Correct Compassion, A. Kirkup.
Craftsmen. Sackville-West.

Crane, Hart
Fish Food. Wheelwright.
Hart Crane. Creeley.
Hart Crane. Symons.
Homage to Hart Crane. Balakian.
Portrait of the Artist with Hart Crane. Wright.
Words for Hart Crane. Lowell.

Cranes (birds)
Crane. Langland.
Crane Is My Neighbour, The. Neilson.
Cranes, The. Po Chü-I.
Herald Crane, The. Garland.
Pet Crane, A. *Unknown.*
Sandhill Crane, The. Austin.

Cranmer, Thomas
Cranmer. Sisson.

Crashaw, Richard
On the Death of Mr. Crashaw. Cowley.

Crayfish
Catching Soft Craws. Vernon.

Crazy Horse (Indian Chief)
Crazy Horse Returns to South Dakota. Elliott.
Death of Crazy Horse, The. Neihardt.
Sound from the Earth, A. Stafford.

Creation
Adam's Morning Hymn. *Fr.* Paradise Lost. Milton.
Almighty Maker God! *Fr.* Sincere Praise. Watts.
Beginning and an End, A. Roditi.
Birth of Sea and Land Life. *Fr.* Kumulipo, The: A Creation Chant. Keaulumoku.
Book of How, The. Moore.
Bowl. Stevens.
Caedmon's Hymn. Caedmon.
Chant out of Doors, A. Wilkinson.
Chant to Io. Paraone.
Creation, The. Alexander.
Creation, The. *Fr.* Genesis. Bible, *O.T.*
Creation, The. *Fr.* Davideis. Cowley.
Creation, The. Johnson.
Creation, The. *Maori.*
Creation. Nicholl.
Creation. Noyes.
Creation, The: According to Coyote. Ortiz.
Creation Myths. Raffel.
Deo Opt. Max. *Fr.* Paraphrase on the Psalms. Sandys.
Father, thy hand/ Hath reared. *Fr.* A Forest Hymn. Bryant.
God of the Granite and the Rose! *Fr.* Reconciliation. Doten.
God, through All and in You All. Longfellow.
In Praise of Creation. Jennings.
Lamentations. Glück.
Old Creation Chant. *Unknown.*
Over all the face of earth/ Main ocean flowed. *Fr.* Paradise Lost. Milton.
Pastoral Hymn, A. Hall.
Praise of Created Things. St. Francis of Assisi.
Pulley, The. Herbert.
Six Periods of Creation, The. *Unknown.*
Song of Creation, The. *Fr.* Vedic Hymns. *Unknown.*
Spacious Firmament on High, The. Addison.
Stately Structure of This Earth, The. Brewster.
Thou Art, O God. Moore.
Tiger, The. *Fr.* Songs of Experience. Blake.
To God, the Architect. Kemp.
Up from the Bed of the River. *Fr.* The Creation. Johnson.
What Is the World. Dryden.
When God had finished the stars and whirl of coloured suns. *Fr.* Ducks. Harvey.
Whilst I beheld the neck o' th' dove. Cary.
Wonderful World, The. Rands.
See also **Cosmology.**

Creatures
Allie. Graves.
Caterpillar. Rossetti.
End-of-Summer Poem. Bennett.
Feather or Fur. Becker.
Four Things. Proverbs. Bible, *O.T.*
Hurt No Living Thing. Rossetti.
Little Black Bug. Brown.
Little Talk. Fisher.
Little Things. Stephens.
Near Dusk. Auslander.
Only My Opinion. Shannon.
See also **Animals.**

Crécy, Battle of (1346)
Crecy. Palgrave.
Eve of Crecy, The. Morris.

Credit. *See* **Installment Buying.**

Cremation
Fire Burial. McInnis.

Crete
Gate. McAleavey.
Paranoia in Crete. Corso.
Queen of Crete, The. Grimes.
Tomb of Lt. John Learmonth, AIF, The. Manifold.

Crew Racing
Crew Poem, A. Blount.
Henly, July 4: 1914–1964. Sissman.
Racing Eight, A. Cuthbertson.

Cricket (game)
At Lord's. Thompson.
Brahma. Lang.
Game of Cricket, The. Belloc.
How McDougal Topped the Score. Spencer.
I ran for a catch. Kernahan.
When the returning sun begins to smile. *Fr.* Cricket; an Heroic Poem. Dance.

Crickets
Animal That Drank Up Sound, The. Laughlin.
Ant and the Cricket, The. *Unknown.*
Cricket, The. Bourne.
Cricket, The. Cowper.
Cricket. No Ch'ŏn-myŏng.
Cricket, The. Tuckerman.
Cricket Kept the House, The. Thomas.
Crickets. McCord.
Crickets. Saroyan.
Crickets. Worth.
Cricket's Story, The. Nason.
On the Grasshopper and Cricket. Keats.
Poems to a Brown Cricket. Wright.
Poetry of Earth, The. Keats.
Splinter. Sandburg.
Spring Cricket. Rodman.
Thinker, The. Delius.
To a Cricket. Bennett.

To the Grasshopper and the Cricket. Hunt.
Winter Cricket. Heath-Stubbs.
Crime and Criminals
Against the Thieves of Liddesdale. Maitland.
Around his open grave from near and far. *Fr.* Convicted. Mills.
Ballad of Billy the Kid, The. Knibbs.
Betty and Dupree. McGhee.
Black Bart. *Unknown.*
"Black Bart, P08." Bierce.
Bold Jack Donahue. *Unknown.*
Boston Burglar, The. *Unknown.*
Bowery, The. Hoyt.
Burglar of Babylon, The. Bishop.
Bushrangers, The. Harrington.
Captain Hall. *Unknown.*
Capture of Edwin Alonzo Boyd, The. Miller.
Claude Allen. *Unknown.*
Cole Younger. *Unknown.*
Crafty Farmer, The. *Unknown.*
Death of Ben Hall, The. Ogilvie.
Dopefiends Trip. Angulo.
Dream of Eugene Aram, The. Hood.
Effort at Speech. Meredith.
Execrators, The. Galler.
Father and Son. Ignatow.
For by forged letters he tried to accuse Parnell. *Fr.* Richard Piggot, the Forger. McGonagall.
Frank James, the Roving Gambler. *Unknown.*
Frankie Silvers. Silvers.
Full and True Account of a Horrid and Barbarous Robbery, A. Byrom.
Gentle Alice Brown. Gilbert.
Geordie. *Unknown.*
Gilderoy. *Unknown.*
He Fell among Thieves. Newbolt.
Highwayman, The. Noyes.
Hills of *Tsa la gi,* The. Conley.
Hustler, The. *Unknown.*
I know some lonely houses off the road. Dickinson.
In the Servants' Quarters. Hardy.
Ipswich Bar. E. W. *and* B. L. Bates.
Jesse James. R. *and* S. V. Benét.
Jim Jones. *Unknown.*
Johnie Armstrong. *Unknown.*
Johnson. *Unknown.*
Marrying the Hangman. Atwood.
Mary Arnold the Female Monster. *Unknown.*
Monologue through Bars. Hubbell.
Morgan. Harrington.
Musgrove. *Unknown.*
Ned Christie. Conley.
Newgate's Garland. Gay.
Peddler and His Wife, The. *Unknown.*
Quaker's Meeting, The. Lover.
Queen of Hearts, The. Mother Goose.
Results of Stealing a Pin, The. *Unknown.*
Robbing and Stealing Blues. *Unknown.*
Sam Bass. *Unknown.*
Sam Hall. *Unknown.*
Shining Night or Dick Daring, the Poacher, A. *Unknown.*
Shooting of John Dillinger outside the Biograph Theater, July 22, 1934, The. Wagoner.
Since Then. Enright.
Somebody Call. Rogers.
Streets of Forbes, The. *Unknown.*
Thief, The. Kunitz.
Thief's Niece, The. Keithley.
Tom Starr. Conley.
Tractor. Sellers.
Twenty-one Years. *Unknown.*
Wild Colonial Boy, The. *Unknown.*
See also **Prisons and Prisoners.**
Crimean War
Balaclava. *Unknown.*
Charge of the Light Brigade, The. Tennyson.
Due of the Dead, The. Thackeray.
Song of the Camp, The. Taylor.
Sonnet on the Crimean War. Forster.
Cripples
Crippled Child at the Window. Cannon.
Cripples. Cassian.
Disabled. Owen.
Faithless Nelly Gray. Hood.
Mrs. McGrath. *Unknown.*
Stumpfoot on 42nd Street. Simpson.
See also **Handicaps and the Handicapped.**
Criticism and Critics
Adonais. Shelley.
And now, kind friends, what I have wrote. Moore.
Apology Addressed to the Critical Reviewers, The. Churchill.
As soon/ Seek roses in December; ice in June. *Fr.* English Bards and Scotch Reviewers. Byron.
Author Consults a Critic and Sells His Manuscript, The. *Fr.* The Signal; or, A Satire against Modesty. Hawling.
Behold! in various throngs the scribbling crew. *Fr.* English Bards and Scotch Reviewers. Byron.
Black Poet, White Critic. Randall.
Choice of Weapons, A. Kunitz.
Critic, A. Landor.
Critic and Poet. Murray.
Critic on the Hearth, The. Sissman.
Critical Fribble, A. *Fr.* The Rosciad. Churchill.
Critics. Crabbe.
Critics, The. Spencer.
Critics. *Fr.* On Poetry: A Rhapsody. Swift.
Critic's Rules, The. *Fr.* Shakespeare; an Epistle to David Garrick, Esq. Lloyd.
Crusty Critics. *Fr.* The Library. Crabbe.
Eminent Critic. Nims.
Envious Critick, The. Wycherley.
Essay on Criticism, An. Pope.
Hendecasyllabics. Tennyson.
In Imitation of Anacreon. Prior.
Interpreters, The. Enright.
Lines to a Don. Belloc.
Modern Critics. Coleridge.
Narcissus and Some Tadpoles. Daley.
Notes on a Certain Terribly Critical Piece. Whittemore.
Now Muse assist me, aptly to describe. *Fr.* Dunciad Minor. Hope.
O you chorus of indolent reviewers. Tennyson.
On Critics. Prior.
On Dennis. Pope.
On First Looking in on Blodgett's Keats's "Chapman's Homer." Starbuck.
Owl-Critic, The. Fields.
Pains, reading, study, are their just pretense. *Fr.* Epistle to Dr. Arbuthnot. Pope.
Perpetuum Mobile. Sitwell.
Pipling. Roethke.
Poet and Critic. *Fr.* Musophilus; or, Defence of All Learning. Daniel.
Poets, The. Wevill.
Poet's Fate, The. Hood.
Popular. Tennyson.
St. Cecilia's Day Epigram, A. Porter.
Saturday Review, The. Greenwell.
Second Epistle to Robert Graham. Burns.
That Idiot, Wordsworth. *Fr.* English Bards and Scotch Reviewers. Byron.
To a Captious Critic. Dunbar.
To a Reviewer Who Admired My Book. Ciardi.
To an Ungentle Critic. Graves.
To Certain Critics. Cullen.
To Christopher North. Tennyson.
To Critics. Herrick.
To Detraction I Present My Poesie. Marston.
To His Noble Friend, Mr. Richard Lovelace, upon His Poems. Marvell.
To My Least Favorite Reviewer. Nemerov.
To the Learned Critic. Jonson.
To the Reviewers. Hood.
Ultra-Germano-Criticasterism. Hunt.
Valentine. Hemingway.
Crocker, Charles
Beneath this mound Charles Crocker now reposes. Bierce.
Crockett, Samuel Rutherford
To S. R. Crockett. *Fr.* Songs of Travel. Stevenson.
Crocodiles
Amphibious Crocodile. Ransom.
Don't Ever Cross a Crocodile. Starbird.
Hard by the lilied Nile I saw. *Fr.* The Last Man. Beddoes.
How Doth the Little Crocodile. *Fr.* Alice's Adventures in Wonderland. "Carroll."
If You Should Meet a Crocodile. *Unknown.*
Lady and Crocodile. Burgess.
Monkeys and the Crocodile, The. Richards.
My Dream. Rossetti.
On the Crocodile. Heyrick.
Purist, The. Nash.

See also **Alligators.**

Crocuses
Crocus, The. Crane.
Crocus. Kreymborg.
Crocus. Murray.
Crocuses, The. Harper.
From a Trench. Bell.
Voice of the Crocus. Hoyer.

Croesus
Oracle at Delphi. Bagg.

Cromwell, Oliver
Cromwell Dead. *Fr.* A Poem upon the Death of Oliver Cromwell. Marvell.
Heroique Stanzas, Consecrated to the Glorious Memory of His Most Serene and Renowned Highnesse, Oliver, Late Lord Protector of This Common-Wealth. Dryden.
Horatian Ode upon Cromwell's Return from Ireland, An. Marvell.
More Power to Cromwell. O'Rahilly.
On the Late Metamorphosis of an Old Picture of Oliver Cromwell's. *Unknown.*
Three Troopers, The. Thornbury.
To the Lord General Cromwell, May 1652. Milton.
While with a strong and yet a gentle hand. *Fr.* A Panegyric to My Lord Protector. Waller.

Croquet
Croquet. Huddle.
Soap Suds. MacNeice.

Cross, The
A. B. C. of Devotion, An. *Unknown.*
Above the Hills of Time. Tiplady.
Cross, The. Pace.
Crucifix, A. *Fr.* Amour. Verlaine.
Dream of the Rood, A. *At. to* Cynewulf.
In Thine Own Heart. Silesius.
Making of the Cross, The. Everson.
Old Rugged Cross, The. Bennard.
Standards of the king go forth, The. Fortunatus.
Steadfast Cross. *Unknown.*
Stick, The. O'Rourke.
Thought, A. Sangster.
To See the Cross at Christmas. Cooper.
See also **Crucifixion, The.**

Crowds
At the Ball Game. Williams.
Center of Attention, The. Hoffman.
Crowds. Schonborg.
I Am the People, the Mob. Sandburg.
Vox Populi. *Fr.* The Medall. Dryden.

Crowns
Coronet, The. Marvell.
La Corona. Donne.

Crows
Billy Magee Magaw. *Unknown.*
Carrion crow sat upon an oak, The. Mother Goose.
Composition in Black and White. Pollitt.
Craw's Killed the Poussie, O, The! *Unknown.*
Crow, The. Canton.
Crow, The. Creeley.
Crow, The. Page.
Crow, crow, get out of my sight. *Unknown.*
Crow on the fence. *Unknown.*
Crow Resting. Pygge.
Crow Sat on the Willow. Clare.
Crow Voices. Tremblay.
Crows. Booth.
Crows. Clark.
Crows, The. Ghose.
Crows. McCord.
Crows. Simic.
Crows. Witherup.
Crows in Spring. Clare.
Flight. Johnston.
Fox and the Crow, The. La Fontaine.
Frog and the Crow, The. *Unknown.*
From a Birch. Wolny.
Haiku: "Crow flew so fast, The." Wright.
Hoggie dead, A! a hoggie dead! a hoggie dead! *Unknown.*
Hooded Crow, The. McOwan.
In Air. Clarke.
Jackdaw, The. Cowper.
My Sister Jane. Hughes.
Night Crow. Roethke.
Note on Master Crow, A. Garrigue.
Preparations. Silko.
Rooks, The. Browne
Rooks. Sorley.
To a Crow. Wilson.
To Be or Not to Be. *Unknown.*
Twa Corbies, The. *Unknown.*
Two Old Crows. Lindsay.

Crucifixion, The
At the Cross. *Unknown.*
At the Crucifixion. *Unknown.*
Ballad of Trees and the Master, A. Lanier.
Calvary. Hallet.
Calvary. Robinson.
Calvary. Stopple.
Choice of the Cross, The. Sayers.
Christ Is Crucified Anew. Moreland.
Crucifixion. Gore-Booth.
Crucifixion. Isbell.
Crucifixion. Peifer.
Crucifying. Donne.
Dream of the Rood, The. *Unknown.*
Early Lynching. Sandburg.
Easter Eve. Cabell.
Fill High the Bowl. Keble.
Garden, The. Beaumont.
Good Friday. Nims.
Good Friday. Rossetti.
Good Friday, 1613. Riding Westward. Donne.
Guard of the Sepulcher, A. Markham.
He Gave Himself for Me. *Unknown.*
Hill, The. Holley.
His Saviour's Words, Going to the Cross. Herrick.
Hours of the Passion, The. *Unknown.*
I Saw One Hanging. *Unknown.*
I should have been too glad, I see. Dickinson.
I Sigh When I Sing. *Unknown.*
In Memory of Two Sons. Stellwagon.
In My Place. Archibald.
In the Deep Museum. Sexton.
Indifference. Studdert-Kennedy.
Killing, The. Muir.
Last Day, The. Derosier.
Leaves of Life, The. *Unknown.*
Look on Him Whom They Pierced, and Mourn. Watts.
Martyr, The. Flohr.
My God, My God, Look upon Me. *Fr.* The Psalm of Christ. Walsh.
Oberammergau. Speyer.
On Our Crucified Lord, Naked and Bloody. Crashaw.
On the Crucifixion. Fletcher.
On the Passion. *Unknown.*
Our Saviour's Love. *Unknown.*
Passion, The. Knevet.
Passion of Jesus, The. *Unknown.*
Robin Redbreast. Doane.
Seven Virgins, The. *Unknown.*
Shield of Achilles, The. Auden.
Simon the Cyrenean. Lyttleton.
Simon the Cyrenian Speaks. Cullen.
Soldiers Bathing. Prince.
Stabat Mater Dolorosa. Jacopone da Todi.
Still Falls the Rain. Sitwell.
That Day. Leax.
There Is a Green Hill Far Away. Alexander.
There Is a Man on the Cross. Cheney.
There Is None to Help. *Fr.* The Psalm of Christ. Walsh.
They Crucified My Lord. *Unknown.*
Thief, The. *Unknown.*
This Crosse-Tree Here. Herrick.
This Very Hour. Reese.
Thou Who Createdst Everything. *Unknown.*
Thy Nail-Pierced Hands. Bowsher.
Upon the Ensignes of Chistes Crucifyinge. Alabaster.
We May Not Know. Alexander.
We'll Never Know. Hoellein.
Were You There When They Crucified My Lord? *Unknown.*
What if this present were the world's last night? *Fr.* Holy Sonnets. Donne.
When I Survey the Wondrous Cross. Watts.
Winds, The. Clemo.
Yes, I Have Been to Calvary. Christiansen.
Yet Listen Now. Carmichael.

Zone of Death. Everson.
See also **Cross, The.**
Cruelty
Secret of Poetry, The. Anderson.
Cruelty to Animals
Beasts Are Very Wise, The. Kipling.
Bells of Heaven, The. Hodgson.
Blinded Bird, The. Hardy.
Elephant, The. Hochman.
Epigram: "Thy nags (the leanest things alive)." Prior.
Formal Application. Baker.
Gallows, The. Thomas.
Nemo Canem Impune Lacessit. Garioch.
Nymph Complaining for the Death of Her Fawn, The. Marvell.
Seven Mexican Children. Schmidt.
Snare, The. Stephens.
S.P.C.A. Sermon. Hemsley.
Thoughts on Capital Punishment. McKuen.
To a Little Boy, Who Had Destroyed a Nest of Young Birds. *Unknown.*
Traverse City Zoo. Harrison.
Village Tale, A. Sarton.
Crusades
Crusade. Belloc.
Jerusalem Delivered, *sels.* Tasso.
Lepanto. Chesterton.
Crusoe, Robinson. *See* **Robinson Crusoe.**
Cuba
Central Park *Some People* (3 P.M.). Morejón.
Farewell to Cuba. Brooks.
Maceo. Lloréns Torres.
On Leaving Cuba, Her Native Land. Gómez de Avellaneda.
Song of Black Cubans. García Lorca.
Cuchulain (Irish legendary hero)
Cuchulain Comforted. Yeats.
Cuchullain's Lament over Fardiad. *Unknown.*
Death of Cuchulain, The. Yeats.
Cuckoldry and Cuckolds
O What's the Bride? "MacDiarmid."
Silly Old Man, The. *Unknown.*
When Daisies Pied and Violets Blue. *Fr.* Love's Labour's Lost. Shakespeare.
See also **Adultery.**
Cuckoos
Cuckoo! Belloc.
Cuckoo, The. Chalmers.
Cuckoo, The. Hopkins.
Cuckoo. Lister.
Cuckoo, The. Locker-Lampson.
Cuckoo, The. Thomas.
Cuckoo, The ("A-walking and a-talking"). *Unknown.*
Cuckoo ("In former days my father and mother"). *Fr.* Riddles (Exeter Book). *Unknown.*
Cuckoo. Young.
Cuckoo, cuckoo,/ What do you do? *Unknown.*
Cuckoo Sings, The. *Fr.* Love's Labour's Lost. Shakespeare.
Cuckoo Song. *Unknown.*
Cuckoos. Young.
Gowk, The. Soutar.
Great Time, A. Davies.
Ingratitude. Thynne.
Koocoo, The. *Unknown.*
Lament for the Cuckoo. Alcuin.
Late Winter. McAuley.
Nightingale, the organ of delight, The. *Unknown.*
Ode: To the Cuckoo. Bruce.
Of the Cuckoo. Bunyan.
Of Use. Heywood.
On the Cuckoo. Quarles.
Oocuck, The. Richardson.
Pallid Cuckoo. Campbell.
Riddle: Cuckoo. *Unknown.*
To the Cuckoo. Bruce.
To the Cuckoo. Logan.
To the Cuckoo. Townsend.
To the Cuckoo. Wordsworth.
Well fare the nightingale. *Unknown.*
Cucumbers
Cautionary Limerick. *Unknown.*
How to Grow Cucumbers. *Fr.* The Task. Cowper.
Cuernavaca, Mexico
View from the Gorge. Belitt.
Cullen, Countee
Countee Cullen. Maleska.
Culloden, Battle of (1746)
Lament for Culloden. Burns.
Lochiel's Warning. Campbell.
Old Scottish Cavalier, The. Aytoun.
Culture
Breakfast for Barbarians, A. MacEwen.
Footnote to Enright's "Apocalypse." Bell.
Cumberland, England
Millom Old Quarry. Nicholson.
Cumberland, Virginia
Cumberland Station. Smith.
Cumberland (ship)
Cumberland, The. Longfellow.
Cumberland and the *Merrimac,* The. *Unknown.*
Cumberland's Crew, The. *Unknown.*
Cunningham, Merce
Merce Cunningham and the Birds. Mueller.
Merce of Egypt. Olson.
Cupboards
Cupboard, The. De la Mare.
Cupid
Cards and Kisses. *Fr.* Alexander and Campaspe. Lyly.
Cheat of Cupid, The; or, The Ungentle Guest. Herrick.
Cupid. Sidney.
Cupid. *Unknown.*
Cupid Drowned. Hunt.
Cupid Far Gone. Lovelace.
Cupid in a Bed of Roses. *Unknown.*
Cupid Stung. Moore.
Cupid the Ploughboy. *Unknown.*
Cupid Ungodded. Shirley.
Cupid's Indictment. *Fr.* Galathea. Lyly.
Damon and Cupid. Gay.
Duel, The. Lovelace.
Eros. Bridges.
Ladies Prayer to Cupid, A. Carew.
Love Arm'd. *Fr.* Abdelazer. Behn.
Love Sleeping. Plato.
Metamorphosis, The. Suckling.
O Cupid! Monarch over Kings. *Fr.* Mother Bombie. Lyly.
O Gentle Love. *Fr.* The Arraignment of Paris. Peele.
Of Cupid. *Fr.* Piers Plainness' Seven Years' Prenticeship. Chettle.
Of His Cynthia. *Fr.* Caelica. Greville.
Plea to Eros. *Unknown.*
Shoot, false Love, I care not. *Unknown.*
Song: "Fool, take up thy shaft again." Stanley.
To Cupid. Drayton.
To the God of Love. Knox.
Venus' Runaway. *Fr.* Hue and Cry after Cupid, The. Jonson.
Warning to Cupid. *Unknown.*
Wounded Cupid, The. Herrick.
Cups
Ode to a Homemade Coffee Cup. Warden.
Curfew
Curfew Must Not Ring Tonight. Thorpe.
Curie, Marie
Marie Curie Contemplating the Role of Women Scientists in the Glow of a Beaker. Frazier.
Power. Rich.
Curiosity
Curiosity. Reid.
Curses
Bagman O'Reilly's Curse. Murray.
Bruadar and Smith and Glinn. *Unknown.*
Cenci's Curse upon His Daughter, The. *Fr.* The Cenci. Shelley.
Curse, The. Donne.
Curse, A. Feldman.
Curse. Greacen.
Curse, The. Synge.
Curse against the Owner, A. Sutter.
Curse for a Nation, A. Browning.
Curse of a Fisherman's Wife. Chalpin.
Curse of Doneraile, The. O'Kelly.
Curse on a Closed Gate, A. Cousins.
Curse on the Mine-Owners, The. *Unknown.*
Curses. Duemer.
Glass of Beer, A. Stephens.
Goblin Market. Rossetti.
I charm thy life. *Fr.* The Curse of Kehama. Southey.
I curse my bearing, childhood, youth. Synge.

Lear's Curse on Goneril. *Fr.* King Lear. Shakespeare.
May the strong curse of crushed affections light. *Fr.* To the Lord Chancellor. Shelley.
Nell Flaherty's Drake. *Unknown.*
Odell. Stephens.
On a Cock at Rochester. Sedley.
Righteous Anger. Stephens.
Rime of the Ancient Mariner, The. Coleridge.
Sam. Hall. *Unknown.*
Skin the Goat's Curse on Carey. *Unknown.*
Some curse that traitor Judas life and limb. Quarles.
Song of the Witches. *Fr.* Macbeth. Shakespeare.
Spell to Destroy Life, A. *Unknown.*
Timon Curses Athens and Mankind. *Fr.* Timon of Athens. Shakespeare.
To His Booke. Herrick.
Traveler's Curse after Misdirection. Graves.

Custer, George Armstrong
Custer ("In this picture/ Custer is wearing"). Baker.
Custer ("You, Custer, you hated"). Baker.
Custer. Stedman.
Custer's Last Charge. Whittaker.
Death of Custer, The. Crawford.
Revenge of Rain-in-the-Face, The. Longfellow.

Cyclamen
Cyclamen, The. Bates.
Sicilian Cyclamens. Lawrence.

Cyclops
And so an easier life our Cyclops drew. *Fr.* Idylls. Theocritus.
Cave we found, but vacant all within, The. *Fr.* The Odyssey. Homer.
Cyclops. *Fr.* Metamorphoses. Ovid.

Cymon
Cymon and Iphigenia. Dryden.

Cynicism
As a Plane Tree by the Water. Lowell.
Cynic, The. Tucker.
Unfortunate Coincidence. Parker.

Cypress Trees
Cypresses. Francis.

Cyprus
Home of Aphrodite, The. *Fr.* Bacchae. Euripides.
Paphos. Durrell.

D

Da Vinci, Leonardo. *See* **Leonardo da Vinci.**

Dachau, Germany
Dachau. Brinnin.

Dachshunds
Daschshund, The. Anthony.

Daedalus
Be Daedalus. Alba.
Now in this while gan Daedalus a wearinesse to take. *Fr.* Metamorphoses. Ovid.

Daffodils
Daffodils. Harding.
Daffodils. Heffernan.
Daffodils. Kikurio.
Daffodils. Reese.
Daffodils. *Unknown.*
Daffodil's Return. Carman.
Divination by a Daffadill. Herrick.
I Show the Daffodils to the Retarded Kids. Sharp.
I Wandered Lonely as a Cloud. Wordsworth.
To Daffodils. Herrick.

Dahlias
Autumn. Lowell.
Dahlias. Colum.
Giant Decorative Dahlia. Holden.

Daisies
Buttercups and Daisies. Howitt.
Daisies, The. Carman.
Daisies. Nowlan.
Daisies. Worth.
Daisy, The. Burns.
Daisy, The. Tennyson.
Daisy. Williams.
Daisy, The. Zaturenska.
Daisy's Song. Keats.
Field Flower, A. Montgomery.
Loss. Ammons.
Of all the floures in the the mede. *Fr.* The Legend of Good Women. Chaucer.
Spring. *Unknown.*
To a Child. Wordsworth.
To a Daisy. Meynell.
To a Mountain Daisy. Burns.
To Daisies. Thompson.
To Daisies, Not to Shut So Soon. Herrick.
To the Daisy ("Bright flower! whose home is everywhere"). Wordsworth.
To the Daisy ("In youth from rock to rock I went"). Wordsworth.

Dali, Salvador
Salvador Dali. Gascoyne.

Damascus, Syria
Gates of Damascus. Flecker.

Damien, Father
Father Damien. Tabb.

Damnation and the Damned
Ah, Faustus,/ Now hast thou but one bare hour to live. *Fr.* Dr. Faustus. Marlowe.
If poisonous minerals, and if that tree. *Fr.* Holy Sonnets. Donne.
Ubi Sunt Qui ante Nos Fuerunt? *Unknown.*

Damocles
Damocles. Graves.

Dams
American Falls. Keeler.
Big Dam. Moses.
Boulder Dam. Sarton.
Bucyrus. Holmes.
Fish Counter at Bonneville, The. Stafford.

Danaë
Gold That Fell on Danae, The. Colony.

Dancing and Dancers
American Bandstand. Waters.
Art of Dancing, The. Jenyns.
Arthur Mitchell. Moore.
Artist, The. Williams.
At a Cowboy Dance. Adams.
Balinda's Dance. Erdich.
Ballad of the Ten Casino Dancers. Meireles.
Ballet under the Stars. Stewart.
Ballroom Dancing Class. McGinley.
Band Played On, The. Palmer.
Belly Dancer. Wakoski.
Bill Haller's Dance. Carr.
Bottled: New York. Johnson.
Castanets. Spencer.
Cat or Stomp. Tohe.
Cowboy's Ball, The. Knibbs.
Dance, The. Roethke.
Dance. Weeden.
Dance, The. Williams.
Dance for Rain, A. Bynner.
Dance Instructions for a Young Girl. Hahn.
Dance of the Abakweta. Danner.
Dance on Pushback. Still.
Dancer, The. Campbell.
Dancer, The. Clarke.
Dancer: Four Poems. Engle.
Dancer's Life, A. Justice.
Dancing. Yang Kuei-fei.
Dancing Girl, A. Osgood.
Dancing School. Holden.
Death of Carmen Miranda, The. Smith.
Deepest Bow, The. Takvan.
Fancy's Knell. Housman.
Fiddler of Dooney, The. Yeats.
Golden Oldie. Mariani.
Gratiana Dancing and Singing. Lovelace.
Harlem Dancer, The. McKay.
Her Dancing Days. Adams.
Imogen. Newbolt.
Javanese Dancers. Symons.
Kearney Park. Soto.
La Mélinite: Moulin-Rouge. Symons.
Lachlan Gorach's Rhyme. *Unknown.*
Little Dancers, The. Binyon.
Little Viennese Waltz. García Lorca.
Lobster Quadrille, The. *Fr.* Alice's Adventures in Wonderland. "Carroll."
Lost Dancer, The. Toomer.
Matisse. Hirsch.

May Day Dancing, The. Nemerov.
Merce Cunningham and the Birds. Mueller.
Merce of Egypt. Olson.
Minuet, The. Dodge.
Mrs. Applebaum's Sunday Dance Class. Schultz.
Muse of the many-twinkling feet! whose charms. *Fr.* The Waltz. Byron.
My Papa's Waltz. Roethke.
Nancy, You Dance. Johnson.
Next Door to Monica's Dance Studio. Smith.
Nijinsky. Ferne.
Of Dancing. Brownjohn.
Off the Ground. De la Mare.
On a Female Rope-Dancer. *Unknown.*
On Her Dancing. Shirley.
On Lydia Distracted. Ayres.
One More Quadrille. Praed.
Orchestra; or, A Poem of Dancing. Davies.
Peg Leg Snelson. Tolson.
Perdita. Coates.
Powwow 79, Durango. Allen.
Quick-Step. Creeley.
Reminiscences of a Dancing Man. Hardy.
Rumba. Tallet.
Seeing Her Dancing. Heath.
Some Semblance of Order. Wright.
Song from a Country Fair. Adams.
South of the Border. Nicholas.
Susie Asado. Stein.
Tarantella. Belloc.
Tullochgorum. Skinner.
Variations on a Theme. Vinz.
Waltz Me Around Again Willie. Cobb.
War Dance, The. Carr.
Watching the Dance. Merrill.
We Dance like Ella Riffs. Rodgers.
Wheel, The. Berry.
When Dutchy Plays the Mouth Harp. Carr.
Window, The. Dobyns.
Zalka Peetruza. Dandridge.
Untune the Sky (UnS). Helen Plotz, ed.
See also **Ballet.**

Dandelions
Americana XVII: A Reminder of William Carlos Williams. Rakosi.
Casual Gold. Uschold.
Dandelion. Annan.
Dandelion. Conkling.
Dandelion Gatherer, The. Francis.
Dandelions. Albee.
Dandelions, The. Cone.
Dandelions. Nemerov.
Dandelions for Chains. Kirsch.
First Dandelion, The. Whitman.
Late Dandelions. Belitt.
Little Dandelion. Bostwick.
Little Dandelion, The. Weeden.
Of Dandelions & Tourists. Rosenblatt.
To the Dandelion. Lowell.

Danes
King of Ulster, The. *Unknown.*
Murrough Defeats the Danes, 994. *Unknown.*

Daniel
Daniel. Lindsay.
Handwriting on the Wall, The. Shaw.

Dante Alighieri
At Dante's Grave. Zussman.
Elegy: "Floods of tears well from my deepest heart, The." Immanuel di Roma.
Fiammetta. Boccaccio.
Man Called Dante, I Have Heard, A. King.
On a Bust of Dante. Parsons.
On the "Vita Nuova" of Dante. Rossetti.
Soul of Dante, The. Michelangelo.
Tribute to Dante, A. Boccaccio.

Daphne
Daphne. Carman.
Daphne. Flanner.
Daphne. Rodman.
Daphne. Sitwell.
Daphne and Apollo. *Fr.* The Metamorphoses. Ovid.
Song of Daphne to the Lute, A. *Fr.* Midas. Lyly.
Story of Phoebus and Daphne Applied, etc., The. Waller.

Dare, Virginia
Peregrine White and Virginia Dare. R. *and* S. V. Benét.

Daredevils
On the Edge at Santorini. Blumenthal.

Darkness
Afraid. De la Mare.
Auld Daddy Darkness. Ferguson.
Dark. Healy.
Dark, The. Heyen.
Flowers of Darkness. Davis.
His Necessary Darkness. Sullivan.
Hymn to Darkness. Norris.
In the Hours of Darkness. Flexner.
Learning to Understand Darkness. Rose.
Out of the Darkness. Armstrong.
Phases of Darkness, The. Petrie.
Three Darks Come Down Together. Francis.

Darling, Grace Horsley
Grace Darling. *Unknown.*

Darwin, Charles
Darwinity. Merivale.
See also **Evolution.**

Dating
Blind Date. Aiken.

Daughters
Beauty of Job's Daughters, The. MacPherson.
Bells for John Whiteside's Daughter. Ransom.
Birthday: Tara Regina. Mosby.
Daughter at Evening, The. Nathan.
Father, The. Finkel.
First Lesson. Booth.
For My Daughter. Koertge.
Gift, The. Darr.
Going to Town. Hogan.
I Have Three Daughters. Stone.
If a daughter you have, she's the plague of your life. *Fr.* The Duenna. Sheridan.
If I Should Ever by Chance. Thomas.
Little Girl, My Stringbean, My Lovely Woman. Sexton.
Little Sleep's-Head Sprouting Hair in the Moonlight. Kinnell.
Louise on the Door-Step. Mackay.
Mama and Daughter. Hughes.
Marina. Eliot.
Midnight, Walking the Wakeful Daughter. Meredith.
Missing My Daughter. Spender.
Mothers, Daughters. Kaufman.
My mother wept loudly. *Fr.* Tiresias. Clarke.
Old Song Resung, An. Graves.
On My First Daughter. Jonson.
Only Daughter, The. *Unknown.*
Pain for a Daughter. Sexton.
Poems for My Daughter. Gregory.
Poet's Welcome to His Love-begotten Daughter, A. Burns.
Prayer for My Daughter, A. Yeats.
Saturday Afternoon, When Chores Are Done. Mullen.
Sonnet: "Daughter to that good Earl, once President." Milton.
This Morning. Stallworthy.
To a Daughter with Artistic Talent. Meinke.
To an Infant Daughter. Clare.
To My Infant Daughter. Winters.
To Our Daughter. Armitage.
With Cindy at Vallecito. McDonald.
Writer, The. Wilbur.

Davenant, Sir William
To Sir William Davenant. Cowley.

David
Abishag. Spire.
After Goliath. Amis.
David and Goliath. Crouch.
David and Jonathan. *Fr.* Davideis. Cowley.
David and Solomon. Naylor.
David Jazz, The. Robinson.
David's Lament for Jonathan. Abelard.
Death of David, The. Bialik.
Goliath and David. Untermeyer.
Harp of David, The. Cohen.
Harp of David, The. "Yehoash."
King David. Benét.
King David and King Solomon. Naylor.
Like David. Preil.
Little David. *Unknown.*
Malcontents, The. *Fr.* Absalom and Achitophel. Dryden.

Saul. Browning.
Song to David, A. Smart.
That Harp You Play So Well. Moore.
Translating. Whitman.
David (statue)
David Homindae. Rosenfeld.
Davidson, John
In Memoriam: John Davidson. Macfie.
Davies, Sir John
Four for Sir John Davies. Roethke.
Davis, Angela
Angela Davis. Cobb.
Davis, Miles
Miles' Delight. Joans.
Davis, Thomas Osborne
Lament for the Death of Thomas Davis. Ferguson.
Davy, Sir Humphry
Sir Humphry Davy. *Fr.* Clerihews. Bentley.
Dawn
Alba. Walcott.
At Dawn. Symons.
Break of Day. Neilson.
But Venus first. *Fr.* First Dream. Sister Juana Inés de la Cruz.
Chanticleer. Austin.
Cock-Crow. Thomas.
Dawn. Dunbar.
Dawn. García Lorca.
Dawn. Logan.
Dawn. Malay.
Dawn. Masefield.
Dawn. Rimbaud.
Dawn. Sherman.
Dawn. *Unknown.*
Dawn. Williams.
Dawn, The. Yeats.
Dawn-Angels. Robinson.
Dawn and Scotch Firs. "Macleod."
Dawn in Inishtrahull. O'Sullivan.
Dawn of Day. *Fr.* The Shepherd's Pipe. Browne.
Dawn on the Lievre, The. Lampman.
Dawns I Have Seen. Gurney.
Daybreak. Longfellow.
Death at Daybreak. Aldrich.
Deirdre's Song at Sunrise. Sister Maura.
Early Morning, The. Belloc.
Early News. Pratt.
Edge of Day, The. Lee.
First Light. Kinsella.
Hark! Hark! the Lark. *Fr.* Cymbeline. Shakespeare.
Hey! Now the Day Dawns. Montgomerie.
I dreamed I saw the crescent moon. *Unknown.*
In gold sandals. Sappho.
Lark Now Leaves His Watery Nest, The. Davenant.
Late Starting Dawn. Brautigan.
Little Morning Music, A. Schwartz.
Mad Song. Blake.
Miracle of the Dawn, The. Cawein.
Morning on the St. John's. Cooper.
Morning Prayer. Aua.
Mountain Vigil. Fraser.
Music of the Dawn. Harrison.
"Now from the east." Masahongva.
Owl, The. Tennyson.
Phoebus, Arise! Drummond of Hawthornden.
Prayer at Dawn. Poteat.
Prelude: "Night was dark, though sometimes a faint star, The." *Fr.* The New Day. Gilder.
Salutation of the Dawn, The. *Unknown.*
Starting at Dawn. Sun Yun-feng.
Summer Dawn. Morris.
Trumpet, The. Thomas.
Very Early. Kuskin.
Wakers, The. Freeman.
Window to the East. Evans.
Wings at Dawn. Auslander.
Winter Daybreak above Venice, A. Wright.
With the Dawn. Irwin.
You tossed a blanket from the bed. *Fr.* Preludes. Eliot.
See also **Morning; Sunrise.**
Day
Day; a Pastoral. Cunningham.
Days. Emerson.
Days. Larkin.
Of the Day Estivall. Hume.
This Day Is Thine. Whinery.
Wee Davie Daylicht. Tennant.
Daydreams
Autumn Road, An. Dresbach.
Celebrant. Mitchell.
Heresy for a Class-Room. Humphries.
Instruction Manual, The. Ashbery.
Mixed Feelings. Ashbery.
See also **Dreams and Dreaming.**
Deafness
Deaf. Bunner.
Deaf. Higgs.
Deaf-and-Dumb School. Delius.
Deaf School. Hughes.
Deafness. Ryan.
Judge Kroll. Greenberg.
Monologue of a Deaf Man. Wright.
Mutterings over the Crib of a Deaf Child. Wright.
On His Own Deafness. Swift.
Speechless. Marston.
To a Deaf and Dumb Little Girl. Coleridge.
Dean, James
For James Dean. O'Hara.
Death and the Dead
Adieu, Farewell Earth's Bliss. *Fr.* Summer's Last Will and Testament. Nashe.
Admiral Death. Newbolt.
After Death. Rossetti.
After Death in Arabia. Arnold.
After Death nothing is, and nothing Death. *Fr.* Troas. Seneca.
After Grave Deliberation. Flynn.
After Grief. Plumly.
After Lorca. Creeley.
After My Death. Bialik.
After Night Flight. Warren.
After Work. Oxenham.
Afterwards. Hardy.
Against the Fear of Death. *Fr.* De Rerum Natura. Lucretius.
Age. Landor.
Alas! 'Tis Very Sad to Hear. Landor.
Algonkian Burial. Bailey.
All Being Well. Gibson.
All the Dead Dears. Plath.
All the Death-Room Needs. Hartnett.
All the Hills and Vales Along. Sorley.
All Things Decay and Die. Herrick.
Alone in the House. Bogin.
Along the Field as We Came By. *Fr.* A Shropshire Lad. Housman.
And Again. Evans.
And Death Shall Have No Dominion. Thomas.
And the Earth Rebelled. Suhl.
And You as Well Must Die, Beloved Dust. Millay.
Andrée Rexroth. Rexroth.
Angel of Death, The. *Unknown.*
Angina Pectoris. Moses.
Annabel Lee. Poe.
Anniverse, The; an Elegy. King.
Anthony. Shore.
Apostrophe to Death. *Fr.* Carmen Paschale. Sedulius.
Archer, The. Smith.
Ariel's Song: "Full fathom five thy father lies." *Fr.* The Tempest. Shakespeare.
Arundel Tomb, An. Larkin.
As He Came near Death. Fisher.
Asleep. Owen.
Aspatia's Song. *Fr.* The Maid's Tragedy. Beaumont *and* Fletcher.
At a Loss. Weil.
At Daybreak. Sassoon.
At Henry's bier let some thing fall out well. *Fr.* Dream Songs. Berryman.
At Last. Whittier.
At Night. Eberhart.
At the Center of Everything Which Is Dying. Goedicke.
At the Grave of My Brother. Stafford.
Aubade: "I work all day, and get half drunk at night." Larkin.
Auld Lang Syne. Chadwick.
Aunt Elsie's Night Music. Oliver.
Aunt Jane. Nowlan.
Autumn. De la Mare.
Autumnus. Sylvester.
Ave atque Vale. *Fr.* Sigismonda and Guiscardo. Dryden.

Away, Delights! *Fr.* The Captain. Fletcher.
Away. Riley.
Bachelor Hall. Field.
Ballad of Dead Ladies, The. Villon.
Ballad of Dead Yankees, The. Petersen.
Ballad of John Cable and Three Gentlemen. Merwin.
Barbara. Smith.
Barbara Allen. Unknown.
Beautiful Youth. Benn.
Because I could not stop for death. Dickinson.
Before the Anaesthetic. Betjeman.
Before the Birth of One of Her Children. Bradstreet.
Belita. Ríos.
Bereft Child's First Night. Bellerby.
Beside the Bed. Mew.
Bess. Stafford.
Between Here and Illinois. Pomeroy.
Beyond. Johnson.
Bid me remember, O my gracious Lord. *Fr.* Death. Coleridge.
Bird of Paradise, The. Davies.
Birthday. Kavanagh.
Blind Date. Aiken.
Blue Sparks in Dark Closets. Snyder.
Blue-eyed was Elf the minstrel. *Fr.* The Ballad of the White Horse: The Harp of Alfred. Chesterton.
Bourne, The. Rossetti.
Boy Wandering in Simms' Valley. Warren.
Bridge of Sighs, The. Hood.
Broken Gull, A. Moore.
Broken Tower, The. Crane.
Buck in the Snow, The. Millay.
Burial. Francis.
Burial. Walker.
Burial, The. *Fr.* The Devil's Law Case. Webster.
Burial of Sir John Moore, The. Wolfe.
Burn Out Burn Quick. Reisen.
Bustle in a house, The. Dickinson.
Call for the Robin Redbreast and the Wren." *Fr.* The White Devil. Webster.
Call Me Not Dead. Gilder.
Can the Circle Be Unbroken? *Unknown.*
Canticle. Berry.
Canto XLVII: "Who even dead, yet hath his mind entire!" Pound.
Celebrating the Mass of Christian Burial. Mathis.
Channel Firing. Hardy.
Charon's Cosmology. Simic.
Child-Bride, The. Oates.
Child Dying, The. Muir.
Choosing a Death. Turner.
Choricos. Aldington.
City Dead-House, The. Whitman.
City in the Sea, The. Poe.
City of the Dead, The. Burton.
Closing Piece. Rilke.
Closing Prayer. Patrick.
Cold Green Element, The. Layton.
Come Away, Come Away, Death. *Fr.* Twelfth Night. Shakespeare.
Coming and Going. Goodman.
Conqueror Worm, The. Poe.
Consolation, The. *Fr.* The Complaint; or, Night Thoughts on Life, Death and Immortality. Young.
Contemplation of Our State in Our Deathbed. *Fr.* Of the Progresse of the Soule; the Second Anniversarie. Donne.
Conversation. Ai.
Cool Tombs. Sandburg.
Coronach. *Fr.* The Lady of the Lake. Scott.
Could I Believe. Milne.
Cover Her Face. Kinsella.
Cross of Snow, The. Longfellow.
Crossing the Bar. Tennyson.
Cultural Presupposition, The. Auden.
Dance of Death, The. Dobson.
Dancing Partners. Child.
Dark Cat, The. Brown.
Dark Cavalier, The. Widdemer.
D'Avalos' Prayer. Masefield.
David in April. Booker.
Day Death Comes, The. Falz.
Dead, The. Blind.
Dead, The. Dudek.
Dead, The. Heavysege.
Dead, The. Smith.
Dead, The. Strand.
Dead, The. Williams.
Dead Coach, The. Tynan.
Dead Knight, The. Masefield.
Dead Man's Dump. Rosenberg.
Dead Ponies. Chamberlain.
Death. Babcock.
Death. Bodenheim.
Death. Brontë.
Death. Coates.
Death. *Fr.* The House of Night. Freneau.
Death. Gond.
Death. Harjo.
Death. Herbert.
Death. Jeffrey.
Death. Jones.
Death. More.
Death. Oppenheim.
Death. Pellew.
Death. Turner.
Death. *Unknown.*
Death. Vaughan.
Death. Williams.
Death. Wright.
Death. Yeats.
Death & Co. Plath.
Death and the Arkansas River. Stanford.
Death and the Lady. Adams.
Death and the Maiden. *Unknown.*
Death and the Plowman. Keyes.
Death and the Three Revellers. *Fr.* The Canterbury Tales: The Pardoner's Tale. Chaucer.
Death Balloon, The. Goedicke.
Death, Be Not Proud. *Tr.* Holy Sonnets. Donne.
Death Bed. Kinsella.
Death Bells. *Unknown.*
Death Circus, The. Tranter.
Death Fugue. Celan.
Death in Hospital, A. Lehmann.
Death in Leamington. Betjeman.
Death in the Home. Moore.
Death Invoked. *Fr.* The Emperor of the East. Massinger.
(Death is a dialogue between). Dickinson.
Death Is a Door. Turner.
Death Is Awful. *Unknown.*
Death of a Bird. Silken.
Death of a Fair Girl. Butler.
Death of a Poet. Causley.
Death of a Whale. Blight.
Death of an Old Man, The. Hamburger.
Death of David, The. Bialik.
Death of Friends, The. Levi.
Death of Moses, The. *Unknown.*
Death of the Craneman, The. Hayes.
Death of the Day. Landor.
Death of the First Man, The. Sullivan.
Death of the Flowers, The. Bryant.
Death of the Hired Man, The. Frost.
Death on a Crossing. Paterson.
Death Rode a Pinto Pony. Montgomery.
Death; She Was Always Here. Wallach.
Death Snips Proud Men. Sandburg.
Death Song, A. Dunbar.
Death Song. Hawker.
Death Sonnet I. Mistral.
Death Stands above Me. Landor.
Death, Thou Hast Seized Me. Luzzatto.
Death Valley Blues. *Unknown.*
Death Was a Woman. Russell.
Death Watchers, The. Ryerson.
Death-Bed, The. Hood.
Death-Bed, The. Sassoon.
Death-Bed Song. *Unknown.*
Death's Blue-eyed Girl. Pastan.
Death's the Classic Look. Ciardi.
Death's Transfiguration. Zangwill.
Death's Warning to Beauty. *Unknown.*
Deceased. Corman.
Deep Sea Soundings. Williams.
Delicate, Plummeting Bodies, The. Dobyns.
Delta Traveller. Wright.
Desideria. Wordsworth.

Destruction of Sennacherib, The. Byron.
Dirge, A: "Why were you born when the snow was falling." Rossetti.
Dirge in Woods. Meredith.
Do Not Go Gentle into That Good Night. Thomas.
Doom Ferry. Quiller-Couch.
Dream, A. Allingham.
Dream, The. *Unknown.*
Dream Fantasy. "Macleod."
Dream of a Decent Death. Borgese.
Drum. Hughes.
During Wind and Rain. Hardy.
Dying. Alvarez.
Dying. Pinsky.
Dying Californian, The. *Unknown.*
Dying Christian to His Soul, The. Pope.
Dying Father's Farewell, The. *Unknown.*
Dying Gaul, The. O'Grady.
Dying Stockman, The. *Unknown.*
Early Purges, The. Heaney.
Earth Changes. Shire.
Earth out of Earth. *Unknown.*
Edge. Plath.
Egoist Dead, The. Brewster.
Elegy: "Death be not proud, thy hand gave not this blow." Bedford.
Elegy: "Fled is the swiftness of all the white-footed ones." Auslander.
Elegy: "My prime of youth is but a frost of cares." Tichborne.
Elegy: "Somebody left the world last night, I felt it." Broumas.
Elegy: "Who keeps the owl's breath? Whose eyes desire?" St. John.
Elegy for a School-Friend. Young.
Elegy for Alfred Hubbard. Connor.
Elegy (for Himself). Rimos.
Elegy for Jack Bowman. Bruchac.
Elegy for Jane. Roethke.
Elegy for My Father. Strand.
Elegy on Gordon Barber. Derwood.
Elegy on Mistress Boulstred. Donne.
Elegy over a Tomb. Herbert of Cherbury.
Elegy to the Memory of an Unfortunate Lady. Pope.
Elephants May Parade before Your House. Gond.
Emancipation. Babcock.
Emperor of Ice-Cream, The. Stevens.
End, The. Owen.
End of Man Is Death, The. Ibn Ezra.
Epigram: Fatum Supremum. *Unknown.*
Epilogue: "That death might not be casual." Singer.
Epistle to a Lady, An. Leapor.
Epitaph: "Here lies the flesh that tried." Driscoll.
Epitaph: "Man who in his life trusts in this world, A." *Unknown.*
Epitaph: "My brother is skull and skeleton now." Montgomerie.
Epitaph: "This is the end of him, here he lies." Levy.
Epitaph. Caecil. Boulstr. Herbert.
Epitaph for a Postal Clerk. Kennedy.
Epitaph of Graunde Amoure, The. Hawes.
Epitaph of Nearchos. Ammianus.
Epitaph on an Army of Mercenaries. Housman.
Epitaph on Elizabeth, L. H. Jonson.
Epitaph on Master Vincent Corbett, An. Jonson.
Epitaph on the Marchioness of Winchester, An. Milton.
Epitaph upon Husband and Wife, Who Died and Were Buried Together, An. Crashaw.
Epitaph upon My Dear Brother, Francis Beaumont, An. Beaumont.
Eve. Rossetti.
Even Such Is Time. Ralegh.
Exequy, The. King.
Exequy: To Peter Allt. Dobbs.
Exile from God. Wheelock.
Exit. MacDonald.
Exit Molloy. Mahon.
Extempore Effusion upon the Death of James Hogg. Wordsworth.
Extreme Unction. Dowson.
Fall Comes in Back-Country Vermont. Warren.
Fall Journey. Stafford.
Falstaff's Song. Stedman.
Family Reunions. Miller.
Farewell, A. *Fr.* Arcadia. Sidney.
Father of all! in Death's relentless claim. *Fr.* A Poem. Holmes.
Fear No More the Heat o' the Sun. *Fr.* Cymbeline. Shakespeare.
Fearful Death. *Unknown.*
Felix Randal. Hopkins.
Finale: Presto. Davison.
Fire and Ice. Frost.
First Death. Justice.
First Death in Nova Scotia. Bishop.
First Grief, The. Hemans.
First of My Lovers, The. Carter.
First Snowfall, The. Lowell.
Fixing to Die. *Unknown.*
Flat One, A. Snodgrass.
Flight, The. Roethke.
For a Dead Lady. Robinson.
For Annie. Poe.
For E. McC. Pound.
For My Funeral. Housman.
For Sleep, or Death. Pitter.
For the Anniversary of My Death. Merwin.
For Zbigniew Herbert, Summer, 1971, Los Angeles. Levis.
Force That through the Green Fuse Drives the Flower, The. Thomas.
Forever. O'Reilly.
Forget about It. Currie.
Forsaken, The. Scott.
Forsaken Garden, A. Swinburne.
Fragment: "No use/ being angry at the dead." Berlind.
Fragment on Death, A. Villon.
Freedom, New Hampshire. Kinnell.
Friends Beyond. Hardy.
From the Antique. Rossetti.
Fugue of Death. Celan.
Funeral. Bennett.
Funeral, The. "M. J."
Funeral Hymn. Howe.
Funeral Poem. Baraka.
Funerall, The. Donne.
Funerall Song, A. *Unknown.*
Futility. Owen.
Gallows, The. Thomas.
Game of Chance, A. Moss.
Garden of Proserpine, The. Swinburne.
Gardener, The. Housman.
Genius of Death, The. Croly.
German Legion, The. Dobell.
Gift of a Skull, The. Skelton.
Giorno dei Morti. Lawrence.
Glories of Our Blood and State, The. *Fr.* The Contention of Ajax and Ulysses. Shirley.
Glory of the Day Was in Her Face, The. Johnson.
Go Down Death. Johnson.
God of all power and might. *Fr.* In Memoriam, A. C. M. L. Spring-Rice.
Going, The. Hardy.
Gone Years, The. Fulton.
"Good Night, Willie Lee, I'll See You in the Morning." Walker.
Good-bye. Emerson.
Goodbye. Kinnell.
Grace to Be Said at the Supermarket. Nemerov.
Grave, A. Moore.
Grave, The. *Unknown.*
Grave, The. Winters.
Grave Clothes. Swenson.
Graves of a Household, The. Hemans.
Hark, Now Everything Is Still. *Fr.* The Duchess of Malfi. Webster.
Haunted Odysseus: The Last Testament. Gregory.
He Came to Visit Me. Seymour-Smith.
Heart asks pleasure first, The. Dickinson.
Heart Burial. Grigson.
Henry My Son. *Unknown.*
Henry's Lament. *Fr.* The Complaint of Rosamond. Daniel.
Here Dead Lie We. Housman.
Here Lies a Lady. Ransom.
Hero Song. Duncan.
Highland Mary. Burns.
Hills of Rest, The. Paine.
His Winding-Sheet. Herrick.
Hour of Death, The. Hemans.
Hours, The. Bishop.
House. For Sale. Clark.
House of Falling Leaves, The. Braithwaite.
How Death Comes. *Unknown.*
How Did You Die? Cooke.
How Great unto the Living Seem the Dead! Heavysege.
How many times these low feet staggered. Dickinson.
Hungry Grass. MacDonagh.
Hymn to God My God, in My Sickness. Donne.
I died for Beauty—but was scarce. Dickinson.
I felt a funeral in my brain. Dickinson.
I Found Her Out There. Hardy.

I Have a Rendezvous with Death. Seeger.
I heard a fly—buzz when I died. Dickinson.
I Hoed and Trenched and Weeded. *Fr.* A Shropshire Lad. Housman.
I Kissed Pa Twice after His Death. Peterson.
I Know a Lovely Lady Who Is Dead. Burt.
I Know Moonrise. *Unknown.*
"I loathe that I did love." *Fr.* The Image of Death. Vaux.
I never hear that one is dead. Dickinson.
I Never Shall Love the Snow Again. Bridges.
I Tell of Another Young Death. Tiempo.
I Thank God I'm Free at Las'. *Unknown.*
I Wage Not Any Feud with Death. *Fr.* In Memoriam A.H.H. Tennyson.
I Want to Die While You Love Me. Johnson.
I Went to Death. *Unknown.*
I Would Like My Love to Die. Beckett.
Ignorance of Death. Empson.
Ikons, The. Baxter.
Illi Morituri. Webster.
Image from Beckett, An. Mahon.
Immortality. "Æ."
Immortality. Ai.
In a Grave-Yard. Braithwaite.
In Memoriam. Gingell.
In Memory of a Friend. Barker.
In Memory of My Dear Grandchild Anne Bradstreet. Bradstreet.
In Memory of My Dear Grandchild Elizabeth Bradstreet. Bradstreet.
In Obitum M.S., X° Maij, 1614. Browne.
In Tenebris. Hardy.
In the House of the Dying. Cooper.
In the thirtieth year of life. Cunningham.
Incident in a Rose Garden. Justice.
Indian Burying Ground, The. Freneau.
Inevitable. Betjeman.
Inheritance. *Unknown.*
Inseparable. Marston.
Invocation of Death. Raine.
Iona; the Graves of the Kings. Jeffers.
Irreconcilables. Gregor.
Irony. Untermeyer.
Is My Team Ploughing. *Fr.* A Shropshire Lad. Housman.
Isaac Leybush Peretz. Halpern.
It Is Her Cousin's Death. Fox.
It was not death, for I stood up. Dickinson.
I've seen a dying eye. Dickinson.
Janet Waking. Ransom.
Journey of the Magi. Eliot.
Journey's End. Wolfe.
Joy of My Life! Vaughan.
Joy, Shipmate, Joy! Whitman.
Just Passing. *Unknown.*
Keys of Morning, The. De la Mare.
Kindertotenlieder. Longley.
Knight, Death, and the Devil, The. Jarrell.
La Chute. Olson.
Lads in Their Hundreds, The. *Fr.* A Shropshire Lad. Housman.
Lament: "I lie in darkness, as the dead shades gather." Hauroa.
Lament: "Listen, children." Millay.
Lament for Barney Flanagan. Baxter.
Lament for Taramoana. Makere.
Lament for the Makaris. Dunbar.
Lamentation, A. Campion.
Lamenting Tauba. Akhyaliyya.
Land o' the Leal, The. Nairne.
Last Confession, A. Yeats.
Last Invocation, The. Whitman.
Last Lines. Brontë.
Last night that she lived, The. Dickinson.
Last Plea. Untermeyer.
Last Quatrain of the Ballad of Emmett Till, The. Brooks.
Last Republicans, The. Clarke.
Last Words. Plath.
Last Years, The. Davies.
Laus Mortis. Knowles.
Leaf after Leaf. Landor.
L'Envoi: "Who findeth comfort in the stars and flowers." *Fr.* Death's Jest Book. Beddoes.
Lesson, The. Lucie-Smith.
Let Me Go Down to Dust. Sarett.
Let Me Live Out My Years. Neihardt.
Let Me Not Die. Pierce.
Letter from a Death Bed. Ciardi.
Letter from the Street. Brush.
Life. Herbert.
Life and Death. Turner.
Life flows to death as rivers to the sea. Cunningham.
Linnet in the Rocky Dells, The. Brontë.
Litany of the Rooms of the Dead. Werfel.
Living among the Dead. Matthews.
Lone Prairie, The. *Unknown.*
Lonesome Valley. *Unknown.*
Lord! if in love, though fainting oft, I have tended thy gracious vine. *Fr.* Last Lines. "Meredith."
Losers. Sandburg.
Losses. Jarrell.
Louise on the Door-Step. Mackay.
Luke Havergal. Robinson.
Lully, Lulley, Lully, Lulley. *Unknown.*
Lycidas. Milton.
Lydia Is Gone This Many a Year. Reese.
Lyke-Wake Dirge, A. *Unknown.*
Lyke-Wake Song, A. Swinburne.
Madam Life's a Piece in Bloom. Henley.
Madrigal: "Your love is dead, lady, your love is dead." Thomas.
Malefic Surgeon, The. Lansing.
Man is a sacred city built of marvelous earth. *Fr.* The Tragedy of Pompey the Great. Masefield.
Man Walking and Singing, A. Berry.
Mansion stood apart in its own ground, The. *Fr.* The City of Dreadful Night. Thomson.
Margaritæ Sorori. Henley.
Maria Wentworth. Carew.
Mater Dolorosa. Barnes.
Maurice, I dreamed of you last night. You wore. *Fr.* Twenty-one Sonnets. Stead.
Memorial Service. Williams.
Memory. Lincoln.
Merlin. Hill.
Messmates. Newbolt.
Midnight Lamentation. Monroe.
Mid-Term Break. Heaney.
Mill, The. Wilbur.
Minor Elegy. Lisboa.
Missing. Pudney.
Missing. Tabb.
Missing. *Unknown.*
Mr. Edwards and the Spider. Lowell.
Mr. Over. Smith.
Monument. Sullivan.
Moriturus. "Madelaine."
Mortality. Devaney.
Mortician's Twelve-year-old Son, The. Ai.
Mortification. Herbert.
Mountain Creed. Rae.
Mowers, The; an Anticipation of the Cholera, 1848. Mackay.
My Days among the Dead Are Past. Southey.
My Dead. Hosmer.
My Death. Smith.
My Death. Zuckmayer.
My Father; October 1942. Stafford.
My Father's Ghost. Wagoner.
My Father's Heart. Friebert.
My Grandfather Dying. Kooser.
My life closed twice before its close. Dickinson.
My Mother's Death. Hemschemeyer.
My Pilgrimage. Ralegh.
Nature. Longfellow.
Nature's Cook. Newcastle.
Necropolis. Shapiro.
Never More Will the Wind. Doolittle ("H. D.").
New Night Thoughts on Death; a Parody. Whitehead.
News. Pomeroy.
Next, Please. Larkin.
Night Is Freezing Fast, The. Housman.
Night-Piece on Death, A. Parnell.
Nirvana. Törel.
No Coward Soul Is Mine. Brontë.
Not Thou but I. Marston.
Not Waving but Drowning. Smith.
Now Spring returns: but not to me returns. *Fr.* Elegy: In Spring. Bruce.
Now the Labourer's Task Is O'er. Ellerton.
O All Down within the Pretty Meadow. Patchen.
O Death. *Fr.* Apocrypha Bible, *O.T.*
O Death, Rock Me Asleep. Boleyn.
O Mariners! Rutledge.

O My Poor Darling. Watson.
Oh sing unto my roundelay. *Fr.* Aella. Chatterton.
Oath, The. Tate.
Obit on Parnassus. Fitzgerald.
Ocean Burial, The. Chapin.
Of Death. *Fr.* Antonius. Pembroke.
Of the Progresse of the Soule; the Second Anniversary. Donne.
Oh! Death. *Unknown.*
Oh, Thou! Who Dry'st the Mourner's Tear. Moore.
Oh, when this earthly tenement. "Ada."
Oh! Why Should the Spirit of Mortal Be Proud? Knox.
Old Familiar Faces, The. Lamb
Old man Dozed, The. The hospital quietened. *Fr.* Sonnets for a Dying Man. Singer.
Old Man Who Is Gone Now, The. Reyes.
Old People Speak of Death, The. Troupe.
Old yew, which graspest at the stones. *Fr.* In Memoriam A. H. H. Tennyson.
Omnia Exeunt in Mysterium. Sterling.
On an Old Woman Who Sold Pots. *Unknown.*
On Death. Keats.
On Death. Killigrew.
On Death. *Fr.* Measure for Measure. Shakespeare.
On His Deceased Wife. Milton.
On Neal's Ashes. Ginsberg.
On the Countess Dowager of Pembroke. Browne.
On the day my father died a flame-tree. *Fr.* Brother Jonathan, Brother Kafka. O'Sullivan.
On the Death of a Prince; a Meditation. Philipott.
On the Death of a Recluse. Darley.
On the Death of Dermondy, the Poet. White.
On the Death of Friends in Childhood. Justice.
On the Death of His Wife. O'Dalaigh.
On the Death of Lisa Lyman. Burt.
On the Death of Mr. William Hervey. Cowley.
On the Death of Neruda. Van Brunt.
On the Death of Parents. Barson.
On the Death of Phillips. *Unknown.*
On the Tombs in Westminster Abbey. Beaumont.
On the University Carrier. Milton.
On Time. Milton.
One dignity delays for all. Dickinson.
One Morning in May; or, The Young Girl Cut Down in Her Prime. *Unknown.*
One of Wally's Yarns. Masefield.
One Who Watches. Sassoon.
One X. Cummings.
Only the Polished Skeleton. Cullen.
Orchids. Minty.
Out of the Cradle Endlessly Rocking. Whitman.
Out of the Hitherwhere. Riley.
Out of the Hurly-Burly. "Adeler."
"Out, Out." Frost.
Overtures to Death. Day Lewis.
Pale Blue Casket, The. Pitcher.
Pardon, The. Wilbur.
Parted Souls. Herbert.
Pause en Route. Kinsella.
Peace. *Fr.* 1914. Brooke.
Peace. Hughes.
Per Iter Tenebricosum. Gogarty.
Piazza Piece. Ransom.
Pierrette in Memory. Griffith.
Pietä. McAuley.
Pipes, The. Lipsitz.
Place of Rest, The. "Æ."
Poem for My Father's Ghost. Oliver.
Poem to My Death. Burgos.
Poet Is Dead, The. Everson.
Poets against the Angel of Death. Webb.
Poor soul, the center of my sinful earth. Sonnets, CXLVI. Shakespeare.
Portrait of One Dead. *Fr.* The House of Dust. Aiken.
Postcard from the Volcano, A. Stevens.
Praematuri. Cole.
Prayer: "Give me a death like Buddha's, let me fall." Moss.
Prayer for the Little Daughter between Death and Burial. Scott.
Prayer in the Prospect of Death, A. Burns.
Precious in the Sight of the Lord. *Unknown.*
Presence, The. Graves.
Price, The. Davidson.
Prophecy. Wylie.
Prospect of Heaven Makes Death Easy, A. Watts.
Prospice. Browning.
Pure Death. Graves.
Rain. Thomas.
Raisin, The. Hall.
Raising of Lazarus, The. Clifton.
Rata blooms explode, the bow-legged tomcat, The. *Fr.* Autumn Testament. Baxter.
Ravens. Hughes.
Reaper, The. Duncan.
Reasonable Affliction, A. Prior.
Reconciliation. Day Lewis.
Reconciliation. Whitman.
Reed-Player, The. MacLeish.
Reflections, Written on Visiting the Grave of a Venerated Friend. Plato.
Refusal to Mourn the Death, by Fire, of a Child in London, A. Thomas.
Remember the Ladies. Lifshin.
Remember. Rossetti.
Remembrance. Brontë.
Reminiscence, A. Brontë.
Remorse. Betjeman.
Requiem. Stevenson.
Requiescat. Arnold.
Requiescat. Wilde.
Responsory, 1948, A. Meron.
Resurgam. Pickthall.
Resurgam. *Unknown.*
Resurrection, The. Taylor.
Retrieval System, The. Kumin.
Reuben, Reuben. Harper.
Revel, The. Dowling.
Revelation, The. Wright.
Rites for a Demagogue. Thwaite.
Rites for Cousin Vit, The. Brooks.
Ron Mason. Tuwhare.
Rope and Drum. Currie.
Roundel of Rest, A. Symons.
Ruin, The. *Unknown.*
Safe in their alabaster chambers. Dickinson.
Said Death to Passion. Dickinson.
Sailing to Byzantium. Yeats.
Sea Canes. Walcott.
Sea of Death, The. Hood.
Sea Ritual, The. *Fr.* Syren Songs. Darley.
Sea Shanty. Dyment.
Secret, The. Kaneko.
Seeds. Oxenham.
Self-Portrait in 2035. Wright.
Sensitive Plant, The. Shelley.
Serious and a Curious Night-Meditation, A. Traherne.
Shape of Death, The. Swenson.
She Dwelt among the Untrodden Ways. *Fr.* Lucy. Wordsworth.
She Was a Phantom of Delight. Wordsworth.
Ship, The. *Unknown.*
Ship of Death, The. Lawrence.
Should You Go First. Rowswell.
Sick Rose, The. *Fr.* Songs of Experience. Blake.
Silent Is the House. Brontë.
Silent Slain, The. MacLeish.
Silver Swan, The. *Unknown.*
Simplify Me When I'm Dead. Douglas.
Sin and Death. *Fr.* Paradise Lost. Milton.
Sister Lou. Brown.
Sitting at Night on the Front Porch. Wright.
Sixty-eighth Birthday. Lowell.
Skeleton at the Feast, The. Roche.
Sleep, The. Browning.
Sleep. Rogers.
Sleeping at Last. Rossetti.
Slumber Did My Spirit Seal, A. *Fr.* Lucy. Wordsworth.
Small Square, The. Andresen.
Smell of death is so powerful, The. Marguerite de Navarre.
Smile, Death. Mew.
So Be My Passing. Henley.
So Might It Be. Galsworthy.
Softly Softly. Shelton.
Soliloquy on Death. Fiawoo.
Soliloquy I. Aldington.
Soliloquy II. Aldington.
Some Late Lark Singing. Henley.
Some Time at Eve. Hardy.
Some wretched creature, savior take. Dickinson.
Song: "Spirit haunts the year's last hours, A." Tennyson.

Song: "When I am dead, my dearest." Rossetti.
Song in Passing, A. Winters.
Song of the Invisible Corpse in the Field. Orr.
Sonnet: Death's Last Will. Drummond of Hawthornden.
Sonnet: "He came in silvern armor, trimmed with black." Bennett.
Sonnet: "It is not death, that sometime in a sigh." Hood.
Sonnet: "Sweet soul, which in the April of thy years." Drummond of Hawthornden.
Sonnet: "There, on the darkened deathbed, dies the brain." Masefield.
Sonnet for My Father. Justice.
Sonnet on the Death of Mr. Richard West. Gray.
Sonnet 21. Goodman.
Soon at Last My Sighs and Moans. Ginsberg.
Space in the Air, A. Silkin.
Sparrow-Hawk's Complaint, The. *Unknown.*
Speculation. Nemerov.
Speech of the Dead, The. Ridler.
Spring and Death. Hopkins.
Springfield Mountain. *Unknown.*
St. James Infirmary. *Unknown.*
Staircase, The. Allen.
Stand Close Around. Landor.
Stanzas: "I'll not weep that thou art going to leave me." Brontë.
Stanzas to——: "Well, some may hate, and some may scorn." Brontë.
Statue, The. Belloc.
Stirrup-Cup, The. Lanier.
Stone Words for Robert Lowell. Eberhart.
Strange Meeting. Owen.
Strangers Are We All upon the Earth. Werfel.
Streets of Laredo, The. *Unknown.*
Strong Son of God, immortal Love. *Fr.* In Memoriam A. H. H. Tennyson.
Suffering. Ehrenstein.
Sunday Morning. Stevens.
Sunlight on the Garden, The. MacNeice.
Suppose in Perfect Reason. Griffin.
Suppose This Moment Some Stupendous Question. Nowlan.
Supreme Death. Dunn.
Sylvester's Dying Bed. Hughes.
Telephoning It. Edmond.
Tell Me You Wandering Spirits. *Unknown.*
Telling the Bees. Reese.
Telling the Bees. Whittier.
Tenancy, The. Gilmore.
Terminus. Emerson.
Test, The. McAlpine.
Tetélestai. Aiken.
Thanatopsis. Bryant.
That Dark Other Mountain. Francis.
That time of year thou mayst in me behold. Sonnets, LXXIII. Shakespeare.
That's Life? Bold.
Then Sings My Soul. Mariani.
There Is No Death. McCreery.
There Is No Reason Why Not to Look at Death. Sward.
Therefore, We Thank Thee, God. Grossman.
There's a certain slant of light. Dickinson.
There's been a death in the opposite house. Dickinson.
These Things to Come. Butler.
Thesis. De Bolt.
They Are All Gone into the World of Light. Vaughan.
They Never Quite Leave Us. Sangster.
Things Dead. Schwob.
This Houre Her Vigill. Iremonger.
This Is a Photograph of Me. Atwood.
This Is My Play's Last scene, Here Heavens Appoint. *Fr.* Holy Sonnets. Donne.
This talking of death in itself is getting over. *Fr.* Brother Jonathan, Brother Kafka. O'Sullivan.
Thomas Iron-Eyes. Walsh.
Thought of Death, A. Flatman.
Thoughts of Phena. Hardy.
Three images of dying stick in my mind like morbid transfers. *Fr.* Letters to Live Poets. Beaver.
Threnody: "Only quiet death." Cuney.
Tie the strings to my life, my Lord. Dickinson.
'Tis the Last Rose of Summer. Moore.
To a Gentleman and Lady on the Death of the Lady's Brother and Sister, and a Child of the Name Avis, Aged One Year. Wheatley.
To an Athlete Dying Young. *Fr.* A Shropshire Lad. Housman.
To Anthea ("If dear Anthea"). Herrick.
To Anthea ("Now is the time"). Herrick.
To Azrael. Baudelaire.
To Be, or Not to Be. *Fr.* Hamlet. Shakespeare.
To Death. Gogarty.
To Death, Castara Being Sicke. Habington.
To His Dying Brother, Master William Herrick. Herrick.
To His Mistress For Her True Picture. Herbert.
To know just how He suffered would be dear. Dickinson.
To One in Paradise. Poe.
To Perilla. Herrick.
To Robin Red-Breast. Herrick.
To S. A. Lawrence.
To Sir William Alexander. Drummond of Hawthornden.
To the Fringed Gentian. Bryant.
To the Holy Spirit. Winters.
To the Memory of Mr. Oldham. Dryden.
To the Reverend Shade of His Religious Father. Herrick.
To Think of Time. Whitman.
To Vera Thompson. Haines.
Tobacconist of Eight Street, The. Eberhart.
Tolerance of Crows, The. Donnelly.
Transfiguration, The. Herrick.
Traveller, A. *Unknown.*
Triviality, A. Cuney.
Truth the Dead Know, The. Sexton.
Turn Again to Life. Hall.
Twa Brothers, The. *Unknown.*
Twa Corbies, The. *Unknown.*
'Twas warm at first like us. Dickinson.
Two Garden Scenes. Burgess.
Two Invocations of Death. Raine.
Two Mysteries, The. Dodge.
Two Societies, The. Wheelock.
Two Sonnets. Sorley.
Two White Horses in a Line. *Unknown.*
Ubi Sunt Qui ante Nos Fuerunt? *Unknown.*
Uncle Claude. Evans.
Uncle Death. Clark.
Unhappy Diary Days. Vizenor.
Unquiet Grave, The. *Unknown.*
Unwelcome. Dovey.
Up-Hill. Rossetti.
Upon a Dying Lady. Yeats.
Upon His Sister-in-Law, Mistress Elizabeth Herrick. Herrick.
Upon Prue, His Maid. Herrick.
Upon the Image of Death. Southwell.
Vacillation. Yeats.
Valley of the Shadow. Galsworthy.
Verses Written in 1872. Stevenson.
Vespers. Mitchell.
Vesta. Whittier.
Victorious Men of Earth. *Fr.* Cupid and Death. Shirley.
Villagers and Death, The. Graves.
Virgo Descending. Wright.
Virtue. Herbert.
Vision, A. Hofmannsthal.
Vital Spark of Heavenly Flame. Pope.
Voice, The. Hardy.
Voices of Heroes. Gregory.
Waiting for the Post. Auchterlonie.
Wake. Spires.
Wake of William Orr, The. Drennan.
Warning. Curnow.
Warning and Reply. Brontë.
Watch, The. Cornford.
Water Island. Moss.
We Watch'd Her Breathing. Hood.
Welcome, Sweet Rest. Wigglesworth.
What Am I Who Dare. Habington.
What Are Years? Moore.
What Has This Bugbear Death. *Fr.* De Rerum Natura. Lucretius.
What If Some Little Paine the Passage Have. *Fr.* The Faerie Queene. Spenser.
What inn is this. Dickinson.
What Profit? Immanuel di Roma.
When All Is Done. Dunbar.
When Death Comes. *Unknown.*
When Death to Either Shall Come. Bridges.
When I Am Dead. Barrie.
When I Am Dead. Wilson.
When I Die. *Fr.* All Flesh Is Grass. Macrow.
When I Have Fears. Keats.
When I Watch the Living Meet. Housman.

When Lilacs Last in the Dooryard Bloom'd. Whitman.
When the Ambulance Came. Morgan.
When the Roll Is Called up Yonder. Black.
When Thou Must Home. Campion.
Where Shall the Lover Rest. *Fr.* Marmion. Scott.
Where the Rainbow Ends. Lowell.
White Notes. Justice.
Who's Most Afraid of Death? Cummings.
Why Fear to Die? Sidney.
Wife a-Lost, The. Barnes.
Wife of Usher's Well, The. *Unknown.*
Winter Solstice—for Frank. Asphodel.
Wisdom of Old Jelly Roll, The. Smith.
With Rue My Heart Is Laden. *Fr.* A Shropshire Lad. Housman.
Within the Veil. Sangster.
Witness to Death. Lattimore.
Woman Mourned by Daughters, A. Rich.
World, The. Creeley.
Writing while My Father Dies. Pastan.
Death in Literature (DL). Robert F. Weir, ed.
Home Book of Verse, The (HBV-2), 3449–3583. Burton Egbert Stevenson, ed.

Death in Childhood
Afraid. De la Mare.
Babes in the Wood, The. *Unknown.*
Bells for John Whiteside's Daughter. Ransom.
Challenge. Murray.
Child Ill, A. Betjeman.
Childless Father, The. Wordsworth.
Child's Wish Granted, The. Lathrop.
Dead Boy. Ransom.
Dead Child, The. Dowson.
Dead Sister, The. Gilman.
Death of a Son. Silkin.
Dying Child, The. Clare.
Dying Child's Request, The. Gould.
Epitaph on S. P., a Child of Queen Elizabeth's Chapel. Jonson.
First Death in Nova Scotia. Bishop.
Funeral. Meyer.
Home Burial. Frost.
In Memory of My Dear Grandchild. Bradstreet.
Little Boy Blue. Field.
Little Elegy. Kennedy.
Little Libbie. Moore.
Lost Children, The. Jarrell.
Mid-Term Break. Heaney.
Of My Dear Son, Gervase Beaumont. Beaumont.
On a Dead Child. Bridges.
On a Dead Child. Middleton.
On a Dying Boy. Bell.
On My First Daughter. Jonson.
On My First Son. Jonson.
On the Death of Friends in Childhood. Justice.
On the Death of His Son. Cothi
On the Death of His Son. Wesley.
On the Death of Mistress Mary Prideaux. Strode.
Papa's Letter. *Unknown.*
Protocols. Jarrell.
Refusal to Mourn the Death, by Fire, of a Child in London, A. Thomas.
Request of a Dying Child. Sigourney.
There Was a Boy. *Fr.* The Prelude. Wordsworth.
Three Years She Grew. Wordsworth.
To a Child in Death. Mew.
Upon a Child That Died. Herrick.
Upon Wedlock, and Death of Children. Taylor.
Vesta. Whittier.
We Are Seven. Wordsworth.

Death in War. *See* **War Dead.**

Death of Animals
Dirge for Small Wilddeath. Moffett.
Draft Horse, The. Frost.
Farewell, A. Flanner.
Gallows, The. Thomas.
Hurt Hawks. Jeffers.
Killing the Rooster. Nelms.
Nymph Complaining for the Death of Her Faun, The. Marvell.
Obituary. Parsons.
Pardon, The. Wilbur.
Traveling through the Dark. Stafford.

Debauchery
Disabled Debauchee, The. Rochester.
Hand-Mirror, A. Whitman.
On Gut. Jonson.
Short Song of Congratulation, A. Johnson.
Village of Balmaquhapple, The. Hogg.

Debt
File-Hewer's Lamentation, The. Mather.
Happy the man, who voide of cares and strife. *Fr.* The Splendid Shilling; an Imitation of Milton. Philips.
If I Should Die Tonight. King.
Love and Debt Alike Troublesome. Suckling.
Promissory Note, The. Taylor.
Remember. *Unknown.*

Decadence
Habitué. Stickney.
Modern Fine Lady, The. Jenyns.
One More Quadrille. Praed.
Taste. Updike.
To a Boy-Poet of the Decadence. Seaman.

Decalogue
Latest Decalogue, The. Clough.
Thoughts on the Commandments. Baker.

Decay
As a Plane Tree by the Water. Lowell.
Boy Wandering in Simms' Valley. Warren.
Disintegration. Shelton.
Finding an Old Newspaper in the Woods. Morgan.
Groundhog, The. Eberhart.
House on the Hill, The. Robinson.
Ivy Green, The. *Fr.* The Pickwick Papers. Dickens.
Junk. Wilbur.
Lion's Skeleton, The. Turner.
Ozymandias. Shelley.
Prescription of Painful Ends. Jeffers.
View from Father's Porch, The. Wright.
Wood-Pile, The. Frost.

December
Bon Mot, A. *Unknown.*
Daft Days, The. Fergusson.
December. Clare.
December. Fisher.
December. Francis.
December. Irwin.
December. Kenny.
December. Rossetti.
December Blues. Pinsky.
December Day, A. Teasdale.
December Stillness. Sassoon.
December Sunset. Holden.
I Heard a Bird Sing. Herford.
In a Drear-nighted December. Keats.
Long Night Moon, The: December. Frost.
My Grandfather Burning Cornfields. Sauls.
Tree in December. Cane.
When dark December glooms the day. *Fr.* Marmion. Scott.

Deception
Word of Encouragement, A. Pope.

Decisions
Fragment thirty-six. Doolittle ("H.D.")
Road Not Taken, The. Frost.
To Be or Not to Be, *parody.* Edmunds.
To Be or Not to Be. *Fr.* Hamlet. Shakespeare.
Se also **Free Will.**

Declaration of Independence.
Emancipation from British Dependence. Freneau.

Decorum
Shepherdess, The. Meynell.

Deer
Any April. Beard.
Buck in the Snow, The. Millay.
Child's Song. Moore.
Color of Many Deer Running, The. Gregg.
Death of a Hind. MacLean.
Deer at the Roadside. *Fr.* Deer on the High Hills—a Meditation. Smith.
Deer in the Bush. Bloch.
Deer, The. Austin.
Deer. Drinkwater.
Deer. No Ch'ŏn-myŏng.
Deer, The. Sheck.
Deer Isle. Booth.
Deer on Pine Mountain, The. Onakatomi no Yoshinobu.
Deer Song. Silko.
Doe at Evening, A. Lawrence.
Envoy: "On Meall nan Con, the Peak of the Dogs." MacLean.

Fallow Deer at the Lonely House, The. Hardy.
Fawn in the Snow, The. Benét.
Four Deer, The. Jones.
How to See Deer. Booth.
Hunting Song. *Unknown.*
In the Falling Deer's Mouth. Levien.
Knole. Sisson.
Landscape, Deer Season. Howes.
Morning Song. Orr.
New Jersey White-tailed Deer. Oates.
Nymph Complaining for the Death of Her Faun, The. Marvell.
Old Man Said, An. Colum.
Poacher, The. *Fr.* The Parlement of the Three Ages. *Unknown.*
Psalm: "In the small beauty of the forest." Oppen.
Runnable Stag, A. Davidson.
Sila. Warren.
Song for the Greenwood Fawn. Salomon.
Stags. Montgomerie.
Traveling through the Dark. Stafford.
Two Look at Two. Frost.
Whoso List to Hunt. Wyatt.
See also **Hunting and Hunters.**

Defeat
Beauty of Israel is slain upon thy high places, The. Bible, *O.T. Fr.* Second Samuel.
First in the Pentathlon. Lucilius.
Last Word, The. Arnold.
Mighty Runner, A. Robinson.
My portion is defeat—today. Dickinson.
Russia 1812. Hugo.
Snapshot for Miss Bricka Who Lost in the Semifinal Round of the Pennsylvania Lawn Tennis Tournament at Haverford, July, 1960. Wallace.
To the Men Who Lose. Scarborough.

Defoe, Daniel
Daniel Defoe. Landor.
To That Most Senseless Scoundrel, the Author of Legion's Humble Address to the Lords. Brown.
Upon the Anonymous Author of Legion's Humble Address to the Lords. Brown.

Degas, Edgar
In the Sitting Room of the Opera. Cannady.
Museum Piece. Wilbur.

Dehumanization
Applicant, The. Plath.
See also **Bureaucracy and Bureaucrats; Oppression; Racial Prejudice; Sexism.**

Deirdre
Deirdre. Stephens.
Deirdre's Farewell to Alba. *Unknown.*
Deirdre's Lament for the Sons of Usnagh. *Unknown.*

Deism
Spacious Firmament on High, The. Addison.
There is no God, as I was taught in youth. *Fr.* Sonnets ("Long, long ago"). Masefield.

Déjà Vu
Once Before. Dodge.
Vision by Sweetwater. Ransom.

Dejection
Dejection; an Ode. Coleridge.
Stanzas Written in Dejection near Naples. Shelley.
See also **Melancholy.**

De la Mare, Walter
Mr. Walter de la Mare Makes the Little Ones Dizzy, *parody.* Hoffenstein.

Delaware
Airwaves. Woessner.
Rodney's Ride. Brooks.

Delaware River
Across the Delaware. Carleton.

Delft, Holland
At Delft. Tomlinson.

Deliverance
I to the Lord from My Distress. *Unknown.*

Delphi, Oracle of
Last Utterance of the Delphic Oracle, The. Simonides.
News for the Delphic Oracle. Yeats.
Oracle at Delphi. Bagg.

Demeter
Appeasement of Demeter, The. Meredith.
Demeter and Persephone. Tennyson.
To Demeter. Fleming.

Democracy
America. Hamilton.
Black Man Speaks, The. Hughes.
Councils. Piercy.
Democracy. *Fr.* Commemoration Ode. Monroe.
Demos. Robinson.
For You O Democracy. Whitman.
Hark! Young Democracy from sleep. *Fr.* Young Democracy. O'Dowd.
On a General Election. Belloc.
See also **Voting and Voters.**

Denmark
King Christian. Evald.
There Is a Charming Land. Oehlenschlager.

Dentistry and Dentists
After the Dentist. Swenson.
Anxiety about Dying. Ostriker.
Dentist, The. Fyleman.
Hands folded like napkins in my lap. Peterson.
Intimations of Mortality. McGinley.
London Evening Post. *Unknown.*
Making an Impression. Jackson.
Next. Koyama.
Ode to a Dental Hygienist. Hooton.

Dentures
Poet's Farewell to His Teeth, The. Dickey.

Denver, Colorado
Camels Have Come. *Unknown.*
Carrier's Address. *Unknown.*
Curtain, The. Gower.
Doing Railroads for *The Rocky Mountain News.* Warman.
Grand Opening of the People's Theatre. Goldrick.
House in Denver. Ferril.
Waltz against the Mountains. Ferril.

Department Stores
Fixture, A. Swenson.
Macy's Poem, The. Reiss.

Deportation
Plane Wreck at Los Gatos. Guthrie.

Depression (economic). *See* **Great Depression.**

Depression (psychological). *See* **Melancholy; Mental Illness.**

Derbyshire, England
Ode Written in the Peak, An. Drayton.
Retirement, The. Cotton.

Descartes, René
Theological. Fadiman.
Whoroscope. Beckett.

Deserts
Death in the Desert, A. Tomlinson.
Death Valley. Lee.
Desert, The. Knibbs.
Desert Bloom. Arnold.
Desert Shipwreck. Jordan.
Desert Song ("There's no hiding here in the glare of the desert"). Dresbach.
Desert Song ("When I came on from Santa Fe"). Galsworthy.
Deserts. Hanes.
Drifting Sands and a Caravan. Langworthy.
New Mexican Desert. Bynner.
Rain in the Dessert. *Fr.* Arizona Poems. Fletcher.
Skull in the Desert, The. Trimpi.
Sleep in the Mojave Desert. Plath.
Spring in the Desert. Merrill.
To the Colorado Desert. Morris.
Toll of the Desert, The. Monroe.
Wind-Song. *Unknown.*
Yuma. Phelps.

Desire
Abstinence sows sand all over. *Fr.* Gnomic Verses. Blake.
Affection and Desire. Ralegh.
Argument, An. Moore.
Arrow of Desire, The. *Unknown.*
At Mid-Ocean. Bly.
Aye Waukin' O! *Unknown.*
Desire. Sidney.
Desire is a witch. Day Lewis.
Desire Is Dead. Lawrence.
Epigram: "Beauty, a silver dew that falls in May." *Unknown.*
Filling her compact & delicious body. *Fr.* Dream Songs. Berryman.
Fire and Ice. Frost.
First Love. Clare.
For My Husband. Voigt.
I Knew a Woman. Roethke.

I turn you out of doors. Chartier.
I'd Want Her Eyes to Fill with Wonder. Patchen.
Inanna's Song. *Unknown.*
Love. Baker.
My Gostly Fader, I Me Confesse. D'Orléans.
Of the Birth and Bringing Up of Desire. De Vere.
Palmer's Ode, The. *Fr.* Never Too Late. Greene.
Quantum Est Quod Desit. Moore.
Question Answer'd, A. *Fr.* Several Questions Answered. Blake.
Rapture, The. Baker.
Re-forming the Crystal. Rich.
Seizure. Sappho.
Shall I come, if I swim? wide are the waves, you see. Campion.
Thou Blind Man's Mark. *Fr.* Astrophel and Stella. Sidney.
Two Songs. Rich.
Uneasy Rider. Wakoski.
White Rose, A. O'Reilly.
See also **Erotic Love; Lust.**

Desolation
Last Visit. Finch.
More than People. *Fr.* A Cleared Land. Fulton.
No Voice of Man. Falconer.
Sgurr Nan Gillean. *Fr.* The Cuillin. MacLean.

De Soto, Hernando
Distant Runners, The. Van Doren.
New Orleans. Harjo.

Despair
Against Hope. *Fr.* The Mistress. Cowley.
Another While. Rosenfeld.
Ashes of Life. Millay.
Better Resurrection, A. Rossetti.
Carrion Comfort. Hopkins.
Cave of Despair, The. *Fr.* The Faerie Queene. Spenser.
City is of Night, The; perchance of Death. *Fr.* The City of Dreadful Night. Thomson.
Coda. Parker.
Collar, The. Herbert.
Cry of the Peoples, The. Brody.
Dance of Despair, The. Bialik.
Darkling Thrush, The. Hardy.
Dead Faith, The. Lea.
Delirium in Vera Cruz. Lowry.
Despair. *Fr.* Caelica. Greville.
Despair. Lindsay.
Despair. Reed.
Despair. *Fr.* The Faerie Queene. Spenser.
Despairing Lover, The. Walsh.
Die My Shriek. Kushniroff.
Divorce of a Lover, The. Gascoigne.
Down, Down, Down. McHugh.
Epistle to the Gentiles. Hayes.
God Our Refuge. Trench.
How Much Longer? Mezey.
I cannot live with you. Dickinson.
I Wake and Feel the Fell of Dark, Not Day. Hopkins.
If Only. Rossetti.
It was not death, for I stood up. Dickinson.
Knife, The. Kaplan.
Koheleth. Untermeyer.
Leaden Echo and the Golden Echo, The. Hopkins.
Lines Written among the Euganean Hills. Shelley.
Lo, thus, as prostrate, "In the dust I write." *Fr.* The City of Dreadful Night. Thomson.
London. Blake.
Lover Compareth His State to a Ship in Perilous Storm Tossed on the Sea, The. Petrarch.
Madrigal: "My thoughts hold mortall strife." Drummond of Hawthornden.
Mariana. Tennyson.
Miserere, My Maker. *Unknown.*
Moses and Jesus. Zangwill.
Mountaineer, The. Nathan.
No Worst, There Is None. Hopkins.
O dull, cold northern sky. Stevenson.
O Heavy Step of Slow Monotony. Toller.
O Powers Celestial, with what sophistry. *Fr.* Parthenophil and Parthenophe. Barnes.
Old-World Thicket, An. Rossetti.
Poem for a Suicide. Economou.
Redeployment. Nemerov.
Remembrance. Slonimski.
Renascence. Millay.
Reunion. Tawney.
Shall the Dead Praise Thee? Macdonald.
She May Have Seen Better Days. Thornton.
Sick Rose, The. *Fr.* Songs of Experience. Blake.
Song: "My silks and fine array." Blake.
Song of Despair. Rangiaho.
Stanzas Written in Dejection near Naples. Shelley.
Tailor, The. Ansky.
To My Generation. Galai.
Tregardock. Betjeman.
'Twas Night. *Unknown.*
Waly, Waly. *Unknown.*
Why Hast Thou Forsaken Me? *Fr.* The Psalm of Christ. Walsh.
Work without Hope. Coleridge.
You buy some flowers for your table. *Fr.* Poems in Praise of Practically Nothing. Hoffenstein.
Youth. Shelton.

Destiny. *See* **Fate.**

Destruction
Deserted Village, The. Goldsmith.
Doomsday. Wylie.
End of Clonmacnois, The. *Unknown.*
Figure for an Apocalypse. Merton.
Grey Eye Weeping, A. O'Rahilly.
Kilcash. *Unknown.*
Lament for the Woodlands. *Unknown.*
Summer Holiday. Jeffers.
Summer Noon: 1941. Winters.

Detectives
Operative No. 174 Resigns. Fearing.

Detroit, Michigan
Coming Home, Detroit, 1968. Levine.
Detroit. Hall.
In Detroit, I walk out Woodward Avenue. Cuscaden.

Devil. *See* **Satan.**

Devonshire, England
Devon to Me. Galsworthy.
Devonshire Scenes. *Fr.* Tamerton Church-Tower, or First Love. Patmore.
Devonshire Walk, A. *Fr.* Britannia's Pastorals. Browne.
Discontents in Devon. Herrick.
Frolic Mariners of Devon, The. *Fr.* Britannia's Pastorals. Browne.
To Dean-bourn, a Rude River in Devon, by Which Sometimes He Lived. Herrick.

Dew
Drop of Dew, A. Halkin.
For a Dewdrop. Farjeon.
On a Drop of Dew. Marvell.
Prayer for Dew. Eleazar ben Kalir.
Quick-falling Dew. Basho.
When the Dews Are Earliest Falling. Clough.

Dewey, George
Dewey and His Men. Rice.
Dewey at Manila. Johnson.
Dewey in Manila Bay. Risley.
Manila. Ware.

Diabetes
Day of the Pancreas, The. McFadden.

Diamonds
Diamond, A. Loveman.
Upon a Diamond Cut in Forme of a Heart . . . Sent in a New-Yeares Gift. Ayton.

Diana
Diana. Ralegh.
Dianae Sumus in Fide. Catullus.
Hymn to Diana. *Fr.* The Golden Age. Heywood.
Hymn to Diana. *Fr.* Cynthia's Revels. Jonson.
We will wait by the chestnut and the ilex tree. *Fr.* Landscape with the Giant Orion: Orion Seeks the Goddess Diana. Sitwell.
See also **Artemis.**

Diaries
Lady's Diary, The. Dibdin.
On a Seven-Day Diary. Dugan.

Dickens, Charles
Dickens in Camp. Harte.
Owed to Dickens, 1956. Burroway.

Dickinson, Emily
Altitudes. Wilbur.
Brief History. Briggs.
Emily Dickinson. Hagerup.
Emily Dickinson. Longley.
Emily Dickinson Postage Stamp. Strongin.
Mystery of Emily Dickinson, The. Bell.

Sisters, The. Lowell.
To Emily Dickinson. Crane.
Visiting Emily Dickinson's Grave with Robert Francis. Bly.
When I Consider. Griffith.
Your Birthday in Wisconsin You Are 140. Berryman.

Dictionaries
Aardvark. Fields.

Dido
Beaten Path, The. Winslow.
Dido's Hunting. *Fr.* The Aeneid. Virgil.
I am that Dido which thou here do'st see. Ausonius.

Dieting
Breakfast Song in Time of Diet. King.
Diet, The. Burge.
I Can't Have a Martini, Dear, but You Take One. Nash.
Jack Sprat could eat no fat. Mother Goose.

Digby, Lady Venetia
Elegie Made by Mr. Aurelian Townshend in Remembrance of the Ladie Venetia Digby. Townshend.
Lady Venetia Digby, The. Jonson.
Picture of Her Mind, The. Jonson.

Dikes
Dykes, The. Kipling.
Leak in the Dike, The. Cary.

Dillinger, John
Shooting of John Dillinger outside the Biograph Theater, July 22, 1934, The. Wagoner.

DiMaggio, Joe
Byron vs. DiMaggio. Meinke.

Dimples
Where Shall the Baby's Dimple Be? Holland.

Dinosaurs
Brontosaurus. Kredenser.
Dinosaur. Hearn.
Dinosaur, The. Junge.
Dinosaur Spring. Waniek.
Dinosaur Tracks in Beit Zayit. Kaufman.
Dinosaurs. Stoloff.
Dinosaurs. Worth.
Ice Dragons. Ackerman.
Long Gone. Prelutsky.
So Big! Fatchen.

Diocletian
Great Diocletian. *Fr.* The Garden. Cowley.

Diogenes
Diogenes. Eastman.
Tomb of Diogenes, the. *Unknown.*

Dionysus
Ambrosia of Dionysus and Semele, The. Graves.
Dionysus. Andresen.
Hail, Dionysos. Randall.

Diplomacy and Diplomats
I Had a Duck-billed Platypus. Barrington.
On Reading the War Diary of a Defunct Ambassador. Sassoon.
Status Symbols. Sostrom.

Dirigibles
Ascension, The: 1925. Brinnin.
Dirigible, The. Bergengren.
Elegy, An. Winters.
Zeppelin. Glaze.

Disarmament
This Excellent Machine. Lehmann.
See also **Militarism; Pacifism and Pacifists.**

Disasters
Albion Battleship Calamity, The. McGonagall.
Ashtabula Disaster, The. Moore.
Blantyre Explosion, The. *Unknown.*
Explosion, The. Larkin.
Gresford Disaster, The. *Unknown.*
Tay Bridge Disaster, The. McGonagall.
Trimdon Grange Explosion, The. Armstrong.

Discipline
Lesson, The. Mariani.

Discontent
Inquietude. Murray.

Discotheques
Disco Chinatown. Kageyama.

Disraeli, Benjamin
To Disraeli. Brooks.

Ditmars, Raymond Lee
Lines to Dr. Ditmars. Robinson.

Dives (Bible)
Dives and Lazarus. *Unknown.*
On Dives. Crashaw.

Diving and Divers
Diver. Francis.
Diver, The. Hayden.
Diver, The. Phocas.
Diver, The. Ross.
Diver. Simpson.
Divers, The. Quennell.
Diving into the Wreck. Rich.
Elegy for a Diver. Booth.
Elegy for a Diver. Meinke.
Fantasia. Livesay.
Fine, a Private Place, A. Ackerman.
High Diver. Francis.

Divorce
Ballad of the Despairing Husband. Creeley.
Betsey and I Are Out. Carleton.
By this he knew she wept with waking eyes. *Fr.* Modern Love. Meredith.
Chance Meeting. Griffin.
Dividing the House. Richardson.
Divorce. Jennings.
Divorce. Noll.
Divorce. Widerberg.
Divorce Dress, The. Finley.
Getting Out. Mathis.
Jamie Douglas. *Unknown.*
Mementos, I: "Sorting out letters and piles of my old." Snodgrass.
On Certain Days of the Year. Simpson.
Poem for a "Divorced" Daughter. Coleman.
Popular Functionary, A. Dibdin.
Power of Innocence, The. "C. G. H."
Songs of Divorce. Green.
Thus piteously Love closed what he begat. *Fr.* Modern Love. Meredith.

Dobson, Austin
On Receiving a Copy of Mr. Austin Dobson's "Old World Idylls." Lowell.

Doctors. *See* **Physicians.**

Dodo Birds
Dodo, The. Belloc.
Dodo. Carlile.
Dodo, The. Lucie-Smith.

Dogs
Ah, Are You Digging on My Grave? Hardy.
Arf, Said Sandy. Stetler.
At the Dog Show. Morley.
At thieves I bark; at lovers wag my tail. *Unknown.*
Back Country. Oates.
Ballad of Master McGrath, A. *Unknown.*
Bandog, The. De la Mare.
Bath, The. Lehmann.
Beth Gêlert; or, The Grave of the Greyhound. Spencer.
Big Dog. Booth.
Bingo. *Unknown.*
Bingo Has an Enemy. Fyleman.
Bishop Doane on His Dog. Doane.
Bliss. Farjeon.
Bony. Ortiz.
Bounce to Fop; an Heroick Epistle from a Dog at Twickenham to a Dog at Court. Pope.
Buccaneer, The. Turner.
Bum. Wedgefarth.
Buying the Dog. Ondaatje.
Cerberus. Van Brunt.
Contentment. Johnson.
Curate Thinks You Have No Soul, The. Lucas.
Cynotaph, The. "Ingoldsby."
Daley's Dorg Wattle. Goodge.
Dame. Astor.
Day was so bright, The. *Fr.* A Dog in the Quarry. Holub.
Dead "Wessex" the Dog to the Household. Hardy.
Denise. Hale.
Der Deitcher's Dog. Winner.
Dog, The. Faber.
Dog, The. Herford.
Dog, The. Iremonger.
Dog. Monro.
Dog. Ransom.
Dog. Smith.
Dog, The. *Unknown.*
Dog Alive. Witt.
Dog Parade, The. Guiterman.

Dogs and Weather. Welles.
Dog's Best Friend Is His Illiteracy, A. Nash.
Dog's Cold Nose, The. Guiterman.
Dog's Death, A. Squire.
Dog's Death. Updike.
Dogs of Santiago. McCarthy.
Elegy on a Lap-Dog, An. Gay.
Elegy on the Death of a Mad Dog, An. *Fr.* The Vicar of Wakefield. Goldsmith.
Epigram Engraved on the Collar of a Dog Given to His Royal Highness. Pope.
Epitaph on True, Her Majesty's Dog, An. Prior.
Epitaph to a Dog. Byron.
Explaining about the Dachshund. Stone.
Extraordinary Dog, The. Turner.
Fashions in Dogs. White.
Fatal Dream, The; or, The Unhappy Favourite. Collins.
Fidelity. Wordsworth.
Flush or Faunus. Browning.
Geist's Grave. Arnold.
German Shepherd. Livingston.
Gift with the Wrappings Off. Counselman.
Gluskap's Hound. Roberts.
Grip, The. Kennelly.
Haiku: "Dog's violent sneeze, The." Wright.
Hairy Dog, The. Asquith.
"Hold." Chalmers.
Hope. Dickey.
I Muse Not. Davison.
I Think I Know No Finer Things than Dogs. Brent.
Incident Characteristic of a Favourite Dog. Wordsworth.
Introduction to Dogs, An. Nash.
Irish Harper and His Dog, The. Campbell.
Island Dogs. Bell.
Jubilate Canis. Jong.
Kaiser Dead. Arnold.
Letter to the City Clerk. Wright.
Lines I Told Myself I Wouldn't Write. Mariani.
Little Black Dog, The. Reynolds.
Little Dog-Angel, A. Holland.
Little Dog under the Wagon, The. *Unknown.*
Little Lost Pup. Guiterman.
Little Puppy. Wetherill.
Lone Dog. McLeod.
Love Me, Love My Dog. Crawford.
Loyal. Matthews.
Macinnes's Mountain Patrol. Patey.
Madness. Dickey.
Madrid, Iowa. Ikan.
Maggie. *Unknown.*
Malemute Dog, A. O'Cotter.
Maltese Dog, A. Blunden.
Montgomery. Evans.
Mother Doesn't Want a Dog. Viorst.
Murgatroyd. Wright.
My Airedale Dog. Mason.
My Dog. Bangs.
My Dog. Chute.
My Dog. Robinson.
My Dog Dash. Ruskin.
My Dog Jock. Carruth.
My Dog Ponto. Masters.
My Dog Tray. Byron.
My Last Terrier. Halsham.
My Puppy. Fisher.
Night Song. Cornford.
Nino, the Wonder Dog. Fuller.
Noctambule. Johnston.
Obituary. Parsons.
Old Blue. *Unknown.*
Old Dog. Souster.
Old Dog. Stafford.
Old Dog in the Ruins of the Graves at Arles, The. Wright.
Old Dog, New Dog. Lea.
Old Dog Tray. Foster.
Old Mother Hubbard. *Unknown.*
Old Rattler. *Unknown.*
On the Death of a Favorite Old Spaniel. Southey.
On the Death of a Lady's Dog. Roscommon.
Ordinary Dog, The. Turner.
Overland to the Islands. Levertov.
Pain. Wrigley.
Pardon, The. Wilbur.
Popular Personage at Home, A. Hardy.
Power of the Dog, The. Kipling.
Puppy. Fisher.
Puppy. Lape.
Puppy and I. Milne.
Rags. Cooke.
Rake. Ratcliffe.
Red Dog, The. Jensen.
Rest in Peace. Funk.
Roger the Dog. Hughes.
Savage Beast, The. Williams.
Scroppo's Dog. Swenson.
Shaggy Dog Story. Steele.
Sheepdog Trials in Hyde Park. Day Lewis.
Shepherd's Dog, The. Norris.
Shlup, shlup, the dog. *Fr.* Six Variations. Levertov.
Sila. Warren.
Simon and the Tarantula. Wright.
Song of the Mischievous Dog, The. Thomas.
Sonnet: To Tartar, a Terrier Beauty. Beddoes.
Stray Dog. Mish.
Stray Dogs, near Écully, Valley of the Rhône. Avison.
Sudden Assertion. Leslie.
Sunning. Tippett.
Supplication of the Black Aberdeen. Kipling.
Timon Speaks to a Dog. Hobsbaum.
To a Bull-Dog. Squire.
To a Dog. Peabody.
To a Dog Injured in the Street. Williams.
To a Spaniel. Landor.
To My Dog "Blanco." Holland.
To My Setter, Scout. Seldon.
To Our House-Dog Captain. Landor.
To robbers furious, and to lovers tame. Johnson.
To Scott. Letts.
Tom's Little Dog. De la Mare.
Towser Shall Be Tied Tonight. *Unknown.*
Train Dogs, The. Johnson.
Tray. Browning.
Tribute to the Memory of the Same Dog. Wordsworth.
Two Dogs. Davidson.
Two Dogs Have I. Nash.
Uncle Dog; the Poet at 9. Sward.
Victor Dog, The. Merrill.
Village Tale, A. Sarton.
Watch-Dog. Brasch.
Wolf and the Dog, The. La Fontaine.
Woodman's Dog, The. *Fr.* The Task. Cowper.
"Word" of a Watch-Dog, The. Sandag.
Your Dog Dies. Carver.
Good Dog Poems (GDP). William Cole, ed.
See also ***individual breeds of dogs (e.g.,*** **Collies**).

Dollhouses
Making a Door. Schmitz.

Dolls
Doll Song. "Carroll."
Dolls, The. Yeats.
Five Poems for Dolls. Atwood.
Lost Doll, The. Kingsley.

Dolphins
Dolphin Seen Alone. Lattimore.
Dolphins, The. Maclaren.
They Say the Sea Is Loveless. Lawrence.

Domitian
Apology for Domitian. Warren.

Don Juan
Aubade: Donna Anna to Juan, Still Asleep. Howard.
Don Giovanni on His Way to Hell. Gilbert.
Don Giovanni on His Way to Hell II. Gilbert.
Don Juan, *sels.* Byron.
Don Juan. Lawrence.
Don Juan in Hell. Baudelaire.
How to Tell Juan Don from Another. Lewis.

Don Quixote
Bridge of Heraclitus, The. Reavey.
Don Quixote. Betts.
Don Quixote. Dobson.
Don Quixote. Ficke.

Donegal. *See* **County Donegal, Ireland.**

Donkeys
Ass, The. Allan.

Big Friend of the Stones. Orlen.
Burro, The. Gibbons.
Burro with the Long Ears. Wetherill.
Donkey, The. Chesterton.
Donkey, The. Roethke.
Donkey, The. *Unknown.*
Donkey. Van Doren.
Donkey and the Lapdog, The. La Fontaine.
Donkeys. Field.
Faith. Dunkels.
Little Donkey, The. Jammes.
Me and Prunes. Sherwood.
Nicholas Nye. De la Mare.
Ol' Jinny Mine, The. Detrick.
Prayer of the Donkey, The. De Gasztold.
Prayer to Go to Paradise with the Donkeys, A. Jammes.
Time Out. Montague.
To a Young Ass. Coleridge.
Turf Carrier on Aranmore. Hewitt.
What the Donkey Saw. Fanthorpe.

Donne, John
Dr. Donne. Alling.
Elegy for Doctor Dunn. Herbert of Cherbury.
Elegy upon the Death of the Dean of Paul's, Dr. John Donne, An. Carew.
Epitaph on Doctor Donne, Deane of Pauls, An. Corbett.
John Donne. Simmons.
John Donne's Statue. Bishop.
Letter to John Donne, A. Sisson.
On Donne's Poetry. Coleridge.
To John Donne. Jonson.
Upon the Death of My Ever Desired Friend Doctor Donne Dean of Pauls. King.

Donnelly, Charles
Of what a quality is courage made. *Fr.* Charles Donnelly. MacDonagh.

Donner Party
Donner Party, The. Keithley.

Donnybrook Fair, Dublin
Humours of Donnybrook Fair, The. O'Flaherty.
Humours of Donnybrook Fair, The. *Unknown.*

Doorbells
Doorbells. Field.

Doors
Delights of the Door, The. Ponge.
Door, The. Tomlinson.
Lockless Door, The. Frost.
Old Essex Door. Hickey.
Terrible Door, The. Monro.

Dormice
Elf and the Dormouse, The. Herford.

Dorset, England
Ad Henricum Wottonem. Bastard.
Domicilium. Hardy.
On Sturminster Footbridge. Hardy.
Once at Swanage. Hardy.
Overlooking the River Stour. Hardy.
Roman Road, The. Hardy.

Dostoyevsky, Feodor
Buzzing Doubt, The. Hill.
Respectable Burgher, The. Hardy.
Will You, Won't You? Van Doren.

Doubt
Buzzing Doubt, The. Hill.
Doubt. Deland.
Doubt. Gregh.
Doubt. *Fr.* In Memoriam A. H. H. Tennyson.
Doubter, The. Gilder.
Doubter's Prayer, The. Brontë.
Dover Beach. Arnold.
Father. Ficke.
Praise Doubt. Van Doren.
Prayer for Living and Dying. La Farge.
Prayer of an Unbeliever. Reese.
Scholfield Huxley. *Fr.* Spoon River Anthology. Masters.
Song of Doubt, A. Holland.
Will You, Won't You? Van Doren.
See also **Agnosticism.**

Douglas, James, 2d Earl of Douglas and Mar
Battle of Otterbourne, The. *Unknown.*

Douglas, Stephen Arnold
Lecompton's Black Brigade. Halpine.

Douglass, Frederick
Frederick Douglass. Cornish.
Frederick Douglass. Dunbar.
Frederick Douglass. Hayden.
Frederick Douglass: 1817-1895. Hughes.

Dove, Arthur Garfield
Studies from Life. Dickey.

Dover, England
At Dover Cliffs. Bowles.
Dover Beach. Arnold.
Dover, the Samphire Cliff. *Fr.* King Lear. Shakespeare.

Doves
Again My Fond Circle of Doves. Hathaway.
Captive Dove, The. Brontë.
Coo-pe-coo. *Unknown.*
Dove. Farber.
Dove, The. MacColl.
Dove Apologizes to His God for Being Caught by a Cat, The. Eaton.
Dove says, Coo, coo, The. Mother Goose.
Dove's Loneliness, The. Darley.
I Had a Dove. Keats.
I have two sparrows white as snow. *Fr.* The Muses' Elysium. Drayton.
Jealousie Is the Rage of a Man. Winchilsea.
Literary Landscape with Dove and Poet. McGinley.
My Doves. Browning.
Nature of the Turtle Dove, The. *Fr.* The Bestiary. *Unknown.*
Parrot and Dove. Landor.
Stockdoves, The. Young.
Turtle-Doves' Nest, The. *Unknown.*
Turtle thus with plaintive crying, The. Gay.
White Dove of the Wild Dark Eyes. Plunkett.
Wings. Bible, *O.T.* *Fr.* Psalms
Wood-Dove's Note, The. Miller.

Down's Syndrome
Almond Tree, The. Stallworthy.
Mongol Quine. Mackie.

Dowries
Arise, Arise. *Unknown.*
Dainty Sang, A. *Fr.* The Gentle Shepherd. Ramsay.
Lass with a Lump of Land. Ramsay.
My Tocher's the Jewel. Burns.

Dowsing
Water-Witch, The. Perry.

Dowson, Ernest
Ernest Dowson. Wheelock.

Dragonflies
Bête Humaine. Young.
Dragonfly, The. Bogan.
Dragonfly, The. Chisoku.
Dragonfly, A. Farjeon.
Dragonfly, The. Nemerov.
Dragonfly, The. Rand.
Hunter's Moon. Sandy.
Lines to a Dragon-Fly. Landor.

Dragons
Death of the Dragon, The. *Fr.* The Faerie Queene. Spenser.
Dragon, The. Spenser.
Dragon Lesson. Hearst.
Gold-tinted Dragon, The. Kuskin.
Jabberwocky. *Fr.* Through the Looking-Glass. "Carroll."
O to Be a Dragon. Moore.
Sir Eglamour, That Worthy Knight. Rowlands.
Tale of Custard the Dragon, The. Nash.
Toaster, The. Smith.

Drake, Sir Francis
Drake's Drum. Newbolt.
Epigram: On Sir Francis Drake. *Unknown.*
Farewell to Sir John Norris and Sir Francis Drake, A. Peele.
Of the Great and Famous Sir Francis Drake. Hayman.
Sir Francis Drake. *Unknown.*
Upon Sir Francis Drake's Return from His Voyage about the World, and the Queen's Meeting Him. *Unknown.*

Drake, Joseph Rodman
On the Death of Joseph Rodman Drake. Halleck.

Drama. *See* **Theater.**

Drayton, Michael
Funeral Elegy on the Death of His Very Good Friend, Mr. Michael Drayton. Cokayne.

Dreams and Dreaming
African Dream. Kaufman.
Aladdin. Lowell.
All Night! Baker.
Ante-natal Dream. Kavanagh.
Archetypes. Bowers.

Beale Street. Hughes.
Big Dream, Little Dream. Simpson.
Birthday Dream, The. Dickey.
Brothers, The. Muir.
Calamity Jane Greets Her Dreams. Lignell.
Cave-Boy, The. Richards.
Chimera. Howes.
Cock and the Hen, The. *Fr.* The Canterbury Tales: The Nun's Priest's Tale. Chaucer.
Crowning of Dreaming John, The. Drinkwater.
Cry of the Dreamer, The. O'Reilly.
Darkness. Byron.
Daybreak. Spender.
Directions for Dreamfishing. Johnston.
Dream, A. Songs of Innocence. Blake.
Dream, The. Byron.
Dream, The. Donne.
Dream, The. Ignatow.
Dream, A. *Fr.* The Fall of Hyperion. Keats.
Dream. Miles.
Dream. Smith.
Dream, The. Spalding.
Dream, The. *Unknown.*
Dream Barker. Valentine.
Dream Deferred. Hughes.
Dream, Dump-Heap, and Civilization. Warren.
Dream Farmer. Boyer.
Dream-Land. Poe.
Dream of Fair Women, A. Amis.
Dream of the Rood, The. *Unknown.*
Dream-Pedlary. Beddoes.
Dreamscape. Booth.
Dream Variations. Hughes.
Dream within a Dream, A. Poe.
Dreamer of Dreams. Carruth.
Dreams. Alexander.
Dreams. Daley.
Dreams. Giovanni.
Dreams. Herrick.
Dreams. Hughes.
Dreams. Poe.
Echo. Rossetti.
Empire of Dreams. Simic.
Epistle to John Hamilton Reynolds. Keats.
Eye of Humility, The. Smith.
Fidelity. Kass.
First of All My Dreams, The. Cummings.
Five Dreams, The. Woods.
Forgotten Dreams. Silvera.
Harlequin of Dreams, The. Lanier.
He Whom a Dream Hath Possessed. O'Sheel.
Hold Fast Your Dreams. Driscoll.
House in the Wood, The. Jarrell.
If Only the Dreams Abide. Scollard.
Illusion. Wilcox.
I'm a Dreamer. Cumbo.
In Your Bad Dream. Hugo.
It's Comforting. Simmons.
Ivory, Coral, Gold, The. Drummond of Hawthornden.
King of Dreams, The. Scollard.
Kitchenette Building. Brooks.
Kubla Khan. Coleridge.
Land of Dreams, The. Blake.
Le Jazz Hot. Hollo.
Le Rêve. Bowers.
Lesson for Dreamers. Janeczko.
Loom of Dreams, The. Symons.
Lotos-Eaters, The. Tennyson.
Lover, Having Dreamed of Enjoying His Love, Complaineth That the Dream Is Not either Longer or Truer, The. Wyatt.
Man Asleep in the Desert. Lux.
Mares of Night. Long.
May Morning. *Fr.* The Book of the Duchess. Chaucer.
Methought I saw my late espoused Saint. Milton.
Miniver Cheevy. Robinson.
Mirage. Rossetti.
Mouth of the Amazon. Gira.
Mowing the Lawn. Bensko.
My Dream. Blockcolski.
My Dream. Rossetti.
My Little Dreams. Johnson.
New Dreams for Old. Rice.
Night a Sailor Came to Me in a Dream, The. Wakoski.
Nightmare. *Fr.* Iolanthe. Gilbert.
Nightmares. Fox.
No One Is Asleep Even While Dreaming. Roberts.
Nocturne in the Women's Prison. Beneyto.
Ode: "We are the music makers." O'Shaughnessy.
On Dreams. Swift.
On His Dead Wife. Milton.
On My Late Dear Wife. Richardson.
Orchard-Pit, The. Rossetti.
Origin of Dreams. Bell.
Pinch of Salt, A. Graves.
Prelude to an Evening. Ransom.
Prowling the Ridge. Minty.
Rain. Murray.
Reverie at Dawn. O'Rahilly.
Rhyme of the Dream-Maker Man, A. White.
Rock-a-by Lady, The. Field.
Scapegoat. Rodgers.
Seafarers tell of the Eastern Isle of Bliss, The. *Fr.* His Dream of the Sky-Land: A Farewell Poem. LiPo.
September. Pastan.
Sleep. Berssenbrugge.
Sleep-Learning. Fainlight.
Sleeping Saint, The. La Follette.
Solutions. Barton.
Song: "Don't Tell Me What You Dreamt Last Night." Adams.
Song: "It autumne was, and on our hemispheare." Drummond of Hawthornden.
Song of the Zambra Dance. Dryden
Sugar-Plum Tree, The. Field.
They Flee from Me. Wyatt.
This was my dream! I saw a Forest. *Fr.* Bad Dreams. Browning.
To Dark Eyes Dreaming. Snyder.
Tonight Everyone in the World Is Dreaming the Same Dream. Litwack.
Trance, The. Spender.
True to a Dream. Petersen.
Undergraduate. Moore.
Vine, The. Herrick.
Vision, The ("Methought I saw as I dream in bed"). Herrick.
Vision, The ("Sitting alone as one forsook"). Herrick.
Waking. Pyle.
Wharf of Dreams, The. Markham.
What Did I Dream? Graves.
Window Sill, The. Graves.
With Kathy at Wisdom. Hugo.
Wynken, Blynken, and Nod. Field.
Yes, wonderful are dreams: and I have known. *Fr.* The Tower of the Dream. Harpur.

Dreiser, Theodore
Homage to Theodore Dreiser on the Centennial of His Birth, *sel.* Warren.

Dress. *See* **Clothing.**

Driftwood
Driftwood. Smythe.
Driftwood Dybbuk. Lefcowitz.
Fires of Driftwood. MacKay.

Drinking
Anacreontic ("Born I was to be old"). Herrick.
Anacreontic to Flip. Tyler.
At the Tavern. *Unknown.*
Auld Lang Syne. Burns.
Awake! for Morning in the Bowl of Night. *Fr.* The Rubáiyát of Omar Khayyám. Omar Khayyám.
Bacchanal. De Vries.
Bacchus's Opinion of Wine, and Other Beverages. *Fr.* Bacchus in Tuscany. Redi.
Back and Side Go Bare, Go Bare. Stevenson.
Ballad of the Drinker in His Pub. Van Wyk Louw.
Ballade of Liquid Refreshment. Bentley.
Bar, The. *Unknown.*
Be Drunken. Baudelaire.
Beer. Arnold.
Beer. Calverley.
Beer Drops. Boyd.
Captain Stratton's Fancy. Masefield.
Catch, A. Aldrich.
Champagne Rosé. Kenyon.
Chevaliers de la Table Ronde. *Unknown.*
Clepsydra. Cotton.
Company One Keeps, The. Dickson.
Cruiskeen Lawn, The. *Unknown.*
Daft Days, The. Fergusson.

Dartmouth Winter-Song. Hovey.
Drink To-day. *Fr.* The Bloody Brother. Fletcher.
Drink with Something in It, A. Nash.
Drinking. *Fr.* Anacreontics. Cowley.
Drinking Song. Brome.
Drinking Song. *Fr.* The Bloody Brother. Fletcher.
Drinking Song. Harrison.
Drinking Song. Stephen.
Drinking Song. Still.
Drinking Song. *Unknown.*
Drinking Song, A. Yeats.
Drinking-Song, against All Sorts of Disputes in Drinking, A. Wycherly.
Drunk Last Night with Friends, I Go to Work Anyway. Dow.
Drunken Dee, The. Scroggie.
Dry. Hoffenstein.
England's Triumph. *Unknown.*
Epicure, The. Cowley.
Face upon the Floor, The. D'Arcy.
Fill the Bowl, Butler. *Unknown.*
Fill the Bumper Fair. Moore.
Finnair Fragment. Hoffmann.
Finnegan's Wake. *Unknown.*
Fishing Drunk. Mondy.
Fragment: "I would to heaven that I were so much clay." *Fr.* Don Juan. Byron.
Frolic, A. Herrick.
Glass of Beer, A. Stephens.
Grape Daiquiri. Koyama.
Had we two met, blythe-hearted Burns. Landor.
Head and Bottle. Thomas.
His Fare-well to Sack. Herrick.
Hymn to Bacchus, A. Herrick.
I drink to forget, but whenever I think. Bold.
I Go to Whiskey Bars. Thompson.
If all be true that I do think. Aldrich.
In New York I got drunk, to tell the truth. *Fr.* A Trip to Four or Fives Towns. Logan.
In the Bar. Vander Molen.
In the 2 A.M. Club, a working man's bar. Peterson.
Indian Macho. Oliver.
Inebriety. Crabbe.
Interview with Doctor Drink. Cunningham.
John Barleycorn. Burns.
Johnson's Ale. *Unknown.*
Judged by the Company One Keeps. *Unknown.*
Jug of Punch, The. McPeake.
Landlord Fill the Flowing Bowl. *Unknown.*
Last Drink, A. *Unknown.*
Let the Toast Pass. Sheridan.
Lilliputian's Beer Song. Winner.
Lips That Touch Liquor. Young.
Lips That Touch Liquor Shall Never Touch Mine, The. Glazebrook.
Liquor and Longevity. *Unknown.*
Little Brown Jug. *At. to* Winner.
Logical Vegetarian, The. Chesterton.
Lord Alcohol. Beddoes.
Love. *Unknown.*
Man in the Moon Drinks Clarret, The. *Unknown.*
McSorley's Bar. Denney.
Mermaid Tavern, The. Keats.
Miniver Cheevy. Robinson.
Mint Julep, The. Hoffman.
Mistaken Resolve, The. Martial.
Mr. Flood's Party. Robinson.
Mr. Francis Beaumont's Letter to Ben Johnson. Beaumont.
Moonshine. *Unknown.*
Now We've Met. *Unknown.*
Nut-brown Ale, The. Marston.
Ode: "Come, let us drink away the time." Cotton.
Ode for a Social Meeting. Holmes.
Of Jolly Good Ale and Old. *Fr.* Gammer Gurton's Needle. Stevenson.
Old Filthy Beer Pail, The. Hall.
Old Keg of Rum, The. *Unknown.*
Old Wife in High Spirits. "MacDiarmid."
O'Tuomy's Drinking Song. O'Tuomy.
Parting Glass, The. Freneau.
Pledge of Spunky Point, The. Hay.
Price of a Drink. Pollard.
Quebec Liquor Commission Store. Klein.
Reason Fair to Fill My Glass, A. Morris.
R-e-m-o-r-s-e. Ade.
Revenue Man Blues. *Unknown.*
Rubáiyát of Omar Khayyám of Naishápúr, The. Omar Khayyám.
Rye Whisky. *Unknown.*
Said the Whiskey Flask. *Unknown.*
Sigh as It Ends. Berryman.
Sir John Barleycorn. *Unknown.*
Song: "Here's to the maiden of bashful fifteen." *Fr.* The School for Scandal. Sheridan.
Song: "Let school-masters puzzle their brain." *Fr.* She Stoops to Conquer. Goldsmith.
Song: "Pints and the pistols, the pike-staves and pottles, The." *At. to* Praed.
Song: "There's a barrel of porter at Tammany Hall." Halleck.
Song in a Siege. Heath.
Song of Ale, A. *Fr.* Gammer Gurton's Needle. *Unknown.*
Stein Song, A. *Fr.* Spring. Hovey.
Stony Brook Tavern. Reed.
Strip Me Naked, or Royal Gin for Ever; a Picture. *Unknown.*
Take a Drink on Me. *Unknown.*
Tale of Lord Lovell, The. *Unknown.*
Tam o' Shanter. Burns.
Terence, This Is Stupid Stuff. *Fr.* A Shropshire Lad. Housman.
There is drink fermented. *Fr.* A Satirical Poem about Drink. Mongol.
Thirsty Earth, The. Cowley.
Three Pigeons, The. Goldsmith.
To Julius. Martial.
To the Fly in My Drink. Wagoner.
Tom Brown. *Unknown.*
Troll the Bowl! *Fr.* The Shoemaker's Holiday. Dekker.
Two Glasses, The. Wilcox.
Up in the Air. Ramsay.
Upon Drinking in a Bowl. Rochester.
Villon's Straight Tip to All Cross Coves. Henley.
Vive la Compagnie (Vive l'Amour). *Unknown.*
Wassail Song. *Unknown.*
Water-Drinker, The. Jonson.
We Be Soldiers Three. *Unknown.*
Welcome to Sack, The. Herrick.
We're All Dry. *Unknown.*
West Sussex Drinking Song. Belloc.
What Matter? *Unknown.*
What Thomas an Buile Said in a Pub. Stephens.
Whenever you drink all night you make. Martial.
Whisky, Drink Divine. O'Leary.
Whiskey Song, A. *Unknown.*
Why I Drink. Aldrich.
Why Liquor of Life? Carolan.
Willie Brew'd a Peck o' Maut. Burns.
Willows, The. Harte.
Wine and Water. Chesterton.
Winter Glass, The. Cotton.
Winter Wish, A. Messinger.
Yellow Bittern, The. Mac Giolla Gunna.
See also. **Alcoholism and Alcoholics; Drunkards.**
Driving and Drivers
Drive Imagining. Vogelsang.
Driver in Italy, The. Christopher.
See also **Automobiles.**
Drought
Drought. Laight.
Drought. Oumar Ba.
Dust Bowl. Davis.
Said Hanrahan. Hartigan.
Sun Drops Red, The. Miller.
Wind/ flattening its gaunt furious self against. *Fr.* The Wind Our Enemy. Marriott.
Drowning
Ballad of the Oysterman, The. Holmes.
Beautiful Swimmer, The. Whitman.
Castaway, The. Cowper.
Dead Man Dragged from the Sea, The. Gardner.
Death by Drowning. Brewster.
Death of a Young Son by Drowning. Atwood.
Drowned, The. Spender.
Drowning is not so pitiful. Dickinson.
Elegy on Gordon Barber. Derwood.
Emmeline Grangerford's "Ode to Stephen Dowling Bots, Dec'd." *Fr.* The Adventures of Huckleberry Finn. "Twain."
Ezra Shank. *Unknown.*
Family. Miles.
Fish Food. Wheelwright.
Floating Bridge. *Unknown.*
Full fathom five thy father lies. *Fr.* The Tempest. Shakespeare.

Jacqueline Gray. Pitchford.
Jimmy Judge. *Unknown.*
Lady in Kicking Horse Reservoir, The. Hugo.
Limbo. Heaney.
Lowlands o' Holland, The. *Unknown.*
Lycidas. Milton.
Mary in the Silvery Tide. *Unknown.*
Near Drowning. Pomeroy.
Not Waving but Drowning. Smith.
Ode on the Death of a Favorite Cat, Drowned in a Tub of Gold Fishes. Gray.
On the Memory of Mr. Edward King, Drown'd in the Irish Seas. Cleveland.
Outlandish Knight, The. *Unknown.*
Samuel Allen. *Unknown.*
Sands of Dee, The. *Fr.* Altar Locke. Kingsley.
Silly Willy. "R. L. B."
Sir Patrick Spens. *Unknown.*
Swan Swims So Bonny, The. *Unknown.*
These Trees Are No Forest of Mourners. Jones.
This Is a Photograph of Me. Atwood.
To Some Millions Who Survive Joseph E. Mander, Senior. Wright.
Water Island. Moss.

Drug Addiction
Addict, The. Rubin.
Addict, The. Sexton.
Aga Khan, The. Orlen.
Babylon Revisited. Baraka.
Blues for Sister Sally. Kandel.
Certain Choices. Shelton.
Class of 19——. Dec.
Cocaine Blues. *Unknown.*
Cocaine Lil. *Unknown.*
Cocteau's *Opium:* 1. Finkel.
Documentary on Airplane Glue, A. Henderson.
Ho. Young.
Idea of Ancestry, The. Knight.
In Praise of Laudanum. Harrison.
Junior Addict. Hughes.
Laudanum. *Unknown.*
Mainline. Ditsky.
"O. D." Gilbert.
Solo for Bent Spoon. Finkel.
Street Song. Gunn.
Stuff. Johnson.
Summer Words of a Sistuh Addict. Sanchez.
To My Daughter the Junkie on a Train. Lorde.
Willie the Weeper. *Unknown.*

Drugs
Discovery of LSD a True Story, The. Hollo.

Drugstores
Drug Clerk, The. Tietjens.
Drug Store. Shapiro.
Drug Store. Weaver.
Saturday Sundae. Scott.

Druids
Hymn to the Sun. Doughty.

Drums
African Dance. Hughes.
Beat! Beat! Drums! Whitman.
Distant Drum, The. Hernton.
Drummer Hodge. Hardy.
I Hate That Drum's Discordant Sound. Scott of Amwell.
La Chute. Olson.
Percussions. Welburn.
Piano and Drums. Okara.
Portrait of Rudy, A. Olumo.
Talking Drums, The. Kyei.

Drunkards
Absinthe-Drinker, The. Symons.
(Alcoholic). Berryman.
Beautiful Brown Eyes. *Unknown.*
Bowery. Ignatow.
Calton Weaver, The. *Unknown.*
Canned Heat Blues. *Unknown.*
Chant Royal of the Dejected Dipsomaniac. Marquis.
Closing Time. Michie.
Dead Drunk Blues. *Unknown.*
Drunk in the Furnace, The. Merwin.
Drunk Last Night. *Unknown.*
Drunkard, The. *Fr.* Proverbs. Bible, *O.T.*
Drunkard, The. Levine.
Drunkard, A. *Unknown.*
Drunkard and the Pig, The. *Unknown.*
Drunkard to His Bottle, A. LeFanu.
Drunkards, The. Lowry.
Drunkard's Doom, The. *Unknown.*
Drunken Man, The. Orlen.
Eclipse. Probst.
Elegy for a Diver. Meinke.
Epigram: "When Bibo thought fit from the world to retreat." Prior.
Epitaph: "Stavro's dead. A truant vine." Durrell.
Extravagant Drunkard's Wish, The. Ward.
Face upon the Floor, The. D'Arcy.
Falling Down to Bed. NorthSun.
Four Nights Drunk. *Unknown.*
He as O, A. Cummings.
Hemmed-in Males. Williams.
I'll Never Get Drunk Any More. *Unknown.*
Interview with Doctor Drink. Cunningham.
Intoxicated Rat, The. *Unknown.*
John Adkins' Farewell. *Unknown.*
Little Brown Jug. *At. to* Winner.
Lost after All. Tillman.
Lying in a Yuma Saloon. Barnes.
Midnight Ramble, The. Woodward.
Miniver Cheevy. Robinson.
Mr. Flood's Party. Robinson.
My Darling Dear, My Daisy Flower. Skelton.
Not a Sous Had He Got. "Ingoldsby."
Note Left in Jimmy Leonard's Shack, A. Wright.
Old Witherington. Randall.
On an Imaginary Journey to the Continent. Porson.
Original Epitaph on a Drunkard. Tyler.
Pig, The. *Unknown.*
Point of No Return. Graves.
Porson's Visit to the Continent. Porson.
Railroad to Hell. *Unknown.*
Red Whiskey. *Unknown.*
Reformed Drunkard. Scannell.
Resentments Composed Because of the Clamor of Town Topers outside My Apartment. Knight.
Rolling English Road, The. Chesterton.
Song-Maker. Endrezze-Danielson.
There is drink fermented. *Fr.* A Satirical Poem about Drink. Mongol.
What Shall We Do with a Drunken Sailor? *Unknown.*
Where He Hangs His Hat. Lee.
Whiskey Johnny. *Unknown.*
Willie's and Nellie's Wish. Moore.
Zimmer Drunk and Alone, Dreaming of Old Football Games. Zimmer.
See also **Alcoholism and Alcoholics.**

Dryads
Dryad Song. Fuller.

Dryden, John
Dear John, whoever now takes pen to write. *Fr.* A Letter to John Dryden. McAuley.
Medal of John Bayes, The. Shadwell.
Panegyric on the Author of "Absalom and Achitophel," A. *Unknown.*
To Mr. Bays. Sackville.

Dublin, Ireland
Arrival: The Capital. O'Grady.
Back to Dublin. Ford.
Dublin. MacNeice.
Dublin Doggerel. Conniff.
Dublin Made Me. MacDonagh.
Herbert Street Revisited. Montague.
Humours of Donnybrook Fair, The. *Unknown.*
Mountown! Thou Sweet Retreat. *Fr.* Mully of Mountown. King.
No Place So Grand. *Unknown.*
Rocky Road to Dublin, The. *Unknown.*

Du Bois, William Edward Burghardt
Booker T. and W. E. B. Randall.
For William Edward Burghardt Du Bois on His Eightieth Birthday. Latimer.
On the Death of William Edward Burghardt Du Bois by African Moonlight and Forgotten Shores. Rivers.
See also **Easter Rebellion.**

Duchamp, Marcel
Nude Descending a Staircase. Kennedy.

Ducks
Duck, The. Digance.
Duck. Donaghy.
Duck, The. King.
Duck, The. Nash.

Duck. Worth.
Duck and the Kangaroo, The. Lear.
Duck-Chasing. Kinnell.
Duck in Central Park. Savage.
Ducks. Bly.
Ducks. Harvey.
Ducks. Hesketh.
Ducks, The. Wilkins.
Ducks at Dawn. Tippett.
Ducks' Ditty. *Fr.* The Wind in the Willows. Grahame.
I had a duck and the young duck died. Stodart-Walker.
Little Duck, The. Joso.
Muscovy Drake, The. Lesoro.
Nearing Winter. Sandeen.
Nell Flaherty's Drake. *Unknown.*
New Duckling, The. Noyes.
Notorious Glutton, The. Taylor.
Prayer of the Little Ducks, The. Gasztold.
Quack! De la Mare.
Regent's Park. Fyleman.
Shooting Ducks in South Louisiana. Tillinghast.
Sing-Song Rhyme. *Unknown.*
Solitary, The. Barnard.
That duck, bobbing up. Joso.
Three Moves. Logan.
Trueblue Gentleman, A. Patchen.
Usually an Old Female is the Leader. Hennen.
When God had finished the stars and whirl of coloured suns. *Fr.* Ducks. Harvey.
Wild Duck, The. Masefield.
Wild Duck's Nest, The. Wordsworth.

Duels
Dowie Houms o' Yarrow, The. *Unknown.*
Duel, The. Field.
Young Barnswell. *Unknown.*

Dulles, John Foster
Just Dropped In. Cole.

Dumas, Alexandre
Lines Written at the Grave of Alexandre Dumas. Bennett.

Dumbness
Child in the Rug, The. Haines.

Dumont, Margaret
To the Lady Portrayed by Margaret Dumont. Hollander.

Dumps
Dump, The. Kuzma.
Rural Dumpheap. Cane.
Town Dump, The. Nemerov.

Dunbar, Paul Laurence
Dunbar. Spencer.
For Paul Laurence Dunbar. *Fr.* Four Epitaphs. Cullen.
Paul Laurence Dunbar. Corrothers.
Paul Laurence Dunbar. Hayden.

Dundee, John Graham of Claverhouse, 1st Viscount (Bonnie Dundee)
Bonny Dundee. *Fr.* The Doom of Devergoil. Scott.
Upon the Death of the Earl of Dundee. Dryden.

Dunes
Sand Dunes. Frost.
Sand Dunes and Sea. Moreland.

Dunkirk, France
Little Boats of Britain, The. Carsley.

Duns Scotus
Duns Scotus. Merton.
Duns Scotus's Oxford. Hopkins.

Dunwich, England
At Dunwich. Thwaite.

Dupree, Frank
Dupree. *Unknown.*

Dürer, Albrecht
Dürer; Innsbruck, 1495. "Malley."
Dürer's Piece of Turf. Krapf.
Knight, Death, and the Devil, The. Jarrell.
Steeple-Jack, The. Moore.

Duse, Eleanora
Eleanora Duse as Magda. Binyon.

Dusk. *See* **Twilight.**

Dust
Common Dust. Johnson.
Dust. "AE."
Dust, The. Hall.
Dust. Spire.
Dust on Spring Street. Grudin.
Praise of Dust, The. Chesterton.
This Quiet Dust. Wheelock.

Dust Storms
Colorado Sand Storm, A. Field.

Dutch, The
Dutch, The. Canning.

Dutch Wars
Fourth Day's Battle, The. *Fr.* Annus Mirabilis. Dryden.
Now van to van the foremost squadrons meet. *Fr.* Annus Mirabilis. Dryden.
Song: Written at Sea, in the First Dutch War, 1665, the Night before an Engagement. Sackville.

Duty
Abraham Davenport. Whittier.
Do It Now! *Unknown.*
Duty. Clough.
Duty. *Fr.* Voluntaries. Emerson.
Duty. Hooper.
Duty. Markham.
Kind of an Ode to Duty. Adams.
Life's Common Duties. Savage.
Ode to Duty. Wordsworth.
Reward of Service. Browning.
So Nigh Is Grandeur. Emerson.
So night is grandeur to man. Cook.
Stopping by Woods on a Snowy Evening. Frost.
Three Fishers, The. Kingsley.

E

Eagles
American Eagle, The. Lawrence.
Dalliance of the Eagles, The. Whitman.
Dead Eagle, The. Campbell.
Eagle. Bowker.
Eagle, The. *Fr.* Transcripts from Nature. "MacLeod".
Eagle. Skelton.
Eagle, The. Tennyson.
Eagle, The. Young.
Eagle and the Beetle, The. La Fontaine.
Eagle and the Mole, The. Wylie.
Eagle Plain. Francis.
Eagles. Woody.
Fire on the Hills. Jeffers.
Inability to Depict an Eagle. Eberhart.
Mole and the Eagle, The. Hale.
Nature of the Eagle, The. *Fr.* The Bestiary. *Unknown.*
Salmon Drowns Eagle. Lowry.
Story of a Well-made Shield, The. Momaday.
White Eagle, The. McDonald.

Ears
Colonel, The. Forché.
Downy Hair. *Fr.* Zen Poems. Stryk.
On Wearing Ears. Harris.
There Are Three Bones in the Human Ear. Endrezze-Danielson.

Earth
Advent. Rossetti.
Anatomy of Monotony. Stevens.
Aspects of the World Like Coral Reefs. Bronk.
Bog Queen. Heaney.
Bonnie Broukit Bairn, The. "MacDiarmid."
Bowl. Stevens.
Common Living Dirt, The. Piercy.
Dust. "Æ."
Earth. Bryant.
Earth. Wheelock.
Earth and Sky. Euripides.
Earth in Spring, The. Halevi.
Earth Is the Lord's, The. Psalms. Bible, *O.T.*
Earth's Answer. Blake.
Epitaph on the World. Thoreau.
Evensong. Moffett.
Eye, The. Jeffers.
First Psalm, The. Brecht.
God's Grandeur. Hopkins.
God's World. Millay.
Hamatreya. Emerson.
Hymn to Earth. Wylie.
I am the poet of the body. *Fr.* Song of Myself. Whitman.
I Never Saw a Moor. Dickinson.

I see a great round wonder rolling through space. *Fr.* Salut au Monde! Whitman.
In No Strange Land. Thompson.
La Guerre. Cummings.
Lute Music. Rexroth.
Magnificat in Transit from the Toledo Airport. Starbuck.
Merchant Marine. Miles.
Moment Please, A. Allen.
My Father's World. Babcock.
Night Falls on China. Auden.
O Earth, Sufficing All Our Needs. Roberts.
O Earth, Turn! Johnston.
O Sweet Spontaneous Earth. Cummings.
On a Wednesday. Aliesan.
On Inhabiting an Orange. Miles.
One Foot in Eden. Muir.
Open Range. Jackson.
Orbiter 5 Shows How Earth Looks from the Moon. Swenson.
Our Mother's Body Is the Earth. McAnally.
Report from a Planet. Lattimore.
This Earth. Minthorn.
To an Old Lady. Empson.
Under the Hill. Eberhart.
Views of Our Sphere. Sandeen.
When Last Seen. Flexner.
Wilt Thou Set Thine Eyes upon That Which Is Not? *Fr.* Emblems. Quarles.
Windy Planet, The. Dillard.
Wonderful World, The. Rands.
World, The. Raine.
World, The. Vaughan.
World's Music, The. "Setoun."

Earthquakes
Crack in the Wall Holds Flowers. Miller.
Earth Tremor in Lugano. Kirkup.
Earthquake. Ford.
Earthquake, The. Zuni.
Ruaumoko—the Earthquake God. Turei.
San Francisco Falling. Markham.
Santa Barbara Earthquake, The. *Unknown.*

Easter
A Song at Easter. Towne.
African Easter. Nicol.
Alleluia! Alleluia! Let the Holy Anthem Rise. *Unknown.*
Alleluia! Christ Is Risen Today. Hopkins.
Assurance. Munson.
Beacon Light. Clark.
Calvary and Easter. "Coolidge."
Christ Is Risen! Dugan.
Christmas Is Really for the Children. Turner.
Cross and the Tomb, The. Flint.
Day of Resurrection, The. John of Damascus.
Down a Sunny Easter Meadow. Turner.
Drizzling Easter Morn, A. Hardy.
Early, Early Easter Day. Fisher.
Easter. Coatsworth.
Easter. Herbert.
Easter. Kilmer.
Easter. King.
Easter. Sabin.
Easter. Whitaker.
Easter Beatitudes. Burkholder.
Easter Carol. Lovejoy.
Easter Communion. Hopkins.
Easter, Day of Christ Eternal. Moore.
Easter Day. Clough.
Easter-Day. Vaughan.
Easter Eve, 1945. Rukeyser.
Easter Hymn. Housman.
Easter Hymn. Vaughan.
Easter Hymn. Wesley.
Easter in the Woods. Frost.
Easter Joy. Turner.
Easter Monday. Farjeon.
Easter Monday. Rossetti.
Easter Morn. *Fr.* Christ's Victory and Triumph. Fletcher.
Easter Morning. *Fr.* Matthew. Bible, *O.T.*
Easter Morning. Spenser.
Easter Night. Meynell.
Easter, 1923. Neihardt.
Easter Poem. Raine.
Easter Snowfall. Behn.
Easter Song, An. "Coolidge."
Easter Sunday. Sedulius Scottus.
Easter Thought. Cox.
Easter Wings. Herbert.
Easter Zunday. Barnes.
Follow Me. Longfellow.
For Our Sakes. Wilde.
Freedom. *Unknown.*
From Bethlehem To Calvary. Nicholson.
Good Friday in My Heart. Coleridge.
He Lives! He Lives to Bless! Stroud.
His Last Week. Lennen.
His Life Is Ours. Stroud.
Hymn of the Resurrection, A. Dunbar.
If a Man Die. Moreland.
If Easter Be Not True. Barstow.
If Easter Eggs Would Hatch. Malloch.
Jesus Lives! Gellert.
Legend of the Easter Eggs, The. O'Brien.
Lent Lily, The. Housman.
Lift Your Glad Voices in Triumph on High. Ware.
Meeting the Easter Bunny. Bennett.
Morning, Noon, And. Truax.
Most glorious Lord of life, that on this day. *Fr.* Amoretti. Spenser.
Not There. *Unknown.*
O Day of Light and Gladness. Hosmer.
Of the Resurrection of Christ. Dunbar.
On Easter Day. Thaxter.
On Easter Morning. Rexford.
Rejoice, Let Alleluias Ring. Schaefer.
Resurrection, The. Brooks.
Resurrection. St. John of Damascus.
Rhyme for Remembering the Date of Easter. Richardson.
Sepulcher, The. Flint.
Seven Stanzas at Easter. Updike.
Some Things That Easter Brings. Parrish.
That Nature is a Heraclitean Fire and of the Comfort of the Resurrection. Hopkins.
Upon an Easter Morning. Farjeon.
Well Pleaseth Me the Sweet Time of Easter. Pound.
What Does Easter Mean to You? Conrad.
Words for a Resurrection. Kennedy.

Easter Island
Easter Island. Scott.

Easter Rebellion (1916)
Dublin Ballad, A: 1916. O'Byrne.
Easter, 1916. Yeats.
Lament for the Poets: 1916. Ledwidge.
Lament for Thomas MacDonagh. Ledwidge.
Rose Tree, The. Yeats.
Veterans, The. MacDonagh.

Eatherly, Claude R.
Song about Major Eatherly, A. Wain.

Eating
Hymn to Comus. Jonson.
Life would be an easy matter. *Fr.* If We Didn't Have to Eat. Waterman.
Methuselah. *Unknown.*
Nightmare of a Cook. Kallman.
When Father Carves the Duck. Wright.
See also **Food; Gluttony and Gluttons.**

Echo (mythology)
Song: "Sweet Echo, sweetest nymph, that liv'st unseen." Milton.
See also **Narcissus (mythology).**

Echoes
Echo. De la Mare.
Echo. Moore.
Echo. *Fr.* Arcadia. Sidney.
Echo. Weston.
Echoes. Grey.
Echoes. Lazarus.
Echoing Cliff, The. Young.
Gentle Echo on Woman, A. Swift.
Splendour Falls, The. *Fr.* Princess, The. Tennyson.

Eclipses
December Eclipse. Lockwood.
Eclipse. Sheehan.
Lunar Eclipse. Scarbrough.

Ecology
All the Smoke. Siegel.
As Yet. Rodríguez Nietzche.
Baby Ten Months Old Looks at the Public Domain, A. Stafford.
Binsey Poplars (Felled 1879). Hopkins.

Buffalo. Brodsky.
Bungaloid Growth. Ellis.
Dead Seal. Purdy.
Dogwood Blossoms. Blue Cloud.
Easier. Harrison.
Ecological Lecture. Raffel.
Evensong. Moffett.
Flower-Fed Buffaloes, The. Lindsay.
Hamatreya. Emerson.
Hard Questions. Tsuda.
Highway Construction. Chapin.
Hymn to Moloch. Hodgson.
Instructions for a Park. Walker.
Inversnaid. Hopkins.
Little Things. Stephens.
Looking at Power. Woessner.
Malediction. Spacks.
Martyred Earth, The. Milne.
Memo to the 21st Century. Appleman.
Moorhen Pond, The. Earley.
Moss-Gathering. Roethke.
Mother Earth; Her Whales. Snyder.
Mystic River. Ciardi.
On the Projected Kendal and Windermere Railway. Wordsworth.
Plans for Altering the River. Hugo.
Poplar-Field, The. Cowper.
Progress. Martin.
Quid Restat. Beebe.
Requiem for a River. Williams.
Smokey the Bear Sutra. *Unknown.*
Song of Cove Creek Dam, The. *Unknown.*
Statement on Our Higher Education. Ransom.
Stranded Whales, The. Dutton.
To a Young Wretch. Frost.
War against the Trees, The. Kunitz.
What Have They Done to the Rain. Reynolds.
When There Were Trees. Willard.
Why the Soup Tastes like the Daily News. Piercy.
Woodman, Spare that Tree. Morris.
Working against Time. Wagoner.
News of the Universe. (NU). Robert Bly, ed.
See also **Pollution.**

Economics and Economists
Forecasting the Economy. Morin.

Eczema
Eczema. Slavitt.

Eden
Adam Fallen. *Fr.* Paradise Lost. Milton.
Adam Lay Ibounden. *Unknown.*
Alas, that ever that speche was spoken. *Unknown.*
Apple, The. Smith.
Banishment, The. *Fr.* Paradise Lost. Milton.
Before the Fall. *Fr.* Paradise Lost. Milton.
Corruption. Vaughan.
Fall, The. Rochester.
Garden, The. Beaumont.
Garden, The. Very.
Lord God Planted a Garden, The. Gurney.
Naming of the Beasts, The. Sparshott.
Old Story, An. Lee.
One Foot in Eden. Muir.
Paradise. *Fr.* Paradise Lost. Milton.
Poisoned Man, The. Dickey.
Rose of Eden, The. Phillips.
Spring. Hopkins.
Symposium, A: Apples. Pastan.
Theology. Hughes.
What Words Have Past. *Fr.* Paradise Lost. Milton.
See also **Adam and Eve.**

Edinburgh, Scotland
Daft-Days, The. Fergusson.
Edinburgh. Guiterman.
Edinburgh. Noyes.
Edinburgh from the Pentland Hills. Scott.
November Night, Edinburgh. MacCaig.
To the Merchantis of Edinburgh. Dunbar.

Edison, Thomas Alva
Progress. Belfrage.

Editors
Editor Whedon. *Fr.* Spoon River Anthology. Masters.
Editor's Tragedy, The. Hankin.

Education
As Joe Gould says in. Cummings.
Campus on the Hill, The. Snodgrass.
Clerk there was of Oxenford also, A. *Fr.* The Canterbury Tales: Prologue. Chaucer.
Cyriack, Whose Grandsire. Milton.
Educational Administration Professor's Prayer, The. Bobango.
Elementary School Classroom in a Slum, An. Spender.
Frost at Midnight. Coleridge.
History of Education. McCord.
Indian Education. Louis.
Lines to a Don. Belloc.
Little Learning, A. *Fr.* An Essay on Criticism. Pope.
Modern Ode to the Modern School. Erskine.
On the Prospect of Planting Arts and Learning in America. Berkeley.
Pains of Education, The. Churchill.
Poem: "In the earnest path of duty." Forten.
Primary Education. McGinley.
So it was./ I broke the copious curls upon my head. *Fr.* Aurora Leigh. Browning.
Supervising Examinations. Lucy.
To David, about His Education. Nemerov.
To whom should you entrust your son. *Fr.* Epigrams. Martial.
University Examinations in Egypt. Enright.
We flee away from cities, but we bring. *Fr.* The Adirondacs. Emerson.
Women. Walker.
Would you your son should be a sot or dunce. *Fr.* Tirocinium; or, A Review of Schools. Cowper.
See also **Colleges and Universities; Scholars and Scholarship; Students; Teaching and Teachers.**

Edward I, King of England
Bard, The. Gray.
Death of King Edward I, The. *Unknown.*
English Retort, The. *Unknown.*
Scots in Berwick, The. *Unknown.*

Edward II, King of England
Four Wise Men on Edward II's Reign. *Unknown.*
This Edward in the Aprill of his age. *Fr.* Piers Gaveston. Drayton.

Edward III, King of England
On the Death of Edward III. *Unknown.*

Edward IV, King of England
King Edward the Fourth and a Tanner of Tamworth. *Unknown.*

Edward VII, King of England
Death of King Edward VII, The. *Unknown.*
Elegy on Albert Edward the Peacemaker. *Unknown.*
New Song on the Birth of the Prince of Wales, A. *Unknown.*

Edwards, Jonathan
After the Surprising Conversions. Lowell.
Mr. Edwards and the Spider. Lowell.
Theology of Jonathan Edwards, The. McGinley.

Eels
Bucket of Sea-Serpents. Ant.
Eel, The. Montale.
Eel, The. Nash.
Eels and Tortoises. *Fr.* Halieutica. Diaper.
Existential. Heyen.
Song of Hate for Eels. Guiterman.

Eggs
Beautiful Poultry. Wedde.
Easter Egg. Kieffaber.
Egg, The. Bowering.
Egg Boiler, The. Brooks.
Egg Thoughts. Hoban.
How the Hen Sold Her Eggs to the Stingy Priest. Willard.
Humpty Dumpty sat on a wall. Mother Goose.
In marble walls as white as milk. Mother Goose.
Inefficacious Egg, The. Bishop.
It's in the Egg. Rosenblatt.
Little Bits of Soft-boiled Egg. Maschler.
Long white barn, A. *Unknown.*
Meg's Egg. Hoberman.
Motherhood. Calverley.
Soft-boiled Egg. Hoban.

Egotism
Ego. Siegel.
Egotist, The. Evans.
Immoral Proposition, The. Creeley.
Invictus. Henley.
Megaceph, chosen to serve the State. *Fr.* The Devil's Dictionary. Bierce.
Talker, The. Van Duyn.
Travelling Companions. Armour.
See also **Individualism.**

Egrets
Egrets. Wright.
Snowy Egret. Weigl.
Two Egrets. Ciardi.
Egypt
Chorus: "Then thus we have beheld." *Fr.* Cleopatra. Daniel.
Egypt. Doolittle ("H. D.").
Egypt's Might Is Tumbled Down. Coleridge.
I Am a Cowboy in the Boat of Ra. Reed.
Nile, The. Hunt.
Ozymandias. Shelley.
Sakhara. Ford.
Snails. Blodgett.
There Is a Dream Dreaming Us. Dubie.
Witch Going Down to Egypt, A. Chalfi.
Eichmann, Adolf
For Adolf Eichmann. Levi.
Peachtree, The. Levertov.
Eichmann. Blazek.
Einstein, Albert
Einstein. MacLeish.
Einstein's Father. Klauck.
Gift to Be Simple, The. Moss.
How Einstein Started It Up Again. Dillard.
It did not last; the Devil howling Ho. Squire.
Poem about Intelligence for My Brothers and Sisters, A. Jordan.
St. Augustine Contemplating the Bust of Einstein. Ackerman.
There's a wonderful family called Stein. *Unknown.*
Eisenhower, Dwight David
Eisenhower's Visit to Franco, 1959. Wright.
Lay of Ike, The. Berryman.
Tentative Description of a Dinner to Promote the Impeachment of President Eisenhower. Ferlinghetti.
Eisenhower, Mamie Doud
Funeral Song for Mamie Eisenhower. Wong.
El Dorado
Eldorado. Poe.
El Greco. *See* **Greco, El**
Elands
Seele im Raum. Jarrell.
Eleanor of Aquitaine
Queen Eleanor's Confession. *Unknown.*
Rose of the World, The. Masefield.
Electric Appliances
Man about the Kitchen, A. Hobson.
Now I Set Me. Herman.
Electricity
Action of Electricity, The. *Fr.* The Economy of Vegetation. Darwin.
Electricity Is Funny! Currier.
Men against the Sky. Haines.
Ohms. Layton.
Pylons, The. Spender.
Elephants
Address to Mr. Cross, of Exeter 'Change, on the Death of the Elephant. Hood.
Beside the Line of Elephants. Becker.
Blind Men and the Elephant, The. Saxe.
Cradle Song of the Elephants. Del Valle.
Death of an Elephant, The. Pagnucci.
Elephant, The. Asquith.
Elephant, The. Belloc.
Elephant, The. Hochman.
Elephant. McFadden.
Elephant, The ("Elephant carries a great big trunk"). *Unknown.*
Elephant ("Tall-topped acacia, you, full of branches"). *Unknown.*
Elephant Is Slow to Mate, The. Lawrence.
Elephant, or the Force of Habit, The. Housman.
Elephant to the Girl in Bertram Mills' Circus, The. Cronin.
Elephants, The. *Unknown.*
Elephants in the Circus. Lawrence.
Elephant's Trunk, The. Wilkins.
Eletelephony. Richards.
Erin (Elephant). *Unknown.*
Gunga. *Fr.* A Circus Garland. Field.
Holding Hands. Link.
Indian Elephant, The. Kaberry.
Oliphaunt. Tolkien.
Rat and the Elephant, The. La Fontaine.
Salute to the Elephant. Apolebieji.
Tit for Tat: A Tale. Aikin.
To a Dead Elephant. Livingstone.
Elevators
Ode to a Vanished Operator In an Automatized Elevator. Rosenfield.
Elgin Marbles
On Seeing the Elgin Marbles. Keats.
Elijah (Bible)
Angel, The. Hayes.
"Eliot, George" (Mary Ann Evans Cross)
On the Deaths of Thomas Carlyle and George Eliot. Swinburne.
Eliot, Thomas Stearns
Chard Whitlow, *parody*. Reed.
Lines for Cuscuscaraway and Mirza Murad Ali Beg. Eliot.
Mr. Eliot's Day. Francis.
Mr. T. S. Eliot Cooking Pasta. Tornai.
T. S. Eliot. Auden.
To T. S. Eliot. Litvinoff.
Verses for the 60th Birthday of T. S. Eliot. Barker.
Vice. Hecht.
Elizabeth, Queen of Bohemia
On His Mistress, the Queen of Bohemia. Wotton.
On His Mistris, the Queen of Bohemia. Wotton.
Elizabeth I, Queen of England
Elizabeth's War with the Christmas Bear: 1601. Dubie.
God Save Elizabeth! Palgrave.
Hymn to Cynthia. Jonson.
In Honour of That High and Mighty Princess Queen Elizabeth of Happy Memory. Bradstreet.
Looking-Glass, The. Kipling.
Songe betwene the Quenes Majestie and Englande, A. Birche.
This Royal Infant. *Fr.* King Henry VIII. Shakespeare.
To Queen Elizabeth. *Fr.* Nosce Teipsum. Davies.
With Fragrant Flowers We Strew the Way. *Fr.* The Honourable Entertainment Given to the Queen's Majesty in Progress at Elvetham, 1591. Watson.
Elizabeth II, Queen of England
Queen Elizabeth. *Unknown.*
Elizabeth, Queen Consort of Henry VII
Rueful Lamentation on the Death of Queen Elizabeth, A. More.
Ellington, Edward Kennedy (Duke)
Day Duke Raised, The. Troupe.
Morning Duke Ellington Praised the Lord and Six Little Black Davids Tapped Danced Unto, The. Dodson.
Perdido, Duke? McGovern.
Elm Trees
Connecticut Elm, The. Swan.
Dilemma of the Elm. Taggard.
Elm, The. Shepard.
Elm's Home, The. Heyen.
Wind in the Elms, The. Miller.
Elopement
Eve of St. Agnes, The. Keats.
Jock of Hazeldean. Scott.
Lord Ullin's Daughter. Campbell.
Skeleton in Armor, The. Longfellow.
Young Lochinvar. *Fr.* Marmion. Scott.
Elphinston, James
Epigram on Elphinstone's Translation of Martial's Epigrams. Burns.
Elves
Darkling Elves, The. Prelutsky.
Elf and the Dormouse, The. Herford.
Elf Night. Rogers.
Elves' Dance, The. *Fr.* The Mayde's Metamorphosis. *Unknown, at. to* Lyly *and to* Ravenscroft.
For a Mocking Voice. Farjeon.
How to Tell Goblins from Elves. Shannon.
How to Treat Elves. Bishop.
Little Elf, The. Bangs.
Man Who Hid His Own Front Door, The. MacKinstry.
Seven Ages of Elf-hood, The. Field.
See also **Fairies.**
Ely, England
Monks of Ely, The. *Unknown.*
Emancipation (1863-1865)
Fifty Years, 1863-1913. Johnson.
Laus Deo! Whittier.
Proclamation, The. Whittier.
Slav'ry Chain. *Unknown.*
Embryos
Dead Embryos. Tóth.
In the Planetarium. Fox.
Woman to Man. Wright.
Emerson, Ralph Waldo
Art in America. Weiss.

Carlyle and Emerson. Schuyler.
Emerson. Alcott.
Emerson. Dodge.
Emerson. *Fr.* A Fable for Critics. Lowell.
Emerson: Last Days at Concord. Gregory.
In the Garden. Schmidt.

Emigration
Adieu to Old England. *Unknown.*
Complaint of the Morpethshire Farmer, The. Bunting.
Gin the Goodwife Stint. Bunting.
Lament of the Irish Emigrant. Sheridan.
Ye Simple Men. Blackie.

Emmet, Robert
Bold Robert Emmet. Maguire.
Oh, Breathe Not His Name. Moore.
She Is Far from the Land. Moore.

Empedocles
Death and Empedocles 444 B.C. Gregory.
Empedocles. Meredith.
Empedocles on Etna. Arnold.
Empedocles on Etna. Mallalieu.

Empire State Building, New York City
Looking at the Empire State Building. Pomeroy.
New York. Wheelock.

Emus
Emus. Fullerton.

Enclosures. *See* **Inclosure Movements**

End of the World
Advice to a Prophet. Wilbur.
Armaments Race. Paterson.
Black Mesa. Rogers.
Call to Order. Burbank.
Conclusion. Nims.
Earth. Wheelcock.
End of the World, The. Bottomley.
End of the World. Hoddis.
End of the World, The. MacLeish.
Epitaph Ending in And, The. Stafford.
Fire and Ice. Frost.
Fundamental Project of Technology, The. Kinnell.
LMFBR. Snyder.
Once by the Pacific. Frost.
Ordinary People in the Last Days. Macpherson.
Seven Days. Rowland.
Sun and Moon. Macpherson.
What If a Much of a Which of a Wind. Cummings.
When I Awoke. Patterson.
See also **Judgment Day.**

Endangered Species
Moschus Moschiferus. Hope.

Endurance
Endurance. Allen.
See also **Fortitude.**

Endymion
Endymion, *sels.* Keats.
Endymion. Longfellow.
Oh, Sleep Forever in the Latmian Cave. Millay.
Phoebe on Latmus. *Fr.* Endimion and Phoebe. Drayton.
Song by Fairies. *Fr.* Endymion. Lyly.

Energy Crisis
Elegy Written in a Country Coal-Bin. Morley.

Engineers
Engineers. Garthwaite.

England
Above the Medway. *Fr.* The Vales of the Medway. Munby.
Adlestrop. Thomas.
Airman Who Flew over Shakespeare's England, The. Plutzik.
America to England. Woodberry.
And Did Those Feet in Ancient Time. *Fr.* Milton. Blake.
Anglicized Utopia. Gilbert.
Britain. *Fr.* The Traveller; or, A Prospect of Society. Goldsmith.
Britannia. *Fr.* The Seasons: Summer. Thomson.
By the River Eden. Raine.
Channel Crossing. Barker.
Christmas. Betjeman.
Coastwise Lights, The. Kipling.
Come to Britain; a Humble Contribution to the Movement. Herbert.
Corrymeela. O'Neill.
Distant View Of England from the Sea. Bowles.
1887. Housman.
Elegy in a Country Churchyard. Chesterton.
England in 1819. Shelley.
England, My England. Henley.
England, Unprepared for War. *Fr.* An Ode to the Country Gentlemen of England. Akenside.
England, 1802. Wordsworth.
England. Cardinal Newman.
England. Channing.
England. *Fr.* The Task. Cowper.
England. Day.
England. Massey.
England. Montgomery.
England. Moore.
England. Newman.
England. *Unknown.*
England's Sovereigns in Verse. *Unknown.*
English Counties. *Unknown.*
English Succession, The. *Unknown.*
English Weather. *Fr.* The Fleece. Dyer.
Eureka! Godley.
Fair England. Cone.
Farewell to England. *Unknown.*
Free Parliament Litany, A. *Unknown.*
Halcyon's Nest, The. *Fr.* Christ's Victory and Triumph. Fletcher.
Happy Britannia. *Fr.* The Seasons: Summer. Thomson.
Home Thoughts, from Abroad. Browning.
Home Thoughts from Abroad. Browning.
Home Thoughts, from Abroad. Browning.
Homes of England, The. Hemans.
Home-Thoughts, from Abroad. Browning.
Home-Thoughts, from the Sea. Browning.
I Have Loved England. *Fr.* The White Cliffs. Miller.
I Traveled among Unknown Men. Wordsworth.
In Good King Charles's Golden Days. *Unknown.*
International Hymn. Huntington.
Italy and Britain. *Fr.* A Letter from Italy. Addison.
Italy. *Fr.* Beppo. Byron.
Jerusalem. *Fr.* Milton. Blake.
Land, The. Kipling.
Land of Hope and Glory. Benson.
Last Buccaneer, The. Kingsley.
Laurel Axe, The. *Fr.* An Apology for the Revival of Christian Architecture in England. Hill.
London, 1802. Wordsworth.
Look for Me on England. Mallalieu.
Look, Stranger, on This Island Now. Auden.
Matlock Bath. Betjeman.
Mercian Hymns, *sels.* Hill.
Mother England. Thomas.
O My Mother Isle! ("Not yet enslaved, not wholly vile"). *Fr.* Ode on the Departing Year. Coleridge.
O my Mother Isle! ("O native Britain!"). *Fr.* Fears in Solitude. Coleridge.
Oak and Olive. Flecker.
Ode Written in the Beginning of the Year 1746. Collins.
Old Liberals, The. Betjeman.
Old Vicarage, Grantchester, The. Brooke.
On a Parisian Boulevard. Stephen.
On Wenlock Edge. Housman.
O'Reilly's Reply. Weber.
Prelude: "Fields from Islington to Marybone, The." *Fr.* Jerusalem. Blake.
Properties of the Shires of England, The. *Unknown.*
Puck's Song. *Fr.* Puck of Pook's Hill. Kipling.
Ravenglass Railway Station, Cumberland. Nicholson.
Return, The. Kipling.
Return, The. Silkin.
Rhymed Mnemonic of the Forty Counties of England. Monat.
Rhyming Prophecy for a New Year. Cooper.
Rolling English Road, The. Chesterton.
Rule, Britannia. *Fr.* Alfred, a Masque. Thomson.
Slaves Cannot Breathe in England. *Fr.* The Task. Cowper.
Soldier, The. *Fr.* 1914. Brooke.
Song: "Old England is eaten by knaves." *Fr.* The Emigrant. McLachlan.
Song of Nidderdale, The. Ratcliffe.
Song of Sherwood, A. Noyes.
Song to the Men of England. Shelley.
Sonnet: England in 1819. Shelley.
South Country, The. Belloc.
Spring in England. Going.
Summer in England, 1914. Meynell.
This England. *Fr.* King Richard, II. Shakespeare.
Thought of a Briton on the Subjugation of Switzerland. Wordsworth.
To England. Moore.

Town Clerk's Views, The. Betjeman.
True-Born Englishman, The. Defoe.
Truth's Complaint over England. Lodge.
We Must Be Free or Die. Wordsworth.
Whack Fol the Diddle. Kearney.
When Spring Comes Back to England. Noyes.
While with a strong and yet a gentle hand. *Fr.* A Panegyric to My Lord Protector. Waller.
Writing in England Now. O'Connor.
You Ask Me, Why, though Ill at Ease. Tennyson.
"You that love England." Lewis.
See also **Civil wars, English.**

England, Church of. *See* **Church of England.**

English, The
Bonne Entente. Scott.
Britannia's Baby. Lawrence.
British Journalist, The. Wolfe.
British, The. Tessimond.
England Expects. Nash.
England's Heart. Tupper.
English, The. *Unknown.*
English Are Frosty, The. *Fr.* The White Cliffs. Miller.
English Are So Nice, The! Lawrence.
English Race, The. *Fr.* The True-born Englishman. Defoe.
Englishman, The. Cook.
Englishmen, The. Gilbert.
Fears in Solitude. Coleridge.
For the Rain It Raineth Every Day. Graves.
How Beastly the Bourgeois Is. Lawrence.
In pious times, ere priestcraft did begin. *Fr.* Absalom and Achitophel. Dryden.
It Is Not to Be Thought Of. Wordsworth.
Mad Dogs and Englishmen. Coward.
Neutral British Gentleman, The. "Kerr."
Nongtongpaw. Dibdin.
Observations in a Cornish Teashop. Rexroth.
Old England Forever and Do It No More. *Unknown.*
Secret People, The. Chesterton.
Soldier, The. *Fr.* 1914. Brooke.
Song to the Men of England. Shelley.
Tragic Guilt. Rhys.
Two Englishmen. Stewart.
Wherever God erects a house of prayer. *Fr.* The True-born Englishman. Defoe.
Why Should I Care for the Men of Thames? Blake.
World Is a Bundle of Hay, The. Byron.
Ye Mariners of England. Campbell.

English Channel
Channel Crossing. Barker.
Outlanders, The. Glaze.

Envy
Envy. *Fr.* The Faerie Queene. Spenser.
Frog Who Would Be an Ox, The. La Fontaine.
Laid in My Quiet Bed. Surrey.
When, in disgrace with Fortune and men's eyes. Shakespeare.
See also **Jealousy.**

Epic Poetry
Critics say that epics have died out, The. *Fr.* Aurora Leigh. Browning.
Epic. Kavanagh.
Epic, The. Tennyson.

Epictetus
To a Friend. Arnold.

Epicureanism
Author Loving These Homely Meats, The. *Fr.* The Scourge of Folly. Davies of Hereford.
Epicure, The. Cowley.

Epigrams
Epigram: "Three things must epigrams, like bees, have all." *Unknown.*
Epigram, An: "Epigram should be, An—if right." Walsh.
Epigram: "What is an Epigram? a dwarfish whole." Coleridge.
Epigrams must be curt, nor seem. Landor.
Faber Book of Epigrams and Epitaphs, The (FaBoEE). Geoffrey Grigson, ed.

Epstein, Sir Jacob
Jacob Epslem. *Unknown.*
On the Night Train from Oxford. Mayo.
There's a wonderful family called Stein. *Unknown.*

Equality
For A' That and A' That. Burns.
Woman to Her Lover, A. Walsh.
See also **Social Class.**

Equanimity
On Even Keel. *Fr.* The Spleen. Green.

Erie, Lake
Autumn Squall—Lake Erie. Russo.
Battle of Erie, The. *Unknown.*
Great lakes Suite, The. Reaney.
Perry's Victory. *Unknown.*

Erie Canal
E-ri-e, The. *Unknown.*
Erie Canal, The. Allen.
Erie Canal, The. *Unknown.*

Erne (river), Ireland
Adieu to Belashanny. Allingham.
Winding Banks of Erne, The. Allingham.

Eros. *See* **Cupid.**

Erosion
Where Dunwich Used to Be. *Fr.* By the North Sea. Swinburne.

Erotic Love
After Love. Kumin.
Amores (after Ovid). Parini.
Any Time, What May Hit You. Hummer.
Candy Man Blues. *Unknown.*
Cherrylog Road. Dickey.
Courtship. O Hehir.
December 18th. *Fr.* Eighteen Days Without You. Sexton.
Drunk as drunk on turpentine. Neruda.
Elegy, The: "Madam, no more! The time has come to eat." Hope.
Enigma. Murphy.
Envy of Poor Lovers, The. Clarke.
Equilibrists, The. Ransom.
Fine, a Private Place, A. Ackerman.
Flea, The. Donne.
Geranium, The. Sheridan.
Girl in the Foreign Movie, The. Goedicke.
Going to Bed. *Fr.* Elegies. Donne.
Goodbye, Sally. Simmons.
His Legs Ran About. Hughes.
I Care Not for These Ladies. Campion.
I gently touched her hand: she gave. *Unknown.*
I Like My Body When It Is With Your Body. *Fr.* Sonnets—Actualities. Cummings.
Imperfect Enjoyment, The. Rochester.
In Days of New. Bartlett.
Incident. Shapiro.
It Fell on a Summer's Day. Campion.
Italian Chest, An. Seiffert.
Last Confession, A. Yeats.
Last Ride Together, The. Browning.
Lee Rigg, The. Fergusson.
Libertine, The. MacNeice.
Love and Sleep. Swinburne.
Love at Roblin Lake. Purdy.
Love Made in the First Age: To Chloris. Lovelace.
Love Poem. Kageyama.
Love Poem: "Isadora, your body charts a course." Wagner.
Love Poem on Theme by Whitman. Ginsberg.
Lover Sheweth How He is Forsaken of Such as He Sometime Enjoyed, The. Wyatt.
Man and Woman. Lee.
May No Man Sleep. *Unknown.*
Morning after. . .Love, The. Cumbo.
Net, The. Rodgers.
New Year's Eve. Lawrence.
New York, Summer. Gilbert.
"Nicest Phantasies Are Shared, The." Coffey.
Night-Piece, to Julia, The. Herrick.
No Platonic Love. Cartwright.
Now Ain't That Love? Rodgers.
Oh! the time that is past. *Unknown.*
On the Happy Corydon and Phyllis. Sedley.
Ovid's Fifth Elegy. *Fr.* Amores. Ovid.
Penal Law. Clarke.
Platonic Love. Cowley.
Player. Dunning.
Poemlove (Fragment). *Fr.* Erotic Suite. Vega.
Privation. Carruth.
Proffered Love Rejected. Suckling.
Queen-Ann's-Lace. Williams.
Rapping Along with Ronda Davis. Cunningham.
Rapture, A. Carew.
Recreation. Lorde.
Rigs o' Barley, The. Burns.

Salmon. Graham.
Shelley and jazz and lieder and love and hymn-tunes. *Fr.* Autumn Journal. MacNeice.
Sleeping with Someone Who Came in Secret. *Fr.* Eleven Tanks. Ise.
Soft, lovely, rose-like lips, conjoined with mine. *Fr.* Parthenophil and Parthenophe. Barnes.
Some Semblance of Order. Wright.
Song, A: "The Night her blackest sables wore." D'Urfey.
Song of Dalliance, A. Cartwright.
Swimmer. Francis.
Terraplane Blues. *Unknown.*
That Day. Sexton.
Three Part Invention. Blackburn.
To a Fine Young Woman. Wycherley.
To His Dear Friend, Bones. Parini.
To His Mistress Going to Bed. Donne.
To remain. Cavafy.
To the Fair Clarinda, Who Made Love to Me, Imagin'd More than Woman. Behn.
To the Tune "Red Embroidered Shoes." Huang O.
To the Tune "Soaring Clouds." Huang O.
Tryst, The. Soutar.
Tubes. Mollin.
Twenty-Year Marriage. Ai.
Uncle Henry. Auden.
Upon Julia's Breasts. Herrick.
Upon My Lady Carlisle's Walking in Hampton Court Garden. Suckling.
Us. Sexton.
Vine, The. Herrick.
We Bear About No Cats' Skins. *Unknown.*
Whilst Alexis Lay Pressed. *Fr.* Marriage a-la-Mode. Dryden.
You held my lotus blossom. Huang O.
See also **Sex.**

Esau
Esau. Kwitko.

Escalators
Escalator, The. Glasgow.

Escapes
Houdini. Mandel.
I'd Leave. Lang.
Manzini; Escape Artist. MacEwen.

Eschatology. *See* **End of the World.**

Eskimos
Al Capone in Alaska. Reed.
Bear Hunting. Aua.
Eskimo Chant. *Unknown.*
For an Eskimo. Dalton.
Hymn to the Air Spirit. Eskimo.
Immoral Arctic, The. Bishop.
Lament for the Dorsets. Purdy.
Magic Word. Jackson.
Manerathiak's Song. *Unknown.*
Self-Portrait. Jackson.
Sila. Warren.
Song of the Trout Fisher, The. Ikinilik.
Walrus Hunting. Aua.
When the Iceworms Nest Again. Service.
Wind Has Wings, The. *Unknown.*

Essex, Robert Devereux, 2nd Earl of
Lementable New Ballad upon the Earle of Essex Death, A. *Unknown.*
Young Earl of Essex's Victory over the Emperor of Germany, The. *Unknown.*

Essex, England
Battle of Maldon. *Unknown.*
Map of the Western Part of the County of Essex in England, A. Levertov.

Esther, Book of (Bible)
Before the Feast of Shushan. Spencer.
Vashti. Harper.

Eternity
Because I could not stop for Death. Dickinson.
Chorus Tertius: Of Time; Eternitie. *Fr.* Mustapha. Greville.
Epitaph for Any New Yorker. Morley.
Eternity. *Fr.* Songs and Ballads. Blake.
Eternity. Herrick.
Eternity. More.
Eternity's Speech against Time. *Fr.* Mustapha. Greville.
Face of the Waters, The. Fitzgerald.
Man Frail, and God Eternal. Watts.
Only news I know, The. Dickinson.
Our journey had advanced. Dickinson.
Pibroch. Hughes.
Where Runs the River? Bourdillon.
World, The. Vaughan.
See also **Immortality.**

Ethiopia
Ode to Ethiopia. Dunbar.
On the Baptized Ethiopian. Crashaw.
Rusted Chain, The. Ben Yeshaq.
Star of Ethiopia. Watkins.

Etiquette
Boy Serving at Table, The. Lydgate.
Etiquette. Gilbert.
How to Get On in Society. Betjeman.
Little Gentleman, The. *Unknown.*
Manners. Van Rensselaer.
Manners at Table When Away from Home. *Unknown.*
Mutual Subjection. *Fr.* Hymns for the Amusement of Children. Smart.
Politeness. Turner.
Respectability. Browning.
Story of Fidgety Philip, The. Hoffmann.
Table Manners. Flagg.
Table Rules for Little Folks. *Unknown.*
Taste. *Fr.* Hymns for the Amusement of Children. Smart.

Eton College
Founder's Day. Bridges.
Ode on a Distant Prospect of Eton College. Gray.

Etruscan Civilization
Cypresses. Lawrence.
Etrusean Tombs. Robinson.
Etruscan Warrior's Head. Henze.

Eucharist
At Communion. L'Engle.
Bread of Heaven, on Thee We Feed. Conder.
Bread of Life, The. Lathbury.
General Communion, A. Meynell.
H. Communion, The. Herbert.
Holy Communion, The. Vaughan.
In Portugal, 1912. Meynell.
Let Us Break the Bread Together. *Unknown.*
Of the Holy Eucharist. *Unknown.*
Receiving Communion. Miller.
Sacrament, The. Donne.
Sacrament of the Altar, The.
"This Do in Remembrance of Me." *Unknown.*
To the Blessed Sacrament. Constable.

Euclid
Euclid. Lindsay.
Euclid Alone Has Looked on Beauty Bare. Millay.

Europa
Europa. Cory.
Europa. Walcott.

Europe
Beyond the Alps. Lowell.
Channel Crossing. Barker.
Europa. Thayer.
Europe and America. Ignatow.
European Night, The. Vinaver.
Farewell to Europe. Pillen.
Ignorant present has scribbed over the past, The. *Fr.* Europe. Dudek.
1945. Cussons.
Of Commerce and Society. Hill.
To Cole, the Painter, Departing for Europe. Bryant.
To Walt Whitman in America. Swinburne.

Eurydice
Death of Eurydice and Orpheus' Journey to Hell, The. *Fr.* Metamorphoses. Ovid.
Eurydice. Gregg.
Orpheus and Eurydice. Browning.
Orpheus to Beasts. Lovelace.

Eurynome
Eurynome. Macpherson.

Eutaw Springs, South Carolina, Battle of (1781)
Battle of Eutaw. Simms.
To the Memory of the Brave Americans. Freneau.

Euthanasia
How Annandale Went Out. Robinson.
Hurt Hawks. Jeffers.
To the Mercy Killers. Randall.

Evangelism
Evangelize! Crocker.
Faith Healer Come to Rabun County. Bottoms.
Few ever came to help you speak or sell. *Fr.* The Fragments. Dale.
Go Tell. *Unknown.*
Revivalist in Boston, A. Rich.

This Child Is the Mother. Oden.
Eve
Adam and Eve. Genesis. Bible, *O.T.*
Adam and Eve. Manger.
Adam and Eve. Sisson.
Adam's Curse. Yeats.
Adam's Dream. Schwartz.
Age of Innocence. Hough.
Circle, A. Spencer.
Eve. Bull.
Eve. *Fr.* Paradise Lost. Milton.
Eve. Fichman.
Eve. Gascoyne.
Eve. Herford.
Eve. Hodgson.
Eve. Rossetti.
Eve. *Unknown.*
Eve. Wolf.
Eve in Old Age. Holland.
Eve in Reflection. MacPherson.
Eve Penitent. *Fr.* Paradise Lost. Milton.
Eves Apologie. Lanier.
Eve's Birth. Chernin.
Eve's Lament. *Unknown.*
Eve's Song in the Garden. Gottlieb.
Eve's Version. Harrison.
First Rain. Akins.
First Wedding in the World, The. Rosenberg.
Fortunate Fall, The. Alvarez.
Good Beasts, The. Barnstone.
Imperial Adam. Hope.
In the Beginning. Sinason.
Jealous Adam. Manger.
Lady's-Maid Song, The. Hollander.
Lament of Eve, The. *Unknown.*
Never Again Would Birds' Song Be the Same. Frost.
Occasional Poem. Housman.
Paradise. Bloch.
Reflection, A. Hood.
Reveille. Hughes.
Rose of Eden, The. Phillips.
She. Wilbur.
Temptation and Fall of Man, The. *Fr.* Genesis. *Unknown.*
Theology. Hughes.
229. Villa.
Waiting for Lilith. Kessler.
See also **Adam and Eve.**
Evening
After Sunset. Conkling.
Autumnal Evening, An. "Macleod."
By the Sea. Wordsworth.
Child's Evening Prayer, A. Coleridge.
Crickets sang, The. Dickinson.
Eunice in the Evening. Brooks.
Evenen in the Village. Barnes.
Evening. Aldington.
Evening, An. Allingham.
Evening. Behn.
Evening. Clare.
Evening. Cotton.
Evening. Doolittle ("H. D.").
Evening. *Fr.* The Task. Cowper.
Evening. Manger.
Evening. Matheson.
Evening. McCrae.
Evening. Miller.
Evening. Sangster.
Evening. Shelley.
Evening. Stephens.
Evening. Vriesland.
Evening and Morning in June, An. *Fr.* Prologues to the Aeneid. Douglas.
Evening and Morning in Winter, An. *Fr.* Prologues to the Aeneid. Douglas.
Evening, as slow thy placid shades descend. Bowles.
Evening at the Farm. Trowbridge.
Evening by the Sea. Swinburne.
Evening Falls, An. Stephens.
Evening Hymn, An. Ken.
Evening Knell, The. *Fr.* The Faithful Shepherdess. Fletcher.
Evening on the Harbor. Tunstall.
Evening Quatrains. Cotton.
Evening Twilight. Baudelaire.
Evening Wind, The. Bryant.
Evening Without Angels. Stevens.
Evensong. Lewis.
Evensong. Stevenson.
February Twilight. Teasdale.
Fields at Evening. Morton.
First-Born Star, The. Arnold.
Gascoigne's Good-Night. Gascoigne.
Georgia Dusk. Toomer.
Grace Before Sleep. Teasdale.
Home-coming. Adams.
In Evening Air. Roethke.
In the Cool of the Evening. Noyes.
Island in the Evening, The. Porter.
It Is a Beauteous Evening. Wordsworth.
Lake in the Sky, The. Haines.
Late, Last Rook, The. Hodgson.
Morning and Evening. Slonimski.
Mountain Evenings. Holme.
Naturalist's Summer Evening Walk, The. White.
Nightfall on Sedgemoor. Young.
November Blue. Meynell.
O God, whose daylight leadeth down. *Fr.* Evening Hymn. Macdonald.
Ode to Evening. Collins.
Priest's Chant, The. *Fr.* The Faithful Shepherdess. Fletcher.
Progress of Evening. Landor.
Shoreham: Twilight Time. Palmer.
Stopping By Woods on a Snowy Evening. Frost.
Summer Evening. De la Mare.
Summer Evening, A. Lampman.
Summer Evening and Night. *Fr.* The Seasons: Summer. Thomson.
Sunken Evening. Lee.
Surprised By Evening. Bly.
'Tis gone, that bright and orbed blaze. *Fr.* Evening. Keble.
To Evening. Collins.
To Mary: It is the Evening Hour. Clare.
To the Evening Star. Blake.
Vespers. Shepard.
Windmill of Evening, The. Reich.
Winter Evening. *Fr.* The Task. Cowper.
Winter Evening. De la Mare.
Winter Evening. Lampman.
Winter evening settles down, The. *Fr.* Preludes. Eliot.
Winter Nightfall. Bridges.
Witnesses. Merwin.
See also **Twilight.**
Evening Star
Evening Star, The. Clare.
Hesperus. Clare.
Lamp in the West, The. Higginson.
Ode to the Evening Star. Akenside.
Song to the Evening Star. Campbell.
To the Evening Star. Blake.
See also **Venus (planet)**
Evers, Medgar
Medgar Evers. Brooks.
Evictions
Oakey Street Evictions, The. Armstrong.
See also **Inclosure Movement.**
Evil
Doth Then the World Go Thus, Doth All Thus Move? Drummond of Hawthornden.
God and the Strong Ones. Widdemer.
Hymn to Evil. Ginsberg.
I Sit and Look Out. Whitman.
On the Origin of Evil. Byrom.
Puritan, The. Shapiro.
Pythoness, The. Raine.
Evolution
Ballade of Evolution, A. Allen.
Children, behold the chimpanzee. Herford.
Darwin on Species. *Unknown.*
Darwinity. Merivale.
Easier. Harrison.
Evolution. Blight.
Evolution. Smith.
Evolution. Swenson.
Evolutionary Hymn. Lewis.
Fossils. Stewart.
Hominization. Holub.
Love Song to Eohippus. Viereck.

Love Song to Lucy. Ehrlich.
Lucy Answers. Ehrlich.
Missing Link, The. Herford.
On Becoming Man. Lister.
On Evolution. Ciardi.
Progress? Auden.
Progression of the Species. Aldiss.
Self-Protection. Lawrence.
Similar Cases. Gilman.
"Time of Man, The." Webb.
Verse for Vestigials. Allen.
See also **Extinction; Genetics.**
Ewing, Patrick
Patrick Ewing Takes a Foul Shot. Ackerman.
Executions
Ballad of Reading Gaol, The. Wilde.
Black and White. Adame.
Bride's Toilette, The. Cortissoz.
Carpenter's Son, The. *Fr.* A Shropshire Lad. Housman.
Clever Tom Clinch Going to Be Hanged. Swift.
Condemned, The. Howland.
Croppy Boy, The. *Unknown.*
Danny Deever. Kipling.
Dunlavin Green. *Unknown.*
Eight o'Clock. Housman.
Electrocution. Ridge.
Electrocution Script. Jacobs.
Elegy: "My prime of youth is but a frost of cares." Tichborne.
Epitaph in Form of a Ballad, The. Villon.
Execution of Cornelius Vane, The. Read.
He Fell among Thieves. Newbolt.
His Metrical Prayer: Before Execution. Graham.
King Charles on the Scaffold. *Fr.* An Horatian Ode upon Cromwell's Return from Ireland. Marvell.
London Fête, A. Patmore.
Mary Hamilton. *Unknown.*
"More Light! More Light!" Hecht.
Night before Larry Was Stretched, The. *Unknown.*
No Speech from the Scaffold. Gunn.
On Himself, upon Hearing What Was His Sentence. Graham.
On Moonlit Heath and Lonesome Bank. *Fr.* A Shropshire Lad. Housman.
Samuel Hall. *Unknown.*
Savage, A. O'Reilly.
Shameful Death. Morris.
Stranger's Song, The. Hardy.
Summons to Execution. *Fr.* The Duchesse of Malfi. Webster.
They brought him one morning. *Fr.* A Rhapsody of Old Men. Tsaloumas.
Verses Composed on the Eve of His Execution. Graham.
Walls Breathe. Mariah.
Woman's Execution, A. King.
Young Windebank. Woods.
See also **Capital Punishment; Hanging.**
Exile
Brumana. Flecker.
By Babel's Streams. Freneau.
By the rivers of Babylon, there we sat down. *Fr.* Psalms. Bible, *O.T.*
Canadian Boat Song, The. *Unknown, at. to.* Galt *and also to* "North."
Canadian Exile, The. Gerin-Lajoie.
Canadien Errant, Un. *Unknown.*
Castaway. Nerber.
Dublin. MacNeice.
Emigrant Song. Ansky.
Exile in Nigeria. Mphahlele.
Exile's Letter. Pound.
Exile's Song, The. Gilfillan.
Look, he is superfluous—for of what use was it to be born? *Fr.* Tristia. Ovid.
Old Vicarage, Grantchester, The. Brooke.
Ovid on the Dacian Coast. Thompson.
Pacifists. Woodcock.
Republic 1939, The. Liddy.
Sun Rises Bright in France, The. Cunningham.
To Cordelia. Stansbury.
Travelogue for Exiles. Shapiro.
Wanderer, The. Field.
Wanderer, The. *Unknown.*
Written in Exile. Raine.
Existentialism
Existentialism. Frankenberg.
Exodus
Exodus. Shapiro.
Exodus from Egypt, The. Ezekielos of Alexandria.
Flowering Without End. *Fr.* Jeremiah. Zweig.
Go Down, Moses. *Unknown.*
Parting of the Red Sea, The. *Fr.* Exodus. *Unknown.*
Sound the Loud Timbrel. Moore.
Exploring and Explorers
Alexander Selkirk. Cowper.
Arabia. Falkner.
Bermudas. Marvell.
Columbus. Miller.
Explorer, The. Kipling.
Explorers as Seen by the Natives. Fetherling.
For the Grave of Daniel Boone. Stafford.
Hakluyt Unpurchased. McDuffee.
New Worlds. *Fr.* Paradise Lost. Milton.
North Pole Story, A. Smedley.
Nuflo do Olano (Who Sailed with Balboa). Mberi.
O Pioneers! Bishop.
On the Discoveries of Captain Lewis. Barlow.
Polar Quest, The. Burton.
Samuel Hearne in Wintertime. Newlove.
Sir Humphrey Gilbert. Longfellow.
Sonnet: "There was an Indian, who had known no change." Squire.
Southward Sidonian Hanno. Allen.
There lies the port; the vessel puffs her sail. *Fr.* Ulysses. Tennyson.
"They made impudent inspection of our Coast." *Fr.* The Great South Land. Ingamells.
To the Virginian Voyage. Drayton.
To the Western World. Simpson.
Two Hundred Years Ago. Drummond.
Voyage West. Macleish.
Extinction
Bedtime Story. MacBeth.
Conspirators, The. Prokosch.
Dodo. Carlile.
Moschus Moschiferus. Hope.
Extreme Unction
Extreme Unction. Dowson.
Eyeglasses
In Grandfather's Glasses. Peters.
News Item. Parker.
Eyes
Armistice. Lodge.
Eye, The. Benedikt.
Eye, The. Herrick.
Eyes. De la Mare.
Eyes. Nicoïdski.
Eyes of Night-Time. Rukeyser.
For Sore Eyes. *Unknown.*
Fury of Hating Eyes, The. Sexton.
Her Eyes. Ransom.
His Lady's Eyes. *Fr.* Caelica. Greville.
Ladies' Eyes Serve Cupid Both for Darts and Fire. "W."
My Father's Eye. Vakalo.
Pretty Twinkling Starry Eyes. *Fr.* The Passionate Shepherd. Breton.
Sight. Davies.
There was a man of our town. Mother Goose.
Three Poems for Your Eyes. McAlpine.
Through a Glass Eye, Lightly. Kizer.
To Her Eyes. Herbert of Cherbury.
Your Eyes Have Their Silence. Barrax.
Ezekiel
'Zekiel Saw de Wheel. *Unknown.*
Ezra
So I Said I Am Ezra. Ammons.

F

Faces
Epigram: "Face that should content me wonders well, A." Wyatt.
Eternal Contour. Smyth.
Face. Toomer.
Face in the Mirror, The. Graves.
Face-Painting of the Caduveo Indians. Dickey.
Faces Seen Once. Dickey.
Looking at Your Face. Kinnell.
Poem about Your Face. Alterman.

Self-Portrait. Cassian.
Sweet mouth, that send'st a musky-rosed breath. Sylvester.
There Is a Garden in Her Face. Campion.

Factories
Ah! leave my harp and me alone. *Unknown.*
Birmingham and Wolverhampton. *Fr.* The Life and Lucubrations of Crispinus Scriblerus. Woodhouse.
Changsha Shoe Factory. Barnstone.
Dream after Touring the Tokyo Tokei. Kogawa.
Factories. Hirsch.
Factories, The. Widdemer.
Factory, The. Cabral.
Factory Girl, The. Phillips.
Factory Girl, The. *Unknown.*
Factory Rainbow, A. Saadi.
Factory Windows Are Always Broken. Lindsay.
Hands. Glasgow.
Iron Industry in Birmingham, The. *Fr.* Edge-Hill; or, The Rural Prospect Delineated and Moralised. Jago.
Jute Mill Song, The. *Unknown.*
Little Factory Girl to a More Fortunate Playmate, The. *Unknown.*
"Oh! isn't it a pity, such a pretty girl as I." Robinson.
On the Closing of Millom Ironworks. Nicholson.
Our Father's Hand. Flint.
Song of a Factory Worker, The. Collins.
Song of the Factory Girls. *Unknown.*

Failure
Abandoned Farmhouse. Kooser.
Battle-Song of Failure. Burr.
Bewick Finzer. Robinson.
Clavering. Robinson.
Consecration, A. Masefield.
Epitaph on a Young Poet Who Died before Having Achieved Success. Lowell.
Failure. Mayo.
Failures. Upson.
Humpty Dumpty. Whitney.
I Think of Him as One Who Fights. Branch.
In the Smoking-Car. Wilbur.
Success is counted sweetest. Dickinson.
To a Friend Whose Work Has Come to Nothing. Yeats.
Victory in Defeat. Markham.

Fairies
Adventure. Benét.
Alice Brand. *Fr.* The Lady of the Lake. Scott.
Ann and the Fairy Song. *Fr.* A Child's Day. De la Mare.
Ariel's Song: "Come unto these yellow sands." *Fr.* The Tempest. Shakespeare.
Ariel's Song: "Where the bee sucks, there suck I." *Fr.* The Tempest. Shakespeare.
Bacchante to Her Babe, The. Tietjens.
Beggar to Mab, the Fairy Queen, The. Herrick.
Best Game the Fairies Play, The. Fyleman.
Bogeyman, The. Prelutsky.
Brownies' Celebration, The. Cox.
Bubbles. Shorey.
By the Moon. *Unknown.*
Changeling, The. Mew.
Cornish Magic. Durell.
Could It Have Been a Shadow? Shannon.
Crab-Apple. Talbot.
Dance, The. Lehmann.
Dancers, The. Deutsch.
Dusk in the Domain. Mackellar.
Elf and the Dormouse, The. Herford.
Elfin Town. Field.
Fairies, The. Allingham.
Fairies. Conkling.
Fairies. Fyleman.
Fairies, The. Herrick.
Fairies. *Fr.* Kensington Garden. Tickell.
Fairies Farewell, The. Corbet.
Fairies Feast, The. Doughty.
Fairies Have Never a Penny to Spend, The. Fyleman.
Fairies of the Caldon-Low, The. Howitt.
Fairies' Shopping, The. Deland.
Fairy Book, The. Brown.
Fairy Book, The. Gale.
Fairy Folk, The. Bird.
Fairy Harpers, The. Dollard.
Fairy Host, The. *Unknown.*
Fairy In Armor, A. Drake.
Fairy Queen, The. *Unknown.*
Fairy Song. Hemans.
Fairy Song. Keats.
Fairy Thorn, The. Ferguson.
Fairy Thrall, The. Byron.
Fairy Voyage, A. *Unknown.*
Fairy Went a-Marketing, A. Fyleman.
Fairy Wings. Howard.
Fairyland. Tagore.
Farewell to the Fairies. Corbet.
Five Little Fairies, The. Burnham.
Goblin, The. Fyleman.
Goblin Market. Rossetti.
Goblinade, A. Jaques.
Godmother. Morden.
Have You Watched the Fairies? Fyleman.
Hob Gobbling's Song. Lowell.
How to Tell Goblins from Elves. Shannon.
How to Treat Elves. Bishop.
I'd Love to Be a Fairy's Child. Graves.
In the Moonlight. O'Conor.
La Belle Dame Sans Merci. Keats.
Last Voyage of the Fairies, The. Adams.
Leprahuan, The. Joyce.
Letter to Elsa, A. Conkling.
Light-Hearted Fairy, The. *Unknown.*
Little Elf, The. Bangs.
Little Orphant Annie. Riley.
Mab the Mistress-Fairy. *Fr.* The Satyr. Jonson.
Mercutio's Queen Mab Speech. *Fr.* Romeo and Juliet. Shakespeare.
Midsummer Magic. Eastwick.
Midsummer Night's Dream, A, *sels.* Shakespeare.
Mr. Moon. Carman.
Oberon's Feast. Herrick.
Oberon's Palace. Herrick.
Of Certain Irish Fairies. Guiterman.
Oh! Where Do Fairies Hide Their Heads? Bayly.
Once When You Were Walking. Wynne.
Others, The. "O'Sullivan."
Overheard on a Saltmarsh. Monro.
Pigwiggin Arms Himself. *Fr.* Nymphidia; or, The Court of Fairy. Drayton.
Plumpuppets, The. Morley.
Proper New Ballad Intituled the Faeryes Farewell; or God-A-Mercy Will, A. Corbett.
Puk-Wudjies. Chalmers.
Queen Mab. Hood.
Queen's Chariot, The. *Fr.* Nymphidia. Drayton.
Rilloby-Rill. Newbolt.
Robin Good-Fellow. *Unknown.*
Sea Princess, The. Pyle.
Shakespeare: The Fairies' Advocate. *Fr.* The Plea of the Midsummer Fairies. Hood.
"She Wandered after Strange Gods." Benét.
Song by Isbrand. *Fr.* Death's Jest Book. Beddoes.
Song of Fairies Robbing an Orchard. *Fr.* Amyntas. Hunt.
Song of Sherwood, A. Noyes.
Song of the Ogres. Auden.
Songs of the Pixies. Coleridge.
Spell, The. Hoyt.
Star That Bids the Shepherd Fold, The. *Fr.* Comus. Milton.
Stocking Fairy. Welles.
Stolen Child, The. Yeats.
Tam Lin's Lady. Lochhead.
Tam Lin. *Unknown.*
There Are No Wolves in England Now. Fyleman.
Thomas the Rhymer. *Unknown.*
Tim, the Fairy. Livesay.
To Mother Fairie. Cary.
Tree Stands Very Straight and Still, The. Wynne.
Twenty Foolish Fairies. Turner.
Very Nearly. Scott-Hopper.
Visitor, The. Chalmers.
Wee Wee Man, The. *Unknown.*
When a Ring's around the Moon. Carr.
When I Was Six. Cross.
White Horses. Howard.
Yesterday in Oxford Street. Fyleman.
Home Book of Verse for Young Folks, The (HBVY), pp. 206–236. Burton Egbert Stevenson, ed.
Why Am I Grown So Cold? Poems of the Unknowable (WSC), pp. 104–121. Myra Cohn Livingston, ed.

See also **Elves; Goblins.**

Fairs
After the Fair. Hardy.
Agricultural Show, Flemington, Victoria, The. "Maurice".
Ballad-Singer, The. *Fr.* At Casterbridge Fair. Hardy.
Bartleme Fair. Stevens.
Blaydon Races. *Unknown.*
Cattle Show. "MacDiarmid."
Coasting toward Midnight at the Southeastern Fair. Bottoms.
Dance, The. Williams.
Dunmow Flitch of Bacon, The. *Unknown.*
Fair at Windgap, The. Clarke.
Fair below Helvellyn, The. *Fr.* The Prelude. Wordsworth.
Fairground. Auden.
Lads in Their Hundreds, The. *Fr.* A Shropshire Lad. Housman.
On the Road to Anster Fair. *Fr.* Anster Fair. Tennant.
Sledburn Fair. *Unknown.*

Fairy Tales
At Hans Christian Andersen's Birthplace, Odense, Denmark. Lindsay.
Frog Prince, The. Smith.
House in the Wood, The. Jarrell.
Märchen, The. Jarrell.
Reading the Brothers Grimm to Jenny. Mueller.
Tam Lin's Lady. Lochhead.
Disenchantments: An Anthology of Modern Fairy Tale Poetry (DFT). Wolfgang Mieder, ed.

Faith
Act of Faith. Trías.
After the Burial. Lowell.
Amazing Grace. Newton.
Apostasy. Aus of Kuraiza.
Argument, An—of the Passion of Christ. Merton.
As a Plane Tree by the Water. Lowell.
At the Round Earth's Imagined Corners. *Fr.* Holy Sonnets. Donne.
Auguries of Innocence. Blake.
Ballad of the Tempest. Fields.
Ballad Which Anne Askew Made and Sang When She Was in Newgate, The. Askew.
Batter My Heart. *Fr.* Holy Sonnets. Donne.
Beginnings of Faith, The. Morris.
Believe and Take Heart. Spalding.
Bishop Blougram's Apology. Browning.
Candle and Book. Walter.
Captain of the Years. Macdougall, Jr.
Carrion Comfort. Hopkins.
Chartless. Dickinson.
Collar, The. Herbert.
Common Inference, A. Gilman.
Confession. Clifton.
Country Faith, The. Gale.
Credo. Jeffers.
Credo. Robinson.
Creed, A. Masefield.
Creed, A. McLeod.
Creeds. Baker.
Death. *Unknown.*
Death in the Desert, A. Browning.
Disappointment. Young.
Discipline. Herbert.
Divine Image, The. *Fr.* Songs of Innocence. Blake.
Doors of the Temple. Huxley.
Doubt. Jackson.
Doubter's Prayer, The. Brontë.
Dover Beach. Arnold.
"Dream is the thought in the ghost, The." *Fr.* A Faith on Trial. Meredith.
Eclipse of Faith, The. Woolsey.
Even Such Is Time. Ralegh.
Evening Contemplation. Doane.
Evensong. Stevenson.
Faith. Bulwer-Lytton.
Faith. Cambridge.
Faith. Daley.
Faith. Howells.
Faith. Kemble.
Faith. Palmer.
Faith. *Fr.* An Essay on Man. Pope.
Faith. Sangster.
Faith. *Fr.* Sonnets. Santayana.
Faith. Tabb.
Faith. Whittier.
Faith. Wilcox.
Faith Came First, The. Carter.
Faith is a fine invention. Dickinson.
Faith of Abraham Lincoln, The. Lincoln.
Faith of Our Fathers. Fabers.
Faith's Difficulty. Maynard.
Faith's Vista. Abbey.
Feathered Faith. *Unknown.*
For the Sleepwalkers. Hirsch.
Generous Creed, A. Phelps.
God and Yet a Man, A? *Unknown.*
God's Grandeur. Hopkins.
Have Faith. Carpenter.
Heaven. Brooke.
Highway, The. Gannett.
His Creed. Herrick.
His Litany to the Holy Spirit. Herrick.
Homeward Journey, The. Aaronson.
Hope Evermore and Believe. Clough.
Hound of Heaven, The. Thompson.
How the Great Guest Came. Markham.
Hymn: "Thou hidden love of God, whose height." Wesley.
Hymn: "When all thy mercies, O my God." Addison.
Hymn for Atonement Day. Halevi.
Hymn of Saint Thomas in Adoration of the Blessed Sacrament, The. Crashaw.
Hymnus. *Fr.* Sarum Primer. *Unknown.*
I know not what shall befall me: God hangs a mist o'er my eyes. *Fr.* Not Knowing. Brainard.
I never lost as much but twice. Dickinson.
I never saw a moor. Dickinson.
If This Were Faith. *Fr.* Songs of Travel. Stevenson.
Impercipient, The. Hardy.
Implicit Faith. *Fr.* May Carols. De Vere.
In a Country Church. Thomas.
"In No Strange Land." Thompson.
In the Hospital. Guiterman.
Incomprehensible, The. Watts.
Inspiration. Thoreau.
Joy and Peace in Believing. Cowper.
Lamb, The. *Fr.* Songs of Innocence. Blake.
Last Lines. Brontë.
Lead, Kindly Light. Cardinal Newman.
Life's Lessons. *Unknown.*
Light in the Darkness. Newman.
Light Shining Out of Darkness. Cowper.
Lord is my shepherd, The; I shall not want. Psalms XXIII. Bible, *O.T.*
Love Song, A. Halevi.
Meditation on Communion with God. Halevi.
Mock On, Mock On, Voltaire, Rousseau. Blake.
My Creed. Cary.
My Creed. Gilder.
My Faith. Acharya.
My Faith Looks Up to Thee. Palmer.
My Spirit Longeth for Thee. Byrom.
Night. *Fr.* Songs of Innocence. Blake.
No Coward Soul Is Mine. Brontë.
O World. *Fr.* Sonnets. Santayana.
Obedience. Macdonald.
Ode: Intimations of Immortality from Recollections of Early Childhood. Wordsworth.
On His Blindness. Milton.
On Time. Milton.
Opportunity. Malone.
Optimism. Wilcox.
Pagan Isms, The. McKay.
Pastoral Hymn. Addison.
Poet's Simple Faith, The. Hugo.
Possession. *Unknown.*
Pray without Ceasing. Browning.
Prayer: "Prayer, the Church's banquet, Angels' age." Herbert.
Prayer, A: "Let me do my work each day." Ehrmann.
Prayer for Faith, A. Michelangelo.
Prayer for Faith, A. Norris.
Problem, The. Emerson.
Read, sweet, how others strove. Dickinson.
Real Presence. Adair.
Recessional. Kipling.
Religion and Doctrine. Hay.
Retreat, The. Vaughan.
Riddle of the World, The. Whittier.
Rocked in the Cradle of the Deep. Willard.
Rugby Chapel. Arnold.

Say Not. Clough.
Sense and Spirit. Meredith.
Shema Yisrael. *Unknown.*
Silence. Towne.
Simple Faith. *Fr.* Truth. Cowper.
Song of Faith, A. Holland.
Stream of Faith, The. Gannett.
Temper, The. Herbert.
Terrible Sons, The. Eleazar ben Kalir.
That which we dare invoke to bless. *Fr.* In Memoriam A. H. H. Tennyson.
That's Faith. Leitner.
There Is No God. *Fr.* Dipsychus. Clough.
There is no God, as I was taught in youth. *Fr.* Sonnets. Masefield.
There Is No Unbelief. Case.
Therefore, We Thank Thee, God. Grossman.
Thou Art Indeed Just, Lord. Hopkins.
Though Mine Eye Sleep Not. *Fr.* The Dead Sea Scrolls. *Unknown.*
Thus man by his own strength to Heaven would soar. *Fr.* Religio Laici. Dryden.
Thy Way, Not Mine. Bonar.
Tide of Faith. *Fr.* A Minor Prophet. "Eliot."
To a Waterfowl. Bryant.
To Be Said at the Seder. Wolfskehl.
To God. Herrick.
To Him Who Is Feared. Eleazar ben Kalir.
To Trust. Pozzi.
Tree in December. Cane.
Trust Him. *Unknown.*
Two Mysteries. Dodge.
Unshrinking Faith. Balhurst.
Victory. *Unknown.*
Visionary, The. Brontë.
Voyagers. Van Dyke.
Weakness of Nature. Froude.
Wise Men and Shepherds. Godolphin.
Wit Wonders. *Unknown.*
You say, but with no touch of scorn. *Fr.* In Memoriam A. H. H. Tennyson.

Faith Healers
Faith Healer Come to Rabun County. Bottoms.

Faithfulness. *See* **Fidelity.**

Falcons
Falcon, The. Lovelace.
Falcon and the Dove, The. Read.
Lover Compareth Himself to the Painful Falconer, The. *Unknown.*
Lux, My Fair Falcon. Wyatt.
Sparrow-Hawk's Complaint, The. *Unknown.*
When the water fowl are found, the falconers hasten. *Fr.* The Parliament of the Three Ages. *Unknown.*
Windhover, The. Hopkins.
Woods and Kestrel. Bells.

Falkland, Lucius Cary, Viscount
Falkland at Newbury, 1643. Conway.

Fall. *See* **Autumn.**

Falmouth, England
Home. Henley.

Fame
After Publication of Under the Volcano. Lowry.
Choice, The. Norris.
Contemporary. Flexner.
Fame. Cantus.
Fame. Mew.
Fame. More.
Fame and Fortune. *Fr.* The Legend of Robert, Duke of Normandy. Drayton.
Fame Makes Us Forward. Herrick.
Greatness. *Unknown.*
He that hath set his headlong heart. *Fr.* The Consolation of Philosophy. Boethius.
Honest Fame. *Fr.* The Temple of Fame. Pope.
I'm nobody! Who are you? Dickinson.
In an Album. Lowell.
Let Us Now Praise Famous Men. *Fr.* Ecclesiasticus. Bible, Apocrypha.
Love of praise, howe'er concealed by art, The. *Fr.* Love of Fame, The Universal Passion. Young.
Ode to Popularity. Praed.
On Fame ("How fever'd is that man"). Keats.
Ozymandias. Shelley.
Perry Zoll. *Fr.* Spoon River Anthology. Masters.
Pillar of Fame, The. Herrick.
Power of Poets, The. *Fr.* Epistle to Elizabeth, Countess of Rutland. Jonson.
Provide Provide. Frost.
Resolve, The. Chudleigh.
Savage Portraits. Marquis.
Settling Some Old Football Scores. Bishop.
Stanzas Written on the Road between Florence and Pisa. Byron.
There is a tall long-sided dame. *Fr.* Hudibras. Butler.
To an Athlete Dying Young. Housman.
To My Friend, Grown Famous. Tietjens.
True and False Glory. *Fr.* Paradise Regained. Milton.
Two Sonnets on Fame. Keats.
Wish, A. Kemble.
See also **Greatness.**

Family Life
Animal Crackers. Morley.
Another Generation. Squire.
Around the Kitchen Table. Gildner.
Ave Maria. O'Hara.
Beneath the Shadow of the Freeway. Cervantes.
Brooklyn Summer. Lipsitz.
Brown Family, The. Thibaudeau.
Childhood. Stanton.
Church Poem. Thomas.
Coming Home. Stone.
Eating Lechon, with My Brothers and Sisters. Cabalquinto.
Eyes, the Blood, The. Meltzer.
Family. MacCaig.
Family. *Unknown.*
Family Court. Nash.
Family Life. *Unknown.*
Folded Flock, The. Meynell.
For My Mother, Feeling Useless. Rankin.
Frank Courtship, The. Crabbe.
From a Childhood. Rilke.
Funnel. Sexton.
Gemwood. Bell.
Good Times. Clifton.
Green Family, The. Thibaudeau.
Heritage. Hogan.
Hot Day and Human Nature, The. Johnston.
House on Buder Street, The. Gildner.
I Come Home Wanting to Touch Everyone. Dunn.
Ice Cream. Wild.
Idea of Ancestry, The. Knight.
In the Old Guerilla War. Pastan.
In the Park. Harwood.
Kitchen Tables. Huddle.
Letter to Peter, A. Chiang.
Let's Be Merry. Rossetti.
Linebacker at Forty, The. Wallace.
Long Island Springs. Moss.
Looking for a Country under Its Original Name. McElroy.
Love between Brothers and Sisters. Watts.
Love Should Grow Up like a Wild Iris in the Fields. Griffin.
Mother. Montoya.
My Father in the Night Commanding No. Simpson.
Nails. Gildner.
Nikki-Rosa. Giovanni.
Nisei Picnic, A. Mura.
Old Man Dreams, The. Holmes.
Rescued Year, The. Stafford.
Somerset Dam for Supper, The. Holmes.
Still Wrestling. Boiarski.
Summer Visitors. Clark.
Sunday Morning. Jenkins.
Survivors. Marcus.
Those Winter Sundays. Hayden.
Verandahs. Brissenden.
What Do They Do? Rossetti.
When Father Carves the Duck. Wright.
Strings: A Gathering of Family Poems (Str). Paul B. Janeczko, ed.

Famine
Famine Song. *Unknown.*
Famine Year, The. Lady Wilde.
Hunger. Binyon.
Maguire is not afraid of death, the Church will light him a candle. *Fr.* The Great Hunger. Kavanagh.

Fancy. *See* **Imagination.**

Fans
Eagle-Feather Fan, The. Momaday.
In Passing. Jonas.

Japanese Fan. Kirkup.
On a Fan That Belonged to the Marquise de Pompadour. Dobson.
Present from the Emperor's New Concubine, A. Pan.
To a Lady, with a Present of a Fan. *Unknown, at. to* Brandling.
Two Triolets. Robertson.
Fargo, North Dakota
Outside Fargo, North Dakota. Wright.
Farming and Farmers
Abandoned Farmhouse. Kooser.
After Winter. Brown.
Anxious Farmer, The. Johnson.
At a Potato Digging. Heaney.
Black Man Talks of Reaping, A. Bontemps.
Boy Wandering in Simms' Valley. Warren.
Canadian Farmer. Bartole.
Code, The. Frost.
Cooney Potter. *Fr.* Spoon River Anthology. Masters.
Corn-Planter. Kenny.
Cotter's Saturday Night, The. Burns.
Country Greeting. Steele.
Country Hirings. *Unknown.*
Country Summer. Adams.
Cupid the Ploughboy. *Unknown.*
Curse, The. Francis.
Dakota Land. *Unknown.*
Death of the Hired Man, The. Frost.
Deserted Homestead, The. Eiseley.
Drover, A. Colum.
Drumdelgie. *Unknown.*
Earth Dweller. Stafford.
Eleven. MacLeish.
Entailed Farm, The. Glassco.
Evening on the Farm. Trowbridge.
Farewell to the Farm. Stevenson.
Farm Child. Thomas.
Farm Hands, The. Laing.
Farm near Norman's Lane, The. Finnin.
Farm Picture, A. Whitman.
Farm Wife. Mitchell.
Farmer. Bailey.
Farmer. Fallon.
Farmer, The. Herbert.
Farmer and the Farmer's Wife, The. Hiebert.
Farmer, The. Stokes.
Farmer. Stryk.
Farmer Comes to Town, The. *Unknown.*
Farmer Is the Man, The. *Unknown.*
Farmers. Percy.
Farmers. Roberts.
Farmer's Boy, The. *Unknown.*
Farmer's Son So Sweet, A. *Unknown.*
Field and Forest. Jarrell.
Field Work. Cockrell.
Floodtide. Touré.
For a Young South Dakota Man. Manfred.
Fruit Rancher, The. Roberts.
Gin the Goodwife Stint. Bunting.
Go Home. McFatter.
God Save the Plough. Sigourney.
Hard Way to Learn. Hearst.
Hay for the Horses. Snyder.
Hayfield, The. *Fr.* The Flowing Summer. Bruce.
Haymaking. Thomas.
Hill Farmer Speaks,The. Thomas.
Hillside Farmer, A. Farrar.
His Grange, or Private Wealth. Herrick.
How was November's melancholy endear'd to me. *Fr.* The Testament of Beauty. Bridges.
Husbandman and Serving-Man, The. *Unknown.*
I Will Go with My Father a-Ploughing. Campbell.
Improved Farm Land. Sandburg.
John Barleycorn. *Unknown.*
Laying By. Williams.
Mad Farmer Stands Up In Kentucky for What He Thinks Is Right, The. Hall.
Man and Machine. Morgan.
Man with the Hoe, The: A Reply. Cheney.
Man with the Hoe, The. Markham.
Manor Farm, The. Thomas.
Marginal Field, The. Spender.
Memoirs of a Spinach-Picker. Plath.
Method of Preserving Hay from Being Mow-Burnt, or Taking Fire, A. *Fr.* Agriculture. Dodsley.
Miss Creighton. Taylor.
Mother. Heaney.
Mowing. Frost.
Mowing, The. Roberts.
My Own Brand. Cuelho.
New-fashioned Farmer, The. *Unknown.*
Northern Farmer: New Style. Tennyson.
Northern Farmer: Old Style. Tennyson.
Now I'm Easy. Bogle.
Old MacDonald Had a Farm. *Unknown.*
On the Debt My Mother Owed to Sears Roebuck. Dorn.
On the Land. Lindquist.
Ox Cart Man. Hall.
Pasture, The. Frost.
Pretty Ploughboy, The. *Unknown.*
Prodigal, The. Bishop.
Putting in the Seed. Frost.
Reapers. Blind.
Reapers. Toomer.
Retired Farmer. Evans.
Retreat of Ita Cagney, The. Hartnett.
Rival, The. Warner.
Robert's Farm. *Unknown.*
Saving the Harvest. Lehmann.
Six Badgers, The. Graves.
Small Farm, A. Hartnett.
Solitary Reaper, The. Wordsworth.
Son, The. Torrence.
Song of the Farmworker. Jahns.
Sower, The. Blind.
Sower, The. Figueroa.
Sower, The. Roberts.
Spraying the Potatoes. Kavanagh.
Spring. McCarriston.
Tenant Farmer. Ward.
Therapy. Poyner.
Times Have Altered, The. *Unknown.*
Todd. Conn.
Vermont Conversation. Hubbell.
Wife's Tale, The. Heaney.
Faber Book of Useful Verse, The (FaBoUs), pp. 36-55. Simon Brett, ed.
Farmworkers
Funeral of Rufino Contreras, The. Schuler.
Meeting at the Local. Parson.
Napa, California. Castillo.
Pickers. Brett.
See also. **Migrant Workers.**
Farragut, David Glasgow
Farragut. Meredith.
River Fight, The. Brownell.
Fashion
Beau's Receipt for a Lady's Dress, The. *Unknown.*
Dandy O, The. *Unknown.*
Dresscessional, A. Wells.
Fashion. Twiss.
Fashion in the 70's. Swenson.
Innocent Country-Maid's Delight, The. *Unknown.*
Lady's Receipt for a Beau's Dress, The. *Unknown.*
Life of a Beau, The. Miller.
Monkey, lap-dog, parrot, and her Grace, The. *Fr.* Isabella; or, The Morning. Williams.
Omar for Ladies, An. Bacon.
On English Monsieur. Jonson.
Time was, an Englishman would join. *Fr.* Of Taste; an Essay. Cawthorn.
What the Choir Sang about the New Bonnet. Morrison.
See also **Clothing.**
Fate
Astrologer Argues Your Death, The. DeGravelles.
Definition of Love, The. Marvell.
Design. Frost.
Destiny. Arnold.
Draft Horse, The. Frost.
Eros Turannos. Robinson.
Eshu, the God of Fate. Yoruba.
Fate. Cooper.
Fate in Incognito. Benedikt.
Flux. Eberhart.
Hap. Hardy.
Invictus. Henley.
Karma. Robinson.

Lachesis. Raine.
Poet's Fate, The. Hood.
Unmanifest Destiny. Hovey.
Waiting. Burroughs.
What Different Dooms Our Birthdays Bring! *Fr.* Miss Kilmansegg and Her Precious Leg. Hood.
Whiplash. Matthews.
Winds of Fate, The. Wilcox.
See also **Fortune.**

Fathers

After Dark. Rich.
After Grief. Plumly.
All My Pretty Ones. Sexton.
American Primitive. Smith.
Ancestor. Baca.
And This Is My Father. Grapes.
Any Man's Advice to His Son. Fearing.
Apples. Waters.
Attic, The. *Fr.* The Flowing Summer. Bruce.
Au Tombeau de Mon Père. McCuaig.
Automobile Mechanics. Baruch.
Because. McAuley.
Becoming a Dad. Guest.
Bee, The. Dickey.
Before the Breaking. Pennington.
Beryl. Lifshin.
Between Here and Illinois. Pomeroy.
Business as Usual. Vinz.
Cage, The. Montague.
Celebration, A. Sarton.
Childless Father, The. Wordsworth.
Clay and Water. Hochman.
Cleaning Up, Clearing Out. Bronson.
Colossus, The. Plath.
Coming and Going. Johnson.
Commander Lowell. Lowell.
Common Light, A. Orlen.
Concertmaster. Burgin.
Country Ways. *Fr.* Impressions of My Father. Masters.
Dad. Feinstein.
Daddy. Clifton.
Daddy. Fyleman.
Daddy. Plath.
Daddy Fell Into the Pond. Noyes.
Dear Old Dad. Shaver.
Death of Fathers, The. Weiss.
December 18, 1975. Hogan.
Desk, The. Bottoms.
Do Not Go Gentle into That Good Night. Thomas.
Efficiency Apartment. Barrax.
Elegy: "I know but will not tell." Dugan.
Elegy for My Father. Moss.
Elegy for My Father. Strand.
Equality, Father! Bruck.
Europe and America. Ignatow.
Everybody Works but Father. McClintock.
Eyes of Flesh, The. Hochman.
Failed Fathers. Turco.
Family Photograph. Vizenor.
Father, The. Finkel.
Father. Frost.
Father. Kaffka.
Father. Kooser.
Father. Livingston.
Father. Pack.
Father. Weston.
Father and Child. Harwood.
Father and Son. Higgins.
Father and Son. Wallace.
Father of My Country, The. Wakoski.
Father Son and Holy Ghost. Lorde.
Father Takes to the Road and Lets His Hair Down. Lau.
Fathers and Sons. *Unknown.*
Father's Story. Roberts.
Father's Testament, A. Ibn Tibbon.
Father's Whiskers. *Unknown.*
Figures of Authority. Watkins.
Fire. 10/78. Plantenga.
First Prelude. Dream in Ohio; the Father. *Fr.* Poem in Progress. Logan.
Fisherman, The. Wells.
Follower. Heaney.
For My Father on His Birthday. Kuzma.
Forgiving My Father. Clifton.
Gardener, The. Wheelock.
Gratulatory to Mr. Ben Johnson for His Adopting of Him to Be His Son, A. Randolph.
Hallelujah: A Sestina. Francis.
He. Koertge.
Heirloom. Klein.
Hospital Window, The. Dickey.
How My Father Died. Ezekiel.
Hudson Hornet. Cook.
I Remember. Sánchez.
I Sit with My Dolls. *Unknown.*
In White Tie. Huddle.
Irish Cliffs of Moher, The. Stevens.
Letter to a Dead Father. Shelton.
Letter to a Young Father in Exile. Logan.
Letters & Other Worlds. Ondaatje.
Lines to My Father. Daiken.
Lines to His Son on Reaching Adolescence. Logan.
Little Father Poem. Bell.
Lost Pilot, The. Tate.
Love from My Father. Clemmons.
Love Song for a Tyrant. Rewey.
Man Who Finds That His Son Has Become a Thief, The. Souster.
Mask of Stone. Johnson.
Melkon. Kherdian.
Middle Age. Lowell.
Missing the Children. Zimmer.
Moss of His Skin, The. Sexton.
My Father. Chalfi.
My Father after Work. Gildner.
My Father Died This Spring. Kyger.
My Father Dreams of Baseball. Lieberman.
My Father in the Night Commanding No. Simpson.
My Father Kept His Cats Well Fed. Sherman.
My Father Moved through Dooms of Love. Cummings.
My Father, My Son. Brinnin.
My Father, Who's Still Alive. Kozer.
My Father's Eye. Vakalo.
My Father's Ghost. Wagoner.
My Father's Heart. Friebert.
My Father's Martial Art. Liu.
My Father's Song. Ortiz.
My Papa's Waltz. Roethke.
1933. Levine.
Not Saying Much. Gregg.
On My First Son. Jonson.
On the Road at Night There Stands the Man. Ravikovitch.
On the Seventh Anniversary of the Death of My Father. Pack.
Origin of Dreams. Bell.
Our Hired Man. Shannon.
Out-of-the-Body Travel. Plumly.
Pa. Dangel.
Parentage. Stafford.
Photograph of My Father in His Twenty-second Year. Carver.
Placing a $2 Bet for a Man Who Will Never Go to the Horse Races Any More. Wakoski.
Playing the Bones. Brewster.
Poem for a "Divorced" Daughter. Coleman.
Poem for My Father, A. Sanchez.
Poem for My Father. West.
Poem for My Father's Ghost. Oliver.
Poem to Help My Father. Richman.
Portrait, The. Kunitz.
Prayer: "She cannot tell my name." Reed.
Quoits. Newsome.
Reformer to His Father, A. Simmons.
Remembering My Father. Holden.
Return, The. MacBeth.
Revelation, The. Wright.
Russian Cradle Song, A. Nomberg.
Secret, The. Kaneko.
Secret Heart, The. Coffin.
Shaving. Wright.
Shore. O Hehir.
Silence. Moore.
Sixth Day, The. Adcock.
Song about My Father. Smither.
Steelworker, The. Brown.
Stonecarver. Oles.
Story of Lava, The. Evans.
Stranger, The. Gelman.

Subway Psalm. Nowlan.
Sum. Nolan.
Sunday Funnies. Keiter.
Sunflowers and Saturdays. Boyd.
That Day. Kherdian.
Those Winter Sundays. Hayden.
To Any Daddy. *Unknown.*
To My Father. Fried.
To My Son, Aged Three Years and Five Months. Hood.
To the Reverend Shade of His Religious Father. Herrick.
To Tony (Aged 3). Wilson.
Toys, The. *Fr.* The Unknown Eros. Patmore.
Trying. Nathan.
Two Hopper. Ikan.
Uncle Robert. Morgan.
Waking. "Maxton."
What For. Hongo.
When Father Came Home for Lunch. Mitsui.
When Father Carves the Duck. Wright.
When Father Slept. Anderson.
Wind's Song, The. "Setoun."
Wonderful Man, A. Fisher.
Worm, The. Barnstone.
Writing while My Father Dies. Pastan.
Youth. Wright.
Zealot without a Face. Dobzynski.
Divided Light: Father and Son Poems (DiL). Jason Shinder, ed.

Fatigue. *See* **Weariness.**

Fauns
Après-Midi d'un faune, L'. Mallarmé.
Faun, The. Pound.
Visitor, The. Chalmers.

Faust
Doctor Faustus was a good man. Mother Goose.
Faust. Ashbery.
Finale. *Fr.* Dr. Faustus. Marlowe.
Progress of Faust, The. Shapiro.
Prologue in Heaven. *Fr.* Faust. Goethe.
Royalties. Enright.

Fawkes, Guy
Gunpowder Plot, The. *Unknown.*
November the Fifth. Clark.
Please to remember. *Unknown.*

Fear
Afraid. De la Mare.
After writing for an hour in the presbytery. *Fr.* Autumn Testament. Baxter.
Deserter, The. Letts.
Fairy Tale, A. Mackenzie.
Fall, The. Reid.
Fear. Camerino.
Fear. Dobyns.
Fear. Peacock.
Fear. Pizarnik.
Fear Test: Integrity of Heroes. Simmons.
Frightened Flier Goes North, The. Kazantzis.
Garden, The. Glück.
I am afraid. *Unknown.*
In Waste Places. Stephens.
Lament for the Non-Swimmers. Wagoner.
News, The. "Sec."
Ode to Fear. Collins.
"Paper Men to Air Hopes and Fears." Francis.
Seein' Things. Field.
Sometimes. Kuzma.
Storm Fear. Frost.

February
At the Nadir. Kennedy.
Brook in February, The. Roberts.
February, Tall and Trim. Gilmore.
February Thaw. Dutton.
February Twilight. Teasdale.
February. Clare.
February. Heath-Stubbs.
February. Sherman.
February. Whitney.
February. Young.
In February. Symonds.
Infant Spring. Shove.
Lent Tending. Shepherd.
Mirror in February. Kinsella.
When. Aldis.

Federal Bureau of Investigation
Award. Durem.

Feet
About Feet. Hillert.
Baby's feet, like sea-shells pink, A. *Fr.* Étude Réaliste. Swinburne.
Feet. Aldis.
Feet. Harry.
Feet, a Sermon. Paul.
House Remembers, The. Francis.
My Mother's Feet. Plumly.

Fellowship. *See* **Brotherhood.**

Feminism
About Women's Liberation. Saucedo.
Ain't I a Woman? Truth.
Breaking Tradition. Mirikitani.
Clubwoman. Smith.
Daughters. Astra.
Emulation, The. Egerton.
Evening in the Suburbs. Barnett.
For the ERA Crusaders. Kennedy.
Free Woman, A. At last free! *Unknown.*
Funeral Song for Mamie Eisenhower. Wong.
Hard Is the Fortune of All Womankind. *Unknown.*
He and She. Ware.
Her Sister. O'Neill.
Housewife's Lament, The. *Unknown.*
How many wise men and heroes. Ch'iu Chin.
Hypocrite Women. Levertov.
I take as my theme, "The Independent Woman." *Fr.* Pro Femina. Kizer.
It's in the Name. Tsui.
It's No Good! Lawrence.
Liberation. Stone.
Little Phoebe. *Unknown.*
Man Within, The. Ewing.
March of the Women, The. Hamilton.
Myth. Rukeyser.
Ninth Symphony of Beethoven Understood at Last as a Sexual Message, The. Rich.
On a Fortification at Boston Begun By Women. Tompson.
Over the fence. Dickinson.
Poem to the Man on My Fire Escape. Wakoski.
Purple, White and Green, The. Morgan-Browne.
Rights of Woman, The. Barbauld.
She Proves the Inconsistency of the Desires and Criticism of Men Who Accuse Women of What They Themselves Cause. Sister Juana Inés de la Cruz.
She Told Me. Kilgore.
Significant Fevers. Fell.
Snapshots of a Daughter-in-Law. Rich.
Soul-Drift. Blind.
Subversive, The. Woo.
There Is a Woman in This Town. Parker.
They lived out in a women's house. *Fr.* The Rime of the Ancient Feminist. Markman.
Things Not of This Union. Gregg.
To Kate, Skating Better than Her Date. Daiches.
To the Ladies. Chudleigh.
To Women. Hugo.
Under Our Own Wings. Wong.
Woman Defending Herself Examines Her Own Character Witness, A. Griffin.
Women Called Bossy Cowboys. Jankola.
Women of My Land. Armstrong.
Women's Degrees. Godley.
Women's Marseillaise, The. Macaulay.
Wonder Woman. Lim.
I Hear My Sisters Saying (IHMS). Carol Konek *and* Dorothy Walters, eds.
No More Masks! (NMM). Florence Howe *and* Ellen Bass, eds.

Fences
Barbed Wire Fence Meditates upon the Goldfinch, A. McKay.
Fence, A. Sandburg.
Fence Wire. Dickey.
How to Build a Ha-ha. *Fr.* The English Garden. Mason.
Old Fence Post. Hanes.
Picket Fence, The. Morgenstern.
Pickety fence, The. McCord.
Snow Fence. Kooser.
See also **Walls.**

Fencing
Extempore Verses upon a Trial of Skill between the Two Great Masters of the Noble Science of Defence, Messrs. Figg and Sutton. Byrom.

Fencing School. Manifold.
For E. McC. Pound.
Fenians
Caoilte. *Unknown.*
Down by the Glenside. Kearney.
Ferns
Bracken Hills in Autumn. "MacDiarmid."
Ferns, The. Baro.
Petrified Fern, The. Branch.
Ferry Boats
Back and Forth. Mitchell.
Crossing Brooklyn Ferry. Whitman.
"Ferry me across the water." *Fr.* Sing-Song. Rossetti.
Ferry Me Across the Water. Rossetti.
Ferry-Boats. Tippett.
Ferryman, The. Rossetti.
Jolly Young Waterman, The. Dibdin.
Letter Written on a Ferry Crossing Long Island Sound. Sexton.
Recuerdo. Millay.
Trip on the Staten Island Ferry, A. Lorde.
Fertilizer
How to Fertilize Soil. *Fr.* The Sugar-Cane. Grainger.
Festivals
Mulberry Street. Herschberger.
Feuds
Lads of Wamphray, The. *Unknown.*
Lord Maxwell's Last Goodnight. *Unknown.*
Massacre of the MacPherson, The. Aytoun.
Rowan County Crew, The. Day.
Fever
Fever 103°. Plath.
Fiddlers and Fiddles
Clabe Mott. Still.
Fiddler, The. Trapnell.
Fiddler Jones. *Fr.* Spoon River Anthology. Masters.
Fiddler of Dooney, The. Yeats.
First Fight. Then Fiddle. Brooks.
First Song. Kinnell.
Green Fiddler, The. Field.
Mountain Whippoorwill, The. Benét.
My Fiddle. Kwitko.
Seven Fiddlers, The. Evans.
Take Down the Fiddle, Karl! Neilson.
'Tis I Go Fiddling, Fiddling. Hopper.
See also **Violins.**
Fidelity
As the Holly Groweth Green. Henry VIII, King of England.
Barbara. Smith.
Born with the Vices. D'Urfey.
Constant Lover, The. Suckling.
Fair Sylvia. *Unknown.*
Let me not to the marriage of true minds. *Fr.* Sonnets. Shakespeare.
Love and Life; a Song. Rochester.
Love Me Little, Love Me Long. Herrick.
Lover Exhorteth His Lady to Be Constant, The. *Unknown.*
Lover's Protestation, A. Lodge.
Love's Last Suit. Davidson.
My Dear and Only Love. Graham, Marquess of Montrose.
Non Sum Qualis Eram Bonae sub Regno Cynarae. Dowson.
Nutbrown Maid, The. *Unknown.*
Polly Oliver's Rambles. *Unknown.*
Promise of a Constant Lover, The. *Unknown.*
Scrutinie, The. Lovelace.
Song, A: "Chloris, when I to thee present." *Unknown.*
Song to Celia, A. Sedley.
There Is a Lady Sweet and Kind. *Unknown.*
Vow to Love Faithfully, Howsoever He Be Rewarded. Surrey.
When men shall find thy flower, thy glory pass. *Fr.* Delia. Daniel.
Woman, Don't Be Troublesome. "Young."
Fields and Pastures
August. Scheele.
Cornfield, The. Roberts.
Deserted Pasture, The. Carman.
Fields at Evening. Morton.
Immortal. Van Doren.
Like a Field Waiting. Chalfi.
Lost. Brand.
Low Fields and Light. Merwin.
Meadow-Field, The. *Fr.* Pleasant Memories. Sangster.
Meadows in Spring, The. Fitzgerald.
Mountain Meadows. Keller.
Mower's Song, The. Marvell.
On Westwell Downs. Strode.
Out in the Fields with God. *At. to* Browning *and to* Guiney.
Pasture, A. Knowles.
Pasture, The. Frost.
Pea-Fields, The. *Fr.* Songs of the Common Day. Roberts.
Poetry Reading, The. Manhire.
Poplar Field, The. Cowper.
Psalm of the Fruitful Field. Klein.
Return, The. Ostenso.
To Meadows. Herrick.
When You Will Walk in the Field. Goldberg.
White Fields. Stephens.
Fiesole, Italy
Fiesolan Idyl. Landor.
Fife (region), Scotland
Gateway to the Sea—St. Andrews, A. Bruce.
Fig Trees
Tapestry Trees. Morris.
Fights
Fist Fight. Cockrell.
Figs
Beware of Figs. Nicophon.
Figs. Lawrence.
No Fig. Booker.
Where the Slow Fig's Purple Sloth. Warren.
Figureheads (ship)
Figurehead, The. Adams.
Filipinos
Lolo died yesterday. Zarco.
Manong Federico Delos Reyes and His Golden Banjo. Robles.
Manong Jacinto Santo Tomas. Robles.
New Manong, The. Syquia.
Pick-up at Chef Rizal Restaurant. Cerenio.
Pinay. Cerenio.
We who carry the endless seasons. Cerenio.
Without Names. Tagami.
You Lovely People. Cerenio.
See also **Philippines.**
Financiers
New Order of Chivalry, A. Peacock.
On a Travelling Speculator. Freneau.
See also **Banking and Bankers.**
Finches
Birdsong. Singer.
Blind Linnet, The. Buchanan.
Epitaphs on Two Piping-Bullfinches of Lady Ossory's, Buried under a Rose-Bush in Her Garden. Walpole.
Finches, The. Murray.
Finches, The. Shapcott.
Green Linnet, The. Wordsworth.
On the Death of Mrs. Throckmorton's Bullfinch. Cowper.
110 Year Old House. Ochester.
Sometimes goldfinches one by one will drop. *Fr.* I Stood Tip-Toe. Keats.
Song: "Where I walk out." Winters.
Fingal's Cave, Scotland
Cave of Staffa, I ("We saw, but surely, in the motley crowd"). Wordsworth.
Cave of Staffa, II ("Ye shadowy beings, that have rights and claims"). Wordsworth.
Fingernails
I Think Sometimes. Hartnett.
Fingers
Bestiary for the Fingers of My Right Hand. Simic.
Finger of Necessity. Barks.
Now It Is Broccoli. Tagami.
This little pig went to market. Mother Goose.
Thumb. Dacey.
Upon the Losse of His Little Finger. Randolph.
Fink, Mike
Shooting of the Cup, The. *Fr.* The Song of Three Friends. Neihardt.
Finland
Finland. Graves.
Reindeer and Engine. Jacobsen.
Finns
Ode to the Finnish Dead. Walsh.
Finnsburg, Battle of
Battle of Finnsburg, The. *Unknown.*
Fionn (legendary king of Fenians)
Generosity. *Unknown.*
Praise of Fionn, The. *Unknown.*
Fir Trees
Epitaph on a Fir-tree. Murphy.

Fir-Tree, The. Thomas.
Firwood. Clare.
Tapestry Trees. Morris.

Fire
Aftermath. Plath.
Armies in the Fire. *Fr.* A Child's Garden of Verses. Stevenson.
Arthur with a lighted taper. *Fr.* Science for the Young. Irwin.
Banking Coal. Toomer.
Barn Fire. Lux.
Barnfire during Church. Bly.
Brooklyn Theater Fire, The. *Unknown.*
Brother Fire. MacNeice.
Burning the Small Dead. Snyder.
Coal Fire in Winter, A. McGrath.
Execration upon Vulcan, An. Jonson.
Feeding the Fire. Finkel.
Fire, The. Buford.
Fire! *Unknown.*
Fire and Ice. Frost.
Fire at Alexandria, The. Weiss.
Fire Down Below. *Unknown.*
Fire of Driftwood, The. Longfellow.
Fire of London, The. *Fr.* Annus Mirabilis. Dryden.
Fire on the Hills. Jeffers.
Fires. Heyen.
Forest Fire, The. Monroe.
Hotel Fire: New Orleans. Ruffin.
Houses Burning; Quebec. Anderson.
Looking West. Stafford.
Lumberyard, The. Herschberger.
Marriage of Heaven and Earth, The. Nemerov.
Milwaukee Fire, The. *Unknown.*
Miramichi Fire, The. *Unknown.*
Mister Charlie. *Unknown.*
My Grandfather Burning Cornfields. Sauls.
My love is like to ice and I to fire. *Fr.* Amoretti. Spenser.
Prairie Fires. Garland.
Scare-Fire, The. Herrick.
Some Verses upon the Burning of Our House, July 10th, 1666. Bradstreet.
Sourdough mountain called a fire in. *Fr.* Myths and Texts: Burning. Snyder.
Staying Ahead. Glass.
Street Fire. Halpern.
Summer Oracle. Lorde.
There's a Fire in the Forest. Ross.
Two Fires, The. Wright.
Where Fire Burns. Cardiff.
Within Us, Too. Grenville.

Fire Engines
F Is the Fighting Firetruck. McGinley.
Fire-Truck, A. Wilbur.
Great Figure, The. Williams.

Firearms. *See* **Guns.**

Firefighters
Habeas Corpus Blues, The. Aiken.

Fireflies
Fireflies. Fawcett.
Fireflies. Fisher.
Fireflies. Hall.
Fireflies. *Fr.* Transcripts from Nature. "MacLeod".
Fireflies in the Garden. Frost.
Firefly Lights His Lamp, The. *Unknown.*
Firefly, The. Nash.
Firefly. Roberts.
Glow-Worm, The. Mercer.
Glow Worm. Robinson.
Glow-Worm, The. Shanks.
Glow-Worm, The. Smith.
How dreamy-dark it is! *Fr.* The Fireflies. Mair.
Lightning Bug. Morgan.
Mower to the Glow-Worms, The. Marvell.
Night-Piece to Julia, The. Herrick.
Very Minor Poet Speaks, A. Valle.

Fireworks
Fireworks. Deutsch.
Fireworks. Reeves.
Fireworks. Worth.
Fourth of July Night. Aldis.
Fourth of July Night. Sandburg.
July 4th. Swenson.
Pinwheel's Song, The. Ciardi.

Fish
Although it's cold no clothes I wear. *Unknown.*
Aquarium. Wright.
Aquarium, San Francisco, The. Sackville-West.
At the Aquarium. Eastman.
Beginning of an Undergraduate Poem. *Unknown.*
Birds and Fishes. Jeffers.
Blow Ye Winds Westerly. *Unknown.*
Crawdad. *Unknown.*
Description of a Strange (and Miraculous) Fish, A. Parker.
Dreaming Trout, The. *Fr.* The Flowing Summer. Bruce.
Eating Fish. Johnston.
Ecological Lecture. Raffel.
Evolution. Blight.
Festoons of Fishes. Kreymborg.
Fish, The. Bishop.
Fish, The. Brooke.
Fish, The. Gustafson.
Fish. Hughes.
Fish, The. Moore.
Fish. Rosenblatt.
Fish. Ross.
Fish. Witt.
Fish in River. *Fr.* Riddles (Exeter Book). *Unknown.*
Fish Story. Armour.
Fish, the Man, and the Spirit, The. Hunt.
Fish With the Deep Sea Smile. Brown.
Fishes, The. *Unknown.*
Fishes' Evening Song. Ipcar.
Flattered Flying Fish, The. Rieu.
Flying Fish, The. Cope.
Flying Fish. Miller.
Flying Fish. Taylor.
Flying Fish, II, The. Gray.
Fun with Fishing. Tietjens.
Gar, The. Bell.
Goose Fish, The. Nemerov.
Great fish's eyes never shut, The. Castellanos.
Grunion. Livingston.
Heaven. Brooke.
How They Brought the Good News by Sea. Farber.
Ichthycide. Rosenblatt.
King of waters, the sea shouldering whale, The. Wood.
Little Fish. Lawrence.
Luscious lobster, with a crabfish raw, The. Wood.
Maldive Shark, The. Melville.
Methods of Cooking Trout. *Fr.* The Art of Angling. Barker.
Minnows. Keats.
Movement of Fish, The. Dickey.
Mrs. Busk. Sitwell.
My Garden, My Daylight. Graham.
Pesci Misti. Aaronson.
Pike, The. Blunden.
Pike. Hughes.
Robbers came to our house, The. *Unknown.*
Sea School. Howes.
Small Fountains. Abercrombie.
Snapper, The. Heyen.
Some Scribbles for a Lumpfish. Johnson.
Starfish. Welles.
Three Movements. Yeats.
To a Baked Fish. Wells.
To the Carp, and Those Who Hunt Her. Hazard.
To the Immortal Memory of the Halibut on Which I Dined This Day, Monday, April 26, 1784. Cowper.
When Howitzers Began. Carruth.
When pleasing heat, and fragrant blooms inspire. *Fr.* Halieuticks. Fish.

Fisher, John, Cardinal (Saint John Fisher)
Cardinal Fisher. Heywood.
Alas, Alack! De la Mare.

Fishing and Fishermen
Angler's Song, The. *Fr.* The Secrets of Angling. Dennys.
Angler, The. Chalkhill.
Angler's Ballad, The. Cotton.
Angler's Invitation, The. Stoddart.
Anglers Song, The. Basse.
Angler's Song, The ("As inward love breeds outward talk"). Walton.
Angler's Wish, An. Van Dyke.
Angler's Wish, The. Walton.
Armstrong Spring Creek. Davis.
As inward love breeds outward talk. *Fr.* The Angler's Song. Blake.
At the Fishhouses. Bishop.

Bait, The. Donne.
Baits for Various Fish. Barker.
Big One, The. Cabalquinto.
Blackfriars. Farjeon.
Blow Ye Winds Westerly. *Unknown.*
Bobber. Carver.
Bold Fishermen, The. *Unknown.*
Caller Herrin'. Nairne.
Canst Thou Draw Out Leviathan with an Hook. Curnow.
Careful Angler, The. Stevenson.
Casting at Night. Hoey.
Caulker, The. Lewis.
Cedar River, The. Gibbons.
Cod-Fisher, The. Lincoln.
Coracle Fishers, The. *Fr.* The Banks of Wye. Bloomfield.
Coromandel Fishers. Naidu.
Crabbing. Levine.
Crane's Ascent, The. Bozanic.
Curse of a Fisherman's Wife. Chalpin.
Did You Ever Go Fishing? *Unknown.*
Don's Holiday. Hamilton.
Drunken Fisherman, The. Lowell.
Elver Fishers. Gurney.
Father Fisheye. Balakian.
Feeling for Fish. Trawick.
Finding a Teacher. Merwin.
Fish, The. Bishop.
Fisherman Casts His Line into the Sea, The. Holland.
Fisherman. Booth.
Fisherman, The. Brown.
Fisherman, The. Bruce.
Fisherman. Francis.
Fisherman, The. McCord.
Fisherman, The. Spicer.
Fisherman, The. Stuart.
Fisherman, The. Yeats.
Fisherman's Luck. Gibson.
Fishermen. Bunting.
Fishermen, The. Theocritus.
Fishermen, The. Whittier.
Fisher's Life, The. *Unknown.*
Fishing Blues. *Unknown.*
Fishing Fleet, The. Colcord.
Fishing Harbour Towards Evening. Kell.
Fishing on a Lake at Night. Bly.
Fishing Pole, The. Davies.
Fishing Season. Vallis.
Fishing. *Maori Oral Tradition.*
Fishing Song, A. Rands.
Flyfisherman in Wartime. Bacon.
Fun with Fishing. Tietjens.
Gar, The. Bell.
Halibut Cove Harvest. Leslie.
Hard Times, But Carrying On. Smith.
How to Catch Trout. Barker. *Unknown.*
Ice-Fishing House, The: Long Lake, Minnesota. Harper.
In the Deep Channel. Stafford.
Instruction in the Art. Booth.
It Is Hard to Catch Trout. Piuvkaq.
Late Afternoon on a Good Lake. Wier.
Limits of Departure, The. Weigl.
Master and Man. Newbolt.
Narrows, The. Bruchac.
Neither Hook nor Line. Bunyan.
Net Menders, The. Vrepont.
Night Fishing for Blues. Smith.
Nocturne: Georgia Coast. Hicky.
Not Being Wise. Elson.
Off to the Fishing Ground. Montgomery.
Old Angler, The. De la Mare.
Old Fisherman, The. Hay.
Old Fisherman with Guitar. Brown.
Once There Were Three Fishermen. *Unknown.*
Out Fishing. Howes.
Out Fishin'. Guest.
Out from Lobster Cove. Reed.
Papio. Chock.
Peter Grimes. *Fr.* The Borough. Crabbe.
Pike, The. Bruce.
Prayer for Fish. Wallace.
Purse-Seine, The. Jeffers.
Rainy Midnight. Gurney.
Reading Plato. Graham.
Reflections of a Trout Fisherman. Demon.
Ritualists, The. Williams.
Running the River Lines. Baker.
Silver Herring Throbbed Thick in My Seine, The. Leslie.
Skipper Ireson's Ride. Whittier.
Skipper-Hermit, The. Rich.
Snacks. Tanaka.
Sockeye Salmon. Hambleton.
Song of the Full Catch. Skinner.
Song of the Trout Fisher, The. Ikinilik.
Summit Lake. Thalman.
Three Fishers, The. Kingsley.
To a Little Boy Learning to Fish. Hoeft.
Trip to the Grand Banks, A. *Unknown.*
Trout, The. Montague.
We are at the hauling then hoping for it. *Fr.* The Nightfishing. Graham.
We'll Go to Sea No More. *Unknown.*
With the Herring Fishers. "MacDiarmid."
Words Are Never Enough. Bruce.
Wetting Our Lines Together (WOLT). Allen Hoey, ed.
See also **Crabs and Crabbing.**

Fisk, James
Jim Fisk. *Unknown.*

Fitts, Dudley
Elegy and Flame. Gregory.

Fitzgerald, Edward
To Edward Fitzgerald. Browning.
To Edward Fitzgerald. Tennyson.

Fitzgerald, F. Scott
Effervescence and Evanescence. Preston.
On Editing Scott Fitzgerald's Papers. Wilson.

Flags
Battle-Flag, The. Davis.
Conquered Banner, The. Ryan.
Foreboding. Rilke.
Que Bonita Bandera (How Beautiful Is the Flag). *Unknown.*
Red Flag, The. Connell.

Flags, United States
American Flag, The. Drake.
Barbara Frietchie. Whittier.
Brother, Lift Your Flag with Mine. Bacon.
Flag, The. Silverstein.
Flag Goes By, The. Bennett.
Flag of the Constellation, The. Read.
Flag Song. Ward.
Flag Speaks, The. Balch.
Flag We Fly, The. Fisher.
God Save the Flag. Holmes.
Hang Out the Flags. Tippett.
I Am the Flag. Jones.
Not of School Age. Frost.
Old Flag, The. Bunner.
Our Country's Emblem. *Unknown.*
Our Flag Forever. Stanton.
Red, White and Blue, The. Shaw.
Song for Our Flag, A. Sangster.
Stand by the Flag. Wilder.
Star-spangled Banner, The. Key.
Toast to the Flag, A. Daly.
Your Flag and My Flag. Nesbit.
You're a Grand Old Flag. Cohan.

Flamingos
Boy in the Roman Zoo. MacLeish.
Turtle and the Flamingo, The. Fields.

Flanders, Belgium
Another Reply To "In Flanders Fields." *At. to* Armstrong.
In Flanders Fields. McCrae.
In Flanders Now. Jaques.
Into Battle. Grenfell.
Old Houses of Flanders, The. Ford.
Reply To in Flanders Fields. Mitchell.

Flapjacks. *See* **Pancakes.**

Flattery
Flattery. *Fr.* Cadenus and Vanessa. Swift.
Fox and the Crow, The. La Fontaine.
One White Hair, The. Landor.
Spider and the Fly, The. Howitt.
When my love swears that she is made of truth. *Fr.* Sonnets. Shakespeare.

Fleas
Cannibal Flea, The. Hood.

Flea, The. Donne.
Flea, The. Young.
Flea Circus at Tivoli, The. Willard.
Fleas, The. De Morgan.
Harlots' Catch. Nichols.
On Donne's Poem "To a Flea." Coleridge.
To a Flea in a Glass of Water. Greig.

Fletcher, John
Prologue to "The Tempest." Vaughan.
To Fletcher Reviv'd. Lovelace.
Upon Master Fletcher's Incomparable Playes. Herrick.
Upon the Dramatick Poems of Mr. John Fletcher. Cartwright.

Flies
Amber Bead, The. Herrick.
Blue-Fly, The. Graves.
Blue-Tail Fly, The. *Unknown.*
Calvus to a Fly. Turner.
Dead Fly. Ní Chuilleanáin.
Death to Us, A. Silken.
Evening Dance of the Grey Flies. Page.
Flesh-Fly and the Bee, The. Patmore.
Flies Love Me. Archer.
Fly, The. Ayres.
Fly, The. *Fr.* Songs of Experience. Blake.
Fly, The. De la Mare.
Fly, The. Googe.
Fly, The. Nash.
Fly, The. Oldys.
Fly, The. Shapiro.
Fly Caught in a Cobweb, A. Lovelace.
Fly in December. Wallace.
Fly That Flew into My Mistress's Eye, A. Carew.
Harriet. Lowell.
I heard a fly buzz—when I died. Dickinson.
Near Dusk. Auslander.
On Finding a Small Fly Crushed in a Book. Turner.
Once Musing as I Sat. Googe.
Spider and the Fly, The. Howitt.
Swarm, The. Moore.
To a Fly, Taken out of a Bowl of Punch. "Pindar."
To a Midge. Nisbet.
To the Fly in My Drink. Wagoner.
Truth. Nemerov.
Upon a Flie. Herrick.

Flight
Feel like a Bird. Swenson.
Flight. Vinal.
High Flight. Magee.

Flirtation
Advice to the Ladies. Somervile.
Disillusion. Burge.
Doris. Congreve.
Flirt, The. Davies.
Flirtation, The. Blumenthal.
Love Song, The. Gurney.
"O Polly, you might have toy'd and kist." *Fr.* The Beggar's Opera. Gay.
Ode, An: "Merchant, to secure his treasure, The." Prior.
Rape of the Lock, The. Pope.
Some Semblance of Order. Wright.
Song by the Wavering Nymph. Behn.
Teasing. Mack.
To His Coy Love. Drayton.

Flodden Field, Battle of (1513)
Flodden. *Fr.* Marmion. Scott.
Lament for Flodden, A. Elliot.
Then the Provost he uprose. *Fr.* Edinburgh after Flodden. Aytoun.

Flood, The
Late Passenger, The. Lewis.
Noah's Prayer. De Gasztold.
Return to Ararat. Halsall.

Floods
Back Water Blues. *Unknown.*
Cabin Creek Flood, The. *Unknown.*
Flood, The. Bell.
Flood. Charles.
Flood. Feldman.
Flood. McGough.
Flood, The. *Fr.* Metamorphoses. Ovid.
High Tide on the Coast of Lincolnshire, The (1571). Ingelow.
High Water Everywhere: I ("Back water done rose around Sumner, now, The)." *Unknown.*
High Water Everywhere: 2 ("Back water at Blytheville)." *Unknown.*
No More the Slow Stream. McLaren.
Rising High Water Blues. *Unknown.*

Florence, Italy
Above the Arno. Swenson.
Daisies of Florence. Raine.
È, The Feasting Florentines. Hoffman.
Florence. Landor.
More Nudes for Florence. Witt.
Night Character. Campana.
Old Bridge at Florence, The. Longfellow.
Old Pictures in Florence. Browning.
San Marco Museum, Florence. Maris Stella.
Santa Maria del Fiore. Clarke.

Florida
But, Still, He. Lucas.
Causeway. Block.
Cuban Refugees on Key Biscayne. Winder.
Developers at Crystal River. Merrill.
Everglade. Cherner.
Florida. Bishop.
Florida. Rakosi.
Florida Road Workers. Hughes.
Floridian Museum of Art, A. Whittemore.
Mullet Snatching. Glass.
Okeechobee. Allison.
Okefenokee Swamp. Hicky.
Sharks, Caloosahatchee River. Pape.

Florists
Old Florist. Roethke.

Flowers
Ann's House. Lourie.
Arise and Pick a Posy. *Unknown.*
Aunt Gladys's Home Movie No. 31, Albert's Funeral. Miller.
Babiaantje, The. Prince.
Baby Seed Song. Nesbit.
Bavarian Gentians. Lawrence.
Behold, O Man. *Fr.* The Faerie Queene. Spenser.
Bloody Cranesbill on the Dunes. Scovell.
Bloom. Kreymborg.
Blossome, The. Donne.
Bouquet in Dog Time. Carruth.
Bouquets. Francis.
Buttercups and Daisies. Howitt.
Chanted Calendar, A. *Fr.* Balder. Dobell.
Charm for Spring Flowers, A. Field.
Cheddar Pinks. Bridges.
Choir of Day, The. Milton. Blake.
City, The. Ignatow.
Columbine, The. Very.
Contemplation upon Flowers, A. King.
Cut Flower, A. Shapiro.
Cycle. Hughes.
Death of the Flowers, The. Bryant.
Derbyshire Bluebells. Sitwell.
Divination by a Daffodil. Herrick.
Earliest Spring. Levertov.
Fear of Flowers, The. Clare.
Flower, The. Herbert.
Flower in the Crannied Wall. Tennyson.
Flower-Cart Man, The. Field.
Flowers. Behn.
Flowers, The. Herbert.
Flowers. Hood.
Flowers. Longfellow.
Flowers, The. Stevenson.
Flowers and Men. Lawrence.
Flowers by the Sea. Williams.
Flowers in the Ward. Neilson.
Flower's Name, The. *Fr.* Garden Fancies. Browning.
Flowers of Middle Summer. *Fr.* The Winter's Tale. Shakespeare.
For the doubling of flowers is the improvement of the gardners talent. *Fr.* Jubilate Agno. Smart.
Fragment: "Flower in the crannied wall." Tennyson.
Fury of Flowers and Worms, The. Sexton.
Gardener to His God, The. Van Duyn.
Geranium, The. Roethke.
Ghost-Flowers. Higginson.
How the Flowers Grow. "Setoun."
I Hoed and Trenched and Weeded. *Fr.* A Shropshire Lad. Housman.
I walked the other day (to spend my hour). Vaughan.
Idle Flowers, The. Bridges.
In Back of the Real. Ginsberg.

In the Field Forever. Wallace.
Iris. Williams.
Kingcups. Sitwell.
Life. Herbert.
Matter of Life and Death, A. Ridler.
Meditation for His Mistresse, A. Herrick.
Mirrorment. Ammons.
Morning Compliments. Dayre.
Nosegay Always Sweet, for Lovers to Send for Tokens of Love at New Year's Tide, or For Fairings, A. Hunnis.
Of Flowers. Loney.
On Clarastella Walking in Her Garden. Heath.
Pearly Everlasting, The. Fewster.
Picture of Little T. C. in a Prospect of Flowers, The. Marvell.
Poem: "Geranium, houseleek, laid in oblong beds." Gray.
Pyxidanthera, The. Bristol.
Quaker Ladies. Cortissoz.
Rhodora, The. Emerson.
Roadside Flowers. Carman.
Round, The. Booth.
Sensitive Plant, The. Shelley.
Some Flowers o' the Spring. *Fr.* The Winter's Tale. Shakespeare.
Someone Gave Him Some Plastic Flowers Once. Shady.
Song: "Primrose in the green forest, The." Deloney.
Spring Flowers from Ireland. McCarthy.
Spring Flowers. *Fr.* The Seasons: Spring. Thomson.
Sundew, The. Swinburne.
Swans, The. Sitwell.
Tiger Lily. McCord
To a Wind-Flower. Cawein.
To Blossoms. Herrick.
To Daffodils. Herrick.
To Mistress Margery Wentworth. *Fr.* The Garlande of Laurell. Skelton.
To Violets. Herrick.
Troll's Nosegay, The. Graves.
Violets, daffodils. Coatsworth.
Vision of the Lamentation of Beulah over Ololon. *Fr.* Milton. Blake.
Vlamertinghe; Passing the Château, July 1917. Blunden.
White coral bells upon a slender stalk. *Unknown.*
Why Flowers Change Color. Herrick.
Wild Thyme, The. *Fr.* Milton. Blake.
Window Boxes. Farjeon.
Woman Looking at a Vase of Flowers. Stevens.
Wonga Vine. Wright.
Woodspurge, The. Rossetti.

Flutes
Amateur Flute, The. *Unknown.*
Elderberry Flute Song. Blue Cloud.
Flute of the Lonely, The. Lindsay.
Flute Player. Gond.
Flute Players. Rabéarivelo.
Khristna and His Flute. Hope.
Lament of the Flutes. Okigbo.
Longing. Gond.
Musical Instrument, A. Browning.
Old Orange Flute, The. *Unknown.*
Shakuhachi. Mitsui.
Tree to Flute. Hajnal.

Flying Dutchman (ship)
Flying Dutchman, The. Robinson.
Flying Dutchman, The. Sullivan.
Flying Dutchman, The. *Unknown.*

Flying Fish
Flying Fish. Fenollosa.

Flying Saucers
Go Fly a Saucer. McCord.

Foals
Birth of the Foal. Juhász.
Foal. Miller.

Fog
Boats in a Fog. Jeffers.
Fog. Binyon.
Fog, The. Davies.
Fog. Sandburg.
Fog-Horn. Clarke.
Fog-Horn. Merwin.
Fog 9/76. Dey.
Haar in Princes Street. Scott.
Haze. Thoreau.
On the Great Fog in London, December 1762. Weeks.
Quiet Fog, The. Piercy.
River-Fog. Kiyowara.
Sea Fog, The. Jacobsen.
Sounding Fog, The. Pulsifer.
White Dusk. Boyd.
See also **Mist.**

Folk Songs. *See* **Ballads and Folk Songs.**

Fontenoy, Battle of (1745)
Fontenoy. Davis.
Fontenoy, 1745. Lawless.

Food
Ad Ministram. Thackeray.
Animal Crackers. Morley.
Another Grace for a Child. Herrick.
Author Loving These Homely Meats, Specially, viz.: Cream, Pancakes, Buttered Pippin-Pies. Davies.
Ballad of Bouillabaisse, The. Thackeray.
Beans, Bacon and Gravy. *Unknown.*
Beauty I Would Suffer For. Piercy.
Butchery. McPherson.
Can Zone; or, The Good Food Guide. Lesser.
Christmas Dinner. Rosen.
Conserves. *Fr.* Joy of Cooking, The. Mus.
Deliver Me, O Lord, from My Daily Bread. Walker.
Dietary Advice. *Unknown.*
Dish for a Poet, A. *Unknown.*
Dried Apple Pies. *Unknown.*
Dunderbeck. *Unknown.*
Elegy, The: "Madam, no more! The time has come to eat." Hope.
Epigram on Fasting. Swift.
Essay on Lunch. Gibson.
Fat Boy's Dream, The. McCann.
Fire, The. Scott.
Food. Valle.
Food and Drink. Untermeyer.
Food of the North. Lawrence.
Goober Peas. *Unknown.*
Gourmet's Love-Song, The. Wodehouse.
Grace for Children. Herrick.
Grace to Be Said at the Supermarket. Nemerov.
Green Corn. *Unknown.*
Hasty Pudding, The. Barlow.
Having Replaced Love with Food and Drink. Wakoski.
High on the Hog. Fields.
Hog Meat. Davis.
How One-Thumb Willie Got His Name. Sellers.
Hymn to Comus. *Fr.* Pleasure Reconciled to Virtue. Jonson.
I Had But Fifty Cents. *Unknown.*
If We Didn't Have to Eat. Waterman.
I'm Hungry! Prelutsky.
Invitation to Lubberland, An. *Unknown.*
Inviting a Friend to Supper. Jonson.
Lasagna. Kennedy.
Last Bite, The. Frost.
Lemon Pie. Guest.
Love Song, A. Tyler.
Methuselah. *Unknown.*
Miss Foggerty's Cake. *Unknown.*
Miss T. De la Mare.
Mix a pancake. Rossetti.
Mountown! Thou Sweet Retreat. *Fr.* Mully of Mountown. King.
My Other Chinee Cook. Stephens.
No Mixed Green Salad for Me, Thanks. Galbraith.
Observations in a Cornish Teashop. Rexroth.
Old Men, The. Reznikoff.
On Tomato Ketchup. *Unknown.*
One Fish Ball. *Unknown.*
Pancake, The. Rossetti.
Peas and Honey. *Unknown.*
Peasant Declares His Love, The. Roumer.
Pesci Misti. Aaronson.
Punkin Pie. Mills.
Quartermaster Store, The. *Unknown.*
Repast. Tiemer-Wille.
Rillons, Rillettes. Wilbur.
Salad, A. Smith.
Salad. Collins.
Sausage. Guest.
Song against Broccoli. Blount.
Song of the Taste. Snyder.
Spectator Ab Extra. Clough.
Stacking Up. Rosenfeld.
Stomach. Norris.
Suet Dumpling, The. *Unknown.*

Survey of Literature. Ransom.
Tale of a Tart, The. Weatherley.
Tamales. "O. Henry."
This Is Just to Say. Williams.
Those Flapjacks of Brown's. Taylor.
Vision that appeared to me, A. *Fr.* The Vision of MacConglinne. MacConglinne.
Watermelons. Simic.
When de Co'n Pone's Hot. Dunbar.
When good King Arthur ruled this land. Mother Goose.
When in Rome. Evans.
Who Among You Knows the Essence of Garlic? Hongo.
Witches' Menu. Nikolay.
See also **Cooking and Cooks; Eating; Gluttony and Gluttons.**

Fools
Epigram: "Sir, I admit your gen'ral rule." Pope.
Epigram: "Yes, every poet is a fool." Prior.
Fool much bit by fleas put out the lights, A. Lovelace.
Fools. *Fr.* Volpone. Jonson.
Fool's Prayer, The. Sill.
Fools, They Are The Only Nation. *Fr.* Volpone. Jonson.
Plays. Landor.
To Fool, or Knave. Jonson.
Tonversation with Baby, A. Bishop.
Upon a Fool. Hoskyns.
See also **Jesters.**

Football
Alumnus Football. Rice.
Autumn Begins in Martins Ferry, Ohio. Wright.
Bee, The. Dickey.
Caught in the Pocket. Barney.
First Practice. Gildner.
Football Game, A. Van Eck.
For the Death of Vince Lombardi. Dickey.
Friendly Game of Football, A. Dyson.
Funky Football. Saunders.
In the Pocket. Dickey.
Linebacker at Forty, The. Wallace.
Nearly Everybody Loves Harvey Martin. Barney.
Passer, The. Abbe.
Revisiting the Field. Pavlich.
Running Back. Smith.
Say Goodbye to Big Daddy. Jarrell.
Settling Some Old Football Scores. Bishop.
Sleeper, The. Field.
Ties. Stuart.
Watching the Jets Lose to Buffalo at Shea. Swenson.
See also **Soccer.**

Ford, Ed ("Whitey")
Poem for Ed "Whitey" Ford, A. Holden.

Ford, Ford Madox
Ford Madox Ford. Lowell.
To Ford Madox Ford in Heaven. Williams.

Ford, Gerald Rudolph
Bouquet for Jerry Ford, A. Marcus.

Forest Fires
Forest Fire, The. Monroe.
Lost Silvertip. Reed.

Foresters
I Have Been a Foster. *Unknown.*
Solitary Woodsman, The. Roberts.
Song of the Forest Ranger, The. Bashford.

Forests
A B C's in Green. Speyer.
Arcana Sylvarum. De Kay.
Ballad of the Trees and the Master, A. Lanier.
Breathing, The. Levertov.
By Canoe through the Fir Forest. Dickey.
Charnwood Forest. *Fr.* Polyolbion. Drayton.
Choir Practice. Crosby.
Christmas in the Wood. Frost.
Dark Forest, The. Thomas.
Dark Wood. Wedde.
Deep in a windless/ wood. Buson.
Departure, The. Whittemore.
Dorus's Song. Sidney.
Ecce in Deserto. Beers.
Enchantment. Cawein.
English Wood, An. Graves.
Font in the Forest, The. Adams.
Forest. Blackwell.
Forest Hymn, A. Bryant.
Gift of Sight. Graves.
Green Roads, The. Thomas.
In a Maple Wood. Schneider.
In a Wood. Hardy.
In November. Lampman.
In the forest, in unexplored. *Fr.* Geography. Dransfield.
In the Redwood Forest. Pomeroy.
In the Woods. Scott.
In Winter in the Woods Alone. Frost.
Inscription for the Entrance to a Wood. Bryant.
Lament for the Woodlands. *Unknown.*
Lost. Wagoner.
November in Ettrick Forest. *Fr.* Marmion. Scott.
O Sweet Woods. *Fr.* Arcadia. Sidney.
On Wenlock Edge the Wood's in Trouble. Housman.
Out of the Earth. Davies.
Piney Woods. Cowley.
Quilled Quilt, a Needle Bed, A. Leithauser.
Sancta Silvarum. Johnson.
Sitting in the Woods: A Contemplation. Moses.
Solitary Woodsman, The. Roberts.
Solitude. Lampman.
Solitude. Savage.
Solitude Late at Night in the Woods. Bly.
Song of the Forest Ranger, The. Bashford.
Sonnet Made upon the Groves near Merlou Castle. Herbert of Cherbury.
Staying Alive. Wagoner.
Stopping by Woods on a Snowy Evening. Frost.
There's a Fire in the Forest. Ross.
Third Song. *Fr.* Polyolbion. Drayton.
Waldeinsamkeit. Emerson.
Walk, The. Ross.
Way through the Woods, The. Kipling.
We flee away from cities, but we bring. *Fr.* The Adirondacs. Emerson.
When in the Woods I Wander All Alone. Hovell-Thurlow.
Woodland Worship. Wetherald.
Woodlands, The. Barnes.
Woodlands. Read.
Woodnotes, I. Emerson.
Woods. Auden.
Woods and Kestrel. Bell.

Forgetfulness
Keeper, The. Carpenter.
Lethe. Doolittle ("H. D.").

Forgiveness
Brazen Tongue. Benét.
Forgiveness. Whittier.
Hymn to God the Father, A. Donne.
Love ("Love bade me welcome; yet my soul drew back"). Herbert.
Outwitted. Markham.
Ten Years and More. Waddington.
'Tis true—they shut me in the cold. Dickinson.

Forks
Fork. Simic.

Forsythia
Aspects of Some Forsythia Branches. Gustafson.
Forsythia Is the Color I Remember. Cherwinski.

Fort Laramie Trail
Laramie Trail. Hanson.

Fortitude
Don't Quit. *Unknown.*
Granma's Words. Palmanteer.
If. Kipling.
Nevertheless. Moore.
Solitude. Wilcox.
Winners, The. *Fr.* The Story of the Gadsbys. Kipling.
Worth While. Wilcox.

Fortune
Author, of His Own Fortune, The. Harington.
Doth Then the World Go Thus, Doth All Thus Move? Drummond of Hawthornden.
Fame and Fortune. *Fr.* The Legend of Robert, Duke of Normandy. Drayton.
Fate. Spalding.
Flowers of the Forest, The. Rutherford.
Fortune. *Fr.* Old Fortunatus. Dekker.
Fortune ("Lady Fortune is both friend and foe, The.") *Unknown.*
Fortune. Wyatt.
Fortune's Treachery. Halevi.
Good Fortune. Heine.
Hap. Hardy.
Hughie at the Inn. Wylie.

Indifference to Fortune. *Fr.* The Castle of Indolence. Thomson.
Lady Fortune, The. *Unknown.*
My Stars. Ibn Ezra.
Now the golden Morn aloft. *Fr.* Ode on the Pleasure Arising from Vicissitude. Gray.
Of Fortune. *Fr.* Cornelia. Kyd.
Rattlesnake Band, The. Conley.
Thomas More to Them That Seek Fortune. More.
To a Mouse on Turning Her Up in Her Nest with the Plough, November 1785. Burns.
To Fortune. More.
To Fortune. Thomson.
When All This All. *Fr.* Caelica. Greville.
See also **Fate; Luck.**

Fortunetellers
All Your Fortunes We Can Tell Ye. Jonson.
Crepe de Chine. Williams.
Fortune-Teller, A. Bynner.
Spaewife, The. Stevenson.

Fossils
Autograph, An. Lowell.
Fossil. Blodgett.
Fossils. Stewart.
Peking Man, Raining. Lorr.
Petrified Fern, The. Branch.

Fotheringay, England
At Fotheringay. Southwell.

Found Poetry (genre)
Some Modern Good Turns. Dibben.

Fountains
Baroque Wall-Fountain in the Villa Sciarra, A. Wilbur.
Drinking Fountain. Chute.
Fountain, The. Davie.
Fountain. Jennings.
Fountain, The. Liasides.
Fountain, The. Lowell.
Fountain, The. Wordsworth.
Fountains, The. Rodgers.
Fountains. Sitwell.
From Rome, for More Public Fountains in New York City. Dugan.
Great Fountains, The. Hébert.
Inscription for a Fountain. "Cornwall."
Nichols Fountain. Miner.
Roman Fountain. Bogan.
Venus of Bolsover Castle, The. Sitwell.

Fourth of July
Brownies' Celebration, The. Cox.
Chippewa Lake Park. Woessner.
Choice. Farrar.
Everyman true to himself as Whitman—and that goes. *Fr.* Brother Jonathan, Brother Kafka. O'Sullivan.
Fatherland, The. Lowell.
Fourth of July. Chute.
Fourth of July. Field.
Fourth of July, The. Pierpont.
Fourth of July Night. Aldis.
Fourth of July Song. Lenski.
Grandfather Watts's Private Fourth. Bunner.
Independence Bell—July 4, 1776. *Unknown.*
Independence Day. Berry.
I've Got a Rocket. *Unknown.*
July 4th. Swenson.
Long as thine Art shall love true love. *Fr.* The Centennial Meditation of Columbia. Lanier.
Red White & Another Ism. Otey.
This is Independence Day. *Fr.* Listen to the People: Independence Day, 1941. Benét.

Fox, Charles James
Lines Composed at Grasmere. Wordsworth.
Nelson, Pitt, Fox. *Fr.* Marmion. Scott.

Foxes
Abnegation. Rich.
Ballad of Red Fox, The. La Follette.
Bold Reynard the Fox. *Unknown.*
False Fox, The. *Unknown.*
Field Trip. Miranda.
Four Little Foxes. Sarett.
Fox, The. Clare.
Fox, The. Day Lewis.
Fox. *Fr.* A Bestiary. Rexroth.
Fox, The. Scheuer.
Fox, The. *Unknown.*
Fox and the Crow, The. La Fontaine.
Fox and the Goose, The. *Unknown.*
Fox and the Grapes, The. La Fontaine.
Fox and the Wolf, The. *Unknown.*
Fox at the Point of Death, The. *Fr.* Fables. Gay.
Fox jumped up one winter's night, A. *Unknown.*
Fox knew well, that before they tore him, The. *Fr.* Reynard the Fox. Masefield.
Fox Went Out One Frosty Night, The. *Unknown.*
Gone. Thompson.
Hunt, The. De la Mare.
Kilruddery Hunt, The. Mozeen.
Listening to Foxhounds. Dickey.
Little Fox, The. Edey *and* Grider.
Night of Wind. Frost.
On old Cold Crendon's windy tops. *Fr.* Reynard the Fox: The Fox Awakes. Masefield.
Owl and the Fox, The. *Unknown.*
Sycophantic Fox and the Gullible Raven, The. Carryl.
Thought-Fox, The. Hughes.
Three Foxes, The. Milne.
Vixen, The. Clare.

Foxgloves
Four and Eight. Wolfe.

France
American to France, An. Miller.
Calais, August 15, 1802. Wordsworth.
England. Moore.
Evil. Rimbaud.
Four Sheets to the Wind and a One-Way Ticket to France. Rivers.
France. *Fr.* The Traveller. Goldsmith.
Grasse: The Olive Trees. Wilbur.
In France. Cornford.
Journey into France, The. *Unknown.*
Kings of France. Lincoln.
Provincia Deserta. Pound.
Rioupéroux. Flecker.
Rouen. Cannan.
Scenes from Carnac. Arnold.
Summer Day, A. *Fr.* Of the Day Estivall. Hume.
St. Aubin d'Aubigné. Dehn.
To France. Chaplin.
Trees on the Calais Road. Blunden.

Francesca, Piero della
See **Piero della Francesca.**

Francesca da Rimini
Ready she sat with one hand to turn o'er. *Fr.* The Story of Rimini. Hunt.

Francis of Assisi, Saint
Blessing of St. Francis, The. Maura.
In Assisi. Blumenthal.
Little Litany to St. Francis, A. Murray.
Love. Graham.
Old Man in the Park. Osborn.
Saint Francis. Bishop.
Saint Francis and the Birds. McFadden.
Saint Francis and the Sow. Kinnell.
St. Francis of Assisi and the Miserable Jews. Wittlin.

Franck, César
At the Symphony. Nathan.
César Franck. Auslander.
During a Chorale by César Franck. Bynner.

Franco, Francisco
Eisenhower's Visit to Franco, 1959. Wright.

Franco-Prussian War
In Time of "The Breaking of Nations." Hardy.
Poster of Our Dazzling Victory at Saarbrucken, A. *Fr.* Eighteen-Seventy. Rimbaud.

Frank, Anne
Day for Anne Frank, A. Williams.
Return to Prinsengracht. Blue-Swartz.

Frankenstein
Bride of Frankenstein, The. Field.
Frankenstein. Field.
Help Is On the Way. Scott.

Frankenthaler, Helen
To Helen Frankenthaler. Cherner.

Franklin, Aretha
Poem for Aretha. Giovanni.

Franklin, Benjamin
Benjamin Franklin. Benét.
On the Death of Benjamin Franklin. Freneau.

Franklin, Sir John
Ballad of Sir John Franklin, A. Boker.
Lady Franklin's Lament. *Unknown.*
Fraternity. *See* **Brotherhood.**
Frederick Augustus, Duke of York
On Prince Frederick. *Unknown.*
Frederick Louis, Prince of Wales
On Prince Frederick. *Unknown.*
Free Will
Free Will. Clark.
Invictus. Henley.
Road Not Taken, The. Frost.
Freedom
Ante-Bellum Sermon, An. Dunbar.
Antiquity of Freedom, The. Bryant.
Assembly: Harlem School. Maleska.
At the Zoo. Zangwill.
Battle-Hymn of the Republic. Howe.
Brave New World. MacLeish.
Country Justice, The. Langhorne.
Dame Liberty Reports from Travel. Pinkney.
Dark Testament. Murray.
Dreaming about Freedom. Baca.
Dublin Ballad, A :1916. "O'Byrne."
Eagles and Isles. Gibson.
Frederick Douglass. Hayden.
Free Nation, A. Markham.
Freedom. *Fr.* The Bruce. Barbour.
Freedom. Hughes.
Freedom Is a Constant Struggle. *Unknown.*
Freedom of the Hills. Fraser.
Harp That Once through Tara's Halls, The. Moore.
I Did but Prompt the Age. Milton.
I Thank God I'm Free at Las'. *Unknown.*
In Exile. Lazarus.
It is not to be thought of that the flood. Wordsworth.
Landscape with Lapwings. Aitchison.
Letter from Italy, to the Right Honourable Charles Lord Halifax, A. Addison.
Liberty. Hay.
Liberty. MacLeish.
Midway. Madgett.
No More Beneath the Oppressive Hand. *Unknown.*
Notes for My Son. Comfort.
Ode: "God save the Rights of Man!" Freneau.
Of the Child with the Bird on the Bush. Bunyan.
Prayers to Liberty. Shaul.
Present Crisis, The. Lowell.
Proem: "I love the old melodious lays." Whittier.
Runagate Runagate. Hayden.
Shine, Republic. Jeffers.
Silkworms, The. Stewart.
Slaves. Lowell.
Song of the Settlers. West.
Sonnet on Chillon. *Fr.* The Prisoner of Chillon. Byron.
Stanzas: When a Man Hath No Freedom to Fight for at Home. Byron.
Stanzas: "When a man hath no freedom to fight for at home." Byron.
They shut me up in prose. Dickinson.
To Althea, from Prison. Lovelace.
To My Father. Ray.
Tree. Otey.
Trumpet of Liberty, The. Taylor.
Twilight of Freedom. Mandelstam.
We Must Be Free or Die. Wordsworth.
When a Man Hath No Freedom to Fight for at Home. Byron.
Whose freedom is by suff'rance, and at will. *Fr.* The Winter Morning Walk. Cowper.
Woke up this Morning with My Mind on Freedom. *Unknown.*
Words Like Freedom. Hughes.
You Ask Me, Why, though Ill at Ease. Tennyson.
Freemasonry
Level and the Square, The. Morris.
Lodge Room Over Simpkins' Store, The. Greenleaf.
Freezers
Hiding Place. Armour.
Freighters
Freight Boats. Tippett.
See also **Cargoes.**
Frémont, John Charles
On Recrossing the Rocky Mountains After Many Years. Frémont.
To John C. Frémont. Whittier.
French, The
Bonne Entente. Scott.
French Cookery. *Fr.* The Fudge Family in Paris. Moore.
French, The, 1870–1871. *Unknown.*
Letter to Wilbur Frohock, A. Hoffman.
Ode: Salute to the French Negro Poets. O'Hara.
To Henrietta, on her Departure for Calais. Hood.
To the French of the Second Empire. Rimbaud.
French Revolution
France: An Ode. Coleridge.
French Revolution, The. *Fr.* The Prelude. Wordsworth.
La Tricoteuse. Thornbury.
Noise of trampling, the wind of trumpets, The. *Fr.* The French Revolution. Blake.
Ode: "God save the Rights of Man!" Freneau.
Freud, Sigmund
Doctor Freud. Lazar.
Freud: Dying in London, He Recalls the Smoke of His Cigar Beginning to Sing. Schevill.
In Memory of Sigmund Freud. Auden.
Sigmund Freud. Nemerov.
Song: "Don't Tell Me What You Dreamt Last Night." Adams.
Wayman in Love. Wayman.
Friars
Against Friars. *Unknown.*
Against the Friars. *Unknown.*
Friar Complains, A. *Unknown.*
Friar of Orders Gray, The. O'Keefe.
Friar of Orders Gray, The. Percy.
Friars' Enormities. *Unknown.*
Friar's Retort, The. *Unknown.*
Friends, Society of
On Barclay's Apology for the Quakers. Green.
Quaker Widow, The. Taylor.
Friendship
After the Quarrel. Dunbar.
Alas! they had been friends in youth. *Fr.* Christabel. Coleridge.
Around the Corner. Towne.
Arrow and the Song, The. Longfellow.
As toilsome I wandered Virginia's woods. Whitman.
Auld Lang Syne. Burns.
Best Friends. Hemschemeyer.
Best Treasure, The. Moment.
Broken Friendship. Coleridge.
Burden, The. Pereira.
Comrades. McGlennon.
Expect no thanks from anyone. Catullus.
Faithful Friend, The. Cowper.
Fame and Friendship. Dobson.
Fellowship. *Unknown.*
Female Friend, The. Whur.
Four Years Were Mine at Princeton. Bishop.
Friend. Brooks.
Friend, A. De Carrion.
Friend, The. Piercy.
Friend, A. Power.
Friend or Two, A. Nesbit.
Friend Who Just Stands By, The. Williams.
Friend Who Never Came. Stafford.
Friends. Durem.
Friends. Goose.
Friends. Stafford.
Friends Come. Clifton.
Friend's Greeting, A. Guest.
Friendship. Coleridge.
Friendship. Craik.
Friendship. Silverstein.
Friendship Game, The. DiCicco.
Friendship in Perfection. Ramsay.
Friendship Is Love Without His Wings. Byron.
Friendship's Mystery; to My Dearest Lucasia. Philips.
Gone. Coleridge.
Grasshopper, The. Lovelace.
He Was a Friend of Mine. *Unknown.*
House by the Side of the Road, The. Foss.
How to Murder Your Best Friend. O Hehir.
I Have a Friend. Spencer.
"I Hear It Said." Young.
I Met This Guy Who Died. Corso.
I Saw in Louisiana a Live-Oak Growing. Whitman.
I Tell of Another Young Death. Tiempo.
If You Have a Friend. *Unknown.*

Interlude. Smith.
I've Gone and Stained with the Color of Love. Acorn.
La Belle Confidente. Stanley.
Letter to a Friend. Thomspson.
Letter to a Jealous Friend. Simmons.
Losing Track. Song.
Love Is Like the Wild Rose-Briar. Brontë.
Loyalty. Braley.
Lux, My Fair Falcon. Wyatt.
Make Friends. Ali Ben Abu Taleb.
Matrix III. Lipman.
Mile with Me, A. Van Dyke.
Modes of the Court, The. *Fr.* The Beggar's Opera. Gay.
Money and a Friend. *Unknown.*
My Familiar. Saxe.
My Gal Sal. Dresser.
My Ramblin' Boy. Paxton.
New Friends and Old Friends. Parry.
O tan-faced prairie-boy. Whitman.
Of Money. Googe.
Of Perfect Friendship. Cheke.
Old Familiar Faces, The. Lamb.
Old-long Syne. *Unknown.*
On Friendship. Whitehead.
On Parting with Moses Ibn Ezra. Halevi.
Poem: "I loved my friend." Hughes.
Reflection: After Visiting Old Friends. Allison.
Remembrance. Shakespeare.
Sonnet: To a Friend. Coleridge.
Sweet Loving Friendship. Bellamy.
They Say That in the Unchanging Place. *Fr.* Dedicatory Ode. Belloc.
Three Friends. *Unknown.*
Time to Talk, A. Frost.
To a Distant Friend. Wordsworth.
To a Friend. Coleridge.
To a Friend. Dawson.
To a Friend. Gullans.
To a Friend. Lowell.
To H. Blake.
To My Excellent Lucasia, on Our Friendship. Philips.
To My Friend. Thompson.
To Phylocles, Inviting Him to Friendship. Philips.
Verses Occasioned by the Death of Dr. Aikman. Thomson.
Verses Written in 1872. Stevenson.
When to the sessions of sweet silent thought. *Fr.* Sonnets. Shakespeare.
With Schoolchildren. Barnstone.
Without My Friends the Day Is Dark. Ibn Ezra.
Written in the Album of a Child. Wordsworth.
Home Book of Verse, The (HBV2), vol. II, pp. 2999–3016. Burton Egbert Stevenson, ed.
Frietchie, Barbara
Barbara Frietchie. Whittier.
Frisbees
Frisbee. Humphries.
Frith, John
From William Tyndale to John Frith. Bowers.
Frog Prince, The
Disenchantments: An Anthology of Modern Fairy Tale Poetry (DFT), pp. 23–41. Wolfgang Mieder, ed.
Frogs
Aesop's Fable of the Frogs. La Fontaine.
Amphibian. Clampitt.
Ascend my shoulders, firmly keep thy seat. *Fr.* The Battle of the Frogs and Mice. *Unknown.*
Between Leaps. Leithauser.
Bullfrog. Hughes.
Bullfrogs. Evans.
Cheers. Merriam.
Death of a Naturalist. Heaney.
Early Frogs, The. Mills.
First Song. Kinnell.
Frog, The. Belloc
Frog, The. *Unknown.*
Frog and the Crow, The. *Unknown.*
Frog and the Golden Ball, The. Graves.
Frog Hunting. Cooley.
Frog Prince, The. Smith.
Froggie Went A-Courtin'. *Unknown.*
Frogs. MacCaig.
Frogs. Simpson.
Frogs' Singing-School, The. Carbell.
Grandfather Frog. Bechtel.
Green Frog at Roadstead, Wisconsin. Schevill.
Haiku: "No need to cling." Joso.
His mansion in the pool. Dickinson.
Marriage of the Frog and the Mouse, The. *Unknown.*
Padda Song, The. *Unknown.*
Peepers in Our Meadow, The. MacLeish.
Rebels from Fairy Tales. Hill.
Small Frogs Killed on the Highway. Wright.
Speckle-black Toad and freckle-green Frog. *Fr.* Thomas à Becket, a Dramatic Chronicle. Darley.
Tin Frog, The. Hoban.
Tree Frog, The. Moore.
Wooing Frog, The. Reeves.
Frontiers
Lay of the Last Frontier. Hersey.
Frontiersmen
Old Scout's Lament, The. Drannan.
Shooting of the Cup, The. *Fr.* The Song of Three Friends. Neihardt.
Stationed Scout, The. Sproull.
Texas Types "The Bad Man." Chittenden.
Tough Cuss From Bitter Creek, A. Adams.
Frost, Robert
For Robert Frost. Kinnell.
Letter to Robert Frost, A. Hillyer.
On the Porch at the Frost Place, Franconia, NH. Matthews.
Robert Frost. Lowell.
Three around the Old Gentleman. Berryman.
"Yes, But. . ." Weiss.
Frost
Apparently with no surprise. Dickinson.
Because I Could Not Dump. Paterson.
Cold Snap. Mangan.
Devonshire Rhyme, A. *Unknown.*
Fairy Artist, The. Garabrant.
First Frost. Curran.
Frost. Davies.
Frost, The. Gould.
Frost. Johnston.
Frost. Pratt.
Frost. Thomas.
Frost at Midnight. Coleridge.
Frost Spirit, The. Whittier.
Frost Warning. McFarland.
Frosted Pane, The. Roberts.
Hard Frost. Young.
Jack Frost. Davis.
Jack Frost. "Setoun."
Jack Frost. Thaxter.
Little Jack Frost. *Unknown.*
Sudden Frost. Wagoner.
Fruit
Full, ripe apple, pear and banana. *Fr.* Sonnets to Orpheus. Rilke.
Goblin Market. Rossetti.
Nevertheless. Moore.
This Is Just to Say. Williams.
Tropics in New York, The. McKay.
Fry, Elizabeth
Friendly Address, A. Hood.
Fuchsia
Fuchsia Hedges in Connacht. Colum.
Fuller, Margaret
Margaret Fuller. Alcott.
On the Death of M. d'Ossoli and His Wife, Margaret Fuller. Landor.
Fulton, Robert
Robert Fulton. Stanford.
Fun
Frolic. "Æ."
Ring-a-Ring. Greenaway.
See also **Play; Pleasure.**
Fundy, Bay of
Arnold, Master of the *Scud.* Carman.
Biftek aux Champignons. Beers.
Funerals
After the Funeral. Graves.
After the Funeral. Thomas.
At a Low Mass for Two Hot-Rodders. Kennedy.
At the Funeral of Great-Aunt Mary. Bly.
Aunt Gladys's Home Movie No. 31, Albert's Funeral. Miller.
Aunt Laura Moves toward the Open Grave of Her Father. De Roche.
Bells for John Whiteside's Daughter. Ransom.
Blouzelinda's Funeral. *Fr.* The Shepherd's Week. Gay.
Bredon Hill. Housman.

Brown Girl Dead, A. Cullen.
Burial. Grigson.
Burial. Walker.
Burial of a Fisherman in Hydra. Schulman.
Burial of Sir John Moore, The. Wolfe.
Choirmaster's Burial, The. Hardy.
Corpse-Bearing. Ashe.
Country Doctor, The. Carleton.
Dead of Winter. Towne.
Deadman's Dirge. *Fr.* Syren Songs. Darley.
Dirge for McPherson, A. Melville.
Dirge without Music. Millay.
Do Nothing till You Hear from Me. Henderson.
Está muy caliente. Bowering.
Finnegan's Wake. *Unknown.*
First Death. Justice.
Funeral, The. De la Mare.
Funeral, The. Donne.
Funeral, The. Dubie.
Funeral at Ansley. Welch.
Funeral Parlor, The. Johnson.
Funeral Pyre, The. *Fr.* Beowulf. *Unknown.*
Funeral Song. *Fr.* The Two Noble Kinsmen. Fletcher.
Ganges, The. Dubie.
How I'd Have It. Stone.
Italian Extravaganza. Corso.
Lenore. Poe.
Lovers, The. Aiken.
My Father's Funeral. Shapiro.
My Grandfather's Funeral. Applewhite.
Night Funeral in Harlem. Hughes.
Obituary. Adeler.
Pauper's Funeral, The. *Fr.* The Village. Crabbe.
Queen's Last Ride, The. Wilcox.
Question, A. Synge.
Sea-Ritual, The. *Fr.* Syren Songs. Darley.
She: At His Funeral. Hardy.
She Plans Her Funeral. Bowman.
Tract. Williams.
Traveler, The. Bottoms.
Upon a Funeral. Beaumont.
Visiting the Dead. Carson.

Furnaces
Drunk in the Furnace, The. Merwin.

Furniture
Address to His Elbow-Chair, New Cloath'd, An. Somervile.
Inventory of the Furniture of a Collegian's Chamber, An. Winstanley.

Fuseli, Henry
Only Man that e'er I knew, The. Blake.

G

Gabriel
Crusader, The. Parker.
Then When I Am Thy Captive, Talk of Chains. *Fr.* Paradise Lost. Milton.

Galahad, Sir
Sir Galahad. Tennyson.

Galatea
Galatea Again. Taggard.
Galatea and Pygmalion. Graves.
Question, A. Livingston.

Galilee, Palestine
In Galilee. Butts.

Galileo
Galileo Galilei. Smith.

Galley Slaves
Galley-Slave, The. Kipling.
Press-Gang, The. *Unknown.*
Song of the Galley-Slaves. Kipling.

Gallipoli Campaign (1915)
War Story. Stallworthy.

Galloway, Scotland
Galloway Shore, The. Tremayne.
Grey Galloway. Cairncross.
In Galloway. Greig.

Gallows
Tyburn and Westminster. Heywood.
See also **Hanging.**

Galoshes
Galoshes. Bacmeister.
Upon Julia's Arctics. Taylor.

Galuppi, Baldassaro
Toccata of Galuppi's, A. Browning.

Galveston, Texas
On Galveston Beach. Howes.
Sailor's Song, A. Harris.

Galway. *See* **County Galway, Ireland.**

Gambling and Gamblers
Camptown Races. Foster.
Crapshooters. Sandburg.
Deathbed, A. *Fr.* The Journey and Observations of a Countryman. Hawthorn.
Gambler, The. *Unknown.*
Gambler's Repentance, The. Gerald, Baron of Offaly.
Gambling. Tyler.
Gamesters All. Heyward.
Great Wager, The. Studdert-Kennedy.
"Gwine to Run All Night; or, De Camptown Races." Foster.
Heathen Chinee, The. Harte.
John Hardy. *Unknown.*
Keno. Wier.
Man Who Broke the Bank at Monte Carlo, The. Gilbert.
Man Who Invented Las Vegas, The. Costanzo.
Nickle Bet, A. Knight.
O, Gambler, Git Up off o' Yo' Knees. *Unknown.*
Off from Swing Shift. Hongo.
On a Distant Prospect of an Absconding Bookmaker. Hamilton.
On the Cards and Dice. Ralegh.
One Time Henry Dreamed the Number. Long.
Placing a $2 Bet for a Man Who Will Never Go to the Horse Races Any More. Wakoski.
Plain Language from Truthful James. Harte.
Rambling, Gambling Man. Houston.
Root Hog or Die. *Unknown.*
Roving Gambler Blues. *Unknown.*
Wednesbury Cocking. *Unknown.*

Games
Billiards. Blauner.
Dunmow Flitch of Bacon, The. *Unknown.*
Game of Consequences, A. Dehn.
Lost Ball, The. Mitchell.
Old Men Pitching Horseshoes. Kennedy.
See also **Card Games; Sports.**

Gandhi, Mohandas Karamchand
In India. Shapiro.
Vaticide. O'Higgins.

Ganges River, India
Ganges, The. Dubie.

Gangs
Black Jackets. Gunn.
Blackstone Rangers, The. Brooks.
Dogchain Gang, The. Rice.

Gangsters
Morning They Shot Tony Lopez, Barber and Pusher Who Went Too Far, 1958, The. Soto.

Gannets
Long-billed Gannets. Emery.
See also **Boobies.**

Ganymede
Ganymede. Plomer.
Ganymede and Helen. *Unknown.*
Jupiter and Ganimede. Heywood.

Garbage and Garbage Men
Man on the Dump, The. Nemerov.
Sarah Cynthia Sylvia Stout Would Not Take the Garbage Out. Silverstein.
Town Dump, The. Nemerov.
Trash Men, The. Bukowski.

García Lorca, Federico
Federico. Guillén.
García Lorca. Dudek.
García Lorca Murdered in Granada. Manifold.
In Memory of García Lorca. Grier.
Poem for Garcia Lorca. Woodcock.

Garda, Lake, Italy
Frater Ave Atque Vale. Tennyson.
There Is a Pool on Garda. Scollard.

Gardens and Gardening
Autumn Garden, An. Carman.
Benedictine Garden, A. Brown.
Broken-Hearted Gardener, The. *Unknown.*

Butterbean Tent, The. Roberts.
Center of the Garden, The. Stanford.
Charleston Garden, A. Bellamann.
Child's Song. Moore.
Come ride and ride to the garden. Gregory.
Contrary Mary. Turner.
Deserted Garden, The. Stanford.
Elegy while Pruning Roses. Wagoner.
Falling Asleep in a Garden. Wagoner.
Fern House at Kew. Dehn.
Flowers. Behn.
For Jim, Easter Eve. Spencer.
Forsaken Garden, A. Swinburne.
Garden, The. Giltinan.
Garden, The. Grimald.
Garden, The. Marvell.
Garden, The. Shirley.
Garden, The. Strand.
Garden, The. Warren.
Garden by Moonlight, The. Lowell.
Garden Fancies. Browning.
Garden in September, The. Bridges.
Garden Lore. Ewing.
Garden Song, A. Dobson.
Garden Song, A. Moore.
Gardener, The. Stevenson.
Gardener, The. Symons.
Gardener to His God, The. Van Duyn.
Gardeners. Ignatow.
Gardens Are All My Heart. Triem.
Glory of the Garden, The. Kipling.
Grace for Gardens. Driscoll.
How to Build a Ha-ha. *Fr.* The English Garden. Mason.
In a Garden. Jennings.
In Green Old Gardens. Fane.
In the Garden. Crosby.
Indolent Gardener, The. Kennedy.
Just after Noon with Fierce Shears. Combs.
Lawn-Mower. Baruch.
Le Jardin. Wilde.
Long Garden, The. Kavanagh.
Lord God Planted a Garden, The. Gurney.
Lost Garden. "Hale."
May Garden. Drinkwater.
Midways of a Walled Garden. *Fr.* Golden Wings. Morris.
Mower against Gardens, The. Marvell.
Mr. Bidery's Spidery Garden. McCord.
Mummies, The. Kumin.
My Garden. Brown.
My Garden. Davies.
My Garden. Lindon.
My Garden Is a Pleasant Place. Driscoll.
My Mother's Garden. Allen.
Old Quin Queeribus. Turner.
Perfect Garden, The. Robertson.
Pruning. *Fr.* Cyder. Philips.
Public Garden, The. Lowell.
Pulling Weeds. Chock.
Roof Garden, The. Moss.
Seeds of Love, The. *Unknown.*
Spring Arithmetic. *Unknown.*
Summer Garden. Akhmatova.
Sunken Garden, The. De la Mare.
Their Lonely Betters. Auden.
Time and the Garden. Winters.
Two Gardens. De Bevoise.
Whatever It Was I Was Saving for My Old Age. Darr.
Who Loves a Garden. Jones.
Widow's Weeds, A. de la Mare.

Garfield, James Abram
At the President's Grave. Gilder.
Bells at Midnight, The. Aldrich.
Charles Guiteau. *Unknown.*
On the Death of President Garfield. Holmes.
President Garfield. Longfellow.

Garfield, John
John Garfield. Christopher.

Gargoyles
527 Cathedral Parkway. Lesser.

Garibaldi, Giuseppe
In Front of a Poster of Garibaldi. Moss.

Garlic
Garlic, The. Meyers.
Garlic. Richardson.
To Maecenas. Horace.

Garrick, David
Retaliation. Goldsmith.

Garrison, William Lloyd
Garrison. Alcott.
To W.L.G. on Reading His "Chosen Queen." Forten.
To William Lloyd Garrison. Whittier.

Gaslight
Ode on Gas, An. *Unknown.*

Gasoline Stations
Filling Station. Bishop.
Hottest Brand Goin'. *Unknown.*
Working at a Service Station, I Think of Shinkichi Takahashi. Finnell.

Gates
Gates. Madeleva.
Nemo Canem Impune Lacessit. Garioch.

Gauguin, Paul
At Pont-Aven, Gauguin's Last Home in France. Grossbardt.
Two Women with Mangoes. Cramer.
Vor a Gauguin Picture zu Singen. Stein.

Gautier, Théophile
Sonnet: "This is the golden book of spirit and sense." Swinburne.

Gaveston, Piers
This Edward in the Aprill of his age. *Fr.* Piers Gaveston. Drayton.

Gawaine, Sir
Sir Gawaine and the Green Knight. Winters.

Gay, John
On Mr. Gay; in Westminster Abbey, 1732. Pope.

Gazelles
Gazelle Calf, The. Lawrence.
Gazelles, The. Moore.

Geese
Aunt Rhody. *Unknown.*
Barnacle Geese. Higham.
Cackle, cackle, Mother Goose. *Unknown.*
Flight of the Geese, The. *Fr.* Songs of the Common Day. Roberts.
Fox and the Goose, The. *Unknown.*
Fox jumped up one winter's night, A. *Unknown.*
Gaggle of Geese, Pride of Lions, A. Moore.
Geese, The. Plutzik.
Gray Goose, The. *Unknown.*
He comes, the pest and terror of the yard. *Fr.* The Farmer's Boy: Summer. Bloomfield.
Late at Night. Stafford.
Night Flight. Whalley.
Old Grey Goose, The. *Unknown.*
Some Geese. Herford.
Something Told the Wild Geese. Field.
Swan and the Goose, The. Aesop.
Three grey geese in a green field grazing. *Unknown.*
To a Goose. Southey.
Wild Geese. Chipp.
Wild Geese. Hart-Smith.
Wild Geese. Peterson.
Wild geese returning, The. Kunimoto.

Gems
Emerald is as green as grass, An. Rossetti.
Mine Argosy from Alexandria. *Fr.* The Jew of Malta. Marlowe.
Stone Diary, A. Lowther.

Generals
Bold General Wolfe. *Unknown.*
General, The. Sassoon.
His Excellency General Washington. Wheatley.

Generosity
Generosity. *Unknown.*

Genetic Engineering
DNA Lab. Spence.
Progression of the Species. Aldiss.

Genetics
Mendel's Law. Meinke.
Neural Folds. Day.
Question, The. Auden.
See also **Evolution.**

Geneva, Switzerland
Geneva. Reid.

Genius
Ben Jonson Entertains a Man from Stratford. Robinson.
Mortified Genius, The. Graeme.

Gentians
Bavarian Gentians. Lawrence.
Fringed Gentians. Lowell.
Gentian. Crane.
God made a little gentian. Dickinson.
To the Fringed Gentian. Bryant.
Gentry
Birth of the Squire, The; an Eclogue. Gay.
Geography and Geographers
Art of Biography, The. Bentley.
Geographers. *Fr.* The Ship of Fools. Brant.
Geography. Farjeon.
Geography. *Fr.* Songs of Education. Chesterton.
Geology
Brevard Fault. Morgan.
Goodnight. Ciardi.
Lyell's Hypothesis Again. Rexroth.
Minerals of Cornwall, Stones of Cornwall. Redgrove.
Pre-Cambrian Shield, The. *Fr.* Towards the Last Spike. Pratt.
What Happened Here Before. Snyder.
Geometry
Plane Geometry. Rounds.
This is now—this was erst. Coleridge.
George, Saint
Carol of St. George, A. *Unknown.*
See also **Euclid.**
George I, King of England
Epigram: "King George, observing with judicious eyes." Trapp.
Epigram: "King to Oxford sent a troop of horse, The." Browne.
Pasquin to the Queen's Statue at St. Paul's. Shippen.
George II, King of England
God Save the King. *Unknown.*
Lilliputian Ode on Their Majesties' Accession, A. Carey.
What mean these loud aerial cracks I hear? *Fr.* Bedlam; a Poem on His Majesty's Happy Escape from His German Dominions. *Unknown.*
George III, King of England
Absolvers, The. *Fr.* A Vision of Judgment. Southey.
England in 1819. Shelley.
George the Third. Bentley.
George the Third. *Fr.* The Vision of Judgment. Byron.
George III Visits Whitbread's Brewery. *Fr.* Instructions to a Celebrated Laureat. "Pindar."
Royal Tour, The. "Pindar."
Saint Peter sat by the celestial gate. *Fr.* The Vision of Judgment. Byron.
George IV, King of England
Epitaph on the Late King of the Sandwich Isles. Praed.
George the Fourth in Ireland. Byron.
George VI, King of England
Praises of King George VI. Ngani.
Georgia
Coasting toward Midnight at the Southeastern Fair. Bottoms.
Coon Hunt, Sixth Month (1955). Lea
Daufuskie. Evans.
Faith Healer Come to Rabun County. Bottoms.
Georgia Dusk. Toomer.
Georgia Towns. Hicky.
In a U-Haul North of Damascus. Bottoms.
In the Marble Quarry. Dickey.
Litany of Atlanta, A. DuBois.
Marching through Georgia. Work.
Nocturne: Georgia Coast. Hicky.
Refugee. Madgett.
Robert Whitmore. Davis.
Roll Call: A Land of Old Folk and Children. Black.
Song of the Chattahoochee. Lanier.
Stumptown Attends the Picture Show. Bottoms.
Talking to the Townsfolk in Ideal, Georgia. Black.
Writing on Napkins at the Sunshine Club, Macon, Georgia, 1971. Bottoms.
Geraniums
Geranium, The. Roethke.
Red Geranium and Godly Mignonette. Lawrence.
Red Geraniums. Clark.
Germans, The
"No Quarrel." Herbert.
Germany
Bingen on the Rhine. Norton.
German Fatherland, The. Arndt.
High Germany. Shanks.
No Offence. Enright.
Nuremberg. Longfellow.
On a German Tour. Porson.
Song of the Cape of Good Hope. Schubart.
To Germany. Sorley.
Walk in Würzburg, A. Plomer.
Weavers. Heine.
Wreathmakertraining. Patten.
Germs
Germ, The. Nash.
Some Little Bug. Atwell.
See also **Bacteria.**
Geronimo
Geronimo. McGaffey.
Gethsemane
Agony in the Garden, The. Hemans.
Christ's Prayer in Gethsemane. *Unknown.*
Gethsemane. Tappan
Gettysburg, Battle of (1863)
Battle of Gettysburg, The. *Fr.* John Brown's Body. Benét.
Battlefield, The. Mifflin.
Gettysburg. Roche.
Gettysburg. Stedman.
Gettysburg Ode, The, *sel.* Taylor.
High Tide at Gettysburg, The. Thompson.
John Burns of Gettysburg. Harte.
Ghana
Cornfields in Accra. Aidoo.
Ghettos
Anglosaxon Street. Birney.
Autobiographical. Klein.
Back to the Ghetto. Glatstein.
Butterfly, The. Friedmann.
Cure All, The. Lee.
Dark People. Cumbo.
Disco Chinatown. Kageyama.
Ghetto Twilight. Brody.
In the Ghetto. Sonnenschein.
Jewish Main Street. Layton.
Poor Christian Looks at the Ghetto, A. Milosz.
Ghost Dance
Indian Ghost Dance and War, The. Prather.
Ghosts
All Souls' Night. Cornford.
Alonzo the Brave and Fair Imogine. *Fr.* The Monk. Lewis.
Apparition, The. Donne.
Barbarossa. Rückert.
Chez Brébant. Durivage.
Colonel Fazackerley. Causley.
Corporal Stare. Graves.
Cruise of the *Mystery,* The. Thaxter.
Cuchulian Comforted. Yeats.
Dark House, The. *Unknown.*
Dido among the Shades. *Fr.* The Aeneid. Virgil.
Fall of J. W. Beane, The. Herford.
False Dawn. De la Mare.
Ghost, The. De la Mare.
Ghost, The. Lowell.
Ghost Boy. Van Doren.
Ghost of a Ghost, The. Leithauser.
Ghost of the Cargo Boat, The. Neruda.
Ghost Story. Thomas.
Ghosts. Behn.
Ghosts. Jennings.
Ghosts. Reid.
Grey Cock, The. *Unknown.*
Greyport Legend, A. Harte.
Haunted House, The. Hood.
Horseman, The. De la Mare.
In the Night. Roberts.
Klabauterwife's Letter. Morgenstern.
Listeners, The. De la Mare.
Little Man, The. Mearns.
Miss Bailey's Ghost. Colman.
My Spirit Will Not Haunt the Mound. Hardy.
Neighbors, The. Garrison.
Old Ghost, The. Beddoes.
Our Little Ghost. Alcott.
Palatine, The. Whittier.
Peter Grimes. *Fr.* The Borough. Crabbe.
Phantom Horsewoman, The. Hardy.
Phantom-Wooer, The. Beddoes.
Poet Haunted, The. Rose.
Poor Ghost, The. Rosetti.
Sally Simpkin's Lament. Hood.

Shadwell Stair. Owen.
Silent Hill. Snyder.
Song by Isbrand. *Fr.* Death's Jest Book. Beddoes.
Sonnet: "They say that shadowes of deceased ghosts." Sylvester.
Souls of the Slain, The. Hardy.
Southern Mansion. Bontemps.
Spooks. Crane.
Story from Another World. Petrie.
Suffolk Miracle, The. *Unknown.*
Superstitious Ghost, The. Guiterman.
Three Ghostesses. *Unknown.*
To a Shade. Yeats.
Town Ghost. Edmond.
Unfortunate Miss Bailey. *Unknown.*
Unhinged the iron gates half open hung. *Fr.* The Haunted House. Hood.
Unquiet Grave, The. *Unknown.*
Village of Erith, The. *Unknown.*
Welsh Incident. Graves.
Whilst some affect the sun and some the shade. *Fr.* The Grave. Blair.
Why He Was There. Robinson.
Wicked Hawthorn Tree, The. Yeats.
Wife of Usher's Well, The. *Unknown.*
William and Margaret. Mallet.
Willis, The. Proudfit.
Why Am I Grown So Cold? Poems of the Unknowable (WSC), Pp. 44–56, 124–142. Myra Cohn Livingston, ed.

Giants
Bean-Stalk, The. Millay.
Being a Giant. Mezey.
Hickenthrift and Hickenloop. Kennedy.
In the Orchard. Stephens.
Sleeping Giant, The. Hall.

Gibbon, Edward
Card of Invitation to Mr. Gibbon, at Brighthelmstone, 1781. Hayley.
Distribution of Honours for Literature. Landor.
Lausanne. Hardy.
Voltaire and Gibbon. *Fr.* Childe Harold's Pilgrimage. Byron.

Gibbs, Josiah Willard
It was much later in his life he rose. *Fr.* Gibbs. Rukeyser.

Gibraltar
At Gibraltar. Woodberry.
Gibraltar. Blunt.
Gibraltar. Trench.

Gifts and Giving
Betsy Jane's Sixth Birthday. Noyes.
Birthday Gifts. Asquith.
Christmas Thank You's. Gowar.
For the Lady Olivia Porter; a Present upon a New Year's Day. Davenant.
Gift. Cohen.
Gift. Hemschemeyer.
Gift, The. Lourie.
Gifts. Snow.
His Gift and Mine. Gurley.
How Long Shall I Give? *Unknown.*
How to Give. *Unknown.*
I've Got a New Book from My Grandfather Hyde. Jackson.
Little Brother's Secret. Mansfield.
My Gift. Rossetti.
Presents. Chute.
Roman Presents. Martial.
Roman Thank-You Letter, A. Martial.

Gilbert, Sir Humphrey
First American Sailors. Rice
Sir Humphrey Gilbert. Longfellow.

Gilbert, Sir William Schwenck
" 'Everybody Works but Father" as W. S. Gilbert Would Have Written It. Burgoyne.

Gilmore, Gary
8:00 A.M. Monday Morning. Welsh.

Ginkgo Trees
Ginkgoes in Fall. Nemerov.
These Green-Going-to-Yellow. Bell.

Ginsberg, Allen
Allen Ginsberg Blesses a Bride and Groom: A Wedding Night Poem. Peters.
For Allen Ginsberg, Who Cut Off His Beard. Pinsker.
He. Ferlinghetti.
Squeal, *parody.* Simpson.

Giorgione
For "A Venetian Pastoral" by Giorgione. Rossetti.

Giotto
Giotto's Campanile. O'Hagan.
To Giotto. Trimpi.

Giraffes
Giraffe, The. Solomon.
Giraffe. *Unknown.*
Giraffes, The. Fuller.
Listen:/ There roams, far away, by the waters of Clead. *Fr.* The Giraffe. Gumileo.
Mr. Giraffe. Lapage.
On the Death of the Giraffe. Hood.
To and on Other Intellectual Poets on Reading That the U.S.A.F. Had Sent a Team of Scientists to Africa. Guthrie.

Girdles
On a Girdle. Waller.
Woman with Girdle. Sexton.

Girls
Advice to a Young Lady. Chesterfield.
Child Next Door, The. Fyleman.
Extremes. Riley.
Felicia Ropps. Burgess.
Girl's Mood, A. Reese.
In the Library. Ochester.
Little Jumping Girls, The. Greenaway.
Narcissa. Brooks.
Ode to a Country Hoyden. "Pindar."
Teen-Ager, A. Snodgrass.
See also **Adolescence; Childhood and Children; Youth.**

Glasgow, Scotland
Glasgow. Smith.
Hail Glasgow! famed for ilka thing. *Fr.* Glasgow. Mayne.

Glassblowers
Epitaph: "Glassblower lies here at rest, A." Morton.
Glass Blower, The. Scully.

Glasses. *See* **Eyeglasses.**

Glencoe, Scotland
Glencoe. Chesterton.
Glencoe. Stewart.
Rannoch, by Glencoe. Eliot.

Globes
School Globe, The. Reaney.

Gloucester, Massachusetts
Evening in Gloucester Harbor. Sargent.
Gloucester Moors. Moody.
Out from Gloucester. Trott.

Gloves
Elinda's Glove. Lovelace.
Glove, The. Bond.
Glove, The. Greig.
Glove, The. *Fr.* Cynthia's Revels. Jonson.
Sonnet: "Here, hold this glove (this milk-white cheveril glove)." Barnfield.
See also **Mittens.**

Glowworms. *See* **Fireflies.**

Gluttony and Gluttons
Eat-It-All-Elaine. Starbird.
Glutton, The. *Fr.* The Vision of Piers Plowman. Langland.
Glutton, The. Oakman.
Glutton, The. Shapiro.
Greedy Jane. *Unknown.*
Hymn to Comus. *Fr.* Pleasure Reconciled to Virtue. Jonson.
Mouse and the Cake, The. Cook.
Notorious Glutton, The. Taylor.
On Gut. Jonson.
Plum-Cake, The. Taylor.
Vulture, The. Belloc.

Glyn, Elinor
Would you like to sin. *Unknown.*

Gnats
Accidentally. Kumin.
Gnat, The. Beaumont.
Gnat on My Paper. Eberhart.
Gnat-Psalm. Hughes.

Gnomes
Gnome, The. Behn.

Gnus
Gnu, The. Belloc.
Gnu Wooing, The. Johnson.
Wildebeest, The. Daly.

Goats
All Goats. Coatsworth.
April. Winters.
Bill Groggin's Goat. *Unknown.*
Care. Murphy.
Goat, The. *Unknown.*

Goat, The. Young.
Goat Paths, The. Stephens.
I Have Got to Stop Loving You. Ai.
Mating the Goats. Barnstone.
Smile of the Goat, The. Herford.
Tracks. Torain.
Goblins
Goblin, The. Fyleman.
How to Tell Goblins from Elves. Shannon.
Little Orphant Annie. Riley.
Overheard on a Saltmarsh. Monro.
See also **Elves; Fairies; Ghosts.**
God
Accepting. Miller.
Adon 'Olam. *Unknown.*
All are but parts of one stupendous whole. *Fr.* An Essay on Man. Pope.
All the Hosts of Heaven. Simeon ben Isaac Ben Abun of Mainz.
All-embracing, The. Faber.
Ancient Thought, The. Kerr.
And Yet. Rhinow.
As due by many titles I resign. *Fr.* Holy Sonnets. Donne.
Ballad for Gloom. Pound.
Batter my heart, three-personed God; for You. *Fr.* Holy Sonnets. Donne.
Be Thankful Unto Him. Psalms. Bible, *O.T.*
Belief in Plan of Thee. Whitman.
Bermudas. Marvell.
Berries, The. Heyen.
Best for Us, The. Burnett.
Bitter-sweet. Herbert.
Bless Him. *Unknown.*
Book of the World, The. Drummond of Hawthornden.
Brahma, the World Idea. *Fr.* The Rig-Veda. *Unknown.*
Brother Ass, Brother Ass, you are full of fancies. *Fr.* Jerusalem Sonnets. Baxter.
Business Man's Prayer, A. Ludlum.
Caliban upon Setebos. Browning.
Canticle: "Ev'n like two little bank-dividing brookes." Quarles.
Canticle of the Sun, The. St. Francis of Assisi.
Child of Loneliness. Gale.
Child's Thought of God, A. Browning.
Christmas Folk Song, A. Reese.
Colin, you can tell my words are crippled now. *Fr.* Jerusalem Sonnets. Baxter.
Collar, The. Herbert.
Contentment. Schlipf.
Cradle Hymn. Luther.
"Daily with You." Flint.
Dark Night, The. St. John of the Cross.
Day After Sunday, The. McGinley.
Deliverance of Jehovah, The. Psalm XXVII. Bible, *O.T.*
Discipline. Herbert.
Divine Abundance. *Unknown.*
Divine Image, The. *Fr.* Songs of Innocence. Blake.
Divine Presence, The. *Fr.* May Carols. De Vere.
Each in His Own Tongue. Carruth.
Easter Wings. Herbert.
Ecclesiastes. Mahon.
Eclogue: Queen Elizabeth's Day. Davidson.
Edom. Watts.
Egocentric. Smith.
End of Being, The. Seneca.
Eternal Goodness, The. Whittier.
Eternal Jew, The. Cohen.
Even-Song. Herbert.
Everlasting Love, The. Flint.
Eyewitness. Hall.
Faith and Sight. King.
Father Knows, The. "F. L. H."
For Eleanor Boylan Talking with God. Sexton.
Friendly Beasts, The. *Unknown.*
From the Batter's Box. Harford.
Fury of Aerial Bombardment, The. Eberhart.
Get Somebody Else. Dunbar.
God. Bradford.
God. *Fr.* Dawn. Monro.
God. Slutsky.
God. Tabb.
God. Wallace.
God Cares. Casterline.
God Cares. Farningham.
God Does Do Such Wonderful Things! Morgan.
God Doeth All Things Well. *Unknown.*
God Don't Never Change. *Unknown.*
God Everywhere. Ibn Ezra.
God Has Pity on Kindergarten Children. Amichai.
God is a distant, stately lover. Dickinson.
God Is at the Anvil. Sarett.
God Is Here Again. Angoff.
God Is in Every Tomorrow. Snow.
God, Is, Like, Scissors. Villa.
God Is Love. Bowring.
God Is There. Isenhour.
God Is with Me. Smith.
God Knows What He's About. *Unknown.*
God Makes a Path. Williams.
God Moves in a Mysterious Way. Cowper.
God of Might, God of Right. *Unknown.*
God of the Earth, the Sky, the Sea. Longfellow.
God of the Living, The. Ellerton.
God Our Father. Faber.
God Poem. Moss.
God Provides. *Fr.* St. Matthew. Bible, *N.T.*
God the Architect. Kemp.
God the Omniscient. Wallace.
God, Whom Shall I Compare to Thee? Halevi.
God's Funeral. Hardy.
God's Grandeur. Hopkins.
God's Love. *Unknown.*
God's Will Is Best. Curtis.
Great Sad One, The. Greenberg.
Hail, Thou great mysterious Being! *Fr.* God. McLachlan.
He Leadeth Me. Gilmore.
He Puts Me to Rest. Ignatow.
He's Got the Whole World in His Hands. *Unknown.*
Hidden Weaver, The. Shepard.
Higher Pantheism, The. Tennyson.
Highest Divinity. *Unknown.*
His Hand Shall Cover Us. Isaac ben Samuel of Dampière.
His Necessary Darkness. Sullivan.
His Plan. *Unknown.*
His Sovereignty. Kalonymos ben Moses of Lucca.
Hitherto and Henceforth. Flint.
Holy God, We Praise Thy Name. Walworth.
Holy of Holies, The. Chesterton.
Hound of Heaven, The. Thompson.
How amiable are thy tabernacles, O Lord of hosts! *Fr.* Psalms. Bible, *O.T.*
Hunchback, The. Bishop.
Hymn: "Mighty fortress is our God, A." Luther.
Hymn: "Now we should praise Heaven-kingdom's guard." Caedmon.
Hymn of Joy. Van Dyke.
Hymn of Unity. *Unknown.*
Hymn to God the Father, A. Donne.
Hypnopompic Poem. Cole.
I am the Reaper. Henley.
I bet God understands about givin up five. Jamal.
I See God. *Unknown.*
I Sing the Mighty Power of God. Watts.
I sought thee round about, O thou my God! *Fr.* Hierarchie of the Blessed Angels. Heywood.
I stood within the heart of God. *Fr.* The Fire Bringer. Moody.
If God Exists. Lipska.
If I Could Trust Mine Own Self. Rossetti.
If We Believed in God. Gibbs.
Ikons, The. Baxter.
Image of God, The. Aldana.
Immanence. Hovey
In Absentia. Mackie.
In the castle of my soul. *Fr.* The Postern Gate. Rauschenbusch.
Incarnatio est maximum donum Dei. Alabaster.
Indian upon God, The. Yeats.
Instantaneous. Ayers.
Invocation, An: "To God, the everlasting, who abides." Symonds.
It Is a Beauteous Evening. Wordsworth.
Jehovah. Zangwill.
Just the Same To-Day. *Unknown.*
Kingdom of God, The. Rab.
Lauds. Berryman.
Let Us with a Gladsome Mind. Milton.
Light Shining Out of Darkness. Borthwick.
Light Shining Out of Darkness. Cowper.
Livid lightnings flashed in the clouds, The. *Fr.* The Black Riders. Crane.
Living God, The. Daniel ben Judah.

Living God, The. Gilman.
Living God, The. Ibn Ezra.
Lord Is King, The. *Unknown.*
Lord is my shepherd, The; I shall not want. *Fr.* Psalms. Bible, *O.T.*
Lord my shepherd, me His sheep, The. *Fr.* A paraphrase upon the Psalms of David. Sandys.
Lord of the World. *Unknown.*
Love of the Father, The. *Unknown.*
Machine Out of the God. Sanders.
Majesty and Mercy of God, The. Grant.
Majesty of God, The. Sternhold.
Man went before a strange god, A. *Fr.* The Black Riders. Crane.
Master of beauty, craftsman of the snowflake. *Fr.* Eleven Addresses to the Lord. Berryman.
Master Weaver, The. *Unknown.*
Mighty Fortress Is Our God, A. Luther.
More than We Ask. Wells.
Morning Hour, The. *Unknown.*
Mr. Edwards and the Spider. Lowell.
My Dog Jock. Carruth.
My Father Knows. Tillett.
My Garden. Brown.
My Gift. Rossetti.
My God, How Wonderful Thou Art. Faber.
"My Grace Is Sufficient for Thee." *Unknown.*
My Hiding Place. Bowsher.
Mysterious Way, The. Cowper.
Mystery, The. Hodgson.
Mystery, The. Hyde.
Nature's Hymn to the Deity. Clare.
New God, The. *Fr.* The New World. Bynner.
No Coming to God without Christ. Herrick.
No Coward Soul Is Mine. Brontë.
No Time for God. Trott.
Noah's Ark. Young.
O God, Our Help in Ages Past. Watts.
O God, unknown, invisible, secure. *Fr.* An Invocation. Symonds.
O Lord, Seek Us. Rossetti.
O Thy Bright Eyes Must Answer Now. Brontë.
O, Thou Eternal One! Derzhavin.
Observer, The. Yates.
Of Gods Omnipotencie. Hume.
Old Repair Man, The. Johnson.
Omnipresence. Hale.
On His Blindness. Milton.
On the Universality and Other Attributes of the God of Nature. Freneau.
151st Psalm, The. Shapiro.
Our God, Our Help. Watts.
Our Rock. Key.
Over to God. Harrigan.
Overlord. Carman.
Parable: November. Tapscott.
Paradox, The. Pereira.
Petition. Auden.
Physics, A. McHugh.
Pied Beauty. Hopkins.
Pillar of the Cloud, The. Newman.
Praise of Created Things. Saint Francis of Assisi.
Prayer: "In the bright bay of your morning,/ O God." Goll.
Prayer: "Lord, what a change within us one short hour." Trench.
Prayer for Every Day. *Unknown.*
Prayer, The: "Wilt thou not visit me?" Very.
Precepts He Gave His Folk. Elijah ben Menahem Hazaken of Le Mans.
Preface, The: "Infinity, when all things it beheld." *Fr.* God's Determinations Touching His Elect. Taylor.
Protection of Jehovah, The. Psalm XXIII. Bible, *O.T.*
Psalm CXXXIX: "O Lord, thou hast searched me, and known me." Pembroke.
Pulley, The. Herbert.
Quite Apart from the Holy Ghost. Mitchell.
Recessional. Kipling.
Revelation. Markham.
Rinsed with Gold, Endless, Walking the Fields. Siegel.
Rose, The. Studdert-Kennedy.
Scapegoat. Rodgers.
Search, The. Clarke.
Secret, The. Cushman.
Seeking God. Dowden.
Send Me. Rossetti.
Shadows, The. Macdonald.
Small gray cloudy louse that nests in my beard, The. *Fr.* Jerusalem Sonnets. Baxter.
Small Song. Shaw.
Some Verses upon the Burning of Our House, July 10th, 1666. Bradstreet.
Song: "My straying thoughts, reduced stay." Collins.
Song of the Wind and the Rain. Ibn Gabirol.
Songs of Kabir. Kabir.
Sonnet: "God and man, though in this amphitheatre." Alabaster.
Sonnet: "Like as the fountain of all light created." Alabaster.
Sonnet XI: "Is God invisible? This very room." Greeff.
Still, Still with Thee. Stowe.
Stupendous God! how shrinks our bounded/ sense. *Fr.* The Omnipresence of the Deity. Montgomery.
Sun-Day Hymn, A. Holmes.
Testimony. Rodgers.
Then Sang Moses and the children of Israel this song unto the Lord. *Fr.* Exodus. Bible, *O.T.*
Then Sings My Soul. Mariani.
"There Is No God," the Wicked Saith. Clough.
There Is Nothing False in Thee. Patchen.
Therefore I will not refrain my mouth. *Fr.* Job. Bible, *O.T.*
There's a Wideness in God's Mercy. Faber.
Third Enemy Speaks. *Fr.* The Magnetic Mountain. Day Lewis.
This Is My Father's World. Babcock
This Moment. Flint.
Thou Art Indeed Just, Lord, If I Contend. Hopkins.
Thou Art of All Created Things. Calderón de la Barca.
Thou Great God. *Unknown.*
Though Mine Eye Sleep Not. *Fr.* The Dead Sea Scrolls. *Unknown.*
To a God Unknown. Eller.
To a Waterfowl. Bryant.
To Heaven. Jonson.
To Men. Wickham.
Transcendence of God, The. *Fr.* Samson Agonistes. Milton.
Transcendence. Hovey
Truant, The. Pratt.
True Hymn, A. Herbert.
True Knowledge. Panatattu.
Twelve Lines About the Burning Bush. Ravitch.
Twenty-third Psalm, The. Herbert.
Ultimate Problems. Stafford.
Under a Wiltshire Apple Tree. De Bary.
Unity of God, The. Panatattu.
Unknown God, The. Watson.
Upon the Burning of Our House. Bradstreet.
Veni Creator Spiritus. *At. to* Charlemagne *and to* Maurus.
Vestigia. Carman.
Voice of God, The. Barnard.
Walking with God. *Unknown.*
Welcome Morning. Sexton.
What the Devil Said. Stephens.
What Thomas an Buile Said in a Pub. Stephens.
When God First Said. Zach.
When I Consider How My Light Is Spent. Milton.
When I Consider Thy Heavens. Psalms. Bible, *O.T.*
When I Was Growing Up. Vogel.
Wherefore Hidest Thou Thy Face, and Holdest Me For Thy Enemie? Quarles.
Whilst I beheld the neck o'th'dove. Cary.
Who? Jaffe.
Whose Hand. *Unknown.*
Wish, that of the living whole, The. *Fr.* In Memoriam A. H. H. Tennyson.
With Thee. Pinkham.
Work of Love, The. Sangster.
Written in Exile. Raine.
Yet Do I Marvel. Cullen.
Your Father Knoweth. *Unknown.*
Zebaoth. Lasker-Schüler.
In Love with Love (ILwL). Anne *and* Christopher Fremantle, eds.

Godiva, Lady
Godiva. Tennyson.
Lady Godiva. Shanks.

Godolphin, Sidney Godolphin, 1st Earl of
Sidney Godolphin. Scollard.

Gods and Goddesses
Dead Pan, The. Browning.
God-Maker, Man, The. Marquis.
Gods, The. Lee.
Gods Are Mighty, The. Van Wyk Louw.
Hertha. Swinburne.
Hymn to Diana. *Fr.* Cynthia's Revels. Jonson.
No Man, If Men Are Gods. Cummings.
Old Gods, The. Muir.

Oshun, the River Goddess. *Yoruba Oral Tradition.*
Queen and Huntress. *Fr.* Cynthia's Revels. Jonson.
River God, The. Smith.
Visit of the Gods, The. Schiller.
Weather of Olympus, The. Graves.
Goebbels, Joseph
Dr. Joseph Goebbels. *Fr.* The Führer Bunker. Snodgrass.
Goethe, Johann Wolfgang von
Goethe and Frederika. Sidgwick.
Goethe's Death Mask. Gregg.
Memorial Verses. Arnold.
Shake, Mulleary, and Go-ethe. Bunner.
Sorrows of Werther, The. Thackeray.
When Goethe's death was told, we said. *Fr.* Memorial Verses. Arnold.
Gogh, Vincent van. *See* **Van Gogh, Vincent.**
Gold
Gold Seekers, The. Richardson.
John Sutter. Winters.
Peck of Gold, The. Frost.
Song For the Pike's Peaker. *Unknown.*
Yellow Witch of Caribou, The. Robertson.
Gold Mining and Miners
Ballad of Chicken Bill, The. Vaughn.
Broken-down Digger, The. *Unknown.*
Californian, The. *Unknown.*
Cleaning Up. Dyson.
Clementine. *Unknown.*
Cremation of Sam McGee, The. Service.
Days of Forty-Nine, The. *Unknown.*
Dead Prospector, The. Chapman.
Dow's Flat. Harte.
Dreary Black Hills, The. *Unknown.*
Golden Gullies of the Palmer, The. *Unknown.*
Gold-Seekers, The. Garland.
Gold Seekers, The. Richardson.
Gold Seeker's Song, The. *Unknown.*
Hit At the Times, A. McGrew.
In the Mines. Swett.
In the Summer of Sixty. *Unknown.*
Joe Bowers. *Unknown.*
Little Johnny Mine, The. Detrick.
Look Out Below! Thatcher.
Lousy Miner. *Unknown.*
Me and Prunes. Sherwood.
Miner's Lament, The. *Unknown.*
Miner's Progress, The. Delano.
Mistress of the Matchless Mine. Robertson.
National Miner, The. *Unknown.*
Ol' Jinny Mine, The. Detrick.
On the Gold Mines. Vilakazi.
Pike's Peakers, The. Greenleaf.
Prospecting Dream. *Unknown.*
San Francisco Company, The. *Unknown.*
Slide At the Empire Mine, The. Wason.
Soliloquy of the Returned Gold Adventurer. "Syntax."
Song: "We came to Tamichi in 1880." Judy and Hammond.
Spell of the Yukon, The. Service.
Sweet Jane. *Unknown.*
When I Went Off To Prospect. *Unknown.*
Golden Age
Age of Gold. Metastasio.
Golden Age, The. Fenollosa.
Happy Too Much. *Fr.* De Consolatione Philosophiæ. Boethius.
Verses on the Prospect of Planting Arts and Learning in America. Berkeley.
Goldenrod
Golden Rod, The. Sherman.
Goldenrod. Eastman.
Goldfinches
Mechanism. Ammons.
Song: "Where I walk out." Winters.
Goldfish
Address to Certain Gold Fishes. Coleridge.
Goldfish, The. Brown.
Goldfish. Monro.
Goldfish. Nemerov.
Prayer of the Goldfish, The. Gasztold.
To Miss — on the Death of Her Goldfish. Meredyth
Goldilocks
In Love with the Bears. Kuzma.
Golem
Bella and the Golem. Ombres.
Golem, The. Reich.
How They Made the Golem. Colombo.
Golf
Afforestation. Wodehouse.
Golf Ball. Delaney.
Golfers. Layton.
Golfer's Rubaiyat, The. Boynton.
I was playing golf that day. *Unknown.*
One Down. Armour.
Poems from Prison. Maloney.
Public Nuisance, A. Arkell.
Quatrain: "Golf links lie so near the mill, The." Cleghorn.
Seaside Golf. Betjeman.
Victory on the Last Green. *Fr.* The Goff; an Heroi-comical Poem. Mathison.
Who Taught Caddies to Count? or, A Burnt Golfer Fears the Child. Nash.
Goliath
David and Goliath. Crouch.
Goliath and David. Untermeyer.
Goliath of Gath. Wheately.
Good Friday
Good Friday. Rossetti.
Good Friday. Smith.
Good Friday. *Unknown.*
Good Friday Evening. Rossetti.
Good Friday in My Heart. Coleridge.
Good Friday, 1613. Riding Westward. Donne.
Poem for Good Friday. Jones.
Praetorium Scene: Good Friday. Lennen.
Tenebrae. Clarke.
Good Hope, Cape of. *See* **Cape of Good Hope.**
Gore-Booth, Eva
In Memory of Eva Gore-Booth and Con Markiewicz. Yeats.
Gorillas
Au Jardin des Plantes. Wain.
Best Loved of Africa. Danner.
Gorilla, The. Hathaway.
Koko. Downer.
Gorse
Lessons from the Gorse. Browning.
Gospel Music
And the Old Women Gathered. Evans.
Gossip
Journal of Society, The. Turner.
Noël Tragique. Guthrie.
People do gossip. Sappho.
People Will Talk. Dodge.
Tattle. Turner.
Tea. Embry.
They Say. Wilcox.
Three Gates. *Unknown.*
See also **Reputation; Rumor.**
Gould, Benjamin Apthorp
Welcome to Dr. Benjamin Apthorp Gould, A. Holmes.
Gout
Definitions of the Word *Gout.* Koyama.
Government
All Things Being Equal. Humphrey.
Chilean Elegies, The: 5. The Interior. Wayman.
God Give Us Men! Holland.
Government. Nihoniho.
Panegyrick to My Lord Protector, A. Waller.
Proper New Ballad, Intituled The Fairies Farewell, A; or, God-a-Mercy Will. Corbet.
Under the Rose. *Unknown.*
Goya y Lucientes, Francisco José de
Church of San Antonio de la Florida, The. Petrie.
In Goya's Greatest Scenes. *Fr.* A Coney Island of the Mind. Ferlinghetti.
La Pesadilla. Penfold.
Grace
Grace. Emerson.
Grace. Patrick.
Love ("Love bade me welcome: yet my soul drew back"). Herbert.
Meditation XXXII: "Thy grace, dear Lord's my golden wrack, I find." *Fr.* Preparatory Meditations. Taylor.
Grackles
Grackle, The. Nash.
Graffiti
Aphrodite Metropolis. Fearing.
From a Lavatory Wall. *Unknown.*

Graffiti. Field.
Graffiti for Lovers. Hall.
Kilroy. Viereck.
Men's Room in the College Chapel, The. Snodgrass.
Observing a Vulgar Name on the Plinth of an Ancient Statue. Landor.
SM. Moss.
Sunny Prestatyn. Larkin.
Thesis, Antithesis, and Nostalgia. Dugan.
To Desi as Joe as Smoky the Lover of 115th Street. Lorde.

Graham, James, Marquess of Montrose. *See* **Montrose, James Graham, 5th Earl and 1st Marquess of**

Graham, Martha
Martha Graham. Lifshin.

Grain Elevators
Grain Elevator. Klein.

Grammar
Grammar in a Nutshell. *Unknown.*
Grammar in Rhyme. *Unknown.*
How a Girl Was Too Reckless of Grammar. Carryl.
Parts of Speech, The. *Unknown.*

Grampian (region), Scotland
Aberdeen Train. Morgan.
Kinnaird Head. Bruce.

Granada, Spain
Conquest of Granada, *sels.* Dryden.

Grand Canyon
At Grand Canyon's Edge. Ray.

Grand Lake, Colorado
Legend of Grand Lake. Westcott.

Grand Pré, Nova Scotia
Low Tide on Grand Pré. Carman.

Grand Rapids, Michigan
Grand Rapids. Moore.

Grandfathers
Blue Lantern. Song.
Card Game, A; Kinjiro Sawada. Ikeda.
Careless/ but not fearless. *Fr.* Urn I: Silent for Twenty-five Years, the Father of My Mother Advises Me. Lew.
Child to His Sick Grandfather, A. Baillie.
Gardeners. Ignatow.
Gooseberries. Wild.
Grampa Schuler. Suckow.
Grandfather. Barnstone.
Grandfather. Bowering.
Grandfather. Coleman.
Grandfather. Harper.
Grandfather in the Old Men's Home. Merwin.
Grandfathers. Castro.
Grandfathers. Shady.
Grandfather's Clock. Work.
Grandfather's Heaven. Nye.
Harmonica Man. Wolny.
I Want to Write a Jewish Poem. Pacernik.
In Grandfather's Glasses. Peters.
In January, 1962. Kooser.
I've Got a new Book from My Grandfather Hyde. Jackson.
Late Gothic. Gotlieb.
Mi Abuelo. Ríos.
My Grandaddy Mostly with His Knife. Huddle.
My Grandfather Burning Cornfields. Sauls.
My Grandfather Dying. Kooser.
Naming. Stroud.
On the Photograph of a Man I Never Saw. Plutzik.
Other Side, The. Reiter.
Pass It On Grandson. Palmanteer.
Poem for My Grandfather. Jacobs.
Poet Imagines His Grandfather's Thoughts on the Day He Died, The. Lum.
Real Story, A. Pastan.
Vignette: 1922. Spingarn.
With My Grandfather. Zelda.
Yahrzeit. Schaeffer.
Zaydee. Levine.
Zeyde. Metz.

Grandmothers
Afternoon with Grandmother. Huff.
Almost Ninety. Whitman.
Anishinabe Grandmothers. Vizenor.
Apology for E.H. Hathaway.
At My Grandmother's. Malouf.
At the Long Island Jewish Geriatric Home. Graham.
Beads, The. Jacinto.
Belita. Ríos.
Both My Grandmothers. Field.
Cupboard, The. De la Mare.
Daguerreotype of a Grandmother. Wright.
For All My Grandmothers. Brant.
For My Grandmother. *Fr.* Four Epitaphs. Cullen.
For My Grandmother, Bridget Halpin. Hartnett.
From My Mother's Home. Goldberg.
Grammer's Shoes. Barnes.
Grandfather's Heaven. Nye.
Grandma Shorba and the Pure in Heart. Manfred.
Grandmamma's Birthday. Belloc.
Grandma's Advice. *Unknown.*
Grandmother. Allen.
Grandmother, The. Berry.
Grandmother. Carlile.
Grandmother. Minarik.
Grandmother. Young Bear.
Grandmother and Grandson. Merwin.
Grandmother Jackson. Jackson.
Grandmother Poems. Chin.
Grandmother, Rocking. Merriam.
Grandmother Sleeps. Bahe.
Grandmothers, The. Oliver.
Grandpa's Picture. Ruffin.
Great-Grandma. Shields.
Green Rain. Livesay.
Growing Old. Henderson.
In Memory of My Arab Grandmother. Zerbe.
In Search of a Short Poem for My Grandmother. Hardeman.
It's All the Same. Davis.
Last Words of My English Grandmother, The. Williams.
Late Gothic. Gotlieb.
Legacies. Giovanni.
Lineage. Walker.
Looking for My Old Indian Grandmother in the Summer Heat of 1980. Glancy.
Love Necessitates. Redmond.
Mardi Gras/Grandmothers—Portrait in Red and Black Crayon. Nolan.
Minuet, The. Dodge.
My Grandmother. Adams.
My Grandmother. Shapiro.
My Grandmother Had Bones. Hemschemeyer.
My Grandmother's Love Letters. Crane.
Nechama. Kaufman.
Point Shirley. Plath.
Quills. Gafford.
Recollection. Big Eagle.
Remedies. Soto.
Room in the Past, A. Kooser.
She Sews Fine Linen. Davis.
Sunday Visiting. Rios.
Thoughts for My Grandmother. Firestone.
To My Grandmother. Locker-Lampson.
Touchstone. Worley.
Victorian Grandmother. Lockwood.
When My Grandmother Died. Cornish.
When the Ambulance Came. Morgan.
Woman of the House, The. Murphy.
Words to Remind Me of Grandmother. Castro Ríos.
Yonosa House. Smith.

Grandparents
Admiral's Daughter, The. Burrows.
Celebration. Sachs.
Insight. Goose.
Long Island Springs. Moss.

Granicus, Battle of (334 B.C.)
How We Heard the Name. Dugan.

Grant, Ulysses Simpson
Achilles Deatheridge. Masters.
Aged Stranger, The. Harte.
Death of Grant, The. Bierce.
In Memory of General Grant. Abbey.
Lee's Parole. Manville.
Vanquished. Browne.

Grapes
American Vineyard. Cousens.
Father and his Children, The. *Unknown.*
Grapes. Maris Stella.
Grapes Making. Adams.
Harvester, The. Lawrence.
Picking Grapes in an Abandoned Vineyard. Levis.

Taste of Purple. Jacobs.
Grass
Blade of Grass Sings to the River, The. Goldberg.
Blades of Grass. Crane.
Cut Grass. Larkin.
Former Barn Lot. Van Doren.
Fragile blades of grass. *Fr.* The Stars. "Ping Hsin."
Grass, The. Bowering.
Grass. Corn.
Grass, The. Dickinson.
Grass. Sandburg.
Grass. Webster.
Grass. *Fr.* Song of Myself. Whitman.
Grass Fingers. Grimké.
Grass on the Mountain, The. Austin.
Grass so little has to do, The. Dickinson.
Grasses. Mills.
Grassroots. Sandburg.
Green Grass Grew All Around, The. *Unknown.*
Long Feud. Untermeyer.
Lying in the Grass. Gosse.
Sad Green. Warner.
Shearing Grass. Redgrove.
Song the Grass Sings, A. Blanden.
Speaks the Whispering Grass. Stuart.
Spring Grass. Sandburg.
Tribute to Grass. Ingalls.
Voice of the Grass, The. Boyle.
Who Maketh the Grass to Grow. *Fr.* Psalms. Bible, *O.T.*
Grasshoppers
Explanation of the Grasshopper, An. Lindsay.
Grasshopper, The. Anacreon.
Grasshopper, The. *Fr.* Anacreontiques. Cowley.
Grasshopper, The. Lovelace.
Grasshopper, The. McCord.
Grasshopper, The. Stanley.
Grasshopper, A. Wilbur.
Grasshopper and the Ant, The. La Fontaine.
Grasshopper Green. *Unknown.*
Grasshopper's Song, The. Bialik.
On the Grasshopper and Cricket. Keats.
Ondt and the Gracehoper, The. *Fr.* Finnegans Wake. Joyce.
Poetry of Earth, The. Keats.
Rilloby-Rill. Newbolt.
R-P-O-P-H-E-S-S-A-G-R. Cummings.
To the Grasshopper and the Cricket. Hunt.
Graves, Morris
Three Poems on Morris Graves' Paintings. Logan.
Graves
Ah, Are You Digging on My Grave? Hardy.
All Souls. Lawrence.
Ample make this bed. Dickinson.
Aodh Ruadh O'Domhnaill. MacGreevy.
Arundel Tomb, An. Larkin.
At White River. Haines.
Beach Burial. Slessor.
Beneath the Mound. Smith.
Bishop Orders His Tomb at Saint Praxed's Church, The. Browning.
Buffel's Kop. Campbell.
Bury Me in a Free Land. Harper.
Burying Ground By the Ties. MacLeish.
Claribel. Tennyson.
Coffin-Worm, The. Pitter.
Cool Tombs. Sandburg.
Cornelia's Song. *Fr.* The White Devil. Webster.
Despair. Levertov.
Dig My Grave. *Unknown.*
Dirge: "We do lie beneath the grass." *Fr.* Death's Jest Book. Beddoes.
Elegy Written in a Country Churchyard. Gray.
Elizabeth. Warner.
Elmer Ruiz. Oresick.
Fame. Browning.
Father Son and Holy Ghost. Lorde.
Giorno Dei Morti. Lawrence.
Grave, The. Blair.
Grave in Ukraine, A. Tchernichowsky.
Graves in Queens. Hugo.
Graveyard, The. Cooper.
In the Grave No Flower. Millay.
Indian's Grave, The. Mountain.
Invocation: "Let me be buried in the rain." Johnson.
Iona; the Graves of the Kings. Jeffers.
Lord Cozens Hardy. Betjeman.
Manhood End. Thwaite.
Meditations on the Sepulchre in the Garden. Doddridge.
My Burial Place. Jeffers.
On a Grave in Christchurch, Hants. Adams.
Prehistoric Burials. Sassoon.
Rain on a Grave. Hardy.
Requiescat. Wilde.
Simpson's Rest. Sipmson.
Sir Walter Scott at the Tomb of the Stuarts in St. Peter's. Milnes.
Snails. Blodgett.
Sonnet Written in the Church-Yard at Middleton, in Sussex. Smith.
Stranger, The. De la Mare.
Temporary Problems. Rubin.
They're Shifting Father's Grave. *Unknown.*
Unknown Dead, The. Timrod.
Unknown Grave, The. Landon.
Unquiet Grave, The. *Unknown.*
Wanderer's Grave, The. Sage.
We do lie beneath the grass. *Fr.* Death's Jest Book. Beddoes.
We do not play on graves. Dickinson.
You Can Dig My Grave. *Unknown.*
Yugoslav Cemetery. Wright.
Graveyards. *See* **Cemeteries.**
Gray, Thomas
Sketch of His Own Character. Gray.
To Mr. Gray on the Publication of His Odes. Garrick.
Great Britain. *See* **England; Scotland; Wales.**
Great Depression
Arizona. *Unknown.*
Beans, Bacon and Gravy. *Unknown.*
34 Blues. *Unknown.*
Working Man Blues. *Unknown.*
Great Lakes
Aubade: Lake Erie. Merton.
Great Lakes of Canada, The. Perry.
Great Lakes Suite. Reaney.
Lake Superior. Goodrich.
Lost. Sandburg.
Maids of Simcoe, The. *Unknown.*
Thousand Islands, The. *Fr.* The St. Lawrence and the Saguenay. Sangster.
Greatness
Great Men Have Been among Us. Wordsworth.
I Think Continually of Those Who Were Truly Great. Spender.
Let Us Now Praise Famous Men. *Fr.* Ecclesiasticus. Bible, *Apocrypha.*
On the Vanity of Earthly Greatness. Guiterman.
Song About Great Men, A. Hamburger.
Song of Greatness, A. Austin.
See also **Fame.**
Greco, El
High Renaissance. Starbuck.
Greece
After Greece. Merrill.
And yet how lovely in thine age of woe. *Fr.* Childe Harold's Pilgrimage. Byron.
At Lindos. Sarton.
Chorus: "World's great age begins anew, The." *Fr.* Hellas. Shelley.
England. Moore.
Greek Transfiguration. Friar.
Invocation to the Genius of Greece. *Fr.* The Pleasures of Imagination. Akenside.
Islands, The. Doolittle ("H. D.").
Isles of Greece, The. Byron.
Isles of Greece, The. *Fr.* Don Juan. Byron.
Isles of Greece, The. Capetanakis.
Marco Bozzaris. Halleck.
Mt. Lykaion. Stickney.
Mycenae. Fisher.
Nemea. Durrell.
On This Day I Complete My Thirty-Sixth Year. Byron.
Patmos. Thomas.
Quality of Air, A. Chapin.
To a Greek Ship in the Port of Dublin. Stanford.
When raging love with extreme pain. Earl of Surrey.
Greed
Avarice. Herbert.
Bird on Nellie's Hat, The. Lamb.
Covetousness. Idley.
Greed Song, The. Goldbarth.
Greed. Blazek.
Greedy Richard. Taylor.

Pardoner's Tale, The. *Fr.* The Canterbury Tales. Chaucer.
To a Covetous Churl. May.
With Mercy for the Greedy. Sexton.
Green (color)
Green. Lawrence.
Green Eye, The. Merrill.
Variables of Green. Graves.
Greene, Graham
Muted Screen of Graham Greene, The. McGinley.
Greene, Nathanael
To the Memory of the Brave Americans. Freneau.
Greenhouses
Big Wind. Roethke.
Child on Top of a Greenhouse. Roethke.
New England Greenhouse. McQuilkin.
Greenland
Greenland Whale Fishery, The. *Unknown.*
Greenwich Village, New York City
Autumn Song on Perry Street. Frankenberg.
Lüchow's and After. Sissman.
Sad Song about Greenwich Village, A. Park.
Thompson Street. McCoy.
Gregory, Lady Augusta
Municipal Gallery Revisited, The. Yeats.
Gregory, Robert
In Memory of Major Robert Gregory. Yeats.
Grenville, Sir Richard
First American Sailors, The. Rice.
Revenge, The. Tennyson.
Greyhounds
Ballad of Master McGrath, A. *Unknown.*
How a Good Greyhound Is Shaped. *Unknown.*
Grief
Adonais. Shelley.
After great pain a formal feeling comes. Dickinson.
After the Burial. Lowell.
Alarum. Koziol.
Alone. Finch.
Alone in an Inn at Southampton, April the 25th, 1737. Hill.
Andrée Rexroth. Rexroth.
Annabel Lee. Poe.
Anniverse, The; an Elegy. King.
Another Weeping Woman. Stevens.
Away loose-reined careers of Poetry! *Fr.* An Elegie upon the Death of the Reverend Mr Thomas Shepard. Oakes.
Bereavement. Browning.
Bread and Music. *Fr.* Discordants. Aiken.
Break, Break, Break. Tennyson.
Brooding Grief. Lawrence.
Bustle in a house, The. Dickinson.
But unto him came swift calamity. *Fr.* Sonnets. Tuckerman.
Calm is the morn without a sound. *Fr.* in Memoriam A. H. H. Tennyson.
Carousel, The. Oden.
Chamber over the Gate, The. Longfellow.
Complaint. Wright.
Confession. Herbert.
Coronach. *Fr.* The Lady of the Lake. Scott.
Cross of Snow, The. Longfellow.
David's Lament for Jonathan. Abélard.
Dear loss! since thy untimely fate. *Fr.* The Exequy. King.
Death of the Flowers, The. Bryant.
Desideria. Wordsworth.
Dirge, A: "Rough wind, that moanest loud." Shelley.
Echo's Song. *Fr.* Cynthia's Revels. Jonson.
Elegy: "Floods of tears well from my deepest heart, The." Immanuel di Roma.
Elegy on a Lady Whom Grief for the Death of Her Betrothed Killed. Bridges.
Elegy on the Death of Her Husband. Howard.
Exequy, The. King.
Eyes that drew from me such fervent praise, The. *Fr.* Sonnets to Laura. Petrarch.
Farewell to the Court. Ralegh.
Finis. Thomson.
First Love. Olds.
For Annie. Poe.
Forsaken. Schneour.
Fountain of tears, river of grief. Pisan.
Funeral Song, A. *Unknown.*
Gathering the Bones Together. Orr.
Gingilee. Halpern.
Girl's Song, A. Tynan.
Glory of the Day Was in Her Face, The. Johnson.
Great grief came over me. Aleqaajik.
Grey Eye Weeping, A. O'Rahilly.
Grief. Berry.
Grief. Browning.
Grief and God. Phillips.
Grief Plucked Me Out of Sleep. King.
Has Sorrow Thy Young Days Shaded? Moore.
He Is Not Dead. Riley.
Home Burial. Frost.
Home-Coming. Ehrenstein.
Homer. Ehrenstein.
I, a Most Wretched Atlas. *Fr.* Homeward Bound. Heine.
I held it truth, with him who sings. *Fr.* In Memoriam A. H. H. Tennyson.
If Ever Hapless Woman Had a Cause. Pembroke.
If in the World There Be More Woe. Wyatt.
In Grandfather's Glasses. Peters.
In the Silent Night. Peretz.
In the Time of Trouble. Clark.
Influence of Time on Grief. Bowles.
Kilcash. *Unknown.*
Kol Nidra. Leiser.
Lament for Art O'Leary, The. *Unknown.*
Lament for Art O'Leary. O'Connell.
Lament for the Woodlands. *Unknown.*
Lament for Yellow-haired Donough, The. *Unknown.*
Lamentations. Brody.
Last Lines. O'Rahilly.
Lycidas. Milton.
Mansion stood apart in its own ground, The. *Fr.* The City of Dreadful Night. Thomson.
Mask of Stone. Johnson.
Meanwhile Achilles, plung'd. *Fr.* The Iliad. Homer.
Missing. Tabb.
Mourning Women. Blind.
Mourning. Marvell.
Music I Heard. *Fr.* Discordants. Aiken.
My Buried Friends. *Unknown.*
My grief on the sea. Cussrooee.
My True Love Hath My Heart and I Have His. Coleridge.
No longer mourn for me when I am dead. *Fr.* Sonnets. Shakespeare.
No Worst, There Is None. Hopkins.
Not Lost, but Gone Before. Norton.
Not Thou but I. Marston.
Nurse No Long Grief. Gilmore.
O might those sighes and teares returne againe. *Fr.* Holy Sonnets. Donne.
Oft in My Thought. D'Orléans.
Oh, Thou! Who Dry'st the Mourner's Tear. Moore.
On Another's Sorrow. *Fr.* Songs of Innocence. Blake.
On His Deceased Wife. Milton.
On My First Son. Jonson.
On My Late Dear Wife. Richardson.
On My Sorrowful Life. Ibn Ezra.
One still dark night, I sat alone and wrote. *Fr.* Sonnets. Tuckerman.
Patrick Sarsfield, Lord Lucan. *Unknown.*
Poet's Lament on the Death of His Wife. Somali.
Receipt to Cure the Vapours, A. Montagu.
Remembrance. Brontë.
Requiescat. Wilde.
Reuben Bright. Robinson.
Sad Shepherd, The. Yeats.
Safe despair it is that raves. Dickinson.
Sleepless Night, A. O'Rahilly.
Slievenamon. *Unknown.*
Slow, Slow, Fresh Fount. *Fr.* Cynthia's Revels. Jonson.
Solitude. Monro.
Song: "When I am dead, my dearest." Rossetti.
Sonnet: "Because my grief seems quiet and apart." Nathan.
Sonnet: "My Soul surcharged with grief now loud complains." Morpurgo.
Sonnet: "No worst, there is none. Pitched past pitch of grief." Hopkins.
Sonnet on the Death of Mr. Richard West. Gray.
Sorrow. De Vere.
Sorrow. Lawrence.
Sorrow. Phillips.
Sorrow Is the Only Faithful One. Dodson.
Spell Against Sorrow. Raine.
Spiritual Isolation. Rosenberg.
Spring and Fall. Hopkins.
Stanzas. Ibn Gabirol.

Strong Son of God, immortal Love. *Fr.* In Memoriam A. H. H. Tennyson.
Swift Floods. Petröczi.
Tears, Idle Tears. *Fr.* The Princess. Tennyson.
Telling the Bees. Whittier.
The Exequy. King.
There Is No Country. Tuwim.
They Are All Gone. Vaughan.
Three Seamstresses, The. Peretz.
To One in Paradise. Poe.
Unquiet Grave, The. *Unknown.*
Valediction: Forbidding Mourning, A. Donne.
Vesta. Whittier.
Victory in Defeat. Markham.
Wanderer, The. *Unknown.*
Weep No More. Fletcher, *and others.*
When I See Another's Pain. Leib.
When Lilacs Last in the Dooryard Bloom'd. Whitman.
When My Dog Died. Littledale.
Widow's Lament in Springtime, The. Williams.
Wine and Grief. Ibn Gabirol.
Women Are Grieving, The. Hogan.
Woodspurge, The. Rossetti.
See also **Mourning.**

Grocers
London Adulterations. *Unknown.*
Song against Grocers, The. Chesterton.

Groundhogs
Drumlin Woodchuck, A. Frost.
Groundhog, The. Eberhart.
Groundhog, The. Shaw.
Groundhog. *Unknown.*
Ground Hog Day. Moore.
Jolly Woodchuck, The. Edey *and* Grider.
Woodchuck Who Lives on Top of Mt. Ritter, The. Simon.
Woodchucks. Kumin.

Grouse
Blackcock, The. Baillie.
Plea for a Plural, A. Lehmann.

Guadalajara, Mexico
Instruction Manual, The. Ashbery.

Guatemala
Below Mount T'ui K'oy, Home of the Gods, Todos Santos Cuchumatán, Guatemalan Highlands. Stroud.
Letter from the Hotel, A. Barnstone.

Guérin, Maurice de
Maurice de Guérin. Egan.

Guernsey
In Guernsey. Swinburne.

Guerriere (ship)
Constitution and the *Guerrière,* The. *Unknown.*

Guerrillas
French and the Spanish Guerrillas, The. Wordsworth.
Requiem for the Croppies. Heaney.

Guest, Edgar A.
Edgar A. Guest Considers "The Good Old Woman Who Lived in a Shoe" and the Good Old Truths Simultaneously. *Fr.* Mother Goose Up-to-Date. Untermeyer.
Edgar Guest. Williams
Lines to a World-Famous Poet Who Failed to Complete a World-Famous Poem; or, Come Clean, Mr. Guest! Nash.

Guests
Doorbells. Field.
Guest, The. *Unknown.*
In the Valley of the Elwy. Hopkins.
See also **Hospitality; Visiting and Visitors.**

Guggenheim, John Simon
No Foundation. Hollander.

Guilt
Christina. MacNeice.
Debt, The. Dunbar.
Guilty. Wilkinson.
Matthew V.29-30. Mahon.
Oedipus. Muir.
Pursuit. Warren.
Song about Major Eatherly, A. Wain.
Why Would I Have Survived? Bruck.

Guinea Hens
Flock of Guinea Hens Seen from a Car, A. Welty.

Guinea Pigs
Guinea-pig Song, A. *Unknown.*

Guitars
Guitar. García Lorca.
Guitarist Tunes Up, The. Cornford.
On Learning to Play the Guitar. Fraser.
On My Old Ramkiekie. Leipoldt.

Guiteau, Charles J.
Charles Guiteau. *Unknown.*

Gulf Stream
Gulf Stream, The. Bellamann.
Gulf Stream. Coolidge.
Song of the Gulf Stream. Ford.
Thoughts in the Gulf Stream. Morley.

Gulls
Alien. MacLeish.
Ballet of the Fifth Year, The. Schwartz.
Desert Gulls. Gillespie.
Dialectics of Flight. Wheelock.
Gull. Smith.
Gull Goes Up, A. Adams.
Gull, it is said, The. Nakasuk.
Gulls. Howes.
Gulls. Muir.
Gulls. Williams.
Gulls and Dreams. Stevenson.
Gulls in an aery morrice. Henley.
Handicapped. Berrigan.
Lines Addressed to a Seagull. Griffin.
Lives of Gulls and Children, The. Nemerov.
Maine Sea Gulls. Hoban.
On the Beach. Cornford.
Predictor of Famine, The. Williams.
Sea Bird to the Wave, The. Colum.
Sea-Birds. Allen.
Sea Gull. Coatsworth.
Seagull, The. Howitt.
Sea-Gull, The. Nash.
Sea Gulls. Pratt.
Sea-Gull, The. *Unknown.*
Seagulls. Francis.
Seagulls. Hubbell.
Seagulls. Updike.
Seagulls on the Serpentine. Noyes.
Sea-Mew, The. Browning.
Sea-ward, white gleaming through the busy scud. Coleridge.
To a Seamew. Swinburne.
Visit from the Sea, A. Stevenson.
Winged Mariner. Howes.

Gum Trees
Gnarled Riverina Gum-Tree, A. Moll.
Snow-Gum, The. Stewart.

Gunpowder Plot. *See* **Fawkes, Guy.**

Guns
A. E. F. Sandburg.
Arms and the Boy. Owen.
Channel Firing. Hardy.
Defensive Position. Manifold.
Grandpa's .45. Ransom.
Guns. Crowe.
Naming of Parts. *Fr.* Lessons of the War. Reed.
Original Sin. Laing.
Pipe Dreams. Bickston.
Shooting, The. Pack.
Technique on the Firing Line. Cassity.
There was a little man, and he had a little gun. Mother Goose.
.38, The. Joans.

Gustavus II (Gustavus Adolphus), King of Sweden
Battle Hymn. Altenburg.
In Answer of an Elegiacall Letter upon the Death of the King of Sweden. Carew.

Guthlac, Saint
Death of Saint Guthlac. *Fr.* Guthlac. Cynewulf.

Guy Fawkes Day. *See* **Fawkes, Guy.**

Guyana
Those Guyana Nights. Foerster.

Gwyn, Nell
Ballad Called the Haymarket Hectors, A. *Unknown.*
Nell Gwynne's Looking-Glass. Blanchard.
Panegyric, A: "Of a great heroine I mean to tell." *Unknown.*

Gymnastics
Watching Gymnasts. Francis.
See also **Acrobats.**

Gypsies
Ballad of Luna, Luna. García Lorca.
Beggars. Carpenter.
Being Gypsy. Young.
Dino Campana and the Bear. Hirsch.
Dreamers, The. Garrison.
Gipsies ("The gipsies seek wide sheltering woods again.") Clare.
Gipsies ("The snow falls deep; the forest lies alone.") Clare
Gipsies, The. "Scrace."
Gorgio Lad. Burr.
Gypsies. *Fr.* The Country Justice. Langhorne.
Gypsies. Nowlan.
Gypsies in the Wood. *Unknown.*
Gypsy, The. Thomas.
Gypsy Countess, The. *Unknown.*
Gypsy Davey. *Unknown.*
Gypsy Girl, The. Alford.
Gypsy-Heart. Bates
Gypsy Jane. Rands.
Gypsy Laddie, The. *Unknown.*
Gypsy Rover, The. *Unknown.*
Gypsy Trail, The. Kipling.
Gyspy Davy, The. *Unknown.*
Idlers, The. Blunden.
Johnny Faa, the Lord of Little Egypt. *Unknown.*
Meg Merrilies. Keats.
Men That Don't Fit In, The. Service.
Outside Dunsandle. Sitwell.
Princess and the Gypsies, The. Cornford.
Scholar-Gipsy, The. Arnold.
Song: "Trip it Gipsies, trip it fine." *Fr.* The Spanish Gypsy. Middleton *and* Rowley.
Where Do the Gipsies Come From? Bashford.
Wraggle Taggle Gipsies, The. *Unknown.*

H

Hafiz
To Hafiz. Aldrich.
Hagar
Hagar and Ishmael. Lasker-Schüler.
Hagar to Ishmael. Eibel.
Haggard, Sir Henry Rider
To R. K. Stephen.
Hail
Ballad of the Strange and Wonderful Storm of Hail, A. *Unknown.*
Haiku: "Why is the hail so wild." Wright.
Hair
Boy with His Hair Cut Short. Rukeyser.
Combing. Cardiff.
Emaricdulfe. "E. C."
For Anne Gregory. Yeats.
For Muh' Dear. Rodgers.
Girl with Long Dark Hair. Gray.
Hair. Gourmont.
Hair. Silverman.
Haircut. Packard.
Haircut. Shapiro.
Hairdresser, The. Hopes.
Her Hair. Baudelaire.
Janette's Hair. Halpine.
Keeping Hair. Wilson.
Lady in the Barbershop, The. Rudnik.
Lavender Cowboy, The. Hersey.
Love. Ostroff.
Maiden and Her Hair, A. Davies.
Oh Who Is That Young Sinner with the Handcuffs on His Wrists? Housman.
On Getting a Natural. Randall.
On Seeing a Hair of Lucretia Borgia. Landor.
Rape of the Lock, The. Pope.
Sam's World. Cornish.
Saturday Afternoon, When Chores Are Done. Mullen.
Song Called "His Hide Is Covered with Hair," The. Belloc.
To Amarantha, That She Would Dishevell Her Haire. Lovelace.
W. W. Jones.
What Guile Is This, That Those Her Golden Tresses. *Fr.* Amoretti. Spenser.
When I Cut My Hair. Green.
Wrapped Hair Bundles. Tauhindauli.
Haiti
Drums of Haiti. Christian.
Haitian Suite. Orr.
On a Bougainvillea Vine in Haiti. Howes.
Hale, Nathan
Nathan Hale. Finch.
Nathan Hale. Partridge.
Nathan Hale. *Unknown.*
Halevi, Judah
"If, Jerusalem, I Ever Should Forget Thee." Heine.
Haley, Alex
For Kinte. La Grone.
Hallam, Arthur Henry
Clevedon Church. Lang.
In Memoriam A. H. H. Tennyson.
Halloween
Black and Gold. Turner.
Ghoulies and Ghosties. *Unknown.*
Hallowe'en. Behn.
Halloween. Burns.
Hallowe'en. Frost.
Halloween. Lawson.
Halloween. Livingston.
Hallowe'en. Mayne.
Halloween. Pomeroy.
Halloween Concert. Fisher.
Hallowe'en Indignation Meeting. Fishback.
Halloween Witches. Holman.
Hist whist. Cummings.
If You've Never. Fowler.
It's Halloween. Prelutsky.
Jack o'Lantern. Ayre.
Lazy Witch. Livingston.
Mr. Macklin's Jack O'Lantern. McCord.
October Magic. Livingston.
On Halloween. Silverstein.
Riddle: What Am I? Aldis.
Skeleton Parade. Prelutsky.
Tam Lin. *Unknown.*
Theme in Yellow. Sandburg.
This Is Halloween. Thompson.
What Night Would It Be? Ciardi.
Hamer, Fannie Lou
Remembering Fannie Lou Hamer. Davis.
Hamlet
Elegy of Fortinbras. Herbert.
Midrash on Hamlet. Landy.
Song, *Hamlet.* Poole.
They All Want to Play Hamlet. Sandburg.
Hammocks
Lesson in Hammocks, A. Schevill.
Hampstead Heath, London
As We Rush, As We Rush in the Train. *Fr.* Sunday at Hampstead. Thompson.
Breath of Hampstead Heath. Thomas.
Sunday on Hampstead Heath. Woodcock.
Hampton Roads, Virginia
Cumberland, The. Longfellow.
Handball
Day and Night Handball. Dunn.
Game Resumed. Lattimore.
Handball Players at Brighton Beach, The. Feldman.
Handel, George Frideric
Epigram on Handel and Bononcini. Byrom.
Handicaps and the Handicapped
Freaks at Spurgin Road Field, The. Hugo.
Hunchback in the Park, The. Thomas.
Near the School for Handicapped Children. Shapcott.
See also **Amputees; Birth Defects; Blindness; Cripples; Deafness; Mental Retardation.**
Hands
Hand, The. Moss.
Hand, The. Thomas.
Hand That Signed the Paper, The. Thomas.
Hands. Aldis.
Hands, The. *Fr.* The Limeratomy. Euwer.
Hands. Finkel.
Hands. Glasgow.
Hands, The. Harrison.
His Lady's Hand. Wyatt.
In the Small Boats of Their Hands. Kircher.

Look to the Back of the Hand. Minty.
Love for a Hand. Shapiro.
Palm of the Hand. Rilke.
This Living Hand. Keats.
Thumb. Dacey.
Your Hands. Grimké.

Handwriting
Lesson in Handwriting, A. Reid.
Writing. Nemerov.

Hanging
Ballade: "Brother humans who live on after us". Villon.
Briton Who Shot at His King, A. Ross.
Captain Hall. *Unknown.*
Clever Tom Clinch Going to Be Hànged. Swift.
Constance Kent. *Unknown.*
Danny Deever. Kipling.
Death-Doomed. Carleton.
Eight o'Clock. Housman.
Four Maries, The. *Unknown.*
Gallows Pole, The. *Unknown.*
Geordie. *Unknown.*
Hang Me, O Hang Me, and I'll Be Dead and Gone. *Unknown.*
Hanging, The. MacDonald.
Hanging Johnny. *Unknown.*
Hanging of Sam Archer, The. *Unknown.*
Jack Hall. *Unknown.*
Jeff Buckner. Beddo.
Kevin Barry: Died for Ireland, 1st November, 1920. *Unknown.*
Life of the Mannings. *Unknown.*
London Fête, A. Patmore.
MacPherson's Farewell. *Unknown.*
Maid Freed from the gallows, The. *Unknown.*
Marrying the Hangman. Atwood.
Murder of Maria Marten, The. *Unknown.*
Night before Larry Was Stretched, The. *Unknown.*
On Bell-Ringers. Voltaire.
On Moonlit Heath and Lonesome Bank. Housman.
One Good Turn Deserves Another. *Unknown.*
Pisanello's Studies of Men Hanging on Gallows. Wheatcroft.
Poor Boy. *Unknown.*
Portent, The. Melville.
Receipt to Cure a Love Fit, A. *Unknown.*
Salvation of Texas Peters, The. Foley.
Sam Hall. *Unknown.*
To His Son. Ralegh.
Two Poems (After A. E. Housman). Kingsmill.
See also **Executions; Lynching.**

Hanks, Nancy
I Saw a Ghost. Boilleau.
Nancy Hanks. R. *and* S. V. Benét.
Nancy Hanks, Mother of Abraham Lincoln. Lindsay.
Out of the Wilderness. Troubetzkoy.
Reply to Nancy Hanks, A. Silberger.

Hannibal
Put Hannibal i'th' scale. *Fr.* Satires. Juvenal.

Hanno
Southward Sidonian Hanno. Allen.

Hansel and Gretel
Disenchantments: An Anthology of Modern Fairy Tale Poetry. (DFT), pp. 59–69. Wolfgang Mieder, ed.

Han-shan
Poem to Han-shan. Stroud.

Hanukkah
Chanuke, O Chanuke. *Unknown.*
Kindle the Taper. Lazarus.
Light Another Candle. Chaikin.
Light the Festive Candles. Fisher.
Mi Y'Malel. *Unknown.*

Happiness
Anatomy of Happiness, The. Nash.
Art of Happiness, The. Young.
Blessing, A. Wright.
Character of a Happy Life, The. Wotton.
Choice, The. Pomfret.
Cliff Klingenhagen. Robinson.
Epistle to Davie, a Brother Poet. Burns.
Example, The. Davies.
Four Things Make Us Happy Here. Herrick.
Good Times. Clifton.
Happiness. Isenhour.
Happiness. Leonard.
Happiness Dependent on Ourselves. *Fr.* The Traveller. Goldsmith.
Happiness Makes Up in Height for What It Lacks in Length. Frost.
Happy Life, The. Martial.
Happy the Man. *Fr.* Odes. Horace.
Happy Thought. Stevenson.
If You Happy Would Be. Fernández.
Joy. Delany.
L'Allegro. Milton.
Ode on Solitude. Pope.
On the South Downs. Teasdale.
Poem: "Ah, I know what happiness is!" Dickinson.
Poetry Is Happiness. Gardiner.
Rarely, Rarely, Comest Thou. Shelley.
Running. Wilbur.
Sensation. Rimbaud.
Summer Mansions. Herschberger.
Wish, A. Rogers.
Wishes. Harjo.
See also **Contentment.**

Harbors and Ports
Cinque Port, A. Davidson.
Fishing Harbour Towards Evening. Kell.
Harbor, The. Sandburg.
Harbor Dawn, The. *Fr.* The Bridge. Crane.
Outward Bound. Aldrich.
Plymouth Harbor. Radford.

Hardin, John Wesley
Wes Hardin: From a Photograph. Carver.

Harding, Warren Gamaliel
Two Poems about President Harding. Wright.

Hardy, Thomas
At Thomas Hardy's Birthplace, 1953. Wright.
Birthday Poem for Thomas Hardy. Day Lewis.
Heart of Thomas Hardy, The. Betjeman.
Luncheon, A. Beerbohm.
Thoughts of Thomas Hardy. Blunden.

Hares
Cowper's Three Hares. Turner.
Ecclesiastes. Langland.
Epitaph on a Hare. Cowper.
Hare, A ("Eyes that glass fear, though fear on furtive foot."). De la Mare.
Hare. Holden.
Hare, The. *Unknown.*
Hare and the Tortoise, The. Serraillier.
Hare in Winter. Piercy.
March Hares. Young.
Poor Wat. *Fr.* Venus and Adonis. Shakespeare.
Two Songs of a Fool. Yeats.
White Hare, The. Bowes-Lyon.
White Hares, The. Lyon.
See also **Rabbits.**

Harlem, New York City
College Formal: Renaissance Casino. Hughes.
Dive. Hughes.
Esthete in Harlem. Hughes.
Harlem (A Dream Deferred). *Fr.* Lenox Avenue Mural. Hughes.
Harlem Freeze Frame. Bethune.
Harlem Gallery: From the Inside. Neal.
Harlem in January. Fields.
Harlem Shadows. McKay.
Harlem Sounds: Hallelujah Corner. Browne.
Harlem Sweeties. Hughes.
Harlem. *Fr.* Lenox Avenue Mural. Hughes.
Jitterbugging in the Streets. Hernton.
Juke Box Love Song. Hughes.
Keep on Pushing. Henderson.
King of Harlem, The. García Lorca.
Lenox Avenue Mural. Hughes.
Lenox Avenue. Alexander.
Night Funeral in Harlem. Hughes.
Prime. Hughes.
Promised Land. Engel.
Puzzled. Hughes.
Sketches of Harlem. Henderson.
Sonnet to a Negro in Harlem. Johnson.
Still Voice of Harlem, The. Rivers.
Train Runs Late to Harlem, The. Rivers.
Under the Edge of February. Cortez.
Walk with De Mayor of Harlem. Henderson.
Young Negro Poet. Hernton.

Harper's Ferry, West Virginia
Harper's Ferry. Rodman.
How Old Brown Took Harper's Ferry. Stedman.

Narrative. Atkins.
Harps and Harpists
Bishop's Harp, The. Mannyng.
Dear Harp of My Country. Moore.
Harp That Once through Tara's Halls, The. Moore.
Harper, The. *Unknown.*
Military Harpist, The. Pitter.
Minstrel Boy, The. Moore.
Harpur, Charles
Extinct Birds. Wright.
Harrison, Benjamin
Historical Reflections. Hollander.
Harvard University
Christo et Ecclesiae. *Fr.* Two Sonnets: Harvard. Holmes.
Experiential Religion. Du Priest.
I Went to See Irving Babbitt. Eberhart.
On the Aristocracy of Harvard. Bossidy.
To the University of Cambridge, in New-England. Wheatley.
Harvest
Antique Harvesters. Ransom.
Bringing in the Sheaves. Shaw.
Dead Harvest, A. Meynell.
Harvest. Cortissoz.
Harvest. Shuford.
Harvest and Consecration. Jennings.
Harvest Home. *Fr.* King Arthur. Dryden.
Harvest Home. Guiterman.
Harvest Poem. Fisher.
Harvest Song. Campbell.
Harvest Song. Toomer.
Harvest Time. Powers.
Harvest Time. Watermeyer.
Harvesting Wheat for the Public Share. Li Chü.
Haying. Herbin.
High Plains Harvest. Morton.
Hock-Cart, or Harvest Home, The. Herrick.
Hurrahing in Harvest. Hopkins.
Potato Harvest, The. Roberts.
Praise of Ceres. *Fr.* The Silver Age. Heywood.
Reaper, The. Allen.
Reapers. Blind.
Reapers. Toomer.
Returning from Harvest. Watkins.
Ripe and Bearded Barley, The. *Unknown.*
Rural Lines after Breughel. Krapf.
Solitary Reaper, The. Wordsworth.
Soon as the harvest hath laid bare the plains. *Fr.* The Thresher's Labour. Duck.
Threshing-Machine, The. Meynell.
Harvey, William
On the Death of Mr. William Harvey. Cowley.
Hashish
Haschish, The. Whittier.
Hasidism
Invocation: "Good morning to you, Lord of the world!" Isaac of Berditshev.
Hate
Beyond Words. Frost.
Enslaved. McKay.
Epitaph of Nearchos. Ammianus.
Fire and Ice. Frost.
Fury's Field. Bodker.
Hate. Stephens.
Hate-Song, A. Shelley.
Hatred. Bennett.
I Hate Harry. Chaikin.
I Saw a Little Girl I Hate. Spilka.
Love and Hate. *Unknown.*
On Love. *Fr.* Twenty-three Tanka. Tamekane.
Soliloquy of the Spanish Cloister. Browning.
Song of Hate. Frances.
Stone Orchard, The. Oates.
Tree of Hatred, The. Moreh.
When I loved you, I can't but allow. Moore.
Tygers of Wrath (TW). X. J. Kennedy, ed.
Hats
Alicia's Bonnet. Pullen.
At the Millinery Shop. Epstein.
Hat Bar. Weston.
My Hat. Smith.
My Infundibuliform Hat. Adams.
My Old Straw Hat. Cook.
Newspaper Hats. Howard.
Quangle Wangle's Hat, The. Lear.
Where Did You Get That Hat? Sullivan.
Haunted Houses
Empty House, The. Hoban.
Ghost House. Frost.
Haunted House. Worth.
Haunted Palace, The. Poe.
House Fear. Frost.
In the Old House. Aiken.
Southern Mansion. Bontemps.
Havana, Cuba
Habana. Bond.
Havana Dreams: Havana. Hughes.
Hawaii
Above the Falls at Waimea. Johnson.
Born was the island. *Unknown.*
Hongo Store, The, 29 Miles Volcano Hilo, Hawaii. Hongo.
Kula . . . a Homecoming. Mark.
Leper, The. Ka-'ehu.
Mango Tree, The. Chock.
My landlady has been to Hawaii. I look at her diamante. *Fr.* Brother Jonathan, Brother Kafka. O'Sullivan.
Poet Imagines His Grandfather's Thoughts on the Day He Died, The. Lum.
Twenty-third Flight. Birney.
Hawks
Afternoon,/ with just enough of a breeze for him to ride it. Sund.
Fieldmouse, A/ crouches low. Sund.
Fish-Hawk, The. Wheelock.
Hawk, The. Knister.
Hawk Is a Woman. Flanner.
Hawk Nailed to a Barn Door. Blue Cloud.
Hawk Roosting. Hughes.
Hurt Hawks. Jeffers.
On the Plains. Brooks.
Red Wing Hawk. Applewhite.
Sparrow Hawk, The. Hoban.
Sparrow-Hawk, A. *Unknown.*
Spring Hawks. Thomas.
Tamer and Hawk. Gunn.
To a Marsh Hawk in Spring. Thoreau.
To the Man-of-War-Bird. Whitman.
Windhover, The. Hopkins.
Wounded Hawk, The. Palmer.
Hawthorn
Hawthorn, The. *Unknown.*
Hawthorn Hedge, The. Wright.
I Bended unto Me. Brown.
Hawthorne, Nathaniel
Hawthorne. Alcott.
Hawthorne. *Fr.* A Fable for Critics. Lowell.
Hawthorne. Longfellow.
Hawthorne Garland, A. Fogle.
On Visiting the Graves of Hawthorne and Thoreau. Very.
Hayden Planetarium (New York City)
Ode to the Hayden Planetarium. Guiterman.
Haydn, Franz Joseph
Allegro: "After a black day, I play Haydn." Tranströmer.
To Haydn. Holcroft.
Haydon, Benjamin Robert
Addressed to Haydon. Keats.
Haze. *See* Fog.
Heads
Head Is a Paltry Matter, The. Di Cicco.
Head, The. Fallon.
Thoughts on One's Head. Meredith.
Health Clubs
At the Spa. Bowden.
Hearne, Samuel
Samuel Hearne in Wintertime. Newlove.
Hearst, Patricia
Dear Patty Dear Tania. Mathews.
Patty Hearst Hoists the Carbine. James.
Hearst, William Randolph
Doxology. Taylor.
Hearts
Heart, The. *Fr.* The Black Riders. Crane.
Heart, The. Ignatow.
Heart. LaBombard.
To a Bad Heart. Reynolds.

To pray for an easy heart is no prayer at all. *Fr.* Autumn Testament. Baxter.
Upon A Diamond Cut in Forme of a Heart . . . Sent in a New-Yeares Gift. Ayton.

Heat
Central Heating System. Spender.
Cold and Heat. Hawaiian.
Cool Web, The. Graves.
Heat. Doolittle ("H. D.").
Heat. Lampman.
Heat. Mackenzie.
January. Voigt.
Pagett, M.P. Kipling.
Shade-seller, The. Jacobsen.

Heaven
About the Heavenly Life. Leon.
And That Will Be Heaven. Paterson.
At Home in Heaven. Montgomery.
At Last. Whittier.
Blessed Damozel, The. Rossetti.
Bower of Bliss, The. *Fr.* The Faerie Queene. Spenser.
Celestial City, The. *Fr.* Christ's Victory and Triumph. Fletcher.
Chartless. Dickinson.
Choir Invisible, The. "Eliot."
Cold Heaven, The. Yeats.
Coming Home with Jesus. Isenhour.
De Glory Road. Wood.
Description of Elizium, The. *Fr.* Muses' Elizium, The. Drayton.
Description of Elysium. Agee.
End of the Way, The. Cole.
Eternal Light. Binney.
Far Land, The. Wheelock.
For a Lady I Know. *Fr.* Four Epitaphs. Cullen.
General William Booth Enters into Heaven. Lindsay.
Glorious Things of Thee Are Spoken. Newton.
God's Residence. Dickinson.
God's Trails Lead Home. Clements.
Gradatim. Holland.
Greater Country, The. Watkins.
"He Will Give Them Back." "Klingle."
He Would Have His Lady Sing. Dolben.
Heaven, Heaven, Heaven Is the Place. Hughes.
Heaven Is Heaven. Rossetti.
Heaven is what I cannot reach. Dickinson.
Heaven Overarches Earth and Sea. Rossetti.
Heaven. Brooke.
Heaven. Herbert.
Heaven. *Fr.* Paradise Lost. Milton.
Heaven. *Unknown.*
Heaven. Watts.
Heaven-Haven. Hopkins.
Heaven's Declare the Glory of God, The. Psalms. Bible, *O.T.*
Heavenly City, The. Smith.
Heavenward. Nairne.
Hierusalem. *Unknown.*
Holy City, The. Weatherly.
Home. Kowit.
Home. Sill.
Home at Last. Chesterton.
Home of the Soul. Gates.
Homeland, The. Haweis.
Hour of Peaceful Rest, The. Tappan.
Hymn for the Close of the Week. Abelard.
I never saw a moor. Dickinson.
I went to heaven. Dickinson.
Ice Cream in Paradise. Hollander.
If There Are Any Heavens. Cummings.
If Thou Indeed Derive Thy Light from Heaven. Wordsworth.
If To Die. Romilu.
Immortal is an ample word. Dickinson.
In Him. Dunbar.
Jerusalem, My Happy Home. *Unknown.*
Jerusalem. Bernard of Cluny.
Jordan ("When first my lines"). Herbert.
Lady I Know, A. Cullen.
Land o' the Leal, The. Nairne.
Land of the Evening Mirage, The. *Unknown.*
Last Landlord, The. Allen.
Leave Me, O Love. Sidney.
Let Us Go Down, the Long Dead Night Is Done. *Fr.* Towards the Source. Brennan.
Life above, the Life on High, The. St. Teresa of Avila.
Life after Death. Pindar.
My Ain Countree. Demarest.
Nearer Home. Cary.
New Jerusalem, The. *Unknown.*
O Mother Dear, Jerusalem. "F. B. P."
O Paradise! O Paradise! Faber.
Oh that I was the Bird of Paradise! *Fr.* Preparatory Meditations before My Approach to the Lord's Supper. Taylor.
One Centred System. *Fr.* The Columbiad. Barlow.
Other World, The. Stowe.
Our Companie in the Next World. *Fr.* Of the Progresse of the Soule; the Second Anniversarie. Donne.
Out of the Hitherwhere. Riley.
Paradise. Faber.
Paradise. Rossetti.
Paradise Lost, *sels.* Milton.
Peace. Vaughan.
Pilgrimage, The. Ralegh.
Port of Many Ships. Masefield.
Prospect of Heaven Makes Death Easy, A. Watts.
Rest Is Not Here. Nairne.
Safely Home. *Unknown.*
Saint Peter sat by the celestial gate. *Fr.* The Vision of Judgment. Byron.
Saints in Glory, The. *Fr.* Divina Commedia: Paradiso. Dante.
Seek Flowers of Heaven. Southwell.
Sister Lou. Brown.
Song: "It Autumne was, and on our hemispheare." Drummond of Hawthornden.
Splendidis Longum Valedico Nugis. Sidney.
Streets of Glory. *Unknown.*
Sunset City, The. Cornwell.
Surprises. *Unknown.*
Theology. Dunbar.
There Is a Land. Watts.
There. Coleridge.
They Are All Gone into the World of Light! Vaughan.
This World Is All a Fleeting Show. Moore.
Tired of Towns. Lang.
True Heaven, The. Hayne.
Up-Hill. Rossetti.
We Are God's Chosen Few. Swift.
We'll Meet Again. Smith.
What is—"Paradise." Dickinson.
Where Is Heaven? Carman.
White Island, The; or, Place of the Blest. Herrick.
World of Light, The. Vaughan.

Hebe
Hebe. Lowell.

Hebrew
Hebrew Lesson. Brod.
Hebrew of Your Poets, Zion, The. Reznikoff.

Hebrides
Beckon Me, Ye Cuillins. Hendrie.
Island of Mull. *Unknown.*
Island of Rhum, The. Ferguson.
Letter to Garber from Skye. Hugo.
Misty Island, The. *Unknown.*
Nightmare on Rhum. Macmillan.
Over the Sea to Skye. Stevenson.
Skye. Gawsworth.
Skye Summer. Donaldson.
There Are Gods. Riley.
View. Munro.
Witch, The. *Fr.* Skye. Gibson.

Hector
Achilles with wild fury in his heart. *Fr.* The Iliad. Homer.
Ballad of Hector in Hades. Muir.
Hector. Iremonger.

Hedgehogs
Hedgehog, The. Bell.
Hedgehog, The. *Fr.* The Shepherd's Calendar. Clare.
Hedgehog. Muldoon.
To a Hedgehog. Thompson.

Heidelberg, Germany
Thinking of Hölderlin. Middleton.

Heine, Heinrich
Century Piece for Poor Heine (1800–1856), A. Logan.
Heinrich Heine. Lewisohn.
Translator to Translated. Pound.
Venus of the Louvre. Lazarus.

Helen of Troy
Ganymede and Helen. *Unknown.*

Helen. Doolittle ("H. D.").
Helen. Valéry.
Helen Grown Old. Lewis.
Helen—Old. MacKay.
Mythmaking. Spivack.
Past Ruin'd Ilion Helen Lives. *Fr.* Ianthe. Landor.
To Helen. Poe.
Under a Lady's Picture. Waller.
Was This the Face. *Fr.* Doctor Faustus. Marlowe.
White Isle of Leuce, The. Read.
White Queen. Fuller.
Helicopters
Flight Plan. Merchant.
Hell
Arrival in Hell. Huch.
Good Man in Hell, The. Muir.
Hell is a city much like London. *Fr.* Peter Bell the Third. Shelley.
Hell. *Unknown.*
Jews in Hell, The. Goldemberg.
Lament of an Idle Demon. Lister.
Paradise Lost, *sels.* Milton
Place of the Damned, The. *Fr.* Paradise Lost. Milton.
Place of the Damned, The. Swift.
Poets of Hell, The. Shapiro.
Simon Legree—A Negro Sermon. *Fr.* The Booker Washington Trilogy. Lindsay.
Strange Meeting. Owen.
Theology. Dunbar.
To Dives. Belloc.
Warm Babies. Preston.
Hell's Angels
Black Jackets. Gunn.
Helmholtz, Hermann Ludwig Ferdinand Von
Hermann Ludwig Ferdinand Von Helmholtz. Meinke.
Heloise. *See* **Abelard and Heloise.**
Hengist
Hengest Cyning. Borges.
Henly, England
Henly, July 4: 1914–1964. Sissman.
Henry I, King of England
White Ship, The. Rossetti.
Henry II, King of England
Epistle of Rosamond to King Henry the Second, The. *Fr.* England's Heroical Epistles. Drayton.
King Henry to Rosamond. *Fr.* England's Heroical Epistles. Drayton.
Queen Eleanor's Confession. *Unknown.*
Henry V, King of England
Agincourt. Drayton.
King Henry Fifth's Conquest of France. *Unknown.*
Once More unto the Breach. *Fr.* King Henry V. Shakespeare.
Henry VIII, King of England
Ballade of the Scottyshe Kynge, A. Skelton.
Henry VIII. Farjeon.
Henry VIII. *Unknown.*
Portrait of Henry VIII, The. Surrey.
Tudor Portrait. Lattimore.
Henry III, King of France
Portrait of Henri III, A. Théodore Agrippa d'Aubigné.
Henry IV, King of France (Henry of Navarre)
Ivry. Macaulay.
Henry the Navigator
Portrait of Prince Henry, The. Clouts.
Prince Henry the Navigator. Clouts.
"Henry, O." (William Sydney Porter)
Knight in Disguise, The. Lindsay.
Hens
Chickens, The. *Unknown.*
Clocking Hen, The. *Unknown.*
Cock and the Hen, The. *Fr.* The Canterbury Tales: The Nun's Priest's Tale. Chaucer.
Cock and the Hen, The. Heywood.
Flock of Guinea Hens Seen from a Car, A. Welty.
Hen, The. Douglas.
Hen Dying. Maclean.
Hen Flower, The. Kinnell.
Hen Under Bay-Tree. Pitter.
Hens. Nowlan.
Hens, The. Roberts.
Hen's Nest. Clare.
Higgledy, piggledy, my black hen. *Unknown.*
Janet Waking. Ransom.
Motherhood. Calverley.
Reverend Henry Ward Beecher, The. Holmes.
See also **Chickens.**
Henschel, Sir George
For the Eightieth Birthday of a Great Singer. Shanks.
Heraclitus
Elegy on Herakleitos. Fitts.
From Heraclitus. Dugan.
Heraclitus. Cory.
That Nature Is a Heraclitean Fire and of the Comfort of the Resurrection. Hopkins.
Herbert, George
On Mr. George Herberts Booke Intituled the Temple of Sacred Poems, Sent to a Gentle-woman. Crashaw.
Herbs
Lines with a Gift of Herbs. Lewis.
Nosegay Always Sweet, for Lovers to Send for Tokens of Love at New Year's Tide, or for Fairings, A. Hunnis.
Old Man. Thomas.
Hercules
Antaeus; a Fragment. Owen.
Heracles. Winters.
Herding
How Low Is the Lowing Herd. Kelly.
See also **Shepherds and Shepherdesses.**
Heresy and Heretics
Epigram: "When doctrines meet with general approbation." Garrick.
Hermaphrodites
Upon an Hermaphrodite. Cleveland.
Hermit Crabs
With the Shell of a Hermit Crab. Wright.
Hermits
Black Jess. Dufault.
Bushed. Birney.
Desire for Hermitage, The. *Unknown.*
Eremites, The. Graves.
Hermit, The. Davies.
Hermit, The. Hsü Pên.
Hermit, The. Moss.
Hermit, The. Ralegh.
Hermitage, The. *Unknown.*
Hermit's Song, A. *Unknown.*
Inscription in a Hermitage. Warton.
Marban, a Hermit Speaks. *Unknown.*
Resolution and Independence. Wordsworth.
Three Hermits, The. Yeats.
Hero and Leander
Hero and Leander. Marlowe.
On a Landscape of Sestos. *Fr.* A Visit to the Art Gallery. Baker.
On Leander's Swimming over the Hellespont to Hero. Warton, the Younger.
Repentance. *Fr.* Hero and Leander. Chapman.
Subjectivity at Sestos. Hubbard.
Written after Swimming from Sestos to Abydos. Byron.
Herod the Great
Children's Ghosts, The. Letts.
Clap Your Hands for Herod. Hanzlik.
Coventry Carol, The. *Unknown.*
Innocents, The. MacPherson.
Innocent's Song. Causley.
Slaughter of the Innocents by Order of King Herod, The. *Fr.* Carmen Paschale. Sedulius.
St. Stephen and Herod. *Unknown.*
Heroes and Heroines
Abdul, the Bulbul Amir. *Unknown.*
Ballad of Heroes, A. Dobson.
Casabianca. Hemans.
Casey at the Bat. Thayer.
Character of the Happy Warrior. Wordsworth.
Charlton Heston. Fried.
Commemorative of a Naval Victory. Melville.
Critics say that epics have died out, The. *Fr.* Aurora Leigh. Browning.
Emily Geiger. *Unknown.*
Gee-Up Dar, Mules. Piper.
Hero, The. Moore.
Hero, The. Nicoll.
Heroes. Creeley.
Heroes, The. Simpson.
Hervé Riel. Browning.
Horatius at the Bridge. *Fr.* Lays of Ancient Rome. Macaulay.
How Sleep the Brave. Collins.
I Think Continually of Those Who Were Truly Great. Spender.
John Maynard. Alger.

Man from the Crowd, The. Foss.
Molly Pitcher. Richards.
New Hunting Song, A. *Unknown.*
Ode: "How sleep the brave, who sink to rest." Collins.
Poem for Heroes, A. Fields.
Settling Some Old Football Scores. Bishop.
Sinfonia Eroica. James.
Sixteen Dead Men. Sigerson Shorter.
Song for the Heroes. Comfort.
Where Are You Now Superman? Patten.
Where, O Where? Bracker.
Who'd Be a Hero (Fictional)? Bishop.
Heroin. *See* **Drug Addiction.**
Herons
Blue Heron, The. Roberts.
Fishing Blue Creek. Scheele.
Great Blue Heron, The. Kizer.
Heron, The. Donaghy.
Heron, The. Hovell-Thurlow.
Heron, The. Murray.
Heron, The. Roethke.
Heron. Walker.
Heron, The. Watkins.
Heron. Booth.
Heron in Swamp. Howard.
Herons, The. Ledwidge.
Herons. *Unknown.*
Incorrigible Music, An. Curnow.
Night Heron. Frost.
Snowy Heron. Ciardi.
Herrick, Robert
To his book's end this last line he'd have placed. Herrick.
Whenas in Jeans, *parody.* Dehn.
Herring
Caller Herrin'. Nairne.
Herrings. *Fr.* Verses for Fruitwomen. Swift.
Red Herring, The. MacBeth.
Smoked Herring, The. Cros.
Hervey, William. *See* **Harvey, William.**
Herzl, Theodor
Theodor Herzl. Zangwill.
Hess, Dame Myra
Jesu, Joy of Man's Desiring. Fitzgerald.
Heston, Charlton
Charlton Heston. Fried.
Hiawatha
Hiawatha's Photographing. "Carroll."
Modern Hiawatha, The. *Fr.* The Song of Milkanwatha. *Unknown.*
Song of Hiawatha, The, *sels.* Longfellow.
What I Think of Hiawatha. Morris.
Hiccups
Charm: Hiccups. *Unknown.*
Hicks, Edward
For Edward Hicks. Helwig.
Highlands of Scotland. *See* **Scottish Highlands.**
Highwaymen
Black Bart. *Unknown.*
"Black Bart, PO8." Bierce.
Bold Jack Donahue. *Unknown.*
Brennan on the Moor. *Unknown.*
Death of Morgan, The. *Unknown.*
Dick Turpin and Black Bess; or, My Bonnie Black Bess. *Unknown.*
Execution of Luke Hutton, The. *Unknown.*
Highwayman, The. Noyes.
Mulberry Mountain. *Unknown.*
Rambling Boy, The. *Unknown.*
Wild Colonial Boy, The. *Unknown.*
Highways. *See* **Roads.**
Hiking and Hikers
Maine Trail, A. McGiffert.
Week-End Naturalist, The. Buchan.
Hilary, Saint
World's Worth. Rossetti.
Hills and Mountains
After Sunset. Conkling.
Afternoon on a Hill. Millay.
Alaskan Mountain Poem 1. Silko.
Alpine. Thomas.
Alpine Spirit's Song. Beddoes.
Among the Finger Lakes. Wallace.
Blue Ridge. Hodges.
Blue Ridge, The. Monroe.
Cheyenne Mountain. Jackson.
Circumambulation of Mt. Tamalpais. Hoyem.
Climbing in Glencoe. Young.
Close-Up. Ammons.
Dark Hills, The. Robinson.
Fable: "Mountain and the squirrel, The." Emerson.
Golgotha Is a Mountain. Bontemps.
Granite Mountain, The. Sarett.
Grass on the Mountain, The. Austin.
Grongar Hill. Dyer.
Hill, A. Hecht.
Hills. Guiterman.
Hills and the Sea, The. Campbell.
I Haunt the Hills that Overlook the Seas. *Fr.* The Testament of a Man Forbid. Davidson.
I Stood Tiptoe upon a Little Hill. Keats.
I Will Lift Up Mine Eyes. *Fr.* Psalms. Bible, *O.T.*
In the Canadian Rockies. Hopper.
In the Mountains on a Summer Day. Li Po.
In the Selkirks. Scott.
Like to these unmeasurable mountains. Sannazaro.
Mid-August at Sourdough Mountain Lookout. Snyder.
Mountain, The. Frost.
Mountain Born. Bost.
Mountain Evenings. Holme.
Mountain sat upon the plain, The. Dickinson.
Mountain That Got Little, The. Stafford.
Mountain to the Pine, The. Hawkes.
Mountains, The. De la Mare.
Mountains. Larcom.
Mountains grow unnoticed, The. Dickinson.
Nocturne of the Self-Evident Presence. MacGreevy.
Old Man Mountain. Noyes.
Olives and Mountains. *Fr.* Aurora Leigh. Browning.
On Middleton Edge. Young.
On the Solitary Fells around Hawkshead. *Fr.* The Prelude. Wordsworth.
Peaks, The. Crane.
Pennines in April. Hughes.
Pilgrimage Song. *Unknown.*
Quantocks, The. Wordsworth.
Schreckhorn, The. Hardy.
Shancoduff. Kavanagh.
Silent Ranges, The. Bird.
Sleeping Giant, The. Hall.
That Dark Other Mountain. Francis.
Three Hills, The. Squire.
To My Mountain. Raine.
Trosachs, The. Wordsworth.
Up to thy summit, Lewesdon, to the brow. *Fr.* Lewesdon Hill. Crowe.
With Hands like Leaves. Still.
Poems of the Scottish Hills (PoSH). Hamish Brown, ed.
See also **Mountain Climbing.**
Himalayas
Hills, The. Grenfell.
Kinchinjunga. Rice.
Hinduism
Indian upon God, The. Yeats.
Mahabalipuram. MacNeice.
Hippopotamuses
Dawn Hippo. Clouts.
Habits of the Hippopotamus. Guiterman.
Hippo, The. Roethke.
Hippopotamothalamion. Wheelock.
Hippopotamus, The. Belloc.
Hippopotamus. Cole.
Hippopotamus, The. Durston.
Hippopotamus, The. Eliot.
Hippopotamus, The. Nash.
Hippopotamus, The. Prelutsky.
I Had a Hippopotamus. Barrington.
I shoot the hippopotamus. Belloc.
Native African Revolutionaries. Jones.
To a Blue Hippopotamus. Kay.
Hiroshige, Ando
Hiroshige. Perlberg.
Hiroshima, Japan
Day after Trinity, The. Oyama.
Dirge for the New Sunrise. Sitwell.
Hiroshima Exit. Kogawa.
Hiroshima Lullaby, A. Langland.
I Come and Stand at Every Door. Hikmet.
Shadow of Cain, The. Sitwell.

Hispanics. *See* **Chicanos; Puerto Ricans.**
History and Historians
Ancient Historian. Wallace-Crabbe.
Ancient History. Guiterman.
Antiquary, The. Campbell.
Cannon Park. St. Germain.
Fall of Rome, The. Auden.
Help from History. Stafford.
History. Francis.
History. Gregor.
Human Greatness. Barclay.
I Shall Laugh Purely. Jeffers.
Incident Here and There, An. Doolittle ("H. D.").
Johnny's Hist'ry Lesson. Waterman.
Lessons in History. Warren.
Living Truth, The. Plumpp.
Meredith Phyfe. *Fr.* The New Spoon River. Masters.
On Sir Nathaniel Wraxall the Historian. Colman, the Younger.
Our History. Coblentz.
Poet Speaks from the Visitors' Gallery, A. MacLeish.
Readings of History. Rich.
There was a time when the stars fell like rain. Tauhindauli.
Urban History. Kallman.
What Happened Here Before. Snyder.
Written in the Beginning of Mezeray's History of France. Prior.
Hitchhiking
Faces. Ciardi.
Fort Wayne, Indiana 1964. Lewis.
Hitchhiker, The. Ai.
Poets Hitchhiking on the Highway. Corso.
Hitler, Adolf
Adolph Hitler Meditates on the Jewish Problem. Hahn.
Hitler, frothy-mouth, wooden-head. Unknown.
Letter to Hitler, A. Laughlin.
Round and Round Hitler's Grave. *Unknown.*
Teahouse. Rinaldi.
Ho Chi Minh
Ballad of Ho Chi Minh. MacColl.
On the Death of Ho Chi Minh. Mandel.
Hobbes, Thomas
Hobbes, 1651. Hollander.
To Mr. Hobbes. Cowley.
Hoboes. *See* **Vagabonds.**
Hoffa, Jimmy
Binding Arbitration. Wrigley.
Hogarth, William
Epitaph on William Hogarth. Johnson.
Hogarth. Churchill.
Hogg, James
Extempore Effusion upon the Death of James Hogg. Wordsworth.
Hogue, La, Battle of (1692)
Hervé Riel. Browning.
Hohenlinden, Battle of (1800)
Hohenlinden. Campbell.
Hokusai, Katsushika
Camden Magpie. McCrae.
Great Wave, The: Hokusai. Finkel.
Great Wave off Kanagwa, The. Egemo.
Hokusai's Wave. Cabral.
Laughing Hyena, by Hokusai, The. Enright.
Holbein, Hans
Fancy Dress. Mackellar.
Holiday, Billie (Eleanora Fagan McKay)
Blues and Bitterness. Bennett.
Day Lady Died, The. O'Hara.
Holidays
Bonne Entente. Scott.
Ceremonies for Candlemasse Eve. Herrick.
Conversation with Washington. Livingston.
Rebolushinary X-mas. Rogers.
Whitmonday. MacNeice.
Our Holidays in Poetry (OHIP). Mildred P. Harrington *and* Josephine H. Thomas, comps.
Poems for the Great Days (PGD). Thomas Curtis Clark *and* Robert Earle Clark, comps.
Poems for Seasons and Celebrations (PoSC). William Cole, ed.
See also **specific holidays.**
Holland. *See* **Netherlands.**
Holly
As the Holly Groweth Green. Henry VIII, King of England.
Highty, tighty, paradighty, clothed in green. *Unknown.*
Holly, The. De la Mare.
Holly against Ivy. *Unknown.*
Holly and Ivy. *Unknown.*
Holly and Mistletoe. Farjeon.
Holly and the Ivy, The. *Unknown.*
Holly Tree, The. Southey.
Itum Paradisum all clothed in green. *Unknown.*
Ivy and Holly. Meyerstein.
Hollyhocks
Hollyhock, A. Sherman.
Hollyhocks, The. Betts.
Hollywood, California
Hollywood. Blanding.
Hollywood. Shapiro.
Holmes, Oliver Wendell
Filling an Order. Trowbridge.
Holmes. *Fr.* A Fable for Critics. Lowell.
Holocaust
Adolph Hitler Meditates on the Jewish Problem. Hahn.
Auschwitz from Colombo. Ranasinghe.
Babi Yar. Ozerov.
Ballade of Beauties. Scott.
Camp in the Prussian Forest, A. Jarrell.
Children of Auschwitz. Korzhavin.
Desnos Reading the Palms of Men on Their Way to the Gas Chambers. Berg.
Extermination of the Jews, The. Bell.
Holocaust 1944. Ranasinghe.
Homeless, The. Hall.
How They Killed My Grandmother. Slutsky.
Letter from Berlin, A. Stallworthy.
"More Light! More Light!" Hecht.
Mother. Tuwim.
Murder of a Community. Weissbort.
1976. Shapiro.
Permanent Delegate, The. Suhl.
Poem for Anton Schmidt, A. Pillen.
Pripet Marshes, The. Feldman.
September Song. Hill.
Shipment to Maidanek. Fogel.
Wall, The. Askenazy.
Holy Baptism. *See* **Baptism.**
Holy Communion. *See* **Eucharist.**
Holy Family
Cherry-Tree Carol, The. *Unknown.*
Swiftly Arose. *Fr.* Song of Myself. Whitman.
What Life Have You. *Fr.* The Rock. Eliot.
Holy Ghost
His Litany to the Holy Spirit. Herrick.
Holy Spirit, Truth Divine. Longfellow.
Holy Grail
Parsifal. Verlaine.
Quest of the Sangraal, The. Hawker.
Vision of Sir Launfal, The. Lowell.
Holy Spirit
Call to Pentecost, A. Tyler.
Hymn to the Holy Spirit. Langton.
Pentecost. Bennett.
Prayer for Pentecost, A. Brown.
Veni, Creator Spiritus. *Unknown.*
Veni, Sancte Spiritus. *Unknown.*
Holy Thursday
Holy Thursday ("Is this a holy thing to see"). *Fr.* Songs of Innocence. Blake.
Holy Thursday (" 'Twas on a holy Thursday, their innocent faces clean"). *Fr.* Songs of Innocence. Blake.
Home
Are You Just Back for a Visit or Are You Going to Stay? Rosenberger.
Auld House, The. Nairne.
Autumn. *Fr.* Seasons of the Soul. Tate.
Autumn. Untermeyer.
Bless This House. Taylor.
Blows the Wind Today. Stevenson.
Considerations. Helwig.
Cricket's Story, The. Nason.
Dearest Spot on Earth, The. Wrighton.
Death of the Hired Man, The. Frost.
Down Home. Outlaw.
Edgar A. Guest Considers the Good "Old Woman Who Lived in a Shoe" and the Good Old Truths Simultaneously. Untermeyer.
Exiled. Millay.
Falmouth. Henley.
Family Prime. Van Doren.

Fire Side, The; a Pastoral Soliloquy. Browne.
Go Home. McFatter.
Going Home. Kenny.
Hame, Hame, Hame. Cunningham.
Hearth and Home. King.
Heart's Content. *Unknown.*
Home. Gibson.
Home. Greenwell.
Home. Guest.
Home. Heidenstam.
Home. Henley.
Home. Nicholson.
Home. *Unknown.*
Home. Van Dyke.
Home Is Where There Is One to Love Us. Swain.
Home on the Range, A. *Unknown.*
Home, Sweet Home, with Variations. Bunner.
Home, Sweet Home. *Fr.* Clari, the Maid of Milan. Payne.
Home! You're Where It's Warm Inside. Prelutsky.
Homecoming. Thompson.
Homecoming in Storm. Kenyon.
Hometown. Cabalquinto.
Homeward Bound. Tooker.
House and Home. Hugo.
House on the Hill, The. Robinson.
House with Nobody in It, The. Kilmer.
In the Inner City. Clifton.
I've Got a Home in That Rock. Patterson.
Last Journey. *Fr.* The Testament of John Davidson. Davidson.
Long Voyage, The. Cowley.
Motels, Hotels, Other People's Houses. Van Brunt.
My Ain Fireside. Hamilton.
My Early Home. Clare.
My Little Lodge. *Unknown.*
My Old Kentucky Home. Foster.
Old Folks at Home. Foster.
Old Home, The. Cawein.
Old Homes. Blunden.
Old House, The. Woodberry.
Old Woman of the Roads, An. Colum.
On the Wide Heath. Millay.
Our children have eaten supper. *Fr.* Missouri Sequence. Coffey.
Our House. Thompson.
Pilgrim from the East, The. Kahn.
Prayer for a Little Home, A. Bone.
Prayer for the Household, A. Stevenson.
Prayer for This House. Untermeyer.
Return of the Native, The. Matthews.
Roofs. Kilmer.
Search. Marriott.
Shiny Little House, The. Hayes.
Song: "Stay, stay at home, my heart, and rest." Longfellow.
Sweet Stay-at-Home. Davies.
Sweetest Home, The. *Unknown.*
Thanksgiving for a Habitat. Auden.
Thanksgiving to God for His House, A. Herrick.
There's Nae Luck about the House. Mickle.
To Hampstead. Hunt.
To S. R. Crockett. Stevenson.
True Riches. Martin.
Urn, The. Cowley.
We'll All Feel Gay. Scott.
West Wind, The. Masefield.
Where He Hangs His Hat. Lee.

Homeless, The
Apology for Vagrants. *Fr.* The Country Justice. Langhorne.
Derelict. Johnson.
Grand Street & the Bowery. Ghitelman.
Hunchback in the Park, The. Thomas.
Letter from the Street. Brush.
Miss Rosie. Clifton.
Old Lady Under the Freeway, The. O Hehir.
Old Woman of the Roads, An. Colum.
Two girls of twelve or so at a table. Reznikoff.

Homer
After Reading Homer. Dolben.
By Deputy. Adcock.
Cure for Poetry, A. *Unknown.*
Development. Browning.
Homer. Ehrenstein.
Homeric Unity. Lang.
Odyssey, The. Lang.
On First Looking into Chapman's Homer. Keats.
Praise of Homer. Chapman.
Seven Wealthy Towns. *Unknown.*
To Homer. Keats.
Tourist. Van Doren.

Homer, Winslow
Winslow Homer, Prisoners from the Front. Blakely.

Homesickness
City Clerk, The. Ashe.
Hame, Hame, Hame. Cunningham.
Home. Chalmers.
Home, Boys, Home. *Unknown.*
Home Thoughts from Abroad. Browning.
Homesick. Lasker-Schüler.
Homesick Blues. Hughes.
Home-Sickness. Brontë.
Homesickness. Lasker-Schüler.
I Wonder How My Home Is. Tewa.
John B. Sails. *Unknown.*
Les Vaches. Clough.
North Country Maid, The. *Unknown.*
Outcast. McKay.
Outside Fargo, North Dakota. Wright.
Tropics in New York, The. McKay.
Un Canadien Errant (An Exiled Canadian). *Unknown.*

Homesteaders
Greer County. Unknown.
Little Old Sod Shanty. *Unknown.*
Starving to Death on a Government Claim. *Unknown.*

Homosexuality and Homosexuals
Against Homosexuality. *Fr.* A View of the Town. In an Epistle to a Friend. Gilbert.
Double Exposure. Young.
Dream. Dobyns.
Ever-fixed Mark, An. Amis.
Feast of Stephen, The. Hecht.
For Freckle-faced Gerald. Knight.
Homosexual Sonnets. Pitchford.
Homosexuality. O'Hara.
Island of Giglio. Norse.
Magnificat. Roberts.
My Dream by Henry James. Ryan.
Of all our bathhouse thieves the cleverest one. Catullus.
Old Age of Michelangelo, The. Prince.
On the Road to the Sea. Mew.
Pair of muscular calves, A. *Fr.* You Must Have Been a Sensational Baby. Norse.
Pick-up at Chef Rizal Restaurant. Cerenio.
Playboy of the Demi-World, The: 1938. Plomer.
Song: "Love a woman? You're an ass!" Rochester.
Sonnet: "Of thee, kind boy, I ask no red and white." Suckling.
Sugar-Candy Bird. Young.
This Form of Life Needs Sex. Ginsberg.
Torso, The: Passages 18. Duncan.
Why We Bombed Haiphong. Holden.
Wholesome. Meredith.
Words for Hart Crane. Lowell.
Penguin Book of Homosexual Verse, The (PeHV). Stephen Coote, ed.

Honesty
Getting By on Honesty. Smith.
Honest Man, An. *Fr.* Essay on Man. Pope.
Honesty. Bonar.
Truth the Best. Turner.

Honey
Bees Awater. Morgan.
I Eat My Peas with Honey. *Unknown.*
What does the bee do? Rossetti.

Honey Eaters
Nesting Time. Stewart.

Honeymoons
Honeymoon, The. *Fr.* Advice to Julia. Luttrell.
Marriage. Corso.

Honeysuckle
Honeysuckle, The. Rossetti.
Wild Honeysuckle, The. Freneau.

Hong Kong
Eyes of Cantonese Schoolmasters Remembered in Hong Kong, The. Barnstone.

Honor
If We Must Die. McKay.
On Honour. Mandeville.
Pastoral of Tasso, A. Daniel.

To Lucasta, Going to the Wars. Lovelace.
Ulysses and the Siren. Daniel.
Hood, Thomas
Elegy on Thomas Hood. Fagg.
On Thomas Hood. Landor.
Thomas Hood. Robinson.
Hooker, Joseph
Hooker's Across. Boker.
Hoopoes
Hoopoe. *Fr.* Nepenthe. Darley.
Hoover Dam
Boulder Dam. Sarton.
Hope
Against Hope. Cowley.
Answer for Hope. Crashaw.
Anticipation. Brontë.
At summer eve, when Heaven's ethereal bow. *Fr.* The Pleasures of Hope. Campbell.
Aubade for Hope. Warren.
"Bottle Should Be Plainly Labeled 'Poison.' " Hay.
Dark Testament. Murray.
Darkling Thrush, The. Hardy.
For a Child. Davis.
For Hope. Crashaw.
Good Man in Hell, The. Muir.
Hold Fast Your Dreams. Driscoll.
Hope. Anderson.
Hope. Brontë.
Hope. Carmichael.
Hope. *Fr.* Il Pastor Fido. Fanshawe.
Hope. *Fr.* The Captivity; an Oratorio. Goldsmith.
Hope. Herbert.
Hope. Howells.
Hope. Hughes.
Hope. Jarrell.
Hope. Mezquida.
Hope and Fear. Swinburne.
Hope is the thing with feathers. Dickinson.
Hope Springs Eternal. *Fr.* An Essay on Man. Pope.
Hopes, The. Fringell.
I dwell in possibility. Dickinson.
Its Ain Drap o' Dew. Ballantine.
Larger Hope, The. *Fr.* In Memoriam A. H. H. Tennyson.
Leaden Echo and the Golden Echo, The. Hopkins.
Lines Written Among the Euganean Hills. Shelley.
Maestro's Barber Shop, The. Vásquez.
Message of the March Wind, The. Morris.
New Every Morning. *Unknown.*
On Hope by Way of Question and Answer betweene Abraham Cowley and Richard Crashaw. Cowley *and* Crashaw.
"Paper Men to Air Hopes and Fears." Francis.
Pause of Thought, A. Rossetti.
Pleasure of Hope, The. *Fr.* An Essay on Man. Pope.
Relics. Wagoner.
Say Not the Struggle Naught Availeth. Clough.
To Hope. *Fr.* Julia, a Novel. Williams.
Work Without Hope. Coleridge.
See also **Optimism.**
Hopi Indians
Builder Kachina: Home-going. Rose.
Death in the Desert, A. Tomlinson.
Flute Song: "Hail, fathers, hail!" *Unknown.*
Hopi Lament. Beghtol.
Hopi Prayer. Beghtol.
Hopi Woman. Spencer.
Pueblo Women I Watched Get Down in Brooklyn. Rose.
Rain all over the cornfields. Lahpu.
To Some Few Hopi Ancestors. Rose.
Hopkins, Gerard Manley
Breakfast with Gerard Manley Hopkins, *parody.* Brode.
Hopper, Edward
Edward Hopper Retrospective, The. Quagliano.
Homage to Edward Hopper. George.
Hopper's "Nighthawks" (1942). Sadoff.
Sunlight in a Cafeteria. Cannady.
Horace
After Horace. Godley.
Allusion to Horace, An; the Tenth Satire of the First Book. Rochester.
Classical Criticism. Richardson.
Horace. Sargent.
Horations, The. Auden.
On First Looking into Loeb's Horace. Durrell.
Horatius
Horatius. *Fr.* Lays of Ancient Rome. Macaulay.
Horn, Cape. *See* **Cape Horn.**
Horse Chestnut Trees
Hampstead; the Horse Chestnut Trees. Gunn.
Horse Chestnut Tree, The. Eberhart.
Horse Racing
At Galway Races. Yeats.
At Grass. Larkin.
Beautiful Horses, The. Hall.
Camptown Races, The. Foster.
Day at the Races, A. Phillips.
Famous Ballad of the Jubilee Cup, The. Quiller-Couch.
Galway Races. *Unknown.*
Grog-an'-Grumble Steeplechase. Lawson.
How We Beat the Favourite. Gordon.
Morning Track, The. Parone.
Morning Workout. Deutsch.
Placing a $2 Bet for a Man Who Will Never Go to the Horse Races Any More. Wakoski.
To A Race Horse at Ascot. Palen.
Tom Fool at Jamaica. Moore.
Horse Shows
Pliny Jane. Luton.
Horseback Riding
Billy Could Ride. Riley.
Boot and Saddle. Browning.
Boy Riding Forward Backward. Francis.
Diverting History of John Gilpin, The. Cowper.
Flying Changes. Wood.
Galloping. Chitty.
Gentled Beast, The. Laing.
Haiku, For Cinnamon. Chaffin.
Horse. Harrison.
How They Brought the Good News from Ghent to Aix. Browning.
Indecision Means Flexibility. Abhau.
Limits of Equitation, The. Winder.
New Skills. Nye.
Night of Spring. Westwood.
Once Upon a Nag. McMahon.
Riding. Grossman.
Riding Lesson. Taylor.
Tallyho-Hum. Nash.
Horseradish
Consumer's Report. Kennedy.
Horses
All Through the Rains. Snyder.
Arab to His Favorite Steed, The. Norton.
At Grass. Larkin.
Birth of the Foal. Juhász.
Blessing, A. Wright.
Blood Horse, The. "Cornwall."
Blue Horses; West Winds. Endrezze-Danielson.
Broncho That Would Not Be Broken, The. Lindsay.
But lo from forth a copse that neighbors by. *Fr.* Venus and Adonis. Shakespeare.
Cariboo Horses, The. Purdy.
Carter, The. *Unknown.*
Circus-postered Barn, The. Coatsworth.
Colts. *Unknown.*
Comanche. Gildner.
Corral, The. Thompson.
Courser, The. *Fr.* Venus and Adonis. Shakespeare.
Cow-ponies. Lesemann.
Cynthia on Horseback. Ayres.
Daniel Webster's Horses. Coatsworth.
Day the Beatles Lost One to the Flesh-eating Horse, The. Kelly.
Dead Ponies. Chamberlain.
Dick Turpin's Ride. *Unknown.*
Distant Runners, The. Van Doren.
Dobbin. Bowering.
Draft Horse, The. Frost.
Dream of Horses, A. Hughes.
Dusk of Horses, The. Dickey.
Elegy on the Death of Dobbin, the Butterwoman's Horse, An. Fawkes.
Flying Change, The. Taylor.
Foal. Miller.
Foal. Watkins.
Gallop of Fire, A. Pitt.
Ghostly Story. Acorn.
Gigantic beauty of a stallion, A. *Fr.* Song of Myself. Whitman.
Glory Trail, The. Clark.

Golden Stallion, The. Thompson.
Gun Teams. Frankau.
Horse, The. *Fr.* Job. Bible, *O.T.*
Horse. Blasing.
Horse, The. Coppard.
Horse, The. Eguren.
Horse. Glück.
Horse. Harrison.
Horse, The. Kicknosway.
Horse, The. Ponge.
Horse. *Fr.* A Bestiary. Rexroth.
Horse. Roberts.
Horse, The. Royde-Smith.
Horse Aboard. Hardy.
Horse and His Rider, The. Baillie.
Horsemen, The. Baro.
Horses. Armour.
Horses. Kipling.
Horses, The ("Barely a twelvemonth after"). Muir.
Horses ("Those lumbering horses in the steady plough"). Muir.
Horses. Riedemann.
Horses. Wellesley.
Horses Aboard. Hardy.
Horses Chawin' Hay. Garland.
Horses Graze. Brooks.
Horses of Marini, The. Van Zyl.
Horses of the sea, The. *Fr.* Sing-Song. Rossetti.
Horses on the Camargue. Campbell.
How They Brought the Good News from Ghent to Aix. Browning.
How to Choose a Horse. *Unknown.*
How We Drove the Trotter. Goodge.
Huckster's Horse, The. Strong.
I know two things about the horse. *Unknown.*
I like to see it lap the miles. Dickinson.
Imperiously he leaps, he neighs, he bounds. *Fr.* Venus and Adonis. Shakespeare.
Inviolable. Hoffman.
Jack and His Pony, Tom. Belloc.
Kentucky Belle. Woolson.
Kentucky Thoroughbred, The. Riley.
Love Song to Eohippus. Viereck.
Lovers, The. Comfort.
Lyarde Is an Old Horse. *Unknown.*
Mare, A. Barnes.
Mares of the Camargue, The. *Fr.* Mirèio. Mistral.
Mare. Thurman.
Milk-Cart Pony, The. Farjeon.
Milkman's Horse, The. *Unknown.*
Mountain Corral. Sorrels.
My Bonny Black Bess. *Unknown.*
My Horses. Jaszi.
Names of Horses. Hall.
Nell. *Fr.* A Row of Stalls. Knister.
New York City—1935. Corso.
Night Mare. Endrezze-Danielson.
Noonday Sun. Jackson.
Old Gray Mare. *Unknown.*
Old Mare, The. Coatsworth.
Old Poulter's Mare. *Unknown.*
Old Timbrook Blues. *Unknown.*
Orchard. Stone.
Pain for a Daughter. Sexton.
Paiute Ponies. Barnes.
Palomino Stallion, The. Nowlan.
Phar Lap in the Melbourne Museum. Porter.
Pinto, The. Wister.
Pony Blues, The. *Unknown.*
Poor Old Horse. *Unknown.*
Prayer of the Old Horse, The. Gasztold.
Racing-Man, The. Herbert.
Rain-in-the-Face. Crow.
Riding a One-eyed Horse. Taylor.
Riding In the Rain. Kumin.
Runaway, The. Frost.
Sail. Quilter.
Say This of Horses. Moody.
She Had Some Horses. Harjo.
Silver. Ammons.
Stallion, The. Merrill.
Steeds. Hiebert.
Stewball. *Unknown.*
Strawberry Roan, The. Fletcher.
Tam Pierce. *Unknown.*
Thracian Filly, The. Anacreon.
Three Colts Exercising in a Six-Acre. Campbell.
Title of a Swift Horse. Mongol.
To the Four Courts, Please. Stephens.
Todd. Conn.
Tom Fool at Jamaica. Moore.
Track, The. Christopher.
Triangular Field, The. Dobyns.
Unbridled Now. LeGear.
Undertaker's Horse, The. Kipling.
War Horse, The. Boland.
What a Proud Dreamhorse. Cummings.
White Horse, The. Lawrence.
White Horse of the Father, White Horse of the Son. Root.
White Horses. Farjeon.
White Horses. Howard.
White Stallion, The. Owen.
White Steed of the Prairies, The. Barber.
Widdecombe Fair. *Unknown.*
Wild Horse Jerry's Story. Howard.
Wild, the Free, The. Byron.
Work Horses. Chase.
Zebra Dun, The. *Unknown.*
Poetry of Horses, The (PH). William Cole, ed.

Horseshoes
Old Men Pitching Horseshoes. Kennedy.

Hospitality
Ballad of East and West, The. Kipling.
Inviting a Friend to Supper. Jonson.
On a Dead Hostess. Belloc.
Yussouf. Lowell.
See also **Guests.**

Hospitals
And This Is My Father. Grapes.
Balance. Schultz.
Benicasim. Warner.
Birthday in the Hospital, A. Jennings.
Cottage Hospital, The. Betjeman.
Days Ago. Hai-Jew.
Death of the Sailor's Wife, The. Barton.
Dedication for a Building. Dugan.
Emergency Room, The. Fisher.
Evening in the Sanitarium. Bogan.
Far Cry After a Close Call, A. Howard.
Field Hospital, The. Muldoon.
Flat One, A. Snodgrass.
Flight. Whitman.
Gramophone Tunes. Dobell.
Hospital, The. Kavanagh.
Hospital, A. Noyes.
Hospital. Shapiro.
Hospital Observation. Symons.
Hospital Visitor, The. Trotter.
Hospital Waiting-Room, The. Davies.
Hospital, The—Retrospections. Mackenzie.
In Hospital. Flecker.
In Hospital. Henley.
In Hospital: Poona (II). Lewis.
In the Children's Hospital. "MacDiarmid."
In the Children's Hospital. Tennyson.
In the Hospital. Guiterman.
Malice of Innocence, The. Levertov.
Mental Cases. Owen.
Microcosmos. Miles.
Night Duty. Dobell.
Notes for the Chart in 306. Nash.
Old Men's Ward. Dean.
Operation, The. Snodgrass.
Red Cross Nurses. Stewart.
St. Vincent's. Merwin.
Screens. Letts.
Semi-Private Room. Nowlan.
Sleeping Pill. O'Hehir.
Slipping Out of Intensive Care. Trefethen.
Stones, The. Plath.
Surgical Ward: Men. Graves.
Talking to Her. O'Sullivan.
To My Sister, from the Twenty-Seventh Floor. Knoll.
Transfusion. Moore.
Tulips. Plath.
Unknown Girl in the Maternity Ward. Sexton.

Viaticum. MacCarthy.
Visit to a Hospital. Chace.
Wait. Steele.
Ward Two. Webb.
Windfall. Mitchell.

Hotels
At a Summer Hotel. Gardner.
At the Algonquin. Moss.
At the End of the Affair. Kumin.
Black Bull of Aldgate. Tennyson.
Casey's Table D'Hote. Field.
Chelsea, The. Walcott.
Coloratura. Page.
Conversation Piece. Graves.
Dolgelley Hotel, The. Hughes.
Enormous Aquarium, The. Santos.
Gramercy Park Hotel. Smith.
Holiday Inn at Bemidji. Vizenor.
Hotels. Donnell.
Irish Hotel. Wevill.
John Carey's Second Song. McGrath.
Lament for Lost Lodgings. McGinley.
Lodging, The. Brown.
On the Ruins of a Country Inn. Freneau.
Registered at the Bordello Hotel (Vienna). Rubin.
Results of a Scientific Survey. Cutler.
Stirling's Hotel. *Unknown.*
Traveler's Rest. Nash.
Up-Hill. Rossetti.
Written at an Inn at Henley. Shenstone.
See also **Motels.**

Hottentots
Midsummer Fantasy. Levy.

Houdini, Harry
Houdini. Mandel.

House Painting
Painters, The. Hemschemeyer.

Housekeeping
Housewife, The. Coblentz.
I Like Housecleaning. Thompson.
When Young Melissa Sweeps. Turner.
See also **Housewives.**

Houses
Abandoned House, The. Hubbell.
After Reading in a Letter Proposals for Building a Cottage. Clare.
Architect. Nicholl.
Architectural Masks. Hardy.
Bless this House. Taylor.
Buildings, The. Berry.
Consecration of the House. Fairbridge.
Corner Lot. Bryan.
Crayon House. Rukeyser.
Deserted House, The. Coleridge.
Directive. Frost.
Empty House, The. De la Mare.
Empty House, The. Monro.
Empty House, The. Spender.
Empty House, The. Williams.
Fire. Carpenter.
Floor and the Ceiling, The. Smith.
For the Rebuilding of a House. Berry.
Ghosts. Jennings.
Ground for the Floor. *Unknown.*
Haunted House, The. Hood.
Hole in the Floor, A. Wilbur.
House, The. Bowering.
House. Browning.
House, The. Creeley.
House, The. Marietta.
House, The. Nelson.
House. O Hehir.
House, The. Van Zyl.
House, The. Williams.
House and Grounds, A. Hunt.
House and Home. Beaumont.
House and Home. Hugo.
House Blessing, A. Cartwright.
House Blessing. Guiterman.
House-hunting. Wagoner.
House on the Hill, The. Robinson.
House with Nobody in It, The. Kilmer.
Houses. Fisher.
Houses. Justice.
Housing Starts. Davison.
Hush, Hush, New House in Charlotte. Schorb.
I know some lonely houses off the road. Dickinson.
I Like Housecleaning. Thompson.
Invites His Nymph to His Cottage. Ayres.
Invocation: "Silent, about-to-be-parted-from house." Levertov.
Jerónimo's House. Bishop.
Little Old Sod Shanty, The. *Unknown.*
Love Song: I and Thou. Dugan.
Mending the Adobe. Carruth.
My house, I say. But hark to the sunny doves. Stevenson.
My House. Krows.
New House, The. McDougall.
New House, The. Thomas.
O Blessed house, that cheerfully receiveth. Spitta.
O Thou Whose Gracious Presence Blest. Benson.
Old Houses of Flanders, The. Ford.
Old Mansion. Ransom.
Old Woman of the Roads, An. Colum.
On a Picture of Your House. Jones.
On Blenheim House. Evans.
On Lord Holland's Seat near Margate, Kent. Gray.
On the Hall at Stowey. Tomlinson.
On the House of a Friend. Logan.
Point Shirley. Plath.
Post Mortem. Harden.
Prayer for This House. Untermeyer.
Quebec Farmhouse. Glassco.
Ruin, The. Tomlinson.
Ruined Cabin, The. King.
Ruined Cottage, The. Wordsworth.
Setting the Table. Aldis.
Some Verses upon the Burning of Our House July 10th, 1666. Bradstreet.
Song for a Little House. Morley.
Sonnet: Written after Seeing Wilton-House. Warton, the Younger.
Thanksgiving to God, for His House, A. Herrick.
To My Friend G. N., from Wrest. Carew.
To Penshurst. Jonson.
To Saxham. Carew.
Up at a Villa—Down In the City. Browning.
Vagabond House. Blanding.
World, The. Herbert.
See also **Home.**

Housewives
Divine Office of the Kitchen, The. Hallack.
Farm Wife. Field.
Gone Is the Sleepgiver. Shuttle.
Housewife, The. Coblentz.
How About. Nelms.
Marks. Pastan.
Occupation: Housewife. McGinley.
On a Tired Housewife. *Unknown.*
Suburban Wife's Song. Hutchinson.
When You Are Gone. Van Winckel.
Woman Driving the Country Squire, The. Dayton.
See also **Housekeeping.**

Housman, Alfred Edward
A. E. Housman and a Few Friends, *parody.* Wolfe.
Mr. Housman's Message. Pound.

Huckleberry Finn
Huck Finn at Ninety, Dying in a Chicago Boarding House Room. Schevill.

Hudson, Henry
Henry Hudson's Quest. Stevenson.
Weepers Tower in Amsterdam, The. Goodman.

Hudson Bay
Empty Threat, An. Frost.

Hudson River
Egyptian Passage, An. Weiss.
Hudson, The. Hellman.
Lordly Hudson, The. Goodman.
Mouth of the Hudson, The. Lowell.

Hughes, Langston
Do Nothing till You Hear from Me. Henderson.
For All Things Black and Beautiful. Rivers.
Langston. Evans.
Langston Blues. Randall.
Langston Hughes. Blockcolski.
Reading Walt Whitman. Forbes.
Rhetoric of Langston Hughes, The. Danner.

Hugo, Victor
To Victor Hugo. Swinburne.
Huguenots
Huguenot, A. Coleridge.
Ivry. Macaulay.
Psalm, The. Bridges.
Human Race. *See* **Mankind.**
Humanism
This *Humanist* whom no beliefs constrained. Cunningham.
Hume, David
On the Author of the *Treatise of Human Nature*. Beattie.
Humility
Blades of Grass, The. Crane.
Clod and the Pebble, The. *Fr.* Songs of Experience. Blake.
Enough! *Fr.* The Pilgrim's Progress. Bunyan.
Happiest Heart, The. Cheney.
House by the Side of the Road, The. Foss.
Hymne in Honour of Those Two Despised Virtues, Charitie and Humilitie, An. More.
Little Things. Fletcher.
Magnanimous, The. Kay.
Non Nobis Domine. Kipling.
O Why Should the Spirit of Mortal Be Proud? Knox.
Resolve, The. Chudleigh.
Shepherd Boy Sings, The. *Fr.* The Pilgrim's Progress. Bunyan.
To Show How Humble. *Unknown.*
Violet, The. Taylor.
Hummingbirds
Container, The. Corman.
Hummingbird, A. Dickinson.
Humming Bird, The. Kemp.
Humming-Bird. Lawrence.
Hummingbird. Littlebird.
Hummingbird. Piercy.
Murmurers, The. Jacobsen.
On Some Humming-Birds in a Glass Case. Turner.
Ritual, The. Gwillim.
Vision. Eberhart.
Humorous Verse
Century of Humorous Verse, 1850–1950, A (CenHV). Robert Lancelyn Green, ed.
Faber Book of Comic Verse, The (FaBoCo). Michael Roberts *and* Janet Adam Smith, eds.
Faber Book of Nonsense Verse, The (FaBoNo). Geoffrey Grigson, ed.
Fireside Book of Humorous Poetry, The (FiBHP). William Cole, ed.
Home Book of Verse for Young Folks, The (HBVY), pp. 162–204. Burton Egbert Stevenson, ed.
Innocent Merriment; an Anthology of Light Verse (InMe). Franklin P. Adams, comp.
Moon Is Shining Bright As Day, The. (MoShBr). Ogden Nash, ed.
New Oxford Book of English Light Verse, The. (NOBL). Kingsley Amis, ed.
Nonsense Anthology, A (NA). Carolyn Wells, ed.
Oxford Book of American Light Verse, The (OBAL). William Harmon, ed.
Oxford Book of Light Verse, The (OxBoLi). W. H. Auden, ed.
Pith and Vinegar (PV). William Cole, ed.
Poems One Line and Longer (POL). William Cole, ed.
Shrieks at Midnight (ShM). Sara *and* John Brewton, eds.
Speak Roughly to Your Little Boy (SpRo). Myra Cohn Livingston, ed.
They've Discovered a Head in the Box for the Bread (TDH). John E. Brewton *and* Lorraine A. Blackburn, comps.
What Cheer (WhC). David McCord, ed.
Humphrey, Hubert Horatio
Hubert Horatio Humphrey (1911–1978). Galvin.
Hunchbacks
Hunchback in the Park, The. Thomas.
Hundred Years War
Agincourt. Drayton.
Ballad of Banners, The. Lehmann.
Ballad of Orleans, A. Robinson.
Before Agincourt. *Fr.* Henry V. Shakespeare.
Creçy. Palgrave.
King Henry Fifth's Conquest of France. *Unknown.*
Hungary
Birth of a Country. Gergely.
Music of Hungary. Aldrich.
Hunger
Colliers' March, The. Freeth.
Encounter with Hunger. Vanderlip.
For an Obligate Parasite. Dugan.
Freemon Hawthorne. Tolson.
Give Me Three Grains of Corn, Mother. Edwards.
Hunger. Binyon.
Hunger. *Unknown.*
Hunger and Thirst. Bishop.
Hunger in New York City. Ortiz.
Late Rising. Prévert.
To starve, or not to starve? that is the question. Ireland.
When I Think of the Hungry People. O-Shi-O.
Hunt, Leigh
Dedication, to Leigh Hunt, Esq. Keats.
Jenny kiss'd me when we met. *Fr.* A Leaden Treasury of English Verse. Dehn.
Sonnet: Written on the Day that Mr. Leigh Hunt left Prison. Keats.
Such Stuff as Dreams. Adams.
To Leigh Hunt, Esq. Keats.
Hunting and Hunters
After the Night Hunt. Dickey.
Ageing Hunter, The. Avane.
A-Hunting We Will Go. *Fr.* Don Quixote in England. Fielding.
All in Green Went My Love Riding. Cummings.
Badger. Clare.
Ballad of Red Fox, The. La Follette.
Beagles. Rodgers.
Bear Hunt, The. Widdemer.
Bear Hunting. Aua.
Blackwater Mountain. Wright.
Blessing the Hounds. Winter.
Bold Reynard the Fox. *Unknown.*
Brother Solon's Hunting Song. D'Urfey.
Buffalo Skinners, The. *Unknown.*
Carmen Possum. *Unknown.*
Chase, The. Cunningham.
Cheerful Horn, The. *Unknown.*
Coon Hunt, Sixth Month (1955). Lea.
Coots. Bruchac.
Death of a Hind. MacLean.
December. Francis.
Decoys, The. Auden.
Deer Hunt. Jerome.
Deer Hunt, Salt Lake Valley. Handley.
Dido's Hunting. *Fr.* The Aeneid. Virgil.
Doe. Dow.
Dream 2: Brian the Still-Hunter. Atwood.
Dressing Game. Schmitz.
Duck Pond at Mini's Pasture, a Dozen Years Later, The. Dow.
Duck. Donaghy.
Field Sports. *Fr.* Windsor Forest. Pope.
First Blood. Stallworthy.
First Hunt, The. Anderson.
For the Opening of the Hunting Season. Bishop.
Fox knew well, that before they tore him, The. *Fr.* Reynard the Fox. Masefield.
Fox-Hunters, The. Elliott.
Good Grease. TallMountain.
Hare-hunting. *Fr.* The Chase. Somerville.
Horse and Rider. Robinson.
Hunt Is Up, The. *Unknown.*
Hunt, The. De la Mare.
Hunt, The. Halpern.
Hunt. La Follette.
Hunt, The. *Fr.* Windsor Forest. Pope.
Hunter, The. Nash.
Hunter, The. Souster.
Hunter of the Prairies, The. Bryant.
Hunter Sees What Is There, The. Jackson.
Hunter Trials. Betjeman.
Hunter's Morning. Littlebird.
Hunters of the Deer, The. Zieroth.
Hunting at Dusk. Cockrell.
Hunting of the Hare, The. Lucas, Duchess of Newcastle.
Hunting Song. Finkel.
Hunting-Song. *Fr.* King Arthur. Hovey.
Hunting Song. Scott.
Hunting Song. *Unknown.*
Hunting Song. *Fr.* Apollo and Daphne. Whitehead.
Hunting with My Father. Absher.
Huntsmen, The. De la Mare.
Hymn to the Air Spirit. Eskimo.
"I dance on all the mountains." *Fr.* Myths and Texts. Snyder.
I Saw a Jolly Hunter. Causley.
In Autumn. Howes.
It's up Glenbarchan's braes I gaed. Scott.
Jabberwocky. "Carroll."

January: Cover Shooting. *Fr.* An Idler's Calender. Blunt.
John Peel. Graves.
Kilruddery Hunt, The. Mozeen.
Kirk Lonegren's Home Movie Taking Place Just North of Prince George, with Sound. Thesen.
Last Hunt, The. Thayer.
Lion Hunts. Beer.
Listening to Foxhounds. Dickey.
Lord Epsom. Belloc.
Lyke as a huntsman, after weary chace. *Fr.* Amoretti. Spenser.
Manlet, The. "Carroll."
March Hares. De la Mare.
Mighty Hunter, The. Worley.
My Woodcock. Chalmers.
Nimble Stag, The. Knox.
Nine Charms against the Hunter. Wagoner.
Nor less the spaniel, skillful to betray. *Fr.* Rural Sports. Gay.
Nymph Complaining for the Death of Her Fawn, The. Marvell.
Of the Stalking of the Stag. Seaman.
Old Dog, New Dog. Lea.
Old Squire, The. Blunt.
On Dressing to Go Hunting. *Unknown.*
On His Mistris That Lov'd Hunting. *Unknown.*
One day that we mustered on Sliabh Truim. Hunt of Sliagh Truim, The. *Unknown.*
Partridges. Masefield.
Poacher, The. *Fr.* The Parlement of the Three Ages. *Unknown.*
Rabbit, The. Davies.
Rabbit-Hunter, The. Frost.
Rainbow. Huff.
Revenge of the Hunted. Ford.
Reynard the Fox. *Unknown.*
Rock Painting. Cope.
Rousing Canoe Song, The. Fraser.
Runnable Stag, A. Davidson.
Rural Lines after Breughel. Krapf.
Scene after Hunting at Swallowfield in Berkshire, A. Davies.
See! from the brake the whirring pheasant springs. *Fr.* Windsor-Forest. Pope.
Shoot, The. *Fr.* Windsor Forest. Pope.
Shooting Ducks in South Louisiana. Tillinghast.
Song of the Rejected Woman. Kibkarjuk.
Sportsman, The. McCord.
Springer Mountain. Dickey.
St. Valentine's Day. *Fr.* The Love Sonnets of Proteus. Blunt.
Stag-Hunt. *Unknown.*
Stories of Snow. Page.
Summons, The. Dickey.
Target Practice. Finkel.
There Faunus and Sylvanus keep their courts. *Fr.* Cooper's Hill. Denham.
Thirteenth Song. *Fr.* Polyolbion. Drayton.
Three Huntsmen, The. *Unknown.*
To Christ Our Lord. Kinnell.
Tracking Rabbits: Night. Barnes.
Usually an Old Female Is the Leader. Hennen.
Walrus Hunting. Aua.
We'll All Go a-Hunting Today. *Unknown.*
What Shines in Winter Burns. Hummer.
When Autumn smiles, all beauteous in decay. *Fr.* Field Sports. Somerville.
When milder autumn summer's heat succeeds. *Fr.* Windsor Forest. Pope.
When we heard the owls at midnight. *Fr.* Songs of Hiawatha. Longfellow.
Whoso List to Hunt. Wyatt.
Winter: East Anglia. Blunden.
Woodchucks. Kumin.
Yolp, Yolp, Yolp, Yolp. *Unknown.*

Huntington, Collis Potter
Here Huntington's ashes long have lain. Bierce.

Hurdy-Gurdies
Barrel-Organ, The. Noyes.
Hurdy-Gurdy Man in Winter. Watkins.
Lines on Hearing the Organ. Calverley.
Organ Grinders' Garden, The. Merryman.

Huron, Lake
Great Lakes Suite, The. Reaney.
Huron, The. Herschberger.

Hurricanes
After the Hurricane. Hazo.
Hurricane, The. Crane.
Hurricane, The. Freneau.
Hurricane. MacLeish.
Hurricane, The. Matos.
Wasn't That A Mighty Storm? *Unknown.*

Husbands
Advice to the Ladies of London in the Choice of Their Husbands. *Unknown.*
After the Golden Wedding. Stephen.
Bridegroom of Cana, The. Picktahll.
Brother-in-Law, The. Rubin.
Henpecked Husband, A. *Unknown.*
Husband with No Courage in Him, The. *Unknown.*
Letter to Daphnis, A. Countess of Winchilsea.
Maiden's Ideal of a Husband, A. *Fr.* The Contrivances. Carey.
Marriage Contract. Rutsala.
One of the Boys. Dacey.
Perfect Husband, The. Nash.
Prowling the Ridge. Minty.
To My Dear and Loving Husband. Bradstreet.

Hyacinths
Admonition for Spring. Mackay.
Babiaantje, The. Prince.
Hyacinths to Feed Thy Soul. *Fr.* The Gulistan. Sadi.

Hyde, Douglas
Burial of an Irish President. Clarke.

Hyenas
Happy Hyena, The. Wells.
Hyaenas, The. Kipling.
Hyena. *Unknown.*
Hyena's Song to Her Children. *Unknown.*

Hymns
American Hymns Old and New (AH). Albert Christ-Janer, Charles W. Hughes, *and* Carleton Sprague Smith, eds.

Hypnotism
Animal Magnetism. Halloran.

Hypocrisy
Address to the Unco Guid, or the Rigidly Righteous. Burns.
American Heartbreak. Hughes.
Hyena. *Unknown.*
At dinner, she is hostess, I am host. *Fr.* Modern Love. Meredith.
Bona de Mortius. Beddoes.
Confessional, The. *Unknown.*
Confessor, The. Belli.
Deserter, The. Letts.
Double Standard, A. Harper.
Epistle from Mrs. Yonge to Her Husband. Montagu.
Ethics for Everyman. Woddis.
Fight to a Finish, A. Ford.
Holy Willie's Prayer. Burns.
Hue and Cry after Fair Amoret, A. Congreve.
Human Relations. Sisson.
Hypocrisy will serve as well. Butler.
Hypocrite Women. Levertov.
Jogger, The: Denver to Kansas City. Ray.
Keep up appearances; there lies the test. *Fr.* Night. Churchill.
Latest Decalogue, The. Clough.
Modes of the Court, The. *Fr.* The Beggar's Opera. Gay.
Next to of Course God America I. Cummings.
Of the Courtier's Life. Wyatt.
She Proves the Inconsistency of the Desires and Criticism of Men Who Accuse Women of What They Themselves Cause. Sister Juana Inés de la Cruz.
Soliloquy of the Spanish Cloister. Browning.
Terrible People, The. Nash.
We Wear the Mask. Dunbar.

I

Ibn Ezra, Abraham ben Meir
Rabbi Ben Ezra. Browning.

Ibn Ezra, Moses
On Parting with Moses Ibn Ezra. Halevi.

Ibsen, Henrik
Fox Who Watched for the Midnight Sun, The. Dubie.

Ibycus
Cranes of Ibycus, The. Lazarus.
Ibycus. Heath-Stubbs.

Icarus
Daedalus. *Fr.* Metamorphoses. Ovid.
I, Icarus. Nowlan.

Icarus. Bottrall.
Icarus. Iremonger.
Icarus. Spender.
Landscape with the Fall of Icarus. Williams.
Lines on Brueghel's *Icarus.* Hamburger.
Musée des Beaux Arts. Auden.
Now in this while gan Daedalus a wearinesse to take. *Fr.* Metamorphoses. Ovid.
Waiting for Icarus. Rukeyser.
Winged Man. Benét.

Ice
Break-up, The. Klein.
Fire and Ice. Frost.
Ice. Aldis.
Ice. Driscoll.
Ice. Roberts.
Ice Castle, The. Harris.
Ice-Floes, The. Pratt.
My love is like to ice and I to fire. *Fr.* Amoretti. Spenser.
Sleet. MacCaig.

Ice Cream
Good Humor Man, The. McGinley.
Ice-Cream Man, The. Field.
Tableau at Twilight. Nash.

Ice Hockey
Rink Keeper's Sestina. Draper.

Ice-Skating. *See* **Skating and Skaters.**

Icebergs
Berg, The. Melville.
Convergence of the Twain, The. Hardy.
Iceberg, The. Roberts.
Icebergs. Foster.
Imaginary Iceberg, The. Bishop.
On the Ice Islands Seen Floating in the German Ocean. Cowper.
Titanic Blues. *Unknown.*

Iceland
Iceland First Seen. Morris.
Journey to Iceland. Auden.

Icicles
Mistakable Identity. Emans.
To an Icicle. Dickinson.

Idaho
American Falls. Keeler.
Bonner's Ferry Beggar. Clark.
Cataldo Mission. Hugo.
Chronicle. Dorn.
Clear Night, Small Fire, No Wind. Saner.
Idaho. *Unknown.*
Way Out in Idaho. *Unknown.*

Identity Crisis
After Love. Kumin.
Agony, An. As Now. Baraka.
Being Somebody. Honig.
Cousin Ella Goes to Town. Lyon.
Exits and Entrances. Madgett.
Give Me Five. Harris.
Heir and Serf. Marquis.
My Son. Stone.
Now or Never. Astra.
Self-Dependence. Arnold.
Woman at the Washington Zoo, The. Jarrell.

Idleness
Idler, The. Jennings.
Land of Indolence, The. *Fr.* The Castle of Indolence. Thomson.
Sluggard, The. Watts.
See also **Sloth.**

Idolatry
Idols. Burton.
Manicheans did no idols make, The. *Fr.* Caelica. Greville.
Three things there be in man's opinion dear. *Fr.* Caelica. Greville.

Iguanas
Mid-Noon in January. *Fr.* Australian Transcripts. "MacLeod."

Illegitimacy
Elsa Wertman. *Fr.* Spoon River Anthology. Masters.
In gayer hours, when high my fancy ran. *Fr.* The Bastard. Savage.
Poet's Welcome to His Love-begotten Daughter, A. Burns.
Practical Woman, A. Hardy.
Unknown Girl in the Maternity Ward. Sexton.

Illinois
Blues for Bessie. O'Higgins.
Canal Street, Chicago. Fixmer.
Early Illinois Winter, An. Kuo.
El-a-noy. *Unknown.*
First Song. Kinnell.
Journey. Thompson.
Lovers of the Poor, The. Brooks.
Making Chicago. Schmitz.
Meyer and I, we drove. Nibbelink.
North Clark Street. Thompson.
Of De Witt Williams on His Way to Lincoln Cemetery. Brooks.
On Clark Street in Chicago. Keithley.
On the Building of Springfield. Lindsay.
On the Upside. Murray.
Planting Trout in the Chicago River. Schmitz.
Shooting of John Dillinger outside the Biograph Theater, The, July 22, 1934. Wagoner.
Sitting in Bib Overalls, Workshirt, Boots on the Monument to Liberty in the Center of the Square, Jacksonville, Illinois. Brodsky.
Trading Chicago. Hartman.
Waiting for Nighthawks in Illinois. Pfingston.
Zoo, The. Logan.

Illiteracy
Illiterate, The. Meredith.
Reading Lesson, The. Murphy.
Sarah Byng. Belloc.

Illness
Adieu, Farewell Earth's Bliss. *Fr.* Summer's Last Will and Testament. Nashe.
Bout with Burning. Miller.
But, O immortals! What had I to plead. *Fr.* Hymn to the Supreme Being on Recovery from a Dangerous Fit of Illness. Smart.
Convalescence. McAuley.
Departure. Lim.
Dialogue between the Soul and Body, A. Marvell.
Far Cry after a Close Call, A. Howard.
Felix Randal. Hopkins.
Flat One, A. Snodgrass.
Gastric. C. T.
Green-Sickness Beauty, The. Herbert of Cherbury.
Household Remedies. *Unknown.*
Hymn of Praise, on a Recovery from Sickness, A. Colman.
Hymn to God My God, in My Sickness. Donne.
Hymn to My God in a Night of My Late Sicknesse, A. Wotton.
Lion, Leopard, Lady. Le Pan.
In Hospital. Henley.
In Praise of Music in Time of Pestilence. Hine.
In Sickness; Written Soon after the Author's Coming to Live in Ireland, upon the Queen's Death, October 1714. Swift.
In Sickness. Swift.
Judgment, The. Spivack.
Land of Counterpane, The. Stevenson.
Letters from a Father. Van Duyn.
Litany in Time of Plague, A. Nashe.
Lumière. Van Brunt.
Medicine. Walker.
Memphis Minnie-Jitis Blues. *Unknown.*
Night Nurse Goes Her Round, The. Gray.
Notes for the Chart in 306. Nash.
Poem: "You are ill and so I lead you away." Purdy.
Song of Sickness, A. Tangikuku.
Tableau. Wright.
To Mary. Cowper.
Tulips. Plath.
Upon Prudence Baldwin Her Sickness. Herrick.
Visiting Hour. Conn.
Waiting for a Second Time. Tauhindauli.
Watch, The. Cornford.

Imagination
Attic, The. Coulette.
Bedpost, The. Graves.
Block City. Stevenson.
Bottle, The. Levine.
Centaur, The. Swenson.
Children, The. Vinz.
Corsons Inlet. Ammons.
Creative Process, The. *Fr.* The Pleasures of Imagination. Akenside.
Delaying Tactics. Wiseman.
Fancy. Keats.
Final Soliloquy of the Interior Paramour. Stevens.
Good Play, A. Stevenson.
Harvest, The. Aberg.
Hold Fast Your Dreams. Driscoll.
Invocation to Fancy. *Fr.* Ode to Fancy. Warton.
Land of Counterpane, The. Stevenson.

Land of Storybooks, The. Stevenson.
Little Exercise. Bishop.
Little Land, The. Stevenson.
Lovers and madmen have such seething brains. *Fr.* A Midsummer-Night's Dream. Shakespeare.
Magnetized. Sze.
Mime. Allen.
Mind's Liberty, The. Davies.
Mr. Nobody. *Unknown.*
Mrs. Alfred Uruguay. Stevens.
O warm, enthusiastic maid. *Fr.* Ode to Fancy. Warton.
Oh, Sleep, Fond Fancy. *Unknown.*
On Imagination. Wheatley.
On the Subject of Poetry. Merwin.
One Day When We Went Walking. Hobbs.
Out of Body. Moore.
Plain Sense of Things, The. Stevens.
Pleasures of Imagination, The. Akenside.
Poem: "O who can ever praise enough." Auden.
Power of Fancy, The. Freneau.
Puella Parvula. Stevens.
Realm of Fancy, The. Keats.
Romance. Turner.
Seein' Things. Field.
Settlers, The. Hemschemeyer.
Ships of Yule, The. Carman.
Sick Child, A. Jarrell.
Snow Man, The. Stevens.
Somewhere. De la Mare.
Talking with Soldiers. Turner.
Tell Me Where Is Fancy Bred. *Fr.* The Merchant of Venice. Shakespeare.
To Imagination. Thomas.
Toad, The. Oliver.
Tricksters. Benét.
Underwood. Moss.
Upon My Lady Carlisle's Walking in Hampton Court Garden. Suckling.
Walking to Sleep. Wilbur.
Warning to Children. Graves.
When the Mississippi Flowed in Indiana. Lindsay.
Windows, The. Merwin.
Yachting in Arkansas. Weeden.

Immigrants
At a Chinaman's Grave. Lum.
Both My Grandmothers. Field.
Chinatown Talking Story. Tsui.
Chinese Camp, Kamloops (circa 1883). Suknaski.
Elegy for Bella, Sarah, Rosie, and All the Others. Dorman.
Europe and America. Ignatow.
Farmer Goes Bersek. Elder.
Foreign Soil. Hai-Jew.
I Am the Little Irish Boy. Thoreau.
Immigrants. Frost.
Immigrants. Nelson.
Immigrants. Turner.
In Exile. Lazarus.
Inheritors, The. Geddes.
Irish Blessing, An. Murray.
My Father. Dalven.
My Polish Grandma. Field.
Nechama. Kaufman.
New Colossus. Lazarus.
No Irish Need Apply. *Unknown.*
Prospective Immigrants Please Note. Rich.
Schwiegermutterlieder. Harrison.
Scum o' the Earth. Schauffer.
Speech for the Repeal of the McCarran Act. Wilbur.
Stanzas On the Emigration to America, and Peopling the Western Country. Freneau.
Who Makes the Journey. Song.
William and Phyllis. *Unknown.*

Immortality
Arjuna said:/ "How shall I in battle against Bhisma." *Fr.* Bhagavad-Gita. *Unknown.*
Because I could not stop for death. Dickinson.
Carried Away. Elder.
Chambered Nautilus, The. Holmes.
Cities and Thrones and Powers. Kipling.
Creed, A. Masefield.
Death. Herbert.
Death, Be Not Proud. *Fr.* Holy Sonnets. Donne.
Dryad Song. Fuller.
Easter Hymn. Vaughan.
Exceptional. Lewis.
Great Victory, The. Gilbert.
His Immortality. Hardy.
Human Life; on the Denial of Immortality. Coleridge.
I Lost the Love of Heaven. Clare.
If My Bark Sink. Dickinson.
Iliad. Wolfe.
Immortal. Teasdale.
Immortal Mind, The. Byron.
Immortality. "AE."
Immortality. Arnold.
Immortality. Dana.
Immortality. Jefferson.
Immortality. Minsky.
Immortality. Reese.
Invite to Eternity, An. Clare.
It is an honorable thought. Dickinson.
Joy, Shipmate, Joy! Whitman.
Kiss of God, The. Studdert-Kennedy.
Lord, It Belongs Not to My Care. Baxter.
My Hereafter. De Long.
New Birth, The. Very.
No Coward Soul. Brontë.
Not marble, nor the gilded monuments. *Fr.* Sonnets. Shakespeare.
O, Lift One Thought. Coleridge.
O may I join the choir invisible. "Eliot."
Ode: Intimations of Immortality from Recollections of Early Childhood. Wordsworth.
Ode on a Grecian Urn. Keats.
Oh, when this earthly tenement. "Ada."
On the Beach, at Night. Whitman.
Of the Progress of the Soule; the Second Anniversarie. Donne.
One day I wrote her name upon the strand. *Fr.* Amoretti. Spenser.
Our Dead. Nichols.
Pilgrimage, The. Ralegh.
Poem in Three Parts. Bly.
Poet and His Book, The. Millay.
Resurrection. Donne.
Resurrection and Immortality. Vaughan.
Sailing to Byzantium. Yeats.
Saon of Acanthus. Symonds.
Shelley's Skylark. Hardy.
Song: "Soules joy, now I am gone." *Unknown, at. to* Pembroke.
Song of Derivations, A. Meynell.
There Is No Death. McCreery.
There Is No Death. *Unknown.*
There is no Death. What seems so is transition. *Fr.* Resignation. Longfellow.
Tithonus. Tennyson.
To a Gentleman and Lady on the Death of the Lady's Brother and Sister, and a Child of the Name Avis, Aged One Year. Wheatley.
To Bring the Dead to Life. Graves.
To Inez Milholland. Millay.
To This Hill Again. Macmillan.
Village Atheist, The. *Fr.* Spoon River Anthology. Masters.
Virtue. Herbert.
Waterfall, The. Vaughan.
We thirst at first—'tis nature's act. Dickinson.
Whispers of Immortality. Eliot.
Wish, A. Kimble.
With you, I know, my offering will find grace. *Fr.* Epistle to Elizabeth, Countess of Rutland. Jonson.

Imperialism
Ave Imperatrix! Wilde.
European Crimes. *Fr.* Gotham. Churchill.
Goodbye Nkrumah. Di Prima.
Hand, The. Fawcett.
Hatred of Men with Black Hair. Bly.
Hope. "O'Connor."
Peace with Honor. Appleman.
Recessional. Kipling.
Remember Suez? Mitchell.
Scythians, The. Blok.
Spirit of the *Maine*, The. Jenks.
When London Calls. Daley.

Impermanence. *See* **Transcience.**

Impotence
Against an Old Lecher. Harington.
Age. Mannes.
And Now You're Ready Who While She Was Here. Cunningham.
Carnation, The. Hannigan.

Disabled Debauchee, The. Rochester.
Faint Heart. Rufinus.
Imperfect Enjoyment, The. Rochester.
Impotence. Knight.
O Dear O. *Unknown.*
One Writing against His Prick. *Unknown.*
Shameful Impotence. *Fr.* Amores. Ovid.
To the Tune "Red Embroidered Shoes." Huang O.
Impressionism
Monet Refuses the Operation. Mueller.
Incest
Chain. Lorde.
Inclosure Movement
Cottager's Complaint, on the Intended Bill for Enclosing Sutton-Coldfield, The. Freeth.
Deserted Village, The. Goldsmith.
Indecision. *See* **Decisions.**
Independence Day. *See* **Fourth of July.**
India
Ajanta. Rukeyser.
Bear on the Delhi Road, The. Birney.
Defence of Lucknow, The. Tennyson.
Documentary. Stroud.
Grand Hotel, Calcutta. Silbert.
Gunga Din. Kipling.
Hot Weather in the Plains—India. Tipple.
In Hospital: Poona (II). Lewis.
In India. Shapiro.
In Springtime. Kipling.
In the Bazaars of Hyderabad. Naidu.
India. Coates.
Introduction, An: "I don't know politics but I know the names." Das.
Pagett, M.P. Kipling.
Passage to India. Whitman.
Signature (II). Stroud.
Studies at Delhi. Lyall.
Woman Painter of Mithila. Mumford.
Indian Summer
Indian Summer. Burr.
Indian Summer. Campbell.
Indian Summer. Dickinson.
Indian Summer. Moodie.
Indian Summer. Tabb.
Indian Summer Day on the Prairie, An. Lindsay
Indian Summer: Vermont. Stevenson.
Prevision. Murray.
Pyre of My Indian Summer, The. Leib.
These are the days when birds come back. Dickinson.
Vermont: Indian Summer. Booth.
Indiana
Fort Wayne, Indiana 1964. Lewis.
Home in Indianapolis. Pflum.
July in Indiana. Fitzgerald.
Memo to the 21st Century. Appleman.
Midwest. Nims.
On the Banks of the Wabash. Dresser.
Sketch for a Morning in Muncie, Indiana. Murray.
South Shore Line. Schlesinger.
Tornado Watch, Bloomington, Indiana. Young.
Valedictory to Standard Oil of Indiana, A. Wagoner.
Indians, American
Adulteries, murthers, robberies, thefts. Williams.
Alice Corbin Is Gone. Sandburg.
American Indian, The. *Unknown.*
Arrowy Dreams. Bynner.
As Brothers Live Together. *Fr.* The Song of Hiawatha. Longfellow.
At Grand Canyon's Edge. Ray.
At Gull Lake: August, 1810. Scott.
Ballad of Ira Hayes. La Farge.
Bars Fight, August 28, 1746. Terry.
Black Hawk in Hiding. Keithley.
Boast not proud English, of thy birth and blood. Williams.
Can I Say. Bird.
Carrier Indians. Belford.
Cattle Thief, The. Johnson.
Caughnawaga Beadwork Seller, The. Lighthall.
Choctaw Chief Helps Plan a Festival In Memory of Pushmataha's Birthday, A. Barnes.
Christmas Comes to Moccasin Flat. Welch.
Church on Comiaken Hill, The. Hugo.
Columbus Reaches Juana, 1492. Gustafson.
Concealment, The: Ishi, the Last Wild Indian. Stafford.
Cottonwood Leaves. Clark.
Crazy Horse Returns to South Dakota. Elliott.
Dakota: October, 1822, Hunkpapa Warrior. Taylor.
Dawn Boy's Song. *Unknown.*
Driving Through the Pima Indian Reservation. Cook.
Dying Indian, The. Warton.
End of the Indian Poems, The. Plumly.
Forsaken, The. Scott.
From his wanderings far to eastward. *Fr.* The Song of Hiawatha. Longfellow.
Further Language from Truthful James. Harte.
Gathering on the Plains, The. Butler.
Ghosts of the Buffaloes, The. Lindsay.
Grass on the Mountain, The. Austin.
Haskell. Bynner.
Hiawatha. Sandy.
Hiawatha's Childhood. *Fr.* The Song of Hiawatha. Longfellow.
I Expected My Skin and My Blood to Ripen. Rose.
I love you better than I love my race. *Fr.* Tecumseh. Mair.
Immigrants. Turner.
In the Oregon Country. Stafford.
Indian. Doriot.
Indian at the Burial-Place of His Fathers, An. Bryant.
Indian Burying Ground, The. Freneau.
Indian Camp. McFatter.
Indian Children. Wynne.
Indian Children Speak. Bell.
Indian Convert, The. Freneau.
Indian Dance. Niven.
Indian Ghost Dance and War, The. Prather.
Indian Graveyard, The. Weeks.
Indian Hunter, The. Cook.
Indian Lass, The. *Unknown.*
Indian Names. Sigourney.
Indian Painting, Probably Paiute, In a Cave Near Madras, Oregon. Ramsey.
Indian Pipe and Moccasin Flower. Guiterman.
Indian Reservation; Caughnawaga. Klein.
Indian School. Russell.
Indian Woman's Death-Song. Hemans.
Indians. Fandel.
Indians Come Down from Mixco, The. Asturias.
Indians on Alcatraz, The. Muldoon.
Indian's Welcome to the Pilgrim Fathers, The. Sigourney.
Inscription: "Eagle, stooping from yon snow-blown peaks, The." Whittier.
La Mâquina a Houston. Dorn.
Lamentable Ballad of the Bloody Brook, The. Hale.
Last Reservation, The. Learned.
Lennox Island. McFadden.
Little Mohee, The. *Unknown.*
Little Papoose. Conkling.
Lords of the Wilderness. Leyden.
Lovewell's Fight. *Unknown.*
Memorial Ode. Buck.
Mending the Adobe. Carruth.
Missouri Traveller Writes Home, A: 1830. Bly.
Native, The. Merwin.
Natives of America, The. Plato.
New Mexican Mountain. Jeffers.
Night at the Napi In Browning, A. Hugo.
Ojistoh. Johnson.
Old Man, the Sweat Lodge. George.
On the Way to the Mission. Scott.
Once we were strong. *Fr.* Tecumseh. Mair.
Pocahontas. Thackeray.
Poem for Nana. Jordan.
Portrait of an Indian. Rashley.
Powwow. Snodgrass.
Pride, The. Newlove.
Prophecy of King Tammany, The. Freneau.
Red Men, The. Sangster.
Remains of an Indian Village. Purdy.
Returned to Say. Stafford.
Santo Domingo Corn Dance. Dickey.
Savage, A. O'Reilly.
Sioux, The. *Unknown.*
Sisseton Indian Reservation, The. Lyons.
Song of Greatness, A. *Unknown.*
Song of the Ancient People, The. Proctor.
Song of the Micmac, The. Howe.
Sonnet: "There was an Indian, who had known no change." Squire.
Speech of the Salish Chief. *Fr.* Damnation of Vancouver. Birney.

Spontaneous Requiem for the American Indian. Corso.
There Was an Indian. Squire.
Thomas Iron-Eyes. Walsh.
To the Driving Cloud. Longfellow.
Ute Lover, The. Garland.
Victory of the Battle of Wounded Knee, The. Parson.
War Dance, The. Carr.
We Are a People. Henson.
Western Trail, The Carr.
What Black Elk Said. Smith.
Who Are They? *Unknown.*
Yonosa House. Smith.
Carriers of the Dream Wheel; Contemporary Native American Poetry (CDW). Duane Niatum, ed.
Songs from This Earth on Turtle's Back (STE). Joseph Bruchac, ed.
That's What She Said: Contemporary Poetry and Fiction by Native American Women (TWSS). Rayna Green, ed.
Voices of the Rainbow (VoR). Kenneth Rosen, ed.

Indigestion
Rondeau of Remorse, A. Johnson.

Individualism
Game of Life, The. Saxe.
I Don't Care. Lenox.
Light Baggage. Walker.
Mission of the Flowers, The. Harper.
Ode Inscribed to W. H. Channing. Emerson.
On Myselfe. Winchilsea.
On Stripping Bark from Myself. Walker.
Self-Dependence. Arnold.
Silence. Moore.
"Think as I Think." Crane.
See also **Egotism.**

Indolence
Castle of Indolence, The. Thomson.
See also **Idleness; Laziness; Sloth.**

Indonesia
Walking down Jalan Thamrin. Brissenden.
See also **Borneo.**

Indulgences
Pardoner's Sermon, The. Lindsay.
Pardoner's Tale, The. *Fr.* The Canterbury Tales. Chaucer.

Industrial Revolution
Deserted Village, The. Goldsmith.
Factory Girl's Come-All-Ye, The. *Unknown.*
My Grandfather's Days. *Unknown.*
Next day they rambled round the town, and swore. *Fr.* Ramble of the Gods through Birmingham. Bisset.
Steam Power. *Fr.* The Botanic Garden. Darwin.
While neighbouring cities waste the fleeting hours. *Fr.* Colebrook Dale. Seward.

Industrial Workers of the World (IWW)
Popular Wobbly, The. Slim.
There Is Power. Hill.

Industrialization
Cornfields in Accra. Aidoo.
Valedictory to Standard Oil of Indiana, A. Wagoner.

Infant Death
Cruel Mother, The. *Unknown.*
Firstborn, The. Soto.
Future Generation. NorthSun.
Gill Boy. Schmitz.
Home Burial. Frost.
Little Shroud, The. Landon.
On a Child Who Lived One Minute. Kennedy.
On a Photo of a Baby Killed in the War. DeFoe.
On an Infant Dying as Soon as Born. Lamb.
On My First Daughter. Jonson.
Pietà. McAuley.
To an Infant Expiring the Second Day of Its Birth. Wright.
Upon a Child That Died. Herrick.
We Assume; on the Death of Our Son, Reuben Masai Harper. Harper.

Infanticide
At Devlin's Siding. Boake.
Mary Hamilton. *Unknown.*
Runaway Slave at Pilgrim's Point, The. Browning.

Infants. *See* **Babies.**

Infidelity
Adultery. Dickey.
Adultery. Dugan.
Along the Field as We Came By. *Fr.* A Shropshire Lad. Housman.
Ballade Against Woman Inconstant, A. Chaucer.
Banks o' Doon, The. Burns.
Bianca among the Nightingales. Browning.
Bird on Nellie's Hat, The. Lamb.
Black Snake. *Unknown.*
By day & also by night & you are. *Fr.* Earthly: Sonnets for Carlos. Wedde.
Caledonia. McElroy.
Chandler's Wife, The. *Unknown.*
Change Thy Mind Since She Doth Change. Essex.
Chop-Cherry. Herrick.
Clever Skipper, The. *Unknown.*
Constant Lover, The. Suckling.
Crowned with flowers, I saw fair Amarillis. *Unknown.*
Demon Lover, The. *Unknown.*
Deposition from Love, A. Carew.
Dionysus. Layton.
Don't Fish in My Sea. *Unknown.*
Early in the Spring. *Unknown.*
Epigram: "When Pontius wished an edict might be passed." Prior.
Epistle from Mrs. Yonge to Her Husband. Montagu.
Faithless Wife, The. García Lorca.
First Lawcase, The. *Unknown.*
Good Bye, My Lady Love. Howard.
Grey Cock, The. *Unknown.*
His Side / Her Side. Skinner.
Host of the Air, The. Yeats.
"If thy wife is small bend down to her &." *Fr.* Earthly: Sonnets for Carlos. Wedde.
I'm Gonna Move to the Outskirts of Town. *Unknown.*
Inconstancy Reproved. Ayton.
Jilted Nymph, The. Campbell.
Letter to a Jealous Friend. Simmons.
Little Cheat, A! Malay.
Little Musgrave and Lady Barnard. *Unknown.*
Little Sparrow. *Unknown.*
Lost Jewel, A. Graves.
Madrigal: "Your love is dead, lady, your love is dead." Thomas.
Matty Groves. *Unknown.*
Mind Reader Blues. *Unknown.*
Newcomer's Wife, The. Hardy.
Non Sum Qualis Eram Bonae sub Regno Cynarae. Dowson.
Ode: "Now I find thy looks were feigned." *Fr.* Phyllis. Lodge.
Of an Heroical Answer of a Great Roman Lady to Her Husband. Harington.
Oh, Think Not I Am Faithful to a Vow! Millay.
Old Devil. *Unknown.*
Old Farmer and His Young Wife. *Unknown.*
Only Jealousy of Emer, The. *Unknown.*
Our Goodman. *Unknown.*
Peach Orchard Mama. *Unknown.*
Pneumonia Blues. *Unknown.*
Poem with the Answer, A. Suckling.
Queen Eleanor's Confession. *Unknown.*
Reaping. Lowell.
Resolving Doubts. Dickey.
Scrutiny, The. Lovelace.
Sigh No More, Ladies, Sigh No More. *Fr.* Much Ado About Nothing. Shakespeare.
Song: "Go and catch a falling star." Donne.
Song: I Promised Sylvia. Rochester.
Song: "Phillis is my only joy." Sedley.
Song: " 'Tis affection but dissembled." Godolphin.
Song: To My Inconstant Mistris. Carew.
Song of Longing. Gond.
Take Back Your Gold. Pritzkow.
Temperaments, The. Pound.
Thursday. Millay.
To His Mistress. Ovid.
To My Inconstant Mistress. Carew.
To the Unconstant Cynthia. Howard.
Trail to Mexico, The. *Unknown.*
Two or Three: a Recipe to Make a Cuckold. Pope.
Upon Scobble: Epigram. Herrick.
Variety, The. Dancer.
What Should I Say. Wyatt.
When Daisies Pied and Violets Blue. *Fr.* Love's Labour's Lost. Shakespeare.
When my love swears that she is made of truth. *Fr.* Sonnets. Shakespeare.
When We Two Parted. Byron.
Who Would Have Thought. *Fr.* The Lover Deceived Writes to His Lady. Howell.
Whoopee Blues. *Unknown.*

Womanizers. Press.
Womans Constancy. Donne.
You All Know the Story of the Other Woman. Sexton.
See also **Adultery.**

Inflation
Cost-of-Living Mother Goose, The. Richardson.
$. Abelardo.

Inge, William Ralph
On Dean Inge. Wolfe.

Ingres, Jean Auguste Dominique
For "Ruggiero and Angelica" by Ingres. Rossetti.

Inheritance
Inheritance. *Unknown.*
Lines to My Father. Daiken.
Michael. Wordsworth.
Remonstrance, A. Gerrard.
Short Song of Congratulation, A. Johnson.
To Geron. Jacob.

Injustice
Abraham Lincoln Walks at Midnight. Lindsay.
Justice Denied in Massachusetts. Millay.
Litany at Atlanta, A. DuBois.
Patty Hearst Hoists the Carbine. James.
Spokane Falls 1874. George.
Tired with all these, for restful death I cry. *Fr.* Sonnets. Shakespeare.
See also **Protest, Social.**

Inkwells
To a Post-Office Inkwell. Morley.

Innisfree, Ireland
Lake Isle of Innisfree, The. Yeats.

Innocence
Auguries of Innocence. Blake.

Inns. *See* **Hotels; Motels.**

Insanity. *See* **Madness; Mental Illness.**

Insects
August Midnight, An. Hardy.
Brief Reflection on the Insect. Holub.
Creatures. Kumin.
Depressed by a Book of Bad Poetry. Wright.
Divine Insect, The. Wheelock.
Insects, The. Willard.
Interlude. Shapiro.
Little Black Bug. Brown.
Motive for Mercy. Milburn.
Nameless One, A. Avison.
Plane Geometer. McCord.
There Ain't No Bugs on Me. *Unknown.*
To a Midge. Nisbet.
Voices of the Air. Mansfield.

Insomnia
Insomnia. Oates.
Insomnia. Piercy.
Insomnia. Thomas.
Insomnia. Zelvin.
Insomnia the Gem of the Ocean. Updike.
Morning Kiss, A. Jones.
Sleeplessness of Our Time. Ford.
Walking to Sleep. Wilbur.

Inspiration
He Whom a Dream Hath Possessed. O'Sheel.
If with light head erect I sing. *Fr.* Inspiration. Thoreau.
Inspiration. Gibson.
Inspiration. Service.
Inspiration. Thoreau.

Installment Buying
I'm Leery of Firms with Easy Terms. Jennison.

Institutionalization
Children Not Kept at Home. Oates.
December 18, 1975. Hogan.
Did They Help Me at the State Hospital for the Criminally Insane? Smith.
Home. Summers.
Home Is the Sailor. McGinley.
Moose Lake State Hospital. Shady.
Mourningsong for Anne. Posner.
Old Folks Home, An. Lake.
Sleepers, The. Kocan
Sons. Polson.
Supremer Sacrifice, The. "Maurice".
To One in Bedlam. Dowson.
Visitors' Parking. Szumigalski.
Light from Another Country, The: Poetry from American Prisons (LFAC). Joseph Bruchac, ed.

Insurance
Epitaph: "Insured for Every Accident." Armour.

Intellect
A Considerable Speck. Frost.
All-seeing Intellect, The. *Fr.* The Purple Island. Fletcher.
At Woodward's Gardens. Frost.
Blue Swallows, The. Nemerov.
Brain is wider than the sky, The. Dickinson.
Freedom for the Mind. Garrison.
Harsh Climate. Simic.
Hymn to Intellectual Beauty. Shelley.
I Remember Galileo. Stern.
In a Hard Intellectual Light. Eberhart.
Lobotomy. Pitchford.
Mind. Wilbur.
Mind, Intractable Thing, The. Moore.
Mind is an Enchanting Thing, The. Moore.
My Mind to Me a Kingdom Is. Dyer.
Of a Contented Mind. Vaux.
On the Birth of His Son. Su Tung-Po.
Perishing Bird, The. Jones.
Pet Panther. Ammons.
Poem about Intelligence for My Brothers and Sisters, A. Jordan.
Question, Is It, The? Bailey.
Reply to the Committed Intellectual. Sparshott.
Riddles. Kirby.
Sonnet: Content and Resolute. Drummond of Hawthornden.
Substance and Shadow. Newman.
Thought. Emerson.
Wandering Lunatic Mind, The. Carpenter.

International Brigade. *See* **Civil War, Spanish.**

Internationalism. *See* **League of Nations; United Nations.**

Internment
Breaking Silence. Mirikitani.
Coming Home from Camp. Kaneko.
Family Album. Kaneko.
Heart Mountain Japanese Relocation Camp, The: 30 Years Later. Levendosky.
In Response to Executive Order 9066: All Americans of Japanese Descent Must Report to Relocation Centers. Okita.
Old Photo, 1942. Uba.
On the Bus. *Fr.* Camp Notes. Yamada.
Relocation. Mura.

Inventors
Darius Green and His Flying-Machine. Trowbridge.
In Tesla's Laboratory. Johnson.
Inventor's Wife, The. Corbett.
Wrights' Biplane, The. Frost.

Investment
Investor's Soliloquy. Ward.

Invisibility
Perils of Invisibility, The. Gilbert.

Iona, Scotland
Iona. Coxe.
Iona. Tennyson.
Iona; the Graves of the Kings. Jeffers.
There Are Gods. Riley.

Iowa
Amazing Grace. Hollo.
Coralville, in Iowa. Bell.
Explanation. Hewitt.
Iowa. Browne.
Letter from Des Moines. Swiss.
Madrid, Iowa. Ikan.
Malcom, Iowa. Itzin.
Mile Hill. Schmitz.
Old Dubuque. Etter.
Old Soldiers Home at Marshalltown, Iowa. Barnes.
Stopping Near Highway 80. Ray.
Tea. Struthers.

Iphigenia
Cymon and Iphigenia. Dryden.
Iphigeneia and Agamemnon. *Fr.* The Hellenics. Landor.

Iran
"Banquet of the Century" in Persepolis, The. Hashmi.
Hostage and His Takers, The. Olds.
Impotence. Knight.
O Realm Bejewelled. Farrokhzad.
Oil and Blood. Kizer.
Wasp. Welsh.

When the Sultan Goes to Ispahan. Aldrich.

Ireland

After Death. Parnell.
Aldfrid's Itinerary through Ireland. *Unknown.*
Andromeda. Roche.
Anglo-Eire Vignette. Stevenson.
Apologia Addressed to Ireland in the Coming Days. Yeats.
Arran. *Unknown.*
Back to Dublin. Ford.
Bard of Armagh, The. *Unknown.*
Brightness of Brightness. O'Rahilly.
Clay is the word and clay is the flesh. *Fr.* The Great Hunger. Kavanagh.
Clonard. Jones.
Cois na Teineadh. Rolleston.
Columcille's Greeting to Ireland. *At. to* Saint Columcille.
Corrib. An Emblem. Davie.
County of Mayo, The. Lavelle.
Cult of the Celtic, The. Deane.
Cushla Ma Chree. Curran.
Dark Rosaleen. *Unknown, at. to* O'Donnell.
Dawning o' the Year, The. Blake.
Dear Harp of My Country. Moore.
Dispossessed Poet. Gibbon.
Down by the Glenside. Kearney.
Downfall of the Gael, The. O'Gnive.
Dublin Made Me. MacDonagh.
Dunlavin Green. *Unknown.*
Easter Week. *Unknown.*
Easter, 1916. Yeats.
Eire. Drennan.
Eireann. *Fr.* Afternoons with Baedeker. Lancaster.
Erin Go Braugh! *Unknown.*
Exile of Erin. Campbell.
Fair Hills of Ireland, The. *Unknown.*
Famine Song. *Unknown.*
First Invasion of Ireland, The. Montague.
Flight of the Earls, The. *Unknown.*
Glorious Twelfth, The. Greacen.
Go to Old Ireland. *Unknown.*
Harp That Once through Tara's Halls, The. Moore.
Hibernia. Howard-Jones.
Hope. *Unknown.*
"I Am of Ireland." Yeats.
In Ireland: By the Pool at the Third Rosses. Symons.
In Memoriam: Francis Ledwidge. O'Conor.
In Spain. Lawless.
Ireland. Johnson.
Ireland. Landor.
Ireland. Shorter.
Ireland. Stuart.
Ireland, Ireland. Newbolt.
Ireland Never Was Contented. Landor.
Ireland Weeping. Livingston.
Ireland with Emily. Betjeman.
Irish Airman Foresees His Death, An. Yeats.
Irish Cliffs of Moher, The. Stevens.
Irish Dancer, The. *Unknown.*
Irish Language, The. Mangan.
Island, The. Jennett.
Johnson's Motor Car. *Unknown.*
Kathaleen Ny-Houlahan. Mangan.
Kennedy. Heffernan.
Kevin Barry. *Unknown.*
King Cahal Mór of the Wine-red Hand. Mangan.
Lament for Banba. O'Rahilly.
Last Lines. O'Rahilly.
Leitrim Woman, A. Donaghy.
Let Erin Remember the Days of Old. Moore.
Maguire is not afraid of death, the Church will light him a candle. *Fr.* The Great Hunger. Kavanagh.
Memory of the Dead, The. Ingram.
Midnight Court, The. Merriman.
Minstrel Boy, The. Moore.
Mr. Gunman. Garbutt.
Municipal Gallery Revisited, The. Yeats.
National Presage. Ingram.
Neutrality. MacNeice.
Nightmare leaves fatigue. *Fr.* Autumn Journal. MacNeice.
Numerous Celts. Squire.
Old Orange Flute. *Unknown.*
On Not Hearing the Birds Sing in Ireland. Colum.
On the Bridge of Athlone: A Prophecy. MacDonagh.
On the Irish Club. Swift.
Once Alien Here. Hewitt.
Orange Lily, The. *Unknown.*
Our Stars Come from Ireland. Stevens.
Parnell. Yeats.
Pastoral Ballad, by John Bull, A. Moore.
Patriot Game, The. Behan.
Poor Scholar of the 'Forties, A. Colum.
Prelude. Synge.
Red Hanrahan's Song about Ireland. Yeats.
Requiem for the Croppies. Heaney.
Reverie at Dawn. O'Rahilly.
Rose Tree, The. Yeats.
September 1913. Yeats.
Shan Van Vocht, The. *Unknown.*
Sixteen Dead Men. Shorter.
Sleepless Night, A. O'Rahilly.
Soggarth Aroon. Banim.
Song for Ireland. P. *and* J. Colclough.
Spenser's Ireland. Moore.
Spring Flowers from Ireland. McCarthy.
Sweet Innisfallen. Moore.
Tara. *Unknown.*
Three accomplishments well regarded in Ireland: a clever. *Fr.* The Triads of Ireland. *Unknown.*
Three Woes, The. De Vere.
To an Irish Blackbird. MacAlpine.
To My Native Land. Mangan.
Traditions. Heaney.
Ulster. Adler.
Valediction. MacNeice.
View of the Present State of Ireland, A. Blunden.
Warning to Conquerors, A. MacDonagh.
Ways of War. Johnson.
Wearing of the Green, The. *Unknown.*
Whack Fol the Diddle. Kearney.
Where the River Shannon Flows. Russell.
Winding Banks of Erne, The. Allingham.
Written in Ireland. Alcock.
Anthology of Irish Literature, An (AnIL). David H. Greene, ed.
Anthology of Irish Verse, An (AnIV). Padraic Colum, ed.
Book of Irish Verse, The (BIrV). John Montague, ed.
Contemporary Irish Poetry (CIP). Anthony Bradley, ed.
Irish Poetry after Yeats (IPY). Maurice Harmon, ed.
Kings, Lords, & Commons; an Anthology from the Irish (KiLC). Frank O'Connor, ed.
New Irish Poets (NeIP). Devin A. Garrity, ed.
1000 Years of Irish Poetry (OnYI). Kathleen Hoagland, ed.
Oxford Book of Irish Verse, The; XVIIth Century–XXth Century (OxBI). Donagh MacDonagh *and* Lennox Robinson, eds.
See also ***Individual Counties listed under, (e.g.)*** **County Donegal, Ireland;** ***also*** **Northern Ireland.**

Ireland, Northern. *See* **Northern Ireland.**

Iris (flower)

Beds of Fleur-de-Lys, The. Gilman.
Blue Flag. Donnelly.
Iris. Williams.
Irises. Colum.
White Iris, A. Barrington.

Irish, The.

Barney McGee. Hovey.
Boys of Wexford, The. *Unknown.*
Civil Irish and Wild Irish. Mac an Bhaird.
Cult of the Celtic, The. Deane.
Dedication: "I speak with a proud tongue of the people who were." MacGill.
Docker. Heaney.
Father O'Flynn. Graves.
Fighting Race, The. Clarke.
Finnegan's Wake. *Unknown.*
Gaeltacht. Hutchinson.
Hibernia. Howard-Jones.
I'll Wear a Shamrock. Davies.
Insular Celts, The. Carson.
Ireland. Hewitt.
Irish. O'Brien.
Irish Airman Foresees His Death, An. Yeats.
Irish Antiquities. Moore.
Irish Blessing, An. Murray.
Irish Grandmother. Edelman.
Irishman in Coventry, An. Hewitt.
Native Irishman, The. *Unknown.*

Ninepenny Fidil, The. Campbell.
No Irish Need Apply. *Unknown.*
O Bruadair. Stephens.
On Behalf of Some Irishmen Not Followers of Tradition. "Æ."
Paddy Works on the Railway. *Unknown.*
Secret Irish, The. Hoey.
Slainthe! MacGill.
Written on the Sense of Isolation in Contemporary Ireland. Greacen.

Irish Republican Army
Last Republicans, The. Clarke.
Tomb of Michael Collins, The. Devlin.

Iron
Humphrey Hardfeature's Descriptions of Cast-Iron Inventions. *Unknown.*
Red Iron Ore. *Unknown.*
Scrap Iron. Durgnat.
Some Good Things to Be Said for the Iron Age. Snyder.

Iron Lungs
Iron Lung, The. Plumly.

Isaac
Akedah, The. Megged.
Isaac. Burnshaw.
Isaac. Guri.
Isaac. Holtz.
Isaac. Jacobs.
Parable of the Old Man and the Young, The. Owen.
Sacrifice, The. Bloch.
Story of Isaac. Cohen.

Ishi
Concealment, The: Ishi, the Last Wild Indian. Stafford.

Ishmael
Hagar and Ishmael. Lasker-Schüler.
Isaac. Jacobs.
Ishmael. Palmer.

Ishtar
Song for Ishtar. Levertov.

Isis
Prayer to Isis. Walsh.

Islands
Aloha. Griffith.
Arran. *Unknown.*
Barred Islands. Booth.
Dead Neck. Standing.
Enviable Isles, The. Melville.
If Once You Have Slept on an Island. Field.
Island, The. Jennett.
Islands. Pomeroy.
Islands. Rukeyser.
Lake Isle of Innisfree, The. Yeats.
Letter from an Island. Brinnin.
On This Island. Auden.
Poet on the Island. Murphy.
Ragged Island. Millay.
Tristan da Cunha. Campbell.

Isle of Man
Braddan Vicarage. Brown.

Isle of Wight, England
At Farringford. *Fr.* To the Rev. F. D. Maurice. Tennyson.
Forsaken Garden, A. Swinburne.
November in the Isle of Wight. *Fr.* Enoch Arden. Tennyson.

Israel
Banner of the Jew, The. Lazarus.
But We Shall Bloom. Guri.
Canaan. Spark.
Déjà Vu. Kaufman.
Hear, O Israel! Spire.
New Ezekiel, The. Lazarus.
Pictures at an Exhibition. Rosenbaum.
Temple, The. Kahn.

Italians, The
I Promessi Sposi. Corman.
Cigarette for the Bambino. Ewart.
Modern Romans, The. Johnson.

Italy
Above Salerno. Murray.
Amours de Voyage, *sels.* Clough.
Byron Recollected at Bologna. *Fr.* Italy. Rogers.
City of Beggars, The. Hayes.
Cypresses. Lawrence.
Daisy, The. Tennyson.
Driver in Italy, The. Christopher.
England. Moore.
Florence. *Fr.* Aurora Leigh. Browning.
Frater Ave atque Vale. Tennyson.
Good-Bye to the Mezzogiorno. Auden.
Hotel Paradiso e Commerciale. Brinnin.
In Ampezzo. Stickney.
Italia, Io Ti Saluto! Rossetti.
Italian Rhapsody. Johnson.
Italian Woman. Wakoski.
Italy. *Fr.* Beppo. Byron.
Italy and Britain. *Fr.* A Letter from Italy. Addison.
Italy of the South. *Fr.* De Gustibus. Browning.
Letter from Italy, to the Right Honourable Charles Lord Halifax, A. Addison.
Life of. . ., The. Weiss.
Lines Written Among the Euganean Hills. Shelley.
Off Viareggio. Pitchford.
Olives and Mountains. *Fr.* Aurora Leigh. Browning.
On an Italian Hillside. Weber.
On the Road to Vicenza. Gustafson.
Perugia. Burr.
Piano di Sorrento. *Fr.* The Englishman in Italy. Browning.
Poem: "So many pigeons at Columbus." Gregor.
Street Melody, A. Cooper.
Super Flumina Babylonis. Swinburne.
Temple at Segesta, The. Henri.
There Is a Pool on Garda. Scollard.
Written in the Euganean Hills, North Italy. Shelley.

Ives, Charles
This is Charles Ives. *Fr.* Ives. Rukeyser.

Ivry, Battle of (1590)
Ivry. Macaulay.

Ivy
Holly against Ivy. *Unknown.*
Holly and Ivy. *Unknown.*
In Praise of Ivy. *Unknown.*
Ivy and Holly. Meyerstein.
Ivy, Chief of Trees. *Unknown.*
Ivy Green, The. *Fr.* The Pickwick Papers. Dickens.
Ivy-Wife, The. Hardy.

J

Jack and Jill
Flight of the Bucket, The. Kipling.
Jack and Jill. Loomis.

Jack-in-the-pulpits
Jack-in-the-Pulpit. Eastwick.

Jackdaws
Jackdaw, The. Bourne.
Jackdaw. Earley.
Jackdaw, The. Cowper.
Of a Daw. Heywood.

Jackrabbits
Jack Rabbit. Stoutenburg.
Jackrabbits. Barker.
To a Jack Rabbit. Barker.

Jackson, Andrew
Andrew Jackson. Benét.
Andrew Jackson. Keller.
Jackson at New Orleans. Rice.
Madam Hickory. Larremore.
Oration, Entitled "Old, Old, Old, Old Andrew Jackson," An. Lindsay.
Three Presidents. Bly.

Jackson, Helen Hunt
Helen Hunt Jackson. Coolbrith.

Jackson, "Hurricane"
On Hurricane Jackson. Dugan.

Jackson, Mahalia
Mahalia. Harper.
When Mahalia Sings. Prettyman.

Jackson, Thomas Jonathan (Stonewall)
Brigade Must Not Know, Sir, The. *Unknown.*
Dying Words of Stonewall Jackson, The. Lanier.
Stonewall Jackson. Flash.
Stonewall Jackson's Way. Palmer.
Under the Shade of the Trees. Preston.

Jacob
Jacob. Lasker-Schüler.
Jacob. Reznikoff.
Jacob. Schwartz.

Jacob and the Angel. Mitchell.
Wrestling Jacob. Wesley.

Jacobites
Farewell, The. Burns.
Jacobite's Exile, 1746, A. Swinburne.
Lament for Culloden. Burns.
Old Scottish Cavalier, The. Aytoun.

Jacopone da Todi
Jacopone da Todi. Arnold.

Jaguars
Jaguars, The. Hughes.
Second Glance at a Jaguar. Hughes.

Jamaica, West Indies
Jam Fa Jamaica. Lynch.
Jamaica Market. Maxwell-Hall.
Two-an'-Six. McKay.

James I, King of England
To His Late Majesty Concerning the True Form of English Poetry. Beaumont.

James II, King of England
Clerical Cabal, The. *Unknown.*
Dialogue between King William and the Late King James on the Banks of the Boyne, A. Blount.
Hounslow Heath. *Unknown.*
Humble Address, The. *Unknown.*
King James II. *Fr.* The Hind and the Panther. Dryden.
Trick for Tyburn, or a Prison Rant, A. *Unknown.*
Upon the King's Voyage to Chatham to Make Bulwarks against the Dutch. *Unknown.*

James IV, King of Scotland
Ballade of the Scottyshe Kynge, A. Skelton.
Then the Provost he uprose. *Fr.* Edinburgh after Flodden. Aytoun.

James, Henry
At the Grave of Henry James. Auden.
Henry James. Stevenson.
Henry James at Newport. Kees.
Jacobean. Fadiman.
My Dream by Henry James. Ryan.

James, Jesse
Jesse James. Benét.
Jesse James ("Jesse James was a lad that killed many a man"). *Unknown.*
Jesse James ("Jesse James was a man who traveled through the land"). *Unknown.*

Jamestown, Virginia
Burning of Jamestown, The. English.
Jamestown. Jarrell.
Ode to Jamestown. Paulding.

January
January. Gibson.
January. Hawley.
January. Heath-Stubbs.
January. Lambdin.
January. Sherman.
January. Updike.
January. Voigt.
January. Williams.
January Is Here. Fawcett.
January Snow. Fisher.
Old January. *Fr.* The Faerie Queene. Spenser.
Song of January. Kennedy.
Weeding in January. Brodsky.
Wind of January, The. Rossetti.

Janus
Janus. Mason.

Japan
Ancestors' Graves in Kurakawa. Kogawa.
Great Wave off Kanagwa, The. Egemo.
Hiking Up Hieizan with Alan Lau/Buddha's Birthday 1974. Hongo.
Hiroshima. Rockwell.
Hokkaido. Trifilio.
Japan That Sank under the Sea. Sato.
Japanesque. Herford.
Japan. Hecht.
Letters from Kazuko (Kyoto, Japan—Summer 1980). Lau.
Snow Party, The. Mahon.
Sunrise in the Hills of Satsuma. Fenollosa.
Walk in Kyoto, A. Birney.

Japanese, The
Breaking Silence. Mirikitani.
Card Game, A; Kinjiro Sawada. Ikeda.
Coming Home from Camp. Kaneko.
Dance Instructions for a Young Girl. Hahn.
Discovery of Tradition, The. Inada.
Heart Mountain Japanese Relocation Camp, The: 30 Years Later. Levendosky.
In a Bar near Shibuya Station, Tokyo. Engle.
In Response to Executive Order 9066: All Americans of Japanese Descent Must Report to Relocation Centers. Okita.
Japanese, The. Nash.
Love Poem. Kageyama.
Obon by the Hudson. Oyama.
Relocation. Mura.
Strings/Himo. Kageyama.
Sushi-Okashi and Green Tea with Mitsu Yashima. Robles.
This Song Shows Me Pictures; Morningside Drive, New York City 1950–1960. Oyama.

Jasmine
White Jessamine, The. Tabb.
Yellow Jessamine. Woolson.

Jason
Golden Fleece, The. Williams.

Jays
Riddle: Jay: *Higora.* *Unknown.*
See also **Blue Jays.**

Jaywalking
J's the Jumping Jay-Walker. McGinley.

Jazz
All That Jazz. Jamal.
Battle Report. Kaufman.
Dear John, Dear Coltrane. Harper.
In a Mist. Young.
Jazz. Brown.
Jazz. Rogers.
Jazz Band in a Parisian Cabaret. Hughes.
Jazz Fantasia. Sandburg.
Jazz of This Hotel, The. Lindsay.
Jazzonia. Hughes.
Lamda. Tolson.
Lester Young. Joans.
Mellow Groove Grave Elegy. Ford.
Mingus. Kaufman.
Reuben, Reuben. Harper.
Satchmo. Tolson.
Song thumbed down a cruiser for a ride, A. *Fr.* The Narrator's Trance. Cunningham.
There were blood spots on the skirt. *Fr.* The Narrator's Trance. Cunningham.
Two Handfuls of *Waka* for Thelonious Sphere Monk (d. Feb. 1982). Lew.
Two Jazz Poems. Hines.
Voodoo on the Un-Assing of Janis Joplin. Rogers.
Walking Parker Home. Kaufman.
Zimmer's Last Gig. Zimmer.

Jealousy
Attempt at Jealousy, An. Tsvetaeva.
Better Answer to Cloe Jealous, A. Prior.
English Padlock, An. Prior.
Face upon the Floor, The. D'Arcy.
Fair Margaret and Sweet William. *Unknown.*
I Can't Think What He Sees in Her. Herbert.
In Oxford City. *Unknown.*
Jealous Lovers, The. Hall.
Jealous Man, A. Graves.
Jealous Man, A. *Unknown.*
Jealous Wife, The. Scannell.
Jealousie Is the Rage of a Man. Countess of Winchilsea.
Jealousy. *Fr.* Elegies. Donne.
Jealousy. Malay.
Jealousy. *Unknown.*
Joe Tinker. Hall.
Letter to a Jealous Friend. Simmons.
Lily of the West, The. *Unknown.*
Lord Thomas and Fair Ellinor. *Unknown.*
Love and Jealousy. Greene.
My Last Duchess. Browning.
She Lay Wrapped. Fox.
Sheffield 'Prentice, The. *Unknown.*
Shooting of Dan McGrew, The. Service.
Song: To My Inconstant Mistress. Carew.
Those Wedding Bells Shall Not Ring Out! Rosenfeld.
To Clarissa. Nugent.
Two Sisters, The. *Unknown.*
Upon a Wife That Dyed Mad with Jealousie. Herrick.
What if jealousy is just a bad dream. Palmer.
Widow's Old Broom, The. *Unknown.*

Wild Bill Jones. *Unknown.*
See also **Envy.**
Jeffers, Robinson
Poet Is Dead, The. Everson.
Jefferson, Thomas
Ballad of the Common Man. Kreymborg.
Brave New World. MacLeish.
Death of Jefferson, The. Butterworth.
Jefferson and Liberty. *Unknown.*
Monticello. Sarton.
Thomas Jefferson. R. *and* S. V. Benét.
Twilight's Last Gleaming. Monks.
Jeffreys of Wem, George Jeffreys, 1st Baron
Lord Chancellors Villanies Discovered, or, His Rise and Fall in the Four Last Years, The. *Unknown.*
Sir T.J.'s Speech to His Wife and Children. *Unknown.*
Jehovah's Witnesses
3-31-70. *Fr.* Journal. Jones.
Jellyfish
Jellyfish, A. Moore.
Jellyfish, The. Root.
Lesson, The. Rubin.
Medusa, The. Davenport.
Jenner, Edward
What Jenner Said on Hearing in Elysium That Complaints Had Been Made of His Having a Statue. Brooks.
Jeremiah (Bible)
Jeremiah. Bynner.
Prophet Jeremiah and the Personification of Israel, The. Ben Kalir.
Jerome, Saint
Jerome. Jarrell.
Leonardo da Vinci's. Moore.
Thunderer, The. McGinley.
Jerusalem
At the Western Wall. Lefcowitz.
By the Rivers of Babylon. *Fr.* Psalms. Bible, *O.T.*
By the Waters of Babylon. *Fr.* Hebrew Melodies. Heine.
Celestial Country, The. *Fr.* De Contemptu Mundi. Neale.
Guide to Jerusalem. Silk.
Heavenly City, The. *Unknown.*
Heavenly Jerusalem, Jerusalem of the Earth. Goldberg.
Holy City, The. Weatherly.
I Return unto Zion. *Fr.* Zechariah. Bible, *O.T.*
If I Forget Thee. Litvinoff.
If, Jerusalem, I Ever Should Forget Thee. Heine.
In the Old City. Fichman.
Jerusalem. Ausländer.
Jerusalem. *Fr.* Milton. Blake.
Jerusalem. Kanalenstein.
Jerusalem. Molodovski.
Jerusalem. Slonimski.
Jerusalem. Vinner.
Jerusalem in the Snow. Bental.
Jerusalem Notebook, A. Shapiro.
Jerusalem, Port City. Amichai.
Jerusalem the Dismembered. Greenberg.
Longing for Jerusalem. Halevi.
Mirrors of Jerusalem, The. Lefcowitz.
New Jerusalem, The. *Unknown.*
O holy Jerusalem, Vision of Peace. *Fr.* Christ. *Unknown.*
Prayer for Redemption. *Unknown.*
Prisoner's Song of Jerusalem, A. *Unknown.*
Shadow of the Old City. Amichai.
Sodom's Sister City. Amichai.
Walk in Jerusalem, Just Like John. *Unknown.*
Wandering Jew Comes to the Wall, The. *Fr.* The Wall of Weeping. Fleg.
See also **Zion.**
Jesters
Cap and Bells, The. Yeats.
Fool's Prayer, The. Sill.
Jester's Sermon, The. Thornbury.
See also **Fools.**
Jesuits
Brébeuf and His Brethren. Scott.
Canto I. *Fr.* The Locusts, or Apollyonists. Fletcher.
Satires upon the Jesuits, *sels.* Oldham.
Jesus Christ
Adam and Eve. Sisson.
Agonie, The. Herbert.
Airy Christ, The. Smith.
All Hail the Power of Jesus' Name. Perronet.
Amid the Din of Earthly Strife. Hawkes.
And Did Those Feet in Ancient Time. *Fr.* Milton. Blake.
Approaches. Macdonald.
Argument, An—of the Passion of Christ. Merton.
Ascension of Our Lord Jesus Christ, The. Smart.
At Prime Jesus was y-led. *Fr.* Hours of the Passion. William of Shoreham.
At the Manger Mary Sings. Auden.
Attraction. *Unknown.*
Away in a Manger. *Unknown.*
Bag, The. Herbert.
Ballad of the Golden Bowl. Hay.
Ballad of the Goodly Fere. Pound.
Ballade of Illegal Ornaments. Belloc.
Barnfloor and Winepress. Hopkins.
Because He Was Tempted. *Unknown.*
Beloved, The. Tynan.
Bitter Withy, The. *Unknown.*
Blessed Name, The. Bethune.
Blessing, and Honor. Bonar.
"Borrowed." *Unknown.*
Bridegroom of Cana, The. Pickthall.
But Thee, but Thee, O sovereign Seer of time. *Fr.* The Crystal. Lanier.
By Him. Jonson.
Carol: "Now is the world withdrawn all." Nemerov.
Carpenter, The. Whiteside.
Carpenter of Galilee, The. Smith.
Carpenter's Son, The. Housman.
Chanticleer. Austin.
Child. Sandburg.
Child My Choice, A. Southwell.
Child's Prayer, A. Thompson.
Christ, The, *sels.* *Cynewulf.*
Christ. Holmes.
Christ, The. Oxenham.
Christ and the Pagan. Tabb.
Christ Complains to Sinners. *Unknown.*
Christ in Flanders. Whitmell.
Christ in the Clay-Pit. Clemo.
Christ in the Universe. Meynell.
Christ Is Coming. Macomber.
Christ, My Beloved. Baldwin.
Christ of Judea, look thou in my heart! *Fr.* Credo. Gilder.
Christ Quiets the Tempest. *Fr.* Carmen Paschale. Sedulius.
Christ, the Man. Davies.
Christ Walking on the Water. Rodgers.
Christ with me, Christ before me, Christ behind me. *Fr.* St. Patrick. Garlick.
Christ's Descent into Hell. Rilke.
Christ's Tear Breaks My Heart. *Unknown.*
Church's One Foundation, The. Stone.
Coming Child, The. Crashaw.
Coming of Christ, The. *Unknown.*
Comrade Jesus. Cleghorn.
Coronet, The. Marvell.
Corpus Christi Carol, The ("Heron flew east, the heron flew west, The"). *Unknown.*
Corpus Christi Carol, The ("Over yonder's park, which is newly begun"). *Unknown.*
Corpus Christi Carol ("Lully, lullay, lully, lullay"). *Unknown.*
Coventry Carol. *Unknown.*
Cradle and the Cross, The. Reitz.
Cradle Hymn. Watts.
Credo. Oxenham.
Dawning, The. Herbert.
Deep Spring. *Unknown.*
Despised and Rejected. Bates.
Devout Prayer of the Passion, A. *Unknown.*
Discerning the Lord's Body. Montgomery.
Divine Love. *Unknown.*
Divine Lover, The. Wesley.
Do We Not Hear Thy Footfall? Carmichael.
Drunken Fisherman, The. Lowell.
Dumbfounding, The. Avison.
E Tenebris. Wilde.
Earliest Christian Hymn. Clement of Alexandria.
Easter Hymn. Housman.
Easter Song, A. *Unknown.*
Ecce Homo. Gascoyne.
El Greco: Espolio. Birney.
Eli, Eli. Wright.
Ex Ore Infantium. Thompson.
Fairest Lord Jesus. *Unknown.*

Father, part of his double interest. *Fr.* Holy Sonnets. Donne.
Father to the Man. Knight.
Feet of Judas, The. McClellan.
For God While Sleeping. Sexton.
For My Brother Jesus. Layton.
From Heaven High I Come to You. Luther.
Fugitive, The. Meynell.
Gentle Jesus, Meek and Mild. Wesley.
Give Me Jesus. *Unknown.*
God is a distant, stately lover. Dickinson.
Great Man, The. Tietjens.
Greatest Person in the Universe, The. Marsh.
Guest, The. *Unknown.*
Happy Man, The. Chesterton.
He. Kunitz.
He Is a Path. *Fr.* Christ's Victory and Triumph. Fletcher.
He Is the Lonely Greatness. Rock.
He Is the Way. *Fr.* For the Time Being; a Christmas Oratorio. Auden.
He Made Us Free. Egan.
He Never Will Forget. "M. G. H."
He Was Not Willing. Meyer.
Head That Once Was Crowned with Thorns, The. Kelly.
Hem of His Garment, The. Hamilton.
Him Evermore I Behold. Longfellow.
His Are the Thousand Sparkling Rills. Alexander.
His Hands. Moreland.
Holy Well, The. *Unknown.*
Hound of Heaven, The. Thompson.
How Sweet the Name of Jesus Sounds. Newton.
How to Hide Jesus. Turner.
Hymn: "Sing, my tongue, the Saviour's glory." St. Thomas Aquinas.
Hymn of the Incarnation, A. *Unknown.*
Hymn to Christ, at the Author's Last Going into Germany, A. Donne.
I Met the Master. *Unknown.*
I Saw a Peacock. *Unknown.*
I See His Blood upon the Rose. Plunkett.
I shall know why, when time is over. Dickinson.
I think the Lord on his axe-chopped cross. *Fr.* Autumn Testament. Baxter.
I Told Jesus. Plumpp.
I Turn to Jesus. Smith.
I Was a Stricken Deer, That Left the Herd. *Fr.* The Task. Cowper.
I Wonder as I Wander. *Unknown.*
If Christ Were Here To-Night. Sangster.
In Christ. *Unknown.*
In-Group. Kearns.
In the Wilderness. Graves.
Inasmuch! Brooks.
Incarnate Love. Tillett.
Incarnation and Passion, The. Vaughan.
Incarnation Poem. Leax.
Inner Light, The. Myers.
Innumerable Christ, The. "MacDiarmid."
Insight. Kearns.
Invocation: "Great-hearted Christ, importunate and mild." *Fr.* The Psalm of Christ. Walsh.
Irony of God. Warner.
Jesu. Herbert.
Jesu Christ, My Leman Swete. *Unknown.*
Jesus. McAuley.
Jesus and His Mother. Gunn.
Jesus and I. Crawford.
Jesus Bids Man Remember. *Unknown.*
Jesus Borned in Bethlea. *Unknown.*
Jesus Christ. Guthrie.
Jesus Contrasts Man and Himself. *Unknown.*
Jesus, Lover of My Soul. Wesley.
Jesus Make Up My Dying Bed. *Unknown.*
Jesus Reassures His Mother. *Unknown.*
Jesus Reproaches His People. *Unknown.*
Jesus, Saviour, Pilot Me. Hopper.
Jesus Shall Reign Where'er the Sun. Watts.
Jesus the Carpenter. Liddell.
Jesus, Thou Joy of Loving Hearts. St. Bernard of Clairvaux.
Jesus! thy Crucifix. Dickinson.
Jesus to Those Who Pass By. *Unknown.*
Joys of Mary, The. *Unknown.*
King Triumphant. Watts.
Lachrimae Verae. *Fr.* Lachrimae. Hill.
Lamb, The. *Fr.* Songs of Innocence. Blake.
Last Supper, The. Rilke.
Last Words of Don Henriquez, The. Schneour.
Legend of Cherries, A. Dalmon.
Little Cradle Rocks Tonight in Glory, The. *Unknown.*
Little Jesus. Thompson.
Lord of the Dance. Carter.
Lost Word of Jesus, A. Van Dyke.
Love. Beaumont.
Lovely was the death. *Fr.* Religious Musings. Coleridge.
Luke XI: Blessed Be the Paps Which Thou Hast Sucked. Crashaw.
Mary and Her Son Alone. *Unknown, at. to* Ryman.
Mediator, The. Browning.
Mercy Pleads for Mankind. *Fr.* Christ's Victory and Triumph. Fletcher.
Messiah, The. *Fr.* Paradise Regained. Milton.
Middle-Time, The. Fowler.
Morning Hymn, A. Wesley.
Moses and Jesus. Zangwill.
Mother and Child. Eastwick.
Mother and Her Son on the Cross, The. *Unknown.*
My Friend. *Unknown.*
My Gift. Rossetti.
My Heart Is Woe. *Unknown.*
My Master Was So Very Poor. Lee.
My Song Is Love Unknown. Crossman.
Mystic Song, A. *Unknown.*
Never Said a Mumbalin' Word. *Unknown.*
New Approach Needed. Amis.
New Heaven, New Warre. Southwell.
New Year's Carol. *Unknown.*
Night. *Fr.* Songs of Innocence. Blake.
No Coming to God without Christ. Herrick.
None of Self and All of Thee. Monod.
Not I. *Unknown.*
O Christ of Olivet, you hushed the wars. *Fr.* The Christ of the Andes. Markham.
O Christ, Who Died. Slemp.
O Come All Ye Faithful. *Unknown.*
O Jesu Parvule. "MacDiarmid."
O Little Town of Bethlehem. Brooks.
O Master-Workman of the Race. Stocking.
O Son of God, Afflicted. *Unknown.*
O Young and Fearless Prophet. Harlow.
On the Bleeding Wounds of Our Crucified Lord. Crashaw.
On the Infancy of Our Savior. Quarles.
On the Safe Side. Dunsany.
Once in Royal David's City. Alexander.
One in Christ. Van Dyke.
Our Christ. Farrington.
Our Lord and Our Lady. Belloc.
Our Master. Whittier.
Out of Bounds. Tabb.
Pair of Wings, A. Hawes.
Palm-Sunday Hymn, A. Herbert.
Passion and Exaltation of Christ, The. Watts.
Passion of Christ, The. Devlin.
Peace. Vaughan.
Peace, Perfect Peace. Bickersteth.
Pietà, The, Rhenish, 14th C., The Cloisters. Van Duyn.
Poet, The. Bynner.
Poor Little Jesus. *Unknown.*
Praise to the Holiest in the height. *Fr.* The Dream of Gerontius. Cardinal Newman.
Protagonist, The. Hopegood.
Question, The. Auden.
Quia Amore Langueo. *Unknown.*
Quintina of Crosses, A. Walsh.
Reality. Havergal.
Redemption. Herbert.
Rime of the Rood, A. O'Donnell.
Rorate Coeli Desuper. Dunbar.
Royal Guest, A. *Unknown.*
Salutation to Jesus Christ. Calvin.
Search, The. Crashaw.
Search, The. Lowell.
Search, The. Vaughan.
Second Coming, The. Clark.
Second Coming, The. Yeats.
Second Crucifixion, The. Le Gallienne.
Second Seeing. Golding.
Sheep and Lambs. Tynan.
Shine Out, Fair Sun, with All Your Heat. *Fr.* The Masque of the Twelve Months. *At. to* Chapman.
Signum Cui Contradicetur. Sister Mary Angelita.
Sometime during eternity. *Fr.* A Coney Island of the Mind. Ferlinghetti.

Song of a Heathen, The. Gilder.
Song of Love for Jesus, A. Rolle.
Sonnet: "By what glass of resemblance may we see." Alabaster.
Soul of Jesus Is Restless, The. Mitchell.
Souls Groan to Christ for Succour, The. Taylor.
Spit in my face you Jews, and pierce my side. *Fr.* Holy Sonnets. Donne.
Spring. Hopkins.
Stigmata. Stoddard.
Strong Son of God, immortal Love. *Fr.* In Memoriam A. H. H. Tennyson.
Sweet Jesu. *Unknown.*
Temple. Donne.
That Holy Thing. Macdonald.
The Man Christ. Lindsey.
There Were Ninety and Nine. Clephane.
This Endris Night. *Unknown.*
Thou Who Taught the Thronging People. Minde.
Three Enemies, The. Rossetti.
To a Crucifix. Wickham.
To God the Son. Constable.
To His Saviour, a Child; a Present, by a Child. Herrick.
To Jesus of Nazareth. Knowles.
To Our Blessed Lord upon the Choice of His Sepulchre. Crashaw.
To the Child Jesus. Van Dyke.
To the Christians. Adams.
To the Young Man Jesus. Dalton.
True Apostolate, The. Weyburn.
Two Songs from a Play. Yeats.
Unchanging Jesus. Massie.
Under Sorrow's Sign. O'Dalaigh.
Unto Us a Son Is Given. Meynell.
Virile Christ, A. Boundy.
Vision of Ita, The. *Unknown.*
Vision of Jesus, The. *Fr.* The Vision of Piers Plowman. Langland.
Voice of Christmas, The. Kemp.
Way, the Truth, and the Life, The. Parker.
Way, The; the Truth; the Life. Porter.
We Bear the Strain of Earthly Care. Davis.
We Would See Jesus. *Unknown.*
What Christ Is to Us. *Unknown.*
When Will He Come? *Unknown.*
White Was His Naked Breast. *Unknown.*
Wilt thou love God, as He thee? then digest. *Fr.* Holy Sonnets. Donne.
Windhover, The. Hopkins.
Woefully Arrayed. *At. to.* Skelton.
Woman. Barrett.
Wonder. Traherne.
Words from an Old Spanish Carol. *Unknown.*
Work. Studdert-Kennedy.
Wreck of the *Deutschland*, The. Hopkins.
Young Poet. O'Higgins.
Young Workman, The. Frear.

Jewelry
Alexandrite Ring, The. Ryan.
Amber Beads. Brown.
Lost Jewel, A. Graves.
Ring, The. Wakoski.
Sparrow and Diamond, The. Green.
To His Ring, Given to His Lady, Wherein Was Graven This Verse, "My Heart Is Yours." Turberville.
Upon a Diamond Cut in Form of a Heart. Ayton.
When Diamonds, Nibbling in My Ears. Davies.
With a Gift of Rings. Graves.
See also **Rings.**

Jews
August 12, 1952. Fishman.
Autobiographical. Klein.
Ballade of Beauties. Scott.
Before Passover. Mayne.
Both My Grandmothers. Field.
Breaking of the Day, The. Davison.
Bury Me in America. Karlen.
But not so odd. Browne.
Chosen People, The. Ewer.
Crowing of the Red Cock, The. Lazarus.
Debate with the Rabbi. Nemerov.
Design for Mediaeval Tapestry. Klein.
For Arthur Gregor. Field.
Genius, The. Cohen.
Hebrew of Your Poets, Zion, The. Reznikoff.
Heirloom. Klein.
Homeless, The. Hall.
In re *Solomon Warshawer.* Klein.
Jew. Randall.
Jew, The. Rosenberg.
Jew to Jesus, The. Frank.
Jewish Cemetery at Newport, The. Longfellow.
Jewish Main Street. Layton.
Jews, The. Herbert.
Jews, The. Vaughan.
Jews at Haifa. Jarrell.
Judaism. Cardinal Newman.
Let Other People Come as Streams. Reznikoff.
Little Sir Hugh. *Unknown.*
"More Light! More Light!" Hecht.
Note in Lieu of a Suicide. Finkel.
151st Psalm, The. Shapiro.
Permanent Delegate, The. Suhl.
Portrait of a Jew Old Country Style. Rothenberg.
Rabbi Ben Ezra. Browning.
Restaurantsri/Geraniums, The. Taggard
Scene of a Summer Morning. Feldman.
Second Generation, The. Rosensaft.
Sir Hugh; or, The Jew's Daughter. *Unknown.*
Still Small Voice, The. Klein.
Story about Chicken Soup, A. Simpson.
Summa Contra Gentiles. Leary.
That Was Then. Gardner.
To Russia. Miller.
Wandering Jew, The. Bridges.
Wandering Jew, The. Mezey.
What Is a Jewish Poem? Sklarew.
World's Justice, The. Lazarus.
Worm, The. Barnstone.
Yiddish Poet. Jacobs.
Treasury of Jewish Poetry, A (TrJP). Nathan Ausubel *and* Marynn Ausubel, eds.
Voices Within the Ark; the Modern Jewish Poets (VWA). Howard Schwartz *and* Anthony Rudolf, eds.

Jezebel
Jezebel. Middleton.
Song for the Clatter-Bones. Higgins.

Joan of Arc
Good Joan, The. Reese.
Joan of Arc. McCrae.
Joan of Arc to the Tribunal. Frisch.
Maid, The. Brégy.
Maid, The. Roberts.
Maid of Arc, The. Bottomley.

Job (Bible)
Beauty of Job's Daughters, The. MacPherson.
Job. Sewell.

Jockeys
Old Jockey, The. Higgins.
See also **Horse Racing.**

Jogging and Joggers. *See* **Running and Runners.**

John, Saint
Peter and John. Wylie.
Song to John, Christ's Friend, A. *Unknown.*

John Bull
World Is a Bundle of Hay, The. Byron.

John Henry (folk hero)
Birth of John Henry, The. Tolson.
John Henry. *Unknown.*
Spike Driver Blues. *Unknown.*

John of Austria
Lepanto. Chesterton.

John the Baptist, Saint
For the Baptist. Drummond of Hawthornden.
John the Baptist. Simpson.
St. John Baptist. O'Shaughnessy.

Johnson, Lionel
In Memory of Major Robert Gregory. Yeats.

Johnson, Lyndon Baines
Gray Oak Twilight, The. Kilgore.
Miltonic Sonnet for Mr. Johnson on His Refusal of Peter Hurd's Official Portrait, A. Wilbur.

Johnson, Samuel
Doctor Johnson. Jenyns.
Epitaph: "Here Johnson lies—a sage by all allow'd." Cowper.
My Marriage with Mrs. Johnson. Gilbert.
To the Oaks of Glencree. Synge.

Jonah
Father Mapple's Hymn. *Fr.* Moby Dick. Melville.

For Lo! My Jonah How He Slumped. Wilson.
I to the Lord from My Distress. *Unknown.*
Jonah. Huxley.
Jonah. *Fr.* Patience. *Unknown.*
Jonah and the Whale. Meynell.
Jonah is Cast into the Sea. *Fr.* Patience. *Unknown.*
Noah an' Jonah an' Cap'n John Smith. Marquis.
Who Did Swallow Jonah? *Unknown.*

Jonathan (Bible)
Beauty of Israel is slain upon thy high places, The. *Fr.* Second Samuel. Bible, *O.T.*

Jones, Casey (John Luther Jones)
Casey Jones (Union). Hill.
Casey Jones. *Unknown.*
Kassie Jones. *Unknown.*

Jones, John Paul
Battle of the *Bonhomme Richard* and the *Serapis*. *Fr.* Song of Myself. Whitman.
Paul Jones. *Unknown.*
Paul Jones—A New Song. *Unknown.*
Paul Jones's Victory. *Unknown.*
Yankee Man-of-War, The. *Unknown.*

Jonson, Ben
Elegy on Ben Jonson, An. Cleveland.
Gratulatory to Mr. Ben Johnson for His Adopting of Him to Be His Son, A. Randolph.
His Prayer to Ben Jonson. Herrick.
Humble Petition of Poor Ben to the Best of Monarchs, Masters, Men, King Charles, The. Jonson.
Let dull and ignorant pretenders art condemn. *Fr.* Upon the Works of Ben Jonson. Oldham.
Ode for Ben Jonson, An. Herrick.
Ode to Himself ("Where do'st thou careless lie"). Jonson.
Prologue to "The Tempest." Vaughan.
Scorne then their censure, who gave out thy wit. *Fr.* To the Memory of Ben Johnson. Mayne.
Sun, Which Doth the Greatest Comfort Bring, The. *Fr.* Mr. Francis Beaumont's Letter to Ben Jonson. Beaumont.
To Ben Jonson. Carew.
To His Friend Ben. Jonson, of His Horace Made English. Herbert of Cherbury.
To My Dead Friend Ben: Johnson. King.
Upon Ben Jonson. Herrick.
Upon Ben Jonson. Waller.

Joplin, Janis
Burying Blues for Janis. Piercy.
Death of Janis Joplin, The. Phillips.
Janis Joplin and the Folding Company. Winters.

Joseph (Bible, *O.T.*)
Pharaoh and Joseph. Lasker-Schüler.
September, the First Day of School. Nemerov.

Joseph, Saint
Cherry Tree Carol. *Unknown.*
Joseph's Suspicion. Rilke.

Joshua
Joshua Fit de Battle of Jericho. *Unknown.*
Joshua's Face. Gilboa.
Moses and Joshua. Lasker-Schüler.

Journalism
British Journalist, The. Wolfe.
Note on Modern Journalism during the Last Campaign. Mayo.
Problems of a Journalist. Kees.
Song: "Closes and courts and lanes." Davidson.
See also **Magazines; Newspapers.**

Journeymen
Journeyman, The. *Unknown.*

Jowett, Benjamin
Balliol Rhymes, *sel.* Beeching.
I am the great Professor Jowett. *Unknown.*

Joy
After the Second Operation. Goedicke.
Answer, The. Teasdale.
Birthday, A. Rossetti.
Blessing, A. Wright.
Delight Song of Tsoai-Talee, The. Momaday.
Eternity. *Fr.* Several Questions Answered. Blake.
First or Last. Hardy.
Hurrahing in Harvest. Hopkins.
In Assisi. Blumenthal.
Infant Joy. *Fr.* Songs of Innocence. Blake.
Joy. Creeley.
Joy. Delany.
Joy. Jeffers.
Joy Sonnet in a Random Universe. Chasin.
L'Allegro. Milton.
Ode to Joy. Hoffman.
Song of Joy. Uvavnuk.
Tidings of Great Joy. *Fr.* St. Luke. Bible, *N.T.*
To the Lord General Cromwell. Milton.
Welcome Morning. Sexton.

Joyce, James
D. H. Lawrence and James Joyce. Wolfe.
Poets of Hell, The. Shapiro.
Ulysses' Library. Daiches.

Judas Iscariot
Apocrypha. Deutsch.
Ballad of Judas Iscariot, The. Buchanan.
Betrayal. Cholmondeley.
Christus Matthaeum et Discipulos Alloquitur. Sherburne.
Descent for the Lost. Child.
Historical Judas, The. Nemerov.
Judas. Miller.
Judas. *Unknown.*
Judas Iscariot. Cullen.
Judas Iscariot. Martin.
Judas Iscariot. Spender.
Judas, Joyous Little Son. Farber.
Judas Sells His Lord. *Unknown.*
Pawns, The. Betts.
Saint Judas. Wright.

Judas Maccabeus
Judas Maccabeus. *Fr.* First Maccabees. Aprocrypha. Bible, *O.T.*

Judges
Beak, The. Smither.
Circuit Judge, The. Masters.
Judge, The. McClane.
Judge Somers. Masters.
Judge with the Sore Rump, The. Tucker.
Killers. Sandburg.
On Rÿneveld, an Unpopular Dutch Judge. *Unknown.*
Roy Bean. *Unknown.*

Judgment Day
Abraham Davenport. Whittier.
At the round earth's imagined corners, blow. *Fr.* Holy Sonnets. Donne.
Auguries of Innocence. Blake.
Blow Gabriel. *Unknown.*
Carol for the Last Christmas Eve. Nicholson.
Cherry Fair, The. *Unknown.*
Crazy Jane on the Day of Judgment. Yeats.
Crowdieknowe. "MacDiarmid."
Day of Judgement, The. Swift.
Day of Judgment, The. Buchanan.
Day of Judgment, The. Watts.
Day of Wrath, The. Saint Columba.
Death. Herbert.
Death and Resurrection. Croly.
Dies Irae. Thomas of Celano.
Doomsday. Herbert.
Fifteen Days of Judgement, The. Evans.
Great Round-up. *Unknown.*
Heavenly Aeroplane, The. *Unknown.*
How long, dear Savior, O how long. Watts.
In Dat Great Gittin'-up Mornin'. *Unknown.*
Jesus Is Coming Soon. *Unknown.*
Judgement. Herbert.
Judgment Day. Oxenham.
Last Judgment, The. *Fr.* Christ. *Unknown.*
My Lord, What a Mourning. *Unknown.*
O Children, Would You Cherish? Dock.
Rapture. Carlson.
Remember the Day of Judgment. *Unknown.*
Rise and Shine. Lattimore.
Second Coming, The. Yeats.
Te Judice. Scott.
Ten thousand times ten thousand. Alford.
Vision of the Day of Judgment. *Fr.* Isaiah. Bible, *O.T.*
Where Shall I Be When de Firs' Trumpet Soun'? *Unknown.*

Judith (Apocrypha)
Judith of Bethulia. Ransom.
Judith Recalls Holofernes. Stanton.

Jugglers
Draw me nere, draw me nere. *Unknown.*
Juggler. Wilbur.
Juggler and the Baron's Daughter, The. *Unknown.*

Juggling Jerry. Meredith.
Julius Caesar. *See* **Caesar, Julius.**
July
Fourth of July, The. Pierpont.
It Is July. Swett.
July. *At. to* Whittier.
July in Indiana. Fitzgerald.
July Meadow. Driscoll.
July: The Succession of the Four Sweet Months. Herrick.
Loud is the Summer's busy song. *Fr.* The Shepherd's Calendar: July. Clare.
Prayer on Fourth of July. Turner.
Smelling the End of Green July. Yates.
That's July. Butts.
Jumping
Little Jumping Girls, The. Greenaway.
June
Cut Grass. Larkin.
Dawning of the Day, The. Mangan.
Earth gets its price for what Earth gives us. *Fr.* The Vision of Sir Launfal. Lowell.
Evening and Morning in June, An. *Fr.* Prologues to the Aeneid. Douglas.
Harebells in June. Wynne.
In June and Gentle Oven. Wilkinson.
In June. Perry.
June. Davies.
June. Feinstein.
June. Fisher.
June. Hopper.
June. Ledwidge.
June ("Over his keys the musing organist"). *Fr.* The Vision of Sir Launfal. Lowell.
June ("What is so rare as a day in June?") *Fr.* The Vision of Sir Launfal. Lowell.
June. MacDonald.
June. Malloch.
June. Rand.
June. Reaney.
June Bracken and Heather. Tennyson.
June Is Bustin' Out All Over. *Fr.* Carousel. Hammerstein.
June Morning. McCrae.
June Night. Hall.
June, 1915. Mew.
June Rapture. Morgan.
June Thunder. MacNeice.
June Twenty-first. Guernsey.
June Twilight. Masefield.
Knee-deep in June. Riley.
Mowing, The. Roberts.
Night in June, A. Scott.
Poem in June. Acorn.
Stay, June, Stay! Rossetti.
Sun Has Long Been Set, The. Wordsworth.
That's June. Butts.
Jungles
At the Edge of the Jungle. Lane.
Jungle. Haring.
Jungle, The. *Fr.* Thailand Railway. Stow.
Song for the Elephant Hunt, The, *sel.* *Unknown.*
Juniper
Juniper. Francis.
Sing a Song of Juniper. Francis.
Junk and Junkyards
Caravati's Junkyard. Morgan.
Cherrylog Road. Dickey.
Drunk in the Furnace, The. Merwin.
In Passing. Jonas.
Junk. Wilbur.
Junkyards. Rayford.
Jupiter (god)
Jupiter and Ganimede. Heywood.
Justice
Carl Hamblin. *Fr.* Spoon River Anthology. Masters.
Country Justice, The. Langhorne.
Death of Justice, The. Hawkins.
"Guilty or Not Guilty?" *Unknown.*
Justice. Hughes.
Net of Law, The. Roche.
Rain It Raineth, The. Bowen.
They Can't Do That. *Unknown.*
Thou Art Indeed Just, Lord. Hopkins.
To Sir Thomas Egerton. Daniel.
Who But the Lord? Hughes.
Youth. "Hope."
See also **Injustice.**
Juvenile Delinquency
We Real Cool. Brooks.

K

Kabbala. *See* **Cabala.**
Kabul, Afghanistan
Ford o' Kabul River. Kipling.
Kafka, Franz
Letter to Kafka. Stanton.
Tribute to Kafka for Someone Taken. Dugan.
Kalakaua (Hawaiian King)
Praise Song for King Kalakaua. *Unknown.*
Kalamazoo, Michigan
Sins of Kalamazoo, The. Sandburg.
Kandinsky, Wassily
Kandinsky: "Improvisation No. 27." Tick.
Kane (Hawaiian God)
O Kane, O Lono of the blue sea. *Unknown.*
Water of Kane, The. *Unknown.*
Kangaroos
Delicate Mother Kangaroo. Lawrence.
Duck and the Kangaroo, The. Lear.
Kangaroo by Nightfall. Macainsh.
Kangaroo. Lawrence.
Kangaroo, The. *Unknown.*
Native Born. Irvin.
Nature Note. Guiterman.
Sing-Song of Old Man Kangaroo, The. Kipling.
Kansas
Birth in a Narrow Room. Brooks.
Ceremony. Stafford.
Crossing Kansas by Train. Justice.
Delphine. Anderson.
Haskell. Bynner.
In Kansas. *Unknown.*
In Lucas, Kansas. Williams.
Kansas Boy. Lechlitner.
Kansas Boys. *Unknown.*
Moonlit Night in Kansas. Contoski.
Piccola Commedia. Wilbur.
Rescued Year, The. Stafford.
Stories from Kansas. Stafford.
Talking across Kansas. Kwon.
Trail into Kansas, The. Merwin.
Wichita Vortex Sutra. Ginsberg.
Kansas City, Kansas and Missouri
Kansas City. Hammerstein.
Kansas City West Bottoms. Dahlberg.
Nichols Fountain. Miner.
Kashmir, India
Light of the Haram, The. *Fr.* Lalla Rookh. Moore.
Katharine of Aragón, Queen of England
Ballad for Katharine of Aragon, A. Causley.
Katmandu, Nepal
Here in Katmandu. Justice.
Katydids
To a Caty-Did. Freneau.
To an Insect. Holmes.
Katzenjammer Kids
Katzenjammer Kids, The. Reaney.
Kavanagh, Patrick
If Ever You Go to Dublin Town. Kavanagh.
Kayaks
Kayak, The. *Unknown.*
Kearny, Philip
Kearny at Seven Pines. Stedman.
Keaton, Buster
Buster Keaton & the Cops. Keithley.
Keats, John
Adonais: An Elegy on the Death of John Keats. Shelley.
After a Lecture on John Keats. Holmes.
At Lulworth Cove a Century Back. Hardy.
For John Keats, Apostle of Beauty. *Fr.* Four Epitaphs. Cullen.
Keats. Longfellow.

Keats. Lord.
Keats. Reese.
Keats to Fanny Brawne. Masters.
October XXIX, 1795. Braithwaite.
Ode on a Grecian Urn Summarized. Skirrow.
On the Death of Keats. Logan.
Posthumous Keats. Plumly.
Rome. Hardy.
To John Keats, Poet, at Springtime. Cullen.
Who Kill'd John Keats? Byron.

Kees, Weldon
Weldon Kees. Levis.

Keller, Helen
Helen Keller. Stedman.
Of One Who neither Sees nor Hears. Gilder.

Kells, Book of
Book of Kells, The. Colum.
Library, The. Logan.

Kempenfelt, Richard
On the Loss of the *Royal George.* Cowper.

Kennedy, John Fitzgerald
Assassination Raga. Ferlinghetti.
Belief. Ammons.
Channel U.S.A.—Live. Stoutenburg.
Down in Dallas. Kennedy.
John Fitzgerald Kennedy. Masefield.
Kennedy. Heffernan.
November Twenty-sixth Nineteen Hundred and Sixty-three. Berry.
Seven Houses, The. Brown.
Thanksgiving, 1963. Kazan.
Three Presidents. Bly.
To J. F. K. 14 Years After. Weaver.
Traction: November 22, 1963. Moss.

Kennedy, Robert Francis
Assassination Raga. Ferlinghetti.
Beyond the Presidency. Gibson.

Kensington Gardens, London
Dead Harvest, A. Meynell.
In Kensington Gardens. Symons.

Kent, England
In Romney Marsh. Davidson.
Memory of Kent, The. Blunden.
On Lord Holland's Seat near Margate, Kent. Gray.
On the Pilgrim's Way in Kent, as It Leads to the Coldrum Stones. Asphodel.
To Penshurst. Jonson.
Tunbridge Wells. Rochester.
See also **Cinque Ports.**

Kent State University, Ohio
Kent State Massacre, The. Warshaw *and* Dane.
Kent State, May 4, 1970. Goodman.
O Whose Are These Children. Snyder.

Kentucky
American Portrait: Old Style. Warren
Girl of Constant Sorrow. Gunning.
Hunters of Kentucky, The. Woodworth.
In the Corn Land. Howard.
Lily of the West. *Unknown.*
Mad Farmer Stands Up in Kentucky for What He Thinks Is Right. Hall.
My Fathers Came from Kentucky. Lindsay.
My Old Kentucky Home. Foster.
Old Athens of the West Is Now a Blue Grass Tour, The. Hall.
Radcliff, Kentucky. Nickens.
Road in Kentucky, A. Hayden.
Tourism. Chaffin.
Walthena. Peck.

Kepler, Johannes
Johannes Kepler. *Fr.* Letters from the Astronomers. Cedering.

Kerouac, Jack
I Met This Guy Who Died. Corso.

Kerry. *See* **County Kerry, Ireland.**

Kesey, Ken
First Party at Ken Keseys with Hell's Angels. Ginsberg.

Kevin, Saint
St. Kevin. Lover.

Kew Gardens, London
Barrel Organ, The. Noyes

Key West, Florida
Hemingway House in Key West, The. Schultz.
Idea of Order at Key West, The. Stevens.

Keys
Keys of Morning, The. De la Mare.
Liberator, The. Coleman.
Skeleton Key. Hollander.

Kibbutzim
Kibbutz Sabbath. Amittai.

Kidd, William
Captain Kidd. *Unknown.*

Kierkegaard, Søren
Kierkegaard, a/ cripple and a Dane. *Fr.* Die Neuen Heiligen. Updike.

Kilcash, Ireland
Kilcash. *Unknown.*

Kildare. *See* **County Kildare, Ireland.**

Killarney, Ireland
Killarney. Falconer.
Killarney. Larminie.

Killdeers
Nesting Ground, The. Wagoner.

Kilmer, Joyce
Joyce Kilmer. Burr.

King, Edward
Lycidas. Milton.
On the Memory of Mr. Edward King Drown'd in the Irish Seas. Cleveland.

King, William, Archbishop of Dublin
Excellent New Song upon His Grace Our Good Lord Archbishop of Dublin, An. Swift.

King, Martin Luther, Jr.
Alabama Bus. *Unknown.*
Assassination. Lee.
Death of Dr. King. Cornish.
Funeral of Martin Luther King, Jr., The. Giovanni.
In Memoriam: Martin Luther King, Jr. Jordan.
King Lives. Boyer.
Martin Luther King. Livingston.
Martin Luther King, Jr. Brooks.
Martin's Blues. Harper.
Stopped in Memphis. Bauer.
White Weekend. Troupe.

King, William Lyon Mackenzie
W. L. M. K. Scott.

King Kong
Fay Wray to the King. Rechter.

King Lear
Lear. Williams.
On Sitting Down to Read "King Lear" Once Again. Keats.

King Philip's War
Lamentable Ballad of the Bloody Brook. Hale.

Kingfishers
Kingfisher, The. Davies.
Kingfisher, The. Kelly.
Kingfisher, The. *Fr.* Upon Appleton House. Marvell.

Kings
And Ride in Triumph through Persepolis. *Fr.* Tamburlaine the Great. Marlowe.
And welcom now (Great Monarch) to your own. *Fr.* Astraea Redux. Dryden.
Apple Dumplings and a King. "Pindar."
Bastard King of England, The. *Unknown.*
Chapter of Kings, The. Collins.
Cloth of Gold. Scott.
Coronation. Jackson.
Elegy on the Late King of Patagonia, An. Hankin.
England's Sovereigns in Verse. *Unknown.*
English Succession, The. *Unknown.*
Epigram: "Here lies a great and mighty king." Rochester.
Extempore Verses Intended to Allay the Violence of Party-Spirit. Byrom.
Fable, A: "In Aesop's tales an honest wretch we find." Prior.
Georges, The. Landor.
Georges, The. Thackeray.
King John and the Abbot of Canterbury. *Unknown.*
Kings and Queens of England, The. *Unknown.*
Kings of France. Lincoln.
Lines on Succession of the Kings of England. *Unknown.*
Model for the Laureate, A. Yeats.
Of the Death of Kings. *Fr.* Richard II. Shakespeare.
Old King Cole was a merry old soul. Mother Goose.
On King Richard the Third, Who Lies Buried under Leicester Bridge. Suckling.
Poor Kings. Davies.
Primacy of Dullness, The. *Fr.* MacFlecknoe. Dryden.
Ribbon Two Yards Wide, A. Kreymborg.
Royal Line, The. Hunt.
Sesostris. Mifflin.

There Lived a King. Gilbert.
Time seems not now beneath his years to stoop. *Fr.* To His Sacred Majesty, a Panegyrick on His Coronation, 1661. Dryden.
Twentieth Song. *Fr.* Polyolbion. Drayton.
Yet If His Majesty, Our Sovereign Lord. *Unknown.*
See also **individual names of kings.**

Kipling, Rudyard
Ballad, A: "As I was walkin' the jungle round, a-killin' of tigers an' time." Carryl.
Rhyme of the Kipperling, The. *Fr.* The Battle of the Bays. Seaman.
To R. K. Stephen.

Kisses
Come Chloe, and Give Me Sweet Kisses. Williams.
Did Not. Moore.
Epigram of Martial, Imitated, An. Williams.
First Kiss, The. Watts-Dunton.
First Kiss of Love, The. Byron.
First time he kissed me, he but only kissed. *Fr.* Sonnets from the Portuguese. Browning.
I Kissed You. *Unknown.*
Jenny Kissed Me. Hunt.
Kiss, A. Drummond of Hawthornden.
Kiss, A. Herrick.
Kiss, The. *Fr.* Cynthia's Revels. Jonson.
Kiss, The. Moore.
Kiss, The. *Fr.* The Angel in the House. Patmore.
Kiss, The. Sexton.
Kiss, The. Smith.
Kiss, The. Teasdale.
Kiss, The. *Unknown.*
Kiss, if you can: Resistance if she make. *Fr.* Art of Love. Ovid.
Kisse, The. Herrick.
Kisses. Campion.
Kisses Desired. Drummond of Hawthornden.
Kisses Loathesome. Herrick.
Kissin'. *Unknown.*
Kissing. Herbert of Cherbury.
Kissing Natalia. Grier.
Lady, A. Snodgrass.
Moth's kiss, first, The! *Fr.* In a Gondola. Browning.
Not alwayes give a melting kiss. *Fr.* Basia. Johannes Secundus.
Poor Is the Life That Misses. *Unknown.*
Rondeau: "Jenny kissed me when we met." Hunt.
Smack in School, The. Palmer.
Some Kisses from *The Kama Sutra.* Williams.
Song: "My love bound me with a kiss." *Unknown.*
Stolen Kiss, A. Wither.
Take, O Take Those Lips Away. Shakespeare.
To a Kiss. "Pindar."
To Anthea. Herrick.
To Celia ("Kiss me, sweet: the wary lover"). Jonson.
To Electra. Herrick.
What They Do to You in Distant Places. Bell.
You Kissed Me. Hunt.

Kissinger, Henry
Mr. Secretary. Patten.

Kitchens
Kitchen Song. Dobbs.
Room in the Past, A. Kooser.

Kites
How the Little Kite Learned to Fly. *Unknown.*
Kite, The. Behn.
Kite. McCord.
Kite, The. O'Keeffe.
Kite, A. *Unknown.*
Kite, completed thus, is borne along, The. *Fr.* The Paper Kite. Bowden.
Kite Days. Sawyer.
Kite Is a Victim, A. Cohen.
Paper Dragons. Schmeltz.
Treehouse. Kooser.

Kittens
Kitten and Falling Leaves, The. Wordsworth.
Kitten, The. Nash.

Klee, Paul
Painter Dreaming in the Scholar's House, The. Nemerov.
Paul Klee. Haines.
Paul Klee. Todd.

Klimt, Gustav
Two Paintings by Gustav Klimt. Graham.

Knife-Grinders
Sparkles from the Wheel. Whitman.

Knight, Etheridge
Brother of My Heart. Kinnell.
Hospital/Poem. Sanchez.

Knighthood and Knights
Brave Knight, A. Dodge.
Bristowe Tragedie; or, The Dethe of Syr Charles Bawdin. Chatterton.
Chivalry at a Discount. Fitzgerald.
Dead Knight, The. Masefield.
Duke of Marlborough, The. *Unknown.*
Gilliflower of Gold, The. Morris.
Golden Wings. Morris.
Haystack in the Floods, The. Morris.
Knight Stained from Battle, The. Herebert.
La Belle Dame sans Merci. Keats.
Lochinvar. *Fr.* Marmion. Scott.
New Order of Chivalry, A. Peacock.
Of the Great and Famous Ever to Be Honoured Knight, Sir Francis Drake, and of My Little-Little Selfe. Hayman.
Outlandish Knight, The. *Unknown.*
Sir Eglamour. *Fr.* The Melancholy Knight. Rowlands.
Sir Gawaine and the Green Knight. Winters.
Sir Roland; a Fragment. Merry.
Tale of Sir Thopas, The. *Fr.* The Canterbury Tales. Chaucer.
True Knight, The. *Fr.* The Pastime of Pleasure. Hawes.
Wandering Knight's Song, The. Lockhart.
"Whilom, as olde stories tellen us." *Fr.* The Knightes Tale. Chaucer.

Knitting
On a Grey-haired Old Lady Knitting at an Orchestral Concert. "Maurice."

Knives
Dagger, The. Borges.

Knowledge
Know Then Thyself. *Fr.* An Essay on Man. Pope.
Knowledge and Reason. *Fr.* Nosce Teipsum. Davies.
Little Learning, A. *Fr.* An Essay on Criticism. Pope.
Man. *Fr.* Nosce Teipsum. Davies.
Marcus Argentarius. Rexroth.
To David, about His Education. Nemerov.
Written upon the Top of Ben Nevis. Keats.

Knoxville, Tennessee
Knoxville, Tennessee. Giovanni.

Koalas
Koala. Ross.

Kollwitz, Kaethe
Death Swoops. Pitchford.

Korean War
H. S. Beeney Auction Sales. Pichaske.
Korea Bound, 1952. Childress.
Ode for the American Dead in Korea. McGrath.
On a Certain Engagement South of Seoul. Carruth.

Koreans
Careless/ but not fearless. *Fr.* Urn I: Silent for Twenty-five Years, the Father of My Mother Advises Me. Lew.

Kosciusko, Thaddeus
Koskiusko. Coleridge.

Krakow, Poland
Waiting for Death. Gebirtig.

Krupa, Gene
Mellow Groove Grave Elegy. Ford.

Ku Klux Klan
Best Dance Hall in Iuke, Mississippi, The. Johnson.
Ku Kluck Klan. Gellert.
Ku Klux. Cawein.
Ku Klux. Hughes.
Night, Death, Mississippi. Hayden.
Special Bulletin. Hughes.

Kubla Khan
Kubla Khan. Coleridge.

Kwan-Yin (Chinese Goddess of Mercy)
Bronze Statuette of Kwan-yin, A. Stork.

Kyoto, Japan
Things to Do around Kyoto. Snyder.

L

La Plata, Missouri
Last Look at La Plata, Missouri. Barnes.

Labor and Laborers
Artisan, The. Brown.

At the Sign-Painter's. Carter.
Behold, O world, the toiling man. *Fr.* The Toiler. Markham.
Black Money. Gallagher.
Boss Machine-Tender after Losing a Son, The. Corrigan.
Burying Ground by the Ties. MacLeish.
Captain Captain. *Unknown.*
Carpenter, The. Macdonald.
Carpenter, The. Whiteside.
Commonwealth of Toil, The. Chaplin.
Contentment; or, The Happy Workman's Song. Byrom.
Description of the Morning, A. Swift.
Digging. Heaney.
Dignity of Labor, The. Bersohn.
Drill Ye Tarriers, Drill. Casey.
Drying-Green, The. Dunn.
Elmer Ruiz. Oresick.
Employee, The. Holzapfel.
England and America, 1863. Milnes.
English Labourer, The. *Unknown.*
Epitaph: "John Bird, a laborer, lies here." Warner.
Equipment. Dunbar.
Factory Girl's Come-All-Ye, The. *Unknown.*
Flirtation, The. Blumenthal.
Florida Road Workers. Hughes.
Forgotten Man, The. Markham.
Foundations of American Industry, The. Hall.
Freighting from Wilcox to Globe. *Unknown.*
Go Down, Old Hannah. *Unknown.*
Going Up and Down. Daniels.
Golden Lot, A. Skipsey.
Gospel of Labor, The. Van Dyke.
Grinders, The; or, The Saddle on the Right Horse. *Unknown.*
Hay for the Horses. Snyder.
Helmet, The. Levine.
Horn Blow, The. Tagami.
Hymn of Labor. Van Dyke.
I Hear America Singing. Whitman.
I Was a Labourer. Jennett.
Ice Handler. Sandburg.
Inspiration. Thoreau.
John Henry. *Unknown.*
Labor. *Unknown.*
Labor and Love. Gosse.
Labor Day. Pomeroy.
Labouring Man, The. *Unknown.*
Landscape Workers. Elliott.
Life-Mosaic. Havergal.
Liftman, The. Evans.
Lining Track. *Unknown.*
Little Song of Work, A. Sprouse.
Little Tommy Yesterday. Glasgow.
Man Carrying Bale. Monro.
Man with the Hoe, The. Markham.
Me Johnny Mitchell Man. *Unknown.*
Mission Tire Factory, 1969. Soto.
Monument. Sullivan.
Moon Is a Diamond, The. Sze.
Morning Work. Lawrence.
Muckers. Sandburg.
My Mother, Who Came from China, Where She Never Saw Snow. Mar.
Now It Is Broccoli. Tagami.
O Son of Man, Thou Madest Known. Littlefield.
Old Bing, The. Green.
Old Flagman, The. Sandburg.
Old Men Working Concrete. Hey.
Paper Cutter, The. Ignatow.
Pat Works on the Railway. *Unknown.*
Pity Poor Labourers. *Unknown.*
Prayer, A: "Let me work and be glad." Garrison.
Preacher and the Slave, The. Hill.
Psalm of Those Who Go Forth before Daylight. Sandburg.
Quatrain: "Golf links lie so near the mill, The." Cleghorn.
Raggedy Man, The. Riley.
Reapers. Toomer.
Reject Jell-O. Day.
Rêveille. Ridge.
Riveter, The. Watts.
Rivets. Olds.
Road, The. Aiken.
Roadmenders' Song, The. Gond.
Serf, The. Campbell.
Servants, The. Wightman.
Shovelling Iron Ore. *Unknown.*
Singing Man, The. Peabody.
Sisyphus. Garioch.
Six o'Clock. Stickney.
So Handy, Me Boys, So Handy. *Unknown.*
Something Has Fallen. Levine.
Song of a Factory Girl. Zaturenska.
Song of the Builders. Murton.
Song of the Lower Classes, The. Jones.
Song of the Shirt, The. Hood.
Song to the Men of England. Shelley.
Sons of Martha, The. Kipling.
Stevedore. Collins.
Stevedores, The. Fletcher.
Stonehouse. Tagami.
Sweepers, The. Whitehead.
Tamping Ties. *Unknown.*
Telephone Lineman. Kroll.
Thatcher, The. Kennelly.
There you sit. Silverstein.
They Who Tread the Path of Labor. Van Dyke.
Thinker, The. Braley.
This Sun Is Hot. *Unknown.*
Three-handed Fugue. Gotlieb.
Tired Worker, The. McKay.
To Be of Use. Piercy.
To Labor. Gilman.
Toads. Larkin.
Toads Revisited. Larkin.
Track-Lining Song. *Unknown.*
Train Runs Late to Harlem, The. Rivers.
True Aristocrat, The. Stewart.
Unaccompanied. Andrews.
United Front. Brecht *and* Eisler.
Unloading Rails. *Unknown.*
Way Out in Idaho. *Unknown.*
We Are the Burden-Bearers! Stidger.
What Grandma Knew. Field.
When through the Whirl of Wheels. Studdert-Kennedy.
Women at Munition Making. Collins.
Women Transport Corps. *Unknown.*
Wood-Cutter's Night Song, The. Clare.
Work. Block.
Work. Lowell.
Work. Studdert-Kennedy.
Work. Van Dyke.
Work; a Song of Triumph. Morgan.
Worker, The. Massey.
Worker, The. Thomas.
Working Class. Warr.
Young Workman, The. Frear.
Saturdays Children: Poems of Work (SaC). Helen Plotz, ed.
Talking Union. Hays, Lampell *and* Seeger.

Labor Day
Labor Day. Pacernick.
Unemployed, The. Roberts.

Labor Unions
Blackleg Miners, The. *Unknown.*
Casey Jones (Union). Hill.
Comrade Jesus. Cleghorn.
Great Day ("One of these mornings bright and fair"). *Unknown.*
Hold the Fort. *Unknown.*
It's a Good Thing to Join a Union. *Unknown.*
Joe Hill. Hayes.
Ludlow Massacre, The. Guthrie.
My Master and I. *Unknown.*
Old Man's Advice, An. *Unknown.*
Picket Line Song, The. *Unknown.*
Popular Wobbly, The. Slim.
Roll the Union On. Williams *and* Hays.
Solidarity Forever. Chaplin.
Talking Union. Hays, Lampell *and* Seeger.
Talking Union: 1964. Sissman.
There Is Power. Hill.
Union Maid. Guthrie.
Union Man. Morgan.
Union Train. Hays, Lampell *and* Seeger.
We Are Building a Strong Union. *Unknown.*
Which Side Are You On? Reese.
You Gotta Go Down (and Join the Union). *Unknown.*
See also **Strikes and Strikers.**

Labrador, Canada
North Labrador. Crane.
Labyrinths
Labyrinth, The. Muir.
Ladybirds
Clock-a-clay. Clare.
Down in the Hollow. Fisher.
Lady Lost. Ransom.
Ladybird. Sansom.
Ladybird, Ladybird, fly away home. Mother Goose.
Ladybirds, The. Lucie-Smith.
Ladybug. Anglund.
Ladybug. Dodat.
Ladybug's Christmas. Farber.
Lines to a Lady-Bird. De Tabley.
Lafayette, Marie Joseph, Marquis de
La Fayette. Coleridge.
La Fayette. Madison.
Lake District, England
On the Solitary Fells around Hawkshead. *Fr.* The Prelude. Wordsworth.
Raised are the dripping oars. *Fr.* The Youth of Nature: Wordsworth's Country. Arnold.
Two Long Vacations: Grasmere. Butter.
Lakes and Ponds
Among the Finger Lakes. Wallace.
Beaver Pond. Marriott.
By Loe Pool. Symons.
Crows, The. Engels.
Goose Pond. Kunitz.
Lake, The. Coxe.
Lake, The. Hughes.
Lake. Simpson.
Lake Chelan. Stafford.
Lake in the Sky, The. Haines.
Lakes. Auden.
Lakeshore. Scott.
Links. Pau-Llosa.
Little Lough, The. Hewitt.
Little Ponds. Guiterman.
Midnight Skaters, The. Blunden.
My Lady the Lake. Davison.
On Autumn Lake. Ashbery.
On Windermere; Bowness Bay and Belle Isle. *Fr.* The Prelude. Wordsworth.
Return to Lake Emily Chequamegon National Forest. Behm.
Road to the Pool, The. Conkling.
Sonnet: Composed by the Side of Grasmere Lake. Wordsworth.
Spring Pools. Frost.
Suicide Pond. McLaughlin.
To Ben, at the Lake. McQueen..
Twice. Finlay.
Unnamed Lake, The. Scott.
Vapour and Blue. Campbell.
Winter Lakes, The. Campbell.
Winter Pond. Belitt.
Lalemant, Gabriel
Brébeuf and His Brethren. Scott.
Père Lalemant. Pickthall.
Lamb, Charles
This Lime-Tree Bower My Prison. Coleridge.
Lamb, Mary
To the Sister of Elia. Landor.
Lambs
First Sight. Larkin.
For a Lamb. Eberhart.
How It Goes On. Kumin.
I Held a Lamb. Worthington.
Lamb, The. *Fr.* Songs of Innocence. Blake.
Lambs. Browne.
Lambs Frolicking Home. Lape.
Mary's Lamb. Hale.
Pallid Cuckoo. Campbell.
Pet Lamb, The. Wordsworth.
Ravens. Hughes.
Sale of the Pet Lamb, The. Howitt.
Searching for Lambs. *Unknown.*
Sheep and Lambs. Tynan.
Wolf and the Lamb, The. La Fontaine.
Lamplighters
Lamplighter, The. "O'Sullivan."
Lamplighter, The. *Fr.* A Child's Garden of Verses. Stevenson.
Light the Lamps Up, Lamplighter! Farjeon.
Lampman, Archibald
Bereavement of the Fields. Campbell.
Lampreys
Lamprey, glowing with uncommon fires, The. *Fr.* Halieutica. Diaper.
To a Young Lady with Some Lampreys. Gay.
Lancashire, England
Lancashire Winter. Connor.
To Saxham. Carew.
Lancelot du Lac
Lancelot. Bontemps.
Lancelot and Guinevere. Gould.
Lancelot and Elaine, *sel.* *Fr.* Idylls of the King. Tennyson.
Landlords and Landladies
Adieu to My Landlady, An. Farewell.
Behold the Deeds. Bunner.
I Want a Tenant; a Satire. O'Keeffe.
Inferno: A New Circle. Ormsby.
Inn That Missed Its Chance, The. Wells.
Landlady. Page.
Landlord's Wife, The. Chin.
Pity the Down-trodden Landlord. Woolf *and* Clayton.
Redemption. Herbert.
Scenery. Joans.
Telephone Conversation. Soyinka.
Landor, Walter Savage
Envoi: "I warmed both hands before the fire of Life." Lewis.
Fable, A. Frere.
For an Epitaph at Fiesole. Landor.
In Memory of Walter Savage Landor. Swinburne.
Landor. Albee.
W. S. Landor. Moore.
Walter Savage Landor. Parker.
Landscape
At Dieppe; Green and Grey. Symons.
Florence. *Fr.* Aurora Leigh. Browning.
In Search of the Picturesque. Combe.
Landscapes. Untermeyer.
Mask. Spender.
Midsummer Day in France. *Fr.* Of the Day Estivall. Hume.
Now. Monroe.
Storm, The. Williams.
View. Munro.
Lang, Andrew
Ballade of Andrew Lang. MacColl.
Language
Aestivation. *Fr.* The Autocrat of the Breakfast Table. Holmes.
Americana IX: "Your correspondent must be kidding when he says." Rakosi.
Ancient Speech, The. *Fr.* Eileann Chanaidh. Raine.
And the whole earth was of one language, and of one speech. *Fr.* Genesis. Bible, *O.T.*
Anthology of Nouns. Tyler.
Antiques. De la Mare.
At a Vacation Exercise. Milton.
Bonne Entente. Scott.
Burning of Paper Instead of Children, The. Rich.
Change, The. O'Bruadair.
Coal. Lorde.
Conversational Reformer, The. Graham.
Cool Web, The. Graves.
Desmet, Idaho, March 1969. Hale.
Dirty Word, The. Shapiro.
Genesis. Higgins.
Grafted Tongue, A. Montague.
Grammar Lesson. Pastan.
Hail native Language, that by sinews weak. *Fr.* At a Vacation Exercise in the College. Milton.
Harp of Renfrewshire, The. Dunn.
Hearing Russian Spoken. Davie.
Hebrew Lesson. Brod.
Hieroglyphic. Sklarew.
Hints on Pronunciation for Foreigners. *Unknown.*
Hogwash. Francis.
Hollow Theasaurus, The. McDonald.
How a Girl Was Too Reckless of Grammar. Carryl.
I Speak, I Say, I Talk. Shapiro.
In Despair He Orders a New Typewriter. Olson.
Irish Language, The. Mangan.
Jutaculla Rock. Morgan.
Koko. Downer.
Language, The. Creeley.
Language has not the power to speak what love indites. Clare.

Language Lesson, 1976. McHugh.
Latin for To-Day. *Unknown.*
Latin Tongue, The. Daly.
Learning to Speak. Wilk.
Little Girl, Be Careful What You Say. Sandburg.
Loving and Liking. Wordsworth.
Makers, The. Nemerov.
Moon, Sun, Sleep, Birds, Live. Patchen.
Naughty Preposition, The. Bishop.
New Style, The. O'Bruadair.
Nigger. Sanchez.
Nothingness. Amir.
Of the Manner of Addressing Clouds. Stevens.
On Reading Mr. Ytche Bashes' Stories in Yiddish. Ehrlichman.
On the Use of Jayshus. Gogarty.
Paradoxes and Oxymorons. Ashbery.
Permanently. Koch.
Persimmons and Plums. Hodges.
Phraseology. Cortez.
Poet. Viereck.
Precious Moments. Sandburg.
Pretty Words. Wylie.
Primer Lesson. Sandburg.
Since When As Ever More. Inada.
Singular Singulars, Peculiar Plurals. Espy.
Spanish Is the Loving Tongue. *Unknown.*
Spell against Spelling, The. Starbuck.
Think'st Thou to Seduce Me Then. Campion.
Tilth. Graves.
To a Thesaurus. Adams.
Traditions. Heaney.
Tree of Silence, The. Miller.
Usk, The. Sisson.
Varitalk. Holbrook.
V-a-s-e, The. Roche.
Very like a Whale. Nash.
Vowels. Rimbaud.
Ways of Pronouncing "Ough." *Unknown.*
What's the Plural? *Unknown.*
When the Wine Was Gone. Aubert.
Why English Is So Hard. *Unknown.*
Words. Finch.
Words. Harpur.
Word. Spender.
Words. *Unknown.*
Words. Williams.

Lanterns
Street Lanterns. Coleridge.

Laocoon
Laocoon. Hall.

Laos
Room above the White Rose, The. Stroud.

Lao-tze
Philosopher, The. Po Chü-i.

Lapwings
Landscape with Lapwings. Aitchison.
O Lapwing! Blake.

Larches
Tamarack. McCarthy.

Larkin, James
Inscription for a Headstone. Clarke.

Larks
Bunch of Larks, The. Leighton.
Caged Skylark, The. Hopkins.
Desert Lark, The. Marais.
Hark, Hark the Lark. *Fr.* Cymbeline. Shakespeare.
Lark, The. Reese.
Lark, The. *Unknown.*
Lark above the Trenches, The. Graham.
Lark Ascending, The. Meredith.
Lark in the Morning, The. *Unknown.*
Lark Now Leaves His Wat'ry Nest, The. Davenant.
Larks. Hinkson.
Lark's Nest, The. Clare.
Lark's Nest, A. Smart.
Lark's Song, The. *Fr.* Milton. Blake.
Lo! Here the Gentle Lark. *Fr.* Venus and Adonis. Shakespeare.
On a Picture by J. M. Wright, Esq. Southey.
Over Salève. Clarke.
Returning, We Hear the Larks. Rosenberg.
Shelley's Skylark. Hardy.
Skylark, The. Hogg.
Skylark, The. Tennyson.
Skylark's Nest, The. Long.
Skylarks. Hughes.
Song: " 'Tis sweet to hear the merry lark." Coleridge.
To a Lark in War-Time. Werfel.
To a Skylark. Shelley.
To a Skylark ("Ethereal minstrel! pilgrim of the sky!"). Wordsworth.
To a Skylark. ("Up with me! up with me into the clouds!"). Wordsworth.
Upon the Lark and the Fowler. Bunyan.
See also **Meadowlarks.**

Las Vegas, Nevada
Man Who Invented Las Vegas, The. Costanzo.
Vegas. Cunningham.

Last Rites. *See* **Extreme Unction.**

Last Supper
Last Supper, The. Williams.

Latimer, Hugh
Latimer's Light. *Unknown.*

Latin
Latin. *Unknown.*
Latin Tongue, The. Daly.
Sum, Es, Est. *Unknown.*

Latter-Day Saints, Church. *See* **Mormons.**

Laughter
American Laughter. Robinson.
Before the Statue of a Laughing Man. Bowie.
Child's Laughter, A. Swinburne.
Early Supper. Howes.
Her Merriment. Davies.
Humorist, The. Preston.
Laugh It Off. Elliot.
Laughing Song. *Fr.* Songs of Innocence. Blake.
Laughter. Crawford.
Laughter. Waddington.
Water Tap. MacCaig.
When God had finished the stars and whirl of coloured suns. *Fr.* Ducks. Harvey.
When You Laugh. Jonker.
Wiggly Giggles. Crossen *and* Covell.
See also **Mirth.**

Laundry and Laundering
Bendix. Updike.
Dolls' Wash, The. Ewing.
Drying-Green, The. Dunn.
In an Iridescent Time. Stone.
Goldfish Wife, The. Hochman.
Laundromat. McCord.
Love Calls Us to the Things of This World. Wilbur.
Mad Scene, The. Merrill.
Old Ellen Sullivan. Welles.
Saturday Morning at the Laundry. Gilbert.
Shepherd's Hut, The. Young.
Storm. Nagy.
Thinking Twice in the Laundromat. Elliott.
Tubby or not tubby—there's the rub. Burnand.
Upon Sudds, a Laundress. Herrick.
Uppon Sudds a Laundresse. Herrick.
Wash Day. Mollin.
Wash-Day Wonder. Faubion.
Washer-Woman, The. Bohanan.
Washerwoman, The. *Fr.* The Woman's Labour; an Epistle to Mr. Stephen Duck. Collier.
Washing Machine, The. Davies.

Laurels
Tapestry Trees. Morris.
To Laurels. Herrick.

Laurentian Mountains, Canada
Laurentian Shield. Scott.

Lavender
I planned to have a border of lavender. Goodman.
Lavender's Blue. *Unknown.*
Lavender's for Ladies. Chalmers.

Lawes, Henry
To Master Henry Lawes, the Excellent Composer of Lyrics. Herrick.
To Mr. H. Lawes on His Airs. Milton.
To Mr. Henry Lawes. Philips.
To Mr. Henry Lawes, Who Had Then Newly Set a Song of Mine, in the Year 1635. Waller.

Lawns
Rolling the Lawn. Empson.

Lawrence, David Herbert
D. H. Lawrence and James Joyce. Wolfe.
Elegy for D. H. Lawrence, An. Williams.
Lawrence, Thomas Edward
There Is No Place to Hide. *Fr.* The T. E. Lawrence Poems. MacEwen.
Void, The. *Fr.* The T. E. Lawrence Poems. MacEwen.
Lawrence, Kansas
Defense of Lawrence, The. Realf.
Lawyers and Law
Briefless Barrister, The. Saxe.
Case at Sessions, A. Landor.
Case to the Civilians, A. *Unknown.*
Conversation in Craven Street, Strand. Smith *and* Rose.
Damages, Two Hundred Pounds. Thackeray.
Erected to the Memory of Mr. Jonathan Gill, Esq. *Unknown.*
Fox may steal your hens, sir, A. *Fr.* The Beggar's Opera. Gay.
Help Wanted. Waldheim.
In the Dock. De la Mare.
International Copyright. Lowell.
Jailhouse Lawyers. Smith.
Judge, The. McClane.
Judge Somers. Masters.
Law like Love. Auden.
Laws of God, the Laws of Man, The. Housman.
Lawyer Clark Blues. *Unknown.*
Lawyers Know Too Much, The. Sandburg.
Legal Fiction. Empson.
Letter to My Daughters, 11. Minty.
London Lickpenny. Lydgate.
Net of Law, The. Roche.
Next bring some lawyers to thy bar. *Fr.* A Hymn to the Pillory. Defoe.
Penal Law. Clarke.
People vs. the People, The. Fearing.
Soldier and a Sailor, The. *Fr.* The Beggar's Opera. Gay.
To Sir Thomas Egerton. Daniel.
Verbatim from Boileau. Pope.
Who doubts? The laws fell down from heaven's height. *Fr.* Virgidemiae. Hall.
Lazarus
Act of Faith. Trías.
Another sate near him. *Fr.* The Vision of Lazarus. Johnson.
Come Out, Lazarus! *Unknown.*
Convert, The. Chesterton.
Dives and Lazarus. *Unknown.*
Karshish, The Arab Physician. Browning.
Raising of the Dead, The. Dobson.
When Lazarus left his charnel-cave. *Fr.* In Memoriam A. H. H. Tennyson.
Lazarus, Emma
Homecoming of Emma Lazarus, The. Kinnell.
Laziness
Epitaph, An: "Interr'd beneath this marble stone." Prior.
Get Up, Get Up. *Unknown.*
Hot-Weather Song, A. Marquis.
I'm Really Not Lazy. Spilka.
Lazy Man's Song. Po Chü-I.
Ode to Work in Springtime. Ybarra.
Personal Song. Arnatkoak.
Sluggard, The. Watts.
Leadership
God, Give Us Men! Holland.
Leader, A. "Æ."
Leaders. *Unknown.*
Masters. Amis.
League of Nations
League of Nations, The. Siegrist.
Lear, Edward
Edward Lear. Auden.
How Pleasant to Know Mr. Lear. Lear.
Lear, King. *See* **King Lear.**
Learning
Chiefe use then in man of that he knowes, The. *Fr.* Of Human Learning. Greville.
Father's Testament, A. Ibn Tibbon.
Fledglings. Meredith.
For a Man Who Learned to Swim When He Was Sixty. Wakoski.
Learning Soul, The. Whittemore.
Lesson, The. Bentley.
Little Learning Is a Dangerous Thing, A. *Fr.* Essay on Criticism. Pope.
My father was a scholar and knew Greek. *Fr.* Development. Browning.
On the Prospect of Planting Arts and Learning in America. Berkeley.
Oyfn Pripetshuk (On the Hearth). Warshawsky.
To a Boy. *Unknown.*
To the Blacksmith with a Spade. O'Sullivan.
Leaves
Auction. Heyen.
Autumn Leaves. Webb.
Autumn Woods. Tippett.
Burning of the Leaves, The. Binyon.
City of Falling Leaves, The. Lowell.
College of Surgeons, The. Stephens.
Come, Little Leaves. Cooper.
Dock-Leaves. Browning.
Fading-Leaf and Fallen-Leaf. Garnett.
Fallen Leaves. Tupper.
Falling Leaves, The. Cole.
Gathering Leaves. Frost.
How the Leaves Came Down. "Coolidge."
Kitten and the Falling Leaves, The. Wordsworth.
L(a. Cummings.
Leaves. Barnes.
Leaves. Davies.
Leaves. Teasdale.
Leaves Do Not Mind at All, The. Wynne.
Leaves in a Frolic, The. *Unknown.*
Leaves like Fish. Cardiff.
Les Etiquettes Jaunes. O'Hara.
Looking Up at Leaves. Howes.
Maple Leaves. Shiko.
Markings. Steele.
My Own House. Ignatow.
New York—Albany. Ferlinghetti.
November Night. Crapsey.
October's Party. Cooper.
Pity of the Leaves, The. Robinson.
Red o'er the forest glows the setting sun. *Fr.* Forest Leaves in Autumn. Keble.
Reply to the Question: "How Can You Become a Poet?" Merriam.
So This Is Autumn. Watt.
Sonnet: Leaves. Barnes.
Two Pictures of a Leaf. Bell.
Watch long enough, and you will see the leaf. *Fr.* Preludes for Memnon. Aiken.
Windfall. Scott.
See also **Autumn.**
Lebanon
As I Came Down from Lebanon. Scollard.
On Lebanon. Gray.
Leda
Leda. Doolittle ("H. D.").
Leda. Rilke.
Leda. Van Duyn.
Leda and the Swan. Friman.
Leda and the Swan. Gogarty.
Leda and the Swan. Yeats.
Leda Reconsidered. Van Duyn.
People do gossip. Sappho.
Renaissance/a Triptych. Minczeski.
Lee, Robert Edward
Lee in the Mountains. Davidson.
Lee to the Rear. Thompson.
Lee's Parole. Manville.
Robert E. Lee. *Fr.* John Brown's Body. Benét.
Robert E. Lee. Howe.
Leeds, England
Poem for Jacqueline Hill. *Unknown.*
Leeuwenhoek, Anton
Microscope, The. Kumin.
Legionnaires' Disease
On the Latest Crisis of Confidence. Jackson.
Legree, Simon
Simon Legree—A Negro Sermon. *Fr.* The Booker Washington Trilogy. Lindsay.
Legs
Amputation, The. Sorrells.
Her Leg. Herrick.
Leg, The. Shapiro.
Legs, The. Graves.
Poem in Which My Legs Are Accepted. Fraser.
Sailor's Apology for Bow-Legs, A. Hood.
Vet's Rehabilitation. Durem.
Leicester, Robert Dudley, Earl of
Epitaph on the Earl of Leicester. Ralegh.

Leif Ericsson
Leif was a man's name. *Fr.* Saga of Leif the Lucky. Allen.
Story of Vinland, The. *Fr.* Psalm of the West. Lanier.
Leinster, Ireland
Carroll's Sword. *Unknown.*
In Leinster. Guiney.
Leisure
Absence of Occupation. *Fr.* Retirement. Cowper.
Gentleman of the Old School, A. Dobson.
Hob upon a Holiday. *Unknown.*
Leisure. Davies.
Pastime. Henry VIII, King of England.
Lemmings
Lemmings, The. Masefield.
Lemonade
Lemonade Stand. Thompson.
Lemons
Lemon. Satz.
Lemons, Lemons. Young.
Lenin, Vladimir Ilyich
Second Hymn to Lenin. "MacDiarmid."
Skeleton of the Future, The. "MacDiarmid."
So I came down the steps. *Fr.* Lenin. Wellesley.
Leningrad, U.S.S.R.
For Leningrad, and My Jewish Ancestors. Rosenberg.
Leningrad Cemetery, Winter of 1941. Olds.
Lent
Children's Lenten Wisdom. Houck.
Easter. Whitaker.
Lent. Rodgers.
To Keep a True Lent. Herrick.
To Search Our Souls. Lanning.
Two Old Lenten Rhymes. *Unknown.*
Leonardo da Vinci
Annunciation, The. Kriel.
For "Our Lady of the Rocks" by Leonardo da Vinci. Rossetti.
Leonardo da Vinci's. Moore.
Leonardo's Secret. Bly.
There Lived a Lady in Milan. Benét.
Leonidas
Death of Leonidas, The. Croly.
Leopards
Leopard. Kreps.
Leopard. Yoruba.
Snow-Leopard, The. Jarrell.
Leopold III, King of the Belgians
Moon and the Night and the Men, The. Berryman.
Leopold, Duke of Albany
Death of Prince Leopold, The. McGonagall.
Lepanto, Battle of (1571)
Lepanto. Chesterton.
Leprechauns
Confession in Holy Week. Morley.
Faith, I Wish I Were a Leprechaun. Ritter.
Singing-Woman from the Wood's Edge, The. Millay.
Leprosy
Leper, The. Ka-'ehu.
Leper, The. Willis.
Lesbians. *See* **Homosexuality and Homosexuals.**
Lesbos, Greece
Night in Lesbos, A. Horton.
Letters
Aunt Maud. *Unknown.*
Burning Love Letters. Moss.
Children's Letters, The. Livesay.
Correspondence School Instructor Says Goodbye to His Poetry Students, The. Kinnell.
Dear Reader. Meinke.
Deceased. Corman.
Destruction of Letters. Deutsch.
Familiar Letter to Several Correspondents, A. Holmes.
Fire a Simple Fire, A. Will.
How to Write a Letter. Turner.
Illiterate, The. Meredith.
Letter, The. Blight.
Letter, The. Tatham.
Letter from Home, A. Minarik.
Letter from Home, A. Oliver.
Letter Is a Gypsy Elf, A. Wynne.
Letter to a Live Poet, A. Brooke.
Letter to a Young Poet. Barker.
Letter to an American Visitor. Comfort.
Letter to Her Husband, A. Bradstreet.
Letter to N.Y. Bishop.
Letter to Paul Celan in Memory, A. Rothenberg.
Letter to Peter, A. Chiang.
Letter to Tina Koyama from Elliot Bay Park. Mitsui.
Letters from Kazuto (Kyoto, Japan—Summer 1980). Lau.
Lines Occasioned by the Burning of Some Letters. Dixon.
Love Letter. Ray.
Midcentury Love Letter. McGinley.
My Grandmother's Love Letters. Crane.
Packet of Letters. Bogan.
Parting, without a Sequel. Ransom.
Postman's Bell Is Answered Everywhere, The. Gregory.
Railway Stationery, The. Koch.
Song Written at Sea. Sackville.
Special Delivery. Montague.
Way I read a letter's this, The. Dickinson.
Wife in London, A. Hardy.
Words, like Spiders. Wolny.
Leukemia
Transparent Man, The. Hecht.
Leven River, Scotland
Ode to Leven Water. Smollett.
Levett, Robert
On the Death of Mr. Robert Levet. Johnson.
Levita, Eliajah
Epitaph: "Stone cries from the wall, The." *Unknown.*
Lewis, Meriwether
On the Discoveries of Captain Lewis. Barlow.
Li Po
On the Subject of Waves. Grier.
Liars. *See* **Lies and Lying.**
Liberace
Liberace. Holden.
Liberalism and Liberals
Lost Leader, The. Browning.
Norris Dam, Tennessee. Rodman.
Liberia
On the Founding of Liberia. *Fr.* Libretto for the Republic of Liberia. Tolson.
Liberty. *See* **Freedom.**
Liberty, Statue of
Barthold: Statue, The. Whither.
Fairest of Freedom's Daughters. Rankin.
Liberty Enlightening the World. Van Dyke.
New Colossus, The. Lazarus.
Statue of Liberty, The. Crooke.
Statue of Liberty, The. Field.
To the Statue. Swenson.
Libraries
Books. *Fr.* The Library. Crabbe.
British Museum Reading Room, The. MacNeice.
Certified Copy. Deagon.
Fire at Alexandria, The. Weiss.
Letter to a Librarian. Layton.
Library, The. Huff.
Public Library. Stevenson.
Reading Room, the New York Public Library. Eberhart.
Scholar II. Deane.
Lice
Immortals, The. Rosenberg.
Louse Crept Out of My Lady's Shift, A. Bottomley.
Louse Hunting. Rosenberg.
Small gray cloudy louse that nests in my beard, The. *Fr.* Jerusalem Sonnets. Baxter.
To a Louse. Burns.
Lidice, Czechoslovakia
Lady of Lidice. Chavez.
Lies and Lying
Ancient Custom, An. Steiger.
Beware, Oh, Take Care. *Unknown.*
Golly, How Truth Will Out! Nash.
Honesty. Wyatt.
Liar, The. *Unknown.*
Lie, The. Kipling.
Lie, The. Ralegh.
Matilda. Belloc.
Merry Christmas. Olson.
Mountain Liars. Hafen.
Song: "Lying is an occupation." Pilkington.
Tony Baloney ("Tony Baloney is fibbing again"). Lee.
Uncle Ananias. Robinson.

Use of Fiction, The. Nye.
When my love swears that she is made of truth. *Fr.* Sonnets. Shakespeare.
Word of Encouragement, A. Pope.

Life
All the World's a Stage. *Fr.* As You Like It. Shakespeare.
Alumnus Football. Rice.
And the days are not full enough. Pound.
Another and the Same. Rogers.
Anyone Lived in a Pretty How Town. Cummings.
April Inventory. Snodgrass.
As One Who Bears beneath His Neighbor's Roof. Hillyer.
Bankrupt. Sayres.
Beach in August, The. Kees.
Before the Beginning of Years. *Fr.* Atalanta in Calydon. Swinburne.
Behind me—dips eternity. Dickinson.
Behold the child, by Nature's kindly law. *Fr.* An Essay on Man. Pope.
Cafes. Smith.
Choice, The. Pomfret.
Choruses from "Hellas." *Fr.* Hellas. Shelley.
Coda. Parker.
Consumer's Report, A. Porter.
De Morte. Wotton.
Dreams. Zangwill.
Easy Does It. Chapin.
Envoy: "They are not long, the weeping and the laughter." Dowson.
Epitaph: "Here dead lie we because we did not choose." Housman.
Esthete in Harlem. Hughes.
Experience. Harford.
Fighting Failure, The. Appleton.
Force That through the Green Fuse Drives the Flower, The. Thomas.
Four Ages of Man, The. Yeats.
Hating Your Life. Morris.
Health. Parker.
Horse Show, The. Williams.
Hound, The. Francis.
Hughie at the Inn. Wylie.
Human Life. De Vere.
Human Seasons, The. Keats.
I Have a Rendezvous with Life. Cullen.
I never cared for Life: Life cared for me. Hardy.
I Shall Not Pass This Way Again. York.
If. Howells.
Illusion. Wilcox.
Immortal Part, The. Housman.
Introduction of the Shopping Cart. Costanzo.
Is Life Worth Living? Austin.
It's in Your Face. *Unknown.*
Joy Is the Blossom. Landor.
Last Chapter, The. De la Mare.
Life. Bacon.
Life. Barbauld.
Life. Dunbar.
Life. Herbert.
Life. Sill.
Life. Treasone.
Life Cycle of Common Man. Nemerov.
Life flows to death as rivers to the sea. Cunningham.
Life of Man, The. Bacon.
Life Sculpture. Doane.
Life's a Funny Proposition after All. Cohan.
Life's a Game. *Unknown.*
Life's Chequer-Board. Oxenham.
Life's Lessons. *Unknown.*
Life's Poor Play. *Fr.* An Essay on Man. Pope.
Little Song of Life, A. Reese.
Live ever here, Lorenzo?—shocking thought! *Fr.* The Complaint. Young.
Lucinda Matlock. *Fr.* Spoon River Anthology. Masters.
Madam Life. Henley.
Madrigal: "This life, which seems so fair." Drummond of Hawthornden.
Making a Man. Waterman.
Matter of Life and Death, A. Ridler.
May It Be. Pasternak.
Mean Old Twister. *Unknown.*
Men Made out of Words. Stevens.
Mother to Son. Hughes.
My Own Epitaph. Gay.
Mystery of Life, The. Gambold.
Naked I reached the world at birth. Palladas.
Nature. Longfellow.
New Territory. Boland.
Next, Please. Larkin.
Nothing. Burgos.
Old Adam, The. Levertov.
Old Man's Idyl, An. Realf.
On Wenlock Edge the wood's in trouble. Housman.
Our life is like a forest, where the sun. *Fr.* Sonnets Written in the Orillia Woods. Sangster.
Our lives are Swiss. Dickinson.
Pale Blue Casket, The. Pitcher.
Pessimist, The. King.
Picture-Show. Sassoon.
Pilgrimage, The. Herbert.
Postscript. Hochman.
Psalm of Life, A. Longfellow.
Quickness. Vaughan.
Rainy Day, The. Longfellow.
River of Life, The. Campbell.
Road Not Taken, The. Frost.
Sea Boy on the Giddy Mast, The. Clare.
Secret in the Cat, The. Swenson.
Sergeant, The. Johnson.
Ships That Pass in the Night. *Fr.* Tales of a Wayside Inn: The Theologian's Tale. Longfellow.
Sic Vita. King.
Song of Life, A. Werfel.
Sonnet: "Lift not the painted veil which those who live." Shelley.
Sonnet: "World's a stage, The. The light is in one's eyes." Belloc.
Sonnet: "You were born; must die; were loved; must love." Spender.
Sower, The. Blind.
Still Here. Hughes.
Sunday Morning. Stevens.
Tears. Reese.
Things, The. Aiken.
This Life. Drummond of Hawthornden.
This life a theater we well may call. Palladas.
This Life Is All Chequer'd with Pleasures and Woes. Moore.
To Robert Louis Stevenson. Henley.
Tomorrow, and Tomorrow, and Tomorrow. *Fr.* Macbeth. Shakespeare.
Two Mysteries, The. Dodge.
Under Sorrow's Sign. O'Dalaigh.
Up-Hill. Rossetti.
Vitae Summa Brevis Spem Nos Vetat Incohare Longam. Dowson.
Voyage of Life, The. *Fr.* Christ. Cynewulf.
Way of the World, The. Wilcox.
We Are Transmitters. Lawrence.
We cannot retrace our steps. Stein.
"We hurry on, nor passing note." Dolben.
What Is Lived. Valle.
What Is Our Life? A Play of Passion. Ralegh.
When I Consider Life. *Fr.* Aureng-Zebe. Dryden.
Whist. Ware.
Willing Suspension, A. Holmes.

Lifeguards
Lifeguard, The. Dickey.

Liffey (river), Ireland
To the Liffey with the Swans. Gogarty.

Light
City Lights. Field.
City Limits, The. Ammons.
Dazzle. Roberts.
Galloway Shore, The. Tremayne.
Hymn to Light. Cowley.
Light. *Fr.* Paradise Lost. Milton.
Light at Equinox. Adams.
Light exists in Spring, A. Dickinson.
Light in the Open Air. Dillard.
Light the Lamps Up, Lamplighter! Farjeon.
Love Poem: "Isadora, your body charts a course." Wagner.
Lumière. Van Brunt.
My Invention. Silverstein.
O Light Invisible, we praise Thee! *Fr.* The Rock. Eliot.
O Virtuous Light. Wylie.
There's a certain slant of light. Dickinson.
To Morris Louis. Cherner.
Uses of Light, The. Snyder.
When the Light Falls. Kunitz.

Lighthouses
Brilliant kernel of the night, The. *Fr.* The Light-Keeper. Stevenson.
Epitaph for a Lighthouse-Keeper's Horse. Morton.
Flannan Isle. Gibson.
I'd Like to Be a Lighthouse. Field.
Lighthouse, The. Anson.
Lighthouse in the Night. Storni.

Lighthouses. Wellesley.
Needles' Lighthouse from Keyhaven, Hampshire, The. Turner.
Skerryvore. Stevenson.
Lightning
At Great Torrington, Devon. *Unknown.*
Dance-Song of the Lightning. *Unknown.*
Haiku: "Lightning Gleam, A." Basho.
Lightning is a yellow fork, The. Dickinson.
Magic Lantern. Stafford.
Miramichi Lightning. Bailey.
She Didn't Even Wave. Ai.
Lightning Bugs. *See* **Fireflies.**
Lilacs
Cut Lilac. Beyer.
Lilac. Flint.
Lilac, The. Wolfe.
Lilacs. Lowell.
With Lilacs. Crandall.
Lilies
Bulb, A. Munkittrick.
How Lilies Came White. Herrick.
Lilies, The. Berry.
Lilies. Colum.
Lilies. Shiko.
Lilly in a Christal, The. Herrick.
Little White Lily. *Fr.* Within and Without. Macdonald.
Mariposa Lily, The. Coolbrith.
Maudle-in Ballad, A. *Unknown.*
On a Bed of Guernsey Lilies. Smart.
On Easter Day. Thaxter.
Orange Lilies. Reaney.
Picking Lilies. *Unknown.*
Tiger Lily. McCord.
Lilies of the Valley
Lilies of the Valley. Silkin.
White coral bells upon a slender stalk. *Unknown.*
Lilith
Anguish'd Doubt Broods over Eden, The. *Fr.* Lilith. Brennan.
Ballad of Adam's First, The. Davis.
Body's Beauty. *Fr.* The House of Life. Rossetti.
Lilith. Fainlight.
Lilith. Feldman.
Lilith. Finkel.
Lilith. Gregg.
Lilith. Grossman.
Lilith. Levi.
Waiting for Lilith. Kessler.
Limbo
Limbo. Coleridge.
Limericks
They've Discovered a Head in the Box for the Bread (TDH). John E. Brewton *and* Lorraine A. Blackburn, eds.
Limestone
In Praise of Limestone. Auden.
Lincoln, Abraham
Abraham Lincoln. Auslander.
Abraham Lincoln. R. *and* S. V. Benét.
Abraham Lincoln. Meigs.
Abraham Lincoln. Stoddard.
Abraham Lincoln. Taylor.
Abrahan Lincoln Walks at Midnight. Lindsay.
Anne Rutledge. *Fr.* Spoon River Anthology. Masters.
At the Lincoln Tomb. Bryant.
Ballad of the Lincoln Penny. Kreymborg.
Booth Killed Lincoln. *Unknown.*
Born without a Chance. Cooke.
Come Back, Lincoln. Piety.
Death of Lincoln, The. Bryant.
February 12, 1809. Burket.
For February Twelfth. Gessner.
Glory of Lincoln, The. Clark.
Hand of Lincoln, The. Stedman.
His Living Monument. Irving.
Honest Abe Lincoln. Shulman.
House in Springfield. Burket.
I Saw a Ghost. Boilleau.
In Hardin County, 1809. Thompson.
Kentucky Birthday; February 12, 1815. Frost.
Let man be free! The mighty word. *Fr.* The Emancipation Group. Whittier.
Lincoln. Ditmars.
Lincoln. Fletcher.
Lincoln. Frank.
Lincoln. Hill.
Lincoln. *Fr.* Ode Recited at the Harvard Commemoration. Lowell.
Lincoln. *Fr.* Commemoration Ode. Monroe.
Lincoln. Trowbridge.
Lincoln. Turner.
Lincoln and Liberty. Hutchinson.
Lincoln and Liberty. Simpson.
Lincoln-Child, The. Oppenheim.
Lincoln, Come Back. Clark.
Lincoln Monument: Washington. Hughes.
Lincoln Statue, The. Collins.
Lincoln, the Man of the People. Markham.
Lincoln's Birthday. Bangs.
Lincoln's Farewell. Lincoln.
Lord Lovel. *Unknown.*
Man of Men, A. Van Noppen.
Martyr, The. Melville.
Master, The. Robinson.
Masterful Man, The. Tyrrell.
Masterpiece, The. Malone.
Nancy Hanks. R. *and* S. V. Benét.
O Captain! My Captain! *Fr.* Memories of President Lincoln. Whitman.
Old Abe Lincoln Came Out of the Wilderness. *Unknown.*
On a Picture of Lincoln. Cheney.
On the Life-Mask of Abraham Lincoln. Gilder.
People's King, The. Allen.
Prairie. Llewellyn.
Remembering Lincoln. Mundorf.
Reply to Nancy Hanks, A. Silberger.
Soul of Lincoln, The. Piety.
Star of Sangamon, The. Allen.
They Will Look for a Few Words. Turner.
Thou Shouldst Be Living at This Hour. West.
To Abraham Lincoln. Piatt.
Tribute, A: "Lincoln, the man who freed the slave." *Unknown.*
Washington and Lincoln. Stafford.
When Lilacs Last in the Dooryard Bloom'd. *Fr.* Memories of President Lincoln. Whitman.
Would I Might Rouse the Lincoln in You All. Lindsay.
Your Glory, Lincoln. Goodman.
Lincolnshire, England
At Lincoln. Adams.
Boston, Lincolnshire. *Unknown.*
High Tide on the Coast of Lincolnshire (1571), The. Ingelow.
Lincolnshire; from the Wolds to the Fens. *Fr.* The Sad Shepherd. Jonson.
Lincolnshire's Holland Speaks of Her Waterfowl. *Fr.* Polyolbion. Drayton.
Lines: "Here often, when a child, I lay reclined." Tennyson.
Lindbergh, Charles
Lindbergh. *Unknown.*
Lindsay, Vachel
To Lindsay. Ginsberg.
Linnets
Green Linnet, The. Wordsworth.
Grey Linnet, The. McCarroll.
I Heard a Linnet Courting. Bridges.
Linnet, The. De la Mare.
To a Linnet in a Cage. Ledwidge.
Lions
Circus Lion. Day Lewis.
Glove and the Lions, The. Hunt.
Jim, Who Ran Away from His Nurse, and Was Eaten by a Lion. Belloc.
King, The. Livingstone.
Lion, The. Belloc.
Lion, The. Howitt.
Lion, The. Lindsay.
Lion, The. Nash.
Lion, The. Prelutsky.
Lion. Smith.
Lion. Swenson.
Lion. *Unknown.*
Lion and Albert, The. Edgar.
Lion and the Wave, The. Allingham.
Lion Hunts. Beer.
Lion is a beast to fight, The. Quiller-Couch.
Lion's Skeleton, The. Turner.
Lucky Lion! Zulu.
O My Poor Darling. Watson.
Song of the Lioness for Her Cub. *Unknown.*
Sunt Leones. Smith.

Lippi, Fra Filippo
Fra Lippo Lippi. Browning.
Lips
Song: "Often I have heard it said." Landor.
Lipscomb, Eugene (Big Daddy)
Say Good-bye to Big Daddy. Jarrell.
Liquids
What Is Liquid. Newcastle.
Lister, Joseph
Chief, The. *Fr.* In Hospital. Henley.
Literature
Can. Lit. Birney.
Canadian Prairies View of Literature, The. Donnell.
Principal British Writers. Goodwin.
Survey of Literature. Ransom.
See also **Authorship and Authors; Criticism and Critics.**
Lithuania, U.S.S.R.
Little House in Lithuania, The. Marshak.
Summer Pogrom. Zwicky.
Vilna. Kulbak.
Little Bighorn, Battle of (1876)
Comanche. Gildner.
Death of Custer, The. Crawford.
Down the Little Big Horn. Brooks.
Little Big Horn. McGaffey.
Miles Keogh's Horse. Hay.
Revenge of Rain-in-the-Face, The. Longfellow.
Little Miss Muffet
Embarassing Episode of Little Miss Muffet, The. Carryl.
Little Miss Muffet. *Unknown.*
Little Red Riding Hood
Coup de Grâce. Hope.
Red Riding Hood. Carryl.
Disenchantments: An Anthology of Modern Fairy Tale Poetry (DFT). Wolfgang Mieder, ed.
Little Rock, Arkansas
Chicago *Defender* Sends a Man to Little Rock, Fall, 1957, The. Brooks.
Livingstone, David
Into the Dark. Monette.
Lizards
Americans Are Afraid of Lizards. Shapiro.
Grey Him. Mariah.
Horned Lizard. Molesworth.
Lizard, The. Gardner.
Lizard. Lawrence.
Lizard, The. Lechlitner.
Lizard, The. Markham.
Lizard. McLean.
Lizard, The. Murray.
Lizard, The. Roethke.
Lizards of La Brea. De Baca.
Note on Lizards' Feet, A. Van Rensselaer.
On a Bougainvillæa Vine in Haiti. Howes.
Recognition. Perry.
Small Lizard, The. Gregg.
Under Creag Mhor. Conn.
Witches' Menu. Nikolay.
Llamas
In Praise of Llamas. Guiterman.
Lama, The. Nash.
Llama, The. Belloc.
Snap Judgement on the Llama, A. Bennett.
Lobsters
In the Case of Lobsters. Morstein.
Lobsters and the Fiddler Crab, The. Forster.
Lobsters in the Window. Snodgrass.
Loch Ness. *See* **Ness, Loch, Scotland.**
Locusts
Coyote and the Locust, The. *Unknown.*
Four Things. *Fr.* Proverbs. Bible, *O.T.*
Locust, The. Cushing.
Locust, The. *Unknown.*
Locust Hunt, The. Murray.
Serenade: "Tin-type tune the locusts make, The." Donnelly.
Log Houses
Old Log House. Tippett.
Lombardi, Vince
For the Death of Vince Lombardi. Dickey.
London, England
About in London. *Fr.* Trivia; or, The Art of Walking the Streets of London. Gay.
Afterlives. Mahon.
Ballad of London, A. Le Gallienne.
Ballad of the Londoner. Flecker.
Barrel-Organ, The. Noyes.
Bells of London, The. *Unknown.*
Breath of Hampstead Heath. Thomas.
Composed upon Westminster Bridge, September 3, 1802. Wordsworth.
Country and Town. Morris.
Countryman's Return, The. Thomas.
Description of a City Shower, A. Swift.
Description of London, A. Bancks.
Description of the Spring in London, A. *Unknown.*
Earth Has Not Anything to Show More Fair. Wordsworth.
Farewell to Kurdistan. Tonks.
Fields from Islington to Marybone, The. *Fr.* Jerusalem. Blake.
Fire of London, The. *Fr.* Annus Mirabilis. Dryden.
Going Up to London. Turner.
Hell is a city much like London. *Fr.* Peter Bell the Third. Shelley.
His Return to London. Herrick.
His Tears to Thamasis. Herrick.
Homage to Wren. MacNeice.
Important Statement. Kavanagh.
Impression de Nuit; London. Douglas.
Impression du Matin. Wilde.
In Honour of the City of London. Dunbar.
In the Dials. Henley.
Kensington Gardens. Verne.
Let dirty streets by paved with flow'ry green. *Fr.* The Comparison. *Unknown.*
Let due civilities be stricty paid. *Fr.* Trivia; or, The Art of Walking the Streets of London. Gay.
Lines on the Mermaid Tavern. Keats.
London. *Fr.* Songs of Experience. Blake.
London. Davidson.
London. *Fr.* Reformation of Manners. Defoe.
London. Johnson.
London. Rowland.
London. Wilson.
London at Night. *Fr.* Trivia; or, The Art of Walking the Streets of London. Gay.
London Bells. *Unknown.*
London Bridge. *Unknown.*
London: 1802. Wordsworth.
London in 1646. Vaughan.
London in War. Dircks.
London Interior. Monro.
London Is a Fine Town. *Unknown.*
London Lickpenny. *Unknown.*
London Snow. Bridges.
London Suburbs. *Fr.* Retirement. Cowper.
London Town. Johnson.
London versus Epping Forest. *Fr.* Child Harold. Clare.
New London, The. *Fr.* Annus Mirabilis. Dryden.
New River Head, a Fragment, The. Dower.
November Blue. Meynell.
Of London Bridge, and the Stupendous Sight, and Structure Thereof. Howell.
Of Walking the Streets by Day. *Fr.* Trivia; or, The Art of Walking the Streets of London. Gay.
Old Song, The. Chesterton.
On St. James's Park, as Lately Improved by His Majesty. Waller.
On the Lord Mayor and Court of Aldermen, Presenting the Late King and Duke of York Each with a Copy of Their Freedoms, Anno Dom. 1674. Marvell.
Piccadilly. Burke.
Poor of London, The. Forster.
Regent's Park Terrace. Spencer.
St. James's Street. Locker-Lampson.
Satire on London, A. Surrey.
Scherzando. *Fr.* London Coluntaries. Hardy.
Simplicity's Song. Wilson.
Solitude and Reason, in the Village. *Fr.* Of Solitude. Cowley.
Song: "Closes and courts and lanes." Davidson.
Song of Fleet Street, A. Werner.
Song of Parting, A. Mackenzie.
Streets. Goldring.
Streets of Laredo, The. MacNeice.
Sunken Evening in Trafalgar Square. Lee.
Symphony in Yellow. Wilde.
To Hampstead. Hunt.
To the City of London. Dunbar.
Troynovant. Dekker.
Tyburn and Westminster. Heywood.

Wandsworth Common. Bromwich.
You are now in London, that great sea, whose ebb and flow. *Fr.* Letter to Maria Gisborne. Shelley.
Young Wordsworth's London, The. *Fr.* The Prelude. Wordsworth.

Lone Ranger, The
Tonto. Koertge.

Loneliness
Acquainted with the Night. Frost.
Alone. Chu Shu-chen.
Alone. De la Mare.
Alone. Manger.
Alone. Sassoon.
Alone by the Road's Edge. O Hehir.
And the Hotel Room Held Only Him. Evans.
Bereft. Frost.
Bereft. Hardy.
Cold Feet in Columbus. Heath.
Consider a Move. Ryan.
Departure's Girl-Friend. Merwin.
Desert Places. Frost.
Dove's Loneliness, The. Darley.
Early Morning. Dow.
Eleanor Rigby. Lennon *and* McCartney.
Eyes That Drew from Me Such Fervent Praise, The. Petrarch.
Five Sense. Wyche.
Fog, The. Coffin.
Fruit of Loneliness. Sarton.
He Resigns. Berryman.
House by the Tracks, A. Etter.
I explain the silvered passing of a ship at night. *Fr.* War Is Kind. Crane.
I Saw in Louisiana a Live-Oak Growing. Whitman.
Interior. Parker.
L(a. Cummings.
Letter to Her Husband, Absent upon Public Employment. Bradstreet.
Little Eclogue. Wylie.
Loneliness. Carruth.
Loneliness. Essex.
Loneliness. *Fr.* The Hill Wife. Frost.
Loneliness. Hashin.
Loneliness. Jenkins.
Loneliness. Werfel.
Loneliness. Young.
Loneliness of the Long Distant Runner, The. Nowlan.
Lonely Road. Abrahams.
Lonely. Modisane.
Lonely. Spire.
Lying here alone. Izumi Shikibu.
Mariana. Tennyson.
Mnemosyne. Stickney.
Most of It, The. Frost.
Mr. Flood's Party. Robinson.
On the Wide Heath. Millay.
One. Rodgers.
Parents-without-Partners Picnic, The. Schaefer.
Poem: "I loved my friend." Hughes.
Poem for Some Black Women. Rodgers.
Search. Souster.
Secret of Poetry, The. Anderson.
Sheep-Herder's Lament, The. Chapman.
Siren Chorus. Darley.
Sleeping Alone. Fickert.
So lonely am I. Ono no Komachi.
Solitude. Monro.
Song: "You're wondering if I'm lonely." Rich.
Sorrow. Chu Shu-chen.
Spring Night. Teasdale.
Stranger in This Land, A. Ashby.
Summary. Sanchez.
To Marguerite. *Fr.* Switzerland. Arnold.
Tonight I'v Watched. Sappho.
Wanderer's Grave, The. Sage.
What Color Is Lonely. Rodgers.
When I'm alone—the words tripped off his tongue. Sassoon.
Wife A-Lost, The. Barnes.

Long Island, New York
Afternoon: Amagansett Beach. Wheelock.
Amagansett Beach Revisited. Wheelock.
Fire Island. Swenson.
In the Hamptons. Morris.
Long Island Springs. Moss.
On the Island. Sissman.

Longfellow, Henry Wadsworth
Henry Wadsworth Longfellow. Dobson.
Hiawatha's Photographing, *parody*. "Carroll."
Higher, *parody*. *Unknown.*
Longfellow's Visit to Venice. Betjeman.
Poe and Longfellow. *Fr.* A Fable for Critics. Lowell.
Shades of Night, The, *parody*. Housman.
Shot at Random, A, *parody*. Lewis.

Longshoremen
Docker. Heaney.

Lookout Mountain, Battle of (1863)
Battle in the Clouds, The. Howells.
Battle of Lookout Mountain, The. Baker.

Loons
Loon, The. Rand.
Loon, The. Sarett.
Loon, The. Street.
Running the River Lines. Baker.

Lorelei
Lorelei. Heine.

Los Angeles, California
Daily I Fall in Love with Waitresses. Fried.
Gary Gotow. Uba.
Lizards of La Brea, The. De Baca.
Los Angeles. Healy.
Watts. Rivers.
Yellow Light. Hongo.
See also **Hollywood, California.**

Lot (Bible)
Half-Way, for One Commandment Broken. Housman.
His Wife. Kaufman.
Lot Later. Nemerov.

Lotus
Egyptian Lotus, The. Eaton.
He Is like the Lotus. *Unknown.*
Lotos-Eaters, The. Tennyson.

Louis XIV, King of France
Satire upon the French King, A. Brown.

Louis XV, King of France
Louis XV. Sterling.

Louis, Madame (daughter of Louis XV of France)
Aux Carmélites. Tynan.

Louis, Morris
To Morris Louis. Cherner.

Louisiana
African in Louisiana. Kyei.
Alcide Pavageau. Williams.
House of the Rising Sun. *Unknown.*
In Louisiana. Paine.
New Orleans. Carruth.
Pine Barrens: Letter Home. Mathis.
Ruston, Louisiana: 1952. Mathis.
Shooting Ducks in South Louisiana. Tillinghast.
Song for New Orleans, A. Keithley.
Southern Season. Claudel.
Vieux Carré. Roberts.
View of Louisiana. Mathis.

L'Ouverture, Toussaint. *See* **Toussaint L'Ouverture, François Dominique.**

Love
Book of Love Poetry, A (BoLoP). Jon Stallworthy, ed.
English Love Poems (EnLoPo). John Betjeman *and* Geoffrey Taylor, eds.
Erotic Poetry (ErPo). William Cole, ed.
Gambit Book of Love Poems, The (GBL). Geoffrey Grigson, ed.
Home Book of Modern Verse, The (HBMV), pp. 74–254. Burton Egbert Stevenson, ed.
Home Book of Verse, The (HBV-1), pp. 474–1290. Burton Egbert Stevenson, ed.
Love (LO). Walter de la Mare, ed.
Love Is Like the Lion's Tooth (LLLT). Frances McCullough, ed.
One Little Room, an Everywhere (OLR). Myra Cohn Livingston, ed.
Uninhibited Treasury of Erotic Poetry, An (UnTE). Louis Untermeyer, ed.

Lovelace, Richard
Footnote to a Famous Lyric, A. Guiney.
To His Noble Friend, Mr. Richard Lovelace, upon His Poems. Marvell.

Lowell, Amy
For Amy Lowell. Cullen.

Lowell, James Russell
Lowell. *Fr.* A Fable for Critics. Lowell.
To John Greenleaf Whittier. Ward.

Lowell, Percival
Observatory Ode, The. Nims.

Lowell, Robert
North Haven. Bishop.
Robert Lowell. O'Connell.
Robert Lowell Is Dead. Gray.
Stone Words for Robert Lowell. Eberhart.
Loyalty
His Golden Locks Time Hath to Silver Turned. *Fr.* Polyhymnia. Peele.
Loyalty. Davies.
Will Ye No Come Back Again? Nairne.
See also **Fidelity.**
Luck
Coming of Good Luck, The. Herrick.
Favour. Fitzgerald.
For Good Luck. Ewing.
Good Luck and Bad. Hay.
Lady Fortune, The. *Unknown.*
Luck. Epstein.
Pain. Södergran.
Stupid Old Myself. Hoban.
See also **Chance; Fate; Fortune.**
Lucknow, India
Defence of Lucknow, The. Tennyson.
Pipes at Lucknow, The. Whittier.
Lucretius
Lucretius. Tennyson.
Luddites
Framework-Knitters Lamentation, The. *Unknown.*
Framework-Knitters Petition, The. Briggs.
Ode to the Framers of the Frame Bill, An. Byron.
Ludlow Massacre (1914)
Ludlow Massacre, The. Guthrie.
Luke, Saint
Saint Luke the Painter. *Fr.* The House of Life. Rossetti.
Lullabies
All through the Night. *Unknown.*
Bed-Time Song. Poulsson.
Bye, baby bunting. Mother Goose.
Christmas Cradlesong, A. Lope de Vega.
Coventry Carol, The. *Unknown.*
Cradle Hymn. Watts.
Dutch Lullaby, A. Field.
Fairies' Lullaby, The. *Fr.* A Midsummer Night's Dream. Shakespeare.
Golden Slumbers. *Fr.* The Pleasant Comedy of Patient Grissell. Dekker.
Good-Night. Taylor.
Holy Innocents. Rossetti.
Hush-a-bye, baby, on the tree-top. Mother Goose.
Italian Lullaby. *Unknown.*
Lady Anne Bothwell's Lament. *Unknown.*
Lover's Lullaby, A. Gascoigne.
Lulla La, Lulla Lulla Lullaby. Byrd.
Mamma Sings. Hoffenstein.
Mary's Song. Causley.
Mouse's Lullaby, The. Cox.
Norse Lullaby. Field.
O sleep, my babe, hear not the rippling wave. *Fr.* Phantasmion. Coleridge.
On a Quiet Conscience. Charles I, King of England.
Our Blessed Lady's Lullaby. Verstegan.
Response. Kaufman.
Rock-a-bye, baby, thy cradle is green. Mother Goose.
Schlof, Bobbeli. *Unknown.*
Sleep, Baby Boy. *Unknown.*
Sleep, Baby, Sleep. *Unknown.*
Sleepy Song, The. Bacon.
Slumber Song. Ledoux.
Sweet and Low. Tennyson.
Sweet Lullaby, A. Breton.
When the Sleepy Man Comes. *Fr.* The Book of the Native. Roberts.
Wynken, Blynken, and Nod. Field.
See also **Cradle Song** *and* **Lullaby** ***in Title and First Line Index.***
Lumbering and Lumbermen
Again the ancient, meaningless. *Fr.* Myths and Texts. Snyder.
At the Cedars. Scott.
Canada-I-O. *Unknown.*
Colley's Run-I-O. *Unknown.*
Farmer and the Shanty Boy, The. *Unknown.*
Frozen Logger, The. *Unknown.*
In Winter in the Woods Alone. Frost.
Jack Haggerty. McGinnis.
Jam on Gerry's Rock, The. *Unknown.*
Jim the Splitter. Kendall.
Johnny Carroll's Camp. *Unknown.*
Jolly Lumbermen, The. *Unknown.*
Lake of the Caogama, The. *Unknown.*
Little Brown Bulls, The. *Unknown.*
Log Jam, The. Drummond.
Lumberman's Alphabet, The. *Unknown.*
Michigan-I-O. *Unknown.*
On Meesh-e-gan. *Unknown.*
Once More a-Lumbering Go. *Unknown.*
Peter Amberley. *Unknown.*
Raftsmen, The. *Unknown.*
Roving Shanty Boy, The. *Unknown.*
Saws Were Shrieking, The. Ross.
Shanty Boys and the Pine, The. *Unknown.*
Shanty Man's Life, A. *Unknown.*
Timber (Jerry the Mule). *Unknown.*
Turner's Camp on the Chippewa. *Unknown.*
When the Drive Goes Down. Malloch.
Wild Mustard River, The. *Unknown.*
Woodman Spare That Tree. Morris.
Woodyards in the Rain. Marriott.
Shantymen and Shantyboys (ShS). William Main Doerflinger, ed.
Lumumba, Patrice
Lumumba's Grave. Hughes.
Lunch
Lunch. Koch.
Lundy's Lane, Battle of (1814)
Battle of Bridgewater, The. *Unknown.*
Lungworms
Autobiography of a Lungworm. Fuller.
Lust
Against Them Who Lay Unchastity to the Sex of Women. *Fr.* Castara. Habington.
Arrowhead Christian Center and No-Smoking Luncheonette. Sylvester.
But for Lust. Pitter.
Conversion. Hewitt.
Cudworth's Undergraduate Oath to a Bare Behind. Owen.
Expense of spirit in a waste of shame, The. *Fr.* Sonnets. Shakespeare.
For X. MacNeice.
Galatea and Pygmalion. Graves.
Hares on the Mountain. *Unknown.*
In Praise of Beverly. Orlen.
It's Just the Same to Me. Hesse.
Late-Flowering Lust. Betjeman.
Nine Times a Night. *Unknown.*
Nymphs and Satyrs. Ewart.
Once-over, The. Blackburn.
Sex without Love. Olds.
Sic et Non. Read.
Slogan, The. Blackburn.
Snake, The. Corke.
To Barba. May.
Toast, A ("Here's to you and here's to me"). *Unknown.*
Two Songs. Rich.
Vine, The. Herrick.
See also **Erotic Love; Seduction; Sex.**
Lutes
Blame Not My Lute, for He Must Sound. Wyatt.
Lover Complaineth the Unkindness of His Love. Wyatt.
Music's Duel. Crashaw.
Of My Lady Isabella Playing on the Lute. Waller.
To His Lute. Drummond of Hawthornden.
When to her lute Corinna sings. Campion.
Luther, Martin
Luther. Auden.
Luxury
Contentment. *Fr.* The Autocrat of the Breakfast Table. Holmes.
Persian Fopperies. Horace.
Lying. *See* **Lies and Lying.**
Lynching
Between the World and Me. Wright.
Bird and the Tree, The. Torrence.
Black Bly. Rosten.
Black Draftee from Dixie. Clifford.
Emmett Till. Emanuel.
Fourteen Men. Gilmore.
Haunted Oak, The. Dunbar.
I Saw Them Lynch. Freeman.
Lynched. Booker.
Lynched Negro. Bodenheim.
Lynching, The. McKay.
Lynching and Burning. St. John.
Nice Day for a Lynching. Patchen.

Night, Death, Mississippi. Hayden.
Plaint. Ford.
So Quietly. Hill.
Song for a Dark Girl. Hughes.
Swimmers, The. Tate.

Lynx
Lesser Lynx, The. Rieu.
Lynx. Ford.
Lynx. Howard.

Lynn, Massachusetts
Bells of Lynn, The. Longfellow.

Lyonesse
Sunk Lyonesse. De la Mare.
When I Set Out for Lyonnesse. Hardy.

Lyrebirds
Lyre-Bird, The. Robinson.
Lyrebirds. Wright.

Lyres
Enchanted Lyre, The. Darley.
Supplication, A. Cowley.

Lysergic Acid (LSD)
Discovery of LSD a True Story, The. Hollo.

M

Macbeth
Macbeth. Horace *and* James Smith.
Macbeth's Dream. Andrew of Wyntoun.

McClellan, George Brinton
How McClellan Took Manassas. *Unknown.*
Victor of Antietam, The. Melville.

McCormack, John
Upon Hearing His High Sweet Tenor Again. Langland.

"MacDiarmid, Hugh" (Christopher Murray Grieve)
To Hugh MacDiarmid. Morgan.

Macdonough, Thomas
Thomas MacDonagh. Ledwidge.

McHenry, Fort
Fort McHenry. *Unknown.*
Star-spangled Banner, The. Key.

Machines
Beautiful Lawn Sprinkler, The. Nemerov.
Bulldozer, The. Francis.
Concrete Mixers. Hubbell.
Crane, The. Tomlinson.
Deus ex Machina. Armour.
Egg and the Machine, The. Frost.
Engine, The: A Manual. Dobberstein.
Horatian Variation. Bacon.
Junkyards. Rayford.
Needs. Ammons.
Nightmare Number Three. Benét.
Now I Set Me. Herman.
Portrait of a Machine. Untermeyer.
Steam Threshing Machine, The. Turner.
Steamboats, Viaducts, and Railways. Wordsworth.
Time for Building, A. Livingston.
To a Steam Roller. Moore.
Washing Machine, The. Davies.

McKinley, William
Assassination of President McKinley, The. Blackburn.
Buffalo. Coates.
Faithful unto Death. Titherington.
McKinley. *Unknown.*
White House Blues. *Unknown.*
Zolgotz. *Unknown.*

MacLeish, Archibald
Omelet of A. MacLeish, The. Wilson.
On a Flimmering Floom You Shall Ride. Sandburg.

"MacLeod, Fiona" (William Sharp)
To William Sharp. Scollard.

McLuhan, Marshall
Taste of Space, The. Smith.

MacNeice, Louis
In Carrowdore Churchyard. Mahon.

McPherson, James Birdseye
Dirge for McPherson, A. Melville.

MacSwiney, Terence James
Terence MacSwiney. "Æ."

Macy's (department store)
Macy's Poem, The. Reiss.

Mad Song (genre)
Fool's Song. Holcroft.
Mad Song. Blake.
Tom o' Bedlam's Song. *Unknown.*

Madness
After Visiting a Home for Disturbed Children. Lipsitz.
Another Poem about the Madness of Women. Wayman.
As other men, so I myself do muse. *Fr.* Idea. Drayton.
Bedlamite, The. Mozeen.
Bushed. Lillard.
Butch Is Back. Box.
Comfort Stop, A. Beyer.
Counting the Mad. Justice.
Division. Ratti.
Evening in the Sanitarium. Bogan.
Flee on Your Donkey. Sexton.
From an Asylum; Kathy Chattle to Her Mother, Ruth Arbeiter. Stevenson.
Hatters, The. McDonald.
Haunted Palace, The. Poe.
Hurry of the Spirits, in a Fever and Nervous Disorders, The. Watts.
I Am. Clare.
In a Dark Time. Roethke.
Letter from a State Hospital. Mundorf.
Lines Written during a Period of Insanity. Cowper.
Loving Mad Tom. *Unknown.*
Mad Gardener's Song, The. *Fr.* Sylvie and Bruno. "Carroll."
Mad Maid's Song, The. Herrick.
Mad Song. Blake.
Mad Song. Levertov.
Mad Woman of Punnet's Town, The. Strong.
Madhouse. Hernton.
Madman, The. Pretorius.
Madman, The. Urdang.
Madman's Song, The. *Fr.* The Duchess of Malfi. Webster.
Madness. *Fr.* The Art of Preserving Health. Armstrong.
Madness. Yoshihara.
Madwoman at Rodmell. Roberts.
Maniac, The. Russell.
Mental Cases. Owen.
Mourningsong for Anne. Posner.
Much madness is divinest sense. Dickinson.
Nebuchadnezzar. Wylie.
Note in a Sanitorium. Amorisi.
On a Painting by Patient B. of the Independence State Hospital for the Insane. Justice.
Ringing the Bells. Sexton.
Scene in a Madhouse. De Vere.
Seele im Raum. Jarrell.
Seventies, The. Beyer.
Sonnet Found in a Deserted Madhouse. *Unknown.*
To One in Bedlam. Dowson.
Vietnamese Girl in the Madhouse, The. Fisher.
Visitors' Parking. Szumigalski.
Visits to St. Elizabeths. Bishop.
Waking in the Blue. Lowell.
What Reward? Letts.
You, Doctor Martin. Sexton.
See also **Mental Illness.**

Madrid, Spain
Segovia and Madrid. Cooke.

Magazines
Alexandrine Magazine, An. Nemerov.
Talk of the Town, The. Fisher.
See also **Journalism; Newspapers.**

Magdalene, Mary. *See* **Mary Magdalene.**

Maggots
Filbert, The. Southey.

Magi
Adoration of the Magi, The. Pilling.
Adoration of the Wise Men, The. Alexander.
Ballad of the Cross, The. Garrison.
Camels of the Kings. Norris.
Carol of the Brown King. Hughes.
Carol of the Three Kings. Merwin.
Gift, The. Williams.
Journey of the Magi, The. Eliot.
Kings and Stars. Erskine.
Kings Came Riding. Williams.
Kings of the East, The. Bates.

Lord When the Wise Men Came from Far. Godolphin.
Lullaby in Bethlehem. Bashford.
Magi, The. Glück.
Magi, The. Yeats.
Mystic Magi, The. Hawker.
Perfect Gift, The. Cooke.
Poem for Epiphany. Nicholson.
Royall Presents. Wanley.
Take Frankincense, O God. *Fr.* Holy Transportations. Fitz-geffry.
Three Holy Kings from Morgenland. Heine.
Three Kings, The. Dario.
Three Kings, The. Longfellow.
Through the Dark the Dreamers Came. Marlatt.
We saw him sleeping in his manger bed. Bullett.
We Three Kings of Orient Are. Hopkins.
Wise Men Ask the Children the Way, The. Heine.

Magic
De Cunjah Man. Campbell.
For the El Paso Weather Bureau. Wild.
Houdini. Mandel.
Jolly Juggler, The. *Unknown.*
La Belle Dame sans Merci. Keats.
Magic. Johnson.
Magical Eraser. Silverstein.
Manzini; Escape Artist. MacEwen.
Sermonette. Reed.
Sorcerer, The. Smith.
Testing-Tree, The. Kunitz.
Two Magicians, The. *Unknown.*
Usk. *Fr.* Landscapes. Eliot.

Magnets
Fable of the Magnet and the Churn, The. Gilbert.

Magnolias
Planting a Magnolia. Snodgrass.
To a Magnolia Flower in the Garden of the Armenian Convent at Venice. Mitchell.

Magpies
Camden Magpie. McCrae.
I crossed the pynot. *Unknown.*
Magpie. Davison.
One for sorrow, two for mirth. *Unknown.*
One is a sign of mischief. *Unknown.*
One is sorrow, two mirth. *Unknown.*
Pie sat on a pear tree, A. *Unknown.*

Magritte, René
Magistrate's Escape, The. Fulton.
Two Windows by Magritte. Roston.

Maguire, Hugh, Lord of Fermanagh
Hugh Maguire. O'Hussey.
O'Hussey's Ode to the Maguire. O'Hussey.

Maguire, Molly
Captain Molly. Collins.

Maia
Fragment of an ode to Maia. Keats.

Mail and Mailmen
Epitaph for a Postal Clerk. Kennedy.
Getting the Mail. Kinnell.
Hope. Jarrell.
Letter Edged in Black, The. *Unknown.*
Night Mail, The. Auden.
Night Mail North, The. Pennell.
Post-Boy, The. *Fr.* The Task. Cowper.
Postman, The. Richards.
Postman, The. *Unknown.*
Six-Horse Limited Mail, The. Fuller.
To the Postmaster General. Redgrove.

Maimonides, Moses
Duel with Verses over a Great Man. *Unknown.*

Maine (State)
Bar Harbor. Garin.
Boothbay Whale, The. *Unknown.*
Exiled. Millay.
For Jean Vincent d'Abbadie, Baron St.-Castin. Nowlan.
Fourth of July in Maine. Lowell.
Jake's Wharf. Booth.
Kineo Mountain. Wright.
Little Ponds. Guiterman.
Lovely Rivers and Lakes of Maine, The. Wallis.
Maine. Booth.
Maine Trail, A. McGiffert.
Miss Ada. Fahy.
Skunk Hour. Lowell.
Stove. Booth.
Summer Storm. Kent.
Tomah Stream. Gorman.
Water. Lowell.
Yankee Cradle. Coffin.

Maine (ship)
Battleship of *Maine.* *Unknown.*
Spirit of the *Maine*, The. Jenks.

Majorca
Andraitx—Pomegranate Flowers. Lawrence.

Malachy, Saint
St. Malachy. Merton.

Malaga, Spain
Famous Fight at Malago, The; or, The Englishmen's Victory over the Spaniards. *Unknown.*
Malaga. Hutchinson.

Malcolm X (Malcolm Little)
Aardvark. Fields.
At That Moment. Patterson.
El-Hajj Malik El-Shabazz. Hayden.
For Brother Malcolm. Spriggs.
For Malcolm: After Mecca. Barrax.
For Malcolm Who Walks in the Eyes of Our Children. Troupe.
For Malcolm X. Alba.
For Malcolm X. Walker.
I Remember. Jackson.
It Was a Funky Deal. Knight.
Malcolm. Clifton.
Malcolm. Cumbo.
Malcolm, a Thousandth Poem. Rivers.
Malcolm X. Brooks.
Malcolm X—An Autobiography. Neal.
My Ace of Spades. Joans.
Poem for Black Hearts, A. Baraka.
Portrait of Malcolm X. Knight.
Sun Came, The. Knight.
They Are Killing All the Young Men. Henderson.

Maldon, Battle of (991)
Battle of Maldon, The. *Unknown.*

Mallards
Solitary, The. Barnard.

Malls. *See* **Shopping Malls.**

Man in the Moon
Moon-Man. Hewett.

Manassas, Battles of. *See* **Bull Run, Battles of.**

Manatees
Developers at Crystal River. Merrill.
Manatee, The. Blyton.

Manchester, England
Manchester Ship Canal, The. *Unknown.*
Murphy in Manchester. Montague.

Manchuria
Manchouli. Empson.

Mandalay, Burma
Mandalay. Kipling.

Mandelstam, Osip
Mandelstam. Young.
Osip Mandelshtam. Layton.

Mandrills
Mandrill, The. Aiken.

Mangan, James Clarence
Clarence Mangan. Kinsella.
Nameless One, The. Mangan.

Mangoes
Mango Tree, The. Chock.

Manhattan. *See* **(New York City)**

Manila Bay, Battle of (1898)
Battle of Manila, The. Hovey.
Captive Ships at Manila, The. Paul.
Manila. Ware.
Manila Bay. Hale.

Manitoba, Canada
Signature. Livesay.
Wilderness Gothic. Purdy.

Mankind
Afterthought. Richardson.
As Concerning Man. Radcliffe.
Autonomous. Van Doren.
Away, Melancholy. Smith.
Beasts, The. *Fr.* Song of Myself. Whitman.
Before the Beginning of Years. *Fr.* Atlanta in Calydon. Swinburne.

Bliss of man, The (could pride that blessing find). *Fr.* An Essay on Man. Pope.
Book, The. Drummond of Hawthornden.
Brief Essay on Man. Guiterman.
Building a Person. Dunn.
Charitas Nimia; or, The Dear Bargain. Crashaw.
Chorus Sacerdotum. *Fr.* Mustapha. Greville.
Collective Portrait, The. Finch.
Common Dust. Johnson.
Consider the Auk. Nash.
Contemplations. Bradstreet.
Corruption. Vaughan.
Day of Judgment, The. Swift.
Divine Image, A. *Fr.* Songs of Experience. Blake.
Divine Image, The. *Fr.* Songs of Innocence. Blake.
Essay on Man, An. Pope.
Fish, the Man, and the Spirit, The. Hunt.
For A' That and A' That. Burns.
Formal Application. Baker.
Four Ages of Man, The. Yeats.
From Stone to Steel. Pratt.
Heavy Bear, The. Schwartz.
Hold a glass of pure water to the eye of the sun. *Fr.* The Glass of Pure Water. "MacDiarmid."
Horror Comic. Conquest.
Human Form Divine, The. Raine.
Human Races, The. Lister.
Human Seasons, The. Keats.
Hymn of Man. Swinburne.
If. Kipling.
In Men Whom Men Condemn as Ill. *Fr.* Byron. Miller.
In Random Fields of Impulse and Repose. Hathaway.
In Shame and Humiliation. Wright.
In the Waiting Room. Bishop.
Inquisitors, The. Jeffers.
"It Was Wrong to Do This," Said the Angel. *Fr.* The Black Riders. Crane.
"Know then thyself, presume not God to scan." *Fr.* An Essay on Man. Pope.
Knowing the heart of man is set to be. *Fr.* To the Lady Margaret Countesse of Cumberland. Daniel.
Last Man, The. Campbell.
Man. *Fr.* Nosce Teipsum. Davies.
Man. Greenberg.
Man. Herbert.
Man ("What a piece of work is a man!"). *Fr.* Hamlet. Shakespeare.
Man. Vaughan.
Man. Wolfe.
Man, Man, Man Is for the Woman Made. *Unknown.*
Man with the Hoe, The. Markham.
Man with the Hoe, The; a Reply. Cheney.
Measure of a Man. *Unknown.*
Measuring a Man. *Unknown.*
Meditatio. Pound.
Men. MacLeish.
Mercy Pleads for Mankind. *Fr.* Christ's Victory and Triumph. Fletcher.
Mystery of Dawn, ere yet the glory streams. *Fr.* The Sirens. Binyon.
Nature of Man, The. Sisson.
Ode on a Distant Prospect of Eton College. Gray.
On Man. Landor.
On the Persistence of Humanity. Fraser.
Pity This Busy Monster, Manunkind. Cummings.
Placed on this isthmus of a middle state. *Fr.* An Essay on Man. Pope.
Progress? Auden.
Progress. Meinke.
Pulley, The. Herbert.
Sans Equity and Sans Poise. *Fr.* Yung Wind. Confucius.
Satire against Mankind, A. Rochester.
Seven Ages of Man. *Fr.* As You Like It. Shakespeare.
Sic Vita. King.
Small Comment. Sanchez.
So, Man? Derwood.
Tetélestai. Aiken.
Timon Curses Athens and Mankind. *Fr.* Timon of Athens. Shakespeare.
Timon Speaks to a Dog. Hobsbaum.
To a Mouse. Burns.
To Men. Wickham.
To My Son Parker, Asleep in the Next Room. Kaufman.
Truant, The. Pratt.
Us. Wyatt.
Vanity of Human Wishes, The: The Tenth Satire of Juvenal Imitated. Johnson.
Weak Is the Will of Man, His Judgment Blind. Wordsworth.
Were I, who to my cost already am. *Fr.* A Satire against Mankind. Rochester.
What would this Man? Now upward will he soar. *Fr.* An Essay on Man. Pope.
Which Is a Proud, and Yet a Wretched Thing. *Fr.* Nosce Teipsum. Davies.
Why I Never Went into Politics. Shelton.
Wild Garden, The. *Fr.* An Essay on Man. Pope.
Wings. Holub.
Wishes of an Elderly Man, The. Raleigh.
Words Made of Water. Singer.
World, The. Vaughan.
World Is a Bundle of Hay, The. Byron.

Mannequins
Mannequins. Epstein.
Manners. *See* **Etiquette.**
Man-of-War Birds
To the Man-of-War Bird. Whitman.
Mansfield, Katherine
Horse in a Field. De la Mare.
Manson, Charles
Who Needs Charlie Manson? Thompson.
Mantegna, Andrea
For "An Allegorical Dance of Women" by Andrea Mantegna. Rossetti.
Mantis. *See* **Praying Mantis.**
Mantle, Mickey
Mantle. Heyen.
Maple Sugar and Maple Syrup
Maple Feast. Frost.
Sugar Weather. McArthur.
Sugaring, The. Klein.
Maps
Harp of Renfrewshire, The. Dunn.
Map, The. Oden.
Map, The. Strand.
Mapmaker on His Art, The. Nemerov.
Mappemounde. Birney.
Maps. Thompson.
Mermaids. *Fr.* The Atlas. Slessor.
Private Letter to Brazil, A. Oden.
Marathon (race)
For the Running of the New York City Marathon. Dickey.
Marathon, Battle of
Persian Version, The. Graves.
Marble
In the Marble Quarry. Dickey.
Island Quarry. Crane.
Marc Antony. *See* **Antony.**
March
Confrontations of March. Dillow.
Counting-out Rhyme for March. Frost.
Daffodils,/ That come before the swallow dares. Shakespeare.
Day before April, The. Davies.
Earliest Spring. Howells.
Four Little Foxes. Sarett.
I saw green banks of daffodil. Tennant.
In like a Lion. Hewitt.
In March. Martin.
Mad Day in March. Levine.
March. Coatsworth.
March. Crane.
March. Dickinson.
March. Guiterman.
March. Hopper.
March. Housman.
March. Loveman.
March. Morris.
March. *Unknown.*
March Snow. McKay.
March, Upstate. Bronk.
March Weather. Swan.
March Wind, The. *Unknown.*
March Winds, The. Houghton.
March Wind. Uschold.
March Winds. Lloyd.
Merry Month of March, The. Wordsworth.
Not Ideas about the Thing but the Thing Itself. Stevens.
Not to March. Hackleman.
Song in March. Simms.
Spring and All. Bauer.
Thorn Leaves in March. Merwin.

Twilight in Middle March, A. Ledwidge.
We like March—his shoes are purple. Dickinson.
Wild March. Woolson.
Winter is long in this climate. Williams.
Written in March. Wordsworth.

Marching and Marches
Away We Go. Fisher.
Marching Song. Stevenson.
See also **Parades.**

Mardi Gras
Mardi Gras. Keithley.
Mardi Gras/Grandmothers—Portrait in Red and Black Crayon. Nolan.

Marduk
Hymn to Marduk, *sels.* *Unknown.*

Margaret, Saint
To Saint Margaret. Constable.

Marigolds
Boldness in Love. Carew.
How Marigolds Came Yellow. Herrick.
Marigold. Garnett.
Marigold. Haines.
Marigold, The. Wither.
Marigolds. Graves.

Marijuana
Smoking Drugs with Strangers. Bowering.

Marin, John
Marin. Booth.

Marin County, California
Clouds of Evening. Jeffers.

Mariners. *See* **Sailing and Sailors.**

Marines. *See* **United States Marine Corps.**

Marion, Francis
Song of Marion's Men. Bryant.
Swamp Fox, The. Simms.

Mark Antony. *See* **Antony.**

Markets
In Saturday Market, there's eggs a-plenty. *Fr.* Saturday Market. Mew.
In the Bazaars of Hyderabad. Naidu.
Market Square. Milne.
Orgy (That Is, Vegetable Market, at Sarno). Labriola.

Markiewicz, Constance Georgine, Countess
In Memory of Eva Gore-Booth and Con Markiewicz. Yeats.

Marlborough, John Churchill, 1st Duke of
But, O my muse, what numbers wilt thou find. *Fr.* The Campaign. Addison.
False Favorite's Downfall, The. *Unknown.*
Satirical Elegy on the Death of a Late Famous General, A. Swift.

Marley, Bob
Elegy for Bob Marley, An. Matthews.

Marlowe, Christopher
Christopher Marlowe. *Fr.* To Henry Reynolds, of Poets and Poesy. Drayton.
Marlowe. Bayldon.

Marriage
About Marriage. Levertov.
Ache of Marriage, The. Levertov.
After the Golden Wedding. Stephen.
Against Marriage. *Unknown.*
All's Well That Ends Well. *Unknown.*
Antiquary. Donne.
Any Wife or Husband. Haynes.
Any Wife to Any Husband. Browning.
Archaeology of Marriage, The. Kumin.
As I am unhappy. Yosano Akiko.
At Potterne, Wilts. *Unknown.*
Auld Robin Gray. Lindsay.
Bachelor Bold and Young. *Unknown.*
Ballad of the Despairing Husband. Creeley.
Ballad upon a Wedding, A. Suckling.
Ballade upon a Wedding, A. Suckling.
Bed, The. Saleh.
Bon Mot, A. *Unknown.*
Brewer's Man, The. Strong.
But That Is Another Story. Justice.
By Vows of Love Together Bound. Fitch.
Caledonia. McElroy.
Call It a Good Marriage. Graves.
Careful Husband, The. *Unknown.*
Come All You Young Ladies and Gentlemen. *Unknown.*
Contention Betwixt a Wife, a Widow, and a Maid, A. Davies.
Couple. Swope.
Crisis, The. Creeley.
Curate's Kindness, The. Hardy.
Daisy Bell. Dacre.
Daughters Will You Marry? *Unknown.*
De Se. Weever.
Dead Bride, The. Hill.
Decade, A. Lowell.
Dedication to My Wife, A. Eliot.
Degli Sposi. Lesser.
Developing a Wife. Taylor.
Dialogue between a Squeamish Cotting Mechanic and His Sluttish Wife, in the Kitchen. *Fr.* Nuptial Dialogues. Ward.
Double Transformation, The. Goldsmith.
Dying Wife to Her Husband, A. Ibn Ezra.
Early Thoughts of Marriage. Cotton.
Eating. Gibbons.
Epigram: "After such years of dissension and strife." Hood.
Epigram: "As Thomas was cudgell'd one day by his wife." Swift.
Epigram: "Here lies my wife: here let her lie!" Dryden.
Epistle from Mrs. Yonge to Her Husband. Montagu.
Epitaph Intended for His Wife. Dryden.
Epitaph upon Husband and Wife Who Died and Were Buried Together, An. Crashaw.
Epithalamion Made at Lincolnes Inne. Donne.
Eros Turannos. Robinson.
Eurynome. Macpherson.
Exequy, An. King.
Family Life. Laing.
Farmer's Bride, The. Mew.
Farmer's Curst Wife, The. *Unknown.*
First Goodbye Letter, The. Simmons.
First Snow of the Year, The. Van Doren.
For a Marriage. Jong.
For a Second Marriage. Merrill.
40——Love. McGough.
Get Up and Bar the Door. *Unknown.*
Girl may not be quite so philosophical as she sounds, The. Gond.
Good and Bad Wives. *Unknown.*
Googs, The. Marquis.
Green Mossy Banks of the Lee, The. *Unknown.*
Groom's Lament, The. Peterson.
Habitation. Atwood.
He Waiata mo Te Kare. Baxter.
He'd Nothing but His Violin. Dallas.
His Being Was in Her Alone. Sidney.
His Mother's Wedding Ring. Crabbe.
Holy Matrimony. Keble.
Home Burial. Frost.
Honeymoon. Albert.
Honeymoon, The. *Fr.* Advice to Julia. Luttrell.
Husbands and Wives. Hershenson.
Hymeneal Song on the Nuptials of the Lady Anne Wentworth and the Lord Lovelace, An. Carew.
Hymeneall Dialogue, An. Carew.
I. *Fr.* Is 5. Cummings.
I Don't Have No Bunny Tail on My Behind. Alta.
I Wish I Was Single Again. *Unknown.*
If Ever I Marry, I'll Marry a Maid. *Unknown.*
If No One Ever Marries Me. Alma-Tadema.
Imitation of Martial, Book II Ep. 105, An. "Captain——."
In our old shipwrecked days there was an hour. *Fr.* Modern Love. Meredith.
Jealous Wife, The. Scannell.
Keep a Good Tongue in Your Head. Parker.
Late Abed. MacLeish.
Les Sylphides. MacNeice.
Letter. Bergman.
Letter to Dafnis, April: 2, 1685. Winchilsea.
Living with Others. Zolynas.
Love and Marriage. Mathew.
Love in a Life. Browning.
Lucky Marriage, The. Blackburn.
Major Macroo. Smith.
Man and Wife. Goodman.
Man and Wife. Sexton.
Man and Wife Is One Flesh. Deagon.
Man May Live Thrice Nestor's Life, A. Norton.
Man Who Married Magdalene, The. Simpson.
Marriage. Clarke.
Marriage. Corso.
Marriage. Gibson.
Marriage. Hall.
Marriage. *Unknown.*

Marriage. Williams.
Marriage, The. Winters.
Marriage and Money. *Fr.* The Happy Pair. Sedley.
Marriage Charm, A. Hopper.
Marriage Contract. Rutsala.
Marriage is a lovely thing. Pisan.
Marriage of Two. Day Lewis.
Marriage Song. Halevi.
Marriage, which might have been a mateship sweet. *Fr.* Woman Free. Wolstenhome-Elmy.
Married and Single Life. *Unknown.*
Married Man Blues. *Unknown.*
Marry the Lass? Greig.
Maternity Gown. Holbrook.
Matrimony. Williams.
Meditation at Kew. Wickham.
Midnight Court, The. Merriman.
Minion Wife, A. *Fr.* Ralph Roister Doister. Udall.
Modern Love. Meredith.
Most Like an Arch This Marriage. Ciardi.
Mother of the Groom. Heaney.
Moving in Winter. Rich.
My Last Duchess. Browning.
My Marriage with Mrs. Johnson. Gilbert.
My Three Wives. *Unknown.*
Needles and pins, needles and pins. *Unknown.*
Nervous Prostration. Wickham.
Nesting. Saleh.
Newly-wedded, The. Praed.
Newlyweds, The. Criswell.
Next at our altar stood a luckless pair. *Fr.* The Parish Register. Crabbe.
No Love, to Love of Man and Wife. Eedes.
Nuptiall Song, or Epithalamie, on Sir Clipseby Crew and His Lady, A. Herrick.
O, love, in your sweet name enough. *Fr.* Essay on Marriage. Finch.
Occasional Poem. Housman.
Ode: "That I have often been in love, deep love." "Pindar."
Of Man and Wife. Eedes.
Old Cloak, The. *Unknown.*
Old-Marrieds, The. Brooks.
On Giles and Joan. Jonson.
On Marriage. Flatman.
On the Marriage of a Virgin. Thomas.
One Wife for One Man. Aig-Imoukhuede.
Our Ship She Lies in Harbour. *Unknown.*
Packin' Trunk Blues. *Unknown.*
Paradise. Birdseye.
Passionate Shepherd to His Love, The. Schwartz.
Plea for Trigamy, A. Seaman.
Poem in Prose. MacLeish.
Prayer for a Marriage, A. Davies.
Prince of Wales' Marriage. *Unknown.*
Prothalamion. Spenser.
Prothalamium. MacDonagh.
Proverb reporteth, no man can deny, The. *Fr.* Tom Tyler and His Wife. *Unknown.*
Quinks, The. Marquis.
Reasonable Affliction, A. Prior.
Red-haired Man's Wife, The. Stephens.
Reject Jell-O. Day.
Rejoice, O Bridegroom! *Unknown.*
Retired Boxer, The. Lucilius.
River-Merchant's Wife, The: A Letter. Li Po.
Robertin Tush. *Unknown.*
Rosy Apple, Lemon or Pear. *Unknown.*
Rural Lass, The. Jemmat.
Sanctum, The. Daly.
Sandgate Girl's Lamentation, The. *Unknown.*
Sign of the Bonny Blue Bell, The. *Unknown.*
Silver Wedding. Hodgson.
Slave Marriage Ceremony Supplement. *Unknown.*
Slice of Wedding Cake, A. Graves.
Socrates Snooks. Ludlow.
Some twenty years of marital agreement. Cunningham.
Song Ballet (I Was Sixteen Years of Age). *Unknown.*
Sonnet Reversed. Brooke.
Stumbling. Lourie.
Suite for Marriage, A. Ignatow.
Tale for Husbands, A. Sidney.
This Winter's Weather It Waxeth Cold. *Unknown.*
Three Seamstresses, The. Peretz.
Three Seasons. Sparshott.
To a Lady on Her Marriage. Bell.
To Be or Not to Be. Edmunds.
To Mary. Bishop.
To My Dear and Loving Husband. Bradstreet.
To My Wife. Stevenson.
To the Ladies. Chudleigh.
To wed, or not to wed? That is the question. *Unknown.*
Together. Lewisohn.
Too Candid by Half. Saxe.
Twenty-Year Marriage. Ai.
Upon the Death of Sir Albertus Morton's Wife. Herbert.
Upon Wedlock, and Death of Children. Taylor.
Wait for Me. Creeley.
Waiting at the Church; or, My Wife Won't Let Me. Leigh.
Washing the Dishes. Morley.
Washing Windows. Wild.
Wasp Sex Myth (One). Hollo.
Wasp Sex Myth (Two). Hollo.
Way Sun Keeps Falling Away from Every Window, The. Lifshin.
Wedded Love. *Fr.* Paradise Lost. Milton.
Wedding-Hymn. Lanier.
Wedding Morn. Lawrence.
Wedding Procession. Emanuel.
Wedding Signs. *Unknown.*
Wedding Song. *Unknown.*
Wedding-Wind. Larkin.
Wedlock; a Satire. Wright.
Westminster Drollery, 1671. Behn.
When Charlie Bowdre married Manuela, we carried them. Ondaatje.
When I Was Single. *Unknown.*
Whistle o'er the Lave O't. Burns.
Whitsun Weddings, The. Larkin.
Who Drags the Fiery Artist Down? Day.
Why Should a Foolish Marriage Vow. *Fr.* Marriage à la Mode. Dryden.
Wife, The. Creeley.
Wife, A. Lewis.
Wife Who Would a Wanton Be, The. *Unknown.*
Wife Wrapt in Wether's Skin, The. *Unknown.*
Winchester Wedding, The. D'Urfey.
Woman Painter of Mithila. Mumford.
Woman to Her Lover, A. Walsh.
Word to Husbands, A. Nash.
World Is Really a Sugarplum House in the Forest, The. Boyajian.
You were young—but that was scarcely to your credit. *Fr.* Monogamy. Gould.
Young Bride's Dream, The. Coghill.
Young Wife, A. Lawrence.
Young Wife, The. Stead.
Faber Book of Useful Verse, The (FaBoUs), pp. 74-80. Simon Brett, ed.
See also **Wedding Songs; Weddings.**

Mars (god)
Ares. Ehrenstein.
Mars and Venus. *Fr.* Tullie's Love. Greene.
To Mars. *Unknown.*

Mars (planet)
Viking 1 on Mars—July 20, 1976. Perlman.

Marshes
Bedford Level. *Fr.* The Fleece. Dyer.
Dingman's Marsh. Moore.
Marsh, The. Snodgrass.
Marsh, New Year's Day, The. Everwine.
Marshes of Glynn, The. Lanier.
Marshlands. Johnson.
Northamptonshire Fens. Clare.
Sunrise in Summer. Clare.

Marsyas
Marsyas. Roberts.

Martens
Dead Marten, The. Landor.
Fisher Cat, The. Eberhart.
On My Pretty Marten. Cotton.

Martha's Vineyard, Massachusetts
Making Port. McKay.

Martí, José
On a Monument to Martí. Roberts.

Martial Arts
My Father's Martial Art. Liu.

Martin, Saint
St. Martin and the Beggar. Gunn.

Martyrs
After the Martyrdom. Iris.
Cardinal Fisher. Heywood.

City of Slaughter, The. Bialik.
Da Silva Gives the Cue. Blumenthal.
Death of Gaudentis. "Harriet Annie."
Elegy: "I die for Your holy word without regret." Gomez.
Fr. Anselm Williams and Br. Leander Neville. Smither.
Here Followeth the Songe of the Death of Mr. Thewlis. *Unknown.*
Hymn to the Name and Honour of the Admirable Saint Teresa, A. Crashaw.
Last Words of Don Henriquez, The. Schneour.
Live here, great heart; and love and dy and kill. *Fr.* The Flaming Heart. Crashaw.
Martyrdom. Learsi.
Martyrdom of Brébeuf and Lalemant, 16 March 1649, The. *Fr.* Brébeuf and His Brethren. Pratt.
Martyrdom of Father Campion. Walpole.
Martyrdom of Mary, Queen of Scots, The. Southwell.
Martyr's Death, A. Menahem.
Martyr's Mass, A. Barrett.
On the Late Massacre in Piedmont. Milton.
Père Lalement. Pickthall.
Song of Four Priests Who Suffered Death at Lancaster, A. *Unknown.*
Sunt Leones. Smith.
These Things I Do Remember. Solomon Ephraim ben Aaron of Lenczicz.
Thy Faithful Sons. Eleazar.
To the Infant Martyrs. Crashaw.
Two Souls. Pickthall.
Upon the Infant Martyrs. Crashaw.
Vanzetti. Buckmaster.
Wallabout Martyrs, The. Whitman.

Marvell, Andrew
Marvell's Ghost. Ayloffe.
Poet of Gardens, The. Henderson.
You, Andrew Marvell. MacLeish.

Marx, Julius ("Groucho")
For the Passing of Groucho's Pursuer. Hollander.
Sort of Elegy, A. Farley.

Marx, Karl
Wayman in Love. Wayman.
Workers Rose on May Day, or Postscript to Karl Marx. Lorde.

Mary, the Virgin
Against Women's Fashions. Lydgate.
Ah (You Say), This Is Holy Wisdom. Doolittle ("H. D.").
Aishah Schechinah. Hawker.
Ane Ballat of Our Lady. Dunbar.
Annunciation. *Fr.* La Corona. Donne.
Annunciation, The. Kriel.
Annunciation, The. Merwin.
Annunciation, The. Muir.
Annunciation, The. *Unknown.*
As I Lay upon a Night. *Unknown.*
Assumption, The. Beaumont.
Assumption. Fallon.
Assumption, The. *Unknown.*
At Dawn the Virgin Is Born. Lope de Vega.
Ave. Rossetti.
Ballad of Our Lady. Dunbar.
Ballade of Illegal Ornaments. Belloc.
Ballade to Our Lady of Czestochowa. Belloc.
Bee, The. Hawkins.
Blessed Virgin Compared to the Air We Breathe, The. Hopkins.
Carol, The: Five Joys of the Virgin. *Unknown.*
Cherry-Tree Carol, The. *Unknown.*
Cradle-Song: "Madonna, Madonnina." Crapsey.
Devout Man Prays to His Relations, The. Herebert.
Epigram to the Queen Then Lying In, An. Jonson.
Expectation, The. Faber.
Five Joys of Mary, The. *Unknown.*
Folds of a White Dress/Shaft of Light. Keenan.
Gift of God, The. Robinson.
He came all so still. *Unknown.*
Hymn to Mary, A. Dunbar.
Hymn to Mary, A. *Unknown.*
Hymn to the Virgin, A. *Unknown.*
Hymn to the Virgin. *At. to* William of Shoreham.
I Have Lighted the Candles, Mary. Patchen.
I Sing of a Maiden. *Unknown.*
In Praise of Mary. *Unknown.*
In the Carpenter's Shop. Teasdale.
In the Glorious Assumption of Our Blessed Lady. Crashaw.
In the Town. *Unknown.*
Jesus and His Mother. Gunn.
Jesus Comforts His Mother. *Unknown.*
L'Annunciazione. O'Gorman.
Leaves of Life, The. *Unknown.*
Ler to Loven as I Love Thee. *Unknown.*
Little Carol of the Virgin, A. Lope de Vega.
Little Hymn to Mary, A. *Unknown.*
Living Room, The. Schnackenberg.
Luke XI: Blessed Be the Paps Which Thou Hast Sucked. Crashaw.
M and A, R and I. *Unknown.*
Maiden That Is Makeless, A. *Unknown.*
Mary and Her Son Alone. *At. to* James Ryman.
Mary at the Cross. McGee.
Mary Complains to Other Mothers. *Unknown.*
Mary Had a Baby. *Unknown.*
Mary Is with Child. *Unknown.*
Mary, Mother of Christ. Cullen.
Mary, Queen of Heaven. *Unknown.*
Mary Tired. Pickthall.
Mary Weeps for Her Child. *Unknown.*
Mary's Girlhood. Rossetti.
Mater Dei. Fallon.
May Magnificat, The. Hopkins.
Mother and Child. Eastwick.
Mother and Her Son on the Cross, The. *Unknown.*
Mother of God, The. Yeats.
Motherhood. Lee.
New Song of Mary, A. *Unknown.*
Now Fade the Rose and Lily-Flower. *Unknown.*
Now Goeth Sonne under Wode. *Unknown.*
O Simplicitas. *Fr.* The Three Songs of Mary. L'Engle.
O Virgin. *Unknown.*
Of One That Is So Fair and Bright. *Unknown.*
On the Assumption. Crashaw.
On the Blessed Virgin's Bashfulness. Crashaw.
On the Glorious Assumption of Our Blessed Lady. Crashaw.
On the Infancy of Our Saviour. Quarles.
Our Lady. Coleridge.
Our Lady in the Middle Ages. Faber.
Our Lady's Lullaby. Verstegan.
Our Lady's Song. *Unknown.*
Our Lord and Our Lady. Belloc.
Penitent Considers Another Coming of Mary, A. Brooks.
Penitent Hopes in Mary, The. *Unknown.*
Quaerit Jesum Suum Maria. Crashaw.
Quia Amore Langueo. *Unknown.*
Quickening, The. Tuttle.
Renaissance/a Triptych. Minczeski.
Rosa Mystica. Hopkins.
Seven Blessings of Mary, The. *Unknown.*
Seven Virgins, The. *Unknown.*
She Sang, Dear Son, Lullay. *Unknown.*
Song to Mary, A. William of Shoreham.
Song to the Virgin, A. *Unknown.*
Spinner, The. O'Donnell.
Star of the Sea. *Fr.* The Ship of Fools. Brant.
Sweet Was the Song. *Unknown.*
Thou maid and mother, daughter of thy Son. *Fr.* The Canterbury Tales: Prologue to the Second Nun's Tale. Chaucer.
To Our Blessed Lady. Constable.
To Our Lady. Henryson.
To the Virgin. Lydgate.
Two Carols to Our Lady. *Unknown.*
Venite Adoremus. Cannon.
Virgin, The. Wordsworth.
Virgin Mary, The. Bowers.
Virgin Mary Had One Son. *Unknown.*
Virgin's Slumber Song, The. Carlin.
Visitation, The. Jennings.
Welcome O Great Mary. *Unknown.*
I Sing of a Maiden (ISi). Sister M. Thérèse, ed.

Mary I, Queen of England
Marigold, The. Forrest.
New Ballade of the Marigolde, A. Forrest.
On the Princess Mary. Heywood.

Mary Magdalen

Mary Magdalene
Lent. Rodgers.
Magdalen. Kingsley.
Magdalen, The. Sherburne.
Marie Magdalene. Herbert.
Marie Magdalens Complaint at Christs Death. Southwell.
Mary Magdalene. Kassia.
Mary Magdalene. Speyer.

Mary Magdalene at the Door of Simon the Pharisee. Rossetti.
Multum Dilexit. Coleridge.
On Mary Magdalen. Drummond.
To Saint Mary Magdalen. Constable.
To St. Mary Magdalen. Hill.
Weeper, The. Crashaw.
Woman. Barrett.

Mary Queen of Scots
Alas! Poor Queen. Angus.
At Fotheringay. Southwell.
Decease, Release: Dum Morior Orior. Southwell.
Martyrdom of Mary, Queen of Scots, The. Southwell.
Mary, Queen of Scots. Bell.
Mary Queen of Scots. Turner.

Maryland
Barbara Frietchie. Whittier.
Battle of Baltimore, The. *Unknown.*
Chesapeake. Kennedy.
Cumberland Station. Smith.
First Precinct Fourth Ward. Epstein.
Fort McHenry. *Unknown.*
Harriet Tubman. Walker.
Hooking the Rainbow. Baldwin.
Incident. Cullen.
L'il Liza Jane. *Unknown.*
Maryland Battalion, The. Palmer.
Maryland Resolves. *Unknown.*
Miss Crustacean. Phillips.
My Maryland. Randall.
Night Song from Backbone Mountain. Epstein.
Purpose of the Chesapeake & Ohio Canal, The. Smith.
Sometimes I Think of Maryland. Braxton.
Stars Shine So Faithfully. Flanders.
Streets of Baltimore. *Unknown.*
Through Baltimore. Taylor.

Masks
On a Celtic Mask by Henry Moore. Gregory.

Masochism
In Francum. Davies.

Massachusetts
Bars Fight, August 28, 1746. Terry.
Beasts of Boston, The. Lowry.
Bells of Lynn, The. Longfellow.
Boston. Bossidy.
Boston Burglar, The. *Unknown.*
Cape Ann. *Unknown.*
Cape Ann: A View. Brinnin.
Cape Code Girls. *Unknown.*
Concord Hymn. Emerson
Connecticut River, The. Denney
Drivers of Boston, The. Gross.
Evening in Tyringham Valley. Gilder.
For the Union Dead. Lowell.
From Gloucester Out. Dorn.
In the Waiting Room. Bishop.
Librarian, The. Olson.
Maximum Poems, The, *sels.* Olson.
Men of Sudbury, The. Baker.
Monument Mountain. Bryant.
Nantucket/Mussels/October. Lewandowski.
Nantucket Skipper, The. Fields.
New Order, The. McGinley.
Nocturne: Homage to Whistler. Feldman.
North Shore. Davison.
Old Age Home, The. Holmes.
On a Fortification at Boston Begun by Women. Tompson.
Point Shirley. Plath.
Provincetown, *sels.* Dudek.
Provincetown, Mass. Shapiro.
Route Six. Kunitz.
Warren's Address at Bunker Hill. Pierpont.

Massacre of the Innocents
Clap Your Hands for Herod. Hanzlik.
Coventry Carol, The. *Unknown.*
Holy Innocents, The. Lowell.
To a Christmas Two-Year-Old. Shaw.

Massacres
And the Earth Rebelled. Suhl.
City of Slaughter, The. Bialik.
Elegy: "Those reckless hosts rush to the wells." Baruch.
Sonnet: On the Late Massacre in Piedmont. Milton.
Summer Pogrom. Zwicky.

Massada
At Masada. Neufeld.
Masada. Mozeson.
Never Again, The. Dobzynski.
On an autumn night, lying restless, far from her broken homeland. *Fr.* Massada. Lamdan.

Masts
Choosing a Mast. Campbell.

Matadors. *See* **Bullfights and Bullfighting.**

Mathematics
Arithmetic. Sandburg.
Counting. Collier.
Even Though. Stone.
Invention of Zero, The. Urdang.
Last Mathematician. Edelstein.
Mortifying Mistake, A. Pratt.
New Maths. Lehrer.
Of the Mathematicians. Matthews.
Power of Numbers, The. *Fr.* Davideis. Cowley.
Song of the Screw. *Unknown.*
Zito the Magician. Holub.
Imagination's Other Place (ImOP). Helen Plotz, ed.
See also **Arithmetic.**

Matisse, Henri
Matisse. Hirsch.
Picasso and Matisse. Francis.
Red Room, The. Berke.

Matterhorn
Zermatt: To the Matterhorn. Hardy.

Matthew, Saint
Christus Matthaeum et Discipulos Alloquitur. Sherburne.

Mausoleums
Lines Written in a Mausoleum. Grant.
Queen of Heaven Mausoleum. Schmitz.
Skeleton of the Future, The. "MacDiarmid."
See also **Cemeteries; Graves; Monuments.**

May
Apple Blossoms. Larcom.
April and May. Robinson.
Baby Seed Song. Nesbit.
Corinna's Going a-Maying. Herrick.
Fairy Music. Ledwidge.
Flute of May, The. Woodbourne.
Fountain in the Park, The. Haley.
Gladness of the May, The. Wordsworth.
Here We Come a-Piping. *Unknown.*
Home-Thoughts, from Abroad. Browning.
In Obitum M.S., X° Maii, 1614. Browne.
In Praise of May. *Unknown.*
Jewish May, The. Rosenfeld.
Judgment of the May, The. Dixon.
Lusty May. *Unknown.*
May. Barnes.
May. Bird.
May. Edwards.
May. Hovell-Thurlow.
May. Neilson.
May. Rossetti.
May. *Unknown.*
May. Updike.
May. Wade.
May and Death. Browning.
May Burden, A. Thompson.
May Carol. *Unknown.*
May Day. Teasdale.
May Day, A. Wotton.
May-Day at Sea. Finerty.
May Day Carol, A. *Unknown.*
May Day Garland, The. Blunden.
May Garden. Drinkwater.
May in the Green-Wood. *Unknown.*
May Is Building Her House. Le Gallienne.
May Magnificat, The. Hopkins.
May Morning. Thaxter.
May Mornings. Eastwick.
May, 1915. Mew.
May Song. *Unknown.*
May Time. Wyatt.
May 10th. Kumin.
Mayers' Song, The. *Unknown.*
Month of May, The. *Fr.* The Knight of the Burning Pestle. Beaumont *and* Fletcher.

O, the Month of May. *Fr.* The Shoemaker's Holiday. Dekker.
Ode in May. Watson.
Old May Song. *Unknown.*
Padstow Night Song, The. *Unknown.*
Poem in May. Hewitt.
Queen of Seasons, The. Newman.
Right as the star of day began to shine. *Fr.* The Golden Targe. Dunbar.
St. Mary's Loch. Faber.
Song: "Oh the charming month of May." Addison.
Song: Sunny shaft did I behold, A. Coleridge.
Song on May Morning. Milton.
Spring in These Hills. MacLeish.
There is but one May in the year. Rossetti.
'Tis Merry in Greenwood. Scott.
To the Lady May. Townsend.
You that in love finde lucke and habundance. Wyatt.

Maya
Two Families. Bell.

Mayflower (ship)
Mayflower, The. Ellsworth.
Mayflower. O'Reilly.

Mayflowers. *See* **Arbutus.**

Mayo. *See* **County Mayo, Ireland.**

Mazepa, Ivan
Mazeppa. Byron.

Mc. ***For names beginning thus, see*** **Mac.**

Mead
Honey-Mead. *Fr.* Riddles (Exeter Book). *Unknown.*

Meadowlarks
Meadow Lark, The. Garland.

Meadows. *See* **Fields and Pastures.**

Meadowsweet
Meadowsweet. Allingham.

Meat
Butchery. McPherson.
Poet and the Butcher, The. Whetham.
Receipt for Stewing Veal, A. Gay.
Recipe: Hare. Archestratus.
Recipe: Sausage. Axionicus.
Roast Beef of Old England, The. *Fr.* Don Quixote in England. Fielding.
Song in Praise of Old English Roast Beef, A. Leveridge.
To Stew a Rump-Steak. *Unknown.*
What Is Veal? *Unknown.*

Meath. *See* **County Meath, Ireland.**

Mechanics
Misery of Mechanics, The. Booth.
Spring Sunday on Quaker Street. Bass.

Medals
After Bourlon Wood. Dircks.
For Valour. Herschel-Clarke.
On a Nomination to the Legion of Honour. *Unknown.*

Medea
Jason and Medea. *Fr.* Confessio Amantis. Gower.
Oh smooth adder/ who with fanged kisses changedst my natural blood. *Fr.* Medea in Athens. Webster.

Medici, Ferdinand de'
Statue and the Bust, The. Browning.

Medici, Lorenzo de'
Statue of Lorenzo de' Medici, The. Nesmith.

Medicine
Calling the Doctor. Holloway.
Chicken Soup Therapy: Its Mode of Action. Hall.
Drinking Song, A. *Unknown.*
Mountain Medicine. Long.
On Hygiene. Belloc.
Plantation Bitters. *Unknown.*
Remedies. Soto.
Simples. Cardiff.
Song for a Lost Art. Brasier.
See also **Hospitals; Illness; Nurses; Physicians.**

Meditation
How to Meditate. Kerouac.

Mediterranean Sea
Mediterranean, The. Tate.
Middle of the World. Lawrence.
Ode to the Mediterranean. *Fr.* Odes. Santayana.

Medusa
Medusa. Bogan.
Medusa. O'Sullivan.
Statue of Medusa, The. Drummond of Hawthornden.

Meiklejohn, Alexander
I read your testimony and I thought. *Fr.* To Alexander Meiklejohn. Beecher.

Melampus
Melampus. Meredith.

Melancholy
Ah Me! Am I the Swaine. Wither.
Authors Abstract of Melancholy, The. *Fr.* The Anatomy of Melancholy. Burton.
Away, Melancholy. Smith.
Broken Heart, The. Beedome.
Charles Carville's Eyes. Robinson.
Dejection. Bridges.
Dejection: An Ode. Coleridge.
Flowers of the Forest, The. Rutherford.
Here I sit in my infested cubicle. Greenwood.
His Litany, to the Holy Spirit. Herrick.
If Only. Rossetti.
Il Penseroso. Milton.
Itylus. Swinburne.
Melancholia. Bly.
Melancholia. Bridges.
Melancholy. *Fr.* Scilla's Metamorphosis. Lodge.
Melancholy. *Fr.* The Nice Valor. Fletcher.
Melancholy. Thomas.
Mirth and Melancholy. Newcastle.
My Sad Self. Ginsberg.
My Spirit Longeth for Thee. Byrom.
Naked Seed, The. Lewis.
Ode on Melancholy. Keats.
Passionate Man's Song, The. *Fr.* The Nice Valour. Fletcher.
Platonick Love. Herbert of Cherbury.
Pleasures of Melancholy, The. Warton.
Pulley, The. Herbert.
Reverie. Marquis.
Sad Child's Song, The. Van Doren.
She Warns Him. Cornford.
Sigh, The. Wanley.
Solitude. Traherne.
Stanzas Written in Dejection, Near Naples. Shelley.
To Melancholy. Winchilsea.
Water Is Wide, The. *Unknown.*
What rage is this? what furour of what kind? Wyatt.
Why So Pale and Wan, Fond Lover? Suckling.
World Is Too Much with Us, The. Wordsworth.
See also **Dejection.**

Meleager
Meleager. *Fr.* Metamorphoses. Ovid.

Melville, Herman
At Melville's Tomb. Crane.
Herman Melville. Aiken.
Herman Melville. Auden.
Letter for Melville 1951. Olson.

Memento Mori
Memento for Mortality, A. Basse.
Upon a Dead Man's Head. Skelton.
Upon the Image of Death. Southwell.

Memnon
Memnon. Scollard.

Memorial Day
Aftermath. McCulloch.
Bitter Question. MacDougall.
Bivouac of the Dead, The. O'Hara.
Blue and the Gray, The. Finch.
Comrade, Remember. Kresensky.
Criminality of War, The. Young.
Dead, The. Brooke.
Decoration Day. Longfellow.
Decoration Day. Sinclair.
For Decoration Day. Hughes.
For Those Who Died. Clark.
From Beyond. Trent.
High Flight. Magee.
How Shall We Honor Them? Markham.
How Sleep the Brave. Collins.
If These Endure. Lorraine.
In Flanders Fields. McCrae.
In Memoriam. Jackson.
In the Name of Our Sons. Gould.
It Is Not Too Late. Trent.
Lament of the Voiceless, The. Everett.
Last Thoughts of a Fighting Man. *Unknown.*

March, The. Squire.
May Thirtieth. *Unknown.*
May 30, 1893. Bangs.
Memorial. Goodman.
Memorial Day. Brooks.
Memorial Day. Garrison.
Memorial Day. Lent.
Mother before a Soldier's Monument, A. Rockett.
O gallant brothers of the generous south. *Fr.* Ode for Decoration Day. Peterson.
On a World War Battlefield. Clark.
Reapers, The. Watt.
Remembering Day. Saunders.
Scapegoats. Breed.
Silent Testimony. Parmenter.
Starred Mother, The. Whitaker.
There Will Be Peace. Pettengill.
Thus Speak the Slain. Holliday.
Toward a True Peace. Trent *and* Cheyney.
Unknown Soldier. Dunn.
We Who Are About to Die. Fey.
We Who Are Dead. Benjamin.
We Whom the Dead Have Not Forgiven. Field.
Why. Freeman.
Youth. Bates.

Memory

After a Journey. Hardy.
Afterwards. Hardy.
Ah, Are You Digging on My Grave? Hardy.
All. Gom.
Ancient to Ancients, An. Hardy.
Animals, The. Muir.
Aspects. MacCaig.
At Ballyshannon, Co. Donegal. Allingham.
August from My Desk. Flint.
Autumn. *Fr.* Seasons of the Soul. Tate.
Babiaantje, The. Prince.
Bachelor Hall. Field.
Barefoot Boy, The. Whittier.
Before the Big Storm. Stafford.
Ben Alder 1963–1977. Hannigan.
Birthplace Revisited. Corso.
Blows the Wind Today. Stevenson.
Boyhood. *Fr.* The Prelude. Wordsworth.
Burning Hills. Ondaatje.
Cameo, The. Millay.
Celandine. Thomas.
Cold Glow: Icehouses. Wojahn.
Collector, The. Flynn.
Companions. Calverley.
Considerations. Helwig.
Crossing. MacLeish.
Crystals like Blood. "MacDiarmid."
Dear Men and Women. Wheelock.
Deja Vu. Mulligan.
Directive. Frost.
Early Influences. *Fr.* The Pleasures of Imagination. Akenside.
Elegy for a Woman Who Remembered Everything. Wagoner.
Embroidery. Jacobs.
Fall Journey. Stafford.
Fire of Drift-Wood, The. Longfellow.
Firefly. Uba.
Fishing, at Coot Shallows. Welch.
Flame-Heart. McKay.
Forget Thee? Moultrie.
Forgettin'. O'Neill.
Forgiven Past, The. Riding.
Gean Trees, The. Jacob.
Grand Hotel, Calcutta. Silbert.
Green Rain. Livesay.
Green Slates. Hardy.
Green Valley, The. Warner.
Heart! We will forget him! Dickinson.
Homecoming Celebration. Catacalos.
Home-Coming. Ehrenstein.
Hours, The. Bishop.
Houses. Justice.
I Don't Remember Anything of Then. O'Hara.
I Remember, I Remember. Hood.
In Memory. Pollitt.
In scenes paternal, not beheld through years. *Fr.* Eyam. Seward.
Journey, The. Ignatow.
Kashmiri Song. "Hope."
Lament for the O'Neills. Montague.
Letter from the Caribbean, A. Howes.
Light of Other Days, The. Moore.
Lines Composed a Few Miles above Tintern Abbey. Wordsworth.
Long, Long Be My Heart with Such Memories Filled. Moore.
Looking at Pictures to Be Put Away. Snyder.
Memontos, I. Snodgrass.
Memories. Whitman.
Memories. Whittier.
Memory. Aldrich.
Memory. Brontë.
Memory. Deutsch.
Memory. *Fr.* The Captivity. Goldsmith.
Memory. Hoyt.
Memory. Landor.
Memory. Lincoln.
Memory, A. Sackville.
Memory as Memorial in the Last. Marshall.
Memory Movie. Webster.
Mill, The. Wilbur.
Mnemosyne. Stickney.
Moments He Remembers, The. Van Doren.
Music I Heard. Aiken.
Music, When Soft Voices Die. Shelley.
My Lost Youth. Longfellow.
October. Kavanagh.
Ode to Memory. Tennyson.
Oft, in the Stilly Night. Moore.
Old Familiar Faces, The. Lamb
Old Oaken Bucket, The. Woodworth.
Old Times Were the Best, The. Riley.
On the Death of Friends in Childhood. Justice.
Out of the Cradle Endlessly Rocking. Whitman.
Out to Old Aunt Mary's. Riley.
Past and Present. Hood.
People, The. Creeley.
Piano. Lawrence.
Rain in my ears: impatiently there raps. *Fr.* Essay on Memory. Fitzgerald.
Ram Time. Heyen.
Recollection. Aldrich.
Recollection Long Ago: Sad Music. Warren.
Recuerdo. Allen.
Remember. Rossetti.
Remember or Forget. Aidé.
Remembering. Angelou.
Remembering. Tóth.
Remembrance. Brontë.
Remembrance. Slonimski.
Reminiscence. Irwin.
Reminiscences of a Dancing Man. Hardy.
Resurrection. Fearing.
Return. Spencer.
Reverie of a Mum. Keesing.
Rhapsody on a Windy Night. Eliot.
Road of Remembrance, The. Reese.
Rock Me to Sleep. Allen.
School Globe, The. Reaney.
Scrapbooks. Giovanni.
Sea-Lands, The. Johns.
Self Portrait 4. Ditlevsen.
Since. Auden.
Song: "Place in thy memory, dearest, A." Griffin.
Sonnet: "When to the sessions of sweet silent thought." Shakespeare.
Special Delivery. Montague.
Stanzas: "Black absence hides upon the past." Clare.
Tears, Idle Tears. *Fr.* The Princess. Tennyson.
Telling the Bees. Whittier.
Ten Days Leave. Snodgrass.
Then and Now. Murray.
Time Reminded Me. Uceda.
Tower, The. Yeats.
Tropics in New York, The. McKay.
Tune, A. Symons.
Twenty Years Ago. Smith.
Two Old Ladies. Sassoon.
Two Years Later. Wieners.
Unknown, The. Laughlin.
Veterans, The. MacDonagh.
Visit to the Author's Paternal Seat, A. *Fr.* The Influence of Local Attachment. Polwhele.

Voice, The. Hardy.
Walls of Ice. Hale.
Warning and Reply. Brontë.
Wedded Memories. Marston.
What lips my lips have kissed, and where, and why. Millay.
What Need Have I for Memory? Johnson.
When Summer's End is Nighing. Housman.
Where Are the Waters of Childhood? Strand.
With Rue My Heart Is Laden. Housman.
Woodman, Spare That Tree. Morris.
World, The. Rutsala.

Memphis, Tennessee
Beale Street, Memphis. Snyder.
Memphis Blues. Brown.

Men
Being with Men. Gregg.
Bird Sings to Establish Frontiers, A. Gilbert.
Cantata for Two Lovers. Sandburg.
Experience. Simmons
Fair Circassian, The. Garnett.
Feast of Stephen, The. Hecht.
Female of the Species, The. Kipling.
Helpmate. Chapin.
Hemmed-in Males. Williams.
How Beastly the Bourgeois Is. Lawrence.
I Fear No Power a Woman Wields. McGaffey.
I Hate Men. Porter.
I Sing the Body Electric. Whitman.
Lover, The; a Ballad. Montagu.
Lure, The. O'Reilly.
Male Rage Poem. Di Cicco.
Manhood. More.
Men. Parker.
Mr. Macklin's Jack O'Lantern. McCord.
Mr. Wells. Roberts.
Never Love Unless You Can. Campion.
Old Men. Ostriker.
Our Hired Man. Shannon.
Rainer Maria Rilke Returns from the Dead to Address the Junior Military School at Sankt Pölten. Engman.
Sail and Oar. Graves.
Sigh No More, Ladies. *Fr.* Much Ado about Nothing. Shakespeare.
Stand, Stately Tavie. *Unknown.*
Stew Meat Blues. *Unknown.*
That Women Are but Men's Shadows. Jonson.
Three Men. *Unknown.*
Tired As I Can Be. *Unknown.*
To Anthea, Who May Command Him Anything (New Style). Cochrane.
Twin Aces. Wilson.
When I am grown to man's estate. Stevenson.
When I Consider Thy Heavens. *Fr.* Psalms. Bible, *O.T.*
Women and Men. Somali.
Word in Edgeways, A. Tomlinson.

Menageries. *See* **Zoos.**

Mencken, Henry Louis
Poem to the Memory of H. L. Mencken. Wormser.

Menopause
Bloody Pause. Astra.

Mental Illness
Bill. Kocan.
Counting the Mad. Justice.
Dementia Praecox. Bishop.
Did They Help Me at the State Hospital for the Criminally Insane? Smith.
Evening in the Sanitarium. Bogan.
Grandeurs of the crazy man alone, The. Roethke.
Hard Rock Returns to Prison from the Hospital for the Criminal Insane. Knight.
Hour of Feeling, The. Simpson.
Lines Written during a Period of Insanity. Cowper.
MANICdepressant. Dammers.
Mental Cases. Owen.
Mental Hospital Garden, The. Williams.
Parents of Psychotic Children, The. Bell.
Patient, The: Rockland County Sanitarium. Hernton.
Ringing the Bells. Sexton.
Schizophrenic. Page.
Servant to Servants, A. Frost.
Simplicity. Simpson.
Sleepers, The. Kocan.
Third Avenue in Sunlight. Hecht.
Visit to the Asylum, A. Millay.
Waking in the Blue. Lowell.
See also **Madness; Psychiatry and Psychiatrists.**

Mental Retardation
Hospital for Defectives. Blackburn.
I Show the Daffodils to the Retarded Kids. Sharp.
Idiot, The. Wilson.
In the Dome Car of the "Canadian." Marty.
Mongol Quine. Mackie.
Retarded Children Find a World Built Just for Them, The. O Hehir.
Retarded Class at F. A. O. Schwarz's Celebrates Christmas, The. Fisher.

Menus
La Carte. Richardson.

Mephistopheles. *See* **Satan.**

Mercenaries
Another Epitaph on an Army of Mercenaries. "MacDiarmid."
Epitaph on an Army of Mercenaries. Housman.

Merchants
Seraph and the Snob, The. Kendall.
Turners Dish of Lentten Stuffe, or, A Galymaufery. Turner.
See also **Business and Businessmen; Clerks.**

Mercury (god)
To Mercury. Kennedy.

Mercury (planet)
To Mercury. Kennedy.

Mercy
Discipline. Herbert.
I opened the window wide and leaned. *Fr.* The Everlasting Mercy. Masefield.
Mercy. *Unknown.*
Ode to Mercy. Collins.
Quality of Mercy Is Not Strain'd, The. *Fr.* The Merchant of Venice. Shakespeare.

Merlin
Merlin and the Gleam. Tennyson.
Merlin & the Snake's Egg. Norris.
Merlin Enthralled. Wilbur.
Merlin. Emerson.

Mermaid Tavern, London
Lines on the Mermaid Tavern. Keats.

Mermaids and Mermen
Ballad by Hans Breitmann. Leland.
Ballad of the Mermaid. Leland.
Clerk Colvill. *Unknown.*
Elegy on a Dead Mermaid Washed Ashore at Plymouth Rock. Hillyer.
Figure-Head, The. Garstin.
Fisherman Writes a Letter to the Mermaid, The. Aiken.
Fisherman's Blunder Off New Bedford, Massachusetts. Ewing.
Forsaken Merman, The. Arnold.
Little Fan. Reeves.
Loreley, The. Heine.
Madness One Monday Evening. Fields.
Mermaid, The. King.
Mermaid, The. Tennyson.
Mermaid, The. *Unknown.*
Mermaiden, A. Hennell.
Mermaidens, The. Richards.
Mermaidens' Vesper-Hymn, The. *Fr.* Syren Songs. Darley.
Mermaids. *Fr.* The Atlas. Slessor.
Mermaids, The. *Fr.* The Faerie Queene. Spenser.
Mermaids and Mermen. *Fr.* The Pirate. Scott.
Merman, The. Tennyson.
Moon-Child, The. Macleod.
My Cabinets Are Oyster-Shells. Duchess of Newcastle.
Old Angler, The. De la Mare.
Rowing, I reach'd a rock—the sea was low. *Fr.* A Vision of the Mermaids. Hopkins.
Sam. De la Mare.
Sea-Maiden, The. De Forest.
Sea-Spell, A (for a Picture). Rossetti.
Silkie o'Sule Skerrie, The. *Unknown.*
Siren Chorus. *Fr.* Syren Songs. Darley.
Song of the Mermaids. Darley.

Merrimac (ship)
Cumberland and the Merrimac, The. *Unknown.*
Men of the *Merrimac,* The. Scollard.
Sinking of the *Merrimac.* Larcom.
Turtle, The. *Unknown.*
See also **Monitor (ship)**

Merry-go-rounds
Carousel, The. Oden.
Green Horse, The. Ramke.
Merry-go-round. Baruch.

Merry-go-round. Hughes.
Merry-go-round. Jenkins.
Merry-go-round. McAuley.
Merry-go-round, The. Rilke.
Merry-go-round. Van Doren.
Messengers
How They Brought the Good News from Ghent to Aix. Browning.
Messiah
Advice to a Prophet. Wilbur.
Ballad of the Days of Messiah. Klein.
Encounter in Safed. Yungman.
Hush, Hush. Leib.
Instructions for the Messiah. Sklarew.
Messiah, The. Yungman.
Messiah-Blower, The. Goodman.
O Hark to the Herald. Eleazar ben Kalir.
Rex Mundi. Gascoyne.
When the Days Grow Long. Bialik.
Metals
Tin-Ore. Malay.
Metaphor
Very Like a Whale. Nash.
Young Housewife, The. Williams.
Meteors and Meteorites
Doesn't It Seem to You. Emin.
Watching the Out-Door Movie Show. Struthers.
Methodism
Hearken, Lady Betty, hearken. *Fr.* The New Bath Guide. Anstey.
Religion and the Lower Classes. *Fr.* The Methodist. Lloyd.
World, the Devil, and Tom Paine, The. *Unknown.*
Methuselah
Man was called Methuselah I remember, The. *Fr.* The Devil and the Angel. Dobson.
Methuselah. *Unknown.*
Metric System
Elegy for Yards, Pounds, and Gallons. Wagoner.
Mexican War
Angels of Buena Vista, The. Whittier.
Fight at the San Jacinto, The. Palmer.
Maid of Monterey, The. *Unknown.*
Monterey. Hoffman.
Santy Anno. *Unknown.*
Mexico
Baja. Stern.
Edge of Town, The. Clamurro.
Finisterra. Winters.
For *Under the Volcano.* Lowry.
In Mexico. Stein.
Indians Come Down from Mixco, The. Asturias.
Instruction Manual, The. Ashbery.
Irapuato. Birney.
Leaving Mexico One More Time. Urdang.
Lesson in Hammocks, A. Schevill.
Lines for a Young Wanderer in Mexico. Logan.
Mexican Scrapbook, A. Oliphant.
Mexican Serenade. Guiterman.
Monte Albán. Stroud.
Mountain Town—Mexico. Grier.
Ponce de León / A Morning Walk. Young.
Sinalóa. Birney.
View from the Gorge. Belitt.
Visions of Mexico While at a Writing Symposium in Port Townsend, Washington. Cervantes.
Xochitepec. Lowry.
Mexico City
Fire Breather, Mexico City, The. Jacinto.
Mexico City Hand Game. Green.
Mexico City, 150 Pesos to the Dollar. Mitsui.
Mice
Ascend my shoulders, firmly keep thy seat. *Fr.* The Battle of the Frogs and Mice. *Unknown.*
Ballad of the Mouse. Wallace.
Cat and Mouse. Hughes.
Change of Heart, A. Hobbs.
Church Mouse, The. Bullett.
City Mouse and the Garden Mouse, The. *Fr.* Sing-Song. Rossetti.
Country Mouse and the City Mouse, The. Sharpe.
Diary of a Church Mouse. Betjeman.
Elf and the Dormouse, The. Herford.
Fieldmouse, The. Alexander.
Field Mouse, The. Sharp.
Fieldmouse, A/ crouches low. Sund.
Four III. Cummings.
Funeral Oration for a Mouse. Dugan.
Hickory, dickory, dock. Mother Goose.
House of the Mouse, The. Mitchell.
I was lying still in a field one day. Gay.
Little Black Bug. Brown.
Magical Mouse, The. Patchen.
Marriage of the Frog and the Mouse, The. *Unknown.*
Me Up at Does. Cummings.
Meadow Mouse, The. Roethke.
Message from a Mouse, Ascending in a Rocket. Hubbell.
Mice. Fyleman.
Mice in the Hay. Norris.
Missing. Milne.
Mouse, The. Coatsworth.
Mouse. Conkling.
Mouse, The. Garrigue.
Mouse, The. Richards.
Mouse and the Cake, The. Cook.
Mouse Dinners, The. Edson.
Mouse in the Wainscot, The. Serraillier.
Mouse Night: One of Our Games. Stafford.
Mouse's Nest. Clare.
Mouse's Petition, The. Barbauld.
Mus Ridiculus Non. Welch.
New Strain. Starbuck.
Of a Mouse and Men. Hovde.
Prayer of the Mouse, The. Gasztold.
Tale of the Upland Mouse and the Burgess Mouse, The. Henryson.
Three Blind Mice. *Unknown.*
To a Mouse, on Turning Her Up in Her Nest, with the Plough, November 1785. Burns.
To the Field Mice. Eberhart.
Two Mice, The. Henryson.
Waltzer in the House, The. Kunitz.
Michaelmas
Michaelmas. Nicholson.
Michelangelo Buonarroti
David Homindae. Rosenfeld.
Death-Bed Reflections of Michel-Angelo. Coleridge.
Love Song of J. Alfred Prufrock, The. Eliot.
Old Age of Michelangelo, The. Prince.
With a Sliver of Marble from Carrara. Wright.
Michigan
Coming Home, Detroit, 1968. Levine.
Detroit. Hall.
Detroit City. Boyer.
End of Summer, The. Minty.
Expanded Want Ad, An. Leithauser.
Foundations of American Industry, The. Hall.
Harry Dunne. *Unknown.*
Hooking the Rainbow. Baldwin.
In Detroit, I walk out Woodward Avenue. Cuscaden.
Lake St. Clair. *Fr.* The Great Lakes Suite. Reaney.
Making Music. Minty.
1913 Massacre, The. Guthrie.
Nocturne: Lake Huron. Kelly.
Pickers. Brett.
Road Along the Thumb and Forefinger, The. Hickey.
That Was Then. Gardner.
Microbes
Lines Written on the Antiquity of Microbes. Gillilan.
Microbe's Serenade, The. Ade.
See also **Bacteria.**
Microscopes
Microscope, The. Kumin.
Midas
King Midas. *Fr.* Metamorphoses. Ovid.
King Midas. Moss.
Ungrateful Garden, The. Kizer.
Middle Age
Autumnal, The. *Fr.* Elegies. Donne.
Ballade of Middle Age. Lang.
Bloody Pause. Astra.
Contented at Forty. Cleghorn.
Cupid tho' all his darts were lost. *Fr.* Cadenus and Vanessa. Swift.
"Dover Beach"—a Note to That Poem. MacLeish.
End of Summer. Kunitz.
Fifty Years Spent. Burt.
From a Correct Address in a Suburb of a Major City. Sorrells.
Game Resumed. Lattimore.
Gentleman of Fifty Soliloquizes, A. Marquis.

Journey towards Evening. McGinley.
Lady's Complaint, The. Heath-Stubbs.
Love Song of J. Alfred Prufrock, The. Eliot.
Loved One, The. Hansen.
Men at Forty. Justice.
Menstruation at Forty. Sexton.
Mezzo Cammin. Longfellow.
Middle Age. Lehmann.
Middle Age. Lowell.
Middle-Age. Jones.
Middle-Aged, The. Rich.
Middle-Aged Conversation. Tessimond.
Middleaged Man, The. Simpson.
Minuet on Reaching the Age of Fifty, A. Santayana.
Next Day. Jarrell.
Now or Never. Astra.
Ode on Celestial Music. Patten.
Phillis's Age. Prior.
Professor Waking, The. Tate.
Rondel for Middle Age. Nicholl.
Stella's Birthday. Swift.
Thirty-Eight. Smith.
To His Love in Middle Age. Brock.

Middle Ages
Middle Ages, The. Haines.
Ode to the Medieval Poets. Auden.

Middlesex, England
Middlesex. Betjeman.
Pax Paganica. Guiney.
Slough. Betjeman.
Twickenham Garden. Donne.

Midgets
Lie Easy in Your Secret Cradle. *Fr.* Wildtrack. Wain.

Midnight
Beneath yon ruined abbey's moss-grown piles. *Fr.* The Pleasures of Melancholy. Warton.
Midnight. Mistral.
Midnight. *Fr.* The Mirror for Magistrates. Sackville.
No Time for Poetry. Fields.

Midsummer
Midsummer Night. Edey.
Song for Midsummer Night. Coatsworth.

Mignonettes
Pitcher of Mignonette, A. Bunner.
Red Geranium and Godly Mignonette. Lawrence.

Migrant Workers
Pastures of Plenty. Guthrie.
Picking Grapes in an Abandoned Vineyard. Levis.
Plane Wreck at Los Gatos. Guthrie.
See also **Farmworkers.**

Migration
Migration. Lane.
To a Waterfowl. Bryant.
Wild Geese. Peterson.

Milan, Italy
Duomo, Milan. *Fr.* View of the Cathedral. Henri.

Militarism
Armaments Race. Paterson.
Cavalier's Song, The. Motherwell.
Channel Firing. Hardy.
Chilean Elegies, The: 5. The Interior. Wayman.
Drum, The. Scott of Amwell.
Mrs Snatcher Thatcher. *Fr.* Jezebel: Her Progress. Hanscombe.
On the Frequent Review of the Troops. "M."
There's Nothing Polite about a Tank. Minarik.
Us. Ignatow.
When the Great Gray Ships Come In. Carryl.

Military Justice
Danny Deever. Kipling.

Military Life. *See* **Army Life.**

Milk and Milking
Breakfast Song, The. Poulsson.
If you wish to live for ever. *Unknown.*
Milke before wine, I would 'twere mine. *Unknown.*
Milking Time. Roberts.
Milkmaid. Lee.

Milkmaids
Blackberry Fold. *Unknown.*
Buxom Young Dairy Maid, The. *Unknown.*
Kitty of Coleraine. Shanly.
To Milk in the Valley Below. *Unknown.*

Milkmen
Milkman, The. Krows.
Milkman, The. "O'Sullivan."

Milkweed
Milkweed. Levine.
Milkweed. Wright.
Open. Bruchac.
To the Milkweed. Mifflin.
Two Voices in a Meadow. Wilbur.

Milky Way, The
Two Coyotes, The. Marietta.

Mill, John Stuart
John Stuart Mill. *Fr.* Clerihews. Bentley.

Millennium
Birthing: 2000. Aguila.
Dawning, The. Vaughan.
End, The. Owen.
Epitaph Ending in And, The. Stafford.
Second Coming, The. Yeats.

Miller, Glenn
Glenn Miller's music is a trunk. Valle.

Miller, Henry
Henry Miller: A Writer. Lem.

Millet, Jean François
Angelus, The. Coates.
Man with the Hoe, The. Markham.

Mills and Millers
Dishonest Miller, The. *Unknown.*
Lesson of the Water-Mill, The. Doudney.
Mill, The. Robinson.
Mill, The. Wilbur.
Mill at Romesdal. Hugo.
Miller, The. Clerk.
Miller, The. Cunningham.
Miller, The. *Unknown.*
Miller and His Sons, The. *Unknown.*
Miller of Dee, The. *Unknown.*
Old Mill, The. English.
Song: "There was a jolly miller once." *Fr.* Love in a Village. Bickerstaffe.
Unfortunate Miller, The. Coppard.
Water Mill, The. Doudney.

Milton, John
Adventurous Muse, The. Watts.
And Did Those Feet in Ancient Time. *Fr.* Milton. Blake.
Extempore to Voltaire Criticising Milton. Young.
How Soon Hath Time. Milton.
Johannes Milton, Senex. Bridges.
Lines Printed under the Engraved Portrait of Milton. Dryden.
London, 1802. Wordsworth.
Milton. Longfellow.
Milton. Mifflin.
Milton. Ray.
Milton by Firelight. Snyder.
Milton's Prayer for Patience. Howell.
Milton's Wife on Her Twenty-third Birthday. Conant-Bissell.
On Mr. Milton's Paradise Lost. Marvell.
On Seeing a Lock of Milton's Hair. Keats.
Poet and the Butcher, The. Whetham.
To Milton. Wilde.
To the Ghost of John Milton. Sandburg.

Milwaukee, Wisconsin
Walking Milwaukee. Witt.

Mind. *See* **Intellect.**

Minerals
Crystals like Blood. "MacDiarmid."
Minerals of Cornwall, Stones of Cornwall. Redgrove.
See also **Metals; Mining and Miners.**

Minerva
To Minerva. Hood.
See also **Athena.**

Mining and Miners
Air Shaft. *Fr.* Poems from the Coalfields. Healy.
Avondale Mine Disaster, The. *Unknown.*
Ballad of a Mine, A. Skelton.
Ballad of Springhill (The Springhill Mine Disaster). MacColl *and* Seeger.
Blackleg Miners, The. *Unknown.*
Burning Mountain. Merwin.
Caliban in the Coal Mines. Untermeyer.
Casey Jones ("Come all you muckers and gather here"). *Unknown.*
Childhood. Brooks.
Christ in the Clay-pit. Clemo.
Coal-Owner and the Pitman's Wife, The. *Unknown.*

Collier, The. Watkins.
Cousin Jack Song. Tregonning.
Curse on the Mine-Owners, The. *Unknown.*
Donibristle Moss Moran Disaster, The. *Unknown.*
Down In a Coal Mine. Geoghegan.
Dreary Black Hills, The. *Unknown.*
Drill Man Blues. Sizemore.
Drilling Missed Holes. Cameron.
Durham Lock-out, The. *Unknown.*
Dynamite Song. *Unknown.*
Explosion, The. Larkin.
For Laurence Jones. Kizer.
Hard-Working Miner, The. *Unknown.*
Hill above the Mine, The. Cowley.
I tell him how it used to be in Paguate. *Fr.* After the Pow-Wow. Littlebird.
I'm Only a Broken-Down Miner. *Unknown.*
In a Night. Savage.
Lament While Descending a Shaft. *Unknown.*
Ludlow Massacre, The. Guthrie.
Miner, The. King.
Miner Boy, The. *Unknown.*
Mineral Point. Dana.
Miners. Wright.
Miner's Lifeguard. *Unknown.*
Mourning Letter, March 29 1963. Dorn.
1913 Massacre, The. Guthrie.
Oh, Give Me the Hills. *Unknown.*
Old Bing, The. Green.
Only a Miner. *Unknown.*
Photo of Miners, A. Galvin.
Photos of a Salt Mine. Page.
Plodder Seam, The. *Unknown.*
Prospecting. Ammons.
Prospecting Dream. *Unknown.*
Ramon. Harte.
78 Miners in Mannington, West Virginia. Phillips.
Song of the Leadville Mine Boss. Cameron.
Strip Mining Pit. Gillespie.
Tramp Miner's Song. *Unknown.*
White Dust, The. Gibson.
See also **Coal Mining and Miners; Gold Mining and Miners.**

Ministers. *See* **Clergy.**

Minnesota
Blessing, A. Wright.
By a Lake in Minnesota. Wright.
California, This Is Minnesota Speaking. Dunn.
Cut. Feela.
Driving toward the Lac Qui Parle River. Bly.
Ice. Ai.
Ice-Fishing House, The: Long Lake, Minnesota. Harper.
Late Lights in Minnesota. Kooser.
Lying in a Hammock at William Duffy's Farm in Pine Island, Minnesota. Wright.
Minneapolis Poem, The. Wright.
Minnesota Camp Grounds. Vizenor.
Minnesota Thanksgiving. Berryman.
Pine Point, You Are. Henry.
Seeing in the Dark. Brennan.
Working near Lake Traverse. Hennen.

Minotaur
Minotaur. Fisher.

Minstrels
Deor's Lament. *Unknown.*
Minstrel, The. Goethe.
Minstrel Boy, The. Moore.
Minstrel's Song. *Fr.* Aella. Chatterton.
Widsith, the Minstrel. *Fr.* Widsith. *Unknown.*

Miracles
Cana. Merton.
Getting Inside the Miracle. Shaw.
Jesus Himself. Burton.
Leave the Miracle to Him. Allan.
Miracles. Aiken.
Miracles. Whitman.
On the Miracle of Loaves. Crashaw.
Religion. Vaughan.
Why I Am Offended by Miracles. Bergman.

Mirages
Into My Heart an Air That Kills. *Fr.* A Shropshire Lad. Housman.
Mirage. *Fr.* Sea Island Miscellany. Blackmur.

Miranda, Carmen.
Carmen Miranda. Polite.

Miró, Joan
Joan Miró ("After that war, when death had gone away"). Todd.
Joan Miró ("Once there were peasant pots and a dry brown hare"). Todd.

Mirrors
Beware: Do Not Read This Poem. Reed.
Furniture: humble, dependent. *Fr.* Habitat. Wright.
Image in a Mirror. Goodman.
In a Glass-Window for Inconstancy. Herbert of Cherbury.
Lady Who Offers Her Looking-Glass to Venus, The. Prior.
Lais now old, that erst attempting lass. Plato.
Lais to Aphrodite. Robinson.
Looking-Glass, A. Carew.
Looking Glass, The. Kipling.
Man and His Image, The. La Fontaine.
Mirror. Chimako.
Mirror. Plath.
Mirror Images. Speer.
Mirrors, The. Andresen.
Mirrors, no one yet has really described. *Fr.* Sonnets to Orpheus. Rilke.
Moments of Vision. Hardy.
Nell Gwynne's Looking-Glass. Blanchard.
On His Mistress Looking in a Glass. Carew.
Results of a Scientific Survey. Cutler.
Shadows in the Water. Traherne.
To a Lady Sitting before Her Glass. Fenton.
Written on a Looking-Glass. *Unknown.*

Mirth
Cyriack, Whose Grandsire. Milton.
Hock-Cart, or Harvest Home, The. Herrick.
L'Allegro. Milton.
Lyric to Mirth, A. Herrick.
To Live Merrily, and To Trust to Good Verses. Herrick.
See also **Laughter.**

Misanthropy
Complete Misanthropist, The. Bishop.
Eagle and the Mole, The. Wylie.
Satire against Mankind, A. Rochester.
Wishes of an Elderly Man, The. Ralegh.

Miscarriages
Vow, The. Hecht.

Misfortune
Hymn to Adversity. Gray.
Ode on the Pleasure Arising from Vicissitude. Gray.
Shrubbery, The. Cowper.
Then hate me when thou wilt; if ever, now. *Fr.* Sonnets. Shakespeare.

Mishima, Yukio
Mysterious East. Cole.

Misogyny
Custer ("You, Custer, you hated"). Baker.
Gentle Echo on Woman, A. Swift.
Love a Woman. Rochester.
Misogynist. Conniff.
Misogynist, The. Morgan.
Tho' You May Boast You're Fairer. *Unknown.*
Upon Some Women. Herrick.
Warning, A. Patmore.
Worst Horror, The. Euripides.

Missionaries
Cry for Light, A. *Unknown.*
From Greenland's Icy Mountains. Heber.
Let Me Go Back. Albright.
Magalu. Johnson.
Martyrdom of Brébeuf and Lalemant, 16 March 1649, The. *Fr.* Brébeuf and His Brethren. Pratt.
Missionary Visits Our Church in Scranton, The. Parini.
Path of the Padres, The. Osborne.
Père Lalement. Pickthall.
Two Families. Bell.
Two Souls. Pickthall.
Wake, Isles of the South. Tappan.
Your Mission. Gates.

Mississippi
Best Dance Hall in Iuka, Mississippi, The. Johnson.
Birthday Poem. Young.
Church Burning; Mississippi. Emanuel.
Delta Farmer in a Wet Summer. Whitehead.
Jackson, Mississippi. Walker.
Janitor, The; Kindergarten, Corinth. *Fr.* Tatoos. Wright.
Mississippi Born. Lomax.
Night, Death, Mississippi. Hayden.

Ocean Springs Missippy. *Fr.* The Song Turning Back on Itself. Young.
Pachuta, Mississippi / A Memoir. Young.
Song Turning Back into Itself 3, The. Young.
Troubador. Simmons.

Mississippi River
Brown River, Smile. Toomer.
Down the Mississippi. Fletcher.
Down the Yellowstone, the Milk, the White and the Cheyenne. *Fr.* The River. Lorentz.
River, The. *Fr.* The Bridge. Crane.
Steamboat Bill. *Unknown.*

Missouri
Childhood. Justice.
Early June. Dickey.
Feral Pioneers. Reed.
Jogging at Dusk. Grossbardt.
Last Look at La Plata, Missouri. Barnes.
Meet Me in St. Louis, Louis. Sterling.
Missouri Town. Palen.
Porpoise, The. Pape.
Riverfront, St. Louis. Knoepfle.
Staying Up on Jack's Fork near Eminence, Missouri. Salisch.
Stockton Lake; Stockton, Missouri. Sanders.
When I Was Conceived. Ryan.

Missouri, River
Foreclosure. Brown.
Missouri Traveller Writes Home, A: 1830. Bly.

Mist
Kythans. McGavin.
Mist. Man.
Mist. Thoreau.
Mist. Young.
Mist and All, The. Willson.
See also **Fog.**

Mistletoe
Mistletoe. De la Mare.
Mistletoe Bough, The. Bayly.
Under the Mistletoe. Cullen.

Mitchell, Martha
Artificial Death, II. James.

Mites
Interlude. Shapiro.

Mithridates the Great
Mithridates. Emerson.

Mittens
Modern Hiawatha, The. Strong.
See also **Gloves.**

Mnemonics
Faber Book of Useful Verse, The (FaBoUs). Simon Brett, ed.

Mobile Bay, Battle of
Bay Fight, The. Brownell.
Craven. Newbolt.
Farragut. Meredith.
Through Fire in Mobile Bay. Unknown.

Mockingbirds
Bird at Night. Hamilton.
Bird-witted. Moore.
Fable of the Talented Mockingbird. Bates.
Lament of a Mocking-Bird. Kemble.
Listen to the Mockingbird. Winner.
Look at Six Eggs. *Fr.* Cornhuskers. Sandburg.
Mocking-Bird, The. Clarke.
Mockingbird, The. Jarrell.
Mocking Bird, The. Lanier.
Mocking-Bird, The. Stanton.
Mocking-Bird, The. Stockard.
Mocking-Bird, The. *Fr.* Out of the Cradle Endlessly Rocking. Whitman.
Mockingbird in Winter. Kroll.
Moonlight Song of the Mockingbird. Hayne.
To the Mocking-Bird. Pike.
To the Mocking-Bird. Wilde.

Models
Ode to a Model. Nabokov.

Moderation
Counsel of Moderation, A. Thompson.

Modern Man
Christ I Wudint Know Normal if I Saw It When. Bissett.
Common Man, The. Smith.
Curtain Speech. Braude.
Dirge: "123 was the number he played but today the number came 321." Fearing.
Every Thing. Monro.
Flying Deeper into the Century. Di Cicco.
For Tony, Dougal, Mick, Bugs, Nick *et al.* Bathgate.
Glengormley. Mahon.
Good Life, A. Watson.
Impotence. Knight.
Life Cycle of Common Man. Nemerov.
Lost Parents. Ferlinghetti.
Make Love Not War. Nemerov.
Modern Architecture. Nathan.
Net and the Sword, The. LePan.
Psychology Today. Jerome.
Quiet Desperation. Simpson.
Season 'Tis, My Lovely Lambs, The. Cummings.
Unknown Citizen, The. Auden.
Wasp Sex Myth (One). Hollo.
Wasp Sex Myth (Two). Hollo.
We're OK. Fuertes.
Who's Who. Auden.

Mojave Desert
In the Mohave. Orr.

Moles
All But Blind. De la Mare.
Anarchist. Dugdale.
Back to Base. Joseph.
Blue Moles. Plath.
Dead Mole, A. Young.
Eagle and the Mole, The. Wylie.
Mole, The. Clare.
Mole, The. Daniells.
Mole, The. Haines.
Mole and the Eagle, The. Hale.
Moles. Stafford.
Star-Nosed Mole, The. Wallace.
Unfortunate Mole, The. Kennedy.

Mona Lisa
At the Louvre. Mayo.
Mona Lisa. Dowden.
Mona Lisa. Pater.

Monaghan. *See* **County Monaghan, Ireland.**

Monasteries
Abbey Asaroe. Allingham.
Decayed Monastery, A. Dermody.
December. Snyder.
Lament for the Priory of Walsingham, A. *Unknown.*
Semblables, The. Williams.
Stanzas from the Grande Chartreuse. Arnold.
Trappist Abbey, The: Matins. Merton.
See also **Monks.**

Monday
Monday morning back to school. McCord.
On a Monday Morning. Tawney.

Monet, Claude
Monet: "Les Nymphéas." Snodgrass.
Monet Refuses the Operation. Mueller.

Money
Am I Thy Gold? *Fr.* Preparatory Meditation, First Series. Taylor.
America. Dumas.
American Primitive. Smith.
As I Sat at the Café. Clough.
Avarice. Herbert.
Basic. Durem.
Behaviour of Money. Spencer.
Christmas Bills. Hatton.
Complaint of Chaucer to His Purse, The. Chaucer.
Dialogue. Nemerov.
Fatigue. Belloc.
Gold. Hood.
Hardship of Accounting, The. Frost.
Her "Allowance"! Gard.
How Five and Twenty Shillings Were Expended in a Week. *Unknown.*
How the Money Rolls In. *Unknown.*
Investor's Soliloquy. Ward.
Jolly Shilling, The. *Unknown.*
Lines on the Back of a Confederate Note. Jonas.
London Lickpenny. Lydgate.
Lyrick for Legacies. Herrick.
Marriage and Money. *Fr.* The Happy Pair. Sedley.
Money. Armour.
Money. Davies.
Money. Nemerov.
Money. Sisson.
Money and a Friend. *Unknown.*

Money Cry, The. Davison.
Money Gets the Mastery. Herrick.
Money Is King. *Unknown.*
Money Is What Matters. *Unknown.*
Money Isn't Everything! Hammerstein.
Money Makes the Mirth. Herrick.
Money! Money! Yoruba.
Montefiore. Bierce.
Munition Wages. Bedford.
My God, How the Money Rolls In. *Unknown.*
My Purse. *Unknown.*
Of a Rich Miser. Turberville.
Of Money. Googe.
Open Letter-Poem-Note to Vincent van G., An. Bernadine.
Parley with His Empty Purse, A. Randolph.
Reckoning, The. Roethke.
Render unto Caesar. Humphries.
Singe we alle and say we thus. *Unknown.*
Song for an Allegorical Play. Ciardi.
Spectator ab Extra. Clough.
Terrible People, The. Nash.
To Their Excellencies the Lords Justices of Ireland, the Humble Petition of Frances Harris, Who Must Starve and Die a Maid If It Miscarries. Swift.
Words, the Words, the Words, The. Williams.
Worry about Money. Raine.
Your Money and Mine. *Unknown.*

Mongolia
For the Cultural Campaign. Jigmed.

Mongolism. *See* **Down's Syndrome.**

Mongooses
Mon-Goos, The. *Fr.* Child's Natural History. Herford.

Monitor (ship)
Cruise of the *Monitor,* The. Boker.
Utilitarian View of the *Monitor's* Fight, A. Melville.

Monk, Thelonious
Two Handfuls of *Waka* for Thelonious Sphere Monk (d. Feb. 1982). Lew.

Monkeys
Ape, the Monkey and Baboon Did Meet, The. *Unknown.*
At Woodward's Gardens. Frost.
Monkeys. Colum.
Monkeys, The. Moore.
Monkeys, The. Thompson.
Monkeys and the Crocodiles, The. Richards.
Monkeys on Mt. Hiei. Shiffert.
Ship of Rio, The. De la Mare.
So Many Monkeys. Edey *and* Grider.
Sonnet on a Monkey, A. Fleming.
Three Monkeys. *Unknown.*
Three Wise Monkeys, The. Davis.

Monks
Bees and Monks. *Fr.* King Arthur and His Round Table. Frere.
Carthusians. Dowson.
Elegy for the Monastery Barn. Merton.
Monasteries. Webb.
Monk and His Pet Cat, The. *Unknown.*
Monk of Casal-Maggiore, The. Longfellow.
Monks. Newman.
Monks at Ards, The. Maybin.
Pangur Ban. *Unknown.*
Pilgrimage. Clarke.
Practical Program for Monks, A. Merton.
Soliloquy of the Spanish Cloister. Browning.
Weak Monk, The. Smith.
See also **Clergy; Monasteries.**

Monmouth, James Scott, Duke of
Advice to the Painter. Prior.
Ballad Called Perkin's Figary, A. *Unknown.*
Dutchess of Monmouth's Lamentation for the Loss of Her Duke, The. *Unknown.*
England's Darling, or, Great Britain's Joy and Hope on That Noble Prince James, Duke of Monmouth. *Unknown.*
Hue and Cry after Blood and Murder, A. *Unknown.*
In pious times, ere priestcraft did begin. *Fr.* Absalom and Achitophel. Dryden.
On the University of Cambridge's Burning the Duke of Monmouth's Picture. Stepney.
Western Rebel, The. *Unknown.*

Monmouth, Battle of (1778)
Battle of Monmouth, The. English.
Battle of Monmouth, The. "R.H."
Molly Pitcher. Richards.

Monroe, Marilyn
Death of Marilyn Monroe, The.

Monsters
Attack of the Crab Monsters. Raab.
Chimera, The. Mombert.
Father and Mother. Kennedy.
Kraken, The. Tennyson.
Scylla and Charybdis. *Fr.* The Odyssey. Homer.
Amazing Monsters (AmMo). Robert Fisher, ed.

Mont Blanc
Hymn before Sunrise, in the Vale of Chamouni. Coleridge.
Mont Blanc. Shelley.

Montana
Armstrong Spring Creek. Davis.
Autobiography, Chapter XII: Hearing Montana. Barnes.
Degrees of Gray in Philipsburg. Hugo.
Elegy to the Sioux. Dubie.
Fishing the Big Hole. Holbrook.
Harlem, Montana: Just off the Reservation. Welch.
In Montana. McCormick.
Lady in Kicking Horse Reservoir, The. Hugo.
Looking at Power. Woessner.
Map of Montana in Italy, A. Hugo.
Montana Eclogue. Stafford.
Montana Pastoral. Cunningham.
Montana Wives. Haste.
Mount Caribou at Night. Wright.
Night at the Napi in Browning, A. Hugo.
Nymphing through Car Windows (East Gallatin). Keeler.
Rosebud. Anderson.
Snapshot of Uig in Montana, A. Hugo.
Turtle Lake. Hugo.
With Kathy at Wisdom. Hugo.

Monterrey, Mexico
Monterey. Hoffman.

Montgomery, Richard
Montgomery at Quebec. Scollard.

Months
Days of the Month, The. Mother Goose.
Four Sweet Months, The. Herrick.
Fourth, eleventh, ninth, and sixth. *Unknown.*
Garden Year, The. Coleridge.
Inst., Ult., and Prox. Herbert.
January brings the snow. Mother Goose.
Labours of the Months. *Unknown.*
Marjorie's Almanac. Aldrich.
Mask of Mutability, The. *Fr.* The Faerie Queene. Spenser.
Months, The. Coleridge.
Months, The. Rossetti.
Months, The. *Unknown.*
September. Jackson.
Thirty days hath November. Grafton.
Thirty Days Hath September. *Unknown.*
'Tis Merry in Greenwood. Scott.

Montreal, Quebec
Bonne Entente. Scott.
Calamity. Scott.
Montreal. Klein.
O God! O Montreal! Butler.
When I'm Going Well. Everson.
Psalm of Montreal, A. Butler.

Montrose, James Graham, 5th Earl and 1st Marquess of
Execution of Montrose, The. Aytoun.

Monuments
Cenotaph, The. Mew.
Cenotaph, The. Roberts.
Church-Monuments. Herbert.
Concord Hymn. Emerson.
For the Union Dead. Lowell.
Inscription for Marye's Heights, Fredericksburg. Melville.
Lines Written on a Seat on the Grand Canal, Dublin. Kavanagh.
Old Bing, The. Green.
Pro Patria. Carrier.
Tenth Armistice Day, The. Ford.
Washington Monument by Night. Sandburg.

Moon
Above the Dock. Hulme.
Academic Moon. Bevington.
Alfonso Churchill. *Fr.* Spoon River Anthology. Masters.
All Other Love Is Like the Moon. *Unknown.*
Another Full Moon. Fainlight.
Apollo 8. Berryman.

April Fool. Hunt.
As when the moon hath comforted the night. *Fr.* The Conspiracy of Charles, Duke of Byron. Chapman.
Aesthetics of the Moon. Anderson.
Auctioneer. Sandburg.
Aware. Lawrence.
Ballad of Downal Baun, The. Colum.
Ballad of Luna, Luna. García Lorca.
Because the Three Moirai Have Become the Three Maries, of Faith, Hope, and Charity. Urdang.
Cat and the Moon, The. Yeats.
Charming the Moon. DenBoer.
Chase, The. Davies.
Clair de Lune. Symons.
Crazed Moon, The. Yeats.
Creation of the Moon, The. *Unknown.*
Crescent Moon. Roberts.
Crescent Moon, The. *Unknown.*
Cynthia. Benlowes.
Dearest Man-in-the-Moon. Jong.
Death of the Moon, The. Wagoner.
Edith Sitwell Assumes the Role of Luna. Francis.
Evening. Aldington.
Farewell to the Moon, A. Ochester.
Flight of Apollo, The. Kunitz.
Flying. Westrup.
Freedom of the Moon, The. Frost.
Full Moon. De la Mare.
Full Moon. Fletcher.
Full Moon. Hayden.
Full Moon. Kinnell.
Full Moon. Wylie.
Full Moon in Malta. Asphodel.
Full Moon; Santa Barbara. Teasdale.
Giving the Moon a New Chance. Stokes.
Glow and beauty of the stars, The. Sappho.
Golden Bird, The. Ingamells.
Golden Moonrise. Braithwaite.
Graham Bell and the Photophone. Montgomery.
Haiku: "Halo of the moon, The." Buson.
Half Moon. García Lorca.
Half Moon Shows a Face of Plaintive Sweetness, The. Rosetti.
Harvest Moon, The. Longfellow.
Heaven's Queene. Ralegh.
Helen in Egypt. Doolittle.
Horseman, The. De la Mare.
How Old's the Moon? *Unknown.*
How to Reach the Moon. Pomerantz.
Hunger Moon. Cooper.
Hymn to Diana. *Fr.* Cynthia's Revels. Jonson.
I Gazed Upon the Cloudness Moon. Brontë.
I Have Cared for You, Moon. Conkling.
I watched the moon around the house. Dickinson.
Images. Campbell.
In a Moonlit Hermit's Cabin. Ginsberg.
In Dispraise of the Moon. Coleridge.
Injured Moon, The. Baudelaire.
Is the Moon Tired? Rossetti.
It Was the Lovely Moon. Freeman.
July Dawn. Bogan.
La Fuite de la Lune. Wilde.
Lady Moon. Milnes.
Lady Moon. Rossetti.
Landing on the Moon. Swenson.
Languishing Moon, The. Sidney.
Last Quarter. Hollander.
Look Down Fair Moon. Whitman.
Lost Playmate, The. Brown.
Lunar Baedeker. Loy.
Lunar Eclipse. Scarbrough.
Lunar Paraphase. Stevens.
Lunar Probe, The. Kumin.
Lunar Tides, The. Zaturenska.
Lune Concrete. Federman.
Madam's Song. Wylie.
Man in the Moon, The. Riley.
Man in the Moon, The. *Unknown.*
Man in the moon came down too soon, The. *Unknown.*
Man in the moon was caught in a trap, The. *Unknown.*
Match with the Moon, A. Rossetti.
Milk-White Moon, Put the Cows to Sleep. Sandburg.
Mr. Moon. Carman.
Moon, The. Creeley.
Moon, The. Davies.
Moon, The. Follen.
Moon. Horovitz.
Moon, The. Ryuho.
Moon and the Yew Tree, The. Plath.
Moon Compasses. Frost.
Moon Eclipse Exorcism. *Unknown.*
Moon Ground, The. Dickey.
Moon in the Water, The. Ryota.
Moon Is a Diamond, The. Sze.
Moon Landing. Auden.
Moon like a flower, The. *Fr.* Songs of Innocence. Blake.
Moon-Madness. Starbuck.
Moon-Man. Hewett.
Moon Man. Valentine.
Moon Poem. Sharp.
Moon Rises, The. García Lorca.
Moon Rock. Mally.
Moon Shadow. Bowering.
Moon Sings, The. *Unknown.*
Moon, So Round and Yellow. Barr.
Moon, Son of Heaven. Kenji.
Moon Song, Woman Song. Sexton.
Moon was but a chin of gold, The. Dickinson.
Moon-Witches. Hughes.
Moonlight. Apollinaire.
Moonlight. De la Mare.
Moonlight. Harjo.
Moonlight. Longfellow.
Moonlight. Moxon.
Moonlight. *Fr.* The Merchant of Venice. Shakespeare.
Moonlight. Verlaine.
Moonlight in Autumn. *Fr.* The Seasons: Autumn. Thomson.
Moonlight on Lake Sydenham. MacDonald.
Moonrise. Hopkins.
Moonrise. Lawrence.
Moonrise. Sherman.
Moon's Ending. Teasdale.
Moon's Orchestra, The. Fletcher.
Moon's the North Wind's Cooky, The. Lindsay.
Moonset. Newbolt.
Moonshot. Kelly.
Moontan. Strand.
Morning Song. Teasdale.
New Moon. *Fr.* The Moon-Bone Cycle. Aborigine.
New Moon, The. Blunden.
New Moon, The. Issa.
New Moon. Lawrence.
New Moon, The. Teasdale.
Niagara. Crapsey.
Night Light. Willard.
Night Song. Cornford.
Night-Walker, The. Gregory.
Nine Bean-Rows on the Moon. Purdy.
O Lady Moon. Rossetti.
Of the Moon. Best.
On Aesthetics, More or Less. Dufault.
On the Eclipse of the Moon of October 1865. Turner.
On the Telescopic Moon. Drennan.
Once Only. Snyder.
One-eyed Bridegroom, The. Urdang.
One Night. Sutherland.
Only a Little Litter. Livingston.
Orbed Maiden. Shelley.
Pan and Luna. Browning.
Partial Eclipse. Snodgrass.
Phases of the Moon. *Fr.* One Word More. Browning.
Poetic Thought. *Unknown.*
Prayer by Moonlight. Swartz.
Prayer to the Young Moon. *Unknown.*
Promontory Moon. Kinnell.
Proposition. Guillén.
Re-Birth. *Unknown.*
Riddle #29: The Moon and the Sun. *Unknown.*
Sadness of the Moon, The. Baudelaire.
Setting of the Moon, The. Leopardi.
Shepherd's Praise of Diana, The. Ralegh.
Shooting at the Moon. Kim Yo-sōp.
Silver. De la Mare.
Simples. Joyce.
Sing a Song of Moonlight. Eastwick.

Singing on the Moon. Hughes.
Song: "Make this night loveable." Auden.
Song for Ishtar. Levertov.
Song of the Moon, A. McKay.
Sonnet of the Moon, A. Best.
Strange Kind (II). Reed.
Sun and Moon. Macpherson.
Sun of the Sleepless! Byron.
Talking to the Moon. Harjo.
This Lunar Beauty. Auden.
Thoughts on the Sight of the Moon. Knight.
To a Solitary Disciple. Williams.
To an Old Lady. Empson.
To Etesia Looking from Her Casement at the Full Moon. Vaughan.
To Night. *Unknown.*
To the Afternoon Moon, at Sea. Rice.
To the Moon. Darley.
To the Moon. Goethe.
To the Moon. Hardy.
To the Moon. *Fr.* Fragments. Shelley.
To the Moon. Smith.
To the Moon. Winters.
To the Moon and Back. Plomer.
To the Moon, 1969. Deutsch.
Tonight the City. Cook.
Turn of the Moon. Graves.
Upon Moon. Herrick.
Vacuum. Miles.
Voyage to the Moon. Dickey.
Voyage to the Moon. MacLeish.
Waning Moon, The. *Fr.* Fragments. Shelley.
Washed in Silver. Stephens.
Wavering planet most stable, The. *Unknown.*
Welcome to the Moon. *Unknown.*
What Semiramis Said. Lindsay.
When Two Suns Do Appear. Sidney.
White Window, The. Stephens.
Who Doth Not See the Measure of the Moon? Davies.
Who Knows If the Moon's. Cummings.
Wind and Silver. Lowell.
Wind and the Moon, The. MacDonald.
Window Frames the Moon, The. Mar.
Winter Moon. Hughes.
With How Sad Steps, O Moon, Thou Climb'st the Skies. *Fr.* Astrophel and Stella. Sidney.
Year Passes, A. Lowell.
You Made It Rain. Saunders.
Young May Moon, The. Moore.
Your soul is a sealed garden, and there go. Verlaine.
Moonstruck; an Anthology of Lunar Poetry (MOON). Robert Phillips, ed.

Moonflowers
To the Moonflower. Betts.

Moonshiners
Kentucky Bootlegger. *Unknown.*
Moonshiner. *Unknown.*
Mountain Dew. *Unknown.*
Real Old Mountain Dew. *Unknown.*

Moore, Henry
On a Celtic Mask by Henry Moore. Gregory.
"Reclining Figure." Hall.
"Twiner," A. Lindon.
Warrior with Shield. Browne.

Moore, Sir John
Burial of Sir John Moore after Corunna, The. Wolfe.

Moore, Marianne
Invitation to Miss Marianne Moore. Bishop.
Marianne Moore (1887–1972). Roseliep.

Moore, Thomas
On Thomas Moore's Poems. *Unknown.*
Recollections of "Lalla Rookh." Trowbridge.
To Thomas Moore. Byron.
Will you come to the bower I have shaded for you? *Fr.* A Reply to Lines by Thomas Moore. Landor.

Moors (people)
War Song of the Saracens, The. *Fr.* Hassan. Flecker.

Moors (geography)
Barren Moors, The. Channing.
Gloucester Moors. Moody.
Ilkla Moor. *Unknown.*
Night on the Downland. Masefield.
On Westwall Downes. Strode.
Rannoch Moor. MacGregor.

Moose
Bull Moose, The. Nowlan.
Moose. Wiljer.

More, Sir Thomas (Saint Thomas More)
Case of Thomas More, The. St. Virginia.

Moreau, Gustave
From Sappho's Death: Three Pictures by Gustave Moreau. Moore.

Morgan, Sir Henry
Morgan. Stedman.

Morgan, John Hunt
Kentucky Belle. Woolson.

Morison, Sir Henry
To the Immortall Memorie, and Friendship of That Noble Paire, Sir Lucius Cary, and Sir H. Morison. Jonson.

Mormons
Brigham Young. *Unknown.*
Desert Gulls. Gillespie.
Fire and Ice. Pettit.
Marching to Utah. *Unknown.*
Mormon Bishop's Lament, The. *Unknown.*
Mormon Immigrant Song, A. *At. to* Hicks.
Nauvoo. Taylor.

Morning
And Love Hung Still. MacNeice.
Aubade: Lake Erie. Merton.
Aubade after the Party. O'Grady.
Awake, Mine Eyes! *Unknown.*
Awaking. Spender.
Ballad of the Morning Streets. Baraka.
Barefoot Days. Field.
Break of Day. Donne.
Call of the Morning, The. Darley.
Calm Morning at Sea. Teasdale.
Cock. Amir.
Cocoa Morning. Kaufman.
Composed upon Westminster Bridge, Sept. 3, 1802. Wordsworth.
Courtier's Good-Morrow to His Mistress, The. *Unknown.*
Dawn. Rimbaud.
Dawn Walk. Hirsch.
Description of the Morning, A. Swift.
Dew. Maiden.
Early. Bennett.
Early Morn. Davies.
Early Morning, The. Belloc.
Early Morning Meadow Song. Dalmon.
Early Rising. Saxe.
Evening and Morning in June, An. *Fr.* Prologues to the Aeneid. Douglas.
Evening and Morning in Winter, An. *Fr.* Prologues to the Aeneid. Douglas.
Frosty Morning, A. *Fr.* The Task. Cowper.
Frosty Morning, A. Davidson.
Full many a glorious morning have I seen. *Fr.* Sonnets. Shakespeare.
Gascoigne's Good-Morrow. Gascoigne.
Get Up. Levine.
Good Morrow. *Fr.* The Rape of Lucrece. Heywood.
Hail, Fair Morning. *Unknown.*
Hark! Hark! the Lark. *Fr.* Cymbeline. Shakespeare.
Hymn: "Framer of the Earth and Sky." Ambrose.
Impression du Matin. Wilde.
In the naked bed, in Plato's cave. Schwartz.
Is It the Morning? Is It the Little Morning? Schwartz.
January Morning, A. Lampman.
January Morning. Williams.
June Morning. McCrae.
Lauds. Auden.
Love Calls Us to the Things of This World. Wilbur.
Matinal. McQueen.
Matins. Levertov.
Mattens. Herbert.
May All Earth Be Clothed in Light. Hitchcock.
Morning. Blake.
Morning. Cunningham.
Morning. Davenant.
Morning. Dickinson.
Morning. Fainlight.
Morning. Gallagher.
Morning. George.
Morning. Keble.
Morning. Taylor.
Morning and Evening. Slonimski.
Morning at the Window. Eliot.

Morning comes to consciousness, The. *Fr.* Preludes. Eliot.
Morning Fog. Duval.
Morning Hymn. Keble.
Morning Hymn, A. Ken.
Morning Kiss, A. Jones.
Morning Light, The. Simpson.
'Morning, Morning. Mathew.
Morning on the Shore. Campbell.
Morning Poem. Beenen.
Morning Prayer. Nash.
Morning Serenade. Cawein.
Morning Song. *Fr.* Senlin, a Biography. Aiken.
Morning Song. DeClue.
Morning Song. Dugan.
Morning Song. Orr.
Morning Sun. MacNeice.
Morning-Watch, The. Vaughan.
Morning Work. Lawrence.
9:00. Hooper.
No Time for Poetry. Fields.
Now, before Shaving. Kramer.
On the Bright Side. Revard.
Pack, Clouds, Away. *Fr.* The Rape of Lucrece. Heywood.
Poem about Morning. Meredith.
Prayer for Dreadful Morning. Root.
Reveille. *Fr.* A Shropshire Lad. Housman.
Right as the star of day began to shine. *Fr.* The Golden Targe. Dunbar.
Satyr's Song. *Fr.* The Faithful Shepherdess. Fletcher.
Sister, Awake! *Unknown.*
Softly, Drowsily. De la Mare.
Song: "Lark now leaves his wat'ry nest, The." Davenant.
Song: "Phœbus arise." Drummond of Hawthornden.
Song: "Rise Lady Mistresse, rise." *Fr.* Amends for Ladies. Field.
Song Form. Baraka.
Sonnet XIII: "Rise up, rise up, Jack Spratt. And you, his wife." Scott.
Summer Morning, A. Field.
Summer Morning. *Fr.* The Seasons: Summer. Thomson.
Summer Morning, A. Wilbur.
Sun Rising, The. Donne.
Sunday. Rutsala.
Sunday Morning. MacNeice.
Sung on a Sunny Morning. Untermeyer.
To Morning. Blake.
Tropical Morning at Sea, A. Sill.
Turning. Finch.
Twenty-two Minutes. Martinez.
Upon Phillis Walking in a Morning before Sun-Rising. Cleveland.
Very Early. Kuskin.
Vigil. Knoll.
Waking Early. Barth.
Waking from Sleep. Bly.
Waking Time. Eastwick.
Wayside Station, The. Muir.
Welcome Morning. Sexton.
What Do I Care for Morning. Johnson.
Will there really be a morning? Dickinson.
Year's at the spring, The. *Fr.* Pippa Passes. Browning.

Morning-Glories
Morning-Glory, The. Coates.

Morocco
Marrakech. Currey.

Morris, William
Rondel: "Behold the works of William Morris." *Unknown.*

Morrison, Norman
Norman Morrison. Mitchell.

Mortality
All the Flowers of the Spring. *Fr.* The Devil's Law-Case. Webster.
April Mortality. Adams.
Because I could not stop for death. Dickinson.
Black Faced Sheep, The. Hall.
Chestnut Casts His Flambeaux, The. Housman.
Clay. Lucas.
Cloud Chamber, The. Sze.
Dead Fly. Ní Chuilleanáin.
Death the Consequence of the Fall. *Fr.* The State of Innocence. Dryden.
Death's Final Conquest. *Fr.* The Contention of Ajax and Ulysses. Shirley.
Epitaph of Graunde Amoure, The. *Fr.* The Pastime of Pleasure. Hawes.
Fear no more the heat o' the sun. *Fr.* Cymbeline. Shakespeare.
Fire in My Meditation Burned. Ainsworth.
His Poetrie His Pillar. Herrick.
Hos Ego Versiculos. Quarles.
In Plague Time. *Fr.* Summer's Last Will and Testament. Nashe.
Life and Death. *Fr.* The Christians Reply to the Philosopher. Davenant.
Life of Man, The. Barnes.
Little Sleep's-Head Sprouting Hair in the Moonlight. Kinnell.
Lord, thou hast been our dwelling place. *Fr.* Psalms XC. Bible, *O.T.*
Man That Lives, The. *Unknown.*
Man's Life. Hammond.
Man's Mortality. *Fr.* Microbiblion. Wastell.
Meditation of a Mariner. Auchterlonie.
Memento for Mortalitie, A. *At. to* Beaumont, *also to* Basse.
Mimnermus in Church. Cory.
My Midnight Meditation. King.
Oh, Why Should the Spirit of Mortal Be Proud? Knox.
Omnia Somnia. Sylvester.
On a Child Who Lived One Minute. Kennedy.
On a Similar Occasion for the Year 1790. Cowper.
On a Similar Occasion for the Year 1792. Cowper.
On the Vanity of Man's Life. *Unknown.*
People. Yevtushenko.
Piazza Piece. Ransom.
Picture of Little T. C. in a Prospect of Flowers, The. Marvell.
Quickness. Vaughan.
Respice Finem. Proctor.
Rueful Lamentation on the Death of Queen Elizabeth, A. More.
Shortness and Misery of Life, The. Watts.
Sic Vita. King.
So, pure and dutiful, she sought that place. *Fr.* Mahabharata. *Unknown.*
Song XI: "Lay your sleeping head, my love." Auden.
Song of Dust, A. De Tabley.
Stanzas Subjoined to the Yearly Bill of Mortality of the Parish of All Saints, Northampton; for the Year 1787. Cowper.
Submission to Afflictive Providences. Watts.
Sunlight on the Garden, The. MacNeice.
Tetélestai. Aiken.
To Evan. Eberhart.
To L. B. S. Scott.
Verses of Mans Mortalitie, with an Other of the Hope of His Resurrection. *Unknown.*
Virtue. Herbert.
Vitae Summa Brevis Spem Nos Vetat Incohare Longam. Dowson.
What's the Life of a Man? *Unknown.*
Winter Term. Brinnin.
World a Hunt, The. Drummond of Hawthornden.

Morticians. *See* **Undertakers.**

Morton, Sir Albertus
Tears at the Grave of Sir Albertus Morton. Herbert.

Mosby, John Singleton
Mosby at Hamilton. Cawein.

Moses
Angels Came a-Mustering, The. *Unknown.*
Burial of Moses, The. Alexander.
Burning Bush, The. Nicholson.
Death of Moses, The. *Unknown.*
Deuteronomy. Bringhurst.
Go Down, Moses. *Unknown.*
Little Moses. *Unknown.*
Moses' Account. Fuest.
Moses and Jesus. Zangwill.
Moses and Joshua. Lasker-Schüler.
Moses on Mount Nebo. Regelson.
Murder of Moses, The. Shapiro.
Oh, Mary Don't You Weep. *Unknown.*
Pharao's Daughter. Moran.
Soliloquy of One of the Spies Left in the Wilderness, A. Hopkins.

Mosquitoes
Baja. Stern.
Mosquito, The. Jones.
Mosquito, The. Lawrence.
Mosquito. Updike.

Moss
Moss. Willard.
Moss-gathering. Roethke.

Motels
In the Motel. Kennedy.
Leaving the Motel. Piercy.
Soliloquy in a Motel. Gibson.
See also **Hotels.**

Mothers
Ad Matrem. Fane.
Adversary, The. McGinley.
Affliction of Margaret, The. Wordsworth.
Apples. Kaufman.

Are All the Children In? *Unknown.*
Arrival of My Mother, The. Wilson.
At My Mother's Bedside. Masters.
At My Mother's Knee. *Unknown.*
Autumn. Untermeyer.
Awful Mother, The. Griffin.
Bad Mother, The. Griffin.
Baking Day. Joseph.
Because. McAuley.
Belief. Miles.
Big Momma. Madhubuti.
Boy's Mother, A. Riley.
Bravest Battle, The. Miller.
Breaking Silence. Mirikitani.
Buckdancer's Choice. Dickey.
C. L. M. Masefield.
Carpenter's Wife, The. *Unknown.*
Certain True Woords Spoken Concerning One Benet Corbett After Her Death. Corbett.
Child Bearers, The. Sexton.
Confession to Settle a Curse. Waldrop.
Cradle Song: "Sleep, my child, my little daughter." *Unknown.*
Cruel Mother, The. *Unknown.*
Disquieting Muses, The. Plath.
Distress. Griffin.
Division of Parts, The. Sexton.
Dream Girl. Snow.
Each Bird Walking. Gallagher.
Emma. Yvonne.
External Element, The. McFadden.
First Love. Dorcey.
First Love. Hemschemeyer.
For an Obligate Parasite. Dugan.
For My Mother. Glück.
For My Mother: Genevieve Jules Creeley. Creeley.
From an Asylum; Kathy Chattle to Her Mother, Ruth Arbeiter. Stevenson.
From the House of Yemanjá. Lorde.
Generation Gap. Wallace.
Getting Down to Get Over. Jordan.
Gift, The. Darr.
Gift, The. *Unknown.*
Gladioli For My Mother. Bernstein.
God's Ideal Mother. Pinkham.
Goodbye. Kinnell.
Hand That Rocks the Cradle Is the Hand That Rules the World, The. Wallace.
Her Eyes Don't Shine Like Diamonds. Marion.
Her Words. Branch.
Home Burial. Frost.
Horse Show, The. Williams.
Housecleaner, The. White.
How's My Boy? Dobell.
Human Geography. Whitman.
I Should Be Ashamed. Uvlunuaq.
I Used to Watch You, Sleeping. *Fr.* My Mother's Birthday. Raine.
I Was the Child. Warren.
In Memory of My Mother. Kavanagh.
Interior. Colum.
International Motherhood Assoc. Hester.
Intruder, The. Kizer.
Jessie Mitchell's Mother. Brooks.
Kaddish. Ignatow.
Kineo Mountain. Wright.
Kitchen Memory, A. Scheele.
Kitchen Song. Dobbs.
Lacking Sense, The. Hardy.
Late Mother, The. Macdonald.
Let Me Go. Gond.
Let's Talk, Mother. Bruck.
Lines on Receiving His Mother's Picture. Cowper.
Lonely Mother, The. Johnson.
Lost Children, The. Jarrell.
Mama and Daughter. Hughes.
Mamma Sings. Hoffenstein.
Mary Complains to Other Mothers. *Unknown.*
Men Tell and Talk. Francisco.
Metamorphoses. Fuller.
Morning Song. Plath.
Mother. Dempster.
Mother. Dow.
Mother. Fyleman.
Mother, The. Gardons.
Mother. Helburn.
Mother. Kelleher.
Mother. Montoya.
Mother. Kiyoko.
Mother, The. Palmer.
Mother. Vincent.
Mother. Widdemer.
Mother and Poet. Browning.
Mother and Son. Heyen.
Mother and Son. Tate.
Mother, Home, Heaven. Brown.
Mother, I Am. Clifton.
Mother Is a Sun, A. Bennett.
Mother o' Mine. Kipling.
Mother of Ten. Strong.
Mother of the Groom. Heaney.
Mother of the House, The. *Fr.* Proverbs. Bible, *O.T.*
Mother-Prayer. Widdemer.
Mother to Son. Hughes.
Mothers. Giovanni.
Mothers. Sexton.
Mothers and Children. Johns.
Mothers—and Others. Wells.
Mothers, Daughters. Kaufman.
Mother's Habits. Giovanni.
Mother's Love. Clapp.
Mother's Nerves. Kennedy.
Mother's Sacrifice, The. Sigourney.
Mother's Song, The. *Unknown.*
Must Be the Season of the Witch. Alurista.
My Mother. Burr.
My Mother. Ledwidge.
My Mother. Taylor.
My Mother. *Unknown.*
My Mother on an Evening in Late Summer. Strand.
My Mother Pieced Quilts. Acosta.
My Mother Takes a Bath. Kageyama.
My Mother Would Be a Falconress. Duncan.
My Mother's Death. Hemschemeyer.
My Mother's Feet. Plumly.
My Mother's Garden. Allen.
My Mother's Hand. *Unknown.*
My Mother's House. Tietjens.
My Mother's Love. *Unknown.*
My Mother's Prayer. O'Kane.
My Nightingale. Ausländer.
My Trundle Bed. Baker.
My Young Mother. Cooper.
Nancy Hanks, Mother of Abraham Lincoln. Lindsay.
New Mothers, The. Shields.
Night and Morning. Aldis.
Night Feeding. Rukeyser.
90th Year, The. Levertov.
Nobody Knows but Mother. Morrison.
Now It Is Broccoli. Tagami.
October. Goren.
Oedipus at San Francisco. Finkel.
Old Arm Chair, The. Cook.
Old Ladies. Dromgoole.
Old Mother Hubbard. *Unknown.*
Olga Poems. Levertov.
On Mother's Day. Fisher.
On the Receipt of My Mother's Picture out of Norfolk. Cowper.
One Who Struggles, The. Toller.
Only One Mother. Cooper.
Pavane for the Passing of a Child. Chester.
Perfect Mother, The. Griffin.
Physical for My Son. Smith.
Picture memory brings to me, A. *Fr.* My Trust. Whittier.
Poem: "I meet Mother on the street." Bruce.
Poem for My Mother. Fox.
Poem for My Mother. Jaeger.
Poem of the Mother. Sklarew.
Poems. Gildner.
Portrait, A. Ashby-Sterry.
Portrait of My Mother on Her Wedding Day. Gilbert.
Queen of the World. *Unknown.*
Question, The. Rukeyser.
Reading Mother, The. Gillilan.
Recollection. Govan.
Recuerdo. Millay.

Reflections. Barrows.
Reunion. Herzberg.
Revelation. Gregory.
Revenge Fable. Hughes.
Reverie of a Mum. Keesing.
Rock Me to Sleep. Allen.
Ruth. McElroy.
She Didn't Even Wave. Ai.
She'd Say. Davey.
Sick Child, The. Stevenson.
Sitting. Griffin.
Somebody's Mother. Brine.
Song for My Mother, A—Her Words. Branch.
Song of Hannah, The. *Fr.* First Samuel. Bible, *O.T.*
Song of the Old Mother, The. Yeats.
Songs My Mother Taught Me. Wagoner.
Sonnet to My Mother. Barker.
Sonnet to My Mother, A. Heine.
Stabat Mater. Hunt.
Stark Country Holidays. Oliver.
Strength and honour are her clothing. *Fr.* Proverbs. Bible, *O.T.*
Teeth. Griffin.
There was an old woman who lived in a shoe. Mother Goose.
Thoughts upon a Walk with Natalie, My Niece, at Houghton Farm. Pulsifer.
Threnody. Ignatow.
Tissue. Griffin.
To My Mother. Brock.
To My Mother. Ginsberg.
To My Mother. Poe.
To My Mother. Rosenberg.
To the Anxious Mother. Malangatana.
To the Mothers. Toller.
To Whom Shall They Go? *Unknown.*
Upon a Young Mother of Many Children. Herrick.
Vacation Trip. Stafford.
Violets for Mother. Kaneko.
Visit. Outlaw.
Wastrel, The. Kauffman.
Way It Is, The. Oden.
What a Friend We Have in Mother. Roat.
When a Girl Looks Down. Smith.
When Mother Reads Aloud. *Unknown.*
Which Loved Best? "Allison."
Whipping, The. Hayden.
Women Hoping for Rain. Tillinghast.
Words from a Bottle. Lee.
Your Mother. Cornish.

Mother's Day
Beautiful Hands. Gates.
Dear Old Mothers. Ross.
Greatest Battle That Ever Was Fought, The. Miller.
Hand That Rocks the Cradle Is the Hand That Rules the World, The. Wallace.
I loved her, one. *Fr.* The Princess. Tennyson.
Identity. Helen.
Love's Tribute. Sturgeon.
Mother. Taylor.
Mother. *Unknown.*
Mother—A Portrait. Fuller.
Mother Love. Alford.
Motherhood. Chworowsky.
Motherhood. Stidger.
Mothers. *Unknown.*
Mother's Name, A. *Unknown.*
Mothers of Men, The. Miller.
My Mother. Nolan.
My Mother. Taylor.
O, Mothers of the Human Race. Whitaker.
Rock Me to Sleep. Allen.
Shrine, The. Dolben.
Wondrous Motherhood. *Unknown.*

Mothers-in-Law
His Mother-in-Law. Parke.
Man Arrested in Hacking Death Tells Police He Mistook Mother-in-Law for Raccoon. Ludvigson.
Mothers-in-Law. Sward.
Prince Robert. *Unknown.*
Unexpected Pleasure, An. *Unknown.*
Unrecorded Speech. Adams.

Moths
Book-Moth. *Fr.* Riddles (Exeter Book). *Unknown.*
Death's-Head Moth. Green.
Getting Older Here. Hauk.
Great Moth, The. Gittings.
Green Moth. Welles.
Lying Awake. Snodgrass.
Moth, The. De la Mare.
Moth-Song. Cortissoz.
Moth-Terror. De Casseres.
Near Dusk. Auslander.
Night Moths, The. Markham.
To a Moth. Thomas.
Tyranny of Moths. Vizenor.
Under the Sign of Moth. Wagoner.
Warning, The. Crapsey.

Motion Pictures
About Motion Pictures. Darr.
Adam, Eve and the Big Apple. Watkins.
At a Private Showing in 1982. Kumin.
At the Movies. Mastin.
Aunt Gladys's Home Movie No. 31, Albert's Funeral. Miller.
Ave Maria. O'Hara.
Bijou. Rutsala.
Buster Keaton. McFee.
Curse of the Cat Woman. Field.
Cut. Feela.
Day with the Foreign Legion, A. Whittemore.
Dear John Wayne. Erdich.
Documentary. Stroud.
Double Feature. Roethke.
Essay in Defense of the Movies. Gibson.
Film, A. Goldbarth.
Frankenstein. Field.
Grace at the Atlanta Fox. Cassity.
Horror Movie. Moss.
If Life's a Lousy Picture, Why Not Leave Before the End. McGough.
Ingmar Bergman's "Seventh Seal." Duncan.
Movie-Going. Hollander.
Movies, The. Gilbert.
Movies for the Home. Moss.
Newsreel. Day Lewis.
Old Movies. Cotton.
Star & Garter Theater. Schmitz.
This world/ is amazingly flat. Gorbanyevskaya.
To the Film Industry in Crisis. O'Hara.
Triple Feature. Levertov.
Vamp Passes, The. Montague.
War Film, A. Hooley.
Western Movies. Jensen.
Where Are You Now Superman? Patten.
While Cecil Snores: Mom Drinks Cold Milk. Cunnigham.
Why I Like Movies. Jones.

Motley, John Lothrop
In Memory of John Lothrop Motley. Bryant.

Motor Boats
Riding In a Motor Boat. Baruch.

Motorcycles and Motorcycling
For Jack Chatham. Carter.
Motorcycle. Pray.
Motorcycle Irene. Spence.
On the Move. Gunn.
Poems of My Lambretta. Goodman.
Unsettled Motorcyclist's Vision of His Death, The. Gunn.
What the Motorcycle Said. Van Duyn.

Mount Saint Helens, Washington
Loo-Wit. Rose.

Mt. Tamalpais
Circumambulation of Mt. Tamalpais. Hoyem.

Mount Vernon, Virginia
Monument and the Shrine, The. Logan.
Mount Vernon, the Home of Washington. Day.

Mountain Beavers
Looking For Mountain Beavers. Wagoner.

Mountain Climbing
Alpine. Thomas.
Climb in Torridon. Macrow.
Climber Surveys His Mountain, The. Ouston.
Climbing in Glencoe. Young.
Climbing Rope, The. Stuart.
Climbing Zero Gully. Morley.
David. Birney.
De Gustibus. Hankin.
Descending. Iremonger.

Doing the Dubhs. *Unknown.*
Finding a Poem. Merriam.
Flower Herding on Mount Monadnock. Kinnell.
Here in Katmandu. Justice.
Hiking Up Hieizan with Alan Lau/Buddha's Birthday 1974. Hongo.
How Small Is Man. Blackie.
In Memoriam. Gingell.
Last Defile, The. Carmichael.
Last of the Grand Old Masters, The. Patey.
Llanberis Summer. Loyd.
Lost Leader, The. Fraser.
Magna. Dutton.
Marriage on a Mountain Ridge. Conn.
Mountain Creed. Rae.
Mountain Days. Fraser.
Mountaineering Bus. McOwan.
O Aa the Manly Sports. Annand.
On Falling. *Fr.* Men on Ice. Greig.
On Looking at an Old Climbing Photograph. Fraser.
On Scafell Pike. Walker.
One Thousand Feet of Shadow. Craig.
Pitch Seven. Brown.
Rock Leader. Bathgate.
Scottish Mountaineering Club Song, The. Stott.
Spring Mountain Climb. Eberhart.
Story, A. Stafford.
Three Girls on a Buttress. Nisbet.
What Called Me to the Heights? Pilkington.
Wingwalking in Oregon. Peterson.
Mountain Lions
Mountain Lion. Lawrence.
Mountain Men
Mountain Liars. Hafen.
Mountains. *See* **Hills and Mountains**
Mourning
Bustle in a house, The. Dickinson.
Elegy for My Father. Moss.
Kaddish. Ginsberg.
Minyan, The. Myers.
Mourn for Yourself. Keating.
Mourning Pablo Neruda. Bly.
Mourning-Song for Rangiaho, A. Herea.
No longer mourn for me when I am dead. Sonnets, LXXI. Shakespeare.
Ode: "Tell me, thou soul of her I love." Thomson.
Thou Lingering Star. Burns.
To the Memory of a Lady. Lyttelton.
Wake of William Orr, The. Drennan.
Yahrzeit. Jaffe.
See also **Funerals; Grief.**
Mouths
Her Mouth. Aldington.
Movies. *See* **Motion Pictures.**
Moving and Movers.
Almost Grown. Ai.
Getting Loaded. Thomas.
Going Away. Nemerov.
In a U-Haul North of Damascus. Bottoms.
Moving. Jarrell.
Moving. Matthews.
Moving. McFatter.
Moving Day. Horne.
Moving In. Engle.
Moving In. Miles.
Moving in Winter. Rich.
Moving Out. Oates.
October 1. Shapiro.
Photograph of Haymaker, 1890. Holden.
Removal from Terry Street, A. Dunn.
Mowing and Mowers
Damon the Mower. Marvell.
Hay-Time; or, The Constant Lovers. A Pastoral. Relph.
Haymaking. Thomas.
Lawn-Mower. Baruch.
Lost. Brand.
Lying in the Grass. Gosse.
Morning-Piece, A; or, An Hymn for the Hay-Makers. Smart.
Mower, The. *Unknown.*
Mower, Against Gardens, The. Marvell.
Mower to the Glowworms, The. Marvell.
Mower's Song, The. Marvell.
Mowing. Frost.
Mowing, The. Roberts.
Needs. Ammons.
Old Field Mowed, An. Meredith.
Old Man with a Mowing Maching. Lord.
Reapers. Toomer.
Scythe Song. Lang.
Tuft of Flowers, The. Frost.
Mozart, Wolfgang Amadeus
Corner Knot, The. Graves.
Mozart. Glatstein.
Mozart, 1935. Stevens.
Mozart's Grave. Mowrer.
Mud
Mud. Boyden.
Muddy Puddle, The. Lee.
Muffins
Aunt Nerissa's Muffin. Irwin.
Muffs
On an Old Muff. Locker-Lampson.
See also **Gloves; Mittens.**
Muhammad Reza Shah Pahlevi
"Banquet of the Century" in Persepolis, The. Hashmi.
Mulberry Trees
Tapestry Trees. Morris.
Mules
Cincerinella Had a Mule. *Unknown.*
Driving the Mule. *Unknown.*
Erie Canal, The. *Unknown.*
Ever Since. Coatsworth.
Kicking Mule, The. *Unknown.*
Mule, The. Barks.
Mule-Train. Sellers.
Mules. Fox-Smith.
Mules. Muldoon.
Mules. Walker.
My Sweetie's a Mule in the Mine. *Unknown.*
Old Balaam. *Unknown.*
Poem to a Mule, Dead Twenty Years. Owen.
Timber (Jerry the Mule). *Unknown.*
Mummies
Address to a Mummy. Smith.
For an Egyptian Boy, Died c. 700 B. C. Baron.
Grauballe Man, The. Heaney.
In the Museum. Gardner.
Punishment. Heaney.
Tollund Man, The. Heaney.
Wanting a Mummy. McPherson.
Mumps
Mumps. Roberts.
Munch, Edvard
Kiss, The. Smith.
Munch's Scream. Hall.
Murasaki Shikibu
For Murasaki. Jacobsen.
Murder and Murderers
After the Murder of Jimmy Walsh. Murray.
Ashland Tragedy, The. Adams.
Assassination. Lee.
Babylon; or, the Bonnie Banks o' Fordie. *Unknown.*
Bad Luck Blues. *Unknown.*
Bad Man Ballad. *Unknown.*
Ballad of a Barber, The. Beardsley.
Ballad of Reading Gaol, The. Wilde.
Ballad of William Bloat, The. *Unknown.*
Bermondsey Tragedy, The. *Unknown.*
Billy Lyons and Stack O'Lee. *Unknown.*
Binnorie. *Unknown.*
Blood Hound Blues. *Unknown.*
Bonny Earl of Murray, The. *Unknown.*
Brockton Murder, The; a Page out of William James. Skinner.
Check to Song. Meredith.
Cheerful Chilterns, The. Sidgwick.
Clerk Saunders. *Unknown.*
Colonel Sharp. *Unknown.*
Constance Kent. *Unknown.*
Constant Farmer's Son, The. *Unknown.*
Coroner's Fury. Strong.
Crime Club. Kees.
Cruel Mother, The. *Unknown.*
Death of Samuel Adams, The. *Unknown.*
Deep Water. *Unknown.*
Delia Holmes. Ruff.
Did Ya Hear? Jamal.

Down in the Willow Garden. *Unknown.*
Edward. *Unknown.*
Ella Speed. *Unknown.*
Ellen Flannery. *Unknown.*
Eulogy for a Tough Guy. Klauck.
Farewell: "Farewell to barn and stack and tree." *Fr.* A Shropshire Lad. Housman.
Florella; or, the Jealous Lover. *Unknown.*
For Andy Goodman—Michael Schwerner—and James Chaney. Walker.
For the One Who Would Take Man's Life in His Hands. Schwartz.
Fragment from the Elizabethans. Bridges-Adams.
Frankie and Johnny. *Unknown.*
Fuller and Warren. Whitecotton.
Go Down You Murderers. MacColl.
Gosport Tragedy, The. *Unknown.*
Hannah Dustin. Coxe.
He Fell Among Thieves. Newbolt.
Hitchhiker, The. Ai.
Homage to Marian Pyszko. Snyder.
How to Change the U. S. A. Edwards.
Hugh of Lincoln. *Unknown.*
I Should Be Ashamed. Uvlunuaq.
If Justice Moved. Sellers.
Indictment, The. Ayer.
Inquest, The. Davies.
It is the cause, it is the cause, my soul. *Fr.* Othello. Shakespeare.
John Adkins' Farewell. *Unknown.*
John Hardy. *Unknown.*
Johnson. *Unknown.*
Kid, The. Ai.
Knoxville Girl. *Unknown.*
Lady Isabella's Tragedy, The. *Unknown.*
Lambkin. *Unknown.*
Lexington Murder, The. *Unknown.*
Life of the Mannings. *Unknown.*
Lily of the West. *Unknown.*
Little Musgrave and Lady Barnard. *Unknown.*
Little Sir Hugh. *Unknown.*
Lizie Wan. *Unknown.*
Loose Woman. Kennedy.
Lord Randal. *Unknown.*
Lula Vires. *Unknown.*
Man Arrested in Hacking Death Tells Police He Mistook Mother-in-Law for Raccoon. Ludvigson.
Man He Killed, The. Hardy.
Mary in the Silvery Tide. *Unknown.*
Mary Wyatt and Henry Green. *Unknown.*
McAffee's Confession. *Unknown.*
McCaffery. *Unknown.*
Murder of Goins, The. *Unknown.*
Murder of Maria Marten, The. *Unknown.*
Murder Pact, The. *Fr.* Macbeth. Shakespeare.
Murdered Girl Is Found on a Bridge, The. Hayman.
Murderer, The. Petrie.
Murderers, The. *Fr.* Macbeth. Shakespeare.
Naomi Wise. *Unknown.*
On the Duke of Buckingham, Slain by Felton, the 23rd August, 1628. Felltham.
One to destroy, is murder by the law. Young.
Oxford Girl, The. *Unknown.*
Pearl Bryan. *Unknown.*
Peddler and His Wife, The. *Unknown.*
Poem for Jacqueline Hill. *Unknown.*
Poor Ellen Smith. *Unknown.*
Poor Omie. *Unknown.*
Porphyria's Lover. Browning.
Pretty Polly. *Unknown.*
Prince Robert. *Unknown.*
Revolutionary Petunias. Walker.
Robin and Gandelein. *Unknown.*
Robin Hood's Death. *Unknown.*
Rose Connoley. *Unknown.*
Sacrifice of a Virgin in the Mayan Ball Court. Dubie.
Sam Hall. *Unknown.*
Scenery. Joans.
Shooting, The. Tohe.
Silvery Tide, The. *Unknown.*
Sir Hugh; or, the Jew's Daughter. *Unknown.*
Sisters, The. Tennyson.
Southern Cop. Brown.
Stab, The. Harney.
Stagolee. *Unknown.*
.38, The. Joans.
To an Avenue Sport. Collins.
To the Spirit of Monahsetah. DeClue.
Tom Dooley. *Unknown.*
Two Sisters, The. *Unknown.*
Upon the Double Murther of King Charles I. Philips.
Wake of William Orr, The. Drennan.
Wexford Girl, The. *Unknown.*
Wild Bill Jones. *Unknown.*
Young Edwin in the Lowlands Low. *Unknown.*
Young Hunting. *Unknown.*

Murfreesboro, Battle of (1862–1863)
Battle of Murfreesboro, The. Cornwallis.

Muses
Admonition to the Muse. Taylor.
His Muse Speakes to Him. Habington.
I now solicit not the Muses nine. *Fr.* A Mock Invocation to Genius. Woty.
Muse, The. Davies.
Muse. Wagoner.
Muse in the New World, The. *Fr.* Song of the Exposition. Whitman.
Muse of Amergin. *Unknown.*
My Muse and I Ere Youth and Spirits Fled. Colman.
Ode to the Muse on Behalf of a Young Poet. Wagoner.
Saint Harmony my patroness. Goodman.
To the Contemporary Muse. Bowers.
To the Muses. Blake.

Museums
Antwerp: Musée des Beaux-Arts. Ross.
At the Museum of Modern Art. Swenson.
At the Natural History Museum. Meredith.
At the Smithsonian. Haley.
Cloisters, The. Yellen.
Floridian Museum of Art, A. Whittemore.
Historical Museum, Manitoulin Island. Mueller.
Homage to the British Museum. Empson.
In a Museum. Deutsch.
In Galleries. Jarrell.
In the Egyptian Museum. Lewis.
In the Local Museum. De la Mare.
In the Museum. Gardner.
More Nudes in Florence. Witt.
Municipal Gallery Revisited, The. Yeats.
Musée des Beaux Arts. Auden.
Museum of the Second Creation, The. McPherson.
Museum Piece. Wilbur.
Museum Piece No. 16228. Watson.
Museums. MacNeice.
National Gallery, The. MacNeice.
Night in the Royal Ontario Museum, A. Atwood.
Pitt-Rivers Museum, Oxford, The. Fenton.
Tutankhamen. Dickey.

Mushrooms
Autumn Mushrooms. Mackenzie.
Fairy Ring, The. Young.
Morels. Smith.
Mushroom Hunting in Late August, Peterborough, N.H. Blumenthal.
Mushroom is the elf of plants, The. Dickinson.
Mushrooms. Plath.
Toadstool Wood, The. Reeves.
Wild Mushroom, The. Snyder.

Music and Musicians
Abt Vogler. Browning.
Alexander's Feast: or, The Power of Music. Dryden.
An die Musik. Malouf.
Anthem for St. Cecilia's Day. Auden.
Apocalypse. Enright.
At a Bach Concert. Rich.
At a Solemn Music. Milton.
At the Band Concert. Brinnin.
At the Symphony. Nathan.
Bagpipe Music. MacNeice.
Bard. Bantock.
Barrel-Organ, The. Noyes.
Battle Report. Kaufman.
Blues Note. Kaufman.
Boy Playing an Organ. Sweeney.
Brahms, The. Morris.
Cadenza. Hughes.
Calyx of the Oboe Breaks, The. Aiken.
Cello, The. Gilder.
Choral Symphony Conductor. Coates.

Church-Musick. Herbert.
Corinna. Campion.
Daybreak in Alabama. Hughes.
Dead Musicians. Sassoon.
Dear John, Dear Coltrane. Harper.
"Duke" and the "Count," The. Fewell.
Entertainment Industry, The. *Fr.* The Vision of Piers Plowman. Langland.
Epitaph upon the Celebrated Claudy Philips, Musician, Who Died Very Poor, An. Johnson.
Evening Musicale. McGinley.
Fiddler of Dooney, The. Yeats.
For a Musician. *Fr.* Hallelujah. Wither.
For the spiritual musick is as follows. *Fr.* Jubilate Agno. Smart.
Four Friends. Ward.
Free Thoughts on Several Eminent Composers. Lamb.
Guide to the Symphony. Kees.
Guitar. Garcia Lorca.
Guitarist Tunes Up, The. Cornford.
Harlem Sounds: Hallelujah Corner. Browne.
Harper, The. *Unknown.*
Here Where Coltrane Is. Harper.
Hex on the Mexican X, A. McCord.
How High the Moon. Jeffers.
Hugging the Jukebox. Nye.
Hymn of Pan. Shelley.
I Was Fair Beat. Garioch.
In a Music-Hall. Davidson.
In Commendation of Music. Strode.
In Memory of Bryan Lathrop. Masters.
In Praise of Music in Time of Pestilence. Hine.
Instruments. Smart.
Jis' Knowin'. Nickens.
Johann Joachim Quantz's Five Lessons. Graham.
Juke Box Love Song. Hughes.
Lamda. Tolson.
Lament for the O'Neills. Montague.
Leit. Rodríguez Frese.
L'Envoi: "Now in a thought, now in a shadowed word." Robinson.
Lost Chord, A. Procter.
Lyre Player, The. George.
Make Music with Your Life. O'Meally.
Melchior Vulpius. Moore.
Military Harpist, The. Pitter.
Mr. Brunt. Siegel.
Monseigneur Plays. Garrison.
Music. Aiken.
Music. Ecclesiasticus. Bible, *O.T.*
Music. Dunbar-Nelson.
Music. Emerson.
Music. Farjeon.
Music. Fletcher.
Music. *Fr.* In Hospital. Henley.
Music. Herrick.
Music. Lowell.
Music. Nye.
Music. Thomas.
Music Alone Shall Live. *Unknown.*
Music in Camp. Thompson.
Music of the Future, The. Herford.
Musical Instrument, A. Browning.
Musician. Bogan.
Musician at His Work, The. Currie.
Musician Returning from a Cafe Audition, A. Minard.
Music's Duel. Crashaw.
New Music. Harwood.
Ninth Symphony of Beethoven Understood at Last as a Sexual Message, The. Rich.
Old Fisherman with Guitar. Brown.
Old Gramophone Records. Kirkup.
Old Tune, An. Lang.
On Hearing a Symphony of Beethoven. Millay.
On Hearing Mrs. Woodhouse Play the Harpsichord. Davies.
On Music. Landor.
On the Death of Phillips. *Unknown.*
Orchestra. Saner.
Orchestra, The. Williams.
Orpheus. Roberts.
Orpheus with his lute made trees. *Fr.* King Henry VIII. Fletcher.
Passions, The. Collins.
Percussions. Welburn.
Peter Quince at the Clavier. Stevens.
Piano, The. Davey.
Piano. Lawrence.
Piano after War. Brooks.
Piano and Drums. Okara.
Piano Practice. Moss.
Piano Recital. Deutsch.
Piper, A. "O'Sullivan".
Piping down the valleys wild. *Fr.* Songs of Innocence: Introduction. Blake.
Poem for the Conguero in D-Yard. Fernandez.
Portrait of Rudy, A. Olumo.
Rubinstein Staccato Etude, The. Dett.
Saxophonetyx. Zarco.
Selfsame Song, The. Hardy.
Seventy Six Trombones. *Fr.* The Music Man. Willson.
Singers to Come. Meynell.
Song for St. Cecilia's Day, 1687, A. Dryden.
Song of the Banjo, The. Kipling.
Sonnet: "My lute be as thou wast when thou didst grow." Drummond of Hawthornden.
Songs, The. Bell.
Sonnet: To Mr. H. Lawes, on His Aires. Milton.
Soul. Graham.
Spanish Johnny. Cather.
Spirits Unchained. Kgositsile.
Stanzas for Music ("There be none of Beauty's daughter's"). Byron.
Stark Country Holidays. Oliver.
Strings in the Earth. *Fr.* Chamber Music. Joyce.
Symphony. Dorn.
This Is Our Music. Leong.
Three Musicians, The. Beardsley.
To———: "Half in the dim light from the hall." Braithwaite.
To a Lad Who Would Wed Himself with Music. Doro.
To His Friend Master R. L., in Praise of Music and Poetry. Barnfield.
To Lucasta. Lovelace.
To Melody. Allen.
To Music: A Song. Herrick.
To Music Bent Is My Retired Mind. Campion.
To Music. Herrick.
To Sheila Playing Haydn. Lynd.
To the One of Fictive Music. Stevens.
Toccata of Galuppi's, A. Browning.
Unrelenting Flood. Matthews.
Victor Dog, The. Merrill.
Violinist, The. Lampman.
Vow. Updike.
We Dance Like Ella Riffs. Rodgers.
When de Saints Go Ma'chin' Home. Brown.
With a Guitar: To Jane. Shelley.
Untune the Sky (UnS). Helen Plotz, ed.

Music Festivals
Woodstock. Mitchell.

Music Halls
In a Music-Hall. Davidson.

Musk Oxen
Arctic Ox, The. Moore.
Long River, The. Hall.
Musk Oxen. Igjugarjuk.
See also **Ovibos.**

Muslims
Hush, Honey. Saunders.

Mussels
Nantucket / Mussels / October. Lewandowski.
There's Life in a Mussel; a Meditation. Farewell.

Mustaches
Mustacheless Bard, A. Coogler.

Mutiny
Captain, The. Tennyson.

Mysticism
In No Strange Land. Thompson.
Kabbalist, The. Eibel.
Mystic, The. Rice.
Mystic, The. Tennyson.
Mystic's Prayer, The. "Macleod."
In Love with Love (ILwL). Anne *and* Christopher Fremantle, eds.

Mythology
Earl of Mar's Daughter, The. *Unknown.*
Echo. *Fr.* Comus. Milton.
Europa. Walcott.
Hellenics, The. Landor.
Myths. Klauck.
Sabrina. *Fr.* Comus. Milton.

Story of Phoebus and Daphne Applyed, The. Waller.
Tithonus. Tennyson.

N

Nabakov, Vladimir
Poem for Vladimir. Ripley.
Nagasaki, Japan
Wedding Day at Nagasaki. Hall.
Names
Adam's Task. Hollander.
Ballade of Ladies' Names. Henley.
Boys' Names. Farjeon.
Changeling VIII. Gunnars.
Choosing a Name. Lamb.
Conversation with God. Hathaway.
Crow, Straight Flier, but Dark. Firestone.
Empty Dwelling Places. Patchen.
Geography: A Song. Moss.
Girls' Names. Farjeon.
How a Girl Got Her Chinese Name. Wong.
Ill Met by Zenith. Nash.
Indian Names. Sigourney.
It's in the Name. Tsui.
John Jacob Jingleheimer Schmidt. *Unknown.*
Lovely Rivers and Lakes of Maine, The. Wallis.
Makers, The. Nemerov.
Mary's a Grand Old Name. Cohan.
Mutual Problem. Cole.
My Baby Has No Name Yet. Kim Nam-jo.
My Name and I. Graves.
Name, The. Rumi.
Names. Aldis.
Names, The. Edmond.
Nomen. Madgett.
Round, The. Booth.
Sing a Song of the Cities. Bishop.
Song for My Name. Hogan.
There. Harmon.
There's a Man Goin' 'Round Takin' Names. *Unknown.*
Well-Intentioned Question, The. Rose.
When I Hear Your Name. Fuertes.
See also **Place Names.**
Namur, Belgium
English Ballad, on the Taking of Namur by the King of Great Britain, 1695, An. Prior.
Nantucket, Massachusetts
Limerick: "That Nantucket Limerick, and What Followed." *Unknown.*
Nantucket. Williams.
Nantucket Whalers. Henderson.
Phenomenal Survivals of Death in Nantucket. Glück.
Napier, Robert Cornelis, 1st Baron Napier of Magdala
Lost Colors, The. Ward.
Naples, Italy
Naples Again. Freeman.
Napoli Again. Hugo.
To Naples. Mallalieu.
Napoleon I
Advice to a Raven in Russia December, 1812. Barlow.
Boney. *Unknown.*
Bonny Bunch of Roses, The. *Unknown.*
Exile at Rest, The. Pierpont.
Funeral of Napoleon I. Hagarty.
Incident of the French Camp. Browning.
Lines Written on Hearing the News of the Death of Napoleon. Shelley.
March to Moscow, The. Southey.
Napoleon. *Fr.* Childe Harold's Pilgrimage. Byron.
Napoleon. De la Mare.
Napoleon and the British Sailor. Campbell.
October 1803. Wordsworth.
Return of Napoleon from St. Helena, The. Sigourney.
St. Helena Lullaby, A. Kipling.
Thought of a Briton on the Subjugation of Switzerland. Wordsworth.
Napoleon III
Napoleon after Sedan. Rimbaud.
Poster of Our Dazzling Victory at Saarbrucken, A. *Fr.* Eighteen-Seventy. Rimbaud.
Napoleonic Wars
Advice to a Raven in Russia. Barlow.
Banks of the Nile, The. *Unknown.*
Battle of the Baltic. Campbell.
Burial of Sir John Moore after Corunna, The. Wolfe.
Casablanca. Hemans.
Eve of Waterloo, The. *Fr.* The Dynasts. Hardy.
Fears in Solitude. Coleridge.
Fighting Téméraire, The. Newbolt.
Incident of the French Camp. Browning.
Johann Gaertner (1793–1887). Gildner.
November, 1806. Wordsworth.
Plains of Waterloo, The. *Unknown.*
Russia 1812. Hugo.
Sonnet: French and the Spanish Guerrillas, The. Wordsworth.
To the Men of Kent. Wordsworth.
Waterloo. *Fr.* Childe Harold's Pilgrimage. Byron.
Waterloo. De Vere.
Year 1812, The. Davie.
Narcissism
Laus Virginitatis. Symons.
Narcissus (mythology)
Farewell to Narcissus. Horan.
Fate of Narcissus, The. *Fr.* Albion's England. Warner.
Narcissus. Gullans.
Narcissus. Petersen.
Narcissus. Voléry.
Narcissus (flower)
Among the Narcissi. Plath.
Window Ledge in the Atom Age. White.
Narcotics. *See* **Drug Addiction.**
Naseby, Battle of (1645)
Battle of Naseby, The. Macaulay.
Nash, Richard (Beau Nash)
On Mr. Nash's Picture at Full Length. Brereton.
Nasturtiums
Big Nasturtiums, The. Hale.
Lines to a Nasturtium (A Lover Muses). Spencer.
Nation, Carry
That Little Hatchet. Butler-Andrews.
Nationalism
Nationalism. Roskolenko.
Nationality. Gilmore.
Nativity, The. *See* **Christmas.**
I Saw a Stable. Coleridge.
Naturalists
Death of a Naturalist. Heaney.
Naturalist's Summer-Evening Walk, The. White.
Week-End Naturalist, The. Buchan.
Nature
A B C's in Green. Speyer.
Alastor. Shelley.
All Nature Has a Voice to Tell. Lawson.
All That's Past. De la Mare.
All the Scenes of Nature Quicken. Smart.
Almighty Maker God! *Fr.* Sincere Praise. Watts.
Amends to Nature. Symons.
And what if all Nature ratify this merciless outrage? *Fr.* Epistle II: To a Socialist in London. Bridges.
Animal, Vegetable and Mineral. Bogan.
As an Old Mercer. Fisher.
Assynt. Gilchrist.
At the Trough. Gregor.
Attraction. Wilcox.
Beatus Vir. Le Gallienne.
Blue Horses. Roberson.
Bonac. Wheelock.
Book of the World, The. Drummond of Hawthornden.
Boyhood. *Fr.* The Prelude. Wordsworth.
Bring me the sunset in a cup. Dickinson.
Change and Immutability. Scroggie.
Chant Out of Doors, A. Wilkinson.
Charms of Nature, The. *Fr.* The Enthusiast. Warton.
Chorus Sacerdotum. Greville.
Christmas Day. Smart.
Comparison and Complaint, The. Watts.
Contemplations. Bradstreet.
Correspondences. Baudelaire.
Corsons Inlet. Ammons.
Cosmic Fabric, The. Polonsky.
Creative Force. Hadden.
Dauncing (bright Lady) then began to be. *Fr.* Orchestra or A Poeme of Dauncing. Davies.
Design. Frost.

Dry Loaf. Stevens.
Each and All. Emerson.
Enthusiast, The: or, The Lover of Nature. Warton.
Eternity of Nature, The. Clare.
Expostulation and Reply. Wordsworth.
Fall of Rome, The. Auden.
Father, thy hand/ Hath reared. *Fr.* A Forest Hymn. Bryant.
Field of Light, A. Roethke.
Foliage. Keble.
For I have lov'd the rural walk through lanes. *Fr.* The Sofa. Cowper.
For My Grandmother, Bridget Halpin. Hartnett.
Force That through the Green Fuse Drives the Flower, The. Thomas.
Friends. Brown.
Give Me the Splendid Silent Sun. Whitman.
Gladness of Nature, The. Bryant.
Glory of Nature, The. Tennyson.
God of the Granite and the Rose! *Fr.* Reconciliation. Doten.
God, through All and in You All. Longfellow.
God's Grandeur. Hopkins.
God's Virtue. Barnes.
God's World. Keeling.
God's World. Millay.
Gravelly Run. Ammons.
Great Nature Is an Army Gay. Gilder.
Green Inn, The. Garrison.
Green Symphony. Fletcher.
Grongar Hill. Dyer.
Groves of Blarney, The. Milliken.
Handiwork of God, The. *Unknown.*
Happy Swain, The. Philips.
Highland Loves. McOwan.
Holding the Mirror Up to Nature. Nemerov.
How to See Deer. Booth.
How was November's melancholy endear'd to me. *Fr.* The Testament of Beauty. Bridges.
Hymn on the Seasons, A. Thomson.
I taste a liquor never brewed. Dickinson.
In a Wood. Hardy.
In Ampezzo. Stickney.
In the Fields. Mew.
Introduction. *Fr.* The Testament of Beauty. Bridges.
Inward Morning, The. Thoreau.
Lessons of Nature, The. Drummond of Hawthornden.
Lines Composed a Few Miles above Tintern Abbey. Wordsworth.
Lines Written in Early Spring. Wordsworth.
Loving and Liking. Wordsworth.
Man in Harmony with Nature. Very.
Manuscripts of God, The. Longfellow.
Marban, a Hermit Speaks. *Unknown.*
Memories of a Dorset Childhood in the 1730's. *Fr.* The Life of Hubert. Cole.
Miracle, The. De la Mare.
Mont Blanc. Shelley.
Morning Hymn of Adam. *Fr.* Paradise Lost. Milton.
Mower against Gardens, The. Marvell.
Musketaquid. Emerson.
My Books I'd Fain Cast Off, I Cannot Read. Thoreau.
Nature. Longfellow.
Nature. Stone.
Nature. Thoreau.
Nature. Very.
Nature and the Poets. *Fr.* The Minstrel. Beattie.
Nature Be Damned. Wilkinson.
Nature in War-Time. Ford.
Nature Is. Prelutsky.
Nature one hour appears a thing unsexed. *Fr.* Contemplation. Thompson.
Nature's Charms. *Fr.* The Minstrel. Beattie.
Nature's Hymn to the Deity. Clare.
Nature's Lineaments. Graves.
Nature's Questioning. Hardy.
Nocturnal Reverie, A. Winchilsea.
O Wearisome Condition of Humanity. Greville.
Ode: Intimations of Immortality from Recollections of Early Childhood. Wordsworth.
Ode: "Spacious firmament on high, The." Addison.
Ode to the Spirit of Earth in Autumn. Meredith.
Old Love, The. Tynan.
On a Bank as I Sate a Fishing. Wotton.
On the Religion of Nature. Freneau.
On the Uniformity and Perfection of Nature. Freneau.
On thy stupendous summit, rock sublime! *Fr.* Beachy Head. Smith.
Oneness of the Philosopher with Nature, The. Chesterton.
Out in the Fields. *Unknown.*
Out-of-Doors. Whitaker.
Out of the Vast. Bamberger.
Over-Heart, The. Whittier.
Pastoral Hymn, A. Hall.
Patience Taught by Nature. Browning.
Pied Beauty. Hopkins.
Pippa's Song. *Fr.* Pippa Passes. Browning.
Pleasures of Imagination, The. Akenside.
Poets Love Nature. Clare.
Possession. *Unknown.*
Prayer, A: "O Earth, O dewy mother, breathe on us." Lampman.
Prayer, A: "Tend me my birds, and bring again." Gale.
Prelude: "Along the roadside, like the flowers of gold." *Fr.* Among the Hills. Whittier.
Prelude: "Still south I went and west and south again." Synge.
Prelude, The; or, Growth of a Poet's Mind, *abr.* Wordsworth.
Proem: "There is no rhyme that is half so sweet." Cawein.
Quiet Work. Arnold.
Rainy Summer, The. Meynell.
Reason for Not Writing Orthodox Nature Poetry. Wain.
Regeneration. Vaughan.
River has not any care, The. *Fr.* Contemplation. Thompson.
Rooftop, The. Gunn.
Rural Sights and Sounds. *Fr.* The Task. Cowper.
St. Philip and St. James. Smart.
Satire Against Mankind, A. Rochester.
Seasons, The. Thomson.
Second Wisdom. Robinson.
Sensitive Plant, The. Shelley.
Sky is low, the clouds are mean, The. Dickinson.
Sky's unresting cloudland, that with varying play, The. *Fr.* The Testament of Beauty. Bridges.
Small Song. Shaw.
Song of Nature. Emerson.
Song Tournement: New Style. Untermeyer.
Sonnet: "Is there a great green commonwealth of Thought." Masefield.
Spring Mountain Climb. Eberhart.
Summer Day, A. Hume.
Sweetness of Nature, The. *Unknown.*
Tables Turned, The. Wordsworth.
Teach me, Father, how to go. Markham.
Thanatopsis. Bryant.
That Nature Is a Heraclitean Fire and of the Comfort of the Resurrection. Hopkins.
Thirteenth Song. *Fr.* Polyolbion. Drayton.
This Is My Father's World. Babcock.
Thou Art, O God. Moore.
Three Kingdoms of Nature, The. Lessing.
To God, the Architect. Kemp.
To Mr. Henry Lawes. Philips.
To Mother Nature. Knowles.
To the River Isca. Vaughan.
'Twas at that hour of beauty when the setting sun. *Fr.* The Testament of Beauty. Bridges.
Vegetable Loves. *Fr.* The Botanic Garden. Darwin.
Vestigia. Carman.
Waking, The. Roethke.
Walking. Traherne.
Why, Lord. Van Doren.
Wilderness, The. Raine.
Wind in the Pine. Sarett.
Wish, that of the living whole, The. *Fr.* In Memoriam A. H. H. Tennyson.
Within the Circuit of This Plodding Life. Thoreau.
Wonderful World, The. Rands.
Wonders of the World. Shelton.
Word, The. Realf.
Work without Hope. Coleridge.
Written in Early Spring. Wordsworth.
Ye green-robed Dyrads, oft at dusky eve. *Fr.* The Enthusiast; or, The Lover of Nature. Warton.
Youth of a Poet, The. *Fr.* The Minstrel; or, The Progress of Genius. Beattie.
Book of Nature Poems, A (BoNaP). William Cole, comp.
Room for Me and a Mountain Lion (RFM). Nancy Larrick, ed.

Nautilus (shell)
Chambered Nautilus, The. *Fr.* The Autocrat of the Breakfast Table. Holmes.

Nauvoo, Illinois
Nauvoo. Taylor.

Navaho Indians
Dawn Boy's Song. *Unknown.*
Juanita, Wife of Manuelito. Ortiz.
Navajo, The. Coatsworth.
Song of the Navajo. Pike.
Naval Battles
Armada, The; a Fragment. Macaulay.
Battle of Actium. *Fr.* The Aeneid. Virgil.
Battle of the *Bonhomme Richard* and the *Serapis*. *Fr.* Song of Myself. Whitman.
Burnt Ship, A. Donne.
Casabianca. Hemans.
Constitution and *Guerriere,* The. *Unknown.*
Fourth Day's Battle, The. *Fr.* Annus Mirabilis. Dryden.
Nabara, The. Day Lewis.
Now van to van the foremost squadrons meet. *Fr.* Annus Mirabilis. Dryden.
Revenge, The. Tennyson.
Song, Written at Sea, in the First Dutch War, 1665, the Night before an Engagement. Sackville.
Utilitarian View of the *Monitor's* Fight, A. Melville.
Word's gone out, and now they spread the main, The. *Fr.* The Spanish Descent. Defoe.
Navarino, Battle of (1827)
Battle of Navarino, The. *Unknown.*
Glorious Victory of Navarino, The! *Unknown.*
Navels
Definition. Shakely.
Navy, France
Ballad for a Boy, A. Cory.
Hervé Riel. Browning.
Navy, Great Britain
Admirals All. Newbolt.
Ballad for a Boy, A. Cory.
Battle of Sole Bay, The. *Unknown.*
Battle of the Baltic, The. Campbell.
Captain, The. Tennyson.
Captain Death. *Unknown.*
Chief Petty Officer. Causley.
Essay on the Fleet Riding in the Downes, An. "J.D."
Famous Fight at Malago, or, The Englishmen's Victory over the Spaniards, The. *Unknown.*
Heart of Oak. Garrick.
Instructions to a Painter. Waller.
Joyful New Ballad, A. Deloney.
Midshipman, The. Falconer.
On the Loss of the *Royal George.* Cowper.
"Revenge," The. Tennyson.
Sailing at Dawn. Newbolt.
Second Advice to a Painter, The. Marvell.
"Soldier an' Sailor Too." Kipling.
Third Advice to a Painter, The. Marvell.
Victory. *Unknown.*
Ye Mariners of England. Campbell.
Navy, Netherlands
Famous Sea-Fight, A. Looke.
Navy, Spain
Famous Sea-Fight, A. Looke.
Navy, United States
Bay Fight, The. Brownell.
Blood Is Thicker than Water. Rice.
Cumberland, The. Longfellow.
Farragut. Meredith.
Fleet at Santiago, The. Russell.
How We Burned the *Philadelphia.* Eastman.
Homing, The. Rooney.
Men behind the Guns, The. Rooney.
Old Ironsides. Holmes.
River Fight, The. Brownell.
Running the Batteries. Melville.
Strong Swimmer, The. Benét.
When the Great Gray Ships Come In. Carryl.
Nazis
Dr. Joseph Goebbels. *Fr.* The Führer Bunker. Snodgrass.
"More Light! More Light!" Hecht.
Mother. Tuwim.
Peachtree, The. Levertov.
Poem Touching the Gestapo. Heyen.
Tailor, The. Garfinkel.
Years Later. Lerner.
Nebraska
Biography. Stanton.
Fort Robinson. Kooser.
Funeral at Ansley. Welch.
July Storm, A: Johnson, Nemaha County, Nebraska. Hahn.
Kinkaiders, The. *Unknown.*
Otoe County in Nebraska. Kloefkorn.
Pornography, Nebraska. McPherson.
Where I Walk in Nebraska. Westerfield.
Wild Pigs. Kooser.
Nebuchadnezzar
Dere's a Han'writin' on de Wall. *Unknown.*
Nebuchadnezzar. Wylie.
Warm Babies. Preston.
Nefertiti
Queen Nefertiti. *Unknown.*
Negro Spirituals
Negro Spiritual. Trott.
O Black and Unknown Bards. Johnson.
Negroes. *See* **Blacks.**
Neighbors
Body, The. Bronk.
Couple Overhead, The. Meredith.
Malediction. McGinley.
Mending Wall. Frost.
Neighbors. Evans.
Neighbors. "Lennox."
Neighbors. Spencer.
New Neighbor, The. Fyleman.
Portrait by a Neighbor. Millay.
Song, A: "Good neighbour, why do you look awry?" *Unknown.*
This and That. Davis.
Welcome. Waldo.
What Life Have You. *Fr.* The Rock. Eliot.
What Thou Lovest Well, Remains American. Hugo.
Winter Saint. Ammons.
Nelson, Horatio Nelson, Viscount
Admirals All. Newbolt.
Ballad of the Good Lord Nelson, A. Durrell.
Battle of the Baltic, The. Campbell.
Death of Nelson, The. *Unknown.*
1805. Graves.
England Expects? Seaman.
Grand Conversation on Brave Nelson. *Unknown.*
Nelson, Pitt, Fox. *Fr.* Patriotism. Scott.
Nelson's Death. *Unknown.*
New Song Composed on the Death of Lord Nelson, A. *Unknown.*
Trafalgar. Palgrave.
Nepal
Here in Katmandu. Justice.
Neptune (god)
Court of Neptune, The. Hughes.
Homeric Hymn to Neptune. Chapman.
In Praise of Neptune. Campion.
Next unto Him Was Neptune Pictured. *Fr.* The Faerie Queene. Spenser.
Neri, Filippo de'. *See* **Philip Neri, Saint.**
Nero
Ave! Nero Imperator. Osborne.
Neruda, Pablo
Last Letter to Pablo. Lowther.
Mourning Pablo Neruda. Bly.
On the Death of Neruda. Cabral.
Two Communist Poets. Layton.
Nerve Gas
At Night. Proctor.
Ness, Loch, Scotland
Monster, The. Lowbury.
Nessie. Hughes.
Nests. *See* **Birds' Nests.**
Netherlands
Character of Holland, The. Marvell.
Dutch April. Halpern.
Dutch Picture, A. Longfellow.
Dutch Seacoast. *Fr.* The Atlas. Slessor.
Leak in the Dike, The. Cary.
Lowlands o' Holland, The. *Unknown.*
Road to Nijmegam, The. Birney.
Such Is Holland! Genestet.
Nettles
Stinging Nettle. Head.
Tall Nettles. Thomas.
Nevada
January 15 as a National Holiday. Revard.
Man Who Invented Las Vegas, The. Costanzo.

Nevada. Gurney.
Reno, *2 a.m.* Hamill.
Vacation. Stafford.
You Are on U.S. 40 Headed West. White.

New Brunswick, Canada
Banks of the Gaspereaux, The. *Unknown.*
Biftek aux Champignons. Beers.
Duffy's Hotel. *Unknown.*
Pea-Fields, The. Roberts.
Saint John, The. Clarke.
Tantramar Revisited. Roberts.
Winter of '73, The. Gorman.

New Deal
CCC, The. Whitbread.

New England
Air Raid. Wild.
Home Thoughts. Shepard.
Hundred Collars, A. Frost
Late Comer. Hastings.
Letters for the New England Dead. Baron.
Lilacs. Lowell.
Mayflower. Aiken.
New England. Percival.
New England. Robinson.
New England Is New England Is New England. Green
New England Sampler, A. Brinnin.
Painter in New England, A. Stork.
Praise of New England. Chubb.
Uppon the First Sight of New-England, June 29, 1638. Tillam.
With Due Deference to Thomas Wolfe. Townsend.
With hearts revived in conceit, new land and trees they eye. *Fr.* Good News from New England. Johnson.
Yankee Poet. Wilson.

New Guinea
New Guinea. McAuley.

New Hampshire
Black Faced Sheep, The. Hall.
Flower Herding on Mount Monadnock. Kinnell.
Freedom, New Hampshire. Kinnell.
Mushroom Hunting in Late August, Peterborough, N.H. Blumenthal.
New Hampshire. *Fr.* Landscapes. Eliot.
New Hampshire. Hall.
On the Porch at the Frost Place, Franconia, NH. Matthews.
Sonnet to Seabrook. Ray.
Spring in New Hampshire. McKay.
Town of Hill, The. Hall.
Winter, New Hampshire. Kherdian.

New Haven, Connecticut
On the Democracy of Yale. Jones.

New Jersey
Corsons Inlet. Ammons.
In a Prominent Bar in Secaucus One Day. Kennedy.
Invention of New Jersey, The. Anderson.
Jersey Bait Shack. Balakian.
Jersey Marsh, The. Galler.
Legend. Weaver.
Looking at Power. Woessner.
Metroliner. DuVall.
New Jersey White-tailed Deer. Oates.
Paterson, *sels.* Williams.
Patroling Barnegat. Whitman.
Route 95 North: New Jersey. Bowman.
Sandy Hook. Houghton.
Thirty Childbirths. Brand.
With the Nuns at Cape May Point. Anderson.

New Mexico
Arrival of My Mother, The. Wilson.
At Mexican Springs. Tohe.
Back Again from Yucca Flats. Kelley.
How to Get to New Mexico. Brandi.
I tell him how it used to be in Paguate. *Fr.* After the Pow-Wow. Littlebird.
It Was a Special Treat. Tapahonso.
Landscape, New Mexico. Robertson.
New Mexican Mountain. Jeffers.
New Mexico. Boyden.
New Mexico and Arizona. Canterbury.
Old Women beside a Church. Wilson.
Progress. Agnew.
Prospectus. Huffstickler.
Sand Painters, The. Belitt.
Santo Domingo Corn Dance. Dickey.
Sound of Morning in New Mexico, The. Kelley.
When the Fairies. Dorn.
Woman, Gallup, N.M. Swenson.

New Orleans, Louisiana
Alcide Pavageau. Williams.
Ballade des Belles Milatraisses. Jonas.
Girod Street Cemetary: New Orleans. Morris.
Letter from the Vieux Carre. Russell.
New Orleans. Carruth.
New Orleans. Harjo.
Song for New Orleans, A. Keithley.
Vieux Carré. Roberts.
Zulu King, The: New Orleans. Copeland.

New Orleans, Battle of (1815)
Battle of New Orleans, The. English.
Hunters of Kentucky. Woodworth.
Jackson at New Orleans. Rice.
To the Defenders of New Orleans. Drake.

New Year
All thro' the Year. *Unknown.*
Another Year Is Dawning. Havergal.
Another Year. Smith.
At Dawn of the Year. Klingle.
At the New Year. Patchen.
At the Portal. Havergal.
Auld Lang Syne. Burns.
Backward—Forward. *Unknown.*
Bells of New Year. Field.
Both my child. Teitoku.
Cheerful Welcome, A. *Unknown.*
Confidence. *Unknown.*
Death of the Old Year, The. Tennyson.
End of the Year, The. Su Tung P'o.
Facing the New Year. Pearse.
Facing the New Year. *Unknown.*
Farewell and Hail! Clark.
Farewell to the Old Year. Farjeon.
For a fresh start. *Fr.* Oraga Haru. Issa.
For the Lady Olivia Porter; a Present upon a New-Years Day. Davenant.
Full knee-deep lies the winter snow. *Fr.* The Death of the Old Year. Tennyson.
Gates of the Year, The. Hull.
"Go Forward." "A. R. G."
God Is Faithful. Havergal.
Happy New Year! Happy New Year! *Unknown.*
Here We Come a-Caroling. *Unknown.*
Hymn for the Eve of the New Year. Gerondi.
"I Am with Thee." Allen.
I Buried the Year. Luff.
In Trust. Dodge.
Invocation for the New Year. Armstrong.
January 1. Pomeroy.
Last Day of the Year (New Year's Eve), The. Droste-Hülshoff.
Lessons of the Year. *Unknown.*
Lord, Make a Regular Man Out of Me. Guest.
Message of the Bell, The. Clark.
Midnight Mass for the Dying Year. Longfellow.
New Leaf, A. Wheeler.
New Time. *Unknown.*
New-Year, The. Cotton.
New Year, The. Craik.
New Year, A. Davies.
New Year. Harada.
New Year, The. Homer-Dixon.
New Year, A. Shorter.
New Year, The. Templeton.
New Year, The. *Unknown.*
New Year Carol, A. *Unknown.*
New Year Prayer, A. Parker.
New Year Song. Hughes.
New Year Wish, A. Havergal.
New Year Wish, A. *Unknown.*
New yeares, expect new gifts: Sister, your Harpe. Jonson.
New Years and Old. Jackson.
New Year's Carol. *Unknown.*
New Year's Day. Field.
New Year's Day. Lowell.
New Year's Eve. Berryman.
New Year's Eve. Hardy.
New Year's Eve, 1938. Nims.
New Year's, 1978. Nemerov.
New Year's Poem. Avison.

New Year's Promise, A. *Unknown.*
New-Year's Sacrifice, A: To Lucinda. Carew.
New Year's Water. *Unknown.*
New Year's Wish, A. "J. H. S."
New Year's Wishes. Havergal.
News! News! Farjeon.
Old and New. *Unknown.*
Old Father Annum. Jackson.
Old Year, The. Clare.
Old Year, The. Urmy.
Old Year and the New, The. Flint.
Old Year's Prayer. The. Irving.
Opening Year, The. *Unknown.*
Parable, A. Kress.
Prayer. Clarke.
Prayer, A: "Through every minute of this day,". Oxenham.
Prayer for a Happy New Year, A. Clarke.
Prayer for the New Year, A. *Unknown.*
Reconsecration. Gould.
Resolutions?—New and Old. Rolfe.
Ring Out the Old, Ring In the New. *Fr.* In Memoriam A. H. H. Tennyson.
Ring out, wild bells, to the wild sky. *Fr.* In Memoriam A. H. H. Tennyson.
Song for December Thirty-first. Frost.
Thought for a New Year. Burket.
To the Countesse of Bedford on New-Yeares Day. Donne.
Up the Hill, Down the Hill. Farjeon.
Upon this happy New Year night. *Fr.* A New Year Idyl. Field.
Wassail Song, The. *Unknown.*
Weary year his race now having run, The. *Fr.* Amoretti. Spenser.
Welcome to the New Year. Farjeon.
Wish for the New Year, A. Brooks.
Year Ahead, The. Powers.
Year's End. Wilbur.

New York (state)
Among the Finger Lakes. Wallace.
At the Long Island Jewish Geriactric Home. Graham.
Breakfast in a Bowling Alley in Utica, New York. Rich.
Canadice Lake. Mondy.
Crossing Raquette Lake at Night. Kuzma.
Early Fall: the Adirondacks. Wright.
E-ri-e, The. *Unknown.*
Erie Canal, The. Allen.
Getting a Poem in the Rain. Lourie.
Grandfather. Harper.
Home Front. Bell.
Long Island Springs. Moss.
Mother and Son. Heyen.
Niagara Falls. Parisi.
Oxford Commination. Leary.
Pearl Harbor Day 1970. Lourie.
Penn Central Station at Beacon, N.Y., The. Ochester.
Raquette River, The, Potsdam, New York; Lying on a Rock Drinking Scotch While My Friends Fish Upstream. Piccione.
Sestina d'Inverno. Hecht.
State of Nature, A. Hollander.
Summer in a Small Town. Gregg.
Those Trees that Line the Northway. Perreault.

New York City
Arrival, New York Harbor. Peters.
Aspects of Robinson. Kees.
At the Battery Sea-Wall. Laube.
Avenue Bearing the Initial of Christ into the New World, The. Kinnell.
B Negative. Kennedy.
Birthday Memorial to Seventh Street, A. Lorde.
Bleat of Protest. Weston.
Bottled: New York. Johnson.
Bowery, The. Hoyt.
City of Orgies. Whitman.
City Roofs. Towne.
Curse, A. Feldman.
Dawn. García Lorca.
Day in the City, A. Sissman.
Dedication for a Building. Dugan.
Early Dutch. Palen.
East River. Thomas.
Epistrophe. Baraka.
Factories. Hirsch.
Give Me the Splendid Silent Sun. Whitman.
Give My Regards to Broadway. Cohan.
Glory. Moore.
High Wind at the Battery. Pomeroy.
Houston and Bowery, 1981. Burns.
Houston Street, N. Y. Baxter.
I Am New York City. Cortez.
I Awoke with the Room Cold. Piercy.
I'd rather listen to a flute. Hoffenstein.
Imprisoned, The. Fitzgerald.
In New York I got drunk, to tell the truth. *Fr.* A Trip to Four or Five Towns. Logan.
John Garfield. Christopher.
Junkie with a Flute in the Rain, A. Fisher.
Last Impression of New York. Mason.
Last Warmth of Arnold, The. Corso.
Letter to N. Y. Bishop.
Madison Square. Glanz-Leyeles.
Mannahatta. Whitman.
Manhattan. Beer.
Manhattan. Hart.
Manhattan Lullaby. Field.
Manhattan Menagerie. Cherwinski.
Metropolitan Nightmare. Benét.
My City. Johnson.
My Sad Self. Ginsberg.
My Son and I. Levine.
New York City. Abbe.
New York City. Bodenheim.
New York in August. Davie.
New York City—1935. Corso.
Nothing but Image. Swilky.
Obon by the Hudson. Oyama.
Ode to New York. Whittemore.
Owed to New York. Newton.
Poem for Edie Sedgwick Who Slept in a Swimming Pool. Brisby.
Poem for the Conguero in D-Yard. Fernandez.
Proud New York. Reed.
Regarding (1) the U. S. and (2) New York. Adams.
Review from Staten Island. Oden.
Riverside Drive, November Fifth. Pollitt.
School Days in New Amsterdam. Guiterman.
Sickness, The. Seidel.
Sidewalks of New York, The. Lawlor *and* Blake.
Sign, The. Blackburn.
Slogan, The. Blackburn.
Snow. Chiang.
Speakers, Columbus Circle. Souster.
Step Away from Them, A. O'Hara.
Steps. O'Hara.
Stone, The. Blackburn.
Storm on Fifth Avenue. Sassoon.
Strawberries. Hughes.
Stumpfoot on 42nd Street. Simpson.
These Green-going-to-Yellow. Bell.
This Song Shows Me Pictures; Morningside Drive, New York City 1950–1960. Oyama.
Times Square Parade. Watson.
To New York. Sédar-Senghor.
Tropics in New York, The: New York. McKay.
Tulips and Addresses. Field.
Tunnel, The. Crane.
Twenty-third Street Runs into Heaven. Patchen.
Under. Bowering.
Walking. O'Hara.
West Forties, The: Morning, Noon, and Night. Sissman.
When Dawn Comes to the City: New York. McKay.
Winter Sketches. Reznikoff.
Workers Rose on May Day, The, or Postscript to Karl Marx. Lorde.
New York: Poems (NYP). Howard Moss, ed.
See also **Bronx, Brooklyn,** *and* **Queens.**

New Yorker, The (magazine)
Talk of the Town, The. Fisher.

New Zealand
East Coast Journey. Baxter.
Farewell to New Zealand. Vaughan-Thomas.
Foxes, The. Frame.
Oxford Book of Contemporary New Zealand Poetry, The (OCNZ). Fleur Adcock, ed.

Newark, New Jersey
Ballgame, The. Baraka.
Newark, for Now (68). Rodgers.

Newfoundland, Canada
Banks of Newfoundland, The. *Unknown.*
Gazeteer of Newfoundland. Harrington.

North Labrador. Crane.
Pleasant Life in Newfoundland, The. Hayman.
Trip to the Grand Banks, A. *Unknown.*
Way of Cape Race, The. Pratt.
Wreckers' Prayer, The. Roberts.

Newfoundland (dog)
Epitaph, An: Inscription on a Monument at Newstead Abbey. Byron.

Newgate Prison, London
Friendly Address, A. Hood.

Newport, Rhode Island
Looking at Wealth in Newport. Schevill.

Newspapers
After the Last Bulletins. Wilbur.
Boston Evening Transcript, The. Eliot.
Carl Hamblin. *Fr.* Spoon River Anthology. Masters.
Carrier's Address. *Unknown.*
Daisy Fraser. *Fr.* Spoon River Anthology. Masters.
Doing Railroads for *The Rocky Mountain News.* Warman.
Editor Whedon. *Fr.* Spoon River Anthology. Masters.
Extras. Burton.
Finding an Old Newspaper in the Woods. Morgan.
Headline History. Plomer.
It Is Dangerous to Read Newspapers. Atwood.
News. Schmitz.
Newsboy. Layton.
Newspaper is a collection of half-injustices, A. *Fr.* War Is Kind. Crane.
Poetry and Thoughts on Same. Adams.
Reading Today's Newspaper. Abbott.
Suggestion Made by the Posters of the *Globe,* A. Rogers.
Sunday Review Section. Wormser.
To a Dead Journalist. Williams.
You cannot hope. Wolfe.
See also **Journalism; Magazines.**

Newton, Sir Isaac
All intellectual eye, our solar round. *Fr.* To the Memory of Sir Isaac Newton. Thomson.
Intended for Sir Isaac Newton. Pope.
Newton. *Fr.* The Prelude. Wordsworth.
Newton to Einstein. Chappell.
Sir Isaac Newton. *Unknown.*

Newts
Newt, The. McCord.

Niagara Falls
Niagara. Crapsey.
Niagara Falls. Parisi.
Niagara Falls Nocturne. Gasparini.

Nicaragua
June 10. Rodríguez.

Nigeria
Ibadan. Clark.
Safari West. Williams.
See also **Civil War, Nigerian.**

Night
A. M.—P. M. Hirschfield.
Acquainted with the Night. Frost.
Acts of Youth, The. Wieners.
Ancient Thought, The. Kerr.
At Arm's Length. Bossert.
At Night. Meynell.
At the Mid Hour of Night. Moore.
Auld Daddy Darkness. Ferguson.
Bagley Wood. Johnson.
Ballad of London, A. Le Gallienne.
Battle, A. Crawford.
Beautiful Night, A. Beddoes.
Black pitchy night, companion of my woe. *Fr.* Idea's Mirrour. Drayton.
Breath of Night, The. Jarrell.
Casting at Night. Hoey.
Check. Stephens.
Children of Night. Shelton.
Church and Church-Yard at Night. *Fr.* The Grave. Blair.
City, The: Midnight. Dawe.
Cold Front. Sharpe.
Colloquy with God, A. Browne.
Come, Sable Night. *Unknown.*
Dark Night, The. St. John of the Cross.
Dark Stag, The. Crawford.
Day Is Done, The. Longfellow.
Day That I Have Loved. Brooke.
Evening. Doolittle ("H. D.").
Falling Asleep. Sassoon.
Flowers of Darkness. Davis.
Four Glimpses of Night. Davis.
God's Dark. Martin.
Going to Sleep in the Country. Moss.
Good Night. Hugo.
Good Night. Pierce.
Hotel in Paris. Trudell.
Hour of Magic, The. Davies.
Hymn to Night. Cane.
Hymn to Night, A. Michelson.
Hymn to the Evening, An. Wheatley.
Hymn to the Night. Longfellow.
I Wake and Feel the Fell of Dark. Hopkins.
If night takes the form of a whale and. Fraire.
In the Dark None Dainty. Herrick.
In the Half-Point Time of Night. Menebroker.
In the Night. Jennings.
Interim. Delany.
Invocation of Comus, The. *Fr.* Comus. Milton.
Last Leave. Newton.
Light the Lamps Up, Lamplighter! Farjeon.
Lucina Schynning in Silence of the Night. Ní Chuilleanáin.
Lux in Tenebris. Hinkson.
Madrigal: "Unhappie Light." Drummond of Hawthornden.
Makes the Little Ones Dizzy. De la Mare.
Meeting at Night. Browning.
Melrose Abbey. *Fr.* The Lay of the Last Minstrel. Scott.
Middle of the Night, The. Kuskin.
Midnight Prayer. Bialik.
Midnight. *Fr.* Blurt, Master-Constable. Middleton.
Midnight. Lampman.
Midnight. Masefield.
Moonlit Apples. Drinkwater.
Night. Benét.
Night. *Fr.* Songs of Innocence. Blake.
Night. Brown.
Night. Camerino.
Night. Coleridge.
Night. *Fr.* The Shadow of Night. Chapman.
Night. Hayes.
Night. Heavysege.
Night. Hoberman.
Night. Hubbell.
Night. Ibn Gabirol.
Night. Jeffers.
Night. Lovelace.
Night. McKay.
Night. Montgomery.
Night. Radcliffe.
Night. Surrey.
Night. Sutu.
Night. Symonds.
Night. Teasdale.
Night, The. Vaughan.
Night. White.
Night. *Fr.* Night Thoughts. Young.
Night's Mardi Gras. Wheeler.
Night Airs. Landor.
Night and Sleep. Patmore.
Night and the Pines. Scott.
Night Comes. De Regniers.
Night Crackles. Woody.
Night Enchantment. Muth.
Night Hymns on Lake Nipigon. Scott.
Night in June, A. Scott.
Night Is Near Gone, The. Montgomerie.
Night of Spring. Westwood.
Night on the Prairie. Sage.
Night-Piece. Patterson.
Night Piece, A. Shanks.
Night Piece. Strand.
Night-Piece, A. *Unknown.*
Night-Piece, A. Wordsworth.
Night-Piece, to Julia, The. Herrick.
Night Up There. Valentine.
Night Will Never Stay, The. Farjeon.
No Difference in the Dark. Herrick.
Nocturnal Reverie, A. Winchilsea.
Nocturnal Sketch, A. Hood.
Nocturnal Sounds. Cumbo.
Nocturne: "Listening for the sound." Lane.
Nocturne: "Red flame flowers bloom and die, The." Garstin.
Nocturne: "This cool night is strange." Bennett.

November Night, Edinburgh. MacCaig.
Now winter nights enlarge. Campion.
O Daedalus, Fly Away Home. Hayden.
Omalos. Warren.
On a Calm Summer's Night. Nicholson.
On the Night in Question. Goedicke.
Out in the Dark. Thomas.
Owl, The. Thomas.
Pine Tree Tops. Snyder.
Questions at Night. Untermeyer.
Reflection of Night, A. Marietta.
Rhapsody on a Windy Night. Eliot.
Rhapsody, Written at the Lakes in Westmorland, A. Brown.
Second Hymn to the Night, The. *Fr.* Hymns of the Night. "Novalis."
Seein' Things. Field.
Shadow of Night, The. Patmore.
Short Night, The. Buson.
Silver. De la Mare.
So Beautiful Is the Tree of Night. Hanson.
Song: "Make this night loveable." Auden.
Song for Past Midnight. Lehmann.
Sound of Night, The. Kumin.
Spring Night. Su Tung-P'o.
Star That Bids the Shepherd Fold, The. *Fr.* Comus. Milton.
Still Life. Whittemore.
Summer Night, A. Arnold.
Suns, planets, stars, in glorious array. *Fr.* Night. Daley.
Thanks from Earth to Heaven. Wheelock.
Time Exposures. Rukeyser.
Tiptoe Night. Drinkwater.
To Night. Shelley.
To Night. *Unknown.*
To Night. White.
Upon a Gloomy Night. *Fr.* The Dark Night of the Soul. Campbell.
Wait till the darkness is deep. Wallāda.
Walking at Night. Hare.
Walking Late. Montague.
Watchman, The. Kingsley.
Watchman, What of the Night? Swinburne.
Winter Night, A. Barnes.
Winter Night. Fitzgerald.
Dusk to Dawn (DuDa). Helen Hill, Agnes Perkins *and* Alethea Helbig, eds.
See also **Evening.**

Nightclubs
Jazz Band in a Parisian Cabaret. Hughes.
Jazzonia. Hughes.
Night Club. Scott.

Nighthawks
Waiting for Nighthawks in Illinois. Pfingston.

Nightingales
As it fell upon a day. *Fr.* The Affectionate Shepherd. Barnfield.
Bianca among the Nightingales. Browning.
Canadian Rossignol, The. Thomson.
Early Nightingale. Clare.
Fields Abroad with Spangled Flowers, The. *Unknown.*
Happy Nightingale, The. *Unknown.*
Hast Thou Heard the Nightingale? Gilder.
Jug, jug! Fair fall the nightingal. Brathwaite.
Music's Duel. Crashaw.
My Nightingale. Ausländer.
Nightingale, The. Akenside.
Nightingale, The. Brathwaite.
Nightingale, The. Clare.
Nightingale, The. Coleridge.
Nightingale, The. Moxon.
Nightingale, The. Petrarch.
Nightingale, The. Sidney.
Nightingale near the House, The. Monro.
Nightingales. Bridges.
Nightingales. Conkling.
No cloud, no relique of the sunken day. *Fr.* The Nightingale. Coleridge.
O Nightingale! Thou Surely Art. Wordsworth.
Ode, An: "As it fell upon a day." Barnfield.
Ode: To the Nightingale. Warton.
Ode to a Nightingale. Keats.
On a Nightingale in April. "Macleod."
On the Cliffs. Swinburne.
On the Death of a Nightingale. Randolph.
Owl against Nightingale. *At. to* Nicholas de Guildford.
Philomel. *Fr.* The Passionate Pilgrim. Barnfield.
Philomela. Arnold.
Philomela. Ransom.
Philomela. Sidney.
Riddle: Nightingale. *Unknown.*
Sparrow-Hawk, A. *Unknown.*
There the voluptuous nightingales. *Fr.* Prometheus Unbound. Shelley.
To a Nightingale. Drummond of Hawthornden.
To the Nightingale. Drummond of Hawthornden.
To the Nightingale. Milton.
To the Nightingale. Winchilsea.
Upon the boughs and tops of trees. *Fr.* Philomela, the Nightingale. Hannay.
When I was in a summer valley. *Fr.* The Owl and the Nightingale. *Unknown.*

Nightmares
Apology for Bad Dreams. Jeffers.
In Your Bad Dream. Hugo.
Nightmare Inspection Tour for American Generals. Ruark.
Original Sin: A Short Story. Warren.
See also **Dreams.**

Nihilism
Nothing. Burgos.
Upon Nothing. Rochester.

Nijinsky, Vaslav
For Nijinsky's Tomb. Cornford.
Friends. Ashbery.
Homage to Vaslav Nijinsky. Kirkup.
Nijinsky. Ferne.
Nijinsky. Tyler.

Nile (river)
Chorus: "Then thus we have beheld." *Fr.* Cleopatra. Daniel.
Nile, The. Hunt.
To the Nile. Keats.
To the Nile. Shelley.

1970s
70 on the 70's: A Decade's History in Verse (SOTS). Richard Snyder *and* Robert McGovern, eds.

Nixon, Richard Milhous
Campaign Promise. Taylor.
Final Curtain. Woddis.
Hallelujah I'm a Bum ("I read in the news, the President said"). Dane *and* Silber.
News from Detroit. Minty.
Nixon at Calvary. Nemerov.

Nkrumah, Kwame
Goodbye Nkrumah. Di Prima.

Noah
And Did the Animals? Van Doren.
Animals in the Ark, The. *Unknown.*
Ballad of the Flood. Muir.
Brother Noah. *Unknown.*
Dog's Cold Nose, The. Guiterman.
Flood, The. Mak.
Hammer, Ring. *Unknown.*
History of the Flood, The. Heath-Stubbs.
Late Passenger, The. Lewis.
Missing Link, The. Herford.
Noah an' Jonah an' Cap'n John Smith. Marquis.
Noah. Bloch.
Noah. Daniells.
Noah's Ark. Young.
Noah's Carpenters. *Unknown.*
Noah's Flood. *Fr.* Genesis. *Unknown.*
Noah's Song. Jones.
Old Ark's A-Moverin', The. *Unknown.*
One More River to Cross. *Unknown.*
Parley of Beasts. "MacDiarmid."
Proust on Noah. Silberschlag.
Rise and Shine. *Unknown.*
Wine and Water. *Fr.* The Flying Inn. Chesterton.

Nobility
My Lord Tomnoddy. Brough.

Noguchi, Isamu
Halfbreed Chronicles; Isamu. Rose.

Nomads
Song of the Sons of Esau, The. Runkle.

Noon
Noon. Clare.
Silent Noon. Rossetti.

Norfolk, England
Coast, The: Norfolk. Cornford.
Horsey Gap. *Unknown.*
Lament for the Priory of Walsingham, A. *Unknown.*

Norfolk. Betjeman.
Normandy
At Dieppe. Symons.
Norman Abbey. *Fr.* Don Juan. Byron.
Two Lovers. Marie de France.
Normandy, Invasion of
Carentan O Carentan. Simpson.
Norris Dam, Tennessee
Norris Dam. Rodman.
North, Christopher (John Wilson)
To Christopher North. Tennyson.
North, Frederick, Earl of Guilford and Baron North.
Lord North's Recantation. *Unknown.*
North Carolina
August Evenings in Hatteras. Glang.
Brevard Fault. Morgan.
Carolinas, The. Ray.
Cottonmouth Country. Glück.
Dog Creek Mainline. Wright.
East Virginia. *Unknown.*
Hill Hunger. West.
It's a debatable land. The winds are variable. *Fr.* Report from the Carolinas. Bevington.
On the Wings of a Dove. Miller.
Suppose a Man. Smith.
Swannanoa Tunnel. *Unknown.*
North Dakota
August from My Desk. Flint.
Outside Fargo, North Dakota. Wright
Sisseton Indian Reservation, The. Lyons.
Something Is Dying Here. McGrath.
North Pole
90 North. Jarrell.
Scientific Proof. Foley.
North Wind
Awake! Oh, north wind. *Fr.* Song of Solomon. Bible, *O.T.*
Blow, Northern Wind. *Unknown.*
Exile in Nigeria. Mphahlele.
Moon's the North Wind's Cooky, The. Lindsay.
North Wind Came Up Yesternight, The. Bridges.
North Wind in October. Bridges.
Northwind. Baro.
Ode to the North-east Wind. Kingsley.
Ode to the Norther. Chittenden.
Northamptonshire, England
Northamptonshire Fens. Clare.
Sunrise in Summer. Clare.
Northern Ireland
Ballymurphy. *Unknown.*
Carrickfergus. MacNeice.
Derry. Deane.
Lines of history. Lines of defiance. *Fr.* A New Siege: An Historical Meditation. Montague.
Lisnagade. *Unknown.*
Northern Ireland: Two Comments. Deane.
Strand at Lough Beg, The. Heaney.
Whatever You Say Say Nothing. Heaney.
See also counties listed under, e.g., **County Tyrone, Northern Ireland.**
Northern Lights. *See* **Aurora Borealis.**
Northumberland, England
Alnwick Castle. Halleck.
At Elsdon. Chatt.
Early Influences. *Fr.* The Pleasures of Imagination. Akenside.
Elsdon. Downie.
Northwest Territories, Canada
I persist in a little fabric between me and the world. *Fr.* The Great Bear Lake Meditations. Yates.
Trees at the Arctic Circle. Purdy.
Noses
Disagreeable Feature, A. Robinson.
Dong with a Luminous Nose, The. Lear.
Hairs in My Nose, The. Boyajian.
My Nose. Aldis.
Of One That Had a Great Nose. Turberville.
Of Tyndarus, That Frumped a Gentlewoman. *Unknown.*
Smell. Williams.
There's a man with a nose. *Fr.* The Devil's Dictionary. Bierce.
To My Nose. Forrester.
Nostalgia
After a Journey. Hardy.
Alone by the Hearth. Arnold.
Ballad of Dead Ladies, The. Villon.
Deserted Home, A. Lysaght.
Family Album, A. Brody.
Farewell: "Not soon shall I forget—a sheet." Tynan.
Home No More Home to Me. Stevenson.
I Remember, I Remember. Larkin.
Lad That Is Gone, A. Stevenson.
Looking for the Buckhead Boys. Dickey.
Miniver Cheevy. Robinson.
Moon behind the Hill, The. *Unknown.*
My Other Me. Litchfield.
Nostalgia. Lawrence.
Oh, Give Us Back the Days of Old. Neale.
Old Familiar Faces, The. Lamb.
Old Furniture. Hardy.
Old-Long-Syne. *Unknown.*
Old Movies. Cotton.
One day when I was a child, long ago. Paley.
Out to Old Aunt Mary's. Riley.
Piano. Lawrence.
Retreat, The. Vaughan.
Straus Park. Stern.
Tears, Idle Tears. *Fr.* Princess, The. Tennyson.
Two Old Gentlemen, The. Wallace.
Voice of the Western Wind. Stedman.
When This Old Hat Was New. *Unknown.*
Nothingness
Neither Here nor There. Rodgers.
See also **Nihilism.**
Notre Dame Cathedral
Notre Dame. Mandelstam.
Notre Dame Perfected by Reflection. Witt.
Nottingham, England
Nottamun Town. *Unknown.*
Nova Scotia, Canada
Ballad of Springhill (the Springhill Mine Disaster). MacColl *and* Seeger.
Building in Nova Scotia. Dunn.
By Cobequid Bay. Fraser.
First Death in Nova Scotia. Bishop.
In the Night Watches. Roberts.
Louisburg. *Unknown.*
Low Tide on Grand Pré. Carman.
On the Late Successful Expedition against Louisburg. Hopkinson
Poem: "About the size of an old-style dollar bill." Bishop.
To Cordelia. Stansbury.
Words Are Never Enough. Bruce.
Novels
Critical Observations. MacLeish.
Who'd Be a Hero (Fictional)? Bishop.
November
Beautiful Ruined Orchard, The. Berrigan.
Dream of November, A. Gosse.
Hearth Song. Johnson.
In November. Aldrich.
In November. Lampman.
Last Days, The. Sterling.
Late November in a Field. Wright.
Marmion. Scott.
Mist and All, The. Willson.
My November Guest. Frost.
Nearing Winter. Sandeen.
No! Hood.
November. Binyon.
November. Bridges.
November. Cary.
November. Cleaveland.
November. Coatsworth.
November. *Fr.* Sonnets to the Seasons. Coleridge.
November. Fisher.
November. Harvey.
November. Hughes.
November. Keble.
November. Rossetti.
November. Stoddard.
November Afternoons. Madeleva.
November Cotton Flower. Toomer.
November Eves. Flecker.
November Garden. Driscoll.
November in Ettrick Forest. *Fr.* Marmion. Scott.
November in the Isle of Wight. *Fr.* Enoch Arden. Tennyson.
November Morning. Stein.
November Night. Crapsey.
November Night, Edinburgh. MacCaig.

November Rain. Uschold.
November Song. Vinz.
November Sun. Daryush.
November Surf. Jeffers.
November through a Giant Copper Beech. Honig.
November Wears a Paisley Shawl. Morris.
Parable: November. Tapscott.
Riverside Drive, November Fifth. Pollitt.
Roses, Revisited, in a Paradoxical Autumn. Cullum.
There's Nothing Like the Sun. Thomas.
Transparence of November, The. Borson.
Weather Vanes. Frost.

Nuclear Accidents
Accident at Three Mile Island. Barnes.
Amish, The. Doreski.
Hershey Kiss. Renner-Tana.
In Distress. Wagoner.
Plumber Arrives at Three Mile Island, The. Stewart.
See also **Radiation and Radiation Sickness.**

Nuclear Energy
Black Mesa. Rogers.
Looking at Power. Woessner.
Sonnet to Seabrook. Ray.
Tar. Williams.

Nuclear War
Advice to a Prophet. Wilbur.
Berceuse. Clampitt.
Blue Alert. Merriam.
Conquerors, The. McGinley.
Fall 1961. Lowell.
Fifteen Million Plastic Bags. Mitchell.
Fundamental Project of Technology, The. Kinnell.
Halflives. Hoffman.
Horses, The. Muir.
How Do You Spell "Missile"?: Preliminary Instructions in the Nuclear Age. Uba.
In a Surrealist Year. *Fr.* A Coney Island of the Mind. Ferlinghetti.
In the Hedge-Back. "MacDiarmid."
Late Lunch, San Antonio. O'Sullivan.
Modern Grimm. Richardson.
Nuclear Land. Tifft.
O nuclear wind, when wilt thou blow. *Fr.* Leaden Treasury of English Verse, A. Dehn.
Of How Scientists Are Often Ahead of Others in Thinking, While the Average Man Lags Behind; and How the Economist (Who Can Only Follow in the Footsteps of the Average Man Looking for Clues to the Future), Remains Thoroughly Out of It. Benedikt.
Post-Mortem, A. Sassoon.
Rose Bay Willow Herb. Ray.
Song about Major Eatherly, A. Wain.
Survivors, The. Hine.
Wedding Day at Nagasaki. Hall.
When the Vacation Is Over for Good. Strand.
Your Attention Please. Porter.
See also **Atomic Bomb; Radiation and Radiation Sickness.**

Nudity and Nudists
"Gross, Coarse, Hideous" (Police Description of My Pictures). Lawrence.
Landscape as a Nude. *Fr.* Frescoes for Mr. Rockefeller's City. MacLeish.
L'Ile du Levant: The Nudist Colony. Howes.
Naked and the Nude, The. Graves.
Naked in Borneo. Swenson.
Nudities. Spire.
Old Nudists, The. Colby.
Playboy. Wilbur.
To His Mistress Going to Bed. *Fr.* Elegies. Donne.

Number Poems (genre)
Cardinal Ideograms. Swenson.

Numbers
Accountant in His Bath, The. Mitchell.
Difference, The. Richards.
One, two,/ Buckle my shoe. Mother Goose.

Nuns
Abbess, The. *Fr.* Marmion. Scott.
Ballad of a Nun, A. Davidson.
Convent, The. O'Sullivan.
Felixstowe, or The Last of Her Order. Betjeman.
Fixture, A. Swenson.
For the Sisters of the Hôtel Dieu. Klein.
Heaven-Haven. Hopkins.
Holy Nunnery, The. *Unknown.*
I am a young girl, gay. *Unknown.*
Intercessors. Clarke.
Maid of Honour, The. Massinger.
Motet: "I am a young girl." *Unknown.*
Mother Marie Therese. Lowell.
Notre Dames des Champs. Synge.
Nuns at Eve. Brinnin.
Nuns in the Wind. Rukeyser.
Sister Rose. Martin.
Territory. Wood-Thompson.
To a Nun. *Unknown.*
To a Severe Nun. Merton.
Vestal, The. *Fr.* Eloise to Abelard. Pope.
Wreck of the *Deutschland*, The. Hopkins.
See also **Convents.**

Nuremberg, Germany
Nuremberg. Longfellow.

Nursery Rhymes
Goosey Goosey Gander—By Various Authors. French.

Nurses
Epigraph to "Drum-Taps." Whitman.
Incident, An. Henderson.
Malice of Innocence, The. Levertov.
Modern American Nursing. Hricz.
Night Nurse Goes Her Round, The. Gray.
Nurse's Song ("When the voices of children are heard on the green/ And laughing"). *Fr.* Songs of Innocence. Blake.
Rivalry. Nowlan.
Staff-Nurse: New Style. *Fr.* In Hospital. Henley.
Staff-Nurse: Old Style. *Fr.* In Hospital. Henley.
Terrible Infant, A. Locker-Lampson.
Wound-Dresser, The. Whitman.

Nursing Homes
At the Nursing Home. Cain.
Sons. Polson.

Nymphs
Nymph Complaining for the Death of Her Fawn, The. Marvell.
Overheard on a Saltmarsh. Monro.
Sabrina. *Fr.* Comus. Milton.
Sea-Nymph's Parting, The. *Fr.* Gebir. Landor.
There are the fair-limbed Nymphs o' the Woods, (Look ye). *Fr.* The Nymphs. Moore.
To the Water Nymphs, Drinking at the Fountain. Herrick.
Water Lady, The. Hood.

O

Oafs
What Kind of a Guy Was He? Nemerov.
Yes, What? Francis.

Oak Trees
At the Woodpile. Henri.
Autumn Scene. Dowling.
Bearded Oaks. Warren.
Brave Old Oak, The. Chorley.
California Oaks, The. Winters.
Girt Woak Tree That's in the Dell, The. Barnes.
Heart of Oak. Luders.
I Saw in Louisiana a Live-Oak Growing. Whitman.
Oak. Child.
Oak, The. Tennyson.
Oak and the Reed, The. La Fontaine.
Spring Oak. Kinnell.
Tapestry Trees. Morris.
To an Oak Tree. *Fr.* Waverley. Scott.
To the Oaks of Glencree. Synge.
Yardley Oak. Cowper.

Oases
Green, Green Is El Aghir. Cameron.
See also **Deserts.**

Oates, Titus
Ballad upon the Popish Plot, A. Gadbury.
Panegyric upon Oates, A. Duke.
Salamanca Doctor's Farewell, The. *Unknown.*
Tragi-Comedy of Titus Oates, The. *Unknown.*

Oban, Scotland
End of the Season on a Stormy Day—Oban. Smith.

Obesity
Blank Verse for a Fat Demanding Wife. Lindsey.
Fat Boy's Dream, The. McCann.
Fat Man, The. Rutsala.

Perils of Obesity, The. Graham.
Obituaries
Funeral Notices. Storni.
Obscenity
Finger of Necessity. Barks.
Obscene Caller, The. Fein.
See also **Pornography.**
Observatories
Greenwich Observatory. Keyes.
See also **Astronomy and Astronomers.**
Obsessions
Juliet. Belloc.
Price of Paper, The. Russ.
Occult, The
Diehard. Moffett.
Séance. King.
Why Am I Grown So Cold? Poems of the Unknowable (WSC). Myra Cohn Livingston, ed.
Occupations
Vocation. Tagore.
What Do They Do? Rossetti.
Ocean. *See* **Sea.**
O'Conaire, Padraic
Padraic O'Conaire, Gaelic Storyteller. Higgins.
O'Connell, Daniel
Dead Tribune, The. McCarthy.
O'Connor, Flannery
Flannery O'Connor. Walters.
O'Connor, Rory
Grave of Rury, The. Rolleston.
October
Autumn Poem. Cronin.
Boys in October. Layton.
Chestnut vendor, The. Szelki.
Especially When the October Wind. Thomas.
Fall. Fisher.
Harvest Home. Guiterman.
Home Thoughts. Shepard.
Impulse of October, The. Moses.
In October. Carman.
In the Month of Green Fire. Himmell.
Late October. Carleton.
Late October. Teasdale.
Mallee in October. Hudson.
Now Blue October. Nathan.
October. Aldrich.
October. Frost.
October. Fyleman.
October. Hahn.
October. Kavanagh.
October. Koeppel.
October. Thomas.
October. Updike.
October Elegy. Gibson.
October in Tennessee. Malone.
October Journey. Walker.
October Morning. Piatt.
October Night. Dean.
October Winds. Randall.
October's Bright Blue Weather. Jackson.
October's Party. Cooper.
October's Song. Farjeon.
Old October. Constable.
Partial Draft. Shaw.
Poem in October. Thomas.
Return to Lake Emily Chequamegon National Forest. Behm.
Snow in October. Dunbar-Nelson.
Tregardock. Betjeman.
Vagabond Song, A. Carman.
Variations on a Late October Day. Mosby.
Winter Watch. Marion.
Octopuses
Octopus. Hilton.
Octopus, The. "MacDiarmid."
Octopus, The. Merrill.
Octopus, The. Nash.
Odin
Descent of Odin, The. *Fr.* The Norse Tongue. Gray.
O'Donnell, Hugh Roe
Aodh Ruadh O'Domhnaill. MacGreevy.
Odysseus. *See* **Ulysses.**
Oedipus
Antigone and Oedipus. Ray.
Incantation to Oedipus. *Fr.* Oedipus. Dryden.
Myth. Rukeyser.
Oedipus. Blackburn.
Oedipus. Ignatow.
Oedipus. Muir.
Oedipus Tyrannus. Sophocles.
Oenone
Oenone's Complaint. *Fr.* The Arraignment of Paris. Peele.
Offa, King of Mercia
Princes of Mercia were badger and raven, The. *Fr.* Mercian Hymns. Hill.
Office Workers
Any Man to His Secretary. Corke.
Back Again, Home. Lee.
Dolor. Roethke.
Love in Brooklyn. Wakeman.
Report, The. Swan.
Return to Work, The. Williams.
Song from a Two-Desk Office. Buck.
Stenographers, The. Page.
What Grandma Knew. Field.
See also **Clerks; Secretaries.**
Officers, Military
Base Details. Sassoon.
Old General, The. *Fr.* Isabella. Williams.
Ogres
Ogres and Pygmies. Graves.
See also **Monsters; Trolls.**
Ohio
Autumn Begins in Martins Ferry, Ohio. Wright.
Blessing at Kellenberger Road. Valian.
Chippewa Lake Park. Woessner.
Cold Feet in Columbus. Heath.
Founders of Ohio, The. Venable.
In Columbus, Ohio. Matthias.
In Response to a Rumor That the Oldest Whorehouse in Wheeling, West Virginia, Has Been Condemned. Wright.
Kent State Massacre, The. Warshaw *and* Dane.
Labor Day. Pacernik.
Magnificat in Transit from the Toledo Airport. Starbuck.
Map Reading. Citino.
Ohio. Updike.
Ohioan Pastoral. Wright.
Shelby County, Ohio. November 1974. Murray.
Taking the Train Home. Matthews.
Waders and Swimmers. Plumly.
Oil Industry
Slick. Hoffman.
Oisin
Bathing of Oisin's Head, The. *Unknown.*
History. Liddy.
Oisin. *Unknown.*
Oisin in the Land of Youth. Comyn.
Wanderings of Oisin, The. Yeats.
When Oisin came back to Ireland. *Fr.* Armageddon, Armageddon. Muldoon.
O'Keefe, Georgia
Only One. Burns.
Okinawa, Japan
Okinawa Kanashii Monogatari. Kudaka.
Picture of Okinawa, A. Schmitz.
Oklahoma
Captive Stone, The. Barnes.
Country-Western Music. Kooser.
Driving into Enid. Van Walleghen.
He Told Me His Name Was Sitting Bull. Harjo.
Last Song, The. Harjo.
Poem near Midway Truck Stop. Henson.
Race Riot, Tulsa, 1921. Olds.
Starving to Death on a Government Claim. *Unknown.*
Old Age
Adios. Babock.
Advice to the Old Beaux. Sedley.
After a Line by John Peale Bishop. Justice.
Against Winter. Feinstein.
Age. Jones.
Age. Landor.
Age. More.
Age and Youth. *Fr.* The Passionate Pilgrim. Shakespeare.
Age in Prospect. Jeffers.

Age Not to Be Rejected. Herrick.
Aged Aged Man, The. *Fr.* Through the Looking-Glass. "Carroll."
Aged Fisherman. Bynner.
Aged Lover Renounceth Love, The. Vaux.
Alas! 'Tis Very Sad to Hear. Landor.
Almost Ninety. Whitman.
Almswomen. Blunden.
Ancient to Ancients, An. Hardy.
April Inventory. Snodgrass.
At Eighty. Stanhope.
At 85. Ardinger.
At the Doors. Der Nistor.
Aunt Alice in April. Matchett.
Auspex. Lowell.
Autumn. Wolfe.
Autumnus. Sylvester.
Baucis and Philemon. Hoskins.
Bean Eaters, The. Brooks.
Bedtime Story, A. Mezey.
Black and glossy as a bee and curled was my hair. Ambapali.
Blue-eyed was Elf the minstrel. *Fr.* The Ballad of the White Horse: The Harp of Alfred. Chesterton.
Boarding, The. Johnson.
Boys, The. Holmes.
Bulldozers. Dec.
Centenarian's Story, The. Whitman.
Chaperon, The. Bunner.
Chard Whitlow. Reed.
Childhood. Cornford.
Chough, The. Reaney.
City Pigeons. Chasin.
Comfort. Widdemer.
Coming of Wisdom with Time, The. Yeats.
Complaint of the Fair Armoress. Villon.
Consider the Lilies. Donnelly.
Conversation. Giovanni.
Crabbed Age and Youth. *Fr.* The Passionate Pilgrim. Shakespeare.
Crows, The. Bogan.
Cry of an Aged One, The. Fraser.
Daguerreotype Taken in Old Age. Atwood.
Danny Murphy. Stephens.
Days Ago. Hai-Jew.
Dear Men and Women. Wheelock.
Disturb me not, O buoyant youths! Maori.
Do Not Go Gentle into That Good Night. Thomas.
Double Ritual. Rainer.
Dust to Dust. De la Mare.
Emancipation. *Unknown.*
Enough! Scully.
Envy the Old. Van Doren.
Ever On. *Unknown.*
Faded Face, The. Hardy.
Failure. Lattimore.
Father William. *Fr.* Alice's Adventures in Wonderland. "Carroll."
First Meditation. *Fr.* Meditations of an Old Woman. Roethke.
Flying Wheel, The. Tynan.
Forerunners, The. Herbert.
Fountain, The. Wordsworth.
From the Crag. Leib.
Gather Ye Rosebuds. Fowler.
Gerontion. Eliot.
Gold Leaves. Chesterton.
Grand Finale. Layton.
Grandfathers, The. Justice.
Grandmother, Rocking. Merriam.
Great-Grandmother, The. Graves.
Grey Woman. Cardiff.
Grow Old Along with Me. *Fr.* Rabbi Ben Ezra. Browning.
Growing Old. Arnold.
Growing Old. Fraser.
Growing Old. *Unknown.*
Growing Old. Wells.
Growing Old. Wilcox.
Growing Older. Wells.
Hag of Beare, The. *Unknown.*
Harmonica Man. Wolny.
Healing. Reisen.
Heavy, Heavy—What Hangs Over? Burke.
His Age. Herrick.
His Golden Locks Time Hath to Silver Turned. *Fr.* Polyhymnia. Peele.
How Old Are You? Fritsch.
How to Be Old. Swenson.
I Followed a Path. Parker.
I Look into My Glass. Hardy.
I Used to Watch You, Sleeping. *Fr.* My Mother's Birthday. Raine.
Ice, The. Gibson.
If I Should Die Before I Wake. Mezey.
I'm Here. *Fr.* Meditations of an Old Woman. Roethke.
"I'm 92," Joe said. Weber.
Image of Death, The. Vaux.
In Respect of the Elderly. Peacock.
In Tenebris. Hardy.
In Time of Gold. Doolittle ("H. D.").
Infirmity. Roethke.
Invisible Man, The. Matthews.
It Is Too Late! *Fr.* Morituri Salutamus. Longfellow.
Jerry an' Me. Rich.
John Anderson, My Jo. Burns.
Laid in My Quiet Bed. Surrey.
Lament of the Lovely Helmet-Dealer. Villon.
Lamentation of the Old Pensioner, The. Yeats.
Last Chapter, The. De la Mare.
Last Leaf, The. Holmes.
Last Words of My English Grandmother, The. Williams.
Late-Flowering Lust. Betjeman.
Late Leaves. Landor.
Leaden Echo and the Golden Echo, The. Hopkins.
Leitrim Woman, A. Donaghy.
Let Me Grow Lovely. Baker.
Letter. Bergman.
Letter from a Girl to Her Own Old Age, A. Meynell.
Letters from a Father. Van Duyn.
Life's Last Scene. *Fr.* The Vanity of Human Wishes. Johnson.
Light and Dark. Howes.
Litany for Old Age, A. Harsen.
Little Boy and the Old Man, The. Silverstein.
Little Old Lady in Lavender Silk, The. Parker.
Long Hill, The. Teasdale.
Love Is Like the Wild Rose-Briar. Brontë.
Loveliest of Trees. Housman.
Lovers, The. Murray.
Man's Going Hence. *Fr.* Human Life. Rogers.
Man's Mortality. *Unknown.*
Medicine. Walker.
Minuet on Reaching the Age of Fifty, A. Santayana.
Miss Creighton. Taylor.
Miss Euphemia. Ransom.
Mr. Flood's Party. Robinson.
Model T. Stoutenburg.
Moonlight. Teasdale.
My Love Is Young. Birney.
Nature. Longfellow.
New Day. Madgett.
Night Thoughts in Age. Wheelock.
90th Year, The. Levertov.
Niño Leading an Old Man to Market. Nathan.
No charm can stay, no medicine can assuage. Landor.
Nod. De La Mare.
Ode on Advancing Age. Dixon.
Of the Last Verses in the Book. Waller.
Oisin. *Unknown.*
Old Adam, The. Levertov.
Old Age. Gond.
Old Age. Sidney.
Old Age. *Fr.* Of the Last Verses in the Book. Waller.
Old Age. Zulu.
Old Age Home, The. Holmes.
Old Age in His Ailing. Melville.
Old Age Pensioner, The. Campbell.
Old age sticks. Cummings.
Old Black Men. Johnson.
Old Couple, The. Green.
Old Crabbed Men. Reeves.
Old Dan'l. Strong.
Old Familiar Faces, The. Lamb.
Old Folk, The. Ditlevsen.
Old Folks Home, An. Lake.
Old General, The. *Fr.* Isabella. Williams.
Old Habitant, An. Call.
Old I Am. Bosman.
Old Jockey, The. Higgins.
Old Ladies. Dromgoole.
Old Lady's Lament for Her Youth, The. Villon.
Old Man, The. Fisher.

Old Man. Jennings.
Old Man, An. Wordsworth.
Old Man Dreams, The. Holmes.
Old Man He Courted Me, An. *Unknown.*
Old Man's Comforts and How He Gained Them, The. Southey.
Old Man's Song, An. Le Gallienne
Old Man's Winter Night, An. Frost.
Old Man's Wish, The. Pope.
Old Men, The. Corman.
Old Men, The. De la Mare.
Old Men, The. Feldman.
Old Men, The. Kipling.
Old Men, The. Lavitz.
Old Men. Nash.
Old Men Admiring Themselves in the Water, The. Yeats.
Old Men and Old Women Going Home on the Street Car. Cullen.
Old Men on the Blue. Ferril.
Old Nudists, The. Colby.
Old Pensioner, The. Yeats.
Old People. Livingston.
Old Seawoman. LeClaire.
Old Soldiers Home at Marshalltown, Iowa. Barnes.
Old Wife in High Spirits. "MacDiarmid."
Old Woman, The. Campbell.
Old Woman. Smith.
Old Woman Awaiting the Greyhound Bus. Niatum.
Old Woman of Beare, The. *Unknown.*
Old woman sits, The. Davis.
Old Women of Toronto. Waddington.
On Falling Asleep to Birdsong. Meredith.
On Growing Old. Masefield.
On His Seventy-fifth Birthday. *Fr.* The Last Fruit off an Old Tree. Landor.
One Flesh. Jennings.
Over the Hill to the Poor-House. Carleton.
Parable of the Old Man and the Young, The. Owen.
Pass we the ills, which each man feels or dreads. *Fr.* Solomon on the Vanity of the World. Prior.
Passing the Masonic Home for the Aged. Scott.
Pause for Breath, A. Hughes.
Peekaboo, I Almost See You. Nash.
Phone Call to Rutherford. Blackburn.
Piazza Piece. Ransom.
Pigeon-Feeders in Battery Park, The. Altrocchi.
Plaudite, The; or End of Life. Herrick.
Poem: "Old man in the crystal morning after snow." Schwartz.
Portrait of a Very Old Man. Carsley.
Prayer: "Lord God of the oak and the elm." Villiers.
Promise of Peace. Jeffers.
Provide, Provide. Frost.
Rabbi Ben Ezra. Browning.
Real Story, A. Pastan.
Reflecting on the Aging-Process. Peters.
Reflections. Crabbe.
Remarks of Soul to Body. Warren.
Requiem, A. Ignatow.
Retirement. *Unknown.*
Rhymes. Steele.
Sad Song, A. *Fr.* The Emperor of the East. Massinger.
Sailing to Byzantium. Yeats.
Sair Fyel'd, Hinny. *Unknown.*
She, to Him. Hardy.
Silly Old Man, The. *Unknown.*
Silver Threads among the Gold. Rexford.
Simon Lee. Wordsworth.
Sixty-eighth Birthday. Lowell.
Smell of Old Newspapers Is Always Stronger after Sleeping in the Sun, The. Lowery.
So What. Appleman.
Song for September. Fitzgerald.
Song from a Country Fair. Adams.
Song of a Woman Abandoned by the Tribe. *Unknown.*
Song on Reaching Seventy. Wheelock.
Sonnet: Anniversary, February 23, 1795. Mason.
Sonnet: "Long time a child, and still a child, when years." Coleridge.
Sons. Polson.
Span of Life, The. Frost.
Spur, The. Yeats.
Strokes. Stafford.
Survivor. MacLeish.
Survivor, The. Thomas.
Temporal. Jonas.
Terminus. Emerson.
That time of year thou mayst in me behold. Sonnets, LXXIII. Shakespeare.
There was an old woman lived under a hill. Mother Goose.
Tithonus. Tennyson.
To a Gentlewoman, Objecting to Him His Grey Hairs. Herrick.
To a Poor Old Woman. Williams.
To Age. Landor.
To an Old Lady. Empson.
To His Mistresses ("Help me! Help me! now I call"). Herrick.
To Mary. Cowper.
To My Ninth Decade. Landor.
To One Being Old. Mitchell.
To Perilla. Herrick.
To Waken an Old Lady. Williams.
Too Late? Longfellow.
Too Late. Ludlow.
Tower, The. Yeats.
Twenty Golden Years Ago. Mangan.
Twilight. Robinson.
Two Old Gentlemen, The. Wallace.
Ulysses. Tennyson.
Uselessness. Wilcox.
Very Old, The. Galloway.
Very Old Woman, A. Eshleman.
Waiting for a Second Time. Tauhindauli.
Warning. Joseph.
Weeksville Women. Loftin.
Welcome Eild. *Unknown.*
When all the world is young, lad. *Fr.* The Water Babies. Kingsley.
When I Am Old. Mason.
When I See Old Men. Souster.
When my love swears that she is made of truth. *Fr.* Love's Labour's Lost. Shakespeare.
When the Sword of Sixty Comes Nigh His Head. Firdausi.
When They Grow Old. Ralph.
When You and I Were Young, Maggie. Johnson.
When You Are Old. Yeats.
When Your Parents Grow Old. Hart.
Whisperer, The. Bullen.
Whom the Gods Love. Bruner.
Wishes of an Elderly Man, The. Raleigh.
Years, The. Wheelock.
Year's End, The. Cole.
Young and Old. *Fr.* The Water Babies. Kingsley.
Youth and Age. Byron.
Youth and Age. Coleridge.
Youth and Age. Surrey.
Youth and Age on Beaulieu River, Hants. Betjeman.
Zeke. Strong.
See also **Pensions; Retirement.**

Old Ironsides. *See* **Constitution (ship)**

Oldham, John
To the Memory of Mr. Oldham. Dryden.

O'Leary, Arthur
Lament for Art O'Leary, The. *Unknown.*

Olive Trees
Olive Tree, The. Baring-Gould.
Olive Trees. Colum.
Tapestry Trees. Morris.

Olympics
First in the Pentathlon. Lucilius.

Omar Khayyám
In a Copy of Omar Khayyám. Lowell.

O'Neill, Owen Roe
Lament for the Death of Eoghan Ruadh O'Neill. Davis.

O'Neill, Shane
Shane O'Neill. MacManus.
Shane O'Neill's Cairn. Jeffers.

Onions
Man in the Onion Bed, The. Ciardi.
Onions. *Fr.* Verses for Fruitwomen. Swift.
Peeling Onions. Rich.
Recipe: Onions. Philemon.

Ontario, Canada
Battle of Bridgewater, The. *Unknown.*
Beast Enough. Billings.
Burning Hills. Ondaatje.
Camping at Thunder Bay. Fedo.
Capital Square. Anderson.
Country North of Belleville, The. Purdy.
Day before Christmas, The. Souster.

Dufferin, Simcoe, Grey. Atwood.
Giant's Tomb in Georgian Bay. "Hale."
Honi Soit Qui Mal Y Pense. Young.
Lake St. Clair. *Fr.* The Great Lakes Suite. Reaney.
Love at Robin Lake. Purdy.
Night Hyms on Lake Nipigon. Scott.
Out of Control; the Quarry. Dewdny.
Renfrew County. *Fr.* May Day Rounds. Finnigan.
River, The; North of Guelph. Jones.
Stranded in My Ontario. Everson.
Temagami. Lampman.
Thousand Islands, The. *Fr.* St. Lawrence and the Saguenay. Songster.
Three Cezannes. Whipple.
Tick Picking in the Quetico. Johnson.
Wilderness Gothic. Purdy.

Opera
Aux Italiens. "Meredith."
Carmen. Levy.
Das Liebesleben. Gunn.
Faust. Ashbery.
Il Janitoro. Ade.
Ill Met by Zenith. Nash.
Italian Opera. Miller.
Lohengrin. Payne.
Matinees. Merrill.
Rigoletto. Levy.
Tannhauser. Levy.
Tannhäuser. Payne.

Ophelia
Ballad of Another Ophelia. Lawrence.
Ophelia. Rimbaud.
Ophelia. Watkins.
Ophelia's Song. Zaturenska.

Opium
Opium Den, The. Malay.
Sonnet to Opium, A; Celebrating Its Virtues. "Orestes."
Willie the Weeper. *Unknown.*

Opossums
Carmen Possum. *Unknown.*
Opossum. Smith.

Opportunity
Opportunity. Braley.
Opportunity. Graham.
Opportunity. Ingalls.
Opportunity. Malone.
Opportunity. *Fr.* The Rape of Lucrece. Shakespeare.
Opportunity. Sill.
Opportunity's Knock. Bishop.
Today. Carlyle.
Water Mill, The. Doudney.

Oppression
Burning of Paper Instead of Children, The. Rich.
Commission. Pound.
Day of the Night, The. Scully.
Determination. Clarke.
For Refugio Talamante. Ochester.
Man with the Hoe, The. Markham.
Oppression. Hughes.
See also **Apartheid; Dehumanization; Sexism; Slavery; Tyranny.**

Optimism
Away, Melancholy. Smith.
Good Time Coming, The. Mackay.
M. Crashaw's Answer for Hope. Crashaw.
Optimism. Wilcox.
Optimist, The. *Unknown.*
Optimist and Pessimist. Wilson.
Pippa's Song. *Fr.* Pippa Passes. Browning.
Protect Me. Adler.
Say Not the Struggle Nought Availeth. Clough.
Tree-Top Road, The. Smith.
Truth. North.
Try the Uplook. *Unknown.*
When the clouds' swoln bosoms echo back the shouts. *Fr.* In Tenebris. Hardy.
Wisdom of Folly, The. Fowler.
See also **Hope.**

Oracles
Hebrew Sibyl, The. Fainlight.
Oracles, The. Housman.

Orange
What Is Orange? O'Neill.

Orange Trees and Oranges
Red-Gold Rain, The. Sitwell.
Smudging. Wakoski.
Tapestry Trees. Morris.

Oratory
Overworked Elocutionist, An. Wells.

Orchards
Among the Orchards. Lampman.
Autumn Orchard. Jacobs.
Good-by and Keep Cold. Frost.
I Have an Orchard. *Fr.* The Tragedy of Dido. Marlowe.
In an Old Orchard. Dufault.
Little Green Orchard, The. De la Mare.
Lost Orchard, The. Masters.
My Orcha'd in Linden Lea. Barnes.
Of an Orchard. Tynan.
Old Apple Trees. Snodgrass.
Orchard, The. Ehrlich.
Orchard. Doolittle ("H. D.").
Orchard at Avignon, An. Robinson.
Orchard Snow. Goodenough.
Through Ruddy Orchards. Oliver.

Orchids
Bee-Orchis, The. Young.
Orchids. Roethke.
Orchids. Wratislaw.

Order
Idea of Order at Key West, The. Stevens.

Oregon (state)
Exodus for Oregon. Miller.
Fish Counter at Bonneville, The. Stafford.
Grand Ronde Valley, The. Higginson.
Indian Painting, Probably Paiute, In a Cave Near Madras, Oregon. Ramsey.
Lines Written in Oregon. Nabokov.
Men against the Sky. Haines.
Oregon Winter. McGahey.
Wingwalking in Oregon. Peterson.

Oregon (ship)
Battle-Song of the *Oregon.* Rice.
Race of the *Oregon,* The. Meehan.
Rush of the *Oregon,* The. Guiterman.

Oregon Trail
Oregon Trail, The. *Unknown.*
Oregon Trail: 1851. Marshall.
Oregon Trail, The: 1843. Guiterman.

Organ-grinders. *See* **Hurdy-gurdies.**

Organs and Organists
Organist, The. Stevens.
Organist, The. *Unknown.*
Organist in Heaven, The. Brown.

Orient (ship)
Brave Old Ship, *The Orient,* The. Lowell.

Original Sin
Adam Lay Ibounden. *Unknown.*
Alas that ever that speche was spoken. *Unknown.*
Corruption. Vaughan.
Ha! Original Sin. Nash.
Original Sin; a Short Story. Warren.

Orioles
Song the Oriole Sings, The. Howells.
To an Oriole. Fawcett.
To hear an oriole sing. Dickinson.

Orion (mythology)
Artemis. *Fr.* Orion. Horne.
We will wait by the chestnut and the ilex tree. *Fr.* Landscape with the Giant Orion: Orion Seeks the Goddes Diana. Sitwell.

Orion (constellation)
Irish Astronomy. Halpine.
Orion. Rich.

Oriskany, Battle of (1777)
Battle of Oriskany, The. Helmer.

Orkney Islands
Above Ben Loyal. Ball.
In Orknay. Fowler.
Lion Gate. Rich.

Ormonde, Elizabeth Preston Butler, Countess of
To the Excellent Pattern of Beauty and Virtue, Lady Elizabeth, Countess of Ormond. Shirley.

Orphans
Babes in the Wood, The. *Unknown.*
Children's Elegy. *Fr.* Eighth Elegy. Rukeyser.

Little Orphant Annie. Riley.
Motherless Children. *Unknown.*
Nobody's Child. Case.
Orphan, The. *Unknown.*
Orphan Boy, The. *Unknown.*
Orphan Boy's Tale, The. Opie.
Orphans. Ray.
Orphan's Song, The. Dobell.
Readen ov a Head-stwone. Barnes.

Orpheus
Death of Eurydice and Orpheus' Journey to Hell, The. *Fr.* Metamorphoses. Ovid.
Greater Music, The. Weiss.
Orpheus. Davie.
Orpheus. Herrick.
Orpheus. Winters.
Orpheus and Eurydice. Browning.
Orpheus in Greenwich Village. Gilbert.
Orpheus in the Underworld. Gascoyne.
Orpheus to Beasts. Lovelace.
Orpheus to Woods. Lovelace.
Orpheus with His Lute. *Fr.* King Henry VIII. *At. to* Fletcher *or* Shakespeare.
Power of Music, The. Lisle.
Thus sung Orpheus to his strings. *Unknown.*

Ospreys
Fish-Hawk, The. Wheelock.
Osprey Suicides, The. Lieberman.

Ostriches
Bored Ostrich, The. *Unknown.*
He "Digesteth Hard Yron." Moore.
Ostrich Is a Silly Bird, The. Freeman.

Ottawa, Ontario
Capital Square. Anderson.

Ottawa River
Deep Dark River. Roberts.

Otterburn, Battle of (1388)
Battle of Otterburn, The. *Unknown.*
Chevy Chase. *Unknown.*

Otters
Otter, The. Heaney.
Otters. Hart-Smith.
Otter, An. Hughes.

Oudenarde, Battle of (1708)
Jack Frenchman's Lamentation. *Unknown.*

Ouija Boards
For My Husband. Voigt.
Voices from the Other World. Merrill.

Ouray, Colorado
Lines on Mountain Villages. "Sunset Joe."

Outlaws. *See* **Crime and Criminals.**

Ovenbirds
Oven Bird, The. Frost.

Overland Trail
Dust of the Overland Trail, The. Adams.

Ovibos
Ovibos, The. Hale.
See also **Musk Oxen.**

Ovid (Publius Ovidius Naso)
Ovid. Pevear.
Ovid on the Dacian Coast. Thompson.
Written in an Ovid. Prior.

Owain Gwynedd, Prince of North Wales
Triumphs of Owen, The. Gray.

Owls
Aziola, The. Shelley.
Bird of Night, The. Jarrell.
Come, doleful owl, the messenger of woe. *Unknown.*
Eyes. Davies.
Father and Child. Harwood.
From a Printed Bill, Fixed in the Beak of One in a Group of Five Stuffed Owls in the Shop Window of a Bird Stuffer, at Richmond, Yorkshire. *Unknown.*
Great Brown Owl, The. Browne.
Hail to Thee, Blithe Owl. Lardner.
Hunter, The. Wallis.
If the Owl Calls Again. Haines.
Leaves that rustled on this oak-crowned hill, The. Wordsworth.
Little Fox, The. Edey *and* Grider.
Materialized into an Owl. Oliver.
Of all the gay birds that e'er I did see. *Unknown.*
Once I was a monarch's daughter. *Unknown.*
Owl. Dufault.
Owl, The. Owen.
Owl. Rokwaho.
Owl, The. Sackville-West.
Owl, The. Smith.
Owl, The. Tennyson.
Owl, The. Thomas.
Owl against Nightingale. *At. to* Nicholas de Guildford.
Owl and the Fox, The. *Unknown.*
Owl and the Pussy-Cat, The. Lear.
Owl Critic, The. Fields.
Owl in the Rabbi's Barn, The. Jaffe.
Owls. Snodgrass.
Owl's Song. Hughes.
Prayer to the Snowy Owl. Haines.
Questioning Faces. Frost.
Song of the Owl, The. Munkittrick.
Sweet Suffolk Owl. *At. to* Vautor.
There came a gray owl at sunset. *Unknown.*
There was an old owl lived in an oak. *Unknown.*
Town Owl. Lee.
When I was in a summer valley. *Fr.* The Owl and the Nightingale. *Unknown.*
White Owl, The. *Fr.* Love in a Valley. Meredith.
Wise Old Owl, A. Richards.
You look at me, a hut or cage contains. *Fr.* Sagesse. Doolittle ("H. D.").

Oxen
Beasts Are Very Wise, The. Kipling.
Crossing the Plains. Miller.
I Have Twelve Oxen. *Unknown.*
My Ox Duke. Dyer.
Old Ox, The. Hamilton.
Ox, The. Webster.
Oxen, The. Hardy.
Oxen: Ploughing at Fiesole. Tomlinson.
Song of Praise for an Ox. Sutskever.
Twelve Oxen, The. *Unknown.*

Oxford, England
Above the High. Grigson.
Almae Matres. Lang.
By Magdalen Bridge, Oxford. Hopkins.
Christ Church Meadows, Oxford. Hall.
Duns Scotus's Oxford. Hopkins.
Epigram on the Refusal of the University of Oxford to Subscribe to His Translation of Homer. Cowper.
How changed is here each spot man makes or fills! *Fr.* Thyrsis. Arnold.
Letter, A. Quiller-Couch.
Masque of Balliol, The, *sels.* Beeching, Mackail, *and* Nichols.
On the Night Train from Oxford. Mayo.
Oxford. Douglas.
Oxford. Johnson.
Oxford Bells. Hopkins.
Oxford Bells. Maris Stella.
Oxford Commination. Leary.
"Oxford Is a Stage." Nolan.
Oxford Nights. Johnson.
Philomela. Ransom.
Pitt-Rivers Museum, Oxford, The. Fenton.
Prologue to the University of Oxford. Dryden.
Scholar-Gipsy, The. Arnold.
Sonnet: To Oxford. Russell.
Spires of Oxford, The. Letts.
To Oxford. Hopkins.
To the University of Oxford, 1674. Dryden.
Trent Again, The. *Fr.* Polyolbion. Drayton.
Verses on Sir Joshua Reynolds's Painted Window at New-College, Oxford. Warton.
Views of the Oxford Colleges. Howes.
Views of the Oxford Colleges. Leary.

Oysters
Ossified Oyster, An. Wells.
Oyster, The. Nash.
Oyster, The. Ponge.
Oysters. Swift.
Walrus and the Carpenter, The. *Fr.* Through the Looking-Glass. "Carroll."

Ozark Mountains
Caves. Baker.

P

Pacific Ocean
Eye, The. Jeffers.
Facing West from California's Shores. Whitman.
Once by the Pacific. Frost.
Pacific Sonnets, *sels.* Barker.
Prayer to the Pacific. Silko.
Remembering That Island. McGrath.
Slow Pacific Swell, The. Winters.
Pacifism and Pacifists
Breakthrough. Sinclair.
Bring 'Em Home. Dane *and* others.
Christmas Eve under Hooker's Statue. Lowell.
Conscientious Objector, The. Shapiro.
Dooley Is a Traitor. Michie.
Dove, The. MacColl.
Education. Barrington.
For the Minority. Peterson.
He Went for a Soldier. Mitchell.
I Just Wanna Stay Home. Silber.
I Sing of Olaf Glad and Big. Cummings.
In the one-two domestic goose one-two one-two step. *Fr.* New Wings for Icarus. Beissel.
I've Got to Know. Guthrie.
Memories of West Street and Lepke. Lowell.
Pacifist, The. Belloc.
Put My Name Down. Silber.
Study War No More. *Unknown.*
That Crazy War. *Unknown.*
Women at Munition Making. Collins.
See also **Conscientious Objectors.**
Paganism and Pagans.
Christ and the Pagan. Tabb.
First and Last Man. McTell.
Plain of Adoration, The. *Unknown.*
Paige, Leroy ("Satchel")
To Satch. Allen.
Pain
After great pain, a formal feeling comes. Dickinson.
Dolores. Swinburne.
Flower, The. Creeley.
For All in Pain. Carmichael.
House of Pain, The. Coates.
I Sit and Look Out. Whitman.
If my vain soul needs blows and better losses. *Fr.* The Christian's New Year Prayer. Wilcox.
Is it not sure a deadly pain. *Unknown.*
It's Just the Same to Me. Hesse.
My Uninvited Guest. Smith.
Never Admit the Pain. Gilmore.
90 North. Jarrell.
No Pleasure without Some Pain. Vaux.
Pain. "Æ."
Pain. Södergran.
Pain for a Daughter. Sexton.
Pain has an element of blank. Dickinson.
Place of Pain in the Universe, The. Hecht.
Postcard from Zamboanga. Esbensen.
Prayer for Pain. Neihardt.
Process. O'Donnell.
Security. O'Donnell.
Solitude. Wilcox.
Sympathizers, The. Miles.
There is a languor of the life. Dickinson.
There is a pain—so utter. Dickinson.
Thirty Childbirths. Brand.
To My New Mistress. Bowie.
Villanelle: "It is the pain, it is the pain, endures." Empson.
Way of Pain, The. Berry.
Paine, Thomas
Democratic Barber, The; or, Country Gentleman's Surprise. Parrish.
God Save Great Thomas Paine. Mather.
Soldier's Friend, The. Canning.
Stanzas: "On the Decease of Thomas Paine, Who Died at New York, on the 8th of June, 1809." Freneau.
Painting and Painters
After two sittings, now our Lady State. *Fr.* The Last Instructions to a Painter. Marvell.
All Too Little on Pictures. Black.
Andrea del Sarto. Browning.
Anonymous Drawing. Justice.
Another November. Plumly.
Backgrounds to Italian Paintings: Fifteenth Century. Ridler.
Bather in a Painting, A. Greene.
Beauty and Sadness. Song.
Card-Dealer, The. Rossetti.
Cardinal's Dog, The. Glassco.
Dance, The. Williams.
Detail from an Annunciation by Crivelli. Dobson.
Early Unfinished Sketch. Clarke.
Elegiac Stanzas. Wordsworth.
Epigram: "The Likeness." Martial.
Face, A. Browning.
Face upon the Floor, The. D'Arcy.
Flemish Primitive. Fraser.
For "A Venetian Pastoral" by Giorgione. Rossetti.
For "An Allegorical Dance of Women" by Andrea Mantegna. Rossetti.
For "Our Lady of the Rocks" by Leonardo da Vinci. Rossetti.
For "Ruggiero and Angelica" by Ingres. Rossetti.
For "The Wine and Circe" by Edward Burne-Jones. Rossetti.
Fra Lippo Lippi. Browning.
Giovanni Da Fiesole on the Sublime; or, Fra Angelico's "Last Judgment." Howard.
History of the World as Pictures, The. Sullivan.
How to Paint a Perfect Christmas. Holub.
I Paint What I See. White.
In an Artist's Studio. Rossetti.
In Santa Maria del Popolo. Gunn.
Joan Brown, about Her Painting. Fraser.
Large Bad Picture. Bishop.
Laughing Hyena, by Hokusai, The. Enright.
Man with the Hoe, The. Markham.
Man with the Hoe, The; a Reply. Cheney.
Meditation on John Constable, A. Tomlinson.
Michelangelo: "The Creation of Adam." Djanikian.
Minor Victorian Painter, A. Hewitt.
Monet Refuses the Operation. Mueller.
Most Expensive Picture in the World, The. Nemerov.
Musée des Beaux Arts. Auden.
Museum Piece. Wilbur.
My Madonna. Service.
My own head. Seen in mirrors. Cleanly axed. *Fr.* Caravaggio Dying, Porto Ercole, July 1610, Aged 36. Lucie-Smith.
Nightmare. *Fr.* The Botanic Garden. Darwin.
Nikos Painting. Hanson.
Nude with Green Chair. Oldknow.
Old Paintings on Italian Walls. Raine.
Old Pictures in Florence. Browning.
On a Fifteenth-Century Flemish Angel. Ray.
On a Painting by Patient B of the Independence State Hospital for the Insane. Justice.
On a Picture by Michele da Verona, of Arion as a Boy Riding upon a Dolphin. Ridler.
Order for a Picture, An. Cary.
Paint Box, The. Rieu.
Painted Head. Ransom.
Painted Passages. Harada.
Painter, The. Ashbery.
Painter Who Pleased Nobody and Everybody, The. Gay.
Painter's Mistress, The. Flecker.
Painting. Jacobs.
Painting the Gate. Swenson.
Painture. Lovelace.
Paul Klee. Haines.
Pictor Ignotus. Browning.
Picturesque; a Fragment. Aiken.
Poem: "About the size of an old-style dollar bill." Bishop.
Poem, The: "Painter of Dante's awful ferry-ride, The." Deutsch.
Politics of Rich Painters, The. Baraka.
Portrait of a Cree. "Hale."
Portrait of Prince Henry, The. Clouts.
Post-Impressionism. Taylor.
Proportions. Stroud.
Remember the Ladies. Lifshin.
Ryder. Haines.
1614 Boren. Hugo.
Squeeze Play. McGinley.
Story of Soutine, A. Schevill.
Studies from Life. Dickey.
Suggested by a Picture of the Bird of Paradise. Wordworth.
Technique. Eaton.

To Cole, the Painter, Departing for Europe. Bryant.
To Mr. Jervas, with Fresnoy's Art of Painting, Translated by Mr. Dryden. Pope.
To S. M. a Young African Painter, on Seeing His Work. Wheatley.
To the Painter Preparing to Draw M. M. H. Shirley.
Unpraised Picture, An. Burton.
West Fifty-seventh Street. Vazakas.
When Sir Joshua Reynolds Died. Blake.
White Fox. Shepard.
Why I Am Not a Painter. O'Hara.
Winter Landscape. Berryman.
With Francis Furini. *Fr.* Parleyings with Certain People of Importance in Their Day. Browning.
Poet Dreaming in the Artist's House, The; Contemporary Poems about the Visual Arts (PoDr). Emilie Buchwald *and* Ruth Roston, eds.

Paleontology
Imitation of Julia A. Moore. "Twain."
See also **Dinosaurs; Evolution; Extinction; Fossils.**

Palestine
In Galilee. Butts.
On Jordan's Bank. Byron.
Palestine. Whittier.
To F. C. in Memoriam Palestine. Chesterton.
See also **Israel.**

Palm Sunday
Donkey, The. Chesterton.
Little Catkins. Blok.
Palm-Sunday Hymn, A. Herbert.

Palm Trees
Palm House, Botanic Gardens. Hetherington.
Palm-Tree, The. Abd-ar-Rahman I.
Palm Tree and the Pines, The. Milnes.
Royal Palm. Crane.
Song of the Palm. Robinson.

Pan (god)
Dead Pan, The. Browning.
God of Sheep, The. *Fr.* The Faithful Shepherdess. Fletcher.
Great God Pan, The. Browning.
Hymn of Pan. Shelley.
Hymn to Pan. *Fr.* Endymion. Keats.
Musical Instrument, A. Browning.
Note from the Pipes, A. Speyer.
Pan and Luna. Browning.
Pan and Syrinx. Rodgers.
Pan in Wall Street. Stedman.
Pan-Pipes. Chalmers.
Pan Piping. Plato.
Pans Anniversarie. Jonson.
Pan's Song. *Fr.* Midas. Lyly.
Sing his praises that doth keep. *Fr.* The Faithful Shepherdess. Fletcher.
Song: "My spirit like a shepherd boy." Sackville-West.
Syrinx. *Fr.* Midas. Lyly.

Panama
Beyond the Chagres. Gilbert.
Panama. Jones.
Panama. Roche.

Panama Canal
Song of Panama, A. Runyon

Pancakes
Mix a Pancake. Rosetti.
Pancake Collector, The. Prelutsky.
Those Flapjacks of Brown's. Taylor.

Pandas
Panda, The. *Fr.* Animals That Stand in Dreams. Elliott.
Panda, The. Smith.

Pansies
Pansy. Newsome.
Yellow Pansy, A. Cone.

Pantheism
Higher Pantheism in a Nutshell, The. *Fr.* The Heptalogia. Swinburne.
Higher Pantheism, The. Tennyson.
It Is a Beauteous Evening, Calm and Free. Wordsworth.
One, The. Kavanagh.

Panthers
In the Night. Roberts.
Panther, The. Nash.
Panther, The. Rilke.

Papacy
Election, An. Marcus.
To Pius IX. Whittier.
See also **Catholicism.**

Parachuting. *See* **Sky Diving and Sky Divers.**

Parades
Flag Goes By, The. Bennett.
Parade. *Fr.* A Circus Garland. Field.
Parade, A. Rose.
Two Hundred Girls in Tights and Halters. Hoffman.
See also **Marching and Marches.**

Paradise. *See* **Heaven.**

Paradise Lost
On Mr. Milton's "Paradise Lost." Marvell.
See also **Milton, John.**

Paranoia
Tryst. Merriam.
Tunnel, The. Strand.
Widow, The. Ludvigson.

Parenthood
Adam. Hecht.
Anacreontic, on Parting with a Little Child. Wesley.
Andre. Brooks.
Any Time. Stafford.
Becoming a Dad. Guest.
Censorship. Ciardi.
Childless. MacNamee.
Dad's Greatest Job. *Unknown.*
Door and Window Bolted Fast. Leib.
Expectant Father, The. Ai.
Father, The. Finkel.
Father Poem. Oppenheimer.
For a Child Expected. Ridler.
For My Daughter. Ochester.
For Sapphires. Rodgers.
Fruit of the Flower. Cullen.
Generations. Awad.
Heart's Needle. Snodgrass.
I am slowly dying, water evaporating. *Fr.* Summer Solstice. Bowering.
Joyful Prophecy. Miller.
Living among the Dead. Matthews.
Name, The. Creeley.
On My First Daughter. Jonson.
On My First Son. Jonson.
On the Birth of His Son. Su Tung-p'o.
Parental Ode to My Son, A. Hood.
Parents. Buckley.
Parents. Meredith.
Parents-without-Partners Picnic, The. Schaefer.
Personal History; for My Son. Todd.
Poet's Welcome to His Love-Begotten Daughter, A. Burns.
Prayer for My Daughter, A. Yeats.
Secret Laughter. Morley.
Separate Parties. Stuart.
Service Supreme. *Unknown.*
Sleep, My Child. Aleichem.
Sonnet to a Friend Who Asked, How I Felt When the Nurse First Presented My Infant to Me. Coleridge.
They Grow Up Too Fast, She Said. O Hehir.
To Evan. Eberhart.
To His Son, Vincent Corbet. Corbet.
To My Children, Fearing for Them. Berry.
Toys, The. Patmore.
Two Parents, Two. "MacDiarmid."
Upon Wedlock and Death of Children. Taylor.
Visit. Coccimiglio.
Way of Pain, The. Berry.
What My Child Learns of the Sea. Lorde.
When Forty Winters. *Fr.* Sonnets. Shakespeare.
Which Shall It Be? Beers.
Wishes for My Son. MacDonagh.

Paret, Benny ("Kid")
Memory of Boxer Benny (Kid) Paret, The. Lima.

Paris, France
A Fauxbourg. *Fr.* Paris in 1815. Croly.
Enigmatic Traveler, The. Vazakas.
Four Sheets to the Wind and a One-Way Ticket to France. Rivers.
Impression de Paris. Wilde.
In a Station of the Metro. Pound.
In Paris. MacDonagh.
Merry Man of Paris, The. Mead.
Mourning Letter from Paris, A. Rivers.
Next Time You Were There, The. Hazo.
104 Boulevard Saint-Germain. Pitchford.
Paris. Garnett.
Paris. Symons.

Paris at Night. Corbière.
Paris by Night. Milbauer.
Paris Nocturne, A. "Macleod."
Paris; the Seine at Night. Divine.
Paris: This April Sunset Completely Utters. Cummings.
Public Holiday: Paris. Horner.
Southeast Ramparts of the Seine, The. Tóth.
Two X. Cummings.
Unromantic Song. Brode.
Woman's Execution, A. King.

Parker, Charlie
Mellowness and Flight. Barlow.
Requiem for "Bird" Parker. Corso.
Walking Parker Home. Kaufman.
Yardbird's Skull. Dodson.

Parks
Back to Life. Gunn.
Ballet under the Stars. Stewart.
Battery Park, High Noon. Belitt.
Central Park. Nemerov.
Central Park, 1916. Stewart.
Crossing the Park. Moss.
Definition of Nature. Redmond.
False Summer, The. Zaturenska.
Fountain in the Park, The. Haley.
In Epping Forest. *Fr.* Child Harold. Clare.
Instructions for a Park. Walker.
Lines Written in Kensington Gardens. Arnold.
London versus Epping Forest. *Fr.* Child Harold. Clare.
On St. James's Park, as Lately Improved by His Majesty. Waller.
On the Fine Arts Garden, Cleveland. Atkins.
Park. Ignatow.
Park, The. Tippett.
Park Pigeons. Cane.
Public Garden, The. Lowell.
Smelling the End of Green July. Yates.
South End. Aiken.
Sunday in the Park. Williams.
Upon the Priory Grove, His Usual Retirement. Vaughan.

Parliament (Great Britain)
And now a fig for the lower house. Cary.
Free Parliament Litany, A. *Unknown.*
On the New Forcers of Conscience under the Long Parliament. Milton.
Stanzas on Seeing the Speaker Asleep in His Chair during One of the Debates of the First Reformed Parliament. Praed.

Parnell, Charles Stewart
Parnell. Kettle.
Parnell. Yeats.

Parnell, Thomas
To Robert Earl of Oxford and Earl Mortimer. Pope.

Parodies
Brand-X Anthology of Poetry, The (BXAP). William Zaranka, ed.
Faber Book of Parodies, The (FaBoPa). Simon Brett, ed.
Innocent Merriment (InMe), pp. 3–79. Franklin P. Adams, ed.
Parodies; an Anthology from Chaucer to Beerbohm—and After (Par). Dwight Macdonald, ed.
Speak Roughly to Your Little Boy (SpRo). Myra Livingston, ed.
Understanding Poetry (UnPo). Cleanth Brooks *and* Robert Penn Warren, eds.
What Cheer; an Anthology of American and British Humorous and Witty Verse (WhC). David McCord, ed.

Parrots
Contrast, The; the Parrot and the Wren. Wordsworth.
Deprecating Parrots. May.
Gossip, The. Halpern.
Little Miss and her Parrot. Marchant.
Obituary. Kees.
Parrot, The. Campbell.
Parrot, The. Flecker.
Parrot, The. Lucie-Smith.
Parrots, The. Gibson.
Parrot's Soliloquy. *Fr.* Speak, Parrot. Skelton.
Poor Poll. Bridges.
"Psittachus Eois Imitatrix Ales ab Indis." Sitwell.
Reflections on the Death of a Parrot. Jacinto.
Sailor to His Parrot, The. Davies.

Parsifal
Parsifal. *Fr.* Amour. Verlaine.
Percivale's Quest. *Fr.* Idylls of the King. Tennyson.
See also **Arthurian Legend.**

Parthenon
On Seeing the Elgin Marbles. Keats.

Parties
After the Party. Wise.
Dancers Inherit the Party, The. Finlay.
False Security. Betjeman.
Feckless Dinner Party, The. De la Mare.
Love Feast, The. Auden.
Office Party. McGinley.
Party, The. Avison.
Party, The. Dunbar.
Party in Winter. Shapiro.

Parting
Adieu. Carlyle.
Adieu to His Mistress. Montgomerie.
Ae Fond Kiss. Burns.
After He Had Gone. Warner.
After the Supper and Talk. Whitman.
Against Parting. Zach.
Already I Feel the Emptiness. *Fr.* Three Songs. Jackson.
And wilt thou leave me thus? Wyatt.
As Firmly Cemented Clam-Shells. Basho.
At Parting. Swinburne.
At the San Francisco Airport. Winters.
Auf Wiedersehen. Lowell.
Before Good-bye. Wolny.
Black-eyed Susan. Gay.
Bright Was the Morning. D'Urfey.
Childe Harold's Farewell to England. *Fr.* Childe Harold's Pilgrimage. Byron.
Chilterns, The. Brooke.
Chloris Farewell. Waller.
Corydon's Farewell, on Sailing in the Late Expedition Fleet. *Unknown.*
Departure, A. Mahon.
Elegie: His Parting from Her. *Fr.* Elegies. Donne.
End Is Now, The. "Madelaine."
Esyllt. Jones.
Even as I Hold You. Walker.
False Cadence. Berger.
Fare Thee Well! Byron.
Farewell, The: "It was a' for our rightful' king." Burns.
Farewell, A: "Oft have I mused, but now at length I find." Sidney.
Farewell, A: "With all my will, but much against my heart." *Fr.* The Unknown Eros. Patmore.
Farewell to Juliet ("I see you, Juliet, still, with your straw hat"). *Fr.* The Love Sonnets of Proteus. Blunt.
Farewell, Unkind! Farewell! to me, no more a father! *Unknown.*
Gesture, The. Libbey.
Go Fetch Me a Pint o' Wine. Burns.
Going Away. Nemerov.
Going to the Warres. Lovelace.
Goodbye. Bloch.
Goodbye. Lewis.
Good-bye My Fancy! Whitman.
Goodbye, My Lover, Goodbye. *Unknown.*
Hence, Hairt, with Her That Must Depairt. Scott.
I will not let thee go. Bridges.
I Will Write. Graves.
If He Let Us Go Now. Williams.
In Time of War. Thanet.
Kathleen Mavourneen. Crawford.
Lament of the Irish Emigrant. Sheridan.
Lament of the Master of Erskine. Scott.
Last Night. Darley.
Leave-Taking, A. Swinburne.
Leaving Raiford. Petaccia.
Lines Written Immediately after Parting from a Lady. Brydges.
Loch Leven. Smith.
Lucasia, Rosania and Orinda Parting at a Fountain, July 1663. Philips.
Maid of Athens, Ere We Part. Byron.
My life closed twice before its close. Dickinson.
No Madam Butterfly. Hajek.
Now That You Too. Farjeon.
On Fanny Godwin. Shelley.
On His Mistress Going from Home. *Unknown.*
On His Mistresse Going to Sea. Cary.
On Leaving Cuba, Her Native Land. Gómez de Avellaneda.
Orinda to Lucasia Parting, October, 1661, at London. Philips.
Our Captain Cried All Hands. *Unknown.*
Parting. Massey.
Parting as Descent. Berryman.
Parting at Morning. Browning.
Parting Hour, The. Custance.
Parting in Wartime. Cornford.

Parting with Lucasia; a Song. Philips.
Parting, without a Sequel. Ransom.
Separation. Arnold.
Since there's no help, come, let us kiss and part. *Fr.* Idea. Drayton.
Soldier Going to the Field, The. Davenant.
Song: "Sweetest love, I do not go." Donne.
Song of Parting, A. Mackenzie.
Taking Leave of a Friend. Li Po.
There Is No Word for Goodbye. TallMountain.
There Is Something. Pope.
To His Lady. Henry VIII, King of England.
To Lucasta, Going beyond the Seas. Lovelace.
To Lucasta, Going to the Wars. Lovelace.
To William Roe. Jonson.
Upon His Leaving His Mistress. Rochester.
Valediction, A. Browning.
Weary Lot is Thine, A. *Fr.* Rokeby. Scott.
West-Country Lover, The. Brown.
When We Two Parted. Byron.
Winter. Wingfield.
Winter's Tale, A. Lawrence.
Words at Farewell. Derian.

Partridges
Another Song of the Same Woman, to Some Partridges, Sent to Her Alive. Pinar.
Partridges. Masefield.

Pasadena, California
On a View of Pasadena from the Hills. Winters.

Passivity
I Never Even Suggested It. Nash.

Passover
Angel, The. Hayes.
Passover Eve. Kruger.
Passover in the Holy Family, The. Rossetti.
Pesach Has Come to the Ghetto Again. Heller.
Seder, 1944. Torberg.
Still Small Voice, The. Klein.

Pasternak, Boris
Last Year's Discussion: The Nobel Russian. McGinley.
Letter to Pasternak. Pomeroy.

Pastoral Verse
Pastoral Poesy. Clare.
To Make a Pastoral: A Receipt. *Unknown.*

Pastures. *See* **Fields and Pastures.**

Pater, Walter
Gemlike Flame, The. Lister.

Paterson, New Jersey
Paterson, *sels.* Williams.

Paths
Crooked Footpath, The. Holmes.
Footpath. Ngatho.

Patience
Disappointment, The. Taylor.
His Answer. Thompson.
On His Blindness. Milton.
Owl, The. Davison.
Patience. Horne.
Patience. Wyatt.
Patience Taught by Nature. Browning.
Patience, Though I Have Not. Wyatt.
Sonnet: "Patience, hard thing! the hard thing but to pray." Hopkins.
Third Wonder, The. Markham.
Waiting. Burroughs.
Waiting Both. Hardy.

Patients
At the Nursing Home. Cain.
In Hospital, *sels.* Henley.
Mental Cases. Owen.
Old Men's Ward. Dean.
Patient, The; Rocland County Sanitarium. Hernton.
See also **Hospitals; Illness; Institutionalization; Mental Illness.**

Patrick, Saint
Bard's Chant. *Fr.* Saint Patrick for Ireland. Shirley.
Birth of Saint Patrick, The. Lover.
Breastplate of St. Patrick, The. *At. to* St. Patrick.
Saint Patrick. Bennett.
St. Patrick's Hymn before Tara. Mangan.
Wearin' of the Green, The. *Unknown.*

Patriotic Songs, American
America. Smith.
America for Me. Van Dyke.
America the Beautiful. Bates.
As Down a Lone Valley. Dwight.
Battle Cry of Freedom, The. Root.
Battle-Hymn of the Republic. Howe.
Bunker Hill. Niles.
Chester. Billings.
Columbia, the Gem of the Ocean. Shaw.
God Bless America. Berlin.
Hail, Columbia. Hopkinson.
Land of the Free. Hosking.
Liberty Song, The. Dickinson.
O Beautiful My Country. Hosmer.
O Lord Our God, Thy Mighty Hand. Van Dyke.
Song for Our Flag, A. Sangster.
Star-spangled Banner, The. Key.
Tenting Tonight. Kittredge.
Tramp! Tramp! Tramp! Root.
Yankee Doodle. *Unknown.*
Yankee Doodle Boy, The. *Fr.* Little Johnny Jones. Cohan.
See also **Patriotic Songs, Confederate.**

Patriotic Songs, Australian
Waltzing Matilda. Paterson.

Patriotic Songs, Canadian
Hymn for Canada, A. Watson.
O Canada! Routhier.

Patriotic Songs, Chinese
Chee Lai! (Arise!). *Unknown.*

Patriotic Songs, Confederate
Dixie ("I wish I was in de land ob cotton"). Emmett.
Dixie ("Southrons, hear your country call you"). Pike.
My Maryland. Randall.

Patriotic Songs, English
Anglo-Saxon Race: A Rhyme For Englishmen. Tupper.
Give a Rouse. *Fr.* Cavalier Tunes. Browning.
God Save the King. Carey.
Heart of Oak. Garrick.
Marching Along. *Fr.* Cavalier Tunes. Browning.
Rule, Britannia! *Fr.* Alfred, a Masque. Thomson.

Patriotic Songs, French
Marseillaise, The. Rouget de Lisle.

Patriotic Songs, German
Watch on the Rhine, The. Schneckenburger.

Patriotic Songs, Italian
Garibaldi Hymn, The. Mercantini.

Patriotic Songs, Scottish
Campbells Are Comin', The. *Unknown.*

Patriotism
America for Me. Van Dyke.
Anglo-Saxon Race: A Rhyme For Englishmen. Tupper.
As One Non-Combatant to Another. Orwell.
Barbara Frietchie. Whittier.
Bleat of Protest. Weston.
Breathes There the Man. *Fr.* The Lay of the Last Minstrel. Scott.
Canadian Boat Song. Cunningham.
Celebrations. Clarke.
Columbia. *Unknown.*
Dear Harp of My Country. Moore.
Dulce et Decorum Est. Owen.
England, My England. Henley.
Fatherland, The. Lowell.
Flag Goes By, The. Bennett.
God Save Elizabeth! Palgrave.
Hame, Hame, Hame. Cunningham.
Harp That Once through Tara's Halls, The. Moore.
Homes of England, The. Hemans.
I Am an American. Lieberman.
I Have Loved England. *Fr.* The White Cliffs. Miller.
I Hear America Singing. Whitman.
In an Age of Fops and Toys. *Fr.* Voluntaries. Emerson.
In Spain. Wyatt.
In Westminster Abbey. Betjeman.
Jingo-Woman, The. Hamilton.
Kid Has Gone to the Colors, The. Herschell.
Killers That Run, The. Cohen.
Marseillaise, The. Rouget de Lisle.
Minority Report. Updike.
New Colossus, The. Lazarus.
Next to of Course God America I. Cummings.
MCMXIV. Larkin.
Non-Combatant. Hamilton.
Patriot, The. Milne.
Patriot Game, The. Behan.
Pat's Opinion of Flags. Brooks.

Pibroch of Donald Dhu. Scott.
Pro Patria Mori. Moore.
Sail On, O Ship of State! *Fr.* The Building of the Ship. Longfellow.
Scots Wha Hae. Burns.
Soldier, The. *Fr.* 1914. Brooke.
Weeping Sad and Lonely (When This Cruel War Is Over). Sawyer.
Yankee Doodle Boy, The. Cohan.

Patrons
Miserly Patron, A. *Unknown.*

Paul, Saint
Our Two Worthies. Ransom.
Paul. Oxenham.
Saul, Afterward, Riding East. Brinnin.

Pavlova, Anna
Glory and the ardour of the stage, The. *Fr.* Elegy on the Death of Mme. Anna Pavlova. Meyerstein.

Pawnbrokers and Pawnshops
New Order of Chivalry, A. Peacock.
Pawnbrokers. Wilkinson.
Pawnshop Window. Grenville.
Street Window. Sandburg.

Peace
A. E. F. Sandburg.
Afterwards. Cole.
And afterwards, when honour has made good. Tree.
"And There Was a Great Calm." Hardy.
And They Shall Beat Their Swords into Plowshares. *Fr.* Micah. Bible, *O.T.*
Annul Wars. Nahman.
As Brothers Live Together. *Fr.* The Song of Hiawatha. Longfellow.
Bells of Peace, The. Fisher.
Bucolic. Merwin.
Bugle Song of Peace. Clark.
Child of Peace, The. Lagerlof.
Church Triumphant, The. Symonds.
Dear Lord and Father of Mankind. Whittier.
Even During War. *Fr.* Letter to the Front. Rukeyser.
Evening Star, The. Carmichael.
Forty Years Peace. Sivan.
He Shall Speak Peace. Clark.
He Shall Speak Peace unto the Nations. Walters.
He Walks at Peace. *Fr.* Tao Teh King. *Unknown.*
Hymnal: "Bringer of sun, arrower of evening, star-begetter and moon-riser." Vinal.
In Distrust of Merits. Moore.
In the End of Days. *Fr.* Isaiah. Bible, *O.T.*
Io! Shirley.
Legend of Versailles, A. Tolson.
Liberty and Peace, a Poem. Wheatley.
Lotos-Eaters, The. Tennyson.
Man unto His Fellow Man. *Fr.* On a Note of Triumph. Corwin.
Message of Peace, A. Longfellow.
More than Flowers We Have Brought. Turner.
My Peace I Give unto You. Studdert-Kennedy.
Not Marching Away to Be Killed. Fuller.
O Brother Man. Whittier.
Ode, upon Occasion of His Majesties Proclamation in the Year 1630, An. *Fr.* Il Pastor Fido. Fanshawe.
Pax. Lawrence.
Peace. *Fr.* 1914. Brooke.
Peace. De la Mare.
Peace. Edman.
Peace. Farjeon.
Peace. Greenberg.
Peace. Herbert.
Peace. Hopkins.
Peace. Jonas.
Peace. Longley.
Peace, The. *Fr.* Advice to Julia. Luttrell.
Peace. Markham.
Peace. Sangster.
Peace. *Unknown.*
Peace. Vaughan.
Peace does not mean the end of all our striving. *Fr.* The Suffering God. Studdert-Kennedy.
Peace on Earth. Sears.
Peace, So That. Kuzma.
Pleading Voices. Katav.
Poet Questions Peace, The. *Fr.* Euthymiae Raptus; or, The Tears of Peace. Chapman.
Prayer to Peace. *Fr.* Cresophontes. Euripides.
Prince of Peace, The. Fosdick.
Prophecy. *Fr.* Locksley Hall. Tennyson.
Reconciliation. Wheelock.
Reconciliation. Whitman.
Reign of Peace, The. Starck.
Season of Phantasmal Peace, The. Walcott.
Shalom Aleichem. *Unknown.*
Song for Simeon, A. Eliot.
Song of the New World. Morgan.
Vine and Fig Tree. Altman.
What a Grand and Glorious Feeling. Wolff.

Peach Trees and Peaches
Artist Draws a Peach, An. Hampl.
Peach, The. Brown.
Peach Tree with Fruit. Colum.

Peacocks
Fragment: "Mark you how the peacock's eye." Hopkins.
On a Peacock. Heyrick.
Peacock and Nightingales. Finch.
Verses under a Peacock Portrayed in Her Left Hand. Greene.
What is it more eyes doth wear. *Unknown.*

Pear Trees and Pears
Pear Tree. Doolittle ("H. D.").
Pear Tree, The. Millay.
Pears. Pastan.
Sadness and Still Life. Ramke.
Sickle Pears (For Glidden Parker). Dodson.
Stone Orchard, The. Oates.
Study of Two Pears. Stevens.
Tapestry Trees. Morris.
To a Blossoming Pear Tree. Wright.

Pearl Diving
Diving for Pearls. Yamamoto.

Peas
I Eat My Peas with Honey. *Unknown.*
Peas. *Unknown.*

Peasants
Cottager's Complaint, The. Freeth.
Exiles. "Æ."
French Peasants. Gibbon.
I Am the Mountainy Singer. Campbell.
Nobleman and Thresherman, The. *Unknown.*
Peasant. Merwin.
Peasant Poet, The. Clare.
Peasants, The. Lewis.
Swiss Peasant, The. Wordsworth.
To His Father on Praising the Honest Life of the Peasant. E'tesami.
Viewing Russian Peasants from a Leningrad-bound Train. Gaess.

Pedantry
On the Edition of Mr. Pope's Works with a Commentary and Notes. Edwards.
Purist, The. Nash.
See also **Scholarship and Scholars.**

Peddling and Peddlers
Autolycus as Peddler. *Fr.* The Winter's Tale. Shakespeare.
Fine Knacks for Ladies. *Unknown.*
Negro Peddler's Song, A. Johnson.
New Brooms. *Fr.* The Three Ladies of London. Wilson.
Oysters. Swift.
Peddler's Caravan, The. Rands.

Pedestrians
J's the Jumping Jay-walker. McGinley.
To a Passer-by. Baudelaire.

Peeping Toms. *See* **Voyeurism.**

Peewees *or* Peewits. *See* **Pewees *or* Pewits.**

Pegasus
Pegasus. Day Lewis.
Pegasus. Kavanagh.

Pelicans
Frigate Pelican, The. Moore.
King and Queen of the Pelicans we. *Fr.* The Pelican Chorus. Lear.
Pelicanaries ("Pelicanaries are homely birds"). Lewis.
Pelicans. Jeffers.
Pelicans My Father Sees, The. Maris Stella.
Reason for the Pelican, The. Ciardi.

Pembroke, Mary Sidney Herbert, Countess of
On the Countess Dowager of Pembroke. Browne.

Pembroke, William, Earl of
To William Earle of Pembroke. Johnson.

Penelope (mythology)
Ancient Gesture, An. Millay.
Penelope, for Her Ulysses' Sake. *Fr.* Amoretti. Spenser.
World as Meditation, The. Stevens.

Penguins
On the Death of an Emperor Penguin in Regent's Park, London. Wright.
Penguin, A. Herford.
Penguin on the Beach. Miller.
View from Here, The. Stafford.
Peninsular War
Burial of Sir John Moore after Corunna, The. Wolfe.
Pennsylvania
Accident at Three Mile Island. Barnes.
All the Smoke. Siegel.
Amish, The. Doreski.
Daybreak on a Pennsylvania Highway. Daunt.
Jurgis Petraskas, the Workers' Angel, Organizes the First Miners' Strike in Exeter, Pennsylvania. Petrosky.
Max Schmitt in a Single Scull. Lattimore.
Missionary Visits Our Church in Scranton, The. Parini.
Pennsylvania Places. Daly.
Pennsylvania Winter Indian 1974. Littlebird.
Pittsburgh. Bynner.
Prophecy in Flame. Howard.
Rulers: Philadelphia. Johnson.
Snake Hill. Parini.
Unseen Fire, An. Cooke.
William Penn/ Was the most level-headed of men. Smith.
Penshurst, England
At Penshurst. Waller.
To Penshurst. Jonson.
Pensions
On Seeing an Officer's Widow Distracted. Barber.
Pluralist and Old Soldier, The. Collier.
See also **Retirement.**
Pentagon (building)
Pentagonia. Bates.
March 2, The. Lowell.
Pentecost
Call to Pentecost, A. Tyler.
Pentecost. Coats.
Whit Sunday. Beaumont.
Whit Sunday. Keble.
Peonies
Selling Ruined Peonies. Yü Hsüan-chi.
Peppertrees
Scenes from the Life of the Peppertrees. Levertov.
Perception
Idea of Order at Key West, The. Stevens.
Thirteen Ways of Looking at a Blackbird. Stevens.
Percivale. *See* **Parsifal.**
Percy, Sir Henry
Battle of Otterburn, The. *Unknown.*
Chevy Chase. *Unknown.*
Perry, Oliver Hazard
On the Death of Commodore Oliver H. Perry. Brainard.
Perry's Victory. *Unknown.*
Perry's Victory—a Song. *Unknown.*
Persephone
Demeter and Persephone. Tennyson.
Garden of Proserpina, The. *Fr.* The Faerie Queene. Spenser.
Gardens of Proserpine, The. Cassity.
Garden of Proserpine, The. Swinburne.
Hymn to Proserpine. Swinburne.
Kore. Creeley.
Proserpina. Campion.
Proserpine at Enna. Bottrall.
Perseus
Medusa. O'Sullivan.
Perseus. MacNeice.
Perseverance
After. Ryan.
Ants at the Olympics, The. Digance.
Carry On! Service.
Cost of Pretending, The. Davison.
Excelsior. Longfellow.
Fighting Failure, The. Appleton.
I Saw a Man. Crane.
Keep a-Goin'. Stanton.
Nevertheless. Moore.
On the Persistence of Humanity. Fraser.
Psalm of Life, A. Longfellow.
Reeds in the Loch Sayis, The. *Unknown.*
Say Not the Struggle Nought Availeth. Clough.
Survivors. Hogan.
Ulysses. Tennyson.
Persia. *See* **Iran.**
Persian Wars
Leonidas. Croly.
On the Spartan Dead at Thermopylae. Simonides.
Persian Version, The. Graves.
Salamis. *Fr.* The Persians. Aeschylus.
Persians
Fie on Eastern Luxury! Horace.
Sohrab's Death. *Fr.* Sohrab and Rustum. Arnold.
Persimmon Trees
Longing for the Persimmon Tree. Brand.
Peru
Of History More Like Myth. Garrigue.
Pessimism
Epitaph on a Pessimist. Hardy.
For a Pessimist. Cullen.
Moments. Allen.
Of Misery. Howell.
Optimist and Pessimist. Wilson.
Pessimist, The. King.
There Are Bad Times Just around the Corner. Coward.
Tom on the Beach. Bruce.
Truth. North.
Violent Storm. Strand.
Worried Skipper, The. Irwin.
Peter, Saint
And the Cock Begins to Crow. Avery.
Domine, Quo Vadis? *Unknown.*
Domine Quo Vadis? Watson.
In the Servants' Quarters. Hardy.
Look, The. Browning.
Meaning of the Look, The. Browning.
Peter and John. Wylie.
St. Peter. Rossetti.
Peter Rabbit
Peter Rabbit. McPherson.
Peterloo Massacre (1819)
England in 1819. Shelley.
Mask of Anarchy, The. Shelley.
Song to the Men of England. Shelley.
Petra, Jordan
Pedra. Burgon.
Petrarch
Petrarch. Carducci.
Petrels
Stormpetrel. Murphy.
Stormy Petrel, The. "Cornwall."
To see the petrel cropping in the farmyard. *Fr.* Sonnets for a Dying Man. Singer.
Petrified Forest National Monument
Fair Warning, A. Mayo.
Pets
Disaster. Calverley.
Epitaph on a Hare. Cowper.
Gerbil Who Got Away, The. Root.
Monk and His Pet Cat, The. *Unknown.*
Ode of Odium on Aquariums. Guiterman.
Open the Door. Edey.
Pet Shop. MacNeice.
Pewees *or* **Pewits**
Pewee, The. Trowbridge.
Two Pewits. Thomas.
Peyote
Peyote Vision. Blockcolski.
Phaeton
Phaeton. Mandel.
Pheasants
Obscure Pleasure of the Indistinct, The. Ramke.
Pheasant, The. Coffin.
See! from the brake the whirring pheasant springs. *Fr.* Windsor-Forest. Pope.
Philadelphia, Pennsylvania
Max Schmitt in a Single Scull. Lattimore.
Philadelphia. *Unknown.*
Rulers: Philadelphia. Johnson.
South Street. Silvera.
Philadelphia (ship)
How We Burned the *Philadelphia.* Eastman.
Philanthropy and Philanthropists
Disagreeable Man, The. Gilbert.
Lines on Being Refused a Guggenheim Fellowship. Whittemore.
Offer, An. Guiterman.

Tribute to the Founder, The. Amis.
See also **Charity.**
Philately
Philatelic Lessons: The German Collection. Spingarn.
Philatelist Royal, The. Graves.
Philip, King (American Indian Chief)
King Philip's Last Stand. Scollard.
Philip Neri, Saint
St. Philip in Himself. Newman.
Philiphaugh, Battle of (1645)
Battle of Philiphaugh, The. *Unknown.*
Philippines
Blue Tropic. Cabalquinto.
Flower Vendor, The. Cabalquinto.
Postcard from Zamboanga. Esbensen.
See also **Filipinos.**
Phillips, Wendell
Wendell Phillips. Alcott.
Wendell Phillips. O'Reilly.
Philodendrons
Woolworth Philodendron, The. Sandy.
Philomela
Philomela. Arnold.
Philosophy and Philosophers
Alexander and the Gymnosophists. *Unknown.*
Dialogue from Plato, A. Dobson.
Dissatisfaction with Metaphysics. Empson.
Epigram: "Philosopher, whom dost thou most affect." Garnett.
Epistemological Rag, The. Burr.
Epistemologist, Over a Brandy, Opining, The. Sargent.
Homage to the Philosopher. Deutsch.
In Defense of Metaphysics. Tomlinson.
Makhno's Philosophers. Manifold.
Metaphysical Amorist, The. Cunningham.
Metaphysics. Herford.
Mock On, Mock On, Voltaire, Rousseau. Blake.
Moorlands of the Not. *Unknown.*
Of the Pythagorean Philosophy. Ovid.
On Philosophers. *Unknown.*
On Philosophy. Goldstein.
On the Death of a Metaphysician. Santayana.
Philosopher, A. Foss.
Philosopher and Her Father, The. Brooks.
Philosopher and the Birds, The. Murphy.
Philosophy, the great and only heir. *Fr.* To the Royal Society. Cowley.
Plato Instructs a Midwest Farmer. Palmer.
Poetry and Philosophy. *Fr.* An Ecologue to Mr. Johnson. Randolph.
Positivists, The. Collins.
Questionings. Hedge.
Reading and Talking. Zukofsky.
To an Old Philosopher in Rome. Stevens.
To the Royal Society. Cowley.
Voltaire at Ferney. Auden.
Phoebus Apollo. *See* **Apollo.**
Phoenix
I Saw a Phoenix in the Wood Alone. *Fr.* The Visions of Petrarch. Spenser.
Lo! I have learned of the loveliest of lands. *Fr.* The Phoenix. *Unknown.*
News of the Phoenix. Smith.
O blest unfabled incense tree. *Fr.* Nepenthe. Darley.
Pheonix, The. Cunningham.
Phoenix, The. Megged.
Phoenix, The. Nash.
Phoenix, The. Sassoon.
Phoenix, The. Spencer.
Phoenix and Turtle, The. Shakespheare.
Phoenix, bird of terrible pride. *Fr.* Mutations of the Phoenix. Read.
Phoenix Self-Born, The. *Fr.* Metamorphoses. Ovid.
Photocopying
Certified Copy. Deagon.
Photography and Photographers
About the Cows. Pfingston.
Album, The. Day Lewis.
Among His Effects We Found a Photograph. Ochester.
Baby Pictures of Famous Dictators. Simic.
Camera. Kooser.
Chinese Camp, Kamloops (circa 1883). Suknaski.
City Afternoon. Ashbery.
Daguerreotype of a Grandmother. Wright.
Developing a Wife. Taylor.
Edward Weston in Mexico City. Dacey.
Family Album, A. Brody.
Family Man, A. Kumin.
Family Portrait. Hood-Adams.
Family Portrait 1933. Oresick.
Glance at the Album, A. Burr.
Grandpa's Picture. Ruffin.
Hiawatha's Photographing. "Carroll."
History of Photography, A. Goldbarth.
Hold My Hand. Pennant.
I Am Not a Camera. Auden.
Instead of Features. Moore.
Lines on a Young Lady's Photograph Album. Larkin.
Mary Ackerman, 1938. Glancy.
Mementos. Snodgrass.
Message to the Photographer Whose Prints I Purchased, A. Williams.
Middle of a War, The. Fuller.
Negatives. Wright.
Old Photo, 1942. Uba.
Old Photographs. Harsent.
On Being Photographed. Gass.
Photo of Miners, A. Galvin.
Photograph in a Stockholm Newspaper for March 13, 1910. Coles.
Photographer. Booth.
Photographer, The. Pfingston.
Photograph. Prettyman.
Photographer, The. Simpson.
Photographer Whose Shutter Died, The. Meissner.
Photographer's Wife, The. Beeler.
Photos, The. Wakoski.
Profile. Wallace.
Six Young Men. Hughes.
Suite of Six Pieces for Siskind, A. Logan.
View by Color Photography on a Commercial Calendar. Williams.
Water Lily, The. Wagoner.
Physicians
Arthur Ridgewood, M.D. Davis.
Better Way, The. Leaf.
Chief, The. *Fr.* In Hospital. Henley.
Clinic: Examination. Conard.
Cold Front, A. Williams.
Correct Compassion, A. Kirkup.
Country Doctor, The. Carleton.
Dispensary, The. Garth.
Doctor Blenn. Bierce.
Dr. Dimity Is Forced to Complain. Macdonald.
Dr. Dimity Lectures on Unusual Cases. Macdonald.
Doctor Rebuilds a Hand, The. Young.
Doctor Who Sits at the Bedside of a Rat, The. Miles.
Doctors' Row. Aiken.
Doctor's Story, The. Carleton.
Epistle, An, Containing the Strange Medical Experience of Karshish, the Arab Physician. Browning.
House-Surgeon. *Fr.* In Hospital. Henley.
Le Médecin Malgré Lui. Williams.
New Doctor, The. "Mix."
New Physician, The. Chalmers.
Ol' Doc' Hyar. Campbell.
Old Doc. Vinz.
On a Quack. *Unknown.*
On Dr Isaac Letsome. *Unknown.*
On Hygiene. Belloc.
On the Death of Dr. Robert Levet. Johnson.
Remedy, Worse Than the Disease, The. Prior.
See, one physician, like a sculler, plies. Jekyll.
Surgery. Burbank.
Though a soldier at present, a doctor of yore. More.
To a Good Physician. Wycherley.
To Doctor Empirick. Jonson.
Wish, A. Arnold.
See also **Medicine; Nurses.**
Physics and Physicists
After Reading a Child's Guide to Modern Physics. Auden.
Causes of Color, The. Jonas.
Concept of Force, The. Sargent.
Entoptic Colours. Goethe.
First and Second Law. Flanders.
First Rainfall. Lightman.
How Einstein Started It Up Again. Dillard.
Life of Particles, The. Benedikt.
Monkish Mind of the Speculative Physicist, The. Ramke.
My Physics Teacher. Wagoner.
Song of the Screw. *Unknown.*

Pianos
A Cappella. Pettit.
Fantasia. Nathan.
Investment, The. Frost.
Piano, The. Davey.
Piano, The. Lawrence.
Piano. Russ.
Piano at Evening. Palea.
Piano Lessons. Wormser.
Piano Tuner, The. Smith.
Player Piano. Updike.
Picasso, Pablo
Father, The. Lattimore.
Picasso and Matisse. Francis.
Picasso's Women. Cabral.
Sleeping Peasants. Janik.
"Twiner," A. Lindon.
What Pablo Picasso Did in "Les Demoiselles d'Avignon." Colombo.
Pickles
Meditation for a Pickle Suite. Dillard.
Ode on a Jar of Pickles. Taylor.
Picnics and Barbecues
Archaeological Picnic, The. Betjeman.
Barbecue Blues. *Unknown.*
Georgia Dusk. Toomer.
Picnic, A. Fisher.
Picnic. Lofting.
Picnic Day. Field.
Picnic: The Liberated. Holman.
Pico della Mirandola, Giovanni
Pico della Mirandola. Mason.
Piedmont, Italy
On the Late Massacre in Piedmont. Milton.
Piero della Francesca
Nativity. Sarton.
Pies
Lemon Pie. Guest.
Melton Mowbray Pork-Pie, A. Le Gallienne.
Pigeons
Fly. Merwin.
Homing. Bowman.
Homing Pigeons. Walker.
Mrs. Peck-Pigeon. Farjeon.
On Seeing a Pigeon Make Love. Hunt.
On Starling Some Pigeons. Turner.
Park Pigeons. Cane.
Pigeon. Fuller.
Pigeons. Kell.
Pigeons. Moore.
Pigeons. Reid.
Pigeons. Whisler.
Trinity Place. McGinley.
Wild Oats. MacCraig.
Wood-Pigeons. Masefield.
Pigs
Again, the year's decline, midst storms and floods. *Fr.* The Farmer's Boy. Bloomfield.
Animals Are Passing from Our Lives. Levine.
Boar, The. Kelly.
Ego. Siegel.
Feed. Knister.
For the Eating of Swine. Jones.
Hare and the Pig, The. Bridgman.
Hog at the Manger. Farber.
Hog-Calling. Blount.
Hog-Calling Competition. Bishop.
I Had a Little Pig. *Unknown.*
Judged by the Company One Keeps. *Unknown.*
Laughing Faces of Pigs, The. Lape.
Little Pig, The. Landau.
Little Piggy. Hood.
Mary Middling. Fyleman.
Melancholy Pig, The. "Carroll."
Moly. Gunn.
Ode to a Pig While His Nose Was Being Bored. Southey.
Ode to the Pig: His Tail. Brooks.
Pig, The. Nash.
Pig, The. *Unknown.*
Pig, The. Young.
Pig Is Never Blamed, A. Deutsch.
Pig Song. Atwood.
Pigs. Cotton.
Pigs, The. Lehmann.
Pigs, The. Taylor.
Pig-Tale, A. *Fr.* Sylvie and Bruno Concluded. "Carroll."
Pindaric on the Grunting of a Hog, A. Wesley.
Poor Man's Pig, The. Blunden.
Roasted Sucking Pig. *Unknown.*
St. Anthony and His Pig; a Cantata. Forrest.
Sow of Feeling, The. Fergusson.
Sow Took the Measles, The. *Unknown.*
State Fair Pigs. Pfingston.
This little pig went to market. Mother Goose.
Three Little Pigs, The. Gatty.
Transubstantiation. Geddes.
Unknown Color, The. Cullen.
View of a Pig. Hughes.
Wart Hog. Skelton.
Wild Boar and the Ram, The. *Fr.* Fables. Gay.
Wild Pigs. Kooser.
Pike, Zebulon Montgomery
Death of General Pike, The. Osborn.
Pike (fish)
Pike, The. Bruce.
Pike. Hughes.
Pike's Peak
Gold Seeker's Song, The. *Unknown.*
Hit at the Times, A. McGrew.
In the Summer of Sixty. *Unknown.*
Pike's Peak. *Unknown.*
Pike's Peakers, The. Greenleaf.
Soliloquy of the Returned Gold Adventurer. "Syntax."
Song for the Pike's Peaker. *Unknown.*
To Pikes Peak. Hills.
Ute Pass. Whitney.
Pilgrim Fathers
Boston Hymn. Emerson.
Children of Light. Lowell.
Courtship of Miles Standish, The. Longfellow.
First Proclamation of Miles Standish, The. Preston.
If I Were a Pilgrim Child. Bennett.
Landing of the Pilgrim Fathers, The. Hemans.
Mayflower, The. Ellsworth.
Pilgrim Fathers, The. Bacon.
Pilgrim Fathers, The. Pierpont.
Uppon the First Sight of New-England, June 29, 1638. Tillam.
Word of God to Leyden Came, The. Rankin.
Pilgrimages and Pilgrims
Bullocky. Wright.
Carcassonne. Nadaud.
Christmas Creek. Kendall.
End of the Way, The. Cole.
Friar of Orders Gray, The. Percy.
General Prologue, The. *Fr.* The Canterbury Tales. Chaucer.
In Canterbury Cathedral. Oldenburg.
O California. Murguía.
O Weary Pilgrims. *Fr.* The Growth of Love. Bridges.
Palmer, The. *Fr.* The Vision of Piers Plowman. Langland.
Passionate Man's Pilgrimage, The. Ralegh.
Pilgrim, The. *Fr.* The Pilgrim's Progress. Bunyan.
Pilgrim, The. Wightman.
Pilgrim at Rome, The. *Unknown.*
Pilgrimage. Clarke.
Pilgrimage, The. Herbert.
Pilgrim's Problem. Lewis.
Pilgrim's Song. Ingemann.
Saint Called "Truth," A. Langland.
Seekers, The. Masefield.
Up-Hill. Rossetti.
Pilots
Irish Airman Foresees His Death, An. Yeats.
Pilot from the Carrier, A. Jarrell.
Prayer for a Pilot. Roberts.
See also **Air Warfare.**
Pinball Machines
Pinball Queen of South Illinois St., The. Tietz.
Pindar
Pindar. Antipater.
Poem Beginning with a Line by Pindar, A. Duncan.
Praise of Pindar, The. Horace.
Pine Island, Minnesota
Lying in a Hammock at William Duffy's Farm in Pine Island, Minnesota. Wright.

Pine Trees
Aspects of the Pines. Hayne.
At Torrey Pines State Park. Mazzaro.
Foxtail Pine. Snyder.
Pine, The. Webster.
Pine at Timber-Line, The. Monroe.
Pine Bough, The. Aldridge.
Pine Gum. Ross.
Pines, The. Lippmann.
Pines, The. Spofford.
Snowing of the Pines, The. Higginson.
Southern Pines. Bishop.
Up in the Pine. Watson.
Pink
What Is Pink? Rossetti.
Pinkham, Lydia
Lydia Pinkham. *Unknown.*
Piombo, Sebastiano del
Geo-Politics. Cardona-Hine.
Pioneers
American History. Moses.
Arrival, The. *Fr.* The Emigrant. McLachlan.
Axe of the Pioneer, The. Crawford.
Ballad of William Sycamore, The. Benét.
Boys of Sanpete County, The. *Unknown.*
Camp within the West, The. Quinn.
Coureurs de Bois. LePan.
Covered Wagon, The. Blakeney.
Crossing the Plains. Miller.
Delphine. Anderson.
Emigrant's Child, The. Sproull.
End of Steel. Saunders.
Face to Face. Rich.
For Jean Vincent d'Abbadie, Baron St.-Castin. Nowlan.
Grandfather. Bowering.
Great-Aunt Rebecca. Brewster.
Handcart Song, The. *Unknown.*
Home Winner, The. Lindberg.
I love you better than I love my race. *Fr.* Tecumseh. Mair.
Lonely Settler, The. *Fr.* The Rising Village. Goldsmith.
New Mexico and Arizona. Canterbury.
Pioneer, The. Field.
Pioneer, The. Guiterman.
Pioneer Mother, The. Fuller.
Pioneer Woman. Crawford.
Pioneer Woman, The—in the North Country. Tietjens.
Pioneers. Clark.
Pioneers. Garland.
Pioneers! O Pioneers! Whitman.
Root Hog or Die. Small.
Rutherford McDowell. Masters.
St. George. Walker.
Settler, The. Street.
Settler in the olden times went forth, A. *Fr.* The Creek of the Four Graves. Harpur.
Silhouette in Sepia. Carr.
Sioux Indians, The. *Unknown.*
Stanzas on the Emigration to America, and Peopling the Western Country. Freneau.
Tempest, The. Smith.
Tittery-Irie-Aye. *Unknown.*
Western Wagons. Benét.
Westward Ho! Miller.
Where the Pelican Builds. Foott.
Wilderness Theme. Mudie.
Woman in the Wagon. The. Robertson.
Women of the West, The. Evans.
Pipers
Piper, A. O'Sullivan.
Piper's Progress, The. "Prout."
Piping down the Valleys Wild. *Fr.* Songs of Innocence. Blake.
Piracy and Pirates
Ballad of Captain Kidd, The. *Unknown.*
Ballad of John Silver, A. Masefield.
Ballad of O'Bruadir, The. Higgins.
Captain Kidd. *Unknown.*
Captain Stratton's Fancy. Masefield.
Captain Ward and the *Rainbow.* *Unknown.*
Derelict. Allison.
Dutch Picture, A. Longfellow.
Flying Cloud, The. *Unknown.*
Henry Martin. *Unknown.*
High Barbaree. *Unknown.*
Last Buccaneer, The. Kingsley.
Last Buccaneer, The. Macaulay.
Morgan. Stedman.
Pirate Don Durk of Dowdee, The. Meigs.
Pirate of High Barbary, The. *Unknown.*
Pirate Story. Stevenson.
Pirate Treasure. Brown.
Pirates. Coatsworth.
Pirates' Fight, The. *Fr.* The Legend of Ghost Lagoon. Schull.
Reformed Pirate, The. Roberts.
Rhyme of the Three Captains, The. Kipling.
Roughchin, the Pirate. Boswell.
Salcome Seaman's Flaunt to the Proud Pirate, The. *Unknown.*
Sir Andrew Barton. *Unknown.*
To the Roving Pirate. Turberville.
Pisa, Italy
Evening: Ponte al Mare, Pisa. Shelley.
Pisanello
Pisanello's Studies of Men Hanging on Gallows. Wheatcroft.
Pitcher, Molly
Molly Pitcher. Richards.
Molly Pitcher. Sherwood.
Pitt, William
Epitaph for William Pitt. Byron.
Nelson, Pitt, Fox. *Fr.* Patriotism. Scott.
Pittsburgh, Pennsylvania
Fort Duquesne. Plimpton.
Pittsburgh. Bynner.
Pity
God's Pity. Driscoll.
Ode to Pity. Collins.
Pity Me Not Because the Light of Day. Millay.
She Is More to Be Pitied than Censured. Gray.
Pius IX, Pope
To Pius IX. Whittier.
Pius XII, Pope
Eugenio Pacelli. Neilson.
Pixies. *See* **Fairies.**
Place Names
American Names. Benét.
American Traveller, The. "Kerr."
Englishman with an Atlas, An; or, America the Unpronounceable. Bishop.
Indian Names. Sigourney.
Localities. Sandburg.
Maiden of Passamaquoddy, The. De Mille.
Names from the War. Catton.
Pennsylvania Places. Daly.
Rivers of the West. "Sunset Joe."
Yankee Cradle. Coffin.
Plague
Adieu, Farewell Earth's Bliss. *Fr.* Summer's Last Will and Testament. Nashe.
Coming of the Plague, The. Kees.
Plains. *See* **Prairies.**
Plantations
Corn-Song, A. Dunbar.
Plants
Air Plant, The. Crane.
Bracken Hills in Autumn. "MacDiarmid."
Caryo's sweet smile Dianthus proud admires. *Fr.* The Loves of the Plants. Darwin.
Cuttings ("Sticks-in-a-drowse droop over sugary loam"). Roethke.
Cuttings ("This urge, wrestle, resurrection of dry sticks"). Roethke.
Giant Decorative Dahlia. Holden.
Green Things Growing. Craik.
Have You Thanked a Green Plant Today. Anderson.
House Plants. McFadden.
Houseplant. Napier.
Jubilate Herbis. Farber.
May 20: Very Early Morning. Shaw.
Moss-Gathering. Roethke.
Nevertheless. Moore.
Prayer, The: "Wilt thou not visit me?" Very.
Rooftop, The. Gunn.
Root Cellar. Roethke.
Sundew, The. Swinburne.
Vegetable Loves. *Fr.* The Loves of the Plants. Darwin.
Woman with Flower. Madgett.
Woodspurge, The. Rossetti.
See also **Flowers, Trees,** *etc.*

Plath, Sylvia
Babysitters, The. Plath.
Cottage Street, 1953. Wilbur.
On the Death of Sylvia Plath. Herzberg.
Your face broods from my table, Suicide. *Fr.* Dream Songs. Berryman.
Plato
Plato, a Musician. Leontius.
Plato in London. Johnson.
Plato Instructs a Midwest Farmer. Palmer.
Spirit of Plato. *Unknown.*
What Then? Yeats.
Platonic Love
Against Platonick Love. *Unknown.*
No Platonic Love. Cartwright.
Platonic Love. Cowley.
Platte River
Trail Beside the River Platte, The. Heyen.
Plattsburgh, Battle of (1814)
Battle of Plattsburg, The. *Unknown.*
Battle of Plattsburg Bay, The. Scollard.
Platypuses
I Had a Duck-billed Platypus. Barrington.
Old Man Platypuses. Paterson.
Platypus, The. Herford.
Play
At the Playground. Stafford.
Ben Plays Hide & Seek in the Deep Woods. Hewitt.
Boy with a Hammer. Hoban.
Chinatown Games. Lum.
Frolic. "Æ."
Hop, Skip, and Jump. Snyder.
Innocent Play. Watts.
Land of Counterpane, The. Stevenson.
Land of Story-Books, The. Stevenson.
Laughing Child. Sandburg.
Nurse's Song ("When the voices of children are heard on the green/ And laughing"). *Fr.* Songs of Innocence. Blake.
Play Time. Blake.
Playing Catch. Moul.
Ring-a-Ring. Greenaway.
Roller Skates. Farrar.
Romping. Ciardi.
Under My Window. Westwood.
Voyage of Jimmy Poo, The. Emanuel.
Playhouses. *See* **Theater and Theaters.**
Playmates
Invisible Playmate, The. Widdemer.
Pleasure
Dialogue, A, between the Resolved Soul, and Created Pleasure. Marvell.
Goblin Market. Rossetti.
Sweet and Sour. *Fr.* Amoretti. Spenser.
To the Blacksmith with a Spade. O'Sullivan.
Pleiades
Pleiades, The. Coatsworth.
Plowing and Plowmen
All Jolly Fellows That Follow the Plough. *Unknown.*
Frightened Ploughman, The. Clare.
Go, Ploughman, Plough. Campbell.
Harry Ploughman. Hopkins.
Horse, The. Kicknosway.
I Will Go with My Father a-Ploughing. Campbell.
On the Plough-Man. Quarles.
Painful Plough, The. *Unknown.*
Ploughboy, The. Clare.
Plougher, The. Colum.
Ploughing on Sunday. Stevens.
Ploughman, The. Thomas.
Ploughman, The. *Unknown.*
Ploughman at the Plough. Golding.
Ploughman, in Imitation of Milton, The. Jones.
Plow, The. Horne.
Plow. *Fr.* Riddles (Exeter Book). *Unknown.*
Plowman, The. Knister.
Plowman's Song. Knister.
Seed. Bosman.
Sod-Breaker, The. Stringer.
Useful Plow, The. *Unknown.*
Plum Trees and Plums
I came to look, and lo. Reinko.
Leave the Top Plums. Chandler.
Little Jack Horner. Mother Goose.
Plum, A. Leib.
Plum Blossoms. Basho.
Plum Blosssoms. Chu Shu-chên.
Plum Tree, The. Reaney.
Plum Trees. Rankō.
Plum Tree by the House, The. Gogarty.
This Is Just to Say. Williams.
'Tis the White Plum Tree. Neilson.
To a Poor Old Woman. Williams.
Wild Plum. Johns.
Word *Plum,* The. Chasin.
Plumbing and Plumbers
Difference, The. King.
Elegy for Alfred Hubbard. Connor.
Murie Sing. Campbell.
Plumber Arrives at Three Mile Island, The. Stewart.
Plutarch
Plutarch. Agathias Scholasticus.
Pluto (planet)
Undiscovered Planet, The. Nicholson.
Plymouth, England
Devonshire Song, A. *Unknown.*
For an Age of Plastics, Plymouth. Davie.
Hardy's Plymouth. Grigson.
Marble-streeted Town, The. Hardy.
Plymouth Harbor. Radford.
Po Chü-i
As I Step over a Puddle at the End of Winter. Wright.
Poaching and Poachers
Antoine and I Go Fishing. Budbill.
Lincolnshire Poacher, The. *Unknown.*
Nottinghamshire Poacher, The. *Unknown.*
Poaching *In Excelsis.* Menzies.
Van Diemen's Land. *Unknown.*
Pocahontas
Last Meeting of Pocahontas and the Great Captain. Preston.
Marriage of Pocahontas, The. Webster.
Pocahontas. Thackeray.
Pocahontas to Her English Husband, John Rolfe. Allen.
Poe, Edgar Allan
Fall of the House of Usher, The. Whittemore.
Goblin Goose, The. *Unknown.*
I would bear a love Platonic to the souls in earthly/ life. *Fr.* Farewell to Earth. Doten.
Poe and Longfellow. *Fr.* A Fable for Critics. Lowell.
Poe's Cottage at Fordham. Boner.
Sonnets (from the Series Relating to Edgar Allan Poe). Whitman.
There comes Emerson first, whose rich words, every one. *Fr.* A Fable for Critics. Lowell.
Tomb of Edgar Poe, The. Mallarmé.
Walt Whitman at the Reburial of Poe. Christopher.
Poetic Meter
Hendecasyllabics. Tennyson.
Metre Columbian, The. *Unknown.*
Metrical Feet: Lesson for a Boy. Coleridge.
Poetry and Poets
Beginnings in Poetry (BiP). William J. Martz, ed.
Fifty Contemporary Poets; the Creative Process (FiCP). Alberta T. Turner, ed.
How Does a Poem Mean? (HoPM). John Ciardi *and* Miller Williams, eds.
Introduction to Poetry, An (InPK). X. J. Kennedy, ed.
Master Poems of the English Language (MasP). Oscar Williams, ed.
Poetry; an Introduction (PAI). Ruth Miller *and* Robert A. Greenberg, eds.
Poems on Poetry; the Mirror's Garland (PP). Robert Wallace *and* James G. Taaffe, eds.
Practical Imagination, The; an Introduction to Poetry (PrIm). Northrop Frye, Sheridan Baker, *and* George Perkins.
Poetspeak; in Their Work, about Their Work (Psk). Paul B. Janeczko, comp.
Sound and Sense; an Introduction to Poetry (SoSe). Laurence Perrine, ed.
Singular Voices; American Poetry Today (SV). Stephen Berg, ed.
Understanding Poetry (UnPo). Cleanth Brooks *and* Robert Penn Warren, eds.
Western Wind; an Introduction to Poetry (WeW). John Frederick Nims, ed.
See also **names of individual poets.**
Pogroms. *See* **Massacres.**
Point Lobos, California
Land's End (Point Lobos, California). Coblentz.
Poison Ivy
Poison Ivy. Gallagher.
Poker
My Poker Girl. Masson.
Newton's Third. Hubbard.

Poker Poem. Pettit.
Rambling, Gambling Man. Houston.
Root, Hog, or Die. *Unknown.*
Twin Aces. Wilson.

Poland
Beast That Rode the Unicorn, The. Meyer.
Good sir, whose powers are these? *Fr.* Hamlet. Shakespeare.
Poland/1931 "The Wedding." Rothenberg.
To the Jews in Poland. Wittlin.

Police
Award. Durem.
Bobby Blue. Drinkwater.
Chicago Allegory. Parker.
Constable Calls, A. Heaney.
Cops and Robbers. Middleton.
Corner. Pomeroy.
Definition for Blk/Children. Sanchez.
Idiot, The. Randall.
I'm the Police Cop Man, I Am. Morrison.
Knock on Wood. Dumas.
Lust. Matthews.
My Policeman. Fyleman.
Negro Hero. Brooks.
Peeler and the Goat, The. *Unknown.*
Poem to a Nigger Cop. Hamilton.
Police Station Ditties. Beerbohm.
Policeman, The. Watts.
Policeman's Lot, The. *Fr.* The Pirates of Penzance. Gilbert.
P's the proud Policeman. McGinley.
Southern Cop. Brown.
Two X. Cummings.
Up against the Wall. Phillips.
Who But the Lord? Hughes.
Wundrfulness uv th Mountees Our Secret Police, Th. Bissett.

Police States
All of a Sudden. Jesús.
"More Light! More Light!" Hecht.
Poem Touching the Gestapo. Heyen.
See also **Nazis.**

Politics and Politicians
Air: "Sportsmen keep hawks, and their quarry they gain, The." *Fr.* Polly; an Opera. Gay.
As I strole the city, oft I. *Fr.* The Legion Club. Swift.
Attorney General, An. Bierce.
Blest statesman he, whose mind's unselfish will. Wordsworth.
Bouquet for Jerry Ford, A. Marcus.
Bryan, Bryan, Bryan, Bryan. Lindsay.
Campaign, The. Miles.
Candidate, The. Ezell.
Candidate's Creed, The. *Fr.* Biglow Papers. Lowell.
Canopus. Taylor.
Civil Service, The. *Fr.* The Vision of Piers Plowman. Langland.
Commonwealth. Bierce.
Daughters of the Horseleech, The. Kunitz.
Dead Statesman, A. Kipling.
Debate in the Sennit, The. *Fr.* The Biglow Papers. Lowell.
Dodger, The. *Unknown.*
Eisenhower's Visit to Franco, 1959. Wright.
Election, The. Pack.
Election Reflection. Jones.
Electrocution Script. Jacobs.
Elegy in a Country Churchyard. Chesterton.
Epigram: "Midas, they say, possessed the art of old." "Pindar."
Epitaph: "We mourn the loss." Bierce.
Epitaph on the Politician. Belloc.
Epitaphs for Prominent Persons, *sels.* McGinley.
Extempore Verses Intended to Allay the Violence of Party-Spirit. Byrom.
Friend of Humanity and the Knife-Grinder, The. Canning.
Gaelic is the conscience of our leaders. *Fr.* A Farewell to English. Hartnett.
Gilbertian Recipe for a Politician. Lindon.
Hubert Horatio Humphrey (1911–1978). Galvin.
Killers That Run, The. Cohen.
Legend of Versailles, A. Tolson.
London Sad London. *Unknown.*
Misconception, A. Lowell.
Mr. Secretary. Patten.
Next to of Course God America I. Cummings.
On a General Election. Belloc.
On the Latest Crisis of Confidence. Jackson.
On Watching Politicians Perform at Martin Luther King's Funeral. Knight.
Political Meeting. Klein.
Politician, A. Cummings.
Politics. Yeats.
Portrait of a Senator. Norman.
Said ("President Johnson to"). Starbuck.
Salesman, A. Cummings.
Senior Members. Lucy.
Similes for Two Political Characters of 1819. Shelley.
Snapshot: Politician. Garrett.
Tall Hat. Daley.
This, the last ornament among the peers. Belloc.
Time's Changes. *Fr.* The Art of Politics. Bramston.
To a Noisy Politician. Freneau.
To Antenor. Philips.
To My Honour'd Kinsman, John Driden, of Chesterton. Dryden.
Tory Pledges. Moore.
W. L. M. K. Scott.
Wharton! the scorn and wonder of our days. *Fr.* Epistle to Sir Richard Temple. Pope.
What Mr. Robinson Thinks. *Fr.* The Biglow Papers. Lowell.
What the Moon Saw. Lindsay.

Pollock, Jackson
Squeeze Play. *Fr.* Spectator's Guide to Contemporary Art. McGinley.

Pollution
Agent Orange. Kiefer.
All the Smoke. Siegel.
Country Stars. Meredith.
E. P. A. Aguila.
Inadequate Aqua Extremis. Walsh.
Rural Dumpheap. Cane.
Slick. Hoffman.
There Was a Young Lady of Rome. Nash.
Unless We Guard Them Well. Merchant.
Urban Pollution. *Fr.* The Art of Preserving Health. Armstrong.
See also **Ecology.**

Polo
Polo Match. Ciardi.

Polyandry
One Wife for One Man. Aig-Imoukhuede.

Pomegranates
Pomegranate, The. Dudek.
Pomegranate. Harada.

Pompadour, Marquise de
On a Fan That Belonged to the Marquise de Pompadour. Dobson.
Pompadour, The. Thornbury.

Pompeii, Italy
At Pompeii. *Fr.* Ode to Naples. Shelley.
Girl of Pompeii, A. Martin.
Volcanoes. Akhmadulina.

Ponce de León, Juan
Ponce de Leon. Thomas Ponds. *See* **Lakes and Ponds**

Ponies
Blessing, A. Wright.
Dapple-Gray. Mother Goose.
For a Shetland Pony Brood Mare Who Died in Her Barren Year. Kumin.
Hey! My Pony. Farjeon.
Hunter Trials. Betjeman.
Ponies, The. Gibson.
Shetland Pony. Lindsay.

Pony Express
Pony Express, The. Thompson.

Pool (game)
8-Ball at the Twilite. Baker.
Kelly. Hershon.
Poolhall, The. Burt.
Rotation. Bond.

Poorhouses
Curate's Kindness, The. Hardy.
In the Workhouse: Christmas Day. Sims.
Over the Hill to the Poor-House. Carleton.

Popcorn
Pop Corn Song, A. Turner.

Pope, Alexander
Epistle to Dr. Arbuthnot. Pope.
Johnson on Pope. Ferry.
Mr. Pope. Tate.
Mr. Pope's Welcome from Greece. Gay.
On the Death of Mr. Pope. *Unknown.*
On the Edition of Mr. Pope's Works with a Commentary and Notes. Edwards.
Spoken Extempore on the Death of Mr. Pope. *Unknown.*
When None Shall Rail. Lewis.

Poplar Trees
Binsey Poplars. Hopkins.
Black Poplar-Boughs. Freeman.
Poplar, The. Aldington.
Poplar. Benn.
Poplar Field, The. Cowper.
Poplar Tree. Colum.
Poplars, The. Garrison.
Poplars. Reed.
Poplars, The. Trotter.
Poplar's Shadow, The. Swenson.
Tapestry Trees. Morris.
See also **Aspen Trees.**
Poppies
Farewell Ballad of Poppies, A. Brudne.
I Love a Flower. Nichols.
Italian Poppies. Spingarn.
In the Poppy Field. Stephens.
November Poppies. Corke.
Ode to the Poppy. Oneil.
Poppies. McPherson.
Poppies. Scheele.
Poppies in July. Plath.
Poppies in October. Plath.
Poppies in the Wheat. Jackson.
Poppy, The. Corman.
White Summer Flower. Merwin.
Wind Flowers. Lockwood.
Porcupines
Porcupine, The. Kinnell.
Porcupines. Wilson.
Pornography
Girl, The/The Girlie Magazine. Gray.
Ode to Pornography. Anderson.
Same Tits. Tate.
Saturday Afternoon at the Movies. Logan.
See also **Obscenity.**
Porter, Cole
Parodies of Cole Porter's "Night and Day." Lardner.
Portland, Maine
My Lost Youth. Longfellow.
Portraits
Art Work. Wallace.
Dorothy Q. Holmes.
Elegie: His Picture. *Fr.* Elegies. Donne.
Enemy's Portrait, The. Hardy.
Faded Pictures. Moody.
"Formerly a Slave." Melville.
In an Artist's Studio. Rossetti.
Likeness, A. Browning.
My Last Duchess. Browning.
My Picture. Procter.
On a Portrait by Copley. Freeman.
On His Portrait. Cowper.
On Mr. Nash's Present of His Own Picture at Full Length. Chesterfield.
On the Portrait of a Woman about to be Hanged. Hardy.
On the Receipt of My Mother's Picture out of Norfolk. Cowper.
Poem: "I do not want only." Thibaudeau.
Portrait. Cummings.
Portrait, The. Rossetti.
Portrait by Alice Neel. Kramer.
Portrait of a Lady in the Exhibition of the Royal Academy. *Fr.* Every Day Characters. Praed.
Rembrandt's Late Self-Portraits. Jennings.
Romney, The. Monroe.
Sonnet on a Family-Picture. Edwards.
Tudor Portrait. Lattimore.
Unwanted. Field.
See also **Painting and Painters.**
Ports. *See* **Harbors and Ports.**
Portugal
Camoes and the Debt. Andresen.
Poseidon. *See* **Neptune.**
Possums. *See* **Opossums.**
Postmen. *See* **Mail and Mailmen.**
Potatoes
Famine Song. *Unknown.*
Potato. Wilbur.
Potatoes. Donnell.
Potatoes' Dance, The. Lindsay.
Spraying the Potatoes. Kavanagh.
Potomac River
All Quiet along the Potomac. Beers.
By the Potomac. Aldrich.
Potomac, The. Shapiro.
Pound, Ezra
After the Release of Ezra Pound. Abse.
Another Canto. Morton.
Asylum. Clark.
Cage, The. Berryman.
Elegy for Ezra. Roseliep.
Epistle to the Rapalloan. MacLeish.
Ezry. MacLeish.
Homage. Highet.
Literary Criticism. Na Gopaleen.
On the Fly-Leaf of Pound's Cantos. Bunting.
Postscript, on a Name. Ratcliffe.
Pound at Spoleto. Ferlinghetti.
Rainuv; a Romantic Ballad from the Early Basque. Widdemer.
Talking of Ezra Pound and long-dead pantos. *Fr.* Fisbo. Nichols.
Poverty
Alice Fell; or, Poverty. Wordsworth.
All Things Be Dear but Poor Mens Labour, or, The Sad Complaint of Poor People. *Unknown.*
Art thou poor, yet hast thou golden slumbers? *At. to* Dekker.
Bad Old Days, The. Rexroth.
Bean Eaters, The. Brooks.
Beggar. Parra.
Between a Contractor and His Wife. *Unknown.*
"Borrowed." *Unknown.*
Boy Trash Picker. Howard.
Brian O Linn. *Unknown.*
By numbers here from shame or censure free. *Fr.* London; a Poem in Imitation of the Third Satire of Juvenal. Johnson.
Challenge, The. Longfellow.
Christmas Day in the Workhouse. Sims.
Christmas 1970. Milligan.
Come, live with me and be my love. Day Lewis.
Country Justice, The. Langhorne.
Dakota Land. *Unknown.*
Debt. Gond.
Dry Loaf. Stevens.
Elementary School Classroom in a Slum, An. Spender.
Enough! Scully.
Esperanza. Scully.
Face of Poverty. Smith.
Facts. Davies.
For A' That and A' That. Burns.
Forgotten Man, The. Markham.
Furnished Lives. Silkin.
Gaffer Gray. Holcroft.
Gin the Goodwife Stint. Bunting.
Gleaner, The. Taylor.
Good Times. Clifton.
"Guilty or Not Guilty?" *Unknown.*
Happy Workhouse and the Good Effects of Industry, The. *Fr.* The Fleece. Dyer.
Hard Time Killin' Floor Blues. *Unknown.*
Heap of Rags, The. Davies.
His Throne Is with the Outcast. Lowell.
Holy Thursday ("Is this a holy thing to see"). *Fr.* Songs of Experience. Blake.
Holy Thursday ("'Twas on a Holy Thursday"). *Fr.* Songs of Innocence. Blake.
Is There For Honest Poverty? Burns.
Jone o'Grinfield. *Unknown.*
Kitchenette Building. Brooks.
Lady Poverty, The. Meynell.
Lady Poverty, The. Underhill.
Lives of Famous Men, The. Gilbert.
London. *Fr.* Songs of Experience. Blake.
London Lickpenny. *At. to* Lydgate.
Lovers of the Poor, The. Brooks.
May poverty, without offence, approach. *Fr.* The Complaints of Poverty. James.
Money in the Bank. Ehrhart.
Moneyless Man, The. Stanton.
My Song. Bialik.
No New Music. Crouch.
One Time Henry Dreamed the Number. Long.
Orphan Girl, The. *Unknown.*
Over the Hill to the Poor-House. Carleton.
Palaces of Gold. Rosselson.

Parish Poor-House, The. *Fr.* The Village. Crabbe.
Parish Poor-Officers, The. *Fr.* A Journey to Hell; or, A Visit Paid to the Devil. Ward.
Parley with His Empty Purse, A. Randolph.
Pauper's Drive, The. Noel.
Photographing the Facade—San Miguel de Allende. Colquitt.
Poor, The. *Fr.* The Country Justice. Langhorne.
Poor, The. Williams.
Poor for Our Sakes. Smith.
Poor Girl's Meditation, The. *Unknown.*
Poor Man Blues. *Unknown.*
Poor Man Pays for All, The. *Unknown.*
Poor Man's Province, The. Wright.
Poor of London, The. Forster.
Poverty. Simic.
Poverty. Traherne.
Poverty, in Imitation of Milton. Jones.
Poverty in London. *Fr.* London. Johnson.
Poverty Knock. *Unknown.*
Praise for Mercies Spiritual and Temporal. Watts.
Pray Remember the Poor. Smart.
Proletarian Portrait. Williams.
Recruit from the Slums, A. Orr.
Red Wig, The. *Unknown.*
Reminder, The. Hardy.
Rich and Poor; or, Saint and Sinner. Peacock.
Ruined Cottage, The. Wordsworth.
Said the Innkeeper. Connolly.
Sale of the Pet Lamb, The. Howitt.
Saturday's Child. Bontemps.
She Was Poor but She Was Honest. *Unknown.*
Shoofly, The. O'Hare.
Slum Dwelling, A. *Fr.* The Borough. Crabbe.
Small Paths. Roland-Holst.
Song, A: "While a thousand fine projects are planned ev'ry day." *Unknown.*
Song of Poverty. Gond.
Sonnet: "Could then the babes from yon unshelter'd cot." Russell.
Starving to Death on a Government Claim. *Unknown.*
Street, The. Soto.
Strictly for Posterity. Simic.
Sunrise of the Poor, The. Wilson.
Sure a Poor Man. Hawaiian.
Things About Comin' My Way. *Unknown.*
Third Wonder, The. Markham.
Thirty Bob a Week. Davidson.
Tin Cup Blues. *Unknown.*
To a Red-Headed Do-Good Waitress. Dugan.
To the Four Courts, Please. Stephens.
Two Boys, The. Lamb.
Village life, and every care that reigns, The. *Fr.* The Village. Crabbe.
We Live in a Rickety House. McLachlan.
West London. Arnold.
What shall I give my children? who are poor. *Fr.* The Children of the Poor. Brooks.
What You Goin' to Do When the Rent Comes 'Round? Sterling.
Winter. Synge.
Worry About Money. Raine.
Ye Simple Men. Blackie.

Prague, Czechoslovakia
My Return to Czechoslovakia. Edmond.

Prairie Dogs
Prairie-Dog Town. Austin.

Prairie Schooners
Conestoga. Murphy.
Covered Wagon, The. Blakeney.
Prairie Schooner, The. Dale.
Western Wagons. Benét.

Prairies
Bury Me Not on the Lone Prairie. *Unknown.*
Bury Me Out on the Prairie. *Unknown.*
Canadian Prairies View of Literature, The. Donnell.
Horizontal World. Saunders.
My Prairies. Garland.
Nebraska. Swan.
Night on the Prairie. Sage.
Plains, The. Dixon.
Prairie. Bates.
Prairie Graveyard. Marriott.
Prairie Spring. Fallis.
Prairie Water Colour, A. Scott.
Prairies, The. Bryant.
Refuge. Sarett.
Stories from Kansas. Stafford.
Summer on the Great American Desert. Sage.
To make a prairie it takes a clover and one bee. Dickinson.
West of Chicago. Dimoff.
Wind of the Prairie. Howes.

Praxiteles
Praxiteles and Phyrne. Story.
Spoken by Venus on Seeing Her Statue Done by Praxiteles. *Unknown.*

Prayer
Abide with Me. Lyte.
After the Rain. Collier.
Another Grace for a Child. Herrick.
Ask, and Ye Shall Receive. Havens.
Be present at our table, Lord. *Unknown.*
Be With Me, Lord. *Fr.* Diary of an Old Soul. Macdonald.
Because We Do Not See. *Unknown.*
Before Sleeping. *Unknown.*
Cell, The. Rostrevor.
Chamber Scene. Willis.
Childless. MacConmidhe.
Child's Grace, A. Herrick.
Child's Prayer, A. Tabb.
Child's Prayer, A. *Unknown.*
Colloquy with God, A. Browne.
Communion. Spicer.
Compline. Greger.
Conversation of Prayer, The. Thomas.
Dark Scent of Prayer, The. Drachler.
Day by Day the Manna Fell. Conder.
De Profundis. *Fr.* Psalm CXXX. Bible, *O. T.*
Death Bed, The. Cuney.
Divine Office of the Kitchen, The. Hallack.
Do I Really Pray? Burton.
Dost Thou Remember Me? Dickinson.
During His Courtship. Wesley.
Ethicks. *Fr.* The Testament of Beauty. Bridges.
Evening Contemplation. Doane.
Evening Hymn, An. Ken.
Evening Prayer, An. Kendall.
Exhortation to Prayer. Cowper.
Father of Heaven, and Him, by whom. *Fr.* A Litanie. Donne.
Fool's Prayer, The. Sill.
Forme of Prayer, A. Quarles.
Gascoigne's Good-Night. Gascoigne.
Glory to Thee, My God, This Night. Ken.
God bless this food, and bless us all. *Unknown.*
God is great and God is good. *Unknown.*
Grass on the Prayer Path. *Unknown.*
Great God, let all my tuneful pow'rs. Heginbothom.
Great God, Thou giver of all good. *Unknown.*
Heaven which art in Heaven Our Father in Heaven. *Fr.* Footnote to the Lord's Prayer. Smith.
Heavenly Father, bless this food. *Unknown.*
His Litany to the Holy Spirit. Herrick.
His Prayer for Absolution. Herrick.
His Prayer to Ben Jonson. Herrick.
His Presence Came like Sunrise. Cushman.
Hour of Prayer, The. Elliot.
Hour of Prayer, The. Hoy.
Housewife, The. Coblentz.
How the Ploughman Learned his Paternoster. *Unknown.*
Huswifery. Taylor.
Hymn to God the Father, A. Donne.
Hymne to God the Father, A. Jonson.
I Dare Not Pray to Thee. Baring.
I rest with Thee, O Jesus. *Fr.* Four Prayers. *Unknown.*
I Thank Thee, Lord. *Unknown.*
Jesus Tender Shepherd. Duncan.
John Wesley's Grace Before Meals. Wesley.
Keep on Praying. Lyon.
Larger Prayer, The. Cheney.
Lead, Kindly Light. Cardinal Newman.
Leave It with Him. *Unknown.*
Letter to the Child Lady Margaret Cavendish Holles-Harley, A. Prior.
Lord, Hear My Prayer. Clare.
Lord, Make a Regular Man Out of Me. Guest.
Lord, speak to me, that I may speak. Havergal.
Matins, or Morning Prayer. Herrick.
More Prayer. *Unknown.*
My Father's Voice in Prayer. Nottage.
My Prayer. Bonar.

My Prayer: "Lord Jesus, make Thyself to me." *Unknown.*
My Prayer: "My life must touch a million lives in some way ere I go." *Unknown.*
Now I Lay me Down to Sleep. *Unknown.*
Now I wake and see the light. Pullen.
O come, our Lord and Saviour. *Unknown.*
O Lord, Seek Us. Rossetti.
Of course I prayed. Dickinson.
Oh! for a Closer Walk with God. Cowper.
Pagan Prayer. Brown.
Paraphrase on Thomas á Kempis. Pope.
Paths of Prayer, The. Roditi.
Payments. O Hehir.
Peaks, The. Crane.
Poet Prays, The. Crowell.
Poet's Prayer. Love.
Poet's Prayer, The. Philipps.
Poet's Prayer. Sussman.
Poet's Prayer, The. *Unknown.*
Pray! Arnold.
Pray! Wells.
Pray, Christian, Pray! *Unknown.*
Pray—Give—Go. Flint.
Pray On! *Unknown.*
Prayer: "As I walk through the streets." Flint.
Prayer: "Be not afraid to pray—to pray is right." Coleridge.
Prayer, A: "Father in Heaven! from whom the simplest flower." Hemans.
Prayer: "I ask good things that I detest." Stevenson.
Prayer: "I know not by what methods rare." Hickok.
Prayer, A: "Let me do my work each day." Ehrmann.
Prayer: "Lo, here a little volume, but great book!" Crashaw.
Prayer, A: "Lord, not for light in darkness do we pray." Drinkwater.
Prayer: "Lord, what a change within us one short hour." Trench.
Prayer: "Master, they say that when I seem." Lewis.
Prayer: "More things are wrought by Prayer." *Fr.* Morte d'Arthur. Tennyson.
Prayer: "Oh! that mine eye might closed be." Ellwood.
Prayer: "Prayer must be grounded on the Word."
Prayer: "Prayer, the church's banquet, angel's age." Herbert.
Prayer: "These are the gifts I ask of thee." Van Dyke.
Prayer: "To Thy continual Presence, in me wrought." Channing.
Prayer: "What a commanding power." Washbourne.
Prayer, The: "Wilt thou not visit me?" Very.
Prayer and Song. Noble.
Prayer at Dawn. O'Shea.
Prayer for All Poets at This Time. Edman.
Prayer for My Daughter, A. Yeats.
Prayer for This House. Untermeyer.
Prayer in Darkness, A. Chesterton.
Prayer Moves the Hand That Moves the World. Wallace.
Prayer of an Unknown Confederate Soldier. *Unknown.*
Prayer of St. Francis of Assisi for Peace. St. Francis of Assisi.
Prayer-Poem, A. Adgar.
Prayers, The. Schwartz.
Prevailing Prayer. Trench.
Psalm CXXX: "Out of the depths have I cried unto thee, O Lord." Wyatt.
Qui Laborat, Orat. Clough.
Quiet Hour, The. Bowman.
Recessional. Kipling.
Right Use of Prayer, The. De Vere.
Rocked in the Cradle of the Deep. Willard.
Scribe's Prayer, The. Guiterman.
Scribe's prayer, The. Service.
Secret Place, The. Pollard.
Secret Place of Prayer, The. Adams.
Sentinel, The. *Unknown.*
Shall the Dead Praise Thee? Macdonald.
Somebody Prayed. *Unknown.*
Sometime, Somewhere. Browning.
Song for Simeon, A. Eliot.
Sonnet: "Bible says Sennacherib's campaign was spoiled, The." Lewis.
Sonnet: "Lord, what a change within us one short hour." Trench.
Stone Too Can Pray. Aiken.
Submission and Rest. *Unknown.*
Supplication. Masters.
Sweet Hour of Prayer. Walford.
Taste of Prayer, The. Seager.
Temple, The. Sisson.
Thanksgiving to God for His House, A. Herrick.
Thy Will Be Done. Flint.
To Begin the Day. *Unknown.*
To Heaven. Jonson.
To the Supreme Being. Buonarroti.
Two Prayers, The. Gillies.
Two Went Up to the Temple to Pray. Crashaw.
Unanswered Prayers. Wilcox.
Unfailing Friend, The. Scriven.
Universal Prayer. Pope.
We thank Thee for the morning light. *Unknown.*
We thank Thee, Lord, for this our food. *Unknown.*
Weakness of Nature. Froude.
What Is Prayer? Montgomery.
What Is Prayer? Robertson.
When I Had Need of Him. Kiser.
When Ol' Sis' Judy Pray. Campbell.
Wherefore Hidest Thou Thy Face, and Holdest Me for Thine Ememy? *Fr.* Emblems. Quarles.
Whirring Wheels. Oxenham.
Who Prayed? *Unknown.*
Without Ceremony. Miller.

Praying Mantis
Chance, The. Holmes.
Confrontation. Hart.
Don't Sit under the Apple Tree with Anyone Else but Me. Pack.
Mantis. McCord.
"Mantis." Zukofsky.
Mantis Friend, The. McHugh.
Praying Mantis. Hoberman.
Praying Mantis, The. Nash.
Praying Mantis Visits a Penthouse, The. Williams.

Preaching and Preachers
Aimee McPherson. *Unknown.*
Mourning Poem for the Queen of Sunday. Hayden.
Music of His Steps, The. Wakefield.
On Hearing a Lady Praise a Certain Rev. Doctor's Eyes. Outram.
Pardoner's Sermon, The. Lindsay.
Street Preacher. MacCaig.
Theology of Jonathan Edwards, The. McGinley.
Three Preachers, The. Mackay.
See also **Clergy.**

Predestination
Disappointment—His Appointment. Young.
"God Is Working His Purpose Out." Ainger.
God's Plans. Smith.
If I Could Trust Mine Own Self. Rossetti.
Life and the Weaver. Dewar.
Our Father's Hand. Flint.
Predestination. *Unknown.*
Predestination and Free Will. *Fr.* The State of Innocence. Dryden.
Subalterns, The. Hardy.

Pregnancy
After Annunciation. Wickham.
Angel. Soto.
Annunciation, The. Pritam.
Bone Poem. Willard.
Buddha in the Womb, The. Jong.
Cell Lay Inside Her Body, The. *Fr.* A Patching Together. Edmond.
Child Waters. *Unknown.*
Cravings during Pregnancy. *Fr.* Paedotrophiae; or, The Art of Bringing Up Children. Saint-Marthe.
Died of Love. *Unknown.*
Early Morning Woman. Harjo.
Early Pregnancy. Shuttle.
Emergency at 8. Hewitt.
Epistle to My Friend J. B., An. Dodsley.
Expectant Mother. Shuttle.
First Pregnancy. Alta.
I loved/ secretly. *Fr.* Carmina Burana. *Unknown.*
I Wish, I Wish. *Unknown.*
Labour of the Brain, Ballad of the Body. Forman.
Maritimes. Shuttle.
Maternity Gown. Holbrook.
Meeting, The. Spivack.
Men Tell and Talk. Francisco.
Metaphors. Plath.
Night Watch. Magid.
Now Jentil Belly Down. *Unknown.*
Now That I Am Forever with Child. Lorde.
Poem for J. Berry.
Poem Wondering if I'm Pregnant. Fraser.
Pregnancy. McPherson.
Pregnant Teenager on the Beach. Balazs.
Sarah Hazard's Love Letter. Ellis.
Song of Cradle-making. Skinner.

To a Child Born in Time of Small War. Sorrells.
Trouble. Wright.
Unborn, The. Finch.
Wait, The. Janowitz.
With Child. Taggard.
Woman to Child. Wright.
Woman's Song. Wright.
Youth Mowing, A. Lawrence.
Prejudice
Moderation. *Fr.* Hymns for the Amusement of Children. Smart.
See also **Racial Prejudice; Sexism.**
Presbyterianism and Presbyterians
Covenanter's Lament for Bothwell Brigg, The. Praed.
Elegy in a Presbyterian Burying-Ground. Wilson.
On the New Forcers of Conscience under the Long Parliament. Milton.
Presbyterian Wedding, The. *Unknown.*
Presbyterians, The. *Fr.* The Hind and the Panther. Dryden.
Presents. *See* **Gifts and Giving.**
Presidency, The (U.S.)
Historical Reflections. Hollander.
Our Presidents. *Unknown.*
Presidents of the United States. *Unknown.*
Presley, Elvis
Painkillers. Gunn.
Sort of Elegy, A. Farley.
Pretzels
Pretzel Man, The. Field.
Pride
Address to the Unco Guid. Burns.
Be not proud of your sweet body. Gond.
Conceited Man, A. Gond.
Do Not, Oh, Do Not Prize. *Unknown.*
Godolphin Horne. Belloc.
It is time that I wrote my will. *Fr.* The Tower. Yeats.
Jolly Juggler, The. *Unknown.*
Naturally. Lorde.
Of all the causes which conspire to blind. *Fr.* An Essay on Criticism. Pope.
On a Proud Fellow. *Unknown.*
Ozymandias. Shelley.
Pointless Pride of Man, The. *Unknown.*
Positive, a Coxcomb. Plomer.
Primer Lesson. Sandburg.
Proper Pride. Lawrence.
Song: "One day the god of fond desire." Thomson.
Priests. *See* **Clergy.**
Primitive Man
Double Ballade of Primitive Man. Tylor *and* Lang.
See also **Cavemen.**
Primroses
Evening Primrose, The. Clare.
Evening Primrose, The. Langhorne.
Primrose, The. Herrick.
Primrose, Being at Montgomery Castle, The. Donne.
To an Early Primrose. White.
To Primroses. Herrick.
Prince Edward Island, Canada
Boys of the Island, The. Gorman.
History of Prince Edward Island, The. Gorman.
Lennox Island. McFadden.
Peter Emberley. Calhoun.
Princes and Princesses
Another Prince Is Born. Mitchell.
Duke Is the Lad to Frighten a Lass, The. Moore.
Everymaid. Oxenham.
Prince of Wales' Marriage. *Unknown.*
Princess and the Gypsies, The. Cornford.
Royal Princess, A. Rossetti.
Princeton, Battle of (1777)
Trenton and Princeton. *Unknown.*
Princeton University
Four Years Were Mine at Princeton. Bishop.
Printing and Printers
Composed in the Composing Room. Adams.
Gas from a Burner. Joyce.
Printer's Error. Wodehouse.
Printing Jenny. Mitchell.
Prior, Matthew
For My Own Monument. Prior.
Senex to Matt. Prior. *Fr.* Two Epigrams. Stephen.
Prisoners of War
Hospital Prison Ship, The. *Fr.* The British Prison Ship. Freneau.
Prisoner of War. Lutz.
Tramp! Tramp! Tramp! Root.
Prisons and Prisoners
Attica Is. Brisby.
Baby, Please Don't Go. *Unknown.*
Ballad of Reading Gaol, The. Wilde.
Been in the Pen So Long. *Unknown.*
Bell-Man, The. Herrick.
Birthday: Tara Regina. Mosby.
Boston Burglar, The. *Unknown.*
Botany Bay. *Unknown.*
Captivity. Rogers.
Cell Song. Knight.
Certain Mercies. Graves.
Chain Gang Blues. *Unknown.*
Chain Gang Trouble. *Unknown.*
Chesspieces. Campbell.
Clonmel Jail. *Unknown.*
Coming of Age in the County Jail. Revard.
Convict, The. Frisch.
Convict of Clonmel, The. *Unknown.*
Convict's Ball, The. Bierce.
Decayed Time. Wahl.
December 18, 1975. Hogan.
Dirty Joke. Klauck.
Down in the Valley. *Unknown.*
Durant Jail, The. *Unknown.*
8:00 A.M. Monday Morning. Welsh.
Elegy Wrote in the Tower, 1554. Harington.
Flowering Bars, The. Donnelly.
For Freckle-faced Gerald. Knight.
Gaol Song, The. *Unknown.*
Girl Held without Bail. Walker.
Hand Me Down My Walking Cane. *Unknown.*
Hard Rock Returns to Prison from the Hospital for the Criminal Insane. Knight.
He did not wear his scarlet coat. *Fr.* The Ballad of Reading Gaol. Wilde.
He Says He Wrote By Moonlight. Aal.
He Sees through Stone. Knight.
High Sheriff Blues. *Unknown.*
Hospital Prison Ship, The. *Fr.* The British Prison Ship. Freneau.
Humours of the King's Bench Prison, a Ballad, The. Howard.
Idea of Ancestry, The. Knight.
If you see my mother, partner, tell her pray for me. Maze.
In Jail. Corretjer.
In Prison. Morris.
In the Cage. Lowell.
In the Prison Pen. Melville.
In Windsor Castle. Surrey.
Inscription. Canning *and* Frere.
It's Almost Done (On a Monday). *Unknown.*
Jailhouse Blues. *Unknown.*
Judge Harsh Blues. *Unknown.*
Keys. Rockwell.
Lean Day in a Convict's Suit, A. Wahl.
Light broke in upon my brain, A. *Fr.* The Prisoner of Chillon. Byron.
Limbo. *Unknown.*
Line-Up, The. Swift.
Little Bird I Am, A. Guyon.
Long Parenthesis, The. Whiteman.
Lord Bateman. *Unknown.*
Loyalty Confin'd. L'Estrange.
Memories of West Street and Lepke. Lowell.
Midnight Special. Leadbelly.
My Crime. *Unknown.*
Nashville Stonewall Blues. *Unknown.*
O Death, Rock Me Asleep. Boleyn.
Officers' Prison Camp Seen from a Troop Train, An. Jarrell.
Ol' Hannah. *Unknown.*
Old Prison, The. Wright.
On Leaving Prison. Leon.
Owslebury Lads, The. *Unknown.*
Parchman Farm Blues. *Unknown.*
Passive Resistance. Bruchac.
Poems from Prisons. Maloney.
Portland County Jail. *Unknown.*
Prison Cell Blues. *Unknown.*
Prison House, The. Paton.
Prisoned in Windsor, He Recounteth His Pleasure There Passed. Surrey.
Prisoner, The. Plomer.
Prisoner of Chillon, The. Byron.
Privation. Carruth.

San Francisco County Jail Cell B-6. Conyus.
Singer in the Prison, The. Whitman.
Song of the Turnkey, The. Smith.
Sonnet: The Cell. Thelwall.
Southern Road. Brown.
Spring. Hogan.
Still, let my tyrants know, I am not doomed to wear. *Fr.* The Prisoner. Brontë.
Stir the Wallaby Stew. *Unknown.*
Street Kid. Niatum.
Sympathy. Dunbar.
There is no chapel on the day. *Fr.* The Ballad of Reading Gaol. Wilde.
To Althea, from Prison. Lovelace.
Visiting Day. Young.
What Is Left? Shakur.
When First unto This Country. *Unknown.*
Wind at Your Door, The. Fitzgerald.
Women's Jail, The. Waddington.
Words from Hell. Helwig.
Written on a Wall at Woodstock. Elizabeth I, Queen of England.
Written on the Walls of His Dungeon. León.
Light from Another Country, The: Poetry from American Prisons (LFAC). Joseph Bruchac, ed.

Privacy
Peek-A-Boo. Lowenstein.
Sexual Privacy of Women on Welfare. Lane.
See also **Solitude.**

Procne
Procne. Quennell.

Procrastination
Delay. Bates.
Getting Started. Hale.
Loss in Delay. Southwell.
Procrastination. *Fr.* Night Thoughts. Young.
When I Get Time. Masson.

Prodigal Son
Prodigal, The. Bishop.

Progress
For the Cultural Campaign. Mongol.
General Summary, A. Kipling.
Into the Future. Witt.
LMFBR. Snyder.
Moon Landing. Auden.
On the Hurry of This Time. Dobson.
Pity This Busy Monster, Manunkind. Cummings.
Plans for Altering the River. Hugo.
Progress. Wilcox.
Similar Cases. Gilman.

Prometheus
Prometheus. Byron.
Prometheus. Mastoraki.
Prometheus Bound. Aeschylus.
Prometheus Unbound. Shelley.
Prometheus, with Wings. Ondaatje.
Wail of Prometheus Bound, The. *Fr.* Prometheus Bound. Aeschylus.

Pronunciation
Literary Squabble, A. Planché.

Propertius, Sextus
Ghost, The. Lowell.
Homage to Sextus Propertius. Pound
Note on Propertius I, 5. Adcock.

Property
Fire. Carpenter.
North, The. McKinnon.
Soul's Liberty. Wickham.
Woman of Three Cows, The. Mangan.

Prophecy and Prophets
Mother Shipton's Prophecies. *At. to* Hindley.
Prophecy, A. Ginsberg.
Prophet, The. Pushkin.
Prophets for a New Day. Walker.
Tiresias. Tennyson.
Word, The. Kahn.
See also **Oracles.**

Proserpina *or* Proserpine. *See* **Persephone.**

Prospectors. *See* **Gold Mining and Miners**

Prostitution and Prostitutes
All-Nite Donuts. Goldbarth.
Amelia Street. Ormsby.
As You Leave Me. Knight.
Beautiful Young Nymph Going to Bed, A. Swift.
Belle de Jour. Melly.
Black Magdalens. Cullen.
Cavalier Lyric. Simmons.
Cell-Mates. Untermeyer.
Comrades in Arms: Conversation Piece. *Unknown.*
Daisy Fraser. *Fr.* Spoon River Anthology. Masters.
Dying Prostitute, The; an Elegy. Holcroft.
Elegy XIII: "I got her in the Black Bull." *Fr.* Under the Eildon Tree. Smith.
Execration against Whores, An. *Fr.* The White Devil. Webster.
For a Masseuse and Prostitute. Rexroth.
Greasy Spoon Blues. Gasparini.
Ho. Young.
House of the Rising Sun. *Unknown.*
Impression du Matin. Wilde.
In Response to a Rumor That the Oldest Whorehouse in Wheeling, West Virginia, Has Been Condemned. Wright.
Lower Court. Baxter.
Net, The. Rodgers.
Old Lady's Lament for Her Youth, The. Villon.
Place Pigalle. Wilbur.
Pro, The. Swenson.
Registered at the Bordello Hotel (Vienna). Rubin.
Ruined Maid, The. Hardy.
Scarlet Woman, The. Johnson.
She-Devil. Goldring.
She Is More to Be Pitied, than Censured. Gray.
Sweet Ethel. Piper.
To a Courtesan a Thousand Years Dead. Eldridge.
Traümerei at Ostendorff's. Laird.
Village-Born Beauty. *Unknown.*
Violent Space, The. Knight.
Waiting for God. *Fr.* Baguio Poems. Roskolenko.

Protest, Social
Adultery. Dugan.
Advice to a Prophet. Wilbur.
After the Industrial Revolution, All Things Happen at Once. Bly.
Ain't Gonna Let Nobody Turn Me Round. *Unknown.*
Alabama Bus. *Unknown.*
Alabama Centennial. Madgett.
America. Ginsberg.
Americana XV: Simplicity. Rakosi.
And you'll say a nation totters. *Fr.* Civil Riot. Cole.
Apostrophe to Man. Millay.
April 1962. Goodman.
Bad Old Days, The. Rexroth.
Burning of Paper Instead of Children, The. Rich.
Chic Freedom's Reflection. Walker.
Chile. Griffin.
Cinque. Hale.
Comments. Kenner.
Covenant, The. Cunnigham.
Custer Lives in Humbolt County. Hale.
Death to Van Gogh's Ear! Ginsberg.
Don Baty, the Draft Resister. Rukeyser.
Don't Want No Hungry Woman. *Unknown.*
Environment. Kearns.
First Fight. Them Fiddle. Ply the Slipping String. Brooks.
For My People. Walker.
For the Student Strikers. Wilbur.
Free Silver. *Unknown.*
Funeral of Rufino Contreras. Schuler.
Girl Held without Bail. Walker.
Hallelujah I'm a Bum ("I read in the news, the President said"). Dane *and* Silber.
Harlem. Hughes.
Home on the Range, February 1962. Dorn.
How Beastly the Bourgeois Is. Lawrence.
I Am Waiting. *Fr.* Oral Messages. Ferlinghetti.
If We Must Die. McKay.
Just Taking Note. Scott.
Keep Your Eyes on the Prize. *Unknown.*
Kent State, May 4, 1970. Goodman.
Labourer's Wife, A. *Fr.* To the Street Piano. Davidson.
Latest Decalogue, The. Clough.
Let Us All Be Unhappy on Sunday. Neaves.
Lovers of the Poor, The. Brooks.
Low Road, The. Piercy.
March 1, The. Lowell.
March 2, The. Lowell.
Mask of Anarcy, The. Shelley.
Memorial Day. Miles.
Montgomery. Cornish.

Much madness is divinest sense. Dickinson.
No More. Clark.
Norman Morrison. Mitchell.
Note to Olga, A (1966). Levertov.
O Whose Are These Children. Snyder.
Ode Inscribed to W. H. Channing. Emerson.
Of Late. Starbuck.
Old Chartist, The. Meredith.
On a Recent Protest against Social Conditions. Posner.
Peace Walk. Stafford.
Picketing Supermarkets. Wayman.
Plot to Assassinate the Chase Manhattan Bank, The. Larsen.
Psalm—People Power at the Die-in. Levertov.
Rich and Poor; or, Saint and Sinner. Peacock.
Salad La Raza. Hale.
Same in Blues. Hughes.
Season 'Tis, My Lovely Lambs, The. Cummings.
Secret People, The. Chesterton.
She Was Poor, But She Was Honest. *Unknown.*
Sit-In, The. Turner.
Song for the Ragged Schools of London, A. Browning.
Song of the Shirt, The. Hood.
Song to the Men of England. Shelley.
Sonnet to Seabrook. Ray.
Stand Up! Lawrence.
Strange Hells. Gurney.
Street Demonstration. Walker.
Thanks to Industrial Essex. Davie.
Thirty Bob a Week. Davidson.
Two X. Cummings.
Un-American Investigators. Hughes.
Unlawful Assembly. Enright.
Until They Have Stopped. Wright.
We Shall Overcome. *Unknown.*
We're Gonna Move When the Spirit Says Move! *Unknown.*
World is a beautiful place, The. *Fr.* Pictures of the Gone World. Ferlinghetti.
Forerunners, The: Black Poets in America (FB). Woodie King, Jr., ed.
Poems of Protest Old and New (PPON). Arnold Kenseth, ed.

Proust, Marcel
Hymn to Proust. Ewart.
Proust on Noah. Silberschlag.

Provence, France
Cocooning, The. *Fr.* Mirèio. Mistral.
Grasse: The Olive Trees. Wilbur.
Visit to Van Gogh, A. Causley.

Psyche
Mythics. Chasin.
Ode to Psyche. Keats.

Psychiatry and Psychiatrists
Analyst. Fisher.
Couch, The. Wright.
Loneliness. McPherson.
Psychiatrist. De Vries.
Their speech, compared with Wisdom and Poetry. *Fr.* Essay on Psychiatrists. Pinsky.
Walking through the Upper East Side. Jong.
See also **Mental Illness.**

Psychoanalysis and Psychoanalysts
Analysands. Randall.
Ballad of the Oedipus Complex. Durrell.
Doctor Freud. Lazar.
Interrogator, The. Jennings.
Notes from an Analyst's Couch. Probst.
Psychoanalysis. Ewart.

Psychological Testing
Catch-22 Test, A. Sellers.
Rorschach. Fargas.

Ptarmigans
Ptarmigan, The. *Unknown.*

Publishing
Jacob Tonson, his Publisher. Dryden.
Publisher's Party. McGinley.

Pudding
Little Pudding. Roberts.

Puerto Ricans
Esperanza. Scully.
Man I Thought You Was Talking Another Language That Day. Cruz.
Puerto Ricans in New York I. Reznikoff.
Puerto Ricans in New York II. Reznikoff.
You're Nothing But a Spanish Colored Kid. Luciano.
Inventing a Word; an Anthology of Twentieth-Century Puerto Rican Poetry (InW). Julio Marzán, ed.

Puerto Rico
African Things. Cruz.
Esperanza. Scully.
Que Bonita Bandera (How Beautiful Is the Flag). *Unknown.*
Why I Can't Write a Poem about Lares. Silén.

Pumpkins
Mr. Macklin's Jack O'Lantern. McCord.
Pumpkin, The. Graves.
Pumpkin. Morgan.
Pumpkins. Cotton.
Saint Pumpkin. Willard.

Punctuality
Time's Fool. Updike.

Punctuation
What Hath Man Wrought Exclamation Point. Bishop.

Punishment
Bitter Withy, The. *Unknown.*
Whipping, The. Hayden.

Punks
Punk Party (They Told Me It Was Literary. . .). Rose.

Puns
Cautionary Verses to Youth of Both Sexes. Hook.

Puppets
Puppet Play, The. Colum.
Puppets. Verlaine.
Street Performers, 1851. Tiller.
Young Master's Account of a Puppet Show. Marchant.

Puppies
Little Puppy. Wetherill.
Puppy. Fisher.
Puppy. Lape.
Puppy and I. Milne.
Vern. Brooks.

Purcell, Henry
Henry Purcell. Hopkins.
On the Death of Mr. Purcell. Dryden.

Puritans and Puritanism
After the Surprising Conversions. Lowell.
On Those That Deserve It. Quarles.
Praise-God Barebones. Cortissoz.
Puritan, The. Shapiro.
Puritan Sonnets. *Fr.* Wild Peaches. Wylie.
Spring Beauties. Cone.
Zealous Puritan, The. *Unknown.*
See also **Calvinism.**

Pushers
Street Song. Gunn.
See also **Drug Addiction.**

Pushkin, Alexander
Natalya Nikolayevna Goncharov. Coles.

Pussy Willows
Little Gray Pussy. *Unknown.*

Pygmalion
Galatea and Pygmalion. Graves.
O gracious Gods, take compassion. *Fr.* The Metamorphosis of Pygmalion's Image. Marston.
Pygmalion seeing these to spend their times. *Fr.* Metamorphoses. Ovid.
Pygmalion's Statue Comes to Life. *Fr.* Metamorphoses. Ovid.
Twixt nature and Pygmalion there might appear great strife. *Fr.* Tottel's Miscellany.

Pygmies
Ogres and Pygmies. Graves.

Pym, John
Pyms Anarchy. *At. to* Jordan.

Pyramids
Innovator, The. Benét.
Pyramis; or The House of Ascent. Hope.

Pyramus and Thisbe
Epitaph of Pyramus and Thisbe. Cowley.
Pyramus and Thisbe. Saxe.

Pythons
Python, The. Belloc.
Python. Yoruba.

Q

Quail
California Quail in January. Jumper.
Quail in Autumn. Smith.

Quail Walk. Miller.
Quakers. *See* **Friends, Society of.**
Quantrill, William Clarke
Quantrell. *Unknown.*
Quarrels
Accusation. Utahania.
After the Quarrel. Dunbar.
Against Quarrelling and Fighting. Watts.
Amantium Irae. Edwards.
City Eclogue, A. "W. J."
Defiance, The. Behn.
Domestic Quarrel. McInerney.
Early Evening Quarrel. Hughes.
His Side / Her Side. Skinner.
Malcontents, The. *Fr.* Absalom and Achitophel. Dryden.
Phillis Knotting. Sedley.
Quarrel, The. Farjeon.
Quarrel. McDougall.
Quarrel, The. Swenson.
Quarrelling. Watts.
Quinks, The. Marquis
Repulse, The. Stanley.
Song; Love Arm'd. Behn.
To One That Pleaded Her Own Want of Merit. Stanley.
Upon Lesbia—Arguing. Cochrane.
When Thou Did Thinke I Did Not Love. Ayton.
Words! Words! Fauset.
See also **Anger.**
Quarries
Green Slates. Hardy.
Millom Old Quarry. Nicholson.
Rockferns. Nicholson.
Quebec (province), Canada
At St. Jerome. Harrison.
Bells of Ste. Anne des Monts, The. Cox.
Bonne Entente. Scott.
Calamity. Scott.
Dawn on the Lièvre, The. Lampman.
Indian Reservation; Caughnawaga. Klein.
Nicolas Gatineau. Bourinot.
Off Rivière du Loup. Scott.
Old Nick in Sorel. O'Grady.
On Autumn Lake. Ashbery.
Quebec Farmhouse. Glassco.
Québec May. Birney.
Sunset at Les Éboulements, A. Lampman.
Wednesday at North Hatley. Gustafson.
When I'm Going Well. Everson.
Quebec (city), Canada
At Quebec. Blewett.
Brave Wolfe. *Unknown.*
Child with Shell. Everson.
House Burning, Quebec. Anderson.
Quebec. Grier.
Queen Anne's Lace
Queen Anne's Lace. Newton.
Queen-Ann's-Lace. Williams.
Queens
Australian Dream, The. Campbell.
Bast. Benét.
Epigram to the Queen, the Lying In, An. Jonson.
Queen Mother to New Queen. Graves.
Queen of the Nile, The. Smith.
Queens. Synge.
See also **individual names of queens.**
Queens, New York City
Day in the City, A. Sissman.
Flushing Meadows, 1939. Hoffman.
Roses of Queens, The. White.
To the Little House. Morley.
Queenston, Battle of (1812)
Battle of Queenstown, The. Banker.
Quests
Credo. Gale.
Desire. "Æ".
I found Thee in my heart, O Lord. *Fr.* New Hymns for Solitude. Dowden.
If There Had Anywhere Appeared. Trench.
Lord, If Thou Art Not Present. Gray.
O Thou/ God of all long desirous roaming. *Fr.* The Song of the Pilgrims. Brooke.
O Thou who bidst the torrent flow. *Fr.* Hymn from the French of Lamartine. Whittier.
Prayer. Pierce.
Pursuit. Warren.
Quest, The. Scudder.
Search. Widdemer.
Seeker in the Night, A. Coates.
Sight and Insight. Slater.
To-Morrow. De Vega.
Why dost Thou shade Thy lovely face? O why. *Fr.* Emblem VII, Book III. Quarles.
World's Desire, The. Benét.
Quilts
Looking at Quilts. Piercy.
My Mother Pieced Quilts. Acosta.
Patchwork Quilt, The. Shorter.
Quilt, The. Levis.
Quilt, The. Newsome.
Spare Quilt, The. Bishop.
Star Quilts. Whiteman.
Quinces
At Times I Feel like a Quince Tree. Quinn.
Quivira
Quivira. Guiterman.

R

Ra. *See* **Amon-Ra**
Rabbis
Baal Shem Tov. Klein.
Bratzlav Rabbi to His Scribe, The. Glatstein.
Debate with the Rabbi. Nemerov.
Rabbi Ben Ezra. Browning.
Rabbi Yom-Tob of Mayence Petitions His God. Klein.
Rabbi Yussell Luksh of Chelm. Glatstein.
Rabbits
Drummer, The. Robinson.
Four Things. *Fr.* Proverbs. Bible, *O.T.*
Hare, The. De la Mare.
Hare and the Pig, The. Bridgman.
Love for a Hare. La Follette.
Meeting the Easter Bunny. Bennet.
Myxomatosis. Larkin.
Rabbit, The. Davies.
Rabbit, The. Durston.
Rabbit, The. King.
Rabbit, The. Roberts.
Rabbit. Robinson.
Rabbit, The. *Unknown.*
Rabbit Cry. Lucie-Smith.
Rabbits. Baruch.
Rabbits' Song outside the Tavern, The. Coatsworth.
Snare, The. Stephens.
Song of the Rabbits outside the Tavern. Coatsworth.
Story in the Snow, A. Crouch.
What Is It? Allen.
White Season. Frost.
See also **Hares.**
Rabelais, François
In Memory of François Rabelais. Moritz.
Rabies
Elegy on the Death of a Mad Dog, An. *Fr.* The Vicar of Wakefield. Goldsmith.
Raccoons
Dance of Gray Raccoon, The. Guiterman.
Diary of a Raccoon. Bennett.
Mill Valley. Livingston.
Raccoon. *Fr.* A Bestiary. Rexroth.
Raccoon on the Road. Brennan.
Raccoon Poem. Palmer.
Raccoons. Fisher.
Rachel
At the Tomb of Rachel. Yehoash.
Rachel's Lament. Zisquit.
Racial Prejudice
And What Shall You Say? Cotter.
Backlash Blues, The. Hughes.
Ballad in Birmingham. Randall.
Birmingham Sunday. Hughes.

Black Poet, White Critic. Randall.
Chicago *Defender* Sends a Man to Little Rock, Fall, 1957, The. Brooks.
Children's Rhymes. Hughes.
Circles. Sandburg.
Coming Home from Camp. Kaneko.
Communication to Nancy Cunard, A. Boyle.
Coon Hunt, Sixth Month (1955). Lea.
Crispus Attucks McCoy. Brown.
Cross. Hughes.
Custer Lives in Humboldt County. Hale.
Day in a Long Hot Summer, A. Kageyama.
Dear John Wayne. Erdich.
Defeat. Bynner.
Everybody but Me. Burroughs.
Family Album. Kaneko.
For a Lady I Know. Cullen.
Grandfather. Harper.
Gulf, The. Walcott.
Hallelujah, I'm a-Travelin'. Raymond.
Hatred of Men with Black Hair. Bly.
Homage to Marian Pyszko. Snyder.
How to Change the U. S. A. Edwards.
Immigration Act of 1924, The. Mar.
In Bloemfontein. Ross.
In re Solomon Warshawer. Klein.
In the Matter of Two Men. Corrothers.
Incident. Cullen.
Indian Children Speak. Bell.
Is It Because I Am Black? Cotter.
Little Black Boy, The. *Fr.* Songs of Innocence. Blake.
Little White Schoolhouse Blues. Lennon.
Look Back. Arnett.
Melting Pot, The. Randall.
Merry-go-round. Hughes.
Moment Please, A. Allen.
Montgomery. Cornish.
No Irish Need Apply. *Unknown.*
Old Lem. Brown.
On being bought from Africa to America. Wheatley.
On Seeing Two Brown Boys in a Catholic Church. Horne.
Once. Walker.
Parasitosis. Davis.
Poem for the Young White Man Who Asked Me How I, an Intelligent, Well-read Person, Could Believe in the War between Races. Cervantes.
Prejudice. Johnson.
Recapitulations. Shapiro.
Runaway Slave at Pilgrim's Point, The. Browning.
Searching, The. Cobb.
Slim Greer. Brown.
Southern Cop. Brown.
Status Quo. Dismond.
Stereo. Lee.
Sure You Can Ask Me a Personal Question. Burns.
Tableau. Cullen.
Telephone Conversation. Soyinka.
There's Somethin'. Small.
Tiger. McKay.
Tripart. Jones.
Ultimate Equality. Durem.
Upstairs Downstairs. Allen.
Vietnam #4. Major.
Warming Up for the Real Thing. Rudolph.
Where? When? Which? Hughes.
White House, The. McKay.
With All Deliberate Speed. Lee.
With the Herring Fishers. "MacDiarmid."
Woodtick. Kogawa.
You Know, Joe. Durem.
You've Got to Be Taught. Hammerstein.
See also Apartheid.
Racing. *See* **Automobile Racing; Crew Racing; Horse Racing; Track Athletics.**
Rackham, Arthur
Inscription for Arthur Rackham's Rip Van Winkle. Flecker.
Radar
Radar. Ross.
Radcliffe, James, 3d Earl of Derwentwater
Lord Derwentwater. *Unknown.*
Radiation and Radiation Sickness
Radiation Leak. Aliesan.
To a Victim of Radiation. Vivante.
See also **Nuclear Accidents; Nuclear War.**
Radio
Airwaves. Woessner.
Elegy for Helen Trent. Leary.
In Memory of Radio. Baraka.
Mr. Vachel Lindsay Discovers Radio. Hoffenstein.
Mixed Media. Schevill.
Not Lost in the Stars. Bliven.
Radio. O'Hara.
Radio under the Bed, The. Whittemore.
Riders. Peavy.
That Radio Religion. Ludlum.
Umbilical. Merriam.
War of the Worlds, The. Rutsala.
Raffles
Midweek. Miles.
Ragworts
Ragwort, The. Clare.
Rahab
Scarlet Thread, The. Henderson.
Railroad Wrecks
Ashtabula Disaster, The. Moore.
Wreck of the Old 97, The. *Unknown.*
Wreck of the Royal Palm, The. *Unknown.*
Railroads
Aberdeen Train. Morgan.
Asleep at the Switch. Hoey.
Burying Ground by the Ties. *Fr.* Frescoes for Mr. Rockefeller's City. MacLeish.
Calling Trains. *Unknown.*
Casey Jones. *Unknown.*
Clitta, Clatta, clatta, clatter. *Fr.* Railroad Song. Chivers.
Conductor Bradley. Whittier.
Crossing. Booth.
D. L. and W.'s Phoebe Snow, The. *Unknown.*
Depot, The. Turco.
Echo Canyon. *Unknown.*
Elevated Train, The. Tippett.
Engine. Tippett.
Engine Driver's Story, The. Wilkins.
Engine 143. *Unknown.*
Engineer's Story, The. *Unknown.*
For Esther. Plumly.
George Allen. *Unknown.*
Guild's Signal. Harte.
Henry K. Sawyer. *Unknown.*
House by the Tracks, A. Etter.
In Texas Grass. Troupe.
In the evening from my window. *Unknown.*
I've Been Workin' on the Railroad. *Unknown.*
Jay Gould's Daughter. *Unknown.*
Joseph Mica. *Unknown.*
Melodic Trains. Ashbery.
Metropolitan Railway, The. Betjeman.
Newport Railway, The. McGonagall.
Night Journey. Roethke.
Observation Car and Cigar. Stafford.
Old Section Boss, The. *Unknown.*
Other Side, The. Reiter.
Oxford and Hampton Railway, The. *Unknown.*
Parting in Wartime. Cornford.
Pat Works on the Railway. *Unknown.*
Railroad, The. Thoreau.
Railroad Bill. *Unknown.*
Railroad Blues, The. *Unknown.*
Railroad Cars Are Coming, The. *Unknown.*
Railway Junction, The. De la Mare.
Railway Stationery, The. Koch.
Red Flag, The. Jackson.
River, The. *Fr.* The Bridge. Crane.
Rock Island Line, The. *Unknown.*
Stop. Wilbur.
To a Locomotive in Winter. Whitman.
Tracks. Schrager.
Train Song. Siebert.
Trains. Tippett.
Travel. Millay.
Utah Iron Horse, The. *Unknown.*
Wabash Cannonball, The. *Unknown.*
Way Out in Idaho. *Unknown.*
What the Engines Said. Harte.
What's the Railroad to Me? Thoreau.
Wreck of the Old 97, The. *Unknown.*

Wreck of the Royal Palm, The. *Unknown.*
See also **Trains.**
Railway Stations
Adlestrop. Thomas.
At Euston. Harbord.
Penn Central Station at Beacon, N.Y., The. Ochester.
Pennsylvania Station. Hughes.
Ravenglass Railway Station, Cumberland. Nicholson.
Striking. Calverley.
Railway Travel
Faintheart in a Railway Train. Hardy.
From a Railway Carriage. Stevenson.
I Rode Southern, I Rode L.&N. *Unknown.*
Rock away, passenger, in the Third Class. *Unknown.*
Rain
About in London. *Fr.* Trivia; or, The Art of Walking the Streets of London. Gay.
After Rain. Thomas.
After the Shower. Lampman.
After Verlaine. Hollo.
All Night I Heard. Moffatt.
And Then It Rained. Van Doren.
April. Shorter.
April Rain. Loveman.
April Rain Song. Hughes.
At Dieppe: Rain on the Down. Symons.
Atavism. Lake.
August Rain. Bly.
Autumn Rain. Lawrence.
Autumn Rain. Rexroth.
Beloved, Let Us Once More Praise the Rain. Aiken.
Biography of Southern Rain. Patchen.
City Rain. Field.
Cloud, The. Shelley.
Cold Irish Earth, The. Skinner.
Conversation with Rain. Gunn.
Dance of the Rain, The. Marais.
Dark and Falling Summer, The. Schwartz.
Dark gray clouds, The. Belting.
Deluge. Clare.
Description of a City Shower, A. Swift.
Down the Rain Falls. Coatsworth.
Fallen Rain. Dixon.
Female Rain. Tohe.
First Rain. Akins.
First Rainfall. Lightman.
Footwear. Justus.
For the Rain It Raineth Every Day. Graves.
Fragment: Rain. Shelley.
Green Rain. Webb.
Haiku: "Winter rain at night." Wright.
Happy are you, whom Quantock overlooks. *Fr.* Brent, a Poem. Diaper.
How Gray the Rain. Coatsworth.
I Saw God Wash the World. Stidger.
In the Middle of August. Hirsch.
In Time of Silver Rain. Hughes.
It Is Raining. Mitchell.
It Rains. Thomas.
It's Raining. Apollinaire.
June Thunder. MacNeice.
Little Rain. Roberts.
Latter Rain, The. Very.
Little Rain, The. Tu Fu.
Little Raindrops. Browne.
Little Raindrops. Hawkshaw.
London Rain. MacNeice.
Male Rain. Tohe.
Mists and Rain. Baudelaire.
Monsoon. Wevill.
Moods of Rain. Scannell.
Ode on Contemplating Clapham Junction. *Fr.* Herman Moon's Hourbook. Middleton.
Old Man Rain. Cawein.
Others. Behn.
Pluviose. Bell.
Prayer for Fine Weather. Leslie.
Prayer for Rain. Jama.
Prayer for Rain. *Unknown.*
Rain. Alling.
Rain, The. Creeley.
Rain, The. Davies.
Rain. DiPasquale.
Rain, The. Hawaiian.
Rain. Henley.
Rain. Henson.
Rain. Kirby.
Rain. Nabokov.
Rain. "O'Sullivan."
Rain. Riley.
Rain. Sears.
Rain. Shaw.
Rain. Stevenson.
Rain. Stoutenburg.
Rain. Thomas.
Rain, The. *Unknown.*
Rain. Williams.
Rain after a Vaudeville Show. Benét.
Rain at Wildwood. Swenson.
Rain Clouds. Long.
Rain for Ka-waik. Allen.
Rain Has Silver Sandals, The. Justus.
Rain in the Southwest. Kelley.
Rain It Raineth, The. Bowen.
Rain Magic Song. Tewa.
Rain Music. Cotter.
Rain on the Cumberlands. Still.
Rain on the Roof. Kinney.
Rain, rain, go away. Mother Goose.
Rain Riders. Scollard.
Rain Sizes. Ciardi.
Rain Song. Loveman.
Rain Song, The. Rogers.
Rainpoem. Dransfield.
Rains of Spring, The. Lady Ise.
Rainy Day Song. Storey.
Rainy Morning. Rivera-Avilés.
Rainy Nights. Thompson.
Rainy Summer, The. Meynell.
Reading in Fall Rain. Bly.
Reprieve. Cormack.
Rhyme of Rain. Holmes.
Santo Domingo Corn Dance. Dickey.
Seven Rainy Months. Plomer.
Shower, A. Izembo.
Shower, The. Vaughan.
Signs of Rain. Jenner.
Soft Day, A. Letts.
Song of the Rain. McCrae.
Sophistication. Miller.
Sower, The. Figueroa.
Spring Rain. Chute.
Sudden Shower. Clare.
Summer Rain. Coleridge.
Summer Rain. Lee.
Summer Rain. Merriam.
Sunday Rain. Updike.
There's a Feeling. Bullwinkle.
Thunderstorm in South Dakota. Boyle.
To Walk in Warm Rain. McCord.
Umbrella Brigade, The. Richards.
Umbrellas. Bennett.
Very Lovely. Fyleman.
Way Through, The. Levertov.
Weathers. Hardy.
Wet Thursday. Kees.
Wet Weather. Low.
What Could Be Lovelier than to Hear. Coatsworth.
What to Do. Wise.
Who Is Tapping at My Window. Deming.
Who Loves the Rain. Shaw.
Winter Rain. Rossetti.
Rain-in-the-Face
On the Big Horn. Whittier.
Revenge of Rain-in-the-Face, The. Longfellow.
Rainbows
Door, The. Strong.
Great Time, A. Davies.
In a Double Rainbow. Littlebird.
Legend. Wright.
My Heart Leaps Up. Wordsworth.
Prisms. Dacey.
Rainbow, The. Davies.
Rainbow, The. De la Mare.
Rainbow, The. Hopkins.

Rainbow, The. McCord.
Rainbow, The. *Fr.* The Angel in the House. Patmore.
Rainbow, The. *Fr.* Sing-Song. Rossetti.
Red and blue and delicate green. *Unknown.*
To the Rainbow. Campbell.
Watergaw, The. "MacDiarmid."
Rainey, Gertrude (Ma)
Dance for Ma Rainey, A. Young.
Ranier, Mount
Mount Ranier. Bashford.
Ralegh, Sir Walter
Britannia and Raleigh. Ayloffe.
Call on Sir Walter Raleigh, A. Piatt.
Elegy, An:"I will not weep, for 'twere as great a sin." King.
Epitaph: On Sir Walter Rawleigh at His Execution. *Unknown.*
Sir Walter Rauleigh His Lamentation. *Unknown.*
Rameau, Jean Philippe
On an Air of Rameau. Symons.
Ramses II, King
Ozymandias. Shelley.
Rape
Ballant o' the Laird's Bath, The. Young.
Blackberry Fold. *Unknown.*
Bride of Frankenstein, The. Field.
Deceptions. Larkin.
Exodus. Probst.
Father of the Victim. Ballard.
Night. Oates.
Rape. Pickard.
Rape. Rabbitt.
Rape Poem. Piercy.
Raped and Revenged. *Fr.* Epitaphs of the War. Kipling.
Raper from Passenack, The. Williams.
Rapist. Terán.
Rapunzel
Disenchantments: An Anthology of Modern Fairy Tale Poetry (DFT), pp. 45–56. Wolfgang Mieder, ed.
Rationalism
Fragment: "Locke fell into a swoon." Yeats.
Mock On, Mock On, Voltaire, Rousseau. Blake.
On the Triumph of Rationalism. Ainger.
Sanctimonious Poets, The. Hölderlin.
See also **Reason.**
Rats
Advancement of Learning, An. Heaney.
Assailant. Raven.
Experiment with a Rat, The. Rakosi.
Freemon Hawthorne. Tolson.
God's Judgment on a Wicked Bishop. Southey.
How to Exterminate Rats. *Fr.* The Sugar-Cane. Grainger.
Intoxicated Rat, The. *Unknown.*
Letters from an Irishman to a Rat. Logue.
Pied Piper of Hamelin, The. Browning.
Rat, The. Davies.
Rat and the Elephant, The. La Fontaine.
Rat Riddles. Sandburg.
Rats. De la Mare.
Reapers. Toomer.
Song of a Rat. Hughes.
Town Rat and the Country Rat, The. La Fontaine.
"Trade" Rat. Wallis.
Two Rats, The. *Unknown.*
Wanted. Silverstein.
What Became of Them? *Unknown.*
Rattlesnakes
Crotalus. Harte.
Massasauga, The. Garland.
Rattlesnake, The. Carr.
Rattlesnake, The. Purdy.
Ravens
Advice to a Raven in Russia. Barlow.
Raven at Lemon Creek Jail. Waltner.
Raven, The. Coleridge.
Raven, The. Poe.
Raven, The. Rich.
Raven, The. Robinson.
Sycophantic Fox and the Gullible Raven, The. Carryl.
Three Ravens, The. *Unknown.*
True Facts of the Case, The. Euwer.
Twa Corbies, The. *Unknown.*
Reading and Readers
Breakfast with Gerard Manley Hopkins. Brode.
Fiction and the Reading Public. Larkin.
House of Readers, A. Miller.
House Was Quiet and the World Was Calm, The. Stevens.
Large Red Man Reading. Stevens.
Learning to Read. Harper.
Old Susan. De la Mare.
On Reading Aloud My Early Poems. Williams.
On Reading Poems to a Senior Class at South High. Berry.
On Sitting Down to Read *King Lear* Once Again. Keats.
Proverbial Philosophy: Of Reading. Calverley.
Reading and Talking. Zukofsky.
Reading Walt Whitman. Forbes.
Study of Reading Habits, A. Larkin.
There is no frigate like a book. Dickinson.
To the Reader. Levertov.
White Autumn. Morgan.
Reagan, Ronald Wilson
Reagan, The. Quick.
Real Estate
At the Grave of a Land-Shark. Moll.
Reality
Angel Surrounded by Paysans. Stevens.
Not Ideas about the Thing but the Thing Itself. Stevens.
Quest for Reality (QFR). Yvor Winters *and* Kenneth Fields, eds.
Reason
Age of Reason, The. Langland.
Eclipse of Faith, The. Woolsey.
Mock On, Mock On, Voltaire, Rousseau. Blake.
On the Triumph of Rationalism. Ainger.
Once Musing as I Sat. Googe.
Reason. Miles.
Reason and Imagination. *Fr.* Milton. Blake.
Reason, the Use of It in Divine Matters. Cowley.
Sanctimonious Poets, The. Hölderlin.
Satire against Mankind, A. Rochester.
To Hell with Commonsense. Kavanagh.
To His Love, That Sent Him a Ring Wherein Was Engraved "Let Reason Rule." Turberville.
See also **Intellect.**
Rebellions and Rebels
Croppy Boy, The. *Unknown.*
Requiem for the Croppies. Heaney.
Rising in the North, The. *Unknown.*
Rising of the Moon, The. *Unknown.*
See also **Revolution.**
Rebirth
After Grief. Plumly.
Ascension Hymn. Vaughan.
Batter my heart, three-personed God; for You. *Fr.* Holy Sonnets. Donne.
Flower, The. Herbert.
For Life I Had Never Cared Greatly. Hardy.
I walked the other day (to spend my hour). Vaughan.
Incubation, The. Zolynas.
Inside Chance, The. Piercy.
Onset, The. Frost.
Renascence. Millay.
Saint Francis and the Sow. Kinnell.
Thou hast made me, and shall thy work decay? *Fr.* Holy Sonnets. Donne.
Recipes
Ballad of Culinary Frustration. McGinley.
Reconciliation
Quarrel, The. Aiken.
Woman's Last Word, A. Browning.
Reconstruction, United States
Mr. Johnson's Policy of Reconstruction. Halpine.
Old Thad Stevens. Porter.
To the Thirty-ninth Congress. Whittier.
Record Players
Gramophone, The. Reaney.
Red
What Is Red? O'Neill.
Red Jacket
Red Jacket. Halleck.
Red Riding Hood. *See* **Little Red Riding Hood.**
Red Sea
Parting of the Red Sea, The. *Fr.* Exodus. *Unknown.*
Red Sea Place in Your Life, The. Flint.
Redbirds. *See* **Cardinals.**
Redding, Otis
Poem for Otis Redding. Thomas.

Redemption
All My Love, Leave Me Not. *Unknown.*
Atonement, The. *Fr.* Paradise Lost. Milton.
Ballad of Barnaby, The. Auden.
Batter My Heart, Three-personed God. *Fr.* Holy Sonnets. Donne.
Carol: "Now is the world withdrawn all." Nemerov.
Charitas Nimia; or, The Dear Bargain. Crashaw.
Cherry Fair, The. *Unknown.*
Done Is a Battle. Dunbar.
Forget. *Fr.* Holy Sonnets. Donne.
Free Grace. Wesley.
Garden, The. Beaumont.
God's Grandeur. Hopkins.
He who would acclaim Cleanness in becoming style. *Fr.* Cleanness. "The Pearl Poet."
His Epitaph. Ralegh.
Hound of Heaven, The. Thompson.
I Am the Way. Meynell.
I Asked for Peace. Dolben.
Lift Up Your Heads, Rejoice. Lynch.
Love. Herbert.
Meditation VIII: "I kenning through astronomy divine." *Fr.* Preparatory Meditations. Taylor.
Most glorious Lord of life, that on this day. *Fr.* Amoretti. Spenser.
On the Crucifixion. Fletcher.
Out of Your Sleep Arise and Wake. *Unknown.*
Pulley, The. Herbert.
Redemption. Herbert.
Regeneration. Vaughan.
Sonnet: "Man, dreame no more of curious mysteries." *Fr.* Caelica. Greville.
Truth from Above, The. *Unknown.*
Wilt thou love God, as He thee? then digest. *Fr.* Holy Sonnets. Donne.
World, The. Herbert.
Redwings
Bay Bank. Ammons.
Redwing, The. Dickinson.
Red-Wing Blackbird, The. Williams.
Redwings. Wright.
Redwood Trees. *See* **Sequoia Trees.**
Reeds
Reeds in the Loch Sayis, The. *Unknown.*
Refugees
Address to the Refugees. Brinnin.
My Polish Grandma. Field.
Refugees. Grade.
Refugees, The. Jarrell.
Refugees. MacNeice.
Refugees, The. Read.
Road to Pengya, The. Tu Fu.
Two Refugees. Marcus.
Regret
Eyes of My Regret, The. Grimké.
Florine. Campbell.
Into My Heart an Air That Kills. Housman.
Love Is Teasing. *Unknown.*
Once. Batterham.
Retreat, The. Vaughan.
Song: "False though she be to me and love." Congreve.
Sonnet: "In minds pure glasse when I my selfe behold." Drummond of Hawthornden.
Sonnet: "When as mans life, the light of human lust." *Fr.* Caelica. Greville.
Text. Wurdemann.
Time Long Past. Shelley.
Reincarnation
Pre-Existence. Hayne.
Reincarnation. Sickels.
Song IV: Sudden Light. *Fr.* The House of Life. Rossetti.
We Have Been Here Before. Bishop.
Reindeer
Reindeer and Engine. Jacobsen.
Rigorists. Moore.
Rejection
Banks o' Doon, The. Burns.
Disdain Returned. Carew.
Dream about Sunsets. Hébert.
I Lov'd Thee Once. Ayton.
Locksley Hall. Tennyson.
Look, Delia, how we esteem the half-blown rose. *Fr.* To Delia. Daniel.
Meditation on a Bone. Hope.
Song: "Farwell ungratefull traytor." *Fr.* The Spanish Friar. Dryden.
To His Forsaken Mistresse. Ayton.
Relativity
How Einstein Started It Up Again. Dillard.
Relativity. Millay.
Relativity. *Unknown.*
Religion
After Lorca. Creeley.
Agnostic's Creed, The. Malone.
And They Were Richt. Garioch.
Antichrist, or the Reunion of Christendom; an Ode. Chesterton.
Awakening, The. Marquis.
Ballade of the Heresiarchs. Belloc.
Bangkok. Scott.
Baroque Gravure, A. Merton.
Bishop's See, The. *Unknown.*
Black Church on Sunday. Mosley.
Blue-eyed was Elf the minstrel. *Fr.* The Ballad of the White Horse: The Harp of Alfred. Chesterton.
Boom! Nemerov.
Brébeuf and His Brethren. Scott.
By plain analogy we're told. Bierce.
Church Going. Larkin.
Church Poem. Thomas.
Church's One Foundation, The. Stone.
Converts, The. Bloch.
Day after Sunday, The. McGinley.
Evangelist, The. Sinclair.
For his religion it was fit. *Fr.* Hudibras. Butler.
Garden of Love, The. *Fr.* Songs of Experience. Blake.
Gimme Dat Ol'-Time Religion. *Unknown.*
Gray Squirrel, The. Wolfe.
Higher Catechism, The. Foss.
Higher Pantheism in a Nutshell, The. *Fr.* The Heptalogia. Swinburne.
Hippopotamus, The. Eliot.
Holy Fair, The. Burns.
How to Hide Jesus. Turner.
How to Start a War. McGinley.
I'm ceded—I've stopped being theirs. Dickinson.
I'm Gonna Run to the City of Refuge. *Unknown.*
In Good King Charles's Golden Days. *Unknown.*
Indian Convert, The. Freneau.
J. Milton Miles. *Fr.* Spoon River Anthology. Masters.
Kind pity chokes my spleen; brave scorn forbids. *Fr.* Satires. Donne.
Lay Preacher Ponders, The. Davies.
Love Lifted Me. Leary.
Matlock Bath. Betjeman.
Mock On, Mock On, Voltaire, Rousseau. Blake.
Moses and Jesus. Zangwill.
My Church. "E. O. G."
Nativity, The. Vaughan.
Old Orange Flute, The. *Unknown.*
On the Late Massacre in Piedmont. Milton.
"Onward Christian Soldiers!" Davis.
Pie in the Sky. *Unknown.*
Preacher and the Slave, The. Hill.
Private Judgement Condemned. *Fr.* The Hind and the Panther. Dryden.
Problem, The. Emerson.
Reason and Revelation. *Fr.* Religio Laici. Dryden.
Religion. Vaughan.
Religion Back Home. Stafford.
Religion of Hudibras, The. *Fr.* Hudibras. Butler.
Respectable Burgher, The. Hardy.
Semblables, The. Williams.
Some keep the Sabbath going to church. Dickinson.
Soul of Jesus Is Restless, The. Mitchell.
Sunday Morning. Stevens.
"They." Sassoon.
Those Guyana Nights. Foerster.
Thus man by his own strength to Heaven would soar. *Fr.* Religio Laici. Dryden.
To Caelia. *Unknown.*
Tradition. *Fr.* Religio Laici. Dryden.
Transcendentalism. *Unknown.*
Vicar of Bray, The. *Unknown.*
We Live in a Rickety House. McLachlan.
Wednesday Night Prayer Meeting. Wright.
When Mahalia Sings. Prettyman.
Wisdom. Yeats.
With Mercy for the Greedy. Sexton.
Written in Exile. Raine.
Year of Our Lord two thousand one hundred and seven, The. *Fr.* An Ecclesiastical Chronicle. Heath-Stubbs.

Religious Life
Affliction. Herbert.
Created, The. Very.
Decay of Piety. Wordsworth.
December. Snyder.
Fire Burns Low, The. Leax.
For man to act as if his soul did see. *Fr.* Christian Ethics. Traherne.
Godly Casuistry. *Fr.* Hudibras. Butler.
Gospel According to You, The. *Unknown.*
Harder Task, The. *Unknown.*
Huswifery. Taylor.
I Am My Beloved's, and His Desire Is towards Me. *Fr.* Emblems. Quarles.
Joy and Peace in Believing. Cowper.
Oh! for a Closer Walk with God. Cowper.
On His Blindness. Milton.
One Thing Needful, The. Reich.
Rabia. *Unknown.*
Resurgam. Bitton.
Sonnet: "When I consider how my light is spent." Milton.
Take Time to Be Holy. Longstaff.
To a Young Gentle-Woman, Councel Concerning Her Choice. Crashaw.
To the Countesse of Bedford on New-Yeares Day. Donne.
Walking with God. Cowper.
What God Hath Promised! Flint.
Whole Armour of God, The. Wesley.
See also **Clergy; Convents; Monasteries; Monks; Nuns; Rabbis.**

Religious Verse
Anthology of Catholic Poets, An (ACP). Shane Leslie, ed.
Best-Loved Religious Poems, The (BLRP). James Gilchrist Lawson, ed.
Earth Is the Lord's, The (EaLo). Helen Plotz, comp.
Eerdmans Book of Christian Poetry (EBCP). Pat Alexander, ed.
Golden Book of Catholic Poetry, The (GoBC). Alfred Noyes, ed.
New Oxford Book of Christian Verse, The (NOCV). Donald Davie, ed.
Oxford Book of Christian Verse, The (OxBoCh). Lord David Cecil, ed.
Speaker's Treasury of 400 Quotable Poems, The (STF). Croft Pentz, ed.
Treasury of Christain Poetry, The (TrCP). Lorraine Eitel, ed.
Treasury of Jewish Poetry, A (TrJp). Nathan Ausubel *and* Marynn Ausubel, eds.
Treasury of Poems for Worship and Devotion, A (TrPWD). Charles L. Wallis, ed.
Treasury of Religious Verse, The (TRV). Donald T. Kauffman, ed.
World's Great Religious Poetry, The (WGRP). Caroline Miles Hill, ed.

Religious Wars
Christians at War. Kendrick.
Sonnet: "Avenge O Lord thy slaughtered saints, whose bones." Milton.

Rembrandt, Harmenszoon van Rijn
Rembrandt's Late Self-Portraits. Jennings.
"Titus, Son of Rembrandt: 1665." Lyons.

Remorse
Brazen Tongue. Benét.
Eternal Lord! Eased of a Cumbrous Load. Buonarroti.
God, to whom we look up blindly. *Fr.* The Poet's Journal. Taylor.
Hymne to God the Father, A. Donne.
Last Prayer, A. Jackson.
Mea Culpa. Carbery.
Pagan Reinvokes the Twenty-Third Psalm, A. Wolf.
Prayer, A: "When I look back upon my life nigh spent." Macdonald.
Prayer in the Prospect of Death, A. Burns.
Remorse is memory awake. Dickinson.
R-E-M-O-R-S-E. Ade.
Remorseis memoryawake. Dickinson.
Resolution. O'Donnell.
'Tis not by guilt the onward sweep. *Fr.* The Fool's Prayer. Sill.
When Oats Are Reaped. Hardy.

Renaissance
Exodus from a Renaissance Gallery. Acton.
Renaissance. Avrett.

Reno, Nevada
Reno, 2 a.m. Hamill.

Renoir, Pierre Auguste
Renoir's Confidences. Pilz.

Repentance
Ash Wednesday. Rossetti.
At the round earth's imagined corners, blow. *Fr.* Holy Sonnets. Donne.
Away Vane World. Montgomerie.
Deeply repentant of my sinful ways. Stampa.
Discipline. Herbert.
Eve Penitent. *Fr.* Paradise Lost. Milton.
Hymn to God the Father, A. Jonson.
Latter Day Psalms. Ashby.
Lord Will Happiness Divine, The. Cowper.
O Lord, I Come Pleading. Lawson.
Psalm LXXIV: "O God, why hast thou cast us off for ever?" Pembroke.
Psalm CXXXIX: "O Lord, thou hast searched me, and known me." Pembroke.
Reconciliation. "Æ."
Relapse, The. Vaughan.
Revival Hymn. *Fr.* Uncle Remus. Harris.
Rock of Ages. Toplady.
Self-Acquaintance. Cowper.
So Little and So Much. Oxenham.

Reptiles
Prayer for Reptiles. Hubbell.

Reputation
Good Name, A. *Fr.* Othello. Shakespeare.
See also **Fame; Gossip; Rumor.**

Rescues
Macinnes's Mountain Patrol. Patey.

Reservations, Indian
Big Fun. Burns.
Builder Kachina: Home-going. Rose.
Indian Reservation; Caughnawaga. Klein.
Pine Point, You Are. Henry.
Turtle Mountain Reservation. Erdich.
Up & Out. NorthSun.

Resorts
Saratoga Ending. Kees.

Restaurants
At the Lavender Lantern. Divine.
Ballad of Bouillabaisse, The. Thackeray.
Eat and Walk. Hall.
Green Estaminet, The. Herbert.
Home Cooking Cafe. Field.
I Had But Fifty Cents. *Unknown.*
La Carte. Richardson.
Lines on the Mermaid Tavern. Keats.
Obscure Pleasure of the Indistinct, The. Ramke.
On a Sunday. Reznikoff.
One Fish Ball. *Unknown.*
Partial Explanation, The. Simic.
R is for the Restaurant. McGinley.
Song: "Sometimes in the fast food kitchen." Lane.
Waiters. Hoberman.

Resurrection, The
Because He Lives. Lathrop.
Christ Is Arisen. Goethe.
Christ's Resurrection and Ascension. Doddridge.
Easter Chorus. *Fr.* Faust. Goethe.
For They Shall See God. Shaw.
Guard of the Sepulcher, A. Markham.
Hymn for Easter Morn. *Unknown.*
I Have Labored Sore. *Unknown.*
Light's Glittering Morn. Neale.
Most glorious Lord of life, that on this day. *Fr.* Amoretti. Spenser.
Not in Vain. *Unknown.*
On the Resurrection of Christ. Dunbar.
Resurrection, The. Brooks.
Seven Stanzas at Easter. Updike.
That Nature is a Heraclitean Fire and of the Comfort of the Resurrection. Hopkins.
That Thou Art Nowhere to Be Found. *Fr.* Diary of an Old Soul. Macdonald.
Triumph. Stearns.

Retirement
Band, The. Dennis.
Blest Retirement. *Fr.* The Deserted Village. Goldsmith.
Day of my double birth, if such the year. *Fr.* Lines Written at Bridgwater, 27 July 1797. Thelwall.
Death. Byatt.
Farewell to Town. Housman.
Garden, The. Marvell.
His Golden Locks Time Hath to Silver Turned. *Fr.* Polyhymnia. Peele.
Home Is the Sailor. McGinley.
Lamentation of the Old Pensioner, The. Yeats.
Nil Admirari. Congreve.
Petition for an Absolute Retreat, The. Winchilsea.
Retirement, The. Cotton.
Retirement, The. Norris.
Retirement, The. *Unknown.*
Solitude. *Fr.* Retirement. Beattie.
Statesman in Retirement, The. *Fr.* Retirement. Cowper.
Swineherd. Ní Chuilleanáin.
Teacher, The. Fisher.

To Retirement. León.
Tomorrow. Collins.
Wish, The. Cowley.
See also **Old Age; Pensions.**

Reunions
All. Gom.
All Legendary Obstacles. Montague.
Auld Lang Syne. Burns.
Eating Lechon, with My Brothers and Sisters. Cabalquinto.
Face to Face. Rich.
Family Reunions. Miller.
Renewal by Her Element. Devlin.
Sailor's Wife, The. Mickle.
Though I get home how late, how late! Dickinson.

Revenge
Achilles with wild fury in his heart. *Fr.* The Iliad. Homer.
Aunt Sponge and Aunt Spiker. Dahl.
Binnorie. *Unknown.*
Brown Girl, The. *Unknown.*
Enslaved. McKay.
Frustration. Parker.
God's Judgment on a Wicked Bishop. Southey.
Heroic Vengeance. *Fr.* Samson Agonistes. Milton.
I Shall Not Care. Teasdale.
I Woke Up. Revenge. Poulin.
If Justice Moved. Sellers.
King Lear Pledges Revenge. *Fr.* King Lear. Shakespeare.
Kissie Lee. Walker.
Laily Worm and the Machrel of the Sea, The. *Unknown.*
Lines on the Execution of King Charles the First. Graham.
O how comely it is and how reviving. *Fr.* Samson Agonistes. Milton.
Pied Piper of Hamelin, The. Browning.
Revenge of Rain-in-the-Face, The. Longfellow.
Tamales. "Henry."
Wild Boar and the Ram, The. *Fr.* Fables. Gay.
William Taylor. *Unknown.*

Revenge, (ship)
Revenge, The. Tennyson.

Revere, Paul
Paul Revere's Ride. *Fr.* Tales of a Wayside Inn: The Landlord's Tale. Longfellow.

Revivalism
Pie in the sky. *Unknown*
Revivalist in Boston, A. Rich.
Revive Us Again. Mackay.
See also **Evangelism; Religion.**

Revolution
Abu. Randall.
And. Gonsalves.
Black People! Jones.
Exhortation: Summer, 1919. McKay.
For My People. Walker.
For Saundra. Giovanni.
Get Stuffed. Alurista.
Great Day, The. Yeats.
Internationale, The. Potter *and* Degeyter.
It Begins Slowly. Bernadine.
June 10. Rodríguez.
Last Poem. Donnelly.
Letter to the Revolution. Griffin.
Militant. Hughes.
My Poem. Giovanni.
O! Start a Revolution. Lawrence.
Old O. O. Blues, The. Young.
Pentecost. Ai.
Radical War Song, A. Macaulay.
Revolutionaries, The. Reed.
Revolutionary. Friel.
Revolutionary Dreams. Giovanni.
Roses and Revolutions. Randall.
Royal Princess, A. Rossetti.
Song in Time of Revolution 1860, A. Swinburne.
Tryptych for Jan Bockelson, A. Simon.
Warning. Hughes.
Whirlwinds of Danger. *Unknown.*

Revolutionary War, American. *See* **American Revolution.**

Reynolds, Henry
For from my cradle you must know that I. *Fr.* To My Most Dearly Loved Friend, Henry Reynolds, Esq. Drayton.

Reynolds, Sir Joshua
Sir Joshua Reynolds. Blake.
Sir Joshua Reynolds. *Fr.* Retaliation. Goldsmith.
Verses on Sir Joshua Reynolds's Painted Window at New College, Oxford. Warton.

Rhinoceroses
Rhinoceros, The. Belloc.
Rhinoceros. Hart-Smith.
Rhinoceros, The. Nash.
Rhinoceros. Stoutenburg.

Rhode Island
Bombardment of Bristol, The. *Unknown.*
Canonicus and Roger Williams. *Unknown.*
Limerick: "But he followed the pair to Pawtucket." *Unknown.*
Looking at Wealth in Newport. Schevill.
Palatine, The. Whittier.
Rhode Island. Meredith.
Roger Williams. Butterworth.
Trout. Hindley.

Rhodora
Rhodora, The. Emerson.

Ribbons
On a Girdle. Waller.

Rice
Manomin. Wolf.

Richard I (Richard Coeur de Lion), King of England
Coeur de Lion to Berengaria. Tilton.

Richard II, King of England
King Richard II, *sels.* Shakespeare.

Richard III, King of England
King Richard III, *sels.* Shakespeare.
On King Richard the Third, Who Lies Buried under Leicester Bridge. Suckling.
Richard III's Speech. *Fr.* Bosworth Field. Beaumont.
Tudor Rose, The. *Fr.* The Ship of Fools. Brant.

Richard, Earl of Cornwall
Song of Lewes, The. *Unknown.*

Richardson, Dorothy M.
Lower Criticism, The. Hollander.

Riches.
See **Wealth.**

Riddles
Anchor. *Fr.* Riddles (Exeter Book). *Unknown.*
As I was going to St. Ives. *Unknown.*
As I went over London Bridge. *Unknown.*
As I went over Tipple Tyne. *Unknown.*
As I went through a garden gap. *Unknown.*
At the end of my yard there is a vat. *Unknown.*
Bishop of Canterbury, The. *Unknown.*
Book-Moth. *Fr.* Riddles (Exeter Book). *Unknown.*
Captain Wedderburn's Courtship. *Unknown.*
Clothes make no sound when I tread ground. *Unknown.*
Cuckoo. *Fr.* Riddles (Exeter Book). *Unknown.*
Devil's Nine Questions, The. *Unknown.*
First Tooth, The. Rands.
Fish in River. *Fr.* Riddles (Exeter Book). *Unknown.*
Four stiff-standers. *Unknown.*
Highty, tighty, paradighty, clothed in green. *Unknown.*
Honey-Mead. *Fr.* Riddles (Exeter Book). *Unknown.*
Horn. *Fr.* Riddles (Exeter Book). *Unknown.*
Humpty Dumpty sat on a wall. *Unknown.*
I am within as white as snow. *Unknown.*
I come more softly than a bird. *Fr.* Rhyming Riddles. Austin.
I Have a Young Sister. *Unknown.*
I washed my face in water. *Unknown.*
I'm called by the name of a man. *Unknown.*
In marble halls as white as milk. *Unknown.*
It is in the rock, but not in the stone. *Unknown.*
Land was white, The. *Unknown.*
Little Nancy Etticoat with a white petticoat. *Unknown.*
Long white barn, A. *Unknown.*
On the Cards and Dice. Ralegh.
On yonder hill there is a red deer. *Unknown.*
Plow. *Fr.* Riddles (Exeter Book). *Unknown.*
Present to a Lady, A. *Unknown.*
Riddle, A: "I am just two and two, I am warm, I am cold." Cowper.
Riddle of Snow and Sun. *Unknown.*
Riddles Wisely Expounded. *Unknown.*
Shield. *Fr.* Riddles (Exeter Book). *Unknown.*
'Twas in heaven pronounced, and 'twas muttered in hell. Fanshawe.
Two legs sat upon three legs. *Unknown.*
Wee man o' leather. *Unknown.*
White bird featherless. *Unknown.*
White bird floats down through the air, A. *Unknown.*
Wild Swan. *Fr.* Riddles (Exeter Book). *Unknown.*

Wind. *Fr.* Riddles (Exeter Book). *Unknown.*
Rifles
A. E. F. Sandburg.
Naming of Parts. *Fr.* Lessons of the War. Reed.
On Teaching David to Shoot. McDonald.
Springfield Calibre Fifty, The. Hanson.
Riley, James Whitcomb
Options. "Henry."
Rilke, Rainer Maria
Rainer Maria Rilke Returns from the Dead to Address the Junior Military School at Sankt Pölten. Engman.
Rilke. Webb.
Rimbaud, Arthur
Birds in the Night. Cernuda.
Death of Rimbaud. Fisher.
Response to Rimbaud's Later Manner. Moore.
Rimbaud. Auden.
Rimbaud and Verlaine, precious pair of poets. *Fr.* Preludes for Memnon. Aiken.
Rings
Alexandrite Ring, The. Ryan.
Ring, The. Mariani.
Ring, The. Pack.
Ring, The. Wakoski.
Ring Poem, The: A Husband Loses His Wedding Band as He Gestures from a Bridge. Dacey.
Ring, so worn as you behold, The. Crabbe.
To His Ring, Given to His Lady. Turberville.
With a Gift of Rings. Graves.
Riots
An Old Woman Remembers. Brown.
Gulf, The. Levertov.
Harlem Riot, 1943. Murray.
House-Top, The. Melville.
Litany of Atlanta, A. Du Bois.
Mr. Roosevelt Regrets. Murray.
New Dance, A. Anderson.
Old Woman Remembers, An. Brown.
On Riots. Leslie.
Riot. Brooks.
Riot, The; or, Half a Loaf Is Better than No Bread. More.
To a Friend in Love during the Riots. Parsons.
Willie B (2). Clifton.
Risorgimento
To Pius IX. Whittier.
Ritsos, Yannis
Two Communist Poets. Layton.
River
River God, The. Smith.
Rivera, Diego
I Paint What I See. White.
Rivers
Above the Medway. *Fr.* The Vales of the Medway. Munby.
Afton Water. Burns.
And There Will I Be Buried. Davidson.
Apostrophe to the Parret. Burrington.
Baptism. Zieroth.
Blade of Grass Sings to the River, The. Goldberg.
Blue-Hole, The. Bell.
Brazos River, The. *Unknown.*
By the River Eden. Raine.
Call of the River Nun, The. Okara.
Course of the Tavy, The. *Fr.* Britannia's Pastorals. Browne.
Crossing the Colorado River into Yuma. Ortiz.
Deep Dark River. Roberts.
Fish Will Swim as Before, The. Spence.
Flood, The. Young.
Going to the Water. Hobson.
"Good-bye," said the river, "I'm going downstream." Nemerov.
Green River. Bryant.
Home of the Naiads, The. *Fr.* The Art of Preserving Health. Armstrong.
I like to see it lap the miles. Dickinson.
In Front of the Seine, Recalling the Rio de La Plata. Ocampo.
In Our Boat. Craik.
Like Ghosts of Eagles. Francis.
Long River, The. Hall.
Low Tide on Grand Pré. Carman.
Meditation at Oyster River. Roethke.
Negro Speaks of Rivers, The. Hughes.
Nicolas Gatineau. Bourinot.
On the Rouge. Souster.
Rapid, The. Sangster.
Rapids at Night. Scott.
Río Grande do Loíza. Burgos.
River, The. *Fr.* The Bridge. Crane.
River. Locke.
River Afram. Opoku.
River Glideth in a Secret Tongue, The. Ostroff.
River God, The. Sitwell.
River God, The. Smith.
River God's Song. Ridler.
River in Asia, A. Grossbardt.
River in the Meadows, The. Adams.
River Is a Piece of Sky, The. Ciardi.
River Lynher, The. *Fr.* Survey of Cornwall. Carew.
River, The; North of Guelph. Jones.
River of Rivers in Connecticut, The. Stevens.
River Rhyme. Williams.
River Roads. Sandburg.
River Song. Brewster.
River That Is East, The. Kinnell.
River-God's Song, The. Beaumont *and* Fletcher.
Rivers. Storer.
Rivers Arise: a Fragment. Milton.
Rivers Come to the Hall of Proteus for the Marriage of the Thames and the Medway, The. *Fr.* The Faerie Queene. Spenser.
Rivers of the West. "Sunset Joe."
Rivers Remember, The. Turner.
Rivers Unknown to Song. Meynell.
Sailing upon the River. *Fr.* The Borough. Crabbe.
Saint John, The. Clarke.
Shenandoah. *Unknown.*
Skykomish River Running. Hugo.
Slip, The. Berry.
"So Have I Spent on the Banks of Ysca Many a Serious Hour." Vaughan.
Song, The: "Do not fear to put thy feet." *Fr.* The Faithful Shepherdess. Fletcher.
Song of the Chattahoochee. Lanier.
Sonnet to the River Lodon. Warton.
Sonnet: To the River Otter. Coleridge.
Stanzas to the Po. Byron.
This Solitude of Cataracts. Stevens.
Tide River, The. *Fr.* The Water Babies. Kingsley.
To Dean Bourn, a Rude River in Devon, by Which Sometimes He Lived. Herrick.
To the River Isca. Vaughan.
To the River Itchin, Near Winton. Bowles.
Trent Again, The. *Fr.* Polyolbion. Drayton.
Tweed and Till. *Unknown.*
Twilight on Tweed. Lang.
Two Rivers. Emerson.
Virginia. *Fr.* Landscapes. Eliot.
Walking to Bellrock. Ondaatje.
Watershed, The. Meynell.
Way to the Sea, The. Lerner.
When the Drive Goes Down. Malloch.
Wilderness Rivers. Coatsworth.
See also **Brooks and Streams.**
Roaches. *See* **Cockroaches.**
Roads
Blessing at Kellenberger Road. Valian.
Bound No'th Blues. Hughes.
Daybreak on a Pennsylvania Highway. Daunt.
Florida Road Workers. Hughes.
Highway, The. Merwin.
King's Highway, The. McGroarty.
Leaving Mendota, 1956. Locke.
Little Road, The. Turner.
Merritt Parkway. Levertov.
Old River Road. Keysner.
Old Roads. Ní Chuilleanáin.
On the Ridgeway. Young.
Path, The. Thomas.
Post-Roads. *Fr.* The Atlas. Slessor.
Road, The. Aiken.
Road, The. Johnson.
Road. Merwin.
Road, The. Muir.
Road, The. Orr.
Road in Kentucky, A. Hayden.
Road Not Taken, The. Frost.
Roads. Brown.
Roads. Field.
Roads Go Ever Ever On. Tolkien.

Rolling English Road, The. Chesterton.
Roman Road, The. Hardy.
Route 29. Brosman.
Song of the Open Road. Nash.
Song of the Open Road. Whitman.
Way through the Woods, The. Kipling.
Working Man, The. Donovan.
You Are on U.S. 40 Headed West. White.
See also **Streets.**

Rob Roy
Rob Roy. *Unknown.*

Robbers. *See* **Crime and Criminals.**

Robert I *or* **Robert the Bruce, King of Scotland.** *See* **Bruce, Robert.**

Robert I, Duke of Normandy
Legend of Robert, Duke of Normandy, The, *sel.* Drayton.

Robert, Elizabeth Madox
For Elizabeth Madox Roberts. Lewis.

Robeson, Paul
Paul Robeson. Brooks.

Robespierre, Maximilien Marie Isidore
Robespierre and Mozart as Stage. Lowell.

Robin Hood
Archer, The. Scollard.
Birth of Robin Hood, The. *Unknown.*
Bold Pedlar and Robin Hood, The. *Unknown.*
Death of Robin Hood, The. *Unknown.*
How Robin Hood Rescued the Widow's Sons. *Unknown.*
In Sherwood lived stout Robin Hood. *Unknown.*
Jolly Pinder of Wakefield, The. *Unknown.*
Little John a Begging. *Unknown.*
Robin Hood. Burr.
Robin Hood. Keats.
Robin Hood and Allen-a-Dale. *Unknown.*
Robin Hood and Guy of Gisborne. *Unknown.*
Robin Hood and Little John. *Unknown.*
Robin Hood and Maid Marian. *Unknown.*
Robin Hood and Queen Katherine. *Unknown.*
Robin Hood and the Beggar. *Unknown.*
Robin Hood and the Bishop. *Unknown.*
Robin Hood and the Bishop of Hereford. *Unknown.*
Robin Hood and the Curtal Friar. *Unknown.*
Robin Hood and the Monk. *Unknown.*
Robin Hood and the Potter. *Unknown.*
Robin Hood and the Tanner. *Unknown.*
Robin Hood and the Three Squires. *Unknown.*
Robin Hood and the Tinker. *Unknown.*
Robin Hood and the Widow's Three Sons. *Unknown.*
Robin Hood Newly Revived. *Unknown.*
Robin Hood Rescuing Three Squires. *Unknown.*
Robin Hood Rescuing Will Stutly. *Unknown.*
Robin Hood's Chase. *Unknown.*
Robin Hood's Death. *Unknown.*
Robin Hood's End. *Unknown.*
Robin Hood's Funeral. Munday.
Robin Hood's Golden Prize. *Unknown.*
Robin Hood's Progress to Nottingham. *Unknown.*
Sherwood. Noyes.
Song: "Weep, weep, ye woodmen! wail." *Fr.* The Death of Robert, Earl of Huntingdon. Munday.
Song of Sherwood, A. Noyes.

Robins
Bird in the Room, The. Lehmann.
Death and Burial of Cock Robin, The. *Unknown.*
Driven in by autumn's sharpening air. *Fr.* The Redbreast. Wordsworth.
Epitaph on a Free but Tame Redbreast. Cowper.
Epitaph on a Robin Redbreast, An. Rogers.
First Robin, The. Leveridge.
Fowls of heaven, The. *Fr.* The Seasons: Winter. Thomson.
I am called by name of man. *Unknown.*
Kill a robin or a wren. *Unknown.*
Little Cock Robin. *Unknown.*
Little Robin Redbreast. *Unknown.*
Little Robin Redbreast sat upon a tree. Mother Goose.
No noise is here, or none that hinders thought. *Fr.* The Robin in Winter. Cowper.
North wind doth blow, The. *Unknown.*
Robin, The. Daniel.
Robin, A. De la Mare.
Robin, The. Scott.
Robin and the redbreast, The. *Unknown.*
Robin at My Window. *Fr.* The Black Bastill; or, A Lamentation of the Kirk of Scotland. Melville.
Robin is the one, The. Dickinson.
Robin Redbreast. Allingham.
Robin Redbreast. Davies.
Robin Redbreast. Doane.
Robin Redbreast. Kunitz.
Robin Redbreast's Testament. *Unknown.*
Robin's Come! Caldwell.
Secret, The. *Unknown.*
Song of the Robin, The. Bergquist.
Three Things to Remember. Blake.
To Robin Red-Breast. Herrick.
What Robin Told. Cooper.
Who killed Cock Robin? *Unknown.*
Why the Robin's Breast Was Red. Randall.

Robinson, Edwin Arlington
T. R. Hall.

Robinson Crusoe
Crusoe. McLaren.
Robinson Crusoe Returns to Amsterdam. *Fr.* Amsterdam. Jammes.
Robinson Crusoe's Story. *Fr.* Davy and the Goblin. Carryl.

Robots
Man from the Top of the Mind, The. Wagoner.

Rochester, John Wilmot, Earl of
Upon the Author of a Play Called *Sodom.* Oldham.

Rock Lilies
Rock-Lily. Robinson.

Rockefeller, John Davison
Compliance. Bierce.

Rockefeller Center, New York City
I Paint What I See. White

Rockets
Enough. Masson.
See also **Space and Space Travel.**

Rocking Chairs
Rocking Chair, The. Klein.

Rocks. *See* **Stones and Rocks.**

Rocky Mountain News
Camels Have Come, The. *Unknown.*
Doing Railroads For *The Rocky Mountain News.* Warman.

Rocky Mountains
David. Birney.
Lines on Mountain Villages. "Sunset Joe."
Moonrise in the Rockies. Higginson.
On Recrossing the Rocky Mountains after Many Years. Frémont.

Rodeos
Bronco Busting, Event #1. Swenson.
Bumper Sticker on His Pickup Said, "I'm a Lover, I'm a Fighter, I'm a Wild Bull Rider," The. Fox.
Closing of the Rodeo, The. Smith.
For Carole. Burns.

Rodin, Auguste
Rodin to Rilke. Grosholz.

Rodney, Caesar
Rodney's Ride. Brooks.

Rodney, George Brydges Rodney, 1st
Rodney's Glory. O'Sullivan.

Roethke, Theodore
Poet on the Island, The. Murphy.
Roethke Plain. Brinnin.
Theodore Roethke. Paley.
Theodore Roethke Foots It. Berry.

Roland
In wrath and grief away the Paynims fly. *Fr.* The Song of Roland. *Unknown.*
Silent Slain, The. MacLeish.
Too-Late Born, The. MacLeish.

Roller Skating
Roller Skates. Farrar.
Stars Shine So Faithfully. Flanders.
We're Racing, Racing down the Walk. McGinley.

Roller-Coasters
Flight of the Roller-Coaster. Souster.

Roman Catholicism. *See* **Catholicism.**

Romanticism
Miniver Cheevy. Robinson.

Rome
Aeneas built, in days of yore. *Fr.* Roman History in Rhyme. Goodwin.
Amours de Voyage, *sels.* Clough.
Da Boy from Rome. Daly.
Epithalamium: "In the streets the crowds go about their business." Halpern.
Hate and Debate Rome through the World Hath Spread. Harington.

Horatius at the Bridge. *Fr.* Lays of Ancient Rome. Macaulay.
Lay of Ancient Rome. Ybarra.
Likeness, A. Cather.
Marcellus. *Fr.* The Aeneid. Virgil.
Piazza di Spagna, Early Morning. Wilbur.
Roma. Rutilius.
Roma Aeterna. Crapsey.
Roman Roman, A. Del Monte.
Rome. *Fr.* Amours de Voyage. Clough.
Rome. Cunningham.
Rome. Hardy.
Rome. *Fr.* Paradise Regained. Milton.
Rome by Metella's Tomb. *Fr.* Childe Harold's Pilgrimage. Byron.
Rome, Conqueror, Conquered. Sylvester.
Rome Remember. Keyes.
Thief, The. Kunitz.
Thou stranger, which for Rome in Rome here seekest. *Fr.* Ruins of Rome. Du Bellay.
Tibur is beautiful, too, and the orchard slopes, and the Anio. Clough.
Villa Sciarra: Rome. Curtis.

Romeo and Juliet
Play, The. *Fr.* The Sentimental Bloke. Dennis.
Silver Dagger, The. *Unknown.*

Romney Marsh, England
In Romney Marsh. Davidson.

Ronsard, Pierre de
Ronsard. DeFord.

Roofing and Roofers
Tar. Williams.
Thatcher. Heaney.
Thatcher, The. Kennelly.

Rooks
Black Rook in Rainy Weather. Plath.

Rooming Houses. *See* **Boarding Houses.**

Roosevelt, Franklin Delano
Danish Wit. Hollander.
Franklin D. Roosevelt's Back Again. *Unknown.*
Homage to Our Leaders. Symons.
President Roosevelt. *Unknown.*
Visitor, The. Bogin.
When Death Came April Twelve 1945. Sandburg.

Roosevelt, Theodore
Great-Heart. Kipling.
Man, A. Scollard.
Sagamore. Robinson.
Star, The; Dedicated to Theodore Roosevelt, Following His Death, January 6, 1919. Smith.
T. R. Hall.
Three Presidents. Bly.

Roosters
Bantams in Pine-Woods. Stevens.
Before the barn door crowing. Gay.
Bonny Grey, the. *Unknown.*
Chanticleer. Austin.
Chauntecleer. *Fr.* The Canterbury Tales: The Nun's Priest's Tale. Chaucer.
Chanticleer. Farrar.
Chanticleer. Irvin.
Chanticleer. Tynan.
Cock Again, the. Kikaku.
Cock and the Hen, The. *Fr.* The Canterbury Tales: The Nun's Priest's Tale. Chaucer.
Cock and the Hen, The. Heywood.
Cock-Crow. Currey.
Cock Crowing in a Poulterer's Shop, A. Ferguson.
Cock-throwing. Lluellyn.
Gamecock. Dickey.
I Have a Gentle Cock. *Unknown.*
Killing the Rooster. Nelms.
Old Grey. Lape.
On a Cock at Rochester. Sedley.
Roosters. Bishop.
Roosters. Coatsworth.
To Be or Not to Be. *Unknown.*
See also **Chickens.**

Rope
On a Rope Maker Hanged. Browne.
Ropewalk, The. Longfellow.

Rosamond (Rosamond Clifford)
Henry's Lament. *Fr.* The Complaint of Rosamond. Daniel.
King Henry to Rosamond. *Fr.* England's Heroical Epistles. Drayton.
"Out from the horror of infernal deeps." *Fr.* The Complaint of Rosamond. Daniel.

Rosary
Rosary, The. Rogers.

Rosemary
Rosemary Spray, The. Góngora.
Time has an end, they say. Doolittle ("H. D.").

Roses
Act, The. Williams.
Ah me, if I grew sweet to man. "Field."
All Night by the Rose. *Unknown.*
Baffled for just a day or two. Dickinson.
Casida of the Rose. García Lorca.
Cliff Rose, The. Fewster.
Elegy while Pruning Roses. Wagoner.
For the Man Who Stole a Rose. Elliot.
Go, Lovely Rose. Waller.
Gold-of-Ophir Roses. Dennen.
How Roses Came Red. Herrick.
I Am Rose. Stein.
Landscape as Metal and Flowers. Scott.
Last Rose of Summer, The. Moore.
Little Rose Tree, The. Field.
Love's Emblem. Clare.
Mystery, The. Hodgson.
Of a Rose, a Lovely Rose. *Unknown.*
One Perfect Rose. Parker.
Poem: "Rose fades, The." Williams.
Rose, The. Browne.
Rose, A. *Fr.* Il Pastor Fido. Fanshawe.
Rose, The. Hammond.
Rose, The. Howell.
Rose, The. Roethke.
Rose, The. Studdert-Kennedy.
Rose and God, The. Stork.
Rose Family, The. Frost.
Rose in the Afternoon. Joseph.
Rose Is a Royal Lady, The. Blanden.
Rose of Eden, The. Phillips.
Rose of May, The. Howitt.
Rose-Bud, The. Broome.
Roses. *Unknown.*
Roses of Sa'adi, The. Desbordes-Valmore.
Roses on the Breakfast Table. Lawrence.
Roses, Revisited, in a Paradoxical Autumn. Cullum.
Said the Rose. Miles.
Sea Rose. Doolittle ("H. D.").
Sick Rose, The. *Fr.* Songs of Experience. Blake.
Song: "What is there hid in the heart of a rose." Noyes.
Southern Gothic. Justice.
Sweet Violets. *Unknown.*
'Tis the Last Rose of Summer. Moore.
To a Withered Rose. Bangs.
To Roses in the Bosom of Castara. *Fr.* Castara. Habington.
To the Rose. *Fr.* Hymns of Astraea. Davies.
To the Rose: A Song. Herrick.
To the Rose upon the Rood of Time. Yeats.
Violet and the Rose, The. Webster.
Violets and Roses. *Unknown.*
White Rose, A. O'Reilly.
Wild Roses. Fawcett.
Wild Roses. Newsome.

Rosh Hashanah
Feast of the Ram's Horn. Shapiro.
This is the autumn and our harvest. *Fr.* New Years'. Reznikoff.

Ross, Betsy
Betsy's Battle-Flag. Irving.

Rothko, Mark
Rothko. Moore.
Sleeping, The. Emanuel.
To Mark Rothko. Cherner.

Rouen, France
Rouen. Cannan.

Rousseau, Henri
Sleeping Gypsy, The. Johnson.

Rousseau, Jean Jacques
Eternity. Blake.
Mock On, Mock On Voltaire, Rousseau. Blake.

Rowing
Eton Boating Song. Cory.
Football and Rowing—An Eclogue. Godley.
Max Schmitt in a Single Scull. Lattimore.

Rowers, The. Benét.
Rowing. Ochester.
See also **Crew Racing.**
Royal George (ship)
On the Loss of the *Royal George.* Cowper.
Royal Society
Philosophy, the great and only heir. *Fr.* To the Royal Society. Cowley.
Royalty
Epitaph on the Late King of the Sandwich Isles. Praed.
Georges, The. Landor.
On a Royal Demise. Hood.
Royal Princess, A. Rossetti.
See also **Kings; Princes and Princesses; Queens.**
Rubens, Peter Paul
Folds of a White Dress/Shaft of Light. Keenan.
Women of Rubens, The. Szymborska.
Rugs
Figure in the Carpet, The. Camp.
Prayer Rug, The. Kennedy.
Ruins
At a Ruined Croft. Manson.
Boy Wandering in Simms' Valley. Warren.
Corner Stone, The. De la Mare.
Crooked bank still winds to something new, The. *Fr.* A Voyage to Tintern Abbey. Davies.
Fall'n, fall'n, a silent heap; her heroes all. *Fr.* The Ruins of Rome. Dyer.
Grapevine, The. Brockman.
Hast Thou Not Seen an Aged Rifted Tower. Coleridge.
House on the Hill, The. Robinson.
House That Was, The. Binyon.
Jade Flower Palace. Tu Fu.
Landscape. *Fr.* The English Garden. Mason.
Love among the Ruins. Browning.
Melrose Abbey. *Fr.* The Lay of the Last Minstrel. Scott.
Netley Abbey, Midnight. Sotheby.
Nettles. Munro.
Newstead Abbey. Byron.
On a Stupendous Leg of Granite, Discovered Standing by Itself in the Deserts of Egypt, with the Inscription Inserted Below. Smith.
Ozymandias. Shelley.
Ravaged Villa, The. Melville.
Remains of an Indian Village. Purdy.
Ruin, The. *Unknown.*
Ruined House, A. Aldington.
Silence. Hood.
Sonnet Written in Tintern Abbey, Monmouthshire. Gardner.
Villages Démolis. Read.
Rukeyser, Muriel
Solitary. Olds.
Rum
Captain Stratton's Fancy. Masefield.
Rumor
My Lady Wind. *Unknown.*
See also **Fame; Gossip; Ruputation.**
Rumpelstiltskin
Disenchantments: An Anthology of Modern Fairy Tale Poetry (DFT), pp. 169–179. Wolfgang Mieder, ed.
Running and Runners
Jogging. Stein.
Jogging at Dusk. Grossbardt.
Mighty Runner, A. Robinson.
Running under Street Lights. White.
Service, The. Johnson.
Song of the Ungirt Runners, The. Sorley.
This Runner. Webb.
To an Athlete Dying Young. Housman.
Rushmore, Mount
Rushmore. Witt.
Russell, Lucy, Countess of Bedford
On Lucy, Countess of Bedford. Jonson.
To Lucy, Countesse of Bedford, with Mr. Donnes Satyres. Jonson.
Russia
Advice to a Raven in Russia. Barlow.
Less Nonsense. Herbert.
Meadowland. *Unknown.*
Requiem 1935–40. Akhmatova.
Russia. Blok.
Russia. Dole.
Russia. Williams.
Shootin' with Rasputin. *Unknown.*
To Russia. Miller.
Viewing Russian Peasants from a Leningrad-bound Train. Gaess.
Why Do You Write about Russia? Simpson.
Russian Revolution
Makhno's Philosophers. Manifold.
Sons of Our Sons, The. Ehrenburg.
Twelve, The. Blok.
Russians
Old Peasant Woman at the Monastery of Zagorsk, The. Schevill.
Rostov. Fraser.
Russo-Turkish War
Last Redoubt, The. Austin.
Rustum
Then Sohrab with his sword smote Rustum's helm. *Fr.* Sohrab and Rustum. Arnold.
Ruth
Ruth. Hood.
Ruth, George Herman ("Babe")
And You Are There. Clark.
Rutledge, Anne
Anne Rutledge. *Fr.* Spoon River Anthology. Masters.
Rydal Water, England
Sunrise on Rydal Water. Drinkwater.
Ryder, Albert Pinkham
Ryder. Haines.
Ryōkan
Ryōkan. Heyen.

S

Sabbath
Attending Church. *Unknown.*
How Sweet Thy Precious Gift of Rest. Menahem ben Makhir of Ratisbon.
Keep Ye Holy Sabbath Rest. *Unknown.*
Light a Candle. Zelda.
Light and Rejoicing to Israel. *Unknown.*
Not on Sunday Night. *Unknown.*
Outgoing Sabbath. *Unknown.*
Princess Sabbath. Heine.
Queen Sabbath. Bialik.
Sabbath. Haan.
Sabbath, My Love. Halevi.
Sabbath of Rest, A. Luria.
Shabbat Morning. Strahan.
Shattered Sabbath. Goldstein.
Softly Fades the Twilight Ray. Smith.
Some keep the Sabbath going to church. Dickinson.
Son-Dayes. Vaughan.
Song of the Sabbath. Molodowsky.
Summer Sabbath. Sampter.
Sunday. Herbert.
Sunday Morning. MacNeice.
Thou Beautiful Sabbath. *Unknown.*
Thrice Welcome First and Best of Days. Chanler.
Voice Out of the Tabernacle, A. Zukofsky.
Welcome, Queen Sabbath. Schneour.
See also **Sunday.**
Sacajawea
Sa-ca-ga-we-a. Proctor.
Sacco-Vanzetti Case
Justice Denied in Massachusetts. Millay.
Sacco-Vanzetti. Halpern.
Sacco Writes to His Son. Lewis.
Vanzetti. Buckmaster.
Sacramento River
Sacramento. *Unknown.*
Sacraments. *See* **Baptism; Eucharist; Extreme Unction; Marriage.**
Sacrifices
Messenger, The. Horovitz.
Scapegoat. Rodgers.
Tollund Man, The. Heaney.
Sadness
Dolor. Roethke.
Sailing and Sailors
Adieu My Lovely Nancy. *Unknown.*
All through the windless night the clipper rolled. *Fr.* Dauber. Masefield.
Ballad of the Tempest. Fields.
Banks of Newfoundland, The. *Unknown.*
Bay of Biscay, The. *Unknown.*
Becalmed. Blight.
Bell-Bottomed Trousers. *Unknown.*

Bermudas. Marvell.
Birlinn Chlann-Raghnaill. MacDonald.
Blood Red Roses. *Unknown.*
Blooming Sally. *Unknown.*
Blow Me Eyes. Irwin.
Blow the Man Down. *Unknown.*
Blow, Ye Winds. *Unknown.*
Boatman's Hymn. *At. to* Magrath.
British Man-of-War, A. *Unknown.*
Brown Robyn's Confession. *Unknown.*
Burial of the Dane, The. Brownell.
Canada-I-O. *Unknown.*
Canto I: "And then went down to the ship." Pound.
Capstan Chantey, A. Brady.
Captain Reece. Gilbert.
Chief Petty Officer. Causley.
Child and the Mariner, The. Davies.
Christmas at Sea. Stevenson.
Coasters, The. Day.
Codfish Shanty, The. *Unknown.*
Coming around the Horn. *Unknown.*
Commemorative of a Naval Victory. Melville.
Crowd, The. Masefield.
Dark-Eyed Sailor, The. *Unknown.*
Darned Mounseer, The. Gilbert.
Dom Pedro, The. *Unknown.*
Dreadnought, The. *Unknown.*
Drowned Sailor. Shaw.
Dutch in the Medway, The. *Fr.* Last Instructions to a Painter. Marvell.
Early, Early in the Spring. *Unknown.*
Enoch Arden. Tennyson.
Epitaph For a Sailor Buried Ashore. Roberts.
Evening on the Broads. Swinburne.
Falmouth. Henley.
Female Sailor, The. *Unknown.*
Fiddler's Green. Roberts.
Fifteen Ships on Georges Banks. *Unknown.*
Flying Cloud, The. *Unknown.*
Forty Singing Seamen. Noyes.
Frankie's Trade. Kipling.
Girls Around Cape Horn, The. *Unknown.*
Golden Vanity, The. *Unknown.*
Good Play, A. Stevenson.
Grandser. Brown.
Gray Swan, The. Cary.
Greenland Whale Fishery, The. *Unknown.*
Grey Funnel Line, The. Tawney.
Hakluyt Unpurchased. McDuffee.
Harp Song of the Dane Women. Kipling.
Hastings Mill. Fox-Smith.
Haul Away, My Rosy. *Unknown.*
Haul on the Bowline. *Unknown.*
Heaving the Lead Line. *Unknown.*
Hell's Pavement. Masefield.
Hervé Riel. Browning.
Homeward Bound. Allingham.
How's My Boy? Dobell.
In the Trades. Smith.
Indian Lass, The. *Unknown.*
I've served my country nine and twenty years. *Fr.* An Humble Wish; off Porto-Sancto, March 29, 1779. Thompson.
Jack Is Every Inch a Sailor. *Unknown.*
Jack Robinson. *Unknown.*
Jack Was Every Inch a Sailor. *Unknown.*
Jim at the Corner. Farjeon.
John Maynard. Alger.
Johnny Todd. *Unknown.*
Jolly Soldier. *Unknown.*
Jovial Marriner, or, The Sea-Man's Renown, The. Playford.
Just as the Tide Was a-Flowing. *Unknown.*
Landlubber's Chantey, The. Stuart.
Last Chantey, The. Kipling.
Leadsman's Song, The. Dibdin.
Life on the Ocean Wave, A. Sargent.
Lightning Flash, The. *Unknown.*
Little Billee. Thackeray.
Long Trail, The. Kipling.
Longshore Intellectual. Lucy.
Lowlands o' Holland, The. *Unknown.*
Manchester Ship Canal, The. *Unknown.*
Mariners' Carol. Merwin.
Mariner's Dream, The. Dimond.
Mariners. Morton.
McAndrew's Hymn. Kipling.
Men behind the Guns, The. Rooney.
Merchant Marine. Miles.
Messmates. Newbolt.
Nautical Ballad, A. *Fr.* Davy and the Goblin. Carryl.
Norse Sailor's Joy. Thorley.
Ocean Burial, The. Chapin.
Ode for a Master Mariner Ashore. Guiney.
Off Rivière du Loup. Scott.
Old Quartermaster, The. Grant.
Old Song Re-sung, An. Masefield.
One of Wally's Yarns. Masefield.
Our Captain stood upon the deck, a spyglass in his hand. *Unknown.*
Over Bright Summer Seas. Hillyer.
Paddy, Get Back. *Unknown.*
Pageant of Seamen, The. Byron.
Peg-Leg's Fiddle. Adams.
Pleasant and Delightful. *Unknown.*
Poor Jack. Dibdin.
Psalm CVII. *Fr.* Psalms. Bible, *O.T.*
Putting to Sea. Bogan.
Quaker Graveyard in Nantucket, The. Lowell.
Rambling Sailor, The. Mew.
Red Iron Ore. *Unknown.*
Reuben Ranzo. *Unknown.*
Rime of the Ancient Mariner, The. Coleridge.
Rolling Home. Mackay.
Rosemary Lane. *Unknown.*
Rounding the Horn. *Fr.* Dauber. Masefield.
Rude Boreas. *Unknown.*
Sacramento. *Unknown.*
Sailing, Sailing. Burr.
Sailing Sailing. Marks.
Sailing to an Island. Murphy.
Sailor, The. Allingham.
Sailor. Hughes.
Sailor, The. MacDonald.
Sailor Boy, The. *Unknown.*
Sailor Cut Down in His Prime, The. *Unknown.*
Sailor Man. Bailey.
Sailors' Alphabet, The.
Sailor's Consolation, The. Dibdin.
Sailor's Consolation. Pitt.
Sailor's Wife, A. Bernhardt.
Salcome Seaman's Flaunt to the Proud Pirate, The. *Unknown.*
Sally Free and Easy. Tawney.
Santy Anno. *Unknown.*
Saucy Sailor, The. *Unknown.*
Say That He Loved Old Ships. Hicky.
Saylors for My Money. Parker.
Schooner *Fred Dunbar*, The. *Unknown.*
Sea, The. "Cornwall."
Sea Dialogue, A. Holmes.
Sea Fever. Masefield.
Sea Gypsy, The. Hovey.
Sea-Fever. Masefield.
Sea-Song, A. Cunningham.
Sea-Voyage from Tenby to Bristol, A. Philips.
Seafarer. MacLeish.
Seafarer, The. Surrey.
Seafarer, The. *Unknown.*
Seumas Beg. Stephens.
Sheep. Davies.
Shepherdess and the Sailor, The. *Unknown.*
Shipman, The. *Fr.* The Canterbury Tales. Chaucer.
Shipmen, The. Hunnis.
Sir Patrick Spens. *Unknown.*
Song for All Seas, All Ships. Whitman.
Song Written at Sea. Sackville.
Sounding. Ferne.
Stony Brook Tavern. Reed.
Storm at Sea. Davenant.
Sweet William. *Unknown.*
Sweet William's Farewell to Black-eyed Susan. Gay.
Tacking Ship off Shore. Mitchell.
Tempest, The. *Unknown.*
Things to Do Around a Ship at Sea. Snyder.
To a Seaman Dead on Land. Boyle.
To Sea, to Sea. *Fr.* Death's Jest Book. Beddoes.
Tom Bowling. Dibdin.
Two Anchors, The. Stoddard.

We'll Go to Sea No More. *Unknown.*
Wet Sheet and a Flowing Sea, A. Cunningham.
What Shall We Do with a Drunken Sailor?. *Unknown.*
What the Red-haired Bo'sun Said. Souter.
Where Lies the Land. *Fr.* Songs in Absence. Clough.
William Taylor. *Unknown.*
Wind Sou'west, The. *Unknown.*
Wynyard Sailor. Mathew.
Yachts, The. Williams.
Yarn of the *Nancy Bell*, The. Gilbert.
Ye Mariners of England. Campbell.
Young Allan. *Unknown.*
American Sea Songs and Chanteys (AmSS). Frank Shay, ed.
Eternal Sea, The (EtS). W. M. Williamson, ed.
Moods of the Sea (MOS). George C. Solley *and* Eric Steinbaugh, eds.
Shantymen and Shantyboys (ShS). William Main Doerflinger, comp.

St. Agnes' Eve
Eve of St. Agnes, The. Keats.
St. Agnes' Eve. Tennyson.

St. Andrews, Scotland
Almae Matres. Lang.
Gateway to the Sea—St. Andrews, A. Bruce.

St. Cecilia's Day. *See* Cecilia, Saint
Song for St. Cecilia's Day, 1687, A. Dryden.

St. Crispin's Day
St. Crispin's Day. *Fr.* Henry V. Shakespeare.

St. Croix (river), Canada
Border River. Bailey.

Saint Helena
St. Helena Lullaby, A. Kipling.

St. John, The Apostle
Death in the Desert, A. Browning.

Saint Keyne's Well, Cornwall
Well of St. Keyne, The. Southey.

St. Louis, Missouri
Meet Me in St. Louis, Louis. Sterling.
Riverfront, St. Louis. Knoepfle.

Saint Lucia
For the Altarpiece of the Roseau Valley Church, Saint Lucia. Walcott.

St. Mark's Eve
Eve of Saint Mark, The. Keats.

St. Patrick
Praise of Fionn, The. *Unknown.*
St. Patrick Was a Gentleman. Bennett.

St. Patrick's Day
Dawn Song—St. Patrick's Day. Storey.
I'll Wear a Shamrock. Davies.
Wearing of the Green. Fisher.

St. Paul's Cathedral
Homage to Wren. MacNeice.

Saint Peter (or, Pierre), Lake, Quebec
Julie Plante, The. Drummond.

St. Valentine's Day. *See* **Valentine's Day.**

Saint-Just, Louis de
Saint-Just 1767-93. Lowell.

Saints
Mrs. Malone. Farjeon.
Nameless Saints, The. Hale.
Saints. Garrett.
Saints in Glory, The. *Fr.* Divina Commedia: Paradiso. Dante.
When the Saints Go Marching In. *Unknown.*

Salamis, Battle of (480 B.C.)
Salamis. *Fr.* The Persians. Aeschylus.

Salem, Massachusetts
Salem. Lowell.
Salem. Stedman.
Salem Witch, A. Clarke.
Ship Comes In, A. Jenkins.

Sales Clerks. *See* **Clerks.**

Salesmen
One Foot in the Door. Elder.
Salesman Is an It That Stinks Excuse, A. Cummings.

Salisbury, England
In a Cathedral City. Hardy.
Salisbury; the Cathedral Close. *Fr.* The Angel in the House. Patmore.

Salmon
Salmon Draught at Inveraray. Nunley.
Salmon Drowns Eagle. Lowry.
Sockeye Salmon. Hambleton.
Weir Bridge. Fallon.

Salt
Ode to Salt. Neruda.
Photos of a Salt Mine. Page.

Salt Lake City, Utah
Salt Lake City. Carruth.

Salvation
Ubi Sunt Qui ante Nos Fuerunt? *Unknown.*
Zion's Sons and Daughters. *Unknown.*

Salvation Army
Away with Rum. *Unknown.*
General William Booth Enters into Heaven. Lindsay.
Karma. Robinson.
We'll Roll the Golden Chariot Along. *Unknown.*

Samarkand
Golden Journey to Samarkand, The. Flecker.
Journey in the Orient. Spaziani.

Samson
Blindness of Samson, The. *Fr.* Samson Agonistes. Milton.
Death of Samson. *Fr.* Samson Agonistes. Milton.
Deliverer, The. *Fr.* Samson Agonistes. Milton.
Epilogue: "All is best, though we oft doubt." *Fr.* Samson Agonistes. Milton.
If I Had My Way. *Unknown.*
Love Letter. Gregory.
My Samsons. Guri.
O Dark, Dark, Dark. *Fr.* Samson Agonistes. Milton.
O, how comely it is, and how reviving. *Fr.* Samson Agonistes. Milton.
Samson. Gilboa.
Samson Fallen. *Fr.* Samson Agonistes. Milton.
Samson Rends His Clothes. Eldan.
Ways of God to Men, The. *Fr.* Samson Agonistes. Milton.

San Francisco, California
After the Cries of Birds. Ferlinghetti.
Ballad of the Hyde Street Grip. Burgess.
Barriers Burned. Field.
City: San Francisco. Hughes.
Frisco's Defi. Hooper.
From Russian Hill. Coolbrith.
Lines Written near San Francisco. Simpson.
Nostalgia. Millard.
Pan-Asian Holiday Tour. Syquia.
Returned to Frisco, 1946. Snodgrass.
San Francisco. Austin.
San Francisco. Roberts.
San Francisco Arising. Markham.
San Francisco Bay. Miller.
San Francisco Falling. Markham.
San Francisco from the Sea. Harte.
San Francisco Poem. Logan.
Scenic. Updike.
Seal Rocks: San Francisco. Conquest.
Trip: San Francisco. Hughes.

San Giorgio Maggiore, Venice (church)
Venetian Scene. Ridler.

San Jacinto, Battle of (1836)
Fight at San Jacinto, The. Palmer.

San Juan Capistrano Mission, California
San Juan Capistrano. Cooper.

Sancho Panza
Sancho. Collin.

Sanctuaries
Sanctuary. Boothroyd.

Sand, George
George Sand. Parker.
To George Sand. Browning.

Sand
Culbin Sands. Young.
I dug and dug amongst the snow. Rossetti.
Sand-between-the-Toes. Milne.
We Lying by Seasand. Thomas.

Sandpipers
Sandpiper. Bishop.
Sandpiper, The. Bynner.
Sandpiper, The. Frost.
Sandpiper, The. Thaxter.
Sandpipers. Egerton.
Summer's Early End at Hudson Bay. Carruth.

Sands, Bobby
Hunger Striker. Franklin.

Sandys, George
To My Honoured Friend Mr. George Sandys. King.
To My Worthy Friend Master Geo. Sands. Carew.

Sanitary Engineering
They're Shifting Father's Grave. *Unknown.*

See also **Sewers.**
Santa Barbara, California
Santa Barbara. Browne.
Santa Barbara Beach. Torrence.
Santa Clara Valley, California.
On the Great Plateau. Wyatt.
Santa Claus
Boy Who Laughed at Santa Claus, The. Nash.
Conversation between Mr. and Mrs. Santa Claus. Bennett.
Kriss Kringle. Aldrich.
Merry Christmas. Olson.
Mrs. Kriss Kringle. Thomas.
Mrs. Santa Claus' Christmas Present. Morris.
Saint Nicholas. Moore.
Santa Claus. De la Mare.
Santa Claus ("He comes in the night!"). *Unknown.*
Santa Claus ("Little fairy snowflakes"). *Unknown.*
Visit from St. Nicholas, A. Moore.
Santa Fe, New Mexico
Spring Morning—Santa Fe. Riggs.
Santa Fe Trail
Effortlessly Democratic Santa Fe Trail. Baird.
Old Santa Fe Trail, The. Burton.
Santa Fe Trail, The. Chapman.
Santayana, George
For George Santayana. Lowell.
To an Old Philosopher in Rome. Stevens.
Upon the Death of George Santayana. Hecht.
Santiago de Cuba, Battle of (1898)
Charge at Santiago, The. Hayne.
Deeds of Valor at Santiago. Scollard.
Santiago. Janvier.
Spain's Last Armada. Rice.
Sappho
Sappho. Cope.
Sappho Rehung. Smith.
Sappho's Tomb. Stringer.
Sisters, The. Lowell.
Summer Matures. Johnson.
Saracens
War Song of the Saracens. Flecker.
Sarah
Sarah. Schwartz.
Sarai. Sherman.
Sarajevo, Yugoslavia
Sarajevo. Durrell.
Saratoga, New York
Field of the Grounded Arms, The. Halleck.
Sardanapulus, King of Assyria
Sardanapulus. Surrey.
Sarsfield, Patrick, Earl of Lucan
Ballad of Sarsfield, A. De Vere.
Farewell to Patrick Sarsfield. *Unknown.*
Sarto, Andrea del
Andrea del Sarto. Browning.
Saskatchewan, Canada
Breathe Dust. Wah.
Double-Headed Snake, The. Newlove.
From the North Saskatchewan. Mandel.
Saskatchewan Dusk. Buckaway.
Verigin, Moving In Alone. Newlove.
Sassafras
Sassafras. Peck.
Witchwood. Justus.
Satan
Address to the Deil. Burns.
After Reading the Life of Mrs. Catherine Stubbs in Isaac Ambrose's "War with the Devils." Hann.
Copy of an Intercepted Despatch from His Excellency Don Strepitoso Diabolo. Moore.
Dark Angel, The. Johnson.
Demon Lover, The. *Unknown.*
Devil, The. *Unknown.*
Devil and the Farmer's Wife, The. *Unknown.*
Devil's Bag, The. Stephens.
Devil's Thoughts, The. Southey *and* Coleridge.
Devil's Walk, The. Southey.
Epilogue: "Truly, my Satan, thou art but a dunce." *Fr.* The Gates of Paradise. Blake.
Hell in Texas. *Unknown.*
Knight Fallen on Evil Days, The. Wylie.
Lament of an Idle Demon. Lister.
Limits of the sphere of dream, The. *Fr.* Faust. Goethe.
Litany to Satan. Baudelaire.
Lucifer. Lawrence.
Lucifer in Starlight. Meredith.
Lucifer in the Train. Rich.
Man's Amazement. *Unknown.*
Overthrow of Lucifer, The. *Fr.* The Purple Island. Fletcher.
Prologue in Heaven. *Fr.* Faust. Goethe.
Satan. *Fr.* Paradise Lost. Milton.
Satan and His Host. *Fr.* Paradise Lost. Milton.
Satan and the Fallen Angels. *Fr.* Paradise Lost. Milton.
Satan Defiant. *Fr.* Paradise Lost. Milton.
Satan's Guile. *Fr.* Paradise Regained. Milton.
Satan's Soliloquy. *Fr.* Paradise Lost. Milton.
Sin and Death. *Fr.* Paradise Lost. Milton.
Sin, Despair, and Lucifer. *Fr.* The Locusts, or Apollyonists. Fletcher.
Sinners, abhor the fiend. *Fr.* The Horrible Decree. Wesley.
Souls Groan to Christ for Succour, The. Taylor.
Three Enemies, The. Rossetti.
To an Artist. Burns.
Tyin' a Knot in the Devil's Tail. Gardner.
Whale, The. *Fr.* Physiologus. *Unknown.*
Satellites
Little Satellite. Krows.
Satie, Erik
Angel. Merrill.
Satie, at the End of Term. Curtis.
Satiric Verse
Anthology of Poems on Affairs of State: Augustan Satirical Verse (APAS). George deF. Lord, ed.
Devil's Book of Verse, The (DBV). Richard Conniff, ed.
Home Book of Verse, The, (HBV-1), pp. 1835-1956. Burton Egbert Stevenson, ed.
Oxford Book of Satirical Verse, The (OBSV). Geoffrey Grigson, ed.
Pith and Vinegar (PV). William Cole, ed.
Saturday
For Saturday. Smart.
Saturday Afternoon, When Chores Are Done. Mullen.
See also **Sabbath.**
Saturday Review, The (magazine)
Saturday Review, The. Cole.
Satyrs
Afternoon of a Faun, The: Eclogue. Mallarmé.
Crackling Twig, The. Stephens.
Satyr, The. Stephens.
Satyr on Elysium lights, A. *Fr.* The Muses' Elysium. Drayton.
Saudi Arabia
In Memory, 1978. Kazantzis.
Saul
Beauty of Israel is slain upon thy high places, The. *Fr.* Second Samuel. Bible, *O.T.*
Dance of Saul with the Prophets, The. Tchernichowsky.
King Saul. Horvitz.
Saul. Alterman.
Saul. Browning.
Saul. Gilboa.
Saul. Lasker-Schüler.
Saul. Sterling.
Saunas. *See* **Baths and Bathing.**
Sausage
Recipe: Sausage. Axionicus.
Sausage. Guest.
Savannah, Georgia
About Savannah. *Unknown.*
Savannah. Burroughs.
Savile, Henry
To Sir Henrie Savile. Jonson.
Savonarola, Girolamo
Old Savonarola was a merry old soul. *Fr.* Merry Old Souls. Bishop.
Savonarola. Beerbohm.
Scarecrows
Dressmaker's Dummy as Scarecrow, The. Howes.
Lonely Scarecrow, The. Kirkup.
Scarecrow, The. De la Mare.
Scarecrow, The. Franklin.
Scarecrow, The. Young.
Schoenberg, Arnold
Ode to Arnold Schoenberg. Tomlinson.
Scholarship and Scholars
Academic Affair. Stockwell.
Academic Curse; an Epitaph. Court.
Ad Chloen, M. A. Collins.

Address to the Scholars of New England. Ranson.
Andrew M'Crie. Murray.
Baccalaureate. McCord.
Be gone ye blockheads, Heraclitus cries. Diogenes Laertius.
Binni the Meshuggener. Siegel.
Classical Criticism. Richardson.
Company of Scholars, The. Bevington.
Dedication for a Book of Criticism. Winters.
Development. Browning.
Dillar, a dollar, a ten o'clock scholar, A. Mother Goose.
Don, The. Howes.
Early Chronology. Sassoon.
End of April, The. Murray.
End of My Sister's Guggenheim, The. Brinnin.
Epilogue: "My bibliography has grown." Wiebe.
For My Students, Returning to College. Williams.
For Scholars and Pupils. Wither.
Giles Johnson, Ph.D. Davis.
Going to School. Shapiro.
Grammarian's Funeral, A. Browning.
He That Never Read a Line. *Unknown.*
I Want to One Morning. Turner.
"If, Jerusalem, I Ever Should Foget Thee." Heine.
Lines on Being Refused a Guggenheim Fellowship. Whittemore.
Lines to a Don. Belloc.
Little Something for William Whipple, A. Oliphant.
Memory of a Scholar. Lattimore.
Morning. Kavanagh.
Of the Manner of Addressing Clouds. Stevens.
Phi Beta Kappa Poem, The. Lattimore.
Plain Language from Truthful James. Harte.
Poor Scholar, The. Ibn Chasdai.
Poor Scholar of the 'Forties, A. Colum.
Professor Gratt. Hall.
Scholar, The. Cornford.
Scholar, The. Southey.
Scholar and the Cat, The. *Unknown.*
Scholar Complains, The. *Unknown.*
Scholar Gipsy, The. Arnold.
Scholar II. Deane.
Scholars. *Unknown.*
Scholar's Life, The. *Fr.* The Vanity of Human Wishes. Johnson.
Scholars, The. Yeats.
Schools. *Fr.* The Borough. Crabbe.
Short History of Twentieth-Century Scholarship. Wain.
Sons of Our Sons, The. Ehrenburg.
Talmud Student, The. Bialik.
To a Friend, on Her Examination for the Doctorate in English. Cunningham.
Two men wrote a lexicon, Liddell and Scott. *Unknown.*
See also **Pedantry; Students; Teaching and Teachers.**

School
Change of School. Smither.
Class of 19—. Dec.
Classroom in October. Lieberman.
Cruel Boys. Soto.
Dancing School. Holden.
Description of a Good Boy, The. Dixon.
Desk, The. Bottoms.
Ecole St. Luc. Fraser.
Elementary School Classroom in a Slum, An. Spender.
End of Term. *Unknown.*
First Departure. Frost.
First Practice. Gildner.
From all the jails the boys and girls. Dickinson.
Getting Back. Thompson.
Ghetto Summer School. Worth.
Goodbye to Regal. Huws.
Haskell. Bynner.
Hickory Stick Hierarchy. Selle.
How a Girl Got Her Chinese Name. Wong.
In School-Days. Whittier.
Janie Swecker and Me and Gone with the Wind. Huddle.
Johnny's Hist'ry Lesson. Waterman.
Kindergarten. Schmitz.
Long Term Suffering. Eberhart.
Mortifying Mistake, A. Pratt.
Nine o'Clock. Pyle.
Not of School Age. Frost.
Ode on a Distant Prospect of Clapham Academy. Hood.
Old Brown Schoolhouse, The. *Unknown.*
Old Man's Thought of School, An. Whitman.
On Reading Poems to a Senior Class at South High. Berry.
Our School Now Closes Out. Dumas.
Overworked Elocutionist, An. Wells.
Public School 168. Brisby.
Public Schools. *Fr.* A Familiar Epistle to J. B. Esq. Lloyd.
Room 000. Stafford.
School-Bell. Farjeon.
School Cadets. Elder.
School Children, The. Glück.
School Days. Cobb.
School Days. Stafford.
School Days/Rule Days. Butler.
Schoolboys in Winter. Clare.
Schoolboy's Lot, A. *Unknown.*
Schools. *Fr.* The Borough. Crabbe.
Schoolyard in April. Koch.
Shapes, Vanishings. Taylor.
Sing-Song Rhyme. *Unknown.*
Small Boy, Dreaming, A. Herzing.
Still sits the schoolhouse by the road. *Fr.* In School-Days. Whittier.
Student, The. Moore.
To the Right Person. Frost.
Tom Brainless as Student and Preacher at College. *Fr.* The Progress of Dulness. Trumbull.
Under All This Slate. Hayford.
Unhappy Schoolboy, The. *Unknown.*
Unteaching, The. Oles.
Wee Hughie. Shane.
Zimmer's Head Thudding against the Blackboard. Zimmer.
Gladly Learn and Gladly Teach; Poems of the School Experience (GLGT). Helen Plotz, comp.
See also **Colleges and Universities.**

Schoolmasters. *See* **Teaching and Teachers.**

Schopenhauer, Arthur
Ballade of Schopenhauer's Philosophy. Adams.

Schubert, Franz
Schubertiana. Tranströmer.

Schwartz, Delmore
I can't get him out of my mind, out of my mind. *Fr.* Dream Songs. Berryman.
This world is gradually becoming a place. *Fr.* Dream Songs. Berryman.
To Delmore Schwartz. Lowell.

Science and Scientists
And, constantly, I seek/ A poetry of facts. *Fr.* The Kind of Poetry I Want. "MacDiarmid."
Apprentices. Munro.
Counting Sheep. Edson.
Dr. Sigmund Freud Discovers the Sea Shell. MacLeish.
Ed and Sid and Bernard. MacDuff.
Exhaustive experimentation. *Unknown.*
Horrid Voice of Science, The. Lindsay.
Into the Future. Witt.
Laboratory Poem. Merrill.
Letter to Alex Comfort. Abse.
Meditations for a Savage Child. Rich.
Ode to Terminus. Auden.
On an Engraving by Casserius. Hope.
Poetry and Science. Turner.
Problems. Scott.
Progress. Lamport.
Purist, The. Nash.
Revelation. Keesing.
Science for the Young. Irwin.
Science, the agile ape, may well. Patmore.
Sonnet to Science. Poe.
Toad, The. Oliver.
True Enough: To the Physicist. Goethe.
V. B. Nimble, V. B. Quick. Updike.
Imagination's Other Place (ImOP). Helen Plotz, ed.
Of Quarks, Quasars, and Other Quirks: Quizzical Poems for the Supersonic Age (QQQ). Sara Brewton, John E. Brewton, *and* John Brewton Blackburn, eds.
Songs from Unsung Worlds (SUW). Bonnie Bilyeu Gordon, ed.

Science Fiction
Discovery of the New World. Revard.
Insect Shuffle Method, The. Tapp.
S F. Leverett.
Science Fiction. Amis.

Scilly Islands
Tresco. Grigson.

Scopes Trial
Bryan's Last Battle. *Unknown.*

See also **Evolution.**
Scorpions
Playing House. Gilbert.
Scorpion, The. Belloc.
Scorpion, The. Plomer.
Scotland
Ballade of the Scottyshe Kynge, A. Skelton.
Birks of Aberfeldy, The. Burns.
Blue Bells of Scotland, The. McVicar *and* Jordan.
Breathes there the man, with soul so dead. *Fr.* The Lay of the Last Minstrel. Scott.
Caledonia. Powell.
Canadian Boat Song, The. Galt.
Come keen Iambicks with your badgers feet. *Fr.* The Rebell Scot. Cleveland.
Cotter's Saturday Night, The. Burns.
Exile's Song, The. Gilfillan.
Inchcape Rock, The. Southey.
Lord Ullin's Daughter. Campbell.
Massacre of the Macpherson, The. Aytoun.
Melrose Abbey. *Fr.* The Lay of the Last Minstrel. Scott.
My Heart's in the Highlands. Burns.
North Sea off Carnoustie. Stevenson.
O Caledonia! *Fr.* The Lay of the Last Minstrel. Scott.
On Scotland. Cleveland.
Patriot, The. *Fr.* The Lay of the Lost Minstrel. Scott.
Scotland. Gray.
Scotland Yet. Riddell.
Scotland's Winter. Muir.
Scots, Wha Hae. Burns.
Sic Transit Gloria Scotia. "MacDiarmid."
Soldier, The. Watson.
Tears of Scotland, The; Written in the Year 1746. Smollett.
To S. R. Crockett. Stevenson.
Upon the Death of the Viscount of Dundee. Dryden.
Vision, The. Defoe.
Young Lochinvar. *Fr.* Marmion. Scott.
Book of Scottish Verse, A (BSV). Maurice Lindsay *and* R. L. Mackie, eds.
Golden Treasury of Scottish Poetry, The (GoTS). "Hugh MacDiarmid," ed.
Oxford Book of Scottish Verse, The (OxBS). John MacQueen *and* Tom Scott, eds.
Poems of the Scottish Hills (PoSH). Hamish Brown, ed.
Scots, The
Border March. *Fr.* The Monastery. Scott.
Call to a Scot, The. Harding.
Gathering, The. *Fr.* Towards the Last Spike. Pratt.
Genealogical Reflection. Nash.
Nature herself doth Scotchmen beasts confess. *Fr.* The Rebel Scot. Cleveland.
Scotland, 1941. Muir.
Scots, Wha Hae. Burns.
Scott, Sir Walter
On Scott's "The Field of Waterloo." *Unknown.*
On the Departure of Sir Walter Scott from Abbotsford, for Naples. Wordsworth.
Sir Walter Scott at the Tomb of the Stuarts in St. Peter's. Milnes.
Yarrow Revisited. Wordsworth.
Young Lochinvar, *parody. Unknown.*
Scott, Winfield
Hero of Bridgewater. Jones.
Scottish Borders
Dreary Change, The. Scott.
Flowers of the Forest, The. Elliot.
North of Berwick. Tremayne.
November in Ettrick Forest. *Fr.* Marmion. Scott.
Sun upon the Weirdlaw Hill, The. Scott.
Village of Balmaquhapple, The. Hogg.
Scottish Highlands
Canadian Boat-Song. *At. to* Galt.
Highland's Swelling Blue, The. *Fr.* The Island. Byron.
In the Highlands. Stevenson.
My Heart's in the Highlands. Burns.
Ode on the Popular Superstitions of the Highlands of Scotland, An. Collins.
Poems of the Scottish Hills (PoSH). Hamish Brown, ed.
Scottsboro Case
Communication to Nancy Cunard, A. Boyle.
Scottsboro. *Unknown.*
Scottsboro, Too, Is Worth Its Song. Cullen.
They Are Ours. Magil.
Trial, The. Rukeyser.
Screams
Landscape of Screams. Sachs.
Munch's Scream. Hall.
Scribes
Scribe, The. *Unknown.*
St. Columcille the Scribe. *Unknown.*
See also **Secretaries; Stenographers.**
Sculpture and Sculptors
Afterbirth. Williams.
Arundel Tomb, An. Larkin.
Before a Statue of Achilles. Santayana.
Burial in the Sand. Sullivan.
Carrara. Murray.
Carved by Obadiah Verity. Welch.
Children and Sir Nameless, The. Hardy.
Convert, The. Danner.
Crack, The. Goldman.
Etruscan Warrior's Head. Henze.
Hans Christian Andersen in Central Park. Sobiloff.
Hiram Powers' "Greek Slave". Browning.
Homage to David Smith. Haines.
Likeness, A. Cather.
Museum-Piece. Brown.
No Swan So Fine. Moore.
O God! O Montreal! Butler.
On a Prize Crucifix by a Student Sculptor. Logan.
On Seeing the Elgin Marbles. Keats.
On the Bust of Helen by Canova. Byron.
Praxiteles and Phryne. Story.
Reclining Figure. Hall.
Rodin to Rilke. Grosholz.
Scrimshaw. Hogan.
Sculptors, The. Purdy.
Statue, The. Fuller.
Statues, The. Yeats.
Statuette: Late Minoan. Day Lewis.
Tulip. Wolfe.
"Twiner," A. Lindon.
Warrior with Shield. Browne.
Sea
Absences. Larkin.
All Day I Hear. Joyce.
Amoris Exsul: In the Bay. Symons.
At Melville's Tomb. Crane.
At Sainte-Marguerite. Stickney.
At the Seaside. Stevenson.
Aunt Zillah Speaks. Palmer.
Ayii, Ayii,/ I walked on the ice of the sea. *Unknown.*
Ayii, Ayii,/ The great sea has set me in motion. *Unknown.*
Bones. Sandburg.
Boundaries. Fleming.
Break, Break, Break. Tennyson.
Breeze is sharp, the sky is hard and blue, The. *Fr.* Sonnets. Tuckerman.
By the Deep Sea. *Fr.* Childe Harold's Pilgrimage. Byron.
By the Sea. Dixon.
By the Sea. Rossetti.
City in the Sea, The. Poe.
Coming Homeward Out of Spain. Googe.
Coming Suddenly to the Sea. Dudek.
Cornwallis. Beyer.
Dancing Sea, The. *Fr.* Orchestra. Davies.
Deep, The. Brainard.
Deep and Dark Blue Ocean. Byron.
Deep Blue Sea. *Unknown.*
Deep-Sea Cables, The. Kipling.
Dover Beach. Arnold.
Down from the Country. Blight.
East Anglian Bathe. Betjeman.
Enigmas. Neruda.
Evening by the Sea. Swinburne.
Eye, The. Jeffers.
Fear Death by Water. Eberhart.
Fishing Fleet, The. Colcord.
Flowers by the Sea. Williams.
From a Rise of Land to the Sea. Hoffmann.
Frozen Ocean, The. Meynell.
Grave, A. Moore.
Gravedigger, The. Carman.
Ground-Swell, The. Pratt.
Had I the Choice. Whitman.
Hall of Ocean Life. Hollander.

Her Heards Be Thousand Fishes. *Fr.* Colin Clout's Come Home Again. Spenser.
High Tide. Untermeyer.
Hills and the Sea, The. Campbell.
Horses of the Sea, The. Rossetti.
I Never Saw a Moor. Dickinson.
I started early—took my dog. Dickinson.
Idea of Order at Key West, The. Stevens.
Iphione. Irwin.
Kraken, The. Tennyson.
La Mer. Wilde.
Last Chantey, The. Kipling.
Lighthouse Keeper's Offspring, The. Broughton.
Lines on the Sea. Laing.
Listening to Beethoven on the Oregon Coast. Carlile.
Look, Stranger, on This Island Now. Auden.
Maggie and Milly and Molly and May. Cummings.
Main-Deep, The. Stephens.
Man Whom the Sea Kept Awake, The. Bly.
Maritimes. Shuttle.
Morality of Poetry, The. Wright.
Neither Out Far nor In Deep. Frost.
Noise of Waters, The. Joyce.
November Surf. Jeffers.
Now is it pleasant in the summer-eve. *Fr.* The Borough. Crabbe.
O Billows Bounding Far. Housman.
Ocean. Jeffers.
Ocean Burial, The. Chapin.
Ocean is a strange, The/ midnight lover. St. Martin.
Ocean Is Like a Wreath, The. Kuapakaa.
Ode to the Sea. Baker.
Offshore Breeze. Acorn.
On a Steamer. Baruch.
On the Sea. Keats.
Once at Swanage. Hardy.
Once by the Pacific. Frost.
One grey and foaming day. *Fr.* Sea Island Miscellany. Blackmur.
Open Sea, The. Meredith.
Oread. Doolittle ("H. D.").
Pattern of Saint Brendan. MacManus.
Pebbles. Melville.
Plague of Dead Sharks. Dugan.
Point Shirley. Plath.
Prayer to the Pacific. Silko.
Quaker Graveyard in Nantucket, The. Lowell.
Sailor's Prayer, A. Morris.
Sea, The. *Fr.* Childe Harold's Pilgrimage. Byron.
Sea, The. "Cornwall."
Sea, The. Crane.
Sea, The. Lawrence.
Sea, The. *Unknown.*
Sea, The. Webb.
Sea and Ourselves at Cape Ann, The. Ferlinghetti.
Sea and the Hills, The. Kipling.
Sea Born. Vinal.
Sea Breeze. Mallarmé.
Sea-Chill. Guiterman.
Sea Dirge, A. "Carroll."
Sea Eats the Land at Home, The. Awoonor.
Sea Fever. Masefield.
Sea Gipsy, The. Hovey.
Sea, The! O the sea! Hawaiian.
Sea Pieces. Fitzgerald.
Sea retains such images, The. *Fr.* Europe. Dudek.
Sea Ritual, The. Darley.
Sea Song, A. Dolben.
Sea Song. Holland.
Sea Sonnet: "Tell me today, when all my tides are gone". Lay.
Sea Surface Full of Clouds. Stevens.
Seafarer, The. *Unknown.*
Sea-Grief. O'Reilly.
Sea-Limits, The. Rossetti.
Sea's Spell, The. Spalding.
Seascape. Auden.
Seascape. Bishop.
Seascape. Spender.
Seascape. Young.
Shell, The. Stephens.
Shore. Miller.
Silences. Pratt.
Sir Patrick Spens. *Unknown.*
Sketch. Sandburg.
Song for All Seas, All Ships. Whitman.
Sonnet Written in the Church-Yard at Middleton, in Sussex. Smith.
Sonnet's Voice, The. Watts-Dunton.
Sound of the Sea, The. Longfellow.
Stanzas: "I will go back to the great sweet mother." *Fr.* The Triumph of Time. Swinburne.
Storm at Sea. *Unknown.*
Storm Tide on Mejit. *Unknown.*
Surf. Morrison.
Thalassa. MacNeice.
There is a pleasure in the pathless woods. *Fr.* Childe Harold's Pilgrimage. Byron.
Tide Rises, the Tide Falls, The. Longfellow.
To Sea. Beddoes.
To the Ocean. *Fr.* Childe Harold's Pilgrimage. Byron.
Told by Seafarers. Kinnell.
Training. Demetrio.
Until I Saw the Sea. Moore.
Uses of Ocean, The. Seaman.
Waking from a Nap on the Beach. Swenson.
Wanderer's Song, A. Masefield.
Waves Gleam in the Sunshine, The. *Fr.* Songs to Seraphine. Heine.
When winds that move not its calm surface sweep. Moschus.
Where shall I go then. *Fr.* Sea Island Miscellany. Blackmur.
Winter Ocean. Updike.
Winter Views Serene. *Fr.* The Borough. Crabbe.
World below the Brine, The. Whitman.
Yachts, The. Williams.
You Will Know When You Get There. Curnow.
Zennor. Ridler.
American Sea Songs and Chanteys (AmSS). Frank Shay, ed.
Eternal Sea, The (EtS). W. M. Williamson, ed.
Moods of the Sea (MOS). George C. Solley *and* Eric Steinbaugh, eds.
See also **Sailing and Sailors.**
Sea Battles. *See* **Naval Battles.**
Sea Chanteys
Black Sailor's Chanty. Keeler.
Shenandoah. *Unknown.*
American Sea Songs and Chanteys (AmSS). Frank Shay, ed.
Shantymen and Shantyboys (ShS). William Main Doerflinger, ed.
Sea Gulls. *See* **Gulls.**
Sea Monsters and Sea Serpents
Great Silkie of Sule Skerrie, The. *Unknown.*
Kraken, The. Tennyson.
Sea Monster. Merwin.
Sea Serpant, The. Irwin.
Sea Serpent Chantey, The. Lindsay.
Sea Shells. *See* **Shells.**
Sea Voyages. *See* **Voyages.**
Seacoasts. *See* **Shores.**
Seafaring and Seafarers. *See* **Sailing and Sailors.**
Sea Hawks
Sea-Hawk. Eberhart.
Seals
Animals. Jeffers.
Dancing Seal, The. Gibson.
Dead Seal Near McClure's Beach, The. Bly.
Dead Seal near McClure's Beach, The. Bly.
Dead Seal. Purdy.
Ice-Floes, The. Pratt.
Performing Seal, The. Field.
Performing Seal, The. *Fr.* A Circus Garland. Field.
Question, A. Cole.
Rookery. Dauenhauer.
Seal, A. *Fr.* Child's Natural History. Herford.
Seal Lullaby. Kipling.
Seal Pups. Dauenhauer.
Seal Rock. Pollitt.
Seals at High Island. Murphy.
Seals in Penobscot Bay, The. Hoffman.
Seals, Terns, Time. Eberhart.
Seal. Smith.
Seamstresses
Three Seamstresses, The. Peretz.
See also **Sewing.**
Seashore. *See* **Shores.**
Seasickness
Channel Passage, A. Brooke.
Seasons
Acceleration near the Point of Impact. Oates.
Against Seasons. Mezey.
Ceremonies for Candlemas Eve. Herrick.

Come Not the Seasons Here. Pratt.
Common Poem, A. Rodgers.
Eskimo Chant. *Unknown.*
Fall, Leaves, Fall. Brontë.
Fall Wind. Stafford.
Four Seasons. Bennett.
Four Seasons, The. Prelutsky.
Four Seasons. *Unknown.*
Four Seasons of the Year, The. Bradstreet.
Human Seasons, The. Keats.
Hundreth Good Poyntes of Husbandry, A. Tusser.
Hymn on the Seasons, A. *Fr.* The Seasons. Thomson.
I Haunt the Hills that Overlook the Sea. *Fr.* The Testament of a Man Forbid. Davidson.
If Only. Rossetti.
In Due Season. Auden.
In Suffolk. *Fr.* The Ancient Mansion. Crabbe.
In the Elegy Season. Wilbur.
January by This Fire. *Unknown.*
January Man. Goulder.
Love Song, A. Hawley.
Mask of Mutability, The. *Fr.* The Faerie Queene. Spenser.
Metamorphosis. Stevens.
November. *Fr.* A Suit of Nettles. Reaney.
Pencil and Paint. Farjeon.
Procession, The. Widdemer.
Seasons, The. Holcroft.
Seasons, The. Humphries.
Seasons. Rossetti.
Seasons of the Soul. Tate.
Solace. Delany.
Solstice. George.
Song: "When daisies pied, and violets blue." *Fr.* Love's Labour's Lost. Shakespeare.
Song for the Seasons, A. Cornwall.
Song of the Seasons. Lofton.
Song of the Seasons, A. Monkhouse.
Still. Meriluoto.
Summer Sunshine. Lathbury.
Through the Year. Cutler.
Weather Factory, The. Turner.
Wheel, The. Yeats.
Winter Will Follow. Dixon.
Winter's Onset from an Alienated Point of View. Dugan.
Year, The. Patmore.
Sing a Song of Seasons (SiSoSe). Sara Brewton *and* John E. Brewton, eds.
Year Around, The (YeAr). Alice I. Hazeltine *and* Elva S. Smith, comps.

Seattle, Washington
Letter to Tina Koyama from Elliot Bay Park. Mitsui.
Our Strange and Lovable Weather. Matthews.

Seaweed
Kelp. Dauenhauer.
Sea-Weed. Lawrence.
Seaweed. Longfellow.
Sea-Weed, The. Pullen.
Seaweeds. McPherson.
Tuft of Kelp, The. Melville.

Second Coming
Daybreak. Smith.
Earth Breaks Up. *Fr.* Christmas Eve and Easter-Day. Browning.
See also Millennium.

Second World War. *See* **World War II.**

Secretaries
Scribe, The. De la Mare.
Secretary, The. Redgrove.
Stenographers, The. Page.
See also **Scribes.**

Secrecy and Secrets
Canal Bank, The. Stephens.
Skeleton in the Cupboard, The. Locker-Lampson.
Winter: My Secret. Rossetti.

Sectarianism
Fragment of an Anti-Papist Ballad. *Unknown.*
No Sects in Heaven. Cleaveland.
Your Church and Mine. Lord.

Security
Abide with Me. Lyte.
Hitherto and Henceforth. Flint.
9:00. Hooper.
Ninetieth Psalm, The. Watts.
Old Woman of the Roads, An. Colum.
Reckoning, The. Roethke.
Safety. *Fr.* 1914. Brooke.
Wish, The. Watkyns.

Seduction
Abroad as I Was Walking. *Unknown.*
As I Walked through the Meadows. *Unknown.*
Dark-Eyed Gentleman, The. Hardy.
Disappointment, The. Behn.
Down by the Riverside. *Unknown.*
Fair Singer, The. Marvell.
Foggy Dew, The. *Unknown.*
Fragment, A: "In Cloe's chamber, she and I." Bancks.
Gently Johnny My Jingalo. *Unknown.*
Invites His Nymph to His Cottage. Ayres.
It Fell on a Summer's Day. Campion.
Leicester Chambermaid, The. *Unknown.*
Naughty Lord and the Gay Young Lady, The. *Unknown.*
Oh No John. *Unknown.*
Posy of Thyme, The. *Unknown.*
Puritan's Ballad, The. Wylie.
Rosemary Lane. *Unknown.*
Seduced Girl. Hedylos.
Seduction. Giovanni.
Seduction. Hall-Evans.
Seventeen Come Sunday. *Unknown.*
She Bewitched Me. Burbidge.
Solitary Canto to Chloris the Disdainful, A. Smith.
To-morrow is Saint Valentine's day. *Fr.* Hamlet. Shakespeare.
Volatile Kerryman, The. O'Sullivan.
Willing Mistress, The. *Fr.* The Dutch Lover. Behn.

Seeds
Avocado Pit, The. Rakosi.
Baby Seed Song. Nesbit.
I Hoed and Trenched and Weeded. *Fr.* A Shropshire Lad. Housman.
Open. Bruchac.
Seed, The. Fisher.
Seed Leaves. Wilbur.
Seed Shop, The. Stuart.
Seeds. De la Mare.

Self
Me. De la Mare.
My Inside-Self. Field.

Selfishness
Legend of the Northland, A. Cary.

Self-Pity
Self-Pity. Lawrence.

Self-Righteousness
Holy Willie's Prayer. Burns.
Religion of Hudibras, The. *Fr.* Hudibras. Butler.

Selkirk, Alexander
Verses Supposed to Be Written by Alexander Selkirk, during His Solitary Abode on the Island of Juan Fernandez. Cowper.

Semele
Ambrosia of Dionysus and Semele, The. Graves.

Semiramis
Fan, The. Sitwell.

Seneca
Seneca. Merton.

Senegal
Double Take at Relais de l'Espadon. Davis.

Senility
Senile. Folk.

Sennacherib, King of Assyria
Destruction of Sennacherib, The. Byron.

Seoul, Korea
Leaving Seoul; 1953. Lew.

Separation
Above the High. Grigson.
Ae Fond Kiss. Burns.
Ancient Couple on Lu Mountain, The. Van Doren.
At the San Francisco Airport. Winters.
Auf Wiedersehen. Hayes.
Autumn, 1914. Webb.
Blessed Damozel, The. Rossetti.
Boudoir Lament. Yü Hsüan-chi.
Brazos River, The. *Unknown.*
Business Trips. Taylor.
By Return Mail. Aldridge.
Complaint of a Young Girl. Wang Chung-ju.
Definition of Love, The. Marvell.
Departure, The. Steele.
Disintegration. Shelton.
Epistle to Miss Blount. Pope.

Excuse of Absence, An. Carew.
Exile. Dowson.
Fare Thee Well. Byron.
Farewell, A. Patmore.
Father's Testament, A. Ibn Tibbon.
Fatima. Tennyson.
First Winter. Harada.
Flowers of the Forest, The. Elliot.
Forsaken. Schneour.
Frisco Whistle Blues. *Unknown.*
Gal I Left behind Me, The. *Unknown.*
Going to Moscow. Edmond.
Goodbye.
Good-bye My Fancy! Whitman.
He Resigns. Berryman.
He Would Not Stay for Me; and Who Can Wonder? Housman.
He's Gone Away. *Unknown.*
I am now so weary with waiting. Stampa.
I have had not one word from her. Sappho.
I let the incense grow cold. Li Ch'ing-chao.
I took leave of my beloved one evening: how I wish. At Taliq.
I Will Write. Graves.
If You Were Here. Marston.
In the Vaulted Way. Hardy.
It's Already Autumn. Pagliarani.
Jealousy. De Vries.
Kashmiri Song. "Hope."
Lake Michigan Blues. *Unknown.*
Last Ride Together, The. Browning.
Leaving of Liverpool, The. *Unknown.*
Let the Wind Blow High or Low. *Unknown.*
Letter to Her Husband, Absent upon Public Employment, A. Bradstreet.
Like the Touch of Rain. Thomas.
Lines for a Friend Who Left. Logan.
Locks and Bolts. *Unknown.*
Long Distance Moan. *Unknown.*
Love, 20 the First Quarter Mile. Fearing.
Meeting, The. Rukeyser.
Memory. *Fr.* Brittania's Pastorals. Browne.
Message. Ginsberg.
Miss You. Cory.
Molly of the North Country. *Unknown.*
My Johnny. *Unknown.*
My life closed twice before its close. Dickinson.
Never Let Your Left Hand Know. *Unknown.*
New Spring. Jiménez.
On Parting with Moses Ibn Ezra. Halevi.
On the Departure Platform. Hardy.
Orinda to Lucasia. Philips.
Out of Sight, Out of Mind. Googe.
Painful Love Song, A. Amichai.
Parting, The. Drayton.
Parting. Halevi.
Parting. Hegori.
Parting. *Fr.* A Chaste Maid in Cheapside. Middleton.
Partings. Jewsbury.
Portrait of a Lady. Eliot.
Retreat, The. Vaughan.
River Merchant's Wife, The: A Letter. Li Po.
Round Her Neck She Wore a Yellow Ribbon. *Unknown.*
Sale. Williams.
Sence You Went Away. Johnson.
Sent from the Capital to Her Elder Daughter. Lady Otomo no Sakanoe.
Separation. Bianchi.
Separation, A. Cory.
Separation. Merwin.
Separation on the River Kiang. Li Po.
Separation on the River Kiang. Pound.
Since there's no help. *Fr.* Idea. Drayton.
Since We Parted. "Meredith."
Socks. Pope.
Song of Longing. Maori.
Spring, The. Cowley.
Spring of Joy Is Dry, The. *Unknown.*
Spring Thoughts Sent to Tzu-an. Yü Hsüan-chi.
Strange. Burnshaw.
Sundered. Barford.
Sundered. Zangwill.
Terrible Door, The. Monro.
That Lonesome Train Took My Baby Away. *Unknown.*
They flee from me that sometime did me seek. Wyatt.
Three Moments. Sherman.
To an Estranged Wife. Young.
To Her in Absence: A Ship. Carew.
To His Lady. Henry VIII, King of England.
To Lucasta, Going beyond the Seas. Lovelace.
To Lucasta, Going to the Wars. Lovelace.
To My Mistress in Absence. Carew.
To Tzu-an. Yü Hsüan-chi.
Tommy's Gone to Hilo. *Unknown.*
Two Letters From Chang-Kan. Li Po.
Upon Your Leaving. Knight.
V-Letter. Shapiro.
Valediction, A. Cartwright.
Valediction. Heaney.
Valediction, A: forbidding mourning. Donne.
Western Wind. *Unknown.*
What I Have. North.
When, dearest, I but think on thee. Felltham.
When We Two Parted. Byron.
When You Go Away. Merwin.
Wife's Lament, The. *Unknown.*
Within the Dream You Said. Larkin.
Writing to Aaron. Levertov.
Year after year I have watched. Li Ch'ing-chao.
You Never Miss the Water. *Unknown.*
You'll Never Miss Your Jelly. *Unknown.*
Your Light. Lee.

Sepoy Rebellion
Defence of Lucknow, The. Tennyson.
Relief of Lucknow, The. Lowell.

September
Another September. Kinsella.
Artist on Penmaenmawr, The. Turner.
For Nicholas, Born in September. Perry.
Man's Bread, A. Peabody.
Pont-y-Wern. *Fr.* Ambarvalia. Clough.
Remember September. Justus.
Rondel for September. Baker.
September. Arnold.
September. Fallis.
September. Jackson.
September. Pastan.
September. Reed.
September Afternoon. Carpenter.
September Days Are Here. Jackson.
September in Australia. Kendall.
September Is Here. Reed.
Sonnet: September, 1815. Wordsworth.
Tell me not here, it needs not saying. Housman.

Sequoia Trees
Kind. Ammons.
Redwoods, The. Simpson.
Thumbprint. Wright.

Sermons
Model Sermon, A. *Unknown.*

Serfs. *See* **Slavery.**

Servants
Ballad of Sally in Our Alley, The. Carey.
Buttons. De la Mare.
Carter, The. *Unknown.*
Country Hirings. *Unknown.*
Country Statutes. *Unknown.*
Domestics. Cumbo.
Elegy: "Nor Hammond's love nor Shenstone's was sincere." MacLaurin.
Familiar Faces, Long Departed. Hillyer.
Famous Flower of Serving-Men, The. *Unknown.*
Husbandman and Serving-Man, The. *Unknown.*
In an Old House. Brown.
Lèse-Majesté. Gorman.
Madam and Her Madam. Hughes.
Odour, The. Herbert.
Old-Time Service. *Fr.* A Fayned Fancy betweene the Spider and the Gowte. Churchyard.
Our Hired Girl. Riley.
Sally in Our Alley. Carey.
Song of Diligence, A. Frazee-Bower.
Summer Morning, A. Wilbur.
To His Maid Prew. Herrick.
To Their Excellencies the Lords Justices of Ireland. The Humble Petition of Frances Harris, Who Must Starve and Die a Maid If It Miscarries. Swift.
Upon Prue, His Maid. Herrick.
Upstairs Downstairs. Allen.

When in Rome. Evans.
Service (plant)
Life of Service, The. Davie.
Shadbush. Rainsford.
Service Stations. *See* **Gasoline Stations.**
Sestina (form)
Figures of Authority. Watkins.
Imperfect Sestina. Webb.
Island in the Evening, The. Porter.
Magician Suspends the Children, The. Oles.
Morning on the St. John's. Cooper.
Murmurers, The. Jacobsen.
Painter, The. Ashbery.
Quintina of Crosses, A. Walsh.
Rink Keeper's Sestina. Draper.
Sestina: "I saw my soul at rest upon a day." Swinburne.
Sestina: "September rain falls on the house." Bishop.
Sestina; Altaforte. Pound.
Sestina d'Inverno. Hecht.
Sestina in Time of Winter. Anderson.
Sestina of the Tramp-Royal. Kipling.
Sestina with Refrain. Shapcott.
Tide Turning. Nims.
Ye Goatherd Gods. Sidney.
Seurat, Georges
Seurat. Sadoff.
Seven Deadly Sins
Dance of the Sevin Deidly Synnis, The. Dunbar
Seven Wonders of the World
Seven Wonders of the World, The. *Unknown.*
Severn River, England
Danube to the Severn gave, The. *Fr.* In Memoriam A. H. H. Tennyson.
Seven Fiddlers, The. Evans.
Severn, The. *Fr.* The Baron's War. Drayton.
Seville, Spain
Seville. Walters.
Sewall, Samuel
Samuel Sewall. Hecht.
Sewers
Municipal. Kipling.
See also **Sanitary Engineering.**
Sewing
Balgu Song. *Unknown.*
Delia Very Angry. *Unknown.*
Huswifery. Taylor.
Leave the Thread with God. *Unknown.*
My Mother Pieced Quilts. Acosta.
Needle, The. Woodworth.
Needle Travel. Patton.
See also **Seamstresses.**
Sex
Adam, Eve and the Big Apple. Watkins.
Against Fruition I. Suckling.
Against Them Who Lay Unchastity to the Sex of Women. Habington.
Beachhead Preachment. Zu-Bolton.
Blank Verse for a Fat Demanding Wife. Lindsey.
Blue Bottle. Hampl.
Brickster, The. *Unknown.*
Bubba Esther, 1888. Whitman.
Canticles to Men. Mannes.
Censorship. Ciardi.
Doing, a filthy pleasure is, and short. Petronius Arbiter.
Fair Ursly, in a merry mood. Annibol Cruceius.
Fine Body. Clare.
Glutton, The. Graves.
Harvest, The. Aberg.
Haven't I said that part of having intercourse. *Fr.* Hmmmm. Scalapino.
How can I help myself, as one woman said to me about wanting. *Fr.* Hmmmm. Scalapino.
I'd Have You, Quoth He. *Unknown.*
If. Lane.
Imitation of Martial, Book II Ep. 105, An. "Captain H——."
Lingam and the Yoni, The. Hope.
Little Ball of Yarn. *Unknown.*
Little Tumescence, A. Williams.
May I Feel Said He. Cummings.
Minotaur, The. Gibb.
Mr. Muscle-On. Kicknosway.
Mock Orange. Glück.
Mower, The. *Unknown.*
Oil and Blood. Kizer.
One Man Down. Ai.
One Writing against His Prick. *Unknown.*
Poet Loves a Mistress, but Not to Marry, The. Herrick.
Poetess's Bouts-Rimés, The. *Unknown.*
Puberty. Wallace.
Question, The. Rukeyser.
Sequence, A. Scalapino.
Source, The. Stallworthy.
Stacking Up. Rosenfeld.
Then. Morgan.
To Electra ("I'll come to thee in all those shapes"). Herrick.
To Hell with Your Fertility Cult. Snyder.
Trooper's Horse, The. *Unknown.*
Two Songs. Rich.
Wanton Seed, The. *Unknown.*
Wayman in Love. Wayman.
Why Can't I Leave You? Ai.
Words from Hell. Helwig.
See also **Erotic Love; Homosexuality and Homosexuals; Lust; Sexualty; Voyeurism.**
Sexism
Advice to Young Ladies. Hope.
Affinity, The. Wickham.
Barbie Doll. Piercy.
Door-Mats. Davies.
Paper Matches. Jiles.
Poem for Jacqueline Hill. *Unknown.*
Poet Recognizing the Echo of the Voice, A. Wakoski.
Snapshots of a Daughter-in-Law. Rich.
What cruel laws depress the female kind. *Fr.* Hypatia. Tollet.
Work of Artiface, A. Piercy.
Sexton, Anne
Anne Sexton. Juergensen.
Rip. Balderston.
Sexuality
Annus Mirabilis. Larkin.
Cry Faugh! Graves.
From Pent-up, Aching Rivers. Whitman.
Seymour, Edward, Duke of Somerset. *See* **Somerset, Edward Seymour, Duke of.**
Seymour, Jane
Death of Queen Jane, The. *Unknown.*
Shadbush. *See* **Service (plant).**
Shadows
Calculation, The. Wagoner.
Child and the Shadow, The. Jennings.
Could It Have Been a Shadow? Shannon.
Countershadow, The. Booth.
Escape. Johnson.
Follow Thy Fair Sun, Unhappy Shadow. Campion.
Her Shadow. Pullen.
I Heard a Noise and Wishèd for a Sight. *Unknown.*
Lecture upon the Shadow, A. Donne.
My Shadow. Stevenson.
Nocturne Varial. Alexander.
On the Croun o Bidean. Annand.
Shadow, The. De la Mare.
Shadow and Substance. *Unknown.*
Shadow Dance. Eastwick.
Shadows, The. Sherman.
Shadows. Tewa.
Shadows among the Ettrick Hills. Addison.
Stopping by Shadows. Fulton.
Swan and Shadow. Hollander.
Tenebris. Grimké.
Shadwell, Thomas
Mac Flecknoe; or, A Satire upon the True-Blue-Protestant Poet T.S. Dryden.
Og and Doeg. *Fr.* Absalom and Achitophel. Dryden.
Thomas Shadwell the Poet. *Fr.* Absalom and Achitophel. Dryden.
Shaftesbury, Anthony Ashley Cooper, 1st Earl of
Achitophel. *Fr.* Absalom and Achitophel. Dryden.
Ballad upon the Popish Plot, A. Gadbury.
Dutchess of Monmouth's Lamentation for the Loss of Her Duke, The. *Unknown.*
Hypocrite, The. Caryll.
In pious times, ere priestcraft did begin. *Fr.* Absalom and Achitophel. Dryden.
Shakers
Arrival, New York Harbour. Peters.
Meditation By Mascoma Lake. Babock.
Shakespeare, William
Archy Confesses. *Fr.* Archy and Mehitabel. Marquis.

At Shakespeare's Grave. Browne.
At the Mermaid Inn. Hildreth.
Before Rereading Shakespeare's Sonnets. Moore.
Ben Jonson Entertains a Man from Stratford. Robinson.
Brush Up Your Shakespeare. Porter.
By Deputy. Adcock.
Charms of Nature, The. Warton.
Cynicus to W. Shakspere. *Fr.* Two Epigrams. Stephen.
Elegy on Shakespeare. Basse.
Epitaph on the Admirable Dramatic Poet, W. Shakespeare, An. Milton.
Found. Shatford.
Guilielmus Rex. Aldrich.
On Mr. Wm. Shakespeare. Basse.
On Shakespeare. Milton.
On Sitting Down to Read "King Lear" Once Again. Keats.
On the Portrait of Shakespeare Prefixed to the First Folio Edition, 1623. Jonson.
Prologue to "The Tempest." Vaughan.
Quotation from Shakespeare, with Slight Improvements, A. "Carroll."
Schoolroom: 158. Warren.
Shake, Mulleary, and Go-ethe. Bunner.
Shakespeare. Arnold.
Shakespeare. Blood.
Shakespeare. Day.
Shakespeare. Watson.
Shakespeare Dead. Holland.
Shakespeare, Possibly, in California. Whittemore.
Thing Is Sex, Ben, The. *Fr.* Tomorrow Is My Birthday. Masters.
To an Artist, to Take Heart. Bogan.
To the Memory of My Beloved Master William Shakespeare. Jonson.
To the Reader. Jonson.
True Genius. *Fr.* Shakespeare, an Epistle to David Garrick, Esq. Lloyd.

Shamans
Morning Star Man. Keithley.
Shaman. Mumford.
Wili Woyi, Shaman, Also Known as Billy Pigeon. Conley.

Shame
Shame. Wilbur.

Shamrocks
Green Little Shamrock of Ireland, The. Cherry.
Shamrock, The. Egan.

Shannon (ship). *See* **Chesapeake (ship)**

Shaped Poetry
Altar, The. Herbert.
Andy-Diana DNA Letter. Weiman.
Brain Coral. Bassen.
Christmas Tree, A. Burford.
Computer's First Christmas Card, The. Morgan.
Dead of Winter. Towne.
Easter Wings. Herbert.
Forsythia. Solt.
40——Love. McGough.
400-Meter Freestyle. Kumin.
Fury Said to a Mouse. *Fr.* Alice's Adventures in Wonderland. "Carroll."
Grasshopper, The. McCord.
Hang Up the Baby's Stocking! *Unknown.*
Headrock. Coffey.
How Everything Happens (Based on a Study of the Wave). Swenson.
I. Cummings.
It's Raining. Apollinaire.
Like Attracts Like. Williams.
Love Knot. *Unknown.*
Marriage. Solt.
Message Clear. Morgan.
Moonshot Sonnet. Solt.
Oil. Mayer.
Parody. Paley Francescato.
Pattern Poem with an Elusive Intruder. Döhl.
Pillar of Fame, The. Herrick.
Rain Down. Solt.
Seal. Smith.
Semen. Paley Francescato.
Sharpbreasted Snake, The. Oliver.
Skeleton Key. Hollander.
State of Nature, A. Hollander.
Swan and Shadow. Hollander.
This crosse-tree here. Herrick.
Tlingit Concrete Poem. Dauenhauer.
Two Tile Beaks. Fonte Boa.
Vitality. Fonte Boa.
Wild Crab. Solt.
Windy Planet, The. Dillard.
Women. Swenson.
You Too? Me Too—Why Not? Soda Pop. Hollander.

Shapiro, Karl
V-Letter to Karl Shapiro in Australia. Rodman.

Sharecroppers
Share-Croppers. Hughes.

Sharks
About the Teeth of Sharks. Ciardi.
Basking Shark. MacCaig.
Birth of a Shark, The. Wevill.
Chivalrous Shark, The. *Unknown.*
Love Is a Shark. Hawaiian.
Maldive Shark, The. Melville.
Nurse Sharks. Matthews.
Rhyme of the Chivalrous Shark, The. Irwin.
Sea-Turtle and the Shark, The. Tolson.
Shark, The. Douglas.
Shark, The. Pratt.
Sharks. Overton.
Shark's Parlor, The. Dickey.
Spirit of Wrath, The. Heyen.

Shaving
Daddy. Fyleman.

Shaw, George Bernard
Epitaph for G. B. Shaw. Beerbohm.
Last words of Shaw, The: "I'm going to die." Bold.

Shaw, Robert Gould
For the Union Dead. Lowell.
My Hero. Brawley.
Ode in Time of Hesitation, An. Moody.
Ode on the Unveiling of the Shaw Memorial on Boston Common, May 31st, 1897, An. Aldrich.
Robert G. Shaw. Ray.

Shay's Rebellion
Radical Song of 1786, A. Honeywood.

Sheep
And, now that every thing may in the proper place. *Fr.* Poly-Olbion. Drayton.
Ariel. Campbell.
At the Trough. Gregor.
Baa, baa, black sheep, have you any wool? Mother Goose.
Bah! De la Mare.
Black Faced Sheep, The. Hall.
Bleat of Protest. Weston.
Child's Pet, A. Davies.
Dead Sheep, The. Young.
Derby Ram, The. *Unknown.*
Eighteen-Ninety. Ship.
Flock at Evening, The. Shepard.
Happy Sheep, The. Thorley.
Homecoming of the Sheep, The. Ledwidge.
How Low Is the Lowing Herd. Kelly.
Lambs Frolicking Home. Lape.
Lambs of Grasmere, 1860, The. Rossetti.
Little Bo-Peep. *Unknown.*
Poor Mailie's Elegy. Burns.
Sheep. Davies.
Sheep. Francis.
Sheep. Hoffenstein.
Sheep. Porter.
Sheep, The. Taylor.
Sheep Fair, A. Hardy.
Sheep in the Rain. Wright.
Sheep in Winter. Clare.
Wild Boar and the Ram, The. *Fr.* Fables. Gay.

Sheepshearing
Banks of the Condamine, The. *Unknown.*
Click Go the Shears, Boys. *Unknown.*
Flash Jack from Gundagai. *Unknown.*
How to Shear Sheep. *Fr.* The Fleece. Dyer.
Shearer's Song, The. *Unknown.*
Sheep Shearing. *Unknown.*

Sheets
Song of the Sheet. *Unknown.*

Shelley, Percy Bysshe
Cor Cordium. Swinburne.
Fishes and the Poet's Hands, The. Yerby.
General Public, The. Benét.
Lines Written in a Blank Leaf of the Prometheus Unbound. Beddoes.
Memorabilia. Browning.
Off Viareggio. Pitchford.
Percy Shelley. Bishop.

Rome. Hardy.
Shelley. *Fr.* Pauline. Browning.
Shelley's Skylark. Hardy.
To Shelley. Landor.
To Shelley. Tabb.

Shells
Chambered Nautilus, The. *Fr.* The Autocrat of the Breakfast-Table. Holmes.
Child with Shell. Everson.
Curious child, who dwelt upon a tract, A. *Fr.* The Excursion. Wordsworth.
Dr. Sigmund Freud Discovers the Sea Shell. MacLeish.
Enduring Music, The. Vinal.
Frutta di Mare. Scott.
Lonely Shell, The. Perry.
Lower Forms of Life. Winter.
Mantelpiece of Shells, A. Todd.
Poem about a Seashell. Crosby.
Sea Shell. Lowell.
See What a Lovely Shell. Tennyson.
Shell, The. Stephens.
Shells. Mahony.
Shells. Raine.
Shell's Song, The. Keats.
Some Small Shells from the Windward Islands. Swenson.
To Lady Anne Fitzpatrick, When about Five Years Old, with a Present of Shells, 1772. Walpole.
Wanderer, The. Field.

Shenandoah River and Shenandoah Valley
Portent, The. Melville.
Shenandoah. *Unknown.*

Shepherds and Shepherdesses
As I Rode Out. *Unknown.*
Black Faced Sheep, The. Hall.
Cassamen and Dowsabell. *Fr.* The Shepherd's Garland. Drayton.
Colin's Complaint. Rowe.
Come, Shepherds, Come! *Fr.* The Faithful Shepherdess. Fletcher.
Coridon and Phillis. *Fr.* Perimedes. Greene.
Coy Shepherdess, or, Phillis and Amintas, The. *Unknown.*
Doris; a Pastoral. Munby.
Eclogue: "Late 'twas in June, the fleece when fully grown." *Fr.* The Shepherd's Garland. Drayton.
Enquiry, The. Dyer.
Faithless Shepherd, A. Clare.
Gorbo and Batte. Drayton.
Green Shepherd, The. Simpson.
Harpalus' Complaint of Phillida's Love. *Unknown.*
Herdmen, The. *Unknown.*
How Pleasant Is This Flowery Plain. *Unknown.*
Hye Nommy Nonny Noe. *Unknown.*
In Praise of His Love. Wotton.
In the Cheviots. Lindsay.
In the Holy Nativity of Our Lord God. Crashaw.
Jolly Shepherd Wat, The. *Unknown.*
Lincolnshire Shepherd, A. *Unknown.*
Little Bo-peep has lost her sheep. Mother Goose.
Long, Long Ago. *Unknown.*
Lyric from a Play, A. *Unknown.*
Michael. Wordsworth.
Moonlight. . .Scattered Clouds. *Fr.* The Farmer's Boy. Bloomfield.
Nod. De la Mare.
Nymphs and Shepherds. *fr.* Arcades. Milton.
Nymph's Reply to the Shepherd, The. Ralegh.
Old Shepherd's Prayer. Mew.
Once I Was a Shepherd Boy. *Unknown.*
Passionate Shepherd to His Love, The. Marlowe.
Pastoral, A: "My time, O ye muses, was happily spent." Byrom.
Pastoral Ballad. Shenstone.
Phyllida's Love-Call to Her Corydon, and His Replying. *Unknown.*
Priest's Chant, The. *Fr.* The Faithful Shepherdess. Fletcher.
Rise Up, Shepherd, and Follow. *Unknown.*
Sheep Country. Pond.
Sheep-herder, The. Clark.
Sheepherder, The. Sarett.
Sheep-herder's Lament, The. Chapman.
Shep'erd Bwoy, The. Barnes.
Shepheards, The. Vaughan.
Shepherd, The. *Fr.* Songs of Innocence. Blake.
Shepherd. Blunden.
Shepherd, The. Gilmore.
Shepherd, The. *Fr.* The Prelude. Wordsworth.
Shepherd and His Flock, The. Mtshali.
Shepherd and Shepherdess. *Fr.* The Passionate Shepherd. Breton.
Shepherd and Shepherdess. Hennell.
Shepherd and the Shepherdess, The. *Unknown.*
Shepherd Boy, The. O'Brien.
Shepherd Left Behind, The. Meigs.
Shepherd Speaks, The. Erskine.
Shepherd Who Stayed, The. Garrison.
Shepherdess. *Fr.* Three Love Poems. Cameron.
Shepherdess, The. Meynell.
Shepherdess and the Sailor, The. *Unknown.*
Shepherds, The. Van Slyke.
Shepherds, The. Vaughan.
Shepherds' Carol. Nicholson.
Shepherd's Holiday. Wylie.
Shepherd's Ode, The. *Fr.* Tullie's Love. Greene.
Shepherd's Song at Christmas. Hughes.
Shepherd's Tale, The. Kirkup.
Shepherd's Wife's Song, The. *Fr.* Greene's Mourning Garment. Greene.
Tenth Eclogue, The. *Fr.* The Shepherd's Garland. Drayton.
Thistledown. Reese.
To His Flocks. *At. to* Constable *and* Chettle.
Tom Farley. Thiele.
Tuesday; or, the Ditty. *Fr.* The Shepherd's Week. Gay.
Twenty-third Psalm, The. Herbert.
Unknown Shepherd's Complaint, The. Barnfield.
Vision of the Shepherds. *Fr.* For the Time Being; a Christmas Oratorio. Auden.
Wandering Shepherdess, The. *Unknown.*
While Shepherds Watched Their Flocks by Night. Tate.
Woodland Revel, A. Urmy.
Ya Se Van Los Pastores. Fitts.
Young Shepherd Bathing His Feet. Clarke.

Sheridan, Philip Henry
Sheridan at Cedar Creek. Melville.
Sheridan's Ride. Read.

Sherman, General William Tecumseh
Marching through Georgia. Work.
Sherman. Gilder.
Sherman's in Savannah. Holmes.
Song of Sherman's March to the Sea. Byers.

Shetlands
Shetland, Hill Dawn. Munro.

Shields
Copper Song, The. Fraser.
Shield. *Fr.* Riddles (Exeter Book). *Unknown.*

Shiloh, Battle of (1862)
Battle of Shiloh, The. *Unknown.*
Drummer Boy of Shiloh, The. *Unknown.*
Shiloh; a Requiem. Melville.

Ships
Aboard at a Ship's Helm. Whitman.
After the Sea-Ship. Whitman.
All Hands Unmoor! *Fr.* The Shipwreck. Falconer.
Ark and the *Dove*, The. Sargent.
Beauty of the Ship, The. Whitman.
Birlinn Chlann-Raghnaill. MacDonald.
Boats in a Fog. Jeffers.
Bonnie Ship *The Diamond,* The. *Unknown.*
Building of the *Long Serpent,* The. *Fr.* Tales of a Wayside Inn. Longfellow.
Building of the Ship, The. Longfellow.
By the Deep Nine. Pearce.
Canto I: "And ten went down to the ship." *Fr.* Cantos. Pound.
Cargoes. Masefield.
Cheer of the *Trenton,* The. Mitchell.
Clipper, The. Day.
Cruise of the *Mystery,* The. Thaxter.
Derelict, The. Foote.
Derelict, The. Kipling.
Derelict. Pullen.
Description of a Ninety Gun Ship. Falconer.
Dismantled Ship, The. Whitman.
Down Below. Aiken.
Fire of Drift-Wood, The. Longfellow.
Freighter. Ruddick.
Frightening. Lewis.
Garden of Ships, The. Stewart.
George Aloe and the *Sweepstake,* The. *Unknown.*
Ghost of the Cargo Boat, The. Neruda.
Godspeed. Spofford.
H. M. S. *Hero.* Roberts.
High Barbaree. *Unknown.*

I saw a ship a-sailing. Mother Goose.
John B. Sails. *Unknown.*
Last Gloucesterman, The. Grant.
Liner She's a Lady, The. Kipling.
Lost Ships. Ferril.
Main-Truck; or, A Leap for Life, The. Morris.
Marina. Eliot.
My Brigantine. *Fr.* The Water Witch. Cooper.
My Ship and I. Stevenson.
Night Boat. Brown.
Nocturne of the Wharves. Bontemps.
Off Rivière du Loup. Scott.
Oil. Snyder.
Old Conservativee, The. Tooker.
Old Figurehead Carver, The. Cody.
Old Ship Riggers. Cody.
Old Ships, The. Flecker.
Old Ships. Ginsberg.
Old Ships. Morton.
On Seeing a Fine Frigate at Anchor in a Bay off Mount Edgecumbe. Carrington.
Passer-by, A. Bridges.
Pictures. Smith.
Revenge, The. Tennyson.
Sails. Sterling.
She Is Far from the Land. Hood.
Ship, The. Squire.
Ship Bottom. Lattimore.
Ship-Builders, The. Whittier.
Ship Comes In, A. Jenkins.
Ship that Never Returned, The. Work.
Ships, The. Maynard.
Ships. Turner.
Ships at Sea. Gray.
Ships in Harbour. Morton.
Ships of Saint John, The. Carman.
Ships of Yule, The. Carman.
Silver Ships. Meigs.
Sir Andrew Barton. *Unknown.*
Sketch. Sandburg.
Song for All Seas, All Ships. Whitman.
South Street. Falkenbury.
Spirit of the *Bluenose,* The. MacIntosh.
Stone Fleet, The. Melville.
Tacking Ship Off Shore. Mitchell.
Tanker. Middleton.
They That Go Down to the Sea. Psalms. Bible, *O.T.*
Titanic Blues. *Unknown.*
Troopship, The. Johnson.
Troopship for France, War II. Bogin.
Wanderer, The. Masefield.
Where Go the Boats? Stevenson.
Where Lies the Land to Which Yon Ship Must Go? Wordsworth.
With Ships the Sea Was Sprinkled. Wordsworth.
Wooden Ships. Morton.
Would you hear of an old-time sea-fight? *Fr.* Song of Myself. Whitman.
Eternal Sea, The (EtS). W. M. Williamson, ed.
See also **Boats; Yachts.**

Shipwrecks
Æolian Harp, The. Melville.
Alec Yeaton's Son. Aldrich.
Asleep in the Deep. Lamb.
Berg, The. Melville.
Brave Old Ship, the *Orient,* The. Lowell.
Castaway, The. Cowper.
Convergence of the Twain, The. Hardy.
Diving into the Wreck. Rich.
Dream of Wrecks, A. *Fr.* Richard III. Shakespeare.
Etiquette. Gilbert.
Final Moments, The. *Fr.* The Titanic. Pratt.
Full Fathom Five. *Fr.* The Tempest. Shakespeare.
Grace Darling. *Unknown.*
How's My Boy? Dobell.
In Memory of the Circus Ship *Euzkera,* Wrecked in the Caribbean Sea, 1 September, 1948. Gibson.
In Wintry Midnight, o'er a Stormy Main. Petrarch.
Inchcape Rock, The. Southey.
Inscription by the Sea, An. *Unknown.*
Isle of Man Shore, The. *Unknown.*
John Maynard. Alger.
Last Words. Hollander.
Loss of the *Cedar Grove,* The. *Unknown.*
Loss of the *Due Dispatch*, The. *Unknown.*
Loss of the *New Columbia*, The. *Unknown.*
Nets on the *Andrea Doria,* The. Tepfer.
Of the Lost Ship. White.
On the Loss of the *Royal George.* Cowper.
One Friday Morn. *Unknown.*
Palatine, The. Whittier.
Pat Cloherty's Version of *The Maisie.* Murphy.
Portland Going Out, The. Merwin.
Rain, and a flurry of wind shaking the pear's white blossom. *Fr.* Twenty-one Sonnets. Stead.
Sea, The. Stoddard.
Second Mate, The. O'Brien.
Shipwreck, The. *Fr.* Don Juan. Byron.
Shipwreck, The. Falconer.
Silent Tower of Bottreaux, The. Hawker.
Sir Patrick Spens. *Unknown.*
Skipper Ireson's Ride. Whittier.
Three Bells, The. Whittier.
Three Fishers, The. Kingsley.
Titanic, The. *Unknown.*
Ulysses in the Waves. *Fr.* The Odyssey. Homer.
White Ship, The. Rossetti.
Wreck, The. De la Mare.
Wreck of the *Deutschland,* The. Hopkins.
Wreck of the *Hesperus*, The. Longfellow.
Wreck of the *Julie Plante*, The. Drummond of Hawthornden.
Yarn of the *Loch Achray,* The. Masefield.
Yarn of the *Nancy Bell*, The. Gilbert.

Shiva
Shiva. Jeffers.

Shoemakers
Amends to the Tailors and Soutars. Dunbar.
Cobbler, The. Chaffee.
Cobbler in Willow Street, The. O'Neil.
Mr. Minnitt.
Shoe Shop. Sutter.
Shoemaker, The. *Unknown.*
Shoemaker's Holiday, The, *sels.* Dekker.

Shoes
Cartload of Shoes, A. Sutskever.
Choosing Shoes. Wolfe.
Footwear. Justus.
Grammer's Shoes. Barnes.
I Have Lost My Shoes. Suasnovar.
It's fun to go out and buy new shoes to wear. Hoberman.
My Boots. Thoreau.
My Mistress's Boots. Locker-Lampson.
My Mother's Shoes. Zychlinska.
New Shoes. Watts.
New Shoes. Wilkins.
Sale. Miles.
Shoes. Robinson.
To a Pair of Egyptian Slippers. Arnold.
Velvet Shoes. Wylie.

Shoplifting
Shoplifters. Stanton.

Shopping and Shops
Christmas Shopping. MacNeice.
Counters. Coatsworth.
Country Store, The. *Unknown.*
Garage Sale. Shapiro.
General Store. Field.
I shop in the streets of my hometown with/ my family. *Fr.* Letters to Live Poets. Beaver.
Junk Shop, The. Coulette.
Market, The. Snyder.
Night: Landing at Newark. Holden.
Ordinary Women I. Hacker.
Pushcart Row. Field.
Saturday Shopping. Edelman.
Shop Windows. Fyleman.
Shopman, The. Farjeon.
Shopping. Nitzche.
Shopping for Midnight. Murray.
Supermarket in California, A. Ginsberg.
To a Salesgirl, Weary of Artificial Holiday Trees. Wright.
To market, to market, to buy a fat pig. Mother Goose.
Winds are bleak, stars are bright. *Fr.* The Victoria Markets Recollected in Tranquillity. "Maurice."
Women at the Market. Figuera Aymerich.

Shopping Malls
Day Begins at Governor's Square Mall. Stokesbury.
Shores
Address to the Vacationers at Cape Lookout, An. Stafford.
At Carmel Highlands. Lewis.
At the Seaside. Stevenson.
"But Still in Israel's Paths They Shine." Revard.
By Cobequid Bay. Fraser.
By the Pacific. Bashford.
By the Pacific Ocean. Miller.
By the Saltings. Walker.
Cliff-top, The. Bridges.
Coastline. Feinstein.
Corsons Inlet. Ammons.
Earliness at the Cape. Deutsch.
East Coast—Canada. Brewster.
Finisterra. Winters.
Fisher's Boy, The. Thoreau.
Giant's Tomb in Georgian Bay. "Hale."
Headland. Ghiselin.
Heron's Bay. Galvin.
I Pray You. *Fr.* Odes to Nea. Moore.
In the Bay. *Fr.* Amoris Exsul. Symons.
Low Fields and Light. Merwin.
Meditation at Oyster River. Roethke.
Moonlight Night; Carmel. Hughes.
Morning on the Shore. Campbell.
On the Beach at Fontana. Joyce.
Patroling Barnegat. Whitman.
Pines and the Sea, The. Cranch.
Provincetown, Mass. Shapiro.
Salt Flats, The. Roberts.
Seaweeds. McPherson.
Shining. Spivack.
Shore, The. St. John.
Shore Scene. Logan.
Shoreline. Barnard.
Some Sound Advice from Singapore. Ciardi.
Suffolk. *Fr.* By the North Sea. Swinburne.
Tide Pools. Smith.
We Lying by Seasand. Thomas.
Winter Shore, The. Wade.
See also **Beaches.**
Show Business
Has Been. Worsley.
See also **Acting and Actors; Motion Pictures; Theater and Theaters.**
Shrews
Masked Shrew, The. Gardner.
Shrew, The. Nash.
Shrimps
Shrimp, A! Black thing as widow's crape. *Fr.* The Shrimp. Browne.
Shrines
Lament for the Priory of Walsingham, A. *Unknown.*
Sonetto XXXV: To Guido Orlando. Cavalcanti.
See also **Mausoleums; Monuments.**
Shropshire, England
On Wenlock Edge. *Fr.* A Shropshire Lad. Housman.
Sibelius, Jean Julius Christian
Program Note on Sibelius. Babcock.
Siberia
Message to Siberia. Pushkin.
Siberia. Mangan.
Sibyl
Sibyl, The. LaBombard.
Sicily
Almond Blossom. Lawrence.
Bare Almond-Trees. Lawrence.
Siciliana: The Landings at Gela. Koehler.
Sickness. *See* **Illness.**
Sidmouth, Henry Addington, Viscount
Similes for Two Political Characters of 1819. Shelley.
Sidney, Sir Philip
Elegy on the Death of Sidney. Dyer.
Epitaph on Sir Philip Sidney. Greville.
Epitaph on Sir Philip Sidney. Ralegh.
Of Sir Philip Sidney. Beaumont.
On Sir Philip Sidney. *Fr.* An Elegy, or Friend's Passion for His Astrophil. Royden.
On the Death of Sir Philip Sidney. Constable.
Such skill, matcht with such courage as he had. *Fr.* Astrophel. Spenser.
To Elizabeth, Countess of Rutland. Jonson.
Siegfried
Battle-Flag of Sigurd, The. Greenwell.
Siena, Italy
Siena. Swinburne.
Sierra Nevada Mountains
Ascent to the Sierras. Jeffers.
Dead in the Sierras. Harte.
Strength through Joy. Rexroth.
Siestas
Mad Dogs and Englishmen. Coward.
Sight
Sight. Gibson.
Silence
After Long Silence. Yeats.
Burke and Wills. Barratt.
Elected Silence. Sassoon.
Gift. Cohen.
Golden Silences. Rossetti.
Night Song at Amalfi. Teasdale.
Pastourelle. Hayes.
Precept of Silence, The. Johnson.
Sea of Silence Exhales Secrets, The. Bialik.
Second Poem the Night-Walker Wrote, The. Goethe.
Silence. Cummings.
Silence. Hageman.
Silence. Hood.
Silence. Moore.
Silence. Turner.
Silences. Pratt.
Sonnet—Silence. Poe.
To Silence. Moore.
Velvet Shoes. Wylie.
Silk
Upon Julia's Clothes. Herrick.
Silkweed
Silkweed. Savage.
Silkworms
Psyche. Very.
Silkworms, The. Stewart.
Silva, Antonio José da
Da Silva Gives the Cue. Blumenthal.
Silver
Silver. De la Mare.
Simhath Torah
Simchas Torah. Rosenfeld.
Simhat Torah. Gordon.
This Feast of the Law. *Unknown.*
Similes
New Song, A. Gay.
See also **Metaphor.**
Simon of Cyrene
Simon the Cyrenean. Lyttelton.
Simon the Cyrenian Speaks. Cullen.
Simplicity
Familiar Epistle, A. Murry.
Ode on Solitude. Pope.
Ode to Simplicity. Collins.
Still to Be Neat. *Fr.* Epicoene; or, The Silent Woman. Jonson.
'Tis the Gift To Be Simple. *Unknown.*
Wreath, A. Herbert.
Sin
Adam Lay Ibounden. *Unknown.*
All My Love, Leave Me Not. *Unknown.*
And Forgive Us Our Trespasses. Behn.
At the round earth's imagined corners blow. *Fr.* Holy Sonnets. Donne.
Attend, Young Friends, While I Relate. *Unknown.*
Authour's Dreame, The. *Fr.* Argalus and Parthenia. Quarles.
Biothanatos. Beaumont.
Christ Complains to Sinners. *Unknown.*
Cinderella. Saunders.
Corruption. Vaughan.
Father Molloy. Lover.
First Confession. Kennedy.
God from His Throne with Piercing Eye. Steward.
Going to Hell. *Unknown.*
Ha! Original Sin! Nash.
High Windows. Larkin.
I am a little world made cunningly. *Fr.* Holy Sonnets. Donne.
I stood upon a high place. *Fr.* The Black Riders. Crane.
I Wake and Feel the Fell of Dark. Hopkins.
If I Could Shut the Gate. *Unknown.*
If poisonous minerals, and if that tree. *Fr.* Holy Sonnets. Donne.

Jehovah Our Righteousness. Cowper.
Lost but Found. Bonar.
Lost Sheep, The. Clephane.
Love ("Love bade me welcome; yet my soul drew back"). Herbert.
Of man's first disobedience, and the fruit. *Fr.* Paradise Lost. Milton.
Oh, If They Only Knew! Mapes.
Original Sin; a Short Story. Warren.
Penitent, The. Taylor.
Portrait of the Artist as a Prematurely Old Man. Nash.
Seven Sins, The. *Unknown.*
Sin ("Lord, with what care hast thou begirt us round!"). Herbert.
Sin and Its Cure. *Unknown.*
Sin of Omission, The. Sangster.
Sinnes Heavie Loade. Southwell.
Sonnet: "Eternall truth, almighty, infinite." *Fr.* Caelica. Greville.
Stains. Garrison.
Sting of Death, The. Scott.
Subject of Heroic Song, The. *Fr.* Paradise Lost. Milton.
There Was One I Met upon the Road. Crane.
They That Have Power to Hurt. *Fr.* Sonnets. Shakespeare.
Two Questions, The. Meynell.
Undo! *Unknown.*
Unpardonable Sin, The. Lindsay.
Vision of Sin, The. Tennyson.
Young People Who Delight in Sin. *Unknown.*
See also **Original Sin, Seven Deadly Sins.**

Sinai, Mount
Two Mountains Men Have Climbed. Starkewather.

Singing and Singers
Aim Was Song, The. Frost.
Alabama. Fields.
All the Hills and Vales. Sorley.
All Which Isn't Singing Is Mere Talking. Cummings.
Ancient Speech, The. *Fr.* Eileann Chanaidh. Raine.
And the Old Women Gathered. Evans.
Aunt Elsie's Night Music. Oliver.
Autumn Song on Perry Street. Frankenberg.
Before I Stumbled. Carlin.
Buckdancer's Choice. Dickey.
Carolers. Westerfield.
Choristers Training. *Unknown.*
Cino. Pound.
Corinne at the Capitol. Hemans. *Unknown.*
Everyone Sang. Sassoon.
Fa La La. *Unknown.*
Fair Singer, The. Marvell.
For M.S. Singing *Fruhlingsglaube* in 1945. Cornford.
Gratiana Dancing and Singing. Lovelace.
Has Been. Worsley.
He paused: the listening dames again. *Fr.* The Lay of the Last Minstrel. Scott.
How to the Singer Comes the Song? Gilder.
Hugging the Jukebox. Nye.
I Am the Mountainy Singer. Campbell.
I Hear America Singing. Whitman.
I Remember How She Sang. Penny.
Idea of Order at Key West, The. Stevens.
Little Tommy Tucker. Mother Goose.
M., Singing. Bogan.
Mourning Poem for the Queen of Sunday. Hayden.
O Black and Unknown Bards. Johnson.
Of Corinna's Singing. Campion.
Old Women Still Sing, The. Rowell.
On Clarastella Singing. Heath.
Owl's Song. Hughes.
Piano. Lawrence.
Poem for a Singer. Acorn.
Rose-cheekt Laura, come. Campion.
Silver Swan, The. *Unknown.*
Singers to Come. Meynell.
Singing. Stevenson.
Singing on the Moon. Hughes.
Singing-Time. Fyleman.
Solitary Reaper, The. Wordsworth.
Song Making. Teasdale.
Songs My Mother Taught Me. Wagoner.
Swans Sing. Coleridge.
Threnody: "Let happy throats be mute." Hayes.
To a Lady Who Did Sing Excellently. Herbert of Cherbury.
To Constantia Singing. Shelley.
To Signora Cuzzoni. Philips.
Tullochgorum. Skinner.
Two Girls Singing. Smith.
Upon Hearing His High Sweet Tenor Again. Langland.
Upon Julia's Voice. Herrick.
When Malindy Sings. Dunbar.
When the Green Woods Laugh. Blake.
When to Her Lute Corinna Sings. Shakespeare.
Who Bids Us Sing? Carpenter.
Why Should I Wander Sadly. Trimberg.
Yonosa House. Smith.
Untune the Sky (UnS). Helen Plotz, ed.
See also **Tenors.**

Sinkholes
Sinkholes. McFatter.

Sioux Indians
Dakota: October, 1822; Hunkpapa Warrior. Taylor.
Elegy to the Sioux. Dubie.
Remember the Promise, Dakotah. Carr.
Rosebud. Anderson.
Sioux, The. Field.

Sirens (mythology)
Nearing Again the Legendary Isle. *Fr.* The Magnetic Mountain. Day Lewis.
Siren Chorus. *Fr.* Syren Songs. Darley.
Siren Song. *Fr.* Songs of the Transformed. Atwood.
Sirens, The. Lipsitz.
Sirens' Song, The. *Fr.* The Inner Temple Masque. Browne.
Ulysses and the Siren. Daniel.

Sirens (warning devices)
Sirens. Coleman.

Siskind, Aaron
Suite of Six Pieces for Siskind, A. Logan.

Sisters
Coloring Margarine. Hathaway.
Dirty-billed Freeze Footy, The. Hemschemeyer.
Goblin Market. Rossetti.
In Go-Cart So Tiny. Greenaway.
Little Blue Shoes. Greenaway.
Little. Aldis.
My Sisters. Storni.
Olga Poems. Levertov.
Our Silly Little Sister. Aldis.
Portait. Fox.
Seal Rock. Baugh.
Sisters. Farjeon.
Sisters. Roberts.
To My Blood Sister. Hemp.
Triolet against Sisters. McGinley.
Two Sisters, The. *Unknown.*

Sisyphus
Sisyphus. Garioch.
Sisyphus. Miles.

Sitting Bull
Song of Sitting Bull. *Unknown.*

Sitwell, Dame Edith
Thin Facade for Edith Sitwell, A. Brinnin.

Skateboarding and Skateboarders
Sidewalk Racer, The; or, On the Skateboard. Morrison.
See also **Roller-skating.**

Skating and Skaters
Boys of These Men Full Speed. Rukeyser.
Ice-Skaters. Olson.
Midnight Skaters, The. Blunden.
On the Frozen Lake. *Fr.* The Prelude. Wordsworth.
Rink Keeper's Sestina. Draper.
Skater, The. Roberts.
Skaters, The. Fletcher.
Skaters, The. Williams.
Skater's Waltz, A. Burr.
Skating. Asquith.
Three Children. *Unknown.*
To Kate, Skating Better than Her Date. Daiches.
What She Wished. Throne.
Wings and Wheels. Turner.
74th Street. Livingston.
See also **Roller-skating.**

Skeetshooting
Working the Skeet House. Eastman.

Skeletons
To a Skeleton. Vardhill.
See also **Bones.**

Skelton, John
John Skelton. Graves.

Skepticism. *See* **Doubt.**
Skiing and Skiers
Aviemore. Waller.
Skier. Francis.
Skiers. *Fr.* In the Mountains. Warren.
Song of the Ski, The. MacDonald.
T-Bar. Page.
Transit. Rich.
White Pass Ski Patrol. Logan.
Winter Trees. Diekman.
Skin
Eczema. Slavitt.
Epiderm. Dransfield.
Flesh. Rice.
Skulls
Scientist, The. Burroway.
Skull in the Desert, The. Trimpi.
Skull of a Neandertal. Cadnum.
Sparrow's Skull, The. Pitter.
Swedenborg's Skull. Watkins.
To a Skull. Jones.
Upon a Dead Man's Head. Skelton.
Yardbird's Skull. Dodson.
See also **Bones.**
Skunks
Skunk, The. Baruch.
Skunk, The. Coffin.
Skunk, The. Dow.
Skunk Hour. Lowell.
We have little animals here. *Fr.* Skunks. Jeffers.
Sky
Battle, A. Crawford.
Broken Sky. Sandburg.
Heaven's Declare the Glory of God, The. *Fr.* Psalms. Bible, *O.T.*
How to Write a Poem about the Sky. Silko.
I Never Saw a Moor. Dickinson.
Psalm XIX. Addison.
Sky, The. Roberts.
Sky, The. Stoddard.
Sky Is Up Above the Roof, The. Verlain.
Skycoast. Hazo.
Sky's unresting cloudland, that with varying play, The. *Fr.* The Testament of Beauty. Bridges.
Spacious firmament on high, The. Addison.
Upper skies are palest blue, The. Bridges.
We will watch the Northern Lights. *Unknown.*
When I Consider Thy Heavens. Psalms. Bible, *O.T.*
White Whales Specked Black. Outlaw.
Winter Galaxy, The. Heavysege.
Winter Heavens. Meredith.
See also **Constellations; Stars.**
Sky Diving and Sky Divers
Parachutist, The. Anderson.
Sky Diver. Stoutenburg.
Sky Diving. Lattimore.
Skye, Isle of, Scotland
Beckon Me, Ye Cuillins. Hendrie.
Skye Summer. Donaldson.
Skye. Gawsworth.
Warning, A. Nicolson.
Skylarks. *See* **Larks.**
Skyscrapers
Building a Skyscraper. Tippett.
Monadnock, The. Fletcher.
Of Man and Nature. Mungin.
On Watching the Construction of a Skyscraper. Raffel.
Skyscraper. Sandburg.
Skyscrapers. Field.
Slander
To the Detracted. Andrews.
Slaughter of the Innocents. *See* **Massacre of the Innocents.**
Slaughterhouses
Point, greatly enlarged, The. *Fr.* A Technical Supplement. Kinsella.
Slaughterhouse Boys, The. Meissner.
Slavery
African Chief, The. Bryant.
Against Slavery. *Fr.* The Task. Cowper.
Bondage. "Innsley."
Breath in My Nostrils. Jeffers.
Creole Slave-Song, A. Thompson.
Dark Testament. Murray.
Death of Slavery, The. Bryant.
Disillusion. Tewa.
Early Losses; a Requiem. Walker.
Enslaved. McKay.
Farewell, The: "Gone, gonesold and gone." Whittier.
Flying Cloud, The. *Unknown.*
Folklore. Dabydeen.
"Formerly a Slave." Melville.
Frederick Douglass. Hayden.
From America. Whitfield.
Fugitive Slaves, The. Very.
Fugitive Slave's Apostrophe to the North Star, The. Pierpont.
Go Down, Moses. *Unknown.*
In Bondage. McKay.
Independence. Faleti.
Jack and Dinah Want Freedom. *Unknown.*
Jim Crack Corn; or the Blue Tail Fly. *Unknown.*
John Cherokee. *Unknown.*
Liberty for All. Garrison.
Lines: "From fair Jamaica's fertile plains." "Ada."
Many Thousand Gone. *Unknown.*
Middle Passage. Hayden.
Mother Dark. Pereira.
My Great-Grandfather's Slaves. Berry.
My Name Was Legion. Swift.
No more, America, in mournful strain. *Fr.* To the Right Honourable William, Earl of Dartmouth, His Majesty's Principal Secretary of State for North America, & C. Wheatley.
No More Auction Block. *Unknown.*
Old Cabin, The. Dunbar.
On Being Brought from Africa to America. Wheatley.
On Liberty and Slavery. Horton.
Poem for My Family. Jordan.
Primitive, The. Lee.
Promises of Freedom. *Unknown.*
Runagate Runagate. Hayden.
Runaway Slave, The. *Fr.* Song of Myself. Whitman.
Runaway Slave at Pilgrim's Point, The. Browning.
Safari West. Williams.
Serf, The. Campbell.
She's Free. Harper.
Simfunny of thee Hold Whorl. Lynch.
Simon Legree—A Negro Sermon. *Fr.* The Booker Washington Trilogy. Lindsay.
Slave, The. Oppenheim.
Slave Auction, The. Harper.
Slave Chase, The. *Unknown.*
Slave Quarters. Dickey.
Slave Singing at Midnight, The. Longfellow.
Slavery Chain Done Broke at Last. *Unknown.*
Slaves. *Fr.* The Sugar Cane. Grainger.
Slaves. Lowell.
Slaves Cannot Breathe in England. *Fr.* The Task. Cowper.
Slave's Dream, The. Longfellow.
Song: "We raise de wheat." *Unknown.*
Song of the Galley-Slaves. Kipling.
Song of the Son. Toomer.
Song to the Runaway Slave. *Unknown.*
Strong Men. Brown.
Suffer, Poor Negro. Diop.
Sweet Meat Has Sour Sauce; or, The Slave-Trader in the Dumps. Cowper.
Sympathy. Dunbar.
Those Who Lost Everything. Diop.
To a Dark Girl. Bennett.
To Sir Toby. Freneau.
To the First of August. Plato.
Tour Guide: La Maison des Esclaves. Dixon.
Trellie. Jeffers.
Wake Nicodemus. Work.
When Israel Was in Egypt's Land. *Unknown.*
Wild Negro Bill. *Unknown.*
Witnesses, The. Longfellow.
Woman's Song, A. McElroy.
Wounded Person, The. *Fr.* Song of Myself. Whitman.
Sleds
Little Red Sled, The. Bush.
Sledding Song, A. Schlichter.
Tracking the Sled, Christmas 1951. Walker.
See also **Sleighs.**
Sleep
At Night. Cornford.
Care-charmer Sleep. *Fr.* To Delia. Daniel.

Care-charmer sleep, sweet ease in restless misery. *Fr.* Fidessa, More Chaste than Kind. Griffin.
Care-Charming Sleep. *Fr.* The Tragedy of Valentinian. Fletcher.
Cares of Majesty, The. *Fr.* King Henry IV, Pt. II. Shakespeare.
Come, Sleep. *Fr.* The Woman-hater. Beaumont.
Come, Sleep! O Sleep, the certain knot of peace. *Fr.* Astrophel and Stella. Sidney.
Country of Water. Ames.
Cradle Song, A. Blake.
Cuddle Doon. Anderson.
Disillusionment of Ten o' Clock. Stevens.
Early Rising. Saxe.
Falling Asleep. Sassoon.
For Sleep, or Death. Pitter.
Grania. *Unknown.*
His Sleep. Urdang.
I Met at Eve. De la Mare.
If Once You Have Slept on an Island. Field.
If You Can't Eat You Got To. Cummings.
In Sleep. Burton.
Insomnia. Bishop.
Insomnia. Piercy.
Insomnia. Tabb.
Invocation to Sleep. *Fr.* The Tragedy of Valentinian. Fletcher.
Laura Sleeping. Cotton.
Lonely Are the Fields of Sleep. Baldwin.
Lullaby: "Beloved, may your sleep be sound." Yeats.
Lullaby: "Sleep, mouseling, sleep." Coatsworth.
Morphine. Heine.
Nap. Van Doren.
Night and Sleep. Patmore.
Nod. De la Mare.
O Sleep. Norton.
Old Lizette on Sleep. Lee.
Pains of Sleep, The. Coleridge.
Quiet Nights, The. Tynan.
Rock-a-by Lady, The. Field.
Sacrament of Sleep, The. Oxenham.
Sandman, The. "Vandegrift."
Sleep and Poetry. Keats.
Sleep, Angry Beauty, Sleep. Campion.
Sleep is a Reconciling. *Unknown.*
Sleep, My Child. Aleichem.
Sleep, Silence' Child, Sweet Father of Soft Rest. Drummond of Hawthornden.
Sleep Sweet. Gates.
Sleep Watch. Henson.
Sleep. Berssenbrugge.
Sleep. Brown.
Sleep, The. Browning.
Sleep. Doty.
Sleep. Martin.
Sleep. *Fr.* Arcadia. Sidney.
Sleep. *Fr.* The Induction to "The Mirror for Magistrates." Sackville.
Sleep. *Fr.* The Woman-Hater. Beaumont *and* Fletcher.
Sleeper, The. Clouts.
Sleeper, The. De la Mare.
Sleeping on Her Couch. Leigh.
Slumber Song. Ledoux.
Song: "See, how like twilight slumber falls." Cotton.
Song: "Sleep, O Sleep." Gay.
Sugar-Plum Tree, The. Field.
Sweet and Low. Tennyson.
To My Wife Asleep. Tick.
To Sleep. Fleming.
To Sleep. Keats.
To Sleep. Osgood.
To Sleep. Smith.
To Sleep. Wordsworth.
Variations on the Word *Sleep*. Atwood.
Walking to Sleep. Wilbur.
We are not wholly blest who use the earth. *Fr.* Dreamland. Mair.
Weep You No More, Sad Fountains. *Unknown.*
When Father Slept. Anderson.
Willie Winkie. Miller.
Wynken, Blynken, and Nod. Field.
45. *Fr.* To Delia. Daniel.

Sleepwalking. *See* **Somnambulism.**

Sleeping Beauty
Disenchantments: An Anthology of Modern Fairy Tale Poetry (DFT), pp. 117-145. Wolfgang Mieder, ed.

Sleet
Sleet Storm. Tippett.

Sleighs
Blue Sleigh. Scott.
Jingle Bells. Pierpont.
Phantoms of the Steppe. Pushkin.
Sleigh Bells at Night. Coatsworth.
Sleighride. Anderson.
See also **Sleds.**

Slides
Sliding. Chute.

Sligo. *See* **County Sligo, Ireland.**

Sloth
Praise of Industry, The. *Fr.* The Castle of Indolence. Thomson.
Sluggard, The. Watts.

Sloths
Sloth, The. Gardner.
Sloth, The. Roethke.
Sloth, The. Romanes.
Three-toed Sloth. Donnelly.

Slugs
Slug in Woods. Birney.
Slug. Roethke.

Slums
Childhood. Latimore.
"Dangerous Condition:" Sign on Inner-City House. Atkins.
East Bronx. Ignatow.
Elementary School Classroom in a Slum, An. Spender.
Feeding the Lions. Jordan.
Get the Gasworks. Ignatow.
Here Is the Abattoir Where. Smith.
In the Barrio. Alurista.
Judeebug's Country. Johnson.
Letter in Winter. Patterson.
Lovers of the Poor, The. Brooks.
On Saint-Urbain Street. Acorn.
Ordinary Women II. Hacker.
Our Barrio. Alurista.
Rat, The. Davies.
Reckoning A.M. Thursday. Turner.
Reflections in a Slum. "MacDiarmid."
Scenery. Joans.
Summertime and the Living. Hayden.
To the New Annex to the Detroit County Jail. Thomas.

Smart, Christopher
History, A. Williams.
To Christopher Smart. Stroud.

Smells
Alien. Hayes.
Cologne. Coleridge.
Dog in Us, The. Barnie.
Epitaph on the Fart in the Parliament House. Hoskyns.
Lady's Dressing Room, The. Swift.
Old Movies. Cotton.
Sense of Smell, The. MacNeice.
Smell. Williams.
Smell My Fingers. Axelrod.
Smell of Fish, The. Meissner.
Smell on the Landing, The. Porter.
Smells. Morley.
Smells. Worth.
Sniff. Frost.
World is full of wonderful smells, The. Gay.

Smelts
Opening the Season. Lewandowski.

Smiles
Egnatius, because his teeth are white. Catullus.
Growing Smiles. *Unknown.*
Hustle and Grin. *Unknown.*
Judy-One. Lee.
Keep Smiling. *Unknown.*
Let Us Smile. Nesbit.
Little Things. *Unknown.*
Only a Smile. *Unknown.*
Philosophy. Dunbar.
Simile for Her Smile, A. Wilbur.
Smile, The. Blake.
Smile. *Unknown.*
Smile, A. *Unknown.*
They Might Not Need Me; But They Might. Dickinson.
Trus' an' Smile. Williams.
Try Smiling. *Unknown.*

Two Smiles. Herford.
Smith, Adam
Adam Smith. *Fr.* Clerihews. Bentley.
Smith, Bessie
Blues for Bessie. O'Higgins.
Homage to the Empress of the Blues. Hayden.
Last Affair; Bessie's Blues Song. Harper.
Smith, David
Homage to David Smith. Haines.
Smith, John
John Smith's Approach to Jamestown. Hope.
Last Meeting of Pocahontas and the Great Captain, The. Preston.
Noah an' Jonah an' Cap'n John Smith. Marquis.
Smith, Joseph
Nauvoo. Taylor.
Smoke
All the Smoke. Siegel.
On the Closing of Millom Ironworks. Nicholson.
Smoke. Thoreau.
Smoke Animals. Bennett.
Song of the Smoke, The. DuBois.
Smoking
He Records a Little Song for a Smoking Girl. Whitehead.
On Giving Up Smoking. *Fr.* A Looking-Glass for Smokers. Spooner.
Smoker, The. Huff.
Smugglers
Smuggler. The. *Unknown.*
Smuggler's Song, A. *Fr.* Puck of Pook's Hill. Kipling.
Snails
After Tempest. MacKaye.
Butterfly and the Snail, The. *Fr.* Fables. Gay.
Considering the Snail. Gunn.
Haughty Snail-King, The. Lindsay.
Housekeeper, The. Bourne.
Housekeeper, The. Lamb.
Little Snail. Conkling.
My Garden. Lindon.
Snail, The. Conkling.
Snail, The. Cowper.
Snail. Drinkwater.
Snail. Eybers.
Snail, The. Herbert.
Snail. Hughes.
Snail, The. Lovelace.
Snail, The. *Unknown.*
Snail's Derby, A. Lee-Hamilton.
Snail's Monologue, The. Morgenstern.
Snails. Aborigine.
Snails. Liagarang.
To a Snail. Moore.
Upon the Snail. Bunyan.
Snakes
Andante of Snakes, The. Symons.
Black Snake, The. Hubbell.
Boy and the Snake, The. Lamb.
Breaking Green. Ondaatje.
Cheers. Merriam.
Cocker of Snooks, A. Gotlieb.
Copperhead, The. Bottoms.
Death of a Snake, The. Plomer.
Dying Viper, A. "Field".
Fastidious Serpent, The. Johnstone.
Five Serpents. Burgess.
Garden Hose, The. Janosco.
Green and Yellow. *Unknown.*
In a Garden. Babcock.
In the Snake Park. Plomer.
In Winter, In My Room. Dickinson.
Lizards and Snakes. Hecht.
Medallion. Plath.
Mountain Bride. Morgan.
Narrow fellow in the grass, A. Dickinson.
On a Little Boy's Endeavouring to Catch a Snake. Foxton.
Pit Viper. Momaday.
Pit Viper. Starbuck.
Poisoned Man, The. Dickey.
Prologue: Moments in a Glade. Stephens.
Python, The. Belloc.
Python. Yoruba.
Rattler, Alert. Ghiselin.
Rattlesnake, The. Carr.
Rattlesnake, The. Wrigley.
Reveille. Hughes.
Serpent, The. Langland.
Serpent, The. Roethke.
Sharpbreasted Snake, The. Oliver.
Silent Snake, The. Hughes.
Silent Snake, The. *Unknown.*
Snake, The. Berry.
Snake. Lawrence.
Snake. Roethke.
Snake Trying, The. Ross.
Snakecharmer. Plath.
Snakes of September, The. Kunitz.
Springfield Mountain. *Unknown.*
Summer. Wakoski.
Time We Climbed Snake Mountain, The. Silko.
To a Fair Lady Playing with a Snake. Waller.
To a Fine Young Woman. Wycherley.
To the Snake. Levertov.
Viper, The. Belloc.
Viper, The. Pitter.
Snapdragons
Snapdragon. Newman.
Sneezing
Haiku: "Dog's violent sneeze, The." Wright.
Sneeze, The. *Fr.* The Limeratomy. Euwer.
Sneeze on a Monday, you sneeze for danger. Mother Goose.
Snipes
To the Snipe. Clare.
Snobbery
Cenotaph, The. Roberts.
Epitaph on a Tuft-Hunter. Moore.
Jingo-Woman, The. Hamilton.
Snoring
Snoring Bedmate, The. *Unknown.*
Snow
After Snow. Clark.
Angels in Winter. Willard.
April Snow, The. Very.
At Liberty. Perlman.
Beautiful Snow, The. Watson.
Because You Asked about the Line between Prose and Poetry. Nemerov.
Brindabella. Stewart.
Cardinal. Howes.
Cynthia in the Snow. Brooks.
Dafydd ap Gwilym Resents the Winter. Humphries.
Dawn Walk. Hirsch.
Desert Places. Frost.
Devonshire Rhyme, A. *Unknown.*
Drove-Road, The. Gibson.
Dust of Snow. Frost.
Easter Snowfall. Behn.
Falling of the Snow, The. Souster.
Falling Snow. *Unknown.*
Faun Sees Snow for the First Time, The. Aldington.
Feathers of Snow. *Unknown.*
Fire in the Snow, The. Watkins.
First Snow in Alsace. Wilbur.
First Snow on an Airfield. Ciardi.
First Snow. Allen.
First Snow. Eastwick.
First Snowfall, The. Lowell.
First Snow. Kooser.
First Winter's Day. Aldis.
For Snow. Farjeon.
Getting Through. Kumin.
Ghosts. Munkittrick.
Home Place, The. Currie.
I come more softly than a bird. *Fr.* Rhyming Riddles. Austin.
In the Snowfall. Mechain.
It sifts from leaden sieves. Dickinson.
January. Coatsworth.
January. Hawley.
Landscape. Purdy.
Lester Tells Wanda and the Big Snow. Zimmer.
Limerick: "There was a young man of Quebec." *Unknown.*
London Snow. Bridges.
Long Lines. Goodman.
Metaphysic of Snow. Finkel.
New Forms. Redgrove.
New Snow. Rowles.
On a Gentlewoman Walking in the Snowe. Strode.
On a Night of Snow. Coatsworth.

On a Snowy Day. Aldis.
On Chloris Walking in the Snow. Strode.
Once in a Lifetime, Snow. Murray.
Onset, The. Frost.
Outside the Door. Wynne.
Patch of Old Snow, A. Frost.
Phantoms of the Steppe. Pushkin.
Presence of Snow. Cane.
Slushy snow splashes and sploshes, The. Hoberman.
Snow. Allen.
Snow. Austin.
Snow. Chiang.
Snow. Coatsworth.
Snow. Crapsey.
Snow. De la Mare.
Snow, The. Dickinson.
Snow, The. Dyment.
Snow, The. Hall.
Snow. Fry.
Snow. Lampman.
Snow. MacNeice.
Snow. Malouf.
Snow. Pomeroy.
Snow. Stone.
Snow. Thomas.
Snow Anthology. Bourinot.
Snow Crystals on Meall Glas. Wilson.
Snow Curlew, The. Watkins.
Snow Fell with a Will. Gillman.
Snow had begun in the gloaming, The. *Fr.* The First Snow-Fall. Lowell.
Snow Harvest. Young.
Snow in New York. Swenson.
Snow in October. Nelson.
Snow in Spring. Eastwick.
Snow in the City. Field.
Snow in the Suburbs. Hardy.
Snow Toward Evening. Cane.
Snow-Bird, The. Sherman.
Snow-bound. Whittier.
Snowfall: Four Variations. Amabile.
Snowfall; a Poem about Spring.
Snowfall in the Afternoon. Bly.
Snowfall. Bernard.
Snowfall. Carducci.
Snowfall, A. Eberhart.
Snowfall, The. Justice.
Snowfall, The. MacLeish.
Snowfall. Tuwhare.
Snowfish, The. Field.
Snowflakes. Behrend.
Snowflakes. Chute.
Snowflakes. Dodge.
Snowflakes. Longfellow.
Snowman, The. Stevens.
Snow-Shower, The. Bryant.
Snowstorm, The. Emerson.
Snowstorm, The. Scott.
Snowstorm. Clare.
Snow Storm, The. Millay.
Snow Storm. Madeleva.
Soft Snow. Blake.
Stopping by Woods on a Snowy Evening. Frost.
Stories of Snow. Page.
Storm Fear. Frost.
Storm in April, A. Wilbur.
There Blooms No Bud in May. De La Mare.
Thin ice/ Free advice. McCord.
To a Snowflake. Thompson.
Upon a Great Shower of Snow That Fell on May-Day, 1654. Washbourne.
Velvet Shoes. Wylie.
Village in Snowstorm. Krapf.
Waiting. Behn.
Wednesday at North Hatley. Gustafson.
When All the World Is Full of Snow. Bodecker.
White bird feartherless floats down through the air, A. *Unknown.*
White Fields. Stephens.
White. Krolow.
Why Does it Snow? Richards.
Willows in the Snow. Tsuru.
Winter. De la Mare.
Winter. Menashe.
Winter Hymn, A—to the snow. Jones.
Winter Poem. Giovanni.
Winter Rune. Coatsworth.
See also **Snowflakes.**

Snow White
Dwarf, The. Locklin.
Disenchantments: An Anthology of Modern Fairy Tale Poetry (DFT), pp. 149–165, 183–186. Wolfgang Mieder, ed.

Snowdrops
Snowdrop, The. De Bary.
Snowdrop. Hughes.
Snowdrops. MacBeth.

Snowflakes
Snowflake on asphodel, clear ice on rose. Aiken.
Snowflake, The. De la Mare.
Snowflakes. Nemerov.
Snowflakes. Sansom.
Watering the Horse. Bly.

Snowmen
Boy at the Window. Wilbur.
Snowman, The. Page.

Soap
How Come? Ignatow.
Soap, the Oppressor. Johnson.

Soccer
Bewteis of the Fute-Ball, The. *Unknown.*
Eureka! Godley.
Football and Rowing—An Eclogue. Godley.
Soccer. Voznesensky.
Stanley Matthews. Ross.

Social Class
Dignity of Labor, The. Bersohn.
False Security. Betjeman.
For a Lady I Know. *Fr.* Four Epitaphs. Cullen.
Garden, The. Pound.
Garden Party, The. Belloc.
Maud Muller. Whittier.
Modest Wit, A. Osborn.
Old Woman, outside the Abbey Theater, An. Strong.
Red Wig, The. *Unknown.*
Song of the Lower Classes, The. Jones.
Uncultivated Accent. *Unknown.*
When Adam Delved. *Unknown.*
Without and Within. Lowell.
Working Class. Warr.
See also **Snobbery.**

Social Protest. *See* **Protest, Social.**

Social Workers
Feeding the Lions. Jordan.

Socialism
Emigrant Song. Ansky.
Why I Voted the Socialist Ticket. Lindsay.

Socrates
Reply of Socrates, The. Thomas.

Sodom
And there came two angels to Sodom at even. *Fr.* Genesis. Bible, *O.T.*
Lot Later. Nemerov.
Lot's Wife. Akhmatova.
Sodom. Grade.
This Place Rumord to Have Been Sodom. Duncan.

Softball
Casey's Daughter at the Bat. Graham.

Soldiers
A Terre. Owen.
Achilles Deatheridge. Masters.
Air Sentry, The. Barrington.
All Day It Has Rained. Lewis.
All the Hills and Vales Along. Sorley.
American Soldier, The. Freneau.
An Army Corps on the March. Whitman.
Another Epitaph on an Army of Mercenaries. "MacDiarmid."
Anthem for Doomed Youth. Owen.
Apologia pro Poemate Meo. Owen.
Aristocrats. Douglas.
Arms and the Boy. Owen.
Army Corps on the March, An. Whitman.
Arthur McBride. *Unknown.*
As Toilsome I Wander'd Virginia's Woods. Whitman.
Ballad: "O What Is That Sound." Auden.
Ballad for the Unknown Soldier. Taylor.
Ballad of East and West, The. Kipling.
Band Played Waltzing Matilda, The. Bogle.

Banks of Claudy, The. *Unknown.*
Banks of the Nile, The. *Unknown.*
Base Details. Sassoon.
Battle Eve of the Irish Brigade, The. Davis.
Before Action. Gellert.
Bingen on the Rhine. Norton.
Blue Bells of Scotland, The. *Unknown.*
Bold Dragoon, A. *Unknown.*
Bold Dragoon, The. *Unknown.*
Bonnets So Blue. *Unknown.*
Boot and Saddle. *Fr.* Cavalier Tunes. Browning.
Boots. Kipling.
Breakfast. Gibson.
British Grenadiers, The. *Unknown.*
Budmouth Dears. *Fr.* The Dynasts. Hardy.
By the Bivouac's Fitful Flame. Whitman.
Caisson Song, The. Gruber.
Calling the Roll. Shepherd.
Canadians. Gurney.
Captain Jinks. *Unknown.*
Cavalry Crossing a Ford. Whitman.
Centenarian's Story, The. Whitman.
Champs D'Honneur. Hemingway.
Chant-Pagan. Kipling.
Charge of the Light Brigade, The. Tennyson.
Charlie He's My Darling. Burns.
Christmas Night of '62. McCabe.
Civil War. Van Dorn.
Comrades. McGlennon.
Cool Web, The. Graves.
Corporal. Bierce.
Cry from the Canadian Hills, A. Leveridge.
Danny Deever. Kipling.
Danny. Cowley.
Death of a Warrior, The. Mastoraki.
Deserter, The. Housman.
Dirge for a Soldier. Boker.
Dirge for One Who Fell in Battle. Parsons.
Disabled. Owen.
Dreamers. Sassoon.
Drummer Boy. Stafford.
Drummer Hodge. Hardy.
Dug-out, The. Sassoon.
Duke of Plaza-Toro, The. Gilbert.
Dulce et Decorum Est. Owen.
Eighth Air Force. Jarrell.
Elegy for a Dead Soldier. Shapiro.
End of World War One, The. Olds.
Epistle from a Half-Pay Officer in the Country to His Friend in London, An. Pack.
Epitaph on an Army of Mercenaries. Housman.
Execution of Cornelius Vane, The. Read.
Exposure. Owen.
Fable of the War, A. Nemerov.
Fallen, The. Scott.
Farewell, The: "It was a' for our rightfu' king." Burns.
Flowers of the Forest, The. Elliot.
For My Torturer, Lieutenant D——. Djabali.
For Our Soldiers Who Fell in Russia. Fortini.
For Soldiers. Gifford.
Forgive Me, Sire. Cameron.
Fulfilment. Nichols.
Gee, But I Want to Go Home. *Unknown.*
General, The. Sassoon.
General's Death, The. O'Connor.
Georgia Volunteer, A. Townsend.
Girl I Left behind Me, The. *Unknown.*
Guard at the Binh Thuy Bridge, The. Balaban.
Gunga Din. Kipling.
Gunner. Jarrell.
Hail and Farewell. Spicer.
Haltersick's Song. *Fr.* Horestes. Pickering.
Happy Warrior, The. Read.
Here Dead Lie We. Housman.
Heroic Heart. Donnelly.
High Germany. *Unknown.*
I Hate That Drum's Discordant Sound. Scott of Amwell.
I Heard a Soldier. Trench.
I Stood with the Dead. Sassoon.
In an Age of Fops and Toys. *Fr.* Voluntaries. Emerson.
In Barracks. Sassoon.
In Flanders Fields. McCrae.
In Memoriam, Private D. Sutherland. Mackintosh.
Infrantryman, An. Blunden.
Insensibility. Owen.
Into Battle. Grenfell.
Into the Salient. Blunden.
Israeli Soldier's Nightmare, An. Carb.
It Was the Last of the Parades. Simpson.
Jester in the Trench, The. Gellert.
Jewish Conscript, The. Frank.
Jimmy's Enlisted, or, the Recruited Collier. *Unknown.*
Johnny, I Hardly Knew Ye. *Unknown.*
Kerry Recruit, The. *Unknown.*
Kid Has Gone to the Colors, The. Herschell.
Kid In Upper 4, The. Metcalf.
Lancashire Lads. *Unknown.*
Lancer. Housman.
Lessons of the War: Naming of Parts. Reed.
Little Giffen. Ticknor.
Lofty Lane. Gerard.
Losers, The. Young.
Man He Killed, The. Hardy.
March in the Ranks Hard-prest, and the Road Unknown, A. Whitman.
March, March, Ettrick and Teviotdale. *Fr.* The Monastery. Scott.
Maunding Souldier, or, The Fruits of Warre Is Beggery, The. *Unknown.*
McCaffery. *Unknown.*
Men behind the Guns, The. Rooney.
Men in Green. Campbell.
Men Who March Away. *Fr.* The Dynasts. Hardy.
Mental Cases. Owen.
Modern Major-General, The. *Fr.* The Pirates of Penzance. Gilbert.
More than Flowers We Have Brought. Turner.
Mrs. McGrath. *Unknown.*
New Mistress, The. *Fr.* A Shropshire Lad. Housman.
Nocturne: "Be thou at peace this night." Davison.
Nostalgia. Shapiro.
O What is That Sound. Auden.
Ode for the American Dead in Korea. McGrath.
Ode Written in the Beginning of the Year 1746. Collins.
Officers' Mess (1916). Monro.
Old Battalion, The. *Unknown.*
Old Soldiers Home at Marshalltown, Iowa. Barnes.
Old Soldiers Never Die. *Unknown.*
Old Souldier of the Queens, An. *Unknown.*
Old Timers. Sandburg.
Oldest Soldier, The. Graves.
On a Very Young, Very Dead Soldier. Gillman.
On the Grave of a Young Cavalry Officer Killed in the Valley of Virginia. Melville.
On the Idle Hill of Summer. Housman.
One of the Regiment. Le Pan.
Orphan Boy, The. *Unknown.*
Parthians, The. *Fr.* Paradise Regained. Milton.
Peasants, The. Lewis.
Plains of Waterloo, The. *Unknown.*
Poem: "Between rebellion as a private study and the public." Donnelly.
Poem for Anton Schmidt, A. Pillen.
Poem of the Conscripted Warrior. Nogar.
Portrait in the Guards, A. Whistler.
Portrait; the Freedom Fighter. Jonas.
Prayer: "Thy blessing on the boysfor time has come." Guri.
Prayer of a Soldier in France. Kilmer.
Prelude: The Troops. Sassoon.
Private of the Buffs, The. Doyle.
Prolonged Sonnet: When the Troops Were Returning from Milan. Niccolò Degli Albizzi.
Quarry, The. Auden.
Rambling Soldier, The. *Unknown.*
Rebel, A. Fletcher.
Recall. Whittemore.
Recessional. Kipling.
Recruit, The. Chambers.
Recruit, The. Housman.
Recruited Collier, The. *Unknown.*
Recruiting Drive. Causley.
Recruiting Sergeant, The. *Unknown.*
Rendezvous. Seeger.
Return, The. Kipling.
Richard III's Speech. *Fr.* Bosworth Field. Beaumont.
Roman Wall Blues. Auden.
Royal Light Dragoon, The. *Unknown.*
Send-off, The. Owen.
Sentry, The. Lewis.

Sergeant-Major Money. Graves.
Shillin' a Day. Kipling.
Sight in Camp in the Daybreak Gray and Dim, A. Whitman.
Silver Tassie, The. Burns.
Sir Dilberry Diddle, Captain of Militia. *Unknown.*
Soldier, The. *Fr.* 1914. Brooke.
Soldier, A. Frost.
Soldier, The. Krige.
Soldier, A. Suckling.
Soldier from the Wars Returning. Housman.
Soldier, Rest! Thy Warfare O'er. *Fr.* The Lady of the Lake. Scott.
Soldier That Has Seen Service, The. *Unknown.*
Soldier: Twentieth Century. Rosenberg.
Soldiers Bathing. Prince.
Soldier's Death, A. *Fr.* The Atheist's Tragedy. Tourneur.
Soldier's Dream, The. Campbell.
Soldier's Dream. Owen.
Soldier's Farewell to Manchester, The. *Unknown.*
Soldier's Prayer, A. Freeman.
Soldier's Song. *Unknown.*
Soldiers who wish to be a hero. *Unknown.*
Somebody's Darling. Lacoste.
Song: "Farewell, adieu, that court-like life!" Pickering.
Song: To all you ladies now at land. Sackville.
Song of the Banjo, The. Kipling.
Sonnet to Negro Soldiers. Cotter.
Souldier Going to the Field, The. Davenant.
Souldiers Farewel to His Love, The. *Unknown.*
Sound of the Drum, The. *Unknown.*
Speaking: the Hero. Pollak.
Spires of Oxford, The. Letts.
Spring Offensive. Owen.
Strange Meeting. Owen.
Street Sounds to the Soldiers' Tread, The. Housman.
Suicide in Trenches. Sassoon.
Tambourine Song for Soldiers Going into Battle. Hind bint Utba.
Taught to Be Polite. Young.
Ten Days Leave. Snodgrass.
There Was an Old Soldier. *Unknown.*
There's Nothing Polite about a Tank. Minarik.
These Fought in Any Case. *Fr.* Hugh Selwyn Mauberley. Pound.
"They." Sassoon.
Three Troopers, The. Thornbury.
Thus spoke to my lady the knight full of care. *Fr.* A Soldier and a Scholar. Swift.
To a Captain in Sinai. Aharoni.
To a Comrade in Arms. Lewis.
To Lucasta, Going to the Wars. Lovelace.
To the Veterans of the Abraham Lincoln Brigade. Taggard.
Tomb of Lt. John Learmonth, A. I. F., The. Manifold.
Tommy. Kipling.
Trooper and Maid, The. *Unknown.*
Trooper's Horse, The. *Unknown.*
Troops, The. Sassoon.
Two Armies. Spender.
Unknown Soldier, The. Lewis.
Unknown Soldier, The. Rose.
Vergissmeinnicht. Douglas.
Veteran, The. Blunden.
Viet Cong Sapper Dies, A. Sossaman.
Volunteer, The. Asquith.
Volunteer, The. Cutler.
Volunteer, The. *Unknown.*
Volunteer's Reply to the Poet, The. *Fr.* Talking Bronco. Campbell.
War-Song of Dinas Vawr, The. *Fr.* The Misfortune of Elphin. Peacock.
When Johnny Comes Marching Home. Gilmore.
When the Assault Was Intended to the City. Milton.
Which Side Am I Supposed to Be On? Auden.
Whisperin' Bill. Bacheller.
Why, Soldiers, Why? *Unknown.*
Widow at Windsor, The. Kipling.
Working Party, A. Sassoon.
Wound-Dresser, The. Whitman.
See also **War.**

Solipsism
Argent Solipsism. Blake.
Good Creatures, Do You Love Your Lives. Housman.

Solitude
Acquainted with the Night. Frost.
Alastor. Shelley.
Alone. Holden.
Anticipation of Sharks. Wakoski.
Bits of Straw. Clare.
Compensation. Jeffers.
Desert Places. Frost.
Deviator, The. Warr.
Eagle and the Mole, The. Wylie.
Earth, ocean, air, beloved brotherhood! *Fr.* Alastor; or, The Spirit of Solitude. Shelley.
Elected Silence. Sassoon.
Enthusiast, The; an Ode. Whitehead.
Face in a Mirror. Anderson.
Garden, The. Marvell.
Goat Paths, The. Stephens.
Going In. Piercy.
Green Inn, The. Garrison.
Hermit, The. Halpern.
How to Eat Alone. Halpern.
Hymn on Solitude. Thomson.
I Am. Clare.
I Met My Solitude. Replansky.
I will not shut me from my kind. *Fr.* In Memoriam A. H. H. Tennyson.
I'm Alone in the Evening. Rosen.
In November. Lampman.
Inniskeen Road; July Evening. Kavanagh.
Invocation: "Earth, ocean, air, beloved brotherhood." *Fr.* Alastor; or, The Spirit of Solitude. Shelley.
Keziah. Brooks.
Lake Isle of Innisfree, The. Yeats.
Lisa. Carrier.
Little Eclogue. Wylie.
Mid-August at Sourdough Mountain Lookout. Snyder.
Most of It, The. Frost.
My Dog Jock. Carruth.
O Sweet Woods. *Fr.* Arcadia. Sidney.
Ode on Solitude. Pope.
Of Solitude. Cowley.
Of Those Who Walk Alone. Burton.
On Looking into Henry Moore. Livesay.
Peter Grimes at Aldeburgh. *Fr.* The Borough. Crabbe.
Petition for an Absolute Retreat, The. Winchilsea.
Prelude: "Still south I went and west and south again." Synge.
Quiet. Pickthall.
Rain. Thomas.
Retirement. Cowper.
Retirement, The. *Unknown.*
Room, The. Day Lewis.
Singles. Waters.
Six Winter Privacy Poems. Bly.
Small Moon. Nemerov.
Solitariness. *Fr.* Arcadia. Sidney.
Solitary, The. Teasdale.
Solitary Life, A. Drummond of Hawthornden.
Solitary Reaper, The. Wordsworth.
Solitude. De la Mare.
Solitude. Grainger.
Solitude. Keats.
Solitude. Lampman.
Solitude. Mollineux.
Solitude. Peterson.
Solitude. Pope.
Solitude. Rilke.
Solitude. Wilcox.
Solitude. *Fr.* The Search after Happiness. More.
Still Life, A. Kessler.
Sun Moon Kelp Flower or Goat. Gregg.
There is a solitude of space. Dickinson.
Thrice Happy He. Drummond of Hawthornden.
To Any M. F. H. Sackville-West.
Tokyo West. Corn.
Under a Wiltshire Apple Tree. De Bary.
Verses: "I am monarch of all I survey." Cowper.
Verses Supposed to Be Written by Alexander Selkirk, during His Solitary Abode on the Island of Juan Fernandez. Cowper.
Wants. Larkin.
When in the Woods I Wander All Alone. Hovell-Thurlow.
Woman Alone. Levertov.
Wood-Cutter's Night Song, The. Clare.

Solomon
David and Solomon. Naylor.
On Woman. Yeats.
Solomon to Sheba. Yeats.
Solomon. Hagedorn.
Solomon. Heine.

Solstices
Toward the Solstice. Rich.
Solzhenitsyn, Alexander
Chekhov Comes to Mind at Harvard. Freeman.
Somalia
Independence. Somali.
Our Country Is Divided. Somali.
Somerset, Edward Seymour, Duke of
On Edward Seymour, Duke of Somerset. *Unknown.*
Somerset, Robert Carr, Earl of
Upon the Sudden Restraint of the Earl of Somerset, Then Falling from Favour. Wotton.
Somerset, England
Apostrophe to the Parret. Burrington.
Brent. Diaper.
Clevedon Church. *Abr. by* Lang.
Looking down on Nether Stowey. Fr. Fears in Solitude. Coleridge.
Nightfall on Sedgemoor. Young.
Quantocks, The. Wordsworth.
Seen from the Quantocks. *Fr.* This Lime Tree Bower My Prison. Coleridge.
Somnambulism
For the Sleepwalkers. Hirsch.
Sonnets
Nuns Fret Not at Their Convent's Narrow Room. Wordsworth.
On a Magazine Sonnet. Loines.
On the Sonnet. Keats.
Scorn Not the Sonnet. Wordsworth.
Sonnet, A: "Sonnet is a moment's monument, A." *Fr.* The House of Life. Rossetti.
Sonnet Sonnet. Engle.
Sonnet, The: "Sonnet is a fruit which long hath slept, The." Symonds.
Sonnet, The: "What is a sonnet? 'Tis the pearly shell." Gilder.
Sonneteering Made Easy. Botsford.
Sonnet's Voice, The. Watts-Dunton.
Untitled Poem, about an Uncompleted Sonnet, An. Pinsker.
Velvet Sonneteers. MacInnes.
What Is a Sonnet? Watkins.
Sonora Desert
Requiem for Sonora. Shelton.
Sons
Affliction of Margaret, The. Wordsworth.
Almond Tree, The. Stallworthy.
Ancient Couple on Lu Mountain, The. Van Doren.
Basketball. Vincent.
Bee, The. Dickey.
Birthday. Yevtushenko.
Breakings. Taylor.
Daedalus. Reid.
Death of a Son. Silkin.
Even the Best. Kizer.
Father, The. Finkel.
Father and Son. Wallace.
Fathers and Sons. *Unknown.*
Field, The. Huddle.
For a Father. Cronin.
For My Father. Potts.
For My Son, Born during an Ice Storm. Jauss.
For Stephen. Brookhouse.
For You, My Son. Gregory.
Fording the River. Deane.
Gemwood. Bell.
Generations. Awad.
It Comes during Sleep. Dow.
Lament of a Man for His Son. Austin.
Letter to a Dead Father. Shelton.
Lost Son, The. Roethke.
Lullaby: "O my son, born on a winter's morn." Nohomaiterangi.
Mothers of Sons. Saunders.
My Mother Would Be a Falconress. Duncan.
Notes for My Son. *Fr.* The Song of Lazarus. Comfort.
Odysseus to Telemachus. Brodsky.
Of My Deare Sonne, Gervase Beaumont. Beaumont.
On My First Son. Jonson.
On the Birth of His Son. Su Tung-P'o.
On the Death of His Son. Wesley.
On the Death of My Son Charles. Webster.
Prayer for My Son, A. Winters.
Prayer for My Son, A. Yeats.
Rowing. Ochester.
Son, The. Torrence.
Sonship. Rezmerski.
Sympathy, a Welcome, A. Berryman.
Then Sohrab with his sword smote Rustum's helm. *Fr.* Sohrab and Rustum. Arnold.
Threnody. Ignatow.
To My Child Carlino. Landor.
To My Little Son. Davis.
To My Son. Byron.
To My Son. Grafflin.
To My Son, Aged Three Years and Five Months. Hood.
To My Unborn Son. Thorne.
Toys, The. Patmore.
Two Prayers, The. Gillies.
Wishes for My Son. MacDonagh.
Yesterday. Merwin.
Divided Light: Father and Son Poems (DiL). Jason Shinder, ed.
Sophocles
Kaire. Eberhart.
To a Friend. Arnold.
Sorrow
Bad Season Makes the Poet Sad, The. Herrick.
Braes of Yarrow, The. Logan.
Bridge, The. Longfellow.
Come, Ye Disconsolate. Moore.
Dark Song. Ammons.
Depths of Sorrow, The. Gond.
Desolate. Massey.
Desolation Is a Delicate Thing. Wylie.
Ettrick. Scott.
Folded Power. Cromwell.
Girl's Song. *Unknown.*
Harp of Sorrow, The. Clifford.
I saw my lady weep. *Unknown.*
I Sit and Look Out. Whitman.
Man of Constant Sorrow. *Unknown.*
Moan, Moan, Ye Dying Gales. Neele.
Narrow Doors, The. Gifford.
O Sorrow! *Fr.* Endymion. Keats.
On a Picture by J. M. Wright, Esq. Southey.
On Another's Sorrow. *Fr.* Songs of Innocence. Blake.
Poem of the Intimate Agony. Burgos.
Rainy Day, The. Longfellow.
Shrubbery, The. Cowper.
Sorrow Is the Only Faithful One. Braithwaite.
Sorrow Is the Only Faithful One. Dodson.
Sorrow. *Fr.* Hymen's Triumph. Daniel.
Spell Against Sorrow. Raine.
Stormy Night in Autumn. Chu Shu-chen.
Tailor Called Sorrow, A. Alver.
Tenth Eclogue, The. *Fr.* The Shepherd's Garland. Drayton.
They Say My Verse Is Sad: No Wonder. Housman.
Time and Grief. Bowles.
To Each His Own. Garvin.
Troubled Woman. Hughes.
With Rue My Heart Is Laden. *Fr.* A Shropshire Lad. Housman.
See also **Grief.**
Soul
Anastasis. Smythe.
Animal Song. McHugh.
Be Still, My Soul, Be Still. *Fr.* A Shropshire Lad. Housman.
Bodies of the young are not the flower, The. *Fr.* Autumn Testament. Baxter.
Caged Skylark, The. Hopkins.
Chambered Nautilus, The. Holmes.
City of the Soul, The. Douglas.
Dialogue, between the Resolved Soul, and Created Pleasure, A. Marvell.
Dialogue between the Soul and Body, A. Marvell.
Dialogue of Self and Soul, A. Yeats.
Doubts. Brooke.
Ecstasy, The. Donne.
Falconer of God, The. Benét.
Gallery, The. Marvell.
Green River, The. Douglas.
Hadrian's Address to His Soul When Dying. Hadrian.
I Know My Soul. McKay.
Indian Burying Ground, The. Freneau.
Invention of Comics, The. Baraka.
Lie, The. Ralegh.
Like to the Arctic Needle. Quarles.
Love Calls Us to the Things of This World. Wilbur.
Most souls, 'tis true, but peep out once an age. *Fr.* Elegy to the Memory of an Unfortunate Lady. Pope.
My Soul Hovers over Me. Tan Pai.

Noiseless Patient Spider, A. Whitman.
Octopus, The. "MacDiarmid."
Oh my black soul! now thou art summoned. *Fr.* Holy Sonnets. Donne.
On a Drop of Dew. Marvell.
Palladium. Arnold.
Peace. Vaughan.
Poor soul, the centre of my sinful earth. *Fr.* Sonnets. Shakespeare.
Rebirth. Machado.
Retreat, The. Vaughan.
Scorpion. Smith.
Soul, The. Cawein.
Soul selects her own society, The. Dickinson.
Soul selects her own society, The. Dickinson.
Soul Speaks, The. Pfeiffer.
Soules Ignorance in This Life and Knowledge in the Next, The. *Fr.* Of the Progresse of the Soule; the Second Anniversarie. Donne.
Souls Groan to Christ for Succour, The. Taylor.
Speculation. Nemerov.
Terrain. Ammons.
Triumphalis. Carman.
True Riches. Watts.
Virtue. Herbert.
Wake. Spires.
What Are Years? Moore.

Sound
All Day I Hear. *Fr.* Chamber Music. Joyce.
Animal That Drank Up Sound, The. Laughlin.
East Hampton: The Structure of Sound. Appleman.
Hermit Wakes to Bird Sounds, The. Kumin.
Hurlygush. Lindsay.
Nocturnal Sounds. Cumbo.
On a Wednesday. Aliesan.
On the Power of Sound. Wordsworth.
Overheard. Levertov.
Sound of Night, The. Kumin.

Soup
Chicken Soup Therapy: Its Mode of Action. Hall.
Story of Augustus, Who Would Not Have Any Soup, The. Hoffman.

Sousa, John Philip
Sousa. Dorn.

South, The
Alas! for the South! Coogler.
Appeal to My Countrywomen, An. Harper.
Childhood. Walker.
Day in a Long Hot Summer, A. Kageyama.
Dixie. Emmet.
Dixie. Pike.
First Families Move Over. Nash.
Georgia Dusk. Toomer.
Good Old Rebel. Randolph.
Invitation to Madison County, An. Wright.
It's a debatable land. The winds are variable. *Fr.* Report from the Carolinas. Bevington.
Legacy: My South. Randall.
My South. West.
Once. Walker.
Slim in Hell. Brown.
Snapshots of the Cotton South. Davis.
Southern Exposures. Murray.
Southern Mansion. Bontemps.
Southern Road, The. Randall.
Southern Ships and Settlers. Benét.
Southerner, The. Shapiro.
When the Mint Is in the Liquor. Ousley.

South Africa
Attend my fable if your ears be clean. *Fr.* The Wayzgoose. Campbell.
Birth of Moshesh, The. Bereng.
In the Gold Mines. Vilakazi.
Incident at Mossel Bay. Balazs.
Marching to Pretoria. *Unknown.*
Me, Colored. Abrahams.
On Some South African Novelists. Campbell.
Pass Office Song. *Unknown.*
Penguin Book of South African Verse, The (PeSA). Jack Cope *and* Uys Krige, eds.

South African War. *See* **Boer War.**

South Carolina
Battle of Charleston Harbor, The. Hayne.
Brother Jonathan's Lament for Sister Caroline. Holmes.
Carolina. Timrod.
Carolina Spring Song. Allen.
Carolinas, The. Ray.
Charleston. Gilder.
Charleston. Timrod.
Charleston Blues. *Unknown.*
Charleston. Hayne.
It's a debatable land. The winds are variable. *Fr.* Report from the Carolinas. Bevington.
Ode: "Sleep sweetly in your humble graves." Timrod.
South Carolina to the States of the North. Hayne.
Sunday in South Carolina. Parham.

South Carolina (ship)
South Carolina, The. *Unknown.*

South Dakota
Beginning the Year at Rosebud, S. D. Whiteman.
Crazy Horse Returns to South Dakota. Elliott.
Dakota Badlands. Landeweer.
For a Young South Dakota Man. Manfred.
Primer Lesson. Vinz.
Rushmore. Witt.
Tourist Guide: How You Can Tell for Sure When You're in South Dakota. Heynen.
Victory of the Battle of Wounded Knee, The. Parson.
Working near Lake Traverse. Hennen.

South Sea Islands
Fun with Fishing. Tietjens.

South Wind
Awake! Oh, north wind. *Fr.* Song of Solomon. Bible, *O.T.*
Moon's the North Wind's Cooky, The. Lindsay.
South Wind, The. Bridges.
South Wind laid his moccasins aside, The. *Fr.* Malcolm's Katie. Crawford.

Southern Cross, The (constellation)
Southern Cross. Melville.

Southey, Robert
Dedication: "Bob Southey! You're a poet, poet laureate." *Fr.* Don Juan. Byron.
Epitaph on Robert Southey. Moore.
On the Death of Southey. Landor.
Vision of Judgment, The. Byron.

Soutine, Chaim
Story of Soutine, A. Schevill.

Soviet Union. *See* Russia.

Space and Space Travel
Achieving Perspective. Rogers.
Apollo 113. Finne.
Asteroid Light, The. *Unknown.*
Astronaut's Choice. Darcy.
Autosonic Door. Thompson.
Canopus. Taylor.
Capsule Philosophy. Lamport.
Christmas 1959 Et Cetera. Barrax.
Cross Spider, The. Swenson.
Doesn't It Seem to You. Emin.
Doorman. Galvin.
Everlasting Astronauts, The. Buchan.
Far Trek. Brady.
Faster Than Light. Buller.
How Strange It Is. Lewis.
Incubation, The. Zolynas.
Interplanetary Limericks. Graham.
Little Bo-Peep. *Fr.* The Space Child's Mother Goose. Winsor.
Message from a Mouse, Ascending in a Rocket. Hubbell.
Moon Landing. Auden.
Moonwalk. Engels.
Not Lost In the Stars. Bliven.
On Shooting Particles beyond the World. Eberhart.
Orbiter 5 Shows How Earth Looks from the Moon. Swenson.
Post Early for Space. Henniker-Heaton.
Probable-Possible, my black hen. *Fr.* The Space Child's Mother Goose. Winsor.
S F. Leverett.
Soft Landings. Sergeant.
Solomon Grundy. *Fr.* The Space Child's Mother Goose. Winsor.
Space. Kennedy.
Space Shuttle. Ackerman.
Space Travel. Krows.
Space-Wanderer's Homecoming. Viereck.
This little pig built a spaceship. *Fr.* The Space Child's Mother Goose. Winsor.
Valentine for Earth. Frost.
Viking 1 on Mars—July 20, 1976. Perlman.
When I Consider Thy Heavens. Bible, *O.T.* Psalms.

Space (outer space)
Spain
And I remember Spain. *Fr.* Autumn Journal. MacNeice.
Castile. Unamuno.
Cordoba. Mendelssohn.
Feller I Know, A. Austin.
In Spain. Lawless.
Madrigal to the City of Santiago. Garcia Lorca.
Monserrat. Collin.
Poem for Garcia Lorca. Woodcock.
Recollections of Burgos. Trench.
Spanish-American War
Battleship of *Maine*. *Unknown.*
Breath on the Oat. Taylor.
Deeds of Valor at Santiago. Scollard.
Dewey at Manila. Johnson.
No Hint of Stain. *Fr.* An Ode in Time of Hesitation. Moody.
Ode in Time of Hesitation, An. Moody.
On a Soldier Fallen in the Philippines. Moody.
Surrender of Spain, The. Hay.
Unmanifest Destiny. Hovey.
When the Great Gray Ships Come In. Carryl.
Spanish Armada
Armada, The. Macaulay.
Armada, 1588, The. Wilson.
Ballade of the Armada, A. Dobson.
Sir Francis Drake; or Eighty-Eight. *Unknown.*
Sir Francis Drake; or Eighty-eight. *Unknown.*
Spanish Civil War. *See* **Civil War, Spanish.**
Spanish Main
Song of the Spanish Main, The. Bennett.
Spanish Needle
Spanish Needle, The. McKay.
Spanish Succession, War of the
Battle of Blenheim, The. Southey.
But, O my muse, what numbers wilt thou find. *Fr.* The Campaign. Addison.
Jack Frenchman's Defeat. Congreve.
Word's gone out, and now they spread the main, The. *Fr.* The Spanish Descent. Defoe.
See also **Blenheim, Battle of**
Spankings
Whipping, The. Hayden.
Sparrows
Because You Asked about the Line between Prose and Poetry. Nemerov.
Bee, the Ant, and the Sparrow, The. Cotton.
City Sparrow. Mayhall.
Dead Sparrow, The. Cartwright.
Did You Ever Hear an English Sparrow Sing? Johnston.
First Surf. Di Pasquale.
Fringilla Melodia, The. Hirst.
Good brother Philip, I have borne you long. *Fr.* Astrophel and Stella. Sidney.
Haiku: "Bitter morning, A." Hackett.
House and Shutter. Turco.
I have two sparrows white as snow. *Fr.* The Muses' Elysium. Drayton.
In the Morning All Over. Stafford.
Lesbia on Her Sparrow. Cartwright.
London Sparrow's If, A. Lindon.
Mr. and Mrs. Spikky Sparrow. Lear.
Of All the Birds That I Do Know. Gascoigne.
Of All the Birds. *Unknown.*
Phyllyp Sparrowe. Skelton.
Song of the Reed Sparrow, The. *Unknown.*
Sparrow, The. Bible, *O.T.* Psalms
Sparrow, The. Williams.
Sparrow and Diamond, The. Green.
Sparrow in Winter. Takahashi.
Sparrows among Dry Leaves. Williams.
Sparrows at the Airport, The. Ostroff.
Sparrow's Feather, A. Barker.
Sparrows in College Ivy. Wolfe.
Sparrows Song, The. *Unknown.*
Survivors. Hogan.
Tell me not of joy: there's none. Cartwright.
They've All Gone South. Miller.
To a Sparrow. Ledwidge.
Upon the Death of His Sparrow; an Elegie. Herrick.
Sparta, Greece
Death of Leonidas, The. Croly.
On the Spartan Dead at Thermopylae. Simonides.
Spas
Tunbridge Wells. Rochester.
Speech
Effort at Speech between Two People. Rukeyser.
Overworked Elocutionist, An. Wells.
See also **Screams; Talk.**
Spelling
I Before E. *Unknown.*
Principal and Principle. *Unknown.*
Spelling Bees
Bananananananananana. Cole.
Spelling Bee at Angels, The. Harte.
Spellman, Francis Cardinal
Dirge. Clarke.
Spender, Stephen
To Stephen Spender. Corsellis.
Spenser, Edmund
Upon Master Edmund Spenser. Beaumont.
Vision upon This Conceit of the Faerie Queene, A. Ralegh.
Sphinx
How subtle-secret is your smile! *Fr.* The Sphinx. Wilde.
Myth. Rukeyser.
Sphinx Speaks, The. Saltus.
Sphinx, The. Brownell.
Sphinx, The. Emerson.
Spiders
Arachne. Aliesan.
Arachne. Cooke.
Arachne. Empson.
Broken, The. Merwin.
Cross Spider, The. Swenson.
Design. Frost.
Discoveries in Arizona. Wright.
Four Things. Bible, *O.T.* Proverbs
Homes, The. Pitkin.
Huntress, The. Johnston.
Image, The. Fuller.
Little City. Horan.
Little Miss Muffet. Mother Goose.
Mr. Edwards and the Spider. Lowell.
Mrs. Spider. Livingston.
Noiseless Patient Spider, A. Whitman.
Of a Spider. Thorley.
Orb Weaver, The. Francis.
Parson's Pleasure. Higgs.
Spider, The. Coffin.
Spider. Colum.
Spider, The. Eberhart.
Spider, The. Eiseley.
Spider. Farber.
Spider, The. Littleton.
Spider, The. MacKenzie.
Spider, The. Whitman.
Spider and the Fly, The. Howitt.
Spider and the Ghost of the Fly, The. Lindsay.
Spider holds a silver ball, The. Dickinson.
Spiders. Ackerman.
Study of a Spider, The. De Tabley.
Tarantula. O Hehir.
To A Spider. Southey.
To the Man Who Watches Spiders. Fox.
Upon a Spider Catching a Fly. Taylor.
Voyage. Donaghy.
Wedding, The. Aiken.
Welcome to This House. George.
White Spider. Garin.
Spies
On Spies. Jonson.
Spinning and Spinners
Song for the Spinning Wheel. Wordsworth.
Spinners at Willowsleigh. Zaturenska.
Spinning. Jackson.
Spinning in April. Peabody.
Spinning Wheel, The. Klein.
Spinning Women. Leonidas of Tarentum.
Spinsters
Eleanor Rigby. Lennon *and* McCartney.
Emily Hardcastle, Spinster. Ransom.
I'll Not Marry at All. *Unknown.*
Miss Gee. Auden.
Miss Loo. De la Mare.
My Aunt. Holmes.

My Mother's Sister. Day Lewis.
Old Ladies, The. Ellis.
Old Maid's Song. *Unknown.*
Single Girl. *Unknown.*
Some Foreign Letters. Sexton.
Spinster's Lullaby. Miller.
Three Sisters. De La Mare.
Waiting, the Hallways under Her Skin Thick with Dreamchildren. Lifshin.
Spiritualists
After the Seance. Clewell.
Spirituals
Negro Spiritual. Trott.
Negro Spirituals. Benét.
O Black and Unknown Bards. Johnson.
Book of American Negro Spirituals, The (BoAN). James Weldon Johnson, ed.
Spittoons
Brass Spittoons. Hughes.
Spohr, Ludwig
Violinist, The. Lampman.
Sports
Confessions of a Born Spectator. Nash.
First Practice. Gildner.
Football Field: Evening. McKellar.
Frisbee. Humphries.
Spartan Wrestler, The. Damagetus.
We Used to Play. Welch.
Where fair Sabrina's wand'ring currents flow. *Fr.* The Bowling-Green. Somerville.
Literature of Sports, A (LiSp). Tom Dodge, ed.
See also **Athletes; Games;** *and* **names of individual sports.**
Spring
Abishag. Fichman.
Admonition for Spring. MacKay.
After Dark Vapours. Keats.
Ah, Sweet Is Tipperary. McCarthy.
Alysoun ("Lenten ys come with love to towne"). *Unknown.*
And When the Green Man Comes. Haines.
Answer to a Child's Question. Coleridge.
April. Teasdale.
April. Thompson.
April, 1885. Bridges.
April Morning, An. Carman.
April Rain Song. Hughes.
As Spring the Winter. Bradstreet.
Aspects of Spring in Greater Boston. Starbuck.
At the Edge of the Bay. Chubb.
Aunt Alice in April. Matchett.
Autumnal Spring Song. Miller.
Baby Seed Song. Nesbit.
Backward Spring, A. Hardy.
Barren Spring. *Fr.* The House of Life. Rossetti.
Bee! I'm expecting you! Dickinson.
Budding Spring. Lindsay.
Budding-Time Too Brief. Stein.
Carolina Spring Song. Allen.
Chansons Innocentes. Cummings.
Chanted Calendar, A. *Fr.* Balder. Dobell.
Cloud, The. Shelley.
Cold Spring, A. Bishop.
Come, Love, Let's Walk. *Unknown.*
Comin' o' the Spring, The. Scott.
Coming. Larkin.
Coming of the Spring, The. Perry.
Daffodils,/ That come before the swallow dares. Shakespeare.
Darling! Because My Blood Can Sing. Cummings.
Dawn. *Unknown.*
Days Too Short. Davies.
Depression before Spring. Stevens.
Description of Spring, Wherein Each Thing Renews, Save Only the Lover. Surrey.
Dress of Spring, The. Justus.
Dying Child, The. Clare.
Eager Spring. Bottomley.
Earliest Spring. Levertov.
Early Spring. Keyes.
Early Spring. Tennyson.
Earth in Spring, The. Halevi.
Echoing Green, The. *Fr.* Songs of Innocence. Blake.
Farewell Frost, or Welcome the Spring. Herrick.
February's Forgotten Mitts. Knister.
Fields of Flanders, The. Nesbit.
Fight of the Year, The. McGough.
First Sight. Larkin.
First Spring Day, The. Rossetti.
First Spring Morning, The. Bridges.
Footsteps of Spring. Bialik.
For Jane Myers. Glück.
For, lo, the winter is past. *Fr.* Song of Solomon. Bible, *O.T.*
For Spring. Jones.
For those first tiny, prayerful-folded hands. *Fr.* A Little Te Deum of the Commonplace. Oxenham.
Four Little Foxes. Sarett.
Four Sweet Months, The. Herrick.
Georgian Spring. Campbell.
Glad Earth. Forbes.
Good-by My Winter Suit. Bodecker.
Green Song. Booth.
Haiku: "Balmy spring wind, A." Wright.
Hark, Hark, the Lark. *Fr.* Cymbeline. Shakespeare.
Hello! Garnett.
Here We Come a-Piping. *Unknown.*
Heresy for a Class-Room. Humphries.
Home Thoughts from Abroad. Browning.
Hope and Faith. Peretz.
How Many Heavens. Sitwell.
I dreaded that first robin, so. Dickinson.
If Ice. Ross.
In a Spring Still Not Written Of. Wallace.
In Earliest Spring. Howells.
In Early Spring. Meynell.
In Springtime. Kipling.
In the Spring. *Fr.* Locksley Hall. Tennyson.
Inside Chance, The. Piercy.
It Was a Lover. *Fr.* As You Like It. Shakespeare.
It's Spring Returning, It's Spring and Love. *Unknown.*
Jonathan Bing Dances for Spring. Brown.
June. Ledwidge.
Kerchoo! Fishback.
Kite Days. Sawyer.
Last Snow. Young.
Late Spring, A. Scully.
Late Spring: a Heaving, a Turning. Gill.
Late Spring, A: Eastport. Booth.
Late Spring Day in My Life, A. Bly.
Laughing Song. *Fr.* Songs of Innocence. Blake.
Lawyer's Invocation to Spring, The. Brownell.
Lenten Is Come with Love to Toune. *Unknown.*
Letter from Germany. Grosholz.
Letter to His Friend Isaac, A. Halevi.
Light exists in Spring, A. Dickinson.
Lines Written in Early Spring. Wordsworth.
Little madness in the spring, A. Dickinson.
Little Song of Spring, A. Austin.
Loveliest of Trees, [the Cherry Now]. Housman.
Love's Emblems. *Fr.* The Tragedy of Valentinian. Fletcher.
Lumber of Spring. Ridler.
Lyric to Spring. Stilwell.
Magdalen Walks. Wilde.
Magic Piper, The. Marsh.
Mardi Gras. Keithley.
May, 1915. Mew.
May 10th. Kumin.
Mayflower. Aiken.
Memory, A. Allingham.
Miracle. Bailey.
Miss Euphemia. Ransom.
Moorburn in Spring. *Unknown.*
New Hampshire. *Fr.* Landscapes. Eliot.
New York in the Spring. Budbill.
Northern Spring, A. Baro.
Now fades the last long streak of snow. *Fr.* In Memoriam A. H. H. Tennyson.
Now Is the High-Tide of the Year. *Fr.* The Vision of Sir Launfal. Lowell.
Now That the Winter's Gone. Carew.
Ode on the Spring, An. Gray.
Ode to Mr. Forbes, An. Ramsay.
Ode to Spring. Brooks.
On a Banc as I Sat a-Fishing; a Description of the Spring. Wotton.
One Morning When the Rain-Birds Call. Roberts.
Page's Road Song, A. Percy.
Peaceful Western Wind, The. Campion.
Pippa's Song. *Fr.* Pippa Passes. Browning.

Poem: "By the road to the contagious hospital." Williams.
Prairie Spring. Fallis.
Prayer for This Day. Flanner.
Prayer in Spring, A. Frost.
Prologue to "The Canterbury Tales." *Fr.* The Canterbury Tales. Chaucer.
Question, The. Shelley.
Rains of Spring, The. Lady Ise.
Return to Spring. Mastin.
Robin's Come! Caldwell.
Russian Spring Song with Minaiev, A. Walsh.
Saint-Henri Spring. Acorn.
Screw Spring. Hoffman.
Seed Leaves. Wilbur.
Seeds. De la Mare.
Song: "Spring lights her candles everywhere." Shove.
Song in Spring. Ginsberg.
Sonnet: "Sweet *Spring*, thou turn'st with all thy goodlie Traine." Drummond.
Sonnet Written at the Close of Spring. Smith.
Soon with the Lilac Fades Another Spring. MacDonogh.
Soote Season, The. Surrey.
Sprin' Fevah. Dandridge.
Spring, The. Barnes.
Spring. *Fr.* Songs of Innocence. Blake.
Spring, The. Carew.
Spring. Charles d'Orléans.
Spring. Chute.
Spring. Cornish.
Spring, The. *Fr.* The Mistress. Cowley.
Spring. De Vere.
Spring. Feirstein.
Spring. Hogan.
Spring. Hopkins.
Spring. Kuskin.
Spring. Larkin.
Spring. Loveman.
Spring. *Fr.* The Biglow Papers; Sunthin' in the Pastoral Line. Lowell.
Spring, The. *Fr.* Alexander and Campaspe. Lyly.
Spring. Mayakovsky.
Spring. McCarriston.
Spring. Millay.
Spring. Nashe.
Spring. Ridge.
Spring. Rodgers.
Spring. Rossetti.
Spring. Sackville-West.
Spring. *Fr.* Love's Labour's Lost. Shakespeare.
Spring. Sitwell.
Spring. Smart.
Spring. Still.
Spring. Surrey.
Spring. *Fr.* In Memoriam A. H. H. Tennyson.
Spring. *Fr.* The Seasons. Thomson.
Spring. Timrod.
Spring. *Unknown.*
Spring; a Formal Ode. Tyuchev.
Spring Again. Wallace.
Spring Air. Derwood.
Spring and All. Williams.
Spring and Death. Hopkins.
Spring and Fall: To a Young Child. Hopkins.
Spring at Fort Okanogan. Wilson.
Spring comes linking and jinking throught the woods, The. *Fr.* Spring. Miller.
Spring Coming. Ammons.
Spring Doggerel. Coghill.
Spring Ecstacy. Reese.
Spring Equinox, The. Ridler.
Spring Goeth All in White. Bridges.
Spring has come again. The earth. Rilke.
Spring in England. Going.
Spring in Hiding. Frost.
Spring in New Hampshire. McKay.
Spring in the Old World. Levine.
Spring in Virginia. Wilson.
Spring in War-Time. Nesbit.
Spring in War-Time. Teasdale.
Spring in Washington. Den Boer.
Spring Is. Katz.
Spring is a recurring astonishment—like poetry. *Fr.* Twenty-one Sonnets. Stead.
Spring Is at Work with Beginnings of Things. Rose.
Spring Is in the Making. Duffy.
Spring Is Like a Perhaps Hand. Cummings.
Spring Landscape. La Follette.
Spring Market. Driscoll.
Spring Morning, A. Clare.
Spring Morning. Lawrence.
Spring Morning: Waking. Seelbinder.
Spring Nocturne. Liessin.
Spring Oak. Kinnell.
Spring Pools. Frost.
Spring Quiet. Rossetti.
Spring Rites. Robbins.
Spring Song. Carman.
Spring Song. Conkling.
Spring Song. McKuen.
Spring Song. Nahum.
Spring Song. O'Brien.
Spring Song, A. *Unknown.*
Spring Song of Aspens. Spencer.
Spring Song of the Birds. James I, King of Scotland.
Spring Song of Tzu-yeh, A. Yen.
Spring: The Lover and the Birds. Allingham.
Spring, the Sweet Spring. *Fr.* Summer's Last Will and Testament. Nashe.
Spring-Tide. *Unknown.*
Springtime in Cookham Dean. Roberts.
Spring too, very soon! Harbingers. Bashō.
Spring Will Come, The. Lowry.
Spring Wind. Turner.
Spring's Arrival. *Unknown.*
Spring's Delights. Sterry.
Starling's Spring Rondel, A. Cousins.
Stay, Spring. Young.
Sumer Is Icumen In. *Unknown.*
Sweet o' the Year, The. Meredith.
"Sweet spring is your." Cummings.
That Sharp Knife. Wolfe.
Thaw. Thomas.
Thaw in the City. Lipsitz.
There Will Come Soft Rains. Teasdale.
Those Trees that Line the Northway. Perreault.
Thou hearest the Nightingale begin the Song of Spring. *Fr.* Milton. Blake.
'Tis Merry in Greenwood. Scott.
To a Nun. *Unknown.*
To Amanda. Thomson.
To be in a place for spring and not have lived its winter. *Fr.* Brother Jonathan, Brother Kafka. O'Sullivan.
To Bring Spring. Keithley.
To John Keats, Poet, at Springtime. Cullen.
To My Sister. Wordsworth.
To Spring. Blake.
To Spring. Smith.
To the Cuckoo. Bruce.
To the Spring. *Fr.* Hymns to Astraea. Davies.
To the Spring Sun. Laughton.
To-day I saw a butterfly. Hooley.
Turn o' the Year. Tynan.
Twilight in Middle March, A. Ledwidge.
Twist-Rime on Spring. Guiterman.
Two Springs. Li Ch'ing-chao.
Vernal Equinox. Johnston.
Vernal Sentiment. Roethke.
Waking Year, The. Dickinson.
Well Pleaseth Me the Sweet Time of Easter. Pound.
When Daffodils Begin to Peer. *Fr.* The Winter's Tale. Shakespeare.
When Daisies Pied. *Fr.* Love's Labour's Lost. Shakespeare.
When Faces Called Flowers Float out of the Ground. Cummings.
When, loosened from the winter's bonds. Nukada.
When Spring came,/ Leaves grew with a green fresh. *Unknown.*
When Spring Comes Back to England. Noyes.
When the Hounds of Spring Are on Winter's Traces. *Fr.* Atalanta in Calydon. Swinburne.
Who Calls. Sayers.
Winter Is Past, The. *Fr.* The Song of Solomon. Bible, *O.T.*
Winter's Cold. Rodgers.
Wise Johnny. Fallis.
Wonder and a Thousand Springs. Percy.
Written in March. Wordsworth.
Year's at the Spring, The. *Fr.* Pippa Passes. Browning.
Year's Awakening, The. Hardy.
Yellow Violet, The. Bryant.

Springfield, Illinois
House in Springfield. Burket.
On the Building of Springfield. Lindsay.
Springfield, Massachusetts
Arsenal at Springfield, The. Longfellow.
Springs
Enchanted Spring, The. Darley.
Spring, The. Fyleman.
Spruce Tree
Spruce. George.
Squash (fruit)
Squash in Blossom. Francis.
Squash (sport)
After a Game of Squash. Albert.
Game Resumed. Lattimore.
Squid
Squid. Blumenthal.
Squid-Jiggin' Ground, The. *Unknown.*
Squills
Blue Squills. Teasdale.
Squirrels
Abandoned House, The. Hubbell.
After Shiki. Eigner.
Conversation. Robinson.
Fable: "Mountain and the Squirrel, The." Emerson.
Fred. McCord.
Gray Squirrel, The. Wolfe.
Joe. McCord.
Migration of the Grey Squirrels, The. Howitt.
Mountain and the Squirrel, The. Emerson.
My Little Neighbor. Mason.
On a Squirrel Crossing the Road in Autumn, in New England. Eberhart.
Sacrifice of a Red Squirrel. Langland.
Squirrel in Sunshine. Cowper.
Squirrel near Library. Taggard.
Squirrel, The. Nash.
Squirrel, The. *Unknown.*
Story of the Baby Squirrel, The. Aldis.
To a Squirrel at Kyle-na-no. Yeats.
Sri Lanka
Auschwitz from Colombo. Ranasinghe.
Coppersmith. Murphy.
Letters and Other Worlds. Ondaatje.
Tea. Struthers.
Stables
More To It Than Riding. Lindon.
Riding Stable in Winter, The. Tagliabue.
Stable, The. Hoffman.
Stagecoaches
Baldy Green. *Unknown.*
Californy Stage. *Unknown.*
Jolly Waggoner, The. *Unknown.*
Ore Stage, The. Knibbs.
Stairs
Choice. Ammons.
Halfway Down. Milne.
On the Staircase. Farjeon.
Stairs. Herford.
Stalin, Joseph
Homage to Our Leaders. Symons.
Less Nonsense. Herbert.
Stamp Collecting. *See* **Philately.**
Stampa, Gaspara
Gaspara Stampa. Benét.
Standish, Miles
Courtship of Miles Standish, The. Longfellow.
Stanley, Sir Henry Morton
Stanley Meets Mutesa. Rubadiri.
Starfish
Daybreak. Kinnell.
Starfish, The. Coffin.
Starfish. Welles.
Stark, John
Marching Song of Stark's Men, The. Hale.
Starlings
Manoeuvre, The. Williams.
Plague of Starlings, A. Hayden.
Rooftop Winter. Thorpe.
Starling, The. Buchanan.
Starling's Spring Rondel, A. Cousins.
Starlings. Jensen.
Starlings. MacCaig.
Stars
Ah! Why, because the Dazzling Sun. Brontë.
At Camino. Sheehan.
Ataraxia. Taylor.
August Night. Roberts.
Awake, oh Heaven, for (lo) the heavens conspire. Tourneur.
Baby Toes. Sandburg.
Beauty of the Stars, The. Ibn Ezra.
Bright Star! Would I Were Steadfast as Thou Art. Keats.
Canopus. Taylor.
Caroline, II: To the Evening Star. Campbell.
Choose Something Like a Star. Frost.
Counting. Johnson.
Country Stars. Meredith.
Daisies. Young.
Darkness. Campbell.
El Hombre. Williams.
Es Stehen Unbeweglich. Heine.
Escape at Bedtime. Stevenson.
Evening Star. Barker.
Evening Star. Poe.
Fallen Star, The. Darley.
Falling Star, The. Teasdale.
Great Bear, The. Hollander.
Heart of Herakles, The. Rexroth.
I Look into the Stars. Draper.
I see the golden hunter go. *Fr.* Songs of the Sea-Children. Carman.
If the Stars Should Fall. Allen.
Immortal Nature. *Fr.* The Botanic Garden. Darwin.
Impressions, Number III. Cummings.
In the Field. Wilbur.
It Is the Stars that Govern Us. Magee.
Kitchen Window. MacDonald.
Little Star, The. *Unknown.*
Lost Lane. Wellesley.
Lucifer in Starlight. Meredith.
Man's Littleness in Presence of the Stars. White.
Martial Cadenza. Stevens.
My Star. Browning.
Nova. Jeffers.
Nox Nocti Indicat Scientiam. *Fr.* Castara. Habington.
On the Beach at Night. Whitman.
Pleiades, The. Coatsworth.
Pole Star. MacLeish.
Silver Sheep. Payne.
Sky Pair, The. Frost.
Slowly, by God's hand unfurled. Furness.
Song to the Evening Star. Campbell.
Speculation. Nemerov.
Star, The. Redpath.
Star, The. Taylor.
Star Drill. Moore.
Star Wish. *Unknown.*
Star-Gazer. MacNeice.
Starlight Night, The. Hopkins.
Star-light, star-bright. Mother Goose.
Starlighter, The. Guiterman.
Starlight. Meredith.
Starre, The. Herbert.
Starry Host, The. *Fr.* God and the Soul. Spalding.
Stars, The. Dodge.
Stars. Hayden.
Stars. Moss.
Stars. Nowlan.
Stars. Teasdale.
Stars Are Glittering in the Frosty Sky, The. Heavysege.
Stars, I Have Seen Them Fall. Housman.
Stars in Apple Cores. Shaw.
Stars of the superior class. *Fr.* The Stars. Smart.
Stars over the Dordogne. Plath.
Stars Wheel in Purple. Doolittle ("H. D.").
Star-talk. Graves.
Summer Stars. Sandburg.
Suns in a skein, the uncut stones of night. *Fr.* Mythological Sonnets. Fuller.
To the Evening Star. Blake.
To the Evening Star. Campbell.
Twinkle, twinkle, little star. Dehn.
Until We Built a Cabin. Fisher.
When I Heard the Learn'd Astronomer. Whitman.
When Sun Doth Rise. Williams.
Winter Galaxy, The. Heavysege.

Winter Heavens. Meredith.
See also **Astronomy and Astronomers; Astrophysics; Constellations; Sky.**
State, The
Fugal Chorus. *Fr.* For the Time-Being. Auden.
Statistics
Meditation on Statistical Method. Cunningham.
Statue of Liberty. *See* **Liberty, Statue of.**
Statues
After Plotinus. Stafford.
Archaic Apollo. Plomer.
Archaic Torso of Apollo. Rilke.
By the Statue of King Charles at Charing Cross. Johnson.
Christmas Eve under Hooker's Statue. Lowell.
Duke of York's Statue, The. Landor.
Figures, The. Creeley.
Frozen Hero, The. Vance.
Green Mountain Boy. Smyth.
Letter to Statues. Brinnin.
Marble Statuette Harpist. Allen.
Nike of Samothrace, The. Morley.
O God! O Montreal! Butler.
On a Statue of Sir Arthur Sullivan. Hamilton.
Ozymandias. Shelley.
Rider Victory, The. Muir.
Spanish Lions, The. McGinley.
Statue, The. Berryman.
Statue, The. Creeley.
Statue of Lorenzo de' Medici, The. Nesmith.
Statue of Medusa, The. Drummond of Hawthornden.
Statues. Raine.
Statues. Wilbur.
Statues, The. Yeats.
Statues in the Public Gardens, The. Nemerov.
Wayside Virgin, The. Mitchell.
Steak
Thoughts of Loved Ones. Fishback.
Steam Baths. *See* **Baths and Bathing.**
Steam Power
Means of Propulsion for Steam-ships. *Fr.* The Steam Engine; or, The Power of Flame. Baker.
Watt's Improvements to the Steam Engine. *Fr.* The Steam Engine; or, The Power of Flame. Baker.
Steam Rollers
To a Steam Roller. Moore.
Steam Shovels
Steam Shovel. Malam.
Steamers. *See* **Ships.**
Steel
Prayers of Steel. Sandburg.
Smoke and steel, *sel.* Sandburg.
See also **Iron.**
Steeples
Steeple-Jack, The. Moore.
To a Solitary Disciple. Williams.
Steers. *See* **Oxen.**
Stein, Gertrude
There's a notable family named Stein. *Unknown.*
They Don't Speak English in Paris. Nash.
Steinberg, Saul
Metamorphoses. Nemerov.
Stenographers
Stenographers, The. Page.
See also **Scribes, Secretaries.**
Stepfathers
Open Roads. Donnell.
Stephen, Saint
Feast o' Saint Stephen, The. Sawyer.
Feast of Stephen, The. Nichols.
St. Stephen and Herod. *Unknown.*
St. Stephen's Day. Dickinson.
Sterne, Laurence
Epitaph on Laurence Sterne. Garrick.
Stevedores. *See* **Longshoremen.**
Stevens, Thaddeus
Old Thad Stevens. Porter.
Stevens, Wallace
Rouse for Stevens, A. Roethke.
So Long? Stevens. Berryman.
Wallace Stevens Gives a Reading. Zinnes.
Stevenson, Robert Louis
Apparition. *Fr.* In Hospital. Henley.
Robert Louis Stevenson. Reese.
Saint R. L. S. Cleghorn.
Seamark, A. Carman.
Stevenson's Birthday. Miller.
Stickball
Of Kings and Things. Morrison.
Still Lifes
Still Life. Bering.
Still Lives. Buchwald.
Stink Bugs
Dusty black beetle, A. Sund.
Stockholm, Sweden
Dear Old Stockholm. Young.
Stockmen
Andy's Gone with Cattle. Lawson.
Ballad of the Drover. Lawson.
Dying Stockman, The. *Unknown.*
Harry Pearce. Campbell.
Man from Snowy River, The. Paterson.
My Mate Bill. Gibson.
Sick Stockrider, The. Gordon.
See also Cowboys;
Stoicism
Old Stoic, The. Brontë.
Stoic. Durrell.
Stonecutters
To the Stone-Cutters. Jeffers.
Stonehenge, England
In Love, at Stonehenge. *Fr.* The Angel in the House. Patmore.
Salisbury Plain and Stonehenge. *Fr.* Guilt and Sorrow. Wordsworth.
Stonehenge. *Fr.* Polyolbion. Drayton.
Stonehenge. *Fr.* The Seven Wonders of England. Sidney.
To My Friend, Dr. Charleton, on His Learned and Useful Works; and More Particularly This of Stone-Heng, by Him Restored to the True Founders. Dryden.
Stones and Rocks
Another Stone Poem. Dacey.
As Rocks Rooted. Hanson.
Crystals Like Blood. "MacDiarmid."
Cutting Edge, The. Levine.
Detail, The. Corman.
How to Amuse a Stone. Shelton.
I've Got a Home in That Rock. Patterson.
Mason, The. Farren.
Minerals of Cornwall, Stones of Cornwall. Redgrove.
Mountain Sculpture. Will.
Path among the Stones, The. Kinnell.
Rock Climbing. Cooper.
Serenity in Stones, The. Ortiz.
Silica Carbonate Rock. Berry.
Stanes. Glen.
Stone, The. Blackburn.
Stone. Mayo.
Stone. Simic.
Stone, The. Vaughan.
Stonetalk. Hamelin.
This Is My Rock. McCord.
Thyme Flowering among Rocks. Wilbur.
To Ailsa Rock. Keats.
To the Stone-Cutters. Jeffers.
Touchstone. Worley.
Two Voices in a Meadow. Wilbur.
Why Stone Does Not Sing by Itself. Endrezze-Danielson.
Stonington, Battle of
Battle of Stonington on the Seaboard of Connecticut, The. Freneau.
Stony Point, Battle of (1779)
Storming of Stony Point, The. Guiterman
Wayne at Stony Point. Scollard.
Storms
Arnold, Master of the *Scud.* Carmen.
Ballad of the Tempest. Fields.
Beginning to Squall. Swenson.
Brainstorm. Nemerov.
Channel Passage, A. Swinburne.
City-Storm. Monro.
Cloud-Flower Lullaby, The. Tewa.
December Storm. Hay.
Eastern Tempest. Blunden.
Elegy: "Somebody left the world last night, I felt it." Broumas.
Epitaph Ending in And, The. Stafford.
Equinox, The. Heyward.
Equinox, The. *Fr.* Seaweed. Longfellow.
First Things First. Auden.

First Winter Storm. Everson.
Found In a Storm. Stafford.
Gale in April. Jeffers.
Golden Hour, The. *Fr.* Lalla Rookh. Moore.
Hailstorm in June 1831, The. Clare.
Hatteras Calling. Aiken.
High o'er the Poop the Audacious Seas Aspire. Falconer.
Hurricane, The. Freneau.
In Cold Storm Light. Silko.
Invocation for a Storm. Hawaiian.
It. Snyder.
Late Light. Blunden.
Lear's Speech to the Storm. *Fr.* King Lear. Shakespeare.
Little Exercise at 4 A.M. Bishop.
Local Storm, A. Justice.
Lord Ullin's Daughter. Campbell.
Low Barometer. Bridges.
Miriam Tazewell. Ransom.
Night Storm. Simms.
On a Sea-Storm nigh the Coast. Steere.
One A.M. Kennedy.
Patroling Barnegat. Whitman.
Presage of Storme. *Fr.* Eugenia. Chapman.
Reefing Topsails. Mitchell.
Safe. Walker.
Snow-Bound. Whittier.
Snowstorm, The. Emerson.
Squall. Moore.
Storm, The. Donne.
Storm, The. Jennings.
Storm, The. Patmore.
Storm, The. Roethke.
Storm, The. Shanks.
Storm, The. Wallace.
Storm, The. Williams.
Storm. Wright.
Storm at Sea. Davenant.
Storm at Sea, A. *Unknown.*
Storm Cone, The. Kipling.
Storm Fear. Frost.
Storm from the East, A. Whittemore.
Storm in April, A. Wilbur.
Storm in Summer, A. Blunt.
Storm is over, the land hushes to rest, The. Bridges.
Storm on the Island. Heaney.
Storm Song. Taylor.
Storm Tide on Mejit. *Unknown.*
Stormy Day, A. Hawaiian.
Stormy Night in Autumn. Chu Shu-chen.
Summer Storm. Johnson.
Summer Storm. Kent.
Summer Storm, A. Whitehead.
Tempest, The. Smith.
Tempest, The. *Unknown.*
Tempest, The. Zaturenska.
That Is All I Heard. Yehoash.
Thunder-Storm, A. Dickinson.
Thunderstorm, A. Lampman.
Thunderstorm in Town, A. Hardy.
Tornado Watch, Bloomington, Indiana. Young.
Tornado. Stafford.
Viking Terror, The. *Unknown.*
Vision of the Sea, A. Shelley.
West Palm Beach Storm, The. *Unknown.*
Wet Night, A. Ryan.
Wind begun to knead the grass, The. Dickinson.
Wind took up the northern things, The. Dickinson.
Winter Storm at Sea, The. *Fr.* The Borough. Crabbe.
Zoe and the Ghosts. Weslowski.
See also **Blizzards**

Story Poems
Best Loved Story Poems (BeLS). Walter E. Thwing, ed.
Dark Tower, The (DTo). Dairine Coffey, ed.
Home Book of Verse for Young Folks, The (HBVY), pp. 397–474. Burton Egbert Stevenson, ed.
Modern Ballads and Story Poems (MoBS). Charles Causley, ed.
100 More Story Poems (OnMSP). Elinor Parker, ed.
Oxford Book of Narrative Verse, The (OBNV). Iona Opie *and* Peter Opie, eds.
Parlour Poetry; a Casquet of Gems (PaPo). Michael Turner, ed.
Story Poems, New and Old (StPo). William Cole, ed.

Storytelling and Storytellers
Andrew's Bedtime Story. Serraillier.
Aunt Sue's Stories. Hughes.
Lost Anchors. Robinson.
Martha. De la Mare.
Mythology. Thompson.
Palace Dancer, Dancing at Last. Green.
Request Number. Sprod.
Stories Relate Life. Shady.
Story-teller, The. Van Doren.
Story Tellers Summer, 1980. Francisco.
To Juan at the Winter Solstice. Graves.

Stowe, Harriet Beecher
Harriet Beecher Stowe. Dunbar.

Stradivari, Antonio
Working with God. *Fr.* Stradivarius. "Eliot."

Strafford, Thomas Wentworth, 1st Earl of
Epitaph on the Earl of Strafford. Cleveland.

Strangers
To You. Whitman.

Strasbourg, France
O Strassburg. *Unknown.*

Strathclyde (region), Scotland
Epistle to William Simpson, Ochiltree. Burns.
Glasgow. Smith.
Greenock. Davidson.
Hail Glasgow! famed for ilka thing. *Fr.* Glasgow. Mayne.
Harp of Renfrewshire, The. Dunn.
Isle of Arran. Reid.

Strawberries
Millions of Strawberries. Taggard.
Original Strawberry. Willard.
Strawberries in November. Neilson.
Strawberries. Hemschemeyer.
Strawberries. Morgan.
Wild Strawberries. Graves.
With Strawberries. Henley.

Strawberry Jam
Strawberry Jam. Justus.

Streams. *See* **Brooks and Streams.**

Street Performers
Fire Breather, Mexico City, The. Jacinto.

Streetcars
Burned Bridge, The. Stone.
Foundered Tram, The. Monro.

Streets
Manhole Covers. Shapiro.
Prayer: "As I walk through the streets." Flint.
Step Away from Them, A. O'Hara.
Street, The. Baro.
See also **Roads.**

Strikes and Strikers
Case for the Miners, The. Sassoon.
Durham Lock-out, The. *Unknown.*
Jurgis Petraskas, the Workers' Angel, Organizes the First Miners' Strike in Exeter, Pennsylvania. Petrosky.
Meeting at the Local. Parson.
Owslebury Lads, The. *Unknown.*
Skyhook. Kizer.
Sons of Saint Crispin, 'tis in vain! *Fr.* Resignation; an Ode to the Journeymen Shoemakers. "Pindar."
Strike, The. *Unknown.*
Striking Times. *Unknown.*

String
Henry King. Belloc.
See also **Rope.**

Striptease
Dancing Sunshine Lounge, The. Rabbit.
Epitaph of a Stripper. Smith.
National Winter Garden. Crane.
Poem as Striptease, The. Dacey
Stripper, The. Probst.
Vegas. Cunningham.

Stroke
Ojisan after the Stroke; Three Notes to Himself. Koyama.
Stroke. Lowery.
Strokes. Stafford.

Strokes
Resurrection of the Right Side. Rukeyser.

Struwwelpeter
Fräulein Reads Instructive Rhymes. Kumin.
Story of Little Suck-a-Thumb, The. Hoffman.

Stuart, Charles Edward (The Young Pretender)
Charlie Is My Darling. Nairne.
O'er the Water to Charlie. Burns.
Old Scottish Cavalier, The. Aytoun.
Will He No Come Back Again? *Unknown.*
Will Ye No Come Back Again? Nairne.
Stuart, James Ewell Brown ("Jeb")
Obsequies of Stuart. Thompson.
Stuart, James Francis Edward (The Old Pretender)
New Song Entitled the Warming Pan, A. *Unknown.*
Stubbs, George
On Looking at Stubbs's Anatomy of the Horse. Lucie-Smith.
Students
Audiences. Hollander.
Campus on the Hill, The. Snodgrass.
Correspondence School Instructor Says Goodbye to His Poetry Students, The. Kinnell.
Discontented Student, The. Tucker.
Elegy for Former Students. Miner.
Elementary School Class Room in a Slum, An. Spender.
Emily Sparks. *Fr.* Spoon River Anthology. Masters.
Etudes. Thomas.
Evening Schoolboys. Clare.
Fledglings. Meredith.
For the Student Strikers. Wilbur.
Foreign Student. Robinson.
Freshmen. Spacks.
Heathen Pass-ee, The. Hilton.
Homework for Annabelle. McGinley.
In a Spring Still Not Written Of. Wallace.
School Girl, The. Venable.
Schoolboy, The. *Fr.* Songs of Experience. Blake.
September, the First Day of School. Nemerov.
Straying Student, The. Clarke.
Student. Miles.
Student, The. Moore.
Student, The. *Unknown.*
Theme for English B. Hughes.
To the University of Cambridge in New England. Wheatley.
University Examinations in Egypt. Enright.
Vulture and the Husbandman, The. Hilton.
We saw three boys. Wordsworth.
See also **Education; Scholars and Scholarship; School.**
Stuttering
Mister Charlie. *Unknown.*
Stutterer. Dugan.
Stuyvesant, Peter
Epitaph for Peter Stuyvesant, Late General of New Netherland. Selyns.
Peter Stuyvesant's New Year's Call. Stedman.
Submarines
Mare Liberum. Van Dyke.
Yellow Submarine. Lennon *and* McCartney.
Suburban Life
Inspiration. Knox.
Suburbs
Commuter's Entry in a Connecticut Diary. Warren.
Decks. Phillips.
Housewife. Miles.
In the Suburbs. Simpson.
London Suburbs. *Fr.* Retirement. Cowper.
Long Island Springs. Moss.
Middlesex. Betjeman.
Northern Suburb, A. Davidson.
Slough. Betjeman.
Snow in the Suburbs. Hardy.
Soliloquy in the Suburbs, A. *Fr.* Eclogue IV: the Poet. Jenner.
Suburb, The. Stevenson.
Suburban Dream. Muir.
Suburban Song. Riddell.
Suburban Sonnet. Harwood.
Suburban Wife's Song. Hutchinson.
Three-handed Fugue. Gotlieb.
To an American Poet Just Dead. Wilbur.
Woman Driving the Country Squire, The. Dayton.
5:32, The. McGinley.
Subways
Approaching Washington Heights. Reiss.
Boy Who Smells Like Cocoa, A. Hershon.
Curse, The. Hollander.
Going Uptown to Visit Miriam. Cruz.
Graffiti. Field.
In a Station of the Metro. Pound.
Metropolitan Railway, The. Betjeman.
Once-Over, The. Blackburn.
One Year to Life on the Grand Central Shuttle. Lorde.
Queen, The. Pitchford.
Rapid Transit. Agee.
Riding the "A." Swenson.
Sing a Song of Subways. Merriam.
Spirit of 34th Street, The. Shriver.
Subway, The. Tate.
Things to Do If You Are a Subway. Katz.
Train to Reflection. O'Neill.
Tubes. Mollin.
Tunnel, The. *Fr.* The Bridge. Crane.
Underground Poetry. Pietri.
Underground, The. Boas.
Walk about the Subway Station. Reznikoff.
Success
After Publication of Under the Volcano. Lowry.
Air: "Flaxen-headed cow-boy, as simple as may be, A." O'Keeffe.
Back to Griggsby's Station. Riley.
Don't Quit. *Unknown.*
Failure. Mayo.
Game of Life, The. Saxe.
If. Kipling.
It Couldn't Be Done. Guest.
Kindly Unhitch That Star, Buddy. Nash.
Measure of Success. *Unknown.*
Names. Enright.
Robert Whitmore. Davis.
Success! Braley.
Success. *Unknown.*
Success is counted sweetest. Dickinson.
To a Friend Whose Work Has Come to Nothing. Yeats.
Villanelle: "Woods we're lost in aren't real, The." Kerr.
Will. Wilcox.
Winners, The. *Fr.* The Story of the Gadsbys. Kipling.
Sudan
Fuzzy-Wuzzy. Kipling.
Sudan. Jackson.
Suez Canal
Suez Crisis, The. Somali.
Suffering
After. Grayson.
Alajire, we ask you to be patient. Yoruba.
All-sufficient Christ, The. Lubke.
Amen. Browning.
And Yet. Sloan.
Convinced by Sorrow. *Fr.* Cry of the Human, The. Browning.
Guide and Friend. *Unknown.*
How Can I Smile? Hodgdon.
I Do Not Ask Thee, Lord. *Unknown.*
I Have Always Found It So. Bell.
Jesus Understands. *Unknown.*
Life's Lessons. *Unknown.*
May God Give Strength. Van Wynen.
Musée des Beaux Arts. Auden.
Our Light Afflictions. *Unknown.*
Passing Through. Flint.
Revelation. Cook.
School of Sorrow, The. Hamilton.
Security. Sangster.
Some Time We'll Understand. Cornelius.
Therefore I will not refrain my mouth. *Fr.* Job. Bible, *O.T.*
Unfailing One, The. Brooks.
Warp and Woof. Halbisch.
Whipping, The. Hayden.
See also **Pain.**
Suffern, New York
House with Nobody in It, The. Kilmer.
Suffolk, England
Evening by the Sea. Swinburne.
In Suffolk. *Fr.* The Ancient Mansion. Crabbe.
Peter Grimes at Aldeburgh. *Fr.* The Borough. Crabbe.
Suffolk. *Fr.* By the North Sea. Swinburne.
Suffolk Shore, The. *Fr.* The Borough. Crabbe.
Where Dunwich Used to Be. *Fr.* By the North Sea. Swinburne.
Suffrage. *See* **Voting and Voters; Woman Suffrage.**
Sugar
Little Brother's Secret. Mansfield.
Suibhne, King
Sweetness of Nature, The. *Unknown.*

Suicide
Abandoned, The. Symons.
Advice of an Efficiency Expert, The. "Young."
After the Surprising Conversions. Lowell.
Along the River. Enright.
Autumn. Shapcott.
Ballade of Suicide, A. Chesterton.
Bridge of Sighs, The. Hood.
Butcher Boy, The. *Unknown.*
Call It a Good Marriage. Graves.
Caroline of Edinboro' Town. *Unknown.*
Center of Attention, The. Hoffman.
Colloquy with Gregory on the Balcony, A. Moss.
Despairing Lover, The. Walsh.
Dispute over Suicide, A. *Unknown.*
Faithless Nelly Gray. Hood.
at Sonezaki. Chikamatsu Monzaemon.
Felo De Se. Blackburn.
Fish Food. Wheelwright.
For Black Poets Who Think of Suicide. Knight.
Good Creatures, Do You Love Your Lives. Housman.
Hart Crane. Symons.
Hemingway House in Key West, The. Schultz.
I Am Going to Sleep (Suicide Poem). Storni.
Immigration Act of 1924, The. Mar.
Japanese Girl with Red Table. Dobyns.
Justice Is Reason Enough. Wakoski.
Lady Lazarus. Plath.
Leap, The. Dickey.
Letters Found near a Suicide. Horne.
Lovers, The. Murray.
Mill, The. Robinson.
Newcomer's Wife, The. Hardy.
Notes Found near a Suicide. Horne.
Of Late. Starbuck.
Of One Self-slain. Towne.
On a Friend's Suicide. Yots.
On the Suicide of a Friend. Whittemore.
On the Threshold. *Unknown.*
Paragraph, A. Carruth.
Passages. Walker.
Poem for a Suicide. Economou.
Poem on the Suicide of My Teacher. Stroud.
Poor Shammes of Berditchev, The. Ratner.
Portrait of One Dead. *Fr.* The House of Dust. Aiken.
Portrait, The. Kunitz.
Résumé. Parker.
Richard Cory. Robinson.
Rooftop. Barnstone.
Rope and Drum. Currie.
Sentiment. Chatterton.
Shooting, The. Tohe.
Shot? So Quick, So Clean an Ending? *Fr.* A Shropshire Lad. Housman.
Six Feet Under. Hale.
Song for a Suicide. Hughes.
Sportsman, The. McCord.
Springboard, The. MacNeice.
Stringer, The. Brasfield.
Suicid/ing(ed) Indian Women. Allen.
Suicide. *Fr.* In Hospital. Henley.
Suicide. MacNeice.
Suicide, The. Oates.
Suicide. Walker.
Suicide in the Trenches. Sassoon.
Suicide in Trenches. Sassoon.
Suicide off Egg Rock. Plath.
Suicide's Note. Hughes.
Suicides of the Rich, The. Contoski.
That Summer. Hemschemeyer.
To be, or not to be: that is the question. *Fr.* Hamlet. Shakespeare.
To D——, Dead by Her Own Hand. Nemerov.
To Friends Who Have Also Considered Suicide. Webb.
To Helen in a Huff. Willis.
Tragedy, A. Marzials.
Two Views of a Cadaver Room. Plath.
Walking on Water. Petaccia.
Wanting to Die. Sexton.
What He Saw. Currie.
Woman Hanging from the 13th Floor Window, The. Harjo.
Sullivan, John L.
John L. Sullivan Enters Heaven. Frost.
Sumac
Sumach Leaves, The. Very.
Summer
A B C's in Green. Speyer.
As imperceptibly as grief. Dickinson.
At a Summer Hotel. Gardner.
August. Thaxter.
Ballade Made in the Hot Weather. Henley.
Beginning, The. Stevens.
Boy's Summer Song, A. Dunbar.
Canticle. Griffith.
Comfort of the Fields. Lampman.
Country Summer. Adams.
Credences of Summer. Stevens.
Cuckoo Song, The. *Unknown.*
Cure All, The. Lee.
Ear Is Not Deaf. Dayton.
End of Summer, The. Millay.
End of Summer. Kunitz.
End-of-Summer Poem. Bennett.
Exeunt. Wilbur.
Fair Summer Droops. *Fr.* Summer's Last Will and Testament. Nashe.
Flowers of Middle Summer. *Fr.* The Winter's Tale. Shakespeare.
For Sue. Hey.
For Summer's Here. Barnett.
Ghetto Summer School. Worth.
Green lane now I traverse, where it goes, The. Clare.
Heat. Lampman.
Heaven Is Heaven. Rossetti.
High Summer on the Mountains. Davies.
Hymn to the Sun. Roberts.
I love at early morn, from new-mown swath. *Fr.* Summer Images. Clare.
In Fields of Summer. Kinnell.
In the Good Old Summertime. Shields.
In the Middle of August. Hirsch.
Knoxville, Tennessee. Giovanni.
Labor of Fields. Coatsworth.
Letters of Summer, The. Buckley.
Lines Written in the Dog-Days. Woty.
Loch Ossian. Scroggie.
Long Summer. Lee.
Love. Browning.
Manitou. Ikan.
Midsummer. Kinsella.
Midsummer. Scully.
Midsummer. Trowbridge.
Midsummer. Wilcox.
Midsummer Noon in the Australian Forest, A. Harpur.
Midsummer Pause. Lape.
Midsummer Song, A. Gilder.
Misericordia. Mead.
Month of the Thunder Moon, The. Doyle.
Mowers, The. Benton.
Musings. Barnes.
My Father Paints the Summer. Wilbur.
Night Enchantment. Muth.
Now Welcom, Somer. *Fr.* The Parlement of Foules. Chaucer.
Of the Day Estivall. Hume.
On a Wet Summer. Bampfylde.
Poem on the End of Sensation. Stange.
Qui Bien Aime a Tard Oublie. Chaucer.
Rainy Summer, The. Meynell.
Rainy Summer. Pitter.
Schoolboy, The. *Fr.* Songs of Experience. Blake.
Secret. Doolittle.
Shall I compare thee to a summer's day? *Fr.* Sonnets. Shakespeare.
Soote Season, The. Surrey.
Summer. Asch.
Summer. Manhire.
Summer. Rossetti.
Summer. Soto.
Summer. *Fr.* The Seasons. Thomson.
Summer. Wilson.
Summer Countries, The. Rago.
Summer Day, A. Hume.
Summer Days. Call.
Summer Days. Daniells.
Summer Days Are Come Again, The. Longfellow.
Summer Evening. De la Mare.
Summer Farm. MacCaig.
Summer Has Come. *Unknown.*
Summer Idyll. Barker.

Summer Images. Clare.
Summer in England, 1914. Meynell.
Summer Is Coming, The. Guinness.
Summer Magic. Hill.
Summer Malison, The. Hopkins.
Summer Matures. Johnson.
Summer Morning. Clare.
Summer Morning, A. Field.
Summer Music. Sarton.
Summer Noon at Sea, A. Sargent.
Summer Rain. Lee.
Summer Sabbath. Sampter.
Summer Song. Nesbit.
Summer Song. Watt.
Summer Stars. Sandburg.
Summer Storm. Montague.
Summer Twilight, A. Turner.
Summer Wind. Bryant.
Summer's Day, A. Hume.
"Summertime and the Living." Hayden.
Tansy for August. Enslin.
Tell All the World. Kemp.
That Summer. Treece.
That Was Summer. Ridlon.
There Were Some Summers. Lux.
These are the days when birds come back. Dickinson.
Thistledown. Reese.
Three Part Invention. Blackburn.
Throstle, The. Tennyson.
To Summer. Blake.
To Summer. Nadel.
Touring. Morton.
Vacation Song. Millay.
Waning Summer. *Fr.* Summer's Last Will and Testament. Nashe.
Wet Summer. Ward.
What Could Be Lovelier than to Hear. Coatsworth.
When Summer took in hand the winter to assail. Surrey.
When Summer's End is Nighing. Housman.
Why Are Our Summer Sports So Brittle? *Unknown.*
Winter Saint. Ammons.

Sumter, Fort, South Carolina
Battle of Mooris' Island, The. *Unknown.*
Fight at Sumter, The. *Unknown.*
On Fort Sumter. *Unknown.*
Sumter. Brownell.
Sumter. Stedman.
Sumter; a Ballad of 1861. *Unknown.*
Sumter's Band. Simmons.
Twilight on Sumter. Stoddard.

Sun
Cock-crowing. Vaughan.
Dream, or the Type of the Rising Sun, A. Adams.
Energy of Light, The. Hay.
Fair sun, if you would have me praise your light. *Fr.* Diana. Constable.
Follow Thy Fair Sun. Campion.
Forecast. Miles.
Give Me the Splendid Silent Sun. Whitman.
Glory, Glory to the Sun. Alford.
Guerdon of the Sun, The. Sterling.
Hint from Voiture. Shenstone.
Hymn of Apollo. Shelley.
Hymn to the Sun. Percy.
I'll tell you how the sun rose. Dickinson.
In Praise of the Sun. "A. W."
Indian Summer Day on the Prairie, An. Lindsay.
Light Is Sweet, The. *Fr.* Ecclesiastes. Bible, *O.T.*
Metric Figure. Williams.
Morning Light. Dudek.
Morning Sun. MacNeice.
Noon Glare. Brennan.
Nova. Jeffers.
November. Harvey.
November Sun. Daryush.
Ol' Hannah. *Unknown.*
On yonder hill there is a red deer. *Unknown.*
Phoebus, Arise. Drummond of Hawthornden.
Riddle #29: The Moon and the Sun. *Unknown.*
Shine Out, Fair Sun. *Unknown.*
Some say the sun is a golden earring. Belting.
Song: "I'd much rather sit there in the sun." Krauss.
Song: "Stay Phoebus, stay." Waller.
Sonnet: "Lamp of heaven's crystal hall that brings the hours." Drummond of Hawthornden.
Summer Sun. Stevenson.
Sun, The. Davis.
Sun. Dickey.
Sun, The. Drinkwater.
Sun, The. Sexton.
Sun, The. *Fr.* Ode to the Setting Sun. Thompson.
Sun, The. Turner.
Sun and Moon. Macpherson.
Sun God, The. De Vere.
Sun, his journey ending in the west, The. *Fr.* Diana. Constable.
Sun Rising, The. Donne.
Sun-Flower, The. Greenwell.
Sunlight. Bruchac.
Sunning. Tippett.
Sun's Perpendicular Rays, The. Mansel.
Sun's Travels, The. Stevenson.
There's Nothing Like the Sun. Thomas.
Thy Rising Is Beautiful. Akhnaton.
To the Sun. Bachmann.
To the Sun. Campbell.
To the Sun from a Flower. Gezelle.
True Account of Talking to the Sun at Fire Island, A. O'Hara.
Welcome to the Sun. *Fr.* The Aeneid. Virgil.
Yesterday I planted garlic. *Fr.* Jerusalem Sonnets. Baxter.

Sunburn
Some Sound Advice from Singapore. Ciardi.

Sunday
Ain't It a Shame. *Unknown.*
Aside. Dugan.
God Made a Trance. *Unknown.*
Morning After. Vinz.
O Day of Rest and Gladness. Wordsworth.
On a Sunday Afternoon. Sterling.
Poor Man's Sunday Walk, The. Mackay.
Sabbath. Burden.
Sabbaths, W. I. Walcott.
Sunday. Coatsworth.
Sunday. Herbert.
Sunday. Miles.
Sunday. Rungren.
Sunday. Rutsala.
Sunday Afternoon. Levine.
Sunday Evenings. Hollander.
Sunday Funnies. Keiter.
Sunday in South Carolina. Parham.
Sunday Morning. *Fr.* The Sabbath. Grahame.
Sunday Morning. Jenkins.
Sunday Morning. MacNeice.
Sunday Night Walk. Souster.
Sundays. Rugo.
When You Have Forgotten Sunday: The Love Story. Brooks.
Written on a Sunday Morning. Southey.
See also **Sabbath.**

Sundews
Sundew, The. Swinburne.

Sundials
Epigram: "I who by day am function of the light." Cunningham.
I am a sundial. Ordinary words. Belloc.
I am a sundial, turned the wrong way round. Belloc.
Motto for a Sundial. *Unknown.*
On a Sundial. Belloc.
On the Needle of a Sundial. Quarles.

Sunflowers
Ah! Sun-Flower. *Fr.* Songs of Experience. Blake.
Relics. Wagoner.
Sun-Flower, The. Greenwell.
Sunflower. Updike.
Sunflowers, The. Stewart.
Sunflowers. Scollard.
Wintered Sunflowers. Snyder.
Yesterday I planted garlic. *Fr.* Jerusalem Sonnets. Baxter.

Sunrise
Ant Sun, The. *Fr.* Herman Moon's Hourbook. Middleton.
Dark Stag, The. Crawford.
Design for a Stream-lined Sunrise. Madeleva.
Earliness at the Cape. Deutsch.
Fingernail Sunrise. Watkins.
Hymn to the Morning, An. Wheatley.
Hymn to the Sunrise. *Unknown.*
Idyl: Sunrise. Ray.

I'll tell you how the sun rose. Dickinson.
Invitation, to Jane, The. Shelley.
Kitchen Window. Ebberts.
Loch Leven. Smith.
Out of the Sea, Early. Swenson.
Pennsylvania Academy of Fine Arts. Kroll.
Plainview: 3. Momaday.
Reveille. *Fr.* A Shropshire Lad. Housman.
Sing a Song of Sunshine. Eastwick.
Song: "Morning opened/Like a rose." Justice.
Sun Rising, The. Donne.
Sunrise. Bennett.
Sunrise. Sangster.
Sunrise at Sea. Atherstone.
Sunrise at Sea. Sargent.
Sunrise at Sea. *Fr.* Tristram of Lyonesse: The Sailing of the Swallow. Swinburne.
Sunrise Call, The. Tewa.
Sunrise in Summer. Clare.
Sunrise on Mansfield Mountain. Brown.
Sunrise Trumpets. Auslander.
Sunset and Sunrise. Dickinson.
Watching the Sun Rise over Mount Zion. Whitman.

Sunset
Acceptance. Frost.
Afterglow. Borges.
Allie. Graves.
Another Sunset. Minczeski.
At Dieppe: After Sunset. Symons.
Cader Idris at Sunset. Turner.
Crickets sang, The. Dickinson.
Dark Hills, The. Robinson.
Datur Hora Quieti. Scott.
December Sunset. Holden.
Descend, Fair Sun! *Fr.* The Masque of the Middle Temple and Lincoln's Inn. Chapman.
Evening Sun, The. Brontë.
Evensong. Dufault.
Evensong. Moffett.
Flock at Evening, The. Shepard.
Great Breath, The. "Æ."
Hesperos, you bring home all the bright dawn disperses. Sappho.
Idyl: Sunset. Ray.
I'll tell you how the sun rose. Dickinson.
Mediterranean. Whitman.
Mise en Scène. Fitzgerald.
Narrows, The. Bruchac.
Ode to the Setting Sun. Thompson.
Of the Going Down of the Sun. Bunyan.
On Its Way. Swenson.
Paris: This April Sunset Completely Utters. Cummings.
Setting Sun, The. Horton.
So Be My Passing. Henley.
Sun Set. Aridjis.
Sun Upon the Weirdlaw Hill, The. Scott.
Sundown. Adams.
Sunset. Bayldon.
Sunset. Bialik.
Sunset, The. Burgess.
Sunset, A. Loveman.
Sunset and Sunrise. Dickinson.
Sunset at Les Éboulements, A. Lampman.
Sunset over the Aegean. *Fr.* The Corsair. Byron.
Sunset Song. Tewa.
Sunset Wings. Rossetti.
Sunsets. Sandburg.
'Twas at that hour of beauty when the setting sun. *Fr.* The Testament of Beauty. Bridges.
You Will Know When You Get There. Curnow.

Superior, Lake
Great Lakes Suite, The. Reaney.
Lake Superior. Goodrich.

Supermarkets
Grace to Be Said at the Supermarket. Nemerov.
Picketing Supermarkets. Wayman.
Supermarket. Holman.
Supermarket in California, A. Ginsberg.
Whistling Willie. Starbird.

Supernatural
Ballad of Douglas Bridge. Carlin.
Ballad of Hell, A. Davidson.
Cold blows the blast the night's obscure. *Fr.* The Maid of the Moor; or, the Water-Fiends. Colman.
Conqueror Worm, The. *Fr.* Ligeia. Poe.
Cremation of Sam McGee, The. Service.
Dream of Aengus Og, The. Cox.
Green Candles. Wolfe.
In No Strange Land. Thompson.
Kilmeny. *Fr.* The Queen's Wake. Hogg.
King o' Spain's Daughter, The. Foster.
Kingdom of God, The. Thompson.
La Belle Dame sans Merci. Keats.
Low Barometer. Bridges.
Pied Piper of Hamelin, The. Browning.
Raven, The. Poe.
Shadows in the Water. Traherne.
Skeleton in Armor, The. Longfellow.
Strange Tree. Roberts.
Ulalume. Poe.
We Still Must Follow. Mayo.
Shrieks at Midnight; Macabre Poems, Eerie and Humorous (ShM). Sara Brewton *and* John E. Brewton, eds.
Why Am I Grown So Cold? Poems of the Unknowable (WSC). Myra Cohn Livingston, ed.

Superstition
Chorus Quintus: Tartarorum. *Fr.* Mustapha. Greville.
Evil Eye, The. Ciardi.
Mountainy Childer, The. Shane.
Ode on the Popular Superstitions of the Highlands of Scotland. Collins.
See a pin and pick it up. *Unknown.*
Superstition. Karibo.

Supper
Animal Crackers. Morley.
Early Supper. Howes.
Eunice in the Evening. Brooks.
Setting the Table. Aldis.

Surfing and Surfers
From the Wave. Gunn.
Surfer, The. Wright.
Surfers at Santa Cruz. Goodman.

Surgery
Before. Henley.
Correct Compassion, A. Kirkup.
Debridement: Operation Harvest Moon: *On Repose.* Harper.
Hard Rock Returns to Prison from the Hospital for the Criminal Insane. Knight.
In the Operating Room. Nowlan.
Surgery. Burbank.
Surgical Ward: Men. Graves.
Tonsilectomy. Rivers.
Under the Catalpa Trees. Young.
See also **Medicine; Physicians.**

Surrealism
Against Surrealism. Wright.
Salvador Dali. Gascoyne.
English and American Surrealist Poetry (EAS). Edward B. Germain, ed.

Surrey, England
Pot Pourri from a Surrey Garden. Betjeman.

Surrey, Henry Howard, Earl of
Earl of Surrey to Geraldine, The. *Fr.* England's Heroical Epistles. Drayton.

Survival
Horses, The. Muir.
Staying Alive. Wagoner.

Susanna
Peter Quince at the Clavier. Stevens.
Susanna and the Elders. Crapsey.
Susanna and the Elders. Gilbert.
Susannah and the Elders. *Unknown.*

Sussex, England
Flood, The. Young.
Green Sussex. *Fr.* Prologue to General Hamley. Tennyson.
Puck's Song. *Fr.* Puck of Pook's Hill. Kipling.
South Country, The. Belloc.
West Sussex Drinking Song. Belloc.
See also **Cinque Parts.**

Sutter, John
John Sutter. Winters.

Swallows
Blue Swallows, The. Nemerov.
Children's Song, The. *Unknown.*
Chimney Swallows. Powers.
First Swallow, The. Smith.

Fly away, fly away over the sea. *Fr.* Sing-Song. Rossetti.
In the Cathedral Close. Dowden.
Itylus. Swinburne.
O Master Masons. Toller.
O My Swallows! Toller.
On Shooting a Swallow in Early Youth. Turner.
Sand Martin, The. Clare.
Swallow, The. Coleridge.
Swallow, The. Cowley.
Swallow Song. Pickthall.
Swallow Tails. Robinson.
Swallows, The. Dickinson.
Swallows. Ferril.
Swallow's Flight, The. Levy.
Swallows over the Camp. Krige.
To a Swallow. Bishop.
To a Swallow Building under Our Eaves. Carlyle.
To the Swallow. Cowper.
Upon the Swallow. Bunyan.

Swamps
Alligator, The. Ravenel.
Poets Agree to Be Quiet by the Swamp. Wagoner.
Walking in a Swamp. Wagoner.

Swan Lake (ballet)
Swan, The. Spender.

Swans
Bereaved Swan, The. Smith.
Black Swan, The. Jarrell.
Clothes make no sound when I tread ground. *Unknown.*
Dark World, A. Scovell.
Dying Swan, The. Tennyson.
Dying Swan, The. *Unknown.*
His Swans. Grigson.
Love the Wild Swan. Jeffers.
No Swan so Fine. Moore.
Prospect of Swans, A. Donnelly.
Riddle: Mute Swan. *Unknown.*
Silver Swan, The. *Unknown.*
Sitting Pretty. Fishback.
Swan, The. Baudelaire.
Swan, The. Gosse.
Swan. Lowbury.
Swan, The. Mallarmé.
Swan, The. Rodgers.
Swan, The. *Unknown.*
Swan and Shadow. Hollander.
Swan and the Goose, The. Aesop.
Swan Bathing, The. Pitter.
Swan, The—Vain Pleasures. Horton.
Swans. Durrell.
Swans, The. Dyment.
Swans, The. Sitwell.
Swans. Speyer.
Swans. *Fr.* An Evening Walk. Wordsworth.
Swan's Feet, The. Scovell.
To the Liffey with the Swans. Gogarty.
Wild Swan. *Fr.* Riddles (Exeter Book). *Unknown.*
Wild Swans. Millay.
Wild Swans at Coole, The. Yeats.
Within the night, above the dark. *Fr.* Swans at Night. Gilmore.

Sweden
Autobiography. Akesson.
Carriage from Sweden, A. Moore.
Evening Walk. Akesson.
Portraits, The. Lenngren.

Sweet Peas
Sweet Peas. Keats.

Swift, Jonathan
Hypocrite Swift. Bogan.
Lines on Swift's Ancestors. Pope.
New Simile in the Manner of Swift, A. Goldsmith.
On Seeing Swift in Laracor. MacNamara.
Sermon on Swift, A. Clarke.
Swift. Schwartz.
Swift's Epitaph. Yeats.
Tryst in Brobdingnag, A. Rich.
Verses on the Death of Dr. Swift, D. S. P. D., Occasioned by Reading a Maxim in Rochefoucauld. Swift.
With a Copy of Swift's Works. *Fr.* Epigrams. Cunningham.

Swimming and Swimmers
Above These Cares. Millay.
Ballade of Boys Bathing. Rolfe.
Bathers. Tiller.
Bathing Song. Ridler.
Diver, The. Herbin.
First Lesson. Booth.
For a Man Who Learned to Swim When He Was Sixty. Wakoski.
I saw him beat the surges under him. *Fr.* The Tempest. Shakespeare.
Idea of a Swimmer. Bloch.
Lakeshore. Scott.
Lament for the Non-Swimmers. Wagoner.
Lesson, The. Krows.
Let Go: Once. Fleming.
Morning Swim. Kumin.
Old Swimmer, The. Morley.
Our Silly Little Sister. Aldis.
Swimmer. Francis.
Swimmer in the Rain. Wallace.
Swimmer of Nemi, The. "Macleod."
Swimmer's Moment, The. Avison.
Swimming. Scollard.
Swimming By Night. Merrill.
Swimming Chenango Lake. Tomlinson.
Under the Boathouse. Bottoms.
Upon Boys Diverting Themselves in the River. Foxton.
Written after Swimming from Sestos to Abydos. Byron.
400-Meter Freestyle. Kumin.
See also **Surfing and Surfers.**

Swinburne, Algernon Charles
After Swinburne. Chesterton.
If. Collins.
Singer Asleep, A. Hardy.

Swings
At the Playground. Stafford.
Backyard Swing. Hale.
Swing, The. Stevenson.
Swing Song, A. Allingham.
Walnut Tree, The. McCord.

Swiss League
Patriot's Pass-Word, The. Montgomery.

Swithin, Saint
St. Swithin. Henderson.

Switzerland
Arnold von Winkelried. Montgomery.
On the Late Massacre in Piemont. Milton.
Thought of a Briton on the Subjugation of Switzerland. Wordsworth.
View by Color Photography on a Commercial Calendar. Williams.

Swords
End of Clonmacnois, The. *Unknown.*

Sydney, Australia
Telling the Cousins. Murray.
Visit of Hope to Sydney Cove, near Botany-Bay. Darwin.

Symbols
Symbols. Roskolenko.
See also **Metaphor; Similes.**

Synagogues
Cry for a Disused Synagogue in Booysens. Hirsch.

Synge, John Millington
In Memory of Major Robert Gregory. Yeats.
Memory, A. Strong.
Municipal Gallery Revisited, The. Yeats.
Synge's Grave. Letts.

Syphilis
Pangloss's Song: A Comic-Opera Lyric. Wilbur.
See also **Veneral Disease.**

Syrinx. *See* **Pan.**

T

Tabor, Elizabeth McCourt
Mistress of the Matchless Mine. Robertson.

Tabor, Horace Austin Warner
Ballad of Chicken Bill, The. Vaughn.

Tabor Grand Opera House, Denver, Colorado
Curtain, The. Gower.

Tagus River, Spain and Portugal
Tagus, Farewell. Wyatt.

Tahiti
Tiara Tahiti. Brooke.
Vor a Gauguin Picture zu Singen. Stein.

Tailors
Amends to the Tailors and Soutars. Dunbar.
Tailor, The. Ansky.
Tailor. Farjeon.
Tailor, The. Leftwich.
Taliesin
Taliesin, *sel.* Hovey
Taliessin's Song of the Unicorn. Williams.
Talk
Controlling the Tongue. Chaucer.
Talk. Stalker.
See also **Speech.**
Talmud, The
Horn, Mouth, Pit, Fire. Dickey.
Pilpul. Kamenetz.
Talmud, The. Frug.
Talmud Student, The. Bialik.
Tamerlane
Tamburlaine the Great, *sels.* Marlowe.
Tamerlane. Poe.
Tammuz
Death of Tammuz, The. Tchernichowsky.
Tammuz. Alterman.
Thammuz. Moody.
Tanagers
Scarlet Tanager, The. Benton.
Scarlet Tanager, The. Mason.
Tanks (vehicle)
"Brighters." Sassoon.
Tannhäuser
Laus Veneris. Swinburne.
Tannhauser. Levy.
Taos, New Mexico
House in Taos, A. Hughes.
Tapestries
Aunt Jennifer's Tiger. Rich.
Beyond the Tapestries. Farber.
Offering of the Heart: Tapestry from Arras, XV Century, The. Humphries.
On a Piece of Tapestry. Santayana.
Tapestry, The. Nemerov.
Tapestry. Simic.
Unicorn and the Lady, The. Garrigue.
Tara, Ireland
Harp That Once through Tara's Halls, The. Moore.
St. Patrick's Hymn Before Tara. Mangan.
Tara Is Grass. *Unknown.*
Tarantulas
Discoveries in Arizona. Wright.
Tasmania
Van Dieman's Land. *Unknown.*
Taste
Alarmed Skipper, The. Fields.
Tate, Allen
Elegy for a Dead Confederate. McGovern.
Tattoos
Pornography, Nebraska. McPherson.
Taverns
At the Cantina. Soto.
Closing Time. Wagoner.
General Elliott, The. Graves.
Glass of Beer, A. Stephens.
Lady of the Ferry Inn. Mechain.
Lines on the Mermaid Tavern. Keats.
Old Wife in High Spirits. "MacDiarmid."
Railroad to Hell. *Unknown.*
Rank. Kirstein.
Singles. Waters.
Will Waterproof's Lyrical Monologue. Tennyson.
8-Ball at the Twilite. Baker.
Taxes
Ballad on the Taxes, A. Ward.
Caged Rats. Elliott.
Inventory, in Answer to the Usual Mandate Sent by a Surveyor of the Taxes, Requiring a Return of the Number of Horses, Servants, Carriages, etc., Kept, The. Burns.
New Song on the Birth of the Prince of Wales, A. *Unknown.*
New Song on the Taxes, The. *Unknown.*
On M. Pitt's Hair-Powder Tax. Burns.
Peace, The. *Fr.* Advice to Julia. Luttrell.
Tax Return. *Unknown.*
Taxes. Lee.
Taxidermy
At the Smithsonian. Haley.
From a Printed Bill, Fixed in the Beak of One in a Group of Five Stuffed Owls in the Shop Window of a Bird Stuffer, at Richmond, Yorkshire. *Unknown.*
In the Taxidermist's Shop. Cedering.
Owl Critic, The. Fields.
Taxis
After Anacreon. *Fr.* Taxi Suite. Welch.
Taxis. Field.
Taxis, The. MacNeice.
Taylor, Bayard
Bayard Taylor. Whittier.
Tayside, Scotland
Rannoch Moor. MacGregor.
Tea
How to Get On in Society. Betjeman.
Poets at Tea, The. Pain.
Pot of Tea. Griffin.
Sassafras Tea. Newsome.
Tea. Embry.
Twinings Orange Pekoe. Moffett.
See also **Teahouses.**
Teaching and Teachers
Academic Moon. Bevington.
America Was Schoolmasters. Coffin.
April Inventory. Snodgrass.
As dusk comes on, I almost hope to meet. *Fr.* A Letter to Charles Townsend Copeland: Le Baron Russell Briggs. Hillyer.
Assignment: Descriptive Essay. Willis.
Campus on the Hill, The. Snodgrass.
Correspondence School Instructor Says Goodbye to His Poetry Students, The. Kinnell.
Creature in the Classroom, The. Prelutsky.
Dear Mrs. McKinney of the Sixth Grade. Kherdian.
Education. Lee.
Emeritus, n. Coulette.
Emily Sparks. *Fr.* Spoon River Anthology. Masters.
Examiner. Scott.
Expecting. Langton.
Eyes of Cantonese Schoolmasters Remembered in Hong Kong, The. Barnstone.
First Day of Teaching. Overstreet.
Flower for a Professor's Garden of Verses. Edman.
Flycatchers. Bridges.
For an Early Retirement. Hall.
Freshmen. Spacks.
Golden Gate: The Teacher. Mastrolia.
Golgotha. Kennedy.
Grouchy Good Night to the Academic Year, A. Pauker.
History of Education. McCord.
Humanities Course. Updike.
I Went to See Irving Babbitt. Eberhart.
Irish Schoolmaster, The. Hood.
James McCosh. Bridges.
Jolly Old Pedagogue, The. Arnold.
Last Word, A. Sarton.
Late Tutorial. Buckley.
Learning. Simpson.
Letter to a Substitute Teacher. Gildner.
Mark Van Doren. Worley.
Miss Ada. Fahy.
Miss Norma Jean Pugh. O'Neill.
Mr. Brunt. Siegel.
No teacher I of boys or smaller fry. Ramsay.
Off to Patagonia. Weiss.
Old Brown Schoolhouse, The. *Unknown.*
Pedagogical Principles. Amoss.
Pedagogue Arraigned. Wain.
Philosophic Pill, The. Gilbert.
Poor Scholar of the 'Forties, A. Colum.
Prayer of a Beginning Teacher. Dunnam.
Prayer of a Teacher. Littlewort.
Professor's Song, A. Berryman.
Purist, The. Nash.
Reuben Pantier. *Fr.* Spoon River Anthology. Masters.
Schoolmaster, The. *Unknown.*
Schoolmaster Abroad with His Son, The. Calverley.
Schoolmaster, give your simple mob a break. *Fr.* Epigrams. Martial.
Schoolmistress, The. Shenstone.
Shapes, Vanishings. Taylor.
Short History of the Teaching Profession, A. Sister Maura.

Small Town. Joyce.
So it was./ I broke the copious curls upon my head. *Fr.* Aurora Leigh. Browning.
Teacher, The. Bevington.
Teacher. Dorman.
Teacher, The. Hill.
Teacher, A. Whittemore.
Teacher's Dream, The. Venable.
Teacher's Prayer, A. Havergal.
Teaching Swift to Young Ladies. Dickey.
To Dr. Swift on His Birthday, 30th November 1721. Johnson.
Turn on the Footlights: The Perils of Pedagogy. Carter.
Upon Fone a School-Master, Epigram. Herrick.
Village Schoolmaster, The. *Fr.* The Deserted Village. Goldsmith.
What Schoolmasters Say. Seymour-Smith.
"When the Students Resisted, a Minor Clash Ensued." Knight.
Gladly Learn and Gladly Teach; Poems of the School Experience (GLGT). Helen Plotz, comp.
See also **Scholars and Scholarship.**

Teahouses
White Conduit House. Woty.
See also **Tea.**

Teamsters
How the Fire Queen Crossed the Swamp. Ogilvie.
See also **Trucks and Truckers.**

Tears
Absolutely Ordinary Rainbow, An. Murray.
And She Washed His Feet with Her Teares, and Wiped Them with the Hairs of Her Head. Sherburne.
Birthday in the Hospital, A. Jennings.
By this he knew she wept with waking eyes. *Fr.* Modern Love. Meredith.
Faery Song. Keats.
Flow Not So Fast. *Unknown.*
Flow, O My Tears! *Unknown.*
Hours of Idleness. Byron.
Hymne, An: "Drop, drop, slow tears." Fletcher.
I Saw My Lady Weep. *Unknown.*
I Weep. Grimké.
In Grandfather's Glasses. Peters.
Lines on the Execution of King Charles the First. Graham, Marquess of Montrose.
Lucasta Weeping. Lovelace.
Man in the Onion Bed, The. Ciardi.
Maxim Revised, A. *Unknown.*
On a Tear. Rogers.
Peeling Onions. Rich.
Rain. Lindsay.
Rosary of My Tears, The. Ryan.
Slow, Slow, Fresh Fount. *Fr.* Cynthia's Revels. Jonson.
Tear, The. Crashaw.
Tears. Browning.
Tears. *Fr.* Glenaveril. Lytton.
Tears. Reese.
Tears. Sitwell.
Tears, Flow No More. Herbert of Cherbury.
Tears, Idle Tears. *Fr.* The Princess. Tennyson.
To Primroses Fill'd with Morning-Dew. Herrick.
Twicknam Garden. Donne.
Valediction, A: Of Weeping. Donne.
Wasted Sympathy, A. Howells.
Weep You No More. *Unknown.*
Weeper, The. Crashaw.
When Lovely Woman. Cary.
When Phoebe form'd a wanton smile. Collins.

Technology
Old Whim Horse, The. Dyson.
The Steam Engine; or, The Power of Flame, *sels.* Baker.
Telephone Poles. Updike.

Tecumseh
Fall of Tecumseh, The. *Unknown.*
Tecumseh, *sels.* Mair.

Teeth
Dentologia; a Poem on the Diseases of the Teeth and Their Proper Remedies, *sels.* Brown.
First Holes Are Fresh. Shipley.
First Tooth, The. C. *and* M. Lamb.
First Tooth, The. Rands.
Good Riddance to Bad Rubbish O at Last. Goodman.
My Teeth. Ochester.
Palace for Teeth, The. Luttinger.
Poet's Farewell to His Teeth, The. Dickey.
Root Canal, The. Piercy.
Teeth. Holub.
Thirty white horses upon a red hill. Mother Goose.
To have it out or not? that is the question. "C. A. W."
To Women, to Hide Their Teeth, if They Be Rotten or Rusty. Herrick.
Twenty white horses on a red hill. *Unknown.*
See also **Dentistry and Dentists; Dentures; Smiles; Toothaches.**

Telegrams
Telegram. Wise.

Telegraph
Electric Telegraph, The. *Fr.* The Steam Engine; or, The Power of Flame. Baker.
On the Completion of the Pacific Telegraph. Very.
To a Vine-clad Telegraph Pole. Untermeyer.

Telemachus
Odysseus to Telemachus. Brodsky.

Telephones
Business Life, The. Ignatow.
Central. Kooser.
Commanding a Telephone to Ring. Anderson.
Dial Tone, The. Nemerov.
Dial Tone. Pollak.
Eletelephony. Richards.
Hello! My Baby. Howard *and* Emerson.
Hot Line. Dunann.
I Am a Victim of Telephone. Ginsberg.
Long Distance. Stafford.
Obscene Caller, The. Fein.
Obscene Phone Call #2. Harjo.
On Seeing a Torn Out Coin Telephone. Robbins.
Simultaneously. Ignatow.
Telephone, The. Field.
Telephone. Shectman.
Telephone Ghosts. Frazier.
Telephone Operator, The. Francis.
Telephone Poles. Updike.
Telephoning It. Edmond.
Your little voice. Cummings.
Your Phone Call at Eight A.M. Harjo.

Television
Addict. Montgomery.
Christmas Myth, 1973. McGovern.
Day the T.V. Broke, The. Jonas.
Death. Byatt.
Electric Cop, The. Cruz.
Jabber-Whacky. Di Caprio.
Jimmy Jet and His TV Set. Silverstein.
Metaphysical Shock while Watching a TV Cartoon. Rice.
Mixed Media. Schevill.
Mousemeal. Nemerov.
Not-so-good Earth, The. Dawe.
Old Lady Watching TV, An. Skinner.
Poem for David Janssen. Smith.
Robin Hood. *Fr.* Speaking of Television. McGinley.
Soaps. Witt.
Tee-Vee Enigma. Raskin.
Teevee. Merriam.
To a Man in a Picture Window Watching Television. Weston.
Watching Television. Bly.
Way of Life, A. Nemerov.
When Daddy Died. Ackerson.
Winning of the TV West, The. Alexander.

Tell, William
Archer, The. Scollard.
Archery. De la Mare.

Temeraire (ship)
Temeraire, The. Melville.

Temperance
Away with Rum. *Unknown.*
Have Courage, My Boy, to Say No! Hilton.
John Barley-Corn, My Foe. Adams.
Temperance Song. *Unknown.*
Temperance. *Unknown.*
We Live in a Rickety House. McLachlan.

Temple, Shirley
Shirley Temple. Michael.

Temptation
All Things Can Tempt Me. Yeats.
Dialogue between the Resolved Soul, and Created Pleasure, A. Marvell.
Quip, The. Herbert.

Ten Commandments
Addendum to the Ten Commandments. *Unknown.*
Covet. Bierce.

Latest Decalogue, The. Clough.
Ten Commandments, The. *Unknown.*
Tennessee
Black Bottom Bootlegger, The. Leiper.
Example of a How a Daily Temporary Madness Can Help a Man Get the Job Done, An. Stone.
Father in Tennessee, A. Simmons.
Hills of Sewanee, The. McClellan.
Knoxville, Tennessee. Giovanni.
October in Tennessee. Malone.
Shiloh; a Requiem. Melville.
Snake-Handling Religious Service. *Fr.* Tatoos. Wright.
Stopped in Memphis. Bauer.
Street Scene—1946. Porter.
Tenantry. Scarbrough.
Tennessee. Brooks.
Tennessee Crickets. Outlaw.
Wake, The. Prunty.
Tennessee Valley Authority
Norris Dam. Rodman.
T. V. A., The. *Unknown.*
Tennis
40——Love. McGough.
Lawn-Tennisonian Idyll, A. *Unknown.*
Near the Base Line. Albert.
Old Pro's Lament, The. Petrie.
Old Tennis Player. Brooks.
Prothalamion. Kumin.
Snapshot for Miss Bricka Who Lost in the Semi-final Round of the Pennsylvania Lawn Tennis Tournament at Haverford, July, 1960, A. Wallace.
Tennyson, Alfred Tennyson, 1st Baron
After Lord Tennyson. Chesterton.
Alfred Lord Tennyson. Whittemore.
Footnote to Tennyson. Bullett.
Lacrimae Musarum. Watson.
Tennyson. Aldrich.
Tennyson. Coates.
Tennyson. Huxley.
Tennyson. Van Dyke.
To Alfred Tennyson. Landor.
Tenors
Schmaltztenor. Branch.
Tents
Benediction for the Tent. Mongol.
Silken Tent, The. Frost.
Thinking of Tents. Whittemore.
Teresa, Saint. *See* **Theresa, Saint.**
Termites
Termite, The. Nash.
Termites. Bell.
Termites. Chock.
Terns
Arctic Tern in a Museum. Newsome.
Gracious Goodness. Piercy.
Seals, Terns, Time. Eberhart.
Terrorism and Terrorists
Disillusionment. Alegria.
Mr. Gunman. Garbutt.
Princess Casamassima, The. Hoffman.
18 West 11th Street. Merrill.
Tesla, Nikola
In Tesla's Laboratory. Johnson.
Texas
Ain't No More Cane on This Brazos. *Unknown.*
At the Airport in Dallas. Mooney
Barbara's Land Revisited—August 1978. Hobson.
Cattle. Nance.
Crêpes Flambeau. Gallagher.
Crossing West Texas. Robertson.
Defeat. Bynner.
Down in Dallas. Kennedy.
Driving North from Kingsville, Texas. Shihab.
Eyes of Texas, The. *Unknown.*
Hell in Texas. *Unknown.*
Homage to Texas. Graves.
Hunting with My Father. Absher.
In Blanco County. Fowler.
Jefferson, Texas. Shihab.
Lament for the Alamo. Guiterman.
Lasca. Desprez.
My Father & the Figtree. Shibab.
People Who Went By in Winter. Stafford.
Tantalus—Texas. Miller.
Texas. Daugherty.
Texas. Lowell.
Texas Ranger, The. Boswell.
Texas Rangers, The. *Unknown.*
Texas Trains and Trails. Austin.
Texas Types—"The Bad Man." Chittenden.
Tornado Watch. Shuttleworth.
Wes Hardin: From a Photograph. Carver.
West Texas. *At. to* Austin.
Yellow Rose of Texas, The. *Unknown.*
Texas Revolution
Defence of the Alamo, The. Miller.
Fight at San Jacinto, The. Palmer.
Valor of Ben Milam, The. Scollard.
See also **Alamo.**
Thackeray, William Makepeace
Adsum. Stoddard.
1864. Howard.
Thames (river), England
Alley, The; an Imitation of Spenser. Pope.
Bab-Lock-Hythe. Binyon.
His Tears to Thamasis. Herrick.
Lines Written near Richmond, upon the Thames, at Evening. Wordsworth.
Lover to the Thames of London, to Favour His Lady Passing Thereon, The. Turberville.
Old Summerhouse, The. De la Mare.
Rivers. Storer.
Rivers Come to the Hall of Proteus for the Marriage of the Thames and the Medway, The. *Fr.* The Faerie Queene. Spenser.
Song of the River Thames, A. *Fr.* Albion & Albanius. Dryden.
Thames from Cooper's Hill, The. *Fr.* Cooper's Hill. Denham.
Thanksgiving
Another Grace for a Child. Herrick.
Are We Thankful? *Unknown.*
Be Thankful. Bullock.
Be Thankful unto Him. Psalms. Bible, *O.T.*
Blessings That Remain, The. Flint.
Child's Grace, A. Burns.
Father in Heaven. *At. to* Emerson.
First Thanksgiving of All. Turner.
For all the wonders of this wondrous world. *Fr.* A Te Deum of the Commonplace. Oxenham.
For all Thy ministries. *Fr.* A Little Te Deum of the Commonplace. Oxenham.
For Beauty, We Thank Thee. Oxenham.
For Everything Give Thanks. Tupper.
For maiden sweetness, and for strength of men. *Fr.* A Little Te Deum of the Commonplace. Oxenham.
For the gladness here where the sun is shining at evening. *Fr.* Our Prayers of Thanks. Sandburg.
For the rosebud's break of beauty. *Fr.* A Thanksgiving. Larcom.
Give Thanks. Tupper.
Giving Thanks. *Fr.* Psalms. Bible, *O. T.*
God, You Have Been Too Good to Me. Stork.
Grace. Emerson.
Grace, A. Tiplady.
Grace at Evening. Guest.
Grace at Evening. Poteat.
Grace for a Child. Herrick.
Gratitude. McGee.
Harvest Home. Alford.
Hymn: "For Summer's bloom and Autumn's blight." *Fr.* Bitter-Sweet. Holland.
Hymn: "Lord, by whose breath all souls and seeds are living." Young.
Hymn of Gratitude. *Unknown.*
I Have a Roof. Jackson.
I Thank You God for Most This Amazing. Cummings.
If I Were a Pilgrim Child. Bennett.
In Every Thing Give Thanks. *Unknown.*
In Thankfull Remembrance for My Dear Husband's Safe Arrivall Sept. 3, 1662. Bradstreet.
Most Acceptable Gift, The. Claudius.
Not Alone for Mighty Empire. Merrill.
Oh come, let us sing unto Jehovah. *Fr.* Psalms. Bible, *O. T.*
One Thousandth Psalm, The. Hale.
Our Prayer. Herbert.
Poet's Grace, A. Burns.
Prayer, A: "Give me work to do." *Unknown.*
Prayer before Meat. Harsen.

Prayer for Thanksgiving, A. Auslander.
Prayer for the Great Family. Snyder.
Song of Thanksgiving. Moreland.
Thank God for Life. *Unknown.*
Thankful Heart. Davis.
Thankfulness. Procter.
Thanks Be to God. Alford.
Thanks for Everything. Tupper.
Thanks to God. Hultman.
Thanksgiving. Best.
Thanksgiving. Brotherton.
Thanksgiving. Coates.
Thanksgiving. Driscoll.
Thanksgiving. Eastwick.
Thanksgiving. Emerson.
Thanksgiving. Herrick.
Thanksgiving. Howells.
Thanksgiving. Ketchum.
Thanksgiving. Morgan.
Thanksgiving. Morris.
Thanksgiving, A. Newman.
Thanksgiving. Osborne.
Thanksgiving. Oxenham.
Thanksgiving. Sangster.
Thanksgiving. Simpson.
Thanksgiving for the Earth. Goudge.
Thanksgiving Magic. Bennett.
Thanksgiving to God, for His House, A. Herrick.
Things I Miss, The. Higginson.
Thy Name We Bless and Magnify. Power.
To the Spirit Great and Good. Hunt.
We Thank Thee. *Unknown.*
Who Maketh the Grass to Grow. *Fr.* Psalms. Bible, *O.T.*
Youth's Thankfulness. Kramer.

Thanksgiving Day
First Thanksgiving, The. Prelutsky.
First Thanksgiving, The. Turner.
Good Thanksgiving, A. Robinson.
Minnesota Thanksgiving. Berryman.
New-England Boy's Song about Thanksgiving Day, The. Child.
Once more the liberal year laughs out. *Fr.* For an Autumn Festival. Whittier.
Pumpkin, The. Whittier.
Thanksgiving Day. Bangs.
Thanksgiving Day. Child.
Thanksgiving in Boston Harbor, The. Butterworth.
Thanksgiving Magic. Bennett.
Thanksgiving Time. *Unknown.*
Thanksgiving Wishes. Guiterman.
Thanksliving. Piety.
Volunteer's Thanksgiving, The. Larcom.
We Thank Thee! Clark.

Thatcher, Margaret
Mrs Snatcher Thatcher. *Fr.* Jezebel: Her Progress. Hanscombe.

Theater and Theaters
Adam, Eve and the Big Apple. Watkins.
At the Comedy. Stringer.
At the Theater. Field.
At the Theater. Herbert.
Curtain! Dunbar.
Elegy in a Theatrical Warehouse. Fearing.
Epilogue at Wallack's, An. Wayland.
Grand Opening of the People's Theatre. Goldrick.
Identities. Young.
Ode (To Himself). Jonson.
Ode to the German Drama. "S."
Old Woman, outside the Abbey Theater, An. Strong.
On Writing for the Stage. Sheffield.
Open Air Performance of "As You Like It," An. Scovell.
Play-House, The. Addison.
Playhouse Key, The. Field.
Prologue Spoken at the Opening of the Theatre in Drury-Lane, 1747. Johnson.
Rehearsal, The. Gregory.
Saved. *Unknown.*

Thebes, Greece
Tiresias. Tennyson.

Theft. *See* **Crime and Criminals.**

Theocritus
For a Copy of Theocritus. Dobson.
Little Theocritus. Paradise.
Theocritus. Fields.
Theocritus. Wilde.
Written on a Fly-Leaf of Theocritus. Thompson.

Theology
Burning Bush, The. Nicholson.
Duns Scotus. Merton.
Grace for Theology. *Fr.* The Vision of Piers Plowman. Langland.
He preached upon "breadth" till it argued him narrow. Dickinson.
Here stood Hypocrisy, in sober brown. *Fr.* The Triumph of Infidelity. Dwight.
Man on the dubious waves of error toss'd. *Fr.* Truth. Cowper.
On Exodus 3:14: "I am that I am." Prior.
Presbyterian Church Government. *Fr.* Hudibras. Butler.
Presbyterian Knight and Independent Squire. *Fr.* Hudibras. Butler.
Respectable Burgher, The. Hardy.
Riddle, The. Brome.
Theologians. De la Mare.

Thera (island), Greece
Santorin. Flecker.

Theresa, Saint, of Avila
Apology for the Foregoing Hymn, An. Crashaw.
Conversation in Avila. McGinley.
Flaming Heart, The. Crashaw.
Hymn to the Name and Honour of the Admirable Saint Teresa, A. Crashaw.
Martyrdom of St. Teresa, The. Hope.
Mould of Castile. Clemo.
Theresa of Avila. Jennings.

Thermopylae, Battle of
Leonidas. Croly.
On the Spartan Dead at Thermopylae. Simonides.
Thermopylae. Thwaites.

Theseus
Labyrinth, The. Muir.
Theseus: A Trilogy. Winters.
Theseus and Ariadne. Graves.
See also **Minotaur.**

Thieves. *See* **Crime and Criminals.**

Third World
Underdeveloped Country, An. Enright.

Thirst
Green, Green Is El Aghir. Cameron.
Hunger and Thirst. Bishop.
Thirsty Poet, The. Philips.
See also Hunger.

Thirty Years War
Ode, upon Occasion of His Majesties Proclamation in the Yeare 1630, An. Fanshawe.

Thistles
Looking at a Dry Canadian Thistle Brought in from the Snow. Bly.
Roadside thistle, eager, The. Basho.
Thistledown. Monro.
Thistles. Hughes.

Thomas, Saint
Hymn of Saint Thomas in Adoration of the Blessed Sacrament, The. Crashaw.

Thomas, Dylan
Contempt for Dylan Thomas. Watson.
Cwmrhydyceirw Elegiacs. Watkins.
Elegy for Dylan Thomas. Sitwell.
True Picture Restored, A. Watkins.
When a Warlock Dies. Gardner.

Thomas, Edward
To Edward Thomas. Lewis.

Thomas, George Henry
Thomas at Chickamauga. Sherwood.

Thomas à Becket, Saint
Becket's Diadem. *Unknown.*
Murder of Saint Thomas of Kent, The. *Unknown.*

Thomas à Kempis
Thomas à Kempis. Bowker.
Thomas à Kempis. Reese.

Thomas Aquinas, Saint
Thomas in the Fields. Moyles.

Thomas the Rhymer (Thomas of Erceldoune)
Thomas the Rhymer. *Unknown.*

Thompson, Francis
On the Death of Francis Thompson. Noyes.
Quiet Singer, The. Towne.

Thomson, James (1700–1748)
Ode Occasioned by the Death of Mr. Thomson. Collins.

Thomson, Tom
Tom Thomson. Bourinot.

Thor
Labors of Thor, The. Wagoner.
Thoreau, Henry David
Alimentary. Fadiman.
Men of Sudbury, The. Baker.
On Visiting the Graves of Hawthorne and Thoreau. Very.
Tears in Spring. Channing.
Thoreau. Alcott.
Thoreau. Jones.
Thoreau's Flute. Alcott.
Thought
Climate of Thought, The. Graves.
Mind Is an Enchanting Thing, The. Moore.
Prayer for Recollection, A. *Unknown.*
Thoughts. Scott.
What Does a Man Think About. Holmes.
See also **Intellect; Reason.**
Thousand Islands, New York and Ontario
Thousand Islands, The. *Fr.* The St. Lawrence and the Saguenay. Sangster.
Three Henrys, War of the. *See* **War of the Three Henrys.**
Three Kings ***or*** **Three Wise Men.** *See* **Magi.**
Three Mile Island, Pennsylvania
Accident at Three Mile Island. Barnes.
Amish, The. Doreski.
Hershey Kiss. Renner-Tana.
Plumber Arrives at Three Mile Island, The. Stewart.
Thrift
The Pin. Taylor.
Thrushes
Blow Softly, Thrush. Taylor.
Brown Thrush, The. Larcom.
Come In. Frost.
Darkling Thrush, The. Hardy.
Joy-Month. Wasson.
Might these be thrushes climbing through almost. Cummings.
My Thrush. Collins.
Northern Water Thrush. Jones.
Overflow. Tabb.
Reminder, The. Hardy.
Throstle, The. Tennyson.
Thrush, The. Austin.
Thrush, The. Benét.
Thrush before Dawn, A. Meynell.
Thrushes. Hughes.
Thrush's Nest, The. Clare.
Thrush's song, The. *Unknown.*
Thunder
Giant Thunder. Reeves.
June Thunder. MacNeice.
Song of the Thunder. *Unknown.*
Thunder in the Garden. Morris.
Thunder over Earth. Colony.
Written in a Thunder Storm July 15th 1841. Clare.
Thyme
Thyme Flowering among Rocks. Wilbur.
Ticonderoga, Battle of (1775)
On the Defeat at Ticonderoga or Carilong. *Unknown.*
Surprise at Ticonderoga, The. Stansbury.
Ticonderoga. Wilson.
Tides
Between the Tides. Councilman.
Herring Weir, The. Roberts.
High Tide on the Coast of Lincolnshire (1571), The. Ingelow.
Low Tide on Grand Pré. Carman.
Quiet Tide near Ardrossan, The. Turner.
Sketch. Sandburg.
Tide, The. Longfellow.
Tide Rises, the Tide Falls, The. Longfellow.
Tide Turning. Nims.
Tide Will Win, The. Leonard.
Tides, The. Bryant.
Tides. Blackwell.
Tigers
Fearful Symmetry. Bunting.
Here She Is. Miller.
O have you caught the tiger? Housman.
There was a young lady of Niger. Monkhouse.
Tiger, The. Belloc.
Tiger, The. *Fr.* Songs of Experience. Blake.
Young Lady of Niger, The. *Unknown.*
Tightrope Walkers. *See* **Acrobats.**
Tightrope Walker. Scannell.
Till, Emmett
Emmett Till. Emanuel.
Last Quatrain of the Ballad of Emmett Till, The. Brooks.
Timber Line
At Timber Line. Mayer.
Timber Line Trees. Holme.
Time
Acceleration near the Point of Impact. Oates.
Alas, How Soon the Hours. Landor.
All That's Bright and Fair. Moore.
And What though Winter Will Pinch Severe. *Fr.* Old Mortality. Scott.
Another Year Come. Merwin.
Anyone Lived in a Pretty How Town. Cummings.
As I Walked out One Evening. Auden.
August. MacNeice.
Awake! for morning in the bowl of night. *Fr.* The Rubáiyát of Omar Khayyám of Naishápúr. Khayyám.
Ballad of Dead Ladies, The. Villon.
Birthday Verses Written in a Child's Album. Lowell.
Birthright. Drinkwater.
Burnt Norton. *Fr.* Four Quartets. Eliot.
Calmly We Walk through This April's Day. Schwartz.
Changes to Corinna, The. Herrick.
Chronology. Cassity.
Cities and Thrones and Powers. *Fr.* Puck of Pook's Hill. Kipling.
Clepsydra. Cotton.
Clock, The. Baudelaire.
Clock in the Square, A. Rich.
Continental Crossing. Thompson.
Counting the Beats. Graves.
Cow Time. Shannon.
Days. Emerson.
Dear Men and Women. Wheelock.
Devouring Time, blunt thou the lion's paws. *Fr.* Sonnets. Shakespeare.
Dialogue betwixt Time and a Pilgrim, A. Townshend.
Digging. Thomas.
During Wind and Rain. Hardy.
Each New Hour's Passage Is the Acolyte. *Fr.* The City of the Soul. Douglas.
Earthly Illusion. Leighton.
Epilogue: "Time is a thing." Spender.
Epitaph: "Even such is Time, which takes in trust." Ralegh.
Eternity's Speech against Time. *Fr.* Mustapha. Greville.
Even Such is Time. Ralegh.
Express Train. Kraus.
Father Father Son and Son. Swan.
Father Time. Ault.
Father William. "Carroll."
Fern Hill. Thomas.
Flying Change, The. Taylor.
For Rhoda. Schwartz.
Force That through the Green Fuse Drives the Flower, The. Thomas.
Four Preludes on Playthings of the Wind. Sandburg.
Four Quartz Crystal Clocks. Moore.
Gallop, Gallop to a Rhyme. Shannon.
Gone in the Wind. Mangan.
Growing Up. Behn.
Harvest to Seduce, A. Cane.
Her Reply. Ralegh.
His Golden Locks Time Hath to Silver Turned. *Fr.* Polyhymnia. Peele.
His Poetry His Pillar. Herrick.
Hour-Glass, The. Herrick.
How Many Seconds in a Minute? Rossetti.
How on Solemn Fields of Space. Daryush.
How Soon Hath Time. Milton.
How Time Consumeth All Earthly Things. *At. to* Proctor.
I Saw from the Beach. Moore.
If I Could Tell You. Auden.
In a Prominent Bar in Secaucus One Day. Kennedy.
In a Rose Garden. Bennett.
In Passing. Shepherd.
In the Fleeting Hand of Time. Corso.
In time the strong and stately turrets fall. *Fr.* Licia. Fletcher.
In Time. Graves.
Influence of Time on Grief. Bowles.
Island of Geological Time, The. Fargas.
Isle of the Long Ago, The. Taylor.
Lamentation of the Old Pensioner, The. Yeats.
Last Leaf, The. Holmes.
Leave Him Now Quiet. Stickney.

Leisure. Davies.
Let It Be Forgotten. Teasdale.
Life. Herbert.
Light Year, The. Ridland.
Like as the waves make towards the pebbled shore. *Fr.* Sonnets. Shakespeare.
Limited. Sandburg.
L'Imprevisibilite. Hippius.
Long Ago, The. Taylor.
Love and Life, A Song. Rochester.
Marjorie's Almanac. Aldrich.
Minute, The. Shapiro.
Moats, The. Yeats.
Moment Please, A. Allen.
Months, The. Rossetti.
Mount, The. Adams.
Mutability. Wordsworth.
Nature, That Washed Her Hands in Milk. Ralegh.
Noise That Time Makes, The. Moore.
North Infinity Street. Aiken.
Nothing Gold Can Stay. Frost.
Nymph's Reply to the Shepherd, The. Ralegh.
O Heavy Step of Slow Monotony. Toller.
Old Clock on the Stairs, The. Longfellow.
Old Furniture. Hardy.
On a Fly Drinking Out of His Cup. Oldys.
On Time. Hughes.
On Time. Milton.
On Wenlock Edge. Housman.
Palindrome. Mueller.
Paradox of Time, The. Dobson.
Passage. Eberhart.
Polo Grounds. Humphries.
Prayer for the New Year, A. Storey.
Proper Sonnet, How Time Consumeth All Things, A. Proctor.
Quod Tegit Omnia. Winters.
River of Life, The. Campbell.
Road, The. Muir.
Rome, Conqueror, Conquered. Sylvester.
Rubáiyát of Omar Khayyám of Naishápúr. Khayyam.
Seven Ages of Man, The. *Fr.* As You Like It. Shakespeare.
Sheep Fair, A. Hardy.
Signature For Tempo. Macleish.
Since brass, nor stone, nor earth, nor boundless sea. *Fr.* Sonnets. Shakespeare.
So, So. Clerke.
Sorrow. Dickinson.
Stillness. Flecker.
Sun-Dial, The. *Fr.* Melincourt. Peacock.
Sunshade, The. Hardy.
Tea Shop, The. Pound.
There Isn't Time. Farjeon.
This Solitude of Cataracts. Stevens.
Thought Suggested by the New Year, A. Campbell.
Thy Beauty Fades. Very.
Tide Rises, the Tide Falls, The. Longfellow.
Time. Creeley.
Time. *Fr.* Licia. Fletcher.
Time. Hodgson.
Time. More.
Time. Shelley.
Time. *Fr.* Hecatompathia. Watson.
Time. Wynne.
Time and Eternity. Bunyan.
Time and Tide. Lamarre.
Time-Clock, The. Towne.
Time, cruel Time, come and subdue that brow. *Fr.* To Delia. Daniel.
Time Eating. Douglas.
Time Has Come, the Clock Says Time Has Come, The. *Fr.* Preludes for Memnon. Aiken.
Time Is the Mercy of Eternity. Rexroth.
Time Passes. Lister.
Time, Real and Imaginary. Coleridge.
Time, the Faithless. Iremonger.
Time time said old King Tut. Marquis.
Time, You Old Gypsy Man. Hodgson.
Timers. Arnstein.
Time's Bright Sand. Finch.
Time's Dedication. Schwartz.
Time's Song. Praed.
To Every Thing There Is a Season. *Fr.* Bible, *O.T.*
To His Coy Mistress. Marvell.
To His Watch, When He Could Not Sleep. Herbert of Cherbury.
To the Virgins, to Make Much of Time. Herrick.
To Think of Time. Whitman.
To Time. "A. W."
Trumpet, The. Ehrenburg.
Unbeseechable, The. Cornford.
Upon Time. Herrick.
Waking Time. Eastwick.
Wayfarer, The. Pearse.
Weaver, The. Burleigh.
What If a Day. Campion.
What Time of Day? *Unknown.*
When I do count the clock that tells the time. *Fr.* Sonnets. Shakespeare.
When I have seen by time's fell hand defaced. *Fr.* Sonnets. Shakespeare.
Who Was It, Tell Me. Heine.
Wild Thyme. Farjeon.
Words in Time. MacLeish.
Yesterday. Chesterman.
You, Andrew Marvell. MacLeish.

***Time* (Magazine)**
Sub-Average *Time* Reader, The. Wittenberg.
Time Like an Ever-rolling Stream. Wodehouse.

Timoshenko, Semyon Konstantinovich
Timoshenko. Keyes.

Tintoretto
Leda and the Swan. Friman.

Tiresias
Judgement of Tiresias, The. Jacob.
My mother wept loudly. *Fr.* Tiresias. Clarke.
Tiresias. Garrett.
Tiresias. Tennyson.

Tisha Ba'Ab
Dirge for the Ninth of Ab. *Unknown.*

Titanic (ship)
Convergence of the Twain, The. Hardy.
Final Moments, The. *Fr.* The Titanic. Pratt.
Great *Titanic*. *Unknown.*
I Sing of Shine. Knight.
Titanic, The. *Unknown.*
Titanic Blues. *Unknown.*

Titans
Den of the Titans, The. *Fr.* Hyperion. Keats.

Tithonus
Tithonus. Tennyson.
Wedding, The. Aiken.

Titian (Tiziano Vecellio)
From Titian's "Bacchanal" in the Prado at Madrid. Moore.

Titmice
Titmouse. De la Mare.
See also **Chickadees.**

Titus (Roman Emperor)
Titus and Berenice. Heath-Stubbs.

Toads
At the Garden Gate. McCord.
Death of a Toad, The. Wilbur.
Delicate the Toad. Francis.
Friend in the Garden, A. Ewing.
History Lesson for My Son. Kooser.
Kissing the Toad. Kinnell.
Little Horned Toad. Wetherill.
Our Mr. Toad. McCord.
Song of Mr. Toad, The. Grahame.
Song of the Toad, The. Burroughs.
Speckle-black Toad and freckle-green Frog. *Fr.* Thomas á Becket, a Dramatic Chronicle. Darley.
Spring Song. Finkel.
Toad, A. Allen.
Toad, The. Corbière.
Toad. Cotton.
Toad, The. Oliver.
Tree-Toad, The. Johns.
Tree Toad, The. Shannon.
Warty Bliggens, the Toad. *Fr.* Archy and Mehitabel. Marquis.

Toasters
Toaster, The. Smith.

Tobacco
Author Loving These Homely Meats, Specially, viz., The: Cream, Pancakes, Buttered Pippin-pies. Davies.
Blest Leaf. Browne.
Come, Sirrah Jack, Ho! *Unknown.*
Farewell to Tobacco. Lamb.
From a Tobacco Wrapper. *Unknown.*

I'll Never Use Tobacco. *Unknown.*
In Imitation of Pope. *Fr.* A Pipe of Tobacco. Browne.
In Imitation of Young. *Fr.* A Pipe of Tobacco. Browne.
Inter Sodales. Henley.
Make three fourths of a cross, and a circle complete. *Unknown.*
Man Has No Smokestack. *Unknown.*
Ode to Tobacco. Calverley.
On Tobacco. Cotton.
On Tobacco. Pestel.
Pernicious Weed. Cowper.
Pipe of Tobacco, The. *At. to* Usher.
Religious Use of Tobacco, A. *At. to* Wisdome.
Said the Whiskey Flask. *Unknown.*
Says the Miner to the Mucker. *Unknown.*
Tobacco. Freneau.
Tobacco. Hemminger.
Tobacco is a filthy weed. *Unknown.*

Toes
Moses. *Unknown.*
Oration on the Toes. Brynes.
See also **Feet.**

Tokyo, Japan
Dream after Touring the Tokyo Tokei. Kogawa.
Ending, The. Engle.

Toledo, Spain
High Bridge above the Tagus River at Toledo, The. Williams.
Toledo. Campbell.

Toller, Ernst
In Memoriam: Ernst Toller. Auden.

Tombs. *See* **Cemeteries; Graves; Mausoleums.**

Tone, Theobald Wolfe
Tone's Grave. Davis.

Tongues
Tongue, The. Strong.

Tools
Hammer. Funkhouser.
Hand Saw. Funkhouser.
His Request. O'Sullivan.

Toothaches
Charm against the Tooth-ache, A. Heath-Stubbs.
Meditation upon the Toothache, A. Lerner.
Root Canal, The. Piercy.
See also **Teeth.**

Toothbrushes
My Six Toothbrushes. McGinley.

Torah, The
Angels Came A-Mustering, The. *Unknown.*
Expounding the Torah. Zukofsky.
Simhat Torah. Gordon.
Talmud Student, The. Bialik.
This Feast of the Law. *Unknown.*

Tories
Suggestion Made by the Posters of the *Globe,* A. Rogers.
Tory Pledges. Moore.

Tornadoes
Mid-Plains Tornado. Bierds.
Sherman Cyclone, The. *Unknown.*
Tornado, The. Russell.
Tornado Watch. Shuttleworth.
Tupelo Destruction, The. *Unknown.*

Toronto, Ontario
Beast Enough. Billings.
Day before Christmas, The. Souster.
Nights Passed on Ward's Island, Toronto Harbour. Fetherling.
Often I sit in the sun and brooding over the city, always. *Fr.* Civil Elegies. Lee.

Tortoises
Baby Tortoise. Lawrence.
Desert Tortoise. Baylor.
Eel and Tortoises. *Fr.* Halieuticks. Diaper.
Elegy for the Giant Tortoises. Atwood.
Giant Tortoise, The. Lucie-Smith.
Hare and the Tortoise, The. Serraillier.
Meditations of a Tortoise Dozing under a Rosetree near a Beehive at Noon While a Dog Scampers about and a Cuckoo Calls from a Distant Wood. Rieu.
Night Thought of a Tortoise Suffering from Insomnia on a Lawn. Rieu.
On Amaryllis, a Tortoyse. Pickthall.
Soliloquy of a Tortoise on Revisiting the Lettuce Beds after an Interval of One Hour While Supposed to Be Sleeping in a Clump of Blue Hollyhocks. Rieu.
To My Tortoise Chronos. Lee-Hamilton.
Tortoise Family Connections. Lawrence.
Tortoise Gallantry. Lawrence.
Tortoise Shell. Lawrence.
Tortoise. De Longchamps.
Tortoise-Shell. Lawrence.

Torture
Day of the Night, The. Scully.
For My Torturer, Lieutenant D——. Djabali.
For Refugio Talamante. Ochester.
Things That Are Worse than Death. Olds.

Touch
Realm of Touching, The. Bold.

Tourism and Tourists
Afternoons with Baedeker. Lancaster.
Ascension, The: 1925. Brinnin.
Burbank with a Baedeker; Bleistein with a Cigar. Eliot.
For the Stranger. Forché.
Importer, An. Frost.
Jumblies, The. Lear.
Letter from the Hotel, A. Barnstone.
Manners. Shiffert.
Niagara Falls. Dugan.
Permanent Tourists, The. Page.
Temple at Segesta, The. Henri.
Thief, The. Kunitz.
Tourism. Chaffin.
Tourist and the Town, The. Rich.
Tourists. Moss.
Trials of a Tourist. Tibble.
Virgins, The. Walcott.

Toussaint L'Ouverture, François Dominique
To Toussaint L'Ouverture. Wordsworth.
Toussaint L'Ouverture. Robinson.

Towns
Be'mi'ster. Barnes.
Good Town, The. Muir.
Small Town. Joyce.
Small Towns. Murguía.
Steeple-Jack, The. Moore.
They're Tearing Down a Town. Strunk.
Up at a Villa—Down in the City. Browning.
See also **Cities; Villages.**

Toys
Block City. Stevenson.
Cirque d'Hiver. Bishop.
Land of Counterpane, The. Stevenson.
Little Boy Blue. Field.
Orange Bears, The. Patchen.
Ships of Yule, The. Carman.
Silver Racer, The. Murphey.
Tin Frog, The. Hoban.
Toy-Maker, The. Colum.
Toys, The. Patmore.
Toys. Sutskever.
Toys Talk of the World, The. Pyle.
What the Toys are Thinking. Wolfe.

Track Athletics
High Jump, The. *Unknown.*
Mighty Runner, A. Robinson.
Pole-Vaulter, The. *Unknown.*
Runner, The. Whitman.

Tractors
New Farm Tractor. Sandburg.

Trafalgar, Battle of
Night of Trafalgar, The. *Fr.* The Dynasts. Hardy.
Trafalgar. Palgrave.
Victory. *Unknown.*

Traffic
Before Disaster. Winters.
Drivers of Boston, The. Gross.
Eclogue: "Whores are afraid to cross the street, The." Bergman.

Traffic Accidents. *See* **Automobile Accidents.**

Traherne, Thomas
Of Thomas Traherne and the Pebble Outside. Clouts.

Trains
Ambulance Train 30. Oman.
Amtrak. Fried.
"Are Ye Right There, Michael?" French.
Ballade of the Old-Time Engine. Vines.
Beautiful Train, The. Empson.
Blurry Cow. Twichell.
By Rail through the Earthly Paradise, Perhaps Bedfordshire. Levertov.

Empties Coming Back. Ponciano.
Engine. Tippett.
Express, The. Spender.
Faintheart in a Railway Train. Hardy.
Flying Crow. *Unknown.*
Four Untitled Poems. Jonas.
Freight Train, The. Bennett.
Freight Train. *Unknown.*
From a Railway Carriage. Stevenson.
Gambler, The. *Unknown.*
Goat, The. *Unknown.*
I like to see it lap the miles. Dickinson.
I Never Saw the Train. Roberts.
In a Train. Bly.
In the Dome Car of the "Canadian." Marty.
In the Train. *Fr.* City Nights. Symons.
Journey, The. Johnson.
Landscape as Metal and Flowers. Scott.
Limited. Sandburg.
Locomotive, The. Dickinson.
Metroliner. DuVall.
Modern Dragon, A. Bennett.
Newport Railway, The. McGonagall.
Night Journey. Roethke.
Night Mail. Auden.
Night Mail North, The. Pennell.
Night Train. Fineran.
Night Train. Stoutenburg.
North Philadelphia, Trenton, and New York. Lattimore.
Number 29. *Unknown.*
Orient Express, The. Jarrell.
Panama Limited, The. *Unknown.*
Passenger Train. Chase.
Praise of a Train. Zulu.
Praises of the Train. Segooa.
Railroad Cars Are Coming, The. *Unknown.*
Railway Train, The. Dickinson.
Regent's Park Terrace. Spencer.
Reindeer and Engine. Jacobsen.
Rhyme of the Rails. Saxe.
Siding near Chillicothe, A. Lattimore.
Smokestack Lightnin'. *Unknown.*
Song of a Train. Davidson.
Song of the Train. McCord.
South Shore Line. Schlesinger.
Starting from San Francisco. Ferlinghetti.
Texas Trains and Trails. Austin.
This Train. *Unknown.*
Three Sunrises from Amtrak. Dolgorukov.
To a Locomotive in Winter. Whitman.
Train, The. Brownjohn.
Train, The. *Unknown.*
Train: Abstraction. Taggard.
Train Blues. Zimmer.
Train Song. Siebert.
Trains. Tippett.
Trains at Midnight. Frost.
Transandean Railway, The. Kretz.
Travel. Millay.
Travelling Backward. Baro.
Vacation. Stafford.
Wabash Cannonball, The. *Unknown.*
Ways of Trains, The. Coatsworth.
Western Town. Shapiro.
Wreck of the Old 97, The. *Unknown.*
900 Miles. *Unknown.*
See also **Railroads.**
Traitors. *See* **Treason and Traitors.**
Tramps. *See* **Vagabonds.**
Transience
Adieu, Farewell Earth's Bliss. *Fr.* Summer's Last Will and Testament. Nashe.
Along the Field as We Came By. *Fr.* A Shropshire Lad. Housman.
Apple, The. *At. to* Plato.
As I Walked Out One Evening. Auden.
Ballad of Dead Ladies, The. Villon.
Blue Girls. Ransom.
Break, Break, Break. Tennyson.
Calmly We Walk Through This April's Day. Schwartz.
Changes to Corinna, The. Herrick.
Corinna's Going a-Maying. Herrick.
Dandelions. Nemerov.
Elegy: He Complains How Soon the Pleasing Novelty of Life Is Over. Shenstone.
Envoy: "They are not long, the weeping and the laughing." Dowson.
Glories of our blood and state, The. *Fr.* Ajax and Ulysses. Shirley.
Grandmother Watching at Her Window. Merwin.
Groundhog, The. Eberhart.
I Know That All beneath the Moon Decays. Drummond of Hawthornden.
If I Could Tell You. Auden.
In a Country Cemetery in Iowa. Kooser.
In Drear-nighted December. Keats.
La Chute. Olson.
Litany in Time of Plague, A. Nashe.
Meditation for His Mistress, A. Herrick.
Mutability. Wordsworth.
Nothing Gold Can Stay. Frost.
"Nox Nocti Indicat Scientiam." *Fr.* Castara. Habington.
Nymph's Reply to the Shepherd, The. Ralegh.
On a Stupendous Leg of Granite, Discovered Standing by Itself in the Deserts of Egypt, with the Inscription Inserted Below. Smith.
On the Vanity of Earthly Greatness. Guiterman.
On Wenlock Edge the Wood's in Trouble. Housman.
Ozymandias. Shelley.
Palinode, A. Bolton.
Ruin, The. *Unknown.*
Shall I compare thee to a summer's day? *Fr.* Sonnets. Shakespeare.
Sic Vita. King.
Sonnet: "I know that all beneath the moon decays." Drummond of Hawthornden.
Sunlight on the Garden, The. MacNeice.
Tears, Idle Tears. Tennyson.
Those Hours When Happy Hours Were My Estate. Millay.
Time's Changes. *Fr.* The Art of Politicks. Bramston.
Time's Times Again. Ammons.
To Blossoms. Herrick.
To Daffodils. Herrick.
To Dianeme. Herrick.
To the Stone-Cutters. Jeffers.
Two Songs from a Play. Yeats.
Virtue. Herbert.
What If a Day, or a Month, or a Year. Campion.
See also **Change.**
Translations and Translators
Difficulties of Translation, The. *Fr.* Prologues to the *Aeneid.* Douglas.
Each poet with a different talent writes. *Fr.* An Essay on Translated Verse, An. Roscommon.
Lesson in Translation, A. Preil.
O thou, whom Poesy abhors. Burns.
On First Looking into Chapman's Homer. Keats.
On the Translation of Anacreon. Walpole.
On Tom Moore's Translation of Anacreon. Erskine.
To His Friend Ben. Jonson, of His Horace Made English. Herbert of , Cherbury.
To His Worthy Friend Doctor Witty upon His Translation of the "Popular Errors." Marvell.
To My Worthy Friend Master George Sandys, on His Translation of the Psalms. Carew.
To the Translation of Palingenius. Googe.
Translation. Lesser.
Translations. Rich.
Translator to Translated. Pound.
Who Translates a Poet Badly. Prada.
Transportation, Penal
Jim Jones. *Unknown.*
Moreton Bay. *Unknown.*
Van Dieman's Land. *Unknown.*
Trapeze Artists
Man on the Flying Trapeze, The. *Unknown.*
Trapping and Trappers
Hare in Winter. Piercy.
Rabbit, The. Davies.
Snare, The. Stephens.
Trash. *See* **Garbage and Garbage Men.**
Traubel, Helen
I Like to Sing Also. Updike.
Traveling and Travelers.
Amtrak. Fried.
Best Road of All, The. Towne.
Commercial Traveller. Edmond.
Driving toward the Lac Qui Parle River. Bly.
End of the Line. Taylor.
Far Trek. Brady.
Farewell, farewell! Before our prow. *Fr.* Dover to Munich. Calverley.

Frightened Flier Goes North, The. Kazantzis.
From a Railway Carriage. Stevenson.
Frontier, The. Hewitt.
Gemwood. Bell.
Good-Night. Thomas.
Hard Traveling. Guthrie.
Hitch Haiku. Snyder.
Home Leave. Howes.
Ijajee's Story. DeClue.
In Foreign Parts. Richards.
Journey into France, The. *Unknown.*
Journey, The. Johnson.
Journey, The. Winters.
Lonely Traveller, The. Brew.
Louise. Smith.
Lunch. Koch.
Melodic Trains. Ashbery.
Movies for the Home. Moss.
Moving between Beloit and Monroe. Noll.
Needle Travel. Patton.
New Horizons. Lysaght.
Night Boat. Brown.
Night Journey. Roethke.
North Philadelphia, Trenton, and New York. Lattimore.
Not That Far. Miller.
October Journey. Walker.
Old Walking Song, The. Tolkien.
On a Subway Express. Firkins.
On the Circuit. Auden.
On the Road through Chang-te. Sun Yün-feng.
Out of the Deepness. Jackson.
Over 2000 Illustrations and a Complete Concordance. Bishop.
Owl and the Pussycat, The. Lear.
Railway Junction, The. De la Mare.
River, The. *Fr.* The Bridge. Crane.
Road to Anywhere, The. Taylor.
Rosy Bosom'd Hours, The. Patmore.
Sestina of the Tramp-Royal. Kipling.
"Sing we the two lieutenants, Parer and M'Intosh." *Fr.* A Time to Dance: The Flight. Day Lewis.
Spencer the Rover. *Unknown.*
Starting from San Francisco. Ferlinghetti.
Stepping Westward. Wordsworth.
There Are So Many Ways of Going Places. Thompson.
They Clapped. Giovanni.
Three Sunrises from Amtrak. Dolgorukov.
Ticket Agent, The. Leamy.
To My Fellow-Mariners, March '53. Whitbread.
Travel. Millay.
Travel. Stevenson.
Travelers, The. Reeves.
Traveler's Curse after Misdirection. Graves.
Traveler's Rest. Nash.
Traveller, The. Auden.
Traveller, The. Berryman.
Traveller Has Regrets, The. Fraser.
Travelling Companions. Armour.
Trip, The. Stafford.
Unexplorer, The. Millay.
Up-Hill. Rossetti.
Waking in Nice. Traxler.
Treason and Traitors.
Ballad of Christmas, A. De la Mare.
Of Treason. Harington.
Treasures
Spanish Waters. Masefield.
Treaties
Hand That Signed the Paper Felled a City, The. Thomas.
Tree, Herbert Beerbohm
To My Father. Tree.
Tree Surgeons
Tree Man. McQuilkin.
Tree Toads. *See* **Toads.**
Trees
Advice to a Forest. Bodenheim.
All That Time. Swenson.
And When the Green Man Comes. Haines.
Autumn Fancies. *Unknown.*
Autumn Fashions. Thomas.
Autumnal Spring Song. Miller.
Ballad of the Trees and the Master, A. Lanier.
Bare Almond-Trees. Lawrence.
Bare Arms of Trees, The. Tagliabue.
Be Different to Trees. Davies.
Bent Tree. Serchuk.
Binsey Poplars (Felled 1879). Hopkins.
Birches. Frost.
Bound. Roethke.
Brooms. Aldis.
Chestnut Avenue at Alton House, The. Tomlinson.
Child's Song in Spring. Nesbit.
Christmas Trees. Frost.
City Tree, The. Crawford.
City Trees. Millay.
Complicity. Gallagher.
Cut It Down. Coleridge.
Departure, A. Mahon.
Dogwood Blossoms. Blue Cloud.
Double Tree, The. Scott.
Every Time I Climb a Tree. McCord.
Fallen Tree, The. Young.
Felled Plane Tree, The. Hajnal.
For the Slender Beech and the Sapling Oak. Peacock.
Foreign Soil. Hai-Jew.
Forester's Song. Coppard.
Four trees—upon a solitary acre. Dickinson.
Gathered at the River. Levertov.
Good Company. Baker.
Great-great Grandma, Don't Sleep in Your Treehouse Tonight. Kennedy.
Green Grass Growing All Around, The. *Unknown.*
Hampstead; the Horse Chestnut Trees. Gunn.
Happy Tree, The. Gould.
He Praises the Trees. *Unknown.*
Heart of the Tree, The. Bunner.
House of the Trees, The. Wetherald.
I Consider the Tree. Buber.
In a Wood. *Fr.* The Woodlanders. Hardy.
In One Place. Wallace.
Injured Maple. Everson.
Juniper. Duggan.
Knife and Sap. Leslie.
Knockmany. Ryan.
Laurel Tree, The. Simpson.
Learning by Doing. Nemerov.
Lines to a Tree. Teller.
Little Epithalamium. Kallman.
Loveliest of Trees. Housman.
Mango Tree, The. Chock.
Mrs. Asquith Tries to Save the Jacarandas. Witt.
Mountain Tree, The. Connell.
Music of a Tree, The. Turner.
New Year for Trees, The. Schwartz.
O Brother Tree. Michelson.
Of All Plants, the Tree. White.
Old Tree, The. Young.
On the day my father died a flame-tree. *Fr.* Brother Jonathan, Brother Kafka. O'Sullivan.
Paradigm. Deutsch.
Pastoral, A: "Wise old apple tree in spring, The." Hillyer.
Plant a Tree. Larcom.
Planting a Tree. Turner.
Planting Trees. Friedlaender.
Progress. Martin.
Proud Trees, The. Kerr.
Pruned Tree, The. Moss.
Roots. Ginsberg.
Rowan, The. Jacob.
Second Shadow. Roethke.
Snow-Gum, The. Stewart.
Song of the Forest Trees. *Unknown.*
Song of the Open Road. Nash.
Song to a Tree. Markham.
Spruce Is Standing Lonely, A. Heine.
Strange Tree. Roberts.
Stump Is Not the Tombstone, The. Seager.
Tapestry Trees. Morris.
Tenebris. Grimké.
These Trees Are No Forest of Mourners. Jones.
This Way Only. Harford.
Three Stanzas About a Tree. Bell.
Timber Line Trees. Holme.
To Sycamores. Herrick.
To the Wayfarer. *Unknown.*
Tree, The. Björnson.

Tree, The. Ehrenburg.
Tree, The. Very.
Tree, The. Winchilsea.
Tree and the Lady, The. Hardy.
Tree at My Window. Frost.
Tree Design, A. Bontemps.
Tree Is Father to the Man, The. Lipsitz.
Tree Party. MacNeice.
Tree Sleeps in the Winter, The. Russell.
Tree Stands Very Straight and Still, The. Wynne.
Trees. Behn.
Trees. Coleridge.
Trees. Hughes.
Trees. Kilmer.
Trees. Merwin.
Trees. Nemerov.
Trees, The. Rich.
Trees and Cattle. Dickey.
Trees and Evening Sky. Momaday.
Trees Are Down, The. Mew.
Trees at Night. Johnson.
Trees at the Arctic Circle. Purdy.
Trees both in hills and plaines, in plenty be. Wood.
Trees in the Garden. Lawrence.
Trees Lose Parts of Themselves inside a Circle of Fog. Ponge.
Trees, Who Are Distant. Warr.
Tulip Tree. Sitwell.
Under the Greenwood Tree. Shakespeare.
Underside of Trees, The. DeClue.
War against the Trees, The. Kunitz.
What Do We Plant? Abbey.
When Mary Goes Walking. Chalmers.
When There Were Trees. Willard.
Willow-Man, The. Ewing.
Winter Trees. Plath.
Wood Music. King.
Woodman, Spare That Tree. Morris.
Yes! I have seen the ancient oak. *Fr.* The Brereton Omen. Hemans.
Yew-Trees. Wordsworth.
See also **names of tree species.**

Trelawny, Edward John
Dedication to "Songs of the Springtides." Swinburne.
Trelawny Lies by Shelley. O'Donnell.

Trelawny, Sir Jonathan
And Shall Trelawny Die? Hawker.
Song of the Western Men, The. Hawker.

Trench Warfare
Aftermath. Sassoon.
Anthem for Doomed Youth. Owen.
Attack. Sassoon.
Battle of the Swamps, The. Graham.
Break of Day in the Trenches. Rosenberg.
Counter-Attack. Sassoon.
Dug-out, The. Sassoon.
Exposure. Owen.
From a Trench. Bell.
Great War, The. Scannell.
In Parenthesis, *sels.* Jones.
In the Trench. Gellert.
It's a Queer Time. Graves.
Lark above the Trenches, The. Graham.
Over the Top. Bristowe.
Pierrot Goes to War. Elliot.
Rear-Guard, The. Sassoon.
Winter Warfare. Rickword.

Trenton, Battle of (1776)
Battle of Trenton, The. *Unknown.*
Trenton and Princeton. *Unknown.*

Trieste, Italy
Three Streets. Saba.

Trilobites
Lay of the Trilobite, The. Kendall.

Trinidad and Tobago
Returning to Store Bay. Howes.
Trinidad, 1958. Mondy.

Trinity, The
Batter my heart, three person'd God; for, you. *Fr.* Holy Sonnets. Donne.
One Divinity of Father, Son, The. *Fr.* On Trinity Sunday. Byrom.
Thrice Holy. Heber.
Trinity, The. *Unknown.*

Triolet (form)
How Great My Grief. Hardy.
To a Fat Lady Seen from the Train. Cornford.
Triolet: "When first we met we did not guess." Bridges.
Triolet against Sisters. McGinley.

Tristan da Cunha (islands)
Tristan da Cunha. Campbell.

Tristram and Isolde
Tristram and Isolt. Marquis.
Tristram of Lyonesse, *sels.* Swinburne.
Tristram's End. Binyon.

Troilus and Cressida
Testament of Cresseid, The. Henryson.
Troilus and Cressida, *sels.* Dryden.
Troilus and Cressida, *sels.* Shakespeare.
Troilus and Criseyde, *sels.* Chaucer.

Trojan War
Aegean. Simpson.
Anger be now your song, immortal one. *Fr.* The Iliad. Homer.
The Iliad, *sels.* Homer.
Leda and the Swan. Yeats.
Menelaus and Helen. Brooke.
Night Encampment outside Troy. Tennyson.
Palladium. Arnold.
Return, The. Muir.
Trojan Horse, The. Drummond of Hawthornden.
Why They Waged War. Bishop.
Young Paris. *Fr.* Posthumous Tales. Crabbe.
See also **Troy.**

Trolleys. *See* **Streetcars.**

Trolls
Kallundborg Church. Whittier.
Stone Troll, The. Tolkien.
Troll, The. Prelutsky.

Trossachs, The (Scotland)
Trosachs, The. Wordsworth.

Trout
It Is Hard to Catch Trout. Piuvkaq.
Reflections of a Trout Fisherman. Demon.
Sanctuary, The. Nemerov.
That Pure Place. Moriarty.
Trout, The. Montague.
Winter Trout. Dickey.

Troy
But Troy, alas, methought above them all. *Fr.* A Mirror for Magistrates (Induction). Sackville.
Ilion, Ilion. Tennyson.
Troy. Flower.
Troy. Muir.
Troy Depicted. *Fr.* The Rape of Lucrece. Shakespeare.
See also **Trojan War.**

Trucks and Truckers
Buffalo. Brodsky.
Country Trucks. Shannon.
Daybreak on a Pennsylvania Highway. Daunt.
F Is the Fighting Firetruck. McGinley.
Julio. Robertson.
Long Lonely Lover of the Highway. Will.
Pancho Villa. Lipsitz.
Song of the Truck. Frankel.
Truck Drivers. Haag.
Trucker, A. Gunn.
Trucks. Tippett.
Water-Truck, The. Lane.
Why Log Truck Drivers Rise Earlier than Students of Zen. Snyder.

Truman, Harry S.
Thinning Out the Grove. Neeld.

Trumpets
How High the Moon. Jeffers.
Lewis Has a Trumpet. Kuskin.

Trust
Hymn of Trust, A. Sargent.
Trust in the Lord: so shalt thou dwell. *Fr.* Psalm XXXVII. Bible, *O. T.*

Truth, Sojourner
I Think I See Her. Fauset.
Oriflamme. Fauset.
Sojourner Truth. *Fr.* Stars. Hayden.
Stars. Hayden.

Truth
Be True. Bonar.
Catch-22 Test, A. Sellers.
Difference between a Lie and the Truth, The. Dessus.
Goddess, The. Levertov.

History of Truth, The. Auden.
How We Learn. Bonar.
I died for beauty—but was scarce. Dickinson.
In a World of Change. Awad.
Invocation. Eastman.
Leaders of the Crowd, The. Yeats.
Lie, The. Ralegh.
Lying. Wilbur.
Magna Est Veritas. *Fr.* The Unknown Eros. Patmore.
1643 "Veritas" 1878. *Fr.* Two Sonnets: Harvard. Holmes.
On Finding the Truth. Very.
Revenge. Nugent.
Saint Called "Truth," A. Langland.
Spectacle of Truth, The. Hewitt.
Standing on Tiptoe. Cameron.
Student. Cheng Min.
Tell all the truth but tell it slant. Dickinson.
To Truth. *Fr.* Solomon. *Unknown.*
Truth. "Æ."
Truth. Chaucer.
Truth, The. Joans.
Truth, The. Lampman.
Truth. Lloyd.
Truth. Masefield.
Truth. McKay.
Truth, crushed to earth, shall rise again. *Fr.* The Battle-Field. Bryant.
Truth is as old as God. Dickinson.
Truth Is Quite Messy, The. Harris.
Truth Never Dies. *Unknown.*
"Truth," said a traveller. *Fr.* The Black Riders. Crane.
Truth, the Invincible. Bryant.
Wayfarer, The. Crane.
With Whom Is No Variableness, neither Shadow of Turning. Clough.

Truxtun, Thomas
Truxton's Victory. *Unknown.*

Tuberculosis
T. B. Blues. *Unknown.*

Tuberoses
Tuberose. Block.

Tubman, Harriet
Harriet Tubman. Walker.
I Like to Think of Harriet Tubman. Griffin.
Runagate, Runagate. Hayden.

Tucson, Arizona
In Old Tucson ("In old Tucson, in old Tucson/ How swift the happy days ran on!"). Hall.
In Old Tucson ("In old Tucson, in old Tucson/ What cared I how the days ran on?"). Conrard.
In Old Tucson ("Within a dobe wall"). Beghtol.

Tugboats
East River. Thomas.
Tugs. Tippett.

Tulip Trees
Tulip Tree. Sitwell.

Tulips
To a Bed of Tulips. Herrick.
Tulips. Colum.
Tulips. Plath.
Tulip. Wallace.
Tulips and Addresses. Field.

Tumbleweeds
Weeds. Stanford.

Turkey
In the Turkish Ward. Balakian.
Thoughts of Loved Ones. Fishback.

Turkeys
Black November Turkey, A. Wilbur.
Melancholy Lay, A. Fleming.
Soliloquy of a Turkey. Dunbar.
Table-Birds. Mackenzie.

Turner, Joseph Mallord William
Turner's Sunrise. Bevington.

Turner, Lana
Poem: "Lana Turner has collapsed!" O'Hara.

Turner, Nat
Ballad of Nat Turner, The. Hayden.
Nat Turner. Allen.
Remembering Nat Turner. Brown.

Turnips
Mr. Finney's Turnip. *Unknown.*
Swedes. Thomas.

Turpin, Richard (Dick Turpin)
Dick Turpin and the Lawyer. *Unknown.*
My Bonny Black Bess. *Unknown.*

Turtle Doves
Phoenix and Turtle, The. Shakespeare.
Turtle-Dove's Nest, The. *Unknown.*
See also **Doves.**

Turtles
Emancipation of George Hector, The (a Colored Turtle). Evans.
Little Turtle, The. Lindsay.
Living Tenderly. Swenson.
Mud Turtle, The. Nemerov.
Sea Turtle. Pope.
Sea-Turtle and the Shark, The. Tolson.
Snapper, The. Heyen.
Tony the Turtle. Rieu.
Tortoise in Eternity, The. Wylie.
Turtle. Lowell.
Turtle, The. Nash.
Turtle's Song, The. *Unknown.*
Zimmer and His Turtle Sink the House. Zimmer.
See also **Tortoises.**

Tuskegee Institute
Tuskegee. Hill.

"Twain, Mark" (Samuel Langhorne Clemens)
When the Mississippi Flowed in Indiana. Lindsay.

Tweed (river), Scotland and England
Twilight on Tweed. Lang.
Two Rivers. *Unknown.*

Twelfth Night
Ballad of the Epiphany. Dalmon.
Brightest and Best of the Sons of Morning. Heber.
Epiphany. Duggan.
In the Glorious Epiphanie of Our Lord God. Crashaw.
Old Christmas Morning. Helton.
Poem for Epiphany. Nicholson.
Twelfth Night. Booth.
Twelve Days of Christmas, The. *Unknown.*

Twickenham, England
Twickenham Ferry. Marzials.
Twicknam Garden. Donne.

Twilight
As Soon as Ever Twilight Comes. De la Mare.
At the Edge of the Day. Urmy.
Back to Life. Gunn.
Beside the Blackwater. O'Conor.
By the Margin of the Great Deep. "Æ."
Children's Hour, The. Longfellow.
Day That I Have Loved. Brooke.
Dusk. Grimké.
Dusk. Lopez-Penha.
Dusk of Horses, The. Dickey.
Georgia Dusk. Toomer.
Gloaming. Bowen.
Half Past Four, October. Hajnal.
His soul stretched tight across the skies. *Fr.* Preludes. Eliot.
Home-coming. Adams.
Invisible Landscape. Wright.
Jogging at Dusk. Grossbardt.
Music at Twilight. Sterling.
Near Dusk. Auslander.
Remembering Home. Petrykewycz.
Saskatchewan Dusk. Buckaway.
Southey Looks out of the Window at Greta Hall. *Fr.* A Vision of Judgement. Southey.
Summer Twilight, A. Turner.
This Is My Hour. Akins.
Twilight. Hall.
Twilight. McCormick.
Twilight at Sea. Welby.
Twilight Calm. Rossetti.
Twilight in Middle March, A. Ledwidge.
Twilight Song. Hunter-Duvar.
Twilight Time. Palmer.
Winter Twilight. Elliot.
Winter Twilight, A. Grimké.
See also. **Evening; Sunset.**

Twins
Autumn. Roberts.
Twins. Graves.
Twins, The. Leigh.
Twins. Matthews.

Twins, The. Shapiro.
Twins, The. Wright.
Tyburn Gallows, London
Tyburn and Westminister. Heywood.
Tyndale, William
From William Tyndale to John Frith. Bowers.
Typing and Typists
Learning to Type. O Hehir.
Please Excuse Typing. Boothroyd.
Typewriter Revolution, The. Enright.
Tyrone. *See* **County Tyrone, Northern Ireland.**
Tyranny
But Man, Proud Man. *Fr.* Measure for Measure. Shakespeare.
Epitaph on a Tyrant. Auden.
Foreign Ruler, A. Landor.
Human Debasement; a Fragment. Rushton.
In New South Wales, as I plainly see. *Fr.* The Devil and the Governor. Forster.
Song to the Men of England. Shelley.
Tyrconnel, Richard Talbot, Duke and Earl of
Ho, broder Teague, dost hear de decree? *Unknown.*
Lilliburlero. Wharton.
Tyrconnel, Rory O'Donnell, Earl of
Lament for the Princes of Tyrone and Tyrconnel, A. *Tr. by* Mangan.
Tyrone, Hugh O'Neill, 2d Earl of
Lament for the Princes of Tyrone and Tyrconnel, A. *Tr. by* Mangan.

U

UFOs. *See* **Flying Saucers.**
Uccello, Paolo
Rout of San Romano, The. White.
Uccello. Corso.
Ugliness
Deformed Mistress, The. Suckling.
John, Tom, and James. Ross.
Portrait. Landor.
Ulster, Ireland
King of Ulster, The. *Unknown.*
Ulysses
And then went down to the ship. *Fr.* The Cantos. Pound.
Calypso. Kell.
Canto XLVII: "Who even dead, yet hath his mind entire!" Pound.
Constant Penelope sends to thee, careless Ulysses! *Unknown.*
Haunted Odysseus: The Last Testament. Gregory.
Lotos-Eaters, The. Tennyson.
Odysseus. Fallon.
Odysseus. Merwin.
Odysseus Dying. Wingfield.
Odysseus to Telemachus. Brodsky.
Odyssey, The, *sels.* Homer.
Odyssey, The. Lang.
Old Ships, The. Flecker.
Return, The ("The doors flapped open in Ulysses' house."). Muir.
Strayed Reveller, The. Arnold.
Ulysses. Graves.
Ulysses. Tennyson.
Ulysses and the Siren. Daniel.
Ulysses Hears the Prophecies of Tiresias. Chapman.
World as Meditation, The. Stevens.
Umbrellas
Elf and the Dormouse, The. Herford.
Haiku: "Just enough of rain." Wright.
Outcast, The. Sanford.
U is for Umbrella. McGinley.
Umbrella, The. Stanford.
Umbrella Brigade, The. Richards.
Umbrellas. Bennett.
Uncles
All Up and Down the Lines. Cooperman.
Aunt Elsie's Night Music. Oliver.
Bobby's First Poem. Gale.
Lolo died yesterday. Zarco.
My Uncle Joe. Smith.
Nobody Loses All the Time. Cummings.
Uncle. Graham.
Uncle. Levine.
Uncle Claude. Evans.
Uncle Jack. Kherdian.
Underground Railroad
Runagate Runagate. Hayden.
Underhill, John
John Underhill. Whittier.
Undertakers
Undertakers. Bierce.
Undertakers' Club, The. *Unknown.*
Underwear
Underwear. Ferlinghetti.
Unemployment
Appeal by Unemployed Ex-Service Men, An. *Unknown.*
Between an Unemployed Artist and His Wife. *Unknown.*
Brother, Can You Spare a Dime. Harburg.
I Don't Want Your Millions Mister. Garland.
Muckers. Sandburg.
Rip the Apple Seller Awakes; or, after 50 Years, the Great Depression (1929–79) Reawakens. Ackerson.
Soup Song. Sugar.
Tiempo Muerto. Alonso.
Tom's Garland. Hopkins.
Trinity Place. McGinley.
Unemployment/Monologue. Jordan.
Young fellow walks about, The. Reznikoff.
Unicorns
Days of the Unicorns, The. Webb.
How to Catch Unicorns. Benét.
Inhuman Henry. Housman.
Late Passenger, The. Lewis.
Lo! in the mute, mid wilderness. *Fr.* Nepenthe. Darley.
Natural History of Dragons and Unicorns My Daughter and I Have Known, A. Root.
Strangers, The. Brown.
Taliessin's Song of the Unicorn. Williams.
Unicorn, The. *Fr.* Nepenthe. Darley.
Unicorn, The. Pitter.
Unicorn, The. Rieu.
Unicorn. Smith.
Unicorn, The. Young.
Unicorn and the Lady, The. Garrigue.
Union of Soviet Socialist Republics. *See* **Russia.**
Unions, Labor. *See* **Labor Unions.**
United Nations
Just Dropped In. Cole.
United States
America. Babcock.
America. *Fr.* The Torch-Bearers. Bates.
America. Creeley.
America. Ginsberg.
America. McKay.
America. Newlove.
America. Smith.
America. Whitman.
America; a Prophecy. Blake.
America Bleeds. Lewis.
America First! Oldham.
America for Me. Van Dyke.
"America, I Love You." Kalmar *and* Ruby.
America Is Great Because. *At. to* De Tocqueville.
America the Beautiful. Bates.
America the Beautiful. Rice.
American Eagle, The. Lawrence.
American Letter. MacLeish.
American Lights, Seen from Off Abroad. Berryman.
American Names. Benét.
Approaching America. Squire.
Blue Meridian, The. Toomer.
Brooklyn Heights. Wain.
Building of the Ship, The. Longfellow.
Center of America, The. Siegel.
Columbia. Dwight.
Columbia. *Unknown.*
Columbia, the Gem of the Ocean. Shaw.
Coming American, The. Foss.
Coming Back to America. Dickey.
Das Kapital. Baraka.
Dear Land of All My Love. *Fr.* The Centennial Meditation of Columbia. Lanier.
Dreaming America. Oates.
Empire Builders. MacLeish.
From My Lai the Thunder Went West. Ryan.
From Paumanok Starting I Fly like a Bird. Whitman.
Gift Outright, The. Frost.

Great Society, The. Bly.
Hail! Columbia. Hopkinson.
History of the U.S., The. Stoner.
I Am Waiting. *Fr.* Oral Messages. Ferlinghetti.
I Hear America Singing. Whitman.
I, Too. Hughes.
In the States. Stevenson.
Inner Part, The. Simpson.
International Hymn. Huntington.
Invocation: "American muse, whose strong and diverse heart." *Fr.* John Brown's Body. Benét.
It Is Time. Joans.
Jefferson and Liberty. *Unknown.*
Land of the Free. Hosking.
Land of the Free. MacLeish.
Land Where Hate Should Die, The. McCarthy.
Last Whiskey Cup, The. Engle.
Lion's Cub, The. Thompson.
Long as thine art shall love true love. *Fr.* The Centennial Meditation of Columbia. Lanier.
Lyric: "From now on kill America out of your mind." Agee.
Map of My Country. Holmes.
Melting Pot, The. Randall.
Men. MacLeish.
Meredith Phyfe. *Fr.* The New Spoon River. Masters.
Millions Are Learning Now. Agee.
Minority Report. Updike.
Mrs. Trollope in America. Bevington.
My America. La Grone.
My Blackness Is the Beauty of This Land. Jeffers.
My Country, Right! Clark.
My country 'tis of thee, *parody.* Bierce.
My Country, to Thy Shore. Williams.
My Land. Davis.
N.Y. to L.A. by Jet Plane. Dorman.
National Hymn. Roberts.
New Colossus, The. Lazarus.
Next to of Course God America I. Cummings.
Night Journey. Roethke.
1492. Lazarus.
Nobody Lives on Arthur Godfrey Boulevard. Costanzo.
O Beautiful, My Country. Hosmer.
O Lord Our God, Thy Mighty Hand. Van Dyke.
Observe the Whole of It. Wolfe.
Ode Recited at the Harvard Commemoration. Lowell.
Oh Mother of a Mighty Race. Bryant.
On a Rhine Steamer. Stephen.
On the Prospect of Planting Arts and Learning in America. Berkeley.
Our Country. Thoreau.
Parting of the Ways, The. Gilder.
Passage to India. Whitman.
Peace Hymn of the Republic. Van Dyke.
Plain-Chant for America. Chapin.
Poem of the Forty-eight States, A. Koch.
Poem, or Beauty Hurts Mr. Vinal. Cummings.
Republic, The. Longfellow.
Sailing from the United States. Merrill.
Serpent Knowledge. *Fr.* An Explanation of America. Pinsky.
Shine, Perishing Republic. Jeffers.
Sleep, My Child. Aleichem.
Song of the Universal. Whitman.
Star of Columbia. Dwight.
This Is America. Clark.
To My Son Parker, Asleep in the Next Room. Kaufman.
To the States. Whitman.
To the Western World. Simpson.
Toast to the Flag, A. Daly.
Unmanifest Destiny. Hovey.
Voice of America 1961, The. Liddy.
Vow, A. Ginsberg.
What Happened Here Before. Snyder.
Wreathmakertraining. Patten.
Yonder. Eberhart.
Gift Outright, The; America to Her Poets (GOA). Helen Plotz, ed.
Patriotic Poems America Loves (PAL). Jean Anne Vincent, ed.
Traveling America with Today's Poets (TAT). David Kherdian, ed.

United States (ship)
United States and *Macedonian,* The ("The Banner of Freedom high floated unfurled"). *Unknown.*
United States and *Macedonian,* The ("How glows each patriot bosom thats boasts a Yankee heart") *Unknown.*

United States Army
Caisson Song, The. Gruber.

United States Marine Corps
Marines' Hymn, The. *Unknown.*

Universe
Black Holes. Perkins.
Christ in the Universe. Meynell.
Man Said to the Universe, A. Crane.
Natural History. Fargas.
Ode on Zero. Pettingell.
Universe, The. Miller.
Universe, The. Swenson.
Universe Is Closed and Has REMs, The. Starbuck.

Universities. *See* **Colleges and Universities.**

Unknown Soldier
Unknown, The. Laughlin.
Unknown Dead, The. Timrod.
Unknown Soldier. Dunn.
Unknown Soldier, The. Rose.
Unknown Warrior. Daryush.

Unwin, Mary
To Mary Unwin. Cowper.
To the Same. Cowper.

Urania
Urania. Arnold.
Urania. Pitter.

Uriel
Uriel. Emerson.

Ursa Major
Great Bear, The. Hollander.
Ursa Major. Kirkup.

Usury
Gombeen, The. Campbell.
With Usura. *Fr.* Cantos. Pound.

Utah
Abandoned Copper Refinery. Gillespie.
Brigham Young. *Unknown.*
Desert Gulls. Gillespie.
Marching to Utah. *Unknown.*
Salt Lake City. Carruth.
Utah. Stevenson.

Ute Indians
Chipeta. Field.
Chipeta's Ride. Taylor.
Legend of Grand Lake. Westcott.
Red Ghosts Chant, The. Spencer.

Utopia
Anglicized Utopia. Gilbert.
Pantisocracy. Coleridge.

Utrillo, Maurice
Utrillo's World. Glassco.

V

Vacation
After Vacation. Hanley.
Any Time. Stafford.
Back Again for the Holidays. *Fr.* Summoned by Bells. Betjeman.
Diverting History of John Gilpin, The. Cowper.
Eunice. Betjeman.
I'm Going to Rocky Island. *Unknown.*
In the Motel. Kennedy.
July Wakes. Pomfret.
Lake Chemo. Rowe.
Last Resort, The. Willson.
Movies for the Home. Moss.
Our Annual Return to the Lake. Hoeft.
Photos from Summer Camp, The. Corpman.
School Is Out. Frost.
Vacation. Stafford.
Vacation Time. Bennett.

Vacuum Cleaner
Vacuum, The. Nemerov.

Vagabonds
African Tramp, The. Haresnape.
Another Academy. Bukowski.
Big Rock Candy Mountain, The. *Unknown.*
Bindlestiff. Piper.
Communion of Saints: The Poor Bastard under the Bridge. Ponsot.

Danville Girl. *Unknown.*
Despised and Rejected. Bates.
Drifters. Dawe.
Dying Hobo, The. *Unknown.*
Eye-Witness. Torrence.
Freeborn Man. MacColl.
Great American Bum, The. *Unknown.*
Hallelujah, Bum Again. *Unknown.*
Hallelujah, I'm a Bum ("Why don't you work"). *Unknown.*
Hard Traveling. Guthrie.
Hobo's Lullaby. Reeves.
Jay Gould's Daughter. *Unknown.*
Joys of the Road, The. Carman.
Lady in the Pink Mustang. Erdich.
November. Hughes.
Old Woman of the Roads, An. Colum.
Raggedy Man, The. Riley.
River, The. *Fr.* The Bridge. Crane.
Road to Vagabondia, The. Burnet.
Romany Gold. Burr.
Sestina of the Tramp-Royal. Kipling.
Song of the Open Road. Whitman.
Sundowner, The. Neilson.
Things of the Spirit. Mason.
To a Vagabond. Woodrow.
Tramp, The. Hill.
Trampwoman's Tragedy, A. Hardy.
Two Hoboes. *Unknown.*
Vagabond, The. Stevenson.
Vagabonds, The. Trowbridge.
Wanderers. Calverley.
Wanderer's Grave, The. Sage.
Wanderer's Song, A. Masefield.
When window-lamps had dwindled, then I rose. *Fr.* The Wanderer. Brennan.

Valentine's Day
Good Bishop Valentine. Farjeon.
Hail, Bishop Valentine. *Fr.* Epithalamion on the Lady Elizabeth and Count Palatine Being Married on St. Valentine's Day. Donne.
Hearts Were Made to Give Away. Wynne.
My Valentine. Parsons.
My Valentine. Stevenson.
Romance. Stevenson.
St. Valentine. Aguila.
St. Valentine. Moore.
Saint Valentine's Day. *Fr.* The Unknown Eros. Patmore.
Sure Sign, A. Turner.
To Clarastella on St. Valentines Day Morning. Heath.
To His Valentine. Drayton.
Tomorrow Is Saint Valentine's day. *Fr.* Hamlet. Shakespeare.
Valentine. "C. W. T."
Valentine. Hall.
Valentine, A. Hammond.
Valentine. Hemingway.
Valentine, A. Richards.
Valentine. Silverstein.
Valentine Promise. *Unknown.*
Valentine to a Little Girl. Newman.
Valentine's Day. Fisher.
Valentines to My Mother, 1880. Rossetti.

Valkyries
Fatal Sisters, The. Gray.
Song of the Valkyries, The. *Unknown.*

Valparaiso, Battle of (1866)
Battle of Valparaiso, The. *Unknown.*

Vampires
Undead, The. Wilbur.
Vampire, The. Kipling.
Voices Answering Back: The Vampires. Raab.

Van Doren, Mark
Ballad of Remembrance, A. Hayden.

Van Gogh, Vincent
Birds of Arles, The. Fisher.
Blue Church, The, Balakian.
Farewell to Van Gogh. Tomlinson.
Following Van Gogh (Avignon, 1982). Puziss.
In the Van Gogh Room. Yamamoto.
Open Letter-Poem-Note to Vincent van G., An. Bernadine.
Potato Eaters, The. Graziano.
Vincent Van Gogh. Smith.
Visit to Van Gogh, A. Causley.

Van Leyden, Lucas
Rilke Speaks of Angels. Donnelly.

Vanbrugh, Sir John
On Sir John Vanbrugh. Evans.
Vanbrug's House. Swift.

Vancouver, British Columbia
Christ Walks in This Infernal District Too. Lowry.
Vancouver Lights. Birney.

Vancouver Island, British Columbia
Lairdless Place, The. Archer.

Vanderbilt, Gloria
Poor Kid. Cole.

Vane, Sir Henry (1613–62)
To Sir Henry Vane the Younger. Milton.

Vanity
Abbey Walk, The. Henryson.
Accomplishments. MacDonald.
Butterfly and the Bee, The. Bowles.
Evening Out, The. Nash.
Goose, affected, empty, vain, A. *Fr.* The Goose and the Swans. Moore.
Here Follows Some Verses upon the Burning of Our House July 10th, 1666. Bradstreet.
Lament for the Makaris. Dunbar.
Litany in Time of Plague, A. Nashe.
Man and His Image, The. La Fontaine.
O Wretch, Beware. Dunbar.
Oak and the Brere, The. *Fr.* The Shepheardes Calender: February. Spenser.
On a Stupendous Leg of Granite, Discovered Standing by Itself in the Deserts of Egypt, with the Inscription Inserted Below. Smith.
On the Vanity of Earthly Greatness. Guiterman.
Our God, Our Help. Watts.
Ozymandias. Shelley.
Palinode, A. Bolton.
Praise of Age, The. Henryson.
Proud Maisie. *Fr.* The Heart of Midlothian. Scott.
Song of Emptiness to Fill Up the Empty Pages Following, A. Wigglesworth.
Spider and the Fly, The. Howitt.
To a Very Beautiful Lady. Todd.
To Vanity. Turner.
Vanity ("The fleet astronomer can bore"). Herbert.
Vanity. Thomson.
Vanity of All Worldly Things, The. Bradstreet.
Vanity of Human Wishes, The. Johnson.
Verses under a Peacock Portrayed in Her Left Hand. Greene.
See also **Pride.**

Vashti
Before the Feast of Shushan. Spencer.
Vashti. Harper.

Vaudeville
Death of Professor Backwards, The. Kennedy.
Vaudeville Dancer. Wheelock.

Vaughan, Henry
At the Grave of Henry Vaughan. Sassoon.
To Henry Vaughan. Smith.

Veeries
Veery, The. Van Dyke.
Veery-Thrush, The. Taylor.

Vegetables
Cauliflower, The. Haines.
For Instance. McAlmon.
Mummies, The. Kumin.
Nocturn Cabbage. Sandburg.
Potato. Wilbur.
Swedes. Thomas.
Vegetables. Farjeon.
Vegetables. Field.
See also **Names of specific vegetables.**

Vegetarians
Flying Bum, The: 1944. Plomer.
Logical Vegetarian, The. Chesterton.

Velázquez, Diego Rodríguez de Silva y
Castilian. Wylie.
Juan de Pareja: Painted by Velázquez. Long.

Veld
Nocturne: "Red Flame flowers bloom and die." Garstin.

Venereal Disease
Buck's Elegy, The. *Unknown.*
Sailor Cut Down in His Prime, The. *Unknown.*
They make a pretty pair of debauchees. Catullus.
See also **Syphilis.**

Venice, Italy
Burbank with a Baedeker; Bleistein with a Cigar. Eliot.
City of Falling Leaves, The. Lowell.
Doves of Venice, The. Hutton.
From a Venetian Sequence. Naudé.
Music in Venice. Simpson.
On the Extinction of the Venetian Republic. Wordsworth.
Toccata of Galuppi's, A. Browning.
Venice. *Fr.* Childe Harold's Pilgrimage. Byron.
Venice. Longfellow.
Venice. Symonds.
Venice. Wright.
Water-Colour of Venice, A. Durrell.
Venus (goddess)
Birth of Venus, The. *Unknown.*
Birth of Venus. Urdang.
Evening Star, The. *Fr.* The Moon-Bone Cycle. *Unknown.*
Infida's Song. *Fr.* Never Too Late. Greene.
Invocation. Watson.
Invocation to the Goddess, The. Wright.
Laus Veneris. Swinburne.
Mars and Venus. *Fr.* Tullie's Love. Greene.
On the Nature of Things. *Fr.* De Rerum Natura. Lucretius.
Prayer to Venus. *Fr.* The Faerie Queene. Spenser.
Queen of Paphos, Erycine, The. *Unknown.*
Song of Venus. Dryden.
Spoken by Venus on Seeing Her Statue Done by Praxiteles. *Unknown.*
Venus Accoutered as Mars. *Unknown.*
Venus againe thou mov'st a warre. *Fr.* Odes. Horace.
Venus and Adonis. Browne.
Venus and Adonis. Shakespeare.
Venus of the Salty Shell. Devlin.
Venus Transiens. Lowell.
See also **Aphrodite.**
Venus (planet)
Hesperus. Clare.
Morning Star, The. Brontë.
Perspective. *Fr.* The Angel in the House. Patmore.
See also **Evening Star.**
Venus of Milo (statue)
Venus of the Louvre. Lazarus.
Veracruz, Mexico
Beach at Veracruz, The. Bowering.
Veracruz. Hayden.
Verdi, Giuseppe
Barrel-Organ, The. Noyes.
Verdun, Battle of (1916)
Littel Song of the Maimed. Péret.
Vergil. *See* **Virgil.**
Verlaine, Paul
Birds in the Night. Cernuda.
Rimbaud and Verlaine, precious pair of poets. *Fr.* Preludes for Memnon. Aiken.
Vermeer, Jan
Lacemaker, The (Vermeer). Marx.
Vermont
Angling, a Day. Kinnell.
Fall Comes in Back-Country Vermont. Warren
Indian Summer: Vermont. Stevenson.
Mating the Goats. Barnstone.
Pearl Harbor Day 1970. Lourie.
Poem to Explain Everything about a Certain Day in Vermont, A. Taggard.
Safe Places. Urdang.
Settling In. Stuart.
Sunrise on Mansfield Mountain. Brown.
Vermont. Cleghorn.
Vermont: Indian Summer. Booth.
Verona, Italy
Map of Verona, A. Reed.
Versailles, France
No Swan So Fine. Moore.
Pompadour, The. Thornbury.
Versailles. Rich.
Vesta
To Vesta. Middleton.
Veterans
By-Products. Wormser.
See also **Soldiers.**
Veterans' Day *or* **Armistice Day.** *See* **Armistice.**
Veterinarians
Vet, The. Boas.
Vice. *See* **Evil; Sin.**
Vicksburg Campaign (1862–63)
Before Vicksburg. Boker.
Running the Batteries. Melville.
Vicksburg (a Ballad). Hayne.
Victoria, Queen of England
1887. Housman.
"Me loving subjects," sez she. *Fr.* The Queen's Afterdinner Speech. French.
Much Distressed. *Unknown.*
On the Jubilee of Queen Victoria. Tennyson.
Queen Victoria. *Unknown.*
To the Queen. *Fr.* Idylls of the King. Tennyson.
Widow at Windsor, The. Kipling.
Vienna, Austria
Little Viennese Waltz. García Lorca.
Vienna, Siege of (1683)
Carrouse to the Emperor, the Royal Pole, and the Much-Wronged Duke of Lorrain, A. *Unknown.*
Vietnam
Advent 1966. Levertov.
Altars in the Street, The. Levertov.
Americana XV: Simplicity. Rakosi.
Asians Dying, The. Merwin.
Ballad of Ho Chi Minh. MacColl.
Ballet. Kaplan.
Black Soldier Remembers, A. Coleman.
Bring 'Em Home. Dane *and others.*
Bring the War Home. Matthews.
Burning Shit at An Khe. Weigl.
Butter. Schmidt.
Condemnation. Thich Nhat Hanh.
Containing Communism. Cobb.
Dirge. Clarke.
Driving through Minnesota during the Hanoi Bombings. Bly.
Fare Thee Well. Siegel.
Framed Photograph, A. *Fr.* Trees, Effigies, Moving Objects. Curnow.
From My Lai the Thunder Went West. Ryan.
Gods in Vietnam. Redmond.
Grey October. "The Critics."
Guard at the Binh Thuy Bridge, The. Balaban.
Homecoming. Dawe.
How Much Longer? Mezey.
In the Mourning Time. Hayden.
It Is Not Enough. Henderson.
Junglegrave. Anderson.
Kilroy. McCarthy.
Lan Nguyen; the Uniform of Death 1971. Mura.
MACV Advisor. Gray.
Memo. Lynch.
Nam. Lowery.
National Security. MacLeish.
Negro Soldier's Viet Nam Diary, A. Martin.
Nine Years after Viet Nam. Quintana.
Norman Morrison. Mitchell.
On a Morning Full of Sun. Appleman.
On a Photo of a Baby Killed in the War. DeFoe.
Poem for Viet Nam. Young Bear.
Poem to My Sister, Ethel Ennis, Who Sang "The Star-spangled Banner" at the Second Inauguration of Richard Milhous Nixon. Jordan.
Problems. Scott.
Remembrance of Things Past. Coleman.
Somewhere near Phu Bai. Komunyakaa.
Song My. Griffin.
Song of Napalm. Weigl.
Starlight Scope Myopia. Komunyakaa.
Teeth Mother Naked at Last, The. Bly.
Tenebrae. Levertov.
To Maynard on the Long Road Home. Ehrhart.
To Whom It May Concern. Mitchell.
Up Rising. *Fr.* Passages. Duncan.
Vapor Trail Reflected in the Frog Pond. Kinnell.
Viet Cong Sapper Dies, A. Sossaman.
Vietnam. Major.
Vietnam #4. Major.
Voice from Danang. Redshaw.
Waiting for the Fire. Appleman.
Waking in the Dark. Livesay.
What Were They Like? Levertov.
Wichita Vortex Sutra. Ginsberg.
Women in Vietnam, The. Paley.

Vigilantes
Lay of the Vigilantes, The. *Unknown.*
Vikings
Battle of Brunanburh. *Unknown.*
Battle of Maldon, The. *Unknown.*
Heap On More Wood! *Fr.* Marmion. Scott.
Heritage, The. Reed.
O'er the Wild Gannet's Bath. Darley.
Skeleton in Armor, The. Longfellow.
Viking, The. Stokes.
Vikings, The. *Unknown.*
Viking Terror, The. *Unknown.*
Village Idiots
Greek Transfiguration. Friar.
Idiot Boy. Hill.
Villages
Our Village—by a Villager. Hood.
Rural Lines after Breughel. Krapf.
See also **Towns.**
Villanelle (form)
Aging Poet, on a Reading Trip to Dayton, Visits the Air Force Museum and Discovers There a Plane He Once Flew, The. Snyder.
And "I Know Why the Caged Bird Sings"; a Villanelle. Mosby.
Beekeeper's Dream, The. Lorr.
Chateau Papineau. Harrison.
Culture in the Slums, II: Villanelle. Henley.
Do Not Go Gentle into That Good Night. Thomas.
Farm Wife. Field.
Freaks at Spurgin Road Field, The. Hugo.
House on the Hill, The. Robinson.
Missing Dates. Empson.
Nothing Gold Can Stay. Farber.
Oedipus, Pentheus. Bromwich.
On the Night Express to Madrid. Dunetz.
One Art. Bishop.
Runes for an Old Believer. Humphries.
Three Towns, The. Nemerov.
Tracking the Sled, Christmas 1951. Walker.
Unknown, The. Davidson.
Villanelle: "It is the pain, it is the pain, endures." Empson.
Villanelle: "It's all a trick, quite easy when you know it." Skeat.
Villanelle: "Like twilight bleeding on a winter day." Nist.
Villanelle: "Proud inclination of the flesh." Laing.
Villanelle, The: "Regard the motion of the villanelle." Harington.
Villanelle: "Time can say nothing but I told you so." Auden.
Villanelle of His Lady's Treasures. Dowson.
Villanelle of Marguerites. Dowson.
Villanelle of Sunset. Dowson.
Waking, The ("I wake to sleep, and take my waking slow.") Roethke.
Villiers de l'Isle-Adam, Philippe Auguste Mathias, Comte de
Villiers de l'Isle-Adam. Huxley.
Villon, François
Ballad of François Villon, A. Swinburne.
Exile. Stroud.
Vilna, Poland
Like Groping Fingers. Sutzkever.
Secret Town, The. Sutzkever.
We Survive! Glick.
Vinci, Leonardo da. *See* **Leonardo da Vinci.**
Vines
Grape-Vine Swing, The. Simms.
Tapestry Trees. Morris.
Vinland
Story of Vinland, The. *Fr.* Psalm of the West. Lanier.
Violence
Be punctual then to know. *Fr.* The Art of Wenching. *Unknown.*
Beating, The. Stanford.
Bloody Sire, The. Jeffers.
Law in the Country of the Cats. Hughes.
Snowy Egret. Weigl.
Street Fight. Monro.
To the Spirit of Monahsetah. DeClue.
Why We Bombed Haiphong. Holden.
Violets
Bay Violets. Sister Maris Stella.
How Violets Came Blue. Herrick.
On a Violet in Her Breast. Stanley.
Sea Violet. Doolittle ("H. D.").
Sonnet: "I had no thought of violets of late." Nelson.
Sweet Violets. *Unknown.*
To a Wood-Violet. Tabb.
To Violets. Herrick.
Violet, The. Story.
Violet, The. Taylor.
Violet and the Rose, The. Webster.
Violets in Thaumantia's Bosome. Sherburne.
White Violet. Osborne.
White Violets. Low.
Yellow Violet, The. Bryant.
Violins
First Fight. Then Fiddle. Brooks.
Old Violin, The. Egan.
On Sivori's Violin. Osgood.
Out-of-the-Body Travel. Plumly.
Second Violinist's Son, The. Gregor.
Violin's Complaint, The. Thayer.
Virgil
To the Ship in Which Vergil Sailed to Athens. Horace.
To Virgil. Tennyson.
Virgil's Tomb. Rogers.
Virgin Islands
Skin Diving in the Virgins. Brinnin.
Virgins, The. Walcott.
Virgin Mary. *See* **Mary, the Virgin.**
Virginia
Abandoned, Overgrown Cemetery in the Pasture near Our House, An. Orr.
As Toilsome I Wander'd Virginia's Woods. Whitman.
Blossom. Plumly.
Blue Ridge. Hodges.
Carry Me Back to Old Virginny. Bland.
Farewell, The. Whittier.
I went to the valley. Clifton.
Jamestown. Jarrell.
Leafless Trees, Chickahominy Swamp. Smith.
Life-long, Poor Browning. Spencer.
Low Fields and Light. Merwin.
Monticello. Sarton.
Monument and the Shrine, The. Logan.
Night Fishing for Blues. Smith.
Night Trip across the Chesapeake and After. Lea.
On a Field at Fredericksburg. Smith.
Perspective and Limits of Snapshots, The. Smith.
Route 29. Brosman.
Shenandoah. *Unknown.*
Snowy Egret. Weigl.
To the Virginian Voyage. Drayton.
Trout Fishing in Virginia. McMahon.
Virginia Beach. Plumly.
Virginia Britannia. Moore.
Virginiana. Johnston.
Virginians of the Valley, The. Ticknor.
Virginity
Advice to Lovers. *Fr.* The Oeconomy of Love; a Poetical Essay. Armstrong.
Alas How Long. *Unknown.*
Best Line Yet, The. Allen.
Beware Fair Maide. *At. to* Sylvester.
Blow Away the Morning Dew. *Unknown.*
Broomfield Hill, The. *Unknown.*
Chastity. *Fr.* Comus. Milton.
Description of Maidenhead, A. *Unknown.*
Dialogue after Enjoyment. Cowley.
First, The. Mannes.
First Time, The. Newlove.
Good Counsell to a Young Maid. Carew.
Honour. Cowley.
In Bertram's Garden. Justice.
In Praise of Virginity. Hroswitha.
Inscription on a Chemise. *Fr.* The Thousand and One Nights. *Unknown.*
Maidenhead. Philips.
My Little Love Lies on the Ground. Paraske.
On the Marriage of a Virgin. Thomas.
Somebody's Child. Moulton.
Temperance and Virginity. *Fr.* Comus. Milton.
To His Lady, Who Had Vowed Virginity. Davison.
To the Virgins, to Make Much of Time. Herrick.
True Maid, A. Prior.
Twa Magicians, The. *Unknown.*
Two Rural Sisters. Cotton.
Virgin Pictured in Profile. Warren.
Where shall Celia fly for shelter. Smart.
Whistle, Daughter, Whistle. *Unknown.*

Virtue
Chant Royal of High Virtue. Quiller-Couch.
Fortune and Virtue. Dekker.
Virtue. Herbert.
Vishnu
Gita Govinda, The, *sels.* Jayadeva.
Visiting and Visitors
Doorbells. Field.
One Poet Visits Another. Davies.
Reunion. Cadsby.
Surprise. Witt.
Visit. Ammons.
Vitamins
Methuselah. *Unknown.*
Vivaldi, Antonio
Vivaldi. Schwartz.
Vocations. *See* **Occupations.**
Vogler, Georg Joseph
Abt Vogler. Browning.
Voices
London. *Fr.* Songs of Experience. Blake.
Upon Julia's Voice. Herrick.
See also **Screams; Speech; Talk.**
Volcanoes
Hongo Store 29 Miles Volcano Hilo, Hawaii, The. Hongo.
Loo-Wit. Rose.
Mount Saint Helens/Loowit; an Indian Woman's Song. Rose.
Peace. Lawrence.
Romance. Turner.
Volcanoes. Akhmadulina.
Voltaire, François Marie Arouet de
Epigram on Voltaire. Young.
Eternity. Blake.
Mock On, Mock On Voltaire, Rousseau. Blake.
On Shakespeare and Voltaire. Holcroft.
Voltaire and Gibbon. *Fr.* Childe Harold's Pilgrimage. Byron.
Voltaire at Ferney. Auden.
Voodoo
Women's Locker Room. Waniek.
Voting and Voters
Ballot, The. Pierpont.
Deliverance. Harper.
Fair and Free Elections. *Unknown.*
Poll. Roberson.
Poor Voter on Election Day, The. Whittier.
Voting Machine. Nathan.
See also **Woman Suffrage.**
Vowels
Genesis of Vowels. Broughton.
On the Vowels—a Riddle. Swift.
Voyages
Canto XLVII: "Who even dead, yet hath his mind entire!" Pound.
Crossing the Atlantic. Sexton.
Helena Embarks for Palestine. *Fr.* Elene. Cynewulf.
It Should Be Easy. Van Doren.
Letter, The. Blackburn.
Miss Emily Brittle Sails for India. *Fr.* The India Guide; or, Journal of a Voyage to the East Indies in 1780. Dallas.
St. Andrew's Voyage to Mermedonia. *Fr.* Andreas. *Unknown.*
To the Virginian Voyage. Drayton.
Voyages. Crane.
What Is. Cummings.
Voyageurs
Canadian Boat Song, A. Moore.
Voyageur. Rashley.
Voyeurism
Fiend, The. Dickey.
Girl in a Window, A. Wright.
Peeper, The. Davidson.
Peeping Tom. Hope.
Sequence, A. Scalapino.
To Dianeme ("Show me thy feet; show me thy legs, thy thighs"). Herrick.
Voyeur. Hardy.
Vuillard, Edouard
Interior with Mme. Vuillard and Son. Fraser.
Mother and Sister of the Artist. Cabral.
Vulcan
Execration upon Vulcan, An. Jonson.
Shield of Achilles, The. Auden.
To Vulcan. Herrick.
Vulcan's Song. *Fr.* Sappho and Phao. Lyly.
Vulpius, Melchior
Melchior Vulpius. Moore.
Vultures
Black Vulture, The. Sterling.
Still, Citizen Sparrow. Wilbur.
Vulture, The. Belloc.
Vulture. Jeffers.
Vulture. Kennedy.
Vulture. *Fr.* A Bestiary. Rexroth.
Vulture of the Plains, The. Garland.
See also **Buzzards.**

W

Wabash River
On the Banks of the Wabash, Far Away. Dresser.
Wagner, Richard
Death of Richard Wagner, The. Swinburne.
Tannhauser. Levy.
Wagner. Brooke.
Wagon Trains
Exodus for Oregon. Miller.
Oregon Trail, The. Guiterman.
Wagon Train, The. Simpson.
See also **Prairie Schooners.**
Wagtails
Little Trotty Wagtail. Clare.
Waiters and Waitresses
Contrary Waiter, The. Parker.
Crêpes Flambeau. Gallagher.
Epitaph on a Waiter. McCord.
Somewhere Else. Rankin.
To a Junior Waiter. Herbert.
Waiting Rooms
In the Waiting Room. Bishop.
Waiting Rooms. Nemerov.
Waiting-Room, The. Fulton.
Wakes
Finigan's Wake. *Unknown.*
Willie's Lyke-Wake. *Unknown.*
Waking
Waking from Sleep. Bly.
Walden Pond, Massachusetts
Walden in July. Junkins.
Waldenses
On the Late Massacre in Piedmont. Milton.
Wales
Artist on Penmaenmawr, The. Turner.
Bard, The. Gray.
Cader Idris at Sunset. Turner.
Carmarthen Bar. Brinnin.
Dafydd ap Gwilym Resents the Winter. Humphries.
Days that Have Been. Davies.
Dysynni Valley, The. Holmes.
For My Ancestors. Humphries.
Grongar Hill. *Fr.* Looking Back. Dyer.
Hiraeth in N.W.3. Vaughan-Thomas.
In Hospital: Poona (I). Lewis.
Llanberis Summer. Loyd.
Mysterious Britain. Clampitt.
O what can you give me? *Fr.* 'Gwalia Deserta. Davies.
On the Welsh Marches. Stone.
Peace in the Welsh Hills. Watkins.
Pont-y-Wern. *Fr.* Ambarvalia. Clough.
Snowdon Sunrise, The. *Fr.* The Prelude. Wordsworth.
Wales. Nicholson.
Wales Visitation. Ginsberg.
We Who Were Born. Lewis.
Welsh Incident. Graves.
Welsh Landscape. Thomas.
See also **Welsh, The.**
Waley, Arthur
Homage to Arthur Waley. Kees.
Walker, William
At the Grave of Walker. Miller.
Walking
How to Walk in a Crowd. Hershon.
Long Walk before the Snows Began, A. Bly.
Long Walks in the Afternoon. Gibson.

One Day When We Went Walking. Hobbs.
Stepping Westward. Wordsworth.
Velvet Shoes. Wylie.
Walking. Van Brunt.
Wall Street, New York City
Pan in Wall Street. Stedman.
Wallace, Sir William
Gude Wallace. *Unknown.*
Wallace, The, *sels.* Henry the Minstrel.
Wallenda, Carl
Last Flight of the Great Wallenda. Hyett.
Wallflowers
Wall-Flower, The. Landor.
Wall-Flower, The. Wergeland.
Walls
Grongar Hill. Dyer.
Mending Wall. Frost.
Old Grey Wall, The. Carman.
Stone Walls. Lippmann.
Wall, The. Phelps.
Wall of China, The. Colum.
Walls. Cavafy.
Walls. Francis.
Ye walls! sole witness of happy sighs. Landor.
See also **Fences.**
Walnuts
I am within as white as snow. *Unknown.*
Raking Walnuts in the Rain. Shannon.
Walnut. Carrera Andrade.
Walruses
Smile of the Walrus, The. Herford.
Walrus Hunting. Aua.
Walsingham, England
Holy Land of Walsingham, The. *Unknown.*
Lament for the Priory of Walsingham. *Unknown.*
Walton, Izaak
Ike Walton's Prayer. Riley.
Farewell, thou busy world, and May. *Fr.* To Mr. Izaak Walton. Cotton.
To My Dear and Most Worthy Friend, Mr. Isaac Walton. Cotton.
Waltzing
My Papa's Waltz. Roethke.
Wanderlust
Afoot and light-hearted I take to the open road. *Fr.* Song of the Open Road. Whitman.
Call of the Spring, The. Noyes.
Drifting. Bushby.
Early One Morning. Thomas.
Forbidden Lure, The. Davis.
How Old Is My Heart. *Fr.* The Wanderer. Brennan.
Land I Came Thro' Last, The. *Fr.* The Wanderer. Brennan.
Long Gone. Brown.
Morning Song. Baker.
Over the Hills and Far Away. Henley.
Poetry of Departures. Larkin.
Prisoners. Mavity.
Sea Fever. Masefield.
Sea Gipsy, The. Hovey.
Ulysses. Tennyson.
Vagabond Song, A. Carman.
Wakeful in the Township. Riddell.
Walking Tour, The. Auden.
Wander-Lovers, The. Hovey.
Wander-Thirst. Gould.
Wanderer, The. Auden.
Wanderer, The. Field.
Wandering. *Unknown.*
Wild Rover. *Unknown.*
Wildness. Wagstaff.
Wang Wei
Note to Wang Wei. Berryman.
War
Absolution. Sassoon.
Advent 1966. Levertov.
After the Killing. Randall.
Aftermath. Sassoon.
Against the Age. Simpson.
Air: "What a charming thing's a battle!" *Fr.* The Recruiting Serjeant. Bickerstaffe.
All, All of a Piece Throughout. *Fr.* The Secular Masque. Dryden.
All Day It Has Rained. Lewis.
All Quiet along the Potomac. Beers.
Alliteration, or The Siege of Belgrade. *Unknown.*
Apologia pro Poemate Meo. Owen.
Apostrophe to Man. Millay.
Apparitions. Clark.
Ares. Ehrenstein.
Aristocrats. Douglas.
Arms and the Boy. Owen.
Arsenal at Springfield, The. Longfellow.
As One Non-Combatant to Another. Orwell.
Ash and the Oak, The. Simpson.
At alarming bell daybreak, before. *Fr.* Site of Ambush. NíChuilleanáin.
At the Center of Everything Which Is Dying. Goedicke.
Attack. Sassoon.
August 1914. Rosenberg.
Awakened War God, The. Widdemer.
Barrage. Aldington.
Battle Hymn of the Republic. Howe.
Battle of Blenheim, The. Southey.
Battle Won Is Lost. George.
Battle-Field, The. Bryant.
Beat! Beat! Drums! Whitman.
Between Two Prisoners. Dickey.
Bivouac of the Dead, The. O'Hara.
Bloody Sire, The. Jeffers.
Boots. Kipling.
Break of Day in the Trenches. Rosenberg.
Breakfast. Gibson.
Burial of Sir John Moore, The. Wolfe.
But We Shall Bloom. Guri.
Bye Baby Bother. Smith.
Call of the Bugles, The. Hovey.
Carrickfergus. MacNeice.
Carroll's Sword. *Unknown.*
Censorship. Waley.
Chances, The. Owen.
Channel Firing. Hardy.
Christmas Letter Home. Fraser.
Chronicler, The. Bergman.
Civil War. Shanly.
Come to the Stone. Jarrell.
Conquerors, The. McGinley.
Consolation in War. Mumford.
Corporal Stare. Graves.
Counting Small-Boned Bodies. Bly.
Crucifix, The. Read.
Cruel War Is Raging, The. *Unknown.*
Daughters of War. Rosenberg.
Dead Musicians. Sassoon.
Deserter, The. Housman.
Disabled. Owen.
Does It Matter? Sassoon.
Dover Beach. Arnold.
Driving Home the Cows. Osgood.
Dry Loaf. Stevens.
Early in the Morning. Simpson.
Elegy on Gordon Barber. Derwood.
English Mother, An. Johnson.
Epigraph to "Drum-Taps." Whitman.
Escape. Graves.
Every Day. Bachmann.
Execution of Cornelius Vane, The. Read.
Exposure. Owen.
Fable of the War, A. Nemerov.
"Faith and Practice." Balaban.
Feast of Blood, The. *Fr.* The Art of War. Fawcett.
Fife Tune. Manifold.
First Snow in Alsace. Wilbur.
Flowers of the Forest, The. Elliot.
For Soldiers. Gifford.
Fortunes of War, The. *Unknown.*
Fury of Aerial Bombardment, The. Eberhart.
Fuzzy-Wuzzy. Kipling.
Galway. MacNeice.
General, The. Sassoon.
Give me this day a faith not personal. *Fr.* More Sonnets at Christmas. Tate.
Glories of Our Blood and State, The. Shirley.
God of us who kill our kind! *Fr.* A Prayer of the Peoples. MacKaye.
Gun Teams. Frankau.
Hame, Hame, Hame. Cunningham.
Henry before Agincourt: October 25, 1415. Lydgate.
Henry Fifth's Address to His Soldiers. *Fr.* King Henry V. Shakespeare.
Hohenlinden. Campbell.

Horses, The. Muir.
How to Kill. Douglas.
How to Start a War. McGinley.
Hugh Maguire. O'Hussey.
I Hate That Drum's Discordant Sound. Scott of Amwell.
I Have a Rendezvous with Death. Seeger.
I have been,/ Three separate times, in war. *Fr.* What Is Truth? Manning.
I Sing of Olaf Glad and Big. Cummings.
I Sit and Sew. Nelson.
I was playing golf that day. *Unknown.*
In Distrust of Merits. Moore.
In the Dordogne. Bishop.
In Time of "The Breaking of Nations." Hardy.
Insensibility. Owen.
Into Battle. Grenfell.
Invocation: "There is no balm on earth." Thomas.
It's a Queer Time. Graves.
Jeannette and Jeannot. Jeffries.
Jewish Conscript, The. Frank.
Just an Old Sweet Song. MacDonagh.
King of Ulster, The. *Unknown.*
Lan Nguyen; the Uniform of Death 1971. Mura.
Last War, The. Amis.
Legion, The. Graves.
Lessons of the War: Naming of Parts. Reed.
Letter to an American Visitor. Comfort.
Life at War. Levertov.
Lilium Regis. Thompson.
Lullaby: "Though the world has slipped and gone." Sitwell.
Mademoiselle from Armentieres. *Unknown.*
Manila. Ware.
March into Virginia, The. Melville.
Marching. Rosenberg.
Memories of a Lost War. Simpson.
Mental Cases. Owen.
Mid-Ocean in War-Time. Kilmer.
Mrs. McGrath. *Unknown.*
Montcalm and Wolfe. *Unknown.*
Munich Elegy No. 1. Barker.
Murrough Defeats the Danes, 994. *Unknown.*
My Company. Read.
My Sweet Old Etcetera. *Fr.* Is 5. Cummings.
Naming of Parts. *Fr.* Lessons of the War. Reed.
National Security. MacLeish.
New Mars, The. Coates.
Next War, The. Graves.
Nightingales Are Not Singing. Dor.
1935. Benét.
No Man Knows War. Rolfe.
Northern Legion, A. Read.
Now with a general peace the world was blest. *Fr.* Astraea Redux. Dryden.
O. T.'s Blues. Cuney.
Oh, It's Nine Years Ago I Was Digging in the Land. *Unknown.*
Old Man and Jim, The. Riley.
On the Lawn at the Villa. Simpson.
On the March. Aldington.
One-and-Twenty. *Unknown.*
One Morning the World Woke Up. Williams.
One Morning We Brought Them Order. Lee.
One to destroy, is murder by the law. Young.
Out of Our Shame. Rosten.
Parable of the Old Man and the Young, The. Owen.
Peasants, The. Lewis.
Permanence of the Young Men, The. Soutar.
Picciola. Newell.
Piece of Shrapnel, A. Ray.
Poets in Time of War. Warr.
Portrait: The Freedom Fighter. Jonas.
Prayer after World War. Sandburg.
Prayer during Battle. Hagedorn.
Prayer for Light. Coblentz.
Prayer for the Age. Broomell.
Prayer from 1936, A. Sassoon.
Prey to Prey. Rowbotham.
Prince of Peace, The. Fosdick.
Protest in the Sixth Year of Ch'ien Fu, A. Ts'ao Sung.
Quintana Lay in the Shallow Grave of Coral. Shapiro.
Recalling War. Graves.
Refugees, The. Read.
Repression of War Experience. Sassoon.
Reveillé. Untermeyer.
Roll-Call. Shepherd.
Rumors. Arkell.
Russians. Douglas.
Scalp Dance Song. Tewa.
Send-Off, The. Owen.
Sestina: Altaforte. Pound.
Show, The. Owen.
Sick Nought, The. Jarrell.
Silent Slain, The. MacLeish.
Sing, Brothers, Sing! Rodgers.
Soldiers Bathing. Prince.
Song: "Pints and the pistols, the pike-staves and pottles, The." *At. to* Praed.
Song in a Siege. Heath.
Sonnet to Britain. Aytoun.
Sons of Our Sons, The. Ehrenburg.
Spring 1942. Fuller.
Spring Offensive. Owen.
Strange Hells. Gurney.
Strength through Joy. Rexroth.
Suicide in Trenches. Sassoon.
Summer in England, 1914. Meynell.
Sunset Horn. O'Higgins.
Sweetness of Nature, The. *Unknown.*
Tan Ta Ra, cries Mars. Wagoner.
Ten Thousand Miles. *Unknown.*
Tenting Tonight. Kittredge.
That Crazy War. *Unknown.*
There Was a Crimson Clash of War. Crane.
There was crimson clash of war. *Fr.* The Black Riders. Crane.
"They." Sassoon.
This is a damned inhuman sort of war. *Fr.* Unseen Fire. Currey.
Three Little Girls. Aldington.
To Germany. Sorley.
To Lucasta, Going to the Wars. Lovelace.
To Nearly Everybody in Europe To-Day. "MacDiarmid."
To the Mothers. Toller.
Too-Late Born, The. MacLeish.
Trafalgar. *Fr.* The Dynasts. Hardy.
Trees on the Calais Road. Blunden.
Triumphs of Owen, The. Gray.
Two Armies. Spender.
Two Sides of War. Rice.
Under the Frontier Post. Wang Chang-ing.
Unpardonable Sin, The. Lindsay.
Valley of the Black Pig, The. Yeats.
Viking Terror, The. *Unknown.*
Villages Démolis. Read.
Vision, A. Dearmer.
Vision of War, A. *Fr.* Induction to a Myrroure for Magistrates. Sackville.
Voices of Heroes. Gregory.
Volunteer's Reply to the Poet, The. *Fr.* Talking Bronco. Campbell.
War. Channing.
War. Ish-Kishor.
War! Lawson.
War. Li Po.
War. McLean.
War. Ostroff.
War. Shelton.
War Comes. Schneour.
War Is Kind, *sels.* Crane.
War Is the Statesman's Game. *Fr.* Queen Mab. Shelley.
War Poetry. *Fr.* Blenheim. Philips.
War Song, A. Bertrans de Born.
War Song. Davidson.
War Song. *Unknown.*
War Song of Dinas Vawr, The. *Fr.* The Misfortunes of Elphin. Peacock.
War Song to Englishmen, A. *Fr.* King Edward the Third. Blake.
Waste. Studdert-Kennedy.
We were glad together in gladsome meads. *Fr.* The Rhyme of Joyous Garde. Gordon.
We Who Are Left. Whalley.
What Kind of War? Rottman.
What the Orderly Dog Saw. Ford.
When Banners Are Waving. *Unknown.*
Which Side Am I Supposed to Be On? Auden.
While We Slept. Wolff.
White Horse, The. Tu Fu.
Why Should Vain Mortals Tremble. Niles.
Winter Warfare. Rickword.
Without Benefit of Declaration. Hughes.

Women at the Corners Stand, The. Golding.
World War. *Unknown.*
Men Who March Away; Poems of the First World War (MMA). I. M. Parsons, ed.
Oxford Book of War Poetry, The (OBWP). Jon Stallworthy, ed.
Scars Upon My Heart (SUMH). Catherine W. Reilly, ed.
War and the Poet (WaaP). Richard Eberhart *and* Selden Rodman, eds.
War Poets, The (WaP). Oscar Williams, ed.
See also **Soldiers** ***and*** **names of specific wars and battles.**

War Casualties
A Terre. Owen.
Broken Soldier, The. Tynan.
Carentan O Carentan. Simpson.
Convalescent, The. Smith.
Despair. Lindsay.
Disabled. Owen.
Fallen. Corbin.
From My Window. Williams.
Futility. Owen.
Gramophone Tunes. Dobell.
Hospital Visitor, The. Trotter.
Incident, An. Henderson.
March in the Ranks Hard-prest, and the Road Unknown, A. Whitman.
Mental Cases. Owen.
Night Duty. Dobell.
Nightmare Inspection Tour for American Generals. Ruark.
Nocturn at the Institute. McElroy.
Pluck. Dobell.
Screens. Letts.
Sestina with Refrain. Shapcott.
Soldier Is Home, The. Neilson.
"They." Sassoon.
To the Memory of Gavin Wilson (Boot, Leg and Arm Maker). Galloway.
Transport of Wounded in Mesopotamia, 1917. Lawrence.
Vision of 400 Sunrises. Schechter.
War Blinded. Dunn.
Wound-Dresser, The. Whitman.
See also **Soldiers.**

War Dead
After Our War. Balaban.
Anthem for Doomed Youth. Owen.
Armistice. Dehn.
As the Team's Head Brass. Thomas.
Astronomy. Housman.
Autumn, 1914. Webb.
Ballad of Heroes, A. Dobson.
Base Details. Sassoon.
Beach Burial. Slessor.
Blue and the Gray, The. Finch.
Bobby Campbell. *Unknown.*
Broken Bodies. Golding.
Burial in Flanders, The. Nichols.
By the Wood. Nichols.
Casualty. Letts.
Cenotaph, The. Mew.
Certain Dead. Haines.
Charge of the Light Brigade, The. Tennyson.
Classic Encounter. Caudwell.
Come Up from the Fields, Father. Whitman.
Concord Hymn. Emerson.
Coronach. *Fr.* The Lady of the Lake. Scott.
Corpses in the Wood. Toller.
Dead, The ("Blow out, you bugles, over the rich dead!"). *Fr.* 1914. Brooke.
Dead Man's Dump. Rosenberg.
Dead on the War Path. Tewa.
Dead, The ("These hearts were woven of human joys and cares"). *Fr.* 1914. Brooke.
Dead Warrior, A. Housman.
Death of a Soldier, The. Stevens.
Death of the Ball Turret Gunner, The. Jarrell.
Drummer Hodge. Hardy.
Due of the Dead, The. Thackeray.
Dulce et Decorum? Jenkins.
Dulce et Decorum. Wilson.
Dulce et Decorum Est. Owen.
Easter Monday. Farjeon.
1887. Housman.
Elegy for a Dead Soldier. Shapiro.
End, The. Owen.
Epitaph: "Underneath this wooden cross there lies." *Fr.* Elegy for a Dead Soldier. Shapiro.
Epitaphs of the War, 1914-18. Kipling.
Fallen, The. Gurney.
Farewell, The: "It was a' for our rightfu' king." Burns.
Fighting Race, The. Clarke.
For the Fallen. Binyon.
For Valour. Herschel-Clarke.
Forgotten Dead, I Salute You. Stuart.
Gallantry. Douglas.
Gervais. Wilson.
Ghouls, The. Hamilton.
Grass. Sandburg.
Greater Love. Owen.
Gunner. Jarrell.
Happy Death. Freeman.
He Never Smiled Again. Hemans.
Here Dead Lie We. Housman.
Hero, The. Sassoon.
Holy Innocents, The. Lowell.
Homecoming. Dawe.
How Sleep the Brave. Collins.
Hunting Civil War Relics at Nimblewill Creek. Dickey.
Hymn to the Fallen. *Unknown.*
I Stood with the Dead. Sassoon.
In Flanders Fields. McCrae.
In Memoriam (Easter 1915). Thomas.
In Memoriam, Private D. Sutherland. Mackintosh.
In Memory of Basil, Marquess of Dufferin and Ava. Betjeman.
Inscription for Marye's Heights, Fredericksburg. Melville.
Johnny, I Hardly Knew Ye. *Unknown.*
Lamentation, A. Campion.
Lamplight. Cannan.
Land, The. Burt.
Landscape with Figures. Douglas.
Leningrad Cemetery, Winter of 1941. Olds.
Light Casualties. Francis.
"Lord, I Owe Thee a Death." Meynell.
Losses. Jarrell.
Lost Army, The. Lawrence.
Lost Colours, The. Ward.
Man He Killed, The. Hardy.
March, The. Squire.
Memo. Lynch.
Memorial Wreath. Randall.
Memory of the Dead, The. Ingram.
Messmates. Newbolt.
Minstrel Boy, The. Moore.
Mother and Poet. Browning.
My Luve's in Germany. *Unknown.*
New Year, 1916. Harrison.
No Man's Land. Bogle.
Nothing to Report. Herschel-Clarke.
Ode: "Sleep sweetly in your humble graves." Timrod.
Ode to the Confederate Dead. Tate.
Ode to the Finnish Dead. Walsh.
Of all who died in silence far away. Tree.
Of what a quality is courage made. *Fr.* Charles Donnelly. MacDonagh.
Old Road to Paradise, The. Widdemer.
On a Field at Fredericksburg. Smith.
On a Soldier Fallen in the Philippines. Moody.
On the idle hill of summer. *Fr.* A Shropshire Lad. Housman.
On the Spartan Dead at Thermopylae. Simonides.
Parson's Job, The. Bedford.
Perhaps. Brittain.
Photographs: A Vision of Massacre. Harper.
Plaque in the Reading Room for My Classmates Killed in Korea, The. Reeve.
Pro Patria. Carrier.
Protocols. Jarrell.
Remembrance Day in the Dales. Ratcliffe.
Rendezvous. Seeger.
Reported Missing. Keown.
Revision. Newton.
Rouge Bouquet. Kilmer.
Sight in Camp in the Daybreak Gray and Dim, A. Whitman.
Six Young Men. Hughes.
Slain. Crosland.
Soldier, The. Brooke.
Soldier in the Park, The. Riddell.
Soldier, Rest! Thy Warfare O'er. *Fr.* The Lady of the Lake. Scott.
Somebody's Darling. Ravenel de la Coste.
Song of the Camp, The. Taylor.
Spires of Oxford, The. Letts.

Strange Meeting. Owen.
There died a myriad. *Fr.* Hugh Selwyn Mauberley. Pound.
To His Love. Gurney.
To My Daughter Betty, the Gift of God. Kettle.
To the Dead of '98. Johnson.
To Tony (Aged 3). Wilson.
Trench Poets. Rickword.
Ultima Ratio Regum. Spender.
Uncle Robert. Morgan.
Unknown Soldier, The. Rose.
Unknown Warrior. Daryush.
Vacant Chair, The. Washburn *and* Root.
Vergissmeinnicht. Douglas.
Vigil Strange I Kept on the Field One Night. Whitman.
Volunteer, The. Asquith.
Volunteer's Grave, A. Percy.
War. Langland.
War Requiem. Rogers.
When the Dead Men Die. O'Neill.
When You See Millions of the Mouthless Dead. Sorley.
White-Throat Sings, A. Eaton.
Wife in London, A. Hardy.
Wind on the Downs, The. Allen.
Young Dead Soldiers, The. MacLeish.
Home Book of Verse, The (HBV2), vol. II, pp. 2301–2326. Burton Egbert Stevenson, ed.
See also **Soldiers.**

War of 1812
Banks of Champlain, The. *Unknown.*
Battle of Bridgewater, The. *Unknown.*
Battle of New Orleans, The. *Unknown.*
Come All You Bold Canadians. *Unknown.*
Constitution and the *Guerrière,* The. *Unknown.*
James Bird. *Unknown.*
Johnny Bull, My Jo, John. *Unknown.*
Shannon and the *Chesapeake,* The. *Unknown.*
Star-spangled Banner, The. Key.
Ye Parliament of England. *Unknown.*

War of the Austrian Succession
Fontenoy. Davis.

War of the Grand Alliance
Hervé Riel. Browning.

War of the Three Henrys
Ivry. Macaulay.

Warblers
Happy Bird, The. Clare.
Maryland Yellow-Throat, The. Van Dyke.

Ward, John
Captain Ward and the *Rainbow.* *Unknown.*

Ward, William George
Valedictory. Tennyson.

Warren, Joseph
Death of Warren, The. Sargent.
Warren's Address at Bunker Hill. Pierpont.

Warren, Robert Penn
In Praise of Robert Penn Warren. Lehman.

Wars of the Roses
Song at the Feast of Brougham Castle. Wordsworth.
Wars of the Roses, The. *Unknown.*

Warsaw, Poland
Conversation with a Countryman. Slonimski.
Willows in Alma-Ata. Wat.

Warsaw Ghetto
Pesach Has Come to the Ghetto Again. Heller.
Poor Christian Looks at the Ghetto, A. Milosz.
Shtil di Nacht (Silent Is the Night). Glik.
Stone and the Blade of Grass in the Warsaw Ghetto, The. Scheinert.
Zog Nit Keynmol (Tell Us No More). *Unknown.*

Warton, Thomas, the Younger
Lines on Thomas Warton's Poems. Johnson.

Warwickshire, England
Dwindling Forest of Arden, The. *Fr.* Polyolbion. Drayton.

Washing
Old Ellen Sullivan. Welles.

Washing Machines
Our Washing Machine. Hubbell.
See also **Laundry and Laundering.**

Washington, Booker Taliaferro
Alabama Earth. Hughes.
Booker T. and W.E.B. Randall.

Washington, George
At Mount Vernon. Clark.
Boy Washington, The. Thompson.
Cameo No. II. Jordan.
Ever Since. Coatsworth.
February 22. Updike.
First Citizen. Roche.
Footnote to History. Coatsworth.
George Washington. Benét.
George Washington. Ingham.
George Washington. Silverstein.
George Washington. Tippett.
Great Virginian, The. *Fr.* Under the Old Elm. Lowell.
His Task—And Ours. Gould.
Imperial Man. *Fr.* Under the Old Elm. Lowell.
Leetla Giorgio Washeenton. Daly.
Mount Vernon. *Unknown.*
Name of Washington, The. Field.
Never to see a nation born. *Fr.* Under the Old Elm. Lowell.
Ours, and All Men's. *Fr.* Under the Old Elm. Lowell.
Patriotic Poem. Wakoski.
Picture People. Bennett.
Rivers Remember, The. Turner.
To His Excellency, General Washington. Wheatley.
Washington. *Fr.* Ode to Napoleon Buonaparte. Byron.
Washington. Goodman.
Washington. *Fr.* Commemoration Ode. Monroe.
Washington. Turner.
Washington. *Unknown.*
Washington. Williams.
Washington and Lincoln. Stafford.
Washington in Love. Berryman.
When Shall We See Thy Like Again? Wingate.
Which Washington? Merriam.
Whom We Revere. *Fr.* Under the Elm. Lowell.
Young Washington. Guiterman.

Washington (state)
Acres of Clams. *Unknown.*
Age, An. Jensen.
American Landscape with Clouds & a Zoo. Anderson.
Bobber. Carver.
Crow Voices. Tremblay.
Eagle, The. Blessing.
Fish Counter at Bonneville, The. Stafford.
Letter with a Black Border. McPherson.
Mid-August at Sourdough Mountain Lookout. Snyder.
Old Man Con. Box.
Our Strange and Lovable Weather. Matthews.
Sourdough mountain called a fire in. *Fr.* Myths and Texts: Burning. Snyder.
Tahola. Hugo.
White Center. Hugo.

Washington, D.C.
Aeneas at Washington. Tate.
D.C. Shapiro.
Effigy. McElhaney.
From Trollope's Journal. Bishop.
Homage to Paul Mellon, I. M. Pei, Their Gallery, and Washington City. Meredith.
It Pleases. Snyder.
July in Washington. Lowell.
Spring in Washington. Den Boer.
View of the Capitol from the Library of Congress. Bishop.
Washington Cathedral. Shapiro.

Washington Monument
Monument and the Shrine, The. Logan.
Washington Monument by Night. Sandburg.
Washington's Monument. *Unknown.*
Washington's Monument, February, 1885. Whitman.

Washington Square, New York City
Villanelle of Washington Square. Roberts.

Wasp (ship, War of 1812)
Ocean-Fight, The. *Unknown.*
Wasp's Frolic, The. *Unknown.*

Wasps
How to Catch Wasps. *Fr.* Cyder. Philips.
New Hampshire, February. Eberhart.
Upon a Wasp Chilled with Cold. Taylor.
Wasp, The. Davidson.
Wasp, The. Hine.
Wasp, The. *Fr.* Transcripts from Nature. "MacLeod".
Wasp. Nowlan.
Wasp, The. Oates.
Wasp, The. Sharp.

Waspish. Frost.
Wasps. Aldis.
Wasps' Nest, The. Macbeth.

Watches
Mr. Coggs, Watchmaker. Lucas.
To His Watch. Hopkins.
To His Watch, When He Could Not Sleep. Herbert of Cherbury.
Watch, The. Cornford.
Watch, The. Swenson.
Watch Repair. Simic.
See also **Clocks.**

Water
Appogiatura. Hayes.
Bucyrus. Holmes.
Come, Happy Children. *Unknown.*
Desire of Water, The. Jarman.
Diviners, The. Oliver.
Gift of Water, The. Garland.
Glass Town, The. Reid.
Green, Green Is El Aghir. Cameron.
Inscription for a Wayside Spring. Cornford.
Like Water down a Slope. Schneour.
Noise of Waters, The. Joyce.
Reflections on Water. Pitchford.
Sound of Water. O'Neill.
There is a stream that flowed before the first beginning. *Fr.* Water. Raine.
To Drink. Mistral.
To the Revd. Mr. —— on His Drinking Sea-Water. Winstanley.
Waiters. Hoberman.
Water. Conkling.
Water. Jabès.
Water. Larkin.
Water. Sexton.
Water-Drinker, The. Johnson.
Water-Images. Osborn.
Water Song. Ibn Gabirol.
Well, The. Levertov.
Well Water. Jarrell.
Wine and Water. Chesterton.
Word of Water, The. Mayo.

Water Lilies
Cherwell Waterlily, The. Faber.
Clote, The. Barnes.
Dog and the Water-Lily. Cowper.
Monet's "Les Nympheas." Snodgrass.
To Paint a Water Lily. Hughes.
Water-Lily, The. Tabb.

Water Ouzels
Water-Ousel. Webb.
Water Ouzel. Matchett.

Waterbeds
Insomnia the Gem of the Ocean. Updike.
Rift Tide. Walsh.

Watercolors
Ghazal: Japanese Paintbrush. Mott.
"That First Gulp of Air We All Took When First Born." Paddock.
Watercolor of Grantchester Meadows. Plath.

Waterfalls
At a Welsh Waterfall. Hopkins.
By Frazier Creek Falls. Snyder.
By the Waterfall. Adler.
Cataract of Lodore, The. Southey.
Falls of Glomach, The. Young.
Fragment: "Cataract, whirling to the precipice, The." Clare.
Leaping Falls. Kinnell.
Waterfall, The. Vaughan.
Waterfall. Welsh.

Waterford. *See* **County Waterford, Ireland.**

Waterfowl
Duck Pond at Mini's Pasture, a Dozen Years Later, The. Dow.
Lincolnshire's Holland Speaks of Her Waterfowl. *Fr.* Polyolbion. Drayton.
Pair, A. Swenson.
To a Waterfowl. Bryant.
To a Waterfowl. Hall.
Water Fowl. Wordsworth.
Willets, The. Swenson.
See also **Ducks; Geese; Swans.**

Watergate
Final Curtain. Woddis.
Watergate. Herschberger.
See also **Mitchell, Martha; Nixon, Richard Milhous.**

Waterloo, Battle of
Eve of Waterloo, The. *Fr.* The Dynasts. Hardy.
Plains of Waterloo, The. *Unknown.*
Waterloo. *Fr.* Childe Harold's Pilgrimage. Byron.
Waterloo. De Vere.

Watermelons
Ode to the Watermelon. Neruda.
Watermelon. Joans.
Watermelons. Simic.

Watertowers
Watertower. Bellg.

Waterwheels
Water-Wheel, The. Clemo.

Watts, Isaac
For the Bicentenary of Isaac Watts. Nicholson.

Watts, Los Angeles, California
Watts. Kaufman.
Watts. Rivers.

Waugh, Evelyn
Elegy: E. W. Sissman.

Waves
"Dover Beach"—a Note to That Poem. MacLeish.
From the Wave. Gunn.
Great Wave off Kanagwa, The. Egemo.
Hokusai's Wave. Cabral.
How Everything Happens. Swenson.
Main-Deep, The. Stephens.
Song of the Wave, A. Lodge.
There Are Big Waves. Farjeon.

Wayne, Anthony
Anthony Wayne. Guiterman.
Wayne at Stony Point. Scollard.

Wayne, John
Considering the Death of John Wayne. Phillips.
Dear John Wayne. Erdich.

Wealth
Art thou poor, yet hast thou golden slumbers? *At. to* Dekker.
Back to Griggsby's Station. Riley.
Beverly Hills, Chicago. Brooks.
Bewick Finzer. Robinson.
Even as the raven, the crow, and greedy kite. *Unknown.*
For A' That and A' That. Brooks.
Good Rich Man, The. Chesterton.
Looking at Wealth in Newport. Schevill.
Lord Finchley. Belloc.
Mrs. Seymour Fentolin. Herford.
Moneyless Man, The. Stanton.
Mornin's Mornin', The. Brennan.
Nation's Wealth, A. *Fr.* The Fleece. Dyer.
On Dives. Crashaw.
On Late-Acquired Wealth. *Unknown.*
Rich and Poor; or, Saint and Sinner. Peacock.
Rich Man and the Poor Man, The. *Unknown.*
Rich Men, Trust Not. Nashe.
Richard Cory. Robinson.
Short Song of Congratulation, A. Johnson.
Spectator Ab Extra. Clough.
Suicides of the Rich, The. Contoski.
To a Millionaire. Lampman.
To Richard Boyle, Earl of Burlington: Of the Use of Riches. *Fr.* Moral Essays. Pope.
Wealth and Wisdom. *Fr.* The Proverbs of Alfred. *At. to* Alfred, King of England.
Worldly Wealth. Watkyns.

Weariness
Song of the Lotos-Eaters. *Fr.* The Lotos-Eaters. Tennyson.
Tired Tim. De la Mare.

Weasels
Dead Weasel, A. Helwig.
Don't Ever Seize a Weasel by the Tail. Prelutsky.
Weasel, The. *Unknown.*

Weather
Bones of Incontention, The. Cohen.
Border Forecast, A. Landles.
Crow on the fence. *Unknown.*
English Weather. *Fr.* The Fleece. Dyer.
Good Weather. Belli.
Hydrographic Report. Frost.
I love snow and all the forms. Shelley.
If the robin sings in the bush. *Unknown.*
Our Strange and Lovable Weather. Matthews.

Self and the Weather, The. Whittemore.
Sunshiny shower, A. *Unknown.*
Weather. Conkling.
Weather of Olympus, The. Graves.
Weather of the World, The. Nemerov.
Weather Rhymes. Brown.
Weather Wisdom. *Unknown.*
Weathergrams are poems of about ten words. Reynolds.
Weathers. Hardy.
Wild geese, wild geese, ganging to the sea. *Unknown.*
Winter's Onset from an Alienated Point of View. Dugan.
Faber Book of Useful Verse, The (FaBoUs), pp. 31-37. Simon Brett, ed.

Weathervanes
Upon the Weathercock. Bunyan.
Weathercock. Jennings.

Weaving and Weavers
Arachne. Aliesan.
Carpet-Weavers' Lament, The. *Unknown.*
Funny Rigs of Good and Tender-hearted Masters. *Unknown.*
General Ludd's Triumph. *Unknown.*
Jone o' Grinfield. *Unknown.*
Life and the Weaver. Dewar.
Linen Weaver, The. *Unknown.*
Macramé. Riley.
Marrakesh Women. Lifshin.
New Bury Loom, The. *Unknown.*
Poor Cotton Weaver, The. *Unknown.*
Poverty Knock. *Unknown.*
Simple Faith. *Fr.* Truth. Cowper.
Tapestry Weavers, The. Chester.
Weave Room Blues. *Unknown.*
Weaver, The. *Unknown.*
Weaver and the Factory Maid, The. *Unknown.*
Weavers. Heine.
Weaver's Life. *Unknown.*
Work of the Weavers, The. *Unknown.*

Webster, Daniel
At Marshfield. Wilkinson.
Daniel Webster's Horses. Coatsworth.
Ichabod. Whittier.
Why did all manly gifts in Webster fail? Emerson.

Webster, John
John Webster. Swinburne.
Whispers of Immortality. Eliot.

Wedding Songs
Away to Twiver, Away, Away! *Unknown.*
Bridal Song. *Fr.* The Maid's Tragedy. Beaumont *and* Fletcher.
Bridal Song. *Fr.* The Masque of the Middle Temple and Lincoln's Inn. Chapman.
Bridal Song, A. *Fr.* The Pleasant Comedy of Patient Grissill. Dekker.
Bridal Song, A. Shelley.
Entertainment, The, or Porch-Verse, at the Marriage of Master Henry Northleigh and the Most Witty Mistress Lettice Yard. Herrick.
Epithalamium: "Come, virgin tapers of pure wax." Crashaw.
Epithalamion: "Look there! *The Lovers/ in the Flowers.*" Schulman.
Epithalamion: "Now al is done; bring home the bride againe." Spenser.
Epithalamium: "Voice that breathed o'er Eden, The." Keble.
Epithalamion: "Ye learned sisters which have oftentimes." Spenser.
Epithalamy to Sir Thomas Southwell and His Lady, An. Herrick.
Good-Night, The, or Blessing. Herrick.
I Mun Be Married a Sunday. *Fr.* Ralph Roister Doister. Udall.
Nuptial Hymn. *Fr.* The Period of Mourning. Peacham.
Nuptial Song, A, or Epithalamy, on Sir Clipsby Crew and His Lady. Herrick.
Phoenix and the Turtle, The. Shakespeare.
Prothalamion: "Calm was the day, and through the trembling air." Spenser.
Ring, The. Pack.
Sergeant's Weddin', The. Kipling.
Song for a Country Wedding. Smith.
Songs from the Masque of the Gentlemen of Gray's-Inne and the Inner Temple. Beaumont.

Weddings
At last the beef appears in sight. *Fr.* The Collier's Wedding. Chicken.
Ballad upon a Wedding, A. Suckling.
Below fair Peebles, on the River's side. *Fr.* A Marriage betwixt Scrape, Monarch of the Maunders, and Blobberlips, Queen of the Gypsies. Pennecuik.
Betrothed. Bogan.
Black Wedding Song, A. Brooks.
Bride, The. Hope.
I Promessi Sposi. Corman.
Lochinvar. *Fr.* Marmion. Scott.
Marriage. Corso.
Portrait of My Mother on Her Wedding Day. Gilbert.
To the Last Wedding Guest. Gregory.
Wedding. Brown.
Wedding Party. Hall.
See also **Marriage.**

Weeds
Bindweed, The. De la Mare.
Knapweed. Benson.
My Aunt. Hughes.
Tumbleweed. Wagoner.

Weekends
Week-End Naturalist, The. Buchan.
Week-End Sonnet No. 1. Monro.

Weeping. *See* **Tears.**

Weight Lifting
Weight Room, The. Rabbitt.

Welfare
Can I Say. Bird.
Feeding the Lions. Jordan.
Home Is the Sailor. McGinley.
Sexual Privacy of Women on Welfare. Lane.
Stamp Blues. *Unknown.*

Wellington, Arthur Wellesley, 1st Duke of
Duke of Wellington, The. *Fr.* Don Juan. Byron.
Lamentation on the Death of the Duke of Wellington. *Unknown.*
Ode on the Death of the Duke of Wellington. Tennyson.
Warden of the Cinque Ports, The. Longfellow.

Wells
At Grandfather's. Bates.
Cleaning the Well. Ruffin.
Jacob's Well. *Unknown.*
Personal Helicon. Heaney.
Song of the Well. *Fr.* Numbers. Bible, *O.T.*
Well, The. Palés Matos.
Well, The: Two Songs. *Unknown.*

Welsh, The
Tragic Guilt. Rhys.
Welshmen of Tirawley, The. Ferguson.
See also **Wales.**

Wenceslaus, Saint
Good King Wenceslas. Neale.

Wentworth, Thomas, Earl of Strafford
Epitaph on the Earl of Strafford. Cleveland.

Werewolves
Beasts. Wilbur.
Were-Wolf. Hawthorne.

Werfel, Franz
Shooting of Werfel, The. Watkins.

Wesley, Charles
Wesley in Heaven. Brown.

Wessex, England
Wessex Heights. Hardy.

West, Mae
Mae West. Field.

West, Richard
Sonnet on the Death of Richard West. Gray.

West (United States)
Arizona Nature Myth. Michie.
Away Out West. Hall.
Far, Far West, The. *Unknown.*
Goin' Back T'morrer. Garland.
Hitch Haiku. Snyder.
Home on the Range. *Unknown.*
Horse Thief, The. Benét.
Let the Rest of the World Go By. Brennan.
Long Road West, The. Knibbs.
Man of the Open West, The. Monroe.
One more rendezvous. *Fr.* The Song of Jed Smith. Neihardt.
Out Where the West Begins. Chapman.
Out Where the West Begins: A Parody. Douglas.
Ruin of Bobtail Bend, The. Adams.
Somewhere West. Jones.
Spanish Johnny. Cather.
Stages on a Journey Westward. Wright.
Westering. Kane.
Western Magic. Austin.
Western Ways. Lattimore.
Westward Ho! Miller.
Westward Ho. *Unknown.*
Wild West. Vinz.

Best Loved Poems of the American West (BPAW). John J. *and* Barbara T. Gregg, eds.
Cowboy Songs and Other Frontier Ballads (CoSo). John A. Lomax *and* Alan Lomax, eds.
New Poetry of the American West (NPAW). Peter Wild *and* Frank Graziano, eds.
19 New American Poets of the Golden Gate (NPGG). Philip Dow, ed.
Poems of the Old West (PoOW). Levette J. Davidson, ed.

West Indies
Beauties of Santa Cruz, The. Freneau.
Indian Maid, The; Demararie, Oct. 27, 1781. Thompson.
Jamaican Bus Ride. Tessimond.
O Carib Isle! Crane.
Sabbaths, W. I. Walcott.
Tales of the Islands. Walcott.

West Virginia
Harpers Ferry. Rodman.
How Old Brown Took Harpers Ferry. Stedman.
In Response to a Rumor That the Oldest Whorehouse in Wheeling, West Virginia, Has Been Condemned. Wright.
Looking Down on West Virginia. Dickson.
Narrative. Atkins.
78 Miners in Mannington, West Virginia. Phillips.
Written at the White Sulphur Springs. Key.

West Wind
Ode to the West Wind. Shelley.
To the Western Wind. Halevi.
To the Western Wind. Herrick.
West Wind, The. Masefield.
Western Wind. *Unknown.*
Wind from the West, A. Watt.

Westminster Abbey
In Westminster Abbey. Betjeman.
On First Entering Westminster Abbey. Guiney.
On the Tombs in Westminster Abbey. *At. to* Beaumont *and to* Basse.
Refusal, A. Hardy.

Weston, Edward
Edward Weston in Mexico City. Dacey.

Whales and Whaling
Al Capone in Alaska. Reed.
And God Created the Great Whales. *Fr.* Paradise Lost. Milton.
Autumn. Carpenter.
Beached Whales off Margate. Dunn.
Bill the Whaler. Lawson.
Blackfish Poem. Acorn.
Blood on the Sails. P. *and* J. Colclough.
Blow Ye Winds in the Morning. *Unknown.*
Blue Whale, The. Watson.
Boothbay Whale, The. *Unknown.*
Brand Fire New Whaling Song Right from the Pacific Ocean. *Unknown.*
Coast of Peru, The. *Unknown.*
Death of a Whale. Blight.
Elegy for 41 Whales Beached in Florence, Ore., June, 1979. Bierds.
Father Mapple's Hymn. *Fr.* Moby Dick. Melville.
For a Coming Extinction. Merwin.
Greenland Whale Fishery, The. *Unknown.*
Jonah and the Whale. Meynell.
Killing a Whale. Gill.
Leviathan. Merwin.
Leviathan: A Poem in Four Movements. Pitchford.
Nantucket Whalers. Henderson.
Norway. Dubie.
Quaker Graveyard in Nantucket, The. Lowell.
Shooting Whales. Strand.
Song of the Hatteras Whale, A. *Unknown.*
Stranded Whales, The. Dutton.
There She Blows! *Unknown.*
Thousand years now had his breed, A. *Fr.* The Cachalot. Pratt.
Triumph of the Whale, The. Lamb.
Waterwitch, The. *Unknown.*
Whale. Benét.
Whale, The. Buson.
Whale, The. *Fr.* The Progress of the Soul. Donne.
Whale, The ("Cethegrande is a fis"). *Unknown.*
Whale, The ("Now I will fashion the tale of a fish"). *Fr.* Physiologus. *Unknown.*
Whale and the *Essex,* The. Sullivan.
Whale at Twilight. Coatsworth.
Whale, His Bulwark, The. Walcott.
Whale Song. Maguire.
Whales. Bates.
Whales, The. Young.
Whales off Wales, The. Kennedy.
Whales Weep Not! Lawrence.
Where Cape Delgado strikes the sea. *Fr.* The Cachalot. Pratt.

Wharves
Bight, The. Bishop.
Down among the Wharves. Jewett.
Jake's Wharf. Booth.
Old Wharves, The. Field.

Wheat
Color in the Wheat. Garland.
Dakota Wheat-Field, A. Garland.
Sheaves, The. Robinson.
Spirit of the Wheat, The. Valentine.

Wheatley, Phillis
Address to Miss Phillis Wheatley, An. Hammon.

Wheelbarrows
Red Wheelbarrow, The. Williams.

Wheeler, Joseph
Wheeler at Santiago. Gordon.

Wheeling, West Virginia
In Response to a Rumor That the Oldest Whorehouse in Wheeling, West Virginia, Has Been Condemned. Wright.

Wheelock, Eleazar
Eleazar Wheelock. Hovey.

Wheels
Junkyards. Rayford.

Whigs (English political party)
Absalom and Achitophel, Pt. I. Dryden.

Whippoorwills
Going to Sleep in the Country. Moss.
Mountain Whippoorwill, The. Benét.

Whiskey
Calton Weaver, The. *Unknown.*
John Barleycorn. *Unknown.*
Kentucky Bootlegger. *Unknown.*
Kentucky Moonshiner. *Unknown.*
Mountain Dew. *Unknown.*
Raftery's Dialogue with the Whiskey. Fallon.
Real Old Mountain Dew. *Unknown.*
Rye Whiskey. *Unknown.*
Whiskey Johnny. *Unknown.*

Whistler, James Abbott McNeill
There's a combative artist named Whistler. Rossetti.
To a Portrait of Whistler in the Brooklyn Art Museum. Cox.
To James McNeill Whistler. Henley.
To Whistler, American. Pound.

White, Peregrine
Peregrine White and Virginia Dare. Benét.

White, William Allen
To William Allen White. Ferber.

White Sulphur Springs, West Virginia
Written at the White Sulphur Springs. Key.

Whitman, Walt
Adhesive Autopsy of Walt Whitman, The. Williams.
After Walt Whitman. Chesterton.
Face on the Daguerreotype. Rosten.
Let us tunnel. *Fr.* Letters to Walt Whitman. Johnson.
Ode to Walt Whitman. García Lorca.
Of W. W. (Americanus). Stephen.
Old Walt. Hughes.
Pact, A. Pound.
Reading Walt Whitman. Forbes.
Sincere Flattery of W. W. Stephen.
Supermarket in California, A. Ginsberg.
To Walt Whitman. MacInnes.
To Walt Whitman in America. Swinburne.
Tribute of Grasses, A. Garland.
Walt Whitman. Carnevali.
Walt Whitman. Honig.
Walt Whitman. Morris.
Walt Whitman. Robinson.
Walt Whitman. Williams.
Walt Whitman at Bear Mountain. Simpson.
Walt Whitman at the Reburial of Poe. Christopher.
Whitman. Honig.
Whitman. Levis.

Whitsunday. *See* **Pentecost.**

Whittier, John Greenleaf
Mr. Whittier. Scott.
Mrs. Judge Jenkins. Harte.
To John Greenleaf Whittier. Ward.
White Magic; an Ode. Braithwaite.

Whittier. *Fr.* A Fable for Critics. Lowell.
Whittier. Sangster.
Whittling
Wonderful Man, A. Fisher.
Widecombe Fair
Widdecombe Fair. *Unknown.*
Widows and Widowers
At first I was given centuries. Atwood.
Brisk Young Widow, A. *Unknown.*
Contention betwixt a Wife, a Widow, and a Maid, A. Davies.
Dear Old Girl. Buck.
Epitaph on the Monument of Sir William Dyer at Colmworth, 1641. Dyer.
Fisher's Widow, The. Symons.
I am a widow, robed in black, alone. Pisan.
Methought I Saw My Late Espoused Saint. Milton.
On Seeing an Officer's Widow Distracted. Barber.
Parents-without-Partners Picnic, The. Schaefer.
Poem for My Dead Husband. Roberts.
Portrait of a Widow. Strauss.
Racer's Widow, The. Glück.
Reasons for and against Marrying Widows. Selyns.
To a Lady on the Death of Her Husband. Wheatley.
Upon the Death of Sir Albert Morton's Wife. Wotton.
Urgency. Sholl.
Widow, The. Davenport.
Widow. Pollak.
Widow, The. Ramsay.
Widow, The. Southey.
Widow in Wintertime, A. Kizer.
Widow Machree. *Fr.* Handy Andy. Lover.
Widow Malone, The. Lever.
Widow Perez, The. Soto.
Widow to Her Son. Smith.
Widower, The. Tyler.
Widows. Masters.
Widow's Lament. *Fr.* Shih Ching. *Unknown.*
Widow's Lament in Springtime, The. Williams.
Wigs
Bald Cavalier, The. *Unknown.*
Wilberforce, William
Sonnet to William Wilberforce, Esq. Cowper.
Wilde, Oscar
Arrest of Oscar Wilde at the Cadogan Hotel, The. Betjeman.
Dead Poet, The. Douglas.
Message, A. Ives.
Wildebeests. *See* **Gnus.**
Wilderness
Above Pate Valley. Snyder.
Among High Hills. Soutar.
Bushed. Birney.
Call of the Wild, The. Service.
Do You Fear the Wind? Garland.
En Route. Scott.
Inversnaid. Hopkins.
Laurentian Shield. Scott.
Lonely Land, The. Smith.
Lords of the Wilderness. Leyden.
North, The. McKinnon.
Okeechobee. Allison.
Oreads. Raine.
Peace of Wild Things, The. Berry.
Poem after a Speech by Chief Seattle, 1855. Brashers.
Poem, 1972. Scroggie.
Pre-Cambrian Shield, The. *Fr.* Towards the Last Spike. Pratt.
Requiem for Sonora. Shelton.
Rocky Acres. Graves.
Staying Alive. Wagoner.
There was a time on this fair continent. *Fr.* Tecumseh. Mair.
Toil of the Trail, The. Garland.
Track into the Swamp, The. Morse.
Wilderness Is Tamed, The. Coatsworth.
Wildflowers
Ghost-Flowers. Higginson.
Kind. Ammons.
Peppergrass. Plumly.
Violet Bank, A. *Fr.* A Midsummer Night's Dream. Shakespeare.
Wildflower. Plumly.
Woodspurge, The. Rossetti.
William II, Emperor of Germany
Kaiser & Co. Rose.
William III, King of England (William of Orange)
Dialogue between King William and the Late King James on the Banks of the Boyne, A. Blount.
Duchess of York's Ghost, The. *Unknown.*
Fable, A: "In Aesop's tales an honest wretch we find." Prior.
Impartial Inspection, The. *Unknown.*
Mourners, The. Higgons.
New Song of an Orange, A. *Unknown.*
On the Late Metamorphosis of an Old Picture of Oliver Cromwell's. *Unknown.*
Panegyric, A: "Hail happy William, thou art strangely great." *Unknown.*
Shash, The. *Unknown.*
Upon the King's Return from Flanders. Hall.
William IV, King of England
Royal Adventurer, The. Freneau.
Williams, Roger
Canonicus and Roger Williams. *Unknown.*
Roger Williams. Butterworth.
Williams, Theodore Samuel (Ted)
Dream of a Baseball Star. Corso.
Williams, William Carlos
Couplets for WCW. Christina.
Doctor Bill Williams. Walsh.
Elegy for W. C. W., the Lovely Man, An. *Fr.* Dream Songs. Berryman.
Letter to William Carlos Williams, A. Rexroth.
Nuances of a Theme by Williams. Stevens.
Out of Your Hands. Weiss.
Phone Call to Rutherford. Blackburn.
To W. C. W. M.D. Kreymborg.
To William Carlos Williams. Kinnell.
W. C. W. Ray.
"Yes, But. . ." Weiss.
Willow Herbs
Rose Bay Willow Herb. Ray.
Willow Trees
Hunting Pheasants in a Cornfield. Bly.
Song, A: "My head on moss reclining." *Unknown.*
To the Willow-Tree. Herrick.
Weeping Willow. Aldridge.
Willow, The. Tu Fu.
Willow Poem. Williams.
Willows, The. Eaton.
Willows. Langland.
Willows in the Snow. Tsuru.
Wills
Extraordinary Will. Jackett.
In the Twentieth Century of My Trespass on Earth. *Fr.* The Dead Shall Be Raised Incorruptible. Kinnell.
Last Will and Testament, A. Winstanley.
Mira's Will. Leapor.
Wiltshire, England
Houseless Downs, The. *Fr.* The Shepherds' Song, Sung before Queen Anne, on the Wiltshire Downs, 11 June 1613. Ferebe.
Prehistoric Burials. Sassoon.
Wiltshire Downs. Young.
Winchester, England
In Praise of Winchester. *Unknown.*
Winchester. Johnson
Winchester, Virginia
Sheridan's Ride. Read.
Wind
Address to a Child During a Boisterous Winter Evening. Wordsworth.
Aim Was Song, The. Frost.
All Day I Hear. Joyce.
Beggar Wind, The. Austin.
Big Wind. Roethke.
Blow, Blow, Thou Winter Wind. *Fr.* As You Like It. Shakespeare.
Cars once steel and green, now old. Zukofsky.
Cook County. MacLeish.
Dirge, A: "Rough wind, that moanest loud." Shelley.
Drummer Boy. Stafford.
Evening Wind, The. Bryant.
Four Winds, The. Leslie.
Four Winds, The. Lüders.
Haiku: "Balmy spring wind, A." Wright.
Hearing the Wind at Night. Swenson.
High Wind at the Battery. Pomeroy.
I Saw the Wind Today. Colum.
Irish Wind, An. Dennis.
January. Williams.
King Wind. Van Doren.
Lake Harriet: Wind. Taylor.

Little Wind. Greenaway.
Mid-Country Blow. Roethke.
Mistral. Howes.
Mountain Wind. Loots.
My Lady Wind. *Unknown.*
Night Wind, The. Field.
O Mighty, Melancholy Wind. Todhunter.
O Thirsty Wind. *Unknown.*
On the Death of Neruda. Van Brunt.
On Wenlock Edge the Wood's in Trouble. Housman.
Piper on the Hill, The. Shorter.
Pirate Wind. Carr.
Prayer to the Wind, A. Carew.
Sleepless at Crown Point. Wilbur.
Small Dark Song. Dacey.
Snow-Storm, The. Emerson.
Solar Signals. Schuck.
Song of the Four Winds, The. *Fr.* The Misfortunes of Elphin. Peacock.
Song to the Wind, A. Taliessin.
Sound of the Wind, The. *Fr.* Sing-Song. Rossetti.
Spring Wind. Turner.
Storm at Sea. *Unknown.*
Strong Wind, A. Clarke.
Summer Wind. Bryant.
Sun Has Set, The. Brontë.
Sweet and Low. Tennyson.
Theory of Wind, A. Goldbarth.
There came a wind like a bugle. Dickinson.
To the Maids Not to Walk in the Wind. *Fr.* The Conquest of Granada. Gogarty.
Villain, The. Davies.
Weather. MacLeish.
Weather of Olympus, The. Graves.
What if a much of a which of a wind. Cummings.
Who Has Seen the Wind? *Fr.* Sing-Song. Rossetti.
Wild Geese, The. Jacob.
Wind/ flattening its gaunt furious self against. *Fr.* The Wind Our Enemy. Marriott.
Wind. Brown.
Wind. Dobell.
Wind, The. Graddon.
Wind. Hughes.
Wind. *Malay.*
Wind, The. Reeves.
Wind, The. Rendall.
Wind, The. Stephens.
Wind, The. Stevenson.
Wind. *Fr.* Riddles (Exeter Book). *Unknown.*
Wind and the Bird, The. *Unknown.*
Wind and the Moon, The. Macdonald.
Wind at Penistone, The. Davie.
Wind begun to knead the grass, The. Dickinson.
Wind Carries Me Free, The. Shady.
Wind Has Wings, The. *Unknown.*
Wind in a Frolic, The. Howitt.
Wind in the Grass. Van Doren.
Wind Is a Cat. Fuller.
Wind Is Blind, The. Meynell.
Wind of the Cliff Ka Hea, The. Thompson.
Wind Song. Sandburg.
Wind tapped like a tired man, The. Dickinson.
Wind That Shakes the Rushes, The. Clare.
Wind-Wolves. Sargent.
Winds. McCrae.
Winds, The. Tusser.
Wind's Head, The. Sweeney.
Wind's Song, The. "Setoun."
Wind's Work. Moore.
Windy Morning. Behn.
Windy Nights. Stevenson.
Windy Planet, The. Dillard.
Windy Trees. Ammons.
Words to the Wind. Di Cicco.
See also **East Wind; North Wind; South Wind; West Wind.**
Windflowers. *See* **Anemones.**
Windhovers. *See* **Falcons.**
Windmills
Mill, The. Heyen.
Windmill, The. De Tabley.
Windmill, The. Longfellow.
Windmill in March. Privett.
Windmill on the Cape. Sieller.
Windmills, The. *Fr.* Arizona Poems. Fletcher.
Window Boxes
Window Boxes. Farjeon.
Windows
Climbing. Epstein.
Kitchen Window. Ebberts.
Window, The. Aiken.
Window. Cherner.
Window to the East. Evans.
Windows, The. Herbert.
Windows in Providence. Barnstone.
W's for Windows. McGinley.
Windsor, Wallace Warfield, Dutchess of
Abdication Street Song. *Unknown.*
Windsor Castle
In Windsor Castle. Surrey.
Windsor Forest, England
Lines Written in Windsor Forest. Pope.
Thy forests, Windsor! and thy green retreats. *Fr.* Windsor Forest. Pope.
Wine
Awake, My Soul. *Fr.* Wine-Songs. Ibn Ezra.
Bacchus. Emerson.
Bacchus's Opinion of Wine, and Other Beverages. *Fr.* Bacchus in Tuscany. Redi.
Bottle of Chianti, The. Souster.
Bring Me the Cup. *Fr.* Wine-Songs. Ibn Ezra.
Bubbling Wine. Abu Zakariya.
Champagne Rosé. Kenyon.
Drink, Friends. *Fr.* Wine-Songs. Ibn Ezra.
Epicure, The. Cowley.
Epilogue: "Poets pour us wine, The." Browning.
Five Arabic Verses in Praise of Wine. *Unknown.*
Fly, The. Ayres.
Forty Pounds of Blackberries Equals Thirteen Gallons of Wine. Hoeft.
Havdolah Wine. Ulinover.
His Fare-Well to Sack. Herrick.
In a Wine Cellar. Daley.
Logic. *Unknown.*
Ode in the Praise of Sack, An. *Unknown.*
On a Honey Bee. Freneau.
Red Wine. Justin.
Spirit of Wine, The. Henley.
Under Leafy Bowers. Al-Harizi.
Welcome to Sack, The. Herrick.
Wine. Lebensohn.
Wine and Water. Chesterton.
Wine Bowl. Doolittle ("H. D.").
Wine upon beer, I counsel thee. *Unknown.*
Wreathe the Bowl. Moore.
Wings
Wings. Psalms. Bible, *O.T.*
Winkelried, Arnold von
Make Way For Liberty. Montgomery.
Winslow, John Ancrum
Eagle and Vulture, The. Read.
Winnipeg, Manitoba
Farewell to Winnipeg. Daniells.
Signature. Livesay.
Winter
Advent. *Fr.* For the Time Being; a Christmas Oratorio. Auden.
Aging. Wakoski.
Alone. De la Mare.
Ancient Music. Pound.
Before Sunrise in Winter. Sill.
Birches. Frost.
Birds at Winter Nightfall. Hardy.
Blue Horses. Roberson.
Blue Winter. Francis.
Calm Winter Sleep. Corke.
Cardinal. Howes.
Child's Winter Evening, A. John.
Cold Blows the Wind. Hamilton.
Cold Fear. Roberts.
Cold Wave Blues. *Unknown.*
Cold winter now is in the wood. Coatsworth.
Colonial Set. Bailey.
Come with Me into Winter's Disheveled Grass. Swenson.
Coming of the Cold, The. Roethke.
Comparison, A. Farrar.
Cover. Frost.
Crumbs. De la Mare.
Cynthia in the Snow. Brooks.

Dartmouth Winter-Song. Hovey.
Death of the Flowers, The. Bryant.
Dirge for the Year. Shelley.
Down swept the chill wind from the mountain peak. *Fr.* The Vision of Sir Launfal. Lowell.
Early Illinois Winter, An. Kuo.
Elegy, An: "In early winter before the first snow." Scovell.
Emmonsail's Heath in Winter. Clare.
End of the Street, The. Haines.
Evening and Morning in Winter, An. *Fr.* Prologues to the Aeneid. Douglas.
Exposure. Owen.
February Twilight. Teasdale.
First Ice of Winter. Shorb.
First Winter. Harada.
Glass World. Donnelly.
Gone Were but the Winter Cold. Cunningham.
Great Frost, The. *Fr.* Trivia. Gay.
Haiku: "Winter rain at night." Wright.
Hillside Thaw, A. Frost.
How One Winter Came in the Lake Region. Campbell.
Hugh Maguire. O'Hussey.
I Walkt the Other Day. Vaughan.
Ice. Roberts.
In Defense of Felons. Mezey.
In Winter. Wallace.
It Is Winter, I Know. Cullen.
Jingle Bells. Pierpont.
Lalique. Porter.
Late Winter. Hall.
Long Walk before the Snows Began, A. Bly.
Love. Browning.
March 1st. Spivack.
Meditation in Winter. Dunbar.
Midnight. Lampman.
Midwinter. Trowbridge.
Midwinter Thaw. Pratt.
My Winter Past. Grier.
New Snow. Rowles.
New Year's Song. Hughes.
Night Is Freezing Fast, The. Housman.
Night was winter in his roughest mood, The. *Fr.* The Winter Walk at Noon. Cowper.
No Possum, No Sop, No Taters. Stevens.
November Night, Edinburgh. MacCaig.
Now Comes the Blast of Winter. *Unknown.*
Now Winter Nights Enlarge. Campion.
Ode to Winter. Campbell.
Old Man's Winter Night, An. Frost.
Old Winter. Noel.
On the Dark, Still, Dry, Warm Weather Occasionally Happening in the Winter Months. White.
One Horse Open Sleigh, The. Pierpont.
Onset, The. Frost.
Out of My Study Window. Whittemore.
Outside the Door. Wynne.
Persia. Sackville-West.
Poem on the End of Sensation. Stange.
Poet in Winter. Lucie-Smith.
Relics. Wagoner.
Remembering the Winter. Bennett.
Robin, The. Daniel.
Sayings from the Northern Ice. Stafford.
Schoolboys in Winter. Clare.
Sestina d'Inverno. Hecht.
Settling In. Stuart.
Shine Out, Fair Sun. *Unknown.*
Signs of Winter. Clare.
Six Winter Privacy Poems. Bly.
Sledding Song, A. Schlichter.
Slushy snow splashes and sploshes, The. Hoberman.
Snow had begun in the gloaming, The. *Fr.* The First Snow-Fall. Lowell.
Snow Man, The. Stevens.
Snow toward Evening. Cane.
Snow-Bound. Whittier.
Snowdrop. Hughes.
Snow-Flakes. Longfellow.
Snowy Night. Haines.
Something Told the Wild Geese. Field.
Song: "I'd much rather sit there in the sun." Krauss.
Song: "Lovely hill-torrents are." Turner.
Song in the Cold Season. Morse.
Song of Winter, A. *Unknown.*
Sonnet: "The winter deepening, the hay all in." Wilbur.
Star-Talk. Graves.
Stopping by Woods on a Snowy Evening. Frost.
Storm at Sea. *Unknown.*
Summer and Winter. Shelley.
Summer Is Gone. *Unknown.*
Thaw. Thomas.
These. Williams.
Thin ice/ Free advice. McCord.
'Tis Winter Now. Longfellow.
To Winter. Blake.
Tree Sleeps in the Winter, The. Russell.
Triolet on a Dark Day. Fishback.
Turning. Finch.
Turning Point. Holshouser.
Tu-Whit To-Who. *Fr.* Love's Labour's Lost. Shakespeare.
Up in the Air. Ramsay.
Up in the Morning Early. Burns.
Velvet Shoes. Wylie.
Walk on a Winter Day. Allen.
What Is Winter? Blunden.
When biting Boreas, fell and doure. *Fr.* A Winter Night. Burns.
When gadding snow makes hillsides white. *Fr.* Winter. Mair.
When Icicles Hang by the Wall. *Fr.* Love's Labour's Lost. Shakespeare.
Where It Is Winter. O'Neil.
White Fields. Stephens.
Widow bird sate mourning for her love, A. Shelley.
Winter. Akhmadulina.
Winter. *Fr.* The Task. Cowper.
Winter. De la Mare.
Winter. Donaghy.
Winter. Douglas.
Winter. Hurnard.
Winter. Jaszi.
Winter. Mair.
Winter. *Fr.* The Unknown Eros. Patmore.
Winter. *Fr.* A Mirror for Magistrates. Sackville.
Winter. Synge.
Winter. *Fr.* The Seasons. Thomson.
Winter. *Unknown.*
Winter. Williams.
Winter, a Dirge. Burns.
Winter Burn. Hill.
Winter Circus. Fisher.
Winter Climb. Eunaich.
Winter Coming On. Bell.
Winter Day. Fried.
Winter Days. Abbey.
Winter Days. Owen.
Winter Evening. De la Mare.
Winter Evening. Lampman.
Winter Fairyland in Vermont. Osgood.
Winter Feast. Frost.
Winter Garden. Gascoyne.
Winter Has Come. *Unknown.*
Winter Hymn, A—to the Snow. Jones.
Winter in Lower Canada. *Fr.* The Emigrant. O'Grady.
Winter in the Fens. Clare.
Winter in the Wood. Eastwick.
Winter Is Icumen In. Smith.
Winter Lakes, The. Campbell.
Winter Landscape. Berryman.
Winter Love. Jennings.
Winter Memories. Thoreau.
Winter Morning. Smith.
Winter: My Secret. Rossetti.
Winter, New Hampshire. Kherdian.
Winter News. Haines.
Winter Night, A. Barnes.
Winter Night. Day Lewis.
Winter Night. Fitzgerald.
Winter Night. Pasternak.
Winter Night, Cold Spell. Nelson.
Winter Nights. Dunetz.
Winter Noon. Teasdale.
Winter Piece, A. Bryant.
Winter-Piece, A. Diaper.
Winter Portrait. Southey.
Winter Remembered. Ransom.
Winter Scene. *Fr.* The Task. Cowper.
Winter Scene, A. Whittemore.

Winter Scene. Young.
Winter Shore, The. Wade.
Winter Sketch. Bourinot.
Winter Sleep. Wylie.
Winter Song. Daiches.
Winter Streams. Carman.
Winter Time. *Fr.* A Child's Garden of Verses. Stevenson.
Winter Twilight, A. Grimkė.
Winter Wakens All My Care. *Unknown.*
Winter without Snow, A. McClatchy.
Winterfall. *Unknown.*
Wintering. Plath.
Winter's Tale, A. Thomas.
Winter's Troops. *Fr.* Winter. Cotton.
Wizard Frost. Sherman.
Words of Finn, The. *Unknown.*
World Winter. Birney.
Year's-End. Wilbur.

Winters, Yvor
To Yvor Winters, 1955. Gunn.

Wisconsin
Crows, The. Engels.
Driving to Sauk City. Woessner.
For the Death of Vince Lombardi. Dickey.
From Garvey's Farm: Seneca, Wisconsin. Hoeppner.
La Crosse at Ninety Miles an Hour. Eberhart.
Walking Milwaukee. Witt.

Wisdom
Art of Happiness, The. Young.
Come, Captain Age. Cleghorn.
Coming of Wisdom with Time, The. Yeats.
For This Is Wisdom. *Fr.* The Teak Forest. "Hope."
Happy Is the Man That Findeth Wisdom. *Fr.* Proverbs. Bible, *O.T.*
Life's Lessons. *Unknown.*
Lost Genius, The. Piatt.
Ode to Wisdom. Carter.
Swarthmore Phi Beta Kappa Poem, The. Lattimore.
Two Voices. Corbin.
Wealth and Wisdom. *Fr.* The Proverbs of Alfred. *At. to* Alfred, King of England.
Where Shall Wisdom Be Found? *Fr.* Job. Bible, *O.T.*
Wisdom. Middleton.
Wisdom. Sobiloff.
Wisdom is the finest beauty of a person. Yoruba.
Word to the Wise, A. Duer.
See also **Reason.**

Wise Men. *See* **Magi.**

Wishes
Bunches of Grapes. De la Mare.
He Wishes for the Cloths of Heaven. Yeats.
I Keep Three Wishes Ready. Wynne.
My Inside-Self. Field.
My Wishes. Healy.
Rathers. Austin.
Reflections at Dawn. McGinley.
Richard Roe and John Doe. Graves.
Star Wish. *Unknown.*
Wishes. Ault.
Wishin' Well, The. Cruickshank.
Wishing. Allingham.

Wit
Ode: Of Wit. Cowley.

Witchcraft and Witches
Against Witches. *Unknown.*
Allison Gross. *Unknown.*
Ballad of the Harp-Weaver, The. Millay.
Ballad of the Hoppy-Toad. Walker.
Broomstick Train, The ("Look out! Look out, boys! Clear the track!"). *Fr.* The Broomstick Train. Holmes.
Demon Lover, The. *Unknown.*
Eight Witches. Lee.
Fable: "Pity the girl with crystal hair." Aiken.
Fatal Sisters, The. Gray.
Hag, The ("The hag is astride"). Herrick.
Hag, The ("The staff is now greased"). Herrick.
Hag-Ridden. Graves.
Her Kind. Sexton.
Her Strong Enchantments Failing. Housman.
In Salem. Clifton.
John Darrow. Davidson.
Korf's Enchantment. Morgenstern.
Lincolnshire; from the Wolds to the Fens. *Fr.* The Sad Shepherd. Jonson.
Little Creature, The. De la Mare.
Mr. Wells. *Fr.* The Sorcerer. Gilbert.
Molly Means. Walker.
Mother Maudlin the Witch. *Fr.* The Sad Shepherd. Jonson.
Queen Nefertiti. *Unknown.*
Ride-by-Nights, The. De la Mare.
Riverman, The. Bishop.
Song of Wandering Aengus, The. Yeats.
Sorceress, The! Lindsay.
Spell, A. *Fr.* Oedipus. Dryden.
Tailor, The. Beddoes.
Tam o' Shanter. Burns.
Thrice Toss These Oaken Ashes in the Air. Campion.
Two Witches. Frost.
Two Witches, The. Graves.
Uncle Mells and the Witches' Tree. Roberts.
Wanteda Witch's Cat. McGee.
What is the opposite of a prince? Wilbur.
Wind on the Hills, The. Shorter.
Witch, A. Barnes.
Witch, The. Coleridge.
Witch, The. Hinkson.
Witch, The. Southey.
Witch o' Fife, The. Hogg.
Witch of East Seventy-Second Street, The. Bishop.
Witch, The! The Witch! Farjeon.
Witchcraft: New Style. Abercrombie.
Witches. Hughes.
Witches, The. *Unknown.*
Witches' Ballad, The. Scott.
Witches' Brew. *Fr.* Macbeth. Shakespeare.
Witches' Charms, The. *Fr.* The Masque of Queens. Jonson.
Witches' Menu. Nikolay.
Witches' Ride, The. Kuskin.
Witch's Ballad, The. Scott.
Witch's Broomstick Spell. *Unknown.*
Witch's Cat, The. Serraillier.
Witch's Chant, A. Hogg.
Witch's Spell, A. *Unknown.*
Witch's Work Song, The. White.
Wizard of Alderley Edge, The. Coe.
Yellow Witch of Caribou, The. Robertson.
Why Am I Grown So Cold? Poems of the Unknowable (WSC), pp. 24–42, 170–185. Myra Cohn Livingston, ed.

Wittgenstein, Ludwig Josef Johann
Philosopher and the Birds, The. Murphy.

Wives
Abroad and at Home. Swift.
After the Golden Wedding. Stephen.
Aged Wino's Counsel to a Young Man on the Brink of Marriage, The. Kennedy.
Alive or Not. Purdy.
Auld Robin Gray. Lindsay.
Ballad of the Despairing Husband. Creeley.
Berry Picking. Layton.
Brewer's Man, The. Strong.
Cinnamon Peeler, The. Ondaatje.
Contention betwixt a Wife, a Widow, and a Maid, A. Davies.
Deil o' Bogie, The. Gray.
Double Transformation, The. Goldsmith.
Dream, The. "Bendo."
Elder's Reproof to His Wife, An. *Somali.*
Exequy, The. King.
Fisherman's Wife, The. Mitchell.
Fishermen's Wives, The. Namanworth.
For My Lover, Returning to His Wife. Sexton.
Fox and the Hare, The. *Unknown.*
Good Woman, The. MacLean.
He Waiata mo Te Kare. Baxter.
House Carpenter's Wife, The. *Unknown.*
Housewife's Lament, The. *Unknown.*
I Married in My Youth a Wife. Cunningham.
Johnny Sands. *Unknown.*
Julia. Rose.
Man May Live Thrice Nestor's Life, A. Norton.
Milton's Wife on Her Twenty-third Birthday. Conant-Bissell.
My Old Wife's a Good Old Cratur. *Unknown.*
My Wife's a Winsome Wee Thing. Burns.
New Wife, The. Gond.
Next Day. Jarrell.

Old Flame, The. Lowell.
On His Deceased Wife. Milton.
On My Wife's Birth-Day. Smart.
On the Death of His Wife. O'Dalaigh.
Peter, Peter, pumpkin eater. Mother Goose.
Poor Man's Work Is Never Done, A. *Unknown.*
Retreat of Ita Cagney, The. Hartnett.
Ruined Cottage, The. Wordsworth.
Scholar's Wife, The. Mernit.
Single Girl. *Unknown.*
Surfaces. Meinke.
Sweet 'n Sour. Lim.
Ten Week Wife. Donovan.
To the Ladies. Chudleigh.
Trusty, Dusky, Vivid, True. Stevenson.
Upon the Death of Sir Albert Morton's Wife. Wotton.
When Adam Was First Created. *Unknown.*
Wife, A. Lewis.
Wife a-Lost, The. Barnes.
Wife a-Prais'd, A. Barnes.
Wife's Lament, The. *Unknown.*
Wish for a Young Wife. Roethke.
Wives in the Sere. Hardy.
Young Housewife, The. Williams.
Seel also **Marriage.**

Wolfe, James
Bold General Wolfe. *Unknown.*
Brave Wolfe. *Unknown.*
Death of Wolfe, The. *Unknown.*

Wolsey, Thomas, Cardinal
Cardinal Wolsey's Farewell. *Fr.* King Henry VIII. Shakespeare.
Colin Clout, *sels.* Skelton.
On Cardinal Wolsey. *Unknown.*
Such a prelate, I trow. *Fr.* Why Come Ye Not to Court. Skelton.

Wolverines
For the Last Wolverine. Dickey.

Wolves
Four Mountain Wolves. Silko.
Fox and the Wolf, The. *Unknown.*
Howling of Wolves, The. Hughes.
Last Wolf, The. TallMountain.
Lobo. Lillard.
Prairie Wolves. Carr.
Wolf. Blue Cloud.
Wolf, The. Durston.
Wolf. *Fr.* A Bestiary. Rexroth.
Wolf and the Dog, The. La Fontaine.
Wolf and the Lamb, The. La Fontaine.
Wolf and the Stork, The. La Fontaine.
Wolf Cry, The. Sarett.
Wolves. Haines.
"Word" of a Wolf Incircled by the Hunt, The. Mongol.

Woman Suffrage
Brother Baptis' on Woman Suffrage. Jonas.
See also **Voting and Voters.**

Wombats
Weary Will. Paterson.
Wombat, The. Nash.

Women
Against Blame of Woman. Desmond.
Against Them Who Lay Unchastity to the Sex of Women. Habington.
Against Women. Juvenal.
Against Women. *Unknown.*
Against Women either Good or Bad. Norton.
Another. In Defence of Their Inconstancie. Jonson.
Another Poem about the Madness of Women. Wayman.
Are Women Fair. Davison.
As Joe Gould says in. Cummings.
At the Theater. Herbert.
Bad Girl Blues. *Unknown.*
Ballade of the Women of Paris. Villon.
Beautiful Black Women. Baraka.
Beautiful Woman Who Sings, The. Allen.
Before Bed. Waldrop.
Belly Dancer. Wakoski.
Beneath the Shadow of the Freeway. Cervantes.
Birds. "O'Sullivan."
Black Sister. Cumbo.
Black Woman. Madgett.
Bookshop Idyll, A. Amis.
Bottle Up and Go. *Unknown.*
Breaking Tradition. Mirikitani.
Bubba Esther, 1888. Whitman.
C. L. M. Masefield.
Cantata for Two Lovers. Sandburg.
Chain Letters. Fulton.
Changed Woman, The. Bogan.
Changes. Bulwer-Lytton.
Characters of Women. *Fr.* Love of Fame. Young.
Charming Woman, The. Sheridan.
Childhood. *Fr.* The Four Ages of Man. Bradstreet.
Colours of Love, The. Devlin.
Combing. Cardiff.
Creatrix. Wickham.
Darby and Joan. Honeywood.
Dark Phrases. Shange.
Dear Old Stockholm. Young.
December: Of Aphrodite. Merwin.
Declaimer, The. Baker.
Dedication of the Cook. Wickham.
Dispraise of Absalom, The. *Unknown.*
Divine Office of the Kitchen, The. Hallack.
Duplicity of Women, The. Lydgate.
Energetic Women. Lawrence.
Epigram on Woman, An. Ayres.
Epistle to a Lady: Of the Characters of Women. *Fr.* Moral Essays. Pope.
Essay on Woman, An. Leapor.
Eve-Song. Gilmore.
Evil Devil Woman. *Unknown.*
Farm Wife. Mitchell.
Farmer's Curst Wife, The. *Unknown.*
Father of Women, A. Meynell.
Faults, Male and Female. *Unknown.*
Female Friend, The. Whur.
Female God, The. Rosenberg.
Female of the Species, The. Kipling.
Fine Young Folly. *Fr.* The Queen of Aragon. Habington.
For love no time has she, or inclination. *Fr.* The Modern Fine Lady. Jenyns.
For Mariella, in Antrona. Simpson.
For We Are All Madwomen. Sweeney.
Foreign Land, The. *Fr.* The Angel in the House. Patmore.
Four Women. Simone.
Freedom Song for the Black Woman, A. Gregory.
Friend Cato. Wickham.
From an Old House in America. Rich.
From Sappho to myself, consider the fate of women. *Fr.* Pro Femina. Kizer.
From the Cavities of Bones. Parker.
Furniture of a Woman's Mind, The. Swift.
Garment of Good Ladies, The. Henryson.
Gentle Echo on Woman, A. Swift.
Glass of Beer, A. Stephens.
Glory of Women. Sassoon.
Green Grow the Rashes. Burns.
Grinding Vibrato. Cortez.
Hand That Rocks the Cradle Is the Hand That Rules the World, The. Wallace.
Heart of a Woman, The. Johnson.
Helpmate. Chapin.
Her Sister. O'Neill.
His Mother-in-Law. Parke.
Home Winner, The. Lindberg.
Hush, Honey. Saunders.
Hypocrite Women. Levertov.
I Am a Black Woman. Evans.
I Knew a Woman. Roethke.
I Know a Lady. Thomas.
I Never Even Suggested It. Nash.
I Shall Not Die for Thee. *Unknown.*
I, Woman. McClaurin.
If the Heart of a Man. *Fr.* The Beggar's Opera. Gay.
If Women Could Be Fair. Vere.
I'll Tell You What a Flapper Is. Freeman.
Impossible to Trust Women. *Unknown.*
In Celebration of My Uterus. Sexton.
In her first passion woman loves her lover. *Fr.* Don Juan. Byron.
In Her Praise. Graves.
In Librum. Davies.
In the Old Guerilla War. Pastan.
Introduction, The. Winchilsea.
It's No Good! Lawrence.
I've Got the Giggles Today. Herbert.
James Alley. *Unknown.*

Jewish Woman, The. Kolmar.
Katie May. *Unknown.*
Kneading. Crooker.
Korean Woman Seated by a Wall, A. Meredith.
Labourer's Wife, A. *Fr.* To the Street Piano. Davidson.
Ladies, The. Kipling.
Lady, Lady. Spencer.
Lady's Dressing Room, The. Swift.
Lady's-Maid's Song, The. Hollander.
Lay Your Arms Aside. Ferriter.
Legend of Viable Women, A. Eberhart.
Let the Toast Pass. *Fr.* The School for Scandal. Sheridan.
Letter from Caroline Herschel (1750–1848). Cedering.
Letter to My Sister. Spencer.
Looking Out. Chasin.
Lord Walter's Wife. Browning.
Lords of Creation, The. *Unknown.*
Lost and Given Over. Brady.
Mabel Kelly. O'Carolan.
Madonna of the Hills. Allen.
Man, Man, Man. *Unknown.*
Man's Woman, A. Davies.
Marie Curie Contemplating the Role of Women Scientists in the Glow of a Beaker. Frazier.
Marrakesh Women. Lifshin.
Maxim Revised, A. *Unknown.*
Mean Drunk Poem. Thesen.
Meditation at Kew. Wickham.
Metamorphoses. Fuller.
Mistresses. *Unknown.*
Mother. Montoya.
My Lady Carenza of the lovely body. *Unknown.*
My Mother's Sister. Day Lewis.
Mynstrelles Songe: Angelles bee wrogte to bee of neidher kynde. *Fr.* Aella. Chatterton.
Nakedness of women, The. Blake.
Negro Woman. Alexander.
Nehi Blues. *Unknown.*
New York Woman, The. Sissman.
Next Day. Jarrell.
No Images. Cuney.
No Second Troy. Yeats.
Ode to a Beautiful Woman. Clark.
Of Women. Edwards.
Of Women. *Fr.* The Thousand and One Nights. Mathers.
Of Women No More Evil. *Unknown.*
Oh, oh, you will be sorry for that word! Millay.
Old Woman, The. Campbell.
Old Women. Deutsch.
On Being a Woman. Parker.
On the Debt My Mother Owed to Sears Roebuck. Dorn.
On Woman. Yeats.
Ordinary Women I. Hacker.
Ordinary Women II. Hacker.
Out on Santa-Fe—Blues. *Unknown.*
Patterns. Lowell.
Peggy Browne. O'Carolan.
Perfect Woman. Wordsworth.
Photographer's Wife, The. Beeler.
Picasso's Women. Cabral.
Piccante. Di Michele.
Pioneer Woman. Crawford.
Poem for Some Black Women. Rodgers.
Portrait d'une Femme. Pound.
Portrait. Bogan.
Prayer for My Daughter, A. Yeats.
Present. Sanchez.
Prologue, The: "To sing of wars, of captains, and of kings." Bradstreet.
Pueblo Women I Watched Get Down in Brooklyn. Rose.
Queen-Ann's-Lace. Williams.
Raising the Flag. Vizenor.
Rape Poem. Piercy.
Rebel Girl, The. Hill.
Ride a cock-horse to Banbury Cross. Mother Goose.
Robbing and Stealing Blues. *Unknown.*
Sail and Oar. Graves.
Saturday Blues. *Unknown.*
Serious Merriment of Women, The. Goedicke.
Shack, The. Miller.
Shall I, Wasting in Despair. *Fr.* Fidelia. Wither.
She. Roethke.
She. Wilbur.
She sweeps with many-colored brooms. Dickinson.
She Walked Unaware. MacDonogh.
She Was a Phantom of Delight. Wordsworth.
Short Haired Woman. *Unknown.*
Sisters, The. Lowell.
Smothered Fires. Johnson.
Snapshots of a Daughter-in-Law. Rich.
Song: "Go and catch a falling star." Donne.
Song: "Ladies, though to your conqu'ring eyes." *Fr.* The Comical Revenge. Etherege.
Song: "Love a woman? You're an ass!" Rochester.
Song: "When lovely woman stoops to folly." *Fr.* The Vicar of Wakefield. Goldsmith.
Song: "With my frailty don't upbraid me." Congreve.
Song: "Woman's face is full of wiles, A." Gifford.
Song of Songs, The. Heine.
Sonnet: Dolce Stil Novo. Ewart.
Sonnet XLI: "I, being born a woman and distressed." Millay.
Streets. Lowell.
Streets of New York, The. Blossom.
Sun Was Slumbering in the West, The. Hood.
Suzie Wong Doesn't Live Here. Mark.
Tame Cat. Pound.
That Reminds Me. Nash.
That Women Are but Men's Shadows. Jonson.
There Has to Be a Jail for Ladies. Merton.
There Is Nothin' like a Dame. Hammerstein.
These Women All. Heath.
This Pretty Woman. *Unknown.*
Three Poems for Women. Griffin.
To a Dark Girl. Bennett.
To a Pretty Girl. Zangwill.
To a Young Lady. Savage.
To Caelia. *Unknown.*
To Daphne and Virginia. Williams.
To Kate, Skating Better Than Her Date. Daiches.
To the Man Who Watches Spiders. Fox.
To Their Excellencies the Lord Justices of Ireland, the Humble Petition of Frances Harris. Swift.
To Women. Hugo.
To Women, as Far as I'm Concerned. Lawrence.
Transit. Rich.
Treat the woman tenderly, tenderly. *Unknown.*
Tribute, The. *Fr.* The Angel in the House. Patmore.
Triolet: "All women born are so perverse." Bridges.
Troubled Woman. Hughes.
Trust in Women. *Unknown.*
Twicknam Garden. Donne.
Two Parents, The. "MacDiarmid."
Two Strange Worlds. Pereira.
Upon Some Women. Herrick.
Vampire, The. Kipling.
Villon's Straight Tip to All Cross Coves. Henley.
Virtuous Wife, The. Trimberg.
Virtuous Woman, The. *Fr.* Proverbs. Bible, *O.T.*
Volcanic Venus. Lawrence.
Warrior Maid, The. Branch.
Washer-Woman, The. Bohanan.
Wasn't your mother a woman? Honnamma.
Way It Was, The. Clifton.
Weeksville Women. Loftin.
What One May and May Not Call a Woman. *Unknown.*
What Women Are Not. *Unknown.*
Why Do We Love. Rudyerd.
Why, Some of My Best Friends Are Women. McGinley.
Wife's Tale, The. Heaney.
Wish, A. Lerner.
Woman. Barrett.
Woman. Layton.
Woman. Malangatana.
Woman. *Fr.* Samson Agonistes. Milton.
Woman ("A comfort but a queer companion"). *Unknown.*
Woman in Sunshine, The. Stevens.
Woman in the Wagon, The. Robertson.
Woman Is a Worthy Thing, A. *Unknown.*
Woman Me. Angelou.
Woman of Three Cows, The. *Unknown.*
Woman Poem. Giovanni.
Woman Waits for Me, A. Whitman.
Woman Who Understands, The. Appleton.
Woman Work. Angelou.
Woman's Answer to the Vampire, A. Blake.

Woman's Arms. Anacreon.
Woman's Song, A. McElroy.
Womanwork. Allen.
Women. Bogan.
Women. Cartwright.
Women. Heath.
Women. Swenson.
Women and Men. Mumin.
Women at the Corners Stand, The. Golding.
Women in Vietnam, The. Paley.
Women Open Cautiously. Lee.
Women Speak Out in Defense of Themselves, The. *Fr.* The Thesmophoriazusae. Aristophanes.
Women's Degrees. Godley.
Women's Longing. *Fr.* Women Pleased. Fletcher.
Wonder Woman. Lim.
Yellow Woman Speaks. Woo.
Yet Cloe sure form'd without a Spot. *Fr.* Moral Essays. Pope.
Young Acacia, The. Bialik.
Black Sister; Poetry by Black American Women, 1746–1980 (BlSi). Erlene Stetson, ed.
Book of Women Poets from Antiquity to Now, A (BoWoP). Aliki Barnstone *and* Willis Barnstone, eds.
Bread and Roses; an Anthology of Nineteenth- and Twentieth-Century Poetry by Women Writers (BrRo). Diana Scott, comp.
I Hear My Sisters Saying; Poems by Twentieth-Century Women (IHMS). Carol Konek *and* Dorothy Walters, ed.
No More Masks! An Anthology of Poems by Women (NMM). Florence Howe *and* Ellen Bass, eds.
Penguin Book of Women Poets, The (PBWP). Carol Cosman, Joan Keefe, *and* Kathleen Weaver, eds.
Salt and Bitter and Good: Three Centuries of English and American Women Poets (SBG). Cora Kaplan, ed.
Scars Upon My Heart: Women's Poetry & Verse of the First World War (SUMH). Catherine W. Reilly, ed.
That's What She Said; Contemporary Poetry and Fiction by Native American Women (TWSS). Rayna Green, ed.
Women Poets in English, The (WPE). Ann Stanford, ed.
Women Poets of the World (WPOW). Joanna Bankier *and* Deirdre Lashgari, eds.
See also **Feminism; Girls.**

Wood
Dark Wood. Wedde.
Old Boards. Bly.
Wood-Pile, The. Frost.
Woodworker's Ballad. Palmer.
Workbox, The. Hardy.

Wood, Grant
Grant Wood's American Landscape. Scott.

Woodchucks. *See* **Groundhogs.**

Woodcocks
My Woodcock. Chalmers.

Woodpeckers
Hewel, or Woodpecker, The. *Fr.* Upon Appleton House. Marvell.
Legend of the Northland, A. Cary.
Woodpecker, The. Roberts.

Woods. *See* **Forests.**

Woodstock, New York
Woodstock. Mitchell.

Wool
Benediction for the Felt. Mongol.
Braid Claith. Fergusson.
Wool Trade, The. *Fr.* The Fleece. Wesley.

Woolf, Virginia
Water-Images. Osborne.

Worcestershire, England
At Arley. Young.
Bredon Hill. Housman.

Words
Coal. Lorde.
Elegy: "In my collection, the words are, we use." Loney.
Feelings about Words. O'Neill.
Glass. Francis.
Idle Words. Landor.
Like Ghosts of Eagles. Francis.
Lost Word. Burden.
Lyrick for Legacies. Herrick.
Meditation at Lagunitas. Hass.
Moon, Sun, Sleep, Birds, Live. Patchen.
Permanently. Koch.
Symbols. Roskolenko.
Threes. Sandburg.
Two Words; a Wedding. Nichol.
Word. Spender.
Word is dead, A. Dickinson.
Word Man, The. Moffi.
Words. Plath.
Words That Speak of Death. Eldan.
Words Words Words. Krysl.
See also **Language.**

Wordsworth, Christopher
On Christopher Wordsworth, Master of Trinity. Kennedy.

Wordsworth, William
Bards, The. De la Mare.
Dedication: "Bob Southey! You're a poet—poet-laureat." *Fr.* Don Juan. Byron.
Fragment in Imitation of Wordsworth. Fanshawe.
He Lived amidst th' Untrodden Ways. Coleridge.
Here Pause: The Poet Claims at Least This Praise. Wordsworth.
In the Lake Country. Wissinger.
Lost Leader, The. Browning.
Memorial Verses. Arnold.
Next comes the dull disciple of thy school. *Fr.* English Bards and Scotch Reviewers. Byron.
On a Portrait of Wordsworth by B. R. Haydon. Browning.
Raised are the dripping oars. *Fr.* The Youth of Nature: Wordsworth's Country. Arnold.
Resolution of Dependence. Barker.
Some of Wordsworth. Landor.
Sonnet, A: "Two voices are there: one is of the deep." Stephen.
To the Poet Wordsworth. Hemans.
To William Wordsworth. Coleridge.
To Wordsworth. Clare.
To Wordsworth. Landor.
To Wordsworth. Shelley.
William Wordsworth. Keyes.
With Wordsworth at Rydal. Fields.
Wordsworth. Lord.
Wordsworth's Grave. Watson.

Work. *See* **Labor and Laborers.**

Work Songs
American Folk Poetry (AmFP). Duncan Emrich, ed.
Blues Line, The (BluL). Eric Sackheim, comp.

Workhouses
Parish Poor-House, The. *Fr.* The Village. Crabbe.

World. *See* **Earth.**

World Federation
For I dipped into the future, far as human eye could see. *Fr.* Locksley Hall. Tennyson.
Universal Republic, The. Hugo.
See also **United Nations.**

World War I
À Terre. Owen.
Aftermath. Sassoon.
And There Was a Great Calm. Hardy.
Another Reply to "In Flanders Fields." Armstrong.
Anthem for Doomed Youth. Owen.
Anzac Cove. Gellert.
Apologia pro Poemate Meo. Owen.
At the Front. Erskine.
August, 1914. Masefield.
August 1914. Rosenberg.
"Blighters." Sassoon.
Break of Day in the Trenches. Rosenberg.
But sweet sister death has gone debauched today and stalks. *Fr.* In Parenthesis. Jones.
Calligram, 15 May 1915. Apollinaire.
Channel Firing. Hardy.
Charing Cross. Roberts.
Christmas: 1924. Hardy.
Christmas Eve in France. Fauset.
Christmas 1914. Harding.
Connaught Rangers, The. Letts.
Corpses in the Wood. Toller.
Counter-Attack. Sassoon.
Death and the Fairies. MacGill.
Disabled. Owen.
Dulce et Decorum Est. Owen.
Dying Patriot, The. Flecker.
End of World War One, The. Olds.
Epicedium. Miller.
Epitaphs of the War, 1914-18. Kipling.
Everyone Sang. Sassoon.
Farmer Remembers the Somme, The. Palmer.

First Division Marches, The. Rice.
For All We Have and Are. Kipling.
Futility. Owen.
Gethsemane. Kipling.
Great War, The. Scannell.
Gun Teams. Frankau.
Home Thoughts in Laventie. Tennant.
In Flanders Fields. McCrae.
In Flanders Fields. *Unknown.*
In Flanders Now. Jaques.
In Memoriam: Easter 1915. Thomas.
In the Dordogne. Bishop.
In Time of "The Breaking of Nations." Hardy.
Irish Airman Foresees His Death, An. Yeats.
Iron Music, The. Ford.
Jezreel. Hardy.
Lighten Our Darkness. Douglas.
Little Car, The. Apollinaire.
Little Saling. Baker.
Little Song of the Maimed. Péret.
Mademoiselle from Armentières. *Unknown.*
Mail Call. Bensko.
MCMXIV. Larkin.
1917–1919. Hoyt.
Parable of the Old Man and the Young, The. Owen.
Peace. *Fr.* 1914. Brooke.
Pity of It, The. Hardy.
Private, A. Thomas.
Rear-Guard, The. Sassoon.
Reply to "In Flanders Fields." Mitchell.
Reprisals. Yeats.
Rouen. Cannan.
Rouge Bouquet. Kilmer.
Sergeant-Major Money. Graves.
Show, The. Owen.
Smoke-Blue Plains, The. Clark.
Soldier, The. *Fr.* 1914. Brooke.
Song of the Dark Ages. Young.
Sonnets Written in the Fall of 1914. Woodberry.
Spring Offensive. Owen.
Star, The. Conkling.
Summer in England, 1914. Meynell.
These Men. Gellert.
They Who Wait. Going.
To a Conscript of 1940. Read.
To the United States of America. Bridges.
Trench Poets. Rickword.
Unscarred Fighter Remembers France, The. Alling.
Vampire, The. Aiken.
Veteran of the Great War, A. Bensko.
Victory in the Cabarets. Untermeyer.
Vlamertinghe; Passing the Château, July 1917. Blunden.
War Story. Stallworthy.
Zonnebeke Road, The. Blunden.
Men Who March Away (MMA). I. M. Parsons, ed.
Scars Upon My Heart: Women's Poetry & Verse of the First World War (SUMH). Catherine W. Reilly, ed.

World War II
Ballad of Banners, The. Lehmann.
Ballad of the D-Day Dodgers. *Unknown.*
Beach Burial. Slessor.
Before Invasion, 1940. Betjeman.
Bella Ciao. *Unknown.*
Bird, The. Simpson.
Black-out. Jeffers.
Breaking. Allan.
Carentan O Carentan. Simpson.
Chez-Nous. Austin.
Children's Crusade 1939. Brecht.
Christmas 1942. Irvin.
D-Dawn. McGarvey.
Death of an Aircraft. Causley.
Death of the Ball Turret Gunner, The. Jarrell.
Eighth Air Force. Jarrell.
El Alamein Revisited. Macnab.
England's Difficulty. Heaney.
Exodus 1940. Wolfenstein.
Firebombing, The. Dickey.
Footnote to Enright's "Apocalypse." Bell.
For Lover Man, and All the Other Young Men Who Failed to Return from World War II. Williams.
Fourth Act. Jeffers.
Full Moon; New Guinea. Shapiro.
Here war is harmless like a monument. *Fr.* Sonnets from China. Auden.
Hitler, frothy-mouth, wooden-head. Maori.
Homecoming. Shapiro.
In a London Schoolroom. Kirkup.
In Distrust of Merits. Moore.
In Westminster Abbey. Betjeman.
Incident on a Front Not Far from Castel di Sangro. Brown.
Kilroy. Viereck.
Landscape with Figures. Douglas.
Leningrad Cemetery, Winter of 1941. Olds.
Less Nonsense. Herbert.
Lilacs and the Roses, The. Aragon.
Little Boats of Britain, The. Carsley.
Losses. Jarrell.
Man unto His Fellow Man. *Fr.* On a Note of Triumph. Corwin.
May-June, 1940. Jeffers.
Moon and the Night and the Men, The. Berryman.
Nerves. Sagittarius.
Neutrality. MacNeice.
Night of Battle. Winters.
Nike. Wazyk.
Norfolk Memorials. Leavenworth.
Notes for a Movie Script. Holman.
On the Pilots Who Destroyed Germany in the Spring of 1945. Spender.
1 September 1939. Berryman.
Ops in a Wimpey. *Unknown.*
Palermo, Mother's Day, 1943. Belvin.
Picture of Okinawa, A. Schmitz.
Picture Postcards. Radnóti.
Pilots, Man Your Planes. Jarrell.
Remembering That Island. MacGrath.
Reverie of a Mum. Keesing.
Scyros. Shapiro.
Second Air Force. Jarrell.
September 1, 1939. Auden.
Sergeant, The. Johnson.
Siciliana: The Landings at Gela. Koehler.
Spring, 1942. Fuller.
Spring Offensive, 1941. Biggs.
Streets of Laredo, The. MacNeice.
Sunday: New Guinea. Shapiro.
There Is Yet Time. Steece.
This Was My Brother. Gould.
Timoshenko. Keyes.
To a Conscript of 1940. Read.
Troopship for France, War II. Bogin.
V-J Day. Ciardi.
Vale from Carthage. Viereck.
Vergissmeinnicht. Douglas.
War. Langland.
Wartime Dawn, A. Gascoyne.
Welcoming Party, A. Montague.
Written in a Time of Crisis. Benét.

World's Fair, 1939
Flushing Meadows, 1939. Hoffman.

Worms
Autobiography of a Lungworm. Fuller.
Christmas Dinner. Rosen.
Fishing Song, A. Rands.
Fury of Flowers and Worms, The. Sexton.
I'd like to be a worm. Gay.
Old Shellover. De la Mare.
Our little kinsmen after rain. Dickinson.
Periphrastic Insult, Not a Banal, A. Cunningham.
Sick Rose, The. *Fr.* Songs of Experience. Blake.
This Is an African Worm. Danner.
To a Worm Which the Author Accidentally Trode Upon. Hawkins.
Wee Little Worm, A. Riley.
Worm, The. Bergengren.
Worm, The. Souster.

Wormwood
Tall Ambrosia. Thoreau.

Worship
All Hail the Power of Jesus' Name. Perronet.
Anthem ("Let us praise our Maker, with true passion extol Him"). Auden.
As Spring the Winter. Bradstreet.
At Mass. Lindsay.
Child My Choice, A. Southwell.
First-Day Thoughts. Whittier.
Floods Clap Their Hands, The. *Fr.* Psalms. Bible, *O.T.*
From All That Dwell below the Skies. Watts.

Gascoigne's Good-Morrow. Gascoigne.
Go, Heart, unto the Lamp of Licht. *Unknown.*
Heavens Declare the Glory of God, The. *Fr.* Psalms. Bible, *O.T.*
Hosanna to Christ. Watts.
Hymn: "Lord, when the wise men came from far." Godolphin.
In the First Cave. Mayne.
Jordan ("Who says that fictions only and false hair"). Herbert.
May 20: Very Early Morning. Shaw.
O my Lord, if I worship you from fear of Hell. Rabi'a the Mystic.
On Christmas-Day. Traherne.
Pied Beauty. Hopkins.
Praise to the holiest in the height. *Fr.* The Dream of Gerontius. Cardinal Newman.
Psalm C: "O be joyful in the Lord, all ye lands." Kethe.
Psalm CIII: "Praise the Lord, O my soul." Lyte.
Psalm CXLVII: "Praise ye the Lord." Pembroke.
Psalm CXLVII: "Praise ye the Lord." Smart.
Some keep Sunday going to church. Dickinson.
Song of Hannah, The. *Fr.* First Samuel. Bible, *O.T.*
Song to David, A. Smart.
Sunday. Herbert.
Temper, The. Herbert.
True Hymn, A. Herbert.
Water and Worship: An Open-Air Service on the Gatineau River. Avison.
Worship. Whittier.
Ye holy Angels bright. *Fr.* A Psalm of Praise. Baxter.
See also **Churches; Prayer; Religion.**

Wotton, Sir Henry
Letter to Sir H. Wotton at His Going Ambassador to Venice. Donne.

Wounded Knee, Battle of
I Expected My Skin and My Blood to Ripen. Rose.

Wreaths
Wreathmakertraining. Patten.

Wren, Sir Christopher
Homage to Wren. MacNeice.
Sir Christopher Wren. *Fr.* Clerihews. Bentley.

Wrens
Contrast, The; the Parrot and the Wren. Wordsworth.
Dove says, Coo, coo, The. Mother Goose.
Jenny Wren. Davies.
Kill a robin or a wren. *Unknown.*
Lark, The ("Malisons, malisons, more than ten"). *Unknown.*
Little Lady Wren. Robinson.
Looking at a Dead Wren in My Hand. Bly.
Robin and the redbreast, The. *Unknown.*
Wren, The. *Unknown.*
Wrens, The. Burke.

Wrestling and Wrestlers
Antaeus; a Fragment. Owen.
Funeral Games for Patroclus, The: Wrestling to a Draw. *Fr.* The Iliad. Homer.
Rasslers, The. Barney.
Ripper Collins' Legacy. Johnson.
Spartan Wrestler, The. Damagetus.
Two Wrestlers. Francis.
Wrestling. Fraser.

Wright, Richard
Mourning Letter from Paris, A. Rivers.
Richard, Richard: American Fuel. Dixon.
To Richard Wright. Rivers.

Writing and Writers
Burning Hills. Ondaatje.
Canadian Prairies View of Literature, The. Donnell.
Dichtung und Wahrheit. Curnow.
John Horace Burleson. *Fr.* Spoon River Anthology. Masters.
Jordan ("When first my lines"). Herbert.
Long Term Suffering. Eberhart.
Mr. Francis Beaumont's Letter to Ben Johnson. Beaumont.
Ode to Himself, An ("Where do'st thou careless lie"). Jonson.
See also **Handwriting.**

Wyatt, Sir Thomas
Divers Thy Death. Surrey.
In Praise of Wyatt's Psalms. Surrey.
In the Rude Age. Surrey.
Note on Wyatt, A. Amis.
Of the Death of Sir T. W. Surrey.
Wyatt Resteth Here. Surrey.

Wye (river), Wales and England
Lines Composed a Few Miles above Tintern Abbey. Wordsworth.
Meandering Wye. *Fr.* The Banks of Wye. Bloomfield.

Wyoming
Accountability. Stafford.
Cutting Wood on Shell Creek. Ehrlich.
Heart Mountain Japanese Relocation Camp, The: 30 Years Later. Levendosky.
Old Photo, 1942. Uba.
Old Trial Town, Cody, Wyoming. Garmon.
Orchard, The. Ehrlich.
Other Women's Children. Waniek.
Rumors of War in Wyoming. Rea.
Sheepherder, The. Sarett.
Snow Country. Etter.
Trestle Bridge, The. Wright.
12 Photographs of Yellowstone. Koertge.
Way of Speaking, A. Ehrlich.

X

X-Rays
After X-Ray. Pastan.
Röntgen Photograph. Eybers.
Walk in Würzburg, A. Plomer.
X-Ray. Ray.
X-Ray. Speyer.

Xantippe
Xantippe. Levy.

Xenophanes
Xenophanes. Emerson.

Y

Yachts
Yachts on the Nile. Spencer.
Yachts, The. Williams.
See also **Boats.**

Yaks
Mad Yak, The. Corso.
Yak, The. Belloc.
Yak, The. *Fr.* Child's Natural History. Herford.
Yak, The. Prelutsky.
Yak, The. Sheard.
Yak. Smith.

Yale University
Mother of Men. Hooker.
On the Democracy of Yale. Jones.
Yale Boola! Hirsh.

Yankees, New York (baseball team)
Ballad of Dead Yankees, The. Petersen.
Baseball and Writing. Moore.

Yarrow *or* Yarrow Water, Scotland
Braes of Yarrow, The. Hamilton.
Braes of Yarrow, The. Logan.
Yarrow Revisited. Wordsworth.
Yarrow Unvisited. Wordsworth.
Yarrow Visited. Wordsworth.

Years
What Are Years? Moore.

Yeats, John Butler
John Butler Yeats. Foster.

Yeats, William Butler
After W. B. Yeats. Chesterton.
Bring Home the Poet. MacDonough.
Circus Animals' Desertion, The. Yeats.
Death of Yeats, The. Barker.
In Memory of W. B. Yeats. Auden.
Letter to David Campbell on the Birthday of W. B. Yeats, 1965, A. Hope.
Ode: "On the Death of William Butler Yeats." Smith.
To W. B. Yeats Who Says That His Castle of Ballylee Is His Monument. Gogarty.
Under Ben Bulben. Yeats.
William Yeats in Limbo. Keyes.
"Young poets, The," he murmured. *Fr.* Yeats in Dublin. Watkins.

Yellow
Symphony in Yellow. Wilde.
Yellow. McCord.
Yellow Light. Hongo.

Yellowstone Park
12 Photographs of Yellowstone. Koerge.

Yesenin, Sergey
Death of the Epileptic Poet Yesenin, The. Boyajian.
Yew Trees
Fallen Yew, A. Thompson.
Moon and the Yew Tree, The. Plath.
Old yew, which graspest at the stones. *Fr.* In Memoriam A. H. H. Tennyson.
Tapestry Trees. Morris.
Yew-Trees. Wordsworth.
Yiddish
Move On, Yiddish Poet. Glatstein.
On Reading Mr. Ytche Bashes' Stories in Yiddish. Ehrlichman.
Where the Cedars. Glatstein.
Yiddish. Herzberg.
Yiddish. Sutskever.
Yiddish Poet. Jacobs.
Yom Kippur
Day of Atonement. Myers.
Kol Nidra. Leiser.
On the Day of Atonement. Amichai.
Riding Westward. Shapiro.
Yom Kippur. Bloch.
Yom Kippur. Chaet.
Yom Kippur. Day.
Yom Kippur. Pastan.
Yom Kippur. Zangwill.
Yom Kippur: Fasting. Whitman.
York, England
Coldness, The. Silkin.
Yorkshire, England
In Teesdale. Young.
Inside the Cave. Grigson.
Sonnet: Composed after a Journey across the Hamilton Hills, Yorkshire. Wordsworth.
Yosemite Valley, California
Now. Monroe.
Young, Andrew
Status Symbols. Sostrom.
Young, Brigham
Brigham Young. *Unknown.*
Mormon Bishop's Lament, The. *Unknown.*
Nauvoo. Taylor.
Young, Lester
Lester Leaps In. Young.
Lester Young. Joans.
Young Men's Christian Association (Y.M.C.A.)
Soldier's Plea for the YMCA, A. Reed.
Young Pretender, The. *See* **Stuart, Charles Edward.**
Younger, Cole
Cole Younger. *Unknown.*
Youth
A'Chuilionn. Hutchison.
Anthem for Doomed Youth. Owen.
Apology for Youth. Madeleva.
Aquellos Vatos. Villanueva.
At Majority. Rich.
At the Doors. Der Nistor.
At 21. Belisle.
Ballade of Lost Objects. McGinley.
Barefoot Boy, The. Whittier.
Bargain. Driscoll.
Bedtime Story, A. Mezey.
Birches. Frost.
Boy Reciter, The. Everett.
Boy's Song, A. Hogg.
Cherries. Schneour.
Crabbed Age and Youth. *Fr.* The Passionate Pilgrim. Shakespeare.
Daedalus. Reid.
Deceptrices, The. Williams.
Dedication to the Generation Knocking at the Door. Davidson.
Description of Beauty, A. Daniel.
Down by the Salley Gardens. Yeats.
English Schoolboy, The. *Fr.* The Play of the Weather. Heywood.
Exit. MacDonald.
Farm Child. Thomas.
Father William. *Fr.* Alice's Adventures in Wonderland. "Carroll."
Fern Hill. Thomas.
Flight of Youth, The. Stoddard.
For Freckle-faced Gerald. Knight.
For My Son on the Highways of His Mind. Kumin.
Furniture. Harris.
Garret, The. Béranger.
Generous Years, The. Spender.
Girl in the Foreign Movie, The. Goedicke.
Green Apples. Randall.
Growing Old. Learned.
Has Sorrow Thy Young Days Shaded? Moore.
Her Dancing Days. Adams.
How Soon Hath Time. Milton.
How to Be Old. Swenson.
I Saw from the Beach. Moore.
In a Spring Still Not Written Of. Wallace.
In an Age of Fops and Toys. *Fr.* Voluntaries. Emerson.
In Memoriam F. A. S. Stevenson.
In Youth Is Pleasure. *Fr.* Lusty Juventus. Wever.
Intimations of Sublimity. *Fr.* The Prelude. Wordsworth.
Lads in Their Hundreds, The. Housman.
Laid in My Quiet Bed. Surrey.
L'Eau Dormante. Aldrich.
Let's away with study. *Fr.* Carmina Burana. *Unknown.*
Life. Crabbe.
Lightly like music running, our blood. Garrigue.
Lines to Do with Youth. Bynner.
Little Boy and the Old Man, The. Silverstein.
Lost Shipmate, The. Roberts.
My Gang. Kerouac.
My Lost Youth. Longfellow.
My Rival. Kipling.
Noone" autumnal this great lady's gaze. Cummings.
O Youth with Blossoms Laden. Peack.
October Redbreast, The. Meynell.
Ode on a Distant Prospect of Eton College. Gray.
Old age sticks. Cummings.
Old Man's Comforts and How He Gained Them, The. Southey.
Old Song Resung, An. Yeats.
Old Swimmin'-Hole, The. Riley.
On Reading Aloud My Early Poems. Williams.
On the Instability of Youth. Vaux.
Our Youth. Ashbery.
Out to Old Aunt Mary's. Riley.
Over the Sea to Skye. Stevenson.
Pachuco Remembered. Villanueva.
Parable of the Old Man and the Young, The. Owen.
Piazza Piece. Ransom.
Pity. Deutsch.
Portrait of a Girl with Comic Book. McGinley.
Reports of Midsummer Girls. Lattimore.
Ringleted Youth of My Love. Hyde.
Schiehallion. Cruickshank.
Schoolboy, The. *Fr.* Songs of Experience. Blake.
Seein' Things. Field.
Seventeen. Holden.
Short Song of Congratulation, A. Johnson.
Since Youth Is All for Gladness. Dresbach.
Snake Hill. Parini.
Song: "When Maidens are young, and in their spring." *Fr.* The Emperor of the Moon. Behn.
Spring Rites. Robbins.
Stanzas Written on the Road between Florence and Pisa. Byron.
Susan to Diana. Cornford.
Talmud Student, The. Bialik.
There I could never be a boy. O'Hara.
There Was a Boy. *Fr.* The Prelude. Wordsworth.
Time's Revenge. Learned.
To a Very Young Lady. Waller.
To Chloe Who Wish'd Her Self Young Enough for Me. Cartwright.
To Youth. Landor.
Trees They Do Grow High, The. *Unknown.*
Unbeliever. Dow.
Unemployment/Monologue. Jordan.
Village of Winter Carols. Lee.
Way I Was, The. Sanchez.
We Poets in Our Youth. Wordsworth.
We Real Cool. Brooks.
"What You See Is Me." Gibbs.
When I Was One-and-twenty. Housman.
World Youth Song. *Unknown.*
Young. Sexton.
Young and Old. *Fr.* The Water Babies. Kingsley.
Young Girl. Huch.
Young Ones, Flip Side, The. Emanuel.
Youth. Cloud.
Youth. Cornford.

Youth. "Hope."
Youth. Hughes.
Youth. Johnson.
Youth. Lodge.
Youth. Rittenhouse.
Youth. Salkeld.
Youth. Shelton.
Youth and Age. Byron.
Youth and Age. Coleridge.
Youth and Age. Surrey.
Youth and Age on Beaulieu River, Hants. Betjeman.
Youth and Beauty. Townshend.
Youth Mowing, A. Lawrence.
Youth Sings a Song of Rosebuds. Cullen.
Youth's the Season. *Fr.* The Beggar's Opera. Gay.

Yucatán, Mexico
Hunter, The. Turner.
Lost in Yucatan. McKeown.

Yugoslavia
Crew Practice on Lake Bled, in Jugoslavia. Scully.
Dubrovnik Poem (Emilio Tolentino). Rudolf.
Seventh Eclogue. Radnoti.

Yukon Territory
At White River. Haines.
Cremation of Sam McGee, The. Service.
Law of the Yukon, The. Service.
Spell of the Yukon, The. Service.

Yuma, Arizona
Crossing the Colorado River into Yuma. Ortiz.

Z

Zacchaeus
On Zacheus. Quarles.

Zambia
Leader, The. Livesay.

Zapata, Emiliano
Pentecost. Ai.

Zebras
Miscegenous Zebra, The. Young.
Zebra. "Dinesen."
Zebra. Smith.
Zebra. *Unknown.*
Zebra Stallion. *Unknown.*
Zebras, The. Campbell.

Zen Buddhism
December. Snyder.
Last Frontier, The. Thomas.
Visit to the Hermitage. Anderson.

Zeppelin's. *See* **Dirigibles.**

Zeus
Europa. Plomer.
Hymn to Zeus. *Fr.* Agamemnon. Aeschylus.
Hymn to Zeus. Cleanthes.
Leda and the Swan. Yeats.
Praise of Zeus. Aratus of Soli.

Zimbabwe
Black and White. Adame.

Zinnias
Zinnias. Worth.

Zion
By the Waters of Babylon. *Fr.* Hebrew Melodies. Heine.
Hebrew of Your Poets, Zion, The. Reznikoff.
Kadia the Young Mother Speaks. Sampter.
Last Words of Don Henriquez, The. Schneour.
Light and Rejoicing to Israel. *Unknown.*
My Heart Is in the East. Halevi.
Ode to Zion. Halevi.
Promised Land, The. Sampter.
Song: "There stands a lonely pine-tree." Heine.
Through These Pale Cold Days. Rosenberg.
To the Western Wind. Halevi.

Zionism
Hatikvah—a Song of Hope. Imber.
Road, The. Schneour.
Theodor Herzl. Zangwill.
Those Zionists. Del Monte.
Zionist Marching Song. Imber.

Zodiac
Signs of the Zodiac, The. Brewer.

Zola, Émile
Zola. Robinson.

Zoos
At the Zoo. Milne.
At the Zoo. Thackeray.
Au Jardin des Plantes. Wain.
Elephant, The. Hochman.
Encounter in the Cage Country. Dickey.
Excuse Us, Animals in the Zoo. Wynne.
False Country of the Zoo. Garrigue.
Further Instructions. O'Sullivan.
Gorilla, The. Hathaway.
In the Snake Park. Plomer.
Invitation to the Zoological Gardens, An. *Unknown.*
Jaguar, The. Hughes.
Jim. Belloc.
Lion. Swenson.
Lion and Albert, The. Edgar.
Menagerie, The. Moody.
On the Death of an Emperor Penguin in Regent's Park, London. Wright.
On Visiting Central Park Zoo. Dugan.
Our Visit to the Zoo. Pope.
Prodigy, The. Herbert.
Traverse City Zoo. Harrison.
Twilight at the Zoo. Rodger.
Van Amburgh's Menagerie. *Unknown.*
Woman at the Washington Zoo, The. Jarrell.
Zoo, The. Logan.
Zoo in the City, The. Allen.

Zulus
Fallen Zulu Commander, The. Van den Heever.
Lalela Zulu. *Unknown.*
Senzangakhona. Zulu.
Those Were the Days. Zulu.
Young viper grows as it sits, The. *Fr.* Shaka. Zulu.
Zulu Girl, The. Campbell.

Zuñi Indians
Songs, The. Zuñi.